THIN PAPER

WEBSTER'S
NEW COLLEGIATE
DICTIONARY

A Merriam-Webster
REG. U.S. PAT. OFF.

BASED ON

WEBSTER'S
NEW INTERNATIONAL
DICTIONARY

SECOND EDITION

G. & C. MERRIAM CO., PUBLISHERS

SPRINGFIELD, MASS., U.S.A.

CONTENTS

PREFACE

History of the Collegiate. WEBSTER'S NEW COLLEGIATE DICTIONARY is an entirely new book — newly edited and typeset and presented in a new format. It will, however, have for many persons the characteristics of an old friend; for it is but the latest member of the century-old MERRIAM-WEBSTER family. For many years MERRIAM-WEBSTER dictionaries have formed a series, in which the unabridged dictionary is the parent work and the COLLEGIATE DICTIONARY the largest abridgment. From each successive revision of the unabridged work new abridged books have sprung. In 1898 the first edition of the COLLEGIATE appeared. Its size, appearance, typography, and, above all, its wealth of material and scholarly presentation quickly won for it a high place in the regard of both general reader and scholar. In 1910 a second edition appeared, followed by new editions or revisions in 1916 (the third), 1931 (the fourth), and 1936 (the fifth). This NEW COLLEGIATE (the sixth) incorporates the best of the time-tested features of its predecessors.

Scope and Format. The general content and over-all plan of the previous edition (WEBSTER'S COLLEGIATE DICTIONARY, *Fifth Edition*) have proved so well adapted to the needs of its users that any attempt to change its essential character and form seemed inadvisable. The editors felt, too, that there were relatively few entries, both in its main vocabulary and in the special sections, that could be omitted without loss to the user of WEBSTER'S NEW COLLEGIATE. At the same time, there were many new terms and meanings, many older terms and meanings of increasing importance or frequency, many abbreviations, and many proper names that must be added in a new edition. The problem was how to retain most of the material of the previous work while adding material essential to the new book without markedly increasing its physical size. The new format of the present book is the answer. The wider page, with its wider column, has enabled the editors to achieve this dual aim within a handy-sized volume.

Typography. The type faces used in this book are those of the NEW INTERNATIONAL, *Second Edition*, for which they were carefully chosen, after extensive experimenting, for their appearance and readability. These type faces have stood the further tests of time and use in the previous edition of the COLLEGIATE.

The General Vocabulary. Once again the vocabulary of the COLLEGIATE has been selected to meet the needs both of the college student and of the general reader seeking clear and accurate, but not encyclopedic, information. Every entry and every definition of the previous edition has been reviewed, and many of them have been revised to incorporate additional, often new, information or to effect improvements in the former presentation. The definitions have for the most part been based on the most recent available information contained in the latest printings of the parent work, WEBSTER'S NEW INTERNATIONAL DICTIONARY, *Second Edition*, with such modifications or adaptations as are required by the smaller scope of the COLLEGIATE. Wherever they are needed and, indeed, as freely as possible within the limitations of the space, phrases and sentences have been given that illustrate the definitions. The literary vocabulary contains many additions, consisting principally of new terms and meanings and some older ones of increased importance or frequency, the inclusion of which is often the direct result of suggestions from users of the previous edition. The NEW COLLEGIATE follows the practice of its predecessors in including only a limited selection of slang, dialectal, and obsolete terms and meanings. Since behind the present work are all the vast resources of the NEW INTERNATIONAL, *Second Edition*, containing some 550,000 vocabulary entries, the problem has been one of selection of terms to be included here. Usefulness has been the criterion.

Special Subjects. The greater emphasis on the vocabularies of technical and scientific fields, which was perhaps the most noticeable difference between the previous edition and earlier COLLEGIATES, has been continued in this NEW COLLEGIATE. The wealth of information prepared by the 207 consulting editors for the NEW INTERNATIONAL, *Second Edition*, has been freely drawn upon and a great deal of new material has been added. Many of the new definitions have been specially prepared or reviewed for the present work by various members of this group of consultants and by others, particularly Dr. Robert A. Hall, Jr., Associate Professor of Linguistics at Cornell University, Dr. Ralph Harper, Instructor in English at Harvard University, Dr. James A. Hootman of the National Advisory Committee for Aeronautics, and Dr. Hans Kohn, Professor of History at Smith College.

In the selection of newer terms for inclusion in this book the important contributions to the language resulting from World War II play a major part. Such terms include not only those in the military field (such as *bazooka, blitzkrieg, foxhole, jeep, kamikaze, Panzer, roadblock*) but also those in many other fields, such as aeronautics, chemistry, electronics, nuclear physics, and medicine.

Trade-marks. Public interest in the status, the pronunciation, and the application of many terms originally coined for use as trade-marks makes such terms a matter of lexical concern. In a dictionary of this scope, however, it is possible to include only a limited number of those trade-marks most likely to be sought by the average dictionary user. All entries suspected of being trade-marks have been investigated in the files of the United States Patent Office at Washington, D. C., and those which the evidence showed to be trade-marks have been defined as such. The inclusion of a term in this dictionary is not, however, to be taken as an expression of the publishers' opinion as to whether or not it is subject to proprietary rights, but only as an expression of their belief that such a term is of sufficiently general use and interest to warrant its inclusion in a work of this kind. No definition in this dictionary is to be regarded as affecting the validity of any trade-mark.

Presentation of Material. Although the presentation of the material conforms to accepted dictionary practices and will in general offer no difficulty to most users of this book, occasional details may raise questions requiring precise answer. The editors, with the help of users of the previous edition, have tried to anticipate and answer all such questions in the section of *Explanatory Notes*, pages xviii–xx. Every user of this book, even the experienced dictionary consulter, will gain much from a reading of these pages.

Order of Definitions. In general the order of definitions follows the practice of the NEW INTERNATIONAL, where the earliest ascertainable meaning is placed first and later meanings are arranged in the order shown to be most probable by dated citations and semantic development. Technical senses, except in a few cases where they are essential elements in this pattern, are placed after nontechnical senses and are arranged according to the alphabetical order of their labels (such as *Bot., Chem., Med.*). This historical arrangement is of especial value to those interested in the development of meanings and offers no difficulty to the user who is merely looking for a particular meaning.

Pronunciation. The pronunciations given in this dictionary are based on those of the NEW INTERNATIONAL, *Second Edition*, and reflect the large body of firsthand information specially gathered for that work from scores of persons in all parts of the United States and elsewhere in the English-speaking world. The pronunciations of the individual entries in the general vocabulary and in the special sections are given in a phonetic alphabet that can be readily understood. A concise key to this MERRIAM-WEBSTER phonetic alphabet is printed at the front and back of the book, just inside the covers, where it can be found most easily and quickly. Users particularly interested in pronunciation are urged to read the *Guide to Pronunciation* (pages vii–xvii), which not only supplements this key by explaining fully each symbol used in the pronunciations but also discusses in some detail many general matters of pronunciation. This material was condensed by Dr. John S. Kenyon, eminent authority on pronunciation, from the fuller treatment prepared by him for the NEW INTERNATIONAL, *Second Edition*.

Etymologies. For vocabulary entries retained from the previous edition the etymologies, with such changes as are required to reflect recent information, are taken over from that book, for which they were condensed from those of the NEW INTERNATIONAL, *Second Edition*. These etymologies were prepared by Dr. E. E. Thompson of the editorial staff in consultation with Dr. Harold H. Bender of Princeton University, chief consultant in etymology, who has written or supervised the writing of the etymologies of new entries as well.

Synonyms. Brief articles discriminating from one another words of closely associated meaning have long been a valuable feature of the COLLEGIATE. In the present book the number of these articles has been increased. The articles, adapted from the fuller treatments in WEBSTER'S DICTIONARY OF SYNONYMS, were prepared by Miss Rose F. Egan, who had a major part in the writing of that book.

Pictorial Illustrations. The wide scope of illustrations that was a feature of previous editions of the COLLEGIATE has been retained in this new work. Many new illustrations have been prepared especially for this work. In general the aim has been to include illustrations not for their decorative quality but for their value in clarifying definitions.

Supplementary Features. Except for the section of *Foreign Words and Phrases*, the material of which has been incorporated in the general vocabulary of this book, the supplementary features of the previous edition have been retained.

The *Pronouncing Gazetteer* gives the spelling, syllabic division, and pronunciation of over seven thousand names and continues to provide information on location, political status or ownership, population, and other statistics (such as length of rivers, height of mountains, area of political divisions, lakes, etc.) in the concise form familiar to users of the COLLEGIATE.

The *Biographical* section gives the spelling, pronunciation, given names, dates, nationality, and a brief indication of achievements or sphere of activity for a selected list of names of persons, ancient and modern, of general interest. The number of entries has been increased to upwards of five thousand.

The list of *Colleges and Universities,* which has proved to be one of the most often consulted of the special sections of the COLLEGIATE, has been completely revised and its basis of selection broadened to include a very much larger number of institutions. The pronunciation and syllabic division of the names of these institutions are given wherever needed.

The lists of *Abbreviations* and of *Given Names* have been revised and many entries have been added.

The section of *Arbitrary Signs and Symbols,* the *Vocabulary of Rhymes,* and the several sections treating *Orthography,* and *Punctuation, Compounds, Capitals, etc.,* and *Preparation of Copy for the Press* have been revised and retained.

Editorial Staff. The editing, checking, proofreading, and similar operations have been carried out by the trained editorial staff of G. & C. MERRIAM COMPANY, many of whom worked not only on the preparation of the previous edition of the COLLEGIATE but also on the NEW INTERNATIONAL, *Second Edition.* An exhaustive list of staff members who contributed to this NEW COLLEGIATE, some by performing essential clerical work and others by preparing or reviewing a few definitions, would serve little purpose; but it would be ungracious not to mention the chief participants in various phases of the work. The reviewing and writing of definitions were done by Dr. Lucius H. Holt, *Managing Editor,* Mr. Edward F. Oakes, *Associate Editor,* and the following *Assistant Editors*: Mr. Hubert P. Kelsey, Dr. Everett E. Thompson, Dr. Edward A. H. Fuchs, Dr. Philip B. Gove, Dr. Donald W. Lee, and Miss Anne M. Driscoll; pronunciations by Miss Elsie Mag and Mr. Edward Artin; synonyms by Miss Rose F. Egan; cross-referencing and checking by Miss Ervina E. Foss; proofreading by Mr. Hubert H. Roe and Miss Rita L. Goyette; the editing of various special sections as follows: *Abbreviations* by Miss Driscoll, *Biographies* by Dr. Gove, *Colleges and Universities* by Dr. Thompson, *Gazetteer* by Dr. Thompson, Dr. Lee, and Miss Foss, *Given Names* and *Rhymes* by Miss Egan, *Orthography, Punctuation, etc.* by Mr. Oakes.

The typesetting and electrotyping have been done by The Riverside Press, whose staff have once again given their hearty co-operation and have assisted with excellent proofreading.

WEBSTER'S NEW COLLEGIATE DICTIONARY represents the results of the collaborative efforts of the permanent MERRIAM-WEBSTER editorial staff, with the assistance of others previously mentioned. It is the product of an organization with the background of more than one hundred years of continuous dictionary-making experience. It is the latest addition to the MERRIAM-WEBSTER series of dictionaries which have served successive generations. We offer it to the user with the conviction that it will serve him well.

John P. Bethel
General Editor.

A GUIDE TO PRONUNCIATION

KEY TO THE SYMBOLS USED IN THE RESPELLING
FOR PRONUNCIATION

REFERENCES. Numbers following the respelling for pronunciation of some words in the Vocabulary refer to sections in this GUIDE.

ACCENTS AND HYPHENS. The principal accent is indicated by a heavy mark (′), and the secondary accent by a lighter mark (′), at the end of the syllable. Syllabic division is indicated by a centered period, except where this is replaced by an accent mark or by a hyphen used to join the members of words written or printed with a hyphen.

FOREIGN SOUNDS for which no special symbols are provided are represented by the nearest English equivalents.

ā, as in āle, fāte, lā′bor, chā′os, chăm′ber (§ 5).
ȧ, " " chȧ·ot′ic, fȧ·tal′i·ty, cor′dȧte (§ 12).
â, " " câre, pâr′ent, com·pâre′, beâr, âir (§ 6).
ă, " " ădd, ăm, făt, ăc·cept′ (§ 7).
ȧ, " " ȧc·count′, in′fȧnt, guid′ȧnce (§ 14).
ä, " " ärm, fär, fä′ther, äh, pälm (§ 8).
á, " " ásk, gráss, dánce, stáff, páth (§ 9).
ȧ, " " so′fȧ, i·de′ȧ, ȧ·bound′, di′ȧ·dem (§ 15).
b, " " ba′by, be, bit, bob, but (§ 17).
ch, " " chair, much; also for tch as in match; for ti as in ques′tion; for te as in right′eous (§ 21).
d, as in day, add′ed; also for ed as in robbed (§ 25).
dụ̇: for du as in ver′dure; for deu as in gran′deur (§§ 25, 118).
ē, as in ēve, mēte, se·rēne′, hē′li·om′e·ter (§ 26).
ẽ, " " hẽre, fẽar, wẽird, deer (dẽr) (§ 27).
ė, " " ė·vent′, dė·pend′, crė·ate′ (§ 35).
ĕ, " " ĕnd, ĕx·cuse′, ĕf·face′ (§§ 28, 29).
ĕ, " " si′lĕnt, pru′dĕnce, nov′ĕl (§ 37).
ẽ, " " măk′ẽr, pẽr·vert′, in′fẽr·ence (§§ 32, 36).
f, " " fill, feel; for ph as in phan′tom, tri′umph; for gh as in laugh (§ 43).
g (always "hard"), as in go, be·gin′; also for gu as in guard; for gue as in plague; for gh as in ghost (§ 44).
gz: for x as in ex·ist′, ex·act′, ex·am′ple (§ 128).
h, as in hat, hen, hide, hot, hurt, a·head′ (§ 49).
hw: for wh as in what, why, where (§ 127).
ī, as in īce, sīght, in·spīre′, ī·de′a, bī·ol′o·gy (§§ 50, 51).
ĭ, " " ĭll, ad·mĭt′, hab′ĭt, pit′y (pĭt′ĭ) (§§ 52, 53).
ĭ, " " char′ĭ·ty, pos′sĭ·ble, dĭ·rect′, A′prĭl (§ 54).
j, " " joke, jol′ly; also for "soft" g, as in gem, gi′ant; for gi and ge as in re·li′gion, pi′geon; for di as in sol′dier; for dg(e) as in edge, judg′ment (§ 59).
k, as in keep, kick; also for "hard" ch, as in cho′rus, ep′och; for "hard" c, as in cube; for ck as in pack; for qu as in con′quer, co·quette′; for que as in pique (§ 60).
ᴋ (small capital): for ch as in German ich, ach, etc. (§ 60).
ks: for x as in vex, ex′e·cute, per·plex′ (§ 128).
kw: for qu as in queen, quit, qual′i·ty (§ 91).
l, as in late, leg, lip, lot, lull, hol′ly (§ 61).
m, " " man, men, mine, hum, ham′mer (§ 64).
n, " " nod, man, man′ner; also for gn as in sign (§ 66).
ɴ (small capital): without sound of its own, indicates the nasal tone (as in French or Portuguese) of the preceding vowel, as in bon (bôɴ), en′sem′ble (äɴ′säɴ′bl′) (§ 67).
ng, as in sing, long, sing′er; also for ngue as in tongue; for n before the sound of k or "hard" g, as in bank, junc′tion, lin′ger, sin′gle, can′ker (§ 68).
ō, as in ōld, nōte, bōld, he′rō, cal′i·cō (§ 69).
ō̇, " " ō̇·bey′, tō̇·bac′co, a·nat′ō̇·my (§ 79).
ô, " " ôrb, lôrd, ôr·dain′; law (lô), bought (bôt), caught (kôt), all (ôl) (§ 71).
ŏ, as in ŏdd, nŏt, tŏr′rid, fŏr′est, pŏs·ter′i·ty (§§ 73 ff.).

ô̇, as in sŏft, dŏg, clŏth, lŏss, cŏst (§ 74).
ŏ̇, " " cŏn·nect′, ŏ̇·cur′, co′lŏn, cŏm·bine′ (§ 80).
oi, " " oil, nois′y, a·void′, goi′ter (§ 82).
ōō, " " fōōd, mōōn, fōōl, nōōn; rude (rōōd), ru′mor (rōō′mẽr) (§ 83).
ŏŏ, as in fŏŏt, wŏŏl; put (pŏŏt), pull (pŏŏl) (§ 85).
ou, " " out, thou, de·vour′ (§ 86).
p, " " pa′pa, pen, pin, pop, put (§ 88).
r, " " rat, red, rip, rod, hor′rid (§§ 92 ff.); also for rh as in rho′do·den′dron, rhom′boid.
s (always voiceless, or "sharp"), as in sit, this, haste; also for "soft" c, as in cell, vice; for sc as in scene, sci′ence; for ss as in hiss (§ 97).
sh, " " she, ship, shop; also for ch as in ma·chine′, chaise; for ce as in o′cean; for ci as in so′cial; for sci as in con′scious; for s as in sure; for se as in nau′seous; for si as in pen′sion; for ss as in is′sue; for ssi as in pas′sion; for ti as in na′tion (§§ 102 ff.).
t, as in to, talk; also for ed as in baked, capped; for th as in thyme, Thom′as (§ 104).
ᵗʰ (voiced): for th as in then, though, this, smooth, breathe (§ 107).
th (voiceless), as in thin, through, wealth, worth, breadth, width (§ 107).
tụ̇: for tu as in na′ture, cul′ture, pic′ture (§ 118).
ū, as in cūbe, pūre, tūne, lūte, dū′ty, hū′man (§§ 112–114).
ụ, as in ụ·nite′, for′mụ·late, hụ·mane′ (§ 118).
û, " " ûrn, fûrl, con·cûr′; her (hûr), fern (fûrn), fir (fûr) (§§ 117, 31); for Ger. ö, oe, as in schön (shûn), Goe′the (gû′tĕ); for Fr. eu, as in jeu (zhû), seul (sûl).
ŭ, as in ŭp, tŭb, stŭd′y, ŭn′der, ŭn·do′ (§ 116).
ŭ, " " cir′cŭs, cau′cŭs, dā′tŭm, cir′cŭm·stance, de′mon (-mŭn), na′tion (-shŭn) (§ 119).
ü: for German ü, as in grün, küm′mel; for French u, as in me·nu′ (mĕ·nü′) (§ 122).
v, as in van, vent, vote, re·voke′, re·vive′ (§ 123); also for f as in of.
w, " " want, win, weed, wood (§ 124); also for u as in per·suade′ (-swäd′) or o as in choir (kwīr).
y, as in yet, yard, yel′low, be·yond′ (§ 131); also for i as in un′ion (-yŭn).
z, as in zone, haze; also for voiced ("soft") s, as in is, lives, wise, mu′sic, ears, figs (§ 132); for x as in Xen′o·phon, xy′lo·phone (§ 128).
zh: for z as in az′ure; for zi as in gla′zier, bra′zier; for s as in pleas′ure, u′su·al; for si as in vi′sion; for ssi as in ab·scis′sion; for g as in rouge, mi·rage′ (§ 133).
′, as in par′don (pär′d′n), eat′en (ēt′′n), e′vil (ē′v′l), indicates that the following consonant is syllabic (§ 38), or, occasionally, indicates unusual consonant combinations, as in Knut (k′nōōt).

(vii)

THE ALPHABET OF THE INTERNATIONAL PHONETIC ASSOCIATION (IPA)

The following symbols have each the sound values shown in the key words. **The IPA symbols and words respelled with them are in square brackets [ ].**

CONSONANTS

[p]	in peep	[θ]	in ether	[tʃ]	in church
[b]	" bib	[ð]	" either	[dʒ]	" judge
[m]	" maim	[f]	" fife	[r]	" rear
[t]	" toot	[v]	" valve	[l]	" lull
[d]	" deed	[s]	" cease	[h]	" hail
[n]	" noon	[z]	" zones	[w]	" wail
[k]	" cook	[ʃ]	" mission	[hw]	" whale
[g]	" gig	[ʒ]	" vision	[j]	" you
[ŋ]	" sing				

NOTE: For convenience in printing, the symbol [g] may be substituted for [ɡ].

VOWELS

[i]	in beet	[ɜ]	in bird as pronounced in southern England and parts of eastern and southern America (only in stressed syllables)
[ɪ]	" sit		
[e]	" chaotic		
[eɪ]	" cave		
[ɛ]	" set		
[æ]	" sat		
[ɑ]	" father		
[a]	" ask as often pronounced in America (between [æ] and [ɑ]. See § 9)	[ɝ]	" bird as pronounced by the majority of Americans (only in stressed syllables)
[ɔ]	" all, horse		
[ɒ]	" sorry as pronounced in England and often in America (between [ɑ] and [ɔ])		
[o]	" notation	[ɚ]	" better as pronounced by the majority of Americans (only in unstressed syllables)
[ou]	" go		
[ʊ]	" pull		
[u]	" pool		
[ʌ]	" sun (used only in stressed syllables)		

[ə] in sofa (only in unstressed syllables)

NOTE: [ɚ] is not a symbol of the IPA, which at present has no unambiguous symbol for the sound.

DIPHTHONGS

[aɪ] in ice · [aʊ] in house · [ɔɪ] in boy
[ɪu] in mute: the symbols [ju] are used when the first element is [j] as in use, instead of [ɪ]

NOTE: [eɪ] and [ou], given above, are also diphthongs, the usual sounds of "long a" and "long o" (see §§ 5, 69).

NON–ENGLISH CONSONANTS

[ç] = ch in German ich and Scottish heich "high" [hiç], the voiceless palatal fricative (§ 60).
[x] = ch in German ach and Scottish loch [lɒx], the voiceless velar fricative (§ 60).

NON–ENGLISH VOWELS

[y] in French pur, German fühlen, — the high-front-round vowel (§ 122).
[ø] " French creuse, German Goethe, — the mid-front-round vowel (§ 117).
[œ] " French seul, German können, — the low-front-round vowel (§ 117).

The symbols [l̩], [m̩], [n̩], [r̩] represent l, m, n, and r sounds that form syllables either alone or with nonsyllabic sounds; as [bæt'l̩, bæt'l̩d, kæz'm̩, kæz'm̩z, fæt'n̩, fæt'n̩d, bɛt'r̩, bɛt'r̩d].

The colon [ː] after a symbol indicates that its sound is long in duration as compared with that of the unmarked symbol. The raised period [ˑ] may be used for intermediate length.

The sign [⊥] after a vowel symbol (as [e⊥]) indicates a pronunciation of it with slightly raised tongue; [⊤] (as [ɛ⊤]), with slightly lowered tongue; [⊢] (as [o⊢]), with slightly advanced tongue; and [⊣] (as [e⊣]), with slightly retracted tongue.

SYMBOLS USED TO INDICATE PRONUNCIATION WITHOUT RESPELLING

To indicate PRONUNCIATION WITHOUT RESPELLING, the table below may be used in connection with the one on p. vii. For indicating PRONUNCIATION BY RESPELLING, however, the table on p. vii is complete in itself and is alone used throughout this dictionary.

The table below is to be used only when any letter of a word has a sound that is represented in the table on p. vii by a different letter. Thus, in the respelling table s is used for one sound only, that in sin or so. To show the z sound of s (as in his) without respelling, the marked s (ṣ) from the table below should be used, — thus, hiṣ. In the table below, the symbols in parentheses are the equivalent symbols from the respelling table.

In digraphs, mark only the letter that is to be regarded as sounded, as in breāk, brĕad, yiēld, veil, etc. Silent e at the end of a syllable, as in fate, etc., need not be marked. ce, ci, sci, se, si, or ti before a vowel, and immediately after an accented syllable, usually have the sound of sh, and need not be marked. Where desirable, any letter regarded as silent may be shown as an unmarked italic. In a few words, the pronunciation can be indicated only by respelling.

ã (= ĕ),	as in	li'ar, cow'ard, mus'tard.
ạ (= ŏ),	" "	what, was, qual'i·ty.
A, ạ (= ô),	" "	all, awe, swarm, talk.
Au, au, aw (= ô),	" "	au'thor, law.
E, ę (= ā),	" "	eight, prey, vein, o·bey'; or (= ā) as in me·lee'.
Ê, ê (= â),	" "	thêre, hêir, whêre·in'.
Ẽ, ẽ (= û),	" "	ẽr'mine, e·tẽr'nal, swẽrve.
Ee, ee (= ē),	" "	eel, feet, fee'ble, un·seen'.
Ew, ew (= ū),	" "	ewe, dew, hewn; or (= o͞o) as in brew.
Ï, ï (= ē),	" "	pïque, ma·chïne', po·lïce'; or (= ĕ) as in fï·as'co.
Ĩ, ĩ (= ē),	" "	vĩr·gin'i·ty, e·lix'ĩr; or (= û) as in ĩrk'some, fĩr, bĩrd.
ǫ (= o͞o),	" "	wǫlf, wǫm'an, wǫl'ver·ine'.
Ọ, ọ (= o͞o),	" "	ọoze, dọ, whọ, tọmb.
Ò, ó (= ŭ),	" "	òth'er, sòn; or (= ŭ) as in wel'còme, wis'dòm.
õ (= ĕ),	" "	mi'nõr; or (= û) as in wõrk.
Ow, ow (= ou),	" "	owl, cow'ard, vow'el.
Oy, oy (= oi),	as in	oys'ter, boy, roy'al, en·joy'.
Ụ, ụ (= o͞o),	" "	rụde, rụ'mor, in·trụde'.
Ụ, ụ (= o͝o),	" "	full, put, push, hand'ful.
Ȳ, ȳ (= ī),	" "	flȳ, skȳ, stȳle, de·fȳ', dȳ'ing.
Y̆, y̆ (= ĭ),	" "	y̆t'tri·a, hy̆mn, lȳr'ic.
ỹ (= ĕ),	" "	sat'ỹr, mar'tỹr; or (= û) as in mỹrrh, mỹr'tle.
Ꞓ, ꞓ (= k),	" "	cat, con·cur'.
Ç, ç (= s),	" "	çell, viçe.
Ꞓh, ꞓh (= k),	" "	ꞓho'rus, ech'o, ep'och.
Çh, çh (= sh),	" "	çhaise, ma·çhine'.
Ḡ, ḡ (= g),	" "	ḡet, be·ḡin', an'ḡer.
Ġ, ġ (= j),	" "	ġem, en'ġine.
dġ (= j),	" "	edġe, bridġe, badġ'er.
ṇ (= ng),	" "	aṇ'chor, iṇk.
ṣ (= z),	" "	iṣ, haṣ, wiṣ'dom.
x (= gz),	" "	ex·ist', ex·am'ple.
x (= ks),	" "	vex, ex'e·cute.
Ph, ph (= f),	" "	phan'tom, sylph.
Qu, qu (= kw),	" "	queen, con'quest.
Wh, wh (= hw),	" "	when, what.

I. PRONUNCIATION OF MODERN ENGLISH

STANDARD PRONUNCIATION

Standard Pronunciation. The term *correct pronunciation* is often used. Yet it is probable that many who use the term would find it difficult to give a precise and clear definition of the sense in which they use it. When the essential facts are considered, "correctness of pronunciation" must be a flexible term. It is perhaps as accurate a definition as can be made to say that a pronunciation is correct when it is in actual use by a sufficient number of cultivated speakers. This is obviously elastic, depending both on knowledge — not always obtainable — of the number of users, and on judgment as to the cultivation of the speakers.

The standard of English pronunciation, so far as a standard may be said to exist, is the usage that now prevails among the educated and cultured people to whom the language is vernacular; but, since somewhat different pronunciations are used by the cultivated in different regions too large to be ignored, we must frankly admit the fact that, at present, uniformity of pronunciation is not to be found throughout the English-speaking world, though there is a very large percentage of practical uniformity.

The function of a pronouncing dictionary is to record as far as possible the pronunciations prevailing in the best present usage, rather than to attempt to dictate what that usage should be. In so far as a dictionary may be known and acknowledged as a faithful recorder and interpreter of such usage, so far and no farther may it be appealed to as an authority.

A further factor in the determination of correct pronunciation is the style of speech, within the same regional form, used for different occasions. The most important of these different styles is what may be called the cultivated colloquial, which has been aptly termed the style of well-bred ease. This is the most used of the standard styles, it is acceptable to every class of society, whether used by them or not, and its sound system represents the main current of progress, change, and unification of the language as a whole.

It is unfortunate that with some the term *colloquial* has somewhat fallen into disrepute, the impression having gained ground that a word marked "Colloquial" in a dictionary or similar work is thereby condemned as not in the best use. See the definition of *colloquial* in the Vocabulary.

In public worship, especially in reading from the Bible, the Prayer Book, or similar authoritative work, the rate of speech is often slower than in ordinary conversation or normal public utterance. The articulation of consonants is more distinct, and the vowels are often of greater length. The unaccented vowels are often sounded as if under secondary accent, as in **vulgate** (vŭl′gāt), **converse**, *v.* (kŏn·vûrs′), **triumvirate** (trī·ŭm′vĭ·rāt), **labor** (lā′bôr), etc. Such pronunciations with full vowel are confined to solemn or other very deliberate style.

§ 1. ACCENT

Accent may be defined as the prominence given to a syllable or a word which makes it stand out to the attention above adjacent syllables or words. Accent that distinguishes the syllables of words is called **word accent**, or **syllabic accent**. Accent that distinguishes words in a group is called **sentence accent**.

The term **stress**, which in a strict sense means force of expiration, is commonly used to mean accent, since it is the principal element of prominence. For clearness, **stress** will here be used as a general term for accent (prominence) both of syllables and words; **accent** will be used only of **word accent**, or **word stress**; while the prominence that distinguishes words in a sense group will here be called **sense stress** (other terms being *sentence stress, sentence accent,* and *emphasis*). Of the various degrees of accent, only the **primary** (′) and the **secondary** (′) need be marked.

§ 2. SHIFTING ACCENT

Shifting Accent. In many words and phrases, chiefly in adjectives and adverbs, the accent is often variable, being stronger on one syllable or the other according to the rhythm of the syllables in the context. Thus, we say, **The room is air′tight′**, but **an air′tight′ room′**.

In addition to the influence of sense stress and sentence rhythm, a number of other causes contribute to shifting and variable accent. One of the most potent of these is the emphasis of contrast. Such a word as **exte′rior** or **inte′rior** by itself has the accent here marked; but when contrasted, these become **ex′terior and in′terior**. So **up′stairs′, down′stairs′,** when contrasted, become **up′stairs′,** etc.

Emphasis of intensity also frequently produces shift of accent, as in **ab′solute′ly,** emphatic form **ab′solute′ly**. It is especially common in adverbs ending in -arily, as **ar′bitrar′ily, nec′essar′ily,** etc. Under emphasis these words are often pronounced **ar′bitrar′ily, nec′essar′ily**.

As a consequence of the various influences mentioned, in actual speech many words in English have no fixed accent.

In this dictionary, as a rule, one accentuation is given, together with a reference (2) to this section. But the accentuation given in words of this sort may not be more "correct" than the one not given: the two merely represent different uses of the word, both equally correct. Usually, compound adjectives are entered in their predicate or absolute form, with even accent. This is taken as the basic form, as it is in most cases the original form, from which the attributive form (′ ′) is shifted. In some instances, however, the unevenly accented form is entered.

§ 3. BRITISH AND AMERICAN ACCENT

British and American Accent. A considerable group of words of French and Latin origin show a historical difference of accentuation in British and American usage. The most numerous of these are words ending in -ary (**necessary**), -ery (**cemetery**), -ory (**dormitory**). In Old French these words had primary accent on -ar-, -er-, -or-, and secondary accent on the second syllable before (**nec′essar′ie,** etc.). In English the secondary accent became the main one, and the former primary became secondary (**nec′essar′y**); or the primary sometimes fell on the third syllable before the secondary (**lab′ora-tor′y**). But recently in southern England the secondary accent has been dropped, and the more usual British pronunciation is now **nĕs′ĕsĕrĭ, dŏr′mĭtĕrĭ,** etc. The older British pronunciation is, however, still frequently heard in England, and it is universal in America, except for the comparatively few instances in which there is recent influence from British practice. Those Americans who have adopted the newer pronunciation have usually done so in only a few of the large number of words of this class so pronounced in England. In England, on the other hand, it has affected all the words of the group. There the loss of the subordinate accent has naturally resulted in the reduction of the syllable that bore it, in some words suppressing it entirely. Hence in England are often heard the pronunciations **mĭl′ĭtrĭ, dĭk′sh′nrĭ, ŏr′d′nrĭ, sĕk′rĕtrĭ**. In a few words the accent has been moved from the first to the second syllable in British usage, as in **labor′atory, axil′lary, corol′lary,** thus preserving the unaccented syllables.

In a group of words ending in -ative (**appreciative, cumulative, legislative,** etc.) often paralleling verbs in -ate, British pronunciation is in a transition state, a subordinate accent, or at least a full vowel, being sometimes retained (**admin′is·tra′tive**), or the accent being lost and the vowel obscured, as in **cumulative** (kū′mū·lȧ·tĭv). In America such words as a rule have the full vowel and a subordinate accent; but when the main accent immediately precedes the syllable in which the **a** occurs, and in a few other words, the syllable is also reduced in American use (**dĕm′ŏn·strȧ′tĭv, ȧ·fûr′mȧtĭv**).

In the small group of words ending in -mony, usage differs in England and America as in those in -ary; as, **testimony** (*Brit.* tĕs′tĭmŭnĭ, *Amer.* tĕs′tĭmō′nĭ).

In a few other words British practice tends to one accent and an obscure vowel where America has two accents and a fuller vowel; as, **melancholy** (*Brit.* mĕl′ȧnkŭlĭ, *Amer.* mĕl′ȧnkŏl′ĭ), **necromancy**.

In compound names in -borough (or -burgh), -bury (or -bery), British practice usually obscures or drops the vowel of the next to the last syllable, as in **Scarborough** (-bŭrŭ; -brŭ). Sometimes an alternating rhythmical secondary accent is heard with full vowel, as in **Canterbury** (kăn′tĕrbĕrĭ; -brĭ; *or* -bĕr′ĭ). In compounds with -berry (**strawberry**) the pronunciation -bĕrĭ; -brĭ is there the rule, though sometimes -bĕr′ĭ is heard. In the eastern United States sometimes the same obscuration is heard in **strawberry, blackberry,** etc., but in the country as a whole the full vowel is used (strô′bĕr′ĭ).

§ 4. STRESSED AND UNSTRESSED MONOSYLLABLES

Stressed and Unstressed Monosyllables. Prepositions (**at, for, from, to,** etc.), auxiliary and copulative verbs (**am, are, can, has, must,** etc.), conjunctions (**and, but, or, than,** etc.), pronouns (**he, her, me, your,** etc.), and occasionally some other words, under the conditions of sense stress may receive any degree of stress from the lowest to the highest. Accordingly the vowels of these words vary from the full and "proper" sound suggested by the spelling to an obscure sound. Note the sounds of **to** in the natural utterance of the sentence, **It began to move to and fro.** In normal speech the unstressed **to** is here pronounced tŭ, while stressed **to** is tōō. Such words, though having only one spelling form as a rule, in actual speech have one stressed pronunciation and one or more unstressed pronunciations, — the difference, though really marked, often passing unnoticed because of the identity of spelling and similarity of meaning.

The stressed form is always used when the word is mentioned alone, not as part of a context; it is therefore necessary, in order to pronounce an unstressed form, to use it naturally, as if unconsciously, in a phrase, clause, or sentence; if pronounced by itself the stressed form will inevitably be spoken. Most of the words have more than one unstressed form, depending partly on the style of speech, partly on the preceding and following sounds, and partly on the rhythmic succession of syllables in the context.

II. THE SOUNDS OF SPOKEN ENGLISH

A

§ 5. ā as in fāte, āle, māk'er, etc., is commonly called "long a." In standard English, ā is not usually a pure, or simple, sound, but is a diphthong, with several closely similar varieties, often beginning with the tongue a little higher than for ĕ (as in mĕt) and moving toward ĭ (as in ĭt). The second element, or vanish, of the ā sound appears in accented syllables in both England and America when the sound is final or before voiced consonants, as in dāy, āle. But in America, before voiceless consonants it is usually not prominent and is sometimes lacking, as in hāte. In unaccented syllables, especially before vowels, the vanish may be absent in both England and America (chă·ot'ic).

The sound (ā) is also otherwise variously represented in the ordinary spelling, as in pain, day, break, veil, obey, and exceptionally in gaol, gauge.

§ 6. â as in câre is a relatively long vowel formerly identical with the ā sound, but gradually lowered by the influence of a following r to a more open front sound, reaching and passing below the position for ĕ in vĕry.

The â sound may be described as a front vowel lying in tongue position between the ĕ in vĕry and the ă in măn. Two principal varieties exist in standard speech; one somewhat nearer acoustically and organically to ĕ than to ă, and the other decidedly nearer to ă than to ĕ. Both varieties are widespread in England and America alike, often occurring with different speakers in the same locality.

The typical occurrence of â is in accented syllables formerly (17th century) containing a long ā sound, of various origin and spelling, before r, as in aware, fare, there, bear, chair, prayer, vary, fairy, various, etc.; and many longer words, as precarious, barbarian.

As stated above, the pronunciation of these words is not uniform in cultivated speech. In America â may still be heard in vâry, bar-bârian, and in names like Sârah, Mâry. Some speakers use a lengthened ĕ sound in Sarah, Hungarian, vary (nearly like vĕry), Mary (nearly like mĕrry), while in such words as spare, compare, they use the lower sound â, as also in wâry, by analogy of awâre, bewâre.

When the vowel is followed by r and another vowel in longer words, the tendency (in America, at least) is toward the short ĕ sound in popular words, as in Maryland (mĕr'ĭ·lănd), necessary (nĕs'ĕ·sĕr'ĭ).

For those words (barbarian, etc.) that may be pronounced with either ā or â, the marking â is used in this dictionary as conforming to the more general tendency to lower the vowel. In Latin words, however, the older ā is retained in accord with the customary more formal and somewhat artificial pronunciation of Latin words and phrases and technical terms: lares (lā'rēz).

Other spellings for â are seen in there, pear, air, heir, prayer, e'er.

§ 7. ă as in hăt, băck, răn'dom, păr'ity, etc., is commonly called "short a." Its spelling is almost invariably a, exceptionally ai, as in plaid.

The standard sound ă is low-front, the mouth being nearly or quite as wide open as for ä in ärt, but the tongue somewhat farther forward and the front (but not the tip) elevated instead of the back, as it is (though less) for ä. This is the sound often popularly called "flat a," with reference to certain supposed acoustic qualities, in contrast to "broad a," as in father.

§ 8. ä occurs in ärm, fär, fä'ther, äh, älms, pälm, with equivalent spellings in hearth, ser'geant, and exceptionally in memoir (mĕm'wär; -wôr).

This sound is classed by some phoneticians as mid-back (unrounded), i. e., made with the back of the tongue in a position midway between high and low, and with the lips not rounded. Others, however, class it as low-back. The Southern British ä is, however, pronounced with the tongue somewhat farther forward than for the usual American ä.

In Southern British and with some Americans the ä sound occurs also in such words as chaff, path, grass, ask, chance, can't, etc. For further treatment, see § 9.

In the larger part of America and Canada the ä sound is used in many words spelled with o, as top, doll, etc., and in words like what, want, etc., with w before a (see §§ 11, 73).

The stressed ä sound in all words except those spelled with o (top) is now a relatively long sound.

The symbol ä is also used to represent a shorter ä sound in unaccented syllables, as in är·tis'tic, cär·toon'; or partly accented syllables, as in är'ti·fi'cial, etc.

§ 9. The symbol á is used in the representation of the pronunciation of certain words in this dictionary. Most such words have á as the final-syllable vowel symbol, immediately followed by the consonant sound ſ, s, th, or v (staff[s], pass[ed], path, halve[s]) or by an n-initial consonant group (branch, chance); or have á as the vowel of a nonfinal syllable, followed by th (rather) or by a consonant group of which the first member is ſ, s, m, or n (after, plaster, sample, answer). In English (but not in foreign) words, á is a symbol with a multiple value, standing for at least three distinct variants that may be heard in the English-speaking world as a whole. The use of á is thus a space-saving device.

By probably more than 90% of American speakers, á words are pronounced with the vowel sound that would be indicated by the symbol ă in the same environment or context.

Often in the speech of eastern New England, less often in the speech of New York City and of Richmond (Virginia), and rarely in other parts of the United States, the á words are pronounced with a sound that is intermediate between the sounds ă and ä.

In Southern British speech the sound usually heard for á is much the same in quality as, and much the same in quantity as or longer than, the vowel usually heard in the United States in pairs like card and cod from speakers who have identical or similar vowels in such pairs.

With speakers who have a sound other than ä in some but not all

members of this group, there is in some words an especially strong tendency to use a vowel other than ă, and in other words an especially strong tendency to use ă rather than another vowel. The first tendency is indicated in the vocabulary by the two variants ä, à in that order (cf. aunt), the second tendency by ă, à in that order (cf. Mass).

The following are the chief English words and word elements marked with à in this dictionary:

advance	can't	distaff	(-)graph	plant
advantage	cask	draft	grasp	plaster
aft(er)	casket	draught	grass	prance
aghast	cast	enchant	half	raft
answer	caste	example	halve	rafter
ask	caster, -or	fast	lance	rasp
aunt	castle	fasten	last	rather
avalanche	chaff	flask	lath	sample(r)
bask	chancel	France	laugh	shaft
basket	chancellor	Frances	-mand	shan't
bath	chancery	Francis	mask	slant
behalf	chandler	gasp	mast	staff
blanch	chant	ghastly	master	stanch
Blanch(e)	clasp	giraffe	nasty	supplant
blast	class	glance	pass	task
branch	craft	glass	past	trance
brass	dance]	graft	pastor	vantage
calf	disaster	grant	path	vast

In foreign words, à represents a sound whose quality is very much like that of the à described in the third paragraph of this section.

§ 10. a as in all, talk, swarm, quar'ter, etc. — otherwise spelled as in haul, caught, draw, awe, and exceptionally in U'tah, Ar'kansas (-sô) — is equivalent to ô in ôrb, bôrn (see § 71), and the symbol ô is used in the respelling for pronunciation, however the sound may be ordinarily spelled; thus, all (ôl), talk (tôk), etc.

When a (ô) occurs in unaccented syllables it is briefer; as in aus-tere', al·though', au·thor'ity. The symbol ô is used both for the short and the long sound. The short ô is the same in quality as accented ô, higher in tongue position than ŏ in ŏdd and more lip-rounded.

§ 11. a as in was, what, wan'der, wal'low, swan, qual'i·ty, etc., is equivalent to ŏ (ŏdd, nŏt) (§ 73), and is represented in the respelling in this dictionary by ŏ; thus, was (wŏz), etc.

a as in any, Thames = ĕ; see § 28.

§ 12. ȧ as in chȧ·ot'ic, fȧ·tal'i·ty, vȧ·ca'tion, ȧ·sex'u·al, and numerous adjectives or nouns in -āte, as cor'dāte, du'pli·cāte, represents a sound called "half-long a," with reference to its ā-like quality, not to its quantity, or duration, which is short. This sound occurs in syllables without primary or secondary accent, with only enough accent (not usually marked) to preserve a recognizable ā quality of the vowel, as in bi·fur'cāte, adj., du'pli·cāte, adj. or n. In standard pronunciation the a in words like duplicate, graduate (n. or adj.) varies from a recognizable ā sound to ĭ. Hence the symbol ȧ in such cases may in practice represent a range of pronunciation from ā to ĭ. The symbol ȧ conveniently distinguishes adjectives and nouns like duplicate, graduate, etc., from the corresponding verbs, which have the full ā sound (du'pli·cāte, grad'u·āte, etc.). In some of the nouns or adjectives an ĭ is usual in familiar speech (dĕl'ĕ·gĭt, dū'plĭ·kĭt; see § 13).

§ 13. In many words, a in a similar situation to the a in cor'dāte, as for example in cottage, is unaccented and is regularly pronounced as ĭ; so in village (vĭl'ĭj), savage (săv'ĭj), homage (hŏm'ĭj). So -ace = ĭs, as in palace, preface, furnace; and -ate = ĭt, as in climate, prelate, separate, adj., etc. In some such endings many speakers replace ĭ with ȧ, as in immediate (ĭ·mē'dĭ·ȧt).

ai and ay in final syllables are likewise often pronounced ĭ in some familiar words, as in always (ôl'wĭz) and regularly in the days of the week, Monday (mŭn'dĭ), etc. Saturday and yesterday are occasionally pronounced săt'ēr·dȧ, yĕs'tēr·dȧ, but ordinarily are săt'ēr·dĭ, yĕs'tēr·dĭ. But when -day has a secondary accent, it is dā' (work'day', week'day'). American pronunciation often retains ā or ȧ where British usually has ĭ, as in delegate.

Unaccented ia is sounded ĭ in parliament (also ȧ), marriage, and often, in colloquial speech, in miniature.

§ 14. ă in unaccented initial syllables, ending in a consonant in the spelling, as in ăb·hor', ab·surd', ac·count', ac·crue', etc.; and in final closed syllables, as in loy'ăl, va'cant, mad'am, myr'i·ad, is more or less obscured in ordinary speech, becoming almost or quite the same as the á in so'fa, i·de'a (§ 15). There is considerable variation according to the style of speech used, whether very formal or familiarly colloquial. Hence as no single symbol can exactly express each variety of sound, the symbol ă is used to suggest a variable sound between the limits of á in so'fa and ă in ag'itate, tending, however, in the majority of words, and especially in familiar speech, to the neutral vowel á. The symbol ă is also used in some open syllables where it is desirable to suggest a tendency toward the ă sound, as in the first a of pha·ryn'geal (fă·rĭn'jē·ăl).

Between certain consonants, articulated in the same or nearly the same place in the mouth, this ă sound may disappear entirely, as in mor'tal, Sa'tan, where in ordinary speech the final consonant usually follows immediately after the preceding one without any vowel whatever. Since in most cases, however, it is possible to pronounce the vowel, such words are often marked with both pronunciations (môr'tăl, -t'l; sā'tăn, -t'n).

§ 15. á as in á·bound', ca·rouse', di'a·dem, so'fa, i·de'a, etc., occurs in open unaccented syllables, including such as the first one of a·bridge', in which two consonants begin the following syllable. In all styles of cultivated speech á has the sound of the neutral vowel. See also § 36.

au

§ 16. The digraph **au** regularly spells the sound **ô** (**lôrd, law**), as in **aught, caught, haul**, etc. When followed by **n** (**haunt, launch, laundry**), it is pronounced **ä** by many speakers, and this is given as an alternative pronunciation in this dictionary. The words **aunt** and **laugh** are never pronounced with **ô**, but with **ä, ȧ**, or **ă** (§ 9).

aw

The digraph **aw**, pronounced as **ô** (**ôrb**), is now the usual form finally and before **k, l**, and **n**; as in **law, hawk, lawn**.

B

§ 17. **b** as in **boy, cab, ebb, rob′ber, a′ble**, etc., is the voiced bilabial oral stop corresponding to **p**, the voiceless bilabial oral stop, and to **m**, the voiced bilabial nasal continuant. All three are lip sounds. **b** is usually silent after **m** in the same syllable, as in **bomb, climb, thumb**, etc. On the other hand, a sounded **b** is excrescent in many words between **m** and **l** or **er**, as in **thimble, timber**. In **debt, doubt, subtle, b** is silent. Initial **b** before other consonants than **l** (**blue**), **r** (**brig**) is silent (**bdellium**).

In Spanish, **b** initially and after **m** or **n** is a lip stop, there being little or no explosive action after it. Medially, esp. between vowels, it is usually not a stop, but a bilabial fricative, a voiced sound made with the lips (but not the tongue back) shaped as for English **w**, and somewhat resembling English **v**, which is a labiodental sound. In fact, the two sounds and their spellings are sometimes interchanged; cf. **Havana, Habana; Cordova, Cordoba**. In this dictionary, Spanish **b** and **v** when initial or after **m** or **n** are indicated by **b** in the respelling, and medial **b** and **v** are transcribed as **v**.

C

§ 18. **c** spells three "soft" sounds and one "hard" sound: (1) The voiceless **s** sound before **e, i**, or **y**, as in **cede, civil, cypress, force**; for this sound it is respelled with **s**, as **cit′y** (**sĭt′ĭ**). It is sometimes written **ç**, when not before **e, i**, or **y**, as in **façade**, regularly so for pronunciation without respelling (**çĭt′y**). (2) The voiceless **sh** sound, as in **vicious, ocean, oceanic**, in which the **c** is combined with the **i** or **e** (see § 103). (3) Rarely, the voiced **z** sound, as in one pronunciation of **sacrifice, suffice** (-**fīz**).

§ 19. **c** is "hard," i. e., = **k**, before any letter but **e, i, y**, or **h** (see **ch**) and when final, as in **can, cup, cry, act, arc, picnic, picnicker**, exceptionally in **sceptic, scirrhous. cc** before **e, i** is pronounced **ks** (**success, vaccinate**); **cc** is pronounced **k** wherever **c** would be so sounded (**accord, accrue**).

§ 20. **c** is silent in **czar** and its derivatives, and in **indict, victuals, muscle, scene**, etc.

ch

§ 21. This digraph has four sounds in English: (1) **ch**, (2) **j**, (3) **sh**, (4) **k**. — (1) The most frequent (**ch**) is approximately **t** + **sh**. Though it is disputed whether **ch** is one or two sounds, in practice it functions as a single speech sound, as in **church**. It is the voiceless correlative of voiced **j**. In most native words **ch** has the sound **ch**, as in **child, chin, much**. It is also (except initially) spelled **tch** (**satchel, catch, watch**, etc.), chiefly after a short vowel; **ti** (**question**); **te** (**righteous**); and **t** before **u** (**nature**); see § 118.

(2) **ch** has been voiced to **j** in certain unaccented syllables. It is so regularly in the traditional pronunciation of -**wich** in English place names: **Greenwich** (**grĭn′ĭj**), **Norwich** (**nŏr′ĭj**). In **knowledge, cabbage, partridge**, the spelling has conformed to the sound. In **spinach** it is pronounced **ch** or **j**.

§ 22. (3) In loan words from modern French, **ch** has the **sh** sound, as in **chagrin, machine, mustache**, etc. In some words borrowed early, as **chivalry**, association with modern French has introduced **sh** for the historically correct **ch**. In **champaign** (level country) British still keeps the pronunciation **chămpān**, while in America the Frenchified pronunciation is usual (**shămpān**). — The **sh** sound of **ch** is indicated without respelling by **ç̇h**.

§ 23. (4) **ch** has the "hard" sound of **k** in most words from Greek, either directly or through Latin, as in **chorus, echo, epoch**; and from Hebrew, as **Chaldea, Enoch**. But some that entered Anglo-Saxon, or came from Old French popular forms, have the **ch** sound, as **church, archbishop, archduke, cherub, chart, Rachel**; but **k** is the sound in **archangel, architect, architrave**. — "Hard" **ch** (= **k**) is indicated without respelling by **ch**.

In Italian, **ch** before **e** and **i** represents **k**. In some words from foreign languages, the corresponding **ch** has a fricative sound. (See § 60.)

§ 24. **ch** is silent in **drachm, schism, yacht, fuchsia** (common plant name).

D

§ 25. **d** as in **day, bed, hard, robbed** is the voiced tongue-point alveolar oral stop, corresponding to **t**, its voiceless correlative. Both are tongue-point sounds, the contact in English being on the upper teeth-ridge (alveoli).

The spelling **d** represents a **t** sound after a voiceless consonant in the same syllable, as in **dropped, talked, puffed**, etc. The past and past participle of **dream, learn, spell** are pronounced either **drĕmt** (§ 89), **lûrnt, spĕlt**, or **drēmd, lûrnd, spĕld**. Pronunciations with **d** are always spelled -**ed** but those with **t** are spelled either -**ed** or -**t**.

In archaic, poetic, or solemn style, the -**ed** sound is often retained, as in **belov′ed brethren**, etc.

d is regularly silent in **handkerchief, handsome**, and, in informal speech, in **grandfather, grandma**, etc. **Wednesday** is ordinarily pronounced **wĕnz′dĭ**.

d is palatalized before **i** and **u** in words like **soldier, verdure** (**sōl′jẽr, vûr′dūr**); see § 118.

dg, dge, see **g**, § 45.

E

§ 26. **ē** as in **ēve, bē, mēte**, etc., is the high-front-tense vowel commonly known as "long **e**." This sound is formed with the tongue in nearly the same position as for **ĭ** (§ 52), but slightly raised and more tense, with the highest part of the tongue farthest forward and nearest the front (or hard) palate of any of the English vowels. The sound **ē** occurs only in syllables of some stress, as in **keep′er, rēclothe′** (cf. **ė**, § 35). It is also otherwise variously represented in the ordinary spelling, as in **feet, beam, de·ceive′, peo′ple, key, Cae′sar, ma·chine′, field, quay, Phoe′be.**

§ 27. **ḗ** in **hḗre, fḗar, drḗar′y, wḗird**, etc., is the high-front-lax (or lowered) vowel when followed by an **r** sound, and corresponds nearly to **ĭ** when followed by an **r** sound. Just as the tongue position of long **ā** is lowered to **â** in **câre** by a following **r** (§ 6), so **ē** is lowered to **ḗ** in **hḗre** by the **r**. As with the sounds **ā** and **â**, dictionaries till recently made no distinction between **ē** and **ḗ**, though the difference between the vowels of **he** and **here** is now obvious.

The words **hero, Nero, zero** are pronounced either with **ḗ** or with **ē**.

In the pronunciation of Latin words (technical terms, etc.) the older **ē** is often retained before **r**, while in the Anglicized adjective the **ḗ** is used.

In a few words, some speakers lower the **ē** as in words where **r** follows, as in **idea** and derivatives, **real** and derivatives, often pronounced **ī·dḗ′*ȧ*, rḗ′*ăl*.**

The vowel **ḗ** is spelled as in **deer, dear, drear′y, mere, bier, weird, fa·kir′** (**f*ȧ*·kḗr′**).

§ 28. **ĕ** as in **ĕnd, pĕt, ĕr′ror**, etc., is the mid-front-lax vowel, slightly lower and laxer than **ā** (**āle**), commonly called "short **e**" but varying considerably in actual length, as, e.g., between **pĕt** and **sĕnd** or **wĕll**. It is otherwise spelled in **heifer, leopard, friend, Aetna, asafoetida, feather, bury, any, Thames, said, says.**

§ 29. Unaccented short **ĕ** in initial syllables of such words as **ex·cuse′, en·large′, es·teem′** varies from a recognizable **ĕ** sound to an **ĭ** sound. Obscuration toward the neutral vowel is also not infrequent among good speakers both in America and England, as **ĕ·fĕkt′**. In medial syllables also, where a deliberate pronunciation often shows **ĕ**, as in **con′cĕn·trate, con′stĕl·la′tion**, obscuration takes place in ordinary speech, as **kŏn′stĕ·lā′sh*ŭ*n.**

§ 30. What was formerly a short **ĕ** also occurs in unaccented final syllables, as in **stream′let, Es′sex, kind′ness, small′est, col′lege**; very often in the plural or the possessive case of nouns ending in a sibilant (**s, z, sh**, etc.), as **hors′es, match′es, Al′ice′s**, etc.; in the third person singular of the present tense of verbs, as **push′es, urg′es**, etc.; in verbs and adjectives like **stat′ed, four–leg′ged**, etc.; and in **breth′ren, kitch′en, wom′en, wool′en** (for another sound of final -**en**, see §§ 37 ff.). These words vary in pronunciation of the **e** from **ĕ** to **ĭ**. In **stream′let, Es′sex** the **ĕ** sound is often heard in deliberate or formal speech, but **ĭ** in more familiar speech, some speakers using **ĭ** in both styles. In the endings seen in **kind′ness, small′est, hors′es, Al′ice′s, urg′es, stat′ed**, and in -**en** of the words given above, the sound of **e** in the familiar type of educated speech has long been **ĭ**.

Some words, however, are pronounced with the neutral vowel in the best speech, as **claret** (**klăr′ĕt**), **diet** (**dī′ĕt**); so with -**e**- in a medial syllable, as in **piety** (**pī′ĕ·tĭ**), etc.

§ 31. **e** in **fern, err, herd, verge, er′mine, in·fer′** is identical with **û** in **ûrn** (§ 117), by which it is represented in respelling in this dictionary.

When an originally short **ĕ** is followed by **r** and a vowel, it usually retains the short **ĕ** sound, as in **vĕr′y, pĕr′il.**

§ 32. Cf. § 36. The sound **ẽ** in the unaccented syllables of **mak′er, ev′er, rev′er·ent, per·form′, in′fer·ence, cav′ern** — otherwise spelled as in **li′ar, e·lix′ir, ac′tor, au′gur, sur·prise′, pres′sure, glam′our, zeph′yr** — is the unaccented vowel corresponding to **û** (§ 117).

In a large number of words the unaccented sound **ẽr** is variously spelled with -**ar**, -**er**, -**ir**, -**or**, -**our**, -**ur**, -**yr**. The final syllables of **bak′er, li′ar, sail′or, au′gur, na′dir**, etc., are sounded with the same vowel **ẽr**, which is established by long usage, unaffected by the various spellings.

§ 33. **e** in **sergeant** = **ä**. **ĕ** before **r** final or followed by a consonant formerly often had the sound of **ä** (**ärm**). A large number of words like **smart, dark, starve, darling, barn, Clark**, etc., were formerly spelled with **er** and pronounced **ĕr** (as in **mĕrry**). In most such words the spelling has also been changed from **er** to **ar** along with the sound change from **ĕr** to **är**. But in some words the old spelling with **er** remains, as **Derby, Berkeley, Berkshire, clerk**, etc. In England the normal pronunciation (**där′bĭ, bärk′lĭ**, etc.) is still used in these words, but a recent spelling pronunciation with **ûr** is often substituted, esp. by those less familiar with them, — commonly so in America. **Heart, hearth, hearken** have a modified earlier spelling. In **Clark** the changed spelling has preserved the **ä**, while in **clerk** (the same word) spelling has won the day for **ûr** in America, and with some speakers in England. Several words have double spellings, and sometimes double pronunciations, as **clerk, Clark; person, parson; Kerr, Carr; sergeant, Sargent**; etc.

§ 34. **e** in **there, where**, spelled also as in **their**, etc. (§ 6), occurs only before **r**, and is identical with **â** in **câre**, by which it is represented in the respelling in this dictionary. It is indicated without respelling by **ê** (**thêre**).

§ 35. Unaccented **ė** in **ė·vade′, crė·ate′, dė·lin′ė·ate**, etc., is shorter than **ē** in **ēve**. This sound in formal or public speaking style is often a high but very brief **ē**, as in **ā′thė·ĭst**, but in colloquial speech, and often in formal speech, it regularly becomes indistinguishable in common words from **ĭ**, as in **ĭllu′sion**. In some familiar words the obscuration of **ė** goes even farther, to the neutral vowel **ĕ**, as in **society** (**sȯ·sī′ĕ·tĭ**), **necessary** (**nĕs′ĕ·sĕr′ĭ**).

§ 36. Unaccented **e** before **r**, as in **mak′ẽr**, is of the same quality as accented **e** in **fern**, but shorter and laxer. Cf. §§ 31, 32.

When **ẽ** is sounded by itself, with no **r** sound, it is the same sound, with slight variations, as some other unaccented vowels; as, **a** in **sofa, e** in **fallen, i** in **terrible**, etc.

Words containing the sound ẽr can be marked without respelling thus: **li′ăr, elix′ĭr, ac′tõr, zeph′ỹr**, etc.

§ 37. *ĕ* as in **concĕntrate, angĕl, momĕnt, quiĕt, systĕm** is obscured in varying degrees in ordinary speech. In the great majority of everyday words, unaccented **e** before **n** or **l**, and in many words in other unaccented position, as in **quiĕt, propriĕty**, is obscured to the neutral vowel in colloquial speech. But as in some cases like **concentrate** the **e** may have the sound of ĕ without artificial effect, the symbol italic *ĕ* may indicate a sound varying from ĕ to the neutral vowel — the latter in the great majority of words. Most words in final **-en** have the obscure vowel, as **freshĕn, fallĕn**, except a few words in which it is frequently pronounced **ĭn**, as **woolen (wo͝ol′ĭn)** (§ 30), or is quite silent, as in **bitten (bĭt′′n)** (§ 38).

§ 38. Unaccented **e** before **n** or **l** often disappears entirely, leaving **n** or **l** to form a syllable alone or with another consonant; as in **eaten (ēt′′n), garden (gär′d′n), model (mŏd′′l), vessel (vĕs′′l)**. Such syllabic consonants are indicated in Webster symbols by an apostrophe before the consonant. When the apostrophe is used, there is no vowel whatever in the syllable. In some words, however, the syllable may be pronounced either with or without a vowel, as in **deafen, freshen, bushel, chapel**, which are accordingly marked **dĕf′ĕn, -′n; chăp′ĕl, -′l**; etc. In many such cases the two pronunciations are possible where only one is given; and where both pronunciations are given for a main word, sometimes only one is given for its derivatives, though both are allowable.

§ 39. e *as a consonant.* When unaccented **e** is closely followed by another vowel having slightly more stress, there is formed a rising diphthong with a consonant **y** sound (or "consonantal" ĭ) as its first element. A preceding **t, d, s,** or **z** sound is often palatalized (esp. in the common words) by the **y** element to **ch, j,** or **sh**, as in **righteous (rī′chŭs), grandeur (grăn′dūr**; *colloq.* **-jẽr**), **ocean (ō′shăn)**. In some cases ē remains a syllabic vowel, as in **Gideon (gĭd′ē·ŭn)**; but often either pronunciation may occur, as in **hideous (hĭd′ē·ŭs; hĭd′yŭs), piteous (pĭt′ē·ŭs; pĭt′yŭs)**; but after **w (aqueous)** or a consonant + **r (vitreous)** the **y** sound is not heard **(ā′kwē·ŭs, vĭt′rē·ŭs)**, though it may occur after **r** alone, as in **calcareous (kăl·kâr′ē·ŭs; -kâr′yŭs)**. Cf. § 58. See § 121.

§ 40. e *silent.* **e** is frequently silent at the end of a word. Final **e** is now written: (1) to show the vowel long, as **cāne, mēte, hōpe** (cf. **căn, mĕt, hŏp**); (2) to show a preceding **c** or **g** "soft," as in **lace, rage** (cf. **lac, rag**); (3) to show **l** or **r** syllabic after other consonants, as in **apple (ăp′′l)**; (4) to follow certain consonants or groups that are not usually written at the end, as in **live, nurse, pulse, bronze**; (5) for various traditional reasons (as a former long vowel, etc.), as in **one, done, fertile**, etc.

The **e** in **-ed** of the past and past participles of verbs is now silent except after **t** or **d (stated, needed**, § 30), though sometimes sounded in poetry or solemn style (§ 25). It is also silent in the ending **-es** of verbs **(goes)** and of nouns **(stones)**, except after sibilants **(tosses, horses**, etc.; see § 30).

ee

§ 41. ee usually spells ē (ēve), as in **see, meet**, etc. Before **r** it is lowered to ē̤ **(hē̤re)**, as in **deer, cheer**, etc. (§ 27). In **been**, it has been shortened to **bĭn**, the standard stressed and unstressed form in America. Many English speakers use stressed **bēn** and unstressed **bĭn**; others use **bēn** or **bĭn** for both. In some other words also **ee** has been shortened to ĭ, as in **breeches, steelyards, sick, rick** (formerly **seek, reek**), though spelling pronunciation tends to restore ē in those still spelled **ee**.

ei, ey

§ 42. ei spells ē (ēve), as in **conceive, leisure**; ā (āle), as in **deign, rein**, etc.; before **r**, â (câre), as in **heir, their**. When final, the spelling is usually **ey**, as in **obey, they**, etc. Unaccented **ei, ey** are sounded ĭ, as in **forfeit (fôr′fĭt), sovereign, money (mŭn′ĭ)**. Words containing this digraph when sounded ē or ā may be marked without respelling as in **de·çēive′, rāin**.

For **eu, ew**, see ū.

F

§ 43. f as in **fame, fly, left, cuff**, etc., is the voiceless lip-teeth fricative consonant, made by forcing the breath out between the lower lip and the upper teeth. Its voiced correlative is **v (vine)**. It is also spelled in native English words with **gh**, as in **laugh, cough**. In Greek derivatives it is spelled **ph**, as in **phantom, photograph, telephone**, etc., and, by imitation, in **nephew**, for older **nevew, neffewe**. In **of** the **f** is pronounced **v**.

G

This letter spells three sounds:

§ 44. (1) "Hard" **g**, as in **gay, go, egg**, the voiced tongue-back velar stop corresponding to **k**, its voiceless correlative, and to **ng**, the voiced tongue-back velar nasal continuant. All three are tongue-back velar sounds, the back of the tongue, by contact with the soft palate, or velum, closing the air passage through the mouth. For **g** and **k** the nasal passage is also closed by the raised velum, while for **ng** it is open.

In modern English **g** is "hard": (a) Always when final: **beg, drug**; and in derivatives from such words: **begging, druggist**, where **g** is doubled to distinguish between, e.g., **ragged (răg′ĕd)** and **raged (rājd)**. (b) Before **a, o, u**, or a consonant in the same syllable: **game, go, gun, lingual, bags** (except in the British **gaol, gaoler**). (c) In words of Germanic origin before **e** and **i**: **get, give**, and in some words of doubtful origin, as **bogy**; and usually when doubled **(muggy, buggy, lagging)**. (d) In a few Hebrew words, as **ge′rah, Gideon**. For **gz** and **gzh** spelled **x**, see under **X**.

"Hard" **g** is also spelled **gh (ghost), gu (guard, guest), -gue (plague)**. It is indicated in respelling by plain **g**, as in **exist (ĕg·zĭst′)**, and without respelling by **g̅ (g̅ŭn)**.

§ 45. (2) "Soft" **g = j** (§ 59). **g** usually is soft in Latin or Romance derivatives before **e, i, y: gem, engine**. At the end of a word this sound is usually spelled **-ge, -dge (rage, judge)**; at the end of a syllable also by **dg (badg′er, judg′ing)**. Like voiceless **tch, dg** occurs after short vowels **(edge**, etc.). "Soft" **g** does not begin native words. It is respelled with **j** in this dictionary, and may be represented without respelling by **ġ**, as in **ġem, enġine**.

§ 46. (3) **g** as in French **mirage = zh**. This sound occurs in a few recent French loan words not fully Anglicized; as **rouge (ro͞ozh), garage**, etc.

§ 47. g is now silent before final **m** or **n (diaphragm, sign, benign)**; inflectional endings do not affect it: **diaphragming (-frăm′ĭng)**; but in such derivatives as **diaphragmatic, signal, benignity, g** is sounded **(-frăg·măt′ĭk, sĭg′năl)**. It is also silent initially before **n (gnat, gnaw)**. For **g** in the digraph **ng**, see § 68.

gh

§ 48. gh in **aghast, ghastly, ghost** is a useless spelling for "hard" **g (go)**. In other English words **gh** has either become silent **(high, bought, caught, eight, bough)** or changed to **f (draught, laugh, cough, rough)**. In **hough, gh** is sounded **k**. In Irish **lough**, etc., **gh** is like Scottish **ch**.

H

§ 49. h in **hate, home, behave**, etc., is often called the aspirate, because it is made with a breathing sound. It is usually voiceless, but sometimes voiced when between vowels. The **h** sound occurs only at the beginning of syllables, and before vowels, or **w**, as in **where (hwâr)**, or **y**, as in **huge (hyo͞oj)**, never at the end of syllables or words.

In native English words at the beginning of accented syllables, even if only slightly accented, **h** is sounded in standard English whenever it is spelled **(har′dy, be·hoove′, green′house′)**.

Words that came from Old French into English had no **h** sound, though the **h** was often spelled, as **hospital, host, exhort, herb, humble, humor, hour**, etc. In the 18th century there was a gradual adoption of the **h** sound where it was spelled in such words. The most popular of the words, however, as **honest, honor, heir, hour**, were in too frequent use to gain the *h*, and are still without it. Others still waver in general usage, as **herb, hostler, homage, humble, humor, hotel**. Those that lost the letter **h** are still without the sound, as **able** (OF. **(h)able**), **ostler, arbor** "bower."

The **h** sound has been dropped at the beginning of most unaccented syllables, as in **shepherd (shĕp′ẽrd), Durham (dûr′ăm), forehead (fŏr′ĕd), vehement (vē′ē·mĕnt), vehicle (vē′ĭ·k′l)**, etc. In many such words spelling pronunciation has partly restored the **h** sound.

In the unstressed forms of **he** the **h** is regularly silent in ordinary speech, as in **They said (h)e would; They met (h)er; I saw (h)is father**; etc. At the beginning of longer words, as **histor′ical, hered′itar′y, h** is commonly pronounced. But usage and sentence rhythm vary, so that either **a** or **an** is written before such words: **a historical, an hereditary**, etc.

I

§ 50. ī as in **īce, tīme, chīld, mīght′y** is commonly called "long **i**." It is also spelled as in **vie, rye, height, eye, aisle, aye** "yes," **sky, buy, choir**. This diphthong ī varies somewhat in both its elements. The last part is often nearer to ĕ than to ĭ. The diphthong in standard American and British speech is virtually the same, with the first element like the **ȧ** of **ȧsk** as sounded in New England and in many British local dialects. A form with the first element the **ä** in **fäther** is also common in both countries.

§ 51. "Long **i**" when not under the main accent, as in **ī·de′a, bī·ol′ogy, dī·am′eter**, is still a diphthong, but somewhat briefer than when fully accented.

§ 52. Accented ĭ, as in **bĭt, ĭll, pĭt′y, ad·mĭt′**, is also spelled as in **sieve, English, pretty, been (bĭn), breeches, threepence (thrĭp′ĕns), women (wĭm′ĕn), busy, build, nymph, hymnal**. This sound is commonly called "short **i**," and is the high-front-lax vowel corresponding to the high-front-tense ē (ēve) (§ 26). The same sound occurs before **r** and a vowel in words like **mĭr′ror, lỹr′ic**.

§ 53. Unaccented ĭ occurs in such words as **hab′ĭt, cab′ĭn, fam′ĭne, ĭn·tend′, trag′ĭ·cal**, etc. When final, its spelling is changed to **-y (cop′y, hap′py)** or **-ey (mon′ey, hon′ey)**. It is represented by various other spellings, as in **senate (sĕn′ĭt), cottage (kŏt′ĭj), surface (-fĭs)** (§ 13), **added (ăd′ĕd, ăd′ĭd), horses (hôr′sĕz, hôr′sĭz), smallest (smôl′ĕst, smôl′ĭst), mountain (moun′tĭn)** (§ 30), **foreign (fŏr′ĭn), circuit (sûr′kĭt), mischief (mĭs′chĭf), guinea (gĭn′ĭ), coffee (kŏf′ĭ), pigeon (pĭj′ŭn, pĭj′ĭn), always (ôl′wāz, ôl′wĭz), carriage (kăr′ĭj)**, etc.

The ĭ of unaccented syllables is not always identical with ĭ of accented **(bĭt′ẽr)**. In America the tendency of final unaccented ĭ or of ĭ immediately preceding another vowel is either to remain like accented **ĭ (bĭt)**, or to vary to a higher tongue position toward ē. Phoneticians generally, however, use the symbol ĭ (or an equivalent) for practical transcription of both accented and unaccented ĭ.

ĭ

§ 54. In longer words unaccented short **i** before an accented syllable **(as′pi·ra′tion)** or after it **(pos′si·ble)** very commonly is retracted further toward the neutral vowel (*ȧ* in **so′fȧ**). But there is great variation in good usage, and since many speakers sound ĭ where others use a sound nearer to *ȧ* in **sofȧ**, and since the same speaker often uses either sound in different styles of speech, an italic "short **i**" (*ĭ*) is used in this dictionary as an intentionally ambiguous symbol indicating that both pronunciations of words so marked are in general good use in England and America. Thus the symbol *ĭ* is used to mark such words as **char*ĭ*ty, van*ĭ*ty, poss*ĭ*ble** (and other words in **-ible**), **princ*ĭ*ple, pol*ĭ*cy, sim*ĭ*lar, an*ĭ*mal, priv*ĭ*lege, Cal*ĭ*fornia, anonymous (-*ĭ*·mŭs)**, etc.; and occasionally in initial or final syllables, as in **d*ĭ*vide, Apr*ĭ*l**, etc.

In a difference so slight and so variable as this, it is difficult to represent usage exactly in every word concerned. The marking here is conservative, ĭ being used only if a pronunciation with ȧ is in unquestioned good use beside ĭ. In many words, therefore, where the symbol ĭ instead of ĭ is used, some speakers would probably pronounce ȧ. Different derivatives of the same stem are not always pronounced alike; thus many speakers who pronounce the **i** in **eradicate** like ȧ, would pronounce it as ĭ in **radical**. Moreover, the words differ according to style: some words have ĭ only in very careful speech (as **polĭcy**), while others may have it also in colloquial speech (as **edĭtor**). In general, the more common words are marked with ĭ (as also certain common endings, as **-ĭty, -ĭble**, even in rarer words), while rarer words are usually marked with ĭ.

§ **55. i** *silent*. In certain unaccented syllables, especially in colloquial speech, **i** often becomes silent before **l** or **n**, which thus becomes a syllable alone or with another consonant; cf. similarly silent **e** (§ 38). Thus in **civil, devil, evil, pupil, basin, cousin, Latin, raisin,** this is regular in colloquial speech (**sĭv′′l, ē′v′l, pū′p′l**, etc.); and in some of them, in all styles of speech (**dĕv′′l, bā′s′n, kŭz′′n**); and likewise when an ĭ sound is otherwise spelled, as in **certain** (**sûr′tĭn; -t′n**), **garden** (**gär′d′n**, occas. **gär′dĭn**); more rarely in initial syllables, as in **sincere** (**sĭn·sēr′; s′n·sēr′**). Likewise in many medial syllables, wherever the phonetic surroundings favor syllabic consonants; as in **easily** (**ēz′ĭ·lĭ; ēz′′l·ĭ**), **ordinary** (**ôr′dĭ·nĕr′ĭ; ôr′d′n·ĕr′ĭ**).

§ **56. -ile, -ile.** The ending **-ile** in words from French or Latin is now pronounced sometimes **ĭl** and sometimes **īl**. The prevailing tendency in England is toward **īl** (**agīle, fertīle**), and in America to **ĭl** (**agĭle, fertĭle**). But there are exceptions, as **gentile** (*n.*) with **īl** in both countries; both **ĭl** and **īl** are heard in America in **infantile, juvenile, mercantile, versatile.** (**Camomile, crocodile, exile, reconcile,** with **īl** in both countries, contain a different suffix.) Some of the more familiar words lose the **i** sound in America (see § 55), as **fertile** (**fûr′tĭl; -t′l**), **futile** (**fū′tĭl; -t′l**), **hostile**, etc.

-ine. The suffix **-ine** of adjectives and nouns, derived directly or through French from Latin **-īnus** and **-ĭnus**, is variously pronounced in English **īn, ĭn,** or **ēn**, partly according to its Latin source, partly by French analogy, partly by English rules of spelling and position of the accent, but chiefly by the analogy of familiar forms; e.g., with **īn** (like **divīne, turpentīne**), with **ĭn** (like **genuĭne, doctrĭne**), or with **ēn** (like **marïne**). No rule without exceptions can be laid down, many words varying in pronunciation with different speakers. British English shows some tendency to **īn** where American has **ĭn**. When it is desired to represent the **ē** sound of **i**, as in **machine, regime**, etc., without respelling, two dots may be placed over the letter: **machïne**, etc.

-ine, -ide. The endings **-ine** and **-ide** in chemical terms are variously pronounced. In the case of **-ine**, usage in America is divided between **ēn** and **ĭn**, very few American chemists using **īn**. The **ēn** pronunciation now distinctly prevails. The pronunciation **īn** prevails among British chemists, but is by no means the only pronunciation in use in England. In the case of **-ide**, especially in those words which have been long in the language, usage decidedly favors **īd**, though **ĭd** is used by many and in a few words, as **amide**, prevails.

In terms ending in **-ine** and **-ide** the pronunciation often varies even in the mouth of the same speaker, and this condition is especially true of teachers, who often are obliged to pronounce such words in the way that seems most likely to avoid confusion of the endings.

§ **57.** Stressed **i** before **r** final or followed by another consonant, as in **bird, fir, vir′gin**, etc., is the same sound as **e** in **fern** (**û**) and **û** in **ûrn**. (Cf. § 31.) In this dictionary it is respelled **û**, as in **stir** (**stûr**).

Unaccented, as in **na′dir, ta′pir, elix′ir**, it is the same sound as **ẽ** in **mak′ẽr**, by which symbol it is respelled. Without respelling, both the stressed and unstressed sounds may be marked **ĩ** (**stĩr, na′dĩr**).

For **ir** + a vowel (**miracle, mirror**, etc.), see § 117.

§ **58. i** *consonant*. The consonant y sound, as in **yet**, may be regarded as an unaccented ĭ (or ē) sound gliding quickly into a following vowel, as in such words as **Indian**, which may be pronounced **ĭn′dĭ·ăn**, or, more rapidly, **ĭn′dyăn**. The increase in speed, with decrease in sonority, converts the vowel ĭ into the consonant **y**, and the two syllabic vowels **ĭ·ă** into a rising diphthong **yă**. Some words are, however, fairly well fixed in usage with **ĭ**, as **serious** (**sēr′ĭ·ŭs**), esp. where **y** would be hard to pronounce, as after a consonant + **r**, as in **pedestrian** (**-dĕs′trĭ·ăn**), or after a **w** sound, as in **colloquial** (**-lō′kwĭ·ăl**) (cf. § 39). Others usually have **y**, as **opinion** (**ō·pĭn′yŭn**), **familiar** (**fȧ·mĭl′yẽr**), etc. Though no exceptionless rules can be stated, there is some tendency in America to keep the syllabic ĭ (which is the older) and in England to change it to nonsyllabic **y**, as in **audience** (**ô′dĭ·ĕns; ôd′yĕns**); but sometimes vice versa, as in **collier** (*Am.* **kŏl′yẽr**; *Brit.* **kŏl′ĭ·ẽr; -yẽr**). The same variation in sound between ĭ and **y** applies to **ē** in similar position, as in **lineal** (**lĭn′ē·ăl; lĭn′yăl**), etc. See § 39.

For **ia** in **carriage**, see § 13.

J

§ **59. j** as in **jar, jest, jute, proj′ect**, etc., is an affricate, or consonantal diphthong, nearly like **d** + **zh**. These two elements blend into a composite sound in which both are somewhat changed. The sound is the voiced correlative of **ch** in **chin** (§ 21). It is also spelled with **g** (**register, magic, clergy**), **ge** (**vengeance, page**), **dg** (**judgment, lodging**), **dge** (**judge, lodge**), **ch** (**Greenwich**, § 21 (2)), **di** (**soldier**), and **dj** (in Oriental words, as **hadj, hadji**). In **hallelujah**, **j** has the sound of **y**, as in Latin and German. In some partly Anglicized words from French, **j** has its modern French sound **zh**, as in **déjeuner** (**dā′zhû′nā′**), etc. See also § 118.

K

§ **60. k** as in **kite, skill, ark, ink, oak** is the voiceless tongue-back velar stop, corresponding to its voiced correlative **g** (§ 44), and to the voiced tongue-back nasal continuant **ng** (**sing**, § 68). All three are tongue-back velar sounds, the back of the tongue making contact with the velum, or soft palate. The **k** sound is also spelled as in **call, account, back, biscuit** (**-kĭt**), **choir, bacchanal, acquire, liquor, queen, hough** (**hŏk**). **k** is also a part of the sounds of **x** in **tax** (**tăks**), **luxury** (**lŭk′shŏŏ·rĭ**), **except** (**ĕk·sĕpt′**).

For excrescent **k**, as in **strength** (**strĕngkth**), see § 68. Initial **k** before **n** is now silent, as in **know, knot, knee.**

A small capital ᴋ is used in the respelling in this dictionary to indicate any of certain palatal or velar fricative sounds, often wrongly called "gutturals," which occur in German, Scottish, Dutch, and other languages. These sounds are of two typical classes: a palatal (front) or velar (back) voiceless fricative. The palatal sound results from a strong current of voiceless breath between the front (hard) palate and the front of the tongue (not the point) pressed close to it. It can be approximated by placing the tip of the tongue behind the lower teeth, pressing the front part toward the front palate, and then whispering forcibly the word **he**. This is the sound of **ch** in German **ich**, hence called the "**Ich–laut**," occurring after consonants and front vowels and initially.

The velar (back) voiceless fricative is made with the back of the tongue pressed close to the roof of the mouth. It may be learned by first pronouncing the "Ich-laut" as above till it is familiar, and then passing from **ĭch** to **äch** with similar forcible whisper and upward and backward pressure of the back part of the tongue. Another method is to begin to say **lock**, taking care not to let the **k** quite cut off the current of breath, continuing the loose **k** sound with a "hawking" sound. This is called the "**Ach–laut**," and occurs in German after back vowels, as **a, o, u.**

These two sounds are familiar in Scottish, the first after front vowels, as in **heich** "high," and the second after back vowels, as in **loch**. Both front and back **ch** sounds are indicated in the respelling by small capital ᴋ, one symbol being sufficient, since the front or back sound in nearly all cases will automatically be determined by the preceding vowel.

L

§ **61. l** as in **leave, low, clay, ill**, etc., is a so-called liquid consonant, formed with the tongue point on the teethridge as for **t, d, n**, the nasal passage being closed and voiced breath passing out at one, or more commonly both, free sides of the tongue. Hence the name **lateral consonant** — usually bilateral, sometimes unilateral. Being a tongue-point alveolar sound (like **t, d, n**), **l** precedes or follows any of these sounds without removal of the tongue point from the teethridge, as in **salt, battle; sold, saddle; coolness, channel** (**chăn′′l**).

§ **62.** "**Clear l**" and "**dark l.**" In sounding **l**, since the sides and back of the tongue are somewhat free to assume various positions while the point remains in contact with the teethridge, there is a large range of variation in the acoustic resonance, so that this consonant may take the "color" of various vowels. The term "**clear l**" has been used to indicate an **l** sound having the resonance of a front vowel **ē, ĭ, ā, ĕ, â, ă,** and "**dark l**" to indicate an **l** with the resonance of a back vowel **ä, ô, ō, ŏŏ, ōō**, or of one of the central vowels **û, ẽ, ŭ**; i. e., **l**'s formed with the tip of the tongue in the **l** position on the teethridge while the rest of the tongue approximates the position of one of these vowels. "Clear **l**" occurs before vowels (**lily, loose**); and "dark **l**" before consonants (**shield**), and when final (**feel**) or syllabic (**battle**).

English initial **l** is "clearer" than final **l**. But even initial **l** in English is not so "clear" as French **l**, which is "clear" in all positions, all "dark **l**'s" having become the vowel **u** or having disappeared in older French. In America, sometimes initial **l** is noticeably "dark."

The acoustic difference between a final dark **l** and **l** preceded by the neutral vowel is not easily perceptible. Hence the difference of sound in **real** (**rē′ăl**) and **reel** (**rēl**), or in **ideal** (**ī·dē′ăl**) and **deal** (**dēl**), is not always observed in ordinary speech. Cf. also **vial** and **vile**.

In certain combinations the **l**, originally sounded, has regularly become silent, as in **would, alms, salmon, half, talk, folk**, etc.

§ **63. l** often forms a syllable by itself, as in **battle** (**băt′′l**), **channel** (**chăn′′l**), **trouble** (**trŭb′′l**); or with other consonants, as in **ruffled** (**rŭf′′ld**), **handled** (**hăn′d′ld**). Some words may be pronounced with either syllabic or nonsyllabic **l**, as **struggling** (**strŭg′′l·ĭng; strŭg′lĭng**), **awfully** (**ô′f′l·ĭ; ô′flĭ**).

M

§ **64. m** as in **me, smile, lamp, drachm** is the voiced lip nasal continuant, formed by bringing the lips together, as for **b** and **p**, at the same time lowering the soft palate, and thus allowing the voice to pass into or through the nasal passage. All three sounds (**m, b, p**) are made with closed lips, and are hence called labials.

§ **65. m** may form a syllable by itself, as in the colloquial expression "**Stop 'em**" (**stŏp′′m**); or with other consonants, as in **chasmed** (**kăz′md**). **m** is, however, less commonly syllabic than **n** and **l**, and in many words in which the spelling suggests syllabic **m**, a vowel often actually intervenes, though not spelled, as in **chasm, prism, spasm,** and the numerous words like **feudalism**. Cf. §§ 63, 67.

N

§ **66. n** as in **none, knit, canny, inn**, etc., is the voiced tongue-point alveolar nasal continuant corresponding to the voiced tongue-point stop **d** and the voiceless tongue-point stop **t**. All three sounds are made with the tongue point on the alveolar ridge (teethridge), and are hence sometimes called alveolar consonants, or, less accurately, dentals.

After **m**, a final **n** is silent (**hymn, solemn**), but before a vowel in derivatives like **hymnology, solemnity**, etc., the **n** is usually sounded (**hĭm·nŏl′ō·jĭ**, etc.). Before a consonant the **n** of **mn** is always silent, as in **condemns, solemnly**. Usage is divided in the participles **damned, damning**, the familiar pronunciation being without **n**; or usage is inconsistent, as in **limner** (**lĭm′nẽr**) beside **condemner** (**kŏn·dĕm′ẽr; -dĕm′nẽr**). In **kiln, limekiln**, the historical pronunciation **kĭl** is used by those familiar with kilns, but **kĭln** is pronounced by some others.

§ **67. n** may form a syllable by itself, as in **cotton** (**kŏt′′n**), **often** (**ŏf′′n**), **prison** (**prĭz′′n**); or with other consonants, as in **garden** (**gär′d′n**), **pardoned** (**pär′d′nd**).

ɴ. A small capital ɴ is used in the respelling in this dictionary to indicate that a *preceding vowel* is pronounced as a *nasal*, as in French **bon** (**bôɴ**). The nasal passage from the throat must be open, but no **n** is pronounced. The tongue point makes no contact with the upper teethridge, as it must do to sound **n**.

ng

§ **68.** The digraph **ng**, as in **sing, singing**, represents the voiced tongue-back velar nasal continuant, corresponding to the voiced tongue-back stop **g**, and the voiceless tongue-back stop **k**. The tongue back touches the velum (soft palate) for all three sounds. In sounding **ng** the contact of the tongue back with the velum prevents the voiced breath from issuing through the mouth, and, the velum being lowered, the sound passes out through the nose.

Though commonly represented by two letters **ng**, this sound is a simple nasal sound, neither **n** nor **g** nor a combination of them.

When followed by a **g** or a **k** sound, **ng** is also spelled with **n**, as in **anger (ăng′gẽr), ink (ĭngk), anxious (ăngk′shŭs), uncle (ŭng′k′l), anchor (ăng′kẽr), conquer (kŏng′kẽr)**. It is represented by **ng** in respelling **(fĭng′gẽr)**, and without respelling by **n̲ (fĭn̲′gẽr, ĭn̲k)**.

The letter **n** now invariably represents the **ng** sound when before a **k** or **g** sound in the same syllable. When **k** or **g** follows in the next syllable, usage varies somewhat. A few words suggest the rule that **ng** is sounded when its syllable is accented; as **con′gress (kŏng′grĕs), con′grega′tion (kŏng′grē·gā′shŭn)** beside **con·gres′sional (kŏn·grĕsh′ŭn·ăl), congrat′ulate (kŏn·grăt′-)**, or **bron′chia (brŏng′kĭ·ȧ)** beside **bronchi′tis (brŏn·kī′tĭs)**; but the rule has many exceptions; as **con′crete (kŏn′krēt), in′crease (ĭn′krēs)**, or **bron·chi′tis** (also **brŏng·kī′tĭs**). In many words usage varies, as in **conclave (kŏn′-; kŏng′-), con′cord, mel′anchol′y**, etc.

Between **ng** and certain other consonants, a **k** or **g** sound is present or absent with different speakers, regardless of the spelling. Thus, **k** is sounded by some in **anxious (ăngk′shŭs), length (lĕngkth), strength (strĕngkth), instinct (ĭn′stĭngkt)**, or **g** in **anxiety (ăngg·zī′ĕ·tĭ)**, and by others it is omitted **(ăng′shŭs, lĕngth**, etc.).

O

§ **69. ō** as in **ōld, nōte, ō′ver**, etc., is the so-called "long **o**" sound. It is also spelled as in **oh, roam, foe, shoul′der, grow, owe, sew, yeo′man, beau, haut′boy, brooch**. When accented, **ō** is usually a diphthong in standard English. It begins with the mid-back-tense vowel, a "pure" **ō** sound, and glides to a vowel resembling **o͝o (go͝od)**. In the speech of South England, however, the prevailing tendency is to begin the **ō** sound with the tongue farther forward toward the central position.

In America the diphthongal character is less marked. Before voiceless consonants, as in **note, oak**, the **ō** is often nearly or quite pure, without the **o͝o** sound, or vanish. In any case, the beginning of the American sound, like that of northerly England, is a back vowel, not advanced, though sometimes slightly lowered toward **ô (ôrb)**. The one symbol **ō** is here used to indicate all standard varieties.

§ **70.** When long **ō** occurs before **r**, it has as its vanish the neutral vowel **ẽ**, representing the fore-glide of the **r**, which is slight in America. Thus the word **more** has the diphthong **(ōẽ) (mōẽr)**. This applies to a large group of words that had a long **ô** (occasionally **o͞o**) in Middle English, as **board, sword, court, pork, borne, coarse, course, before, door, oar, story**, and many others. These are to be distinguished from another large group now pronounced with **ô**, as **border, horse, lord**, etc., which had a short **ŏ** in Middle English. In the prevailing speech of South England these two classes of words have fallen together, both having the sound **ô**. This is a recent change. In all other parts of England there are cultivated speakers who keep such words apart in sound.

In the pronunciation of America as a whole the distinction between **hoarse** and **horse** is still made naturally. It is, however, disappearing in the speech of some in America who are influenced by Southern British practice. The **ō** sound in **hoarse** is not, however, identical with that in **hōpe**, but it is acoustically much nearer to that of **hōpe** than to that of **hôrse**. Some speakers also use a sound midway between **ō** and **ô** for both groups of words.

§ **71.** The sound of **ô** as in **ôrb, lôrd, ôr′der** is also spelled with **a** in **all, talk, swarm**; by **au** in **fault, haul, caught**; by **aw** in **law, dawn, awful**; by **ou** in **fought, trough**; by **oa** in **broad**; by **ag** in **Magdalen (môd′lĭn)**; by **i** in **memoir (mĕm′wôr)**; and by **u** in one pronunciation of **sure (shôr**, § 84). This vowel is described as the low-back-tense rounded vowel, which may be long, as in **law**, or relatively short, as in **auspi′cious**. But its articulation is not uniform. In South England the typical sound is made with the back of the tongue in a low (but not the lowest) position and decidedly rounded lips (nearly or quite as closely as for **ō**), the British sound to an American ear often suggesting (but not reaching) a pure **ō**. The American sound is made with less lip rounding, often very slight — only a little compression at the corners — in which case a little higher position of the tongue and jaw helps to distinguish the **ô** sound from the low-back unrounded **ä (ärm)**.

The sound **ô** is respelled in this dictionary with **ô (ôrb)**; when spelled with **a, au, aw**, it may be indicated without respelling by **a̤ (ca̤ll, fa̤ult, la̤w)**.

§ **72.** When **o** is followed by final **r (for, abhor)**, or by **r** and a consonant **(horse, forty)**, its normal sound is **ô** when it is not **ō** as in **fōrd** (§ 70), or is not obscured by lack of stress as in **actor (ăk′tẽr)**. When the **r** sound is followed by a vowel, as in **moral, sorry**, its regular sound is **ŏ (mŏr′ăl, sŏr′ĭ)** if it is not **ō** as in **glory (glō′rĭ)**. But derivatives from words like **abhôr (abhorring**, etc.), although the **r (rr)** is followed by a vowel, usually keep the **ô** of the stem **(abhôrring, abhôrrer)**. In America this commonly is extended also to less immediate derivatives, such as **abhôrrent, abhôrrence**. But in British use and sometimes in American, these are pronounced with **ŏ (abhŏrrent, abhŏrrence)**.

§ **73. ŏ** as in **nŏt, ŏdd, bŏg, dŏff, prŏp′er, prŏb′able**, spelled also with **(w)a-** as in **want, wan′der, wash, watch**, is commonly called "short **o**." As now pronounced in South England, this is a low-back-lax rounded vowel, the tongue being in the position lowest and farthest back, and the lips having "open rounding," a degree of aperture only slightly less than the open unrounded position for **ä** in **fä′ther**. Since Southern British **ô** has a higher tongue position and is much more closely lip-rounded, the sounds **ŏ** and **ô** are there quite distinctly different sounds, not the short and long of the same sound.

The **ŏ** sound is sometimes found in syllables with little stress, as in **car′bon, can′not, ma′cron**.

The rounded **ŏ** sound described above is not in general use in America. It is used by a considerable part of the inhabitants of eastern New England, by many in New York City, and to a considerable extent in the South. Words historically containing "short **o**" in general American pronunciation are mostly pronounced either with **ä** or with **ô**, not with the intermediate **ŏ**. Some of these variations are discussed in the following section. It is convenient to represent the "short **o**" by **ŏ**, which may thus indicate, for American pronunciation, either the true "short **o**" or the unrounded variety **ä**.

§ **74. ŏ̂.** The following words containing a voiceless fricative (except **sh**), viz., **off, oft, often, croft, loft, soft, soften, cough, trough**; (a) **cross, loss, toss, cost, frost, lost; broth, cloth, froth**, are prevailingly pronounced with **ô** in southern England, though **ŏ** is also heard. In **moss, moth, coffee, offer, office, officer, ô** is also heard there, but **ŏ** prevails; while only **ŏ**, as a rule, is pronounced in **doff, scoff, boss, dross, floss, gloss, Goth, profit, prophet, accost, Boston, gossip, gospel, hostile, possible**, and most other two-syllable words of the group. In Southern British also words with **au** (= **ô**) before **s (Austin, Austria, austere)** are often sounded with **ŏ (ŏs′tĭn**, etc.).

In the most general type of American pronunciation the **ô** sound prevails in all the one-syllable words above (except **doff** (rare) and **Goth** (cf. **Gŏthic**)), and also in the words **coffee, offer, office, officer, Boston**. But it must be remembered that American **ô** is not the closely rounded, **ō**-like vowel of British, being, in fact, not far from British **ŏ**. In the other two-syllable words the unrounded **ŏ** (= **ä**) prevails. But with those speakers in America who normally or frequently use a true **ŏ**, the latter sound is used in some or all of these words.

The variation in the sound of **o** in this class of words is indicated in this dictionary by the combined symbol **ŏ̂**, suggesting either **ô** or **ŏ**.

In another group of words having "short **o**" followed by an **r** sound (spelled **r** or **rr**), as **moral, sorry**, etc., usage in England is fairly uniform in the use of **ŏ**. In America the influence of the **r** (often slightly rounded) has made **ŏ** or **ô** in these words much commoner than the unrounded **ŏ (ä)**, which is rare in these words. The more general sound in America in these is an **ô** of moderate length and more like **ŏ** than is British **ô**, — as in **sorry, moral, forest**, etc. The same tendency is seen in the **wa-** words, as **warrant, warrior, quarrel, quarry**, the most general American pronunciation being with **ô**, though **ŏ** is fairly frequent. When the **r** is final **(war)** or followed by a consonant **(warm)**, the pronunciation is everywhere **ô (wôr, wôrm)**, etc., just as in **abhôr, hôrse**.

In a group of other words with **o**, as **bob, knob, rob, sob; God, rod; bog, dog, fog, frog, hog, log, catalogue; doll**, American usage is quite variable. The most frequent pronunciations are with the unrounded **ŏ (bäg, näb**, etc.), except in **dog, log, catalogue**, which more commonly have **ô**. In all these words, the true **ŏ** is, of course, proper, but most American speakers to whom the true **ŏ** is not native are likely to pronounce **ô** in attempting **ŏ**.

In words like **long, song, tongs, wrong**, and in **gone**, British speech has **ŏ**, but the more general American pronunciation is **lông, gône**, etc. In these words the unrounded **ŏ** is seldom heard.

§ **75. o** in **ado, do, lose, move, prove, to, tomb, two, who** is an occasional spelling for the **o͞o** sound **(fo͞od)**, which is represented in respelling in this dictionary by **o͞o**, or may be indicated without respelling by **o̤ (do̤)**.

§ **76. o** in **wolf, woman (wo͝om′ăn), Worcester (wo͝os′tẽr)**, etc., is an occasional spelling for **o͝o (fo͝ot)**, respelled in this dictionary with **o͝o**. It may be indicated without respelling by **o̦ (wo̦lf)**.

§ **77. o** in **son (sŭn), come, dove, front, honey, London, some, tongue, won**, etc., spells the **ŭ** sound **(sŭn)**. In some of the rarer words the **ŏ** or **ō** sound has been adopted from the spelling (§ 3), as in **cŏmbat, constable (kŭn′stȧ·b′l; kŏn′-), wont (wŭnt; wōnt)**. The **ŭ** sound of **o** may be marked without respelling by **ȯ (sȯn)**.

§ **78. o** in **work, worm, worse, attorney**, etc. (chiefly in native words after **w**), is equivalent to **û** in **ûrn**. It may be indicated without respelling by **ŏ (wŏrk)**.

§ **79. ȯ** as in the unaccented syllables of **ȯ·bey′, pȯ·et′ic, e′gȯ·ism**, etc., represents a shorter variety of **ō** sound, without the vanish, or **o͝o** sound, occurring in unaccented syllables. It is also used to represent a more obscure vowel sound, in ordinary colloquial speech becoming the neutral vowel **ŭ**, as in **anat′ȯmy, biol′ȯgy, pȯta′to**, etc.

§ **80. ŏ** in **cŏm·pact′, cŏn·form′** represents an unaccented sound which ranges from a full **ŏ** sound **(stŏp)** to the obscure neutral vowel in nation **(nā′shŭn)**. It occurs in a very large number of words which in ordinary speech regularly have the neutral vowel, as in **ŏccur, cŏnnect, recŏllect**, etc., which are marked with **ŏ** to show that the **ŏ** sound has been obscured.

§ **81. o** as in the unaccented syllables of **nation (nā′shŭn), lem′on, hand′some, gal′lop, big′ot**, etc., always has the obscure sound, the neutral vowel. The symbol **ŭ** is used in this dictionary to respell **u** or **o** when the full **ŭ** or **ŏ** sound is not a normal pronunciation. Compare the two **o**'s in **oblivion (ŏb·lĭv′ĭ·ŭn)**.

For **o** in **actor** = **ẽ**, see §§ 32, 36.

In some words **o** may become quite silent, being replaced by a syllabic consonant, as in **button (bŭt′′n), idol (ī′d′l), pardoner (pär′d′n·ẽr)**; or with loss of a syllable, as in **reckoning (rĕk′nĭng), chocolate (chŏk′lĭt)**.

oi and oy

§ **82. oi** in **oil, boil**, etc., is a diphthong consisting of **ô + ĭ**, the elements being pronounced in a single wave of sound **(ô′ĭ)**. It is used in the respelling always with this value.

oi sometimes represents other sounds, as in **cham′ois, choir**.

oy regularly has the sound of **oi** as in **oil**. The sound of **oi** when final is commonly represented, in the ordinary spelling, by **oy**, as in **boy (boi)**, and sometimes when medial, as in **royal (roi′ăl)**.

oo

§ 83. oo in modern English represents most commonly the sounds **o͞o** in **fo͞od** and **o͝o** in **fo͝ot**, by which these sounds, however spelled, are represented in the respelling. The letters **oo** also spell the sounds of **ŭ** in **flood, blood,** and **ō** in **door, floor, brooch.**

o͞o as in **fo͞od, fo͞ol, no͞on, pro͞of** — otherwise spelled as in **rude** (§ 114), **group, drew, fruit, do, canoe, rheum, maneuver, blue** — is the high-back-tense rounded vowel. Sometimes, esp. in South England, it is slightly diphthongal, beginning a trifle more open and ending closer.

§ 84. Before **r** (**moor, poor, tour, sure**) the **o͞o** sound is somewhat lowered by the **r** so as to become nearly or quite **o͝o** (**mo͝or, po͝or, to͝or, sho͝or**). Cf. the lowering effect of **r** in **hēre, câre.** The same lowering effect is also seen in the last part of the diphthongal sound spelled with long **ū** = **yo͞o** before **r**. Words like **endūre′, Eu′rope, secū′rity** (§ 114) are commonly pronounced **ĕn·dyo͝or′** (**-do͝or′**), **yo͝or′ŭp, sē·kyo͝or′ĭ·tĭ.** In Southern British speech words like **poor, sure,** etc., are pronounced either **pōr, shōr,** or **pôr, shôr.**

§ 85. The sound **o͝o**, as in **fo͝ot, bo͝ok, co͝ok, cro͝ok,** etc., also spelled as in **full** (**fo͝ol**), **wolf** (**wo͝olf**), **would** (**wo͝od**), is the high-back-lax rounded vowel, with tongue slightly lower and less tense than for **o͞o** and lips less closely rounded.

The pronunciation with **o͝o** is well agreed on in the words **bo͝ok, bro͝ok, co͝ok, cro͝ok, fo͝ot, go͝od, ho͝od, ho͝ok, lo͝ok, no͝ok, ro͝ok, sho͝ok, sto͝od, to͝ok, wo͝od, wo͝ol.**

In the following words, cultivated usage is divided between **o͞o** and **o͝o**: **broom, coop, groom, hoof, hoop, pooh, roof, room, root, snook, soon, soot, spoon, whoop, whooping cough.**

ou

§ 86. ou is the regular spelling for the diphthong in **out.** The **ou** sound in standard British and American is a diphthong beginning with **ȧ** (**ȧsk**) and ending with (or near) **o͝o**, sometimes about **ō**.

Other sounds represented by the letters **ou** in English are: **ō** (**soul**), **o͞o** (**soup**), **o͝o** (**should**), **ô** (**bought**), **ŭ** (**double**), **ŏ** (**hough**), **û** (**journey**); and unaccented, ***ŭ*** (**grievous**), **ō̤** (**borough**), **ẽ** (**glamour**).

ow

§ 87. When final, the diphthong **ou** is usually spelled **ow** (**cow, now**), sometimes also medially (**scowl, howl**). Likewise when **ou** is sounded **ō** (**soul**) it is spelled **ow** finally (**know, tow**) and sometimes medially (**bowl**). Unaccented at the end of such words as **sparrow, follow,** etc., the generally accepted pronunciation is **ō** (**fŏl′ō,** etc.).

For **oy**, see **oi** (§ 82).

P

§ 88. p as in **pay, play, happy, cup,** etc., is the voiceless lip stop, corresponding to the voiced lip stop **b** (§ 17), and the voiced nasal lip continuant **m** (§ 64). All three sounds are made with closed lips.

p is silent in **raspberry** (**răz′bĕr′ĭ**), **cupboard, receipt, corps;** and also in the commoner Greek derivatives **psalm** (**säm**), **psalter, pneumatic, pneumonia,** etc. In less common words, as **pseudo-, Psyche, pterodactyl,** etc., some pronounce the **p.**

§ 89. The **p** sound is often excrescent, as in **Thompson, glimpse,** etc. The same excrescent sound often occurs when it is not spelled, as in **warmth** (**wôrmpth**), **dreamt, comfort, triumph,** though usage varies in this, as it does also when the letter **p** is spelled, as in **em(p)ty, glim(p)se, jum(p)ed, sem(p)stress, etc.**

ph

§ 90. ph as in **phantom,** etc., usually spells the **f** sound (**far**), chiefly in Greek derivatives, as **phantom, sylph, philosophy,** etc. Exceptionally, it has the sound **v**, as in **Stephen,** and in **nephew** as pronounced by some. In **diphthong, triphthong, diphtheria, naphtha,** etc., **ph** is often sounded **p**, but **f** is usual. Initially before **th** (**phthalin**) **ph** is more often silent: **thăl′ĭn; fthăl′ĭn.**

Q

§ 91. q is regularly followed by **u**, with the sound of **kw** in native words, as **quell, quake.** In loan words **qu** is also usually **kw** (**quite, conquest**), but is sometimes **k**, as in **liquor** (**lĭk′ẽr**), **coquette** (**kō·kĕt′**). Final **-que** is sounded **k**, as in **unique** (**ū·nēk′**).

R

§ 92. The letter **r** in **rate, very, far, feared, hurt, better,** etc., spells a variety of sounds, the chief of which are described here.

(I) **Description of r.** (1) The original English **r**, at least before vowels, was a **tongue-point trill.** The audible sound consists both of voice and the tongue-point vibrations.

(2) **Uvular r** (**velar r**, less properly, **guttural r**) is made by the combined sound of voice and rapid vibrations of the uvula against the back of the tongue raised toward the velum, or soft palate.

(3) **Fricative r** is made with the tongue raised to a position similar to that for the tongue-point trill, but with the point not vibrating. The point is close enough to the front palate to cause audible friction of the voiced breath between.

(4) **Frictionless continuant r** is formed by a tongue position much like that of fricative **r**, but with the tongue sufficiently withdrawn from the front palate to eliminate the fricative sound. Though similar in tongue position to fricative **r**, the difference is fundamental, no sound but voice being heard. It is vowellike in sound.

(5) **Retroflex r** is a further modification of the fricative and frictionless **r**, in that the tongue point is further turned up toward the hard palate, in some cases being bent back, or "retroflexed." Here, too, there is no sound but voice. Organically, (4) and (5) are characterized by a gliding movement of the tongue to or from a vowel.

(6) If the tongue be held in the position for (4) or (5) and the voice sounded without change of tongue position, an "r-colored" vowel will result. This is the vowel **û** (stressed) and **ẽ** (unstressed) of general American pronunciation.

§ 93. (II) **Occurrence of r.** (1) **Trilled r** is still used by Scottish speakers of standard English, though not invariably in all positions of the word. It is also occasionally pronounced between vowels by Englishmen, usually with a single flip of the tongue. The trilled **r** is still common with Welsh speakers of English and in Irish and Scotch dialect. The point-trilled **r** is regular in German standard speech, and is common in some types of French. It is also regular in Welsh, Italian, and Spanish.

(2) **Uvular r** is found in English chiefly in Northumbrian dialect, but not at all in standard English. The uvular trill, or a strong fricative ("uvular scrape") articulated at the same point, is regular for Parisian standard French, and is also common in Germany.

(3) **Fricative** or (4) **Frictionless continuant r** is the usual one in standard Southern British. In so-called fricative **r**, the fricative element is often a minor one.

(5) Some degree of **retroflex r** is common with educated speakers in northern, western, and southwestern England, and is regular in the greater part of America and Canada. In regions where **r** is sounded finally and before consonants, retroflex **r** often affects the quality of a preceding vowel. In the most general type of educated American speech the **r** coincides with the vowel **û** (**hûrt**) and with the corresponding unstressed vowel **ẽ** (**pẽrceive**); i. e., the vowel is pronounced for its whole duration with the tongue in the raised position for **r** — the so-called retroflex, or "r-colored," vowel, no further consonant **r** being added. This is the only vowel in standard American English so affected.

Loss of r. In the standard speech of southern England, of eastern New England, of New York City, of most of the southern United States, and of some speakers in the cities of Canada (esp. eastern), **r** is sounded only before a vowel in the same or a closely following word, the letter **r** being retained in the spelling. The following will illustrate: **fear** (**fēẽ**), **are** (**ä**), **arm** (**äm**), **form** (**fôẽm, fôm**), **bore** (**bōẽ**), **far away** (**fär *ȧ*wā′**), **here and there** (**hēẽr *ă*n thâẽ**), **here they are** (**hēẽ thā ä**). When an **r** sound is thus retained before a vowel of the next word, it is called **linking r.**

§ 94. As a result of sounding **r** only before a vowel, many words, spelled with final **r**, exist in two forms but in one spelling, as seen in **here I am** (**hēẽr ī ăm**), **here they are** (**hēẽ thā ä**), according as a vowel follows or not. Hence any word that ends in **ẽ** (as does (**hēẽ**)), such as **idea** (**ī·dē′*ȧ***), etc., is likely to be treated like those that end in **r**, and hence to take an **r** sound when a vowel follows. Thus the speaker says, **a good idea** (***ȧ*** **go͝od ī·dē′*ȧ***), but **the idea of it** (**thē ī·dē′ẽr ŏv ĭt**). This is called **intrusive r**, and is common in England and eastern America, less so in the southern United States.

§ 95. Since speakers of some types of standard speech pronounce **r** where others do not, in this dictionary all **r**'s are marked in the respelling for pronunciation as being pronounced, with the understanding that those who omit **r** except before vowels will in these cases pronounce it or omit it just as they would when it appears in the ordinary spelling.

S

§ 96. The letter **s** spells four different sounds, two voiceless and two voiced; viz.: (1) **s** as in **sun** (**sŭn**), (2) **z** as in **easy** (**ēz′ĭ**), (3) **sh** as in **sure** (**sho͝or**), and (4) **zh** as in **vision** (**vĭzh′*ŭ*n**).

§ 97. (1) The usual method of forming English **s** as in **sun** is with the tip and blade of the tongue pressed close to the upper teethridge, and the point drawn into itself so as to form a very narrow, tubelike channel between the tip and the teethridge. A thread of voiceless breath forced through this channel strikes the points of the teeth (esp. the lower) and produces the characteristic "hissing" sound. It cannot be made with the mouth wide open, since the air stream does not then strike the lower teeth. Some speakers place the tip of the tongue behind the lower teeth, pressing the front of the tongue toward the teethridge to form the channel.

Voiceless **s** is heard in **see, so, small, basis, yes, hats,** etc. It is otherwise spelled as in **pass, cell, rice, scene, schism, tax, quartz.** It is silent in **aisle, isle, island, Carlisle, corps** (**kōr**), **chamois, rendezvous, debris, viscount, demesne, apropos, Grosvenor,** and with varying frequency in **bas-relief, Arkansas, Illinois, St. Louis, Louisville.**

§ 98. (2) Voiced **s** has the sound of **z** and is formed like voiceless **s** with the addition of voice. It is heard in **easy, resolve, has, is, ribs.** (Initial **s** does not spell **z.**) This sound of **s** is respelled in this dictionary with **z**, as in **ribs** (**rĭbz**), and may be indicated without respelling by **s̤** (**rĭbs̤**).

Two principal sources of voiced **s** (originally always voiceless) are: (**a**) Lack of stress, as in the unaccented syllables of words like **Mary's** (**mâr′ĭz**), **roses,** etc., or in the frequently unstressed words **is, was, has,** etc. (**b**) Voice assimilation between voiced sounds, as in **observe, pansy, easy;** also in **refuse, lose,** etc., where final **e** was once sounded, and hence **s** was between vowels.

In certain nouns and adjectives spelled in the same way, the **s** sound was originally final, as it still is, as **abuse** (*n.*), **loose** (*adj.*). Hence some pairs of verbs and nouns or adjectives are distinguished by the sound of **z** or **s**, however spelled, as **close:** *v.* (**klōz**), *adj.* (**klōs**) — **house:** *v.* (**houz**), *n.* (**hous**) — **use:** *v.* (**ūz**), *n.* (**ūs**); etc.

§ 99. The ending **-s** or **-es** in the plural of nouns (**ships, bushes**), or in the possessive case (**Jack's, George's**), or in verbs (**eats, goes**), is pronounced according to the preceding sound. After voiceless sounds except sibilants (**s, sh, ch**) it is pronounced **s**; as in **ships, Ruth's, takes.** After voiced sounds except sibilants (**z, zh, j**) it is pronounced **z**; as in **ribs, trees, Tom's, Joe's; digs, goes.** After sibilants, voiced or voiceless, it is pronounced **ĕz, ĭz** (§ 30); as in **losses** (**lŏs′ĕz**), **roses** (**rōz′ĕz**); **Grace's** (**grās′ĭz**), **thrush's** (**thrŭsh′ĭz**); **ceases** (**sēs′ĕz**), **gazes** (**gāz′ĕz**).

§ 100. (3) **s** has the **sh** sound when it is palatalized by a following **ĭ** or **y** sound (however spelled), as in **mansion** (**măn′sh*ŭ*n**), **censure** (**sĕn′shẽr**), **nauseous** (**nô′sh*ŭ*s**). See § 103.

§ 101. (4) Likewise voiced **s** (= **z**) has the sound **zh** when palatalized by a following **ĭ** or **y** sound, as in **vision** (**vĭzh′*ŭ*n**), **measure** (**mĕzh′ẽr**). See further in § 103.

sh

§ 102. sh as in **sharp, rashly, bush,** etc., is pronounced with the tip and blade of the tongue approaching the hard palate a little farther back than for **s**. The aperture is wider laterally, so that the current of air passing over the tongue is more spread out like a waterfall than for **s**, in which it is like a jet. The main body of the tongue is also higher toward the roof of the mouth. The broader stream of air rushes against the teeth much as for **s**, the mouth requiring to be nearly closed. The position of the tongue is on the whole similar to that for **y**; hence **sh** and its voiced correlative **zh** are often called palatal sounds, and are, in fact, often the result of palatalization (§ 103).

The sound spelled **sh** is not a combination of **s** and **h**, contains no **s** or **h** sound, and is a simple sound. It does often result from pronouncing **s** next to a **y** sound, but when it becomes **sh** it ceases to be either **s** or **y** and becomes a different, simple sound. It is now also spelled as in **machine, chandelier, schist (shĭst), issue, mission, conscience, special, anxious.** See § 103.

When **s** and **h** are in separate syllables, each has its own sound, as in **sheepshead (shēps′hĕd′).** In some names, ignorance has led to a wrong division and pronunciation that have come into good use, as in **Lewisham** (= **Lewis** + **ham**), often pronounced **lū′ĭsh·ăm** for the historically correct **lū′ĭs·ăm.**

§ 103. The words **issue, mission, conscience,** etc., mentioned above (§ 102), contain instances of palatalization of **s** to **sh**. The condition for this is a consonant **y** sound following the **s**, and followed by an unstressed or lightly stressed vowel. In words like **conscience, special, nauseous,** etc., this **y** sound was earlier an unaccented **ĭ** or **ē** sound (still so spelled), which by lack of stress became a **y** sound, just as unaccented **ĭ** in **Indian (ĭn′dĭ·ăn)**, may become **y (ĭn′dyăn)**, as explained in § 58. The sound **s** is thus, as the tongue anticipates the position for (palatal) **y**, transformed into the palatalized **sh** sound (cf. § 102, first ¶). Regardless of the spelling, when these combinations of *sound* occur, the palatalization takes place, as in **anxious (x = ks), nauseous.** So, too, before **ū**, as in **issue**, though the **y** sound is not spelled at all, it is yet a part of the pronunciation of **ū**, and the palatalization takes place as usual: **ĭsh′ū, ĭsh′o͞o.** The corresponding palatalization also takes place when the first sound is voiced **s (z)**, which is changed to **zh**, the voiced correlative of **sh**; as in **vision (vĭzh′ŭn)**, etc.

In some words, after the **ĭ** or **ē** has become **y** and been absorbed into the **sh** or **zh** sound **(mission, vision)**, it has sometimes been restored, as seen in **Asia (ā′zhȧ)** but **Asiatic (ā′zhĭ·ăt′ĭk)**, etc. This is partly due to analogy, partly to spelling, and no doubt partly to the rhythm of utterance. Thus the rhythm of **ā′zhăt′ĭk** is a trifle difficult, owing to the adjacent accent, so that the more natural alternating rhythm is apt to be substituted (or kept from the beginning): **ā′zhĭ·ăt′ĭk.**

T

§ 104. t as in **tie, note, apt, matter,** etc. — also spelled as in **Thomas, walked,** or without spelling in **eighth (ātth)** — is the voiceless tongue-point alveolar stop, corresponding to the voiced tongue-point alveolar stop **d**, and to the voiced tongue-point alveolar nasal continuant **n**. All three are made with the tongue point on the upper teeth-ridge, as also is **l**. See § 25.

t in words like **question** is palatalized to **ch** as **d** in **soldier** is to **j**. See §§ 103, 118.

§ 105. t is silent in **Matthew, mortgage, hautboy, chasten, listen, castle, soften,** etc.; and commonly in combinations like **sit down, must go** — esp. when between two consonants.

§ 106. An excrescent **t** is pronounced in **against** (formerly **agains**), **amongst** (formerly **amongs**), **midst, pennant.**

th

§ 107. th spells the tongue-point dental (or interdental) fricative, voiceless, as in **thin, ether, tooth,** or voiced, as in **th̶is, eith̶er, smooth̶,** the symbol **th** being used in this dictionary for the voiceless, and **th̶** for the voiced sound. In forming **th, th̶,** the point of the tongue lightly touches the backs or the points of the upper teeth, in some cases protruding a trifle between upper and lower teeth, while breath hisses through with a fricative sound — the only sound when **th** is voiceless, and combined with voice when it is voiced **(th̶is).**

When spelled with final **th**, the sound is usually voiceless (except in **bequeath̶, booth̶, mouth̶,** *v.*, **smooth̶, with̶**); when final and voiced, it is usually spelled **-the (bath̶e).**

The **th** sound is a simple sound, made with a single tongue position, not a combination of **t** and **h** sounds.

§ 108. Certain nouns ending in **th** have **th** in the singular **(mouth)** and **th̶z** in the plural **(mouth̶z)**, etc. After a short vowel, there is a tendency to voiceless **th**, as in the plurals **breaths, deaths,** etc., and likewise after consonants, as in **breadths, months,** etc. But the usage is divided in some words, as in **truths (tro͞oth̶z; -ths), youths,** etc.; and some words with long vowel regularly have voiceless **-ths**, as **heaths, growths.** In **cloths**, a modern formation, some speakers distinguish **clŏth̶z** "pieces of cloth" from **clŏths** "kinds of cloth."

Initial **th** in pronominal words **(the, this, then, there,** etc.) is now voiced **(th̶is,** etc.). In the word **with** usage is divided, the voiceless form being especially apt to occur before voiceless consonants **(with certainty, with feeling,** etc.).

§ 109. The **th** is voiced in several verbs, as **bath̶e, loath̶e, teeth̶e,** in which the final **-e** was once sounded. It is likewise voiced in the verbs **bequeath̶, mouth̶, smooth̶,** though the **-e** is no longer written. Thus the voiced **th̶** constitutes a distinction between nouns or adjectives and verbs; as **bath, bath̶e; mouth, mouth̶.**

§ 110. th has the sound of **t** in **thyme, Thomas, Esther.**

When **t** and **h** are in separate syllables, each has its own sound, as in **nut′hatch′.** Through ignorance, or reverence for the spelling, a **th** sound has become standard in some such words; as **Waltham (wôl′thăm;** *Brit.* **wôl′tăm, -thăm).**

ti

§ 111. ti in **nation, patience, martial,** etc., has the sound of **sh (shine).** In **bestial (bĕs′chăl)**, etc., **ti** has a **ch** sound.

U

§ 112. ū as in **ūse, lūte, dispūte,** etc., is commonly called "long **u.**" It is otherwise spelled as in **beauty, feud, pew, queue, lieu, view, cue, suit, yule, yew, you.** The sound marked **ū** is chiefly used in syllables having a full stress **(cūbe)**, or a subordinate accent, whether marked or not, as in **in′ter·view′er (ĭn′tẽr·vū′ẽr), per′fūme.** When quite unaccented, a different symbol **(ů)** is used (§ 118).

§ 113. The sound of **ū** varies both with different speakers and according to neighboring sounds. The main element of **ū** is the sound **o͞o (fo͞od)**, commonly with slightly forward tongue position. Preceding this is usually the sound of **y (yes)**, or a more vowellike sound **ĭ (ĭll)**, the tongue being somewhat retracted. After certain sounds, the initial element is much lightened or absent, leaving only **o͞o.** (See § 114.)

§ 114. The **ū** sound, however spelled, varies in cultivated speech according to the phonetic nature of the preceding sound. The same condition, with some modifications, also affects the unaccented **ů** (§ 118).

(1) When the **ū** sound is initial, the **y** sound is always fully heard in all types of cultivated English, as in **use (ūz), union (ūn′yŭn), ewe (ū), eulogy (ū′lō·jĭ)**; the **y** is written in the phonetically identical sound in **yew (yo͞o), yule (yo͞ol), youth (yo͞oth). y** is also sounded whenever unaccented **ů** is initial, as in **ůtility,** etc.

(2) After **b (beauty), c (cube), f (few), g (gew′gaw), h (human), k (Kew), m (mute), p (pure), v (view),** the sound **ū** is regular, and **o͞o** is not used. Thus there is no confusion between pairs like **beauty–booty; cue–coo; feud–food; hew–who;** etc.

(3) After **s (assume), z (resume), th (enthusiast)** — tongue-point fricatives — though the same pronunciations as in (2) are in accepted use, cultivated speakers in both England and America often suppress the first element of the **ū**, leaving **o͞o** alone: **(ă·so͞om′,** etc.). This is often criticized, but is in widespread use.

(4) After **d (duty), t (tune), n (new)** — tongue-point stops and nasal — the **ū** sounds are also accepted generally, but here too in America, at least, the **o͞o** sound is widely used by the educated. It is to be observed, however, that the **o͞o** in these words is formed with the tongue farther forward, and that **suit, duty,** thus pronounced, are not accurately represented by the spellings "soot" and "dooty," and do not exactly rhyme with **shoot, booty.**

(5) After **l (lute)** usage is divided both in England and in America, the pronunciations **lūte** and **lo͞ot** both being in good use. However, when another consonant precedes the **l** in the same syllable, as in **blue, blew, in·clude′,** etc., the **o͞o** sound is regular. But if the consonant is in the preceding syllable, as in **ab·lu′tion,** the pronunciation is like that of **lūte.** Thus in the word **flu′ent,** the marking is **flo͞o-,** while in **af′flu·ent,** it is **ăf′lů·ĕnt.**

(6) After **ch (chew)** and **j (June)** the first element of **ū** is likewise usually omitted **(cho͞o, jo͞on).** But after the palatalized sounds **ch** and **j** there is apt to be a noticeable **ĭ** glide to the following vowel, and the pronunciations often resemble **(chū, jūn).**

Likewise after the simple sounds **sh** and **zh**, as in **sure, usu′rious,** the **y** element usually disappeared when **sh** or **zh** was palatalized from **s** or **z.** But **ū** is sometimes heard, as in **usu′rious (ů·zho͝or′ĭ·ŭs, ů·zhū′rĭ·ŭs)**; and when unaccented, in **issue (ĭsh′ů, ĭsh′o͞o).**

(7) After **r** the **y** element is now completely silent in standard speech, as in **rule (ro͞ol), brew (bro͞o), crew, prune, true, threw,** etc. But the **o͞o** with tongue forward is still common in these words, though they are regularly marked with **o͞o** in the respelling in this dictionary (or without respelling, may be indicated by **u̧**, as in **ru̧le**). By this advanced **o͞o**, often also with prefixed retracted **ĭ**, many Americans preserve the historical distinction in sound between **rude** and **rood, rheum–room, threw–through, chews–choose, lute–loot,** etc.

(8) When **ū** occurs before **r**, the **o͞o** element of the **ū** sound is commonly lowered to **o͝o** just as is the simple **o͞o** sound, in such words as **Europe, fury, bureau, mural, cure, mature, endure.** Attention is often called to it in the Vocabulary by a reference to this section or to § 84. Thus a common pronunciation of the foregoing words is: **yo͝or′ŭp, fyo͝or′ĭ, byo͝or′ō,** etc. The lowered sound **o͝o** is especially evident after those consonants where the first (y-) element is sometimes omitted, as in **sure (sho͝or), rural (ro͝or′ăl), jury (jo͝or′ĭ).**

Just as there is a tendency in Southern British speech to change **o͝o** before **r** into **ō** or **ô**, likewise the second element of **ū (yo͞o)** in **pure, endure,** etc., varies to **ō** or **ô (pyo͝or, pyōr, pyôr; ĕn·dyo͝or′, ĕn·dyōr′, ĕn·dyôr′;** etc.).

§ 115. u as in **pull, bull, push,** etc. — otherwise spelled as in **wolf, wood, woman** — has the sound of **o͝o** in **foot** (§ 85), being respelled in this dictionary with **o͝o** (§ 76). It may be represented without respelling by **u̧ (pu̧ll)** or **o̧ (wo̧lf).** This is the high-back-lax rounded vowel made with the back of the tongue raised toward the velum, and with lips rounded a little less than for **o͞o.** The same sound of **u** is heard in **sure** and in **sugar.**

§ 116. ŭ as in **sŭn, ŭn′der, ŭn·do′** — otherwise spelled as in **son, in′come, does, flood, dou′ble, two′pence (tŭp′ĕns)** — is the "short **u**" sound. For the frequent spelling with **o (dove, won, done),** see § 77. As pronounced generally in America, this is a central unrounded vowel, the highest part of the tongue being a little lower and farther back than for the **ȧ** in **sofȧ** or **ẽ** in **bettẽr.**

§ 117. û as in **ûrn, hûrt, hûrl** is the vowel already mentioned in § 31, being the accented form corresponding to unaccented **ẽ** (§ 32). It is a central vowel, made with the tongue intermediate in position between front and back, although it varies somewhat with different speakers and when it occurs in different positions. The sound **û** is otherwise spelled in **fern, err, heard, sir, word, journal, myrrh.**

The sound **û** occurs also in syllables with only a slight accent, often not marked, as in **bûr·lesque′.** There is often a choice between **û** and **ẽ** according to speed of utterance or difference of usage **(bûr·lĕsk′, bẽr-).** Wherever **û** is frequently heard in such lightly accented syllables, they are marked with the symbol **û**, it being understood that, when entirely unaccented, the sound changes, without a sharp dividing line, to **ẽ.**

When **û**, or its equivalent, is followed by **r** or **rr** and a vowel, as in **hurry, courage, worry,** usage is divided as to the sound of the vowel. The earlier sound in such words corresponded to the present **û**, and this is preserved as the usual pronunciation in America. But in the prevailing speech of England this sound has become **ŭ**, often somewhat modified by the following **r** so as to differ somewhat from **ŭ** in **sŭn, come,** etc. An intermediate type is also heard in America, acoustically between **û** and **ŭ**, but **û** is also common even with those speakers whose speech in some respects resembles British, esp. in the Southern States.

When words like **fûr, cûr, stir, err,** etc., take a vowel suffix, as in **furry, erring,** etc., they retain the **û** of the stem. The word **erring** is also sometimes pronounced **ĕr′ĭng** — esp. in **unerring** — both probably influenced by **ĕrror, ĕrrant;** but **ûr′ĭng** is more usual.

The symbol **û** is also used in this dictionary to respell French words like **jeu**, having the mid-front rounded vowel, and **jeune**, having the low-front rounded vowel; or German words like **schön**, with mid-front rounded vowel, or **können**, with low-front rounded vowel. The tongue for these sounds is somewhat farther forward than for English **û**, which is usually not rounded.

§ 118. **ū** as in **ūnite, insūlar, natūre, verdūre,** etc., represents a modification of **ū** (§§ 112–114) in unaccented syllables. The sound **ū** differs from **ū** in taking as its second element either the lower **o͝o**, or a briefer form of **o͞o**, the same word often varying between a brief **o͝o** or **o͞o** according to conditions of speed, sense stress, or sentence rhythm.

The treatment of the first element of **ū** is much like that of accented **ū**, according to the preceding consonants. When initial, the **y** sound is invariably heard, as in **ūnite, ūsurp, eugenic,** etc. After **s, y** is sometimes lost, as in **sūpreme,** often **(so͞o·prēm′)**, etc. In familiar speech the vowel is often obscured to (*ŭ*) — **(s*ŭ*·prēm′,** etc.). After **ch (virtuous (vûr′tū·*ŭ*s)), j (judicious (jo͞o·dĭsh′*ŭ*s)), sh (sexual (sĕk′sho͞o·*ă*l)), zh (visual (vĭzh′ū·*ă*l)),** the **y** is often lost; but, as in accented syllables, there is some wavering. After **r (prudential (pro͞o·dĕn′sh*ă*l))**, and a consonant + **l**, the **y** is regularly lost. In unaccented syllables, however, the preceding consonant often belongs phonetically to the syllable before the **ū**, as in **val′ū·a′tion**, with the result that the **ū** is phonetically initial, and thus takes a clear **y** sound (as above): **(văl′ū·ā′sh*ŭ*n).** Compare **re·pūte′** with **rep′ū·ta′tion, sa·lūte′** with **sal′ū·ta′tion.** With these compare **af′fluence (ăf′lū·ĕns)**, in which the first element of **ū** is much less like **y**. Likewise after **r** in a preceding syllable the **y** sound is often clear, as in one pronunciation of **erudite (ĕr′ū·dīt), garrulous (găr′ū·l*ŭ*s).** So with partly accented **ū** in **Matthew (măth′ū)**, with clear **y** sound.

For the difference between **flu′ent (flo͞o′ĕnt)** and **af′flūent,** see § 114 (5).

So far as the second element of the unaccented **ū** is not already lowered to **o͝o** by lack of stress, it undergoes the same lowering effect of a following **r** that is seen in accented **ū** (**endūre′**), or in simple **o͞o** (**po͝or**); as in **ūranium, dūration,** etc. See §§ 84, 114 (8).

Before **u** in words like **censure** the **s** sound is palatalized to **sh**, and in words like **measure** the **z** sound is palatalized to **zh**, the **s** and **z** combining with the initial **y** element of the **u**. In the common words of this sort the **u** is reduced in ordinary speech to **ẽ** when before **r**, as in **censure (sĕn′shẽr), measure (mĕzh′ẽr).** Other examples are **sensuous (sĕn′sho͞o·*ŭ*s), visual (vĭzh′ū·*ă*l; -o͞o·*ă*l).** Initial **s** is not thus palatalized, however, as in **supreme (sū·prēm′; s*ŭ*·prēm′), superior,** etc., and occasionally when medial, as in **consular (kŏn′sū·lẽr; kŏn′s*ŭ*·lẽr,** the first element of **ū** being weakened or lost).

In words like **nature, verdure,** the off-glide of the **t** or **d** combines with the first element of **ū** to form a sound that varies from **ty** or **dy** to a completely palatalized **ch** or **j**. The last is the natural pronunciation in general use by unaffected speakers in all the common words. This palatalization is indicated in the pronunciation by the tie bar **tū, dū.**

This palatalization also takes place before the partly accented **ū**, as in **virtue (vûr′tū, vûr′cho͞o),** etc. But before fully accented **tū, dū,** it does not occur in standard speech (**tūne, dūty,** etc.).

§ 119. *ŭ* in the unaccented syllables of **circ*ŭ*s, dat*ŭ*m, s*ŭ*bmit, circ*ŭ*mstance** — otherwise spelled as in **porpoise (pôr′p*ŭ*s), pious, dungeon, righteous, gracious, atom, irksome, nation,** etc. — represents the obscuration of a **u** or an **o** sound to the stage of the neutral vowel, the usual italic letter indicating the obscuration.

§ 120. A silent **u** occurs after **g**, as in **guard, guess, rogue,** etc. In these cases **u** does not form a digraph with a following vowel, but is a mere sign of "hard" **g**.

In the common adjective ending **-ful (awful, careful,** etc.), the **u** is regularly silent in familiar speech, the **l** thus becoming syllabic (**ô′f′l, kâr′f′l**). The noun ending **-ful**, as in **cupful**, etc., is pronounced with the vowel **o͝o**.

§ 121. **u** *with consonant value.* The letter **u** is an equivalent spelling for **w**, esp. after **q (= k)** or **g (quality, quite, language,** etc.); occasionally elsewhere, as in **persuade, suave, suite.**

§ 122. **ü** as in French **menu (mē·nü′)**, German **grün**, etc., occurs only in foreign loan words not yet naturalized. The French sound may be imitated by firmly rounding the lips as if to pronounce **o͞o (mo͞on)**, and then, while holding the lips in this position, pronouncing **ē (ēve)**. The German sound is in some words the same as the French, in others it is approximately **ĭ (ĭll)** pronounced with somewhat less rounding of the lips.

V

§ 123. **v** as in **vain, vivid, ever, live, valve, wolves** — spelled **ph** in **Stephen** (also **Steven**), **nephew (nĕf′ū; nĕv′ū)**, and **f** in **of (ŏv)** — is the voiced lip-teeth fricative consonant corresponding to voiceless **f** (§ 43).

v in Spanish is like Spanish **b** in pronunciation. See § 17.

W

§ 124. **w** as in **we, worse, dwarf, twice** — spelled also **u (persuade, queen), o (memoir (mĕm′wär), choir (kwīr))** — is a combined lip and tongue sound, the lips being rounded and the tongue back raised as for **o͞o** or **o͝o**. It may be regarded as a gliding sound, made while the lips and tongue are moving toward the position of the following vowel. It is classed as a *semivowel*.

§ 125. The consonant **w** sound occurs only before vowels. It is now silent before **r (write, wren,** etc.). The letter is often written finally, as in **snow, know,** and **now.** In **snow** it is not needed, for **ō** alone spells the same sound, as in **go.** In **now,** however, **w** is essential, representing the second element of the diphthong **ou** in **out.** Omission of **w** would change **now** to **nō.** The group **aw(e)** is the final form for the spelling **au.**

§ 126. Besides being silent before **r (write)**, **w** is also silent before vowels in two classes of instances: (1) When not initial, **w** coalesced with its closely related **o͞o** or **o͝o** sound, as in **two (to͞o,** formerly **two͞o), who (ho͞o,** formerly **hwo͞o), sword (sōrd,** formerly **swo͞ord).** Initially **w** remains before **o͞o**, as in **wound (wo͞ond; wound), woo, womb,** etc. (2) Before the vowels of unaccented syllables or unstressed words **w** regularly disappeared, as in **answer (ân′sẽr), toward (tōrd), boatswain (bō′s′n), I'll go** (from **I′ will go′**), and the endings **-wich** and **-wick** of place names — **Woolwich (wo͝ol′ĭj), Warwick (wŏr′ĭk).** Many such silent **w**'s have been restored by spelling pronunciation. In **one, once, w** is sounded but not spelled.

wh

§ 127. **wh** as in **which, when, whale,** etc., represents either **h + w** or a voiceless **w** sound. Voiceless **w** and **hw** sound very much alike. The symbol **hw** is commonly used for either sound.

w for **hw** is now usual in standard Southern British speech. In Scotland, in Ireland, in North England, and in America, **hw** is the usual pronunciation, though the **w** sound appears to be spreading in America.

X

§ 128. The letter **x** spells six sounds in English: (1) **ks**, as in **box, exclaim′,** etc.; (2) **gz**, as in **exact′, exist′, exag′gerate,** etc.; (3) **ksh**, as in **an′xious (ăngk′sh*ŭ*s), lux′ury (lŭk′sho͞o·rĭ);** (4) **gzh**, as in **luxu′rious (lŭg·zho͝or′ĭ·*ŭ*s);** (5) **z**, in **anxi′ety (ăng·zī′ĕ·tĭ)** and initially in Greek derivatives, as **xy′lophone (zī′lō-),** etc.; (6) **sh**, as in one pronunciation of **anx′ious (ăng′sh*ŭ*s).** In **except′ (ĕk·sĕpt′), exscind′ (ĕk·sĭnd′),** the **s** element of **x** has merged with the **s** sound of the **c**, or **sc**. In (3), (4), and (6) the **s** or **z** element of **x** has been palatalized by the following **ĭ**, or by the **y** element of **ū** or **û** (§ 103).

It will be seen in the above examples that when **x** immediately follows an accented vowel **(ex′it, lux′ury)**, or is followed by a consonant sound **(exclaim′)**, it is voiceless **(ks, ksh, sh)**; when it immediately follows an unaccented vowel **(exact′, exhort′, luxu′rious, anxi′ety)**, it is voiced **(gz, gzh, z)**.

But the analogy of differently accented forms of related words disturbs this natural phonetic tendency; thus **luxu′rious** is also pronounced **lŭk·sho͝or′ĭ·*ŭ*s**, by analogy of **lux′ury;** and conversely, **lux′ury** is sometimes **lŭg′zho͞o·rĭ.** Moreover, less familiar words are likely to have **ks** from the spelling, or from a foreign pronunciation, as in **axil′la,** etc. **Exhaust′ (ĕg·zôst′)** and **exhort′ (ĕg·zôrt′)** are regular, the **h** being silent; so is **exhale′,** being **ĕg·zāl′,** if **h** is silent, but **ĕks·hāl′** if it is sounded, **ks** being regular before a consonant sound.

Y

§ 129. **y** in English spells one consonant **(yes)** and the following four vowels: (1) **ī (sky, defy, style,** etc.); (2) **ĭ (lyric, nymph, pity, ready** (§ 130), etc.); (3) **û (myrrh, myrtle,** etc.); (4) **ẽ (martyr, zephyr,** etc.). **y** (or **ey**) is the regular spelling for the final sounds **ī (fly)** and **ĭ (ready, money).** These sounds of **y** may be indicated without respelling as in **skȳ, nўmph, mÿrrh, martỹr.**

§ 130. Unaccented final **y** as in **ready**, or **ey** as in **money**, varies considerably from accented **ĭ**. For this variation and for that of medial **y (analysis)**, the equivalent of medial unaccented **ĭ (charĭty)**, see §§ 53, 54.

§ 131. As a consonant, **y** is the typical palatal semivowel, formed with the front of the tongue, behind the tip (which is lowered), near or touching the hard palate. It corresponds to the sound of **j** in German and Latin. English **y** differs from that of German and some other European languages in having no fricative or other sound but voice. It is analogous to **w** in being a gliding sound (§ 124). It is spelled **y** in **year, you, beyond,** etc.; **i** in **poniard, union,** etc.; **e** in **feud (fūd), linear (lĭn′ē·ẽr; lĭn′yẽr); j** in **hallelujah; g** in **vignette.** It is sounded without being spelled by a separate letter in **use, unite, value,** etc.

Like **w**, consonant **y** can occur only before vowels, not at the end of words. When written at the end of words, it is: (1) a vowel **(ready)**; (2) a diphthong **(sky)**; (3) the "vanish" of the partial diphthong **ā (day, they)**; or (4) the second element of a full diphthong **oi (boy).** Unlike **w, y** by itself can spell a vowel **(ready)** or a diphthong **(sky).**

Z

§ 132. **z** as in **zeal, hazy, buzz,** etc., is the voiced tongue-point alveolar fricative continuant corresponding to voiceless **s** (§ 97). **z** is often spelled with **s**, as in **busy, his, ears, robs, roses,** etc. It is rarely spelled **sc** (one pronunciation of **discern**) or **c** (one pronunciation of **suffice, sacrifice**).

§ 133. **z** as in **azure, seizure, grazier,** etc., has the sound of **zh**, the voiced correlative of **sh**. The same sound is spelled **s** in **vision, measure,** etc. In the foregoing, the **zh** sound results from the palatalization of **z** before **i** or **y** (§ 103). **zh** is also spelled in French derivatives by **g (rouge)** and by **j (bijou)**. It forms the second element of the consonantal diphthong **j** (nearly **d + zh**).

RULES FOR THE PRONUNCIATION OF LATIN ENTRIES

Vowels not followed by a consonant in the same syllable are to be pronounced long (ā, ē, ī, ō, ū), and vowels followed by a consonant in the same syllable are to be pronounced short (ă, ĕ, ĭ, ŏ, ŭ), unless the respelling for pronunciation indicates otherwise. Consonants have the same value as in similar situations in English unless the respelling indicates otherwise. For those who prefer to pronounce the Latin entries according to the "Roman" method, the syllabification as indicated, together with the rules for such pronunciation as set forth in the Latin grammars, will be a sufficient guide.

EXPLANATORY NOTES

A careful reading of the following Explanatory Notes will enable the user of this dictionary to locate quickly and easily the answers to his questions and will make plain the significance of the different kinds of type, the labels, the symbols, and the other conventions that make possible its compactness and fullness.

The regular order of arrangement of the parts of the entries in this dictionary is as follows (although, of course, not every entry has all of these parts): 1. The vocabulary entry. 2. The pronunciation, in parentheses. 3. The part of speech. 4. Inflectional forms. 5. The etymology, in square brackets. 6. The definition or definitions. 7. Synonyms and Antonyms. 8. Run-on entries.

In the following paragraphs, numbered to correspond with the numbers in the above list, each of these parts of the entry is discussed in detail with illustrations, usually in the form of references to entries in the *Vocabulary*. The sections numbered 9 and 10 deal with special types of composite entries calling for special interpretation; section 11 deals with pictorial illustrations.

---

1. The **Vocabulary Entry** (the term to be defined) is printed in heavy-faced type. The spelling, accent, syllabic division, hyphenation, variant forms, and capitalization are shown in the entry.

If the entry is a word of more than one syllable, the syllables are indicated by a centered period [·], or by a heavy accent [′] or a light accent [′]. Each of these indicates the end of a syllable — the point where a word should be divided at the end of a line in writing and printing. The accents also show on what syllables the stress falls in pronouncing a word. In hyphened words, the hyphen marks a syllabic division of the word.

When more than one spelling or form is given, the one printed first is in general to be preferred. If the forms are of equal or nearly equal standing, they are separated by a comma (**canyon, cañon; sextet, sextette; inward, inwards**) or by the word *or* (see 1st **plane; sandbox tree; heath grass; real estate**). If one form is distinctly preferable, the second form is usually preceded by the word "Also" (see **envelope,** *n.*) or its status is otherwise plainly indicated (see **moonlit, candelabrum**). Spellings proper in British use are regularly set off by a comma from the American spellings in vocabulary entries (**analyze, analyse; peddler, pedlar**). See *British Spelling Preferences*, page 1147.

Proper Names and **Proper Adjectives** either are entered with a capital letter or are treated otherwise to show the capitalization (see **illuminati**). Nouns which are proper nouns in one or more senses, but common nouns in other senses, have the facts shown by bracketed notes (see **dharma**).

Prefixes (such as **pre-, sub-, un-**), **Suffixes** (such as **-ation, -hood, -ness**), and **Combining Forms** (such as **paleo-, -plasty**) are entered and defined. See also § 9, below.

Foreign Words are indicated by prefixed parallel bars (see ‖**Autobahn,** ‖**flâneur**). These are terms that occur frequently in speech and in print in English, but are not generally considered to be Anglicized. While parallel bars are affixed to these words indicating them to be commonly italicized in printing and writing, italic type for these words in this dictionary is precluded by use of italics for several other purposes.

2. The **Pronunciation** is given, in parentheses, following the vocabulary entry. In the pronunciation,

the word is respelled in the WEBSTER phonetic alphabet. (A working key to this alphabet is printed inside the covers at the front and back of this book; and a full key on page vii.) In the pronunciation respelling, a heavy accent mark [′] is placed after the syllable on which the chief stress falls in pronouncing the word; a light accent mark [′] is placed after a syllable on which there is a lighter, or secondary, stress; and a centered period [·] is placed after the syllables on which there is no stress.

In the pronunciation respelling the syllabic division sometimes differs from that of the heavy-faced entry because in the heavy-faced entry the division is according to printers' usage; in the pronunciation respelling, the division is according to speech; thus:

dou′ble (dŭb′'l), **mi·li′tia** (mĭ·lĭsh′á),

spe′cial (spĕsh′ăl), **vi′sion** (vĭzh′ŭn).

Figures within the parentheses with the pronunciation refer to sections of the *Guide to Pronunciation* in the Introduction, where additional information is given regarding the pronunciation of the word or the group of words to which it belongs.

A part or the whole of a pronunciation is often omitted when it is the same as that of a word immediately preceding and may be readily supplied from such preceding entry.

Accents and syllabic division only are given for some phrases and compounds, and for some derivatives ending in common suffixes such as *-ess, -ing, -ist, -less, -ment, -ship*, if the pronunciation is perfectly regular and can therefore easily be learned from the separate parts.

When two or more pronunciations are recorded the general rule has been to place first the one that has been selected as preferable. Each form entered, however, has the support of good usage, and in some cases this usage is nearly or quite equally divided. Specific variations of usage have been indicated by limiting words, as *often, sometimes*, etc.

Further explanations will be found on page vii and following.

3. The name of the **Part of Speech** follows the pronunciation or (if no pronunciation is given) the entry word. The part of speech is given as an italic abbreviation: *n.* for *noun, v.* for *verb, adj.* for *adjective, pron.* for *pronoun*, etc. (see list of abbreviations, page xxi). When the entry consists of two or more separate words it is not labeled except, for clarity, in a few instances,

(xviii)

chiefly the proper nouns and adjectives run on after entries in the *Gazetteer* (as at **Nova Scotia**).

Occasionally the same entry is labeled as belonging to two or more parts of speech; thus:

ago, *adj. & adv.*

asthma, *n*. . . . — **asthmatic**, *adj. & n.*

If a verb is both transitive and intransitive and has more than one meaning, the *transitive* and *intransitive* meanings are usually separated and labeled *v. t.* and *v. i.* respectively, the second label being preceded by a heavy dash (see **break, conduct**). If the transitive and intransitive definitions of a verb can be combined without ambiguity or confusion, the label is *v. t. & i.*, for *verb transitive and intransitive* (see **concentrate, recite**).

4. Inflectional Forms (as the plural of a noun, the past tense and the participles of a verb, and the comparative and superlative forms of an adjective or adverb [see COMPARISON, 2, in *Vocab.*]) are given, in SMALL CAPITALS (see **mouse, shake,** *v.*), when they are irregular or present difficulties of spelling or pronunciation.

The plural of nouns is indicated by the prefixed italic abbreviation *pl.* Plurals formed regularly, by the addition of *s* or *es* (see *Orthography*, § 12), are not ordinarily given. Plurals of compounds (such as compounds of *man* and *berry*) are often omitted when they are formed in the same way as the plurals of the main word. If a noun has the same form in both singular and plural, the label is *n. sing. & pl.* (see **deer**). When two (or more) plurals are given, the first is in general to be preferred. When different plurals are used for different senses of a word the usage is plainly indicated (see **antenna, genius**). See also the note at the entry of **plural** in the *Vocabulary*.

When a verb is entered without principal parts, such omission means that the past tense and past participle are formed by adding *-ed* (see **climb**) or, if the verb ends in a mute *e*, by dropping the *e* and adding *-ed* (see **unite**). Principal parts formed otherwise are shown in SMALL CAPITALS. The principal parts of verbs are separated by semicolons. When three forms are given (see **blow**) the first is the past tense; the second, the past participle; the third, the present participle. When only two forms are given (see **abase**) the first is both past tense and past participle. If alternative forms are given for any of the principal parts, these are set off from one another by commas (see **bereave**) or by words like *or* and *also* (see **level**). In complex situations, italic labels (*past; past part.;* and *pres. part.*) are added for complete clarity (see **cleave**). In the case of compound verbs formed from a verb whose principal parts are shown, a cross reference to the latter is often given instead of repeating the principal parts (see **befall**). For obvious compounds beginning with *re-*, no principal parts are given; readers should consult the main verb.

5. The **Etymology**, in square brackets, precedes the definition. For the meanings of abbreviations in the etymology, see list of abbreviations, page xxi. The following familiar conventions are used:

In the etymology the words in italic type are those, whether English or foreign, from which the vocabulary word is derived; definitions of the italicized words are printed in roman type:

cipher, *n.* [OF. *cifre* zero . . .]

When the only etymology is [F.], [L.], or the like, or when the etymology begins with F., OF., etc., followed by a comma, the source word in French or Latin is spelled in the same way as the English word:

front, *n.* [OF., forehead, . . .]

Occasionally, only the language source is given, the label being then preceded by "from" or "through." Intermediate steps in an etymology are sometimes omitted, being indicated by the words "deriv. of" (derivative of) or "ult. fr." (ultimately from):

almond, *n.* [From OF., ult. fr. L. *amygdala*, . . .]

Any prefix, suffix, or combining form used without definition will be found defined in its alphabetical place:

geology, *n.* [*geo-* + *-logy.*]

In the case of many words descended originally from Latin or Greek, the etymology gives also the primary Latin or Greek constituents of the word:

coleopterous, *adj.* [Gr. *koleopteros,*
fr. *koleos* sheath + *pteron* wing.]

In words of Chinese origin, the small superior figures refer to the four tones of the Peking dialect, which is the accepted standard of speech:

ginseng, *n.* [Chin. (Pek.) *jen²-shen¹.*]

These tones are pitched in different keys to facilitate the recognition of many words that have the same sound.

The history of a word is in general traced back as far as it can be with certainty. Thus if a Middle English word is the only etymology given, the source of the Middle English word is either unknown or doubtful:

wiggle, *v. i.* [ME. *wigelen* to totter, reel.]

In accordance with these conventions, the etymology of **curfew** [OF. *cuevrefu, covrefeu,* fr. *covrir* to cover + *feu* fire, fr. L. *focus* hearth.] will be read "*curfew* is from the Old French word spelled either *cuevrefu* or *covrefeu,* which is derived from the Old French words *covrir* meaning 'to cover' and *feu* meaning 'fire'; *feu* is from the Latin word *focus* meaning 'hearth.'"

6. The **Definition** follows the etymology. Heavy-faced Arabic numerals (**1., 2., 3.,** etc.) are used to number definitions when the meanings are numerous or are quite divergent from one another. Heavy-faced letters (**a, b, c**) are used to group meanings that are very closely related; thus, several special senses (as in *Botany* definitions) may be separately lettered and placed under one number. In general, the technical and scientific senses are arranged in the alphabetical order of their subject labels. So far as possible the order of definitions is that of the historical order of development of the meanings of a word.

a. Various kinds of cross references sometimes take the place of a definition. A mere spelling variant is entered thus:

cañon. Var. of CANYON.

A common term having the same meaning as some more technical term fully defined at its own place or a technical term having the same meaning as a common term fully defined is often entered in one of these two ways:

founder, *n.* *Veter.* = LAMINITIS.

pertussis, *n.* *Med.* Whooping cough.

A term whose meaning is recorded under the entry of some other term is (if it seems to require separate entry at its own alphabetical place) entered thus:

Desdemona, *n.* See OTHELLO.

b. Labels, or italic epithets, are prefixed (often in abbreviated form: see page xxi) to many definitions. *Subject Labels* (as *Law, Radio, Bot.*) show the department of knowledge in which the word or the meaning occurs; *Usage Labels* (as *Colloq.*, *Dial.*, *Slang*) show its status in actual usage; *Geographical Labels* indicate the area in which (only or chiefly) it is used. When such labels follow the number or letter introducing a definition, they apply only to that definition; when they precede a number or letter they apply to everything that follows them.

c. Cross References, printed in SMALL CAPITALS, are made in order to guide the reader to further information. In such references in both the definitions and the etymologies: "See" leads to information that is either highly important or essential to an understanding of the meaning (see **boldface**, *n.*; and the etymology of **foible**); "Cf." means "compare," and leads to useful, interesting, or related material (see **impetus**, 1; and the etymology of **nib**, *n.*). For the use of cross references in connection with synonyms and antonyms, see § 7, below.

A cross reference to one of two or more entries that are spelled alike, especially when the entries belong to the same part of speech, is sometimes by number thus:

lamiaceous, *adj.* . . . See 1st MINT.

When the entries are of different parts of speech, a cross reference to one is usually made by part-of-speech label, thus:

field of force. = FIELD, *n.*, 10.

Cross references to entries in the *Biographical Names* and *Gazetteer* sections of the back matter are indicated by means of the abbreviations *Biog.* and *Gaz.* in the reference.

7. The Synonymy, when given, is placed at the end of the entry and is introduced by the label **Syn.** Sometimes, it consists merely of a "word-finding" list of words of similar meaning, often with semicolons separating words that are synonyms in one sense from those that are synonyms in another sense. Sometimes the synonymy contains a full treatment of the distinction in meanings of a group of words, the words to be discriminated being printed in heavy-faced type (see **bodily**). A synonymy of this kind is printed as a separate paragraph, in distinctive type.

In the synonymy, a cross reference directs the reader to the entry where a full treatment is to be found. Thus, at **defame** the cross reference "See MALIGN" indicates that in the synonymy at **malign** the word *defame* is discussed.

Antonyms, when given, are in light-faced type, following the synonyms, and are introduced by the label **Ant.** The differences in meaning among antonyms are often discussed under the synonymy of another word to which a cross reference is given.

8. Run-on Entries are placed at the end of the paragraphed entries, with an intervening light dash. Such entries are usually derivative adjectives, adverbs, and nouns, and are of such a character that their meaning is easily inferred from the definition of the word to which they are attached (see **colonize**).

Often, when the run-on entry is the same word as the main entry but used as a different part of speech and requiring definition, the run-on entry consists only of a short heavy dash and the part-of-speech label (see **best**). The heavy dash is to be interpreted as standing for all spellings of the entry word if more than one is given (as: **color, colour**, *n.* . . . — *v. t.*).

In the *Gazetteer*, many proper adjectives and nouns derived from geographical names, and requiring no definition because their meaning is obvious, are run on after the appropriate entry chiefly for their spelling and pronunciation.

9. Lists of Self-explanatory Combinations are inserted frequently after prefixes and combining forms, and similar lists of combinations and phrases are sometimes given after nouns and adjectives (see **non-**, **over-**, **micro-**, **air**). These lists record the existence of hundreds of idiomatically formed expressions, and answer the question whether the terms included (and similar terms) are to be written or printed as hyphened compounds, as solid compounds, or as two words.

These self-explanatory lists are rather illustrative than exhaustive. The list, for example, at **cross** shows the various ways of combining but by no means all existing combinations. The lists serve also as guides in the use of prefixes and combining forms, most of which, like *hyper-* and *multi-*, are free for use in forming new compounds at need.

10. Compounds and Phrases. Many two-word and three-word compounds, such as those consisting of an adjective (or an attributive noun) and a noun are given main vocabulary entry in their alphabetical place (see **flying buttress**, **mountain sheep**, **shore bird**). Combinations that belong naturally with some main vocabulary entry have generally, however, been treated at that entry. Thus, the terms *blue crane* and *sandhill crane* are both covered at the entry **crane** and not at their own alphabetical places. (See also **covenant**, **year**.) This method of treatment has permitted the inclusion of information about many two-word and three-word entries, especially names of varieties of plants and animals, that would otherwise have been omitted for lack of space.

Verb phrases are given following the entry of their verb, a group of such phrases being generally printed as a block paragraph alphabetically arranged (see **fall** and **make**).

Prepositional phrases are run on, following an em dash, after the most important word of the phrase.

11. Illustrations. The ratio of the size of figures of plants and animals shown in illustrations to natural size is usually indicated by a fraction in parentheses, as **whale** ($\frac{1}{300}$), that is, the natural overall length is 300 times the 1½ inches of the figure, or 37½ feet. Where the illustration is larger than natural size, this fact is indicated by a multiple in parentheses, as **flea** ($\times 8$), that is, the natural size is one eighth that of the figure shown.

ABBREVIATIONS USED IN THIS WORK

For a more extensive list of abbreviations see pages 998 ff.

ab. ....about
abbr., abbrev. .abbreviated, abbreviation
abl. ....ablative
acc(us). .....accusative
A.D. ....anno Domini
adj. ....adjective
adv. ....adverb, adverbial
AF. ....Anglo-French
Af., Afr. ....Africa, African
Agr(ic). .....Agriculture
Alg. ....Algebra
alt. ....altitude
Alta. ....Alberta
A.M. ....ante meridiem
Am(er). ......America, American
amb. ....ambassador
Am. Sp. ......American Spanish
Anal. ....Analytic, Analysis
Anat. ....Anatomy
Anc., anc. ...Ancient
Angl. ....Anglican, Anglicized
Anglo-Ind. ...Anglo-Indian
Anglo-Ir. ....Anglo-Irish
Anglo-Lat. ...Anglo-Latin
Anon. ....Anonymous
Ant. ....Antonym
Anthropol. ...Anthropology
Antiq. ....Antiquity, Antiquities
appar. ....apparently
Ar. ....Arabic
A. R. ....Autonomous Region
Arab. ....Arabian, Arabic
Aram. ....Aramaic
Arch. ....Architecture
Archaeol. ....Archaeology
Arith. ....Arithmetic
Armen. ....Armenian
art. ....article
AS., A.-S. ....Anglo-Saxon
assoc. ....associate(d), association
A.S.S.R. .....Autonomous Soviet Socialist Republic
Assyr. ....Assyrian
Assyr.-Bab. ..Assyro-Babylonian
Astrol. ......Astrology
astron. ......astronomer
Astron. ......Astronomy
at. no. ......atomic number
attrib. ......attributive(ly)
at. wt. ......atomic weight
aug., augm. ..augmentative
Austral. .....Australia, Australasia
auxil. ....auxiliary
av. ....average
A.V. ....Authorized Version
av(oir). ......avoirdupois

b. ....born
Bab. ....Babylonian
bacteriol. ...bacteriologist
Bacteriol. ...Bacteriology
Bank. ....Banking
bbl. ....barrel
B.C. ....before Christ
bd. ....board
bdl. ....bundle
Belg. ....Belgian
bet. ....between
Bib. ....Bible, Biblical
Bibliog. .....Bibliography
biochem. .....biochemist
Biochem. .....Biochemistry
Biog. ....Biographical Names (section of the back matter)
Biogeog. .....Biogeography
Biol. ....Biology
Bk. ....Book
Bot. ....Botany, Botanical
bpl. ....birthplace
Br. ....British
Braz. ....Brazilian
Bret. ....Breton

Brit. ....Britain, British
bro(s). ......brother(s)
B.T.U. ....British Thermal Unit
bu. ....bushel(s)
Bulg. ....Bulgarian

c. ....circa (L., about), cent(s), century, cubic
C. ....Centigrade
Can. ....Canada, Canadian
Can. F. ......Canadian French
Cant. ....Cantonese
cap(s). ......capital(s)
Capt., capt. .Captain
Carp. ....Carpentry
Cath. ....Catholic
c.c., cc. .....cubiccentimeter(s)
Celt. ....Celtic
Cen., cen. ...Central
Cen. Amer. ...CentralAmerica(n)
cent(s). .....century(-ries)
cf. ....confer (L., compare)
cg. ....centigram(s)
C.G.S. ....centimeter-gram-second
ch., chap. ...chapter
Ch. ....Church
Chald. ....Chaldean
chem. ....chemist
Chem. ....Chemistry
Chin. ....Chinese
Chino-Jap. ...Chino-Japanese
Ch. of Eng. ..Church of England
Chron. ....Chronicles
Civ. Engin. ..Civil Engineering
cl. ....centiliter(s)
Class. ....Classical
cm. ....centimeter(s)
Co(s)., co(s). .County(-ties)
Col. ....Colonel, Colossians
Coll. ....College
coll., collect. .collective
colloq. ......colloquial(ly)
com. ....common(ly)
Com. ....Commerce
comb. ....combination
comp. ....composition, compound
compar. ......comparative
Confed. ......Confederate
Cong. ....Congregational
conj. ....conjunction
contr. ....contraction, contracted, contrasted
Cor. ....Corinthians
correl. ....correlative
corresp. ......corresponding
corrupt. .....corruption, corrupted
cos ....cosine
cosec ....cosecant
cot ....cotangent
Cr. ....Credit, Creditor
Craniol. .....Craniology
Criminol. ....Criminology
Crystallog. ..Crystallography
cu., cub. ....cubic
cwt. ....hundredweight

d. ....day, denarius, -rii (L., penny, pence), died
D. ....Dutch
Dan. ....Danish, Daniel
dat. ....dative
dau. ....daughter
D. Bib. ......Douay Bible
def. ....definition, definite
deg. ....degrees
Dent. ....Dentistry
dep. ....deposed
Dept., dept. .Department
deriv. ....derived, derivative
Deut. ....Deuteronomy
Dial., dial. ..Dialect, Dialectal
diam. ....diameter
Dict. ....Dictionary

dim. ....diminutive
disc. ....discovered
Dist., dist. ..District
disting. ......distinguished
Div. ....Division
do. ....ditto
doz. ....dozen
dr. ....dram(s)
Dr. ....Debit, Debtor, Doctor
dram. ....dramatist
Dram. ....Dramatic
Du. ....Dutch
dwt. ....pennyweight
Dyn. ....Dynamics

E. ....English, East(ern)
East. ....Eastern
Eccl(es). .....Ecclesiastical
Eccles. ....Ecclesiastes
Ecclus. ......Ecclesiasticus
Ecol. ....Ecology
econ. ....economist
Econ. ....Economics
ed. ....edition
educ. ....educator
Educ. ....Education
e.g. ....exempli gratia (L., for example)
Egypt. ....Egyptian
Egyptol. .....Egyptology
Elec. ....Electric, Electrical
Embryol. .....Embryology
e.m.f. ....electromotive force
emp(s). ......emperor(s)
Encyc. ....Encyclopedia
Eng. ....England, English
Engin. ....Engineering
Entom(ol). ...Entomology
Eph. ....Ephesians
Epis., Episc. .Episcopal
equiv. ....equivalent
erron. ....erroneous(ly)
esp. ....especially
est. ....estimate, estimated
estab. ....established
etc. ....et cetera
Eth. ....Ethiopic
Ethnog. ......Ethnography
Ethnol. ......Ethnology
ety., etym. ...etymology
Ex. ....Exodus
exc. ....except
Exch. ....Exchange
excl. ....excluding
exclam. ......exclamation
Ezek. ....Ezekiel

f. ....feminine, fluid
F., Fahr. ....Fahrenheit
F. ....French
fem. ....feminine
ff. ....following
fig. ....figurative(ly)
Fig(s)., fig(s). .Figure(s)
Finn. ....Finnish
fl. ....flourished
Flem. ....Flemish
form. ....formerly
Fort. ....Fortification
fr. ....from
Fr. ....French
freq. ....frequentative, frequently
Fris. ....Frisian
Fr. W. Africa .French West Africa
ft. ....foot, feet
Furn. ....Furniture
fut. ....future

g. ....gram(s)
G. ....German
Gael. ....Gaelic
gal(s). ......gallon(s)
Gal. ....Galatians
Gallo-Lat. ...Gallo-Latin
Gaz. ....Gazetteer
gen. ....general, generally, genitive
Gen. ....General, Genesis

Geneal. ......Genealogy
Geo. ....George
Geog. ....Geography
Geol. ....Geology
Geom. ....Geometry
Ger. ....German(y)
Gk. ....Greek
Goth. ....Gothic
gov. ....governor
Govt. ....Government
gr. ....grain(s)
Gr. ....Greek
Gram. ....Grammar
Gr.Brit. ......Great Britain
Gun. ....Gunnery

h. ....hour(s)
H. ....hardness
ha. ....hectare(s)
Hab. ....Habakkuk
Hag. ....Haggai
Heb. ....Hebrew(s)
Her. ....Heraldry
HG. ....High German
Hind. ....Hindustani
hist. ....historian
Hist. ....Historical, History
hl. ....hectoliter(s)
H.M. ....His (or Her) Majesty('s)
Horol. ....Horology
Hort. ....Horticulture
Hos. ....Hosea
h.p. ....horsepower
hr. ....hour(s)
Hung. ....Hungarian
Hydraul. .....Hydraulic(s)
Hydrog. ......Hydrography
Hymnol. ......Hymnology

i. ....intransitive
I. ....Island(s), Isle
ibid. ....ibidem (L., in the same place)
Icel. ....Icelandic
id. ....idem (L., the same)
i. e. ....id est (L., that is)
Illit. ....Illiterate
illust. ....illustrated
Illust. ....Illustration
Immunol. .....Immunology
imp. ....imperfect
imper. ....imperative
impers. ......impersonal
in. ....inch(es)
Inc. ....Incorporated
incl. ....including, inclusive
incor. ....incorrect(ly)
incorp. ......incorporated
ind. ....independent
Ind. ....India(n), Indiana
indef. ....indefinite
indic. ....indicative
inf., infin. ...infinitive
Inorg. ....Inorganic
Ins. ....Insurance
inst. ....instant
intens. ....intensive
interj. ....interjection
Internat. .....International
interrog. .....interrogatory, interrogative
Introd. ....Introduction
Ion. ....Ionic
Ir. ....Irish, Ireland
Iran. ....Iranian
Ire., Irel. ....Ireland
irreg. ....irregular(ly)
Is. ....Islands
Isa. ....Isaiah
Isl(s). ......Island(s)
It., Ital. ....Italian
ital. ....italics

Jap. ....Japanese
Jas. ....James
Jav. ....Javanese
Jer. ....Jeremiah
Join. ....Joinery
Josh. ....Joshua
Judg. ....Judges

(xxi)

kg.	kilogram(s)
km.	kilometer(s)
l	line
l.	line, liter(s)
L.	Late, Low
L.	Latin
Lam.	Lamentations
lat.	latitude
Lat.	Latin
lb(s).	pound(s)
l.c.	lower case [small letter(s)]
Lett.	Lettish
Lev.	Leviticus
LG.	Low German
LGr.	Late Greek
Lieut., lieut.	Lieutenant
Ling.	Linguistics
liq.	liquid
lit.	literal, literally
Lit.	Literature
Lith.	Lithuanian
Lithog.	Lithography
ll	lines
LL.	Late Latin
log	logarithm
long.	longitude
m.	masculine, meter(s), mile(s), minute(s)
M.	meridies (L., noon)
M.	Middle, Medieval, Monsieur
Macc.	Maccabees
Mach.	Machinery
Mal.	Malachi
manuf.	manufacturer
Manuf.	Manufacture, Manufacturing
Mar.	Maritime
masc.	masculine
math.	mathematician
Math.	Mathematical, Mathematics
Matt.	Matthew
MD.	Middle Dutch
ME.	Middle English
Mech.	Mechanical, Mechanics
Med.	Medicine, Medical
memo.	memorandum
Metal.	Metallurgy
Meteorol.	Meteorology
Mex.	Mexico, Mexican
Mex. Sp.	Mexican Spanish
MF.	Middle French
Mfg., mfg.	Manufacturing
mg.	milligram(s)
MGr.	Medieval Greek
MHG.	Middle High German
mi.	mile(s)
Mic.	Micah
Micros.	Microscopy
Mid.	Middle
Mil., mil.	Military
min.	minute(s)
Mineral.	Mineralogy, Mineralogical
MIr.	Middle Irish
misc.	miscellaneous
mistrans.	mistranslation
ml.	milliliter(s)
ML.	Medieval Latin
MLG.	Middle Low German
mm., mm.	millimeter(s)
Mod., mod.	Modern
Mod. Gr.	Modern Greek
Moham.	Mohammedan
MS(S).	Manuscript(s)
Mt(s).	Mount(s), Mountain(s)
munic.	municipality
Mus.	Music
Myth(ol).	Mythology
n.	noun
N.	New, North, Northern
Nah.	Nahum
N. Am(er).	North America(n)
nat.	natural
Nat. Hist.	Natural History
Naut.	Nautical
Nav.	Navy, Naval
Navig.	Navigation
N.E.	Northeast, New England
Neh.	Nehemiah
Neth.	Netherlands
neut.	neuter
New Eng.	New England
NGr.	New Greek
NHeb.	New Hebrew, Neo-Hebraic
N. Ireland	Northern Ireland
NL.	New Latin
No.	North, number
no.	number
N. of Eng.	North of England
nom.	nominative
Nor(w).	Norwegian
Norm.	Norman
North.	Northern
nov.	novelist
N.S.	New Style, Nova Scotia
N.S.W.	New South Wales
N.T.	New Testament
Num.	Numbers
Numis.	Numismatics
N.W.	Northwest
N.Z.	New Zealand
O.	Old
O	oxygen
Obad.	Obadiah
obj(ect).	objective
Obs.	Obsolete
occas.	occasionally
Occult.	Occultism
Oceanog.	Oceanography
O.D.	Old Dutch
ODan.	Old Danish
OE., O.E.	Old English
OF.	Old French
OHG.	Old High German
OIr.	Old Irish
ON.	Old Norse
ONF.	Old North French
op. cit.	opere citato (L., in the work quoted)
OPer.	Old Persian
Ophth(almol).	Ophthalmology
opp.	opposed, opposite
OPr.	Old Provençal
Org. Chem.	Organic Chemistry
orig.	origin, original(ly)
Ork.	Orkney
Ornith(ol).	Ornithology
OS.	Old Saxon
O.S.	Old Style
OSlav.	Old Slavic
O.T.	Old Testament
OW.	Old Welsh
Oxf. E. D.	Oxford English Dictionary
oz.	ounce(s)
p	page
p.	page
Paleobot.	Paleobotany
Paleog.	Paleography
Paleontol.	Paleontology
par(a).	paragraph
Parl.	Parliament(ary)
part.	participial, participle
pass.	passive
Pat., pat.	Patent, patented
Pek.	Pekingese
Penin(s).	Peninsula(s)
Per.	Persian
perf.	perfect
perh.	perhaps
pers.	person, personal
Pers.	Persian
pert.	pertaining
Pet.	Peter
Petrog.	Petrography
Petrol.	Petrology
Pg.	Portuguese
Pharm.	Pharmacy
Phil.	Philippians
Philem.	Philemon
Phil. I., Phil. Is.	Philippine Islands
Philol.	Philology
philos.	philosopher
Philos.	Philosophy
Phil. Sp.	Philippine Spanish
Phonet.	Phonetics
Phonog.	Phonography
Photog.	Photography
phr.	phrase
Phys.	Physical, Physics
Physiog.	Physiography
physiol.	physiologist
Physiol.	Physiology
Phytogeog.	Phytogeography
P.I.	Philippine Islands
pk.	peck(s)
pl.	plural, plate
plup.	pluperfect
P.M.	post meridiem
Poet.	Poetic, Poetical
Pol.	Polish
Pol(it).	Political
polit.	political, politician
pop.	population
Port.	Portuguese
poss.	possessive
pp., pp	pages
Pr.	Provençal
P.R.	Puerto Rico
Prac.	Practice
prec.	preceding
pred.	predicate
pref.	prefix
prep.	preposition
pres.	present
Pres., pres.	President
pres. part.	present participle
pret.	preterit
prin.	principal, principally
Print.	Printing
priv.	privative
prob.	probably
pron.	pronoun, pronunciation
pron'd.	pronounced
prop.	proper(ly)
Pros.	Prosody
Prot.	Protestant
prov(s).	province(s)
Prov.	Proverbs
pseud.	pseudonym
psychol.	psychologist
Psychol.	Psychology
Psychopathol.	Psychopathology
pt.	pint(s), part
pub.	published
qt.	quart(s)
q.v.	quod vide (L., which see)
R.	Rare, Reaumur
rad	radius, radial
R.C.	Roman Catholic
R.C.Ch.	Roman Catholic Church
redupl.	reduplication
ref.	reference
refl., reflex.	reflexive
Refrig.	Refrigeration
Ref. Sp.	Reformed Spelling
rel.	relative
Relig.	Religion
Rep.	Representative, Republic
resp.	respectively
Rev.	Revelation, Reverend, Revised, Revolution
Rhet.	Rhetoric
Rom.	Roman(s)
R.R.	Railroad
Rs.	Reis, rupees
R.S., R. Sp.	Reformed Spelling
R.S.F.S.R.	Russian Soviet Federated Socialist Republic
Russ.	Russian
R.V.	Revised Version
Ry.	Railway
s.	second(s), section, shilling(s)
S.	South, Southern
S. Afr.	South Africa(n)
S. Afr. D.	South African Dutch
Sam.	Samuel
S. Am(er).	South America(n)
Sax.	Saxon
sc.	scilicet (L., to wit)
Scand.	Scandinavian
Schol.	Scholastic(ism)
Scot.	Scottish, Scotland
Sculp.	Sculpture
S.E.	Southeast
sec	secant
sec., sect.	section
Sec., Secy.	Secretary
Seismol.	Seismology
seq.	sequente (L., following)
Serb.	Serbian
Shak.	Shakespeare
Shet.	Shetland
sin	sine
sing.	singular
Skr.	Sanskrit
Slav.	Slavonic
So.	South
sociol.	sociologist
Sociol.	Sociology
Sol.	Solomon
Sou., South.	Southern
sp.	species
Sp., Span.	Spanish
Sp. Am(er).	Spanish America(n)
specif.	specific(ally)
sp. gr.	specific gravity
sq. m.	square mile(s)
S.S.R.	Soviet Socialist Republic
St.	Saint
Ste.	Sainte
sub.	suburb
subj.	subjunctive
suff.	suffix
superl.	superlative
Surg.	Surgery
Surv.	Surveying
Sw., Swed.	Swedish
S.W.	Southwest
syn.	synonymous
Syn.	Synonym(s)
Syr.	Syriac
t.	transitive, troy
Tag.	Tagalog
tan	tangent
Technol.	Technology
Teleg.	Telegraphy
Teleph.	Telephony
Ter(r).	Territory
Test.	Testament
Teut.	Teutonic
Theat.	Theatrical
theol.	theologian
Theol.	Theology
Theos.	Theosophy
Thermodyn.	Thermodynamics
Thess.	Thessalonians
Tim.	Timothy
trans.	transitive
trans., transl.	translated, translation, translator
Treas., treas.	Treasury
Trig.	Trigonometry
Turk.	Turkish
U.	University
Ukrain.	Ukrainian
ult.	ultimate(ly), ultimo
UN	United Nations
uncert.	uncertain
Univ., univ.	University
U.S.	United States
U.S.A.	United States Army, United States of America
U.S.N.	United States Navy
U.S.S.	United States Ship
U.S.S.R.	Union of Soviet Socialist Republics
usu.	usually
v.	verb, versus
Var(s)., var(s).	Variant(s)
Veter.	Veterinary
v. i.	verb intransitive
Vict.	Victoria
viz.	videlicet (L., namely)
VL.	Vulgar Latin
voc.	vocative
Vocab.	Vocabulary
vol(s).	volume(s)
vs.	versus
v. t.	verb transitive
W.	Welsh, West
West.	Western
W. Ind.	West Indies
wt.	weight
yd(s).	yard(s)
Yugo.	Yugoslav(ian)
Zech.	Zechariah
Zeph.	Zephaniah
zool.	zoologist
Zool.	Zoology

A
DICTIONARY
OF
THE ENGLISH LANGUAGE

A

A B C

A, a (ā), *n.; pl.* A's, A's, As, as, aes (āz). **1.** The first letter of the English alphabet. A comes from Latin A, which came from Greek A (*alpha*), which in turn was derived from the first letter of the Phoenician alphabet. **2.** The sound of this letter A. In Modern English the letter represents various sounds. See *Pron.*, § 5. **3.** *Music.* **a** The sixth tone in the model major scale (that of C), or the first of its relative minor scale. **b** A key or string producing this tone; also, a symbol for the tone. See PITCH, *Illust.* **4.** As a *symbol*, the first in order or of its class. — **A 1** (ā' wŭn'). See A ONE.

a (ā; *emphatic* ā), *adj.*, or *indefinite article.* [Shortened fr. AN, *adj.*] **1.** One; some particular; one kind of. **2.** Any; each; the same. **3.** [Deriv. fr. AS. *an, on.*] In, to, or for each; as, twice a week. ☞ *A* is used before words beginning with a consonant sound (see AN, *adj.*).

a (ā), *prep.,* **a–** (ā–), *prefix.* [AS. *an, on.*] On; in; at; as in abed, asleep, nowadays, aloud, *a* hunting.

a– (à–). A prefix. **1.** From Anglo-Saxon *ā–*, often having intensive significance, as in arise. **2.** From Anglo-Saxon *of*, orig. meaning *off*, as in adown. **3.** Reduced form of Latin *ad*, to, as in ascribe. **4.** = AB– (before *p, m, v*). **5.** (*pron.* ă–; ā–; ā–) [Gr. *an–* not, *a–* before consonants.] Denoting –*less, not, without, un–*, as in abyss, agnostic, asexual, asymmetric. Called *alpha privative.*

a, a' (ä; ô), *adj.* *Scot.* All.

a (ā), *v.* Unemphatic form of HAVE.

A–1, A–2, A–3, A–4. *Air Force, U. S.* The four sections of the executive officer's staff. Cf. S-1, S-2, etc.

aard'vark (ärd'värk'), *n.* [S. Afr. D., earth pig.] A large burrowing nocturnal African mammal with extensile tongue, powerful claws, large ears, and heavy tail that feeds largely on termites. Its genus (*Orycteropus*) is sole representative of an order (Tubulidentata).

aard'wolf (ärd'wŏolf'), *n.* [D., earth wolf.] A hyenalike quadruped (*Proteles cristata*) of South Africa. It feeds on carrion and insects.

Aar'on (âr'ŭn), *n.* The first high priest of the Jews; brother of Moses.

Ab (ăb; äb), *n.* [Heb.] See JEWISH CALENDAR.

ab– (ăb–; äb–), **abs–**, *a–.* A prefix from Lat. *ab–*, signifying *from, away, off, away from*, as in abduct, absonant, abscond, avert.

a'ba (ä'bä), *n.* [Ar. *'abā'.*] A fabric woven from the hair of camels or goats; also, a loose sleeveless garment worn by Arabs.

a'ba·cá' (ä'bä-kä'), *n.* [Tag.] Manila hemp; also, the plant that yields this fiber.

a·back' (à-băk'), *adv.* [AS. *on bæc* at, on, or toward the back.] **1.** *Archaic.* Backward; back. **2.** *Naut.* Backward against the mast; with sails pressed back, as by head winds, checking headway. Hence, **to be taken aback**, to be surprised and checked or disconcerted.

ab'a·cus (ăb'à-kŭs), *n.; pl.* ABACI (-sī), -CUSES (-kŭs-ĕz; -īz). [L., fr. Gr. *abax.*] **1.** An instrument for performing calculations by sliding counters along rods or in grooves. **2.** *Arch.* The uppermost member or division of a capital. See IONIC, *Illust.*

A·bad'don (à-băd'ŭn), *n.* [Heb. *ābaddōn* destruction.] **1.** The place of the lost in Sheol; the bottomless pit. **2.** The angel of the bottomless pit; Apollyon. *Rev.* ix. 11.

Abacus, 1 (showing total of 123,456).

a·baft' (à-baft'; 9), *prep.* [*a–* on + ME. *baft*, fr. AS. *bæftan*, fr. *be* by + *æftan* behind.] *Naut.* Behind; toward the stern from; to the rear of. — *adv.* *Naut.* Toward or at the stern; aft; astern.

ab'a·lo'ne (ăb'à-lō'nē), *n.* [Origin uncert.] Any of a genus (*Haliotis*) of rock-clinging gastropod mollusks with a flattened shell of slightly spiral form, lined with mother-of-pearl and having a row of apertures along its outer edge; — called also *ear shell.*

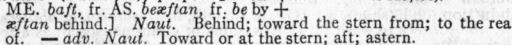
Abalone Shell. (⅒₂)

a·ban'don (à-băn'dŭn), *v. t.;* A·BAN'DONED (-dŭnd); A·BAN'DON·ING. [OF. *abandoner*, fr. *a* (L. *ad*) + *bandon* jurisdiction, fr. LL. *bandum* public proclamation.] **1.** To give up with the intent of never again claiming one's rights or interests in; to give over or surrender completely; to desert. **2.** To give (oneself) up without attempt at self-control, as to grief. **3.** *Obs.* To banish; expel. *Shak.* — **a·ban'don·er**, *n.* — **ment**, *n.*
Syn. (1) Abandon, desert, forsake mean to quit absolutely. **Abandon** emphasizes leaving a person or thing to the mercy of someone or something else; **desert** implies previous occupation, companionship, or guardianship, and sometimes, culpability; **forsake** implies a breaking off of a close association whether by repudiation, renunciation, or the like. — **Ant.** Reclaim. (2) See RELINQUISH.

a·ban'don (à-băn'dŭn; F. à'bäN'dôN'), *n.* [F.] A yielding to natural impulses; careless freedom or ease.

a·ban'doned (à-băn'dŭnd), *adj.* **1.** Forsaken. **2.** Given up to vice; irreclaimably wicked; irredeemable. — **Syn.** Profligate, dissolute, reprobate. — **Ant.** Reclaimed: redeemed, regenerate.

à bas (ä bä'). [F.] Down with; — in disapprobation.

a·base' (à-bās'), *v. t.;* A·BASED (à-bāst'); A·BAS'ING (-bās'ĭng). [OF. *abaissier.* See BASE, *adj.*] To lower; bring down; cast down; now only specif.: to lower or reduce in rank, estimation, etc.; to degrade; as, rascals so abased. — **a·base'ment**, *n.*
Syn. Abase, demean, debase, degrade, humble, humiliate mean to lower a person in his own estimation or in that of others. **Abase** suggests loss, often a voluntary loss, of dignity or prestige; **demean**, loss of social standing by an unsuitable act or association; **debase**, a deterioration, especially of moral standards or character; **degrade**, the taking of a step or steps downward, sometimes in rank but more often on the road to moral degeneration; **humble** suggests a being forced to realize one's own littleness or impotence, usually without loss of self-respect, thus differing from humiliate, which always implies mortification or deep shame. — **Ant.** Exalt.

a·bash' (à-băsh'), *v. t.* [OF. *esbahir*, fr. L. *ex* out + *bah*, interj. of astonishment. In ME. somewhat confused with *abase.*] To destroy the self-possession or self-confidence of; to confuse or confound. — **Syn.** See EMBARRASS. — **Ant.** Embolden: reassure. — **a·bash'ment**, *n.*

a·bate' (à-bāt'), *v. t.;* A·BAT'ED (-bāt'ĕd; -ĭd); A·BAT'ING. [OF. *abatre, abattre*, fr. *a* to + *batre, battre*, to beat.] **1.** *Obs. exc. Law.* To demolish; to put an end to; to quash; as, to abate a nuisance or action. **2.** To reduce in amount, degree, intensity, etc.; to diminish; as, to *abate* a tax or one's zeal. **3.** *Archaic.* **a** To reduce as in size or value. **b** To deprive (a person of something). **c** To blunt (a point or edge). **4.** To deduct; omit; as, to *abate* part of a price. — **Syn.** See DECREASE. — **Ant.** Augment. — *v. i.* To become less; specif.: **a** To be defeated, or come to nought, as a writ. **b** To diminish or become less intense or violent; as, the disease is *abating*; a storm *abates* in fury. —
a·bat'a·ble (à-bāt'à-b'l), *adj.* — **a·bat'er** (-bāt'ẽr), *n.*
Syn. Abate, subside, wane, ebb agree in meaning to die down in force and intensity. **Abate** stresses the idea of progressive diminution, as of a wind; **subside**, the cessation of turbulence or agitation, as of waves; **wane**, the fading or weakening of something good, such as interest; **ebb**, the recession or gradual loss of that which fluctuates, such as one's vitality or a passion. — **Ant.** Revive.

a·bate'ment (à-bāt'mĕnt), *n.* Act of abating, or state of being abated; diminution; mitigation; also, amount abated; deduction.

ab·a·tis (ăb'à-tĭs or, *esp. Brit.*, à-băt'ĭ), *n. sing. & pl.* [F., fr. *abattre* to fell.] A defense formed of felled trees the sharpened ends of whose branches face the enemy.

A battery (ā). *Radio.* An electric battery used to heat the filament serving as cathode in an electron tube.

ab'at·toir' (ăb'à-twär'), *n.; pl.* -TOIRS (-twärz'). [F., fr. *abattre* to fell.] A slaughterhouse.

ab·ax'i·al (ăb-ăk'sĭ-ăl), *adj.* [*ab–* + L. *axis* axle.] Situated out of, or directed away from, the axis.

ab'ba·cy (ăb'à-sĭ), *n.; pl.* -CIES (-sĭz). [LL. *abbatia.*] Dignity, estate, jurisdiction, or term of tenure of an abbot.

Ab·bas'side (ă-băs'īd; ăb'à-sīd), *n.* Any member of the dynasty (750–1258) of caliphs claiming descent from Abbas, uncle of Mohammed. See OMMIAD. — *adj.*

ab·ba'tial (ă-bā'shǎl), *adj.* Pert. to an abbot or abbey.

ab·bé' (ă-bā'), *n.* [F.] A title given in France to anyone who wears the garb of a secular ecclesiastic, including many clerics not in holy orders.

ab'bess (ăb'ĕs; -ĭs), *n.* [Through OF. fr. LL. *abbatissa*, fem. of *abbas* abbot.] A woman who is the superior or head of a convent of nuns.

ab'bey (ăb'ĭ), *n.; pl.* ABBEYS (-ĭz). [Through OF. fr. LL. *abbatia*, fr. *abbas* abbot.] **1.** A monastery ruled by an abbot or a convent ruled by an abbess. **2.** The church of a monastery. — **Syn.** See CLOISTER.

ab'bot (ăb'ŭt), *n.* [AS. *abbod, abbad*, fr. L. *abbas, abbatis*, fr. Gr. *abbas*, fr. Aram. *abbā* father.] The superior or head of an abbey for men. — **ab'bot·cy** (-sĭ), *n.* — **ab'bot·ship**, *n.*

ab·bre'vi·ate (ă-brē'vĭ-āt), *v. t.;* -AT'ED (-āt'ĕd; -ĭd); -AT'ING. [L. *abbreviatus*, past part. of *abbreviare.* See ABRIDGE.] To make briefer; to reduce or shorten, as words, by contraction or by omission (*Maryland* to *Md., article* to *art.*), sometimes by substitution (*ounce* to *oz.*). — **Syn.** See SHORTEN. — **Ant.** Elongate, lengthen. — **ab·bre'vi·a'tor**, *n.*

ab·bre'vi·a'tion (ă-brē'vĭ-ā'shŭn), *n.* Act or result of abbreviating; an abbreviated form of a word or phrase. Abbreviated to *Abbr.* Cf. CONTRACTION.

A B C (ā'bē'sē'); *pl.* A B C's (-sēz'). **1.** The first three letters of the alphabet; *pl.*, the whole alphabet. **2.** The rudiments of any subject; as, the *A B C* of finance. **3.** The initial letters of *Argentina, Brazil, Chile*; as, the *A B C* powers.

abd- (ăbd-). [Ar. *'abd* slave, servant.] A word often compounded in Semitic languages with a name or epithet of the Deity to form proper names; as, *Abd*-er-Rahman (Servant of the Merciful One).

Ab·di′as (ăb·dī′ăs). *Douay Bib.* Obadiah. See BIBLE.

ab′di·cate (ăb′dĭ·kāt), *v. i.;* -CAT′ED (-kāt′ĕd; -ĭd); -CAT′ING. [L. *abdicatus*, past part. of *abdicare*, fr. *ab-* + *dicare* to proclaim.] To give up or relinquish formally, as sovereign power; to renounce; to surrender, as a trust, duty, right, etc. — *v. i.* To relinquish or renounce a throne, high office, dignity, or function. — **ab′di·ca·ble** (ăb′dĭ·kȧ·b'l), *adj.* — **ab′di·ca′tion** (-kā′shŭn), *n.* — **ab′di·ca′tor** (-kā′tẽr), *n.*

Syn. **Abdicate, renounce, resign** mean to give up a position of trust, honor, or glory. **Abdicate** implies a giving up of sovereign or inherent power; **renounce**, frequently used in place of *abdicate*, often suggests sacrifice for a greater end; **resign** implies the giving up of an unexpired office or trust. — **Ant.** Usurp.

ab·do′men (ăb·dō′mĕn; ăb′dō·mĕn), *n.* [L.] **1.** The part of the body between the thorax and the pelvis; the belly; also, the cavity of this part of the trunk, containing the stomach, intestines, liver, etc. **2.** The posterior section of the body, behind the thorax, in insects and crustaceans. See INSECT, *Illust.* — **ab·dom′i·nal** (ăb·dŏm′ĭ·năl), *adj.* — **ab·dom′i·nal·ly**, *adv.*

ab·dom′i·nous (ăb·dŏm′ĭ·nŭs), *adj.* Big-bellied.

ab·duce′ (ăb·dūs′), *v. t.* [L. *abducere*, fr. *ab-* + *ducere* to lead.] To draw or conduct away.

ab·du′cent (ăb·dū′sĕnt), *adj. Physiol.* Abducting; — opposed to *adducent*.

ab·duct′ (ăb·dŭkt′), *v. t.* [L. *abductus*, past part. of *abducere* to lead away.] **1.** To take away surreptitiously by force; usually, to kidnap; as, to *abduct* a child or a voter. **2.** *Physiol.* To draw away, as a limb, from a position near or parallel to the median axis, as in raising the arm laterally. — **ab·duc′tor** (ăb·dŭk′tẽr), *n.*

ab·duc′tion (ăb·dŭk′shŭn), *n.* Act of abducting, or state of being abducted; specif., under statutory law, the unlawful taking away of a woman for marriage or for immoral purposes; — as distinguished from *kidnaping*.

a·beam′ (ȧ·bēm′), *adv. Naut.* On a line at right angles with a ship's keel; opposite the middle of a ship's side.

a′be·ce·dar′i·an (ā′bē·sē·dâr′ĭ·ăn), *n.* [ML. *abecedarius*, fr. the names of the first four letters of the alphabet.] **1.** One who is learning the alphabet; hence, a tyro. **2.** One who teaches the rudiments of learning. — *adj.* Alphabetical; rudimentary. — **a′be·ce′da·ry** (ā′bē·sē′dȧ·rĭ), *n.* & *adj.*

a·bed′ (ȧ·bĕd′), *adv.* In bed; to childbed.

A′bel (ā′bĕl; -b'l), *n. Bib.* The second son of Adam and Eve, slain by his elder brother Cain. *Gen.* iv.

a·bele′ (ȧ·bēl′; ā′bĕl), *n.* [Through D. & OF. fr. a dim. of L. *albus* white.] The white poplar (see POPLAR).

a′bel·mosk′ (ā′bĕl·mŏsk′), *n.* [From NL. *Abelmoschus*, the genus, fr. Ar. *abu-al-misk* father (source) of musk. See MUSK.] A yellow-flowered bushy herb (*Abelmoschus moschatus*) of the mallow family, native to tropical Asia and the East Indies, whose musky seeds are used in perfumery.

Ab′er·deen′ An′gus (ăb′ẽr·dēn′ ăng′gŭs). An animal of a breed of black hornless beef cattle originating in Scotland.

ab·er′rant (ăb·ĕr′ănt), *adj.* [L. *aberrans*, *-antis*, pres. part. of *aberrare*, fr. *ab-* + *errare* to wander.] **1.** Wandering; straying from the right way; deviating from truth, rectitude, propriety, etc. **2.** Exceptional; abnormal. — **ab·er′rance** (-ăns), **ab·er′ran·cy** (-ăn·sĭ), *n.*

ab′er·ra′tion (ăb′ẽr·ā′shŭn), *n.* **1.** Act of being aberrant; deviation, esp. from what is right, natural, or normal. **2.** Disorder of the mind. **3.** *Astron.* A small periodic change of position in heavenly bodies, due to the combined effect of the motion of light and the motion of the observer. **4.** *Optics* The convergence to different foci, by a lens or mirror, of rays of light emanating from one and the same point, or the deviation of such rays from a single focus. ***Spherical aberration*** is due to the spherical form of the lens or mirror, giving different foci for central and marginal rays; ***chromatic aberration***, or ***chromatism***, is due to the differences in refraction of the colored rays of the spectrum, those of each color having a distinct focus.

a·bet′ (ȧ·bĕt′), *v. t.;* A·BET′TED; A·BET′TING. [OF. *abeter*, fr. *a* to + *beter* to bait (as a bear).] To encourage, support, or countenance, esp. an offender or the commission of an offense. — **Syn.** See INCITE. — **Ant.** Deter. — **a·bet′ment**, *n.*

a·bet′tor, a·bet′ter (ȧ·bĕt′ẽr), *n.* One who abets.

‖**ab ex′tra** (ăb ĕks′trȧ). [L.] From without; extrinsic.

a·bey′ance (ȧ·bā′ăns), *n.* [AF., fr. OF. *abeance* expectation, fr. *a* to + *baer, beer*, to gape.] *Chiefly in **in abeyance**.* **1.** *Law.* Expectancy; condition of an inheritance pending determination of rightful owner or title. **2.** Temporary suppression; suspension.

a·bey′ant (-ănt), *adj.* In abeyance. — **Syn.** See LATENT.

ab·hom′i·na·ble (ăb·hŏm′ĭ·nȧ·b'l), *adj.* Abominable. *Obs.*

ab·hor′ (ăb·hôr′), *v. t.;* AB·HORRED′ (-hôrd′); AB·HOR′RING. [L. *abhorrere*, fr. *ab-* + *horrere* to bristle, shudder.] To shrink with shuddering from; to regard with horror or detestation. — **Syn.** See HATE. — **Ant.** Admire: enjoy. — **ab·hor′rer**, *n.*

ab·hor′rence (ăb·hôr′ĕns; -hŏr′ĕns), *n.* Act or state of abhorring; that which is abhorred.

ab·hor′rent (-ĕnt), *adj.* **1.** Feeling or showing abhorrence. **2.** Contrary or repugnant; — with *to*. **3.** Arousing strong dislike or aversion; abominable. — **Syn.** See HATEFUL: REPUGNANT. — **ab·hor′rent·ly**, *adv.*

a·bide′ (ȧ·bīd′), *v. i.; past & past part.* A·BODE′ (-bōd′), -BID′ED (-bīd′ĕd; -ĭd), *past part.* rarely -BID′DEN (-bĭd′'n), *pres. part.* A·BID′ING (-bīd′ĭng). [AS. *ābīdan*, fr. *ā-* + *bīdan* to bide.] **1.** To stay; to continue in a place; to dwell; sojourn. **2.** To remain stable or fixed in some state; to continue. — **Syn.** See STAY: CONTINUE. — *v. t.* **1.** To wait for; to await expectantly. **2.** To face or submit to without shrinking. **3.** To bear patiently; submit to; tolerate. **4.** [Confused with ABY to pay for.] To stand the consequences of; to suffer for. — **Syn.** See BEAR. — **a·bid′er** (ȧ·bīd′ẽr), *n.*

abide by. **a** To keep faithful to; to adhere to. **b** To accept as valid and take the consequences of.

a·bid′ing (ȧ·bīd′ĭng), *adj.* Continuing; lasting. — **a·bid′ing·ly**, *adv.*

Ab′i·gail (ăb′ĭ·gāl), *n.* [Heb. *Abīgayil.*] **1.** *Bib.* The wife of Nabal. 1 *Sam.* xxv. **2.** [*not cap.*] A lady's waiting maid.

a·bil′i·ty (ȧ·bĭl′ĭ·tĭ), *n.; pl.* -TIES (-tĭz). [Through OF. fr. L. *habilitas* aptness, fr. *habilis* apt. See ABLE.] Quality or state of being able; power to perform, whether physical, moral, intellectual, or legal; capacity; skill or competence; sufficiency of power, skill, etc.; in *pl.*, faculties; talents.

‖**ab in·i′ti·o** (ăb ĭ·nĭsh′ĭ·ō). [L.] From the beginning.

‖**ab in′tra** (ăb ĭn′trȧ). [L.] From within.

ab′i·o·gen′e·sis (ăb′ĭ·ō·jĕn′ĕ·sĭs), *n.* [NL., fr. *a-* not + *bio-* + *-genesis*.] = SPONTANEOUS GENERATION. — **ab′i·o·ge·net′ic** (-jĕ·nĕt′ĭk), **ab′i·o·ge·net′i·cal** (-ĭ·kăl), *adj.* — **ab′i·o·ge·net′i·cal·ly**, *adv.* — **ab′i·og′e·nist** (ăb′ĭ·ŏj′ĕ·nĭst), *n.*

ab·ir′ri·tant (ăb·ĭr′ĭ·tănt), *n. Med.* A medicine that removes or relieves irritation. — **ab·ir′ri·tant**, *adj.*

ab′ject (ăb′jĕkt; ăb·jĕkt′), *adj.* [L. *abjectus*, past part. of *abjicere* to throw away, fr. *ab-* + *jacere* to throw.] **1.** *Archaic.* Cast down; lowlying. *Milton.* **2.** Sunk to a low condition; cast down in spirit or hope; servile. — **Syn.** See MEAN. — **Ant.** Exalted: imperious. — **ab·jec′tion** (ăb·jĕk′shŭn), *n.* — **ab·ject′ly** (ăb·jĕkt′lĭ; ăb′jĕkt·lĭ; 2), *adv.* — **ab·ject′ness** (-nĕs; -nĭs; 2), *n.*

ab·jure′ (ăb·jo͝or′), *v. t.;* AB·JURED′; AB·JUR′ING. [L. *abjurare* to deny upon oath, fr. *ab-* + *jurare* to swear.] **1.** To renounce upon oath; forswear; disavow; as, to *abjure* allegiance or a claim. **2.** To renounce or reject with solemnity; recant; repudiate; as, to *abjure* a former belief. — **ab′ju·ra′tion** (ăb′jo͞o·rā′shŭn), *n.* — **ab·jur′a·to′ry** (ăb·jo͞or′ȧ·tō′rĭ), *adj.* — **ab·jur′er** (-ẽr), *n.*

Syn. **Abjure, renounce, forswear, recant, retract** mean to repudiate irrevocably. **Abjure** implies repudiation of an oath or vow or, sometimes, of something generally accepted; **renounce** often equals *abjure* but sometimes carries the meaning of *disclaim* or *disown;* **forswear** often implies the act of going back upon one's word, sometimes with intent to deceive or, more often, an abjuration; **recant** stresses the withdrawal of something professed or taught, **retract** the withdrawal of a promise, an offer, a charge, or the like. — **Ant.** Pledge (*allegiance, etc.*): elect (*a means, etc.*).

ab′lac·ta′tion (ăb′lăk·tā′shŭn), *n.* Act or process of weaning.

ab·la′tion (ăb·lā′shŭn), *n.* [L. *ablatio*, fr. *ablatus*, past part. to *auferre* to carry away.] Removal, specif. by surgery.

ab′la·tive (ăb′lȧ·tĭv), *adj.* [F. or L.; F. *ablatif, ablative*, fr. L. *ablativus*, fr. *ablatus*. See ABLATION.] *Gram.* Designating or pertaining to a case of the noun, in Latin and Sanskrit, expressing the relations of *removal* or *direction away* which are expressed for English nouns by *from*, and in Latin also the senses of *with, by, at*, and *in*. — *n.* The ablative case, or a form in that case. Abbr. *abl.*

ablative absolute. A Latin noun and its adjunct both in the ablative case, forming an adverbial phrase expressing time, cause, or circumstance (*se sciente*, wittingly).

ab′laut (ăb′lout; *G.* äp′lout), *n.* [G., off-sound.] The systematic variation of the root vowel in related words, indicating a change of use or meaning (*ride, rode, ridden; sing, song*), — an Indo-European phenomenon.

a·blaze′ (ȧ·blāz′), *adv.* & *adj.* On fire; gleaming; ardent.

a′ble (ā′b'l), *adj.;* A′BLER (ā′blẽr); A′BLEST (-blĕst; -blĭst). [OF., fr. L. *habilis* that may be easily held or managed, apt, fr. *habere* to have, hold.] **1.** Having sufficient power, skill, or resources of any kind to accomplish an object; capable; competent. **2.** Having intellectual qualifications, or strong mental powers; showing mastery in some department of knowledge or affairs; talented; clever.

Syn. **Able, capable, competent, qualified** come into comparison when they mean having power or fitness for work. **Able** suggests ability above the average as revealed in promise or performance; **capable** stresses qualities which fit one for work but seldom imply a special ability; **competent** and **qualified** imply the experience or training for a definite employment. — **Ant.** Inept.

-a·ble (-ȧ·b'l). Also **-i·ble** (-ĭ·b'l), **-ble** (-b'l). [F., fr. L. *-abilis, -ibilis, -bilis*.] An adjective suffix used: **a** Passively with implication of *capacity, fitness*, or *worthiness* to be acted upon, as in read*able*, capable of being read, eat*able*, fit to be eaten. **b** In the sense of *tending to, given to, favoring, causing, able to*, or *liable to*, as in peace*able*, given to peace, perish*able*, liable to perish.

☞ The form *-ible* occurs mostly with words going back directly to Latin verbs in *-ere, -ire*. The form *-able*, occurring originally in words formed on Latin verbs in *-are*, has been adopted in English as the form for use with native verbs and nouns. In adjectives from the French, *-able* often represents French *-able* for Latin *-ibilis* (mov*able*).

a′ble–bod′ied (ā′b'l·bŏd′ĭd; ā′b'l·bŏd′ĭd; 2), *adj.* Having a sound, strong body.

a′ble–bod′ied sea′man. See SEAMAN.

ab′le·gate (ăb′lĕ·gāt), *n.* A papal envoy on a special mission, as to convey insignia of office to a newly named cardinal.

able seaman. See SEAMAN, *n.*, 1.

a′blins, a′blings (ā′blĭnz), *adv. Scot.* Perhaps.

a·bloom′ (ȧ·blo͞om′), *adj.* & *adv.* Blooming.

ab′lu·ent (ăb′lū·ĕnt), *adj.* & *n.* [L. *abluens*, pres. part.] = DETERGENT.

a·blush′ (ȧ·blŭsh′), *adj.* Blushing.

ab·lu′tion (ăb·lū′shŭn), *n.* [OF. or L.; OF., fr. L. *ablutio*, fr. *abluere*, fr. *ab-* + *luere* to wash.] **1.** A washing or cleansing, specif. as a religious rite. **2.** The liquid used in cleansing. — **ab·lu′tion·ar′y** (-ĕr′ĭ or, *esp. Brit.*, -ẽr·ĭ), *adj.*

a′bly (ā′blĭ), *adv.* In an able manner; with great ability.

ab′ne·gate (ăb′nē·gāt), *v. t.;* -GAT′ED (-gāt′ĕd; -ĭd); -GAT′ING. [L. *abnegatus*, past part. of *abnegare*, fr. *ab-* + *negare* to deny.] To deny and reject; to abjure; renounce. — **ab′ne·ga′tor** (-gā′tẽr), *n.*

ab′ne·ga′tion (-gā′shŭn), *n.* A denial; a renunciation; self-denial.

ab·nor′mal (ăb·nôr′măl), *adj.* [From *anormal*, after L. *abnormis*, fr. *ab-* + *norma* rule.] Deviating from the normal condition, or from the norm or average; markedly or strangely irregular. — **ab·nor′mal·ly**, *adv.*

ab′nor·mal′i·ty (ăb′nôr·măl′ĭ·tĭ), *n.; pl.* -TIES (-tĭz). **1.** Abnormal state or quality. **2.** Something abnormal, as a malformation or aberration.

ab·nor′mi·ty (ăb·nôr′mĭ·tĭ), *n.; pl.* -TIES (-tĭz). Abnormality; hence, a monstrosity.

a·board′ (ȧ·bōrd′; 70), *adv.* **1.** On board; into or within a boat or railway car. **2.** Alongside; as, close *aboard*. — *prep.* On board of.

a·bode′ (ȧ·bōd′), *n.* [From ABIDE.] **1.** Continued stay in a place; sojourn. **2.** Abiding place; dwelling.

a·bode′, *past & past part.* of ABIDE.

a·bol′ish (ȧ·bŏl′ĭsh), *v. t.* [F. *abolir*, fr. L. *abolere*, prob. fr. *aboles-*

cere to perish, fr. *ab-* + *alescere* to grow.] **1.** To do away with wholly; to annul; abrogate; as, to *abolish* a law or custom, taxes, or folly. **2.** *Poetic.* To destroy (a physical object). — **a·bol′ish·a·ble,** *adj.* — **a·bol′ish·er,** *n.* — **a·bol′ish·ment,** *n.*

Syn. **Abolish, annihilate, extinguish** are comparable when they mean to make nonexistent. **Abolish** takes for its object things which are the outgrowth of law, custom, and conditions of human existence; **annihilate,** anything material or immaterial that can be wiped out of existence. **Extinguish** stresses the power of the cause to overwhelm or suppress more than it does the result.

ab′o·li′tion (ăb′ō·lĭsh′ŭn), *n.* [L. *abolitio.*] **1.** Act of abolishing, or state of being abolished; an abrogation; utter destruction. **2.** Specif., *Hist.*, the abolishing of slavery. — **ab′o·li′tion·ar′y** (-ĕr′ĭ; -ēr·ĭ; 3), *adj.*

ab′o·li′tion·ism (-ĭz′m), *n.* The system of principles or measures favoring abolition, esp. of Negro slavery. — **ab′o·li′tion·ist** (-ĭst), *n.* & *adj.*

ab′o·ma′sum (ăb′ō·mā′sŭm), *n.*; *pl.* -MASA (-sȧ); **ab′o·ma′sus** (-sŭs), *n.*; *pl.* -MASI (-sī). [NL., fr. L. *ab-* + *omasum* bullock's tripe.] The fourth or digestive stomach of a ruminant. See RUMINANT, *Illust.*

A′–bomb′ (ā′bŏm′), *n.* See ATOMIC BOMB.

a·bom′i·na·ble (ȧ·bŏm′ĭ·nȧ·b′l), *adj.* [OF., fr. L. *abominabilis.*] **1.** Worthy of, or causing, abhorrence; detestable; loathsome. **2.** Disagreeable; unpleasant. — **Syn.** See HATEFUL. — **a·bom′i·na·ble·ness,** *n.* — **a·bom′i·na·bly** (-blĭ), *adv.*

a·bom′i·nate (-nāt), *v. t.*; -NAT′ED (-nāt′ĕd; -ĭd); -NAT′ING. [L. *abominatus*, past part. of *abominari* to deprecate as ominous, fr. *ab-* + *omen* a foreboding.] To detest in the highest degree; abhor. — **Syn.** See HATE. — **Ant.** Esteem; enjoy. — **a·bom′i·na′tor** (-nā′tēr), *n.*

a·bom′i·na′tion (-nā′shŭn), *n.* **1.** Extreme disgust and hatred; abhorrence; detestation; loathing. **2.** That which is abominable; anything hateful or shamefully vile.

‖**à bon mar′ché′** (à bôɴ′ mȧr′shā′). [F.] At a bargain; cheap.

a·boon′ (ȧ·bōōn′), *prep.* & *adv.* *Chiefly Dial.* Above.

ab′o·rig′i·nal (ăb′ō·rĭj′ĭ·năl), *adj.* **1.** First; original; native from the beginning or from a very early time. **2.** Of or pertaining to aborigines. — **Syn.** See NATIVE. — *n.* An aborigine. — **ab′o·rig′i·nal·ly,** *adv.*

ab′o·rig′i·ne (ăb′ō·rĭj′ĭ·nē), *n.*; *pl.* -RIGINES (-nēz). [L. *Aborigines*, esp. those who originally (*ab origine*) inhabited Latium. See ORIGIN.] **1.** One of the earliest known inhabitants of a country; one of the native race. **2.** *pl.* The original fauna and flora of a geographical area.

‖**ab o·ri′gi·ne** (ăb ō·rĭj′ĭ·nē). [L.] From the origin or beginning.

a·bort′ (ȧ·bôrt′), *v. i.* [L. *abortare*, fr. *abortus*, past part. of *aboriri*, fr. *ab-* + *oriri* to rise, be born.] **1.** *Med.* To give birth prematurely. **2.** *Biol.* To become checked in development, so as to remain rudimentary or shrink away.

a·bor′ti·cide (ȧ·bôr′tĭ·sīd), *n.* [L. *abortus* + *-cide.* See ABORT.] *Med.* **a** Act of destroying a fetus in the womb. **b** An agent that destroys the fetus and causes abortion.

a·bor′ti·fa′cient (-fā′shĕnt), *adj.* & *n.* [L. *abortus* + *faciens* making.] Producing, or that which produces, abortion.

a·bor′tion (ȧ·bôr′shŭn), *n.* [L. *abortio*, fr. *aboriri.* See ABORT.] **1.** The expulsion of the mammalian fetus prematurely, particularly at any time before it is viable; miscarriage. **2.** Any immature product of an untimely birth; a monstrosity. **3.** Any project or action that fails to attain full development. **4.** *Biol.* Arrest of development of an organ; also, an aborted organ. — **a·bor′tion·al,** *adj.*

a·bor′tion·ist (-ĭst), *n.* One who produces criminal abortions.

a·bor′tive (ȧ·bôr′tĭv), *adj.* **1.** Born prematurely. **2.** Coming to nought; ineffectual; unsuccessful. **3.** *Biol.* Imperfectly formed; rudimentary. **4.** *Med.* **a** Causing abortion. **b** Cutting short the course of a disease. — **a·bor′tive·ly,** *adv.* — **a·bor′tive·ness,** *n.*

‖**à bouche ou·verte′** (à bōōsh′ ōō′vĕrt′). [F.] With open mouth; hence, eagerly; uncritically.

a·bought′ (ȧ·bôt′), *past* & *past part.* of ABY.

a·bou′li·a (ȧ·bōō′lĭ·ȧ), **a·bou′lic.** Vars. of ABULIA, ABULIC.

a·bound′ (ȧ·bound′), *v. i.* [OF. *abonder*, fr. L. *abundare* to abound, fr. *ab-* + *undare* to rise in waves, fr. *unda* wave.] **1.** To be in great plenty, quantity, or number; to be prevalent. **2.** To be copiously supplied; to teem; — with *in* or *with*; as, a stream *abounding* in fish. — **a·bound′ing,** *adj.* — **a·bound′ing·ly,** *adv.*

a·bout′ (ȧ·bout′), *adv.* [AS. *abūtan, onbūtan*, fr. *on* on + *būtan*, fr. *be* by + *ūtan* outside, fr. *ūt* out.] **1.** On all sides; around. **2.** In circuit; around the outside. **3.** Here and there; around. **4. a** Approximately. **b** *Colloq.* Almost; as, *about* frozen. **5.** To a reversed position; half around; as, to face *about.* **6.** In rotation; as, turn *about* is fair play. **7.** *Colloq.* Near; in the vicinity. — *adj.* Stirring or moving from place to place; astir; up; as, able to be *about* again. — *prep.* **1.** All round; on every side of. **2.** In the immediate neighborhood of; near; by or on (one's person). **3.** Over or upon different parts of; here and there in. **4.** Near; not far from; as, *about* this time tomorrow. **5.** Engaged in; intent upon. **6.** On the point or verge of; in the act of; — before an infinitive or gerund. **7.** Concerning; with regard to. **8.** Appertaining to; as, something sly *about* her.

a·bout′–face′, *n.* A reversal of position or attitude.

a·bout′–face′, *v. i.* To execute an about-face.

a·bout′–ship′, *v. i.* To place a ship on the other tack.

a·bove′ (ȧ·bŭv′), *adv.* [AS. *on* on + *bufan*, fr. *be* by + *ufan* above.] **1.** In a place above something; overhead. **2.** Earlier in order; higher in the same page; hence, in a foregoing page; — sometimes used in combinations, as in **a·bove′–cit′ed, –men′tioned, –named′, –said′.** **3.** Superior in rank or power. — *prep.* **1.** In or to a higher place than; higher than; over. **2.** Superior to in any respect; surpassing; beyond; as, things *above* comprehension; specif., too high-minded to stoop to. **3.** Surpassing in number or quantity; more than. — *adj.* Being above; situated, said, written, or the like, above; foregoing. — *n.* That which is above.

a·bove′board′ (ȧ·bŭv′bōrd′; 70), *adv.* & *adj.* Above the board or table; without concealment or deception.

a·bove′ground′ (-ground′; 2), *adv.* & *adj.* Above the surface of the ground; hence, not dead and buried; alive.

‖**ab o′vo** (ăb ō′vō). [L.] From the egg; hence, from the beginning.

ab′ra·ca·dab′ra (ăb′rȧ·kȧ·dăb′rȧ), *n.* [L.] A mystical word supposed, when written triangularly and worn on an amulet, to ward off diseases; hence, a pretended spell; jargon.

ab·ra′dant (ăb·rā′dănt), *adj.* & *n.* [OF.] = ABRASIVE.

ab·rade′ (ăb·rād′), *v. t.* & *i.*; AB·RAD′ED (-rād′ĕd; -ĭd); AB·RAD′ING. [L. *abradere, abrasum*, to scrape off, fr. *ab-* + *radere* to scrape.] To rub off; to wear away by friction. — **Syn.** Excoriate, chafe, fret, gall. — **ab·rad′er** (-rād′ẽr), *n.*

A′bra·ham (ā′brȧ·hăm), *n.* [Heb.] *Bib.* The first of the patriarchs and father of the Hebrews. *Gen.* xi. ff.

a·bran′chi·an (ā·brăng′kĭ·ăn), *adj.* Also **a·bran′chi·al, a·bran′chi·ate, a·bran′chi·ous.** [See A- not; BRANCHIA.] *Zool.* Without gills.

ab·ra′sion (ăb·rā′zhŭn), *n.* [L. *abrasio*, fr. *abradere* to abrade.] The act of abrading, as of a coin by circulation; specif., a wearing away of the skin in small shreds by friction; also, an abraded surface.

ab·ra′sive (-sĭv), *adj.* Tending to abrade. — *n.* A substance used for abrading, as for grinding, polishing, etc.

‖**à bras ou′verts′** (à brȧ′-zōō′vâr′). [F.] With open arms; cordially.

ab′re·ac′tion (ăb′rē·ăk′shŭn), *n.* [*ab-* + *reaction*, after G. *abreagierung.*] *Psychoanalysis.* The removal of a complex or suppressed desire, as by talking it out. See CATHARSIS. — **ab′re·act′** (-ăkt′), *v. t.*

a·breast′ (ȧ·brĕst′), *adv.* & *adj.* **1.** Side by side. **2.** Up to a certain level or line; equally advanced; even.

‖**a′bri′** (ȧ′brē′), *n.*; *pl.* ABRIS (ȧ′brēz′; *F.* ȧ′brē′). [F.] A shelter, as a dugout, a shed, or a cavity in a hillside.

a·bridge′ (ȧ·brĭj′), *v. t.*; A·BRIDGED′ (-brĭjd′); A·BRIDG′ING. [OF. *abregier*, from L. *abbreviare*, from *ad-* + *breviare* to shorten, fr. *brevis* short.] To reduce in compass, leaving still relatively complete; specif.: **a** To make shorter; to diminish; curtail; as, to *abridge* a visit or distance. **b** To shorten by using fewer words, yet retaining the sense; to condense. **c** To deprive; to cut off; as, to *abridge* a person of his rights. — **Syn.** See SHORTEN. — **Ant.** Expand. — **a·bridge′a·ble, a·bridg′a·ble** (-brĭj′ȧ·b′l), *adj.* — **a·bridged′,** *adj.* — **a·bridg′er,** *n.*

a·bridg′ment, a·bridge′ment (ȧ·brĭj′mĕnt), *n.* **1.** Act of abridging, or state of being abridged. **2.** A reduced form of a work, retaining the general sense and unity of the original.

Syn. **Abridgment, abstract, brief, synopsis, conspectus, epitome** mean a condensed treatment. **Abridgment** suggests reduction in compass with retention of relative completeness; **abstract,** a summary of points of a treatise or proposed treatment; **brief,** an abstract covering arguments, especially in law; **synopsis** and **conspectus,** an ordered presentation of salient points of a subject or treatise enabling the reader to apprehend it at a glance; **epitome,** the briefest possible statement giving a complex whole in miniature. Cf. COMPENDIUM.

a·broach′ (ȧ·brōch′), *adv.* & *adj.* Broached; in a condition for letting out liquor; hence, afoot; astir.

a·broad′ (ȧ·brôd′), *adv.* **1.** At large; widely; broadly. **2.** Outside a certain confine; as, to walk *abroad.* **3.** Beyond the bounds of a country. **4.** Before the public at large; as, mischief is *abroad.* **5.** Astray; wide of the mark.

ab′ro·ga·ble (ăb′rō·gȧ·b′l), *adj.* Capable of being abrogated.

ab′ro·gate (ăb′rō·gāt), *v. t.* [L. *abrogatus*, past part. of *abrogare* to repeal, fr. *ab-* + *rogare* to propose.] To annul by an authoritative act; to abolish. — **Syn.** See NULLIFY. — **ab′ro·ga′tion** (-gā′shŭn), *n.* — **ab′ro·ga′tive** (-gā′tĭv), *adj.* — **ab′ro·ga′tor** (-gā′tẽr), *n.*

ab·rupt′ (ăb·rŭpt′), *adj.* [L. *abruptus*, past part. of *abrumpere*, fr. *ab-* + *rumpere* to break.] **1.** Broken off; very steep or craggy, as promontories. **2.** Sudden; hasty; unceremonious. **3.** Having sudden transitions from one subject to another; unconnected; as, an *abrupt* style. **4.** *Bot.* Suddenly terminating, as if cut off. — **Syn.** See STEEP; PRECIPITATE (**Ant.** deliberate). — **ab·rupt′ly,** *adv.* — **ab·rupt′ness,** *n.*

ab·rup′tion (ăb·rŭp′shŭn), *n.* A sudden breaking off or away.

abs-. A form of AB-.

ab′scess (ăb′sĕs; 30), *n.* [L. *abscessus* a going away, gathering of humors, deriv. of *abs-* + *cedere* to go.] A collection of pus, in any part of the body, usually due to infection by bacteria. Cf. ULCER.

ab′scessed (ăb′sĕst), *adj.* Having an abscess.

ab·scind′ (ăb·sĭnd′), *v. t.* To cut asunder. *Rare.*

ab·scis′sa (ăb·sĭs′ȧ), *n.*; *pl.* -SAS (-ȧz), -SAE (-ē). [L., fem. of *abscissus*, past part. of *abscindere* to cut off, fr. *ab-* + *scindere* to rend, cut.] *Geom.* One of the elements of reference by which a point, as of a curve, is referred to a system of fixed rectilineal co-ordinate axes. See ORDINATE, *Illust.*

ab·scis′sion (-sĭzh′ŭn), *n.* [L. *abscissio.*] Act or process of cutting off, or putting an end to; state of being cut off.

ab·scond′ (ăb·skŏnd′), *v. i.* [L. *abscondere* to hide, fr. *abs-* + *condere* to store.] To depart clandestinely; to steal off and secrete oneself. — **Syn.** Decamp, flee, fly, escape. — **ab·scond′er,** *n.*

ab′sence (ăb′sĕns; -s′ns), *n.* [F., fr. L. *absentia.*] **1.** State of being absent; failure to be present. **2.** Want; lack. **3.** Abstraction (of mind). — **Ant.** Presence.

ab′sent (-sĕnt; -s′nt), *adj.* [F., fr. L. *absens, absentis*, pres. part. of *abesse*, fr. *ab-* + *esse* to be.] **1.** Being away from a place; not present. **2.** Not existing; lacking. **3.** Inattentive to what is passing; as, an *absent* air. — **ab′sent·ly,** *adv.* — **ab′sent·ness,** *n.*

ab·sent′ (ăb·sĕnt′), *v. t.* To withdraw (oneself) to such a distance as to prevent intercourse. — **ab′sen·ta′tion** (ăb′sĕn·tā′shŭn), *n.*

ab′sen·tee′ (ăb′sĕn·tē′), *n.* One who is absent, or who absents himself, from his country, office, post, duty, etc.; specif., a landholder who lives in a country or district away from his estate. — **ab′sen·tee′,** *adj.*

ab′sen·tee′ism (-ĭz′m), *n.* State or practice of an absentee; specif.: **a** The practice of absenting oneself from the district where one's estate is situated. **b** The practice by an employee or group of employees of being absent from work, esp. when such absences are continued or often repeated.

ab′sent–mind′ed (ăb′sĕnt·mīn′dĕd; -dĭd; 2), *adj.* So preoccupied in mind as to fail to respond to the ordinary demands on one's attention; absent. — **ab′sent–mind′ed·ly,** *adv.* — **ab′sent–mind′ed·ness,** *n.*

ab′sinthe, ab′sinth (ăb′sĭnth), *n.* [F. *absinthe.*] **1.** The common wormwood (*Artemisia absinthium*). **2.** A green alcoholic liquor containing oils of wormwood and anise, and other aromatics. Its continued use causes nervous derangement.

ab′sinth·ism (ăb′sĭnth·ĭz′m; ăb·sĭnth′-), *n.* *Med.* A diseased condition due to the excessive use of absinthe.

‖**ab′sit o′men** (ăb′sĭt ō′mĕn). [L.] May there be no (ill) omen, or harm (from a word just used or from an action).

ab′so·lute (ăb′sō·lūt), *adj.* [L. *absolutus*, past part. of *absolvere.* See ABSOLVE.] **1.** Free from imperfection; perfect. **2.** Free from mixture; pure; as, *absolute* alcohol. **3.** Positive; certain; also, authorita-

tive; peremptory. **4.** Free from limit, restriction, or qualification; as, an *absolute* monarch, veto, or gift. **5.** Determined in itself and not by anything outside itself; not dependent or relative; ultimate; intrinsic; as, *absolute* moral law; *absolute* knowledge. **6.** Measuring or representing the distance from an aircraft to the ground or water beneath. **7.** *Gram.* **a** Standing apart from its usual construction with another word or other words; as, an *absolute* construction (this being the case, let us go); "ours" is the *absolute* form of "our." **b** Standing with no object expressed; — said of a transitive verb. **8.** *Physics.* **a** Independent of arbitrary standards of measurement. **b** Pert. to, or derived in the simplest manner from, the fundamental units of length, mass, and time; as, *absolute* electric units. **c** Pert. to the absolute-temperature scale; as, 10° *absolute.*
— n. That which is absolute; esp. [*cap.*], with *the,* all reality considered as the final or total fact, or existence. — **ab′so·lute·ly** (ăb′sō·lūt·lĭ; *emphatic also* ăb′sō·lūt′lĭ), *adv.* — **ab′so·lute·ness,** *n.*

absolute music. Music expressively self-sufficient and structurally intelligible without aid of text or program. Cf. PROGRAM MUSIC.

absolute pitch. *Music.* **a** The position of a tone in reference to the whole range of pitch or to a standard scale, conceived as independently determined by its rate of vibration. See PITCH, *Illust.* **b** A sense of, or memory of, absolute pitch; as, that singer has *absolute pitch.*

absolute scale. See KELVIN SCALE.

absolute temperature. *Physical Chemistry.* Temperature measured in degrees centigrade from approximately –273.1° C. (–459.6° F.), which is the **absolute zero.**

ab′so·lu′tion (ăb′sō·lū′shŭn), *n.* [See ABSOLVE.] **1.** An absolving, or setting free from guilt, sin, or penalty; forgiveness. **2.** *Eccl.* **a** A remission of sins imparted or pronounced by a priest, esp. in the sacrament of penance. **b** *R.C.Ch.* A releasing from censures, as from excommunication.

ab′so·lut·ism (ăb′sō·lūt·ĭz′m), *n.* **1.** The doctrine of that which is absolute, or without limitations; specif., the doctrine or existence of unconditional power vested esp. in an autocrat; despotism. **2.** Absoluteness; positiveness. — **ab′so·lut·ist** (-ĭst), *n. & adj.* — **ab′so·lu·tis′tic** (-lū·tĭs′tĭk), *adj.*

ab·solve′ (ăb·sŏlv′ *or, esp. Brit.,* ăb·zŏlv′), *v. t.* [L. *absolvere* to set free, fr. *ab-* + *solvere* to loose.] **1.** To set free, or release, as from some obligation or from the consequences of guilt. **2.** To remit (an offense). — **Syn.** See EXCULPATE. — **ab·solv′a·ble,** *adj.* — **ab·sol′vent,** *adj. & n.* — **ab·solv′er,** *n.*

ab′so·nant (ăb′sō·nănt), *adj.* [L. *ab-* + *sonans* sounding.] Discordant; contrary; unreasonable.

ab·sorb′ (ăb·sôrb′), *v. t.* [F. *absorber,* fr. L. *absorbere,* fr. *ab-* + *sorbere* to suck in.] **1.** *Archaic.* To swallow up. **2.** Hence, to cause to disappear or lose identity. **3.** To suck up, as does a sponge; to take in (a gas, heat, light, etc.). **4.** To engross or engage wholly. **5.** To receive without a recoil or other effect; as, a sound-*absorbing* surface. — **ab·sorb′a·bil′i·ty,** *n.* — **ab·sorb′a·ble,** *adj.* — **ab·sorb′er,** *n.*
Syn. **Absorb, imbibe, assimilate** mean to take something in so as to become imbued with it. **Absorb,** which often implies a soaking up, may connote a loss of identity in that which is taken in or an enrichment of that which takes in; **imbibe,** which more often implies a process such as drinking in, usually suggests a learning effortlessly or unconsciously; **assimilate** suggests an incorporation into the substance of the body (in any sense) or into the mind of that which takes in. — **Ant.** Exude.

ab·sorbed′ (ăb·sôrbd′), *adj.* Buried or plunged in some thought or pursuit. — **Syn.** See INTENT. — **ab·sorb′ed·ly** (-sôr′bĕd·lĭ; -bĭd·lĭ), *adv.* — **ab·sorb′ed·ness,** *n.*

ab·sor′be·fa′cient (ăb·sôr′bē·fā′shĕnt), *adj.* [L. *absorbere* to absorb + L. *faciens, -entis,* pres. part. of *facere* to make, do.] Tending to produce absorption. **— n.** *Med.* Any agent promoting absorption.

ab·sorb′ent (ăb·sôr′bĕnt), *adj.* Having the power or capacity to take in, esp. by suction; absorptive. **— n.** A substance that absorbs. — **ab·sorb′en·cy** (-bĕn·sĭ), *n.*

ab·sorb′ing (-bĭng), *adj.* Engrossing. — **ab·sorb′ing·ly,** *adv.*

ab·sorp′tion (ăb·sôrp′shŭn), *n.* [L. *absorptio.*] **1.** Act or process of absorbing or of being absorbed; specif.: **a** Assimilation; as, the *absorption* of a smaller tribe. **b** The passage of digested food through the epithelial cells of the alimentary canal into the blood or lymph. **2.** Entire engrossment of the mind. — **ab·sorp′tive** (-tĭv), *adj.* — **ab·sorp′tive·ness, ab′sorp·tiv′i·ty** (ăb′sôrp·tĭv′ĭ·tĭ), *n.*

ab·stain′ (ăb·stān′), *v. i.* [From OF., fr. L. *abstinere, abstentum,* to keep from, fr. *ab-, abs-* + *tenere* to hold.] To withhold oneself from participation; to refrain voluntarily, esp. from indulgence of the appetites; — with *from.* — **Syn.** See REFRAIN. — **Ant.** Indulge.

ab·stain′er, *n.* One who abstains, esp. from the use of intoxicating liquors; as, a total *abstainer.*

ab·ste′mi·ous (ăb·stē′mĭ·ŭs), *adj.* [L. *abstemius.*] Sparing in use of food and drink; abstinent; also, marked by abstinence. — **ab·ste′mi·ous·ly,** *adv.* — **ab·ste′mi·ous·ness,** *n.*

ab·sten′tion (ăb·stĕn′shŭn), *n.* [F.] An act, or the practice, of abstaining. — **ab·sten′tious** (-shŭs), *adj.*

ab·sterge′ (ăb·stûrj′), *v. t.;* -STERGED′ (-stûrjd′); -STERG′ING (-stûr′jĭng). [F. or L.; F. *absterger,* fr. L. *abstergere, -tersum,* fr. *ab-, abs-* + *tergere* to wipe.] To clean, as by wiping; hence, to purge. — **ab·ster′sion** (-stûr′shŭn), *n.*

ab·ster′gent (-stûr′jĕnt), *adj.* Cleansing; detergent. **— n.** A cleansing substance, as soap.

ab′sti·nence (ăb′stĭ·nĕns), *n.* [OF., fr. L. *abstinentia,* fr. *abstinere.* See ABSTAIN.] **1.** Voluntary forbearance, esp. from indulgence of appetite or from eating certain foods; abstention. **2.** Habitual abstaining from intoxicating beverages; — called also *total abstinence.* — **ab′sti·nent,** *adj.* — **ab′sti·nent·ly,** *adv.*

ab′stract (ăb′străkt; ăb·străkt′; 2), *adj.* [L. *abstractus,* past part. of *abstrahere* to draw from, separate, fr. *ab-, abs-* + *trahere* to draw.] **1. a** Considered apart from any application to a particular object; as, *abstract* truth. **b** Ideal; abstruse. **c** *Math.* Used without reference to a thing or things; as, the *abstract* number 10. **2.** Of words, names, etc., not concrete: **a** Expressing a quality apart from any object (*honesty, whiteness*). **b** General, as opposed to particular (*reptile*). **3.** Dealing with a subject in its theoretical considerations only. **4.** *Art.* Presenting or characterized by nonrepresentational designs depicting no recognizable thing, only geometric figures, or abstruse diagrams, or mechanical or amorphous creations. — **Ant.** Concrete. — **ab′stract·ly,** *adv.* — **ab′stract·ness,** *n.*

ab′stract (ăb′străkt), *n.* **1.** That which comprises or concentrates in itself the essential qualities of a larger thing or of several things. **2.** A summary or an epitome. **3.** An abstract term or idea; also, with *the,* that which is abstract. — **Syn.** See ABRIDGMENT. — ***in the abstract.*** With reference to theoretical considerations only; apart from practical or actual conditions.

ab·stract′ (ăb·străkt′), *v. t.* **1.** To withdraw; separate; take away; specif., to disengage (the mind, attention, etc.). **2.** To separate by the operation of the mind, as the notion of dimension from that of space. **3.** To take dishonestly; purloin. **4.** (*pron.* ăb′străkt) To epitomize; summarize; abridge. — **Syn.** Detach, disengage. — **Ant.** Insert, introduce. — **ab·stract′er,** *n.*

ab·stract′ed (ăb·străk′tĕd; -tĭd), *adj.* Absent-minded. — **ab·stract′ed·ly,** *adv.* — **ab·stract′ed·ness,** *n.*

ab·strac′tion (ăb·străk′shŭn), *n.* **1.** Act of abstracting, or state of being abstracted. **2.** A withdrawal from worldly objects. **3.** An abstract idea or term; loosely, a theory; a visionary notion. **4.** Absence or absorption of mind. **5.** Abstract quality or character. **6.** *Art.* **a** An abstract composition; — often called ***pure abstraction.*** **b** A composition or creation suggested by a concrete object or organic figure which is transformed by the artist into a nonrepresentational design with recognizable elements, irregular curved lines, graded tones, etc.; — often called ***near abstraction.*** Cf. COLLAGE.

ab·strac′tion·ism (-ĭz′m), *n.* The principles or ideals of abstract art; also, the creation of abstractions (see ABSTRACTION, 6).

ab·strac′tive (ăb·străk′tĭv), *adj.* Able or tending to abstract. — **ab·strac′tive·ly,** *adv.* — **ab·strac′tive·ness,** *n.*

abstract of title. *Law.* An epitome of the successive conveyances upon which title to a piece of land rests. In England the vendor or mortgagor is required to furnish an abstract to the vendee or mortgagee at his own expense; in the United States, this is customary.

ab·stric′tion (ăb·strĭk′shŭn), *n.* [L. *ab-* + *strictio* a binding tight.] *Bot.* Formation of spores by the cutting off of portions of the sporophore through the growth of dividing partitions.

ab·struse′ (ăb·strōōs′), *adj.* [L. *abstrusus,* past part. of *abstrudere* to conceal, fr. *abs-* + *trudere* to thrust.] **1.** *Obs.* Concealed. *Milton.* **2.** Difficult to comprehend; recondite. — **ab·struse′ly,** *adv.* — **ab·struse′ness,** *n.*

ab·surd′ (ăb·sûrd′), *adj.* [F. *absurde,* fr. L. *absurdus* harsh-sounding, absurd.] Contrary to reason; obviously inconsistent with truth, opinions generally held, or common sense; ridiculously incongruous. — **Syn.** Foolish, silly, preposterous. — **ab·surd′ly,** *adv.* — **ab·surd′ness,** *n.*

ab·surd′i·ty (ăb·sûr′dĭ·tĭ), *n.; pl.* -TIES (-tĭz). **1.** Quality or state of being absurd. **2.** That which is absurd.

a·bu′li·a (ȧ·bū′lĭ·ȧ), *n.* [NL., fr. Gr. *a-* not + root of *boulesthai* to will; cf. Gr. *aboulia* thoughtlessness.] *Psychol.* Loss of will power. — **a·bu′lic** (-lĭk), *adj.*

a·bun′dance (ȧ·bŭn′dăns), *n.* [From OF., fr. L. *abundantia,* fr. *abundare.* See ABOUND.] **1.** An overflowing fullness; ample sufficiency; great plenty. **2.** Affluence.

a·bun′dant (-dănt), *adj.* [From OF., fr. L. *abundans,* pres. part. of *abundare.* See ABOUND.] Existing in or possessing abundance; abounding. — **Syn.** See PLENTIFUL. — **Ant.** Scarce. — **a·bun′dant·ly,** *adv.*

abundant year. See JEWISH CALENDAR.

‖**ab ur′be con′di·ta** (ăb ûr′bē kŏn′dĭ·tȧ) [L.] From the founding of the city (Rome) — about 753 B.C.; — used by the Romans in reckoning dates. Abbr. *A.U.C.*

a·buse′ (ȧ·būz′), *v. t.* [F. *abuser,* fr. L. *abusus,* past part. of *abuti* to abuse, fr. *ab-* + *uti* to use.] **1.** To put to a wrong or bad use; to misapply; as, to *abuse* one's authority. **2.** To use ill or maltreat, as prisoners; to tax excessively, as one's patience. **3.** *Archaic.* To deceive. **4.** To revile; reproach coarsely; disparage. — **Syn.** Misuse, mistreat, maltreat, ill-treat, outrage. — **Ant.** Respect, honor. — **a·bus′er** (ȧ·būz′ẽr), *n.*

a·buse′ (ȧ·būs′), *n.* [F. *abus.*] **1.** Improper treatment or use; misuse. **2.** Physical ill treatment; injury. **3.** A corrupt custom; offense. **4.** Vituperative words; coarse, insulting speech. **5.** *Obs.* Deception.
Syn. **Abuse, vituperation, invective, obloquy, scurrility, billingsgate** mean vehemently expressed condemnation. **Abuse,** the general term, stresses the offensiveness of the language used or, now often, of its connotations; **vituperation,** an overwhelming of someone with a torrent of abuse; **invective,** in no way weakening the implication of the vehemence in attack, suggests logical presentation, usually in public, often in a good cause; **obloquy** suggests defamation and consequent disgrace; **scurrility** and **billingsgate** stress offensiveness and foulness of the language rather than skill in attack. — **Ant.** Adulation.

a·bu′sive (ȧ·bū′sĭv), *adj.* **1.** Wrongly used; perverted. **2.** Given to or tending to abuse; practicing abuse. **3.** Containing, or serving for, abuse. — **Syn.** Vituperative, scurrilous, opprobrious, contumelious. — **a·bu′sive·ly,** *adv.* — **a·bu′sive·ness,** *n.*

a·but′ (ȧ·bŭt′), *v. i.;* A·BUT′TED; A·BUT′TING. [Through OF. *abouter, aboter,* to fix the limits of, fr. *a-* to + *boter, buter,* to push, of LG. origin. See BUTT to strike with the head.] To touch, as contiguous estates, along a border or with a projecting part; to terminate or lean at a point of contact; — with *on, upon,* or *against.* Cf. ADJACENT. **— v. t.** To border on; touch. — **a·but′ter,** *n.*

a·bu′ti·lon (ȧ·bū′tĭ·lŏn), *n.* [NL., fr. Ar. *aubūtīlūn.*] *Bot.* Any of a genus (*Abutilon*) of plants of the mallow family, with, usually, lobed leaves and showy, solitary, bell-shaped flowers; also, the flower of this plant.

a·but′ment (ȧ·bŭt′mĕnt), *n.* **1.** Act or place of abutting. **2.** *Arch.* The part of a buttress, pier, wall, etc., which receives thrust, as of an arch or strut; specif., of a bridge, the support at either extreme end; — distinguished from *pier.* Cf. BRIDGE, *Illust.*

a·but′tal (ȧ·bŭt′ăl), *n.* **1.** *pl.* The boundaries of lands. **2.** Position or state of abutting.

a·but′ting, *adj.* That abuts. — **Syn.** See ADJACENT.

a·by′, a·bye′ (ȧ·bī′), *v. t. & i.; past & past part.* A·BOUGHT′ (ȧ·bôt′). [AS. *ābycgan* to pay for.] *Archaic.* **1.** To pay or atone (for). **2.** To endure; last.

a·bysm′ (ȧ·bĭz′m), *n.* [OF. *abisme,* fr. L. *abyssus.* See ABYSS.] An abyss. "The dark backward and *abysm* of time." *Shak.*

a·bys′mal (ȧ·bĭz′măl), *adj.* Pertaining to or resembling an abyss; bottomless; profound. — **Syn.** See DEEP. — **a·bys′mal·ly,** *adv.*

a·byss′ (ȧ·bĭs′), *n.* [L. *abyssus,* fr. Gr. *abyssos* bottomless, fr. *a-* not + *byssos* bottom.] **1.** The bottomless gulf or chaos of old cosmogonies. **2.** Any deep immeasurable space, chasm, or void; hence, infinite time; a vast intellectual or moral depth.

a·byss′al (ȧ·bĭs′ăl), *adj.* **1.** Unfathomable. **2.** Pertaining to the bottom waters of the ocean depths.

ac-. The Latin assimilated form of AD- before *c* or *q*, as in *acquire.*

-ac. [F. or L. or Gr.; F. *-aque,* fr. L. *-acus,* fr. Gr. *-akos.*] A suffix in adjectives and derivative nouns taken or formed from Greek or Latin, as in elegi*ac*; — equivalent to *-ic.*

a·ca′cia (ȧ·kā′shȧ), *n.* [L., fr. Gr. *akakia;* orig., a thorny tree found in Egypt.] **1.** *Bot.* A woody shrub or tree (genus *Acacia*) of the mimosa family, with pinnate leaves and ball-like clusters of white or yellow flowers. The species are found throughout warm parts of the world; some yield valuable gums (e.g., gum arabic) and tanning extracts (e.g., some kinds of catechu). See WATTLE, *n.*, 5. **2.** *U.S.* = LOCUST, 3 **a**. **3.** Gum arabic.

ac′a·deme′ (ăk′ȧ·dēm′), *n.* *Poetic.* Academy (sense 1).

ac′a·dem′ic (ăk′ȧ·dĕm′ĭk), **ac′a·dem′i·cal** (-ĭ·kăl), *adj.* **1.** Pertaining or belonging to an academy, college, or university, or to colleges, etc. **2.** Literary, classical, or liberal, rather than technical or professional; as, an *academic* course. **3.** Conforming to scholastic traditions or rules; conventional; as, *academic* verse. **4.** Theoretical and not expected to produce a practical result; as, an *academic* discussion. — **Syn.** Pedantic, bookish, scholastic: theoretical, speculative. — **ac′a·dem′i·cal·ly,** *adv.*

ac′a·dem′ic, *n.* A member of a college or university.

ac′a·dem′i·cals (-ĭ·kălz), *n. pl.* Academic garb.

a·cad′e·mi′cian (ȧ·kăd′ē·mĭsh′ăn), *n.* A member of an academy for promoting science, art, or literature.

ac′a·dem′i·cism (ăk′ȧ·dĕm′ĭ·sĭz′m), *n.* Also **a·cad′e·mism** (ȧ·kăd′ē·mĭz′m), *n.* Adherence to conventional manner and theme; formalism.

a·cad′e·my (ȧ·kăd′ē·mĭ), *n.; pl.* -MIES (-mĭz). [From F., fr. L. *academia,* fr. Gr. *akadēmeia.*] **1.** [*cap.*] A grove near Athens where Plato and his followers met; hence, Plato's school or philosophy. **2.** An institution of higher learning; a college or university; now, a secondary school under trustees or a proprietor. **3.** A place of training; a school. **4.** A society of learned men united to advance art or science.

ac′a·leph (ăk′ȧ·lĕf), **ac′a·lephe** (-lēf), *n.* [Gr. *akalēphē* nettle.] Any of a group (Acalephae) of coelenterates including the jellyfishes, hydroids, and their allies.

ac′an·tha′ceous (ăk′ăn·thā′shŭs), *adj.* *Bot.* **a** Prickly. **b** Belonging to the acanthus family (Acanthaceae) of herbs, shrubs, and trees typified by the acanthus.

a·can′tho- (ȧ·kăn′thō-), **acanth-.** [Gr. *akantha* a thorn.] A combining form meaning *thorn, thorny, spine, spiny.*

a·can′tho·ceph′a·lan (-sĕf′ȧ·lăn), *n.* [*acantho-* + Gr. *kephalē* head.] *Zool.* Any of a class (Acanthocephala) of intestinal worms having the proboscis armed with recurved spines. They absorb food through the body wall. — **a·can′tho·ceph′a·lan,** *adj.*

a·can′thoid (ȧ·kăn′thoid), *adj.* [*acanth-* + *-oid.*] Shaped like a spine; spiny; spinous.

ac′an·thop′ter·yg′i·an (ăk′ăn·thŏp′tēr·ĭj′ĭ·ăn), *adj.* [*acantho-* + Gr. *pterygion* fin.] *Zool.* Of or pertaining to a division (Acanthopterygii) of teleost fishes, including most spiny-finned fishes, as basses, perches, mackerels, and some soft-finned fishes. — *n.* An acanthopterygian fish.

a·can′thous (ȧ·kăn′thŭs), *adj.* Spinous.

a·can′thus (-thŭs), *n.; pl.* -THUSES (-ĕz; -ĭz), -THI (-thī). [L., fr. Gr. *akanthos,* fr. *akantha* thorn.] **1.** *Bot.* Any of a genus (*Acanthus*) of prickly herbs (family Acanthaceae, the acanthus family) of the Mediterranean region. **2.** *Arch.* An ornamentation patterned after leaves of the acanthus, as in the Corinthian capital.

Acanthus, 2.

‖**a ca′pi·te ad cal′cem** (ā kăp′ĭ·tē ăd kăl′sĕm). [L.] From head to heel; from head to foot.

‖**a cap·pel′la** (ä käp·pĕl′lä). [It.] In chapel style; that is, unaccompanied; — of choral music.

‖**a ca·pric′cio** (ä kä·prēt′chō). [It.] *Music.* At the performer's pleasure with regard to interpretation; — a direction.

ac′a·ri′a·sis (ăk′ȧ·rī′ȧ·sĭs), *n.* [NL.] Infestation with acarids, or mites, or any resulting diseased condition.

ac′a·rid (ăk′ȧ·rĭd), *n.* [Gr. *akari* mite, tick.] *Zool.* One of an order (Acarina) of arachnids including the mites and ticks.

ac′a·roid (-roid), *adj.* [See -OID.] Resembling a mite.

acaroid resin *or* **gum.** See GRASS TREE **a**.

a·car′pel·ous, a·car′pel·lous (ā·kär′pĕl·ŭs), *adj.* *Bot.* Having no carpels.

a·car′pous (ā·kär′pŭs), *adj.* [Gr. *akarpos,* fr. *a-* not + *karpos* fruit.] *Bot.* Not producing fruit; sterile.

a·cat′a·lec′tic (ā·kăt′ȧ·lĕk′tĭk), *adj.* [LL. *acatalecticus,* fr. Gr. *akatalēktos* not defective at the end.] *Pros.* Not defective in the last foot. — *n.* An acatalectic verse.

a·cau′dal (ā·kô′dăl; -d'l), **a·cau′date** (-dāt), *adj.* [*a-* not + *caudal, caudate.*] Tailless.

ac′au·les′cent (ăk′ô·lĕs′ĕnt), *adj.* Also **a·cau′line** (ā·kô′lĭn; -līn), **a·cau′lose** (-lōs), **a·cau′lous** (-lŭs). [See A- not; CAULESCENT.] *Bot.* Having no visible stem. — **ac′au·les′cence** (-lĕs′ĕns), *n.*

ac·cede′ (ăk·sēd′), *v. i.* [L. *accedere* to approach, accede, fr. *ad-* + *cedere* to move, yield.] **1.** To enter upon an office or dignity; attain; — with *to.* **2.** To give one's adherence; hence, to agree or assent, as to an opinion or proposal. — **Syn.** See ASSENT. — **Ant.** Demur. — **ac·ced′ence** (-sēd′ĕns; -'ns), *n.* — **ac·ced′er** (-sēd′ẽr), *n.*

ac·cel′er·a·ble (ăk·sĕl′ẽr·ȧ·b'l), *adj.* Capable of acceleration.

ac·cel′er·an′do (ăk·sĕl′ẽr·ăn′dō; *It.* ät·chā′lā·rän′dō), *adv. & adj.* [It.] *Music.* Gradually faster; — a direction.

ac·cel′er·ant (ăk·sĕl′ẽr·ănt), *adj.* Accelerating. — *n.* One who or that which accelerates; specif., *Chem.,* a catalyst.

ac·cel′er·ate (-āt), *v. t.* [L. *acceleratus,* past part. of *accelerare,* fr. *ad-* + *celerare* to hasten, fr. *celer* quick.] **1.** To cause to move faster. **2.** To quicken the natural or ordinary progression or process of. **3.** To bring about at an earlier point of time, as one's departure. **4.** *Mech.* To cause to undergo acceleration. — *v. i.* To move or act faster. — **Syn.** Speed, quicken. — **Ant.** Retard, decelerate.

ac·cel′er·a′tion (-ā′shŭn), *n.* **1.** Act or process of accelerating, or state of being accelerated. **2.** *Mech.* Change of velocity, or the rate of such change, as regards either speed or direction, or both. Retardation is called *deceleration,* or *negative acceleration.*

acceleration of gravity. *Physics.* The acceleration of a freely falling body due to the attraction of gravity, expressed as the rate of increase of velocity per unit of time (32.17 feet per second per second at the sea level in latitude 45°).

ac·cel′er·a′tive (ăk·sĕl′ẽr·ā′tĭv; -ȧ·tĭv), *adj.* Also **ac·cel′er·a·to′ry** (-ȧ·tō′rĭ *or, esp. Brit.,* -tẽr·ĭ). Relating to, or tending to cause, acceleration; adding to velocity.

ac·cel′er·a′tor (-ā′tẽr), *n.* One who or that which accelerates; specif.: **a** On automobiles, a foot-operated throttle. **b** (*pron.* ăk·sĕl′ẽr·ā′tẽr; *L.* ăk·sĕl′ẽr·ā′tôr) *Anat.* Any muscle or nerve that hastens a motion. **c** *Chem.* A substance that hastens a reaction. **d** *Physics.* Any device used to impart high speeds to charged particles.

ac·cel′er·om′e·ter (-ŏm′ē·tẽr), *n.* A device for measuring acceleration, as of a moving vehicle.

ac′cent (ăk′sĕnt *or, esp. Brit.,* ăk′sĕnt), *n.* [F., fr. L. *accentus* (trans. of Gr. *prosōidia,* cf. PROSODY), fr. *ad-* + *cantus* a singing, fr. *canere* to sing.] **1.** An articulative effort giving prominence to one syllable of a word or group of words over adjacent syllables; also, the prominence so given. Cf. STRESS. See *Pron.,* § 1. **2.** A mark used with a letter or group of letters to indicate the nature and place of the spoken accent or, esp. in European languages, the quality of sound of the letter marked. **3.** Modulation of the voice in speaking; as, a foreign *accent.* **4.** *Poetic.* A word; *pl.,* speech. **5.** Distinctive mode of expression; distinguishing character, as of a painter. **6.** A mark placed at the right hand of a letter or number, and a little above it: **a** *Math.* To distinguish either different variables or different values of the same variable, as in y', y''; — usually called *prime, double prime.* **b** To denote minutes or seconds of a degree or of time, as in 2′ 21″ (two minutes twenty-one seconds), or feet or inches, as in 6′ 10″ (six feet ten inches). **7.** *Music.* **a** A stress or special emphasis upon a tone, or a mark indicating this. **b** The principle of regularly recurring stresses which serve to distribute a succession of pulses into equal groups or measures. **8.** *Pros.* Rhythmically significant stress; the beat in poetic rhythm; ictus; the mark indicating this.

ac·cent′ (ăk·sĕnt′; ăk′sĕnt), *v. t.* **1.** (*pron. usually* ăk′sĕnt) To express the accent of (either by the voice or by a mark). **2.** To accentuate; emphasize.

ac·cen′tu·al (ăk·sĕn′tū·ăl), *adj.* Of, pertaining to, characterized by, or formed by, accent; specif., *Pros.,* syllabic accent. Cf. QUANTITATIVE. — **ac·cen′tu·al′i·ty** (-ăl′ĭ·tĭ), *n.* — **ac·cen′tu·al·ly,** *adv.*

ac·cen′tu·ate (-āt), *v. t.* [ML. *accentuatus,* past part. of *accentuare.*] To accent; emphasize; intensify. — **ac·cen′tu·a′tion** (-ā′shŭn), *n.*

ac·cept′ (ăk·sĕpt′), *v. t.* [From F., fr. L. *acceptare,* freq. of *accipere,* fr. *ad-* + *capere* to take.] **1.** To receive (a thing offered) with a consenting mind. **2.** To receive with favor; to approve. **3.** To receive or admit and agree to; to assent to; as, I *accept* your excuse. **4.** To understand; as, how are these words to be *accepted?* Hence, to receive as true; believe. **5.** In a deliberative body, to receive (a report, as from a committee) in acquittance of a duty imposed. **6.** To engage oneself by a favorable reply to (an invitation). **7.** *Com.* To receive as obligatory and promise to pay, as a bill of exchange. — *v. i.* To make acceptance; — with *of.* — **Syn.** See RECEIVE. — **Ant.** Reject, decline.

ac·cept′a·ble (ăk·sĕp′tȧ·b'l), *adj.* Capable, worthy, or sure of being accepted; agreeable; welcome. — **ac·cept′a·bil′i·ty** (-bĭl′ĭ·tĭ), **ac·cept′a·ble·ness,** *n.* — **ac·cept′a·bly,** *adv.*

ac·cept′ance (-tăns), *n.* [OF.] **1.** Act of accepting; esp., favorable reception; approval. **2.** State or quality of being accepted; acceptableness. **3.** *Com.* **a** An assent and engagement by the person on whom a bill of exchange is drawn to pay it when due according to terms stated. **b** An accepted bill, esp. a bill of exchange; as, a trade *acceptance,* a bank *acceptance.* **4.** *Law.* An agreeing, either expressly or by conduct, to the act or offer of another so that a contract is concluded and the parties become bound.

ac·cept′an·cy (-tăn·sĭ), *n.* Acceptance.

ac·cept′ant (-tănt), *adj.* Accepting; receiving.

ac′cep·ta′tion (ăk′sĕp·tā′shŭn), *n.* [F.] **1.** *Archaic.* Acceptance. **2.** The meaning in which a word or expression is understood, or generally received. — **Syn.** See MEANING.

ac·cept′ed (ăk·sĕp′tĕd; -tĭd), *adj.* **1.** Generally believed in or approved. **2.** Acknowledged as an obligation, with promise of payment, as a bill of exchange.

ac·cept′er (-tẽr), *n.* One who accepts; a taker.

ac·cep′tor (ăk·sĕp′tẽr; -tôr), *n.* [L.] One who or that which accepts; specif., one who accepts a bill of exchange, or the like.

ac′cess (ăk′sĕs; *formerly* ăk·sĕs′), *n.* [OF. *acces,* fr. L. *accessus,* fr. *accedere.* See ACCEDE.] **1.** Approach; admittance; admission; accessibility; as, to gain *access;* easy of *access;* also, an advance or approaching. **2.** A means, place, or way of approach. **3.** An attack or fit of disease. **4.** A fit of passion; an outburst; as, an *access* of fury or of zeal. **5.** Increase by addition; accession. *Milton.* **6.** *Eccl.* Approach to God through Jesus Christ (*Rom.* v. 2; *Eph.* ii. 18, iii. 12); — in titles of prayers.

ac·ces′sa·ry (ăk·sĕs′ȧ·rĭ), *adj. & n.* Accessory.

☞ Etymologically the noun is primarily *accessary,* the adj. *accessory;* but present usage favors *accessory* for both.

ac·ces′si·ble (-ĭ·b'l), *adj.* **1.** Usable for access. **2.** Easy of access; also, open to the influence (of); as, a mind *accessible* to reason. **3.** Obtainable; as, all the data *accessible.* — **ac·ces′si·bil′i·ty** (-bĭl′ĭ·tĭ), *n.* — **ac·ces′si·bly,** *adv.*

ac·ces′sion (ăk·sĕsh′ŭn), *n.* [L. *accessio.*] **1.** A coming to or near; approach. **2.** Act of acceding and becoming joined; also, assent. **3.** Increase by something added; as, an *accession* of wealth; also, that which is added; as, a list of *accessions* to a library. **4.** The act of coming to or reaching a throne, an office, or a condition, as manhood. **5.** *Law.* Addition to property by growth, increase, or labor. — *v. t.* To record (data concerning accessions). — **ac·ces′sion·al,** *adj.*

ac′ces·so′ri·al (ăk′sĕ·sō′rĭ·ăl; 70), *adj.* Of or pertaining to, or of the nature of, accession or an accessory.

ac·ces′so·ry (ăk·sĕs′ō·rĭ), *adj.* **1.** Aiding or contributing in a secondary way; as, *accessory* sounds in music. **2.** Of a person, assisting or aiding as a subordinate; privy; as, made *accessory* to an offense. **3.** *Petrog.* Present in a minor amount and not essential as a constituent. — **Syn.** Auxiliary, contributory, subsidiary, adjuvant.

— *n.; pl.* -RIES (-rĭz). **1.** That which contributes subordinately to an effect; an adjunct or accompaniment. **2.** Any article or device that adds to the convenience or effectiveness of something else but is not essential; an appurtenance; attachment. **3.** *Law.* One who, not being present, contributes as an assistant to the commission of an offense (**accessory before the fact**), or one who aids or shelters an offender with the intent to defeat justice (**accessory after the fact**). — **ac·ces'so·ri·ly**, *adv.* — **ac·ces'so·ri·ness**, *n.*

‖**ac·ciac'ca·tu'ra** (ät·chäk'kä·tōō'rä), *n.* [It., fr. *acciaccare* to crush.] *Music.* The short appoggiatura, written with a stroke through the stem of the note and performed as quickly as possible.

ac'ci·dence (ăk'sĭ·dĕns), *n.* [For *accidents*, L. *accidentia*, neut. pl., accidental or nonessential properties.] That part of grammar dealing with inflections.

ac'ci·dent (-dĕnt), *n.* [F., fr. L. *accidens*, *-entis*, pres. part. of *accidere* to happen, fr. *ad-* + *cadere* to fall.] **1.** An event that takes place without one's foresight or expectation, esp. one of an afflictive or unfortunate character; a casualty; as, an *accident* to a locomotive. **2.** Chance; contingency; also, a contingent circumstance, relation, etc. **3.** A quality, esp. one not in the essence or specific nature of a thing. **4.** *Geog. & Astron.* A surface irregularity or unevenness. — **Syn.** Chance, hazard, luck, fortune. — **Ant.** Design, intent.

ac'ci·den'tal (-dĕn'tăl; -t'l), *adj.* **1.** Happening by chance or unexpectedly. **2.** Nonessential; incidental; as, songs *accidental* to a play. **3.** *Music.* Pertaining to or designating an accidental.

Syn. **Accidental, fortuitous, contingent, casual, incidental, adventitious** mean not expected, or outside of the regular order of things. **Accidental** sometimes stresses chance, sometimes nonessentiality (as, an *accidental* meeting; an *accidental* value); **fortuitous** so strongly suggests chance that it often connotes absence of a cause (as, a *fortuitous* concourse of atoms); **contingent** suggests possibility of happening, but emphasizes uncertainty (as, a *contingent* result); **casual** implies lack of premeditation or an appearance of indifference (as, a *casual* glimpse); **incidental** implies a secondary or nonessential character that requires some forethought (as, *incidental* expenses); **adventitious** implies a lack of relation to the original and intrinsic character of a thing (as, *adventitious* importance).

— *n.* **1.** A property not essential; a nonessential; anything happening accidentally. **2.** *Music.* Any sharp, flat, natural, double sharp, or double flat occurring in the course of a composition, after the key signature.

— **ac'ci·den'tal·ly**, *adv.* — **ac'ci·den'tal·ness**, *n.*

ac·cip'i·tral (ăk·sĭp'ĭ·trăl), *adj.* Of, like, or pert. to a hawk.

ac·cip'i·trine (-trĭn; -trīn), *adj.* [L. *accipiter* hawk.] Hawklike; raptorial; like or belonging to the birds of prey.

ac·claim' (ă·klām'), *v. t.* [L. *acclamare*, fr. *ad-* + *clamare* to cry out.] **1.** To applaud. **2.** To declare or proclaim by acclamations; as, to *acclaim* him king. **3.** To shout; to call out loudly; as, to *acclaim* my joy. — *v. i.* To shout applause. — **Syn.** Extol, laud, praise, eulogize. — *n.* Acclamation; applause. — **ac·claim'er**, *n.*

ac'cla·ma'tion (ăk'lȧ·mā'shŭn), *n.* [L. *acclamatio*.] **1.** Act of acclaiming; that which is uttered in acclaiming; loud applause. **2.** In parliamentary usage, the act or method of voting orally. — **ac·clam'a·to'ry** (ă·klăm'ȧ·tō'rĭ *or, esp. Brit.,* -tĕr·ĭ), *adj.*

ac·cli'mate (ă·klī'mĭt; ăk'lĭ·māt), *v. t. & i.* [F. *acclimater*, fr. *à* to + *climat* climate.] To habituate, or become habituated, to a climate not native; to acclimatize. — **Syn.** Inure, season, harden. — **ac·cli'mat·a·ble** (ă·klī'mĭt·ȧ·b'l), *adj.* — **ac'cli·ma'tion** (ăk'lĭ·mā'shŭn; ăk'lī-), *n.*

ac·cli'ma·tize (ă·klī'mȧ·tīz), *v. t. & i.* = ACCLIMATE. — **ac·cli'ma·tiz'a·ble** (-tīz'ȧ·b'l), *adj.* — **ac·cli'ma·ti·za'tion** (-tĭ·zā'shŭn; -tī·zā'-), *n.* — **ac·cli'ma·tiz'er** (-tīz'ẽr), *n.*

ac·cliv'i·ty (ă·klĭv'ĭ·tĭ), *n.; pl.* -TIES (-tĭz). [L. *acclivitas*, fr. *acclivis*, *acclivus*, ascending, fr. *ad-* + *clivus* a hill.] Slope or inclination of the earth, as the side of a hill, considered as ascending; an upward slope; — opposed to *declivity*. — **ac·cliv'i·tous** (-tŭs), *adj.*

ac·cli'vous (ă·klī'vŭs), *adj.* [L. *acclivus*.] Sloping upward.

ac'co·lade' (ăk'ō·lād'; -läd'), *n.* [F., fr. It., fr. *accollare* to embrace, fr. L. *ad* to + *collum* neck.] **1.** An embrace; specif., a ceremony or salutation used to mark the conferring of knighthood, as by a tap on the shoulder with the blade of a sword; a salutation or rite performed to mark the recognition of special merit, etc.; also, an award. **2.** *Music.* A brace, or line used as a brace, to join two or more staffs carrying simultaneous parts.

ac·com'mo·date (ă·kŏm'ō·dāt), *v. t.* [L. *accommodatus*, past part. of *accommodare*, fr. *ad-* + *commodare* to make fit, help, fr. *com-* + *modus* measure, proportion.] **1.** To render fit or correspondent; to adapt; as, to *accommodate* ourselves to circumstances. **2.** To bring into agreement or harmony; as, to *accommodate* differences. **3.** To furnish with something desired, needed, or convenient; to favor; oblige; specif., to furnish sleeping quarters, and often food, for. **4.** To hold without crowding or inconvenience; as, the car *accommodates* five persons. — *v. i.* To adapt oneself; to make adjustment. — **Syn.** See ADAPT: CONTAIN.

ac·com'mo·dat'ing (-dāt'ĭng), *adj.* Affording, or disposed to afford, accommodation; obliging. — **ac·com'mo·dat'ing·ly**, *adv.*

ac·com'mo·da'tion (-dā'shŭn), *n.* **1.** Act of accommodating, or state of being accommodated; adaptation; adjustment. **2.** Willingness to accommodate; obligingness. **3.** Adjustment of differences; settlement. **4.** Whatever supplies a want or affords ease, refreshment, or convenience; — often in *pl.;* as, the *accommodations* (that is, lodgings and food) at a hotel. **5.** Short for ACCOMMODATION TRAIN. **6.** *Com.* **a** A loan. **b** An accommodation bill. **7.** *Physiol.* The automatic adjustment of the eye for seeing at different distances. — **ac·com'mo·da'tion·al**, *adj.*

accommodation bill, draft, *or* **note.** A bill, draft, or note made, drawn, accepted, or endorsed by one person for another without consideration, to enable that other to raise money or obtain credit thereby.

accommodation ladder. *Naut.* A light ladder or stairway hung over the side of a ship at the gangway for use in ascending from, or descending to, small boats.

accommodation train. *U.S.* A train stopping at all or nearly all stations.

ac·com'mo·da'tive (ă·kŏm'ō·dā'tĭv), *adj.* Tending to accommodate; accommodating. — **ac·com'mo·da'tive·ness**, *n.*

ac·com'pa·ni·ment (ă·kŭm'pȧ·nĭ·mĕnt), *n.* **1.** That which accompanies as a circumstance or an ornament, or to give symmetry. **2.** *Music.* An instrumental part or parts designed to support or enrich a voice or instrument or a melody.

ac·com'pa·nist (-nĭst), *n.* One who accompanies; esp., one who plays or sings an accompaniment.

ac·com'pa·ny (-nĭ), *v. t.;* -NIED (-nĭd); -NY·ING. [From OF., fr. *a* to + *compaing*, *compain*, companion.] **1.** To cause to be attended by or as by a companion; as, he *accompanied* the advice with a warning. **2.** To go with or attend as a companion or associate. **3.** To occur in association with. **4.** *Music.* To play or sing an accompaniment to or for. — **ac·com'pa·ny·ist** (-nĭ·ĭst), *n.*

Syn. **Accompany, attend, conduct, escort, convoy** mean to go along with someone or something. **Accompany** implies closeness of association and, with a personal subject, equality of status; **attend** implies a waiting upon one (often as a subordinate) in order to serve one; **conduct** usually retains the implication of guidance, even with an impersonal subject; **escort** and **convoy** add to *accompany* the implication of protection, especially for journeys on land and sea, *escort* usually being preferred for the former, and *convoy* for the latter. *Escort* also refers to the accompaniment of a lady or ladies by a man.

ac·com'plice (ă·kŏm'plĭs), *n.* [*ac-* (prob. fr. the article *a*) + *complice*.] An associate in guilt.

ac·com'plish (ă·kŏm'plĭsh), *v. t.* [OF. *acomplir*, fr. L. *ad* to + *complere* to fill up, complete.] **1.** To bring to an issue of full success; to effect; fulfill. **2.** To attain to or cover in traversing, as time or distance. **3.** To equip thoroughly, as with accouterments or refinements. — **Syn.** See PERFORM. — **Ant.** Undo. — **ac·com'plish·a·ble**, *adj.* — **ac·com'plish·er**, *n.*

ac·com'plished (-plĭsht), *adj.* **1.** Completed; effected. **2.** Complete in acquirements as the result of training.

ac·com'plish·ment (ă·kŏm'plĭsh·mĕnt), *n.* **1.** Accomplishing; completion. **2.** That which is accomplished. **3.** That which completes or equips thoroughly; an element in excellence of mind, or elegance of manners, acquired by education or training. — **Syn.** See ACQUIREMENT.

ac·cord' (ă·kôrd'), *v. t.* [Through OF. & LL., fr. L. *ad* to + *cor*, *cordis*, heart.] **1.** *Archaic.* To bring into agreement; to reconcile; also, to settle or adjust. **2.** To grant as suitable or proper; as, to *accord* due praise to one. — *v. i.* To agree; correspond; be in harmony. — **Syn.** See AGREE (**Ant.** conflict): GRANT (**Ant.** withhold). — *n.* **1.** Agreement; concurrence; harmony; specif., harmony of sounds; concord. **2.** A reaching of agreement; specif., an informal political agreement between governments. **3.** Voluntary or spontaneous impulse to act; volition; as, of one's own *accord*. — **ac·cord'a·ble**, *adj.* — **ac·cord'er**, *n.*

ac·cord'ance (ă·kôr'dăns), *n.* **1.** Agreement; conformity; as, in *accordance* with a rule. **2.** Act of according.

ac·cord'ant (-dănt), *adj.* Agreeing; consonant; also, correspondent. — **ac·cord'ant·ly**, *adv.*

ac·cord'ing (ă·kôr'dĭng), *adj.* Agreeing. — *adv.* Accordingly. — ***according as.*** Conformably as; proportionately as. — ***according to.*** **a** Agreeably to; in conformity with. **b** As attested or declared by.

ac·cord'ing·ly, *adv.* **1.** Conformably. **2.** In natural sequence; consequently; so.

ac·cor'di·on (ă·kôr'dĭ·ŭn), *n.* [See ACCORD.] *Music.* A small, portable, keyed wind instrument in which the wind is forced upon free metallic reeds by means of a bellows. — *adj.* Folding like the bellows of an accordion. — **ac·cor'di·on·ist**, *n.*

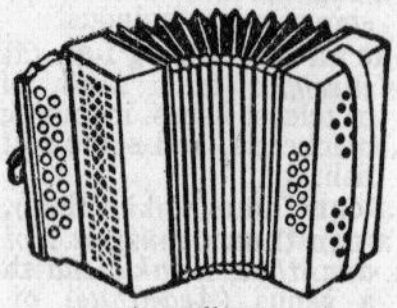

Accordion.

ac·cost' (ă·kŏst'; 74), *v. t.* [F. *accoster*, fr. LL. *accostare*, fr. L. *ad* to + *costa* rib, side.] **1.** To approach; make up to. **2.** To speak first to; to greet. — *n.* Greeting.

ac·couche'ment (ȧ·kōōsh'mäN; -mĕnt), *n.* [F.] Lying-in; delivery in childbed.

ac'cou·cheur' (ăk'ōō·shûr'), *n.* [F., masc.] An obstetrician.

ac'cou·cheuse' (-shûz'), *n.* [F., fem.] A midwife.

ac·count' (ă·kount'), *v. t.* [From OF., fr. *a* to + *conter* to count, fr. L. *computare*.] **1.** To assign. **2.** To value, estimate, or hold in opinion; to deem; as, to *account* a man wise. — *v. i.* **1.** To render, or state the terms of, an account; as, he must *account* to the treasurer. **2.** To answer in judgment; — with *for*. **3.** To be responsible for causing death, capture, or the like; — with *for*.

— *n.* **1.** A reckoning; computation. **2.** A record or reckoning of debit and credit, esp. in money, usually with a balance; as: a balanced statement of receipts and expenditures of a given period; the series of items under one heading in a company's ledger; a reckoning of charged purchases and credits rendered periodically. Abbr. *a/c* or *acct.* **3.** Any collection of items to be balanced; as, to settle *accounts* with an enemy. **4.** A statement and explanation, as of one's discharge of responsibilities. **5.** Advantage; profit; as, to turn to *account*. **6.** A statement in general of reasons, causes, grounds, etc., explanatory of some event; loosely, reason, ground, or motive. **7.** A statement of facts; narrative; report. **8.** **a** Estimation; judgment. **b** Importance; value; as, of small *account*. — ***on account of.*** For the sake of; by reason of.

ac·count'a·ble (ă·koun'tȧ·b'l), *adj.* **1.** Liable to be called to account; answerable. **2.** Capable of being accounted for; explicable. — **Syn.** See RESPONSIBLE. — **ac·count'a·bil'i·ty** (-bĭl'ĭ·tĭ), **ac·count'a·ble·ness**, *n.* — **ac·count'a·bly**, *adv.*

ac·count'an·cy (-tăn·sĭ), *n.* Accountant's art or occupation.

ac·count'ant (-tănt), *n.* **1.** One who is liable to render account. **2.** One who is skilled in, keeps, or adjusts accounts. See CERTIFIED PUBLIC ACCOUNTANT. — **Syn.** See BOOKKEEPER. — **ac·count'ant·ship**, *n.*

ac·count'ing (ă·koun'tĭng), *n.* Art or system of making up or stating accounts; the body of principles underlying the keeping and explanation of business accounts. Accounting draws from the results furnished by the bookkeeper inferences as to the condition and conduct of the business.

ac·cou'ter, ac·cou'tre (ă·kōō'tẽr), *v. t.;* -TERED, -TRED (-tẽrd); -TER·ING (-tẽr·ĭng), -TRING (-trĭng; -tẽr·ĭng). [F. *accoutrer*.] To furnish with dress or equipments, esp. for military service; to equip. — **Syn.** See FURNISH.

ac·cou'ter·ment, ac·cou'tre·ment (ă·kōō'tẽr·mĕnt; -trĕ·mĕnt), *n.* **1.** *pl.* Trappings; equipment; specif., a soldier's outfit other than clothes and weapons. **2.** Act or process of accoutering; state of being accoutered.

ac·cred'it (ă·krĕd'ĭt), *v. t.* [From F., fr. *à* to + *crédit* credit.] **1.** To put or bring into credit; to sanction. **2.** To send with letters credential; to authorize, as a delegate. **3.** To believe; accept as valid. **4.** To vouch for officially; to certify as of a (prescribed or desirable) standard; as, an *accredited* college. **5.** To credit (sense 4). — **Syn.** See APPROVE.

ac·crete′ (ă·krēt′), *v. i.* [L. *accretus*, past part. of *accrescere* to increase.] To become attached by accretion. — *adj.* Accreted; *Bot.*, grown together.

ac·cre′tion (ă·krē′shŭn), *n.* **1.** Growth; specif., organic growth; also, increase by external addition; a growing together of parts that are naturally separate. **2.** The result of such growth or accumulation; also, the matter added. **3.** Concretion; coherence. **4.** *Law.* Increase or extension of the boundaries of land by action of natural forces. — **ac·cre′tive** (-tĭv), *adj.*

ac·cru′al (ă·kro͞o′ăl), *n.* The process of accruing; that which accrues.

accrual basis. The method of keeping accounts which shows expenses incurred and income earned for a given period, although such expenses and income may not have been actually paid or received in cash.

ac·crue′ (ă·kro͞o′), *v. i.* [From F. *accrue*, n., fr. OF., fr. L. *accrescere*, fr. *ad-* + *crescere* to grow.] **1.** To come (to someone) by way of increase or advantage. **2.** To be added by ordered growth by way of increase or decrease; as, *accrued* interest on invested money. — **-ment**, *n.*

ac·cul′tu·ra′tion (ă·kŭl′tū̇·rā′shŭn), *n.* [*ac-* + L. *cultura* culture.] The process of absorbing new cultural traits, esp. by transference from another group or people.

ac·cum′bent (ă·kŭm′bĕnt), *adj.* [L. *accumbens, -entis*, pres. part.] Reclining; lying against something; as, *accumbent* cotyledons. — **ac·cum′ben·cy** (-bĕn·sĭ), *n.*

ac·cu′mu·late (ă·kū′mū·lāt), *v. t.* [L. *accumulatus*, past part. of *accumulare*, fr. *ad-* + *cumulare* to heap.] To heap or pile up; to collect or bring together. — **Syn.** Amass, hoard. — *v. i.* To increase in quantity or number. — **ac·cu′mu·la·ble** (-lȧ·b'l), *adj.*

ac·cu′mu·la′tion (-lā′shŭn), *n.* Process or act of accumulating; state of being accumulated; that which is accumulated; specif., addition of earnings or profits, otherwise distributable as dividends, to the active capital of a corporation.

ac·cu′mu·la′tive (ă·kū′mū·lā′tĭv; -lȧ·tĭv), *adj.* Tending to, characterized by, or produced by, accumulation; cumulative. — **ac·cu′mu·la′tive·ly**, *adv.* — **ac·cu′mu·la′tive·ness**, *n.*

ac·cu′mu·la′tor (-lā′tẽr), *n.* [L.] One who or that which accumulates; specif.: **a** An apparatus for storing energy. **b** A shock absorber. **c** *Brit.* A storage battery.

ac′cu·ra·cy (ăk′ū·rȧ·sĭ), *n.* State or quality of being accurate; freedom from mistake or error; precision; exactness.

ac′cu·rate (-rĭt), *adj.* [L. *accuratus*, past part. & adj., fr. *accurare* to take care of, fr. *ad-* + *curare* to take care, fr. *cura* care.] In exact or careful conformity to truth, or to some standard, esp. as the result of care; exact. — **Syn.** See CORRECT. — **Ant.** Inaccurate. — **ac′cu·rate·ly**, *adv.* — **ac′cu·rate·ness**, *n.*

ac·curs′ed (ă·kûr′sĕd; ă·kûrst′; 30), **ac·curst′** (ă·kûrst′), *adj.* Cursed; execrated; damned; execrable; detestable. — **ac·curs′ed·ly**, *adv.* — **ac·curs′ed·ness**, *n.*

ac·cus′al (ă·kūz′ăl), *n.* Accusation.

ac′cu·sa′tion (ăk′ū·zā′shŭn), *n.* **1.** Act of accusing; arraignment. **2.** That of which one is accused; charge; allegation.

ac·cu′sa·tive (ȧ·kū′zȧ·tĭv), *adj.* [F. or L.; F. *accusatif*, fr. L. *accusativus*, a trans. of Gr. *aitiatikos*, fr. *aitiatos* caused. See ACCUSE.] *Gram.* Designating or pert. to the case which marks primarily the immediate object of the action or influence expressed by a verb, or of the motion or tendency indicated by a preposition; — in English commonly called *objective.* — *n.* The accusative case, or a form in that case. Abbr. *accus., acc.* — **ac·cu′sa·ti′val** (-tī′văl), *adj.* — **ac·cu′sa·tive·ly**, *adv.*

ac·cu′sa·to′ri·al (ă·kū′zȧ·tō′rĭ·ăl; 70), *adj.* Of or relating to an accuser.

ac·cu′sa·to′ry (ă·kū′zȧ·tō′rĭ *or, esp. Brit.*, -tẽr·ĭ), *adj* Pertaining to, containing, or of the nature of, accusation.

ac·cuse′ (ă·kūz′), *v. t.* [From OF., fr. L. *accusare* to call to account, fr. *ad-* + *causa* cause, lawsuit.] To charge with a fault or offense; to blame; censure. — **Syn.** Charge, incriminate, indict, impeach, arraign. — **ac·cus′er** (ă·kūz′ẽr), *n.* — **ac·cus′ing·ly**, *adv.*

ac·cused′ (ă·kūzd′), *adj.* Charged with an offense; — esp. in ***the accused***, the defendant in a criminal case.

ac·cus′tom (ă·kŭs′tŭm), *v. t.* [From OF., fr. *a* to + *costume* custom.] To make familiar by use; to habituate, familiarize, or inure.

ac·cus′tomed (-tŭmd), *adj.* **1.** Usual; customary. **2.** Wont; used; — followed by an infinitive. — **Syn.** See USUAL.

ace (ās), *n.* [OF. *as*, fr. L. *as, assis*, unity, unit, copper coin.] **1.** A single point or spot on a card or die; a card so marked. **2.** A particle; atom; jot. **3.** In certain games, a point won by a single stroke. **4.** A combat pilot who has downed at least five enemy airplanes; — originated in World War I. **5.** One who excels at anything. — *adj.* Of first rank, or surpassing, in excellence.

-a′ce·a (-ā′shē·ȧ). [L., neut. pl. of suffix *-aceus.*] A plural suffix used in zoology in names of orders and classes See -ACEOUS.

-a′ce·ae (-ā′sē·ē). [L., fem. pl. of suffix *-aceus.*] A plural suffix used in botany in names of families and, formerly, orders. See -ACEOUS.

a·ce′di·a (ȧ·sē′dĭ·ȧ), *n.* [LL., fr. Gr. *akēdia*, fr. *a-* not + *kēdos* care.] **a** Sloth, — one of the seven deadly sins. **b** Spiritual torpor and apathy.

A·cel′da·ma (ȧ·sĕl′dȧ·mȧ), *n.* [L., fr. Gr. *Akeldama*, fr. Syr. *ōkēl damō* the field of blood.] The scene of the suicide of Judas (*Acts* i. 18); hence, any scene of bloodshed.

a·cen′tric (ā·sĕn′trĭk), *adj.* Not centered; without center.

-a′ceous (-ā′shŭs). [L. suffix *-aceus.*] An adjective suffix signifying *pertaining* or *belonging to, of the nature of, resembling, like*, as in herb*aceous*, herblike. It is regularly used in zoology and botany to form adjectives corresponding to nouns in *-acea, -aceae.*

a·ceph′a·lous (ā·sĕf′ȧ·lŭs), *adj.* [From L., fr. Gr. *akephalos*, fr. *a-* not + *kephalē* head.] Headless; hence, without a leader.

‖**a·ce′quia** (ä·sā′kyä), *n.* [Sp.] An irrigating trench.

ac′er·ate (ăs′ẽr·āt), *adj.* Needle-shaped; acerose.

a·cerb′ (ȧ·sûrb′), *adj.* [L. *acerbus*, fr. *acer* sharp.] Sour, bitter, and harsh to the taste, as unripe fruit; sharp and harsh.

ac′er·bate (ăs′ẽr·bāt), *v. t.* [L. *acerbatus*, past part. of *acerbare*, fr. *acerbus* sour.] To sour; embitter; irritate.

a·cer′bi·ty (ȧ·sûr′bĭ·tĭ), *n.; pl.* -TIES (-tĭz). [From F., fr. L. *acerbitas.*] **1.** Sourness of taste, with bitter and puckery quality, as of unripe fruit. **2.** Harshness, bitterness, or severity, as of language. — **Syn.** See ACRIMONY.

ac′er·ose (ăs′ẽr·ōs), **ac′er·ous** (-ŭs), *adj.* [L. *acerosus* chaffy, and L. *acus* needle; both akin to L *acer* sharp.] *Bot.* Needle-shaped; having a sharp, rigid point, as the leaf of a pine tree. See LEAF, *Illust.* (1).

a·cer′vate (ȧ·sûr′vāt), *adj* [L. *acervatus*, past part. of *acervare* to heap up.] Heaped, or growing in heaps or closely compacted clusters. — **a·cer′vate·ly**, *adv.*

acet-. = ACETO-.

ac′e·tab′u·lum (ăs′ē·tăb′ū·lŭm), *n.; pl.* -LA (-lȧ). [L., a little saucer for vinegar, fr. *acetum* vinegar.] The cup-shaped socket in the hipbone. — **ac′e·tab′u·lar** (-lẽr), *adj.*

ac′e·tal (ăs′ē·tăl), *n.* [*acetic* + *al*dehyde.] *Chem.* Any of a class of compounds characterized by the grouping $>C(OR)_2$ and obtained esp. by heating aldehydes or ketones with alcohols.

ac′et·am′ide (ăs′ĕt·ăm′ĭd· ȧ·sĕt′ȧ·mĭd; -ĭd; -mīd), *n.* Also **-am′id.** [*acetic* + *amide.*] *Chem.* A white crystalline solid, CH_3CONH_2, the amide of acetic acid.

ac′et·an′i·lide (ăs′ĕt·ăn′ĭ·lĭd; -līd), *n.* Also **-lid.** [*ace*tic + *anil*ine + *-ide.*] *Chem.* A white crystalline solid, $CH_3CONHC_6H_5$, derived from aniline and acetic acid, and used in medicine for dulling pain and abating fever.

ac′e·tate (ăs′ē·tāt), *n.* [L. *acetum* vinegar.] *Chem.* **1.** A salt or ester of acetic acid. **2.** Cellulose acetate or one of its products (as a textile fiber, yarn, or fabric).

a·ce′tic (ȧ·sē′tĭk), *adj.* [L. *acetum* vinegar.] Of, pert. to, or producing vinegar; designating acetic acid.

acetic acid. A compound, CH_3COOH, which in the pure state is a colorless, pungent, biting liquid congealing in cool weather. Vinegar contains 4½–12 per cent of acetic acid.

a·cet′i·fy (ȧ·sĕt′ĭ·fī), *v. t. & i.;* -FIED (-fīd); -FY′ING. [L. *acetum* vinegar + *-fy.*] To turn into acetic acid or vinegar. — **a·cet′i·fi·ca′tion** (-fĭ·kā′shŭn), *n.* — **a·cet′i·fi′er** (-fī′ẽr), *n.*

ac′e·tim′e·ter (ăs′ē·tĭm′ē·tẽr), *n.* = ACETOMETER.

ac′e·to- (ăs′ē·tō-; ȧ·sē′tō-), **acet-.** [L. *acetum* vinegar.] A combining form denoting *connection with*, or *derivation from, acetic acid* or *acetyl*, as in *aceto*meter.

ac′e·tom′e·ter (ăs′ē·tŏm′ē·tẽr), *n.* [*aceto-* + *-meter.*] An instrument for estimating the amount of acetic acid in any solution of it, esp. in vinegar. — **ac′e·tom′e·try** (-trĭ), *n.*

ac′e·tone (ăs′ē·tōn), *n.* [*acetic* + *-one.*] *Chem.* **a** A volatile, fragrant, liquid ketone, CH_3COCH_3, used as a solvent for many organic compounds. It is found in urine, esp. in diabetes. **b** Any ketone. — **ac′e·ton′ic** (-tŏn′ĭk), *adj.*

ac′e·tose (-tōs), *adj.* Sour like vinegar; acetous.

ac′e·tous (ăs′ē·tŭs; ȧ·sē′tŭs), *adj.* [L. *acetum* vinegar.] Pertaining to, or producing, vinegar; sour; acid.

a·ce′tum (ȧ·sē′tŭm), *n.* [L.] *Pharm.* Vinegar.

a·ce′tyl (ȧ·sē′tĭl; ăs′ē·tĭl), *n.* [*acetic* + *-yl.*] *Chem.* The radical, CH_3CO, of acetic acid. — **ac′e·tyl′ic** (ăs′ē·tĭl′ĭk), *adj.*

a·cet′y·lene (ȧ·sĕt′ĭ·lēn), *n.* *Chem.* A colorless gaseous hydrocarbon, HC:CH, formed by the direct union of carbon and hydrogen in the electric arc, by the action of water on certain carbides, etc. In a burner it produces a brilliant white diffusive light, and combined with oxygen is used for welding (see OXYACETYLENE).

A·chae′an (ȧ·kē′ăn), **A·cha′ian** (-kā′yăn; -kī′ăn), *adj.* [L. *Achaeus, Achaius*, fr. Gr. *Achaios.*] Of or pert. to Achaia or ancient Greece. — *n.* One of the people of Achaia; a Greek.

A·cha′tes (ȧ·kā′tēz), *n.* [L.] A faithful companion of Aeneas in Vergil's *Aeneid*; hence, a faithful friend.

ache (āk), *v. i.;* ACHED (ākt); ACH′ING (āk′ĭng). [AS. *acan.*] **1.** To suffer continued pain. **2.** *Colloq.* To be possessed with painful yearning. — *n.* [AS. *æce, ece.*] Continued pain, as distinguished from twinges. — **Syn.** Pain, pang, smart, throe, twinge, stitch. — **ach′ing·ly**, *adv.*

☞ The verb was spelled *ake* (*pron.* äk, āk) until confused, about 1700, with the noun *ache* (*pron.* äch, āch).

a·chene′ (ā·kēn′), *n.* Also **a·kene′.** [Gr. *a-* not + *chainein* to gape.] *Bot.* A small, dry, one-seeded fruit which ripens without bursting its thin outer sheath, or pericarp, as the fruit of the buttercup. — **a·che′ni·al** (ā·kē′nĭ·ăl), *adj.*

Ach′er·on (ăk′ẽr·ŏn), *n.* [L., fr. Gr. *Acherōn.*] *Myth.* The River of Woe in Hades; hence, the nether world.

‖**à che·val′** (ȧ shē·vȧl′). [F.] Literally, on horseback; hence, astride.

a·chieve′ (ȧ·chēv′), *v. t.* [OF. *achever* to finish, fr. *a* to + *chief* end, head, fr. L. *caput* head.] **1.** To carry to a termination; to bring to a successful conclusion; to perform. **2.** To end; kill. *Shak.* **3.** To obtain, or gain, as the result of exertion; to attain; as, to *achieve* greatness. — *v. i.* To attain a desired end or aim. — **Syn.** See PERFORM: REACH (**Ant.** miss). — **a·chiev′a·ble**, *adj.* — **a·chiev′er**, *n.*

a·chieve′ment (-mĕnt), *n.* **1.** Act of achieving; accomplishment. **2.** Anything achieved, esp. by valor, boldness, or praiseworthy exertion; a feat. — **Syn.** See FEAT.

A·chil′les (ȧ·kĭl′ēz), *n.* [L., fr. Gr. *Achilleus.*] The hero of Homer's *Iliad*, who became the Greek ideal of youthful strength, beauty, and valor. He was fatally wounded by Paris's arrow, which pierced his heel, where alone he was vulnerable. — **Ach′il·le′an** (ăk′ĭ·lē′ăn), *adj.*

Achilles' tendon. The strong tendon joining the muscles in the calf of the leg to the bone of the heel.

ach′la·myd′e·ous (ăk′lȧ·mĭd′ē·ŭs), *adj.* [*a-* not + Gr. *chlamys, -ydos*, cloak.] *Bot.* Having no perianth.

a·chon′drite (ā·kŏn′drīt), *n.* A stony meteorite without small rounded grains or spherules.

ach′ro·mat′ic (ăk′rō·măt′ĭk), *adj.* [Gr. *achrōmatos* colorless, fr. *a-* not + *chrōma, -atos*, color.] **1.** *Optics.* Refracting light without decomposing it into its constituent colors; giving images practically free from extraneous colors. **2.** *Biol.* **a** Not readily colored by the usual staining agents. **b** Composed of achromatin. **3.** *Music.* Without accidentals or modulation. **4.** Colorless. — **ach′ro·mat′i·cal·ly** (-ĭ·kăl·ĭ), *adv.* — **a·chro′ma·tic′i·ty** (ā·krō′mȧ·tĭs′ĭ·tĭ), *n.* — **a·chro′ma·tism** (ā·krō′mȧ·tĭz′m), *n.*

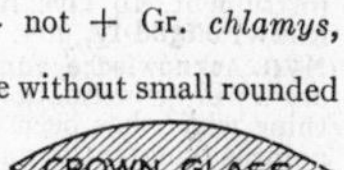

Achromatic Lens.

a·chro′ma·tin (ā·krō′mȧ·tĭn), *n.* *Biol.* The substance of the cell nucleus not readily colored by basic stains.

a·chro′ma·tize (-tīz), *v. t.* To deprive of color; to make achromatic.

a·chro′ma·tous (ā·krō′mȧ·tŭs), *adj.* [See ACHROMATIC.] Lacking, or deficient in, color; as, *achromatous* blood.

a·chro′mic (-mĭk), **a·chro′mous** (-mŭs), *adj.* [Gr. *achrōmos* colorless, fr. *a-* not + *chrōma* color.] Free from color; colorless.

a·cic′u·la (ȧ·sĭk′ū·lȧ), *n.; pl.* -LAE (-lē). [L., dim. of *acus* needle]

A needlelike spine, bristle, or crystal. — **a·cic′u·lar** (ȧ·sĭk′ū·lẽr), *adj.* — **a·cic′u·lar·ly**, *adv.* — **a·cic′u·late** (-lāt), **a·cic′u·lat′ed** (-lāt′ĕd; -ĭd), *adj.*

a·cic′u·lum (ȧ·sĭk′ū·lŭm), *n.; pl.* -LUMS (-lŭmz), -LA (-lȧ). [NL.] **a** = ACICULA. **b** *Zool* A seta.

ac′id (ăs′ĭd), *adj.* [F. or L.; F. *acide,* fr. L. *acidus,* fr. *acere* to be sour.] **1.** Sour, sharp, or biting to the taste; tart; also, sour-tempered; biting; as, *acid* intelligence. **2.** Of, pertaining to, or of the nature of an acid; having one of the reactions characteristic of acids. **3.** *Metal.* Pertaining to, or made by, a process (**acid process**), as in steelmaking, in which the furnace is lined with acidic, or highly siliceous, material, and acidic slag is added to the molten charge; — opp. to *basic.* **4.** *Petrog.* Rich in silica. — **Syn.** See SOUR.

— *n.* **1.** A sour substance. **2.** *Chem.* Any one of a class of substances which typically are soluble in water, sour in taste, and redden litmus; according to modern views, a compound containing hydrogen replaceable by positive elements or radicals to form salts, or a compound that dissociates in aqueous solution with the production of hydrogen ions, or still more recently, a compound or ion that can give protons (hydrogen ions) to some other substance.

☞ Names of oxygen acids end ordinarily in *-ic* and their corresponding salts in *-ate.* Salts formed from *-ous* acids take the ending *-ite;* as, potassium chlor*ite.*

ac′id–fast′, *adj.* Not easily decolorized by acids or other agents when stained. — **ac′id–fast′ness**, *n.*

ac′id–form′ing, *adj.* Forming acid; of foods, yielding a preponderance of acid residue after combustion.

a·cid′ic (ă·sĭd′ĭk), *adj* Acid-forming; as, silicon is the chief *acidic* element of rocks; also, rich in silica.

a·cid′i·fy (-ĭ·fī), *v. t. & i.;* -FIED (-fīd); -FY′ING. [L. *acidus* acid + *-fy.*] To make or become acid; to convert into an acid. — **a·cid′i·fi′a·ble** (-fī′ȧ·b'l), *adj.* — **a·cid′i·fi·ca′tion** (-fĭ·kā′shŭn), *n.*

ac′i·dim′e·ter (ăs′ĭ·dĭm′ē·tẽr), *n.* [L. *acidus* acid + *-meter.*] *Chem.* An apparatus or solution for ascertaining the strength or the amount of acid present. — **ac′i·dim′e·try** (-trĭ), *n.* — **ac′i·di·met′ric** (-dĭ·mĕt′rĭk), **ac′i·di·met′ri·cal** (-rĭ·kăl), *adj.*

a·cid′i·ty (ă·sĭd′ĭ·tĭ), *n.; pl.* -TIES (-tĭz). **1.** Quality or state of being acid or sour. **2.** Degree of sourness. **3.** Hyperacidity.

ac′id·ly (ăs′ĭd·lĭ), *adv.* In an acid manner; bitingly.

ac′id·ness, *n.* Acidity.

ac′i·doph′i·lus milk (ăs′ĭ·dŏf′ĭ·lŭs). Milk fermented by bacteria (species *Lactobacillus acidophilus*) and used therapeutically to change the intestinal flora.

ac′i·do′sis (ăs′ĭ·dō′sĭs), *n.* [NL., fr. E. *acid* + *-osis.*] *Med.* An abnormal state of reduced alkalinity of the blood and of the body tissues. — **ac′i·dot′ic** (-dŏt′ĭk), *adj.*

acid test. A severe or decisive test, as of authenticity.

a·cid′u·late (ă·sĭd′ū·lāt), *v. t.* To make acidulous.

a·cid′u·lent (-lĕnt), *adj.* Acidulous.

a·cid′u·lous (-lŭs), *adj.* [L. *acidulus,* dim. of *acidus* sour.] Slightly sour; subacid; sourish. — **Syn.** See SOUR.

ac′i·er·ate (ăs′ĭ·ẽr·āt), *v. t.* [F. *acier* steel + *-ate.*] To convert into steel; as, to *acierate* iron by cementation. — **ac′i·er·a′tion** (-ā′shŭn), *n.*

ac′i·form (ăs′ĭ·fôrm), *adj.* [L. *acus* needle + *-form.*] Shaped like a needle.

ac′i·nac′i·form (ăs′ĭ·năs′ĭ·fôrm), *adj.* [L. *acinaces* a short sword + *-form.*] *Bot.* Scimitar-shaped; — of a leaf.

a·cin′i·form (ȧ·sĭn′ĭ·fôrm), *adj.* [L. *acinus* a grape, grapestone + *-form.*] **a** Having the form of a cluster of grapes. **b** Full of small kernels like a grape.

ac′i·nous (ăs′ĭ·nŭs), *adj.* Also **ac′i·nose** (-nōs). [L. *acinosus,* fr. *acinus* grapestone.] Consisting of or containing acini.

ac′i·nus (ăs′ĭ·nŭs), *n.; pl.* -NI (-nī). [L., grape, grapestone.] **1.** *Bot.* **a** An individual drupelet in a multiple fruit, as in the blackberry. **b** A berry, esp. a grape. **c** A small bony kernel, as a grapestone. **2.** *Anat.* One of the smallest sacs of a racemose gland.

-a′cious (-ā′shŭs). [L. *-ax, -acis* + *-ous.*] A compound suffix meaning *given to, abounding in, tending to,* as in pugn*acious,* fall*acious,* mend*acious.*

-ac′i·ty (-ăs′ĭ·tĭ). [F. *-acité,* fr. L. *-acitas.*] The noun suffix corresponding to *-acious.*

ack′–ack′ (ăk′ăk′), *adj.* [Pron. of letters *AA,* orig. by British signalers for telephoning.] = ANTIAIRCRAFT. — *n.* An antiaircraft gun or its fire; also, collectively, antiaircraft guns or their fire.

ac·knowl′edge (ăk·nŏl′ĕj; -ĭj; *or, esp. Brit.,* -nŏ′lĕj; -lĭj), *v. t.;* -EDGED (-ĕjd; -ĭjd); -EDG·ING. [For *aknowledge,* as if fr. L. *ad-, ac-,* to. See 4th A; KNOWLEDGE.] **1.** To recognize as a fact or as one's own; to admit as true or as pertinent; to confess; as, to *acknowledge* a necessity or one's faults; to *acknowledge* oneself to be the author. **2.** To admit the claims or authority of; to recognize **3.** To own with gratitude or as a benefit or as imposing obligation; to express thanks for; as, to *acknowledge* a favor, a compliment, or service; to report receipt of (a letter, check, gift, etc.). **4.** To own as genuine; to assent to, as a legal instrument, to give it validity. — **ac·knowl′edge·a·ble**, *adj.* — **ac·knowl′edged·ly**, *adv.* — **ac·knowl′edg·er** (-ĕj·ẽr; -ĭj·ẽr), *n.*

Syn. **Acknowledge, admit, own, avow, confess** mean to disclose against one's will or inclination. **Acknowledge** implies the disclosure of something which has been or might be concealed; **admit** implies that the point is reluctantly granted or conceded; **own** implies acknowledgment of something in relation to oneself; **avow,** as here compared, implies open declaration when silence may be preferable; **confess** usually implies acknowledgment of something known to be wrong, but it may imply deference to the opinion of others.

ac·knowl′edg·ment, ac·knowl′edge·ment (ăk·nŏl′ĕj·mĕnt; -ĭj·mĕnt), *n.* **1.** Act of acknowledging; specif., *Law,* a declaration or avowal of one's act or a fact to give it legal validity, esp. before a duly qualified public officer. **2.** A thing done or given by way of recognition of something, as a favor, communication, etc., received; specif., *Law,* the formal certificate made by an officer before whom one has acknowledged a deed.

a·clin′ic (ā·klĭn′ĭk), *adj.* [Gr. *a-* not + *klinein* to incline.] Without inclination or dipping; — of the imaginary line near the equator on which the magnetic needle has no dip.

ac′me (ăk′mē), *n.* [Gr. *akmē* point, prime.] The top or highest point; as, the *acme* of perfection. — **Syn.** See SUMMIT.

ac′ne (ăk′nē), *n.* [NL.] Any of several skin diseases involving the oil glands and hair follicles and marked by inflamed pustules or pimples, in man chiefly on the face or shoulders.

a·cock′ (ȧ·kŏk′), *adv.* [*a-* on + *cock* a turn or tilt.] In cocked fashion.

a·cold′ (ȧ·kōld′), *adj.* Cold.

ac′o·lyte (ăk′ō·līt), *n.* [From ML., fr. Gr. *akolouthos* follower, attendant.] **1.** *R.C.Ch.* **a** One who holds the highest of the four minor orders. **b** A boy who serves a priest at Mass. **2.** An assistant.

‖**à compte** (à kônt′). [F.] On account; in part payment.

ac′o·nite (ăk′ō·nīt), *n.* [L. *aconitum,* fr. Gr. *akoniton.*] Any aconitum, esp. the common monkshood (*Aconitum napellus*); also, *Pharm.,* a sedative extract from this.

ac′o·ni′tum (-nī′tŭm), *n.* [L.] *Bot.* Any of a genus (*Aconitum*) of blue- or purple-flowered poisonous herbs of the crowfoot family (Ranunculaceae), the species of which are called *monkshood* or *wolfsbane;* also, *Pharm.,* aconite.

a′corn (ā′kôrn; ā′kẽrn), *n.* [AS. *æcern,* fr. *æcer* field, acre.] The nut, or fruit, of the oak. See OAK, *Illust.*

acorn squash. A ridged, somewhat acorn-shaped, dark-green winter squash about four to six inches in width, with sweet, yellow to orange flesh.

acorn tube. *Radio.* A very small vacuum tube, resembling an acorn in shape, used at extremely high frequencies.

‖**à corps per′du′** (à kôr′ pĕr′dü′). [F.] Literally, with lost body; impetuously; desperately.

a·cot′y·le′don (ā·kŏt′ĭ·lē′dŭn), *n.* [See A- not; COTYLEDON.] *Bot.* A plant without cotyledons, as the dodder. — **a·cot′y·le′don·ous** (-lē′dŭn·ŭs; -lĕd′ŭn·ŭs), *adj.*

a·cous′tic (ȧ·kōōs′tĭk; ȧ·kous′-), *adj.* [From F., fr. Gr. *akoustikos* relating to hearing, fr. *akouein* to hear.] Pertaining to the sense or organs of hearing, to sound, or to the science of sounds; auditory. — *n.* A medicine or agent to assist hearing.

a·cous′ti·cal (-tĭ·kăl), *adj.* Of or pertaining to acoustics; serving to aid hearing.

a·cous′ti·cal·ly, *adv.* of ACOUSTIC, ACOUSTICAL.

ac′ous·ti′cian (ăk′ōōs·tĭsh′ăn; ăk′ous-), *n.* One versed in acoustics.

a·cous′tics (ȧ·kōōs′tĭks; ȧ·kous′-), *n. sing. & pl.;* see -ICS. **1.** *Physics.* The science of sound, including its production, transmission, and effects. **2.** *Arch.* The sum of the qualities that determine the value of an auditorium as to distinct hearing.

‖**à cou′vert′** (à kōō′vâr′). [F.] In cover; under cover; sheltered.

ac·quaint′ (ă·kwānt′) *v. t.* [Through OF. & LL. fr. L. *ad* to + *cognitus* past part. of *cognoscere* to know.] **1.** To furnish or give personal, experiential knowledge of; to make (one) to know; — followed by *with.* **2.** To communicate notice to; inform. — **Syn.** See INFORM.

ac·quaint′ance (ă·kwān′tăns), *n.* **1.** Personal knowledge (of a person or thing) which results from becoming acquainted; — implying more than *recognition,* but less than *fellowship, friendship,* or *intimacy.* **2.** A person or persons with whom one is acquainted. — **ac·quaint′ance·ship**, *n.*

ac·quaint′ed (ă·kwān′tĕd; -tĭd), *adj.* Having acquaintance; possessed of personal knowledge of someone or something; — with *with.*

ac′qui·esce′ (ăk′wĭ·ĕs′), *v. i.;* -ESCED′ (-ĕst′); -ESC′ING (-ĕs′ĭng). [From F., fr. L. *acquiescere,* fr. *ad-* + *quiescere* to be quiet, fr. *quies* rest.] To accept or comply tacitly or passively without implying assent or agreement; to accept as inevitable or indisputable; — often with *in.* — **Syn.** See ASSENT. — **ac′qui·esc′ing·ly**, *adv.*

ac′qui·es′cence (-ĕs′ĕns; -'ns), *n.* Act or state of acquiescing.

ac′qui·es′cent (-ĕs′ĕnt; -'nt), *adj.* Acquiescing or disposed to acquiesce. — **ac′qui·es′cent·ly**, *adv.*

ac·quire′ (ă·kwīr′), *v. t.* [L. *acquirere, acquisitum,* fr. *ad-* + *quaerere* to seek.] To gain by any means, usually by one's own exertions; to get as one's own. — **Syn.** See GET. — **ac·quir′a·ble** (-kwīr′ȧ·b'l), *adj.* — **ac·quir′er**, *n.*

ac·quire′ment (-mĕnt), *n.* **1.** Act of acquiring. **2.** That which is acquired; an attainment.

Syn. **Acquirement, acquisition, attainment, accomplishment** are comparable when they mean a power or skill won through exertion or effort. **Acquirement** implies an achieving through constant endeavor at self-cultivation; **acquisition** emphasizes avidity in effort and the inherent value of that gained; **attainment** suggests a distinguished achievement; **accomplishment,** a skill that makes for effectiveness, especially socially.

ac′qui·si′tion (ăk′wĭ·zĭsh′ŭn), *n.* [L. *acquisitio,* fr. *acquirere.*] **1.** Act of acquiring. **2.** A thing acquired. — **Syn.** See ACQUIREMENT.

ac·quis′i·tive (ă·kwĭz′ĭ·tĭv), *adj.* Given to, or strongly desirous of, acquiring; avid. — **Syn.** See COVETOUS. — **-ly**, *adv.* — **-ness**, *n.*

ac·quit′ (ă·kwĭt′), *v. t.;* AC·QUIT′TED; AC·QUIT′TING. [From OF., fr. L. *quietare* to appease. See AD-; QUIT.] **1.** To discharge, as a debt; to pay off. **2.** To set free or discharge (from an accusation, obligation, or burden); to pronounce not guilty; — often with *of;* as, *acquitted* of arson or of evil intentions. **3.** Reflexively: **a** To clear (oneself). *Shak.* **b** To conduct (oneself); as, the soldier *acquitted* himself well. — **Syn.** See EXCULPATE (**Ant.** convict): BEHAVE. — **ac·quit′ter**, *n.*

ac·quit′tal (ă·kwĭt′ăl; -'l), *n.* **1.** Act of acquitting; exculpation; also, discharge of a duty. **2.** *Law.* A setting free by legal process from the charge of an offense.

ac·quit′tance (-ăns; -'ns), *n.* **1.** Act of acquitting, now usually the clearing off of a debt or obligation. **2.** A writing evidencing a discharge; a receipt in full.

acr-. = ACRO-.

a′cre (ā′kẽr), *n.* [AS. *æcer.*] **1.** Orig., a tilled or enclosed field; as, God's *acre* (a burial ground); *pl.,* lands; estate. **2.** A measure of land. See MEASURE, *Tables* 3 & 4.

a′cre·age (-ĭj), *n.* Acres collectively; area in acres.

a′cre–foot′, *n.* *Irrigation Engin.* A unit of volume of water equal to the volume of a prism one foot high with a base one acre in area; 43,560 cubic feet or 1,233.5 cubic meters.

a′cre–inch′, *n.* One twelfth of an acre-foot.

ac′rid (ăk′rĭd), *adj.* [L. *acer* sharp.] **1.** Sharp and harsh or bitterly pungent to the taste; irritating or corrosive. **2.** Bitterly irritating to the feelings; of caustic temper. — **ac′rid·ly**, *adv.* — **ac′rid·ness**, *n.*

ac′ri·dine (ăk′rĭ·dēn; dĭn), *n.* [*acrid* + *-ine.*] *Chem.* A colorless, crystalline compound, $C_{13}H_9N$, occurring in coal tar. It is the parent substance of certain artificial dyes (**acridine dyes**) and drugs.

a·crid′i·ty (ă·krĭd′ĭ·tĭ), *n.* Quality of being acrid; acrimony.

ac′ri·mo′ni·ous (ăk′rĭ·mō′nĭ·ŭs), *adj.* Angry and bitter; caustic; as,

acrimonious dispute. — **Syn.** See ANGRY. — **ac′ri·mo′ni·ous·ly,** *adv.* — **ac′ri·mo′ni·ous·ness,** *n.*

ac′ri·mo′ny (ăk′rĭ·mō′nĭ *or, esp. Brit.,* -mŭn·ĭ), *n.; pl.* -NIES (-nĭz). [F. or L.; F., fr. L. *acrimonia,* fr. *acer* sharp.] Harsh or biting sharpness, as of temper or language; pungency.

Syn. **Acrimony, acerbity, asperity** mean temper or language marked by angry or resentful irritation. **Acrimony** stresses anger with rising bitterness and a power to sting or blister; **acerbity** implies sourness as well as bitterness, sometimes as shown in words but, more often, in mood; **asperity** suggests quickness of temper and sharpness of resentment, but rarely bitterness. — **Ant.** Suavity.

ac′ro- (ăk′rō-). [Gr. *akros* highest, outermost.] A combining form denoting *pertaining to the tip* or *to extremes* or *to the extremities.*

ac′ro·bat (ăk′rō·băt), *n.* [F. *acrobate,* fr. Gr. *akrobatos* walking on tiptoe, climbing aloft, fr. *akros* highest + *-batos,* fr. *bainein* to go.] One who performs gymnastic feats; a tumbler; gymnast. — **ac′ro·bat′ic** (-băt′ĭk), **ac′ro·bat′i·cal** (-ĭ·kăl), *adj.* — **ac′ro·bat′i·cal·ly,** *adv.* — **ac′ro·bat′ics** (-ĭks), *n.;* see -ICS. — **ac′ro·bat′ism** (-ĭz′m), *n.*

ac′ro·car′pous (ăk′rō·kär′pŭs), *adj.* [Gr. *akrokarpos* bearing fruit at the top, fr. *akros* highest + *karpos* fruit.] *Bot.* Bearing fruit at the apex of the main stem.

ac′ro·dont (ăk′rō·dŏnt), *adj.* [*acr-* + *-odont.*] *Zool.* **a** Consolidated with the summit of the alveolar ridge without sockets; — said of teeth. **b** Having acrodont teeth; — opposed to *pleurodont.*

ac′ro·drome (ăk′rō·drōm), **a·crod′ro·mous** (*ȧ*·krŏd′rō·mŭs), *adj.* [See ACRO-; -DROME.] *Bot.* Having the principal nerves, or veins, terminating at the leaf tip.

ac′ro·gen (ăk′rō·jĕn), *n.* [*acro-* + *-gen.*] *Bot.* A plant of the highest class of cryptogams, including the ferns, mosses, and liverworts, which have the growing point at the summit or apex. — **a·crog′e·nous** (*ȧ*·krŏj′ē·nŭs), *adj.* — **a·crog′e·nous·ly,** *adv.*

a·cro′le·in (*ȧ*·krō′lē·ĭn), *n.* [L. *acer* sharp + *olēre* to smell.] *Chem.* A colorless liquid aldehyde, C_3H_4O, of pungent odor, obtained by dehydration of glycerol or destructive distillation of fats.

ac′ro·meg′a·ly (ăk′rō·mĕg′*ȧ*·lĭ), *n.* [*acro-* + Gr. *megas, megalou,* big.] *Med.* Chronic hyperpituitarism marked by progressive enlargement of hands, feet, and face. — **-me·gal′ic** (-mē·găl′ĭk), *adj.*

a·cron′i·cal, a·cron′y·cal (*ȧ*·krŏn′ĭ·kăl), *adj.* Also **-chal** (-kăl). [Gr. *akronychos* at nightfall.] *Astron.* Occurring at nightfall, or sunset. — **-cal·ly, -chal·ly,** *adv.*

ac′ro·nym (ăk′rō·nĭm), *n.* [*acr-* + *-onym* (fr. Gr. *onyma* name).] A word formed from the initial letters or syllables of the successive parts of a compound term (*asdic, radar*). — **ac′ro·nym′ic** (ăk′rō·nĭm′ĭk), **a·cron′y·mous** (*ȧ*·krŏn′ĭ·mŭs), *adj.* — **a·cron′y·mize** (*ȧ*·krŏn′ĭ·mīz), *v. i. & t.*

ac′ro·pho′bi·a (ăk′rō·fō′bĭ·*ȧ*), *n.* [NL., fr. *acro-* + *-phobia.*] *Med.* Morbid dread of being at a great height.

a·crop′o·lis (*ȧ*·krŏp′ō·lĭs), *n.; pl.* -LISES (-ĕz; -ĭz), -LEIS (-līs). [L., fr. Gr. *akropolis,* fr. *akros* highest + *polis* city.] The upper fortified part or citadel of a Greek city, esp. that of Athens (***the Acropolis***).

ac′ro·spire (ăk′rō·spīr), *n.* [*acro-* + Gr. *speira* anything twisted.] *Bot.* The spiral plumule in germinating grain.

a·cross′ (*ȧ*·krŏs′; 74), *adv. & prep.* [*a-* on, in + *cross.*] Crosswise (of); to or on the opposite side (of); over.

a·cros′tic (*ȧ*·krŏs′tĭk), *n.* [Gr. *akrostichis, akrostichion,* fr. *akros* extreme + *stichos* order, line.] A composition, usually in verse, in which one or more sets of letters, when taken in order, form words. — **a·cros′tic, a·cros′ti·cal** (-tĭ·kăl), *adj.* — **a·cros′ti·cal·ly,** *adv.*

ac′ro·tism (ăk′rō·tĭz′m), *n.* [*a-* not + Gr. *krotos* a beating.] *Med.* Failure or defect of pulsation. — **a·crot′ic** (*ȧ*·krŏt′ĭk), *adj.*

a·cryl′ic (*ȧ*·krĭl′ĭk), *or* **ac′ry·late** (ăk′rĭ·lāt), **res′in.** [L. *acer* sharp + *-yl* + *-ic.*] Any of a group of glasslike thermoplastic resins made by polymerizing esters of ***acrylic acid*** ($C_3H_4O_2$, a liquid with an odor like acetic acid) or ***methacrylic acid*** ($C_4H_6O_2$, a colorless crystalline substance). ***Methacrylate resins,*** used as transparent molding materials, are derivatives of methacrylic acid.

ac′ry·lo- (ăk′rĭ·lō-), **acryl-.** *Chemistry.* Combining form for *acrylic,* as in **ac′ry·lo·ni·trile′** (ăk′rĭ·lō·nī·trĭl′; ăk′rĭ·lō·nī·trĕl′), acrylic nitrile.

act (ăkt), *n.* [F. and L.; F. *acte,* fr. L. *actus* a doing, and *actum* a thing done, fr. *agere* to drive, do.] **1.** That which is done; the exercise of power, or the effect whose cause is power exerted; a deed. **2.** The decision of a legislative body (disting. from *bill,* def. 3), or of a court, etc.; a decree, edict, law, judgment, resolve, award. **3.** A formal writing stating that something has been done; as, an *act* of sale. **4.** Process of doing; action; as, taken in the *act.* **5.** One of the principal divisions of a play or dramatic work; hence, one of the parts of a variety program. **6.** *Metaph.* A state of reality or real existence as opposed to a possibility or possible existence. — **Syn.** See ACTION.

— *v. t.* [L. *actus,* past part. of *agere* to drive, lead, do; but influenced by E. *act,* n.] **1.** *Obs.* To actuate. **2.** To perform as an actor; as, *acting* the role of Iago; hence, to play the part of, as if in a play; to personate; as, to *act* the jester. **3.** To feign; to simulate. — **Syn.** Represent, impersonate. — *v. i.* **1.** To perform on the stage; as, to *act* in a play; hence, to behave as if acting a part; also, of plays, to admit of being performed. **2.** To conduct oneself or behave; as, to *act* with modesty; to bear oneself as being or as if being; as, to *act* wise. **3.** To exert one's powers in a way to bring about an effect; to do something; as, he chose to *act* first and think after. **4.** To serve or operate in fulfillment of a special function; as, to *act* as mediator; the brakes failed to *act.* **5.** To produce an effect or influence, esp. a change in the condition of something; as, the pancreatic juice *acts* on all classes of food. **6.** To render a decision or award, as by vote of a legislature or by judicial decree. — **Syn.** Function, work, operate, behave. — **act′a·bil′i·ty** (ăk′tȧ·bĭl′ĭ·tĭ), *n.* — **act′a·ble,** *adj.*

Ac·tae′on (ăk·tē′ŏn), *n.* [L., fr. Gr. *Aktaiōn.*] *Class. Myth.* A huntsman who, having surprised Diana bathing, was changed into a stag, and killed by his own hounds.

ACTH (ā′sē′tē′āch′). *Abbr.* for adrenocorticotropic hormone.

actin-. = ACTINO-.

ac′ti·nal (ăk′tĭ·năl; ăk·tī′năl), *adj.* [Gr. *aktis aktinos,* ray.] *Zool.* Pert. to the part of a radiate animal from which the tentacles or arms radiate and where the mouth is situated; — hence often equivalent to *oral.*

act′ing (ăk′tĭng), *adj.* **1.** Actively functioning. **2.** Doing duty temporarily or for another; as, an *acting* mayor. **3.** Of a version of a play, prepared with directions to actors; also, actable.

ac·tin′i·a (ăk·tĭn′ĭ·*ȧ*), *n.; pl.* -IAE (-ē), -IAS (-*ȧ*z). [NL., fr. Gr. *aktis, aktinos,* ray.] Any sea anemone or related animal. — **ac·tin′i·an** (-ăn), *adj. & n.*

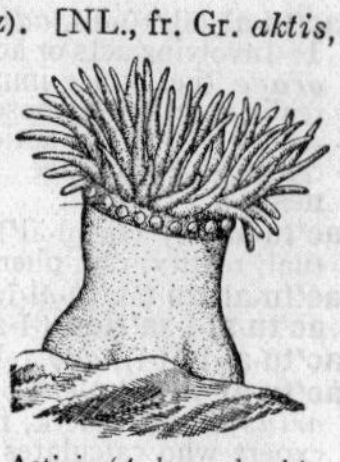

Actinia (*A. bermudensis*). (¼)

ac·tin′ic (ăk·tĭn′ĭk), *adj.* Of, pertaining to, or exhibiting actinism; as, **actinic ray,** any of the rays exhibiting actinism. — **ac·tin′i·cal·ly** (-ĭ·kăl·ĭ), *adv.*

ac·tin′i·form (ăk·tĭn′ĭ·fôrm), *adj.* Having a radiated form; like a sea anemone.

ac′tin·ism (ăk′tĭn·ĭz′m), *n.* [Gr. *aktis, aktinos* ray.] The property of radiant energy (found especially in the shorter wave lengths of the spectrum) by which chemical changes are produced, as in light-sensitive photographic emulsions.

ac·tin′i·um (ăk·tĭn′ĭ·ŭm), *n.* [NL.] *Chem.* A radioactive element discovered by Debierne in 1899 in pitchblende. Symbol, *Ac;* at. no., 89; at. wt., 227.

ac′ti·no- (ăk′tĭ·nō-), **actin-.** [Gr. *aktis, aktinos,* ray of light.] A combining form designating *ray* or *rays, radiated structure;* — used, specif., to denote: **a** *Relation to actinism, actinic effect,* as in **ac′ti·no·chem′is·try.** **b** *Zool. Radiated structure.* **c** *Pertaining to* or *caused by actinic radiation* (as X-ray radiation), as in **ac′ti·no·der′ma·ti′tis, ac′ti·nos′co·py, ac′ti·no·ther′a·py.**

ac·tin′o·graph (ăk·tĭn′ō·grăf), *n.* [*actino-* + *-graph.*] *Photog.* An actinometer (sense 2).

ac′ti·noid (ăk′tĭ·noid), *adj.* [*actin-* + *-oid.*] Raylike; radiated, as an actinia.

ac′ti·nol′o·gy (ăk′tĭ·nŏl′ō·jĭ), *n.* [*actino-* + *-logy.*] The science of rays of light, esp. as to their chemical effects.

ac′ti·nom′e·ter (-nŏm′ē·tẽr), *n.* [*actino-* + *-meter.*] **1.** An instrument for measuring the direct heating power of the sun's rays. **2.** An instrument for measuring the actinic power of a light source; *Photog.,* a form of this instrument for calculating suitable exposure time. — **ac′ti·nom′e·try** (-trĭ), *n.* — **ac′ti·no·met′ric** (-nō·mĕt′rĭk), **ac′ti·no·met′ri·cal** (-rĭ·kăl), *adj.*

ac′ti·no·mor′phic (ăk′tĭ·nō·môr′fĭk), **ac′ti·no·mor′phous** (-fŭs), *adj.* [*actino-* + *-morphic, -morphous.*] *Biol.* = RADIOSYMMETRICAL.

ac′ti·no·my′ces (-mī′sēz), *n.* A bacterial parasite (genus *Actinomyces*), one species of which (*Actinomyces bovis*) causes **ac′ti·no·my·co′sis** (-mī·kō′sĭs), a chronic infectious disease of cattle and swine, and also man, characterized by local suppurating tumors, esp. about the jaw and lungs.

ac′ti·no·zo′an (-zō′ăn), *n. & adj.* [*actino-* + Gr. *zōion* animal.] = ANTHOZOAN.

ac′tion (ăk′shŭn), *n.* [OF., fr. L. *actio,* fr. *agere* to do.] **1.** The act or process of producing an effect or performing a function; the doing of something; as, an emergency requiring *action;* a press in *action.* **2.** The effecting of an alteration by means of force or some natural power; as, *action* of water on rocks. **3.** **a** An act; thing done; also, enterprise or efficiency in a generic sense; as, a man of *action.* **b** *pl.* Habitual deeds; hence, conduct; behavior. **4.** The mode of acting or functioning, as of an actor, typewriter, etc. **5.** The event or series of events, either real or imaginary, forming the subject of a play, poem, etc. **6.** A mechanism; as, the breech *action* of a gun; the *action* in a piano. See GUNLOCK, *Illust.* **7.** *Law.* A legal proceeding by which one demands or enforces one's right in a court of justice. **8.** *Mil. & Nav.* Combat in war; also, a battle. **9.** *Painting & Sculp.* Attitude or position as suggestive of movement or of the sentiment or passion depicted.

Syn. (1) **Action, act, deed** mean something done or effected. **Action** implies a process which takes time and involves more than one step; **act** usually implies a single accomplishment, complete in itself; as, the rescue of a shipwrecked crew is a heroic *action;* the launching of the lifeboat is a brave *act.* **Deed** often connotes that the act is illustrious or an achievement.
(2) See BATTLE.

ac′tion·a·ble (ăk′shŭn·*ȧ*·b'l), *adj.* Subject to, or affording ground for, an action or suit at law. — **ac′tion·a·bly,** *adv.*

ac′ti·vate (ăk′tĭ·vāt), *v. t.* To make active; specif.: **a** *Chem.* To render (molecules) capable of reacting or (enzymes) of promoting reaction; also, to make (substances) radioactive. **b** To render (sewage) active with aerobic bacteria by prolonged aeration so that the purification of sewage added later is hastened. **c** To treat (charcoal or carbon), as by heating in steam, to enhance its adsorptive property, as for purifying water or for use as an absorbent in gas masks. **d** *U. S. Army.* To set up or institute formally (a unit, as a division). — **ac′ti·va′tion** (-vā′shŭn), *n.* — **ac′ti·va′tor** (-vā′tẽr), *n.*

ac′tive (ăk′tĭv), *adj.* [F. or L.; F. *actif,* fr. L. *activus,* fr. *agere* to act.] **1.** Communicating or causing action or change; as, *active* powers of the mind. **2.** Quick in physical movement; as, an *active* gait. **3.** In action; working; in force; as, an *active* volcano. **4.** Given to action; energetic; busy; as, an *active* mind. **5.** Requiring or implying action or exertion; as, *active* service. **6.** Brisk; lively; as, an *active* demand. **7.** Implying rapid action; progressive; as, an *active* disease. **8.** *Accounting.* Productive; as, *active* assets. **9.** *Bookkeeping.* Bearing interest; as, an *active* bond. **10.** *Gram.* Pertaining to or designating: **a** The form, or voice, of the verb which represents the subject as the agent or doer of the action expressed by the verb (the wind *blows*); — distinguished from *passive.* **b** A verb used transitively. **c** A verb expressing action (*strike, run*) as distinct from mere existence or state. Cf. NEUTER. — **Syn.** Operative, live, dynamic. — **ac′tive·ly,** *adv.* — **ac′tive·ness,** *n.*

active service. *Mil.* **a** Service in the field against an enemy. **b** Service upon the **active list,** comprising all officers performing, or available for, military or naval duties.

ac·tiv′i·ty (ăk·tĭv′ĭ·tĭ), *n.; pl.* -TIES (-tĭz). **1.** State of action, or quality of being active; as: **a** Physical motion; agility. **b** Vigorous or energetic action. **c** Natural or normal function. **2.** An active agent or force; a force that actuates. **3.** An instance of being active; a sphere of action; as, social *activities.*

act of God. *Law.* An inevitable accident; such an interruption of the usual course of events that no experience, foresight, or care which might reasonably be expected could have foreseen or guarded against it.

ac′tor (ăk′tẽr), *n.* **1.** A doer. **2.** A theatrical or motion-picture performer. — **ac′tress** (-trĕs; -trĭs), *n.*

Acts (ăkts), *n. pl., construed as sing.* Short for **Acts of the Apostles,** a book of the New Testament (see BIBLE).

ac'tu·al (ăk'tū·ăl), *adj.* [OF. *actuel*, fr. LL. *actualis*, fr. *actus* act.] **1.** Involving acts or actions. *Obs.*, except in ***actual sin*** and ***actual grace*** (i.e., grace impelling man to do good). **2.** Existing in act or reality; real; — opposed to *potential, virtual, theoretical, hypothetical*, etc. **3.** In action at the time being; as, caught in the *actual* crime. — **Syn.** See REAL. — **Ant.** Ideal; imaginary. — **ac'tu·al·ness**, *n.*

ac'tu·al'i·ty (ăk'tū·ăl'ĭ·tĭ), *n.*; *pl.* -TIES (-tĭz). **1.** State of being actual; reality, esp. phenomenal reality. **2.** *pl.* Actual conditions.

ac'tu·al·ize (ăk'tū·ăl·īz), *v. t.* To make actual; to realize in action. — **ac'tu·al·i·za'tion** (-ĭ·zā'shŭn; -ī·zā'-), *n.*

ac'tu·al·ly (-ĭ), *adv.* In act or in fact; really.

ac'tu·ar'y (ăk'tū·ĕr'ĭ *or, esp. Brit.*, -ĕr·ĭ), *n.*; *pl.* -IES (-ĭz). [L. *actuarius* copyist, clerk, fr. *actus* act.] **1.** A registrar or clerk. **2.** An expert who calculates insurance risks and premiums. — **ac'tu·ar'i·al** (-âr'ĭ·ăl), *adj.* — **ac'tu·ar'i·al·ly**, *adv.*

ac'tu·ate (ăk'tū·āt), *v. t.* [ML. *actuatus*, past part. of *actuare*, fr. L. *actus* act.] To put into action; to incite to action; to arouse. — **Syn.** See MOVE. — **ac'tu·a'tion** (-ā'shŭn), *n.* — **ac'tu·a'tor** (-ā'tẽr), *n.*

ac'u·ate (ăk'ū·āt), *adj.* [L. *acus* needle.] Sharpened; pointed.

a·cu'i·ty (ȧ·kū'ĭ·tĭ), *n.* [F. *acuité*, fr. ML. *acuitas*.] Sharpness or acuteness.

a·cu'le·ate (ȧ·kū'lē·āt), *adj.* Also **a·cu'le·at'ed** (-āt'ĕd; -ĭd). [L. *aculeatus*, fr. *aculeus*.] Having a sting; having, or beset with, prickles, or sharp points; hence, stinging; incisive.

a·cu'le·us (-ŭs), *n.*; *pl.* -LEI (-ī). [L., dim. of *acus* needle.] **1.** *Bot.* A prickle, as of the rose. **2.** *Zool.* A sting.

a·cu'men (ȧ·kū'mĕn), *n.* [L., fr. *acuere* to sharpen.] Acuteness of mind; keenness in intellectual or practical matters. — **Syn.** See DISCERNMENT.

a·cu'mi·nate (-mĭ·nāt), *adj.* [L. *acuminatus*, past part. of *acuminare* to sharpen.] Tapering to a slender point; pointed. See LEAF, *Illust.* (7). — (-nāt), *v. t.* To render sharp or keen. — **a·cu'mi·na'tion** (-nā'shŭn), *n.*

ac'u·punc'ture (ăk'ū·pŭngk'tūr), *n.* [L. *acus* needle + *punctura* a pricking.] A puncturing of bodily tissue, as for relief of pain. — (ăk'ū·pŭngk'tūr), *v. t.* To treat with acupuncture.

a·cute' (ȧ·kūt'), *adj.* [L. *acutus*, past part. of *acuere* to sharpen.] **1.** Sharp at the end; pointed; — opposed to *blunt* or *obtuse*. See LEAF, *Illust.* **2.** Perceiving, using, or demanding minute distinctions; penetrating; keen; — opposed to *dull, obtuse*, or *stupid*. **3.** High or shrill; — opposed to *grave* or *low*. **4.** Acting keenly on the senses; sharp; as, *acute* pain. **5.** Susceptible to slight impressions; as, *acute* eyesight. **6.** Constituting a crisis; crucial; as, an *acute* shortage. **7. a** Of less than 90°; — of an angle. See ANGLE, *Illust.* **b** Having one or more acute angles; as, an *acute* triangle. See TRIANGLE, *Illust.* **8.** Marked with an acute accent; as, an *acute* e (é). **9.** *Med.* Attended with symptoms of some severity, and coming speedily to a crisis; — opposed to *chronic*. — **a·cute'ly**, *adv.* — **a·cute'ness**, *n.*

Syn. (1) See SHARP. — **Ant.** Obtuse.

(2) **Acute, critical, crucial** are synonyms when they mean full of uncertainty to those concerned. **Acute** stresses intensification of symptoms, conflicting emotions, or the like, to the culmination or breaking point (as, the controversy had reached the *acute* stage); **critical** adds to *acute* implications of imminent change, of concomitant suspense, and of decisiveness in the outcome (as, she is at the *critical* point in her illness); **crucial**, in discriminating use, suggests a crossing or dividing of the ways, and a test or trial involving the determination of a course or direction (as, he is now at the *crucial* stage of his career).

acute accent. A mark (′) used to indicate stressed or accented syllables, the quality or quantity of a vowel or consonant sound, a rising inflection, etc.

-a·cy (-ȧ·sĭ). A suffix denoting *quality, state, office*, etc., as in efficacy, primacy, piracy, accuracy.

a·cy'clic (ā·sī'klĭk; -sĭk'lĭk), *adj.* [*a-* not + *cyclic*.] Not cyclic; not arranged in cycles or whorls.

ad (ăd), *n.*; *pl.* ADS (ădz). *Colloq.* An advertisement.

ad-. A prefix from Lat. *ad*, to, expressing *motion, direction*, or *change to* or *toward, adherence* or *addition, proximity*, or merely *intensification*; as in admit, adjunct, admixture, administer. It appears as *ad-* before a vowel, and before *d, h, j, m, v*; as *a-* before *sc, sp*, and *st*; before *c, f, g, l, n, p, q, r, s*, and *t*, it is assimilated to *ac-* (before *c* or *q*), *af-, ag-*, etc., as in *af*fix, assimilate, etc.

ad'age (ăd'ĭj), *n.* [F., fr. L. *adagium*.] A saying which has obtained credit by long use. — **Syn.** Saying, saw, maxim, proverb, motto.

a·da'gio (ȧ·dä'jō), *adv.* [It.] *Music & Dancing.* Slowly; in an easy, graceful manner. — *n.*; *pl.* -GIOS (-jōz). **1.** A composition in adagio tempo; a slow movement, as of a symphony. **2.** In ballet dancing, a slow duet dance in which the woman performs balancing feats on her toes and flies slowly through the air with the aid of her partner.

Ad'am (ăd'ăm), *n.* [Heb. *Ādām*.] **1.** As related in Genesis (i–v), the first man. **2.** "Original sin"; human frailty. — **A·dam'ic** (ȧ·dăm'ĭk), **A·dam'i·cal** (-ĭ·kăl), *adj.* — **A·dam'i·cal·ly**, *adv.*

Ad'am (ăd'ăm), *adj.* Designating a style of furniture or of architecture introduced in the 18th century by the brothers Adam, in England. Adam furniture is characterized by straight lines, surface decoration, and use of conventional designs such as festooned garlands and medallions.

Ad'am-and-Eve', *n.* The puttyroot.

ad'a·mant (ăd'ȧ·mănt *or, esp. Brit.*, -mănt), *n.* [OF., fr. L. *adamas, adamantis*, the hardest metal, fr. Gr. *adamas, -antos*, fr. *a-* not + *daman* to subdue.] **1.** An imaginary stone of impenetrable hardness; formerly, the diamond. **2.** An unbreakable obstacle; impenetrable hardness. **3.** [ME., fr. confusion with L. *adamare* to love.] *Obs.* Loadstone. — *adj.* Impenetrably hard; hence, unyielding; obdurate. — **Syn.** See INFLEXIBLE. — **ad'a·man·te'an** (ăd'ȧ·măn·tē'ăn), *adj.*

ad'a·man'tine (ăd'ȧ·măn'tĭn; -tīn; -tēn), *adj.* **1.** Of or like adamant; incapable of being broken, dissolved, or penetrated; immovable. **2.** *Mineral.* Like the diamond in hardness or luster.

Ad'am's ap'ple (ăd'ămz). The projection in the front of the neck formed by the largest cartilage of the larynx.

Ad'am's-nee'dle, *n.* Yucca.

a·dapt' (ȧ·dăpt'), *v. t.* [F. *adapter*, fr. L. *adaptare*, fr. *ad-* + *aptare* to fit, fr. *aptus* fit.] To make suitable; to fit, or suit; to adjust.

Syn. **Adapt, adjust, accommodate, conform, reconcile** mean to bring one into correspondence with another. **Adapt** specifically implies modification to meet new conditions, sometimes connoting pliability or readiness; **adjust** implies a bringing into as exact or close a correspondence as exists between the parts of a mechanism, but suggests more tact or more ingenuity in the agent; **accommodate** implies, more than *adjust*, a yielding or giving in to the demands or requirements of the other; **conform** (often intransitive or reflexive) implies a bringing into accordance with a pattern, example, or principle; **reconcile** implies the demonstration, to one's own or another's satisfaction, of the consistency or congruity of things that are, or seem to be, incompatible.

a·dapt'a·ble (ȧ·dăp'tȧ·b'l), *adj.* That can be adapted or can easily adapt itself. — **Syn.** See PLASTIC. — **a·dapt'a·bil'i·ty** (-bĭl'ĭ·tĭ), **a·dapt'a·ble·ness**, *n.*

ad'ap·ta'tion (ăd'ăp·tā'shŭn), *n.* **1.** Act or process of adapting, or state of being adapted. **2.** Adjustment to environmental conditions; specif.: **a** *Physiol.* Adjustment of a sense organ, as the eye, to the intensity or quality of stimulation, as of light, temperature, or pressure. **b** *Biol.* Modification of an animal or plant (or of its parts or organs) fitting it more perfectly for existence under the conditions of its environment. **3.** An adapted form or structure. — **ad'ap·ta'tion·al**, *adj.* — **ad'ap·ta'tion·al·ly**, *adv.*

a·dapt'er, a·dap'tor (ȧ·dăp'tẽr), *n.* One who or that which adapts; as: **a** Any device for connecting two pieces of apparatus. **b** Any attachment for adapting apparatus for uses not originally intended.

a·dap'tion (ȧ·dăp'shŭn), *n.* = ADAPTATION. — **a·dap'tion·al**, *adj.*

a·dap'tive (-tĭv), *adj.* Tending to or showing adaptation. — **a·dap'tive·ly**, *adv.* — **a·dap'tive·ness**, *n.*

A·dar' (ȧ·där'; ā'där), *n.* [Heb. *Adār*.] See JEWISH CALENDAR.

‖**ad a'stra per a'spe·ra** (ăd ăs'trȧ pûr ăs'pĕr·ȧ). [L.] To the stars by hard ways; — the motto of Kansas.

add (ăd), *v. t.* [L. *addere* to add to, join.] **1.** To join or unite so as to increase the number, augment the quantity, or enlarge the magnitude; — with *to*. **2.** To combine into one sum or quantity. **3.** To append, as a statement; to say further. — *v. i.* **1.** To make an addition. **2.** To perform mathematical addition. — **Syn.** Annex, subjoin. — **add'er**, *n.*

ad'dax (ăd'ăks), *n.* [L., an animal with twisted horns; of African origin.] A large light-colored antelope (*Addax nasomaculata*) of Arabia, Syria, and northern Africa.

add'ed line (ăd'ĕd; -ĭd). *Music.* A ledger line.

ad'dend (ăd'ĕnd; ă·dĕnd'), *n.* *Math.* A number or quantity to be added to another, the *augend*. See SUM, *n.*, 5.

ad·den'dum (ă·dĕn'dŭm), *n.*; *pl.* -DA (-dȧ). [L.] **1.** A thing to be added; an addition. **2.** A supplement to a book; an appendix.

ad'der (ăd'ẽr), *n.* [AS. *nǣdre* adder, snake. *Adder*, without initial *n-*, arose through the incorrect division of *a nadder* as *an adder*.] **a** The common venomous viper (*Vipera berus*) of Europe; also, any other terrestrial viper (see VIPER, 1 **a**) of the family Viperidae, as the ***puff adder*** (*Bitis arietans*) of Africa. **b** In North America, any of several harmless snakes, as the ***blowing, puffing***, or ***spreading adder*** (= HOGNOSE SNAKE) and the ***checkered, milk***, or ***spotted adder*** (= MILK SNAKE). **c** Any of several venomous snakes, as the krait, and the ***death adder*** (*Acanthophis antarctica*) of Australia.

ad'der's-mouth' (ăd'ẽrz·mouth'), *n.* **a** Any small terrestrial orchid (genus *Malaxis*) having greenish, inconspicuous flowers. **b** The snakemouth.

ad'der's-tongue' (-tŭng'), *n.* **1.** A fern (genus *Ophioglossum*, family Ophioglossaceae) whose fruiting spike resembles a serpent's tongue. **2.** Rattlesnake plantain. **3.** The dogtooth violet *Erythronium albidum*.

add'i·ble (ăd'ĭ·b'l), *adj.* Capable of being added.

ad·dict' (ă·dĭkt'), *v. t.* [L. *addictus*, past part. of *addicere* to adjudge, devote, fr. *ad-* + *dicere* to say.] To apply habitually, as one's mind to speculation; to give (oneself) up or over, as to versifying, as a constant practice; to habituate.

ad'dict (ăd'ĭkt), *n.* One who is addicted to a habit, esp. to the taking of some drug.

ad·dict'ed (ă·dĭk'tĕd; -tĭd), *adj.* Given up or over (to a practice). — **ad·dict'ed·ness**, *n.*

ad·dic'tion (ă·dĭk'shŭn), *n.* State of being addicted; also, habituation, esp. to drugs.

Ad'di·son's dis·ease' (ăd'ĭ·s'nz). [After Thomas *Addison* (1793–1860), of London.] *Med.* An anemic emaciated condition causing a peculiar brown skin, and due to disease of the suprarenal glands.

ad·dit'a·ment (ă·dĭt'ȧ·mĕnt), *n.* [L. *additamentum*.] An addition; a thing added.

ad·di'tion (ă·dĭsh'ŭn), *n.* [OF., fr. L. *additio*, fr. *addere*.] **1.** Act, process, or instance of adding; also, anything added; increase; accession. **2.** *Obs. exc. Law.* A designation, esp. of a person's status, added to his name; as, John Doe, *Gent.* **3.** A part added to a building, to a real-estate development, or the like. **4.** *Math.* The process of combining two or more numbers so as to obtain a number called their sum. It is denoted by the sign +. — **Syn.** Accretion, increment, accession.

ad·di'tion·al (-ăl), *adj.* Added; coming by way of addition; extra; supplementary. — **ad·di'tion·al·ly**, *adv.*

ad'di·tive (ăd'ĭ·tĭv), *adj.* [L. *additivus*.] Characterized by, produced by, or admitting, addition; to be added. — **ad'di·tive·ly**, *adv.*

ad'dle (ăd''l), *adj.* [AS. *adela* filth.] **1.** Rotten and putrid; — of an egg. **2.** Empty as an addle egg; unsound or confused; muddled; — of talk or brains. Sometimes used in combinations, as in **ad'dle·brained'**, **ad'dle·head'ed, ad'dle·pat'ed.** — *v. t. & i.* To make or grow addle; to muddle.

ad·dress' (ă·drĕs'), *v. t.*; -DRESSED' (-drĕst') or -DREST'; -DRESS'ING. [OF. *adrecier* to straighten, address, fr. *a* to + *drecier* to straighten, arrange. See DRESS, *v.*] **1.** *Obs.* To put right; arrange. **2.** *Obs.* To prepare; array. **3.** *Obs.* To aim or shape the course of; to dispatch; also, to betake (oneself). **4.** To direct the effort or attention of, as in endeavor to achieve an aim; to apply; devote; as, to *address* oneself or one's powers to a task. **5.** To direct, as a speech, petition, etc. (*to* anyone, *to* an audience); as, to *address* a petition to Congress. **6.** To direct speech or a communication to; as, to *address* an audience; — also reflexive. **7.** To write an address (sense 5 **a**) on, as a letter; to direct. **8.** To use a set form in accosting or greeting; as, How does one *address* a governor? **9.** *Com.* To consign or entrust, as to an agent. **10.** *Golf.* To adjust the club head behind (the ball) in making ready for a stroke. **11.** *Law.* To unseat or remove (a judge) as unworthy of office, though not liable to impeachment, by executive order in accordance with a formal petition (called an **ad·dress'** [ă·drĕs'; ăd'rĕs]) from the legislature. — *v. i. Obs.* **1.** To prepare. **2.** To direct speech or attentions.

ad·dress′ (ă·drĕs′ *or, esp. in sense* 5, ăd′rĕs), *n.* **1.** *Obs.* Preparation. **2.** *Obs.* An addressing oneself or one's words to a person. **3.** Skillful management; dexterity; adroitness. **4.** A formal communication, either written or spoken; a lecture. **5. a** The directions for delivery of a letter, package, etc., esp. as written, stamped, or printed on an outer surface; a superscription. **b** A place where a person may be communicated with. **6. a** Bearing; deportment. **b** Manner of speaking to another; delivery; as, a man of pleasing *address.* **7.** Attention in the way of courtship; — now usually in *pl.* — **Syn.** See TACT.

ad′dress·ee′ (ăd′rĕs·ē′), *n.* One to whom anything is addressed.

ad·dress′er (ă·drĕs′ẽr), *n.* Also **ad·dres′sor** (ă·drĕs′ẽr; -ôr). One who addresses.

Ad·dres′so·graph (ă·drĕs′ō·graf; 9), *n.* A trade-mark applied to a machine for addressing letters, etc., that prints each address separately from characters embossed on a plate.

ad·duce′ (ă·dūs′), *v. t.;* -DUCED′ (-dūst′); -DUC′ING (-dūs′ĭng). [L. *adducere, adductum,* to lead to, fr. *ad-* + *ducere* to lead.] To bring forward or offer as an argument or consideration which bears on a statement or case; to cite; as, to *adduce* proof. — **ad·duc′er** (-dūs′ẽr), *n.* — **ad·duc′i·ble** (-ĭ·b'l), **ad·duce′a·ble** (-ȧ·b'l), *adj.*

Syn. Adduce, advance, allege, cite mean to bring forward for proof. Adduce implies facts, evidence, instances, etc., offered as proof or in support of something stated; advance implies, on the other hand, the presentation of a theory, a claim, a proposal, or the like, for consideration or acceptance; allege implies a recital of facts intended to be proved, but sometimes the word suggests that this is not possible; cite, more concrete and definite than *adduce,* suggests the use of an authority, a specific instance, etc., in support.

ad·du′cent (ă·dū′sĕnt), *adj.* [L. *adducens,* pres. part.] *Physiol.* Adducting; — opposed to *abducent.*

ad·duct′ (ă·dŭkt′), *v. t.* [See ADDUCE.] *Physiol.* To draw toward the median line or axis or, sometimes, together. — **ad·duc′tive** (-dŭk′tĭv), *adj.*

ad·duc′tion (ă·dŭk′shŭn), *n.* An adducing or adducting.

ad·duc′tor (-tẽr), *n.* *Anat.* An adducting muscle.

-ade (-ād, *generally; sometimes* -äd, *or* -ăd). [F. *-ade,* fr. Sp., Pg., or Pr. *-ada,* or It. *-ata,* fr. LL. *-ata.*] A noun suffix signifying: **a** *Act* or *action,* as in cannonade. **b** *Result* or *product* (of an action); *thing made;* as in lemonade. **c** A *person* or *aggregate concerned in an action* or *process,* as in brigade.

ad′e·no- (ăd′ē·nō-), **ad′en-.** [Gr. *adēn, adenos,* a gland.] A combining form denoting *gland, glandular,* as in **ad′e·nal′gi·a, ad′e·nec′to·my, ad′e·ni′tis, ad′e·no·log′i·cal, ad′e·nol′o·gy, ad′e·not′o·my** (see -ALGIA, -ECTOMY, etc.).

ad′e·noid (ăd′ē·noid), *adj.* [Gr. *adenoeidēs* glandular, fr. *adēn* gland. See -OID.] *Anat.* **a** Like or pertaining to a gland. **b** Of, like, or pertaining to lymphoid tissue. — *n.* An abnormally enlarged mass of lymphoid tissue at the back of the pharynx obstructing breathing through the nose; — usually in *pl.* — **ad′e·noi′dal** (-noi′dăl; -d'l), *adj.*

ad′e·no′ma (ăd′ē·nō′mȧ), *n.; pl.* -MATA (-nō′mȧ·tȧ), -MAS (-mȧz). [NL., fr. *aden-* + *-oma.*] *Med.* A benign tumor of glandlike structure or of glandular origin. — **ad′e·nom′a·tous** (-nŏm′ȧ·tŭs; -nō′mȧ·tŭs), *adj.*

a·den′o·sine (ȧ·dĕn′ō·sēn; -sĭn), *n.* [*adenine* a chemical with inserted *os* from *ribose.*] *Biochem.* A compound, $C_{10}H_{13}N_5O_4$, isolated from muscle. Its derivative **adenosine triphosphate,** abbr. *ATP,* occurs in muscle extract and is important in sugar metabolism.

ad′ept (ăd′ĕpt; ă·dĕpt′), *n.* [L. *adeptus* having obtained (sc. *artem*), that has obtained an art, past part. of *adipisci* to obtain, fr. *ad-* + *apisci* to attain.] One fully skilled or well versed in anything; a proficient.

a·dept′ (ă·dĕpt′), *adj.* Thoroughly proficient; expert. — **Syn.** See PROFICIENT. — **Ant.** Inept. — **a·dept′ly,** *adv.* — **a·dept′ness,** *n.*

ad′e·qua·cy (ăd′ē·kwȧ·sĭ), *n.* State or quality of being adequate; sufficiency for a purpose.

ad′e·quate (ăd′ē·kwĭt), *adj.* [L. *adaequatus,* past part. of *adaequare,* fr. *ad-* + *aequare* to make equal, fr. *aequus* equal.] **1.** Equal to or sufficient for some (specific) requirement; proportionate or correspondent. **2.** Such as is lawfully and reasonably sufficient. — **Syn.** See SUFFICIENT. — **Ant.** Inadequate. — **ad′e·quate·ly,** *adv.* — **-ness,** *n.*

a·der′min (ā·dûr′mĭn), *n.* [*a-* not + Gr. *derma* skin + *-in.*] Vitamin B_6 (see VITAMIN).

‖**ad e·un′dem (gra′dum)** (ăd ē·ŭn′dĕm grā′dŭm). [L.] To the same (rank); — said esp. of the admission of a student of one university to the same rank at another without an examination.

‖**à deux** (à dû′). [F.] Of, for, or between two; — used of familiar relations between two persons; as, a dinner *à deux.*

‖**ad ex·tre′mum** (ăd ĕks·trē′mŭm). [L.] To the extreme; at last.

ad·here′ (ăd·hēr′), *v. i.* [L. *adhaerere, adhaesum,* fr. *ad-* + *haerere* to stick.] **1.** To stick fast or cleave, as a glutinous substance does; to become joined or united, as by sticking, growth, etc.; to cling. **2.** To hold, be attached, or devoted; specif., to give support by some act of aid; as, one *adheres* to a party or faith. **3.** *Obs.* To be consistent; to agree. *Shak.* — **Syn.** See STICK.

ad·her′ence (ăd·hēr′ĕns), *n.* Quality, act, or state of adhering; specif., steady or firm attachment; fidelity, as to party or principle.

Syn. Adherence, adhesion are distinguished in present usage. The tendency prevails to confine adhesion to physical attachment, adherence to mental or moral attachment. But the distinction is not rigorously enforced.

ad·her′ent (-ĕnt), *adj.* **1.** Sticking; clinging; adhering. **2.** Attached or joined, though naturally or normally separate; adnate. — *n.* One who adheres; a follower. — **Syn.** See FOLLOWER. — **ad·her′ent·ly,** *adv.*

ad·he′sion (ăd·hē′zhŭn), *n.* [F. *adhésion,* fr. L. *adhaesio,* fr. *adhaerere.*] **1.** The adhering or sticking together of substances in contact with each other. **2.** Adherence; also, agreement to adhere; concurrence. **3.** *Med.* Union of surfaces normally separate by the formation of new tissue resulting from an inflammatory process. **4.** *Physics.* The molecular attraction exerted between the surfaces of bodies in contact. See COHESION. — **Syn.** See ADHERENCE.

ad·he′sive (-sĭv), *adj.* **1.** Sticky; tenacious, as glutinous substances. **2.** Tending to adhere; prepared for adhering. — *n.* An adhesive substance, as glue, cement. — **ad·he′sive·ly,** *adv.* — **ad·he′sive·ness,** *n.*

ad·hib′it (ăd·hĭb′ĭt), *v. t.* [L. *adhibitus,* past part. of *adhibere* to apply.] **1.** To admit or bring in. **2.** To apply or administer. **3.** To attach or affix. — **ad′hi·bi′tion** (ăd′hĭ·bĭsh′ŭn), *n.*

‖**ad hoc** (ăd hŏk′). [L.] For this case alone; special.

‖**ad ho′mi·nem** (hŏm′ĭ·nĕm). [L.] To the man; — of an argument directed at one's prejudices rather than one's intellect.

ad′i·a·bat′ic (ăd′ĭ·ȧ·băt′ĭk; ā′dī-), *adj.* [Gr. *adiabatos* not passable, fr. *a-* not + *dia* through + *bainein* to go.] Occurring without loss or gain of heat. Cf. ISOTHERMAL.

ad′i·an′tum (ăd′ĭ·ăn′tŭm), *n.* [L., fr. Gr. *adianton* maidenhair, fr. *a-* not + *diainein* to wet.] *Bot.* Any of a large genus (*Adiantum*) of plants, the maidenhair ferns, having much-divided fronds and short, margined sori.

ad′i·a·ther′man·cy (ăd′ĭ·ȧ·thûr′măn·sĭ), *n.* [*a-* not + *diathermancy.*] Imperviousness to heat waves. Cf. OPACITY.

a·dieu′ (ȧ·dū′; *F.* à·dyû′), *interj.* [F., fr. L. *ad Deum* to God.] Goodby; farewell. — *n.; pl.* ADIEUS (ȧ·dūz′), ADIEUX (à·dyû′). A farewell; a leave-taking.

ad in′fi·ni′tum (ăd ĭn′fĭ·nī′tŭm). [L.] Without limit.

ad in′te·rim (ĭn′tẽr·ĭm). [L.] In the meantime; in or for an interim; as, appointed to serve *ad interim;* an *ad interim* report. — **Syn.** Temporary, provisional, acting, supply.

‖**a·dios′** (ä·thyōs′; *Angl.* ăd′ĭ·ōs′), *interj.* [Sp.] Adieu.

ad′i·po·cere′ (ăd′ĭ·pō·sēr′), *n.* [L. *adeps, adipis,* fat + *cera* wax.] A waxy brownish substance generated in dead bodies long buried or immersed in moisture.

ad′i·pose (ăd′ĭ·pōs), *adj.* [L. *adeps, adipis,* fat.] Of animal fat; fatty. — *n.* The fat stored in the cells of loose connective tissue distributed through an animal's body. — **ad′i·pose·ness, ad′i·pos′i·ty** (-pŏs′ĭ·tĭ), *n.*

ad′it (ăd′ĭt), *n.* [L. *aditus,* fr. *adire, aditum,* fr. *ad-* + *ire* to go.] **1.** An entrance; *Mining,* a nearly horizontal passage from the surface. **2.** Admission; access.

ad·ja′cen·cy (ă·jā′sĕn·sĭ), *n.* **1.** Quality or state of being adjacent; contiguity. **2.** That which is adjacent.

ad·ja′cent (-sĕnt), *adj.* [L. *adjacens, -entis,* pres. part. of *adjacere* to lie near, fr. *ad-* + *jacere* to lie.] Lying near, close, or contiguous; neighboring; bordering; juxtaposed. — **ad·ja′cent·ly,** *adv.*

Syn. Adjacent, adjoining, contiguous, abutting mean in close proximity. Adjacent may or may not imply contact but it always implies absence of anything of the same kind in between; adjoining always implies meeting and touching at some point or line; contiguous adds to *adjoining* the implication of meeting and touching on all or most of one side; abutting suggests a bordering on or contact with something else, often with the implication of the end of a property line.

ad′jec·ti′val (ăj′ĕk·tī′văl; ăj′ĕk·tĭv·ăl; ăj′ĭk-), *adj.* Of or relating to, or of the nature of, an adjective. — **ad′jec·ti′val·ly,** *adv.*

ad′jec·tive (ăj′ĕk·tĭv; ăj′ĭk-), *n.* [L. *adjectivum* (sc. *nomen*), neut. of *adjectivus* that is added, fr. *adjicere* to add to, fr. *ad-* + *jacere* to throw.] **1.** *Gram.* A word used with a noun or noun equivalent to denote a quality of the thing named, or something attributed to it (a *wise* ruler), or to define its range of application (*any* men), or to specify a thing as distinct from something else (*these* holes). Abbr. *adj.* **2.** A dependent; an accessory. — *adj.* **1.** *Gram.* Of the nature of or having the function of an adjective; adjectival; as, an *adjective* pronoun (*their* son). **2.** Not standing by itself; dependent. **3.** Relating to procedure; — of law. **4.** *Dyeing.* Requiring or employing a mordant; — opposed to *substantive.* — **ad′jec·tive·ly,** *adv.*

ad·join′ (ă·join′), *v. t.* [From OF., fr. L. *adjungere,* fr. *ad-* + *jungere* to join.] To lie contiguous to; to be in contact with; to abut upon. — *v. i.* To lie or be next, esp. in actual contact along a line.

ad·join′ing, *adj.* Contiguous. — **Syn.** See ADJACENT.

ad·journ′ (ă·jûrn′), *v. t.* [From OF., fr. LL. *adiurnare,* fr. *ad-* + *jurnus,* fr. L. *diurnus* daily, fr. *dies* day.] To put off or defer to another day or place, or indefinitely; to close or suspend for the day. — *v. i.* To suspend a session, esp. of business, for resumption at another time or place, or indefinitely; as, a court *adjourns* sine die.

Syn. Adjourn, prorogue, dissolve, as used of public bodies, mean to suspend business. Adjourn implies suspension of deliberations, usually for a brief period, and their resumption at the next meeting (except for something to the contrary in the rules of procedure); prorogue implies the ending of a session of a parliament or the like by the crown or its representative, with the result that all bills not enacted are quashed and can be taken up only as new matter at a succeeding session; dissolve implies that the body ceases to exist as there constituted.

ad·journ′ment (-mĕnt), *n.* Act of adjourning, or state of being adjourned; also, the interval for which a body adjourns.

ad·judge′ (ă·jŭj′), *v. t.;* AD·JUDGED′ (-jŭjd′); AD·JUDG′ING. [OF. *ajugier,* fr. L. *adjudicare,* fr. *ad-* + *judicare* to judge.] **1.** To decide, determine, or pronounce judicially; to order or decree. **2.** To sentence; condemn; — now with *to.* **3.** To award or grant judicially in a case of controversy. **4.** *Now Rare.* To deem as an act of private judgment; as, to *adjudge* a man happy.

ad·ju′di·cate (ă·jōō′dĭ·kāt), *v. t.* & *i.* [See ADJUDGE.] To hear or try, and determine judicially; to settle by judicial decree; to adjudge; to act as judge. — **ad·ju′di·ca′tive** (-kā′tĭv; -kȧ·tĭv), *adj.* — **ad·ju′di·ca′tor** (-kā′tẽr), *n.*

ad·ju′di·ca′tion (-kā′shŭn), *n.* **1.** An adjudicating. **2.** A judicial decision or sentence; specif., a decree in bankruptcy.

ad′junct (ăj′ŭngkt), *adj.* [L. *adjunctus,* past part. of *adjungere.* See ADJOIN.] Attending; consequent. — *n.* **1.** Something joined or added to another thing, but not essentially a part of it; as, charters with their *adjuncts.* **2.** A person joined to another in some duty or service; colleague; associate. **3.** *Gram.* A word or phrase added to qualify the force of another word or other words, esp. such an added word or phrase as distinguished from an essential element of the sentence. Thus, in "A merry heart goes all the day," *merry* is an adjunct to the subject, and *all the day* an adjunct to the predicate verb of the sentence. **4.** *Logic.* A nonessential quality. — **Syn.** Appendage, appurtenance, accessory. — **ad·junc′tive** (ă·jŭngk′tĭv), *adj.*

ad′ju·ra′tion (ăj′ōō·rā′shŭn), *n.* **1.** Act of adjuring; an earnest appeal. **2.** A solemn oath or swearing. — **ad·jur′a·to′ry** (ă·jōōr′ȧ·tō′rĭ *or, esp. Brit.,* -tẽr·ĭ), *adj.*

ad·jure′ (ă·jōōr′), *v. t.* [F. or L.; F. *adjurer,* fr. L. *adjurare, adjuratum,* to swear to; later, to adjure.] To charge, bind, or command, solemnly, as if under oath, or under penalty of a curse; to appeal to solemnly; to entreat earnestly. — **Syn.** See BEG. — **ad·jur′er, ad·ju′ror** (ă·jōōr′ẽr), *n.*

ad·just′ (ă·jŭst′), *v. t.* [F. *ajuster,* fr. *à* to + *juste* just, fr. L. *justus* just, right.] **1.** To settle; to free from differences or discrepancies; to bring to a satisfactory state, so that parties are agreed; as, to *adjust* accounts or differences with clients. **2.** To make exact; to fit; to make correspondent or conformable; to bring into proper relations; as, to *adjust* a garment to the body, or behavior to circumstances, or oneself to one's environment. **3.** To regulate, or reduce to system, as the orthography of a text. **4.** To bring to a true relative position, as the parts of an instrument; to regulate for use, as a carburetor. **5.** *Insurance.* To determine the amount to be paid under a policy in settlement of (a loss or claim). — **Syn.** See ADAPT. — *v. i.* To adapt or conform oneself. — **ad·just'a·ble,** *adj.* — **ad·just'a·bly,** *adv.* — **ad·just'er, ad·jus'tor** (ă·jŭs'tẽr), *n.*

ad·just'ment (ă·jŭst'mĕnt), *n.* **1.** Act or process of adjusting, or state of being adjusted; the establishing of a satisfactory relationship, as representing harmony, conformance, adaptation, or the like; the bringing of a thing or things into proper or exact position or condition. **2.** A means, as a mechanism, by which things are adjusted one to another; as, an *adjustment* for focusing a microscope. **3.** *Com.* The calculation and settlement of the shares to be had or borne by various parties in respect of a joint liability, claim, loss, or payment.

ad'ju·tant (ăj'ŏŏ·tănt), *n.* [L. *adjutans,* pres. part. of *adjutare* to help.] **1.** A helper; assistant. **2.** In present-day armies, a staff officer in charge of the official correspondence, records of personnel, preparation and distribution of orders, etc., of a command. Abbr. *Adj., Adjt.* **3.** A large stork (*Leptoptilus dubius*), common in India. It is also called **adjutant bird, adjutant crane, adjutant stork.** — **ad'ju·tan·cy** (-tăn·sĭ), *n.*

adjutant general; *pl.* ADJUTANTS GENERAL. **1.** In the U. S. Army, an adjutant under the commander of a corps area, expeditionary force, division, or higher tactical unit. **2.** A military officer having administrative charge of the militia of a state or territory. — **The Adjutant General.** *U. S.* The chief officer in the **Adjutant General's Department** of the U. S. Army, the department of records, orders, and correspondence. See INSIGNIA, *Illust.*

ad'ju·vant (ăj'ŏŏ·vănt), *adj.* [L. *adjuvans,* pres. part. of *adjuvare* to aid.] Helping; helpful. — **Syn.** Auxiliary, subsidiary, contributory. — *n.* **1.** An assistant. **2.** That which aids or modifies something, as a subsidiary ingredient in a medicine.

ad'-lib' (ăd'lĭb'), *v. i. & t.;* -LIBBED' (-lĭbd'); -LIB'BING. [Short for *ad libitum.*] *Slang.* To insert (lines not in the script); to play or sing (music not in the written score).

ad lib'i·tum (ăd lĭb'ĭ·tŭm). [L.] **1.** At pleasure; as one wishes; as far as one desires. **2.** *Music.* To be interpreted, varied, or omitted according to the performer's feeling and taste. Abbr. *ad lib.*

ad·meas'ure (ăd·mĕzh'ẽr), *v. t.* To determine the proper share or apportionment of.

ad·meas'ure·ment (-mĕnt), *n.* **1.** An admeasuring. **2.** Dimensions.

Ad·me'tus (ăd·mē'tŭs), *n.* *Gr. Myth.* Husband of Alcestis (which see).

ad·min'i·cle (ăd·mĭn'ĭ·k'l), *n.* [L. *adminiculum* support.] **1.** A help; an auxiliary. **2.** *Law.* Corroborative or explanatory proof. — **ad'mi·nic'u·lar** (ăd'mĭ·nĭk'ū·lẽr), *adj.*

ad·min'is·ter (ăd·mĭn'ĭs·tẽr), *v. t.* [From OF., fr. L. *administrare,* fr. *ad-* + *ministrare* to serve.] **1.** To manage or direct the execution, application, or conduct of; as, to *administer* public affairs. **2.** To dispense or serve out, as relief or justice. **3.** To apply, as a remedy; to give, as a dose or something beneficial; hence, to give by way of punishment or reproof. **4.** To tender, as an oath. **5.** *Law.* To settle, as an estate. — **Syn.** See EXECUTE. — *v. i.* **1.** To contribute; to bring aid or supplies; to minister. **2.** To manage affairs; specif., *Law,* to perform the office of administrator. — **ad·min'is·tra·ble** (-trȧ·b'l), *adj.* — **ad·min'is·trant** (-trănt), *adj. & n.*

ad·min'is·trate (-trāt), *v. t.* To administer.

ad·min'is·tra'tion (-trā'shŭn), *n.* **1.** Act or process of administering; specif., dispensing or tendering to another, esp. according to a prescribed formula or rite; as, *administration* of justice, an oath, a sacrament. **2.** The performance of the executive duties of an institution, business, or the like. **3.** The activity of the state in the exercise of its political powers; in a narrower sense, the activity of the executive and judiciary departments, or esp. of the executive alone, in the conduct of government. **4.** The persons collectively who are entrusted with the execution of laws; the chief magistrate and his cabinet or council. **5.** The term during which an administrative officer or body holds office. **6.** *Law.* The management and disposal, under legal authority, of the estate of a deceased person, or of an infant, lunatic, etc.

ad·min'is·tra'tive (ăd·mĭn'ĭs·trā'tĭv *or, esp. Brit.,* -trȧ·tĭv), *adj.* Of or having to do with administration, esp. management; executive. — **ad·min'is·tra'tive·ly,** *adv.*

ad·min'is·tra'tor (ăd·mĭn'ĭs·trā'tẽr), *n.* [L.] **1.** One who administers; esp., one who administers affairs. **2.** *Law.* A person who is legally vested with the right of administration of an estate, esp. of an estate belonging to a minor, to a lunatic, or to a testator having no competent executor. — **ad·min'is·tra'tor·ship,** *n.* — **ad·min'is·tra'trix** (-trā'trĭks), *n. fem.; pl.* -TRATRICES (-trā·trī'sēz; -trā'trĭ·sēz). — **ad·min'is·tra'tress** (-trā'trĕs), *n. fem.*

ad'mi·ra·ble (ăd'mĭ·rȧ·b'l), *adj.* [F., fr. L. *admirabilis.*] Having qualities to excite wonder united with approbation; deserving the highest esteem. — **ad'mi·ra·ble·ness,** *n.* — **ad'mi·ra·bly,** *adv.*

ad'mi·ral (ăd'mĭ·răl), *n.* [OF. *a(d)miral,* fr. Ar. *amīr-al-* commander of the, in titles; early confused with L. *admirabilis* admirable.] **1.** *Hist.* The commander in chief of a country's navy. **2.** A naval officer of highest rank comprising in the U. S. Navy four grades, fleet admiral of the U. S. Navy (not over four at one time; insignia 5 silver stars), admiral (4 stars), vice-admiral (3 stars), rear admiral (2 stars), and in the British Navy, admiral of the fleet, admiral, vice-admiral, rear admiral. **3.** The ship which carries the admiral; the flagship. **4.** Any of several handsome nymphalid butterflies. — **ad'mi·ral·ship',** *n.*

ad'mi·ral·ty (-tĭ), *n.; pl.* -TIES (-tĭz). **1.** The office or jurisdiction of an admiral. **2.** The department or officers having authority over naval affairs. **3.** The court having jurisdiction of maritime questions and offenses; also, maritime law. **4.** [*cap.*] The building in which the lords of the Admiralty, in England, transact business.

ad'mi·ra'tion (ăd'mĭ·rā'shŭn), *n.* **1.** *Archaic.* Wonder. **2.** Marveling esteem accompanied by gratification and delight; also, observation attended by such esteem; as, *admiration* of a landscape. **3.** That toward which such esteem is directed.

ad·mire' (ăd·mīr'), *v. t.* [L. *admirari,* fr. *ad-* + *mirari* to wonder.] **1.** *Archaic.* To regard with wonder or astonishment. **2.** To regard with wondering esteem accompanied by pleasure and delight; to look at or upon with an elevated feeling of pleasure. **3.** To esteem or regard highly; as, *admired* but not approved. — **Syn.** See REGARD. — **Ant.** Abhor. — **ad·mir'er** (-mīr'ẽr), *n.* — **ad·mir'ing,** *adj.* — **ad·mir'ing·ly,** *adv.*

ad·mis'si·ble (ăd·mĭs'ĭ·b'l), *adj.* **1.** That may be allowed or conceded; — of ideas or propositions. **2.** Worthy to be admitted. — **ad·mis'si·bil'i·ty** (-bĭl'ĭ·tĭ), **ad·mis'si·ble·ness,** *n.* — **ad·mis'si·bly,** *adv.*

ad·mis'sion (ăd·mĭsh'ŭn), *n.* [L. *admissio.*] **1.** The action of admitting or the fact of being admitted or received, esp. into a position or class, a privileged group, or the like; the right to enter a place or school, into society, etc.; entrance; access. **2.** Acceptance into an office. **3.** The granting of an argument or position not fully proved; concession. **4.** A fact, point, or statement admitted. **5.** Fee paid at or for entering. — **Syn.** See ADMITTANCE.

Admission Day. A legal holiday commemorating the day of admission as a state of the United States, — Feb. 14 in Arizona, Sept. 9 in California, Oct. 31 in Nevada.

ad·mis'sive (ăd·mĭs'ĭv), *adj.* Implying an admission.

ad·mit' (ăd·mĭt'), *v. t.;* AD·MIT'TED; AD·MIT'TING. [L. *admittere, admissum,* fr. *ad-* + *mittere* to send.] **1.** To suffer to enter; to grant entrance to, whether into a place, the mind, or consideration; as, to *admit* a friend into one's confidence; to have capacity to receive or allow entrance to; as, a dock *admitting* two boats. **2.** To allow to enter on an office or to enjoy a privilege; as, *admitted* to bail. **3.** To allow; permit; also, to permit as compatible; as, this law *admits* no exceptions. **4.** To accept as valid; to acknowledge or assent to, as an allegation; to concede; own; as, he *admitted* his responsibility; an *admitted* error. **5.** To give a right of entrance to; as, this ticket *admits* one. — **Syn.** See RECEIVE (**Ant.** eject, expel): ACKNOWLEDGE. — *v. i.* **1.** To give entrance or access. **2.** To grant; allow; permit; — with *of;* as, to *admit* of two interpretations. — **ad·mit'ted·ly,** *adv.*

ad·mit'tance (-ăns), *n.* **1.** Act of admitting. **2.** Permission to enter; admission; also, actual entrance; reception. **3.** *Elec.* The reciprocal impedance.

Syn. **Admittance, admission** mean permitted entrance, but **admittance** is usually confined to entrance to a locality or building, **admission** to something that carries with it rights, privileges, obligations, or the like, such as a church, a society, a country as the home of a nation, a theater for the purpose of seeing a play, etc.

ad·mix' (ăd·mĭks'; ăd-), *v. t. & i.* To add by mixing; mix.

ad·mix'ture (-tūr), *n.* [L. *admiscere, admixtum,* fr. *ad-* + *miscere* to mix.] **1.** A mixing; a mixture. **2.** That which is added to anything by mixing.

ad·mon'ish (ăd·mŏn'ĭsh), *v. t.* [From OF., fr. L. *admonere* to remind, warn, fr. *ad-* + *monere* to warn.] **1.** To warn of a fault; to reprove gently or kindly, but seriously; to exhort; also, to put (one) in mind of something forgotten, by way of a warning or exhortation; as, he was *admonished* not to go. **2.** To enjoin by a warning; as, to *admonish* silence. — **Syn.** See REPROVE. — **ad·mon'ish·er,** *n.* — **ad·mon'ish·ment,** *n.*

ad'mo·ni'tion (ăd'mō·nĭsh'ŭn), *n.* [OF. *amonition,* fr. L. *admonitio,* fr. *admonere.*] Gentle or friendly reproof; counseling against fault or oversight; warning.

ad·mon'i·tor (ăd·mŏn'ĭ·tẽr), *n.* [L.] An admonisher.

ad·mon'i·to'ry (-tō'rĭ *or, esp. Brit.,* -tẽr·ĭ), *adj.* That conveys admonition.

ad'nate (ăd'nāt), *adj.* [L. *adnatus,* past part. of *adnasci* to grow to or on.] *Bot. & Zool.* Congenitally grown together; — said esp. of unlike parts. — **ad·na'tion** (ăd·nā'shŭn), *n.*

‖**ad nau'se·am** (ăd nô'shē·ăm; nô'sē·ăm). [L.] To nausea; so as to disgust.

a·do' (ȧ·dōō'), *n.* [ME. *at do,* northern form for *to do.*] Doing; trouble; fuss. — **Syn.** See STIR.

a·do'be (ȧ·dō'bĭ), *n.* [Sp.] **1.** An unburnt brick dried in the sun. **2.** Earth from which unburnt bricks are made; hence, any alluvial or playa clay in desert regions. **3.** A structure made of such bricks or clay. — **a·do'be,** *adj.*

ad'o·les'cence (ăd'ō·lĕs'ĕns), *n.* The state or process of growing up from childhood to manhood or womanhood; youth, or the period of life between puberty and maturity.

ad'o·les'cent (-ĕnt), *adj.* [L. *adolescens, -entis,* pres. part. of *adolescere* to grow up.] **1.** Growing from childhood to maturity; in a state of adolescence. **2.** Of or characteristic of adolescence or an adolescent. — *n.* An adolescent person.

A·do'nis (ȧ·dō'nĭs; ȧ·dŏn'ĭs), *n.* [L., fr. Gr. *Adōnis.*] **1.** *Class. Myth.* A beautiful youth loved by Aphrodite. In youth he was slain by a wild boar. So great was Aphrodite's grief that the gods required him to spend only part of the year in Hades. **2.** A very beautiful young man.

a·dopt' (ȧ·dŏpt'), *v. t.* [F. *adopter,* fr. L. *adoptare,* fr. *ad-* + *optare* to choose.] **1.** To take by choice into some relationship, such as that of heir, friend, citizen, etc.; to take voluntarily (a child of other parents) as one's own child. **2.** To take and apply or put into practice as one's own (what is not so naturally). **3.** *Parl. Practice.* To accept, as a report, in acquittance of a duty imposed. — **a·dopt'a·ble,** *adj.* — **a·dopt'er,** *n.*

Syn. **Adopt, embrace, espouse** mean to make one's own that which in some fashion one owes to another. **Adopt** implies accepting that of which one is not the begetter, author, or the like; **embrace** implies acceptance, usually joyful acceptance, of that which one figuratively takes to one's bosom; **espouse** implies an attachment suggesting the closeness of marriage, such as sharing the same fortunes or misfortunes.

a·dop'tion (ȧ·dŏp'shŭn), *n.* [F. or L.; F. *adoption,* fr. L. *adoptio.*] Act of adopting, or state of being adopted.

a·dop'tive (ȧ·dŏp'tĭv), *adj.* Made or acquired by adoption; tending or inclined to adopt. — **a·dop'tive·ly,** *adv.*

a·dor'a·ble (ȧ·dōr'ȧ·b'l; 70), *adj.* **1.** Worthy to be adored; worthy of fervent devotion. **2.** *Colloq.* Exquisitely charming. — **a·dor'a·bil'i·ty** (-bĭl'ĭ·tĭ), **a·dor'a·ble·ness,** *n.* — **a·dor'a·bly,** *adv.*

ad'o·ra'tion (ăd'ō·rā'shŭn), *n.* **1.** Act of paying honor to a divine being. **2.** Homage paid to one held in high esteem.

a·dore' (ȧ·dōr'; 70), *v. t.* [F. *adorer,* fr. L. *adorare,* fr. *ad-* + *orare* to speak, pray.] **1.** To worship or honor as a deity or as divine. **2.** To feel or express reverent admiration for; to regard with fervent devotion and affection; to idolize. — **Syn.** See REVERE. — **a·dor'er** (ȧ·dōr'ẽr), *n.*

a·dorn' (ȧ·dôrn'), *v. t.* [From OF., fr. L. *adornare,* fr. *ad-* + *ornare* to embellish.] **1.** To deck or dress with ornaments; to set off to advantage. **2.** To add to the beauty, splendor, or attractiveness of.

Syn. **Adorn, decorate, ornament, embellish, beautify, deck, garnish**

mean to enhance in appearance. **Adorn** implies not only a heightening of background or setting but beauty in that which enhances; **decorate** suggests relieving plainness or monotony of background by contributing beauty of color or design to it; **ornament** implies something added which sets off a thing to advantage; **embellish** implies the addition of ornament for the sake of effect; **beautify** adds to *embellish* a suggestion of counterbalancing plainness or ugliness; **deck** implies the addition of something that contributes to the gaiety, splendor, or showiness of something; **garnish** adds to *deck* the suggestion of a final touch for use.

a·dorn′ment (ȧ·dôrn′mĕnt), *n.* An adorning; decoration; also, that with which one is adorned.

‖**ad pa′tres** (ăd pā′trēz). [L.] (Gathered) to his fathers; dead.

‖**ad quem** (kwĕm′). [L.] At or to which; — opposed to *a quo.*

‖**ad rem** (rĕm′). [L.] To the thing or matter in hand.

ad·re′nal (ăd·rē′năl), *adj.* [*ad-* + *renal.*] *Anat.* Adjacent to the kidneys; specif., pertaining to or derived from the **adrenal glands** or **bodies**, paired ductless glands commonly called *suprarenal glands.* — *n.* An adrenal gland.

Ad·ren′al·in (ăd·rĕn′ăl·ĭn), *n.* A trade-mark applied to a crystalline compound, $C_9H_{13}NO_3$, prepared from suprarenal extract; hence [*usually not cap.; commonly* **ad·ren′al·ine** (-ĭn; -ēn)], this compound, used as a heart stimulant, for arresting hemorrhage, etc.

ad·re′no·cor′ti·co·trop′ic (ăd·rē′nō·kôr′tĭ·kō·trŏp′ĭk), *adj.* [*adreno-* (fr. *adrenal,* adj.) + *cortico-* (fr. *cortical*) + *-tropic.*] Affecting the cortex of the adrenal glands, as in **adrenocorticotropic hormone**, a compound produced by the pituitary gland, having a stimulatory effect on the cortex of the adrenal glands.

a·drift′ (ȧ·drĭft′), *adj.* Afloat without moorings or anchor, at the mercy of wind and waves. — **a·drift′**, *adv.*

a·droit′ (ȧ·droit′), *adj.* [F., fr. *à* to + *droit* right, fr. L. *directus.* See DIRECT.] Dexterous in the use of the hands or in the exercise of the mental faculties; ready in invention or execution. — **Syn.** See DEXTEROUS (**Ant.** maladroit): CLEVER (**Ant.** stolid). — **-ly**, *adv.* — **-ness**, *n.*

‖**à droite** (á drwȧt′). [F.] To or on the right (hand).

ad′sci·ti′tious (ăd′sĭ·tĭsh′ŭs), *adj.* [L. *adscitus,* past part. of *adsciscere* to take knowingly, fr. *ad-* + *sciscere* to seek to know, fr. *scire* to know.] Supplemental; additional; adventitious.

ad′script (ăd′skrĭpt), *adj.* [L. *adscriptus,* past part. of *adscribere* to enroll.] Written after; as, iota *adscript.*

ad·scrip′tion (ăd·skrĭp′shŭn), *n.* Ascription.

ad·sorb′ (ăd·sôrb′), *v. t.* [L. *ad* to + *sorbere* to suck in.] To condense and hold by adsorption. — **ad·sorb′ent**, *adj. & n.*

ad·sorp′tion (-sôrp′shŭn), *n.* [See ADSORB.] The adhesion, in an extremely thin layer, of the molecules of gases, of dissolved substances, or of liquids, to the surfaces of solid bodies with which they are in contact; — distinguished from *absorption.* — **ad·sorp′tive** (-tĭv), *adj. & n.*

ad·su′ki bean (ăd·sōō′kĭ; ăd·zōō′-). Var. of ADZUKI BEAN.

‖**ad′sum** (ăd′sŭm). [L.] I am present; — used esp., as at school, as an answer to a roll call.

ad′u·lar′i·a (ăd′ū·lâr′ĭ·ȧ), *n.* [From *Adula,* a mountain group in Switzerland.] A translucent variety of feldspar. It is the moonstone of commerce.

ad′u·late (ăd′ū·lāt), *v. t.* [L. *adulatus,* past part. of *adulari.*] To flatter in a servile way; to praise obsequiously and fulsomely. — **ad′u·la′tion** (-lā′shŭn), *n.* — **ad′u·la′tor** (-lā′tẽr), *n.* — **ad′u·la·to′ry** (-lȧ·tō′rĭ *or, esp. Brit.,* -tẽr·ĭ), *adj.*

a·dult′ (ȧ·dŭlt′; ăd′ŭlt), *adj.* [L. *adultus,* past part. of *adolescere* to grow up, fr. *ad-* + *alescere* to grow.] Grown to full size and strength; matured. — *n.* A person, animal, or plant that has reached maturity. In civil law the term is applied to males after the age of fourteen and to females after twelve.

a·dul′ter·ant (ȧ·dŭl′tẽr·ănt), *n.* An adulterating substance or agent. — *adj.* Adulterating.

a·dul′ter·ate (-āt), *v. t.* [L. *adulteratus,* past part. of *adulterare,* fr. *ad-* + *alter* other, different.] To corrupt, debase, or make impure by an admixture of a foreign or a baser substance; to prepare, esp. for sale, with an ingredient included which is not part of the professed substance, or, according to certain statutes, with an essential ingredient abstracted, or with a defect artificially concealed, or under conditions of exposure to disease, or so as to simulate a better article. — **a·dul′ter·a′tor** (-ā′tẽr), *n.*

a·dul′ter·ate (ȧ·dŭl′tẽr·āt), *adj.* **1.** Adulterous. **2.** Adulterated; spurious.

a·dul′ter·a′tion (-ā′shŭn), *n.* **1.** Process of adulterating; condition of being adulterated. **2.** An adulterated product.

a·dul′ter·er (ȧ·dŭl′tẽr·ẽr), *n.* One, esp. a man, who commits adultery. — **a·dul′ter·ess**, *n.*

a·dul′ter·ine (-ĭn; -īn), *adj.* Proceeding from or relating to adultery or adulteration; spurious.

a·dul′ter·ous (-ŭs), *adj.* Guilty of, given to, or pertaining to, adultery; illicit. — **a·dul′ter·ous·ly**, *adv.*

a·dul′ter·y (-ĭ), *n.; pl.* -TERIES (-ĭz). [L. *adulterium.*] Voluntary sexual intercourse by a married man with another than his wife or by a married woman with another than her husband. Cf. FORNICATION.

a·dult′hood (ȧ·dŭlt′ho͝od), *n.* State or time of being an adult.

ad·um′brate (ăd·ŭm′brāt; ăd′ŭm·brāt), *v. t.* [L. *adumbratus,* past part. of *adumbrare,* fr. *ad-* + *umbrare* to shade, fr. *umbra* shadow.] **1.** To give a shadowy or sketchy representation of; to indicate by a vague disclosure. **2.** To foreshadow vaguely. **3.** To overshadow. — **ad′um·bra′tion** (ăd′ŭm·brā′shŭn), *n.* — **ad·um′bra·tive** (ăd·ŭm′brȧ·tĭv), *adj.* — **ad·um′bra·tive·ly**, *adv.*

a·dunc′ (ȧ·dŭngk′), **a·dun′cous** (ȧ·dŭng′kŭs), *adj.* [L. *aduncus,* fr. *ad-* + *uncus* hooked, hook.] Curved inward; hooked. — **a·dun′ci·ty** (-dŭn′sĭ·tĭ), *n.*

a·dust′ (ȧ·dŭst′), *adj.* [L. *adustus,* past part. of *adurere* to burn, fr. *ad-* + *urere* to burn.] **1.** Burnt or scored; dried up with heat; sunburnt. **2.** Atrabilious; gloomy.

ad va·lo′rem (ăd vȧ·lō′rĕm). [L.] Literally, according to the value; — esp. of a duty or charge laid upon goods at a certain rate per cent upon their invoiced value. Abbr. *ad val.*

ad·vance′ (ăd·våns′; 9), *v. t.;* AD·VANCED′ (-vånst′); AD·VANC′ING (-vån′sĭng). [With *d,* as if fr. L. *ad* to, fr. OF. *avancier, avancer,* fr. L. *ab* away + *ante* before.] **1.** To bring or move forward. **2.** To accelerate the growth or progress of; to forward; as, to *advance* a scheme. **3.** To raise to a higher rank; promote. **4.** *Archaic.* To raise or elevate, as one's eyelids. **5.** To make earlier, as an event or date; to hasten. **6.** To bring to view or notice; to offer or propose, as arguments. **7.** To raise in rate, as prices. **8.** To furnish, as money or other value, before it is due, or in aid of an enterprise; to supply beforehand.

Syn. (1) **Advance, promote, forward, further** here mean to move or put ahead. **Advance** stresses effective assistance or force, as in hastening a process bringing about a desired end, etc.; **promote** stresses an encouraging or fostering, but sometimes an advancing in grade or in rank; **forward** (as here considered) implies an impetus that forces something ahead; **further** suggests a removal of obstacles or obstructions in the way of a desired advance. — **Ant.** Retard. (2) See ADDUCE.

— *v. i.* **1.** To move or go forward. **2.** To increase or make progress in any respect; as, to *advance* in knowledge. **3.** To rise in rank, office, or consequence. **4.** To rise in rate; as, prices have *advanced.*

Syn. Advance, progress, as intransitive verbs, mean to move forward in space or time or toward an objective. **Advance** implies little more; **progress** carries implications of a process, a circuit, a cycle, or of an evolution, that give it greater definiteness and character. — **Ant.** Recede.

— *n.* **1.** An advancing; progress. **2.** Improvement or progression, as in knowledge or rank. **3.** A rise in price or value. **4.** Approach made to form an acquaintance, adjust a difference, etc.; an overture; tender; — usually in *pl.* **5.** A furnishing of something before an equivalent is received (as money or goods); money or value supplied beforehand. — ***in advance.*** **a** In front. **b** Before receiving an equivalent. — *adj.* Placed, sent, issued, etc., or going, in advance.

ad·vanced′ (ăd·vånst′), *adj.* **1.** Moved or set in the van or front; in advance as to time or place of what is in course, use, etc. **2.** Far on, as in life, time, or course. **3.** In the front or before others, as regards progress or ideas; as, *advanced* views.

ad·vance′ment (ăd·våns′mĕnt), *n.* Act of advancing; progression; furtherance; promotion to a higher position.

ad·van′tage (ăd·vån′tĭj; 9), *n.* [OF. *avantage,* fr. *avant* before, fr. L. *ab* + *ante.*] **1.** Superiority of state or position; — often with *of* or *over.* **2.** Any condition, circumstance, opportunity, or means particularly favorable to success, or to any desired end; as, the *advantages* of an alliance. **3.** That which is gained from superiority of state or position; hence, benefit; as, information to one's *advantage.* **4.** Interest of money. **5.** *Tennis.* The first point won after deuce, or the score for it. — ***to advantage.*** So as to better the impression or opportunity. — *v. t.;* -TAGED (-tĭjd); -TAG·ING (-tĭj·ĭng). To give an advantage to; to further; promote; benefit; profit.

ad′van·ta′geous (ăd′văn·tā′jŭs), *adj.* Of or conferring advantage; favorable; profitable; useful. — **Syn.** See BENEFICIAL. — **Ant.** Disadvantageous. — **ad′van·ta′geous·ly**, *adv.* — **ad′van·ta′geous·ness**, *n*

ad·vec′tion (ăd·vĕk′shŭn), *n.* [L. *advectio,* fr. *advehere* to carry to, fr. *ad* to + *vehere* to carry.] *Meteorol.* The horizontal shifting of a mass of air, considered especially as a means of the transfer of heat. — **ad·vec′tive** (-tĭv), *adj.*

Ad′vent (ăd′vĕnt *or, esp. Brit.,* -vĕnt), *n.* [L. *adventus,* fr. *advenire, adventum,* to reach, arrive, fr. *ad-* + *venire* to come.] **1.** The period including the four Sundays before Christmas. **2.** The Nativity. **3.** The coming of Christ as judge on the Last Day; — called also *Second Advent.* **4.** [*not cap.*] Any coming; arrival; approach. — **Syn.** See ARRIVAL.

Ad′vent·ism (ăd′vĕn·tĭz′m), *n.* The doctrine that the second coming of Christ and the end of the world (or age) are near at hand.

Ad′vent·ist (-tĭst), *n.* A believer in the doctrine of Adventism; a member of a religious body emphasizing this doctrine (as the ***Evangelical Adventists***, the ***Advent Christian Church***, and the ***Seventh-day Adventist Denomination***).

ad′ven·ti′ti·a (ăd′vĕn·tĭsh′ĭ·ȧ), *n.* [L. *adventicia,* neut. pl. of *adventicius.*] An external covering of an organ, especially of a blood vessel.

ad′ven·ti′tious (ăd′vĕn·tĭsh′ŭs), *adj.* [L. *adventicius.*] **1.** Added extrinsically; not essentially inherent; acquired, accidental, or casual. **2.** *Biol.* Out of the usual place; arising sporadically; as, an *adventitious* bud. **3.** *Philol.* Not historically an organic part of a word (*t* in *against*). — **Syn.** See ACCIDENTAL. — **Ant.** Inherent. — **ad′ven·ti′tious·ly**, *adv.* — **ad′ven·ti′tious·ness**, *n.*

ad·ven′tive (ăd·vĕn′tĭv), *adj. Bot.* Growing spontaneously, but not native; as, an *adventive* weed. — *n. Bot.* An imperfectly naturalized exotic.

Advent Sunday. The first Sunday in Advent (sense 1).

ad·ven′ture (ăd·vĕn′tūr), *n.* [OF. *aventure,* fr. L. *adventura,* fr. *advenire.* See ADVENT.] **1.** *Obs.* **a** Chance; fortune; luck. **b** Risk or jeopardy. **2.** The encountering of risks; hazardous enterprise. **3.** A bold undertaking, in which hazards are to be met and the issue hangs upon unforeseen events; a daring feat. **4.** A remarkable experience. **5.** A mercantile or speculative enterprise or hazard; a venture. — *v. t.* To risk, or expose to hazard; also, to venture upon; to dare. — *v. i.* **1.** To venture or hazard oneself; as, *adventuring* upon paths unknown. **2.** To take the risk.

ad·ven′tur·er (-tūr·ẽr), *n.* One who adventures; esp.: **a** One who engages in new and perilous enterprises. **b** A soldier of fortune.

ad·ven′ture·some (ăd·vĕn′tūr·sŭm), *adj.* Venturesome.

ad·ven′tur·ess (-tūr·ĕs; -ĭs), *n.* A female adventurer; a woman who seeks position or livelihood by equivocal means.

ad·ven′tur·ous (-tūr·ŭs), *adj.* **1.** Inclined to adventure; prone to embark on hazardous enterprises. **2.** Attended with risk; requiring courage; — applied esp. to acts. — **ad·ven′tur·ous·ly**, *adv.* — **ad·ven′tur·ous·ness**, *n.*

Syn. Adventurous, venturous, venturesome, daring, daredevil, rash, reckless, temerarious, foolhardy mean exposing oneself to danger more than is required by good sense or courage. **Adventurous** implies a willingness to incur risks or hazards, but not necessarily imprudence; **venturous** and, even more, **venturesome** apply more often to acts than to spirit and carry a stronger suggestion of imprudence; **daring** stresses fearlessness in courting danger; **daredevil** stresses ostentation in daring; **rash** stresses great imprudence in encountering danger, and **reckless** utter heedlessness of consequences; **temerarious** not only implies recklessness but a very faint chance of success; **foolhardy** suggests a recklessness that is wholly inconsistent with good sense.

ad′verb (ăd′vûrb), *n.* [L. *adverbium,* fr. *ad-* + *verbum* word, verb.] *Gram.* A qualifier of a verb or of another qualifier, whether adjective, adverb, or qualifying phrase or clause, or of verbal nouns. The greater number of English adverbs are formed by adding to adjectives and participles the suffix *-ly* (high*ly*; loving*ly*). Abbr. *adv.* — *adj.* Adverbial.

ad·ver′bi·al (ăd·vûr′bĭ·ăl), *adj. Gram.* Of, pertaining to, or containing an adverb or adverbs; of the nature of, or taking the force of, an adverb. — **ad·ver′bi·al·ly**, *adv.*

‖**ad ver′bum** (ăd vûr′bŭm). [L.] To a word; verbatim.

ad'ver·sar'y (ăd'vẽr·sĕr'ĭ *or, esp. Brit.*, -sẽr·ĭ), *n.; pl.* -IES (-ĭz). [L. *adversarius.*] One turned against another or others with a design to oppose or resist him or them; an antagonist; enemy; foe. — **Syn.** See OPPONENT. — **Ant.** Ally.

— ***the Adversary.*** The Devil; Satan.

ad·ver'sa·tive (ăd·vûr'să·tĭv), *adj.* [L. *adversativus.*] Expressing contrariety, opposition, or antithesis; as, an *adversative* conjunction (*but*). — *n.* An adversative word or proposition. — **ad·ver'sa·tive·ly,** *adv.*

ad·verse' (ăd·vûrs'; ăd'vûrs; 2), *adj.* [OF. *avers*, fr. L. *adversus*, past part. of *advertere* to turn to. See ADVERT.] **1.** Acting against, or in a contrary direction; antagonistic; as, *adverse* winds. **2.** In hostile opposition to one's interests; unpropitious; calamitous; afflictive; as, *adverse* circumstances. **3.** Placed opposite. **4.** *Bot.* Turned toward the stem or axis. Cf. AVERSE. — **ad·verse'ly,** *adv.* — **ad·verse'ness,** *n.*

Syn. **Adverse, antagonistic, counter, counteractive** mean so opposed as to cause interference. **Adverse** applies to something that is unfavorable, often fatal in its effects, to another person or thing; **antagonistic** usually implies mutual opposition and either hostility or incompatibility; **counter** applies to forces coming from opposite directions and into contact with each other, with either resulting conflict or tension (as, *counter* currents in a stream often produce whirlpools; the *counter* influences of freedom and authority shape character); **counteractive** implies an opposition between two things or of one thing to another that nullifies or neutralizes the effect of each other or of the other (as, the *counteractive* effects of certain drugs; to destroy a bad influence by a *counteractive* good influence). — **Ant.** Propitious.

ad·ver'si·ty (ăd·vûr'sĭ·tĭ), *n.; pl.* -TIES (-tĭz). A state of being adversely circumstanced; a condition of destitution or affliction; — implying previous well-being; also, a stroke of ill fortune. — **Syn.** See MISFORTUNE.

ad·vert' (ăd·vûrt'), *v. i.* [For *avert*, fr. F. *avertir*, fr. L. *advertere* to turn (the mind) to, fr. *ad-* + *vertere* to turn.] To turn the mind or attention; to refer; allude; — with *to.*

ad·vert'ent (ăd·vûr'tĕnt), *adj.* Attentive; heedful. — **ad·vert'ence** (-tĕns), *n.* — **ad·vert'en·cy** (-tĕn·sĭ), *n.* — **ad·vert'ent·ly,** *adv.*

ad'ver·tise (ăd'vẽr·tīz; ăd'vẽr·tīz'), *v. t.* Also **ad'ver·tize.** [From F., fr. L. *advertere* to turn to. See ADVERT.] **1.** To inform; notify; hence, to warn; — often with *of* before the subject of information; as, to *advertise* a man of his loss. **2.** To announce publicly, esp. by a printed notice or by radio broadcast; hence, to call public attention to, esp. by emphasizing desirable qualities, in order to arouse a desire to purchase or invest. **3.** To make conspicuous. — *v. i.* To issue or sponsor advertising. — **ad'ver·tis'er, ad'ver·tiz'er** (ăd'vẽr·tīz'ẽr; ăd'vẽr·tīz'ẽr), *n.*

ad·ver'tise·ment (ăd·vûr'tĭz·mĕnt; -tĭs·mĕnt; *or, esp. U.S.*, ăd'vẽr·tīz'mĕnt), *n.* Also **ad·ver'tize·ment.** [F. *avertissement*, formerly also *advertissement*, a giving notice.] A public notice, as in some public print, by poster, by samples, etc. Abbr. *ad., adv., advt.*

ad'ver·tis'ing (ăd'vẽr·tīz'ĭng), *n.* Also **ad'ver·tiz'ing.** **a** Any form of public announcement intended to aid directly or indirectly in the sale of a commodity, in securing employment, etc. **b** The business of preparing and circulating advertisements.

ad·vice' (ăd·vīs'), *n.* [OF. *avis* opinion, fr. L. *ad* to + *visum*, past part. of *videre* to see.] **1.** Recommendation regarding a decision or course of conduct; as, to obtain professional *advice.* **2.** Information or notice given; intelligence; as, late *advices* from France.

Syn. **Advice, counsel** mean a recommendation as to a decision, a course of conduct, or the like: their corresponding verbs **advise, counsel,** mean to make such a recommendation. **Advice** and **advise** imply real or pretended knowledge or experience, often professional or technical, on the part of the one who recommends; **counsel** often stresses the fruit of wisdom or deliberation and presupposes weightier occasions, or more authority, or more concern in the one who advises, than do the other words.

ad·vis'a·ble (ăd·vīz'ă·b'l), *adj.* Proper to be advised or to be done; prudent. — **Syn.** See EXPEDIENT. — **ad·vis'a·bil'i·ty** (-bĭl'ĭ·tĭ), **ad·vis'a·ble·ness,** *n.* — **ad·vis'a·bly,** *adv.*

ad·vise' (ăd·vīz'), *v. t.* [OF. *aviser*, fr. LL. *advisare*, fr. L. *ad* to + *visum.* See ADVICE.] **1.** To give advice to; to recommend (a course of action) to; to counsel; warn. **2.** To give information or notice to; to apprise; inform; — often with *of.* — **Syn.** See under ADVICE. — *v. i.* To take counsel; consult; — followed by *with;* as, to *advise* with friends. — **ad·vis'er, ad·vi'sor** (-vīz'ẽr), *n.*

ad·vised' (ăd·vīzd'), *adj.* Thought out; considered; as, badly *advised* conduct. — **ad·vis'ed·ly** (ăd·vīz'ĕd·lĭ; -ĭd·lĭ), *adv.* — **ad·vis'ed·ness,** *n.*

ad·vise'ment (ăd·vīz'mĕnt), *n.* Careful consideration; deliberation; as, taken under *advisement.*

ad·vi'so·ry (ăd·vī'zō·rĭ), *adj.* Having or exercising power to advise; pertaining to or containing advice; as, an *advisory* council or capacity. — **ad·vi'so·ri·ly** (-rĭ·lĭ), *adv.*

‖**ad vi'vum** (ăd vī'vŭm). [L.] To that which is alive; to the life.

ad'vo·ca·cy (ăd'vō·kă·sĭ), *n.* [OF. *advocacie.*] Act of advocating, pleading for, or supporting.

ad'vo·cate (ăd'vō·kāt), *n.* [OF. *avocat*, fr. L. *advocatus*, past part. of *advocare* to call to, call to one's aid, fr. *ad-* + *vocare* to call.] **1.** One who pleads the cause of another, as before a tribunal or judicial court; a counselor. **2.** One who defends or espouses any cause by argument; a pleader; as, an *advocate* of free trade; also, an intercessor.

ad'vo·cate (-kāt), *v. t.* To plead in favor of; to support, vindicate, or recommend publicly. — **Syn.** See SUPPORT. — **ad'vo·ca'tor** (-kā'tẽr), *n.*

ad'vo·ca'tion (-kā'shŭn), *n.* A summoning; advocacy.

ad·voc'a·to'ry (ăd·vŏk'ă·tō'rĭ; -tẽr·ĭ; ăd'vō·kā'tẽr·ĭ), *adj.* Of or pertaining to an advocate.

‖**ad'vo·ca'tus di·a'bo·li** (ăd'vō·kā'tŭs dī·ăb'ō·lī). [L.] = DEVIL'S ADVOCATE.

ad·vow'son (ăd·vou'zŭn), *n.* [From OF., fr. L. *advocatio.*] *Eng. Law.* The patronage of a church living.

ad'y·na'mi·a (ăd'ĭ·nā'mĭ·ă), *n.* [NL., fr. Gr. *adynamia* want of strength, fr. *a-* not + *dynamis* strength.] *Med.* Lack or loss of the vital powers, caused by disease.

ad'y·nam'ic (ăd'ĭ·năm'ĭk; ā'dĭ-), *adj.* Characterized by feebleness of the vital powers or by absence of force.

ad'y·tum (ăd'ĭ·tŭm), *n.; pl.* -TA (-tă). [L., fr. Gr. *adyton*, deriv. of *a-* not + *dyein* to enter.] The innermost sanctuary in ancient temples, open only to priests; hence, a sanctum.

adz, adze (ădz), *n.* [AS. *adesa* ax, hatchet.] A cutting tool differing from an ax in having an arching blade set at right angles to the handle.

1 Carpenter's Adz with flat head; 2 Ship carpenter's Adz with spur head; 3 Cooper's Adz; 4 Canoe or Spout Adz.

ad·zu'ki bean (ăd·zōō'kĭ). [Jap. *adzuki.*] An annual bushy bean (*Phaseolus angularis*) grown in Japan and China for food.

ae (ā), *adj. Scot.* One.

ae, æ. A Latin diphthong (corresponding to Greek *ai*), in English usually retained (or restored) in proper names and in scientific terms (*Caesar, archaeology*) but in familiar words generally replaced by *e.*

ae-. For many words in *ae-*, see preferred forms in *e-.*

ae'ci·o·stage' (ē'sĭ·ō·stāj'), *n.* Also **ae·cid'i·o·stage'** (ē·sĭd'ĭ·ō-). [*aecium* + *stage.*] *Bot.* The stage in the life cycle of a typical rust characterized by the production of aecia. Cf. UREDOSTAGE, TELIOSTAGE.

ae'ci·um (ē'shĭ·ŭm; -sĭ·ŭm), *n.; pl.* -CIA (-shĭ·ă; -sĭ·ă). Also **ae·cid'i·um** (ē·sĭd'ĭ·ŭm). [NL., fr. Gr. *aikia* injury.] *Bot.* The spore fruit formed during the aeciostage of a rust and producing chainlike series of spores capable of infecting the same host.

a·ë'des (ā·ē'dēz), *n.* [NL., fr. Gr. *aēdēs* odious, fr. *a-* not + *hēdys* sweet.] Any of a genus (*Aëdes*) of mosquitoes including the mosquito (*A. aegypti*) which transmits yellow fever and dengue. Cf. ANOPHELES, CULEX.

ae'dile (ē'dīl), *n.* Also **e'dile.** [L. *aedilis*, fr. *aedes* temple, public building.] A Roman official in charge of public works and games, police, and the grain supply.

Ae·ge'an (ē·jē'ăn), *adj.* [L. *Aegaeus*, fr. Gr. *Aigaios.*] Pertaining to the prehistoric civilization of the islands of the Aegean Sea, esp. in the Bronze Age (3000–1100 B.C.).

‖**ae'ger** (ē'jẽr), *adj.* [L.] Sick; — used on a sick excuse in English universities. — *n.* A note certifying sickness as an excuse.

Ae'gir (â'gĭr; ē'jĭr), *n.* [ON.] *Teut. Myth.* God of the sea. His wife, ***Ran,*** is the death deity of the sea.

ae'gis (ē'jĭs), *n.* Also **e'gis.** [L. *aegis*, fr. Gr. *aigis.*] **1.** *Gr. Antiq.* An accouterment, shaggy and tasseled, ascribed in Homer to Zeus; later, a breast ornament bordered with serpents, ascribed to Athena. **2.** A shield or protection. **3.** Patronage; sponsorship; auspices.

Ae·gis'thus (ē·jĭs'thŭs), *n.* See CLYTEMNESTRA.

‖**ae·gro'tat** (ē·grō'tăt), *n.* [L., he is sick.] *Eng. Univs.* **a** A medical certificate certifying illness. **b** The unclassified degree granted to a candidate prevented by illness from attending the examinations.

-ae'mi·a (-ē'mĭ·ă). Var. of -EMIA.

Ae·ne'as (ē·nē'ăs), *n.* [L., fr. Gr. *Aineias.*] Son of Anchises and Aphrodite, in Homeric legend a chief defender of Troy, and hero of Vergil's ***Ae·ne'id*** (ē·nē'ĭd; ē'nē·ĭd), which recounts his wanderings from Troy to Latium and his part in the wars preceding the legendary founding of Rome.

Ae·o'li·an (ē·ō'lĭ·ăn), *adj.* Also **E·o'li·an.** **1.** Of or belonging to Aeolis, or to its inhabitants or their language; Aeolic. **2.** Of Aeolus. **3.** [*not cap.*] Borne or produced by the wind; as, *aeolian* rock sculpture. — *n.* **1.** A member of a group of Greek tribes of Thessaly and Boeotia which colonized Lesbos and the adjacent coast of Asia Minor, named from them ***Ae'o·lis*** (ē'ō·lĭs) or ***Ae·o'li·a*** (ē·ō'lĭ·ă). **2.** Aeolic.

aeolian harp *or* **lyre.** A box fitted with strings tuned in unison, on which the wind produces musical tones.

Ae·ol'ic (ē·ŏl'ĭk), *adj.* Also **E·ol'ic.** Aeolian. — *n.* The Aeolic dialect; — also used attributively. See GREEK, *n.*, **4.**

ae'o·lo·trop'ic (ē'ō·lō·trŏp'ĭk), *adj.* [Gr. *aiolos* changeful + *-tropic.*] *Physics.* Showing different properties as to velocity of light transmission, conductivity, compressibility, etc., in different directions; not isotropic. — **ae'o·lot'ro·py** (-lŏt'rō·pĭ), **ae'o·lot'ro·pism** (-pĭz'm), *n.*

Ae'o·lus (ē'ō·lŭs), *n.* [L., fr. Gr. *Aiolos.*] *Class. Myth.* **a** The god having dominion over the winds. **b** A king of Thessaly.

ae'on, e'on (ē'ŏn), *n.* [L. *aeon*, fr. Gr. *aiōn* space of time, lifetime.] An immeasurably or indefinitely long period of time.

ae·o'ni·an (ē·ō'nĭ·ăn), *adj.* [Gr. *aiōnios.*] Everlasting.

‖**ae'quo a'ni·mo** (ē'kwō ăn'ĭ·mō). [L.] With even mind; calmly.

a'er·ate, a'ër·ate (ā'ẽr·āt), *v. t.* [L. *aer* air. See AIR, *v.*] **1.** To combine or charge with gas, usually with carbon dioxide. **2.** To impregnate with common air, as soil. **3.** To oxygenate (the blood) by respiration. **4.** To pass (milk) in a thin layer over a surface so that odors are absorbed into the air. — **a'er·a'tion, a'ër·a'tion** (-ā'shŭn), *n.*

a'er·a'tor, a'ër·a'tor (ā'ẽr·ā'tẽr), *n.* Specif.: **a** Any apparatus used for aerating a liquid. **b** A fumigator used to bleach grain, destroying fungi and insects.

‖**ae're per·en'ni·us** (ē'rē pẽr·ĕn'ĭ·ŭs). [L.] More lasting than brass (or bronze).

a·e'ri·al, a·ë'ri·al (ā·ēr'ĭ·ăl; âr'ĭ·ăl), *adj.* [L. *aerius*, fr. Gr. *aerios.* See AIR.] **1.** Of the air, or atmosphere; inhabiting or found in the air; produced by or performed in the air; lofty. **2.** Consisting of air. **3.** Resembling air; airy; light as air. **4.** Hence, unsubstantial; ethereal; as, *aerial* distinctions. **5.** Growing or existing in the air rather than underground or in water; as, *aerial* roots. **6.** Of or pertaining to aircraft; designed for, or operating from or against, aircraft. **7.** Operating or operated high overhead upon, or by means of, elevated cables, rails, etc. — *n. Radio.* An antenna. — **a·e'ri·al·ly, a·ë'ri·al·ly,** *adv.*

a·e'ri·al·ist, a·ë'ri·al·ist (ā·ēr'ĭ·ăl·ĭst), *n.* One who performs feats in the air or above the ground, as on a trapeze.

a'er·ie, a'ër·ie (ā'ẽr·ĭ; ēr'ĭ), *n.* [OF. *aire* nest, origin, perh. fr. L. *ager* field.] **1.** The nest of a bird, esp. of a bird of prey, as an eagle, on a crag; also, a brood of birds of prey. **2.** Figuratively, a human dwelling place on a height.

a'er·if'er·ous, a'ër·if'er·ous (ā'ẽr·ĭf'ẽr·ŭs), *adj.* [L. *aer, aeris*, air + *-ferous.*] Conveying air.

a'er·i·form', a'ër·i·form' (ā'ẽr·ĭ·fôrm'), *adj.* Having the form or nature of air; gaseous; hence, unreal.

a'er·i·fy, a'ër·i·fy (-fī), *v. t.;* -FIED (-fīd); -FY'ING. [L. *aer, aeris*, air + *-fy.*] **1.** To infuse or force air into. **2.** To change into an aeriform state, specif. into vapor, as in a carburetor. — **a'er·i·fi·ca'tion, a'ër·i·fi·ca'tion** (-fĭ·kā'shŭn), *n.*

a'er·o, a'ër·o (ā'ẽr·ō; âr'ō), *adj.* Of, concerned with, or devoted to, aircraft or aeronautics; as, an *aero* club.

a'er·o-, a'ër·o- (ā'ẽr·ō- *or, esp. in popular words,* âr'ō-), **aer-, aër-.**

[Gr. aēr, aeros, air.] A combining form denoting: **a** *Air, aerial*, as in **a′er·o·pho·tog′ra·phy**. **b** *Gas* or *gases*, as in *aero*therapeutics.
☞ For each of the combinations given below in the preferred form in *aero-* there is a variant form in *aëro-*.
a′er·o·bat′ics (ā′ēr·ō·băt′ĭks; âr′ō-), *n.;* see -ICS. [*aero-* + acro*batics*.] Performance of stunts, as nose dives, etc., in an airplane, glider, or the like. — **a′er·o·bat′ic** (-băt′ĭk), *adj.*
a′er·obe (ā′ēr·ōb), *n.; pl.* -OBES (-ōbz). Also **a′er·o′bi·um** (-ō′bĭ·ŭm); *pl.* -OBIA (-ȧ). [*aero-* + Gr. *bios* life. Cf. MICROBE.] *Biol.* An organism, esp. one of certain bacteria, which lives only in the presence of oxygen. Cf. ANAEROBE.
a′er·o′bic (-ō′bĭk; -ŏb′ĭk), *adj.* *Biol.* **a** Living or active only in the presence of oxygen. **b** Pertaining to, or induced by, aerobes; as, *aerobic* fermentation.
a′er·o·bi·ol′o·gy (ā′ēr·ō·bī·ŏl′ō·jĭ), *n.* That branch of biology which deals with air-borne bacteria, viruses, pollen, plant spores, and the like.
a′er·o·do·net′ics (ā′ēr·ō·dō·nĕt′ĭks; âr′ō-), *n.;* see -ICS. [*aero-* + Gr. *donētos* shaken, fr. *donein* to shake.] *Aeronautics.* The science of gliding and soaring flight.
a′er·o·drome′ (ā′ēr·ō·drōm′; âr′ō-), *n.* [*aero-* + *-drome* as in hippo*drome*.] *Chiefly Brit.* An airport.
a′er·o·dy·nam′ics (ā′ēr·ō·dī·năm′ĭks; -dĭ-; âr′ō-), *n.;* see -ICS. The branch of dynamics which treats of the motion of air and other gases and of the forces acting on bodies in motion through air or on fixed bodies in a current of air (or other gas). — **a′er·o·dy·nam′ic** (-ĭk), **a′er·o·dy·nam′i·cal** (-ĭ·kăl), *adj.* — **a′er·o·dy·nam′i·cist** (-ĭ·sĭst), *n.*
a′er·o·dyne′ (ā′ēr·ō·dīn′), *n.* [See AERO-; DYNE.] *Aeronautics.* A heavier-than-air aircraft which derives its lift in flight from the forces resulting from its motion through the air.
a′er·o·em′bo·lism (-ĕm′bō·lĭz′m), *n.* *Med.* A condition, similar to caisson disease, induced by rapid ascent to high altitudes and due to the formation of nitrogen bubbles in the blood and spinal fluid.
a′er·o·gram′ (ā′ēr·ō·grăm′; âr′ō-), *n.* [*aero-* + *-gram*.] **1.** A message conveyed by aircraft or by radio. **2.** The record made by an aerograph.
a′er·o·graph′ (-grȧf′), *n.* [*aero-* + *-graph*.] = METEOROGRAPH.
a′er·og′ra·phy (ā′ēr·ŏg′rȧ·fĭ), *n.* [*aero-* + *-graphy*.] Description of the air or atmosphere. — **a′er·og′ra·pher** (-fēr), *n.* — **a′er·o·graph′ic** (-ō·grăf′ĭk), **a′er·o·graph′i·cal** (-ĭ·kăl), *adj.*
a′er·o·lite′ (ā′ēr·ō·līt′), *n.* [*aero-* + *-lite*.] A stony meteorite. — **a′er·o·lit′ic** (-lĭt′ĭk), *adj.*
a′er·ol′o·gy (-ŏl′ō·jĭ), *n.* [*aero-* + *-logy*.] **a** The branch of physics treating of the atmosphere. **b** *Meteorol.* Study of the phenomena of the free air as revealed by kites, balloons, airplanes, and clouds. — **a′er·o·log′ic** (-ō·lŏj′ĭk), **a′er·o·log′i·cal** (-ĭ·kăl), *adj.* — **a′er·ol′o·gist** (-ŏl′ō·jĭst), *n.*
a′er·o·ma·rine′ (ā′ēr·ō·mȧ·rēn′), *adj.* [*aero-* + *marine*.] Of or pert. to aerial navigation above the sea or ocean.
a′er·o·me·chan′ic (-mē·kăn′ĭk), *n.* A mechanic or mechanician expert in the art and practice of aeronautics.
a′er·o·me·chan′ics (-mē·kăn′ĭks), *n.;* see -ICS. The science of the equilibrium and motion of air or an aeriform fluid, including aerodynamics and aerostatics. — **a′er·o·me·chan′ic** (-ĭk), **a′er·o·me·chan′i·cal** (-ĭ·kăl), *adj.*
a′er·o·me′te·or·o·graph′ (ā′ēr·ō·mē′tē·ŏr·ō·grȧf′; -mē′tē·ŏr′-; âr′ō-), *n.* A meteorograph, especially one adapted for use on an aircraft.
a′er·om′e·ter (ā′ēr·ŏm′ē·tēr), *n.* [*aero-* + *-meter*.] An instrument for ascertaining the weight or density of air or other gases. — **a′er·om′e·try** (-trĭ), *n.* — **a′er·o·met′ric** (-ō·mĕt′rĭk), *adj.*
a′er·o·naut (ā′ēr·ō·nôt; âr′ō·nôt), *n.* [F. *aéronaute*, fr. Gr. *aēr* air + *nautēs* sailor.] One who operates or travels in an airship or a balloon.
a′er·o·nau′tic (-nô′tĭk), **a′er·o·nau′ti·cal** (-tĭ·kăl), *adj.* Pertaining to aeronautics or aeronauts. — **a′er·o·nau′ti·cal·ly**, *adv.*
a′er·o·nau′tics (-nô′tĭks), *n.;* see -ICS. The science that treats of the operation of aircraft; also, the art or science of operating aircraft.
a′er·o·neu·ro′sis, a′ër·o·neu·ro′sis (ā′ēr·ō·nū·rō′sĭs), *n.* [NL., fr. *aero-* + *neurosis*.] *Med.* A nervous disorder of aviators caused by emotional stress and characterized by restlessness, pains in the abdomen, diarrhea, etc.
a′er·o–o·ti′tis me′di·a (ā′ēr·ō·ō·tī′tĭs mē′dĭ·ȧ). [*aero-* + *otitis* + NL. *media* middle.] *Med.* Inflammation of the middle ear resulting from pressure difference between this part and the surrounding atmosphere, as in high-altitude flying.
a′er·o·phore′ (ā′ēr·ō·fōr′; 70), *n.* [*aero-* + *-phore*.] A portable apparatus containing compressed air for respiration.
a′er·o·phyte′ (-fīt′), *n.* *Bot.* An epiphyte.
a′er·o·plane′ (ā′ēr·ō·plān′; âr′ō-), *n.* An airplane.
a′er·o·scope′ (ā′ēr·ō·skōp′), *n.* [*aero-* + *-scope*.] *Biol.* An apparatus for collecting spores, dust, bacteria, etc., suspended in the air. — **a′er·o·scop′ic** (-skŏp′ĭk), *adj.*
a′er·o·sol′ (ā′ēr·ō·sŏl′; -sōl′), *n.* [*aero-* + 4th *sol*.] *Phys. Chem.* A suspension of fine solid or liquid particles in air or gas, as smoke, fog, or mist.
A′er·o·sol′, *n.* A trade-mark applied to a detergent, emulsifier, and wetting agent.
a′er·o·stat′ (-stăt′), *n.* [F. *aérostat*, fr. Gr. *aēr* air + *statos* placed.] *Aeronautics.* Any aircraft embodying a container filled with a gas lighter than air, and supported by the buoyancy of the surrounding air.
a′er·o·stat′ic (-stăt′ĭk), **a′er·o·stat′i·cal** (-ĭ·kăl), *adj.* **1.** Of or pertaining to aerostatics; pneumatic. **2.** Used, or for use, in aerostats; as, *aerostatic* gases. **3.** Aeronautic; as, an *aerostatic* voyage.
a′er·o·stat′ics (-stăt′ĭks), *n.;* see -ICS. The science that treats of the equilibrium of gaseous fluids and of the equilibrium of solid bodies immersed in them.
a′er·o·sta′tion (-stā′shŭn), *n.* [F. *aérostation* the art of using aerostats.] **1.** Aerostatics. **2.** The art or science of operating lighter-than-air aircraft.
a′er·o·ther′a·peu′tics (-thĕr′ȧ·pū′tĭks), *n.;* see -ICS. Also **a′er·o·ther′a·py** (-thĕr′ȧ·pĭ). [*aero-* + *therapeutics, therapy*.] Treatment of disease by the use of air or other gases in various ways.
a′er·y, a′ër·y (ā′ēr·ĭ; âr′ĭ), *adj.* [See AIR.] Aerial.
a′er·y, a′ër·y (ā′ēr·ĭ; ē̇r′ĭ). Var. of AERIE, a nest.
aes-, aet-. For many words in *aes-* and *aet-* (as **aes′ti·vate, ae′ti·o·log′i·cal**), see the preferred forms in *es-, et-*.
Aes′cu·la′pi·an (ĕs′kū·lā′pĭ·ăn), *adj.* Of or pertaining to Aesculapius, the Roman god of medicine (the Greek *Asklēpios*); relating to the healing art; medical; medicinal. — *n.* A physician.

Ae′sir (ā′sĭr; ē′sĭr), *n. pl.* [ON., pl. of *āss* god.] The chief gods of the Teutonic pantheon. The Aesir included: Odin (Woden), Thor (Donar), Tyr (Tiu), Balder, Forseti, Heimdall, and other lesser gods. See RAGNAROK, LOKI.
aes′thete (ĕs′thēt *or, esp. Brit.*, ēs′thēt), **es′thete** (ĕs′-), *n.* [Gr. *aisthētēs* one who perceives.] One who makes much or overmuch of the sense of the beautiful.
aes·thet′ic (ĕs·thĕt′ĭk *or, esp. Brit.*, ēs-), **es·thet′ic** (ĕs-), *adj.* Also **aes·thet′i·cal, es·thet′i·cal** (-ĭ·kăl). **1.** Of or pertaining to aesthetics. **2.** Of or pertaining to the beautiful, as distinguished from the moral and, esp., the useful; as, a purely *aesthetic* reaction. **3.** Appreciative of, or responsive to, the beautiful in art or nature; manifesting taste; as, an *aesthetic* race or age. — **Syn.** See ARTISTIC.
aes·thet′i·cal·ly, es·thet′i·cal·ly, *adv.* of AESTHETIC, -ICAL.
aes′the·ti′cian (ĕs′thē·tĭsh′ăn; ēs′-), **es′the·ti′cian** (ĕs′-), *n.* One versed in, or professionally occupied with, aesthetics.
aes·thet′i·cism (ĕs·thĕt′ĭ·sĭz′m *or, esp. Brit.*, ēs-), **es·thet′i·cism** (ĕs-), *n.* **1.** Devotion to the principles of beauty and good taste as basic, with moral principles regarded as derivative. **2.** Susceptibility to aesthetic influences.
aes·thet′ics (ĕs·thĕt′ĭks *or, esp. Brit.*, ēs-), **es·thet′ics** (ĕs-), *n.;* see -ICS. [Gr. *aisthētikos* perceptive, esp. by feeling, fr. *aisthanesthai* to perceive, feel.] The branch of philosophy dealing with the beautiful, chiefly with respect to theories of its essential character, tests by which it may be judged, and its relation to the human mind; also, the branch of psychology treating of the sensations and emotions evoked by the fine arts and belles-lettres.
a·far′ (ȧ·fär′), *adv.* From, at, or to a great distance.
a·feard′, a·feared′ (ȧ·fērd′), *adj.* *Archaic & Dial.* Afraid.
af′fa·ble (ăf′ȧ·b′l), *adj.* [F., fr. L. *affabilis*, fr. *affari* to speak to, fr. *ad-* + *fari* to speak.] **1.** Easy to speak to; courteous and amiable in response to another's address; sociable. **2.** Mild and gracious; — of mien. — **Syn.** See GRACIOUS. — **af′fa·bil′i·ty** (-bĭl′ĭ·tĭ), **af′fa·ble·ness**, *n.* — **af′fa·bly**, *adv.*
af·fair′ (ă·fâr′), *n.* [OF. *afaire*, fr. *a faire* to do, fr. L. *ad* to + *facere* to do. See FACT.] **1.** That which is done or is to be done; matter; concern; as, a difficult *affair* to manage; business of any kind; — often in *pl.;* as, a talent for *affairs*. **2.** A proceeding or action; also, a material thing; — used with intentional vagueness; as, involved in a disgraceful *affair;* living in a dilapidated *affair;* also, a fight; a duel. **3.** Short for LOVE AFFAIR.
‖**af′faire′** (ȧ′fâr′), *n.* [F.] Short for ‖**af′faire′ d'a′mour′** (dȧ′mo͞or′) or ‖**af′faire′ de cœur** (dē kûr′), a love affair.
‖**af′faire′ d'hon′neur′** (dô′nûr′). [F.] An affair of honor; a duel.
af·fect′ (ă·fĕkt′), *v. t.* [F. and L.; F. *affecter*, fr. L. *affectare*, freq. of *afficere* to apply (oneself) to, fr. *ad-* + *facere* to do.] **1.** *Archaic.* To aspire to the possession or achievement of. **2.** *Archaic.* To have affection for. *Shak.* **3.** To be fond of using, frequenting, wearing, etc.; as, to *affect* loud neckties. **4.** To frequent or haunt; — used esp. of animals and plants. **5.** To tend toward by natural disposition; to tend to assume, as a crystalline form. **6.** To make a display of liking, adopting, or following after; to cultivate ostentatiously; as, to *affect* a particular author; to *affect* an Oxford accent. **7.** To assume the character or appearance of; to pretend or feign; as, to *affect* indifference. — **Syn.** See ASSUME. — **af·fect′er**, *n.*
af·fect′ (ă·fĕkt′), *v. t.* [L. *affectus*, past part. of *afficere* to do to, attack.] To lay hold of or attack (as a disease does); to act, or produce an effect, upon; to impress or influence (the mind or feelings).
Syn. **Affect, influence, touch, impress, strike, sway** mean to produce an effect upon a person or comparable thing. **Affect** presupposes a stimulus powerful enough to elicit a response or reaction; **influence** presupposes an agent or agency that affects a person or thing, in some degree changing his or its nature, character, or behavior; **touch** suggests vividly close contact or the force of impact, often connoting stirring, arousing, harming, or the like; **impress** usually implies depth and lastingness of effect; **strike** implies suddenness or sharpness of response; **sway** implies the pressure or control of some force that is unresisted or irresistible and resulting changes in character, opinions, etc.
— *n.* **1.** *Obs.* Inward feeling or disposition. **2.** (*pron.* ăf′ĕkt) *Psychol.* Feeling, emotion, and desire as factors in determining thought and conduct; — from German *Affekt*.
af′fec·ta′tion (ăf′ĕk·tā′shŭn), *n.* **1.** *Obs.* A striving after; aspiration toward. **2.** An attempt to assume or exhibit what is not natural or real; an instance of this, esp. in speech or behavior. — **Syn.** See POSE.
af·fect′ed (ă·fĕk′tĕd; -tĭd), *adj.* [From AFFECT to assume.] **1.** Assumed artificially; as, an *affected* accent; pretended; feigned; as, *affected* indifference. **2.** Pretending to possess what is not natural or real. **3.** Inclined or attached, as to religion. — **af·fect′ed·ly**, *adv.* — **af·fect′ed·ness**, *n.*
af·fect′ed, *adj.* [From AFFECT to lay hold of.] **1.** Afflicted or tainted, as by disease; as, *affected* with gout. **2.** Impressed; moved.
af·fect′ing, *adj.* **1.** *Obs.* Given to false show. **2.** Moving, or fitted to excite, the emotions. — **Syn.** See MOVING. — **af·fect′ing·ly**, *adv.*
af·fec′tion (ă·fĕk′shŭn), *n.* [F. See AFFECT to assume.] **1.** A feeling or emotion, now usually a moderate one. **2.** Bent of mind; natural impulse swaying the mind; disposition. **3.** A settled good will; zealous or tender attachment; love; as, filial *affection;* — often in the *pl.* **4.** *Obs.* Affectation. **5.** A condition, state, or mode of being which is not essential or unalterable; as, the *affections* of time and place. **6.** An attribute; a property; as, figure, weight, etc., are *affections* of bodies. **7.** *Psychol.* The feeling aspect of consciousness, as in pleasure, displeasure, or any emotion; — contrasted with *cognition* and *conation*. — **Syn.** See FEELING.
af·fec′tion, *n.* [F. See AFFECT to lay hold of.] **1.** Act of affecting, or acting upon; state of being affected. **2.** A bodily state; esp., an abnormal bodily state; disease; as, a pulmonary *affection*.
af·fec′tion·al (-ăl), *adj.* Of or pertaining to the affections.
af·fec′tion·ate (-ĭt), *adj.* **1.** *Obs.* Unreasonably or favorably disposed. **2.** Having, proceeding from, or indicating affection or warm regard; loving; tender. — **Syn.** Loving, devoted, fond, doting. — **af·fec′tion·ate·ly**, *adv.* — **af·fec′tion·ate·ness**, *n.*
af·fec′tive (ă·fĕk′tĭv), *adj.* **1.** Emotional; also, of language, fitted for transmitting emotion. **2.** *Psychol.* Pertaining to affection or affect; as, subordinating *affective* life. — **af′fec·tiv′i·ty** (ăf′ĕk·tĭv′ĭ·tĭ), *n.*
af′fen·pin′scher (äf′ĕn·pĭn′shēr), *n.* [G., fr. *affe* monkey + *pinscher*.] A small dog of a breed with stiff red, gray, or black coat, pointed ears, chin tuft, and mustache.
af′fer·ent (ăf′ēr·ĕnt), *adj.* [L. *afferens*, pres. part. of *afferre*, fr. *ad-*

+ *ferre* to bear.] *Physiol.* Bearing or conducting inward; of nerves, conveying impulses toward a nerve center; — opposed to *efferent.*

af′fet·tuo′so (äf′făt·twō′sō), *adj.* [It.] *Music.* Tender or affecting; with sentiment; — a direction.

af·fi′ance (ă·fī′ăns), *n.* [From OF., fr. LL. *affidare*, fr. *ad-* + *fidare* to trust, fr. L. *fides* faith.] **1.** Trust; reliance; faith. **2.** Plighted faith; marriage contract. — *v. t.* To promise solemnly, esp. (oneself or another) in marriage; to betroth.

af·fi′ant (-ănt), *n.* *Law. U. S.* A deponent.

af′fi·da′vit (ăf′ĭ·dā′vĭt), *n.* [LL. & ML., he has made oath, perfect tense of *affidare*. See AFFIANCE.] A sworn statement in writing, esp. one made upon oath before an authorized officer.

af·fil′i·ate (ă·fĭl′ĭ·āt), *v. t.*; -AT′ED (-āt′ĕd; -ĭd); -AT′ING. [L. *affiliatus*, past part. of *affiliare* to adopt as son, fr. *ad-* + *filius* son.] **1.** To adopt or receive into a family as a son; hence, to unite or attach in a close connection, often as a member or branch; as, to *affiliate* the soul to God; railroads *affiliated* through stock ownership or lease. **2.** To fix the paternity of (an illegitimate child); hence, to ascribe (a child) as offspring; — with *to.* **3.** To trace the origin of (something); to father; — with *to* or *upon;* as, to *affiliate* Greek art upon Egypt. — *v. i.* To connect or associate oneself; — followed by *with.* — (-ăt), *n.* An affiliated person; an associate. — **af·fil′i·a′tion** (-ā′shŭn), *n.*

af·fined′ (ă·fīnd′), *adj.* [F. *affiné*, fr. *affin*, fr. L. *affinis*.] **1.** Joined in affinity. **2.** *Rare.* Bound by obligation. *Shak.*

af·fin′i·ty (ă·fĭn′ĭ·tĭ), *n.*; *pl.* -TIES (-tĭz). [OF. *afinité*, fr. L. *affinitas*, fr. *affinis* related by marriage, fr. *ad-* + *finis* end, border.] **1.** Relationship by marriage; — disting. from *consanguinity.* **2.** Kinship generally; relation; conformity; connection; as, the *affinity* of languages. **3.** A spiritual relationship or attraction held to exist between certain persons, esp. persons of opposite sex; also, one who exerts such attraction. **4.** *Biol.* A relation between species or higher groups dependent on resemblance in the whole plan of structure, and indicating community of origin. **5.** *Chem.* The attractive force exerted in different degrees between atoms, which causes them to enter into and remain in combination. — **Syn.** See ATTRACTION: LIKENESS.

af·firm′ (ă·fûrm′), *v. t. & i.* [From OF., fr. L. *affirmare*, fr. *ad-* + *firmare* to make firm, fr. *firmus* firm.] **1.** To confirm or ratify; to assert as valid. **2.** To assert positively; to aver; — opposed to *deny.* **3.** *Law.* To testify to, or declare, by affirmation; to make affirmation. — **Syn.** See ASSERT. — **Ant.** Deny. — **af·firm′a·ble**, *adj.* — **af·firm′a·bly**, *adv.* — **af·firm′ance**, *n.* — **af·firm′ant**, *n. & adj.* — **af·firm′er**, *n.*

af′fir·ma′tion (ăf′ẽr·mā′shŭn), *n.* **1.** Confirmation of anything established; ratification. **2.** Assertion; also, an averment; as, an *affirmation* of its quality. **3.** *Law.* A solemn declaration, made under the penalties of perjury, by a person who conscientiously declines taking an oath. This is in law equivalent to an oath.

af·firm′a·tive (ă·fûr′mȧ·tĭv), *adj.* **1.** That affirms; asserting that the fact is so; answering "yes" to a question; — opposed to *negative;* as, an *affirmative* answer or vote. **2.** *Logic.* Affirming that the predicate is true of the subject. See NEGATIVE, *adj.* — *n.* **1.** That which affirms; that side of a question which affirms or maintains a proposition stated; as, forty votes for the *affirmative.* **2.** A word or phrase expressing affirmation or assent (*yes; that is so;* etc.). — **af·firm′a·tive·ly**, *adv.*

af·fix′ (ă·fĭks′), *v. t.*; AF·FIXED′ (ă·fĭkst′) or AF·FIXT′; AF·FIX′ING. [ML. *affixare*, fr. L. *affixus*, past part. of *affigere* to fasten to, fr. *ad-* + *figere* to fasten.] **1.** To fix or fasten in any way; to attach physically; as, to *affix* a seal; hence, to impress (a stamped seal). **2.** To add at the close or end; to append; as, to *affix* one's name. **3.** To attach or connect with; as, to *affix* blame to a person. — **Syn.** See FASTEN.

af′fix (ăf′ĭks), *n.* That which is affixed; a prefix or suffix.

af·fix′ture (ă·fĭks′tūr), *n.* Act of affixing; attachment.

af·fla′tus (ă·flā′tŭs), *n.* [L., fr. *afflare, afflatum*, to breathe or blow on.] A divine imparting of knowledge; overmastering or supernatural impulse. — **Syn.** See INSPIRATION.

af·flict′ (ă·flĭkt′), *v. t.* [From OF., fr. L. *afflictus*, past part. of *affligere* to cast down, fr. *ad-* + *fligere* to strike.] **1.** *Obs.* To strike down; to overthrow. *Milton.* **2.** To inflict some great injury or hurt upon, causing continued pain or mental distress; to trouble grievously. — **af·flict′er**, *n.*

Syn. **Afflict, try, torment, torture, rack, grill** mean to inflict something upon a person which he finds hard to bear. **Afflict** implies not only the infliction of pain or suffering but also of acute annoyance, embarrassment, or the like; **try** suggests the imposition of something that imposes a strain on one's powers of endurance or is a severe test of one's stamina or self-control; **torment** suggests persecution and also the repeated infliction of suffering or annoyance; **torture** adds to *torment* the implication of causing to writhe; **rack**, that of straining or wrenching, but both suggest excruciating suffering; **grill** implies tortures suggestive of being broiled over a fire. — **Ant.** Comfort.

af·flic′tion (ă·flĭk′shŭn), *n.* **1.** State of being afflicted. **2.** The cause of continued pain of body or mind, as illness, losses, etc.; also, a grievous distress. — **Syn.** Trial, tribulation, visitation, cross.

af·flic′tive (ă·flĭk′tĭv), *adj.* Giving pain; causing continued or repeated pain or grief. — **af·flic′tive·ly**, *adv.*

af′flu·ence (ăf′lū·ĕns), *n.* [F., fr. L. *affluentia*.] **1.** A flowing to or toward; influx; as, an *affluence* of strangers. **2.** An abundant supply, as of thought, words, etc.; profusion; also, abundance of property; opulence.

af′flu·ent (-ĕnt), *adj.* [F., fr. L. *affluens, -entis*, pres. part. of *affluere* to flow to, fr. *ad-* + *fluere*.] **1.** Flowing abundantly. **2.** Abundant; copious; as, *affluent* in idioms. **3.** Well supplied with material possessions. — **Syn.** See RICH. — *n.* A tributary stream. — **af′flu·ent·ly**, *adv.*

af′flux (ăf′lŭks), *n.* [ML. *affluxus*, fr. L. *affluere*.] A flowing, or anything that flows, toward a junction.

af·ford′ (ă·fōrd′; 70), *v. t.* [AS. *geforthian, forthian*, to further, accomplish, afford, fr. *forth* forth, forward.] **1.** To incur, stand, or spare without serious detriment (as to financial condition, health, reputation, etc.); — used chiefly in the infinitive; as, he cannot *afford* to repeat scandal; also, to spare the price of; as, to be able to *afford* a new coat. **2.** To give forth; yield; as, olives *afford* oil. **3.** To give or provide, esp. as a natural consequence; as, a good life *affords* consolation in old age. — **Syn.** See GIVE. — **af·ford′a·ble**, *adj.*

af·for′est (ă·fŏr′ĕst; 30), *v. t.* [ML. *afforestare*, fr. *ad-* + *forestare*. See FOREST.] To convert into hunting land under forest laws; to forest. — **af·for′est·a′tion** (-ĕs·tā′shŭn), *n.*

af·fran′chise (ă·frăn′chīz), *v. t.* [F. *affranchir*, fr. *à* to + *franc* free.] To free from bondage or obligation.

af·fray′ (ă·frā′), *v. t.* [OF. *effreer, esfreer*, orig., to disquiet, fr. L. *ex* out + a Germanic word for "peace."] *Archaic.* To alarm; to frighten. — *n.* **1.** A tumultuous assault or quarrel; a brawl. **2.** *Law.* The fighting of two or more persons, in a public place, to the terror of others.

af′fri·cate (ăf′rĭ·kĭt), *n.* [L. *affricatus*, past part. of *affricare* to rub against, fr. *ad-* + *fricare* to rub.] *Phonet.* A stop, or explosive, followed by a slow separation of the articulating organs, so that the last part is a fricative, or spirant, with corresponding organic position (*th* in *eighth*). — **af·fric′a·tive** (ă·frĭk′ȧ·tĭv), *adj. & n.*

af·fright′ (ă·frīt′), *v. t.* [Orig. past part., fr. AS. *āfyrhtan* to terrify.] *Archaic.* To terrify. — *n.* *Archaic.* **1.** Sudden terror, or a cause of it. **2.** A terrifying.

af·front′ (ă·frŭnt′), *v. t.* [OF. *afronter* to strike on the forehead, to confront, fr. LL. *affrontare* to strike against, fr. L. *ad* to + *frons* forehead, front.] **1.** To offend by disrespect; to insult to the face by demeanor or language; also, to cause to feel affront. **2.** To face in defiance; to confront; as, to *affront* death. **3.** *Archaic.* To front or border upon. — **Syn.** See OFFEND. — **Ant.** Gratify. — *n.* **1.** *Obs.* An encounter. *Milton.* **2.** A deliberately offensive act or word. **3.** An offense to one's self-respect; an indignity. — **af·front′er**, *n.*

Syn. **Affront, insult, indignity** mean a speech or action that has the intent or the effect of dishonoring. **Affront** implies a designed and usually open mark of disrespect; **insult** usually implies an attack intended to humiliate or degrade; **indignity** suggests something that outrages one's personal dignity.

af·fu′sion (ă·fū′zhŭn), *n.* [L. *affusus*, past part. of *affundere* to pour to.] Act of pouring a liquid upon.

Af′ghan (ăf′găn; -găn), *n.* **1.** A native of Afghanistan. **2.** The chief language of Afghanistan. See PASHTO. **3.** [*not cap.*] A kind of worsted blanket or wrap. **4.** A Turkoman carpet of long pile, woven in geometric designs. — *adj.* Of or pert. to Afghanistan or the Afghans.

Afghan hound. A swift hunting dog of an old breed from the Near East, about 26 inches in height, having fine, thick, silky hair and a long silky topknot.

af·ghan′i (ăf·găn′ĭ), *n.* A silver coin and the monetary unit of Afghanistan, divided into 100 puls; — called also **afghani rupee.**

a·field′ (ȧ·fēld′), *adv.* **1.** To, in, or on the field. **2.** Away from home; hence, out of the way; astray.

a·fire′ (ȧ·fīr′), *adj.* On fire.

a·flame′ (ȧ·flām′), *adj.* Flaming; glowing.

a·float′ (ȧ·flōt′), *adj.* **1.** Floating; on board ship. **2.** In general circulation; as, a rumor is *afloat.* **3.** Adrift; without guide. **4.** Flooded; as, the decks are *afloat.*

a·flut′ter (ȧ·flŭt′ẽr), *adj.* Fluttering.

‖à fond (à fôɴ′). [F.] To the bottom; thoroughly; wholly.

a·foot′ (ȧ·fo͝ot′), *adv. & adj.* **1.** On foot. **2.** In action; astir; as, mischief *afoot.*

a·fore′ (ȧ·fōr′; 70), *adv., prep., & conj.* [AS. *onforan, ætforan.* See A-, 1; FORE.] *Archaic, Dial., & Naut.* Before.

a·fore′said′ (-sĕd′), *adj.* Said or named before or above.

a·fore′thought′ (-thôt′), *adj.* Premeditated; designed; as, malice *aforethought.* — *n.* Premeditation.

a·fore′time′ (-tīm′), *adv.* Formerly. — *adj.* Former.

a for′ti·o′ri (ā fôr′shĭ·ō′rī; 70). [L.] With the greater force; all the more; — said of a conclusion which, as compared with some other, is even more certain or necessary.

a·foul′ (ȧ·foul′), *adv. & adj.* In collision; in a tangle.

Afr-. = AFRO-, as in **Af′ra·mer′i·can.**

a·fraid′ (ȧ·frād′), *adj.* [Old past part. of *affray*.] Filled with fear or apprehension. — **Syn.** See FEARFUL.

af′reet (ăf′rēt; ȧ·frēt′), *n.* [Ar. *'ifrīt*.] *Arabic Myth.* A powerful evil jinni, demon, or monstrous giant.

a·fresh′ (ȧ·frĕsh′), *adv.* Anew; again.

Af′ri·can (ăf′rĭ·kăn), *adj.* Also **Af′ric** (ăf′rĭk). Of or pertaining to Africa. — *n.* A native of Africa; one ethnologically of an African race.

African languages. See LANGUAGE, *Table.*

African lily. See AGAPANTHUS.

Af′ri·kaans′ (ăf′rĭ·käns′), *n.* A language developed in South Africa from seventeenth-century Dutch; — called also *South African Dutch.*

Af′ri·ka′ner (-kä′nẽr), *n.* [D.] A South African of Dutch or Huguenot descent; a Boer.

af′rit (ăf′rēt; ȧ·frēt′). Var. of AFREET.

Af′ro- (ăf′rō-), **Afr-.** [L. *Afer* African.] A combining form denoting *African, African and,* as in **Af′ro–A′si·at′ic.**

Af′ro–A·mer′i·can, *adj.* Pertaining to American Negroes. — *n.* An American Negro.

aft (áft; 9), *adv.* [AS. *æftan* behind.] *Naut.* Near, toward, or in the stern of a vessel; astern; abaft.

aft′er (áf′tẽr; 9), *adv.* [AS. *æfter* after, behind. The ending *-ter* is an old comparative suffix, and *after* is a compar. of *of, off.*] Subsequently in time or place; behind; afterward. — *prep.* **1.** Behind in place; — often used with the same noun preceding and following to denote repetition or succession; as, wave *after* wave. **2.** Moving toward from behind; following, as in search of; hence, concerning; in behalf of; as, to look *after* workmen. **3.** Subsequent to; following the expiration of. **4.** Subsequent to and in view of; as, *after* all our advice. **5.** Below in rank; next to in order. **6.** In imitation of; in the characteristic manner of; also, in honor of. **7.** In conformity with the nature of. — *adj.* **1.** Next; subsequent; succeeding; second. **2.** Hinder; nearer the rear; usually, *Naut.*, toward the stern of the ship. — *conj.* Subsequently to the time when; later than.

aft′er·birth′ (áf′tẽr·bûrth′), *n.* The placenta and membranes with which the fetus is connected, expelled after delivery.

aft′er·brain′ (-brān′), *n.* See HINDBRAIN.

aft′er·burn′er (-bûr′nẽr), *n.* An auxiliary burner attached to the exhaust pipe of a turbojet engine for injecting fuel into the hot exhaust gases and burning it to provide extra thrust.

aft′er·care′ (-kâr′), *n.* Care of patients after treatment, or of convalescents.

aft′er·clap′ (-klăp′), *n.* An unlooked-for, usually disagreeable, stroke or blow resulting from or following an affair supposedly at an end.

aft′er·damp′ (-dămp′), *n.* An irrespirable gas remaining after an explosion of firedamp in mines.

aft′er·deck′ (-dĕk′), *n.* The part of a deck abaft midships.

aft′er–din′ner (-dĭn′ẽr; 2), *adj.* Following dinner or a banquet.

aft′er·ef·fect′ (áf′tẽr·ĕ·fĕkt′), *n.* **1.** An effect that follows its cause after an interval. **2.** *Med.* A secondary result coming on after the subsidence of the first effect.

aft′er·glow′ (-glō′), *n.* A glow of refulgence remaining where a light has disappeared, as in the sky after sunset.

aft′er·im′age (-ĭm′ĭj), *n.* *Psychol.* A sensation occurring after the stimulus causing it has ceased.

aft′er·math (-măth), *n.* [*after* + *math* a mowing.] **1.** A second mowing; a second-growth crop; rowen. **2.** A consequence or consequences; esp., disastrous consequences; as, the *aftermath* of war.

aft′er·most (-mōst; -mŭst), *adj. superl.* [AS. *æftemest*, orig. a superl. of *of*, with superl. endings *-te, -me, -st*. See -MOST.] **1.** Hindmost; last. **2.** *Naut.* Nearest the stern.

aft′er·noon′ (áf′tẽr·nōōn′; 9), *n.* The time between noon and evening. — **aft′er·noon′** (áf′tẽr·nōōn′; 2), *adj.*

aft′er·piece′ (áf′tẽr·pēs′), *n.* **1.** A piece performed after a play. **2.** The after timber of a rudder built of wood.

aft′er·shaft′ (áf′tẽr·shàft′), *n.* *Zool.* An accessory plume arising from the posterior side of the stem of the feathers of many birds. See FEATHER, *Illust.*

aft′er·taste′ (-tāst′), *n.* A taste which remains in the mouth after eating or drinking.

aft′er·thought′ (-thôt′), *n.* Reflection after an act; a later or subsequent thought or expedient.

aft′er·time′ (-tīm′), *n.* Time after the present; the future.

aft′er·ward (-wẽrd), **aft′er·wards** (-wẽrdz), *adv.* [AS. *æfterweard*, adj., behind.] At a later time; subsequently.

aft′er·world′ (-wûrld′), *n.* A future or subsequent world.

a·gain′ (*ȧ*·gĕn′ *or, esp. Brit.*, *ȧ*·gān′), *adv.* [AS. *ongēan, ongegn, agēn*, against, again.] **1.** In return; back; as, bring us word *again*. **2.** Another time; once more; anew. **3.** In addition; besides; as, half as much *again*. **4.** On the other hand. **5.** Moreover; further.

a·gainst′ (*ȧ*·gĕnst′ *or, esp. Brit.*, *ȧ*·gānst′), *prep.* [AS. *ongegn, ongēanes.*] **1.** Abreast of; opposite to; facing; toward. **2.** From an opposite direction, so as to strike or touch; in contact or collision with. **3.** In the opposite direction to the motion or course of; as, to swim *against* the current. **4.** In opposition to; counter to, as in competition, in contrariety to; hence, adverse to; as, *against* reason. **5.** For resisting; as, severe measures *against* disease. **6.** In preparation or provision for. **7.** As compared or contrasted with.

a·ga′ma (*ȧ*·gā′m*ȧ*), *n.* [NL., fr. Sp. *agama*, of Cariban origin.] Any of a genus (*Agama*) of partly herbivorous Old World lizards. Many are of changeable colors.

Ag′a·mem′non (ăg′*ȧ*·mĕm′nŏn), *n.* A king of Mycenae, the son of Atreus and brother of Menelaus, and leader of the Greeks in the Trojan War. See ATREUS, CLYTEMNESTRA.

a·gam′ic (*ȧ*·găm′ĭk), *adj.* [See AGAMOUS.] *Biol.* **a** Asexual. **b** Developing or reproducing without impregnation by the male. — **a·gam′i·cal·ly** (-ĭ·kăl·ĭ), *adv.*

ag′a·mo·gen′e·sis (ăg′*ȧ*·mō·jĕn′ē·sĭs), *n.* [NL., fr. Gr. *agamos* unmarried + *-genesis*.] *Biol.* **a** Parthenogenesis. **b** Asexual reproduction. — **ag′a·mo·ge·net′ic** (-jē·nĕt′ĭk), *adj.*

ag′a·mous (ăg′*ȧ*·mŭs), *adj.* [Gr. *agamos* unmarried, fr. *a-* not + *gamos* marriage.] *Bot.* Cryptogamous.

ag′a·pan′thus (ăg′*ȧ*·păn′thŭs), *n.* [NL., fr. Gr. *agapē* love + *anthos* flower.] Any of several African plants (genus *Agapanthus*) of the lily family, cultivated for their umbels of blue or purple flowers, as the African lily (*A. africanus*).

a·gape′ (*ȧ*·gāp′; *ȧ*·găp′), *adj.* Gaping, as with wonder.

ag′a·pe (ăg′*ȧ*·pē), *n.* A love feast among the primitive Christians, observed with prayers and songs, scripture reading, etc.

a′gar (ä′gär; ăg′är; ā′gär), *n.* **a** = AGAR-AGAR. **b** A culture medium using agar-agar; as, blood *agar*.

a′gar–a′gar (ä′gär·ä′gär; ăg′är·ăg′är; ā′gär·ā′gär), *n.* [Malay.] A gelatinous substance obtained mostly as translucent strips or as a white powder from certain seaweeds (red algae), as the Ceylon moss. It is used as a solidifying agent in culture media.

a·gar′ic (*ȧ*·găr′ĭk; ăg′*ȧ*·rĭk), *n.* [L. *agaricum*, fr. Gr. *agarikon*.] *Bot.* Any of the gill fungi (Agaricaceae), esp. one of a genus (*Agaricus*) characterized by brown spores and including the common edible type (*Agaricus campestris*, the meadow mushroom; see MUSHROOM); also, any of several shelflike fungi. See FUNGUS, *Illust.* — **a·gar′i·ca′ceous** (*ȧ*·găr′ĭ·kā′shŭs), *adj.*

ag′ate (ăg′ĭt; ăg′*ȧ*t), *n.* [F., fr. L. *achates*, fr. Gr. *achatēs*.] **1.** A variegated chalcedony, having its colors arranged in stripes, in clouds, etc. **2.** Something made of, or fitted with, agate; as: **a** The drawplate used by gold-wire drawers. **b** A bookbinder's burnisher. **c** A child's marble of agate. **3.** A diminutive person; — in allusion to the small figures cut in agate for rings and seals. *Shak.* **4.** *Magic.* A talismanic stone, used esp. as an amulet guarding its wearer from all dangers. **5.** *Print.* A size of type (5½ point); — called *ruby* in England. See TYPE.

ag′ate·ware′ (-wâr′), *n.* **1.** Pottery veined and mottled to resemble agate. **2.** An enameled iron or steel ware.

‖**à gauche** (á gōsh′). [F.] To or on the left (hand).

a·ga′ve (*ȧ*·gā′vē), *n.* [NL., fr. L., fr. Gr. *Agauē*, prop. fem. of *agauos* illustrious, noble.] Any of a genus (*Agave*) of plants of the amaryllis family, having spiny-margined leaves and flowers in tall candelabralike panicles, including the common fleshy-leaved century plant of tropical America and the sisal.

Agave (*A. americana*). (1/60)

a·gaze′ (*ȧ*·gāz′), *adj.* Gazing.

age (āj), *n.* [OF. *aage*, fr. L. *aetas*, fr. *aevitas*, fr. *aevum* lifetime, age.] **1.** That part of a being's or thing's existence extending from the beginning to any given time; as, his *age* is now ten years. **2.** The whole time of a being's existence; a lifetime; as, the *age* of a dog is from 10 to 15 years. **3.** The time of life at which some particular qualification, power, or capacity arises or vests; as, to reach school *age*. **4.** Specif.: Mature age; full age, or majority, which at the common law is fixed at 21 years, or in some states at 18 years for women; as, to come of *age*. **5.** One of the stages of life; as, middle *age*. **6.** A particular period of time in the history of man, esp. with reference to cultural evolution, or in the history of the earth; as, the golden or coal *age*; the *Age* of Reptiles (Mesozoic). **7.** The period spanned by anyone's lifetime; one's contemporaries collectively; hence, a generation. **8.** In poker, the right belonging to the player to the left of the dealer, under certain conditions, to have the last say; the player in this position. **9.** *Psychol.* An individual's development, educational, mental, anatomical, etc., measured in (number of) years requisite for like development of an average child. Thus, the measure of a person's development mentally (***mental age***), or his progress physically (***anatomical age, physiological age***) often varies from his actual age (***chronological age***). — **Syn.** See PERIOD. — *v. i. & t.*; AGED (ājd); AG′ING, AGE′ING (āj′ĭng). To become old; to show or impart the characteristics of increasing age, as weakness, maturity, or crystalline or chemical change.

-age (-ĭj; 13). [F. & OF. *-age*, fr. LL. *-aticum*.] A suffix used to form nouns denoting: **a** Something in the relationship of appurtenance, function, or the like, and esp. the collection, aggregate, or sum total of things in, or arising from, such relationship, as in post*age*, aver*age*, shrink*age*, mile*age*. **b** Act or process, as in pass*age*, marr*iage*. **c** State, condition, rank, dignity, or the like, as in pastor*age*. **d** Place of abode, as in orphan*age*. **e** A fee for the use of something or for some (specified) service, as in tow*age*.

a′ged (ā′jĕd; -jĭd; *in sense* 1 **b** *& in compounds*, ājd), *adj.* **1.** Grown old; specif.: **a** Of an advanced age. **b** Having attained a (specified) age; as, a man *aged* forty years. **c** *Phys. Geog.* Well advanced toward reduction to base level. **2.** Belonging to old age; as, *aged* wrinkles. — **Syn.** Old, elderly, superannuated. — **a′ged·ly** (ā′jĕd·lĭ; -jĭd·lĭ), *adv* — **a′ged·ness**, *n.*

a·gee′ (*ȧ*·jē′), *adj. & adv.* *Dial.* Awry; ajar.

age′less (āj′lĕs; -lĭs), *adj.* That never grows old; timeless.

age′long′ (-lŏng′), *adj.* Long as an age; everlasting.

a′gen·cy (ā′jĕn·sĭ), *n.*; *pl.* -CIES (-sĭz). **1.** Faculty or state of acting or of exerting power; action; instrumentality. **2.** Office or function of an agent, or factor; relation between a principal and his agent. **3.** The place of business or the district of an agent. **4.** An establishment for executing business in behalf of others, as at a distance; as, an employment *agency*. — **Syn.** See MEANS.

a·gen′da (*ȧ*·jĕn′d*ȧ*), *n. pl.*; *sing.* -DUM (-dŭm). [L., neut. pl. of gerundive of *agere* to do.] **1.** Things to be done. **2.** Memoranda of things to be done, as items of business or discussion to be brought up at a meeting. **3.** *Theol.* Matters of practical duty; — disting. from *credenda*.

a′gent (ā′jĕnt), *adj.* [L. *agens, agentis*, pres. part. of *agere* to drive, lead, act, do.] *Archaic.* Acting; — opposed to *patient*.

a′gent, *n.* [F. and L.; F. *agent*, fr. L. *agere*.] **1.** A power that acts; a moving force; as, by some other than human *agent*. **2.** One who acts or performs an act or who has power to act; as, a free moral *agent*. **3.** That which produces or will produce a certain effect; an active cause; also, esp. *Chem.*, a substance or element capable of producing a reaction. **4.** A means or instrument. **5.** One who acts for, or in the place of, another, by authority from him. Abbr. *agt.* **6.** *Colloq.* A traveling salesman.

Syn. (1) See MEANS.

(2) **Agent, factor, attorney, deputy, proxy** mean one who transacts business for another. **Agent** is the general term covering this idea; **factor**, in present usage, names an agent transacting business for a landlord or for a group of producers; **attorney**, now used chiefly of a professional legal agent (*attorney at law*), still applies to one given legal authority (*power of attorney*) to act as one's agent; **deputy** implies the delegation of powers or duties from a superior and responsibility to him; **proxy** implies authorization as a substitute when a promise, a vote, or the like, is to be made for the principal.

a·gen′tial (ā·jĕn′shăl), *adj.* **1.** Of or pertaining to an agent or agency. **2.** Also **a′gen·ti′val** (ā′jĕn·tī′văl; ā′jĕn·tĭv·ăl). Expressive of an agent; as, an *agentival* noun.

‖**a′gent′ pro′vo′ca′teur′** (á′zhäN′ prô′vô′ká′tûr′); *pl.* AGENTS PROVOCATEURS (á′zhäN′ prô′vô′ká′tûr′). [F.] One employed to associate himself with members of a group, and by pretended sympathy with their aims encourage them to commit illegal or harmful acts, esp. so that they may be caught and punished.

ag′er·a′tum (ăj′ẽr·ā′tŭm; *ȧ*·jĕr′*ȧ*·tŭm), *n.* [NL., fr. Gr. *agēraton* (a plant), fr. *a-* not + *gēras* old age.] Any of a large genus (*Ageratum*) of tropical American herbs of the thistle family, having small heads of blue or white flowers; also, any of several other blue-flowered plants of the thistle family.

Ag·ge′us (ă·gē′ŭs), *n.* *Douay Bible.* Haggai. See BIBLE.

ag·glom′er·ate (ă·glŏm′ẽr·āt), *v. t. & i.* [L. *agglomeratus*, past part. of *agglomerare*, fr. *ad-* + *glomerare* to form into a ball.] To gather into a ball or mass; to cluster; mass. — (-āt), *adj.* Agglomerated; *Bot.*, collected into a mass but not coherent, as a head of flowers. — (-āt), *n.* **1.** A collection, mass, or heap. **2.** *Geol.* A rock composed of volcanic fragments of various sizes and degrees of angularity.

ag·glom′er·a′tion (-ā′shŭn), *n.* **1.** Act of massing together. **2.** A clump or cluster of things gathered into a ball or mass. — **ag·glom′er·a′tive** (ă·glŏm′ẽr·ā′tĭv; -*ȧ*·tĭv), *adj.*

ag·glu′ti·nant (ă·glōō′tĭ·nănt), *adj.* Uniting, as glue; causing adhesion. — *n.* Any viscous substance that causes objects to adhere.

ag·glu′ti·nate (-nāt), *adj.* [L. *agglutinatus*, past part. of *agglutinare* to glue to a thing, fr. *ad-* + *glutinare* to glue, fr. *gluten* glue.] **1.** United with glue or as with glue. **2.** *Philol.* Agglutinative. — (-nāt), *v. t.* To unite, or cause to adhere, as with glue or other viscous substance; to unite by adhesion.

ag·glu′ti·na′tion (-nā′shŭn), *n.* **1.** Act of agglutinating, or state of being agglutinated. **2.** That which is composed of agglutinated parts. **3.** *Immunol.* A reaction in which cells, as bacteria or blood corpuscles, suspended in a liquid collect into clumps whenever the cell suspension is treated with serum immunized against cells of the same kind and species. **4.** *Philol.* A combination or running together of primitive words into compounds, in which the form and meaning of the constituent parts undergo little or no change.

ag·glu′ti·na′tive (ă·glōō′tĭ·nā′tĭv; -n*ȧ*·tĭv), *adj.* **1.** Causing, or produced by, agglutination; adhesive. **2.** *Philol.* Formed or characterized by agglutination.

ag·glu′ti·nin (ă·glōō′tĭ·nĭn), *n.* *Immunol.* An organic substance producing agglutination.

ag′gra·da′tion (ăg′r*ȧ*·dā′shŭn), *n.* [*ag-* (= *ad-*) + *gradation*.] *Phys. Geog.* Modification of the earth's surface in the direction of uniformity of grade, or slope, by deposition, as in a river bed. Cf. DEGRADATION.

ag·grade′ (ă·grād′), *v. t.* To build up by aggradation.

ag′gran·dize (ăg′răn·dīz; ă·grăn′dīz), *v. t.* [F. *agrandir*, fr. *à* to + *grandir* to increase, fr. L. *grandire*, fr. *grandis* great.] **1.** To make great or greater, as in power, rank, honor, or wealth. **2.** To make appear great or greater; to exalt; to embellish or exaggerate. — **Syn.** Magnify, exalt. — **ag·gran′dize·ment** (ă·grăn′dĭz·mĕnt), *n.* — **ag′gran·diz′er** (ăg′răn·dīz′ēr), *n.*

ag′gra·vate (ăg′rȧ·vāt), *v. t.* [L. *aggravatus*, past part. of *aggravare*, fr. *ad-* + *gravare* to burden.] **1.** *Obs.* To make heavy or heavier; to increase. **2.** To make worse or more severe or more offensive; to intensify. **3.** *Now Dial.* To exasperate; irritate. — **Syn.** See INTENSIFY. — **Ant.** Alleviate. — **ag′gra·vat′ing** (-vāt′ĭng), *adj.* — **ag′gra·vat′ing·ly**, *adv.* — **ag′gra·va′tive** (-vā′tĭv), *adj.*

ag′gra·va′tion (-vā′shŭn), *n.* **1.** Act of aggravating, or state of being aggravated. **2.** An act or circumstance that increases the gravity or seriousness of a thing, as a calamity or crime. **3.** Exaggerated representation. **4.** *Now Dial.* Provocation; irritation.

ag′gre·gate (ăg′rē·gāt), *adj.* [L. *aggregatus*, past part. of *aggregare*, fr. *ad-* + *gregare* to collect.] **1.** Formed by collection of particulars into a mass or sum. **2. a** *Bot.* Clustered together in a dense mass or head. **b** *Geol.* Composed of mineral crystals, or of mineral or rock fragments.

— (-gāt), *v. t.* **1.** To collect or unite into a mass or sum. **2.** *Colloq.* To amount in the aggregate to.

— (-gāt), *n.* **1.** A mass, assemblage, or sum of particulars. **2.** Any hard inert material for mixing in graduated fragments with a cementing material to form concrete, or the like. **3.** *Agrology.* A clustered mass of individual soil grains or particles, of any shape and ranging in size from a microscopic granule to a clod several inches in diameter; — usually considered the basic structural unit of soil. — **Syn.** See SUM. — ***in the aggregate.*** Collectively; together. — **ag′gre·gate·ly**, *adv.* — **ag′gre·gate·ness**, *n.*

ag′gre·ga′tion (ăg′rē·gā′shŭn), *n.* An aggregating; union into a mass or sum; state of being aggregated; a collection; an aggregate.

ag′gre·ga′tive (ăg′rē·gā′tĭv), *adj.* Taken together; tending to aggregate or form an aggregation; collective.

ag·gress′ (ă·grĕs′), *v. i.* [L. *aggressus*, past part. of *aggredi* to approach, fr. *ad-* + *gradi* to step, go. See GRADE.] To commit the first act of hostility or offense; to begin a quarrel.

ag·gres′sion (ă·grĕsh′ŭn), *n.* [F., fr. L. *aggressio*.] A first or unprovoked attack, or act of hostility; also, the practice of attack or encroachment. — **Syn.** Attack, offense, offensive.

ag·gres′sive (ă·grĕs′ĭv), *adj.* Tending to, or characterized by, aggression; as, an *aggressive* war; disposed to attack or encroach; self-assertive; also, enterprising; as, an *aggressive* sales manager. — **ag·gres′sive·ly**, *adv.* — **ag·gres′sive·ness**, *n.*

Syn. **Aggressive, militant, assertive, self-assertive, pushing** mean conspicuously or obtrusively energetic. **Aggressive** implies the disposition to dominate, sometimes by indifference to others' rights, but now, more often, by determined, forceful prosecution of one's ends; **militant** also implies a fighting disposition, but suggests not self-seeking but extreme devotion to a cause, movement, etc.; **assertive** and **self-assertive** stress self-confidence and boldness (in the case of the latter, bumptiousness) in action and in expressing oneself; **pushing**, sometimes close to *aggressive*, more often implies officiousness, offensive intrusiveness, or the like.

ag·gres′sor (-ēr), *n.* [L.] One who aggresses; an assailant.

ag·grieve′ (ă·grēv′), *v. t.* [From OF., fr. L. *aggravare* to make heavy. See AGGRAVATE.] To give pain or sorrow to; to afflict; hence, to injure in one's rights; — now commonly used in the passive. — **Syn.** See WRONG.

ag·grieved′ (ă·grēvd′), *adj.* Distressed; having a grievance; specif., *Law*, adversely affected in respect of legal rights.

a·ghast′ (ȧ·gȧst′; 9), *adj.* [ME. *agast*, *agasted*, past part. of *agasten* to terrify.] Terrified; struck with amazement.

ag′ile (ăj′ĭl; -īl), *adj.* [F., fr. L. *agilis*, fr. *agere* to move.] Quick, dexterous, and easy in moving; deftly nimble; also, mentally quick. — **ag′ile·ly**, *adv.* — **ag′ile·ness**, *n.* *Rare.*

Syn. **Agile, nimble, brisk, spry** mean acting or moving with alacrity. **Agile** implies dexterity and ease in the use of one's limbs or one's wits; **nimble** suggests surpassing lightness and swiftness of action or thought; **brisk** suggests liveliness, animation, or vigor of movement; **spry** stresses alacrity that is a sign of (often surprising) vigor or health.

a·gil′i·ty (ȧ·jĭl′ĭ·tĭ), *n.* [F. *agilité*, fr. L. *agilitas*.] Quality or state of being agile; nimbleness; activity.

ag′i·o (ăj′ĭ·ō; ā′jĭ·ō), *n.; pl.* AGIOS (-ōz). [It. *aggio*.] *Com.* **a** A premium or percentage paid for the exchange of one currency for another; also, an allowance or deduction for depreciation of coin by wear. **b** Sometimes, the premium or discount on foreign bills of exchange.

ag′i·o·tage (ăj′ĭ·ō·tĭj), *n.* [F.] Exchange business; also, stockjobbing; speculative buying or selling of stocks.

ag′i·tate (ăj′ĭ·tāt), *v. t.* [L. *agitatus*, past part. of *agitare* to put in motion, fr. *agere* to move.] **1.** To move with a violent, irregular action; to set or keep in motion. **2.** To stir up or excite; to perturb. **3.** To discuss with excitement and earnestness. **4.** To contrive busily; to devise; plot. **5.** To excite public discussion over, esp. with a view to bringing about a change. — *v. i.* To make an agitation; to stir up discussion. — **Syn.** See SHAKE; DISCOMPOSE. — **ag′i·tat′ed·ly** (-tāt′ĕd·lĭ; -ĭd·lĭ), *adv.*

ag′i·ta′tion (-tā′shŭn), *n.* Act of agitating; state of being agitated.

‖**a′gi·ta′to** (ä′jē·tä′tō), *adj.* [It.] *Music.* Restless, hurried, and agitated in manner; — a direction.

ag′i·ta′tor (ăj′ĭ·tā′tēr), *n.* [L.] One that agitates; specif.: **a** One who stirs up social agitation. **b** An implement or apparatus for shaking or mixing.

A·gla′ia (ȧ·glā′yȧ; ȧ·glī′ȧ), *n.* *Gr. Myth.* One of the Graces.

ag′let (ăg′lĕt; -lĭt), **ai′glet** (ā′glĕt; -glĭt), *n.* [F. *aiguillette* point, fr. LL., dim. of L. *acus* needle, pin.] The metal tag of a lace; a tag or pendent ornament of the points, braids, or cords once used in dress. Cf. AIGUILLETTE.

a·gley′ (ȧ·glē′; ȧ·glī′; ȧ·glā′), *adv.* [*a-* + *gley* squint, to squint.] *Chiefly Scot. & N. of Eng.* Aside; askew.

a·glit′ter (ȧ·glĭt′ēr), *adj.* Glittering.

a·glow′ (ȧ·glō′), *adj.* Glowing.

ag′nail (ăg′nāl), *n.* [AS. *angnægl*, fr. *ang* (in comp.) compressed, painful + *nægl*, *nægel*, nail.] A sore under or around the nail; also, a hangnail.

ag′nate (ăg′nāt), *n.* [F., fr. L. *agnatus*, past part. of *agnasci* to be born in addition to, fr. *ad-* + *nasci* to be born.] A relative whose relationship is exclusively through males or, sometimes, through the father's side. — *adj.* **1.** Related through males only or through the father. Cf. COGNATE. **2.** Allied; akin. — **ag·na′tion** (ăg·nā′shŭn), *n.*

Ag′ni (ŭg′nĭ), *n.* [Skr., fr. *agni* fire.] The Vedic god of the altar fire, mediator between the gods and men.

ag·nize′ (ăg·nīz′), *v. t.* To recognize; acknowledge. *Archaic.*

ag·no′men (ăg·nō′mĕn), *n.; pl.* AGNOMINA (-nŏm′ĭ·nȧ). [L., fr. *ad-* + *nomen* name.] **1.** *Rom. Antiq.* An additional cognomen, as in honor of some achievement. **2.** A nickname. — **ag·nom′i·nal** (-nŏm′ĭ·năl), *adj.*

ag·nos′tic (-nŏs′tĭk), *n.* [Gr. *agnōstos* unknowing, unknown, fr. *a-* not + *gignōskein* to know. See GNOSTIC.] One who professes agnosticism. — **Syn.** See ATHEIST. — **ag·nos′tic, ag·nos′ti·cal** (-tĭ·kăl), *adj.*

ag·nos′ti·cism (-nŏs′tĭ·sĭz′m), *n.* **1.** The doctrine that neither the existence nor the nature of God, nor the ultimate origin of the universe, is known or knowable; — distinguished from *atheism*. **2.** Any doctrine which affirms that all knowledge is relative and therefore uncertain.

Ag′nus De′i (ăg′nŭs dē′ī). [L., Lamb of God; — applied by John the Baptist to Christ (*John* i. 29).] **1.** An image or representation of a lamb as an emblem of Christ, esp. one bearing a cross or a banner. **2.** *R.C.Ch.* **a** A small disk of wax stamped with the figure of a lamb and blessed by the Pope. **b** A triple prayer in the sacrifice of the Mass, beginning with the words "Agnus Dei"; also, the accompanying music. **3.** In churches of the Anglican Communion, an anthem beginning "O Lamb of God."

a·go′ (ȧ·gō′), *adj. & adv.* [ME. past part. of *agon*, fr. AS. *āgān* to pass away.] Past; gone by; in the past.

a·gog′ (ȧ·gŏg′), *adj.* [OF. *engogues* merry, lively.] Keyed up with eager desire or interest.

-a·gogue (-ȧ·gŏg; 74). [Gr. *agōgos* leading, fr. *agein* to lead.] A combining form in the sense of *inducing, dispelling,* or *guiding,* in adjectives and agent nouns, as in emmen*agogue*.

ag′on (ăg′ōn; -ŏn), *n.; pl.* AGONES (ȧ·gō′nēz). [Gr. *agōn*. See AGONY.] *Gr. Antiq.* A struggle or contest, specif. one in athletics, chariot or horse racing, music, or literature, at a public festival.

a·gone′ (ȧ·gŏn′; 74), *adj. & adv.* *Archaic.* Ago; gone by.

a·gon′ic (ȧ·gŏn′ĭk), *adj.* [Gr. *agōnos* without angles, fr. *a-* not + *gōnia* an angle.] **1.** Not forming an angle. **2.** Designating an imaginary line passing through points where a compass needle is in equilibrium in a true north-and-south plane, showing no magnetic declination. See VARIATION, *Illust.*

ag′o·nis′tic (ăg′ō·nĭs′tĭk), **ag′o·nis′ti·cal** (-tĭ·kăl), *adj.* [Gr. *agōnistikos*.] **1.** Pertaining to the ancient Greek contests (**a·go′nes** [ȧ·gō′nēz]) in athletics, chariot racing, music, etc.; hence, combative. **2.** Strained for effect.

ag′o·nize (ăg′ō·nīz), *v. t.* [F. *agoniser*, fr. ML. *agonizare*, fr. Gr. *agōnizesthai* to struggle.] To cause to suffer agony; to torture. — *v. i.* **1.** To writhe with agony; to suffer anguish. **2.** To strive desperately. — **ag′o·niz′ing·ly** (-nīz′ĭng·lĭ), *adv.*

ag′o·ny (ăg′ō·nĭ), *n.; pl.* -NIES (-nĭz). [Through OF. and L., fr. Gr. *agōnia* a contest, fr. *agōn* assembly at games, contest for a prize, fr. *agein* to celebrate.] **1.** Extreme pain of mind or body; anguish; torture. **2.** Intensity or a sudden or violent display (of joy, delight, etc.). **3.** Death struggle. **4.** Violent striving. — **Syn.** See DISTRESS.

agony column. *Chiefly Brit.* A newspaper column devoted to personal advertisements, esp. those relating to lost relatives or friends.

ag′o·ra (ăg′ō·rȧ), *n.; pl.* -RAE (-rē). [Gr.] An assembly; hence, the place of assembly, esp. the market place, in an ancient Greek city.

ag′o·ra·pho′bi·a (ăg′ō·rȧ·fō′bĭ·ȧ), *n.* [NL., fr. Gr. *agora* market place + *-phobia*.] *Psychopathol.* Morbid dread of crossing, or being in the midst of, open spaces. Cf. CLAUSTROPHOBIA.

a·gou′ti (ȧ·gōō′tĭ), *n.; pl.* AGOUTIS, AGOUTIES (-tĭz). Also **a·gou′ty.** [F. *agouti*, fr. Sp. *aguti*, fr. Guarani *acuti*.] A rodent of the cavy, or guinea-pig, family (esp. *Dasyprocta aguti*), about the size of a rabbit, common in tropical America.

a·graffe′ (ȧ·grăf′), *n.* Also **a·grafe′.** [F. *agrafe*, fr. *agrafer* to hook, fasten.] A hook used as a fastening or clasp on armor or costumes by catching it into a loop or ring.

‖**à grands frais** (à grän′ frĕ′). [F.] At great expense.

Ag′ra·pha (ăg′rȧ·fȧ), *n. pl.* [Gr. *agrapha* (sc. *rhēmata*) unwritten sayings.] Sayings attributed to Jesus, which, though not found in the canonical gospels, were current in early Christian tradition or writings. Cf. LOGIA.

a·graph′i·a (ȧ·grăf′ĭ·ȧ), *n.* [NL. See A- not; -GRAPHY.] *Psychopathol.* A form of aphasia characterized by loss of ability to write. — **a·graph′ic** (-ĭk), *adj.*

a·grar′i·an (ȧ·grâr′ĭ·ăn), *adj.* [L. *agrarius*, fr. *ager* field.] **1.** Pertaining to fields or lands, or their tenure. **2.** Organized or designed to promote agricultural interests. — *n.* One who favors equal or a more equitable division of land.

a·grar′i·an·ism (-ĭz′m), *n.* Theory or practice of an equitable division of landed property; principles, agitation, or acts favoring a redistribution of land, or the establishment by law of conditions more favorable to the general use and occupation of land.

a·gree′ (ȧ·grē′), *v. t.* [From OF. *agreer*, fr. *a* to, at + *gre* will, pleasure, fr. L. *gratum*.] To admit; concede; — now usually with a noun clause. — *v. i.* **1.** To yield assent or favor; to become favorable or compliant; accede; — usually followed by *to* (for things), *with* (for persons); as, to *agree* to a proposal. **2.** To be in harmony, as in opinion or action; to concur; as, all *agree* as to the need. Specif., to get on well together. **3.** To come to terms or to a common understanding, esp. in settling a difference or in determining a price. **4.** Of things associated for comparison, to be conformable; to resemble; coincide; as, a picture that *agrees* with the original; two scales *agree*. **5.** To be or prove suited, congruous, or adapted; as, sweets do not *agree* with everyone. **6.** *Gram.* To correspond in respect of inflectional gender, number, case, or person.

Syn. (1) See ASSENT.

(2) **Agree, concur, coincide** mean to come into, or be in, harmony regarding a matter of opinion. **Agree** implies unison or a complete accord, sometimes after discussion; **concur** implies a specific or definite agreement as arrived at through a vote as made a basis for action, or the like; **coincide** applies more often to opinions, judgments, etc., that are in agreement, than to persons. — **Ant.** Disagree, differ.

(3) **Agree, square, conform, accord, comport, harmonize, correspond** mean

to exist or go together without conflict. **Agree** implies a relation that reveals no discrepancies, no inequalities, no untoward effect, etc.; **square** suggests an exact, often mathematically exact, agreement; **conform** stresses agreement in essentials; **accord** stresses a fitness of one thing to or for the other; **comport** stresses a lack of incongruity; **harmonize** and **correspond** suggest differences, but *harmonize* stresses their blending to produce an agreeable effect, and *correspond* stresses their matching, complementing, or answering to each other.

a·gree′a·bil′i·ty (ȧ·grē′ȧ·bĭl′ĭ·tĭ), *n.* Agreeableness.

a·gree′a·ble (ȧ·grē′ȧ·b'l), *adj.* **1.** Pleasing, either to the mind or senses; pleasant; as, *agreeable* manners or companions; fruit *agreeable* to the taste. **2.** Ready to agree or consent; as, to be *agreeable* to a plan. **3.** Agreeing or suitable; conformable; in accordance or conformity; according; — followed by *to* or *with;* as, conduct *agreeable* to our standards; *agreeable* to the order of the day, the House took up the report. — **Syn.** See PLEASANT. — **Ant.** Disagreeable. — **a·gree′a·ble·ness,** *n.* — **a·gree′a·bly** (-blĭ), *adv.*

a·greed′ (ȧ·grēd′), *adj.* Settled by common consent.

a·gree′ment (ȧ·grē′mĕnt), *n.* [OF. *agrement.*] **1.** State or act of agreeing; harmony of opinion, action, or character; concurrence; concord; conformity. **2.** *Law.* **a** An exchange of promises; mutual understanding, arrangement, or stipulation. **b** The language or a writing embodying reciprocal promises. Cf. CONTRACT.

‖**a′gré′mens′** (ȧ′grā′mäɴ′), *n. pl.* Also ‖**a′gré′ments′** (-mäɴ′). [F.] Agreeable or ornamental qualities; amenities; embellishments.

a·gres′tic (ȧ·grĕs′tĭk), *adj.* [L. *agrestis,* fr. *ager* field.] Rural; rustic; unpolished.

ag′ri·cul′ture (ăg′rĭ·kŭl′tūr), *n.* [F., fr. L. *agricultura,* fr. *agri,* gen. of *ager* field + *cultura* cultivation.] The art or science of cultivating the ground; the production of crops and livestock on a farm; farming. — **ag′ri·cul′tur·al** (-kŭl′tūr·ăl), *adj.* — **ag′ri·cul′tur·al·ly,** *adv.*

ag′ri·cul′tur·ist (-kŭl′tūr·ĭst), **ag′ri·cul′tur·al·ist** (-ăl·ĭst), *n.* One versed or trained in agriculture.

ag′ri·mo′ny (ăg′rĭ·mō′nĭ *or, esp. Brit.,* -mŭn·ĭ), *n.; pl.* -NIES (-nĭz). [OF. *aigremoine,* fr. L. *agrimonia,* for *argemonia,* fr. Gr. *argemōnē.*] **a** A common yellow-flowered herb (genus *Agrimonia*) of the rose family, having toothed leaves and burlike fruits. **b** Any of several similar plants; as, the hemp *agrimony.*

ag′ri·ol′o·gy (ăg′rĭ·ŏl′ō·jĭ), *n.* [Gr. *agrios* savage + *-logy.*] The comparative study of primitive customs. — **ag′ri·o·log′i·cal** (-ō·lŏj′ĭ·kăl), *adj.* — **ag′ri·ol′o·gist** (-ŏl′ō·jĭst), *n.*

ag′ro·bi·ol′o·gy (ăg′rō·bī·ŏl′ō·jĭ), *n.* [Gr. *agros* soil + *biology.*] The study of plant nutrition and growth and crop production in relation to soil control. — **ag′ro·bi′o·log′ic** (-bī′ō·lŏj′ĭk), **-log′i·cal** (-ĭ·kăl), *adj.* — **ag′ro·bi′o·log′i·cal·ly,** *adv.* — **ag′ro·bi·ol′o·gist** (-bī·ŏl′ō·jĭst), *n.*

a·grol′o·gy (ȧ·grŏl′ō·jĭ), *n.* [Gr. *agros* soil + *-logy.*] That branch of agricultural science which treats of soils. — **ag′ro·log′ic** (ăg′rō·lŏj′ĭk), **ag′ro·log′i·cal** (-ĭ·kăl), *adj.*

ag′ro·nom′ic (ăg′rō·nŏm′ĭk), **ag′ro·nom′i·cal** (-ĭ·kăl), *adj.* Of, pertaining to, or devoted to the pursuit of agronomy.

ag′ro·nom′ics (-ĭks), *n.; see* -ICS. Agronomy.

a·gron′o·my (ȧ·grŏn′ō·mĭ), *n.* [Gr. *agronomos,* fr. *agros* field + a derivative of *nemein* to distribute, manage.] The theory and practice of field-crop production and soil management. — **a·gron′o·mist** (-mĭst), *n.*

ag′ros·tol′o·gy (ăg′rŏs·tŏl′ō·jĭ), *n.* [Gr. *agrōstis,* a kind of grass + *-logy.*] That branch of systematic botany treating of the grasses.

a·ground′ (ȧ·ground′), *adv. & adj.* On the ground; of a ship or vessel, lodged on the ground or a shoal; stranded.

a′gue (ā′gū), *n.* [OF. *ague,* fr. ML. (febris) *acuta,* fr. L. *acutus* sharp.] **1.** *Med.* A fever of malarial character attended by paroxysms which occur at regular intervals. **2.** A chill, or state of shaking, as with cold. — **a′gu·ish** (ā′gū·ĭsh), *adj.* — **a′gu·ish·ly,** *adv.*

a′gue·weed′ (-wēd′), *n.* **a** Boneset. **b** The five-flowered gentian (*Gentiana quinquefolia*).

ah (ä), *interj.* An exclamation expressive of regret, contempt, delight, etc., according to the manner of utterance.

a·ha′ (ä·hä′), *interj.* An exclamation expressing triumph, mixed with derision or irony, or simple surprise.

A′hab (ā′hăb), *n.* *Bib.* One of Israel's greatest kings.

‖**à haute voix** (à ōt′ vwà′). [F.] Out loud; aloud.

a·head′ (ȧ·hĕd′), *adv.* [*a-* on, in + *head.*] At or toward the front or an earlier time; in advance.

a·hoy′ (ȧ·hoi′), *interj.* [*a* as an interj. + *hoy.*] *Naut.* A term used in hailing; as, Ship *ahoy!*

Ah′ri·man (ä′rĭ·măn), *n.* [Per.] *Zoroastrianism.* The evil spirit, coeval with Ormazd.

a·hun′gered (ȧ·hŭng′gērd), *adj.* Pinched with hunger.

ai (ä′ē), *n.; pl.* AIS (ä′ēz). [Pg., fr. Tupi *ai.*] A three-toed sloth (*Bradypus tridactylus*) of South America. See SLOTH.

ai′blins (ā′blĭnz). Var. of ABLINS.

aid (ād), *v. t. & i.* [OF. *aider,* fr. L. *adjutare,* freq. of *adjuvare,* fr. *ad-* + *juvare* to help.] To help; to further. — **Syn.** See HELP. — *n.* **1.** Help. **2.** Also **aide.** One who or that which promotes or helps in something done; helper; assistant. **3.** *Eng. Hist.* An extraordinary subsidy or tax; also, an exchequer loan. **4.** *Feudal Law.* A pecuniary tribute paid by a vassal to his lord. — **aid′er,** *n.*

A·i′da (ä·ē′dȧ), *n.* The title and heroine (an Ethiopian princess) of an opera by Verdi, first produced in 1871.

aide (ād), *n.* [F.] An assistant; an aid; specif., a military or naval officer acting as assistant to a superior.

aide′-de-camp′, aid′-de-camp′ (ād′dē·kămp′; ād′dē·käɴ′), *n.; pl.* AIDES-DE-CAMP, AIDS-DE-CAMP (ādz′-). [F. *aide de camp* camp assistant.] *Mil.* An officer attached to the person of a general to assist him in his duties, transmit orders, and collect information.

ai′glet (ā′glĕt; ā′glĭt), *n.* = AGLET.

ai·grette′ (ā·grĕt′; ā′grĕt), *n.* [F.] **1.** An egret. **2.** A plume or tuft for the head, made of feathers, of gems, etc.

ai·guille′ (ā·gwēl′; ā′gwēl), *n.* [F., a needle.] **1.** A needle-shaped peak of rock. **2.** A boring instrument.

ai′guil·lette′ (ā′gwĭ·lĕt′), *n.* [F.] An aglet; specif., one of the ornamental tags, cords, or loops on some uniforms.

ail (āl), *v. t.* [AS. *eglan* to trouble, pain.] To affect with pain or uneasiness; — used impersonally; as, something *ails* him. — **Syn.** Trouble, distress. — *v. i.* To be ill or indisposed or in trouble.

ai·lan′thus (ā·lăn′thŭs), *n.* [NL., fr. *aylanto,* i.e., tree of heaven, name of the tree in the Moluccas.] *Bot.* Any of a small Asiatic genus (*Ailanthus*) of chiefly tropical trees and shrubs typifying a family (Simaroubaceae, the ailanthus family) having bitter bark, mainly pinnate leaves, and small 3–5-merous flowers with a prominent disk. The ailanthus has terminal panicles of ill-scented greenish flowers. — **ai·lan′thic** (-thĭk), *adj.*

ai′ler·on (ā′lēr·ŏn), *n.* [F., dim. of *aile* wing.] A hinged or pivoted control flap on an airplane, usually part of a wing, for rolling the craft on its longitudinal axis. See AIRPLANE, *Illust.*

ail′ment (āl′mĕnt), *n.* Bodily infirmity, esp. a malady that is not an acute disease; also, a mental uneasiness.

aim (ām), *v. i. & t.* [From OF., fr. *a* (L. *ad*) to + *esmer* to estimate, aim, fr. L. *aestimare* to estimate.] **1.** *Obs.* To calculate; guess. *Shak.* **2.** To point or direct (a missile, or a weapon that propels a missile) toward an object or spot with intent to hit it; to direct (an act, a blow, a satire, or the like) at an object, as a person or a vice, so as to effect it. **3.** To direct one's endeavor or effort to the achievement of a purpose; — followed by *at;* as, to *aim* at success. **4.** To intend or purpose; also, to endeavor or strive; — followed by an infinitive; as, to *aim* to please.
— *n.* **1.** *Obs.* Guess. **2.** The act of aiming a weapon, missile, action, discourse, or the like; the line of sighting. See SIGHT, *Illust.* **3.** The point intended to be hit, or object intended to be attained. **4.** Intention; design. — **Syn.** See INTENTION.

aim′less, *adj.* Without aim or purpose. — **aim′less·ly,** *adv.* — **aim′less·ness,** *n.*

ain (ān). Scot., N. of Eng., & Ir. var. of ONE, OWN.

‖**aî′né′,** *adj. masc.,* ‖**aî′née′** (ĕ′nā′), *fem.* [F.] Elder; senior; — often after proper names.

ain't (ānt). Contraction of *are not,* and used also for *am not, is not, has not,* and *have not;* — now used in dialect or illiterate speech.

Ai′nu (ī′nōō), *n.* A member of an indigenous race of Japan, having light-colored skin and features of a European cast.

air (âr; ār), *adv. & adj.* [See ERE.] *Scot.* Before; early.

air (âr), *n.* [OF. *air,* fr. L. *aer,* fr. Gr. *aēr* air, mist.] **1.** The invisible, odorless, and tasteless mixture of gases which surrounds the earth. **2.** Air in motion; light breeze; hence, breath or breathing. **3.** Utterance abroad; publicity; as, to give *air* to a view. **4.** A surrounding or pervading influence or condition; as, an *air* of poverty. **5.** Outward appearance of a thing; semblance; as, imparted with an *air* of secrecy. **6.** Characteristic attitude, action, or mien; as, to inspect with the *air* of a connoisseur. **7.** An artificial or affected manner; haughtiness; as, to put on *airs.* **8.** [F., fr. It. *aria.*] *Music.* **a** The chief melody or part, as in chorals, or the voice part carrying it. **b** Tune; — a popular use. **9.** *Radio.* Figuratively, the medium of transmission of radio waves; as, to go on the *air* (to begin broadcasting). — **Syn.** See POSE.

☞ COMBINATIONS are:

air-bind, *v.*	**air-driven**	**airscape**
air-blown	**air-dry,** *v.*	**air-season,** *v.*
air-borne	**air-filled**	**air-shy,** *adj.*
air-braked	**air-hardening,** *adj.*	**airsick**
air-breathing, *adj.*	**air-lance,** *v.*	**airsickness**
air-bred	**airless**	**air-slake,** *v.*
air-built	**airlike**	**air-twisted**
air-cure, *v.*	**air-pervious**	**airward**
air-drawn	**airphobia**	**airwards**
air-dried	**airproof,** *adj. & v.*	**air-wise,** *adj.*

— ***in the air.*** **a** Prevalent without traceable origin, as rumors. **b** In an unsettled or perturbed state.
— *v. t.* **1.** To expose to the air, as for cooling, refreshing, etc.; to ventilate. **2.** To expose for public notice; to display ostentatiously. — **Syn.** See EXPRESS.
— *adj.* **1.** Of, conducting, or supplying air, as in:

air blast	**air duct**	**air passage**
air cock	**air filter**	**air shaft**
air compressor	**air gauge**	**air vent**
air drain	**air meter**	**air well**

2. Holding or restraining air, as for cushioning effect, or confining air, esp. compressed air, as in:

air bed	**air jacket**	**air space**
air cushion	**air pillow**	**air trap**
air cylinder	**air plug**	**air valve**

3. Operating or operated by air or, esp., by the force of compressed air; pneumatic; as in:

air drill	**air injection**	**air shovel**
air gun	**air lance**	**air sprayer**
air hammer	**air lift**	**air system**
air hoist	**air rifle**	**air thermometer**

4. Of or pertaining to navigation of the air; done by means of, or used by, aircraft; as in:

air attack	**air harbor**	**air photography**
air base	**air log**	**air route**
air bus	**air map**	**air service**
air fleet	**air ministry**	**air station**

air bladder *or* **cell.** A sac containing air or gas, present in most fishes and in certain animals and plants, as for adjusting the specific gravity of the body or assisting respiration.

air brake. *Mach.* A brake operated by a piston driven by compressed air. In the usual types, air is pumped into reservoirs connected to brake cylinders by triple valves and when released actuates pistons which move the brake levers. See WESTINGHOUSE BRAKE.

air′brush′ (âr′brŭsh′), *n.* A kind of atomizer for applying paint or protective coating in a spray.

air castle. = CASTLE IN THE AIR.

air chamber. Any chamber or cavity filled with air, esp., *Hydraulics,* one serving by its elasticity to equalize the flow of a liquid.

air′-con·di′tion (âr′kŏn·dĭsh′ŭn), *v. t.* To equip with an apparatus for air conditioning; also, to subject to the process of air conditioning.

air conditioning. A process of washing, humidifying, and dehumidifying air before it enters a room, hall, building, etc. — **air′-con·di′tioned,** *adj.* — **air conditioner.**

air′-cool′, *v. t.* Specif., to cool the cylinders of (a motor) by air without the use of any intermediate medium. — **air′-cooled′,** *adj.*

air′craft′ (âr′krȧft′), *n. sing. & pl.* Any weight-carrying structure for navigation of the air, designed to be supported either by the buoyancy of the structure or by the dynamic action of the air against its surfaces.

aircraft carrier. *Nav.* A ship designed to carry aircraft and so constructed that aircraft can be launched from it and landed on it.

air′crew′ (âr′krōō′), *n.* The crew manning an aircraft. See WINGS, *Illust.*

air′drome′ (âr′drōm′), *n.* [*air* + *-drome.*] An airport.

air′–dry′ (-drī′), *adj.* Dry to such a degree that no further moisture is given up on exposure to air.

Aire′dale′ (âr′dāl′), *n.* [From the *dale* of the *Aire,* Yorkshire.] A large terrier of a breed with hard and wiry coat, black or grizzled on back and sides, and tan elsewhere.

air′field′ (âr′fēld′), *n.* The field of an airport.

air′foil′ (-foil′), *n.* [*air* + *foil.*] *Aeronautics.* Any surface, as a wing or rudder, designed to obtain reaction upon its surfaces from the air through which it moves.

air force [*usually caps.*]. The military organization of a nation for air warfare; as, the *Air Force* of the United States, created by Act of Congress 1947 from the principal aviation components of the U. S. Army.

air frame. The structure of an airplane without the power plant.

air gas. Producer gas.

air′head′ (âr′hĕd′), *n.* *Mil.* An area in hostile territory secured by paratroops. Cf. BEACHHEAD, RAILHEAD.

air hole. **1.** A hole to admit or discharge air; a spot not frozen over in the ice. **2.** Any condition of the atmosphere, as a local down current, that causes an airplane to drop suddenly.

air′i·ly (âr′ĭ·lĭ), *adv.* In an airy manner; lightly; jauntily.

air′i·ness (âr′ĭ·nĕs; -nĭs), *n.* State or quality of being airy.

air′ing (âr′ĭng), *n.* **1.** An exposure to air, as for drying. **2.** A walk, ride, drive, or run in the open air.

air lane. A path through the air, esp. one made easy for aerial navigation by steady winds.

air letter. **1.** An airmail letter. **2.** *U. S.* A sheet of paper designed for folding and sealing, with the message written on the inside, so as to form an envelope with the address, sometimes a printed airmail stamp, and markings on the outside, for airmail delivery.

air′lift′ (âr′lĭft′), *n.* A supply line operated by aircraft; also, air transportation. — *v. t.* To transport by air.

air line. **1.** A straight line, as through the air; a beeline. **2.** *Aeronautics.* Commonly **air′line′** (âr′līn′), *n.* **a** A system of transportation by aircraft, or the equipment with which the system operates. **b** The company operating such a system. **c** The route covered.

air′–line′, *adj.* Straight; direct; as, an *air-line* road.

air lock. An intermediate chamber between the outer air and the working chamber of a pneumatic caisson.

air′mail′ (âr′māl′), *n.* **a** The system of transporting mail by aircraft. **b** Equipment so used. **c** Mail so transported. — **air′mail′**, *adj.*

air′mail′, *v. t.* To transport by airmail.

air′man (âr′măn), *n.* One engaged in the navigation or maintenance of aircraft; specif., *U. S.*: an enlisted man or woman in the U. S. Air Force; *U. S. Navy*, an enlisted man taking training in aviation.

air mass. *Meteorol.* A body of air extending hundreds of miles and often as high as the stratosphere, and maintaining as it travels nearly uniform conditions of temperature and humidity at any level.

Air Medal. *Mil., U. S.* A decoration, established 1942, awarded for meritorious achievement in aerial flight.

air′–mind′ed (âr′mīn′dĕd; -dĭd; 2; 30), *adj.* Interested in, or favorably disposed toward, the use and improvement of aircraft; interested in aviation. — **air′–mind′ed·ness**, *n.*

air′plane′ (âr′plān′), *n.* A fixed-wing aircraft, heavier than air, which is driven by a screw propeller or by a high-velocity rearward jet and supported by the dynamic reaction of the air against its wings. A ***pusher airplane*** is one with the propeller in the rear of the main supporting surfaces; a ***tractor airplane*** is one with the propeller forward.

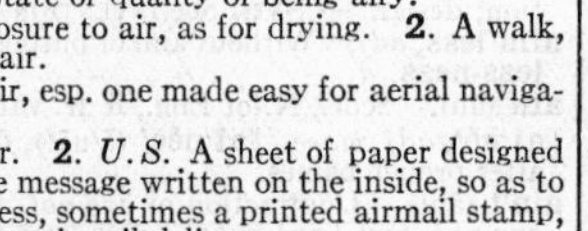

Airplane (single-seat, single-engine). 1 Spinner; 2 Propeller; 3 Cowling (and Cowl Flaps); 4 Air Scoop; 5 Cockpit; 6 Radio Antenna Mast; 7 Leading Edge of Wing; 8 Pitot-static Tube; 9 Fin; 10 Tab; 11 Aileron; 12 Rudder; 13 Retractable Landing Gear; 14 Fuselage; 15 Trailing Edge of Wing; 16 Retractable Tail Wheel; 17 Stabilizer; 18 Elevator; 19 Tabs.

☞ The form *airplane* has been officially adopted by the U. S. Army, Navy, and Air Force, Bureau of Standards, etc.; *aeroplane* is still generally used by British writers.

air plant. An epiphyte.

air pocket. = AIR HOLE, 2.

air′port′ (âr′pōrt′; 70), *n.* A place, either on land or on water, where aircraft may land to discharge or receive cargo and passengers, make repairs, or take in fuel.

air post. Airmail.

air pump. A pump for exhausting air from a vessel or closed space; also, a pump for compressing air, or for drawing or forcing it through other apparatus.

air raid. A raid made by one or more military aircraft, esp. for destruction by dropping bombs. — **air raider.**

air sac. *Zool.* One of the spaces, in different parts of the bodies of birds, filled with air and connected with the air passages of the lungs.

air′screw′ (âr′skrōō′), *n.* A screw, or screw propeller, designed to operate in air; specif., *Eng.*, an airplane propeller.

air′ship′ (âr′shĭp′), *n.* A form of mechanically driven aircraft, lighter than air, having a means of controlling the direction of its motion. Airships are distinguished as: ***rigid***, when the form is maintained by a rigid structure contained within the envelope; ***nonrigid***, or ***flexible***, when the form is maintained by the pressure of the contained gas; and ***semirigid***, when the form is maintained by means of a rigid or jointed keel and the pressure of the contained gas.

air sleeve, air sock, air tee. = WIND CONE.

air speed. The speed of an aircraft with relation to the air, as distinguished from its speed with relation to the earth.

air′strip′ (âr′strĭp′), *n.* See STRIP.

airt (ârt; ărt), **airth** (ârth; ărth), *n.* [Gael. & Ir. *āird.*] *Chiefly Scot.* Point of the compass. — *v. t.* To direct.

air′tight′ (âr′tīt′; 2), *adj.* **1.** So tight as to be impermeable to air. **2.** Hence, impenetrable; leaving no loophole for an opponent; as, an *airtight* defense or argument.

air train. An aircraft towing one or more transport gliders.

air vesicle. *Bot.* A greatly inflated air space, often occurring in aquatic plants, and serving as an aid in floating.

air′way′ (âr′wā′), *n.* **1.** A passage for a current of air, often underground. **2.** A designated or traveled way or route along which aircraft may ply from airport to airport, esp. one equipped with navigational aids. **3.** A channel of a designated radio frequency for broadcasting or other radio communication.

air′wom′an (-wŏŏm′ăn), *n., fem.* of AIRMAN.

air′wor′thy (-wûr′thĭ), *adj.* *Aeronautics.* Fit for operation in the air; able to bear the strains of flight, to withstand storms, etc., as an airplane. — **air′wor′thi·ness**, *n.*

air′y (âr′ĭ), *adj.;* AIR′I·ER (-ĭ·ẽr); AIR′I·EST. **1.** Relating or belonging to air; performed in air; atmospheric; high in air; aerial. **2.** Open to the free circulation of air; breezy. **3.** Resembling air in elasticity or lightness. Hence: **a** Light in movement or manner; esp., sprightly; vivacious. **b** Delicate and graceful as air; ethereal. **4.** Resembling air in its immaterial character; without reality; empty; visionary. **5.** *Now Colloq.* Having an affected manner; affectedly grand.

aisle (īl), *n.* [OF. *ele* wing, wing of a building, fr. L. *ala* wing, armpit. The pron. and spelling seem to be due to confusion with *isle.*] *Arch.* **1.** A lateral subdivision of a church or other building, flanking the nave, choir, or transept and set off by rows of columns or piers. See GOTHIC, *Illust.* **2.** By extension, a nave. **3.** Also (perhaps from confusion with *alley*), a passage into which the pews of a church or the seats of an assembly room, as a theater, open. — **aisled** (īld), *adj.*

ait (āt), *n.* [ME. *æit, eyt.*] *Eng.* An islet in a river or lake.

aitch (āch), *n.; pl.* AITCHES (āch′ĕz; -ĭz). [See H.] The letter *h, H.* — *adj.* Having the shape of capital H.

aitch′bone′ (āch′bōn′), *n.* Also **edge′bone′** (ĕj′bōn′). [From *nachebone*, fr. ME. and OF. *nache, nage*, fr. L. *natis* buttock. For loss of *n*, cf. ADDER.] The bone of the rump; also, the cut of beef containing this bone.

a·jar′ (ȧ·jär′), *adj.* [ME. *on char* on the turn, fr. AS. *cerr, cyrr*, turn.] Slightly opened; — esp. of doors.

a·jar′, *adj.* [*a-* + *jar.*] In discord; out of harmony.

A′jax (ā′jăks), *n.* [L., fr. Gr. *Aias.*] **1.** One of the Greek heroes in Homer's *Iliad*, who killed himself because the armor of Achilles was awarded to Odysseus. **2.** The swiftest of the Greeks before Troy, except Achilles; — called specif. **Ajax the Less.**

a·jee′ (ȧ·jē′). Var. of AGEE.

ake (āk), **a·kene′.** Vars. of ACHE, ACHENE.

a·kim′bo (ȧ·kĭm′bō), *adj. & adv.* [ME. *in kenebowe.*] With the hand on the hip and the elbow turned outward.

a·kin′ (ȧ·kĭn′), *adj.* [*a-* (for *of*) + *kin.*] **1.** Of the same kin; consanguineous. **2.** Allied by nature; of the same kind. — **Syn.** See SIMILAR. — **Ant.** Alien.

-al (-ăl). [F. or L.; F. *-al, -el*, fr. L. *-alis*, forming adjectives from nouns.] **1.** An adjective suffix denoting *belonging to, of* or *pertaining to, having the character of, appropriate to*, as in autumn*al*, mur*al*, norm*al*, reg*al*, or*al*, etc. **2. a** A suffix appearing in nouns which were originally adjectives used substantively, or which have been formed on the analogy of such nouns, as in riv*al*, anim*al*, ov*al*, sign*al*. **b** [OF. *-aille*, fr. L. *-alia*, neut. pl. of *-alis.*] A suffix used to form nouns of action from verbs, as in arriv*al*, acquitt*al*. **3.** (*pron.* -ăl; -ăl) [From *al*dehyde.] *Chem.* A suffix indicating the *presence of the aldehyde group*, as in acet*al*, chlor*al*.

a′la (ā′lȧ), *n.; pl.* ALAE (ā′lē). [L., a wing.] A wing, or winglike process or part; as, the *alae* of the nose, of the sacrum, of certain seeds (maple, ash, etc.).

à la (ä lä; ä lȧ), *or* ‖**à la** (à là), *fem.;* ‖**à l′**, *masc. & fem.;* ‖**au** (ō), *masc.; pl.* AUX (ō). [F.] **a** After, or according to, the; as, *à la* mode, according to the fashion. **b** After the (style or fashion of); as, *à la* Hollywood.

al′a·bam′ine (ăl′ȧ·băm′ēn; -ĭn), *n.* [*Alabama* + *-ine.*] *Chem.* Element 85, reported in monazite sand (but its presence not confirmed); — a proposed name. Cf. ASTATINE.

‖**à l′a′ban′don′** (à lȧ′bäɴ′dôɴ′). [F.] Carelessly; in disorder.

al′a·bas′ter (ăl′ȧ·bȧs′tẽr; 9), *n.* [From OF., fr. L. *alabaster*, fr. Gr. *alabastros, alabastos.*] *Mineral.* **a** A compact gypsum, of fine texture, and usually white and translucent. **b** A hard, compact calcite, somewhat translucent, and sometimes beautifully banded. — *adj.* Of or resembling alabaster; specif., having a nearly white color and a diffusing surface. — **al′a·bas′trine** (-bȧs′trĭn), *adj.*

‖**à la bonne heure** (à là bôn′ ûr′). [F.] At a good time; well and good; all right.

à la carte (ä lä kärt′; ä lȧ). [F.] By the bill of fare; dish by dish with a stated price for each; — contrasted with *table d'hôte.*

a·lack′ (ȧ·lăk′), **a·lack′a·day′** (-ȧ·dā′), *interj.* *Archaic.* An exclamation of deprecation, sorrow, or regret.

a·lac′ri·tous (ȧ·lăk′rĭ·tŭs), *adj.* Characterized by alacrity.

a·lac′ri·ty (-tĭ), *n.* [L. *alacritas*, fr. *alacer* lively, eager.] A cheerful readiness or promptitude; briskness. — **Syn.** See CELERITY.

A·lad′din (ȧ·lăd′ĭn), *n.* A youth in *The Arabian Nights* who gets a magic lamp and ring, the rubbing of which brings two frightful jinn, who do the owner's bidding.

‖**à la fran′çaise′** (à là fräɴ′sâz′). [F.] After the French style.

al′a·me′da (ăl′ȧ·mā′dȧ), *n.* [Sp., fr. *álamo* poplar.] A public promenade bordered with trees, esp. poplars.

al′a·mo (ăl′ȧ·mō; ä′lȧ·mō), *n.; pl.* -MOS (-mōz). In the southwestern United States, a poplar tree.

a′la·mode′ (ä′lȧ·mōd′; ăl′ȧ·mōd′), *adj., or* **à la mode** (ä lä mōd′; ä lȧ). [F. *à la mode* after the fashion.] **1.** According to the fashion; fashionable. **2.** *Cookery.* **a** Larded and braised, and simmered with vegetables in a sauce; — of beef. **b** Served with a mound of ice cream; as, pie *alamode.* — *n.* A thin, glossy silk for hoods, scarves, etc.

‖**à l′an′glaise′** (à läɴ′glâz′). [F.] After the English fashion or style.

al′a·nine (ăl′ȧ·nēn; -nĭn), *n.* Also **al′a·nin.** [*al*dehyde + *-ine.* The *-an-* is an insertion.] *Chem.* A white crystalline amino acid, $C_3H_7NO_2$, formed as a cleavage product of proteins, and in other ways.

a′lar (ā′lẽr), *adj.* [L. *alaris*, fr. *ala* wing.] Like, pertaining to, or having, a wing or ala; also, axillary.

a·larm′ (ȧ·lärm′), *n.* [OF. *alarme*, fr. It. *all' arme* to (the) arms. See ARMS.] **1.** A summons to arms; also, formerly, a sudden attack. *Shak.* **2.** Any sound or information for notifying of danger; a warning of danger. **3.** A device for making a noise as a warning or for awaking persons. **4.** Sudden surprise with fear excited by apprehension of danger. **5.** *Fencing.* A sharp stamp made with the foot advanced. — **Syn.** See FEAR. — *v. t.* **1.** To give notice to (anyone) of approaching danger; to rouse to vigilance. **2.** To surprise with apprehension of danger.

alarm clock. A clock which can be so set as to cause an alarm to ring at an indicated time. See ALARM, *n.*, 3.

a·larm′ing, *adj.* Exciting alarm. — **a·larm′ing·ly**, *adv.*

a·larm′ist (ȧ·lär′mĭst), *n.* One prone to sound or excite alarms, esp.

needlessly; pessimist; scaremonger. — **a·larm′ism** (ȧ·lär′mĭz'm), *n.* — **a·larm′ist** (-mĭst), *adj.*

alarm reaction. *Physiol.* The complex of reactions of an organism to stress (as injury, chilling) marked by increased adrenal cortical activity, increased circulating leucocytes, changes in blood volume, etc.

a·lar′um (ȧ·lăr′ŭm; ȧ·lär′ŭm), *n.* Archaic var. of ALARM.

a′la·ry (ā′lȧ·rĭ; ăl′ȧ·rĭ), *adj.* [L. *alarius*, fr. *ala* wing.] Of or pertaining to wings; also, wing-shaped.

a·las′ (ȧ·lȧs′; 9), *interj.* [OF., fr. *a* interj. (L. *ah*) + *las* weary, wretched (that I am), fr. L. *lassus* weary.] An exclamation expressing sorrow, pity, or apprehension of evil.

A·las′ka cod (ȧ·lăs′kȧ). See COD.

a′late (ā′lāt), **a′lat·ed** (-lāt·ĕd; -ĭd), *adj.* [L. *alatus*, fr. *ala* wing.] **1.** Winged; having wings. **2.** *Bot.* Furnished with winglike expansions. — **a·la′tion** (ā·lā′shŭn), *n.*

alb (ălb), *n.* [ML. *alba*, fr. L. *albus* white.] *Eccl.* A full-length white linen vestment with close sleeves, worn at the Eucharist. See VESTMENT, *Illust.*

al′ba·core (ăl′bȧ·kōr), *n.; pl.* ALBACORES (-kōrz), sometimes ALBACORE. See PLURAL, *Note.* [Pg. *albacor*, fr. Ar. *al-bakr* the young camel.] **a** A large open-sea mackerellike fish (*Germo alalunga*) having long pectoral fins. **b** The tunny; — called also ***great albacore***. **c** Any of several related smaller fishes, as the bonitos, etc.

Al·ba′ni·an (ăl·bā′nĭ·ăn), *adj.* Of or pertaining to Albania or its inhabitants or their language. — *n.* **1.** A native of Albania. They are generally considered to be descendants of the ancient Illyrians, mixed with Slavs and Greeks. **2.** The language of the Albanians, supposed to be descended from the ancient Illyrian. It has borrowed heavily from Latin, Italian, and other languages of southeastern Europe.

al·ba′ta (ăl·bā′tȧ), *n.* [L., whitened.] A silverlike alloy.

al′ba·tross (ăl′bȧ·trŏs), *n.* [Corrupt. (after L. *albus* white) fr. *alcatras* frigate bird, fr. Pg. *alcatraz* cormorant, albatross, orig. pelican.] Any of several web-footed birds (genus *Diomedea* and allied genera) related to the petrels. They are the largest of sea birds.

Albatross. (1/35)

al·be′it (ôl·bē′ĭt), *conj.* [ME. *albeit, al be it,* all though it be.] Even though; although.

Al′ber·ich (äl′bĕr·ĭк), *n.* [G.] In German legend, the all-powerful king of the dwarfs and chief of the Nibelungs.

al·bes′cent (ăl·bĕs′ĕnt; -'nt), *adj.* [L. *albescens*, pres. part.] Becoming white or whitish. — **al·bes′cence** (-ĕns; -'ns), *n.*

Al′bi·gen′ses (ăl′bĭ·jĕn′sēz), *n. pl.* [ML., fr. *Albi* a city of France.] A religious sect of southern France, arising in the 11th century and exterminated by the crusades and the Inquisition. — **Al′bi·gen′si·an** (-sĭ·ăn; -shăn), *adj.*

al·bi′no (ăl·bī′nō *or, esp. Brit.,* -bē′nō), *n.; pl.* -NOS (-nōz). [Pg., orig. whitish, fr. *albo* white, fr. L. *albus*.] **1. a** A person having a congenital deficiency of pigment in the skin, hair, and eyes. Albinos in extreme cases have skin of a milky color, very light hair, and eyes with a deep-red pupil and pink or blue iris. **b** In Mexico, an octoroon. **2.** Any animal or plant similarly deficient in pigment. — **al·bin′ic** (ăl·bĭn′ĭk), *adj.* — **al′bi·nism** (ăl′bĭ·nĭz'm; -bē·nĭz'm), *n.* — **al′bi·nis′tic** (ăl′bĭ·nĭs′tĭk), *adj.*

Al′bi·on (ăl′bĭ·ŭn), *n.* [L., of Celtic origin.] *Poetic.* England.

al′bite (ăl′bīt), *n.* [L. *albus* white.] *Mineral.* A triclinic feldspar, usually white, found in granite. It is a sodium aluminum silicate, $NaAlSi_3O_8$. — **al·bit′ic** (ăl·bĭt′ĭk), *adj.*

al′bum (ăl′bŭm), *n.* [L., neut. of *albus* white.] **1.** A register for visitors' names; a visitors' book. **2.** A blankbook in which to insert autographs, photographs, stamps, etc.

al·bu′men (ăl·bū′mĕn), *n.* [L., fr. *albus* white.] **a** The white of an egg. See EGG, *Illust.* **b** *Bot.* Nutritive parenchyma. **c** Albumin.

al·bu′men·ize (-īz), *v. t.* To cover, saturate, or treat with albumen. — **al·bu′men·i·za′tion** (-ĭ·zā′shŭn; -ī·zā′-), *n.*

al·bu′min (ăl·bū′mĭn), *n.* *Biochem.* Any of a class of proteins forming an important constituent of the serum of the blood, and found also in milk, muscle, egg, and in many vegetable tissues and fluids. They are rich in sulfur and complex in structure. Albumins were formerly regarded as different occurrences of a single substance, called at first *albumen* because erroneously supposed to exist nearly pure in white of egg.

al·bu′mi·nate (ăl·bū′mĭ·nāt), *n.* **a** A member of either of two classes of nearly insoluble proteins, obtained by the action of acids and alkalies on the albumins. **b** A compound formed by the union of an albumin with another substance.

al·bu′mi·noid (-noid), *n.* [*albumin* + *-oid*.] *Biochem.* **a** Protein, in its broad sense. **b** Any of a number of substances resembling the true proteins and including collagen (gelatin), keratin, etc. — *adj.* Resembling albumin. — **al·bu′mi·noi′dal** (-noi′dăl; -d'l), *adj.*

al·bu′mi·nous (-nŭs), *adj.* Also **al·bu′mi·nose** (-nōs). Pertaining to, containing, of the nature of, or like albumen or albumin.

al·bu′mi·nu′ri·a (-nū′rĭ·ȧ), *n.* [NL., fr. *albumin* + *-uria*.] Presence of albumin in the urine, often symptomatic of kidney disease. — **al·bu′mi·nu′ric** (-rĭk), *adj.*

al′bu·mose (ăl′bū·mōs), *n.* [From ALBUMIN.] *Biochem.* Any of a class of proteoses formed from the albumins.

al·bur′num (ăl·bûr′nŭm), *n.* [L., fr. *albus* white.] *Bot.* The young, soft wood of a dicotyledonous stem, consisting of living tissues near the cambium and outside the heartwood.

alc-. For many words in *alc-*, see the forms spelled ALK-.

Al·ca′ic (ăl·kā′ĭk), *adj.* Pertaining to Alcaeus, a lyric poet of Mytilene, about 600 B.C., or to the meter which he invented. — *n.* An Alcaic verse, either: the ***greater Alcaic***, ⏑̆ ⁝ – ⏑ | – ⏑ | – ⏑ ⏑ | – ⏑ | – ⏑ | – ^, or the ***lesser Alcaic***, – ⏑ ⏑ | – ⏑ ⏑ | – ⏑ | – ⏑ .

al·caide′ (ăl·kād′; *Sp.* äl·kä′ē·thā), **al·cayde′**, *n.* [Sp. *alcaide*, fr. Ar. *al-qā'id* the leader, fr. *qāda* to lead.] **1.** Among Spaniards or Moors, a commander of a fortress. **2.** A jailer.

al·cal′de (ăl·kăl′dē), *n.* [Sp., fr. Ar. *al-qāḍī* the judge, fr. *qaḍa* to decide, judge.] In Spanish use, a mayor of a town who exercises in addition certain judicial powers.

al·caz′ar (ăl·kăz′ẽr; *Sp.* äl·kä′thär), *n.* [Sp. *alcázar*, fr. Ar. *al-qaṣr* the castle, fr. L. *castrum*.] A fortress; also, a palace.

Al·ces′tis (ăl·sĕs′tĭs), *n.* [L., fr. Gr. *Alkēstis*.] Wife of Admetus, king of Thessaly, whose life she preserved by dying in his stead. Hercules brought her back from Hades.

al′che·mist (ăl′kē·mĭst), *n.* One given to the study or practice of alchemy. — **al′che·mis′tic** (-mĭs′tĭk), **al′che·mis′ti·cal** (-tĭ·kăl), *adj.*

al′che·mize (-mīz), *v. t.* To change by alchemy; transmute.

al′che·my (ăl′kē·mĭ), *n* [OF. *alkemie*, fr. ML. *alchimia*, fr. Ar. *al-kīmiyā'*, prob. ult. fr. the Gr. *chymeia* a mingling, fr. *chymos* juice, because chemistry was orig. the art of extracting medicinal juices from plants.] **1.** The medieval chemical science, the great objects of which were to transmute base metals into gold and to discover the universal cure for diseases and means of indefinitely prolonging life. **2.** Power to transform, or act or process of transforming, something common into something precious. — **al·chem′ic** (ăl·kĕm′ĭk), **al·chem′i·cal** (-ĭ·kăl), *adj.* — **al·chem′i·cal·ly**, *adv.*

al′chi·my, al′chy·my (ăl′kĭ·mĭ). Vars. of ALCHEMY.

Al·ci′des (ăl·sī′dēz), *n.* Hercules, whose stepfather was named Alcaeus.

Alc·me′ne (ălk·mē′nē), *n.* Mother of Hercules by Zeus.

al′co·hol (ăl′kō·hŏl), *n.* [ML., fr. Ar. *al-kuḥl* a powder for painting the eyelids; hence, from the fineness of this powder, highly rectified spirits, a signification unknown in Arabia. Sp. *alcohol* has both meanings.] **1.** A colorless, volatile, inflammable liquid, C_2H_5OH, which is the intoxicating principle in fermented and distilled liquors; — called also *ethyl alcohol* and *ethanol*. **2.** *Chem.* Any one of a class of compounds analogous to common, or ethyl, alcohol in constitution, as: *methyl alcohol*, or *wood alcohol*, CH_3OH (see METHANOL); *amyl alcohol*, $C_5H_{11}OH$, the principal constituent of fusel oil.

al′co·hol′ic (-hŏl′ĭk), *adj.* Of or pertaining to alcohol; containing or using alcohol; caused by alcohol. — *n.* A person addicted to excessive use of alcoholic liquors.

al′co·hol·ism (ăl′kō·hŏl·ĭz'm), *n.* A diseased condition caused by excessive use of alcoholic liquors; dipsomania.

al′co·hol·ize (-īz), *v. t.* **1.** To refine to an essence; to rectify. **2.** To treat with or saturate with alcohol; hence, to put under the influence of alcoholic liquor. — **al′co·hol′i·za′tion** (-hŏl′ĭ·zā′shŭn; -ī·zā′-), *n.*

al′co·hol·om′e·ter (-ŏm′ē·tẽr), *n.* [*alcohol* + *-meter*.] Any instrument for determining the alcoholic strength of liquids. — **al′co·hol·om′e·try** (-trĭ), *n.*

Al′co·ran′ (ăl′kō·rän′; -răn′), *n.* [F. *alcoran*, fr. Ar. *alqur'ān*, orig. the recitation, reading. Cf. KORAN.] The Koran.

al′cove (ăl′kōv), *n.* [Deriv. fr. Ar. *al-qubbah* arch, vault.] **1.** A recessed portion of a room; esp., a recess to contain a bed, or a recess in a library. **2.** A summerhouse.

Al·cy′o·ne (ăl·sī′ō·nē), *n.* [L., fr. Gr. *Alkyonē*.] *Astron.* The brightest star in the Pleiades.

Al·deb′a·ran (ăl·dĕb′ȧ·răn), *n.* [Ar. *al-dabarān*, fr. *dabar* to follow; because it follows the Pleiades.] *Astron.* A red star of the first magnitude, in the eye of Taurus. It is the brightest star in the Hyades.

al′de·hyde (ăl′dē·hīd), *n.* [Abbr. fr. *al*cohol *dehyd*rogenatum, alcohol deprived of its hydrogen.] *Chem.* A colorless, mobile, and very volatile liquid, CH_3CHO, obtained from alcohol by moderate oxidation; also, any one of a class of compounds of which this is the type.

al′der (ôl′dẽr), *n.* [AS. *aler, alor*.] *Bot.* Any of a genus (*Alnus*) of trees or shrubs of the birch family growing in moist ground. The wood is used by turners, and the bark in dyeing and tanning. Alders have toothed leaves and conelike fruit.

al′der·man (ôl′dẽr·măn), *n.; pl.* -MEN (-mĕn). [AS. *aldormon, ealdorman*, fr. *ealdor* a parent, head of a family (fr. *eald, ald*, old) + *man*.] **1.** In Anglo-Saxon history, one governing a territory as viceroy. **2. a** In English and Irish cities and boroughs, a magistrate ranking next below the mayor; properly, the chief officer of a ward. **b** In the United States, a member of the governing body of a city. This body is usually the higher of two "houses" (a board of *aldermen* and a board of *common councilmen*). Abbr. *Ald.* *Aldm.* — **al′der·man′ic** (-măn′ĭk), *adj.*

Al′dine (ôl′dīn; ăl′dīn), *adj.* *Bibliog.* **1.** Printed or published by Aldus Manutius or his family (about 1494–1597), of Venice, known by the sign of an intertwined anchor and dolphin. **2.** Designating certain elegant editions of English works, and certain styles of display type. — *n.* An Aldine book, edition, or type.

ale (āl), *n.* [AS. *alu, ealu*.] **1.** A fermented liquor brewed, esp. by rapid fermentation, from an infusion of malt with the addition of hops. **2.** *Eng.* A country festival, so called from the liquor drunk.

a′le·a·to′ry (ā′lē·ȧ·tō′rĭ *or, esp. Brit.,* -tẽr·ĭ), *adj.* [L. *aleatorius*, fr. *alea* chance.] **1.** *Law.* Depending on an uncertain event or contingency as to both profit and loss. Aleatory contracts include lottery agreements, wagering and insurance contracts, etc. **2.** *Sociol.* Pert. to, or resulting from, luck.

a·lee′ (ȧ·lē′), *adv. & adj.* *Naut.* On or toward the lee.

ale′house′ (āl′hous′), *n.* A house where ale is retailed.

a·lem′bic (ȧ·lĕm′bĭk), *n.* [OF. *alambic*, fr. Ar. *al-inbīq* the still, fr. Gr. *ambix* a cup, cap of a still.] An apparatus formerly used in distillation; hence, anything serving to distill and refine; as, the *alembic* of a poet's imagination. Cf. STILL, *Illust.*

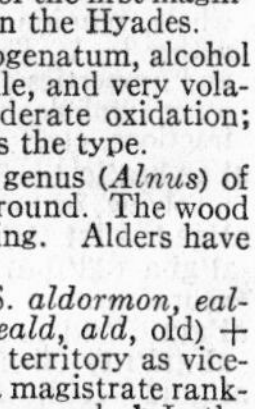

Alembic. *a* Head; *b* Cucurbit; *c* Receiver; *d* Lamp.

a·lert′ (ȧ·lûrt′), *adj.* [F. *alerte*, earlier *à l'erte* on the watch, fr. It. *all' erta*, prop. (standing) on a watchtower or height, fr. *erta* a lookout, declivity, fr. *erto* steep, deriv. of L. *erigere*. See ERECT.] **1.** Watchful; ready or quick to understand or to act. **2.** Brisk; nimble. — **Syn.** See WATCHFUL: INTELLIGENT. — *n.* *Mil.* An alarm to prepare for action, or against gas; specif.: **a** An alarm to warn of the approach of hostile aircraft. **b** The period of time during which the alarm is in effect. **c** The state of vigilance of those warned by the signal. — *v. t.* To call to a state of readiness for an air raid. — **a·lert′ly**, *adv.* — **a·lert′ness**, *n.*

— ***on the alert.*** On the lookout for danger; ready to act.

-a′les (-ā′lēz). [L.] Feminine plural suffix used to form the New Latin names of *orders* of plants.

a·leu′rone (ȧ·lū′rōn), *n.* [Gr. *aleuron* flour.] *Bot. & Biochem.* Protein matter occurring in the form of minute grains (**aleurone grains**) in seeds, and forming a special external layer (**aleurone layer**) in cereals. — **al′eu·ron′ic** (ăl′ū·rŏn′ĭk), *adj.*

Al′e·ut (ăl′ē·o͞ot), *n.* A member of either of two tribes of Eskimauan linguistic stock, native to the Aleutian Islands.

ale′wife′ (āl′wīf′), *n.; pl.* -WIVES (-wīvz′). **1.** A woman who keeps an alehouse. **2.** [Perh. a different word, of Amer. Indian origin.] A shadlike food fish (*Pomolobus pseudoharengus*) of the herring family (Clupeidae), abundant on the Atlantic coast.

Al′ex·an′dri·an (ăl′ĕg·zăn′drĭ·ăn), **Al′ex·an′drine** (-drĭn *or, esp. Brit.*, -drīn), *adj.* **1.** Of or pertaining to Alexandria in Egypt or Alexander the Great. **2.** = HELLENISTIC, 1.

al′ex·an′drine (ăl′ĕg·zăn′drĭn *or, esp. Brit.*, -drīn), *n.* [F. *alexandrin;* because used in OF. poems on Alexander the Great.] A verse consisting regularly of six iambics with the caesura after the third. — **al′ex·an′drine,** *adj.*

al′ex·an′drite (-drīt), *n.* [After *Alexander* II of Russia.] *Mineral.* A grass-green variety of chrysoberyl which shows a columbine-red color by artificial light.

a·lex′i·a (ȧ·lĕk′sĭ·ȧ), *n.* [NL., fr. *a-* not + Gr. *lexis* speech.] *Psychopathol.* A form of aphasia characterized by loss of ability to read; word blindness.

a·lex′in (ȧ·lĕk′sĭn), *n.* [Gr. *alexein* to ward off.] *Immunol.* **a** A defensive substance, found normally in the body, capable of destroying bacteria, as distinguished from an antitoxin. **b** = COMPLEMENT, *n.*, 4.

a·lex′i·phar′mic (ȧ·lĕk′sĭ·fär′mĭk), *adj.* [Gr. *alexipharmakos*, fr. *alexein* to keep off + *pharmakon* poison.] Expelling or counteracting poison; antidotal. — **a·lex′i·phar′mic,** *n.*

al·fal′fa (ăl·făl′fȧ), *n.* [Sp., fr. Ar. *alfisfiṣah.*] An important deep-rooted forage plant (*Medicago sativa*) of the pea family, adapted to widely varying conditions of climate and soil; lucerne. It is grown principally for hay.

Alfalfa.

al·fil′a·ri′a (ăl·fĭl′ȧ·rē′ȧ), **al·fil′e·ri′a** (-ĕ·rē′ȧ), *n.* [Mex. Sp., fr. Sp. *alfiler* pin, fr. Ar. *al-khilāl* thorn.] A European weed (*Erodium cicutarium*) of the geranium family, grown for forage in western America; — called also **al·fil′e·ril′la** (-ĕ·rĭl′ȧ; -rē′yȧ), **al·fil′e·ril′lo** (-rē′yō). See GERANIUM, 2.

‖**al fi′ne** (äl fē′nā). [It.] To the end.

al·for′ja (ăl·fôr′jȧ; *Sp.* äl·fôr′hä), *n.* [Sp.] **a** A saddlebag. **b** A wallet; hence, a cheek pouch.

al·fres′co (ăl·frĕs′kō), *adv. & adj.* [It. *al fresco* in or on the fresh.] In the open air; open-air.

al′ga (ăl′gȧ), *n.; pl.* ALGAE (-jē). [L.] Any plant of a group (Algae) comprising practically all seaweeds, as rockweed, sea lettuce, etc., and allied fresh-water or nonaquatic forms, as pond scums, stoneworts, etc. The group comprises the classes Cyanophyceae (the ***blue-green algae***), Zygophyceae (greenish in color), Chlorophyceae (***green*** and ***yellow-green algae***), Phaeophyceae (***brown algae***), and Rhodophyceae (***red algae***). — **al′gal** (-găl), *adj.*

al′gar·ro′ba (ăl′gă·rō′bȧ), *n.* [Sp., fr. Ar. *al-kharrūbah.*] **a** The carob; also, its edible beans or pods. **b** The common mesquite; also, its sweet, pulpy pods.

al′ge·bra (ăl′jĕ·brȧ), *n.* [It., fr. Ar. *al-jabr* reduction of parts to a whole, reunion of broken parts, bonesetting, fr. *jabara* to bind together.] **1.** That branch of mathematics which treats of the relations and properties of numbers by means of letters, signs of operation, and other symbols, including solution of equations, polynomials, continued fractions, etc. **2.** A treatise on this science.

al′ge·bra′ic (-brā′ĭk), **al′ge·bra′i·cal** (-ĭ·kăl), *adj.* Of, pertaining to, involving, or found in algebra. — **al′ge·bra′i·cal·ly,** *adv.*

al′ge·bra′ist (ăl′jĕ·brā′ĭst), *n.* One versed in algebra.

-al′gi·a (-ăl′jĭ·ȧ). [Gr. *algos* pain.] A suffix meaning *pain*, as in neur*algia.*

al′gid (ăl′jĭd), *adj.* [F. *algide*, fr. L. *algidus* cold.] Cold; chilly. — **al·gid′i·ty** (ăl·jĭd′ĭ·tĭ), *n.*

al′goid (-goid), *adj.* [*alga* + *-oid.*] Like an alga.

Al′gol (ăl′gŏl; ăl·gŏl′), *n.* [Ar. *al-ghūl* the ghoul, ogre.] *Astron.* A fixed star in the constellation Perseus, remarkable for its periodic variation in brightness, which is due to eclipses by a dark satellite.

al′go·lag′ni·a (ăl′gō·lăg′nĭ·ȧ), *n.* [NL., fr. Gr. *algos* pain + *lagneia* lust.] Pleasure in inflicting or suffering pain. — **al′go·lag′nic** (-nĭk), *adj.* — **al′go·lag′nist** (-nĭst), *n.*

al·gol′o·gy (ăl·gŏl′ō·jĭ), *n.* [*alga* + *-logy.*] *Bot.* The study or science of algae, or seaweeds. — **al′go·log′i·cal** (ăl′gō·lŏj′ĭ·kăl), *adj.* — **al·gol′o·gist** (ăl·gŏl′ō·jĭst), *n.*

al·gom′e·ter (ăl·gŏm′ē·tẽr), *n.* [Gr. *algos* pain + *-meter.*] An instrument for measuring the smallest pressure that induces pain. — **al·gom′e·try** (-trĭ), *n.* — **al′go·met′ric** (ăl′gō·mĕt′rĭk), **al′go·met′ri·cal** (-rĭ·kăl), *adj.*

Al·gon′ki·an (ăl·gŏng′kĭ·ăn), *adj. & n.* **1.** Algonquian. **2.** *Geol.* Proterozoic.

Al·gon′qui·an (-kĭ·ăn), *adj.* Pertaining to or designating the most extensive of the linguistic families of North American Indians, including the Arapaho, Blackfoot, Cree, Ojibway, Abnaki, Micmac, Sac, Delaware, Massachuset, and Shawnee. — *n.* **1.** An Indian of any Algonquian tribe. **2.** The Algonquian family of languages. See LANGUAGE, *Table.*

Al·gon′quin (ăl·gŏng′kĭn), *n.* An Indian of an Algonquian tribe formerly living near the mouth of the Ottawa River; loosely, any Algonquian.

al′go·pho′bi·a (ăl′gō·fō′bĭ·ȧ), *n.* [NL., fr. Gr. *algos* pain + *-phobia.*] Morbid fear of pain.

al′gor (ăl′gôr), *n.* [L., cold, *n.*] *Med.* A sensation of coldness occurring in the early stages of a fever; a chill.

al′go·rism (ăl′gō·rĭz′m), *n.* [OF. *algorisme*, fr. ML. *algorismus*, fr. Ar. *al-Khuwārizmī*, surname of a 9th-century arithmetician.] **1.** The art of calculating by means of nine figures and zero; arithmetic. **2.** The art of calculating with any species of notation; as, the *algorisms* of fractions, surds, etc.

al′go·rithm (-rĭth′m), *n.* = ALGORISM.

Al·ham′bra (ăl·hăm′brȧ), *n.* [Sp., fr. Ar. *al-ḥamrā′* the red (house).] The alcazar of the Moorish kings at Granada.

Al′ham·bresque′ (ăl′hăm·brĕsk′), *adj.* Made or decorated after the fanciful style of the ornamentation in the Alhambra.

a′li·as (ā′lĭ·ăs), *adv.* [L., fr. *alius* other.] In full **a′li·as dic′tus** (dĭk′tŭs). Otherwise; otherwise called. — *n.; pl.* ALIASES (-ăs·ĕz; -ĭz). Another name; an assumed name.

A′li Ba′ba (ä′lē bä′bȧ). In *The Arabian Nights*, a woodcutter who enters the cave of the Forty Thieves by the use of the magic password *Sesame.*

al′i·bi (ăl′ĭ·bī), *n.; pl.* ALIBIS (-bīz). [L., elsewhere, fr. *alius* other.] The plea or fact of having been, at the alleged time of the commission of an act, elsewhere than at the alleged place of commission; hence, *Colloq.*, any excuse. — **Syn.** See APOLOGY.

al′i·ble (ăl′ĭ·b′l), *adj.* [L. *alibilis*, fr. *alere* to nourish.] Nutritive; nourishing. — **al′i·bil′i·ty** (-bĭl′ĭ·tĭ), *n.*

al′i·dade (ăl′ĭ·dād), **-dad** (-dăd), *n.* [F., fr. ML. *alhidada*, fr. Ar. *al-'iḍādah* the revolving radius of a circle.] That part of any optical, surveying, or measuring instrument which comprises the indicator, verniers, microscopes, etc. See SEXTANT, *Illust.*

al′ien (āl′yĕn; ā′lĭ·ĕn; 58), *adj.* [OF., fr. L. *alienus*, fr. *alius* another.] **1.** Belonging or pertaining to another; strange; foreign; esp., not belonging or owing allegiance to the same country; belonging to the citizens of a foreign state. **2.** Wholly different in nature; incongruous; unsympathetic; adverse; — with *to* or *from;* as, conceptions *alien* to science. — **Syn.** See EXTRINSIC. — **Ant.** Akin. — *n.* **1.** A person of another family, race, or nation. **2.** A foreign-born resident of a country in which he does not possess the privileges of a citizen. **3.** One excluded from certain privileges; one estranged, as from royal favor. — **Syn.** Foreigner, stranger. — *v. t.* To alienate; to estrange; to transfer, as property.

al′ien·a·ble (-ȧ·b′l), *adj.* That may be alienated. — **al′ien·a·bil′i·ty** (-bĭl′ĭ·tĭ), *n.*

al′ien·age (-ĭj), *n.* Status of an alien.

al′ien·ate (-āt), *v. t.* [L. *alienatus*, past part. of *alienare* to alienate, fr. *alienus* alien.] **1.** To convey or transfer to another, as title or property. **2.** To make inimical or indifferent where devotion or attachment formerly existed. **3.** To divert, as affection or confidence. — **Syn.** See ESTRANGE. — **Ant.** Unite. — **al′ien·a′tor** (-ā′tẽr), *n.*

al′ien·a′tion (-ā′shŭn), *n.* **1.** Act of alienating; state of being alienated. **2.** [Cf. L. *alienatus a se* alienated from himself, insane.] Specif., mental derangement; insanity.

al′ien·ee′ (-ē′), *n.* One to whom property is transferred.

al′ien·ism (āl′yĕn·ĭz′m; ā′lĭ·ĕn-), *n.* **1.** Status of an alien. **2.** The study or treatment of diseases of the mind.

al′ien·ist (-ĭst), *n.* [F. *aliéniste.* Cf. ALIENATION, 2.] A specialist in diseases of the mind; a psychiatrist.

al′ien·or (-ẽr; -ôr′), *n.* One who alienates property.

a′lif (ä′lĭf), *n.* The first letter of the Arabic alphabet (ا).

al′i·form (ăl′ĭ·fôrm; ā′lĭ-), *adj.* [L. *ala* wing + *-form.*] Wing-shaped; winglike.

a·light′ (ȧ·līt′), *v. i.;* A·LIGHT′ED, sometimes A·LIT′ (ȧ·lĭt′); A·LIGHT′ING. [AS. *ālīhtan*, deriv. of *līht, lēoht*, light (in weight).] **1.** To spring down or get down; to dismount. **2.** To descend from the air and settle, or rest, as on a roof. **3.** To come or chance; — with *upon* or *on.*

a·light′, *adj.* [*a-* on + *light*, or orig. past part. deriv. of AS. *ālīhtan* to light.] Lighted; lighted up; in a flame.

a·lign′, a·line′ (ȧ·līn′), *v. t. & i.;* A·LIGNED′, A·LINED′ (-līnd′); A·LIGN′ING, A·LIN′ING. [F. *aligner*, fr. *à* (L. *ad*) to + *ligne* (L. *linea*) line.] To adjust or form to a line; to range or form in line; to bring into line, esp. on the side of, or against, a cause. — **Syn.** See LINE. — **a·lign′er, a·lin′er** (ȧ·līn′ẽr), *n.*

a·lign′ment, a·line′ment (-mĕnt), *n.* **1.** Act of aligning or state of being aligned; formation in line; also, the line so formed. **2.** *Engin.* The ground plan, as of a railroad, in distinction from the grades or profile.

a·like′ (ȧ·līk′), *adj.* [AS. *onlīc* or *gelīc.*] Having resemblance or similarity; similar; without difference; — now used only predicatively. — **Syn.** See SIMILAR. — *adv.* In the same manner, form, or degree; in common; equally.

al′i·ment (ăl′ĭ·mĕnt), *n.* [L. *alimentum*, fr. *alere* to nourish.] Food; nutriment; hence, sustenance; means of support. — **Syn.** See FOOD. — (-mĕnt), *v. t.* To give aliment to. — **al′i·men′tal** (-mĕn′tăl; -t'l), *adj.* — **al′i·men′tal·ly,** *adv.*

al′i·men′ta·ry (-mĕn′tȧ·rĭ), *adj.* **1.** Of or pertaining to the function of nutrition; nutritious. **2.** Supplying sustenance.

alimentary canal. *Anat.* The tubular food-carrying passage extending from the mouth to the anus.

al′i·men·ta′tion (ăl′ĭ·mĕn·tā′shŭn), *n.* Act or process of affording nutriment; state or mode of being nourished.

al′i·men′ta·tive (-mĕn′tȧ·tĭv), *adj.* Nutritive.

al′i·mo′ny (ăl′ĭ·mō′nĭ *or, esp. Brit.*, -mŭn·ĭ), *n.* [L. *alimonia* sustenance, fr. *alere* to nourish.] **1.** Maintenance; means of living. **2.** An allowance made by a man to a woman pending or after her divorce or legal separation from him.

‖**à l'im′pro′viste′** (à lăN′prô′vēst′). [F.] On a sudden; unexpectedly; unawares.

a·line′, a·line′ment, a·lin′er. Vars. of ALIGN, etc.

Al′i·oth (ăl′ĭ·ŏth), *n.* A star of the first magnitude in the handle of the Big Dipper. See URSA MAJOR, *Illust.*

al′i·ped (ăl′ĭ·pĕd), *adj.* [L. *alipes*, fr. *ala* wing + *pes* foot.] Wing-footed, as the bat. — **al′i·ped,** *n.*

al′i·phat′ic (ăl′ĭ·făt′ĭk), *adj.* [Gr. *aleiphar, aleiphatos*, oil, fat.] *Chem.* Of, pertaining to, or derived from fat; fatty; — of compounds having an open-chain structure.

‖**a′li·quan′do bo′nus dor′mi·tat Ho·me′rus** (ăl′ĭ·kwŏn′dō bō′nŭs dôr′mĭ·tăt hō·mē′rŭs). [L.] Even good Homer sometimes nods.

al′i·quant (ăl′ĭ·kwănt), *adj.* [L. *aliquantus* some, moderate, fr. *alius* other + *quantus* how great.] *Math.* Designating a part of a number or quantity that does not divide the number or quantity without leaving a remainder; thus, 5 is an *aliquant* part of 16; — opposed to *aliquot.*

al′i·quot (-kwŏt), *adj.* [L., some, several, fr. *alius* other + *quot* how many.] *Math.* Designating a part of a number that divides the number without a remainder. — **al′i·quot,** *n.*

‖**a′lis vo′lat pro′pri·is** (ā′lĭs vō′lăt prō′prĭ·ĭs). [L.] She flies with her own wings; — motto of Oregon.

a·lit′ (ȧ·lĭt′), *past & past part.* of ALIGHT.

a′li·un′de (ā′lĭ·ŭn′dē), *adv. & adj.* [L.] From another source; from elsewhere; as, a case proved *aliunde.*

a·live′ (ȧ·līv′), *adj.* [ME. *on live*, fr. AS. *on līfe* in life.] (Used only predicatively or postpositively.) **1.** Having life; living. **2.** In a state of action; in force or operation; unextinguished; existent; as, to keep the fire *alive.* **3.** Having susceptibility; easily impressed; sensitive. **4.** Sprightly; lively; brisk. **5.** Exhibiting the activity and motion of many living beings; swarming; as, a thicket *alive* with insects. — **Syn.** See LIVING: AWARE.

a·liz′a·rin (ȧ·lĭz′ȧ·rĭn), *n.* Also **a·liz′a·rine** (-rĭn; -rēn). [F. *alizarine.*] **1.** *Chem.* A dye, $C_{14}H_6O_2(OH)_2$, formerly prepared from madder, now from anthracene, and forming when pure a reddish-yellow powder or orange-red crystals. It produces the Turkey reds, and shades of pink, chocolate, etc., with different mordants. **2.** Any of a group of dyes, of various hues, similarly derived from anthraquinone.

al′ka·hest (ăl′kȧ·hĕst), *n.* [ML. *alchahest*, prob. pseudo-Arabic coinage by Paracelsus.] The fabled "universal solvent" of the alchemists; a menstruum capable of dissolving all substances.

al′ka·les′cent (ăl′kȧ·lĕs′ĕnt; -′nt), *adj.* Slightly alkaline. — **al′ka·les′cence** (-ĕns; -′ns), **al′ka·les′cen·cy** (-ĕn·sĭ; -′n·sĭ), *n.*

al′ka·li (ăl′kȧ·lī; -lĭ), *n.; pl.* -LIES or -LIS (-līz; -lĭz). [Deriv. of Ar. *al-qili* ashes of saltwort.] **1.** *Chem.* **a** Originally, a soluble salt obtained from the ashes of plants, largely potassium or sodium carbonate. **b** Hence, any substance having marked basic properties like the above salts (characteristic acid taste, ability to neutralize acids, etc.). The stronger alkalies are caustic (the hydroxides of sodium, potassium, ammonium, etc.) In the widest sense *alkali* includes also lime, magnesia, alkaloids (formerly called *vegetable alkalies*), etc. **2.** *Geol. & Agric.* A soluble mineral salt present in some soils of arid regions in quantity detrimental to agriculture.
— *adj.* Of or containing an alkali; alkaline.

al′ka·li·fy (ăl′kȧ·lĭ·fī; ăl·kăl′ĭ·fī), *v. t. & i.;* -FIED (-fīd); -FY′ING. To make alkaline. — **al′ka·li·fi′a·ble** (-fī′ȧ·b′l), *adj.*

alkali metal. Any metal of the family including lithium, sodium, potassium, rubidium, and cesium.

al′ka·lim′e·ter (ăl′kȧ·lĭm′ē·tẽr), *n.* [*alkali* + *-meter.*] An instrument to ascertain the strength of alkalies, or the quantity of alkali in a mixture. — **al′ka·lim′e·try** (-trĭ), *n.*

al′ka·line (ăl′kȧ·līn; -lĭn; *chemists generally prefer* -lĭn, *but in popular use* -līn *prevails*), *adj.* Of, pertaining to, or having the properties of an alkali.

alkaline earths. *Chem.* The oxides of barium, calcium, and strontium (the **alkaline–earth metals**).

al′ka·lin′i·ty (ăl′kȧ·lĭn′ĭ·tĭ), *n.* Quality, state, or degree of being alkaline; power of combining with an acid to form a salt.

al′ka·lize (ăl′kȧ·līz), *v. t. & i.* [F. *alcaliser.*] To render alkaline. — **al′ka·li·za′tion** (-lĭ·zā′shŭn; -lī·zā′-), *n.*

al′ka·loid (ăl′kȧ·loid), *n.* [*alkali* + *-oid.*] *Chem.* An organic substance of alkaline properties, esp. one occurring naturally in plants and animals; an organic base; specif., a plant base, as distinguished from other types, as leucomaine and ptomaine. — **al′ka·loid, al′ka·loi′dal** (-loi′dăl; -d′l), *adj.*

al′ka·lo′sis (-lō′sĭs), *n.* [*alkali* + *-osis.*] *Med.* A condition of increased alkalinity of the blood and tissues.

al′ka·net (ăl′kȧ·nĕt), *n.* [Sp. *alcaneta*, dim. of *alcana*, fr. Ar. *al-ḥinnā′* the henna.] **1.** **a** A European plant (*Alkanna tinctoria*) of the borage family; also, its root. **b** The bugloss *Anchusa officinalis.* **c** Any of several plants (genus *Lithospermum*) of the borage family. **2.** A red dyestuff prepared from **al·kan′nin** (ăl·kăn′ĭn), an amorphous powder made from alkanet root.

Al′ko·ran′ (ăl′kō·răn′; -rän′). Var. of ALCORAN.

al′kyd res′in (ăl′kĭd). [*alk*ali + *-yl* + acid.] Any of a group of thermoplastic synthetic resins prepared esp. by the reaction of certain alcohols, as glycerol, with certain acids, as phthalic used as surface coatings, etc.

all (ôl), *adj.* [AS. *all, eall*, pl. *alle, ealle.*] **1.** The whole of; — referring to amount, quantity, extent, duration, quality, or degree; as, *all* the wheat; specif., as much as, or the greatest, possible; as, in *all* kindness. **2.** The whole number or sum of. **3.** Every member or individual component of; each one of; as, *all* men are mortal. **4.** Any whatever; as, beyond *all* doubt. **5.** Only; nothing but; as, ten dollars, *all* profit. **6.** *Dial., U.S.* Entirely gone or disposed of; — used predicatively. — **Syn.** See WHOLE. — *adv.* **1.** Wholly; completely. **2.** Exclusively; solely; as, a sum spent *all* for amusement. **3.** Exceedingly; very. **4.** Apiece; each; as, the score is two *all.* — *pron., sing. & pl.* The whole number, quantity, or amount; as, *all* of us are ready; also, everything or everybody; as, free to *all.* — *n.* The whole of one's possessions; as, he squandered his *all.* — ***at all.*** In any way or respect; to the least extent or degree; under any circumstances; — used for reinforcement or emphasis, esp. in negative or interrogative sentences. — ***in all.*** Altogether; all told. — ***once (and) for all.*** For all contingencies; finally.

‖**al′la bre′ve** (äl′lä brā′vā). [It., according to the *breve.*] *Music.* Duple or quadruple measure in which the beat is represented by the half note. Indicated by 𝄵.

Al′lah (ăl′ȧ; ŏl·lä′h′), *n.* [Ar. *Allāh*, contr. of *al-ilāh* the god.] The Supreme Being of the Mohammedans.

all′–A·mer′i·can, *adj.* Exclusively American; representing the whole United States.

Al′lan–a–Dale′ (ăl′ăn·ȧ·dāl′), *n.* In English ballads, a youth who, aided by Robin Hood, breaks up the wedding of his sweetheart to an old knight, and marries her himself.

al·lan′to·is (ă·lăn′tō·ĭs), *n.* [NL., fr. earlier *allantoides*, fr. Gr. *allantoeidēs* sausage-shaped, fr. *allas* sausage + *eidos* form.] *Anat.* An organ of the embryos of reptiles, birds, and mammals, which in most mammals develops into part of the umbilical cord and unites with the chorion, forming the placenta. — **al′lan·to′ic** (ăl′ăn·tō′ĭk), *adj*

‖**al′lar·gan′do** (äl′lär·gän′dō), *adj.* *Music.* Gradually slower and louder.

all′–a·round′, *adj.* = ALL-ROUND.

‖**al′la vos′tra sa·lu′te!** (äl′lä vôs′trä sä·lōō′tā). [It.] To your health!

al·lay′ (ă·lā′), *v. t.* [AS. *ālecgan*, fr. *ā-* + *lecgan* to lay.] **1.** To make quiet or put at rest; to cause to subside or be still; to pacify or appease; to quell; calm. **2.** To lessen the force or severity of; alleviate. — **Syn.** See RELIEVE. — **al·lay′er,** *n.*

all but. Very nearly; almost.

all clear. A signal that hostile aircraft are retiring.

al′le·ga′tion (ăl′ē·gā′shŭn), *n.* [OF., fr. L. *allegatio*, fr. *allegare, -gatum*, to send a message, cite, fr. *ad-* + *legare* to send.] **1.** Act of alleging. **2.** That which is alleged; a formal averment; also, an assertion unsupported and by implication unsupportable.

al·lege′ (ă·lĕj′), *v. t.;* AL·LEGED′ (-lĕjd′); AL·LEG′ING (-lĕj′ĭng). [OF. *esligier* to buy, prop., to free from legal difficulties, fr. L. *ex* out + *litigare* to quarrel, sue.] **1.** To declare as if under oath; to state positively but without proof; to affirm; to assert. **2.** To produce or urge as support, or as a reason, excuse, or the like. **3.** *Archaic.* To cite. — **Syn.** See ADDUCE. — **Ant.** Contravene, (*in law*) traverse. — **al·lege′a·ble,** *adj.* — **al·leg′er** (-lĕj′ẽr), *n.*

al·leg′ed·ly (ă·lĕj′ĕd·lĭ), *adv.* By, or according to, allegation.

al·le′giance (ă·lē′jăns), *n.* [ME. *alegeaunce*, fr. *a-* to + OF. *ligeance*, fr. *lige, liege*, liege.] **1.** The relation of a feudal vassal to his superior, or liege lord; the duty of fidelity to one's king, government, or sovereign state. **2.** Devotion or loyalty to that which is entitled to obedience or service and respect. — **Syn.** See FIDELITY.

al·le′giant (ă·lē′jănt), *adj.* Loyal. *Shak.*

al′le·gor′ic (ăl′ē·gŏr′ĭk), **al′le·gor′i·cal** (-ĭ·kăl), *adj.* Belonging to, occurring in, constituting, or containing allegory or an allegory. — **al′le·gor′i·cal·ly,** *adv.*

al′le·go′rist (ăl′ē·gō′rĭst *or, esp. Brit.,* gẽr·ĭst), *n.* A writer of allegory.

al′le·go·ris′tic (-gō·rĭs′tĭk), *adj.* Allegorizing; attributing allegorical significance; interpreting as an allegory.

al′le·go·rize (ăl′ē·gō·rīz *or, esp. Brit.,* -gẽr·īz), *v. t.* **1.** To form or turn into allegory. **2.** To treat, understand, or interpret as allegorical. — *v. i.* To form or use allegory. — **al′le·gor′i·za′tion** (-gŏr′ĭ·zā′shŭn; -ī·zā′-), *n.* — **al′le·go·riz′er** (-gō·rīz′ẽr), *n.*

al′le·go′ry (-gō′rĭ *or, esp. Brit.,* -gẽr·ĭ), *n.; pl.* -RIES (-rĭz). [F. or L.; F. *allégorie*, fr. L. *allegoria*, fr. Gr. *allēgoria* description of one thing under the image of another.] **1.** The veiled presentation, in a figurative story, of a meaning metaphorically implied but not expressly stated. Allegory is prolonged metaphor, in which typically a series of actions are symbolic of other actions, as in Bunyan's *Pilgrim's Progress.* **2.** An instance of such presentation; hence, an emblem.

al′le·gret′to (ăl′ē·grĕt′ō), *adj.* [It., dim. of *allegro.*] *Music.* Quicker than andante, but not so quick as allegro. — *n.* A movement in allegretto tempo.

al·le′gro (ä·lā′grō), *adj.* [It., merry, gay, fr. L. *alacer.*] *Music.* Brisk; lively. — *adv.* Briskly. — *n.* A movement in allegro tempo; a fast movement, as of a symphony.

al·lele′ (ă·lēl′), *n.* Also **al·lel′** (ă·lĕl′). = ALLELOMORPH. — **al·le′lic** (-lē′lĭk; -lĕl′ĭk), *adj.* — **al·le′lism** (-lē′lĭz′m; -lĕl′ĭz′m), *n.*

al·le′lo·morph (ă·lē′lō·môrf; ă·lĕl′ō-), *n.* [Gr. *allēlōn* of one another + *-morph.*] *Biol.* **a** Either of a pair of alternative, contrasting Mendelian characters, as roughness and smoothness of hair coat in guinea pigs. See MENDEL'S LAW. **b** The gene which gives rise to the character. — **al·le′lo·mor′phic** (-môr′fĭk), *adj.* — **-phism** (-fĭz′m), *n.*

al′le·lu′ia (ăl′ē·lū′yȧ), *n. & interj.* [L., fr. Gr. *allēlouia*, fr. Heb. *hallĕlū-yāh* praise ye Jehovah.] Hallelujah; — the form esp. used in liturgies.

‖**al′le·mande′** (ȧl′mäɴd′; ăl′ē·mănd′), *n.* [F., fr. *allemand* German.] **1.** One of several German dances in duple or quadruple measure, in which partners hold hands through all evolutions. **2.** Music for such a dance.

al′ler·gen (ăl′ẽr·jĕn), *n.* [*allergy* + *-gen.*] *Immunol.* A substance causing allergy or causing it to become manifest.

al′ler·gen′ic (-jĕn′ĭk), *adj.* [*allergy* + *-genic.*] Inducing allergy.

al′ler·gy (ăl′ẽr·jĭ), *n.* [Gr. *allos* other + *ergon* work.] **1.** *Immunol.* The altered degree of susceptibility caused by a primary inoculation or treatment and manifested in reaction to a subsequent inoculation or treatment with the same germ or serum, as in anaphylaxis. **2.** *Med.* Popularly, excessive sensitiveness to certain substances, as germs, pollen, food, hair, or cloth, to mental or emotional excitement, or to physical conditions, as excessive cold, which are harmless to most people. Thus, contact with feathers or the eating of certain food may cause hives in a person who has an *allergy* for these substances. **3.** *Slang.* A feeling of antipathy or repugnance. — **al·ler′gic** (ă·lûr′jĭk), *adj.*

al·le′vi·ate (ă·lē′vĭ·āt), *v. t.* [L. *alleviatus*, past part. of *alleviare*, fr. *ad-* + *levis* light.] To lighten or lessen (physical or mental troubles); to mitigate. — **Syn.** See RELIEVE. — **Ant.** Aggravate. — **al·le′vi·a′tion** (-ā′shŭn), *n.* — **al·le′vi·a′tor** (-ā′tẽr), *n.* — **al·le′vi·a·to′ry** (-ȧ·tō′rĭ *or, esp. Brit.,* -tẽr·ĭ), *adj.*

al·le′vi·a′tive (ă·lē′vĭ·ā′tĭv; -ȧ·tĭv), *adj.* Tending to alleviate; palliative. — *n.* That which alleviates.

al′ley (ăl′ĭ), *n.; pl.* ALLEYS (-ĭz). [OF. *alee* a going, fr. *aler* to go, fr. L. *ambulare.*] **1.** A walk in a garden or park, bordered by trees or bushes. **2.** A narrow lane between buildings, esp. through the middle of a city block, giving access to the rear of buildings. **3.** A place for playing at bowls, skittles, or the like.

al′ley (ăl′ĭ), *n.; pl.* ALLEYS (-ĭz). [Contr. of *alabaster*, of which it was orig. made.] A choice playing marble.

al′ley·way′ (-wā′), *n.* An alley, esp. between buildings.

All Fools′ Day. The first day of April, a day on which playful tricks are practiced.

all fours. **1.** All four legs of a quadruped; the two legs and two arms of a person; — formerly **all four.** **2.** *Card Playing.* Seven-up. — ***on all fours.*** Evenly; also, on the same footing.

all hail. All health; — a salutation.

All′hal′lows (ôl′hăl′ōz), **All′hal′low·mas** (-ō·mȧs), *n.* All Saints' Day, November 1st. — **All′hal′low·tide′** (-ō·tīd′), *n.*

all′heal′ (ôl′hēl′), *n.* **a** The valerian. **b** The selfheal.

al′li·a′ceous (ăl′ĭ·ā′shŭs), *adj.* *Bot.* Of or pertaining to the genus (*Allium*) or the family (Alliaceae) containing the garlic, onion, and leek; having the smell of garlic or onions.

al·li′ance (ă·lī′ăns), *n.* [OF. *aliance.* See ALLY.] **1.** State of being allied; act of allying or uniting; a union of interests, esp. between families by marriage, and between states, esp. independent ones, by compact or treaty. **2.** Any union by relationship in qualities, as between religion and morals; affinity. **3.** A connection for mutual advantage between any groups or bodies, as between the farm and labor blocs. — **Syn.** League, coalition, confederacy, federation.

al·lied′ (ă·līd′), *adj.* Joined in alliance; — with reference to the Allies, usually *cap.* Also, related; as, *allied* genera.

al′li·ga′tor (ăl′ĭ·gā′tẽr), *n.* [Sp. *el lagarto* the lizard (*el lagarto de Indias*, the cayman or American crocodile), fr. L. *lacertus* lizard.] **1.** Any of several crocodilians (genus *Alligator* and allied genera) in which the snout is shorter and broader than in the crocodiles, and the teeth of the lower jaw shut into pits instead of into marginal notches. They are mainly American. See CAYMAN. **2.** A machine or device having a strong movable jaw like an alligator's. **3.** *Mil.* A flat-bottomed armed and partly armored vehicle, open at the top, traveling on two endless metal belts having finlike extensions, by means of which it is propelled on land or water, used esp. for landing troops. **4.** *Cant.* A nonmusician devotee of swing.

alligator pear. The avocado.

alligator snapper, terrapin, tortoise, *or* **turtle.** See TURTLE, 1.

al·lit′er·ate (ă·lĭt′ẽr·āt), *v. i. & t.* To form an alliteration; to speak or arrange alliteratively.

al·lit′er·a′tion (-ā′shŭn), *n.* [ML. *alliteratio.* See AD-; LETTER.] Repetition of the same sound at the beginning of two or more consecutive words or of words near one another; specif., recurrence of the same

consonant sound or of vowel sounds initially in accented syllables of verse, as in "In a somer seson whan soft was the sonne."
al·lit′er·a′tive (ă·lĭt′ẽr·ā′tĭv; -*ȧ*·tĭv), *adj.* Pert. to, or characterized by, alliteration. — **al·lit′er·a′tive·ly**, *adv.* — **al·lit′er·a′tive·ness**, *n.*
al′li·um (ăl′ĭ·ŭm), *n.* [L. *alium, allium,* garlic.] *Bot.* A plant, bulb, or flower of a large genus (*Allium*) of bulbous herbs of the lily family (Liliaceae), including the onion, garlic, chive, leek, and shallot.
al′lo- (ăl′ō-). [Gr. *allos* other.] A combining form denoting *differentiation from the normal, extraneousness,* or *reversal.*
al′lo·ca·ble (ăl′ō·k*ȧ*·b′l), *adj.* That can be allocated; assignable to a particular account or period of time.
al′lo·cate (ăl′ō·kāt), *v. t.* [ML. *allocatus,* past part. of *allocare,* fr. L. *ad* to + *locare* to place.] To distribute as a share, part, or the like; to assign; apportion; also, to locate. — **Syn.** See ALLOT.
al′lo·ca′tion (-kā′shŭn), *n.* The act of distributing; allotment or apportionment; in accounting, apportionment of business expenses to the account of the particular departments; specif., government apportionment and distribution of available materials among producers.
al′lo·cu′tion (-kū′shŭn), *n.* [L. *allocutio,* fr. *alloqui* to speak to.] An address; a hortatory or authoritative address.
al′lod, al·lo′di·al, al·lo′di·um. Vars. of ALOD, etc.
al·log′a·my (ă·lŏg′*ȧ*·mĭ), *n* [*allo-* + *-gamy.*] *Bot.* Cross-fertilization. — **al·log′a·mous** (-mŭs), *adj.*
al·lom′er·ism (ă·lŏm′ẽr·ĭz′m), *n.* [*allo-* + Gr. *meros* part.] *Chem. & Mineral.* Variability in chemical constitution without variation in crystalline form. — **al·lom′er·ous** (-ŭs), *adj.*
al′lo·morph (ăl′ō·môrf), *n.* [*allo-* + *-morph.*] *Mineral.* **a** Any of two or more distinct crystalline forms of the same substance, or the substance having such forms; thus, carbonate of lime occurs in the *allomorphs* calcite and aragonite. **b** A variety of pseudomorph which has undergone partial or complete change or substitution of material; thus, limonite is often an *allomorph* after pyrite. — **al′lo·mor′phic** (-môr′fĭk), *adj.* — **al′lo·mor′phism** (-fĭz′m), *n.*
al′lo·morph, *n.* [Gr. *allos* the one, the other + *morpheme.*] *Ling.* One of two or more forms that a given morpheme has at different points in a language, as the *-es* (ĭz) of *dishes,* the *-s* (z) of *dreams,* the *-s* (s) of *traps,* and the vowel modification distinguishing *teeth* from *tooth.*
al′lo·nym (ăl′ō·nĭm), *n.* [*allo-* + Gr. *onyma* name.] The name of another person assumed by an author.
al′lo·path (ăl′ō·păth), **al·lop′a·thist** (ă·lŏp′*ȧ*·thĭst), *n.* One who practices allopathy.
al·lop′a·thy (ă·lŏp′*ȧ*·thĭ), *n.* [*allo-* + *-pathy.*] The theory or system of medical practice which combats disease by the use of remedies producing effects different from those produced by the disease treated. Also, erroneously, the system of medical practice making use of all measures which have proved of value in the treatment of disease. Cf. HOMEOPATHY. — **al′lo·path′ic** (ăl′ō·păth′ĭk), *adj.* — **-i·cal·ly**, *adv.*
al′lo·phane (ăl′ō·fān), *n.* [Gr. *allophanēs* appearing otherwise; — so called because its appearance changes before the blowpipe.] *Mineral.* A hydrous aluminum silicate, amorphous, translucent, and of various colors.
al′lo·phone (ăl′ō·fōn), *n.* [*allo-* + *phone* sound.] *Phonet.* A nondistinctive variant of a phoneme; as, the variants of *p* in "pit" (aspirated) and "spit" (unaspirated) are *allophones.*
al·lot′ (ă·lŏt′), *v. t.*; AL·LOT′TED; AL·LOT′TING. [OF. *aloter,* fr. *a* (L. *ad*) + *lot* lot.] **1.** To distribute by lot. **2.** To distribute in portions; to assign or set apart as a share, lot, or part.
Syn. Allot, assign, apportion, allocate mean to give as one's share, one's portion, or the like. **Allot,** unless qualified, implies haphazard or arbitrary selection; **assign** stresses authoritative and fixed allotment and it too carries no clear hint of an even division; **apportion** implies a principle of fair division, such as proportionateness; **allocate,** used chiefly in reference to money, property, etc., suggests a fixed appropriation to a person or group for a particular use.
al·lot′ment (-mĕnt), *n.* An allotting or that which is allotted; apportionment; a share allotted to one.
al′lo·trope (ăl′ō·trōp), *n.* *Chem* An allotropic form.
al′lo·trop′ic (-trŏp′ĭk), **al′lo·trop′i·cal** (-ĭ·kăl), *adj.* Of, pertaining to, or exhibiting allotropy. — **al′lo·trop′i·cal·ly**, *adv.* — **al′lo·tro·pic′i·ty** (-trō·pĭs′ĭ·tĭ), *n.*
al·lot′ro·py (ă·lŏt′rō·pĭ; ăl′ō·trō′pĭ), **al·lot′ro·pism** (ă·lŏt′rō·pĭz′m), *n.* [Gr. *allotropia* variety, fr. *allos* other + *tropos* direction, way, fr. *trepein* to turn.] *Chem.* The phenomenon of the existence of an element, or sometimes compound, in two or more different forms. Thus carbon occurs in the forms of the diamond, graphite, lampblack, and charcoal.
‖**all′ ot·ta′va** (äl′-lŏt·tä′vä). [It.] *Music.* To be performed an octave higher or lower according as *all' ottava* (or its abbreviation *8va*) appears above or below the staff.
al·lot′tee′ (ă·lŏt′ē′), *n.* One to whom allotment is made.
all′–out′ (ôl′out′), *adj.* Exerting all energy and employing every resource; as, an *all-out* offensive; hence, loosely, thoroughgoing.
all′o′ver (ôl′ō′vẽr), *adj.* Covering the entire surface, as of a fabric; — said of designs, figuration, etc. — **all′o′ver**, *n.*
al·low′ (ă·lou′), *v. t.* [OF. *alouer* to place, use, assign, fr. L. *allocare;* confused with OF. *alouer* to approve, fr. L. *allaudare* to extol.] **1.** To approve of; to sanction. **2.** To admit or concede, as the truth of a report. **3.** To recognize as a right or privilege; to assign as a share or award; to grant as appropriate for any purpose, esp. in restricted quantity; as, the law *allows* it; to *allow* a boy spending money. **4.** To permit by way of concession; to grant license to; as, no smoking *allowed;* to *allow* oneself luxuries. **5.** To suffer by neglecting to restrain or prevent. **6.** To grant as a deduction or an addition; esp., to abate or deduct; as, to *allow* a gallon for leakage. **7.** To assign (an amount of time, money, etc.) for a particular purpose; as, to *allow* an hour for lunch. — **Syn.** See LET. — *v. i.* **1.** To approve, admit, or concede. **2.** To take into consideration; — with *for;* as, to *allow* for shrinkage.
al·low′a·ble (-*ȧ*·b′l), *adj.* Permissible; not forbidden; not improper. — **al·low′a·bly** (-blĭ), *adv.*
al·low′ance (-ăns), *n.* **1.** Act of allowing; authorization; sanction. **2.** That which is allowed; share or portion allotted. **3.** Specif., a sum of money granted periodically as a bounty, as to a dependent, or the like. **4.** Abatement; deduction; specif.: **a** *Com.* A customary deduction from the gross weight of goods, as tare and tret. **b** *Coinage.* = TOLERANCE, 4. **5.** *Sports.* A concession or privilege accorded by the rules to a contestant to make his chance more nearly equal with that of his competitors. — *v. t.*; -ANCED (-ănst); -ANC·ING (-ăn·sĭng). To put upon a fixed allowance (esp. of food).
al·low′ed·ly (ă·lou′ĕd·lĭ; -ĭd·lĭ), *adv.* By allowance, admittedly.
al·loy′ (ă·loi′; ăl′oi), *n.* [F. *aloi,* fr. OF. See ALLOY, *v.*] **1.** State as to being mixed with base metals; comparative purity; fineness. **2.** A substance composed of two or more metals or, by extension, of a metal and a nonmetal, intimately united, usually by being fused together and dissolving in each other when molten; also, the state of union of the components. **3.** A metal mixed with a more valuable metal to give durability or some other desired quality. **4.** Admixture of anything that debases; an alien or impairing element or part.
— (ă·loi′), *v. t.* [OF. *aloier, alier,* to combine, fr. L. *alligare.* See ALLY, *v.*] **1.** To reduce the purity of by mixing with a less valuable metal; as, to *alloy* silver with copper. **2.** To mix so as to form an alloy. **3.** To abate, impair, or debase by mixture; to allay; as, to *alloy* pleasure with misfortunes.
all right. *Colloq.* Satisfactory or satisfactorily; correct.
all′–round′ (ôl′round′; 2), *adj.* Extending all round; complete; having general ability, serviceability, or excellence. *Colloq.* — **Syn.** See VERSATILE.
All Saints′ Day. A church feast, observed November 1st.
all′seed′ (ôl′sēd′), *n.* Any of several many-seeded plants, as knotweed, goosefoot, etc.
All Souls′ Day. *R.C.Ch.* November 2d, a day of solemn supplication for all the souls in Purgatory.
all′spice′ (ôl′spīs′), *n.* The berry of a tree (*Pimenta officinalis*) of the myrtle family, the **allspice tree,** of the West Indies; also, the mildly pungent and aromatic spice prepared from it; pimento.
all told. Everything counted; in all.
al·lude′ (ă·lūd′), *v. i.* [L. *alludere* to play with, fr. *ad-* + *ludere* to play.] To refer indirectly or by suggestion; to make covert mention; — followed by *to;* as, the story *alludes* to a recent transaction. — **Syn.** See REFER.
al·lure′ (ă·lūr′), *v. t. & i.* [OF. *aleurrer, alurer,* fr. *a* (L. *ad*) + *leurre* lure.] To tempt or draw by a lure or bait, that is, by the offer of some good, real or apparent; to entice. — **Syn.** See ATTRACT. — **Ant.** Repel. — **al·lure′ment**, *n.* — **al·lur′er** (-lūr′ẽr), *n.*
al·lur′ing (-lūr′ĭng), *adj.* That allures; enticing; tempting. — **al·lur′ing·ly**, *adv.* — **al·lur′ing·ness**, *n.*
al·lu′sion (ă·lū′zhŭn), *n.* [L. *allusio,* fr. *alludere* to play with.] **1.** An alluding; an implied indication or indirect reference; a hint; as, a covert *allusion* to his pride. **2.** An indirect reference by passing mention or quotation to something generally familiar.
al·lu′sive (-sĭv), *adj.* Making allusion; containing an allusion. — **al·lu′sive·ly**, *adv.* — **al·lu′sive·ness**, *n.*
al·lu′vi·al (ă·lū′vĭ·ăl), *adj.* Pertaining to or composed of alluvium; found in alluvium. — *n.* Alluvial soil; in Australia, gold-bearing alluvial soil.
alluvial fan *or* **cone.** The alluvial deposit of a stream where it issues from a gorge upon an open plain. See DELTA.
al·lu′vi·on (ă·lū′vĭ·ŏn), *n.* [F., fr. L. *alluvio,* fr. *alluere* to wash against, fr. *ad-* + *luere* to wash.] **1.** Wash of water against the shore. **2.** An inundation. **3.** Alluvium. **4.** *Law.* An accession to land by gradual addition, as by deposit of alluvium. It belongs to the owner of the land to which it is added. Cf. AVULSION
al·lu′vi·um (-ŭm), *n.*; *pl.* -VIUMS (-ŭmz), -VIA (-*ȧ*). [L., neut. of *alluvius* alluvial.] Soil, sand, gravel, or similar detrital material deposited by running water.
al·ly′ (ă·lī′), *v. t. & i.*; AL·LIED′ (-līd′); AL·LY′ING. [OF. *alier,* fr. L. *alligare* to bind to, fr. *ad-* + *ligare* to bind.] (Generally used passively or reflexively.) **1.** To unite, or form a connection between, as families by marriage, or states by treaty; to join by an alliance; — often with *to* or *with.* **2.** To connect or form a relation between by similitude, resemblance, friendship, or love.
— (ă·lī′; ăl′ī; *see note below*), *n.*; *pl.* ALLIES (-līz′; -īz). **1.** One, esp. a sovereign or state, united to another by treaty or league; a confederate, associate. **2.** Specif. [*pl.; usually cap.*] **a** The nations in alliance against the Central Powers in World War I. **b** = UNITED NATIONS. **3.** Anything akin to another by structure or the like; as, the mosses and their *allies.* **4.** Anything associated with another as a helper; an auxiliary; as, showing science as an *ally* of religion.
☞ The difference in accent often depends on the position of the word in a sentence; also, the plural form is perhaps more generally accented on the final syllable than the singular is.
al′lyl (ăl′ĭl), *n.* [L. *allium* garlic + *-yl.*] *Chem.* An unsaturated univalent radical, C_3H_5, compounds of which are found in the oils of garlic and mustard. — **al·lyl′ic** (ă·lĭl′ĭk), *adj.*
allyl resin. Any of a group of transparent abrasion-resistant resins derived from **allyl alcohol,** C_3H_5OH, a colorless pungent liquid used in organic synthesis.
al′ma, al′mah (ăl′m*ȧ*). Vars. of ALME, ALMEH.
al′ma·gest (ăl′m*ȧ*·jĕst), *n.* [*sometimes cap.*] [OF. & ML. *almageste,* fr. Ar. *al-majusti,* fr. Gr. *megistē* (sc. *syntaxis*) the greatest (composition).] **1.** The celebrated astronomical work by Claudius Ptolemy (about A.D. 140) of Alexandria. **2.** Any of various similar medieval works, as on astrology or alchemy.
Al′ma Ma′ter (ăl′m*ȧ* mā′tẽr; äl′m*ȧ* mä′tẽr). [L.] Literally, fostering mother, as Cybele, Ceres, etc., among the Romans. Hence [*usually not cap.*], one's university, college, or school.
al′ma·nac (ôl′m*ȧ*·năk), *n.* [ML. *almanac, -nach,* fr. Sp. Ar. *almanākh* almanac, calendar, fr. Ar. *al* the + *manākh* climate.] A book or table containing a calendar of days, weeks, and months, to which astronomical data and various statistics are often added, such as the times of sunset and sunrise, changes of the moon, etc.
al′man·dine (ăl′măn·dēn; -dĭn), *n.* [For *alabandine,* fr. L. *alabandina,* after *Alabanda,* a town in Caria.] **a** Almandite. **b** See SPINEL.
al′man·dite (-dīt), *n.* [See ALMANDINE.] A deep-red variety of garnet, esp. the gem. Chemically, it is $Fe_3Al_2(SiO_4)_3$.
al′me, al′meh (ăl′mĕ), *n.* [Ar. *'ālimah* (fem.) learned (in music).] An Egyptian singing and dancing girl
al·me′mar (ăl·mē′mär), *n.* [Ar. *al-minbar* the pulpit.] A platform in a Jewish synagogue, bearing the reading desk from which are read the Pentateuch and the Prophets.
al·might′y (ôl·mīt′ĭ), *adj.* [AS. *ealmihtig, ælmihtig,* fr. *eall* all + *mihtig* mighty.] **1.** Originally, having power over all; as, ***the Almighty,*** God. **2.** Unlimited in might; omnipotent. — **al·might′i·ly**, *adv.* — **al·might′i·ness**, *n.*

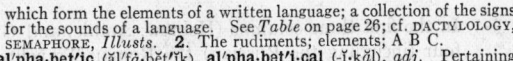

al'mond (ä'mŭnd; ăm'ŭnd), *n.* [From OF., ult. fr. L. *amygdala,* fr. Gr. *amygdalē.*] **1.** A small tree (*Prunus amygdalus,* syn. *Amygdalus communis*) of the peach family, resembling the peach in flowers. **2.** The fruit (a drupe) of this tree, esp. its ellipsoidal, nutlike kernel. **3.** Any of several similar fruits or the trees producing them. **4.** The color biscuit.

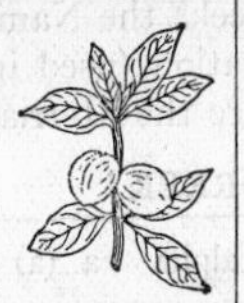

Almond Leaves and Fruit.

al'mond–eyed' (-īd'), *adj.* Having the narrow, slant, almond-shaped eyes characteristic of Mongolians.
al'mon·er (ăl'mŭn·ẽr; ä'mŭn-), *n.* [OF. *almosnier, aumosnier,* fr. *almosne* alms, fr. L. *eleemosyna.* See ALMS.] One who dispenses alms for another, as for an institution or for a prince.
al'mon·ry (-rĭ), *n.* A place where alms are dealt out.
al'most (ôl'mōst; *emphatic or isolated, also* ôl·mōst'; 2), *adv.* [AS. *ealmǣst, ælmǣst,* quite the most, almost all.] Nearly; well-nigh; all but; a little short of.
alms (ämz), *n. sing. & pl.* [AS. *ælmysse,* fr. L. *eleemosyna,* fr. Gr. *eleēmosynē,* fr. *eleos* compassion.] **1.** *Archaic.* Charity; work of mercy. **2.** Anything given gratuitously to relieve the poor; a charitable gift. — **alms'giv'er** (-gĭv'ẽr), *n.* — **alms'giv'ing** (-gĭv'ĭng), *n.*
alms'house' (-hous'), *n.* A house for the use of the poor.
alms'man (-măn), *n.; fem.* **alms'wom'an** (-wŏŏm'ăn). **a** A recipient of alms. **b** *Rare.* A giver of alms.
al'ni·co (ăl'nĭ·kō), *n.* A powerful permanent magnet alloy containing as essential ingredients iron, nickel, and aluminum, also sometimes cobalt and copper.
a·lo'di·um, al·lo'di·um (ă·lō'dĭ·ŭm), *n.* Also **al'od, al'lod** (ăl'ŏd). [ML., of G. origin.] *Law.* Land held in absolute independence, without being subject to any rent, service, or acknowledgment to a superior; — opposed to *feud.* — **a·lo'di·al, al·lo'di·al,** *adj.*
al'oe (ăl'ō), *n.; pl.* ALOES (-ōz). [L. *aloë,* fr. Gr. *aloē* aloe.] **1.** *pl.* The fragrant wood of an East Indian tree (*Aquilaria agallocha*) of the mezereon family. **2.** Any of a large genus (*Aloe* [*pron.* ăl'ō·ē]) of succulent plants, chiefly South African, of the lily family (Liliaceae). They have basal leaves and spicate flowers. **3.** *pl.* The dried juice of the leaves of several species of the aloe, used as a purgative and tonic; — syntactically singular. — **al'o·et'ic** (ăl'ō·ĕt'ĭk), *adj. & n.*
a·loft' (ȧ·lôft'; 74), *adv.* [*a-* on + *loft,* which prop. meant *air.*] **1.** On high; in the air; high above the ground. **2.** *Naut.* In the top; on or to the higher yards or rigging.
‖**a·lo'ha** (ä·lō'hä), *n.* [Hawaiian.] *Hawaii.* **a** Love; affection; kindness. **b** Greetings; farewell; — a salutation.
al'o·in (ăl'ō·ĭn), *n. Chem. & Pharm.* A bitter, yellow, crystalline, purgative substance obtained from the aloe.
a·lone' (ȧ·lōn'), *adj.* [*all* + *one.* ME. *al one* all alone, where *one* is fr. AS. *ān* one, alone.] (The adjective *alone* usually follows its noun.) **1.** Apart from others; all by oneself; solitary. **2.** Exclusive of others; without anyone or anything else; only. **3.** Unique; matchless; as, she is *alone* in worth. — *adv.* Solely; simply; exclusively.
Syn. **Alone, solitary, lonely, lonesome, lone, forlorn, desolate** mean apart from others. **Alone** stresses the objective fact of being entirely by oneself; **solitary** stresses the feeling of lack of close companionship; **lonely** adds to *solitary* a suggestion of longing for companionship; **lonesome** heightens the implication of dreariness; **lone** is chiefly poetical; **forlorn** and **desolate** are applied to persons and places but, though both emphasize dreariness and dismalness, *desolate* usually implies a sharper and more poignant sense of loneliness than does *forlorn.*
a·long' (ȧ·lŏng'; 74), *prep.* [AS. *andlang.*] Lengthwise of; parallel to the length or boundary of, and usually beside or on; progressively through. — *adv.* **1.** In a line with the length or side of something; as, cottages *along* by the lake. **2.** In a line, or with progressive motion; onward; forward; as, to pass *along* an inheritance. **3.** In company; together; as, liberty that exists *along* with order. **4.** In one's or another's company; with one; as, he carries a gun *along.*
a·long', *adv.* [AS. *gelang* owing to.] *Obs. exc. Dial.* In ***along of, along on,*** owing to.
a·long'shore' (-shōr'; 70), *adv.* Along the shore or coast.
a·long'side' (-sīd'; -sīd'; 2), *adv. & prep.* Along or by the side (of); side by side with; in association and keeping pace with.
a·loof' (ȧ·lōōf'), *adv.* [*a-* on + *loof,* prob. fr. D. *loef* luff, in *te loef* to windward.] At or from a distance, but within view. — *adj.* Removed in distance, or in interest or feeling; reserved. — **Syn.** See INDIFFERENT. — **a·loof'ly,** *adv.* — **a·loof'ness,** *n.*
al'o·pe'ci·a (ăl'ō·pē'shĭ·ȧ; -sĭ·ȧ), *n.* [L., fr. Gr. *alōpekia* mange of foxes, fr. *alōpēx* fox.] Loss of the hair; baldness.
a·loud' (ȧ·loud'), *adv.* Loudly; with the speaking voice.
a·low' (ȧ·lō'), *adv. Now Chiefly Naut.* Below.
a·low', a·lowe' (ȧ·lō'; ȧ·lou'), *adv. & adj. Dial.* Ablaze.
alp (ălp), *n.* [L. *Alpes* the Alps.] A very high mountain; specif. [*cap.*], one of the peaks in ***the Alps,*** a mountain system in south central Europe.
al·pac'a (ăl·păk'ȧ), *n.* [Sp. *alpaca, alpaco, paco,* fr. Quechua *alpaca, allpaca, paco.*] **1.** A llama with fine long woolly hair, domesticated in Peru. **2.** Wool of the alpaca, or a thin kind of cloth made of it.

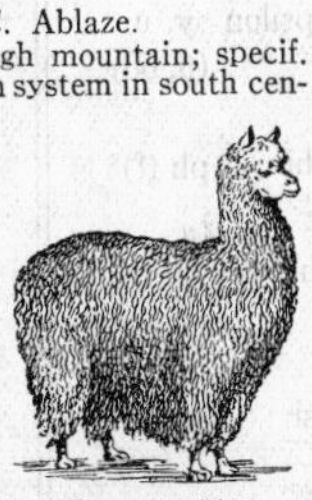

Alpaca. (1/40)

al'pen·glow' (ăl'pĕn·glō'), *n.* A reddish glow seen near sunset or sunrise on the summits of mountains.
al'pen·horn' (-hôrn'), **alp'horn'** (ălp'-), *n.* [G.] A straight wooden horn 7 to 15 feet long, with upturned, flaring mouth, used by the Swiss.
al'pen·stock' (ăl'pĕn·stŏk'), *n.* [G.] A long iron-pointed staff used in mountain climbing, esp. in the Alps.
al·pes'trine (ăl·pĕs'trĭn), *adj.* [L. *alpestris.*] **1.** Pertaining to alps or the Alps. **2.** *Bot.* Subalpine.
al'pha (ăl'fȧ), *n.* [L., fr. Gr.] **1.** The first letter (Α, α) of the Greek alphabet. See A. **2.** The first or beginning; formerly, the chief. **3.** A symbol used variously, as: **a** *Astron.* To designate the chief or brightest star of a constellation. **b** *Chem.* To indicate the position of substituting atoms or groups in certain compounds; as, α-naphthol.
al'pha and o·me'ga. The beginning and end. *Rev.* i. 8.
al'pha·bet (ăl'fȧ·bĕt *or, esp. Brit.,* -bĭt), *n.* [L. *alphabetum,* fr. Gr. *alpha* + *bēta,* the first two Greek letters.] **1.** The letters of a language arranged in the customary order; a series or set of letters or signs which form the elements of a written language; a collection of the signs for the sounds of a language. See *Table* on page 26; cf. DACTYLOLOGY, SEMAPHORE, *Illusts.* **2.** The rudiments; elements; A B C.
al'pha·bet'ic (ăl'fȧ·bĕt'ĭk), **al'pha·bet'i·cal** (-ĭ·kăl), *adj.* Pertaining to, making use of, or furnished with, the letters of an alphabet; following or according to the order of the alphabet. — **al'pha·bet'i·cal·ly,** *adv.*
al'pha·bet·ize (ăl'fȧ·bĕt·īz; -bĭt·īz), *v. t.* To arrange alphabetically; to furnish with an alphabet. — **Syn.** See ASSORT. — **al'pha·bet'i·za'tion** (-bĕt'ĭ·zā'shŭn; -ī·zā'-), *n.* — **al'pha·bet·iz'er** (-bĕt·īz'ẽr; -bĭt·īz'ẽr), *n.*
alpha particle. *Physics & Chem.* The nucleus of a helium atom, carrying a positive charge of 2 and ejected at high speed in certain radioactive disintegrations.
alpha privative. See A-, 5.
alpha ray. A stream of alpha particles.
alpha test. An intelligence test originally used in the United States Army in 1917–1918. It consists mostly of printed questions on number relations, verbal relations, judgment, and general information. Cf. BETA TEST.
Al·phe'us (ăl·fē'ŭs), *n.* See ARETHUSA.
alp'horn' (ălp'hôrn'), *n.* An alpenhorn.
Al'pine (ăl'pīn; -pĭn), *adj.* [L. *Alpinus.*] Of, pert. to, or like the Alps or [*not cap.*] an alp.
Al'pin·ism (ăl'pĭn·ĭz'm), *n.* Mountain climbing in the Alps. — **Al'pin·ist** (-ĭst), *n.*
al·read'y (ôl·rĕd'ĭ; 2), *adv.* [*all* + *ready.*] Prior to some specified time, either past, present, or future; previously.
al'right' (ôl'rīt'), *adv.* All right. The form *alright,* though often used, is not recognized by authorities as proper.
Al·sa'tian (ăl·sā'shăn), *adj.* Of or pertaining to Alsatia, that is: (1) Alsace, France; (2) Whitefriars, London, which was long a sanctuary for insolvent debtors and lawbreakers. — *n.* An inhabitant of Alsace or of Alsatia.
al'sike clo'ver, *or* **al'sike** (ăl'sĭk; -sīk), *n.* [From *Alsike,* Sweden.] See CLOVER, 1.
al'si·na'ceous (ăl'sĭ·nā'shŭs), *adj.* Of or relating to the family (Alsinaceae, order Chenopodiales) of chickweeds, having small perfect flowers and capsular fruits.
Al Si·rat' (ăl sĕ·rät'; *Ar.* ăs sĕ·rät'). [Ar. *al-sirāṭ* the road.] **a** In the Koran, the "right way" of religion. **b** In Moslem tradition, the bridge over the infernal fire to Paradise.
al'so (ôl'sō), *adv.* [From AS., lit., all so; hence, "quite so."] In addition; as well; besides; too.
al'so–ran' (-răn'), *n.* **a** A horse that finishes a race behind the money-winning contestants (usually, the first three). **b** Any contestant that fails to win a prize or points.
alt (ălt), *adj.* [It. *alto.*] *Music.* High in pitch; specif., in the first octave above the treble staff.
Al·ta'ic (ăl·tā'ĭk), **Al·ta'ian** (ăl·tā'yăn; -tī'ăn), *adj.* Pertaining to the Altai Mountains of Central Asia, or designating peoples or languages of the Ural-Altaic group, esp. those of the Turkic, Tungusic, and Mongolic subfamilies.
Al·ta'ir (ăl·tä'ĭr), *n.* [Ar. *al-ṭā'ir* the flier or bird.] The first magnitude star Alpha (α) Aquilae.
al'tar (ôl'tẽr), *n.* [AS., fr. L. *altare.*] **1.** A raised structure, or any structure or place, on which sacrifices are offered or incense is burned in worship of a deity, ancestor, etc. **2.** The Communion table.
al'tar·piece' (-pēs'), *n.* A work of art to decorate the space above and behind an altar.
alt·az'i·muth (ălt·ăz'ĭ·mŭth), *n.* [*alti*tude + *azimuth.*] *Astron.* An instrument for observing the azimuth and altitude of a celestial body.
al'ter (ôl'tẽr), *v. t.* [From F., fr. ML. *alterare,* fr. L. *alter* other.] **1.** To make different without changing into something else; to vary; to modify. **2.** *Dial., U.S.* To geld. — *v. i.* To become different; to vary. — **Syn.** See CHANGE, *v.* — **al'ter·a·bil'i·ty** (-ȧ·bĭl'ĭ·tĭ), *n.* — **al'ter·a·ble** (-ȧ·b'l), *adj.* — **al'ter·a·bly** (-blĭ), *adv.*
al'ter·ant (ôl'tẽr·ănt), *adj.* Altering; alterative. — *n.* Anything that alters; *Dyeing,* a reagent used to vary a shade.
al'ter·a'tion (-ā'shŭn), *n.* **1.** Act of altering, or state of being altered. **2.** The result of altering; a modification.
al'ter·a·tive (ôl'tẽr·ā'tĭv; -ȧ·tĭv), *adj.* Causing alteration; specif., *Med.,* gradually changing, or tending to change, a morbid state into one of health. — *n.* An alterative medicine or treatment.
al'ter·cate (ôl'tẽr·kāt; ăl'-), *v. i.* [L. *altercatus,* past part. of *altercari,* fr. *alter* another.] To contend in words; to dispute with zeal, heat, or anger; to wrangle.
al'ter·ca'tion (-kā'shŭn), *n.* A noisy or angry dispute; wrangle. — **Syn.** See QUARREL.
al'ter e'go (ăl'tẽr ē'gō; ĕg'ō). [L.] Literally, a second I; a second self; specif., a confidential friend; a bosom friend.
‖**al'ter i'dem** (ī'dĕm). [L.] A selfsame other one; a second self; alter ego.
al'tern (ôl'tẽrn; ăl'-), *adj.* [L. *alternus,* fr. *alter* another.] Acting by turns; alternate.
al'ter·nate (ôl'tẽr·nĭt; ăl'-; ôl·tûr'nĭt; ăl-), *adj.* [L. *alternatus,* past part. of *alternare* to alternate, fr. *alternus,* fr. *alter* other.] **1.** Occurring or succeeding by turns; by turns first one and then the other; hence, reciprocal. **2.** Every other; every second; as, read the *alternate* lines. **3.** *Bot.* **a** Distributed, as leaves, singly at different heights on the stem; not opposite. **b** Alternated with, or disposed at intervals between, other organs. — **Syn.** See INTERMITTENT. — *n.* A substitute; one designated to take the place of another, if necessary, in performing a duty. — **al'ter·nate·ly,** *adv.*
al'ter·nate (ôl'tẽr·nāt; ăl'-), *v. t.* To perform by turns, or in succession; to interchange regularly; to cause to alternate. — *v. i.* **1.** To happen, succeed, or act by turns, or in alternation; to follow reciprocally; as, the flood and ebb tides *alternate* with each other. **2.** To vary by turns. **3.** *Elec.* **a** To reverse periodically in direction of flow; — said of currents. **b** To produce, or be operated by, a current that alternates.
al'ter·nat'ing cur'rent (-nāt'ĭng). *Elec.* A periodic conduction current that reverses its direction at regular intervals. Abbr. *A.C.* or *a.c.*
al'ter·na'tion (-nā'shŭn), *n.* Act of alternating; alternate position, succession, performance, or occurrence.
alternation of generations. *Biol.* A method of reproduction in which the immediate descendants are unlike the parent, and organisms of a given type are produced only with every second generation, or after the lapse of several generations. In its simplest form, in certain in-

CHIEF FOREIGN ALPHABETS

In the first three columns (Hebrew, Arabic, and Greek) the Names of the Letters are shown, in the first four (including the Russian) the Roman Transliteration (used in the Etymologies in this dictionary) is given, and in all the columns, in parentheses, are the Merriam-Webster Pronunciation Symbols.

HEBREW[1]

Letter	Name	Transliteration	Pronunciation
א	aleph	'	(1)
ב	beth	b, bh	(b)
ג	gimel	g, gh	(g)
ד	daleth	d, dh	(d)
ה	he	h	(h)
ו	vau	w, v	(w)
ז	zayin	z	(z)
ח	cheth	ḥ	(ĸ)
ט	teth	ṭ	(t)
י	yodh	y	(y)
כ	caph	k, kh	(k)
ל	lamedh	l	(l)
מ	mem	m	(m)
נ	nun	n	(n)
ס	samekh	s	(s)
ע	'ayin	'	(1)
פ	pe	p, ph	(p)
צ	sadhe	ts	(s sharp)
ק	koph	q	(k)
ר	resh	r	(r)
שׂ	sin	ś	(s)
שׁ	shin	sh	(sh)
ת	tav	t, th	(t)

ARABIC[2]

Letter	Name	Transliteration	Pronunciation
ا	alif	'(3)	(4)
ب	bā'	b	(b)
ت	tā'	t	(t)
ث	thā'	th	(th)
ج	jīm	j	(j)
ح	ḥā'	ḥ	(h)
خ	khā'	kh	(ĸ)
د	dāl	d	(d)
ذ	dhāl	dh	(t͟h)
ر	rā'	r	(r)
ز	zāy	z	(z)
س	sīn	s	(s)
ش	shīn	sh	(sh)
ص	ṣād	ṣ	(s)
ض	ḍād	ḍ	(t͟h)
ط	ṭā'	ṭ	(t)
ظ	ẓā'	ẓ	(z)
ع	'ayn	'	(5)
غ	ghayn	gh	(ĸ)
ف	fā'	f	(f)
ق	qāf	q	(k)
ك	kāf	k	(k)
ل	lām	l	(l)
م	mīm	m	(m)
ن	nūn	n	(n)
ه	hā'	h	(h)
و	wāw	w	(w)
ي	yā'	y	(y)

GREEK[6]

Letter	Name	Transliteration (Pronunciation)
Α α	alpha	a (ä)
Β β	beta	b (b)
Γ γ	gamma	g (g)
Δ δ	delta	d (d)
Ε ε	epsilon	e (ĕ)
Ζ ζ	zeta	z (z)
Η η	eta	ē (ā)
Θ θ	theta	th (th)[7]
Ι ι	iota	i (ē)
Κ κ	kappa	k (k)
Λ λ	lambda	l (l)
Μ μ	mu	m (m)
Ν ν	nu	n (n)
Ξ ξ	xi	x (ks)
Ο ο	omicron	o (ŏ)
Π π	pi	p (p)
Ρ ρ	rho	r, rh (r)
Σ σ ς	sigma	s (s)
Τ τ	tau	t (t)
Υ υ	upsilon	y, u (ü, o͞o)
Φ φ	phi	ph (f)[8]
Χ χ	chi	ch (k, ĸ)[9]
Ψ ψ	psi	ps (ps)
Ω ω	omega	ō (ō)

RUSSIAN[10]

Letter	Transliteration	Pronunciation
А а	a	(ȧ)
Б б	b	(b, p)
В в	v	(v, f)
Г г	g	(g, k)
Д д	d	(d)
Е е	e	(yā, ā, yô, yō, yĕ, ĕ)
Ж ж	zh	(zh, sh)
З з	z	(z)
И и Й й	i, ĭ	(ē, y)
І і[10]	i	(ē)
К к	k	(k)
Л л	l	(l)
М м	m	(m)
Н н	n	(n)
О о	o	(ō, ŏ)
П п	p	(p)
Р р	r	(r)
С с	s	(s)
Т т	t	(t)
У у	u	(o͞o)
Ф ф	f	(f)
Х х	kh	(ĸ)
Ц ц	ts	(ts)
Ч ч	ch	(ch, tsh)
Ш ш	sh	(sh)
Щ щ	shch	(shch)
Ъ ъ[10]	*	
Ы ы	y	(wē, üē, ĭ)
Ь ь	e, —, '†	(ĕ, —)
Ѣ ѣ[10]	ye	(yĕ, ĕ)
Э э[10]	e	(ĕ)
Ю ю	yu	(yo͞o [ū])
Я я	ya	(yȧ, yā, ĕ)
Ѳ ѳ[10]	f	(f)
Ѵ ѵ[10]	y	(ē)

* marks nonpalatalization
† marks palatalization

GERMAN

Letter	Pronunciation
𝔄 𝔞	(ä)
𝔄̈ 𝔞̈	(â, ĕ)
𝔅 𝔟	(b, p)
ℭ 𝔠	(k, ts, s)
ℭ𝔥 𝔠𝔥	(ĸ)
𝔇 𝔡	(d, t)
𝔈 𝔢	(ā, ĕ)
𝔉 𝔣	(f)
𝔊 𝔤	(g, ĸ, k)
ℌ 𝔥	(h)
ℑ 𝔦	(ē, ĭ)
𝔍 𝔧	(y)
𝔎 𝔨	(k)
𝔏 𝔩	(l)
𝔐 𝔪	(m)
𝔑 𝔫	(n)
𝔒 𝔬	(ō, ŏ, ô)
𝔒̈ 𝔬̈	(û)
𝔓 𝔭	(p)
𝔔 𝔮	(k) Only in qu (pron. kv)
ℜ 𝔯	(r)
𝔖 𝔰 ſ	(z, s)
𝔖𝔠𝔥 𝔰𝔠𝔥	(sh)
𝔗 𝔱	(t)
𝔘 𝔲	(o͞o, o͝o)
𝔘̈ 𝔲̈	(ü)
𝔙 𝔳	(f, v)
𝔚 𝔴	(v)
𝔛 𝔵	(ks)
𝔜 𝔶	(ē, ĭ, ü)
ℨ 𝔷	(ts)

1. Hebrew *aleph* is a glottal stop (a slight catch in the voice); *'ayin* is a pharyngeal sound which has no English equivalent. 2. In the names of the Arabic letters *ā*, *ī*, and *ū* respectively are pronounced like *a* in *father*, *i* in *machine*, *u* in *rude*. 3. Represented by a macron when used as a sign of vowel length. 4. As a consonant, pronounced like Hebrew *aleph*. 5. Pronounced like Hebrew *'ayin*. 6. See ALPHA, BETA, GAMMA, etc., in Vocab. 7, 8, 9. In classic Greek, about like *th*, *ph*, *kh*, in *hothouse*, *uphill*, *inkhorn*. 10. In the reformed orthography, ѣ is replaced by е, э partly by е, і and ѵ by и, and ѳ by ф; and ъ is omitted at the ends of words.

vertebrate animals and certain plants, the generation reproducing sexually (*sexual generation*) is followed by one or more generations (*asexual generations*) which reproduce asexually (*asexual reproduction*), as by budding or fission.

al·ter′na·tive (ôl·tûr′nȧ·tĭv; ăl-), *adj.* **1.** Offering a choice of two (or, loosely, several) things; offering for choice a second thing or proposition. **2.** *Gram.* Implying that the terms it connects are to be taken not together, but one in place of the other; as, *or* is an *alternative* conjunction. — *n.* **1.** An opportunity for choice between two things, courses, or propositions, either of which may be chosen, but not both; also, a proposition to choose between two, so that if one is rejected the other must be taken; also, either of two things, courses, etc., so offered to one's choice. **2.** Loosely, a choice or offer of choice among more than two things or courses; hence, one of the things so offered. — **Syn.** See CHOICE. — **al·ter′na·tive·ly,** *adv.* — **al·ter′na·tive·ness,** *n.*

al′ter·na′tor (ôl′tẽr·nā′tẽr; ăl′-), *n.* *Elec.* An electric generator or dynamo for producing alternating currents.

al·the′a, al·thae′a (ăl·thē′ȧ), *n.* [L. *althaea*, fr. Gr. *althaia* marsh mallow.] A shrub (*Hibiscus syriacus*) of the mallow family, with showy flowers; the rose of Sharon.

alt′horn′ (ălt′hôrn′), *n.* Also **alto horn.** An instrument of the saxhorn family, used in bands where it often replaces the French horn.

al·though′, al·tho′ (ôl·thō′), *conj.* [*all* + *though.*] **a** Granting or supposing that; even if. **b** In spite of the fact that; though.

al′ti·graph (ăl′tĭ·grăf), *n.* An altimeter equipped with a recording mechanism.

al·tim′e·ter (ăl·tĭm′ē·tẽr; ăl′tĭ·mē′tẽr), *n.* [L. *altus* high + *-meter.*] Any instrument for taking altitudes, as, in navigation, etc., a quadrant or sextant, or, in aviation, an aneroid barometer marked in feet, yards, or meters. — **al·tim′e·try** (-trĭ), *n.*

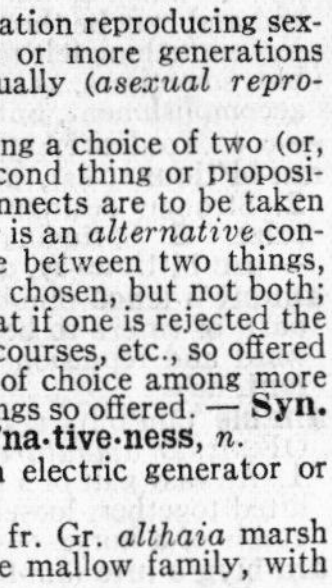

Airplane Altimeter, reading an indicated altitude of 500 feet. 1 Barometer scale, reading 29.92 inches of mercury; 2 Setting Knob.

al′ti·tude (ăl′tĭ·tūd), *n.* [L. *altitudo*, fr. *altus* high.] **1.** The vertical, or perpendicular, elevation of an object above a given level, esp. sea level. **2.** A position or region at a height; as, mountain *altitudes.* **3.** Elevation, or an exalted position, as regards rank, power, etc. **4.** *Astron.* The angular elevation of a celestial object above the horizon. **5.** *Geom.* The perpendicular distance from the base of a figure to the summit. — **Syn.** See HEIGHT. — **al′ti·tu′di·nal** (-tū′dĭ·năl), *adj.*

al′to (ăl′tō), *n.; pl.* -TOS (-tōz), -TI (*It.* äl′tē). [It., high, fr. L. *altus.*] *Music.* **a** The part sung by the highest male voices, or, now usually, by the lowest female voices, that is, the contralto. **b** An alto voice or singer. **c** A viola. **d** An althorn. — *adj.* Belonging to the alto or an alto; having the range of an alto; composed for or rendered by an alto.

al′to–cu′mu·lus (ăl′tō·kū′mū·lŭs), *n.* [L. *altus* high + *cumulus.*] *Meteorol.* A fleecy cloud formation consisting of large whitish globular cloudlets with shaded portions. See MACKEREL SKY; CLOUD, *Illust.*

al′to·geth′er (ôl′tōō·gĕth′ẽr), *adv.* [ME. *altogedere*, fr. *al* all + *togedere.* See TOGETHER.] Wholly; thoroughly; also, on the whole. — *n.* A whole; tout ensemble.

alto horn. See ALTHORN.

al′to–re·lie′vo (ăl′tō·rē·lē′vō), *n.; pl.* -VOS (-vōz). Also ‖**al′to–ri·lie′vo** (äl′tō·rē·lyā′vō), *n.; pl.* ALTI-RILIEVI (äl′tē·rē·lyā′vē). [It. *alto rilievo.*] See RELIEF, *n.*, 6.

al′to–stra′tus (ăl′tō·strā′tŭs), *n.* [L. *altus* high + *stratus.*] *Meteorol.* A cloud formation similar to cirro-stratus, but heavier and at a lower level. See CLOUD, *Illust.*

al′tru·ism (ăl′trōō·ĭz′m), *n.* [F. *altruisme*, fr. *autrui* other people, fr. *autre* another, fr. L. *alter.*] Regard for, and devotion to, the interests of others; — opposed to *egoism* and *selfishness.*

al′tru·ist (-ĭst), *n.* One who adheres to or practices altruism.

al′tru·is′tic (-ĭs′tĭk), *adj.* Pertaining to or given to altruism; unselfish. — **al′tru·is′ti·cal·ly** (-tĭ·kăl·ĭ), *adv.*

al′u·del (ăl′ū·dĕl), *n.* [F., fr. Sp., fr. Ar. *al-uthāl.*] *Chem.* One of the pear-shaped pots, open at both ends, fitted one above another to form a condenser in sublimation.

al′u·la (-lȧ), *n.; pl.* -LAE (-lē). [NL., dim. of L. *ala* wing.] *Zool.* The bastard wing of birds. — **al′u·lar** (-lẽr), *adj.*

al′um (ăl′ŭm), *n.* [OF., fr. L. *alumen* alum.] **1.** Potassium aluminum sulfate, $KAl(SO_4)_2.12H_2O$, called ***potash alum;*** also, ammonium aluminum sulfate, $NH_4Al(SO_4)_2.12H_2O$, called ***ammonia alum.*** The two, often called ***common alum,*** are used as an emetic and as an astringent and styptic. **2.** *Chem.* Any of a series of double salts isomorphous with potash alum; as, chrome alum (which see). **3.** Aluminum sulfate.

a·lu′mi·na (ȧ·lū′mĭ·nȧ), *n.* [L. *alumen, aluminis,* alum.] *Chem.* Aluminum oxide, Al_2O_3, occurring native as corundum, including sapphire, ruby, emery, etc.

a·lu′mi·nif′er·ous (-nĭf′ẽr·ŭs), *adj.* [L *alumen* alum + *-ferous.*] Containing alum or aluminum.

al′u·min′i·um (ăl′ū·mĭn′ĭ·ŭm), *n.* Aluminum (which see).

a·lu′mi·nize (ȧ·lū′mĭ·nīz), *v. t.* To treat or coat with aluminum.

a·lu′mi·no·ther′my (ȧ·lū′mĭ·nō·thûr′mĭ), *n.* [*aluminum* + Gr. *thermē* heat.] *Metal.* The production of great heat and strong chemical reduction by oxidizing finely divided aluminum with oxygen taken from another metal.

a·lu′mi·nous (ȧ·lū′mĭ·nŭs), *adj.* [L. *aluminosus*, fr. *alumen* alum.] Of or containing alum or aluminum.

a·lu′mi·num (ȧ·lū′mĭ·nŭm), **al′u·min′i·um** (ăl′ū·mĭn′ĭ·ŭm), *n.* [NL. See ALUMINA.] A bluish silver-white malleable metal, noted for its lightness (sp. gr., about 2.7) and resistance to oxidation. Symbol, *Al;* at. no., 13; at. wt., 26.98. It is the most abundant metallic element, but is found in nature only in combination. — *adj.* Belonging to or made of aluminum; containing aluminum.

☞ *Aluminum* is in common use in the United States; *aluminium* is used in Great Britain and by some chemists in the United States.

aluminum sulfate. A colorless salt, $Al_2(SO_4)_3$, made commercially by treating bauxite or kaolin with sulfuric acid, used in purifying water, sizing paper, tawing skins, etc.

a·lum′nus (ȧ·lŭm′nŭs), *n. masc.; pl.* -NI (-nī); **a·lum′na** (-nȧ), *fem.; pl.* -NAE (-nē). [L., a foster child, pupil, fr. *alere* to nourish.] A member of a school or college class that has been graduated.

al′um·root′ (ăl′ŭm·rōōt′; 85), *n.* **a** Any of several North American herbs (genus *Heuchera*) of the saxifrage family, esp. *H. americana,* whose root has astringent properties. **b** The crane's-bill *Geranium maculatum.* See GERANIUM, 1.

A·lun′dum (ȧ·lŭn′dŭm), *n.* A trade-mark applied to a material resembling corundum and made by fusing alumina in an electric furnace.

al′u·nite (ăl′ū·nīt), *n.* [F.] *Mineral.* A hydrous potassium aluminum sulfate, $K(AlO)_3(SO_4)_2.3H_2O$, occurring in crystalline or massive forms. H., 3.5–4.

al·ve′o·lar (ăl·vē′ō·lẽr; ăl′vē·ō·lẽr), *adj.* **1.** Of, pertaining to, or resembling alveoli. **2.** *Anat.* **a** Pertaining to the part of the jaws where the sockets for the teeth are situated; as, *alveolar* pyorrhea (see PYORRHEA). **b** Pertaining to the air cells of the lungs. **3.** *Phonet.* Formed with the tongue touching, or near, the alveoli.

al·ve′o·late (-lāt), **al·ve′o·lat′ed** (-lāt′ĕd; -ĭd), *adj.* Pitted like a honeycomb. — **al·ve′o·la′tion** (-lā′shŭn), *n.*

al·ve′o·lus (ăl·vē′ō·lŭs), *n.; pl.* -LI (-lī). [L., dim. of *alveus* a hollow.] **1.** *Anat. & Zool.* A small cavity or pit, as a socket for a tooth, an air cell of the lungs, an acinus of a compound gland, a cell or compartment of a honeycomb, etc. **2.** *pl. Phonet.* The ridge just above and behind the upper front teeth.

al′vine (ăl′vĭn; -vīn), *adj.* [L. *alvus* belly.] *Med.* Of or pertaining to the belly or the intestines.

al′way (ôl′wā; *archaic* ôl′wā′), *adv. Archaic.* Always.

al′ways (ôl′wāz; -wĭz), *adv.* [*all* + *way.*] At all times; invariably; uniformly; ever; perpetually; on every occasion.

a·lys′sum (ȧ·lĭs′ŭm), *n.* [NL., fr. Gr. *alysson*, name of a plant.] **1.** *Bot.* Any of a genus (*Alyssum*) of Old World herbs of the mustard family (Brassicaceae), having small yellow racemose flowers. **2.** Sweet alyssum.

AM, A.M., a–m, a.m. (ā′ĕm′). Amplitude modulation. See FREQUENCY MODULATION.

am (ăm; 4). [AS. *am, eom.*] See BE.

am′a·da·vat′ (ăm′ȧ·dȧ·văt′), *n.* [From *Ahmadabad*, India.] A small Indian songbird (*Sporaeginthus amandava*) often caged and kept for fighting.

am′a·dou (ăm′ȧ·dōō), *n.* [F.] = PUNK, *n.*, 2.

a′mah (ä′mȧ; ăm′ȧ), *n.* [Anglo-Ind., fr. Pg. *ama.*] In the Orient, a nurse; esp., a wet nurse; also, any female servant.

a·main′ (ȧ·mān′), *adv.* [*a-* on + *main* power.] **1.** With might. **2.** At full speed; also, in great haste. **3.** Greatly.

Am′a·lek·ite (ăm′ȧ·lĕk·īt; ȧ·măl′ĕ·kīt), *n.* [Heb. *'Amālēqī.*] One of a marauding Bedouin tribe of Syria who, according to Genesis xxxvi. 12, were descended from Esau.

a·mal′gam (ȧ·măl′găm), *n.* [Through F. & ML. fr. Ar. *al-malgham*, fr. Gr. *malagma* poultice, fr. *malassein* to soften, fr. *malakos* soft.] **1.** An alloy of mercury with another metal or metals; specif., a native alloy with silver. Amalgams are either solid or liquid according to the proportion of mercury present. They are used in tooth cements, in silvering mirrors, etc. **2.** A compound or union of different things.

a·mal′gam·ate (ȧ·măl′gȧ·māt), *v. t. & i.* **1.** To unite in an amalgam. **2.** To combine into a uniform whole, as two races. — **Syn.** See MIX. — **a·mal′gam·a·ble,** *adj.*

a·mal′gam·a′tion (ȧ·măl′gȧ·mā′shŭn), *n.* **1.** Act or process of amalgamating, or state of being amalgamated. **2.** The result of amalgamating. **3.** A merger, as of societies or corporations. See MERGER **b.** — **a·mal′gam·a′tive** (-măl′gȧ·mā′tĭv), *adj.*

Am′al·thae′a, Am′al·the′a (ăm′ăl·thē′ȧ), *n.* [L. *Amalthea*, fr. Gr. *Amaltheia.*] *Gr. & Rom. Myth.* The nurse of Zeus, described as a goat. The *horn of Amalthaea* was one of the goat's horns, which became filled with whatever its possessor wished, hence called the ***horn of plenty,*** or ***cornucopia.***

am′a·ni′ta (ăm′ȧ·nī′tȧ), *n.* [NL., fr. Gr. *amanitai* a sort of fungus.] Any of various white-spored fungi (genus *Amanita*), mostly very poisonous, as the fly agaric and the death cup (see these terms).

a·man′u·en′sis (ȧ·măn′ū·ĕn′sĭs), *n.; pl.* -SES (-sēz). [L., fr. *a, ab* + *manus* hand.] One employed to write from dictation, or to copy manuscript; a secretary.

am′a·ranth (ăm′ȧ·rănth), *n.* [From L., fr. Gr. *amarantos* amaranth, unfading, fr. *a-* not + *marainein* to wither.] **1.** *Poetic.* An imaginary unfading flower. **2.** Any of a large genus (*Amaranthus*), type of a family (Amaranthaceae, the amaranth family) of plants, including pigweeds, and also many species cultivated for their green, purple, or crimson flowers, as prince's-feather and love-lies-bleeding. **3.** A deep purple; also, a purplish pink.

am′a·ran′thine (-răn′thĭn; -thīn), *adj.* **1.** Of or pertaining to amaranth. **2.** Unfading; undying. **3.** Purplish.

am′a·relle′ (ăm′ȧ·rĕl′), *n.* A cultivated sour cherry of any of several types distinguished from the morellos by their colorless juice. See CHERRY, 1.

Am′a·ryl′lis (-rĭl′ĭs), *n.* [L., in sense 1, fr. Gr. *Amaryllis, -idos.*] **1.** In pastorals, a shepherdess sweetheart. **2.** [*not cap.*] Any of several plants of a large family (Amaryllidaceae, the amaryllis family, order Liliales) having perfect, often handsome, flowers, including the narcissus and agave; specif., the belladonna lily (*Amaryllis belladonna*). — **am′a·ryl′li·da′ceous** (-rĭl′ĭ·dā′shŭs), *adj.*

a·mass′ (ȧ·măs′), *v. t.* [F. *amasser*, fr. L. *ad* to + *massare* to lump, fr. L. *massa* mass.] To collect into a mass or heap; to gather a great quantity of; now, esp., to collect for oneself, as a fortune. — **Syn.** Accumulate, hoard. — **a·mass′a·ble,** *adj.* — **a·mass′er,** *n.* — **a·mass′ment,** *n.*

a·mate′ (ȧ·māt′), *v. t.* [OF.] *Archaic.* To daunt.

am′a·teur′ (ăm′ȧ·tûr′; ăm′ȧ·tūr; ăm′ȧ·tūr), *n.* [F., fr. L. *amator* lover, fr. *amare* to love.] **1.** One who cultivates a particular pursuit, study, or science, from taste, without pursuing it professionally; also, a dabbler. **2.** In sports and esp. athletics, one who is not rated as a professional.

Syn. **Amateur, dilettante, dabbler, tyro** (*or* **tiro**) mean one who follows a pursuit without proficiency or a professional purpose. Both **amateur** and **dilettante** originally implied a taste or liking for something rather than an expert knowledge of it. *Amateur* now often refers to one practicing an art without mastery of its essentials. In sports, however, the word does not suggest lack of skill but the status of one who plays without remuneration. *Dilettante,* on the other hand, now often implies elegant trifling in the arts, but many still use the term to name the lover of art rather than its skilled practitioner. **Dabbler** always implies desultory habits of work and lack of persistence; **tyro** implies inexperience and audacity with resulting incompetence or crudeness.

— (ăm′ȧ·tûr′; ăm′ȧ·tûr; ăm′ȧ·tūr; 2), *adj.* Of or of the status of an amateur; engaged in or performed by amateurs. — **am′a·teur′ish** (-ĭsh), *adj.* — **am′a·teur′ish·ly,** *adv.* — **am′a·teur′ish·ness,** *n.* — **am′a·teur′ism** (-ĭz′m), *n.* — **am′a·teur′ship,** *n.*

A·ma′ti (ä·mä′tē), *n.* A violin made by a member of the Amati family of Cremona (16th and 17th centuries).

am′a·tive (ăm′ȧ·tĭv), *adj.* [L. *amatus,* past part. of *amare* to love.] Disposed to love or to sexual passion. — **am′a·tive·ly,** *adv.* — **am′a·tive·ness,** *n.*

am′a·tol (ăm′ȧ·tōl; -tŏl), *n.* [*ammonia* + *tol*uene.] An explosive consisting of ammonium nitrate and trinitrotoluene.

am′a·to′ry (ăm′ȧ·tō′rĭ *or, esp. Brit.,* -tẽr·ĭ), **am′a·to′ri·al** (-tō′rĭ·ăl; 70), *adj.* [L. *amatorius.*] Pertaining to, producing, or expressing, sexual love. — **Syn.** Amorous, erotic.

am′au·ro′sis (ăm′ô·rō′sĭs), *n.* [NL., fr. Gr. *amaurōsis,* fr. *amauros* dark, dim.] *Med.* Decay of sight occurring without perceptible external change. — **am′au·rot′ic** (-rŏt′ĭk), *adj.*

‖**a max′i·mis ad mi′ni·ma** (ā măk′sĭ·mĭs ăd mĭn′ĭ·mȧ). [L.] From the greatest to the least.

a·maze′ (ȧ·māz′), *v. t.* [AS. *āmasian.* See MAZE.] **1.** *Obs.* To bewilder; perplex. *Shak.* **2.** To overwhelm with bewildered wonder; astound; astonish greatly. — **Syn.** See SURPRISE. — *n.* Bewilderment arising from fear, surprise, or wonder. — **a·mazed′** (ȧ·māzd′), *adj.* — **a·maz′ed·ly** (ȧ·māz′ĕd·lĭ), *adv.* — **a·maz′ed·ness,** *n.* — **a·maz′ing,** *adj.* — **a·maz′ing·ly,** *adv.*

a·maze′ment (-mĕnt), *n.* **1.** *Obs.* Mental stupefaction; bewilderment; consternation. **2.** State of being amazed; overwhelming wonder.

Am′a·zon (ăm′ȧ·zŏn; -zŭn), *n.* [L., fr. Gr. *Amazōn.*] **1.** *Gr. Myth.* A member of a race or nation of female warriors with whom the Greeks repeatedly warred. **2.** [*not cap.*] A tall, strong, masculine woman; a virago. **3.** Also **Amazon ant.** An ant of a genus (*Polyergus*) of slave-making ants of Europe and America.

Am′a·zo′ni·an (-zō′nĭ·ăn), *adj.* **1.** Pertaining to, like, or befitting an Amazon; hence, of women, masculine; warlike. **2.** Of or pertaining to the river Amazon or its valley.

am′a·zon·ite (ăm′ȧ·zŭn·īt), *n.* [From the river *Amazon.*] An apple-green or verdigris-green variety of microcline.

am′bage (ăm′bĭj), *n.; pl.* AMBAGES (ăm′bĭ·jĕz; -jĭz; *L.* ăm·bā′jēz). [OF., fr. L. *ambages,* fr. *ambi-, amb-,* about + *agere* to drive.] **1.** Formerly, an ambiguity or circumlocution; *pl.,* winding paths. **2.** Hence, *pl.,* roundabout or circuitous proceedings or ways. — **am·ba′gious** (ăm·bā′jŭs), *adj.* — **am·ba′gious·ly,** *adv.* — **am·ba′gious·ness,** *n.*

am·ba′ry, am·ba′ri (ăm·bä′rē), *n.* [Hind. *ambārā, ambārī.*] A valuable East Indian fiber plant (*Hibiscus cannabinus*); also, its fiber, used in ropemaking.

am·bas′sa·dor (ăm·băs′ȧ·dẽr), **em·bas′sa·dor** (ĕm-), *n.* [F. *ambassadeur,* fr. It. *ambasciatore,* fr. Pr. *ambaisador,* fr. *ambaisada* embassy.] **1.** An envoy or minister of state; now usually only **ambassador extraordinary,** a minister of high rank sent on a mission by one sovereign or state to another. **2.** A minister of the highest rank accredited to a foreign government or sovereign as the official representative of his own government or sovereign; — formerly called **ambassador ordinary. 3.** An official messenger. — **am·bas′sa·do′ri·al** (-dō′rĭ·ăl; 70), *adj.* — **am·bas′sa·dor·ship′,** *n.*

am·bas′sa·dress (-drĕs; 30), *n.* A female ambassador; also, the wife of an ambassador.

am′bas·sage (ăm′bȧ·sĭj), **am′bas·sy** (-sĭ). Vars. of EMBASSAGE, EMBASSY.

am′ber (ăm′bẽr), *n.* [OF. *ambre,* fr. Ar. *'anbar* ambergris.] **1.** *Mineral.* A yellowish to brownish translucent fossil resin. It takes a fine polish, and by friction becomes strongly electric. It is used for pipe mouthpieces, beads, etc., and as a basis for a fine varnish. **2.** A color, reddish-yellow in hue, of medium saturation and high brilliance. See COLOR. — *adj.* Made of or resembling amber; amber-colored.

am′ber·gris (-grēs; -grĭs), *n.* [F. *ambre gris* gray amber.] A waxy substance found floating in tropical seas, and as a morbid secretion in the sperm whale, whence it is all believed to come. It is valued in perfumery.

am′ber·oid (ăm′bẽr·oid), **am′broid** (ăm′broid), *n.* Any amberlike material made from small pieces of amber, or other resins, united by heat and pressure.

am′bi- (ăm′bĭ-). [L. *ambo* both.] A combining form meaning *both,* as in **am′bi·lat′er·al,** *adj.*

‖**am′bi·ance′** (äɴ′byäɴs′), *n.* Environment; surroundings; esp., in decorative art, the totality of motives, patterns, or accessories surrounding and enhancing the central motif or design.

am′bi·dex′ter (ăm′bĭ·dĕk′stẽr), *adj.* [ML., fr. L. *ambo* both + *dexter* right, *dextra* (sc. *manus*) the right hand.] Using both hands with equal ease; hence, belonging to both sides; double-dealing. — *n.* An ambidextrous person; a double-dealer. — **am′bi·dex·ter′i·ty** (-dĕks-tĕr′ĭ·tĭ), *n.*

am′bi·dex′trous (-strŭs), *adj.* **1.** Using both hands with equal ease. **2.** Unusually dexterous; versatile. **3.** Practicing or siding with both parties; double-dealing. — **am′bi·dex′trous·ly,** *adv.* — **am′bi·dex′trous·ness,** *n.*

am′bi·ent (ăm′bĭ·ĕnt), *adj.* [L. *ambiens,* pres. part. of *ambire* to go around, fr. *amb-* around + *ire* to go.] **1.** Moving round. **2.** Encompassing on all sides.

am′bi·gu′i·ty (ăm′bĭ·gū′ĭ·tĭ), *n.; pl.* -TIES (-tĭz). [L. *ambiguitas.*] Ambiguousness in meaning; also, an ambiguous word or expression.

am·big′u·ous (ăm·bĭg′ū·ŭs), *adj.* [L. *ambiguus,* fr. *ambigere* to wander about, waver, fr. *amb-* around + *agere* to drive.] **1.** Doubtful or uncertain, esp. from obscurity or indistinctness; also, inexplicable. **2.** Capable of being understood in two or more possible senses; equivocal. — **Syn.** See OBSCURE. — **am·big′u·ous·ly,** *adv.* — **am·big′u·ous·ness,** *n.*

am′bit (ăm′bĭt), *n.* [L. *ambitus* circuit, fr. *ambire* to go around.] **1.** Circuit or compass. **2.** Bounds or limits.

am′bi·tend′en·cy (ăm′bĭ·tĕn′dĕn·sĭ), *n.* [*ambi-* + *tendency.*] *Psychol.* The state of having along with each tendency a countertendency.

am·bi′tion (ăm·bĭsh′ŭn), *n.* [F., fr. L. *ambitio* a going around (for votes), fr. *ambire.* See AMBIENT.] An eager or inordinate desire for preferment, honor, superiority, power, or attainment; also, an object of such desire.

Syn. Ambition, aspiration, pretension mean strong desire for advancement. **Ambition** suggests personal advancement or preferment as its end and may be thought of as good or bad; **aspiration** implies as its object something felt to be above one, and is often thought of as uplifting but, sometimes, as presumptuous; **pretension** suggests ardent desire for accomplishment, but little assurance of innate capacity.

— *v. t.* To desire ambitiously or covetously.

am·bi′tious (-ŭs), *adj.* **1.** Possessing, or controlled by, ambition. **2.** Strongly desirous; as, *ambitious* of fame or of winning or to win a prize. **3.** Springing from, or indicating, ambition; also, pretentious. — **am·bi′tious·ly,** *adv.* — **am·bi′tious·ness,** *n.*

am·biv′a·lence (ăm·bĭv′ȧ·lĕns), *n.* [*ambi-* + L. *valens, -entis,* pres. part. of *valere* to be strong, be worth.] Simultaneous attraction toward and repulsion from an object, person, or action. — **am·biv′a·lent,** *adj.*

am′ble (ăm′b'l), *v. i.;* AM′BLED (-b'ld); AM′BLING (-blĭng). [From OF., fr. L. *ambulare* to walk, go.] To go at an amble. — *n.* [F.] **1.** An easy gait of a horse in which the legs of each side alternately are lifted together; loosely, an easy gait. **2.** A movement suggesting the amble of a horse. — **am′bler** (-blẽr), *n.*

am·blyg′o·nite (ăm·blĭg′ō·nīt), *n.* [Gr. *amblys* obtuse + *gōnia* angle + *-ite;* — from its obtuse angle of cleavage.] *Mineral.* A mineral, technically a lithium aluminum fluophosphate, $Li(AlF)PO_4$, found commonly in white cleavable masses.

am′bly·o′pi·a (ăm′blĭ·ō′pĭ·ȧ), *n.* [NL., fr. Gr. *amblyōpia,* fr. *amblys* blunt, dim + *ōps* eye.] *Med.* Incipient amaurosis. — **am′bly·op′ic** (-ŏp′ĭk), *adj.*

am′bo (ăm′bō), *n.; pl.* AMBOS (-bōz). [ML., fr. Gr. *ambōn.*] A large pulpit and reading desk, in early Christian churches.

Am·boi′na wood (ăm·boi′nȧ). The mottled and curly wood of a tree (*Lingoum indicum*) of the pea family of India and Malaysia.

am′broid. Var. of AMBEROID.

am·bro′si·a (ăm·brō′zhĭ·ȧ; -zĭ·ȧ; 103), *n.* [L., fr. Gr. *ambrosia,* fr. *ambrotos* immortal, fr. *a-* not + *brotos* mortal.] **1.** *Gr. & Rom. Myth.* The substance which, with nectar, formed the food and drink of the gods, making immortal those who partook of it. **2.** Anything exquisitely gratifying in taste or scent. **3.** Ragweed. **4.** Beebread.

am·bro′si·a′ceous (-zĭ·ā′shŭs), *adj.* *Bot.* Belonging to the ragweed family. See RAGWEED.

am·bro′si·al (ăm·brō′zhĭ·ăl; -zĭ·ăl), *adj.* **1.** Belonging to or worthy of the gods; divine. **2.** Delighting the senses of taste or smell. — **am·bro′si·al·ly,** *adv.*

am·bro′si·an (-zhĭ·ăn; -zĭ·ăn), *adj.* Ambrosial.

Am·bro′si·an (-zhĭ·ăn; -zĭ·ăn), *adj* Of or pertaining, or ascribed, to St. Ambrose; as, the **Ambrosian chant,** the plain song of the Milanese liturgy, including antiphonal Psalm chants.

am′bro·type (ăm′brō·tīp), *n.* [Gr. *ambrotos* immortal + *-type.*] An early type of photograph made on glass by backing a thin negative with a black surface.

am′bry (ăm′brĭ), *n.; pl.* -BRIES (-brĭz). [From OF., fr. L. *armarium* chest, cupboard, orig. for arms, fr. L. *arma* arms.] A repository; specif., a cupboard or pantry.

ambs′ace′ (āmz′ās′; ămz′-), *n.* [OF. *ambes* both (fr. L. *ambo*) + *as* ace.] Double aces, the lowest throw at dice; hence, bad luck; the least thing or particle possible.

am′bu·la′crum (ăm′bū·lā′krŭm), *n.; pl.* -LACRA (-krȧ). [L., an alley or covered way.] *Zool.* One of the radial areas of echinoderms, along which run the principal nerves, blood vessels, and water tubes. — **am′bu·la′cral** (-krăl), *adj.*

am′bu·lance (ăm′bū·lăns), *n.* [F., fr. *hôpital ambulant,* fr. L. *ambulare* to walk.] **1.** A mobile hospital following an army in the field. **2.** A vehicle equipped for transporting those who are wounded, injured, or sick.

ambulance chaser. A person employed by a lawyer to solicit the damage-suit business of the victim of an accident; also, a lawyer employing such a person. *Colloq., U. S.*

am′bu·lant (ăm′bū·lănt), *adj.* Moving about; ambulatory.

am′bu·late (-lāt), *v. i.* [L. *ambulare* to walk.] To walk; to move about. — **am′bu·la′tion** (-lā′shŭn), *n.*

am′bu·la·to′ry (ăm′bū·lȧ·tō′rĭ *or, esp. Brit.,* -tẽr·ĭ), *adj.* **1.** Of or pertaining to walking; adapted to walking; occurring while walking. **2.** Moving from place to place; movable. **3.** *Law.* Alterable. **4.** *Med.* Able to walk about; not bedridden. — *n.; pl.* -RIES (-rĭz). *Arch.* A sheltered place to walk in.

am′bus·cade′ (ăm′bŭs·kād′), *n.* [F. *embuscade,* fr. *embusquer* to ambush.] An ambush; specif., *Mil.,* a body of troops lying in ambush; also, the place of ambush. — *v. t. & i.* To post or wait in an ambuscade. — **am′bus·cad′er** (-kād′ẽr), *n.*

am′bus·ca′do (-kā′dō), *n.* Ambuscade. *Archaic.*

am′bush (ăm′bo͝osh), *n.* [OF. *embusche,* fr. the verb. See AMBUSH, *v.*] **1.** A post or tactical trap of troops in wait, concealed for the purpose of attacking an enemy by surprise; hence, a device to entrap. **2.** The troops so posted. — *v. t.* [OF. *embuissier, embuschier,* to go into the woods, fr. *busche,* ult. of Teut. origin.] **1.** To station in ambush. **2.** To attack from an ambush; to waylay. — *v. i.* To lie in ambush. — **am′bush·er,** *n.* — **am′bush·ment,** *n.*

a·me′ba, a·me′bic, etc. Vars. of AMOEBA, AMOEBIC, etc.

‖**âme dam′née′** (äm′ dä′nā′). [F.] A damned, or lost, soul; hence, a devoted tool of another person.

a·meer′. Var. of AMIR.

a·mel′io·rant (ȧ·mēl′yō·rănt), *n.* That which ameliorates.

a·mel′io·rate (-rāt), *v. t. & i.* [L. *ad* to + *meliorare* to make better.] To make or grow better; to improve; to meliorate. — **Syn.** See IMPROVE. — **a·mel′io·ra·ble** (-rȧ·b'l), *adj.* — **a·mel′io·ra′tor** (-rā′tẽr), *n.*

a·mel′io·ra′tion (-rā′shŭn), *n.* **1.** Act of ameliorating or state of being ameliorated; improvement. **2.** *Can. Law.* A betterment. — **a·mel′io·ra′tive** (-mēl′yō·rā′tĭv; -rȧ·tĭv), *adj.*

a′men′ (ā′mĕn′; *often* ä′mĕn′ — *always in singing*), *interj.* [AS., fr. L. *amen,* fr. Gr. *amēn,* fr. Heb. *āmēn* certainly, truly.] So be it; — used in solemn ratification, as of a creed or prayer, or colloquially as an expression of approval. — (ā′mĕn′), *n.* The word *amen* or its use. — (ā′mĕn′), *adv.* Verily.

A′men (ä′mĕn), **A′mon** (ä′mŏn), *n.* [Egypt. *Āmen,* prop., the hidden.] *Egypt. Relig.* The local deity of Thebes, ram-headed god of life and reproduction, later as **A′men–Ra′** (-rä′) united with the sun-god to become a supreme deity, with the other gods as his members or parts.

a·me′na·ble (ȧ·mē′nȧ·b'l; -mĕn′ȧ·b'l), *adj.* [F. *amener* to lead up, bring, fr. *à* (L. *ad*) + *mener* to lead, fr. LL. *minare* to drive (animals), fr. L. *minari* to threaten, to project.] **1.** Liable to be brought to account or judgment; answerable. **2.** Capable of submission for test; as, *amenable* to the laws of a science. **3.** Readily brought to yield or submit; as, he is *amenable* to persuasion. — **Syn.** See RESPONSIBLE: OBEDIENT. — **a·me'na·bil'i·ty** (-bĭl'ĭ·tĭ), *n.* — **a·me'na·ble·ness,** *n.* — **a·me'na·bly,** *adv.*

a'men' cor'ner (ā'mĕn'). **1.** In a church, a conspicuous corner occupied by fervent worshipers. **2.** Any room or corner used for confidential political discussion.

a·mend' (ȧ·mĕnd'), *v. t.* [OF. *amender,* fr. L. *emendare,* fr. *e* (*ex*) out + *mendum, menda,* fault.] **1.** To free from faults; correct; specif., to emend (a text); formerly, to repair or restore. **2.** To change or modify in any way for the better; to improve; to better; hence, to change or alter in any way, esp. in phraseology; as, to *amend* a statement. **3.** Specif., in parliamentary procedure, to alter (as a bill) formally by some addition or modification. — *v. i.* To reform oneself. — **Syn.** See CORRECT. — **a·mend'a·ble,** *adj.* — **a·mend'er,** *n.*

a·mend'a·to'ry (ȧ·mĕn'dȧ·tō'rĭ *or, esp. Brit.,* -tẽr·ĭ), *adj.* Corrective.

a'mende' ho'no'ra'ble (ȧ'mäNd' ô'nô'rȧ'bl'; *formerly* ȧ·mĕnd' ŏn'ẽr·ȧ·b'l). [F.] A formal and humiliating acknowledgment of offense and apology made to another, originally in reparation of his injured honor.

a·mend'ment (ȧ·mĕnd'mĕnt), *n.* **1.** An alteration or change, esp. for the better; correction of a fault or faults; reformation of life by quitting vices. **2.** In parliamentary or legislative procedure, any alteration made or proposed to be made in a bill, motion, or constitution, or clause thereof, by adding, changing, substituting, or omitting.

a·mends' (ȧ·mĕndz'), *n. sing. & pl.* [OF. *amendes,* pl. of *amende.*] **1.** Compensation for a loss or injury; recompense; reparation; as, full *amends* was made. **2.** *Obs.* Improvement in health.

a·men'i·ty (ȧ·mĕn'ĭ·tĭ; ȧ·mē'nĭ·tĭ), *n.; pl.* -TIES (-tĭz). [F. *aménité,* fr. L. *amoenitas,* fr. *amoenus* pleasant.] **1.** Quality of being pleasant or agreeable; civility; suavity. **2.** An act, pursuit, civility, feature, or the like, expressive of, or conducive to, pleasantness or smoothness of social intercourse; — esp. *pl.* **3.** Attractiveness and value of real estate for purely residential purposes or of any structure as constituting a home; hence, a feature conducive to such attractiveness and value.

a·men'or·rhe'a, a·men'or·rhoe'a (ā·mĕn'ō·rē'ȧ), *n.* [NL., fr. *a-* not + Gr. *mēn* month + *rhein* to flow.] *Med.* Abnormal absence or suppression of the menstrual discharge.

‖**a men'sa et tho'ro** (ā mĕn'sȧ ĕt thō'rō). Also, formerly, **a men'sa et to'ro** (tō'rō). [L.] Literally, from table and bed; from bed and board; — used to designate a kind of divorce which discharges husband and wife from the duty of living together.

am'ent (ăm'ĕnt; ā'mĕnt), *n.* Also **a·men'tum** (ȧ·mĕn'tŭm); *pl.* AMENTA (-tȧ). [L. *amentum* thong, strap.] *Bot.* A spikelike flower cluster in which the flowers have no petals but grow in close circular rows on a slender stalk, as in the alder, willow, birch, and poplar; — commonly called *catkin.* See INFLORESCENCE, *Illust.* — **am'en·ta'ceous** (ăm'ĕn·tā'shŭs), *adj.* — **a·men'ti·form** (ȧ·mĕn'tĭ·fôrm), *adj.*

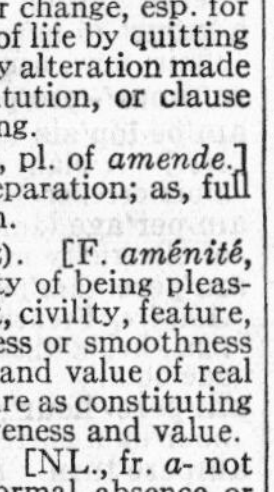

Aments. *a, a, a* Staminate Aments; *b* Pistillate Ament.

a·men'ti·a (ā·mĕn'shĭ·ȧ), *n.* [L.] **1.** Mental deficiency. **2.** Temporary confusional insanity, sometimes a sequel of infectious fevers.

am'en·tif'er·ous (ăm'ĕn·tĭf'ẽr·ŭs), *adj.* [L. *amentum* + *-ferous.*] *Bot.* Bearing aments.

a·merce' (ȧ·mûrs'), *v. t.;* A·MERCED' (ȧ·mûrst'); A·MERC'ING (-mûr'sĭng). [AF. *amercier,* fr. *a merci* at the mercy of.] **1.** To punish by a pecuniary penalty the amount of which is left to the discretion of the court. **2.** To punish; mulct. — **a·merce'a·ble,** *adj.* — **a·merce'ment,** *n.* — **a·merc'er,** *n.*

A·mer'i·can (ȧ·mĕr'ĭ·kăn), *adj.* [After *Americus* Vespucius.] **1.** Of or pertaining to America or the United States. **2.** *Ethnol.* Designating that division of mankind which comprises the Indians of North and South America. — *n.* **a** An American aborigine. **b** Any native or inhabitant of America. **c** A citizen of the United States.

A·mer'i·ca'na (-kā'nȧ; -kä'nȧ; -kăn'ȧ), *n. pl.* [*America* + *-ana.*] A collection of literary, ethnographic, historical, or other similar facts, documents, etc., relating to America.

American Beauty. A hybrid perpetual rose with deep-pink to crimson flowers. It is the floral emblem of the District of Columbia.

American cheese. Cheddar cheese made in America.

American cowslip. See SHOOTING STAR.

American football. See FOOTBALL, 2.

A·mer'i·can·ism (ȧ·mĕr'ĭ·kăn·ĭz'm), *n.* **1.** Attachment or loyalty to the United States, its traditions, interests, or ideals. **2.** An American custom or characteristic. **3.** A word or phrase peculiar to English as developed in the United States.

American ivy. See VIRGINIA CREEPER.

A·mer'i·can·ize (-īz), *v. t. & i.* To assimilate to the Americans in customs, speech, etc.; to bring into conformity with, or to develop, American methods or characteristics. — **-i·za'tion** (-ĭ·zā'shŭn; -ī·zā'-), *n.*

American Legion. A patriotic organization of naval and military veterans, both male and female, of the two world wars, incorporated by act of Congress, Sept. 16, 1919 (amended July 9, 1946).

American party. See KNOW-NOTHING, 2.

American pitcher-plant family. See SARRACENIA.

American plan. In hotels, a plan by which guests pay for both rooms and board by the day, week, or other period; — contrasted with *European plan.*

American Revised Version, American Standard Version. See BIBLE.

American Revolution. See REVOLUTION, 5.

American sable. See MARTEN, 1.

am'er·i'ci·um (ăm'ẽr·ĭsh'ĭ·ŭm; -ĭs'ĭ·ŭm), *n.* [NL., fr. the two *Americas* + *-ium.*] A metallic element artificially produced by bombardment of uranium with high-energy helium ions in the cyclotron. Symbol, *Am;* at. no., 95.

Am'er·ind' (ăm'ẽr·ĭnd'), *n.* [*American* + *Indian.*] An American Indian or Eskimo. — **Am'er·in'di·an** (-ĭn'dĭ·ăn), **Am'er·in'dic** (-dĭk), *adj.*

ames'ace'. Var. of AMBSACE.

am'e·thyst (ăm'ē·thĭst), *n.* [From OF., fr. L. *amethystus,* fr. Gr. *amethystos* a remedy for drunkenness, the amethyst, supposed to have this power, fr. *a-* not + *methyein* to be drunken.] **1.** *Mineral.* **a** A clear purple or bluish-violet variety of crystallized quartz, much used as a jeweler's stone. **b** In full ***Oriental amethyst.*** Purple sapphire (see SAPPHIRE, 1 **b**). **2.** A color, blue-red in hue, of medium saturation and low brilliance. See COLOR. — **am'e·thys'tine** (-thĭs'tĭn; -tīn), *adj.*

am'e·tro'pi·a (ăm'ē·trō'pĭ·ȧ), *n.* [NL., fr. Gr. *ametros* irregular + *-opia.*] *Med.* Abnormal refractive condition of the eye, as in myopia, astigmatism, etc. — **am'e·trop'ic** (-trŏp'ĭk), *adj.*

Am·for'tas (äm·fôr'täs), *n.* See PARSIFAL, KLINGSOR.

Am·har'ic (ăm·hăr'ĭk; ăm·hä'rĭk), *n.* The official and court language of Ethiopia (Abyssinia), a language of the Ethiopic group. — **Am·har'ic,** *adj.*

a'mi·a·ble (ā'mĭ·ȧ·b'l; 58), *adj.* [F., fr. L. *amicabilis* friendly, fr. *amicus* friend.] **1.** *Archaic.* Admirable; also, desirable. **2.** Having, or characterized by, sweetness of temper, kindheartedness, etc., which causes one to be liked; good-naturedly complaisant. — **a'mi·a·bil'i·ty** (-bĭl'ĭ·tĭ), *n.* — **a'mi·a·ble·ness,** *n.* — **a'mi·a·bly,** *adv.*

Syn. (1) See LOVABLE.

(2) **Amiable, good-natured, obliging, complaisant** mean manifesting the desire or disposition to please. **Amiable** implies qualities that inspire liking, such as friendliness, affability, sweet temper; **good-natured** implies a disposition to please and to be pleased with; sometimes, an indifference to being imposed upon; **obliging** stresses a readiness to be helpful, often as a sign of amiability; **complaisant,** in careful use, implies a courteous or merely amiable desire to please or to be agreeable.

am'i·an'thus (ăm'ĭ·ăn'thŭs), *n.* [L. *amiantus,* fr. Gr. *amiantos lithos,* a greenish stone like asbestos, fr. *a-* not + *miainein* to stain.] *Mineral.* Fine silky asbestos.

am'i·ca·ble (ăm'ĭ·kȧ·b'l), *adj.* [L. *amicabilis.*] Friendly; proceeding from, or exhibiting, friendliness; peaceable. — **am'i·ca·bil'i·ty** (-bĭl'ĭ·tĭ), *n.* — **am'i·ca·ble·ness,** *n.* — **am'i·ca·bly,** *adv.*

Syn. Amicable, neighborly (*or* **neighbourly**), **friendly** mean exhibiting a spirit of good will. **Amicable** frequently implies that the parties concerned are not disposed to quarrel or are at peace with each other; **neighborly** implies a disposition to live on good terms with those in proximity; **friendly** more positively implies cordial relations, often suggesting warmth of feeling.

am'ice (ăm'ĭs), *n.* [OF. *amis,* fr. L. *amictus* a cloak.] An oblong piece of white linen worn about the neck and shoulders under the alb and chasuble, by priests at Mass. See VESTMENT, *Illust.*

‖**a·mi'cus cu'ri·ae** (ȧ·mī'kŭs kū'rĭ·ē). [L.] *Law.* Literally, a friend of the court; hence, in practice, a party who suggests or states some matter of law for the court's assistance.

‖**a·mi'cus hu·ma'ni ge'ne·ris** (hū·mā'nī jĕn'ẽ·rĭs). [L.] A friend of the human race; a philanthropist.

‖**a·mi'cus us'que ad a'ras** (ŭs'kwē ăd ā'răs). [L.] A friend as far as to the altars, i.e., except in what is contrary to one's religion.

a·mid' (ȧ·mĭd'), *prep.* In the midst of. See AMIDST.

am'ide (ăm'ĭd; -īd), *n.* Also **am'id.** [*ammonia* + *-ide.*] *Chem.* A compound resulting from replacement of an atom of hydrogen in ammonia by an element or radical, or of one or more atoms of hydrogen in ammonia by univalent acid radicals. — **a·mid'ic** (ȧ·mĭd'ĭk), *adj.*

am'i·din (ăm'ĭ·dĭn), *n.* [F. *amidon* starch, fr. L. *amylum.*] *Chem.* The supposed soluble principle of starch.

a·mi'do (ȧ·mē'dō; ăm'ĭ·dō), *adj.,* **a·mi'do-** (-dō-), *prefix.* [From AMIDE.] *Chem.* **a** Pertaining to or containing the group NH_2 united to a radical of acid character; — disting. from *amino, amino-.* **b** Less correctly, = AMINO, AMINO-.

a·mi'do·gen (ȧ·mē'dō·jĕn; ȧ·mĭd'ō·jĕn), *n.* [*amido-* + *-gen.*] *Chem.* The radical NH_2, which is known only in combination in amides and amines.

am'i·dol (ăm'ĭ·dōl; -dŏl), *n.* [*amide* + *-ol,* 1.] *Chem.* A salt (commonly the dihydrochloride) of 2,4-di-amino phenol, $C_6H_3(NH_2)_2OH$, used in photography as a developer, for dyeing furs, etc.

a·mid'ships (ȧ·mĭd'shĭps), *adv.* Also **a·mid'ship.** *Naut.* In or toward the middle of a ship between stem and stern.

a·midst' (ȧ·mĭdst'), **a·mid'** (ȧ·mĭd'), *prep.* [AS. *on middan* in the middle, fr. *midde* the middle. See MIDST.] In or into the midst or middle of; among.

‖**a·mi'go** (ä·mē'gō), *n.; pl.* -GOS (-gōs; *E.* -gōz). [Sp., fr. L. *amicus.*] A friend; specif., a friendly native.

a·mine' (ȧ·mēn'; ăm'ĭn), *n.* Also **am'in.** [*ammonia* + *-ine.*] *Chem.* Any of a class of compounds derived from ammonia by replacement of hydrogen by one or more univalent hydrocarbon radicals.

a·mi'no (ȧ·mē'nō; ăm'ĭ·nō), *adj.,* **a·mi'no-** (-nō-), *prefix.* [From AMINE.] *Chem.* Pertaining to or containing the group NH_2 united to a radical other than an acid radical, as in **a·mi'no·ben'zene;** — distinguished from *amido, amido-.*

amino acid. *Chem.* Any acid containing the amino group, NH_2. Some thirty have been isolated from proteins, of which they are the chief components.

a·mi'no·ben·zo'ic ac'id (ȧ·mē'nō·bĕn·zō'ĭk; ăm'ĭ·nō-). *Org. Chem.* Any of three crystalline acids $H_2NC_6H_4CO_2H$. The yellowish-red *para* (*p-*) acid, a growth vitamin of the B group, is found in yeast, bran, etc., and also made synthetically. It is sometimes called the "anti-gray-hair vitamin." Abbr. *PABA, paba.*

a·mi'no·plast' (ȧ·mē'nō·plăst'; ăm'ĭ·nō-), *n.* [*amino-* + Gr. *plastos* formed.] A synthetic resin made from amino or amido compounds. — **a·mi'no·plas'tic** (-plăs'tĭk), *adj.*

a·mi'no·py'rine (-pī'rēn; -rĭn), *n.* [*amino-* + anti*pyretic* + *-ine.*] *Pharm.* A white crystalline powder, $C_{13}H_{17}N_3O$, used as an antipyretic and anodyne.

a·mir', a·meer' (ȧ·mēr'), *n.* [See EMIR.] A Mohammedan noble, esp. a prince of Afghanistan.

Am'ish (ăm'ĭsh; ä'mĭsh), *adj.* Of or pertaining to, or named from, Jacob Amen, or Ammann, a strict Mennonite of the 17th century; hence, pertaining to or designating his followers. — *n. Eccl. Hist.* Collectively, the Amish Mennonites.

a·miss' (ȧ·mĭs'), *adv.* [*a-* + *miss.*] Astray; faultily; improperly. — *adj.* Beside the mark; faulty; improper; — used in the predicate.

am'i·to'sis (ăm'ĭ·tō'sĭs), *n.* [NL., fr. *a-* not + *mitosis.*] *Biol.* Cell division in which there is first a simple cleavage of the nucleus without change in its structure, followed by the division of the cytoplasm; direct cell division; — opposed to *mitosis.* — **am'i·tot'ic** (-tŏt'ĭk), *adj.*

am'i·ty (ăm'ĭ·tĭ), *n.; pl.* AMITIES (-tĭz). [F. *amitié,* fr. OF., fr. L. *amicus* friendly.] Friendship; friendly relations, esp. between nations. — **Syn.** Friendship, comity, good will. — **Ant.** Enmity.

am'me'ter (ăm'mē'tẽr; ăm'ē·tẽr), *n.* [*ampere* + *-meter.*] *Elec.* An instrument for measuring electric current.

am'mi·a'ceous (ăm'ĭ·ā'shŭs), *adj.* Belonging to the carrot family (Ammiaceae, syn. Apiaceae); apiaceous. See CARROT.

am'mine (ăm'ēn; ă·mēn'), *n.* [ammonia + 2d -ine.] *Chem.* **a** A molecule of ammonia, NH_3, as it exists in certain complex compounds called **am·mi'no com'pounds** (ă·mē'nō; ăm'ĭ·nō). **b** An ammino compound.

Am'mon (ăm'ŏn), *n.* [L., fr. Gr. *Ammōn*, fr. Egypt. *Āmen*.] **1.** *Egypt. Relig.* Amen, the deity. **2.** *Class. Relig.* An epithet of Zeus and Jupiter as worshiped in Egypt and Libya.

am·mo'ni·a (ă·mō'nĭ·ȧ; -mōn'yȧ), *n.* [From sal *ammoniac*.] **1.** *Chem.* A colorless gaseous compound of nitrogen and hydrogen, NH_3, of extremely pungent smell and taste. Ammonia can easily be condensed by cold and pressure to a colorless liquid boiling at −33.3° C. **2.** Popularly, the aqueous solution of the gas; — called also *aqua ammoniae, ammonia water*, and *spirits of hartshorn*.

am·mo'ni·ac (ă·mō'nĭ·ăk), *n., or* **gum ammoniac.** [F., fr. L., fr. Gr. *ammōniakon* a gum said to distill from plants growing near the temple of Jupiter *Ammon*.] The aromatic gum resin of a Persian herb (*Dorema ammoniacum*) of the carrot family. It is used as an expectorant and stimulant, and as a cement.

am'mo·ni'a·cal (ăm'ō·nī'ȧ·kăl), *adj.* Also **am·mo'ni·ac.** Of or pertaining to ammonia; containing, or having the properties of, ammonia.

am·mo'ni·ate (ă·mō'nĭ·āt), *v. t.* To combine with ammonia.

am·mon'ic (ă·mŏn'ĭk; ă·mō'nĭk), *adj.* Also **am·mon'i·cal** (-ĭ·kăl). Of or pertaining to ammonia or the radical ammonium.

am·mon'i·fi·ca'tion (ă·mŏn'ĭ·fĭ·kā'shŭn), *n.* [*ammonia* + *-fication*.] **1.** Impregnation with ammonia or ammonium compounds. **2.** Decomposition with production of ammonia, esp. by the action of bacteria on nitrogenous organic matter. — **am·mon'i·fy** (ă·mŏn'ĭ·fī), *v. t. & i.*

am'mo·nite (ăm'ō·nīt), *n.* [L. cornu *Ammonis* horn of Ammon.] *Paleontol.* Any of numerous fossil shells of cephalopods having the form of a flat spiral, especially abundant in the Mesozoic age.

am·mo'ni·um (ă·mō'nĭ·ŭm), *n.* *Chem.* A strongly basic radical, NH_4, whose compounds resemble those of the alkali metals. When ammonia reacts with acids, the salts of ammonium are formed, as **ammonium chloride** (*or* **sal ammoniac**), NH_4Cl, used as a source of ammonia, **ammonium nitrate**, NH_4NO_3, used in explosives and as a fertilizer, **ammonium sulfate**, $(NH_4)_2SO_4$, used as a fertilizer and as a source of ammonium compounds.

ammonium hydroxide. *Chem.* A compound, NH_4OH, formed when ammonia dissolves in water, and existing only in solution.

am'mu·ni'tion (ăm'ū·nĭsh'ŭn), *n.* [F. *amunition*, formerly used for *munition*. See MUNITION.] **1.** In warfare, the projectiles thrown against an enemy, such as bullets, shells, grenades, and bombs, with their necessary propellants, detonators, fuses, and primers. **2.** Any material that may be used in attack or defense.

am·ne'si·a (ăm·nē'zhĭ·ȧ; -zĭ·ȧ), *n.* [NL., fr. Gr. *amnēsia* forgetfulness.] Loss of memory due to brain injury, shock, fever, repression, etc.; also, a gap in one's memory. — **am·ne'sic** (-sĭk; -zĭk), **am·nes'tic** (-nĕs'tĭk), *adj.*

am'nes·ty (ăm'nĕs·tĭ), *n.; pl.* -TIES (-tĭz). [From L., fr. Gr. *amnēstia* a forgetting, deriv. of *a-* not + *mnasthai* to remember.] **1.** Forgetfulness; an overlooking. **2.** An act of sovereign power granting oblivion, or a general pardon, for a past offense. — *v. t.* To grant amnesty to.

am'ni·on (ăm'nĭ·ŏn), *n.; pl.* -NIONS (-ŏnz), -NIA (-ȧ). [Gr., the membrane round the fetus, dim. of *amnos* lamb.] *Anat. & Zool.* A thin membrane forming a closed sac surrounding the embryos of reptiles, birds, and mammals. It contains a serous fluid, the **am'ni·ot'ic flu'id** (ăm'nĭ·ŏt'ĭk), in which the embryo is immersed. Cf. CHORION.

a·moe'ba (ȧ·mē'bȧ), *n.; pl.* -BAE (-bē), -BAS (-bȧz). Also **a·me'ba** (ȧ·mē'bȧ); *pl.* -BAS (-bȧz), -BAE (-bē). [NL., fr. Gr. *amoibē* change.] *Zool.* One of the simplest known forms of animal life, a protozoan of a genus (*Amoeba*) comprising several species of aquatic naked rhizopods common in fresh-water pools. An amoeba consists of a microscopic nucleated mass of protoplasm, perpetually changes its shape by protruding portions of its body, and nourishes itself by enveloping minute organisms and fragments of food. — **a·moe'ban** (-băn), *adj.*

a·moe'bic, a·me'bic (ȧ·mē'bĭk), *adj.* Like or pertaining to an amoeba; caused by amoebae or amoebalike organisms.

amoebic dysentery. A tropical form of dysentery, usually ulcerative, caused by amoebae (*Endamoeba histolytica*).

a·moe'boid, a·me'boid (ȧ·mē'boid), *adj.* Like an amoeba, esp. in movements or changes of shape.

a·mok' (ȧ·mŏk'). Var. of AMUCK.

a·mo'le (ä·mō'lā), *n.* [Sp., fr. Nahuatl *amulli* soap.] Any part of a plant possessing cleansing properties and used for soap; also, any of a number of plants so used.

A'mon (ä'mŏn). Var. of AMEN.

a·mong' (ȧ·mŭng'), **a·mongst'** (ȧ·mŭngst'), *prep.* [ME. *among*, fr. AS. *on* in + *gemang* a crowd, mingling, fr. *gemengan* to mingle.] **1.** In or through the midst of; surrounded by; in company or intercourse with; as, the immigrants *among* us. **2.** In the number or class of; as, wittiest *among* poets. **3.** By or through the aggregate of; as, discontent *among* the ignorant. **4.** In shares to each of; as, divided *among* the heirs. **5.** By the common or joint action of; through the reciprocal action of; as, to quarrel *among* themselves.

a·mon'til·la'do (ȧ·mŏn'tĭ·lä'dō; -lyä'dō), *n.* [Sp.] A dry pale sherry.

a·mor'al (ā·mŏr'ăl; ă-), *adj.* [*a-* not + *moral*.] Without a sense of moral responsibility; as, *amoral* morons; specif., outside the sphere in which moral distinctions or judgments apply. — **a'mo·ral'i·ty** (ā'mō·răl'ĭ·tĭ; ăm'ō-), *n.* — **a·mor'al·ly,** *adv.*

am'o·ret'to (ăm'ō·rĕt'ō; *It.* ä'mō·rāt'tō), *n.; pl.* -TI (-tē). Also ‖**a'mo·ri'no** (ä'mō·rē'nō), *n.; pl.* -NI (-nē). [It., dim. of *amore* cupid.] An infant cupid.

am'o·rist (ăm'ō·rĭst), *n.* [L. *amor* love.] One addicted to amours; a gallant.

am'o·rous (ăm'ō·rŭs), *adj.* [OF., fr. LL. *amorosus* loving, fr. L. *amor* love, fr. *amare* to love.] **1.** Inclined to love; having a propensity to love, esp. sexual enjoyment; tenderly affectionate. **2.** In love; enamored; — often with *of*. **3.** Of, relating to, caused by, or productive of love. — **Syn.** Amatory, erotic. — **am'o·rous·ly,** *adv.* — **am'o·rous·ness,** *n.*

‖**a'mor pa'tri·ae** (ā'mŏr pā'trĭ·ē; păt'rĭ·ē). [L.] Love of one's fatherland.

a·mor'phism (ȧ·mŏr'fĭz'm), *n.* Amorphous quality.

a·mor'phous (-fŭs), *adj.* [Gr. *amorphos*, fr. *a-* not + *morphē* form.] **1.** Having no determinate form; shapeless. **2.** Specif.: **a** *Bot. & Zool.* Without developed structural organization. **b** *Geol.* Without division in parts, as by stratification or cleavage. **c** *Chem.* Uncrystallized. **3.** Of anomalous character or form; as, treatises *amorphous* in style. — **a·mor'phous·ly,** *adv.* — **a·mor'phous·ness,** *n.*

a·mort' (ȧ·mŏrt'), *adj.* [F. *à* to + *mort* death.] Lifeless.

am'or·ti·za'tion (ăm'ēr·tĭ·zā'shŭn; ȧ·mŏr'tĭ·zā'shŭn; -tī·zā'-), *n.* Act or process of amortizing; also, the sums devoted thereto.

am'or·tize (ăm'ēr·tīz; ȧ·mŏr'tīz; ȧ·mŏr'tĭz), *v. t.* [ML. *amortisare, admor-*, or F. *amortir*, fr. L. *ad* to + *mors* death.] **1.** To convey or sell in mortmain, i.e., to a corporation, esp. to an ecclesiastical corporation. See MORTMAIN. **2.** To provide for the gradual extinction of (a future obligation) in advance of maturity, esp. by periodical contributions to a sinking fund adequate to discharge a debt or make a replacement when it becomes necessary. — **am'or·tiz'a·ble** (ăm'ēr·tīz'ȧ·b'l; ȧ·mŏr'tĭz·ȧ·b'l; ȧ·mŏr'tĭz-), *adj.*

A'mos (ā'mŏs), *n.* [Heb. *'Āmōs*, lit., borne (by God).] **a** A Hebrew prophet of the 8th century B.C. **b** A book of the Old Testament (see BIBLE).

a·mount' (ȧ·mount'), *v. i.* [OF. *amonter* to increase, ascend, fr. *amont* upward, fr. L. *ad montem* to the mountain.] To rise, reach, or extend in quantity, number, effect, substance, or influence; — used with *to*. — *n.* **1.** The sum total of two or more sums or quantities; the aggregate. **2.** A principal sum and the interest thereon. **3.** The whole effect, substance, value, significance, or result; as, the *amount* of the testimony is this. **4.** A quantity; as, a surprising *amount* of patience. Abbr. *amt.* — **Syn.** See SUM.

a·mour' (ȧ·mōōr'; ă·mōōr'; 84), *n.* [F., fr. L. *amor* love.] A love affair; now, usually, an intrigue; an illicit love affair.

‖**a'mour'–pro'pre** (ȧ'mōōr'prô'pr'), *n.* [F.] Self-esteem.

am'pe·lop'sis (ăm'pĕ·lŏp'sĭs), *n.* [NL., fr. Gr. *ampelos* vine + *-opsis*.] A plant of the genus (*Parthenocissus*) which includes the Virginia creeper.

am·per'age (ăm·pēr'ĭj; ăm·pâr'ĭj), *n.* *Elec.* The strength of a current of electricity measured in amperes.

am'pere (ăm'pēr; ăm·pâr'), ‖**am'père'** (äN'pâr'), *n.* [After A. M. *Ampère*, French physicist.] *Elec.* The practical unit of electric current, being that produced by one volt acting through a resistance of one ohm.

am'pere–hour', *n.* *Elec.* The quantity of electricity delivered in one hour by a current of one-ampere strength.

ampere turn. *Elec.* The magnetomotive force round one turn of wire of a helical coil carrying an electric current of one-ampere strength.

am'per·sand (ăm'pēr·sănd; ăm'pēr·sănd'), *n.* [Corrupt. of *and per se and*, i. e., *&* by itself makes *and*.] The character &, *&*, or &.

am·phet'a·mine (ăm·fĕt'ȧ·mēn; -mĭn), *n.* [From alpha-methyl-beta-phenyl-ethyl-amine.] *Pharm.* A substance (chemically synthetic racemic alpha-methyl-beta-phenyl-ethyl-amine), used as an inhalant and in solution as a spray in head colds, hay fever, etc.

am'phi- (ăm'fĭ-). [Gr.] A prefix signifying *both, of both kinds, on both sides, about, around*, as in *amphi*bious.

am'phi·ar·thro'sis (-är·thrō'sĭs), *n.* [NL., fr. *amphi-* + Gr. *arthrōsis* articulation.] *Anat.* Articulation admitting slight motion. It includes *symphysis* and *syndesmosis*.

Am·phib'i·a (ăm·fĭb'ĭ·ȧ), *n. pl.* [NL. See AMPHIBIOUS.] *Zool.* A class of vertebrates, intermediate in many characters between the fishes and reptiles, including the frogs, toads, newts, salamanders, and their allies. They are mostly oviparous and pass through an aquatic larval stage (tadpole stage) in which they have gills, afterwards losing the gills and breathing by lungs.

am·phib'i·an (-ăn), *adj.* Amphibious (in any sense); specif., *Zool.*, belonging to the Amphibia. — *n.* **1.** An amphibian animal or plant; specif., *Zool.*, one of the Amphibia. **2.** An airplane designed to rise from and alight on either land or water. **3.** Also **amphibian tank.** = ALLIGATOR, 3.

am'phi·bi·ot'ic (ăm'fĭ·bī·ŏt'ĭk), *adj.* [*amphi-* + Gr. *biōtikos* pert. to life.] Terrestrial in one stage of existence and aquatic in another.

am·phib'i·ous (ăm·fĭb'ĭ·ŭs), *adj.* [Gr. *amphibios* living a double life, fr. *amphi* of both kinds + *bios* life.] **1.** Able to live both on land and in water, as frogs, beavers, and some plants. **2.** Pertaining to, or adapted for, both land and water. **3.** Of a mixed nature; partaking of two natures. **4.** *Mil.* Executed by co-ordinated action of land, sea, and, sometimes, air forces organized for invasion; as, *amphibious* operations; also, trained or organized for such action; as, *amphibious* forces. — **am·phib'i·ous·ly,** *adv.* — **am·phib'i·ous·ness,** *n.*

am'phi·bole (ăm'fĭ·bōl), *n.* [F., fr. Gr. *amphibolos* doubtful.] *Mineral.* A silicate of calcium and magnesium and, often, iron, manganese, etc. Asbestos, hornblende, and tremolite are varieties. — **am'phi·bol'ic** (-bŏl'ĭk), *adj.*

am'phi·bol'ic (-bŏl'ĭk), *adj.* **1.** Of or pertaining to amphibology; ambiguous; equivocal. **2.** *Med.* Uncertain or fluctuating.

am·phib'o·lite (ăm·fĭb'ō·līt), *n.* A rock consisting essentially of amphibole. When schistose, it is usually known as a *hornblende schist*.

am'phi·bol'o·gy (ăm'fĭ·bŏl'ō·jĭ), *n.; pl.* -GIES (-jĭz). Also **am·phib'o·ly** (ăm·fĭb'ō·lĭ). [LL. *amphibologia*, for *amphibolia*, fr. Gr. *amphibolia*, with the ending *-logia* as if fr. Gr. *amphibolos* ambiguous + *logos* speech.] A phrase or proposition susceptible of more than one interpretation, esp. as ambiguous in grammatical construction; also, the ambiguity so caused. — **am·phib'o·log'i·cal** (ăm·fĭb'ō·lŏj'ĭ·kăl; ăm'fĭ·bō-), *adj.*

am'phi·brach (ăm'fĭ·brăk), *n.* [L. *amphibrachys*, fr. Gr. *amphibrachys* short at both ends.] *Pros.* A foot of three syllables, the middle one long, or accented, the others short, or unaccented (⏑ – ⏑).

am·phic'ty·on (ăm·fĭk'tĭ·ŏn; -ŭn), *n.* [From L., fr. Gr. *amphiktyones*, pl., prob. orig. *amphiktiones* dwellers around, neighbors.] *Gr. Hist.* A deputy to the council or congress held by an amphictyony.

am·phic'ty·o·ny (ăm·fĭk'tĭ·ō·nĭ), *n.; pl.* -NIES (-nĭz). [Gr. *amphiktyonia*.] *Gr. Hist.* An association of neighboring communities for protecting a common religious center. — **-ty·on'ic** (-ŏn'ĭk), *adj.*

am'phi·go'ry (ăm'fĭ·gō'rĭ; -gēr·ĭ), *n.; pl.* -RIES (-rĭz), **am'phi·gou'ri** (-gōō'rĭ), *n.; pl.* -RIS (-rĭz). [F. *amphigouri*.] A nonsense verse or composition. — **am'phi·gor'ic** (-gŏr'ĭk), *adj.*

am·phim'a·cer (ăm·fĭm'ȧ·sēr), *n.* [From L., fr. Gr. *amphimakros*, fr. *amphi* at both ends + *makros* long.] *Gr. & Lat. Pros.* A foot of three syllables, the middle one short and the others long (– ⏑ –).

am'phi·mix'is (ăm'fĭ·mĭk'sĭs), *n.* [NL., fr. *amphi-* + Gr. *mixis* a mingling.] *Biol.* **a** Union of the germ plasm of two individuals in sexual reproduction. **b** Interbreeding.

Am·phi'on (ăm·fī'ŏn), *n.* A son of Zeus and Antiope. He built the walls of Thebes by charming the stones into place with a lyre given to him by Hermes.

am'phi·ox'us (ăm'fĭ·ŏk'sŭs), *n.* [NL., fr. *amphi-* + Gr. *oxys* sharp.] *Zool.* Any lancelet.

am'phi·pod (ăm'fĭ·pŏd), *n.* [*amphi-* + *-pod.*] Any crustacean of a large group (Amphipoda) comprising the sand fleas and allied forms. — **am'phi·pod**, *adj.*

am·phip'ro·style (ăm·fĭp'rō·stīl; ăm'fĭ·prō'stīl), *adj.* [L. *amphiprostylos*, fr. Gr. *amphiprostylos.*] *Arch.* Having columns at each end only. — *n.* An amphiprostyle building. — **am·phip'ro·sty'lar** (ăm·fĭp'rō·stī'lẽr), *adj.*

am'phis·bae'na (ăm'fĭs·bē'nȧ), *n.* [L., fr. Gr. *amphisbaina*, fr. *amphis* on both ends + *bainein* to go.] **1.** *Myth.* A fabled serpent with a head at each end, moving either way. **2.** A tropical limbless lizard with head and tail nearly indistinguishable. — **-bae'nic** (-nĭk), *adj.*

am·phis'ci·ans (ăm·fĭsh'ĭ·ănz; -fĭsh'ănz), **am·phis'ci·i** (-fĭsh'ĭ·ī), *n. pl.* [Gr. *amphiskios* throwing a shadow both ways.] The inhabitants of the tropics.

am'phi·sty'lar (ăm'fĭ·stī'lẽr), *adj.* [*amphi-* + Gr. *stylos* pillar.] *Arch.* Having columns at both ends or on both sides.

am'phi·the'a·ter, -the'a·tre (ăm'fĭ·thē'ȧ·tẽr; -thē'ȧ·tẽr), *n.* [From L., fr. Gr. *amphitheatron*, fr. *amphi* on both sides + *theatron* theater.] An oval or circular building with rising tiers of seats about an open space called the *arena;* also, a level surrounded by hills; a rising gallery in a theater. — **am'phi·the·at'ric** (-thē·ăt'rĭk), **am'phi·the·at'ri·cal** (-rĭ·kăl), *adj.* — **am'phi·the·at'ri·cal·ly**, *adv.*

Am'phi·tri'te (ăm'fĭ·trī'tē), *n.* *Gr. Myth.* A Nereid, wife of Poseidon and goddess of the sea.

Am·phit'ry·on (ăm·fĭt'rĭ·ŏn; -ŭn), *n.* **1.** *Gr. Myth.* The husband of Alcmene, in whose guise Zeus visits her, feasts her, and becomes the father of Hercules. **2.** Hence, a host whose identity is in doubt.

am'pho·ra (ăm'fō·rȧ), *n.; pl.* -RAE (-rē). [L., fr. Gr. *amphoreus*, *amphiphoreus*, a jar with two handles, fr. *amphi* on both sides + *phoreus* bearer, fr. *pherein* to bear.] *Gr. Antiq.* A jar or vase with a large egg-shaped body, narrow cylindrical neck, and two handles rising nearly to the level of the orifice. Cf. AMPULLA.

am'pho·ter'ic (ăm'fō·tĕr'ĭk), *adj.* [Gr. *amphoteros* both.] Partly one and partly the other; specif.: *Chem.* **a** Capable of reacting either as electropositive or as electronegative. **b** Capable of reacting either as an acid or as a base.

am'ple (ăm'p'l), *adj.* [F., fr. L. *amplus.*] **1.** Of large size, extent, capacity, volume, or scope; spacious; roomy. **2.** Sufficient to satisfy or gratify; more than adequate. **3.** Gratifyingly copious in matter or style; as, an *ample* narrative. — **Syn.** See PLENTIFUL. — **Ant.** Meager. — **am'ple·ness**, *n.*

am·plex'i·caul (ăm·plĕk'sĭ·kôl), *adj.* [L. *amplexus* encircling + *caulis* stem.] *Bot.* Clasping or embracing a stem, as a leaf. See the *Illust.*

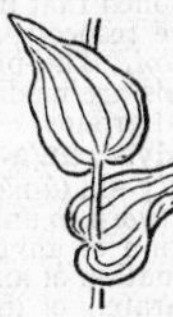

Amplexicaul Leaves.

am'pli·a'tion (ăm'plĭ·ā'shŭn), *n.* [L. *ampliatio*, fr. *ampliare* to widen, fr. *amplus* ample.] Enlargement; amplification.

am'pli·dyne (ăm'plĭ·dīn), *n.* [*ampli*fier + *dyne.*] *Elec.* A direct-current generator which through the unique use of compensating coils and a short circuit across two of its brushes precisely controls a large power output whenever a small power input is varied in the field winding of the generator.

am'pli·fi·ca'tion (ăm'plĭ·fĭ·kā'shŭn), *n.* **1.** Act of amplifying; increase; enlargement; extension. **2.** The matter by which a statement is amplified; an amplified statement. — **am·plif'i·ca·to'ry** (ăm·plĭf'ĭ·kȧ·tō'rĭ; ăm'plĭ·fĭ·kā'tẽr·ĭ), *adj.*

am'pli·fi'er (ăm'plĭ·fī'ẽr), *n.* One who or that which amplifies; specif., *Elec.*, a device to amplify electric impulses, usually including one or more electron tubes.

am'pli·fy (-fī), *v. t.;* -FIED (-fīd); -FY'ING. [F. *amplifier*, fr. L. *amplificare.* See AMPLE; -FY.] **1.** To enlarge, as by discussion; to treat copiously by adding particulars, illustrations, etc.; to expand. **2.** To render more extended, important, or the like; also, to exaggerate. **3.** *Elec. & Radio.* To increase, as current or voltage, through control, as by means of electron tubes, of a larger amount of power than that originally present. — *v. i.* To speak or write with amplification; to dilate upon details; expatiate. — **Syn.** See EXPAND. — **Ant.** Condense.

am'pli·tude (-tūd), *n.* [L. *amplitudo.*] **1.** State or quality of being ample; extent, esp. of surface or space; size. **2.** Largeness, in a figurative sense; breadth; abundance; fullness, as of intellectual powers. **3.** *Astron.* The arc of the horizon between the true east or west point and the foot of the vertical circle passing through any star or object; the complement of azimuth. **4.** *Elec.* The maximum departure of the value of an alternating current or wave from the average value. **5.** *Physics.* The extent of a vibratory movement, as of a pendulum, measured from the mean position to an extreme.

amplitude modulation. See FREQUENCY MODULATION.

am'ply (ăm'plĭ), *adv.* In an ample manner or degree.

am·poule' (ăm·po͞ol'), *n.* Also **am'pule** (ăm'pūl), **am'pul** (ăm'pŭl). [F. *ampoule*, fr. L. *ampulla.*] A small hermetically sealed vessel for holding a solution, usually a single dose, for hypodermic injection.

am·pul'la (ăm·pŭl'ȧ), *n.; pl.* -LAE (-ē). [L., dim. of *ampora*, *amphora.*] **1.** *Rom. Antiq.* A flask of glass or earthenware, having a more or less globular body and usually two handles. Cf. AMPHORA. **2.** *Biol.* A membranous sac or vesicle, as the dilatation at one end of each semicircular canal of the ear. **3. a** A cruet for the wine and water at Mass. **b** The vase holding holy oil for chrism, unction, or coronation. **4.** = AMPOULE. — **am·pul'lar** (-ẽr), *adj.*

am'pul·la'ceous (ăm'pŭ·lā'shŭs), *adj.* Like an ampulla; bladderlike.

am'pu·tate (ăm'pū·tāt), *v. t.* [L. *amputatus*, past part. of *amputare*, fr. *am-* (= *ambi-*) around + *putare* to cut.] To prune or cut off; *Surg.*, to cut off (a limb or projecting part); — usually distinguished from *excise.* — **am'pu·ta'tion** (-tā'shŭn), *n.* — **am'pu·ta'tor**, *n.*

am'pu·tee' (ăm'pū·tē'), *n.* [See -EE.] One who has had a limb or limbs amputated.

am·ri'ta, am·ree'ta (ŭm·rē'tȧ), *n.* [Skr. *amṛta.*] *Hinduism.* Food of the gods, conferring immortality.

Am'stutz (äm'shto͝ots), *n.* [After Walter *Amstutz*, its inventor.] *Skiing.* A coil spring attached at the ankle for holding the ski close against the heel.

amt (ämt), *n.; pl.* AMTER (äm'tẽr), AMTS (ämts). [Dan., fr. G. *amt.*] Administrative territorial division in Denmark; a county.

Am'torg (ăm'tôrg), *n.* [Russ. *Am*erikanskaya American + *torg*ovlya trade.] A Russian trading company incorporated (1924) in the United States to conduct operations in commodities between Russia and the United States.

a·muck' (ȧ·mŭk'), **a·mok'** (ȧ·mŏk'), *adj.* [Malay *amoq* furious.] Possessed with homicidal mania. — *adv.* In a frenzied, murderous manner. — *n.* (Usually *amok.*) A nervous seizure peculiar to the Malays, resulting in a murderous frenzy. — ***run amuck.*** To rush out in a state of frenzy and attack everyone met; to assail recklessly.

am'u·let (ăm'ū·lĕt; -lĭt), *n.* [F. and L.; F. *amulette*, fr. L. *amuletum.*] An ornament, gem, or scroll worn as a charm against evils, and often inscribed with a magic incantation. — **Syn.** See FETISH.

a·muse' (ȧ·mūz'), *v. t.* [OF. *amuser* to cause to muse or waste time, fr. LL. *musus* muzzle, mouth. See A-, 3; MUSE, *v.*] **1.** *Obs.* To engage the attention of; also, to bewilder. **2.** *Archaic.* To divert the attention of in order to deceive; to beguile; delude. **3.** To entertain or occupy pleasurably; to divert. — **a·mus'a·ble** (-mūz'ȧ·b'l), *adj.* — **a·mus'er**, *n.*

Syn. **Amuse, divert, entertain, recreate** mean to cause or enable one to pass time pleasantly or agreeably. **Amuse** stresses engagement of one's attention, usually in leisure, by that which engrosses one or keeps one in good humor; **divert** implies the distraction of the attention from that which preoccupies it, such as business, worry, etc.; **entertain** usually suggests the activities of others to amuse or to divert; **recreate** (commonly in form *recreation*) implies a change in occupation or an indulgence in diversions for the sake of relaxation or refreshment.

a·mused' (ȧ·mūzd'), *adj.* Pleasingly diverted; expressing amusement. — **a·mus'ed·ly** (ȧ·mūz'ĕd·lĭ; -ĭd·lĭ), *adv.*

a·muse'ment (ȧ·mūz'mĕnt), *n.* [F.] **1.** Entertainment, esp. when characterized by quiet mirth. **2.** That which amuses or entertains.

a·mus'ing (ȧ·mūz'ĭng), *adj.* Giving amusement; diverting. — **a·mus'ing·ly**, *adv.* — **a·mus'ing·ness**, *n.*

a·mu'sive (ȧ·mū'zĭv; -sĭv), *adj.* Tending to amuse.

a·myg'da·la (ȧ·mĭg'dȧ·lȧ), *n.; pl.* -LAE (-lē). [L., an almond.] **1.** An almond. **2.** *Anat.* One of the tonsils.

a·myg'da·la'ceous (-lā'shŭs), *adj.* Belonging to the peach family (Amygdalaceae) of trees and shrubs. See PEACH, *n.*, 1.

a·myg'da·lin (ȧ·mĭg'dȧ·lĭn), *n.* A white crystalline glucoside, $C_{20}H_{27}NO_{11}$, found in the bitter almond, a variety (*Amygdalus communis amara*) of the common almond.

a·myg'da·line (-lĭn; -līn), *adj.* **1.** Pertaining to or resembling an almond or almonds. **2.** *Anat.* Of or pertaining to an amygdala, or tonsil.

a·myg'da·loid (-loid), *n.* [Gr. *amygdalon* almond + *-oid.*] *Petrog.* Any igneous rock containing small cavities filled with deposits of different minerals, as chalcedony or calcite.

a·myg'da·loid, a·myg'da·loi'dal (-loi'dăl; -d'l), *adj.* [Gr. *amygdaloeidēs.*] **1.** Almond-shaped. **2.** Of, or of the nature of, amygdaloid.

am'yl (ăm'ĭl; ā'mĭl), *n.* [L. *am*ylum starch + *-yl.*] *Chem.* A univalent hydrocarbon radical, C_5H_{11}, existing in several isomeric modifications, compounds of which occur in fusel oil, fruit essences, etc.

am'y·la'ceous (ăm'ĭ·lā'shŭs), *adj.* [See AMYL.] Pertaining to, or of the nature of, starch; starchy.

amyl alcohol. See ALCOHOL, 2.

am'yl·ase (ăm'ĭ·lās), *n.* *Biochem.* Any of the enzymes that accelerate the hydrolysis of starch and glycogen to maltose, as in saliva and in germinating seeds.

am'yl·ene (ăm'ĭ·lēn), *n.* *Chem.* Any of a group of eight isomeric hydrocarbons, C_5H_{10}, of the ethylene series.

a·myl'ic (ȧ·mĭl'ĭk), *adj.* *Chem.* Of or pertaining to amyl.

a·myl'o·gen (-ō·jĕn), *n.* [*amylum* + *-gen.*] That part of the starch granule or granulose which is soluble in water.

am'y·loid (ăm'ĭ·loid), **am'y·loi'dal** (-loi'dăl; -d'l), *adj.* Like or containing amylum.

am'y·loid, *n.* A nonnitrogenous starchy food.

am'y·lol'y·sis (-lŏl'ĭ·sĭs), *n.* [*amylum* + *-lysis.*] *Chem.* Conversion of starch into soluble products, as dextrins and sugar, esp. by enzymes. — **am'y·lo·lyt'ic** (-lō·lĭt'ĭk), *adj.*

am'y·lop'sin (-lŏp'sĭn), *n.* [*amylum* + *trypsin.*] *Biochem.* An enzyme present in the pancreatic juice.

am'yl·ose (ăm'ĭ·lōs), *n.* *Chem.* Any of the carbohydrates of more complex composition $(C_6H_{10}O_5)_x$ which are decomposable by hydrolysis into simple sugars, as cellulose, or obtained by hydrolysis of starch, as dextrin.

am'y·lum (ăm'ĭ·lŭm), *n.* [L. See AMYL.] Starch.

an (ăn; *emphatic* ăn; 4), *adj.*, or *indefinite article.* [AS. *ān* one, the same word as the numeral. See ONE.] One; some one; — indicating the singular number of its noun without emphasis.

☞ In present usage *an* is invariably the form of the indefinite article before words beginning with a vowel sound, as *an* hour, *an* oak; and *a* is invariably, except as noted below, the form before words beginning with a consonant sound, as *a* table, *a* woman, *a* year, *a* unit, *a* eulogy, such *a* one, *a* history, *a* historian. Some writers, however, use *an* before words beginning with *h* in an unaccented syllable, as *an* historian, *an* hotel; and British writers often use *an* before such words as *union*, *euphony*, *euphonic*, etc., beginning with the sound of *y* (ū = yo͞o).

an, an' (ăn), *conj.* **1.** *Now Dial.* And. **2.** *Archaic.* If.

an-. [Gr.] = A-, not, without; — used before vowels and *h*, as in *an*esthesia, *an*hydrous.

-an (-ăn). [F. and L.; F. *-ain*, *-en*, fr. L. *-anus.*] A suffix having the general sense of *belonging* or *pertaining to*, primarily forming adjectives, of which many are also used substantively; as in Europe*an*, Berkelei*an*, hum*an*, sylv*an*. It is often used in zoology to form singulars for the plural group names in *-a*, *-ae*, etc., as in crustace*an*.

an'a- (ăn'ȧ-). [Gr. *ana* on; in comp., on, up.] A prefix in words derived or formed from Greek (sometimes through Low Latin and French), denoting: **a** *Up; upward.* **b** *Backward.* **c** *Again; anew.* **d** *Greatly; excessively.*

-a'na (-ā'nȧ; -ä'nȧ; -ăn'ȧ). [Neut. pl. ending of Latin adjectives in *-anus.*] A suffix added to proper names to form nouns denoting *items of bibliography, anecdotes, literary gossip*, or other facts or pieces of information, *concerning the designated subject*, as in Americ*ana*.

a'na (ā'nȧ; ä'nȧ), *n.* [From -ANA.] A collection, originally of the memorable sayings of a person, later of items of information relative to a subject of curious interest.

an'a (ăn'ȧ), *adv.* [Gr. *ana* (used distributively).] *Pharm.* Of each an equal quantity; — used in prescriptions.

an'a·bae'na (ăn'ȧ·bē'nȧ), *n.; pl.* -NAS (-năz). [NL., fr. Gr. *anabainein* to go up.] *Bot.* An individual or a mass of individuals of a genus (*Anabaena*) of minute fresh-water blue-green algae that often contaminate reservoirs, causing a fishy taste and odor.

An'a·bap'tist (ăn'ȧ·băp'tĭst), *n.* *Eccl. Hist.* One of a party arising in 1523 in Zurich among followers of Zwingli which rejected infant baptism, held the church to be composed of true Christians baptized on confession of faith, and advocated separation of church and state. — **An′a·bap′tism** (ăn′ȧ·băp′tĭz′m), *n.* — **An′a·bap′tist** (-tĭst), *adj.*

an′a·bas (ăn′ȧ·băs), *n.* [NL., fr. Gr. *anabas*, part. of *anabainein* to go up.] Any of a genus (*Anabas*) of small perchlike fresh-water spiny-finned fishes of southeastern Asia and Africa. One species (*A. scandens*), called *climbing fish*, can travel considerable distances overland, and is said to climb trees.

a·nab′a·sis (ȧ·năb′ȧ·sĭs), *n.; pl.* -SES (-sēz). [Gr., fr. *anabainein* to go up.] **1.** A military advance into a country. **2.** [*cap.*] The march of the younger Cyrus against Artaxerxes, narrated by Xenophon in a history, the *Anabasis.*

an′a·bat′ic (ăn′ȧ·băt′ĭk), *adj.* [Gr. *anabatikos* skilled in mounting, fr. *anabainein.*] Upward-moving; — of air currents or winds.

a·nab′o·lism (ȧ·năb′ō·lĭz′m), *n.* [Gr. *anabolē* something heaped up, fr. *ana-* + *bolē* a stroke.] *Biol.* Constructive metabolism; — opposed to *catabolism.* See METABOLISM. — **an′a·bol′ic** (ăn′ȧ·bŏl′ĭk), *adj.*

an′a·branch (ăn′ȧ·brȧnch), *n.* [*ana*stomosing + *branch.*] A diverging branch of a river which re-enters the main stream; also, a branch which loses itself in sandy soil.

an′a·car′di·a′ceous (-kär′dĭ·ā′shŭs), *adj.* [From NL. *Anacardiaceae*, fr. Gr. *ana* similar to + *kardia* heart; — the fruit being likened to a bird's heart.] Belonging to the sumac family (Anacardiaceae) of trees and shrubs. See SUMAC.

a·nach′ro·nism (ȧ·năk′rō·nĭz′m), *n.* [Gr. *anachronismos*, fr. *anachronizein* to refer to a wrong time, fr. *ana-* + *chronos* time.] **1.** An error in chronology by which events are misplaced in regard to each other, esp. the antedating of an event, custom, or the like. **2.** Anything incongruous in point of time with its surroundings.

a·nach′ro·nis′tic (-nĭs′tĭk), **a·nach′ro·nis′ti·cal** (-tĭ·kăl), *adj.* Of the nature of, or involving, anachronism.

a·nach′ro·nous (ȧ·năk′rō·nŭs), *adj.* Out of place in point of time. — **a·nach′ro·nous·ly**, *adv.*

an′a·clas′tic (ăn′ȧ·klăs′tĭk), *adj.* [Gr. *anaklan* to bend back and break, to reflect (light), fr. *ana-* + *klan* to break.] *Optics.* Pertaining to, or produced by, refraction.

an′a·cli′nal (-klī′năl; -n′l), *adj.* [*ana-* + Gr. *klinein* to incline.] *Geol.* Having a course opposed to the dip of the underlying rocks; — opposed to *cataclinal.*

an′a·clit′ic (-klĭt′ĭk), *adj.* [Gr. *anaklinein* to lean upon.] Characterized by dependence; leaning; specif., *Psychoanalysis*, characterized or qualified by dependence of the libido upon another instinct, such as hunger.

an′a·co·lu′thon (-kō·lū′thŏn), *n.; pl.* -THA (-thȧ). [Gr. *anakolouthos*, *-on*, not following, wanting sequence, fr. *an-* not + *akolouthos* following.] *Gram.* Abandonment in the midst of a sentence of one type of construction in favor of one grammatically different; also, such a sentence. — **an′a·co·lu′thic** (-thĭk), *adj.*

an′a·con′da (ăn′ȧ·kŏn′dȧ), *n.* [Origin unknown; perh. Ceylonese.] **1.** Orig., a python of Ceylon, perhaps *Python molurus.* **2.** A large snake (*Eunectes murinus*) of the boa family of tropical South America. **3.** Loosely, any large snake that crushes its prey. Cf. BOA, 2; BOA CONSTRICTOR, 2; PYTHON, 4.

A·nac′re·on′tic (ȧ·năk′rē·ŏn′tĭk), *adj.* Pert. to Anacreon, Ionian Greek poet, or his light and graceful lyrics; hence, convivial; amatory. — *n.* A poem like Anacreon's lyrics.

an′a·cru′sis (ăn′ȧ·kro͞o′sĭs), *n.* [NL., fr. Gr. *anakrousis*, fr. *anakrouein* to push up or back, fr. *ana-* + *krouein* to strike.] *Pros.* One or two unstressed syllables prefixed to a verse properly beginning with an accented syllable, hence applied to the initial notes in music beginning on a nonaccent or weak accent.

an′a·cul′ture (ăn′ȧ·kŭl′tūr), *n.* [*ana-* + *culture.*] *Bacteriol.* A mixed culture; — said esp. of cultures containing various strains of pathogenic organisms used in the preparation of autogenous vaccines.

an′a·dem (ăn′ȧ·dĕm), *n.* [L. *anadema*, fr. Gr. *anadēma*, deriv. of *ana* up + *dein* to bind.] *Poetic.* A chaplet; garland.

an′a·di·plo′sis (-dĭ·plō′sĭs), *n.* [L., fr. Gr. *anadiplōsis*, fr. *ana-* + *diploun* to double.] *Rhet.* Repetition of a word, esp. the last word, of one clause at the beginning of the next (Rely on his *honor* — *honor* such as his?).

a·nad′ro·mous (ȧ·năd′rō·mŭs), *adj.* [Gr. *anadromos* running upward, fr. *ana-* + *dromos* a running, fr. *dramein* to run.] *Zool.* Ascending rivers from the sea, at certain seasons, for breeding, as shad; — opp. to *catadromous.*

a·nae′mi·a, a·nae′mic. Vars. of ANEMIA, ANEMIC.

an·a′er·obe, an·a′ër·obe (ăn·ā′ēr·ōb), *n.* Also **an·a′er·o′bi·um** (-ō′bĭ·ŭm); *pl.* -OBIA (-ȧ). [NL. *anaerobium*, fr. *an-* not + *aero-* + Gr. *bios* life.] *Biol.* An anaerobic organism, esp. one of certain bacteria.

an·a′er·o′bic, an·a′ër·o′bic (-ō′bĭk; -ŏb′ĭk), *adj.* *Biol.* **a** Living or active in the absence of free oxygen; as, *anaerobic* bacteria. **b** Pertaining to or induced by anaerobes; as, *anaerobic* fermentation.

an′aes·the′si·a, -thet′ic, etc. Vars. of ANESTHESIA, etc.

an′a·glyph (ăn′ȧ·glĭf), *n.* [Gr. *anaglyphos* wrought in low relief, fr. *ana-* + *glyphein* to engrave.] **1.** Any sculptured, chased, or embossed ornament worked in low relief, as a cameo. **2.** A picture combining two images of the same object recorded from different points of view, as images of the right and left eyes, one image in one color being superposed upon the second image in a contrasting color. Viewed through a device (**an′a·glyph′o·scope** [-glĭf′ō·skōp]) consisting of a pair of light filters, the anaglyph produces a stereoscopic effect. — **an′a·glyph′ic** (-glĭf′ĭk), *adj.* — **an′a·glyp′tic** (-glĭp′tĭk), *adj.*

an′a·go′ge (ăn′ȧ·gō′jē), *n.* [NL., fr. Gr. *anagōgē* a leading up, fr. *ana-* + *agōgē* a leading, fr. *agein* to lead.] The mystical or spiritual meaning or application of words.

an′a·gog′ic (-gŏj′ĭk), *adj.* **1.** Also **an′a·gog′i·cal** (-ĭ·kăl). Of or involving anagoge; mystical. **2.** *Psychoanalysis.* Pertaining to the striving of inner psychic forces toward progressive ideals. — **an′a·gog′i·cal·ly**, *adv.*

an′a·go′gy (ăn′ȧ·gō′jĭ; -gŏj′ĭ), *n.* = ANAGOGE.

an′a·gram (ăn′ȧ·grăm), *n.* [From NL., fr. Gr. *anagrammatismos*, fr. *anagrammatizein* to transpose letters, fr. *gramma* letter.] A word or phrase made by transposing the letters of another. — **an′a·gram·mat′ic** (-grȧ·măt′ĭk), **an′a·gram·mat′i·cal** (-ĭ·kăl), *adj.* — **an′a·gram′ma·tize** (-grăm′ȧ·tīz), *v. t.*

an′a·grams (ăn′ȧ·grămz), *n. pl., construed as sing.* A game in which players compete in forming words from letters drawn from a stock.

a′nal (ā′năl), *adj.* Pert. to, or situated near, the anus.

an·al′cime (ăn·ăl′sĭm; -sīm), *n.* [*an-* not + Gr. *alkimos* strong.] *Mineral.* A white or slightly colored zeolite, crystalline or massive.

an·al′cite (ăn·ăl′sīt; ăn′ăl·sīt), *n.* [Gr. *analkēs* weak + *-ite.*] Analcime.

an′a·lects (ăn′ȧ·lĕkts), **an′a·lec′ta** (-lĕk′tȧ), *n. pl.* [Gr. *analekta*, fr. *analegein* to collect, fr. *ana-* + *legein* to gather.] A collection of miscellaneous literary passages; as, the *Analects* of Confucius.

an′a·lep′tic (-lĕp′tĭk), *adj.* & *n.* [Gr. *analēptikos* restorative.] *Med.* Restorative; giving strength.

an′al·ge′si·a (ăn′ăl·jē′zĭ·ȧ; -sĭ·ȧ), *n.* [NL., fr. Gr. *analgēsia*, fr. *an-* not + *algēsis* sense of pain.] Insensibility to pain.

an′al·ge′sic (-jē′sĭk; -jĕs′ĭk), *adj.* Of or producing analgesia. — *n.* An agent for producing analgesia.

an′a·log (ăn′ȧ·lŏg), Var. of ANALOGUE.

an′a·log′ic (ăn′ȧ·lŏj′ĭk), *adj.* Of or pertaining to analogy.

an′a·log′i·cal (-ĭ·kăl), *adj.* Founded on, or of the nature of, analogy; expressing or implying analogy. — **an′a·log′i·cal·ly**, *adv.*

a·nal′o·gist (ȧ·năl′ō·jĭst), *n.* One who reasons from analogy; one who seeks analogies.

a·nal′o·gize (-jīz), *v. i.* To employ, or reason by, analogy; to show analogy.

a·nal′o·gous (-gŭs), *adj.* [L. *analogus*, fr. Gr. *analogos* according to a due ratio, proportionate, fr. *ana-* + *logos* ratio.] **1.** Having analogy; corresponding in some respects to something else. **2.** *Biol.* Having the relation of an analogue. — **Syn.** See SIMILAR. — **a·nal′o·gous·ly**, *adv.* — **a·nal′o·gous·ness**, *n.*

an′a·logue (ăn′ȧ·lŏg), *n.* [F.] **1.** That which is analogous to some other thing. **2.** *Biol.* An organ similar in function to an organ of another animal or plant, but different in structure and origin; thus, the gill in a fish is the *analogue* of the lung in a quadruped.

analogue computer. A type of calculating machine that operates with numbers represented by directly measurable quantities as voltages, resistances, rotations, etc.

a·nal′o·gy (ȧ·năl′ō·jĭ), *n.; pl.* -GIES (-jĭz). **1.** A relation of likeness, *between* two things or *of* one thing *to* or *with* another, consisting in the resemblance not of the things themselves but of two or more attributes, circumstances, or effects. **2.** *Biol.* Correspondence in function between organs or parts of different structure and origin; — distinguished from *homology.* **3.** *Logic.* A form of inference in which it is reasoned that if two (or more) things agree with one another in one or more respects, they will (probably) agree in yet other respects. **4.** *Philol.* The principle or process in accordance with which existing words are modified or new words created in conformity with familiar word groups. — **Syn.** See LIKENESS.

an′a·lyse, an′a·lys′er, etc. Vars. of ANALYZE, etc.

a·nal′y·sis (ȧ·năl′ĭ·sĭs), *n.; pl.* -SES (-sēz). [ML., fr. Gr. *analysis*, fr. *analyein* to unloose, to resolve, fr. *ana* up + *lyein* to loose.] **1.** Separation of anything into constituent parts or elements; also, an examination of anything to distinguish its component parts or elements, separately or in their relation to the whole. **2.** A form of statement, as a syllabus, exhibiting the results of a process of analysis. **3.** *Chem.* **a** The separation of compound substances, by chemical processes, into their constituents. **b** The determination of one or more ingredients of a substance either as to kind (***qualitative analysis***) or amount (***quantitative analysis***). **4.** *Math.* **a** The investigation of problems by the methods of algebra. **b** Generally, any of those methods that are based on considerations of number and the theory of limits, as opposed to geometric intuition. **5.** *Psychoanalysis.* Diagnosis and treatment. — **Syn.** Resolution, dissection, breakdown.

an′a·lyst (ăn′ȧ·lĭst), *n.* One skilled or occupied in making analyses.

an′a·lyt′ic (ăn′ȧ·lĭt′ĭk), **an′a·lyt′i·cal** (-ĭ·kăl), *adj.* [From ML., fr. Gr. *analytikos.*] **1.** Of or pertaining to analysis or analytics; resolving into elements or constituent parts. **2.** Treating of, or given to the use of, analysis. — **an′a·lyt′i·cal·ly**, *adv.*

analytical table. *Bot.* & *Zool.* = KEY, *n.*, 9 **a.**

analytic geometry. *Math.* Geometry subjected to analytic treatment by means of the convention of co-ordinates.

an′a·lyt′ics (ăn′ȧ·lĭt′ĭks), *n.;* see -ICS. **1.** The science of analysis, esp. as a subdivision of logic. **2.** = ANALYTIC GEOMETRY.

an′a·lyze, an′a·lyse (ăn′ȧ·līz), *v. t.* **1.** To separate or resolve into elements or constituent parts. **2.** To separate mentally the parts of (a whole) so as to reveal their relation to it and to one another; as, to *analyze* an economic theory. **3.** To study the factors of (a situation, problem, or the like) in detail, in order to determine the solution or outcome. **4.** To subject to scientific or grammatical analysis. — **an′a·lyz′a·ble, an′a·lys′a·ble** (-līz′ȧ·b′l), *adj.* — **an′a·lyz′er, an′a·lys′er** (-līz′ēr), *n.* — **an′a·ly·za′tion, an′a·ly·sa′tion** (-lĭ·zā′shŭn; -lī·zā′shŭn), *n.*

Syn. Analyze, resolve, dissect, break down mean to divide a complex whole or unit into its components or constituents. **Analyze** presupposes a personal agent and an attempt to discover the true nature or inner relationships of something that does not superficially reveal them, such as a material substance, an intellectual construction, or the like; **resolve** may or may not presuppose a personal agent, and it usually suggests an actual separation into elements or parts (as, oxygen and hydrogen, into which the water is being *resolved* by an electric current); **dissect** literally implies a separation into component parts but, figuratively, a searching analysis; **break down**, the most concrete of these terms, implies a reduction to simpler parts or divisions (thus, proteins are *broken down* by enzymes into amino acids).

an·an′drous (ăn·ăn′drŭs), *adj.* [*an-* not + *-androus.*] *Bot.* Having no stamens.

An′a·ni′as (ăn′ȧ·nī′ȧs), *n.* A follower of the apostles who with his wife, Sapphira, was struck down for lying (*Acts* v); hence, a liar.

an′a·paest (ăn′ȧ·pĕst *or, Brit.,* -pēst), **an′a·pest**, *n.* [From L., fr. Gr. *anapaistos* an anapest, i. e., a dactyl reversed, fr. *ana-* + *paiein* to strike.] *Pros.* **a** A metrical foot consisting of three syllables, the first two short or unaccented, the last long or accented (L. *dĕ·ĭ·tās*; E. *in·ter·vene′*). **b** A line consisting of anapaests. — **an′a·paes′tic** (-pĕs′tĭk *or, Brit.,* -pēs′tĭk), *adj.*

an′a·phase (ăn′ȧ·fāz), *n.* [*ana-* up + *phase.*] *Biol.* A stage in mitosis (following the metaphase) in which the halves of the chromosomes move to the opposite poles of the spindle. Cf. TELOPHASE.

a·naph′o·ra (ȧ·năf′ō·rȧ), *n.* [L., fr. Gr. *anaphora*, fr. *ana-* + *pherein* to carry.] *Rhet.* Repetition of a word or words at the beginning of successive clauses.

an·aph′ro·dis′i·ac (ăn·ăf′rō·dĭz′ĭ·ăk), *adj.* [*an-* not + Gr. *aphrodisiakos* of venery.] *Med.* Capable of lessening sexual desire. — *n.* An anaphrodisiac agent.

an′a·phy·lax′is (ăn′ȧ·fĭ·lăk′sĭs), n. [NL., fr. ana- + -phylaxis as in prophylaxis.] Med. Excessive susceptibility; esp., protein sensitization, caused by a prior introduction of the same protein into the body. — **an′a·phy·lac′tic** (-lăk′tĭk), adj.

an′a·plas′ty (ăn′ȧ·plăs′tĭ), n. [Gr. anaplastos, fr. anaplassein to remodel, fr. ana again + plassein to form.] Plastic surgery. — **an′a·plas′tic** (-plăs′tĭk), adj.

an′arch (ăn′ärk), n. [Gr. anarchos rulerless, fr. an- not + archē beginning, government.] An anarchic leader.

an·ar′chic (ăn·är′kĭk), **an·ar′chi·cal** (-kĭ·kăl), adj. Pertaining to, involving, or of the nature of anarchy; tending to produce anarchy. — **an·ar′chi·cal·ly**, adv.

an′arch·ism (ăn′ärk·ĭz′m), n. **1.** The theory that all government is an evil. Proudhon (1809–65), "Father of Anarchism," advocated a social organization based on common ownership and free agreements. At its worst, anarchism stands for a terroristic resistance to all present government and social order. **2.** Advocacy or practice of anarchistic principles; esp., anarchistic revolution; nihilism; terrorism.

an′arch·ist (ăn′ärk·ĭst), n. One who advocates anarchy or believes in anarchism; a terrorist; a nihilist. — **an′arch·ist, an′ar·chis′tic** (-kĭs′tĭk), adj.

an′arch·y (ăn′är·kĭ), n. [Gr. anarchia.] **1.** The state of society where there is no law or supreme power; a state of political disorder. **2.** A state of confusion or disorder.

Syn. Anarchy, chaos, lawlessness mean a breakdown in law or order. Anarchy implies total absence or suspension of government; chaos, the utter negation of law or order; lawlessness, a prevalent or habitual disregard of law or order.

an·ar′thri·a (ăn·är′thrĭ·ȧ), n. [NL., fr. an- not + Gr. arthron joint.] Inability to articulate words as a result of brain lesion.

an·as′tig·mat′ic (ăn·ăs′tĭg·măt′ĭk), adj. [an- not + astigmatic.] Optics. Not astigmatic; — said esp. of photographic compound lenses consisting of a converging and a diverging lens in which the astigmatism of one is nullified by the equal and opposite astigmatism of the other. See LENS, Illust. (2).

a·nas′to·mose (ȧ·năs′tō·mōz), v. t. & i. To connect or intercommunicate by anastomosis; inosculate; interjoin.

a·nas′to·mo′sis (-mō′sĭs), n.; pl. -SES (-sēz). [NL., fr. Gr. anastomōsis opening, deriv. of ana- + stoma mouth.] **1.** Biol. The union of one vessel or hollow organ with another so as to form intercommunication, as a union between blood vessels, parts of the intestine, or veins of leaves; inosculation. **2.** Union or intercommunication of any system or network. — **a·nas′to·mot′ic** (-mŏt′ĭk), adj.

a·nas′tro·phe (ȧ·năs′trō·fē), n. [Gr. anastrophē, deriv. of ana- + strephein to turn.] Rhetoric. Inversion of the usual order of words ("Blessed are the meek").

an′a·tase (ăn′ȧ·tās), n. [Gr. anatasis a stretching out; — in allusion to the length of its crystals.] Mineral. = OCTAHEDRITE.

a·nath′e·ma (ȧ·năth′ē·mȧ), n.; pl. -MAS (-mȧz). [L. anathema, fr. Gr. anathēma anything devoted, esp. to evil, a curse, fr. anatithenai to set up as a votive gift, dedicate, fr. ana- + tithenai to set.] **1.** A solemn ban or curse pronounced by ecclesiastical authority, and accompanied by excommunication; hence, denunciation of anything as accursed. **2.** An imprecation. **3.** Any person or thing cursed by ecclesiastical authority; hence, any object of intense dislike or of loathing. — **Syn.** See EXECRATE. — **a·nath′e·ma·ti·za′tion** (-tĭ·zā′shŭn; -tī·zā′-), n.

a·nath′e·ma·tize (-tīz), v. t. & i. To pronounce an anathema (against). — **Syn.** See EXECRATE. — **a·nath′e·ma·ti·za′tion** (-tĭ·zā′shŭn; -tī·zā′-), n.

an′a·tom′ic (ăn′ȧ·tŏm′ĭk), **an′a·tom′i·cal** (-ĭ·kăl), adj. Of, pert. to, or dealing with anatomy. — **an′a·tom′i·cal·ly**, adv.

a·nat′o·mist (ȧ·năt′ō·mĭst), n. **1.** A person skilled or versed in anatomy. **2.** An analyst.

a·nat′o·mize (-mīz), v. t. To dissect, so as to display or examine the structure and use of the parts; hence, to analyze. — **a·nat′o·mi·za′tion** (-mĭ·zā′shŭn; -mī·zā′-), n.

a·nat′o·my (ȧ·năt′ō·mĭ), n.; pl. -MIES (-mĭz). [From F., fr. L., fr. Gr. anatomē dissection, fr. ana- + temnein to cut.] **1.** The art of dissecting, or artificially separating, the different parts of any animal or plant, to ascertain their position, relations, structure, and function. **2.** The science, or branch of morphology, which treats of the structure of animals or plants. **3.** The structural make-up of an organism or any of its parts. **4.** The art of dividing anything to examine its parts; analysis. **5.** A skeleton.

a·nat′ro·pous (ȧ·năt′rō·pŭs), adj. [ana- + -tropous.] Bot. Having the ovule inverted at an early period in its development, so that the micropyle is bent down to the funicle, to which the body of the ovule is united.

a·nat′to. Var. of ANNATTO.

-ance (-ăns), **-an·cy** (-ăn·sĭ), **-ence** (-ĕns), **-en·cy** (-ĕn·sĭ). [F. -ance, -ence, fr. L. -antia, -entia.] Suffixes forming nouns and meaning: **1.** Act or fact of doing what the verbal root denotes; as, assistance (act of assisting); sometimes implying some modification, as of continuance, manner, etc.; as in, emergence from obscurity; his first sudden appearance among them was followed by repeated appearances. **2.** State, condition, or quality of being, pl., instances of being, what the root word denotes (in these senses more distinctly specified, in modern English, by the variants -ancy, -ency); as in violence (condition or quality of being violent); compliancy (cf. compliance); fluency (cf. confluence); sometimes also with special implication of continuance, manner, etc.; as in, elegance of dress; unexcused absences. **3.** Concrete fact or thing; as in, standing on an eminence; Formosa was once a dependency of Japan.

an′ces·tor (ăn′sĕs′tẽr or, Brit., ăn′sĭs-), n. [OF. ancestre, fr. L. antecessor one who goes before, fr. antecedere to go before, fr. ante before + cedere to go.] **1.** One from whom a person is descended, esp. at a distance of time; a forefather; — opposed to descendant. **2.** Precursor. **3.** Biol. A progenitor (as one living in an earlier geological period) of a more recent or existing species or group. **4.** Law. One from whom an estate has descended; — the correlative of heir. — **Syn.** Forebear, progenitor. — **an′ces′tress** (-trĕs; 30), n.

an·ces′tral (ăn·sĕs′trăl; formerly ăn′sĕs-), adj. Of, pertaining to, derived from, or possessed by, an ancestor or ancestors; as, ancestral estates. — **an·ces′tral·ly**, adv.

an′ces·try (ăn′sĕs′trĭ or, Brit., ăn′sĭs-), n. **1.** Ancestral lineage; hence, birth or honorable descent. **2.** A series of ancestors. — **Syn.** Ancestry, lineage, pedigree mean one's progenitors collectively or their quality or character. **Ancestry,** in precise use, evokes the image of a family tree branching and ramifying the further it ascends; in looser but good use, it suggests one's progenitors in general, known

or unknown; **lineage** stresses descent in line: it evokes the image of a list of persons who in order of generation are descended from a single ancestor (thus, any group of persons who trace their derivation back to a common ancestor are of the same lineage, although their ancestry may be widely different); **pedigree** implies known and recorded ancestry and is applicable not only to persons but to animals and plants propagated under controlled conditions.

An·chi′ses (ăn·kī′sēz; ăng-), n. [Gr. Anchisēs.] See AENEAS.

an′chor (ăng′kẽr), n. [AS. ancor, fr. L. ancora, anchora, fr. Gr. ankyra.] **1.** An instrument that is attached to a ship or other vessel by a cable, and that, being cast overboard, lays hold of the earth by a fluke or hook and thus holds the vessel in a particular place. A 5th BOWER, SHEET ANCHOR. **2.** Anything regarded as a sure support. **3.** Anything serving a purpose like that of the ship's anchor, as an arrangement of timber to hold a dam fast, a metal tie, a cramp, etc. — v. t. **1.** To place at anchor; to secure by an anchor. **2.** To fix or fasten. — v. i. To cast anchor; to come to rest; to fix.

Anchor, 1.
1 Ring.
2 Stock.
3 Shank.
4 Bill.
5 Fluke, or Palm.
6 Arm.
7 Throat.
8 Crown.

an′chor·age (-ĭj), n. **1.** Act of anchoring, or condition of lying at anchor. **2.** A place suitable for anchoring or where ships anchor; a hold for a vessel's anchor; also, a secure hold for a heavy pull. **3.** A means of security. **4.** A toll for anchoring.

an′cho·ress (ăng′kō·rĕs; 30), n. A female anchorite.

an′cho·rite (-rīt), **an′cho·ret** (-rĕt), n. [Through F. & L., fr. Gr. anachōrētēs, fr. anachōrein to go back, fr. ana- + chōrein to give place.] One who renounces the world to live in seclusion, usually for religious reasons; hermit; recluse. Cf. CENOBITE. — **an′cho·rit′ic** (-rĭt′ĭk), **an′cho·ret′ic** (-rĕt′ĭk), adj.

anchor knot. See KNOT, Illust. (14).

an·cho′vy (ăn·chō′vĭ; ăn′chō·vĭ), n.; pl. -VIES (-vĭz), sometimes AN-CHOVY. See PLURAL, Note, 3. [Sp. anchova.] Any of a number of small herringlike fishes, esp. one (Engraulis encrasicholus) of the Mediterranean, used for pickling, sauces, etc.

an·chu′sa (ăng·kū′sȧ), n. [NL., fr. L. anchusa alkanet, fr. Gr. anchousa.] Bot. Bugloss.

an·chu′sin (-sĭn), n. Chem. Alkannin.

an′chy·lose, an′chy·lo′sis, etc. Vars. of ANKYLOSE, etc.

‖**an′cienne′ no′blesse′** (äⁿ′syĕn′ nō′blĕs′). [F.] Literally, old-time nobility; those French families ennobled before the Revolution of 1789.

‖**an′cien′ ré′gime′** (äⁿ′syäⁿ′ rā′zhēm′). [F.] The former political and social system, esp. that existing in France before the Revolution of 1789.

an′cient (ān′shĕnt), adj. [OF. (& F.) ancien, fr. L. antea, ante, before.] **1.** Old; specif.: **a** Archaic. Aged. **b** Existing or handed down from remote antiquity. **c** Venerable; hoary; also, antique; old-fashioned. **2.** Belonging to times long past; specif.: **a** Belonging to the historical period beginning with the earliest known civilizations (those of Egypt and Chaldea) and generally taken as extending to the fall of the Western Roman Empire (A.D. 476). **b** Pertaining to the ancients or to their times; as, ancient history. — **Syn.** See OLD. — **Ant.** Modern. — n. **1.** An aged living being. **2.** One who lived in antiquity; pl., the civilized peoples of antiquity, esp. the classical nations. **3.** One of the classical authors. — **an′cient·ly**, adv. — **an′cient·ness**, n.

an′cient, n. [Corrupt. fr. ensign.] Archaic. **a** An ensign. **b** The bearer of an ensign. Shak.

Ancient of Days. The Deity; — a Biblical title.

an′cient·ry (ān′shĕnt·rĭ), n. Ancientness; antiquity.

an′cil·lar′y (ăn′sĭ·lĕr′ĭ or, esp. Brit., ăn·sĭl′ȧ·rĭ, ăn′sĭ·lẽr·ĭ), adj. [L. ancillaris, fr. ancilla female servant.] Subservient or subordinate; auxiliary.

an·cip′i·tal (ăn·sĭp′ĭ·tăl; -t'l), adj. [L. anceps, ancipitis, two-headed, fr. an- for ambi- on both sides + caput head.] Bot. Two-edged, as certain flattened stems.

an′con (ăng′kŏn), n.; pl. ANCONES (ăng·kō′nēz). [L., fr. Gr. ankōn elbow.] **1.** Anat. The elbow. **2.** Arch. A corbel supporting a cornice; a console. See CONSOLE, Illust.

-an·cy. See -ANCE.

an′cy·los′to·mi′a·sis (ăn′sĭ·lŏs′tō·mī′ȧ·sĭs), n. [NL., fr. Ancylostoma (Gr. ankylos crooked + stoma mouth) + -iasis.] Med. A severe anemia caused by the sucking of blood from the small intestine by large numbers of certain parasitic nematode worms (esp. of the genera Ancylostoma and Necator); uncinariasis; hookworm disease.

and (ănd; unstressed, ănd, ăn, etc.; 4), conj. [AS. and.] **1.** A particle expressing the general relation of connection or addition, used to conjoin word with word, phrase with phrase, clause with clause. **2.** Obs. If. — **and so forth.** And others or more of the same or of similar kind; further in the same or similar manner. The abbreviation etc. (et cetera), or &c., is often read and so forth.

An′da·lu′sian (ăn′dȧ·lū′zhăn; -shăn), adj. Of Andalusia or its people. — n. **1.** One of the people of Andalusia. **2.** A domestic fowl of a breed similar to the Leghorn.

an′da·lu′site (ăn′dȧ·lū′sīt), n. Mineral. A silicate of aluminum, Al_2SiO_5, usually in thick orthorhombic prisms.

an·dan′te (än·dän′tā; ăn·dăn′tĕ), adj. [It., lit., going.] Music. Moderately slow, but flowing; quicker than larghetto. — n. A piece or movement in andante tempo. — adv. In andante tempo.

an′dan·ti′no (än′dän·tē′nō), adj. [It., dim. of andante.] Music. Quicker than andante, but not so quick as allegretto. — n. A piece or movement in andantino tempo. — adv. In andantino tempo.

An·de′an (ăn·dē′ăn; ăn′dē·ăn), adj. Of or like the Andes.

an′des·ite (ăn′dĕs·īt), n. [From the Andes Mts.] An extrusive, dark-grayish rock, essentially an acid plagioclase.

and′i′ron (ănd′ī′ẽrn), n. [OF. andier.] One of a pair of metal supports for firewood on a hearth, each consisting of a horizontal bar mounted on short legs and having a vertical shaft surmounting the front end; a firedog.

and/or. Either and or or.

an′dra·dite (ăn′drȧ·dīt), n. [After J. B. de Andrada e Silva (1763?–1838), Brazilian geologist.] A variety of garnet, chemically Ca_3Fe_2, occurring in various colors.

an′dro- (ăn′drō-), **andr-.** [Gr. anēr, andros, man.] A combining form signifying: **a** Man, man and, as in **an·droph′a·gous,** man-eating. **b** Male, masculine. **c** Anther or stamen.

An′dro·clus, An′dro·cles (ăn′drō·klŭs, -klēz), *n.* A Roman slave of the 1st century A.D., said to have been spared in the arena by a lion from whose foot he had extracted a thorn years before in Africa.

an·droe′ci·um (ăn·drē′shĭ·ŭm; -sĭ·ŭm), *n.; pl.* -CIA (-ȧ). [NL., fr. *andr-* + Gr. *oikos* house.] The stamens in the flower of a seed plant. See FLOWER, *Illust.* — **an·droe′cial** (-shăl), *adj.*

an′dro·gen (ăn′drō·jĕn), *n.* [*andro-* + *-gen.*] *Biochem.* Any substance capable of inducing masculine characteristics, as a male sex hormone. — **an′dro·gen′ic** (-jĕn′ĭk), *adj.*

an·drog′y·nous (ăn·drŏj′ĭ·nŭs), *adj.* [L. *androgynus,* fr. Gr. *androgynos,* fr. *anēr, andros,* man + *gynē* woman.] **1.** Hermaphroditic. **2.** *Bot.* Bearing both staminate and pistillate flowers in the same cluster. — **an·drog′y·ny** (-nĭ), *n.*

An·drom′a·che (ăn·drŏm′ȧ·kē), *n.* [L., fr. Gr. *Andromachē.*] In Homer's *Iliad,* the devoted wife of Hector.

An·drom′e·da (ăn·drŏm′ē·dȧ), *n.* [L., fr. Gr. *Andromedē.*] **1.** *Gr. Myth.* An Ethiopian princess who was chained to a cliff for a monster to devour but was rescued by Perseus, who married her. **2.** *genitive* -DAE (-dē). A northern constellation directly south of Cassiopeia, between Pegasus and Perseus.

an′dro·sphinx (ăn′drō·sfĭngks), *n.* See SPHINX, 3.

an·dros′ter·one (ăn·drŏs′tēr·ōn), *n.* [*andro-* + *sterol* + *-one.*] *Biochem.* A male sex hormone, a hydroxyketone, $C_{19}H_{30}O_2$, found esp. in human male urine.

-an′drous (-ăn′drŭs). [Gr. *anēr, andros,* man.] *Bot.* A combining form denoting *having* (so many or such) *stamens,* as in mon*androus,* gyn*androus.*

An′dva·ri (än′dwä·rē), *n.* [ON.] In the Eddas, a dwarf whom Loki robs of his treasure and a ring.

ane (ān), **anes** (āns). Dial. vars. of ONE, ONCE.

a·near′ (ȧ·nēr′), *adv. & prep. Poetic & Dial.* Near.

an′ec·dot′age (ăn′ĕk·dōt′ĭj; ăn′ĭk-), *n.* **1.** Anecdotes collectively. **2.** The age when a person becomes addicted to anecdotes; — a punning formation.

an′ec·do′tal (-dō′tăl; -dō′tăl; -t′l), *adj.* Characteristic of or containing anecdotes; as, *anecdotal* conversation.

an′ec·dote (ăn′ĕk·dōt; ăn′ĭk-), *n.* [F., fr. Gr. *anekdotos* not published, fr. *an-* not + *ekdotos* given out.] A narrative, usually brief, of an interesting, often amusing, incident or event. — **an′ec·dot′ist** (-dōt′ĭst), *n.*

an′ec·dot′ic (-dŏt′ĭk), **an′ec·dot′i·cal** (-ĭ·kăl), *adj.* **a** Of, of the nature of, or containing anecdotes. **b** Given to telling anecdotes.

a·nele′ (ȧ·nēl′), *v. t.* [ME. *anelien,* fr. *an* on + AS. *ele* oil, fr. L. *oleum.*] *Archaic.* To give extreme unction to.

an′e·lec′tric (ăn′ē·lĕk′trĭk), *adj.* [*an-* not + *electric.*] *Physics.* Not becoming electrified by friction.

a·ne′mi·a, a·nae′mi·a (ȧ·nē′mĭ·ȧ), *n.* [NL., fr. Gr. *anaimia,* fr. *a-, an-,* not + *haima* blood.] *Med.* A condition in which the red corpuscles of the blood are reduced in number or deficient in hemoglobin, causing pallor, shortness of breath, and palpitation of the heart.

a·ne′mic, a·nae′mic (ȧ·nē′mĭk; ȧ·nĕm′ĭk), *adj.* **1.** Of, pert. to, or affected with anemia; bloodless. **2.** Lacking vigor or vitality; weak.

an′e·mo- (ăn′ē·mō-). [Gr. *anemos.*] A combining form meaning *wind* or *inhalation.*

a·nem′o·graph (ȧ·nĕm′ō·grăf), *n.* [*anemo-* + *-graph.*] A recording anemometer. — **a·nem′o·graph′ic** (-grăf′ĭk), *adj.*

an′e·mol′o·gy (ăn′ē·mŏl′ō·jĭ), *n.* [*anemo-* + *-logy.*] The science of the wind. — **an′e·mo·log′i·cal** (-mō·lŏj′ĭ·kăl), *adj.*

an′e·mom′e·ter (-mŏm′ē·tēr), *n.* [*anemo-* + *-meter.*] An instrument for measuring the force or velocity of the wind; a wind gauge. — **an′e·mo·met′ric** (-mō·mĕt′rĭk), **an′e·mo·met′ri·cal** (-rĭ·kăl), *adj.*

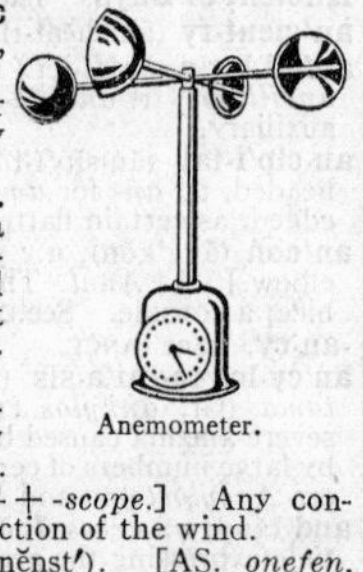
Anemometer.

an′e·mom′e·try (-mŏm′ē·trĭ), *n.* Act or process of ascertaining the force or velocity of the wind.

a·nem′o·ne (ȧ·nĕm′ō·nē), *n.* [L., fr. Gr. *anemōnē,* fr. *anemos* wind.] **1.** Any of a large genus (*Anemone*) of the crowfoot family (Ranunculaceae) having lobed or divided leaves and showy flowers without petals but with conspicuous, often colored, sepals. **2.** A sea anemone. See ACTINIA, *Illust.*

an′e·moph′i·lous (ăn′ē·mŏf′ĭ·lŭs), *adj.* [*anemo-* + *-philous.*] *Bot.* Fertilized by wind-borne pollen. — **an′e·moph′i·ly** (-lĭ), *n.*

a·nem′o·scope (ȧ·nĕm′ō·skōp), *n.* [*anemo-* + *-scope.*] Any contrivance for indicating and recording the direction of the wind.

a·nent′ (ȧ·nĕnt′), *prep.* Also **a·nenst′** (-nĕnst′). [AS. *onefen, onemn,* fr. *an, on,* on + *efen* even, equal.] **1.** *Now Dial.* Beside. **2.** About; concerning.

an′er·gy (ăn′ēr·jĭ), *n.* [NL. *anergia,* fr. Gr. *an-* not + *ergon* work.] *Med.* Lack of energy; specif., *Immunol.,* a condition in which an acquired immunity is reduced or lost.

an′er·oid (ăn′ēr·oid), *adj.* [Gr. *a-* not + *nēros* wet, moist + *-oid.*] Containing no liquid. — *n.* An aneroid barometer.

aneroid barometer. A barometer in which the action of atmospheric pressure in bending a metallic surface is made to move a pointer. Cf. ALTIMETER, *Illust.*

an′es·the′si·a, an′aes·the′si·a (ăn′ĕs·thē′zhĭ·ȧ; -zhȧ; -zĭ·ȧ), *n.* [Gr. *anaisthēsia* insensibility, fr. *an-* not + *aisthēsis* feeling.] Entire or partial loss of feeling or sensation; a state of paralysis of the sensory apparatus produced by disease, by hypnotism, or by administration of certain drugs, gases, etc. Anesthesia is *general* when (as from inhalation of ether) it affects the entire body; *local* when produced by a locally active agent, like cocaine; *block* or *conduction* when produced by blocking nerve impulses from the affected part; *spinal* when the anesthetic is injected under the dura mater of the spinal cord.

an′es·thet′ic, an′aes·thet′ic (ăn′ĕs·thĕt′ĭk), *adj.* **1. a** Capable of producing anesthesia. **b** Characterized by, or connected with, anesthesia. **2.** (*pron.* ăn′ĕs-) Hence, obtuse; — with *to.* — *n.* An agent that produces anesthesia.

an·es′the·tist, an·aes′the·tist (ăn·ĕs′thē·tĭst), *n. Med.* One who administers anesthetics.

an·es′the·tize, an·aes′the·tize (-tīz), *v. t. Med.* To subject to anesthesia. — **an′es·thet′i·za′tion, an′aes·thet′i·za′tion** (ăn′ĕs·thĕt′ĭ·zā′shŭn; ăn·ĕs′thē·tĭ-), *n.*

a·neuch′ (ȧ·nōōk′). Scot. var. of ENOUGH.

an′eu·rin (ăn′ū·rĭn; ȧ·nū′rĭn), *n.* [*a-* not + *neur-* + vitamin.] Vitamin B_1 (see VITAMIN).

an′eu·rysm (ăn′ū·rĭz′m), *n.* Also **an′eu·rism.** [Gr. *aneurysma* an opening, fr. *ana-* + *eurys* wide.] *Med.* A permanent abnormal blood-filled dilatation of an artery, resulting from disease of the vessel wall. — **an′eu·rys′mal, an′eu·ris′mal** (-rĭz′măl), *adj.*

a·new′ (ȧ·nū′), *adv.* [*a-* for *of* + *new.*] Over again; in a new form.

an·frac′tu·os′i·ty (ăn·frăk′tū·ŏs′ĭ·tĭ), *n.; pl.* -TIES (-tĭz). **1.** Anfractuous quality. **2.** A sinuous channel, course, etc.

an·frac′tu·ous (ăn·frăk′tū·ŭs), *adj.* Also **an·frac′tu·ose** (-ōs). [L. *anfractuosus,* fr. *anfractus* a winding, fr. *an-* for *ambi-* + *frangere, fractum,* to break.] Full of windings and turnings; sinuous; tortuous.

an′ga·ry (ăng′gȧ·rĭ), *n.* [L. *angaria* service to a lord.] *Internat. Law.* A right of a belligerent in case of necessity to seize, use, or destroy property of neutrals.

an′gel (ān′jĕl), *n.* [OF. *angele,* fr. L. *angelus,* fr. Gr. *angelos* messenger.] **1.** In theology, a supernatural messenger of God; a spiritual, celestial being, superior to man in power and intelligence; hence: **a** A messenger, as of spring or of death. **b** A person resembling an angel in goodness, innocence, or loveliness. **c** A conventionalized representation of a white-robed winged figure, of human form. **2.** Attendant spirit; genius; as, one's good *angel.* **3.** *Slang.* A nonprofessional backer of a venture, a player, or a political candidate. **4.** An English gold coin, issued 1470–1634, showing the archangel Michael slaying the dragon. **5.** *Christian Science.* A message from Truth and Love; the inspiration of goodness, purity, and immortality, counteracting all evil, sensuality, and mortality. *Mary Baker Eddy.*

angel cake *or* **angel food.** A white spongecake made of flour, sugar, and whites of eggs.

an′gel·fish′ (-fĭsh′), *n.; pl.,* see FISH. **a** Either of two raylike sharks (*Squatina squatina* and *S. dumeril*) with pectoral fins that extend horizontally like wings when spread. **b** Any of several compressed, bright-colored teleost fishes (family Chaetodontidae) of warm seas. **c** A small S. Amer. fish (*Pterophyllum scalare*) with silvery, black-barred body and large fins, a favorite aquarium fish; — called also *scalare.*

an·gel′ic (ăn·jĕl′ĭk), **an·gel′i·cal** (-ĭ·kăl), *adj.* Belonging to angels; resembling, characteristic of, or of the nature of, an angel; heavenly; saintly. — **an·gel′i·cal·ly,** *adv.*

an·gel′i·ca (ăn·jĕl′ĭ·kȧ), *n.* [NL.] Also **an′ge·lique′** (ăn′jē·lēk′). Any of a large genus (*Angelica*) of herbs of the carrot family, esp. one species (*A. archangelica*) whose roots and fruit furnish the **angelica oil** used as a flavoring for liqueurs and as a perfume.

angelica tree. The Hercules'-club.

angelo-. A combining form for *angel,* as in **an′gel·ol′o·gy.**

An′ge·lus (ăn′jē·lŭs), *n.* [L. See ANGEL.] *R.C.Ch.* **a** A devotion commemorating the Incarnation, said at morning, noon, and evening, at the sound of a bell called the **Angelus bell. b** The Angelus bell.

an′ger (ăng′gēr), *n.* [ON. *angr* affliction, sorrow.] **1.** *Obs.* Trouble; affliction; also, physical pain. **2.** *Dial.* Inflammation of a wound, sore, etc. **3.** A strong passion or emotion of displeasure, and usually antagonism, excited by a sense of injury or insult.

Syn. Anger, ire, rage, fury, indignation, wrath mean emotional excitement induced by intense displeasure. **Anger,** the comprehensive term of this group, suggests, apart from the context, neither a definite degree of intensity nor outward manifestation; **ire,** now regarded as literary or affected, suggests great intensity and its exhibition in looks, acts, or words; **rage** implies loss of self-control from violence of emotion, often connoting a temporary mental derangement; **fury,** even more than *rage,* implies an overmastering passion verging on madness; **indignation** stresses a deep, intense, often righteous, anger aroused by that which one considers mean, shameful, or the like; **wrath** may imply either rage or indignation as its emotional basis, but it also implies a desire or intent to avenge or punish, or to get revenge.

— *v. t.* [ON. *angra.*] **1.** To excite to anger; to enrage; provoke. **2.** *Dial.* To cause to smart; to inflame.

an′ger·ly (-lĭ), *adv. Archaic.* Angrily.

An′ge·vin (ăn′jē·vĭn), **An′ge·vine** (-vĭn; -vīn), *adj.* [F. *Angevin.*] Of or pertaining to Anjou or to the Plantagenets. — *n.* A native or inhabitant of Anjou; also, a member of an Angevin royal house.

an·gi′na (ăn·jī′nȧ; *L.* ăn′jĭ·nȧ), *n.* [L., quinsy, fr. Gr. *anchonē* a throttling.] *Med.* Any inflammatory affection of the throat or fauces, as quinsy or croup, esp. one producing suffocative spasms.

an·gi′na pec′to·ris (pĕk′tō·rĭs). [L.] A painful disease characterized by a sense of suffocation in the chest; — so named from a sense of suffocating contraction within the chest.

an′gi·o- (ăn′jĭ·ō-; *classical* ăn·jĭ′ō- *is little used*). [Gr. *angeion* a vessel.] A combining form denoting *a seed vessel, blood vessel,* or *lymph vessel;* as in **an′gi·o·car′pous,** *Bot.,* having fruit enclosed within an external covering; **an′gi·ol′o·gy,** science of the blood vessels and lymphatics.

an′gi·o′ma (ăn′jĭ·ō′mȧ), *n.; pl.* -OMATA (-ō′mȧ·tȧ), -OMAS (-ō′mȧz). [NL., fr. *angi(o)-* + *-oma.*] A tumor chiefly of dilated blood or lymph vessels. — **an′gi·om′a·tous** (-ŏm′ȧ·tŭs; -ō′mȧ·tŭs), *adj.*

an′gi·o·sperm′ (ăn′jĭ·ō·spûrm′), *n.* [*angio-* + *-sperm.*] Any plant of a class (Angiospermae) having the seeds in a closed ovary. Cf. GYMNOSPERM. — **an′gi·o·sper′mous** (-spûr′mŭs), *adj.*

an′gle (ăng′g′l), *n.* [AS. *angel, angul.*] *Archaic.* A fishhook or fishing tackle. — *v. i.;* -GLED (-g′ld); -GLING (-glĭng). **1.** To fish with an angle (fishhook), or with hook and line. **2.** To use artifice or wiles, as in order to gain an end; to fish.

an′gle, *n.* [OF., fr. L. *angulus* angle, corner.] **1.** The figure formed by the coming together in a point of two lines, or the space bounded on two sides by such lines. **2.** *Math.* **a** A measure of the amount of turning necessary to bring one line or plane into coincidence with or parallel to another. **b** A solid angle, trihedral angle, or the like. **3.** A projecting or sharp corner; an angular fragment or space. **4.** A point of view; also, aspect; phase. **5.** A special approach or point of attack or of technique for attaining an end, as for writing a distinctive news story, probing a mystery, or promoting an enterprise or one's own interest. — **Syn.** See PHASE. — *v. t.* **1.** To turn, bend, or move at an angle or in angles. **2.** To warp in presenting so as to favor the writer's or the reader's personal, class, racial, or other bias; as, to *angle* the news; to class-*angle* a story. — *v. i.* **1.** To turn at an angle. **2.** To proceed at an angle.

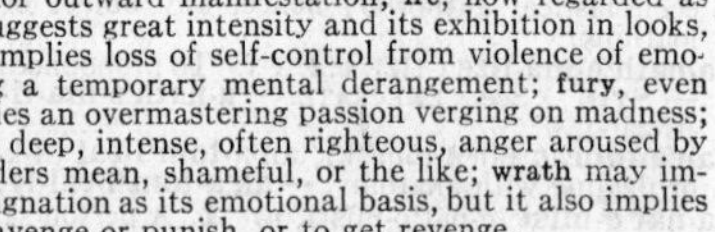

Angles. 1 Obtuse; 2 Acute; 3 Right.

an′gled (ăng′g'ld), *adj.* Having an angle or angles; as, right-*angled*, many-*angled*.

angle iron. A bent piece of iron used for joining parts of a structure at an angle; specif., a bar of L section, used in structural ironwork.

angle of attack. *Aeronautics.* The acute angle between the direction of the relative wind and the chord of an airfoil.

an′gle·pod′ (ăng′g'l·pŏd′) *n.* Any of several plants (genus *Vincetoxicum*) of the southern United States, having angled pods.

an′gler (ăng′glẽr), *n.* **1.** One who angles. **2.** A marine fish (*Lophius piscatorius*) with a very large flattened head and wide mouth, having a lure on its head and fleshy mouth appendages with which to attract smaller fishes as prey.

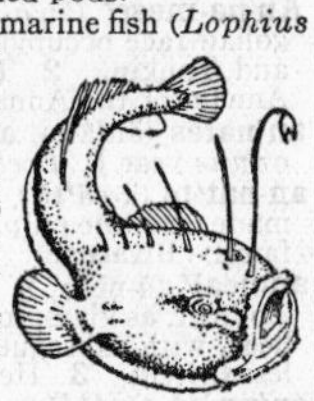
Angler, 2. (1/30)

An′gles (ăng′g'lz), *n. pl.* [L. *Angli*, fr. Teut.] A Germanic people who with Saxons and Jutes conquered England in the 5th century A.D. From their name come the words *England* and *English*. — **An′gli·an** (-glĭ·ăn), *adj. & n.*

an′gle·site (ăng′g'l·sīt), *n.* [From the Isle of *Anglesey*.] Lead sulfate, $PbSO_4$, occurring massive or in orthorhombic crystals.

an′gle·worm′ (ăng′g'l·wûrm′), *n.* An earthworm.

An′gli·can (ăng′glĭ·kăn), *adj.* [ML. *Anglicanus*.] Of or pertaining to England or the English nation; specif., pertaining to, or connected with, the Church of England and churches holding essentially the same faith, order, and worship with it, as the Protestant Episcopal Church in the United States. This body of churches is called the **Anglican Communion.** — *n.* One who acknowledges the faith and order common to the Anglican churches. — **An′gli·can·ism** (-ĭz'm), *n.*

‖**An′gli·ce** (ăng′glĭ·sē), *adv.* [ML.] In English; Anglicized; as, Livorno, *Anglice* Leghorn.

An′gli·cism (ăng′glĭ·sĭz'm), *n.* **1.** An idiom or trait peculiarly English. **2.** The quality of being typically English.

An′gli·cist (-sĭst), *n.* An Anglist; esp., a student of English linguistics.

An′gli·cize, an′gli·cize (-sīz), *v. t. & i.* To render or become conformable to English idiom, usage, etc. — **An′gli·ci·za′tion, an′gli·ci·za′tion** (-sĭ·zā′shŭn; -sī·zā′-), *n.*

An′gli·fy (-fī), *v. t.;* -FIED (-fīd); -FY′ING. To Anglicize.

an′gling (ăng′glĭng), *n.* The act of one who angles; specif., the art of fishing with hook and line, esp. for sport.

An′glist (ăng′glĭst), *n.* A specialist in the study of England, the English language, English institutions, customs, etc.

An·glis′tics (ăng·glĭs′tĭks), *n.;* see -ICS. Linguistic study of English.

An′glo- (ăng′glō-). [LL. *Angli* the English.] A combining form equivalent to *English*, or *English and;* — in adjectives referring esp. to international relations (as in **An′glo-E·gyp′tian**) and in nouns referring esp. to natives or residents of foreign descent or to the language composed of both elements (as in **An′glo-I′rish**).

An′glo-A·mer′i·can, *adj.* **a** Pertaining jointly to England and America, esp. the United States, or to their peoples. **b** Pertaining to Anglo-Americans. — *n.* An American, esp. a citizen of the United States, of English origin or descent.

An′glo-Ca·thol′i·cism (-kȧ·thŏl′ĭ·sĭz'm), *n.* The doctrines and practices of those in the Anglican Communion who maintain (1) that Catholicity is inherent in a church whose episcopate can trace its line of descent from the apostles (see APOSTOLIC SUCCESSION) and whose faith is agreed by all Catholics to be revealed truth, and (2) that any church of the Anglican Communion is such a church, its method of church government and its doctrine remaining unchanged by the Reformation. — **An′glo-Cath′o·lic** (-kăth′ō·lĭk; -kăth′lĭk), *n. & adj.*

An′glo-French′, *adj.* **a** Pertaining jointly to England and France or to their peoples. **b** Relating to Anglo-French. — *n.* Old French as used in England after the Norman Conquest.

An′glo-In′di·an (-ĭn′dĭ·ăn), *adj.* Of or pertaining to the English in India, or the English and East Indian peoples, languages, customs, etc., or to their relations. — *n.* One of the English race born or resident in the East Indies. Specif., in India (officially adopted by the government of India in 1911), a person of mixed European and Indian parentage or descent. Cf. EURASIAN, *n.*

An′glo·ma′ni·a (ăng′glō·mā′nĭ·ȧ), *n.* Excessive fondness for English customs, institutions, etc. — **An′glo·ma′ni·ac** (-ăk), *n.*

An′glo-Nor′man, *n.* **a** One of the Normans who lived in England after the Conquest. **b** The French language of Normandy as used in England from the Conquest to about 1154. — **An′glo-Nor′man,** *adj.*

An′glo·phile (ăng′glō·fīl; -fĭl), **An′glo·phil** (-fĭl), *n.* [*Anglo-* + *-phile, -phil*.] One who greatly admires or favors England and things English.

An′glo·phobe (-fōb), *n.* [*Anglo-* + *-phobe*.] One who is averse to England and things English.

An′glo·pho′bi·a (-fō′bĭ·ȧ), *n.* [*Anglo-* + *-phobia*.] Intense dread of, or aversion to, England or the English.

An′glo-Sax′on, *n.* [ML. *Anglo-Saxones*.] **1.** Usually *pl.* A member of the nation created by the consolidation of Low German tribes that invaded England in the 5th and 6th centuries, together with native and Danish elements, which continued as the ruling power of England until the Norman Conquest. **2.** A member of, or a descendant from, the mixed race which forms the English nation. **3.** The language brought into England by the Germanic invaders and there developed by the Anglo-Saxons; Old English; hence, the inherited Teutonic element of English. See ENGLISH, *n.*, 2; INDO-EUROPEAN LANGUAGES, *Table*.
— *adj.* Of or pertaining to the Anglo-Saxons or their language, or to a people largely descended from Anglo-Saxons.

An·go′ra (ăng·gō′rȧ), *n.* Also **An·go′la** (-gō′lȧ). [From *Angora*, capital of Turkey.] **1. a** A fabric of Angora wool or an imitation of it. **b** A soft fluffy yarn or fabric made wholly or in part of the hair of the Angora rabbit. **2.** Short for *Angora cat, goat,* or *rabbit*.

Angora cat. A long-haired variety of the domestic cat.

Angora goat. A variety of the domestic goat, having long silky hair, **Angora wool,** which is the true mohair.

Angora rabbit. A rabbit of a long-haired domestic breed sometimes raised for the fine wool which it produces. The common, and preferred, type is white with red eyes, but other colors are known.

an′gos·tu′ra (ăng′gŏs·tōōr′ȧ; -tū′rȧ), *n.* [Sp., fr. *Angostura*, in Venezuela.] An aromatic bitter bark used as a tonic and febrifuge, obtained from a South American tree (*Cusparia angostura*) of the rue family.

an′gry (ăng′grĭ), *adj.;* AN′GRI·ER (-grĭ·ẽr); AN′GRI·EST. [From ANGER.] **1.** Inflamed and painful, as a sore. **2.** Touched with, or stirred by, anger; showing vexation or resentment; enraged; wrathful. **3.** Indicative of, or proceeding from, anger; as, *angry* words; also appearing or acting as if moved by anger; threatening; as, an *angry* sky. — **an′gri·ly** (ăng′grĭ·lĭ), *adv.* — **an′gri·ness** (-nĕs; 30), *n.*

Syn. **Angry, irate, indignant, wrathful, acrimonious** mean feeling or showing passionate or ill-tempered displeasure. **Angry,** which usually implies inflamed looks, words, or the like, is applicable not only to men and to beasts but also to things which suggest a comparable condition; **irate,** applied only to persons, their looks, acts, or words, suggests even greater exhibition of feeling than *angry;* **indignant** implies sufficiency of provocation and righteousness of anger; **wrathful** usually connotes more justification than *irate* and greater vehemence in expression than *indignant;* **acrimonious,** usually applied to intercourse and utterances, adds to *angry* implications of an irreconcilable difference of opinion and of increasing bitterness.

ang′strom u′nit, *or* **ang′strom** (ăng′strŭm; *Swed.* ông′strûm), *n.* [After A. J. *Ångström* (1814–74), Sw. physicist.] *Physics.* A minute unit of length equal to one ten-thousandth of a micron or one hundred-millionth of a centimeter, used in expressing the length of light waves. Symbol, λ. Abbr. *A.*, *A.U.*, *Å.*, *Å.U.*

an′guish (ăng′gwĭsh), *n.* [OF. *anguisse, angoisse*, fr. L. *angustia* narrowness, difficulty, distress, fr. *angustus* narrow, difficult, fr. root of *angere* to press together.] Extreme pain, either of body or mind; excruciating distress. — **Syn.** See SORROW. — *v. i. & t.* To suffer, or cause to suffer, anguish.

an′guished (-gwĭsht), *adj.* Produced or accompanied by anguish; as, an *anguished* conscience, shriek, or protest.

an′gu·lar (ăng′gū·lẽr), *adj.* [L. *angularis*.] **1.** Having an angle or angles; forming an angle; sharp-cornered. **2.** Measured by an angle. **3.** Having the bones prominent from leanness. **4.** Stiff in character or manner; as, *angular* politeness. — **-lar·ly,** *adv.* — **-lar·ness,** *n.*

an′gu·lar′i·ty (-lăr′ĭ·tĭ), *n.* Quality of being angular; also, *pl.*, angular outlines.

an′gu·late (ăng′gū·lāt), **an′gu·lat′ed** (-lāt′ĕd; -ĭd), *adj.* [L. *angulatus*, past part. of *angulare* to make angular.] Having angles; angled; as, *angulate* leaves. — **an′gu·late·ly,** *adv.*

an′gu·la′tion (-lā′shŭn), *n.* Angular formation or shape.

an·gus′ti- (ăng·gŭs′tĭ-). [L. *angustus*.] A combining form meaning *narrow*, as in **an·gus′ti·fo′li·ate.**

an′gus·tu′ra (ăng′gŭs·tōōr′ȧ; -tū′rȧ). Var. of ANGOSTURA.

an·hy′drate (ăn·hī′drāt), *v. t.* To dehydrate. — **an′hy·dra′tion** (ăn′hī·drā′shŭn), *n.*

an·hy′dride (ăn·hī′drīd; -drĭd), *n.* Also **-drid.** [See ANHYDROUS.] *Chem.* **a** An oxide of a nonmetallic element or an organic radical, capable of forming an acid by uniting with the elements of water, or of being formed from an acid by the abstraction of water. **b** A compound formed by abstraction of water.

an·hy′drite (-drīt), *n.* *Mineral.* Anhydrous calcium sulfate, $CaSO_4$, usually massive, and white or slightly colored.

an·hy′dro- (ăn·hī′drō-), **anhydr-.** [See ANHYDROUS.] A combining form from Greek *anydros*, waterless, denoting: *Chem. An anhydride* (sense **b**) *of a* (specified) *compound*, as in **an·hy′dro·glu′cose.**

an·hy′drous (-drŭs), *adj.* [Gr. *anydros* waterless, fr. *an-* not + *hydōr* water.] Destitute of water, esp. water of crystallization; as, *anhydrous* salts.

a′ni (ä′nē), *n.;* *pl.* ANIS (-nēz). [Sp. *ani*, Pg. *ani*, fr. Tupi *ani, anú*.] Any of three species of black birds of the cuckoo family (Cuculidae), of the warmer parts of America.

an′il (ăn′ĭl), *n.* [F., fr. Pg., fr. Ar. *al-nīl* the indigo plant, fr. Skr. *nīlī* indigo, fr. *nīla* dark blue.] **a** A West Indian shrub (*Indigofera suffruticosa*) of the pea family, one of the sources of indigo. **b** Indigo.

an′ile (ăn′īl; -ĭl; ā′nīl), *adj.* [L. *anilis*, fr. *anus* an old woman.] Old-womanish; infirm. — **a·nil′i·ty** (ȧ·nĭl′ĭ·tĭ), *n.*

an′i·line (ăn′ĭ·lĭn; -līn; -lēn), *n.* Also **-lin.** [From ANIL.] *Chem.* An oily poisonous basic liquid, $C_6H_5NH_2$, colorless when pure, now chiefly made from nitrobenzene, used in making dyes.

aniline dye. **a** Any dye made with the use of aniline. **b** Hence, any of various dyes related chemically to the foregoing. **c** Popularly, any synthetic organic dye.

an′i·mad·ver′sion (ăn′ĭ·măd·vûr′shŭn; -zhŭn), *n.* [L. *animadversio*. See ANIMADVERT.] A remark, esp. one by way of criticism, usually of censure; also, adverse criticism.

Syn. **Animadversion, stricture, aspersion, reflection** (*or* **reflexion**) mean an adverse criticism. **Animadversion** implies a motive of deep-seated prejudice or ill will and a carping disposition; **stricture** always implies censure which may be ill-natured or judicious; **aspersion** imputes a slanderous character to the criticism; **reflection** usually implies indirect aspersion or a defamatory imputation that may be inferred from what has been said.

an′i·mad·vert′ (-vûrt′), *v. i. & t.* [L. *animadvertere*, fr. *animus* mind + *advertere* to turn to. See ADVERT.] **1.** To take notice; to observe. **2.** To remark by way of criticism; to express censure; — with *on* or *upon*.

an′i·mal (ăn′ĭ·măl), *n.* [L., fr. *animalis* animate, fr. *anima* breath, soul.] **1.** Any member of the group of living beings typically capable of spontaneous movement and rapid motor response to stimulation, as distinguished from a *plant*. See CLASSIFICATION, 2. **2.** One of the lower animals; a brute or beast, as distinguished from *man*. — *adj.* **1.** Of, relating to, resembling, or derived from, animals or their characteristics. **2.** Pertaining to the sentient nature of man, as distinguished from his rational or spiritual nature. **3.** Sensual; carnal. — **Syn.** See CARNAL.

‖**a′ni·mal bi′pes im·plu′me** (ăn′ĭ·măl bī′pēz ĭm·plōō′mē). [L.] A two-legged animal without feathers; man.

an′i·mal′cu·la (ăn′ĭ·măl′kū·lȧ), *n., pl.* of ANIMALCULUM.

an′i·mal′cu·lae (-lē), *n. pl.* [As if fr. a L. fem. sing. *animalcula*.] = ANIMALCULA.

an′i·mal′cule (-kūl), *n.* [L. *animalculum*, dim. of *animal*.] **1.** *Obs.* A tiny animal, as a fly. **2.** A minute animal, invisible, or nearly so, to the naked eye, as a paramecium or rotifer. — **an′i·mal′cu·lar** (-kū·lẽr), *adj.*

an′i·mal′cu·lum (-kū·lŭm), *n.;* *pl.* **-LA** (-lȧ). [NL.] An animalcule.

animal heat. *Physiol.* The heat generated in the body of a living animal by oxidation within the cells.

animal husbandry. The breeding, judging, care, and production of farm animals. — **animal husbandman.**

an′i·mal·ism (ăn′ĭ·măl·ĭz′m), *n.* **1.** Animal qualities; sensuality; also, the exercise of animal qualities. **2.** The doctrine that men are mere nonspiritual animals. — **an′i·mal·ist** (-ĭst), *n.* — **an′i·mal·is′tic** (-ĭs′tĭk), *adj.*

an′i·mal′i·ty (-măl′ĭ·tĭ), *n.* **1.** Animal nature or vitality. **2.** The animal part of man's nature. **3.** The animal world.

an′i·mal·ize (ăn′ĭ·măl·īz), *v. t.* **1.** To convert into animal matter by assimilation. **2.** To sensualize. — **an′i·mal·i·za′tion** (-ĭ·zā′shŭn; -ī·zā′-), *n.*

an′i·mal·ly, *adv.* As to bodily qualities; physically.

animal magnetism. Mesmerism; hypnotism or hypnotic power.

animal spirits. Vivacity arising from physical health and energy.

an′i·mate (ăn′ĭ·māt), *v. t.* [L. *animatus*, past part. of *animare*, fr. *anima* breath, soul.] **1.** To give natural life to; to make alive. **2.** To give spirit or vigor to; to inspirit; also, to stimulate; rouse. **3.** To impart an appearance of life to; as, to *animate* a cartoon. **4.** To actuate; prompt. — **Syn.** See QUICKEN. — (-măt), *adj.* Endowed with life; living; also, lively. — **Syn.** See LIVING. — **an′i·mat′er** (-māt′ẽr), *n.*

an′i·mat′ed (-māt′ĕd; -ĭd), *adj.* **1.** Alive or seeming alive. **2.** Full of life or spirit; indicating animation; lively. — **Syn.** See LIVING: LIVELY. — **an′i·mat′ed·ly,** *adv.*

animated cartoon *or* **drawing.** A series of drawings with slight progressive changes, made and arranged to be photographed and projected like a motion picture.

an′i·mat′ing (-māt′ĭng), *adj.* Causing animation; lifegiving; inspiriting; rousing. — **an′i·mat′ing·ly,** *adv.*

an′i·ma′tion (-mā′shŭn), *n.* **1.** The action of animating, or state of being animate; quality of being animated. **2.** Preparation of animated cartoons.

‖**a′ni·ma′to** (ä′nē·mä′tō), *adj.* [It.] *Music.* Animated.

an′i·ma′tor (ăn′ĭ·mā′tẽr), *n.* [L.] Animating agent.

an′i·mé (ăn′ĭ·mā; -mē), *n.* [F. *animé, animi*, through Sp. & Pg. fr. Tupi *ananim* resin.] Any of various resins or oleoresins; as: **a** Copal, esp. a soft variety. **b** Elemi.

an′i·mism (ăn′ĭ·mĭz′m), *n.* [L. *anima* soul.] **1.** The belief that all objects possess a natural life or vitality or are endowed with indwelling souls; specif.: **a** Belief ascribing conscious life to all natural objects, or to nature in general. **b** Belief that men, animals, all plants, stones, etc., are inhabited by souls which may exist in a separate state. **2.** The doctrine that the soul is the vital organizing principle of the physical universe. — **an′i·mist** (-mĭst), *n.* & *adj.* — **-mis′tic** (-mĭs′tĭk), *adj.*

‖**a′ni·mis o′pi·bus′que pa·ra′ti** (ăn′ĭ·mĭs ŏp′ĭ·bŭs′kwē pȧ·rā′tī). [L.] Prepared in minds and resources; — one of the mottoes of South Carolina. Cf. DUM SPIRO, SPERO.

an′i·mos′i·ty (ăn′ĭ·mŏs′ĭ·tĭ), *n.*; *pl.* -TIES (-tĭz). [F. *animosité*, fr. L. *animositas*.] Ill will, often resentment, tending toward hostile action. — **Syn.** See ENMITY.

an′i·mus (ăn′ĭ·mŭs), *n.* [L., mind.] **1.** Animating or actuating spirit; disposition (to do or effect something); intention. **2.** A feeling of hostility or hatred; animosity. — **Syn.** See ENMITY.

an′i′on (ăn′ī′ŏn), *n.* [Gr. *aniōn*, neut. *anion*, pres. part. of *anienai* to go up.] *Physical Chem.* A negative ion; — so called because in electrolysis it travels to the anode. See ION.

an′ise (ăn′ĭs), *n.* [OF. *anis*, fr. L. *anisum*, fr. Gr. *anison* dill, anise.] An herb (*Pimpinella anisum*) of the carrot family, having carminative and aromatic seeds; also, aniseed.

an′i·seed (ăn′ĭ·sēd; ăn′ĭs·sēd′), *n.* The seed of the anise, yielding an oil (**anise oil**) used in liqueurs.

an′is·ei·ko′ni·a (ăn′ĭs·ī·kō′nĭ·ȧ), *n.* [NL., fr. Gr. *anisos* unequal + *eikōn* image.] *Med.* A condition in which the image of an object formed in one eye differs in size or shape from the image of the same object formed in the other eye.

an′i·sette′ (ăn′ĭ·zĕt′; -sĕt′), *n.* [F.] A colorless sweet liqueur flavored with aniseed.

an·i′so- (ăn·ī′sō-). [Gr. *anisos* unequal. See AN-; ISO-.] A combining form denoting *unequal, dissimilar*, as in **an·i′so·dac′ty·lous**, having the toes dissimilar.

an′i·som′er·ous (ăn′ī·sŏm′ẽr·ŭs), *adj.* [*aniso-* + *-merous.*] *Bot.* Having the number of floral organs in each whorl unequal, as four petals and six stamens.

an·i′so·met′ric (ăn·ī′sō·mĕt′rĭk), *adj.* [*an-* not + *isometric.*] Not isometric; having unsymmetrical parts.

an·i′so·trop′ic (-trŏp′ĭk), *adj.* [*an-* not + *isotropic.*] Not isotropic; as: **a** *Physics.* Exhibiting different properties when tested along axes in different directions. **b** *Plant Physiol.* Assuming different positions in response to the action of external stimuli. — **an′i·sot′ro·py** (ăn′ī·sŏt′rō·pĭ), *n.*

an′ker·ite (ăng′kẽr·īt), *n.* [After Prof. *Anker* of Austria.] A mineral related to dolomite, but containing much iron.

ankh (ăngk), *n.* [Egypt. *ānkh* life, prosperity.] A T-shaped cross surmounted by a loop, used as a sacred emblem, symbolizing life; — called also *crux ansata*.

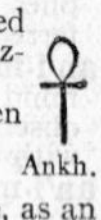
Ankh.

an′kle (ăng′k'l), *n.* [AS. *anclēo, anclēow.*] The joint between the foot and the leg; also, the region of this joint; the tarsus.

an′kle·bone′ (-bōn′), *n.* = ASTRAGALUS, 1.

an′klet (ăng′klĕt; -klĭt), *n.* **1.** Something embracing the ankle, as an ornamental ring, a shoe strap, a fetter, or a supporting brace. **2.** A woman's, man's, or child's sock reaching slightly above the ankle. **3.** A woman's or child's low shoe having one or more straps at the ankle.

an′kus (ŭng′kŭsh), *n.* [Hind., fr. Skr. *aṅkuśa.*] *India.* An elephant goad with a sharp spike and hook.

an′ky·lose (ăng′kĭ·lōs), *v. t.* & *i.* To stiffen or to unite by ankylosis.

an′ky·lo′sis (-lō′sĭs), *n.* [NL., fr. Gr. *ankylōsis*, fr. *ankyloun* to stiffen, fr. *ankylos* crooked.] **1.** *Med.* Stiffness or fixation of a joint caused by fibrous or bony tissue in the joint space. **2.** *Anat. & Zool.* The union of bones or hard parts to form a single bone or part. — **an′ky·lot′ic** (-lŏt′ĭk), *adj.*

an′ky·los′to·mi′a·sis (ăng′kĭ·lŏs′tō·mī′ȧ·sĭs). Var. of ANCYLOSTOMIASIS.

an′lace (ăn′lās), *n.* [OF. *alenas* dagger.] A long, tapering medieval dagger.

‖**An′la·ge** (än′lä·gĕ), *or* **an′la·ge,** *n.*; *pl.* ANLAGEN (-lä·gĕn), ANLAGES (-gĕz). [G., foundation, fr. *an* on + *liegen* to lie.] **1.** The foundation or rudiment; specif., *Biol.*, the first massing of cells in an embryo, recognizable as the commencement of a developing part or organ. **2.** Bent; inclination; proclivity.

an′na (ăn′ȧ), *n.* [Hind. *ānā.*] A nickel coin of India and Pakistan. See MONEY, *Tables.*

an′nal·ist (ăn′ăl·ĭst), *n.* A writer of annals; also, a historian. — **an′nal·is′tic** (-ĭs′tĭk), *adj.*

an′nals (ăn′ălz; -′lz), *n. pl.*; *sing.* ANNAL (ăn′ăl; -′l). [L. pl. *annales* (sc. *libri*) chronicles, fr. *annus* year.] **1.** A relation of events in chronological order, by years. **2.** Historical records; chronicles; history. **3.** *sing.* The record of a single event or of the events of a single year. **4.** A periodic publication, containing records of discoveries, transactions of societies, etc.

An′na·mese′ (ăn′ȧ·mēz′; -mēs′), *n.* **1.** *sing. & pl.* One of a Mongolian race occupying Cochin China and the coast regions of Annam and Tonkin. **2.** The Annamese language. — *adj.* Of or pert. to Annam or the Annamese.

an′nates (ăn′āts), **an′nats** (-ăts), *n. pl.* [F. *annate*, fr. ML., fr. L. *annus* year.] *Eccl. Law.* The first fruits of a benefice.

an·nat′to (ä·nä′tō), *n.* [Of Cariban origin.] A yellowish-red dyestuff made from the pulp around the seeds of a tropical tree (*Bixa orellana*, family Bixaceae).

an·neal′ (ă·nēl′), *v. t.* [AS. *anǣlan*, fr. *an* on + *ǣlan* to burn.] **1.** To heat, as glass, in order to fix laid-on colors. **2.** To subject to high heat, with subsequent cooling, so as to soften thoroughly and render less brittle. **3.** Hence, to temper or toughen, as the mind.

an′ne·lid (ăn′ĕ·lĭd), *n.* [F. *annélide*, deriv. of L. *anellus* a ring.] *Zool.* Any of a phylum (Annelida) including the earthworms, marine worms, leeches, and their allies, having typically an elongated segmented body. — *adj.* Of or belonging to the annelids. — **an·nel′i·dan** (ă·nĕl′ĭ·dăn), *adj.* & *n.*

an·nex′ (ă·nĕks′), *v. t.* [From F., fr. L. *annexus*, past part. of *annectere* to bind to, fr. *ad-* + *nectere* to tie.] **1.** *Archaic.* To join (one thing to another); to subjoin. **2.** To append; also, to affix. **3.** To attach as a qualification, consequence, etc.; as, to *annex* a penalty. **4.** To unite (one thing, usually smaller, to another), as in use or ownership; as, he *annexed* ten acres to his farm. **5.** *Slang.* To obtain or take for oneself. — **Syn.** Append, add. — **an·nex′a·ble,** *adj.* — **an′nex·a′tion** (ăn′ĕk·sā′shŭn), *n.* — **an′nex·a′tion·ist,** *n.*

an′nex (ăn′ĕks; ă·nĕks′), *n.* Something annexed; as: **a** An additional stipulation or statement to a writing. **b** A subsidiary building, or wing, to a building.

‖**an′nexe′** (ȧ′nĕks′), *n.* [F.] An annex (esp. in sense **b**).

an·nex′ment (ă·nĕks′mĕnt), *n.* An appendage. *Shak.*

an·ni′hi·la·ble (ă·nī′ĭ·lȧ·b'l; -hĭ·lȧ·b'l), *adj.* Capable of being annihilated. — **an·ni′hi·la·bil′i·ty** (-bĭl′ĭ·tĭ), *n.*

an·ni′hi·late (ă·nī′ĭ·lāt; -hĭ·lāt), *v. t.* [L. *annihilatus*, past part. of *annihilare*, fr. *ad-* + *nihilum, nihil*, nothing.] **1.** To reduce to nothing; to cause to cease to exist; to destroy completely; to exterminate. **2.** To make void or of no effect; as, to *annihilate* an argument. — **Syn.** See ABOLISH. — **an·ni′hi·la′tion** (-lā′shŭn), *n.* — **an·ni′hi·la′tive** (-lā′tĭv), *adj.* — **an·ni′hi·la′tor** (-lā′tẽr), *n.*

an′ni·ver′sa·ry (ăn′ĭ·vûr′sȧ·rĭ), *adj.* [L. *anniversarius*, fr. *annus* year + *vertere, versum*, to turn.] **1.** Commemorated at the same date each year. **2.** Of or pertaining to an anniversary. — *n.*; *pl.* -RIES (-rĭz). **1.** The annual return of the day of a past event, esp. some notable event. **2.** An anniversary celebration.

☞ For names of particular wedding anniversaries, see WEDDING.

‖**an′no ae·ta′tis su′ae** (ăn′ō ē·tā′tĭs sū′ē). [L.] In the year of his (or her) age.

an′no Dom′i·ni (dŏm′ĭ·nī). [ML., in the year of (our) Lord, i. e., Jesus Christ.] In the (specified) year of the Christian Era. Abbr. A.D.; as, A.D. 1949.

‖**an′no mun′di** (mŭn′dī). [L.] In the year of the world; — used in reckoning dates from the supposed period of the creation, esp. as fixed by Ussher at 4004 B.C.

an′no·tate (ăn′ō·tāt), *v. t.* [L. *annotatus*, past part. of *annotare* to annotate, fr. *ad-* + *notare* to mark.] To furnish with notes, usually critical or explanatory. — *v. i.* To make annotations. — **an′no·ta′tor** (-tā′tẽr), *n.*

Syn. **Annotate, gloss** mean to add or append comment to a text. **Annotate** implies furnishing a text with critical, historical, or explanatory notes touching any word, passage, or detail in need of such comment; **gloss** implies supplying a text with definitions of difficult words or phrases.

an′no·ta′tion (-tā′shŭn), *n.* **1.** Act of annotating. **2.** A note added by way of comment or explanation.

an·nounce′ (ă·nouns′), *v. t.*; -NOUNCED′ (-nounst′); -NOUNC′ING (-noun′sĭng). [From OF., fr. L. *annuntiare*, fr. *ad-* + *nuntiare* to relate, fr. *nuntius* messenger.] **1.** To give public notice, or first or anticipatory notice, of; to publish; proclaim; herald. **2.** To give evidence of. **3.** To give notice of the arrival or presence of. — **Syn.** See DECLARE.

an·nounce′ment (-mĕnt), *n.* Act of announcing; also, a proclamation, public notification, or advertisement.

an·nounc′er (ă·noun′sẽr), *n.* One who or that which announces; specif., *Radio & Television*, one engaged by a radio or television broadcasting station or by a commercial sponsor to introduce programs and performers and to interpolate explanatory remarks or needed continuity and to identify the station.

‖**an′no ur′bis con′di·tae** (ăn′ō ûr′bĭs kŏn′dĭ·tē). [L.] Literally, in the year of the founded city; — used, after the time of Augustus, to express the date since the founding of Rome (753 B.C.). Abbr. *A.U.C.*

an·noy′ (ă·noi′), *n.* [AF. *anoi, anui* (OF. *enui*, F. *ennui*), fr. L. *in odio* in hatred.] *Archaic.* An annoyance. — *v. t.* **1.** To disturb or irritate, esp. by repeated acts; to vex. **2.** To molest; harass; as, to *annoy* an army by impeding its march. — *v. i.* To be troublesome or irritating. — **an·noy′er,** *n.*

Syn. (1) **Annoy, vex, irk, bother** mean to upset a person's nerves. **Annoy** stresses loss of equanimity or patience by being forced to endure something obnoxious or unpleasant for the time being; **vex** implies greater provocation and stronger disturbance, and it usually connotes anger but may suggest deep perplexity or worry; **irk** emphasizes difficulty in enduring and resulting weariness of spirit; **bother** may imply bewilderment or intense worry, but it always suggests interference with one's comfort or peace of mind.
(2) See WORRY.

an·noy′ance (-ăns), *n.* **1.** Act of annoying; state of being annoyed; vexation. **2.** A nuisance.

an·noy′ing, *adj.* That annoys; molesting; vexatious. — **an·noy′ing·ly,** *adv.* — **an·noy′ing·ness,** *n.*

an′nu·al (ăn′ū·ăl), *adj.* [From OF., fr. L. *annualis*, fr. *annus* year.] **1.** Reckoned by the term of a year; as, an *annual* stipend. **2.** Occurring once each year; yearly. **3.** Lasting only one year or one growing season; valid for one year. **4.** Performed in a year. — *n.* **1.** A publication appearing yearly. **2.** A plant which completes its growth in a single year. Symbol, ○, ⊙, or ①. — **an′nu·al·ly,** *adv.*

annual ring. Any of the rings seen in cross sections of the stems of most trees and shrubs, marking annual growth.

an·nu′i·tant (ă·nū′ĭ·tănt), *n.* A beneficiary of an annuity.

‖**an′nu·it coep′tis** (ăn′ū·ĭt sĕp′tĭs). [L.] He (God) has smiled on our undertakings; — a motto on the reverse of the great seal of the United States, adapted from *Aeneid* ix, 625.

an·nu′i·ty (ă·nū′ĭ·tĭ), *n.; pl.* -TIES (-tĭz). [F. *annuité*, fr. ML., fr. L. *annus* year.] **1.** An amount, esp. of money, payable yearly or, by extension, at other regular intervals. **2.** The right to receive or the obligation to pay an annuity (in sense 1).

an·nul′ (ă·nŭl′), *v. t.;* -NULLED (-nŭld′); -NUL′LING. [From OF., fr. LL. *annullare*, fr. L. *ad-* + *nullus* none, *nullum*, neut., nothing.] **1.** To reduce to nothing; to annihilate. **2.** To make void, as legal rights, laws, established rules. — **Syn.** See NULLIFY. — **an·nul′la·ble,** *adj.*

an′nu·lar (ăn′ū·lẽr), *adj.* [L. *annularis*, *anularis*, fr. *annulus*, *anulus*, ring.] Of the form of, or forming, a ring; ring-shaped. — **an′nu·lar′i·ty** (-lăr′ĭ·tĭ), *n.* — **an′nu·lar·ly,** *adv.*

annular eclipse. An eclipse in which a thin ring of sunlight is visible encircling the dark moon.

annular ligament. A ringlike ligament encircling the wrist or ankle.

an′nu·late (ăn′ū·lāt), **an′nu·lat′ed** (-lāt′ĕd; -ĭd), *adj.* Furnished with, or composed of, rings; ringed.

an′nu·la′tion (-lā′shŭn), *n.* Formation of rings; a ring.

an′nu·let (ăn′ū·lĕt), *n.* [L. *annulus*.] A little ring; specif., *Arch.*, a small molding or ridge forming a ring.

an·nul′ment (ă·nŭl′mĕnt), *n.* An annulling; invalidation.

an′nu·lose (ăn′ū·lōs), *adj.* [L. *annulus* ring.] Ringed.

an′nu·lus (ăn′ū·lŭs), *n.; pl.* -LI (-lī), -LUSES (-lŭs·ĕz; -ĭz). [L.] A ring; a ringlike part, structure, marking, or space.

an·nun′ci·ate (ă·nŭn′shĭ·āt; -sĭ·āt), *v. t.* [L. *annuntiatus*, past part. of *annuntiare*.] To announce.

an·nun′ci·a′tion (ă·nŭn′sĭ·ā′shŭn; -shĭ·ā′shŭn; 103), *n.* **1.** Act of announcing; announcement. **2. a** [*usually cap.*] The announcement of the Incarnation, made by the angel Gabriel to the Virgin Mary; also, a representation of this in art. **b** [*cap.*] The festival celebrated (March 25th) in memory of this; Lady Day.

an·nun′ci·a′tor (ă·nŭn′shĭ·ā′tẽr; -sĭ·ā′tẽr), *n.* An announcer; specif., an electrically controlled signal board or indicator.

‖**an′nus mi·ra′bi·lis** (ăn′ŭs mĭ·răb′ĭ·lĭs). [L.] Wonderful year; — applied to various noted years, esp. 1666, the year of the plague and great fire in London.

a·no′ci·as·so′ci·a′tion (ȧ·nō′sĭ·ă·sō′sĭ·ā′shŭn; -shĭ·ā′shŭn), *n.* Also **a·no′ci·a′tion** (ȧ·nō′sĭ·ā′shŭn; ȧ·nō′shĭ-). [*a-* not + L. *nocere* to injure + E. *association*.] *Surg.* A method of preventing the shock and exhaustion incident to surgical operations by physiological disconnection between the field of operation and the nervous system, as by means of local anesthetic or sharp dissection.

an′ode (ăn′ōd), *n.* [Gr. *ana* up + *hodos* way.] *Elec.* The positive pole or electrode of an electrolytic cell, vacuum tube, etc. Cf. CATHODE. — **an·od′ic** (ăn·ŏd′ĭk), *adj.*

an′od·ize (ăn′ŏd·īz; -ōd-), *v. t.* [*anode* + *-ize*.] *Metal.* To subject (a metal) to electrolytic action as the anode of a cell in order to coat it with a protective film.

an′o·dyne (ăn′ō·dīn), *adj.* [L. *anodynus*, fr. Gr. *anōdynos* free from pain, fr. *an-* not + *odynē* pain.] Serving to assuage pain; soothing. — *n.* An anodyne medicine or agent.

a·noint′ (ȧ·noint′), *v. t.* [OF. *enoint*, past part. of *enoindre*, fr. L. *inungere*, fr. *in* on + *ungere*, *unguere*, to anoint.] **1.** To smear or rub over with oil or an unctuous substance; also, to spread over, as oil. **2.** To pour oil upon, as a sacred rite, esp. for consecration. **3.** *Humorous.* To baste; thrash. — **a·noint′er,** *n.* — **a·noint′ment,** *n.*

a·nom′a·lism (ȧ·nŏm′ȧ·lĭz′m), *n.* An anomaly.

a·nom′a·lis′tic (-lĭs′tĭk), *adj.* Pertaining to an anomaly or, *Astron.*, to the anomaly.

a·nom′a·lous (ȧ·nŏm′ȧ·lŭs), *adj.* [L. *anomalus*, fr. Gr. *anōmalos* irregular, fr. *an-* not + *homalos* even.] **1.** Deviating from a general rule, method, or analogy; abnormal. **2.** Out of keeping with accepted notions of fitness or order; also, inconsistent with what would naturally be expected. — **Syn.** See IRREGULAR. — **a·nom′a·lous·ly,** *adv.* — **a·nom′a·lous·ness,** *n.*

a·nom′a·ly (-lĭ), *n., pl.* -LIES (-lĭz). [L. *anomalia*, fr. Gr. *anōmalia*. See ANOMALOUS.] **1.** Deviation from the common rule; irregularity. **2.** Anything anomalous; something out of keeping, esp. with accepted notions of fitness or order. **3.** *Astron.* The angular distance of a planet from its perihelion, as seen from the sun.

a·non′ (ȧ·nŏn′), *adv.* [Lit., in one (moment), fr. AS. *on* in + *ān* one.] **1.** *Archaic.* Straightway; at once. **2.** Soon; presently. **3.** At another time. — *interj. Obs.* Coming!

an′o·nym (ăn′ō·nĭm), *n.* **1.** A person who retains anonymity or is of unknown name. **2.** A pseudonym.

an′o·nym′i·ty (-nĭm′ĭ·tĭ), *n.* Quality or state of being anonymous; anonymousness.

a·non′y·mous (ȧ·nŏn′ĭ·mŭs), *adj.* [Gr. *anōnymos* without name, fr. *an-* not + *onyma*, *onoma*, name.] Bearing or giving no name; of unknown or unavowed authorship or donorship. Abbr. *anon.* — **a·non′y·mous·ly,** *adv.* — **a·non′y·mous·ness,** *n.*

a·noph′e·les (ȧ·nŏf′ĕ·lēz), *n.* [NL., fr. Gr. *anōphelēs* hurtful.] Any of a genus (*Anopheles*) of mosquitoes which are secondary hosts of the malaria parasite, and which transmit malaria to man. See MALARIA; cf. AËDES, CULEX.

a′no·rak (ä′nō·räk), *n.* [Greenland Esk. *ánoráq*.] A hooded jacket of skin or cloth, worn in the arctic.

an·or′thite (ăn·ôr′thīt), *n.* [Gr. *an-* not + *orthos* straight (*orthē*, sc. *gōnia*, right angle).] *Mineral.* A white, grayish, or reddish feldspar, $CaAl_2(SiO_4)_2$, occurring in many igneous rocks. — **an′or·thit′ic** (ăn′ôr·thĭt′ĭk), *adj.*

an·or′tho·site (-thō·sīt), *n.* [F. *anorthose*, a feldspar + *-ite*.] A granular plutonic igneous rock composed chiefly of a soda-lime feldspar, as labradorite.

an·os′mi·a (-ŏz′mĭ·ȧ; -ŏs′mĭ·ȧ), *n.* [NL., fr. *an-* not + Gr. *osmē* smell.] *Med.* Loss or impairment of the sense of smell. — **an·os′mic** (-mĭk), *adj.*

an·oth′er (ă·nŭth′ẽr), *adj.* [*an* a, one + *other*.] **1.** Being one more in addition; being one more of the same kind. **2.** Being one different, distinct, or separate from the one considered; not the same. **3.** Some other and later; as, come *another* day. — *pron.* **1.** One more; an additional one. **2.** Any or some different person or thing; someone or something else.

an·oth′er–guess′ (-gĕs′), *adj.* [Corrupt. of *another-gates*, fr. *another* + *gate* way.] *Archaic.* Of another sort.

an′ox·e′mi·a, an′ox·ae′mi·a (ăn′ŏk·sē′mĭ·ȧ), *n. Med.* An abnormal condition due to deficient aeration of the blood. — **an′ox·e′mic, an′ox·ae′mic** (-sē′mĭk; -sĕm′ĭk), *adj.*

an·ox′i·a (ăn·ŏk′sĭ·ȧ), *n.* [NL., fr. *an-* not + *oxygen* + *-ia*.] *Med.* Oxygen deprivation or deficiency, as of certain tissues.

an·ox′ic (-ŏk′sĭk), *adj. Med.* Of or pertaining to anoxia.

an′sate (ăn′sāt), *adj.* [L. *ansatus*, fr. *ansa* a handle.] Having a handle or handle-shaped part.

ansate cross. The ankh (which see).

‖**An′schluss** (än′shlo͝os), *n.* [G., lit., a joining.] Union; specif., incorporation of Austria into the German Reich (1938).

an′ser·ine (ăn′sẽr·īn; -ĭn), *adj.* Also **an′ser·ous** (-ŭs). [L. *anserinus*, fr. *anser* goose.] Of, pertaining to, or resembling, a goose; hence, stupid.

an′swer (àn′sẽr; 9), *n.* [AS. *andswaru*, fr. *and-* against + *swerian* to swear.] **1.** A reply, as to a question, call, or argument; also, a correct reply. **2.** A responsive or retaliatory action; as, another kick was his only *answer*. **3.** A reply to a charge; specif., *Law*, a counterstatement of facts made in reply to the charges of the complainant in his bill. **4.** The solution of a problem. **5.** *Music.* A version of a theme restated in a different voice, so as to give a sense of consequent or complement.

— *v. i.* **1.** To make an answer, as to a question, a charge, etc. **2.** To act in response, as to a request or to a controlling action or instrument; as, the guitar *answered* to his touch. **3.** To be accountable or undertake responsibility; also, to make amends. **4.** To be in conformity or in correspondence; as, actions that *answer* to his appearance. **5.** To be adequate; to serve the purpose.

— *v. t.* **1.** To make answer to (a question, remark, charge, etc.). **2.** To act in response to (a request, summons, or directing action or instrument); as, a ship *answers* her helm. **3.** To meet successfully by way of explanation, justification, or the like; to comply with, fulfill, or satisfy, as a claim or need. **4.** To atone for. **5.** To be or act in conformity to; to correspond to; to suit. **6.** To be equivalent to or serve for.

Syn. Answer, respond, reply, rejoin, retort mean to give that which is necessary in return, as to a question, a request, a call, or the like. **Answer** implies the giving of the service or attention demanded by one's situation or office or required by courtesy; **respond** implies a proper reaction, often spontaneously or without resistance, to any stimulus; **reply** implies a return that covers the same ground as a question, a charge, an argument, or a salute, and is a more explicit term than *answer;* **rejoin**, in current use, often implies an answer to an unspoken but inferred question or to an objection; **retort** suggests a response to an explicit or implicit charge, criticism, or the like, that is, in effect, retaliatory.

an′swer·a·ble (àn′sẽr·ȧ·b′l), *adj.* **1.** Liable to be called to account; accountable; responsible. **2.** *Archaic.* Suitable; corresponding; accordant; adequate. **3.** Capable of being refuted. — **Syn.** See RESPONSIBLE. — **an′swer·a·ble·ness,** *n.* — **an′swer·a·bly,** *adv.*

ant (ănt), *n.* [ME. *ante*, *amete*, *emete*, fr. AS. *æmete*.] Any of certain insects, constituting a family (Formicidae, order Hymenoptera); an emmet; a pismire. All ants live in communities, usually burrowing in the ground or in wood. The males have wings and are short-lived, the females or queens are wingless when adult, the neuters are wingless and comprise the workers and soldiers. Cf. TERMITE.

Ants (Winged Male and Worker, or Neuter).

ant- (ănt-). = ANTI-, against, as in:

antanemic **antarthritic** **antasthmatic**

-ant (-ănt). [OF. *-ant*, fr. L. *-antem*, *-entem*, acc. pres. part. ending, nom. *-ans*, *-ens*.] A suffix used to form: **a** Adjectives, often clearly with the force of a present participle, as in err*ant*, defi*ant*. **b** Nouns denoting *a person* or *thing acting as an agent*, as in claim*ant*, serv*ant*.

an′ta (ăn′tȧ), *n.; pl.* ANTAE (-tē). [L.] *Arch.* A species of pier produced by thickening a wall at its termination, treated architecturally as a pilaster, with capital and base.

ant·ac′id (ănt·ăs′ĭd), *n.* [*ant-* + *acid*.] *Med.* A remedy for acidity, as an alkali or absorbent. — *adj.* Counteracting acidity.

An·tae′us (ăn·tē′ŭs), *n.* [L., fr. Gr. *Antaios*.] *Gr. Myth.* A giant wrestler who was invincible while he touched the earth, his mother. Hercules strangled him while holding him off the ground. — **An·tae′an** (-ăn), *adj.*

an·tag′o·nism (ăn·tăg′ō·nĭz′m), *n.* [Gr. *antagōnisma*, deriv. of *anti* against + *agōn* contest.] **1.** Active opposition or resistance; counteraction or contrariety of things or principles; also, an opposing agent or principle. **2.** *Biol.* The sum of the mutual interference between dissimilar organisms occupying or attempting to occupy the same ecological niche. — **Syn.** See ENMITY.

an·tag′o·nist (-nĭst), *n.* **1.** One who contends with another, esp. in combat; adversary. **2.** A counteracting muscle. — **Syn.** See OPPONENT.

an·tag′o·nis′tic (-nĭs′tĭk), *adj.* Acting in antagonism; hostile; counteracting. — **Syn.** See ADVERSE. — **an·tag′o·nis′ti·cal·ly,** *adv.*

an·tag′o·nize (ăn·tăg′ō·nīz), *v. t.* **1.** To act in opposition to; to counteract. **2.** To incur or provoke the hostility of. — **Syn.** See OPPOSE.

ant·al′ka·li (ănt·ăl′kȧ·lī; -lĭ), *n.; pl.* -LIES or -LIS (-līz; -lĭz). [*ant-* + *alkali*.] An agent that counteracts alkalinity. — **ant·al′ka·line** (-līn; -lĭn), *adj. & n.*

ant·arc′tic (ănt·ärk′tĭk; *formerly spelled, and still sometimes pronounced,* antar′tic), *adj.* [Through OF. & L., fr. Gr. *antarktikos*, fr. *anti* opposite + *arktos* bear.] Relating to the South Pole or to the region near it. The **Antarctic Circle** is a parallel of latitude distant from the pole 23° 30′. See ZONE, *Illust.* — *n.* The antarctic regions.

An·tar′es (ăn·târ′ēz), *n.* [Gr. *Antarēs*, fr. *anti* similar to + *Arēs* Mars. So called from its color.] *Astron.* A giant red star of very low density, the brightest star in Scorpio.

ant bear. The great anteater (*Myrmecophaga jubata*) of South America, having shaggy gray fur with a black band across the breast and white stripe on the shoulder.

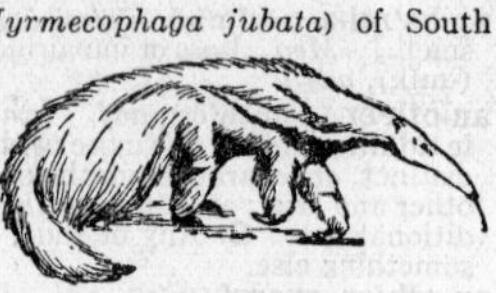
Ant Bear. (1/60)

an′te (ăn′tē), *n.* [L., before.] *Poker.* **a** A player's stake put into the pool after he sees his hand but before he draws other cards. **b** A stake put in by each player before he sees his hand, as in a jack pot. — *v. t. & i.*; AN′TED (-tēd); AN′TE·ING (-tē·ĭng). To stake (the ante); — often with *up*; hence, to pay one's part; also, to pay.

an′te- (ăn′tē-). [L. *ante* before.] A prefix denoting *before*, specif.: **a** *Preceding, in front of, prior to, pre-*; as in:

ante-Christian	antenatal	anteprandial
antehuman	ante-Norman	anteprohibition
antemarital	antenuptial	ante-Victorian
antemundane	anteorbital	antewar

b *Prior, anticipatory, anterior, fore-*; as in:

antechapel	antedawn	anteporch
antecloset	antehall	anteport
antecourt	antenumber	antespring

ant′eat′er (ănt′ēt′ẽr), *n.* Any of several mammals that feed largely or entirely on ants; esp.: **a** Any of certain edentates with the mouth modified for this purpose, having a long narrow snout, a long tongue, and enormous salivary glands, as the ant bear, the tamandua, and the pangolins. See ANT BEAR, *Illust.* **b** The echidna. **c** The aardvark.

an′te bel′lum (ăn′tē bĕl′ŭm). [L.] Before the war; esp., *U. S.*, before the Civil War. — **an′te–bel′lum**, *adj.*

an′te·cede′ (ăn′tē·sēd′), *v. t.* [L. *antecedere*, fr. *ante* + *cedere* to go.] To precede in time or place.

an′te·ced′ence (-sēd′ĕns), *n.* **1.** Priority; precedence. **2.** *Astron.* Retrogression.

an′te·ced′ent (-sēd′ĕnt), *adj.* [L. *antecedens, -entis*, pres. part. of *antecedere*.] **1.** Going before in time; prior; preceding. **2.** *Gram.* Standing in the relation of antecedent. — **Syn.** See PRECEDING. — *n.* **1.** That which goes before in time; that which precedes. **2.** *pl.* The earlier events of one's life; previous principles, conduct, course, history; also, ancestry. **3.** *Gram.* A noun or noun equivalent, whether word, phrase, or clause, referred to by a personal or relative pronoun. **4.** *Logic.* The conditional clause in a hypothetical proposition. **5.** *Math.* The first term of a ratio, as the term *a* in the ratio *a* : *b*, the second, *b*, being the *consequent*. — **Syn.** See CAUSE. — **an′te·ced′ent·ly**, *adv.*

an′te·ces′sor (ăn′tē·sĕs′ẽr; ăn′tē-), *n.* One that goes before; predecessor.

an′te·cham′ber (ăn′tē·chām′bẽr), *n.* [Through F. & It., fr. L. *ante* before + *camera* vault. See CHAMBER.] A chamber or room before a chief room, and leading into it, in which persons wait for audience; an outer chamber.

an′te·choir′ (-kwīr′), *n.* *Arch.* A space, enclosed or reserved for the clergy and choristers, at the entrance to a choir.

an′te·date′ (-dāt′), *n.* A date used in antedating.

an′te·date′ (ăn′tē·dāt′; ăn′tē·dāt′), *v. t.* **1.** To date as of a time prior to that of execution; as, to *antedate* a check; hence, to assign, as an event, to an earlier date. **2.** To anticipate; take before the true time. **3.** To precede in time; come before in date.

an′te·di·lu′vi·an (ăn′tē·dĭ·lū′vĭ·ăn; -dĭ·lū′-), *adj.* Of or pert. to the period before the Deluge; hence, antiquated. — *n.* An antediluvian person; hence, one behind the times.

an′te·fix (ăn′tē·fĭks), *n.*; *pl.* -FIXES (-fĭk′sĕz; -sĭz). [L. *antefixus*, adj.] *Class. Arch.* **a** An ornament at the eaves, concealing the ends of the joint tiles of the roof. **b** An ornament of the molding of a cornice. — **an′te·fix′al** (-fĭk′săl), *adj.*

an′te·lope (ăn′tē·lōp), *n.*; *pl.* -LOPE (-lōp), -LOPES (-lōps). See PLURAL, *Note*, 6. [From OF., fr. Gr. *antholops, -opos.*] **1.** *Zool.* Any of a group of ruminants constituting, with the oxen, sheep, and goats, a family (Bovidae), disting. from the true oxen chiefly by their lighter and more graceful build, and by their upwardly and backwardly directed horns. See HARNESSED ANTELOPE; cf. PRONGHORN. **2.** Leather from antelope hide.

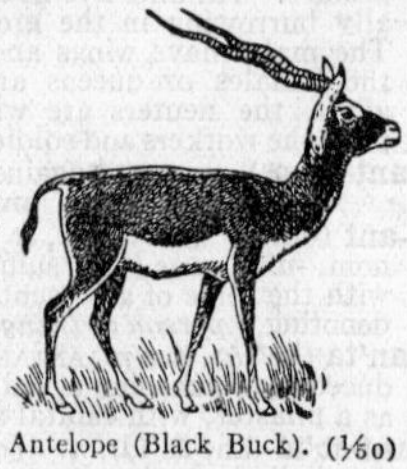
Antelope (Black Buck). (1/60)

an′te me·rid′i·em (ăn′tē mē·rĭd′ĭ·ĕm). [L.] Before noon. Abbr. A.M. or a.m. — **an′te·me·rid′i·an** (-ăn), *adj.*

an′te mor′tem (môr′tĕm). [L.] Before death; — often used adjectively; as, an *ante-mortem* statement.

an·ten′na (ăn·tĕn′ȧ), *n.*; *pl.* -NAE (-ē), (in *Radio* sense) -NAS (-ȧz). [NL., a feeler, horn of an insect, fr. L. *antenna* sail yard.] **1.** *Zool.* A movable, segmented organ of sensation on the head of insects, myriapods, and crustaceans. In insects they are popularly called *horns* and also *feelers*. See HYMENOPTERON, INSECT, *Illusts.* **2.** *Radio.* The portion, usually a wire or wires, of a radio station or receiving set, for radiating waves into space or receiving them from space.

an·ten′nule (-ūl), *n.* A small antenna or similar appendage.

an′te·past (ăn′tē·pȧst), *n.* [*ante-* + L. *pastus* pasture, food.] A foretaste.

an′te·pen′di·um (-pĕn′dĭ·ŭm), *n.*; *pl.* -PENDIA (-ȧ). [ML., fr. L. *ante* + *pendere* to hang.] *Eccl.* **a** The hanging or screen in front of an altar; frontal. **b** A pulpit cloth.

an′te·pe′nult (-pē′nŭlt; -pē·nŭlt′), *n.* [L. *antepaenultima* (sc. *syllaba*) antepenultimate. See PENULT.] *Pros.* The third syllable of a word, counting from the end, as *-syl-* in mono*syl*lable. — **an′te·pe·nul′ti·mate** (-pē·nŭl′tĭ·māt), *adj. & n.*

an·te′ri·or (ăn·tēr′ĭ·ẽr), *adj.* [L., compar. of *ante* before.] **1.** Before, or toward the front, in place; — opposed to *posterior*. **2.** Before in time; prior; antecedent. — **Syn.** See PRECEDING. — **an·te′ri·or′i·ty** (-ŏr′ĭ·tĭ), *n.* — **an·te′ri·or·ly**, *adv.* — **an·te′ri·or·ness**, *n.*

an′ter·o- (ăn′tẽr·ō-). [As if fr. a L. *anterus*.] *Anat.* A combining form meaning *anterior, front*; as in **an′ter·o·in·fe′ri·or**, *adj.*, in front and below; **an′ter·o·pos·te′ri·or**, *adj.*, from front to back or from head to tail.

an′te·room′ (ăn′tē·ro͞om′), *n.* A room before, or forming an entrance to, another, and often used as a waiting room.

an′te·type′ (-tīp′), *n.* An earlier type; a prototype.

ant·he′li·on (ănt·hē′lĭ·ŏn; ăn·thē′-), *n.*; *pl.* -LIA (-ȧ), -LIONS (-ŏnz). [NL., fr. Gr. *anthēlion*, fr. *anti* against + *hēlios* sun.] *Meteorol.* The brightish-white spot on the parhelic circle opposite the sun, a rare species of halo.

an′thel·min′tic (ăn′thĕl·mĭn′tĭk; ănt′hĕl-), *adj.* [*anti-* + Gr. *helmins, -inthos*, worm.] *Med.* Expelling or destroying intestinal worms. — *n.* An anthelmintic remedy.

an′them (ăn′thĕm), *n.* [AS. *antefen*, fr. ML., fr. Gr. *antiphōnon* antiphon, anthem, deriv. of *anti* over against + *phōnē* sound, voice.] **1.** Formerly, a hymn sung responsively; now, a sacred choral composition, with words usually from the Scriptures. **2.** A hymn or song of praise or glorification; as, a national *anthem*. — *v. t.* *Poetic.* To celebrate with anthems.

an·the′mi·on (ăn·thē′mĭ·ŏn), *n.*; *pl.* -MIA (-ȧ). [NL., fr. Gr. *anthemion* flower.] An ornament of floral or foliated forms arranged in a radiating cluster, but always flat, as in relief sculpture or painting. See IONIC, *Illust.*

an′ther (ăn′thẽr), *n.* [Through F. & L., fr. Gr. *antherōs* flowery, fr. *anthos* flower.] *Bot.* In seed plants, the part of the stamen which develops and contains pollen. See FILAMENT, VERSATILE, SPIKELET, *Illusts.*

an′ther·id′i·um (-ĭd′ĭ·ŭm), *n.*; *pl.* -IDIA (-ȧ). [NL., fr. *anther* + *-idion* (a Gr. dim. ending).] *Bot.* The male sexual organ in cryptogams. — **an′ther·id′i·al** (-ăl), *adj.*

an·the′sis (ăn·thē′sĭs), *n.* [NL., fr. Gr. *anthēsis* bloom.] The period or state of expansion in a flower; full bloom.

an′tho·cy′a·nin (ăn′thō·sī′ȧ·nĭn), *n.* Also **an′tho·cy′an** (-sī′ăn). [Gr. *anthos* flower + *kyanos* blue.] *Biochem.* Any of a class of soluble glucoside pigments producing reddish or purplish coloring in flowers and plants.

an·tho′di·um (ăn·thō′dĭ·ŭm), *n.*; *pl.* -DIA (-ȧ). [NL., fr. Gr. *anthōdēs* flowerlike.] *Bot.* In plants of the thistle family: **a** The capitulum or head, formerly called a *compound flower*. **b** The involucre.

an·thol′o·gize (ăn·thŏl′ō·jīz), *v. i. & t.* To compile an anthology; to put into an anthology.

an·thol′o·gy (-jĭ), *n.*; *pl.* -GIES (-jĭz). [Gr. *anthologia*, deriv. of *anthos* flower + *legein* to gather.] Originally, a collection of choice passages of literature, epigrams, or the like; now, any collection of literary works, in verse or prose or both, representative of an age, a national literature, a literary type, an author, or the like. — **an′tho·log′i·cal** (ăn′thō·lŏj′ĭ·kăl), *adj.* — **an·thol′o·gist** (ăn·thŏl′ō·jĭst), *n.*

an′tho·phore (ăn′thō·fōr; 70), *n.* [Gr. *anthophoros* flower-bearing.] *Bot.* An elongated section of the receptacle between the calyx and corolla in some plants, forming a stalk on which the gynoecium and corolla are borne, as in the pinks.

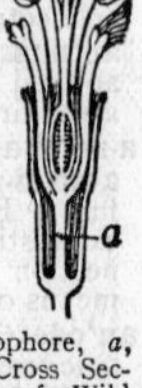
Anthophore, *a*, in Cross Section of Wild Pink (*Silene pennsylvanica*). (3/4)

an′tho·tax′y (ăn′thō·tăk′sĭ), *n.* [Gr. *anthos* flower + *-taxy*.] *Bot.* The arrangement of flowers in a cluster.

an′tho·zo′an (-zō′ăn), *n.* [Gr. *anthos* flower + *zōion* animal.] *Zool.* Any of a class (Anthozoa) of marine coelenterates, the corals, sea anemones, etc., including polyps with radial partitions. — **an′tho·zo′an**, *adj.*

an′thra·cene (ăn′thrȧ·sēn), *n.* [Gr. *anthrax* coal.] *Chem.* A crystalline hydrocarbon, $C_6H_4C_2H_2C_6H_4$, obtained with naphthalene from coal-tar distillation.

an′thra·cite (-sīt), *n.* [L. *anthracites* a kind of bloodstone, fr. Gr. *anthrakitēs* like coals, fr. *anthrax, -akos*, coal.] A hard natural coal, of high luster, differing from bituminous coal in containing little volatile matter. — **an′thra·cit′ic** (-sĭt′ĭk), *adj.*

an·thrac′nose (ăn·thrăk′nōs), *n.* [Gr. *anthrax, -akos*, carbuncle + *nosos* disease.] *Plant Pathol.* Any of certain plant diseases, typically producing ulcerlike lesions, and caused by several species of fungi.

an′thra·coid (ăn′thrȧ·koid), *adj.* Resembling anthrax.

an′thra·qui·none′ (-kwĭ·nōn′; -kwĭn′ōn), *n.* [*anthracene* + *quinone*.] *Chem.* A yellow crystalline ketone, $C_6H_4(CO)_2C_6H_4$, obtained by oxidation of anthracene.

an′thrax (ăn′thrăks), *n.* [L., fr. Gr. *anthrax* coal, carbuncle.] *Med. & Veter.* **a** A carbuncle. **b** A malignant pustule, a characteristic lesion of the disease anthrax. **c** An infectious, and usually fatal, bacterial disease of animals, esp. cattle and sheep, and occasionally of man. **d** The microorganism (*Bacillus anthracis*) causing the disease.

an′thro·po- (ăn′thrō·pō-), **anthrop-**. [Gr. *anthrōpos*.] A combining form meaning *human being, man.*

an′thro·po·cen′tric (-sĕn′trĭk), *adj.* **1.** Assuming man as the center or ultimate end. **2.** Interpreting natural processes or phenomena, as animal instincts, in terms of man or the human mind.

an′thro·po·gen′e·sis (-jĕn′ē·sĭs), **an′thro·pog′e·ny** (-pŏj′ē·nĭ), *n.* The science or study of the origin and development of man. — **an′thro·po·ge·net′ic** (-pō·jē·nĕt′ĭk), *adj.*

an′thro·pog′ra·phy (ăn′thrō·pŏg′rȧ·fĭ), *n.* Anthropology treating of the distribution of the human race, as distinguished by physical character, language, customs, etc. — **an′thro·po·graph′ic** (-pō·grăf′ĭk), *adj.*

an′thro·poid (ăn′thrō·poid), *adj.* [Gr. *anthrōpoeidēs.*] Resembling man; — applied esp. to certain apes. — *n.* An anthropoid ape. See APE, *n.*, 1.

an′thro·pol′o·gy (-pŏl′ō·jĭ), *n.* [*anthropo-* + *-logy.*] The science of man; specif.: **a** The science of the human organism. **b** The science of man in relation to physical character, distribution, origin, classification, and relationship of races, environmental and social relations, and culture. **c** The materials or subject matter of this science. — **an′thro·po·log′i·cal** (-pō·lŏj′ĭ·kăl), *adj.* — **an′thro·po·log′ic** (-ĭk), *adj.* — **an′thro·po·log′i·cal·ly**, *adv.* — **an′thro·pol′o·gist** (-pŏl′ō·jĭst), *n.*

an′thro·pom′e·try (-pŏm′ē·trĭ), *n.* Science of measuring the human body and its parts. — **an′thro·po·met′ric** (-pō·mĕt′rĭk), **an′thro·po·met′ri·cal** (-rĭ·kăl), *adj.*

an′thro·po·mor′phism (ăn′thrō·pō·môr′fĭz′m), *n.* [See ANTHROPOMORPHOUS; -ISM.] Representation or conception of God, or of a god, with human attributes; also, ascription of human characteristics to things not human. — **an′thro·po·mor′phic** (-fĭk), *adj.* — **an′thro·po·mor′phist** (-fĭst), *n. & adj.*

an′thro·po·mor′phize (-fīz), *v. t. & i.* To attribute a human form or personality to.

an′thro·po·mor′pho·sis (-môr′fō·sĭs; -môr·fō′sĭs), *n.* Metamorphosis into human form.

an′thro·po·mor′phous (-môr′fŭs), *adj.* [Gr. *anthrōpomorphos* of human form, fr. *anthrōpos* man + *morphē* form.] Human in form.

an′thro·pon′o·my (ăn′thrō·pŏn′ō·mĭ), *n.* Also **an′thro·po·nom′ics** (-pō·nŏm′ĭks); see -ICS. [*anthropo-* + Gr. *nomos* law, rule.] The science of human behavior. — **an′thro·po·nom′i·cal** (-pō·nŏm′ĭ·kăl), *adj.*

an′thro·poph′a·gi (ăn′thrō·pŏf′ȧ·jī), *n. pl.; sing.* -AGUS (-gŭs). [L., fr. Gr. *anthrōpophagos* man-eating, fr. *anthrōpos* man + *phagein* to eat.] Man-eaters; cannibals.

an′thro·poph′a·gite (-jīt), *n.* A cannibal.

an′thro·poph′a·gous (-gŭs), *adj.* Feeding on human flesh.

an′thro·poph′a·gy (-jĭ), *n.* The eating of human flesh.

an′ti (ăn′tī; -tĭ), *n.; pl.* ANTIS (-tīz; -tĭz). *Colloq.* A person opposed to a practice, law, policy, movement, or the like.

an′ti- (ăn′tĭ-), **ant-**. [Gr. *anti-*, *ant-*, combining form of *anti* against.] A prefix signifying *opposite, against, instead, counter*, used in forming nouns and adjectives. Special implications of sense are: **a** *Rivalry* or *supplanting*, often *spuriousness*, as in:

antibishop	antiduke	antipope

b *Hostility* or *opposition in opinions* or *practice*, as in:

antiadministration	antilabor	antisaloon
antialcoholism	antileague	antislavery
anti-American	antilynching	antisocial
anti-Bolshevik	anti-Masonic	antisocialistic
anti-Christian	antimonarchic	anti-Trinitarian
anticlerical	antinationalistic	antivaccination
anti-imperialist	antinoise	antivivisection
anti-intellectual	antirent	antiwar

c *Oppositeness in position* or *direction; reverse;* as in:

antipedal	antipetalous	antisepalous
antiperistalsis	antipole	antisolar

d *Opposition in effect; preventive of* or *operative against; counteractive;* as in:

antibacterial	antiferment	antitheft
anticoagulant	antifriction	antitrust
anticorrosive	antiglare	antizymotic

e *Un-; in-; non-; spuriously;* as in:

antigrammatical	antilogical	antiwarlike

f *Med. Preventive* or *curative of; allaying; neutralizing;* also, *an agent* or *remedy against;* as in:

antiberiberi	antimalarial	antirachitic
antibilious	antineuritic	antirheumatic
anticatarrhal	antipestilential	antiscorbutic
antidermatitis	antiplastic	antispasmodic
antidiphtheritic	antipruritic	antisyphilitic
antifebrile	antipyic	antivenin
antihemorrhagic	antipyretic	antixerophthalmic
antihydropic	antipyrotic	antodontalgic

an′ti·air′craft′ (ăn′tĭ·âr′krȧft′), *adj. Mil.* Used for defense against aircraft, as a gun, battery, shell, etc. Cf. ACK-ACK.

an′ti·ar (ăn′tĭ·är), *n.* [Jav. *antjar.*] A poisonous gum resin from the upas tree, or an arrow poison made from it.

an′ti·bi·ot′ic (ăn′tĭ·bī·ŏt′ĭk), *n.* [*anti-* + *biotic.*] An antibacterial substance produced by a living organism, esp. by a bacterium or a fungus. — **an′ti·bi·ot′ic**, *adj.* — **an′ti·bi·ot′ics** (-ĭks), *n.;* see -ICS.

an′ti·bod′y (ăn′tĭ·bŏd′ĭ), *n.; pl.* -BODIES (-ĭz). [*anti-* + *body.*] *Chem. & Immunol.* **a** A substance, as an anticatalyst or antitoxin, that opposes the action of another substance. **b** Any of various bodies or substances in the tissues or fluids, as blood or serum, of an organism, which act in antagonism to specific foreign bodies such as toxins or the bacteria producing the toxins. Agglutinins, antitoxins, precipitins, etc., are antibodies. Cf. ANTIGEN.

an′tic (ăn′tĭk), *adj.* [It. *antico* ancient, fr. L. *antiquus.*] **1.** Grotesque; bizarre; — of painting, sculpture, etc. **2.** Grotesquely or ludicrously fantastic, as in appearance or behavior. — *n.* **1.** A grotesquely fanciful carving or sculpture, now esp. of the human face or figure. **2.** An instance of grotesquely ludicrous behavior; a caper. **3.** A buffoon or merry-andrew; the fool of the old play. — *v. i.;* AN′TICKED, AN′TICKT (-tĭkt); AN′TICK·ING. To perform antics.

an′ti·cat′a·lyst (ăn′tĭ·kăt′ȧ·lĭst), *n.* A substance that retards a chemical reaction; a negative catalytic agent. See CATALYSIS.

an′ti·cath′ode (-kăth′ōd), *n.* **a** The anode in a vacuum discharge tube. **b** The target in an X-ray tube.

an′ti·chlor (ăn′tĭ·klōr; 70), *n.* [*anti-* + *chlorine.*] *Chem.* Any substance used in removing the excess of chlorine or bleaching liquor left in paper pulp or textile fibers after bleaching. — **an′ti·chlo·ris′tic** (-klō·rĭs′tĭk), *adj.*

an′ti·christ′ (-krīst′), *n.* [OF. *antecrist*, fr. L., fr. Gr. *Antichristos*, fr. *anti-* + *Christos.*] **1.** One who denies or opposes Christ; specif. [*cap.*], a great antagonist, expected to fill the world with wickedness, but to be conquered forever by Christ at his second coming. **2.** A false Christ.

an·tic′i·pant (ăn·tĭs′ĭ·pănt), *adj.* Anticipating; expectant; — with *of.* — *n.* One who anticipates.

an·tic′i·pate (-pāt), *v. t.* [L. *anticipatus*, past part. of *anticipare* to anticipate, fr. *ante* + a deriv. of *capere* to take.] **1.** To take up, use, or introduce ahead of time; as, to *anticipate* one's thoughts. **2.** To deal with before another; preclude or prevent by prior action; as, to *anticipate* arrest by flight; to be before (another) in doing or acting; forestall; as, death *anticipated* the executioner. **3.** To foresee and do beforehand; as, to *anticipate* his wishes; also, to indicate beforehand. **4.** To experience beforehand; as, to *anticipate* pleasure; also, to expect; as, to *anticipate* disaster. **5.** *Finance.* **a** To spend or use (money) before it is properly available. **b** To pay (an obligation) before the due date. — **Syn.** See PREVENT: FORESEE.

an·tic′i·pa′tion (-pā′shŭn), *n.* **1.** Act of anticipating or state of being anticipated; also, that which is anticipated. **2.** Intuitive preconception; intuition; a priori knowledge. **3.** Expectation; foretaste; as, *anticipations* of joy. **4.** *Law.* The taking or alienation, as by assignment, of the income of a trust estate before it is due. **5.** *Music.* The rhythmically premature entry of one or more tones of a succeeding chord, forming a temporary melodic dissonance. — **Syn.** See PROSPECT.

an·tic′i·pa′tive (ăn·tĭs′ĭ·pā′tĭv; -pȧ·tĭv), *adj.* That anticipates or is given to anticipation. — **an·tic′i·pa′tive·ly**, *adv.*

an·tic′i·pa′tor (-pā′tẽr), *n.* One who anticipates.

an·tic′i·pa·to′ry (-pȧ·tō′rĭ *or, esp. Brit.,* -pā′tẽr·ĭ, -pȧ·tẽr·ĭ), *adj.* Anticipating; of the nature of anticipation.

an′ti·clas′tic (ăn′tĭ·klăs′tĭk), *adj.* [*anti-* + Gr. *klastos* broken, fr. *klan* to break.] *Math.* Having opposite curvatures at a given point, that is, curved convexly along a longitudinal plane section and concavely along the perpendicular section; — of a surface. Cf. SYNCLASTIC.

an′ti·cli′max (-klī′măks), *n.* **1.** *Rhet.* A sentence or passage in which the ideas fall off in dignity or importance at the close. **2.** Any event, esp. the last of a series, that is strikingly or ridiculously less important than what precedes. — **an′ti·cli·mac′tic** (-klī·măk′tĭk), *adj.*

an′ti·cli′nal (ăn′tĭ·klī′năl; -n'l), *adj.* [*anti-* + Gr. *klinein* to incline.] Inclining in opposite directions; specif., *Geol.*, of or pertaining to an anticline. Cf. SYNCLINAL.

an′ti·cline (ăn′tĭ·klīn), *n.* *Geol.* An upfold or arch of stratified rock in which the beds or layers dip in opposite directions from the crest.

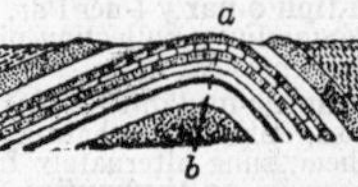

Anticline (Cross Section of Strata); *ab* Axial Plane.

an′tic·ly (ăn′tĭk·lĭ), *adv.* Oddly; grotesquely.

an′ti·cy′clone (ăn′tĭ·sī′klōn), *n.* *Meteorol.* **a** A condition of the atmosphere opposite to that of a cyclone in character as regards direction of the wind and distribution of barometric pressure; also, the high-pressure area where this condition centers. **b** An atmospheric disturbance on the edge of the area. — **an′ti·cy·clon′ic** (-sī·klŏn′ĭk), *adj.*

an′ti·dote (ăn′tĭ·dōt), *n.* [From L., fr. Gr. *antidoton*, deriv. of *anti* against + *didonai* to give.] **1.** A remedy to counteract the effects of poison; — used with *against, for*, or *to.* **2.** Whatever tends to counteract the evil that something else might produce. — **an′ti·dot′al** (ăn′tĭ·dōt′ăl; ăn′tĭ·dō′tăl; -t'l), *adj.*

an′ti·en′er·gis′tic (ăn′tĭ·ĕn′ẽr·jĭs′tĭk), *adj.* Reacting in opposition to applied energy; — opp. to *synergistic.*

an′ti·fed′er·al·ist (-fĕd′ẽr·ăl·ĭst), *n.* One who opposes a federative government; specif. [*cap.*], a member of the party which opposed (1787–89) the adoption of the Constitution of the United States. — **an′ti·fed′er·al** (-fĕd′ẽr·ăl), *adj.* — **an′ti·fed′er·al·ism** (-ĭz'm), *n.*

an′ti·freeze′ (-frēz′), *n.* A substance having a low freezing point. It is either added to the cooling liquid in the radiator of an internal-combustion engine or used as the cooling medium, to prevent the freezing up of the cooling system during cold weather.

an′ti·gen (ăn′tĭ·jĕn), *n.* [*anti-* + *-gen.*] *Immunol.* A substance, as a toxin, enzyme, or the like, which when introduced into the body stimulates the production of an antibody. They are usually proteins. — **an′ti·gen′ic** (-jĕn′ĭk), *adj.*

An·tig′o·ne (ăn·tĭg′ō·nē), *n.* The heroic daughter of Oedipus and Jocasta, who performed funeral rites over the body of her brother Polynices against the command of her uncle Creon, King of Thebes.

an′ti·he′lix (ăn′tĭ·hē′lĭks), *n.; pl.* ANTIHELICES (-hĕl′ĭ·sēz), -HELIXES (-hē′lĭk·sĕz; -sĭz). *Anat.* The curved elevation of cartilage within or in front of the helix. See EAR, *Illust.*

an′ti·his′ta·mine (ăn′tĭ·hĭs′tȧ·mēn; -mĭn), *n.* [*anti-* + *histamine.*] *Biochem.* Any of several compounds used to treat certain allergic reactions and cold symptoms, presumably by inactivating histamine. — **an′ti·his′ta·min′ic** (-mĭn′ĭk), *adj. & n.*

an′ti·knock′ (-nŏk′), *n.* A substance which when added to, or used as, the fuel of an internal-combustion engine prevents knocking in the combustion process.

an′ti·log′a·rithm (-lŏg′ȧ·rĭth'm; -rĭth'm), *n.* *Math.* The number corresponding to a logarithm.

an·til′o·gy (ăn·tĭl′ō·jĭ), *n.; pl.* -GIES (-jĭz). [Gr. *antilogia*, fr. *antilogos* contradictory, fr. *anti* against + *legein* to speak.] A contradiction in terms or ideas.

an′ti·ma·cas′sar (ăn′tĭ·mȧ·kăs′ẽr), *n.* A cover to protect the back or arms of a chair, sofa, etc., orig. from Macassar oil from the hair; a tidy.

an′ti·mask′, -masque′ (ăn′tĭ·mȧsk′; 9), *n.* In Jacobean masks (type of drama), an additional mask, usually preceding the main mask, introduced for contrast, esp. comic or grotesque.

an′ti·mere (-mēr), *n.* [*anti-* + *-mere.*] *Zool.* One of opposite corresponding parts symmetrical with respect to the main axis, as the halves of bilaterally symmetrical animals or parts; — distinguished from *metamere.* — **an′ti·mer′ic** (-mĕr′ĭk), *adj.* — **an·tim′er·ism** (ăn·tĭm′ẽr·ĭz'm), *n.*

an′ti·mo′nic (-mō′nĭk; -mŏn′ĭk), *adj.* *Chem.* Pertaining to, or derived from, antimony in its valence of five.

an′ti·mo′ni·ous (-mō′nĭ·ŭs), *adj.* *Chem.* Pertaining to, or derived from, antimony in its valence of three.

an′ti·mon·soon′ (-mŏn·sōōn′), *n.* *Meteorol.* The upper, contrary-moving current of the atmosphere over a monsoon.

an′ti·mo′ny (ăn′tĭ·mō′nĭ *or, esp. Brit.,* -mŭn·ĭ), *n.* [ML. *antimonium.*] An element of metallic appearance and crystalline structure, tin-white in color, hard and brittle, used chiefly in alloys to give hardness and the property of expanding on solidification. Its prominent valences are three and five. Its compounds are used in medicine, as pigments, etc. Symbol, *Sb* (*stibium*); at. no., 51; at. wt., 121.76. — **an′ti·mo′ni·al** (-mō′nĭ·ăl), *adj. & n.*

an′ti·mo·nyl (ăn′tĭ·mō·nĭl; -nĕl), *n.* *Chem.* A univalent radical, SbO, composed of antimony and oxygen, which forms a series of salts.

an′ti·node′ (ăn′tĭ·nōd′), *n.* *Physics.* That point of a vibrating body which lies midway between two adjacent nodes. See NODE, *Illust.*

an′ti·no′mi·an (-nō′mĭ·ăn), *n.* [*often cap.*] *Eccl. Hist.* One who holds that, under the gospel dispensation, the moral law is of no use or obligation, faith alone being necessary to salvation. — **an′ti·no′mi·an**, *adj.* — **an′ti·no′mi·an·ism** (-ĭz'm), *n.*

an·tin′o·my (ăn·tĭn′ō·mĭ), *n.; pl.* -MIES (-mĭz). [From L., fr. Gr. *antinomia*, fr. *anti-* + *nomos* law.] **1.** Opposition of one law or rule to another. **2.** *Metaph.* A contradiction between two principles each taken to be true, or between inferences correctly drawn from such principles.

‖**an′ti·pas′to** (än′tē·päs′tō), *n.* [It.] A relish or appetizer; hors d'oeuvres.

an′ti·pa·thet′ic (ăn′tĭ·pȧ·thĕt′ĭk), **-i·cal** (-ĭ·kăl), *adj.* **1.** Instinctively averse (to). **2.** Arousing or manifesting antipathy. — **-i·cal·ly**, *adv.*

an·tip′a·thy (ăn·tĭp′ȧ·thĭ), *n.; pl.* -THIES (-thĭz). [From L., fr. Gr. *antipatheia*, fr. *anti-* + *pathein* to suffer.] **1.** Originally, contrariety or opposition in feeling; now, settled aversion or dislike; repugnance; distaste. **2.** A person or thing for whom one has an antipathy. — **Syn.** See ENMITY.

an′ti·pe′ri·od′ic (ăn′tĭ·pēr′ĭ·ŏd′ĭk), *adj.* Preventive of periodic attacks of a disease, as in intermittent fevers. — *n.* An antiperiodic remedy.

an′ti·per′son·nel′ (-pûr′sŏ·nĕl′), *adj.* *Mil.* Designed to destroy or obstruct individuals or patrols of ground troops; as, *antipersonnel* shells.

an′ti·phlo·gis′tic (-flō·jĭs′tĭk), *adj.* *Med.* Counteracting inflammation. — *n.* An antiphlogistic agent or diet.

an′ti·phon (ăn′tĭ·fŏn), *n.* [See ANTHEM.] **1.** A musical response, as in a chant. **2.** A piece of devotional verse or prose responsively sung as a part of the liturgy. **3.** A verse or verses said or sung before and after the psalms.

an·tiph′o·nal (ăn·tĭf′ō·năl; -n'l), *n.* An antiphonary. **—** *adj.* Pertaining to or like an antiphon; responsive as in antiphony. **— an·tiph′o·nal·ly,** *adv.*

an·tiph′o·nar′y (-nĕr′ĭ *or, esp. Brit.,* -nẽr·ĭ), *n.; pl.* -IES (-ĭz). A book containing a collection of antiphons, esp. those of the breviary, with their musical notes.

an·tiph′o·ny (ăn·tĭf′ō·nĭ), *n.; pl.* -NIES (-nĭz). **1.** A musical response; also, antiphonal chanting or singing. **2.** A musical piece, as an anthem, sung alternately by a choir or congregation divided into two parts. **— an′ti·phon′ic** (ăn′tĭ·fŏn′ĭk), *adj.*

an·tip′o·des (ăn·tĭp′ō·dēz), *n. pl.* [L. pl., fr. Gr. *antipous* with the feet opposite, fr. *anti* against + *pous, podos,* foot.] **1.** *Rare.* Those who live on the side of the globe diametrically opposite. **2.** The parts of the globe diametrically opposite; hence, **an′ti·pode** (ăn′tĭ·pōd), *sing.,* anything exactly opposite. **3.** The exact opposite or contrary; — used as *sing.* and *pl.* **— an·tip′o·dal** (-dăl; -d'l), *adj.* **— an·tip′o·de′an** (ăn·tĭp′ō·dē′ăn; ăn′tĭ·pō·dē′ăn), *adj. & n.*

an′ti·pope′ (ăn′tĭ·pōp′), *n.* One elected, or claiming to be, pope in opposition to the pope canonically chosen.

an′ti·quar′i·an (ăn′tĭ·kwâr′ĭ·ăn), *adj.* Pert. to antiquaries or antiquities. **—** *n.* An antiquary. **— an′ti·quar′i·an·ism** (-ĭz′m), *n.*

an′ti·quar′y (ăn′tĭ·kwĕr′ĭ *or, esp. Brit.,* -kwẽr·ĭ), *n.; pl.* -IES (-ĭz). [L. *antiquarius.*] A student of old times through their relics; one who collects or studies antiquities.

an′ti·quate (ăn′tĭ·kwāt), *v. t.* [L. *antiquatus,* past part. of *antiquare,* fr. *antiquus* ancient.] **1.** To make old, or obsolete. **2.** To bring into conformity with the antique. **— an′ti·qua′tion** (-kwā′shŭn), *n.*

an′ti·quat′ed (-kwāt′ĕd; -ĭd), *adj.* Grown old; superannuated; hence, bygone; outmoded; old-fashioned. **— Syn.** See OLD.

an·tique′ (ăn·tēk′), *adj.* [F., fr. L. *antiquus, anticus,* old, ancient, fr. *ante* before.] **1.** Old; venerable; of olden times. **2.** Old, as respects the present age or modern time; antiquated. **3.** Belonging to antiquity, esp. to ancient Greece and Rome. **4.** Of a bygone style or time; archaic; old-fashioned. **5.** Among the oldest of its class, etc.; early; as, an *antique* highboy. **6.** *Print.* Designating a style of display type. **— Syn.** See OLD. **—** *n.* **1.** In general, anything very old; esp., a relic or object of ancient art. **2.** A piece of furniture, tableware, or the like, made at a much earlier period than the present. **3.** *Print.* Antique type. See TYPE, *n.,* 9. **—** *v. t.;* AN·TIQUED′ (-tēkt′); AN·TI′QUING (-tē′kĭng). To finish in antique style; give an appearance of age to. **— an·tique′ly,** *adv.* **— an·tique′ness,** *n.*

an·tiq′ui·ty (ăn·tĭk′wĭ·tĭ), *n.; pl.* -TIES (-tĭz). **1.** Ancient times, esp. those before the Middle Ages. **2.** Quality of being ancient; ancientness; great age. **3.** The people of ancient times, collectively. **4.** A relic, monument, coin, manuscript, etc., of ancient times; — usually in *pl.*

an′ti·re·mon′strant (ăn′tĭ·rē·mŏn′strănt), *n.* One opposed to remonstrance; specif. [*cap.*], one of the Dutch Calvinistic party that opposed the Remonstrants.

an′tir·rhi′num (ăn′tĭ·rī′nŭm), *n.* [NL., fr. Gr. *antirrhinon* snapdragon, fr. *anti-* like + *rhis, rhinos,* nose.] Any of a large genus (*Antirrhinum*) of herbs of the figwort family, with bright-colored irregular flowers. See SNAPDRAGON.

an′ti–Sem′i·tism (ăn′tĭ·sĕm′ĭ·tĭz′m; -sē′mĭ·tĭz′m), *n.* Opposition to, hatred of, or agitation against, Jews. **— an′ti–Sem′ite** (-sĕm′īt; -sē′mīt), *n.* **— an′ti–Se·mit′ic** (-sē·mĭt′ĭk), *adj.*

an′ti·sep′sis (ăn′tĭ·sĕp′sĭs), *n.* [NL. See ANTI-; SEPSIS.] State of being antiseptic; antiseptic methods, processes, etc.

an′ti·sep′tic (-tĭk), *adj.* Opposing sepsis, putrefaction, or decay; having the properties of an antiseptic; pertaining to, or characterized by the use of, antiseptics; as, *antiseptic* surgery. Cf. ASEPTIC. **—** *n.* A substance that checks the growth or action of microorganisms; — used esp. of agents applied to living tissue. **— an′ti·sep′ti·cal** (-tĭ·kăl), *adj.* **— an′ti·sep′ti·cal·ly,** *adv.*

an′ti·sep′ti·cize (-tĭ·sīz), *v. t.* To render antiseptic; to treat with antiseptics; as, to *antisepticize* a wound.

an′ti·se′rum (ăn′tĭ·sēr′ŭm), *n.* *Immunol.* A serum containing antibodies. Cf. ANTITOXIN.

an·tis′tro·phe (ăn·tĭs′trō·fē), *n.* [L., fr. Gr. *antistrophē,* deriv. of *anti-* + *strephein* to turn.] In the Greek choral dance and choral song (see ODE), a part answering to a previous strophe. **— an′ti·stroph′ic** (ăn′tĭ·strŏf′ĭk), *adj.*

an′ti·tank′ (ăn′tĭ·tăngk′; 2), *adj.* *Mil.* Designed to destroy, or to be used against, tanks; as, an *antitank* gun.

an·tith′e·sis (ăn·tĭth′ē·sĭs), *n.; pl.* -SES (-sēz). [L., fr. Gr. *antithesis,* deriv. of *anti-* + *tithenai* to set.] **1.** *Rhet.* An opposition or contrast of ideas, emphasized by the positions of the contrasting words (*fair* and *foul*). **2.** Opposition; contrast; also, the direct opposite; a contrary; as, his temperament is the very *antithesis* of mine.

an′ti·thet′ic (ăn′tĭ·thĕt′ĭk), **an′ti·thet′i·cal** (-ĭ·kăl), *adj.* Containing or characterized by antithesis. **— Syn.** See OPPOSITE. **— an′ti·thet′i·cal·ly,** *adv.*

an′ti·tox′ic (-tŏk′sĭk), *adj.* **1.** Counteracting poison. **2.** Pertaining to or of the nature of an antitoxin.

an′ti·tox′in (-sĭn), *n.* Also **an′ti·tox′ine.** *Immunol.* An antibody formed in the body as a result of the introduction of a toxin (specif., an exotoxin), and capable of neutralizing the specific toxin which stimulated its production. Diphtheria antitoxin is produced by injecting horses with the toxin of the disease, the resulting serum obtained from them being used to counteract diphtheria in human beings.

an′ti·trades′ (ăn′tĭ·trādz′), *n. pl.* *Meteorol.* **a** The prevailing westerly winds of middle latitudes. **b** The westerly winds above (higher than) the trade winds.

an·tit′ra·gus (ăn·tĭt′rȧ·gŭs; ăn′tĭ·trā′gŭs), *n.* [NL., fr. Gr. *antitragos.*] A prominence of the external ear. See EAR, *Illust.*

an′ti·trust′ (ăn′tĭ·trŭst′), *adj.* Opposed to trusts, or combinations made to control or centralize industries, trade, etc.

an′ti·type (ăn′tĭ·tīp), *n.* [Gr. *antitypos* of corresponding form.] **1.** That which corresponds to or is foreshadowed in the type. See TYPE, *n.,* 2. **2.** An opposite type; a countertype. **— an′ti·typ′ic** (-tĭp′ĭk), **an′ti·typ′i·cal** (-ĭ·kăl), *adj.*

an′ti·ven′in (ăn′tĭ·vĕn′ĭn), *n.* [*anti-* + L. *venenum.* See VENIN.] An antitoxin to a venin; also, an antiserum containing such antitoxin.

ant′ler (ănt′lẽr), *n.* [From OF., fr. L. *ante* before + *oculus* eye.] The entire horn, or any branch of the horn, of an animal of the deer family. See HORN, 1. **— ant′lered** (-lẽrd), *adj.*

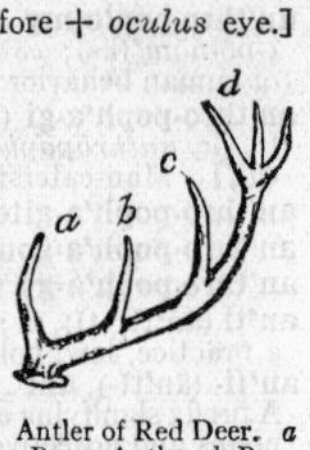

Antler of Red Deer. *a* Brow Antler; *b* Bay, or Bez, Antler; *c* Royal Antler; *d* Surroyal, or Crown, Antlers.

ant lion. Any of certain neuropterous insects (*Myrmeleon* and related genera, order Neuroptera) having net-veined wings and jaws adapted for chewing, the larva of which digs a conical pit, lying in which it catches insects, esp. ants.

an′to·nym (ăn′tō·nĭm), *n.* [Gr. *antōnymia* a word used in place of another, fr. *anti-* + *onoma, onyma,* word.] A word so opposed in meaning to another word that it negates or nullifies every single one of its implications; as, "good" is the *antonym* of "bad"; — contr. with *synonym.* **— an·ton′y·mous** (ăn·tŏn′ĭ·mŭs), *adj.* **— Syn.** See OPPOSITE. **— an·ton′y·my** (-mĭ), *n.*

an′tre (ăn′tẽr), *n.* [F., fr. L. *antrum.*] *Archaic.* A cave.

an·trorse′ (ăn·trôrs′), *adj.* [NL. *antrorsus,* fr. *antero-* + L. *versus* turned.] *Biol.* Directed forward or upward; — opposed to *retrorse, postrorse.* **— an·trorse′ly,** *adv.*

an′trum (ăn′trŭm), *n.; pl.* ANTRA (-trȧ). [L., fr. Gr. *antron.*] A cavern or cavity; esp., *Anat.,* a sinus; as, the maxillary *antrum* leading into the nasal cavity.

ANTU. *Abbr.* for the chemical alpha-naphthyl-thiourea, $C_{11}H_{10}N_2S$, produced as a gray powder for use as a rat poison. Also written **an′tu** (ăn′tōō).

A·nu′bis (ȧ·nū′bĭs), *n.* [L.] *Egypt. Relig.* A jackal god of the necropolis, conductor (with Thoth) of the dead.

an·u′ran (ă·nū′răn), *adj. & n.* [*an-* not + Gr. *oura* tail.] *Zool.* Salientian.

an·u′ri·a (ă·nū′rĭ·ȧ), *n.* [NL., fr. *an-* not + *-uria.*] *Med.* Absence, or defective excretion, of urine; — called also **an′u·re′sis** (ăn′ū·rē′sĭs).

an·u′rous (ă·nū′rŭs), *adj.* Tailless, as the frogs and toads.

a′nus (ā′nŭs), *n.* [L.] *Anat. & Zool.* The posterior opening of the alimentary canal.

an′vil (ăn′vĭl), *n.* [AS. *anfilt, onfilti.*] **1.** A block, usually of iron, steel-faced and of characteristic shape, on which metal is shaped, as by hammering. **2.** Anything resembling an anvil in shape or use; specif.: **a** *Anat.* The incus. **b** The fixed jaw in a measuring instrument. **c** The lower contact of a telegraphic key. **—** *v. t.;* -VILED (-vĭld) or -VILLED; -VIL·ING or -VIL·LING. To form or shape on an anvil; hammer out; as, *anviled* armor.

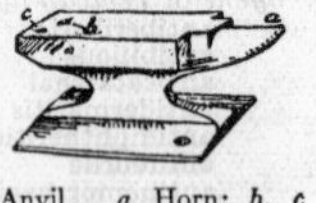

Anvil. *a* Horn; *b, c* Holes for Set Chisels, Swage Blocks, etc.

anx·i′e·ty (ăng·zī′ĕ·tĭ), *n.; pl.* -TIES (-tĭz). [L. *anxietas,* fr. *anxius.* See ANXIOUS.] Painful uneasiness of mind over an impending or anticipated ill; state or an instance of being anxious; solicitous desire. **— Syn.** See CARE.

anx′ious (ăngk′shŭs; ăng′shŭs), *adj.* [L. *anxius,* fr. *angere* to cause pain, choke.] **1.** Disquieted over a possible or impending ill; concerned or solicitous as to something future or unknown; as, *anxious* for news; *anxious* about one's health. **2.** Accompanied with or causing anxiety; worrying; as, *anxious* cares; these are *anxious* times. **3.** Earnestly desirous; as, *anxious* to please. **— Syn.** See EAGER. **— anx′ious·ly,** *adv.* **— anx′ious·ness,** *n.*

an′y (ĕn′ĭ), *adj.* [AS. *ǣnig,* fr. *ān* one.] **1.** Being one (or, *pl.,* some) indiscriminately of whatever kind; no matter what one; as, ask *any* uniformed man; lest *any* marks show. **2.** Being one (or, *pl.,* some) indiscriminately of whatever quality; not none; no matter how great or small; as, to win at *any* cost; also, every; as, *any* help I can get. **3.** That is unmeasured or unlimited; as, *any* quantity you ask. **4.** Appreciable; — with a negative; as, not for *any* length of time. **—** *pron., sing. & pl.* Any person or persons; any single one; any instance, quantity, or amount; as, *any* of several methods. **—** *adv.* To any extent; in any degree; at all.

an′y·bod′y (-bŏd′ĭ; -bŭd·ĭ), *pron.* Any person; anyone.

an′y·how (ĕn′ĭ·hou), *adv.* In any way or manner whatever; at any rate; in any event; haphazard.

an′y·one (-wŭn), *pron.* Any person indiscriminately; anybody; — often written as two words, but to be disting. from *any one,* any single person or thing.

an′y·thing (-thĭng), *pron.* Any object, act, state, event, or fact whatever; something or other; aught. **—** *n.* Thing of any kind. **—** *adv.* In any measure; anywise; at all.

anything but. Not at all or in any respect.

an′y·way (ĕn′ĭ·wā), *adv.* Anywise; at all; in any case; anyhow.

an′y·ways (-wāz), *adv.* Anywise; also, *Dial.,* in any case.

an′y·where (-hwâr), *adv.* In or to any place or point.

an′y·wise (-wīz), *adv.* In any wise or way; at all.

An′zac (ăn′zăk), *n.* *Colloq.* A member of the Australian and New Zealand Army Corps in World War I; — formed from the initials. **— An′zac,** *adj.*

A one (ā′ wŭn′). Usually written **A 1.** **a** A symbol designating a first-class vessel. **b** Also **A number 1.** *Colloq.* Excellent; first-rate.

a′o·rist (ā′ō·rĭst), *adj.* [Gr. *aoristos* indefinite, fr. *a-* not + *horizein* to define.] *Gram.* Designating a tense of the Greek verb denoting that the action took place in unspecified past time, without implication of continuance or repetition. **—** *n.* The aorist tense.

a′o·ris′tic (-rĭs′tĭk), *adj.* **a** Indefinite; undetermined. **b** Of or pertaining to the aorist tense.

a·or′ta (ā·ôr′tȧ), *n.; pl.* -TAS (-tȧz), -TAE (-tē). [NL., fr. Gr. *aortē,* fr. *aeirein* to lift.] The great trunk artery which carries blood from the heart to be distributed by branch arteries through the body. See HEART, *Illust.* **— a·or′tal** (-tăl; -t'l), *adj.* **— a·or′tic** (-tĭk), *adj.*

a′ou·dad (ä′ōō·dăd), *n.* [F., fr. Moorish *audad.*] A wild sheep (*Ammotragus lervia*) of North Africa.

‖à ou′trance′ (à ōō′träns′). [F.] To excess; to the utmost; to the death; unsparingly.

ap-. = APO-.

a·pace′ (ȧ·pās′), *adv.* At a quick pace; swiftly.

A·pach′e (ȧ·păch′ē), *n.; pl.* APACHES (-ēz), APACHE (-ē). **1.** An Indian of a nomadic warlike Athapascan tribe formerly ranging in southwestern North America. **2.** (ȧ·päsh′; ȧ·păsh′; *F.* à′pash′) [F.] [*not cap.*] One of a gang of criminals of the Parisian underworld.

‖a′pa·ge Sa′ta·nas *or* **Sa′tha·nas!** (ăp′ȧ·jē săt′ȧ·năs, săth′ȧ·năs). [L.] Get thee hence, Satan!

ap′a·nage. Var. of APPANAGE.

a′pa·re′jo (ä′pä·rā′hō), *n.; pl.* -JOS (-hōz). [Sp.] A packsaddle of stuffed leather or canvas.

a·part′ (*ȧ*·pärt′), *adv.* [OF. *a part*, fr. *a* (L. *ad*) + *part* part.] **1.** Separately, as regards place or time; as, to live *apart.* **2.** Separately in consideration or function; independently; as, each argument considered *apart.* **3.** Aside; as, jesting *apart.* **4.** In two or more parts; to pieces. — *adj.* Separate; dissociated; — used predicatively.

a·part′heid (*ȧ*·pärt′hāt; -hīt), *n.* [S. Afr. D., fr. *apart* separate (fr. F. *à part* aside) + *-heid* (akin to E. *-hood*).] Separation of the races; specif., in South Africa, a policy of segregation and political and economic discrimination against non-European groups.

a·part′ment (*ȧ*·pärt′m*ĕ*nt), *n.* [F. *appartement*, fr. It. *appartamento*, deriv. fr. *a parte* apart.] A suite or set of rooms, esp. one occupied as a dwelling; sometimes, a single room. Abbr. *apt.* Cf. FLAT, *n.*

apartment house. A residential building containing a number of apartments.

ap′a·thet′ic (ăp′*ȧ*·thĕt′ĭk), **ap′a·thet′i·cal** (-ĭ·k*ă*l), *adj.* Lacking normal feeling or interest; indifferent; phlegmatic; listless. — **Syn.** See IMPASSIVE. — **Ant.** Alert. — **ap′a·thet′i·cal·ly,** *adv.*

ap′a·thy (ăp′*ȧ*·thĭ), *n.; pl.* APATHIES (-thĭz). [F. or L.; F. *apathie*, fr. L., fr. Gr. *apatheia*, fr. *a-* not + *pathos* suffering.] **1.** Want of feeling; lack of passion, emotion, or excitement. **2.** Indifference to what appeals to feelings or interest.

ap′a·tite (ăp′*ȧ*·tīt), *n.* [Gr. *apatē* deceit; it was often mistaken for other minerals.] *Mineral.* Calcium phosphate-fluoride, $CaFCa_4(PO_4)_3$, or, less commonly, phosphate-chloride, $CaClCa_4(PO_4)_3$, occurring variously in six-sided prisms, granular masses, or with fibrous structure, etc.

ape (āp), *n.* [AS. *apa.*] **1.** *Zool.* **a** Any monkey (sense 1 **a**). **b** Narrowly, one of the larger tailless Old World forms (see MONKEY, 1 **b**). Those most nearly related to man are called ***anthropoid apes***, as the gibbon, chimpanzee, orang-utan, and gorilla. **2.** An imitator. — *v. t.* To mimic. — **Syn.** See COPY.

a·peak′ (*ȧ*·pēk′), *adv. & adj.* *Naut.* In a vertical line.

‖a′per′çu′ (*ȧ*′pĕr′sü′), *n.; pl.* APERÇUS (-süz′; *F.* -sü′). [F.] A brief or detached view; survey; sketch. — **Syn.** See COMPENDIUM.

a·pe′ri·ent (*ȧ*·pēr′ĭ·*ĕ*nt), *adj.* [L. *aperiens*, pres. part. of *aperire* to uncover, open.] *Med.* Gently moving the bowels; laxative. — *n.* An aperient medicine or food.

a·pe′ri·od′ic (ā·pēr′ĭ·ŏd′ĭk), *adj.* [*a-* not + *periodic.*] **1.** Of irregular occurrence; not periodic. **2.** *Physics.* Not having periodic vibrations; deadbeat. — **a·pe′ri·o·dic′i·ty** (-ō·dĭs′ĭ·tĭ), *n.*

‖a′pé′ri′tif′ (*ȧ*′pā′rē′tēf′), *n.* [F.] A short alcoholic drink taken before a meal as an appetizer.

a·per′i·tive (*ȧ*·pĕr′ĭ·tĭv), *adj. & n.* Aperient.

ap′er·ture (ăp′ẽr·tūr), *n.* [L. *apertura*, fr. *aperire.* See APERIENT.] **1.** An opening; gap; cleft; hole. **2.** The opening admitting light, as in a camera. **3.** *Optics.* The inside diameter of the ring holding the object glass of an optical instrument, as a telescope.

Syn. **Aperture, interstice, orifice** mean a passage through or in and out. **Aperture** applies to any opening such as a crack, cleft, or window, in an otherwise solid wall or the like; **interstice** applies to any unfilled gap, space, or interval in a fabric (in its widest sense) or in a mass; **orifice** applies to any opening that suggests a mouth or a vent.

ap′er·y (āp′ẽr·ĭ), *n.; pl.* APERIES (-ĭz). Apish action.

a·pet′al·ous (ā·pĕt′*ă*l·*ŭ*s), *adj.* Having no petals.

a′pex (ā′pĕks), *n.; pl.* APEXES (-pĕk·sĕz; -sĭz), APICES (ăp′ĭ·sēz; ā′pĭ-). [L., summit.] **1.** The tip, point, or angular summit of anything; a vertex. **2.** The point of culmination, crisis, or climax. — **Syn.** See SUMMIT.

aph-. = APO-.

a·phaer′e·sis (*ă*·fĕr′ē·sĭs *or, esp. Brit.*, -fē′rē·sĭs), **a·pher′e·sis** (*ă*·fĕr′ē·sĭs), *n.* [L., fr. Gr. *aphairesis*, deriv. of *apo* from + *hairein* to take.] *Gram.* The dropping of a letter or syllable from the beginning of a word (*mid* for *amid*). — **aph′ae·ret′ic, aph′e·ret′ic** (ăf′ē·rĕt′ĭk), *adj.*

aph′a·nite (ăf′*ȧ*·nīt), *n.* [Gr. *aphanēs* invisible + *-ite.*] *Petrog.* Any dark rock of such close texture that its separate grains are invisible to the naked eye. — **aph′a·nit′ic** (-nĭt′ĭk), *adj.*

a·pha′si·a (*ă*·fā′zhĭ·*ȧ*; -zh*ȧ*), *n.* [NL., fr. Gr. *aphasia*, fr. *a-* not + *phanai* to speak.] Loss or impairment of the power to use or understand speech resulting from brain lesion or, sometimes, from functional or emotional disturbance. — **a·pha′si·ac** (-zĭ·ăk), *adj. & n.* — **a·pha′sic** (-zĭk; -sĭk), *adj. & n.*

a·phe′li·on (*ă*·fē′lĭ·*ŏ*n; -fēl′y*ŏ*n), *n.; pl.* APHELIA (-lĭ·*ȧ*; -fēl′y*ȧ*). [Gr. *apo* + *hēlios* sun.] *Astron.* That point of a planet's or comet's orbit most distant from the sun; — opposed to *perihelion.*

a·phe′li·ot′ro·pism (*ă*·fē′lĭ·ŏt′rō·pĭz′m), *n.* [See APO-; HELIOTROPISM.] *Biol.* Tropism involving a turning away from sunlight. Cf. HELIOTROPISM. — **a·phe′li·o·trop′ic** (-ō·trŏp′ĭk), *adj.*

aph′e·sis (ăf′ē·sĭs), *n.* [Gr., a letting go, fr. *aphienai* to let go, fr. *apo* off + *hienai* to send.] *Gram.* The gradual loss of a short unaccented initial vowel. — **a·phet′ic** (*ă*·fĕt′ĭk), *adj.*

a′phid (ā′fĭd; ăf′ĭd), *n.* Any plant louse (see LOUSE, 2) of the family Aphididae, living on plants and sucking their juices; as, the rose *aphid* or aphis. — **a·phid′i·an** (*ă*·fĭd′ĭ·*ă*n), *adj. & n.*

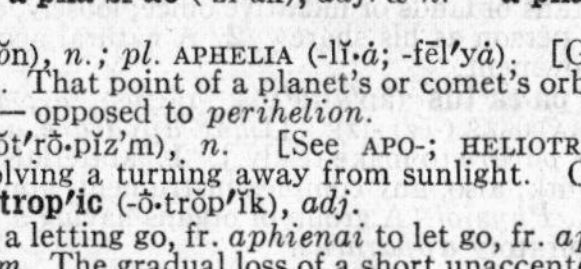

Aphid (*Aphis mali*), much enlarged. *a* Winged adult male; *b* Wingless female.

a′phis (ā′fĭs; ăf′ĭs), *n.; pl.* APHIDES (ăf′ĭ·dēz). [NL.] An aphid.

a·pho′ni·a (ā·fō′nĭ·*ȧ*), *n.* [NL., fr. Gr. *aphōnia*, fr. *aphōnos* voiceless, fr. *a-* not + *phōnē* voice.] Loss of voice due to paralysis of the vocal cords.

a·phon′ic (-fŏn′ĭk), *adj.* **1.** *Phonet.* **a** Having no sound or pronunciation. **b** Voiceless. **2.** Pert. to, or characterized by, aphonia.

aph′o·rism (ăf′ō·rĭz′m), *n.* [From F., fr. Gr. *aphorismos* definition, pithy sentence, fr. *aphorizein* to define, fr. *apo-* + *horizein* to separate.] A short pithy sentence, stating a general doctrine or truth; loosely, a maxim. — **Syn.** Saying, saw, proverb, adage.

aph′o·rist (-rĭst), *n.* A writer or utterer of aphorisms.

aph′o·ris′tic (-rĭs′tĭk), *adj.* Of the nature of an aphorism; abounding in, or given to, aphorisms. — **aph′o·ris′ti·cal·ly** (-tĭ·k*ă*l·ĭ), *adv.*

aph′o·rize (ăf′ō·rīz), *v. i.* To make aphorisms.

a·pho′tic (ā·fō′tĭk), *adj.* [Gr. *aphōs, aphōtos.*] Lightless; as, the *aphotic* region of the ocean depths.

aph′ro·dis′i·ac (ăf′rō·dĭz′ĭ·ăk), *adj.* [Gr. *aphrodisiakos* pert. to sensual love, fr. *Aphroditē* Aphrodite.] Exciting sexual desire; provocative of, or inclined to, venery. — *n.* That which (as a drug, or certain foods) excites to venery.

Aph′ro·di′te (-dī′tē), *n.* [Gr. *Aphroditē.*] **1.** *Gr. Relig.* The goddess of love and beauty, identified by the Romans with Venus. **2.** A brown, black-spotted butterfly (*Argynnis aphrodite*) of the U.S.

a·phyl′lous (ā·fĭl′*ŭ*s), *adj.* [Gr. *aphyllos*, fr. *a-* not + *phyllon* leaf.] *Bot.* Destitute of foliage leaves, as cacti. — **a·phyl′ly** (-ĭ), *n.*

a′pi·a′ceous (ā′pĭ·ā′sh*ŭ*s), *adj.* [L. *apium* parsley.] Ammiaceous.

a′pi·an (ā′pĭ·*ă*n), *adj.* [L. *apianus.*] Of a bee or bees.

a′pi·ar′i·an (-âr′ĭ·*ă*n), *adj.* Relating to beekeeping or bees.

a′pi·a·rist (ā′pĭ·*ȧ*·rĭst), *n.* One who keeps an apiary.

a′pi·ar′y (ā′pĭ·ĕr′ĭ *or, esp. Brit.*, -ẽr·ĭ), *n.; pl.* APIARIES (-ĭz). [L. *apiarium*, fr. *apis* bee.] Place where bees are kept; a collection of hives or colonies of bees kept for their honey.

ap′i·cal (ăp′ĭ·k*ă*l; ā′pĭ-), *adj.* [L. *apex, apicis*, tip or summit.] Belonging to an apex; being at or near the tip. — **ap′i·cal·ly,** *adv.*

ap′i·ces (ăp′ĭ·sēz; ā′pĭ-), *n. pl.* of APEX.

a·pic′u·late (*ȧ*·pĭk′ū·lāt), *adj.* *Bot.* Terminated abruptly, as a leaf, by a small, distinct point.

a′pi·cul′ture (ā′pĭ·kŭl′tūr), *n.* [L. *apis* bee + E. *culture.*] Beekeeping, esp. as an industry. — **a′pi·cul′tur·al** (-kŭl′tūr·*ă*l), *adj.* — **a′pi·cul′tur·ist** (-kŭl′tūr·ĭst), *n.*

a·piece′ (*ȧ*·pēs′), *adv.* [*a* + *piece.* See A, *adj.*, 2.] To or for each by itself; each; as the share of each.

‖à pied (*ȧ* pyā′). [F.] On foot.

A′pis (ā′pĭs), *n.* [L., fr. Gr., fr. Egypt. *Hep, Hāpi.*] A sacred bull worshiped by the ancient Egyptians.

ap′ish (āp′ĭsh), *adj.* Like an ape in appearance or manner; prone to servile imitation; fantastically silly or affected. — **ap′ish·ly,** *adv.* — **ap′ish·ness,** *n.*

a·piv′o·rous (ā·pĭv′ō·r*ŭ*s), *adj.* [L. *apis* bee + *-vorous.*] *Zool.* Feeding upon bees; — said of certain birds.

a′pla·cen′tal (ā′pl*ȧ*·sĕn′t*ă*l; ăp′l*ȧ*-), *adj.* Having or developing no placenta.

ap′la·nat′ic (ăp′l*ȧ*·năt′ĭk), *adj.* [*a-* not + Gr. *planatikos* wandering.] *Optics.* Corrected for spherical aberration. See ABERRATION, *n.*, 4.

ap′lite (ăp′līt), *n.* [Gr. *haploos* simple + *-ite.*] *Petrog.* A fine-grained granite consisting chiefly of quartz and feldspar. — **ap·lit′ic** (ăp·lĭt′ĭk), *adj.*

a·plomb′ (*ȧ*·plŏm′; *F.* *ȧ*′plôN′), *n.* [F., fr. *à* to + *plomb* lead.] Literally, perpendicularity; hence, self-assurance; self-possession. — **Syn.** See CONFIDENCE.

ap·ne′a, ap·noe′a (ăp·nē′*ȧ*), *n.* [NL., fr. *a-* not + Gr. *pnoē, pnoiē*, breath.] *Med.* **a** Partial suspension of breath. **b** Asphyxia; suffocation. — **ap·ne′al, ap·noe′al** (-*ă*l), **ap·ne′ic, ap·noe′ic** (-ĭk), *adj.*

ap′o- (ăp′ō-), **ap-, aph-.** [Gr., fr. *apo*, prep.] A prefix signifying *from, away from, off*, as in *apogee*; or *asunder, detached, separate*, as in *apocarpous.*

a·poc′a·lypse (*ȧ*·pŏk′*ȧ*·lĭps), *n.* [From L., fr. Gr. *apokalypsis*, fr. *apokalyptein* to uncover, fr. *apo-* + *kalyptein* to cover.] **1.** [*cap.*] The last book of the New Testament, otherwise called *The Revelation of St. John the Divine.* See BIBLE. **2.** Anything viewed as a prophetic revelation. — **a·poc′a·lyp′tic** (-lĭp′tĭk), **a·poc′a·lyp′ti·cal** (-tĭ·k*ă*l), *adj.* — **a·poc′a·lyp′ti·cal·ly,** *adv.*

ap′o·carp (ăp′ō·kärp), *n.* *Bot.* An apocarpous gynoecium.

ap′o·car′pous (-kär′p*ŭ*s), *adj.* [*apo-* + *-carpous.*] *Bot.* Having the carpels separate, as in the buttercup; — opp. to *syncarpous.* — **ap′o·car′py** (ăp′ō·kär′pĭ), *n.*

ap′o·chro·mat′ic (-krō·măt′ĭk), *adj.* [*apo-* + *chromatic.*] *Optics.* Free from chromatic and spherical aberration. See ABERRATION, *n.*, 4.

a·poc′o·pate (*ȧ*·pŏk′ō·pāt), *v. t.* [NL. *apocopatus*, past part. of *apocopare* to cut off, fr. L. *apocope.*] *Gram.* To cut short by apocope. — **a·poc′o·pa′tion** (-pā′sh*ŭ*n), *n.*

a·poc′o·pe (-pē), *n.* [L., fr. Gr. *apokopē* a cutting off.] *Gram.* Omission of the last sound or syllable of a word.

A·poc′ry·pha (*ȧ*·pŏk′rĭ·f*ȧ*), *n. pl.*, but also sometimes used as *sing.*, with *pl.* APOCRYPHAS (-f*ȧ*z). [LL. *apocryphus* apocryphal, fr. Gr. *apokryphos* hidden, spurious, deriv. fr. *apo-* + *kryptein* to hide.] **1.** [*not cap.*] Writings or statements of doubtful authorship or authority. **2.** Specif.: **a** In Roman Catholic use, pseudepigrapha. **b** Commonly, the fourteen books of the Old Testament in the Vulgate that were taken from the Septuagint but are not found in Hebrew, now excluded from the Authorized Version. See BIBLE. **c** Christian gospels, epistles, and apocalypses not admitted to the New Testament.

a·poc′ry·phal (*ȧ*·pŏk′rĭ·f*ă*l), *adj.* **1.** [*cap.*] Of or like the Apocrypha. **2.** Not canonical; unauthentic; spurious. — **Syn.** See FICTITIOUS. — **a·poc′ry·phal·ly,** *adv.* — **a·poc′ry·phal·ness,** *n.*

a·poc′y·na′ceous (*ȧ*·pŏs′ĭ·nā′sh*ŭ*s), *adj.* [Gr. *apokynon* dogbane (*apo-* + *kyōn, kynos*, dog) + *-aceous.*] *Bot.* Belonging to the dogbane family (Apocynaceae). See DOGBANE.

ap′o·dal (ăp′ō·d*ă*l; -d′l), **ap′od** (ăp′ŏd), *adj.* [Gr. *apous, apodos*, footless, fr. *a-* not + *pous, podos*, foot.] **1.** Having no feet. **2.** *Zool.* Destitute of pelvic fins, as the eels.

ap′o·dic′tic (ăp′ō·dĭk′tĭk), **ap′o·deic′tic** (-dīk′tĭk), **ap′o·dic′ti·cal** (-dĭk′tĭ·k*ă*l), **ap′o·deic′ti·cal** (-dīk′tĭ·k*ă*l), *adj.* [From L., fr. Gr. *apodeiktikos*, deriv. of *apo-* + *deiknynai* to show.] *Logic.* Involving or expressing necessary truth; absolutely certain; also, clearly demonstrable. — **ap′o·dic′ti·cal·ly, ap′o·deic′ti·cal·ly,** *adv.*

a·pod′o·sis (*ȧ*·pŏd′ō·sĭs), *n.; pl.* -SES (-sēz). [L., fr. Gr. *apodosis*, deriv. of *apo-* + *didonai* to give.] *Gram.* The conclusion in a conditional sentence, expressing the result; — distinguished from *protasis.*

a·pog′a·my (*ȧ*·pŏg′*ȧ*·mĭ), *n.* [*apo-* + *-gamy.*] *Bot.* Development of a sporophyte from a gametophyte without fertilization. Cf. PARTHENOGENESIS, 2. — **ap′o·gam′ic** (ăp′ō·găm′ĭk), **a·pog′a·mous** (*ȧ*·pŏg′*ȧ*·m*ŭ*s), *adj.*

ap′o·gee (ăp′ō·jē), *n.* [F. and L.; F. *apogée*, fr. L., fr. Gr. *apogaion*, deriv. of *apo-* + *gaia, gē*, earth.] **1.** *Astron.* That point in the orbit of the moon at the greatest distance from the earth; — opposed to *perigee.* **2.** The farthest or highest point; culmination; apex. — **ap′o·ge′al** (ăp′ō·jē′*ă*l), **ap′o·ge′an** (-*ă*n), *adj.*

ap′o·ge·ot′ro·pism (-jē·ŏt′rō·pĭz′m), *n.* *Bot.* Tropism involving a bending up or away from the earth. Cf. GEOTROPISM. — **ap′o·ge′o·trop′ic** (-jē′ō·trŏp′ĭk), *adj.*

A·pol′lo (*ȧ*·pŏl′ō), *n.* [L. *Apollo, -linis*, fr. Gr. *Apollōn.*] **1.** *Gr. Relig.* The god of manly youth and beauty, of poetry, music, and oracles; the twin of Artemis. He was also god of healing; in late times, he was identified with the sun-god Helios. **2.** A young man of graceful beauty.

A·pol′lyon (ȧ·pŏl′yŭn; -ĭ·ŭn), *n.* [Gr. *apollyōn* destroying, fr. *apollyein, apollynai,* to destroy utterly.] The angel of the bottomless pit. In *Pilgrim's Progress,* he appears as a fiend overcome by Christian.

a·pol′o·get′ic (ȧ·pŏl′ō·jĕt′ĭk), **a·pol′o·get′i·cal** (-ĭ·kăl), *adj.* [F. or L.; F., fr. L., fr. Gr. *apologētikos,* fr. *apologeisthai* to speak in defense of. See APOLOGY.] Said, written, or done by way of apology; also, regretfully excusing or acknowledging. — **a·pol′o·get′i·cal·ly,** *adv.*

a·pol′o·get′ics (-ĭks), *n.*; see -ICS. Systematic argumentative discourse in defense, esp. of the divine origin and authority of Christianity.

ap′o·lo′gi·a (ăp′ō·lō′jĭ·ȧ), *n.* [L.] An apology (esp. in sense 1). — **Syn.** See APOLOGY.

a·pol′o·gist (ȧ·pŏl′ō·jĭst), *n.* One who apologizes or who argues in defense of a cause, policy, institution, or the like; specif., one who argues in defense of Christianity.

a·pol′o·gize (-jīz), *v. i.* To make an apology. — **a·pol′o·giz′er** (-jīz′ẽr), *n.*

ap′o·logue (ăp′ō·lŏg), *n.* [F., fr. L. *apologus,* fr. Gr. *apologos.*] A short fictitious or allegorical story intended to convey a useful lesson or a moral; a fable.

a·pol′o·gy (ȧ·pŏl′ō·jĭ), *n.; pl.* -GIES (-jĭz). [F. or L.; F., fr. L., fr. Gr. *apologia,* fr. *apo-* + *logos* speech.] **1.** Something said or written in defense or justification of what appears to others to be wrong, or of what may be liable to disapprobation. **2.** An acknowledgment intended as a reparation, or expressive of regret, for some improper, injurious, or discourteous remark or act. **3.** That which serves as an excuse for the absence of something; a makeshift.

Syn. **Apology, apologia, excuse, plea, pretext, alibi** mean an explanation or defense of an act, policy, view, or the like. **Apology,** and now especially **apologia,** in strict use imply no admission of guilt or error but a desire to make clear the grounds for some course, belief, or the like; **excuse** always implies an intent to remove or avoid blame, as for a neglect of duty or a violation of a rule; **plea** stresses a feigned apology intended to win understanding or sympathy; **pretext** invariably suggests subterfuge and the offering of one reason or motive in place of the true one; **alibi,** in colloquial use, designates a plausible rather than true excuse.

ap′o·mix′is (ăp′ō·mĭk′sĭs), *n.* [NL., fr. *apo-* + Gr. *mixis* a mingling.] *Biol.* Reproduction without any form of sexual union, as parthenogenesis and apogamy. — **ap′o·mic′tic** (-mĭk′tĭk), **ap′o·mic′ti·cal** (-tĭ·kăl), *adj.*

ap′o·mor′phine (ăp′ō·môr′fēn; -fĭn), **ap′o·mor′phi·a** (-môr′fĭ·ȧ), *n.* Also **-phin.** [*apo-* + *morphine, morphia.*] An artificial crystalline alkaloid, $C_{17}H_{17}NO_2$, made from morphine. It is a powerful emetic.

ap′o·neu·ro′sis (-nū·rō′sĭs), *n.; pl.* -ROSES (-sēz). [Gr. *aponeurōsis,* fr. *aponeuroun* to pass into a tendon. See NEUROSIS.] *Anat.* Any of the thicker and denser of the deep fasciae (bundles of connective tissue) which cover, invest, and form the terminations and attachments of certain muscles. They differ from tendons only in being flat and thin. — **ap′o·neu·rot′ic** (-rŏt′ĭk), *adj.*

ap′o·pemp′tic (-pĕmp′tĭk), *adj.* [Gr. *apopemptikos,* fr. *apopempein* to send away.] Sung or addressed to one departing; valedictory. — **ap′o·pemp′tic,** *n.*

a·poph′a·sis (ȧ·pŏf′ȧ·sĭs), *n.* [NL., fr. Gr. *apophasis* denial, fr. *apophanai* to speak out, deny.] *Rhet.* Mention of something in disclaiming intention to mention it (I will not speak of his unsavory past).

ap′o·phthegm (ăp′ō·thĕm), **ap′o·phtheg·mat′ic** (-thĕg·măt′ĭk), etc. Vars. of APOTHEGM, etc.

a·poph′y·ge (ȧ·pŏf′ĭ·jē), *n.* [Gr. *apophygē* escape, in arch. a curve (see def.), fr. *apopheugein* to flee away, fr. *apo-* + *pheugein* to flee.] *Arch.* The small concave spread, or curve, at the top or bottom of the shaft of a column where it joins the capital or the base.

a·poph′yl·lite (ȧ·pŏf′ĭ·līt; ăp′ō·fĭl′īt), *n.* [*apo-* + Gr. *phyllon* leaf; — from its exfoliation before the blowpipe.] A hydrous potassium calcium silicate closely related to the zeolites, usually in transparent square prisms or white or grayish masses.

a·poph′y·sis (ȧ·pŏf′ĭ·sĭs), *n.; pl.* -SES (-sēz). [NL., fr. Gr., offshoot.] A projecting part of a bone, esp. of a vertebra.

ap′o·plec′tic (ăp′ō·plĕk′tĭk), *adj.* Of, relating to, or causing apoplexy; affected with, inclined to, or symptomatic of apoplexy. — **ap′o·plec′ti·cal** (-tĭ·kăl), *adj.* — **ap′o·plec′ti·cal·ly,** *adv.*

ap′o·plec′tic, *n.* One liable to, or having, apoplexy.

ap′o·plex′y (ăp′ō·plĕk′sĭ), *n.* [OF. *apoplexie,* fr. L., fr. Gr. *apoplēxia,* fr. *apoplēssein* to cripple by a stroke, fr. *apo-* + *plēssein* to strike.] Sudden diminution or loss of consciousness, sensation, and voluntary motion, caused by the rupture or obstruction of an artery of the brain.

a·port′ (ȧ·pōrt′; 70), *adv.* *Naut.* On or toward the left side.

ap′o·si′o·pe′sis (ăp′ō·sī′ō·pē′sĭs), *n.* [L., fr. Gr. *aposiōpēsis,* fr. *aposiōpan* to be quite silent.] *Rhet.* A breaking off suddenly, as if unwilling to express one's mind (His conduct — but I cannot speak of that). — **ap′o·si′o·pet′ic** (-pĕt′ĭk), *adj.*

a·pos′ta·sy (ȧ·pŏs′tȧ·sĭ), *n.; pl.* -TASIES (-sĭz). [Through F. & L., fr. Gr. *apostasia* a defection, deriv. of *apo-* + *stēnai* to stand.] Abandonment of what one has voluntarily professed; total desertion of principles or faith.

a·pos′tate (-tāt), *n.* One who has forsaken the faith, principles, or party to which he before adhered. — **a·pos′tate,** *adj.*

a·pos′ta·tize (-tȧ·tīz), *v. i.* To commit apostasy.

a pos·te′ri·o′ri (ā′ pŏs·tē′rĭ·ō′rī). [L., fr. *a* (*ab*) from + *posterior* latter.] *Logic.* Characterizing the kind of reasoning deriving propositions from observation of facts or arriving at principles by generalization from facts; hence, designating what can be known only through experience. Cf. A PRIORI.

a·pos′til, a·pos′tille (ȧ·pŏs′tĭl), *n.* [F. *apostille.*] A marginal note; an annotation.

a·pos′tle (ȧ·pŏs′'l), *n.* [From OF., fr. L., fr. Gr. *apostolos* one sent forth, deriv. of *apo-* + *stellein* to send.] **1.** One of the twelve disciples of Christ sent forth to preach the gospel. The original twelve, according to a harmonized list, included Simon Peter, Andrew, James and John (sons of Zebedee), Philip, Bartholomew, Matthew (or Levi), Thomas (or Didymus), James (son of Alphaeus), Jude (or Thaddaeus), Simon the Cananaean, and Judas Iscariot. Matthias was chosen by lot to take the place of Judas. Paul, though not of the twelve, was equal with them in office and dignity. Barnabas, the companion of Paul on his first missionary journey, is sometimes called an apostle. **2.** One who resembles the apostles as the first advocate of a great moral reform. **3.** One of a council of twelve men in the Mormon Church, ordained to the highest order of priesthood, standing next in authority to the First Presidency (see PRESIDENCY, 4). — **a·pos′tle·ship,** *n.*

A·pos′tles' Creed (ȧ·pŏs′'lz). A widely used creed, anciently ascribed to the Twelve Apostles, beginning "I believe in God the Father Almighty, Maker (Creator) of heaven and earth: and in Jesus Christ his only Son our Lord."

a·pos′to·late (ȧ·pŏs′tō·lāt), *n.* Office or mission of an apostle.

ap′os·tol′ic (ăp′ŏs·tŏl′ĭk), **ap′os·tol′i·cal** (-ĭ·kăl), *adj.* **1.** Of or pertaining to an apostle, or the apostles, their times, or their spirit; according to their doctrines. **2.** [*often cap.*] Papal; as, *apostolic* indulgences. — **ap′os·tol′i·cism** (-ĭ·sĭz'm), **a·pos′to·lic′i·ty** (ȧ·pŏs′tō·lĭs′ĭ·tĭ), *n.*

Apostolic Fathers. A 2d-century collection of writings supposedly by personal followers of the apostles.

apostolic succession. *Eccl.* Uninterrupted succession or descent from the apostles by regular and successive ordinations of bishops, held to be necessary for valid administration of the sacraments, transmission of orders, etc.

a·pos′tro·phe (ȧ·pŏs′trō·fē), *n.* [L., fr. Gr. *apostrophē* a turning away, deriv. of *apo-* + *strephein* to turn.] *Rhet.* A feigned turning from one's audience to address directly a person or thing, or an abstract idea or imaginary object. — **ap′os·troph′ic** (ăp′ŏs·trŏf′ĭk), *adj.*

a·pos′tro·phe, *n.* [F., fr. L. *apostrophus* apostrophe, omitting of a letter, fr. Gr. *apostrophos.* See 1st APOSTROPHE, with which this word was confused.] The mark ['] used, in writing and printing, to indicate: **a** Omission of one or more letters or figures (*ne'er* for *never*). **b** The possessive case, originating in this use as a late 17th-century innovation under the misconception that the *-s* possessive represented a contraction of *his* as in "George his hat." **c** The plural of letters and figures (two a's and three 7's). **d** The close of a quotation. See QUOTATION MARK. — **ap′os·troph′ic,** *adj.*

a·pos′tro·phize (-fīz), *v. t. & i.* **1.** To address by or in apostrophe. See 1st APOSTROPHE. **2.** To contract by apostrophe; to mark with an apostrophe [']. See 2d APOSTROPHE.

a·poth′e·car′ies' meas′ure (ȧ·pŏth′ē·kĕr′ĭz; -kẽr·ĭz). A system of fluid measures used by apothecaries. See MEASURE, *Table* 12.

apothecaries' weight. A system of weights, used for compounding medical prescriptions. See WEIGHT, *Tables* 3 & 4.

a·poth′e·car′y (ȧ·pŏth′ē·kĕr′ĭ *or, esp. Brit.,* -kẽr·ĭ), *n.; pl.* -IES (-ĭz). [From OF., fr. LL. *apothecarius,* fr. L. *apotheca* storehouse, fr. Gr. *apothēkē,* deriv. of *apo-* + *tithenai* to put.] A pharmacist; druggist; also formerly, in England, a medical practitioner having the right to prescribe as well as sell drugs. — **Syn.** See DRUGGIST.

ap′o·the′ci·um (ăp′ō·thē′shĭ·ŭm; -sĭ·ŭm), *n.; pl.* -CIA (-ȧ). [NL., fr. Gr. *apothēkē* storehouse.] *Bot.* In lichens and certain fungi, the disklike or cuplike body containing the spore sacs. — **ap′o·the′cial** (-thē′shăl), *adj.*

ap′o·thegm, ap′o·phthegm (ăp′ō·thĕm), *n.* [Gr. *apophthegma* thing uttered, apothegm, deriv. of *apo-* + *phthengesthai* to speak.] A short, pithy, and instructive saying; a sententious precept or maxim. — **ap′o·theg·mat′ic** (-thĕg·măt′ĭk), **ap′o·theg·mat′i·cal** (-ĭ·kăl), *adj.*

ap′o·them (ăp′ō·thĕm), *n.* [Gr. *apo* + *thema* that which is placed.] *Math.* The perpendicular from the center to one of the sides of a regular polygon.

a·poth′e·o′sis (ȧ·pŏth′ē·ō′sĭs; ăp′ō·thē′ō·sĭs), *n.; pl.* -OSES (-sēz). [L., fr. Gr. *apotheōsis,* fr. *apotheoun* to deify.] **1.** Deification. **2.** Glorification; also, a glorified ideal; as, he was the very *apotheosis* of chivalry. — **a·poth′e·o·size** (ȧ·pŏth′ē·ō·sīz; ăp′ō·thē′ō·sīz), *v. t.*

Ap′pa·la′chian tea (ăp′ȧ·lā′chăn; -lăch′ăn). **a** The leaves of either of two shrubs (*Ilex glabra* and *I. vomitoria*) of the eastern United States, locally used as a tea; also, either of the two plants. **b** The withe rod.

ap·pall′, ap·pal′ (ă·pôl′), *v. t.;* AP·PALLED′ (-pôld′); AP·PALL′ING. [OF. *apallir, apalir,* to grow or make pale, fr. *a* to + *pale* pale.] To overwhelm or discourage with fear or horror; to dismay; shock. — **Syn.** See DISMAY.

ap·pall′ing, *adj.* Such as to appall or cause consternation. — **Syn.** See FEARFUL. — **ap·pall′ing·ly,** *adv.*

ap′pa·nage, ap′a·nage (ăp′ȧ·nĭj), *n.* [F. *apanage,* fr. OF. *apaner* to nourish, deriv. of L. *ad* to + *panis* bread.] **1.** The provision made by a sovereign or prince for the younger members of his family, as by a grant of lands or lucrative office; loosely, any property appropriated by a person as his share. **2.** A natural accompaniment, adjunct, or endowment.

ap′pa·ra′tus (ăp′ȧ·rā′tŭs; -răt′ŭs), *n.; pl.* -RATUS (-rā′tŭs; -răt′ŭs), -RATUSES (-ĕz; -ĭz). [L., fr. *apparare, apparatum,* to prepare, fr. *ad-* + *parare* to make ready.] **1.** Materials, implements, etc., for a given work; also, any complex instrument, appliance, or piece of machinery. **2.** *Physiol.* A group of organs having a common function; as, the respiratory *apparatus.*

‖**ap′pa·ra′tus cri′ti·cus** (ăp′ȧ·rā′tŭs krĭt′ĭ·kŭs). [L.] **a** A set of reference books for use in literary work. **b** Supplementary data, esp. variant readings, provided as a basis for critical study of a text.

ap·par′el (ă·păr′ĕl), *v. t.;* AP·PAR′ELED (-ĕld) or -ELLED; AP·PAR′EL·ING or -EL·LING. [OF. *apareillier* to prepare, fr. L. *apparare.* See APPARATUS.] To dress or clothe; to attire; to adorn. — *n.* **1.** Clothing or garments; dress; attire; raiment. **2.** That which adorns; as, gay *apparel* of spring. **3.** *Naut.* A ship's outfit, as rigging, guns, etc.

ap·par′ent (ă·păr′ĕnt; ă·pâr′-), *adj.* [OF. *aparant,* pres. part. of *aparoir.* See APPEAR.] **1.** Open to view; visible. **2.** Clear or manifest to the understanding; evident. **3.** Appearing as actual to the eye or mind (distinguished from, but not necessarily opposed to, *actual, true,* or *real*); seeming. **4.** Of an heir, having an indefeasible right to succeed to a title or estate. **5.** *Law.* Having such an appearance of reality as to appear reasonably true under the circumstances. — **ap·par′en·cy** (-ĕn·sĭ), *n.* — **ap·par′ent·ly,** *adv.* — **ap·par′ent·ness,** *n.*

Syn. (1) See EVIDENT.
(2) **Apparent, illusory, seeming, ostensible** mean not really that which it seems to be. **Apparent** stresses appearance to unaided senses that is not borne out by science or greater knowledge; **illusory** emphasizes the result of a false impression brought about by sense limitations, the exercise of the imagination, or the like; **seeming** implies a character in the thing observed that makes it have the appearance (sometimes through intent) of something else; **ostensible,** applied chiefly to aims, motives, character, etc., suggests merely that they are not those declared, preferred, or avowed.

ap′pa·ri′tion (ăp′ȧ·rĭsh′ŭn), *n.* [F., fr. L. *apparitio,* fr. *apparēre.*

See APPEAR.] **1.** Appearance. **2.** A thing appearing, esp. when unexpected or unusual. **3.** Something preternatural, as a ghost, specter, or phantom. — **ap′pa·ri′tion·al,** *adj.*

ap·par′i·tor (ă·păr′ĭ·tẽr; -tôr), *n.* [L., fr. *apparēre.*] Formerly, an officer present to execute the order of the magistrate, judge, or court.

ap·peal′ (ă·pēl′), *v. t.* [From OF., fr. L. *appellare* to approach, invoke.] *Law.* To take an appeal of (a cause or case); also, *Hist.*, to accuse. — *v. i.* **1.** *Law.* To make an appeal. **2.** To call upon another to decide a question, vindicate one's rights, conduct, taste, etc.; to call upon one, esp. earnestly, for aid, support, or sympathy. **3.** To call forth a sympathetic response; to prove attractive. — *n.* **1.** *Law.* A proceeding by which a cause is brought from an inferior to a superior court for re-examination or review and reversal, retrial, or modification; also, *Hist.*, a criminal accusation before a legal tribunal. **2.** A call upon a person, a faculty of mind, or any kind of authority, for proof or decision in one's favor; as, the *appeal* to reason or to force; also, a call or entreaty for aid, support, or sympathy. **3.** An address or quality that arouses or evokes sympathetic response. — **Syn.** Prayer, petition, plea, suit. — **ap·peal′a·bil′i·ty** (-*à*·bĭl′ĭ·tĭ), *n.* — **ap·peal′a·ble** (-*à*·b′l), *adj.* — **ap·peal′er,** *n.* — **ap·peal′ing,** *adj.* — **ap·peal′ing·ly,** *adv.*

ap·pear′ (ă·pēr′; 27), *v. i.* [OF. *aparoir,* fr. L. *apparēre* to appear, fr. *ad-* + *parēre* to come forth.] **1.** To come or be in sight; become visible. **2.** To attend before some authority, tribunal, or superior, to answer a charge, plead a cause, etc. **3.** To become clear to the mind; be obvious or manifest; reveal itself. **4.** To come before the public or into public view, as a book or actor. **5.** To seem; as, to *appear* to be what one is not; also, to look; as, he *appears* tired.

ap·pear′ance (-ăns), *n.* **1.** The action or an instance of appearing; an occurrence. **2.** *Law.* The actual coming into court of either of the parties in an action or lawsuit. **3.** Manner of appearing; look; aspect; mien. **4.** Semblance; external show or pretense; as, the *appearance* of working; to keep up *appearances.* **5.** A thing seen; a phenomenon; an apparition. **6.** *Philos.* The phenomenal as opposed to the real.

ap·pease′ (ă·pēz′), *v. t.* [OF. *apaisier,* fr. *a* to + *pais* peace, fr. L. *pax, pacis.*] **1.** To pacify, often by satisfying; quiet; calm; soothe; allay. **2.** To conciliate by political, economic, or other considerations; — now usually signifying a sacrifice of moral principle in order to avert aggression; as, an attempt to *appease* the Nazi rulers was made at Munich in 1938. — **Syn.** See PACIFY. — **ap·peas′a·ble** (-pēz′*à*·b′l), *adj.* — **ap·pease′ment,** *n.* — **ap·peas′er,** *n.*

‖**ap′pel′** (*à*′pĕl′), *n.* [F., prop., a call.] *Fencing.* A smart tap or stamp of the foot, orig. as a warning of attack.

ap·pel′lant (ă·pĕl′ănt), *adj.* [F.] Appealing; appellate. — *n.* One who appeals, as from a judicial decision.

ap·pel′late (-āt), *adj.* [L. *appellatus,* past part.] Pertaining to, or taking cognizance of, appeals; vested with the power to review, reverse, etc., the decision of another tribunal; as, *appellate* jurisdiction; *appellate* court.

ap′pel·la′tion (ăp′ĕ·lā′shŭn), *n.* **1.** Act of calling by a name. **2.** A name or designation.

ap·pel′la·tive (ă·pĕl′*à*·tĭv), *adj.* **1.** *Gram.* Common, as opposed to proper. **2.** Of, relating to, or inclined to, the giving of names; as, the *appellative* faculty of children. — *n.* **1.** = COMMON NOUN (see COMMON, *adj.*, 8 **d**). **2.** An appellation or title.

ap′pel·lee′ (ăp′ĕ·lē′), *n.* [F. *appelé,* past part.] *Law.* One against whom an appeal is taken; respondent.

ap·pel′lor (ă·pĕl′ôr; ăp′ĕ·lôr′), *n.* [OF. *apeleor.*] *Law.* One who appeals (accuses) another of a crime.

ap·pend′ (ă·pĕnd′), *v. t.* [F. *appendre,* fr. L. *appendĕre,* fr. *ad-* + *pendĕre* to hang.] **1.** To attach; affix. **2.** To attach as an accessory; add as a supplement. — **Syn.** Add, annex, subjoin.

ap·pend′age (ă·pĕn′dĭj), *n.* **1.** Something appended to a principal or greater thing. **2.** *Biol.* A subordinate part; an external organ or limb. — **Syn.** Appurtenance, adjunct. — **ap·pend′aged** (-dĭjd), *adj.*

ap·pend′ant (-dănt), **ap·pend′ent** (-dĕnt), *adj.* **1.** Associated as an attendant circumstance. **2.** *Law.* Annexed or belonging as a subsidiary right. **3.** Attached as an appendage. — *n.* Anyone or anything, as a right or inheritance, that is appendant; a dependency.

ap′pen·dec′to·my (ăp′ĕn·dĕk′tō·mĭ), *n.* [*appendix* + *-ectomy.*] Surgical removal of the vermiform appendix.

ap·pen′di·ces (ă·pĕn′dĭ·sēz), *n., pl.* of APPENDIX.

ap·pen′di·ci′tis (ă·pĕn′dĭ·sī′tĭs), *n.* [NL. See APPENDIX; -ITIS.] *Med.* Inflammation of the vermiform appendix.

ap·pen′di·cle (ă·pĕn′dĭ·k′l), *n.* [L. *appendicula,* dim. of *appendix.*] A small appendage.

ap′pen·dic′u·lar (ăp′ĕn·dĭk′ū·lẽr), *adj.* *Anat. & Zool.* Of or pert. to an appendicle, an appendage, or a limb; as, the **appendicular skeleton,** the skeleton of the limbs, as opp. to *axial skeleton.*

ap·pen′dix (ă·pĕn′dĭks), *n.; pl.* -DIXES (-dĭk·sĕz; -sĭz), -DICES (-dĭ·sēz). [L. *appendix, -dicis,* fr. *appendĕre* to append.] **1.** Matter added to a book but not essential to its completeness, as a bibliography, notes, or tabular matter. **2.** *Aeronautics.* The tube at the bottom of a balloon, used for inflation. **3.** *Anat. & Zool.* An outgrowth or process; specif., the vermiform appendix. — **Syn.** Supplement, addendum.

ap′per·ceive′ (ăp′ẽr·sēv′), *v. t.* [OF. *aperceivre,* fr. L. *ad* to + *percipere, perceptum,* to perceive. See PERCEIVE.] **1.** *Obs.* To perceive. **2.** *Psychol.* To recognize; interpret (new ideas, knowledge, etc.) in terms of what is already known.

ap′per·cep′tion (-sĕp′shŭn), *n.* [F. *aperception.*] Perception characterized by clearness and by the relating of what is now presented to previously acquired knowledge. — **ap′per·cep′tive** (-tĭv), *adj.*

ap′per·tain′ (ăp′ẽr·tān′), *v. i.* [From OF., fr. L. *appertinere,* fr. *ad-* + *pertinere.* See PERTAIN.] To belong or pertain, as appropriate, or as a possession, attribute, part, or right.

ap′pe·ten·cy (ăp′ē·tĕn·sĭ), *n.; pl.* -CIES (-sĭz). Also **ap′pe·tence** (-tĕns). [L. *appetentia,* fr. *appetere* to strive after, long for. See APPETITE.] **1.** Fixed and strong desire; appetite. **2.** Affinity, as between chemicals. **3.** Instinctive propensity in animals to perform certain actions, as sucking.

ap′pe·tite (ăp′ē·tīt), *n.* [From OF., fr. L. *appetitus,* fr. *appetere* to strive after, long for, fr. *ad-* + *petere* to seek.] **1.** An inherent or habitual desire or propensity for some personal gratification, either of body or mind; craving. **2.** Desire for, or relish of, food or drink.

ap′pe·tiz′er (ăp′ē·tīz′ẽr), *n.* A small portion of food or drink before, or as the first course of, a meal; an apéritif.

ap′pe·tiz′ing (-tīz′ĭng), *adj.* Tempting to the appetite. — **ap′pe·tiz′ing·ly,** *adv.*

Ap′pi·an Way (ăp′ĭ·ăn). The great paved highway from ancient Rome through Capua to Brundisium, now Brindisi, begun by *Appius* Claudius Caecus, about 312 B.C.

ap·plaud′ (ă·plôd′), *v. i.* [L. *applaudere,* fr. *ad-* + *plaudere* to clap the hands.] To express approbation loudly, emphatically, or significantly, esp. by clapping the hands. — **Syn.** Cheer, hurrah, huzza, root. — *v. t.* **1.** To show approval of, esp. by clapping the hands. **2.** To praise; approve. — **ap·plaud′er,** *n.*

ap·plause′ (ă·plôz′), *n.* [L. *applaudere, applausum,* to applaud.] Approbation publicly expressed; marked commendation. — **ap·plau′sive** (-plô′sĭv), *adj.*

ap′ple (ăp′'l), *n.* [AS. *æppel, æpl.*] **1.** The fleshy, usually round, red or yellow edible fruit of any tree of the genus *Malus,* typifying a family (Malaceae, the apple family) which includes also the quince, pear, and hawthorn; also, the tree. In North America, commercial varieties include: Astrachan, Baldwin, Ben Davis, Delicious, Fameuse or snow apple, Gravenstein, Grimes Golden, Jonathan, McIntosh, Northern Spy, Oldenburg, Wealthy, Winesap. Cf. CRAB APPLE, GREENING, PIPPIN. The blossom is the State flower of Arkansas and Michigan. **2.** Any fruit or other vegetable production suggestive of an apple; as, love *apple* (tomato); oak *apple.*

ap′ple·jack′ (-jăk′), *n.* *U. S.* Brandy distilled from cider; also, a beverage produced by freezing hard cider.

apple of discord. A subject of contention and envy, so called from the golden apple inscribed "for the fairest" which the goddess of discord threw into an assembly of the gods. Hera, Athena, and Aphrodite claimed it. Zeus referred the decision to Paris, son of King Priam of Troy. Paris awarded it to Aphrodite, who in return enabled him to carry off Helen, most beautiful of women, from her husband Menelaus. The Greeks won back Helen for Menelaus after a ten-year struggle known as the Trojan War.

Ap′ple·ton lay′er (ăp′'l·tŭn [-t'n] lā′ẽr). [After E. V. *Appleton* (b. 1892), Eng. physicist.] *Radio.* Formerly, one of the layers of the ionosphere.

ap·pli′ance (ă·plī′ăns), *n.* **1.** *Obs.* Compliance. **2.** Application. **3.** A piece of apparatus; instrument; device. — **Syn.** See IMPLEMENT.

ap′pli·ca·ble (ăp′lĭ·k*à*·b'l; ă·plĭk′*à*·b'l), *adj.* Capable of being applied; fit; suitable. — **Syn.** See RELEVANT. — **ap′pli·ca·bil′i·ty** (ăp′lĭ·k*à*·bĭl′ĭ·tĭ), **ap′pli·ca·ble·ness,** *n.* — **ap′pli·ca·bly,** *adv.*

ap′pli·cant (ăp′lĭ·kănt), *n.* One who applies for something.

ap′pli·ca′tion (-kā′shŭn), *n.* [F., fr. L. *applicatio.* See APPLY.] **1.** Act of applying; specif.: **a** Act of laying on or administering; as, the *application* of heat. **b** Use in a particular case or for a practical purpose; as, the *application* of a theory. **c** Close attention. **d** Act of petitioning; as, frequent *applications* for help. **2. a** That which is used in applying, as a remedial device. **b** An appeal or petition, esp. as written or presented; as, an *application* for employment. **3.** Capacity of being practically used; relevancy; as, *application* of words. — **Syn.** See ATTENTION.

ap′pli·ca′tive (ăp′lĭ·kā′tĭv; -k*à*·tĭv), *adj.* Tending or suited to application; applicatory; practical.

ap′pli·ca′tor (-kā′tẽr), *n.* An applier; specif., any device for applying medicine to the nose, throat, or other cavity.

ap′pli·ca·to′ry (-k*à*·tō′rĭ *or, esp. Brit.,* -tẽr·ĭ), *adj.* Having the property of applying; serving for application.

ap·plied′ (ă·plīd′), *adj.* Put to practical use; specif., using and adapting abstract principles and theory in connection with concrete problems, esp. with a utilitarian aim; — disting. from *pure* or *theoretical;* as, *applied* science.

ap·pli′er (ă·plī′ẽr), *n.* One who or that which applies.

ap′pli·qué′ (ăp′lĭ·kā′), *adj.* [F.] Applied or laid on, as figures cut from one fabric and sewed or pasted on another; also, done or made in this way; as, *appliqué* work. — *n.* Ornamentation so applied or for so applying. — *v. t.;* AP′PLI·QUÉD′ (-kād′); -QUÉ′ING. To apply appliqué to; apply as appliqué.

ap·ply′ (ă·plī′), *v. t.;* -PLIED′ (-plīd′); -PLY′ING. [OF. *aplier,* fr. L. *applicare* to attach to, fr. *ad-* + *plicare* to fold.] **1.** To place in contact; to put on, adjust, or direct; as, to *apply* liniment. **2.** To put to use, esp. in a particular case; as, to *apply* a rule; devote to a particular purpose; bring to bear practically, as knowledge. **3.** To use, connect with, or pronounce, as suitable or relative; as, to *apply* an epithet. **4.** To engage with close attention; devote assiduously; as, to *apply* oneself to a task. — *v. i.* **1.** To have some connection or bearing; to be pertinent. **2.** To make request or application, as to a friend for aid.

ap·pog′gia·tu′ra (ă·pŏj′*à*·tōōr′*à*; -tū′r*à*), *n.* [It., fr. *appoggiare* to lean, rest.] *Music.* An accessory tone preceding an essential tone, as an embellishment of melody. It is generally written as a note of smaller size.

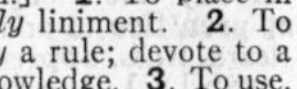

Appoggiatura.

ap·point′ (ă·point′), *v. t.* [OF. *apointier* to prepare, arrange, deriv. of L. *ad* to + *punctum* a point.] **1.** To fix or establish, as by decree, order, or agreement; to constitute; ordain; prescribe; as, to *appoint* a day for trial. **2.** To assign, designate, or set apart, by authority; to place in office; as, to *appoint* a friend to a post. **3.** To furnish in all points; equip; fit out; — chiefly used as a past participle; as, a well-*appointed* house. **4.** *Obs.* To censure or arraign. **5.** *Law.* To direct the disposition of (property) to a person by virtue of power of appointment. — **Syn.** See FURNISH. — *v. i.* **1.** *Archaic.* To make an engagement; also, to determine or purpose. **2.** To exercise power of appointment. — **ap·point′er,** *n.*

ap·point′ee′ (ă·poin′tē′), *n.* A person appointed or to whom an appointment is made.

ap·poin′tive (ă·poin′tĭv), *adj.* Relating to or subject to appointment.

ap·point′ment (ă·point′mĕnt), *n.* **1.** Act of appointing; as: **a** A directing or ordaining. **b** Designation of a person to hold an office or discharge a trust; as, *appointment* of trustees. **c** *Law.* Designation by virtue of power of appointment of a person to enjoy (property) subject to the power. See POWER, *n.*, 7. **2.** That which is appointed or that to which one is appointed; esp.: **a** Any arrangement for a meeting; an engagement. **b** An office, station, or position. **c** Now usually *pl.* Equipment, as for a hotel.

ap·poin′tor (ă·poin′tẽr; ă·poin′tôr′), *n.* See POWER, *n.*, 7.

ap·por′tion (ă·pōr′shŭn; 70), *v. t.* [MF. *apportionner,* fr. *a-* to + *portionner.* See PORTION.] To divide and assign in just proportion; distribute proportionally; portion out. — **Syn.** See ALLOT.

ap·por′tion·ment (-mĕnt), *n.* Act or result of apportioning.

ap·pos′a·ble (ă·pōz′*à*·b'l), *adj.* Capable of being apposed; specif., capable of moving so as to touch with its tip the tip of any finger; — said of the thumb.

ap·pose' (ă·pōz'), *v. t.* [F. *apposer* to set to, fr. *à* (L. *ad*) + *poser* to put, place. See POSE.] To place opposite or before; to put, apply, or add (one thing *to* another).

ap'po·site (ăp'ō·zĭt), *adj.* [L. *appositus*, past part. of *apponere* to put to, fr. *ad-* + *ponere* to put. See POSITION.] Highly pertinent or appropriate. — **Syn.** See RELEVANT. — **ap'po·site·ly**, *adv.* — **ap'po·site·ness**, *n.*

ap'po·si'tion (-zĭsh'ŭn), *n.* **1.** Act of apposing, or state of being apposed. **2.** *Gram.* The setting of a second word beside a first as an adjunct term (Peter *the Hermit*); more strictly, the setting of one beside the other as a loose attributive with the force of a condensed clause (Philip, *King* of Macedon); also, the relationship so established. **3.** *Plant Physiol.* In the growth of the cell wall, the deposition of formative material in successive layers. Cf. INTUSSUSCEPTION. — **ap'po·si'tion·al**, *adj.* — **ap'po·si'tion·al·ly**, *adv.*

ap·pos'i·tive (ă·pŏz'ĭ·tĭv), *adj.* Of or relating to apposition; in apposition; also, = DESCRIPTIVE, 2 **b**. — *n.* An adjunct in apposition.

ap·prais'al (ă·prāz'ăl), *n.* Act of appraising, esp. by one authorized; also, an estimated value set upon property.

ap·praise' (ă·prāz'), *v. t.* [*ad-* + *praise.*] To set a value on, as goods; to estimate the amount of (a loss); hence, to judge as to quality, status, etc. — **Syn.** See ESTIMATE. — **ap·prais'a·ble** (-prāz'ȧ·b'l), *adj.* — **ap·praise'ment**, *n.*

ap·prais'er (-prāz'ẽr), *n.* One who appraises; specif., one vested with authority to determine the value of property.

ap·pre'ci·a·ble (ă·prē'shĭ·ȧ·b'l), *adj.* Sufficient in amount or extent to be recognized or estimated; as, an *appreciable* quantity. — **Syn.** See PERCEPTIBLE. — **ap·pre'ci·a·bly** (-blĭ), *adv.*

ap·pre'ci·ate (-āt; 103), *v. t.* [L. *appretiatus*, past part. of *appretiare* to appraise, fr. *ad-* + *pretiare* to prize, fr. *pretium* price.] **1.** To set a just value on; to esteem fully the worth of. **2.** To be grateful for. **3.** To be sensitive to the aesthetic values of; as, to *appreciate* music. **4.** To be fully aware of; to recognize; as, to *appreciate* a difficulty. **5.** To raise the value of; — opposed to *depreciate.* — *v. i.* To rise in value. — **ap·pre'ci·a'tor** (-ā'tẽr), *n.* — **ap·pre'ci·a·to'ry** (-ȧ·tō'rĭ *or, esp. Brit.*, -tẽr·ĭ), *adj.*

Syn. (1) See UNDERSTAND.
(2) **Appreciate, value, prize, treasure, cherish** mean to hold in high estimation. **Appreciate**, in discriminating use, implies sufficient understanding to admire or enjoy a thing's excellence but, in looser use, may imply merely warm admiration or enjoyment; **value**, that a thing is rated highly or as worth more; **prize**, that one takes deep pride in or sets great store by it; **treasure**, that one protects it from loss as something precious to one; **cherish**, that one loves it especially and gives it special care and attention.

ap·pre'ci·a'tion (ă·prē'shĭ·ā'shŭn; -sĭ·ā'shŭn; 103), *n.* **1.** The action of appreciating. **2.** A favorable critical estimate. **3.** Awareness or perception, esp. of aesthetic value. **4.** A rise in value.

ap·pre'ci·a'tive (ă·prē'shĭ·ā'tĭv; -ȧ·tĭv), *adj.* Having or showing appreciation. — **ap·pre'ci·a'tive·ly**, *adv.* — **ap·pre'ci·a'tive·ness**, *n.*

ap'pre·hend' (ăp'rē·hĕnd'), *v. t.* [F. or L.; F., fr. L. *apprehendere*, fr. *ad-* + *prehendere, prehensum*, to seize.] **1.** *Obs.* To seize. **2.** To arrest. **3.** To become aware of or perceive. **4.** To grasp with the understanding; to recognize the meaning of. **5.** To anticipate, esp. with anxiety, dread, or fear. — **Syn.** See FORESEE. — *v. i.* **1.** To think; to grasp. **2.** To be apprehensive.

ap'pre·hen'si·ble (ăp'rē·hĕn'sĭ·b'l), *adj.* Capable of being apprehended. — **ap'pre·hen'si·bil'i·ty** (-bĭl'ĭ·tĭ), *n.*

ap'pre·hen'sion (-hĕn'shŭn), *n.* **1.** Act of apprehending; specif.: **a** Arrest. **b** A grasping with the mind; perception. **c** Distrust or fear of future misfortune or evil. **2.** The result of apprehending mentally; opinion; idea. **3.** The power of conceiving ideas; understanding. — **Syn.** Misgiving, foreboding, presentiment.

ap'pre·hen'sive (-sĭv), *adj.* **1.** Capable of apprehending, or quick to do so; discerning. **2.** Anticipative of something unfavorable; fearful; as, *apprehensive* for one's life. — **Syn.** See FEARFUL. — **ap'pre·hen'sive·ly**, *adv.* — **ap'pre·hen'sive·ness**, *n.*

ap·pren'tice (ă·prĕn'tĭs), *n.* [From OF. *aprentis*, fr. *apprendre* to learn, fr. L. *apprendere, apprehendere*, to comprehend. See APPREHEND.] **1.** One bound by legal agreement (indenture) to serve another for a certain time with a view to learning an art or trade in consideration of instruction and, formerly, of maintenance. **2.** Hence, one who is learning, esp. by practical experience under skilled workers, and often without pay, an art, trade, or calling. **3.** A beginner; tyro; novice. — *v. t.*; -TICED (-tĭst); -TIC·ING (-tĭs·ĭng). To bind, indenture, or set to work as an apprentice. — **ap·pren'tice·ment**, *n.* — **ap·pren'tice·ship**, *n.*

ap·pressed' (ă·prĕst'), *adj.* *Bot. & Zool.* Pressed close to, or lying flat against, something.

ap·prise' (ă·prīz'), *v. t.* Also **ap·prize'**. [F. *appris*, fem. *apprise*, past part. of *apprendre* to learn, teach, inform.] To give notice to; to inform. — **Syn.** See INFORM.

ap·prize', ap·prise' (ă·prīz'), *v. t.* [OF. *aprisier*, fr. same ultimate source as E. APPRAISE.] To appraise.

ap·proach' (ă·prōch'), *v. i.* [OF. *aprochier*, fr. LL. *appropiare*, fr. L. *ad-* + *propiare* to draw near.] To come or go near; also, to approximate. — *v. t.* **1.** To come near to in space, time, character, or quality. **2.** To take preliminary steps toward, as a task; to make advances to. — *n.* **1.** Act of approaching; an approximation; as, an *approach* to accuracy. **2.** The taking of preliminary steps to accomplishment, acquaintance, etc.; advances; as, new lines of *approach.* **3.** A means of approaching, as a way or passage; an access. **4.** *Golf.* A stroke, not from a tee, for the putting green.

ap·proach'a·ble (-ȧ·b'l), *adj.* **a** Accessible. **b** Easily approached, esp. in speech. — **ap·proach'a·bil'i·ty** (-bĭl'ĭ·tĭ), *n.*

ap'pro·bate (ăp'rō·bāt), *v. t.* [L. *approbatus*, past part. of *approbare.*] To approve; sanction officially.

ap'pro·ba'tion (-bā'shŭn), *n.* **1.** *Obs.* Proof. **2.** Act of approving; approval; sanction; commendation.

ap'pro·ba·to'ry (ăp'rō·bȧ·tō'rĭ; -bā'tō·rĭ), *adj.* Approving, or implying approbation.

ap·pro'pri·a·ble (ă·prō'prĭ·ȧ·b'l), *adj.* Capable of being appropriated.

ap·pro'pri·ate (-ĭt), *adj.* [L. *appropriatus*, past part. of *appropriare*, fr. *ad-* + *propriare* to appropriate, fr. *proprius* one's own, proper.] Belonging peculiarly; specially suitable; fit; proper; as, words *appropriate* to the theme. — **Syn.** See FIT. — **ap·pro'pri·ate·ly**, *adv.* — **ap·pro'pri·ate·ness**, *n.*

ap·pro'pri·ate (-āt), *v. t.* **1.** To take exclusive possession of; as, to *appropriate* a piece of property. **2.** To set apart for, or assign to, a particular person or use; as, to *appropriate* money for the navy. — **Syn.** See ARROGATE. — **ap·pro'pri·a'tor** (-ā'tẽr), *n.*

ap·pro'pri·a'tion (-ā'shŭn), *n.* **1.** Act of appropriating, as for oneself or for a particular person or use. **2.** That which is appropriated, esp. money set apart by formal action to a specific use.

ap·pro'pri·a'tive (ă·prō'prĭ·ā'tĭv; -ȧ·tĭv), *adj.* Appropriating; of appropriating tendency. — **ap·pro'pri·a'tive·ness**, *n.*

ap·prov'al (ă·prōōv'ăl), *n.* **1.** Act of approving; approbation; sanction. **2.** Specif., examination to determine suitability for acceptance; as, goods sent on *approval*, that is, subject to refusal.

ap·prove' (ă·prōōv'), *v. t.* [From OF., fr. L. *approbare*, fr. *ad-* + *probare* to approve.] **1.** To sanction officially; to ratify; confirm; accept as satisfactory. **2.** To have or express a favorable opinion of; as, to *approve* his choice. **3.** To demonstrate or display actually or practically. **4.** *Rare or Obs.* **a** To corroborate; authenticate. **b** To test. **c** To convict. — *v. i.* To judge favorably. — **ap·prov'a·ble** (ă·prōōv'ȧ·b'l), *adj.* — **ap·prov'er**, *n.* — **ap·prov'ing·ly**, *adv.*

Syn. **Approve, endorse** (*or* **indorse**), **sanction, accredit, certify** mean to have or express a favorable opinion of. **Approve** sometimes means no more than this, but it may imply esteem or admiration; **endorse** adds to *approve* the implication of backing or supporting as by an explicit statement; **sanction** implies both approval and authorization; **accredit** and **certify** now usually imply official endorsement as a result of a thing's conformity to high standards.

ap·prox'i·mal (ă·prŏk'sĭ·măl), *adj.* *Anat.* Contiguous; as, *approximal* surfaces of teeth.

ap·prox'i·mate (ă·prŏk'sĭ·mĭt), *adj.* [L. *approximatus*, past part. of *approximare*, fr. *ad-* + *proximare* to come near.] **1.** Situated near or close together; also, nearly resembling. **2.** Near to correctness; nearly exact. Abbr. *approx.* — **ap·prox'i·mate·ly**, *adv.*

ap·prox'i·mate (-māt), *v. t.* **1.** To bring near; cause to approach. **2.** To come near to; as, beauty that *approximates* perfection. — *v. i.* To approach; — often with *to.*

ap·prox'i·ma'tion (ă·prŏk'sĭ·mā'shŭn), *n.* **1.** A drawing, or being, near. **2.** An approach to a correct estimate, conception, etc., or to a given quantity, quality, etc.

ap·pur'te·nance (ă·pûr'tē·năns), *n.* [AF. *apurtenance.* See APPERTAIN.] **1.** That which belongs to something else; adjunct. **2.** Something incident to a chief or principal thing, as a right of way to land. **3.** *pl.* Formerly, apparatus. — **Syn.** Appendage, adjunct.

ap·pur'te·nant (-nănt), *adj.* Pertaining or belonging legally; pertinent; incident. — *n.* An appurtenance.

A'pra (ä'prä), *n.* [Sp. *A*lianza *P*opular *R*evolucionaria *A*mericana (Popular American Revolutionary League).] A Peruvian political party advocating division of landed estates, domestic social reform, and co-operation among Latin-American countries. — **A'prism** (ä'prĭz'm), *n.*

a·prax'i·a (ȧ·prăk'sĭ·ȧ), *n.* [NL., fr. Gr. *apraxia* inaction.] *Med.* Loss or impairment of ability to execute complex co-ordinated movements.

‖**a'près' moi** (*or* **nous**) **le dé'luge'** (ȧ'prĕ' mwȧ' [nōō'] lẽ dā'lüzh'). [F.] After me (or us) the deluge; — attributed usually to Louis XV of France.

a'pri·cot (ā'prĭ·kŏt; ăp'rĭ-), *n.* [F. *abricot*, through Pg. and Ar., fr. Gr. *praikokion*, fr. L. *praecoquum*, neut. of *praecoquus, praecox*, early ripe.] **1.** The oval, orange-colored fruit of a tree (*Prunus armeniaca*) of the peach family, in flavor resembling both peach and plum; also, the tree itself. **2.** A color, red-yellow in hue, of medium saturation and high brilliance. Cf. COLOR.

A'pril (ā'prĭl), *n.* [L. *aprilis.*] The fourth month of the year, having 30 days. Abbr. *Apr., Apl.*

April fool. One who is sportively imposed upon on the first day of April, All Fools' Day.

a pri·o'ri (ā' prĭ·ō'rī; prĭ·ō'rĭ; ä' prĭ·ō'rē). [L., fr. *a* (*ab*) + *prior* former.] **1.** *Logic.* Characterizing the kind of reasoning deducing consequences from definitions or principles regarded as self-evident; deductive; deductively; as, an *a priori* argument; hence, designating that which can be known by reason alone and not through experience. Cf. A POSTERIORI. **2.** Presumptive; presumptively; without examination. — **a'pri·or'i·ty** (-ŏr'ĭ·tĭ), *n.*

a'pron (ā'prŭn; *formerly generally, and still often*, ā'pẽrn), *n.* [OF. *naperon*, dim. of *nape*, cloth, tablecloth, fr. L. *mappa* napkin, table napkin. *Apron*, without initial *n-*, arose through the incorrect division of *a napron* as *an apron.*] **1.** An article of dress, of cloth, leather, or the like, worn on the fore part of the body, to protect the clothes, or as a covering. **2.** Something like, or suggestive of, an apron; as: **a** A piece of waterproof cloth used as a protection from rain, etc., as before the seat of a vehicle. **b** A covering, as of sheet metal, to protect parts of machinery. **c** A shield of planking, brushwood, or the like, below a dam, along a sea wall, etc. **d** *Theater.* The part of the stage in front of the proscenium arch. **e** *Aeronautics.* An extensive hard-surfaced area in front of a hangar. **f** An endless belt for conveying material of any kind. **g** A flap on which paper pulp is led from the strainer. **h** A thick fold of skin on the neck or breast of a ram. See SHEEP, *Illust.*

ap'ro·pos' (ăp'rō·pō'), *adv.* [F. *à propos*, fr. *à* to + *propos* purpose.] **1.** Opportunely; seasonably. **2.** With respect (to); to the purpose; suitably; as, *apropos* of our talk. **3.** By the way; incidentally; — used absolutely. — *adj.* Pertinent; to the point. — **Syn.** See RELEVANT.

‖**à pro'pos' de rien** (ȧ prô'pō' dẽ ryăN'). [F.] Apropos of nothing; not to the purpose; irrelevant.

apse (ăps), *n.*; *pl.* APSES (ăp'sĕz; -sĭz). [See APSIS.] **1.** *Arch.* A projecting part of a building, esp. of a church, usually semicircular in plan. **2.** *Astron.* An apsis.

ap'sis (ăp'sĭs), *n.*; *pl.* APSIDES (-sĭ·dēz; ăp·sī'dēz). [L. *apsis*, fr. Gr. *hapsis* (also *apsis*), *hapsidos*, a fastening, hoop, arch.] **1.** *Astron.* In an orbit, the point at which the distance of the body from the center of attraction is either greatest (***higher apsis***) or least (***lower apsis***). **2.** *Arch.* An apse. — **ap'si·dal** (ăp'sĭ·dăl; -d'l), *adj.*

apt (ăpt), *adj.* [L. *aptus.*] **1.** Fit; suited; suitable; specif., to the point; pat; as, *apt* remarks. **2.** Habitually tending; likely. **3.** Inclined; disposed; as, I am *apt* to hurry. **4.** *Archaic.* Ready; prepared. **5.** Quick to learn; dexterous; as, an *apt* pupil. — **Syn.** See FIT: QUICK. — **apt'ly**, *adv.* — **apt'ness**, *n.*

ap'ter·al (ăp'tẽr·ăl), *adj.* *Zool.* Apterous.

ap'ter·ous (-ŭs), *adj.* [Gr. *apteros* wingless, fr. *a-* not + *pteron* wing.] **a** *Zool.* Without wings. **b** *Bot.* Without winglike expansions, as petioles, stems, or seeds.

ap′ter·yx (ăp′tẽr·ĭks), *n.; pl.* -YXES (-ĭk·sĕz; -sĭz). [NL., fr. Gr. *a-* not + *pteryx* wing.] *Zool.* Any of a genus (*Apteryx*) of New Zealand flightless birds having a flat breastbone and grayish-brown hairlike plumage; a kiwi. A few survive under government protection.

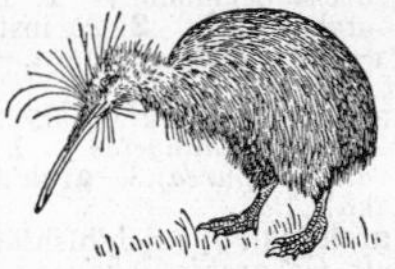

Apteryx. (1/35)

ap′ti·tude (ăp′tĭ·tūd), *n.* [F., fr. ML., fr. L. *aptus* apt.] **1.** Readiness in learning; aptness. **2.** Suitability for a purpose. **3.** Natural disposition or tendency; as, oil has an *aptitude* to burn. **4.** Natural, or potential, capacity or ability. — **Syn.** See GIFT.

aq′ua (ăk′wȧ; ā′kwȧ), *n.; pl.* AQUAE (ăk′wē; ā′kwē), AQUAS (ăk′wȧz; ā′kwȧz). [L.] Water; — used in pharmacy in the sense of *a solution of a volatile substance in water.*

aq′ua am·mo′ni·ae (ă·mō′nĭ·ē). [NL.] = AMMONIA, 2.

aq′ua·cade (ăk′wȧ·kād), *n.* [*aqua* + *-cade.*] An elaborately staged water spectacle consisting of exhibitions of swimming and diving, acrobatics, and group evolutions, with musical accompaniment.

aq′ua for′tis (fôr′tĭs). Also **aq′ua·for′tis**, *n.* [L., strong water.] Nitric acid.

aq′ua·lung′ (ăk′wȧ·lŭng′; ăk′-), *n.* [*aqua* + *lung.*] An underwater breathing device made of one or more cylinders of compressed air and a watertight face mask.

aq′ua·ma·rine′ (ăk′wȧ·mȧ·rēn′; ā′kwȧ-), *n.* [L., *aqua marina* sea water.] **1.** A transparent beryl, typically bluish green, used as a gem. **2.** A color, green-blue in hue, of low saturation and medium brilliance. See COLOR.

aq′ua·plane′ (ăk′wȧ·plān′; ā′kwȧ-), *n.* [*aqua* + *-plane* as in air*plane.*] A wide board towed behind a speeding motorboat and ridden by a person standing on it. Cf. SURFBOARD. — **aq′ua·plane′**, *v. i.*

aq′ua pu′ra (ăk′wȧ pū′rȧ; ā′kwȧ). [L.] *Pharm.* Pure water.

aq′ua re′gi·a (rē′jĭ·ȧ). [L., royal water.] A mixture of nitric and hydrochloric acids, which dissolves gold or platinum.

aq′ua·relle′ (ăk′wȧ·rĕl′), *n.* [F., fr. It. *acquerella*, fr. *acqua* water, fr. L. *aqua.*] A drawing in water color, esp. transparent water color.

aq′ua·rel′list (-rĕl′ĭst), *n.* One who draws or makes aquarelles.

a·quar′i·um (ȧ·kwâr′ĭ·ŭm), *n.; pl.* -IUMS (-ŭmz), -IA (-ȧ). [L., neut. of *aquarius* relating to water.] **1.** An artificial pond, or a tank of water, in which living aquatic animals or plants are kept. **2.** A place or establishment for the care and exhibition of such aquatic collections.

A·quar′i·us (-ĭ·ŭs), *n.; gen.* AQUARII (-ĭ·ī). [L., water carrier, fr. *aqua.*] **a** A constellation south of Pegasus, pictured as a man pouring water. **b** The eleventh sign [♒] of the zodiac. See ZODIAC.

a·quat′ic (ȧ·kwăt′ĭk; -kwŏt′ĭk), *adj.* [L. *aquaticus.* See AQUA.] **1.** Growing or living in, or frequenting, water; as, *aquatic* plants or birds. **2.** Performed in or on water; as, *aquatic* sports. — *n.* **1.** An aquatic animal or plant. **2.** *pl.; see* -ICS. Aquatic sports or exercises.

aq′ua·tint′ (ăk′wȧ·tĭnt′; ā′kwȧ-), *n.* [It. *acqua tinta* dyed water.] Etching with aqua fortis, giving the effect of a water color or India-ink drawing; also, the engraving so made. — *v. t.* To etch by aquatint.

a′qua·vit′ (äk′vȧ·vēt′; äk′vȧ·vēt′), *n.* [Nor., Dan., & Sw. *aquavit, akvavit*, fr. L. *aqua vitae* water of life.] A clear Scandinavian brandy made by redistilling neutral spirits, with caraway flavoring.

aq′ua vi′tae (ăk′wȧ vī′tē; ā′kwȧ). [L., water of life.] Formerly, alcohol; hence, brandy or other ardent spirit.

aq′ue·duct (ăk′wē·dŭkt), *n.* [L. *aquaeductus*, fr. *aquae*, gen. of *aqua* water + *ductus* a leading.] **1.** **a** Any conduit for water, esp. one for a large quantity of flowing water. **b** A structure for conveying a canal over a river or hollow. **2.** *Anat.* A canal or passage in a part or organ.

a′que·ous (ā′kwē·ŭs; ăk′wē-), *adj.* **1.** **a** Of or like water; watery. **b** Made from, by, or with water; as, an *aqueous* solution. **2.** *Anat.* Designating a limpid fluid (the **aqueous humor**) occupying the space between the crystalline lens and the cornea of the eye. See EYE.

aq′ui·cul′ture (ăk′wĭ·kŭl′tụ̄r; ā′kwĭ-), *n.* = HYDROPONICS.

aq′ui·fer (ăk′wĭ·fẽr), *n.* [*aqui-* (fr. L. *aqua* water) + *-fer.*] *Geol.* A water-bearing bed or stratum of earth, gravel, or porous stone.

Aq′ui·la (ăk′wĭ·lȧ), *n.; gen.* -LAE (-lē). [L., eagle.] A northern constellation in the Milky Way, southerly from Lyra and Cygnus.

aq′ui·le′gi·a (ăk′wĭ·lē′jĭ·ȧ; ā′kwĭ-), *n.* [NL., prob. fr. L. *aquila* eagle.] A columbine.

aq′ui·line (ăk′wĭ·līn; -lĭn), *adj.* [L. *aquilinus*, fr. *aquila* eagle.] **1.** Of or like an eagle. **2.** Hooked, like the beak of an eagle.

‖**a quo** (ā kwō′). [L.] From which. Cf. AD QUEM.

ar (är), *n.* Var. of *are* (see METRIC SYSTEM, *Table* 3).

-ar (-ẽr). [ME. *-er*, fr. OF. *-er, -ier*, fr. L. *-aris;* akin to *-alis.* Cf. -AL.] **1.** An adjective suffix signifying *belonging* or *pertaining to, like, of the nature of*, as in consul*ar*, nucle*ar*. **2.** A noun suffix representing Latin *-arius, -arium*, or more commonly its French form *-ier*, equiv. to *-ary*, as in burs*ar*, mort*ar*, etc. See -ARY.

Ar′ab (ăr′ăb), *n.* [F. *Arabe*, through L. & Gr., fr. Ar. *ʽArab.*] **1.** A Semite of the race that from earliest times occupied the Arabian peninsula, thence spread and intermixed with native races of North Africa, India, Malaysia, etc. **2.** A horse used by the natives of Arabia; specif., a horse of a breed noted for its graceful build, speed, intelligence, and spirit. **3.** = STREET ARAB. — *adj.* Arabian.

ar′a·besque′ (ăr′ȧ·bĕsk′), *n.* [F., fr. It., fr. *Arabo* Arab.] **1.** A kind of ornamentation consisting of a fantastic interlacing pattern of flowers, foliage, or fruit, often with figures of men and animals (except in Arabic art), sometimes geometric in character, sometimes flowing. **2.** A ballet dancer's posture bending forward on one leg, with the corresponding arm extended horizontally forward, the other arm and leg backward. — *adj.* Relating to, or exhibiting, arabesque.

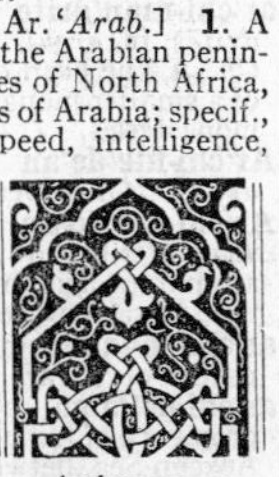

Arabesque.

A·ra′bi·an (ȧ·rā′bĭ·ăn), *adj.* Of or pertaining to Arabia or Arabs. — *n.* **a** A native of Arabia. **b** = ARAB, 2.

Arabian camel. See CAMEL.

Ar′a·bic (ăr′ȧ·bĭk), *adj.* [L. *Arabicus.*] **1.** = ARABIAN. **2.** [*not cap.*] *Chem.* Designating a colorless, amorphous, soluble acid (**ar′a·bic acid** [ăr′ȧ·bĭk] *or* **ar′a·bin** [ăr′ȧ·bĭn]). See GUM ARABIC. — *n.* The (Semitic) language of the Arabs, the prevailing speech of Arabia, Jordan, Lebanon, Syria, Iraq, Egypt, and North Africa. See LANGUAGE, *Table.*

Arabic numerals *or* **figures.** See NUMBER, *Table.*

Ar′ab·ist (ăr′ăb·ĭst), *n.* One versed in Arabic.

ar′a·ble (ăr′ȧ·b'l), *adj.* [F. or L.; F., fr. L. *arabilis*, fr. *arare* to plow.] Fit for, or cultivated by, plowing or tillage. — *n.* Arable land. — **ar′a·bil′i·ty** (-bĭl′ĭ·tĭ), *n.*

Ar′a·by (ăr′ȧ·bĭ), *n.* *Archaic.* Arabia.

a·ra′ceous (ȧ·rā′shŭs), *adj.* [See ARUM.] *Bot.* Belonging to the arum family (Araceae). See ARUM.

A·rach′ne (ȧ·răk′nē), *n.* [L., fr. Gr., fr. *arachnē* a spider.] *Gr. Myth.* A Lydian girl turned into a spider by Athena for presuming to compete with her in weaving.

a·rach′nid (-nĭd), *n.* [Gr. *arachnē* spider.] *Zool.* Any of a class (Arachnida) of arthropods comprising mostly air-breathing invertebrates, including the spiders and scorpions, mites, and ticks, having a segmented body divided into two regions, the anterior one bearing four pairs of legs but no antennae. — *adj.* Of or pertaining to an arachnid. — **a·rach′ni·dan** (-nĭ·dăn), *adj. & n.*

a·rach′noid (-noid), *adj.* [Gr. *arachnoeidēs* like a cobweb, fr. *arachnē* spider, spider's web. See -OID.] **1.** Cobweblike. **2.** *Anat.* Designating a thin membrane of the brain and spinal cord, between the dura mater and pia mater. **3.** **a** *Bot.* Covered with, or composed of, soft loose hairs or fibers; cobwebby. **b** *Zool.* Arachnidan. — *n.* **a** *Anat.* The arachnoid membrane. **b** An arachnid.

a·rag′o·nite (ȧ·răg′ō·nīt; ăr′ȧ·gŏn·īt), *n.* [From *Aragon*, in Spain.] *Mineral.* A mineral composed, like calcite, of calcium carbonate, $CaCO_3$, but differing from calcite in its orthorhombic crystallization, greater density, less distinct cleavage, etc.

a·ra′li·a′ceous (ȧ·rā′lĭ·ā′shŭs), *adj.* *Bot.* Belonging to the ginseng family (Araliaceae). See GINSENG.

Ar′a·mae′an, Ar′a·me′an (ăr′ȧ·mē′ăn), *n.* [From L., fr. Gr. *Aramaios*, fr. Heb. *Arām.*] **a** One of a large Semitic group occupying the Biblical Aram and neighboring territories. **b** The language of the Aramaeans. — **Ar′a·mae′an, Ar′a·me′an**, *adj.*

Ar′a·ma′ic (-mā′ĭk), *n.* A group of languages and dialects of the Aramaean branch of the Semitic languages of which the most important are the Syriac, Biblical and Palestinian Aramaic, and Samaritan. The tongue spoken by Jesus was Aramaic. See LANGUAGE, *Table.* — **Ar′a·ma′ic**, *adj.*

A·rap′a·ho, A·rap′a·hoe (ȧ·răp′ȧ·hō), *n.; pl.* -HO or -HOE (-hō), or -HOES (-hōz). An Indian of a warlike nomadic tribe of the Algonquian stock, now mostly settled in Oklahoma and Wyoming.

ar′a·pai′ma (ăr′ȧ·pī′mȧ), *n.* [Pg., of Tupian origin.] A large-scaled river fish (*Arapaima gigas* family Osteoglossidae) of South America. It becomes fifteen feet long.

a′ra·ro′ba (ä′rȧ·rō′bȧ), *n.* [Pg.] **1.** Goa powder. **2.** A Brazilian tree (*Centrolobium robustum*) of the pea family, with handsomely striped wood.

A·rau′can (ȧ·rô′kăn), *n.* Language of the Araucanians.

Ar′au·ca′ni·an (ăr′ô·kā′nĭ·ăn), *n.* An Indian of a distinct linguistic stock formerly occupying central Chile and adjacent Argentina. See LANGUAGE, *Table.* — **Ar′au·ca′ni·an**, *adj.*

ar′au·ca′ri·a (ăr′ô·kā′rĭ·ȧ), *n.* [NL.] Any of a genus *Araucaria*) of South American or Australian trees of the pine family.

A′ra·wak (ä′rä·wäk), *n.* An Indian of the Arawakan stock. Typically short of stature and light in color, they are agriculturists, living in fixed villages, cultivating cassava, etc. — **A′ra·wak**, *adj.*

A′ra·wa′kan (-wä′kăn), *adj.* Of or pertaining to the most extensive American Indian linguistic family, comprising about ninety tribes. They formerly occupied the coast of northeastern South America, all of the West Indies, and a small area in southwestern Florida, but are now found chiefly in northern South America. See LANGUAGE, *Table.*

ar′ba·lest (är′bȧ·lĕst; -lĭst), **ar′ba·list** (-lĭst), *n.* [OF. *arbaleste, arcbaleste*, fr. L. *arcuballista*, fr. *arcus* bow + *ballista* a military engine.] A crossbow consisting of a steel bow set in a shaft of wood. — **ar′ba·lest′er** (-lĕs′tẽr), **ar′ba·list′er** (-lĭs′tẽr), *n.*

ar′bi·ter (är′bĭ·tẽr), *n.* [L.] **1.** A person having power to decide a dispute; a judge; arbitrator. **2.** Any person having absolute power of judging and determining.

‖**ar′bi·ter e′le·gan′ti·ae** (är′bĭ·tẽr ĕl′ē·găn′shĭ·ē) *or* **e′le·gan′ti·a′rum** (-ā′rŭm). [L.] Literally, judge of elegance; — applied by Tacitus to Petronius; hence, a judge or authority in matters of taste.

ar′bi·tra·ble (är′bĭ·trȧ·b'l), *adj.* Subject to decision by arbitration; referable to an arbitrator.

ar′bi·trage (är′bĭ·trĭj), *n.* [F.] **1.** Arbitration. **2.** (*pron.* är′bĭ·trĭj; är′bĭ·träzh′) *Com.* Purchasing in one market for immediate sale in another at a higher price.

ar′bi·tral (är′bĭ·trăl), *adj.* [L. *arbitralis.*] Of or pertaining to arbiters or arbitration; as, *arbitral* jurisdiction.

ar·bit′ra·ment (är·bĭt′rȧ·mĕnt), *n.* [OF. *arbitrement.*] **1.** Right or power of deciding for oneself. **2.** Act of deciding as an arbiter; arbitration. **3.** An arbitrator's award.

ar′bi·trar′y (är′bĭ·trĕr′ĭ *or, esp. Brit.,* -trẽr·ĭ), *adj.* [L. *arbitrarius*, fr. *arbiter.*] **1.** Decided or fixed at the discretion of an arbiter or judge; as, an *arbitrary* award. **2.** Fixed or arrived at through will or caprice; decisive but unreasoned; as, too *arbitrary* as a critic. **3.** Despotic; absolute; as, an *arbitrary* ruler. — **ar′bi·trar′i·ly** (-ĭ·lĭ; *emphatic also* -trâr′ĭ·lĭ), *adv.* — **ar′bi·trar′i·ness** (-ĭ·nĕs; -nĭs), *n.*

ar′bi·trate (är′bĭ·trāt), *v. t.* [L. *arbitratus*, past part. of *arbitrari* to make a decision, fr. *arbiter.*] **1.** To hear and decide as arbiter or arbitrator; hence, to decide or determine. **2.** To submit to arbitration. — *v. i.* To act as arbitrator. — **ar′bi·tra′tive** (-trā′tĭv), *adj.*

ar′bi·tra′tion (-trā′shŭn), *n.* Act of arbitrating; esp., the hearing and determination of a cause in controversy by a person or persons either chosen by the parties involved or appointed. — **ar′bi·tra′tion·al**, *adj.*

ar′bi·tra′tor (är′bĭ·trā′tẽr), *n.* **1.** A person, or one of two or more persons, chosen to settle a difference between parties in controversy; an arbiter. **2.** An arbiter (sense 2).

ar′bor, ar′bour (är′bẽr), *n.* [ME. *herber* a garden of herbs, fr. OF. *herbier*, fr. L. *herbarium.*] **1.** *Obs.* A plot of grass; a garden; an orchard. **2.** A latticework trellis or bower of, or covered with, vines or branches for shade.

ar′bor (är′bẽr; -bôr), *n.; pl.* ARBORS (-bẽrz; -bôrz); in sense 1, ARBORES (är′bō·rēz). [L., a tree, a beam.] **1.** *Bot.* A tree. **2.** [F. *arbre* tree, axis.] (*pron.* är′bẽr) *Mech.* **a** A main shaft or beam. **b** A spindle or axle of a wheel. **c** A shaft or bar for holding cutting tools.

Arbor Day. A day in late April or early May appointed, in most states of the United States, for planting trees.

ar·bo′re·al (är·bō′rē·ăl; 70), *adj.* **1.** Of, pertaining to, or like a tree or trees. **2.** Inhabiting or frequenting trees.

ar′bored, ar′boured (är′bẽrd), *adj.* Provided with an arbor; lined with trees; embowered; as, an *arbored* walk.

ar·bo're·ous (är·bō'rē·ŭs; 70), *adj.* [L. *arboreus*, fr. *arbor* tree.] Wooded; arborescent; arboreal.

ar'bo·res'cent (är'bō·rĕs'ĕnt; -'nt), *adj.* [L. *arborescens*, pres. part. of *arborescere* to become a tree, fr. *arbor* tree.] Resembling a tree in growth, structure, or appearance; treelike. — **ar'bo·res'cence** (-ĕns; -'ns), *n.* — **ar'bo·res'cent·ly**, *adv.*

ar'bo·re'tum (-rē'tŭm), *n.; pl.* -RETUMS (-tŭmz), -RETA (-tȧ). [L., a place grown with trees.] A place where trees and shrubs are cultivated for scientific or educational purposes.

ar'bo·ri·cul'ture (är'bō·rĭ·kŭl'tṳr), *n.* [L. *arbor* tree + *cultura* culture.] Cultivation of trees and shrubs. — **ar'bo·ri·cul'tur·al** (-kŭl'-tṳr·ăl), *adj.* — **ar'bo·ri·cul'tur·ist**, *n.*

ar'bor·i·za'tion (är'bẽr·ĭ·zā'shŭn; -ī·zā'shŭn), *n.* Formation of a treelike figure or arrangement; also, such a figure.

ar'bor·ous (är'bẽr·ŭs), *adj.* Of, pert. to, or formed by trees.

ar'bor·vi'tae (är'bẽr·vī'tē), *n.*, *or* **ar'bor vi'tae**. [L. *arbor vitae* tree of life.] **1.** Any of certain evergreen trees (esp. of genus *Thuja*) of the pine family, usually with scalelike, closely overlapping, or compressed leaves, often grown for ornament and hedges, as the common American species *T. occidentalis*. See CEDAR. **2.** (In this sense *arbor vitae.*) *Anat.* A treelike structure or arrangement, as of nervous tissue in the cerebellum.

ar'bour (är'bẽr). Var. of ARBOR, bower.

ar·bu'tus (är·bū'tŭs; *L.* är'bū·tŭs), *n.* [L., the strawberry tree, of uncert. origin.] **1.** Any of a genus (*Arbutus*) of shrubs and trees of the heath family, with white flowers and scarlet berries. **2.** Short for ***trailing arbutus***, a related trailing plant (*Epigaea repens*) of eastern North America, with fragrant pinkish flowers, blooming in early spring. It is the State flower of Massachusetts.

arc (ärk), *n.* [OF., fr. L. *arcus* bow, arc.] **1.** A bowlike curve or an object having such a curvature. **2.** *Astron.* The apparent arc described, above (***diurnal arc***) or below (***nocturnal arc***) the horizon, by the sun or other celestial body. **3.** *Geom.* A portion of a curved line, as of a circle (see CIRCLE, *Illust.*). **4.** *Elec.* A sustained luminous glow or bow of light formed between two incandescent electrodes. — *v. i.;* ARCED (ärkt) or ARCKED; ARC'ING (är'kĭng) or ARCK'ING. *Elec.* To form an electric arc.

ar·cade' (är·kād'), *n.* [F., fr. Pr., fr. L. *arcus* bow, arch.] **1.** *Arch.* **a** A series of arches with their columns or piers. See GOTHIC, *Illust.* **b** A long, arched building or gallery. **2.** An arched or covered way or avenue, as between shops. — *v. t.* To form as, or furnish with, an arcade or arcades; — esp. in *part. adj.*, AR·CAD'ED (-kād'ĕd; -ĭd).

Ar·ca'di·a (är·kā'dĭ·ȧ), *n.* Also, *Poetic*, **Ar'ca·dy** (är'kȧ·dĭ). [L., fr. Gr. *Arkadia.*] A mountainous district of Greece, celebrated as the abode of a simple contented pastoral people; hence, any scene of simple pleasure and quiet. — **Ar·ca'di·an** (-ăn), *adj. & n.*

ar·ca'num (är·kā'nŭm), *n.; pl.* -CANA (-nȧ). [L., fr. *arcanus* closed, secret, fr. *arca* chest, box, fr. *arcere* to enclose.] **1.** A secret; mystery; — usually in *pl.;* as, the *arcana* of political intrigue. **2.** A secret remedy; elixir.

‖**arc'-bou'tant'** (år'bōō'täɴ'), *n.; pl.* ARCS-BOUTANTS (år'bōō'täɴ'). [F.] *Arch.* A flying buttress.

arch (ärch), *n.* [OF. *arche.* Cf. ARCADE.] **1.** *Arch.* A structural member, usually curved and made up of separate wedge-shaped solids,

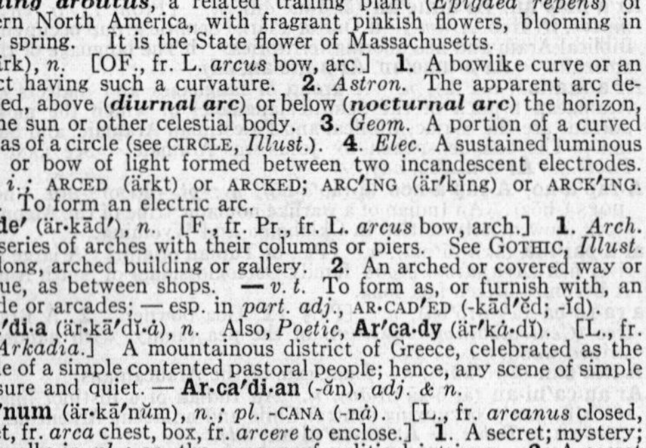

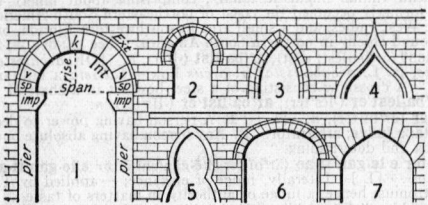

Arches. 1 Round (*Ext* Extrados; *Int* Intrados; *imp* Impost; *k* Keystone; *sp* Springer; *v* Voussoir); 2 Horseshoe; 3 Lancet; 4 Ogee; 5 Trefoil; 6 Basket-handle; 7 Tudor. Cf. SKEWBACK, *Illust.*

with their joints at right angles to the curve, used to span an opening and capable of supporting weight from above. **2.** Any place covered by an arch; an archway. **3.** Something like or functioning as an arch. **4.** Any curve or structure in the form of an arch; as, *Anat.*, the branchial *arches.* — *v. t.* **1.** To cover, or provide, with an arch or arches. **2.** To form or bend into the shape of an arch. — *v. i.* To form into an arch.

arch- (ärch-, *except in* archangel *and derivatives*). [AS. *arce-, erce-*, fr. L. *arch-, archi-*, fr. Gr. *arch-, archi-*. See ARCHI-.] A prefix used in titles and descriptive appellations, meaning *chief, principal, great*, as in *arch*bishop, *arch*duke.

arch (ärch), *adj.* [See ARCH-.] **1.** Chief; eminent. **2.** [From the use of *arch* in **arch'rogue', arch'wag'**, etc.] Cunning or sly; now usually, sportively mischievous; roguish. — *n. Obs.* A chief.

Ar·chae'an (är·kē'ăn). Var. of ARCHEAN.

ar'chae·o- (är'kē·ō-). [Gr. *archaios*, fr. *archē* beginning.] A combining form meaning *ancient, primitive*, referring specifically to antiquities, etc., as in *archaeology.*

ar'chae·ol'o·gist, ar'che·ol'o·gist (-ŏl'ō·jĭst), *n.* A specialist in archaeology.

ar'chae·ol'o·gy, ar'che·ol'o·gy (-jĭ), *n.* [Gr. *archaiologia*, fr. *archaios* ancient + *logos* discourse.] **1.** The scientific study of the material remains of past human life and activities, such as fossil relics, artifacts, monuments, etc. **2.** The materials of this science; the remains of the culture of a people; as, the *archaeology* of the Incas. — **-o·log'i·cal** (-ō·lŏj'ĭ·kăl), **-o·log'ic**, *adj.* — **-o·log'i·cal·ly**, *adv.*

ar'chae·op'ter·yx (är'kē·ŏp'tẽr·ĭks), *n.* [NL., fr. *archaeo-* + Gr. *pteryx* wing.] A primitive reptilelike bird (genus *Archaeopteryx*) of the Upper Jurassic period of Europe.

Ar'chae·o·zo'ic (-ō·zō'ĭk). Var. of ARCHEOZOIC.

ar·cha'ic (är·kā'ĭk), *adj.* [Gr. *archaikos* old-fashioned, fr. *archaios* ancient.] **1.** Of an earlier or more primitive time; antiquated. **2.** Obsolete in ordinary language but retained in special context, as in Biblical and legal expressions, in poetry, etc. — **Syn.** See OLD.

archaic smile. An expression, resembling a smile, peculiar to Greek sculpture until about 500 B.C.

ar'cha·ism (är'kā·ĭz'm), *n.* [Gr. *archaismos*, fr. *archaios* ancient, fr. *archē* beginning.] **1.** The use of archaic speech, style, etc.; also, archaic style. **2.** An instance of archaic usage. **3.** Anything archaic. — **ar'cha·ist** (-ĭst), *n.* — **ar'cha·is'tic** (-ĭs'tĭk), *adj.* — **ar'cha·ize** (-īz), *v. t. & i.*

arch'an'gel (ärk'ān'jĕl; 2), *n.* [OF. or L.; OF., fr. LL. *archangelus*, fr. Gr. *archangelos.*] **1.** A chief angel. **2.** The angelica (*Angelica atropurpurea*). — **arch'an·gel'ic** (-ăn·jĕl'ĭk), **arch'an·gel'i·cal** (-ĭ-kăl), *adj.*

arch'bish'op (ärch'bĭsh'ŭp; 2), *n.* [From AS., fr. LL. *archiepiscopus*, fr. Gr. *archiepiskopos.*] A chief bishop; a prelate at the head of an ecclesiastical province, or one of equivalent honorary rank. Abbr. *Abp.*, or *abp.* — **arch'bish'op·ric** (-rĭk), *n.*

arch'dea'con (-dē'kŭn; -k'n; 2), *n.* [AS. *arcediacon*, fr. LL. *archidiaconus*, fr. Gr. *archidiakonos.*] A chief deacon, next in rank below a bishop. — **arch'dea'con·ate** (-ăt), *n.* — **arch'dea'con·ship**, *n.*

arch'di'o·cese (-dī'ō·sēs; -sĭs), *n.* Diocese of an archbishop. — **arch'di·oc'e·san** (-dī·ŏs'ĕ·săn), *adj.*

arch'du'cal (-dū'kăl), *adj.* Of or pert. to an archduke or archduchy.

arch'duch'y (ärch'dŭch'ĭ), *n.; pl.* -IES (-ĭz). Territory of an archduke or archduchess.

arch'duke' (-dūk'; 2), *n.* **a** A title formerly assumed by the rulers of Lorraine, Brabant, Austria, etc. **b** A prince of the former imperial family of Austria. — **arch'duch'ess** (-dŭch'ĕs; -ĭs; 2), *n.*

Ar·che'an, Ar·chae'an (är·kē'ăn), *adj.* [Gr. *archaios* ancient, fr. *archē* beginning.] *Geol.* Ancient; pertaining to or designating the oldest known group of rocks.

arched (ärcht), *adj.* Made as, or with, an arch or curve.

ar'che·gone (är'kē·gōn), *n.* *Bot.* An archegonium.

ar'che·go'ni·ate (är'kē·gō'nĭ·āt), *adj.* Bearing archegonia.

ar'che·go'ni·um (är'kē·gō'nĭ·ŭm), *n.; pl.* -NIA (-ȧ). [NL., fr. Gr. *archegonos* the first of a race.] *Bot.* The flask-shaped female sex organ in bryophytes and pteridophytes and some gymnosperms. It contains the egg which develops into the sporophyte. — **ar'che·go'ni·al** (-ăl), *adj.*

arch'en'e·my (ärch'ĕn'ĕ·mĭ), *n.* A principal enemy; specif., Satan, the enemy of mankind.

ar·chen'ter·on (är·kĕn'tẽr·ŏn), *n.* [*archi-* + Gr. *enteron* intestine.] See GASTRULA.

ar'che·o- (är'kē·ō-). Var. of ARCHAEO-.

ar'che·ol'o·gy, ar'che·o·log'i·cal, ar'che·ol'o·gist, etc. Vars. of ARCHAEOLOGY, etc.

Ar'che·o·zo'ic (är'kē·ō·zō'ĭk), *adj.* [*archeo-* (var. of *archaeo-*) + Gr. *zōē* life + *-ic.*] Of, pert. to, or designating the earliest division of geological history, the era of the Archean group of rocks. — **Ar'che·o·zo'ic**, *n.*

arch'er (är'chẽr), *n.* [OF. *archier*, fr. L. *arcarius*, fr. *arcus* bow.] **1.** A bowman; one who uses the bow and arrow. **2.** [*cap.*] *Astron.* = SAGITTARIUS.

arch'er·y (-ĭ), *n.* **1.** Art, practice, or skill of shooting with bow and arrows. **2.** An archer's outfit of bows, arrows, etc. **3.** Archers collectively.

ar'che·spore (är'kē·spōr; 70), **ar'che·spo'ri·um** (-spō'rĭ·ŭm), *n.* [*arche-* (= *archi-*) + *spore.*] *Bot.* The cell or group of cells that gives rise to the spore mother cells.

ar'che·type (är'kē·tīp), *n.* [From L., fr. Gr. *arche-* (= *archi-*) + *typos* stamp, pattern.] The original pattern of which all things of the same species are representations or copies; original idea, model, or type; prototype. — **ar'che·typ'al** (-tīp'ăl; -'l), **ar'che·typ'i·cal** (-tĭp'ĭ·kăl), **ar'che·typ'ic** (-tĭp'ĭk), *adj.*

arch'fiend' (ärch'fēnd'), *n.* The chief fiend, esp. Satan.

ar'chi- (är'kĭ-). [L., fr. Gr. *archi-*, a prefix fr. same root as *archein* to be first, *archē* beginning, *archos* chief. Cf. ARCH-.] A prefix denoting: **a** *Chief*, as in *archi*tect. **b** *Anat. & Biol. Primitive, original*, as in *archi*carp.

ar'chi·blast (-blăst), *n.* [*archi-* + *-blast.*] *Biol.* **a** The formative material of an ovum, or egg. **b** The epiblast.

ar'chi·carp (-kärp), *n.* [*archi-* + *-carp.*] *Bot.* The female sex organ in ascomycetous fungi, consisting normally of a filamentous portion (the trichogyne) and a basal fertile portion (the ascogonium).

ar'chi·di·ac'o·nal (-dī·ăk'ō·năl; -n'l), *adj.* Of or pert. to an archdeacon or his office. — **ar'chi·di·ac'o·nate** (-nāt), *n.*

ar'chi·e·pis'co·pal (-ē·pĭs'kō·păl), *adj.* Of or pert. to an archbishop or his office. — **ar'chi·e·pis'co·pate** (-pāt), *n.*

archiepiscopal cross. See CROSS, *Illust.* (3).

ar'chil (är'kĭl; -chĭl), *n.* [OF. *orchel, orcheil*, fr. or akin to It. *orcella, orcello.*] A violet dye obtained from several lichens; also, a plant yielding it.

ar'chi·mage (är'kĭ·māj), *n.* [NL. *archimagus*, fr. *archi-* + L. *magus.* See MAGI.] A great magician or enchanter.

ar'chi·man'drite (-măn'drīt), *n.* [From ML., fr. LGr. *archimandritēs*, fr. *archi-* (E. *arch-*) + *mandra* an enclosed space.] *Eastern Ch.* **a** The head of a larger monastery; — contr. with *hegumen*, head of a smaller monastery. **b** A title bestowed upon heads of a number of monasteries.

Ar'chi·me'de·an (är'kĭ·mē'dē·ăn; -mē·dē'ăn), *adj.* [L. *Archimedeus.*] Of or pertaining to Archimedes.

Ar'chi·me'de·an, *or* **Ar'chi·me'des', screw** (är'kĭ·mē'dēz). A device, attributed to Archimedes, consisting of a tube bent spirally around an axis, or of a coarse screw incased in an open cylinder, and used to raise water for irrigation purposes.

ar'chi·pe·lag'ic (är'kĭ·pē·lăj'ĭk), *adj.* Of or pertaining to, or of the nature of, an archipelago.

ar'chi·pel'a·go (-pĕl'ȧ·gō), *n.; pl.* -GOES, -GOS (-gōz). [It. *arcipelago*, prop., chief sea, fr. Gr. *archi-* + *pelagos* sea.] **1.** [*cap.*] The Aegean Sea, between Greece and Asia Minor. It is studded with small islands. **2.** Any sea or broad sheet of water interspersed with islands; also, such a group of islands.

ar'chi·plasm (är'kĭ·plăz'm), *n.* Archoplasm.

ar'chi·tect (är'kĭ·tĕkt), *n.* [From L., fr. Gr. *architektōn* chief artificer, master builder, fr. *archi-* + *tektōn* workman.] **1.** A person skilled in, or a professional student of, architecture; one who designs and oversees the construction of buildings. **2.** A contriver, designer, or maker.

ar'chi·tec·ton'ic (är'kĭ·tĕk·tŏn'ĭk), *adj.* **1.** Of or pertaining to an architect or architecture; architectural. **2.** Resembling architectural work, as in structure or texture. — *n.; also* **ar'chi·tec·ton'ics** (-ĭks). **1.** The science of architecture. **2.** Structural design; structural skill.

ar′chi·tec′tur·al (är′kĭ·tĕk′tūr·ăl), *adj.* Of, pertaining to, or conforming with the rules of, architecture. — **ar′chi·tec′tur·al·ly**, *adv.*

ar′chi·tec′ture (är′kĭ·tĕk′tūr), *n.* [F., fr. L. *architectura.*] **1.** Art or science of building, esp. houses, churches, bridges, etc. **2.** A method or style of building. **3.** Construction, in general; frame or structure; workmanship. **4.** Architectural product or work.

ar′chi·trave (är′kĭ·trāv), *n.* [F., fr. It., fr. *archi-* + *trave* beam, fr. L. *trabs.*] *Arch.* **a** The lowest division of an entablature, resting on the column, esp. in classical architecture; epistyle. See ORDER, *Illust.* **b** Molding above and on both sides of a door or other square opening.

ar·chi′val (är·kī′văl; är′kĭv·ăl; är′kĭ·văl), *adj.* Of, pertaining to, or contained in, archives or records.

ar′chive (är′kīv), *n.; pl.* ARCHIVES (-kīvz). [F. *archives,* pl., fr. L. *archivum, archium,* fr. Gr. *archeion* government house, *ta archeia* archives, fr. *archē* first place, government.] **1.** *pl.* A place for keeping public records. Formerly also in *sing.* **2.** *pl.* Public records. Also in *sing.*

ar′chi·vist (är′kĭ·vĭst; är′kīv·ĭst), *n.* A keeper of archives or records.

ar′chi·volt (är′kĭ·vōlt), *n.* [It. *archivolto, arcovolta.*] *Arch.* Molding or other ornaments around the sides and top of a curved opening, as an arch.

arch′ly (ärch′lĭ), *adv.* In an arch manner; roguishly.

arch′ness, *n.* The quality of being arch; roguishness.

ar′chon (är′kŏn; -kŭn), *n.* [L., fr. Gr. *archōn, archontos,* pres. part. of *archein* to rule.] **1.** A chief magistrate of ancient Athens. **2.** A ruler or presiding officer.

ar′cho·plasm (är′kō·plăz′m), *n.* [See ARCHON; -PLASM.] *Biol.* The supposed special substance from which the asters and spindles are developed in mitotic cell division, and of which they consist. Cf. TROPHOPLASM. — **ar′cho·plas′mic** (-plăz′mĭk), *adj.*

arch′priest′ (ärch′prēst′; 2), *n.* A chief priest; specif.: *Eccl. Hist.* **a** In early times, a priest who acted as the chief assistant or as the vicar of a bishop in a cathedral, later called *dean;* also, a priest in charge of the clergy in a large town, later called *rural dean.* **b** The head of the Roman Catholic secular clergy in England, from 1598 to 1623, when he was succeeded by a vicar apostolic. — **arch′priest′hood**, *n.* — **arch′priest′ship**, *n.*

arch′way′ (ärch′wā′), *n.* A way or passage under an arch; also, an arch over a passage.

-archy. [Gr. *-archia,* fr. *archos* chief.] A suffix meaning *a rule, ruling,* as in mon*archy,* a rule of one.

ar′ci·form (är′sĭ·fôrm), *adj.* Having the form of an arch; curved.

arcked, arck′ing. See ARC, *v.*

arc lamp *or* **light.** *Elec.* An electric lamp with which light is produced by an arc made when a current passes between two incandescent electrodes surrounded by gas.

arc′tic (ärk′tĭk; *formerly spelled, and still sometimes pronounced,* ar′tic), *adj.* [OF. *artique,* fr. L., fr. Gr. *arktikos,* fr. *arktos* a bear, also a constellation so called.] Pertaining to, or situated under, the northern constellation called the *Bear;* relating to, or characteristic of, the North Pole or the region near it; polar; frigid. The **Arctic Circle** is a parallel of latitude 23° 27′ distant from the North Pole. The **Arctic zone** is the North Frigid Zone (see ZONE, *n.*). — *n.* **1.** The Arctic Circle; the arctic pole or regions. **2.** A waterproof overshoe.

arctic fox. See FOX

arctic seal. Rabbit fur processed to simulate seal.

Arc·tu′rus (ärk·tū′rŭs), *n.* [L., fr. Gr. *Arktouros,* fr. *arktos* bear + *ouros* ward, guard.] A giant fixed star of the first magnitude in Boötes; Alpha (α) Boötis.

ar′cu·ate (är′kū·āt), **ar′cu·at′ed** (-āt′ĕd; -ĭd), *adj.* [L. *arcuatus,* past part. of *arcuare* to bow.] Curved like a bow.

-ard (-ẽrd), **-art** (-ẽrt). [OF.; akin to E. *hard.*] A suffix of many words, usually denoting *one who does something excessively* or *something discreditable,* as in cow*ard,* bragg*art,* drunk*ard.*

ar′deb (är′dĕb), *n.* [Ar.] A unit of capacity used in Egypt and most Islamic countries, varying from about 7.5 bushels to 4 quarts at different places. The ardeb of the Egyptian customs is 5.447 imperial, or 5.619 U. S., bushels.

ar′den·cy (är′dĕn·sĭ), *n.* Ardor; vehemence.

ar′dent (-dĕnt), *adj.* [OF. *ardant,* fr. L. *ardens, -entis,* pres. part. of *ardere* to burn.] **1.** Hot or burning; fiery. **2.** Glowing; shining. **3.** Warm; passionate; eager; — said of affections or passions. — **Syn.** See IMPASSIONED. — **ar′dent·ly**, *adv.*

ardent spirits. Strong distilled liquors, as brandy.

ar′dor, ar′dour (är′dẽr), *n.* [From OF., fr. L. *ardor,* fr. *ardere* to burn.] **1.** Burning heat; fire; flame. **2.** Warmth of emotion; zeal. **3.** *pl. Obs.* Bright or effulgent spirits. — **Syn.** See PASSION.

ar′du·ous (-dū·ŭs), *adj.* [L. *arduus* steep, high.] **1.** Steep and lofty; hard to climb. **2.** Difficult; laborious. **3.** Strenuous; energetic. — **Syn.** See HARD. — **ar′du·ous·ly**, *adv.* — **ar′du·ous·ness**, *n.*

are (är; ȧ). [AS. (Northumbrian) *aron.*] See BE.

are (âr; är), *n.* [F., fr. L. *area.*] See METRIC SYSTEM, *Table* 3.

a′re·a (ā′rē·ȧ; âr′ē·ȧ), *n.; pl.* AREAS (-ȧz) or, chiefly in *Biol.,* AREAE (-ē) [L., a broad piece of level ground.] **1.** Any flat surface, as of the ground. **2.** An areaway. **3.** A particular extent of surface (see MEASURE, *Tables* 3 & 4; METRIC SYSTEM, *Tables* 2 & 3); a space on the surface, as of an organism; a region; tract on the earth. **4.** Extent; scope. **5.** A part of the cerebral cortex having a particular function. **6.** *Geom.* The surface extent of any figure. — **a′re·al** (-ăl), *adj.*

a′re·a·way′ (-wā′), *n.* A sunken space affording access, air, and light to a cellar or basement.

ar′e·ca (ăr′ē·kȧ; ȧ·rē′kȧ), *n.* [NL. *areca,* fr. Pg., fr. Malayalam *adekka.*] Also **areca palm.** **a** The betel palm. **b** Any of several related palms, grown for ornament.

a·re′na (ȧ·rē′nȧ), *n.; pl.* -NAS (-nȧz), -NAE (-nē). [L. *arena, harena,* sand, sandy place.] **1.** *Rom. Antiq.* The area, usually sanded, in an amphitheater, where gladiatorial contests, etc., took place. **2.** Place of public contest or exertion; sphere of action.

ar′e·na′ceous (ăr′ē·nā′shŭs), *adj.* [L. *arenaceus.*] *Petrog., etc.* Sandy or largely of sand; of the nature of, or growing in, sand.

arena theater. A theater having the acting area in the center of the auditorium with the audience seated on all sides.

ar′e·nic′o·lous (ăr′ē·nĭk′ō·lŭs), *adj.* [L. *arena* sand + *-colous.*] *Zool.* Inhabiting, or burrowing in, sand.

aren't (ärnt). A colloquial contraction of *are not.*

a·re′o·la (ȧ·rē′ō·lȧ), *n.; pl.* -LAE (-lē), -LAS (-lȧz). [L., dim. of *area.*] A small area, esp. about something, as about a vesicle or pustule; also an interstice, as between leaf veins. — **a·re′o·lar** (-lẽr), *adj.* — **a·re′o·late** (-lāt), *adj.* — **ar′e·o·la′tion** (ăr′ē·ō·lā′shŭn; âr′-), *n.*

ar′e·ole (ăr′ē·ōl; âr′-), *n.* [F. *aréole.*] An areola.

ar′e·om′e·ter (ăr′ē·ŏm′ē·tẽr; âr′-), *n.* [Gr. *araios* thin, rare + *-meter.*] *Physics.* A hydrometer.

Ar′e·op′a·gite (ăr′ē·ŏp′ȧ·jīt; -gīt), *n.* [L. *Areopagites,* fr. Gr. *Areiopagitēs.*] A member of the court of the Areopagus. — **Ar′e·op′a·git′ic** (-jĭt′ĭk), *adj.*

Ar′e·op′a·gus (-gŭs), *n.* [L., fr. Gr. *Areiopagos,* and *Areios pagos,* hill of Ares (Mars' Hill).] A hill west of the Acropolis, Athens, where sat a high court; also, the court.

A′res (ā′rēz; âr′ēz), *n.* [L., fr. Gr. *Arēs.*] The Greek god of war, son of Zeus and Hera, and lover (or consort) of Aphrodite. The Romans identified him with Mars.

a·rête′ (ȧ·rāt′), *n.* [F., lit., fishbone, ridge, sharp edge, fr. L. *arista* beard of grain.] A sharp and rugged crest of a mountain range or of a subsidiary ridge between two mountain gorges.

Ar′e·thu′sa (ăr′ē·thū′zȧ; -sȧ), *n.* [L., fr. Gr. *Arethousa.*] **1.** *Class. Myth.* A wood nymph who, pursued by the Peloponnesian river-god Alpheus, was changed by Artemis into a stream which ran under the sea and emerged in Sicily as a fountain, still pursued by the river. **2.** [*not cap.*] Any of a genus (*Arethusa*) of bog orchids with a single linear leaf and solitary purple flower.

ar′gal (är′găl). Var. of ARGOL.

ar′ga·li (är′gȧ·lĭ), *n.; pl.* ARGALI, ARGALIS (-lĭz). See PLURAL, *Note,* 6. Also **ar′gal** (-găl). [Mongolian.] A large Asiatic wild sheep (*Ovis ammon*), remarkable for its large horns. The name has been applied to other wild sheep, as the bighorn of America.

ar′gent (är′jĕnt), *n.* [F., fr. L. *argentum* silver.] *Archaic.* Silver; figuratively, whiteness. — *adj.* Of silver; silvery; white; shining.

ar·gen′te·ous (är·jĕn′tē·ŭs), *adj.* [L. *argenteus.*] Silvery.

ar·gen′tic (-tĭk), *adj. Chem.* Pertaining to, derived from, or containing (usually univalent) silver.

ar′gen·tif′er·ous (är′jĕn·tĭf′ẽr·ŭs), *adj.* [L. *argentum* silver + *-ferous.*] Producing or containing silver.

ar′gen·tine (är′jĕn·tĭn; -tīn), *adj.* Pertaining to, or like, silver; silvery. — *n.* Silver; also, any of various metals resembling it.

ar′gen·tite (-tīt), *n.* [L. *argentum* silver.] *Mineral.* Native silver sulfide, Ag_2S, a mineral of metallic luster and dark lead-gray color. It is a valuable ore of silver.

ar′gen·tol (-tōl; -tŏl), *n.* [L. *argentum* silver + *-ol,* 2.] *Pharm.* A yellow compound ($C_9H_5N(OH)SO_3Ag$), used as an antiseptic dusting compound.

ar·gen′tous (är·jĕn′tŭs), *adj. Chem.* Of or containing silver in higher proportion than in argentic compounds.

ar′gil (är′jĭl), *n.* [F. *argile,* fr. L. *argilla* white clay, fr. Gr. *argilla,* fr. *argos* white.] Clay; esp., potter's clay.

ar′gil·la′ceous (är′jĭ·lā′shŭs), *adj.* Clayey.

ar′gil·lif′er·ous (-lĭf′ẽr·ŭs), *adj.* [L. *argilla* white clay + *-ferous.*] Producing or abounding in clay.

ar′gil·lite (är′jĭ·līt), *n.* [Gr. *argillos* clay + *-lite.*] *Petrog.* An argillaceous rock, differing from shale in being metamorphosed, and from slate in having no slaty cleavage.

Ar′give (är′jīv; -gīv), *adj.* [L. *Argivus.*] Of or pertaining to the Achaean city of Argos or the surrounding territory of Argolis; hence (after Homer), of or pert. to the Greeks. — *n.* A Greek of Argos, or freely, any Greek.

Ar′go (är′gō), *n.* [L., fr. Gr. *Argō.*] **1.** *Gr. Myth.* See ARGONAUT. **2.** *gen.* ARGUS (-gŭs). A large constellation in the Southern Hemisphere, through which the Milky Way passes, lying principally between Canis Major and the Southern Cross.

ar′gol (är′gŏl), **ar′gal** (-găl), *n.* Crude tartar.

ar′gon (-gŏn), *n.* [NL., fr. Gr. *argon,* neut. of *argos* inactive.] *Chem.* A colorless, odorless, gaseous element occurring in the air, volcanic gases, etc. Symbol, *A;* at. no., 18; at. wt., 39.944.

Ar′go·naut (är′gō·nôt), *n.* [From L. & Gr., fr. Gr. *Argō* Argo + *nautēs* sailor.] **1.** *Gr. Myth.* One of the band of heroes who sailed with Jason, in the ship *Argo,* to Colchis after the Golden Fleece. **2.** *U. S.* One of those who went to California (1848–49) in search of gold shortly after its discovery there. **3.** [*not cap.*] *Zool.* The paper nautilus. See NAUTILUS, 2. — **Ar′go·nau′tic** (-nô′tĭk), *adj.*

ar′go·sy (är′gō·sĭ), *n.; pl.* -SIES (-sĭz). [Earlier *ragusy,* fr. *ragusa,* meaning orig. a vessel of Ragusa.] A large ship; esp., a great merchant vessel; a fleet of vessels.

ar′got (-gō; -gŏt), *n.* [F.] The conventional slang of a group, esp. of thieves or vagabonds. — **Syn.** See DIALECT.

ar′gue (är′gū), *v. i.* [OF. *arguer,* fr. L. *argutare,* freq. of *arguere* to make clear.] **1.** To offer reasons for or against something; reason; as, we *argued* about the case. **2.** To dispute (*with*); as, to *argue* with a friend. — *v. t.* **1.** To prove; indicate; as, many laws *argue* many sins. **2.** To debate or discuss; to treat by reasoning. **3.** To maintain or contend (*that*). **4.** To persuade by reasons; to dispose of by argument. — **Syn.** See DISCUSS. — **ar′gu·a·ble** (-gū·ȧ·b'l), *adj.* — **ar′gu·er**, *n.*

ar′gu·fy (är′gū·fī), *v. t. & i.* [*argue* + *-fy.*] *Colloq. & Dial.* To argue pertinaciously.

ar′gu·ment (-mĕnt), *n.* [OF., fr. L. *argumentum.*] **1.** *Archaic.* Proof; evidence. **2.** A reason or reasons offered in proof; reasoning. **3.** Discourse designed to convince or to persuade. **4.** Argumentation; discussion; disputation. **5.** The subject matter or topic of anything; also, an abstract or summary, as of a book. **6.** *Obs.* Matter of dispute. **7.** *Math.* One of the independent variables upon whose value that of a function depends.

ar′gu·men·ta′tion (-mĕn·tā′shŭn), *n.* **1.** Act or process of forming reasons, making inductions, drawing conclusions, and applying them to the case in discussion. **2.** Writing based on or embodying such a process. **3.** Debate; discussion.

ar′gu·men′ta·tive (-mĕn′tȧ·tĭv), *adj.* **1.** Relating to argument; controversial. **2.** Given to argument; disputatious. — **ar′gu·men′ta·tive·ly**, *adv.* — **ar′gu·men′ta·tive·ness**, *n.*

‖**ar′gu·men′tum** (är′gū·mĕn′tŭm), *n.; pl.* -TA (-tȧ). [L.] *Logic.* An argument, proof, or appeal to reason.

Ar′gus (är′gŭs), *n.* [L., fr. Gr. *Argos.*] **1.** *Gr. Myth.* A hundred-eyed monster set to watch Io. See IO. **2.** A watchful guardian.

Ar′gus–eyed′ (-īd′), *adj.* Vigilantly observant.

ar·gyr′o·dite (är·jĭr′ō·dīt), *n.* [Gr. *argyrōdēs* rich in silver.] *Mineral.* A steel-gray mineral of metallic luster, composed of silver, germanium, and sulfur (Ag_6GeS_6).

Ar'gy·rol (är'jĭ·rōl; -rŏl), *n.* A trade-mark for silver vitellin, a silver-protein compound. The aqueous solution is used as a local antiseptic.

a'ri·a (ä'rĭ·ȧ; âr'ĭ·ȧ), *n.* [It., ult. fr. L. *aer* air.] *Music.* An air, melody, or tune; esp., an elaborate, accompanied melody sung by a single voice in operas, cantatas, etc.

-a'ri·a (-ā'rĭ·ȧ). [NL., fr. L. *-arius.*] A plural noun suffix used to form generic and group names, esp. in botany and zoology (as in *Calceolaria*).

Ar'i·ad'ne (ăr'ĭ·ăd'nē), *n.* [L., fr. Gr. *Ariadnē.*] *Gr. Myth.* Minos's daughter, who gave Theseus a ball (or clew) of thread to guide him out of the labyrinth (see MINOTAUR). She fled with him, but he abandoned her.

Ar'i·an (âr'ĭ·ăn), *adj.* [L. *Arianus.*] Of or pertaining to Arius or his doctrines, esp. the doctrine that Christ was not the eternal Son of God, nor of the same substance. — *n.* An adherent of these doctrines. — **Ar'i·an·ism** (-ĭz'm), *n.*

Ar'i·an (âr'ĭ·ăn; är'yăn). Var. of ARYAN.

-ar'i·an (-âr'ĭ·ăn). A compound suffix, forming adjectives and nouns from nouns ending in *-ary* and *-aria.* See -AN.

ar'id (ăr'ĭd), *adj.* [L. *aridus*, fr. *arere* to be dry.] **1.** Without moisture; dry; barren. **2.** Lacking in interest or life. — **Syn.** See DRY. — **a·rid'i·ty** (ȧ·rĭd'ĭ·tĭ), *n.*

Ar'i·el (âr'ĭ·ĕl), *n.* [Heb. *Arī'ēl* lioness of God.] **1.** In Shakespeare's *Tempest*, an airy, prankish spirit, changing shape at will to serve Prospero, his master. **2.** *Astron.* The inner satellite of Uranus.

ar'i·el (âr'ĭ·ĕl), *n., or* **ariel gazelle.** [Ar. *aryal*, var. of *ayyil* stag.] A gazelle (*Gazella arabica*) of Arabia.

A'ri·es (ā'rĭ·ēz; âr'ĭ·ēz), *n.; gen.* ARIETIS (ȧ·rī'ĕ·tĭs). [L., ram.] **a** A constellation between Pisces and Taurus, pictured as a ram. **b** The first sign [♈] of the zodiac, which the sun enters about the 21st of March. See ZODIAC.

ar'i·et'ta (ăr'ĭ·ĕt'ȧ), *n.* Also **ar'i·ette'** (-ĕt'). [It. *arietta*, dim. of *aria;* F. *ariette*, fr. It.] A short aria, or air.

a·right' (ȧ·rīt'), *adv.* Rightly; correctly.

ar'il (ăr'ĭl), *n.* [ML. *arilli* dry grapes.] *Bot.* An exterior covering or appendage of certain seeds, developing as an outgrowth from the stalk of an ovule. The scarlet coating of the seeds of the climbing bittersweet is a true aril. — **ar'il·late** (ăr'ĭ·lāt), *adj.*

ar'il·lode (ăr'ĭ·lōd), *n.* *Bot.* A false aril, an aril originating from the orifice instead of from the stalk of an ovule. The mace of the nutmeg is an arillode.

a·rio'so (ä·ryō'sō), *adj.* [It.] *Music.* Melodious in the style of an air or aria. — *n.* An arioso passage. — *adv.* In aria style.

-ar'i·ous (-âr'ĭ·ŭs). [From L. *-arius* + E. *-ous.*] An adjective suffix in words of Latin origin, meaning *pertaining to* or *connected with*, as in greg*arious*, vic*arious*.

a·rise' (ȧ·rīz'), *v. i.;* A·ROSE' (-rōz'); A·RIS'EN (-rĭz''n); A·RIS'ING (-rīz'ĭng). [AS. *ārīsan*, fr. *ā* + *rīsan* to rise.] **1.** To rise; get up; ascend. **2.** To spring up; originate; to come into being or notice. **3.** To proceed; issue. — **Syn.** See SPRING.

a·ris'ta (ȧ·rĭs'tȧ), *n.; pl.* -TAE (-tē). [L.] An awn or bristlelike appendage.

a·ris'tate (-tāt), *adj.* [L. *aristatus*, fr. *arista* awn.] **a** *Bot.* Awned. **b** *Zool.* Having a slender or spiny tip.

a·ris'to- (ȧ·rĭs'tō-). [Gr. *aristos.*] A combining form meaning *best*, as in *aristo*cracy.

ar'is·toc'ra·cy (ăr'ĭs·tŏk'rȧ·sĭ), *n.; pl.* -CIES (-sĭz). [From L., fr. Gr. *aristokratia*, fr. *aristos* best + *kratein* to be strong, rule.] **1.** Rule by the best; hence, government by a relatively small privileged class; also, the ruling body of such a government. **2.** Any form of government in which the ruling power is vested in a minority consisting, presumably, of those best qualified to rule; also, a state having such a government. **3.** The nobles or chief persons in a state; a privileged class. **4.** Those regarded as superior to the rest of the community, as in rank, wealth, or intellect.

a·ris'to·crat (ȧ·rĭs'tō·krăt; ăr'ĭs·tō·krăt), *n.* **1.** One of the aristocracy. **2.** One who has the sympathies, habits, and temper of mind common among a ruling class. **3.** One who favors an aristocracy as a form of government. — **Syn.** Gentleman, patrician.

a·ris'to·crat'ic (ȧ·rĭs'tō·krăt'ĭk; ăr'ĭs-), *adj.* Also **a·ris'to·crat'i·cal** (-ĭ·kăl). **1.** Of or pertaining to an aristocracy; as, an *aristocratic* party. **2.** Partaking of or characteristic of a ruling or privileged class; patrician. **3.** Socially exclusive; snobbish. — **a·ris'to·crat'i·cal·ly,** *adv.*

a·ris'to·lo'chi·a'ceous (ȧ·rĭs'tō·lō'kĭ·ā'shŭs), *adj.* [L. *aristolochia* a plant useful in childbirth, fr. Gr. *aristolocheia*, fr. *aristos* best + *locheia* childbirth.] *Bot.* Belonging to the birthwort family (Aristolochiaceae). See BIRTHWORT.

Ar'is·to·te'li·an (ăr'ĭs·tō·tē'lĭ·ăn; -tēl'yăn), *adj.* Of or pert. to Aristotle (Gr. *Aristotelēs*), the Greek philosopher (384–322 B.C.). — *n.* A follower of Aristotle; an adherent of Aristotle's theories; also, loosely, one who exhibits that tendency to emphasize the empirical and particular, or to be scientific rather than metaphysical, which is supposed to characterize Aristotle as contrasted with Plato. — **Ar'is·to·te'li·an·ism** (-ĭz'm), *n.*

Aristotelian logic. The logic of Aristotle, the central achievement of which was the doctrine of the syllogism; also, the traditional or formal logic following the line of development inaugurated by Aristotle.

a·ris'to·type (ȧ·rĭs'tō·tīp), *n.* [*aristo-* + *-type.*] *Photog.* A process using silver salts in collodion or gelatin; also, a print so made.

a·rith'me·tic (ȧ·rĭth'mĕ·tĭk), *n.* [From OF., fr. L., fr. Gr. *arithmētikē* (sc. *technē*), fr. *arithmētikos* arithmetical, fr. *arithmein* to number, fr. *arithmos* number.] **1.** The art of computation by the use of positive real numbers. **2.** The science of positive real numbers. **3.** A book containing the principles of this science.

ar'ith·met'i·cal (ăr'ĭth·mĕt'ĭ·kăl), **ar'ith·met'ic** (-ĭk), *adj.* Of or pert. to, or according to the rules of, arithmetic; as, **arithmetical mean** (see MEAN, *n.*, 5); **arithmetical progression** *or* **series** (see PROGRESSION, 4). — **ar'ith·met'i·cal·ly,** *adv.*

a·rith'me·ti'cian (ȧ·rĭth'mĕ·tĭsh'ăn; ăr'ĭth-), *n.* One skilled in arithmetic.

‖**a ri've·der'ci** (ä rē'vā·dār'chē). [It.] Till we meet again; au revoir.

ark (ärk), *n.* [AS. *arc*, *earc*, fr. L. *arca*, fr. *arcere* to enclose.] **1.** *Obs. exc. Dial.* A chest or coffer. **2.** *Jewish Hist.* The oblong chest occupying the most sacred place in the sanctuary, in which were the two tables of stone containing the Ten Commandments; — called also **ark of the covenant.** **3.** The vessel in which Noah and his family were preserved during the Deluge (*Gen.* vi); hence, any place of refuge. **4.** *Colloq., U.S.* A large, uncomfortable building.

arles (ärlz), *n. pl.* *Scot. & N. of Eng.* Earnest money.

arm (ärm), *n.* [AS. *arm*, *earm.*] **1.** A human upper limb, esp. the part between the shoulder and the wrist. **2.** Anything like or corresponding to an arm; as: **a** The forelimb of a vertebrate, as of a bear. **b** A limb of an invertebrate animal. **c** A branch, as of a tree. **d** A slender part of a structure, machine, instrument, etc., projecting from a trunk, axis, or fulcrum. **e** *Naut.* The end of a yard; also, the part of an anchor from the crown to the fluke. See ANCHOR, *Illust.* **f** An inlet of water, as from the sea. **g** A support for the elbow, at the side of a chair, the end of a sofa, etc. **h** A sleeve. **3.** Power; might; as, the *arm* of the law; also, support. — ***at arm's length.*** At a good distance. — ***with open arms.*** Cordially.

arm (ärm), *n.* [See ARMS.] **1.** *Mil.* **a** A weapon of offense or defense. See ARMS. **b** A combatant branch of an army. **2.** An organized branch of national defense, as the navy.

arm, *v. t.* [OF. *armer*, fr. L. *armare*, fr. *arma*, pl., arms. See ARMS.] **1.** To furnish with weapons of offense or defense. **2.** To cover or furnish with any strengthening or protective covering. **3.** To fortify, in a moral sense. **4.** To equip or fit out for action or operation. — **Syn.** See FURNISH. — *v. i.* To provide oneself with arms, or means of attack or resistance.

ar·ma'da (är·mā'dȧ; är·mä'dȧ), *n.* [Sp., fr. L. *armata*, fr. *armare* to arm.] **1.** A fleet of armed ships; specif. [*cap.*], the ***Spanish, or Invincible, Armada***, sent by Philip II of Spain against England in 1588. It was in great part destroyed by the English fleet and by storms. **2.** A fleet of military airplanes.

ar'ma·dil'lo (är'mȧ·dĭl'ō), *n.; pl.* -LOS (-ōz). [Sp., dim. of *armado* armed.] A burrowing, chiefly nocturnal, edentate mammal (family Dasypodidae) of South and tropical America, having the body encased in an armor of small bony plates. When attacked, some species can curl up into a ball, presenting the armor on all sides. The ova always undergo two preliminary divisions, resulting in the birth of identical quadruplets.

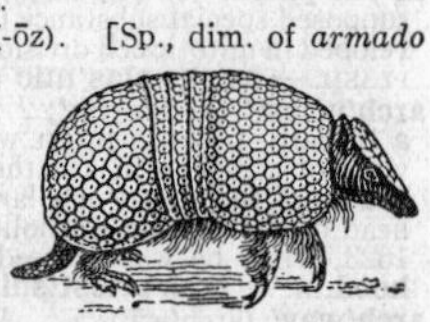

Armadillo (*Tolypeutes tricinctus*). (1/16)

Ar'ma·ged'don (är'mȧ·gĕd'ŭn), *n.* [L. *Armagedon* (Vulgate), fr. Gr. *Armageddōn, Harmagedōn.*] **1.** The place of a great battle to be fought out on "the great day of God" between the powers of good and evil (*Rev.* xvi. 16); — so called probably with reference to the actual battlefield of Megiddo, Palestine. **2.** Any great final conflict.

ar'ma·ment (är'mȧ·mĕnt), *n.* [L. *armamentum*, fr. *armare* to arm.] **1.** *Mil.* The aggregate of a nation's military strength. **2.** All the guns, torpedoes, small arms, etc., of a ship, fortification, or coast-defense system. **3.** Equipment, or act of equipping, for hostile action.

ar'ma·ture (-tūr), *n.* [F. or L.; F., fr. L. *armatura*, fr. *armare* to arm.] **1.** Armor, esp. that worn for the protection and defense of the body; hence, a covering suggestive of such armor; as: **a** A covering of flat wire wound about a cable. **b** *Biol.* An organ or structure for offense or defense, as teeth, thorns, etc. **2.** *Magnetism.* A piece of soft iron or steel used to connect the poles of a magnet or of adjacent magnets. **3.** *Elec.* **a** The movable part of a dynamo or motor, consisting essentially of coils of wire around an iron core. When the armature moves through the magnetic field between the pole pieces, an electric current is induced (as in the dynamo); when a current is passed through the coils they are caused by electromagnetic induction to move through this field (as in the motor). See DYNAMO, MAGNETO, *Illusts.* **b** The movable part of a relay or electric bell, moving in a variable magnetic field. — *v. t.* *Elec.* To furnish with an armature.

arm'chair' (ärm'châr'; ärm'châr'), *n.* A chair with arms. — *adj.* Comfortably remote from actual conditions; lacking first-hand knowledge; as, *armchair* strategists.

Ar·me'ni·an (är·mē'nĭ·ăn; -mēn'yăn), *adj.* Of or pert. to Armenia or Armenians or their language.

Ar·me'ni·an, *n.* **1.** An individual of a Caucasic people dwelling chiefly in Armenia. **2.** The language of the Armenian people, belonging to the Thraco-Phrygian subfamily of Indo-European languages. Its 38-letter alphabet is traditionally ascribed to the patriarch Mesrob of the 4th century A.D. See INDO-EUROPEAN LANGUAGES, *Table.*

ar'met (är'mĕt), *n.* [F., dim. of *arme* arm.] A type of medieval helmet. See HELMET, *Illust.* (10, 11).

arm'ful (ärm'fo͝ol), *n.; pl.* ARMFULS (-fo͝olz). As much as the arm can hold.

arm'hole' (-hōl'), *n.* **1.** The armpit; axilla. **2.** A hole for the arm in a garment.

ar·mif'er·ous (är·mĭf'ĕr·ŭs), *adj.* [L. *armifer*, fr. *arma* arms + *ferre* to bear.] Bearing arms or weapons.

ar'mi·ger (är'mĭ·jĕr), *n.; pl.* ARMIGERI (är·mĭj'ĕ·rī). [L., armor-bearer.] **1.** = ESQUIRE, 1. **2.** One next in degree to a knight, and entitled to armorial bearings. — **ar·mig'er·al** (-ăl), *adj.*

ar·mig'er·ous (är·mĭj'ĕr·ŭs), *adj.* Bearing (heraldic) arms.

ar'mil·lar'y (är'mĭ·lĕr'ĭ; är·mĭl'ȧ·rĭ), *adj.* [L. *armilla* bracelet.] Consisting of rings or circles; as, an **armillary sphere,** an old astronomical device composed of rings representing the positions of important circles of the celestial sphere.

arm'ing, *n.* **a** Offensive or defensive equipment. **b** Heraldic arms. **c** A part or fitting put upon a thing to complete it or fit it for action.

Ar·min'i·an (är·mĭn'ĭ·ăn; 58), *adj.* Of or pertaining to James Arminius (1560–1609), a Dutch protestant against the tenets of strict Calvinism. The theology of the Wesleyans of Great Britain and Methodists of America is Arminian. — *n.* A follower of Arminius. — **Ar·min'i·an·ism** (-ĭz'm), *n.*

ar·mip'o·tent (är·mĭp'ō·tĕnt), *adj.* [L. *armipotens.*] Mighty in battle.

ar'mi·stice (är'mĭ·stĭs), *n.* [F., after *solstice*, fr. L. *arma* arms + *stare, statum*, to stand still.] A brief cessation of arms, by convention; a temporary suspension of hostilities, by agreement; a truce.

Armistice Day. November 11, the anniversary of an armistice in 1918 ending hostilities of World War I; — now called *Veterans Day.*

arm'let (ärm'lĕt; -lĭt), *n.* **1.** A small arm, as of the sea. **2.** A bracelet or band for the upper arm.

ar·moire' (är·mwär'), *n.* [F. See AMBRY.] A large cupboard or clothespress, usually ornate.

ar′mor, ar′mour (är′mẽr), *n.* [From OF., fr. L. *armatura.*] **1.** Defensive arms for the body; any clothing or covering worn to protect one's person in battle. Cf. 2d MAIL, 1. **2.** Anything thought of as an offensive or defensive weapon; as, the *armor* of virtue. **3.** Protective covering, usually steel plates, on ships, forts, airplanes, etc. **4.** Any similar protective covering, as a diver's suit, the plates of an armadillo, etc. **5.** *Mil.* Armored forces and vehicles collectively. — *v. i. & t.* To put armor on.

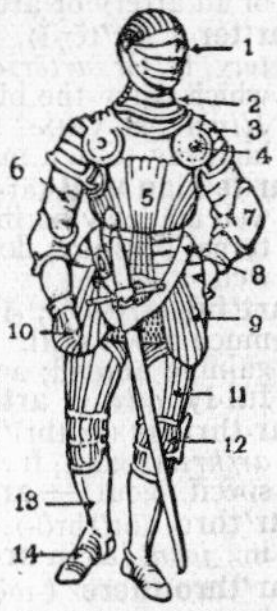

Plate Armor. 1 Helmet; 2 Gorget; 3 Shoulderpiece; 4 Pallette; 5 Breastplate; 6 Brassart; 7 Elbowpiece; 8 Skirt of Tasses; 9 Tuille; 10 Gauntlet; 11 Cuisse; 12 Kneepiece; 13 Jambeau; 14 Solleret.

ar′mor–clad′, ar′mour–clad′, *adj.* Sheathed in armor. — *n.* A vessel so protected.

ar′mor·er, ar′mour·er (är′mẽr·ẽr), *n.* **1.** One who makes or repairs armor or arms. **2.** One who has the care of arms and armor, as of a ship or regiment; also, one of a ground crew charged with repair and service of aircraft armament.

ar·mo′ri·al (är·mō′rĭ·ăl; 70), *adj.* Belonging to or bearing heraldic arms.

Ar·mor′ic (är·mŏr′ĭk), **Ar·mor′i·can** (-ĭ·kăn), *adj.* [L. *Armorica.*] Of Armorica (now Brittany) or its people or their language. — *n.* A native or the language of Armorica.

ar′mor·y, ar′mour·y (är′mẽr·ĭ), *n.; pl.* -IES (-ĭz). [Prob. fr. *armor,* but confused with F. *armoiries* heraldic emblems. Cf. AMBRY.] **1.** *Archaic.* Armor. **2.** A place where arms and instruments of war are deposited, esp., *U. S.*, a large building including also a drill hall, office, etc. **3.** *U. S.* A factory (usually one belonging to the government) where rifles, pistols, etc., are made. **4.** That branch of heraldry which treats of coat armor. **5.** *Archaic.* Armorial bearings.

arm′pit′ (ärm′pĭt′), *n.* The hollow, or pit, beneath the junction of the arm and shoulder; the axilla.

arms (ärmz), *n. pl.* [OF. pl. *armes,* fr. L. *arma* arms.] **1.** Instruments or weapons of offense or defense. **2.** The exploits of war; military service or science. **3. a** The hereditary heraldic devices of a family. **b** Similar devices adopted by governments.

ar′my (är′mĭ), *n.; pl.* -MIES (-mĭz). [F. *armée,* fr. L. *armata,* fr. *armare* to arm.] **1. a** A large organized body of men armed for war. **b** A unit capable of independent action, consisting conventionally of a headquarters, two or more corps, and auxiliary troops and trains; — called also *field army.* **c** The complete military organization of a nation for land warfare. **2.** A body of persons organized to advance a cause. **3.** A great number; host; array. — **Syn.** Host, legion, multitude.

army ant. = FORAGING ANT.

army worm. The larva of a certain noctuid moth (*Cirphis,* syn. *Leucania, unipuncta*), or, often, of other related species. They travel in great armies, destroying grass, grain, and other crops.

ar′ni·ca (är′nĭ·kȧ), *n.* [NL.] **1.** Any of many herbs (genus *Arnica*) of the aster family, some having bright-yellow ray flowers. **2.** The rhizome and roots of one species (*Arnica montana*), used as a counterirritant; also, a tincture derived from them.

ar′oid (ăr′oid; âr′-), *adj.* [*arum* + *-oid.*] *Bot.* Belonging to the arum family. See ARUM. — *n.* A plant of this family. — **a·roi′de·ous** (ȧ·roi′dē·ŭs), *adj.*

a·roint′ (ȧ·roint′), *v. i.* Begone; — with *thee. Shak.*

a·ro′ma (ȧ·rō′mȧ), *n.* [L., fr. Gr. *arōma.*] **1.** *Obs.* Spice. **2.** A distinctive, agreeable fragrance or odor, as of plants or other substances. **3.** A characteristic quality; flavor. — **Syn.** See SMELL.

ar′o·mat′ic (ăr′ō·măt′ĭk), *adj.* Also **ar′o·mat′i·cal** (-ĭ·kăl). **1.** Of, pertaining to, or containing aroma; fragrant; spicy; pungent. **2.** *Chem.* Derived from, or characterized by the presence of, the benzene ring; — said of a large class of cyclic organic compounds, many of which are odorous. — *n.* An aromatic plant, drug, or medicine. — **ar′o·mat′i·cal·ly,** *adv.*

a·ro′ma·tize (ȧ·rō′mȧ·tīz), *v. t.* To render aromatic.

a·rose′ (ȧ·rōz′), *past* of ARISE.

a·round′ (ȧ·round′), *adv.* **1.** In circumference; in, along, or through a circuit. **2.** On all sides at once; close about; here and there on every side. **3.** *Colloq., U. S.* **a** Here and there in the vicinity. **b** Nearby. **c** Backward. — *prep.* **1.** Along the circumference or circuit of. **2.** Close about on all sides of; enveloping; encompassing. **3.** *Colloq., U. S.* **a** Here and there about. **b** On another side of. **c** Not far from in amount, number, etc.

a·rouse′ (ȧ·rouz′), *v. t. & i.* [*a-* + *rouse.*] To excite to action from a state of rest; to rouse.

ar·peg′gio (är·pĕj′ō), *n.; pl.* -GIOS (-ōz). [It., deriv. of *arpa* harp.] *Music.* Production of the tones of a chord in rapid succession, as in playing the harp, and not simultaneously; a chord thus played.

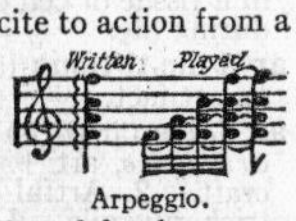

Arpeggio.

ar′pent (är′pĕnt; *F.* ȧr′päN′), *n.* [F.] **1.** An old French land measure of varying value, esp. one equal to .84 acre still common in parts of Canada. **2.** A linear measure, equal to about 11.5 rods, used locally in Canada.

ar′que·bus, ar′que·bus·ier′, etc. Vars. of HARQUEBUS, etc.

ar′rack (ăr′ăk), *n.* [Ar. *'araq.*] A spirit distilled in the East from rum; sometimes, any ardent spirit.

ar·raign′ (ă·rān′), *v. t.* [Through OF., fr. L. *ad* to + *ratio* reason, LL., cause, judgment.] **1.** *Law.* To call (a prisoner) before a court to answer to an indictment. **2.** To call to account, or accuse, as if before a court of public opinion, good taste, etc. — **Syn.** Charge, accuse, indict. — *n.* Arraignment; as, the clerk of the *arraigns.* — **ar·raign′ment** (-mĕnt), *n.*

ar·range′ (ă·rānj′), *v. t.;* -RANGED′ (-rānjd′); -RANG′ING (-rān′jĭng). [From OF., fr. *a* to + *rengier, rangier.* See RANGE, *v.*] **1.** To put in proper order; dispose in the manner intended or best suited for the purpose. **2.** To adjust; settle; determine. **3.** *Music.* To adapt (a composition) to voices or instruments for which it was not originally written. — **Syn.** See ORDER. — *v. i.* To come to an agreement, understanding, or settlement. — **ar·rang′er** (ă·rān′jẽr), *n.*

ar·range′ment (-mĕnt), *n.* [F.] **1.** Act, manner, or result of arranging, or state of being arranged; disposition; adjustment. **2.** Preparatory agreement or settlement. **3.** Something made by arranging parts or things together; a combination; as, an *arrangement* in gray and white.

ar′rant (ăr′ănt), *adj.* [Var. of ERRANT.] **1.** Wandering; vagrant; — now only in *arrant thief.* **2.** Out-and-out; confirmed; hence, notoriously or pre-eminently bad. — **ar′rant·ly,** *adv.*

ar′ras (ăr′ăs), *n.* [From *Arras,* France.] **1.** Tapestry; hence, any textile in tapestry weave. **2.** A wall hanging or screen of tapestry.

ar·ray′ (ă·rā′), *v. t.* [From OF., fr. L. *ad* to + a stem of Teut. origin (whence OF. *rei, roi,* order, arrangement).] **1.** To dispose in order, as troops; marshal. **2.** To adorn with dress; clothe; attire. — **Syn.** See LINE. — *n.* **1.** Order; a regular and imposing arrangement; hence, order of battle. **2.** The whole body of persons placed in order; hence, a body of soldiers. **3.** An imposing series of things; as, an *array* of figures. **4.** Dress; rich or beautiful apparel.

ar·ray′al (ă·rā′ăl), *n.* Act of arraying; also, array.

ar·rear′ (ă·rēr′), *n.* [OF. *ariere,* fr. L. *ad* to + *retro* backward.] **1.** *Archaic.* The rear. **2.** That which is unpaid but due; — commonly in *pl.* **3.** That held in reserve.

— ***in or into arrears or arrear.*** Backward; in debt.

ar·rear′age (-ĭj), *n.* [OF. *arerage.*] **1.** *Obs.* Indebtedness. **2.** State of being in arrears. **3.** That which remains unpaid and overdue; arrears. **4.** A reserve.

ar·rest′ (ă·rĕst′), *n.* [OF. *arest,* fr. *arester,* fr. L. *ad* at + *restare* to stop.] **1.** Act of stopping from further motion; check. **2.** Seizure by any force, physical or moral. **3.** *Law.* Taking or keeping in custody by authority of law. **4.** *Mach.* A device for arresting something. — *v. t.* **1.** To stop; check. **2.** To catch or lay hold upon; capture. **3.** To seize and fix; hold; as, to *arrest* the eyes or attention. **4.** *Law.* To take or keep (a person or chattels) in custody by authority of law; to apprehend; attach. **5.** *Med.* To render inactive; as, *arrested* tuberculosis. — **ar·rest′er, ar·res′tor,** *n.* — **ar·rest′ment,** *n.*

ar·rest′ing (ă·rĕs′tĭng), *adj.* Striking; impressive.

ar·ride′ (ă·rīd′), *v. t.* [L. *arridere,* fr. *ad-* + *ridere* to laugh.] To please; gratify.

‖**ar′rière′–ban′** (ȧ′ryâr′bäN′; *E.* ăr′ĭ·âr·băn′ *or* ăr′ĭ·ẽr-), *n.* [F.] A proclamation, as of the French kings, calling their vassals to arms; also, the body of such vassals.

‖**ar′rière′–pen′sée′** (ȧ′ryâr′päN′sā′), *n.* [F.] An undisclosed intention or meaning; a mental reservation.

ar′ris (ăr′ĭs), *n.* [OF. *areste,* fr. L. *arista* beard of grain, fishbone.] *Arch.* The sharp edge formed by the meeting of two surfaces, esp. in moldings.

ar·riv′al (ă·rīv′ăl), *n.* **1.** Act of arriving. **2.** Act of gaining an object or state; attainment; as, *arrival* at a conclusion. **3.** The person or thing arriving or which has arrived.

Syn. **Arrival, advent** mean the reaching of a destination. **Arrival** usually implies precedent movement; **advent,** sometimes, a momentous or conspicuous arrival but more often an appearance upon a scene.

ar·rive′ (ă·rīv′), *v. i.* [OF. *ariver,* deriv. of L. *ad* to + *ripa* shore, bank.] **1.** *Obs.* To come to shore or port; to land. **2.** To reach a place; as, to *arrive* at home. **3.** To gain an object; attain a state by effort, study, etc.; as, to *arrive* at a conclusion. **4.** To come; — said of time. **5.** To attain success or recognition. Cf. ARRIVÉ. — *v. t. Archaic.* To reach; come to.

‖**ar′ri·vé′** (ȧ′rē′vā′), *n.* [F.] One who has attained success (often in a derogatory sense); a parvenu.

ar·ro′ba (är·rō′bä), *n.* [Sp. & Pg., fr. Ar. *al-rub'* the quarter (of weight).] **1. a** A Spanish weight used in Mexico, South America, etc., usually equal to 25.36 lb. avoirdupois, or 11.51 kg. **b** An old Portuguese weight used in Brazil, 32.38 lb. avoirdupois, or 14.69 kg. **2.** A liquid measure of varying value, used in Spain and some of her former possessions.

ar′ro·gance (ăr′ō·găns), *n.* Also **ar′ro·gan·cy** (-găn·sĭ). [OF., fr. L. *arrogantia.*] A sense of superiority which manifests itself in an overbearing manner; presumption in claiming rank, dignity, or power.

ar′ro·gant (-gănt), *adj.* [OF., fr. L. *arrogans,* pres. part.] **1.** Making, or disposed to make, exorbitant claims of rank, estimation, or importance; haughty. **2.** Proceeding from, or characterized by, arrogance. — **Syn.** See PROUD. — **ar′ro·gant·ly,** *adv.*

ar′ro·gate (-gāt), *v. t.* [L. *arrogatus,* past part. of *arrogare* to appropriate to oneself, fr. *ad-* + *rogare* to ask.] **1.** To assume, or claim as one's own, unduly, proudly, or presumptuously. **2.** To ascribe to another unduly. — **ar′ro·ga′tion** (-gā′shŭn), *n.*

Syn. **Arrogate, usurp, pre-empt, appropriate, confiscate** mean to seize highhandedly. **Arrogate** implies insolence, presumption, and the exclusion of others; **usurp** implies unlawful or wrongful intrusion into the place of another and the seizure of what is his (or its) by right, custom, or law; **pre-empt** implies beforehandedness in taking something desired or needed by others; **appropriate** stresses making something one's own but often suggests unlawful methods of seizure; **confiscate** always implies seizure through the exercise of authority.

‖**ar′ron′disse′ment′** (ȧ′rôN′dēs′mäN′), *n.; pl.* -MENTS (-mäN′). [F.] **a** The largest division of a French department. It is divided into cantons. **b** A subdivision of Paris.

ar′row (ăr′ō), *n.* [AS. *arwe, earh.*] **1.** The missile weapon used with a bow. It usually has a pointed head and slender shaft, feathered at the end. **2.** A mark (→) like an arrow, indicating direction.

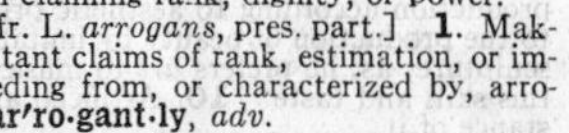

Arrow. 1 Head; 2 Shaft; 3 Feather; 4 Butt; 5 Nock.

ar′row·head′ (ăr′ō·hĕd′), *n.* **1.** The striking end of an arrow, usually separate and wedge-shaped. **2.** Anything resembling an arrowhead; as: **a** A stroke or mark, as on a drawing, to mark a limit, indicate a note, etc.; specif., a stroke used in the cuneiform characters. **b** The dart of an egg-and-dart molding. **3.** *Bot.* Any plant of a genus (*Sagittaria*) having leaves shaped like arrowheads.

ar′row·root′ (-ro͞ot′; 85), *n.* **1.** A tropical American plant of the genus *Maranta,* typifying the family Marantaceae (the arrowroot family), having tuberous rootstocks, esp. *M. arundinacea,* whose roots yield a nutritive starch. **2.** The starch yielded by this plant; also, a similar starch from other plants, as the coontie and curcuma.

ar′row·wood′ (-wo͝od′), *n.* Any of several shrubs having tough plant shoots, formerly used to make arrows, as, in the United States, the sorrel tree and certain viburnums.

ar′row·y (ăr′ō·ĭ), *adj.* Consisting or full of arrows; like, or suggestive of, an arrow; swift; darting.

ar·roy′o (ă·roi′ō), *n.; pl.* -OS (-ōz). [Sp.] A watercourse; also, a small, often dry, gully or channel.

ar′se·nal (är′sē·năl; -n'l), *n.* [It. *arsenale* dock, fr. Ar. *dār al-ṣinā'ah* court or house of industry.] A public establishment for making and storing arms and military equipment; hence, figuratively, a storehouse.

ar′se·nate (är′sē·nāt), *n.* A salt or ester of **ar·sen′ic ac′id** (är·sĕn′ĭk), H_3AsO_4.

ar′se·ni′a·sis (är′sē·nī′ȧ·sĭs), *n.* [NL.] *Med.* Arsenism.

ar′se·nic (är′sē·nĭk; -s'n·ĭk; *or, esp. Brit.,* ärs′nĭk), *n.* [OF., fr. L. *arsenicum,* fr. Gr. *arsenikon, arrhenikon,* yellow orpiment, ult. fr. Per.] **1.** One of the elements, a solid, brittle, very poisonous substance of tin-white to steel-gray color and metallic luster. Symbol, *As;* at. no., 33; at. wt., 74.91. **2.** A white or transparent highly poisonous substance, **ar′se·nic tri·ox′ide,** As_2O_3 (or As_4O_6); — called also *white arsenic.* It is used industrially and medicinally.

ar·sen′ic (är·sĕn′ĭk), *adj.* *Chem.* Pertaining to or containing arsenic; — of compounds in which arsenic is pentavalent.

ar·sen′i·cal (är·sĕn′ĭ·kăl), *adj.* Of, pertaining to, or containing arsenic. — *n.* A preparation containing arsenic.

ar′se·nide (är′sē·nīd; -nĭd), *n.* *Chem.* A binary compound of arsenic with a positive element or radical.

ar·se′ni·ous (är·sē′nĭ·ŭs), **ar′se·nous** (är′sē·nŭs), *adj.* Pertaining to, consisting of, or containing arsenic, esp. trivalent arsenic.

ar′se·nism (är′sē·nĭz'm), *n.* Chronic arsenical poisoning.

ar′se·nite (är′sē·nīt), *n.* A salt or ester of arsenious acid.

ar·se′niu·ret′ed, ar·se′niu·ret′ted (är·sē′nū·rĕt′ĕd; är·sĕn′ū-; 30), *adj.* Combined with arsenic; as, *arseniureted* hydrogen (arsine).

ar′se·no·py′rite (är′sē·nō·pī′rīt; är·sĕn′ō-), *n.* [*arsenic* + *pyrite.*] *Mineral.* A hard, tin-white or grayish iron sulfarsenide, FeAsS, occurring in crystals, or in masses or grains; — called also ***arsenical pyrites.*** It is the chief ore of arsenic, sometimes containing gold, cobalt, or nickel.

‖**ars est ce·la′re ar′tem** (ärz ĕst sē·lā′rē är′tĕm). [L.] It is true art to conceal art, i.e., to make an artistic production appear natural.

ar·sine′ (är·sēn′; är′sēn; -sĭn), *n.* [From ARSENIC.] *Chem.* A colorless, inflammable, extremely poisonous gas, AsH_3, with an odor like that of garlic; also, any of its derivatives.

ar′sis (är′sĭs), *n.; pl.* ARSES (-sēz). [L., fr. Gr. *arsis* a lifting.] **1.** *Pros.* **a** Originally, the unstressed part of a foot. **b** Now, the accented syllable of a foot; — from a misunderstanding of the Greek. **2.** *Music.* The unaccented part of the measure; — opposed to *thesis.*

‖**ars lon′ga, vi′ta bre′vis** (ärz lŏng′gȧ, vī′tȧ brē′vĭs). [L.] Art is long, but life is short; — Latin form of the first aphorism of Hippocrates.

ar′son (är′s'n), *n.* [OF., fr. L. *ardere, arsum,* to burn.] *Law.* The malicious burning of a dwelling house or outhouse of another man (by common law a felony); the similar burning of other property, including one's own house.

ar′son·ist (är′s'n·ĭst), **ar′son·ite** (-īt), *n.* One who commits arson.

ars·phen′a·mine (ärs·fĕn′ȧ·mēn; -ȧ·mĭn), *n.* [*arsenic* + *phenyl* + *amine.*] *Pharm.* A light-yellow, readily oxidizable, hygroscopic powder ($C_{12}H_{12}N_2O_2As_2.2HCl + 2H_2O$), used as a specific remedy for syphilis, relapsing fever, etc.; — orig. known as "606" and marketed under the trade-mark *Salvarsan.*

‖**ars po·e′ti·ca** (ärz pō·ĕt′ĭ·kȧ). [L.] Art of poetry.

art (ärt), *n.* [OF., fr. L. *ars, artis.*] **1.** Skill in performance, acquired by experience, study, or observation; knack. **2.** Human contrivance or ingenuity, as in adapting natural things to man's use. **3.** A branch of learning; a science; esp., one, as grammar or logic, serving chiefly as a discipline or as an instrument of knowledge; specif., *pl.,* those branches of learning taught in the academic course of colleges; as, master of *arts.* **4.** Learning or the field of learning. **5.** The general principles of any branch of learning or of any craft; as, the *art* of war. **6.** Systematic application of knowledge or skill in effecting a desired result; also, an occupation requiring such knowledge or skill; a craft; as, industrial *arts.* **7.** Skillful plan; device; also, cunning; artifice. **8.** *Obs.* Magical skill. *Shak.* **9. a** Application of skill and taste to production according to aesthetic principles; specif., such application to the production of beauty by imitation or design, as in painting and sculpture; as, he prefers *art* to music. **b** That which is produced by this skill and taste. **10.** Artificial and studied behavior; also, an instance of it.

Syn. Art, skill, cunning, artifice, craft mean the faculty of performing or executing that which is devised. **Art** is so variable in meaning that it is the synonym of each of the others which, on the other hand, are not always synonymous among themselves. *Art* is often used interchangeably with **skill** when both imply proficiency or expertness in the exercise or practical application of knowledge; *art* also comes close to **cunning** in the older underogatory sense of the second word when both imply inventive power, capacity for perfection in execution, etc.: it may also be used in place of **artifice** when mechanical skill in contriving, devising, etc., is connoted; *art* and **craft** may be used interchangeably only when they imply subtlety and ingenuity in workmanship. But *art* less often than *craft* suggests trickery or guile.

art (ärt). *Archaic.* 2d person pres. indic. sing. of BE.

-art (-ērt). See -ARD.

ar′tal (är′täl), *n., pl.* of ROTL; — often used incorrectly as a *sing.*

ar′te·fact (är′tē·făkt). Var. of ARTIFACT.

ar·tel′ (är·tĕl′; *Russ.* ŭr·tyĕl′), *n.* [Russ. *artel′,* fr. It. *artieri,* pl., artisans.] In Russia in the nineteenth century, an association of independent laborers for collective work with division of profits.

Ar′te·mis (är′tē·mĭs), *n.* [L., fr. Gr. *Artemis.*] In ancient Greek religion, an Olympian goddess of varied attributes; in myth and art, most typically the virgin huntress, goddess of wild nature, who is associated with the moon as her twin brother, Apollo, is with the sun; — by the Romans identified with Diana.

ar′te·mis′i·a (-mĭz′ĭ·ȧ; -mĭsh′ĭ·ȧ), *n.* [L., mugwort, fr. Gr. *artemisia.*] Any of a genus (*Artemisia*) of herbs and shrubs of the aster family, including the sagebrush and wormwood.

ar·te′ri·al (är·tēr′ĭ·ăl), *adj.* **1.** Of, pert. to, or of the nature of an artery or arteries. **2.** Designating the bright-red blood, as that in most arteries, which has been oxygenated by the lungs or gills. Cf. VENOUS.

ar·te′ri·al·ize (-īz), *v. t.* To transform (venous blood) into arterial blood by oxygenation, as in the lungs. — **ar·te′ri·al·i·za′tion** (-ĭ·zā′shŭn; -ī·zā′-), *n.*

ar·te′ri·o- (är·tē′rĭ·ō-). A combining form, Greek *artērio-,* from *artēria,* artery, denoting also *arterial, arterial and,* as in **ar·te′ri·ol′o·gy,** the branch of science which treats of the arteries; **ar·te′ri·ot′o·my.**

ar·te′ri·o·scle·ro′sis (är·tē′rĭ·ō·sklē·rō′sĭs), *n.* [NL., fr. Gr. *artēria* artery + *sclerosis.*] *Med.* Abnormal thickening and hardening of the walls of the arteries, occurring mostly in old age. — **ar·te′ri·o·scle·rot′ic** (-rŏt′ĭk), *adj.*

ar′te·ri′tis (är′tē·rī′tĭs), *n.* [NL., fr. *artery* + *-itis.*] Inflammation of an artery or arteries.

ar′ter·y (är′tēr·ĭ), *n.; pl.* ARTERIES (-ĭz). [L. *arteria* windpipe, artery, fr. Gr. *artēria.*] **1.** *Anat.* One of the tubular branching vessels which carry the blood from the heart through the body. See HEART, *Illust.;* cf. VEIN. **2.** A channel of communication, as a river, canal, or highway (esp. a main highway).

ar·te′sian well (är·tē′zhăn; -zĭ·ăn). [F. *artésien* pert. to Artois.] A well made by boring into the earth till water is reached which, from internal pressure, flows up like a fountain; hence, *U. S.,* any deep bored well.

art′ful (ärt′fo͝ol; -f'l), *adj.* **1.** *Archaic.* Performed with or showing much art or skill. **2.** Artificial; imitative. **3.** Skillful or ingenious in gaining an end; adroit; hence, crafty; wily. — **Syn.** See SLY. — **art′ful·ly,** *adv.* — **art′ful·ness,** *n.*

ar·thri′tis (är·thrī′tĭs), *n.; pl.* ARTHRITIDES (-thrĭt′ĭ·dēz). [L., fr. Gr. *arthritis* gout, fr. *arthron* joint.] *Med.* Inflammation of the joints; specif., gout. — **ar·thrit′ic** (-thrĭt′ĭk), **ar·thrit′i·cal** (-ĭ·kăl), *adj.*

ar′thro- (är′thrō-), **arthr-.** [Gr. *arthron.*] A combining form meaning *joint,* as in **ar·thral′gi·a, ar·throl′o·gy.**

ar′thro·mere (-mēr), *n.* [*arthro-* + *-mere.*] *Zool.* One of the body segments of jointed animals.

ar′thro·pod (-pŏd), *n.* [*arthro-* + *-pod.*] *Zool.* A member of a phylum (Arthropoda) consisting of animals with articulated body and limbs. The insects, arachnids, and crustaceans are its most important classes. — **ar′thro·pod,** *adj.* — **ar·throp′o·dal** (är·thrŏp′ō·dăl), **ar·throp′o·dous** (-dŭs), *adj.*

ar′thro·spore (-spōr), *n.* [*arthro-* + *spore.*] *Bot.* A thick-walled vegetative resting cell often formed in nostocs and related species. — **ar′thro·spor′ic** (-spŏr′ĭk), **ar·thros′po·rous** (är·thrŏs′pō·rŭs), *adj.*

Ar·thu′ri·an (är·thū′rĭ·ăn), *adj.* Of or pertaining to King Arthur, a legendary sixth-century king of Britain, or his knights. See ROUND TABLE.

ar′ti·choke (är′tĭ·chōk), *n.* [It. *articiocco.*] **1.** A tall thistlelike herb (*Cynara scolymus*) or its edible flower head, which is cooked as a vegetable. **2.** = JERUSALEM ARTICHOKE.

ar′ti·cle (är′tĭ·k'l), *n.* [OF., fr. L. *articulus,* dim. of *artus* joint.] **1.** A distinct portion of any writing consisting of two or more particulars, or treating of various topics; as, an *article* in the Constitution; hence, a clause in a contract, treaty, indictment, or the like; a concise statement; as, *articles* of partnership; *articles* of faith. **2.** *Archaic.* **a** Subject; matter; concern. **b** Precise point of time; as, in the *article* of death. **3.** A literary composition forming an independent portion of a magazine, encyclopedia, etc. **4.** A distinct detail or particular, as of news or conduct. **5.** A thing of a particular class or kind; a commodity. **6.** *Gram.* Any of the words *a, an, the,* or their equivalents in other languages, used before nouns to limit their application. — *v. t.;* -CLED (-k'ld); -CLING (-klĭng). **1.** To formulate or set forth in articles or distinct particulars. **2.** To bind by articles of covenant; as, he was *articled* to a solicitor.

Articles of Confederation. See CONFEDERATION, 3.

ar·tic′u·lar (är·tĭk′ū·lēr), *adj.* [L. *articularis.*] Of or pertaining to a joint or joints; as, an *articular* disease.

ar·tic′u·late (-lāt), *adj.* [L. *articulatus,* past part. of *articulare* to utter distinctly, prop., to divide into joints.] **1.** Jointed; segmented. **2.** Expressed or formulated clearly or systematically; distinct. **3.** Divided into words and syllables; distinctly uttered; spoken so as to be intelligible; as, *articulate* speech. **4.** Able to speak; esp., able to speak intelligibly or expressively. — **ar·tic′u·late·ly,** *adv.* — **ar·tic′u·late·ness,** *n.*

ar·tic′u·late (-lāt), *v. i.* **1.** To join by articulation. **2.** *Obs.* To make terms. *Shak.* **3.** To utter articulate sounds; to enunciate. — *v. t.* **1.** To joint; to unite by a joint or joints. **2.** To utter in distinct syllables or words; as, to *articulate* a word. — **ar·tic′u·la′tive** (-lā′tĭv; -lȧ·tĭv), *adj.* — **ar·tic′u·la′tor** (-lā′tēr), *n.*

ar·tic′u·la′tion (-lā′shŭn), *n.* **1.** Act or manner of jointing; also, state of being jointed; articulateness. **2.** Utterance of articulate sounds, as in pronunciation. **3.** An articulate utterance or an elementary sound, esp. a consonant. **4.** *Anat. & Zool.* **a** A joint or juncture between bones or cartilages in the skeleton of a vertebrate. **b** A movable joint between rigid parts of any animal. **5.** *Bot.* **a** A joint between two separable parts, as the base of a leafstalk. **b** A node or the interval between two nodes.

ar′ti·fact (är′tĭ·făkt), *n.* [L. *ars, artis,* art + *facere, factum,* to make.] **1.** *Archaeol.* A product of human workmanship, esp. of simple primitive workmanship. **2.** *Biol.* A structure or appearance in a tissue or cell due to death or the use of reagents, and not present during life.

ar′ti·fac·ti′tious (är′tĭ·făk·tĭsh′ŭs), *adj.* Possessing the character of an artifact.

ar′ti·fice (är′tĭ·fĭs), *n.* [F., fr. L. *artificium,* fr. *artifex* artificer, fr. *ars, artis,* art + *facere* to make.] **1.** *Obs.* Workmanship; handicraft. **2.** Artful or skillful contriving; ingenuity. **3.** Hence, craft; trickery; guile. **4.** An ingenious expedient; hence, an artful stratagem or trick. — **Syn.** See ART: TRICK.

ar·tif′i·cer (är·tĭf′ĭ·sēr), *n.* **1.** A skilled or artistic worker; a mechanic; craftsman, as a silversmith. **2.** *Mil.* One who prepares the shells, fuses, etc., in a military laboratory. **3.** One who makes or contrives; deviser; inventor.

ar′ti·fi′cial (är′tĭ·fĭsh′ăl), *adj.* **1. a** Made or contrived by art; — opposed to *natural.* **b** Made to resemble a raw material; synthetic; as, *artificial* silk. **2.** Feigned; fictitious; also, affected in manners. **3.** *Obs.* Artful; cunning; crafty. *Shak.* **4. a** *Bot.* Cultivated; not indigenous. **b** *Nat. Hist.* Based on characters not indicating natural relationships; as, an *artificial* key (cf. KEY, 9 a). — **ar′ti·fi′ci·al′i·ty** (-fĭsh′ĭ·ăl′ĭ·tĭ), *n.* — **ar′ti·fi′cial·ly,** *adv.* — **ar′ti·fi′cial·ness,** *n.*

Syn. Artificial, factitious, synthetic mean not brought into being by nature but by art or effort. **Artificial** is applicable to anything that is not the result of natural conditions but is, in a sense, a human creation (as, the family is a natural society but the state is an *artificial* society) but especially to that which has its counterpart in nature (as, *artificial* ice; *artificial* flowers); **factitious** applies to emotions, states of mind, reasons, etc., which are not naturally caused but which seem "trumped up," "worked up," or "cooked up" (as, to create a *factitious* demand; a *factitious* vogue); **synthetic** is applicable to any manufactured substance or to any natural substance so treated that it acquires the appearance or qualities of another and may be used in place of it (as, *synthetic* silk; *synthetic* rubber).

artificial horizon. 1. *Astron.* = HORIZON, 3 c. 2. *Aeronautics.* An instrument, based upon a gyroscope, designed to furnish a surface constantly perpendicular to the vertical and therefore parallel to the horizon.

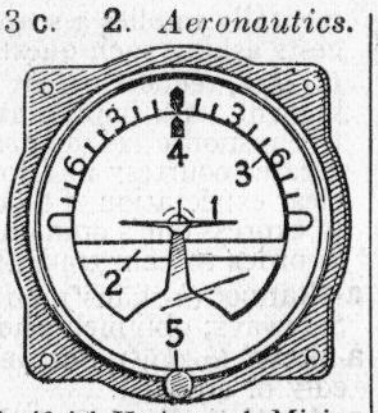

Artificial Horizon. 1 Miniature Airplane; 2 Horizon Bar; 3 Degree of Bank Scale (in 10's of degrees); 4 Pointer; 5 "Caging" (or inactivating) Knob.

ar·til′ler·y (är·tĭl′ẽr·ĭ), *n.* [OF. *artillerie,* fr. *artiller* to equip, fortify.] 1. *Obs.* Munitions of war. 2. Specif.: Missile engines and weapons, as catapults, arbalests, slings, bows, etc., with their missiles. 3. Mounted guns, in distinction from small arms; cannon; ordnance. 4. That branch of the army which handles the artillery. See COAST ARTILLERY, FIELD ARTILLERY. 5. The science of gunnery. — **ar·til′ler·ist** (-ĭst), *n.* — **ar·til′ler·y·man** (-ĭ·măn), *n.*

ar′ti·o·dac′tyl (är′tĭ·ō·dăk′tĭl), *adj.* [Gr. *artios* even + *daktylos* finger, toe.] *Zool.* Having an even number of toes (two or four), as the ox, deer, pig, etc. — *n.* An artiodactyl-hoofed mammal (order Artiodactyla). Cf. PERISSODACTYL. — **ar′ti·o·dac′ty·lous** (-tĭ·lŭs), *adj.*

ar′ti·san (är′tĭ·zăn; *Brit.* är′tĭ·zăn′), *n.* [F., fr. It. *artigiano.*] 1. *Obs.* An artist. 2. One trained in some mechanic art or trade.

art′ist (är′tĭst), *n.* [F. *artiste,* fr. *art* art. See ART, *n.*] 1. *Obs.* **a** One versed in learned arts. **b** An artisan. **c** A schemer. 2. One specially skilled in the practice of a manual art or occupation, as cooking. 3. An artiste. 4. One who professes and practices an art in which conception and execution are governed by imagination and taste; a person skilled in one of the fine arts.

ar·tiste′ (är·tēst′; *F.* ȧr′tēst′), *n.* [F.] **a** A professional singer or dancer. **b** An adept at cooking, millinery, etc.; — orig. jocose.

ar·tis′tic (är·tĭs′tĭk), **ar·tis′ti·cal** (-tĭ·kăl), *adj.* Of or pertaining to art or artists; showing taste or skill. — **ar·tis′ti·cal·ly,** *adv.*

Syn. Artistic, aesthetic, though often applied to identical terms, differ in meaning. Artistic stresses the point of view of one who produces art and thinks in terms of one who creates a beautiful thing; aesthetic, the point of view of one who loves art and thinks of it in terms of the effect a work of art has upon him. *Artistic* implies an urge to create; *aesthetic,* a delight in contemplating that which has been created.

art′ist·ry (är′tĭs·trĭ), *n.* 1. Pursuit of art. 2. Artistic quality of effect or workmanship; artistic ability.

art′less (ärt′lĕs; -lĭs), *adj.* 1. Lacking art, knowledge, or skill; uncultured. 2. **a** Made without skill; rude. **b** Free from artificiality; natural; as, *artless* grace. 3. Free from guile or craft; simple and sincere; ingenuous. — **Syn.** See NATURAL. — **Ant.** Artful. — **art′less·ly,** *adv.* — **art′less·ness,** *n.*

art′y (är′tĭ), *adj. Colloq.* Showily imitative of art; aspiring to be artistic; — used disparagingly.

ar′um (âr′ŭm; ā′rŭm), *n.* [L., fr. Gr. *aron.*] **a** *Bot.* Any plant of a genus (*A′rum* [*pron.* ā′rŭm]), type of the family Araceae, the arum family, having the flowers in a fleshy spike subtended by a leafy bract. The genus includes the cuckoopint. **b** *Hort.* Any of several related plants, as the jack-in-the-pulpit.

a·run′di·na′ceous (ȧ·rŭn′dĭ·nā′shŭs), *adj.* [L. *arundinaceus,* fr. *arundo* reed.] Of, pert. to, or like a reed.

a·rus′pex (ȧ·rŭs′pĕks; ăr′ŭs·pĕks). Var. of HARUSPEX.

-ary (-ẽr′ĭ *or, esp. Brit.,* -ẽr·ĭ). [L. *-arius, -arium,* whence also OF. *-ier,* AF. *-er,* and F. *-aire* in learned words.] A suffix forming: 1. Adjectives, with the sense of *pertaining to, connected with,* as in arbitr*ary,* mercen*ary.* 2. Nouns, with the sense of: **a** *A person belonging to* or *engaged in,* as in not*ary.* **b** *A thing belonging to* or *connected with; a place for;* as in avi*ary.*

-ary. [L. *-aris.*] An adjective suffix denoting *pertaining to, of the nature of,* as in capill*ary;* — a variant of -AR.

Ar′y·an (âr′ĭ·ăn; är′yăn), *n.* [Skr. *ārya* noble, member of the upper castes.] 1. A member of that Caucasian race one branch of which early occupied the Iranian plateau, while another branch entered India and amalgamated with the primitive inhabitants. 2. A member of the people which spoke the parent language from which the Indo-European languages are derived; loosely, in ethnology, an Aryan-speaking individual of the Caucasian race. 3. The assumed parent tongue of the Indo-European languages (which see). 4. In the Nazi ideology, a member of a supposed superior Caucasian race without admixture, esp. with no Semitic strain. — **Ar′y·an,** *adj.*

Ar′y·an·ize (-īz), *v. t.* In the Nazi ideology, to clear of non-Aryan, esp. Semitic, personnel, control, etc.

ar′y·te′noid (ăr′ĭ·tē′noid), *adj.* [Gr. *arytainoeidēs* shaped like a ladle.] *Anat.* Pertaining to or designating: **a** Two small laryngeal cartilages to which the vocal cords are attached. **b** Either of a pair of small muscles or an unpaired muscle of the larynx. — *n.* An arytenoid cartilage or muscle. — **ar′y·te·noi′dal** (-tē·noi′dăl; -d′l), *adj.*

as (ăz; *unstressed,* ăz; 4), *adv.* [AS. *eal swā,* lit., all so; hence, quite so.] 1. To the same extent; in equal degree; equally; — modifying an adjective or adverb; as, to run *as* fast as I could. 2. For instance; — used to introduce examples and illustrative phrases.

— *conj.* 1. To the same degree in which; in the same manner in or with which; — followed by a clause or by a noun or pronoun representing an incomplete clause; as, just as fast *as* I could run; there's no one I despise so bitterly *as* him; deaf *as* a post; do *as* I do; *as* you sow, so shall you reap. See LIKE, *conj., Note.* 2. During the time that; while. 3. Since; it being the case that. 4. Whereby to effect the following result, namely; — followed by an infinitive with *to;* as, so clearly guilty *as* to preclude doubt; be so good *as* to ring. 5. Though; as, strong *as* he is.

— *pron.* 1. That, who, which; — after *such* or *same* as antecedents; as, in the same fraternity *as* my brother. 2. A fact, practice, etc., which; as, he was a foreigner, *as* we observed at once.

— *prep.* In the idea, character, condition, or capacity of; as, to appear *as* Hamlet; to get a job *as* janitor; *as* a rule.

— ***as good as.*** Tantamount to; practically. — ***as if, as though.*** As one would, or as would be the case, if. — ***as it were.*** Much as if it were actually so; in a way. — ***as long as.*** Since; inasmuch as. — ***as such.*** Intrinsically considered. — ***as to*** *or* ***for.*** Also, ***as regards.*** In regard to. — ***as well.*** In addition; besides; also, as well as not, i. e., better. — ***as well as.*** Equally with; no less than. — ***as yet.*** Until now; hitherto.

as (ăs), *n.; pl.* ASSES (ăs′ĕz; -ĭz; *L.* ăs′ēz). [L.] 1. The Roman libra, or pound. 2. A Roman bronze coin, orig. weighing about a pound, reduced finally to half an ounce.

as′a·fet′i·da, as′a·foet′i·da (ăs′ȧ·fĕt′ĭ·dȧ), *n.* [NL. *asa* (fr. Per. *azā* mastic) + L. *foetidus* fetid.] The fetid gum resin of various Oriental plants (genus *Ferula*) of the carrot family, used in medicine as an antispasmodic.

as·bes′tos (ăs·bĕs′tŏs; ăz-), **as·bes′tus** (-tŭs), *n.* [L. *asbestos* (NL. *asbestus*) a kind of mineral unaffected by fire, fr. Gr. *asbestos* inextinguishable.] *Mineral.* A grayish or greenish variety of amphibole, occurring in long, delicate fibers, or in fibrous masses. It is noncombustible, nonconducting, and chemically resistant, and is used in fireproof curtains, roofing, etc. — *adj.* Made of or from, or chiefly of, asbestos. — **as·bes′tine** (-tĭn), *adj.*

As·ca′ni·us (ăs·kā′nĭ·ŭs), *n.* The son of Aeneas.

as′ca·rid (ăs′kȧ·rĭd), *n.* [Gr. *askaris* an intestinal worm.] *Zool.* Any nematode worm of a family (Ascaridae, type genus *Ascaris*) including the common roundworm (*A. lumbricoides*), parasitic in the human intestine.

as·cend′ (ă·sĕnd′), *v. i. & t.* [L. *ascendere,* fr. *ad-* + *scandere* to climb, mount.] 1. To go or move upward; mount; — opposed to *descend.* 2. Figuratively, to proceed from a lower to a higher position, degree, or the like; to rise. — **as·cend′a·ble, as·cend′i·ble,** *adj.*

Syn. Ascend, mount, climb, scale mean to move upward to or toward the top of something. Ascend implies little more than progressive upward movement; mount always distinctly implies reaching the top; climb suggests effort and the use of hands, feet, gears, or the like; scale suggests an even more difficult feat than *climb.* — **Ant.** Descend.

as·cend′ance (ă·sĕn′dăns), **as·cend′ence** (-dĕns), *n.* Ascendancy.

as·cend′an·cy (-dăn·sĭ), **as·cend′en·cy** (-dĕn·sĭ), *n.* Governing or controlling influence; domination. — **Syn.** See SUPREMACY.

as·cend′ant (-dănt), *n.* Also, less properly, **as·cend′ent** (-dĕnt). 1. *Astrol.* The aspect of the stars at a particular time, esp. at one's birth; horoscope; — supposed to have a commanding influence on a person's life and fortune. 2. Place of, or state of having, commanding power or influence; ascendancy; pre-eminence; as, to be in the *ascendant.* — *adj.* 1. Rising above the eastern horizon; hence, rising. 2. Superior; predominant; ruling. 3. *Bot.* Directed upwards, as a stem.

as·cend′ing, *adj.* 1. Rising. 2. *Bot.* **a** Rising obliquely upwards, esp. from a prostrate base. **b** Racemose.

as·cen′sion (ă·sĕn′shŭn), *n.* [OF., fr. L. *ascensio,* fr. *ascendere.*] 1. Act of ascending; a rising. 2. [*cap.,* with *the.*] The visible ascending of Jesus on the fortieth day after his resurrection. *Acts* i. 9. 3. *Astron.* See RIGHT ASCENSION.

as·cen′sion·al (-ăl; -′l), *adj.* Of or relating to ascension or ascent; as, the *ascensional* power of a balloon.

Ascension Day. The Thursday forty days after Easter, on which is commemorated Christ's ascension.

as·cen′sive (ă·sĕn′sĭv), *adj.* Rising or tending to rise.

as·cent′ (ă·sĕnt′), *n.* [Formed like *descent.* See ASCEND.] 1. Act of rising; rise. 2. Advancement in status or esteem. 3. A going up; as, the *ascent* of Mont Blanc. 4. An upward slope; acclivity. 5. Degree of upward slope; as, the road has an *ascent* of five degrees.

as′cer·tain′ (ăs′ẽr·tān′), *v. t.* [OF. *acertener,* fr. *a* to + *certain* certain.] To find out or learn for a certainty, by trial, examination, or experiment; to get to know. — **Syn.** See DISCOVER. — **as′cer·tain′a·ble,** *adj.* — **as′cer·tain′ment** (-mĕnt), *n.*

as·cet′ic (ă·sĕt′ĭk), *adj.* [Gr. *askētikos,* fr. *askein* to exercise.] Given to strict self-denial, esp. for the sake of spiritual or intellectual discipline; also, of, characteristic of, or befitting an ascetic. — **Syn.** See SEVERE. — *n.* A person who leads an ascetic life or practices asceticism.

as·cet′i·cal (-ĭ·kăl), *adj.* Pertaining to asceticism; ascetic.

as·cet′i·cal·ly, *adv.* of ASCETIC, ASCETICAL.

as·cet′i·cism (ă·sĕt′ĭ·sĭz′m), *n.* 1. The condition, practice, or mode of life of ascetics. 2. Doctrine that through self-torture or self-denial one can discipline himself to reach a high state, spiritually or intellectually. 3. A disciplinary course of conduct pursued as a means to a higher ideal.

as·cid′i·an (ă·sĭd′ĭ·ăn), *n.* [See ASCIDIUM.] *Zool.* **a** Any of an order (Ascidiacea) of simple or compound tunicates. Cf. SEA SQUIRT. **b** Sometimes, any tunicate.

as·cid′i·um (-ŭm), *n.; pl.* -IA (-ȧ). [NL., deriv. of Gr. *askos* bag.] *Bot.* A pitcher-shaped or flask-shaped organ or appendage of a plant, as the leaf of the pitcher plant.

as·ci′tes (ă·sī′tēz), *n.* [L., fr. Gr. *askitēs* (sc. *nosos* disease), fr. *askos* bladder, belly.] *Med.* Dropsy of the abdomen.

as·cle′pi·a·da′ceous (ăs·klē′pĭ·ȧ·dā′shŭs), *adj.* [Deriv. of L. *asclepias,* a certain plant.] *Bot.* Belonging to the milkweed family (Asclepiadaceae). See MILKWEED.

As·cle′pi·a·de′an (-dē′ăn), *adj.* Of or designating a variety of verse so called after the Greek poet Asclepiades.

As·cle′pi·us (ăs·klē′pĭ·ŭs), *n.* [Gr. *Asklēpios.*] In Homer, a physician; later, the Greek god of the healing art. See AESCULAPIAN.

as′co·carp (ăs′kō·kärp), *n.* [Gr. *askos* bladder + *-carp.*] *Bot.* In certain ascomycetes, the spherical, discoid, or cup-shaped body containing the asci and constituting the mature fruit. — **as′co·car′pous** (-kär′pŭs), *adj.*

as′co·go′ni·um (-gō′nĭ·ŭm), *n.; pl.* -NIA (-ȧ). [NL., fr. Gr. *askos* bladder + root of *gignesthai* to be born.] *Bot.* **a** The fertile portion of the archicarp in ascomycetes. **b** Sometimes, the archicarp itself. — **as′co·go′ni·al** (-ăl), *adj.*

as′co·my·cete′ (-mī·sēt′), *n.; pl.* -CETES (-sēts′; *not to be confused with the Latin class name* As′co·my·ce′tes). *Bot.* An ascomycetous fungus.

as′co·my·ce′tous (-sē′tŭs), *adj.* [Gr. *askos* bladder + *mykēs, mykētos,* fungus.] *Bot.* Belonging to a class (Ascomycetes) of higher fungi having their spores formed in asci, or spore sacs. The class includes the yeasts, molds, mildews, truffles, morels, etc.

a·scor′bic ac′id (ā·skôr′bĭk). [*a-,* 5 + *scorbutic* + *-ic.*] Vitamin C (see VITAMIN).

as′co·spore (ăs′kō·spōr; 70), *n.* [Gr. *askos* bladder + *spore.*] *Bot.* One of the spores contained in an ascus. — **as′co·spor′ic** (-spŏr′ĭk), **as·cos′po·rous** (ăs·kŏs′pō·rŭs; ăs′kō·spō′rŭs), *adj.*

as′cot (ăs′kŏt), *n.* A broad neck scarf tied to appear as in the illustration. — *adj.* [*cap.*] Pertaining to the famous racecourse and horse races at Ascot Heath, in Berkshire, England.

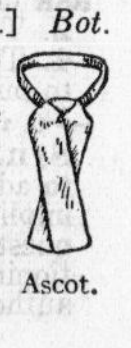
Ascot.

as·cribe′ (ăs·krīb′), *v. t.* [L. *ascribere* to ascribe, fr. *ad-* + *scribere* to write.] 1. To attribute, impute, or assign, as to a cause or source or author; as, his death was *ascribed* to a poison; a play *ascribed* to Shakespeare. 2. To attribute, as a quality; to consider or allege to belong. — **as·crib′a·ble** (ăs·krīb′*ȧ*·b'l), *adj.* — **as·crip′tion** (-krĭp′shŭn), *n.*

Syn. **Ascribe, attribute, impute, assign, refer, credit** mean to lay something to one's [person or thing] account. One **ascribes** to a person or thing something inferred or conjectured; one **attributes** something believed on good grounds to belong or to be appropriate to him or it; one **imputes** when one ascribes definitely and, often, by way of accusation, something to a person or, less often, a thing; one **assigns** something, such as a quality, a reason, or an origin, when one deliberately ascribes it to a person or thing and, usually, places it in a class, under a description, or the like; one **refers** a thing when one assigns it to the class to which it belongs or to its ultimate origin or cause; one **credits** someone *with* something, or something *to* someone, when one ascribes the thing to a person or another thing as its agent, source, or explanation.

as′cus (ăs′kŭs), *n.; pl.* ASCI (ăs′ī). [NL., fr. Gr. *askos* a bladder.] *Bot.* The membranous oval or tubular spore sac in ascomycetes.

as′dic (ăz′dĭk), *n.* [From the *A*nti-*S*ubmarine *D*etection *I*nvestigation *C*ommittee.] See SONAR.

-ase (-ās; -āz). [From ending of *diastase.*] *Biochem.* A suffix used in forming the names of enzymes, often by being added to the name, or part of the name, of a substance decomposed by the enzyme, as in amyl*ase*, prote*ase*, ur*ease*.

a·sep′sis (*ȧ*·sĕp′sĭs; ā-), *n.* [NL., fr *a-* not + *sepsis.*] State of being aseptic; also, aseptic methods, processes, etc.

a·sep′tic (-tĭk), *adj.* [*a-* not + *septic.*] Preventing or not involving sepsis; specif., free or freed from pathogenic microorganisms; as, *aseptic* surgery, characterized by precautions for the exclusion of bacteria, as distinguished from *antiseptic* surgery. — *n.* An aseptic preparation. — **a·sep′ti·cal·ly** (-tĭ·kăl·ĭ), *adv.*

a·sex′u·al (ā·sĕk′shŏŏ·ăl; *see* SEXUAL), *adj.* Having no sex; without sexual action. — **a·sex′u·al·ly**, *adv.*

asexual generation, asexual reproduction. See ALTERNATION OF GENERATIONS.

a·sex′u·al·ize (ā·sĕk′shŏŏ·ăl·īz), *v. t.* To render incapable of reproduction, as by castration. — **a·sex′u·al·i·za′tion** (-ĭ·zā′shŭn; -ī·zā′-), *n.*

As′gard (ăs′gärd), **As′garth** (-gärth), **As′gar′dhr** (-gär′thẽr), *n.* [ON. *āsgarthr*, fr. *āss* god + *garthr* yard.] *Norse Myth.* The abode or citadel of the gods, situated at the zenith and reached only by the bridge Bifrost.

ash (ăsh), *n.* [AS. *æsc.*] A timber and shade tree (genus *Fraxinus*) of the olive family, having pinnate leaves, thin furrowed bark, and ash-colored branchlets; also, its tough elastic wood. See SAMARA, *Illust.*

ash, *n., sing. of* ASHES. **1.** The solid residue left when combustible material is thoroughly burned at not too high a temperature. **2.** The color of wood ashes; a deathly pallor.

☞ *Ash* is used in the singular in connection with chemical, technical, and geological products; as, soda *ash.*

a·shamed′ (*ȧ*·shāmd′), *adj.* Affected by shame; also, reluctant through anticipation of shame; as, *ashamed* to beg. — **a·sham′ed·ly** (*ȧ*·shām′ĕd·lĭ; -ĭd·lĭ), *adv.*

A·shan′ti, A·shan′tee (*ȧ*·shăn′tĭ), *n.; pl.* -TIS, -TIES (-tĭz); -TEES (-tĭz). One of a native warlike race of Negroes of West Africa; also, their language.

ash can. **a** A metal receptacle for refuse. **b** *Slang.* A depth charge.

ash′en (ăsh′ĕn; -'n), *adj.* Of or pertaining to the ash tree, or made of its wood.

ash′en, *adj.* Of or resembling ashes; ash-colored.

Ash′er (ăsh′ẽr), *n. Bib.* See JACOB.

ash′es (ăsh′ĕz; -ĭz), *n. pl.* [AS. *asce, æsce, axe.*] **1.** The earthy or mineral parts of combustible substances remaining after combustion; specif., the remains of the human body after cremation or disintegration. **2.** Ruins or last traces, as of a civilization. **3.** Fine lava thrown out by a volcano. **4.** Mythical symbol contested for in international cricket matches, orig. and specif. between England and Australia.

ash gray. A color, greenish-yellow in hue, of low saturation and very high brilliance. See COLOR. — **ash′-gray′,** *adj.*

Ash′ke·naz′im (ăsh′kē·năz′ĭm), *n. pl.* [Heb.] The Jews of middle and northern Europe, as opposed to the Sephardim. — **Ash′ke·naz′ic** (-ĭk), *adj.*

ash′lar (ăsh′lẽr), *n.* Sometimes **ash′ler.** [From OF., fr. L. *axis*, for *assis*, plank, board.] Hewn or squared stone; also, a similar dressed stone, used for facing; masonry made of either.

a·shore′ (*ȧ*·shōr′; 70), *adv. & adj.* On or to the shore.

Ash′to·reth (ăsh′tō·rĕth), *n.; pl.* ASHTAROTH (-t*ȧ*·rōth; -rŏth). [Heb.] The goddess Astarte.

A′shur (ä′shŏŏr), *n.* The chief deity of the Assyrian pantheon, the god of military prowess and empire.

Ash Wednesday. The first day of Lent. See LENT; EASTER, *Table.*

ash′y (ăsh′ĭ), *adj.;* ASH′I·ER (-ĭ·ẽr); ASH′I·EST. **1.** Pertaining to, or composed of, ashes. **2.** Ashen; deadly pale.

A′sian (ā′zh*ă*n; ā′sh*ă*n), *adj. & n.* Asiatic.

A′si·at′ic (ā′zhĭ·ăt′ĭk; ā′shĭ-), *adj.* Of, pertaining to, or characteristic of Asia or its inhabitants. — *n.* A native, or one of the people, of Asia.

Asiatic beetle. A Japanese beetle (*Anomala orientalis*), introduced into Hawaii and New England, destructive of sugar cane and grass roots.

Asiatic cholera. See CHOLERA.

a·side′ (*ȧ*·sīd′), *adv.* **1.** To or toward the side; as, to step *aside.* **2.** Away; out of the way; as, to take or lay *aside.* **3.** Apart (by way of exclusion); as, jesting *aside.* — *n.* Something spoken aside, as a stage player's remark which the other players are supposed not to hear.

as′i·nine (ăs′ĭ·nīn), *adj.* [L. *asininus*, fr. *asinus* ass.] Of an ass; also, like an ass, as in stupidity or obstinacy. — **Syn.** See SIMPLE. — **as′i·nine·ly,** *adv.* — **as′i·nin′i·ty** (-nĭn′ĭ·tĭ), *n.*

ask (ȧsk; 9), *v. t.* [AS. *āscian, ācsian.*] **1.** To inquire of; question. **2.** To request; petition; solicit. **3.** To demand, claim, or expect. **4.** To need or call for; — of things. **5.** *Colloq.* To publish (banns); to publish banns of (a person or persons). **6.** To invite. — *v. i.* **1.** To make inquiry. **2.** To request or petition. — **ask′er,** *n.*

Syn. (1) **Ask, question, interrogate, query, inquire** (*or* **enquire**) mean to address a person in an attempt to elicit information. **Ask** merely implies the putting of a question; **question** usually suggests asking one question after another; **interrogate** suggests formal or systematic questioning; **query**, often used in place of *ask*, usually implies a desire for authoritative information or the resolution of a doubt; **inquire** fundamentally implies a search for facts or truth, but often specifically suggests asking such questions.

(2) **Ask, request, solicit** mean to seek to obtain by making one's wants known. **Ask** implies expectation of a response, especially an affirmative response (as, he *asked* the close attention of all); **request** suggests greater courtesy and formality and, so, is preferable when there is no clear expectation of a favorable response (as, to *request* an opportunity to express one's opinion); **solicit** implies calling attention to something in order to gain trade, subscriptions, or the like.

a·skance′ (*ȧ*·skăns′), *adv.* Also **a·skant′** (*ȧ*·skănt′). [Origin uncert.] Sideways; obliquely; hence, with disdain, envy, or distrust.

a·skew′ (*ȧ*·skū′), *adv. & adj.* [See SKEW.] Awry; to one side; crookedly or crooked.

a·slant′ (*ȧ*·slȧnt′; 9), *adv.* Slantingly; obliquely. — *adj.* Slanting. — *prep.* In a slanting direction over; athwart.

a·sleep′ (*ȧ*·slēp′), *adj. & adv.* **1.** In or into a state of sleep or inactivity; dormant. **2.** Dead. **3.** Numbed.

a·slope′ (*ȧ*·slōp′), *adv.* Slopingly; aslant. — *adj.* Sloping.

As′mo·de′us (ăz′mō·dē′ŭs; ăs′-), *n.* In Jewish demonology, an evil spirit; later, the king of the demons.

asp (ăsp), *n.* [L. *aspis*, fr. Gr. *aspis.*] A small venomous snake of Egypt, probably the horned viper (*Cerastes cornutus*), noted as being the means of Cleopatra's death. The name is also applied to other poisonous snakes, as the common European viper.

asp, *n. Poetic.* The aspen.

as·par′a·gus (ăs·păr′*ȧ*·gŭs), *n.* [L., fr. Gr. *asparagos, aspharagos.*] **1.** Any of a large genus (*Asparagus*) of Old World perennial plants of the lily-of-the-valley family, having much-branched stems and minute scalelike leaves. **2.** The tender shoots of one species (*A. officinalis*) of these plants, used as food.

as′pect (ăs′pĕkt), *n.* [L. *aspectus*, fr. *aspicere, aspectum*, to look at, fr. *ad-* + *spicere, specere*, to look.] **1.** *Rare.* Act of looking at; gaze. **2.** Position facing a particular direction; also, the part so facing. **3.** Look; countenance; mien; air. **4.** Appearance; view; — of objects, etc. **5.** State or phase in which anything appears or may be regarded. **6.** *Astrol.* The situation of planets or stars with respect to one another, or the visual angle of their light rays. **7.** *Gram.* In some languages, an inflectional category of the verb indicating action or state as beginning, continuing, terminating, etc.; hence, in languages without such an inflectional category, action or state expressed by the verb viewed as being inceptive, continued, completed, etc. In English, aspect is indicated chiefly by the meaning of the verb (to *begin, remain, stop*), by the progressive form (*is playing, singing*), or by an adverbial modifier used with the verb (to stand *up*, ride *away*). **8.** *Mech.* A view of a plane of an airplane from a given direction, usually from above; more exactly, the manner of presentation of a plane to a fluid (as the air) through which it is moving or to a current. — **Syn.** See PHASE.

as·pec′tu·al (ăs·pĕk′tū·ăl), *adj. Gram.* Of or pertaining to aspect.

as′pen (ăs′pĕn; ȧs′-; 9), *n.* [AS. *æsp, æps.*] Any of several poplars (esp. *Populus tremula* of Europe and *P. tremuloides* and *P. grandidentata* of North America) having leaves with flattened petioles, so that they flutter in the lightest wind. — *adj.* Of or resembling the aspen; hence, quivering; tremulous.

as′per (ăs′pẽr), *n.* [F. *aspre* or It. *aspero*, fr. MGr. *aspron, aspros*, white (new).] A Turkish money of account, 120th part of a piaster.

As·per′ges (ăs·pûr′jēz), *n.* [L., thou shalt sprinkle.] *Eccl.* **a** The ceremony of sprinkling altar, clergy, and people with holy water. **b** The anthem "Asperges me, Domine," etc., intoned during this ceremony.

as′per·gil′lum (ăs′pẽr·jĭl′ŭm), *n.; pl.* -LA (-*ȧ*), -LUMS (-ŭmz). [ML., fr. L. *aspergere.* See ASPERSE.] A brush or perforated globe, used for sprinkling holy water.

as′per·gil′lus (-ŭs), *n.; pl.* -LI (-ī). [ML. & NL. See ASPERGILLUM.] *Bot.* Any of certain fungi of a genus (*Aspergillus*, family Aspergillaceae) with brushlike sporophores. They include the common molds.

as·per′i·ty (ăs·pĕr′ĭ·tĭ), *n.; pl.* -TIES (-tĭz). [F. or L.; F. fr. L. *asperitas*, fr. *asper* rough.] **1.** Roughness; in *pl.*, rough places. **2.** Harshness; rigor; inclemency; sharpness of temper. — **Syn.** See ACRIMONY.

as·perse′ (ăs·pûrs′), *v. t.* [L. *aspersus*, past part. of *aspergere* to sprinkle, fr. *ad-* + *spargere* to strew.] **1.** *Now Rare.* To sprinkle; besprinkle. **2.** To bespatter with foul reports or false and injurious charges; to vilify; calumniate. — **Syn.** See MALIGN.

as·per′sion (-pûr′shŭn; -zhŭn), *n.* **1.** Act of aspersing. **2.** A sprinkling, shower, or spray. **3.** A calumnious remark; calumny. — **Syn.** See ANIMADVERSION.

as′per·so′ri·um (ăs′pẽr·sō′rĭ·ŭm), *n.; pl.* -RIA (-*ȧ*), -RIUMS (-ŭmz). [ML.] **a** The stoup or other holy-water vessel. **b** An aspergillum.

as′phalt (ăs′fôlt; -fălt), *n.* [F. *asphalte*, through LL., fr. Gr. *asphaltos.*] **1.** *Mineral.* A brown to black bitumen found in natural beds (natural or native asphalt), and also obtained as a residue from petroleums, etc. (artificial asphalt); mineral pitch. **2.** An asphaltic composition, used in paving, etc. — *v. t.* To cover or impregnate with asphalt. — **as′phalt,** *adj.* — **as·phal′tic** (ăs·fôl′tĭk; ăs·făl′-), *adj.*

as′pho·del (ăs′fō·dĕl), *n.* [From L., fr. Gr. *asphodelos.* See DAFFODIL.] **a** Any of a genus (*Asphodelus*) of plants of the lily family. Several species are cultivated for their flowers. **b** A plant belonging to any of several related genera (as *Asphodeline*). The asphodel of the early English and French poets was the daffodil. The asphodel of the Greek poets is supposed to be a narcissus.

as·phyx′i·a (ăs·fĭk′sĭ·*ȧ*), *n.* [NL., fr. Gr. *asphyxia*, fr. *a-* not + *sphyzein* to throb.] Suspended animation due to deficiency of oxygen and excess of carbon dioxide in the blood.

as·phyx′i·ant (-*ă*nt), *adj.* Producing asphyxia; asphyxiating. — *n.* An asphyxiating agent.

as·phyx′i·ate (-āt), *v. t.* To induce asphyxia in; to suffocate. — **as·phyx′i·a′tion** (-ā′shŭn), *n.* — **as·phyx′i·a′tor** (-ā′tẽr), *n.*

as′pic (ăs′pĭk), *n.* [F.] *Chiefly Poetic.* The asp.

as′pic, *n.* [F., fr. Pr. *espic*, fr. L. *spica* ear, spike.] A lavender (*Lavandula spica*), yielding a volatile oil.

as′pic, *n.* [F.] A savory meat jelly used to garnish meat or fish or to make a mold of meat, fish, etc.

as′pi·dis′tra (ăs′pĭ·dĭs′tr*ȧ*), *n.* [NL., fr. Gr. *aspis* shield + *astron* star.] An Asiatic plant (*Aspidistra lurida*), of the lily-of-the-valley family, with large basal leaves, often grown as a house plant.

as·pir′ant (ăs·pīr′*ă*nt; ăs′pĭ·r*ă*nt), *adj.* Aspiring. — *n.* [F.] One who aspires.

as′pi·rate (ăs′pĭ·rĭt), *n.* [L. *aspiratus*, past part. of *aspirare*, fr. *ad-* + *spirare* to breathe.] *Gram. & Phonet.* **a** The sound of *h*, or the letter *h;* also, any similar sound, as the Greek rough breathing, or the character representing it. **b** A sound followed by, or combined with, the sound of *h*, or a breath glide like *h*. — *adj.* Pronounced with an aspirate; accompanied by an *h* sound. — (-rāt), *v. t.* **1.** To pronounce with a breathing or aspirate. **2.** To draw by suction. **3.** *Med.* To treat by aspiration.

as′pi·ra′tion (ăs′pĭ·rā′shŭn), *n.* **1.** Act of breathing; a breath. **2.** Act of aspiring: **a** A desiring ardently; strong wish. **b** A longing for what is elevated or above one. — **Syn.** See AMBITION.

as′pi·ra′tion, *n.* **a** Pronunciation or addition of an aspirate; also, the aspirate or its symbol. **b** A drawing out by suction; specif., *Med.*, the removal of an abnormal fluid content from a cavity by means of an aspirator.

as′pi·ra′tor (ăs′pĭ·rā′tēr), *n.* **1.** Any apparatus, as a suction pump, for producing a movement of fluids by suction. **2.** *Med.* An instrument for the removal, by suction, of the abnormal fluid content of body cavities, cysts, etc.

as·pir′a·to′ry (ăs·pīr′ȧ·tō′rĭ *or, esp. Brit.,* -tēr·ĭ), *adj.* Pertaining to, or serving for, aspiration (i.e., breathing or suction).

as·pire′ (ăs·pīr′), *v. i.* [F. *aspirer*, fr. L. *aspirare*.] **1.** To desire with eagerness; to seek to attain something high or great; to long; — with *to* or *after*. **2.** To rise; tower; soar. — **as·pir′er** (-pīr′ēr), *n.*

as′pi·rin (ăs′pĭ·rĭn), *n.* [From acetyl + *spir*aeic acid (old name for salicylic acid) + *-in*.] *Pharm.* A white crystalline compound, the acetyl or acetate of salicylic acid, $C_9H_8O_4$, used as a remedy for pain or fever. *Aspirin* was originally a trade-mark.

a·squint′ (ȧ·skwĭnt′), *adv. & adj.* With the eye askance.

ass (ȧs; 9), *n.* [AS. *assa*.] **1.** Any of several quadrupeds (genus *Equus*), smaller than the horse, and having a shorter mane, shorter hair on the tail, and long ears; the donkey. The domestic ass is patient, slow, and sure-footed, and has become the type of obstinacy and stupidity. **2.** A dull, stupid person; a dolt.

as′sa·fet′i·da, as′sa·foet′i·da. Vars. of ASAFETIDA.

as′sa·gai, as′se·gai (ăs′ȧ·gī, ăs′ē-), *n.* [Pg. *azagaia*, of Berber origin.] **1.** A slender hardwood spear, usually tipped with iron, used by tribes in South Africa; a kind of light javelin. **2.** A South African tree (*Curtisia faginea*) of the dogwood family, from whose wood these spears were once made.

as·sai′ (ä·sä′ē), *n.* [Pg. *assahy*, fr. Tupi.] A slender Brazilian palm (*Euterpe edulis*) with dark-purple edible fruit; also, a drink or flavoring made from the fruit.

‖**as·sai′** (äs·sä′ē), *adv.* [It.] Very; enough.

as·sail′ (ă·sāl′), *v. t.* [From OF., fr. L. *ad* to + *salire* to leap.] To attack violently, esp. by repeated blows, words, etc.; to assault. — **Syn.** See ATTACK. — **as·sail′a·ble,** *adj.* — **as·sail′er,** *n.*

as·sail′ant (-ănt), *n.* One who assails.

as·sas′sin (ă·săs′ĭn), *n.* [F., fr. It. *assassino*, fr. Ar. *hashshāshīn* those addicted to *hashīsh* hemp.] **1.** [*cap.*] One of a Mohammedan secret order, which, at the time of the crusades, practiced secret murder, committed under the influence of hashish. **2.** One who kills by surprise or by secret or treacherous assault; esp., a hired or appointed murderer.

as·sas′si·nate (ă·săs′ĭ·nāt), *v. t.* [ML. *assassinatus*, past part. of *assassinare*.] **1.** To kill by surprise or by secret or treacherous assault. **2.** To injure or destroy, as reputation. — **Syn.** See KILL. — **as·sas′si·na′tor** (-nā′tēr), *n.*

as·sas′si·na′tion (-nā′shŭn), *n.* Act of assassinating; a killing by treacherous violence.

assassin bug. Any of certain insects constituting a family (Reduviidae, order Hemiptera), living mostly by sucking the blood of other insects.

as·sault′ (ă·sôlt′), *n.* [From OF., deriv. of L. *ad* to + *saltus* a leaping, fr. *salire* to leap.] **1.** A violent onset or attack; onslaught, literally, as by means of blows, weapons, etc., or figuratively, as by words, arguments, etc. **2.** *Law.* An apparently violent attempt, or a willful offer with force or violence, to do hurt to another, without the actual doing of the hurt threatened, as by lifting the fist or a cane in a threatening manner; as, guilty of *assault* and battery; including, in Scots law, the actual doing of the hurt, that is, a *battery*. **3.** The crime of rape; — a euphemism. **4.** *Mil.* The final phase of an attack. — **Syn.** Attack, onslaught, onset. — *v. t.* To make an assault upon; to attack. — **Syn.** See ATTACK. — *v. i.* To make an assault. — **as·sault′er,** *n.*

assault, *or* **storm, boat.** *Mil.* A lightly armored portable boat, equipped with outboard motor and holding 11 men, for gaining a foothold on an enemy-held riverbank or for supporting a ponton bridge.

as·say′ (ă·sā′; *in senses* 2 & 3, *also* ăs′ā, *esp. when used attributively*), *n.* [OF. *asai, essai*, trial. See ESSAY, *n.*] **1.** *Obs.* Trial; attempt; essay. **2.** Examination and determination as to weight, measure, quality, etc.; test. **3.** Analysis, as of an ore, drug, etc., to determine the presence or absence of one or more ingredients. **4.** The substance to be assayed; also, the tabulated result of assaying. — (ă·sā′), *v. t. & i.* **1.** To try; attempt; also, formerly, to test. **2.** To subject to assay, or analysis. **3.** To appraise critically. — **Syn.** See ATTEMPT. — **as·say′er,** *n.*

as′se·gai. Var. of ASSAGAI.

as·sem′blage (ă·sĕm′blĭj), *n.* [F.] **1.** Act of assembling; state of being assembled. **2.** A collection of individuals, or of particular things; an aggregation; as, a political *assemblage*. **3.** The fitting together of parts and pieces, as of machinery.

as·sem′ble (-b'l), *v. t.*; -BLED (-b'ld); -BLING (-blĭng). [From OF., fr. L. *assimulare* to bring together, fr. *ad-* + *simul* together.] **1.** To collect into one place or body; convoke; congregate. **2.** To fit together the parts of. — *v. i.* To meet together; convene; congregate. — **Syn.** See GATHER. — **as·sem′bler** (-blēr), *n.*

as·sem′bly (ă·sĕm′blĭ), *n.*; *pl.* -BLIES (-blĭz). [OF. *assemblee*.] **1.** A gathering of persons, esp. for deliberation and legislation, or for worship; a concourse. **2.** [*cap.*] Specif., the legislature or the popular branch of it; — in some states of the United States called *General Assembly*. **3.** Act of coming together; state of being assembled. **4.** *Mil.* A signal, as by drum, for troops to assemble, or fall in. **5.** The act or process of building up a complete unit, as a motor vehicle, from parts already manufactured; also, a collection of parts assembled in such a process.

assembly line. A grouping of machines, equipment, and workers so that work passes from operation to operation in direct line until the product is assembled.

as·sem′bly·man (-măn), *n.* A member of an assembly, esp. [*cap.*] of the lower branch of a state legislature.

as·sent′ (ă·sĕnt′), *v. i.* [OF. *assenter*, fr. L. *assentare, -ari*, fr. *assentire*, fr. *ad-* + *sentire* to feel, think.] **1.** To give or express one's concurrence, acquiescence, or compliance; to consent. **2.** To admit a thing as true; give adherence to a proposition or point of view.

Syn. Assent, consent, accede, acquiesce, agree, subscribe mean to concur with what someone else has proposed. **Assent** implies an act of understanding and applies to opinions or propositions; **consent** involves the will or the feelings and indicates compliance with what is requested or desired; **accede** implies a yielding of assent or consent; **acquiesce** implies tacit acceptance or forbearance of opposition; **agree** usually implies previous difference of opinion or attempts at persuasion but always suggests final concurrence; **subscribe** not only implies consent or assent, but hearty approval. — **Ant.** Dissent.

— *n.* Act of assenting; agreement, as with a proposal.

as′sen·ta′tion (ăs′ĕn·tā′shŭn), *n.* Ready assent, esp. when insincere or obsequious.

as·sen′tor (ă·sĕn′tēr), *n.* One who assents; specif., *Eng. Law*, one of the voters, in addition to the proposer and seconder, required to endorse the nomination of a candidate.

as·sert′ (ă·sûrt′), *v. t.* [L. *assertus*, past part. of *asserere* to join to oneself, claim, maintain, fr. *ad-* + *serere* to join.] **1.** To state positively; affirm; aver. **2.** To maintain; vindicate a claim or title to; as, to *assert* one's rights.

Syn. (1) Assert, declare, affirm, aver, protest, avouch, avow mean to state positively either in anticipation or in the face of denial or objection. **Assert** implies such sureness that the speaker or writer is indifferent to evidence; **declare**, as here considered, adds to *assert* the implication of open or public statement; **affirm** implies conviction of truth and willingness to stand by one's statement because of evidence, experience, or faith; **aver** suggests complete confidence and certitude; **protest** (see also OBJECT) stresses emphasis in affirmation, especially in the face of doubt or contradiction; **avouch** and **avow** impute authority or personal knowledge to the one who makes a statement.
(2) See MAINTAIN.

assert oneself. To claim or vindicate one's rights or position; to demand and compel recognition.

as·sert′er, as·ser′tor (ă·sûr′tēr), *n.* One who asserts.

as·ser′tion (ă·sûr′shŭn), *n.* The act of asserting; specif., a positive declaration or averment.

as·ser′tive (-tĭv), *adj.* Disposed to assertion; positive; aggressive. — **Syn.** See AGGRESSIVE. — **as·ser′tive·ly,** *adv.* — **as·ser′tive·ness,** *n.*

as·ser′to·ry (ă·sûr′tō·rĭ), *adj.* Affirming.

ass'es' bridge (ăs′ĕz; -ĭz; 30). [Trans. of L. *pons asinorum*.] *Humorous.* The proposition that "The angles at the base of an isosceles triangle are equal to one another."

as·sess′ (ă·sĕs′), *v. t.* [From OF., fr. LL. *assessare* to value for taxation, fr. L. *assidēre, assessum*, to sit by, in LL. to assess.] **1.** To fix the rate or amount of; as, to *assess* damages at $150. **2.** To apportion (a sum payable) in the nature of a tax, fine, etc. **3.** To impose (a tax, fine, etc.) on or upon; to tax. **4.** To set a value on; to appraise; specif., to make a valuation or official estimate of (property) for the purpose of taxation; as, *assessed* valuation is often less than market value. — **Syn.** See ESTIMATE. — **as·sess′a·ble,** *adj.*

as·sess′ment (-mĕnt), *n.* **1.** Act of assessing. **2.** Amount or value assessed.

as·ses′sor (ă·sĕs′ēr), *n.* [From OF., fr. L. *assessor*, lit., one who sits beside.] **1.** One who sits by another, as next in dignity, or as an adviser. **2.** One appointed to assess property for taxation. — **as′ses·so′ri·al** (ăs′ĕ·sō′rĭ·ăl; 70), *adj.*

as′set (ăs′ĕt), *n.* **1.** Any item of value owned. **2.** That which is a resource; as, character is an *asset*.

as′sets (ăs′ĕts), *n. pl.* [From OF. (pl. of *asset* thing assigned), fr. *asseter* to assign, set, fr. VL. *adsidere*, fr. *ad* at + *sedere* to seat.] **1.** *Law.* **a** The property of a deceased person subject by law to payment of his debts and legacies. **b** The entire property of a person, corporation, or estate, applicable to payment of his or its debts. **2.** The items on the balance sheet of a business showing the book value of its resources, as real property, cash, etc., at any given date.

as·sev′er·ate (ă·sĕv′ēr·āt), *v. t.* [L. *asseveratus*, past part. of *asseverare* to assert seriously, fr. *ad-* + *severus* severe.] To affirm or aver positively or earnestly. — **as·sev′er·a′tion** (-ā′shŭn), *n.*

as′si·du′i·ty (ăs′ĭ·dū′ĭ·tĭ), *n.*; *pl.* -TIES (-tĭz). Quality or state of being assiduous; diligence.

as·sid′u·ous (ă·sĭd′ū·ŭs), *adj.* [L. *assiduus*, fr. *assidēre* to sit near, fr. *ad-* + *sedēre* to sit.] Performed with constant diligence or attention; persistent; devoted; attentive; unremitting. — **Syn.** See BUSY. — **as·sid′u·ous·ly,** *adv.* — **as·sid′u·ous·ness,** *n.*

as·sign′ (ă·sīn′), *v. t.* [OF. *assigner*, fr. L. *assignare*, fr. *ad-* + *signare* to mark, designate, fr. *signum* mark.] **1.** To appoint; prescribe. **2.** To fix, specify, or designate; to determine authoritatively or exactly. **3.** To allot; apportion. **4.** To ascribe, as a motive; allege, as a reason. **5.** *Law.* To transfer or make over (property) to another, esp. for the benefit of creditors. — **Syn.** See ALLOT: ASCRIBE. — *v. i.* *Law.* To assign property. — *n.* An assignee; as, payable to his *assigns*.

as·sign′a·ble (-ȧ·b'l), *adj.* That may be assigned; as, an *assignable* reason. — **as·sign′a·bil′i·ty** (-bĭl′ĭ·tĭ), *n.* — **as·sign′a·bly,** *adv.*

as′sig·nat (ăs′ĭg·năt; *F.* ȧ′sē′nyȧ′), *n.* [F., fr. L. *assignatus*, past part. See ASSIGN, *v.*] A note issued as currency by the French Revolutionary government (1790–95) and based on the security of the lands which had been appropriated by the state.

as′sig·na′tion (ăs′ĭg·nā′shŭn), *n.* **1.** An assigning; apportionment; assignment. **2.** That which is assigned. **3.** An appointment for a meeting, esp. a love tryst; — now commonly in a bad sense.

as′sign·ee′ (ăs′ĭ·nē′), *n.* *Law.* A person to whom an assignment is made; also, one appointed to perform a duty, enjoy some right, etc.

as·sign′er (ă·sīn′ēr), **as′sign·or′** (ăs′ĭ·nôr′), *n.* One who assigns, or makes an assignment.

as·sign′ment (ă·sīn′mĕnt), *n.* **1.** The act of assigning; the fact of being assigned; also, that which is assigned. **2.** *Law.* Transfer of a title or interest by writing; also, the written instrument by which such transfer is effected. **3.** A duty or piece of work allotted as the responsibility of a particular person or group. — **Syn.** See TASK.

as·sim′i·la·ble (ă·sĭm′ĭ·lȧ·b'l), *adj.* That may be assimilated. — **as·sim′i·la·bil′i·ty** (-bĭl′ĭ·tĭ), *n.*

as·sim′i·late (-lāt), *v. t.* [L. *assimilatus*, past part. of *assimilare*, fr. *ad-* + *similare* to make like, fr. *similis* like.] **1.** To make similar or alike. **2.** To liken; to compare. **3.** To appropriate and incorporate into the substance of the appropriating body; to absorb; as, food is *assimilated* by the body; the community *assimilated* persons of many nationalities. — **Syn.** See ABSORB. — *v. i.* To be or become assimilated. — *n.* That which is assimilated.

as·sim′i·la′tion (ă·sĭm′ĭ·lā′shŭn), *n.* 1. Act or process of assimilating. 2. *Phonet.* Conformation of a sound, usually a consonant, to a neighboring sound, as when the voiced *b* of *gooseberry* voices the preceding *s* to a *z*-sound. 3. a *Physiol.* The conversion or incorporation of nutritive material into the fluid or solid substance of the body. b *Bot.* Photosynthesis together with root absorption.

as·sim′i·la′tive (ă·sĭm′ĭ·lā′tĭv), *adj.* Tending to, characterized by, or causing assimilation. — **as·sim′i·la′tive·ness**, *n.*

as·sim′i·la·to′ry (-là·tō′rĭ; -tẽr·ĭ), *adj.* Assimilative.

as·sist′ (ă·sĭst′), *v. i.* [F. *assister*, fr. L. *assistere*, fr. *ad-* + *sistere* to cause to stand, fr. *stare* to stand.] 1. To lend aid; help. 2. *A Gallicism.* To be present as a spectator. 3. *Sports.* To make an assist. — *v. t.* To give support to; help; aid; succor. — **Syn.** See HELP. — **Ant.** Hamper. — *n.* Act or instance of assisting; specif., *Sports*, act of a player who helps another, as in making a put-out in baseball or in scoring a goal in ice hockey.

as·sist′ance (ă·sĭs′tăns), *n.* [F.] Help; aid; support.

as·sist′ant (-tănt), *adj.* That assists; helping; specif., acting as a subordinate; as, *assistant* clerk. — *n.* 1. One who assists; a helper. 2. A means of help; an aid.

as·size′ (ă·sīz′), *n.* [OF. *assise* session, settlement, deriv. of L. *assidēre* to sit by, fr. *ad-* + *sedēre* to sit.] 1. Literally, an assembly; hence, a decree or enactment made by it. 2. *Hist.* A statute or ordinance regulating weights and measures, or the weight, measure, proportions of ingredients, or price of articles sold in the market. 3. A fixed or customary standard of number, quantity, quality, weight, measure, etc.; as, rent of *assize*. 4. A judicial inquest; an action to be decided thereat; the writ for instituting it, or the verdict rendered by the jury. 5. Usually *pl.* a The periodical sessions of the judges of the superior courts in every county of England. b The time or place of holding a court of assize; the court; a session of it.

as·so′ci·a·ble (ă·sō′shĭ·à·b′l; -shà·b′l; -sĭ·à·b′l), *adj.* [F.] Capable of being associated, esp. associated in thought or feeling. — **as·so′ci·a·bil′i·ty** (-bĭl′ĭ·tĭ), *n.*

as·so′ci·ate (ă·sō′shĭ·āt; -sĭ·āt), *v. t.* [L. *associatus*, past part. of *associare*, fr. *ad-* + *sociare* to join, fr. *socius* companion.] 1. To join as a friend, companion, partner, or confederate; as, to *associate* others with us in business. 2. To join; combine; as, gold *associated* with copper. 3. To connect in thought, as ideas. — *v. i.* To unite in company; to be or go together as companions; also, to unite in action; join for a common purpose. — **Syn.** See JOIN.

— (-āt), *adj.* 1. Closely joined with another, as in interest, action, office, etc.; as, an *associate* judge. 2. Accompanying; concomitant; as, *associate* virtues. 3. Admitted to some, but not to all, rights and privileges; as, an *associate* member.

— (-āt), *n.* 1. One associated with another, as in an undertaking. 2. One often in company with another, implying intimacy or equality. 3. Anything closely or usually connected with another. 4. One having an interest in common with another, as a partner, a confederate, a colleague in office, etc.; specif., an associate member of an association or institution. — **Syn.** Companion, crony, pal, comrade.

as·so′ci·a′tion (-sĭ·ā′shŭn; -shĭ·ā′shŭn; 103), *n.* 1. An associating, or state of being associated; confederation; fellowship. 2. A body of persons organized for some common purpose; as, a scientific *association*. Abbr. *assoc., assn.* 3. *Psychol.* Any mental connection established by a process of learning. — **as·so′ci·a′tion·al**, *adj.*

association football. See FOOTBALL, 2.

as·so′ci·a′tive (ă·sō′shĭ·ā′tĭv; ă·sō′sĭ-; -à·tĭv), *adj.* Tending to, inducing, or characterized by association. — **as·so′ci·a′tive·ly**, *adv.*

as·soil′ (ă·soil′), *v. t.* [From OF., fr. L. *absolvere*. See ABSOLVE.] *Archaic.* 1. To absolve. 2. To expiate.

as′so·nance (ăs′ō·năns), *n.* [F., fr. L. *assonans*, pres. part. of *assonare* to correspond to in sound, fr. *ad-* + *sonare* to sound, fr. *sonus* sound.] 1. Resemblance of sound in words or syllables. 2. *Pros.* A correspondence in sound of one word with another in the accented vowel and those that follow, the consonants of the two words being unlike; as, *story* and *holy*. — **as′so·nant** (-nănt), *adj. & n.*

as·sort′ (ă·sôrt′), *v. t.* [F. *assortir*, fr. *à* to + *sorte* sort, kind. See SORT.] 1. To distribute into classes; classify. 2. To make up of a variety of goods; as, to *assort* a cargo. — *v. i.* 1. To be adapted; to suit. 2. To consort or associate (with). — **as·sort′er** (ă·sôr′tẽr), *n.*

Syn. **Assort, sort, classify, alphabetize, pigeonhole** mean to arrange according to some system or method. **Assort** implies division into groups but, apart from the context, suggests no clear principle of arrangement; **sort** comes close to *assort* but is less formal or technical in use; **classify** more often is used of things that fall into intellectual categories than to those which can be physically grouped; **alphabetize** applies only to material that lends itself to arrangement in alphabetical order; **pigeonhole** is a picturesque term implying an assorting or classifying that suggests a distribution similar to that of putting in pigeonholes, or compartments in a desk, a file, etc.

as·sort′ed (ă·sôr′tĕd; -tĭd), *adj.* Classified; made up of various sorts; hence, miscellaneous.

as·sort′ment (ă·sôrt′mĕnt), *n.* 1. Act of assorting; also, assorted condition. 2. A group formed by assorting.

as·suage′ (ă·swāj′), *v. t.*; -SUAGED′ (-swājd′); -SUAG′ING (-swāj′ĭng). [From OF., fr. L. *ad* to + *suavis* sweet.] To ease or lessen, as heat, pain, or grief; to appease or pacify, as passion; to satisfy or quench, as appetite or thirst. — **Syn.** See RELIEVE. — **as·suage′ment**, *n.*

as·sua′sive (ă·swā′sĭv), *adj.* Mitigating; soothing.

as·sume′ (ă·sūm′), *v. t.* [L. *assumere*, fr. *ad-* + *sumere* to take, fr. *sub* under + *emere* to take, buy.] 1. To take into association, partnership, service, use, etc.; as, the board *assumed* a new member. 2. To take to or upon oneself; as, the amoeba *assumes* various shapes; to *assume* new duties. 3. To pretend to possess; affect; feign. 4. To appropriate; usurp. 5. To take for granted; suppose. — **as·sum′a·ble** (-sūm′à·b′l), *adj.*

Syn. **Assume, affect, pretend, simulate, feign, counterfeit, sham** mean to put on a false or deceptive appearance. **Assume** often implies a pardonable motive rather than an intent to deceive; **affect** implies a show of possessing or using, sometimes for effect, sometimes out of genuine liking; **pretend** implies overt profession or exhibition of that which is false; **simulate** suggests an assumed appearance by imitating the signs; **feign** implies more invention than *pretend*, less specific imitation of life than *simulate*; **counterfeit** implies the highest degree of verisimilitude of any of these words; **sham** implies the lowest degree that fools only the gullible.

as·sumed′ (ă·sūmd′), *adj.* a Appropriated. b Supposed. c Pretended; make-believe. d Fictitious.

as·sum′ing (ă·sūm′ĭng), *adj.* Pretentious or presumptuous. — *n.* Pretension; presumption.

as·sump′sit (ă·sŭmp′sĭt; ă·sŭm′sĭt), *n.* [L., he undertook.] *Law.* 1. An action on contract to recover damages for a breach of contract. 2. A promise or contract, not under seal, on which such action may be brought.

as·sump′tion (-shŭn), *n.* 1. The taking up of a person into heaven; specif. [*cap.*], the taking up of the Virgin Mary; also, a church feast (August 15) commemorating this. 2. Act of taking for or upon oneself; also, appropriation; usurpation. 3. Arrogance. 4. Act of taking for granted; supposition; also, the thing assumed; a supposition.

as·sump′tive (-tĭv), *adj.* Assumed; characterized by assumption; assuming; arrogant.

as·sur′ance (ă·shŏŏr′ăns), *n.* 1. An assuring; a pledge or guarantee. 2. Insurance. See INSURANCE. 3. State of being assured or sure; specif.: a Security; safety. b Certitude; certainty. 4. Firmness of mind; confidence; self-reliance. 5. Impudence; audacity. — **Syn.** See CERTAINTY; CONFIDENCE.

as·sure′ (ă·shŏŏr′; 84), *v. t.* [From OF., fr. LL., fr. L. *ad* to + *securus* secure.] 1. *Obs.* To make safe. 2. To secure, as against change or risk; insure (see INSURE). 3. To confirm; give confidence to; as, his kindly manner *assured* them. 4. To make (one) sure or certain; as, he *assures* them of his regret. 5. To state confidently to; as, I *assure* you that it is true. 6. To make (a thing) certain; as, to *assure* the presence of the prisoner. — **Syn.** See ENSURE. — **as·sur′a·ble** (ă·shŏŏr′à·b′l), *adj.*

as·sured′ (ă·shŏŏrd′), *adj.* 1. Made sure; insured; sure; indubitable. 2. Confident; also, bold to excess. — *n.* a In property insurance, the party in whose favor a policy stands. b The person whose life is insured. — **as·sur′ed·ly** (ă·shŏŏr′ĕd·lĭ), *adv.* — **as·sur′ed·ness**, *n.*

as·sur′er (ă·shŏŏr′ẽr), *n.* One who assures; an insurer.

as·sur′gent (ă·sûr′jĕnt), *adj.* [L. *assurgens*, pres. part., fr. L. *assurgere* to rise up.] Ascending; specif., *Bot.*, rising obliquely; — said of stems. — **as·sur′gen·cy** (-jĕn·sĭ), *n.*

As·syr′i·an (ă·sĭr′ĭ·ăn), *adj.* Of or pertaining to Assyria, the Assyrians, or their language. — *n.* 1. An individual of an ancient Semitic race forming the Assyrian nation; — often including Babylonian Semites. 2. The language of the Assyrians.

As·syr′i·ol′o·gy (-ŏl′ō·jĭ), *n.* [*Assyria* + *-logy*.] The science or study of the antiquities, language, etc., of ancient Assyria. — **As·syr′i·ol′o·gist** (-jĭst), *n.*

As·tar′te (ăs·tär′tē), *n.* [L., fr. Gr. *Astartē*.] The Phoenician goddess of fertility and of sexual love, the west Semitic form of Ishtar.

a·stat′ic (ā·stăt′ĭk), *adj.* [*a-* not + *static*.] 1. Not stable or steady. 2. *Physics.* Not taking a fixed or definite position or direction; as, two suspended parallel magnetic needles of equal but opposed magnetic moments are *astatic*. — **-i·cal·ly** (-ĭ·kăl·ĭ), *adv.* — **-i·cism** (-ĭ·sĭz′m), *n.*

as′ta·tine (ăs′tà·tēn; -tĭn), *n.* [Gr. *astatos* unstable.] *Chem.* An unstable element of the halogen family, discovered by bombarding bismuth with alpha particles. Symbol, *At*; at. no., 85.

as′ter (ăs′tẽr), *n.* [L., fr. Gr. *astēr* star. See STAR.] 1. Any of various, chiefly fall-blooming, leafy-stemmed herbs (genus *Aster* and closely allied genera) typifying a very large family (Carduaceae, the aster or thistle family), distinguished by heads containing tubular flowers or both tubular and ray flowers. It includes the ***New England aster*** (*Aster novae-angliae*) of eastern North America, with showy purplish flowers; the ***China aster***, any of various garden annuals derived from the Chinese herb *Callistephus chinensis;* and the ***golden aster*** (genus *Chrysopsis*, esp. *C. mariana*), of America, so called from its yellow rays. 2. *Biol.* A star-shaped figure of achromatic substance found chiefly in cells dividing by mitosis; a cytaster. It consists of a central mass, the *centrosphere* or *attraction sphere*, which in animal and some plant cells often contains a *centrosome*, and radiating fibers called the **aster rays**.

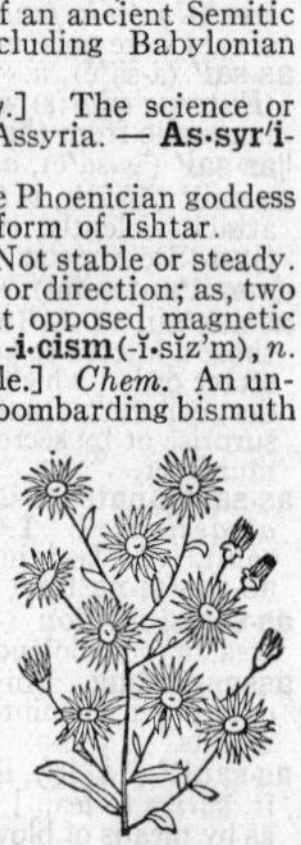
Aster (*A. novae-angliae*). (1/8)

-as′ter (-ăs′tẽr). [Gr. *astēr*.] A suffix meaning *star*, used in *Biol.:* a For structural names, as in di*aster*. b For generic names, as in Ge*aster* (see EARTHSTAR).

-as′ter. [L.] A suffix denoting originally *diminution* or *partial resemblance* (as in ole*aster*), now usually *inferiority* (as in poet*aster*).

as′ter·a′ceous (ăs′tẽr·ā′shŭs), *adj.* *Bot.* Carduaceous.

as·te′ri·at′ed (ăs·tē′rĭ·āt′ĕd; -ĭd), *adj.* [Gr. *asterias* starred.] *Cryst.* Exhibiting asterism. See ASTERISM, 2.

as′ter·isk (ăs′tẽr·ĭsk), *n.* [From L., fr. Gr. *asteriskos*, dim. of *astēr* star.] 1. The figure of a star [*], used in printing and writing to refer to a marginal note, etc., to indicate omission of letters or words, to mark a word or item as of some special character, etc. 2. Anything shaped like a star. — *v. t.* To mark with an asterisk; to star.

as′ter·ism (-ĭz′m), *n.* [Gr. *asterismos*.] 1. *Astron.* a A constellation. b A small group of stars. 2. *Cryst.* The optical phenomenon of a star-shaped figure exhibited by some crystals by reflected light, as in star sapphire, or by transmitted light, as in some mica. 3. *Print.* Three asterisks placed thus, ⁂, for special reference.

a·stern′ (à·stûrn′), *adv.* 1. Behind a vessel; in the rear. 2. Backward; to the rear.

a·ster′nal (ā·stûr′năl; -n′l), *adj.* [See A- not.] *Anat.* a Unattached to the sternum, as the floating ribs. b Having no sternum, as snakes and turtles.

as′ter·oid (ăs′tẽr·oid), *adj.* [Gr. *asteroeidēs*, fr. *astēr* star. See -OID.] 1. Starlike. 2. Of or like a starfish. — *n.* 1. *Astron.* A starlike body; esp., one of many small planets with orbits between Mars and Jupiter. 2. *Zool.* = STARFISH. — **as′ter·oi′dal** (-oi′dăl; -d′l), *adj.* — **as′ter·oi′de·an** (-dē·ăn), *adj. & n.*

as·the′ni·a (ăs·thē′nĭ·à; ăs′thē·nī′à), *n.* [NL., fr. Gr. *astheneia*, fr. *a-* not + *sthenos* strength.] *Med.* Lack or loss of strength; debility.

as·then′ic (ăs·thĕn′ĭk), *adj.* a *Med.* Pertaining to asthenia; weak; debilitating. b *Anthropol.* Characterized by slender build and slight muscular development. — *n.* An asthenic person.

asth′ma (ăz′mà; ăs′mà; *see note below*), *n.* [Gr., short-drawn breath.] A disease characterized by difficulty of breathing, accompanied with a wheezing sound, a sense of constriction in the chest, a cough, and expectoration. — **asth·mat′ic** (ăz·măt′ĭk; ăs-), *adj. & n.* — **asth·mat′i·cal** (-ĭ·kăl), *adj.* — **asth·mat′i·cal·ly**, *adv.*

☞ ăz′mà, ăs′mà, ăsth′mà, and ăst′mà are all in current good use, but ăz′mà decidedly prevails in America.

as′tig·mat′ic (ăs′tĭg·măt′ĭk), *adj.* Affected with, pertaining to, or correcting astigmatism; as, *astigmatic* lenses.

a·stig′ma·tism (*à*·stĭg′m*à*·tĭz′m), *n.* [*a-* not + Gr. *stigma, stigmatos,* prick of a pointed instrument, spot.] A defect of an optical system, as a lens, or of the eye, in consequence of which rays from one point of an object are not brought to a single focal point, thus causing imperfect images or indistinctness of vision.

a·stir′ (*à*·stûr′), *adj.* Stirring; active; out of bed.

a·stom′a·tous (ā·stŏm′*à*·tŭs; ā·stō′m*à*-), *adj.* *Biol.* Not possessing a stoma or stomata.

as·ton′ied (ăs·tŏn′ĭd), *adj.* *Archaic.* Dazed; dismayed.

as·ton′ish (ăs·tŏn′ĭsh), *v. t.* [OF. *estoner,* fr. L. *ex* out + *tonare* to thunder.] To strike with sudden fear or wonder; astound; amaze. — **Syn.** See SURPRISE. — **as·ton′ish·er,** *n.* — **as·ton′ish·ing,** *adj.* — **as·ton′ish·ing·ly,** *adv.*

as·ton′ish·ment (-mĕnt), *n.* **1.** State of one astonished; esp., amazement. **2.** An object causing such an emotion.

as·tound′ (ăs·tound′), *adj.* [ME., past part. of *astonen* to astonish.] *Archaic.* Astounded. — *v. t.* To stun with bewildered wonder. — **Syn.** See SURPRISE. — **as·tound′ing,** *adj.* — **as·tound′ing·ly,** *adv.*

as′tra·chan (ăs′tr*à*·kăn), *n.* **1.** Var. of ASTRAKHAN. **2.** [*cap.*] *Hort.* An apple of Russian origin, having white and red varieties.

a·strad′dle (*à*·străd′'l), *adj.* Straddling; astride.

As·trae′a (ăs·trē′*à*), *n.* [L., fr. Gr. *Astraia,* fr. *astraios* starry.] *Gr. Myth.* Goddess of justice, the last of the divinities to leave the earth at the end of the golden age.

as′tra·gal (ăs′tr*à*·găl), *n.* [L. *astragalus,* fr. Gr. *astragalos.*] **1.** The astragalus, or anklebone. **2.** *Arch.* A small convex molding of rounded surface. See MOLDING, *Illust.* — **as·trag′a·lar** (ăs·trăg′*à*·lẽr), *adj.*

as·trag′a·lus (ăs·trăg′*à*·lŭs), *n.; pl.* -LI (-lī). [L. See ASTRAGAL.] **1.** *Anat.* One of the proximal bones of the tarsus of the higher vertebrates. In man it is called the *talus* or *anklebone.* **2.** *Arch.* An astragal.

as′tra·khan (ăs′tr*à*·kăn), *n.* Also **as′tra·chan.** [From *Astrakhan,* Russia.] **1.** The long curled fur or skin of young karakul lambs. See PERSIAN LAMB; KARAKUL, 2. **2.** A rough cloth imitating it, or a substitute made from mohair.

as′tral (ăs′trăl), *adj.* [L. *astralis,* fr. *astrum* star, fr. Gr. *astron.*] **1.** Pertaining to, coming from, or like the stars; starry. **2.** *Alchemy.* Determined in its character or kind by an emanation from the planets; as, *astral* gold. **3.** *Biol.* Of or pertaining to an aster; as, *astral* rays. **4.** *Theos.* Consisting of, belonging to, or designating a kind of supersensible substance alleged to be next above the tangible world in refinement; as, *astral* spirits.

a·stray′ (*à*·strā′), *adv.* Out of the right way. — *adj.* Straying; wrong.

as·trict′ (ăs·trĭkt′), *v. t.* [L. *astrictus.* See ASTRINGE.] To bind up; confine; restrict; also, to bind by a moral or legal obligation. — **as·tric′tion** (-trĭk′shŭn), *n.*

as·tric′tive (-trĭk′tĭv), *adj. & n.* Astringent. — **as·tric′tive·ly,** *adv.* — **as·tric′tive·ness,** *n.*

a·stride′ (*à*·strīd′), *adj.* With the legs striding, or one leg on each side; astraddle. — *prep.* Astride of.

as·tringe′ (ăs·trĭnj′), *v. t.;* -TRINGED′ (-trĭnjd′); -TRING′ING (-trĭn′jĭng) [L. *astringere,* past part. *astrictus,* fr. *ad-* + *stringere* to draw tight.] To bind fast; constrict; compress.

as·trin′gen·cy (-trĭn′jĕn·sĭ), *n.* Quality of being astringent.

as·trin′gent (-jĕnt), *adj.* [L. *astringens,* pres. part.] **1.** Shrinking, and driving the blood from, the tissues; binding; contracting; styptic. **2.** Stern; austere. — *n.* An astringent medicine or substance.

as′tro- (ăs′trō-). [Gr. *astron* star.] A combining form meaning *of* or *pertaining to the stars.*

as′tro·dome′ (ăs′trō·dōm′), *n.* A transparent dome in the upper surface of an aircraft, from within which celestial observations are made.

as′tro·labe (-lāb), *n.* [From OF. and ML., fr. Gr. *astrolabon,* fr. *astron* star + *lambanein* to take.] A compact instrument for observing the positions of celestial bodies, now superseded by the sextant.

as·trol′o·ger (ăs·trŏl′ō·jẽr), *n.* One who practices astrology.

as·trol′o·gy (-jĭ), *n.* [From F., fr. L., fr. Gr. *astrologia,* deriv. of *astron* star + *logos* discourse.] **1.** *Obs.* Practical astronomy. **2.** The pseudo science which treats of the influences of the stars upon human affairs, and of foretelling terrestrial events by their positions and aspects. — **as′tro·log′ic** (ăs′trō·lŏj′ĭk), **as′tro·log′i·cal** (-ĭ·kăl), *adj.* — **as′tro·log′i·cal·ly,** *adv.*

as·tron′o·mer (ăs·trŏn′ō·mẽr), *n.* One versed in astronomy; one who makes observations of celestial phenomena.

as′tro·nom′i·cal (ăs′trō·nŏm′ĭ·kăl), **as′tro·nom′ic** (-ĭk), *adj.* **1.** Of or pertaining to astronomy. **2.** Enormously or inconceivably large, like the quantities used in astronomy. — **as′tro·nom′i·cal·ly,** *adv.*

as·tron′o·my (ăs·trŏn′ō·mĭ), *n.* [From OF., fr. L., fr. Gr. *astronomia,* fr. *astron* star + *nemein* to distribute, arrange.] **1.** The science which treats of the celestial bodies, their magnitudes, motions, constitution, etc. **2.** A treatise on this science.

as′tro·pho·tog′ra·phy (ăs′trō·fō·tŏg′r*à*·fĭ), *n.* The application of photography to astronomical investigations. — **as′tro·pho′to·graph′ic** (-fō′tō·grăf′ĭk), *adj.*

as′tro·phys′i·cist (-fĭz′ĭ·sĭst), *n.* A specialist in astrophysics.

as′tro·phys′ics (-fĭz′ĭks), *n.;* see -ICS. [*astro-* + *physics.*] The science that deals principally with the constitution of the celestial bodies. — **as′tro·phys′i·cal** (-ĭ·kăl), *adj.*

as′tro·sphere (ăs′trō·sfēr; 27), *n.* *Biol.* **a** The centrosphere. **b** The entire aster exclusive of the centrosome.

as·tu′cious, as·tu′tious (ăs·tū′shŭs), *adj.* [F. *astucieux.*] Astute.

as·tute′ (ăs·tūt′), *adj.* [L. *astutus,* fr. *astus* craft.] Shrewdly discerning and sagacious; acute; wily. — **Syn.** See SHREWD. — **as·tute′ly,** *adv.* — **as·tute′ness,** *n.*

As·ty′a·nax (ăs·tī′*à*·năks), *n.* *Gr. Myth.* Son of Hector and Andromache, hurled by the Greeks from the walls of Troy, that he might not restore the kingdom as predicted.

a·sty′lar (ā·stī′lẽr), *adj.* [*a-* not + Gr. *stylos* pillar.] *Arch.* Without columns or pilasters.

a·sun′der (*à*·sŭn′dẽr), *adv.* [*a-* on + *sunder;* AS. *on sundran.*] Into parts; into different pieces; as, to cut it *asunder.* — *adj.* Situated apart; as, wide *asunder* in meaning.

A′sur (ä′so͝or). Var. of ASHUR.

a·sy′lum (*à*·sī′lŭm), *n.; pl.* -LUMS (-lŭmz), -LA (-l*à*). [L., fr. Gr. *asylon,* fr. *asylos* inviolable, fr. *a-* not + *sylon* right of seizure.] **1.** An inviolable sanctuary giving shelter to criminals and debtors, as anciently a temple or altar, etc. **2.** Any place of retreat and security; shelter. **3.** Protection afforded by such sanctuary or place of retreat. **4.** An institution for relief of the destitute or afflicted, esp. one for the insane.

a·sym′me·try (ā·sĭm′ē·trĭ), *n.* [Gr. *asymmetria.*] Lack of symmetry. — **a′sym·met′ric** (ā′sĭ·mĕt′rĭk; ăs′ĭ-), **a′sym·met′ri·cal** (-rĭ·kăl), *adj.* — **a′sym·met′ri·cal·ly,** *adv.*

as′ymp·tote (ăs′ĭm·tōt; ăs′ĭmp-), *n.* [Gr. *asymptōtos,* fr. *a-* not + *sympiptein* to fall together.] *Math.* A line that is the limiting position which the tangent to a curve approaches, as the point of contact recedes indefinitely along an infinite branch of the curve.

as′ymp·tot′ic (-tŏt′ĭk), **as′ymp·tot′i·cal** (-ĭ·kăl), *adj.* *Math.* Of or pertaining to an asymptote. — **as′ymp·tot′i·cal·ly,** *adv.*

a·syn′chro·nous (ā·sĭng′krō·nŭs), *adj.* Not synchronous. — **a·syn′chro·nism** (-nĭz′m), *n.*

as′yn·det′ic (ăs′ĭn·dĕt′ĭk), *adj.* Using asyndeton; not joined by conjunctions. — **as′yn·det′i·cal·ly** (-ĭ·kăl·ĭ), *adv.*

a·syn′de·ton (*à*·sĭn′dē·tŏn), *n.* [L., deriv. of Gr. *a-* not + *syndetos* bound together.] *Rhet.* Omission of the conjunctions which ordinarily join co-ordinate words or clauses (*I came, I saw, I conquered*).

at (ăt; ăt; 4), *prep.* [AS. *æt.*] Primarily, *at* expresses the relation of *presence or contact in space or time,* or of *direction toward.* Hence, it implies: **1.** Simple presence in, on, or by, or near to; as, *at* the center; *at* home; *at* hand; sick *at* heart; out *at* the elbows. **2.** Direction, terminal point, or end; — with verbs of motion; as, enter *at* the north door; aim *at* a mark; be angry *at* one; to guess *at.* **3.** Relation of employment or action; as, *at* work; *at* meat (eating); *at* the controls; what are you *at?* clever *at* skating. **4.** Situation in an active or passive state; as, the stag *at* bay; *at* war; *at* ease; *at* your service; *at* random. **5.** Relation of source, cause, or occasion; as, merry *at* the sight; *at* short notice; *at* one's hands. **6.** Position in a series or scale; relative order, degree, rate, or value; as, with the mercury *at* 80°; *at* first; *at* best; *at* full speed; sold *at* six shillings. Symbol, in *Commerce,* @. — ***at one.*** In concord or friendship; in agreement; agreed.

☞ Idiomatic usage when indicating place: *at* a local point, as *at* an institution, office, meeting, and *at* a town or city regarded as a point along a course or on a map, also *at* a street number; *in* the interior as of a county, district, or building, and *in* a town or city regarded as an area or scene implying destination or permanent stay or one's personal familiar locale, also according to British usage, *in* a street; *on* a side, boundary, coast, and *on* a street, *on* the north, *on* or *at* one's right.

at′a·bal (ăt′*à*·băl), *n.* [Sp., fr. Ar. *al-ṭabl* the drum.] A kettledrum; a kind of tabor, used by Moors.

At′a·brine (ăt′*à*·brĭn; -brēn), *n.* A trade-mark applied to the antimalarial drug quinacrine dihydrochloride.

at′a·ghan (ăt′*à*·găn). Var. of YATAGHAN.

At′a·lan′ta (ăt′*à*·lăn′t*à*), *n.* [L., fr. Gr. *Atalantē.*] *Gr. Myth.* A heroine, beautiful and fleet of foot. In Boeotian legend she challenges her suitors to a race, death being the penalty of defeat, her hand the prize. Hippomenes defeats her, dropping on the course three golden apples given him by Aphrodite, which Atalanta stoops to pick up.

at′a·man (ăt′*à*·măn), *n.* = HETMAN.

at′a·mas′co lil′y (ăt′*à*·măs′kō). [Virginian *attamusco,* lit., stained with red.] Any of a genus (*Zephyranthes*) of American bulbous plants of the amaryllis family, with pink, white, or yellowish flowers.

at′a·vism (ăt′*à*·vĭz′m), *n.* [L. *atavus* ancestor.] *Biol.* **a** Recurrence in an organism or in any of its parts of a form typical of ancestors more remote than the parents, due, usually, to recombination of ancestral genes. **b** An individual or character manifesting such recurrence; a throwback or reversion. — **at′a·vist** (-vĭst), *n.* — **at′a·vis′tic,** *adj.*

a·tax′i·a (*à*·tăk′sĭ·*à*), *n.* [NL., fr. Gr. *ataxia,* fr. *ataktos* out of order, fr. *a-* not + *taktos* ordered.] *Med.* Lack of normal co-ordination of parts, esp. inability to co-ordinate voluntary muscular movements. See LOCOMOTOR ATAXIA. — **a·tax′ic** (-sĭk), *adj. & n.*

a·tax′ite (ā·tăk′sīt), *n.* *Petrog.* A volcanic rock whose components have no definite arrangement.

ate (āt; *Brit. commonly* ĕt), *past* of EAT.

A′te (ā′tē), *n.* [Gr. *atē.*] **a** [*not cap.*] Blind impulse leading men on to ruin; — personified, as in Greek tragedy. **b** A goddess of infatuation, variously regarded as a daughter of Zeus or Eris (strife).

-ate (-āt; -ăt; -ĭt). [L. *-atus,* the noun ending.] A suffix used to form: **1.** Nouns denoting office or function, or the persons having it, as in tribun*ate,* episcop*ate.* **2.** Participial nouns; as, leg*ate,* one deputed; mand*ate,* something commanded. **3.** [L. *-atum,* neut. of *-atus.*] *Chem.* Names of the salts and esters formed from those acids whose names end in *-ic* (except a few whose names begin with *hydro-, hydr-,* as hydrocyanic, hydriodic); as, sulf*ate* from sulfur*ic* acid, nitr*ate* from nitr*ic* acid, etc. It is also used in the case of a few other compounds; as, methyl*ate.*

-ate (-āt; -ăt; -ĭt). [From L. *-atus,* the past part. ending of 1st conj. verbs.] A suffix used to form: **1.** Participial adjectives equivalent to those formed by the ending *-ed,* as in desol*ate,* sed*ate,* orn*ate,* temper*ate.* Causative verbs are formed from such adjectives. **2.** Adjectives based on nouns, with the sense *possessing* or *characterized by having,* esp. in *Bot.* and *Zool.,* as in chord*ate,* branchi*ate.* **3.** (*pron.* -āt) Verbs formed (on the analogy of causative verbs from adjectives in *-ate*) by Englishing Latin verbs of the 1st conjugation, as in fascin*ate,* vener*ate,* concentr*ate,* etc., or by adding the suffix to Latin, or sometimes other, elements where no corresponding Latin verb exists, as in capacit*ate.* **4.** (*pron.* -āt) *Chem.* Verbs with the meaning *to combine, impregnate,* or *treat with,* as in: camphor*ate,* to combine or impregnate with camphor; chlorin*ate.*

at′e·brin (ăt′ē·brĭn), *n.* The antimalarial drug quinacrine dihydrochloride.

at′el·ier (ăt′ĕl·yā; *F.* à′tē·lyā′), *n.* [F.] A workshop; a studio.

‖a tem′po (ä tĕm′pō). [It.] *Music.* In time; — used to direct a return to the regular rate of speed.

Ath′a·bas′can (ăth′*à*·băs′kăn), *n.* An Indian of a tribe living about Lake Athabaska and belonging to the Athapascan linguistic family. — **Ath′a·bas′can,** *adj.*

ath′a·na′si·a (ăth′*à*·nā′zhĭ·*à*; -zh*à*), *n.* Also **a·than′a·sy** (*à*·thăn′*à*·sĭ) [Gr. *athanasia,* fr. *a-* not + *thanatos* death.] Deathlessness; immortality.

Ath′a·na′sian (ăth′*à*·nā′zhăn; -shăn), *adj.* Of or pertaining to Athanasius (d. 373), bishop of Alexandria, who advocated the Homoousian doctrine against Arianism.

Athanasian Creed. A Latin confession of faith, of unknown authorship but originating probably in the 5th or 6th century. It has been bracketed with the Apostles' and the Nicene creeds in certain Western churches since the 13th century.

Ath'a·pas'can (ăth'ȧ·păs'kăn), *adj.* Pertaining to or designating an extensive linguistic family of North American Indians including the Athabascans, Navahos, and Apaches. — *n.* An Athapascan Indian.

a'the·ism (ā'thē·ĭz'm), *n.* [Gr. *atheos* without god, fr. *a-* not + *theos* god.] **1.** Disbelief in, or denial of, the existence of a supreme being; — disting. from *agnosticism* and opposed to *theism.* **2.** Godlessness.

a'the·ist (-ĭst), *n.* [F. *athéiste.*] **1.** One who holds to atheism. **2.** A godless person.

Syn. **Atheist, agnostic, deist, freethinker, unbeliever, infidel** mean one who rejects some or all of the essential doctrines of religion. An **atheist** is one who denies the existence of God; an **agnostic** is one who withholds belief because he does not know and is unwilling to accept as proof the evidence of revelation and spiritual experience; **deist,** in the historical sense, is one who rejects the conception of a supreme being as ruler and guide of men, but still believes in one as the creator and final judge of men; **freethinker** suggests loss of faith and a belief only in that which seems rational or credible; **unbeliever,** more negative than *freethinker,* carries no implication of a substitute for faith; **infidel,** less specific than the others, usually means one belonging to a religion (such as Mohammedanism) who rejects the Christian and, usually, the Jewish conception of God.

a'the·is'tic (-ĭs'tĭk), **a'the·is'ti·cal** (-tĭ·kăl), *adj.* Pert. to, characterized by, or given to atheism; also, impious. — **a'the·is'ti·cal·ly,** *adv.*

ath'el·ing (ăth'ĕl·ĭng), *n.* [AS. *ætheling* noble, fr. *æthelo* nobility, good family.] An Anglo-Saxon prince or nobleman; esp., the heir apparent or a prince of the royal family.

A·the'na (ȧ·thē'nȧ), **A·the'ne** (-nē), *n.* [Gr. *Athēnē.*] *Gr. Relig.* One of the greater Olympian deities, pre-eminent as a civic goddess, wise in industries of peace and arts of war; — often called ***Pallas*** or ***Pallas Athena*** and by the Romans identified with Minerva.

ath'e·nae'um, ath'e·ne'um (ăth'ē·nē'ŭm), *n.* [L. *Athenaeum,* fr. Gr. *Athēnaion* a temple of Athena at Athens.] **1.** *Rom. Antiq.* A school of oratory, jurisprudence, and poetry, founded by Hadrian. **2.** A literary or scientific association or club. **3.** A building or an apartment where a library, periodicals, and newspapers are kept for use.

a·ther'ma·nous (ā·thûr'mȧ·nŭs), *adj.* [Gr. *a-* not + *thermainein* to heat.] Not transmitting radiant heat; — opposed to *diathermanous.* — **a·ther'man·cy** (-măn·sĭ), *n.*

a·thirst' (ȧ·thûrst'), *adj.* **1.** Thirsty. **2.** Eager; longing. — **Syn.** See EAGER.

ath'lete (ăth'lēt), *n.* [L. *athleta,* fr. Gr. *athlētēs,* fr. *athlein* to contend for a prize, fr. *athlos* contest, *athlon* prize.] Anyone trained or fit to contend in exercises requiring physical agility, stamina, etc.

ath·let'ic (ăth·lĕt'ĭk), *adj.* **1.** Of or pertaining to athletes or athletics. **2.** Befitting an athlete; strong; robust. **3.** Having the physique of an athlete. **4.** *Anthropol.* Characterized by long limbs, large chest, and strong muscles; — disting. from *asthenic* and *pyknic.* **5.** Used by athletes. — **-i·cal·ly** (-ĭ·kăl·ĭ), *adv.* — **-i·cism** (-ĭ·sĭz'm), *n.*

athletic foot. Also **athlete's foot.** Ringworm of the foot or feet, often acquired by athletes in gymnasiums.

ath·let'ics (ăth·lĕt'ĭks), *n. sing. & pl.;* see -ICS. **a** Athletic exercises; the games and sports of athletes; — usually construed as *pl.* **b** Skill or activity in athletic exercises; — usually construed as *sing.*

ath'o·dyd (ăth'ō·dĭd), *n.* [aero- + *th*ermo*dy*namic + *d*uct.] *Aeronautics.* A jet engine consisting essentially of a continuous duct, or tube, of varying diameter which admits air at the forward end, adds heat to it by the combustion of fuel, and discharges it from the after end. The ram-jet engine is an athodyd.

at home *or* **at-home'** (ăt·hōm'), *n.* A reception for guests at one's home.

ath'ro·cyte (ăth'rō·sīt), *n.* [Gr. *athroos* collected + *-cyte.*] Any cell capable of picking up foreign material and storing it in granular form in its cytoplasm. — **ath'ro·cy·to'sis** (-sī·tō'sĭs), *n.*

a·thwart' (ȧ·thwôrt'; *naut.* ȧ·thôrt'), *adv.* [*a-* on + *thwart.*] **1.** Across, esp. obliquely. **2.** So as to thwart. — *prep.* **1.** Across; hence, in opposition to. **2.** *Naut.* Across the length or course of.

a·tilt' (ȧ·tĭlt'), *adj.* **1.** Tilting, as in a tourney. **2.** In the position of a cask tilted.

-a'tion (-ā'shŭn). [F. or L.; F. *-ation,* fr. L. *-ationem.* See -TION.] A suffix forming nouns, often equivalent to the verbal substantive in *-ing.* Most of these nouns have verbs in *-ate;* as, allitera*tion;* many are derived through the French; as, informa*tion;* many are formed on verbs ending in *-ize;* as, civiliza*tion;* some, on native verbs; as, flirta*tion.* They denote: **1.** *Action* (from the active verb senses); *act of doing* (what the verbal root denotes); as, visita*tion,* act of visiting. **2.** *State* or *quality* (from passive and neuter verb senses and from participial adjectives); *state, condition, quality,* or *degree of being* (what the root word denotes); as, men need occupa*tion* (condition of being occupied). **3.** *Concrete result* or *thing* (transferred by causal association from verb senses); as, decora*tions* (things that decorate); discolora*tion* (product of discoloring).

-ative. [F. or L.; F. *-atif,* fem. *-ative,* fr. L. *-ativus.*] A suffix, with the sense of *tending to, of the nature of, relating to,* forming adjectives chiefly from verbs in *-ate* and nouns in *-ty.*

At'kins, Tommy. See TOMMY ATKINS.

At'lan·te'an (ăt'lăn·tē'ăn), *adj.* [L. *Atlantēus.*] Pertaining to, or resembling, Atlas; strong.

at·lan'tes (ăt·lăn'tēz), *n. pl.; sing.* ATLAS (ăt'lăs). [L. See ATLAS.] *Arch.* Figures or half figures of men, used as supporting columns or pilasters; telamones. Cf. CARYATID.

At·lan'tic (ăt·lăn'tĭk), *adj.* [L. *Atlanticus.*] **1.** Of or pert. to Atlas. **2.** Designating, pert. to, or bordering upon, the Atlantic Ocean.

Atlantic Charter. A declaration (made August 14, 1941, at a meeting in the North Atlantic) by President Roosevelt and Prime Minister Churchill of eight principles in the national policies of the U. S. and Great Britain, including disavowal of territorial aggrandizement, restoration of sovereign rights and self-government, equal access to raw materials, freedom of the seas, disarmament of aggressor nations.

Atlantic, *or* **Atlantic standard, time.** See STANDARD TIME.

At·lan'tis (ăt·lăn'tĭs), *n.* A traditional island west of the Pillars of Hercules, said by the ancients to have been sunk beneath the ocean by an earthquake.

At'las (ăt'lăs), *n.; pl.* (except in sense 2) ATLASES (-ĕz; -ĭz). [L. *Atlas, -antis,* fr. Gr. *Atlas,* fr. root of *tlēnai* to bear.] **1.** *Gr. Myth.* In Homer, a divinity in charge of the pillars which upheld the heavens; usually, a Titan forced to support the heavens on his head and hands; later, a king metamorphosed into a lofty mountain. Hence, the bearer of a great burden. **2.** [*not cap.*] Sing. of ATLANTES. **3.** [*not cap.*] *Anat.* The first vertebra of the neck. **4.** [*not cap.*] A collection of maps in a volume; — said to have been named from a picture of Atlas supporting the world. **5.** [*not cap.*] A work in which subjects are exhibited in a tabular form or arrangement. **6.** [*not cap.*] A large size of paper.

At'li (ăt'lē), *n.* [ON. *Atli* Attila.] *Norse Myth.* A king who marries Gudrun after Sigurd's death. She slays him to avenge his treachery to her brothers.

at'man (ät'măn), *n.* [Skr. *ātman* breath, self.] *Hinduism.* **a** The life principle, soul, or individual essence. **b** [*cap.*] The universal ego whence all individual selves arise.

atmo-. [Gr. *atmos.*] A combining form meaning *steam, vapor,* as in *atmo*sphere.

at'mos·phere (ăt'mŏs·fēr; 27), *n.* [*atmo-* + Gr. *sphaira* sphere.] **1.** The whole mass of air surrounding the earth; also, the gaseous envelope of any celestial body; as, the *atmosphere* of Mars. **2.** A surrounding or pervading influence; as, the social *atmosphere* of a place. **3.** The air in any locality; as, a moist *atmosphere.* **4.** The aesthetic tone or mood of, or harmony of effects in, a work of art; as, a novel rich in *atmosphere.* **5.** *Physics.* The pressure of the air at sea level (about 14.7 pounds to the square inch), used as a unit.

at'mos·pher'ic (-fĕr'ĭk), *adj.* **1. a** Of or pertaining to the atmosphere; as, *atmospheric* air, *atmospheric* pressure. **b** Caused, or operated on, by the atmosphere; pneumatic; as, an *atmospheric* engine. **2.** Of, possessing, or imparting, atmosphere or an atmosphere. — **at'mos·pher'i·cal** (-ĭ·kăl), *adj.* — **at'mos·pher'i·cal·ly,** *adv.*

at'mos·pher'ics (-ĭks), *n. pl., or* **atmospheric disturbances.** *Radio.* = STATIC.

at'oll (ăt'ŏl; ȧ·tŏl'), *n.* [Maldivian *atolu.*] A coral island or islands, consisting of a reef surrounding a lagoon.

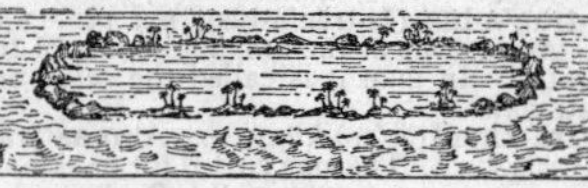

Atoll.

at'om (ăt'ŭm), *n.* [From L., fr. Gr. *atomos* uncut, indivisible, as n., atom, fr. *a-* not + *tomos* cut.] **1.** One of the minute particles postulated in atomism. **2.** A particle; jot. **3.** *Chem. & Physics.* The smallest particle of an element. See ATOMIC THEORY.

a·tom'ic (ȧ·tŏm'ĭk), *adj.* Also **a·tom'i·cal** (-ĭ·kăl). **1.** Of or pert. to atoms, atomic energy, or atomic bombs. **2.** Very minute; tiny. **3.** *Phys. Chem.* Separated into atoms; as, *atomic* hydrogen. — **-i·cal·ly,** *adv.*

atomic, *or* **atom, bomb.** Also **A'–bomb'** (ā'bŏm'), *n.* A bomb whose violent explosive power is due to the sudden release of atomic energy. The release results from the splitting, or fission, of heavy nuclei (plutonium, uranium) by bombardment with particles (neutrons).

atomic energy. Energy liberated by changes in the nucleus of an atom, as by fission of a heavy nucleus or condensation of light nuclei into heavier ones with accompanying loss of mass.

at'o·mic'i·ty (ăt'ō·mĭs'ĭ·tĭ), *n.* **1.** *Chem.* **a** Valence. **b** The number of atoms in the molecule of an element. **c** The number of replaceable atoms or groups in the molecule of a compound. **2.** *Physics & Chem.* The state of consisting of atoms.

atomic mass. *Chem.* The relative mass of an atom, expressed on the scale O^{16} (oxygen) = 16. For each isotope its value is very close to an integer called the *mass number.*

atomic number. *Chem.* A number, experimentally determined, denoting the position of an element in a series of increasing complexity (starting with 1 for hydrogen). See ELEMENT, *Table.* An arrangement of the elements in the order of these numbers and with regard to the periodic variation in their properties is called the *periodic table* (which see). Abbr. *at. no.*

atomic pile. See PILE, *n.,* 5.

atomic theory *or* **hypothesis.** *Chem. & Physics.* The theory that all material substances are composed of minute particles or atoms of a limited number of kinds; hence, any theory concerning the structure of the atom. According to modern discoveries, the atom is now regarded not as an ultimate particle but as a system consisting of a small dense nucleus having a positive electric charge of 1 to 92 or more (depending on the kind of atom) and 1 to 92 or more electrons surrounding it in concentric "shells." The nucleus is considered a combination of protons and neutrons. Atoms of the same element can have different weights (see ISOTOPE) but resemble one another very closely in chemical properties. See ELEMENT, PERIODIC TABLE.

atomic weight. *Chem. & Physics.* The relative weight of the atom of an element, referred to that of some element, as oxygen or hydrogen, as standard. The usual chemical standard is 16 for oxygen (the natural mixture of isotopes). Abbr. *at. wt.* See ELEMENT, *Table.*

at'om·ism (ăt'ŭm·ĭz'm), *n.* *Philos.* The doctrine that the universe is composed of simple, indivisible, and minute particles (atoms). — **at'om·ist** (-ĭst), *n. & adj.* — **at'om·is'tic** (-ĭs'tĭk), *adj.*

at'om·ize (-īz), *v. t.* **1.** To reduce to atoms or to fine particles, usually in a spray; hence, **at'om·iz'er** (-īz'ẽr), *n.* **2.** To view or treat as made up of discrete or atomistic units.

atom smasher. Popularly, any of the accelerators used in nuclear physics, as a cyclotron or a Van de Graaff generator.

at'o·my (ăt'ō·mĭ), *n.; pl.* -MIES (-mĭz). An atom; mite.

at'o·my, *n.* [For *anatomy,* taken as *an atomy.*] *Obs. exc. Jocular.* A skeleton. *Shak.*

a·ton'al (ā·tōn'ăl; -'l), *adj.* [See A- not.] *Music.* Characterized by atonality. — **a·ton'al·ly,** *adv.*

a·ton'al·ism (-ĭz'm), *n.* *Music.* The quality of atonality as a principle of composition. — **a·ton'al·is'tic** (-ĭs'tĭk), *adj.*

a'to·nal'i·ty (ā'tō·năl'ĭ·tĭ), *n.* [See A- not.] *Music.* Absence of tonality, — the characteristic of a style of composition in which the material is organized without reference to key or tonal center, using impartially the tones of the chromatic scale in a strongly dissonant way.

a·tone' (ȧ·tōn'), *v. i. & t.* [From *at one* (see under AT), with pron. ōn as in ME.] **1.** *Obs.* To reconcile or make reconciliation. **2.** To make amends, as for an offense or deficiency; to expiate. — **a·ton'er** (-tōn'ẽr), *n.*

a·tone'ment (-mĕnt), *n.* **1.** *Archaic.* Concord; reconciliation. **2.** Satisfactory reparation for an offense or injury; — with *for.* **3.** The redeeming effect of Christ's incarnation, sufferings, and death; also, reconciliation between God and men, esp. through Christ. **4.** *Christian Science.* The exemplification of man's unity with God, whereby man reflects divine Truth, Life, and Love. *Mary Baker Eddy.*

Atonement, Day of. See *Yom Kippur*, under JEWISH HOLIDAYS.
a·ton'ic (ȧ·tŏn'ĭk), *adj.* **1.** *Med.* Characterized by atony; as, an *atonic* disease. **2.** *Gram.* Unaccented; as, an *atonic* syllable. **3.** *Phonet.* Without tone or vocality; voiceless. — *n.* **1.** *Gram.* A word or syllable with no accent. **2.** *Phonet.* A voiceless consonant.
at'o·ny (ăt'ō·nĭ), *n.* [From ML., fr. Gr. *atonia* slackness, deriv. of *a-* not + *tonos* tone.] **1.** *Med.* Lack of tone, or vital energy; weakness of the system or of an organ. **2.** *Phonet.* Weakness from lack of stress, or accent.
a·top' (ȧ·tŏp'), *adj. & adv.* On, at, or to the top. — *prep.* On the top of.
at'ra·bil'ious (ăt'rȧ·bĭl'yŭs), *adj.* [From L. *atra bilis* black bile.] Affected by "black bile," or melancholy; hypochondriac. — **at'ra·bil'i·ar** (-ĭ·ẽr), *adj.* — **at'ra·bil'ious·ness**, *n.*
A'treus (ā'trōōs; ā'trē·ŭs), *n.* A king of Mycenae, son of Pelops and father of Agamemnon and Menelaus (hence called the **A·tri'dae** [ȧ-trī'dē]). His brother Thyestes seduced his wife and plotted his death. Atreus, feigning reconciliation, killed three sons of Thyestes and served them to him at a banquet.
a·trip' (ȧ·trĭp'), *adj.* *Naut.* Just hove clear of the ground; aweigh; — of an anchor.
a'tri·um (ā'trĭ·ŭm; ä'-), *n.; pl.* ATRIA (-ȧ). [L.] **1.** *Rom. Antiq.* The chief room in a house. **2.** *Anat. & Zool.* Any of various cavities or chambers; esp., the main part of an auricle of the heart or, sometimes, the entire auricle. See HEART, *Illust.*
a·tro'cious (ȧ·trō'shŭs), *adj.* [L. *atrox, atrocis,* cruel, fierce.] **1.** Savagely brutal; outrageously cruel or wicked. **2.** *Colloq.* Very bad; abominable. — **Syn.** See OUTRAGEOUS. — **a·tro'cious·ly**, *adv.* — **a·tro'cious·ness**, *n.*
a·troc'i·ty (ȧ·trŏs'ĭ·tĭ), *n.; pl.* -TIES (-tĭz). State or quality of being atrocious; also, an atrocious deed.
a·troph'ic (ȧ·trŏf'ĭk), *adj.* Relating to atrophy.
at'ro·phied (ăt'rō·fĭd), *adj.* Wasted; emaciated.
at'ro·phy (-fĭ), *n.* [From L., fr. Gr. *atrophia*, fr. *a-* not + *trephein* to nourish.] **1.** A wasting away from lack of nourishment or from disuse. **2.** *Biol.* Arrested development of a part or organ incidental to the normal development of an animal or plant. — *v. i. & t.;* -PHIED (-fĭd); -PHY·ING. To undergo, or cause to undergo, atrophy.
at'ro·pine (ăt'rō·pēn; -pĭn), *n.* Also **at'ro·pin.** [From *Atropa*, generic name of belladonna.] A poisonous, white, crystalline alkaloid, $C_{17}H_{23}NO_3$, extracted from belladonna and other nightshades, used to dilate the pupil of the eye, to relieve spasms, etc.
at'ro·pism (-pĭz'm), *n.* Poisoning by atropine.
At'ro·pos (ăt'rō·pŏs), *n.* [Gr., fr. *atropos* not turning, inflexible.] *Gr. Myth.* One of the Fates (see FATE, *n.,* 4).
ATS (ā'tē'ĕs'; ăts). The Auxiliary Territorial Service, women's auxiliary to the British Army from 1941, incorp. into the Army in 1949 as the *WRAC.*
at'ta·bal (ăt'ȧ·băl). Var. of ATABAL.
at·tach' (ă·tăch'), *v. t.* [OF. *atachier,* fr. *a* to + a word akin to E. *tack* a small nail.] **1.** To take by legal authority, esp. under a writ, as a means of enforcing payment of a debt. **2.** *Obs.* To take; attack. **3.** To bind; fasten; tie; connect. **4.** To bind by personal ties, as of affection, sympathy, etc. **5.** To assign by authority; to appoint. **6.** To attribute; ascribe; as, to *attach* importance to an event. **7.** To associate as a property or adjunct. — **Syn.** See FASTEN. — **Ant.** Detach. — *v. i.* To adhere; be attached. — **at·tach'a·ble**, *adj.*
at'ta·ché' (ăt'ȧ·shā' *or, Brit.,* ă·tăsh'ā; *F.* ȧ'tȧ'shā'), *n.* [F.] A member of the diplomatic staff of an ambassador or minister.
at·tached' (ă·tăcht'), *past part. & part. adj.* of ATTACH, *v.* Hence, specif., *Zool.,* permanently fixed when adult, as a barnacle or oyster; — opp. to *free-swimming.*
at·tach'ment (ă·tăch'mĕnt), *n.* **1.** *Law.* An attaching by legal process; also, the writ commanding such seizure. **2.** State of being attached by personal ties; fidelity; regard. **3.** An attaching or being attached by physical connection, as an adjunct, or by association. **4.** That by which one thing is attached to another; as, the *attachments* of a muscle. **5.** Something attached; some adjunct attached to an instrument, machine, or other object. — **Syn.** Affection, love.
at·tack' (ă·tăk'), *v. t.* [F. *attaquer,* fr. It. *attaccare,* of the same origin as F. *attacher.* See ATTACH.] **1.** To fall upon with force; to assault. **2.** To assail with unfriendly speech or writing; censure. **3.** To set to work upon; tackle. **4.** To begin to affect; to begin to act upon injuriously. — *v. i.* To make an onset or attack.
Syn. **Attack, assail, assault, bombard, storm** mean to make an onset upon. **Attack** implies aggression or aggressiveness and literally or figuratively the initiation of a struggle with the person or thing to be mastered; **assail** implies an attempt to break down resistance by repeated blows, shots, thrusts, etc.; **assault** always suggests direct confrontation and an attempt to overpower by suddenness and violence of onslaught; **bombard,** literally to assail with bombs or shells, in extended use carries a strong implication of continuous pestering; **storm** suggests an attempt to sweep from the path every obstacle to victory.
— *n.* **1.** Act of attacking; onset; assault; — opposed to *defense.* **2.** Offensive or antagonistic action; specif., an access of disease or fit of sickness. **3.** A setting to work upon some task, etc.; beginning of action. **4.** A body of persons participating in an offensive action. **5.** *Music.* Initiation of performance, esp. with respect to the degree of unanimity with which a phrase is begun by the several performers in an ensemble group. — **Syn.** Assault, onslaught, onset.
at·tain' (ă·tān'), *v. t.* [From stem of OF. *ataindre,* fr. L. *attingere,* fr. *ad-* + *tangere* to touch, reach.] **1.** To achieve or accomplish, or reach by effort; gain; compass; as, to *attain* one's ends. **2.** To reach or come to by progression or motion; arrive at; as, to *attain* a ripe old age. — **Syn.** See REACH. — *v. i.* To come or arrive by motion, growth, or effort; reach; — usually with *to* or *unto.*
at·tain'a·ble (-ȧ·b'l), *adj.* That may be attained. — **at·tain'a·bil'i·ty** (-bĭl'ĭ·tĭ), *n.* — **at·tain'a·ble·ness**, *n.*
at·tain'der (ă·tān'dẽr), *n.* [OF. *ataindre* to accuse, convict.] **1.** Act of attainting, or state of being attainted; also, result of attainting; specif.: **a** Extinction of the civil rights and capacities of a person, on sentence of death or outlawry. A ***bill of attainder*** is a legislative act which inflicts the consequences of attainder without a judicial trial. Cf. CORRUPTION OF BLOOD. **b** *Shak.* Dishonor.
at·tain'ment (ă·tān'mĕnt), *n.* **1.** Act of attaining. **2.** That which is attained; a mental acquirement. — **Syn.** See ACQUIREMENT.
at·taint' (ă·tānt'), *v. t.;* -TAINT'ED; -TAINT'ING. *Archaic past part.* AT-TAINT'. [OF. *ataint,* past part. of *ataindre.* See ATTAINDER.] **1.** **a** To prove guilty. **b** *Archaic.* To accuse. **2.** To affect by attainder. **3.** *Rare.* To affect or infect; taint; corrupt. **4.** To stain; sully; disgrace. — *n.* **1.** *Archaic.* A touch; a touch in tilting. **2.** Attainder. **3.** A stain or taint; disgrace.
at·tain'ture (ă·tān'tūr), *n.* Attainder; also, disgrace.
at'tar (ăt'ẽr), *n.* [Per. *'atar,* fr. Ar. *'itr* perfume, essence.] A perfume obtained from flowers; esp., a fragrant volatile oil distilled from rose petals, esp. of the damask rose.
at·tem'per (ă·tĕm'pẽr), *v. t.* [OF. *atemprer,* fr. L. *attemperare.* See AD-; TEMPER.] **1.** To reduce, modify, or moderate by mixture; regulate, as temperature. **2.** To soften; soothe; temper. **3.** To accommodate; attune.
at·tempt' (ă·tĕmpt'; 89), *v. t.* [OF. *atenter,* fr. L. *attentare* to attempt, fr. *ad-* + *tentare, temptare,* to touch, try.] **1.** To make trial or experiment of; try; endeavor to do; as, to *attempt* to sing. **2.** *Archaic.* To tempt. **3.** To try to subdue; attack; assail; as, to *attempt* a man's life. — *n.* Act of attempting; trial, or endeavor; esp., an unsuccessful effort; also, an attack; assault. — **at·tempt'a·ble** (-tĕmp'tȧ·b'l), *adj.*
Syn. **Attempt, try, endeavor** (*or* **endeavour**), **essay, assay, strive, struggle** mean to make an effort to accomplish an end. **Attempt** implies an actual beginning of or venturing upon, often also suggesting failure; **try,** in precise use, suggests effort or experiment made in the hope of ascertaining facts or of testing or proving something (as, to *try* to find a better method); **endeavor** heightens the implications of exertion and difficulty; **essay** and the now less common **assay** imply great difficulty but also suggest tentative effort or experiment; **strive** and **struggle** carry not only implications of great exertion but of greater opposition to be overcome, *strive* specifically suggesting persistence, and *struggle* suggesting straining.
at·tend' (ă·tĕnd'), *v. t.* [OF. *atendre,* fr. L. *attendere* to stretch (sc. *animum*) to apply the mind to, fr. *ad-* + *tendere* to stretch.] **1.** *Archaic.* To heed; listen to; as, *attend* my words. **2.** To care for; take charge of; as, to *attend* machinery. **3.** To go or stay with, as a servant; to visit, as a doctor; escort; wait on; serve. **4.** To be present with; accompany; as, *attended* with ill effects. **5.** To be present at; as, to *attend* church. **6.** *Archaic.* To wait for; await. — **Syn.** See ACCOMPANY. — *v. i.* **1.** To apply the mind; pay attention; listen; as, *attend* to these directions. **2.** To apply oneself; as, *attend* strictly to business. **3.** To take charge (of); look (after); as, I 'll *attend* to the matter. **4.** To be ready for service; to wait; as, to *attend* upon the committee. **5.** *Obs.* To wait; stay; delay.
at·tend'ance (ă·tĕn'dăns), *n.* **1.** Act or fact of attending. **2.** The persons attending; specif.: **a** Retinue; attendants. **b** The persons, or number of persons, present on a given occasion.
at·tend'ant (-dănt), *adj.* Attending; accompanying; following as a consequence; as, *attendant* circumstances or evils. — *n.* **1.** One who attends. **2.** That which accompanies; a concomitant.
at·tent' (ă·tĕnt'), *adj.* [L. *attentus,* past part. of *attendere.* See ATTEND, *v.*] Attentive; heedful. — *n.* Attention. *Obs.* — **at·tent'ly**, *adv.*
at·ten'tion (ă·tĕn'shŭn), *n.* [L. *attentio.*] **1.** Act or state of attending or heeding; special consideration. **2.** Power of giving attention (in sense 1). **3.** Observation with a view to action; notice; observant care. **4.** An act of civility or courtesy; specif., often *pl.,* the addresses of one who is courting. **5.** *Mil.* The attitude of readiness for action on receiving orders, assumed in response to the command "attention."
Syn. **Attention, study, concentration, application** mean the direct focusing of the mind upon something. **Attention** is applicable to the faculty or power as well as to the act but carries, apart from the context, no implication of quality or duration; **study,** on the other hand, stresses continuity and closeness of attention, as in acquiring knowledge, the analysis of something complex or confusing, or the like; **concentration** emphasizes the centering of attention on one thing to the exclusion of everything else; **application** usually suggests persistence in fixing one's attention and assiduity in the performance of what is required.
at·ten'tive (-tĭv), *adj.* **1.** Heedful; intent; observant. **2.** Heedful of the comfort of others; courteous. **3.** Paying attentions as one courting. — **Syn.** See THOUGHTFUL. — **at·ten'tive·ly**, *adv.* — **at·ten'tive·ness**, *n.*
at·ten'u·ant (ă·tĕn'ū·ănt), *adj.* [L. *attenuans,* pres. part. of *attenuare.* See ATTENUATE.] *Med.* Making thin, as fluids; diluting; attenuating. — *n.* A diluent.
at·ten'u·ate (-āt), *v. t.* [L. *attenuatus,* past part. of *attenuare,* fr. *ad-* + *tenuare* to make thin, fr. *tenuis* thin.] **1.** To make thin or slender. **2.** To thin in consistency; dilute; rarefy. **3.** To lessen the amount, force, or value of; weaken. **4.** *Bacteriol.* To reduce the virulence of; as, an *attenuated* strain. — *v. i.* To become thin, fine, or less. — (-ăt), *adj.* Attenuated. — **at·ten'u·a·ble** (-ȧ·b'l), *adj.* — **at·ten'u·a'tion** (-ā'shŭn), *n.*
at·test' (ă·tĕst'), *v. t.* [F. *attester,* fr. L., fr. *ad-* + *testari* to bear witness, fr. *testis* witness.] **1.** To affirm to be true or genuine; specif., to authenticate by signing as a witness; also, authenticate officially. **2.** To be proof of; to manifest. **3.** To put (one) on oath. — *v. i.* To bear witness; testify; — often with *to.* — *n.* Testimony; attestation. — **at·test'ant** (ă·tĕs'tănt), *adj. & n.* — **at'tes·ta'tion** (ăt'ĕs·tā'shŭn), *n.*
at'tic (ăt'ĭk), *n.* [In sense **a** fr. F. *attique,* orig. meaning Attic.] *Arch.* **a** A low story or wall above the main order of a façade, in the classical styles. **b** A room or rooms behind that part of the exterior; hence, the part of a building next below the roof.
At'tic (ăt'ĭk), *adj.* [L. *Atticus,* fr. Gr. *Attikos.*] **1.** Of or pertaining to Attica, or Athens, in Greece; Athenian. **2.** Marked by qualities characteristic of the Athenians; — applied to literary or artistic style, simple, pure, and refined; classical. See GREEK, *n.,* 4. — *n.* **1.** An Athenian. **2.** The dialect of Attica, noted for its purity and elegance; standard Greek.
At'ti·cism, at'ti·cism (ăt'ĭ·sĭz'm), *n.* A peculiarity or characteristic of Attic Greek. See ATTIC, *n.,* 2.
At'ti·cize, at'ti·cize (-sīz), *v. t. & i.* [Gr. *attikizein.*] To conform to the language, customs, etc., of Attica.
Attic salt, Attic wit. Poignant, delicate wit.
at·tire' (ă·tīr'), *v. t.* [OF. *atirier.*] To dress; array; adorn; esp., to clothe with elegant or splendid garments. — *n.* **1.** Dress; clothes; ornamental clothing. **2.** The antlers, or antlers and scalp, of a stag or buck.
at·tire'ment (-mĕnt), *n.* Attire.
at'ti·tude (ăt'ĭ·tūd), *n.* [F., deriv. of L. *aptus* suited.] **1.** Posture;

position assumed or studied to serve a purpose; as, a threatening *attitude.* **2.** Position or bearing as indicating action, feeling, or mood; as, keep a firm *attitude;* hence the feeling or mood itself; as, a kindly *attitude.*

at′ti·tu′di·nize (ăt′ĭ·tū′dĭ·nīz), *v. i.* To assume attitudes; pose.

at·torn′ (ă·tûrn′), *v. i.* [OF. *atorner* to direct, attorn, fr. *a* to + *torner* to turn.] **a** *Feudal Law.* To turn or transfer homage and service to another as lord. **b** *Modern Law.* To agree to become tenant to another as owner or landlord. — **at·torn′ment,** *n.*

at·tor′ney (ă·tûr′nĭ), *n.; pl.* -NEYS (-nĭz). [OF. *atorné,* past part.] **1.** *Obs.* A deputy or agent. **2.** *Law.* One who is legally appointed by another to transact any business for him; specif., a legal agent (an **attorney at law**) qualified to act for suitors and defendants in legal proceedings. Abbr. *atty.* — **Syn.** See AGENT: LAWYER. — **at·tor′ney·ship,** *n.*

at·tor′ney gen′er·al (ă·tûr′nĭ jĕn′ẽr·ăl); *pl.* ATTORNEYS GENERAL or ATTORNEY GENERALS. *Law.* The chief law officer of the state, empowered to act in all litigation in which the law-executing power is a party, and to advise the supreme executive whenever required.

at·tract′ (ă·trăkt′), *v. t.* [L. *attractus,* past part. of *attrahere,* fr. *ad-* + *trahere* to draw.] **1.** To draw to; cause to approach or adhere; act upon by attraction. **2.** To draw by influence of an aesthetic or emotional kind; fix, as the mind, attention, etc.; invite; allure; as, to *attract* admirers. — *v. i.* To exercise attraction. — **at·tract′a·ble,** *adj.* — **at·tract′a·ble·ness,** *n.*

Syn. **Attract, allure, charm, fascinate, bewitch, enchant, captivate** mean to draw another compellingly or irresistibly. **Attract** is broader in its meaning than the others, referring not only to persons but to things, and usually suggests a quality such as magnetism in that which draws, or an affinity for or a susceptibility to in the one that is drawn; **allure** implies enticement by that which is fair, pleasing, seductive, or the like; **charm** implies a power in the agent to cast a spell over the person or thing affected, compelling him or it to respond; **fascinate, bewitch, enchant** likewise suggest a magical influence, but *fascinate* tends to stress the ineffectiveness of resistance, *bewitch* a succumbing to the influence, and *enchant* ecstatic admiration; **captivate** implies merely an attraction that evokes delight or admiration.

at·trac′tion (ă·trăk′shŭn), *n.* **1.** Act, process, property, or power of attracting; specif., personal charm. **2.** An attractive quality, object, or feature. **3.** *Physics.* A force acting mutually between particles of matter, tending to draw them together and resisting their separation.

Syn. **Attraction, affinity, sympathy** mean the relationship existing between things (sometimes persons) that are involuntarily or naturally drawn together. **Attraction** implies the possession by one thing of a quality, or qualities, that pulls another thing to it, often into contact or adherence; **affinity** implies the possession by the thing that is drawn of a susceptibility (a predisposition, a natural inclination, etc.), for it that forces it to approach or come into contact with the other; **sympathy** implies a reciprocal or natural relation between things that are susceptible to the same influences; as, *attraction* is the force by which a magnet draws iron to it; iron is one of the few metals that have an *affinity* for the magnet; the tides rise and fall in *sympathy* with the moon.

at·trac′tive (-trăk′tĭv), *adj.* Having the power or quality of attracting; specif., charming. — **at·trac′tive·ly,** *adv.* — **at·trac′tive·ness,** *n.*

at·trac′tor (-tẽr), *n.* One who or that which attracts.

at′tra·hent (ăt′rȧ·hĕnt), *adj.* [L. *attrahens,* pres. part. of *attrahere.* See ATTRACT, *v.*] Attracting; drawing.

at·trib′ute (ă·trĭb′ūt), *v. t.* [L. *attributus,* past part. of *attribuere,* fr. *ad-* + *tribuere* to bestow.] To ascribe by way of cause, inherent quality, interpretation, authorship, or classification; as, a disease *attributed* to filth; to *attribute* power to a charm. — **Syn.** See ASCRIBE. — **at·trib′ut·a·ble,** *adj.* — **at·trib′ut·er** (-ū·tẽr), **-u·tor** (-ū·tẽr), *n.*

at′tri·bute (ăt′rĭ·būt), *n.* **1.** That which is attributed, as a quality or character ascribed to, or inherent in, a person or thing; as, mercy is an *attribute* of God. **2.** *Obs.* Reputation. **3** *Gram.* A word, esp. an adjective, ascribing a quality (to some person or thing). **4.** *Painting & Sculp.* A conventional symbol of office, character, or identity, added to any particular figure; as, a club is the *attribute* of Hercules. — **Syn.** See QUALITY.

at′tri·bu′tion (-bū′shŭn), *n.* Act of attributing; also, an ascribed quality, character, or right.

at·trib′u·tive (ă·trĭb′ū·tĭv), *adj.* **1.** Attributing; pertaining to, or of the nature of an attribute. **2.** *Gram.* Of an adjective or other adjunct word, standing before its qualified noun to denote the qualification as assumed instead of predicated (*yellow* gold; the *village* school); — disting. from *predicate* or *predicative* (gold is *yellow*). — *n.* *Gram.* An attributive word. — **at·trib′u·tive·ly,** *adv.* — **at·trib′u·tive·ness,** *n.*

at·trite′ (ă·trīt′), *adj.* [L. *attritus,* past part. of *atterere,* fr. *ad-* + *terere* to rub.] Worn down by friction. *Obs.*

at·trit′ed (-trīt′ĕd; -ĭd), *adj.* Worn down by friction.

at·tri′tion (ă·trĭsh′ŭn), *n.* **1.** Act of rubbing together; friction; also, act of wearing down or grinding down by friction. **2.** The gradual wearing down, as of resources; as, a war of *attrition.* **3.** *Theol.* Grief for sin arising from imperfect motives, as fear of punishment.

at·tune′ (ă·tūn′), *v. t.* [*ad-* + *tune.*] To bring into harmony; tune.

a·twain′ (ȧ·twān′), *adv.* [*a-* on + *twain.*] *Archaic.* In twain; asunder; in two.

at·weel′ (ăt·wēl′), *adv.* [Contr. of *I wat* (*wot*) *well.*] *Scot.* I wot well; surely; truly.

a·typ′ic (ā·tĭp′ĭk), **a·typ′i·cal** (-ĭ·kăl), *adj.* [See A- not.] Not of typical character; irregular; unlike the type. — **a·typ′i·cal·ly,** *adv.*

‖**au** (ō). [F.] See À LA.

‖**au′bade′** (ō′băd′), *n.* [F.] Piece of music to be played or sung at dawn; hence, any morning concert; a lyric piece suggesting morning.

‖**au′berge′** (ō′bĕrzh′; ō′-), *n.* [F.] An inn.

‖**au′ber′giste′** (ō′bĕr′zhēst′; ō′-), *n.* [F.] An innkeeper.

au′burn (ô′bẽrn), *adj.* [From OF., fr. ML. *alburnus* whitish, fr. L. *albus* white.] **a** Reddish-brown. **b** Of the color auburn. — *n.* A color, red-yellow in hue, of low saturation and low brilliance. See COLOR.

‖**au con′traire′** (ō′ kôɴ′trâr′). [F.] On the contrary.

‖**au cou′rant′** (ō′ kōō′räɴ′). [F.] In or with the current; hence, well-informed; up-to-date.

auc′tion (ôk′shŭn), *n.* [L. *auctio,* lit., an increasing, fr. *augere, auctum,* to increase.] **1.** A public sale of property to the highest bidder, esp. a sale by a person licensed for the purpose.

☞ In the United States, the more prevalent expression is "to sell, or put up, *at* auction"; in England, "to sell *by,* or put up *to,* auction."

2. *Card Playing.* **a** In certain games, the bidding; specif., in bridge, the bidding for the privilege of naming the trump, or no-trump. **b** A variety of bridge (**auction bridge**) in which the players bid for the privilege of naming the trump, or no-trump.

— *v. t.* To sell at auction; — often with *off.*

auc′tion·eer′ (ôk′shŭn·ēr′), *n.* A person who sells, or makes a business of selling, at auction. — *v. t.* To auction.

au·da′cious (ô·dā′shŭs), *adj.* [F. *audacieux,* fr. L. *audacia* audacity, fr. *audax, -acis,* bold.] **1.** Intrepidly daring; spirited; adventurous. **2.** Showing contempt for the restraints of law, religion, or decorum. **3.** Inspiring audacity. — **-ly,** *adv.* — **-ness,** *n.*

au·dac′i·ty (ô·dăs′ĭ·tĭ), *n.* Quality or state of being audacious; venturesomeness; effrontery. — **Syn.** See TEMERITY.

au′di·ble (ô′dĭ·b′l), *adj.* [ML. *audibilis,* fr. L. *audire* to hear.] Heard or capable of being heard. — **au′di·bil′i·ty** (-bĭl′ĭ·tĭ), *n.* — **au′di·ble·ness,** *n.* — **au′di·bly,** *adv.*

au′di·ence (ô′dĭ·ĕns; ôd′yĕns; 58), *n.* [OF., fr. L. *audientia,* fr. *audire* to hear.] **1.** Act or state of listening. **2.** Opportunity of being heard; admittance to a hearing. **3.** A formal hearing or interview. **4.** An assembly of hearers; hence, the reading public of an author, or an assembly of spectators.

au′di·ent (ô′dĭ·ĕnt), *adj.* [L. *audiens.*] Listening.

au′dile (ô′dĭl; -dīl), *adj.* [L. *audire* to hear.] Auditory. — *n.* *Psychol.* One whose mental imagery is auditory rather than visual or motor. Cf. MOTILE, *n.;* VISUALIZER.

au′di·o (ô′dĭ·ō), *adj.* [L. *audire* to hear.] **1.** Auditory; hence, **audio–,** *auditory and,* as in **au′di·o–vis′u·al.** **2.** *Elec.* Of or pertaining to currents or frequencies corresponding to normally audible sound waves which are of frequencies approximately from 15 to 20,000 per second; as, **au′di·o–fre′quen·cy.** **3.** *Television.* Pertaining to or used in the transmission or reception of sound; — contrasted with *video.*

au′di·om′e·ter (ô′dĭ·ŏm′ē·tẽr), *n.* [L. *audire* to hear + *-meter.*] *Acoustics.* An instrument for measuring the power of hearing or the audibility or intensity of sounds. — **au′di·om′e·try** (-trĭ), *n.*

au′di·o·phile (ô′dĭ·ō·fīl; -fĭl), *n.* [L. *audire* to hear + *-phile.*] One who is enthusiastic about sound reproduction, especially music from high-fidelity broadcasts or recordings.

au′di·phone (ô′dĭ·fōn), *n.* [L. *audire* to hear + *-phone.*] An instrument which, placed against the teeth, conveys sound vibrations to the auditory nerve and enables the deaf to hear more or less distinctly.

au′dit (ô′dĭt), *n.* [L. *auditus* a hearing, fr. *audire* to hear.] **1.** A formal or official examination and verification of accounts. **2.** An account as adjusted by auditors; final statement of account. **3.** **a** *Obs.* An audience. **b** *Archaic.* A judicial examination. — *v. t.* **1.** To examine and verify, as an account. **2.** To attend (a course) as an auditor (def. 4). — *v. i.* To make an audit.

au·di′tion (ô·dĭsh′ŭn), *n.* [F., fr. L. *auditio.*] **1.** Power, sense, or faculty of hearing. **2.** A hearing, esp. one to try out a speaker or a musical performer. **3.** Something heard. — *v. t.* To try out in an audition or auditions, esp. for fitness to participate in radio or opera. — *v. i.* To demonstrate one's ability in an audition.

au′di·tive (ô′dĭ·tĭv), *adj.* Auditory.

au′di·tor (-tẽr), *n.* **1.** A hearer or listener. **2.** A person authorized to audit or examine accounts. **3.** A person appointed to hear certain judicial proceedings. **4.** *Educ.* One who listens to a course of lectures without working for credit.

au′di·to′ri·um (-tō′rĭ·ŭm; 70), *n.; pl.* -RIUMS (-ŭmz), -RIA (-ȧ). [L.] **1.** The part of a church, theater, or other public building assigned to the audience. **2.** A room, hall, or building used for lectures, etc.

au′di·to′ry (ô′dĭ·tō′rĭ *or, esp. Brit.,* -tẽr·ĭ), *n.* [L. *auditorium.*] **1.** = AUDIENCE, 4. **2.** An auditorium. — *adj.* Of or pertaining to hearing or the sense or organs of hearing. See EAR, *Illust.*

‖**au fait** (ō′ fĕ′). [F.] Expert; familiar with the facts (of).

‖**Auf′klä′rung** (ouf′klā′rōōng), *n.* [G.] Enlightenment (sense 2).

‖**au fond** (ō′ fôɴ′). [F.] At bottom; essentially.

‖**auf Wie′der·seh′en** (ouf′ vē′dẽr·zā′ĕn; -zān′). [G.] Till we meet again; — a form of farewell.

Au·ge′an (ô·jē′ăn), *adj.* [L. *Augeas,* fr. Gr. *Augeias.*] **1.** *Gr. Myth.* Of or pertaining to Augeas, king of Elis, whose stable contained an enormous number of oxen, and was uncleaned for many years. Hercules cleaned it in a day by diverting through it the rivers Alpheus and Peneus. **2.** Exceedingly filthy or corrupt.

au′gend (ô′jĕnd; ô·jĕnd′), *n.* A number or quantity to which another (the *addend*) is to be added. See SUM, *n.,* 5.

au′ger (ô′gẽr), *n.* [AS. *nafugār,* fr. *nafu* nave of a wheel + *gār* spear; prop., a nave borer. *Auger,* without initial *n-,* arose through the incorrect division of *a nauger* as *an auger.*] A carpenter's tool for boring holes larger than those bored by a gimlet; hence, any of various augerlike instruments or devices.

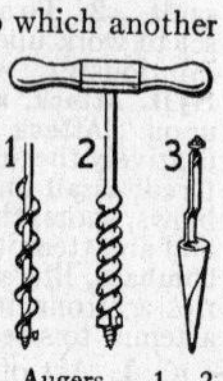

Augers. 1, 2 Screw Augers; 3 Tapering Pod Auger.

aught (ôt), *n.* [AS. *āwiht,* fr. *ā* ever + *wiht* creature, thing.] **1.** Any least part; anything. **2.** [*a naught,* taken as *an aught.*] In arithmetic, a cipher. — *adv.* At all; to any extent.

aught (ôᴋt), *n.* [AS. *æht,* fr. *āgan* to own.] *Obs. exc. Scot.* Property; possession.

aught′lins (ôᴋt′lĭnz), *adv.* [*aught* + *-lings, -lins,* an adv. suffix.] *Scot.* In the least; at all.

au′gite (ô′jīt), *n.* [L. *augites,* fr. Gr. *augitēs,* fr. *augē* brightness.] An aluminous variety of pyroxene, usually black or dark-green, occurring in igneous rocks such as basalt; sometimes, any pyroxene. — **au·git′ic** (ô·jĭt′ĭk), *adj.*

aug·ment′ (ôg·mĕnt′), *v. t.* [F. *augmenter,* fr. L. *augmentare,* fr. *augmentum,* fr. *augere* to increase.] **1.** To enlarge or increase in size, amount, or degree; make bigger. **2.** *Gram.* To add an augment to. — *v. i.* To increase. — **Syn.** See INCREASE. — **aug·ment′a·ble,** *adj.* — **aug·ment′er,** *n.*

aug′ment (ôg′mĕnt), *n.* **1.** Increase. **2.** *Gram.* A vowel prefixed, or a lengthening of the initial vowel, to mark past time, as in Greek and Sanskrit verbs.

aug′men·ta′tion (ôg′mĕn·tā′shŭn), *n.* Act of augmenting; state of being augmented; that which augments.

aug·ment′a·tive (ôg·mĕn′tȧ·tĭv), *adj.* Having the quality or power of augmenting; specif., *Gram.,* expressing with augmented force, or augmenting the force of, the idea of the original word. — *n.* An augmentative word or affix.

‖**au grand sé′rieux′** (ō′ gräɴ′ sā′ryû′) [F.] In all seriousness.

au gra′tin′ (ō′ grȧ′tăɴ′; *Angl.* ō, *or* ô, grăt′′n). [F.] *Cookery.* With a browned covering of bread crumbs, often mixed with butter or cheese; as, potatoes *au gratin.*

au′gur (ô′gẽr), *n.* [L.] **1.** *Rom. Relig.* A member of the highest class of official diviners of ancient Rome; an auspex. Cf. HARUSPEX. **2.** A soothsayer; diviner.

au′gur, *v. t.* [L. *augurari.*] To foretell, as from omens; prognosticate. — *v. i.* **1.** To make an augury; prognosticate. **2.** To foretell or indicate an issue; as, it *augurs* well or ill; it *augurs* of success. — **Syn.** See FORETELL.

au′gu·ry (ô′gū·rĭ), *n.; pl.* -RIES (-rĭz). [L. *augurium.*] **1.** Art or practice of auguring; divination. **2.** An omen; prognostication; presage; foreboding.

au·gust′ (ô·gŭst′; 2), *adj.* [L. *augustus.*] **1.** Of venerably majestic grandeur; stately; imposing. **2.** Of majestic dignity; imposingly exalted. — **Syn.** See GRAND. — **au·gust′ly,** *adv.* — **au·gust′ness,** *n.*

Au′gust (ô′gŭst), *n.* [After *Augustus* Caesar.] The eighth month of the year, having 31 days. Abbr. *Aug.*

Au·gus′tan (ô·gŭs′tăn), *adj.* Of or pertaining to Augustus Caesar or his age, or any age likened to his; hence, correct in taste; classical. — *n.* A writer in an Augustan age.

Augustan age. In a national literature, the period of its highest state of purity and refinement; — so called because the reign of Augustus Caesar (27 B.C.–A.D. 14) was the golden age of Roman literature.

Au′gus·tin′i·an (ô′gŭs·tĭn′ĭ·ăn), *adj.* **1.** Of or pertaining to St. Augustine, bishop of Hippo in northern Africa, or his doctrines, esp. absolute predestination and the immediate efficacy of grace. **2.** Designating any of several orders deriving their name from St. Augustine. — *n.* A follower of St. Augustine; specif.: **a** A member of an Augustinian order. **b** One who accepts the views of Augustine on predestination and grace. — **Au′gus·tin′i·an·ism** (-ĭz′m), **Au·gus′tin·ism** (ô·gŭs′tĭn·ĭz′m), *n.*

‖**au jus** (ō′ zhü′). [F.] Served in gravy, or juice of the meat.

auk (ôk), *n.* [From Scand.; cf. Sw. *alka* auk, Dan. *alke,* ON. *ālka.*] Any of a family (Alcidae) of diving birds which breed in the colder parts of the Northern Hemisphere, esp. the flightless ***great auk*** (*Plautus impennis*), now extinct, the ***razor-billed auk*** (*Alca torda*) and the ***little auk*** (= DOVEKIE **b**).

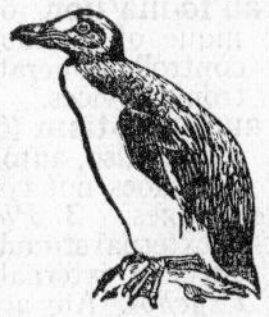

Great Auk. (1/30)

auk′let (ôk′lĕt; -lĭt), *n.* [*auk* + *-let.*] Any of several small auks (*Aethia* and allied genera) of the North Pacific coasts.

‖**au lait** (ō′ lĕ′). [F.] With milk.

auld (ôld; äld). Dial. var. of OLD.

auld lang syne (ôld lăng sīn; ōld; zīn). Literally, old long since; hence, times long past; the (good) old times.

au′lic (ô′lĭk), *adj.* [L. *aulicus,* fr. Gr. *aulikos,* fr. *aulē* hall, court.] Of or pertaining to a court; as, the **Aulic Council,** a supreme court established in 1501 by the Holy Roman Emperor Maximilian I.

‖**au na′tu′rel′** (ō′ nȧ′tü′rĕl′). [F.] **1.** Naturally; to the life; in the nude. **2.** Cooked simply.

aunt (änt; ȧnt; 9), *n.* [OF. *ante,* fr. L. *amita* father's sister.] The sister of one's father or mother; also, an uncle's wife. Cf. CONSANGUINITY, *Illust.*

au′ra (ô′rȧ), *n.; pl.* AURAS (-rȧz), AURAE (-rē). [L., breeze, air, fr. Gr. *aura.*] **1.** Any subtle, invisible emanation or exhalation; as, the *aura,* or scent, of flowers. **2.** A distinctive atmosphere surrounding a person; as, an *aura* of sanctity. **3.** *Elec.* A draft, or motion of the air, caused by electric repulsion, as when the air near a charged metallic point is set in motion. — **au′ral** (-răl), *adj.*

au′ral (-răl), *adj.* [L. *auris* ear.] Of or pertaining to the ear or the sense of hearing; as, *aural* medicine or surgery.

au′rar (oi′rär), *n., pl.* of EYRIR.

‖**au′re·a me′di·o·cri·tas** (ô′rē·ȧ mē′dĭ·ŏk′rĭ·tăs; mĕd′ĭ-). [L.] The golden mean; — adapted from Horace (*Odes,* II. x. 5).

au′re·ate (ô′rē·āt), *adj.* [L. *aureatus,* fr. *aureus* golden, fr. *aurum* gold.] Like gold in resplendence.

au′re·ole (ô′rē·ōl), *n.* Also **au·re′o·la** (ô·rē′ō·lȧ). [L. *aureola* (fem. adj.) of gold (sc. *corona* crown), dim. of *aureus.*] **1.** = GLORY, *n.,* 7. **2.** *Meteorol.* The luminous area surrounding the sun, as when seen through mist; also, a corona.

au′re·o·my′cin (ô′rē·ō·mī′sĭn), *n.* [*aureo*faciens + Strepto*myces* + *-in.*] *Biochem.* An antibiotic isolated from a soil microorganism (*Streptomyces aureofaciens*), effective against certain diseases in animals and man.

au re·voir′ (ō′ rē·vwär′). [F., lit., to the seeing again.] Good-by till we meet again.

au′ri- (ô′rĭ-). A combining form, Latin *auri-,* from *aurum,* gold.

au′ri- (ô′rĭ-). [L. *auris.*] A combining form meaning *ear,* as in **au′ri·scope, au·ris′co·py.**

au′ric (ô′rĭk), *adj.* [L. *aurum* gold.] **1.** Of, pertaining to, or containing, gold. **2.** *Chem.* Derived from gold; — of compounds in which gold is trivalent.

au′ri·cle (ô′rĭ·k'l), *n.* [L. *auricula,* dim. of *auris* ear.] **1.** The external ear; pinna. **2.** Either of the two chambers of the heart that receive the blood from the veins and force it into the ventricles; atrium. See HEART, *Illust.* **3.** *Bot. & Zool.* An earlike lobe or process.

au·ric′u·la (ô·rĭk′ū·lȧ), *n.; pl.* -LAE (-lē), -LAS (-lȧz). [L., ear. See AURICLE.] **1.** A yellow-flowered Alpine primrose (*Primula auricula*); bear's-ear. **2.** An auricle.

au·ric′u·lar (-lẽr), *adj* **1.** Of or pertaining to the ear or sense of hearing. **2.** Told in the ear; told privately; as, *auricular* confession. **3.** Known by the sense of hearing; as, *auricular* evidence. **4.** *Anat.* Pertaining to an auricle. — *n. Zool.* One of the loose-webbed feathers overlying the opening of the ear of birds; — usually in *pl.*

au·ric′u·late (-lāt), *adj.* Having ears or earlike appendages or lobes.

au·rif′er·ous (ô·rĭf′ẽr·ŭs), *adj.* Gold-bearing, as ores.

Au·ri′ga (ô·rī′gȧ), *n.; gen.* AURIGAE (-jē). [L., charioteer.] A constellation between Perseus and Gemini.

au′rist (ô′rĭst), *n.* [L. *auris.*] One skilled in treating ear disorders.

au′rochs (ô′rŏks), *n. sing. & pl.* [G. *auerochs.*] The European bison (*Bison bonasus*), once widely distributed, but now nearly extinct.

au·ro′ra (ô·rō′rȧ; 70), *n.; pl.* AURORAS (-rȧz), rarely AURORAE (-rē). [L.] **1.** The rising light of morning; dawn of day. **2.** [*cap.*] The Roman personification of dawn. Cf. Eos. **3.** The aurora borealis or aurora australis. **4.** Rise; dawn; beginning. — **au·ro′ral** (ô·rō′răl), *adj.* — **au·ro′ral·ly,** *adv.* — **au·ro′re·an** (-rē·ăn), *adj.*

au·ro′ra aus·tra′lis (ôs·trā′lĭs). [L.] A phenomenon in the Southern Hemisphere corresponding to the aurora borealis in the Northern.

au·ro′ra bo′re·a′lis (bō′rē·ā′lĭs; -ăl′ĭs). [L.] A luminous phenomenon, usually consisting of streamers of light, visible only at night, and supposed to be of electrical origin; the northern lights. It is best seen in the arctic regions.

au′rous (ô′rŭs), *adj.* **1.** Containing gold. **2.** *Chem.* Derived from gold; — of compounds in which gold is univalent.

au′rum (-rŭm), *n.* [L.] Gold. Symbol, *Au* (no period).

aus′cul·tate (ôs′kŭl·tāt), *v. i. & t.* To practice auscultation; to examine by auscultation. — **aus′cul·ta′tor** (-tā′tẽr), *n.* — **aus·cul′ta·to′ry** (ôs·kŭl′tȧ·tō′rĭ *or, esp. Brit.,* -tẽr·ĭ), *adj.*

aus′cul·ta′tion (-tā′shŭn), *n.* [L. *auscultatio,* fr. *auscultare* to listen.] Act of listening; specif., listening to sounds within the body, esp. the chest and abdomen, to detect disorders or pregnancy. — **aus′cul·ta′tive** (ôs′kŭl·tā′tĭv; ôs·kŭl′tȧ·tĭv), *adj.*

‖**Aus′gleich** (ous′glĭk), *n.; pl.* -GLEICHE (-glĭk·ĕ). [G.] Agreement; compromise; — applied specif. to various treaties between Austria and Hungary.

aus′pex (ôs′pĕks), *n.; pl.* AUSPICES (-pĭ·sēz). [L. See AUSPICE.] *Rom. Relig.* An augur. See AUGUR, *n.,* 1.

aus′pi·cate (ôs′pĭ·kāt), *v. t.* To begin or enter upon as if with auspices; inaugurate.

aus′pice (ôs′pĭs), *n.; pl.* AUSPICES (-pĭ·sēz; -sĭz). [F., fr. L. *auspicium,* fr. *auspex* a bird seer, augur, fr. *avis* bird + *specere, spicere,* to see.] **1.** A sign, or observation for signs, used in augury, as the flight of birds. **2.** An omen (usually favorable) as to the future. **3.** Protection; patronage and care; — usually in *pl.;* as, under the *auspices* of the king. — **aus·pi′cial** (ôs·pĭsh′ăl), *adj.*

aus·pi′cious (ôs·pĭsh′ŭs), *adj.* [See AUSPICE.] **1.** Affording an auspice, esp. a favorable one; hence, favoring; propitious. **2.** Fortunate; prosperous. — **Syn.** See FAVORABLE. — **aus·pi′cious·ly,** *adv.* — **aus·pi′cious·ness,** *n.*

aus′ten·ite (ôs′tĕn·īt), *n.* [After Sir W. Roberts-*Austen,* English metallurgist.] *Metal.* A solid solution of carbon or iron carbide in iron, determined microscopically as a constituent of steel under certain conditions. — **aus′ten·it′ic** (-ĭt′ĭk), *adj.*

Aus′ter (ôs′tẽr), *n.* [L.] South wind; hence, the south.

aus·tere′ (ôs·tẽr′), *adj.* [OF. *austere,* fr. L. *austerus,* fr. Gr. *austēros,* fr. *auein* to parch.] **1.** Sour or harsh to the taste. **2.** Rigorous; stern; severe or strict; as, an *austere* mode of life. **3.** Unadorned; severely simple. **4.** Grave; somber. — **Syn.** See SEVERE. — **aus·tere′ly,** *adv.* — **aus·tere′ness,** *n.*

aus·ter′i·ty (-tĕr′ĭ·tĭ), *n.; pl.* -TIES (-tĭz). **1.** Austere quality, manner, mode of life, or style; esp., cold or dissipassionate reserve or rigorous self-denial; asceticism. **2.** *Usually pl.* An austere practice. **3.** Enforced or extreme economy; as, the British *austerity* program.

aus′tral (ôs′trăl), *adj.* [L. *australis,* fr. *auster* south wind.] **1.** Southern. **2.** [*cap.*] Australian.

Aus·tra′lian (ôs·trāl′yăn), *adj.* Of Australia or its inhabitants; — often prefixed to plant and animal names to denote species resembling those designated by the noun. — *n.* **1.** An aborigine of Australia. **2.** A native or citizen of the Australian commonwealth.

Australian ballot. A ballot, first used in South Australia, on which the names of all the candidates appear and in the marking and polling of which secrecy is compulsorily maintained.

Aus′tral·orp′ (ôs′trȧ·lôrp′), *n.* [*Austral*ia + *Orp*ington.] A type of black Orpington developed in Australia, valuable as egg layers.

Aus′tro- (ôs′trō-). A combining form for *Austria,* as in **Aus′tro-Hun·gar′i·an.**

Aus′tro·ne′sian (ôs′trō·nē′zhăn; -shăn), *adj.* [From NL. *Austronesia* South Sea Islands.] Designating or belonging to a family of agglutinative languages spoken in Malaysia and Oceania (but excluding the Australian, Papuan, and Negrito languages). The Indonesian languages constitute its most highly developed subfamily. See LANGUAGE, *Table.*

au′ta·coid (ô′tȧ·koid), *n.* [Gr. *autos* self + *akos* remedy + *-oid.*] *Physiol.* A specific organic substance, as a hormone, formed in one part of the body and transported by body fluids or the sap, and activating the cells of another part. — **au′ta·coi′dal** (-koi′dăl; -d'l), *adj.*

au′tarch·y (ô′tär·kĭ), *n.* [Gr. *autarchia* autocracy.] **a** Absolute sovereignty; autocratic rule. **b** By confusion, = AUTARKY. — **au·tar′chic** (ô·tär′kĭk), **au·tar′chi·cal** (-kĭ·kăl), *adj.*

au′tar·ky (ô′tär·kĭ), *n.* [Gr. *autarkeia.*] National economic self-sufficiency; a policy of establishing independence of imports from other countries. — **au·tar′kic** (ô·tär′kĭk), **au·tar′ki·cal** (-kĭ·kăl), *adj.* — **au′tar·kist** (ô′tär·kĭst), *n. & adj.*

‖**aut Cae′sar aut ni′hil** (*or* **nul′lus**) (ôt sē′zẽr ôt nī′hĭl, nŭl′ŭs). [L.] Either a Caesar or nothing (or nobody), i. e., all or nothing.

au·te′cious (ô·tē′shŭs), **au·te′cism** (-sĭz′m). Vars. of AUTOECIOUS, AUTOECISM.

au·then′tic (ô·thĕn′tĭk), *adj.* [From OF., fr. L. *authenticus,* fr. Gr. *authentikos,* fr. *authentēs* one who does anything with his own hand.] **1.** Authoritative. **2.** Having a genuine origin or authority; genuine; real; as, an *authentic* paper. **3.** Trustworthy; credible; true; as, an *authentic* report. — **au·then′ti·cal** (-tĭ·kăl), *adj.* — **au·then′ti·cal·ly,** *adv.*

Syn. **Authentic, genuine, veritable, bona fide** mean exactly that which the thing in question is said to be. **Authentic** implies accordance with fact or actuality, thereby implying full trustworthiness (as, an *authentic* record); **genuine** implies accordance with an original or type, there being no admixture, no adulteration, no counterfeiting, or the like (as, a *genuine* wolfhound; *genuine* maple sirup); **veritable** always implies correspondence with truth and is usually employed in asseveration regarding particular instances (as, "Though Christ be the *veritable* Son of God" —*Quiller-Couch*); **bona fide** is used in place of *authentic* or *genuine* but always when good faith is questioned (as, a *bona fide* sale of securities).

au·then′ti·cate (-tĭ·kāt), *v. t.* **1.** To render authentic; give authority to, as by legal proof. **2.** To prove authentic; determine as genuine. — **Syn.** See CONFIRM. — **au·then′ti·ca′tion** (-kā′shŭn), *n.*

au′then·tic′i·ty (ô′thĕn·tĭs′ĭ·tĭ), *n.* Quality or state of being authentic; genuineness.

au′thor (ô′thẽr), *n.* [OF. *autor,* fr. L. *auctor,* fr. *augere* to increase, produce.] **1.** The maker of anything; creator; originator. **2.** One who composes or writes something, as a book; composer; writer. — **au′thor·ess,** *n.* — **au·tho′ri·al** (ô·thō′rĭ·ăl; 70), *adj.*

au·thor′i·tar′i·an (ô·thŏr′ĭ·târ′ĭ·ăn), *adj.* Advocating the principle of obedience to authority as opposed to individual liberty. Cf. TO-

TALITARIAN. — *n.* One who advocates this principle. — **au·thor′i·tar′i·an·ism** (ô·thŏr′ĭ·târ′ĭ·ăn·ĭz′m), *n.*

au·thor′i·ta′tive (ô·thŏr′ĭ·tā′tĭv), *adj.* 1. Having, or proceeding from, authority; entitled to obedience, credit, or acceptance; as, *authoritative* teachings. 2. Having an air of authority; dictatorial; peremptory. — **au·thor′i·ta′tive·ly**, *adv.* — **au·thor′i·ta′tive·ness**, *n.*

au·thor′i·ty (ô·thŏr′ĭ·tĭ), *n.; pl.* -TIES (-tĭz). [OF. *autorité*, fr. L. *auctoritas.*] 1. Legal or rightful power; a right to command or to act; jurisdiction. 2. A person, board, or commission having power in a particular field; as, the Port *Authority.* 3. Government; those exercising power or command; — chiefly in *pl.* 4. One claimed, or appealed to, in support of opinions, actions, measures, etc.; hence: **a** Testimony; witness. **b** A precedent; previous decision of a court. **c** A book or its author. **d** Justification; warrant. 5. Power due to opinion or esteem; influence of character, station, mental or moral superiority, or the like. — **Syn.** See POWER; INFLUENCE.

au′thor·i·za′tion (ô′thẽr·ĭ·zā′shŭn; -ī·zā′shŭn), *n.* Act of authorizing; sanction; warrant.

au′thor·ize (ô′thẽr·īz), *v. t.* 1. To clothe with authority or legal power; to commission; as, *authorized* agents. 2. To empower; permit; as, *authorize* him to act. 3. To establish by authority, as by precedent; sanction; as, customs *authorized* by time. 4. To justify; to furnish a ground for. — **au′thor·iz′er** (-īz′ẽr), *n.*

au′thor·ized (ô′thẽr·īzd), *adj.* **a** Possessed of, or endowed with, authority. **b** Sanctioned or approved by authority.

Authorized Version. Also **King James Bible.** A revision of the English Bible executed under King James I (published 1611). Abbr. *A.V.* See BIBLE.

au′thor·ship (ô′thẽr·shĭp), *n.* 1. Profession of writing books, articles, etc. 2. Origination, esp. of a literary work; instigation; as, *authorship* of a crime.

au′tism (ô′tĭz′m), *n.* [*auto-* + *-ism.*] *Psychol.* Absorption in phantasy to the exclusion of interest in reality. — **au′tist** (-tĭst), *n.* — **au·tis′tic** (ô·tĭs′tĭk), *adj.*

au′to (ô′tō), *n. Colloq.* Short for AUTOMOBILE.

au′to- (ô′tō-). 1. [Gr. *autos.*] A combining form meaning *self*, as in *auto*biography. 2. A shortened form of *automobile*, meaning *automotive*, as in *auto*truck.

‖**Au′to·bahn′** (ou′tō·bän′), *n.; pl.* -BAHNEN (-bä′nĕn). [G., auto road.] In Germany, a road with double traffic lanes in each direction and with no restriction upon speed.

au′to·bi·og′ra·phy (ô′tō·bī·ŏg′rȧ·fĭ; -bĭ-), *n.; pl.* -PHIES (-fĭz). A biography written by the subject of it; memoirs of one's life written by oneself. — **au′to·bi·og′ra·pher** (-fẽr), *n.* — **au′to·bi′o·graph′ic** (-bī′ō·grăf′ĭk), **-graph′i·cal** (-ĭ·kăl), *adj.* — **-graph′i·cal·ly**, *adv.*

au′to·bus′ (ô′tō·bŭs′), *n.* An automobile omnibus.

au′to·cade (ô′tō·kād), *n.* = MOTORCADE.

au′to·chrome (ô′tō·krōm), *n.* [*auto-* + Gr. *chrōma* color.] A kind of plate for color photography. — **au′to·chro′my** (-krō′mĭ), *n.*

au·toch′thon (ô·tŏk′thŏn), *n.; pl.* -THONS (-thŏnz), -THONES (-thō·nēz). [L., fr. Gr. *autochthōn* from the land itself, fr. *autos* self + *chthōn* earth, land.] 1. One sprung from the ground which he inhabits; an aborigine; native. 2. An indigenous plant or animal.

au·toch′tho·nous (-thō·nŭs), *adj.* Indigenous; native; aboriginal. — **au·toch′tho·nous·ly**, *adv.* — **au·toch′tho·ny** (-nĭ), *n.*

au′to·clave (ô′tō·klāv), *n.* [F., fr. *auto-* + L. *clavis* key.] An apparatus for sterilizing, cooking, etc., by superheated steam under pressure; a pressure cooker. — *v. t.* To sterilize, cook, etc., by autoclave.

au′to·co·her′er (-kō·hēr′ẽr; 27), *n. Radio.* A self-restoring coherer, formerly used as a detector.

au·toc′ra·cy (ô·tŏk′rȧ·sĭ), *n.; pl.* -CIES (-sĭz). [Gr. *autokrateia.* See AUTOCRAT.] 1. Independent or self-derived power; absolute supremacy. 2. Uncontrolled authority of an autocrat; supreme government by an individual; also, a state or community under such a government.

au′to·crat (ô′tō·krăt), *n.* [Gr. *autokratēs*, fr. *autos* self + *kratos* strength.] An absolute sovereign; a monarch ruling by claim of absolute right; a despot; hence, one who rules with undisputed sway in any company or relation.

au′to·crat′ic (-krăt′ĭk), **au′to·crat′i·cal** (-ĭ·kăl), *adj.* Of, pertaining to, or of the nature of, autocracy or an autocrat; absolute; despotic. — **au′to·crat′i·cal·ly**, *adv.*

au′to–da–fé′ (ô′tō·dȧ·fā′; ou′-), *n.; pl.* AUTOS-DA-FÉ (ô′tōz-; ou′tōz-). [Pg., act of the faith.] The ceremony accompanying the pronouncement of judgment by the Inquisition, followed by the execution by the secular authorities; hence, the execution, esp. the burning, of a heretic.

‖**au′to de fe** (ou′tō thā fā′). [Sp.] Auto-da-fé.

au′to·de·tec′tor (ô′tō·dē·tĕk′tẽr), *n.* An autocoherer.

au′to·dyne (ô′tō·dīn), *adj.* [*auto-* + *dyne.*] *Radio.* Designating a type of heterodyne in which the auxiliary current is generated in the rectifying device. — **au′to·dyne**, *n.*

au·toe′cious (ô·tē′shŭs), *adj.* [*auto-* + Gr. *oikia* dwelling.] *Biol.* Passing through all life stages on the same host, as certain parasitic fungi. Cf. HETEROECIOUS. — **au·toe′cism** (-sĭz′m), *n.*

au′to·er′o·tism (ô′tō·ĕr′ō·tĭz′m), *n.* Also **au′to·e·rot′i·cism** (-ē·rŏt′ĭ·sĭz′m; -ĕr·ŏt′-). [*auto-* + *erotism, eroticism.*] *Psychol.* **a** Erotic impulse of spontaneous origin. **b** Sex gratification obtained from the self. — **au′to·e·rot′ic** (-ē·rŏt′ĭk; -ĕr·ŏt′ĭk), *adj.*

au·tog′a·my (ô·tŏg′ȧ·mĭ), *n.* [*auto-* + *-gamy.*] Self-fertilization, as, *Biol.*, of a flower by its own pollen or of an animal by self-produced gametes. — **au·tog′a·mous** (-mŭs), *adj.*

au′to·gen′e·sis (ô′tō·jĕn′ē·sĭs), *n.* = SPONTANEOUS GENERATION.

au′to·ge·net′ic (-jē·nĕt′ĭk), *adj.* Self-generated; specif., *Biol.*, pert. to autogenesis. — **au′to·ge·net′i·cal·ly** (-ĭ·kăl·ĭ), *adv.*

au·tog′e·nous (ô·tŏj′ē·nŭs), *adj.* [Gr. *autogenēs.* See AUTO-; -GENOUS.] 1. Self-generated; produced independently of external aid; endogenous. 2. Of origin within oneself; specif., derived from the patient; as, an *autogenous* vaccine; — opposed to *heterogenous.*

au·tog′e·ny (-nĭ), *n.* Self-generation.

Au′to·gi′ro (ô′tō·jī′rō), *n.* A trade-mark for a type of aircraft, heavier than air, in which the wings are supplemented by a system of revolving blades hinged to a vertical shaft. Cf. HELICOPTER.

au′to·graph (ô′tō·grăf; 9), *n.* [From L., fr. Gr. *autographos* autographic, fr. *autos* self + *graphein* to write.] That which is written with one's own hand; an original, or author's, manuscript; a person's own signature or handwriting. Cf. HOLOGRAPH. — *v. t.* 1. To write with one's own hand. 2. To write one's signature in or on. — **au′to·graph′ic** (-grăf′ĭk), **au′to·graph′i·cal** (-ĭ·kăl), *adj.* — **au′to·graph′i·cal·ly**, *adv.* — **au·tog′ra·phy** (ô·tŏg′rȧ·fĭ), *n.*

au′to·hyp·no′sis (ô′tō·hĭp·nō′sĭs), *n.* [NL.] Self-induced hypnosis. Cf. AUTOSUGGESTION.

au′to·in·fec′tion (-ĭn·fĕk′shŭn), *n.* [*auto-* + *infection.*] *Med.* Infection having an origin within the body.

au′to·in·oc′u·la′tion (-ĭn·ŏk′ū·lā′shŭn), *n.* 1. Inoculation with virus from one's own body. 2. Spread of infection from a focus of disease to other parts of the same body.

au′to·in·tox′i·ca′tion (-ĭn·tŏk′sĭ·kā′shŭn), *n. Med.* Poisoning, or state of being poisoned, from toxic substances produced in the body.

au′to·load′ing (ô′tō·lōd′ĭng), *adj. Firearms.* Semiautomatic.

au·tol′y·sis (ô·tŏl′ĭ·sĭs), *n.* [NL., fr. *auto-* + *-lysis.*] *Biochem.* Process of self-digestion in plant and animal tissues, esp. after separation from the organism to which they belong, as in fruit after picking or in meat after slaughtering. — **au′to·ly′sin** (ô′tō·lī′sĭn), *n.* — **au′to·lyt′ic** (-lĭt′ĭk), *adj.*

au′to·mat (ô′tō·măt), *n.* [G. See AUTOMATON.] A restaurant in which orders are delivered to patrons from slot machines.

au·tom′a·ta (ô·tŏm′ȧ·tȧ), *n., pl.* of AUTOMATON.

au′to·mat′ic (ô′tō·măt′ĭk), *adj.* [See AUTOMATON.] 1. Having an inherent power of action. 2. Self-acting or self-regulating; — esp. of machinery or mechanical devices. 3. *Firearms.* That employs either gas pressure or force of recoil and mechanical spring action in ejecting the empty cartridge case after the first shot, loading the next cartridge from the magazine, firing and ejecting that cartridge, and repeating the above cycle as long as the pressure on the trigger is maintained or until the ammunition is exhausted; as, some rifles can be changed, by throwing a lever, from semiautomatic to full *automatic;* so-called automatic American pistols are autoloading, but none is *automatic.* See RIFLE, *Illust.* 4. Not voluntary; not depending on the will; mechanical; as, *automatic* movements; *automatic* reasoning. 5. *Psychol.* Performed without conscious intention; as, *automatic* writing. — **Syn.** See SPONTANEOUS. — *n.* A machine or apparatus that operates automatically; esp., an automatic firearm. — **au′to·mat′i·cal·ly** (-ĭ·kăl·ĭ), *adv.*

automatic pilot. = GYROPILOT.

au′to·ma′tion (ô′tō·mā′shŭn), *n.* [*automatic* + *-ion.*] 1. The technique of making a process or system automatic. 2. Automatically controlled operation of an apparatus, process, or system, esp. by electronic devices.

au·tom′a·tism (ô·tŏm′ȧ·tĭz′m), *n.* 1. State or quality of being automatic; also, automatic action. 2. *Philos.* The theory that consciousness does not control action, but is a mere adjunct of physiological changes. 3. *Physiol.* The power or fact of moving (1) independently of external stimuli, as the beating of the heart, or (2) directly from the effect of external stimuli but independently of conscious control. 4. *Psychol.* Any action performed without the doer's intention or knowledge; an automatic action. 5. *Surrealism.* Suspension of the conscious mind in order to release for expression the repressed ideas and images of the unconscious. — **au·tom′a·tist** (-tĭst), *n.*

au·tom′a·ton (ô·tŏm′ȧ·tŏn), *n.; pl.* -TA (-tȧ), -TONS (-tŏnz). [Gr., neut. of *automatos* self-acting.] 1. A thing regarded as capable of spontaneous action. 2. A self-moving machine, esp. one imitating the actions of men, birds, etc. 3. A person acting mechanically, esp. one unintelligently following a routine. Cf. ROBOT.

au′to·mo′bile (ô′tō·mō′bĭl; -bēl), *adj.* [*auto-* + *mobile.*] Containing means of propulsion within itself; pertaining to an automobile.

au′to·mo·bile′ (ô′tō·mō·bēl′; ô′tō·mō·bēl′; ô′tō·mō′bēl), *n.* [F.] An automobile vehicle or mechanism; esp., a self-propelled vehicle suitable for use on a street or roadway. — **au′to·mo·bil′ist** (-mō·bēl′ĭst; -mō′bĭl·ĭst), *n.*

au′to·mo′tive (ô′tō·mō′tĭv), *adj.* Self-propelling; automobile; hence, concerned with self-propelling vehicles or machines.

au′to·nom′ic (-nŏm′ĭk), *adj.* 1. Autonomous. 2. *Physiol. & Anat.* Acting independently of volition; specif., designating that part of the peripheral nervous system of vertebrates which regulates the involuntary responses, esp. those concerned with nutritive, vascular, and reproductive activities. See NERVOUS SYSTEM. 3. *Plant Physiol.* Due to internal causes or influences; spontaneous. — **au′to·nom′i·cal** (-ĭ·kăl), *adj.* — **au′to·nom′i·cal·ly**, *adv.*

au·ton′o·mist (ô·tŏn′ō·mĭst), *n.* An advocate of autonomy.

au·ton′o·mous (-mŭs), *adj.* [Gr. *autonomos*, fr. *autos* self + *nomos* law.] 1. Of or pertaining to an autonomy. 2. Independent in government; self-governing; also, without outside control. 3. *Biol.* Existing independently; responding, or reacting, independently of the whole. 4. *Plant Physiol.* Autonomic. — **Syn.** See FREE. — **-ly**, *adv.*

au·ton′o·my (-mĭ), *n.* Quality or state of being autonomous; right of self-government; — opposed to *heteronomy;* also, a self-governing state.

au′to·nym (ô′tō·nĭm), *n.* Literally, one's own name; — opposed to *pseudonym;* hence, a book published under an author's own name.

au′to·phyte (ô′tō·fīt), *n.* [*auto-* + *-phyte.*] *Bot.* A plant not dependent upon organized food materials such as occur in humus. Cf. SAPROPHYTE.

au′to·pi′lot (ô′tō·pī′lŭt), *n.* [*automatic pilot.*] = GYROPILOT.

au′to·plas′ty (ô′tō·plăs′tĭ), *n. Surg.* The repairing of lesions with tissue from the same body. — **au′to·plas′tic** (-plăs′tĭk), *adj.*

au′top·sy (ô′tŏp·sĭ; ô′tŭp-), *n.; pl.* -SIES (-sĭz). [Gr. *autopsia*, fr. *autoptos* seen by oneself, fr. *autos* self + *optos* seen.] Inspection, and partial dissection, of a dead body to learn the cause of death, nature and extent of disease, etc.; post-mortem examination; necropsy.

au′to·ra′di·o·graph′ (ô′tō·rā′dĭ·ō·grăf′; 9), *n.* = RADIOAUTOGRAPH. — **au′to·ra′di·og′ra·phy** (-ŏg′rȧ·fĭ), *n.*

au′to·sta·bil′i·ty (ô′tō·stȧ·bĭl′ĭ·tĭ), *n. Mech.* Stability due to automatic action of self-operative mechanism; also, stability due to inherent qualities, as shape.

au′to·sug·ges′tion (ô′tō·sŭg·jĕs′chŭn; -sŭ·jĕs′chŭn), *n.* Self-suggestion as disting. from suggestion coming from another, esp. in hypnotism. It sometimes produces functional disturbance. — **-tive** (-tĭv), *adj.*

au′to·tox·e′mi·a, au′to·tox·ae′mi·a (-tŏk·sē′mĭ·ȧ), *n.* [NL. See AUTO-; TOXEMIA.] Autointoxication.

au′to·tox′i·co′sis (-tŏk′sĭ·kō′sĭs), **au′to·tox′is** (-tŏk′sĭs), *n.* = AUTOINTOXICATION.

au′to·tox′in (-tŏk′sĭn), *n.* Any toxin produced within the body.

au′to·trans·form′er (-trăns·fôr′mẽr), *n.* = COMPENSATOR, 2.

au′to·troph′ic (-trŏf′ĭk), *adj.* Self-nourishing; — of plants capable of photosynthesis. Cf. HETEROTROPHIC. — **au′to·troph** (ô′tō·trŏf), *n.* — **au·tot′ro·phy** (ô·tŏt′rō·fĭ), *n.*

au′to·truck′ (ô′tō·trŭk′), *n.* A motor-driven truck.

au′to·type′ (-tīp′), *n.* 1. A facsimile. 2. *Photog.* The carbon process; also, a picture made by it. — **au′to·typ′ic** (-tĭp′ĭk), *adj.* — **au′to·typ′y** (ô′tō·tīp′ĭ), *n.*

au'tumn (ô'tŭm), *n.* [From OF., fr. L. *autumnus.*] **1.** The season between summer and winter; — in America commonly called *fall.* **2.** Time of maturity or decline. — **au'tumn,** *adj.*

au·tum'nal (ô·tŭm'năl; -n'l), *adj.* **1.** Of, belonging to, or peculiar to, autumn; as, the *autumnal* equinox or point (see EQUINOX, 1). **2.** Past middle life. — **au·tum'nal·ly,** *adv.*

au'tun·ite (ô'tŭn·īt), *n.* [From *Autun,* France.] *Mineral.* A lemon-yellow uranium calcium phosphate occurring in tabular crystals and micalike scales It is radioactive.

‖**aux** (ō). [F.] See À LA.

‖**aux armes!** (ō'-zärm'). [F.] To arms!

aux·il'ia·ry (ôg·zĭl'yȧ·rĭ), *adj.* [L. *auxiliarius,* fr. *auxilium* help, aid.] **1.** Conferring help or aid; assistant; supporting. **2.** Subsidiary; also, additional. **3.** Serving to supplement or take the place of; as, an *auxiliary* power station. **4.** Equipped with an engine or other power to supplement the motive power of sails; as, an *auxiliary* sloop. — **Syn.** Subsidiary, accessory, subservient, adjuvant. — *n.; pl.* -RIES (-rĭz). **1.** One who assists; an auxiliary group, device, etc. **2.** Foreign troops in the service of a nation at war; — in *pl.* **3.** An auxiliary verb. **4.** An auxiliary boat or vessel.

auxiliary verb. *Gram.* A verb (as *have, be, may, do, shall* and *will, can, must,* in English) which helps to form the voices, moods, tenses, etc., of other verbs.

aux'i·mone (ôk'sĭ·mōn), *n.* [Gr. *auximos* promoting plant growth.] *Plant Physiol.* Any of certain substances considered necessary, though only in small quantities, for the vigorous growth of plants.

aux'in (ôk'sĭn), *n.* [Gr. *auxein* to increase + *-in.*] *Plant Physiol.* Any of a group of substances which promote plant growth by cell elongation, bring about root formation, and cause bud inhibition and other effects.

a·va', a·va'' (ȧ·vä'), *adv.* *Chiefly Scot.* Of all; at all.

a·vail' (ȧ·vāl'), *v. i.* [ME. *availen,* fr. OF. *a-* to + *valoir* to be worth, fr. L. *valere* to be strong, to be worth.] To be of use; to answer the purpose; to have strength, force, or efficacy sufficient to accomplish the object in mind. — *v. t.* To be of advantage to; profit; benefit; help; as, how can that *avail* me? — ***avail oneself of.*** To make use of; to take advantage of. — *n.* **1.** Profit; benefit. **2.** Advantage toward success; usefulness for a purpose; as, of *avail;* to little *avail.* — **Syn.** Use, service, advantage, profit.

a·vail'a·bil'i·ty (ȧ·vāl'ȧ·bĭl'ĭ·tĭ), *n.; pl.* -TIES (-tĭz). Quality or state of being available; also, available person or thing.

a·vail'a·ble (ȧ·vāl'ȧ·b'l), *adj.* **1.** *Obs.* Effectual; beneficial. **2.** *Law.* Valid; as, an *available* plea. **3.** Such as one may avail oneself of; usable. **4.** Having the requisite political associations and circumstantial qualifications for winning election to office; — of a political candidate. **5.** At disposal; accessible or attainable; obtainable; handy. — **a·vail'a·ble·ness,** *n.* — **a·vail'a·bly,** *adv.*

av'a·lanche (ăv'ȧ·lȧnch; 9), *n.* [F., prob., under influence of *avaler* to descend, *aval* downward, deriv. of L. *labi* to slip, glide.] **1.** A large mass of snow and ice, or of earth, rock, etc., in swift motion down a mountainside or over a precipice. **2.** A sudden, great, or overwhelming descent of anything; as, an *avalanche* of words.

Av'a·lon, Av'al·lon (ăv'ȧ·lŏn), *n.* [F.] In medieval, esp. Arthurian, romance, an ocean island, believed to be near the terrestrial paradise.

a·vant'-garde' (ä·vänt'gärd'), *n.* [F., vanguard.] In any art, the most daring of the experimentalists and innovators of original and startlingly unconventional designs, ideas, or techniques during a particular period. — **a·vant'-gard'ist** (-gär'dĭst), *n.*

av'a·rice (ăv'ȧ·rĭs), *n.* [OF., fr. L. *avaritia,* fr. *avarus* avaricious.] Inordinate desire for wealth; — implying both miserliness and greed.

av'a·ri'cious (-rĭsh'ŭs), *adj.* Actuated by avarice; greedy of gain. — **Syn.** See COVETOUS. — **av'a·ri'cious·ly,** *adv.* — **av'a·ri'cious·ness,** *n.*

a·vast' (ȧ·văst'), *v. t. & i.* [Origin unknown.] *Naut.* Cease; stop; stay; as, avast heaving!

av'a·tar' (ăv'ȧ·tär'), *n.* [Skr. *avatāra* descent.] **1.** *Hindu Relig.* Incarnation of a deity; — chiefly associated with Vishnu. **2.** Incarnation; embodiment; manifestation. **3.** Exaltation into an object of worship or a cult.

a·vaunt' (ȧ·vônt'; ȧ·vänt'), *adv.* [F. *avant,* fr. L. *ab* away + *ante* before.] Begone; depart; — used interjectionally.

a've (ā'vē; ä'vā), *interj.* [L., hail, be well.] Hail! also, Farewell! — *n.* **1.** The salutation *ave;* esp. [*cap.*], an Ave Maria. **2.** [*cap.*] The time for saying Aves.

‖**a've at'que va'le!** (ā'vē ăt'kwē vā'lē). [L.] Hail and farewell!

a·vel'lan (ȧ·vĕl'ăn; ăv'ĕl·ăn), *adj.* [L. *avellana* a filbert.] *Her.* In the form of four unhusked filberts; — said of a cross. See CROSS, *Illust.* (14).

A've Ma·ri'a (ä'vā mä·rē'ä), **A've Ma'ry** (ā'vē mā'rĭ; mâr'ĭ). [L. *ave* hail, *Maria* Mary.] **1.** The salutation of Gabriel and of Elisabeth to the Virgin Mary, combined, as now used in the Roman Catholic Church, with a prayer to her as Mother of God. **2.** A particular time, when the people repeat the Ave Maria. **3.** One of the small beads of a rosary by which Ave Marias are counted.

av'e·na'ceous (ăv'ē·nā'shŭs), *adj.* [L. *avenaceus,* fr. *avena* oats.] Of or resembling oats or the oat grasses.

a·venge' (ȧ·vĕnj'), *v. t.;* -VENGED' (-vĕnjd'); -VENG'ING (-vĕn'jĭng). [OF. *avengier,* fr. L. *ad* to + *vindicare* to claim, avenge.] To take vengeance for or on behalf of; to exact satisfaction for. — *v. i.* To take vengeance. — **a·veng'er** (ȧ·vĕn'jẽr), *n.* — **a·veng'ing,** *adj.*

Syn. **Avenge, revenge** mean to inflict punishment on one who has wronged oneself or another. **Avenge** is now preferred when one is thought of as visiting just or merited punishment on a wrongdoer, **revenge** when one is thought of as getting even or paying back in kind or degree.

av'ens (ăv'ĕnz; -ĭnz), *n.* [OF. *avence.*] Any of a genus (*Geum*) of perennial herbs of the rose family, having white, purple, or yellow flowers; a geum; esp., the common avens, or herb bennet (*G. urbanum*) or the purple, or water, avens (*G. rivale*). See BENNET, 2.

av'en·tail, av'en·tayle (ăv'ĕn·tāl), *n.* **1.** An adjustable flap of a hood of mail armor, covering the chin and secured to the hood. **2.** = VENTAIL.

Av'en·tine (ăv'ĕn·tīn; -tĭn), *n.* [L. *Aventinus.*] One of the seven hills of Rome (see SEVEN HILLS), in early times an asylum for refugees. — **Av'en·tine,** *adj.*

a·ven'tu·rine (ȧ·vĕn'tū·rēn; -rĭn), *n.* Also **a·ven'tu·rin** (-rĭn). [From F., fr. It. *avventurina,* fr. *avventura* chance.] **1.** A kind of glass containing particles of copper (***gold aventurine***), of chromic oxide, Cr_2O_3 (***green aventurine***), or of ferric oxide. **2.** *Mineral.* A translucent quartz, spangled throughout with scales of mica or other mineral.

av'e·nue (ăv'ē·nū), *n.* [F., fr. *avenir* to come to, fr. L. *advenire,* fr. *ad-* + *venire* to come.] **1.** An opening or passageway by which a place may be reached; a way of approach or of exit; as, an *avenue* of escape. **2.** Any broad passageway, often one bordered on each side by trees. **3.** A street; esp., a wide and beautiful street. Abbr. *Av.* or *Ave.*

a·ver' (ȧ·vûr'), *v. t.;* -VERRED' (-vûrd'); -VER'RING. [F. *avérer,* deriv. of L. *ad* to + *verus* true.] **1.** *Law.* To avouch or verify; prove or justify. **2.** To affirm confidently; declare positively. — **Syn.** See ASSERT.

av'er·age (ăv'ẽr·ĭj; ăv'rĭj), *n.* [F. *avarie* damage to ship or cargo, port dues, fr. It. *avaria,* fr. Ar.] **1.** Any of sundry small charges, as port charges, defrayed by the master of a vessel. **2.** A loss less than total to cargo or ship, or a charge arising from it, or the proportionate distribution of it among all interested parties. **3.** A mean value, medial sum or quantity, made out of unequal sums or quantities; an arithmetical mean. Abbr. *av.* **4.** An estimate of or approximation to an arithmetical mean; loosely, the usual, typical, or most often encountered thing, happening, or person of a considerable number.

Syn. **Average, mean, median, norm** mean something that represents a middle point between extremes. **Average,** as here considered, is applied to a quotient obtained by dividing the sum total of figures by the number of those figures; thus, the *average* of the 20 apple pickers is 25 bushels a day; his *average* (i. e., average mark) is 85; **mean,** in general, represents a figure midway between two extremes; thus, the *mean* of temperature for a day is reached by adding the minimum and the maximum together and dividing that number by 2; **median,** a term of statistics, usually applies to the figure or quantity that represents the point at which there are as many instances below as there are above it (thus, the *average* of a group of persons earning 3, 4, 5, 8, and 10 dollars a day is 6 dollars, whereas the *median* is 5 dollars); **norm** now means the computed or estimated average of performance or achievement for a group, class, or grade; thus, studies in a certain grade are based upon the accepted *norm* for children of that age, experience, etc.

— *adj.* **1.** *Mar. Law.* Assessed according to the laws of average (def. 2). **2.** Equaling an arithmetical mean; as, the *average* rainfall; also, approximating an arithmetical mean; usual; as, the *average* Englishman. — **Syn.** Medium, fair, mediocre.

— *v. i.;* -AGED (-ĭjd; -rĭjd); -AG·ING (-ĭj·ĭng; -rĭj·ĭng). **1.** To do, get, etc., as an average sum or quantity; as, to *average* eight hours of work a day; also, to amount to, or be, on an average; as, these poles *average* ten feet in length. **2.** *Exchanges.* To buy or sell additional shares, commodities, etc., so as to obtain a more favorable average price. — *v. t.* **1.** To find the mean of; reduce to a mean. **2.** To divide among a number, proportionately; as, to *average* a loss.

a·ver'ment (ȧ·vûr'mĕnt), *n.* Act of averring, or that which is averred; affirmation; positive assertion.

A·ver'nus (ȧ·vûr'nŭs), *n.* [L.] The infernal regions; — so called after a small deep lake in Italy, the vapors of which were fabled to kill birds. — **A·ver'nal** (-năl; -n'l), *adj.*

Av'er·ro'ism (ăv'ẽ·rō'ĭz'm), *n.* The doctrines of the Arab philosopher Averroës (ibn-Rushd), 1126–1198. — **Av'er·ro'ist** (-ĭst), *n. & adj.* — **Av'er·ro·is'tic** (-rō·ĭs'tĭk), *adj.*

a·verse' (ȧ·vûrs'), *adj.* [L. *aversus,* past part. of *avertere.* See AVERT.] **1.** Having an aversion; disliking; unwilling; — usually followed by *to* or *from, to* being now the more frequent; as, *averse* to war. **2.** *Bot.* Turned away from the stem or axis. Cf. ADVERSE. — **Syn.** See DISINCLINED. — **a·verse'ly,** *adv.* — **a·verse'ness,** *n.*

a·ver'sion (ȧ·vûr'zhŭn; -shŭn), *n.* **1.** Act of turning away. **2.** A state of mind in which attention to an object is coupled with dislike of it and desire of turning from it; dislike; repugnance. **3.** A settled dislike; antipathy. **4.** An object of dislike or repugnance.

a·vert' (ȧ·vûrt'), *v. t.* [L. *avertere,* fr. *a, ab,* from + *vertere* to turn.] To turn aside, or away; to ward off, or prevent, the occurrence or effects of. — **Syn.** See PREVENT. — **a·vert'i·ble, a·vert'a·ble,** *adj.*

A·ver'tin (ȧ·vûr'tĭn), *n.* A trade-mark for tribromoethanol.

A'ves (ā'vēz), *n. pl.* [L., pl. of *avis* bird.] *Zool.* The class of vertebrates consisting of the birds. See BIRD.

A·ves'ta (ȧ·vĕs'tȧ), *or* **Zend'-A·ves'ta** (zĕnd'-), *n.* [Prop., the *Avesta,* or sacred text, and its *zend,* or interpretation.] The sacred books of the ancient Zoroastrian religion and of the modified form of it which still survives among the Parsis of Persia and India.

A·ves'tan (-tăn), *adj.* Of or pertaining to the Avesta or the language of the Avesta. — *n.* The language of the Avesta. See INDO-EUROPEAN LANGUAGES, *Table.*

a'vi·an (ā'vĭ·ăn), *adj.* Of or pertaining to Aves or birds.

a'vi·ar'y (-ĕr'ĭ *or, esp. Brit.,* -ẽr·ĭ), *n.; pl.* -IES (-ĭz). [L. *aviarium,* fr. *avis* bird.] A place, as a house, for keeping birds confined.

a'vi·ate (ā'vĭ·āt; ăv'ĭ-), *v. i.* [From AVIATOR.] To fly, or navigate the air, in an airplane, or heavier-than-air aircraft.

a'vi·a'tion (-ā'shŭn), *n.* [F., fr. L. *avis* bird.] The art or practice of operating heavier-than-air aircraft.

aviation badge. See WINGS.

a'vi·a'tor (ā'vĭ·ā'tẽr; ăv'ĭ-), *n.* The operator or pilot of a heavier-than-air aircraft, as an airplane or a seaplane. — **a'vi·a'tress** (-trĕs; -trĭs), **a'vi·a'trix** (-ā'trĭks), *n.*

a'vi·cul'ture (ā'vĭ·kŭl'tūr), *n.* [L. *avis* bird + *cultura* culture.] Rearing and care of birds. — **a'vi·cul'tur·ist** (-kŭl'tūr·ĭst), *n.*

av'id (ăv'ĭd), *adj.* [L. *avidus,* fr. *avēre* to long for.] Craving eagerly; keenly eager; greedy. — **Syn.** See EAGER. — **av'id·ly,** *adv.*

av'i·din (ăv'ĭ·dĭn), *n.* [*avidity* (for biotin) + *-in* as in *protein.*] A protein found in white of egg, which combines with biotin and renders it inactive.

a·vid'i·ty (ȧ·vĭd'ĭ·tĭ), *n.* **1.** Extreme eagerness; greediness; avarice. **2.** *Chem.* The strength of an acid or base, dependent on its degree of dissociation; sometimes, affinity.

a'vi·fau'na (ā'vĭ·fô'nȧ), *n.* [NL., fr. L. *avis* bird + E. *fauna.*] *Zool.* The birds, or all the kinds of birds, considered collectively, of a region. — **a'vi·fau'nal** (-năl), *adj.*

av'i·ga'tion (ăv'ĭ·gā'shŭn), *n.* The science or art of conducting aircraft in flight from one point to another. — **av'i·gate** (ăv'ĭ·gāt), *v. i.* — **av'i·ga'tor** (-gā'tẽr), *n.*

A·vil'ion (ȧ·vĭl'yŭn), *n.* Var. of AVALON.

‖**a vin'cu·lo ma'tri·mo'ni·i** (ā vĭng'kū·lō măt'rĭ·mō'nĭ·ī). [L.] *Law.* From the bond of marriage; an absolute divorce.

‖**a·vion'** (ȧ'vyôN'), *n.* [F.] An airplane.

a·vi'so (ȧ·vī'zō), *n.; pl.* -SOS (-zōz). [Sp.] **1.** Information; notification. **2.** A dispatch boat.

a·vi′ta·min·o′sis (ā·vī′tȧ·mĭn·ō′sĭs; ā′vī·tăm′ĭ·nō′sĭs), *n.* [*a-* not + *vitamin* + *-osis.*] A morbid condition due to a lack or deficiency of vitamins in the food.

av′o·ca′do (ăv′ō·kä′dō), *n.; pl.* -DOS (-dōz). [Corrupt. (perh. by Sp. *bocado* tidbit) fr. Sp. *aguacate, ahuacate,* fr. Nahuatl *ahuacatl, auacatl,* the fruit.] The pulpy, green or purple edible fruit of certain tropical American trees of the laurel family (genus *Persea*); an alligator pear; also, the tree.

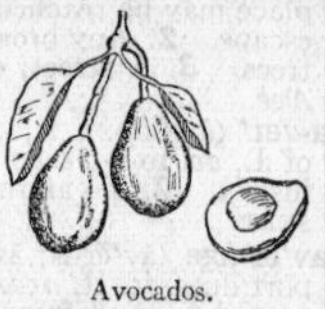

Avocados.

av′o·ca′tion (ăv′ō·kā′shŭn), *n.* [L. *avocatio,* fr. *avocare, avocatus,* fr. *a, ab,* away + *vocare* to call.] **1.** Diversion of attention. **2.** A subordinate occupation; a hobby. **3.** Customary employment; vocation; usual pursuits; — a use now preferably avoided, to preserve the useful distinction from *vocation.*

a·voc′a·to′ry (ȧ·vŏk′ȧ·tō′rĭ *or, esp. Brit.,* -tẽr·ĭ), *adj.* Summoning away or back; as, an *avocatory* letter.

av′o·cet, av′o·set (ăv′ō·sĕt), *n.* [F. *avocette,* fr. It. *avocetta.*] Any of several shore birds (genus *Recurvirostra*) having long legs, webbed feet, and a slender upwardly curved bill.

a·void′ (ȧ·void′), *v. t.* [From OF., fr. *es* (L. *ex*) + *vuidier, voidier,* to empty. See VOID, *adj.*] **1.** *Obs.* To empty; void; expel. **2.** To make void; annul; vacate; specif., *Law,* to defeat, evade, or invalidate, as a plea. **3.** To keep away from; shun; abstain from; as, to *avoid* evil. — **Syn.** See ESCAPE. — **Ant.** Face. — **a·void′a·ble,** *adj.*

a·void′ance (-ăns), *n.* **1.** *Obs.* An emptying; ejection. **2.** The state of being or becoming vacant; — said esp. of a benefice. **3.** Act of annulling; annulment. **4.** Act of avoiding or keeping clear of.

av′oir·du·pois′ (ăv′ẽr·dŭ·poiz′; ăv′ẽr·dŭ·poiz′), *n.* [ME. *avoir de pois, aver de peis,* goods of weight, fr. OF. *aveir, avoir,* goods, and *peis, pois,* weight, fr. L. *pensum.*] **1.** Avoirdupois weight. Abbr. *av., avdp.,* or *avoir.* **2.** *Colloq.* Weight; heaviness.

avoirdupois weight. The system in common use in English-speaking countries for weighing all commodities except precious stones, precious metals, and drugs. See WEIGHT, *Tables* 1 & 4.

‖**à vo′tre san′té′** (à vô′trĕ säN′tā′). [F.] To your health.

a·vouch′ (ȧ·vouch′), *v. t.* [From OF., fr. LL. *advocare* to recognize the existence of a thing, advocate, fr. L. *advocare* to call to, fr. *ad-* + *vocare* to call.] **1.** To assert positively; affirm openly. **2.** Vouch for; guarantee. **3.** Avow; sanction. — **Syn.** See ASSERT.

a·vow′ (ȧ·vou′), *v. t.* [OF. *avouer,* fr. L. *advocare* to call upon. See AVOUCH.] To declare openly; own or acknowledge frankly. — **Syn.** See ASSERT; ACKNOWLEDGE. — **a·vow′er,** *n.*

a·vow′al (-ăl), *n.* An open declaration; frank acknowledgment.

a·vowed′ (ȧ·voud′), *adj.* Openly acknowledged or declared; admitted. — **a·vow′ed·ly** (ȧ·vou′ĕd·lĭ; -ĭd·lĭ), *adv.* — **a·vow′ed·ness,** *n.*

a·vul′sion (ȧ·vŭl′shŭn), *n.* [L. *avulsio.*] **1.** A forcible separation; also, part torn off. **2.** *Law.* The sudden removal of land from the estate of one man to that of another, as by a sudden change in a river, the property thus separated continuing in the original owner. Cf. ALLUVION.

a·vun′cu·lar (ȧ·vŭng′kū·lẽr), *adj.* [L. *avunculus* uncle.] Of or pertaining to, or like, an uncle or, humorously, a pawnbroker.

a·wait′ (ȧ·wāt′), *v. t.* [ONF. *awaitier,* fr. *a* to + *waitier* to watch. See WAIT.] **1.** *Obs.* To watch for. **2.** To wait for; expect. **3.** To be in store for; be ready or in waiting for. — *v. i.* To wait; to stay or be in waiting.

a·wake′ (ȧ·wāk′), *adj.* Not sleeping or lethargic; roused from sleep; vigilant; alert. — **Syn.** See AWARE.

a·wake′ (ȧ·wāk′), *v. i.;* A·WOKE′ (-wōk′) or A·WAKED′ (-wākt′); A·WAKED′ or A·WOKE′; A·WAK′ING (-wāk′ĭng). *Obs. past parts.* A·WOK′EN, A·WAK′EN. [AS. *āwæcnan* (past *āwōc*), and *āwacian* (past *āwacode*).] To cease to sleep; come out of sleep, or a sleeplike state; as, to *awake* to danger. — *v. t.* To rouse from sleep or a sleeplike state; awaken; give new life to; stir up.

a·wak′en (ȧ·wāk′ĕn), *v. t. & i.* [AS. *āwæcnan, āwæcnian,* v. i., fr. *on-* + *wæcnan* to wake.] To rouse from sleep, or from torpor, indifference, etc.; to awake. — **a·wak′en·ing,** *adj. & n.*

a·ward′ (ȧ·wôrd′), *v. t.* [ONF. *eswarder,* fr. *es* (L. *ex*) + *warder* (OF. *garder*) to observe, keep.] **1.** To give by sentence or judicial determination; assign; apportion; adjudge; as, to *award* heavy damages. **2.** To confer or bestow upon. — **Syn.** See GRANT. — *n.* **1.** A judgment; the decision of arbitrators. **2.** That which is awarded, as a prize or honor. — **a·ward′a·ble,** *adj.* — **a·ward′er,** *n.*

a·ware′ (ȧ·wâr′), *adj.* [AS. *gewær,* fr. *wær* wary.] Apprised; informed; cognizant; conscious; as, *aware* of the enemy. — **-ness,** *n.*

Syn. **Aware, cognizant, conscious, sensible, alive, awake** mean having knowledge of something that is not obvious or apparent. **Aware** usually implies vigilance in observing or in drawing inferences from what one sees, hears, etc.; **cognizant** implies special or certain knowledge, as from firsthand sources; **conscious** implies awareness of something when one allows it to enter his mind and usually fixes his attention upon it; **sensible** implies the operation of something like a sixth sense; **alive** adds to *sensible* the implication of acute sensitiveness to something; **awake** implies that one has become alive to something and is on the alert.

a·wash′ (ȧ·wŏsh′), *adv. & adj.* **1.** Washed by waves or tide. **2.** Floating in the water. **3.** Overflowed by water.

a·way′ (ȧ·wā′), *adv.* [AS. *aweg, anweg, onweg,* fr. *on* on + *weg* way.] **1.** From a place; hence; as, go *away.* **2.** Far; as, *away* below the average. **3.** Aside; off; in another direction; as, inclined *away* from the sun. **4.** From one's possession; as, give one's heart *away.* **5.** Out of existence; as, echoes dying *away.* **6.** On; continuously; as, to work *away.* **7.** *Colloq.* Without delay; straightway; as, sing *away.* **8.** By ellipsis of the verb, equivalent to an imperative: Go, come, or take away; as, *away* with it. — *adj.* **1.** Absent; gone; as, he is *away* from home. **2.** At a distance; distant.

awe (ô), *n.* [ON. *agi.*] **1.** *Obs.* Great fear; terror. **2.** *Archaic.* Power to inspire dread or fear. **3.** Profound and reverent dread inspired by deity. **4.** Veneration; solemn wonder. — *v. t.;* AWED (ôd); AW′ING (ô′ĭng). To inspire with awe; control or check by inspiring awe. — **awe′-strick′en, awe′-struck′,** *adj.*

a·wea′ry (ȧ·wẽr′ĭ), *adj.* Wearied.

a·weath′er (ȧ·wĕth′ẽr), *adv. & adj.* *Naut.* On or toward the weather, or windward, side; as, helm *aweather!*

a·wee′ (ȧ·wē′), *adv.* *Chiefly Scot.* A little (while).

a·weigh′ (ȧ·wā′), *adj.* *Naut.* Just clear of the ground, so that a vessel can make headway; atrip; — of an anchor.

awe′less, *adj.* Var. of AWLESS.

awe′some (ô′sŭm), *adj.* Causing, or expressive of, awe or terror. — **awe′some·ly,** *adv.* — **awe′some·ness,** *n.*

aw′ful (ô′fo͝ol; -f′l), *adj.* [*awe* + *-ful.*] **1.** Filling with awe; profoundly impressive; terrible; appalling. **2.** Filled with awe. **3.** *Colloq.* Ugly; very bad; ludicrous; shocking; very great; as, an *awful* coat; *awful* manners. — **Syn.** See FEARFUL. — **aw′ful·ness,** *n.*

aw′ful·ly (ô′fo͝ol·ĭ; *in sense* 2 *generally* ô′flĭ), *adv.* **1.** In a manner inspiring awe; terribly; sublimely. **2.** *Colloq.* In a manner highly distasteful; exceedingly; very.

a·while′ (ȧ·hwīl′), *adv.* For a while; for a short time.

aw′in (ô′ĭn). Scot. var. of OWN.

awk′ward (ôk′wẽrd), *adj.* [ON. *öfugr* (neut. *öfukt*) turning the wrong way + E. *-ward.*] **1.** *Obs.* Perverse; untoward. **2.** Not dexterous; unskillful; clumsy. **3.** Wanting in ease, grace, or effectiveness; ungraceful. **4.** Not adapted to its purpose; unhandy; unwieldy; as, *awkward* tools. **5.** Embarrassing; inconvenient. **6.** Hard to manage; hazardous. — **awk′ward·ly,** *adv.* — **awk′ward·ness,** *n.*

Syn. **Awkward, clumsy, maladroit, inept, gauche** mean ill-adapted to easy or graceful movement. **Awkward** is the most widely applicable of these terms: it may suggest unhandiness, inconvenience, lack of muscular control, lack of tact, embarrassment, and the like (as, an *awkward* tool, arrangement, gait, response, or situation); **clumsy** implies in general stiffness and heaviness, and so may connote inflexibility, unwieldiness, bungling, or the like; **maladroit** and **inept** imply lack of mental or social dexterity, *maladroit* suggesting a tendency to make things awkward, and *inept* a lack of aptness that leads to futile or absurd situations, remarks, or the like; **gauche** suggests a lack of social graces, often connoting shyness, inexperience, or ill breeding.

awl (ôl), *n.* [AS. *awel, al, æl.*] A pointed instrument for piercing small holes, as in leather or wood.

aw′less, awe′less (ô′lĕs; -lĭs; 30), *adj.* Without awe; irreverent; fearless.

awl′-shaped′ (ôl′shāpt′), *adj.* Shaped like an awl; specif., *Bot.,* subulate.

aw′mous (ô′mŭs), *n.* *Scot. & Dial.* Alms.

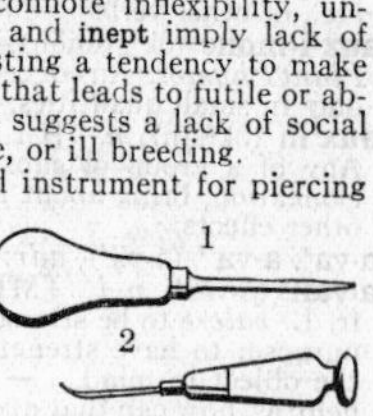

1 Awl; 2 Sewing Awl.

awn (ôn), *n.* [ON. *ögn,* pl. *agnir.*] *Bot.* One of the slender bristles constituting the beard of a head of barley, oats, some wheat, and other grasses; hence, any small pointed process. Cf. WHEAT, *Illust.* — **awned** (ônd), *adj.* — **awn′less,** *adj.*

awn′ing (ôn′ĭng), *n.* **1.** A rooflike cover, usually of canvas, extended over or before a place. **2.** A shelter resembling an awning.

a·woke′ (ȧ·wōk′), **a·wok′en** (-wōk′ĕn). See AWAKE.

a·wry′ (ȧ·rī′), *adv. & adj.* [*a-* on, in + *wry.*] **1.** Turned to one side; not straight; askew. **2.** Aside from truth; perversely or perverse.

ax, axe (ăks), *n.; pl.* AXES (ăk′sĕz; -sĭz). [AS. *eax, æx, acas.*] A cutting tool for felling trees, and chopping, splitting, or hewing wood. It consists of an edged head fixed to a handle, the edge or edges being parallel to the handle. — *v. t.* **1.** To trim or dress with an ax. **2.** To remove or kill as if with an ax.

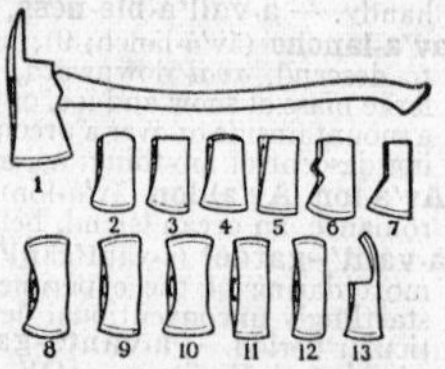

Ax. 1 Fireman's Ax. 2–7 Other Single-bit Ax Patterns: 2 Michigan; 3 Yankee; 4 Connecticut; 5 Wedge; 6 Rockaway; 7 Hudson Bay. 8–13 Double-bit Patterns: 8 Crown, or Michigan; 9 Western, or Pennsylvania; 10 Peeling; 11 Wedge; 12 Puget Sound Falling; 13 Forester's. See also HATCHET, *Illust.*

ax′es (ăk′sēz), *n., pl.* of AXIS.

ax′i·al (ăk′sĭ·ăl), *adj.* Of, pertaining to, or of the nature of an axis; around, in the direction of, or along an axis. — **ax′i·al·ly,** *adv.*

axial skeleton. The skeleton of the head and trunk; — opp. to *appendicular skeleton.*

ax′il (ăk′sĭl), *n.* [L. *axilla* armpit.] *Bot.* The angle between a branch or leaf and the axis from which it arises.

ax′ile (ăk′sĭl; -sīl), *adj.* *Bot.* Of, or situated in, the axis.

ax·il′la (ăk·sĭl′ȧ), *n.; pl.* AXILLAE (-ē). [L.] The armpit.

ax′il·lar (ăk′sĭ·lẽr; ăk·sĭl′ẽr), *adj.* Axillary. — *n.* *Zool.* One of the innermost feathers lining the undersurface of the wing.

ax′il·lar′y (ăk′sĭ·lĕr′ĭ; ăk·sĭl′ȧ·rĭ), *adj.* **1.** *Anat.* Of or pertaining to the axilla. **2.** *Bot.* Situated in, growing from, or pertaining to an axil. — *n.; pl.* AXILLARIES (-ĭz). An axillary feather; an axillar.

ax′i·ol′o·gy (ăk′sĭ·ŏl′ō·jĭ), *n.* [Gr. *axios* worthy + *-logy.*] The theory and study of values, primarily of intrinsic values, as those in ethics, aesthetics, and religion (the good, the beautiful, the holy), but also of instrumental values, as those in economics. — **ax′i·o·log′i·cal** (-ō·lŏj′ĭ·kăl), *adj.* — **ax′i·ol′o·gist** (-ŏl′ō·jĭst), *n.*

ax′i·om (ăk′sĭ·ŭm), *n.* [From L., fr. Gr. *axiōma,* fr. *axioun* to think worthy, fr. *axios* worthy.] **1.** An accepted maxim. **2.** *Logic & Math.* A statement of a self-evident truth; thus, the statement that the whole is greater than any of its parts is an *axiom.* **3.** An established principle which is universally received; as, the *axioms* of science.

ax′i·o·mat′ic (ăk′sĭ·ō·măt′ĭk), **ax′i·o·mat′i·cal** (-ĭ·kăl), *adj.* Of, pertaining to, or having the nature of an axiom; self-evident. — **ax′i·o·mat′i·cal·ly,** *adv.*

ax′is (ăk′sĭs), *n.; pl.* AXES (-sēz). [L. *axis* axis, axle.] **1.** A straight line, real or imaginary, passing through a body that actually or supposedly revolves upon it; as, the earth's *axis.* **2.** Any lengthwise central line, real or imaginary, around which parts of a body are symmetrically arranged, as the spinal column (skeletal *axis*) in man, the stem of a plant, a central line or part in a mathematical figure or in a building plan. **3.** An alliance entered into between two or more major powers to confirm their solidarity of interest and insure collaboration and mutual support; specif., the fascist nations of World War II, Germany, Italy, Japan, and the puppet governments of Croatia, Slovakia, and Romania, allied against the United Nations; hence, loosely, any coalition of forces to form a bloc. **4.** *Aeronautics.* Any of three fixed lines of reference, mutually perpendicular, one being parallel to the axis of the propeller. **5** *Anat.* The second vertebra of the neck, which serves as a pivot for the head to turn upon. **6.** *Crystallog.* One of several imaginary lines assumed in describing the position of the planes by which a crystal is bounded. **7.** *Fine Arts.* An imaginary line to which the different parts of a design are referred; also, an actual line in a working drawing, used as a basis for measurements.

ax′is, *n.* [L.] A deer (*Cervus,* subgenus *Axis, axis*) of India and other parts of southern Asia, having rusine antlers and white-spotted body; — called also **axis deer.**

axis of abscissas, axis of ordinates. See ORDINATE.

axis of a curve. *Geom.* A straight line that bisects at right angles a system of parallel chords. It thus divides the curve into two symmetrical portions, as in the parabola, which has one such axis, the ellipse, which has two, or the circle, which has an infinite number. The two axes of the ellipse are the *major axis* and the *minor axis*, and the two axes of the hyperbola are the *transverse axis* and the *conjugate axis*.

ax'le (ăk's'l), *n.* [ME. *axel* in *axeltre*, fr. ON. *öxultrē*, fr. *öxull* axle + *trē* tree.] **1.** The pin or spindle on which a wheel revolves, or which revolves with a wheel. See SIMPLE MACHINE, *Illust.* **2.** An axletree. **3.** *Archaic.* An axis.

ax'le·tree' (-trē'; -trĭ), *n.* [ON. *öxultrē.*] A transverse nonrotating bar or shaft connecting the opposite wheels of a car or carriage.

Ax'min·ster (ăks'mĭn'stẽr), *n.,* or **Axminster carpet.** A hand-woven carpet imitating Oriental rugs, formerly made (1755–1835) in Axminster, England; also, a machine-made carpet resembling it, using a chenille weft.

ax'o·lotl (ăk'sō-lŏt'l), *n.* [Sp. *axolotl, ajolote,* fr. Nahuatl *axolotl* servant of water.] Any of several larval salamanders (genus *Amblystoma*), found in the mountain lakes of Mexico and the western United States. They are esteemed as food in Mexico.

ax'on (ăk'sŏn), *n.* Also **ax'one** (ăk'sōn). *Anat. & Physiol.* A nerve-cell process which, as a rule, conducts impulses away from the cell body. Cf. DENDRITE, 2.

ax'seed' (ăks'sēd'), *n.* A European vetchlike herb (*Coronilla varia*) naturalized in the eastern United States, with umbels of pink-and-white flowers and sharp-angled pods.

ay (ā), *interj.* [F. *ai, ahi,* ay.] Ah! Alas!

ay. Var. of AYE.

a'yah (ä'yȧ), *n.* [Hind. *āya, āyā,* fr. Pg. *aia.*] *India.* A native nursemaid or lady's maid.

aye, ay (ā), *adv.* [ON. *ei.*] *Archaic & Dial.* Always; ever; continually.

aye, ay (ī), *adv.* Yes; yea. — *n.* An affirmative vote.

aye'–aye' (ī'ī'), *n.* [F., fr. Malagasy *aiay.*] A nocturnal lemur (*Daubentonia madagascariensis*) found in Madagascar.

Ay'ma·ra' (ī'mä-rä'), *n.* **a** An Indian of an important South American linguistic family, whose descendants are found in Bolivia and Peru. They developed an advanced pre-Incan culture. **b** The language of the Aymaras, still spoken in various dialects but largely superseded by Quechua. — **Ay'ma·ran'** (-rän'), *adj.*

Ayr'shire (âr'shĭr; -shẽr), *n.* One of a hardy breed of dairy cattle, originating in Ayrshire, Scotland, varying in color from white to red or brown.

‖**a·yun'ta·mien'to** (ä-yōōn'tä-myän'tō), *n.; pl.* -TOS (*Sp.* -tōs). [Sp.] **1.** A municipal government. **2.** The townhouse; the seat of a municipal government.

az-. = AZO-.

a·zal'ea (ȧ-zāl'yȧ), *n.* [NL., fr. Gr. *azaleos* dry; — because supposed to grow best in dry ground.] **1.** Any of a large genus (*Azalea*, *pron.* ȧ-zā'lē-ȧ) of flowering shrubs of the heath family, closely related to the rhododendron but with funnel-shaped corollas and deciduous leaves. The native American species *A. nudiflora,* the **pinkster flower,** *A. viscosa,* the **swamp azalea, honeysuckle,** or **pink,** and *A. lutea* are commonly cultivated. **2.** The flower of any of these shrubs. **3.** Any of several other fragrant-flowered plants or their flower; — usually with a qualifying adjective; as, the yellow-flowered **bush honeysuckle** (genus *Diervilla*), or the **wild honeysuckle.**

‖**a·zan'** (ȧ-zän'), *n.* [Ar. *ădhān.*] The Mohammedan call to prayer, usually uttered by the muezzin, five times a day, from the minaret of a mosque.

A·za'zel (ȧ-zā'zĕl; ăz'ȧ-zĕl), *n.* [Heb. *'Azāzēl,* lit., entire removal.] The legendary leader of those sons of God who (*Gen.* vi. 2–4) took wives among the daughters of men. Milton makes him an associate of Satan.

az'i·muth (ăz'ĭ-mŭth), *n.* [F. *azimut,* fr. Ar. *al-sumūt.*] *Astron. & Geod.* An arc of the horizon measured clockwise between a fixed point on the horizon (the south point or north point) and the vertical circle (which see) passing through the center of an object; as, the *azimuth* of a star. — **az'i·muth'al** (-mŭth'ăl; ăz'ĭ-mū'thăl; -mū'thăl), *adj.* — **az'i·muth'al·ly,** *adv.*

az'i·muth'al e'qui·dis'tant pro·jec'tion. A map projection of the surface of the earth so centered at any given point that a straight line

radiating from the center to any other point represents the shortest dis-

Azimuthal Equidistant Projection, centered on Washington, D.C.
1 London; 2 Algiers; 3 Moscow; 4 Buenos Aires; 5 Tokyo; 6 Auckland.

tance (that is, an arc of a great circle) and can be measured to scale.

az'ine (ăz'ēn; ā'zēn; ăz'ĭn), *n.* Also **az'in.** [*az-* + *-ine.*] *Chem.* **a** Any of a class of compounds containing a nitrogenous six-membered ring; as, triazine. Cf. AZOLE. **b** Any of a class of nitrogenous compounds formed by the action of hydrazine on aldehydes or on ketones.

az'o- (ăz'ō-; ā'zō-), **az-.** [From AZOTE.] *Chem.* A combining form meaning *nitrogen.* Specif., it denotes the presence of a group of two nitrogen atoms, -N:N-, attached on either side to carbon, as in **az'o·ben'zene** ($C_6H_5N:NC_6H_5$). The typical compounds containing this group are the parents of numerous dyes. — **az'o** (ăz'ō; ā'zō), *adj.*

a·zo'ic (ȧ-zō'ĭk; ā-), *adj.* [Gr. *a-* not + *zōē* life.] Without life. Specif., *Geol.,* pert. to or designating geologic time which antedates life. Cf. ARCHEOZOIC.

az'ole (ăz'ōl; ȧ-zōl'), *n.* [From AZOTE.] *Chem.* Any of a large class of compounds characterized by a five-membered ring which contains one or more atoms of nitrogen; as, diazole, triazole, etc. Cf. AZINE.

az'ote (ăz'ōt; ȧ-zōt'), *n.* [F., fr. Gr. *a-* not + *zōē* life; — because it is incapable of supporting life.] Nitrogen.

az'oth (ăz'ōth), *n.* [Ar. *al-zāwūq* the quicksilver.] *Alchemy.* **a** Mercury, formerly regarded as the first principle of metals. **b** The universal remedy of Paracelsus.

a·zo'to·bac'ter (ȧ-zō'tō-băk'tẽr), *n.* [*azoto-* meaning *azote,* nitrogen + *-bacter,* from *bacteria.*] *Bacteriol.* Any of a genus (*Azotobacter*) of large, rod-shaped or spherical bacteria, occurring in soil and sewage, which fix atmospheric nitrogen.

Az'ra·el (ăz'rā-ĕl), *n.* [Ar., fr. Heb. *'Azar'ēl.*] *Jewish & Moham. Relig.* The angel of death, who watches over the dying, and separates soul from the body.

Az'tec (ăz'tĕk), *n.* **1.** An Indian of the Nahuatlan tribe which founded the Mexican Empire conquered by Cortes in 1519. **2.** Any Indian of the territories under Aztec influence. **3.** Nahuatl. — *adj.* Of or relating to the Aztecs.

Az'tec·an (-ăn), *adj.* Of or pertaining to the Aztecs; also, pertaining to or designating the linguistic stock of the Aztecs; Nahuatlan.

az'ure (ăzh'ẽr; ā'zhẽr), *n.* [OF. *azur, asur,* fr. Ar. *lāzaward,* fr. Per. *lāzhuward.*] **1.** *Her.* Blue, represented in engraving by horizontal lines. **2.** Blue, strictly the blue of the clear sky; also, a pigment or dye of this color. **3.** The blue vault above; the unclouded sky. — *adj.* Like the blue of the clear sky; cloudless.

az'u·rite (ăzh'ū-rīt), *n.* **a** *Mineral.* Blue basic carbonate of copper, $2CuCO_3.Cu(OH)_2$. It is an ore of copper. **b** A semiprecious stone derived from it.

az'y·gous (ăz'ĭ-gŭs), *adj.* [Gr. *azygos,* fr. *a-* not + *zygon* yoke.] *Anat.* Odd; not one of a pair; as, the *azygous* muscle of the uvula.

B

B, b (bē), *n.; pl.* B's, ʙ's, Bs, ʙs (bēz). **1.** The second letter of the English alphabet. B comes from Latin B, which came from Greek B (beta), which in turn came into Greek from the Phoenician. **2.** The sound of this letter. See *Pron.,* § 17. **3.** *Music.* **a** The seventh tone in the model major scale (that of C). **b** A symbol for producing this tone; also, a symbol for this tone. See PITCH, *Illust.* **4.** As a *symbol,* the second in order or of its class.

ba (bä), *n.* *Egypt. Relig.* The immortal soul, which eventually returns to a preserved body to revivify it.

baa (bä; bȧ), *v. i. & n.* Bleat, as (or of) a sheep.

Ba'al (bā'ăl), *n.; pl.* BAALIM (bā'ăl-ĭm), BAALS. [Heb., fr. Phoenician *ba'al* lord.] Any of a number of local deities of the ancient Semitic peoples, in general regarded as authors of the soil's fertility and of the increase in flocks.

Ba'al·ism (bā'ăl-ĭz'm), *n.* Worship of Baal; idolatry. — **Ba'al·ist** (-ĭst), **Ba'al·ite** (-īt), *n.*

Bab (băb), *n.* [Per.] A short form of the title, *Bāb-ud-Dīn* (Per.) Gate of the Faith), assumed by the founder of Babism, Mirza Ali Mohammed of Shiraz (1819–50).

ba·bas·su' (bä'bȧ-sōō'), *n.* [Pg., fr. (assumed) Tupi *babassu.*] A gigantic palm (*Orbignya speciosa*) of northeastern Brazil, with hard-

shelled nuts yielding a valuable oil (**babassu oil**) widely used in the manufacture of soap.

bab'bitt (băb'ĭt), *n.* Babbitt metal; also, a Babbitt-metal lining. — *v. t.* To line or furnish with babbitt.

Bab'bitt, *n.* A business or professional man who adheres to the social and ethical standards of his group; — used derogatorily, in allusion to the hero of *Babbitt,* a novel (1922) by Sinclair Lewis.

Bab'bitt met'al. [After Isaac *Babbitt* (1799–1862), Am. inventor.] A white antifriction alloy, esp. one composed of copper, antimony, and varying proportions of tin.

bab'ble (băb'l), *v. i.;* -BLED (-'ld); -BLING (-lĭng). [ME.] **1.** To talk as a little child or idiot, indistinctly, meaninglessly, or incoherently. **2.** To talk idly or foolishly; to chatter. **3.** To make sounds like a continuous prattle; as, the brook *babbles* over rocks. **4.** To utter indistinctly or incoherently. — *v. t.* **1.** To disclose by too free talk; to blab; as, to *babble* a secret. — *n.* **1.** Idle talk; senseless chatter. **2.** Prattle. **3.** Babbling noises; continuous murmur. — **bab'ble·ment,** *n.* — **bab'bler** (băb'lẽr), *n.*

babe (bāb), *n.* **1.** A baby. **2.** A naïve, inexperienced person.

Ba'bel (bā'bĕl; -b'l), *n.* [Heb. *Bābel,* fr. Assyr.-Bab.] **1.** A city and tower in the land of Shinar, the scene of the confusion of languages

(*Gen.* xi. 9). **2.** A structure impossibly lofty; a visionary scheme. **3.** [*often not cap.*] A place or scene of noise or confusion; also, a confusion of cries, voices, or languages.
Bab'i (bäb'ē), *n.* **a** Babism. **b** A Babist. — **Bab'i,** *adj.*
ba'bies'–breath' (bā'bĭz·brĕth'), *n.* Also **ba'by's–breath'**. **a** The gypsophila *Gypsophila paniculata*, having clusters of small, fragrant, white or pink flowers. **b** Any of several plants with similar flowers, as the grape hyacinth.
bab'i·ru'sa, bab'i·rus'sa (băb'ĭ·rōō'sȧ; bä'bĭ-), *n.* [Malay *bābī* hog + *rūsa* deer.] An East Indian hoglike quadruped (*Babirussa babirussa*) with curved tusks.
Bab'ism (bäb'ĭz'm), *n.* The doctrine of a religious sect in Persia, founded in 1844–45, forbidding concubinage and polygamy, mendicancy, the use of intoxicating liquors and drugs, and slave dealing. See BAB. — **Bab'ist** (-ĭst); *n.* & *adj.* — **Bab'ite** (-īt), *adj.*
ba'boo, ba'bu (bä'bōō), *n.* [Hind. *bābū*.] *India.* **a** A Hindu gentleman. **b** A Hindu title corresponding to *Mr.* or *Esquire.* **c** A native clerk who writes English; — often applied disparagingly to any native having more or less education in English. — **-ism** (-ĭz'm), *n.*
ba·boon' (bă·bōōn'), *n.* [OF. *babuin*, prob. fr. *baboue* grimace.] Any of certain large African and Asiatic apes (of *Papio* and allied genera) having doglike muzzles and short tails. See CHACMA, 2d DRILL, MANDRILL. — **ba·boon'ish,** *adj.*
ba·bul' (bä·bōōl'; bä'bōōl), *n.* [Per. *babūl* a species of mimosa.] Any of several gum-yielding acacias; specif., an Egyptian species (*Acacia vera*).
ba·bush'ka (bȧ·bōōsh'kȧ), *n.* [Russ., grandmother.] A kerchief for the head, usually folded triangularly; also, a small, close-fitting cap.
ba'by (bā'bĭ), *n.*; *pl.* BABIES (-bĭz). [ME. *baby, babi.*] **1.** An infant. **2.** The youngest of a group. **3.** A diminutive person or thing; also, an infantile, childish person. — *adj.* **1.** Of or for a baby; as, *baby* clothes. **2.** Babylike; babyish; infantile; as, a *baby* act. **3.** Very small of its kind; as, a *baby* grand (piano). — *v. t.*; BA'BIED (-bĭd); BA'BY·ING. To treat as a baby; to humor. — **Syn.** See INDULGE. — **ba'by·hood,** *n.* — **ba'by·ish,** *adj.* — **ba'by·like',** *adj.*
ba'by blue'–eyes'. A Californian herb (*Nemophila insignis*) having blue flowers marked with dark spots.
baby farming. The boarding of infants for pay. — **baby farm, farmer.**
Bab'y·lon (băb'ĭ·lŏn), *n.* [L., fr. Gr. *Babylōn*, fr. Heb. *Bābel.* See BABEL.] **1.** An ancient Semitic city in the Euphrates Valley, which about 2225 B.C. was the richest and most magnificent of cities. **2.** Any center of luxury and wickedness. **3.** A place of captivity or exile; — in allusion to the fifty-year captivity of the Jews (**Babylonian captivity**) from 597 B.C. by Nebuchadnezzar. — **Bab'y·lo'nish** (-lō'nĭsh), *adj.*
Bab'y·lo'ni·an (-lō'nĭ·ăn), *adj.* **1.** Of or characteristic of Babylon or Babylonia. **2.** Scarlet; — in reference to *Revelation* xvii. — *n.* An inhabitant or the language of the ancient kingdom of Babylonia.
ba'by's'–breath'. Var. of BABIES'-BREATH.
baby sitter. One who is engaged, usually for pay and for a few hours only, to care for children, esp. in the children's own home while the parents or usual guardians are out. — **ba'by–sit',** *v. i.*
Ba·car'di (bȧ·kär'dē), *n.* A trade-mark for rum manufactured by a Cuban family named Bacardí.
bac'ca·lau're·ate (băk'ȧ·lô'rē·ăt), *n.* [ML. *baccalaureus* a bachelor of arts, corrupted fr. *baccalaris*, under the influence of L. *laurus* laurel. See BACHELOR.] **1.** The degree of bachelor conferred by universities and colleges. **2.** Also **baccalaureate sermon.** A sermon delivered to a graduating class at commencement.
bac'ca·rat', bac'ca·ra' (băk'ȧ·rä'; băk'ȧ·rä), *n.* [F.] A French gambling card game. Cf. CHEMIN DE FER, 2.
bac'cate (băk'āt), *adj.* [L. *baccatus*, fr. *bacca* berry.] **1.** Pulpy throughout, like a berry; berrylike. **2.** Bearing berries.
Bac'chae (băk'ē), *n. pl.* **1.** The women companions of Dionysus (Bacchus) in his journeys through the East. **2.** The women participants in the Dionysia. Cf. MAENAD.
bac'cha·nal (băk'ȧ·năl; -n'l), *adj.* Pertaining to Bacchus; bacchanalian. — *n.* **1.** A devotee of Bacchus; one who celebrates the Bacchanalia; a reveler; carouser. **2.** *pl.* The Bacchanalia. **3.** An orgy.
Bac'cha·na'li·a (-nā'lĭ·ȧ; -nāl'yȧ), *n. pl.* [L., neut. pl. fr. *bacchanalis* bacchanal.] **1.** A Roman festival of Bacchus, celebrated with frenzied dancing, singing, and revelry. Cf. DIONYSIA. **2.** [*not cap.*] A drunken feast; an orgy.
bac'cha·na'li·an (-nā'lĭ·ăn; -nāl'yăn), *adj.* Of or characteristic of Bacchanalia or bacchanals. — *n.* A bacchanal (def. 1). — **bac'cha·na'li·an·ism** (-ĭz'm), *n.*
bac'chant (băk'ănt), *n.*; *pl.* BACCHANTS (-ănts), BACCHANTES (bă·kăn'tēz). [L. *bacchans, -antis*, pres. part.] A votary of Bacchus; a bacchanal. — **bac'chant,** *adj.* — **bac·chan'tic** (bă·kăn'tĭk), *adj.*
bac·chante' (bă·kănt'; bȧ·kăn'tē), *n.* [F.] A female attendant or devotee of Bacchus; a maenad.
Bac'chic (băk'ĭk), **Bac'chi·cal** (-ĭ·kăl), *adj.* **1.** Of or pertaining to Bacchus (or Dionysus) or his rites. **2.** [*often not cap.*] Jovial or riotous with intoxication.
Bac'chus (băk'ŭs), *n.* [L.; cf. Gr. *Bakchos.*] The Greek god of wine; Dionysus.
bac·cif'er·ous (băk·sĭf'ẽr·ŭs), *adj.* [L. *baccifer*, fr. *bacca* berry + *ferre* to bear.] Bearing berries.
bac'ci·form (băk'sĭ·fôrm), *adj.* [L. *bacca* berry + *-form.*] Having the form of a berry.
bac·civ'o·rous (băk·sĭv'ō·rŭs), *adj.* [L. *bacca* berry + *-vorous.*] Eating, or subsisting on, berries.
bach (băch), *n.* *Slang.* Short for BACHELOR. — *v. i.* *Slang.* To live like a bachelor; — often with *it.*
bach'e·lor (băch'ĕ·lẽr), *n.* [OF. *bacheler* young man, fr. ML. *baccalaris* tenant, of Celt. origin.] **1.** A young knight serving under the standard of another; hence, a knight bachelor (which see). **2.** One who has had the first, or lowest, academic degree conferred on him by a college or university; a college graduate; as, a *bachelor* of arts (abbr. *A.B.* or *B.A.*). **3.** A man who has not married. **4. a** The crappie. **b** Any male animal, esp. a young male fur seal, when without a mate during the breeding time. — **bach'e·lor·hood',** *n.* — **bach'e·lor·ship',** *n.*
bach'e·lor's–but'ton (băch'ĕ·lẽrz·bŭt'n), *n.* Any of several flowers the heads of which resemble buttons, esp. the bluebottle (def. 1 **a**) and the knapweed.
bac'il·lar'y (băs'ĭ·lĕr'ĭ *or, esp. Brit.*, bȧ·sĭl'ẽr·ĭ), *adj.* Also **ba·cil'lar** (bȧ·sĭl'ẽr; băs'ĭ·lẽr). [L. *bacillum* little staff.] **1.** Rod-shaped; consisting of small rods or rodlike bodies. **2.** *Bacteriol.* Of, resembling, or produced by bacilli.

ba·cil'li·form (bȧ·sĭl'ĭ·fôrm) *adj.* Rod-shaped; bacillary.
ba·cil'lus (bȧ·sĭl'ŭs), *n.*; *pl.* -CILLI (-ī). [NL., for L. *bacillum*, dim. of L. *baculum* rod.] **1.** Any of a genus (*Bacillus*) of straight, rod-shaped, aerobic bacteria forming endospores which make little change in the shape of the rod, as *B. anthracis*, which causes anthrax. **2.** Hence, any rod-shaped bacterium; as, the comma *bacillus.* See BACTERIA. **3.** Loosely, any of the bacteria, esp. if disease-producing.
bac'i·tra'cin (băs'ĭ·trā'sĭn), *n.* [*Bac*illus subtilis + Margaret *Tracy*, child in whose wounded tibial tissue the bacillus was found + *-in.*] *Biochem.* An antibiotic isolated from a bacillus (*Bacillus subtilis*), effective against certain bacteria and viruses.
back (băk), *n.* [AS. *bæc.*] **1.** The hinder part of the body, or, in most animals, the upper part, extending from the neck to the end of the backbone. **2.** Hence: **a** Power of bearing burdens; as, he has a strong *back.* **b** Body as an object to be clothed, etc.; person; as, she puts all she earns on her *back.* **c** The part of a garment that covers the back. **3.** Backbone; as, he has broken his *back.* **4.** The hinder part; the rear; as, the *back* of the leg; the upper part or side; as, the *back* of the hand; the part that does not face one or is not the face; the farther or reverse side; as, the *back* of a hill. **5.** Something at or on the back for a support, a backing, a lining, or for some special purpose; as, the *back* of a chair. **6.** In certain games, a position, originally a defensive one, behind the front line of players; also, a player stationed in such a position.
— *v. t.* **1.** To give material or moral support to; to uphold; to second; — often with *up.* **2.** To bet on the success of. **3.** To mount. **4.** To write upon the back of; to countersign. **5.** To drive, force, or cause to move or act, backward. **6.** To make or form a back for; put a back to; as, to *back* a wall with bricks. **7.** To form the back of; to be at the back of; as, cliffs *back* the beach. — **Syn.** See SUPPORT. — *v. i.* **1.** To move, go, or flow back; — often with *up.* **2.** To shift counterclockwise, as the wind; — opposed to *veer.* — **Syn.** See RECEDE.
back and fill. **1.** To manage sails so that they alternately catch the wind and lie idle, thereby keeping the boat in a river channel and floating with the current. **2.** To take opposite positions alternately. — ***back out, back down.*** *Colloq.* To retreat or withdraw from a promise, engagement, or contest; to recede. — ***back water.*** **1.** To reverse the action of the oars, paddles, etc. **2.** To retract; to withdraw.
— *adj.* **1.** Being at the back; away from the front, face, or center; rear; remote. **2.** Of the past; overdue; as, *back* rent; not current; as, a *back* issue. **3.** Moving or operating from the back, or backward; returning; as, *back* freight **4.** *Phonet.* Pronounced with closure or narrowing of the oral passage at, or toward, the back of the mouth; guttural; velar (ō, ōō, g in *go*).
back, *adv.* [From ABACK.] **1.** At, to, or toward the back; backward; behind in place or time. **2.** To a former place, condition, owner, etc.; as, to march *back.* **3.** In concealment or reserve; as, to keep *back* the truth. **4.** In return, requital, or retort; as, to talk *back.* **5.** As if not said, made, or given; so as to repudiate; as, to take *back* a charge.
back (băk), *n.* [D. *bak*, fr. F. *bac.*] A shallow vat or tub, esp. one used by brewers or dyers.
back'bite' (băk'bīt'), *v. t.* & *i.* To speak evil of (one absent); to slander. — **back'bit'er** (-bīt'ẽr), *n.*
back'board' (-bōrd'), *n.* A board which forms a back or backing, or which supports a back.
back'bone' (-bōn'), *n.* **1.** The column of bones (vertebrae) in the back which sustains the frame; the spine. **2.** Anything like a backbone in formation or function. **3.** Firmness; determination; as, he lacks *backbone.* — **Syn.** See FORTITUDE.
back cloth, back'drop' (băk'drŏp'), *n.* A painted cloth or a drop curtain at the back of a scene or stage.
back'cross' (-krŏs'), *v. t.* & *i.* To cross (a first-generation hybrid) with one of its parents. — *n.* An instance of this.
back'door' (-dōr'; 70), *adj.* Clandestine.
backed (băkt), *adj.* Made with a back; having, or fitted with, a back.
back'er (băk'ẽr), *n.* One that backs, or supports.
back'fall' (băk'fôl'), *n.* A falling back; that which falls back; specif., *Wrestling*, a fall on the back.
back'fire' (-fīr'), *n.* **1.** A fire that checks an advancing fire by clearing an area before it. **2.** A premature explosion in a cylinder, or an explosion in the intake or exhaust passages, of a gas or oil engine. **3.** An explosion to the rear of a firearm. — *v. i.* To make a backfire.
back'gam'mon (băk'găm'ŭn; băk'găm'ŭn), *n.* [Prob. fr. *back*, adv + *gammon* game, because the men are often set *back.* See GAME.] A game played with pieces on a double board in which the throwing of dice determines the moves. — (băk'găm'ŭn), *v. t.* To beat by getting a gammon.

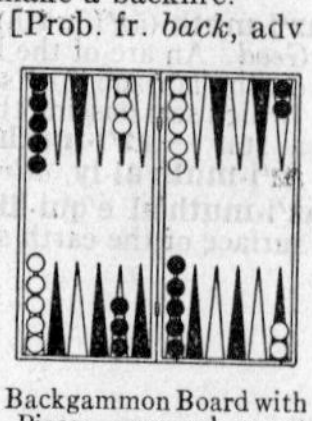

Backgammon Board with Pieces arranged as at Beginning of a Game.

back'ground' (băk'ground'), *n.* **1.** The scenery or ground behind something seen or represented; — opposed to *foreground.* **2.** The part of a painting, etc., representing what lies behind objects in the foreground. **3.** That which is behind something historically, logically, etc.; as, the *background* of the American Revolution. **4.** An inconspicuous position; as, to keep in the *background.* **5.** The sum of one's experience, training, education, etc. **6.** Music or sound effects employed to accompany a dialogue, recital, or other performance.
back'hand' (-hănd'), *n.* **1.** A backhand stroke; also, manner of playing, or position when playing, such strokes. **2.** Handwriting whose up-and-down strokes slant downward to the right. — *adj.* **1.** Backhanded. **2.** *Tennis, Rackets, etc.* Of a stroke, made with the back of the hand turned in the direction of the stroke; hence, made with the arm across the body at the moment of hitting; — opp. to *forehand.*
back'hand'ed (băk'hăn'dĕd; -dĭd), *adj.* **1. a** Made, as a blow or stroke, with the back of the hand. **b** *Tennis, Rackets, etc.* Backhand. **2.** Insincere; sarcastic; as, a *backhanded* compliment. **3.** Written in backhand. **4.** Twisted or laid in a direction opposite to the usual one; as, *backhanded* rope. — **back'hand'ed·ly,** *adv.* — **back'hand'edness,** *n.*
back'ing (băk'ĭng), *n.* **1.** Support or aid; backers, collectively. **2.** Endorsement. **3.** That which forms the back of anything, often giving strength or stability.
back'lash' (-lăsh'), *n.* A sudden and violent backward movement or reaction, as the recoil of waves or the rebound of a falling tree; specif.: **a** In machinery, jarring reaction, or striking back, caused in badly fitting machinery by irregularities in velocity or a reverse of motion; also, a play or movement in the connected parts resulting from looseness. **b** A snarl in the part of a fishing line that is wound on the reel.

back'lins (băk'lĭnz), *adv.* *Chiefly Scot.* Backwards.

back'log' (băk'lŏg'; 74), *n.* **1.** The large log of wood at the back of a hearth fire. **2.** *Colloq.* **a** *Com.* A reserve of unfilled orders. **b** Loosely, any sustaining reserve.

back'saw' (-sô'), *n.* A saw with a blade stiffened by an added metallic back.

back'set' (băk'sĕt'), *n.* **1.** A setback; reverse. **2.** An eddy; countercurrent.

back'sheesh, back'shish. Vars. of BAKSHEESH.

back'side' (băk'sīd'), *n.* The posteriors; rump.

back'slide' (băk'slīd'; băk'slīd'), *v. i.*; -SLID' (-slĭd'); -SLID'DEN (-slĭd''n) or -SLID'; -SLID'ING (-slīd'ĭng). To slide back; to lapse morally or in the practice of religion. — **back'slid'er** (-slīd'ẽr), *n.*

back'spin' (băk'spĭn'), *n.* Backward rotary motion, as one imparted to a golf ball or a billiard ball.

back'stage' (-stāj'), *adv.* **a** On the stage or in the dressing rooms behind the curtain. **b** Upstage; at or toward the rear of the stage. — **back'stage'**, *adj.*

back stairs. **1.** Stairs in the rear or away from the front, used esp. by servants, or, in a palace, by other than state visitors. **2.** An underhanded or intriguing way or course.

back'stairs' (băk'stârz'), **back'stair'** (-stâr'), *adj.* Secret; clandestine; as, a *backstairs* intrigue.

back'stay' (-stā'), *n.* **1.** An aft-slanting stay for the masts, extending from the mastheads to the side of a ship. **2.** A back-supporting or back-strengthening device.

back'stitch' (-stĭch'), *n.* A stitch made by setting the needle back of the end of the last stitch, and bringing it out an equal distance in front of the end. See STITCH, *Illust.* — *v. t. & i.* To sew with backstitches.

back'stop' (-stŏp'), *n.* Anything placed at the back to serve as a stop; as: **a** A screen or fence behind home base (properly at least 90 feet) on a baseball field or behind either base line of a tennis court. **b** *Colloq.* A player, such as a baseball catcher, who stops the ball delivered by a pitcher, bowler, etc. **c** A part, as a pawl, that prevents backward movement beyond a certain point.

back'stretch' (-strĕch'), *n.* In a race track, the part opposite to the homestretch.

back'stroke' (-strōk'), *n.* **1.** A return, reverse, or backhanded stroke. **2.** A stroke executed by a swimmer lying on his back; esp., a racing stroke like an inverted crawl.

back'swept' (-swĕpt'), *adj.* Characterized by a sweepback; — said of the wing of an airplane.

back'sword' (-sōrd'; 70), *n.* **1.** A single-edged sword; — now usually called *broadsword.* **2.** A singlestick. **3.** A fencer with the backsword. — **back'sword'ing**, *n.* — **back'sword'man, back'swords'man** (-sōrdz'măn), *n.*

back talk. Impudent or argumentative reply, esp. from a junior or a subordinate.

back'ward (băk'wẽrd), **back'wards** (-wẽrdz), *adv.* [*back*, adv. + *-ward, -wards.*] **1.** Toward the back or rear; also, on the back. **2.** With the back foremost; as, to ride *backward.* **3.** In a contrary or reverse way, order, or direction; not forward; as, to read *backwards.* **4.** Toward past events; in the past. **5.** From a better to a worse state.

back'ward, *adj.* **1.** Directed or turned backward; made or done in the opposite or reverse direction; as, a *backward* glance. **2.** Situated toward the back. **3.** Not advancing or progressing normally; behindhand in growth, development, mentality, etc.; as, a *backward* season; a *backward* child. **4.** Reluctant; bashful; loath; as, not *backward* in asking favors. — *n.* The part behind or past; as, "the dark *backward* and abysm of time" (*Shak.*). — **back'ward·ly**, *adv.* — **back'ward·ness**, *n.*

back'wash' (băk'wŏsh'), *n.* **1.** Water thrown back by paddle wheels, oars, etc **2.** An agitation resulting from some action or occurrence.

back'wa'ter (-wô'tẽr; -wŏt'ẽr), *n.* **1.** Water turned back, as by a dam, opposing current, or the tide; an accumulation of water so turned or held back. **2.** An isolated, backward place; a stagnant condition.

back'woods' (-wŏŏdz'), *n. pl.* Forests or partly cleared grounds on the frontiers or away from cities. — **back'wood', back'woods'**, *adj.* — **back'woods'man** (-măn), *n.*

ba'con (bā'kŭn; -k'n), *n.* [OF., fr. OHG. *bacho, bahho,* flitch of bacon, ham.] **1.** The back and sides of a pig, salted and smoked. **2.** *Colloq.* Reward, profits, or prize.

Ba·co'ni·an (bā·kō'nĭ·ăn), *adj.* Of or pertaining to Lord Bacon (1561–1626) or his works or doctrines. — *n.* One who accepts Baconian doctrines or the Baconian theory.

Baconian theory. The theory that Lord Bacon was the author of Shakespeare's dramatic works.

bac·te'ri·a (băk·tēr'ĭ·ȧ), *n. pl.* [NL See BACTERIUM.] A large, widely distributed group of typically one-celled microorganisms (class Schizomycetes), chiefly parasitic or saprophytic. They exhibit three chief typical shapes: spherical (*coccus*), rod-shaped (*bacillus*), spiral and threadlike (*spirillum*). Many bacteria are disease-producing; many are active in processes such as fermentation, the conversion of dead organic matter into soluble food for plants, and the fixing of atmospheric nitrogen.

bac·te'ri·al (băk·tēr'ĭ·ăl), *adj.* Pert. to or consisting of bacteria; resulting from or caused by bacteria; as, *bacterial* infection. — **bac·te'ri·al·ly**, *adv.*

bac·te'ri·cide (-ĭ·sīd), *n.* [*bacterium* + *-cide.*] Anything that destroys bacteria. — **bac·te'ri·cid'al** (-sīd'ăl; 2), *adj.*

bac'te·rin (băk'tẽ·rĭn), *n.* [*bacterium* + *-in.*] *Immunol.* A bacterial extract; a bacterial vaccine.

bac·te'ri·ol'o·gy (băk·tēr'ĭ·ŏl'ō·jĭ), *n.* [*bacterium* + *-logy.*] The science which deals with the study of bacteria. — **bac·te'ri·o·log'i·cal** (-ō·lŏj'ĭ·kăl), *adj.* — **bac·te'ri·o·log'i·cal·ly**, *adv.* — **bac·te'ri·ol'o·gist** (-ŏl'ō·jĭst), *n.*

bac·te'ri·ol'y·sis (-ŏl''·sĭs), *n.* [NL., fr *bacterium* + *-lysis.*] **a** Chemical decomposition brought about by bacteria without the addition of oxygen. **b** The destruction or dissolution of bacterial cells. — **bac·te'ri·o·lyt'ic** (-ō·lĭt'ĭk), *adj.*

bac·te'ri·o·phage (băk·tēr'ĭ·ō·fāj), *n.* [*bacterium* + Gr. *phagein* to eat.] A bacteria-destroying agent, normally present in the intestinal tract of man and animals, esp. those recovering from a bacterial disease, and in blood, urine, etc.

bac·te'ri·os'co·py (-ŏs'kō·pĭ), *n.* [*bacterium* + *-scopy.*] Microscopic examination or investigation of bacteria. — **bac·te'ri·o·scop'ic** (-ō·skŏp'ĭk), **bac·te'ri·o·scop'i·cal** (-ĭ·kăl), *adj.* — **bac·te'ri·os'co·pist** (-ŏs'kō·pĭst), *n.*

bac·te'ri·o·stat'ic (băk·tēr'ĭ·ō·stăt'ĭk), *adj.* [*bacterium* + *-static* (see STATIC).] *Bacteriol.* Inhibiting the growth of bacteria without destroying them. — **bac·te'ri·o·sta'sis** (-stā'sĭs), *n.*

bac·te'ri·um (băk·tēr'ĭ·ŭm), *n.* [NL., fr. Gr. *baktērion*, dim. of *baktron* a staff.] Sing. of BACTERIA.

bac'ter·ize (băk'tẽr·īz), *v. t.* To subject to, or modify by, bacterial action; as, *bacterized* peat. — **bac'ter·i·za'tion** (-ĭ·zā'shŭn; -ī·zā'-), *n.*

bac'ter·oid (băk'tẽr·oid), **bac'te·roi'dal** (-tẽ·roi'dăl; -d'l), *adj.* [*bacterium* + *-oid.*] Resembling bacteria.

bac'ter·oid, *n.* *Bot.* An enlarged, branched bacterium, such as those found in the tubercles of leguminous plants.

Bac'tri·an (băk'trĭ·ăn), *adj.* Of or pertaining to Bactria, a satrapy of ancient Persia; as, the two-humped, or *Bactrian*, camel (see CAMEL).

ba·cu'li·form (bȧ·kū'lĭ·fôrm; băk'ū-), *adj.* [L. *baculum* rod + *-form.*] Rod-shaped; as, *baculiform* chromosomes.

bad (băd), *adj.*; *compar.* WORSE (wûrs); *superl.* WORST (wûrst). [ME. *bad, badde,* prob. fr. AS. *bæddel* hermaphrodite.] **1.** Morally evil; wicked. **2.** Defective; below standard; as, a *bad* correspondent; worthless; as, a *bad* debt; faulty; incorrect; as, *bad* grammar. **3. a** Inadequate; unfit; as, the light is *bad.* **b** Unfavorable; as, *bad* news. **4.** Disagreeable; unpleasant; as, a *bad* taste. **5.** Injurious or deleterious; hurtful; as, *bad* for the health. **6.** Ill; sick; in pain; as, to feel *bad.* **7.** Distressed; sorry; as, to feel *bad* about one's mistake. **8.** Severe; as, a *bad* cold. **9.** Not valid; void; not in legal form. **10.** Spoiled; decayed; as, *bad* eggs. — **bad'ly**, *adv.* — **bad'ness**, *n.*

Syn. **Bad, evil, ill, wicked, naughty** mean in some degree reprehensible. **Bad** may imply reprehensibility in any degree; **evil**, a uniformly stronger term than *bad*, is now seldom directly applied to persons but to their acts, words, etc., and usually carries a baleful or sinister connotation; **ill**, as a synonym of *evil*, occurs chiefly in a few combinations, such as *ill* will, *ill* nature; **wicked** implies actual violation of moral law, though it is occasionally used humorously; **naughty**, once serious, is now trivial and applied chiefly to children.

bad, *n.* That which is bad; a bad condition.

bad, *adv.* *Colloq.* In a bad manner or in a bad way.

bad. Archaic past of BID.

bad blood. Bitter feeling; hatred; resentment.

bad'der·locks (băd'ẽr·lŏks), *n.* A large black seaweed (*Alaria esculenta*) often eaten as a vegetable in Europe.

bade (băd), *past* of BID.

badge (băj), *n.* [ME. *bage, bagge.*] **1. a** A distinctive device worn as a sign of one's office, one's membership, etc. **b** *Mil.* An award for attainment, proficiency, or qualification, as in marksmanship. **2.** Outward sign; characteristic mark; also, emblem. — *v. t.*; BADGED (băjd); BADG'ING (băj'ĭng). To mark with a badge.

badg'er (băj'ẽr), *n.* [Earlier *bageard.*] **1. a** A burrowing mammal (genus *Meles* or *Taxidea*) with short, thick legs, and long claws on the forefeet. **b** The fur or pelt of this animal. **2.** In Australia: **a** The wombat. **b** The bandicoot. **3.** A brush made of badger's hair. **4.** [*cap.*] *U.S.* A native or inhabitant of Wisconsin (nicknamed the **Badger State**). — *v. t.* To bait as a badger; to tease or annoy; to harass by nagging, etc. — **Syn.** See BAIT.

bad'i·nage' (băd'ĭ·näzh'; băd'ĭ·näzh; băd'ĭ·nĭj), *n.* [F., fr. *badiner* to joke, fr. *badin* a joker, fool, fr. Pr. *badin.*] Playful raillery; banter.

Syn. **Badinage, persiflage, raillery** mean a kind of banter. **Badinage** implies banter that is delicate and playful; **persiflage**, that is derisive but not cutting; **raillery**, that is keen and, often, sarcastic in ridiculing.

bad'lands' (băd'lăndz'), *n. pl.* [Cf. BAD LANDS, in *Gaz.*] Regions where erosion has carved soft rocks into intricate and fantastic shapes and where vegetation is scanty.

bad'min'ton (băd'mĭn't'n), *n.* [From the name of the seat of the duke of Beaufort in England.] **1.** Claret mixed with soda water and sweetened. **2.** A court game in which a lightweight racket is used to bat a shuttlecock back and forth over a net. See SHUTTLECOCK, *Illust.*

Bae'de·ker (bā'dĕ·kẽr), *n.* A guidebook of the series established by Karl Baedeker; loosely, any guidebook.

baff (băf), *n.* [Scot.] **1.** *Scot.* A blow; a stroke. **2.** *Golf.* A stroke in which the sole of the club hits the ground and drives the ball aloft. — **baff**, *v. t. & i.*

baf'fle (băf''l), *v. t.*; BAF'FLED (-'ld); BAF'FLING (-lĭng). **1.** *Obs.* **a** To disgrace. **b** To cheat; delude. **2.** To check or defeat by perplexing; to frustrate the efforts of or at; as, beauty that *baffles* description. **3.** To beat back or about; to check or turn in its course; as, the ship was *baffled* by wind and weather. — **Syn.** See FRUSTRATE. — *v. i.* To struggle in vain; as, a ship *baffles* with the winds. — *n.* **1.** A baffling; a baffled state. **2.** A plate, wall, screen, etc., used to deflect, check, or otherwise regulate the flow of a gas, a liquid, sound waves, etc. — **baf'fle·ment**, *n.* — **baf'fler** (băf'lẽr), *n.* — **baf'fling** (-lĭng), *adj.* — **baf'fling·ly**, *adv.*

baff'y (băf'ĭ), *n.* [See BAFF.] *Golf.* A wooden club having a short shaft and a deep face with much loft.

bag (băg), *n.* [ME. *bagge*, fr. ON. *baggi.*] **1.** A sack or pouch, used for holding anything. **2.** Specif.: **a** A purse. **b** A suitcase. **c** A gamebag; hence, the quantity of game or fish bagged. **3.** A pouchlike object; as: **a** A dependent fold of skin containing a gland or other organ, as the udder of a cow. **b** A sac or cavity within the body for containing a fluid or secretion; as, the honey *bag* of a bee. **c** The part of anything that bags; as, the *bag* of a sail. **d** *Colloq.* A loose garment, esp., *pl.*, trousers. — *v. i.*; BAGGED (băgd); BAG'GING. To swell or bulge like a full bag. — *v. t.* **1.** To cause to swell; to distend. **2.** To put into or cover with a bag, as game. **3.** To kill or capture in hunting. **4.** To seize; to get possession of. — **Syn.** See CATCH.

ba·gasse' (bȧ·gȧs'), *n.* [F.] The residue of sugar cane or sugar beets after the juice has been extracted.

bag'a·telle' (băg'ȧ·tĕl'), *n.* [F., fr It. *bagattella.*] **1.** A trifle. **2.** A game played with a cue and balls on an oblong board having at one end cups, or cups and arches.

bag'gage (băg'ĭj), *n* [F. *bagage*, fr. OF. *bague* bundle.] **1.** The trunks, valises, etc., which one carries on a journey; — now usually called *luggage* by the English. **2.** The clothes, tents, and effects of every kind, of an army. **3.** Formerly, a wanton; a prostitute; now, an artful, pert young woman.

bag'gie (băg'ĭ; bĕg'ĭ), *n.* *Chiefly Scot.* The belly.

bag'ging (băg'ĭng), *n.* Cloth or similar material for bags.

bag'gy (băg'ĭ), *adj.*; -GI·ER (-ĭ·ẽr); -GI·EST. Loose or puffed out like a bag. — **bag'gi·ly**, *adv.* — **bag'gi·ness**, *n.*

bag′man (băg′măn), *n.* **a** *Brit.* A commercial traveler. **b** A sorter, checker, etc., of mailbags.

bagn′io (băn′yō; bän′yō), *n.; pl.* -IOS (-yōz). [It. *bagno* bath, fr. L. *balneum.*] **1.** An Italian or Turkish bathhouse. **2.** An Oriental prison for slaves. **3.** A brothel.

bag′pipe′ (băg′pīp′), *n.* Sometimes *pl.* A musical wind instrument consisting of a leather bag, a valve-stopped tube, and three or four sounding pipes. — **bag′pip′er** (-pīp′ẽr), *n.*

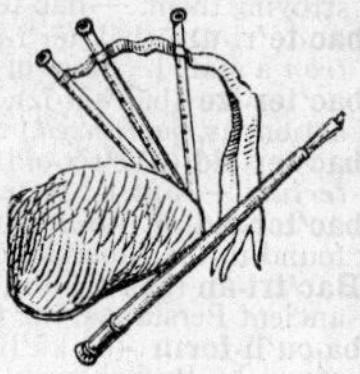
Bagpipe.

ba·guette′ (bă·gĕt′), *n.* Also **ba·guet′.** [F *baguette,* fr. It., fr. L. *baculum, baculus,* stick, staff.] **1.** *Arch.* A molding, like the astragal but smaller; a bead. **2.** A gem cut in the form of a long, narrow rectangle; also, the form itself.

bag′wig′ (băg′wĭg′), *n.* A wig the back hair of which was enclosed in a silk bag. — **bag′-wigged′** (-wĭgd′), *adj.*

bag′worm′ (băg′wûrm′), *n.* The larva of any of several moths (family Psychidae), the **bagworm moths**, which, in the larval state, construct a baglike case of silk, bits of leaves, twigs, etc.

bah (bä), *interj.* An exclamation expressive of extreme contempt.

‖**ba·ha′dur** (bȧ·hô′dŏŏr; bȧ·hä′-), *n.* [Hind. *bahādur* hero, champion.] A title of respect given in India to European officers and other important personages.

Ba·ha′i (bȧ·hä′ē; *Per.* bă·hä·ē′), *n.; pl.* BAHAIS (-hä′ēz). [Per. *bahā* splendor, fr. Ar. *bahā′.*] An adherent of **Ba·ha′ism** (bȧ·hä′ĭz′m), a religious system succeeding Babism and founded in 1863 by Mirza Husayn Ali, entitled "Bahaullah," or "the Splendor of God." Bahaism emphasizes the spiritual unity of mankind. — **Ba·ha′i,** *adj.* — **Ba·ha′ist** (bȧ·hä′ĭst), *n. & adj.*

baht (bät), *n.; pl.* BAHTS (bäts), BAHT. [Siamese *bāt.*] The silver monetary unit of Thailand. See MONEY, *Tables.*

bail (bāl), *n.* [OF. *bail,* fr. *baillier* to deliver, fr. L. *bajulare* to keep in custody, fr. *bajulus* burden bearer.] **1.** *Law.* The security given for the due appearance of a prisoner in order to obtain his release from imprisonment. **2.** The person or persons who give such security; also, the release effected by them. — *v. t. Law.* **a** To deliver (goods, etc.) in trust for a special purpose. **b** To let out on bail; more often, to procure the release of by giving bail.

bail, *n.* [F. *baille* a bucket, pail.] A bucket or vessel used in bailing water out of a boat. — *v. t. & i.* To lade; to dip and throw; also, to lade water from. — ***bail out.*** To jump from an aircraft in flight in order to make a parachute descent.

bail, *n.* [ME. *beyl,* fr. ON. *beygla.*] **1.** A hoop or ring; a half hoop for supporting something, as the cover of a wagon. **2.** The arched handle of a kettle, pail, etc. — *v. t.* To provide with hoops.

bail, *n.* [OF. *bail,* fr. L. *bajulus* burden bearer.] **1.** *Obs.* **a** Usually *pl.* An outer defense of stakes; a palisade. **b** An outer wall of a feudal castle; hence, the space it enclosed; a court. **2.** *Cricket.* Either of two crosspieces placed across the top of the stumps. **3.** A bar, pole, or partition separating animals in an open stable.

bail′a·ble (bāl′ȧ·b'l), *adj.* Capable of being bailed; specif., *Law,* entitled to seek release on bail; also, admitting of bail; as, a *bailable* offense.

bail′ee′ (bāl′ē′), *n.* The person to whom goods are bailed

bail′er (bāl′ẽr), *n.* A person or thing that bails out water.

bai′ley (bā′lĭ), *n.; pl.* -LEYS (-lĭz). [ME. *baily.*] *Hist.* The bail of a castle, or a court enclosed by it; — retained in proper names, as the *Old Bailey* (in London).

Bai′ley bridge. [After Donald Coleman *Bailey,* British engineer, its designer.] A bridge designed for rapid construction from interchangeable latticed panels of electrically welded high-tensile steel which are coupled into girders with alloy steel pins and laid double or triple or superposed to suit the span and load.

bail′ie (bāl′ĭ), *n.* **1.** *Now Dial.* A bailiff. **2.** *Scot.* An officer corresponding to the English alderman.

bail′iff (bāl′ĭf), *n.* [OF. *baillif* custodian, fr. L. *bajulus* porter.] **1.** In England, an officer representing a lord, or esp. the king, in a given district, and charged, usually, with the collection of revenues, the administration of justice, etc.; now, the title of the chief magistrates of various towns and of the keepers of some royal castles. **2.** A sheriff's deputy. **3.** An overseer, understeward, or agent of an estate. **4.** *Eng.* A magistrate; — applied to various non-English officials.

bail′i·wick (bāl′ĭ·wĭk), *n.* [*bailie, bailiff* + *wick* a village.] **1.** The office or jurisdiction of a bailie or bailiff. **2.** Figuratively, one's special province or domain.

bail′ment (bāl′mĕnt), *n.* *Law.* The action of bailing a person, goods or money.

bail′or′ (bāl′ôr′; bāl′ẽr), *n.* *Law* One who delivers goods or money to another in trust.

bails′man (bālz′măn), *n.* *Law.* A bail or surety.

‖**bain′-ma′rie′** (băn′mȧ′rē′), *n.; pl.* BAINS-MARIE (băn′-). [F.] A double boiler.

Bai·ram′ (bī·räm′; bī′räm), *n.* [Turk. *baïrām.*] Either of two Mohammedan festivals held after Ramadan.

bairn (bârn; bärn), *n.* [AS. *bearn.*] *Scot. & N. of Eng.* A child.

bait (bāt), *n.* [ON. *beita* food, *beit* pasture.] **1.** Anything, such as food, used in luring to a hook, trap, etc.; also, a poisonous material distributed where it will be eaten by and kill noxious creatures, as rats or insects. **2.** A lure; a temptation. **3.** A halt for rest or to take food. — *v. t.* [ME. *baiten, beyten,* fr. ON. *beita,* orig., to cause to bite.] **1.** To harass or torment with dogs for sport; as, to *bait* a bear; also, to attack and worry, as dogs, by biting and tearing. **2.** To persecute or exasperate with wanton, malicious, or persistent attacks; as, he was mercilessly *baited* by his fellow workers. **3.** To feed, esp. upon the road; as, to *bait* horses. **4.** To allure; to entice. **5.** To furnish with bait, as a trap. **6.** To spread bait upon (land). — *v. i.* **1.** To feed; — of animals. **2.** To halt, as for food or rest. — **bait′er,** *n.*

Syn. Bait, badger, heckle, hector, chevy (*or* **chivy, chivvy**), **hound** mean to torment or harass a person by efforts to break him down. **Bait,** originally to set dogs upon to bite and worry an animal, now implies wanton cruelty or delight in persecution; **badger,** originally to bait a badger that is trapped, now implies a pestering that drives a person to confusion or frenzy; **heckle** implies persistent questioning of a speaker to confuse him or utterly discomfit him; **hector** always carries an implication of bullying, but now, even more, of spirit-breaking scolding or nagging; **chevy** and **hound** stress relentless chasing, but *chevy* carries a stronger implication of persecution by teasing, and *hound* of persistent efforts to break down.

baith (bāth). Scot. & dial. var. of BOTH.

baize (bāz), *n.* [For *bayes,* pl. fr. OF. *baie,* fr. *bai* bay-colored.] **1.** A coarse, long-napped fabric, usually of wool and dyed in plain colors. **2.** A drape, cloth, etc., of baize.

bake (bāk), *v. t.* [AS. *bacan.*] **1.** To cook in a dry heat, esp. in an oven. **2.** To dry or harden by subjecting to heat; as, to *bake* bricks. **3.** *Obs.* To make solid or hard; to cake. *Shak.* — *v. i.* **1.** To prepare baked foods; as, to *bake* on Tuesdays. **2.** To become dry and hard when heated. — *n.* **1.** Act, process, or result of baking. **2.** *Scot.* A biscuit or cracker. — **bak′er** (bāk′ẽr), *n.*

Ba′ke·lite (bā′kĕ·līt; bāk′līt), *n.* A trade-mark applied to a synthetic resin. Its uses are similar to those of hard rubber and celluloid.

bake′meat′ (bāk′mēt′), *n., or* **baked meat** (bākt). **1.** *Obs.* Baked pastry. *Shak.* **2.** Loosely, any cooked food.

bak′er's doz′en (bāk′ẽrz). Thirteen.

bak′er·y (bāk′ẽr·ĭ), *n.* A place where baking, esp. of bread, cakes, and pastry, is done; also, a shop for retailing bread, cakes, etc.

bak′ing pow′der (bāk′ĭng). A mixture of baking soda and an acid substance such as cream of tartar, with a "filling" of starch or flour, used as a leavening agent in making quick breads, cake, etc.

baking soda. Sodium bicarbonate, $NaHCO_3$.

bak′sheesh, bak′shish (băk′shēsh), *n.* [Per. *bakhshīsh,* fr. *bakhshīdan* to give.] In the Near East, a gratuity; a tip.

BAL (băl), *n.* [From *British Anti-Lewisite.*] *Chem.* A compound, $C_3H_8OS_2$, developed as an antidote against lewisite but now used against other arsenicals and against mercurials.

Ba′laam (bā′lăm), *n.* *Bib.* The prophet who, rebuked by the ass he rode, was bidden to curse Israel but blessed it instead (*Num.* xxii-xxiv).

bal′a·lai′ka (băl′ȧ·lī′kȧ), *n.* [Russ. *balalayka.*] *Music.* A triangle-shaped instrument of the guitar kind, used esp. in Russia.

bal′ance (băl′ăns), *n.* [OF., fr. L. *bilanx, bilancis,* having two scales, fr. *bis* twice + *lanx* plate, scale.] **1.** An instrument for weighing; esp., a beam or lever supported exactly in the middle, having two scales or pans of equal weight suspended from its ends. **2.** Such a balance as the emblem of Justice or of Fortune making decisions; hence, any means of determining human values; as, to be weighed in the *balance* and found wanting. **3.** A counterbalancing weight, force, influence, etc. **4.** State of equipoise, as between weights, different elements, or opposing forces; equilibrium; steadiness; as, to disturb one's emotional *balance.* **5.** An equality between the totals of the two sides of an account; as, to bring accounts to a *balance;* also, an excess or an amount in excess on either side of an account; as, *balance* (abbr. *bal.*) due; to have a *balance* in the bank. **6.** Act of balancing, as in weighing, judging, dancing, etc. **7.** *Colloq.* The remainder; the rest. **8.** [*cap.*] The constellation Libra. **9.** A vibrating wheel that operates with a hairspring to regulate the movement of a timepiece.
— *v. t.;* -ANCED (-ănst); -ANC·ING (-ăn·sĭng). **1.** To weigh in a balance. **2.** To weigh by comparing; to estimate the relative weight, importance, value, etc., of; as, to *balance* one's chances of success and failure. **3.** To counterbalance; to set off; to offset; as, the losses *balance* the gains. **4.** To bring to an equipoise or state of equilibrium; to stabilize; to poise evenly; as, to *balance* a plate on the end of a cane. **5.** To equal in number, weight, force, or value; to be or make proportionate to; as, work, play, and rest should *balance* each other; also, to proportion properly the parts, elements, etc., of; as, to *balance* one's diet. **6.** To compute the difference, if any, between the debits and credits of (an account); to arrange or prove, as an account or a book of accounts, so that the sum of the debits equals the sum of the credits. **7.** To pay the amount due on; to settle; as, to send a check to *balance* one's account. **8.** *Dancing.* To move toward, and then back from, reciprocally; as, to *balance* partners. — *v. i.* **1.** To be equally weighted; as, the scales *balance.* **2.** To be equal in value, amount, etc.; as, the debits and credits *balance.* **3.** To fluctuate; to waver. **4.** To balance partners in dancing. — **Syn.** See COMPENSATE.

bal′anced (băl′ănst), *adj.* In a state or condition of balance.

balanced sentence. A compound sentence in which the co-ordinate clauses are correspondent in structure.

balanced surface. *Aeronautics.* A surface, such as an aileron, part of which is in front of its pivot.

balance of power. Among neighboring sovereign states, such an equilibrium of ability to wage war that no one state can with impunity dominate the others.

balance of trade. **1.** Formerly, the net amount of precious metals shipped from one country to another during a fixed period. **2.** The difference between the total exports and total imports of a country. It is "favorable" if there is an excess in favor of exports.

bal′anc·er (băl′ăn·sẽr), *n.* **1.** One who or that which balances. **2.** Specif.: **a** An acrobat. **b** *Radio.* An appliance used with a direction finder to improve the sharpness of the direction indication. **c** In certain dipterous insects, one of the club-shaped organs (halteres).

balance sheet. *Bookkeeping.* A statement of the financial condition, as of a corporation, at a given date.

balance wheel. A wheel to balance or regulate motion.

bal′as (băl′ăs; bā′lăs), *n., or, now usually,* **balas ruby.** [OF. *balais,* fr. Ar. *balakhsh,* fr. Per. *Badakhshān,* where this ruby is found.] See SPINEL.

ba·la′ta (bȧ·lä′tȧ; băl′ȧ·tȧ), *n.* [Sp.] The bully tree *Mimusops globosa;* also, its milky juice, which when dried forms an elastic gum, **balata gum,** used for insulating telephone cables, in making belting, golf balls, etc.

bal·bo′a (băl·bō′ä; băl·bō′ȧ), *n.* [Sp.] The silver monetary unit of Panama, equivalent to the United States dollar.

bal·brig′gan (băl·brĭg′ăn), *n.* [From *Balbriggan,* Ireland.] A knitted cotton fabric used for hosiery and underwear.

bal′co·ny (băl′kō·nĭ), *n.; pl.* -NIES (-nĭz). [It. *balcone.*] **1.** A platform, enclosed by a parapet or a railing, projecting from the wall of a building. **2.** A projecting gallery in the interior of a theater, auditorium, etc.

bald (bôld), *adj.* [ME. *balled.*] **1.** Destitute of its natural or usual covering, as of hair on the head, nap, awns, feathers, foliage, trees, etc.; as, *bald* wheat (see WHEAT, *Illust.*). **2.** Destitute of ornament; unadorned; bare; plain. **3.** Undisguised; forthright. — **Syn.** See BARE. — **bald′ly,** *adv.* — **bald′ness,** *n.*

bal′da·chin (băl′dȧ·kĭn), *n.* Also **bal′da·quin.** [F. *baldaquin,* fr. It. *baldacchino,* fr. *Baldacco* Baghdad (see *Gaz.*), whence these silks came.] **1** A rich medieval fabric of silk and gold. **2.** A canopy of baldachin or other fabric, borne in ecclesiastical processions, placed over an altar, or the like. **3.** *Arch.* A canopylike structure generally erected over an altar.

bald coot. See COOT.
bald cypress. See CYPRESS, 2.
bald eagle. See EAGLE, 1.
Bal'der (bôl'dẽr), **Bal'dr** (*Icel.* bäl'd'r), *n.* [ON. *Baldr.*] *Teut. Myth.* The son of Odin and Frigg, god of light and peace, and of the good, beautiful, eloquent, and wise.
bal'der·dash (bôl'dẽr·dăsh), *n.* **1.** *Obs.* A worthless mixture of liquors. **2.** Senseless jargon; nonsense.
bald'head' (bôld'hĕd'), *n.* **1.** A bald-headed person. **2.** Any of certain birds with a whitish patch on the head.
bald'–head'ed (-hĕd'ĕd; -ĭd; 2; 30), *adj.* Having a bald spot on the head.
bald'pate' (bôld'pāt'), *n.* A baldhead. *Shak.* — **bald'pate', bald'–pat'ed** (-pāt'ĕd; -ĭd; 2; 30), *adj.*
bal'dric (bôl'drĭk), *n.* [OF. *baudrei, baldrei,* perh. of Teut. origin and ult. fr. L. *balteus* belt.] A belt, usually richly ornamented and worn over one shoulder, to support a sword, bugle, etc.
Bald'win (bôld'wĭn), *n.* A slightly acid, yellowish-red variety of winter apple of northeastern North America.
bale (bāl), *n.* [AS. *bealu, balu.*] **1.** *Now Chiefly Poetic.* Dire evil; a malign influence. **2.** Woe; sorrow.
bale, *n.* [OF. *bale, balle,* fr. OHG. *balla.*] A large bundle of goods; esp., a large, closely pressed package of merchandise, bound, and usually wrapped; as, a *bale* of cotton. — *v. t.;* BALED (bāld); BAL'ING (bāl'ĭng). To make up into a bale or bales. — **bal'er** (bāl'ẽr), *n.*
bale, *n. Archaic.* A balefire.
bale, bal'er (bāl'ẽr). Vars. of BAIL, BAILER.
ba·leen' (bȧ·lēn'), *n.* [OF. *baleine* whale and whalebone, fr. L. *balaena* whale.] Whalebone. See WHALEBONE, *Illust.*
bale'fire' (bāl'fīr'), *n.* [AS. *bǣlfȳr* the fire of the funeral pile, fr. *bǣl* fire, flame + *fȳr* fire.] **1.** A great or blazing fire in the open air; a bonfire. **2.** *Obs.* A funeral pyre. **3.** A signal fire.
bale'ful (-fo͝ol; -f'l), *adj.* [AS. *bealoful.*] **1.** Deadly or pernicious in influence. **2.** *Archaic.* Woeful; sorrowful. — **Syn.** See SINISTER. — **bale'ful·ly,** *adv.* — **bale'ful·ness,** *n.*
Bal'four Dec'la·ra'tion (băl'fo͝or). A declaration by Lord Balfour (Nov. 2, 1917) that the British government favored a national home for the Jewish people in Palestine, without prejudice to the civil and religious rights of the existing non-Jewish communities.
bal'is·tra'ri·a (băl'ĭs·trā'rĭ·ȧ), *n.* [ML.] *Fort.* An opening for discharging arrows. See BARTIZAN, *Illust.*
balk (bôk), *n.* [AS. *balca* ridge.] **1.** A ridge of land left unplowed as a dividing line or through carelessness. **2.** A blunder or slip. **3.** A hindrance or disappointment; check; as, to proceed without *balks.* **4.** A rough-squared length of timber; beam; rafter; a tie beam of a house. **5.** In sports, the failure of a player to complete a motion begun; esp., in baseball, any illegal motion of the pitcher, while in position, as if to throw without throwing the ball. **6.** That part of a billiard or bagatelle table between a balk line and the nearest cushion; in the balk-line game, any of the eight outside divisions of the table made by the four balk lines. — *v. t.* **1.** *Obs.* **a** To make balks in (land). **b** To heap up in piles. *Shak.* **2.** To pass by; specif., to let slip; to fail to use, seize, etc.; as, to *balk* an opportunity. **3.** To check or frustrate; foil; disappoint; bilk; as, to be *balked* of one's prey. — **Syn.** See FRUSTRATE. — *v. i.* To stop short and stand still; to refuse to proceed. — **balk'er,** *n.* — **balk'ing,** *n. & adj.* — **balk'ing·ly,** *adv.*
Bal'kan (bôl'kăn), *adj.* Of or pertaining to the Balkan Peninsula, the Balkan mountain range, or the people of the Balkan States. See *Gaz.*
Bal'kan·ize (bôl'kăn·īz), *v. t.* To break up into small hostile states, like the Balkan States, esp. in the period of the Balkan wars (1912–13). — **Bal'kan·i·za'tion** (-ĭ·zā'shŭn; -ī·zā'-), *n.*
balk line (bôk). **1.** A line across a billiard or bagatelle table, marking a limit within which the cue balls are placed in beginning a game. **2.** In billiards, one of four lines drawn parallel to the cushions, dividing the table into nine compartments, used in playing the **balk'–line' game.** **3.** In field sports, a line the crossing of which counts as a trial.
balk'y (bôk'ĭ), *adj.;* -I·ER (-ĭ·ẽr); -I·EST. Apt to balk; balking. — **Syn.** See CONTRARY.
ball (bôl), *n.* [ME. *bal, balle,* fr. ON. *böllr.*] **1.** Any round or roundish body or mass; esp., a round or oval body used in various games. **2.** The globe or earth; as, the terrestrial *ball.* **3.** A game in which a ball is thrown, kicked, or knocked; esp., baseball. **4.** In certain games, a ball delivered, as by throwing, bowling, etc., in a certain way; esp., in baseball, a pitched ball, not struck at by the batsman, that fails to pass over the home base not higher than the batsman's shoulder or lower than his knee, or that touches the ground before passing over the home base. **5.** A globular missile; now, esp., a solid spherical or elongated missile for a cannon, rifle, etc.; — often used collectively; as, powder and *ball.* **6.** A roundish protuberance at the base of the thumb or great toe. **7.** *Obs.* = ORB, 5. *Shak.* — *v. t.* To form or wind into a ball; as, to *ball* cotton. — *v. i.* To form or gather into a ball.
ball, *n.* [F. *bal,* fr. OF. *baler* to dance, fr. LL. *ballare.*] A large and formal assembly for social dancing.
bal'lad (băl'ăd), *n.* [OF. *balade,* fr. Pr. *balada* a dancing song, fr. *balar* to dance.] **1.** A simple song; esp., a romantic song having the same melody for each stanza; also, a ballad (sense 2) set to music. **2.** A popular short narrative poem in typically simple stanzas; esp., such a poem of unknown authorship which recounts a legendary or traditional event and passes orally from one generation to another. — *v. i.* To make or sing ballads.
bal·lade' (bă·läd'; *F.* bȧ'läd'), *n.* [F. See BALLAD.] **1.** A poetic form derived from the French, having usually three stanzas in each of which the same rhymes recur in the same order. Each stanza ends with a refrain and the entire poem with an envoy. **2.** A musical composition of poetic character, usually for piano or orchestra.
bal'lad·ry (băl'ăd·rĭ), *n.* Ballad poetry.
ball'–and–sock'et joint. A joint in which a ball moves within a socket, so as to admit of rotary motion in every direction within certain limits. In anatomy, the hip is a notable example of this type of joint.

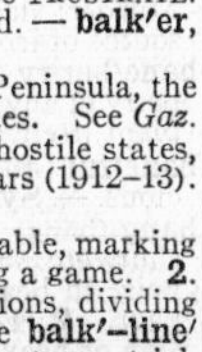
Ball-and-socket Joint (in section).

bal'last (băl'ăst), *n.* [LG., fr. Dan. *barlast,* fr. *bar* bare + *last* load, cargo.] **1.** Any heavy substance used in a vessel or balloon to improve its stability, or to control the draft of the boat or the ascent of the balloon. **2.** That which gives stability in character, conduct, or the like. **3.** Broken stone or gravel, used in making roadbeds solid and in making concrete. — *v. t.* **1.** To steady with or as with ballast; to stabilize; also, to fill or fill in with ballast. **2.** *Archaic.* To load or weigh down. — **bal'last·er,** *n.*
ball bearing. *Mach.* A bearing in which the revolving part turns upon loose, hardened steel balls, thus converting sliding friction into rolling friction; also, one of the balls in such a bearing. Cf. ROLLER BEARING. — **ball'–bear'ing** (*see Pron.,* § 2), *adj.*
ball cock. An automatic device consisting essentially of a valve and a floating ball at the end of a lever, the rise or fall of the ball causing the lever to shut or open the valve.
bal'le·ri'na (băl'ĕ·rē'nȧ; *It.* bäl'lā·rē'nä), *n.; pl.* -RINAS (băl'ĕ·rē'nȧz), -RINE (bäl'lā·rē'nā). [It.] A professional female dancer, esp. a ballet dancer.
bal'let (băl'ā; bă·lā'), *n.* [F., fr. It. *balletto,* dim. of *ballo* dance.] **1.** A theatrical dance; specif., a pantomimic dance executed by a group, esp. of women. **2.** A kind of artistic dancing marked by great variety, intricacy, and expressiveness in its movements. **3.** The performers of a ballet.
bal·let'o·mane (bă·lĕt'ō·măn), *n.* One who delights in ballets; a devotee of ballets; — a French neologism.
ball'–flow'er (bôl'flou'ẽr), *n. Arch.* An ornament resembling a ball placed in a hollowed trefoil, quatrefoil, etc.

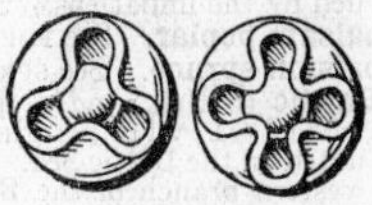
Ball-flowers.

bal·lis'ta (bă·lĭs'tȧ), *n.; pl.* -TAE (-tē). [L., fr. Gr. *ballein* to throw.] An ancient military engine, often shaped like a crossbow, for hurling large missiles at an angle. Cf. CATAPULT, 1.
bal·lis'tic (bă·lĭs'tĭk), *adj.* [*ballista* + *-ic.*] Of or pertaining to ballistics.
bal·lis'tics (-tĭks), *n.;* see -ICS. The science which studies the laws governing the motion of projectiles shot from artillery or firearms, or (**ballistics of bombs**) of bombs dropped from aircraft. — **bal'lis·ti'cian** (băl'ĭs·tĭsh'ăn), *n.*
bal'lo·net' (băl'ō·nĕt'), *n.* [F. *ballonnet,* dim. of *ballon* balloon.] A compartment of variable volume within the interior of a balloon or airship, for controlling its ascent or descent and for maintaining pressure on the outer envelope.
‖**bal'lon' d'es'sai'** (bȧ'lôɴ' dĕ'sĕ'). [F.] Literally, a trial balloon; hence, a proposal or statement made public to test opinion.
bal·loon' (bă·lo͞on'), *n.* [F. *ballon,* fr. It. *ballone, pallone,* fr. *balla, palla,* ball.] **1.** A nonporous bag of tough, light material filled with heated air or a gas lighter than air so as to rise and float in the atmosphere; a nondirigible aerostat. **2.** A toy consisting of a baglike rubber casing that can be inflated with air or gas. **3.** The outline enclosing words represented as coming from the mouth of a pictured figure, as in cartoons. — *v. t.* To inflate; to distend, as a cavity or canal of the body. — *v. i.* **1.** To go up or voyage in a balloon. **2.** To expand, or puff out, like a balloon. — *adj.* Puffed out; much inflated or distended; as, a *balloon* sleeve. — **bal·loon'er,** *n.* — **bal·loon'ist,** *n.*
balloon sail. *Naut.* A large light sail set in addition to, or in place of, an ordinary light sail, as a balloon foresail or jib, set usually between the fore-topmast head and the end of the bowsprit or jib boom.
balloon tire. A pneumatic tire with flexible carcass and large cross section, that lessens shocks because of low-pressure inflation.
balloon vine. A tropical American vine (*Cardiospermum halicacabum*) of the soapberry family, bearing large ornamental bladdery pods.
bal'lot (băl'ŭt), *n.* [It. *ballotta,* fr. *balla* ball.] **1.** Originally, a little ball used for secret voting; now, a printed or written slip used in secret voting. See AUSTRALIAN BALLOT. **2.** Act or system of voting by means of ballots, by use of voting machines, etc. **3.** Total of votes cast at an election or in a given territory. **4.** *New Zealand.* Selection for compulsory military service; draft. — *v. i. & t.;* BAL'LOT·ED; BAL'LOT·ING. **1.** To vote, vote upon, or decide by ballot. **2.** To select by ballot or by casting lots. — **bal'lot·er,** *n.*
bal·lotte'ment (bă·lŏt'mĕnt; *F.* bȧ'lôt'mäɴ'), *n.* [F.] *Med.* A sharp upward pushing against the uterine wall with a finger, for diagnosing pregnancy by feeling the return impact of the displaced fetus; also, a similar procedure for diagnosing floating kidney.
ball'–point', *adj.* Having as a writing point a tiny steel ball rotating freely against an inking magazine; — of a pen.
ball'room' (bôl'ro͞om'), *n.* A room for balls or dancing.
ball valve. A valve in which a ball regulates the aperture by its rise and fall through suction and its own weight.
bal'ly·hoo (băl'ĭ·ho͞o; băl'ĭ·ho͞o'), *n.* [From *Ballyhooly,* village in County Cork, Eire.] *Slang.* Noisy demonstration to attract attention; sensational writing and propaganda. — **bal'ly·hoo'** (băl'ĭ·ho͞o'; băl'ĭ·ho͞o'), *v. t. & i.;* -HOOED' (-ho͞od'; -ho͞od'); -HOO'ING.
bal'ly·rag'. Var. of BULLYRAG.
balm (bäm), *n.* [From OF., fr. L. *balsamum* balsam, fr. Gr. *balsamon.*] **1.** Any balsamic resin, esp. that from a genus (*Commiphora*) of small tropical evergreen trees. **2.** An aromatic oil, ointment, etc., for anointing, soothing, and healing. **3.** An aromatic perfume. **4.** Any of certain plants of the mint family (esp. of the genera *Melissa* and *Monarda*); specif.: **a** The ***garden balm*** or ***bee balm*** (*Melissa officinalis*), cultivated as a garden herb and bee plant. **b** The ***Oswego tea*** or ***bee balm*** (*Monarda didyma*) with showy scarlet flowers. **5.** A healing, soothing agency or influence.
balm of Gil'e·ad (gĭl'ē·ăd; -ăd). **1.** A small evergreen African and Asiatic tree (*Commiphora meccanensis*) yielding a fragrant balsam; also, this balsam. **2.** Balsam fir (see FIR). **3.** Balsam poplar (see POPLAR).
Bal·mor'al (băl·mŏr'ăl), *n.* [From *Balmoral* Castle, in Aberdeen Co., Scotland.] **1.** A kind of woolen petticoat worn below a looped-up skirt. **2.** [*usually not cap.*] A kind of laced boot. **3.** A round flat cap with projecting top all around.
Bal'mung (bäl'mo͝ong), *n.* [G.] Siegfried's sword.
balm'y (bäm'ĭ), *adj.;* -I·ER (-ĭ·ẽr); -I·EST. Having balm or the qualities of balm; aromatic; soothing; refreshing; mild. — **balm'i·ly,** *adv.* — **balm'i·ness,** *n.*
bal'ne·ol'o·gy (băl'nē·ŏl'ō·jĭ), *n.* [L. *balneum* bath + *-logy.*] The science of bathing, or esp. of the therapeutic use of natural mineral waters.
ba·lo'ney (bȧ·lō'nĭ). Var. of BOLONEY.
bal'sa (bôl'sȧ; bäl'sȧ), *n.* [Sp.] **1.** An American tropical tree (*Ochroma lagopus*) of the silk-cotton family, yielding light strong wood used for floats, airplanes, etc.; — called also *corkwood* or *West Indian corkwood.* **2.** A raft or float; specif., a raft made of two cylinders of metal or wood joined by a framework, used for lifesaving and landing through surf.

bal'sam (bôl'săm), *n.* [L. *balsamum.* See BALM.] **1.** An aromatic and, commonly, oily and resinous substance flowing from certain plants; esp., any of several resinous substances containing benzoic or cinnamic acid and used as expectorants, some also as stomachics and in cough sirups, etc., as **balsam of Pe·ru'** (pĕ·rōō'; pē-) from a tropical American tree (*Myroxylon pereirae*) of the pea family and **balsam of To·lú'** (tō·lōō') from a related tree (*M. balsamum*). **2.** Any of various preparations containing resinous substances and having a balsamic odor, as balm of Gilead. **3.** A balsam-yielding tree, as the balsam fir (see FIR, CANADA BALSAM). **4.** Any impatiens, esp. the common garden species (*Impatiens balsamina*). **5.** A balm for mind or body.

balsam fir. See FIR.

bal·sam'ic (bôl·săm'ĭk; băl-), *adj.* Of, belonging to, or characteristic of balsam; containing balsam.

bal'sam·if'er·ous (bôl'sȧ·mĭf'ẽr·ŭs; băl'-), *adj.* [*balsam* + *-ferous.*] Producing balsam.

bal'sa·mi·na'ceous (bôl'sȧ·mĭ·nā'shŭs; băl'-), *adj.* [Gr. *balsaminē* balsam plant.] Belonging to a family (Balsaminaceae) of plants typified by the impatiens. See IMPATIENS.

balsam poplar. See POPLAR.

balsam spruce. See SPRUCE, 2.

Bal'tic (bôl'tĭk), *adj.* [ML. mare *Balticum*, fr. L. *Baltia* Scandinavia.] **1.** Of or pertaining to the Baltic Sea or the Baltic States; situated on the Baltic Sea. See *Gaz.* **2.** Belonging to or designating the western branch of the Balto-Slavic languages. See INDO-EUROPEAN LANGUAGES, *Table.*

Bal'ti·more o'ri·ole (bôl'tĭ·mōr; 70). See ORIOLE, 2.

Bal'to- (bôl'tō-). A combining form for *Baltic*, denoting *Baltic and*, as in **Bal'to-Slav'ic** (designating a subfamily of the Indo-European languages), **Bal'to-Sla·von'ic.** See INDO-EUROPEAN LANGUAGES, *Table.*

Ba·lu'chi (bȧ·lōō'chē), *n. sing. & pl.* **1.** An inhabitant of Baluchistan. **2.** The Iranian language of Baluchistan. See INDO-EUROPEAN LANGUAGES, *Table.*

bal'us·ter (băl'ŭs·tẽr), *n.* [Through F. fr. It., fr. L. *balaustium* wild pomegranate flower, fr. Gr. *balaustion;* — from the similarity of form.] An upright support of a rail, in the railing of a staircase, balcony, etc.; a banister.

bal'us·trade' (băl'ŭs·trād'; băl'ŭs·trād), *n.* [F., fr. It. *balaustrata.*] A row of balusters topped by a rail; banisters.

||**bam·bi'no** (bäm·bē'nō; băm-), *n.; pl.* -NI (-nē). [It.] A child or baby; specif., a representation in art of the infant Christ.

bam·boo' (băm·bōō'), *n.* [Malay *bambu.*] Any of various woody or treelike grasses of the genus *Bambusa* or other related genera, as *Arundinaria, Dendrocalamus.* The hollow stems of some bamboos are used for building, furniture, poles, canes, etc. Young shoots are used for food.

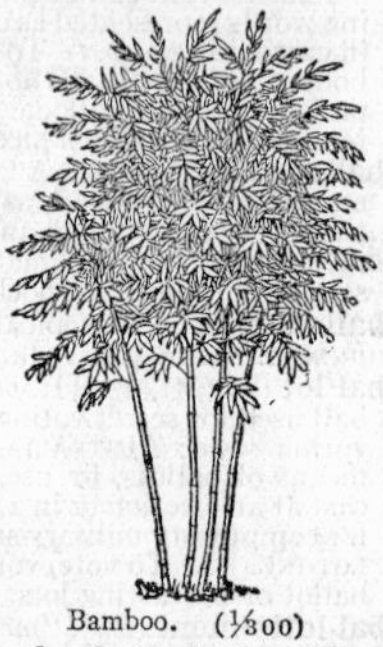
Bamboo. (1/300)

bam·boo'zle (băm·bōō'z'l), *v. t. & i.;* -ZLED (-z'ld); -ZLING (-zlĭng). *Colloq.* To trick; hoax; hornswoggle; also, to perplex; baffle. — **bam·boo'zle·ment,** *n.* — **bam·boo'zler** (-zlẽr), *n.*

ban (băn), *v. t.;* BANNED (bănd); BAN'NING. [AS. *bannan* to summon by proclamation.] **1.** To curse; to denounce; to condemn. **2.** To prohibit as evil or as doing evil; to proscribe; forbid, as by official order; as, to *ban* a play; to *ban* a group from demonstrating. — **Syn.** See EXECRATE. — *n.* [From *ban*, v., and fr. OF. *ban*, fr. LL. *bannum*, of Teut. origin.] **1.** A proclamation; now, in *pl.*, var. of BANNS. **2.** Formerly, a summoning of vassals to military service; also, the body thus summoned. **3.** *Eccl.* Interdict; excommunication. **4.** Curse; malediction. **5.** Proscription by law or authority; status of being officially prohibited or outlawed. **6.** Public disapproval or condemnation.

ban (băn), *n.* [Serbo-Croatian *bān* lord, ruler.] Governor; — an ancient Hungarian and a modern Croatian and Slavonian title.

ban (bän), *n.; pl.* BANI (bä'nĭ). [Romanian.] See MONEY, *Tables* (Romania).

ba'nal (bā'năl; bȧ·năl'; -näl'; băn'ăl), *adj.* [F., fr. *ban* an ordinance.] Lacking freshness and vigor because commonplace or hackneyed; trite; flat; as, a *banal* remark. — **Syn.** See INSIPID. — **ba·nal'i·ty** (bȧ·năl'ĭ·tĭ), *n.* — **ba'nal·ly,** *adv.*

ba·nan'a (bȧ·năn'ȧ *or, esp. Brit.,* -nä'nȧ), *n.* [Sp. & Pg. *banana.*] A large herbaceous perennial tropical plant (*Musa sapientum*) that bears fruit in compact hanging clusters; also, its edible fruit. It typifies a family (Musaceae, the banana family) of tropical trees or treelike herbs.

banana oil. a A colorless liquid ester, amyl acetate, $CH_3CO_2C_5H_{11}$, of agreeable odor, like that of bananas or pears. It is used as a solvent and in the manufacture of artificial fruit essences. **b** A lacquer containing amyl acetate.

ban'at, ban'ate (băn'ăt), *n.* The territory governed by a ban.

band (bănd), *n.* [ME. *band, bond*, fr. ON. *band.* In senses 5 to 7 fr. F. *bande.*] **1.** *Archaic.* A fetter, shackle, or the like. **2.** Something which ties or holds things together; as, a rubber *band.* **3.** A bond; a tie; as, *bands* of matrimony. **4.** A flat narrow strip around, across, or up and down something. **5.** A strip of fabric at the neck, wrist, waist, etc., of a garment to finish, strengthen, bind, adorn, etc.; — usually in combination; as, waist*band;* hat*band.* **6.** A neckband or collar; esp.: **a** An ornamental upstanding collar worn around 1600. **b** Usually ***falling band.*** A plain turned-down collar worn by Puritans in England and America. **c** Usually in *pl.* A pair of strips hanging at the neck opening of some legal, academic, and clerical gowns. The white lawn bands of clerical dress are called ***Geneva bands.*** **7.** A company of persons united for a common purpose. **8.** A company of performers on musical, esp. wind and percussion, instruments. **9.** *Radio.* A range of frequencies or wave lengths. — **Syn.** Company, troop, troupe. — *v. t. & i.* **1.** To bind or tie with a band; to encircle or mark with a band. **2.** To unite in a troop, company, etc.; to confederate.

band'age (băn'dĭj), *n.* [F., fr. *bande.*] A strip of woven material used in dressing and binding up wounds, etc.; also, any similarly used strip or band. — *v. t.;* -AGED (-dĭjd); -AG·ING (-dĭj'ĭng). To bind, dress, or cover with a bandage. — **band'ag·er** (-dĭ·jẽr), *n.*

ban·dan'na (băn·dăn'ȧ), **ban·dan'a** (băn·dăn'ȧ *or, esp. Brit.,* -dä'nȧ), *n.* [Hind. *bāndhnū* a certain mode of dyeing.] A large, usually red or blue, figured handkerchief.

band'box' (bănd'bŏks'), *n.* A light box of pasteboard or thin wood for holding collars (bands), caps, hats, etc.

ban·deau' (băn·dō'; băn'dō), *n.; pl.* -DEAUX (-dōz'; -dōz). [F.] A narrow band; esp., a fillet for the hair.

ban'de·role, ban'de·rol (băn'dĕ·rōl), *n.* [F. *banderole*, fr. It. *banderuola* a little banner.] **1.** A little banner, flag, or streamer. **2.** A ribbon bearing an inscription or a device; a scroll representing such a ribbon. **3.** *Arch.* A sculptured band, often bearing an inscription. **4.** A small flag displayed at funerals of great men.

ban'di·coot (băn'dĭ·kōōt), *n.* [Telugu *pandi-kokku* pig rat.] **a** A very large rat (*Nesokia bandicota*) of India and Ceylon. **b** Any of a genus (*Perameles*) of small, active, insect-eating marsupials, found esp. in Australia.

ban'dit (băn'dĭt), *n.; pl.* -DITS, -DITTI (băn·dĭt'ĭ). [It. *bandito* outlaw, past part. of *bandire* to banish.] An outlaw; hence, a brigand; a lawless marauder. — **ban'dit·ry,** *n.*

band'mas'ter (bănd'mȧs'tẽr; 9), *n.* Conductor of a musical band.

ban'dog' (băn'dŏg'; 74), *n.* [*band* + *dog.*] A watchdog or ferocious dog kept tied and chained; hence, a mastiff; a bloodhound.

ban'do·leer', ban'do·lier' (băn'dō·lēr'; 27), *n.* [F. *bandoulière*, fr. Sp. *bandolera*, fr. *banda* band.] **1.** A broad belt worn slung over the shoulder and used for suspending or supporting heavy articles, esp. cartridges in loops or pockets. **2.** An ammunition box carried on such a belt.

ban'do·line (băn'dō·lēn; -lĭn), *n.* [F.] A glutinous pomade for dressing the hair.

ban·dore' (băn·dōr'; băn'dōr; 70), *n.* [Through Sp. or Pg., fr. L. *pandura, pandurium*, a musical instrument of three strings, fr. Gr. *pandoura.*] An old lutelike musical instrument.

band saw. A saw in the form of an endless belt running over pulleys.

bands'man (băndz'măn; bănz'-), *n.* A member of a band, esp. of musicians.

band'stand' (bănd'stănd'; băn'-), *n.* A stand, usually roofed, in which a band may play an outdoor concert.

band wagon. 1. A high ornate wagon in which a band rides, as in a circus parade. **2.** *Colloq.* An imaginary vehicle thought of as carrying a band of leaders, as political leaders, whose candidate or cause has captivated the populace; as, to get on the *band wagon*, that is, to espouse publicly such a candidate or cause.

ban'dy (băn'dĭ), *v. t.;* -DIED (-dĭd); -DY·ING. [F. *bander* to bandy, *se bander* to band together.] **1.** To toss to and fro, as or as if a ball. **2.** To exchange, esp. in rapid succession; as, to *bandy* blows. **3.** To pass from mouth to mouth; to discuss; as, the story was *bandied* about. — *v. i. Now Rare.* **a** To contend. **b** To band together. — *n.; pl.* -DIES (-dĭz). **1.** An old form of tennis or a stroke in this game. **2.** A kind of field hockey; also, the bent stick used in this game. — *adj.* Curved laterally, esp. with the convex side outward; as, *bandy* legs. — **ban'dy-leg'ged** (-lĕg'ĕd; -ĭd; -lĕgd'; 30), *adj.*

bane (bān), *n.* [AS. *bana* murderer.] **1.** That which destroys life; esp., deadly poison; — now only in rats*bane*, hen*bane*, etc. **2.** *Obs.* Murder; death. **3.** Ruin; woe; esp., destroying or ruining cause; source of irreparable harm. — *v. t. & i.* To poison; to harm.

bane'ber'ry (bān'bĕr'ĭ; -bẽr·ĭ), *n.; pl.* -RIES (-ĭz). The acrid poisonous berry of any plant of the genus *Actaea* of the crowfoot family; also, the plant itself.

bane'ful (-fōōl; -f'l), *adj.* **1.** Poisonous; noxious. **2.** Ruinous; pernicious. — **Syn.** See PERNICIOUS. — **bane'ful·ly,** *adv.* — **-ful·ness,** *n.*

bang (băng), *v. t.* [ON. *banga* to hammer.] To beat, thump, strike, shut, etc., with a loud resounding noise. — *v. i.* To make a loud noise in beating, striking, etc. — *n.* **1.** A resounding blow or impact. **2.** Energy; dash; go. **3.** A sudden loud noise as of an explosion or heavy impact. — *adv.* With a bang.

bang, *v. t.* To cut short and squarely across, as front hair or a horse's tail. — *n.* A fringe of banged hair.

bang. Var. of BHANG.

ban'ga·lore' tor·pe'do (băng'gȧ·lōr'). [From *Bangalore*, city of India.] A long iron pipe, containing TNT, fitted with a detonating cap and long fuse, which is thrust forward and exploded for cutting wire entanglements or for detonating buried mines.

bang'board' (băng'bōrd'; 70), *n.* A sidepiece mounted above the far sidepiece of a wagon, from which the ears of corn tossed by a husker rebound into the wagon.

bang'kok (băng'kŏk), *n.* **1.** A straw grown in Bangkok. **2.** An unblocked shape or hat of finely woven bangkok.

ban'gle (băng'g'l), *n.* [Hind. *bangrī* bracelet, bangle.] An ornamental bracelet or anklet.

ba'ni (bä'nĭ), *n., pl.* of BAN, a coin.

ban'ian (băn'yăn), *n.* [From Skr. *vaṇij* merchant.] **1.** One of a caste of Hindu merchants who abstain from eating meat. **2.** A loose shirt, gown, or jacket worn in India. **3.** Var. of BANYAN.

ban'ish (băn'ĭsh), *v. t.* [OF. *banir*, fr. LL. *bannire*, fr. *bannum* proclamation.] **1.** To condemn to leave a country by sovereign authority. **2.** To drive out from a home, a wonted place, or the like; to expel; dismiss; as, to *banish* suspicion. — **ban'ish·er,** *n.* — **ban'ish·ment,** *n.*

Syn. **Banish, exile, deport, transport** mean to remove by authority or force from a state or country. **Banish** implies compulsory removal from a country (which may or may not be one's own); **exile** may imply compulsory removal or an enforced, sometimes voluntary, absence from one's own country; **deport** implies sending out of the country a person whose presence is considered inimical to the public welfare or who has not lawfully entered that country; **transport** implies banishment to a penal colony, or the like, of a person convicted of a given crime.

ban'is·ter (băn'ĭs·tẽr), *n.* [Corrupt. fr. BALUSTER.] A baluster; *pl.*, the balustrade of a staircase.

ban'jo (băn'jō), *n.; pl.* -JOS, -JOES (-jōz). [Corrupt. fr. *bandore.*] A stringed musical instrument having a neck like a guitar and a body like a tambourine. — *adj.* Having the shape of, or shaped like, a banjo; as, a *banjo* clock. — **ban'jo·ist,** *n.*

bank (băngk), *n.* [ME. *banke*, of Scand. origin.] **1.** A mound, pile, or ridge, esp. of earth. **2.** A steep acclivity or slope, as of a hill, etc. **3.** Rising ground bordering a lake, river, sea, etc., or forming the edge of a cutting or other hollow; specif., *Mining*, the ground at the top of a shaft. **4.** An elevation under the sea; a shoal, shelf, or shallow; as, the *banks* of Newfoundland. **5.** The lateral inclination of an airplane, as when it rounds a curve. **6.** The cushion of a billiard table. — *v. t.* **1.** To raise or form a bank about; to embank. **2.** To heap or pile in a bank. **3.** To cover (a fire) with fresh fuel and to reduce the draft of air, so as to hold in an inactive state. **4.** To incline (an airplane) laterally when rounding a curve. **5.** To build (a curve, as of a road) with the bed inclined laterally upward toward the outside edge. **6.** *Billiards & Pool.* To drive (a ball) to the bank, or cushion; specif., to pocket (the object ball) by playing it against a cushion or cushions. — *v. i.* **1.** To rise in or form a bank or banks. **2.** To bank an airplane.

bank (băngk), *n.* [ME. *banck*, prob. fr. OF. *banc*, of G. origin.] **1.** A bench for rowers in a galley; also, a tier of oars. **2.** A group or series of objects arranged near together; as, a *bank* of electric lamps. **3.** A tier or row of keys belonging to a keyboard. Cf. TYPEWRITER, *Illust.* — *v. t.* To group in a bank.

bank, *n.* [F. *banque*, fr. It. *banca*, orig., bench, table, counter, of G. origin, akin to E. *bench.*] **1.** *Obs.* The table or counter of a money-changer. **2.** Formerly, a fund, esp. a joint fund, for use in business; now, the fund of the dealer or banker in a gambling game. **3.** An establishment for the custody, loan, exchange, or issue of money, for the extension of credit, and for facilitating the transmission of funds by drafts or bills of exchange. **4.** In dominoes and the like, a fund of pieces from which the players draw. **5.** A storage place for any reserve supply; as, a blood *bank.* — *v. i.* **1.** To keep a bank or, in gambling, to keep the bank. **2.** To deposit money in a bank. **3.** *Colloq.* To rely; to count; — with *on* or *upon;* as, to *bank* on a person's honesty. — *v. t.* To deposit in a bank.

bank'a·ble (băngk'ȧ·b'l), *adj.* Receivable as good at a bank.

bank, *or* **bank'er's, ac·cept'ance.** A bill of exchange or draft drawn on and accepted by a bank or banker.

bank annuities. Consols; — the legal name.

bank cod. See COD.

bank discount. The interest at the given rate on the face of a bill or note, from time of discounting until maturity.

bank'er (băngk'ẽr), *n.* A man or vessel employed in cod fishery on the Newfoundland banks.

bank'er, *n.* A sculptor's or mason's workbench.

bank'er, *n.* [After F. *banquier.*] **1.** A person or corporation that conducts a bank. **2.** *Gambling.* One who keeps the bank.

bank'er's ac·cept'ance (băngk'ẽrz). = BANK ACCEPTANCE.

banker's, *or* **bank, bill.** A bill of exchange drawn by one bank on another.

bank holiday. **1.** In Great Britain, a legal holiday. **2.** A period when banks in general are closed.

bank'ing (băngk'ĭng), *n.* Business of a bank or a banker.

bank night. A copyrighted form of lottery conducted by proprietors of motion-picture theaters with a drawing of prizes for distribution among patrons who have registered and are present at an appointed evening performance.

bank note. A promissory note issued by a bank, payable to bearer on demand but without interest, and circulating as money. In England, specif., a Bank of England note.

bank paper. **1.** Bank notes, collectively. **2.** Bankable commercial paper, as discountable notes.

bank rate. Discount rate fixed by a central bank or banks.

bank'rupt (băngk'rŭpt), *n.* [After L. *rupta*, fr. It. and F.; F. *banqueroute*, fr. It. *banca rotta*, lit., broken bank.] **1.** Any person whose property becomes liable to administration under a **bankrupt law,** or law regulating persons unable to pay their debts and protecting their creditors; now, specif., a person who is insolvent or has done any of the acts (such as a transfer of his property actually or constructively fraudulent) which entitle his creditors to have his estate administered for their benefit. **2.** One judicially declared a bankrupt. **3.** One wanting in resources or qualities of a specified kind; as, a moral *bankrupt.* — *adj.* **1.** Being a bankrupt; insolvent. **2.** Destitute of, or wholly lacking (something once possessed or something one should possess). **3.** Relating to bankrupts or bankruptcy. — *v. t.* To make bankrupt; to reduce to bankruptcy; impoverish. — **Syn.** See DEPLETE.

bank'rupt·cy (-rŭpt·sĭ; -rŭp·sĭ), *n.; pl.* -CIES (-sĭz). **1.** State of being actually or legally bankrupt. **2.** Complete impoverishment or failure, as of courage.

bank'si·a (băngk'sĭ·ȧ), *n.* [NL., after Sir Joseph *Banks*, Eng. naturalist.] An Australian evergreen tree or shrub (genus *Banksia*, family Proteaceae) with alternate leathery leaves and yellowish flowers in dense cylindrical heads.

Bank'side' (băngk'sīd'), *n.* The bank of the Thames at Southwark, opposite the old city of London, where theaters were located in Shakespeare's time.

ban'ner (băn'ẽr), *n.* [From OF., fr LL. *baneria, banderia*, fr. *bandum* banner.] **1.** A flag, originally the standard of a king, feudal lord, or the like, now of a nation, state, organization, etc. **2.** Figuratively, something symbolizing one's principles, or the like. — *adj.* Foremost; leading; surpassing; as, the *banner* class.

ban'ner·et (băn'ẽr·ĕt), *n.* [OF. *baneret.*] *Hist.* Orig., a knight leading vassals under his own banner, in rank next to a baron; hence, the title of such a knight.

ban'ner·et', ban'ner·ette' (băn'ẽr·ĕt'), *n.* A small banner.

ban'ner·ol (băn'ẽr·ōl), *n.* A banderole.

ban'nis·ter (băn'ĭs·tẽr), *n.* Var. of BANISTER.

ban'nock (băn'ŭk), *n.* [Gael. *bannach.*] *Scot. & Dial.* A kind of oatmeal or barley cake baked on a griddle.

banns (bănz), *n. pl.* Also **bans.** [See 1st BAN.] Public announcement, esp. in church, of a proposed marriage.

ban'quet (băng'kwĕt; -kwĭt), *n.* [F., fr. an It. dim. of *banco* bench.] A feast, often ceremonious and followed by speeches. — *v. t. & i.;* -QUET·ED; -QUET·ING. To entertain or be entertained at a banquet. — **ban'quet·er,** *n.*

ban·quette' (băng·kĕt'), *n.* [F.] **1.** *Fort.* A raised way along the inside of a parapet or trench for gunners. See BASTION, *Illust.* **2.** A benchlike upholstered seat. **3.** A sidewalk.

Ban'quo (băng'kwō; -kō), *n.* In Shakespeare's *Macbeth*, a Scottish thane and fellow general with Macbeth. After his murder his ghost appears to Macbeth.

bans (bănz). Var. of BANNS.

ban'shee, ban'shie (băn'shē; băn·shē'), *n.* [Gael. *beanshīth*, fr. Gael. & Ir. *bean* woman + Gael. *sīth* fairy.] *Ir. & Scot.* A female spirit whose wailings forewarn families of the coming death of a member.

bant (bănt), *v. i.* *Humorous.* To practice a reducing diet; — so called from William Banting, a London undertaker.

Ban'tam (băn'tăm), *n.* [From *Bantam*, Java.] **1.** A miniature fowl of any of many dwarf breeds, as ***Cochin Bantam, Brahma Bantam.*** **2.** [*not cap.*] A person of diminutive stature and combative disposition. **3.** [*not cap.*] See JEEP.

ban'tam, *adj.* Like a bantam; diminutive; saucy

ban'tam·weight' (-wāt'), *n.* A boxer of a weight not exceeding 118 pounds.

ban'ter (băn'tẽr), *v. t.* [Origin unknown.] To ridicule lightly and good-naturedly; to rally; to chaff. — *v. i.* To banter a person. — *n.* Bantering language; ridicule. — **ban'ter·er,** *n.* — **ban'ter·ing·ly,** *adv.*

bant'ling (bănt'lĭng), *n.* [G. *bänkling* a bastard.] A young child or infant; esp., a bastard.

Ban'tu' (băn'tōō'), *n.; pl.* BANTU (-tōō'), BANTUS (-tōōz'). A member of one of the great family of Negroid tribes occupying equatorial and southern Africa. The Bantu languages constitute the most important linguistic family in Africa south of the Sahara. See LANGUAGE, *Table.* — **Ban'tu',** *adj.*

ban'yan (băn'yăn; -yăn), *n.* [From the use of the space under the tree as a market place by banians.] An East Indian tree (*Ficus bengalensis*) of the mulberry family, whose branches send out aerial roots that grow down to the soil and form additional trunks.

ban'zai' (bän'zä'ē; -zī'), *interj.* [Jap., ten thousand years, forever.] *Japan.* A shout of felicitation.

banzai attack *or* **charge.** A reckless, usually suicidal, bayonet charge by Japanese soldiers in formation or in mass to the accompaniment of yells of "banzai."

ba'o·bab (bā'ō·băb; bä'ō-), *n.* [Source unknown.] A broad-trunked African timber tree (*Adansonia digitata*) of the silk-cotton family, which bears a gourdlike fruit. See MONKEY BREAD.

bap·tis'i·a (băp·tĭz'ĭ·ȧ; -tĭzh'ĭ·ȧ), *n.* [NL., from Gr. *baptisis* a dipping, alluding to the use of certain species in dyeing.] Any of a genus (*Baptisia*) of North American flowering plants of the pea family (Fabaceae). Species are known also as *wild indigo, false indigo,* etc.

bap'tism (băp'tĭz'm), *n.* **1.** *Eccl.* Act or ceremony of baptizing; specif., a sacrament by whose reception one becomes a Christian or a member of a Christian church. **2.** Any act or experience that, like baptism, purifies, initiates, etc. **3.** *Christian Science.* Purification by Spirit; submergence in Spirit. *Mary Baker Eddy.* — **bap·tis'mal** (băp·tĭz'măl), *adj.* — **bap·tis'mal·ly,** *adv.*

baptism of fire. **1.** Spiritual baptism. *Acts* ii. 3, 4; *Matt.* iii. 11. **2.** Martyrdom. **3.** A severe ordeal; specif., a soldier's first exposure to enemy fire.

Bap'tist (băp'tĭst), *n.* **1.** A baptizer; specif., with *the*, John, the forerunner of Christ. **2.** A member of a denomination of Christians who maintain that baptism should be administered to believers only. Nearly all Baptists hold that baptism should be by immersion only.

bap'tis·ter·y (băp'tĭs·tẽr·ĭ), **bap'tist·ry** (-trĭ), *n.; pl.* -TERIES (-ĭz), -RIES (-trĭz). [L. *baptisterium*, fr. Gr. *baptistērion.*] **a** A part of a church, either a separate building or a section, containing a font, used for baptismal service. **b** In modern Baptist and some other churches, a tank used for immersion in baptism.

bap·tize' (băp·tīz'), *v. t.* [F. *baptiser*, fr. L. *baptizare*, fr. Gr. *baptizein*, fr. *baptein* to dip in water.] **1.** To dip or immerse in water, or to pour or sprinkle water upon, as a religious rite; to administer baptism to. **2.** To cleanse, purify, initiate, etc. **3.** To give a name to at baptism; to christen. — *v. i.* To administer baptism. — **bap·tiz'er** (-tīz'ẽr), *n.*

bar (bär), *n.* [OF. *barre*, fr. LL. *barra.*] **1.** A piece of wood or metal, long in proportion to its breadth and thickness, such as one used for a lever, support, barrier, or fastening. **2.** A bar-shaped or block-shaped piece of something; also, the quantity in such a piece; as, a *bar* of gold or of soap. **3.** A band, stripe, or broad shaft, as of light or color. **4.** An obstruction; a barrier; an obstacle; as, a sand *bar;* a *bar* to health. **5.** The railing enclosing the place about the judge where prisoners are stationed, or where business is transacted in civil cases. **6.** Hence: **a** The court; a court or system of courts; — usually in phrases ***at bar or at the bar;*** as, to plead at the *bar.* **b** Any tribunal; as, the *bar* of public opinion. **7.** Formerly, in English Inns of Court, a barrier setting apart the seniors, before which students when qualified were called to debate; hence, barristers or lawyers collectively; also, their profession. **8.** A counter at which liquor or food is served or merchandise is sold and the place behind it; hence, a place having such a counter. **9.** The space in front of the molar teeth of a horse in which the bit is placed; also, the solid mouthpiece of a bit. **10.** A corded, knotted, or buttonholed bride in needle-point lace. **11.** *Her.* A set of horizontal stripes crossing the shield or any charge of it. **12.** *Law.* Destruction of an action or claim; also, the plea or objection which effects such destruction. **13.** *Music.* One of the vertical lines across a staff dividing it into equal measures of time; also, a pair of these, called a ***double bar,*** marking the end of a movement or piece. **14.** *Veter.* See HOOF, *Illust.* — *v. t.;* BARRED (bärd); BAR'RING. **1.** To fasten, surround, confine, or obstruct by or as if by bars. **2.** To mark with bars; to stripe. **3.** To prohibit entrance to, use of, etc.; to exclude; rule out; object to.

bar, *prep.* Except; save; excluding; as, *bar* none.

Bar·ab'bas (bȧ·răb'ăs; bär·ăb'ăs), *n.* The prisoner chosen for release in preference to Christ (*Matt.* xxvii. 15–21).

Ba·rac'a (bȧ·răk'ȧ), *n.* [Heb. *Berakah* blessing.] An international organization of young men's Bible classes.

barb (bärb), *n.* [OF. *barbe*, fr. L. *barba* beard.] **1.** *Obs.* A beard. **2.** = BARBEL, 1. **3.** A plaited linen covering for the throat, worn by some nuns. **4.** A catching and holding projection curving backward from the point of an arrow, fishhook, etc.; hence, any sharp projection with its point similarly oblique. **5.** One of the side branches of the shaft of a feather. See FEATHER, *Illust.* **6.** *Bot.* A hair or bristle ending in a hook. — *v. t.* To furnish with a barb or barbs.

barb (bärb), *n.* [F. *barbe*, fr It. *barbero.*] **1.** A horse of a stock native to Barbary. **2.** A pigeon of a domestic breed related to the carrier pigeons.

bar·bar'i·an (bär·bâr'ĭ·ăn), *n.* [See BARBAROUS.] **1.** A foreigner; — used depreciatively by ancient Greeks, Romans, etc., of one outside the pale of their civilization. **2.** A man in a rude, uncivilized state. **3.** A civilized person without, or out of sympathy with, culture. — *adj.* Of or characteristic of barbarians. — **bar·bar'i·an·ism** (-ĭz'm), *n.*

Syn. **Barbarian, barbarous, barbaric, savage** mean characteristic of uncivilized man. **Barbarian** expresses little more than this; **barbarous** tends to express the harsher or more brutal side of uncivilized life; **barbaric** suggests the crudeness of taste and fondness for gorgeous display characteristic of uncivilized peoples; **savage** implies a more primitive state than *barbarian*, and greater harshness or fierceness than *barbarous*.

bar·bar'ic (bär·băr'ĭk), *adj.* [Through OF. fr. L. *barbaricus*, fr. Gr. *barbarikos*.] **1.** Uncivilized or having a primitive civilization; rude; as, *barbaric* empires. **2.** Showing lack of restraint or refinement; wild, showy, or exuberant; as, *barbaric* magnificence. — **Syn.** See BARBARIAN.

bar'ba·rism (bär'bȧ·rĭz'm), *n.* **1.** The use of words, etc., not accepted as standard; also, such a word or phrase. Cf. IMPROPRIETY, 3; SOLECISM, 1. **2.** A state of society between savagery and civilization; as, nations reverting to *barbarism*. **3.** Barbaric culture, manners, living conditions, etc.

bar·bar'i·ty (bär·băr'ĭ·tĭ), *n.; pl.* -TIES (-tĭz). **1.** Cruelty; inhumanity; also, an inhuman act. **2.** Barbaric taste.

bar'ba·rize (bär'bȧ·rīz), *v. i. & t.* To become or to make barbarous. — **bar'ba·ri·za'tion** (-rĭ·zā'shŭn; -rī·zā'-), *n.*

bar'ba·rous (-rŭs), *adj.* [L. *barbarus*, fr. Gr. *barbaros* strange, foreign, slavish, rude.] **1.** Not classical or pure; full of barbarisms; — of language. **2.** Foreign; non-Hellenic, non-Roman, etc. **3.** Living in, or characterized by, barbarism; barbaric. **4.** Showing barbarity; mercilessly harsh. **5.** Harsh-sounding; raucous. — **Syn.** See BARBARIAN; FIERCE. — **bar'ba·rous·ly**, *adv.* — **bar'ba·rous·ness**, *n.*

Bar'ba·ry ape (bär'bȧ·rĭ). A tailless ape (*Simia sylvana*) of North Africa and Gibraltar, the only monkey inhabiting Europe. It is often trained by showmen.

bar'bate (bär'bāt), *adj.* [L. *barbatus*, fr. *barba* beard.] Bearded; *Bot.*, beset with long stiff hairs.

bar'be·cue (bär'bē·kū), *n.* [Sp. *barbacoa* an elevated frame, fr. Taino *barbacoa*.] A hog, ox, or other large animal roasted or broiled whole for a feast; also, a feast at which a barbecue is served. — *v. t.;* -CUED (-kūd); -CU'ING (-kū'ĭng). **1.** To roast or broil whole, as an ox or hog. **2.** To cook (meat or fish) in thin slices in a highly seasoned vinegar sauce. **3.** To roast or grill (esp. pork or beef) slowly in sizable pieces before an open fire, on a gridiron or revolving spit or in a trench, often drenching with a sauce of vinegar, salt, and pepper.

barbed (bärbd), *adj.* Furnished with a barb or barbs; as, **barbed wire**, a wire or a strand of twisted wires armed with barbs at regular intervals.

bar'bel (bär'bĕl), *n.* [OF., fr. LL. *barbellus*, dim. of L. *barbus*, fr. *barba* beard.] **1.** A slender tactile process on the lips of certain fishes. **2.** A European fresh-water fish (*Barbus fluviatilis*) of the carp family, with four barbels on its upper jaw; also, any of various other fishes of this genus.

bar'bel·late (bär'bĕ·lāt; bär·bĕl'āt), *adj.* [See BARB beard.] *Bot.* Having short, stiff, hooked bristles or hairs.

bar'ber (bär'bẽr), *n.* [OF. *barbeor*, fr. L. *barba* beard.] One whose occupation it is to shave or trim the beard, and to cut and dress the hair, of his patrons. Formerly barbers also practiced surgery and dentistry and were called **bar'ber–sur'geons**. — *v. t.* To shave, cut, or dress the beard or hair of.

bar'ber'ry (bär'bĕr'ĭ; -bĕ·rĭ), *n.; pl.* -RIES (-ĭz). [OF. *berbere*, fr. ML. *berberis, barbaris*, fr. Ar. *barbārīs*.] A shrub (genus *Berberis*) typifying a family (Berberidaceae, the barberry family) having spines, yellow flowers, and oblong red berries.

bar'bet (bär'bĕt; -bĭt; 30), *n.* [F., fr. *barbe* beard.] **1.** A variety of small poodle, having long curly hair. **2.** Any of numerous nonpasserine tropical birds (families Capitonidae or Bucconidae) having a stout bill beset with bristles.

bar·bette' (bär·bĕt'), *n.* [F.] **1.** *Fort.* A mound of earth or a platform on which guns are mounted. **2.** On war vessels, a parapet of fixed armor protecting a gun platform.

bar'bi·can (bär'bĭ·kăn), *n.* [From OF., fr. ML. *barbacana*, fr. Ar. *barbakh-khānah*.] An outer defensive work of a city or castle, esp. a tower or towers at a gate or bridge.

bar'bi·cel (-sĕl), *n.* [Dim. fr. L. *barba* beard.] One of the small processes on the barbules of feathers. See FEATHER.

bar'bi·tal (-tôl; -tăl), *n.* [From BARBITURIC.] A white crystalline powder (chemically diethyl-barbituric acid) used as a hypnotic. Its sodium salt, **barbital sodium** ($C_8H_{11}O_3N_2Na$), is similarly used.

bar'bi·tu'rate (bär'bĭ·tū'rāt; bär·bĭt'ū·rāt), *n.* [*barbituric* + 1st *-ate*, 3.] *Chem.* A salt or ester of barbituric acid; specif., one of a large group of drugs used as sedatives, hypnotics, etc.

bar'bi·tu'ric (bär'bĭ·tū'rĭk), *adj.* [From Usnea *barbata*, beard lichen + *uric* acid.] *Chem.* Pertaining to, or designating, a crystalline acid, $CH_2(CO.NH)_2CO$, derivatives of which are used as soporifics.

bar'bule (bär'būl), *n.* [L. *barbula*.] A minute barb; specif., one of the processes that fringe the barbs of a feather. See FEATHER.

barb'wire' (bärb'wīr'), *n.* = *barbed wire*, under BARBED, *adj.*

bar'ca·role, bar'ca·rolle (bär'kȧ·rōl), *n.* [Through F. & It., fr. It. *barca* barge.] *Music.* **a** A popular melody sung by Venetian gondoliers. **b** Music imitating such a song.

bard (bärd), *n.* [Of Celt. origin.] **1.** A professional poet, whose occupation was composing and singing songs about heroes; a scop. **2.** A poet; as, the *bard* of Avon (Shakespeare). — **bard'ic** (bär'dĭk), *adj.*

bard, barde (bärd), *n.* [F. *barde*, fr. Sp., fr. Ar.] A piece of armor for a horse. — *v. t.* To equip with bards.

bard'y (bär'dĭ), *adj. Scot.* Pert; insolent; bold.

bare (bâr), *adj.* [AS. *bær*.] **1.** Without clothes or covering, esp. the usual covering; naked; nude. **2.** Fully revealed; unconcealed; exposed. **3.** Empty; emptied or nearly emptied; stripped; as, a room *bare* of furniture. **4.** Including no excess; leaving nothing to spare; mere; as, elected by a *bare* majority. **5.** Plain; unadorned; bald; as, to tell the *bare* truth. **6.** Threadbare. *Shak.* — *v. t.* To make or lay bare. — **bare'ness**, *n.*

Syn. **Bare, naked, nude, bald, barren** mean deprived of naturally or conventionally appropriate covering. **Bare** implies the removal of that which is additional, superfluous, dispensable, or the like; **naked** suggests absence of covering, especially of protective or ornamental covering, but it may imply a state of nature, of physical beauty, of destitution, of shameful publicity, of admirable modesty, or the like; **nude** comes close to *naked*, but because of its association with undraped figures in art the word has slight aesthetic or ethical connotations; **bald** implies absence or seeming absence of natural covering, but in extended use implies a conspicuous or colorless bareness; **barren** implies an absence of natural or appropriate coloring that displays a thing's impoverishment, aridity, or the like.

bare (bâr). Archaic past tense of BEAR.

bare'back' (bâr'băk'), *adv. & adj.* On an unsaddled horse.

bare'faced' (bâr'fāst'; 2), *adj.* **1.** With uncovered face; unmasked. **2.** Without concealment; hence, shameless; audacious; as, a *barefaced* lie. — **bare'fac'ed·ly** (-fās'ĕd·lĭ; -ĭd·lĭ; -fāst'lĭ), *adv.* — **bare'fac'ed·ness** (-nĕs; -nĭs), *n.*

bare'fit (bâr'fĭt), *adj. Scot.* Barefooted.

bare'foot' (bâr'fo͝ot'), **bare'foot'ed** (-fo͝ot'ĕd; -ĭd; 30), *adj. & adv.* With the feet bare.

ba·rege' (bȧ·rāzh'; -rĕzh'), *n.* [F. *barège*, fr. *Barèges*, the town.] A gauzelike fabric of wool, or of silk and wool, or of cotton and wool.

bare'head'ed (bâr'hĕd'ĕd; -ĭd; 2; 30), **bare'head'**, *adj. & adv.* With bare head; hatless. — **bare'head'ed·ness**, *n.*

bare'ly, *adv.* **1.** Nakedly. **2.** Without concealment. **3.** *Archaic.* Merely. **4.** Only just; with nothing to spare; as, he *barely* escaped.

bare'sark (bâr'särk), *n.* [Corrupt. of *berserk*, as if *bare* + *sark* shirt.] A berserker. — *adv.* Without shirt of mail.

bar'fly' (bär'flī'), *n.* A tippler who habitually loiters in barrooms.

bar'gain (bär'gĭn), *n.* [OF. *bargaigne*.] **1.** An agreement between parties to a transaction settling what each shall give and receive; a contract regarding terms of sale and purchase; as, to make a *bargain*. **2.** Such an agreement viewed in its results; as, he made a bad *bargain*; esp., an advantageous agreement; as, bought at a *bargain*. **3.** A thing purchased or purchasable cheaply; as, a counter displaying *bargains*. — ***into the bargain***. Over and above what is stipulated. — *v. i.* **1.** To try to get, buy, or sell something on good terms; to haggle. **2.** To make a bargain; to come to terms. — *v. t.* To barter; trade. — ***bargain for***. To expect or plan for; count on. — **bar'gain·er**, *n.* — **bar'gain·or'** (bär'gĭn·ôr'; bär'gĭn·ẽr), *n.*

barge (bärj), *n.* [OF., fr. LL. *barga*.] **1.** *Obs.* A sailing vessel; a bark. **2.** Any of various boats or vessels; as: **a** A roomy boat, usually flat-bottomed, used chiefly on rivers and canals. **b** *Nav.* A large powerboat, supplied to the flag officer of a flagship. **c** A pleasure boat; esp., an elegantly furnished boat of state; a houseboat. — *v. t.;* BARGED (bärjd); BARG'ING (bär'jĭng). To carry by barge. — *v. i.* To move slowly and lumberingly; hence, *Colloq.*, to lurch clumsily; to thrust oneself boorishly.

barge'board' (-bōrd'; 70), *n.* A decorative board covering the face of a projecting gable rafter. Cf. GABLE, *Illust.*

barge couple. One of the two rafters covered by bargeboards.

barge course. The tiling on the sloping edges of a gable roof.

bar'gee' (bär'jē'), *n. Eng.* A bargeman.

barge'man (bärj'măn), *n.* The man who manages a barge; also, one of the crew of a barge.

bar'ghest (bär'gĕst), *n.* A kind of goblin, portending misfortune.

bar'ic (băr'ĭk), *adj. Chem.* Of or pertaining to barium.

bar'ic, *adj.* [Gr. *baros* weight.] *Physics.* Of or pertaining to weight, esp. the weight or pressure of the atmosphere as measured by the barometer; barometric.

ba·ril'la (bȧ·rĭl'ȧ), *n.* [Sp. *barrilla*.] **1.** Either of two European species (*Salsola kali* and *S. soda*) of saltwort. **2.** An impure soda ash from these saltworts, formerly used in making soap, glass, etc.

bar'ite (bâr'īt; bā'rīt), *n.* See BARIUM SULFATE.

bar'i·tone, bar'y·tone (băr'ĭ·tōn), *n.* [F. *baryton* or It. *baritono*, fr. Gr. *barytonos*, fr. *barys* heavy + *tonos* tone.] *Music.* **a** A male voice between bass and tenor and partaking somewhat of the quality of both. Its compass is about A to f'. **b** A man having such a voice. **c** A brass wind instrument of the tuba family, keyed in B♭, with a range from E to c'. — *adj.* Having the compass and quality of a baritone voice.

bar'i·um (bâr'ĭ·ŭm; bā'rĭ·ŭm), *n.* [NL., fr. Gr. *barys* heavy.] A chemical element of the alkaline-earth group, in the free state a silver-white malleable metal, occurring only in combination. Symbol, *Ba*; at. no., 56; at. wt., 137.36.

barium sulfate. *Chem.* A compound, $BaSO_4$, occurring as *barite* and formed artificially as a heavy white insoluble precipitate, used as a pigment and as a filler in paper, rubber, etc. Barite, a common mineral in metallic veins, is, from its high specific gravity (4.3–4.6), often called *heavy spar*.

bark (bärk), *n.* [Of Scand. origin.] **1.** The tough external covering of a woody perennial stem or root. **2.** Tanbark, or spent bark. **3.** Peruvian bark, or cinchona. — *v. t.* **1.** To treat with an infusion of bark; to tan. **2.** To strip the bark from; to peel; specif., to girdle. **3.** To abrade or rub off the skin from; as, to *bark* one's heel. **4.** To cover or enclose with, or as with, bark.

bark (bärk), *v. i.* [AS. *beorcan*.] **1.** To make the short, loud, explosive noise characteristic of some canines, esp. dogs. **2.** To make a similar noise or cry; as, the guns *barked*. **3.** To shout or speak sharply, threateningly, or in an abrupt, snappish manner. **4.** *Slang.* To solicit patronage, as for a cheap show, by crying out its merits at the entrance. **5.** *Colloq.* To cough hoarsely. — *v. t.* To utter with a bark. — ***bark up the wrong tree***. To misdirect one's attack. — *n.* A barking cry or sound.

bark, barque (bärk), *n.* [F. *barque*, fr. It. *barca*, fr. L. *barca*.] **1.** Formerly, any small sailing vessel or boat; now, *Poet.*, any sailing vessel or boat. **2.** *Naut.* A three-masted vessel, with foremast and mainmast square-rigged, and mizzenmast fore-and-aft-rigged.

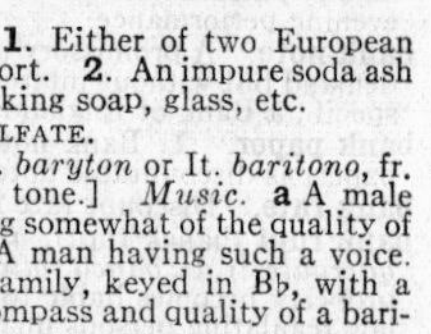

Bark, 2.

bar'keep'er (bär'kēp'ẽr), *n.* One who keeps or tends a bar for the sale of liquors.

bark'en·tine, bar'quen·tine (bär'kĕn·tēn), *n.* [See BARK boat.] *Naut.* A three-masted vessel having the foremast square-rigged and the others fore-and-aft-rigged.

bark'er (bär'kẽr), *n.* A person, machine, etc., that removes or prepares bark. Cf. SPUDDER.

bark'er, *n.* An animal, a person, or a thing that barks; esp., a person who barks at an entrance to a show.

bark'y (bär'kĭ), *adj.;* -I·ER (-kĭ·ẽr); -I·EST. Covered with, containing, or resembling bark.

bar'ley, bar'ly (bär'lĭ), *interj.* [Corrupt. of F. *parlez*, E. *parley*.] *Scot. & Dial.* A cry for a truce, used in games.

bar'ley (bär'lĭ), *n.* [AS. *bærlic*.] A cereal grass (genus *Hordeum*) having the flowers in dense spikes with long awns, differing from wheat in having three spikelets at each joint of the rachis; also, its seed or grain, used in malt beverages and in breakfast foods and stock feeds.

bar'ley–bree' (-brē'), *n.* *Chiefly Scot.* Liquor made from barley; whisky; also, strong ale.

bar′ley·corn′ (bär′lĭ·kôrn′), *n.* **1.** A grain, or corn, of barley. **2.** An old measure of length; one third of an inch.

Bar′ley·corn′, John. A humorous personification of barley as the source of malt liquor or of whisky; hence, the liquor.

barm (bärm), *n.* [AS. *beorma.*] Yeast formed on brewing liquors.

bar′maid′ (bär′mād′), *n.* A waitress or tapstress in a bar.

bar′man (-măn), *n.; pl.* BARMEN (-mĕn). *Brit.* A barkeeper.

Bar′me·cide (bär′mē·sīd), *n.* One of the **Bar′me·cides** (-sīdz), a wealthy Persian family, one member of which, as is told in the *Arabian Nights*, invited a hungry beggar to a feast and made a pretense of serving and eating imaginary viands. Hence: **Barmecide feast,** any illusion of plenty.

‖**bar miz′vah** *or* **mitz′vah** (bär′ mĭts′vä). [Heb. *bar mitswāh,* lit., son of command.] *Hebrew Law.* **1.** A boy who has completed his thirteenth year, the age of responsibility and religious duty. **2.** The ceremony of recognizing one as such a person.

barm′y (bär′mĭ), *adj.;* BARM′I·ER (-mĭ·ēr); -I·EST. Full of barm or froth; hence, flighty; foolish.

barn (bärn), *n.* [AS. *berern, bern,* fr. *bere* barley + *ern, ærn,* a close place.] **1.** A covered building for storing grain, hay, etc., and also, in the United States, for stables, etc. **2.** A building used for housing horses, vehicles, etc.

Bar′na·bas (bär′nȧ·bȧs), *n.* *Bib.* Surname of Joseph, a Levite of Cyprus, companion of St. Paul on his first missionary journey.

bar′na·cle (bär′nȧ·k′l), *n.* [ME. *bernak, bernacle,* fr. OF. *bernac* snaffle.] **1.** *pl.* An instrument for pinching a horse's nose, and thus restraining him. **2.** *pl. Colloq., Eng.* Spectacles.

bar′na·cle, *n.* [F. *bernicle.*] **1.** A barnacle goose. **2.** Any of numerous marine crustaceans (order Cirripedia), having feathery appendages (cirri) for gathering food, and found attached to rocks, the ***rock barnacles,*** or to floating logs and ships' bottoms, the ***goose barnacles.*** **3.** One who clings like a barnacle.

barnacle goose. A European goose (*Branta leucopsis*) that breeds in the far north, related to, but larger than, the brant.

Barn′burn′er (bärn′bûr′nēr), *n.* [In allusion to the fable of the man who burned his barn to rid it of rats.] *U.S. Hist.* A member of the radical reform section of the Democratic party in New York 1845–52.

barn′storm′ (bärn′stôrm′), *v. i.* [*barn* + *storm,* v.] *Orig. U.S.* **1.** To perform plays in barns where a theater is lacking; hence, to play, make political speeches, etc., in small towns or in the country. **2.** To pilot one's airplane, for a livelihood, in irregular sight-seeing flights with passengers or in exhibition stunts, in an unscheduled itinerant course esp. in rural districts. — *v. t.* To tour in the practice of barnstorming. — **barn′storm′er,** *n.* — **barn′storm′ing,** *n. & adj.*

barn′yard′ (-yärd′), *n.* A yard belonging to a barn.

bar′o·gram (băr′ō·grăm), *n.* A barographic tracing.

bar′o·graph (-grȧf; 9), *n.* [Gr. *baros* weight + *-graph.*] An automatic instrument for recording variations of atmospheric pressure; a self-registering barometer. — **bar′o·graph′ic** (-grăf′ĭk), *adj.*

ba·rom′e·ter (bȧ·rŏm′ē·tēr), *n.* [Gr. *baros* weight + *-meter.*] **1.** An instrument for determining atmospheric pressure and hence for judging probable changes of weather, for ascertaining the height of an ascent, etc.; a weatherglass. In its simplest form (***cup, or cistern, barometer***) it consists of a graduated glass tube filled with mercury and inverted in a cup or cistern containing mercury, the height of the column of mercury in the tube varying in response to changes in atmospheric pressure. Cf. ANEROID BAROMETER. **2.** That which registers fluctuations, as in public opinion. — **bar′o·met′ric** (băr′ō·mĕt′rĭk), **bar′o·met′ri·cal** (-rĭ·kăl), *adj.* — **bar′o·met′ri·cal·ly,** *adv.* — **ba·rom′e·try** (bȧ·rŏm′ē·trĭ), *n.*

bar′on (băr′ŭn), *n.* [OF., acc. of *ber,* of Teut. origin.] **1.** *Eng. Hist.* Originally, a tenant holding immediately of the king or other feudal superior; hence, a peer of the realm. **2.** In Great Britain, a member of the lowest grade of the peerage; one of the hereditary nobility entitled to be addressed as "Lord" and to sit in the House of Lords; also, the grade or rank itself. **3.** A nobleman of similar rank on the Continent and in Japan. **4.** *Colloq., U.S.* A powerful industrialist, etc. **5.** A cut of beef, etc., comprising the undivided loins.

bar′on·age (-ĭj), *n.* **1.** The whole body of barons. **2.** Dignity or rank of a baron.

bar′on·ess (-ĕs; -ĭs; 30), *n.* A baron's wife; also, a lady who holds the baronial title in her own right.

bar′on·et (băr′ŭn·ĕt; -ĭt), *n.* A hereditary dignity or degree of honor next below a baron and above a knight; also, a holder of this dignity. Baronets are commoners and have "Sir" prefixed to their Christian names. Abbr. *Bart.* or *Bt.;* as, Sir Walter Scott, *Bart.*

bar′on·et·age (-ĭj), *n.* **1.** State or rank of a baronet. **2.** Baronets collectively.

bar′on·et·cy (-sĭ), *n.; pl.* -CIES (-sĭz). Rank of baronet.

ba·rong′ (bä·rŏng′), *n.* [Native name.] A thick-backed, thin-edged knife or sword used by Moros.

ba·ro′ni·al (bȧ·rō′nĭ·ăl; 58), *adj.* Of, pert. to, or befitting a baron or the baronage.

bar′o·ny (băr′ō·nĭ), *n.; pl.* -NIES (-nĭz). [OF. *baronie.*] Domain, lordship, dignity, or rank of a baron.

ba·roque′ (bȧ·rōk′; -rôk′), *adj.* [F.] **1.** Irregular in form; — said esp. of a pearl. **2.** *Arch.* **a** Of, pertaining to, or designating the style of art and architecture prevailing from about 1550 to late in the 18th century, characterized by the use of curved and contorted forms **b** As used by some writers, equivalent to *rococo.* **3.** Grotesque; in corrupt taste. — *n.* Baroque work or style.

bar′o·scope (băr′ō·skōp), *n.* [Gr. *baros* weight + *-scope.*] Any instrument showing changes in atmospheric pressure, as by the rise and fall of particles of certain substances in suspension in a vial of liquid; a weatherglass. — **bar′o·scop′ic** (-skŏp′ĭk), **bar′o·scop′i·cal** (-ĭ·kăl), *adj.*

ba·rouche′ (bȧ·rōōsh′), *n.* [Through G. & It., fr. L. *birotus* two-wheeled, fr. *bi-* (= *bis*) twice + *rota* wheel.] A four-wheeled carriage with a driver's seat in front, two double seats inside facing each other, and a folding top.

barque, bar′quen·tine. Vars. of BARK, ship; BARKENTINE.

bar′rack (băr′ăk), *n.* [F. *baraque,* through It. & Sp., perh. fr. LL. *barra* bar.] Usually in *pl.* **1.** *Mil.* A building or set of buildings for lodging soldiers, esp. when in garrison. **2.** A plain and large building such as a row of houses joined together, or a barnlike structure. — *v. t. & i.* To lodge in barracks.

bar′rack (băr′ăk), *v. i. & t.* *Chiefly Austral.* To give partisan support, as by cheering one side and jeering the other; to decry; to jeer. — **bar′rack·er,** *n.*

bar′ra·coon′ (băr′ȧ·kōōn′), *n.* [Sp. *barraca.*] An enclosure or barrack for temporary confinement of slaves or by extension, of convicts, etc.

bar′ra·cu′da (băr′ȧ·kōō′dȧ), *n.; pl.* -DA, -DAS (-dȧz). Also **bar′ra·cou′ta** (-kōō′tȧ); *pl.* -TA, -TAS (-tȧz). See PLURAL, *Note.* [Sp.] Any of several voracious pikelike marine fishes (genus *Sphyraena*). The ***great barracuda*** (*S. barracuda*) of the West Indies, Florida, etc., is often six feet or more long and is dangerous to man.

bar′rage (bär′ĭj; băr′-), *n.* [F.] An artificial obstruction placed in a watercourse to increase its depth or to divert it.

bar·rage′ (bȧ·räzh′; -räj′; *Brit.* băr′äzh), *n.* [F., in *tir de barrage* barrage fire.] **1.** *Mil.* A barrier, esp. of artillery shellfire, laid on an area close to friendly troops for protection by impeding enemy movements and fire, or advancing at a fixed rate to precede attacking infantry. **2.** A concentrated delivery of speech or writing. — *v. t. & i.* To deliver a barrage (upon).

barrage balloon. A captive balloon used to support wires or nets as protection against air attack.

bar′ra·mun′da (băr′ȧ·mŭn′dȧ), **bar′ra·mun′di** (-dĭ), *n.; pl.* -DA, -DAS (-dȧz); -DI, -DIS (-dĭz), -DIES (-dĭz). See PLURAL, *Note,* 5. [Native Australian name.] = CERATODUS.

bar·ran′ca (bȧ·răng′kȧ), *n.* [Sp.] A ravine with steep sides; also, a steep bank or bluff.

bar′ra·tor (băr′ȧ·tēr), *n.* Also **bar′ra·ter.** [OF. *barateor* deceiver, fr. *barater* to deceive.] One guilty of barratry.

bar′ra·try (-trĭ), *n.* [F. *baraterie.*] **1.** The purchase or sale of office or preferment in church or state. Cf. SIMONY. **2.** *Mar. Law.* A fraudulent breach of duty on the part of a master of a ship, to the injury of the owner of the ship or cargo. **3.** *Law.* Persistent incitement of litigation. — **bar′ra·trous** (-trŭs), *adj.* — **-trous·ly,** *adv.*

barred (bärd), *adj.* Having, marked by, or divided off by, a bar or bars; ribbed or striped transversely.

barred Rock. See PLYMOUTH ROCK.

bar′rel (băr′ĕl), *n.* [OF. *baril.*] **1.** A round bulging vessel or cask, of greater length than breadth, and having flat ends or heads. **2.** The quantity constituting a full barrel. See MEASURE, *Table* 11. **3.** A drum or cylinder or similarly round part, hollow or solid; specif.: **a** The case holding the mainspring of a watch or clock. **b** The metal tube of a gun. **c** The part of a fountain pen or of a pencil containing the ink or the lead. **d** The cylinder in which a piston travels. **e** The body of a windlass or a capstan. **f** The hollow part of the shaft of a feather. See FEATHER, *Illust.* **g** The upper inside part of a bell. See BELL, *Illust.* — *v. t.;* -RELED (-ĕld) or -RELLED; -REL·ING or -REL·LING. To put or to pack in a barrel or barrels. — *v. i. Colloq.* To move at high speed; — esp. of vehicles; as, the airplane came *barreling* in.

barrel chair. An upholstered easy chair with a high solid rounded back suggestive of a barrel with upright staves.

barrel house. *Slang. U.S.* A low drinking place.

barrel organ. A musical instrument having a revolving cylinder with pegs which open valves that admit air from a bellows to pipes. Cf. HAND ORGAN.

barrel roll. *Aviation.* An aerial maneuver in which a complete revolution about the longitudinal axis is made.

bar′ren (băr′ĕn), *adj.* [OF. *brehaing,* fem. *brehaigne, baraigne.*] **1.** Incapable of producing offspring; sterile; — of females or of a mating. **2.** Not producing fruit, seed, vegetation, etc.; bare; infertile. **3.** Without interest, information, or charm; arid. **4.** Unproductive; unprofitable; empty; as, a *barren* scheme. **5.** Dull; stupid. — **Syn.** See STERILE: BARE. — *n.* **1.** A tract of barren land. **2.** Level tracts of land, poorly forested and commonly having light sandy soil; as, pine *barrens;* — usually in *pl.* — **bar′ren·ly,** *adv.* — **bar′ren·ness,** *n.*

Barren Grounds *or* **Lands.** The treeless plains, or tundras, of northern Canada, esp. near Hudson Bay, sparsely inhabited by Eskimos and a few trappers.

bar′ret (băr′ĕt; -ĭt), *n.* [F. *barrette* fr. It. *berretta.*] A kind of small cap; esp., a biretta.

bar·rette′ (bä·rĕt′; bȧ·rĕt′), *n.* [F., dim. of *barre* bar.] A clasp or bar for holding a woman's hair in place.

bar′ri·cade′ (băr′ĭ·kād′), *n.* [F., fr. It. *barricata,* deriv. of *barra* bar.] **1.** *Mil.* A fortification, as in a street, hastily made of anything that will obstruct progress. **2.** Any barrier obstructing passage. — *v. t.* To fortify or close with a barricade or barricades; obstruct.

bar′ri·ca′do (băr′ĭ·kā′dō), *n.; pl.* -DOES (-dōz). A barricade. — *v. t.;* -DOED (-dōd); -DO·ING. To barricade.

bar′ri·er (băr′ĭ·ēr), *n.* [OF. *barriere,* fr. *barre* bar.] **1.** A fence, stockade, or other obstacle in a passage or way, to stop an enemy. **2.** Any obstruction; anything that hinders approach or attack; as, a mountain *barrier;* a *barrier* to social progress. **3.** *Hist. pl.* **a** A tournament in which combatants fought on foot with a railing (*barrier*) between them. **b** The palisades enclosing the lists of a tournament. **4.** A fortress or fortified town on a frontier. **5.** Any limit or boundary; as, the *barrier* between instinct and reason. **6.** In a race track, the movable gate at the starting line. **7.** [*sometimes cap.*] An extension of the antarctic continental ice sheet into the sea, resting partly on the bottom.

barrier reef. A coral reef roughly parallel to a shore, but separated from it by a lagoon.

bar′ring (bär′ĭng), *prep.* Excepting; as, *barring* accident.

bar′ri·o (bär′rē·ō), *n.* [Sp.] *Phil. I.* A village or subdivision of a municipality.

bar′ris·ter (băr′ĭs·tēr), *n.* [From 1st BAR.] *Eng.* A counsel admitted to plead at the bar in the superior courts of law, as distinguished from a *solicitor.* — **Syn.** See LAWYER.

bar′room′ (bär′rōōm′; 85), *n.* A room containing a bar or counter at which liquors are sold.

bar′row (băr′ō), *n.* [AS. *beorg, beorh,* hill, mound.] **1.** A hill; — now only in names of hills. **2.** A large sepulchral mound; a tumulus.

bar′row, *n.* [AS. *bearg, bearh.*] A castrated male hog.

bar′row, *n.* [From AS. *beran* to bear.] A support having handles, and with or without a wheel, on which things can be transported. Cf. HANDBARROW, WHEELBARROW.

bar sinister. Erroneously, a baton, heraldic mark of bastardy; — probably by confusion with *bend sinister.*

bar′tend′er (bär′tĕn′dēr), *n.* A man who serves liquor at a bar.

bar′ter (bär′tēr), *v. i.* [OF. *barater* to cheat, exchange.] To traffic or trade by direct exchange of one commodity for another. — *v. t.* To trade or exchange (goods or services). — *n.* Act or practice of bartering; also, the thing bartered. — **bar′ter·er,** *n.*

bar′ti·zan (bär′tĭ·zăn; bär′tĭ·zăn′), *n.* *Arch.* A small overhanging structure for lookout or defense; — a word used by Scott.

Bart′lett (bärt′lĕt; -lĭt; 30), *n.* A leading American variety of pear, which originated in England about 1770, and was distributed in America by Enoch Bartlett, of Dorchester, Mass.

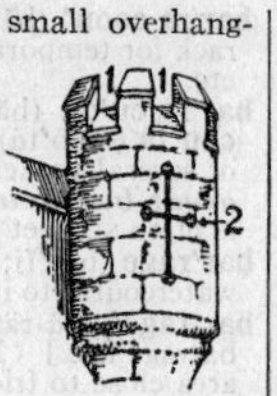

Bartizan. 1, 1 Crenels; 2 Balistraria.

Bar′uch (bâr′ŭk; bā′rŭk), *n.* A book of the Old Testament in the Douay Version, and of the Apocrypha. See BIBLE.

ba·ry′ta (bȧ·rī′tȧ), *n.* [Gr. *barys* heavy.] *Chem.* Barium monoxide; — equiv. in phrases to *barium.* — **ba·ryt′ic** (-rĭt′ĭk), *adj.*

ba·ry′tes (bȧ·rī′tēz), *n.* [Gr. *barys* heavy.] Barite.

bar′y·tone (băr′ĭ·tōn), *n.* [Gr. *barytonos.*] *Greek Gram.* A word with no accent on the last syllable, a grave accent being understood. — **bar′y·tone,** *adj.*

bar′y·tone. *Music.* Var. of BARITONE.

bas′al (bās′ăl; -′l), *adj.* **1.** Relating to, situated at, or forming the base; also, basic; fundamental. **2.** *Bot.* Situated at or growing from the base of the stem; radical; — opp. to *cauline.* **3.** *Med.* Designating, or serving to induce, an initial state of unconsciousness forming the basis for supplemental anesthetization, as in **basal anesthesia.** **4.** *Physiol.* Of, pertaining to, or essential for maintaining, the lowest natural level for continued vital activity in an organism. — **bas′al·ly,** *adv.*

basal metabolism. *Biochem. & Physiol.* The metabolism of an organism in the fasting and resting state, when it uses just enough energy to maintain vital cellular activity, respiration, and circulation, as measured by the rate, called the **basal metabolic rate,** at which heat is given off.

ba·salt′ (bȧ·sôlt′; băs′ôlt; bā′sôlt), *n.* [L. *basaltes* a dark marble found in Ethiopia.] A dark-gray to black, dense to fine-grained igneous rock, consisting of basic plagioclase (usually labradorite), augite, and usually magnetite. — **ba·sal′tic** (bȧ·sôl′tĭk), *adj.*

‖**bas bleu** (bä′ blû′). [F.] A bluestocking; a learned or literary lady.

bas′cule (băs′kūl), *n.* [F., a seesaw.] *Mech.* An apparatus in which one end is counterbalanced by the other, on the principle of the seesaw, or by weights, as in the **bascule bridge,** a counterpoised or balanced drawbridge.

base (bās), *n.; pl.* BASES (bās′ĕz; -ĭz; 30). [F., fr. L. *basis,* fr. Gr. *basis* a stepping, step, a base, pedestal, fr. *bainen* to go.] **1.** The bottom of anything, considered as its support; foundation. **2.** The fundamental part of a thing; groundwork. **3.** The chief ingredient of anything, viewed as its fundamental constituent. **4.** A point or line from which a start is made; specif., a line in surveying serving as the origin for computations. **5.** A starting place or goal in various games; specif., one of the four stations in baseball. **6.** *Arch.* The lower part of a wall, pier, or column, when treated as a separate feature, or especially ornamented; the lower part of a complete architectural design. See DADO, ORDER, *Illusts.* **7.** That part of an organ by which it is attached to the organism. **8.** *Chem.* A compound, as lime or ammonia, capable of reacting with acids to form salts; specif., the hydroxide of a positive element or radical; in modern terms, a compound that yields hydroxyl ions, OH^-, in aqueous solution, or still more recently, a compound or ion that can combine with a proton (hydrogen ion). **9.** *Geom.* The line or surface constituting that part of a figure on which it is supposed to stand. **10.** *Gram. & Philol.* A root; stem; theme. **11.** *Her.* The lower part of the field. See ESCUTCHEON. **12.** *Math.* The number with reference to which a mathematical table is constructed. **13.** *Mil. & Nav.* The locality on which a force relies for supplies or from which it initiates operations.

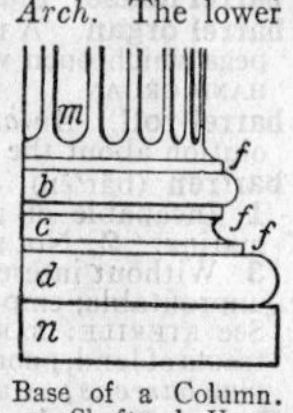

Base of a Column. *m* Shaft; *b* Upper Torus; *c* Scotia; *d* Lower Torus; *f, f, f* Fillets; *n* Plinth.

Syn. **Base, basis, foundation, ground, groundwork** mean that upon which something rests as its support. **Base** in its most general sense equals *bottom* but, more specifically, implies a broad bottom by which something is held up or stabilized (as, a pillar's *base*); **basis,** on the other hand, though carrying practically the same meaning, is rarely applied to a material thing (as, the *basis* of his belief); **foundation** may be used in place of *base* or *basis,* but it more definitely implies a solid or secure support (as, a building's *foundation;* the *foundation* of democracy); **ground** applies to a material, a substance, a surface, etc., upon which another thing is built or against which it is displayed (as, the pattern is worked on a net *ground*); **groundwork** comes close to *foundation* but is used chiefly in a figurative sense (as, to serve as a *groundwork* of good habits).

— *adj.* That constitutes a base; as, a *base* color or line.

— *v. t.* **1.** To form, make, or serve as a base for. **2.** To put on a base or basis; to found; to establish, as an argument or conclusion; — used with *on* or *upon.*

base (bās), *adj.* [OF. *bas* low, fr. LL. *bassus* thick, short, low.] **1.** *Archaic.* Of little, or less than the usual, height. **2.** *Obs.* Low in place or position. **3.** Deep or grave in sound. See BASS. **4.** *Archaic.* Of humble birth; lowly; illegitimate by birth. **5.** Inferior, poor, or debased in quality; specif., alloyed with inferior metal; as, *base* coin. **6.** Not classical; — of language. **7.** Morally low; ignoble. **8.** Menial; degrading; servile. **9.** Of little comparative value, as metals inferior to gold and silver; — opposed to *precious.* **10.** Designating: **a** A metal or alloy, as zinc, lead, or brass, relatively inferior in certain properties, esp. resistance to corrosion or infusibility; — opposed to *noble.* **b** A metal to which a coating or plating is applied. **c** The chief metal of an alloy. **11.** *Eng. Law.* Servile; held by villenage; as, *base* tenure; *base* tenant.

Syn. **Base, low, vile** mean contemptible because beneath what is expected of man. **Base** usually implies indignation aroused by the setting of self-interest ahead of duty or honor; **low,** an outrage of one's sense of what is decent or proper for even the most ignorant of men; **vile** often suggests disgusting foulness or depravity.

base (bās), *n. & adj.* = 2d BASS, the usual spelling.

base′ball′ (bās′bôl′), *n.* A game of ball, developed from the game of rounders, and so called from the four bases or stations which designate the circuit which each player must endeavor to complete in order to score a run; also, the ball used in this game. Cf. SOFTBALL.

base′board′ (-bōrd′; 70), *n.* A board situated at, or forming, the base of something.

base′born′ (bās′bôrn′; 2), *adj.* **1.** Of low parentage; plebeian. **2.** Born out of wedlock. **3.** Vile; mean.

base′-burn′er, *n.* A stove in which the fuel is fed from a hopper as the lower layer is consumed.

base hit. *Baseball.* A hit by which the batsman makes first base without error by an opponent, except when a base runner is forced out by the play.

base′less, *adj.* Without a base or foundation; groundless.

base level. The level below which a land surface cannot be reduced by running water.

base′ly, *adv.* In a base manner; dishonorably; shamefully.

base′man (bās′măn), *n.* Also **base man.** A man stationed at a base; — in combinations, as in *first baseman.*

base′ment (bās′mĕnt), *n.* **1.** The lowest or basal part of anything. **2.** *Arch.* The lower part of the wall or walls of a building; also, the story behind this part. **3.** The floor in a building next below the principal floor.

base′ness (-nĕs; -nĭs; 30), *n.* Quality or condition of being base; also, an act or trait morally base.

ba′sen·ji′ (bā′sĕn·yē′), *n.* [S. Afr. D. *basenji* bush thing.] A rather small, compact, chestnut-brown dog of an African hunting breed that rarely barks.

bash (băsh), *v. t.* *Dial. & Slang.* To strike heavily; smash; slug. — *n.* *Dial. & Slang.* A heavy blow.

ba·shaw′ (bȧ·shô′), *n.* [See PASHA.] Turkish title of honor, now written *pasha;* hence, a magnate or grandee.

bash′ful (băsh′fo͝ol; -f′l), *adj.* Very or excessively modest; shy; diffident; retiring; as, a *bashful* child; indicating excessive modesty; as, *bashful* looks. — **Syn.** See SHY. — **Ant.** Forward, brazen. — **bash′ful·ly,** *adv.* — **bash′ful·ness,** *n.*

bash′i-ba·zouk′ (băsh′ĭ·bȧ·zo͞ok′), *n.* [Turk. *bāshī-bōzuq* one of disordered head.] *Hist.* A soldier belonging to irregular Turkish troops, notoriously turbulent and cruel.

ba′si·ate (bā′sĭ·āt), *v. t. & i.* [L. *basiare* to kiss.] To kiss. — **ba′si·a′tion** (-ā′shŭn), *n.* *Both Rare.*

bas′ic (bās′ĭk), *adj.* **1.** Of or pertaining to the base or essence; fundamental; as, a *basic* fact; constituting a basis; as, a *basic* wage. **2.** *Chem.* Relating to, having the character of, or containing a base; specif.: **a** Having the base-forming constituents present in excess; as, *basic* salts. **b** Alkaline in reaction. **3.** *Metal.* Pertaining to, or made by, a process (**basic process**), as in steelmaking, in which the furnace is lined with basic material, as magnesite, dolomite, etc., and basic slag is added to the molten charge; — opp. to *acid.* **4.** *Petrog.* Designating a rock poor in silica, as one containing less than 52 per cent.

bas′i·cal·ly (-ĭ·kăl·ĭ), *adv.* Fundamentally; essentially.

Bas′ic Eng′lish (*see Pron.,* § 2). Also **Bas′ic,** *n.* A simplified system of learning English through a vocabulary of 850 most essential words, devised by C. K. Ogden.

ba·sic′i·ty (bā·sĭs′ĭ·tĭ), *n.* *Chem.* Quality, state, or degree of being a base.

basic slag. A slag low in silica and high in base-forming oxides, a by-product of steel manufacture, used as a fertilizer.

ba·sid′i·o·my·cete′ (bȧ·sĭd′ĭ·ō·mī·sēt′), *n.* *Bot.* A basidiomycetous fungus.

ba·sid′i·o·my·ce′tous (-sē′tŭs), *adj.* [From *Basidiomycetes,* fr. *basidium* + Gr. *mykēs, myketos,* fungus.] *Bot.* Belonging to a large class (Basidiomycetes) of fungi including rusts and smuts, mushrooms, puffballs, etc. Cf. BASIDIUM.

ba·sid′i·um (bȧ·sĭd′ĭ·ŭm), *n.; pl.* BASIDIA (-ȧ). [NL., dim. fr. Gr. *basis* base.] *Bot.* A form of spore-bearing organ (conidiophore) characteristic of all basidiomycetous fungi, bearing a fixed number (usually four) of asexual spores (conidia). — **ba·sid′i·al** (-ăl), *adj.*

ba′si·fixed′ (bā′sĭ·fĭkst′), *adj.* *Bot.* Attached or fixed by the base.

bas′il (băz′ĭl; -′l), *n.* [OF. *basile,* fr. ML. *basilicum,* fr. Gr. *basilikos* royal, fr. *basileus* king.] Any of several plants of the mint family, esp. the common basil, or ***sweet basil*** (*Ocimum basilicum*), and ***bush basil*** (*O. suave*), the leaves of which are used in cookery.

bas′i·lar (băs′ĭ·lẽr), *adj.* Also **bas′i·lar′y** (-lẽr′ĭ *or, esp. Brit.,* -lẽr·ĭ). *Anat.* Relating to, or situated at, the base, esp. of the skull.

ba·sil′i·ca (bȧ·sĭl′ĭ·kȧ; -zĭl′ĭ·kȧ), *n.; pl.* -CAS (-kȧz), rarely -CAE (-sē). [L., fr. Gr. *basilikē* (sc. *oikia,* or *stoa*), fr. *basilikos.* See BASIL.] **1.** *Rom. Antiq.* An oblong public hall of exchange or assembly. **2.** An early Christian church building of simple oblong type, with a clerestory. **3.** *R.C.Ch.* A title given by the pope to certain churches as a special honor. — **ba·sil′i·can** (-kăn), *adj.*

ba·sil′ic vein (bȧ·sĭl′ĭk). *Anat.* A large vein of the upper arm.

bas′i·lisk (băs′ĭ·lĭsk; băz′-), *n.* [L. *basiliscus,* fr. Gr. *basiliskos* little king, kind of serpent, lizard, or dragon whose breath, or even look, was fatal. Cf. COCKATRICE. **2.** Any of several tropical American lizards (genus *Basiliscus*), allied to the iguanas, having a membranous bag on the head that can be filled with air, and an erectile crest along the back.

ba′sin (bā′s′n), *n.* [OF. *bacin,* fr. LL. *bacchinus,* fr. *bacca* water vessel.] **1.** A wide hollow utensil, usually circular and with sloping sides, for holding water, etc.; any similar vessel used in the arts, etc. **2.** The quantity a basin holds. **3.** Any basinlike hollow, depression, or enclosure containing water, as a pond, a dock for ships, etc. **4.** The tract of country drained by a river and its tributaries; — called ***river basin.*** **5.** A great depression in the surface of the lithosphere, occupied by an ocean; — called ***ocean basin.*** — **ba′sined** (-s′nd), *adj.*

bas′i·net (băs′ĭ·nĕt), *n.* [OF. *bassinet, bacinet,* little basin.] A kind of light steel helmet. See HELMET, *Illust.*

ba′si·on (bā′sĭ·ŏn), *n.* [Gr. *basis* a base.] *Craniol.* The middle of the anterior margin of the foramen magnum. Cf. GNATHIC INDEX.

ba′sis (bā′sĭs), *n.; pl.* BASES (-sēz). [L. See BASE foundation.] **1.** Foundation; base. **2.** Principal component. **3.** Groundwork; fundamental principle. — **Syn.** See BASE.

bask (bȧsk; 9), *v. i. & t.* [ON. *bathask* to bathe oneself.] To lie in warmth, as in sunshine; to be exposed, or to expose, to comfortable warmth.

bas′ket (bȧs′kĕt; -kĭt; 9; 30), *n.* [ME.] **1.** A container made of interwoven osiers, rushes, splints, or other flexible material. **2.** The contents of a basket. **3.** Something resembling a basket, as in shape or use; specif., in basketball, a goal. **4.** *Aeronaut.* The box or cage suspended from a balloon to carry passengers, ballast, etc.

bas′ket·ball′ (bȧs′kĕt·bôl′; -kĭt-; 9; 30), *n.*, *or* **basket ball.** An indoor game played with an inflated ball and elevated basketlike goals; also, the ball used.

basket chair. A deep wicker armchair with back and arms in one.

basket hilt. A hilt with a covering wrought like a basket to protect the hand. — **bas′ket–hilt′ed,** *adj.*

Basket Maker. One of the earliest of the known prehistoric inhabitants (approx. 1000–500 B.C.) of the southwestern United States and adjacent parts of Mexico.

bas′ket·ry (bȧs′kĕt·rĭ; bȧs′kĭt-), **bas′ket·work′** (-wûrk′), *n.* The art of making baskets; work consisting of plaited osiers or twigs.

basket weave. A style of weave in which the pattern has the appearance of a plaited basket.

ba′son (bā′sŭn; -s'n). Var. of BASIN; — now only in ecclesiastical use.

ba′so·phil′ic (bā′sō·fĭl′ĭk), **ba·soph′i·lous** (bā·sŏf′ĭ·lŭs), *adj. Biol.* Staining readily with basic stains.

Basque (băsk), *n.* [F.] **1.** One of a people, of a peculiar ethnical type, inhabiting the Pyrenees region on the Bay of Biscay; also, their unique agglutinative language. **2.** [*not cap.*] A fitted jacketlike waist. — **Basque,** *adj.*

bas′–re·lief′ (bä′rē·lēf′; bä′rē·lēf′; băs′-), *n.* [F., fr. *bas* low + *relief* raised work.] See RELIEF, *n.*, 6.

bass (băs), *n.; pl.* BASS, sometimes BASSES (-ĕz; -ĭz; 30). See PLURAL, *Note.* [Corrupt. of *barse* perch, fr. AS. *bears, bærs.*] **a** The European perch (*Perca fluviatilis*). **b** Any of numerous edible spiny-finned fishes, as the common ***sea bass*** (*Labrax lupus*) of southern Europe, the fresh-water ***largemouthed black bass*** (*Huro floridana*), ***smallmouthed black bass*** (*Micropterus dolomieu*), and ***calico bass*** (*Pomoxis sparoides*) of the central and eastern United States, and the marine ***black sea bass*** (*Centropristes striatus*) and ***striped bass*** (*Roccus saxatilis*) of eastern North America, and the ***white sea bass*** (*Atractoscion nobilis*) of the California coast.

bass (bās), *n.; pl.* BASSES (-ĕz; -ĭz; 30). [From *base*, influenced in spelling by F. *basse*, It. *basso.*] **1.** A bass, or deep, sound or tone. **2.** *Music.* **a** The lowest part in harmonic or polyphonic music, or a male voice singing such a part, having a compass of about E to e′. **b** A singer or instrument having such a voice, part, or compass. — *adj.* Deep or grave in tone; of low pitch.

bass (băs), *n.* **1.** Bast fiber. **2.** Linden; basswood.

bass clef (bās). See CLEF.

bass drum (bās). *Music.* The largest kind of drum, having two heads and emitting a deep, grave sound. See DRUM, *Illust.*

bas′set (băs′ĕt; -ĭt), *n.* A game at cards, resembling faro, and widely popular in the 18th century.

bas′set (băs′ĕt; -ĭt), *n. Geol. & Mining.* The outcropping edge of a stratum; an outcrop. — *v. i.* To crop out.

bas′set, *n.*, *or* **basset hound.** [F. *basset.*] A short-legged hunting dog of French origin.

basset horn. [F. *cor de basset.*] A tenor clarinet in F.

bass horn (bās). *Music.* A tuba.

bas′si·net′ (băs′ĭ·nĕt′; băs′ĭ·nĕt), *n.* [F., dim. of *bassin* basin.] A wicker basket, hooded at one end, used as a cradle; also, a child's perambulator of similar shape.

bass′ist (bās′ĭst), *n.* One who plays a bass instrument.

bas′so (băs′ō; *It.* bäs′sō), *n.; pl.* BASSOS (băs′ōz), BASSI (bäs′sē). [It., fr. LL. *bassus.*] Bass; a bass singer.

bas·soon′ (bă·sōōn′), *n.* [F. *basson.*] *Music.* A wind instrument of the double-reed kind, having a lower pitch than the oboe. A large type, an octave lower in pitch than the common type, is called ***double, or contra, bassoon.***

bas′so pro·fun′do (băs′ō prō·fŭn′dō). [It. *profondo* deep.] A deep, heavy bass voice with a compass extending to about C or D below the bass staff; a person having such a voice.

bas′so–re·lie′vo (-rē·lē′vō), ‖**bas′so–ri·lie′vo** (bäs′sō·rē·lyâ′vō), *n.* [It. *basso-rilievo.*] See RELIEF, *n.*, 6.

bass viol (bās). *Music.* A viola da gamba, predecessor of the cello.

bass′wood′ (băs′wŏŏd′), *n.* **a** Any of a genus (*Tilia*, esp. *T. glabra*) of trees of the linden family; a linden; also, its wood. **b** Incorrectly, the tulip tree or its wood.

bast (băst), *n.* [AS. *bæst.*] **1.** *Bot.* Phloem. **2.** Any of certain strong woody fibers obtained esp. from the phloem of various plants, as the linden, used in making ropes, cordage, etc.

bas′tard (băs′tẽrd), *n.* [OF.] **1.** An illegitimate child. **2.** Something spurious or irregular or of bad or questionable origin. — *adj.* **1.** Illegitimate by birth. **2.** Not genuine; spurious; false. **3.** Of an unusual, abnormal, or nonstandard form, shape, or size; as, *bastard* type. **4.** Of a kind similar to, but inferior to or less typical than, the standard; — chiefly in plant and animal names.

bas′tard·ize (băs′tẽr·dīz), *v. t.* To declare or prove to be a bastard; hence, to debase. — **bas′tard·i·za′tion** (-dĭ·zā′shŭn; -dī·zā′-), *n.*

bas′tard·ly, *adj.* Bastardlike; baseborn; spurious.

bastard wing. The process of a bird's wing corresponding to the thumb; the alula. It bears a few short quills.

bas′tar·dy (băs′tẽr·dĭ), *n.* **1.** Illegitimacy. **2.** The procreation of a bastard child.

baste (bāst), *v. t.* [OF. *bastir*, of Teut. origin.] To sew loosely or with long stitches, esp. to hold the work temporarily; to tack.

baste, *v. t.* [From past part., fr. OF. *basser* to moisten slightly.] *Cookery.* To moisten (roasting meat, etc.) with melted butter, fat, pan drippings, etc.

baste, *v. t.* [ON. *beysta.*] To beat; cudgel; hence, to lash with the tongue.

bas·tille′, bas·tile′ (băs·tēl′; *F.* bȧs′tē′y′), *n.* [F. *bastille* fortress, fr. Pr. *bastida*, fr. *bastir* to build.] **1.** *Feud. Fort.* A defensive tower or elevated work. **2.** A castle or fortress in Paris (***the Bastille***), used as a prison until stormed (July 14, 1789 — ***Bastille Day***) and demolished by the populace. **3.** A prison, esp. one despotically used.

bas′ti·nade′ (băs′tĭ·nād′). Var. of BASTINADO.

bas′ti·na′do (-nā′dō), *n.; pl.* -DOES (-dōz). [Sp. *bastonada*, fr. *baston* a stick.] **1.** A blow with a stick or cudgel; also, a cudgel. **2.** The Oriental punishment of beating an offender on the soles of his feet. — *v. t.;* -DOED (-dōd); -DO·ING (-dō·ĭng). To administer a bastinado to.

bast′ing (bās′tĭng), *n.* **a** Action of one who bastes. **b** Thread used in basting. **c** Liquid used in basting meat, etc. **d** A severe beating.

bas′tion (băs′chŭn; băs′tĭ·ŭn), *n.* [F., fr. It. *bastione*, fr. *bastia* bastion, fr. *bastire* to build.] **1.** *Fort.* A work projecting outward from the main enclosure, with two flanks. **2.** A fortification; strong defense. — **bas′tioned** (-chŭnd), *adj.*

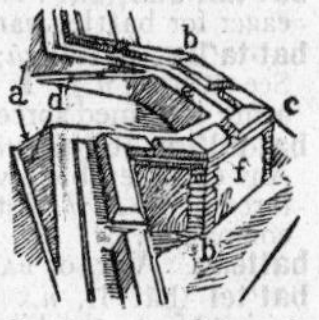

Bastion. *a* Gorge; *b, b* Flanks; *c* Salient Angle; *d* Ramps; *e* Banquette; *f* Face. Extending from the Flanks (*b, b*) are the Curtains.

bat (băt), *n.* [AS. *batt.*] **1.** A stout, solid stick; a club; a club with one end thicker or broader than the other, used in baseball, cricket, etc. **2.** In some games, a racket. **3.** In cricket, baseball, etc., a batsman; batter; also, act of or turn at batting. **4.** A lump, piece, mass, or wad, as of clay or plaster. **5.** Usually ***batt.*** Cotton batting of a poor grade used for filling mattresses, etc.; — usually in *pl.* **6.** *Colloq.* A stroke; a sharp blow; also, rate of motion; speed. **7.** *Slang.* A spree. — *v. t.;* BAT′TED; BAT′TING. To strike or hit with or as with a bat. — *v. i.* To use a bat, as in baseball; specif., to take one's turn at bat.

bat, *n.* [Corrupt. fr. ME. *bakke*, appar. of Scand. origin.] **1.** Any of an order (Chiroptera) of placental mammals with forelimbs modified to form wings. They are the only mammals capable of true flight. **2.** A gliderlike bomb which after being released from an aircraft in flight is automatically guided to the target by its own radar device.

bat, *v. t.* [Cf. 2d BATE.] To wink (the eye).

batch (băch), *n.* [AS. *bacan* to bake.] **1.** The quantity of bread baked at one time. **2.** A quantity of material for one operation, as of dough for a baking; specif., *Glass Mfg.*, the mixture of raw materials which by fusion is converted into glass. **3.** A quantity produced at one operation. **4.** A group of persons or things of the same kind or taken at one time; a lot.

bate (bāt), *v. t.* [From ABATE.] To lessen by retrenching, deducting, or reducing; abate; hence, to lower, moderate, etc.; as, to *bate* one's breath. — *v. i.* To waste away. *Shak.*

bate, *v. i.* [F. *battre de l'aile* or *des ailes.*] To beat the wings with impatience; — said of the falcon, hawk, etc.

bate, *n.* A bath, originally of dung, used by tanners after liming, to remove the lime and soften the hides. — **bate,** *v. t.*

ba·teau′ (bă·tō′), *n.; pl.* BATEAUX (-tōz′). [F., fr. OF. *batel*, fr. *bat*, fr. AS. *bāt.*] *U.S. & Canada.* A light flat-bottomed boat tapering toward the ends, adapted for use on rivers.

bat′fish′ (băt′fĭsh′), *n.; pl.*, see FISH. [From BAT the animal.] Any of several fishes, as a pediculate fish (*Ogcocephalus vespertilio*) of the West Indies, the flying gurnard (*Dactylopterus volitans*) of the Atlantic, and a Californian sting ray (*Aëtobatus californicus*).

bat′fowl′ (-foul′), *v. i.* [From BAT a stick.] To capture birds at night by driving them toward a light, where they are netted.

bath (bȧth; 9), *n.; pl.* BATHS (bȧthz). [AS. *bæth.*] **1.** Act of subjecting the body, or part of it, for cleanliness, comfort, health, etc., to water, vapor, hot air, mud, or the like. Cf. TURKISH BATH. **2.** Water or other medium for bathing. **3.** Any liquid in which objects are immersed so that it may act upon them; also, the receptacle holding the liquid. **4.** State of being covered with a fluid, as sweat. *Shak.* **5.** A place where persons may bathe; *Colloq.*, a bathroom. **6.** A receptacle for water in which to bathe. **7.** A building arranged, as in apartments, for bathing; also (esp. in *pl.*), the elaborate establishments of antiquity providing facilities for bathing and recreation. **8.** *Chem., etc.* A medium, as water, air, sand, or oil, for regulating the temperature of anything placed in or upon it; also, the vessel containing such medium. — *v. t. & i.* To immerse in a bath.

☞ COMBINATIONS are:

bathrobe	**bathroom**	**bathtub**

bath (băth), *n.* [Heb.] An ancient Hebrew liquid measure, corresponding to the ephah of dry measure.

Bath brick (bȧth). [From *Bath*, Eng.] An unbaked brick of siliceous material, used to scour and polish metals.

Bath chair. A kind of hooded chair on wheels, as used by invalids at Bath, England.

bathe (bāth), *v. t.* [AS. *bathian.*] **1.** To wash by immersion, as in a bath; to subject to a bath. **2.** To lave; wet. **3.** To moisten with a liquid. **4.** To apply water or some liquid to; as, to *bathe* the eyes. **5.** To surround, or envelop; as, *bathed* in sunshine. — *v. i.* **1.** To bathe oneself; take a bath; hence, go swimming. **2.** To immerse oneself as if in a bath. — *n. Chiefly Brit.* A swim. — **bath′er** (bāth′ẽr), *n.* — **bath′ing** (bāth′ĭng), *n.*

ba·thet′ic (bȧ·thĕt′ĭk), *adj.* Characterized by bathos.

bath′house′ (bȧth′hous′), *n.* **1.** A house for bathing. **2.** A cabin or apartment, as at a beach, where bathers dress.

bath′o·lith (băth′ō·lĭth), **bath′o·lite** (-līt), *n.* [Gr. *bathos* depth + *-lith, -lite.*] *Geol.* A great mass of intruded igneous rock, which stopped in its rise considerably below the surface. — **bath′o·lith′ic** (-lĭth′ĭk), **bath′o·lit′ic** (-lĭt′ĭk), *adj.*

ba·thom′e·ter (bȧ·thŏm′ē·tẽr), *n.* [Gr. *bathos* depth + *-meter.*] An instrument for measuring depths in water.

ba′thos (bā′thŏs), *n.* [Gr., depth.] **a** Dull and low commonplaceness of matter or style. **b** False pathos; strained pathetic effect. **c** An anticlimax; comedown.

bath′y- (băth′ĭ-). [Gr. *bathys* deep.] A combining form meaning *deep* or, specif., *deep-sea*, as in: **bath′y·al,** deep-sea; **bath′y·sphere,** a diving sphere for deep-sea observation.

ba′tik (bä′tēk; bȧ·tēk′), **bat′ik** (băt′ĭk), *n.* [Malay *batik.*] A method of executing color designs, as on fabric, by coating with wax parts not to be dyed; also, a design so executed or a fabric so decorated. — **ba′tik,** *v. t.;* BA′TIKED (bä′tēkt; bȧ·tēkt′); BA′TIK·ING.

bat′ing (bāt′ĭng), *prep.* With the exception of; excepting.

ba·tiste′ (bă·tēst′), *n.* [F.] A fine cotton fabric.

bat′man (băt′măn), *n.* In the British army, an officer's orderly.

ba·ton′ (bă·tŏn′; bȧ′tôN′; băt′'n), *n.* [F. *bâton*, fr. OF., fr. LL. *bastum* stick.] **1.** A staff borne as a symbol of office. **2.** *Her.* A bend, esp. a narrow bend. A baton with its ends cut off became a mark of bastardy in late heraldry and was borne sinisterwise. **3.** *Music.* The stick or wand with which a leader beats time, as for an orchestra.

ba·tra′chi·an (bȧ·trā′kĭ·ăn), *adj.* [Gr. *batracheios* of a frog, fr. *batrachos* frog.] Relating to or like the frogs and toads; amphibian; narrowly, salientian. — **ba·tra′chi·an,** *n.*

bats′man (băts′măn), *n.* The one who wields a bat, as in baseball, cricket, etc.; specif., one whose turn it is to bat.

batt (băt). Var. of 1st BAT, *n.*, 5.
bat′tail·ous (băt′ĭ·lŭs), *adj.* [OF. *bataillos.*] *Archaic.* Arrayed or eager for battle; warlike.
bat·ta′lia (bă·tăl′yȧ; bă·täl′yȧ), *n.* [It. *battaglia*, fr. L. *battalia.* See BATTLE, *n.*] **1.** *Archaic.* Order of battle. **2.** *Obs.* A marshaled army or armed force.
bat·tal′ion (bă·tăl′yŭn), *n.* [F. *bataillon*, fr. It. *battaglione.*] **1.** Any considerable division of an army organized to act together; in *pl.*, forces. **2.** *Mil.* A tactical unit, as of a headquarters and two or more companies.
batteau. Var. of BATEAU; — now more common than *bateau*.
bat′tel (băt′'l), *n.* *Oxford Univ., Eng.* College accounts for provisions from the kitchen and buttery; also, loosely, the whole college accounts; — only in *pl.*, except adjectively. — *v. i.* To have such an account. — **bat′tel·er**, *n.*
bat′ten (băt′'n), *v. i.* [ON. *batna* to grow better.] To thrive; grow fat. — *v. t.* To make fat; fatten.
bat′ten, *n.* [F. *bâton* stick, staff.] **1.** A strip of sawed lumber, used for flooring, etc. **2.** A strip of wood used for nailing across two other pieces, to cover a crack, stiffen a spar, etc. — *v. t.* To furnish or fasten with battens; as, to *batten* down the hatches. — **bat′ten·er**, *n.*
bat′ter (băt′ẽr), *v. t.* [OF. *batre, battre.* The Eng. word is prob. in part freq. from *bat* to strike.] **1.** To beat with successive blows; beat so as to bruise, shatter, or demolish. **2.** To wear or impair as by hard usage. — *v. i.* To beat repeatedly, esp. with violence. — *n.* **1.** A semiliquid mixture, as for cake or biscuit, of flour, liquid, etc.; — dist. from *dough*. **2.** *Print.* A bruise on the face of a plate or of type in the form; also, the faces or type so injured.
bat′ter, *v. i. & t.* To slope gently backward, as a wall. — *n.* An inward upward slope of the outer face of a wall.
bat′ter, *n.* One who wields a bat; a batsman.
bat′ter·ing-ram′, *n.* *Mil.* An engine of antiquity usually consisting of a huge beam having a head of iron (sometimes in the shape of a ram's head) and mounted or hung so as to be used to beat down walls.
bat′ter·y (băt′ẽr·ĭ), *n.*; *pl.* -TERIES (-ĭz). [F. *batterie*, fr. *battre* to beat.] **1.** Act of battering. **2.** Apparatus used in battering. **3.** A number of similar machines, devices, or articles arranged in a group or set. **4.** *Baseball.* The pitcher and catcher together. **5.** *Elec.* **a** A combination of apparatus for producing a united electric effect; as, a *battery* of Leyden jars. **b** A group of two or more cells connected together, for furnishing electric current; as, a dry *battery*; storage *battery* (see these entries). **6.** *Law.* The unlawful beating of another. It includes every willful, angry and violent, or negligent touching of another's person or clothes or anything attached to his person or held by him. See ASSAULT, 2. **7.** *Mil.* **a** Any emplacement where artillery is mounted. **b** Two or more pieces of artillery under a single command. **c** The smallest and basic unit of organization of field artillery. **8.** *Nav.* The guns, or any group of the guns, of a warship.
bat′tik (băt′ĭk). Var. of BATIK.
bat′ting (băt′ĭng), *n.* **1.** Act of one who bats; the use of a bat. **2.** Cotton or wool in sheets, for use in quilts, etc.
bat′tle (băt′'l), *n.* [OF. *bataille* battle, battalion, fr. L. *battalia, battualia*, the fighting and fencing exercises of soldiers and gladiators, fr. *battuere* to beat.] **1.** A general encounter between armies or ships; engagement. **2.** A combat between two individuals. **3.** Fighting or as of armed forces; war. **4.** *Archaic.* A battalion.
Syn. Battle, engagement, action mean a hostile meeting between opposing forces. **Battle** is commonly used of a general and prolonged combat; an **engagement** may be a general encounter, as between entire armies, or a minor encounter, as between subdivisions or outposts; **action** stresses the idea of active, frequently sharp, offensive and defensive operations.
☞ COMBINATIONS are:

battle cry **battlefield** **battleground**

— *v. i.*; -TLED (-'ld); -TLING (-lĭng). To contend in or as in battle; hence, to struggle. — *v. t.* To fight.
bat′tle, *v. t.* *Obs. exc. Poetic.* To equip with battlements.
bat′tle–ax′, bat′tle–axe′, *n.* *Mil.* A kind of broadax formerly used as an offensive weapon.
battle clasp. See CLASP.
battle cruiser. A warship of dreadnought size and of the highest speed and heaviest battery, but without the heavy armor protection of the dreadnought.
bat′tle·dore (băt′'l·dōr; 70), *n.* [Appar. fr. Pr. *batedor* an instrument for beating.] A light flat bat or racket used in striking a shuttlecock in an old game; also, the game often known as *battledore and shuttlecock.* — *v. t. & i.* To toss back and forth.
bat′tle·ment (-mĕnt), *n.* [ME. *batilment, batelment.*] A parapet with open spaces, surmounting the walls of ancient fortified buildings, later used as a decorative feature. — **bat′tle·ment·ed** (-mĕn·tĕd; -tĭd), *adj.*

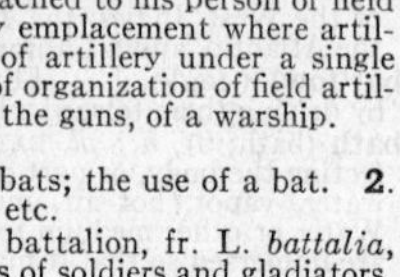

Battlements. *A, A* Merlons; *B, B* Crenels; *C* Machicolations.

bat′tle·plane′ (-plăn′), *n.* A fast, high-powered military airplane, mounting a gun or guns.
bat′tle·ship′ (-shĭp′), *n.* *Nav.* One of a class of the largest and most heavily armed and armored vessels. Cf. DREADNOUGHT, 3 **b**.
battle star. See STAR, *n.*, 6 **a**.
bat′tle·wag′on (-wăg′ŭn), *n.* *Slang.* A battleship.
bat·tue′ (bă·tōō′; bă·tū′; *F.* bȧ′tü′), *n.* [F., fr. *battre* to beat.] **1.** *Hunting.* Act of beating woods, bushes, etc., for game; act of capturing game so driven; also, the game. **2.** Wanton slaughter, as of helpless crowds.
bat′ty (băt′ĭ), *adj.* **1.** Batlike. **2.** *Slang.* Crazy; foolish.
bau′ble (bô′b'l), *n.* [OF. *baubel, babel*, fr. *belbel*, fr. L. *bellus* pretty.] **1.** A trifling piece of finery; a gewgaw. **2.** *Hist.* The fool's scepter. **3.** *Obs.* A toy; plaything.
Bau′cis and Phi·le′mon (bô′sĭs, fĭ·lē′mŏn). *Class. Myth.* An aged Phrygian woman and her husband, rewarded for entertaining Zeus and Hermes traveling in disguise.
bau′de·kin (bô′dē·kĭn), **baud′kin** (bôd′kĭn), *n.* Baldachin (fabric).
bau′drons (bô′drŭnz), *n.* *Scot. & N. of Eng.* A cat.
bauk′ie (bôk′ĭ; bäk′ĭ), **bauk′ie·bird′** (-bûrd′), *n.* *Scot.* A bat.
baulk (bôk). Var. of BALK.
Bau′mé′ (bō′mā′), *adj.* Designating or conforming to scales used by Antoine Baumé, French chemist, in graduating his hydrometers.
bau′son (bô′s'n), *n.* [OF. *baucent, bauçant*, spotted with white.] *Archaic.* A badger.
bau′sond (-s'nd), **bau′son–faced′** (-s'n·făst′), *adj.* [See BAUSON.] *Chiefly Scot.* Having a white spot or streak, esp. on the forehead; — of animals.
baux′ite (bôks′īt; bouks′īt; bō′zīt), *n.* [F., fr. *Baux*, near Arles, France.] *Mineral.* A ferruginous aluminum hydroxide, essentially $Al_2O_3.2H_2O$, but consisting of several minerals occurring in oölitic masses and in earthy form.
‖**ba′var′dage′** (bȧ′vȧr′dȧzh′), *n.* [F.] Prattle; twaddle.
Ba·var′i·an (bȧ·vâr′ĭ·ăn), *adj.* Of or pertaining to Bavaria or the Bavarians. — *n.* A native of Bavaria; also, the High German dialect of Bavaria. See INDO-EUROPEAN LANGUAGES, *Table.*
baw·bee′ (bô·bē′; bô′bē), *n.* *Dial., Brit.* A halfpenny.
baw′cock′ (bô′kŏk′), *n.* [From F. *beau* fine + *coq* cock (the bird).] A fine fellow; — jocose and familiar. *Shak.*
bawd (bôd), *n.* [OF. *baud, baude*, bold, merry, of Teut. origin.] A procurer or, now esp., a procuress.
bawd′ry (bôd′rĭ), *n.* **1.** *Archaic.* Practice or business of a bawd. **2.** *Obs.* Illicit intercourse. **3.** Obscenity.
bawd′y (bôd′ĭ), *adj.*; BAWD′I·ER (-ĭ·ẽr); BAWD′I·EST. **1.** Characteristic of a bawd. **2.** Obscene; lewd. — **bawd′i·ly**, *adv.* — **bawd′i·ness**, *n.*
bawl (bôl), *v. i.* [Icel. *baula* to low, bellow, or ML. *baulare* to bark.] **1.** To cry out with a loud, full sound; shout. **2.** To cry loudly, as from pain; howl. — *v. t.* To proclaim with a loud voice, as a hawker. — *n.* A loud, prolonged cry; an outcry. — **bawl′er**, *n.*
baw′s'nt (bô′s'nt). Var. of BAUSOND.
baw′tie, baw′ty (bô′tĭ), *n.* *Scot.* **a** A dog. **b** A hare.
bay (bā), *n.* [OF. *baie*, fr. LL. *baia.*] **1.** *Geog.* An inlet of the sea, similar to but usually smaller than a gulf. **2.** A recess or indentation, as that formed by part of a plain within a curve in a hill range.
bay, *n.* [OF. *baée* an opening (F. *baie*), fr. *baer, beer*, to be open.] **1.** A principal compartment of a part or of the whole of a structure, as marked off by beams, pillars, buttresses, etc. **2.** A compartment in a barn, for hay or grain in the stalk; also, one for a special purpose; as, a horse *bay*. **3.** *Aeronaut.* **a** The section of a truss included between the transversely adjacent sets of struts or bulkheads. **b** Any of several compartments in the fuselage of an aircraft; specif., ***bomb bay***, a compartment on the underside between the wings, with doors swinging down and out through which bombs are dropped from their racks. **4.** *Arch.* A window with its usual setting of framing, as jambs, window back, etc.; also, a bay window. **5.** *Naut.* The forward part of a ship on each side between decks, often used as a ship's hospital. See SICK BAY.
bay, *n.* [OF. *baie*, fr. L. *baca.*] **1.** The laurel *Laurus nobilis*; hence, in *pl.*, garland bestowed for victory, anciently consisting of laurel branches. **2.** Any of several shrubs or trees resembling the laurel, as certain magnolias.
bay, *v. i.* [OF. *baier, abaier.*] To bark, esp. with deep, prolonged tones, as a dog in the chase. — *v. t.* **1.** To bark at. **2.** To utter by barking. **3.** To pursue with barking. **4.** To bring or drive to bay. — *n.* **1.** The barking of dogs. **2.** [OF. *abai*, prop. the extremity to which the stag is reduced when surrounded by the barking dogs.] State or position of one obliged to face an antagonist or a difficulty, when escape is impossible; as, an animal at *bay*. **3.** State or position of one checked in pursuit or aggression; as, to hold an adversary at *bay*.
bay, *adj.* [OF. *bai*, fr. L. *badius.*] Reddish-brown; — chiefly of horses. — *n.* **1.** An animal of a bay color; esp., a bay horse. **2.** A brown, red-yellow in hue, of low saturation and low brilliance. See COLOR.
ba′ya·dere′ (bä′yȧ·dēr′; -dâr′), *adj.* Striped transversely in sharply contrasted colors. — *n.* Bayadere fabric or design.
bay antler. [See BEZ ANTLER.] See ANTLER, *Illust.*
bay′ard (bā′ẽrd), *adj.* [OF., bay horse, fr. *bai* bay + *-ard.* See BAY reddish-brown; — ARD.] Bay-colored; — esp. of a horse. — *n.* **1.** A bay horse. **2.** [*cap.*] (*Fr. pron.* bȧ′yȧr′) In certain old French romances, a wonderful bay steed. **3.** Any horse; — a mock heroic name.
Bay′ard (bā′ẽrd), *n.* A gentleman of high courage and honor; — so called in allusion to the Chevalier Bayard (1473?–1524), the knight "sans peur et sans reproche" (without fear and without reproach).
bay′ber′ry (bā′bĕr′ĭ; -bĕr·ĭ), *n.* **a** The fruit of the bay tree. **b** A West Indian tree (*Pimenta racemosa*) related to the allspice tree. Its yellow, aromatic essential oil, **bay oil**, is used in bay rum (which see). **c** The wax myrtle or its fruit. **d** A hardy shrub (*Myrica pensylvanica*) of the Northern Hemisphere, sometimes cultivated for ornament.
Ba·yeux′ tap′es·try (bā·yōō′; *F.* bȧ′yû′). [From *Bayeux*, vil. in northern France.] A long narrow strip of embroidered linen, of the 11th century, reputedly made by the wife of William the Conqueror.
bay′o·net (bā′ō·nĕt; -nĭt), *n.* [From F.; — bayonets were first made at Bayonne, France.] *Mil.* A weapon of the dagger kind made to be fitted on the muzzle end of a musket or rifle. — *v. t.*; -NET′ED; -NET′ING. **1.** To stab with a bayonet. **2.** To compel or drive by the bayonet. — *v. i.* To use a bayonet.
bay′ou (bī′ōō; bī′ō), *n.*; *pl.* BAYOUS (-ōōz; -ōz). [Amer. F., of Muskhogean origin.] A creek, secondary watercourse, or minor river, tributary to another river or other body of water; — the regular term in the lower Mississippi basin and in the Gulf-coast region.
bay rum (bā). A fragrant cosmetic and medicinal liquid, originally distilled from the leaves of the West Indian bayberry, now chiefly prepared from essential oils, alcohol, and water.
bay seal. Rabbit fur processed to simulate seal.
Bay State. Massachusetts; — a nickname, from its former name, The Colony of Massachusetts Bay.
bay tree. The laurel *Laurus nobilis.*
bay window. *Arch.* A windowed bay or recess in a room.
bay′wood′ (bā′wŏŏd′), *n.* A mahogany (*Swietenia macrophylla*) from the Gulf of Campeche, softer and lighter than true mahogany.
ba·zaar′ (bȧ·zär′), *n.* Also **ba·zar′**. [Ultimately fr. Per. *bāzār.*] **1.** In the East, a market place or assemblage of shops. **2.** Any similar establishment for the sale of goods. **3.** A fair for the sale of fancy wares, toys, etc.
ba·zoo′ka (bȧ·zōō′kȧ), *n.*; *pl.* BAZOOKAS (-kȧz). [Prob. from fancied resemblance to the sound contraption used by Bob Burns, radio come-

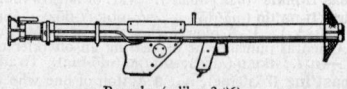

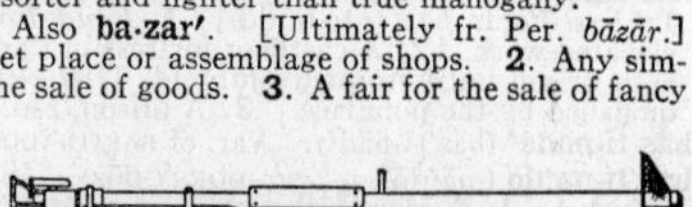
Bazooka (caliber 2.36).

dian.] *Mil., U. S.* A portable, electrically fired rocket launcher consisting of a tube 54–61 inches long, about 3 inches in diameter, and open at both ends, with sights and shoulder frame, which launches a rocket-propelled projectile similar to a small aerial bomb. The projectile is effective against tank armor.

ba·zoo′ka·man (bȧ·zōō′kȧ·măn) *or* **ba·zoo′kier′** (bȧ·zōō′kēr′), *n. Mil.* A man charged with the firing of a bazooka.

B battery (bē). An electric battery connected in the plate circuit of an electron tube to cause the flow of electron current in the tube.

BCG vaccine. [Bacillus *C*almette-*G*uérin, fr. Albert L. C. Calmette (1863–1933) and Camille Guérin (b. 1872), French bacteriologists.] A preparation of tuberculosis bacilli which have been weakened by growth on ox bile, used to vaccinate human beings against tuberculosis.

bdel′li·um (dĕl′ĭ·ŭm; -yŭm), *n.* [L., fr. Gr. *bdellion.*] **1.** A substance mentioned in the Bible (*Gen.* ii. 12, and *Num.* xi. 7), variously taken to be a gum or resin, a precious stone, or a pearl. **2.** A gum resin, similar to myrrh, obtained from various trees (genus *Commiphora,* family Burseraceae).

be (bē; 4), *v. i.;* WAS (wŏz); BEEN (bĭn *or, esp. Brit.,* bēn); BE′ING. Conjugation: indic. pres. sing., 1st person ***am,*** 2d [thou] ***art,*** [you] ***are,*** 3d ***is,*** pl. ***are;*** indic. past sing., 1st & 3d ***was,*** 2d [thou] ***wast,*** also ***wert,*** pl. ***were;*** subjunctive pres. ***be,*** past ***were,*** 2d sing. also ***wert.*** [ME. *been, beon,* fr. AS. *bēon* to be.] **1.** As copulative verb: **a** To coincide in identity with; to equal; as, Carl *is* my brother. **b** To signify or represent; as, let "x" *be* ten. **c** To belong under the description or to the class of; as, I *am* sick. **2.** A substantive verb: **a** To exist or have reality; to live; as, I think, therefore I *am.* **b** To maintain a certain position or condition; to remain; as, to *be* at ease. **c** To occur; as, the fight *was* here. **d** To belong or befall; as, woe *be* to you. **3.** As auxiliary verb: **a** With the past part. of trans. verbs to form the passive voice and of certain intrans. verbs to form a perfect tense; as, to *be* elected; the sun *was* risen. **b** With the pres. part. in progressive forms; as, they *are* hastening. **c** With the infin. to express intention; as, he *is* to be hanged.

be- (bē-). [AS. *be,* and in accented form *bī.*] A prefix forming: **1.** Verbs (from verbs) with a reinforcing sense of *about* or *over,* or with a meaning of *all around, on all sides, all over,* as in:

beclasp	**bedim**	**beslobber**
bedabble	**bescreen**	**besprinkle**
bedash	**bescribble**	**bewrap**

2. Intensive verbs (from verbs) with the sense of *thoroughly, completely, violently, repeatedly,* as in:

bedazzle	**bedrench**	**besmear**
bedrabble	**bemuddle**	**bethump**

3. Intensive verbs (from verbs) and a few adjectives with the sense of *excessively, ostentatiously,* with implied ridicule, as in: **be·laud′, be·rib′boned.**

4. Verbs with the sense of *away from;* as, *be*reave. **5.** Transitive verbs (from verbs) implying action done *for, to, at, on, by, over, against,* as in:

becrawl	**beleap**	**besmile**
begroan	**bemurmur**	**beweep**

6. Verbs (from adjectives or nouns) with the force of *to make* or *to cause to be;* — often with implied ridicule, as in:

becripple	**befoul**	**bespouse**

7. Verbs (from nouns) with the sense *to name,* as in:

bebrother	**belady**	**berascal**

8. Transitive verbs, esp. in the past participle, and a few adjectives (from nouns) with the force of *to affect with* or *by means of, to treat with, to provide with* or *cover with;* — often with an implication of excess or ridicule, as in:

bedew	**begem**	**besmoke**
beflag	**beglue**	**besnow**
begabled	**bejewel**	**bespangle**

beach (bēch), *n.* [Origin uncert.] **1.** Pebbles collectively; shingle. **2.** The shore of the sea or of a lake, washed by the waves; strand. — *v. t. & i.* To run or drive (as a boat) upon a beach; to strand.

beach′comb′er (-kōm′ẽr), *n.* **1.** *Amer.* A comber (def. 2). **2.** A loafer or vagrant along the seacoast; esp., a white man living as a loafer on any of the islands of the Pacific.

beach flea. Any of numerous amphipod crustaceans (family Orchestiidae) living on ocean beaches, and leaping like fleas.

beach′head′ (bēch′hĕd′), *n.* **1.** An area on a hostile shore secured and defended by an advance force to cover the landing of troops or supplies. **2.** Loosely, any initial advance position or foothold to be used as vantage ground for exploitation.

beach wagon. A station wagon.

beach′y (bēch′ĭ), *adj.* Pebbly; shingly.

bea′con (bē′kŭn; -k′n), *n.* [AS. *bēacen, bēcen.*] **1.** A signal, esp. a signal fire on a pole, building, or other eminence. **2.** A watchtower or signal station. **3.** A signal or mark erected on an eminence near the shore to guide mariners. **4.** Something or someone serving as a signal, as of guidance or warning. **5.** = RADIO BEACON. — *v. t. & i.* To furnish with, or shine as, a beacon.

bead (bēd), *n.* [ME. *bede* prayer, prayer bead, fr. AS. *bed, gebed,* prayer.] **1.** *Obs.* (A) prayer. **2.** A small perforated ball strung with others, and used in a rosary or for ornament; hence, *pl.,* the (or a) rosary. **3.** Any small globular body; as: **a** One of the effervescent bubbles in a liquor, or the foam or head formed by them. **b** A drop of sweat or other liquid. **c** A small knob of metal on a firearm near the muzzle, used for a front sight (whence ***to draw a bead on,*** to aim at). Cf. SIGHT, *Illust.* **d** In assaying, the globule of precious metal got by cupellation. **4.** One of the strips around the inner periphery of a pneumatic tire shaped for engaging the rim of the wheel. **5.** *Arch.* A small projecting molding of rounded surface (see MOLDING, QUIRK, *Illusts.*); hence, any of various pieces as a parting strip, having a section somewhat like such a molding. **6.** *Chem.* A glassy drop of flux, as borax, used as a solvent and color test before the blowpipe. — *v. t.* To put beads or beading on; arrange as strung beads. — *v. i.* To form beads or beadlike bubbles.

bead′house′, bede′house′ (bēd′hous′), *n.* An almshouse whose inmates were obligated to pray for their benefactors.

bead′ing (bēd′ĭng), *n.* **1.** Material, or a part or a piece, consisting of a bead or beads. **2.** A beaded molding. **3.** An openwork trimming. **4.** Beadwork.

bea′dle (bē′d′l), *n.* [OF. *bedel* (F. *bedeau*), of Teut. origin.] **1.** An official attendant whose office it is to walk before dignitaries; a macebearer; specif., an officer in a university who precedes processions of officers and students; — spelled *bedel* at Oxford, *bedell* at Cambridge. **2.** *Chiefly Brit.* An inferior parish officer having a variety of duties, as to keep order in church, execute orders of the vestry, etc.

bea′dle·dom (bē′d′l·dŭm), *n.* Redtapism; stupid officialism.

bead′roll′ (bēd′rōl′), *n.* **1.** *R.C.Ch.* A catalogue of persons for the rest of whose souls prayers are to be said. *Hist.* **2.** Any catalogue; series.

beads′man, bedes′man (bēdz′măn), *n.* **1.** A man who prays, esp. one paid to pray for his benefactor. **2.** *Eng.* A poor man supported in a beadhouse. **3.** *Scot.* A licensed beggar. — **beads′wom′an** (-wŏŏm′ăn), *n. fem.*

bead′work′ (bēd′wûrk′), *n.* **1.** Ornamental work in beads. **2.** *Joinery.* Beading (def. 2).

bead′y (bēd′ĭ), *adj.* **1.** Beadlike; small, round, and glistening. **2.** Covered or ornamented with or as with beads.

bea′gle (bē′g′l), *n.* [ME. *begle.*] A small, short-legged, smooth-coated hound with pendulous ears.

beak (bēk), *n.* [OF. *bec,* fr. LL. *beccus,* of Celt. origin.] **1.** The bill or nib of a bird or of some other animal, as a turtle, esp. one with the upper mandible curved downward over the lower (see BILL, *Illust.*); hence, *Slang,* the nose of a person. **2.** Anything beaklike, as the tapering tube of a retort, the spout of a vessel, etc. **3.** *Arch.* A continuous slight projection ending in an arris or narrow fillet; that part of a drip from which the water is thrown off. See MOLDING, *Illust.* **4.** *Bot. & Zool.* A beaklike process or part. **5.** *Nav.* A metal-shod beam projecting from the prow of an ancient galley, to pierce the vessel of an enemy. — **beaked** (bēkt; bēk′ĕd; -ĭd), *adj.*

beak, *n. Slang, Brit.* **1.** A magistrate. **2.** At Eton, a master.

beak′er (bēk′ẽr), *n.* [ON. *bikarr,* fr. LL. *becarium.*] **1.** A large widemouthed drinking cup, sometimes on a standard; also, a beakerful. **2.** A deep, openmouthed, thin vessel of glass, copper, etc., often with a projecting lip, used by chemists and others.

beam (bēm), *n.* [AS. *bēam.*] **1.** Any large and relatively long piece of timber or metal prepared for use. **2.** That part of a plow to which the standard, colter, etc., are attached. See PLOW, *Illust.* **3.** A cylinder of wood in a loom, on which the warp is wound; also, one on which the cloth is wound. **4.** The bar of a balance from which the scales hang. **5.** A principal horizontal timber or metal support of a building or ship. **6.** The main stem of an antler. **7.** A ray or collection of parallel rays emitted, as from the sun or other luminous body; as, a *beam* of light or of heat. **8.** A ray; a gleam; as, a *beam* of comfort. **9.** *Aeronautics.* In full ***radio beam.*** A constant unidirectional radio signal transmitted for the guidance of pilots. Cf. RADIO BEACON. Hence: ***fly, or ride, the beam,*** to fly an airplane exactly on the course indicated by a radio beam; so, ***on the beam.*** **10.** *Naut.* The extreme breadth of a vessel at the widest part. Hence: ***on the beam,*** in a line with the beams, or at right angles with the keel. **11.** *Radio.* **a** The effective range of a microphone or loud-speaker; as, in the *beam.* **b** The angle at which a microphone or loud-speaker functions best. **12.** *Steam Engines.* A lever having an oscillating motion on a central axis, connected at one end with the piston rod from which it receives motion, and at the other with the crank or its equivalent.

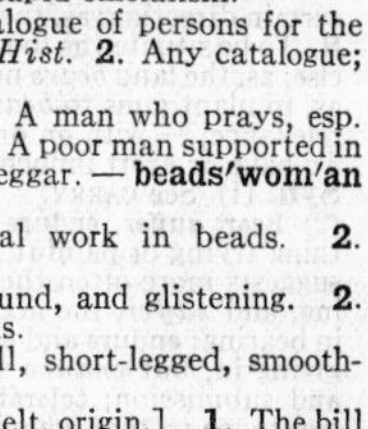

Radio Beam, showing quadrants of signal pattern.

— *v. t.* **1.** To send forth; emit, as light. **2.** *Radio.* To aim (a broadcast) by means of directional antennas; as, programs *beamed* at Britain. — *v. i.* **1.** To emit beams of light; shine. **2.** To look or smile with joy.

beam′-ends′, *n. pl. Naut.* The ends of a ship's beams. — ***on her beam-ends.*** Of a ship, inclined so much on one side that her beams approach a vertical position. — ***on one's beam-ends.*** At the end of one's material resources.

beam′ing (bēm′ĭng), *adj.* Emitting beams; radiant. — **Syn.** See BRIGHT. — **beam′ing·ly,** *adv.*

beam′ish (-ĭsh), *adj.* Beaming.

beam′y (-ĭ), *adj.* **1.** Emitting beams of light. **2.** Resembling a beam; massive. **3.** Having horns or antlers. **4.** *Naut.* Having considerable beam.

bean (bēn), *n.* [AS. *bēan.*] **1. a** Orig., the large, smooth, kidney-shaped edible seed borne severally in long pods by the legume *Vicia faba,* the ***broad bean;*** hence also, the similar seed of various related plants of the pea family (esp. of the genus *Phaseolus*), as the *kidney bean, Lima bean, string bean* (see these terms). **b** Any plant bearing these seeds or the pod containing them. **2.** Any of various other plants, or their beanlike seeds or fruits; as, the castor *bean;* a coffee *bean.* **3.** *Slang.* **a** Head; brain. **b** *Chiefly Brit.* Fellow; chap.

bean beetle. = MEXICAN BEAN BEETLE.

bean caper. A small tree (*Zygophyllum fabago*) of the Levant, typifying a family (Zygophyllaceae, the bean-caper family), distinguished by stipulate leaves and axillary pentamerous flowers. Its flower buds are used as capers.

bean′o (bēn′ō), *n.* **1.** *Slang.* A treat; spree. **2.** [From *bean,* after keno, lotto.] A variety of keno; — called also *bingo.*

bean tree. 1. A handsome Australian tree (*Castanospermum australe*) having yellow flowers and large pods containing edible chestnut-like seeds. **2.** Any of various trees bearing similar pods, as the laburnum or the catalpa.

bear (bâr), *v. t.; past* BORE (bōr), formerly BARE (bâr); *past part.* BORNE (bōrn), BORN (bôrn) (used in passive forms of verb in sense *give birth to,* when not followed by *by*); *pres. part.* BEAR′ING. [AS. *beran.*] **1.** To support and move; carry. **2.** To be equipped, furnished, or marked with; to have as belonging, distinguishing, identifying, or characterizing; as, to *bear* a sword, an inscription, a title, a good reputation, or an evil look. **3.** To bring forth; produce; yield; also, give birth to. **4.** To support the weight of; sustain; hold up. **5.** To endure; tolerate; suffer. **6.** To press; thrust; drive; as, the boat was *borne* backward by the wind. **7.** To disseminate; as, to *bear* tales. **8.** To render or give; as, to *bear* testimony. **9.** To conduct by accompanying; as, crowds *bore* the hero home. **10.** To carry or hold (one's body or a part of it) or conduct (oneself) in a given manner; as, to *bear* one's head high; to *bear* oneself with dignity. **11.** To exercise as a power, function, or right; as, to *bear* rule. **12.** To hold in the mind; to harbor; as, to *bear* a grudge. **13.** To assume or carry on as a duty, a responsibility, etc.; as, to *bear* one's part, or the costs. **14.** To have when compared, related, or the like; as, the ratio which one thing *bears*

to another. **15.** To admit or permit of; to be able to sustain; as, your words *bear* only one interpretation. — *v. i.* **1.** To endure with patience; — often with *up* or *with*. **2.** To bear children, fruit, or the like. **3.** To press; — with *on, upon,* or *against*. **4.** To move or incline in a certain direction; as, the road *bears* to the right. **5.** To carry burdens. **6.** To be situated as to the point of compass, with respect to something else; as, the land *bears* north by east. **7.** To be directed; to be pointed; as, to plant guns to *bear* upon a trench. **8.** To relate, refer, or have relevance; — with *on* or *upon*; as, facts that *bear* on a question. **9.** To have or exert influence or force; as, to bring pressure to *bear*.
Syn. (1) See CARRY.
(2) **Bear, suffer, endure, abide, tolerate, stand** mean to sustain something trying or painful. **Bear** and **suffer** are often very close, but *bear* suggests more often the power to sustain than the manner of sustaining, and *suffer*, the acceptance of affliction than patience or courage in bearing; **endure** and **abide** imply long-continued trials borne without giving in, but *endure* suggests firmness of mind and *abide*, patience and submission; **tolerate** and **stand** usually imply overcoming one's resistance to that which is distasteful or antagonistic.
bear out. To corroborate; to confirm. — ***bear up.*** To keep up one's courage. — ***bear with.*** To endure; to be indulgent to.

bear (bâr), *n.* [AS. *bera.*] **1.** A large, heavy mammal (family Ursidae) with long shaggy hair, rudimentary tail, and plantigrade feet, as the European ***brown bear*** (*Ursus arctos*), the large creamy-white ***polar bear*** (*U. maritimus*) of arctic regions, the large powerful usually brownish-yellow ***grizzly bear*** (*U. horribilis*) of western North America, the American ***black bear*** (*Euarctos americanus*) and its chestnut-colored variety the ***cinnamon bear***. **2.** Anything likened to a bear; specif. [*cap.*], *Astron.*, see URSA MAJOR, URSA MINOR. **3.** An uncouth, surly, or morose person. **4.** A person who sells securities, foreign exchange, or commodities in the expectation of buying them at a lower price later; esp., one who speculates for a decline by selling short. **5.** *Mach.* A portable punch press. — *v. t.* To try to depress the price of, or prices in. — *adj.* Of, pertaining to, or influenced by stock-market bears; hence, falling; as, a *bear* market.

bear, bere (bēr), *n.* [AS. *bere.*] *Chiefly Scot.* Barley.

bear'a·ble (bâr'ȧ·b'l), *adj.* Capable of being borne or endured; tolerable. — **bear'a·ble·ness,** *n.* — **bear'a·bly,** *adv.*

bear'bait'ing (bâr'bāt'ĭng), *n.* The sport of setting dogs on a chained bear. — **bear'bait'er** (-ẽr), *n.*

bear'ber'ry (-bĕr'ĭ; -bẽr·ĭ), *n.* **a** A trailing evergreen plant (*Arctostaphylos uva-ursi*) with tonic, astringent foliage, and red berries. **b** The large cranberry (*Oxycoccus macrocarpus*). **c** A deciduous holly (*Ilex decidua*) of the southern United States.

beard (bērd), *n.* [AS. *beard.*] **1.** The hair that grows on a man's face, — often excluding the mustache. **2.** A beardlike appendage or tuft, as the long hairs on the chin of a goat, the awns of a flower head of grain (see WHEAT, *Illust.*), etc. **3.** *Print.* The part of a type between the face and the body. See TYPE, *Illust.* — *v. t.* **1.** To take by the beard; to pull the beard of. **2.** To confront in defiance; to encounter boldly. **3.** To furnish with a beard. — **beard'less,** *adj.* — **beard'less·ness,** *n.*

beard'ed (bēr'dĕd; -dĭd), *adj.* Having a beard; awned.

beard'tongue' (bērd'tŭng'), *n.* = PENTSTEMON.

bear'er (bâr'ẽr), *n.* One that bears, sustains, or carries; as: **a** A pallbearer. **b** A tree or plant yielding fruit. **c** One holding a check, draft, or the like, specif. one made payable "to bearer."

bear garden. A place for baiting bears and for other rough pastimes; hence, a place or scene of rowdiness.

bear grass. *Southern & Western U.S.* Any of several species of *Yucca* (see YUCCA) with grasslike foliage; also, any of several plants with grasslike foliage (as *Camassia esculenta*).

bear'ing (bâr'ĭng), *n.* **1.** Manner of carrying or comporting oneself; carriage; behavior. **2.** The power or time of bearing offspring or fruit. **3.** That which is borne; a crop. **4.** An object, surface, or point that supports. **5.** Capacity to endure. **6.** The situation or direction of one point or object with respect to another, or to the points of the compass; as, to lose one's *bearings* and go astray. **7.** One of the ways in which a thing affects or is affected by other things; relationship; as, to consider a matter in all its *bearings*. **8.** Purport; meaning. **9.** That part of any member of a building that rests upon its supports. **10.** Any one of the emblems or charges in an escutcheon or coat of arms; as, armorial *bearings*. Cf. ESCUTCHEON, *Illust.* **11.** *Mach.* A part in which a journal, gudgeon, pivot, pin, or the like, turns.
Syn. Bearing, deportment, demeanor (*or* **demeanour**), **mien, manner, carriage** mean the way in which or the quality by which a person outwardly manifests his personality or breeding. **Bearing,** the most general of these words, now usually implies characteristic posture or way of holding oneself; **deportment** suggests one's actions or behavior as formed by breeding or training; **demeanor** suggests one's attitude as expressed in one's behavior to others; **mien** implies reference both to bearing and demeanor; **manner** implies characteristic behavior, with reference esp. to one's attitude, gesture, or address; **carriage** comes close to *bearing*, specifically implying posture in standing or walking.

bearing rein. = CHECKREIN, 1.

bear'ish (bâr'ĭsh), *adj.* **1.** Bearlike in manner or actions; rough; gruff. **2.** Depressing or tending to depress prices in the exchanges. — **bear'ish·ly,** *adv.* — **bear'ish·ness,** *n.*

bear's'-ear' (bârz'ēr'), *n.* The auricula (*Primula auricula*).

bear's'-foot', *n.* See HELLEBORE, 1.

bear'skin' (bâr'skĭn'), *n.* **1.** The skin or fur of a bear. **2.** A cap made of bearskin.

bear'wood' (-wŏŏd'), *n.* = CASCARA BUCKTHORN, under CASCARA, 1.

beast (bēst), *n.* [OF. *beste,* fr. LL. *besta,* for L. *bestia.*] **1.** Any four-footed animal; esp., one of the larger animals; as, a **beast of burden,** an animal used to carry burdens; **beast of prey,** an animal that preys on other animals. **2.** Animal nature in man; as, the *beast* in us. **3.** One showing or swayed by his animal nature; as, a drunken *beast*. — **Syn.** Animal, brute.

beast'ly (-lĭ), *adj.*; -LI·ER (-lĭ·ẽr); -LI·EST. **1.** Of, pertaining to, or like beasts. **2.** Of or characteristic of man's animal nature; sensual; bestial. **3.** *Colloq.* Abominable; disgusting. — **beast'li·ness,** *n.*

beat (bēt), *v. t.*; BEAT; BEAT'EN (bēt''n) or BEAT; BEAT'ING. [AS. *bēatan.*] **1.** To strike repeatedly so as to impel, thresh, mix, sound, etc.; as, to *beat* a drum, eggs, etc. **2.** To produce or to get (into or out of) by or as by repeated blows. **3.** To tread, as a path. **4.** To thrash. **5.** To dash against repeatedly, as waves, rain, etc. **6.** To flap vigorously. **7.** To overcome; defeat; vanquish; also, to surpass. **8.** To measure or mark off by strokes; as, to *beat* time. **9.** To range over, striking bushes, etc., to rouse game; as, to *beat* a wood. **10.** *Colloq.* **a** To baffle; mystify. **b** To get ahead of. **c** To cheat; defraud. **11.** *Mil.* To sound by beat, as of a drum; as, to *beat* an alarm. — **Syn.** (1) Pound, pummel, thrash, thresh, buffet, baste, belabor: (2) see CONQUER. — *v. i.* **1.** To strike, pound, dash, etc., repeatedly and with force; as, to *beat* on a door; rain *beats* on the pavement. **2.** To pulsate; vibrate; throb; as, the heart *beats* regularly. **3.** To sound when struck; as, the drums *beat*. **4.** *Colloq.* To win the victory. **5.** To undergo beating, as eggs. **6.** To seek game by beating a field, wood, etc. **7.** *Mil.* To drum. **8.** *Music & Acoustics.* To make a beat (see BEAT, *n.*, 8). **9.** *Naut.* To make progress to windward, as by tacking.
beat about, or around, the bush. To make an approach to a subject or the like in a roundabout manner. — ***beat the air or wind.*** To strike wide of the mark, to no purpose or against no opponent.
— *n.* **1.** A stroke or blow, usually in series. **2.** In a timepiece, the stroke or sound made by the action of the escapement. **3.** A throb; a pulsation; also, its sound. **4.** A regularly traversed round; as, a watchman's *beat*. **5.** *Local, U.S.* An administrative subdivision, as of a county. **6.** *Slang.* An unprincipled sponger; as, a dead *beat*. **7.** *Colloq.* One that beats, or surpasses; as, I've never seen his *beat*. **8.** *Acoustics & Music.* A sudden swelling or reinforcement of a sound, recurring at regular intervals and produced by the interference of sound waves of slightly different periods of vibration; also, the pulsation or throbbing so produced. **9.** *Music.* **a** The regularly recurring and periodically accented pulse or throb which constitutes the unit of measurement in all measured music. **b** The rise or fall of the hand, baton, foot, etc., in marking such beats. **10.** *Newspapers.* Publication of news before competitors. **11.** *Physics & Radio.* Each of the pulsations of amplitude, recurring at regular intervals, produced by the union of sound or radio waves, or electric currents, having slightly different frequencies. — **beat'er,** *n.*

beat (bēt), *adj.* [Prop. past part.] *Slang.* Exhausted.

beat'en (bēt''n), *adj.* **1.** Made smooth by treading; hence, customary; as, the *beaten* track. **2.** Hammered thin or fine, or into a required shape. **3.** Mixed or lightened by beating; whipped; as, *beaten* biscuit. **4.** Vanquished; baffled; also, exhausted.

beat'er (-ẽr), *n.* **1.** An instrument or device for beating; as, an egg *beater*. **2.** One who beats for game.

be'a·tif'ic (bē'ȧ·tĭf'ĭk), *adj.* Imparting or manifesting bliss or joy.

be·at'i·fi·ca'tion (bē·ăt'ĭ·fĭ·kā'shŭn), *n.* **1.** Act of beatifying; state of being beatified. **2.** *R.C.Ch.* The second stage in canonization, in which a person is declared entitled to public religious honor and to be called *Blessed*. Cf. VENERABLE, 1; CANONIZE, 1.

be·at'i·fy (bē·ăt'ĭ·fī), *v. t.*; -FIED (-fīd); -FY'ING. [L. *beatificare,* fr. *beatus* happy + *facere* to make.] **1.** To make supremely happy. **2.** *R.C.Ch.* To declare the beatification of.

be·at'i·tude (-tūd), *n.* [L. *beatitudo.*] **1.** Consummate bliss; blessedness. **2.** Any of the eight or nine declarations (***the Beatitudes***) made in the Sermon on the Mount (*Matt.* v. 3–12), beginning "Blessed are" (as, "Blessed are the poor in spirit").

Be'a·trice (bē'ȧ·trĭs), *n.* [L. *beatrix* she that makes happy.] **1.** (bē'ȧ·trĭs; *It.* bā·ä·trē'chā) A Florentine lady immortalized by Dante in his *New Life* and his *Divine Comedy*. **2.** See BENEDICK, 1.

beau (bō), *n.*; *pl.* BEAUX (bōz; *F.* bō), BEAUS (bōz). [F., a fop, fr. *beau* fine, beautiful, fr. L. *bellus* pretty, fine.] **1.** A man of fashion; dandy. **2.** A suitor or lover; admirer; escort. — **beau'ish,** *adj.*

Beau Brum'mell (bō' brŭm'ĕl). A dandy; — after George Bryan Brummell, an intimate of George IV and leader of fashion.

Beau'fort's scale (bō'fẽrts). A scale devised by Sir Francis Beaufort, R.N., in 1805, in which the strength of the wind is indicated by numbers from 0 to 12. See *Illust.*, below.

Beaufort number	Name	Miles per hour	Map symbol	Description
0	Calm	Less than 1	o	Calm; smoke rises vertically
1	Light	1-3		Direction of wind shown by smoke but not by wind vanes
2	Light	4-7		Wind felt on face; leaves rustle; ordinary vane moved by wind
3	Gentle	8-12		Leaves and small twigs in constant motion; wind extends light flag
4	Moderate	13-18		Raises dust and loose paper; small branches are moved
5	Fresh	19-24		Small trees in leaf begin to sway; crested wavelets form on inland waters
6	Strong	25-31		Large branches in motion; telegraph wires whistle; umbrellas used with difficulty
7	Strong	32-38		Whole trees in motion; inconvenience felt in walking against wind
8	Gale	39-46		Breaks twigs off trees; generally impedes progress
9	Gale	47-54		Slight structural damage occurs; chimney pots and slate removed
10	Whole Gale	55-63		Trees uprooted; considerable structural damage occurs
11	Whole Gale	64-75		Very rarely experienced; accompanied by widespread damage
12	Hurricane	Above 75		Devastation occurs

‖**beau geste** (bō′ zhĕst′); *pl.* BEAUX GESTES (bō′ zhĕst′). [F.] Graceful gesture; often, a merely ingratiating act or offer.
beau i·de′al (bō′ ī·dē′ăl); *pl.* BEAUX, or BEAUS, IDEAL (bōz). [F. *le beau* the beautiful, beauty + *idéal* ideal.] **1.** Ideal beauty. **2.** The beautiful model; the perfect type; — from an incorrect translation.
beau monde (bō′ mŏnd′; *F.* môNd′). [F.] The world of fashion.
beau′te·ous (bū′tē·ŭs; 58), *adj.* Beautiful, esp. sensuously beautiful. — **beau′te·ous·ly**, *adv.* — **beau′te·ous·ness**, *n.*
beau·ti′cian (bū·tĭsh′ăn), *n.* One whose business is to take care of and beautify clients' hair, hands, or complexion.
beau′ti·ful (bū′tĭ·fo͝ol; -f'l), *adj.* Having the qualities which constitute beauty; full of beauty; exciting sensuous or aesthetic pleasure. — **beau′ti·ful·ly**, *adv.* — **beau′ti·ful·ness**, *n.*
Syn. **Beautiful, lovely, handsome, pretty, bonny, comely, fair** mean pleasing one sensuously or aesthetically. **Beautiful** is applied only to that which excites the keenest of pleasure, not only to the senses but to the mind and soul; **lovely** also suggests more than sensuous pleasure, but it usually implies keen emotional delight; **handsome** suggests rather an approval of a person or thing conforming to one's conception of that which is symmetrical, elegant, well-proportioned, or the like; **pretty**, in contrast, applies to that which pleases by its delicacy, grace, charm, or the like; **bonny** implies approbation of a person's or thing's looks but may connote nothing more than healthiness or plumpness; **comely**, in present usage, suggests a measure of good looks or physical attractiveness; **fair** applies to that which gives delight because of the purity, flawlessness, or freshness of its beauty.
beau′ti·fy (-fī), *v. t. & i.*; -FIED (-fīd); -FY′ING. [*beauty* + *-fy.*] To make or become beautiful; to adorn; embellish. — **Syn.** See ADORN. — **beau′ti·fi·ca′tion** (-fĭ·kā′shŭn), *n.* — **beau′ti·fi′er** (-fī′ẽr), *n.*
beau′ty (bū′tĭ), *n.*; *pl.* -TIES (-tĭz). [From OF., fr. L. *bellus* pretty.] **1.** That quality or aggregate of qualities in a thing which gives pleasure to the senses or pleasurably exalts the mind or spirit; physical, moral, or spiritual loveliness. **2.** A beautiful person or thing, esp. a beautiful woman. **3.** A particular grace, ornament, or excellence; anything beautiful; as, the *beauties* of nature.
beauty shop, parlor, *or* **salon.** An establishment, or department in an establishment, where a woman may have her beauty enhanced, as by having her face massaged or her hair waved.
beauty spot. **1.** = PATCH, *n.*, 2. **2.** A nevus or mole.
beaux (bōz; *F.* bō), *n.*, *pl.* of BEAU.
‖**beaux–arts** (bō′-zȧr′), *n. pl.* [F.] The fine arts.
‖**beaux′–es′prits′** (bō′-zĕs′prē′), *n.*, *pl.* of BEL-ESPRIT.
beaux yeux (bō′-zyû′). [F.] Beautiful eyes; hence, attractive looks.
bea′ver (bē′vẽr), *n.* [AS. *beofor.*] **1.** An amphibious rodent (genus *Castor*) having webbed hind feet and a broad, flat tail, noted for building dams to protect its underwater lodges or winter houses. Cf. CASTOR. **2.** The fur of the beaver. **3.** A hat made of this fur or of a fabric imitating it. **4.** A heavy fabric of felted wool or of cotton napped on both sides.
bea′ver, *n.* [OF. *baviere* beaver, orig., a bib, fr. *bave* saliva.] Originally, the piece of armor which protected the lower part of the face; later, the visor. See HELMET, *Illust.*
Beaver State. Oregon; — a nickname.
be·bee′ru (bē·bē′ro͞o), *n.* [Sp. & Pg. *bibiru.*] See GREENHEART.
be′bop′ (bē′bŏp′), *n.* [Vocal imitation of a staccato two-tone phrase distinctive of this music.] Jazz of a style diverging away from hot jazz and four-to-the-bar rhythm and characterized by flatted fifths, descending sequences of minor sevenths, added and unfamiliar chords, and by the upbeat accent, octave jumps, free use of double time, grace notes, and passing notes. — **be′bop′per** (-bŏp′ẽr), *n.*
be·calm′ (bē·käm′), *v. t.* **1.** To calm. **2.** *Naut.* To hold (a ship) motionless for lack of wind.
be·came′ (bē·kām′), *past* of BECOME.
be·cause′ (bē·kôz′; -kŏz′), *conj.* [ME., fr. *by* + *cause.*] By or for the cause that; for the reason that; since.
because of. By reason of; on account of.
bec′ca·fi′co (bĕk′ȧ·fē′kō), *n.*; *pl.* -COS (-kōz). [It., fr. *beccare* to peck + *fico* fig.] Any small migrant warbler netted in Italy for food.
bé′cha·mel′ sauce (bā′shȧ′mĕl′). [F., after Louis de *Béchamel*, steward of Louis XIV.] A rich white sauce of butter, flour, stock, seasoning, and, usually, cream.
be·chance′ (bē·chȧns′; 9), *v. i. & t.*; -CHANCED′ (-chȧnst′); -CHANC′ING (-chȧn′sĭng). To befall; to chance.
be·charm′ (bē·chärm′), *v. t.* To put under a charm.
‖**bêche–de–mer** (bâsh′dē·mâr′), *n.* [F., lit., caterpillar of the sea.] **1.** A trepang. **2.** A lingua franca, chiefly English, used by Europeans and natives of the western Pacific. Cf. CHINOOK, PIDGIN.
Bech′u·a′na (bĕch′o͞o·ä′nȧ), *n.*; *pl.* -ANA, -ANAS (-nȧz). A member of one of the Bantu tribes dwelling between the Orange and Zambezi rivers, Africa.
beck (bĕk), *n.* [ON. *bekkr.*] *Eng.* A brook.
beck, *n.* **1.** A beckoning gesture; hence, bidding; as, to be at one's *beck* and call. **2.** *Chiefly Scot.* Bow; curtsy. — *v. i. & t. Archaic.* To beckon; to make a beck.
beck′et (bĕk′ĕt; -ĭt), *n.* *Naut.* A device for holding something in place, such as a bracket or a pocket; esp., a grommet or a loop of rope with a knot at one end to catch in an eye at the other.
becket bend. *Naut.* A sheet bend. See KNOT, *Illust.* (34).
beck′on (bĕk′ŭn), *v. i. & t.* [AS. *bȳcnian, bēacnian*, fr. *bēacen* a sign.] To summon or signal by a gesture, as by a nod or a motion of the finger; hence, to invite or lure with silent force. — *n.* A beckoning gesture. — **beck′on·er**, *n.* — **beck′on·ing·ly**, *adv.*
be·cloud′ (bē·kloud′), *v. t.* To obscure, as with clouds.
be·come′ (bē·kŭm′), *v. i.*; BE·CAME′; BE·COME′; BE·COM′ING. [AS. *becuman* to come to, to happen.] **1.** To happen. **2.** To come to be; as, a caterpillar *becomes* a butterfly. **3.** *Chiefly Philos.* To undergo change or development. — *v. t.* To suit or be suitable to; to accord with the character, appearance, nature, etc., of; as, gay clothes *become* her. — ***become of.*** To be the state or place of; to be the fate of.
be·com′ing (bē·kŭm′ĭng), *adj.* Appropriate; suitable; as, *becoming* words; befitting one's style, coloring, etc.; as, a *becoming* dress. — **be·com′ing·ly**, *adv.* — **be·com′ing·ness**, *n.*
Becque·rel′ rays (bĕk·rĕl′; *F.* bĕ′krĕl′). [After A. H. *Becquerel*, Fr. physicist.] The rays emitted by a radioactive substance.
bed (bĕd), *n.* [AS. *bed, bedd.*] **1.** An article of furniture to sleep or take rest in or on, usually a bedstead with springs, mattress, and bedding; specif.: **a** The mattress or flat sack filled with some soft material; as, a feather *bed.* **b** A bedstead; as, an iron *bed.* **2.** Any sleeping or resting place; as, to make a *bed* on the floor. **3.** Marriage bed; hence, conjugal relations. **4.** A plat or level piece of ground prepared for plants. **5.** A surface serving as a base; as: **a** The bottom of any body of water. **b** The superficial earthwork, or ballast, of a railroad. **c** A foundation for a machine, or a rigid support to which the working parts are usually secured. **d** *Masonry.* (1) The place or material in which a block or brick is laid. (2) The lower surface of a brick or tile; also, the upper or lower surface of a stove in position. **6.** A mass or heap suggestive of a bed; as, a *bed* of ashes; also, a layer or stratum; as, a *bed* of sandstone.
☞ COMBINATIONS and PHRASES are:

bedchamber	bedmaker	bedsock
bedcover	bedmaking	bedspread
bedfellow	bedmate	bedspring
bedframe	bed pad	bedstand
bed lamp	bedpost	bedtick
bed light	bedquilt	bedtime
bed linen	bedroom	bed warmer

— *v. t.*; BED′DED; BED′DING. **1.** To put to bed; to lodge for the night. **2.** To cohabit with. **3.** To furnish with a bed or bedding. **4.** To plant or arrange in beds. **5.** To fix in a foundation or matrix; to embed; as, *bedded* on rock. **6.** To lay flat, in order, or in layers or strata. **7.** To make a bed in or for; as, to *bed* up soil for cotton. — *v. i.* **1.** To go to bed. **2.** To form a bed, a bedlike layer, etc.
be·daub′ (bē·dôb′), *v. t.* **1.** To daub over; to besmear. **2.** To overload with ornament, flattery, etc.
bed′bug′ (bĕd′bŭg′), *n.* A wingless bloodsucking hemipterous insect (*Cimex lectularius*), sometimes infesting houses and esp. beds.

Bedbug. Enlarged.

bed′clothes′ (-klōthz′; *colloq.* -klōz′), *n. pl.* Blankets, sheets, coverlets, etc., for a bed.
bed′der (bĕd′ẽr), *n.* **1.** A bedmaker. **2.** A bedding plant.
bed′ding (-ĭng), *n.* **1.** Materials for a bed, such as a mattress and its bedclothes; also, litter, such as straw and hay. **2.** Material in which something is embedded. **3.** *Geol.* Stratification. — *adj.* Suitable for garden beds, esp. decorative beds; as, *bedding* plants.
bede (bēd). Var. of BEAD, prayer; — obs. except in combinations, as **bede′house′, bedes′man.**
be·deck′ (bē·dĕk′), *v. t.* To deck out; to adorn; to grace.
be·del′, be·dell′ (bē·dĕl′). Vars. of BEADLE.
be·dev′il (bē·dĕv′'l), *v. t.*; -ILED or -ILLED (-'ld); -IL·ING or -IL·LING. **1.** To control by or as by a devil; to bewitch. **2.** To confuse utterly; to bemuddle. **3.** To drive to distraction; to torment. **4.** To change so as to spoil; to corrupt. — **be·dev′il·ment**, *n.*
Bed′ford cord (bĕd′fẽrd). A fabric with heavy lengthwise ribs.
be·dight′ (bē·dīt′), *v. t.*; *past & past part.* BE·DIGHT′. *Archaic.* To deck out; array; equip; adorn.
Bed′i·vere′ (bĕd′ĭ·vēr′), **Sir.** A knight of the Round Table, who witnessed the departure of the dying Arthur for the vale of Avalon.
be·diz′en (bē·dĭz′'n; -dī′z'n), *v. t.* To dress out, esp. tawdrily or with vulgar finery. — **be·diz′en·ment**, *n.*
bed′lam (bĕd′lăm), *n.* [ME. *Bedlem, Bethlem*, Bethlehem.] **1.** [*cap.*] The hospital of St. Mary of Bethlehem in London, long used as a hospital for lunatics. **2.** A lunatic. **3.** A lunatic asylum. **4.** Any place or scene of wild uproar and confusion. — *adj.* Of or characteristic of a madhouse. — **bed′lam·ize** (-īz), *v. t.*
bed′lam·ite (-īt), *n.* Inmate of a madhouse; a lunatic.
Bed′ling·ton ter′ri·er (bĕd′lĭng·tŭn). [From *Bedlington*, Northumberland, Eng.] A swift, game, rough-coated terrier weighing about 22–24 pounds.
bed molding. *Arch.* The molding of a cornice immediately below the corona and above the frieze; also, any molding below a deep projection. Cf. ORDER, *Illust.*
Bed′ou·in (bĕd′o͝o·ĭn; -ēn), *n.* [F. *bédouin*, fr. Ar. *badāwi*, pl. of *badawi, badwi*, dweller in the desert.] **1.** A nomadic Arab of the Arabian, Syrian, or North African deserts. **2.** A nomad. — *adj.* Pertaining to the Bedouins; nomad. — **Bed′ou·in·ism** (-ĭz'm), *n.*
bed′pan′ (bĕd′păn′), *n.* **1.** A pan for warming beds. **2.** A shallow chamber pot used by a sick person in bed.
bed′plate′ (-plāt′), *n.* A plate or framing used as a bed or support for something, as the foundation framing or plate of a machine or an iron plate forming a bottom for a furnace.
be·drag′gle (bē·drăg′'l), *v. t.*; see DRAGGLE. To draggle.
bed′rid′ (bĕd′rĭd′), **bed′rid′den** (-'n), *adj.* [AS. *bedreda, bedrida*, fr. *bed, bedd*, bed + *rida* a rider.] **1.** Confined to bed by sickness or infirmity. **2.** Worn out; decrepit.
bed′rock′ (bĕd′rŏk′), *n.* **1.** The solid rock underlying superficial formations. **2.** A solid foundation. **3.** Lowest level; bottom.
bed′roll′ (-rōl′), *n.* Bedding rolled up for carrying.
bed′room′ (-ro͞om′; 85), *n.* A room furnished with a bed and intended primarily to be slept in.
bed′side′ (-sīd′), *n.* Place beside the bed, esp. of a sick or dying person. — **bed′side′**, *adj.*
bed′sore′ (bĕd′sōr′; 70), *n.* A sore due to pressure against the bed, esp. common in wasting diseases.
bed′stead (bĕd′stĕd; -stĭd), *n.* A framework of a bed.
bed′straw′ (-strô′), *n.* An herb (genus *Galium*) having angled stems, opposite or whorled leaves, and small flowers, once used as straw for beds.
bed′ward (-wẽrd), **bed′wards** (-wẽrdz), *adv.* Toward bed.
bee (bē), *n.* [AS. *bēo.*] **1.** Originally, the honey-producing insect *Apis mellifera* (see HONEYBEE); now, broadly, any of numerous membranous-winged, pollen-gathering insects (superfamily Apoidea), differing from the closely related wasps in their more heavily built, hairy bodies and sucking (as well as biting) mouth parts. See HYMENOPTERON, *Illust.* Most bees, as the *honeybee* and *bumblebee*, live in highly organized colonies and are called ***social bees***; but some, as the *carpenter bee*, do not live in colonies and are called ***solitary bees.*** **2.** A fixed or fantastic notion; — esp. in phrase ***a bee in one's bonnet.*** **3.** *Orig. U. S.* A neighborly gathering for work or competition; as, a quilting *bee*; a spelling *bee.*
bee (bē), *n.* Also **bee block.** [AS. *bēah* ring.] A piece of hardwood bolted to the side of the bowsprit, sometimes having metal sheaves for reeving the fore-topmast stays.
bee balm. See BALM, *n.*, 4.

bee beetle. A beetle (*Trichodes apiarius*) infesting hives.
bee′bread′ (bē′brĕd′), *n.* A yellowish-brown bitter substance consisting of pollen, stored up in honeycomb cells and used, mixed with honey, by the bees as food.
beech (bēch), *n.; pl.* BEECHES (-ĕz; -ĭz). [AS. *bēce.*] **a** A hardwood timber tree (genus *Fagus*) typifying a family (Fagaceae, the beech family), including the oak and the chestnut. The beech has smooth gray bark, typically deep-green foliage, and an edible nut (**beech′nut′**). **b** The wood of this tree. — **beech′en,** *adj.*
beech′drops′ (-drŏps′), *n.* **a** A low wiry plant (*Epiphegus virginiana*), parasitic on beech roots. **b** The squawroot (*Conopholis americana*).
bee eater. Any of a family (Meropidae) of brightly colored, slender-billed, insectivorous birds.
beef (bēf), *n.* [OF. *boef, buef,* fr. L. *bos, bovis,* ox.] **1.** *pl.* BEEVES (bēvz), or, *esp. in U. S.,* BEEFS. An ox, cow, or bull, in a full-grown or nearly full-grown state; esp., an ox (steer) or cow fattened for food. **2.** The flesh of an ox or cow. **3.** *Colloq.* Human flesh; brawn. — *v. i. Slang.* To complain.
beef′eat′er (-ēt′ẽr), *n.* **1.** One who eats beef. **2.** One of the yeomen of the royal guard, in England.
bee fly. Any of numerous flies (family Bombyliidae), many of which resemble bees.
beef′steak′ (bēf′stāk′), *n.* A cut of beef, esp. from the hindquarter, for broiling or frying.
beef′-wit′ted (-wĭt′ĕd; -ĭd; 2), *adj.* Stupid.
beef′y (bēf′ĭ), *adj.;* -I·ER (-ĭ·ẽr); -I·EST. Having much beef; fleshy; brawny; stolid. — **beef′i·ness,** *n.*
bee gum. *U. S.* A hollow gum tree in which wild bees hive or from which hives are made; hence, a beehive. Cf. GUM, *n.,* 6.
bee′hive′ (bē′hīv′), *n.* A hive for bees. See HIVE, *Illust.* — *adj.* Shaped like a beehive; as, a *beehive* (coke) oven.
Beehive State. Utah; — a nickname alluding to the device on the state seal.
beek (bēk), *v. t. & i. Scot.* To warm; bask; also, to shine brightly. — *n. Scot.* A basking.
bee′keep′ing (bē′kēp′ĭng), *n.* The process or art of raising bees; apiculture. — **bee′keep′er** (-ẽr), *n.*
bee′line′ (bē′līn′), *n.* The shortest line to a place, as that pursued by a bee laden with honey to its hive.
Be·el′ze·bub (bē·ĕl′zē·bŭb), *n.* [L., fr. Gr. *Beelzeboub,* fr. Heb. *Ba'al zĕbūb* Lord of Flies.] **1.** The prince of demons; the Devil. **2.** A leading devil. **3.** In Milton's *Paradise Lost,* the fallen angel ranking just below Satan.
bee martin. The kingbird, which occasionally eats bees.
been (bĭn *or, esp. Brit.,* bēn), *past part.* of BE.
bee plant. Any plant much frequented by bees for nectar; specif.: **a** A heavy-scented herb (*Cleome serrulata*) with pink flowers. **b** Any figwort (genus *Scrophularia*).

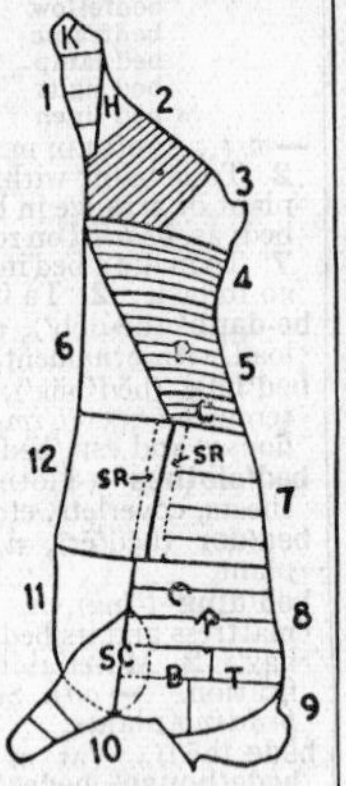

Beef Cuts.
1 Hind Shank (*K* Knuckle).
2 Round (*H* Heel of Round).
3 Rump.
4 Loin End (Sirloin Steaks).
5 Short Loin (*C* Club Steaks, *P* Porterhouse Steaks).
6 Flank.
7 Rib (*SR* Short Ribs).
8 Chuck (*B* Bottom Chuck, *CR* Chuck Rib, and *T* Top Chuck Roasts).
9 Neck.
10 Foreshank (*SC* Shoulder Clod).
11 Brisket.
12 Plate (*SR* Short Ribs).

beer (bēr), *n.* [AS. *bēor.*] **1.** A fermented liquor brewed, esp. by slow fermentation, from malt or from a mixture of malt and malt substitutes and flavored with hops or other bitter. **2.** Any of various fermented but undistilled liquors; as, spruce *beer.* **3.** *U. S.* Any of certain nonalcoholic carbonated drinks; as, root *beer.*
beer and skittles. Drink and play; easygoing enjoyment.
beer′y (bēr′ĭ), *adj.;* -I·ER (-ĭ·ẽr); -I·EST. Of, like, affected by, or caused by beer. — **beer′i·ness,** *n.*
beest′ings, biest′ings (bēs′tĭngz), *n. pl.* [AS. *bȳsting.*] The first milk given by a cow after calving.
bees′wax′ (bēz′wăks′), *n.* The wax secreted by bees for making the honeycomb. — *v. t. & i.* To wax with beeswax.
bees′wing′ (-wĭng′), *n.* A film of tartar scales formed in port and some other wines after long keeping.
beet (bēt), *n.* [AS. *bēte,* fr. L. *beta.*] **1.** A biennial plant (genus *Beta,* of the goosefoot family) with oval stalked leaves and juicy root, cultivated as a garden vegetable (with red root) or as a source of sugar (the ***sugar beet,*** with white root), or for forage (the mangel-wurzel). **2.** Its edible root (called by the British **beet′root′**) or its young leaves cooked for food (called fully **beet greens**). Cf. CHARD.
beet, beete (bēt), *v. t.* [AS. *bētan.*] *Dial.* To mend; also, to kindle or renew (a fire).
bee′tle (bē′t'l), *n.* [AS. *bētel, bītel,* mallet.] **1.** A heavy hammering or ramming instrument, usually with a wooden head. **2.** A wooden pestle, bat, or masher, in domestic use. **3.** A machine in which fabrics are finished by being hammered over rollers. — *v. t.;* BEE′TLED (-t'ld); BEE′TLING (-tlĭng). To beat, drive, ram, or finish with a beetle. — **bee′tler** (-tlẽr), *n.*
bee′tle, *n.* [AS. *bitula,* fr. *bītan* to bite.] **1.** Any coleopterous insect having four wings, the outer pair (elytra) being stiff cases which cover the others when they are folded. **2.** Popularly, any of various insects, as a cockroach, more or less resembling a true beetle.

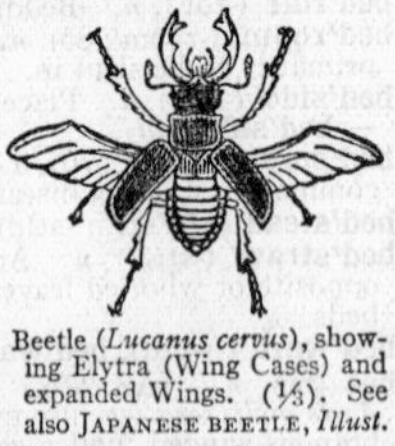

Beetle (*Lucanus cervus*), showing Elytra (Wing Cases) and expanded Wings. (⅓). See also JAPANESE BEETLE, *Illust.*

bee′tle, *adj.* Projecting; lowering; as, *beetle* brows. — *v. i.* To jut.
beet leafhopper. A leafhopper (*Eutettix tenellus*) that transmits a serious virus disease to sugar beets and other plants in the western U. S.
bee′tle-browed′ (-broud′), *adj.* [ME. *bitelbrowed.*] Having overhanging eyebrows; hence, scowling; lowering.
bee′tle·head′ (-hĕd′), *n.* [*beetle* a mallet + *head.*] A stupid fellow.
bee tree. **1.** A hollow tree in which bees nest. **2.** The basswood (genus *Tilia*), whose flowers are rich in nectar.
beet′root′ (bēt′rōōt′), *n.* See BEET, 2.
beet sugar. Sugar made from beets. See BEET, 1; SUGAR, 1.
beeves (bēvz), *n., pl.* of BEEF.
bee wolf. The larva of the bee beetle.
be·fall′ (bē·fôl′), *v. i. & t.;* see FALL. [AS. *befeallan,* fr. *be-* + *feallan* to fall.] To come to pass; to happen (to).
be·fit′ (bē·fĭt′), *v. t.;* see FIT. To be suitable to; to suit; become. — **be·fit′ting,** *adj.* — **be·fit′ting·ly,** *adv.*
be·fog′ (bē·fŏg′), *v. t.;* see FOG. To make foggy; to obscure.
be·fool′ (bē·fōōl′), *v. t.* **1.** To delude or lead into error; to deceive. **2.** To treat as a fool; to call (one) fool.
be·fore′ (bē·fōr′; 70), *adv.* [AS. *beforan,* fr. *be-* + *foran* before.] **1.** In front; on the front side; as, to go on *before.* **2.** In time past; previously; as, it never happened *before.* **3.** Earlier; sooner; as, come at six, not *before.* — *prep.* **1.** In front of; ahead of; also, forward of, as in *before the mast* (see under MAST). **2.** Preceding in time; as, the centuries *before* Christ. **3.** In the future of; in store for; as, success is *before* him. **4.** Preceding in order, rank, right, or worth; as, put safety *before* all else. **5.** In presence or sight of; face to face with; as, to stand *before* the judge. **6.** Under the cognizance or jurisdiction of; as, the case *before* the court. — *conj.* **1.** Previous to the time when; as, look *before* you leap. **2.** Sooner than; rather than; as, he will starve *before* he will steal.
be·fore′hand′ (-hănd′), *adv.* In advance, as by way of forethought; as, to arrive *beforehand.* — *adj. Archaic.* Forehanded.
be·fore′time′ (-tīm′), *adv.* Formerly; aforetime.
be·foul′ (bē·foul′), *v. t.* To make foul; to soil.
be·friend′ (bē·frĕnd′), *v. t.* To act as a friend to; to aid.
be·fud′dle (bē·fŭd′'l), *v. t.;* see FUDDLE. To confuse, as with liquor; to muddle.
beg (bĕg), *v. t.;* BEGGED (bĕgd); BEG′GING. [AF. *begger,* fr. OF. *begard* mendicant.] **1.** To ask for as a charity, esp. habitually or from house to house. **2.** To ask earnestly for or of; to beseech; as, to *beg* a favor; to *beg* a person to grant a favor. **3.** To assume without proof; as, to ***beg the question,*** to assume the truth of something in question. — *v. i.* **1.** To ask alms or charity; to live by asking alms. **2.** To make petition; to make an earnest or polite request.
Syn. **Beg, entreat, beseech, implore, supplicate, adjure, importune** mean to ask or request urgently. **Beg** suggests earnestness or insistence, especially in asking a favor; **entreat** implies an effort to persuade or overcome resistance in another; **beseech** implies great eagerness and, often, anxiety or solicitude; **implore** adds to *beseech* the suggestion of greater urgency or more manifest anguish; **supplicate,** the suggestion of fervent prayer or of a prayerful attitude; **adjure** implies an injunction as well as a plea, and, in some cases, the invocation of something sacred; **importune** suggests repeated attempts to break down resistance and, often, annoying pertinacity.
be·gan′ (bē·găn′), *past* of BEGIN.
be·get′ (bē·gĕt′), *v. t.; past* -GOT′ (-gŏt′), *Archaic* -GAT′ (-găt′); *past part.* -GOT′TEN (-gŏt′'n), -GOT′; *pres. part.* -GET′TING. [AS. *begitan* to get, fr. *be-* + *gitan* to get.] **1.** To procreate as a sire; generate. **2.** To produce as an effect; to cause. — **be·get′ter,** *n.*
beg′gar (bĕg′ẽr), *n.* **1.** One who begs; esp., one who lives by asking alms; a mendicant. **2.** A pauper. **3.** A rogue; rascal; — often playful; as, a good-hearted little *beggar.* — *v. t.* **1.** To reduce to beggary; impoverish. **2.** To exhaust or exceed the powers of; as, to *beggar* description. — **beg′gar·dom** (-dŭm), *n.* — **beg′gar·hood,** *n.*
beg′gar·ly (-lĭ), *adj.* Like or befitting a beggar; extremely indigent; mean. — **Syn.** See CONTEMPTIBLE. — **beg′gar·li·ness,** *n.*
beg′gar's-lice′, beg′gar-lice′, *n. sing. & pl.* The prickly or adhesive fruits of stickseeds, tick trefoils, and bedstraws; also, any of these plants.
beg′gar-ticks′, beg′gar's-ticks′, *n. sing. & pl.* **1.** The achenes of any bur marigold; also, the plant itself. **2.** Beggar's-lice.
beg′gar·weed′ (bĕg′ẽr·wēd′), *n.* **a** Any of various plants that grow in waste ground, as knotweed and certain dodders, spurries, and tickseeds. **b** A West Indian forage plant (*Desmodium tortuosum*), of the pea family, cultivated in the southern United States.
beg′gar·y (-ĭ), *n.; pl.* -GARIES (-ĭz). **1.** State of being a beggar; penury. **2.** Beggars collectively; also, a resort of beggars.
Beg′hard (bĕg′ẽrd; bē·gärd′), *n.* [ML. *beghardus, begardus,* OF. *begard.*] A member of one of many semimonastic associations of laymen founded in the 13th century in Flanders; a Beguin. Cf. BEGUINE.
be·gin′ (bē·gĭn′), *v. i.;* BE·GAN′ (-găn′); BE·GUN′ (-gŭn′); BE·GIN′NING. [AS. *beginnan.*] **1.** To do the first act or the first part of an action; to take the first step; start. **2.** To come into existence; to originate. **3.** To be or do in the least degree; as, it does not *begin* to meet the specifications. — *v. t.* **1.** To set about; start; commence. **2.** To found, originate, invent, etc.; as, the Phoenicians *began* alphabetic writing. — **be·gin′ner,** *n.*
Syn. **Begin, commence, start, initiate, inaugurate** mean to set something going or in progress. **Begin** and **commence** are practically identical in meaning, but traditional good use supports the choice of *commence* in reference to court proceedings, religious and other ceremonies, military operations, and the like; **start** suggests a setting out from a particular point on a journey, course, etc., often, but not necessarily, after inaction or waiting; **initiate** implies the taking of the first step or steps as in a process and carries no suggestion of an end or ending; **inaugurate** retains from its more common sense of *induct* a hint of a ceremonial beginning, and is often no more than a pretentious term for *begin.* — **Ant.** End.
be·gin′ning (-ĭng), *n.* **1.** The commencement; the start. **2.** A point in space or time at which a thing begins. **3.** One of the earliest acts or products of something which has a history; as, the *beginnings* of English poetry. **4.** The first cause; origin; as, God is the *beginning* of all things.
be·gird′ (bē·gûrd′), *v. t.;* see GIRD. [AS. *begyrdan.*] To bind with a band or girdle; to gird; hence, to encompass.
beg′ohm′ (bĕg′ōm′), *n. Elec.* A unit of resistance equal to one billion ohms, or one thousand megohms.
be·gone′ (bē·gŏn′; 74), *v. i.* Go away; depart; — chiefly imperative.
be·go′ni·a (bē·gō′nĭ·ȧ; -nyȧ), *n.* [NL., after Michel *Bégon,* governor of Santo Domingo.] A tropical flowering plant (genus *Begonia*), typifying a family (Begoniaceae, the begonia family), with unsymmetrical ornamental leaves.
be·got′ (bē·gŏt′), **be·got′ten** (-'n). See BEGET.
be·goud′ (bē·gōōd′; -gŏŏd′), *Scot. past* of BEGIN.
be·grime′ (bē·grīm′), *v. t.* To soil with grime or dirt.
be·grudge′ (bē·grŭj′), *v. t.;* see GRUDGE. **1.** To grumble at; envy the possession of. **2.** To grudge. — **be·grudg′ing·ly,** *adv.*
be·guile′ (bē·gīl′), *v. t.* **1.** To delude by guile or craft; to deceive. **2.**

To deprive by guile; to cheat; — with *of* or *out of*. **3.** To charm; to divert; also, to while away. — **Syn.** See DECEIVE; WHILE. — **be·guile′ment,** *n.* — **be·guil′er** (bē·gīl′ẽr), *n.*
Beg′uin (bĕg′ĭn; *F.* bā′găɴ′), *n.* [F. *béguin.*] A Beghard.
Beg′uine (bĕg′ēn; bā′gēn′), *n.* [F. *béguine*, fr. OF. *begard.*] A member of one of certain religious communities dating from the 13th century, composed of laywomen who do not take vows, and retain property and independence.
be′guine′ (bā′gēn′), *n.* [F. dial., a dance, fr. F. *béguin* flirtation.] A vigorous popular dance of the islands of Saint Lucia and Martinique, which somewhat resembles the rumba.
be′gum (bē′gŭm), *n.* [Hind. *begam.*] **1.** *India.* A Mohammedan lady of high rank, as a princess. **2.** *Eng.* An Anglo-Indian heiress.
be·gun′ (bē·gŭn′), *past part.* of BEGIN.
be·half′ (bē·häf′; -hȧf′; 9), *n.* [ME. *on-behalve* in the name of, fr. AS. *healf* half, side, part.] Side; benefit; interest; support; defense; — in prepositional phrases; as, ***in, or on, behalf of; in, or on, one's behalf.***
be·have′ (bē·hāv′), *v. t.* To conduct, esp. properly; comport; — used reflexively; as, *behave* yourself. — *v. i.* **1.** To act; to conduct oneself or itself; as, to *behave* well or ill; also (without a qualifying word), to act or conduct oneself well or properly; as, you must *behave.* **2.** To act in relation to environment; to react. See BEHAVIOR, 2.
Syn. Behave, conduct, demean, deport, comport, acquit mean, when used reflexively, to cause oneself to act or do something in a given way. **Behave** implies meeting a standard, usually a standard of what is proper or decorous; **conduct** implies action or behavior that shows the extent of one's power to direct or control oneself; **demean** suggests conduct, bearing, attitude, or the like, which answers a given description; **deport** implies behavior that shows how far one conforms to rules of discipline, the proprieties, or the like; **comport** suggests conduct or behavior as measured by what is expected or required of a person in a certain class, position, or the like; **acquit** suggests conduct or action calculated to win approval or disapproval, or to meet expectations.
be·hav′ior, be·hav′iour (bē·hāv′yẽr), *n.* **1.** Mode of conducting oneself; deportment. **2.** The way in which an organism, organ, or substance acts, esp. in response to a stimulus; as, the *behavior* of glands; activity or change in relation to environment; as, the *behavior* of steel under stress.
be·hav′ior·ism (-ĭz′m), *n. Psychol.* The doctrine that psychological theories should be based on the publicly observable data of the actions of organisms and exclude introspective data or references to consciousness and mind. — **be·hav′ior·ist** (-ĭst), *n. & adj.* — **be·hav′ior·is′tic** (-ĭs′tĭk), *adj.*
be·head′ (bē·hĕd′), *v. t.* To sever the head from; decapitate.
be·held′ (bē·hĕld′), *past & past part.* of BEHOLD.
be·he′moth (bē·hē′mŏth; bē′hē·mŏth; -mōth), *n.* [Heb. *behēmōth*, intens. pl. of *behēmāh* beast.] An animal, probably the hippopotamus, described in *Job* xl. 15–24.
be·hest′ (bē·hĕst′), *n.* [AS. *behǣs* promise.] A command; a mandate.
be·hind′ (bē·hīnd′), *adv.* [AS. *behindan*, fr. *be-* + *hindan* hind.] **1.** Back in place or time; as, to stay *behind.* **2.** Not yet brought forward; still to come; as, there is stronger evidence *behind.* **3.** Backward in progress, performance, etc.; behindhand; as, to fall *behind* in school. **4.** Late; slow; as, the clock runs *behind.* **5.** In a backward direction. — *adj.* Following, as in a procession; as, the car *behind.* — *prep.* **1.** In a place, state, or time, gone or departed from by (the one or ones referred to); as, he left nothing *behind* him. **2.** Inferior to, as in dignity, rank, or knowledge. **3.** After in time; later than. **4.** After in place; on or at the back side of; as, to look *behind* the door. **5.** Backing up; supporting; as, his father is *behind* him in this venture. **6.** Not yet disclosed about; still unknown about; as, there is something sinister *behind* this strike.
be·hind′hand′ (-hănd′), *adv. & adj.* Behind, as in progress, in payments, etc.; backward; in arrears.
be·hold′ (bē·hōld′), *v. t.;* BE·HELD′; BE·HELD′, *Archaic* BE·HOLD′EN (-hōl′d′n); BE·HOLD′ING. [AS. *behealdan* to hold, fr. *be-* + *healdan* to hold.] To have or keep in sight; look at; watch; now, usually, to see. — **Syn.** See, view, survey, observe, descry, discern. — *interj.* Look! Lo! — **be·hold′er,** *n.*
be·hold′en (-hōl′d′n), *adj.* Bound in gratitude; indebted.
be·hoof′ (bē·hōōf′), *n.* [ME. *to bihove* for the use of, fr. AS. *behōf* advantage.] Advantage; benefit; interest; use.
be·hoove′ (-hōōv′), **be·hove′** (-hōv′; *form.* -hōōv′), *v. t.* [AS. *behōfian* to have need of. See BEHOOF.] To be necessary for, esp. as a duty or obligation; to be proper for, or incumbent upon; — chiefly in impersonal use; as, it *behooves* you to go. — *v. i.* To be needful or incumbent; — chiefly in impersonal use.
beige (bāzh), *n.* [F.] **1.** A soft woolen dress fabric, orig. of undyed, unbleached wool. **2.** The natural color of unbleached wool or cotton. — *adj.* Of the color beige.
be′ing (bē′ĭng), *n.* **1.** Existence; specif., conscious existence; as, things brought into *being* by generation. **2.** Substance, nature, or essence of anything existent; as, love of life was the core of his *being.* **3.** One that exists; specif.: **a** [*cap.*] God; — with various qualifying adjectives, as *Supreme, Infinite,* etc. **b** A living person. **4.** *Philos.* That which exists as an actuality or entity in time or space, in idea or matter; also, that which is logically conceivable, and hence capable of existence. **5.** The fullness of life or perfection possible to a thing that exists; as, *being* is the end of becoming.
Bel (bāl; bĕl), *n.* [Babylon. *Bel.*] One of the chief gods of ancient Babylonian religion.
bel (bĕl), *n.* [After A. G. *Bell*, inventor of the telephone.] Ten decibels. See DECIBEL.
be·la′bor, be·la′bour (bē·lā′bẽr), *v. t.* **1.** *Obs.* To work carefully at or upon. **2.** To beat soundly; to drub; hence, to assail verbally. — **Syn.** Baste, beat, pummel.
Bel and the Dragon. A book of the Apocrypha. See BIBLE.
be·lat′ed (bē·lāt′ĕd; -ĭd), *adj.* **a** *Archaic.* Overtaken by night or darkness. **b** Delayed beyond the usual time; late. — **be·lat′ed·ly,** *adv.* — **be·lat′ed·ness,** *n.*
be·lay′ (-lā′), *v. t. & i.;* BE·LAYED′ (-lād′); BE·LAY′ING. [Prob. fr. D. *beleggen.*] **1.** *Naut.* To make a turn or turns with (as a rope) round a pin (**be·lay′ing pin**), cleat, etc., in order to hold secure; also, to make fast by so doing; — often used imperatively in **belay that, or belay there,** make fast; hence, *Collog.*, quit; that's enough. **2.** *Mountain Climbing.* To take a secure stance and serve as a belay to (another climber). — *n.* A knob of rock, a bush, or some other object round which a running rope may be passed as a safeguard.

‖**bel can′to** (bĕl kän′tō). [It.] Literally, beautiful song; specif., a style of singing, characterized by virtuosity and beauty of sound, developed in 17th- and 18th-century Italian opera.
belch (bĕlch), *v. i.* [AS. *bealcian.*] **1.** To eject wind or gas spasmodically from the stomach through the mouth; to eruct. **2.** To eject its contents, as a gun. **3.** To issue spasmodically; to gush out, as flames from a volcano. — *v. t.* To eject, esp. violently; to throw up or out; to cast forth; emit spasmodically. — *n.* A belching; that which is belched. — **belch′er,** *n.*
beld (bĕld). Scot. var. of BOLD.
bel′dam, bel′dame (bĕl′dăm), *n.* [From *bel-* (F. *bel, belle,* fair, beautiful) + *dame.*] **1.** A grandmother. **2.** An old woman, esp. one ugly or loathsome; a hag.
be·lea′guer (bē·lē′gẽr), *v. t.* [D. *belegeren*, fr. *be-* (= E. *be-*) + *leger* bed, camp, army.] To blockade by surrounding with an army; to besiege; hence, to encompass.
bel′em·nite (bĕl′ĕm·nīt), *n.* [Gr. *belemnon* dart.] A conical fossil shell of an extinct cephalopod. See THUNDERSTONE.
‖**bel′-es′prit′** (bĕl′ĕs′prē′), *n.; pl.* BEAUX-ESPRITS (bō′-zĕs′prē′). [F.] A person of fine mind and delicate, graceful wit.
bel′fry (bĕl′frĭ), *n.; pl.* -FRIES (-frĭz). [OF. *berfrei, berfroi,* fr. OHG. *bergfrid*, lit., guard peace.] **1.** A tower; esp., the separate or attached bell tower of a church or other building; a campanile. **2.** A room in a tower for a bell; also, a cupola, turret, or the like, used for the same purpose. — **bel′fried** (-frĭd), *adj.*
bel′ga (bĕl′gȧ), *n.* Formerly, from 1926 to end of World War II, a monetary unit of Belgium established for use in foreign exchange.
Bel′gae (bĕl′jē), *n. pl.* [L.] A people who, in Caesar's time, occupied northern France and Belgium.
Bel′gian (bĕl′jăn; -jĭ·ăn), *n.* **1.** A native or inhabitant of Belgium. Cf. FLEMING, WALLOON. **2.** A breed of strong, heavy draft horses, usually roan or chestnut, originating in Belgium. — **Bel′gian,** *adj.*
Belgian hare. One of a breed of small, dark-red rabbits.
Bel′gic (bĕl′jĭk), *adj.* Of or pert. to the Belgae or the Netherlands or Belgium.
Bel·gra′vi·a (bĕl·grā′vĭ·ȧ; 58), *n.* A fashionable residence district in the West End of London; hence, aristocratic society. — **Bel·gra′vi·an** (-ăn), *adj. & n.*
Be′li·al (bē′lĭ·ăl; bēl′yăl), *n.* [Heb. *belīya'al* without use or profit.] **1.** A word in the Scriptures and in rabbinical and Apocryphal literature, commonly taken as meaning "worthlessness," or "destruction." In the New Testament the name became identified with *Satan.* **2.** In Milton's *Paradise Lost*, one of the fallen angels.
be·lie′ (bē·lī′), *v. t.;* see LIE. [AS. *belēogan.*] **1.** To tell lies about; to calumniate. **2.** To misrepresent; as, his words *belie* his true feelings. **3.** To be false or unfaithful to; as, to *belie* one's principles; also, to prove to be false; as, his acts *belie* his professions. — **be·li′er** (-lī′ẽr), *n.*
be·lief′ (bē·lēf′), *n.* [AS. *gelēafa*, or fr. a lost n. in *be-.*] **1.** The state or habit of mind of one who believes; faith; confidence; trust; as, to be without *belief* in God. **2.** A conviction or persuasion of truth; intellectual assent; as, claims unworthy of *belief.* **3.** The thing believed; specif., a tenet, or the body of tenets; doctrine; creed. **4.** *Eccl.* A statement of beliefs; a creed; specif. [*cap.*], the Apostles' Creed.
Syn. (1) **Belief, faith, credence, credit** mean the act or mental state of one who assents to something proposed for acceptance. **Belief** and **faith,** though often used interchangeably, are not quite parallel, for *belief* may or may not imply certitude in the one who assents and *faith,* in its older religious and Scriptural sense, always does even when there is no evidence or proof. In current use, *faith* often suggests credulity and overreadiness to accept. **Credence** stresses assent without implying, apart from the context, weak or strong grounds for belief or credulity or its absence; **credit** implies assent on other grounds than direct proof, usually that of a reputation for truth in the one who proposes something for acceptance.
(2) See OPINION.
be·lieve′ (bē·lēv′), *v. i.* [AS. *belēfan, belīfan.*] **1.** To have faith or confidence; — usually with *in* or *on*; as, to *believe* in a person. **2.** To have convictions, esp. religious convictions. **3.** To think; to judge; as, to *believe* meanly of one's neighbor. — *v. t.* To accept as true; also, to have as one's convictions or opinion. — **be·liev′a·ble,** *adj.* — **be·liev′er,** *n.* — **be·liev′ing·ly,** *adv.*
be·like′ (bē·līk′), *adv. Archaic.* Probably; perhaps.
be·lit′tle (bē·lĭt′'l), *v. t.;* -LIT′TLED (-'ld); -LIT′TLING (-lĭng). To make seem little or less; to depreciate; minimize. — **Syn.** See DECRY.
be·live′ (bē·līv′), *adv. Scot.* Forthwith; quickly; soon.
bell (bĕl), *n.* [AS. *belle.*] **1.** A hollow metallic vessel, typically shaped like an inverted cup with flaring mouth, that vibrates and gives forth a ringing sound when struck. **2.** Specif.: **a** A bell, as of a clock, rung to tell the hours; also (usually in *pl.*), the stroke of such a bell, esp. on shipboard. **b** The time so indicated; on shipboard, a half hour: 4, 8, and 12 o'clock are marked by 8 bells; 4.30, 8.30 and 12.30 o'clock by 1 bell; and so on until 8 bells. **3.** Anything in the form of a bell; as: **a** The corolla of a flower. **b** The flaring mouth of a trumpet or other wind instrument. — *v. t.* **1.** To provide with a bell. **2.** To make bell-mouthed, or flaring. — *v. i.* To take the form of a bell; to flare. — ***bell the cat.*** To do a daring or risky deed; — from the fable of the mice who resolved to hang a bell upon the cat's neck, but found none bold enough to do it.

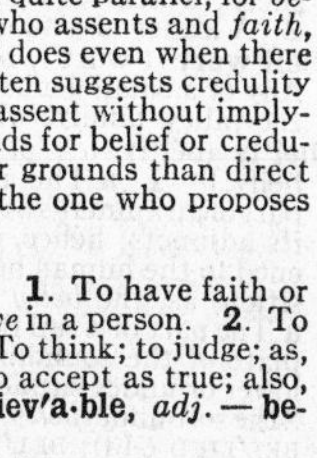

Bell (cross section). *B* Clapper or Tongue; *C* Cannon; *D* Yoke; *M* Mouth; *P* Sound bow; *S* Shoulder; *T* Barrel.

bell, *v. i. & t.* [AS. *bellan.*] To bellow, as deer in rutting time. — *n.* A bellow; a booming sound, as that of the bittern.
bel′la·don′na (bĕl′ȧ·dŏn′ȧ), *n.* [It., lit., fine lady.] **1.** A European poisonous plant (*Atropa belladonna*), of the nightshade family, having reddish bell-shaped flowers and shining black berries; the deadly nightshade. The root and leaves are used in medicine as a narcotic and anodyne, and as a powerful mydriatic. **2.** The belladonna lily.
belladonna lily. A South African bulbous plant (*Amaryllis belladonna*) or its rose-colored lilylike flower.
bell′bird′ (bĕl′bûrd′), *n.* Any of several birds whose notes are likened to the sound of a bell, as (*Local, U. S.*) the wood thrush.
bell′boy′ (-boi′), *n.* A hotel or club employee who answers calls for service by bell or telephone.
bell buoy. See BUOY, 1.
belle (bĕl), *n.* [F., fem. of *bel, beau.* See BEAU.] A beautiful, charming, and much-admired young woman.

Bel·leek′ ware (bĕ·lēk′), *or* **Bel·leek′**, *n.* [From *Belleek*, N. Ireland.] A porcelainlike kind of decorative pottery with a high gloss, which is sometimes iridescent.

Bel·ler′o·phon (bĕ·lĕr′ō·fŏn; -fŭn), *n.* A mythological Corinthian hero who slew the Chimera with the aid of Pegasus.

belles′-let′tres (bĕl′lĕt′r′), *n. pl.* [F.] Literature of aesthetic as distinguished from informational or utilitarian value; esp., poetry, literary essays, drama, and fiction. — **bel′le·tris′tic** (bĕl′lĕ·trĭs′tĭk), *adj.*

bell′flow′er (bĕl′flou′ẽr), *n.* Any of a genus (*Campanula*) typifying a family (Campanulaceae, the bellflower family), having an acrid juice, alternate leaves, and rather showy regular flowers; a campanula.

bell′hop′ (-hŏp′), *n.* *Slang, U. S.* A bellboy.

bel′li·cose (bĕl′ĭ·kōs; bĕl′ĭ·kōs′), *adj.* [L. *bellicosus*, fr. *bellicus* of war, fr. *bellum* war.] Inclined to contention; warlike. — **Syn.** See BELLIGERENT. — **bel′li·cose·ly**, *adv.* — **bel′li·cos′i·ty** (-kŏs′ĭ·tĭ), *n.*

bel·lig′er·ence (bĕ·lĭj′ẽr·ĕns), *n.* Quality of being belligerent; act of waging war.

bel·lig′er·en·cy (-ĕn·sĭ), *n.* The status of a belligerent; warfare between belligerent powers.

bel·lig′er·ent (-ĕnt), *adj.* [L. *belligerans*, pres. part. of *belligerare* to wage war, deriv. of *bellum* war + *gerere* to wage.] **1.** Waging war; also, of or relating to fighting nations or persons. **2.** Tending to war; intent on or provoking conflict; also, openly hostile in tone.

Syn. **Belligerent, bellicose, pugnacious, quarrelsome, contentious, litigious** mean having or taking an aggressive attitude. **Belligerent** usually implies engagement in actual hostility, or an actively hostile mood or temper; **bellicose**, more often applied to a state of mind or temper, suggests a disposition or readiness to fight or stir up a fight; **pugnacious** applies especially to disposition or character, but it does not suggest a readiness to fight without good cause so evident in **quarrelsome; contentious** implies perversity of temper and persistence in dispute; **litigious** implies a fondness for legal contention.

— *n.* A belligerent nation or person. — **bel·lig′er·ent·ly**, *adv.*

bell jar. A type of glass vessel open at the bottom and closed at the top like a bell.

bell′man (bĕl′măn), *n.* A bell ringer, as a town crier.

bell metal. A variety of bronze, consisting usually of three to four parts of copper to one of tin, used for making bells.

bell′mouthed′ (-mouth̶d′; -moutht′), *adj.* Having a flaring mouth.

Bel·lo′na (bĕ·lō′nȧ), *n.* [L., fr. *bellum* war.] Roman goddess of war.

bel′low (bĕl′ō), *v. i.* [AS. *bylgan*.] **1.** To make a hollow loud noise or roar like that of a bull. **2.** To bawl; to clamor. — *v. t.* To emit with such a sound; — with *out* or *forth*. — *n.* A bellowing sound. — **bel′low·er** (-ō·ẽr), *n.*

bel′lows (bĕl′ōz; -ŭs), *n. sing. & pl.* [AS. *belg, belig*, bag, bellows, belly. *Bellows* is prop. a pl. and the orig. sense is bag.] **1.** An instrument, utensil, or machine which by alternate expansion and contraction draws in air through a valve or orifice and expels it through a tube, for various purposes, as blowing fires, ventilating mines, or filling the pipes of an organ with wind. **2.** The lungs. **3.** The expansible part of a photographic camera. See KODAK, *Illust.*

Hand Bellows.

bell′weth′er (bĕl′wĕth̶′ẽr), *n.* **1.** A wether, or male sheep, which leads the flock, with a bell on its neck. **2.** A leader of a thoughtless crowd.

bell′wort′ (-wûrt′), *n.* *Bot.* **a** A bellflower. **b** *U. S.* Any of a small genus (*Uvularia*) of herbs of the lily-of-the-valley family, with yellow, drooping, bell-shaped flowers.

bel′ly (bĕl′ĭ), *n.; pl.* BELLIES (-ĭz). [AS. *belg, belig*, bag, bellows, belly.] **1. a** The abdomen or the abdominal cavity. **b** The under part of an animal's body. **2.** The womb; uterus. **3.** The stomach and its adjuncts; hence, appetite for food. **4.** The part of anything likened to the human belly, as in protuberance, hollowness, or central position; as, the *belly* of a flask; the *belly* of a curved timber; specif.: **a** The part of a sail that swells out when filled with wind. **b** The upper plate of the sounding box of instruments of the violin class. **5.** A lower or under surface, as opposed to the upper surface or the back; as, "the soft under*belly* of Europe" (*Winston S. Churchill*). — *v. t. & i.;* BEL′LIED (-ĭd); BEL′LY·ING. To swell or bulge out.

bel′ly·band′ (-bănd′), *n.* A band that passes around or across the belly, as under a horse's belly to hold the shafts. See HARNESS, *Illust.*

bel′ly·land′ (-lănd′), *v. i.* To land an airplane without use of landing gear, that is, on the underside of the fuselage.

be·long′ (bē·lŏng′; 74), *v. i.* [*be-* + ME. *longen* to belong.] Usually construed with *to*. **1.** To be connected (with) as an adjunct, attribute, function, duty, part, or the like. **2.** To be the property (of). **3.** To be attached or bound (to) or connected (with) by some relation, as of birth, allegiance, residence, membership, or appropriateness. **4.** To be properly classified (among); — with *to, in, under, with.*

be·long′ing (bē·lŏng′ĭng), *n.* **1.** A thing or person that belongs to one. **2.** *pl.* Goods or effects.

be·love′ (bē·lŭv′), *v. t.; past part.* BE·LOVED′ (-lŭvd′). To love; — now only in passive, with *of* (*Poetic*) and *by.*

be·lov′ed (bē·lŭv′ĕd; -ĭd; bē·lŭvd′), *adj.* Dearly loved; dear to the heart. — *n.* One who is dearly loved.

be·low′ (bē·lō′), *adv.* [*be-* by + *low*, adj.] **1.** In a lower place, with respect to any object; beneath. **2.** On earth. **3.** In Hades; in hell. **4.** Lower on a page; hence, in some part following. **5.** On or to a lower floor or deck. **6.** In or to a lower rank. — *prep.* **1.** Lower than in place, rank, value, etc.; inferior to; beneath. **2.** Unworthy of.

Bel·shaz′zar (bĕl·shăz′ẽr), *n.* [Heb. *Bēlshatstsar.*] *Bib.* The last king of Babylon. See *Daniel* v.

belt (bĕlt), *n.* [AS. *belt.*] **1.** A broad strip of leather, cloth, or the like, worn around one's person. **2.** Any encircling strip, stripe, or series of things resembling or suggesting a belt (sense 1). **3. a** An area specially adapted by its climate, soil, etc., to the growth of certain animals or plants; as, the cotton *belt*. **b** *Biogeog.* An area distinctively characterized by its species or forms of life; as, a pine *belt*. **c** *Slang, U. S.* A region marked by the prevalence of some type of inhabitant or of some oddity, condition, etc.; as, the goiter *belt*. **4.** *Geog.* A narrow strait. **5.** *Mach.* A broad, flexible, endless band that passes around two or more pulleys, cylinders, cones, or the like, for communicating motion, conveying material, etc. **6.** *Shipbuilding.* A row of armor plates along the water line. — ***below the belt.*** Lower down than the waistline; hence, unfairly. — *v. t.* **1. a** To encircle, stripe, or invest with or as with a belt. **b** To gird by means of a belt. **c** To gird on. **2.** To encompass. **3.** To beat with a strap; hence, to strike.

Bel′tane (bĕl′tān), *n.* [Gael. *bealltainn, bealltuinn.*] **1.** May 1st (Old Style). **2.** The Celtic May-day festival.

belt′ed (bĕl′tĕd; -tĭd), *adj.* **1.** Encircled by, or secured with, a belt; girt with a belt as an honorary distinction; as, a *belted* earl. **2.** Marked with a band; as, *belted* cattle.

belt′ing, *n.* Material for belts; also, belts collectively.

be·lu′ga (bĕ·lōō′gȧ), *n.* **1.** [Russ., fr. *belyĭ* white.] A white sturgeon (*Acipenser huso*) of the Black Sea and Caspian Sea. **2.** [Russ. *belukha* or *beluga.*] A cetacean (*Delphinapterus leucas*) of the dolphin family, white when adult, and about ten feet long.

bel′ve·dere′ (bĕl′vē·dẽr′; bĕl′vē·dẽr; *It.* bĕl′vā·dā′rā), *n.* [It., fr. *bello, bel*, beautiful + *vedere* to see.] **1.** In Italian architecture, a building commanding a fine prospect. **2.** A cigar of a certain shape, shorter than a corona and with both ends slightly less thick. See CIGAR.

be′ma (bē′mȧ), *n.; pl.* BEMATA (-mȧ·tȧ). [Gr. *bēma* step, platform.] In Eastern churches, that part containing the altar and the structure combining the bishop's throne and clergy stalls.

be·mean′ (bē·mēn′), *v. t.* To abase; to lower (oneself).

be·mire′ (-mīr′), *v. t.* To fix in the mire; to befoul.

be·moan′ (-mōn′), *v. t.* [AS. *bemǣnan.*] To express deep grief for by moaning; to lament. — *v. i.* To lament. — **Syn.** See DEPLORE.

be·mock′ (bē·mŏk′; 74), *v. t.* To mock; to mock at. *Shak.*

be·muse′ (bē·mūz′), *v. t.* To stupefy.

be·mused′ (-mūzd′), *adj.* Dazed; also, absorbed; musing.

ben (bĕn), *adv. & prep.* [AS. *binnan*, fr. *be-* by + *innan* within, *in* in.] Within. *Scot.* — *adj.* Inner. — *n.* The parlor.

ben (bĕn), *n.* [Ar. *bān* the ben tree.] The seed of certain tropical trees (genus *Moringa*, family Moringaceae), yielding a fluid nondrying oil used in perfumery.

be·name′ (bē·nām′), *v. t.; past part.* -NAMED′ (-nāmd′), -NEMPT′ (-nĕmpt′), -NEMPT′ED. *Archaic.* To name; to call.

bench (bĕnch), *n.* [AS. *benc.*] **1.** A long seat for two or more persons. **2.** A thwart or seat in a boat. **3.** A long worktable. **4.** The seat where the judges sit in court; hence, the office or dignity of a judge; also, the persons who sit as judges, collectively; a court; as, the opinion of the full *bench*. **5.** A seat where officials sit together in the exercise of their duties; hence, the officials themselves, or the dignity of their office; as, the Treasury *bench*. **6.** A platform on which a dog is placed at a dog show; hence, a dog show. **7.** A level surface of ground, rock, etc., raised and narrow; specif., a topographic terrace or shelf, esp. a former shore line of a river or lake; an elevated shelf in a mine working. **8.** *Sports.* A seat where the members of each team await their turn at bat, an opportunity to play, etc.

— *v. t.* **1.** To furnish with a bench or benches. **2.** To seat on a bench, esp. a bench of justice. **3.** To exhibit (dogs) on a bench. **4.** *Sports.* To keep (a player) on the bench or to recall (a player) to the bench. See BENCH, *n.*, 8. — *v. i.* To sit on a seat of justice. *Shak.*

bench′er (bĕn′chẽr), *n.* One who sits on or works at a bench; as: **a** An oarsman. **b** *Eng. Law.* One of the senior and governing members of an Inn of Court.

bench clamp, hook, *or* **stop.** A clamp, hook, or stop to hold work on a carpenter's bench.

bench mark. A mark affixed to a permanent object in tidal observations, or in survey, to furnish a datum level.

bench show. An exhibition of small animals, esp. dogs, in competition for prizes on the basis of points of physical formation or condition. Cf. FIELD TRIAL.

bench warrant. A warrant issued by a presiding judge or by a court against a person guilty of some contempt or indicted for some crime.

bend (bĕnd), *v. t.;* BENT, or, *Archaic*, BEND′ED; BEND′ING. [AS. *bendan.*] **1.** Originally, to strain to tension by a band or string, as a bow or catapult. **2.** *Naut.* To fasten, as one rope to another or a sail to its yard or stay. **3.** *Archaic.* To strain or make tense; — with *up*. *Shak.* **4.** To strain or move (something rigid) out of a straight line; to crook or curve; as, to *bend* the knee. **5.** To direct by turning or deflecting, as one's steps; hence, to incline; to dispose. **6.** To cause to bow, stoop, or yield. **7.** To apply closely or with interest; to direct. — *v. i.* **1.** To be moved or strained out of a straight line or away from a given line; to crook or be curving; to bow. **2.** To curve over from upright; of persons, to stoop. **3.** To bend the body in submission or reverence; to bow; to yield; submit. **4.** *Archaic.* To direct oneself; turn. *Shak.* **5.** To have a direction or inclination away from the straight line or any given line; to trend. **6.** To apply oneself closely or vigorously; as, to *bend* to the oars. — **Syn.** See CURVE. — *n.* **1.** Act of bending; a turn or deflection from a straight or given line; state of being bent. **2.** A bent thing; a bent part, as of a river; a curve; bow. **3.** *pl. Naut.* The wales of a ship. **4.** *pl. Colloq.* Caisson disease.

bend, *n.* [AS. *bend.*] **1.** [OF. *bende, bande* (F. *bande*). See BAND.] *Her.* A band aslant and athwart. **2.** *Leather.* The half of a butt, or a hide trimmed of the thinner parts. See HIDE, *Illust.* **3.** A knot by which one rope is fastened to another or to some object. See KNOT.

Ben Da′vis (bĕn dā′vĭs). An American variety of red winter apple of excellent keeping but inferior eating qualities.

Ben Day process (bĕn′ dā′). [After *Benjamin Day* (1838–1916), New York printer.] A method of mechanical reproduction of shadings, tints, or screens, applied by a photographer to a drawing, negative, or a metal plate before it is etched. Ben Day techniques can also be applied to a drawing as art work by pasting a transparent sheet bearing black or white dots, lines, screens, etc., over certain areas before the picture is photographed and made into a printing plate.

bend′er (bĕn′dẽr), *n.* **1.** One who or that which bends, as a pair of pliers. **2.** *Slang.* **a** *Eng.* A sixpence. **b** *U. S.* A drunken spree.

bend sinister. *Her.* A bend drawn from the sinister side, wrongly supposed to represent bastardy. Cf. BATON, BAR SINISTER, ESCUTCHEON.

be·neath′ (bē·nēth′), *adv.* [AS. *beneothan, benythan*, fr. *be-* + *neothan, nythan*, downward, beneath.] **1.** In a lower place than some other place. **2.** Directly below something; under a covering; underneath. — *prep.* **1.** Lower than, in place; specif., directly under; also, at the foot of. **2.** Under (something superior or oppressive). **3.** Lower than, in rank, excellence, etc.; hence, unworthy of.

ben′e·dic′i·te (bĕn′ē·dĭs′ĭ·tē; -dī′sĭ·tē), *interj.* [L. (imperative pl.), bless ye.] Bless you! — *n.* **1.** Grace at table. **2.** [*cap.*] The canticle "Benedicite, omnia opera Domini," or "O all ye works of the Lord, bless ye the Lord."

Ben′e·dick (bĕn′ē·dĭk), *n.* [See BENEDICTUS.] **1.** In Shakespeare's *Much Ado*, a confirmed bachelor who marries Beatrice after a courtship which is a contest of wit and raillery. **2.** [*not cap.*] A benedict.

ben′e·dict (-dĭkt), *n.* [See BENEDICK.] A married man; usually, a man newly married, esp. one long a bachelor.

Ben'e·dic'tine (bĕn'ē·dĭk'tĭn; -tēn; -tīn), *n.* [F. *bénédictin.*] **1.** A monk or a nun of one of the congregations following the rule of St. Benedict and especially devoted to scholarly, literary, and artistic pursuits. **2.** (*pron.* -tēn) A trade-mark applied to a dark-brown cordial made of brandy, sugar, and aromatic herbs. — **Ben'e·dic'tine,** *adj.*

ben'e·dic'tion (-dĭk'shŭn), *n.* [L. *benedictio.* See BENISON.] **1.** Act of blessing; a blessing; specif.: **a** The short blessing, by a minister or priest, with which public worship is closed. **b** *R.C.Ch.* The rite of solemnly blessing and often formally dedicating to God. **2.** Realized blessedness; state of grace.

ben'e·dic'to·ry (-tō·rĭ), *adj.* Of or expressing benediction.

Ben'e·dic'tus (-dĭk'tŭs), *n.* [L., blessed.] Either of two canticles beginning *Benedictus* in the Vulgate (*Matt.* xxi. 9 and *Luke* i. 68); also, a musical setting for either.

ben'e·fac'tion (-făk'shŭn), *n.* [L. *benefactio,* fr. *benefacere* to do good to one, fr. *bene* well + *facere* to do.] The act of benefiting or a benefit conferred; esp., a charitable donation.

ben'e·fac'tor (bĕn'ē·făk'tẽr; bĕn'ē·făk'tẽr), *n.* [L.] One who confers a benefaction, benefit, or benefits.

ben'e·fac'tress (-trĕs; -trĭs), *n.* A woman benefactor.

be·nef'ic (bē·nĕf'ĭk), *adj.* [L. *beneficus.*] Beneficent.

ben'e·fice (bĕn'ē·fĭs), *n.* [OF., fr. L. *beneficium,* fr. *beneficus* beneficent.] **1.** A feudal estate in lands; a fief. **2.** An ecclesiastical living or church preferment, esp. a rectory, vicarage, or perpetual curacy. — *v. t.* To invest with a benefice. — **ben'e·ficed** (-fĭst), *adj.*

be·nef'i·cence (bē·nĕf'ĭ·sĕns; -s'ns), *n.* [F. or L.; F. *bénéficence,* fr. L. *beneficentia,* fr. *beneficus.*] **1.** Active goodness, kindness, charity. **2.** A beneficent act or gift.

be·nef'i·cent (-sĕnt; -s'nt), *adj.* **1.** Doing or producing good. **2.** Productive of benefit. — **be·nef'i·cent·ly,** *adv.*

ben'e·fi'cial (bĕn'ē·fĭsh'ăl), *adj.* **1.** Conferring benefits; conducive to well-being or welfare. **2.** Receiving for one's own benefit; as, the *beneficial* owner. — **ben'e·fi'cial·ly,** *adv.* — **ben'e·fi'cial·ness,** *n.*

Syn. **Beneficial, advantageous, profitable** mean bringing good or gain. **Beneficial** implies especially the promotion of health or well-being; **advantageous,** the conducing of superiority or of a good end; **profitable,** the yielding of useful or lucrative returns. — **Ant.** Detrimental.

ben'e·fi'ci·ar'y (bĕn'ē·fĭsh'ĭ·ĕr'ĭ; -fĭsh'ẽr·ĭ), *adj.* Holding, or held, by feudal tenure; of or pert. to the holding of a benefice. — *n.; pl.* -IES (-ĭz). **1.** One who holds a benefice. **2.** One who receives a benefit or advantage; specif.: **a** *Law.* The person designated to receive the income of a trust estate. **b** The person who is to receive the proceeds or benefits accruing under a policy of insurance, an annuity, etc.

ben'e·fit (bĕn'ē·fĭt), *n.* [AF. *benfet* (OF. & F. *bienfait*), fr. L. *benefactum,* fr. *bene* well + *factum,* past part. of *facere* to do.] **1.** Act of kindness; gift; benefaction. **2.** Whatever promotes welfare; advantage; profit; specif., pecuniary advantage or profit. **3.** A theatrical performance, a concert, etc., the proceeds of which are given to some particular person or purpose. **4.** Pecuniary help in time of sickness, old age, or the like. — *v. t.;* -FIT'ED also -FIT'TED; -FIT'ING also -FIT'TING. To be beneficial to. — *v. i.* To receive benefit; to profit.

benefit of clergy. **1.** *Law.* The privilege, claimed by the medieval church, of demanding a trial and punishment by an ecclesiastical court for one of the clergy when accused of crime before a temporal court. **2.** The ministration or sanction of the church.

Ben'e·lux (bĕn'ĕ·lŭks), *n.* [From *Be*lgium + *Ne*therlands + *Lux*embourg.] A tripartite customs union, formed in 1947 by Belgium, the Netherlands, and Luxembourg.

be·nempt' (bē·nĕmpt'), **be·nempt'ed.** See BENAME.

be·nev'o·lence (bē·nĕv'ō·lĕns), *n.* **1.** The disposition to do good; charitableness. **2.** An act of kindness; charity given. **3.** *Eng. Hist.* A forced levy on subjects by several kings on pretense of prerogative.

be·nev'o·lent (-lĕnt), *adj.* [From OF., fr. L. *benevolens, -entis,* fr. *bene* well + *volens,* pres. part. of *volo* I will, I wish.] Disposed to promote the prosperity and happiness of others; kind; charitable. — **be·nev'o·lent·ly,** *adv.*

Ben'gal cat'e·chu (bĕn'gôl; bĕng'-). See CATECHU.

Ben·gal'i (bĕn·gôl'ē; bĕng-), *n.* **1.** A native of Bengal. **2.** The language of Bengal. The literary language borrows from Sanskrit very freely. See INDO-EUROPEAN LANGUAGES. *Table.* — *adj.* Of or pert. to Bengal.

ben'ga·line (bĕng'gȧ·lēn; bĕng'gȧ·lēn'), *n.* [F.] A corded fabric made of silk and wool or silk and cotton.

Ben'gal light (bĕn'gôl; bĕng'-). A blue light or fire used in theaters, in signaling, etc.

be·night'ed (bē·nīt'ĕd; -ĭd), *adj.* [From *benight,* v., obs. in active.] **1.** Overtaken by night or darkness. **2.** Involved in or due to moral darkness or ignorance. — **be·night'ed·ness,** *n.*

be·nign' (bē·nīn'), *adj.* [From OF., fr. L. *benignus,* fr. *bene* well + root of *genus* kind.] **1.** Of a gentle disposition; gracious. **2.** Manifesting kindness and gentleness; kindly; hence, favorable. **3.** *Med.* Of a mild character; — opp. to *malignant;* as, a *benign* tumor. — **Syn.** See KIND. — **be·nign'ly,** *adv.*

be·nig'nan·cy (bē·nĭg'năn·sĭ), *n.* Benignant quality.

be·nig'nant (-nănt), *adj.* [From *benign,* after *malignant.*] Kindly (to inferiors or dependents); gracious; benign. — **Syn.** See KIND. — **be·nig'nant·ly,** *adv.*

be·nig'ni·ty (-nĭ·tĭ), *n.* **1.** Quality of being benign; esp., gentle disposition. **2.** A kind deed; a favor.

ben'i·son (bĕn'ĭ·z'n; -s'n), *n.* [From OF., fr. L. *benedictio,* fr. *benedicere* to bless, fr. *bene* well + *dicere* to say.] Blessing; benediction.

Ben'ja·min (bĕn'jȧ·mĭn), *n.* *Bib.* See JACOB.

ben'ja·min, *n.* [Corrupt. of *benjoin.*] Var. of BENZOIN.

ben'most (bĕn'mōst; -mŭst), *adj.* *Scot.* Innermost.

ben'ne (bĕn'ē), *n.* [Malay *bĕne* grain, seed.] = SESAME, 1.

ben'net (bĕn'ĕt; -ĭt), *n.* [F. *benoîte,* fr. ML. *benedicta,* fr. fem. of L. *benedictus,* past part., blessed.] **1.** = HERB BENNET (see AVENS). **2.** Either of two American species of avens (*Geum virginianum* and *G. canadense*).

bent (bĕnt), *adj.* **1.** Changed by bending; no longer straight; crooked. **2.** Strongly inclined toward something, so as to be resolved, determined, bound, or set.

bent, *n.* [See BEND.] **1.** Inclination in a particular direction; tendency. **2.** A leaning or bias; proclivity; tendency of mind; disposition; as, a *bent* for politics. **3.** Degree of tension, as of a bow or a spring; hence, power of endurance; capacity; — used in "to the top of one's *bent.*" — **Syn.** See GIFT.

bent (bĕnt), *n.* [AS. *beonot-* (in place names).] **1.** *sing. & pl.* A stalk of stiff, coarse grass. **2.** Also **bent grass.** Any of numerous stiff, wiry grasses, as the dog's-tail grass; in America, any of a large genus (*Agrostis*) of grasses having a panicle with small one-flowered spikelets, esp. redtop. **3.** *Archaic.* An unenclosed pasture; a moor; a heath.

Ben'tham·ism (bĕn'thăm·ĭz'm; bĕn'tăm-), *n.* Utilitarianism as taught by Jeremy Bentham, in which the morality of actions is estimated by their utility. "The greatest happiness of the greatest number" was Bentham's criterion of moral goodness. — **Ben'tham·ite** (-īt), *n.*

ben'thos (bĕn'thŏs), *n.* [NL., fr. Gr. *benthos* depth of the sea.] The bottom of the sea, esp. of the deep oceans; hence, *Biol.:* **a** The fauna and flora of the sea bottom. Cf. PLANKTON. **b** Fresh-water bottom-dwelling organisms collectively. — **ben·thon'ic** (bĕn·thŏn'ĭk), *adj.*

‖**ben tro·va'to** (bĕn' trō·vä'tō). [It.] Well conceived or invented; hence, substantively, a felicitous expression.

be·numb' (bē·nŭm'), *v. t.* [AS. *beniman,* fr. *be-* + *niman* to take. See NUMB.] To make torpid; to deprive of sensation or sensibility; to numb; stupefy; deaden.

benz·al'de·hyde (bĕn·zăl'dē·hīd), *n.* [*benzene* + *aldehyde.*] *Chem.* A colorless, nonpoisonous, aromatic liquid, C_6H_5CHO, the chief constituent of the essential oils of bitter almonds and peach kernels.

Ben'ze·drine (bĕn'zē·drēn, -drĭn; bĕn·zĕd'rĭn), *n.* A trade-mark applied to amphetamine.

ben'zene (bĕn'zēn; bĕn·zēn'), *n.* [From BENZOIN.] *Chem.* A volatile, inflammable, colorless liquid hydrocarbon, C_6H_6, of ethereal odor, used as an illuminant, as a solvent for fats and resins, and as a material in making dyes, etc.

benzene ring *or* **nucleus.** *Chem.* A ring of six carbon atoms believed to exist in the aromatic compounds. In benzene, six hydrogen atoms are attached to the ring; substitution of one or more of these by other atoms or groups gives the various benzene derivatives. Two carbon atoms in union with the substituting atoms or groups may be either adjacent, or separated by another carbon atom, or opposite in the ring. These positions are known respectively as the *ortho* (*o*), *meta* (*m*), and *para* (*p*) positions.

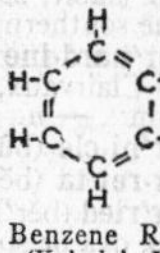

Benzene Ring (Kekule's Formula).

ben'zi·dine (bĕn'zĭ·dēn; -dĭn), *n.* [From BENZINE.] *Chem.* A base, $NH_2C_6H_4C_6H_4NH_2$, prepared from nitrobenzene and crystallizing in silvery scales, used in making dyes.

ben'zine (bĕn'zēn; bĕn·zēn'; bĕn'zĭn), *n.* A volatile inflammable liquid derived from petroleum and used in cleaning, dyeing, painting, etc., and as a motor fuel.

ben'zo·ate (bĕn'zō·āt), *n.* A salt or ester of benzoic acid.

benzoate of soda. Sodium benzoate.

ben·zo'ic (bĕn·zō'ĭk), *adj.* *Chem.* **a** Pertaining to, or obtained from, benzoin. **b** Designating a white crystalline acid (**benzoic acid,** $C_6H_5CO_2H$), occurring in benzoin, cranberries, etc., used as an antiseptic and preservative.

ben'zo·in (bĕn'zō·ĭn; bĕn·zō'ĭn; bĕn'zoin), *n.* [Earlier also *benjoin,* fr. F., through Sp., Pg., & It., fr. Ar. *lubān jāwī* frankincense of Jawa (early name for Sumatra).] **1.** A balsamic resin from a tree of the storax family (*Styrax benzoin*) of Sumatra and Java. It is used in making benzoic acid, as a stimulant and expectorant, and as a perfume. It is called also *benjamin.* **2.** *Bot.* Any plant of a small genus (*Benzoin*) of aromatic shrubs or, rarely, trees of the laurel family, one of which (*B. aestivale*) is known as the *spicebush, spicewood,* or *benjamin bush.* **3.** *Chem.* A white crystalline compound, $C_{14}H_{12}O_2$, made from benzaldehyde.

ben'zol (bĕn'zōl; -zŏl), *n.* *Chem.* A volatile liquid hydrocarbon obtained in the refinement of coal tar, containing benzene and similar compounds, and widely used in dyes.

ben'zo·phe·none' (bĕn'zō·fē·nōn'), *n.* [*benz*ene + *phen*ol + *-one.*] A colorless crystalline ketone, $C_6H_5COC_6H_5$, produced chiefly by the distillation of calcium benzoate.

ben'zo·yl (bĕn'zō·ĭl; -ēl), *n.* *Chem.* A univalent radical, C_6H_5CO, of which benzoic acid is the hydroxide.

ben'zyl (-zĭl; -zēl), *n.* [*benzene* + *-yl.*] *Chem.* The univalent radical $C_6H_5CH_2$, of which toluene is the hydride.

Be'o·wulf (bā'ō·wo͝olf), *n.* The title and warrior hero of an Anglo-Saxon epic poem dating from the 8th century.

be·paint' (bē·pānt'), *v. t.* To cover with paint; to tinge.

be·queath' (bē·kwēth'), *v. t.* [AS. *becwethan* to say, bequeath, fr. *be-* + *cwethan* to say.] **1.** To give or leave by will; — now more appropriately of personalty, as *devise* is of realty. **2.** To hand down; to transmit. **3.** *Archaic.* To offer; commit. — **be·queath'al** (-ăl), *n.*

be·quest' (bē·kwĕst'), *n.* [ME. *biqueste,* corrupt. fr. *biquide,* fr. *be-* + AS. *cwide* a saying, fr. *cwethan* to say.] Act of bequeathing; also, that which is left by will.

be·rate' (-rāt'), *v. t.* *U.S.* To chide vehemently. — **Syn.** See SCOLD.

Ber'ber (bûr'bẽr), *n.* A Hamite of northern Africa west of Tripoli; the Hamitic dialect spoken there. See LANGUAGE, *Table.* — **Ber'ber,** *adj.*

ber'ber·ine (bûr'bẽr·ēn; -ĭn), *n.* Also **-in.** [From genus name *Berberis.* See BARBERRY.] *Chem.* A yellow crystalline alkaloid, $C_{20}H_{17}NO_4$, or $C_{20}H_{19}NO_5$, used as a tonic and antiperiodic.

‖**ber'ceuse'** (bĕr'sûz'), *n.; pl.* BERCEUSES (*F.* -sûz'). [F.] A lullaby; hence, a song or musical composition of a similar soothing character.

bere (bẽr). Var. of BEAR, barley.

be·reave' (bē·rēv'), *v. t.;* -REAVED' (-rēvd'), -REFT' (-rĕft'); -REAV'ING. [AS. *berēafian.*] **1.** To deprive, dispossess, make destitute; — with *of* before the person or thing taken away. In the past tense or past part. *bereaved* is not used in reference to immaterial objects; as, *bereaved* (less usually *bereft*) by death of a relative; *bereft* of hope. **2.** *Obs.* To take away. — **be·reave'ment,** *n.*

Ber'e·ni'ce's Hair (bẽr'ē·nī'sēz). Coma Berenices.

be·ret' (bĕ·rā'; bĕ'rā; *F.* bȧ'rĕ'), *n.* [F. *béret,* fr. Pr. *berret,* fr. L. See BIRETTA.] A round, flat, visorless cap of soft material, originally worn by Basque peasants.

berg (bûrg), *n.* **1.** A great mass of ice. Short for ICEBERG. **2.** (*pron.* bûrg; *D.* bĕrk) [D.] *S. Afr.* A mountain.

ber'ga·mot (bûr'gȧ·mŏt), *n.* [Through F. & It., fr. Turk. *beg-armūdi,* lit., prince's pear.] **1.** A minor variety of pear. **2.** **a** A pear-shaped orange (*Citrus bergamia*) whose rind yields an essential oil used in perfumery. **b** Any of several mints.

Berg'son·ism (bĕrg'sŭn·ĭz'm), *n.* The philosophy of Henri Bergson, a French philosopher, representing the world as a process of "creative evolution" in which the novelty of the successive phenomena is the significant fact. — **Berg·so'ni·an** (bĕrg·sō'nĭ·ăn), *adj.* & *n.*

be·rhyme′, be·rime′ (bē·rīm′), *v. t.* **a** To mention in rhyme or verse; to rhyme about. **b** To put into rhyme.

ber′i·ber′i (bĕr′ĭ·bĕr′ĭ), *n.* [Singhalese *beri* weakness.] An Oriental disease, characterized by multiple neuritis, producing general debility and a painful rigidity. It is caused by insufficiency of vitamin B_1 in the diet and commonly results from the exclusive use of polished rice.

Berke·le′ian (bûrk·lē′ăn; bärk-), *adj.* Of or relating to Bishop Berkeley or his system of idealism, based upon the proposition that so-called material things exist only in being perceived. — *n.* One who believes in this idealism. — **Berke·le′ian·ism**, *n.*

berke′li·um (bûrk′lĭ·ŭm), *n.* [NL., fr. *Berkeley*, Calif. (location of the Univ. of Calif., where it was discovered) + *-ium.*] *Chem.* A radioactive element discovered by bombarding americium 241 with helium ions. Symbol, *Bk*; at. no., 97.

Berk′shire (bûrk′shĭr; *Brit. generally* bärk′shĭr; -shĕr), *n.* [From *Berkshire*, Eng.] An animal of a breed of medium-sized swine, black with white markings.

ber·lin′ (bûr·lĭn′; bûr′lĭn), *n.* [From *Berlin*, Germany.] **1.** A four-wheeled, two-seated, covered carriage having a rear platform for footmen. **2.** Usually **ber·line′** (*pron.* bûr·lĭn′; *F.* bĕr′lēn′). An enclosed automobile body having at the rear of the driver's seat a glass partition with movable window. **3.** [*sometimes cap.*] Short for **Berlin wool**, worsted yarn made from fine merino wool.

berm, berme (bûrm), *n.* [F. *berme*, fr. D. *berm.*] A narrow shelf, path, or ledge, as along the top of a scarp or along a road.

Ber·mu′da grass (bĕr·mū′dȧ). A grass (*Cynodon dactylon*) of trailing habit, spreading from stolons, valued for lawns and pastures in the southern United States, in India, and elsewhere.

Ber′nard·ine (bûr′nĕr·dĭn; -dēn), *adj.* Of or pertaining to St. Bernard of Clairvaux, or the branch of Cistercian monks instituted (1115) by him. — *n.* A Bernardine monk.

ber′ni·cle (bûr′nĭ·k'l), *n., or* **bernicle goose**. The barnacle goose.

ber·ret′ta (bĕ·rĕt′ȧ). Var. of BIRETTA.

ber′ried (bĕr′ĭd), *adj.* **1.** Furnished with berries; baccate. **2.** Carrying ova or spawn; — of lobsters and crabs.

ber′ry (bĕr′ĭ), *n.; pl.* BERRIES (-ĭz). [AS. *berie, berige.*] **1.** Any pulpy fruit of small size, irrespective of its structure, as the strawberry, raspberry, checkerberry, hagberry, and hip of the rose. **2.** *Bot.* Any simple fruit having a pulpy or fleshy pericarp, as the currant, grape, gooseberry, cranberry, tomato, or banana. **3.** The dry seed or kernel of certain plants; as, the coffee *berry*. **4.** One of the eggs of a fish or lobster. — *v. i.;* BER′RIED (-ĭd); BER′RY·ING. **1.** To bear berries. **2.** To gather or seek berries.

‖**Ber·sa·glie′re** (bār·sä·lyâ′rā), *n.; pl.* -RI (-rē). [It., fr. *bersaglio* a mark.] *Mil.* In the Italian army, a member of a certain infantry corps organized (about 1850) as sharpshooters or riflemen.

ber′serk (bûr′sûrk), *n.* A berserker. — (bûr′sûrk; bûr·sûrk′), *adj.* Frenzied; enraged. — (bûr′sûrk; bûr·sûrk′), *adv.* In frenzied rage.

ber′serk·er (bûr′sûr·kĕr), *n.* [ON. *berserkr.*] In Norse folklore, one of a class of warriors who in battle were seized with a frenzy, howled, bit their shields, foamed at the mouth, and were believed invulnerable.

berth (bûrth), *n.; pl.* BERTHS (bûrths; *esp. Brit.*, bûrthz). [From root of *bear* to produce.] **1.** *Naut.* **a** Sufficient room to maneuver under way or to swing at anchor; as, to give a wide *berth* to. **b** The place where a ship lies at anchor, or at a wharf. **2.** An allotted place; situation or billet. **3.** A bunk, as in a ship or railway car. — *v. t.* To give a berth to. — *v. i.* Of a ship, to come to a berth.

ber′tha (bûr′thȧ), *n.* [From *Bertha*, proper name, deriv. fr. OHG.] A kind of deep collar, as of lace, falling from the neckline of a dress.

Ber′til′lon′ sys′tem (bĕr′tē′yôɴ′; bûr′tĭ·lŏn). [After Alphonse *Bertillon* (1853–1914), French anthropologist.] A system for identification of persons by a description based on anthropometric measurements, notes of markings, color, impression of thumb lines, etc.

ber′yl (bĕr′ĭl), *n.* [OF. *beryl*, fr. L. *beryllus*, fr. Gr. *bēryllos.*] A silicate of beryllium and aluminum, $Be_3Al_2(SiO_3)_6$, of great hardness, occurring in hexagonal prisms, commonly green or bluish green, of which aquamarine and emerald are varieties. — **ber′yl·line** (-ĭ·lĭn; -līn), *adj.*

be·ryl′li·um (bĕ·rĭl′ĭ·ŭm), *n.* [NL., fr. *beryl.*] A rare metallic element (called also *glucinum*) occurring always in combination. Symbol, *Be* (also *Gl*); at. no., 4; at. wt., 9.013.

Bes (bĕs), *n.* [Egypt. *besa.*] *Egypt. Relig.* A god averting the evils of omens and witchcraft, and a god of pleasure.

be·seech′ (bē·sēch′), *v. t.;* BE·SOUGHT′ (-sôt′), also BE·SEECHED′ (-sēcht′); BE·SEECH′ING. [ME. *bisechen, biseken*, fr. *be-* + *sechen, seken*, to seek.] **1.** To entreat with urgency; to supplicate. **2.** To ask earnestly for; to beg; crave. — **Syn.** See BEG. — **be·seech′er**, *n.* — **be·seech′ing**, *adj.* — **be·seech′ing·ly**, *adv.* — **be·seech′ing·ness**, *n.*

be·seem′ (bē·sēm′), *v. i.* To be seemly or fitting. — *v. t.* To befit; become; as, it ill *beseems* you to boast.

be·set′ (bē·sĕt′), *v. t.;* see SET. [AS. *besettan.*] **1.** To set or stud with ornaments. **2.** To set upon on all sides; perplex; harass. **3.** To hem in; surround. — **be·set′ment**, *n.*

be·set′ting, *adj.* Persistently assailing; — of sin or danger.

be·show′ (bē·shō′), *n.* A North Pacific food fish (*Anoplopoma fimbra*); — called also *candlefish* and *coalfish*.

be·shrew′ (bē·shrōō′), *v. t.* *Archaic.* To curse; to call down evil upon.

be·side′ (bē·sīd′), *adv.* [ME. *biside*, fr. *be-* by + *side.*] In addition; besides. — *prep.* **1.** At or by the side of; near by; hence, compared with. **2.** Over and above. **3.** To one side or wide of; aside from; as, *beside* the question.

☞ *Beside* is now used, with rare exceptions, as a preposition only. *Besides* is also used as a preposition, but chiefly as an adverb.

— ***beside oneself.*** Out of one's wits or senses; crazy.

be·sides′ (bē·sīdz′), *adv.* Over and above; in addition; else. See BESIDE, *Note.* — *prep.* Over and above; in addition to; other than.

be·siege′ (bē·sēj′), *v. t.;* see SIEGE. To beset or surround with armed forces; to lay siege to; beleaguer; beset. — **be·sieg′er** (-sēj′ĕr), *n.*

be·smear′ (bē·smēr′), *v. t.* [AS. *besmierwan.*] To smear.

be·smirch′ (bē·smûrch′), *v. t.* To smirch or soil; sully.

be′som (bē′zŭm), *n.* [AS. *besma.*] **1.** A broom of twigs, esp. of birch or heather; a broom. **2.** The broom (*Cytisus*).

be·sot′ (bē·sŏt′), *v. t.;* BE·SOT′TED (-ĕd; -ĭd); BE·SOT′TING. To make sottish, dull, or stupid; to stupefy; to muddle with drunkenness or infatuation. — **be·sot′ted**, *adj.*

be·sought′ (bē·sôt′), *past & past part.* of BESEECH.

be·spat′ter (bē·spăt′ĕr), *v. t.* To spatter.

be·speak′ (bē·spēk′), *v. t.;* see SPEAK. [AS. *besprecan* to speak about.] **1.** To speak or arrange for beforehand; to engage, or stipulate for, against a future time. **2.** *Archaic.* To address. **3.** To betoken; to indicate, as by appearances. **4.** To foretell; to give evidence of.

be·spoke′ (bē·spōk′), *past & past part.* of BESPEAK. — *adj. Eng.* Custom; as, *bespoke* clothes, tailors.

be·spread′ (bē·sprĕd′), *v. t.;* see SPREAD. To spread thickly.

be·sprent′ (bē·sprĕnt′), *adj.* [ME. *bespreynt*, past part., deriv. fr. AS. *besprengan.*] *Poetic.* Sprinkled over.

be·sprin′kle (bē·sprĭng′k'l), *v. t.* To sprinkle.

Bes′se·mer proc′ess (bĕs′ĕ·mĕr). [After Sir Henry *Bessemer*, Eng. engineer.] A process of making steel (**Bessemer steel**) from cast iron by burning out carbon and other impurities through the agency of a blast of air forced through the molten metal. The special type of furnace used in the process is called a **Bessemer converter**.

best (bĕst), *adj.; superl.* of GOOD [AS., contr. fr. *betest, betst.* See BETTER.] **1.** Having good qualities in the highest degree. **2.** Most productive of good; most advantageous, serviceable, etc.; as, what is *best* to do? **3.** Most; largest; as, the *best* part of a week. — *adv.; superl.* of WELL. **1.** In the best way; to the most advantage. **2.** In the best or highest degree; to the fullest extent; most. — *n.* **1.** That which is best; the best part. **2.** Best clothing. **3.** Best state, or course of action; utmost. — *v. t* To get the better of; overmatch; outstrip.

be·stead′ (bē·stĕd′), *adj.* [See BE-; STEAD, *n.*] Placed; situated; circumstanced. — *v. t.* [*be-*, 2 + *stead*, v.] To serve; assist; avail.

bes′tial (bĕst′yăl; bĕs′chăl), *adj.* [OF., fr. L. *bestialis*, fr. *bestia* beast.] **1.** Belonging to beasts. **2.** Having the qualities of a beast; specif.: **a** Brutish; irrational. **b** Beastly; sensual; degradedly carnal. — **bes′tial·ly**, *adv.*

bes′ti·al′i·ty (bĕs′tĭ·ăl′ĭ·tĭ; bĕs′chĭ-), *n.* **1.** Bestial nature; brutality. **2.** Bestial indulgence; a bestial action.

bes′tial·ize (bĕst′yăl·īz; bĕs′chăl-), *v. t.* To make bestial.

bes′ti·ar′y (bĕs′tĭ·ĕr′ĭ *or, esp. Brit.*, -ẽr·ĭ), *n.; pl.* -IES (-ĭz). [ML. *bestiarium.*] A medieval moralizing or allegorical treatise on beasts or their habits.

be·stir′ (bē·stûr′), *v. t. & i.;* see STIR. [AS. *bestyrian* to heap up.] To stir up; to rouse to vigorous action.

best man. The principal groomsman at a wedding.

be·stow′ (bē·stō′), *v. t.* **1.** To use; to apply; as, time well *bestowed*. **2.** *Archaic.* **a** To set or place. **b** To deposit; to stow. **c** To quarter; to lodge. **3.** To give or confer in marriage. **4.** To give; confer; impart; — often with *on* or *upon*. — **Syn.** See GIVE. — **be·stow′al** (-ăl), *n.*

be·strad′dle (bē·străd′'l), *v. t.* To bestride.

be·strew′ (bē·strōō′), *v. t.;* see STREW. [AS. *bestrēowian.*] To strew or scatter over; to lie scattered over.

be·stride′ (bē·strīd′), *v. t.;* see STRIDE. [AS. *bestrīdan.*] **1.** To ride, sit, or stand astride of; bestraddle. **2.** To stride over or across.

bet (bĕt), *n.* [Prob. fr. ME. *abet* abetting.] **1.** That which is laid, staked, or pledged, as between two parties, upon the event of a contest or any contingent issue; wager; also, the act of giving such a pledge. **2.** A thing to wager on; as, the gray is the best *bet* to win. — *v. t. & i.;* BET, also BET′TED (-ĕd; -ĭd); BET′TING. To stake upon the event of a contingent issue; to wager.

be′ta (bē′tȧ; bā′tȧ), *n.* [Gr. *bēta.*] **1.** The second letter (Β, β) of the Greek alphabet. **2.** A symbol used variously; as: **a** *Astron.* To designate the second brightest star of a constellation. **b** *Chem.* To indicate the position of substituting atoms or groups in certain compounds; as, β-naphthol.

be′ta·ine (bē′tȧ·ēn; bē·tā′ēn; -ĭn), *n.* Also **be′ta·in**. [From *Beta*, generic name of the beet.] *Chem.* A sweetish, nonpoisonous, crystalline base, $C_5H_{11}NO_2$, occurring in beet juice and other plant substances and in putrefying flesh.

be·take′ (bē·tāk′), *v. t.;* see TAKE. To deliver over or commit. *Obs.* — ***betake oneself.*** To have recourse (*to*); resort; go.

be′ta par′ti·cle (bē′tȧ; bā′tȧ). *Physics.* An electron, as emitted in beta rays. See BETA RAY.

beta ray. A stream of high-speed electrons emitted in certain radioactive disintegrations.

beta test. *Psychol.* An intelligence test similar to the alpha test but without use of written or spoken language.

be′ta·tron (bē′tȧ·trŏn; bā′tȧ-), *n.* [*beta* (ray) + elec*tron.*] *Physics.* An apparatus in which electrons are accelerated to high speeds by electromagnetic means, so that they form a narrow beam of beta rays that is used especially to generate high-voltage X rays and to transmute elements.

be′tel (bē′t'l), *n.* [Pg. *betle, bétel*, fr. Tamil *veṭṭilai.*] A climbing species of pepper (*Piper betle*). Cf. BETEL PALM.

Be′tel·geuse (bē′t'l·jōōz; bĕt′'l·jûz), **Be′tel·geux**, *n.* [F. *Bételgeuse*, fr. Ar.] A variable red giant star of the first magnitude, near one shoulder of Orion; Alpha (α) Orionis.

betel palm. An Asiatic pinnate-leaved palm (*Areca catechu*), bearing the **betel nut**, an orange-colored nutlike drupe with an outer fibrous husk, which is used as a vermifuge and myotic, and, in the East, wrapped with a little lime in leaves of the betel, serves as a masticatory.

bête noire (bāt′ nwär′; *F.* bât′ nwȧr′). [F., black beast.] A person or object of fear or aversion; bugbear.

beth′el (bĕth′ĕl), *n.* [Heb. *bēth'el* the house of God.] **1.** A hallowed spot. *Gen.* xxviii. 19. **2.** A place of worship for seamen; also, *Eng.*, a chapel for nonconformists.

be·think′ (bē·thĭngk′), *v. t.;* see THINK. [AS. *bethencan.*] To call to mind; to recall; to think; to consider; — generally reflexive. — *v. i.* *Archaic.* To consider; reflect.

Beth′le·hem (bĕth′lē·ĕm; -hĕm), *n.* [Heb. *Bēth-leḥem* the house of food.] **1.** A town in Judea, birthplace of Jesus. **2.** = BEDLAM, 1 & 3.

be·thought′ (bē·thôt′), *past & past part.* of BETHINK.

be·tide′ (bē·tīd′), *v. i. & t.* [ME. *bitiden*, fr. *bi-, be-* + *tiden*, fr. AS. *tīdan* to happen, fr. *tīd* time.] To happen (to); befall; as, woe *betide* you!

be·times′ (bē·tīmz′), *adv.* [*be-* (for *by*) + *time;* that is, by the proper time.] **1.** In good season or time; early. **2.** In a short time; speedily.

‖**bê·tise′** (bā′tēz′), *n.* [F.] Silliness; folly; stupidity; an act or a piece of foolishness.

be·to′ken (bē·tō′kĕn), *v. t.* **1.** To foreshow by present signs; presage. **2.** To give evidence of; show. — **be·to′ken·er**, *n.*

bet′o·ny (bĕt′ō·nĭ), *n.; pl.* -NIES (-nĭz). [F. *bétoine*, fr. L. *betonica, vettonica.*] Any of a genus (*Betonica*) of plants of the mint family, esp. the ***purple, or wood, betony*** (*B. officinalis*) of Europe.

be·took′ (bē·tŏŏk′), *past* of BETAKE.

be·tray′ (bē·trā′), *v. t.* [*be-* + OF. *traïr* to betray, fr. L. *tradere*.] **1.** To deliver to an enemy by treachery or fraud, in violation of trust; as, an officer *betrayed* the city. **2.** To be a traitor to; to prove faithless or treacherous to, as to a trust or one who trusts; to fail or desert in a moment of need. **3.** To lead into error, sin, or danger. **4.** To seduce (as under promise of marriage) and then abandon. **5.** To reveal unintentionally; as, to *betray* one's ignorance. **6.** To show or to indicate, as what is not at first obvious. **7.** To disclose in violation of confidence, as government secrets. — **Syn.** See REVEAL. — *v. i.* To betray one. — **be·tray′al**, *n.* — **be·tray′er**, *n.*

be·troth′ (bē·trŏth′; -trōth′), *v. t.* [See BE-; TROTH.] To engage or promise in marriage; to affiance. — **be·troth′ment**, *n.*

be·troth′al (-ăl), *n.* Act of betrothing, or fact of being betrothed; a mutual contract for a future marriage.

bet′ter (bĕt′ẽr), *adj.; used as compar. of* GOOD. [AS. *betera*, adj., and *bet*, adv.] **1.** Having good qualities in a greater number or degree than another; superior; as, a *better* man. **2.** Preferable in regard to value, use, fitness, rank, safety, etc. **3.** Greater; larger; as, the *better* part of an hour. **4.** Improved in health. — *v. t.* **1.** To improve or ameliorate; as, to *better* a situation; to increase the amount or good qualities of. **2.** To improve the condition or circumstances of, esp. as regards health or worldly welfare. **3.** To surpass in excellence; to exceed; excel; as, to *better* expectation. — **Syn.** See IMPROVE. — **Ant.** Worsen. — *n.* **1.** That which is better. **2.** A superior, as in merit, social standing, etc.; — usually in *pl.* **3.** Advantage, superiority, or victory; — usually with *of*. — *adv.; used as compar. of* WELL. **1.** In a more excellent manner. **2.** In a higher or greater degree; more.

bet′ter, bet′tor (bĕt′ẽr), *n.* One who bets; a wagerer.

bet′ter·ment (bĕt′ẽr·mĕnt), *n.* **1.** A making better; improvement. **2.** *Law.* An improvement of an estate which renders it better than mere repairing would do.

bet′u·la′ceous (bĕt′ū·lā′shŭs), *adj.* [L. *betula* birch tree.] Belonging to the birch family (Betulaceae). See BIRCH.

be·tween′ (bē·twēn′), *prep.* [AS. *betwēonan*, *betwēonum*, fr. *be-* by + a form fr. AS. *twā* two.] **1.** In the space or interval which separates. **2.** From one to another of; joining; as, the bond *between* man and man. **3.** In common to; by the united action of; as, they killed six *between* them. **4.** With reference to, or involved in, the interrelation or interaction of; as, war *between* nations. **5.** In point of comparison of; as, to choose *between* courses. — *adv.* In an intermediate space or interval.

be·tween′brain′ (-brān′), *n.* See FOREBRAIN.

be·tween′times′ (-tīmz′), *adv.* Betweenwhiles.

be·tween′whiles′ (-hwīlz′), *adv.* At or during intervals.

be·twixt′ (bē·twĭkst′), *prep.* [AS. *betweox*, *betweohs*, *betweoh*, fr. *be-* by + a form fr. AS. *twā* two.] Between. — *adv.* Between. *Rare*, exc. in **betwixt and between**, in a midway position.

Beu′lah (bū′lȧ), *n.* Short for LAND OF BEULAH.

bev′a·tron (bĕv′ȧ·trŏn), *n.* [*b*illion *e*lectron *v*olts + *a*tom + *-tron* as in elec*tron*.] *Physics.* An apparatus similar to the synchrotron, designed for accelerating protons and other charged particles to a level greater than ten billion electron volts.

bev′el (bĕv′ĕl), *n.* **1.** The angle which one surface or line makes with another when they are not at right angles; also, the slant or inclination of such surface or line. **2.** An instrument consisting of two rules or arms jointed together and opening to any angle, for adjusting surfaces of work to a given inclination; — called also **bevel square**. — *v. t.*; -ELED (-ĕld) or -ELLED; -EL·ING or -EL·LING. To cut or shape to a bevel angle. — *v. i.* To incline; slant. — *adj.* Having the slant of a bevel.

bevel gear. *Mach.* One of a pair of toothed wheels whose working surfaces are inclined to nonparallel axes.

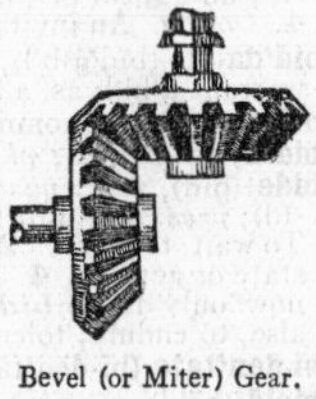

Bevel (or Miter) Gear.

bev′er·age (bĕv′ẽr·ĭj), *n.* [OF. *bevrage*, fr. *beivre* to drink, fr. L. *bibere*.] Liquid for drinking; drink.

bev′y (bĕv′ĭ), *n.; pl.* BEVIES (-ĭz). **1.** A company, esp. of women. **2.** A flock, esp. of quail.

be·wail′ (bē·wāl′), *v. t.* & *i.* To express deep sorrow (for); to lament; wail (over). — **Syn.** See DEPLORE.

be·ware′ (bē·wâr′), *v. i.* & *t.* [*be*, imper. of verb *to be* + *ware*, adj.] To be on one's guard (against); — commonly followed by *of, lest, how, that not*.

be·wil′der (bē·wĭl′dẽr), *v. t.* [*be-* + *wilder*.] **1.** To cause to lose one's bearings. **2.** To perplex or confuse, esp. by a complexity, variety, or multitude of objects or considerations. — **Syn.** See PUZZLE. — **be·wil′der·ing**, *adj.* — **be·wil′der·ing·ly**, *adv.* — **be·wil′der·ment**, *n.*

be·wil′dered (-dẽrd), *adj.* Lost and perplexed; confused; puzzled; confusingly tangled. — **be·wil′dered·ly**, *adv.*

be·witch′ (bē·wĭch′), *v. t.* **1.** To affect (esp. to injure) by witchcraft or sorcery. **2.** To charm; to fascinate. — **Syn.** See ATTRACT. — **be·witch′er**, *n.* — **be·witch′er·y**, *n.*

be·witch′ing, *adj.* Fascinating; enchanting; captivating; charming. — **be·witch′ing·ly**, *adv.*

be·witch′ment (-mĕnt), *n.* Act or power of bewitching; also, state of being bewitched; a spell that bewitches.

be·wray′ (bē·rā′), *v. t.* [*be-* + AS. *wrēgan* to accuse, betray.] *Archaic.* To expose; betray; reveal; disclose.

bey (bā), *n.* [Turki *beg*.] **1.** A governor of a district in the Turkish dominions; also, a title of courtesy, abolished by law 1934. **2.** The title of the rulers of Tunisia since about 1705. It is still held by the head of the ruling family under the French.

bey′lic, bey′lik (bā′lĭk), *n.* The jurisdiction of a bey.

be·yond′ (bē·yŏnd′; bē·ŏnd′), *adv.* [AS. *begeondan*, prep. and adv., fr. *be-* + *geond* yond, yonder.] Farther away; yonder. — *prep.* **1.** On or to the farther side of; later than. **2.** Out of the reach or of sphere of; past; as, *beyond* medical aid. **3.** Above, as in dignity, excellence, or quality of any kind; as, lovely *beyond* expression. **4.** Over and above. — *n.* That which lies outside immediate experience, interests, etc. — ***the beyond.*** The hereafter.

bez′ant (bĕz′ănt; bē·zănt′), *n.* [OF. *besan*, *besant*, fr. L. *Byzantius* Byzantine.] **1.** = SOLIDUS, **1 a**. **2.** A flat disk used in architectural ornament.

bez antler *or* **point** (bĕz; bāz). [L. *bis* twice (through OF. *bes-*).] See ANTLER, *Illust.*

bez′el (bĕz′ĕl), *n.* [From an old form of F. *biseau* sloping edge.] **1.** A sloping edge or face, esp. on a cutting tool. **2.** *Jewelry.* **a** The oblique side or face of a cut gem; specif., the upper faceted portion of a brilliant, projecting from the setting. See BRILLIANT, *Illust.* **b** The part of a setting that holds a gem. **3.** The grooved rim or flange in which a watch crystal is set.

be·zique′ (bĕ·zēk′), *n.* [F. *bésigue*.] A card game similar to pinochle but using 64 cards.

be′zoar (bē′zōr; 70), *n.* [F. *bézoard*, through Pg. or Sp., fr. Ar., fr. Per. *pād-zahr*, fr. *pād* protecting (against) + *zahr* poison.] **1.** *Obs.* An antidote. **2.** Any of various concretions found chiefly in the alimentary organs of certain ruminants and once believed to counteract poisons.

be·zo′ni·an (bē·zō′nĭ·ăn), *n.* [It. *bisogno*, prop., need.] A recruit or raw soldier; a beggarly fellow or scoundrel.

Bha′ga·vad-Gi′ta (bŭg′ȧ·vȧd·gē′tä), *n.* [Skr. *Bhagavadgītā* the Song of the Blessed One.] A philosophical dialogue inserted in the *Mahabharata*, containing a divine revelation from Krishna and constituting the supreme devotional scripture of India.

bhang, bang (băng), *n.* [Hind. *bhāng*, *bhang*, fr. Skr. *bhaṅgā*.] **a** *India.* The hemp (*Cannabis sativa*). **b** A narcotic and intoxicant made of its dried leaves and twigs.

bhees′ty, bhees′tie (bēs′tĭ), *n.* [Hind. *bhīstī*, fr. Per. *bihishtī*, lit., one from heaven.] *India.* A water carrier.

bi- (bī-). [L.] A prefix, forming adjectives and their derivative nouns, denoting in general *two*, and specif.: **1.** *Two, twice, doubly*, as in *bi*dentate, *bi*serrate, *bi*convex; also, *showing* or *combining two different* or *distinguishable elements*, as in **bi·ra′cial, bi′par′ty**. **2.** *Lasting* or *occurring every two*, as in *bi*ennial, appearing every two years; *bi*weekly. **3.** *Occurring* or *coming twice*, as in *bi*weekly, twice a week. In this sense equiv. to *semi-*, which is preferable to avoid ambiguity. **4.** *Anat.* Indicating *connection with*, or *relation to, each of two symmetrically paired parts* or *points*, as in **bi′al·ve′o·lar, bi-il′i·ac, bi·mas′toid.** **5.** *Chem.* **a** In older names, denoting *the presence of two atoms, two equivalents* or *a double proportion*, of the constituent to the name of which it is prefixed, as in *bi*carbonate, *bi*sulfate (salts formed with twice as much acid as is required for a neutral salt), *bi*chloride (now dichloride). *Bi-* and *di-* were sometimes interchangeable, but *di-* is now usually preferred. **b** In organic chemistry, denoting *the doubling of a radical* or *molecule*, as in *bi*phenyl.

bi·an′gu·lar (bī·ăng′gū·lẽr), *adj.* Having two angles.

bi·an′nu·al (-ăn′ū·ăl), *adj.* Occurring twice a year. Cf. BIENNIAL. — **bi·an′nu·al·ly**, *adv.*

bi′as (bī′ăs), *n.* [F. *biais*.] **1.** A diagonal line of seam, cut, or stitching across a fabric. **2.** A propensity or prepossession; bent; prejudice. **3.** *Bowls.* The lopsided shape of a bowl, causing it to swerve when rolled; also, the tendency of the bowl to swerve, or the impulse causing this. **4.** *Elec.* The direct voltage in the grid circuit of an electron tube. — **Syn.** See PREDILECTION. — ***on the bias.*** Diagonally; obliquely to the texture. — *adj.* Cut or shaped on the bias; as, a *bias* yoke. — *adv.* Obliquely; diagonally; hence, awry. — *v. t.*; BI′ASED or BI′ASSED (bī′ăst); BI′AS·ING or BI′AS·SING. To give a bias to; to prejudice. — **Syn.** See INCLINE.

bi′au·ric′u·lar (bī′ô·rĭk′ū·lẽr), **bi′au·ric′u·late** (-lāt), *adj.* Having two auricles.

bi·ax′i·al (bī·ăk′sĭ·ăl), *adj.* Having two axes. — **bi·ax′i·al·ly**, *adv.*

bib (bĭb), *v. t.* & *i.*; BIBBED (bĭbd); BIB′BING. [L. *bibere*.] To drink; sip; tipple. — *n.* **1.** A cloth or plastic shield tied under a child's chin to protect the clothes. **2.** A top of an apron or of overalls that extends above the waist in front. — **bib′less**, *adj.*

bi·bas′ic (bī·bās′ĭk), *adj.* Dibasic.

bibb (bĭb), *n.* *Naut.* A sidepiece of timber bolted to the hounds of a mast to support the trestletrees.

bib′ber (bĭb′ẽr), *n.* A tippler; — chiefly in composition.

bib′cock′ (-kŏk′), *n.* A faucet having a bent-down nozzle.

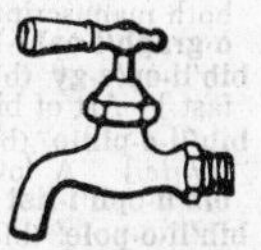

Bibcock.

‖**bi′be·lot′** (bē′blō′; *E.* bĭb′lō), *n.* [F.] A small decorative article of virtu.

bi′-bi·va′lent (bī′bī·vā′lĕnt; bī·bĭv′ȧ·lĕnt), *adj.* *Chem.* Of an electrolyte, that dissociates into two bivalent ions.

Bi′ble (bī′b'l), *n.* [OF., fr. L. *biblia*, fr. Gr. *biblia*, pl. of *biblion*, dim. of *biblos* book, papyrus.] **1.** The book made up of writings accepted by Christians as inspired by God and of divine authority; the Scriptures, including the Old and New Testaments. A pre-Christian Greek translation (the ***Septuagint***) of the Hebrew Old Testament and the Greek version of the New Testament form the Bible in use in the Orthodox Church and some other Eastern churches. The ***Vulgate***, a Latin version made by St. Jerome and others in the 4th century, is the basis of the English translation, completed in 1610, popularly known as the ***Douay Bible or Version*** and of a translation of the New Testament now current in the United States, used by Roman Catholics. The ***Authorized Version, or King James Bible***, published in 1611, and its revisions the ***Revised Version*** (English), completed in 1885, the ***American Revised Version*** (otherwise called ***American Standard Version***), completed in 1901, and the ***Revised Standard Version***, a revision of the American Standard Version and Authorized Version completed in 1952, are the chief English translations in Protestant use. Certain books or parts of books which are in the Vulgate, but which are omitted from the Protestant versions of the Old Testament because not found in the Hebrew Scriptures, form a separate collection called the ***Apocrypha.***

THE BOOKS OF THE OLD TESTAMENT

Canonical Books of the Authorized Version

(Douay Version names are given wherever they differ from those of the Authorized Version)

Genesis*	1 Kings	Esther
Exodus*	*D.V.* 3 Kings	Job
Leviticus*	2 Kings	Psalms
Numbers*	*D.V.* 4 Kings	Proverbs
Deuteronomy*	1 Chronicles	Ecclesiastes
Joshua*	*D.V.* 1 Paralipomenon	Song of Solomon
D.V. Josue	2 Chronicles	*D.V.* Canticle of Canticles
Judges*	*D.V.* 2 Paralipomenon	
Ruth	Ezra	Isaiah
1 Samuel	*D.V.* 1 Esdras	*D.V.* Isaias
D.V. 1 Kings	Nehemiah	Jeremiah
2 Samuel	*D.V.* 2 Esdras,	*D.V.* Jeremias
D.V. 2 Kings	alias Nehemias	Lamentations

* Collectively, the first five books of the Old Testament are called the Pentateuch, the first six the Hexateuch, the first seven the Heptateuch

Ezekiel	D.V. Abdias	Zephaniah
D.V. Ezechiel	Jonah	D.V. Sophonias
Daniel	D.V. Jonas	Haggai
Hosea	Micah	D.V. Aggeus
D.V. Osee	D.V. Micheas	Zechariah
Joel	Nahum	D.V. Zacharias
Amos	Habakkuk	Malachi
Obadiah	D.V. Habacuc	D.V. Malachias

THE BOOKS OF THE NEW TESTAMENT

Matthew	Ephesians	Hebrews
Mark	Philippians	James
Luke	Colossians	1 Peter
John	1 Thessalonians	2 Peter
Acts of the Apostles	2 Thessalonians	1 John
Romans	1 Timothy	2 John
1 Corinthians	2 Timothy	3 John
2 Corinthians	Titus	Jude
Galatians	Philemon	Revelation
		D.V. Apocalypse

THE PROTESTANT APOCRYPHA

Tobit	In the D.V., Tobias, a canonical book following Nehemiah, or 2 Esdras.
Judith	In the D.V. a canonical book following Tobias.
Esther (in part)	In the D.V., chapters 11–16 of Esther.
Wisdom of Solomon	In the D.V., Wisdom, a canonical book following the Canticle of Canticles.
Ecclesiasticus, or Wisdom of Jesus, Son of Sirach	In the D.V., Ecclesiasticus, a canonical book following Wisdom.
Baruch	In the D.V., a canonical book following Lamentations.
Song of the Three Children	In the D.V., part of chapter 3 of Daniel.
Susanna	In the D.V., chapter 13 of Daniel.
Bel and the Dragon	In the D.V., chapter 14 of Daniel.
1 & 2 Maccabees	In the D.V., 1 & 2 Machabees, canonical books at the end of the Old Testament.
1 & 2 Esdras	Not in the D.V.
Prayer of Manasses	Not in the D.V.

2. A book containing the sacred writings of any religion. **3.** [*not cap.*] A book looked upon as authoritative.

Bib′li·cal (bĭb′lĭ·kǎl), *adj.* Of, pertaining to, derived from, or in accord with the Bible. — **Bib′li·cal·ly**, *adv.*

Bib′li·cist (-sĭst), *n.* One versed in the Bible; also, one who adheres to the letter of the Bible.

bib′li·o- (bĭb′lĭ·ō-). [Gr. *biblion*.] A combining form meaning *book* or *books*, or *the Bible*, as in **bib′li·ol′a·ter**, **bib′li·ol′a·trous**, **bib′li·ol′a·try**, **bib′li·o·man′cy**, **bib′li·o·ma′ni·a**, **bib′li·o·ma′ni·ac**, *adj. & n.*, **bib′li·o·ma·ni′a·cal** (see -LATRY, -MANCY, -MANIA).

bib′li·o·film′ (bĭb′lĭ·ō·fĭlm′), *n.* A microfilm used esp. for photographing pages of books, etc.

bib′li·og′ra·pher (-ŏg′rá·fẽr), *n.* Also **bib′li·o·graph′** (bĭb′lĭ·ō·grȧf′). [Gr. *bibliographos*, fr. *biblion* book + *graphein* to write.] One who writes bibliography or is versed in bibliography.

bib′li·og′ra·phy (-fĭ), *n.; pl.* -PHIES (-fĭz). **1.** The history or description of books and manuscripts, with notices of the editions, the dates of printing, etc. **2.** A list of writings relating to a given subject or author. **3.** The systematic historical and technical study of writings, both manuscripts and books. — **bib′li·o·graph′ic** (-ō·grăf′ĭk), **bib′li·o·graph′i·cal** (-ĭ·kǎl), *adj.*

bib′li·op′e·gy (bĭb′lĭ·ŏp′ẽ·jĭ), *n.* [*biblio-* + Gr. *pēgnynai* to make fast.] Art of binding books.

bib′li·o·phile (bĭb′lĭ·ō·fīl; -fĭl), **bib′li·o·phil** (-fĭl), *n.* [*biblio-* + *-phile*.] A lover of books. — **bib′li·oph′i·lism** (-ŏf′ĭ·lĭz′m), *n.* — **bib′li·oph′i·list** (-lĭst), *n.*

bib′li·o·pole′ (bĭb′lĭ·ō·pōl′), *n.* [From L., fr. Gr. *bibliopōlēs*, fr. *biblion* book + *pōlēs* seller.] One who sells books, esp. rare or curious books. — **bib′li·op′o·ly** (-ŏp′ō·lĭ), *n.* — **bib′li·op′o·list** (-lĭst), *n.*

bib′li·o·the′ca (-thē′ká), *n.* A library.

bib′li·ot′ics (bĭb′lĭ·ŏt′ĭks), *n.; see* -ICS. [*biblio-* + Eng. adj. suffix *-otic*; — coined by Persifor Frazer (1844–1909), Am. scientist.] The science of handwriting analysis, esp. the study of documents and of writing materials, as for determining genuineness or authorship. — **bib′li·ot′ic** (-ĭk), *adj.* — **bib′li·o·tist** (bĭb′lĭ·ō·tĭst), *n.*

Bib′list (bĭb′lĭst; bī′blĭst), *n.* **1.** One who makes the Bible the sole rule of faith. **2.** A Biblical scholar.

bib′u·lous (bĭb′ṵ·lŭs), *adj.* [L. *bibulus*, fr. *bibere* to drink.] **1.** Highly absorbent, as a sponge. **2.** Addicted to drink; tippling. — **bib′u·lous·ly**, *adv.* — **bib′u·lous·ness**, *n.*

bi·cam′er·al (bī·kăm′ẽr·ǎl), *adj.* Consisting of two chambers, or legislative branches.

bi·cap′su·lar (-kăp′sṵ·lẽr), *adj. Bot.* Having two capsules or a two-celled capsule.

bi·car′bon·ate (-kär′bǒn·āt), *n.* An acid carbonate.

bicarbonate of soda. Sodium bicarbonate.

bice (bīs), *n.* [OF. *bis* dark gray.] The color of malachite (**bice green**) or of azurite (**bice blue**), or a pigment from these.

bi·cen′te·nar′y (bī·sĕn′tē·nĕr′ĭ; bī′sĕn′tē·nă·rĭ; -tē′nȧ·rĭ), *adj.* Of or pertaining to two hundred, esp. two hundred years. — *n.* A bicentennial.

bi′cen·ten′ni·al (bī′sĕn·tĕn′ĭ·ǎl), *adj.* **1.** Consisting of two hundred years. **2.** Occurring every two hundred years. — *n.* The two-hundredth anniversary, or its celebration.

bi·ceph′a·lous (bī·sĕf′á·lŭs), *adj.* [*bi-* + *-cephalous*.] Having two heads.

bi′ceps (bī′sĕps), *n.* [L., two-headed, fr. *bis* twice + *caput* head.] A muscle having two heads or origins; esp.: **a** The large flexor muscle of the front of the upper arm. **b** The large flexor muscle of the back of the upper leg.

bi·chlo′ride (bī·klō′rīd; -rĭd), *n.* Also **bi·chlo′rid**. **1.** Dichloride. In a loose use, **bichloride of mercury**, or mercuric chloride, HgCl₂.

bi·chro′mate (-krō′māt), *n. Chem.* A salt of dichromic acid, esp. po-

tassium dichromate or sodium dichromate. — *v. t.* To treat or combine with a bichromate.

bi·cip′i·tal (bī·sĭp′ĭ·tǎl; -t′l), *adj.* [L. *biceps, bicipitis*. See BICEPS.] Having two heads or origins, as certain muscles; pertaining to a biceps muscle.

bick′er (bĭk′ẽr), *v. i.* **1.** To contend petulantly; wrangle. **2.** To move quickly and unsteadily; quiver; flicker. — *n.* Petulant quarreling; a wrangle. — **bick′er·er**, *n.*

bick′er (bĭk′ẽr), *n.* [See BEAKER.] *Scot.* A kind of wooden bowl for porridge, liquor, etc.

Bi′col (bē′kōl). Var. of BIKOL.

bi·col′or, bi·col′our (bī′kŭl′ẽr), **bi·col′ored, bi·col′oured** (-ẽrd), *adj.* [L. *bicolor*.] Of two colors.

bi·con′cave (bī·kŏn′kāv; bī′kŏn·kāv′; -kŏng′kāv; 2), *adj.* Concave on both sides. See LENS, *Illust.*

bi·con′vex (bī·kŏn′vĕks; bī′kŏn·vĕks′), *adj.* Convex on both sides. See LENS, *Illust.*

bi′corn (bī′kôrn), *adj.* [L. *bicornis*, fr. *bi-* + *cornu* horn.] Two-horned; crescentlike.

bi·cor′nu·ate (bī·kôr′nṵ·āt), *adj.* Bicorn.

bi′cron (bī′krŏn; bĭk′rŏn), *n. Physics.* A unit equal to one billionth (.000,000,001) of a meter. Symbol, μμ.

bi·cus′pid (bī·kŭs′pĭd), *adj.* Also **bi·cus′pi·date** (-pĭ·dāt). [See BI-; CUSPIDATE.] Having or ending in two points, as teeth, leaves, etc.

bi·cus′pid, *n.* In man, either of the two double-pointed teeth on each side of each jaw. See TOOTH, *n., Illust.*

bi′cy·cle (bī′sĭk·'l), *n.* [F., fr. *bi-* + Gr. *kyklos* circle, wheel.] A light vehicle having two wheels one behind the other, a steering handle, a saddle seat or seats, and pedals by which it is propelled. — **bi′cy·cle**, *v. i.* — **bi′cy·cler** (-lẽr), *n.* — **bi′cy·clist** (-lĭst), *n.*

bi·cy′clic (bī·sī′klĭk; -sĭk′lĭk), *adj.* Also **bi·cy′cli·cal** (-klĭ·kǎl). Consisting of, or arranged in, two cycles.

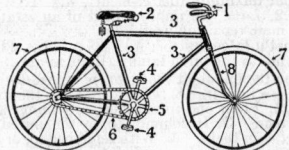

Bicycle. 1 Handle Bar; 2 Saddle; 3, 3, 3 Frame; 4, 4 Pedals; 5 Sprocket Wheel; 6 Chain; 7, 7 Tires; 8 Fork.

bid (bĭd), *v. t.; past* BADE (băd), BID, *Archaic* BAD; *past part.* BID′DEN (bĭd′'n), BID; *pres. part.* BID′DING. [From AS. *biddan*, but early confused with AS. *bēodan* to offer, command. Bid now has the form of ME. *bidden* to ask, but the meaning of ME. *beden* to command.] **1.** [*past & past part.* BID.] To offer as a price, whether for payment or acceptance, as at an auction; as, to *bid* a dollar. **2.** To order; command. **3.** *Chiefly Dial.* To invite; request to come. **4.** To express or utter, as a wish or greeting. **5.** [*past & past part.* BID.] *Card Playing.* To make a bid of or in. — **Syn.** See COMMAND. — *v. i.* To make a bid; as, to *bid* for votes.

bid beads. To say prayers; loosely, to say the rosary. — **bid fair.** To seem likely. — **bid in.** In an auction, to overbid, in the interest of the owner, the highest offer made. — **bid up.** In an auction, to raise the price of by bids.

— *n.* **1.** Act of one who bids; an offer or that which is offered, as at an auction; also, in some card games, an announcement of what a player proposes to undertake, such as the winning of a certain number of tricks. **2.** An attempt or effort to win, achieve, or attract; often specif., an appeal or plea, as for sympathy. **3.** One's turn at bidding. **4.** *Colloq.* An invitation. — **bid′der**, *n.*

bid′da·ble (bĭd′á·b'l), *adj.* **1.** Obedient; docile. **2.** Strong enough to warrant a bid; as, a *biddable* card hand.

bid′ding, *n.* A command; an invitation or summons.

bid′dy (bĭd′ĭ), *n.; pl.* -DIES (-ĭz). A hen or chicken.

bide (bīd), *v. i.; past* BODE (bōd); *past & past part.* BID′ED (bīd′ĕd; -ĭd); *pres. part.* BID′ING (bīd′ĭng). [AS. *bīdan*.] *Archaic & Dial.* **1.** To wait; to tarry. **2.** To remain in a place; stay. **3.** To continue in a state or action. **4.** To dwell or sojourn. — *v. t.* **1.** To wait for; — now only in *to bide one's time.* **2.** To encounter; withstand; also, to endure; tolerate. — **bid′er** (bīd′ẽr), *n.*

bi·den′tate (bī·dĕn′tāt), *adj.* Two-toothed.

bield (bēld), *n. & v. Scot.* Shelter.

‖**bien en′ten·du′** (byăN′-näN′täN′dü′). [F.] Well understood; of course.

bi·en′ni·al (bī·ĕn′ĭ·ǎl; 58), *adj.* [L. *biennalis*, fr. *biennium* a space of two years, fr. *bis* twice + *annus* year.] **1.** Taking place once in two years; as, a *biennial* election. Cf. BIANNUAL. **2.** Continuing or lasting for two years, as certain plants producing leaves the first year of their life and fruit and seeds the second. — *n.* **1.** A biennial event or occurrence. **2.** A biennial plant. — **bi·en′ni·al·ly**, *adv.*

bi·en′ni·um (bī·ĕn′ĭ·ŭm), *n.; pl.* -NIA (-á). [L.] A period of two years.

‖**bien·ve·nue′** (byăN′vė·nü′), *n.* [F.] Welcome.

bier (bẽr), *n.* [AS. *bær*.] **1.** A litter; now, specif., the frame on which a coffin is placed, or borne to the grave. **2.** The coffin and its stand.

biest′ings (bēs′tĭngz). Var. of BEESTINGS.

bi·fa′cial (bī·fā′shǎl), *adj.* **1.** Having two fronts or faces, as the god Janus. **2.** *Bot.* Dorsiventral.

bi·far′i·ous (bī·fâr′ĭ·ŭs), *adj.* [L. *bifarius*, fr. *bi-* + *fari* to speak.] **1.** *Rare.* Twofold. **2.** Pointing two ways, as opposite leaves. — **bi·far′i·ous·ly**, *adv.*

biff (bĭf), *n.* A blow. — *v. t.* To hit. *Both Slang, U. S.*

bif′fin (bĭf′ĭn), *n.* [For *beefing*, from being red like raw beef.] *Eng.* A red variety of cooking apple.

bi′fid (bī′fĭd), *adj.* [L. *bifidus*, fr. *bi-* + root of *findere* to cleave.] Divided into two equal lobes or parts by a median cleft. — **bi·fid′i·ty** (bī·fĭd′ĭ·tĭ), *n.* — **bi′fid·ly**, *adv.*

bi·fi′lar (bī·fī′lẽr), *adj.* Two-threaded; involving the use of two threads. — **bi·fi′lar·ly**, *adv.*

bi·flag′el·late (-flăj′ẽ·lāt), *adj.* Having two long, narrow, whiplike appendages.

bi′flex (bī′flĕks), *adj.* Bent in two directions; having two bends.

bi·fo′cal (bī·fō′kǎl), *adj.* Having two foci, as an eyeglass lens having one part that corrects for near, and another for distant, vision. — *n.* A bifocal glass or lens.

bi·fo′li·ate (bī·fō′lĭ·āt), *adj.* Two-leaved.

bi·fo′li·o·late (bī·fō′lĭ·ō·lāt; bī′fō·lĭ′ō·lāt), *adj.* *Bot.* Having two leaflets, as some compound leaves.
bi′form′ (bī′fôrm′), *adj.* Also **bi′formed′** (-fôrmd′; 2). [L. *biformis*, fr. *bi-* + *forma* shape.] Having two forms; combining characteristics of two forms, as a satyr.
Bif′rost (bēf′rŏst), *n.* [ON. *bifröst.*] *Norse Myth.* The rainbow bridge connecting Asgard and Midgard.
bi′fur·cate (bī′fẽr·kāt; bī·fûr′kāt), *v. t. & i.* To divide into two branches; to fork. — **bi′fur·cate** (bī′fẽr·kāt; bī·fûr′kāt), *adj.* — **bi′fur·cate·ly**, *adv.* — **bi′fur·ca′tion** (bī′fẽr·kā′shŭn), *n.*
big (bĭg), *adj.*; BIG′GER; BIG′GEST. [ME. *big, bigge.*] **1.** *Now Rare.* Strong; mighty. **2.** Large in size, bulk, extent, etc. **3.** Pregnant; swelling; teeming. **4.** Of the voice, full and loud. **5.** Important; imposing. **6.** Magnanimous. — **Syn.** See LARGE. — **Ant.** Little. — **big, big′ly**, *adv.* — **big′ness**, *n.*
big, bigg (bĭg), *v. t.* [ON. *byggja.*] *Dial.* To build.
big′a·mist (bĭg′ȧ·mĭst), *n.* One guilty of bigamy.
big′a·mous (-mŭs), *adj.* [ML. *bigamus.*] Guilty of bigamy; involving bigamy. — **big′a·mous·ly**, *adv.*
big′a·my (-mĭ), *n.* [From OF., fr. ML. *bigamus*, fr. *bi-* + Gr. *gamos* marriage.] The act of ceremonially marrying one person when already legally married to another. Cf. MONOGAMY, DIGAMY.
big′ar·reau′ (bĭg′ȧ·rō′; bĭg′ȧ·rō), *n.* Also **big′a·roon′** (bĭg′ȧ·rōōn′). [F. *bigarreau*, fr. *bigarré* variegated.] A cultivated sweet cherry, having firm flesh. See CHERRY, 1.
Big Ben. The great bell attached to the "Westminster clock" in the Parliament clock tower, London.
bi′ge·ner (bī′jē·nẽr), *n.* [L. See BI-; GENUS.] A bigeneric hybrid.
bi′ge·ner′ic (bī′jē·nĕr′ĭk), *adj.* Of or pert. to two genera; as, a *bigeneric* hybrid, one between species of different genera.
bigg, big (bĭg), *n.* [ME. *big, bigge*, fr. ON. *bygg.*] *Dial. Eng.* The four-rowed variety of barley.
big′gin (bĭg′ĭn), *n.* [F. *béguin.*] **1.** A child's cap; a hood; a nightcap. **2.** *Eng.* The coif of a serjeant-at-law.
big′gin, big′ging (bĭg′ĭn), *n.* [See BIG, *v.*] *Scot. & Dial.* A building; a house.
big′horn′ (bĭg′hôrn′), *n.*; *pl.* -HORN, -HORNS. See PLURAL, *Note*, 6. The wild sheep (*Ovis canadensis*) of the Rocky Mountains. See MOUNTAIN SHEEP.

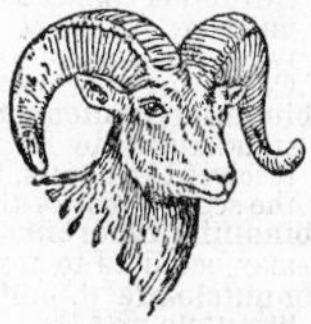

Bighorn. (1/25)

bight (bīt), *n.* [AS. *byht.*] **1.** A corner, bend, or angle; a hollow. **2.** The middle part of a rope; a loop, or double part, of a rope. **3.** A bend or curve, as in a river or a mountain chain; specif., a bend in a coast, forming an open bay; also, the bay itself; as, the *Bight* of Benin. — *v. t.* To fasten with a bight or bights; also, to lay or fasten in bights.
big·no′ni·a (bĭg·nō′nĭ·ȧ), *n.* [NL., after the Abbé *Bignon.*] Any of a genus (*Bignonia*) of American and Japanese woody vines with compound leaves and tubular flowers. The genus typifies the family Bignoniaceae (see TRUMPET CREEPER). — **big·no′ni·a′ceous** (-ā′shŭs), *adj.*
big′ot (bĭg′ŭt), *n.* [F., bigot, hypocrite (in OF. a name once given to the Normans in France).] One obstinately or intolerantly devoted to his own church, party, belief, or opinion.
big′ot·ed (-ĕd; -ĭd), *adj.* So obstinately attached to some creed, opinion, or practice as to be illiberal or intolerant. — **big′ot·ed·ly**, *adv.*
big′ot·ry (-rĭ), *n.* State of mind of a bigot; also, acts or beliefs ensuing from such a state.
big top. The top of the main tent of a circus; hence, the main tent; also, the circus.
big tree. The giant sequoia. See SEQUOIA.
big′wig′ (bĭg′wĭg′), *n.* *Humorous.* A person of consequence.
bi·hour′ly (bī·our′lĭ), *adj.* Once in two hours.
bi′jou (bē′zhōō; bē′zhōō′), *n.*; *pl.* BIJOUX (bē′zhōōz; bē′zhōōz′). [F.] An exquisitely wrought trinket; a jewel.
bi·jou′te·rie (bē·zhōō′tē·rē; *F.* bē′zhōō′trē′), *n.* [F.] Bijoux, collectively; also, articles of virtu.
bi′ju·gate (bī′jōō·gāt; bī·jōō′gāt), **bi′ju·gous** (-gŭs), *adj.* [L. *bi-* + *jugatus* joined.] *Bot.* Having two pairs of leaflets; — said of a pinnate leaf.
bike (bīk), *n.* *Chiefly Scot.* A nest of wild bees, wasps, etc.; a swarm; hence, a swarm or crowd of people.
bike (bīk), *n. & v.* *Colloq.* Short for BICYCLE.
Bi′kol, Bi′col (bē′kōl), *n.* One of a Christian Malayan people of southeastern Luzon and adjacent islands.
bi·la′bi·al (bī·lā′bĭ·ăl), *adj.* **1.** Bilabiate. **2.** Of certain consonants, formed or articulated with the aid of both lips, as *p, b, m.* — *n.* A bilabial consonant.
bi·la′bi·ate (-āt), *adj.* *Bot.* Having two lips, as some corollas.
bil′an·der (bĭl′ăn·dẽr; bī′lăn-), *n.* [D. *bijlander*, fr. *bij* by + *land* land.] A small two-masted merchant vessel, used esp. for coasting or on canals, as in Holland.
bi·lat′er·al (bī·lăt′ẽr·ăl), *adj.* **1.** Having, arranged upon, or relating to, two sides, esp. two corresponding or complementary sides; as, the *bilateral* symmetry of the body; *bilateral* descent. **2.** Affecting reciprocally both sides or parties; as, a *bilateral* contract or treaty. **3.** Bilaterally symmetrical. — **bi·lat′er·al·ism** (-ĭz′m), *n.* — **bi·lat′er·al·ly**, *adv.* — **bi·lat′er·al·ness**, *n.*
bil′ber′ry (bĭl′bĕr′ĭ; -bẽr·ĭ), *n.*; *pl.* -RIES (-ĭz). [Dan. *böllebær.*] **1.** The European whortleberry (*Vaccinium myrtillus*). **2.** Any of several other species of blueberry (genus *Vaccinium*).
bil′bo (bĭl′bō), *n.*; *pl.* -BOES (-bōz). [From *Bilbao*, Spain.] **1.** *Hist.* A rapier; a sword. **2.** A long bar or bolt of iron with sliding shackles, used as a fetter; — used in *pl.*
bilch (bĭlch), *n.* [Orig. unknown.] The dormouse.
bile (bīl), *n.* [F., fr. L. *bilis.*] **1.** The yellow, or greenish, viscid fluid secreted by the liver. In old physiology, ***yellow bile*** (choler) and ***black bile*** (melancholy) constituted two of the four humors. See HUMOR, 2 **a**. **2.** Choler; ill-humor.
bilge (bĭlj), *n.* [Var. of BULGE.] **1.** The protuberant part of a cask. **2.** *Naut.* **a** That part of a ship's underwater body extending outward from the keel to the point where the sides rise vertically. **b** Internally, the bottom of the hull. **3.** Short for **bilge water**, foul water that collects in the hull bottom; hence, *Slang*, anything, esp. utterances, stale or worthless. — *v. i. & t.*; BILGED (bĭljd); BILG′ING (bĭl′jĭng). **1.** *Naut.* To fracture or suffer fracture in the bilge; to leak or cause to leak because of such a fracture. **2.** To bulge or cause to bulge.
bilge keel. Also **bilge piece.** A keel secured for a distance along a ship about at the turn of the bilge on either side, to check rolling.
bilg′y (bĭl′jĭ), *adj.* Having the smell of bilge water.
bil′har·zi′a·sis (bĭl′här·zī′ȧ·sĭs), *n.* [NL., fr. *Bilharzia* a genus of blood flukes + *-iasis.*] = SCHISTOSOMIASIS.
bil′i·ar′y (bĭl′ĭ·ĕr′ĭ; -ẽr·ĭ; -yẽr·ĭ), *adj.* [F. *biliaire*, fr. L. *bilis* bile.] Conveying bile; as, a *biliary* duct; pert. to bile, the bile ducts, or the gall bladder; as, the *biliary* tract.
bi·lin′e·ar (bī·lĭn′ē·ẽr), *adj.* Of or pertaining to two lines; as, *bilinear* co-ordinates.
bi·lin′gual (bī·lĭng′gwăl), *adj.* [L. *bilinguis*, fr. *bi-* + *lingua* tongue, language.] Of, containing, expressed in, or using, two languages; as, a *bilingual* dictionary; a *bilingual* nation. — **bi·lin′gual·ism** (-ĭz′m), *n.* — **bi·lin′gual·ly**, *adv.*
bi·lin′guist (-gwĭst), *n.* One versed in two languages.
bil′ious (bĭl′yŭs), *adj.* [L. *biliosus*, fr. *bilis* bile. See BILE.] **1.** Of or pertaining to the bile. **2.** Suffering from or resulting from excess of bile or disordered functioning of the liver. **3.** Characteristic or suggestive of a bilious person or condition; as: **a** Choleric; ill-tempered. **b** Sickly in color or appearance. — **bil′ious·ly**, *adv.* — **bil′ious·ness**, *n.*
-bil′i·ty (-bĭl′ĭ·tĭ). A noun termination corresponding to *-ble*, as in vulner*ability*, possi*bility*.
bilk (bĭlk), *v. t.* **1.** To evade payment of. **2.** To frustrate; disappoint; also, to deceive; defraud. — *n.* **1.** A hoax. **2.** An untrustworthy person; a cheat. — **bilk′er**, *n.*
bill (bĭl), *n.* [AS. *bile.*] **1.** The beak or nib of a bird. **2.** A similar

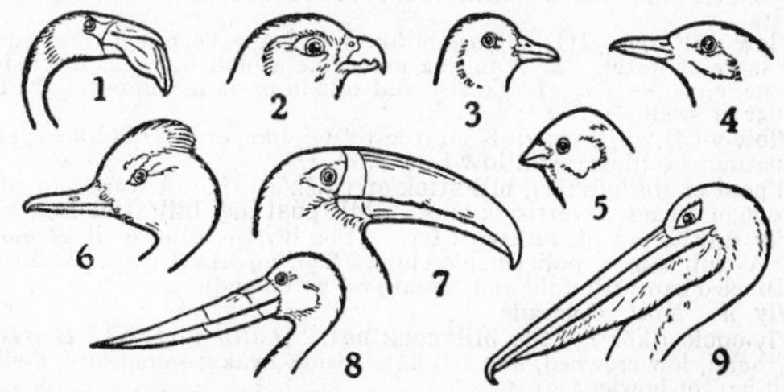

Bills of Birds. 1 Flamingo; 2 Hawk; 3 Pigeon; 4 Thrush; 5 Finch; 6 Duck (Merganser); 7 Toucan; 8 Spoonbill; 9 Pelican.

beak in other animals. — *v. i.* To join bills, as doves; to caress in fondness.
bill (bĭl), *n.* [AS. *bill, bil.*] **1.** *Hist.* A military weapon consisting of a long staff terminating in a hook-shaped blade. **2.** Also **bill′hook′** (-hŏŏk′). A cutting or pruning implement with a hooked point. **3.** Also **bill′man** (-măn). One who wields a bill. **4.** The end of an anchor fluke or of a yard. See ANCHOR, *Illust.*
bill, *n.* [AF. *bille*, Anglo-Lat. *billa*, fr. ML. *bulla* document, seal, fr. L. *bulla* bubble, boss.] **1.** *Obs.* A written document, orig. under seal. **2.** *Rare.* A document containing a petition. **3.** A draft of a law presented to a legislature for enactment; — disting. from *act* (def. 2). **4.** A placard, poster, or handbill. **5.** A statement of particulars or items; a list; as, a *bill* of (legal) exceptions; specif.: **a** A printed program, esp. for a theatrical entertainment; hence, the entertainment itself. **b** An itemized account of indebtedness for goods sold, services rendered, etc. **6. a** Short for BILL OF EXCHANGE. **b** A promissory note; specif., *U. S.*: (1) A piece of paper money, as a bank note, treasury note, etc. (2) An individual or business note; as, *bills* receivable. **7.** *Law.* A declaration in writing stating some wrong the complainant has suffered from the defendant, or a breach of law by some person. — *v. t.* **1.** To make a bill or list of. **2.** To submit a bill to. **3.** To advertise, as by bills or posters; also, to placard with bills. — **bill′er**, *n.*
bil′la·bong′ (bĭl′ȧ·bŏng′), *n.* [Native name.] *Australia.* A blind channel leading out from a river; also, any backwater that forms a stagnant pool.
bill′board′ (bĭl′bōrd′; 70), *n.* *Naut.* A projection or ledge fixed on the bow of a vessel for the anchor to rest on.
bill′board′, *n.* A flat surface, as of a panel, wall, or fence, on which bills are posted; also, a bulletin board.
bill′bug′ (-bŭg′), *n.* Any of various weevils which feed upon the roots of cereal crops; — from their long snouts.
bil′let (bĭl′ĕt; -ĭt), *n.* [OF. *billette, bullette*, dim. of *bulle*, fr. ML. *bulla.*] **1.** *Archaic.* A note; a short letter. **2.** A written order or ticket; specif., *Mil.*, an official requisition upon a person for the lodging of a soldier. **3.** Quarters or place to which one is assigned, as by a billet; hence, berth; position; appointment. — *v. t.* **1.** *Mil.* To direct by a billet where to lodge; hence, to quarter. **2.** To assign a billet to. **3.** To serve with a billet. — **bil′let·er**, *n.*
bil′let, *n.* [OF. *billete*, dim. of *bille* log, round stick, fr. ML. *billia.*] **1.** A small stick of wood, as for firewood. **2.** An ornament in Norman moldings, resembling a billet of wood. **3.** A bar of metal; specif., a length of semifinished iron or steel about 1½ to 4 in. square.
bil′let-doux′ (bĭl′ā·dōō′; *F.* bē′yĕ′dōō′), *n.*; *pl.* BILLETS-DOUX (bĭl′ā·dōōz′; *F.* bē′yĕ′dōō′). [F., fr. *billet* note + *doux* sweet, fr. L. *dulcis.*] A love letter or note.
bill′fish′ (bĭl′fĭsh′), *n.*; *pl.*, see FISH. **a** Any of various fishes with bill-shaped jaws, as a gar or a spearfish.
bill′fold′ (-fōld′), *n.* A folding pocketbook for bills.
bill′head′ (-hĕd′), *n.* A blank with a business address at the top and spaces beneath for billing charges.
bill′hook′ (-hŏŏk′), *n.* See 2d BILL, 2.
bil′liard (bĭl′yẽrd), *n.* **1.** Attributive form of BILLIARDS, as in **billiard ball, table**. **2.** *Colloq.*, *U. S.* A carom.
bil′liards (bĭl′yẽrdz), *n.* [F. *billard* billiards, fr. OF. *billart* staff, cue, fr. *bille* log.] Any of several games played on an oblong table surrounded by an elastic ledge or cushions, with balls impelled by a cue. Cf. *balk-line game*, under BALK LINE, 2; POOL, *n.*, 2. — **bil′liard·ist**, *n.*
bil′lings·gate′ (bĭl′ĭngz·gāt′ *or, esp. Brit.*, -gĭt; -gĕt), *n.* [From a former city gate of London.] **1.** [*cap.*] A London fish market which became notorious for foul and abusive language. **2.** Coarsely abusive language; coarse vituperation. — **Syn.** See ABUSE.
bil′lion (bĭl′yŭn), *n.* [F., fr. L. *bis* twice, in imitation of *million* million.] **a** In French and American numeration, a thousand millions

(1,000,000,000); — *billion* being the usual American term, **milliard** the usual French term. **b** In British and German numeration, a million millions (1,000,000,000,000). See NUMERATION. — **bil′lion,** *adj.* — **bil′lionth** (bĭl′yŭnth), *adj. & n.*

bil′lion·aire′ (bĭl′yŭn·âr′; 2), *n.* One whose wealth is a billion or more, as of francs or dollars.

bill′man (bĭl′măn), *n.* See 2d BILL, 3.

bill of exchange. An unconditional written order from one person to another to pay to some person designated a certain sum of money therein named; a draft. Abbr. *B/E* or *b. e.*

bill of fare. A list of the dishes, as in a restaurant, that are to be served at a meal; a menu; also, figuratively, a program.

bill of health. A certificate attesting the state of health as to infectious diseases of a ship's company and of a port, given to a ship's master at the time of departure.

bill of lading. A paper listing goods shipped and acknowledging their receipt, signed by the agent of the owner of a vessel or issued by a common carrier. Abbr. *B/L* or *b. l.*

bill of rights. [*often caps.*] A summary of rights and privileges claimed by a people; specif.: **a** The declaration presented by the lords and commons of England to the prince and princess of Orange in 1689. **b** The first ten amendments to the Constitution of the United States.

bill of sale. A formal instrument for the conveyance or transfer of title to goods and chattels. Abbr. *B/S* or *b. s.*

bil′lon (bĭl′ŭn), *n.* [F.] An alloy of silver with more than its weight of copper, tin, or the like; hence, gold or silver heavily alloyed with base metal.

bil′low (bĭl′ō), *n.* [ON. *bylgja* billow.] **1.** A wave, esp. a great wave or surge of water. **2.** A rolling mass like a high wave, as of cloud, flame, etc. — *v. i.* **1.** To rise and roll in or as in billows. **2.** To bulge or swell.

bil′low·y (-ĭ), *adj.;* -I·ER (-ĭ·ẽr); -I·EST. Of, like, or full of billows; undulating; swelling. — **bil′low·i·ness,** *n.*

bill′post′er (bĭl′pōs′tẽr), **bill′stick′er** (-stĭk′ẽr), *n.* A workman who posts, or affixes, advertising bills. — **bill′post′ing, bill′stick′ing,** *n.*

bil′ly (bĭl′ĭ), *n.; pl.* BILLIES (-ĭz). [For *Willie,* dim. of *William.*] **1.** A club, esp. a policeman's club. **2.** *Orig. Australia.* A tin or enameled can with a lid and, usually, a wire handle.

bil′ly, *n. Dial.* Comrade.

bil′ly·cock′ (-kŏk′), *n., or* **billycock hat.** [*bully* + *cock.*] *British.* A round, low-crowned, soft felt hat; a wide-awake; sometimes, a stiff felt hat, or bowler.

billy goat. *Colloq.* A male goat.

bi·lo′bate (bī·lō′bāt), **bi·lo′bat·ed** (-bāt·ĕd; -ĭd), *adj.* Divided into two lobes.

bi·loc′u·lar (-lŏk′ū·lẽr), **bi·loc′u·late** (-lāt), *adj.* Divided into two cells or compartments.

bil′sted (bĭl′stĕd), *n. U. S.* The sweet gum (see GUM).

bil′tong′ (bĭl′tŏng′), *n.* [S. Afr. D.] *S. Afr.* Jerked meat.

bi·man′u·al (bī·măn′ū·ăl), *adj.* Done with or requiring the use of both hands. — **bi·man′u·al·ly,** *adv.*

bi·men′sal (-mĕn′săl; -s′l), *adj.* Bimonthly.

bi·mes′ter (bī·mĕs′tẽr), *n.* [L. *bimestris* of two months, fr. *bi-* + L. *mensis* month.] A period of two months.

bi·mes′tri·al (-mĕs′trĭ·ăl), *adj.* Lasting two months; also, bimonthly.

bi′me·tal′lic (bī′mĕ·tăl′ĭk), *adj.* [From F. *bimétallique* and E. *bi-* + *metallic.*] **1.** Composed of two different metals. **2.** Using a double metallic standard (as gold and silver) for coins or currency; of or pertaining to bimetallism.

bi·met′al·lism (bī·mĕt′ăl·ĭz′m), *n.* The use for coins or currency of two metals (as gold and silver) to form at the same time, in combination with each other at a ratio fixed by law, the standard of value. Cf. MONOMETALLISM. — **bi·met′al·list** (-ĭst), *n.*

bi′mil·len′ni·um (bī′mĭ·lĕn′ĭ·ŭm), *n.* [NL., fr. *bi-* + NL. *millennium.*] Two thousand years, or a two thousandth anniversary.

bi′mo·lec′u·lar (bī′mō·lĕk′ū·lẽr), *adj. Chem.* Pert. to or formed from two molecules.

bi·month′ly (bī·mŭnth′lĭ), *adj.* Occurring, done, or coming, once in two months. — *n.* A bimonthly publication. — *adv.* Once in two months.

bin (bĭn), *n.* [AS. *binn, binne,* manger, crib.] A box or receptacle for storage. — *v. t.;* BINNED (bĭnd); BIN′NING. To put into a bin.

bin-. = BI-; — used before vowels, as in *bin*aural.

bi′na·ry (bī′nȧ·rĭ), *adj.* [L. *binarius,* fr. *bini* two by two, two at a time, fr. root of *bis* twice.] **1.** Compounded, consisting of, or characterized by two things or parts. **2.** *Chem.* Composed of two elements, of an element and a radical that acts as an element, or of two such radicals; as, *binary* salts. — *n.; pl.* -RIES (-rĭz). That which is constituted of two things or parts; specif., *Astron.,* a binary star.

binary star. *Astron.* A stellar system consisting of two suns that revolve about its common center of mass. Cf. DOUBLE STAR.

bi′nate (bī′nāt), *adj.* [L. *bini* two by two.] *Bot.* Double; growing in pairs or couples. — **bi′nate·ly,** *adv.*

bin·au′ral (bĭn·ô′răl), *adj.* [*bin-* (= BI-) + *aural.*] Having two ears; relating to or used by both ears; involving the use of both ears.

bind (bīnd), *v. t.;* BOUND; BIND′ING. [AS. *bindan,* past tense *band, bundon,* past part. *bunden.*] **1.** To tie or confine with a cord, band, etc.; hence, to confine, restrain, hold, or restrict as if by a band; as, frost *binds* the streams. **2.** To cause to cohere; to unite into a solid or fluid mass; as, to use tar to *bind* the gravel for a path. **3.** To cover as with a bandage; bandage; — sometimes with *up;* as, to *bind* up a wound. **4.** To make fast (a thing) *about* or *upon* something, as by tying; as, to *bind* a belt about one. **5.** To constipate; as, certain drugs *bind* the bowels. **6.** To protect, strengthen, or decorate by a band or binding; as, to *bind* the edge of a carpet. **7.** To sew or fasten together and enclose in a cover; as, to *bind* a book. **8.** To put under constraint or obligation with respect to performance; as, to *bind* oneself by a promise; he was *bound* over to keep the peace; specif., *Law,* to place under legal obligation to serve; to indenture; as, to be *bound* out to service. **9.** To make irrevocable or obligatory, as by giving a pledge or earnest; as, to *bind* a bargain. — *v. i.* **1.** To tie up anything; as, to reap and *bind.* **2.** To form a stiff or coherent mass. **3.** To be hindered in movement, natural action, etc. **4.** To have the effect of confining, restraining, constraining, uniting, etc.; as, a promise that *binds.* — *n.* **1.** That which binds or ties; act of binding; state of being bound. **2.** *Music.* A tie.

bind′er (bīn′dẽr), *n.* **1.** One who binds; specif., a bookbinder. **2.** A band, tie, cord, ligature, etc. **3.** A substance that binds, as tar or cement. **4.** A mechanical device or machine for binding. **5.** A written instrument binding parties to an agreement. **6.** A cover or other device for holding together loose papers, etc.

bind′er·y (bīn′dẽr·ĭ), *n.; pl.* -ERIES (-ĭz). A place where books are bound; a bookbinder's establishment.

bind′ing, *n.* **1.** The act of one that binds. **2.** Material used in binding books, garments, etc. **3.** *Skiing.* The set of fastenings, usually of straps, sometimes with metal brackets and clamps, for holding the toe of the boot firm on the ski. — *adj.* That binds; esp., obligatory. — **bind′ing·ly,** *adv.* — **bind′ing·ness,** *n.*

binding energy. *Physics & Chem.* The quantity of energy required to disintegrate an atomic nucleus completely into its constituent particles.

bind′weed′ (bīnd′wēd′), *n.* See CONVOLVULUS.

bine (bīn), *n.* [Var. of BIND.] Any twining stem, or flexible shoot, as of the hop; hence: **a** Bindweed. **b** The woodbine (*Lonicera*).

Bi·net′ (bē′nā′; *F.* bē′nĕ′), *or* **Bi·net′–Si·mon′** (-sē′môɴ′), **test.** [After its French devisers.] An intelligence test consisting orig. of tasks graded for children up to twelve years but later extended in range.

bing (bĭng), *n.* [ON. *bingr.*] *Now Dial.* A heap.

bing, *v. i. Old Slang.* To go. *Scott.*

binge (bĭnj), *n. Colloq.* A spree.

bin′go (bĭng′gō), *n.* = BEANO, 2.

bin′na·cle (bĭn′ȧ·k′l), *n.* [From earlier *bittacle,* through Pg., fr. L. *habitaculum* dwelling place.] *Naut.* A case, box, or stand containing a ship's compass (set in gimbals), and a lamp for use at night.

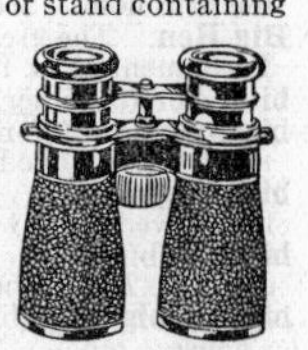
Binoculars.

bin·oc′u·lar (bĭn·ŏk′ū·lẽr; bī·nŏk′-), *adj.* Pertaining to both eyes; using, or adapted to the use of, both eyes. — *n.* Also **bin·oc′u·lars.** A binocular microscope, telescope, opera glass, or the like. — **bin·oc′u·lar′i·ty** (-lăr′ĭ·tĭ), *n.* — **bin·oc′u·lar·ly,** *adv.*

bi·no′mi·al (bī·nō′mĭ·ăl), *n.* [*bi-* + Gr. *nomos* law, rule.] **1.** *Alg.* An expression consisting of two terms connected by the sign plus (+) or minus (−). **2.** *Biol.* A species name consisting of two terms. See BINOMIAL NOMENCLATURE. — *adj.* Consisting of or pert. to binomials. — **bi·no′mi·al·ly,** *adv.*

binomial nomenclature. *Biol.* The system of nomenclature, first standardized by Linnaeus, in which each species (of animals and plants) receives two names, the first being that of the genus to which it belongs, the second that of the species itself.

binomial theorem. *Alg.* The theorem by means of which a binomial may be raised to any power without performing the multiplications.

bi·nu′cle·ate (bī·nū′klē·āt), *adj.* Also **bi·nu′cle·at′ed** (-āt′ĕd; -ĭd), **bi·nu′cle·ar** (-ẽr). Having two nuclei.

bi′o- (bī′ō-), **bi-.** [Gr. *bios* life, mode of life.] A combining form denoting *relation to,* or *connection with, life, vital phenomena,* or *living organisms;* often, *biological; physiological;* as in:

biocentric	**biolinguistics**	**biophysiology**
bioclimatic	**biomagnetism**	**biopsychic**
bioclimatology	**biomicroscopy**	**biopsychology**
bioeconomic	**bio-osmosis**	**bioreaction**
bioelectric	**biophysics**	**biosocial**
biogeography	**biophysiography**	**biosociological**

bi′o–as·say′ (bī′ō·ȧ·sā′; -ăs′ā), *n.* Estimation of the strength of a drug, etc., by testing its effects on a living organism, as by feeding to rats. — (-ȧ·sā′), *v. t.* To test by bio-assay.

bi′o·cat′a·lyst (-kăt′ȧ·lĭst), *n.* [*bio-* + *catalyst.*] A substance which activates or stimulates a biochemical reaction, as insulin; a coenzyme, a vitamin, or a hormone.

bi′o·chem′is·try (-kĕm′ĭs·trĭ), *n.* Chemistry that deals with the chemical compounds and processes occurring in organisms (plants and animals). — **bi′o·chem′ic** (-ĭk), **bi′o·chem′i·cal** (-ĭ·kăl), *adj.* — **bi′o·chem′i·cal·ly,** *adv.* — **bi′o·chem′ist** (-ĭst; 2), *n.*

bi′o·dy·nam′ics (-dī·năm′ĭks; -dĭ-), *n.;* see -ICS. [*bio-* + *dynamics.*] Physiology treating of the active vital phenomena of organisms; — opp. to *biostatics.* — **bi′o·dy·nam′ic** (-ĭk), **-i·cal** (-ĭ·kăl), *adj.*

bi′o·e·col′o·gy (bī′ō·ē·kŏl′ō·jĭ), *n.* [*bio-* + *ecology.*] The branch of ecology that deals with the interrelations and interactions of plants and animals. — **bi′o·ec′o·log′ic** (-ĕk′ō·lŏj′ĭk; -ē′kō-), **-i·cal** (-ĭ·kăl), *adj.* — **-i·cal·ly,** *adv.* — **bi′o·e·col′o·gist** (-ē·kŏl′ō·jĭst), *n.*

bi′o·gen′e·sis (-jĕn′ē·sĭs), **bi·og′e·ny** (bī·ŏj′ē·nĭ), *n.* [*bio-* + *-genesis, -geny.*] *Biol.* **1.** The development of life from pre-existing life. **2.** The supposed tendency for stages in the evolutionary history of a race to briefly recur during the development and differentiation of an individual of that race. — **bi′o·ge·net′ic** (-jē·nĕt′ĭk), **bi′o·ge·net′i·cal** (-ĭ·kăl), *adj.* — **bi′o·ge·net′i·cal·ly,** *adv.*

Bi′o·graph (bī′ō·grăf; 9), *n.* A trade-mark for an early type of motion-picture recorder and projector.

bi·og′ra·pher (bī·ŏg′rȧ·fẽr; bĭ-), *n.* A writer of biography.

bi·og′ra·phy (bī·ŏg′rȧ·fĭ; bĭ-), *n.; pl.* -PHIES (-fĭz). [Gr. *biographia,* fr. *bios* life + *graphein* to write.] **1.** The written history of a person's life. **2.** Biographical writings collectively or as a literary genre. — **bi′o·graph′ic** (bī′ō·grăf′ĭk), **-i·cal** (-ĭ·kăl), *adj.* — **-i·cal·ly,** *adv.*

bi′o·log′i·cal (bī′ō·lŏj′ĭ·kăl), *adj.* Also **bi′o·log′ic** (-ĭk). **1.** Of or pertaining to biology or life and living processes. **2.** Used in or produced by applied biology; as, *biological* supplies. — *n. Pharm.* A biological product. — **bi′o·log′i·cal·ly,** *adv.*

biological warfare. Warfare involving the use of living organisms, especially disease germs, and toxic substances produced by them, against men, animals, or plants; also, warfare involving the use of synthetic chemicals harmful to plants.

bi·ol′o·gism (bī·ŏl′ō·jĭz′m), *n. Philos.* A system or doctrine formulated from the biological point of view, or based on biological modes of explanation; also, adherence to such a doctrine or point of view.

bi·ol′o·gy (bī·ŏl′ō·jĭ), *n.* [*bio-* + *-logy.*] **1.** The science of life; the branch of knowledge which treats of living organisms. **2.** Plant and animal life, as of a region; also, biological history, laws, or phenomena; as, the *biology* of a wasp. — **bi·ol′o·gist** (-jĭst), *n.*

bi′o·lu′mi·nes′cence (bī′ō·lū′mĭ·nĕs′ĕns; -′ns), *n.* [*bio-* + *luminescence.*] The emission of light from living organisms as the result of internal oxidative changes. — **bi′o·lu′mi·nes′cent** (-ĕnt; -′nt), *adj.*

bi·om′e·try (bī·ŏm′ē·trĭ), *n.* [*bio-* + *-metry.*] **a** Calculation of the probable duration of human life. **b** Also **bi′o·met′rics** (bī′ō·mĕt′rĭks); see -ICS. *Biol.* The science of statistics applied to biological observations. — **bi′o·met′ric** (bī′ō·mĕt′rĭk), **bi′o·met′ri·cal** (-rĭ·kăl), *adj.* — **bi′o·met′ri·cal·ly,** *adv.*

bi′o·nom′ics (bī′ō·nŏm′ĭks), *n.*; see -ICS. [*bio-* + *-nomics* as in *economics.*] Ecology. — **bi′o·nom′ic** (-ĭk), **bi′o·nom′i·cal** (-ĭ·kăl), *adj.* — **bi′o·nom′i·cal·ly**, *adv.* — **bi·on′o·mist** (bī·ŏn′ō·mĭst), *n.*

bi′op·sy (bī′ŏp·sĭ), *n.* [See BIO-; -OPSIS.] *Med.* The removal and examination (usually microscopic) of a piece of tissue from the living body, esp. for diagnosis.

bi′o·scope (bī′ō·skōp), *n.* A motion-picture projector.

-bi·o′sis (-bī·ō′sĭs). [NL., fr. Gr. *biōsis* way of life.] *Biol.* A combining form denoting *a* (specified) *mode of living*, as in sym*biosis*.

bi·os′o·phy (bī·ŏs′ō·fĭ), *n.* [*bio-* + *-sophy.*] A system of spiritual self-education developed by Dr. Frederick Kettner, of New York. — **bi′o·soph′i·cal** (bī′ō·sŏf′ĭ·kăl), *adj.*

bi′o·sphere′ (bī′ō·sfēr′), *n.* The sphere of living organisms penetrating the lithosphere, hydrosphere, and atmosphere.

bi′o·stat′ics (bī′ō·stăt′ĭks), *n.*; see -ICS. Physiology treating of the structure of organisms in relation to their functions; — opp. to *biodynamics.* — **bi′o·stat′ic** (-ĭk), **bi′o·stat′i·cal** (-ĭ·kăl), *adj.*

bi′o·syn′the·sis (-sĭn′thē·sĭs), *n. Biochem.* The synthesis of a chemical compound by a living organism.

bi·o′ta (bī·ō′tȧ), *n.* [NL.] The flora and fauna of a region.

bi·ot′ic (bī·ŏt′ĭk), *adj.* Also **bi·ot′i·cal** (-ĭ·kăl). [Gr. *biōtikos* pert. to life.] *Biol.* Relating to life; biological.

-bi·ot′ic. A combining form for *biotic*, denoting *having a* (specified) *mode of life.* Cf. -BIOSIS.

biotic potential. The productive capacity in respect to living things of a region, soil type, etc.

bi′o·tin (bī′ō·tĭn), *n.* [Gr. *bios* life + *-in* (with euphonic *t*).] A member of the vitamin-B complex. See VITAMIN.

bi′o·tite (bī′ō·tīt), *n.* [After J. B. *Biot*, French naturalist.] A species of mica, usually black or dark green, forming a common constituent of crystalline rocks. It is a silicate of iron, magnesium, potassium, and aluminum. H., 2.5–3. Sp. gr., 2.7–3.1. — **bi′o·tit′ic** (-tĭt′ĭk), *adj.*

bi′o·type (-tīp), *n.* [*bio-* + *-type.*] *Biol.* A genotypic race or group of organisms. — **bi′o·typ′ic** (-tĭp′ĭk), *adj.*

bi′pack′ (bī′păk′), *n.* A pack of two separate films with the emulsions in contact, each sensitive to a different color, for single exposure.

bip′a·rous (bĭp′ȧ·rŭs), *adj.* [*bi-* + *-parous.*] **1.** *Zool.* Bringing forth two young at a birth. **2.** *Bot.* Having dichotomous branching.

bi·par′ti·san (bī·pär′tĭ·zăn), *adj.* Representing, or composed of members of, two parties. — **bi·par′ti·san·ship′**, *n.*

bi·par′tite (bī·pär′tīt), *adj.* [L. *bipartitus*, past part. of *bipartire.*] **1.** Having two parts; having two correspondent parts, one for each of two parties; as, a *bipartite* contract. **2.** *Bot.* Divided into two parts almost to the base, as a leaf. — **bi·par′tite·ly**, *adv.* — **bi′par·ti′tion** (bī′pär·tĭsh′ŭn; -pẽr·tĭsh′ŭn), *n.*

bi′ped (bī′pĕd), *n.* [L. *bipes*, fr. *bi-* + *pes, pedis*, foot.] A two-footed animal, as man. — **bi′ped, bi′pe·dal** (bī′pē·dăl; -d′l; -pĕd·′l; bĭp′ē-), *adj.*

bi·phen′yl (bī·fĕn′ĭl; -fē′nĭl), *n.* A white crystalline hydrocarbon, $C_6H_5.C_6H_5$. Its molecule consists of a doubled phenyl group.

bi·pin′nate (-pĭn′āt), *adj. Bot.* Twice pinnate, that is, having pinnate pinnae, as a leaf.

bi′plane′ (bī′plān′), *n.* An airplane with two main supporting planes, in typical forms one above the other.

bi′pod (bī′pŏd), *n.* [*bi-* + *-pod* as in tri*pod.*] A two-legged stand or mount, as for a trench mortar.

bi·po′lar (bī·pō′lẽr), *adj.* **1.** Having or pert. to two poles; as, *bipolar* dynamos. **2.** Pert. to the polar regions. **3.** Having two diametrically opposed natures, views, etc. — **bi′po·lar′i·ty** (bī′pō·lăr′ĭ·tĭ), *n.*

bi·quad′rate (bī·kwŏd′rāt), *n. Math.* The fourth power, or the square of the square. — **bi′quad·rat′ic** (bī′kwŏd·răt′ĭk), *adj.*

bi·ra′di·al (-rā′dĭ·ăl), *adj.* Both bilateral and radial in arrangement.

birch (bûrch), *n.*; *pl.* BIRCHES (bûr′chĕz; -chĭz). [AS. *birce, bierce, beorc.*] **1.** A timber tree of the genus *Betula*, most species having a hard close-grained wood, and outer bark consisting of membranous, easily separable layers. Common species include: the ***white birch*** of Europe (*B. alba*); the related ***white birch*** of North America (*B. papyrifera*), called also ***paper birch or canoe birch***, whose white bark is often worked into fancy articles, as baskets; the ***American gray birch*** of North America (*B. populifolia*), common as a second-growth forest tree; the ***western paper birch*** of western North America (*B. fontinalis*), called also ***gray birch***; the ***yellow birch*** of North America (*B. lutea*), whose strong light-brown wood is used for furniture, buttons, etc. The genus typifies a family (Betulaceae, the birch family) distinguished by simple leaves, monoecious flowers, and one-seeded nutlike fruit and including also the alder (genus *Alnus*) and the hazel (*Corylus*). **2.** The wood or timber of the birch. **3.** A birch twig or twigs for flogging. — *v. t.* To flog with a birch. — **birch, birch′en** (bûr′chĕn), *adj.*

bird (bûrd), *n.* [ME. *brid, bred, bird*, young bird, bird, fr. AS. *bridd.*] **1.** *Obs.* The young of any feathered vertebrate. **2.** Any member of a class (Aves) of warm-blooded vertebrates, distinguished from all other animals by the body being more or less completely covered with feathers. **3.** A game bird; also, the shuttlecock in badminton. **4.** A clay pigeon. **5.** A fellow or guy, esp. a queer one. **6.** *Slang.* A hissing or jeering in disapproval; as, to get, or give one, the *bird.* — *v. i.* **1.** To catch or shoot birds. **2.** To observe or identify wild birds in their natural environment.

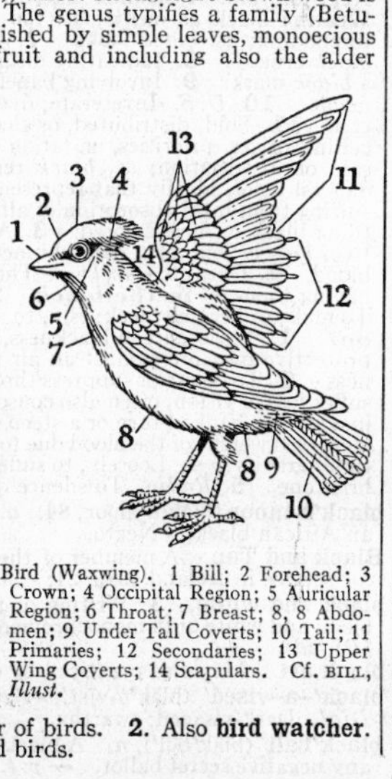

Bird (Waxwing). 1 Bill; 2 Forehead; 3 Crown; 4 Occipital Region; 5 Auricular Region; 6 Throat; 7 Breast; 8, 8 Abdomen; 9 Under Tail Coverts; 10 Tail; 11 Primaries; 12 Secondaries; 13 Upper Wing Coverts; 14 Scapulars. Cf. BILL, *Illust.*

bird′call′ (-kôl′), *n.* The call of a bird, or a sound or instrument imitative of one.

bird cherry. See CHERRY.

bird dog. A gun dog trained to hunt birds.

bird′er (bûr′dẽr), *n.* **1.** A breeder of birds. **2.** Also **bird watcher.** One who observes or identifies wild birds.

bird grass. a The knotgrass *Polygonum aviculare.* **b** A European forage grass (*Poa trivialis*) naturalized in eastern North America.

bird′house′ (bûrd′hous′), *n.* A box for birds to rest in or an aviary.

bird′ie (bûr′dĭ), *n.* **1.** Dim. of BIRD. **2.** *Golf.* A score of one stroke less than par on a hole. Cf. EAGLE, *n.*, 5.

bird′lime′ (bûrd′līm′), *n.* [*bird* + *lime* viscous substance.] **1.** A sticky substance, usually made from the bark of the holly *Ilex aquifolium*, smeared on twigs to snare small birds. **2.** Hence, anything that ensnares. — *v. t.* To smear or snare with birdlime; to ensnare.

bird′man′ (-măn′; -măn), *n.* **1.** One who deals with birds, as a fowler, ornithologist, etc. **2.** *Colloq.* An aviator.

bird of paradise. Any of a number of brilliantly colored, plumed, oscine birds (family Paradiseidae) inhabiting New Guinea and the adjacent islands.

bird of passage. A migratory bird or (*Colloq.*) person

bird of prey. Any carnivorous bird of a group consisting of hawks, eagles, etc., and owls.

bird pepper. See PEPPER, 3.

bird′s′–eye′ (bûrdz′ī′), *n.* **1.** Any of numerous plants having small, bright-colored flowers. **2.** A cotton fabric woven in a bird's-eye design; also, the design. — *adj.* **1.** Seen from above, as if by a flying bird; hence, cursory; as, a *bird's-eye* view. **2.** Marked with spots resembling birds' eyes; as, *bird's-eye* maple.

bird′s′–foot′, bird′–foot′, *n.* **1.** Any of numerous plants having leaves or flowers resembling the foot of a bird; — commonly used attributively. **2.** Specif., any of several plants of the pea family, having bent and jointed pods.

bird's–foot fern. **1.** The tropical American fern *Cheilanthes radiata.* **2.** A rock brake (*Pellaea ornithopus*) of the Pacific coast of North America.

bird's–foot trefoil. Any of a genus (*Lotus*, esp *L corniculatus*) of European plants with clawlike pods.

bird's–foot violet. A common violet (*Viola pedata*) of the eastern United States, with pedate leaves and large, pansylike flowers. It is the State flower of Wisconsin.

bird′s′–nest′, *n.* The nest of various swifts (genus *Collocalia*) of southern Asia, made chiefly of the dried glutinous secretion of their salivary glands, used chiefly in making soup.

bird watcher. See BIRDER, 2.

bird′wom′an (bûrd′wo͝om′ăn), *n. Colloq.* An aviatress.

bi′reme (bī′rēm), *n.* [L. *biremis*, fr. *bi-* + *remus* oar.] A galley with two banks of oars, — common in the early classical period.

bi·ret′ta (bĭ·rĕt′ȧ), **ber·ret′ta** (bĕ·rĕt′ȧ), *n.* [It. *berretta*, fr. LL., a cap, dim. of L. *birrus* a cloak with a hood.] A square cap with three projections above the crown, worn by Roman Catholic clergymen. The pope's is white, a cardinal's scarlet, a bishop's purple, other clerics' black. Cf. ZUCCHETTO.

birk (bûrk; bĭrk), **birk′en.** *Scot. & Dial. Eng.* Vars. of BIRCH, BIRCHEN.

birk′ie (bûr′kĭ; bĭr′kĭ), *n Scot.* A lively or assuming fellow.

birl (bûrl), *v. t. & i.* To spin; also, to whirr.

birle (bûrl; bĭrl), *v. t. & i.* [AS. *byrlian* to pour out.] *Now Dial.* To pour (beer or wine); to ply with drink.

birr (bûr), *n.* [ON. *byrr* wind.] **1.** Force, as of the wind or of an onslaught; impetus; also, energy; vigor. **2.** A whirring sound. — *v. i.*; BIRRED (bûrd); BIRR′ING. To make or move with a birr.

birse (bûrs; *Scot.* bĭrs), *n.* [AS. *byrst.*] *Chiefly Scot.* **a** Bristle or bristles. **b** Temper.

birth (bûrth), *n.* [ME. *burth, birth*, appar. of Scand. origin.] **1.** Act or fact of coming into life, or of being born; also, act of bringing forth. **2.** That which is born or produced. **3.** Lineage; extraction; descent; sometimes, high or noble birth or descent. **4.** One's state, position, vocation, etc., by inheritance or natural gift; as, a poet by *birth.* **5.** Origin; beginning.

birth control. Control or limitation of the number of children born, esp. by preventing, or lessening the frequency of, impregnation, as by the use of contraceptives.

birth′day′ (bûrth′dā′), *n.* **1.** Day of birth or origin. **2.** The anniversary of this day; hence, a year of life.

birth′mark′ (-märk′), *n.* Some peculiar mark or blemish on the skin at birth; a nevus. — **birth′mark′**, *v. t.*

birth′place′ (-plās′), *n.* Place of birth or origin

birth rate. The number of births per hundred or per thousand persons in a given group during a given time.

birth′right′ (-rīt′), *n.* Any right acquired by birth. — **Syn.** See HERITAGE.

birth′root′ (-ro͞ot′; 85), *n.* Any of various trilliums (esp. *Trillium erectum*) having an astringent rootstock.

birth′stone′ (-stōn′), *n.* A precious stone considered as appropriate to, or symbolizing the influences due to, the month of one's birth or, occasionally, the day of the week on which one was born.

birth′wort′ (-wûrt′), *n.* **1.** Any of several species of a genus (*Aristolochia*, typifying a family, Aristolochiaceae, the birthwort family) of herbs or woody vines, the aromatic roots of which are reputed to aid in childbirth. **2.** Birthroot.

bis (bĭs), *adv.* [L. *bis* twice, fr. root of *duo* two.] Twice; — used as a direction to repeat, or as a mark of repetition.

Bi·sa′yan (bē·sä′yăn). Var. of VISAYAN.

bis′cuit (bĭs′kĭt), *n.*; *pl.* BISCUITS, BISCUIT. [F., fr. L. *bis* twice + *coctus*, past part. of *coquere* to cook.] **1.** A kind of unleavened bread, plain, sweet, or fancy, formed into flat cakes, and baked hard. In British use *biscuit* is applied to what are called in U. S. *crackers* and *cookies.* **2.** *U. S.* A kind of raised bread baked in small shapes cut or dropped from dough leavened with baking powder, soda, yeast, etc. **3.** *Ceramics.* Unglazed pottery after the first firing. **4.** A very light tan color.

‖**bise** (bēz), *n.* [F.] A cold dry north wind of southern France, Switzerland, and Italy.

bi′sect′ (bī′sĕkt′), *v. t.* [L. *bi-* + *secare, sectum*, to cut.] To divide into two parts; specif., *Geom.*, into two equal parts. — *v. i.* To fork, as a road; to cross. — **bi·sec′tion** (bī·sĕk′shŭn), *n.* — **bi·sec′tion·al** (-ăl; -′l), *adj.* — **bi·sec′tion·al·ly**, *adv.*

bi·sec′tor (bī·sĕk′tẽr), *n.* One that bisects; esp., *Geom.*, a straight line that bisects an angle or a line segment.

bi·sec′trix (-trĭks), *n.*; *pl.* -TRICES (bī′sĕk·trī′sēz). A bisector; specif., a line bisecting the angle between the optic axes of a biaxial crystal.

bi·ser′rate (bī·sĕr′ăt), *adj.* **a** *Bot.* Doubly serrate; having the serrations serrate. **b** *Zool.* Serrate on both sides.

bi·sex′u·al (-sĕk′shōō·ăl; 118), *adj.* Of or pert. to both sexes; specif., hermaphrodite, as some animals and plants.

bish′op (bĭsh′ŭp), *n.* [AS. *bisceop, biscop*, fr. L. *episcopus* overseer, bishop, fr. Gr. *episkopos*, fr. *epi* over + *skopos* inspector.] **1**. In some churches, a clergyman of the highest order, usually the head of a diocese or the administrative superior of a district. **2**. A spiritual overseer or director. **3**. A beverage of port wine, oranges or lemons, and sugar. **4**. *U.S.* Formerly, a woman's bustle. **5**. *Chess.* A piece moving diagonally any number of unoccupied squares. Abbr. *B*

bish′op·ric (-rĭk), *n.* [AS. *bisceoprīce*, fr. *bisceop* bishop + *rīce* dominion.] **1**. A diocese. **2**. Office of a bishop.

bish′op's-cap′ (bĭsh′ŭps·kăp′), *n.* = MITERWORT **a**.

bisk (bĭsk). Var. of BISQUE.

bis′muth (bĭz′mŭth; bĭs′mŭth), *n.* [G.] One of the chemical elements, a brittle, grayish-white metal with reddish tinge. Symbol, *Bi*; at. no., 83; at. wt., 209.00. — **bis′muth·al** (-mŭth·ăl), *adj.* — **bis·mu′thic** (bĭz·mū′thĭk; -mŭth′ĭk; bĭs-), *adj.* — **bis′muth·ous** (bĭz′mŭth·ŭs; bĭs′-), *adj.*

bi′son (bī′s'n; -z'n), *n. sing. & pl.* [F., fr. L. *bison*, fr. OHG. *wisunt*.] A large, shaggy-maned, oxlike quadruped (genus *Bison*), having short horns and heavy forequarters with a large hump; specif.: **a** The European aurochs (*B. bonasus*). **b** The American buffalo (*B. bison*).

bisque (bĭsk), *n.* [F.] In certain games, odds of a point, or (in golf) a stroke or strokes, or (in croquet) an extra turn, to be taken when desired.

bisque, *n.* [Corrupt. of *biscuit*.] **1**. *Ceramics.* Biscuit. **2**. A color, red-yellow in hue, of low saturation and high brilliance. Cf. COLOR.

bisque, *n.* [F.] **1**. A rich soup of shellfish or of the flesh of birds or rabbits; now also, a rich cream soup thickened with a purée, as of tomato. **2**. A rich ice cream containing powdered nuts or macaroons. — **Syn.** See SOUP.

bis·sex′tile (bĭ·sĕks′tĭl; -tīl), *adj.* [L. *bissextilis*.] Containing or designating the extra day (now generally Feb. 29) added in leap year. — *n.* Leap year.

bis′ter, bis′tre (bĭs′tĕr), *n.* [F. *bistre*.] A dark-brown pigment used in water color; also, its color.

bis′tort (bĭs′tôrt), *n.* [L. *bis* + *tortus*, past part. of *torquere* to twist.] A European herb (*Bistorta bistorta*); also, a related American species (*B. bistortoides*). The twisted root is used as an astringent.

‖**bi′stro′** (bē′strō′; *Angl.* bĭs′trō), *n.* [Parisian argot.] A small or unpretentious wineshop or eating place.

bi·sul′cate (bī·sŭl′kāt), *adj.* **1**. Two-grooved. **2**. Cloven.

bi·sul′fate (-fāt), *n.* *Chem.* An acid sulfate. See BI-, 5.

bi·sul′fide (-fīd; -fĭd), *n.* Also **bi·sul′fid.** Disulfide.

bi·sul′fite (-fīt), *n.* *Chem.* An acid sulfite. See BI-, **5.**

bi′sym·met′ri·cal (bī′sĭ·mĕt′rĭ·kăl), **bi′sym·met′ric** (-rĭk), *adj.* Doubly symmetrical; specif., *Bot.*, see SYMMETRICAL, 2 **a**. — **bi·sym′me·try** (bī·sĭm′ē·trĭ), *n.*

bit (bĭt), *n.* [AS. *bite* a bite, biting.] **1**. The part of a bridle, usually of steel, which is inserted in a horse's mouth. **2**. Anything that curbs or restrains. **3**. The part of a key which enters the lock and acts upon the bolt and tumblers. See KEY, *Illust.* **4**. The biting or cutting edge or part of a tool; also, the tool itself or the cutting piece in a compound tool; specif.: **a** The cutting iron of a plane. **b** A tool for drilling or boring, used in a brace, a drilling machine, etc. See DRILL, *Illust.* — *v. t.;* BIT′TED; BIT′TING. **1**. To put a bridle or bit on; to check. **2**. To form a bit on (a key).

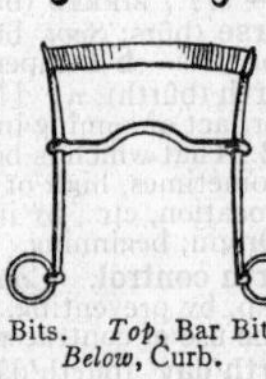

Bits. *Top*, Bar Bit; *Below*, Curb.

bit, *n.* [AS. *bita.*] **1**. A bite; a morsel; now, usually, a very small piece, portion, quantity, or amount; a mite; a whit. **2**. Somewhat; something in a small way; as, he is a *bit* of a poet. **3**. *Colloq.* **a** A short time; a little while. **b** A small coin; also (*U.S.*), 12½ cents, as in ***two bits*** (25 cents, or a quarter dollar). **4**. A small part or role, as in a motion picture.

bi·tar′trate (bī·tär′trāt), *n.* An acid tartrate. See BI-, 5.

bitch (bĭch), *n.* [AS. *bicce.*] **1**. The female of the canine kind. **2**. *Vulgar.* A woman, esp. a lewd woman. — *v. i. Slang.* To complain.

bite (bīt), *v. t.; past* BIT (bĭt); *past part.* BIT′TEN (bĭt′'n), *Colloq.* BIT; *pres. part.* BIT′ING (bīt′ĭng). [AS. *bītan*.] **1**. To seize with the teeth, jaws, or with a jawlike organ, so as to enter, nip, or grip the thing seized; also, to wound, pierce, sting, etc., with a fang, a proboscis, or similar organ. **2**. To cut or pierce, as with an edged weapon. **3**. To cause to smart, sting painfully, etc.; as, winds that *bite* the cheeks. **4**. To grip and hold firmly. **5**. To corrode; to eat into; as, acid *bites* an etcher's plate. **6**. To impress deeply. **7**. To cheat or take in; also, to catch by trickery or a sudden turn of events. — *v. i.* **1**. To bite or have the habit of biting something. **2**. To have biting power or effect; as, mustard *bites;* the anchor *bites*. **3**. To take a bait, as fish; hence, to respond to a lure, esp. a deceitful lure.

bite the dust or ground. To fall fatally wounded.

— *n.* **1**. Act or manner of biting. **2**. A morsel; as much as is taken at once by biting. **3**. Food; esp., *Colloq.*, a snack. **4**. A wound made by biting. **5**. The hold or grip by which friction is created or purchase obtained; also, the surface or surfaces which create such a bite. **6**. A biting sensation or impression. — **bit′er** (bīt′ĕr), *n.*

bite′wing′ (bīt′wĭng′), *n.* *Dentistry.* A type of X-ray film having a fin for biting upon to hold it in place during exposure, that shows the crowns of upper and lower teeth simultaneously.

bit′ing (bīt′ĭng), *adj.* That bites; sharp; cutting; sarcastic; caustic. — **Syn.** See INCISIVE. — **bit′ing·ly**, *adv.* — **bit′ing·ness**, *n.*

bit′stock′ (bĭt′stŏk′), *n.* A stock for rotating a bit; a brace.

bitt (bĭt), *n.* *Naut.* A fixed, vertical timber or metal casting, usually one of a pair, for securing hawsers, cables, and other lines. — *v. t.;* BITT′ED; BITT′ING. To put around the bitts, as a cable.

bit′ten (bĭt′'n), *past part.* of BITE.

bit′ter (bĭt′ĕr), *adj.* [AS. *biter*.] **1**. Having or designating a peculiarly acrid, astringent, or disagreeable taste like that of an infusion of hops. **2**. Distasteful; distressing; painful; poignant. **3**. Expressing grief or pain; as, *bitter* tears. **4**. Piercingly harsh or cruel; stinging; caustic; acrimonious. — *adv.* Bitterly; bitingly. — *n.* **1**. Something bitter. **2**. = BITTERS. **3**. A bitter quality or taste. — *v. t. & i.* To make, or become, bitter. — **bit′ter·ish**, *adj.* — **bit′ter·ly**, *adv.* — **bit′ter·ness**, *n.*

bitter cress. See CRESS.

bitter end. [See BITT, *n.*] *Naut.* The inboard end, as of a cable.

bitter end. The last extremity, however painful or calamitous. Hence, *Colloq.*, **bit′ter–end′er**, one who will not compromise or yield.

bit′tern (bĭt′ĕrn), *n.* [OF. *butor*, fr. L. *butio* bittern (of imitative origin) + *taurus* ox.] Any member of a subfamily (Botaurinae) of small and medium-sized herons, notable for their booming cries.

bit′tern, *n.* [From BITTER, *adj.*] The bitter mother liquor in saltworks after the salt has crystallized out.

bitter principle. *Chem.* Any of various neutral substances of strong bitter taste, as aloin, extracted from plants.

bit′ter·root′ (bĭt′ĕr·rōōt′; 85), *n.* A Rocky Mountain plant (*Lewisia rediviva*) of the purslane family, having handsome pink flowers, adopted as the State flower of Montana.

bit′ters (bĭt′ĕrz), *n. pl.* A liquor, generally spirituous, in which a bitter herb, leaf, or root has been macerated.

bit′ter·sweet′ (bĭt′ĕr·swēt′; 2), *n.* **1**. A sprawling poisonous plant (*Solanum dulcamara*) having purple flowers and oval coral-red berries, and a taste at first sweetish and then bitter. **2**. A North American woody vine (*Celastrus scandens*) having clusters of small greenish flowers succeeded by yellow capsules which open when ripe, disclosing scarlet arils; — called also ***climbing bittersweet.*** — *adj.* Bitter and sweet; pleasant yet painful.

bit′ter·weed′ (bĭt′ĕr·wēd′), *n.* Any of several American plants containing a bitter principle; as: **a** Ragweed. **b** A horseweed (*Leptilon canadense*). **c** A sneezeweed (*Helenium tenuifolium*).

bi·tu′men (bĭ·tū′mĕn; bī-; bĭt′ū-), *n.* [L. *bitūmen*.] Originally, mineral pitch, or asphalt (see ASPHALT); now, any of a number of inflammable mineral substances, including hard, brittle asphalts, semisolid mineral tars, petroleum, and naphthas. — **bi·tu′mi·nize** (bĭ·tū′mĭ·nīz; bī-), *v. t.* — **bi·tu′mi·ni·za′tion** (-nĭ·zā′shŭn; -nī·zā′-), *n.* — **bi·tu′mi·noid** (-noid), *adj.*

bi·tu′mi·nous (bĭ·tū′mĭ·nŭs; bī-), *adj.* Having the qualities of, impregnated or compounded with, or containing bitumen; as, **bituminous coal**, soft coal, which yields, when heated, considerable volatile bituminous matter.

bi·va′lence (bī·vā′lĕns; bĭv′ȧ·lĕns), **bi·va′len·cy** (-lĕn·sĭ), *n.* Quality or state of being bivalent.

bi·va′lent (-lĕnt), *adj.* [*bi-* + L. *valens*, pres. part. See VALENCE.] **1**. *Chem.* Having a valence of two. See VALENCE. **2**. *Biol.* Double; — said of homologous chromosomes when two are associated in synapsis. — *n.* A bivalent chromosome.

bi′valve′ (bī′vălv′), *n.* An animal with a two-valved shell, as a clam or oyster. — *adj.* Having a shell composed of two valves; having two valves or valvelike parts. — **bi·val′vu·lar** (bī·văl′vū·lĕr), *adj.*

biv′ouac (bĭv′wăk; bĭv′ōō·ăk), *n.* [F., fr. G. *beiwache, beiwacht*, fr. *bei* by + *wachen* to watch.] An encampment for a short stay, under improvised shelter or none. — *v. i.;* BIV′OUACKED (-wăkt; -ōō·ăkt); -OUACK′ING. To encamp, as for the night, without tents or housing.

bi·week′ly (bī·wēk′lĭ), *adj.* Occurring or appearing every two weeks; fortnightly; also, semiweekly. See BI-, 2 & 3. — *n.* A biweekly publication. — **bi·week′ly**, *adv.*

bi·year′ly (-yēr′lĭ), *adj.* Occurring twice a year. See BI-, 3.

bi·zarre′ (bĭ·zär′), *adj.* [F., fr. It., fr. Sp. *bizarro* gallant, fr. Basque *bizar* beard, whence the meaning manly, brave.] Odd, extravagant, or eccentric in style or mode; involving sensational contrasts or striking incongruities. — **Syn.** See FANTASTIC. — **bi·zarre′ly**, *adv.* — **bi·zarre′ness**, *n.*

bi·zon′al (bī·zōn′ăl; -'l), *adj.* Combining two zones or pertaining to two combined zones. — **bi′zone′** (bī′zōn′), *n.*

blab (blăb), *v. t. & i.;* BLABBED (blăbd); BLAB′BING. To reveal (secrets or trifles) without reserve or discretion; to tattle; also, to chatter indiscreetly. — *n.* **1**. One who blabs; a telltale. **2**. Chatter; taletelling. — **blab′ber**, *n.*

black (blăk), *adj.* [AS. *blæc*.] **1**. Destitute of light, or incapable of reflecting it; devoid of color or so dark as to have no distinguishable color; — opposed to *white.* **2**. Enveloped in darkness; devoid of light; hence, utterly dismal or gloomy; as, the future looked *black.* **3**. Having dark skin, hair, and eyes; specif., pertaining or belonging to a race characterized by dark pigmentation, including Negroes, Negritos, and Australian natives. **4**. Soiled with dirt; foul. **5**. Wearing black garments; as, the *black* knight. **6**. Sullen; hostile; foreboding; as, *black* looks. **7**. Foully or outrageously wicked; as, *black* cruelty. **8**. Indicating disgrace or dishonor, or culpability; as, a *black* mark. **9**. Involving baneful or forbidden practices; as, *black* magic. **10**. *U.S.* Inveterate; dyed-in-the-wool; as, a *black* Republican. **11**. Sold, distributed, or charged in violation of official quotas, ceiling prices, priorities, or ration restrictions, or conducted for such sale or distribution; as, *black* rent; *black* market. — *n.* **1**. The darkest color, ideally that represented by total absence of light or resulting from total absorption of all light rays. See COLOR. **2**. Something black or dark-colored. **3**. A Negro, Negrito, or Australian native; loosely, one of a dark-skinned race or one having some Negro blood. **4**. *Chess & Checkers.* The dark-colored men; also, the player having them. — ***in the black.*** Showing a net profit. — *v. t. & i.* To make or become black; esp., to apply blacking to (shoes). — ***black out.*** **1**. To obscure in blackness, esp. by extinguishing all lights as a protective measure against an air raid; also, to be engulfed in blackness. **2**. To delete or suppress through censorship. **3**. *Aviation.* To suffer loss of vision, often also consciousness, for an interval of seconds, in a steeply banked turn or a steep pull-out from a dive, because of the increased weight of the blood due to centrifugal force, often five or more times gravity. **4**. Loosely, to suffer a lapse of consciousness, usually a brief one. **5**. *Radio.* To silence or to jam (radio transmission).

black′a·moor (blăk′ȧ·mōōr; 84), *n.* [*black* + *Moor*.] A black; esp., an African black; a Negro.

Black and Tan. A member of the constabulary recruited in England for service in Ireland 1919–21; — from the uniform.

black and white. **1**. Writing or print. **2**. Drawing or printing in black and white or in monochrome. — **black′–and–white′** (*see Pron.*, § 2), *adj.*

black art. Magic as practiced by conjurers and witches.

black′–a–vised′ (blăk′ȧ·vīst′; -vīzd′), **black′–a–viced′** (-vīst′), *adj.* *Dial.* Dark-visaged; swarthy.

black′ball′ (blăk′bôl′), *n.* A black object used as a negative in voting; any negative secret ballot. — *v. t.* To vote against by or as by the use of a blackball; esp., to vote to exclude from membership; hence, to ostracize. — **black'ball'er**, *n.*

black bear. See 2d BEAR, 1.

black'ber'ry (blăk'bĕr'ĭ; -bĕr·ĭ), *n.* [AS. *blæc berie.*] The berrylike fruit of any of various brambles (genus *Rubus*) of the rose family, usually black or dark purple when ripe; also, the plant. See BRAMBLE, RASPBERRY.

blackberry lily. A garden plant (*Belamcanda chinensis*) with lily-like leaves and flower clusters, whose capsule discloses, when ripe, a blackberrylike mass of seeds.

black'-billed' cuck'oo (-bĭld'). See CUCKOO.

black bindweed. 1. A common European twining vine (*Tamus communis*). 2. A twining herb (*Bilderdykia convolvulus*) naturalized in America from Europe, and frequently a troublesome weed.

black'bird' (blăk'bûrd'), *n.* Any of a number of different birds so called because the males are largely or entirely black; as: **a** In England, a common thrush (*Turdus merula*); — also called *merl.* **b** In America, the ***rusty blackbird*** (*Euphagus carolinus*), the ***red-winged blackbird*** (*Agelaius phoeniceus*), with a patch of bright scarlet on the wing coverts of the male, the grackle, the cowbird, etc.

black'board' (-bōrd'; 70), *n.* A dark smooth surface, as of slate, used for writing, drawing, etc., with chalk or crayons.

black book. A book containing a black list. — ***to be in one's black books.*** To be out of one's favor; to be in disgrace with one.

black'boy' (blăk'boi'), *n.* *Australia.* = GRASS TREE **a.**

black brant. See BRANT.

black buck. The common medium-sized antelope (*Antilope cervicapra*) of India. See ANTELOPE, *Illust.*

black'cap' (blăk'kăp'), *n.* **1.** Any of several birds with black crowns, esp. a small European warbler (*Sylvia atricapilla*), the chickadee, etc. **2.** The black raspberry (*Rubus occidentalis*). See RASPBERRY.

black caracara. See CARACARA.

black cherry. See CHERRY.

black'cock' (-kŏk'), *n.* The male of the black grouse.

black cohosh. See COHOSH.

black'damp' (-dămp'), *n.* Chokedamp.

Black Death. A very virulent form of plague which ravaged Asia and Europe in the 14th century.

black diamonds. Coal.

black dog. The spirit of ill-humor or melancholy; as, to be under the *black dog.*

black'en (blăk'ĕn), *v. t.* **1.** To make black or dark. **2.** To defame; to sully. — *v. i.* To grow black or dark. — **black'en·er**, *n.*

black'-eyed' Su'san (blăk'īd'). A coneflower, or yellow daisy (*Rudbeckia hirta*), having yellow to orange rays and dark conical disks. It is the State flower of Maryland. See RUDBECKIA.

black'face' (blăk'fās'), *n.* **1. a** A Negro minstrel, or an actor made up for a Negro role. **b** Theatrical entertainment by Negroes or by persons with blacked faces. **2.** *Printing.* A type with thick black lines, as clarendon. — **black'face'**, *adj.*

black'fel'low (blăk'fĕl'ō), *n.* An Australian aborigine.

black'fish' (-fĭsh'), *n.; plural,* see FISH. **1.** Any one of several small, toothed whales (genus *Globicephala*) found in large schools. **2.** Any of various dark-colored fishes, as the tautog, the black sea bass (*Centropristes striatus*), etc. **3.** A small food fish (*Dallia pectoralis*) of Alaska and Siberia, remarkable for its ability to revive after having been long frozen.

black flag. The flag of a pirate, often bearing a skull and crossbones as an emblem of piracy.

black fly. **a** Any of several small, venomous, two-winged flies (genus *Simulium*) having aquatic larvae. **b** An insect (*Aleurocanthus woglumi*) destructive of citrus fruit trees.

Black'foot' (blăk'fŏŏt'), *n.; pl.* BLACKFEET (-fēt') or, collectively, BLACKFOOT. An Indian of an Algonquian group dwelling in Alberta and Montana.

black fox. See FOX.

Black Friar. A Dominican.

black gnat. *Angling.* An artificial fly with dark-gray wings, black chenille body, and black hackle. Cf. FLY, *Illust.*

black grouse. A large grouse (*Lyrurus tetrix*) of Europe and western Asia. The male (*blackcock*) is black with white wing patches; the female is barred and mottled.

black'guard (blăg'ärd), *n.* [*black* + *guard.*] **1.** *Obs.* The scullions and lower menials of a great household. **2.** A person who uses scurrilous language, or treats others with foul abuse; also, an unprincipled perpetrator of personal injury by foul or corrupt means; a scoundrel. — *v. t.* To revile or abuse scurrilously. — **black'guard**, *adj.* — **black'guard·ism** (-ĭz'm), *n.* — **black'guard·ly**, *adj. & adv.*

black gum. See GUM, 5 **a.**

Black Hand. [A trans. of Sp. *mano negra.*] **a** A former Spanish anarchistic society. **b** An Italian criminal society, originating about 1868, members of which formed the nucleus of a lawless or blackmailing society in the United States.

black haw. A shrub (*Viburnum prunifolium*) bearing cymes of white flowers and bluish-black drupes; also, the related sheepberry (*V. lentago*).

black'head' (blăk'hĕd'), *n.* **1.** A scaup duck. **2.** *Med.* A small plug of fatty matter (sebum) blocking the duct of a sebaceous gland, esp. on the face; a comedo. **3.** *Veter.* A fatal infectious disease of turkeys, peafowl, etc., attacking liver and intestines.

black'heart' (-härt'), *n.* **1.** A heart cherry having a dark flesh and skin. **2.** Any plant disease, as of potato tubers, in which the central tissues blacken.

black hole. A prison dungeon; — from the Black Hole of Calcutta, a small cell into which 146 English prisoners were thrust on the night of June 20, 1756. Only 23 survived until morning.

black'ing, *n.* A preparation that makes things black, esp. one for giving a black luster to boots and shoes, or to stoves.

black'ish, *adj.* Somewhat black. — **black'ish·ly**, *adv.*

black'jack' (blăk'jăk'), *n., or* **black jack.** **1.** A capacious vessel for beer, ale, etc., originally of tar-coated leather. **2.** Caramel, or burnt sugar, used to color wines, spirits, etc. **3.** A pirate flag; the black flag. **4.** *Chiefly U. S.* A small leather-covered club weighted at the head and having an elastic shaft. **5.** A common oak (*Quercus marilandica*) of the eastern United States, with black bark. **6.** *Cards.* = VINGT-ET-UN. **7.** *Mining.* The mineral sphalerite, or zinc blende. — *v. t.* To strike with a blackjack; also, to coerce by threatening.

black knot. A destructive fungus disease of plum and cherry trees, characterized by black, knotty growths on the branches; also, a similar disease, as of the gooseberry.

black lead (lĕd). Graphite.

black'leg' (blăk'lĕg'), *n.* **1.** An infectious, usually fatal, disease, esp. of young cattle. **2.** *Colloq.* A swindler; esp., a dishonest gambler. **3.** *Brit.* A strikebreaker; scab. **4.** A destructive disease of cabbage.

black letter. A style of type. See TYPE.

black'-let'ter, *adj.* **1.** Printed in black letter. **2.** Inauspicious; unlucky; as, *black-letter* days. Cf. RED-LETTER, *adj.*

black list. A list of persons, firms, etc., regarded as suspect or as deserving of censure or adverse discrimination.

black'-list', *v. t.* To put in or on a black list.

black'ly (blăk'lĭ), *adv.* In a black manner; darkly, in color; gloomily; threateningly; atrociously.

black magic. Witchcraft.

black'mail' (-māl'), *n.* [*black* + *mail* payment.] **1.** A tribute anciently exacted on the Scottish border by freebooting chiefs for immunity. **2.** Extortion by intimidation, esp. by threats of public exposure. — *v. t.* To exact blackmail from. — **black'mail'er**, *n.*

Black Ma·ri'a (mȧ·rī'ȧ). *Colloq.* The vehicle, orig. a black closed wagon, in which prisoners are transported to or from jail.

black'-mar'ket, *v. i.* To operate a black market (see BLACK, *adj.*, 11).

black' mar'ket·eer' (mär'kĕ·tēr') *or* **mar'ket·er.** Also **black'et·eer'** (blăk'ĕ·tēr'). An operator in a black market. — **black'-mar'ket·eer'**, *v. i.*

Black Monk. A Benedictine monk.

black'ness, *n.* Quality or state of being black.

black nightshade. See NIGHTSHADE.

black oak. Any of several American oaks with dark bark or foliage; esp., a large timber tree (*Quercus velutina*) of the eastern United States. See QUERCITRON; OAK, *Illust.*

black'out' (blăk'out'), *n.* A blacking out or condition of being blacked out. See *black out,* under BLACK, *v.*

black pepper. See PEPPER, 1 **a.**

black point. A disease of cereal grains caused by bacteria and fungi that blackens the embryo ends and often impairs germination.

black'poll' (blăk'pōl'), *n., or* **blackpoll warbler.** A North American warbler (*Dendroica striata*) having the top of the head of the male bird black when in full plumage.

black poplar. See POPLAR.

Black Rod. In full ***Gentleman Usher of the Black Rod.*** **a** The usher to the Chapter of the Garter, who is also usher to the House of Lords. **b** An usher in the legislature of British colonies.

black sheep. A black-fleeced sheep among normally white-fleeced sheep; hence, a scapegrace.

Black'shirt' (blăk'shûrt'), *n.* **a** One of the Italian Fascisti, whose uniform included a distinctive black shirt. **b** A member of any nationalistic organization of similar principles, as the Schutzstaffel.

black'smith' (blăk'smĭth'), *n.* [*black* (from the color of the metal) + *smith.*] A smith who forges iron. Cf. WHITESMITH.

black snake, *or* **black'snake'** (-snāk'), *n.* **1.** Any of several snakes of a black or very dark color, esp. either of two harmless snakes (*Coluber constrictor* and *Elaphe obsoleta*) of the United States. **2.** A long tapering braided whip of rawhide or leather.

black squirrel. See SQUIRREL, 1 **a.**

black'-tailed' deer (blăk'tāld'). A deer (*Odocoileus columbianus*) of British Columbia, Oregon, Washington, etc. Cf. DEER.

black tea. See TEA, *n.*, 1 **b.**

black'thorn' (blăk'thôrn'), *n.* **a** A European spiny tree (*Prunus spinosa*) of the peach family. **b** Any of several American hawthorns.

black vomit. *Med.* **a** A copious vomiting of dark-colored matter, usually blood. It is one of the most serious symptoms in yellow fever. **b** Yellow fever.

Black'wall hitch (blăk'wôl). See KNOT, *Illust.* (17).

black'wa'ter fe'ver (blăk'wô'tẽr; -wŏt'ẽr). *Med.* A malarial fever of the tropics, marked by bloody urine.

black widow. The female of a common American spider (*Latrodectus mactans*); — so called from its shining black body and its habit of devouring its mate. Its bite is exceedingly poisonous.

blad'der (blăd'ẽr), *n.* [AS. *blǣdre, blǣddre.*] **1** *Anat. & Zool.* A membranous sac serving as the receptacle of some fluid or containing gas; as, an air *bladder;* the gall *bladder;* often, specif., the urinary bladder. **2.** A vesicle or blister. **3.** Anything inflated, empty, or unsound. **4.** *Bot.* A distended membranaceous pericarp.

bladder campion. See CAMPION.

blad'der·nose' (blăd'ẽr·nōz'), *n.* The hooded seal.

blad'der·nut' (-nŭt'), *n.* The bladderlike seed pod of any of a genus (*Staphylea*) of shrubs of the North Temperate Zone; also, the plant.

bladder worm. The bladderlike larval stage of a tapeworm; a cysticercus. Cf. COENURUS, HYDATID, SCOLEX.

blad'der·wort' (blăd'ẽr·wûrt'), *n.* Any of certain aquatic or bog plants (*Utricularia* and related genera) with small insect-catching bladders (ascidia) on the leaves.

blad'der·y (-ĭ), *adj.* Having bladders; bladderlike.

blade (blād), *n.* [AS. *blæd* leaf, blade (of an oar).] **1.** *Bot.* **a** A leaf of a plant, esp. of an herb; — now chiefly of grass and cereals. **b** The expanded portion of a leaf; the lamina. **2.** The cutting part of an instrument; as, the *blade* of a knife or a sword; hence, a sword or swordsman. **3.** An object or part suggestive of the blade of a leaf, sword, etc.; as, the *blade* of an oar, propeller, etc. **4.** Any of various flat anatomical parts; as, the shoulder *blade,* or scapula. **5.** A sharp-witted, dashing, wild, or reckless fellow. **6.** *Phonet.* The upper flat part of the tongue behind the tip, or point. — **blad'ed** (blād'ĕd; -ĭd), *adj.*

blae (blā; blē), *adj.* [ON. *blār.*] *Obs. exc. Dial.* Dark-blue; livid.

blain (blān), *n.* [AS. *blēgen.*] An inflammatory swelling or sore. Cf. CHILBLAIN.

blam'a·ble (blām'ȧ·b'l), *adj.* Faulty; culpable. — **blam'a·ble·ness**, *n.* — **blam'a·bly** (-blĭ), *adv.*

blame (blām), *v. t.* [OF. *blasmer,* fr. L. *blasphemare* to blaspheme, LL. also to blame, fr. Gr. *blasphēmein* to speak ill, blaspheme, fr. *blasphēmos* evil-speaking.] **1.** To censure; find fault with; reproach. **2.** To accuse; hold responsible; — often with *for.* **3.** *Colloq.* To place the blame or responsibility for; — with *on* or *upon.* — **Syn.** See CRITICIZE. — *n.* **1.** Expression of disapprobation; censure. **2** *Archaic.* Culpability; fault; sin. **3.** Responsibility, as for error; as, to shift the *blame.*

blame'a·ble (blām'ȧ·b'l). Variant of BLAMABLE.

blame′ful (blām′fo͝ol; -f'l), *adj.* **1.** Censorious. **2.** Blameworthy.
blame′less, *adj.* Free from blame or fault. — **blame′less·ly,** *adv.* — **blame′less·ness,** *n.*
blame′wor′thy (blām′wûr′thĭ), *adj.* Deserving blame; culpable; reprehensible. — **blame′wor′thi·ness** (-thĭ·nĕs; -nĭs), *n.*
Syn. Blameworthy, guilty, culpable mean deserving recompense for that which is sinful or criminal. Blameworthy implies that a person, his act, or his work merits reproach, censure, or even severe punishment; guilty implies the just charging with responsibility for a delinquency, a crime, a sin, or the consciousness that one is responsible therefor; culpable applies sometimes to the person found guilty of an act deserving severe censure or condemnation but it may also apply to a condition, practice, or the like, for which one is responsible or which leads to an accident, crime, etc.
blanc′ fixe′ (blän′ fēks′). [F.] Barium sulfate, $BaSO_4$, prepared as a heavy white powder, used as a filler in paper, rubber, and linoleum, as a pigment, etc.
blanch (blȧnch; 9), *v. t.* [OF. *blanchir,* fr. *blanc* white.] **1.** To take the color out of and make white; bleach. **2.** To bleach (plants) by excluding the light, as with earth; as, to *blanch* celery. **3.** To whiten by removing the skin, as by scalding; as, to *blanch* almonds; to scald, as meat. **4.** To give a white luster to (silver, before stamping, in coining), with acids, etc. **5.** To cover (sheet iron or steel) with a coating of tin. **6.** To render ashen or pale; as, fear *blanches* the cheek. — *v. i.* To grow or become white or pale. — **Syn.** See WHITEN. — **blanch′er,** *n.*
blanch, *adj.* **1.** *Obs.* White; pale. **2.** *Her.* Argent; silver.
blanc·mange′ (blȧ·mänzh′; -mänzh′), *n.* [F. *blancmanger,* lit., white food.] A dessert made from gelatinous or starchy substances and milk, and shaped in a mold.
bland (blănd), *adj.* [L. *blandus.*] **1.** Smooth and soothing; gentle; as, a *bland* smile. **2.** Not drastic or irritating; not stimulating; as, a *bland* oil, climate. — **Syn.** See SUAVE (**Ant.** brusque): SOFT. — **bland′ly,** *adv.* — **bland′ness,** *n.*
blan′dish (blăn′dĭsh), *v.t. & i.* [OF. *blandir,* fr. L. *blandiri,* fr. *blandus* mild, flattering.] To flatter gently; cajole. — **blan′dish·er,** *n.* — **blan′dish·ment,** *n.*
blank (blăngk), *adj.* [OF. *blanc,* fem. *blanche,* fr. OHG. *blanch* shining, bright, white.] **1.** Of a white or pale color; colorless. **2.** Free from writing, printing, or marks; — said of checks, official documents, etc. **3.** Appearing, or causing to appear, dazed, confounded, or discomfited; nonplused; as, *blank* dismay. **4.** Empty; void; fruitless; as, a *blank* day. **5.** Lacking characteristics that give variety; as, a *blank* stretch of road; a *blank* future. **6.** Lacking animation; expressionless; vacant; as, *blank* faces. **7.** Showing a plain or unbroken surface where an opening, notch, or the like, is usual, esp. as a result of being unfinished; as, a *blank* key, one without slots; a *blank* arch, arcade, etc., that is, a semblance of one without an opening. — **Syn.** See EMPTY. — *n.* **1.** A void space, as in a written or printed instrument; hence, an interval void of consciousness, action, etc.; a void. **2.** A sheet, card, paper, etc., not printed or written on, or one with blank spaces to be filled in. **3.** The bull's-eye of a target; hence, anything aimed at. **4.** A dash (—) denoting an omission; — usually a euphemism for a curse, etc. **5.** A piece of material prepared to be made into something, as a coin or key, by a further operation. — *v. t.* **1.** To obstruct; close up; obscure; blot; as, to *blank* out an entry. **2.** *Sports.* To keep from scoring. **3.** To punch from a sheet or flat piece of stock, as with a die; — often with *out.* — **blank′ly,** *adv.* — **blank′ness,** *n.*
blank′book′ (blăngk′bo͝ok′), *n.* A book of blank pages or of blanks.
blank endorsement. An endorsement (of commercial paper) by writing only the name of the endorser on the back, which makes the paper payable to bearer.
blan′ket (blăng′kĕt; -kĭt), *n.* [OF. *blankete, blanquette, blanchet,* dim. of *blanc* white.] **1.** A broad piece of a woven fabric, often thick or heavy, as of wool, for use as a bed covering, as a robe, etc. **2.** A layerlike covering; as, a *blanket* of snow. **3.** Anything suggestive of a blanket in appearance or use. — *v. t.* **1.** To cover with or as with a blanket. **2.** To toss in a blanket, as by way of punishment. **3.** To obscure, interrupt, extinguish, etc.; as, to *blanket* radio signals by powerful interference. **4.** To cover, or make to apply to, uniformly, despite wide separation or diversity among the elements included; as, freight rates that *blanket* a whole region. — *adj.* Including or covering a group or class; effective or applicable in all instances or contingencies; as, a *blanket* price; *blanket* insurance.
blan′ket·flow′er (-flou′ẽr), *n.* = GAILLARDIA.
blanket stitch. A buttonhole stitch worked wide apart on the edge of materials too thick to hem. See STITCH, *Illust.*
blank verse. Unrhymed verse; specif., the unrhymed iambic pentameter of English dramatic and epic poetry.
blare (blâr), *v. i. & t.* [ME. *blaren, bloren,* to cry, weep.] To sound loud and harsh, as a trumpet; proclaim loudly. — *n.* **1.** The harsh noise of, or one like that of, a trumpet. **2.** Dazzling brilliance, as of color.
blar′ney (blär′nĭ). [From *Blarney,* village and castle near Cork, Eire.] Smooth, wheedling talk; cajoling flattery. — *v. t.* To influence or gain by blarney; wheedle.
Blarney stone. A stone in Blarney Castle, near Cork, Ireland, said to make those who kiss it proficient in blarney.
bla·sé′ (blä·zā′; blä′zā; *F.* blä′zā′), *adj.* [F., past part. of *blaser.*] Having one's taste and interest so dulled by overindulgence that one is unable to enjoy things that appeal to most people.
blas·pheme′ (blăs·fēm′), *v. t.* [L. *blasphemare.* See BLAME, *v.*] **1.** To speak of or address with impious irreverence. **2.** To revile; abuse. — *v. i.* To utter blasphemy. — **blas·phem′er** (-fēm′ẽr), *n.*
blas′phe·mous (blăs′fē·mŭs), *adj.* Uttering blasphemy; profane. — **blas′phe·mous·ly,** *adv.* — **blas′phe·mous·ness,** *n.*
blas′phe·my (-mĭ), *n.; pl.* -MIES (-mĭz). [From OF., fr. L. *blasphemia,* fr. Gr. *blasphēmia.*] **1.** In Jewish law, cursing or reviling God or the king, who was God's representative; in later usage, pronouncing the forbidden name of God (see TETRAGRAMMATON). **2.** Indignity offered to God in words, writing, or signs; also, act of claiming the attributes or prerogatives of deity. **3.** Irreverence toward anything regarded as sacred.
Syn. Blasphemy, profanity, swearing, cursing mean impious or irreverent speech. Blasphemy applies strictly to any intentional utterance defying or offering indignity to the Supreme Being; profanity applies to all impious or irreverent references to holy persons or things; swearing implies indulgence in profane, often meaningless, oaths; cursing is not always distinguished from *swearing* but more often implies invoking disaster or calamity upon the object of one's wrath.
blast (blȧst; 9), *n.* [AS. *blǣst.*] **1.** A violent gust of wind. **2.** The sound made by blowing a wind instrument; as, a *blast* on a horn; also, the sound produced at one breath; also, the sound made by a steam whistle or the like. **3.** A sudden pernicious effect, as if by a noxious wind, esp. on animals and plants. **4.** A forcible stream of air or other gas from an orifice, as from a bellows, organ, etc.; hence, the continuous blowing to which one charge of ore or metal is subjected in a furnace. **5.** The exhaust steam from an engine; also, the draft created. **6.** An explosion or violent detonation, as of the discharge of dynamite; also, the charge used for this purpose. **7.** The violent windlike effect consisting of a wave of increased followed by a wave of decreased atmospheric pressure, produced by an explosion, esp. of a bomb. — *v. i.* To become withered or blighted. — *v. t.* **1.** To injure as by a noxious wind; blight; shrivel; hence, ruin or destroy. **2.** To shatter by an explosive.
-blast (-blăst). [Gr. *blastos* sprout.] A combining form meaning *a sprout* or *shoot; germ;* also, *embryonic; formative;* as in epi*blast,* odonto*blast.*
blast′ed (blȧs′tĕd; -tĭd), *adj.* **1.** Blighted; withered. **2.** Confounded; accursed; detestable.
blas·te′ma (blăs·tē′mȧ), *n.; pl.* -TEMATA (-tē′mȧ·tȧ). [NL., fr. Gr. *blastēma* bud.] *Embryol.* The primitive basis of an organ yet unformed, from which it grows.
blast furnace. A furnace in which combustion is forced by a current of air under pressure, esp. in the smelting of ores. Cf. REVERBERATORY FURNACE, OPEN-HEARTH.
blast′ie (blȧs′tĭ), *n. Scot.* A tiny, blasted creature; a dwarf.
blast′ment (blȧst′mĕnt), *n.* A blasting process or influence.
blas′to- (blăs′tō-), **blast-.** [Gr. *blastos.*] A combining form meaning *sprout, shoot,* used in biology, botany, etc., to indicate *connection with* or *relation to, a bud, budding, a germ,* and esp. *the early stages of the embryo.*
blas′to·coele (-sēl), *n.* The cavity of the blastula. See BLASTULA, *Illust.*
blas′to·derm (-dûrm), *n. Embryol.* A membrane formed by the repeated segmentation of the blastomeres; specif., that formed by the actively segmenting part of the eggs of most vertebrates. — **blas′to·der′mic** (-dûr′mĭk), *adj.*
blas′to·disk, blas′to·disc (-dĭsk), *n.* = GERMINAL DISK.
blas′to·gen′e·sis (blăs′tō·jĕn′ē·sĭs), *n. Biol.* **a** Reproduction by budding. **b** The theory of the transmission of inherited characters by germ plasm; — opp. to *pangenesis.*
blas′to·mere (blăs′tō·mēr), *n.* [*blasto-* + *-mere.*] Any of the cells formed as a result of the first few cell divisions of the egg. See BLASTULA, *Illust.* — **blas′to·mer′ic** (-mĕr′ĭk), *adj.*
blas′to·pore (-pōr; 70), *n. Embryol.* See GASTRULA. — **blas′to·por′ic** (-pŏr′ĭk), *adj.*
blas′to·sphere (-sfēr), *n. Embryol.* A blastula.
blas′tu·la (blăs′tū·lȧ), *n.; pl.* -LAE (-lē). [NL., dim. fr. Gr. *blastos* sprout.] *Embryol.* A form of embryo in the early development of many animals, typically a single layer of cells arranged spherically around a central closed cavity (the *blastocoele*). Cf. GASTRULA. — **blas′tu·lar** (-lẽr), *adj.*

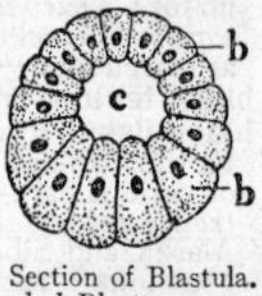

Section of Blastula. *b, b* Blastomeres; *c* Blastocoele. Much enlarged.

blat (blăt), *v. i.; BLAT′TED; BLAT′TING.* [Variant of BLEAT.] To cry, as a calf or sheep; to bleat. — *v. t. Colloq.* To utter raucously; blurt foolishly.
bla′tan·cy (blā′tăn·sĭ), *n.* Blatant quality; anything blatant.
bla′tant (-tănt), *adj.* **1.** Brawling; clamorous; noisy. **2.** Offensively obtrusive; coarse. **3.** Bellowing; also, bleating; as, *blatant* herds. — **Syn.** See VOCIFEROUS. — **bla′tant·ly,** *adv.*
blate (blāt), *adj. Scot.* Bashful; sheepish; also, slow.
blath′er (blăth′ẽr), *v. i. & t.* Also **bleth′er** (blĕth′ẽr). [ON. *blathra.*] To talk foolishly. — *n.* Foolish talk.
blath′er·skite (-skīt), *n.* **1.** *Colloq.* A blustering or noisy talkative fellow. **2.** The ruddy duck.
blau′bok′ (blou′bŏk′), *n.; pl.* -BOK, sometimes -BOKS (-bŏks′). See PLURAL, *Note,* 6. [D. *blauwbok,* lit., blue buck.] **a** A South African antelope (*Hippotragus leucophaeus*), now exterminated. **b** Any of a genus (*Cephalophus*) of South African antelopes, some of which are no larger than a hare.
blaw (blô), *v. t. & i. Scot. & Dial. Eng.* To blow.
blaze (blāz), *n.* [AS. *blæse, blase.*] **1.** An intensely burning fire. **2.** Intense, direct light accompanied with heat; as, the *blaze* of noon. **3.** An active display of any quality; outburst; as, a *blaze* of wrath. **4.** Splendor; effulgence; glare; as, a *blaze* of jewels.
Syn. Blaze, flame, flare, glare, glow mean a brightly burning light or fire. Blaze implies great activity in burning, especially thorough kindling of material and the radiation of intense light or heat; flame suggests a darting tongue of fire fanned by rapidly burning gas or vapor; flare implies a flame or flames darting up suddenly against a dark background or from a dying fire; glare implies the emission or reflection of a very bright light; glow also suggests the emission of light, but it also connotes absence of flame, radiance without effulgence and, often, warmth and duration.
— *v. i.* **1.** To burn with bright flame; glow. **2.** To be resplendent or conspicuous, as with light. — *v. t.* **1.** To cause to blaze; to burn. **2.** To shine with; be resplendent with.
blaze (blāz), *v. t.* [ME. *blasen,* fr. MD. *blasen.*] **1.** *Obs.* To blow as with a trumpet. **2.** To make public far and wide; render conspicuous; as, *blaze* a matter abroad.
blaze, *n.* [From MLG. *blase,* or other LG. dial.] **1.** A white mark on the face of an animal, esp. a white stripe running down the face to the lips. **2.** A spot made on a tree by chipping off a piece of the bark. — *v. t.* To mark (a tree, path, trail, etc.) by blazes.
blaz′er (blāz′ẽr), *n.* **1.** Anything that blazes or glows. **2.** A light jacket, usually bright-colored, for wear at tennis, cricket, or other sport.
blaz′ing star (blāz′ĭng). **1.** *Obs.* A comet. **2.** A brilliant center of attraction; cynosure. **3.** Any of several American plants having conspicuous flower clusters, as: **a** A plant (*Chamaelirium luteum*) of the bunchflower family. **b** The button snakeroot.
bla′zon (blā′z'n), *n.* [OF. *blason* shield, coat of arms.] **1.** A heraldic shield; also, a coat of arms. **2.** The proper description or depiction of heraldic or armorial bearings. **3.** Ostentatious display or

description; show. — *v. t.* **1.** To depict or inscribe in colors; display. **2.** To deck; adorn. **3.** *Her.* To describe (heraldic or armorial bearings) in technical language; popularly, to delineate (armorial bearings). — **bla′zon·er,** *n.* — **bla′zon·ment,** *n.*

bla′zon·ry (blā′z′n·rĭ), *n.* **1.** = BLAZON, *n.*, 2. **2.** A coat of arms; an armorial bearing or bearings. **3.** Artistic or brilliant representation or display.

-ble. See -ABLE.

bleach (blēch), *v. t.* [AS. *blǣcan.*] To make white or whiter; blanch; whiten. — *v. i.* To grow white or lose color; whiten. — **Syn.** See WHITEN. — *n.* **1.** Act or process of bleaching; also, a chemical for bleaching. **2.** Color, or degree of whiteness, obtained by bleaching.

bleach′er (blēch′ẽr), *n.* **1.** A worker or machine that bleaches. **2.** *U.S.* A seat for spectators at outdoor games, or the section (orig. roofless) containing such seats; — usually *pl.*

bleach′er·y (-ĭ), *n.*; *pl.* -ERIES (-ĭz). A place or an establishment where bleaching is done.

bleach′ing pow′der. A powder for bleaching; specif., chloride of lime.

bleak (blēk), *n.* A small European river fish (*Alburnus lucidus*) of the carp family.

bleak, *adj.* **1.** Exposed and, usually, desolate; swept by cold winds. **2.** Cold and cutting; bitter; as, a *bleak* blast. **3.** Cheerless; depressing; as, a *bleak* outlook. — **bleak′ish,** *adj.* — **bleak′ly,** *adv.* — **bleak′ness,** *n.*

blear (blēr), *v. t.* [ME. *bleren.*] To make somewhat sore or watery, as the eyes; to dim, as the sight; hence, to deceive; hoodwink. — *adj.* **1.** Dim with water or rheum; — said of the eyes. **2.** Causing or caused by dimness of sight; dim. — **blear′-eyed′** (-īd′; 2), *adj.*

blear′y (blēr′ĭ), *adj.* Somewhat blear; blear-eyed. — **blear′i·ness** (-ĭ·nĕs; -nĭs), *n.*

bleat (blēt), *v. i.* [AS. *blǣtan.*] To make the noise of, or one like that of, a sheep, goat, or, rarely, a calf; hence, to blather; also, to talk complainingly; whine. — *v. t.* To utter with a bleat. — *n.* The cry of a sheep, goat, or calf, or a similar sound; hence, blather; also, whining talk. — **bleat′er,** *n.* — **bleat′ing·ly,** *adv.*

bleb (blĕb), *n.* A vesicle; blister; bubble. — **bleb′by** (blĕb′ĭ), *adj.*

bleed (blēd), *v. i.*; BLED (blĕd); BLEED′ING. [AS. *blēdan,* fr. *blōd* blood.] **1.** To emit blood; specif., to lose or shed one's blood by a wound or so as to die; as, to *bleed* for one's country. **2.** To feel anguish, pain, or sympathy; as, my heart *bleeds* for him. **3.** To withdraw blood from the body; let blood. **4.** To issue, as blood from an incision. **5.** To exude water, or sap, as an injured tree. **6.** *Colloq.* To pay or lose money; have money extorted. **7.** To diffuse or run when wetted, as dyes. **8.** *Bookbinding, etc.* To bleed a page, or the like; also, to be bled. — *v. t.* **1.** To let blood from. **2.** To lose or exude, as sap. **3.** *Colloq.* To draw or extort money from. **4.** To draw the sap from (a tree). **5.** To drain or empty of liquid, gas, or other contents that will run out. **6.** *Bookbinding, etc.* To trim the edge of (a page margin, plate, etc.) so as to cut into printed or engraved matter. — *n.* **1.** Bleeding. **2.** A page, plate, or the like that has been bled; also, the part trimmed off in bleeding. — *adj.* Bled; printed to the edge without margin.

bleed′er (-ẽr), *n.* One that bleeds; specif., a hemophiliac.

bleed′ing heart. A garden plant (*Dicentra spectabilis*) of the fumitory family, with racemes of deep-pink, drooping, heart-shaped flowers.

blel′lum (blĕl′ŭm), *n.* *Scot.* A talkative idler.

blem′ish (blĕm′ĭsh), *v. t.* [OF. *blesmir,* fr. a Teut. stem akin to G. *blass* pale.] To injure or impair; mar; sully. — *n.* Any mark of deformity or injury; imperfection.

Syn. Blemish, defect, flaw mean an imperfection. Blemish suggests something external or superficial, such as a spot or a stain; defect, the lack or want (not always visible) of something essential to completeness or perfection; flaw, a small defect in continuity or cohesion, such as a crack or a break.

blench (blĕnch), *v. i.* [AS. *blencan* to deceive.] To shrink; start back or aside; quail. — **Syn.** See RECOIL. — **blench′er,** *n.*

blench, *v. i. & t.* To grow pale; whiten; blanch.

blend (blĕnd), *v. t.*; BLEND′ED, *also* BLENT (blĕnt); BLEND′ING. [ME. *blenden,* fr. ON. *blanda.*] **1.** To mix or mingle; now, to combine or associate so that the separate things mixed, or the line of demarcation, cannot be distinguished. **2.** To prepare by mingling different varieties or grades; — of wine, coffee, tobacco, etc. — *v. i.* To unite intimately; pass or shade insensibly into each other, as colors; merge; harmonize. — **Syn.** See MIX. — **Ant.** Resolve. — *n.* **1.** A thorough mixture; blending; also, a product, as a tobacco or coffee, prepared by blending. **2.** Also **blend word.** *Linguistics.* = PORTMANTEAU WORD.

blende (blĕnd), *n.* [G., fr. *blenden* to blind.] **a** Sphalerite. **b** Any of several minerals, chiefly metallic sulfides, with somewhat bright but nonmetallic luster.

Blen′heim span′iel (blĕn′ĭm; -ĕm). [From *Blenheim* Palace, Eng.] See SPANIEL.

blen′ni·oid (blĕn′ĭ·oid), *adj.* [*blenny* + *-oid.*] *Zool.* Of, pertaining to, or resembling the blennies.

blen′ny (blĕn′ĭ), *n.*; *pl.* -NIES (-ĭz). [L. *blennius,* fr. Gr. *blennos,* fr. *blenna* slime, mucus.] Any of numerous jugular, chiefly salt-water fishes (family Blennidae and allies), found about rocky shores.

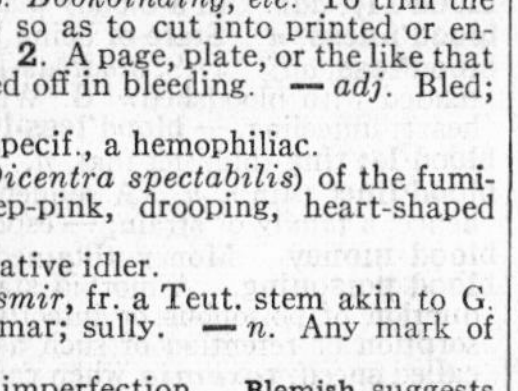

Ocellated Blenny, or Butterfly Fish (*Blennius ocellaris*). (½)

bleph′a·ro- (blĕf′ȧ·rō-), **blephar-.** [Gr. *blepharon.*] A combining form meaning *eyelid,* as in **bleph′a·ri′tis, bleph′a·rot′o·my** (see -ITIS, -TOMY).

bles′bok′ (blĕs′bŏk′), *n.* Also **bles′buck′** (-bŭk′). [S. Afr. D. *blesbok,* fr. D. *bles* a blaze on the forehead + *bok* buck.] A South African antelope (*Damaliscus albifrons*), resembling the bontebok.

bless (blĕs), *v. t.*; BLESSED (blĕst; *archaic* blĕs′ĕd; -ĭd; *cf.* BLESSED, *adj.*), BLEST; BLESS′ING. [AS. *blētsian, blēdsian, bloedsian,* orig. to consecrate with blood, fr. *blōd* blood.] **1.** To consecrate or hallow by religious rite or word; make or pronounce holy. **2.** To make happy; confer prosperity or happiness upon. **3.** To pray for the happiness of; invoke or confer beneficial attributes upon. **4.** To make the sign of the cross upon or over. **5.** To guard; keep; protect; as, God *bless* me. **6.** To praise, or glorify.

bless′ed (blĕs′ĕd; -ĭd; *sometimes, as in verse,* blĕst, *but usually only when spelled* blest), *adj.* **1.** Hallowed; holy. **2.** Favored with blessings; blissful; joyful. **3.** Enjoying, or pertaining to, spiritual happiness; *R.C.Ch.,* beatified. **4.** Cursed; damned; — used euphemistically, ironically, etc.; as, not a *blessed* drop of rain. — **bless′ed·ly,** *adv.*

bless′ed·ness, *n.* Blessed state or quality.

bless′ing, *n.* **1.** Act of one who blesses; a benediction; a grace. **2.** A means of happiness or welfare; a beneficent gift. **3.** In analogous or derived senses: **a** *Bib.* A gift; — a Hebraism. *Gen.* xxxiii. 11. **b** Praise; worship. **c** A cursing; — used euphemistically.

blest (blĕst), *adj.* Blessed.

blet (blĕt), *n.* [F. *blet, blette,* soft from being too ripe.] A type of internal decay in fruit.

bleth′er (blĕth′ẽr). Var. of BLATHER; dial. var. of BLADDER.

blew (blōō; 114), *past* of BLOW.

blight (blīt), *n.* **1.** Any disease or injury of plants resulting in withering, cessation of growth, and death of parts, as leaves, without rotting. **2.** Any insect causing blight, as certain aphids. **3.** That which frustrates one's plans or withers one's hopes; that which impairs or destroys. **4.** State or result of being blighted. — *v. t.* To affect with blight; blast; hence, to ruin; frustrate. — *v. i.* To be affected by blight; blast.

blight′y (blīt′ĭ), *n.* [Hind. *wilāyat* (foreign) country, England.] *Brit. Slang.* **a** [*often cap.*] England; home; as, back to *blighty.* **b** A soldier returned home, or something, as a wound or furlough, that takes one home.

blimp (blĭmp), *n.* [From Type *B* of *limp* dirigible.] *Colloq.* A small nonrigid airship. See AIRSHIP.

blind (blīnd), *adj.* [AS.] **1.** Sightless. **2.** Lacking discernment; unable or unwilling to understand or judge; as, *blind* to faults. **3.** Made without reason or discrimination; as, a *blind* choice. **4.** Apart from intelligent direction or control; as, *blind* chance. **5.** Insensible; as, a *blind* stupor; hence, drunk. **6.** Made or done without the aid of sight of objects or facts comprising the chief means of guidance or judgment; as, *blind* flying; a *blind* lead at bridge. **7.** For sightless persons; as, *blind* asylum. **8.** Unintelligible; also, illegible; as, *blind* writing. **9.** Concealed; covered; as, a *blind* ditch. **10.** Having but one opening, as an alley; closed at one end; as, the *blind* gut, or caecum. **11.** Not open for light or passage; blank; as, a *blind* wall. **12.** *Hort.* Abortive; also, producing leaves instead of flowers or fruit; as, *blind* bulbs. — *adv.* Blindly; esp., to the point of insensibility; as, *blind* drunk. — *v. t.* **1.** To make blind. **2.** To dazzle. **3.** To obscure; darken; also, to hide; conceal. **4.** To dim; outshine. — *n.* **1.** Something to hinder sight or keep out light; a screen; a cover, as a window shutter, a blinder for a horse, etc. **2.** A place or means of concealment; ambush. **3.** Something to mislead one, or to conceal a covert design; a subterfuge; also, an undercover agent or decoy. — **blind′ly,** *adv.* — **blind′ness,** *n.*

blind′er (blīn′dẽr), *n.* **1.** One that blinds. **2.** A flap on a horse's bridle to prevent sight of objects at his side (see HARNESS, *Illust.*); a blinker; winker; hence, an obstruction to sight or discernment.

blind′fish′ (blīnd′fĭsh′), *n.*; *pl.*, see FISH. Any of several small fishes with vestigial, functionless eyes, found in the waters of caves, etc.

blind′fold′ (-fōld′; 25), *v. t.* [AS. *blind* blind + *fellan* to fell, strike down (influenced by *fold*).] To cover the eyes of, as with a bandage; to hinder from seeing, either physically or mentally; as, *blindfolded* by prejudices. — *adj.* Having the eyes covered; blinded; hence, heedless; reckless; as, *blindfold* fury.

blind gut. = CAECUM.

blind′ing, *adj.* Making blind or as if blind; obscuring.

blind′man's buff (blīnd′mănz). [See BUFF a buffet.] A game of tag in which the person who is "it" is blindfolded.

blind pig. *Slang, U. S.* = BLIND TIGER.

blind spot. **1.** The point in the retina, not sensitive to light, where the optic nerve enters. See EYE, *Illust.* **2.** An area in one's discernment where one fails to exercise understanding, judgment, etc. **3.** *Radio.* A locality in which radio reception is markedly poor.

blind′sto′ry (blīnd′stō′rĭ), *n.*; *pl.* -RIES (-rĭz). *Arch.* A story without windows; specif., the triforium of a Gothic church without windows in the outer wall.

blind tiger. *Slang.* A place that sells intoxicants illegally.

blind′worm′ (-wûrm′), *n.* A small, burrowing, snakelike lizard with minute eyes, esp. the species *Anguis fragilis* of Europe, popularly believed to be blind; the slowworm.

blink (blĭngk), *v. i.* [ME. *blenken* and D. *blinken.*] **1.** To look or glance; glimpse. **2.** To look with half-shut, winking eyes; as, *blinking* in the strong light. **3.** To wink. **4.** To shine, esp. intermittently; twinkle. **5.** To condone; look evasively; — with *at.* — **Syn.** See WINK. — *v. t.* **1.** To shut out of sight; avoid, or purposely evade; shirk; as, to *blink* the facts. **2.** To cause to blink. — *n.* **1.** *Chiefly Scot.* A glimpse or glance. **2.** Glimmer; sparkle; as, a *blink* of light. **3.** A winking, as at a sudden glare; a wink. **4.** A whiteness about the horizon due to the reflection of light from ice at sea; iceblink.

blink′er (blĭngk′ẽr), *n.* **1.** One that blinks; esp., a blinking light used as a warning signal. **2.** A blinder for horses. **3.** *pl.* A type of goggles.

bliss (blĭs), *n.* [AS. *blis, blīths,* fr. *blīthe* blithe.] **1.** Blithesomeness; gladness. **2.** Exalted happiness; heavenly joy. **3.** A cause of bliss or felicity.

bliss′ful (-fōōl; -f′l), *adj.* Full of, characterized by, or causing bliss. — **bliss′ful·ly,** *adv.* — **bliss′ful·ness,** *n.*

blis′ter (blĭs′tẽr), *n.* [MD. *bluyster,* or fr. OF. *blestre,* fr. ON. *blāstr* a swelling, a blast.] **1.** A vesicle of the skin containing watery matter or serum. **2.** Any similar enclosed raised spot resembling a blister (sense 1); as, a *blister* on a leaf; a paint *blister.* **3.** A blistering plaster or other agent; a vesicatory. **4.** A gunner's or observer's cockpit protruding from the fuselage of an aircraft and often covered by a transparent dome. **5.** *Nav.* = BULGE, 3. — *v. i.* To be affected with a blister or blisters. — *v. t.* **1.** To raise a blister or blisters upon. **2.** To affect as by blistering; hence, to beat or lash; to scorch with words. — **blis′ter·y** (-ĭ), *adj.*

blister beetle. **a** A beetle which, when dried and powdered, is used to raise blisters on the skin, esp. one called by druggists ***cantharis*** or ***Spanish fly,*** a brilliant green beetle (*Lytta vesicatoria*) of southern Europe, the source of cantharides. **b** Any of the soft-bodied beetles of the family (Meloidae) to which the cantharis belongs, some being injurious to vegetables.

blister copper. *Metal.* Metallic copper of a black, blistered surface, the final product of converting copper matte. It is about 96–99 per cent pure.

blister rust. *Plant Pathol.* Any of certain diseases of pine trees caused by rust fungi (genus *Cronartium*), producing blisters externally; as, the white-pine *blister rust.*

blister steel. Crude steel formed from wrought iron by cementation; — so called from its blistered surface.

blithe (blīth; blīth), *adj.* [AS. *blīthe* blithe, kind.] Merry in disposition; joyous; glad; cheerful; exhibiting lighthearted gaiety. — **Syn.** See MERRY. — **blithe′ly,** *adv.*

blith′er (blĭth′ẽr), *v. i.* To blather. *Dial.*, exc. in part. adj. **blith′er·ing;** as, a *blithering* idiot.

blithe′some (blīth′sŭm; blīth′-), *adj.* Cheery; gay; merry. — **blithe′some·ly,** *adv.* — **blithe′some·ness,** *n.*

blitz (blĭts). *Colloq.* shortening of BLITZKRIEG, *n., adj., & v.*

blitz′bug′gy (blĭts′bŭg′ĭ), *n. U. S. Army Slang.* A light speedy vehicle, esp. the half-ton truck or the jeep.

blitz′krieg′ (blĭts′krēg′; *G.* -krēk′), *n.* [G., lit., lightning war.] **a** *Mil.* War conducted with lightninglike speed and force; specif., a violent surprise offensive by massed air forces and mechanized ground forces in close co-ordination, designed to destroy the enemy's aviation, munitions, communication lines, industry, and transport. The technique of the blitzkrieg was expounded by the Italian general Giulio Douhet and first employed effectively by the Germans against Poland (Sept., 1939). **b** Any sudden overpowering attack, as by propaganda. — *adj.* Of, pert. to, of the nature of, or like blitzkrieg. — *v. t. Colloq.* To subject to, or overpower with, a blitzkrieg.

bliz′zard (blĭz′ẽrd), *n.* **1.** A severe and prolonged snowstorm. **2.** A cold high wind filled with fine snow.

bloat (blōt), *v. t.* **1.** To make turgid, or cause to swell, as with air or liquid. **2.** To inflate; puff up; make vain. — *v. i.* To grow turgid; puff out; swell. — *n.* **1.** *Slang.* One that is bloated; a drunkard. **2.** *Veter.* Flatulent distention of the abdomen, esp. in the ox and horse, arising from eating watery foods and eating too rapidly.

bloat, *v. t.* To cure (herrings) in smoke. See BLOATER.

bloat′er (-ẽr), *n.* A large fat herring cured by being salted, smoked, and half dried. Cf. KIPPER **b**.

blob (blŏb), *n.* **1.** A small viscid drop, globule, or lump; hence, a daub, as of color. **2.** A sound as of a bubble breaking, or of something, as a fish, breaking through the surface of the water. — *v. t.;* BLOBBED (blŏbd); BLOB′BING. To mark as with a blob; to splotch; blot. — *v. i.* To boil or bubble; also, to make a sound as of breaking the surface of water.

bloc (blŏk), *n.* [F., block, lump.] **1.** *Politics.* **a** In Europe, a combination of groups or parties for a common cause or object. **b** In the U. S., a combination of members of different parties for a similar purpose, esp. in Congress; as, the farm *bloc.* **2.** A number or group of any political or racial units; a combination; as, the Central European *bloc.*

block (blŏk), *n.* [OF. *bloc,* fr. MD. *blok.*] **1.** A bulky, usually solid piece of wood, stone, or the like, usually with one or more flat faces. **2.** The wooden block (sense 1) on which condemned persons are beheaded. **3.** A stand for that which is sold at auction. **4.** A mold or form upon which articles are shaped or displayed. **5.** A grooved pulley or sheave in a frame or shell provided with a hook, eye, or strap, by which it may be attached; as, a **block and tackle,** a set of such blocks, with ropes, etc., for hoisting or hauling. **6.** A quantity, number, or section of things dealt with as a unit. **7.** A row of houses or shops, esp. when built in contact, so as to form one building. **8.** A city square; also, the length of one side of such a square. **9.** A blockhead. **10.** A blocking; a hindrance; obstacle. **11.** *Med.* Blocking, as of a nerve; as, *block* anesthesia; nerve *block.* **12.** *Printing.* An engraved block or stamp from which impressions are made. **13.** *Railroads.* See BLOCK SYSTEM. **14.** *Sports.* An obstruction of an opponent's play.

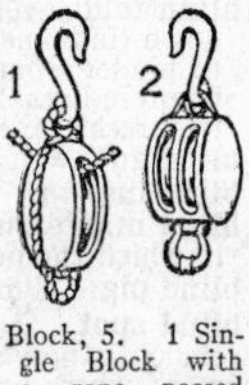

Block, 5. 1 Single Block with a rope passed through the Swallow and over the Sheave; 2 Double Block.

— *v. t.* **1.** To obstruct so as to prevent passage or progress; also, to blockade. **2.** To mark or indicate the outline or chief lines of; as, to *block* out a plan; *block* in a figure in a drawing. **3.** To shape on, or stamp with, a block; as, to *block* a hat. **4.** To secure, support, or provide with blocks. **5.** *Finance.* **a** To prevent by legislation or governmental edict the exchange of (certain funds in the national currency) for any foreign currency; as, *blocked* credits in London that cannot be used by the owner for purchase of dollars or South American currency. Cf. FREEZE, *v. t.*, 7. **b** To restrict by governmental edict the manner in which a foreigner may spend (legally owned bank balances or currency) or may collect (an account); as, certain German *blocked* marks were spendable only in the purchase of designated goods and services in Germany; China created a limited quantity of *blocked* currency, usable only for transfer, not convertible into cash. **c** To restrict (a bond or savings account) by a provision deferring payment for a specified time, as until after the end of a war. **6.** *Med. & Physiol.* To prevent (a nerve, etc.) from transmitting impulses, as by injecting an anesthetic. **7.** *Sports.* **a** To stop (a ball) with a bat without attempting to hit, esp. in cricket. **b** To obstruct or interfere with, as a play or player. — **Syn.** See HINDER. — *v. i.* To act in opposition or by interference, as in boxing, football, cricket, etc. — **block′er** (blŏk′ẽr), *n.*

block·ade′ (blŏk·ād′), *n.* **1.** The shutting up of a place by troops or ships so as to prevent ingress or egress. **2.** By extension, restrictive measures to obstruct communication and cut off commerce with an enemy. **3.** The force maintaining a blockade. **4.** An obstruction to passage. — *v. t.* To subject to a blockade. — **block·ad′er** (-ād′ẽr), *n.*

block·ade′-run′ner (-rŭn′ẽr), *n.* A vessel or person that runs through a blockade. — **block·ade′-run′ning,** *n.*

block′bust′er (blŏk′bŭs′tẽr), *n. Slang.* A huge high-explosive demolition bomb, usually of two, four, or six tons in weight, designed to be dropped from an airplane.

block′head′ (blŏk′hĕd′), *n.* A stupid fellow.

block′house′ (-hous′), *n.* **1.** *Mil.* Formerly, a structure of heavy timbers, for military defense, with sides pierced for gunfire and often a projecting upper story; now, a small defensible building for protection against enemy fire. **2.** A house of squared logs.

block′ish, *adj.* Like a block; stupid; dull. — **block′ish·ly,** *adv.* — **block′ish·ness,** *n.*

block letter. *Print.* **a** A large wooden type or letter. **b** A type or letter without serifs. Cf. GOTHIC, *n.*

block plane. See PLANE, *Illust.* (5).

block system. *Railroads.* A system by which a track is divided into short sections, or blocks, as of three or four miles, and trains are so run by signal apparatus (**block signals**) that no train enters a block until the preceding train has left it.

block tin. Commercial tin, cast in blocks and partly refined.

block′y (blŏk′ĭ), *adj.* **1.** Filled with, or characterized by, blocks or patches. **2.** Heavily or squarely built; chunky.

blond, blonde (blŏnd), *adj.* [F., fair, light.] **1.** Of a fair color; light-colored. **2.** *Anthropol.* Having yellowish-brown, flaxen, or light-auburn hair, blue or gray eyes, and pale or rosy-white skin. — **blond′ness, blonde′ness,** *n.*

blond (blŏnd), *n. masc.*, **blonde** (blŏnd), *fem.* [F.] **1.** A blond person. **2.** (Usually *blonde.*) A silk bobbin lace originally the color of raw silk, now usually bleached or dyed.

blood (blŭd), *n.* [AS. *blōd.*] **1.** The fluid, commonly red in vertebrates, which circulates in the heart, arteries, and veins of animals, carrying nourishment and oxygen to all parts of the body, and bringing away waste products. **2.** Lifeblood; hence, life. **3.** The shedding of blood; taking of life; as, deeds of *blood.* **4.** Stock; lineage; specif., royal lineage; as, a prince of the *blood.* **5.** Relationship by descent from a common ancestor (called ***half blood*** when through one parent only, and ***whole blood*** when through both parents); kinship; hence, kindred; kinsman. **6.** Honorable birth or descent. **7.** Temper; state of the passions; as, stir up bad *blood.* **8.** A man of fire or spirit; a gay showy man; a rake. **9.** Animal appetite; fleshly nature. **10.** The juice of anything, esp. if red. **11.** *Stock Breeding.* Descent from parents of recognized breed; specif., in horses, Thoroughbred breeding. — *v. t.* **1.** *Archaic.* To make bloody. **2.** To give (as hounds or an army) a taste or sight of blood.

blood bank. See 3d BANK, *n.*, 5.

blood count. A counting of the number of corpuscles, usually of each kind, in a definite volume of blood.

blood′cur′dling (blŭd′kûr′dlĭng), *adj.* Congealing, or tending to congeal, the blood through fear or horror.

blood′ed (blŭd′ĕd; -ĭd), *adj.* Also **blood.** **1.** Of pure blood or approved breed; of the best stock. **2.** Having (a specified type or sort of) blood or temperament; as, blue-*blooded;* cold-*blooded.*

blood′fin′ (blŭd′fĭn′), *n.* A small South Amer. fish (*Aphyocharax rubripinnis*), silvery with deep-red fins, often kept in the tropical aquarium.

blood group. *Physiol.* One of several types (four according to most classifications) into which blood may be divided on the basis of the compatibility of its corpuscles and serum with the serum and corpuscles respectively of other individuals.

blood′guilt′y (blŭd′gĭl′tĭ), *adj.* Guilty of murder or bloodshed. — **blood′guilt′i·ness** (-gĭl′tĭ·nĕs; -nĭs), *n.*

blood heat. *Physiol.* The normal temperature of the blood.

blood′hound′ (-hound′), *n.* A hound of a large and powerful breed, remarkable for acuteness of smell.

blood′i·ly, *adv.* In a bloody manner.

blood′i·ness, *n.* State of being bloody.

blood′less, *adj.* [AS. *blōdlēas.*] **1.** Destitute of blood. **2.** Not attended with bloodshed. **3.** Without spirit or activity. **4.** Cold of heart; unfeeling. — **blood′less·ly,** *adv.* — **blood′less·ness,** *n.*

blood′let′ting (blŭd′lĕt′ĭng), *n.* Phlebotomy; bleeding.

blood′line′ (-līn′), *n.* A sequence of direct ancestors in a pedigree; hence, a family or strain; — esp. of animals.

blood money. Money obtained at the cost of another's life.

blood poisoning. A morbid state of the blood caused by the introduction of poisonous or infective matters from without, or the absorption or retention of such as are produced in the body itself; — called specif. ***toxemia*** when caused by absorption of toxins alone, as of pathogenic bacteria, ***septicemia*** when bacteria as well as their toxins are absorbed and circulate in the blood, ***pyemia*** when associated with development of multiple abscesses in the body.

blood pressure. *Physiol.* The pressure of the blood on the walls of the blood vessels, esp. the arteries, which varies in amount according to age and physical condition.

blood pudding *or* **sausage.** A kind of sausage with a large proportion of blood, so that it is almost black in color.

blood′root′ (blŭd′rōōt′; 85), *n.* A plant (*Sanguinaria canadensis*) of the poppy family, having a red root and red sap and bearing a solitary lobed leaf and white flower in early spring; — called also *puccoon, redroot, bloodwort,* and *turmeric.* See SANGUINARIA.

blood′shed′ (-shĕd′), *n.* Also **blood′shed′ding.** The shedding of blood, esp. human blood; slaughter.

blood′shot′ (blŭd′shŏt′), *adj.* [*blood* + *shot* variegated.] Red and inflamed; suffused with blood; — of eyes.

blood′stain′ (-stān′), *n.* A discoloration caused by blood. — **blood′stain′,** *v. t.* — **blood′stained′** (-stānd′), *adj.*

blood′stone′ (-stōn′), *n.* A green chalcedony sprinkled with red spots, as if of blood; — called also *heliotrope.*

blood′suck′er (-sŭk′ẽr), *n.* **1.** Any animal that sucks blood; esp., a leech. **2.** An extortioner; vampire.

blood′thirst′y (-thûrs′tĭ), *adj.* Eager to shed blood; cruel. — **blood′thirst′i·ly,** *adv.* — **blood′thirst′i·ness,** *n.*

blood type. A blood group.

blood vessel. Any vessel or canal in an animal in which blood circulates, as an artery, vein, or capillary.

blood′wort′ (-wûrt′), *n.* **a** Any plant of a family (Haemodoraceae, the bloodwort family) having a deep-red coloring matter in the roots. **b** A European dock (*Rumex sanguineus*) with red-veined leaves. **c** Bloodroot.

blood′y (blŭd′ĭ), *adj.;* BLOOD′I·ER (-ĭ·ẽr); BLOOD′I·EST. [AS. *blōdig.*] **1.** Containing or like blood; of the nature of, pertaining to, or in the blood. **2.** Smeared or stained with blood. **3.** Involving bloodshed; sanguinary; as, a *bloody* battle. **4.** Bloodthirsty; murderous. **5.** *Vulgar, Brit.* Infamous; — a low epithet. — *v. t.;* BLOOD′IED (-ĭd); BLOOD′Y·ING. To make bloody; to stain with blood.

bloody shirt. The bloodstained shirt of a slain man, used to incite vengeance; hence, any symbol similarly used.

bloom (blōōm), *n.* [AS. *blōma* lump.] *Metal.* **a** A mass of wrought iron from the forge or puddling furnace. **b** A bar of iron or steel hammered or rolled from an ingot.

bloom, *n.* [ON. *blōm, blōmi.*] **1. a** A blossom; flower of a seed plant. See BLOSSOM. **b** The flowering state; as, roses in *bloom.* **2.** A state or time of beauty, freshness, and vigor. **3.** The rosy color of the cheek; flush; glow. **4.** The delicate, powdery coating on some fruits or leaves; also, a surface coating suggestive of this; as, the *bloom* on new coins. — *v. i.* **1.** To produce or yield blossoms; blossom;

flower. **2.** To be in a state of youthful beauty and freshness. **3.** To be rosy or warm-colored; to glow. — *v. t.* **1.** To cause to blossom or flourish. **2.** To bestow a bloom upon; to make blooming or radiant; to impart a bloom to.

bloom'er (blōōm'ẽr), *n.* [After Mrs. Amelia *Bloomer*, an American, who advocated the costume.] **1.** A former costume for women, consisting of a short skirt and loose trousers gathered at the ankles. **2.** *pl.* Loose trousers gathered at the knee, used by women in sports; also, a woman's undergarment of similar design.

bloom'er·y (blōōm'ẽr·ĭ), *n.* A furnace and forge in which wrought-iron blooms are made.

bloom'ing, *adj.* **1.** Blossoming; flowering. **2.** Thriving in health, beauty, and vigor. — **bloom'ing·ly**, *adv.*

bloom'y (blōōm'ĭ), *adj.* **1.** Full of bloom; flowery; as, a *bloomy* spray. **2.** Covered with bloom, as fruit.

blos'som (blŏs'ŭm), *n.* [AS. *blōstm, blōsma, blōstma.*] **1.** The flower of a seed plant; bloom; hence, mass of bloom; state of bearing flowers. *Blossom* is more commonly used than *flower* or *bloom* when the reference is to plants producing edible fruits. **2.** A blooming period or stage of development. — *v. i.* **1.** To flower; to bloom. **2.** To flourish and prosper. — **blos'som·y**, *adj.*

blot (blŏt), *n.* [OF. *blotte, bloutte*, a clod or clot of earth.] **1.** A spot or stain, as of ink. **2.** An obliteration of something written or printed; an erasure. **3.** A spot on a reputation; a disgrace; a blemish. — *v. t.*; BLOT'TED (-ĕd; -ĭd); BLOT'TING. **1.** To spot, stain, or bespatter. **2.** To impair; mar. **3.** To stain with infamy; disgrace. **4.** To obliterate; efface; — usually with *out;* as, to *blot* out writing. **5.** To obscure; eclipse. **6.** To dry, as writing, with blotting paper or sand. — **Syn.** See ERASE. — *v. i.* **1.** To make a blot or blots, as of ink. **2.** To take a blot or become blotted; as, this paper *blots* easily.

blot, *n.* **1.** *Backgammon.* A single man left exposed. **2.** A weak or exposed point.

blotch (blŏch), *n.* [OF. *bloche* a clod of earth.] **1.** A blot or spot, as of color or ink. **2.** *Med.* A large pustule, or a coarse eruption. — *v. t. & i.* To cover with blotches; to make or cause a blotch. — **blotch'y** (-ĭ), *adj.*

blot'ter (blŏt'ẽr), *n.* **1.** A piece of blotting paper. **2.** A book in which entries of occurrences are made as they take place; as, a police *blotter.*

blot'ting pa'per. A kind of soft, spongy, unsized paper used esp. to absorb ink from freshly written manuscript.

blouse (blouz; blous; *F.* blōōz), *n.* [F.] **1.** A loose shirtlike overgarment reaching about to the knees. **2.** The undress uniform coat of the United States Army. **3.** A loose waist, usually belted; a shirtwaist.

blow (blō), *v. i.*; BLEW (blōō; 114); BLOWN (blōn); BLOW'ING. [AS. *blōwan* to blossom.] To flower; bloom. — *v. t.* To cause to blossom; put forth (blossoms). — *n.* A display, esp. of blossoms; state of blossoming; mass of blossoms.

blow, *v. i.*; BLEW; BLOWN; BLOW'ING. [AS. *blāwan* to blow, as wind.] **1.** To move, as air, esp. rapidly or with power. **2.** To send forth a forcible current of air or gas, as from a bellows. **3.** To sound on being blown into, as a trumpet. **4.** To produce a noise by blowing; as, whistles *blow.* **5.** To pant; puff. **6.** To talk loudly; boast. **7.** Of whales, etc., to eject the moisture-laden air from the lungs through the blowholes or blowhole. **8.** To be carried or moved by the wind. **9.** *Elec.* To melt; — of a fuse.
— *v. t.* **1.** To force a current of air upon, as with the mouth. **2.** To cause to sound, as a trumpet or organ. **3.** To spread by report; publish; disclose. **4.** To drive by a current of air; impel; as, *blown* ashore. **5.** To inflate, as with pride; puff up. **6.** To form by inflation, as with air. **7.** To clear of contents, as by forcing air through. **8.** To deposit eggs or larvae upon or in (meat, etc.). **9.** To burst, shatter, or destroy by an explosion; — with *up, down, open*, etc. **10.** To put out of breath; to cause to blow from fatigue. **11.** *Slang.* **a** To curse; confound; as, *blow* it! **b** To spend (money), esp. freely; also, to treat (oneself or another).
blow hot and cold. To favor a thing at one time and treat it coldly at another; — from a fable of Aesop. — ***blow over.*** To pass away without effect; cease; as, the trouble *blew over.* — ***blow up.*** **1.** To explode; burst; as, to *blow up* a fort. **2.** To increase in intensity; as, a gale *blew up.* **3.** To scold; abuse; as, to *blow up* a person. **4.** *Colloq.* To enlarge (a picture, etc.), as by projection.

blow (blō), *n.* **1.** A blowing, esp. a violent blowing, of the wind; a gale. **2.** Act of forcing air from the mouth or nose, or through or from some instrument. **3.** A boast; also, boasting; *Slang*, a boaster. **4.** *Metal.* A single heat or operation of the Bessemer converter; also, the quantity of metal so operated upon.

blow, *n.* [ME. *blaw, blowe.*] **1.** A forcible stroke with the hand, fist, or some instrument. **2.** A sudden or forcible act or effort; assault. **3.** A sudden calamity; something that causes suffering or loss (esp. when sudden).

blow'er (blō'ẽr), *n.* **1.** One that blows; specif., a device for producing a current, as of air. **2.** *Slang.* A braggart.

blow'fish' (blō'fĭsh'), *n.*; *pl.*, see FISH. **a** A puffer, or any similar fish that can inflate its body. **b** *Southern U. S.* The walleyed pike.

blow'fly' (-flī'), *n.* Any of various true flies that deposit their eggs or maggots on meat, in wounds, etc.; esp., the bluebottle *Calliphora erythrocephala.*

blow'gun' (-gŭn'), *n.* A tube through which an arrow or other projectile may be impelled by the force of the breath.

blow'hole' (-hōl'), *n.* **1.** A hole for the escape of air or gas; air hole. **2.** A nostril or spiracle in the top of the head of a whale or other cetacean. **3.** A hole in the ice to which whales, seals, etc., come to breathe.

blow'ing, *n.* **1.** A noise caused by the forcible ejection of air, steam, or gas. **2.** A sound produced by the vibration of the nostrils in some horses (called ***high blowers***) during breathing. It is not an unsoundness.

blown (blōn), *past part.* of BLOW, to blossom. Specif.: *adj.* Opened; in bloom or having bloomed; as, a full-*blown* rose.

blown, *past part.* of BLOW, to propel air. Specif.: *adj.* **1.** Swollen; distended; puffed up with gas, as cattle gorged with green food. **2.** Out of breath; tired. **3.** Flyblown. **4.** Formed by means of a blowtube, blowpipe, etc.

blow'off' (blō'ŏf'), *n.* **1.** A blowing off of steam, water, etc., or an apparatus for this. **2.** *Slang.* A braggart.

blow'out' (-out'), *n.* **1.** Act of blowing out; also, the place where something has been blown out; esp., a bursting, as of a tire, or a hole made by bursting. **2.** *Slang.* A hearty meal; also, a big social affair.

blow'pipe' (-pīp'), *n.* **1.** A small tubular instrument for directing a jet of air or other gas into a fire or flame so as to concentrate and increase the heat; also, a similar instrument, used in anatomy and zoology for revealing or cleaning a cavity. **2.** A blowgun or blowtube.

blow'torch' (-tôrch'), *n.* A small lamp or torch with a device to intensify combustion by means of a blast.

blow'tube' (-tūb'), *n.* **1.** A blowgun, or similar instrument. **2.** *Glass Mfg.* A long iron or steel tube on the end of which the workman gathers a quantity of molten glass, and through which he blows to expand or shape it.

blow'up' (-ŭp'), *n.* **1.** An explosion; outburst, as of temper. **2.** *Colloq.* An enlargement, as of a picture.

blow'y (-ĭ), *adj.* Windy. — **blow'i·ness**, *n.*

blowz'y (blouz'ĭ), *adj.* Also **blowzed** (blouzd). Coarse and ruddy-faced; fat, ruddy, and disheveled; frowzy.

blub'ber (blŭb'ẽr), *n.* **1.** The fat of whales and other large marine mammals from which oil is obtained. **2.** The action of blubbering. — *v. i.* To weep so as to disfigure the face. — *v. t.* **1.** To swell, disfigure, or wet (the face) with tears. **2.** To utter tearfully; — with *out.* — *adj.* Swollen; as, *blubber* lips. — **blub'ber·ing·ly**, *adv.*

blub'ber·y (-ĭ), *adj.* **1.** Swollen; protuberant. **2.** Like blubber; gelatinous and quivering. **3.** Rich in blubber; fat.

blu'cher (blōō'chẽr; -kẽr), *n.* **1.** A kind of half boot, named from the Prussian general Blücher. **2.** A shoe in which the quarters extend a short distance over the vamp, their inner edges being loose and lacing across the tongue.

bludg'eon (blŭj'ŭn), *n.* A short clublike weapon with one end loaded or thicker than the other. — *v. t. & i.* To hit with or as if with a bludgeon; to coerce. — **bludg'eon·er** (-ẽr), **bludg'eon·eer'** (-ēr'), *n.*

blue (blōō; 114), *adj.* [ME. *bleu, blew*, fr. OF. *bleu*, of Teut. origin.] **1.** Of the color blue. **2.** Specif.: **a** Of a cool color of low saturation, without redness or glare; — said esp. of a flame. **b** Of the skin, livid, esp. with cold or from a blow. **c** Designating venous blood, which shows blue through the skin. **3.** Figuratively: **a** Suggestive of devils and the flames of hell-fire; as, the air was *blue* with oaths. **b** Low in spirits; melancholy. **c** *Colloq.* Gloomy in prospect; as, things looked *blue.* **d** *Colloq.* Of a woman, literary; learned. Cf. BLUESTOCKING. **e** Morally rigorous or severe; puritanical; as, *blue* laws. **4.** Wearing blue. — *n.* **1.** Any of several colors whose hue is or resembles that of the zenith of the clear sky; any color in that portion of the color spectrum lying between green and violet (reddish blue). **2.** Any pigment or dye that colors blue; also, a powder or bluing for use in laundering. **3.** With *the.* **a** The sky. **b** The sea. **4.** Something blue, as a badge or a poker chip. **5.** A person whose blue uniform, coat, badge, etc., shows military, political, collegiate, or other allegiance. **6.** A bluestocking. **7.** *pl.* See BLUES. — *v. t. & i.*; BLUED (blōōd); BLU'ING or BLUE'ING. To make or turn blue. — **blue'ly**, *adv.* — **blue'ness**, *n.*

blue'back' salm'on (blōō'băk'). A salmon (*Oncorhynchus nerka*) found in Alaskan rivers and as far south as the Columbia River, considered as next below the quinnat salmon in economic importance.

Blue'beard' (blōō'bẽrd'; 114), *n.* A man who murders one wife after another; — from the hero of a popular story.

blue'bell' (-bĕl'), *n.* **1.** Any of various bellflowers, esp. *Campanula rotundifolia*, called also ***bluebell of Scotland*** *or* ***harebell.*** **2.** Any of various plants bearing blue bell-shaped flowers: **a** The European wood hyacinth or grape hyacinth. **b** A low tufted New Zealand plant of the bellflower family. **3.** The blue-flowered columbine.

blue'ber'ry (-bĕr'ĭ; -bẽr-ĭ), *n.* The edible blue or blackish berry of any of several species of plants (genus *Vaccinium*) of the huckleberry family; also, the plant. See HUCKLEBERRY.

blue'bird' (-bûrd'), *n.* **1.** Any of several North American songbirds (genus *Sialia*) blue above, related to the robin. **2.** [*cap.*] A member of the junior organization of Camp Fire Girls, for girls eight to ten.

blue blood. The blood of noble or aristocratic families, or a person of such blood; — used first in Spain, where light-complexioned persons claimed freedom from Moorish or Jewish admixture. — **blue'-blood'ed** (-blŭd'ĕd; -ĭd; 2), *adj.*

blue'bon'net (blōō'bŏn'ĕt; -ĭt), *n.*, *or* **blue bonnet.** **1.** A broad, flat Scottish cap of blue wool, or one wearing such a cap; hence, a Scot. **2.** *Bot.* **a** The bluebottle *Centaurea cyanus.* **b** Either of two lupines with blue flowers, one species of which (*Lupinus subcarnosus*) is the State flower of Texas.

blue book, *or, in sense 2*, **blue'book'** (blōō'bŏŏk'), *n.* **1.** *Eng.* A parliamentary publication; — so called from its blue paper covers. **2.** *Colloq., U. S.* **a** A register or directory of persons of social prominence. **b** A blue-covered booklet used in writing college examinations.

blue'bot'tle (-bŏt''l), *n.* **1.** **a** A European carduaceous plant (*Centaurea cyanus*) having flower heads with blue, pink, or white bottle-shaped rays; — called also *bachelor's button* and *cornflower.* It is common in grainfields. **b** Any of several other plants with blue flowers, as some bellflowers and squills. **2.** Any of several species of true flies, having a steel-blue abdomen or body and making a loud buzzing noise in their flight; esp., a blowfly (*Calliphora erythrocephala*), or an iridescent coppery fly (genus *Lucilia*).

blue'cap' (-kăp'), *n.* **1.** A titmouse (*Parus caeruleus*). **2.** A Scot. Cf. BLUEBONNET, 1.

blue chip. **1.** A high-value poker chip. **2.** A high-priced quality stock valued esp. for its high security.

blue'coat' (blōō'kōt'), *n.* One dressed in blue, as a soldier, sailor, policeman, or, in England, an almsman. — **blue'-coat'ed**, *adj.*

blue cohosh. See COHOSH.

blue comb. Also **blue comb disease.** A severe disease of domestic fowl resembling Bright's disease of man.

blue'-curls' (-kûrlz'), *n.*, *or* **blue curls.** **1.** Any plant of a genus (*Trichostema*) of the mint family, having irregular blue flowers. **2.** A selfheal (*Prunella vulgaris*).

blue devil. **1.** A baleful demon. **2.** *pl.* Apparitions seen during delirium tremens; hence, very low spirits.

Blue Eagle. An emblem representing an eagle with spread wings, printed in dark blue, adopted by the National Recovery Administration (1933–35) as official insignia and authorizing mark.

blue'-eyed' grass (blōō'īd'). Any of various plants (genus *Sisyrinchium*) of the iris family, having grasslike foliage and delicate blue flowers.

blue'fish' (blōō'fĭsh'), *n.*; *pl.*, see FISH. **1.** A very active and voracious fish (*Pomatomus saltatrix*), allied to the mackerel, bluish above and silvery below, an important food fish along the U. S. Atlantic coast. **2.** Any of various other fishes; as: **a** A Californian weakfish (*Eriscyon* *parvipinnis*). **b** A small Californian food fish (*Girella nigricans*). **c** The saury (*Scombresox saurus*).

blue flag. **a** The common iris (*Iris versicolor*) of the eastern United States. It is the State flower of Tennessee. **b** Any blue-flowered species of *Iris*.

blue fox. See FOX, 1 **a**.

blue′gill′ (blōō′gĭl′), *n.* A sunfish (*Helioperca incisor*) of the Mississippi drainage and the Great Lakes region, esteemed as a food fish.

blue′grass′ (-gràs′; 9), *n.* **1.** Any of several grasses (genus *Poa*) having bluish-green culms; esp., a valuable pasture grass (*P. pratensis*) called ***Kentucky bluegrass***. **2.** [*cap.*] With *the*. The bluegrass region of central Kentucky, where fine horses are bred.

Bluegrass State. Kentucky; — a nickname.

blue′-green′ al′gae (blōō′grēn′). See ALGA.

blue gum. See GUM, 5 **a** (3).

blue′hearts′ (blōō′härts′), *n. sing. & pl.* A blue-flowered herb (*Buchnera americana*) with rough, hairy foliage.

blue′ing, blue′ish, etc. Vars. of BLUING, BLUISH, etc.

blue′jack′ (-jăk′), *n.* **1.** Blue vitriol (see VITRIOL). **2.** An inferior oak (*Quercus cinerea*) of the southern United States.

blue′jack′et (-jăk′ĕt; -ĭt), *n.* An enlisted man in the navy.

blue jay. **1.** The common jay (*Cyanocitta cristata*) of eastern North America, with handsome crest, and upper parts chiefly bright blue. **2.** In the western United States, any of various other jays, largely blue in color.

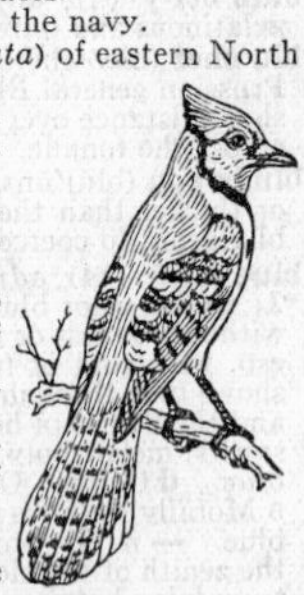

Blue Jay (*C. cristata*). (1/8)

blue laws. Certain laws of extreme rigor enacted in the early days of New Haven colony; hence, any puritanical laws.

blue moon. A period as incalculably long as that between recurrences of an exceedingly rare phenomenon.

Blue′nose′ (blōō′nōz′), *n.* A native of the Canadian Maritime Provinces; esp., a Nova Scotian.

blue′-pen′cil (blōō′pĕn′sĭl; -s′l), *v. t.* To edit, or excise from, with a blue pencil; — originally of printer's copy.

blue peter. [Corrupt. of *blue repeater*, a British signal flag.] *Naut.* A blue flag with a white square in the center, used as a signal for sailing, to recall boats, etc.

blue point. An oyster from a bed near Blue Point, Long Island, much used for eating raw; hence, any similar oyster.

blue′print′ (blōō′prĭnt′), *n.* **1.** A photographic print, white on a bright-blue ground, used for copying maps, architectural plans, etc. **2.** A thoroughly plotted and co-ordinated program of action, as for mobilization. **3.** A key pattern of action or undeveloped master plan, as for a world government. — *v. t.* To make a blueprint of.

blue′-red′, *n.* The hue of the color cycle exactly intermediate between blue and red, that is, equally resembling and differing from the primary hues blue and red. See COLOR.

blue ribbon. **1.** The ribbon worn by members of the Order of the Garter, the highest order of British knighthood. **2.** The highest honor or award. **3.** The badge of some temperance societies.

blue′-rib′bon ju′ry *or* **pan′el.** A special panel of jurors, selected for special qualifications, which may be called to sit in important, esp. criminal, cases.

blues (blōōz; 114), *n.* [Short for *blue devils*.] **1.** *Colloq.* Low spirits; a fit of melancholy. **2.** A type of song written in a characteristic key with melancholy words and syncopated rhythms.

blue′-sky′ law. *Colloq.* A law enacted to protect the investing public; — from a legislator's remark that some companies sought to "capitalize the blue skies."

blue′stock′ing (blōō′stŏk′ĭng), *n.* A literary or pedantic woman; — originally one of a group whose gatherings were attended by a literary lion wearing blue stockings instead of the conventional black silk. — **blue′stock′ing·ism** (-ĭz′m), *n.*

blue′stone′ (-stōn′), *n.* **1.** Blue vitriol (see VITRIOL). **2.** A bluish-gray building or paving stone; specif., a sandstone quarried near the Hudson River.

blue streak. *Colloq.* Speed like that of a lightning flash.

blu′et (blōō′ĕt; -ĭt), *n.* [F., dim. of *bleu* blue.] An American plant (*Houstonia caerulea*) of the madder family, with bluish flowers and tufted stems.

blue′wood′ (blōō′wŏŏd′), *n.* A chaparral shrub (*Condalia obovata*), family Rhamnaceae, of western Texas and northern Mexico.

blue′y (blōō′ĭ), *n.* *Australia.* A bushman's blanket, shirt, or blouse, often blue; also, a swagman's bundle. — ***to hump bluey.*** *Slang.* To carry a swag; hence, to travel in the bush, esp. in search of work.

bluff (blŭf), *adj.* **1.** Having a broad, flattened front. **2.** Rising steeply with a broad, flat or rounded front, as a coast. **3.** Roughly but good-naturedly frank; unceremonious; outspoken. — *n.* A high, steep bank; a cliff. — **bluff′ly,** *adv.* — **bluff′ness,** *n.*

Syn. **Bluff, blunt, brusque, curt, crusty, gruff** mean abrupt and unceremonious in speech and manner. **Bluff** connotes outspokenness, rough good nature, and unconventionality that bespeak sincerity yet scorn of politeness; **blunt,** directness and plain speaking that suggest lack of consideration of others' feelings; **brusque,** a real or apparent sharpness of manner and ungraciousness of speech; **curt,** disconcerting shortness or apparently rude conciseness of utterance; **crusty,** a forbidding exterior and a manner marked by asperity or acerbity that sometimes belies real kindness of heart; **gruff,** a surliness and roughness of manner accompanied by curt and hoarse or guttural utterance.

bluff (blŭf), *v. t.* **1.** In poker, to deter or try to deter (one) from betting by a show of assurance. **2.** To deter or frighten by a pretense of strength or resources; also, to deceive; fool. — *v. i.* To bluff a person; to deceive. — *n.* Act of bluffing; one who bluffs. — **bluff′er,** *n.*

blu′ing, blue′ing (blōō′ĭng; 114), *n.* A laundering preparation of indigo or the like for counteracting the yellowish tinge of linen or cotton.

blu′ish (blōō′ĭsh), *adj.* Somewhat blue. — **blu′ish·ness,** *n.*

blun′der (blŭn′dẽr), *v. i.* [ME. *blunderen, blondren,* to stir, confuse, blunder.] **1.** To move confusedly or clumsily; to flounder and stumble. **2.** To make a serious error or commit a fault, through ignorance, stupidity, overconfidence, or confusion. — *v. t.* **1.** To utter awkwardly, stupidly, or confusedly; — usually with *out*. **2.** To mismanage; bungle. — *n.* A gross error or mistake. — **Syn.** See ERROR. — **blun′der·er,** *n.* — **blun′der·ing·ly,** *adv.*

blun′der·buss (blŭn′dẽr·bŭs), *n.* [Corrupt. fr. D. *donderbus* thunder box, gun.] **1.** An obsolete short firearm with a large bore and, usually, a flaring muzzle, capable of holding a number of balls. **2.** A stupid blunderer.

blunge (blŭnj), *v. t.;* BLUNGED (blŭnjd); BLUNG′ING (blŭn′jĭng). [Cf. *plunge* and *blend*.] To beat up or mix in water, as clay to form slip. — **blung′er** (blŭn′jẽr), *n.*

blunt (blŭnt), *adj.* [Early ME.] **1.** Insensitive; obtuse in feeling or perception. **2.** Dull in understanding; not acute. **3.** Having a thick edge or point; dull; not sharp or keen. **4.** Abrupt in address; tactlessly curt or frank. — **Syn.** See DULL: BLUFF. — *v. t. & i.* **1.** To make or become blunt. **2.** To impair in force, keenness, or susceptibility. — **blunt′ly,** *adv.* — **blunt′ness,** *n.*

blur (blûr), *v. t.;* BLURRED (blûrd); BLUR′RING. **1.** To obscure, soil, or blemish by smearing; to smudge; hence, to sully. **2.** To make dim or indistinct to the sight; as, haze *blurred* the horizon; also, to dim; to cloud; as, tears *blurred* her vision. — *v. i.* To become blurred; to make blurs. — *n.* **1.** A smear or stain which obscures without effacing. **2.** A blot or cloud, as upon one's name. **3.** Something obscurely or dimly seen, understood, etc. — **blur′ry,** *adj.*

blurb (blûrb), *n.* [Coined by Gelett Burgess.] *Colloq.* A fulsome commendation, esp. in advertising.

blurt (blûrt), *v. t.* To utter suddenly and unadvisedly or impulsively; as, to *blurt* out a secret. — **blurt,** *n.*

blush (blŭsh), *v. i.;* BLUSHED (blŭsht) or BLUSHT; BLUSH′ING. [ME. *bluschen,* fr. AS. *blyscan* to shine, be red, *āblysian* to blush, fr. *blysa* torch, flame.] **1.** To become red, esp. in the cheeks or face, as from shame, modesty, or confusion; to flush. **2.** To have a rosy or fresh color; to bloom. **3.** To feel shame; — often with *at* or *for*. — *v. t.* **1.** To redden. **2.** To express by blushing. — *n.* **1.** A glance; look; — now only in *at* or *on (the) first blush*. **2.** A suffusion of the cheeks in blushing. **3.** A red or rosy tint. — *adj.* Ruddy; of the color of a blush. — **blush′er,** *n.* — **blush′ful** (-fŏŏl; -f′l), *adj.* — **blush′ing·ly,** *adv.*

blus′ter (blŭs′tẽr), *v. i.* **1.** To blow fitfully with violence and noise, as wind; to be windy and boisterous, as the weather. **2.** To talk or act with noisy violence; to swagger, storm, or rage. — *v. t.* To affect or bring about by blustering. — *n.* A noisy, violent wind, storm, commotion, fit of anger, etc.; also, the noise or confusion of this. — **blus′ter·er,** *n.* — **blus′ter·ing·ly,** *adv.* — **blus′ter·ous** (-ŭs), *adj.* — **blus′ter·y,** *adj.*

blype (blīp), *n.* *Scot.* A piece or shred, as of skin.

B′nai B′rith (b′nā b′rēth; b′rĭs; *colloq.* brĭth). [Heb. *benāi berīth* sons of the covenant.] A Jewish fraternity founded in New York City in 1843.

bo′a (bō′ȧ), *n.; pl.* BOAS (-ȧz). [L., a kind of water serpent.] **1.** Any of a genus (*Boa,* typical of the family Boidae) of nonvenomous tropical American snakes which crush their prey, including the boa constrictor (def. 1). **2.** Popularly, any large snake that crushes its prey; a constrictor. Cf. ANACONDA, 3; BOA CONSTRICTOR, 2; PYTHON, 4. **3.** A long, round scarf of fur, feathers, etc., for the neck.

boa constrictor. **1.** A tropical American snake (*Constrictor,* syn. *Boa, constrictor*), which attains great length and crushes its prey in its coils. **2.** Loosely, any large snake that crushes its prey. Cf. ANACONDA, 3; BOA, 2; PYTHON, 4.

Bo′a·ner′ges (bō′ȧ·nûr′jēz), *n. pl.* [Gr. *boanerges,* prob. the Aram. equivalent of Heb. *benāi regesh,* explained as "sons of thunder."] **1.** An appellation given by Christ to James and John. *Mark* iii. 17. **2.** Construed as *sing.* (with pl. *-ges* or *-gesses*). Any declamatory and vociferous preacher or orator.

boar (bōr; 70), *n.* [AS. *bār*.] **1.** The uncastrated male of swine. See SWINE, 1. **2.** A (male or female) wild hog (*Sus scrofa*) of continental Europe, southwestern Asia, and northern Africa, from which most domestic swine have been derived; — called specif. *wild boar*.

board (bōrd; 70), *n.* [AS. *bord* board, plank.] **1.** A piece of sawed lumber of little thickness and of a length greatly exceeding its width. Cf. QUARTERSAW, *Illust.* **2.** A square or oblong piece of thin wood or other material used for some special purpose; as, a molding *board*. **3.** Pasteboard; as, a book bound in *boards*. **4.** *pl.* The stage in a theater. **5.** A table; esp., a table for food. **6.** Food; meals; sometimes, meals and lodging. **7.** A table at which a council or court is held; hence, a council, or authorized assembly; as, a *board* of trade. — *v. t.* **1.** To cover with boards or boarding; as, to *board* a house. **2. a** To furnish with meals, or with meals and lodgings, for compensation. **b** To place where board is provided for compensation. — *v. i.* To be furnished with board (def. 6), esp. meals.

board, *n.* [AS. *bord* border, margin.] **1.** The border, side, or edge of anything; as, the sea*board*. **2.** *Naut.* **a** The side of a ship. Cf. SHIPBOARD. **b** The stretch which a ship makes on one tack in beating. — ***by the board.*** Overboard. — ***go by the board.*** To go overboard; hence, to be lost, discarded, ignored, etc. — ***on board.*** Aboard a ship, train, or the like. — *v. t.* **1.** To come up against or alongside of (a ship), as for attacking. **2.** To go on board of, as a ship or a train. **3.** To accost. — *v. i.* *Naut.* To tack.

board′er (bōr′dẽr), *n.* **1.** One who boards, or is provided with board (def. 6). **2.** One who boards a ship.

board foot. A unit of lumber measurement one foot long, one foot wide, and one inch thick, or its equivalent. Abbr. *bd. ft.* (sing. & pl.).

board′ing, *n.* Boards, collectively; a covering of boards.

board′ing·house′ (bōr′dĭng·hous′), *n.* A house at which persons are boarded.

boarding school. A school in which pupils are boarded and lodged as well as taught.

board measure. Measurement in board feet.

board of trade. **1.** [*caps.*] *Eng.* An administrative department concerned with the international, commercial, and industrial policy of the government. **2.** *U. S.* A body of men organized for the advancement and protection of business interests.

board rule. A measuring stick with various scales, for finding without calculation the number of board feet in a board, joist, or the like.

board′walk′ (bōrd′wôk′), *n.* *U. S.* **1.** A walk constructed of planking. **2.** A promenade, orig. of planking, along a beach.

boar′fish′ (bōr′fĭsh′; 70), *n.; pl.,* see FISH. Any of several fishes which have a projecting hoglike snout.

boar′hound′ (-hound′), *n.* A large dog, specif. the great Dane, used in hunting wild boars.

boar′ish, *adj.* Swinish; cruel; lecherous. — **boar′ish·ly,** *adv.* — **boar′ish·ness,** *n.*

boart. Var. of BORT.

boast (bōst), *v. i.* [ME. *bosten, boosten*, v., *bost, boost*, n.] To vaunt oneself or one's possessions; to brag. — *v. t.* **1.** To brag of; extol. **2.** To possess or display, esp. with pride; — often ironical; as, the state *boasts* its good roads; the room *boasts* only a broken chair.

Syn. **Boast, brag, vaunt, crow** mean to give vent to one's pride in oneself, one's accomplishments, or the like. **Boast**, the general term, usually imputes exaggeration, ostentatiousness, or vaingloriousness to the one who vents his pride; **brag**, more colloquial than *boast*, implies more conceit and more glorying in what one can do, as well as in what one is, or has, or has done; **vaunt**, more literary than the others, usually connotes more pomp and bombast than *boast* and less crudeness or naïveté than *brag;* **crow** implies exultant boasting or blatant bragging. — *n.* **1.** Act or instance of boasting. **2.** A cause of boasting; an occasion of pride or exultation. — **boast'er**, *n.* — **boast'ful** (-fo͝ol; -f'l), *adj.* — **boast'ful·ly**, *adv.* — **boast'ful·ness**, *n.* — **boast'ing·ly**, *adv.*

boast, *v. t.* *Stonecutting & Sculp.* To shape roughly with a broad chisel (**boast'er**), in preparation for finer work.

boat (bōt), *n.* [AS. *bāt*.] **1.** A small open vessel or craft for use on the water, usually moved by oars or paddles; hence, any vessel for navigating the water. **2.** A boat-shaped utensil or device; as, a gravy *boat*. — *v. t.* To place, transport, or traverse in a boat. — *v. i.* To go by boat or, for pastime, in a boat.

☞ COMBINATIONS are:

boatbuilder **boathouse** **boatload**

boat'bill' (-bĭl'), *n.* A South American wading bird (*Cochlearius cochlearia*), related to the night herons.

boat'er (bōt'ẽr), *n.* **1.** One who boats. **2.** *Eng.* A type of straw hat.

boat hook. A pole-handled hook, with a point on the back, used to pull or push a boat, raft, log, etc., into place.

boat'ing, *n.* Act or pastime of one who boats. — **boat'ing**, *adj.*

boat'man (bōt'măn), **boats'man** (bōts'-), *n.* A man who manages or deals in boats. — **boat'man·ship**, *n.*

boat'swain (bō's'n *or, esp. as a literary word*, bōt'swān'), *n.* Sometimes **bo'sun.** On a war vessel, a warrant officer in charge of the rigging, anchors, cables, etc.; on some merchant ships, a superior seaman having similar duties.

boat train. A train scheduled to connect with a boat.

bob (bŏb), *v. t.;* BOBBED (bŏbd); BOB'BING. [OF. *bober* to trick.] **1.** To cheat; filch. **2.** To mock or delude; to make sport of. — *n.* A jeer; taunt; trick.

bob (bŏb), *n.* [ME. *bob, bobbe*, bunch, *boben, bobben*, to strike.] **1.** *Now Dial.* A bunch or cluster, as of leaves, flowers, or grapes. **2.** A ball or weight hanging from a rod, line, etc.; as, the *bob* of a pendulum. **3.** A short, jerking motion; as, a *bob* of the head. **4.** The refrain of a song; specif., a short, abrupt one. **5.** A blow; a rap. **6. a** A horse's docked tail. **b** A woman's or child's short haircut. **7.** *pl.* BOB. *Colloq., Eng.* A shilling. **8. a** A bobsled. **b** A bob skate. **9.** *Angling.* A knot or bunch of worms, rags, etc., used for bait; also, a float. — *v. t.;* BOBBED (bŏbd); BOB'BING. **1.** To strike with a quick, light blow; to tap. **2.** To cause to move with a bob, jerk, or shake; as, to *bob* one's head; also, to make with a bob; as, to *bob* a curtsy. **3.** To cut (hair) in the style of a bob. — *v. i.* **1.** To make a bob, as with the head. **2.** To swing or move with a short, jerky motion. **3.** To angle with a bob. — **bob'ber**, *n.*

bobbed (bŏbd), *adj.* **1.** Having, or formed into, a bob. **2.** Cut short, as hair; docked.

bob'ber·y (bŏb'ẽr·ĭ), *n.; pl.* -IES (-ĭz). [Anglo-Ind.] Hubbub.

bob'bin (bŏb'ĭn), *n.* [F. *bobine.*] **1.** One of the small pins or cylinders which are stuck in a pillow so as to form a design and round which threads are plaited in making **bobbin lace.** Cf. NEEDLE-POINT. **2.** A spool or reel used to hold yarn or thread, as in sewing machines; also, a reel for or of insulated wire. **3.** A fine cord or narrow braid.

bob'bi·net' (bŏb'ĭ·nĕt'; bŏb'ĭ·nĕt), *n.* [*bobbin* + *net*.] A hexagonal-meshed cotton or silk net or lace.

bob'ble (bŏb''l), *v. & n.* *Colloq.* Fumble.

bob'by (bŏb'ĭ), *n.; pl.* -BIES (-ĭz). [After Sir *Robert* Peel, who reorganized the London police.] *Colloq., Eng.* A policeman.

bob'by pin (bŏb'ĭ). A flat wire hairpin with prongs pressing close together, originally for use with bobbed hair.

bob'by-sox'er (bŏb'ĭ·sŏk'sẽr), *n.* An adolescent girl, esp. in the early teens; — from the wearing of ankle socks, or **bobby socks.** — **bob'by-sox'** *or* **bob'by-socks'** (-sŏks'), *adj.*

bob'cat' (bŏb'kăt'), *n.* See PLURAL, *Note*, 3. See LYNX.

bob'o·link (bŏb'ō·lĭngk), *n.* [Earlier *boblincoln;* named from its call.] An American migratory bird (*Dolichonyx oryzivorus*) noted for its rollicking song. In the fall it collects in flocks in rice fields of southern U. S., where it is known as *ricebird* or *reedbird.*

bob skate. A skate with double runners.

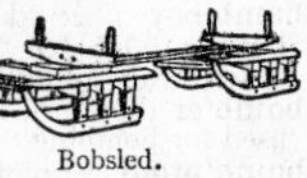

Bobsled.

bob'sled' (bŏb'slĕd'), *n.* Also **bob'sleigh'** (-slā'). *U. S.* A short sled, usually coupled with another, or a compound sled so formed. — *v. i.;* see SLED. To coast or ride on a bobsled.

bob'stay' (-stā'), *n.* *Naut.* A stay to hold the bowsprit down.

bob'tail' (-tāl'), *n.* A bobbed tail or a horse or dog with one. — *adj.* Having the tail cut short; hence, deficient; abbreviated. — *v. t.* To dock the tail of; curtail.

bob veal. The veal of a newborn or unborn calf.

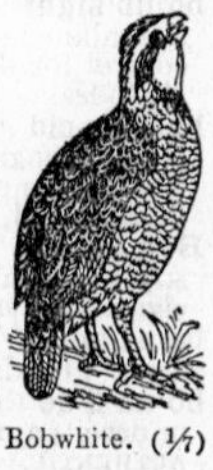

Bobwhite. (1/7)

bob'white' (bŏb'hwīt'), *n.* [From the note.] Any of various North American quails (genus *Colinus*); — often called *partridge* in the southern United States.

bo·cac'cio (bō·kä'chō), *n.* [It. *boccaccio.*] A large rockfish (*Sebastodes paucispinis*), abundant on the California coast.

‖**boc'cie** (bôt'chā), *n. pl.* Also **boc'ce** (-chā). [It., pl., bowls.] An Italian variety of the game of bowls.

Boche, boche (bôsh; bŏsh), *n.* [F. (slang), fr. *caboche* head, hard head.] *Slang.* A German.

bock (bŏk), *n., or* **bock beer.** [G. *bockbier*, corrupt. of *einbecker bier*, from *Einbeck* in Germany.] A kind of beer brewed, usually in the spring, from a strong wort.

bode (bōd), *v. t. & i.* [AS. *bodian* to announce, tell, fr. *boda* messenger.] To presage by signs; to foreshow something; portend. — **bode'ment**, *n.*

bode, *past & obsolete past part.* of BIDE.

bod'ice (bŏd'ĭs), *n.* [Prop. pl. of BODY.] **1.** *Obs.* A corset; stays. **2.** A woman's laced outer garment resembling a corset; also, a close-fitting jacketlike waist.

bod'ied (bŏd'ĭd), *adj.* Having or provided with a body, or a material form; — often in combination, as in able-*bodied.*

bod'i·less (-ĭ·lĕs; -lĭs), *adj.* Incorporeal; immaterial.

bod'i·ly (-ĭ·lĭ), *adj.* **1.** Corporeal; material; as, *bodily* existence. **2.** Of or pertaining to the body; physical; as, *bodily* ills. — *adv.* As one body; entirely; completely.

Syn. **Bodily, physical, corporeal, corporal, somatic** mean specifically of or pertaining to the human body. **Bodily** suggests opposition to *mental* or *intellectual;* **physical**, as here considered, does not carry so strong a suggestion as *bodily* of an organic structure, and is vaguer or less explicit in its reference (as, *physical* well-being is often the result of freedom from *bodily* ailments); **corporeal** suggests the substance or matter of which the body is composed (as, *corporeal* presence); **corporal**, once close to *corporeal*, now applies only to things which affect the body (as, *corporal* punishment); **somatic**, because of freedom from theological and poetic connotations, is now often preferred by scientists to *bodily* and *corporeal*, with an implied opposition to *psychical.*

bod'ing (bōd'ĭng), *n. & adj.* Foreboding.

bod'kin (bŏd'kĭn), *n.* [ME. *boydekyn* dagger.] **1.** A dagger or stiletto. **2.** A stilettolike implement, esp. one for punching holes in cloth. **3.** A stiletto-shaped ornamental hairpin. **4.** A large-eyed blunt needle, for drawing tape, ribbon, etc., through a loop or a hem.

Bo·do'ni (bō·dō'nē), *n.* A style of type devised by the Italian printer Giambattista Bodoni (1740–1813). Its modern form is known as **Bodoni book.** See TYPE, *n.*, 9.

bod'y (bŏd'ĭ), *n.; pl.* BODIES (-ĭz). [AS. *bodig.*] **1.** The total organized substance of an animal or plant, whether living or dead; the physical organism; specif., a corpse. **2.** The trunk, or main part, as distinguished from the limbs and the head; hence, the main, central, or principal part, as of an army, a building, vehicle, airplane, etc. **3.** Specif.: **a** The main part of a document or journal, as distinguished from titles, preambles, appendixes, etc. **b** *Print.* See TYPE, *Illust.* **4. a** *Now Chiefly Dial.* A person. **b** *Law.* The person. **5.** That part of a garment covering the body or trunk. **6.** A mass or portion of matter distinct from other masses; as, a *body* of cold air. **7.** Consistency; substance; compactness of texture; fullness or richness, as of flavor. **8.** A unit formed of a number of persons or things; a collective whole; as, a *body* of troops; a *body* of laws; a legislative *body.* — *v. t.;* BOD'IED (-ĭd); BOD'Y·ING. To furnish with or as with a body; to embody.

body corporate. *Law.* A corporation.

bod'y·guard' (bŏd'ĭ·gärd'), *n.* A guard to protect or defend the person; hence, retinue; attendants.

body politic. A group organized for government; specif., a state (def. 8).

body snatching. *Law.* The unauthorized removal of a dead body from the grave. — **body snatcher.**

Boe·o'tian (bē·ō'shăn), *adj.* Of or pert. to Boeotia, noted for its dull-witted people; hence, stupid. — *n.* A person who is Boeotian by race or mentality.

Boer (bo͝or; *E.* bōr), *n.* [D., a farmer.] A South African of Dutch or Huguenot descent; esp., a rural descendant of the early Dutch settlers. — **Boer**, *adj.*

Bo'fors gun (bō'fôrz; *Swed.* bo͞o'fôrs). A double-barreled 40 mm. automatic antiaircraft gun firing an explosive projectile 120 times per minute, — originally made at the Bofors munition works of Alfred Nobel in Sweden.

bog (bŏg; 73), *n.* [Ir. & Gael. *bog* soft, moist.] A quagmire filled with decayed moss and other vegetable matter; wet spongy ground; as, a peat *bog;* a cranberry *bog.* — *v. t. & i.;* BOGGED (bŏgd); BOG'GING. To sink, as into a bog; to mire. — **bog'gish**, *adj.* — **bog'gish·ness**, *n.*

bog asphodel. Either of two bog herbs (*Narthecium ossifragum* of Europe and *N. americanum* of the United States) of the bunchflower family, resembling the true asphodel.

bo'gey (bō'gĭ), *n.; pl.* BOGEYS (-gĭz). **1.** Var. of 1st BOGY and of 2d BOGIE. **2.** *Golf.* A given score or number of strokes, for each hole or a course, against which players compete; also, one stroke over par.

bog'gle (bŏg''l), *v. i.;* BOG'GLED (-'ld); BOG'GLING (-lĭng). [See BOGLE.] **1.** To shy suddenly in alarm; hence, to hesitate through fear, scruples, indecision, etc. **2.** To dissemble; to exhibit shiftiness. **3.** To work clumsily; to bungle. — *n.* **1.** Act of boggling. **2.** A scruple; difficulty; demur; also, blunder; botch. — **bog'gler** (-lẽr), *n.*

bog'gy (-ĭ), *adj.;* -GI·ER (-ĭ·ẽr); -GI·EST. Consisting of, or containing, a bog or bogs; swampy. — **bog'gi·ness** (-ĭ·nĕs; -nĭs), *n.*

bo'gie (bō'gĭ), *n.; pl.* BOGIES (-gĭz). Var. of 1st BOGY.

bo'gie, *n.* Also **bo'gy** *or* **bo'gey.** **1.** *Chiefly N. of Eng.* A low, strongly built cart. **2.** *British.* A railway truck. **3.** One of the weight-carrying wheels on the inside perimeter of the tread of a tank, serving to keep the treads in line. See TANK, *Illust.*

bo'gle (bō'g'l; bŏg''l), *n.* Also, *Dial.*, **bog'gle** (bŏg''l). [Scot. and North. Eng. *bogle, bogill, bugill*, specter.] A bogy; goblin; specter.

bog'trot'ter (bŏg'trŏt'ẽr), *n.* One who lives in or roves over bogs; formerly, a type of Irish vagabond.

bo'gus (bō'gŭs), *adj.* Spurious; sham.

bog'wood' (bŏg'wo͝od'), *n.* The black, ebonylike wood of oak (**bog oak**) and other trees preserved in peat bogs.

bo'gy (bō'gĭ), *n.; pl.* BOGIES (-gĭz). Also **bo'gey, bo'gie.** [From *bog*, var. of *bug* a bugbear.] An object of superstitious fear; esp., a bugbear.

bo'gy. Var. of 2d BOGIE.

bo·hea' (bō·hē'), *n.* [From *Wu-i*, name of the hills in China where this tea is grown.] Black tea (see TEA, 1 **b**), esp. of a superior grade, but later of an inferior kind.

Bo·he'mi·a (bō·hē'mĭ·ȧ; 58), *n.* **1.** See *Gaz.* **2.** A community of Bohemians. See BOHEMIAN, *n.*, 3.

Bo·he'mi·an (bō·hē'mĭ·ăn; 58), *n.* **1.** A native of Bohemia. **2.** A gypsy, thought to be from Bohemia. **3.** One of a class of artists, intellectuals, etc., who adopt a mode of life in protest against, or indifference to, the common conventions of society, esp. in social relations. — **Bo·he'mi·an**, *adj.* — **Bo·he'mi·an·ism** (-ĭz'm), *n.*

Bohemian Brethren. A Christian body, Unitas Fratrum, organized in 1467 in Bohemia by followers of Peter Chelčický, reformist writer. See MORAVIAN, 2.

boil (boil), *v. i.* [OF. *boillir*, fr. L. *bullire*, fr. *bulla* bubble.] **1.** To generate, through the action of heat, bubbles of vapor which rise and agitate the mass; — of a liquid. **2.** To be agitated by or as if by such boiling; to seethe. **3.** To become hot or stirred up; as, his blood *boils* with anger. **4.** To be in, and to undergo the action of, boiling liquid; as, the meat is *boiling*. — *v. t.* **1.** To cook, cleanse, etc., in boiling water or other liquid; as, to *boil* potatoes; to *boil* clothes. **2.** To heat to the boiling point, or so as to cause to bubble; as, to *boil* water. **3.** To form or separate by boiling or evaporation involving bubbling; as, to *boil* sugar or salt. — *n.* Act or state of boiling.

boil (boil), *n.* [Influenced by *boil*, v., or by D. *buil.*] A localized swelling of the skin caused by infection in a skin gland, having a hard central core, and characterized by inflammation and the formation of pus; a furuncle. Cf. CARBUNCLE.

boiled din′ner (boild). Boiled beef (usually corned beef) and cabbage with other boiled vegetables, usually potato, carrots, turnip, beets.

boiled oil. An oil whose drying properties have been increased by heating, usually with driers.

boil′er (boil′ẽr), *n.* **1.** One that boils. **2.** A vessel in which anything is boiled. **3.** That part of a steam generator in which water is converted into steam, consisting usually of metal shells, headers, and tubes that form the container for the steam and water under pressure.

boil′ing point. The temperature at which a liquid boils. For water at sea level, barometer 30 in., it is 212° F. (100° C.).

bois′ter·ous (bois′tẽr·ŭs), *adj.* [ME. *boistous.*] **1.** *Obs.* **a** Coarse. **b** Rough. **c** Strong. **d** Massive. **2.** Tumultuously violent; furious; as, *boisterous* winds. **3.** Noisy and unrestrained, esp. in jollity. — **Syn.** See VOCIFEROUS. — **bois′ter·ous·ly,** *adv.* — **bois′ter·ous·ness,** *n.*

bo′la (bō′lȧ), *n.* Also **bo′las** (-lȧs). [Sp.] A missile weapon consisting of balls of stone, iron, etc., attached to the ends of a thong or cord, used for hurling at and entangling an animal, as by the Gauchos.

bo′lar (bō′lẽr), *adj.* Of or pertaining to bole; clayey.

bold (bōld), *adj.* [AS. *bald, beald.*] **1.** Forward to meet danger; venturesome. **2.** Too forward; taking undue liberties; lacking proper modesty or restraint. **3.** Exhibiting or requiring daring; audacious; as, a *bold* plan; also, strikingly unconventional; as, *bold* views. **4.** *Obs.* Confident; assured. **5.** Steep; abrupt; as, a *bold* shore. **6.** Standing out prominently; conspicuously clear, sharp, etc.; as, a peak's *bold* outlines. **7.** Of printing type: **a** Bold-faced. **b** Boldface. — **Syn.** Intrepid, audacious, courageous, brave, dauntless, valiant. — **Ant.** Cowardly. — *n. Print.* **a** Boldface. **b** Bold-faced type. — **bold′ly,** *adv.* — **bold′ness,** *n.*

bold′face′ (-fās′), *n. Print.* See TYPE. — **bold′face′,** *adj.*

bold′-faced′ (-fāst′; 2), *adj.* **1.** Bold in manner or expression; indecorously forward. **2.** *Print.* Having a conspicuous or heavy face; — of type. Abbr. *b. f.*

bole (bōl), *n.* [ON. *bolr.*] The trunk or stem of a tree.

bole, *n.* [L. *bolus* clay, lump, fr. Gr. *bōlos.*] Any of several varieties of friable earthy clay.

bole, *n. Scot.* An unglazed opening in the wall of a building; also, a wall recess or cupboard.

bo·le′ro (bō·lâr′ō), *n.* [Sp.] **1.** A Spanish dance in ¾ time or the music for it. **2.** A loose, waist-length jacket open at the front.

bol′i·var (bŏl′ĭ·vẽr; *Sp.* bō·lē′vär), *n.; pl.* BOLIVARS (-vẽrz), BOLIVARES (*Sp.* bō′lē·vä′rās). [Amer. Sp., after Simón *Bolívar.* See *Biog.*] A silver coin and monetary unit of Venezuela. See MONEY, *Tables.*

bo·liv′i·a′no (bō·lĭv′ĭ·ä′nō), *n.; pl.* -NOS (-nōz). [Amer. Sp.] The gold monetary unit of Bolivia. See MONEY, *Tables.*

boll (bōl), *n.* [AS. *bolla.*] The pod or capsule of a plant, esp. of flax or cotton.

bol′lard (bŏl′ẽrd), *n.* An upright wooden or metal post, as in a boat or on a dock, around which to fasten a rope.

boll weevil (bōl). A grayish weevil (*Anthonomus grandis*) about a quarter of an inch long, which infests the cotton plant, puncturing, and laying its eggs in, the squares and bolls.

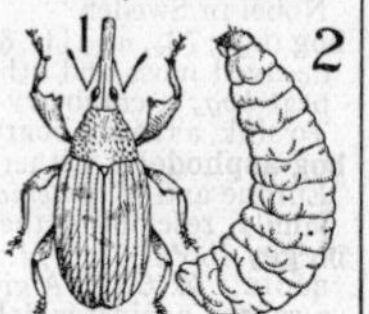

Boll Weevil. 1 Imago; 2 Larva. (× 3)

boll′worm′ (bōl′wûrm′), *n.* The larva of a moth (*Heliothis armigera*), which devours bolls or unripe pods of cotton, and also feeds on corn ears, beans, etc.

bo′lo (bō′lō), *n.; pl.* -LOS (-lōz). [Sp.] A large Philippine single-edged knife.

Bo·lo′gna sau′sage, *or* **Bo·lo′gna** (bō·lō′nyȧ; -nȧ; *colloq.* -nĭ), *n.* A large sausage made of beef, veal, and pork, enclosed in a casing, smoked, and cooked.

bo′lo·graph (bō′lō·grăf), *n.* [Gr. *bolē* stroke + *-graph.*] A photographic record secured with the bolometer.

bo·lom′e·ter (bō·lŏm′ē·tẽr), *n.* [Gr. *bolē* stroke + *-meter.*] *Physics.* An electrical instrument for measuring minute quantities of radiant heat, esp. in the spectrum, by changes in resistance of a blackened platinum strip exposed to the radiations. — **bo′lo·met′ric** (bō′lō·mĕt′rĭk), *adj.*

bo·lo′ney (bō·lō′nĭ), *n.* **1.** Bologna sausage. **2.** *Slang, U. S.* Something pretentious but worthless; bunk; hooey.

Bol′she·vik, bol′she·vik (bŏl′shĕ·vĭk; bōl′-), *n.; pl.* BOLSHEVIKI (bŏl′shĕ·vē′kē; -vĭk′ē; bōl′-), BOLSHEVIKS (bŏl′shĕ·vĭks; bōl′-). [Russ. *bolshe* the larger; — because the Bolsheviki orig. were the majority group of the party.] **a** An adherent of the majority wing (the **Bolsheviki**) of the Russian Social Democratic party, which under Lenin's leadership stressed a more extremist revolutionary Marxism than the Mensheviki (minority wing). In 1919 the Bolshevik party was renamed Communist party. **b** A Bolshevist. — **Bol′she·vik, bol′she·vik,** *adj.* — **-vik·ism** (-ĭz'm), *n.*

Bol′she·vism, bol′she·vism (-vĭz'm), *n.* Doctrines, tactics, or practices of or like those of the Bolsheviki; Bolshevist form of government.

Bol′she·vist, bol′she·vist (-vĭst), *n.* A Bolshevik; hence, any radical, esp. one who believes in the overthrow of capitalism by force. — **Bol′she·vist, bol′she·vist, -vis′tic** (-vĭs′tĭk), *adj.* — **-vis′ti·cal·ly** (-tĭ·kăl·ĭ), *adv.*

Bol′she·vize, bol′she·vize (-vīz), *v. t.* To make Bolshevist; to imbue with Bolshevism. — **-vi·za′tion** (-vĭ·zā′shŭn; -vī·zā′-), *n.*

bol′ster (bōl′stẽr), *n.* [AS.] **1.** A long, narrow pillow or cushion, esp. one that extends from side to side of a bed. **2.** Something resembling a bolster, as in shape, softness, or use as a support; specif., *Arch.*, a rounded projection (see IONIC, *Illust.*). — *v. t.* **1.** To support with a bolster or pillow. **2.** To support, hold up, or maintain; esp., to support with difficulty or effort; — often with *up.* — **bol′ster·er,** *n.*

bolt (bōlt), *v. t.* [OF. *buleter*, fr. MHG. *biuteln* to sift.] **1.** To sift or separate, as bran from flour, as by means of a sieve. **2.** To examine and separate, as if by sifting.

bolt (bōlt), *n.* [AS.] **1.** A shaft or missile intended to be shot from a crossbow or catapult, as an arrow or dart; esp., a short, stout, blunt-headed arrow. **2.** Hence: **a** An attack, argument, charge, etc., delivered with the suddenness or force of a bolt. **b** A flash of lightning; a thunderbolt. **3.** A boltlike, often cylindrical, thing; as: **a** A cylindrical jet; as, a *bolt* of water. **b** A sliding bar used in fastening a door; also, the part of a lock shot or withdrawn by the key. See LOCK, *Illust.* **c** A pin or rod, esp. of steel, to fasten or hold something in place, often having a head at one end and a screw thread on the other. Cf. NUT, *n.*, 3. **d** A compact package or roll of cloth, usually about 40 yards. **e** A roll of wallpaper, usually 15 or 16 yards. **4.** [From the verb, below.] Act of bolting; as: **a** A running away. **b** *U. S.* A refusal to support a nomination, policy, etc., of one's party.

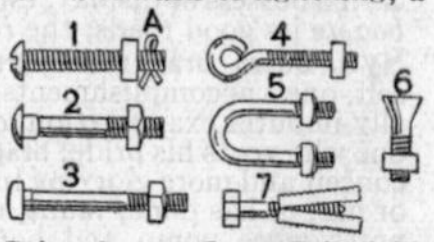

Bolts, 3 c. 1 Stove Bolt (with Cotter Pin, *A*); 2 Carriage Bolt; 3 Machine Bolt; 4 Eyebolt; 5 U Bolt; 6 Plow Bolt; 7 Expansion Bolt.

— *v. i.* **1.** To start forth like a bolt or arrow; dart. **2.** To dart off or away; flee. **3.** To strike like a bolt. **4.** To bolt food. **5.** *U. S.* To bolt one's political party. — *v. t.* **1.** To fasten or secure with or as with a bolt or bolts. **2.** To shoot; discharge; drive forth; dislodge. **3.** To blurt; — often with *out.* **4.** To swallow without chewing. **5.** To form in or make up into a bolt or bolts. **6.** *U. S.* To refuse to support, as a policy of one's political party. — *adv.* In the manner of a bolt; suddenly; straight.

bolt′er (bōl′tẽr), *n.* One that bolts; specif., an instrument or machine for bolting flour, meal, etc.

bolt′er, *n.* One that bolts; as: **a** A horse given to running away. **b** *U. S.* A voter who refuses to support his party.

bolt′head′ (bōlt′hĕd′), *n.* **1.** The head of a bolt. **2.** *Old Chem.* = MATRASS **a.**

bolt′rope′ (bōlt′rōp′), *n.* A strong rope stitched to the edges of a sail, awning, etc.

bo′lus (bō′lŭs), *n.* [L.] A rounded mass of anything; esp., a large pill for a horse.

bomb (bŏm; *by some*, bŭm), *n.* [F. *bombe*, fr. It., fr. L. *bombus* a noise, fr. Gr. *bombos.*] **1.** *Mil.* A projectile, containing a high-explosive charge, propelled at low velocities by a mortar or other thrower or dropped from an aircraft. **2.** Any similar missile or device; as, a dynamite *bomb.* — *v. t. & i.* To bombard; to drop bombs (upon).

bom′ba·ca′ceous (bŏm′bȧ·kā′shŭs), *adj.* [LL. *bombax* cotton.] Belonging to the silk-cotton family (Bombacaceae). See SILK-COTTON TREE.

bom′bard (bŏm′bärd), *n.* [F. *bombarde*, fr. L. *bombus.* See BOMB.] **1.** The earliest kind of cannon, throwing stones and other missiles. **2.** A small war vessel with bomb-throwing mortars.

bom·bard′ (bŏm·bärd′; bŭm-), *v. t.* **1.** To attack with artillery; to throw shells, bombs, etc., at or into. **2.** To assail vigorously or persistently. **3.** *Physics.* To subject (a body) to the impingement of small particles or rays; also, to cause (small particles or rays) to impinge upon; to impinge upon. — **Syn.** See ATTACK. — **bom·bard′er,** *n.* — **bom·bard′ment,** *n.*

bom′bard·ier′ (bŏm′bẽr·dēr′), *n.* [F.] **1.** *Hist.* A man or vessel that bombards. **2.** *Mil.* A noncommissioned officer in the British artillery. **3.** A member of a bomber crew whose duty it is to guide the plane in the run over the target by means of the bombsight and to release the aerial bombs. See WINGS, *Illust.*

bom′bar·don (bŏm′bẽr·dŏn; bŏm·bär′-), *n.* [It. *bombardone.*] *Music.* **a** A deep-toned wind instrument of the double-reed family, predecessor of the bassoon and double bassoon. **b** An organ stop of similar quality. **c** A bass or contrabass tuba.

bom′bast (bŏm′băst), *n.* [OF. *bombace* cotton, fr. LL. *bombax.*] **1.** *Hist.* Soft fibrous stuff used for padding. **2.** Inflated, pretentious language; fustian; rant. — *adj.* Bombastic.

Syn. **Bombast, rhapsody, rant, fustian** mean high-flown, high-sounding speech or writing. **Bombast** implies grandiosity which so outruns the thought that the attention is distracted from the matter; **rhapsody** designates a kind of ecstatic or effusive utterance governed by the feelings rather than logical thought; **rant** and **fustian** are applicable to bombast and rhapsody at their worst, *rant* stressing extravagance and violence of expression, and *fustian*, banality or preposterousness.

bom·bas′tic (bŏm·băs′tĭk), **bom·bas′ti·cal** (-tĭ·kăl), *adj.* Characterized by, or given to, bombast; high-sounding. — **bom·bas′ti·cal·ly,** *adv.*

Bom′bay′ cat′e·chu (bŏm′bā′; bŏm·bā′). See CATECHU.

bom′ba·zine′, bom′ba·sine′ (bŏm′bȧ·zēn′; bŏm′bȧ·zēn; bŭm′-), *n.* [F. *bombasin*, fr. LL. *bombasinum, bombycinum*, a cotton or silk texture.] A twilled dress fabric having a silk or cotton warp and a worsted filling.

bomb bay. See 2d BAY, 3 **b.**

‖**bombe** (bônb), *n.* [F.] A melon or a round mold lined with one kind of ice cream and filled with another.

bomb′er (bŏm′ẽr), *n.* One that bombs; specif., an aircraft of a type used for bombing.

bomb′proof′ (-prōōf′; 2), *adj.* Secure against the explosive force of bombs. — *n.* A structure or shelter, often underground, that explosive shells will not penetrate.

bomb′shell′ (-shĕl′), *n.* A bomb; also, a devastating surprise.

bomb′sight′ (-sīt′), *n.* A sighting device for aiming aerial bombs; esp., a combined optical aiming and calculating mechanism and gyroscopic control for dropping aerial bombs precisely upon a target from high altitudes.

bom′by·cid (bŏm′bĭ·sĭd), *n.* [L. *bombyx* silkworm.] A moth or larva belonging to a family (Bombycidae) of lepidopterous insects, including the silkworms of the genus *Bombyx* and their near allies. — **bom′by·cid,** *adj.*

Bon (bōn), *n.* [Jap.] A Japanese festival, July 13–16, when ancestral spirits are supposed to revisit the household altars; — called by foreigners *Feast of Lanterns.*

bo′na·ci′ (bō′nä·sē′), *n.* [Amer. Sp. *bonasí.*] Any of several groupers of Florida, the West Indies, etc.

bo′na fi′de (bō′nȧ fī′dē). [L.] In or with good faith; without fraud or deceit; authentic; genuine; as, a *bona fide* transaction. — **Syn.** See AUTHENTIC.

bo·nan′za (bō·năn′zȧ), *n.* [Sp., prop., calm, fair weather, prosperity, fr. L. *bonus* good.] An exceptionally rich ore deposit or pocket in veins carrying gold and silver; hence, *Colloq., U. S.*, anything yielding a large return in money.

Bo'na·part'ist (bō'nȧ·pär'tĭst), *n.* An adherent or partisan of Napoleon Bonaparte, his policy, or the dynasty founded by him. — **Bo'na·part·ism** (-pärt·ĭz'm), *n.*

bon'bon' (bŏn'bŏn'; *F.* bôN'bôN'), *n.* [F., fr. *bon bon* very good, fr. *bon* good.] **1.** A small candy having a center of, and coated with, fondant. **2.** See CRACKER, 4.

bond (bŏnd), *n.* [AS. *bonda, bunda,* husband, householder, fr. ON. *bōndi,* fr. *būa* to dwell.] *Obs.* A serf. — *adj.* In serfdom; enslaved; not free or a freeman.

bond, *n.* [ME., var. of BAND a fastening.] **1.** *Archaic.* Now *pl.* That which binds or restrains; fetter, shackle, etc.; hence, confinement. **2.** A binding force or influence; a tie; as, *bonds* of love. **3.** A binding agreement; covenant. **4.** Something which binds, joins, etc.; specif.: **a** A band; ligament. **b** Connection made by overlapping adjacent parts of a structure; also, a timber, stone, or brick used for such connection. **c** A substance which blends, fuses, etc ; a binder. **5** *Obs.* Moral or political duty or obligation. **6.** One who acts as bail or surety. **7.** A writing under seal by which a person binds himself to pay a certain sum on or before an appointed day. **8.** Such an instrument, or, loosely, any interest-bearing certificate, issued by a government or corporation. **9.** A kind of firm, uncalendered paper. **10.** *Chem.* A mechanism by means of which atoms are held together in a molecule; — usually indicated in formulas by a line (—) or a dot (.). **11.** *Com.* The state of goods being manufactured, stored, or transported under the care of bonded agencies until duties or taxes are paid; as, goods in *bond.* **12.** *Insurance.* An agreement under which a person or corporation (as an insurance company) becomes surety to pay, within stated limits, for financial loss caused to another by the act or default of a third person or by some contingency over which the principal may have no control. — *v. t.* **1.** In building, to place or arrange (materials, as the bricks of a wall) so as to secure solidity. **2.** To place under bond; specif : **a** To secure the payment of the duties and taxes on by giving a bond. **b** To issue bonds secured by mortgage upon (property). **c** To convert into a debt secured by bonds. **d** *Colloq., U. S.* To provide a bond (sense 12) for or cause to provide such a bond; as, to *bond* an employee. **3.** To bind together or connect by or as by bonds. — *v. i.* To hold together or solidify by or as by a bond or a binder. — **bond'er,** *n.*

bond'age (bŏn'dĭj), *n.* **1.** *Hist.* Villein service or tenure; thralldom. **2.** Serfdom; slavery. **3.** Subjection to compulsion, as of an appetite or duty. — **Syn.** See SERVITUDE.

bond'ed (bŏn'dĕd; -dĭd), *adj.* Placed under, covered by, or operating under bond or a bond; as, a *bonded* official.

bond'hold'er (bŏnd'hōl'dẽr), *n.* A person who holds a bond, as of a corporation. — **bond'hold'ing,** *adj. & n.*

bond'maid' (-mād'), *n.* A female slave or bond servant.

bond'man (-măn), *n.* **1.** *Hist.* A peasant; a churl. **2.** *Archaic.* A serf; a man slave.

bond servant. A slave; also, one bound to service without wages.

bonds'man (bŏndz'măn; 25), *n.* **1.** A bondman. **2.** *Law.* A surety on a bond.

bond'stone' (bŏnd'stōn'), *n.* *Masonry.* A stone running through a wall to bind it together.

bond'wom'an (-wo͝om'ăn), *n.* A woman slave.

bone (bōn), *n.* [AS. *bān.*] **1.** One of the hard pieces or parts of the skeleton of most vertebrates. **2.** The hard tissue of which the adult skeleton of most vertebrates is largely composed. **3.** A bone with meat adhering to it; as, a soup*bone.* **4.** *pl.* The skeleton; by extension, the body. **5.** Any of various hard animal substances or structures, as whalebone. **6.** Something originally or usually made of bone, ivory, or the like; as, in *pl.,* dice, clappers, etc. **7.** *pl.* One who performs with clappers; specif., one of the end men in a Negro minstrel performance. — *v. t.* To remove bones from; as, to *bone* a fish; also, to put bones or steels in; as, to *bone* a corset.

bone black, *or* **bone'black'** (bōn'blăk'), *n.* The black substance obtained by calcining bones in closed vessels.

bone china. China made with an admixture of the white residue (**bone ash**) of bones calcined in air.

bone'head' (bōn'hĕd'), *n.* *Slang.* A stupid person. — **bone'head'ed·ness,** *n.*

bone meal. Fertilizer or feed made of crushed or ground bone.

bon'er (bōn'ẽr), *n.* **1.** One that bones. **2.** *Slang.* A stupid, often ridiculous, mistake or blunder.

bone'set' (bōn'sĕt'), *n.* Any of several herbs (genus *Eupatorium*) of the aster family; esp., a species (*E. perfoliatum*) with opposite leaves and white-rayed flower heads, used as a diaphoretic and tonic; — called also *thoroughwort* and *agueweed.*

bon'fire' (bŏn'fīr'), *n.* [Orig., a fire of bones, i. e., for consuming corpses.] A large fire built in the open air.

bon'go (bŏng'gō), *n.; pl.* BONGOS (-gōz). Any of three large reddish or brown white-striped African antelopes (genus *Boöcercus*).

‖**bon gré, mal gré** (bôN' grā', mȧl' grā'). [F.] Whether with good or with bad grace; willy-nilly.

bon'ho·mie', bon'hom·mie' (bŏn'ō·mē'; *F.* bô'nô'mē'), *n.* [F.] Good nature; pleasant and easy manner.

Bon'i·face (bŏn'ĭ·fās), *n.* The sleek, jolly landlord in Farquhar's *Beaux' Stratagem;* hence, an innkeeper.

bon'i·ness (bōn'ĭ·nĕs; -nĭs), *n.* Quality of being bony.

bo·ni'to (bō·nē'tō), *n.; pl.* -TOS, -TOES (-tōz). [Sp.] Any of several marine fishes, esp. of certain species allied to the mackerel.

‖**bon jour** (bôN' zho͞or'). [F.] Good day; good morning.

bon mot (bôN' mō'); *pl.* BONS MOTS (bôN' mōz'; *F.* mō'). [F., fr. *bon* good + *mot* word.] A witty remark or riposte; a piquant, adroit, or happy expression.

‖**bonne** (bôn, *almost* bŭn), *n.* [F., prop., good woman.] A maid-servant; a nursemaid.

‖**bonne foi** (bôn' fwȧ'). [F.] Good faith.

bon'net (bŏn'ĕt; -ĭt), *n.* [OF. *bonet, bonnet,* fr. ML. *abonnis* a kind of cap.] **1.** A soft woolen cap worn by men in Scotland. **2.** A covering for the head, usually one kept in place by ribbons or strings tied under the chin, now worn chiefly by children. **3.** A headdress analogous to a bonnet, as the feathered headdress of an American Indian. **4.** Something resembling a bonnet in shape or use; as: **a** A cover for an open fireplace, or a cowl to increase a chimney's draft. **b** The hood of an automobile. **c** A metal covering for valve chambers (see VALVE, *Illust.*), jackets, cylinders, etc. **d** [Cf. F. *bonnette.*] *Naut.* An additional piece of canvas laced to the foot of a jib or foresail in moderate winds. — *v. t.* To provide or dress with a bonnet.

bonnet pepper. See PEPPER, 3.

‖**bon'net' rouge** (bô'nĕ' ro͞ozh'). [F.] The red cap of extremists in the French Revolution; hence, a revolutionist. Cf. SANS-CULOTTE.

bon'ny (bŏn'ĭ), *adj.;* -NI·ER (-ĭ·ẽr); -NI·EST. Also **bon'nie.** [Prob. fr. OF. *bon* good, fr. L. *bonus.*] Handsome; beautiful; also, *Dial.,* plump; healthy. — **Syn.** See BEAUTIFUL. — **bon'ni·ly,** *adv.* — **bon'ni·ness,** *n.*

bon'ny·clab'ber (-klăb'ẽr), *n.* [Ir. *bainne* milk + *clabar* mire, clabber.] Coagulated sour milk; clabber.

‖**bon soir** (bôN' swȧr'). [F.] Good evening; — a salutation.

bon'spiel (bŏn'spēl; -spĕl), *n.* [Scot.] A match between curling clubs.

bon'te·bok' (bŏn'tē·bŏk'), *n.* See PLURAL, *Note,* 6. [D., lit., spotted buck.] A South African purplish-red antelope (*Damaliscus pygargus*) with white face and rump.

bon ton (bôN' tôN'). [F., good tone, manner.] Fashionable manner or style; good breeding; hence, high society.

bo'nus (bō'nŭs), *n.* [L. *bonus* good.] **1.** Something given in addition to what is usual or strictly due; specif.: **a** A premium given for a loan, or for a charter or other privilege granted to a company. **b** Money, or an equivalent, given in addition to an agreed compensation. **2.** Money, insurance, or the like, granted by a government to its discharged soldiers. **3.** *Finance.* A premium, or gift, usually of stock, by a corporation, as to a stockholder. **4.** *Insurance. Eng.* A dividend.

‖**bon vi'vant'** (bôN' vē'väN'); *pl.* BONS VIVANTS (*F.* bôN' vē'väN'). [F., fr. *bon* good + *vivant,* pres. part. of *vivre* to live.] A lover of good living, esp. of the table. — **Syn.** See EPICURE.

‖**bon voy'age'** (bôN' vwȧ'yȧzh'). [F.] A good journey or trip; — a farewell phrase.

bon'y (bōn'ĭ), *adj.;* BON'I·ER (-ĭ·ẽr); BON'I·EST. **1.** Consisting of or like bone or bones; full of or pertaining to bones. **2.** Having large or prominent bones.

bonze (bŏnz), *n.* [F., fr. Pg. *bonzo,* fr. Jap. *bonzō.*] A Buddhist monk of the Far East, orig. of Japan.

bon'zer (bŏn'zẽr), *adj.* [Said to be a corruption of *bonanza.*] *Slang, Australia.* First-rate.

boo (bo͞o), *n.* An exclamation used to startle, esp. children; also, an expression of contempt, disapproval, etc. — *v. i. & t.;* BOOED (bo͞od); BOO'ING. To utter, or assail with, boos.

boob (bo͞ob), *n.* *Slang.* A stupid person; booby.

boo'by (bo͞o'bĭ), *n.; pl.* -BIES (-bĭz). [Sp. *bobo,* fr. L. *balbus* stammering.] **1.** A dunce; a stupid fellow. **2.** Also **booby gannet.** Any of a genus (*Sula*) of tropical sea birds, allied to but smaller than the gannets. **3.** In card playing, etc., the player whose score is lowest.

booby trap. **1.** A trap consisting of a pail of water so placed over a door as to drench a person opening the door, — a schoolboy trick. **2.** *Mil.* A concealed grenade or mine attached to some harmless-looking object and set to explode when this object is disturbed by an unwary person. **3.** Any trap for the unwary.

bood (bo͝od), *v.* *Scot.* (It) behooved; also, must; ought.

boo'dle (bo͞o'd'l), *n.* **1.** *Contemptuous, U. S.* A collection or lot of persons; caboodle; — esp. in phrase *kit and boodle.* **2.** Bribe money; graft; also, swag.

boog'ie-woog'ie (bo͝og'ĭ·wo͝og'ĭ; bo͞o'gĭ·wo͞o'gĭ), *n.* [From *boogie,* Slang, a Negro performer + rhyming imitative sound.] A primitive-sounding percussive style of playing blues on the piano, characterized by a persistent bass rhythm and florid figurations of a simple melody often in contrary motion to the bass.

book (bo͝ok), *n.* [AS. *bōc;* akin to Goth. *boka* a letter, in pl. book, writing, and to AS. *bōc, bēce,* beech; because the Saxons and Germans in general wrote runes on pieces of beechen board.] **1.** A written or printed narrative or record, or series of them; esp., a literary composition. **2.** A set of sheets, as of wood, ivory, or paper, strung or bound together; as, a loose-leaf note*book.* **3.** A major division of a treatise or literary work; as, six *books* of the *Aeneid.* **4.** [*cap.*] The Bible; also [*not cap.*], one of its subdivisions. **5.** Anything that may be studied like a book; as, the *book* of nature. **6.** A libretto; hence, the text of a play. **7.** A packet, as of stamps or gold leaf. **8.** A record of bets, esp. of bets on horse races. **9.** *Card Playing.* A certain number of tricks or of cards forming a set, won or held by one side.

☞ COMBINATIONS and PHRASES are:

bookbinder	booklover	bookshop
bookbindery	bookrack	bookstack
bookbinding	bookrest	bookstall
bookcase	bookseller	bookstand
bookcraft	bookshelf	bookstore

— ***by the book.*** According to a book regarded as authoritative; in the prescribed way; as, to speak *by the book.* — ***in one's bad books.*** In disfavor with one. — ***in one's books,*** *or* ***in one's good books.*** In favor with one. — ***on the books.*** Enrolled. — ***one for the book(s).*** A feat or fact worthy of entry in the record books.

— *v. t. & i.* To enter, write, or register in a book or list, esp. so as to engage service, passage, or accommodation.

— *adj.* **1.** That is shown by books of account; as, *book* profit. **2.** Acquired from books; as, *book* learning.

book end. A supporting device for the end of a row of books.

book'ish, *adj.* **1.** Fond of, or learned in, books. **2.** Characterized by, or affecting, literary form or precision; literary; hence, formal; pedantic. — **book'ish·ly,** *adv.* — **book'ish·ness,** *n.*

book'keep'er (bo͝ok'kēp'ẽr), *n.* One who keeps accounts; one whose business or profession is bookkeeping.

Syn. Bookkeeper, accountant. A **bookkeeper** keeps a regular, accurate record of business transactions by making proper entries in books kept for this purpose. An **accountant** is a skilled bookkeeper who may be employed to organize or set up a system of records or to investigate or report upon the financial condition of an organization.

book'keep'ing, *n.* Art or practice of keeping a systematic record of business transactions; art of keeping accounts.

book'let (-lĕt; -lĭt), *n.* A little book; specif., one in paper covers.

book'mak'er (-māk'ẽr), *n.* **1.** A compiler or publisher of books. **2.** Also **book'ie** (bo͝ok'ĭ). A professional receiver of bets.

book'mark' (-märk'), *n.* A marker for finding a page in a book.

book'mo·bile (bo͝ok'mō·bēl), *n.* [*book* + auto*mobile.*] An autotruck with shelves of books serving as an itinerant library or bookstore.

book of account. **1.** A book for keeping accounts, esp. one of original entry. **2.** *pl.* The records, vouchers, etc., required for an audit.

Book of Common Prayer. The service book of the Anglican Communion.

book′plate′ (bo͝ok′plāt′), *n.* A label placed upon or in a book, showing its ownership or its position in a library.
book review. A critical account of a book, usually of a recent book. — **book reviewer.** — **book reviewing.**
book value. The value of anything as shown by the books of account of the business owning it; specif., of stock, the value as indicated by the excess of assets over liabilities.
book′worm′ (bo͝ok′wûrm′), *n.* **1.** Any of various insect larvae which feed on the binding and paste of books. **2.** One unusually devoted to reading or studying books.
boom (bo͞om), *v. i.* [Imitative.] **1.** To make a hollow sound, as waves or cannon; to cry with a hollow note, as a bittern; hum. **2.** To have a rapid growth in market value or in popular favor; to develop rapidly in resources and population. — *v. t.* **1.** To give forth with a resonant or booming sound; — usually with *out.* **2.** To cause a rapid growth or increase of, as in favor, value, or resources. — *n.* **1.** A hollow roar; also, a hollow cry. **2.** A strong, rapid, and expanding growth in market value, development, favor, etc.; as, a *boom* in real estate. — *adj.* Participating in or maintained by a boom; as, *boom* prices.
boom, *n.* [D., tree, pole, beam, bar.] **1.** *Naut.* A long pole or spar used esp. to extend the bottom of a sail. **2.** *Logging.* **a** A line of connected floating timbers, as across a river or enclosing a water area to keep logs ready for the sawmill from floating away; also, the enclosed area. **b** An obstruction, as of floating logs, retarding the flow of a stream. **3.** *Mach.* A long spar or beam projecting from the mast of a derrick, to support or guide the body to be lifted. See DERRICK, *Illust.*
boom′er·ang (bo͞om′ẽr·ăng), *n.* [From native name in Australia.] **1** A curved or angular club used, mainly by the natives of Australia, as a missile weapon. It can be thrown so that its flight will bring it back near the place whence it was thrown. **2.** Hence, something that reacts to the damage of its user. — *v. i.* To make an unintended reversal in direction so as to visit its damaging effect on the originator.

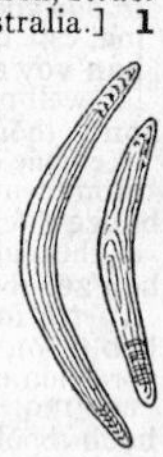
Boomerangs.

boon (bo͞on), *n.* [ON. *bōn* petition.] **1.** *Obs.* A prayer; request. **2.** *Archaic.* Something asked or granted as a favor; a favor; gift. **3.** A benefit enjoyed; a blessing.
boon, *adj.* [F. *bon,* fr. L. *bonus.*] **1.** Kind; bounteous; benign. **2.** Jovial; convivial; congenial; as, a *boon* companion.
boon′dog′gle (bo͞on′dŏg′'l), *n.* [Coined 1925 by Robert H. Link, Scoutmaster, Rochester, N. Y.] **a** A looped cord or lanyard of plaited varicolored leather strips made by boy scouts to be worn as a neckerchief slide or as a hatband. **b** Any handicraft article, esp. of leather or wicker, fashioned for utility. **c** Any unnecessary and wasteful project. — *v. i.* To engage in making boondoggles; derogatorily, to engage in useless or frivolous occupations. — **boon′dog′gler** (-dŏg′lẽr), *n. U. S.*
boor (bo͝or), *n.* [D. *boer* farmer, boor.] **1.** A peasant; rustic; esp., a clownish countryman. **2.** A Dutch, German, or Russian peasant; [*cap.*] a Boer. **3.** A rude, ill-bred, or clownish person.
boor′ish (-ĭsh), *adj.* Like a boor; clownish; uncultured; unmannerly. — **boor′ish·ly,** *adv.* — **boor′ish·ness,** *n.*
Syn. **Boorish, churlish, loutish, clownish** mean uncouth in manners or appearance. **Boorish** implies rudeness of manner, insensitiveness to others' feelings, or unwillingness to make oneself agreeable; **churlish** implies surliness, irresponsiveness, and ungraciousness; **loutish,** applicable especially to hulky youths and men, usually suggests stupidity, clumsiness, and, sometimes, abjectness of demeanor; **clownish** suggests, generally, ignorance or simplicity, ungainliness of movement, and, often, a propensity for absurd antics. — **Ant.** Gentlemanly.
boost (bo͞ost), *v. t.* **1.** *Colloq.* To lift or push from below; hence, to help forward; advance; as, to *boost* a candidate. **2.** *Slang.* To commend highly; — opp. to *knock.* **3.** To increase as in force, pressure, amount. **4.** *Elec.* To raise the voltage of or across (a system or circuit). — **Syn.** See LIFT. — *v. i. Slang.* To be vigorous in commendation. — *n. Colloq.* A push that aids one in rising or advancing.
boost′er (bo͞os′tẽr), *n.* One who or that which boosts. Specif.: **a** *Elec.* An instrument or machine for regulating or modifying the electromotive force in an electric circuit, as a dynamo inserted in a distribution system. **b** *Med.* Any substance that increases the effectiveness of a medicament; esp., a supplementary dose of an immunizing agent to increase existing immunity; — called also *booster dose.*
boot (bo͞ot), *n.* [AS. *bōt.*] **1.** *Archaic.* Remedy; relief. **2.** *Now Dial.* Something given to equalize an exchange. **3.** *Obs.* Profit; advantage; avail; use. — ***to boot.*** In addition; over and above; besides. — *v. t. Obs.* To remedy; enrich; benefit. — *v. i.* To be of avail.
boot, *n.* [OF. *bote* (F. *botte*).] **1.** An article of apparel, usually of leather, for the foot and more or less of the leg. See SHOE, *n.,* 1. **2.** A bootlike instrument of torture for the leg. **3.** A protective sheath or casing; specif.: **a** A partial covering for the hoof and leg of a horse, to prevent injury from interference. **b** In a reed pipe of an organ, the compartment containing the reed. **4.** An apron or cover (of leather or rubber cloth) for the driving seat of a vehicle, to protect it from rain and mud. **5.** A storage compartment, as at the rear of the body of an automobile. **6.** A kick; *Slang,* a discharge or dismissal. **7.** A pneumatic rubber tubular cell. **8.** A recruit sworn into the U. S. Navy or Marine Corps, and in initial training. Hence, **boot camp.** — *v. t.* **1.** To put boots on. **2.** To torture with the boot. **3.** To kick with a booted foot; hence, *Slang,* to eject; discharge. **4.** *Baseball.* To fumble; as, to *boot* the ball.
boot, *n.* [Cf. BOOT profit.] *Archaic.* Booty; spoil.
boot′black′ (-blăk′), *n.* One who shines boots or shoes.
boot′ed (bo͞ot′ĕd; -ĭd), *adj.* **1.** Wearing boots, esp. for riding. **2.** *Zool.* Having a horny, bootlike covering; — of the tarsus of some birds.
boot′ee′ (bo͞o′tē′), *n.* A kind of boot with a short leg; specif., an infant's boot of knitted wool.
Bo·ö′tes (bō·ō′tēz), *n.; gen.* BOÖTIS (-tĭs). [L., fr. Gr. *boōtēs* herdsman, fr. *bous,* gen. *boos,* ox.] *Astron.* A northern constellation containing the bright star Arcturus.
booth (bo͞oth *or, esp. Brit.,* bo͞oth), *n.; pl.* BOOTHS (bo͞othz; bo͞oths). [Prob. fr. ODan. *bōth.*] **1.** A frail, temporary house or shed. **2.** A covered compartment or temporary structure at a fair, polling place, etc.
boot′jack′ (bo͞ot′jăk′), *n.* A V-shaped device for use in pulling off boots.
boot′lace′ (-lās′), *n. Chiefly Brit.* A lace for a boot.
boot′leg′ (-lĕg′), *n.* **1.** The upper part of a boot. **2.** *Slang, U. S.* Bootlegged liquor. — *v. t.;* see LEG. *Slang.* **1.** To carry (liquor) illegally on the person; hence, to sell, make, or transport (liquor) illegally. **2.** To produce, sell, or distribute, illicitly or without approval; as, to *bootleg* books; hence, to smuggle, as aliens. — *v. i. Slang.* To bootleg liquor; also, to bootleg milk, aliens, etc. — *adj. Slang.* **1.** Bootlegged; hence, illicit; surreptitious. **2.** Of or dealing with bootlegging. — **boot′leg′ger** (-lĕg′ẽr), *n.*
boot′less (bo͞ot′lĕs; -lĭs), *adj.* [From BOOT profit.] Unavailing; useless. — **boot′less·ly,** *adv.* — **boot′less·ness,** *n.*
boot′lick′ (bo͞ot′lĭk′), *v. t. & i. Slang, U. S.* To flatter; toady. — **boot′lick′er** (-ẽr), *n.*
boots (bo͞ots), *n.; pl. in form, but construed as a sing.* A servant, as at a hotel, who shines boots and shoes.
boot tree. A device inserted in a boot or shoe to preserve its original form; a shoe tree.
boo′ty (bo͞o′tĭ), *n.* [F. *butin.*] **1.** Plunder, esp. spoil taken in war. **2.** Any rich gain, however taken. — **Syn.** See SPOIL.
booze (bo͞oz), *v. i.* [Var. of BOUSE.] *Colloq.* To drink intoxicating liquor to excess. — *n. Colloq.* A spree; also, liquor. — **booz′er** (bo͞oz′ẽr), *n.* — **booz′y** (-ĭ), *adj.*
bop (bŏp), *n.* = BEBOP. — **bop′pist** (bŏp′ĭst), *n.*
bo′ra (bō′rȧ), *n.* [It., dial. var. of *borea* north wind, fr. L. *boreas.*] A violent, cold, northerly wind of the Adriatic.
bo·rac′ic (bō·răs′ĭk), *adj.* Boric; as, *boracic* acid.
bor′age (bûr′ĭj; bŏr′ĭj), *n.* [From OF., fr. ML. *borrago.*] A rough-hairy blue-flowered European herb (*Borago officinalis*), used medicinally and as a salad. The genus *Borago* typifies a family (Boraginaceae, the borage family) including the heliotrope and forget-me-not. — **bo·rag′i·na′ceous** (bō·răj′ĭ·nā′shŭs), *adj.*
bo′rate (bō′rāt), *n. Chem.* A salt or ester of boric acid. — (-rāt), *v. t.* To mix or impregnate with borax or boric acid; as, *borated* talc.
bo′rax (-răks), *n.* [F., fr. Ar. *bawraq, būraq,* fr. Per. *būrah.*] A crystalline, slightly alkaline borate of sodium, $Na_2B_4O_7$, used as a flux, cleansing agent, antiseptic, etc.
Bor′deaux′ (bôr′dō′; *when used attrib. often* bôr′dō′, *as in B. mixture*), *n.* Wine from the Bordeaux region, France, including white varieties, as the sauternes, and red varieties, usually called *claret.*
Bordeaux mixture. Also **Bor′deaux′,** *n.* A fungicide composed of blue vitriol (copper sulfate), lime, and water.
bor′del (bôr′dĕl), *n.* [F., fr. OF. *borde* hut, cabin, of Teut. origin.] A brothel.
bor·del′lo (bôr·dĕl′ō), *n.* [It.] A brothel.
bor′der (bôr′dẽr), *n.* [OF. *bordure,* fr. *border* to border, fr. *bord* a border, of Teut. origin.] **1.** The outer part or edge; margin. **2.** A boundary or frontier; specif. [*cap.*], that between England and Scotland. **3.** An ornamental or finishing strip or stripe along or near the edge, as of a garment, around printed matter, etc. **4.** A narrow strip of grass, flowers, shrubs, etc., as along a walk.
Syn. **Border, margin, verge, edge, rim, brim, brink** mean a line or narrow space which marks the outermost bound of a thing. **Border** is that part of a surface which marks its boundary line; **margin** usually denotes a border of definite width or distinguished in some other way; **verge** applies chiefly to the line which sharply marks the limit or termination of a thing; **edge** is the sharply defined terminating line made by the converging of two surfaces, as of a blade or a box; **rim** applies to the verge or edge of something circular or curving; **brim,** to the inner and upper rim of a hollow vessel or the like; **brink,** to the edge of something that falls steeply.
— *v. t.* **1.** To make or furnish with a border. **2.** To touch at the edge or boundary; bound; fringe; as, a forest *borders* the lake. — *v. i.* To touch at the edge or boundary; adjoin; as, Iowa *borders* on Missouri; hence, to touch; verge; as, to *border* upon insanity. — **bor′der·er,** *n.*
‖**bor′de·reau′** (bôr′dĕ·rō′), *n.; pl.* -REAUX (-rō′). [F.] A detailed note or memorandum of account, esp. one containing an enumeration of documents.
bor′der·land′ (bôr′dẽr·lănd′), *n.* Land adjacent to a border; also, that which borders or fringes, or forms a border between two things; as, the *borderland* of science.
border line. A boundary line or line of demarcation.
bor′der·line′ (bôr′dẽr·līn′), *adj.* Situated or being on a border line; specif., *Psychol.,* on the line of demarcation between normal and abnormal.
bor′dure (bôr′dųr), *n.* [F. See BORDER.] *Her.* A border surrounding the shield.
bore (bōr; 70), *v. t.* [AS. *borian.*] **1.** To make a hole in, esp. with a rotary tool, as an auger or gimlet; as, to *bore* a plank. **2.** To form or construct by boring; as, to *bore* a hole, well, or tunnel. **3.** To make (a passage) by laborious effort; as, to *bore* one's way through a crowd. **4.** To weary by tedious iteration or dullness, or by forcing one's presence upon; as, the book *bored* me. — *v. i.* To bore a hole; as, insects that *bore* into trees. — *n.* **1.** A hole made by boring, or an opening like or likened to one so made. **2.** An internal cylindrical cavity, as of a pipe, tube, or gun; specif., in modern breech-loading ordnance, that part of the interior tube in front of the breechblock. **3.** The size of a hole; specif., the interior diameter of a tube or gun barrel. In shotguns, *bore* = *gauge* (def. 5); in other firearms *bore* = *caliber* (def. 1 **b**). **4.** A person or thing that wearies by prolixity or dullness.
bore, *n.* [ON. *bāra* wave.] *Phys. Geog.* **a** A tidal flood with high abrupt front, due to a rapidly narrowing inlet or channel, as at the mouth of the Amazon. **b** Loosely, a very high and rapid tidal flow, as in the Bay of Fundy.
bore (bōr; 70), *past tense & obs. past part.* of BEAR.
bo′re·al (bō′rē·ăl), *adj.* [L. *borealis.*] Of or pertaining to Boreas; hence, northern.
Bo′re·as (bō′rē·ăs), *n.* **1.** *Gr. Myth.* The god of the north wind. **2.** The north wind personified.
bore′dom (bōr′dŭm; 70), *n.* State or fact of being bored.
bor′er (bōr′ẽr), *n.* One who or that which bores, as a tool, the shipworm, any of certain insects or larvae (as the corn *borer,* which see), etc.
bo′ric (bō′rĭk; 70), *adj. Chem.* Of or containing boron.
boric acid. Any acid derived from boron trioxide, B_2O_3; specif., a white crystalline compound, $B(OH)_3$, obtained from its salts.
bor′ing (bōr′ĭng; 70), *n.* **1.** Act or process of one who or that which bores. **2.** A hole made by boring; a bore. **3.** A chip or cutting made by boring; — usually in *pl.*
born (bôrn), *past part.* of BEAR. — *adj.* **1.** Brought into existence by or as by birth. Abbr. (with dates) *b.* **2.** Having from birth a certain character; inborn; as, a *born* liar.
borne (bōrn; 70), *past part. & part. adj.* of BEAR.

bor′ne·ol (bôr′nē·ōl; -ŏl), *n.* [*Borneo* + *-ol.*] *Chem.* A kind of camphor, $C_{10}H_{17}OH$, existing in three optically different varieties, which closely resembles true camphor.

born′ite (bôr′nīt), *n.* [After I. von *Born*, Austrian mineralogist.] *Mineral.* A brittle, metallic-looking sulfide of copper and iron, Cu_5FeS_4. It is a valuable ore of copper.

bo′ron (bō′rŏn; 70), *n.* [See BORAX.] *Chem.* A nonmetallic element occurring only in combination, as in borax and boric acid. Symbol, *B*; at. no., 5; at. wt., 10.82.

boron carbide. *Chem.* A black crystalline compound, B_6C, the hardest substance known except the diamond, made in the electric furnace.

bo′ro·sil′i·cate (bō′rō·sĭl′ĭ·kāt), *n.* *Chem.* A salt of any of several hypothetical acids (**bo′ro·si·lic′ic ac′ids** [-sĭ·lĭs′ĭk]), occurring naturally as tourmaline, etc.

bor′ough (bûr′ō), *n.* [AS. *burh, burg*, fortified place or town.] **1.** *A.-S. & Early Eng. Hist.* A fortified group of houses forming a town with special duties and privileges. **2.** *Eng. Law.* **a** A town, or urban constituency, that sends a member or members to Parliament. **b** A town incorporated for purposes of self-government. **3. a** *Local, U. S.* A form of municipal corporation in general like an incorporated town or village. **b** One of the five political divisions of Greater New York.

bor′ough-Eng′lish, *n.* *Eng. Law.* A custom or right by which lands and tenements descend to the youngest son, or sometimes to the youngest daughter or collateral heir. Cf. PRIMOGENITURE.

bor′row (bŏr′ō), *v. t.* [AS. *borgian*, fr. *borg, borh*, pledge.] **1.** To receive with the implied or expressed intention of returning the same or giving an equivalent; — opposite of *lend.* **2.** *Arith.* In subtraction, to take (one) from the next higher denomination in order to add it to the next lower. **3.** To appropriate for one's own use; as, to *borrow* an idea. **4.** To steal; — a euphemism. — *v. i.* To borrow something. — *n.* **1.** *Hist.* A pledge; surety. **2.** A borrowing; also, something borrowed. — **bor′row·er** (-ō·ẽr), *n.*

Bors (bôrs; bôrz), **Sir.** An Arthurian knight. See GRAIL.

borsch (bôrsh; *Russ. also* bôrshch), **borsht** (bôrsht), **bortsch** (bôrch), *n.* [Little Russian *borshch.*] A Russian soup of several ingredients colored with red beet juice.

bort (bôrt), *n.* Also **bortz** (bôrts). Material consisting of imperfectly crystallized or coarse diamonds, or fragments made in cutting good diamonds. — **bort′y** (bôr′tĭ), *adj.*

bor′zoi (bôr′zoi; bôr·zoi′; *Russ.* bŭr·zoi′), *n.* [Russ. *borzoy*, fr. *borzoy* swift.] The Russian wolfhound (see WOLFHOUND).

bos′cage (bŏs′kĭj), *n.* [OF., grove, fr. ML. *boscus* thicket.] A growth of trees or shrubs; a thicket.

bosch′bok′ (bŏsh′bŏk′; *D.* bŏs′-), *n.* [D., fr. *bosch* wood + *bok* buck.] See HARNESSED ANTELOPE.

bosh (bŏsh), *n.* [Turk.] *Colloq.* Empty talk; trash.

bosk (bŏsk), *n.* [See BOSKET.] A thicket; small wood.

bos′kage (bŏs′kĭj). Var. of BOSCAGE.

bos′ket, bos′quet (-kĕt; -kĭt), *n.* [F. *bosquet.*] A thicket.

bosk′y (bŏs′kĭ), *adj.* **1.** Woody or bushy. **2.** Caused by boscage; as, *bosky* shadows. — **bosk′i·ness** (-kĭ·nĕs; -nĭs), *n.*

bos′om (bo͝oz′ŭm; bo͞o′zŭm), *n.* [AS. *bōsm.*] **1.** The breast of a human being. **2.** The breast, considered as the seat of the passions, affections, and thoughts. **3.** Embrace; loving enclosure. **4.** Anything suggestive of the breast; as, the *bosom* of the earth. **5.** The part of a dress, shirt, etc., worn upon the breast; as, a shirt *bosom.* — *v. t.* **1.** To enclose or carry in the bosom; cherish. **2.** To conceal; embosom. — *adj.* **1.** Of or pertaining to the bosom. **2.** Intimate; beloved; as, a *bosom* friend.

boss (bŏs; 74), *n.* [OF. *boce* (F. *bosse*).] **1.** Any protuberant part; a round, swelling part or body, as a knoll of rock or a pad for smoothing; as, a *boss* of wood. **2.** A knoblike ornamental process; stud; as, the *boss* of a shield. **3.** *Arch.* A projecting part, as an ornamental block at the intersection of ribs in Gothic vaulting. See GOTHIC, *Illust.* **4.** *Mech.* The enlarged part of a shaft. — *v. t.* **1.** To emboss. **2.** To ornament with bosses; to stud.

boss, *n.* [D. *baas* master.] **1.** *Colloq.* A master or superior, as a foreman or manager. **2.** *Slang, U. S.* A professional politician who controls votes or dictates measures. — *v. t.* *Colloq.* To direct or superintend, esp. officiously. — *v. i.* *Colloq.* To be master. — **boss,** *adj.*

boss (bŏs), *adj.* *Scot., N. of Eng., & Ir.* Hollow; empty.

boss (bŏs; bŏs), **bos′sy** (bŏs′ĭ; bŏs′ĭ), *n.* *U. S.* A cow or calf.

boss′y (bŏs′ĭ), *adj.* Ornamented with bosses; studded.

boss′y, *adj.* *Colloq.* Inclined to play the boss.

bos′ton (bŏs′tŭn; 74), *n.* [From *Boston*, Mass.] **1.** [Through F.] A game at cards. **2.** A form of waltz.

Boston bag. A handbag for books, papers, etc., held closed by a handle on each side of the top opening.

Boston fern. A fern (*Nephrolepis exaltata bostoniensis*) with drooping, usually much-divided leaves, derived from the tropical *sword fern* (*N. exaltata*) with long sword-shaped pinnate fronds.

Boston terrier *or* **Boston bull.** A dog of a small, smooth-coated breed, originating as a cross between a bulldog and bull terrier. It is brindle with white markings.

bo′sun (bō′s′n). Var. of BOATSWAIN.

bot, bott (bŏt), *n.* The larva of the botfly, esp. the species infesting the horse.

bo·tan′i·cal (bō·tăn′ĭ·kăl), *adj.* Also **bo·tan′ic** (-ĭk). Of or pertaining to plants; relating to botany. — **bo·tan′i·cal·ly,** *adv.*

bot′a·nist (bŏt′ȧ·nĭst), *n.* A specialist in botany or in any branch of it; a student of plants.

bot′a·nize (-nīz), *v. i.* To collect plants for investigation; to study plants, esp. in the field. — *v. t.* To explore for botanical purposes. — **bot′a·niz′er** (-nīz′ẽr), *n.*

bot′a·ny (-nĭ), *n.*; *pl.* (in sense 3) BOTANIES (-nĭz). [F. *botanique*, adj. & n., fr. Gr. *botanikos* botanical, fr. *botanē* plant, fr. *boskein* to feed.] **1.** The science of plants; biology dealing with plant life. Cf. CLASSIFICATION, 2. **2.** Plant life, as of a region; as, the *botany* of Labrador; the properties and life phenomena exhibited by a plant, plant type, or group; as, the *botany* of an orchid. **3.** A book which treats of the science of botany.

botch (bŏch), *n.* [ONF. *boche*, OF. *boce.*] *Obs. exc. Dial.* A tumor.

botch, *v. t.* [ME. *bocchen.*] **1.** To repair; mend; esp., to patch clumsily. **2.** To make, express, or perform in a bungling manner; to mar. — *n.* **1.** Bungling or clumsy work; a bungle. **2.** A patch clumsily put on. — **botch′er,** *n.* — **botch′er·y,** *n.*

botch′y (bŏch′ĭ), *adj.* Full of botches; botched; poorly done.

bote (bōt), *n.* [Old form of *boot*; — used in composition; see BOOT remedy.] *Obs. exc. Hist.* Boot (remedy).

bot′fly′ (bŏt′flī′), *n.* [From BOT.] Any of many dipterous insects (family Oestridae) whose larvae are parasitic on horses, sheep, etc. See BOT.

both (bōth), *adj. & pron.* [ME. *bothe, bathe*, fr. ON. *bāthir.*] The one and the other; the two; as, *both* horses ran away; *both* gave us trouble. — *conj.* As well; not only; equally; as, *both* America and England.

both′er (bŏth′ẽr), *v. t.* [Origin unknown.] **1.** To bewilder, as with noise; confuse. **2.** To annoy; worry; perplex. — **Syn.** See ANNOY. — *v. i.* To feel care or anxiety; to make or take trouble. — *n.* **1.** A state of perplexity or annoyance. **2.** Trouble; worry; inconvenience. **3.** Fuss; disturbance.

both′er·a′tion (-ā′shŭn), *n.* *Colloq.* Act of bothering or state of being bothered; also, a thing that bothers.

both′er·some (bŏth′ẽr·sŭm), *adj.* Causing bother.

both′y (bŏth′ĭ; bōth′ĭ), *n.*; *pl.* -IES (-ĭz). *Scot.* A hut.

bot′o·née, bot′o·né (bŏt′ō·nā), *adj.* *Her.* Furnished with knobs or buttons; — said of a cross. See CROSS, *Illust.* (12).

bo tree (bō). [Singhalese *bo*, fr. Skr. *bodhi*, prop., enlightenment; akin to *buddha.*] The pipal tree; specif. [*cap.*], the sacred tree at Buddh Gaya under which Gautama (see BUDDHA) is said to have received the heavenly light.

bot′ry·oid (bŏt′rĭ·oid), **bot′ry·oi′dal** (-oi′dăl), *adj.* [Gr. *botryoeidēs*, fr. *botrys* a cluster of grapes. See -OID.] Having the form of a bunch of grapes. — **bot′ry·oi′dal·ly,** *adv.*

bott (bŏt). Var. of BOT.

bot′tle (bŏt′'l), *n.* [OF. *bouteille*, fr. LL. *buticula, butticula.*] **1.** A hollow vessel of glass, earthenware, or the like, with a narrow neck or mouth, and without handles. **2.** The contents of a bottle; amount a bottle contains; hence, with *the:* **a** Intoxicating liquor. **b** Milk in a bottle; as, brought up on *the bottle.* — *v. t.*; BOT′TLED (-'ld); BOT′TLING (-lĭng). To put into bottles; enclose in or as in a bottle. — **bot′tler** (bŏt′lẽr), *n.*

bot′tle, *n.* [OF. *botel*, dim. of *botte* bundle.] *Obs. exc. Dial.* A bundle, esp. of hay.

bot′tle·neck′ (bŏt′'l·nĕk′), *n.* Figuratively, a narrow passageway; a place, stage, or condition that checks progress in a process.

bot′tle·nose′ (-nōz′), *n.* Any of several cetaceans of the dolphin family, esp. one (*Tursiops truncatus*) common in the North Atlantic; — called also **bot′tle-nosed′ dol′phin** (-nōzd′). See DOLPHIN, 1.

bot′tom (bŏt′ŭm), *n.* [AS. *botm.*] **1.** The bed of a body of water; as, the *bottom* of a stream. **2.** The part of anything under and supporting the contents or bulk; as, the *bottom* of a chair; the under surface; base; hence, *Colloq.*, the buttocks. **3.** The lowest part of anything; the foot; as, the *bottom* of a tree; hence, the remotest or innermost part, as of a lane or bay. **4.** That which is, or serves as, a groundwork or foundation; basis; as, to get to the *bottom* of the matter. **5.** Chiefly in *pl.* Low alluvial land along a river; — called also **bottom land.** **6.** *Naut.* The part of a ship ordinarily under water; hence, a ship. — *v. t.* **1.** To furnish with a bottom, as a chair. **2.** To found or build upon; to base; — with *on* or *upon.* **3.** To reach the bottom of; to understand fully. — *v. i.* **1.** To be based or grounded; — usually with *on* or *upon.* **2.** To reach or impinge against the bottom, as when a piston strikes the end of a cylinder. — *adj.* Of or pertaining to the bottom; as, *bottom* rock; fundamental; lowest; as, *bottom* prices.

bottom drawer. See HOPE CHEST.

bot′tom·less (bŏt′ŭm·lĕs; -lĭs), *adj.* Without a bottom; hence, unfathomable; as, the **bottomless pit,** or hell.

bot′tom·ry (-rĭ), *n.* [From BOTTOM ship, after D. *bodemerij.*] *Mar. Law.* A contract by which a ship is hypothecated as security for repayment (upon a successful termination of the voyage) of a loan for the use of the ship.

bot′u·lism (bŏt′ū·lĭz'm), *n.* [L. *botulus* sausage + *-ism.*] *Med. & Veter.* Poisoning by the toxin of a bacillus (*Clostridium botulinum*) which may infect preserved food, esp. sausages, canned meat, silage, etc. The toxin is destroyed in five minutes by heat at 212° F.

‖**bou′clé′** (bo͞o′klā′), *adj.* [F., buckled.] Of fabrics, woven so as to have a knotted and curled appearance.

bou′doir (bo͞o′dwär; -dwôr), *n.* [F., fr. *bouder* to pout, be sulky.] A small private room, esp. one belonging to a lady.

‖**bouffe** (bo͞of), *adj.* *Music.* Comic. See OPÉRA BOUFFE.

bou′gain·vil′lae·a, bou′gain·vil′le·a (bo͞o′gĭn·vĭl′ē·ȧ), *n.* [NL., after L. A. de *Bougainville*, French navigator.] A plant of a genus (*Bougainvillaea*) of ornamental tropical American woody vines, with brilliant purple, red, etc., floral bracts.

bough (bou), *n.* [AS. *bōg, bōh*, bough.] **1.** A branch of a tree, esp. a main branch. **2.** *Archaic.* A gallows. — **Syn.** See SHOOT.

bough′pot′ (bou′pŏt′; *dial.* bo͞o′pŏt′), *n.* Also **bow′pot′.** A vase for cut flowers or boughs; also, a bouquet.

bought (bôt), *past & past part.* of BUY.

bought′en (bôt′'n), *adj.* [See 2d -EN.] *Now Dial.* Purchased; not homemade; as, a *boughten* shirt.

bou′gie′ (bo͞o′zhē′; bo͞o′zhē), *n.* [F., fr. *Bougie*, town of Algeria.] **1.** A wax candle. **2.** *Med.* **a** A tapering instrument for introduction into the esophagus, urethra, etc. **b** A suppository.

bouil′la·baisse′ (bo͞o(l)′yȧ·bās′; *F.* bo͞o′yȧ′bâs′), *n.* [F.] A highly seasoned fish chowder, of two kinds of fish.

bouil′lon′ (bo͞o′yôɴ′; bo͝ol′yŭn; bo͝ol·yŏn′), *n.* [F., fr. *bouillir* to boil.] A clear soup, typically made from beef. — **Syn.** See SOUP.

bouk (bo͝ok), *n.* [AS. *būc* belly.] *Scot.* Trunk of the body.

boul′der, bowl′der (bōl′dẽr), *n.* Any detached and rounded or worn mass of rock, larger than a cobblestone.

boule (bo͞ol), *n.* [F., ball.] A pear-shaped mass of some substance (as sapphire, spinel, or rutile) that is formed synthetically in a special furnace.

bou′le (bo͞o′lē), *n.* [Gr. *boulē.*] **1.** *Gr. Antiq.* A legislative council of elders or chiefs; a senate. **2.** [*cap.*] The lower house of the parliament in modern Greece.

boule, boule′work′ (bo͞ol′wûrk′). Vars. of BUHL, BUHLWORK.

bou′le·vard (bo͞o′lĕ·värd; bo͞ol′ĕ-; *or, esp. Brit.,* bo͞ol′vär; -värd), *n.* [F., fr. MLG. *bolwerk.*] **1.** Originally, the flat top of a rampart. **2.** A broad avenue in or around a city, esp. one laid out with trees, turf, etc.; hence, a broad thoroughfare. Abbr. *Blvd.*

‖**bou′le·ver′se·ment′** (bo͞ol′vĕr′sĕ·mäɴ′; *E.* bo͞ol·vûrs′mĕnt), *n.* [F.] Complete overthrow; convulsion; disorder.

boul'ter (bōl'tẽr), *n.* A long fishing line with many hooks.
boun (boun; bōōn), *v. t. & i.* *Archaic.* To prepare; betake (oneself).
bounce (bouns), *v. t.;* BOUNCED (bounst); BOUNC'ING (boun'sĭng). [ME. *bunsen.*] **1.** To bump, thump, or bang. **2.** To cause to bound or rebound; sometimes, to toss. **3.** *Slang, Orig. U. S.* To eject violently, as from a room; to discharge unceremoniously, as from employment. — *v. i.* **1.** To strike or thump, so as to rebound, or to make a sudden noise; *Now Dial.*, to knock loudly. **2.** To leap or spring suddenly; bound. — *n.* **1.** A heavy, sudden, often noisy, blow or thump. **2.** A sudden leap or bound; a rebound. **3.** Bluster; brag; swagger; boast. **4.** *Colloq.* Resilient spirit; verve; resilience. **5.** *Slang, U. S.* A peremptory discharge or expulsion. — *adv.* Suddenly.
bounc'er (boun'sẽr), *n.* **1.** One that bounces. **2.** *Colloq.* A boaster; bully; liar; also, a big lie. **3.** Something big; as, the fish was a *bouncer.* **4.** *Slang, U. S.* A man employed at a theater, hotel, etc., to eject disorderly persons.
bounc'ing (-sĭng), *adj.* Stout; buxom; also, big.
bouncing Bet *or* **Bess.** The soapwort.
bounc'ing-pin' in'di·ca'tor. An indicator for detecting and measuring, by means of a bouncing pin, the presence and intensity of detonation in internal-combustion engines.

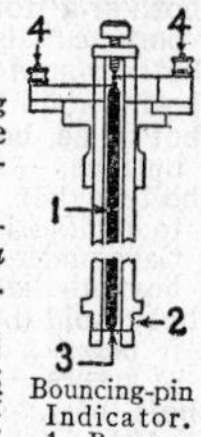

Bouncing-pin Indicator. 1 Bouncing Pin; 2 Threads; 3 Diaphragm; 4, 4 Terminals.

bound (bound), *adj.* [Past part. of ME. *bounen* to prepare, fr. *boun* prepared, fr. ON. *būinn*, past part. of *būa* to dwell, prepare.] **1.** *Archaic.* Prepared; ready. **2.** Intending to go; going; as, a ship *bound* for China.
bound, *n.* [OF. *bonne, bonde, bodne*, fr. ML. *butina.*] **1.** The limiting line; hence, that which limits; a confine; boundary; limit; as, ambition without *bound;* out of *bounds.* **2.** Borderland; also, the tract within bounds; domain. — *v. t.* **1.** To set limits to; confine. **2.** To form a boundary of; enclose; circumscribe. **3.** To name the boundaries of.
bound, *v. i.* [F. *bondir* to leap, rebound, resound.] **1.** To move with a sudden spring or leap, or with a succession of springs or leaps. **2.** To rebound, as a ball. — *v. t.* To cause to rebound; to bounce. — **Syn.** Skip, lope, ricochet. — *n.* **1.** A leap; spring; jump. **2.** A rebound; a bounce, as of a ball.
bound, *past & past part.* of BIND. — *adj.* **1.** Restrained or fastened by a band, bond, or the like; tied; confined. **2.** Destined; certain; — followed by the infinitive; as, a plan *bound* to succeed. **3.** Under legal or moral restraint or obligation. **4.** Constipated; costive. **5.** Enclosed in a binding or cover, as a book. **6.** *Colloq., U. S.* Resolved; as, I am *bound* to do it. — ***bound up in.*** Entirely devoted to; inseparable from.
bound'a·ry (boun'dȧ·rĭ), *n.; pl.* -RIES (-rĭz). [From BOUND a limit.] That which indicates or fixes a limit or extent; that which marks a bound, as of a territory.
boundary layer. *Mechanics.* The region of retarded fluid flow near the surface of a body moving through the fluid or past which the fluid moves.
bound'en (boun'dĕn), *adj.* [Old past part. of BIND.] **1.** Under obligation, as for a favor; obliged; beholden. **2.** Obligatory; binding.
bound'er (-dẽr), *n.* **1.** One who determines bounds. **2.** *Colloq.* A vulgar person of obtrusive manners.
bound form. *Ling.* A linguistic form which cannot be used alone with meaning. Thus, all affixes and such roots as -ceive in "receive" and -mit in "permit" are *bound forms.* Cf. FREE FORM, MORPHEME.
bound'less, *adj.* Without bounds; vast. — **-ly,** *adv.* — **-ness,** *n.*
boun'te·ous (boun'tē·ŭs), *adj.* [OF. *bontif*, fr. *bonté.* See BOUNTY.] **1.** Characterized by bounty; liberal; munificent; as, a *bounteous* giver. **2.** Liberally bestowed; plentiful; ample; as, a *bounteous* harvest. — **boun'te·ous·ly,** *adv.* — **boun'te·ous·ness,** *n.*
boun'ti·ful (boun'tĭ·fŏŏl; -f'l), *adj.* **1.** Full of bounty; free in giving; liberal. **2.** Plentiful; abundant. — **Syn.** See LIBERAL. — **boun'ti·ful·ly,** *adv.* — **boun'ti·ful·ness,** *n.*
boun'ty (-tĭ), *n.; pl.* -TIES (-tĭz). [OF. *bonté* goodness, fr. L. *bonitas*, fr. *bonus* good.] **1.** Liberality in giving; generosity. **2.** That which is given liberally; also, yield. **3.** A reward, esp. one given by a government; specif.: **a** A gift to induce men to enter the army or navy. **b** A subsidy to encourage. **c** A recompense for destroying noxious animals.
bou·quet' (bōō·kā'; bō·kā'), *n.* [F., fr. OF. *boschet*, dim. of *bois*, ML. *boscus.*] **1.** A bunch of flowers; a nosegay. **2.** The distinctive aroma of a wine; hence, any aroma. — **Syn.** See FRAGRANCE.
Bour'bon (bōōr'bŭn), *n.* **1.** A member of the French family of Bourbon, derived from Baron Aimar of the 9th century, whose descendants founded dynasties in France (Henry IV), Spain (Philip V), and Naples (Charles III). **2.** A ruler, politician, etc., who clings obstinately to ideas adapted to a past order. — **Bour'bon·ism** (-ĭz'm), *n.*
bourbon whisky. Originally, whisky produced from corn in Bourbon (*pron.* bûr'bŭn) County, Kentucky; a similar whisky from corn, or with rye or malt added.
bour'don (bōōr'd'n; bōr'-; 70), *n.* [F. See BURDEN a refrain.] *Music.* **a** A drone bass, as in a bagpipe. **b** An organ stop, usually of 16-foot pitch. See STOP, *n.*
bourg (bōōr; bōōrg), *n.* [F.] A town or village; specif.: **a** One neighboring a castle. **b** One on the Continent, as distinguished from an English town. **c** A market town.
bour·geois' (bōōr·zhwä'; bōōr'zhwä), *n. masc., sing. & pl.* [F., fr. *bourg* town.] **1.** In France, a person of middle rank in society, as of the shopkeeping class; hence, any person of middle class. **2.** Among radical socialists, a person with private property interests. — *adj.* Belonging to or characteristic of the bourgeoisie; hence: **a** Engrossed in material interests. **b** Conservative; hidebound. **c** Capitalistic.
bour·geois' (bûr·jois'), *n.* A size of type. See TYPE.
bour·geoise' (bōōr·zhwäz'; *F.* bōōr'zhwȧz'), *n. & adj.; pl.* BOURGEOISES (*F.* bōōr'zhwȧz'). Fem. of BOURGEOIS.
‖**bour'geoi'sie'** (bōōr'zhwȧ'zē'), *n.* [F.] Bourgeois people; the middle class.
bour'geon (bûr'jŭn). Var. of BURGEON.
bourn, (bōrn; bōrn), *n.* [AS. *burna.*] A stream.
bourn, bourne (bōrn; bōōrn; 70), *n.* [F. *borne.*] **1.** *Archaic.* A bound; boundary; limit. **2.** A goal; destination. **3.** Domain; realm; — an erroneous use.
bourse (bōōrs), *n.* [F., purse, exchange, fr. LL. *bursa.*] An exchange; esp. [*cap.*], the stock exchange of Paris, or of various other European cities.
bour'tree (bōōr'trē), *n.* *Dial.* A European elder (*Sambucus nigra*).
bouse (bous; bouz), *v. t. & i.* *Naut.* To pull or haul with a tackle.
bouse (bōōz; bouz), *n.* [ME. *bous*, fr. MD. *buse* a cup, beaker.] Drink, esp. alcoholic drink; also, a carouse. See BOOZE. — *v. i. & t.* [ME. *bousen*, fr. MD. *būsen, bousen.*] To drink; carouse. — **bous'y** (bōōz'ĭ; bouz'ĭ), *adj.*
bout (bout), *n.* **1.** A going and returning, as in mowing; a turn. **2.** A conflict; contest; trial; round; set-to.
bou'ton·niere' (bōō'tŏ·nyâr'), *n.* [F. *boutonnière* buttonhole.] A flower or bouquet worn in a buttonhole.
‖**bouts'-ri'més'** (bōō'rē'mā'; *E.* -māz'), *n. pl.* [F.] Literally, rhymed ends; rhyming words or syllables to which verses are to be written; also, verses written to such rhymed ends.
bo'vine (bō'vīn; -vĭn), *adj.* [LL. *bovinus*, fr. *bos, bovis*, ox, cow.] Of or pertaining to, or like, the ox or cow; oxlike; hence, sluggish and patient; dull; as, a *bovine* temperament. — *n.* A bovine animal.
bow (bou), *v. i.* [AS. *būgan.*] **1.** *Now Dial.* To bend; curve. **2.** To submit or yield; as, to *bow* to authority. **3.** To bend the head, knee, or body, in reverence, submission, civility, or assent. — *v. t.* **1.** To cause to incline; bend. **2.** To bend, as the head or body, in respect, gratitude, assent, submission, or condescension. **3.** To prostrate; depress; crush. **4.** To express by bowing; as, to *bow* one's thanks; to usher (*in* or *out*) with bowing. — *n.* An inclination of the head, or a bending of the body, in reverence, respect, civility, etc.
bow (bō), *n.* [AS. *boga.*] **1.** A rainbow. **2.** A weapon made of a strip of wood, or other elastic material, with a cord to connect the two ends when bent, by means of which an arrow is propelled. Cf. LONGBOW, CROSSBOW, ARBALEST. **3.** A bowman, or archer. **4.** Anything bent or curved; a bend. **5.** A bow-shaped contrivance or implement; as: **a** *Now Dial.* An oxbow. **b** A frame for the lens of spectacles or eyeglasses; also, a curved sidepiece passing over the ear to support spectacles. **c** A metal ring or loop forming a handle, as in a key or pair of scissors. **6.** A knot, esp. an ornamental slipknot, formed by doubling a ribbon or string into one or two loops. **7.** *Music.* An implement (originally curved), with a number of horsehairs stretched from end to end, used in playing on an instrument of the violin class; also, a stroke of this bow. — *adj.* Bent like a bow; bowed. — *v. t. & i.* **1.** To bend like a bow; curve; as, the wall *bows* inwards. **2.** *Music.* To play with a bow.

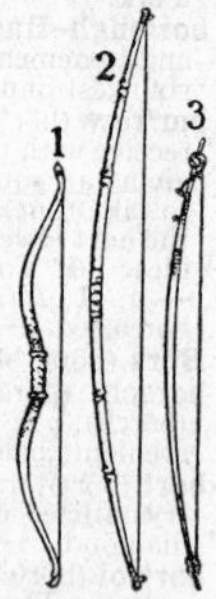

Bows, 2. 1 Classical (Cupid's); 2 African Cane; 3 Brazilian Indian.

bow (bou), *n.* [Of LG. or Scand. origin.] **1.** The forward part of a vessel; hence, the forward end of an airship. **2.** One who rows in the bow of a boat. — **bow,** *adj.*
Bow bells (bō' bĕlz'). The bells of Bow Church, or St. Mary-le-Bow (so called from the bows or arches of its steeple), nearly in the center of London.
bowd'ler·ize (boud'lẽr·īz), *v. t.* [After Thomas *Bowdler*, who published an expurgated Shakespeare in 1818.] To expurgate, as a book, by omitting or modifying parts considered indelicate. — **bowd'ler·i·za'tion** (-ĭ·zā'shŭn; -ī·zā'-), *n.* — **bowd'ler·ism** (-ĭz'm), *n.*
bow'el (bou'ĕl), *n.* [OF. *boel*, fr. L. *botellus* a small sausage, dim. of L. *botulus* sausage.] **1.** An intestine; entrail, esp. of man; gut; — usually in *pl.* **2.** *pl.* *Archaic.* The seat of pity or kindness; tenderness; compassion. **3.** *pl.* The interior of anything, as of the earth. — *v. t.;* -ELED (-ĕld) or -ELLED; -EL·ING or -EL·LING. To disembowel.
bow'er (bou'ẽr), *n.* One who or that which bows.
bow'er (bō'ẽr), *n.* A performer with a bow on the violin, etc.
bow'er (bou'ẽr), *n.* [G. *bauer* a peasant, fr. OHG. *gibūro;* from the figure sometimes used for the knave in cards.] See EUCHRE, *n.*
bow'er, *n.* [AS. *būr*, fr. the root of AS. *būan* to dwell.] **1.** A rustic cottage or retreat. **2.** A leafy shelter of boughs, vines, etc.; an arbor. — *v. t.* To embower; enclose.
bow'er, *n.* *Naut.* Either of two anchors (***best bower*** and ***small bower***) carried at the bow of a vessel. Cf. SHEET ANCHOR.
bow'er-bird' (-bûrd'), *n.* Any of certain oscine birds of the Australian region that build *bowers*, or *runs*, used as playhouses and to attract the females, not as nests.
bow'er·y (bou'ẽr·ĭ), *adj.* Like a bower; full of bowers.
bow'er·y, *n.; pl.* -ERIES (-ĭz). [D. *bouwerij*, fr. *bouwer* farmer.] **1.** A farm or plantation with its buildings (among the Dutch settlers of N. Y.). **2.** [*cap.*] A wide street in lower New York City, formerly notorious for cheap resorts, tawdry display, etc.
bow'fin' (bō'fĭn'), *n.* A voracious ganoid fish (*Amia calva*), of little value as food, of the Great Lakes, Mississippi Valley, etc.
bow'head' (bō'hĕd'), *n.* See RIGHT WHALE.
bow'ie knife (bō'ĭ; bōō'ĭ). [After its reputed inventor, Col. James *Bowie* (d. 1836).] A stout, straight, single-edged hunting knife. See KNIFE, *Illust.* (18).
bow'knot' (bō'nŏt'; 2), *n.* A type of knot with loops. See KNOT, *Illust.*
bowl (bōl), *n.* [AS. *bolla.*] **1.** A concave vessel, usually hemispherical, to hold liquids, etc. **2.** A drinking vessel for wine, liquors, etc.; hence, convivial drinking. **3.** The contents of a bowl. **4.** The bowl-shaped part of anything. **5.** A bowl-shaped amphitheater.
bowl (bōl), *n.* [F. *boule*, fr. L. *bulla* bubble.] **1.** A ball for rolling on a level surface in play, esp. one so weighted or shaped as to give it a bias. **2.** A delivery of the ball in bowling. **3.** *Mach.* A cylindrical roller or drum. — *v. i.* **1.** To play bowls. **2.** To roll a ball on a flat surface, as in the game of bowls. **3.** To move rapidly and smoothly, as in a vehicle. **4.** *Cricket.* To deliver the ball to the batsman with a smooth movement of the unflexed arm. — *v. t.* **1.** To roll or deliver, as a bowl or cricket ball. **2.** To pelt or strike with anything rolled; — often with *over, down.* **3.** To roll or carry smoothly on or as on wheels. **4.** *Cricket.* To put out (a batsman) by bowling; — often with *out.* — **bowl'er,** *n.*
bowl'der (bōl'dẽr). Var. of BOULDER.
bow'leg' (bō'lĕg'), *n.* A crooked leg, esp. one bowed outward. — **bow'leg'ged** (-lĕg'ĕd; -ĭd; -lĕgd'; 2), *adj.*
bowl'er (bōl'ẽr), *n.* [From BOWL a ball.] A derby (hat).
bow'line (bō'lĭn; -līn), *n.* **1.** *Naut.* A rope used to keep the weather edge of the sail taut forward. **2.** A bowline knot. See KNOT, *Illust.* (5, 6, 7, 8). — ***on a bowline,*** *Naut.* Close-hauled.
bowl'ing (bōl'ĭng), *n.* Bowls, now esp. tenpins.
bowling alley. An alley for bowling, now esp. at tenpins.
bowling crease. See CREASE, *n.*, 2.
bowling green. A greensward or ground for playing bowls.
bowls (bōlz), *n. pl., construed as sing.* **a** A game played with biased

balls on a plat of greensward, the aim being to roll the balls near a stationary ball (the *jack*). **b** Ninepins, skittles, or tenpins.

bow'man (bō'măn), *n.* An archer.

bow'man (bou'măn), *n.* One who rows at the bow of a boat; — called usually **bow oar.**

bown, bowne (boun). Vars. of BOUN.

bow'pot' (bou'pŏt'; *dial.* bōō'-). Var. of BOUGHPOT.

bowse. Var. of BOUSE.

bow'shot' (bō'shŏt'), *n.* The distance traversed by an arrow shot from a bow, approximately 400 yards for the English longbow formerly used in war.

bow'sprit (bou'sprĭt; bō'-), *n.* [ME. *bouspret.* See BOW of a ship; SPRIT.] *Naut.* A large spar projecting forward from the bow of a vessel.

bow'string' (bō'strĭng'), *n.* The string of a bow. — *v. t.;* -STRINGED' (-strĭngd') or -STRUNG' (-strŭng'); -STRING'ING. To strangle with a bowstring.

bowstring hemp. See SANSEVIERIA.

bow window (bō). A bay window, esp. a curved one.

bow'yer (bō'yẽr), *n.* **a** One who makes or sells bows. **b** *Chiefly Poetic.* An archer.

box (bŏks), *n.* A slap on the ear; a cuff. — *v. t.* **1.** To strike with the hand. **2.** To engage in boxing with. — *v. i.* To fight with the fists; to engage in boxing.

box, *n.* [AS., fr. L. *buxus,* fr. Gr. *pyxos.*] An evergreen shrub or small tree (genus *Buxus,* esp. *B. sempervirens,* family Buxaceae), used for hedges and borders; boxwood.

box, *n.* [AS., fr. L. *buxus* boxwood, anything made of boxwood.] **1.** A receptacle of firm material with, typically, four sides, a bottom, and a cover. **2.** The quantity that a box contains. **3.** The carrying part of a wagon. **4.** A present in a box; a gift; esp., a Christmas gift. **5.** A limited compartment, as in the theater; also, its occupants. **6.** A stall for a horse. **7.** The driver's seat on a carriage or coach. See COACH, *Illust.* **8.** A boxlike shed; as, a sentry *box.* **9.** A small country house; as, a shooting *box.* **10.** A recess cut into a tree to collect sap or resin. **11.** A predicament; as, to get in a tight *box.* **12.** *Baseball.* The space where the pitcher stands; also, that for the batter. **13.** *Mach.* A boxlike receptacle, as a journal bearing. — *v. t.* **1.** To furnish with boxes, as a wheel. **2.** To enclose in or as in a box; confine; stow. **3.** *Arch.* To enclose with boarding, lathing, etc., so as to bring to a required form. **4.** *Naut.* To boxhaul. — ***box the compass.*** *Naut.* To name the thirty-two points of the compass in their order; hence, to make a complete turn.

box'ber'ry (-bĕr'ĭ; -bẽr·ĭ), *n.* **1.** The wintergreen *Gaultheria procumbens.* **2.** *Local, U. S.* The partridgeberry *Mitchella repens.*

box calf. A kind of calfskin tanned with chrome salts; — so called from the square markings on the grain.

☞ *Box* thus applied to leather, etc., is a trade-mark.

box'car' (bŏks'kär'), *n.* *Railroads.* A roofed freight car, usually with sliding doors in the sides.

box coat. **1.** A thick overcoat for driving. **2.** A plain loose overcoat, fitted only at the shoulders.

box elder. Any maple having compound leaves, esp. a species (*Acer negundo*) of the eastern United States.

box'er (bŏk'sẽr), *n.* One who boxes.

box'er, *n.* A compact, medium-sized, fawn or brindle, short-haired dog of a breed originating in Germany.

Box'er, *n.* A member of a Chinese secret society (literally, "righteous harmony band," mistakenly interpreted as "righteous harmonious fists," hence *Boxers*), which in 1900 spread through the northern provinces of China in an uprising culminating in a siege of the legations in Peking.

box'haul' (bŏks'hôl'), *v. t.* *Naut.* To put (a square-rigged vessel) on the other tack by luffing and then veering short round on her heel. Cf. TACK, *v. t.,* 4.

box'ing, *n.* Fighting with the fists, esp. when they are covered with padded gloves.

box'ing, *n.* **1.** Act of enclosing in a box. **2.** A boxlike enclosure; casing. **3.** Material used for boxes, casings, etc.

Boxing Day. In Great Britain, the first weekday after Christmas, a legal holiday on which Christmas boxes are given to postmen, etc.

boxing glove. A heavily padded glove or mitten, usually weighing not less than five ounces, worn in boxing.

box kite. A kite consisting of two rectangular boxes, open on two sides.

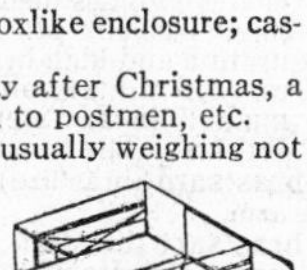

Box Kite.

box office. *Theaters.* The office where admission tickets are sold.

box spring. A bedspring consisting of spiral springs attached to a base, in a boxlike frame, and covered with a thin mattress.

box tail. *Aeronautics.* In a flying machine, a tail or rudder, usually fixed, resembling a box kite.

box'thorn' (bŏks'thôrn'), *n.* Any of a genus (*Lycium*) of plants of the nightshade family, with evergreen leaves and ornamental flowers or berries.

box'wood' (-wŏŏd'), *n.* The very close-grained, heavy, tough, hard wood of the box (*Buxus*); also, the plant itself.

boy (boi), *n.* [ME. *boi.*] **1.** A male child from birth to puberty; youth; familiarly, a man. **2.** A male servant; specif., as in the Far East, a male servant, or a man, of a native race. — **boy'hood** (-hŏŏd), *n.* — **boy'ish** (-ĭsh), *adj.* — **boy'ish·ly,** *adv.* — **boy'ish·ness,** *n.*

bo·yar' (bō·yär'; boi'ẽr), **bo·yard'** (bō·yärd'; boi'ẽrd), *n.* [Russ. *boyarin.*] **1.** A member of a Russian aristocratic order (abolished by Peter the Great) next below that of the ruling princes. **2.** One of a privileged class in Romania.

boy'cott (boi'kŏt), *v. t.* [From Capt. *Boycott,* a land agent in Mayo, Ireland, so treated in 1880.] **1.** To combine against in a policy of nonintercourse; to withhold social or business intercourse from, in disapproval or for coercion. **2.** To refrain by concerted action from using or purchasing. — *n.* Process or instance of boycotting.

boy scout. A member of an organization of boys, founded in England in 1908 by Sir R. S. S. Baden-Powell to promote good citizenship by creating in boys a spirit of civic duty and of usefulness to others, and by training them in handicrafts, woodcraft, and the like; a member of a similar organization, specif. of "The Boy Scouts of America" (incorporated Feb. 8, 1910). Cf. CUB, *n.,* 4; GIRL SCOUT.

boy'sen·ber'ry (boi's'n·bĕr'ĭ; boi'z'n-), *n.* [After Rudolph *Boysen,* the originator.] A huge blackberrylike fruit with raspberrylike flavor; also, the plant, a trailing bramble developed in California by crossing certain blackberries and raspberries.

bra (brä), *n.* Short for BRASSIÈRE.

‖**Bra'ban'çonne', La** (lȧ brȧ'băN'sôn'). [F.] The Belgian national anthem, composed during the revolution of 1830, the words probably by one Jenneval, the music by François van Campenhout.

brab'ble (brăb''l), *v. i.;* BRAB'BLED (-'ld); BRAB'BLING (-lĭng). *Now Dial.* To dispute noisily. — *n.* Contentious chatter. — **brab'ble·ment,** *n.*

brace (brās), *n.* [OF., the two arms, embrace, fathom, fr. L. *brachia* the arms (stretched out), pl. of *brachium* arm.] **1.** *Obs.* Armor for the arm; hence, warlike preparation. **2.** *Mach.* A curved instrument or handle for rotating a bit.

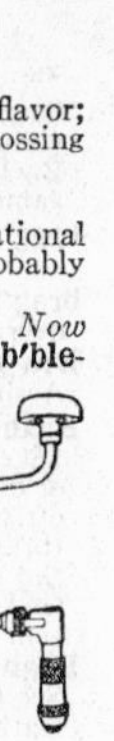

Brace, 2.

brace (brās), *v. t.;* BRACED (brāst); BRAC'ING (brās'ĭng). [OF. *bracier* to embrace.] **1.** To bind or tie; to fasten tightly. **2.** To draw tight or into a state of tension; to strain; as, to *brace* the nerves, a bow, a drum. **3.** To place in a position for resisting pressure; to support so as to give firmness; as, he *braced* himself against the crowd; hence, to stimulate. **4.** To furnish or support with braces. **5.** *Naut.* To move around by means of braces. — *v. i.* *Colloq.* To rouse one's energies or courage; — with *up.* — *n.* **1.** That which connects or fastens, as a clamp or buckle. **2.** A cord, ligament, or rod for producing or maintaining tension. **3.** That which supports anything firmly, or gives rigidity or power of resistance; a prop; a support for shoulders, back, a leg, etc. **4.** *pl. Brit.* Suspenders for trousers. **5.** A pair; a couple, as of ducks or pistols, facetiously of persons; — orig. of dogs. **6.** *Arch. & Engin.* A piece of material used to transmit, divert, or resist weight or pressure. **7.** *Print. & Music.* A character ({) connecting two or more words or lines to be taken together, or two or more staffs the parts on which are to be performed simultaneously; also, the group of staffs so connected. Cf. BRACKET, *n.,* 4. **8.** *Naut.* A rope rove through a block at the end of a yard to swing it horizontally.

brace'let (brās'lĕt; -lĭt), *n.* [OF., dim. of *bracel* armlet, fr. L. *brachiale,* fr. *brachium.*] **1.** An ornamental band or chain worn about the arm, chiefly by women. **2.** *Jocose.* A handcuff.

brac'er (brās'ẽr), *n.* [OF. *brasseure.*] **a** = BRASSART. **b** A guard for the arm or wrist in archery or fencing.

brac'er, *n.* [From BRACE, *v.*] That which braces, binds, or makes firm; a brace; also, *Slang,* a stimulating drink.

brach (brăch; brăk), *n.* Also **brach'et** (brăch'ĕt; -ĭt). [OF. *brachet.*] *Archaic.* A bitch of the hound kind.

bra'chi·al (brā'kĭ·ăl; brăk'ĭ·ăl), *adj.* [L. *brachialis.*] Pertaining to the arm or an armlike process.

bra'chi·ate (-āt), *adj.* *Bot.* Having widely spreading branches arranged in alternate pairs, as the maple.

bra'chi·o- (brā'kĭ·ō-; brăk'ĭ·ō-), **brachi-.** [L. *brachium* arm.] *Anat.* A combining form denoting *the arm; connection with the arm; brachial and;* as in **bra'chi·al'gi·a, bra·chif'er·ous, bra'chi·o·cru'ral, bra'chi·ot'o·my** (see -ALGIA, -FEROUS, etc.).

bra'chi·o·pod' (-pŏd'), *n.* [*brachio-* + *-pod.*] *Zool.* One of a class (Brachiopoda) of animals having bivalve shells within which is a pair of "arms" bearing tentacles by which a current of water is made to bring microscopic food to the mouth. — **bra'chi·o·pod',** *adj.*

bra'chi·um (brā'kĭ·ŭm; brăk'ĭ·ŭm), *n.;* *pl.* BRACHIA (-ȧ). [L., arm.] *Anat. & Zool.* The upper part of the arm or forelimb from shoulder to elbow.

brach'y- (brăk'ĭ-). [Gr. *brachys.*] A combining form meaning *short, abnormally short,* as in **brach'y·dac'ty·ly, bra·chyp'ter·ous, brach'y·stom'a·tous** (see -DACTYLY, etc.).

brach'y·ce·phal'ic (-sē·făl'ĭk), **brach'y·ceph'a·lous** (-sĕf'ȧ·lŭs), *adj.* [*brachy-* + Gr. *kephalē* head.] *Craniom.* Short-headed or broad-headed, having a cephalic index of more than 80. See CEPHALIC INDEX. — **brach'y·ceph'a·ly** (-sĕf'ȧ·lĭ), *n.*

brach'y·dome (brăk'ĭ·dōm), *n.* *Cryst.* See DOME, 4.

brach'y·u'ran (brăk'ĭ·ū'răn), *adj.* [*brachy-* + Gr. *oura* tail.] Of or pertaining to a suborder (Brachyura) of decapod crustaceans consisting of the common crabs. — *n.* A brachyuran crustacean. — **brach'y·u'rous** (-rŭs), *adj.*

brac'ing (brās'ĭng), *adj.* Imparting strength or tone; invigorating.

brack'en (brăk'ĕn), *n.* Any large, coarse fern; esp., the common brake; also, a growth of brakes.

brack'et (-ĕt; -ĭt), *n.* [F. *braguette* codpiece, deriv. of L. *bracae* breeches.] **1.** An overhanging member projecting from a wall or other body to support weight falling outside of the wall, or a similar piece to strengthen an angle; — the general term for all projecting supports, as the brace, console, corbel, strut. **2.** A shelf or set of shelves so supported. **3.** A gas or electric fixture, or a lamp holder, projecting from a wall, column, or the like. **4.** **a** One of the pair of marks [ ], used in writing and printing to enclose matter, chiefly as extraneous or merely incidental to the context. **b** = BRACE, 7. **5.** *Math.* A vinculum. **6.** A part of a list enclosed within a brace or bracket; hence, a class of taxpayers graded according to income. — *v. t.* **1.** To place within brackets; to connect by or furnish with a bracket or brackets. **2.** To couple together as of the same class.

brack'ish (brăk'ĭsh), *adj.* Saltish, as water in saline soil; hence, distasteful; nauseous. — **brack'ish·ness,** *n.*

bract (brăkt), *n.* [L. *bractea* a thin plate of metal.] *Bot.* **a** A leaf from the axil of which a flower or floral axis arises. See COMPOSITE, CORYMB, INVOLUCRE, *Illusts.* **b** A leaf borne on the floral axis itself, esp. one subtending the flower or flower cluster. — **brac'te·al** (brăk'tē·ăl), *adj.* — **brac'te·ate** (-āt), *adj.* — **bract'ed** (brăk'tĕd; -tĭd), *adj.*

brac'te·o·late (brăk'tē·ō·lāt), *adj.* Furnished with bractlets.

bract'let (brăkt'lĕt; -lĭt), *n.* A bract on the floral axis; — called also **brac'te·ole** (brăk'tē·ōl).

brad (brăd), *n.* [ON. *broddr* any pointed piece of iron or steel.] **a** A thin nail, of the same thickness throughout, but tapering in width, and slightly headed. **b** A slender wire nail with a small, deep, round head. Cf. NAIL, *Illust.*

brad'awl' (brăd'ôl'), *n.* A straight awl with chisel edge used to make holes for brads, screws, etc.

brae (brā; brē), *n.* [ON. *brā* eyelash.] *Dial.* A hillside; slope; bank, as of a river valley.

brag (brăg), *v. i.;* BRAGGED (brăgd); BRAG'GING. [OF. *braguer* to flaunt, brag.] To talk boastfully; to boast. — *v. t.* To boast of; to vaunt. — **Syn.** See BOAST. — *n.* **1.** A boast or boasting; bragging. **2.** The thing which is boasted of. **3.** A braggart. **4.** An old card game resembling poker. — **brag′ger**, *n.*

brag′ga·do′ci·o (brăg′*à*·dō′shĭ·ō; 58), *n.; pl* -OS (-ōz). **1.** A braggart; a swaggerer. **2.** Empty boasting; brag.

brag′gart (brăg′ẽrt), *n.* [OF. *bragard* flaunting, vain, bragging.] An overweening boaster. — *adj.* Overweeningly boastful.

Bra′gi (brä′gē), **Bra′ge** (-gĕ), *n.* [ON.] *Norse Myth.* One of the Aesir, god of poetry, and husband of Ithunn.

Brah′ma (brä′m*à*), *n.* *Hindu Religion.* **1.** Also **Brah′man** (-măn). [Skr. *brahman*, neut., prayer, impersonal spirit.] The supreme soul or essence of the universe, immaterial, uncreated, illimitable, timeless, often described as being, intelligence, and bliss. **2.** Also **Brahm** (brăm). In reformed theistic Hinduism, God conceived as comprising the trinity, Brahma, Vishnu, and Siva. **3.** [Skr. *Brahman*, masc., God Brahma.] The first member of the Hindu trinity, the personification of the supreme Brahma and conceived as the creator of the world.

Brah′ma (brä′m*à*; *popularly* brā′m*à*), *n.* [From *Brahmaputra*. See *Gaz.*] A very large domestic fowl of an Asiatic breed having feathered legs.

Brah′man (brä′măn), *n.; pl.* -MANS (-mănz). [Skr. *brāhmaṇa*, masc.] A Hindu of the highest or sacerdotal caste. Cf. KSHATRIYA, VAISYA, SUDRA. — **Brah·man′ic** (brä·măn′ĭk), **Brah·man′i·cal** (-ĭ·kăl), *adj.*

Brah′man·ism (-ĭz′m), *n.* The system of doctrines and institutions of the Brahmans and orthodox Hindus, marked by pantheistic conceptions and the anticipation of blessedness in the extinction of desire, and, socially, by the caste system. — **Brah′man·ist** (-ĭst), *n.*

Brah′min (brä′mĭn), *n.* **1.** A Brahman. **2.** A highly cultured person; an intellectual, esp. one who is supercilious or exclusive; — used satirically.

Brah·min′ic (brä·mĭn′ĭk), **Brah′min·ism, Brah′min·ist.** Vars. of BRAHMANIC, etc.

braid (brād). Scot. var. of BROAD.

braid (brād), *v. t.* [AS. *bregdan* to move to and fro, to weave.] **1.** To weave, interlace, or entwine together, as three or more strands; to plait. **2.** To bind (the hair) with a string or band. **3.** To trim, ornament, or outline with braid. — *n.* **1.** A plait, band, or narrow fabric formed by intertwining different strands; specif., a plait of hair so formed. **2.** A band or ribbon for binding the hair. **3.** A narrow cordlike fabric used for binding, etc.

braid′ing, *n.* Braids collectively.

brail (brāl), *n.* [OF. *braiol, braioel, braiel*, a band placed around the breeches, fr. *braies*, pl., breeches, fr. L. *braca, bracae.*] *Naut.* A rope fastened to the leech or corner of a sail, by which the sail can be hauled up or in, as in furling. — *v. t.* To haul by the brails; — with *up.*

Braille (brāl), *n.* [*also not cap.*] A system of printing or transcribing for the blind in which the characters are represented by raised dots. It was invented in 1829 by Louis Braille.

brain (brān), *n.* [AS. *bragen, brægen.*] **1.** In vertebrate animals, the large mass of nerve tissue enclosed in the skull or cranium. It consists of (1) nerve cells (gray matter) and (2) nerve fibers (white matter). In man it comprises two anterior cerebral hemispheres, the outer layer or cortex of which is regarded as the seat of consciousness, a dorsal cerebellum, the posterior medulla oblongata, and minor structures. See FOREBRAIN, MIDBRAIN, HINDBRAIN. Hence, in many invertebrates, a ganglion (nerve center) of corresponding position and function. **2.** Now usually *pl.* Understanding; intellect; intelligence. — *v. t.* To dash out the brains of.

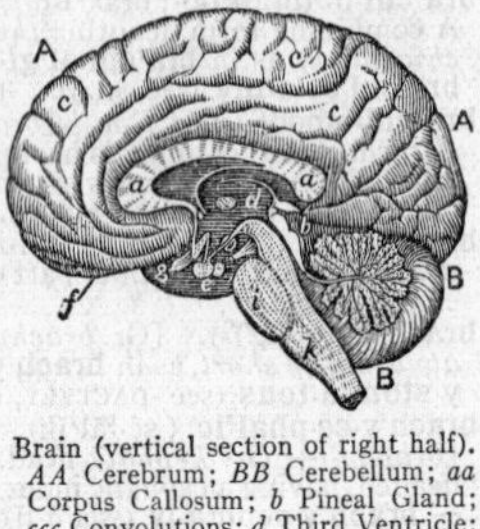

Brain (vertical section of right half). *AA* Cerebrum; *BB* Cerebellum; *aa* Corpus Callosum; *b* Pineal Gland; *ccc* Convolutions; *d* Third Ventricle; *e* Pituitary Body; *f* Olfactory Lobe; *g* Optic Nerve; *i* Pons Varolii; *k* Medulla Oblongata.

brain′less, *adj.* Without understanding; silly; thoughtless; witless. — **brain′less·ly**, *adv.* — **brain′less·ness**, *n.*

brain′pan′ (brān′păn′), *n.* = CRANIUM **b.**

brain′sick′ (-sĭk′), *adj.* Disordered, or resulting from disorder, in the understanding. — **brain′sick′ness**, *n.*

brain storm. Popularly, any transitory agitation or confusion of mind.

brain′wash′ing, *n.* The forcible replacement of one group of political ideas by another group, esp. through indoctrination and mental torture. — **brain′wash′**, *v. t.*

brain wave. **1.** A hypothetical vibration assumed to explain telepathy. **2.** Rhythmic fluctuations of voltage between parts of the brain resulting in the flow of an electric current; also, the current. **3.** *Colloq.* A flash of inspiration.

brain′y (brān′ĭ), *adj.;* BRAIN′I·ER (-ĭ·ẽr); BRAIN′I·EST. *Colloq.* Having brains; intelligent. — **brain′i·ness**, *n.*

braise (brāz), *v. t.* [F. *braiser*, fr. *braise* coals.] To cook (meat) by searing in fat, and then simmering in a covered dish with scant moisture.

brake (brāk), *n.* [ME., fern.] Any of a genus (*Pteridium*) of ferns, esp. one species (*P. aquilinum*) having ternately compound fronds.

brake, *n.* A thicket; brushwood.

brake, *n.* [ME., fr. LG. *brake* an instrument for breaking flax, fr. the root of E. *break.*] **1.** An instrument for bruising the woody part of flax or hemp so that it may be separated from the fiber. **2.** Any of various rolling or crushing instruments. **3.** Any device for retarding or stopping motion, as of a wheel, esp. by friction. — *v. t.* **1.** To crush or break (flax or hemp) in a brake. **2.** To apply a brake to; to retard by a brake. — *v. i.* To operate a brake or brakes.

brake (brāk). Var. of BREAK, a carriage.

brake. Archaic past of BREAK.

brake′man (brāk′măn), *n.* Also, *Brit.*, **brakes′man** (brāks′-). A man employed to operate brakes, as on a freight train.

bram′ble (brăm′b′l), *n.* [AS. *brēmel, brembel, bræmbel.*] Any of a genus (*Rubus*) of shrubs of the rose family, often prickly, including the raspberry and blackberry; esp., the common English blackberry (*Rubus fruticosus*); hence, any rough, prickly shrub. — **bram′bly** (-blĭ), *adj.*

bran (brăn), *n.* [OF. *bren.*] The broken coat of the seed of cereal grain, separated from the flour or meal by sifting or bolting.

branch (brȧnch; 9), *n.* [OF. *branche*, fr. LL. *branca* paw, claw.] **1.** A stem growing from the trunk or from a bough of a tree or shrub; a limb; *Bot.*, a shoot or secondary stem growing from the main stem. **2.** Any division extending like a branch, as of an antler or chandelier. **3.** A member or part of any complex body or work; a distinct section, subdivision, or department; as, a *branch* of the military service. **4.** A subordinate local office or part of a central system, as of a post office. **5.** A division of a family descended from a particular ancestor. **6.** *Ethnol.* A class in the subdivision of linguistic families. Cf. GROUP, *n.*, 3 **c.** **7.** *Geog.* A ramification of a river; as: **a** A stream flowing out of a river, as in a delta. **b** A stream flowing out of, and then rejoining, a river. **c** A tributary. **d** *Local, U. S.* A brook, run, or rivulet. — **Syn.** See SHOOT. — *v. i.* **1.** To shoot or spread in branches; separate into branches; put forth branches. **2.** To spring off or out from the main branch or stem; to diverge; to deviate. — *v. t.* **1.** To embroider with figures of flowers or foliage. **2.** To divide into branches. — ***branch out.*** To extend one's activities; to do anything on a larger scale.

bran′chi·a (brăng′kĭ·*à*), *n.; pl.* BRANCHIAE (-ē). [L., fr. Gr. *branchia*, pl. of *branchion.*] *Zool.* A gill. — **bran′chi·al** (-ăl), *adj.* — **bran′chi·ate** (-āt), *adj.*

bran′chi·o·pod′ (brăng′kĭ·ō·pŏd′), *n.* [Gr. *branchia* gills + *-pod.*] Any of a group (Branchiopoda) of aquatic crustaceans typically having a long body, a carapace, and many pairs of leaflike appendages. — **bran′chi·o·pod′**, *adj.*

brand (brănd), *n.* [AS. *brand, brond*, brand, sword.] **1.** A stick or piece of wood partly burned, whether burning or not. **2.** *Poetic.* A sword. **3.** A mark put upon criminals with a hot iron; hence, any mark of infamy; a stigma. **4. a** A mark made by burning with a hot iron, as upon an animal to designate ownership, or upon a container to designate the quality, manufacturer, etc., of the contents. **b** A similar identifying mark made in any other way, as a trade-mark; hence, quality, grade, class, or make of goods; as, a good *brand* of flour. **5.** An iron used for branding. — *v. t.* **1.** To place a brand upon. **2.** To mark as infamous; stigmatize. — **brand′er**, *n.*

brand goose. See BRANT.

bran′dish (brăn′dĭsh), *v. t.* [OF. *brandir*, fr. *brand* a sword, of Teut. origin.] To shake or wave, usually menacingly. — **Syn.** See SWING. — *n.* A flourish, as with a weapon. — **bran′dish·er**, *n.*

brand′ling (brănd′lĭng), *n.* [See BRAND, *n.;* 1st -LING.] A yellowish dunghill earthworm having brownish-purple rings, used as bait by anglers.

brand′-new′, *adj.* Conspicuously new; bran-new.

bran′dy (brăn′dĭ), *n.; pl.* -DIES (-dĭz). [From older *brandywine, brandwine*, fr. D. *brandewijn*, fr. *branden* to burn, distill + *wijn* wine.] **a** A spirituous liquor distilled from wine. Cf. COGNAC, EAU DE VIE. **b** A similar liquor distilled from the fermented juice of a fruit; as, apricot *brandy*. — *v. t.;* -DIED (-dĭd); -DY·ING. To flavor, blend, or treat with brandy.

bran′gle (brăng′g′l), *n.* & *v.* *Dial.* Wrangle; squabble.

brank (brăngk; *dial* brȧngk), *n.* [F. *branques*, pl.] **1.** *pl. Scot.* & *Ir.* A bridle with wooden sidepieces. **2.** Usually *pl.* An instrument having a triangular piece entering the mouth, formerly used for correcting scolding women.

brank′ie (brȧng′kĭ), *adj.* *Scot.* Gaudy; spruce.

bran′-new′. Var. of BRAND-NEW.

brant (brănt), *n. sing.* & *pl.;* see PLURAL, *Note*, 3. A wild goose, esp. one of a genus (*Branta*) of (typically) small dark geese, as the Canada goose, the common European species (*B. bernicla;* called also *brand goose*), that of eastern North America (*B. bernicla hrota*), and the ***black brant*** (*B. nigricans*) of the Pacific coast. Cf. BARNACLE GOOSE.

brash (brăsh; *dial.* brȧsh), *n.* **1.** *Chiefly Dial.* A fit of sickness; rash. **2.** Rubbish, as clippings of hedges or fragments of ice afloat. — (brăsh), *adj.* **1.** Of timber, brittle. **2.** *Colloq.* Tactlessly hasty or rash; hence, saucy; impudent. — **brash′y**, *adj.* — **brash′i·ness**, *n.*

bra′sier (brā′zhẽr). Var. of BRAZIER.

bra·sil′e·in, bras′i·lin. Vars. of BRAZILEIN, BRAZILIN.

brass (brȧs; 9), *n.* [AS. *bræs.*] **1.** An alloy consisting essentially of copper and zinc in variable proportions. Cf. BRONZE. **2.** *Colloq.* **a** *Orig. Dial.* Money; cash. **b** Impudence; bold assurance. **3.** An engraved brass memorial plate. **4.** A brass utensil, ornament, or the like; — chiefly *pl.* **5.** A color, reddish-yellow in hue, of medium saturation and high brilliance. See COLOR. **6.** The officers of high rank, esp. top military officers. **7.** *Mach.* One of the brass, bronze, or gunmetal linings or steps in a bearing. **8.** *Music.* Also **brass′es** (brȧs′ĕz; -ĭz). The brass winds (see WIND INSTRUMENT).

bras′sard (brăs′ärd), *n.* [F.] A brassart; also, a badge worn on the arm.

bras′sart (brăs′ẽrt), *n.* [F. *brassard*, fr. *bras* arm.] Armor for the upper arm from shoulder to elbow. See ARMOR, *Illust.*

brass hat. *Soldiers' Slang* A general or staff officer; — from the ornamental gold braid on the cap.

bras′si·ca′ceous (brăs′ĭ·kā′shŭs), *adj.* [L. *brassica* cabbage.] Belonging to the mustard family (Brassicaceae). See MUSTARD.

brass′ie, brass′y (brȧs′ĭ), *n.; pl.* -IES (-ĭz). *Golf.* A wooden club soled with brass. See GOLF, *Illust.*

bras·sière′ (br*à*·zẽr′; brăs′ĭ·âr′), *n.* [F.] A form of woman's underwaist, worn to support the breasts. Cf. BRA.

brass winds (brȧs wĭndz). See WIND INSTRUMENT.

brass′y (brȧs′ĭ), *adj.;* BRASS′I·ER (-ĭ·ẽr); BRASS′I·EST. **1.** Of or adorned with brass. **2.** Impudent; brazen. **3.** Having the nature, appearance, or sound of brass. — **brass′i·ly**, *adv.* — **brass′i·ness**, *n.*

brat (brăt), *n.* [AS. *bratt* covering, fr. OIr.] *Dial.* **a** Coarse clothing. **b** A coarse apron; a bib. **c** A film, as on porridge.

brat (brăt), *n.* [From BRAT clothing.] A child; — usually contemptuous.

brat′tice (brăt′ĭs), *n.* [ME. *bretasce* parapet, fr. OF. *bretesche* wooden tower, fr. ML. *brittisca*, fr. AS. *Brittisc* British.] **1.** *Fort.* Formerly, a temporary breastwork or gallery erected as or on an advanced work. **2.** A partition; esp., *Mining:* **a** A wall of separation in a shaft or gallery for controlling ventilation. **b** Planking to support a roof. — *v. t.;* -TICED (-ĭst); -TIC·ING (-ĭs·ĭng). To provide with a brattice.

brat′tle (brăt′′l), *n.* & *v.* *Scot.* Clatter; rattle; scamper.

bra·va′do (br*à*·vä′dō), *n.; pl.* -DOES or -DOS (-dōz). [Sp. *bravada, bravata*, boast, brag. See BRAVE, *adj.*] Expression or action simulating bravery.

brave (brāv), *adj.* [F., fr. It. *bravo*, (orig.) fierce, wild, fr. L. *barbarus.*] **1.** Characterized by courage. **2.** *Archaic.* Superior; excellent. **3.** Making a fine show or display. — **Syn.** Courageous, valiant, dauntless, intrepid, bold. — **Ant.** Craven. — *n.* **1.** A brave person. **2.** *Archaic.* **a** A challenge; a defiance. **b** A bully; a bravo. **3.** A North American Indian warrior. — *v. t.* **1.** To encounter with courage; defy; dare. **2.** *Obs.* To make showy. **3.** To make brave; to embolden. — *v. i.* To vaunt or boast. — **brave′ly,** *adv.* — **brave′ness,** *n.*

brav′er·y (brāv′ẽr·ĭ), *n.* **1.** Intrepid courage. **2.** Brave show; fine dress.

bra′vo (brä′vō; brā′vō), *n.; pl.* -VOES, -VOS (-vōz), -VI (brä′vē). [It.] A desperado; esp., a hired assassin. — (brä′vō), *interj.* Well done! Excellent! — *n.; pl.* BRAVOS (-vōz). An exclamation of "bravo."

bra·vu′ra (brȧ·vū′rȧ; -vōō′rȧ), *n.* [It.] **1.** A show of daring or brilliancy. **2.** A florid, brilliant style of music.

braw (brô; brä), *adj.* *Chiefly Scot.* **a** Well-dressed. **b** Good; fine. — **braw′ly** (-lĭ), **braw′lie** (-lĭ), **braw′lys** (-lĭs), *adv.*

brawl (brôl), *v. i.* [ME. *braulen* to quarrel, boast, *brallen* to cry, make a noise.] **1.** To quarrel or fight noisily. **2.** To make a loud confused noise, as a stream running over stones. — *n.* Noisy quarrel or fight; a wrangle; also, a noise likened to wrangling. — **brawl′er,** *n.*

brawl, *n.* [F. *branle* a sort of dance.] An old dance in duple measure, mimetic, and accompanied by singing.

brawn (brôn), *n.* [OF. *braon* fleshy part, muscle, of Teut. origin.] **1.** Full, strong muscles, esp. of the arm or leg; muscular strength. **2.** The flesh of a boar, esp. when pickled or potted, as headcheese.

brawn′y (brôn′ĭ), *adj.;* BRAWN′I·ER (-ĭ·ẽr); BRAWN′I·EST. Muscular; fleshy; strong. — **Syn.** Muscular, burly, husky, sinewy. — **Ant.** Scrawny. — **brawn′i·ness,** *n.*

braws (brôz; bräz), *n. pl.* *Chiefly Scot.* Fine clothes.

brax′y (brăk′sĭ), *n.* An infectious bacterial disease of sheep, resembling anthrax.

bray (brā), *v. i.* [OF. *braire* to cry (F. *braire* to bray).] To utter a loud harsh cry; — now chiefly of the ass, or donkey. — *v. t.* To utter harshly. — *n.* A harsh cry, esp. of an ass; any loud, harsh, grating sound. — **bray′er;** *n.*

bray, *v. t.* [OF. *breier* (F. *broyer*), of Teut. origin.] **a** To pound, rub, or grind fine. **b** To spread thin, as printer's ink with a hand roller. — **bray′er,** *n.*

braze (brāz), *v. t.* [AS. *bræsian,* fr. *bræs* brass.] To make, cover, or ornament with or as if with brass.

braze (brāz), *v. t.* [F. *braser,* fr. *braise* live coals, of Teut. origin.] To solder with any alloy relatively infusible, esp. with hard solder or with brass. — **braz′er** (brāz′ẽr), *n.*

bra′zen (brā′z'n), *adj.* [AS. *bræsen.*] **1.** Made of brass or bronze; like brass, esp. in strength or color. **2.** Sounding harsh and loud, like resounding brass. **3.** Impudent; shameless. — *v. t.* **1.** To face brazenly; — usually with *out* or *through.* **2.** To make bold or brazen. — **bra′zen-faced′** (-fāst′), *adj.* — **bra′zen·ly,** *adv.* — **bra′zen·ness,** *n.*

bra′zier (brā′zhẽr; 58), *n.* [ME. *brasiere.*] One who works in brass.

bra′zier, *n.* [F. *brasier,* fr. *braise* live coals.] A pan for holding burning coals.

bra·zil′ (brȧ·zĭl′; *formerly, and still in Eng. dial.,* brăz′ĭl), *n.* [ME. *brasil,* fr. OF. *bresil* (or Sp., Pg. *brasil*), fr. the stem of *braise* glowing coals. The wood was named from its reddish color, and the country Brazil was named from the wood.] Brazilwood or the red dyestuff obtained from it. See BRAZILIN.

braz′i·lin (brăz′ĭ·lĭn), *n.* *Chem.* A compound, $C_{16}H_{14}O_5$, extracted from brazilwood as a yellow crystalline powder, and, on exposure to the air, oxidized to the red crystalline dye **bra·zil′e·in** (brȧ·zĭl′ē·ĭn), $C_{16}H_{12}O_5$.

Bra·zil′ nut (brȧ·zĭl′). An oily 3-angled nut, the seed of the fruit of the **Bra·zil′-nut′ tree** (*Bertholletia excelsa*), family Lecythidaceae.

bra·zil′wood′ (brȧ·zĭl′wŏŏd′), *n.* [See BRAZIL.] **1.** The heavy dyewood of an East Indian redwood (*Caesalpinia sappan*); sapanwood. **2.** The similar wood of various tropical American trees of the senna family (esp. of genus *Caesalpinia*).

breach (brēch), *n.* [From OF. *breche* (of Teut. origin) and fr. AS. *bryce.*] **1.** A breaking, or being broken. **2.** A breaking or infraction of a law, or of any obligation or tie; violation; as, a *breach* of contract. **3.** *Archaic.* A bruise; a wound. **4.** A hernia. **5.** A gap made by breaking or battering, as in a wall. **6.** A breaking of waters, as over a vessel; the waters themselves; surge; surf. **7.** A breaking up of amicable relations. **8.** The leap of a whale out of water. — *v. t.* To make a breach in. — *v. i.* To leap out of water, as a whale.

breach of promise. Violation of one's plighted word, esp. of a promise to marry.

bread (brĕd), *n.* [AS. *brēad* fragment, morsel, bread.] **1.** An article of food made from flour or meal by moistening, kneading, and baking. **2.** *Eccl.* A portion of bread; wafer. **3.** Food; sustenance; as, to earn one's *bread.* — *v. t.* *Cookery.* To cover with bread crumbs.

bread and butter. Bread spread with butter; hence, *Colloq.,* livelihood. Hence: **bread′-and-but′ter,** *adj.* **1.** Boyish or girlish; juvenile. **2.** Workaday; prosaic.

bread′-and-but′ter let′ter. A letter of thanks for hospitality.

bread′bas′ket (brĕd′bȧs′kĕt; -kĭt), *n.* **1.** A basket for bread. **2.** A major cereal-producing region. **3.** *Slang.* The stomach. **4.** *Slang.* A large bomb that explodes in mid-air releasing many smaller bombs.

bread′fruit′ (-frōōt′), *n.* *Bot.* **a** The large round fruit of a tall Polynesian tree (*Artocarpus altilis*) of the mulberry family. When baked it resembles bread. **b** The tree bearing this fruit.

bread′root′ (-rōōt′), *n.* The nutritious root of a western U. S. hairy plant (*Psoralea esculenta*) of the pea family; psoralea.

bread′stuff′ (-stŭf′), *n.* Grain or flour; also, bread.

breadth (brĕdth), *n.* [AS. *brǣdu,* fr. *brād* broad.] **1.** Distance or measure from side to side of any surface; width. **2.** Anything considered with reference to, or measured by, its breadth; as, a *breadth* of cloth. **3.** Spaciousness or extent. **4.** Largeness or liberality, as of views. **5.** *Art.* Quality of having the details so massed as to produce an impression of largeness and unity.

breadth′ways′ (-wāz′), **breadth′wise′** (-wīz′), *adv.* See -WAYS.

bread′win′ner (brĕd′wĭn′ẽr), *n.* The member of a family whose labor supplies its food; also, a means of livelihood.

break, brake (brāk), *n.* A high-swung pleasure vehicle carrying six or more passengers, driver, and footman.

break (brāk), *v. t.;* *past* BROKE (brōk), *Archaic* BRAKE (brāk); *past part.* BRO′KEN (brō′kĕn); *pres. part.* BREAK′ING. [AS. *brecan.*] **1.** To separate into parts as a result of concussion or of stress; to strain apart suddenly and violently; as, to *break* new ground; to *break* one's neck. **2.** To destroy, impair, disable, or overcome by or as if by breaking; as, to *break* a set; to *break* ranks; to *break* a strike. **3.** To destroy the tone, firmness, or resiliency of; as, to *break* one's spirit; to *break* a horse to harness; specif.: **a** To bankrupt; ruin. **b** To cashier; degrade; dismiss. **c** To invalidate (a will) by action at law. **4.** To lay open by or as if by breaking; to lay or force open and to pass in or out; to penetrate. **5.** Hence, of immaterial things: **a** To transgress or violate. **b** To disclose; divulge. **c** To impart; broach. **6.** To sever the continuity of; as, to *break* silence; to *break* an electric circuit. **7.** To diminish the force of, as of a fall. **8.** To cause in (one) the discontinuance (of a habit or practice). **9.** *Sports.* To exceed (a record). — *v. i.* **1.** To come apart or divide into two or more pieces, usually with suddenness and violence; of waves, to curl over and fall in foam. **2.** To emerge or depart by breaking bonds or restraints; to burst forth violently, as a storm. **3.** To open by pressure from within, as a seed vessel. **4.** To fail, weaken, or succumb as if by breaking; as, their ranks *broke;* his health *broke.* **5.** To disintegrate or dissolve; as, the cream *breaks* in the churn; to decompose partially. **6.** To cease to have relations; hence, to terminate friendship. **7.** To make an abrupt change in a course, as in gait; to undergo an entire reversal. **8.** To change from one register to another, as a voice. **9.** To come suddenly (into sight or notice); to dawn. **10.** Of fish, to leap out of the water. **11.** *Exchanges.* To fall suddenly and markedly in price. **12.** *Phonet.* To undergo conversion into a diphthong, as Anglo-Saxon *æ* before *r* into *ea.* ***break down.*** **a** To demolish or destroy; hence, to overwhelm; crush. **b** To separate into component parts, substances, or the like; to divide into categories; to analyze. **c** To collapse; give way. — **Syn.** See ANALYZE. — ***break in.*** **a** To force in, as a door. **b** To train; discipline, as a horse. **c** To enter forcibly; also, to interrupt. — ***break on the wheel.*** To execute by stretching upon a wheel and breaking the limbs with an iron bar. — ***break up.*** To dissolve; to put an end to. — *n.* **1.** Act of breaking; rupture; fracture; also, the action of breaking in or breaking forth; irruption; as, a *break* for freedom; *break* of day. **2.** Effect of breaking; condition produced by breaking; a gap, rent, or breach. **3.** *Slang, U.S.* An awkward social blunder or embarrassing remark; also, a chance, good or bad; as, a lucky, or a bad, *break.* **4.** *Elec.* An opening or lack of continuity in a circuit. **5.** *Exchanges, U.S.* A sudden and abrupt decline of prices. **6.** *Music.* The point where one register changes to another. **7.** *Pros.* A caesura. **8.** *Sports.* **a** An opening shot, as in billiards. **b** A sequence of successful shots, as in billiards; a run. **c** Deviation of a pitched or bowled ball. **d** *Tenpins.* A failure to get a strike or a spare on a frame. **9.** A brief interruption of work for temporary relaxation.

break′a·ble (brāk′ȧ·b'l), *adj.* Capable of being broken.

break′age (-ĭj), *n.* **1.** Act or result of breaking; a break; articles broken. **2.** An allowance for things broken.

break′bone′ fe′ver (brāk′bōn′). Dengue.

break′down′ (-doun′), *n.* **1.** A breaking that causes a collapse, as of machinery or health. **2.** Chemical decomposition. **3.** A noisy, rapid, shuffling dance. **4.** Division into categories; analysis; classification; specif., division (of a job or operation) into several distinct processes.

break′er (brāk′ẽr), *n.* [Prob. fr. Sp. *barrica.*] A small water cask.

break′er, *n.* **1.** One who or that which breaks; specif., a machine or plant for breaking coal. **2.** A wave breaking into foam, as against the shore. **3.** Also **breaker strip.** In tires, a strip of fabric under the tread for extra protection of the carcass. See TIRE, *Illust.*

break′fast (brĕk′fȧst), *n.* [*break* + *fast.*] **1.** The first meal in the day. **2.** A meal after fasting. — *v. i. & t.* To eat, or furnish with, breakfast.

break′neck′ (brāk′nĕk′), *adj.* Involving risk of life.

break′through′ (-thrōō′), *n.* **1.** Act or place of breaking through an obstruction. **2.** *Mil.* An offensive thrust that penetrates and carries beyond a defensive zone.

break′up′ (-ŭp′), *n.* Disruption; dispersion; dissolution.

break′wa′ter (-wô′tẽr; -wŏt′ẽr), *n.* A structure for breaking the force of waves, as to protect a harbor or beach.

bream (brēm), *n.* [F. *brême,* fr. OF. *bresme,* of Teut. origin.] **1.** A European fresh-water fish (*Abramis brama*) of the carp family; also, any of certain allied fishes. **2.** **a** Any sparoid fish (see SPAROID); — called specif. ***sea bream.*** **b** Any of various fresh-water sunfishes (genus *Lepomis*).

bream (brēm), *v. t.* [D. *brem* broom.] *Naut.* To clean (a ship's bottom) by heating and scraping.

breast (brĕst), *n.* [AS. *brēost.*] **1.** The fore or ventral part of the body, between the neck and the abdomen; the bosom; hence, a piece of clothing or armor covering this part. **2.** A mammary gland; a teat. **3.** The seat of consciousness, esp. of the emotions; hence, secret thought. **4.** Anything resembling or likened to the human breast; as, the *breast* of a hill. **5.** In a plow, the front part of the moldboard. **6.** *Mining.* = FACE, 17. — *v. t.* To meet with the breast; to struggle with or oppose manfully.

breast′bone′ (brĕst′bōn′; 2), *n.* The sternum. See THORAX, *Illust.*

breast drill. A portable drill with a plate which is pressed by the breast in forcing the drill against the work.

breast fast *or* **line.** *Naut.* A large rope to fasten the midship part of a vessel, as to a wharf.

breast′plate′ (brĕst′plāt′), *n.* **1.** A plate of metal covering the breast as defensive armor. See ARMOR, *Illust.* **2.** *Jewish Antiq.* A vestment of the high priest, set with twelve gems for the twelve tribes of Israel. **3.** The plate of a breast drill. **4.** *Zool.* = PLASTRON, 2.

breast′work′ (-wûrk′), *n.* *Fort.* A defensive work of moderate height, usually one hastily thrown up.

breath (brĕth), *n.* [AS. *brǣth* odor, scent, breath.] **1.** A vapor given off; an exhalation, as of steam; now, a fragrant emanation, or air charged with it. **2.** A very slight breeze. **3.** Air inhaled and exhaled in respiration. **4.** Power of respiration; hence, life. **5.** A single respiration; hence: **a** A single act or instant; as, in the same *breath.* **b** Anything unsubstantial and transient. **6.** Act or power of breathing naturally or freely; as, out of *breath;* also, time to breathe; respite. **7.** That which is produced by the breath, as a film of moisture condensed upon a cold object; utterance or speech, esp. a single utterance; hence, the slightest effort; a trifle. **8.** *Phonet.* Expiration of air with the glottis wide open, as in making the sounds *f, s, p, t,* etc. — ***under one's breath.*** In low tones; in a whisper.

breathe (brēth), *v. i.;* BREATHED (brēthd); BREATH′ING (brēth′ĭng). **1.** To exhale fragrance. **2.** To inhale and exhale air; to respire; hence, to pause; also, to draw the breath of life; to live. **3.** To pass like breath; exhale; blow gently. — *v. t.* **1.** To exhale, as fragrance. **2.** To inject by breathing; to infuse; — with *into.* **3.** To inhale and exhale; hence: **a** To utter, esp. softly; whisper. **b** To express; manifest. **4.** To permit to take breath; to let rest. **5.** To promote free respiration in; exercise. **6.** To put out of breath. **7.** *Phonet.* To utter without voice. — **breath'a·ble** (brēth'ȧ·b'l), *adj.*

breathed (brĕtht; brēthd), *adj.* *Phonet.* Voiceless.

breath'er (brēth'ẽr), *n.* **1.** One who breathes. **2.** *Colloq.* That which puts one out of breath or stimulates breathing, as exercise. **3.** A pause for breath.

breath'ing (brēth'ĭng), *n.* **1.** Respiration; hence: **a** Pause for breath. **b** Utterance. **2.** Air in gentle motion. **3.** The sound sometimes expressed by the letter *h.* **4.** *Greek Gram.* A mark to indicate aspiration or its absence. See ROUGH BREATHING, SMOOTH BREATHING.

breath'less (brĕth'lĕs; -lĭs), *adj.* **1.** Without breath; hence, dead. **2.** Out of breath; spent. **3.** Holding the breath, on account of fear, expectation, or intense interest. **4.** Motionless; without a breeze. — **breath'less·ly**, *adv.* — **breath'less·ness**, *n.*

breath'-tak'ing (brĕth'tāk'ĭng), *adj.* That takes one's breath; startling; thrilling.

breath'y (brĕth'ĭ), *adj.* Accompanied with, or characterized by, noticeably audible emission of breath.

brec'ci·a (brĕch'ĭ·ȧ; brĕsh'ĭ·ȧ), *n.* [It.] A rock composed of angular fragments cemented together.

bred (brĕd), *past & past part.* of BREED.

brede (brēd), *n.* *Archaic.* A braid; also, embroidery.

bree (brē), *n.* [AS. *brīw.*] *Scot.* Broth; liquor.

breech (brēch *or, now dial.,* brĭch), *n.* [See BREECHES.] **1.** The buttocks. **2.** The hinder or lower part; esp.: **a** The rear part of a firearm, behind the bore. **b** The bottom of a block or pulley. — (brēch; brĭch), *v. t.* To furnish with breeches or a breech; figuratively, to cover (as if with breeches).

breech'block' (brēch'blŏk'), *n.* In the mechanism of breech-loading firearms, the steel block which closes the rear of the bore against the force of the charge. See GUNLOCK, *Illust.*

breech'cloth' (-klôth'; *cf.* BREECH, *n.*), *n.* Also **breech'clout'** (-klout'). A cloth worn around the breech.

breech delivery. *Obstet.* Delivery of a fetus with the breech appearing first.

breech'es (brĭch'ĕz; -ĭz), *n. pl.* [AS. *brēc*, pl. of *brōc* breech, breeches.] **1.** Smallclothes. **2.** *Colloq.* Trousers.

breeches buoy. A pair of canvas short-legged breeches depending from a ring-shaped or beltlike life buoy running upon a hawser stretched from the ship to the shore or from one ship to another, designed primarily for rescuing persons.

breech'ing (brĭch'ĭng; brēch'-), *n.* The part of a harness which passes around the breech of a horse. See HARNESS, *Illust.*

breech'load'er (brēch'lōd'ẽr), *n.* A breech-loading firearm.

breech'-load'ing, *adj.* Receiving the charge at the breech.

breed (brēd), *v. t.;* BRED; BREED'ING. [AS. *brēdan* to nourish, cherish.] **1.** To produce (offspring) by hatching or gestation. **2.** To engender; give rise to; produce; as, to *breed* discontent; a land that *breeds* stout men. **3.** To propagate, as any kind of stock; as, to *breed* cattle or dogs; hence, to propagate by artificial pollination. **4.** To bring up; to nurse and foster. — **Syn.** Generate, reproduce, beget, propagate. — *v. i.* **1.** To bear and nourish young. **2.** To be produced or multiplied; originate. **3.** To raise a breed. — *n.* **1. a** A race or variety of animals related by descent and similar in most characters; race; stock. **b** A group of domestic animals (or of plants), developed and controlled by human intervention, having distinctive characteristics as in shape or color. *Breed* in this sense designates a more extensive group than *strain* and does not imply traceable descent from a particular individual. **2.** In general, class; sort; kind. — **breed'er**, *n.*

breed'ing, *n.* **1.** Act of generating. **2.** Nurture; formation of manners. **3.** Knowledge of, or training in, the ceremonies and polite observances of society. **4.** Propagation of plants or animals.

breeks (brēks; brĭks). Colloq. & dial. var. of BREECHES.

breeze (brēz), *n.* [AS. *briosa.*] *Now Dial.* A gadfly.

breeze, *n.* [F. *brise*, possibly a var. of *bise.*] **1. a** A light, gentle wind. **b** *Meteorol.* Any wind of a velocity up to 38 miles per hour (U. S. Weather Bureau wind scale). Breezes are classified as ***light*** (up to 7 miles per hour), ***gentle*** (8–12 mph), ***moderate*** (13–18 mph), ***fresh*** (19–24 mph), and ***strong*** (25–38 mph). Cf. GALE, BEAUFORT'S SCALE. **2.** *Colloq.* **a** A flurry of temper or excitement; a quarrel. **b** A whisper; rumor.

breeze, *n.* [F. *braise* cinders, live coals. See BRAZE to solder.] Bits of refuse left in making coke or charcoal.

breez'y (brēz'ĭ), *adj.;* BREEZ'I·ER (-ĭ·ẽr); -I·EST. **1.** Characterized or swept by breezes. **2.** Fresh; airy; vivacious. — **breez'i·ly**, *adv.* — **breez'i·ness**, *n.*

breg'ma (brĕg'mȧ), *n.; pl.* -MATA (-mȧ·tȧ). [Gr., front of the head.] The junction of the coronal and sagittal sutures at the top of the skull. — **breg·mat'ic** (brĕg·măt'ĭk), *adj.*

Bren gun (brĕn). [*Br*no, city in Czechoslovakia + *En*field, town in England.] A light gas-operated and air-cooled machine gun fired from the shoulder.

brent (brĕnt), *adj.* *Scot.* Of the forehead: high; also, unwrinkled.

brent. Var. of BRANT.

breth'ren (brĕth'rĕn; -rĭn), *n.* A plural of BROTHER.

Bret'on (brĕt'ŭn; *F.* brē·tôN'), *adj.* [F.] Of or relating to Brittany (or Bretagne) or the Bretons. — *n.* **1.** A native of Brittany (or Bretagne). **2.** The Brythonic language of the Armorican Bretons, akin to Cornish and distinct from Welsh. See INDO-EUROPEAN LANGUAGES, *Table.*

breve (brēv), *n.* [It. *breve* or F. *brève*, fr. L. *brevis* short.] **1.** A curved mark [˘] used to indicate a short vowel or syllable. **2.** = BRIEF, *n.*, 1. **3.** *Law.* A writ (= BRIEF, 3 **a**). **4.** In modern music, a note equivalent to two whole notes (semibreves). See NOTE, *n.*, 11 **a**.

bre·vet' (brē·vĕt' *or, esp. Brit.,* brĕv'ĕt; -ĭt), *n.* [F., fr. L. *brevis* short.] *Mil.* A commission giving an officer higher nominal rank than that for which he receives pay. — *adj. Mil.* Taking or conferring rank by brevet. — *v. t.;* BRE·VET'TED or BREV'ET·ED; BRE·VET'TING or BREV'ET·ING. *Mil.* To confer rank upon by brevet.

brev'i- (brĕv'ĭ-). [L. *brevis.*] A combining form meaning *short*, as in **brev'i·pen'nate**, short-winged, **brev'i·ros'trate**, short-beaked.

bre'vi·ar'y (brē'vĭ·ĕr'ĭ *or, esp. Brit.,* -ẽr·ĭ; brĕv'ĭ-), *n.; pl.* -ARIES (-ĭz). [L. *breviarium* abridgment, fr. *breviarius* abridged, fr. *brevis* short.] *Eccl.* A book containing the daily prayers for the canonical hours.

bre·vier' (brē·vēr'), *n.* [Prob. orig. used in printing a *breviary.*] *Print.* A size of type (8 points) See TYPE.

brev'i·ty (brĕv'ĭ·tĭ), *n.; pl.* -TIES (-tĭz). [L. *brevitas*, fr. *brevis* short.] **1.** Shortness of duration; briefness of time. **2.** Expression in few words; conciseness

brew (broo; 114), *v. t.* [AS. *brēowan.*] **1.** To prepare, as beer, from malt and hops, by steeping, boiling, and fermentation, or by infusion and fermentation. **2.** To foment or prepare as if by brewing; to plot; concoct; as, to *brew* mischief. — *v. i.* **1.** To brew beer. **2.** To be mixing, forming, or gathering, as a storm. — *n.* **1.** Process or result of brewing. **2.** That which is brewed, esp. a beverage. — **brew'er**, *n.*

brew'age (broo'ĭj), *n.* Malt liquor; drink brewed; brewing.

brew'er·y (broo'ẽr·ĭ), *n.; pl.* -ERIES (-ĭz). The building and apparatus where brewing is carried on.

brew'ing, *n.* **1.** Act or process of preparing liquors which are brewed, as beer and ale. **2.** A brew.

brew'is (broo'ĭs), *n.* [ME. *brewes, brouwys, browesse*, fr. OF. *brouet*, dim. of *breu, bro.* Cf. BROSE.] **1.** Pot liquor. **2.** Bread soaked in pot liquor, broth, etc.

bri'ar (brī'ẽr), **bri'ar·wood'**, etc. Vars. of BRIER, etc.

Bri·ar'e·an (brī·âr'ē·ăn), *adj.* *Gr. Myth.* Of or like **Bri·ar'e·us** (-ŭs), a monster of a hundred hands; hence, many-handed.

bribe (brīb), *n.* [OF., a lump of bread, scraps, leavings, *briber, brimber*, to beg.] **1.** A price, reward, gift, or favor bestowed or promised with a view to pervert the judgment or corrupt the conduct of a person in a position of trust. **2.** That which seduces; seduction; allurement. — *v. t.* To give a bribe to; to induce or influence, or to gain, by a bribe. — *v. i.* To give a bribe to a person; to practice bribery. — **brib'a·ble** (brīb'ȧ·b'l), *adj.* — **brib'a·bil'i·ty** (-bĭl'ĭ·tĭ), *n.* — **brib'er** (brīb'ẽr), *n.*

brib'er·y (brīb'ẽr·ĭ), *n.; pl.* -ERIES (-ĭz). Act or practice of giving or taking a bribe.

bric'-a-brac' (brĭk'ȧ·brăk'), *n.* [F. *bric-à-brac.*] Curious or antique articles of virtu; odd knickknacks.

brick (brĭk), *n.* [F. *brique*, fr. MD. *bricke* brick.] **1.** A building and paving material made by molding clay into blocks while moist and hardening them in the sun or by fire. **2.** *pl.* BRICKS or, *collectively*, BRICK. An individual molded block of the above material, usually rectangular, in U. S. averaging 2¼ × 3¾ × 8 inches. **3.** A block of any material, or any mass, of similar size and shape; as, a *brick* of ice cream. Cf. GOLD BRICK. **4.** *Colloq.* A person of sterling qualities. — *adj.* **a** Made of bricks. **b** Brick-red. — *v. t* To lay or pave or close, with bricks.

brick'bat' (brĭk'băt'), *n.* **1.** A fragment of a brick, esp. one used as a missile. **2.** An insult or aspersion hurled at one

brick'kiln' (-kĭl'; -kĭln'), *n.* A kiln in which bricks are burned; a pile of green bricks, arched to be burned.

brick'lay'ing (-lā'ĭng), *n.* The act or occupation of laying or building with bricks. — **brick'lay'er**, *n.*

brick'le (brĭk''l), *adj.* [ME. *brekil, brokel, bruchel*, fr. AS. *brecan.*] *Dial.* Brittle; fragile.

brick red. A color, red-yellow in hue, of low saturation and medium brilliance See COLOR. — **brick'-red'**, *adj.*

brick'work' (brĭk'wûrk'), *n.* Work of or with bricks.

brick'yard' (-yärd'), *n.* A place where bricks are made.

brid'al (brīd'ăl; -'l), *n.* [AS. *brȳdealo;* see BRIDE, ALE, 2.] A wedding. — *adj.* Pert. to a bride or a wedding.

bridal wreath. A cultivated spiraea (*Spiraea prunifolia*), having copious umbels of small white flowers, appearing in spring.

bride (brīd), *n.* [F.] **1.** A loop, bar, or tie, in needlework, etc. **2.** A bonnet string.

bride, *n.* [AS. *brȳd.*] A woman newly married, or about to be married.

bride'groom' (brīd'groom'; 85), *n.* [AS. *brȳdguma*, fr. the stems of AS. *brȳd* bride + *guma* man. The second *r* in *bridegroom* is due to confusion with, or substitution of, *groom.*] A man newly married, or about to be married.

brides'maid' (brīdz'mād'), *n.* A woman who attends a bride at her wedding.

bride'well (brīd'wĕl; -wĕl), *n.* A jail; prison; — from a former penitentiary near St. Bride's Well in London.

bridge (brĭj), *n.* [AS. *brycg, bricg.*] **1.** A structure erected over a depression or an obstacle, as over a river, roadway, railroad, etc., carrying a roadway for passengers, vehicles, etc. **2.** Anything bridgelike n form or position; specif.: **a** The upper bony part of the nose. **b** = PONS VAROLII. **3.** A low separating wall, usually of firebrick, in a furnace. **4.** *Billiards & Pool.* The hand, or a contrivance consisting of a notched piece at the end of a thin wooden rod, used as a cue rest in making a shot. **5.** [Appar. from the dealer's *bridging*, or passing, the declaration of trumps to his partner.] *Card Games.* **a** A card game derived from whist and superseded by auction bridge. **b** Auction bridge. **c** Contract bridge. **6.** *Dentistry.* A device for securing artificial teeth by anchorage to natural teeth. **7.** *Elec.* A device in which the current-detecting instrument is bridged across or connected across two branches of the circuit. **8.** *Music.* The movable arch at right angles to the strings of a violin, guitar, etc., serving to raise them. See VIOLIN, *Illust.* **9.** *Naut.* A platform elevated above the rail and

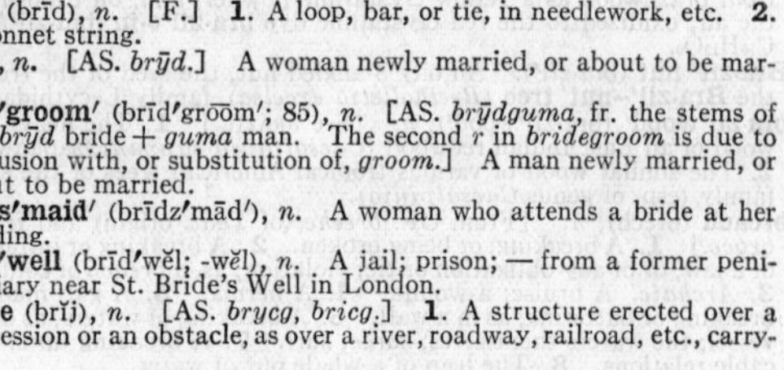

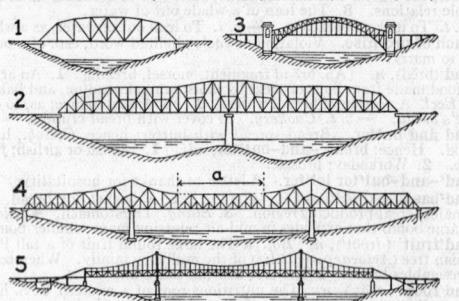

Bridges. 1 Simple Truss; 2 Continuous Truss; 3 Steel Arch; 4 Cantilever (*a* Suspended Span); 5 Suspension.

extending across or over the deck of a vessel. Cf. DECK, *Illust.* **10.** *Railroads.* A gantry. — *v. t.;* BRIDGED (brĭjd); BRIDG′ING (brĭj′ĭng). To build or make a bridge or bridges on or over. — **bridge′a·ble,** *adj.*

bridge′board′ (brĭj′bōrd′), *n.* = STRING, *n.*, 8 **b.** See STAIR, *Illust.*

bridge′head′ (-hĕd′), *n.* A locality on the enemy's side of a stream, fortified to protect a bridge site, ford, or defile; by extension, *Mil.*, an advanced position seized in hostile territory, formerly only on a coast but now also inland, and defended as a foothold for invasion forces or for further advance.

bridge′work′ (-wûrk′), *n.* **1.** Bridge construction. **2.** A dental bridge or bridges.

bri′dle (brī′d'l), *n.* [AS. *brīdel, brigdils.*] **1.** The headgear with which a horse is governed and restrained, consisting of a headstall, a bit, and reins. See BIT, HARNESS, *Illusts.* **2.** A restraint; curb; check. **3.** = BRANK, 2. **4.** *Anat.* A frenum. **5.** *Mach.* A strip of metal joining two parts in a machine or restraining their motion. **6.** *Naut.* A span of two chain cables of a moored ship, joined by a swivel. **7.** Act of bridling, or of assuming a dignified or offended air.

bri′dle (brī′d'l), *v. t.;* BRI′DLED (-d'ld); BRI′DLING (-dlĭng). [AS. *brīdlian.*] **1.** To put a bridle upon. **2.** To restrain or guide with or as with a bridle — **Syn.** See RESTRAIN. — *v. i.* To hold up the head and draw in the chin, as an expression of pride, scorn, or pique. — **bri′dler** (-dlẽr), *n.*

bridle path. A path allowing, or open only to, saddle horses and pack horses.

bri·doon′ (brĭ·dōōn′), *n.* [F. *bridon.*] *Mil.* The snaffle and rein of a bridle having both snaffle and curb bits.

Brie cheese (brē). A soft cheese of Brie, France, ripened by mold or, as made in America, ripened by bacteria.

brief (brēf), *adj.* [OF. *bref,* fr. L. *brevis.*] **1.** Short in duration. **2.** Concise; terse; succinct; also, curt; abrupt.

Syn. **Brief, short** mean lacking length. **Brief** refers primarily to duration, **short** to either duration or linear extent, but *brief,* when applied to duration, usually implies condensation, and *short,* sudden stoppage, curtailment, or the like; as, he made his speech as *brief* as possible; he cut his speech *short.* — **Ant.** Prolonged, protracted.

— *adv. Now Rare.* Briefly; in brief.

— *n.* **1.** An official letter, specif. a papal letter less formal than a bull. **2.** A short statement, oral or written; hence, a summary. **3.** *Law.* **a** A writ. **b** An abridgment or concise statement of a client's case, made out for the instruction of counsel. **c** A statement of the heads or points of a legal argument; — short for **brief of argument. d** An abstract or abridgment of deeds to a property; — short for **brief of title. e** *Colloq.* A client; also, a case at law. **4.** *or* **briefs,** *n. pl.* Very short underpants. — **Syn.** See ABRIDGMENT. — ***in brief.*** Concisely; in short. — ***to hold a brief for.*** To advocate.

— *v. t.* **1.** To make a brief, abstract, or abridgment of. **2.** *Eng.* To instruct by a brief; hence, to retain as counsel. **3.** To give (fliers, etc.) final precise instructions for a mission. **4.** To coach thoroughly in advance. — **brief′ly,** *adv.* — **brief′ness,** *n.*

brief case. A flat, flexible leather case or bag suitable for carrying legal briefs flat and unfolded.

brief′less, *adj.* Having no brief; without clients.

bri′er, bri′ar (brī′ẽr), *n.* [AS. *brēr, brǣr.*] **1.** Any plant with a woody stem bearing thorns or prickles (esp. of the genera *Rosa, Rubus,* or *Smilax*). **2.** A mass of brier bushes; a twig of a brier. — **bri′er·y, bri′ar·y** (-ĭ), *adj.*

bri′er, bri′ar, *n.* [F. *bruyère* heath, heather.] **1.** The tree heath (*Erica arborea*) of southern Europe, the root of which is used for making pipes. **2.** A pipe of brierwood.

bri′er·root′, bri′ar·root′ (-rōōt′; 85), *n.* Brierwood.

bri′er·wood′, bri′ar·wood′ (-wŏŏd′), *n.* **1.** The root wood of the brier *Erica arborea,* used esp. in making tobacco pipes. **2.** A pipe made of this wood.

brig (brĭg), *n.* [Short for BRIGANTINE.] *Naut.* A two-masted, square-rigged vessel. Cf. HERMAPHRODITE BRIG, *Illust.*

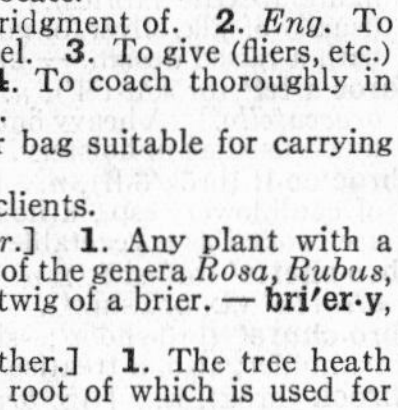

Brig.

brig, *n.* **a** On a United States man-of-war, the place of confinement for offenders. **b** *Humorous.* A guardhouse.

brig (brĭg). Dial. var. of BRIDGE.

bri·gade′ (brĭ·gād′), *n.* [F., fr. It. *brigata,* fr. *brigare* to fight.] **1.** *Mil.* A large body of troops; specif., a unit composed basically of a headquarters and two or more regiments. It is the normal command of a brigadier general. Cf. DIVISION, 9. **2.** Any body of persons organized for acting or marching together under authority; as, a fire *brigade.* — *v. t.* **1.** *Mil.* To form into a brigade. **2.** To arrange in a group; classify.

brig′a·dier′ (brĭg′ȧ·dẽr′), *n.* [F.] **1.** *U.S.Army.* A brigadier general. **2.** *Brit. Army.* **a** An officer of any rank temporarily in command of a brigade. **b** A brigadier general. *Brigadier general* was dropped from official British usage after World War I, and *brigadier* adopted in 1928.

brigadier general; *pl.* BRIGADIER GENERALS. *Mil.* A commissioned officer who ranks above a colonel and below a major general. Abbr. *Brig. Gen.* Cf. BRIGADE, 1.

brig′and (brĭg′ănd), *n.* [F., fr. It. *brigante,* fr. *brigare* to fight, fr. *briga* strife, of Celt. origin.] A lawless fellow who lives by plunder, usually a member of a band; a bandit. — **brig′and·age** (-ăn·dĭj), *n.* — **brig′and·ism** (-dĭz'm), *n.*

brig′an·dine (brĭg′ăn·dēn; -dīn), *n.* [F., fr. It. *brigantina,* fr. *brigare.*] Medieval body armor of scales or plates.

brig′an·tine (-tēn; -tīn), *n.* [F. *brigantin,* fr. It. *brigantino,* orig., a piratical vessel.] **a** A two-masted, square-rigged vessel, differing from a brig in not carrying a square mainsail. **b** Sometimes, a hermaphrodite brig. See BRIG, HERMAPHRODITE BRIG, *Illusts.*

bright (brīt), *adj.* [AS. *beorht, bryht.*] **1.** Radiating or reflecting light; shining; — opposed to *dark;* hence, radiant with happiness, good fortune, etc.; as, a *bright* future. **2.** Illustrious; glorious. **3.** Resplendent with charms; as, *bright* beauty. **4.** Of a color, of high saturation or brilliance. **5.** Intelligent; clever; also, lively; cheerful. — *n. Poetic.* Splendor; brightness. — **bright′ly,** *adv.* — **bright′ness,** *n.*

Syn. **Bright, brilliant, radiant, luminous, lustrous, beaming** mean shining or glowing with light. **Bright** applies to things that shed light or are pervaded by light (as, a *bright* lamp, star, day, night); **brilliant** implies conspicuous or intense brightness (as, a *brilliant* gem or smile); **radiant** properly implies emission or seeming emission of rays of light; **luminous** implies emission of light, but not of rays, and so is applicable to anything that shines, as by reflected light or in the dark; **lustrous** applies to objects the surface of which reflects light; **beaming,** though literally implying emission of beams of light, is more often used figuratively of something from which light seems to stream.

bright′en (brīt′'n), *v. t. & i.* To make bright or brighter (in various senses); as: **1.** To shine or cause to shine. **2.** To make or become cheerful; as, his face *brightened.*

Bright's′ dis·ease′ (brīts). [After Dr. Richard *Bright,* of London.] *Med.* Any of several diseases of the kidney attended with albumin in the urine. See NEPHRITIS.

bright′work′ (brīt′wûrk′), *n.* Polished metal objects or parts, as on the deck of a ship or on an automobile.

brill (brĭl), *n.; pl.* BRILL, BRILLS (brĭlz). See PLURAL, *Note.* A European flatfish (*Bothus rhombus*) allied to the turbot.

bril′liance (brĭl′yăns), **bril′lian·cy** (-yăn·sĭ), *n.* **1.** Brilliant quality; brightness; splendor; also, intellectual keenness. **2.** That one of the three attributes of a color without which it cannot exist (except that black is considered to have zero brilliance), and in respect of which it may be classed as equivalent to some member of the series of grays ranging from black (as the zero member) to white; roughly, the degree of resemblance to white or difference from black. See COLOR.

bril′liant (-yănt), *adj.* [F. *brillant,* pres. part. of *briller* to shine, sparkle, fr. It. *brillare.*] **1.** Sparkling; very bright. **2.** Distinguished by qualities which excite admiration; splendid. — **Syn.** See BRIGHT. — **bril′liant·ly,** *adv.* — **bril′liant·ness,** *n.*

bril′liant, *n.* **1.** *Jewelry.* A diamond or other gem cut in a particular form with numerous facets so as to have especial brilliancy; also, the form itself. **2.** *Print.* A small size of type (3½ or 4 points) See TYPE.

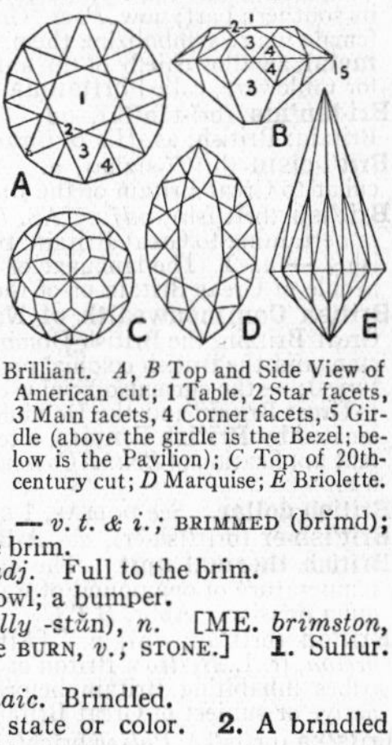

Brilliant. *A, B* Top and Side View of American cut; 1 Table, 2 Star facets, 3 Main facets, 4 Corner facets, 5 Girdle (above the girdle is the Bezel; below is the Pavilion); *C* Top of 20th-century cut; *D* Marquise; *E* Briolette.

bril′lian·tine′ (brĭl′yăn·tēn′; brĭl′-yăn·tēn′), *n.* [F. *brillantine.*] **1.** An oily dressing used to gloss the hair. **2.** A dress fabric, of mohair and cotton, glossy on both sides, resembling alpaca but of superior quality.

Brill's′ dis·ease′ (brĭlz). [After Nathan E. *Brill* (1860–1925), Am. physician.] *Med.* An acute infectious disease, now considered to be a mild form of typhus.

brim (brĭm), *n.* [ME. *brim, brimme.*] **1.** The edge or margin of anything, esp. of water. **2.** The rim, border, or upper edge of a cup, dish, or any hollow vessel. **3.** The rim of a hat. — **Syn.** See BORDER. — *v. t. & i.;* BRIMMED (brĭmd); BRIM′MING. To fill or be filled to the brim.

brim′ful′ (brĭm′fōōl′; brĭm′fōōl; 2), *adj.* Full to the brim.

brim′mer (brĭm′ẽr), *n.* A brimful bowl; a bumper.

brim′stone′ (brĭm′stōn′; *Brit. usually* -stŭn), *n.* [ME. *brimston, bremston, bernston, brenston.* See BURN, *v.;* STONE.] **1.** Sulfur. **2.** A spitfire; virago.

brin′ded (brĭn′dĕd; -dĭd), *adj. Archaic.* Brindled.

brin′dle (brĭn′d'l), *n.* **1.** Brindled state or color. **2.** A brindled animal. — **brin′dle,** *adj.*

brin′dled (-d'ld), *adj.* [Dim. of BRINDED.] Having dark streaks or spots on a gray or tawny ground; streaked.

brine (brīn), *n.* [AS. *brȳne.*] **1.** Water saturated or strongly impregnated with common salt; pickle; hence, any strong saline solution. **2.** The ocean; the water of an ocean, sea, or salt lake. — *v. t.* To treat with brine; esp., to steep or saturate in brine. — **brin′ish** (brīn′-ĭsh), *adj.*

Bri·nell′ ma·chine′ (brĭ·nĕl′). [After J. A. *Brinell* (1849–1925), Sw. engineer.] An apparatus for measuring the hardness of metals. A steel ball is pressed with a standard pressure (usually 3,000 kilograms) into the specimen under test, the resistance to penetration (**Brinell hardness**) being expressed by a number (**Brinell number**) denoting the applied pressure in kilograms divided by the spherical area of indentation in square millimeters.

bring (brĭng), *v. t.; past & past part.* BROUGHT (brôt); *pres. part.* BRING′ING. [AS. *bringan.*] **1.** To cause to come with oneself, as by conveying, leading, or carrying; — the opposite of *take.* **2.** Figuratively, to cause to come, come along, or come about. **3.** To induce; to persuade; as, *brought* to forgive. **4.** *Law.* To prefer, as a charge; institute, as an action. **5.** To advance; adduce, as an argument. **6.** To procure in exchange; to sell for; fetch; as, what does coal *bring* per ton? — **bring′er,** *n.*

bring about. To cause to take place; to accomplish. — ***bring forth.*** To give birth to; produce. — ***bring forward.*** To introduce; produce to view. — ***bring home.*** To prove conclusively. — ***bring home the bacon.*** *Colloq., U. S.* To win the prize sought; to secure the desired results. — ***bring round.*** To cause (one) to change his opinions or conduct; to win (one) over, esp. gradually. — ***bring to.*** To resuscitate, as a fainting person. — ***bring to bear.*** To cause to apply or have influence. — ***bring to book.*** To compel to give an account. — ***bring to terms.*** To compel to agree, assent, or submit. — ***bring up.*** To rear; educate.

brink (brĭngk), *n.* [ME. *brink, brenk,* appar. of Scand. origin.] The edge, margin, or border at the top of a steep place; as, the *brink* of a precipice; hence, bank, as of a river; also, verge; borderline; as, on the *brink* of disaster. — **Syn.** See BORDER.

brin′y (brīn′ĭ), *adj.;* BRIN′I·ER (-ĭ·ẽr); BRIN′I·EST. Of or like brine; salty. — **brin′i·ness** (-ĭ·nĕs; -nĭs), *n.*

bri·oche′ (brē·ōsh′; brē′ōsh; *F.* brē′ôsh′), *n.* [F.] A light roll made from yeast dough rich with eggs and butter.

bri′o·lette′ (brē′ō·lĕt′), *n.* [F.] An oval or pear-shaped diamond cut in triangular facets. See BRILLIANT, *Illust.*

bri·quette′ (brĭ·kĕt′), *n.* [F., dim. of *brique* brick.] A mass of coal or ore dust pressed into a brick-shaped block; — also spelled **bri·quet′.**

bri·sance′ (brĭ·zäns′), *n.* [F. *brisant,* pres. part. of *briser* to break.] The shattering effect shown by explosives such as nitroglycerin and guncotton.

Bri·se′is (brĭ·sē′ĭs), *n.* In the *Iliad,* Achilles' captive, taken away from him by Agamemnon to replace Chryseis (which see), thus originating the feud between the two heroes.

Bri'sing·a·men' (brē'sĭng·ä·mĕn'), *n.* See FREYA

brisk (brĭsk), *adj.* **1.** Full of life; keenly alive or alert. **2.** Of actions, rapid and animated; energetic. **3.** Of the air, sharply or freshly invigorating; as, a *brisk* day; of liquors, effervescing; sparkling — **Syn.** See AGILE. — **Ant.** Sluggish. — *v. t. & i.* To make or become brisk; to enliven. — **brisk'ly,** *adv.* — **brisk'ness,** *n.*

bris'ket (brĭs'kĕt; -kĭt), *n.* [ME. *brusket.*] In quadrupeds used as food and in domestic animals, the breast or lower part of the chest. See BEEF, PORK, DOG, *Illusts.*

bris'ling (brĭz'lĭng), *n.* [Nor.] A small sardinelike European fish which is packed in oil for food.

bris'tle (brĭs''l), *n.* [AS. *byrst.*] One of the short, stiff, coarse hairs on the back and sides of swine; hence, any short, stiff hair or hairlike growth. — *v. i.;* BRIS'TLED (-'ld); BRIS'TLING (-lĭng). **1. a** To rise or stand stiff or erect; — of hair, quills, etc. **b** To raise the bristles, as an angry hog. **2.** To take on an aggressive attitude, as that of an animal bristling. **3.** To appear as if covered with bristles; as, to *bristle* with difficulties — *v. t.* **1.** To cause to stand up, as the bristles of an angry hog. **2.** To furnish with bristles. **3.** To ruffle. — **bris'tly** (-lĭ), *adj.*

bris'tle·tail' (-tāl'), *n.* Any of various insects (orders Thysanura and Entotrophi) with two slender caudal bristles.

Bris'tol board (brĭs't'l). [From *Bristol*, Eng.] A kind of fine pasteboard, made with a smooth but usually unglazed surface.

brit (brĭt), *n. sing. & pl.* **a** The young of the common herring, or sometimes, any of certain small schooling fishes of similar appearance. **b** Minute marine crustaceans, etc., upon which whalebone whales feed.

Bri·tan'ni·a (brĭ·tăn'ĭ·ȧ; -yȧ), *n.* [L.] **1.** Orig., Great Britain, esp. its southern part; now, *Poet.*, Great Britain and the dominions, or the female figure symbolizing them. **2.** [*not cap.*] Short for **britannia metal,** an alloy chiefly of tin, antimony, and copper. It is largely used for tableware, called **britannia ware.**

Bri·tan'nic (brĭ·tăn'ĭk), *adj* [L. *Britannicus.*] Of or pert. to Britain; British; as, His *Britannic* Majesty.

Brit'i·cism (brĭt'ĭ·sĭz'm), *n.* A linguistic usage, word, or idiom peculiar to Great Britain or the British.

Brit'ish (brĭt'ĭsh), *adj.* [AS. *Brittisc, Bryttisc.* Cf. BRITON.] Of or pertaining to Great Britain, the British Commonwealth, or the British. — *n.* **1.** The language of the ancient Britons; Cymric. **2.** The people of Great Britain or of the British Commonwealth.

British Commonwealth of Nations *or* **British Commonwealth.** Great Britain, the British Dominions, the republics of India and Pakistan, and the British colonial possessions (colonies, protectorates, territories); — the current official use. In earlier use the term applied only to Great Britain and the Dominions, the colonial possessions being designated by **British Empire,** a term originally coextensive with the current application of *British Commonwealth* but now passing out of official use.

British dollar. See DOLLAR, 1 **c.**

Brit'ish·er (brĭt'ĭsh·ẽr), *n.* A British subject.

British thermal unit. The quantity of heat required to raise the temperature of one pound of water 1° F. at or near its point of maximum density. Abbr. *B.T.U.*

Brit'on (brĭt'ŭn; -'n), *n.* [After L. *Brito*, fr. ME. *Breton*, fr. F. *breton*, fr. L. *Britto* a Briton or Breton.] **1.** A member of one of the tribes inhabiting Britain before the Anglo-Saxon invasions. **2.** A native or subject of Great Britain, esp. an Englishman.

brits'ka (brĭts'kȧ; *Polish* brĭch'kä), *n.* Also **britz'ka, britz'ska.** [Pol. *bryczka.*] A long roomy carriage with a calash top.

brit'tle (brĭt''l), *adj.* [From AS. *brēotan* to break.] Easily broken or snapped; hence: **a** Insecure; not lasting; as, *brittle* promises. **b** Irritable; as, a *brittle* temper. — **Syn.** See FRAGILE. — **brit'tle·ness,** *n.*

broach (brōch), *n.* [OF. *broche*, fr. Celtic.] Any of various pointed tools, implements, or parts, such as a spit for roasting meat, a tool for tapping casks, a reamer, etc. — *v. t.* **1.** *Obs.* To stab; to pierce, as with a spit. **2.** To tap; to pierce, as a cask, in order to draw the liquor; hence, to let out; to shed, as blood. **3.** To open for the first time, as stores, a mine, etc. **4.** To utter; publish first; introduce as a topic of conversation. — **Syn.** See EXPRESS.

broach (brōch), *v. i. & t. Naut.* To veer; — used only in the phrase ***broach to,*** to veer suddenly into the wind, so as to lay the sails aback, and risk capsizing.

broad (brôd), *adj.* [AS. *brād.*] **1.** Wide; extended in breadth. **2.** Extending far and wide; spacious; as, the *broad* sea. **3.** Extended, in the sense of diffused or expanded; open; clear; full. **4.** Plain; obvious; as, a *broad* hint. **5.** Of language: **a** Of dialectal nature, esp. in pronunciation. **b** Coarse; indelicate; as, a *broad* joke **c** Unrestrained; outspoken. **6.** Free; unrestricted; as, *broad* farce. **7.** Liberal; catholic; as, a *broad* man. **8.** Extended in amount or range; extensive; as, education in the *broadest* sense. **9.** Main and essential; as, the *broad* aspects of the case. **10.** *Phonet.* **a** Of a vowel, uttered with a wide opening between the tongue and palate (*a* in *father; a* in *man*). **b** Of the vowel *a*, sounded as in *father*, as contrasted with the *a* in *man*.

Syn. **Broad, wide, deep** mean having horizontal extent. **Broad** and **wide** apply to surfaces also thought of as having length or height when they are measured or viewed from side to side (as, a screen five feet *broad; wide* ribbon); *wide, broad,* and, as here considered, **deep** may be used of surfaces or areas that spread away from one (as, a flower border four feet *wide* or *broad* or, preferably, *deep*). In general, *broad* is preferred when full horizontal extent is considered (as, *broad* shoulders), *wide* when the horizontal extent of an aperture or opening is in mind (as, a *wide* mouth), and *deep* when horizontal extent backward is suggested (as, a *deep* lot; a *deep* cavern).

— *adv.* Broadly; widely; — in phrases; as *broad* awake.

— *n.* **1.** The broad part of anything, as of the hand. **2.** *Eng.* An expansion of a river; a flooded fen. **3.** *Slang.* A woman; a "skirt."

broad arrow. **1.** An arrow with a broad head **2.** A mark (see the *Illust.*) placed upon British ordnance and government property, and upon the uniform worn by convicts.

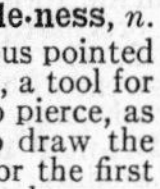
Broad Arrow, 2.

broad'ax', broad'axe' (brôd'ăks'), *n.* An ax with a broad blade, as any of various battle-axes, or a type of ax used for hewing timber.

broad bean. The bean *Vicia faba.* See BEAN.

broad'bill' (brôd'bĭl'), *n.* **1.** = SCAUP DUCK. **2.** = SHOVELER, 2.

broad'brim' (-brĭm'), *n.* **1.** A hat with a broad brim, as one worn by Quakers. **2.** [*cap.*] *Humorous.* A Quaker.

broad'cast' (-kȧst'; 9), *adj.* **1.** Cast in all directions, as seed from the hand in sowing. **2.** *Radio & Television.* Transmitted by broadcasting. — *n.* **1.** A casting or scattering in all directions, as in sowing seed by hand. **2.** *Radio & Television.* **a** Broadcasting as a medium of transmission. **b** The material broadcast; also, a single program of such material. — *adv.* So as to scatter or be scattered in all directions; specif., so as to reach by radio or television transmission an unlimited number of receiving stations. — *v. t.;* BROAD'CAST' (also, *Radio*, -CAST'ED); -CAST'ING. **1.** To scatter or sow broadcast. **2.** *Radio & Television.* To send out broadcast from a radio or television transmitting station. — *v. i.* To broadcast a program, etc. — **broad'cast'er,** *n.*

Broad Church. In churches of the Anglican Communion, a party holding liberal views as to doctrine and fellowship. — **Broad'-Church',** *adj.* — **Broad Churchman.**

broad'cloth' (brôd'klŏth'; 74), *n.* **a** A fine napped and calendered woolen cloth. **b** A fine grade of cotton or silk cloth, having a firm, smooth surface.

broad'en (-'n), *v. i. & t.* To grow or make broad; to widen.

broad'-gauge' (-gāj'; 2), **broad'-gauged'** (-gājd'), *adj.* Having a gauge wider than the usual or standard gauge; hence, broad-minded; liberal. See GAUGE, *n.*, 9.

broad hatchet. See HATCHET, *Illust.*

broad jump. *Athletics.* A jump for distance. Cf. HIGH JUMP.

Broad'leaf' (brôd'lēf'), *n.* Any of a group of varieties of cigar tobaccos having broad leaves.

broad'ly (brôd'lĭ), *adv.* In a broad manner.

broad'-mind'ed (-mīn'dĕd; -dĭd; 2), *adj.* Tolerant of liberal views. — **broad'-mind'ed·ly,** *adv.* — **broad'-mind'ed·ness,** *n.*

broad'side' (brôd'sīd'), *n.* **1.** *Naut.* **a** The side of a ship above the water line, from the bow to the quarter. **b** All the guns, collectively, that can be trained to fire to one side of a ship; also, their simultaneous discharge. **2.** A broad surface of any object, as of a house, an animal, etc. **3.** *Colloq.* A volley of abuse. **4.** *Print.* A sheet of paper containing one large page, or printed on one side only.

broad'sword' (-sōrd'), *n.* A sword with a broad blade for cutting rather than thrusting; esp., a claymore.

broad'tail' (-tāl'), *n.* **1.** Also **broadtail sheep.** A type of fat-tailed sheep native to Asia Minor. See KARAKUL, 1. **2.** The fur or skin of a very young, often prematurely born, broadtail lamb. It is flat and wavy and resembles moiré silk. See KARAKUL, 2.

broad'wife' (-wīf'), *n.* The wife of a slave belonging to a different owner. *Hist., Southern U. S.*

Brob'ding·nag (brŏb'dĭng·năg), *n.* Incorrectly, **Brob'dig·nag** (-dĭg-). In Swift's *Gulliver's Travels,* an imaginary country where everything is on an enormous scale. — **Brob'ding·nag'i·an** (-năg'ĭ·ăn), *adj. & n.*

bro·cade' (brō·kād'), *n.* [Sp. *brocado;* cf. ML. *brocare* to prick, to figure (textile fabrics).] A rich fabric with a raised design woven usually of silk, silver, or gold, or of all three of these; loosely, any fabric with a raised design. — **bro·cad'ed** (-kād'ĕd; -ĭd), *adj.*

broc'a·tel' (brŏk'ȧ·tĕl'), *n.* Also **broc'a·telle'.** [F. *brocatelle*, fr. It. *broccatello.*] A heavy figured fabric, usually of silk and linen, formerly much used as upholstery.

broc'co·li (brŏk'ō·lĭ), *n.* [It., pl. of *broccolo* sprout.] A hardy type of cauliflower; esp., a nonheading form whose green tops and stalks are cooked as a vegetable.

bro·chette' (brō·shĕt'), *n.* [F.] A small spit or skewer. — ***en bro·chette'*** (äN brô'shĕt'). [F.] On a brochette.

bro·chure' (brō·shoor'; -shür'), *n.* [F., fr. *brocher* to stitch.] A pamphlet; also, a treatise or article in pamphlet form.

brock (brŏk), *n.* [AS. *broc*, of Celt. origin.] The European badger (*Meles meles*); — sometimes, because of the animal's offensive smell, used as an opprobrious epithet. Cf. SKUNK.

brock'et (brŏk'ĕt; -ĭt), *n.* See RED DEER.

bro'gan (brō'găn; brō·găn'), *n.* A brogue (shoe).

brogue (brōg), *n.* *Scot.* Trick; fraud.

brogue (brōg), *n.* [Ir. & Gael. *brōg.*] Orig., a stout, coarse shoe worn in Ireland and the Scottish Highlands; hence: **a** A heavy hobnailed shoe of blucher cut **b** A strong low shoe for ordinary wear.

brogue, *n.* [Ir. *barrōg* a grip, a hold, a bond (on the tongue).] A dialect pronunciation, esp. as in the Irish pronunciation of English.

broi'der (broi'dẽr), *v. t.* [F. *broder*, Pr. *broidar*, of Teut. origin.] *Archaic.* To embroider. — **broi'der·y,** *n.*

broil (broil), *v. t.* [OF. *bruillir*, fr. *bruir*, of Teut. origin.] **1.** To cook by direct exposure to radiant heat, as on a gridiron over live coals; to grill. **2.** To subject to great (commonly direct) heat. — *v. i.* To be subjected to heat, as meat over a fire. — *n.* **1.** Act or state of broiling; an excessive heat. **2.** Something broiled.

broil, *n. & v.* [F. *brouiller* to disorder.] Brawl.

broil'er (broil'ẽr), *n.* **1.** One who or that which broils. **2.** A utensil, as a gridiron, used in broiling. **3.** A chicken or other bird fit for broiling. **4.** *Colloq.* A very hot day.

broil'ing, *adj.* That broils; scorching; very hot.

bro'kage (brō'kĭj), *n.* The business or pay of a broker; brokerage; — now chiefly in ***marriage brokage.***

broke (brōk), *past & archaic & poetic past part.* of BREAK. Hence: *adj. Slang.* Out of funds; bankrupt.

bro'ken (brō'kĕn), *past part.* of BREAK; specif.: *adj.* **1.** Violently shattered. **2. a** Fractured or ruptured; as, a *broken* leg. **b** Violated by transgression; as, a *broken* vow. **c** Interrupted; as, *broken* sleep. **d** Made infirm or weak, as by disease, age, etc. **e** Subdued; crushed; as, a *broken* spirit. **f** Bankrupt. **3.** Imperfectly spoken, esp. by a foreigner; as, *broken* English. — **bro'ken·ly,** *adv.* — **bro'ken·ness,** *n.*

bro'ken·heart'ed (-här'tĕd; -tĭd; 2), *adj.* Having the spirits depressed; crushed by grief or despair.

broken wind. *Veter.* The heaves (see HEAVE, *n.*, 4). — **bro'ken-wind'ed** (-wĭn'dĕd; -dĭd; 2), *adj.*

bro'ker (brō'kẽr), *n.* [ONF. *brokeor* (OF. *brocheor*), fr. *brokier* (*brochier*) to broach; — orig., a broacher, retailer of wine.] **1.** *Eng.* A dealer in secondhand goods. Cf. PAWNBROKER. **2.** One who, for a commission or fee, brings parties together and assists in negotiating contracts between them. **3.** A dealer in money, notes, bills of exchange, etc. **4.** A dealer in securities, esp. stocks and bonds such as are dealt in by stock exchanges; a stockbroker.

bro'ker·age (-ĭj), *n.* The business of a broker; also, the fee or commission for transacting business as a broker.

bro'mal (brō'măl), *n.* [G., fr. *brom* bromine + *al*kohol alcohol.] *Chem.* An oily, colorless fluid, CBr_3COH, obtained by the action of bromine on alcohol.

bro′mate (brō′māt), *n.* *Chem.* A salt of bromic acid. — *v. t.* *Pharm.* To treat or combine with bromine; brominate.

brome grass, *or* **brome** (brōm), *n.* [L. *bromos,* fr. Gr. *bromos,* a kind of oats.] Any of a large genus (*Bromus*) of grasses having large, often drooping spikelets. Most species are troublesome weeds. See 3d CHESS.

bro·me′li·a′ceous (brō·mē′lĭ·ā′shŭs), *adj* [After Olaf *Bromel* (1639–1705), Sw. botanist.] *Bot.* Belonging to the pineapple family (Bromeliaceae). See PINEAPPLE.

bro′mic (brō′mĭk), *adj.* *Chem.* Of or containing bromine, esp. in its valence of five; as, **bromic acid,** $HBrO_3$.

bro′mide (brō′mīd; -mĭd), *n.* Also **bro′mid.** **1.** *Chem.* A binary compound of bromine with another element or a radical. Bromides are much used in medicine (as sedatives) and the arts; as, ***potassium bromide,*** KBr, of biting, saline taste, used as a sedative and in photography; ***silver bromide*** AgBr, very sensitive to light and used in photography. **2.** *Slang.* **a** A commonplace or tiresome person. **b** A flat, commonplace statement or notion. — **bro·mid′ic** (brō·mĭd′ĭk), *adj.*

bro′mi·nate (brō′mĭ·nāt), *v. t.* *Chem.* To bromate.

bro′mine (brō′mēn; -mĭn), *n.* Also **bro′min.** [Gr. *brōmos* bad smell.] *Chem.* An element, normally a deep-red caustic liquid emitting an irritating, reddish-brown, ill-smelling vapor. Symbol, *Br;* at. no., 35; at. wt., 79.916.

bro′mism (brō′mĭz'm), *n.* *Med.* A diseased condition produced by the excessive use of bromine or its compounds.

bro′mize (-mīz), *v. t.* To treat with bromine.

bron′chi (brŏng′kī), *n., pl.* of BRONCHUS.

bron′chi·a (brŏng′kĭ·ȧ; 58), *n. pl.* [NL., fr. Gr. *bronchia,* pl.] *Anat.* The bronchial tubes, esp. the subdivisions of the bronchi. — **bron′chi·al** (-ăl), *adj.*

bron′chi·al tube. Any of the bronchi or their branches.

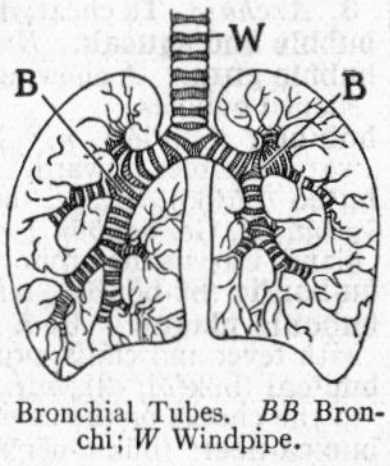

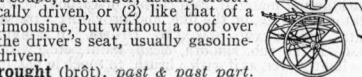

Bronchial Tubes. *BB* Bronchi; *W* Windpipe.

bron·chi′tis (brŏn·kī′tĭs; brŏng-), *n.* [NL., fr. *bronch(o)-* + *-itis.*] *Med.* Inflammation, acute or chronic, of the bronchial tubes. — **bron·chit′ic** (-kĭt′ĭk), *adj.*

bron′cho (brŏng′kō). Var. of BRONCO.

bron′cho- (brŏng′kō-). [Gr. *bronchos* windpipe.] A combining form denoting *connection with,* or *relation to, the bronchi,* as in **bron′cho·pneu·mo′ni·a, bron′cho·cele, bron′chor·rha′gi·a, bron·chos′to·my, bron·chot′o·my** (see -CELE, -RRHAGIA, -STOMY, -TOMY).

bron′cho·scope (-skōp), *n.* [*broncho-* + *-scope.*] *Med.* A narrow tubular instrument used for inspecting the large bronchi, and to remove foreign bodies from them or to treat other morbid conditions. — **bron·chos′co·py** (brŏn·kŏs′kō·pĭ; brŏng-), *n.*

bron′chus (brŏng′kŭs), *n.; pl.* -CHI (-kī). [NL., fr. Gr. *bronchos* windpipe.] *Anat.* One of the subdivisions, esp. the two primary divisions, of the trachea, or windpipe. See BRONCHIAL TUBE, *Illust.*

bron′co, bron′cho (brŏng′kō), *n.; pl.* -COS, -CHOS (-kōz). [Sp. *bronco* wild.] A small, half-wild horse or pony of western North America. Cf. CAYUSE, 2; MUSTANG.

bron′co·bust′er, bron′cho·bust′er (-bŭs′tẽr), *n.* *Slang, U. S.* One who breaks broncos; hence, a cowboy.

bron′to·sau′rus (brŏn′tō·sô′rŭs), *n.* [NL., fr. Gr *brontē* thunder + *-saurus.*] Any of a genus (*Brontosaurus,* order Sauropoda) of American Jurassic dinosaurs which attained a length of over 65 feet and a height of 12 feet. See DINOSAUR, *Illust.*

Bronx cheer (brŏngks). [From the *Bronx,* borough of N. Y. City.] *Slang, U. S.* An insulting explosive noise made with lips and tongue to express contempt. Cf. RASPBERRY, 2.

bronze (brŏnz), *n.* [F., fr. It. *bronzo,* fr. ML. *brundium.*] **1.** An alloy chiefly of copper and tin. **2.** A statue, bust, etc., of bronze. **3.** A brown, yellowish red-yellow in hue, of low saturation and medium brilliance. See COLOR. — *v. t.* To give the appearance of bronze to; to make of bronze color. — **bronz′y** (brŏn′zĭ), *adj.*

Bronze Age. **a** A period of man's cultural development following the Stone Age and characterized by varied use of bronze, as in tools, weapons, etc. **b** [*not caps.*] *Myth.* The age of violence and warfare after the silver age.

bronzed grack′le (brŏnzd). See GRACKLE.

Bronze Star Medal. *Mil., U. S.* A decoration in the form of a bronze star awarded for heroic or meritorious achievement or service, not involving aerial flight during operations against an enemy.

broo (brōō; *Scot.* brû, brü), *n.* *Scot., N. of Eng., & Ir.* Broth; juice; water.

brooch (brōch; brōōch), *n.* [Var. of BROACH, *n.*] An ornamental clasp, with a tongue, pin, or loop for attaching it.

brood (brōōd), *n.* [AS. *brōd.*] **1.** The young of animals, esp. of such as breed from eggs. **2.** **a** The young of birds, etc., hatched or cared for at one time. **b** The offspring of the same mother; progeny. **3.** A female animal kept for breeding purposes. Cf. STUD, *n.* **4.** A particular kind; species. — *v. t.* **1.** To sit on or incubate (eggs) for the purpose of hatching them; hence, to hatch. **2.** To think anxiously or moodily upon; to ponder. — *v. i.* **1.** To sit on eggs or cover young with the wings; — of hens; hence, to sit quietly, as if brooding. **2.** To dwell continuously or moodily on a subject; — usually with *over* or *on;* as, to *brood* over one's wrongs. — *adj.* Kept for breeding purposes; as, a *brood* mare. Cf. STUD, *adj.*

brood′er (-ẽr), *n.* **1.** A person or animal that broods. **2.** A building, cage, or the like, which can be artificially heated, used for raising chicks and other young fowl.

brood′y (-ĭ), *adj.* **a** Of hens, inclined to brood. **b** Contemplative; moody.

brook (brŏŏk), *n.* [AS. *brōc.*] A stream smaller than a river or creek, esp., a primary stream rising directly, as from a spring, and not fed by tributaries.

brook, *v. t.* [AS. *brūcan* to use, enjoy.] To bear; endure; tolerate; — chiefly with a negative.

brook′ite (brŏŏk′īt), *n.* *Mineral.* Titanium dioxide, TiO_2, occurring in orthorhombic crystals commonly brown and translucent, or brown to black and opaque.

brook′let (-lĕt; -lĭt), *n.* A little brook.

broom (brōōm; 85), *n.* [AS. *brōm.*] **1.** *Bot.* **a** Any of several European shrubs of the pea family; specif., the plant *Cytisus scoparius,* which has long slender branches, small leaves, and showy yellow flowers; also, any other species of *Cytisus.* **b** Any of several species of *Genista.* **2.** An implement for sweeping or brushing, originally one made of twigs of broom; a besom. — *v. t.* To sweep with or as with a broom. — **broom′y,** *adj.*

broom′corn′ (-kôrn′), *n.* A tall sorghum which has a jointed stem bearing a stiff-branched elongated panicle, used for making brooms and brushes.

broom′rape′ (-rāp′), *n.* **a** Any of various leafless herbs (family Orobanchaceae, the broomrape family, esp. genus *Orobanche*) growing as parasites on the roots of other plants. **b** = INDIAN PIPE.

broom′stick′ (-stĭk′), *n.* The handle of a broom.

brose (brōz), *n.* [ME. *brouwys, browesse.* See BREWIS.] *Scot.* A dish made by pouring some boiling liquid on meal (esp. oatmeal) and stirring it.

broth (brŏth; 74), *n.* [AS.] Liquid in which meat, and often barley, rice, etc., have been gently boiled; thin soup. — **Syn.** See SOUP.

broth′el (brŏth′ĕl; brŏth′ĕl; -′l), *n.* [ME., fr. AS. *brēothan* to ruin, destroy, past part. *brothen.*] A house of lewdness or ill fame.

broth′er (brŭth′ẽr), *n.; pl.* -ERS (-ẽrz), also BRETHREN. [AS. *brōthor.*] **1.** A male considered in his relation to another person or animal having the same parents (***whole brother***), or one parent only in common (***half brother***). Cf. SIB, *n.,* 3. **2.** A kinsman of a common family, fatherland, or race; in a more general sense, a fellow man, fellow member of a profession, trade-union, etc. **3.** *Eccl.* **a** [*cap.*] A member of one of numerous congregations of men, commonly not in holy orders, and now, esp., engaged in hospital or school work. **b** A member of a men's religious order who is not preparing for, or not yet ready for, holy orders; as, a lay *brother.* — *v. t.* To address or treat as a brother.

broth′er·hood (brŭth′ẽr·hŏŏd), *n.* **1.** State or quality of being brothers or a brother. **2.** An association for any purpose, as a society of monks; a fraternity, guild, etc. **3.** The whole body of persons engaged in the same business or profession; as, the legal *brotherhood.*

broth′er–in–law′, *n.; pl.* BROTHERS-IN-LAW. The brother of one's husband or wife; also, the husband of one's sister.

Broth′er Jon′a·than. *Humorous.* The United States.

broth′er·ly (brŭth′ẽr·lĭ), *adj.* Of or pertaining to brothers; becoming to brothers; kind; affectionate; as, *brotherly* love. — *adv.* As a brother; affectionately; kindly. — **broth′er·li·ness,** *n.*

brougham (brōōm; brōō′ŭm; brō′ŭm), *n.* [After Lord *Brougham* (1778–1868).] **1.** A light, closed carriage, with seats inside for two or four. **2.** An automobile having a closed body either (1) like that of a coupé, but larger, usually electrically driven, or (2) like that of a limousine, but without a roof over the driver's seat, usually gasoline-driven.

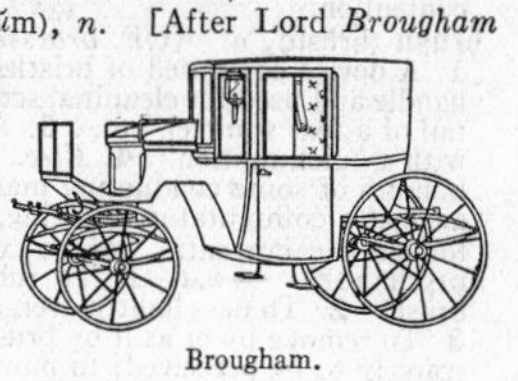
Brougham.

brought (brôt), *past & past part.* of BRING.

brow (brou), *n.* [AS. *brū.*] **1.** The eyebrow. **2.** The edge or projecting upper part of a steep place; as, the *brow* of a hill. **3.** The forehead. **4.** The general air of the countenance; formerly, effrontery; boldness.

brow antler *or* **tyne.** See ANTLER, *Illust.*

brow′beat′ (brou′bēt′), *v. t.; see* BEAT. To depress or abash with haughty, stern looks or speech; to bully.

brown (broun), *adj.* [AS. *brūn.*] Of the color brown; also, tanned or of dark complexion. — *n.* **1.** Any color of a group averaging red-yellow in hue, of low saturation and low brilliance. See COLOR. **2.** A pigment or dye that colors brown. — *v. t. & i.* To make or become brown.

brown algae. See ALGA.

brown bear. See 2d BEAR, 1.

brown Betty. A baked pudding of apples and bread crumbs in layers.

brown bread. Dark-colored bread: **a** Bread made from graham flour. **b** *U. S.* Steamed bread made usually of rye and Indian meal, graham or wheat flour, molasses, soda, and milk or water; — often called ***Boston brown bread.***

brown coal. Lignite.

brown hackle. *Angling.* An artificial fly with body of peacock herl, and bushy brown legs. Cf. FLY, *Illust.*

Brown′i·an movement *or* **motion** (broun′ĭ·ăn). [After Robert Brown (1773–1858), Scot. botanist.] The peculiar random movement exhibited by microscopic particles when suspended in liquids or gases, caused by the impact of the molecules of fluid surrounding the particle.

brown′ie (broun′ĭ), *n.* **1.** A good-natured goblin supposed to perform helpful services by night. **2.** In full **brownie scout.** A member of a division of the Girl Scouts for girls from 7 to 10 years. **3.** A kind of small chocolate cake containing nuts.

Brown′ing au′to·mat′ic ri′fle (broun′ĭng). [After the Amer. inventor John M. *Browning.*] A gas-operated, air-cooled, portable automatic machine rifle fed from a magazine and mechanically capable of firing 200 to 350 rounds a minute. Abbr. *BAR.* See RIFLE, *Illust.*

brown′ish (broun′ĭsh), *adj.* Somewhat brown.

brown′out′ (broun′out′), *n.* **a** *Australia.* A partial blackout. **b** *U. S.* A dimming of street lights and of lighting of advertising displays, store windows, theater marquees, and the like, largely for conserving fuel supplies.

brown rot. A disease of stone and pome fruits caused by certain fungi (genus *Sclerotinia,* esp. *S. fructicola*).

Brown′shirt′ (broun′shûrt′), *n.* [G. *Braunhemd.*] In Germany, a member of the Sturmabteilung.

brown′stone′ (broun′stōn′), *n.* A reddish-brown sandstone used for building.

brown study. A mood of serious absorption; reverie.

brown sugar. See SUGAR, 1.

Brown Swiss. An animal of a hardy breed of dairy cattle.

brown′–tail′ moth. Also **brown′tail′** (broun′tāl′), *n.* A tussock moth (*Euproctis chrysorrhea*) injurious to trees.

browse (brouz), *n.* [OF. *brost, broust,* sprout, shoot.] Tender shoots, twigs, and leaves, fit for food for cattle. — *v. t. & i.* **1.** To eat or nibble off as browse. **2.** To graze. **3.** To read here and there in a book or in a library. **4.** To casually inspect goods offered for sale, as in a store. — **brows′er** (brouz′ẽr), *n.*

bru′cel·lo′sis (brōō′sĕ·lō′sĭs), *n.* [NL., fr. *Brucella*, a genus of bacteria + *-osis.*] *Med.* Undulant fever.

bruc′ine (brōōs′ēn; -ĭn), *n.* Also **bruc′in** (-ĭn). [After James *Bruce*, Scot. traveler.] *Pharm.* A poisonous alkaloid, $C_{23}H_{26}N_2O_4$, found, with strychnine, in the seeds of nux vomica and other plants of the genus *Strychnos.* See STRYCHNOS.

bru′in (brōō′ĭn), *n.* [D., brown.] A bear.

bruise (brōōz), *v. t.* [AS. *brȳsan* and OF. *bruisier* to break, shiver, of Celt. origin.] **1.** To inflict a bruise on; to contuse. **2.** To crush, as in a mortar; to pulverize. **3.** Figuratively, to wound or hurt, as the feelings. — *v. i.* **1.** To inflict a bruise or bruises. **2.** To show the effects of bruises. — *n.* **1.** A surface injury to flesh, without laceration, produced by a blunt instrument or a collision; a contusion. **2.** An injury, as to the feelings.

bruis′er (brōōz′ẽr), *n.* A professional boxer; a pugilist.

bruit (brōōt), *n.* [F., fr. LL. *rugitus* a roar, and the source of F. *braire.*] *Archaic.* **a** Clamor; din. **b** Report; rumor. — *v. t Now Chiefly Passive.* To rumor or noise.

brul′yie, brul′zie (brōōl′ĭ; brül′yĭ), *n.* [See BROIL a brawl.] *Scot. & N. of Eng.* A disturbance; a broil.

‖**Bru′maire′** (brü′mâr′), *n.* [F.] See REVOLUTIONARY CALENDAR.

bru′mal (brōō′măl), *adj.* [L. *brumalis*, fr. *bruma* winter.] Of or pertaining to winter; winterlike.

brume (brōōm), *n.* [F., mist, winter, fr. L. *bruma* winter.] *Poetic.* Mist; fog. — **bru′mous** (brōō′mŭs), *adj.*

brum′ma·gem (brŭm′ȧ·jĕm), *adj.* [From *Birmingham*, Eng., a great manufactory of gilt toys, etc.] *Slang.* Showy but trashy.

bru·net′, bru·nette′ (brōō·nĕt′), *adj.* [F. *brunet, brunette*, dim. of *brun*, fem. *brune*, brown, fr. OHG. *brūn.*] Of dark complexion and brown or black hair and eyes.

bru·net′, *n. masc.*, **bru·nette′**, *fem.* A person displaying predominant brunet traits.

Brun′hild (brōōn′hĭlt), *n.* [G. *Brunhilde.*] In the *Nibelungenlied*, a queen whom Siegfried wins and tames for Gunther. When she learns the deceit from Siegfried's wife, Kriemhild, she induces Hagen to murder Siegfried.

Brünn·hil′de (brün·hĭl′dĕ), *n.* See SIEGFRIED.

brunt (brŭnt), *n.* **1.** *Obs.* An onset; attack. **2.** The force (of a blow) or the shock (of an attack); also, the chief stress or strain in any contention.

brush (brŭsh), *n.* [OF. *broisse* (F. *brosse*), prob. of Teut. origin.] **1.** A device composed of bristles, wire, etc., set in a suitable back or handle and used for cleaning, scrubbing, painting, etc. **2.** The bushy tail of a fox, squirrel, etc. **3.** Act of brushing; a rubbing or grazing with a quick motion. **4.** *Elec.* **a** One of two or more plates, rods, or bundles of some conducting material, esp. copper or carbon, bearing against a commutator, slip ring, or the like, and providing a passage for electric current. See DYNAMO, MAGNETO, *Illusts.* **b** = BRUSH DISCHARGE. — *v. t.* **1.** To rub, smooth, clean, paint, etc., with a brush. **2.** To pass lightly over, as if with a brush; to touch in passing. **3.** To remove by or as if by brushing. — *v. i.* To move so lightly as scarcely to be perceived; to move so as to graze, skim over, or sweep anything. — **brush′y**, *adj.*

brush, *n.* [OF. *broche, broce, brouce.*] **1.** Branches of trees lopped off; brushwood. **2.** A thicket of shrubs, bushes, small trees, etc. — **brush′y**, *adj.*

brush, *v. i.* [ME. *bruschen* to rush.] To move nimbly in haste; to rush. — *n.* A short, brisk skirmish. — **Syn.** See ENCOUNTER.

brush discharge. A luminous, feathery discharge of electricity between two terminals, with a hissing sound but without a spark.

brush′-off′ (brŭsh′ôf′), *n.* Also **brush′off′**. A curt or offhand dismissal; as, to give an applicant the *brush-off.*

brush′wood′ (brŭsh′wŏŏd′), *n.* [From BRUSH branches.] The wood of small branches, esp. when cut or broken; also, a thicket of shrubs and small trees.

brusk. Var. of BRUSQUE.

brusque (brŭsk; *F.* brüsk), *adj.* [F., fr. It. *brusco* brusque, rough, fr. L. *bruscum, bruscus*, butcher's-broom.] Rough and short in manner; abrupt. — **Syn.** See BLUFF. — **brusque′ly**, *adv.* — **brusque′ness**, *n.*

‖**brus′que·rie′** (brüs′kĕ·rē′), *n.* [F.] Brusqueness.

Brus′sels car′pet (brŭs′′lz). [From *Brussels*, Belgium.] A carpet made of colored worsted yarns fixed in a web of strong linen thread. The worsted is drawn up in loops to form the pattern.

Brussels lace. Any lace made in Brussels; specif., a kind of bobbin lace in which the pattern is made first, and the ground put in around it afterwards.

Brussels sprouts. The edible small green heads, or "sprouts," borne on the stem of the plant *Brassica oleracea gemmifera;* also, the plant. See CABBAGE.

‖**brut** (brüt), *adj.* [F.] Of wines, dry; specif., of champagne, with one per cent or less of liqueur.

bru′tal (brōō′tăl; -t′l), *adj.* Of or pertaining to a brute; brutish; hence, savage; cruel; also, coarse; gross. — **bru′tal·ly**, *adv.*

bru·tal′i·ty (brōō·tăl′ĭ·tĭ), *n.; pl.* -TIES (-tĭz). State or quality of being brutal; savageness; also, a brutal act.

bru′tal·ize (brōō′tăl·īz), *v. t.* **1.** To make brutal, unfeeling, or inhuman. **2.** To treat brutally. — *v. i.* To become like a brute. — **bru′tal·i·za′tion** (-ĭ·zā′shŭn; -ī·zā′-), *n.*

brute (brōōt), *adj.* [F. *brut*, masc., *brute*, fem., rough, rude, fr. L. *brutus* irrational.] **1.** Not possessing reason; unthinking; as, a *brute* beast. **2.** Without life or sensibility; inanimate; soulless; as, the *brute* powers of nature. **3.** Of, relating to, or characteristic of a brute beast; hence: **a** Brutal; cruel; savage. **b** Coarse; sensual. — *n.* **1.** A beast. **2.** A brutal person. **3.** The animal passions and appetites in man. — **Syn.** Animal, beast.

bru′ti·fy (brōō′tĭ·fī), *v. t. & i.* To brutalize.

brut′ish (brōōt′ĭsh), *adj.* Of, relating to, or like a brute or brutes; irrational; stupid; gross. — **brut′ish·ly**, *adv.* — **brut′ish·ness**, *n.*

Bryn′hild (brün′hĭlt), *n.* [ON. *Brynhildr.*] *Norse Myth.* A Valkyrie who, disobeying Odin, is condemned to become a mortal. Sigurd wakes her from her enchanted sleep but afterwards forgets her and marries Gudrun. Brynhild procures the murder of Sigurd, but slays herself with the same sword and is burned on the same pyre.

bry·ol′o·gy (brī·ŏl′ō·jĭ), *n.* [Gr. *bryon* moss + *-logy.*] The branch of botany which relates to the bryophytes (mosses and liverworts). — **bry′o·log′i·cal** (brī′ō·lŏj′ĭ·kăl), *adj.* — **bry·ol′o·gist** (brī·ŏl′ō·jĭst), *n.*

bry′o·ny (brī′ō·nĭ), *n.; pl.* -NIES (-nĭz). [L. *bryonia*, fr. Gr. *bryōnia*, fr. *bryein* to swell.] Any of a genus (*Bryonia*) of tendril-bearing vines of the gourd family, with large leaves and red or black fruit, as ***white bryony*** (*B. alba*).

bry′o·phyte (-fīt), *n.* [Gr. *bryon* moss + *-phyte.*] Any of the mosses or liverworts (phylum Bryophyta). — **bry′o·phyt′ic** (-fĭt′ĭk), *adj.*

bry′o·zo′an (brī′ō·zō′ăn), *adj.* [Gr. *bryon* moss + *zōē* life.] *Zool.* Belonging to a class (Bryozoa) of aquatic, mostly marine, animals which reproduce by budding and usually form permanently attached colonies, often of a branched, mosslike form. — **bry′o·zo′an**, *n.*

Bryth′on (brĭth′ŏn), *n.* [W.] A member of the British branch of Celts; a Briton; a Cymric-speaking Celt.

Bry·thon′ic (brĭ·thŏn′ĭk), *adj.* **1.** Of or pert. to the Brythons. **2.** Of, pert. to, or designating that division of the Celtic languages including Welsh, Cornish, and Breton. Cf. GOIDELIC — *n.* The Cymric or Brythonic branch of the Celtic languages. See INDO-EUROPEAN LANGUAGES, *Table.*

bu′ba·lis (bū′bȧ·lĭs), *n.* Also **bu′bal, bu′bale** (-băl). [NL. *bubalis*, fr. Gr. *boubalis* an African antelope.] A large antelope (*Alcelaphus buselaphus*) of Egypt, the Sahara, Arabia, and Syria, closely related to the hartebeest.

bub′ble (bŭb′′l), *n.* **1.** A globule of air or gas within a liquid. **2.** A thin film of liquid inflated with air or gas; as, to blow soap *bubbles.* **3.** A globule of air, or a globular vacuum, in a transparent solid; as, *bubbles* in window glass. **4.** Anything that wants firmness, solidity, or reality; a false show; a delusive scheme. **5.** A bubbling, as of boiling or flowing water; also, a sound like that of bubbling. **6.** A burp by a baby. — *v. i.;* BUB′BLED (-′ld); BUB′BLING (-lĭng). **1.** To rise in, or form, bubbles; to foam. **2.** To run or pour out with a gurgling noise, as if forming bubbles. **3.** To burp; — said of a baby. — *v. t.* **1.** To send out in, or as in, bubbles; to cause to bubble. **2.** To burp (a baby). **3.** *Archaic.* To cheat; deceive; delude. — **bub′bly** (-lĭ), *adj.*

bubble and squeak. *Eng.* Beef and cabbage fried together.

bubble gum. A chewing gum which can be blown into large balloon-shaped bubbles.

bub′bler (bŭb′lẽr), *n.* A drinking fountain from which a stream of water bubbles upward.

bu′bo (bū′bō), *n.; pl.* -BOES (-bōz). [LL., the groin, swelling in the groin, fr. Gr. *boubōn.*] *Med.* An inflammatory swelling of a lymph gland, esp. in the groin.

bu·bon′ic (bū·bŏn′ĭk), *adj.* Of, or attended with, buboes.

bubonic plague. *Med.* A pestilence in which sufferers are afflicted with fever and chills, prostration, and buboes.

buc′cal (bŭk′ăl; -′l), *adj.* [L. *bucca* cheek.] *Anat.* Of or pertaining to the cheeks or the cavity of the mouth.

buc′ca·neer′ (bŭk′ȧ·nēr′), *n.* [F. *boucanier*, fr. *boucaner* to smoke meat on a wooden frame.] A pirate; esp., one of the freebooters preying upon early Spanish-American vessels and settlements, in the 17th and 18th centuries.

bu·cen′taur (bū·sĕn′tôr), *n.* [Gr. *bous* ox + *kentauros* centaur.] **1.** A fabulous monster, half ox, half man. **2.** [It. *bucentoro.*] State barge of Venice, used annually by the doge in the ceremony of the marriage of the Adriatic.

Bu·ceph′a·lus (bū·sĕf′ȧ·lŭs), *n.* [L., fr. Gr. *boukephalos*, lit., ox-headed.] The war horse of Alexander the Great.

buck (bŭk), *n.* *Now Dial.* **1.** Lye or suds in which clothes are washed. **2.** The cloth, clothes, etc., so washed; a wash. — *v. t. Now Dial.* To wash (clothes) in lye or suds.

buck, *n.* [AS. *bucca, buc*, he-goat.] **1.** The male of deer or antelopes, or of goats, hares, rabbits, and rats; — not properly applied to the male of the elk or moose (called *bull*) or red deer (which see). **2.** A dashing fellow; a dandy. **3.** *Colloq., U. S.* A male Indian or Negro. **4.** [From the verb.] The act, or an instance, of bucking; specif., *Amer. Football*, a charge into the opposing rush line. **5.** *Poker.* A counter or other object, possession of which by the dealer requires a jack pot. The buck goes to the winner of each jack pot. Hence, ***to pass the buck***, to shift a responsibility to someone else.

buck, *v. i.* **1.** To spring with a quick plunging leap; — said of a horse or mule. **2.** *Colloq., U. S.* To charge against something as if butting; as, to *buck* against fate. **3.** *Colloq.* To start or move jerkily, as an engine. — *v. t.* **1.** To throw by bucking. **2.** *Colloq.* To butt; also, to oppose; resist. **3.** *Amer. Football* To charge into (the opponents' line). — **buck′er**, *n.*

buck up. *Colloq.* **a** To dress up. **b** To take heart.

buck (bŭk), *adj.* Male; as, *buck* shad.

buck, *n.* [D. *zaagbok* sawbuck.] **1.** *U. S.* A sawhorse; a sawbuck. **2.** *Gymnastics.* A short, thick, leather-covered vaulting block, usually adjustable for height.

buck, *n.* *Slang, U. S.* A dollar.

buck and wing. An American Negro clog dance with winglike steps.

buck′a·roo′ (bŭk′ȧ·rōō′; bŭk′ȧ·rōō′), *n.* Also **buck·ay′ro** (bŭk·ā′rō). [Corrupt. of Amer. Sp. *vaquero* cowboy.] *Western U. S. & Canada.* A broncobuster; a cowboy.

buck bean. A plant (*Menyanthes trifoliata*) growing in bogs, and having racemes of white or purplish flowers.

buck′board′ (bŭk′bōrd′; 70), *n.* A four-wheeled driving vehicle having a springy platform carrying the seat.

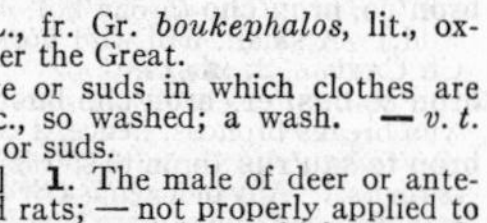
Buckboard.

buck·een′ (bŭk·ēn′), *n.* In Ireland, a young man aping the style of living of the rich.

buck′et (bŭk′ĕt; -ĭt), *n.* [OF. *buket*, fr. AS. *būc* vessel, pitcher.] **1.** A vessel for catching, holding, or carrying water, sap, or other liquids, or salt, coal, ashes, etc.; a pail. **2.** Hence, something resembling a bucket, as one of the cups of an endless-belt type of conveyer, the valved piston of a lifting pump, the scoop of a dredge, etc. — *v. t.* **1.** To draw or lift in or as if in buckets. **2.** To ride (a horse) hard or mercilessly; hence, *Colloq.*, to drive or push forward hurriedly. — *v. i.* **1.** *Colloq., Eng.* To drive or push forward rapidly; to hurry. **2.** *Stock Dealing.* To deal with (an order) in or as in a bucket shop. — **buck′et·ful**, *n.*

bucket seat. A low separate seat with rounded back, for one person, often hinged for tipping or folding forward, chiefly used in automobiles and airplanes.

bucket shop. An office where facilities are given for making bets in the form of orders or options based on current exchange prices of securities or commodities, without any actual buying or selling of the property.

buck′eye′ (bŭk′ī′), *n.* [*buck* animal + *eye;* — from the appearance of the seed.] **1.** Any of several shrubs and trees of the same genus (*Aesculus*) as the horse chestnut, esp. *A. glabra.* **2.** [*cap.*] *Colloq., U.S.* A native of Ohio, the **Buckeye State**; — a nickname.

buck fever. *Colloq., U.S.* Excitement at the sight of game, such as often unnerves a novice in hunting.

buck′hound′ (bŭk′hound′), *n.* The Scottish deerhound.

buck′ish, *adj.* Dandified; impetuous. — **buck′ish·ly,** *adv.*

buck′le (bŭk′'l), *n.* [OF. *bocle, boucle,* boss of a shield, fr L. *buccula,* dim. of *bucca* cheek; this boss resembling a cheek.] **1.** A fastening for two loose ends, as of a belt or strap. **2.** A similar device of ornamental design, as on women's shoes. **3.** *Archaic.* A crisp curl of hair. — *v. t.;* BUCK′LED (-'ld); BUCK′LING (-lĭng). **1.** To fasten with a buckle. **2.** To apply (oneself) with vigor. — *v. i.* **1.** To prepare oneself for an undertaking, as, orig., by buckling on the armor; hence, to apply oneself with vigor; — often with *to* or *down to.* **2.** To struggle; grapple; contend.

buck′le, *v. t. & i.* To bend permanently; to become distorted; to crumple up; as, the freight train *buckled* in the middle. — *n.* A distortion, as a bulge, bend, kink, or twist in a beam, a tube, etc.

buck′ler (bŭk′lẽr), *n.* [OF. *boucler* a shield with a boss, fr. *bocle, boucle,* boss. See 1st BUCKLE.] **1.** A kind of shield worn on one of the arms to protect the front of the body. **2.** Figuratively, one who or that which protects or defends. — *v. t.* To shield or defend.

buck′o (bŭk′ō), *n.; pl.* BUCKOES (-ōz). A bully.

buck private. *Slang, U.S.* A private soldier, esp. a new recruit.

buck′ra (bŭk′rȧ), *n.* [In a Calabar coast dial. *mākara, mbākara.*] A white man; master. — *adj.* White; white man's; strong; good. *Both Orig. Negro Dial.*

buck′ram (bŭk′răm), *n.* [OF. *boquerant,* fr. Per *Buchāra* Bokhara] **1.** Formerly, a fabric of fine linen or cotton for garments **2. a** A coarse cloth of linen or hemp, stiffened with sizing. **b** A similar cloth of cotton, used for binding books, for wrappers, etc. **3.** Stiffness; precise formality. — *adj.* Made of buckram; hence, stiff; precise. — *v. t.* To strengthen with buckram; also, to make pretentious.

buck′saw′ (bŭk′sô′), *n.* A saw set in a deep H-shaped frame, used for sawing wood on a sawbuck, or sawhorse. See SAW, *Illust.*

buck′shee (bŭk′shē; bŭk′shē′), *adj.* [See BAKSHEESH.] *Brit. Army Slang.* Free of charge; gratis.

buck′shot′ (bŭk′shŏt′), *n.* A coarse leaden shot for large game, between .24 and .36 inch in diameter.

buck′skin′ (bŭk′skĭn′), *n.* **1.** The skin of a buck. **2.** A strong soft leather, usually yellowish or grayish. **3.** Cream-white, closely woven woolen cloth (**buckskin cloth**). **4. a** *pl.* Breeches made of buckskin. **b** A person clothed in buckskin, esp. [*cap.*] an American soldier of the Revolutionary War. **c** A buckskin-colored horse. — **buck′skin′,** *adj.*

buck′tail′ (-tāl′), *n.* *Angling.* An artificial fly made of hairs from the tail of a deer, or similar material. See LURE, *Illust.*

buck′thorn′ (-thôrn′), *n.* **1.** Any of a genus (*Rhamnus,* type of the family Rhamnaceae, the buckthorn family) of trees or shrubs, some of which have thorny branches. See CASCARA, 1. **2.** A tree (*Bumelia lycioides*) of the southern United States, of the sapodilla family.

buck′tooth′ (-tōōth′), *n.* Any tooth that juts out.

buck′wheat′ (-hwēt′), *n.* [*buck* beech tree + *wheat.*] **1.** An herb of the genus *Fagopyrum* typifying a family (Polygonaceae, the buckwheat family) characterized by mostly entire leaves with stipules forming a sheath around the stem, and apetalous flowers arranged in spikes. It is cultivated as a food plant. **2.** The triangular seed of this plant ground into flour (**buckwheat flour**).

bu·col′ic (bū·kŏl′ĭk), *adj.* [L. *bucolicus,* fr. Gr. *boukolikos,* fr. *boukolos* cowherd, herdsman.] Pastoral; rustic. — **Syn.** See RURAL — *n.* **1.** A pastoral poem; an eclogue or idyl. **2.** *Humorous.* A rustic; a farmer. — **bu·col′i·cal** (-ĭ·kăl), *adj.* — **bu·col′i·cal·ly,** *adv.*

bud (bŭd), *n.* [ME. *budde.*] **1.** *Bot.* An undeveloped shoot or stem; a small axillary or terminal protuberance on the stem of a plant, consisting of rudimentary foliage or floral leaves. Cf. CION. **2.** A person or thing not yet mature. **3.** *Bot. & Zool.* A protuberance of a part of the body which develops into a new organism; a gemma. — *v. i.;* BUD′DED; BUD′DING. To put forth buds; to develop, as a bud; hence, to be like a bud in youth and freshness, or growth and promise. — *v. t.* **1.** To put forth as buds; to cause to bud. **2.** *Hort.* To insert a bud of (a specified variety, etc.) into an opening in the bark of a different stock, esp. for propagating desired varieties; as, to *bud* a rose. Cf. GRAFT, *v. t.,* 1. — **bud′der,** *n.*

Bud′dha (bŏŏd′ȧ), *n.* [Skr. *buddha* awakened, enlightened.] The title of an incarnation of self-abnegation, virtue, and wisdom, in the form of a religious teacher of the Buddhists who has been deified, esp. Gautama Siddhartha (563–483 B.C.), founder of Buddhism.

Bud′dhism (-ĭz'm), *n.* The religion of central and eastern Asia based upon the doctrine of Gautama Buddha teaching that *nirvana,* escape from liability to suffering and from mortality, is the highest goal attainable, and that the way of escape is the "Eightfold Path" of right belief, right resolve, right word, right act, right life, right effort, right thinking, right meditation. — **Bud′dhist** (-ĭst), *n. & adj.* — **Bud·dhis′tic** (bŏŏd·ĭs′tĭk), *adj.*

bud′dle (bŭd′'l; *dial.* bŏŏd′'l), *n.* [E. *dial.,* to cleanse ore, also a vessel for this purpose.] *Mining.* An inclined trough or plane on which crushed ore is washed.

bud·dle′ia (bŭd·lē′ȧ; bŭd′lē·ȧ), *n.* [NL., after Adam *Buddle* (d. 1715), Eng. botanist.] Any of a genus (*Buddleia*) of showy shrubs or trees (family Loganiaceae) of warm regions, with clusters of yellow or violet flowers.

bud′dy (bŭd′ĭ), *n.; pl.* -DIES (-ĭz). *Colloq., U.S.* Companion; mate pal.

budge (bŭj), *n.* A fur prepared from lambskin dressed with the wool outward. — *adj.* **1.** Lined with budge, as a scholar's gown. **2.** *Dial.* Austere; pompous; solemn.

budge (bŭj), *v. t. & i.;* BUDGED (bŭjd); BUDG′ING (bŭj′ĭng). [F. *bouger* to stir, fr. L. *bullire.* See BOIL, *v.*] To move or stir in spite of inertia or disinclination; — usually with a negative.

budg′er·i·gar′ (bŭj′ẽr·ē·gär′), *n.* [Australian (Port Jackson dial.), fr. *budgeri* good + *ga, gar,* bird.] An Australian parakeet (*Melopsittacus undulatus*) that has become a popular cage bird, often taught to talk and bred in a great variety of colors and patterns.

budg′et (bŭj′ĕt; -ĭt), *n.* [F. *bougette* bag, wallet, dim. of OF. *boge, bouge,* leather bag, fr. L. *bulga.*] **1.** A bag or sack with its contents; hence, a stock or store. **2.** A financial statement of estimated income and expenses of a country for a period of time; also, a plan for financing a government, based on such a statement. **3.** A similar statement or plan in a state or city government, a business, or the like. **4.** Loosely, the cost of operation, living, etc.; as, a minimum weekly *budget* for a family of five. — *v. t.* To put or allow for in a budget. — **budg′et·ar′y** (bŭj′ĕ·tẽr′ĭ *or, esp. Brit.,* -tẽr·ĭ), *adj.* — **budg′et·er,** *n.*

budg′ie (bŭj′ĭ). Short for BUDGERIGAR.

bud scale *or* **sheath.** *Bot.* One of the scalelike leaves which form the external covering of a bud in winter. They often have dense coatings of hair, gum, or resin.

bud sport. A bud mutation or variation.

bud variation. *Biol. & Hort.* Marked deviation from the normal in the development of a shoot from the bud; a sport developed from a bud, as a red-flowered branch on a white-flowered plant. Bud variation involving genetic change is called **bud mutation.**

buff (bŭf), *n.* [Formerly *buffe* buff, buffalo, fr. F. *buffle* buffalo.] **1.** A superior leather prepared from the skin of the buffalo, or of the ox, elk, etc. **2.** A military coat of buff leather. **3.** *Colloq.* The bare skin; as, to strip to the *buff.* **4.** A color, yellowish red-yellow in hue, of medium saturation and high brilliance. See COLOR. **5.** A stick of wood covered with leather and used in buffing or polishing. **6.** A buffing wheel. — *adj.* **1.** Made of or like buff. **2.** Of the color of buff. — *v. t.* **1.** To polish with a buff, buffer, buffing wheel, or the like. **2.** To give a buff or velvety surface to (leather); also, to color or stain buff.

buff, *n.* [OF. *buffe.* See BUFFET a blow.] A buffet; a blow. *Now Dial.,* exc. in "blindman's *buff.*"

buf′fa·lo (bŭf′ȧ·lō), *n.; pl.* -LOES, -LOS (-lōz), -LO. [Pg. *búfalo* or It. *buffalo, bufalo,* fr. L. *bufalus, bubalis,* a kind of African stag or gazelle, also the buffalo or wild ox, fr. Gr. *boubalos,* fr. *bous* ox.] **1.** Any of several species of wild ox, as the ***water buffalo*** (*Bubalus bubalis*) of India, now domesticated in most of the warm parts of Asia and adjacent islands, the ***Cape buffalo*** (*Syncerus caffer*) of Africa, and the American bison (see BISON). **2. a** A robe of buffalo skin. **b** A buffalo fish. — *v. t. Slang, U.S.* To bamboozle; bluff.

buffalo berry. a The edible scarlet berry of either of two shrubs (*Shepherdia argentea* and *S. canadensis,* family Elaeagnaceae) of the western United States, having silvery foliage. **b** Either of these shrubs; — called also **buffalo bush.**

buffalo bug. = CARPET BEETLE.

buffalo fish. Any of several large fishes of the sucker family, found chiefly in the Mississippi Valley.

buffalo grass. A low-growing grass (*Buchloë dactyloides*) very common on former feeding grounds of the bison in the western United States.

buffalo moth. The larva of the carpet beetle (which see).

buff′er (bŭf′ẽr), *n.* [From BUFF to deaden the shock. See BUFFET a blow.] Anything, such as a fender or bumper, serving to deaden a shock or bear the brunt of a collision.

buff′er, *n.* A worker or machine that buffs or polishes something; specif., a polisher, as for fingernails.

buffer state A small independent state lying between two larger, usually rival, states.

buf′fet (bŭf′ĕt; -ĭt), *n.* [OF., a slap in the face, fr. *buffe* blow.] A blow, as with the hand; a slap. — *v. t.* **1.** To strike; slap. **2.** To strike repeatedly; also, to strive with or contend against. — *v. i.* **1.** To strike; contend. **2.** To make one's way, as by blows or struggling. — **buf′fet·er,** *n.*

buf·fet′ (bŏŏ·fā′; bŭ·fā′; bōō·fā′; *Brit. usu.* bŭf′ĕt, -ĭt *for senses* 1 & 2, bōōf′ā *for sense* 3), *n.* [F.] **1.** A sideboard, often without a mirror. **2.** A cupboard or set of shelves for the display of plate, china, etc. **3.** A counter for refreshments, as at a railroad station. — (bōō·fā′; bŭ·fā′; bōō·fā′; *see the noun*), *adj.* Served from a buffet rather than at a table; hence, without formal service; as, a *buffet* supper.

buff′ing wheel (bŭf′ĭng). *Mach.* A wheel covered with buff leather, muslin, or the like, and used in polishing metal products.

buf′fle·head′ (bŭf′'l·hĕd′), *n.* [From obs. *buffle* buffalo + *head.*] A small North American duck (*Charitonetta albeola*), allied to the goldeneye.

‖**buf′fo** (bōōf′fō), *n. masc.; pl.* BUFFI (-fē). [It.] A male singer of comic roles in opera, often a basso.

buf·foon′ (bŭ·fōōn′; bŭ-), *n.* [F. *bouffon,* fr. It. *buffone.*] A man who makes a business of amusing others by tricks, ludicrous gestures, etc.; a clown. — **Syn.** Fool, zany, jester. — **buf·foon′er·y** (-ẽr·ĭ), *n.* — **buf·foon′ish,** *adj.*

bug (bŭg), *n.* [ME. *bugge;* akin to E. *big.*] **1.** *Obs.* A bugbear; bogy. **2. a** *U.S. & Dial. Eng.* In popular language, an insect of almost any kind, esp. a beetle, or an insect which creeps or crawls like a beetle; as, the potato *bug.* **b** The bedbug. **c** *Slang.* A microorganism, esp. one producing disease. **3.** *Slang, U.S.* A defect in apparatus or in its operation.

bug′a·boo′ (bŭg′ȧ·bōō′), *n.* [*bug* goblin + *boo,* interj.] An imaginary object of fright; a bugbear; a bogy.

bug′bane′ (bŭg′bān′), *n.* A perennial herb (*Cimicifuga racemosa*) with flowers supposed to be distasteful to insects.

bug′bear′ (-bâr′), *n.* [*bug* goblin + *bear* the animal.] An imaginary goblin or specter, used to excite needless fear, as in children; now, any object of dread.

bug′ger (bŭg′ẽr; bŏŏg′-), *n.* [F. *bougre,* fr. ML. *Bulgarus* a Bulgarian, also a heretic, sodomite.] **1.** A sodomite. **2.** A low wretch; also, sportively, chap; person.

bug′ger·y (-ĭ), *n.* Sodomy.

bug′gy (bŭg′ĭ), *adj.* Infested with bugs.

bug′gy, *n.; pl.* -GIES (-ĭz). A light single-seated, usually one-horse vehicle or carriage having four wheels (U. S. type) or two wheels (English type).

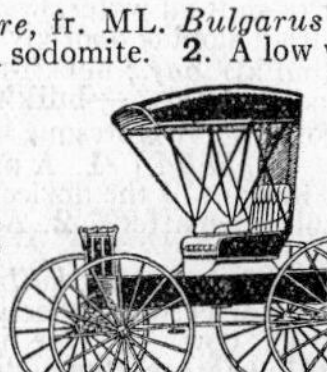

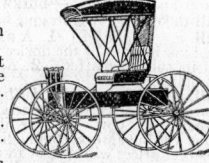

Buggy.

bug′house′ (bŭg′hous′), *n. Slang, U.S.* An insane asylum. — *adj. Slang, U.S.* Insane.

bu′gle (bū′g'l), *n.* [F., fr. L. *bugula.*] Any of a genus (*Ajuga,* esp. *A. reptans*) of plants of the mint family, with spikes of blue flowers, adventive in the United States.

bu′gle, *n.* [OF., fr. L. *buculus* a steer, dim. of *bos* ox.] **1.** A horn used by hunters. **2.** *Music.* A brass-wind instrument with a cupped mouthpiece like the trumpet but having a shorter and more conical tube. It is sometimes keyed. — *v. i. & t.*; BU'GLED (-g'ld); BU'GLING (-glĭng). To sound a bugle; to summon by or as by a bugle call. — **bu'gler** (bū'glẽr), *n.*

bu'gle (bū'g'l), *n.* A long glass bead, often black, used in a dress trimming. — **bu'gle**, *adj.* — **bu'gled** (-g'ld), *adj.*

bu'gle·weed' (bū'g'l·wēd'), *n.* **a** Any of a genus (*Lycopus*) of mints, esp. one (*L. virginicus*) which is mildly narcotic and astringent. **b** The wild indigo *Baptisia tinctoria.*

bu'gloss (bū'glŏs), *n.* [Through F. & L. fr. Gr. *bouglōssos* oxtongue, fr. *bous* ox + *glōssa* tongue.] Any of a genus (*Anchusa*, esp. *A. officinalis*) of rough-hairy plants of the borage family.

bug'seed' (bŭg'sēd'), *n.* A fleshy annual herb (*Corispermum hyssopifolium*) having flat, oval seeds.

buhl (bōōl), **buhl'work'** (-wûrk'), *n.* [After A. C. *Boulle* (1642–1732), French cabinetmaker.] *Furniture.* Decoration in which tortoise shell, yellow metal, white metal, etc., are inlaid, forming scrolls and other designs; also, an article so decorated.

buhr (bûr). Var. of 2d BURR, buhrstone.

buhr'stone', **burr'stone'** (bûr'stōn'), *n.* Any siliceous rock used for millstones; also, a millstone cut from such rock.

build (bĭld), *v. t.*; BUILT (bĭlt); BUILD'ING. *Archaic past & past part.* BUILD'ED. [AS. *byldan* to build, fr. *bold* house.] **1.** To unite materials in order to fabricate or make; erect; construct. **2.** To create or produce gradually as a result of effort, system, etc.; as, to *build* up a practice. **3.** To establish; found; as, to *build* an argument on facts. — *v. i.* **1.** To perform the act, or to practice the business, of building something. **2.** To rest or depend, as on a foundation; rely. — *n.* Form or mode of construction; general figure; make. — **build'er**, *n.*

build'er's knot. See KNOT, *Illust.* (23).

build'ing, *n.* **1.** A structure which is built, esp. for permanent use, as a house, factory, etc. Abbr. *bldg.* **2.** The art or the work of assembling materials into such structures.

buird'ly (bürd'lĭ), *adj. Scot.* Strong; athletic.

bulb (bŭlb), *n.* [L. *bulbus*, fr. (or akin to) Gr. *bolbos.*] **1.** A bud, usually underground, consisting of a short, thick stem sending out roots from below, and bearing overlapping, scalelike leaves, as in the lily, onion, or tulip. **2.** A fleshy tuber or corm resembling a bulb; as, a dahlia *bulb.* **3.** Any plant or flower having a bulb or developing from a bulb. **4.** A bulb-shaped part; as, the *bulb* of a thermometer; the *bulb* of a horse's hoof (see HOOF, *Illust.*); specif., *Anat.*: **a** A rounded mass, part, or end enlargement; as, the *bulb* of the urethra. **b** The medulla oblongata. **5.** A detachable incandescent lamp (see INCANDESCENT LAMP, *Illust.*); also, an electron tube. — **bul·ba'ceous** (bŭl·bā'shŭs), *adj.* — **bulb'ar** (bŭl'bẽr), *adj.* — **bulb·if'er·ous** *adj.* — **bulb'ous**, *adj.*

bul'bil (bŭl'bĭl), *n.* A small or secondary bulb; esp., an aerial deciduous bud, produced in the leaf axils, as in the tiger lily, or replacing the flowers, as in some onions.

bul'bul (bōōl'bōōl), *n.* [Per. & Ar.] **1.** A Persian songbird, probably a kind of nightingale (*Luscinia golzii*). **2.** Any of a group of Asiatic or East African oscine birds (family Pycnonotidae), feeding on fruits, berries, and insects.

Bul·gar'i·an (bŭl·gâr'ĭ·ăn; bōōl-), *n.* Also **Bul'gar** (bŭl'gär; bōōl'-). **1.** One of the people of Bulgaria, linguistically related to the eastern branch of the Slavs. **2.** The language of the Bulgarians, written in a modified Russian alphabet. See INDO-EUROPEAN LANGUAGES, *Table.* — *adj.* Of or pertaining to Bulgaria, the Bulgarians, or their language.

bulge (bŭlj), *n.* [OF. *boulge, bouge*, fr. L. *bulga* leathern bag.] **1.** The bilge of a vessel, or of a cask. **2.** A swelling, protuberant part, as in a wall. **3.** *Nav.* A watertight structure added outside the hull of a vessel to protect it, as against torpedoes or mines; a blister. **4.** *Slang.* Advantage, esp. one slight but telling; — chiefly in ***to get, or have, the bulge on.*** — **Syn.** See PROJECTION. — *v. i. & t.*; BULGED (bŭljd); BULG'ING (bŭl'jĭng). To be, or cause to be, protuberant; to bend outward; to swell or jut out.

bu·lim'i·a (bū·lĭm'ĭ·ȧ), *n.* [NL., fr. Gr., fr. *bous* ox + *limos* hunger.] A disease characterized by perpetual, insatiable hunger. — **bu·lim'ic** (-ĭk), **bu·lim'i·ac** (-ĭ·ăk), *adj.*

bulk (bŭlk), *n.* [ME. *bulke, bolke*, fr. ON. *bulki* heap, cargo.] **1.** *Now Rare.* **a** Heap; pile. **b** Body, trunk, or frame. **2.** Magnitude; volume; greatness of size; as, to increase in *bulk.* **3.** A mass; an aggregate; — esp. in ***in bulk***, a mass of some product not packaged, bottled, etc., for the trade. **4.** The largest or major portion; as, the *bulk* of an estate.

Syn. **Bulk, mass, volume** mean the aggregate that forms a body or unit, especially with reference to its size or amount. **Bulk** always implies an aggregate that is inordinately large, heavy, or numerous (as, the *bulk* of the mountain; the *bulk* of mankind); **mass**, an aggregate made by piling together things of the same kind (as, the *mass* of voters; the *mass* of legislation); **volume**, an aggregate without outline, but thought of as rolling, flowing, or subject to fluctuation (as, the *volume* of water; the *volume* of traffic).

— *v. i.* **1.** To swell; expand; — with *up.* **2.** To have a bulky form or appearance; hence, to loom large, as in significance or importance; as, his fame *bulks* large. — *v. t.* **1.** To swell; stuff; — with *out.* **2.** To pile in a heap, as fish or tobacco.

bulk'head' (bŭlk'hĕd'), *n.* **1.** Any upright partition separating compartments, as on a vessel. **2.** A structure of wall to resist rock pressure, or to shut off water, fire, gas, etc. **3.** *U. S.* A projecting framework with a sloping door giving access to a cellar stairway, shaft, etc.

bulk'y (bŭl'kĭ), *adj.*; BULK'I·ER (-kĭ·ẽr); -I·EST. Of great bulk or size; large and unwieldy. — **bulk'i·ness**, *n.*

bull (bōōl), *n.* A grotesque blunder in language.

bull, *n.* [L. *bulla.*] **1.** A papal letter sealed with a bulla, or with a red-ink imprint of the device on the bulla, because of the significance of its subject matter. **2.** An imperial edict, as of the Holy Roman Empire.

bull, *n.* [AS. *bula* bull, *bulluc* bullock.] **1.** The male of any bovine species or of certain other animals, as the elk, moose, elephant, or whale. Cf. COW. **2.** One like a bull, as in size or loud roaring. **3.** One who buys stock, commodities, etc., with the expectation that their market prices will rise, or to effect such a rise. **4.** *Slang, U. S.* **a** A policeman; a detective. **b** Suave talk; also bunk; nonsense. **5.** [*cap.*] *Astron.* Taurus. — *v. t. & i.* To affect or act as a bull; esp., to try to raise prices (of or in). — *adj.* **a** Male. **b** Large of its kind. **c** Rising; as, a *bull* market.

bul'la (bōōl'ȧ; bŭl'ȧ), *n.*; *pl.* BULLAE (-ē). [L. See 2d BULL.] **1.** A round leaden seal attached to the papal bulls. **2.** *Anat.* A hollow, rounded, bony prominence, as the **bul'la tym'pa·ni** (tĭm'pȧ·nī) [NL.], situated beneath the ear opening in many mammals. **3.** *Med.* A blister; a vesicle.

bul'late (bōōl'āt; bŭl'-), *adj.* [L. *bullatus*, fr. *bulla* bubble.] Appearing blistered; puckered; as, a *bullate* leaf.

bull'bat' (bōōl'băt'), *n.* The nighthawk *Chordeiles minor.*

bull'dog' (bōōl'dŏg'; 74), *n.* **1.** One of a breed of short-haired dogs of compact, muscular build and great courage, having an undershot lower jaw and weighing at maturity from 40 to 50 lbs. **2.** Formerly, a cannon; also, a pistol; now, a large-calibered, short-barreled revolver. **3.** *Eng.* **a** A sheriff's officer. **b** A university proctor's attendant. — *adj.* Characteristic of, or like, a bulldog; tenacious; stubborn. — *v. t.* To throw (a steer) by seizing its horns and twisting its neck.

bull'doze' (-dōz'), *v. t.* **1.** *Orig. U. S.* To restrain or coerce by violence or threats; intimidate or bully. **2.** To move, clear, gouge out, or level off by pushing with a bulldozer. **3.** To force (as one's way) as if with a bulldozer. **4.** *U. S.* To bulldog (a steer).

bull'doz'er (-dōz'ẽr), *n.* **1.** One who bulldozes. **2.** A tractor-propelled earth-moving vehicle having a broad blade or ram attached in front, for clearing land, building roads and airfields, and the like.

bul'let (bōōl'ĕt; -ĭt), *n.* [F. *boulette* a small ball, *boulet* cannon ball, dim. of *boule* ball.] **1.** A small ball. **2.** A missile, usually of lead, to be discharged from a firearm. — **bul'let·proof'** (*see Pron.*, § 2), *adj.*

bul'le·tin (bōōl'ĕ·tĭn; -t'n), *n.* [F., deriv. of It. *bulla* an edict, fr. L. *bulla.*] **1.** A brief statement of news to the public, esp. as issued by an acknowledged authority. Cf. COMMUNIQUÉ. **2.** A periodical, esp. the organ of an association. — *v. t.* To announce by a bulletin.

bull'fight' (bōōl'fīt'), **bull'fight'ing**, *n.* A spectacle in which men excite, and fight with, a bull or bulls in an arena (*bull ring*) for public amusement. — **bull'fight'er**, *n.*

bull'finch' (-fĭnch'), *n.* **1.** A European bird (*Pyrrhula pyrrhula*) allied to the grosbeaks, having red cheeks, breast, and throat; also, any of several related birds. **2.** Any gray grosbeak (see GROSBEAK).

bull'finch', *n.* A hedge too high for a mounted hunter to leap.

bull'frog' (-frŏg'), *n.* See FROG, 1.

bull'head' (-hĕd'), *n.* **1.** Any of various large-headed fishes; esp.: **a** Any of several catfishes (genus *Ameiurus*) of the U. S., esp. the common species *Ameiurus nebulosus.* **b** The miller's-thumb. **c** The sculpin. **2.** A bullheaded person.

bull'head'ed (-hĕd'ĕd; -ĭd; 2), *adj.* Headstrong; obstinate.

bul'lion (bōōl'yŭn), *n.* [D. *bulioen, billioen*, alloyed gold or silver, fr. F. *billon* ingot, bullion.] **1.** Gold or silver, considered merely as so much metal; specif., gold or silver in bars or ingots. **2.** Lace or fringe of gold thread.

bull'ish (bōōl'ĭsh), *adj.* **1.** Of or like a bull; also, bullheaded. **2.** Causing or tending to cause rise in prices in the exchanges; as, *bullish* news; hence, rising; as, a *bullish* market. — **bull'ish·ly**, *adv.* — **bull'ish·ness**, *n.*

Bull Moose. *U. S.* A member of the Progressive party, or a follower of Theodore Roosevelt, in 1912.

bull'ock (bōōl'ŭk), *n.* [AS. *bulluc* young bull.] **a** *Obs.* A young bull. **b** An ox or steer.

bull pen. **1.** A pen for a bull or bulls. **2.** *Colloq.* **a** The barracks in a lumbering camp. **b** *Western U. S.* An enclosure in which prisoners are kept in time of riot. **c** *Baseball.* A place where pitchers to be used in an emergency are kept warmed up and at practice during a game.

bull'pout' (bōōl'pout'), *n.* The common bullhead (*Ameiurus nebulosus*) or a related catfish.

bull ring. See BULLFIGHT.

bull'-roar'er, *n.* **1.** A slat of wood tied to a thong, making an intermittent roaring when whirled, and used in some savage religious rites. **2.** A toy of similar form.

bull's'-eye' (bōōlz'ī'), *n.* **1.** A thick disk of glass inserted in a roof, ship's side, etc., to let in light; also, a circular opening for air or light. **2.** A kind of hard globular candy. **3.** The center of a target, or a shot which hits it; hence, any successful hit. See SIGHT, TARGET, *Illusts.* **4.** A lens of short focal distance or a lantern with such a lens. See LANTERN, *Illust.* **5.** *Naut.* A small circular or oval wooden block without sheaves, having a groove around it and a hole through it.

bull terrier. A strong, white, short-haired terrier of a breed supposed to have developed from a crossing of the bulldog and the white English terrier.

bull'whip' (bōōl'hwĭp'), *n.* A rawhide whip with plaited lash fifteen to twenty-five feet long.

bul'ly (bōōl'ĭ), *n.*, *or* **bully beef.** [Prob. fr. F. *bouilli* boiled beef, fr. *bouillir* to boil.] Pickled or canned beef.

bul'ly (bōōl'ĭ), *n.*; *pl.* -LIES (-ĭz) **1.** **a** *Obs.* Sweetheart. **b** *Archaic.* Good fellow; fine chap. **2.** A blustering, browbeating fellow; one cruel to others weaker than himself. **3.** Specif.: **a** A prostitute's protector. **b** *Archaic.* A hired ruffian or bravo. — *adj.* **1.** Jovial; dashing; good or gallant; — esp. in *bully boy*, a term of address. **2.** *Colloq.* Fine; first-rate. — *interj. Colloq.* Well done! Bravo! — *v. t. & i.*; -LIED (-ĭd); -LY·ING. To act the bully (toward). — **Syn.** Intimidate, browbeat, cow.

bul'ly·rag' (bōōl'ĭ·răg'), *v. t.* To torment by teasing.

bully tree. [From *bullet tree*, corrupt. of *balata* + *tree.*] Any of several West Indian trees of the sapodilla family, esp. one (*Mimusops globosa*) which yields balata gum.

bul'rush' (bōōl'rŭsh'), *n.* [ME. *bulrysche, bolroysche.*] **1.** Any of several large rushes growing in wet land or in water; esp.: **a** A tall sedge (*Scirpus lacustris*). **b** In England, the cattail *Typha latifolia.* **c** In America, the common rush (*Juncus effusus*). **2.** In Egypt and in Mosaic writings, the papyrus.

bul'wark (bōōl'wẽrk), *n.* [LG. *bolwerk.*] **1.** A solid, wall-like defensive structure; a rampart. **2.** Any strong support, defense, or safeguard. **3.** The side of a ship above the upper deck; — usually *pl.* — *v. t.* To fortify or secure with or as with a bulwark.

bum (bŭm; bōōm), *v. i. & n. Dial* Hum; din.

bum (bŭm), *n.* [ME. *bom.*] *Now Vulgar.* The buttocks.

bum (bŭm), *v. i.*; BUMMED (bŭmd); BUM'MING. *Slang, U. S.* To lead an idle, dissolute life; also, to sponge. — *v. t. Slang, U. S.* To obtain by sponging. — *n. Slang, U. S.* A spree; also, a drunken loafer. — **bum'mer**, *n.*

bum'bail'iff (bŭm'bāl'ĭf), *n.* A bailiff; — contemptuous.

bum'ble·bee' (bŭm'b'l·bē'), *n.* [ME. *bumblen* to hum (freq. of *bum* to hum) + *bee.*] Any of numerous species of large true bees (genus *Bombus*); — from their humming noise when in flight.

bum'boat' (bŭm'bōt'), *n.* A boat for conveying provisions, fruit, etc., for sale, to vessels in port or offshore.
bum'kin (bŭm'kĭn). Var. of BUMPKIN.
bump (bŭmp), *v. t.* **1.** To strike, knock, or thump. **2.** To collide with or cause to collide. **3.** *Slang.* To displace, as from one's job, airplane reservation, etc. — *v. i.* To bump something. — ***bump off.*** *Slang.* To kill.
— *n.* **1.** A heavy blow made by colliding; also, a jolt. **2.** A swelling resulting from a bump. **3.** *Phrenol.* One of the protuberances on the cranium associated with the various mental faculties.
bump'er (bŭmp'ẽr), *n.* **1.** A cup or glass filled to the brim. **2.** *Colloq.* A whopper. — *v. t.* To fill to the brim; also, to toast with a bumper. — *adj. Colloq.* Unusually large, good, or successful; as, a *bumper* crop.
bump'er, *n.* **1.** One who or that which bumps. **2.** A device for absorbing shock or, sometimes, preventing damage, as in a collision; specif., a bar or set of bars attached to either end of an automobile.
bump'kin (bŭmp'kĭn), *n.* [Prob. fr. D. *bommekijn* a small cask.] An awkward country fellow.
bump'kin (bŭmp'kĭn), *n.* [Prob. fr. Flem., D. *boomken* little tree.] *Naut.* A projecting beam or boom.
bump'tious (bŭmp'shŭs), *adj.* Offensively conceited; self-assertive. — **bump'tious·ly,** *adv.* — **bump'tious·ness,** *n.*
bump'y (bŭmp'ĭ), *adj.;* -I·ER (-ĭ·ẽr); -I·EST. Characterized by bumps or bumping; causing jolts; as, *bumpy* air. — **bump'i·ly,** *adv.* — **bump'i·ness,** *n.*
bun, bunn (bŭn), *n.* **1.** A kind of bread or roll; esp., a slightly sweetened raised biscuit. **2.** A coiled knot of hair.
bu'na, Bu'na (bū'nȧ; bōō'-), *n.* [G., fr. *Bu*tadien + *Na*trium the element sodium.] A synthetic rubber developed in Germany, made by polymerization of butadiene. **buna N** is a copolymer of butadiene and acrylonitrile (C_3H_3N, a colorless liquid); **buna S** is a copolymer of butadiene and styrene. See GR–S.
bunch (bŭnch), *n.* [ME. *bunche.*] **1.** *Now Rare.* A protuberance; hump. **2.** A cluster or tuft; as, a *bunch* of grapes. **3.** An aggregate of things of the same kind; as, a *bunch* of orders. — *v. i. & t.* To form a bunch; to form into a bunch or bunches; to gather in an aggregate. — **bunch'y** (bŭn'chĭ), *adj.*
bunch'ber'ry (-bĕr'ĭ; -bẽr·ĭ), *n.* See CORNEL **b.**
bunch'flow'er (-flou'ẽr), *n.* A tall herb (*Melanthium virginicum*) bearing a panicle of small greenish flowers; also, any other species of this genus. The genus typifies a family (Melanthaceae, the bunchflower family; order Liliales) distinguished from the lily family by the absence of bulbs.
bun'co (bŭng'kō). Var. of BUNKO.
bun'combe, bun'kum (bŭng'kŭm), *n.* [From *Buncombe,* a county of North Carolina.] *Colloq.* Speechmaking to please constituents, or gain applause; anything said or done for mere show; hence, nonsense.
bund (bŭnd), *n.* [Hind. *band.*] **1.** *India.* An embankment. **2.** *China, Japan, etc.* An embanked thoroughfare along a waterfront.
‖**Bund** (bōōnt; *Angl.* bŭnd, bōōnd), *n.; pl.* BÜNDE (bün'dĕ). [G.] **1.** A league or confederacy of states, as the Federal Republic of Germany. **2.** Also **bund;** *pl.* BUNDS (bŭndz; bōōndz). An association of people, specif. a political organization, as the former pro-Nazi German-American Bund.
Bun'des·rat' (bōōn'dĕs·rät'), *n.* [G.] A federal council; as: **a** The upper house in the legislature of the former German empire and of the Federal Republic of Germany. **b** The federal executive council of Switzerland.
Bun'des·tag' (-täk'), *n.* [G.] The lower house of parliament of the Federal Republic of Germany.
bun'dle (bŭn'd'l), *n.* [ME. *bundel,* fr. MD. *bondel, bundel.*] **1.** A number of things tied or rolled together to form a bunch, package, parcel, etc. Abbr. *bdl.* **2.** A collection; group; lot. **3.** A band of mostly parallel fibers, as of nerves or muscles; a fasciculus. **4.** *Bot.* A fascicle composed primarily of conducting tissue traversing roots, stems, leaves, etc. **5.** *Linguistics.* A number of isoglosses running in the same general direction, whether coinciding, diverging, converging, or crossing each other. — **Syn.** Parcel, package, pack. — *v. t.;* BUN'DLED (-d'ld); BUN'DLING (-dlĭng). **1.** To assemble or tie in a bundle. **2.** To hustle or hurry unceremoniously. — *v. i.* **1.** To hustle. **2.** *Hist.* To occupy the same bed without undressing; — said of a man and woman, esp. during courtship. — **bun'dler** (-dlẽr), *n.*
bung (bŭng), *n.* [MD. *bonge,* dial.] **1.** The stopper of the opening in the bilge of a cask. **2.** Also **bung'hole'** (bŭng'hōl'). The opening stopped by a bung. — *v. t.* **1.** To stop with a bung. **2.** *Slang.* To bruise so as to unfit for action.
bun'ga·low (bŭng'gȧ·lō), *n.* [Bengali *bānglā.*] A dwelling of a type first developed in India, usually one-storied, with low sweeping lines and a wide veranda.
bun'gle (bŭng'g'l), *v. i. & t.;* BUN'GLED (-g'ld); BUN'GLING (-glĭng). To act, work, make, or perform in a clumsy manner. — *n.* Something bungled. — **bun'gler** (-glẽr), *n.* — **bun'gling·ly,** *adv.*
bun'ion (bŭn'yŭn), *n.* An enlargement from chronic inflammation of the small sac on the first joint of the great toe.
bunk (bŭngk), *n.* A case or frame attached to a wall to serve as a bed, as in a ship; a berth. — *v. i. Colloq.* To occupy or share a bed.
bunk, *n. Colloq.* **1.** Buncombe. **2.** Bunko.
bunk'er (bŭngk'ẽr), *n.* [Scot. *bunker, bunkart,* a bench, or low chest, serving for a seat.] **1.** A large bin; esp., a compartment on shipboard for storing coal. **2.** *Golf.* An obstacle; specif.: **a** A rough or sandy spot in a depression. **b** *U. S.* Any raised obstruction of earth, usually with a sand trap in front of it. — *v. t. Golf.* To drive into a bunker.
bunk'er, *n.* [G.] *Mil.* A bombproof chamber of steel and concrete with embrasures for cannon fire, which is sunk in the ground as a defensive work, usually at a distance from a main fort or as one of a series; also, a dugout buttressed and roofed with logs, revetted with earth, drums of sand, metal junk, etc., and having gun slits.
bunk'house' (bŭngk'hous'), *n.* A rough, simple building providing sleeping quarters, usually bunks, esp. for construction workers.
bun'ko, bun'co (bŭng'kō), *n.; pl.* -KOS, -COS (-kōz). A swindling game or scheme. — *v. t.;* BUN'KOED, -COED (-kōd); BUN'KO·ING, -CO·ING. To swindle by a bunko game or scheme; to cheat.
bun'kum (bŭng'kŭm). Var. of BUNCOMBE.
bunn (bŭn). Var. of BUN.
bun'ny (bŭn'ĭ), *n.; pl.* -NIES (-ĭz). A rabbit; — a pet name.
Bun'sen (bŭn's'n; *Ger.* bōōn'zĕn), *or* **Bun'sen's, burn'er.** A gas burner, invented by R. W. Bunsen of Heidelberg, consisting typically of a straight tube with small holes at the bottom where air enters and mixes with the gas, thus producing a blue, intensely hot flame.
bunt (bŭnt), *n.* **1.** The bagging portion of a fishing net. **2.** The middle part of a square sail; the part of a furled sail gathered up in a bunch at the center of the yard.
bunt, *n.* A smut destructive of the kernels of wheat, with ill-smelling spores.
bunt. *v. t. & i.* **1.** To butt with horns; to push by shoving or bumping. **2.** *Baseball.* To bat or tap (the ball) lightly within the infield by meeting it with a loosely held bat and no swing. — *n.* A butt, push, etc.; also, *Baseball,* a bunted ball or a hit made by bunting. — **bunt'er,** *n.*
bun'tine (bŭn'tĭn). Var. of 2d BUNTING.
bun'ting (bŭn'tĭng), *n.* [Scot. *buntlin,* ME. *bunting, buntyle.*] Any of various stout-billed birds (*Emberiza* and allied genera), usually included in the finch family.
bun'ting, *n.* [ME. *bonten* to sift.] A thin woolen stuff, used chiefly for flags or patriotic decorations; also, a cotton stuff imitating this; hence, flags collectively.
bunt'line (bŭnt'lĭn; -līn), *n.* [*bunt* part of a sail + *line.*] *Naut.* One of the ropes attached to the foot of a square sail, to haul the sail up to the yard for furling.
buoy (bōō'ĭ; boi), *n.* [MD. *boeie* (D. *boei*), fr. OF. *boie* (F. *bouée*).] **1.** *Naut.* A float; esp., a floating object moored to the bottom, to mark a channel, anchor, shoal, rock, etc. A ***nun buoy*** is conical in shape; a ***can buoy*** is truncated or flat; a ***spar buoy*** is a spar anchored at one end; a ***bell buoy,*** bearing a bell which is rung by the action of the waves, usually marks shoals or rocks; a ***whistling buoy,*** similarly operated, marks shoals or channel entrances. **2.** = LIFE BUOY. — *v. t. & i.* **1.** To keep from sinking in a fluid; to keep afloat; hence, to sustain or raise. **2.** To mark by or as by a buoy or buoys.

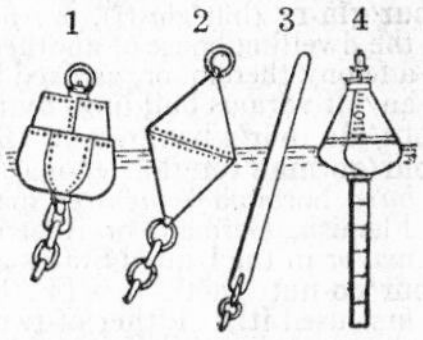

Buoys. 1 Can Buoy; 2 Nun Buoy; 3 Spar Buoy; 4 Whistling Buoy.

buoy'an·cy (bōō'yăn·sĭ; boi'ăn·sĭ), *n.* **1.** The quality of being able to float, as on water or in air. **2.** Power of supporting a floating body; the upward force exerted upon an immersed or floating body by a fluid. **3.** Resilience of spirit; sprightliness.
buoy'ant (bōō'yănt; boi'ănt), *adj.* Having or manifesting buoyancy. — **buoy'ant·ly,** *adv.*
bu·pres'tid (bū·prĕs'tĭd), *n.* [Gr. *bouprēstis,* a poisonous beetle.] Any of a large family (Buprestidae) of beetles with short notched antennae and long bodies tapering at the rear.
bur (bûr), *n.* [ME. *burre, borre,* burdock.] **1.** Any rough or prickly envelope of a fruit, as of the chestnut and burdock. **2.** Any weed that bears burs. **3.** Something that clings like a bur. **4.** Var. of BURR. — *v. t.* To remove burs from; as, to *bur* wool in cleaning
Bur'ber'ry (bûr'bĕr'ĭ; -bẽr·ĭ), *n.* [After *Burberrys,* Ltd., London.] A trade-mark applied to specially treated fabrics and to garments, especially rainproof topcoats.
bur'ble (bûr'b'l), *v. i. Colloq.* **a** To bubble. **b** To jabber. — *n.* **1.** A bubble or bubbling. **2.** *Aeronautics.* The breaking up of the streamline flow of air about a body, as over a wing when an airplane attempts to climb too steeply.
bur'bot (-bŏt), *n.;* see PLURAL, *Note,* 6. [F. *bourbotte* (after *bourbe* mud), fr. *barbote,* fr. *barbe* beard.] Either of two fresh-water fishes allied to the cod, having barbels on the nose and chin: (1) *Lota lota* of Europe; (2) *Lota maculosa* of New England, the Great Lakes, and northward; — called also *ling, eelpout,* or *cusk.*
burd (bûrd), *n. Archaic.* A lady; young woman.
bur'den (bûr'd'n), *n.* Also **bur'then** (-thĕn). [AS. *byrthen.*] **1.** Thing borne; load; hence, care; responsibility. **2.** Something borne with difficulty; a heavy obligation, expense, etc.; encumbrance. **3.** The bearing of loads; as, a beast of *burden.* **4.** Capacity of a vessel for carrying cargo; weight of the cargo; as, a ship of a hundred tons *burden.* — *v. t.* To load; encumber with weight; oppress.
bur'den, *n.* [ME. *burdoun* bass in music, fr. OF. *bourdon.*] **1.** *Music.* The bass; also, a droning undersong or accompaniment. **2.** The refrain or chorus of a song. **3.** Main theme; central idea; gist; as, the *burden* of her plea.
burden of proof. The obligation of the side that affirms in a suit, an argument, etc., to prove its case or contentions.
bur'den·some (bûr'd'n·sŭm), *adj.* Grievous to be borne; oppressive. — **Syn.** See ONEROUS. — **bur'den·some·ly,** *adv.* — **-some·ness,** *n.*
bur'dock' (bûr'dŏk'), *n.* [*bur* + *dock* the plant.] Any plant of a genus (*Arctium,* esp. *A. lappa*) of the aster family, with burlike flower heads.
bu'reau (bū'rō; *Brit. usually* bū·rō'), *n.; pl.* BUREAUS (-rōz; -rōz'), BUREAUX (*E. pron.* -rōz; -rōz'). [F., office, desk, cloth covering for desks or tables, fr. OF. *burel* woolen cloth, fr. *bure.*] **1. a** *Eng.* A writing desk or table with drawers. **b** *U. S.* A chest of drawers, usually low and with a mirror, for a bedroom. **2.** A business office. **3.** A government department or office, or one of its subdivisions, for the transaction of business. **4.** A business establishment for exchanging information, making contacts, etc.; as, an employment *bureau.*
bu·reauc'ra·cy (bū·rŏk'rȧ·sĭ; bū·rō'krȧ·sĭ), *n.; pl.* BUREAUCRACIES (-sĭz). [F. *bureaucratie.* See -CRACY.] **1.** A system of carrying on the business of government by means of bureaus, each controlled by a chief; also, government by bureau heads and their superior administrative officers. **2.** Hence, officialism in government; rigid, formal measures or routine procedure in administration. **3.** Government officials, collectively.
bu'reau·crat (bū'rō·krăt), *n.* An official of a bureau, esp. one pursuing a narrow and arbitrary routine. — **bu'reau·crat'ic** (-krăt'ĭk), *adj.* — **bu'reau·crat'i·cal·ly** (-ĭ·kăl·ĭ), *adv.*
bu·rette', bu·ret' (bū·rĕt'), *n.* [F., can, cruet, dim. of *buire* flagon.] *Chem.* A graduated glass tube, usually with a small aperture and stopcock, for delivering measured quantities of liquid or for measuring the liquid or gas received or discharged.
burg (bûrg), **burh** (bōōrk), *n.* [AS. *burh, burg.*] Orig., a fortified town; now: **a** *Eng.* A borough. **b** *Colloq., U. S.* A town; city.
-burg (-bûrg), **-burgh** (-bûrg; *Brit.* -bŭ·rŭ, -brŭ, -bŭr'ŭ). [See BOROUGH.] A suffix meaning a *burgh* or *borough,* often in place names, as in Harris*burg,* Edin*burgh,* Pitts*burgh.*

bur'gage (bûr'gĭj), *n.* [From BURG.] A form of tenure in which lands, chiefly town lands, are held from the king or other lord at a small rental or for watching and warding.

bur'gee (bûr'jē), *n.* [OF. *burgeis.*] *Naut.* A swallow-tailed or triangular flag.

bur'geon (bûr'jŭn), *n.* [OF. *burjon* (F. *bourgeon*).] A bud; sprout. — *v. i.* To send forth buds, branches, or any new growth; to sprout; hence, to grow forth or come out.

bur'gess (bûr'jĕs; -jĭs), *n.* [OF. *burgeis,* fr. *burc* fortified town, fr. LL. *burgus* fort, city.] **1.** An inhabitant or, strictly, a freeman, of a borough; a citizen. **2.** **a** *Eng.* The person elected to represent a borough, corporate town, or university in Parliament. **b** Before the Revolution, a representative in the popular branch (***House of Burgesses***) of the legislature of Virginia; — now called *delegate.*

burgh (bûrg; *Scot.* bŭr'ŭ), *n.* [See BOROUGH.] A borough; esp., a kind of incorporated Scottish town.

burgh'er (bûr'gẽr), *n.* A freeman of a burgh or borough.

bur'glar (bûr'glẽr), *n.* [ML. *burglator, burgulator,* fr. LL. *burgus* fortified place.] One guilty of burglary.

bur·glar'i·ous (bûr-glâr'ĭ·ŭs), *adj.* Of the nature of, involving, or addicted to burglary. — **bur·glar'i·ous·ly,** *adv.*

bur'glar·ize (bûr'glẽr·īz), *v. t.* *Colloq.* To rifle by burglary.

bur'gla·ry (bûr'glȧ·rĭ), *n.; pl.* -RIES (-rĭz). *Law.* Forcible entry into the dwelling house of another, in the nighttime, with intent to commit a felony therein, or, as fixed by some statutes, such forcible entry into any of various buildings by night or day.

bur'gle (bûr'g'l), *v. t. & i.* *Humorous.* To burglarize.

bur'go·mas'ter (bûr'gō·mȧs'tẽr; 9), *n.* [After D. *burgemeester,* fr. *burg* borough + *meester* master.] A chief magistrate of a Dutch, Flemish, German, or Austrian municipal town, corresponding to a mayor in the United States and England.

bur'go·net (-nĕt), *n.* [F. *bourguignotte,* because the Burgundians first used it.] Either of two types of 16th-century helmet, similar to the morion and armet, respectively.

bur'goo (bûr'gōō; bûr·gōō'), *n.* **1.** Thick gruel; porridge. **2.** A stew or thick soup of meat and vegetables, orig. served at barbecues and picnics.

bur'grave (bûr'grāv), *n.* [G. *burggraf,* fr. *burg* fortress town + *graf* count.] *Ger. Hist.* Originally, the appointed commander of a burg; later, the hereditary lord of a burg and an attached domain.

Bur'gun·dy (bûr'gŭn·dĭ), *n.; pl.* BURGUNDIES (-dĭz). **1.** Any red or white wine made in Burgundy. **2.** A color, bluish-red in hue, of low saturation and very low brilliance. Cf. COLOR.

burh (bŏŏrk). Var. of BURG.

bur'i·al (bĕr'ĭ·ăl), *n.* [ME. *buryel, beriel,* fr. AS. *byrgels.*] Act of burying; interment; sepulture.

bur'i·er (bĕr'ĭ·ẽr), *n.* One who buries.

bu'rin (bū'rĭn), *n.* [F.] **1.** A pointed steel cutting tool used by engravers and marble workers; a graver. **2.** Manner or style of execution of an engraver.

burke (bûrk), *v. t.* [After William *Burke* of Edinburgh, executed for the crime in 1829.] **1.** To murder by suffocation, or with few marks of violence, in order to obtain a body to be sold for dissection. **2.** To dispose of quietly, as by suppressing or shelving.

burl (bûrl), *n.* [OF. *bourle* tuft of wool, fr. *bourre,* fr. L. *burra* a shaggy garment.] **1.** A knot or lump in thread or cloth. **2.** An excrescence, often a flattened hemisphere in form, growing on the trunks of many trees; also, veneer made from such excrescences. — *v. t.* To dress or finish (cloth), esp. by freeing it from burls. — **burl'er,** *n.*

bur'lap (bûr'lăp), *n.* Also **bur'laps** (-lăps). A fabric of jute, hemp, or, sometimes, flax, for bagging, curtains, etc.

burled (bûrld), *adj.* Having burls; as, *burled* walnut.

bur·lesque' (bûr·lĕsk'), *n.* [F., fr. It. *burlesco,* fr. *burla* jest, mockery.] **1.** Literary, dramatic, or other imitation which makes a travesty of that which it represents. **2.** *U. S.* A type of theatrical entertainment, now consisting of short turns, characterized by broad humor and slapstick. — **Syn.** See CARICATURE. — *adj.* Of, pert. to, characterized by, or characteristic of burlesque. — *v. t.* To mock or make ludicrous by burlesque. — *v. i.* To employ burlesque. — **bur·les'quer** (-lĕs'kẽr), *n.*

Bur'ley, *or* **bur'ley** (bûr'lĭ), *n.* [Prob. from surname *Burley.*] A thin-bodied tobacco, light-colored when cured, grown in Kentucky and neighboring states.

bur'ly (bûr'lĭ), *adj.;* BUR'LI·ER (-lĭ·ẽr); -LI·EST. [ME. *burly, borlich.*] Large or stout of body; also, heavily built and rough; bulky and bluff. — **Syn.** Husky, brawny, muscular. — **bur'li·ly,** *adv.* — **bur'li·ness,** *n.*

bur marigold. Any of a genus (*Bidens*) of coarse herbs of the aster family, whose burs adhere to clothing.

Bur'mese' (bûr'mēz'; -mēs'; 2), *n.* **1.** *sing. & pl.* A native, or natives, of Burma. **2.** The language of the Burmese, belonging to the Indo-Chinese family. See LANGUAGE, *Table.* — **Bur'mese',** *adj.*

burn (bûrn), *n.* [See BOURN a stream.] *Chiefly Scot. & Dial.* A brook; a rivulet.

burn (bûrn), *v. i.;* BURNED (bûrnd) *or* BURNT; BURN'ING. [AS. *bærnan, bernan,* v. t.] **1.** To be on fire; to give forth light and heat during combustion. **2.** To feel, or to appear, as if on fire or excessively heated; as, to *burn* with anger. **3.** To be charred, scorched, scalded, withered, etc., by the action of fire or heat. **4.** *Chem.* To undergo combustion of any kind. — *v. t.* **1.** To consume or destroy with flames or heat. **2.** To injure or change destructively by fire or heat; to scald, scorch, singe, etc. **3.** To make or produce by means of fire or heat; as, to *burn* a hole. **4.** To subject to the action of fire or heat in order to perfect, condition, etc.; as, to *burn* clay for pottery; specif., to cauterize. **5.** To affect in a way that is like or suggests the action of fire or heat; as, to *burn* the mouth with pepper. **6.** *Chem.* To cause to undergo combustion. — *n.* **1.** A hurt, injury, or effect caused by burning. **2.** The process, operation, or result of burning.

burn'er (bûr'nẽr), *n.* One that burns; specif., the part of a lamp, furnace, etc., where the flame is produced.

bur'net (bûr'nĕt; -nĭt), *n.* [OF. *burnete, brunete,* dim. of *brun* brown.] Any of a genus (*Sanguisorba,* esp. *S. canadensis*) of herbs of the rose family, with odd-pinnate stipulate leaves and spikes of apetalous flowers.

burn'ing bush. Any of several plants; esp., either of two American shrubs (*Evonymus americanus* and *E. atropurpureus*) bearing bright red capsules.

burning glass. A convex lens for producing an intense heat by converging the sun's rays.

bur'nish (bûr'nĭsh), *v. t.* [OF. *burnir, brunir,* to make brown, polish, fr. *brun* brown, fr. OHG. *brūn.*] To make shiny or lustrous, esp. by rubbing; polish. — *n.* Effect of burnishing; gloss. — **bur'nish·ment,** *n.* — **bur'nish·er** (-ẽr), *n.*

bur·noose', bur·nous' (bûr·nōōs'; bûr'nōōs), *n.* [F. *burnous,* fr. Ar. *burnus.*] A hooded cloak, worn by Arabs and Moors.

burn'sides' (bûrn'sīdz'), *n. pl.* *Colloq., U. S.* Side whiskers, orig. as worn by Gen. A. E. Burnside; sideburns.

burnt (bûrnt), *past & past part.* of BURN.

burp (bûrp), *n.* [Imitative.] A belch. — *v. i.* To belch; eruct. — *v. t.* To help (a baby) expel a pocket of gas from the stomach, esp. by patting or rubbing the back.

burr (bûr), *n.* **1.** Var. of BUR. **2.** Any rounded knot or excrescence on a tree. **3.** A small washer put on the end of a rivet before it is swaged down. **4.** A roughness, esp. on the edge of something made by drilling, turning, etc.; a rough or thin edge, ridge, or the like. **5.** A whir; a rough humming sound. **6.** *Dent.* (Usually **bur.**) A small drill for excavating a tooth cavity. **7.** *Phonet.* A pronunciation of *r* by trilling the uvula against the back of the tongue; hence, any rough pronunciation. — *v. i.;* BURRED (bûrd); BURR'ING. **1.** To speak with a burr. **2.** To whir. — *v. t.* **1.** **a** To form into a burr or rough edge. **b** To remove rough edges from. **2.** To pronounce with a burr.

burr, buhr (bûr), *n.* Buhrstone.

bur reed. Any of a genus (*Sparganium,* family Sparganiaceae) of plants with globose burlike fruit.

bur'ro (bûr'ō; bŏŏr'ō), *n.; pl.* BURROS (-ōz). [Sp.] A donkey, esp. a small one used as a pack animal.

bur'row (bûr'ō), *n.* [Akin to BOROUGH.] A hole in the ground made by certain animals, as rabbits, for shelter and habitation; a similar passage, excavation, or place of retreat; a shelter. — *v. i.* **1.** To excavate a hole, as in the earth, esp. one to lodge in; to penetrate or work one's way under the surface. **2.** To lodge in a burrow, as rabbits; hence, to hide, as in a deep or concealed place. — *v. t.* **1.** To make burrows in; construct by burrowing. **2.** To conceal (oneself) in or as in a burrow. — **bur'row·er,** *n.*

burr'stone' (bûr'stōn'). Var. of BUHRSTONE.

bur'sa (bûr'sȧ), *n.; pl.* -SAE (-sē), -SAS (-sȧz). [LL. See BURSE.] *Anat. & Zool.* A sac or saclike cavity. — **bur'sal** (-săl), *adj.*

bur'sar (-sẽr), *n.* [ML. *bursarius,* fr. *bursa* purse. See BURSE.] A treasurer, as of a college.

bur'sa·ry (bûr'sȧ·rĭ), *n.; pl.* -RIES (-rĭz). [ML. *bursaria.*] **1.** The treasury of a college or monastery. **2.** *Brit.* A scholarship in a university or school; an exhibition (def. 4).

‖**Bur'schen·schaft'** (bŏŏr'shĕn·shäft'), *n.; pl.* -SCHAFTEN (-shäf'tĕn). [G.] In Germany, an association of university students formed to support liberal ideas.

burse (bûrs), *n.* [F. *bourse,* fr. LL. *bursa.* See BOURSE.] **1.** A purse. **2.** *Obs.* = BOURSE. **3.** A scholarship in a university, etc. **4.** *R.C.Ch.* A case of silk or brocade, in which the folded corporal is carried to and from the altar.

bur'seed' (bûr'sēd'), *n.* See STICKSEED.

bur'ser·a'ceous (bûr'sẽr·ā'shŭs), *adj.* *Bot.* Designating or belonging to the torchwood family (Burseraceae). See TORCHWOOD.

bur'si·form (bûr'sĭ·fôrm), *adj.* [LL. *bursa* purse + *-form.*] Shaped like a purse.

bur·si'tis (bûr·sī'tĭs), *n.* [NL., fr. *bursa* + *-itis.*] *Med.* Inflammation of a bursa.

burst (bûrst), *v. i.;* BURST; BURST'ING. [AS. *berstan.*] **1.** To break apart or into pieces from impact or from pressure from within; to explode. **2.** To give way from an excess of emotion; as, his heart will *burst* with grief; also, to give vent suddenly to a repressed feeling, desire, etc.; as, to *burst* into tears. **3.** To emerge, enter, issue, etc., suddenly or as if by breaking through obstacles or limitations; as, he *burst* into the room. **4.** To be filled to the breaking point; to be overloaded, etc.; as, barns *bursting* with grain. — *v. t.* To cause to burst; also, to make by or as by bursting; as, to *burst* a hole in something. — *n.* **1.** Act of bursting; explosion; outbreak. **2.** Result of bursting; a break; breach; rupture. **3.** A spurt. **4.** *Mil.* **a** A brief intensive fire, or period of fire, as of rifles or artillery. **b** A series of shots fired from an automatic gun by one pressure on the trigger. **c** A visible puff accompanying the blast of an antiaircraft shell. — **burst'er,** *n.*

bur'then (bûr'thĕn), **bur'then·some,** etc. Vars. of BURDEN, etc.

bur'ton (bûr't'n), *n.* Any of several kinds of hoisting tackle, usually one with a single and a double block.

bur'weed' (bûr'wēd'), *n.* Any of certain plants having burlike fruit, as the cocklebur, burdock, etc.

bur'y (bĕr'ĭ), *v. t.;* BUR'IED (-ĭd); BUR'Y·ING. [ME. *burien, berien,* fr. AS. *byrgan.*] **1.** To cover out of sight, as a corpse in a grave; to inter with funeral ceremonies; inhume. **2.** To cover over so as to conceal. **3.** To put away out of sight or forever; as: **a** To remove, as oneself, from companionship. **b** To abandon, as a grudge. **c** To submerge or engross; — with *in;* as, *buried* in grief. — **Syn.** See HIDE.

bus (bŭs), *n.; pl.* BUSES, BUSSES (bŭs'ĕz; -ĭz). [From omni*bus.*] An omnibus; motor coach.

bus bar. One of the main bars or conductors carrying an electric current.

bus boy. A restaurant waiter's assistant; also, a man or boy employed to remove soiled dishes and clean up after patrons in an eating place.

bus'by (bŭz'bĭ), *n.; pl.* -BIES (-bĭz). A headdress worn in the British Army by hussars, artillerymen, and engineers, and by hussars generally.

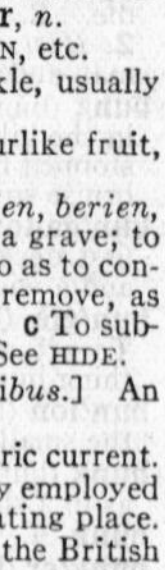
Busby.

bush (bŏŏsh), *n.* [ME. *busch, busk.*] **1.** **a** A shrub; esp., a thick, densely branched shrub. **b** A cluster of shrubs. **2.** Uncleared or uncultivated country; esp., woodland or land covered with shrubby vegetation; specif., *Australia,* the area or areas of arid scrub-covered country in certain interior districts. See SCRUB, 1. **3.** A shrub or branch, esp. a branch of ivy, hung out at vintners' doors, or as a tavern sign; hence, a tavern sign. **4.** A bushlike mass, as of hair or feathers; specif., the tail, or brush, of a fox. — *v. t.* To support, mark, protect, etc., by setting bushes. — *v. i.* To branch or cluster thickly.

bush, *n.* *Mach.* Bushing, a metal lining. See STUFFING BOX, *Illust.* — *v. t.* To furnish with a bushing.

bush'buck' (-bŭk'), *n.* See HARNESSED ANTELOPE.

bush cranberry. The cranberry tree (see CRANBERRY, 2 a).

bush'el (bŏŏsh'ĕl; -'l), *n.* [OF. *boissel,* fr. *boisse* a measure of grain, of Celt. origin.] **1.** A dry measure; also, a weight assumed as its equivalent. See MEASURE, *Table* 10. **2.** A vessel holding a bushel.

bush'el (bo͝osh'ĕl; -'l), *v. t. & i.*; -ELED (-ĕld; -'ld) or -ELLED; -EL·ING or -EL·LING. *Tailoring.* To repair or put in order, as men's garments. — **bush'el·er, bush'el·ler** (-ẽr), **bush'el·man** (-măn), *n.*

‖**Bu'shi·do'** (bo͞o'shē·dō'; *Jap.* bo͞osh'dō'), *n.* [Jap. *bushi* warrior + *dō* way, principle.] The code of chivalry in feudal Japan.

bush'ing (bo͝osh'ĭng), *n.* [From 2d *bush*, fr. D. *bus* a box, fr. Gr. *pyxis*.] **1.** *Mach.* A detachable metal lining, used as a bearing for a shaft, axle, etc., to reduce friction. Cf. JOURNAL, 5. **2.** *Elec.* An insulating part, usually a lining.

Bush'man (bo͝osh'măn), *n.*; *pl.* -MEN (-mĕn). **1.** One of a race of nomadic hunters of South Africa. **2.** [*not cap.*] A woodsman; specif., *Australia*, one who lives in the "bush."

bush'mas'ter (-màs'tẽr), *n.* A tropical American snake (*Lachesis mutus*), the largest venomous snake in the New World.

bush'rang'er (-rān'jẽr), *n.* One who ranges, or hides in, the bush; esp., *Australia*, a highwayman.

bush'whack'er (-hwăk'ẽr), *n.* *U. S.* One accustomed to beat about or travel through bushes; — applied specif. to certain Confederate guerrillas in the Civil War; hence, a guerrilla. — **bush'whack'ing**, *n.*

bush'y (bo͝osh'ĭ), *adj.*; -I·ER (-ĭ·ẽr); -I·EST. [From 1st BUSH.] **1.** Full of, or overgrown with, bushes. **2.** Thick and spreading, like a bush. — **bush'i·ness**, *n.*

bus'i·ly (bĭz'ĭ·lĭ), *adv.* In a busy manner.

busi'ness (bĭz'nĕs; -nĭs), *n.* [*busy* + *-ness*.] **1.** *Obs.* Busyness. **2.** One's rightful work or personal concern; as, attend to *business*; hence, justifiable reason for meddling or the like; as, he had no *business* to do that. **3.** One's particular, esp. one's regular, work, occupation, or employment. **4.** Affair; matter; as, it was a strange *business*. **5.** In the theater, the details in acting or in staging a play usually left to the discretion of actors or director. **6.** Mercantile pursuit or transactions; trade; commerce; as, he prefers *business* to law. **7.** A commercial or industrial enterprise; as, to sell one's *business*. **8.** Custom; patronage; as, to increase *business* by advertising.

Syn. (1) See WORK.

(2) **Business, commerce, trade, industry, traffic,** as here compared, mean a form of activity that has for its end the supplying of commodities. **Business,** often an inclusive term, specifically names the combined activities of those engaged in the purchase or sale of commodities or in related financial transactions; **commerce** and **trade,** of those engaged in the exchange and transportation of commodities; **industry,** of those producing commodities, especially by manufacturing, processing, etc., on so large a scale that problems of labor and capital are involved; **traffic,** of those engaged in the operation of public carriers, such as railroads, ships, bus lines, etc.

busi'ness·like' (-līk'), *adj.* Displaying the efficiency, system, etc., desirable in business; practical.

busi'ness·man' (-măn'), *n.* One in business, esp. on his own account; one familiar with business methods.

busk (bŭsk; *Scot.* bo͞osk), *v. t.* [ON. *būask* to make oneself ready.] *Chiefly Scot.* To prepare; make ready.

bus'kin (bŭs'kĭn), *n.* [Prob. fr. OF. *brousequin, broissequin*.] **1.** A half boot. **2. a** = COTHURNUS **a**. **b** Hence, tragedy, or tragic drama. Cf. SOCK, 1.

bus'man's hol'i·day (bŭs'mănz). A holiday spent in following or observing the practice of one's usual occupation.

buss (bŭs; *dial.* bo͝os), *n. & v. t. & i.* *Dial.* Kiss; smack.

buss (bŭs). Var. of BUS, omnibus.

bus'ses (bŭs'ĕz; -ĭz), *n.*, *pl.* of BUS.

buss'es (bŭs'ĕz; -ĭz), *n.*, *pl.* of BUSS.

bust (bŭst), *n.* [F. *buste*, fr. It. *busto*.] **1.** A piece of sculpture representing the head, neck, and more or less of the shoulders and breast of a person. **2.** The part of the human figure between the neck and waist; the chest.

bust, *v. t. & i.*; BUST'ED; BUST'ING. **1.** *Inelegant.* To burst. **2.** *Slang, U. S.* **a** To make or become bankrupt. **b** To break or tame, as a bronco. **c** To hit or strike, as with the fist. **d** To demote in rank. — *n.* **1.** *Dial.* A burst. **2.** *Slang.* **a** A spree. **b** A flat failure.

bus'tard (bŭs'tẽrd), *n.* [From OF., fr. L. *avis tarda*, lit., slow bird.] Any of a family (Otididae) of Old World and Australian game birds, related to both the cranes and plovers; esp., the ***great bustard*** (*Otis tarda*), the largest European land bird.

bust'er (bŭs'tẽr), *n.* **1.** *Slang.* **a** Something huge or stupendous. **b** *U. S.* One who breaks (horses); as, a bronco*buster*. **c** *U. S.* One who breaks up; as, a trust *buster*. **2.** A fierce wind; specif., *Australia*, a cold southerly wind of sudden violence.

bus'tle (bŭs''l), *v. i. & t.*; BUS'TLED (-'ld); BUS'TLING (-lĭng). To move with fussy or noisy activity, often with more haste than purpose. — *n.* Stir or commotion of bustling. — **Syn.** See STIR. — **bus'tling·ly**, *adv.*

bus'tle, *n.* A pad or framework formerly worn beneath a woman's skirt just below the back of the waist.

bus'y (bĭz'ĭ), *adj.*; BUS'I·ER (-ĭ·ẽr); -I·EST. [AS. *bysig, bisig*.] **1.** Engaged in some occupation or work; not idle or at leisure. **2.** Full of business, activity, etc.; as, a *busy* life; also, constantly active or in motion; as, *busy* hands. **3.** Officious; meddling. **4.** *U. S.* In use; — said of a telephone line.

Syn. **Busy, industrious, diligent, assiduous, sedulous** mean actively engaged or occupied in work. **Busy** may imply nothing more than that the person or thing referred to is engaged or in use but, ordinarily, it implies temporary or habitual engrossment in activity; **industrious** implies characteristic or habitual devotion to work; **diligent,** earnest application to some specific object or pursuit; **assiduous,** studied and unremitting; **sedulous,** painstaking and persevering, application to what is one's business or end. — **Ant.** Idle.

— *v. t. & i.*; BUS'IED (bĭz'ĭd); BUS'Y·ING. [AS. *bysgian, bisgian*.] To make, keep, or be, busy; to occupy or be occupied.

bus'y·bod'y (-bŏd'ĭ), *n.*; *pl.* -IES (-ĭz). An officious or inquisitive person; a meddler.

bus'y·ness (bĭz'ĭ·nĕs; -nĭs), *n.* Quality or state of being busy, or active, meddlesome, etc.

but (bŭt; 4), *prep.* [AS. *būtan* without, on the outside, except, besides, fr. *be-* + *ūtan* outward, without, fr. *ūt* out.] **1.** *Now Scot.* Without; lacking; outside of. **2.** Except; specif.: **a** With the exception of; as, all escaped the fire *but* me. **b** Other or otherwise than; as, he cannot *but* hear.

— *conj.* **1.** Connecting co-ordinate elements: **a** With this exception, namely; as, "whence all *but* he had fled." **b** On the contrary; yet; notwithstanding; as, poor *but* proud. **2.** Introducing a subordinate clause: **a** If not; unless. **b** On the probability that; as, it is ten to one *but* he will escape. **c** Except that; when not; as, it never rains *but* it pours. **d** That not; as, not so stupid *but* he could drive a bargain. **3.** That; — after *no, not, never,* etc., or (often with *that*) *doubt, question,* etc.; as, there is no question *but* he will succeed. **4.** Than; — after a comparative, or *other, otherwise, else.*

— *adv.* **1.** *Now Scot.* Outside; without; specif., *Scot.*, in or into the but, or outer room. **2.** Only; merely; barely; as, he was *but* a youth. **3.** Precisely; just; even; — emphasizing brevity, recentness, or nearness; as, I saw him *but* a moment ago. **4.** There being no less, or no more, objectionable alternative; as, he can *but* kill us. **5.** On the contrary; regardless of that; be that as it may; yet; rather; — used as a connective introducing a sentence.

— (bŭt), *n.* The conjunction *but*; also, an objection, restriction, or the like, such as is often introduced by *but*.

— *pron.* That not; who not. "Nobody *but* has his fault." *Shak.*

but (bŭt), *n.* *Scot.* An outer apartment or kitchen.

bu'ta·di'ene (bū'tȧ·dī'ēn; -dī·ēn'), *n.* [*butane* + *di-* + *-ene* as in *benzene*.] *Chem.* Either of two isomeric hydrocarbons, C_4H_6; specif., 1,3-butadiene, a gas used in making synthetic rubber.

bu'tane (bū'tān; bū·tān'), *n.* [L. *butyrum* butter. See BUTTER.] *Chem.* Either of two isomeric, inflammable, gaseous hydrocarbons, C_4H_{10}, of the methane series.

bu'ta·nol (bū'tȧ·nōl; -nŏl), *n.* *Chem.* Butyl alcohol.

bu'ta·none (bū'tȧ·nōn), *n.* *Chem.* A colorless inflammable liquid, C_4H_8O, used in organic synthesis and as a solvent.

butch'er (bo͝och'ẽr), *n.* [OF. *bochier, bouchier*, fr. ML. *bucola, bucida*, slayer of cattle.] **1.** One who slaughters animals, or dresses their flesh, for market; also, a dealer in meat. **2.** One guilty of ruthless, extensive, or brutal murder or killing. **3.** A botcher. **4.** *U. S.* A vendor, esp. on trains; as, a candy *butcher*. — *v. t.* **1.** To slaughter as a butcher does. **2.** To botch. — **butch'er·er**, *n.*

butch'er·bird' (-bûrd'), *n.* See SHRIKE.

butch'er·ly, *adj.* Like a butcher; hence, savage; bloody.

butch'er's-broom' (bo͝och'ẽrz·bro͞om'), *n.* A European leafless plant (*Ruscus aculeatus*) bearing stiff-pointed leaflike branches (*cladophylls*) and greenish flowers succeeded by red berries.

butcher's saw. See SAW, *Illust.*

butch'er·y (bo͝och'ẽr·ĭ), *n.*; *pl.* -ERIES (-ĭz). **1.** A slaughterhouse. **2.** The business of a butcher. **3.** Wholesale, barbarous, or cruel slaughter.

but'ler (bŭt'lẽr), *n.* [OF. *bouteillier* bottle bearer, cupbearer.] A manservant having charge of the wines and liquors; now, usually, a head servant, who has charge of the plate, glass, etc. — **but'ler·ship**, *n.*

but'ler's pan'try (bŭt'lẽrz). A service room between kitchen and dining room.

butt (bŭt), *n.* [Through F. & Pr., fr. LL. *buttis*.] **1.** A large cask, esp. for wine or beer. **2.** As a measure of capacity, two hogsheads; now commonly, for malt liquors, 108 imperial gals. (129.7 gals. U. S.). Cf. PIPE, 7; TUN, 2.

butt, *n.* [ME. *but, butte*, in various senses. Sense 1 prob. of Teut. origin; senses 2, 3, 5, 6, fr. OF. *but* goal, aim; sense 4 partly fr. F. *butte* mound. Several different stems have fallen together both in French and in English.] **1.** The thicker end (of anything) or the part at the bottom, source, or the like; as, the *butt* of a spear or of a ham (see PORK, *Illust.*). **2.** *Obs.* A bound; goal; end. **3.** One who is the object, as of jest, abuse, etc. **4.** A mound of earth or the like, as one to catch projectiles from artillery, rifles, etc., in target practice, or, in archery, one on which a target is set. **5.** *Now pl.* A range for target shooting. **6.** Loosely, any mark or target. **7.** A push, thrust, or sudden blow, as one given by the head of an animal. **8.** *Carp.* A kind of hinge. **9.** *Leather Trade.* The part of a hide or skin corresponding to the animal's back and sides. See HIDE, *Illust.*

— *v. i.* [Sense 1 is fr. OF. *boter* to push.] **1.** To strike or thrust, now esp. by pushing with the head or horns; hence, to go or drive headfirst. **2.** To jut, run, or project; — with *out, into*, etc. **3.** To abut; — with *on, against*, etc. — *v. t.* **1.** To strike, esp. with the head or horns; to drive or push by such butting. **2.** To abut or cause to abut; — with *on, upon, against*. **3.** To join end to end without overlapping. Cf. BUTT JOINT.

butte (būt), *n.* [F.] An isolated hill or small mountain with steep or precipitous sides.

but'ter (bŭt'ẽr), *n.* [AS. *butere*, fr. L. *butyrum*, fr. Gr. *boutyron*.] **1.** The solidified fat of milk, obtained from cream or milk usually by churning. **2.** A butterlike substance; as: **a** Any of certain concrete fatty oils remaining nearly solid at ordinary temperatures; as, *butter* of cacao. **b** A butterlike product made by grinding nuts, stewing fruits, etc.; as, ***peanut butter, apple butter***. **3.** *Colloq.* Flattery; blarney. — *v. t.* To cover or spread with or as with butter; hence, *Colloq.*, to flatter.

but'ter-and-eggs', *n.* Any of several plants having flowers of two shades of yellow; esp., the common toadflax (*Linaria vulgaris*), and the owl's-clover (*Orthocarpus erianthus*) of California.

but'ter·ball' (bŭt'ẽr·bôl'), **but'ter·box'** (-bŏks'), *n.* = BUFFLEHEAD.

butter bean. **a** See STRING BEAN. **b** *Southern U. S.* The Lima bean.

but'ter·cup' (bŭt'ẽr·kŭp'), *n.* See CROWFOOT, 1.

but'ter·fat' (-făt'), *n.* The natural fat of milk, the chief constituent of butter, consisting essentially of a mixture of glycerides, chiefly butyrin, olein, and palmitin.

but'ter·fin'gered (-fĭng'gẽrd), *adj.* *Colloq.* Apt to let things fall or slip through the fingers; careless.

but'ter·fin'gers (-fĭng'gẽrz), *n.* *Colloq.* A butterfingered person.

but'ter·fish' (-fĭsh'), *n.*; *pl.*, see FISH. Any of several fishes with a slippery coating of mucus, as the dollarfish or the gunnel.

but'ter·fly' (-flī'), *n.* [AS. *buterflēge, buttor-flēoge*.] **1.** Any of certain slender-bodied diurnal insects (order Lepidoptera) with large, broad, usually brightly colored wings. See MOTH. **2.** One as bright, light, etc., as a butterfly.

butterfly bush. = BUDDLEIA.

butterfly fish. Any of various fishes, so called from their variegated colors, or broad winglike fins, or both; as: **a** The ocellated blenny (see BLENNY, *Illust.*). **b** = FLYING GURNARD. **c** Any of a family (Chaetodontidae) of small, brilliantly colored, spiny-finned fishes of tropical seas, having a narrow deep body, and fins partly covered with scales.

butterfly valve. *Mach.* **a** A type of double clack valve (see CLACK VALVE). **b** A damper or throttle valve in a pipe, consisting of a disk turning on a diametral axis.

butterfly weed. **a** An orange-flowered showy milkweed (*Asclepias tuberosa*). The root is diaphoretic and expectorant. **b** A prairie plant (*Gaura coccinea*) of the evening-primrose family, with irregular scarlet flowers.

but'ter·ine (bŭt'ẽr·ēn; -ĭn), *n.* Artificial butter, or oleomargarine, esp. when made with addition of butter.

but'ter·milk' (-mĭlk'), *n.* The liquid left after churning out butter.

but'ter·nut' (-nŭt'), *n.* **1. a** The edible nut of an American tree (*Juglans cinerea*) of the walnut family. **b** The tree itself. **2.** The souari nut. **3. a** *pl. Southern U. S.* A kind of brown overalls. **b** *Slang.* A Confederate soldier or partisan in the Civil War; — from the brown homespun clothes of Confederate soldiers.

but'ter·scotch' (bŭt'ẽr·skŏch'), *n.* A kind of candy, mainly composed of brown sugar and butter. — *adj.* Flavored with the ingredients of butterscotch; as, *butterscotch* sauce.

butter tree. One of several trees the seeds of which yield a butterlike substance, esp. the shea tree and the mahua.

but'ter·weed' (-wēd'), *n.* Any plant so called from its yellow flowers or smooth soft foliage; as: **a** The horseweed. **b** An American ragwort (*Senecio glabellus*).

but'ter·wort' (-wûrt'), *n.* Any of a genus (*Pinguicula*, family Lentibulariaceae) of plants; — so called on account of the mucilage secreted by the leaves to capture insects.

but'ter·y (bŭt'ẽr·ĭ), *adj.* Resembling butter; containing, or spread with, butter; hence, *Colloq.*, flattering.

but'ter·y (bŭt'ẽr·ĭ; bŭt'rĭ), *n.; pl.* BUTTERIES (-ĭz; -rĭz). [OF. *boterie* place for keeping bottles, prop. a place for keeping casks, or *butts.*] **1.** A storeroom for liquors; also, a room for provisions. **2.** In some English colleges, a room where ale, bread, etc., are kept for sale to students.

butt joint. *Structural Engin.* Any joint made by fastening the parts together end to end without overlap, and often strengthened, as with a strap or straps.

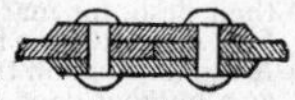
Butt Joint.

but'tock (bŭt'ŭk), *n.* [From BUTT end.] The part at the back of the hip, which in man forms one of the protuberances on which he sits; in *pl.*, the rump.

but'ton (bŭt''n), *n.* [OF. *boton* button, bud.] **1.** A knob, disk, or the like, to fasten together different parts of an article of clothing by being attached to one part and passing through a hole or loop (*buttonhole*) in the other. **2.** A buttonlike part or growth in plants, as a bud, the hip of a rose, etc. **3.** A small knob or device like a button. **4.** *Assaying.* A small globule of metal remaining after fusion. **5.** *Fencing.* A guard on the tip of a foil. **6.** *Boxing Slang.* The point of the chin. — *v. t.* To furnish with, or fasten with, a button or buttons. — *v. i.* To admit of being buttoned.

but'ton·ball' (-bôl'), *n.* See 1st PLANE, *n.*

but'ton·bush' (-bo͝osh'), *n.* A North American shrub (*Cephalanthus occidentalis*) having globular flower heads.

but'ton·hole' (-hōl'), *n.* The hole or loop for a button (see BUTTON, *n.*, 1). — *v. t.* **1.** To hold by the button or buttonhole; hence, to detain in talk. **2.** To furnish with buttonholes; to work with a buttonhole stitch.

buttonhole stitch. A closely worked loop stitch used to make a firm finish on the edge of material, as in buttonholes. See STITCH, *Illust.*

but'ton·hook' (-ho͝ok'), *n.* A hook to draw buttons through buttonholes.

button snakeroot. Any of a genus (*Liatris*) of plants of the aster family, with long spikes of buttonlike flower heads; — called also *blazing star.*

button tree. See 1st PLANE, *n.*

but'ton·wood' (bŭt''n·wo͝od'), *n.* See 1st PLANE, *n.*

but'ton·y (-ĭ), *adj.* Ornamented with buttons; buttonlike.

but'tress (bŭt'rĕs; -rĭs), *n.* [OF. *bouterez*, fr. *bouter, boter*, to thrust.] **1.** *Arch.* A projecting structure to support a wall or building, esp. to receive lateral pressure acting at a particular point in a single direction. Cf. ABUTMENT; see GOTHIC, *Illust.* **2.** A support; prop; as, the *buttress* of public opinion. **3.** Something resembling a buttress, as: **a** A projecting part of a hill. **b** A horny protuberance on a horse's hoof at the heel where the wall bends inward and forward. See HOOF, *Illust.* — *v. t.* To furnish or support with a buttress; prop.

butt shaft. A barbless or a blunt arrow.

butt'stock' (bŭt'stŏk'), *n.* *Firearms.* The part of the stock in the rear of the breech mechanism.

butt weld. A butt joint made by welding.

bu'tyl (bū'tĭl), *n.* [L. *butyrum* butter + *-yl.*] **1.** *Chem.* Any of four isomeric univalent organic radicals, C_4H_9. With hydroxyl they form **butyl alcohols**, C_4H_9OH. **2.** [*cap.*] A registered trade-mark applied to a synthetic rubber made by copolymerization of isobutylene and either butadiene or isoprene.

bu'tyl·ene (bū'tĭ·lēn), *n.* [From *butyl.*] *Chem.* Any of three isomeric hydrocarbons, C_4H_8, of the ethylene series.

bu'tyr·a'ceous (bū'tẽr·ā'shŭs), *adj.* [L. *butyrum* butter.] Having the qualities of, like, or yielding, butter.

bu'tyr·al (bū'tẽr·ăl), *n.* [*butyr*aldehyde + acet*al.*] *Chem.* An acetal of butyraldehyde.

bu'tyr·al'de·hyde (-ăl'dē·hīd), *n.* [*butyric* + *aldehyde.*] *Chem.* A colorless liquid, C_3H_7CHO, made from butyl alcohol and otherwise, used in making synthetic resins, butyric acid, etc.

bu'tyr·ate (bū'tẽr·āt), *n.* A salt or ester of butyric acid.

bu·tyr'ic (bū·tĭr'ĭk), *adj.* *Chem.* **a** Pertaining to, or derived from, butter. **b** Designating a colorless liquid acid (**butyric acid**, $C_3H_7CO_2H$) of unpleasant odor, occurring free in perspiration, etc.

bu'tyr·in (bū'tẽr·ĭn), *n.* A glyceryl ester of butyric acid.

bux'om (bŭk'sŭm), *adj.* [ME. *buxum, buhsum*, pliable, fr. root of AS. *būgan* to bend + *-sum* (see 1st -SOME).] **1.** *Archaic.* Compliant; obedient. **2.** Having health, vigor, and comeliness; plump and rosy. **3.** *Archaic.* Gay; blithe. — **bux'om·ly**, *adv.* — **bux'om·ness**, *n.*

buy (bī), *v. t.;* BOUGHT (bôt); BUY'ING. [AS. *bycgan.*] **1.** To acquire (property) by giving a price; purchase; — opposed to *sell.* **2.** To obtain at a price, cost, or sacrifice; as, to *buy* pleasure with pain. **3.** To redeem, as by a ransom; — chiefly in a theological sense. **4.** To constitute the purchasing equivalent of; as, that which no gold can *buy.* **5.** To hire or bribe; as, to *buy* a public official. — *v. i.* To perform the act of buying something.

buy off. To induce to abstain, or secure the release of, by some consideration. — ***buy out.*** To purchase the share or interest of.

buy, *n.* **1.** A buying. **2.** *Colloq.* A thing bought or to be bought, esp. at a profit or advantage; a bargain.

buy'er (bī'ẽr), *n.* One who buys, as a purchasing agent.

buzz (bŭz), *v. i.* [Of imitative origin.] **1.** To make a low, continuous, humming or sibilant sound, like that made by bees. **2.** To murmur; whisper. **3.** To be filled with a low hum or murmur; as, the room *buzzed* with excitement. — *v. t.* **1.** To utter or give forth with a buzz; — chiefly derogatory, as of busy and incessant talk. **2.** To cause to buzz; as, a fly *buzzing* its wings. **3.** To fly an airplane low and fast over; as, to *buzz* troops. — *n.* **1.** A continuous humming sound, as of bees; confused murmur or hum. **2.** A whisper or rumor.

buzz, *v. t.* *Eng.* To empty to the last drop in drinking.

buz'zard (bŭz'ẽrd), *n.* [OF. *busard*, fr. *buison* (whence F. *buse*), fr. L. *buteo.*] **1.** Any of numerous heavy, slow-flying hawks (*Buteo* and allied genera), as the common European species (*B. buteo*) and the North American ***hen hawks*** *B. borealis, B. lineatus,* and *B. platypterus.* **2.** Any of various other birds of prey, as the ***bald buzzard*** (= OSPREY, 1), ***honey buzzard*** (*Pernis apivorous*, of Europe), ***moor buzzard*** (see 2d HARRIER, 2), and, esp., the ***turkey buzzard*** (which see). **3.** *Slang.* A contemptible or rapacious person.

buzz bomb. See ROBOT BOMB.

buzz'er (bŭz'ẽr), *n.* One that buzzes, as an electric signal device.

buzz saw. A circular saw. See SAW, *Illust.*

by (bī; 4), *prep.* [AS. *bī, big*, near to, by, of, from, after, according to.] **1.** In proximity to; near; also, toward; as, east *by* north. **2.** Along, over, or through; as, go *by* the road. **3.** In, on, or at; as, perils *by* sea. **4.** Past; near to and then on beyond; as, he passed *by* him. **5.** Near or through as regards time; as, *by* day; also, not later than; as, *by* two o'clock. **6.** To the amount of; — involving comparison; as, better *by* far. **7.** According to; with; after. **8.** With respect to; as, he did well *by* her. **9.** Through the medium of; as, to hang *by* a thread. **10.** With the witness or sanction of; — used in oaths.

— ***by and by.*** Presently; pretty soon; before long. — ***by the way.*** Incidentally; also, in addition.

by (bī), *adv.* **1.** Near; at hand. **2.** Near in passing; past; beyond; as, a bird flew *by.* **3.** Aside; apart; as, to put *by.* — *adj.* Apart from the common or main. See BYE. — *n.* Variant of BYE.

by-. A combining form of: **1.** The adverb *by*, meaning *near at hand* or *near in passing;* as, **by'pass'er.** **2.** The adjective *by* used with nouns: Aside or apart from the main or common; out of the way; as, *by*path; hence, secondary; extra; incidental; as, *by*play; *by*-product.

by'-and-by', *n.* A future time or occasion.

by'-blow', *n.* **1.** An indirect blow. **2.** An illegitimate child.

bye (bī), *n.* [See BY, *prep.*] **1.** Something aside or secondary. *Obs.*, except in *by the bye.* **2. a** *Cricket.* A run made upon a ball which the batsman allows to pass. **b** In various sports, after pairs are drawn, the position or turn of one left without an opponent, who advances to the next round without playing. **c** *Golf.* The hole or holes of a course remaining unplayed at the end of a match. — ***by the bye;*** also, ***by the by.*** In passing; by the way.

bye, by (bī), *adj.* Secondary; incidental; as, a *bye* consideration.

bye-. Var. of BY-, as in **bye'-e·lec'tion.**

by'-e·lec'tion, *n.* An election held between regular elections, usually to fill a vacancy.

Bye'lo·rus'sian (byĕ'lō·rŭsh'ăn), *adj. & n.* = WHITE RUSSIAN. See RUSSIAN, *n.*, 1 & 2.

by'gone' (bī'gŏn'; 74), *adj.* Past; gone by; belonging to the past. — *n.* Something gone by or past.

by'law', bye'law' (bī'lô'), *n.* [Prob. fr. AS. *by̆* village. See LAW.] A law or regulation made by a public or private corporation or an association or unincorporated society for the regulation of its own local or internal affairs or its dealings with others, or for the government of its members; as, village *bylaws;* the *bylaws* of a club. The bylaws of a municipal corporation (in the U. S. oftener called *ordinances*) are true laws; those of other corporations are rather agreements of the members.

by'-line', *n.* **1.** = SIDE LINE, 2 **b.** **2.** *Journalism.* The line at the head of an article telling *by* whom it was written.

by'name' (bī'nām'), *n.* A secondary name; a nickname.

by'pass', *n.* **1.** A passage to one side, as a road to deflect traffic. **2. a** *Mach.* An auxiliary passage, as for a pipe; a secondary outlet. **b** *Elec.* A shunt. — *v. t.* **a** To make a circuit or detour round; as, a boulevard *bypassing* cities. **b** To neglect or ignore deliberately in order to reach or confront another objective beyond; to circumvent; as, wartime power to *bypass* the democratic right of habeas corpus; to evade; as, the issue of conscription was *bypassed* at the convention. **c** *Mil.* To pass round and beyond (an enemy stronghold), avoiding frontal attack in favor of subsequent envelopment.

by'past' (bī'påst'), *adj.* Past; gone by. Cf. BYGONE.

by'path' (-påth'; 9), *n.* A side, private, or indirect path.

by'play' (-plā'), *n.* Action aside or apart, as in conversation; on the stage, action apart from the main action.

by'-prod'uct, *n.* Something produced secondarily or in addition to the main product in manufacture; hence, a secondary, often an unexpected or unintended, result; as, epidemics are a *by-product* of war.

byre (bīr), *n.* [AS. *by̆re.*] A cow barn.

by'road' (bī'rōd'), *n.* A side road or one not a main road.

By·ron'ic (bī·rŏn'ĭk), *adj.* Having the characteristics, or in the style, of Byron or his writings, which are marked by the portrayal of pride, cynical scorn, irony, and remorse.

bys'sus (bĭs'ŭs), *n.; pl.* BYSSUSES (-ĕz; -ĭz), BYSSI (-ī). [L. *byssus* fine flax, linen, or cotton, fr. Gr. *byssos.*] **1.** A valuable and fine fabric, probably linen, made by the ancients. **2.** *Zool.* A tuft of filaments by which certain bivalves, as the mussel, fasten to rocks.

by'stand'er (bī'stăn'dẽr), *n.* One who stands near; one present at, but not taking part in, some activity.

by'street' (-strēt'), *n.* A side street; a quiet street off the main thoroughfare.

by'way' (-wā'), *n.* A byroad or a bypath.

by'word' (-wûrd'), *n.* [AS. *bīword.*] **1.** A proverb or proverbial saying. **2.** A person or thing taken proverbially as a type; — usually in a bad sense; hence, an object of scorn. **3.** A nickname. **4.** A word or phrase often used, as for emphasis, affectation, etc.; a pet expression.

By·zan'tine (bĭ·zăn'tĭn; -tīn; bī-; bĭz'ăn·tēn; -tīn), *adj.* **1.** Of, pertaining to, or characteristic of Byzantium (later Constantinople, now Istanbul) or the Byzantine Empire. **2.** *Arch.* Designating a style of architecture developed in the Byzantine Empire chiefly in the 5th and 6th centuries, characterized by a central dome over a square space, with mosaic incrustation and marble veneering of the walls. — *n.* A native or inhabitant of Byzantium.

C

C, c (sē), *n.; pl.* C's, c's, Cs, cs (sēz). **1.** The third letter of the English alphabet. C comes through Latin from Greek, which took it from Phoenician. **2.** The sound of this letter. See *Pron.*, § 18. **3.** [*cap.*] In Roman numerals, 100. **4.** Anything having the shape of the letter C. **5.** *Music.* **a** The keynote of the normal or "natural" major scale, which has neither flats nor sharps in its signature; also, the third note of its relative minor scale (that of A minor). **b** Any symbol representing this tone. See PITCH, *Illust.* **c** A key or string producing this tone. **6.** As a *symbol*, the third in order or of its class.

ca' (kä; kô). Scot. var. of CALL, CALF.

Caa'ba. Var. of KAABA.

cab (kăb), *n.* Also **kab.** [Heb. *qab*, fr. *qābab* to hollow.] A Hebrew dry measure approximately equal to two quarts.

cab, *n.* [From CABRIOLET.] **1. a** A type of closed carriage, usually a public vehicle; a cabriolet. **b** A taxicab. **2. a** The covered part of a locomotive serving as shelter for engineer and fireman. **b** The driver's compartment in a motor truck.

ca·bal' (kȧ·băl'), *n.* [F. *cabale*, fr. ML. *cabala* cabala, fr. Heb. *qabbālāh*, lit., the received or traditional lore.] **1.** The secret artifices of a few persons united in a close design; intrigue. **2.** A secret association of a few designing persons; a junto. — **Syn.** See PLOT. — *v. i.;* CA·BALLED' (-băld'); CA·BAL'LING. [F. *cabaler.*] To unite in or form a cabal; to intrigue.

cab'a·la (kăb'ȧ·lȧ; kȧ·bä'lȧ), *n.* [ML. See CABAL.] **1.** A kind or system of occult theosophy or mystical interpretation of the Scriptures among Jewish rabbis and certain medieval Christians. **2.** Secret or esoteric doctrine or science, in general; occultism. — **cab'a·lism** (kăb'ȧ·lĭz'm), *n.* — **cab'a·list** (-lĭst), *n.* — **ca·bal'ic** (kȧ·băl'ĭk), **cab'a·lis'tic** (kăb'ȧ·lĭs'tĭk), **cab'a·lis'ti·cal** (-tĭ·kăl), *adj.*

‖**ca'bal·le'ro** (kä'vä·lyā'rō; 17), *n.; pl.* -ROS (*Sp.* -rōs). [Sp.] A knight or cavalier; gentleman.

ca·ba'na (kȧ·băn'(y)ȧ), *n.* [Sp. *cabaña.*] A beach shelter resembling a cabin, usually with an open side facing the sea.

cab'a·ret (kăb'ȧ·rĕt; *in sense* 2, *usually* kăb'ȧ·rā'; kăb'ȧ·rā), *n.* [F.] **1.** Orig., a tavern. **2.** A café or restaurant whose patrons are entertained by performers who dance or sing, as in certain French taverns; hence, an entertainment of this nature.

cab'bage (kăb'ĭj), *n.* [ONF. (& F.) *caboche* head.] **1.** A leafy vegetable of many varieties, derived from a European plant (*Brassica oleracea*) of the mustard family (see MUSTARD). The common cabbage (*B. oleracea capitata*) is a short-stemmed plant with a mass of leaves, usually green, forming a dense head. Other vegetables derived from *B. oleracea* include cauliflower and broccoli, Brussels sprouts, kale, collard, kohlrabi. **2.** The terminal bud of certain palm trees, often eaten as a vegetable; — called also ***palm cabbage.*** — *v. i.;* -BAGED (-ĭjd); -BAG·ING (-ĭj·ĭng). To form a head like that of the cabbage.

cab'bage, *v. t. & i.* To purloin; pilfer. — *n.* Pieces of cloth cut off in cutting out garments and kept, or cabbaged, by tailors as perquisites.

cabbage palm. Any palm whose terminal bud is eaten as a vegetable, as the **cabbage palmetto** (see PALMETTO) and various Australian fan palms. Some are called also **cabbage tree.**

cab'ba·la, cab'ba·lism, etc. Vars. of CABALA, etc.

cab'by (kăb'ĭ), *n.; pl.* -BIES (-ĭz). *Colloq.* A cabman.

ca'ber (kā'bẽr), *n.* [Gael. *cabar.*] A beam; a pole, esp. one used in Gaelic games for tossing as a trial of strength.

cab'in (kăb'ĭn), *n.* [F. *cabane*, fr. Pr., fr. LL. *capanna.*] **1.** A small house, esp. a rude one. **2.** *Naut.* **a** A private room on a ship for officers or passengers. **b** On a small vessel, a compartment below deck affording accommodation or shelter for passengers or crew. **c** *U.S. Navy.* The quarters of the captain, admiral, or chief of staff. **3.** A closed cockpit of an airplane. — *v. i. & t.* To lodge or confine in or as in a cabin.

cabin boy. A boy whose duty is to wait on the officers and cabin passengers of a ship.

cabin class. A class of accommodations in a passenger vessel, superior to tourist class (which see) and inferior to first class (which see). *Cabin class* was formerly used for *first class.* — **cabin–class,** *adj. & adv.*

cabin cruiser. See CRUISER, 3.

cab'i·net (kăb'ĭ·nĕt; -nĭt), *n.* [F.] **1.** A case, set of drawers, or cupboard to contain jewels, specimens, or other articles. **2.** A small room or private apartment; a boudoir. **3.** A private room for consultations, esp. of a sovereign's confidential advisers. **4.** [*often cap.*] A body of advisers, esp. the advisory council of a sovereign or the chief executive. — *adj.* **1.** Of or pertaining to a cabinet. **2.** Suitable for a cabinet, small room, or piece of furniture.

cab'i·net·mak'er (-māk'ẽr), **cab'i·net·work'er** (-wûr'kẽr), *n.* One whose occupation is to make or do fine woodwork (**cab'i·net·work'**).

ca'ble (kā'b'l), *n.* [F. *câble*, fr. Pr. *cable*, fr. LL. *capulum, caplum*, a rope.] **1.** A strong fiber rope, esp. one of ten or more inches in circumference; hence, a very strong wire rope or a chain used for hauling, fastening, suspension bridges, etc. **2.** A cable's length (see MEASURE, *Table* 9). **3.** A cablegram. **4.** *Elec.* **a** A waterproof insulated bundle of wires, often twisted around a core, as for submarine telegraphy. **b** In full ***electric cable.*** An insulated wire or flexible built-up conductor for transmitting a current. — *v. t. & i.;* CA'BLED (-b'ld); CA'BLING (-blĭng). To telegraph by a cable (def. 4).

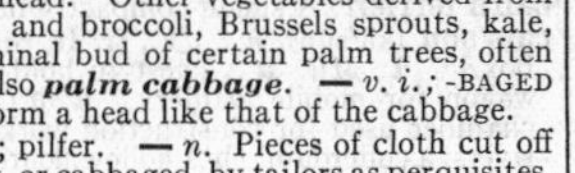

Submarine Cable, cut away to show two conductors, insulation, lead sheathing, jute packing, and armor of steel wires.

cable car. A car made to be moved on a **cable railway** by an endless cable operated by a stationary motor.

ca'ble·gram (kā'b'l·grăm), *n.* [*cable* + *-gram.*] A message sent by a submarine telegraphic cable.

ca'ble–laid' (-lād'), *adj.* *Ropemaking.* Composed of three ropes laid together left-handed, each containing three strands.

ca'blet (kā'blĕt; -blĭt), *n.* [Dim. of *cable.*] A cable-laid rope less than ten inches in circumference.

cab'man (kăb'măn), *n.* One who drives a cab.

ca·bob' (kȧ·bŏb'), *n.* [Per. & Hind. *kabāb.*] Now *pl.* In the Orient, meat roasted in small pieces on a skewer and seasoned; also, in India, roast meat in general.

ca'bo·chon' (kȧ'bô'shôN'), *n.* [F.] *Jewelry.* A stone cut in convex form, polished but not faceted; also, the style itself. Such stones are said to be cut *cabochon*, or [F.] ***en cabochon*** (äN).

ca·boo'dle (kȧ·bōō'd'l), *n.* *Slang.* A collection; lot; as, the whole *caboodle* of them. Cf. BOODLE, 1.

ca·boose' (kȧ·bōōs'), *n.* **1.** *Naut.* A deck room for cooking; galley. **2.** *U.S. Railroads.* A car attached to a freight or construction train for workmen or the train crew.

cab'o·tage (kăb'ō·tĭj; *F.* kȧ'bô'tȧzh'), *n.* [F.] **1.** Coastal navigation. **2.** Restriction of air transport within the boundaries of a country to domestic carriers.

ca·bril'la (kȧ·brĭl'ȧ; kä·brē'yä), *n.* [Sp., prawn.] Any of various edible fishes; specif., the red hind (*Epinephelus guttatus*) or other grouper.

cab'ri·ole (kăb'rĭ·ōl), *n.* [F.] *Furniture.* A curved leg ending in an ornamental foot, frequent in Queen Anne and Chippendale furniture.

cab'ri·o·let' (kăb'rĭ·ō·lā'), *n.* [F., fr. *cabrioler, caprioler*, fr. It., deriv. of L. *caper* he-goat.] **1.** A light one-horse two-seated carriage; a cab. **2.** An automobile with a folding top and glass windows.

ca' can'ny (kä, *or* kô, kăn'ĭ). [Scot. *ca'* call. See CALL, *v. i.*, 4.] *Orig. Eng. Labor Slang.* A deliberate slackening by workmen in rate of production.

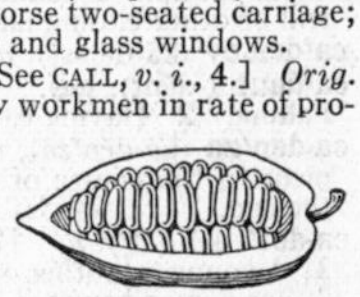

Cacao Pod, showing seeds.

ca·ca'o (kȧ·kā'ō; kȧ·kä'ō), *n.; pl.* CACAOS (-ōz). [Sp., fr. Nahuatl *cacahuatl*, the seed.] **1.** A South American tree (*Theobroma cacao*) of the chocolate family, now cultivated in the West Indies, Mexico, etc. **2.** The dried and partly fermented seeds (**cacao,** *or* **cocoa, beans**) of this tree, used chiefly in making cocoa and chocolate. They yield a yellowish fat (**cacao,** *or* **cocoa, butter**), used in candy, etc. See CHOCOLATE, COCOA.

cach'a·lot (kăsh'ȧ·lŏt; -lō), *n.* [F., fr. Sp. *cachalote.*] The sperm whale.

cache (kăsh), *n.* [F., fr. *cacher* to hide.] **a** A hole in the ground, or a hiding place, esp. one used by explorers for storing provisions or implements. **b** That which is hidden in a cache. — *v. t. & i.* To put, hide, or store, in a cache.

ca·chet' (kă·shā'; kăsh'ā; *F.* kȧ'shĕ'), *n.* [F., fr. *cacher* to hide.] **1.** A seal, as of a letter. **2.** A peculiar distinctive character or quality. **3.** *Pharm.* A capsule. **4.** *Philately.* A design printed or stamped on mail.

ca·chex'i·a (kȧ·kĕk'sĭ·ȧ), *n.* Also **ca·chex'y** (-sĭ). [L. *cachexia*, fr. Gr. *kachexia*, fr. *kakos* bad + *hexis* condition.] A condition of general ill health, bodily or mental. — **ca·chec'tic** (-kĕk'tĭk), **ca·chec'ti·cal** (-tĭ·kăl), *adj.*

cach'in·nate (kăk'ĭ·nāt), *v. i.* [L. *cachinnare.*] To laugh loudly or immoderately. — **cach'in·na'tion** (-nā'shŭn), *n.*

ca'chou' (kȧ'shōō'), *n.* [F. See CATECHU.] **1.** Catechu. **2.** An aromatic pill or pastille used to sweeten the breath.

ca·chu'cha (kȧ·chōō'chȧ), *n.* [Sp.] A gay Andalusian solo dance, in ¾ time, done with castanets.

ca·cique' (kȧ·sēk'), *n.* [Sp., of Arawakan origin.] **1.** A native chief in the West Indies, Peru, Mexico, Philippines, etc.; hence, U.S., a political boss. **2.** Any of numerous tropical American orioles (genus *Cacicus* or allied genera) having the base of the bill expanded into a frontal shield.

cack'le (kăk''l), *v. i.;* CACK'LED (-'ld); CACK'LING (-lĭng). [ME. *cakelen.*] **1.** To make the sharp broken noise or cry of a hen. **2.** To giggle; prattle. — *v. t.* To utter with cackles. — **cack'le,** *n.* — **cack'ler** (-lẽr), *n.*

cac'o- (kăk'ō-), **cac-.** [Gr. *kakos.*] A combining form meaning *bad; specif.*, in medicine, *diseased, deformed.*

cac'o·de'mon, cac'o·dae'mon (kăk'ō·dē'mŏn), *n.* [Gr. *kakodaimōn*, lit., bad daemon.] An evil spirit; a demon.

cac'o·dyl (kăk'ō·dĭl; -dĕl), *n.* [Gr. *kakōdēs* ill-smelling (fr. *kakos* bad + *ozein* to smell) + *-yl.*] *Chem.* **a** An arsenical radical, $As(CH_3)_2$, whose compounds are noted for their vile smell and poisonous properties. **b** A polymer of the radical, or $As_2(CH_3)_4$, a colorless poisonous liquid of offensive odor. — **cac'o·dyl'ic** (-dĭl'ĭk), *adj.*

cac'o·ë'thes (kăk'ō·ē'thēz), *n.* [L., fr. Gr. *kakoēthēs* of ill habits.] An insatiable desire; mania; as, ‖**ca'co·ë'thes scri·ben'di** (skrĭ·bĕn'dī), itch for writing.

cac'o·gen'ics (-jĕn'ĭks), *n.;* see -ICS. [*caco-* + eu*genics.*] The study, or the process, of race deterioration, as from the mating of inferior stock. — **cac'o·gen'ic** (-ĭk), *adj.*

cac'o·mis'tle (kăk'ō·mĭs''l), **cac'o·mix'le** (-mĭs''l; -mĭk's'l), *n.* [Sp. *cacomixtle*, fr. Nahuatl *tlacomiztli.*] A carnivore (*Bassariscus astutus*), related to and resembling the raccoon; also, its fur or pelt.

ca·coph'o·ny (kă·kŏf'ō·nĭ), *n.; pl.* -NIES (-nĭz). [Gr. *kakophōnia*, fr. *kakos* bad + *phōnē* sound.] Harsh or discordant sound, or an instance of it; hence, dissonance; discord; — opp. to *euphony.* — **ca·coph'o·nous** (-nŭs), *adj.*

cac'tus (kăk'tŭs), *n.; pl.* CACTI (-tī), -TUSES (-tŭs·ĕz; -ĭz). [L., a kind of prickly plant, fr. Gr. *kaktos.*] Any plant of a family (Cactaceae, the cactus family) having fleshy stems and branches with scales or spines instead of leaves. — **cac·ta'ceous** (kăk·tā'shŭs), *adj.*

cad (kăd), *n.* [From CADET.] **1.** *Obs. Eng.* A conductor of an omnibus. **2.** A person without gentlemanly instincts; a bounder.

ca·das'tral (kȧ·dăs'trăl), *adj.* [F.] Of or pertaining to a cadastre; of or pert. to landed property, esp. as to its extent, value, and ownership; as, a **cadastral survey,** a survey for the purpose of making a cadastre, hence, one made on a large scale.

ca·das'tre, ca·das'ter (kȧ·dăs'tẽr), *n.* [F. *cadastre.*] An official register of the quantity, value, and ownership of real estate, used in apportioning taxes.

ca·dav'er (kȧ·dăv'ẽr; -dā'vẽr), *n.* [L., fr. *cadere* to fall.] A dead body, esp. a human one, as for dissection; a corpse.

ca·dav'er·ous (kȧ·dăv'ẽr·ŭs), *adj.* Of or pertaining to, or having the qualities of, a cadaver; esp., pale; ghastly; also, gaunt and haggard. — **ca·dav'er·ous·ly,** *adv.* — **ca·dav'er·ous·ness,** *n.*

cad'die, cad'dy (kăd'ĭ), *n.* [F. *cadet.*] **1.** One who waits about for chances to do odd jobs. **2.** An attendant who carries a golf player's clubs, etc. — *v. i.;* CAD'DIED (-ĭd); CAD'DY·ING. To serve as a caddie.

cad′dis, cad′dice (kăd′ĭs), *n.* [ME. *caddas*, Scot. *caddis* lint, *caddes* a kind of woolen cloth.] Worsted yarn; specif., a worsted ribbon or binding for garters, etc.

cad′dis, cad′dice, *n.* A caddis worm.

caddis fly. Any of an order (Trichoptera) of four-winged insects having aquatic larvae, called **caddis worms**, which live in, and drag about, a silken case covered with bits of shell, gravel, etc.

cad′dish (kăd′ĭsh), *adj.* Like a cad; lowbred and presuming. — **cad′dish·ly,** *adv.* — **cad′dish·ness,** *n.*

cad′dy (kăd′ĭ), *n.; pl.* -DIES (-ĭz). [Malay *kātī* weight of 1⅓ pounds.] A small box, can, or chest, orig. one for tea.

cad′dy (kăd′ĭ). Variant of CADDIE.

cade (kād), *adj.* Left by the mother and bred by hand; pet; as, a *cade* lamb or colt.

cade, *n.* [F., fr. Pr.] A European juniper (*Juniperus oxycedrus*). Its wood yields by distillation a dark, tarry liquid, **cade oil,** used locally in treating skin diseases.

-cade (-kād). A suffix formed from the final syllable of *cavalcade*, meaning *procession, parade*, as in motor*cade*.

ca′dence (kā′dĕns), *n.* [F., fr. It., fr. L. *cadere* to fall.] **1.** Rhythmical flow of language; rhythm. **2.** The measure or beat of any rhythmical motion, as dancing. **3.** *Music.* **a** A concluding strain. **b** A trill or other closing embellishment. — **ca′denced** (-dĕnst), *adj.*

ca′den·cy (kā′dĕn·sĭ), *n.* Cadence.

ca′dent (-dĕnt), *adj.* [L. *cadens, -entis*, pres. part.] **1.** *Archaic.* Falling. **2.** Having cadence.

ca·den′za (kȧ·dĕn′zȧ), *n.* [It.] *Music.* A flourish or flight of ornament in the course of an aria, concerto, etc., commonly just before the end.

ca·det′ (kȧ·dĕt′), *n.* [F. (in sense 1), fr. LL. dim. of L. *caput* head.] **1.** A younger brother or son; youngest son; a younger branch of a family, or a member of it. **2.** Formerly, a gentleman who enlisted in a regiment, as a volunteer private, to acquire military skill and obtain a commission. **3.** A young man in training for military or naval service; specif., a student at a military or naval school, as at West Point. Cf. MIDSHIPMAN, 2. — **ca·det′ship,** *n.*

ca′dette′ (kȧ′dĕt′), *n.* *New Zealand.* A woman appointed to the civil service after a competitive examination.

cadge (kăj; kāj), *v. t. & i.;* CADGED (kăjd; kājd); CADG′ING. **1.** *Dial.* To carry; also, to peddle. **2.** *Colloq.* To beg or sponge; also, to live by begging or sponging. — **cadg′er,** *n.*

ca′di (kä′dĭ; kā′dĭ), *n.; pl.* CADIS (-dĭz). [Ar. *qāḍī.*] An inferior magistrate or judge among the Mohammedans.

cad′mi·um (kăd′mĭ·ŭm), *n.* [NL., fr. L. *cadmia* calamine, fr. Gr. *kadmeia.*] A tin-white, malleable, ductile metallic element. Symbol, *Cd;* at. no., 48; at. wt., 112.41.

Cad′mus (kăd′mŭs), *n.* [L., fr. Gr. *Kadmos.*] *Gr. Myth.* A prince of Phoenicia who slew a dragon and sowed its teeth. From these sprang armed men who fought together till but five were left. They, with Cadmus, founded Thebes. Cadmus is said to have introduced the alphabet into Greece. — **Cad·me′an** (kăd·mē′ăn), *adj.*

ca′dre (kä′dẽr; *mil. also* kăd′rē; *F.* kä′dr′), *n.* [F. *cadre*, fr. It. *quadro*, fr. L. *quadrus* square, fr. *quatuor* four.] A frame or framework; specif., skeleton organization, as of a military unit.

ca·du′ce·us (kȧ·dū′sē·ŭs), *n.; pl.* -CEI (-sē·ī). [L.] **1.** A herald's staff of office; specif., the staff of Hermes, or Mercury. **2.** Hermes' staff as a symbol of a physician or medical corps. — **ca·du′ce·an** (-sē·ăn), *adj.*

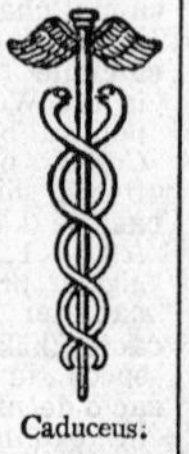
Caduceus.

ca·du′ci·ty (-sĭ·tĭ), *n.* [F. *caducité*, fr. L. *caducus.* See CADUCOUS.] **1.** Perishableness. **2.** Senility.

ca·du′cous (kȧ·dū′kŭs), *adj.* [L. *caducus* falling, fr. *cadere* to fall.] **1.** Falling off; dropping away; *Bot.*, falling off very early; — opp. to *persistent.* Cf. FUGACIOUS, DECIDUOUS. **2.** Transitory; fleeting.

cae·cil′i·an (sē·sĭl′ĭ·ăn), *n.* [L. *caecilia* a kind of lizard, fr. *caecus* blind.] *Zool.* Any of a genus (*Caecilia*) of wormlike burrowing amphibians chiefly of tropical countries.

cae′co- (sē′kō-), **caec-.** A combining form denoting *the caecum*, as in **cae·cec′to·my** (sē·sĕk′tō·mĭ), **cae·cos′to·my** (-kŏs′tō·mĭ), **cae·cot′o·my** (-kŏt′ō·mĭ) (see -ECTOMY, -STOMY, -TOMY).

cae′cum (sē′kŭm), *n.; pl.* -CA (-kȧ). [L. *caecus* blind.] *Anat. & Zool.* A cavity open at one end, as the blind end of a canal or duct; esp., the blind pouch or sac in which the large intestine begins, and into which the ileum opens from one side; the blind gut. — **cae′cal** (-kăl), *adj.*

Cae′li·an (sē′lĭ·ăn), *n.* One of the seven hills of Rome. See SEVEN HILLS.

cae′no- (sē′nō-). Var. of CENO- or of COENO-.

caes′al·pin′i·a′ceous (sĕz′ăl·pĭn′ĭ·ā′shŭs; sĕs′-), *adj.* [After Andrea *Cesalpino*, It. botanist.] *Bot.* Belonging to the senna family (Caesalpiniaceae). See SENNA.

Cae′sar (sē′zẽr), *n.* [L.] **1.** The cognomen of Gaius Julius Caesar; hence: **a** Title given to the Roman emperor. **b** An emperor of the Holy Roman Empire; a kaiser. **2.** Any emperor or autocrat. — **Cae·sar′e·an** (sē·zâr′ē·ăn), **Cae·sar′i·an** (-ĭ·ăn), *adj.*

Cae·sar′e·an sec′tion *or* **op′er·a′tion.** *Surg.* The operation of taking a child from the uterus by cutting through the walls of the abdomen and uterus; — so called from the belief that Julius Caesar was so delivered.

Cae′sar·ism (sē′zẽr·ĭz′m), *n.* Absolute government such as that of a Roman Caesar; imperialism.

cae′si·um (sē′zĭ·ŭm). *Chem.* Var. of CESIUM.

caes′pi·tose, caes′pi·tose·ly. Vars. of CESPITOSE, etc.

cae·su′ra (sē·zū′rȧ; -sū′rȧ), *n.; pl.* -RAS (-rȧz), -RAE (-rē). [L., division, stop, fr. *caedere, caesum*, to cut off.] **1.** In Greek and Latin prosody, a break in a verse caused by the ending of a word within a foot; — loosely used to include diaeresis. A caesura is commonly marked ‖. Thus:

Arma vi|rumque ca|no ‖ Tro|jae qui | primus ab | oris.

2. In modern prosody, a rhythmic break, usually a sense pause, about the middle of a verse. **3.** *Music.* A pause marking a rhythmic point of division in a melody. — **cae·su′ral** (-răl), *adj.*

‖**ca′fé′** (kȧ′fā′), *n.* [F., fr. It. *caffè.*] **1.** Coffee. **2.** [*as an English word*] (*pron.* kă·fā′) A coffeehouse; restaurant; in the United States, a barroom.

‖**ca′fé′ au lait** (kȧ′fā′ ō′ lĕ′). [F.] Coffee with milk, esp. hot milk in about equal proportions.

‖**ca′fé′ noir** (kȧ′fā′ nwȧr′). [F.] Black coffee.

caf′e·te′ri·a (kăf′ē·tẽr′ĭ·ȧ), *n.* [Amer. Sp., coffee shop.] *U. S.* A restaurant at which patrons serve themselves at a counter, taking the food to tables to eat.

caf′fe·ine (kăf′ē·ĭn; -ēn; -ĭn), *n.* Also **caf′fe·in.** A stimulant alkaloid, $C_8H_{10}N_4O_2$ in coffee, tea (see THEINE), kola, etc.

caf′tan (kăf′tăn; kȧf·tän′), *n.* [Turk. *qaftān.*] A long-sleeved gown fastened by a girdle, worn in the Levant.

cage (kāj), *n.* [OF., fr. L. *cavea* cavity, cage, fr. *cavus* hollow.] **1.** A box or enclosure, wholly or partly of openwork, for confining birds or other animals. **2.** *Archaic.* A place of confinement, as for malefactors. **3.** Anything like a cage in form or purpose; specif., the box or enclosed platform of an elevator, or lift. **4.** *Baseball.* A place enclosed for practice. **5.** *Hockey, etc.* The structure used for a goal, typically a framework with a net. **6.** *Ordn.* An openwork steel support for guns.
— *v. t.;* CAGED (kājd); CAG′ING (kāj′ĭng). **1.** To confine in or as in a cage. **2.** *Sports.* To put or drive into a cage, as a ball.

cage′ling (kāj′lĭng), *n.* A bird confined in a cage.

cage′y (kāj′ĭ), *adj.* *Slang.* Wary; shrewdly knowing.

‖**Ca′gou′lard′** (kȧ′gōō′lȧr′), *n.* [F., fr. *cagoule* hood.] *France.* A member of a secret terroristic organization (Comité Secret d'Action Révolutionnaire) active from about 1937 to the World War II period.

‖**ca′hier′** (kȧ′yā′; kȧ·hẽr′), *n.* [F., fr. L. *quaternum* (see QUIRE). The sheets of manuscript were folded into four parts.] **1.** A number of sheets of paper, etc., put together, as for binding. **2.** A memorial (def. 2); also, a report.

Ca′hill (kä′hĭl; kā′hĭl), *n.* [After a Dublin fly maker.] *Angling.* An artificial fly with tan speckled wings, gray wool body, brown hackle, gold tag, and brown speckled tail. Cf. FLY, *Illust.*

ca·hoot′ (kȧ·hōōt′), *n.* *Slang.* Partnership; collusion; — chiefly in ***in cahoots.*** — ***to go cahoots.*** To go shares.

cai′man (kā′măn). Var. of CAYMAN.

Cain (kān), *n.* The brother of Abel; hence, a murderer.

Cai′no·zo′ic (kī′nō·zō′ĭk; kā′-). Var. of CENOZOIC.

ca·ïque′ (kä·ēk′), *n.* [F., fr. It. *caicco*, fr. Turk. *qāyiq.*] **1.** A light skiff or rowboat much used on the Bosporus. **2.** A Levantine sailing vessel of larger size.

‖**Ça i′ra′** (sȧ′ ē′rȧ′). [F.] A French popular song of the Revolution, with the refrain "*ça ira*" ("it will go on"). Cf. CARMAGNOLE, 3; MARSEILLAISE.

caird (kârd; *Scot.* kārd), *n.* [Gael. & Ir. *ceard* a tinker.] *Scot.* A traveling tinker; a tramp.

cairn (kârn), *n.* [Gael, *carn*, gen. *cairn*, a heap.] A heap of stones raised for a memorial, a landmark, etc.

cairn′gorm′ (kârn′gôrm′), *n., or* **Cairngorm stone.** *Mineral.* A yellow or smoky-brown variety of quartz crystal, found esp. on Mt. Cairngorm, Scotland.

cairn terrier. A small, compactly built Scottish terrier.

cais′son (kā′sŭn), *n.* [F., fr. It. *cassone*, fr. *cassa*, fr. L. *capsa* case, box.] **1.** *Mil.* **a** A chest to hold ammunition. **b** An ammunition wagon for mobile artillery. **2. a** *Civ. Engin.* A watertight box or chamber used for construction work under water, as in harbors and rivers; a cofferdam. **b** A hollow floating box or boat used as a floodgate for a dock or basin. **c** A camel (def. 2) for floating a sunken vessel. **3.** *Arch.* = COFFER, 5.

caisson disease. A disease, sometimes fatal, marked by neuralgic pains and paralysis, induced by too rapid decrease in air pressure after a stay in compressed atmosphere, as in caissons, diving bells, etc.; — called colloq. (*the*) *bends.* Cf. AEROEMBOLISM.

cai′tiff (kā′tĭf), *adj.* [ONF. *caitif* captive, mean, fr. L. *captivus.*] Base; wicked and mean; despicable. — *n.* A base, despicable person; a mean and wicked man.

caj′e·put (kăj′ē·pŭt), *n.* **a** Var. of CAJUPUT. **b** A tree (*Umbellularia californica*) of the laurel family, with aromatic evergreen leaves.

ca·jole′ (kȧ·jōl′), *v. t. & i.* [F. *cajoler.*] To deceive with, or persuade by, artful flattery, specious promises, or the like; to wheedle; coax. — **ca·jole′ment,** *n.* — **ca·jol′er** (-jōl′ẽr), *n.*

ca·jol′er·y (-jōl′ẽr·ĭ), *n.; pl.* -ERIES (-ĭz). Act or practice of cajoling; wheedling; coaxing.

Ca′jun (kā′jŭn), *n.* [Corrupt. of ACADIAN.] In Louisiana, a person reputed to be of Acadian French descent.

caj′u·put (kăj′ŭ·pŭt), *n.* [Malay *kāyupūtih*, fr. *kāyu* tree + *pūtih* white.] An East Indian tree (*Melaleuca leucadendron*) of the myrtle family, yielding a pungent greenish oil used chiefly as a local application in skin diseases.

cake (kāk), *n.* [ME., fr. ON. *kaka.*] **1.** A small mass of dough, sometimes unleavened, baked on both sides; also, hashed meat, fish, mashed potatoes, etc., packed into a small mass and baked. **2.** A sweetened mixture of flour and other ingredients, baked in a loaf or mass. **3.** A griddlecake; pancake. **4.** Matter congealed or molded into a solid mass, esp. into a rather flat form; as, a *cake* of soap. — *v. t. & i.* To form or harden into a cake or mass.

cake′walk′ (-wôk′), *n.* Orig., a form of entertainment among American Negroes in which a prize of a cake was given for the most accomplished steps and figures in walking; later, a stage dance developed from these. — *v. i.* To do, or walk as in, a cakewalk. — **cake′walk′er,** *n.*

Cal′a·bar′ bean (kăl′ȧ·bär′; kăl′ȧ·bär). The poisonous seed of a tropical African woody vine (*Physostigma venenosum*) of the pea family, used as a myotic, and in tetanus and in strychnine poisoning.

cal′a·bash (kăl′ȧ·băsh), *n.* [F. *calebasse*, fr. Pr. *carbassa*, *carabasso.*] **1.** A gourd, esp. the common bottle gourd (see GOURD), from the necks of which tobacco pipes are made. **2.** The hard-shelled fruit of a tropical American tree of the trumpet-creeper family (**calabash tree**) used for making drinking utensils, bailers, etc.; also, the tree itself (*Crescentia cujete*).

cal′a·ber, cal′a·bar (kăl′ȧ·bẽr), *n.* [F. *Calabre* Calabria.] Orig., a brown squirrel fur from Calabria, Italy; now, in commerce, the gray fur of a Siberian squirrel.

cal′a·boose (kăl′ȧ·bōōs; kăl′ȧ·bōōs′), *n.* [Sp. *calabozo* dungeon.] *Local, U. S.* A prison; a jail.

ca·la′di·um (kȧ·lā′dĭ·ŭm), *n.* [NL., fr. Malay *kalādi*, name of a plant.] Any of a genus (*Caladium*, esp. *C. bicolor*) of tropical American ornamental plants of the arum family, with handsome, variously colored leaves.

cal′a·man′der wood (kăl′ȧ·măn′dẽr). The hazel-brown, black-striped wood of certain East Indian trees (genus *Diospyros*, esp. *D. hirsuta*), related to the ebony.

cal′a·mine (kăl′ȧ·mīn; -mĭn), *n.* [F., fr. ML., fr. L. *cadmia.*] **a** Hydrous zinc silicate, $(ZnOH)_2SiO_3$. **b** *Chiefly Brit.* Native zinc carbonate, $ZnCO_3$; smithsonite.

cal′a·mint (kăl′ȧ·mĭnt), *n.* [From OF., fr. L. *calamintha*, fr. Gr. *kalaminthē.*] Any of a genus (*Clinopodium*, syn. *Calamintha*) of mints, esp. one of the North Temperate Zone (*C. calamintha*), often called **calamint balm.**

ca·lam′i·tous (kȧ·lăm′ĭ·tŭs), *adj.* [F. *calamiteux*, fr. L. *calamitosus.*] Producing, or attended with, calamity; disastrous. — **ca·lam′i·tous·ly**, *adv.* — **ca·lam′i·tous·ness**, *n.*

ca·lam′i·ty (-tĭ), *n.; pl.* -TIES (-tĭz). [F. *calamité*, fr. L. *calamitas.*] **1.** A state of deep distress or misfortune; misery. **2.** Any great misfortune. — **Syn.** See DISASTER. — **Ant.** Boon.

cal′a·mus (kăl′ȧ·mŭs), *n.; pl.* -MI (-mī). [L., a reed.] **1.** The sweet flag (*Acorus calamus*) or its aromatic root. **2.** *Zool.* The barrel or quill of a feather. See FEATHER, *Illust.*

ca·lash′ (kȧ·lăsh′), *n.* [F. *calèche*, fr. Czech *kolesa* wheels, carriage.] **1.** A light low-wheeled carriage with a top or hood. **2.** = CALÈCHE, 2. **3.** A carriage hood or top that can be thrown back. Cf. CHAISE, VICTORIA, *Illusts.* **4.** A large hood formerly worn.

cal′a·thus (kăl′ȧ·thŭs), *n.; pl.* -THI (-thī). [L., fr. Gr. *kalathos.*] *Gr. Antiq.* A flaring basket, often carried on the head, with fruits. It is a symbol of fruitfulness.

cal·ca′ne·us (kăl·kā′nē·ŭs), *n.* Also **cal·ca′ne·um** (-ŭm). [LL. (& L.), heel.] One of the tarsal bones; in man, the great bone of the heel.

cal′car (kăl′kär), *n.; pl.* -CARIA (kăl·kā′rĭ·ȧ). [L., a spur, fr. *calx, calcis*, heel.] *Bot. & Zool.* A spur. — **cal′ca·rate** (-kȧ·rāt), **cal′ca·rat′ed** (-rāt′ĕd; -ĭd), *adj.*

cal·car′e·ous (kăl·kâr′ē·ŭs), *adj.* [L. *calcarius* pert. to lime. See CALX.] Of the nature of, consisting of, or containing calcite, or calcium carbonate; also, containing calcium; as, *calcareous* soils.

cal′ce·o·la′ri·a (kăl′sē·ō·lā′rĭ·ȧ), *n.* [NL., fr. L. *calceolarius* shoemaker, fr. *calceolus*, a dim. of *calceus* shoe.] Any of a genus (*Calceolaria*) of tropical American plants of the figwort family, having pouch-shaped flowers.

‖**cal′ces** (kăl′sēz), *n., pl.* of CALX.

Cal′chas (kăl′kȧs), *n.* [L., fr. Gr. *Kalchas.*] In the *Iliad*, a priest of Apollo in the Greek army before Troy.

cal′ci- (kăl′sĭ-). A combining form, Latin *calci-*, from *calx, calcis*, lime, denoting also *calcium* or *calcium salts.*

cal′cic (kăl′sĭk), *adj.* [L. *calx, calcis*, lime.] *Chem.* Derived from, or containing, calcium or lime.

cal′ci·cole (kăl′sĭ·kōl), *n.* [L. *calci-* + *colere* to cultivate, dwell.] *Bot.* A plant normally growing on calcareous soils. — **cal·cic′o·lous** (kăl·sĭk′ō·lŭs), *adj.*

cal·cif′er·ol (kăl·sĭf′ĕr·ōl; -ŏl), *n.* [*calcif*erous + ergoster*ol.*] *Biochem.* Vitamin D_2 (see VITAMIN).

cal·cif′er·ous (kăl·sĭf′ĕr·ŭs), *adj.* Also **cal·cif′ic** (-ĭk), *adj.* [L. *calx, calcis*, lime + *-ferous.*] Producing, or having, calcite.

cal′ci·fi·ca′tion (kăl′sĭ·fĭ·kā′shŭn), *n.* **1.** Process of calcifying; deposition of insoluble lime salts in a tissue, etc. **2.** A calcified structure.

cal′ci·fuge (kăl′sĭ·fūj), *n.* [L. *calci-* + *fugere* to flee.] *Bot.* A plant not normally growing on calcareous soils. — **cal·cif′u·gous** (kăl·sĭf′ū·gŭs), *adj.*

cal′ci·fy (kăl′sĭ·fī), *v. t. & i.*; -FIED (-fīd); -FY′ING. To make or become stony or calcareous by the deposit or secretion of lime salts.

cal′ci·mine (kăl′sĭ·mīn; -mĭn), *n.* Also **kal′so·mine** (kăl′sō-). [L. *calx, calcis*, lime.] A white or colored wash for a ceiling or other interior plastering. — *v. t.* To wash or cover with calcimine.

cal·cine′ (kăl·sīn′; kăl′sīn; -sĭn), *v. t. & i.* [F. *calciner*, fr. L. *calx, calcis*, lime.] **1.** To make or become powdery by action of heat. **2.** To oxidize, as by heat. **3.** To frit. — **cal′ci·na′tion** (kăl′sĭ·nā′shŭn), *n.* — **cal·cin′a·to′ry** (kăl·sĭn′ȧ·tō′rĭ; -tĕr·ĭ; kăl′sĭn-), *adj. & n.*

cal′ci·phile (kăl′sĭ·fīl; -fĭl), *n.* [*calci-* + *-phile.*] = CALCICOLE. — **cal·ciph′i·lous** (kăl·sĭf′ĭ·lŭs), **cal′ci·phil′ic** (kăl′sĭ·fĭl′ĭk), *adj.*

cal′ci·phobe (kăl′sĭ·fōb), *n.* [*calci-* + *-phobe.*] = CALCIFUGE. — **cal·ciph′o·bous** (kăl·sĭf′ō·bŭs), **cal′ci·pho′bic** (kăl′sĭ·fō′bĭk; -fŏb′ĭk), *adj.*

cal′cite (kăl′sīt), *n.* [L. *calx, calcis*, lime.] *Mineral.* Calcium carbonate, $CaCO_3$, crystallized in hexagonal form, thus distinguished from aragonite. It includes common limestone, chalk, and marble.

cal′ci·um (kăl′sĭ·ŭm), *n.* [NL., fr. L. *calx, calcis*, lime.] *Chem.* A silver-white soft metallic element occurring only in combination. Symbol, *Ca;* at. no., 20; at. wt., 40.08.

calcium carbide. A crystalline solid, CaC_2, often resembling gray limestone, used for generating acetylene, etc.

calcium carbonate. A solid, $CaCO_3$, occurring in nature as calcite and aragonite and found also in plant ashes, bones, shells, etc., and widely used in making lime and portland cement.

calcium chloride. A crystalline compound, $CaCl_2$, used, in its anhydrous state as a white porous solid, as a drying agent, to lay dust, etc.

calcium cyanamide. Also **-id.** *Chem.* A compound, $CaCN_2$, obtained in impure, cokelike form by passing dry nitrogen over calcium carbide at 1200° C. (2190° F.), and used as a fertilizer and as a source of other nitrogen compounds.

calcium light. = LIMELIGHT, *n.*, 1.

calcium phosphate. See PHOSPHATE.

calc′-sin′ter (kălk′sĭn′tĕr), *n.* [G. *kalksinter*, fr. *kalk* lime + *sinter* sinter.] Calcareous sinter.

calc′-spar′, calc′spar′ (-spär′), *n.* Calcite.

calc′-tu′fa (-tōō′fȧ; -tū′fȧ), **calc′-tuff′** (-tŭf′), *n.* Calcareous tufa.

cal′cu·la·ble (kăl′kū·lȧ·b′l), *adj.* **1.** Subject to, or ascertainable by, calculation. **2.** Dependable; reliable.

cal′cu·late (-lāt), *v. t.* [L. *calculatus*, past part. of *calculare* to calculate, fr. *calculus* a stone used in reckoning, fr. *calx, calcis*, limestone.] **1.** To determine by mathematical processes. **2.** To design or adapt for a purpose; as, *calculated* to succeed. **3.** *Colloq., U. S.* To plan; expect; "reckon."

Syn. **Calculate, compute, estimate, reckon** mean to determine something mathematically. **Calculate** is preferred when highly intricate processes are followed and when the result, because of difficulties involved, is problematical; **compute** is the simpler term, implying a simpler arithmetical process and an exact result; **estimate**, as here compared, is used only of costs, etc., determined in advance and, therefore, usually implies approximate exactness in the result; **reckon**, often colloquial for *compute*, usually implies a rough-and-ready process, such as mental figuring.

— *v. i.* **1.** To forecast consequences; estimate. **2.** To count or rely; with *on.*

cal′cu·lat′ing (-lāt′ĭng), *adj.* Making calculations; hence, given to contrivance or forecasting of what will promote self-interest; scheming; as, a *calculating* disposition, person.

cal′cu·la′tion (kăl′kū·lā′shŭn), *n.* **1.** Act or process, or result, of calculating; computation; reckoning; also, forecast. **2.** Deliberate prudence; studied care; discretion. — **cal′cu·la′tive** (kăl′kū·lā′tĭv), *adj.*

cal′cu·la′tor (kăl′kū·lā′tĕr), *n.* [L.] **1.** One who calculates. **2.** A book of tables for facilitating computation. **3.** A machine for the mechanical performance of mathematical operations; — called also **calculating machine.**

cal′cu·lous (-lŭs), *adj.* *Med.* Caused or characterized by a calculus or calculi.

cal′cu·lus (-lŭs), *n.; pl.* -LI (-lī). [L. See CALCULATE.] **1.** A concretion (def. 2 **a**) formed in the body, as in the bladder or kidneys; a stone. **2.** *Math.* **a** A method of computation; any process of reasoning by the use of symbols; any branch of mathematics involving calculation. **b** Specif., a method of analysis, usually called ***differential calculus*** when dealing with the rate of change of a variable function, and ***integral calculus*** when concerned with the theory and application of integrals, their evaluation, derivation, etc.

‖**cal·de′ra** (käl·dā′rä), *n.* [Sp., caldron.] *Geol.* A large crater formed by the collapse of the central part of a volcano.

cal′dron, caul′dron (kôl′drŭn), *n.* [ONF. *caudron, cauderon*, fr. L. *caldarius* suitable for warming, fr. *calidus* warm, fr. *calere* to be warm.] A large kettle or boiler.

‖**ca′lèche′** (kȧ′lĕsh′), *n.; pl.* CALÈCHES (-lĕsh′ĕz; -ĭz; *F.* -lĕsh′). Also **ca·leche′** (kȧ·lĕsh′). [F.] **1.** = CALASH, 1. **2.** In Quebec (City) a two-wheeled vehicle with a folding hood or top.

cal′e·fa′cient (kăl′ē·fā′shĕnt), *adj.* [L. *calefaciens*, pres. part. of *calefacere* to make warm.] Making warm; heating. — *n.* A calefacient remedy.

cal′e·fac′tion (-făk′shŭn), *n.* [L. *calefactio.*] A warming; state of being warmed. — **cal′e·fac′tive** (-tĭv), *adj.* — **cal′e·fac′to·ry** (-tō·rĭ), *adj.*

cal′en·dar (kăl′ĕn·dĕr), *n.* [L. *calendarium* an account book, fr. *calendae, kalendae*, calends.] **1.** A system of fixing the divisions of time, as years, months, weeks, and days, adapted to the purposes of civil life. See CHINESE CALENDAR, GREGORIAN CALENDAR, JEWISH CALENDAR, JULIAN CALENDAR, MOHAMMEDAN CALENDAR, PERPETUAL CALENDAR, REVOLUTIONARY CALENDAR, ROMAN CALENDAR; cf. also HOLIDAY, MONTH, YEAR. **2.** A tabular register of the divisions of a given year, referring the days of each month to the days of the week. **3.** Formerly, a guide or direction; pattern. **4.** An orderly list; schedule; specif.: **a** A list of causes to be tried in court. **b** A list of canonized saints, martyrs, or the like. **c** *Brit.* A university or college catalogue. See CATALOGUE, 2 **c.** — *v. t.* To enter or write in a calendar; to register.

cal′en·der (-dĕr), *n.* [F. *calandre*, prob. ult. fr. L. *cylindrus* cylinder.] A machine for calendering cloth, rubber, paper, etc. — *v. t.* To press, as cloth, rubber, paper, etc., between rollers to make it smooth and glossy, or to water it. — **cal′en·der·er**, *n.*

cal′en·der, *n.* [Per. *qalandar.*] One of a Sufistic order of wandering mendicant dervishes.

cal′ends, kal′ends (kăl′ĕndz), *n. pl.* [L. *kalendae, calendae*, calends.] See ROMAN CALENDAR.

ca·len′du·la (kȧ·lĕn′dṳ·lȧ), *n.* [NL., fr. L. *calendae* the calends, when the plant was supposed to blossom.] Any of a small genus (*Calendula*) of herbs of the aster family, natives of temperate regions; a pot marigold.

cal′en·ture (kăl′ĕn·tṳr), *n.* [F., fr. Sp., fr. L. *calere* to be warm.] Any of various fevers, formerly so called, occurring in the tropics, caused by exposure to excessive heat.

ca·les′cent (kȧ·lĕs′ĕnt; -′nt), *adj.* [L. *calescens*, pres. part. of *calescere*, incho. of *calere* to be warm.] Growing warm; increasing in heat. — **ca·les′cence** (-ĕns; -′ns), *n.*

calf (käf; kȧf; 9), *n.; pl.* CALVES (kävz; kȧvz). [AS. *cealf.*] **1.** The young of the cow, or of the bovine family of quadrupeds; also, the young of some other large mammals, as of the elephant, rhinoceros, hippopotamus, moose, red deer, and whale. **2.** Leather made of the skin of the calf; esp., a fine, light-colored bookbinder's leather. **3.** *Colloq.* An awkward or silly youth. **4.** A small mass of ice set free from a coast glacier or from an iceberg or floe.

calf, *n.; pl.* CALVES. [ON. *kālfi.*] The fleshy hinder part of the leg below the knee.

calf love. *Colloq.* Transitory affection felt by a boy or a girl for one of the opposite sex; puppy love.

calf's′-foot′ jel′ly (kävz′fo͝ot′; kȧvz′-; *less commonly*, käfs′-; kȧfs′-). Jelly made from calves' feet; gelatin.

calf′skin′ (käf′skĭn′; kȧf′-), *n.* The hide or skin of a calf; also, the superior kind of leather made of the skin.

Cal′i·ban (kăl′ĭ·băn; -bān), *n.* A savage and deformed slave of Prospero in Shakespeare's *Tempest.*

cal′i·ber, cal′i·bre (kăl′ĭ·bĕr), *n.* [F. *calibre*, fr. It., fr. Ar. *qālib* a form, mold.] **1.** *Gun.* **a** The diameter of a bullet or other projectile. **b** The diameter of the bore, as of a cannon or other firearm. See 1st BORE, *n.;* cf. GAUGE, *n.*, 5. **2.** The diameter of a round body; esp., the internal diameter of a hollow cylinder. **3.** Capacity of mind; hence, degree of excellence or importance; quality; ability.

cal′i·brate (-brāt), *v. t.* To ascertain the caliber of, as of a thermometer tube; also, to determine, rectify, or mark the graduations of. — **cal′i·bra′tion** (-brā′shŭn), *n.* — **cal′i·bra′tor** (-brā′tĕr), *n.*

cal′i·ces (kăl′ĭ·sēz), *n., pl.* of CALIX.

‖**ca·li′che** (kä·lē′chā), *n.* [Amer. Sp., fr. Sp. *caliche* a pebble in a brick, a flake of lime.] **a** Crude sodium nitrate, $NaNO_3$, of the Chilean deposits. **b** A crust of calcium carbonate, $CaCO_3$, formed on stony soil in arid regions.

cal′i·co (kăl′ĭ·kō), *n.; pl.* -COES or -COS (-kōz). [So called because first imported from *Calicut*, India.] **1.** Originally, any cotton cloth from India and the East. **2.** Later, any of various cotton stuffs of European make. **3.** *Eng.* Plain white cotton cloth. **4.** *U. S.* Cheap cotton cloth printed with a figured pattern. — *adj.* **1.** Made of calico. **2.** *Colloq., U. S.* Looking like calico; spotted.

cal′i·co·back′ (-kō·băk′), *n.* **a** The calico bass (see BASS **b**). **b** A hemipterous insect (*Murgantia histrionica*) which injures cabbages and other garden plants.

calico bush, flower, *or* **tree.** *U. S.* = MOUNTAIN LAUREL.

ca′lif, cal′if·ate, etc. Vars. of CALIPH, etc.
Cal′i·for′nia pop′py (kăl′ĭ·fôrn′yȧ; -fôr′nĭ·ȧ). Any herb of a genus (*Eschscholtzia*) of the poppy family, esp. one species (*E. californica*) whose yellow-orange flower is the State flower of California.
California rosebay. See RHODODENDRON.
cal′i·for′ni·um (kăl′ĭ·fôr′nĭ·ŭm), *n.* [NL., fr. *California* (after the university and state where it was discovered) + *-ium*.] *Chem.* A radioactive element discovered by bombarding curium 242 with helium ions. Symbol, *Cf*; at. no., 98.
ca·lig′i·nous (kȧ·lĭj′ĭ·nŭs), *adj.* [L. *caliginosus*.] Dim; dark; obscure. — **ca·lig′i·nos′i·ty** (-nŏs′ĭ·tĭ), *n.*
cal′i·pash (kăl′ĭ·păsh; kăl′ĭ·păsh′), *n.* A fatty, gelatinous, dull-greenish, edible substance next to the upper shell of a turtle.
cal′i·pee (kăl′ĭ·pē; kăl′ĭ·pē′), *n.* The fatty, gelatinous, light-yellow substance attached to the lower shell of a turtle, esteemed as a delicacy.
cal′i·per, cal′li·per (kăl′ĭ·pẽr), *n.* [Corrupt. fr. CALIBER.] **1.** Usually *pl.* An instrument with two legs, usually curved, fastened together with a rivet or a screw or with a spring and pivot. They are used for determining the thickness or diameter of objects or the distance between surfaces, etc. An ***outside caliper*** measures external, an ***inside caliper*** internal, dimensions. **2.** A graduated rod or rule (**caliper rule**) with one fixed and one sliding jaw, used for making similar measurements. Cf. MICROMETER CALIPER, *Illust.* — *v. t.* To measure by or as by calipers.

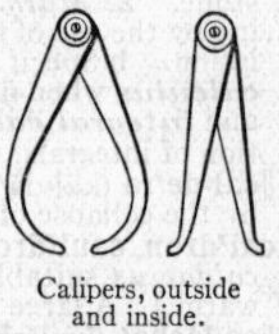

Calipers, outside and inside.

ca′liph, ca′lif (kā′lĭf; kăl′ĭf), *n.* [OF. *calife*, fr. Ar. *khalīfah*.] Successor (i. e., of Mohammed); — a title assumed by temporal and spiritual rulers in Mohammedan countries.
cal′iph·ate (kăl′ĭ·fāt; kā′lĭ-), *n.* Office or dominion of a caliph.
cal′i·sa′ya bark (kăl′ĭ·sā′yȧ). [Sp. *calisaya*.] The yellow bark of a cinchona (*Cinchona calisaya* or *C. ledgeriana*), which yields quinine.
cal′is·then′ics, *or, more properly but less usually*, **cal′lis·then′ics** (kăl′ĭs·thĕn′ĭks), *n.*; see -ICS. [Gr. *kallos* beauty + *sthenos* strength.] **a** The science of bodily exercise without apparatus or with light hand apparatus, to promote strength and gracefulness; — usually construed as *sing.* **b** Exercises of this sort; — usually construed as *pl.* — **cal′is·then′ic** (-ĭk), **cal′is·then′i·cal** (-ĭ·kăl), *adj.*
ca′lix (kā′lĭks; kăl′ĭks), *n.*; *pl.* CALICES (kăl′ĭ·sēz). [L.] **1.** Var. of CALYX. **2.** A cup; esp., *Eccl.*, a chalice.
calk, caulk (kôk), *v. t.* [From ONF., fr. L. *calcare*, fr. *calx* heel.] **1.** To drive tarred oakum, or cotton twist or wicking, into the seams between the planks of (a ship, boat, etc.), to prevent leaking. **2.** *Mech.* To tighten (a joint formed by overlapping plates) by driving the edge of one plate into the surface of the other. **3.** To stop up the crevices of, as of windows.
calk (kôk), *n.* A tapered metal piece projecting downward on the shoe of a horse or an ox, to prevent slipping; also, *U. S.*, a similar device worn on the sole of a shoe. — *v. t.* **1.** To furnish with calks, to prevent slipping. **2.** To wound with a calk, as a horse's leg.
calk′er, caulk′er (kôk′ẽr), *n.* **1.** One who calks ships, etc. **2.** *Mach.* A tool for calking.
call (kôl), *v. t.* [AS. *ceallian*.] **1.** To utter in a loud or distinct voice; hence, to read over (a list of names) loudly; to announce, esp. with authority; as, to *call* a halt. **2.** To summon with a call; also, *Archaic*, to invite or bid. **3.** To bring into action or discussion, as a case in court. **4.** To invoke; to appeal to. **5.** To rouse from sleep or summon to get up by a call. **6.** To attract (animals) by an imitative call. **7.** To communicate with by telephone. **8.** To convoke, as Congress. **9.** To summon to a particular duty, office, or employment. **10.** To demand payment of, esp. by formal notice; as, to *call* a loan. **11.** To demand presentation of for payment; as, to *call* an issue of bonds. **12.** To give a name to; to address by a specified name. **13.** To regard or characterize as of a certain kind. **14.** To estimate, reckon, or consider as being; as, they *call* it ten miles. **15.** *Billiards, Pool, etc.* To name or designate the particulars (as to the balls, the pocket, etc.) of (a shot). **16.** *Poker.* To summon, as to a show of hands, by an equal bet. — *v. i.* **1.** To speak in a loud distinct voice; to cry; shout. **2.** To make a call or brief visit. **3.** To get into contact with a person over the telephone. **4.** *Scot.* To go; proceed; — esp. in *ca′ canny*. **5.** *Card Playing* To make a demand of some kind, as for a card, or, in poker, as for a show of hands. — **Syn.** See SUMMON.
call back. **a** To summon back; to recall. **b** To revoke or retract. **c** To telephone in answer to a telephone call. — ***call down.*** **a** To cause or invoke to descend. **b** *Slang.* To rebuke or censure; to scold.
— *n.* **1.** Act of calling with the voice; esp., a shout; cry. **2.** A summons or invitation; a bidding; as: **a** A summons or signal on a drum, bugle, or pipe, etc. **b** A notice summoning persons to their work, as actors to rehearsal; a summons. **c** Act of signaling, as by a bell, to summon a person to listen at a telephone. **3.** A requirement or appeal; also, the occasion of the requirement; demand; claim; specif., a duty, need, or occasion. **4.** The cry of a bird or other animal. **5.** The call of a roll; a roll call. **6.** A short, usually formal, visit. **7.** A name or thing called or indicated by calling; as, his *call* was heads. **8.** *Card Playing.* Act of calling. **9.** *Com.* The right which one party buys of another to demand a certain amount of stock, grain, or other commodity, at a fixed price, at or within a certain time agreed on. **10.** *Eccl.* An invitation to become the pastor or minister of a church. **11.** *Finance.* **a** A demand for the payment of money. **b** A demand for presentation for payment, as of a bond. **12.** *Hunting.* A tone or a strain blown on the horn to encourage hounds or signal hunters. — ***on call.*** *Stock Exch. & Finance.* Subject, as a call loan, to demand for payment or return without previous notice.
cal′la (kăl′ȧ), *n.*, *or* **calla lily.** A house plant (*Zantedeschia aethiopica*) of the arum family, with a white showy spathe and yellow spadix.
call′a·ble (kôl′ȧ·b′l), *adj.* Capable of being called; *Finance*, subject to a demand for presentation for payment.
cal′lant (kȧl′ănt), **cal′lan** (-ăn), *n.* [MD. *calant* fellow, fr. OF. *chalant*.] *Scot.* A boy; lad.
call′boy′ (kôl′boi′), *n.* **1.** A bellboy; page. **2.** *Theater.* A boy who summons actors to go on stage.
call′er (kôl′ẽr), *n.* A person or thing that calls.
cal′ler (kăl′ẽr; kȧl′ẽr), *adj.* *Scot.* Fresh; in good condition; also, cool.
cal′let (kăl′ĕt; kȧl′ĕt; -ĭt), *n.* *Dial.* A trull; prostitute.
cal·lig′ra·phy (kă·lĭg′rȧ·fĭ), *n.* [Gr. *kalligraphia*.] **1.** Fair or elegant writing or penmanship. **2.** Handwriting in general. — **cal·lig′ra·pher** (-fẽr), *n.* — **cal′li·graph′ic** (kăl′ĭ·grăf′ĭk), *adj.* — **cal·lig′ra·phist** (kă·lĭg′rȧ·fĭst), *n.*
call′ing (kôl′ĭng), *n.* **1.** The action of the verb *call* (in any sense); a call. **2.** One's usual occupation; vocation; trade. **3.** A state of sexual excitement; — used specif. of the female cat. — **Syn.** See WORK.
calling card. = VISITING CARD.
Cal·li′o·pe (kă·lī′ō·pē), *n.* [L., fr. Gr. *Kalliopē*, fr. *kallos* beauty + *ops, opos*, voice.] **1.** *Gr. Myth.* The Muse who presides over eloquence and heroic poetry. **2.** [*not cap.*] (*pron.* kă·lī′ō·pē; *popularly* kăl′ĭ·ōp) A musical instrument consisting of a series of whistles, played by keys arranged as in an organ.
cal′li·op′sis (kăl′ĭ·ŏp′sĭs), *n.* [NL.] A coreopsis.
cal′li·pash, cal′li·per. Vars. of CALIPASH, etc.
cal′lis·then′ic, cal′lis·then′ics, etc. Vars. of CALISTHENIC, etc.
Cal·lis′to (kă·lĭs′tō), *n.* *Astron.* The so-called fourth (really the fifth) satellite of Jupiter. See GANYMEDE, 3.
cal′li·thump′ (kăl′ĭ·thŭmp′), *n.* *U. S.* A boisterous, discordantly noisy parade or burlesque serenade; a charivari or shivaree. — **cal′li·thump′i·an** (-thŭm′pĭ·ăn), *adj. & n.*
call loan. *Stock Exch.* A loan which may be terminated on demand of either party at any time; a demand loan.
call market. The market for lending money on call.
call money. Money loaned or ready to be loaned on call.
cal·los′i·ty (kă·lŏs′ĭ·tĭ), *n.*; *pl.* -TIES (-tĭz). **1.** State or quality of being callous; callousness. **2.** = CALLUS, 1.
cal′lous (kăl′ŭs), *adj.* [L. *callosus*, fr. *callum, callus*, callous skin.] **1.** Having a callus; hardened; indurated. **2.** Hardened in sensibility, feeling, etc.; unfeeling. — *v. t. & i.* To make or become callous. — **cal′lous·ly**, *adv.* — **cal′lous·ness**, *n.*
cal′low (kăl′ō), *adj.* [AS. *calu*.] **1.** Destitute of feathers; unfledged. **2.** Immature; green; as, a *callow* youth. — **Syn.** See RUDE.
call rate. The interest rate charged on call loans.
call to quarters. A bugle call fifteen minutes before taps, at which signal soldiers must repair to quarters. *U. S. Army.*
cal′lus (kăl′ŭs), *n.*; *pl.* CALLUSES (-ĕz; -ĭz). [L. See CALLOUS.] **1.** A hard thickened area on the skin or on the bark of a plant; a callosity. **2.** A substance exuded around the fragments of a broken bone, ultimately converted into true bone. **3.** *Bot.* The soft tissue which forms over any wounded or cut surface of a stem. — *v. i.* To form a callus.
calm (käm), *n.* [F. *calme*, fr. It. *calma*, fr. LL. *cauma* heat, fr. Gr. *kauma* burning heat.] Freedom from motion, agitation, or disturbance; — orig. of weather, winds, or waves; hence, tranquillity; quiet. — *adj.* **1.** In a state of calm; still; quiet. **2.** Undisturbed by passion or emotion; not agitated or excited. — **calm′ly**, *adv.* — **calm′ness**, *n.* — **calm′y**, *adj.*

Syn. **Calm, tranquil, serene, placid, peaceful** mean free from all that disturbs or excites. **Calm**, primarily applied to sea or weather, implies freedom from agitation of any sort; **tranquil** suggests a more settled composure, a more inherent quiet than *calm*; **serene** implies a lofty and unclouded tranquillity; **placid** suggests an unruffled appearance; **peaceful** implies repose, or attainment of undisturbed tranquillity.

— *v. t. & i.* To make or become calm, peaceful, or quiet; to quiet.
cal′ma·tive (kăl′mȧ·tĭv; käm′ȧ-), *adj. & n.* Sedative.
cal′o·mel (kăl′ō·mĕl), *n.* [Gr. *kalos* beautiful + *melas* black.] Mercurous chloride, Hg_2Cl_2, much used in medicine as a mercurial, purgative, and anthelmintic.
ca·lor′ic (kȧ·lŏr′ĭk), *n.* [L. *calor* heat.] **1.** *Old Chem.* The principle of heat, a supposed form of matter to which the phenomena of heat were formerly ascribed. **2.** Heat. — *adj.* Of or pert. to caloric.
cal′o·rie (kăl′ō·rĭ), *n.* Also **cal′o·ry.** [F. *calorie*, fr. L. *calor* heat.] Any of several thermal units: **a** The amount of heat required at a pressure of one atmosphere to raise the temperature of one gram of water one degree centigrade; — called ***small calorie.*** **b** The amount of heat required to raise one kilogram of water one degree centigrade; 1000 small calories; — called ***large, or great, calorie.*** It is used as a unit in expressing the heat-producing or energy-producing value of food. The statement that a tablespoonful of honey contains about one hundred *calories* means that when oxidized in the tissues of the body it will release that amount of energy to be expended in bodily activities.
cal′o·rif′ic (-rĭf′ĭk), *adj.* [L. *calorificus*, fr. *calor* heat + *facere* to make.] Producing heat; heating.
cal′o·rim′e·ter (-rĭm′ē·tẽr), *n.* [L. *calor* heat + *-meter*.] *Physics.* An apparatus for measuring quantities of heat, as those developed by friction, combustion, etc. — **cal′o·ri·met′ric** (kăl′ō·rĭ·mĕt′rĭk; kȧ·lŏr′ĭ-), **cal′o·ri·met′ri·cal** (-rĭ·kăl), *adj.* — **cal′o·ri·met′ri·cal·ly**, *adv.* — **cal′o·rim′e·try** (kăl′ō·rĭm′ē·trĭ), *n.*
ca·lotte′ (kȧ·lŏt′), *n.* [F., fr. Pr. or It.] A close cap without visor or brim; a plain skullcap; esp., *Eccl.*, a zucchetto.
cal′o·yer (kăl′ō·yẽr; kȧ·loi′ẽr), *n.* [F., fr. NGr. *kalogeros*, lit., good old man.] A monk of the Eastern Church.
cal′pac, cal′pack (kăl′păk), *n.* [Turk. *qalpāq*.] A large cap of sheepskin, felt, or the like, worn chiefly by Turks and Armenians.
cal′trop (kăl′trŏp), **cal′trap** (-trăp), *n.* [ONF. *kauketrape*. See CALK to stop up; TRAP a snare.] **1.** *Mil.* An instrument with four iron points so disposed that, any three of them being on the ground, the other projects upward. **2.** *Bot.* Any of several plants with spined, caltroplike fruit or flower heads; as: **a** The star thistle. **b** Any of certain herbs (genera *Tribulus* and *Kallstroemia*) allied to the bean caper. **c** The water caltrop.

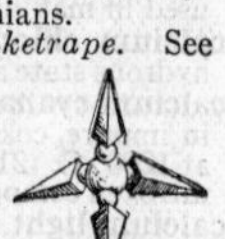

Caltrop, 1.

cal′u·met (kăl′ū·mĕt), *n.* [F., fr. L. *calamus* reed.] The ceremonial long-stemmed pipe of the North American Indians; — often called *peace pipe.*
ca·lum′ni·ate (kȧ·lŭm′nĭ·āt), *v. t.* [L. *calumniatus*, past part. of *calumniari* to calumniate.] To accuse falsely and maliciously of a crime or offense. — **Syn.** See MALIGN. — **ca·lum′ni·a′tor** (-ā′tẽr), *n.*
ca·lum′ni·a′tion (-ā′shŭn), *n.* Act of calumniating; slandering; aspersion; also, a calumny.
ca·lum′ni·a·to′ry (kȧ·lŭm′nĭ·ȧ·tō′rĭ; -tẽr·ĭ), *adj.* Also **ca·lum′ni·a′tive** (-ā′tĭv). Calumnious.
ca·lum′ni·ous (-ŭs), *adj.* Marked by or given to calumny; slanderous; defamatory. — **ca·lum′ni·ous·ly**, *adv.*
cal′um·ny (kăl′ŭm·nĭ), *n.*; *pl.* -NIES (-nĭz). [F. and L.; F. *calomnie*, fr. L. *calumnia*, fr. *calvi* to deceive.] False accusation of a crime or offense, maliciously reported to injure another; calumniation; slander.
Cal′va·ry (kăl′vȧ·rĭ), *n.* [L. *calvaria* a bare skull, deriv. of *calvus* bald.] **1.** The place, outside of the ancient city of Jerusalem, where Christ was crucified. *Luke* xxiii. 33. **2.** [*not cap.*; *pl.* CALVARIES (-rĭz).] An open-air representation, often on a hill, of the crucifixion

of Christ. **3.** An experience of intense, esp. mental, suffering. Cf. GETHSEMANE, 2.

Calvary cross. See CROSS, *Illust.* (2).

calve (käv; kȧv), *v. i.* [AS. *cealfian.*] **1.** To bring forth a calf. **2.** To bring forth young. **3.** To separate or break so that a calf or calves become detached; — said of an iceberg or glacier. — *v. t.* **1.** To bring forth, as a calf. **2.** To let become detached, as a berg from an iceberg or glacier.

calves (kävz; kȧvz), *n., pl.* of CALF.

Cal′vin·ism (kăl′vĭn·ĭz′m), *n.* The doctrines of the French theologian John Calvin (1509–64), including election or predestination, limited atonement, total depravity, irresistibility of grace, and the perseverance of the saints. Calvinism especially emphasizes the sovereignty of God in the bestowal of grace. Cf. ARMINIAN.

Cal′vin·ist (-ĭst), *n.* A follower of Calvin; an adherent of Calvinism. — **Cal′vin·ist,** *adj.* — **Cal′vin·is′tic** (-ĭs′tĭk), *adj.*

calx (kălks), *n.; pl.* CALXES (kălk′sĕz; -sĭz), CALCES (kăl′sēz). [L. See CHALK.] *Chem.* The friable residue left when a metal or mineral has been subjected to calcination or combustion.

cal′y·ces (kăl′ĭ·sēz; kā′lĭ-), *n., pl.* of CALYX.

cal′y·cine (kăl′ĭ·sĭn; -sīn), *adj.* Also **ca·lyc′i·nal** (kȧ·lĭs′ĭ·năl; -n′l). Pertaining to or resembling a calyx.

cal′y·cle (kăl′ĭ·k′l), *n.* [L. *calyculus* small bud, dim. of *calyx.*] **1.** *Bot.* An epicalyx. **2.** *Zool.* A calyculus.

ca·lyc′u·lus (kȧ·lĭk′ū·lŭs), *n.; pl.* -LI (-lī). [L.] *Anat. & Zool.* A small cup-shaped structure, as a taste bud, or a cavity of a coral containing the polyps.

Cal′y·do′ni·an boar hunt (kăl′ĭ·dō′nĭ·ăn). *Gr. Myth.* The pursuit of the boar sent by the goddess Artemis to ravage Calydon (see *Gaz.*) and finally slain by Meleager.

Ca·lyp′so (kȧ·lĭp′sō), *n.* [L., fr. Gr. *Kalypsō.*] **1.** In the *Odyssey,* a sea nymph who kept Odysseus seven years on her island, Ogygia. **2.** [*not cap.*] *Hort.* An orchid (genus *Cytherea*) growing in bogs and having a single white flower variegated with purple, pink, and yellow.

ca·lyp′so (kȧ·lĭp′sō), *n.; pl.* -SOS (-sōz). [Origin uncert.] A ballad-like improvisation in African rhythm, often a satire on current events, composed and sung by natives of Trinidad, B.W.I., at an annual pre-Lenten carnival.

ca·lyp′tra (kȧ·lĭp′trȧ), *n.* [NL., fr. Gr. *kalyptra* a covering for the head.] *Bot.* **a** The female sex organ (archegonium) of a liverwort or moss, carried in some mosses on top of the capsule as a thin hood. **b** Any caplike covering of a flower or fruit.

ca′lyx (kā′lĭks; kăl′ĭks), *n.; pl.* CALYXES (-ĕz; -ĭz), CALYCES (kăl′ĭ·sēz; kā′lĭ-). [L., fr. Gr. *kalyx.*] *Bot.* The external, usually green or leafy, part of a flower, contrasted with the inner showy portion, or *corolla;* the outer perianth. When the perianth consists of one series (as in the anemone) it is commonly called a *calyx,* and the *corolla* is then said to be wanting. The calyx may have distinct segments (*sepals*), or these may be united into a cup. Cf. INVOLUCRE; see FLOWER, *Illust.*

cam (kăm), *n.* [D. *kam* comb, MD. *cam.*] *Mach.* A rotating or sliding piece or projection, as on a wheel, either for imparting desired peculiar movement to a roller moving against its edge, to a pin free to move in a groove on its face, etc., or for receiving motion from such a roller, pin, etc. Cams are widely used to give complicated and exactly timed movements, as in a sewing machine, the valve gear of a gas engine, etc.

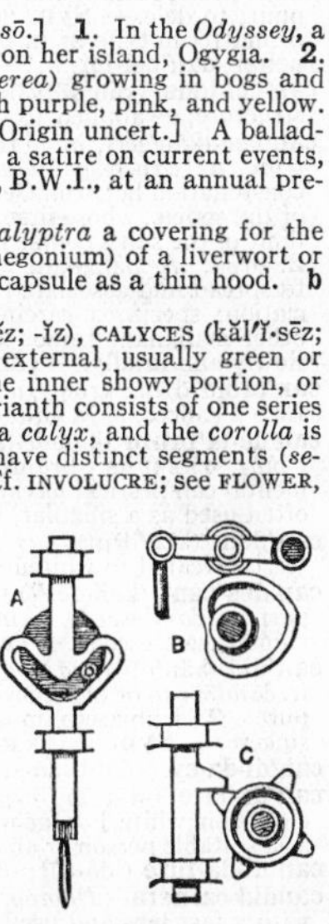

Cams. *A* Needle-bar Cam; *B* Heart Cam; *C* Cam Wheel.

ca′ma·ra′de·rie (kä′mȧ·rä′dē·rē), *n.* [F.] The good will that exists between comrades; good-fellowship.

cam′a·ril′la (kăm′ȧ·rĭl′ȧ; *Sp.* kä′mä·rē′lyä), *n.* [Sp.] **1.** A small chamber, as a king's private audience chamber. **2.** A group of secret advisers; a cabal.

cam′ass (kăm′ăs), *n.* Also **cam′as.** [Amer. Indian name.] **a** Any of a genus (*Camassia,* esp. *C. quamash*) of scapose herbs of the lily family, of the western United States. The bulbs are eaten by Indians. **b** = DEATH CAMASS.

cam′ber (kăm′bēr), *n.* [OF. *cambre* bent, curved.] **1.** Slight convexity of a part or structure, as of a ship's deck or of a road. **2.** A timber having a camber. **3.** A setting of the front wheels of an automobile closer together at the bottom than at the top. **4.** *Aeronautics.* The convexity of the curve of an airfoil from its chord. — *v. t. & i.* To give camber to; to have camber.

cam′bist (-bĭst), *n.* [F. *cambiste,* fr. It. *cambista,* fr. *cambiare* to exchange.] One who deals in bills of exchange, or who is skilled in the science and practice of exchange; also, a book giving the exchange values of moneys, weights, and measures of various countries.

cam′bi·um (kăm′bĭ·ŭm), *n.* [LL., exchange.] *Bot.* The soft formative tissue which gives rise to new tissues (wood, bark, etc.), esp. in the stems and roots of dicotyledonous and gymnospermous shrubs and trees. It usually forms a layerlike sheath beneath the epidermis and continually produces new phloem and xylem.

Cam′bri·an (kăm′brĭ·ăn), *adj.* **1.** Of or relating to Cambria; Welsh. **2.** *Geol.* Of, pert. to, or designating the earliest period of the Paleozoic era, or the system of rocks formed in this period. Plant fossils are scarcely recognizable, but every great animal type except the vertebrate is represented in the fossils of the Cambrian. — **Cam′bri·an,** *n.*

cam′bric (kām′brĭk), *n.* [From *Cambrai* (Flemish *Kamerik*), a city of France.] **1.** A fine, thin, white fabric made of linen. **2.** A similar closely woven cotton fabric.

cambric tea. A beverage of very weak tea, milk, and sugar.

came (kām), *past* of COME.

came (kām), *n.* A grooved rod of cast lead, used, as in stained glass, to hold together the panes or quarries.

cam′el (kăm′ĕl; -′l), *n.* [From AS. and ONF., fr. L. *camelus,* fr. Gr. *kamēlos,* of Sem. origin.] **1.** Either of two large ruminant mammals used, for carrying burdens and for riding, in the desert regions of Asia and Africa. The ***Arabian camel*** (*Camelus dromedarius*), often called ***dromedary,*** has one large hump on the back; the ***Bactrian camel*** (*C. bactrianus*), a central Asiatic species, has two humps. **2.** A watertight structure used to lift vessels, etc., in water, by sinking it, attaching it to the object to be raised, and then pumping out the water; a caisson (def. 2 **c**).

cam′el·back′ (-băk′), *n.* An uncured compound of rubber similar to the rubber from which new tires are made but made of much reclaimed or synthetic and little crude rubber, used for retreading or recapping pneumatic tires.

cam′el·eer′ (kăm′ĕl·ēr′), *n.* A camel driver.

ca·mel′li·a (kȧ·mĕl′ĭ·ȧ; *also commonly* -mēl′yȧ), *n.* [NL., after G. J. *Kamel,* or *Camelli,* a Jesuit.] A greenhouse shrub (*Thea japonica*) of the tea family, with glossy evergreen leaves and red or white double roselike flowers.

ca·mel′o·pard (kȧ·mĕl′ō·pärd *or, esp. Brit.,* kăm′ĕl·ō·pärd′), *n.* [L. *camelopardus,* fr. Gr. *kamēlopardalis,* fr. *kamēlos* camel + *pardalis* pard.] **1.** The giraffe. **2.** [*cap.*] A northern constellation between Cassiopeia and Ursa Major.

Cam′e·lot (kăm′ĕ·lŏt), *n.* In the Arthurian legends, the place where King Arthur had his palace and court.

cam′el's hair. 1. The hair of the camel, or a substitute for it, as hair from squirrels' tails (used for paintbrushes). **2.** Cloth made of camel's hair or a mixture of camel's hair and wool, usually light tan in color and of soft silky feel. — **cam′el's–hair′,** *adj.*

Cam′em·bert′ (kăm′ĕm·bâr′; *F.* kȧ′mäɴ′bâr′), *n., or* **Camembert cheese.** A soft unpressed cheese orig. made in the vicinity of Camembert, near Argentan, France.

cam′e·o (kăm′ē·ō), *n.; pl.* CAMEOS (-ōz). [It. *cammeo.*] **1.** A precious or semiprecious stone, a shell, or the like, carved in relief on layers of different colors, the figure being cut in one layer and another layer serving as background. **2.** Carving or sculpture of this type; — opp. to *intaglio.*

cam′er·a (kăm′ēr·ȧ), *n.; pl.* -ERAS (-ȧz), -ERAE (-ē). [L. See CHAMBER.] **1.** A chamber; specif.: **a** *Law.* A judge's chamber. **b** The legislative or council chamber in Italy. **2. a** A camera obscura. **b** *Photog.* A closed box or similar chamber through the aperture (usually having a lens) of which the image of an object is recorded on a light-sensitive material. Cf. KODAK, *Illust.* **c** *Television.* The part of a transmitting apparatus in which the image of the scene to be televised is formed for conversion into electrical impulses. — ***in camera.*** *Law.* **a** In the judge's chamber; in private. **b** Privately; secretly. — **cam′er·al** (-ăl), *adj.*

cam′er·a lu′ci·da (kăm′ēr·ȧ lū′sĭ·dȧ). [LL. *camera* chamber + L. *lucidus, lucida,* lucid, light.] *Optics.* An instrument which, by means of mirrors, or a prism, causes a virtual image of an external object to appear as if projected upon a plane surface, so that the outlines may be traced. It is generally used with the microscope.

cam′er·a ob·scu′ra (ŏb·skū′rȧ). [LL. *camera* chamber + L. *obscurus, obscura,* dark.] *Optics.* A darkened chamber having an aperture (usually with a lens) through which light from external objects enters to form an image on the surface opposite.

ca′mion′ (kȧ′myôɴ′), *n.* [F.] **a** A low wagon; dray. **b** A truck; motor truck, esp. one used to carry cannon.

cam′i·sa′do (kăm′ĭ·sā′dō), *n.* Also **cam′i·sade′** (-sād′). [F. *camisade.*] *Archaic. Mil.* A night attack, orig. one in which the soldiers wore white shirts for identification.

ca·mise′ (kȧ·mēs′), *n.* [Ar. *qamīṣ,* fr. LL. *camisia.*] A light loose shirt, smock, or tunic.

cam′i·sole (kăm′ĭ·sōl), *n.* [F.] **1.** A jacket or jersey with sleeves, formerly worn by men. **2.** A short negligee jacket for women. **3.** A loose-fitting underwaist.

cam′let (kăm′lĕt; -lĭt), *n.* [F. *camelot.*] **1.** A costly smooth-surfaced fabric, made in Asia of camel's hair or Angora wool. **2.** A garment of this material.

cam′o·mile, cham′o·mile (kăm′ō·mīl), *n.* [Through F. & L., fr. Gr. *chamaimēlon,* lit., earth apple.] Any of a genus (*Anthemis*) of plants of the aster family, esp. the common European species (*A. nobilis*), having strong-scented foliage and flower heads which contain a bitter medicinal principle used as an antispasmodic, a diaphoretic, etc.

Ca·mor′ra (kȧ·mŏr′ȧ; *It.* kä·môr′rä), *n.* [It.] A secret organization formed about 1820 at Naples, Italy, and used for practicing extortion, violence, etc. — **Ca·mor′rism** (-ĭz′m), *n.* — **Ca·mor′rist** (-ĭst), *n.*

cam′ou·flage (kăm′ŏŏ·fläzh), *n.* [F., fr. *camoufler* to disguise.] **1.** The disguising of a camp, battery, ship, etc., as by paint, screens, or the like; also, the disguise so applied. **2.** Any disguise or deceptive expedient. — (kăm′ŏŏ·fläzh′; kăm′ŏŏ·fläzh), *v. t. & i.;* -FLAGED′ (-fläzhd′; -fläzhd); -FLAG′ING (-fläzh′ĭng; -fläzh′ĭng). To disguise by camouflage. — **cam′ou·flag′er** (-fläzh′ēr; -fläzh′ēr), *n.*

camp (kămp), *n.* [F., fr. It., fr. L. *campus* plain, field.] **1.** The ground or spot on which tents, huts, etc., are erected for shelter, as for an army. **2. a** A collection of tents, huts, or other shelters; an encampment. **b** A single tent, cabin, or the like, used on a vacation or outing. **c** *Western U. S.* A town, esp. one new and hastily formed, around a mine of gold, silver, etc. **3.** The body of persons encamped. **4.** Military service or life; as, a product of *camp* and court. **5.** A body of partisans seeking to promote any theory, doctrine, etc.; also, a strongly defended position. — *v. i.* [F. *camper.*] To pitch or prepare a camp; encamp. — *v. t.* To put into camp; also, to accommodate.

☞ COMBINATIONS are:

campcraft **campfire** **campground**

cam·pa′gna (käm·pä′nyä), *n.* [It.] An open level plain; now, specif. [*cap.*], the one surrounding Rome, Italy.

cam·paign′ (kăm·pān′), *n.* [Through F. & It., fr. ML. *campania* level country, fr. *campus* field.] **1.** A connected series of military operations forming a distinct stage in a war. **2.** A connected series of operations to bring about some desired result; as, an advertising *campaign.* — *v. i.* To serve in, or go on, a campaign. — **cam·paign′er,** *n.*

campaign medal. See SERVICE MEDAL.

cam′pa·ni′le (kăm′pȧ·nē′lē; *It.* käm′pä·nē′lā), *n.; pl.* -NILES (-nē′lēz), -NILI (-nē′lē). [It., fr. It. & LL. *campana* bell.] *Arch.* A bell tower, esp. one built separate from a church; a belfry (def. 1).

cam′pa·nol′o·gy (kăm′pȧ·nŏl′ō·jĭ), *n.* [LL. *campana* bell + *-logy.*] The science of bells; art of ringing bells, as in change ringing (which see). — **cam′pa·nol′o·ger** (-jēr), **cam′pa·nol′o·gist** (-jĭst), *n.*

cam·pan′u·la (kăm·păn′ū·lȧ), *n.* [NL., dim. of *campana* bell.] A bellflower.

cam·pan′u·la′ceous (-lā′shŭs), *adj.* Belonging to the bellflower family (Campanulaceae). See BELLFLOWER.

cam·pan′u·late (kăm·păn′ū·lāt), *adj.* Bell-shaped.

Camp′bell·ite (kăm′ĕl·īt; kăm′bĕl-), *n.* See DISCIPLES OF CHRIST.

camp′er (kămp′ēr), *n.* One who camps.

camp′fire′ girl (kămp′fīr′). A member of "The Camp Fire Girls, Inc.," an American organization of girls from 7 to 18.

camp follower. A civilian, male or female, accompanying an army, as a sutler, servant, etc.
cam′phene (kăm′fēn; kăm·fēn′), *n.* A solid terpene, $C_{10}H_{16}$, resembling camphor in appearance and odor.
cam′phire (kăm′fīr), *n.* Henna.
cam′phol (kăm′fōl; -fŏl), *n.* *Chem.* Borneol.
cam′phor (kăm′fẽr), *n.* [From F., through ML. and Ar., fr. Malay *kāpūr.*] **1.** A tough, gumlike, crystalline compound, $C_{10}H_{16}O$, obtained from the wood and bark of the large evergreen **camphor tree** (*Cinnamomum camphora*), now grown in most warm countries. Cf. BORNEOL. Camphor is used in medicine as a diaphoretic, stimulant, and sedative, in celluloid manufacture, in pyrotechny, etc. **2.** Any of certain alcoholic and ketonic derivatives of terpenes. — **cam·phor′ic** (kăm·fŏr′ĭk), *adj.*
cam′phor·ate (-āt), *v. t.* To impregnate or treat with camphor; as, **cam′phor·at′ed oil** (-āt′ĕd; -ĭd), a solution of camphor in cottonseed oil used to allay irritation.
camphor ball. = MOTH BALL.
camphor ice. A waxy preparation (cerate) made chiefly of camphor, white wax, spermaceti, and castor oil.
cam′pi·on (kăm′pĭ·ŭn), *n.* Any of various plants (genera *Lychnis* and *Silene*) of the pink family, as the European crimson-flowered ***rose campion*** (*L. coronaria*), and the ***bladder campion,*** *or* ***cowbell*** (*S. latifolia*), having bluish-green leaves and white flowers with much-inflated calyx.
camp meeting. A religious gathering held, usually by Methodists, for conducting a series of religious services in the open air or in a tent in some retired spot.
cam′po (kăm′pō; *It.* käm′pō), *n.; pl.* -PI (-pē; -pē). [It.] In Italy, an open place in a town, sometimes smaller than a piazza.
cam′po·ree′ (kăm′pō·rē′), *n.* [*camp* + jamb*oree.*] A gathering of boy scouts representing a section of a country or nation, — distinguished from a national or international gathering or *jamboree.*
‖**cam′po san′to** (käm′pō sän′tō). [It., holy field.] A cemetery.
camp′stool′ (kămp′stōōl′), *n.* A folding stool.
cam′pus (kăm′pŭs), *n.* [L., a field.] **1.** *Rom. Antiq.* An open space or field, as for martial exercises, public shows, etc. **2.** *U. S.* The grounds of a college or school containing the main buildings or within the main enclosure.
cam′shaft′ (kăm′shȧft′), *n.* *Mach.* A shaft on which a cam is secured, or of which a cam forms an integral part.
cam wheel. A wheel acting as a cam. See CAM, *Illust.*
can (kăn; 4), *v.; pres. sing., 1st & 3d pers.* CAN, *2d* CANST (kănst), *pl.* CAN; *past* COULD (kŏŏd). [AS. *cunnan.* The present *I can* (AS. *ic cann*) was orig. a past.] **1.** *v. t. & i. Obs.* To have knowledge (of); as, "For he *can* the craft" (Chaucer); "Thou *canst* well of woodcraft" (*Scott*). **2.** As an auxiliary verb followed by an infinitive without *to:* (1) To be physically or intellectually able; (2) to have the necessary physical or mental courage; (3) to be enabled by law, agreement, or circumstances; (4) to be capable or to be possible subject or object of (a specified action); as, time wasted *can* never be replaced; (5) *Colloq.,* to have permission; as, *can* I be excused? **3.** As a substitute verb: To be able to do, make, etc.; as, he has done all that he *can.*
☞ *Can* expresses primarily positive power of acting, thence possibility of acting, a higher degree of circumstantial possibility than *may* in similar use; *may* expresses primarily permission or sanction, thence varying degrees of possibility. But *can* in colloquial use and informal writing expresses permission, often in positive statements, quite generally in place of *may* in questions and in negative expressions.
can (kăn), *n.* [AS. *canne.*] **1.** A drinking cup; a vessel for holding liquids. **2.** A vessel or case of tinned iron or of sheet metal; a tin; also, a jar, crock, or the like; as, a *can* of tomatoes; an oil *can.* — *v. t.;* CANNED (kănd); CAN′NING. **1.** To put in a can or cans; to preserve by sealing in cans, jars, etc. Cf. TIN, *v. t.,* 2. **2.** *Slang, U. S.* **a** To cease doing, making, or using. **b** To discharge; dismiss.
Ca′naan (kā′năn; kā′nyăn), *n.* [L. *Chanaan,* fr. Gr. *Chanaan,* fr. Heb. *Kena'an.*] The Land of Promise of the Israelites, a region corresponding vaguely to modern Palestine; hence, paradise. — **Ca′naan·ite** (-īt), *n.* — **Ca′naan·it′ic** (-ĭt′ĭk), *adj.* — **Ca′naan·it′ish** (-īt′ĭsh), *adj.*
Can′a·da bal′sam (kăn′ȧ·dȧ). The turpentine yielded by the balsam fir (see FIR). It is a yellowish viscid liquid, solidifying in time to a transparent mass, and is much used as a transparent cement, esp. in microscopy.
Canada goose. The common wild goose (*Branta canadensis*) of North America, chiefly gray and brownish, with black head and neck. See BRANT.
Canada jay. A jay (*Perisoreus canadensis*) of northern North America, having gray and sooty plumage and no crest.
ca·naille′ (kȧ·nāl′; *F.* kȧ′nä′y′), *n.* [F., fr. It. *canaglia,* orig. a pack of dogs, fr. L. *canis* dog.] The lowest class of people; the rabble; riffraff.
ca·nal′ (kȧ·năl′), *n.* [F., fr. L. *canalis.*] **1.** *Obs.* Any watercourse or channel. **2.** An artificial channel filled with water, designed for navigation, for irrigating land, etc. **3.** Any of various faint, narrow, seasonal markings on the planet Mars, — thought by many astronomers to be due to vegetation. **4.** *Anat. & Zool.* A duct; a tubular passage; as, the alimentary *canal.* See EAR, *Illust.* — *v. t.;* CA-NALLED′ (-năld′); CA·NAL′LING. To construct a canal through or across; to provide with canals.
ca·nal′boat′ (-bōt′), *n.* A boat for use on a canal.
can′a·lic′u·late (kăn′ȧ·lĭk′ū·lāt), *adj.* Also **can′a·lic′u·lat′ed** (-lāt′ĕd; -ĭd). [L. *canaliculatus* channeled.] Having one or more channels or grooves, as the leafstalks of most palms.
can′a·lic′u·lus (-lŭs), *n.; pl.* -LI (-lī). [L., dim. of *canalis* channel.] *Anat. & Zool.* A minute canal, esp. in bone. — **can′a·lic′u·lar** (-lẽr), *adj.*
ca·nal′i·za′tion (kȧ·năl′ĭ·zā′shŭn; kăn′ȧ·lī-; kăn′ȧ·lĭ-), *n.* **1.** Act of canalizing. **2.** A system of canals or conduits. **3.** *Med. & Surg.* A method of draining wounds by the formation of canals without the insertion of tubes.
ca·nal′ize (kȧ·năl′īz; kăn′ȧ·līz), *v. t.* **1.** To construct a canal through or across; to make into or like a canal. **2.** To provide an outlet for, as emotion. **3.** To direct into certain channels; to give a fixed character or scope to. — *v. i.* **1.** To flow in or into a channel. **2.** *Med.* To develop new paths, as new capillaries in a clot in a blood vessel.
can′a·pé (kăn′ȧ·pā; -pĭ), *n.* [F., orig., a couch with mosquito curtains. See CANOPY.] An appetizer consisting of a piece of bread or toast, or a cracker, topped with caviar, anchovies, or other tasty food.
ca·nard′ (kȧ·närd′ *or, esp. Brit.,* -när′), *n.* [F., prop., a duck.] An extravagant or absurd report or story set afloat to delude the public.
ca·nar′y (kȧ·nâr′ĭ), *n.; pl.* CANARIES (-ĭz), orig. sometimes used for the sing. in senses 1–3. [Through F. & Sp., fr. L. *insula Canaria,* one of the Canary Islands, so called from its large dogs, fr. L. *canis* dog.] **1.** A lively old French dance. **2.** Wine made on the Canary Islands, similar to madeira. **3.** Short for **canary bird,** a small finch (*Serinus canarius*), native to the Canary Islands, the Azores, Madeira, etc., now the commonest cage bird in all parts of the world. **4.** Short for **canary yellow,** a color, reddish-yellow in hue, of medium saturation and high brilliance. See COLOR.
canary seed. The seeds of **canary grass** (*Phalaris canariensis*) of the Canary Islands, used as food for cage birds.
ca·nas′ta (kȧ·năs′tȧ), *n.* [Sp., lit., basket.] A variety of rummy, using two decks shuffled together with four jokers and all deuces wild, in which game (5000 points) is made chiefly by building sets of seven of a kind called "canastas."
can buoy. See BUOY, 1.
can′can (kăn′kăn; *F.* kän′kän′), *n.* [F., lit., scandal.] A rollicking modern dance of French origin characterized by high kicking.
can′cel (kăn′sĕl; -s'l), *v. t.;* -CELED (-sĕld; -s'ld) or -CELLED; -CEL·ING or -CEL·LING. [From F., fr. L. *cancellare* to make like a lattice, to cross out, fr. *cancelli* lattice, dim. of *cancer* lattice.] **1.** To strike out or cross out with a line or lines, as a word, a passage, or the whole of a writing; to delete; to erase; hence, specif., of legal documents, to annul, or make void or invalid, by such marking, or (by extension) in any way. **2.** To annul or destroy; to revoke or recall. **3.** To neutralize or counterbalance; to compensate for. **4.** To cross or mark (a postage stamp, etc.) to show that it has been used. **5.** *Math.* To remove (a common divisor), as from numerator and denominator; to remove (equivalents) on opposite sides of an equation or account. **6.** *Print.* To suppress or omit; to dele. — **Syn.** See ERASE. — *n.* *Print.* **a** The suppression of matter in type or in print. **b** The part thus suppressed. — **can′cel·er, can′cel·ler,** *n.* — **can′cel·la′tion** (kăn′sĕ·lā′shŭn), *n.*
can′cel·lous (kăn′sĕ·lŭs), *adj.* *Anat.* Having a spongy or porous structure; — applied to certain bony tissue.
can′cer (kăn′sẽr), *n.* [L., crab, ulcer, a sign of the zodiac.] **1.** *Astron.* **a** [*cap.*] *genitive* CANCRI (kăng′krī). A northern zodiacal constellation between Gemini and Leo. **b** The fourth sign [♋ or ♋] of the zodiac, whose first point is the summer solstice, or the northern limit of the sun's course in its declination. See ZODIAC; TROPIC, *n.,* 1. **2.** *Med.* A malignant growth of tissue, usually ulcerating, tending to spread and associated with general ill health and progressive emaciation; specif., a carcinoma, or a sarcoma, or, esp. formerly, any other malignant tumor growth. **3.** A malignant evil that corrodes slowly and fatally. — **can′cer·ous** (-ŭs), *adj.*
can′croid (kăng′kroid), *adj.* **1.** *Zool.* Resembling a crab. **2.** *Med.* Like a cancer; as, a *cancroid* tumor.
can′de·la′brum (kăn′dĕ·lā′brŭm; -lā′brŭm; -lăb′rŭm), *n.; pl.* -LABRA (-brȧ), -LABRUMS (-brŭmz). [L., fr. *candela* candle.] A large ornamental candlestick, having several branches. The form *candelabra* is often used as a singular, with pl. *candelabras.*
can′dent (kăn′dĕnt), *adj.* [L. *candens,* pres. part. of *candēre* to glitter.] Heated to whiteness; glowing.
can·des′cent (kăn·dĕs′ĕnt; -'nt), *adj.* [L. *candescens, -entis,* pres. part. of *candescere,* v. incho. fr. *candēre* to shine.] Glowing; dazzling; incandescent. — **can·des′cence** (-ĕns; -'ns), *n.*
can′did (kăn′dĭd), *adj.* [F. or L.; F. *candide,* fr. L. *candidus* white, fr. *candēre* to be of a glowing white.] **1.** White; hence, *Archaic,* clear; pure. **2.** Unbiased; impartial. **3.** Frank; straightforward; patently sincere. — **Syn.** See FRANK. — **can′did·ly,** *adv.* — **can′did·ness,** *n.*
can′di·da·cy (kăn′dĭ·dȧ·sĭ), *n.* State of being a candidate.
can′di·date (-dāt *or, esp. Brit.,* -dĭt), *n.* [L. *candidatus,* prop., clothed in white.] One who offers himself, or is put forward by others, as a suitable person or an aspirant for an office, privilege, or honor.
can′di·da·ture (-dȧ·tūr; -dā′tūr), *n.* Candidacy.
candid camera. *Photog.* **a** A camera, usually of small size, equipped with a fast lens and used for taking informal pictures and pictures of unposed subjects, often without their knowledge. **b** Loosely, a miniature camera. — **candid photograph, candid photography.**
can′died (kăn′dĭd), *adj.* **1.** Preserved in or with sugar; as, *candied* fruits; also, coated with sugar. **2.** Converted wholly or partly into sugar; as, *candied* sirup. **3.** Honeyed; sweet; flattering.
can′dle (kăn′d'l), *n.* [AS. *candel,* fr. L. *candela,* fr. *candēre* to shine.] **1.** A slender cylindrical body of tallow (***tallow candle***), of wax or paraffin (***wax candle***), of spermaceti (***sperm candle***), or the like, containing a wick, burned to furnish light. **2.** Something resembling a candle in shape or use; as, a sulfur *candle* for fumigating. **3.** *Photom.* A unit of luminous intensity approximately equal to the intensity of light from a ⅞-inch sperm candle burning at the rate of 120 grains per hour; — called also ***standard candle.*** The ***international candle*** is the international unit of luminous intensity, being the light emitted by five square millimeters of platinum at the temperature of solidification. See CANDLE POWER, FOOT-CANDLE, LUMEN. — *v. t.;* CAN′DLED (-d'ld); CAN′DLING (-dlĭng). To test or examine (esp. eggs) by holding between the eye and a light, originally candlelight, to detect staleness, blood clots, etc. — **can′dler** (-dlẽr), *n.*
☞ COMBINATIONS are:

candlemaker	**candlestick**	**candlewick**

can′dle·ber′ry (-bĕr′ĭ), *n.* **a** The fruit of the candlenut or the wax myrtle. **b** Either of these trees.
can′dle·fish′ (-fĭsh′), *n.; pl.,* see FISH. **1.** A marine food fish (*Thaleichthys pacificus*) of the North Pacific coast, allied to the smelt. It is so oily that when dried it may be used as a candle. **2.** The beshow.
can′dle–foot′, *n.* *Photom.* = FOOT-CANDLE.
can′dle·light′ (kăn′d'l·līt′), *n.* **a** The light of a candle or candles; artificial illumination. **b** Nightfall; twilight
Can′dle·mas (-mȧs), *n.* [AS. *candelmæsse.*] **1.** The religious feast celebrated on February 2d, commemorating the Purification of the Virgin Mary; — so called because candles for the altar or other sacred uses are blessed on that day. **2.** Also **Candlemas Day.** The day or date of this feast. See GROUND-HOG DAY.
can′dle·nut′ (-nŭt′), *n.* The fruit of a tree or shrub (*Aleurites moluccana*) of the spurge family, found in the Pacific islands, used by the natives as a candle; also, the tree itself.
can′dle·pin′ (-pĭn′), *n.* A slender candlelike tenpin used in one form (**candlepins**) of the game of tenpins.
candle power. Luminous intensity, as of a lamp, expressed in standard or international candles. Abbr. *c.p.*

can′dle·wick′ bed′spread′ (kăn′d'l·wĭk′). A bedspread of unbleached cotton, having a pattern hooked in with wicking.

can′dle·wood′ (-wo͝od′), *n.* **1.** Pine or other resinous wood. **2.** Any of several resinous trees, as the ocotillo.

can′dor, can′dour (kăn′dẽr), *n.* [F. and L.; F. *candeur*, fr. L. *candor*, fr. *candēre*. See CANDID.] **1.** *Obs.* Whiteness; purity. **2.** *Obs.* Kindliness. **3.** A disposition to fairness; impartiality. **4.** Outspokenness; frankness.

can′dy (kăn′dĭ), *n.; pl.* CANDIES (-dĭz). [From *sugar candy*, fr. F. *sucre candi*, deriv. of Ar. *qand* cane sugar.] **1.** Sugar crystals or a hard crystalline mass formed by evaporating or boiling cane sugar, a sirup, or the like; also, a confection covered with these crystals or broken from this mass. **2.** *Chiefly U.S.* A food product made from sugar, varied by addition of fruits, nuts, chocolate, etc. — *v. t.;* CAN′DIED (-dĭd); CAN′DY·ING. **1.** To conserve or preserve by boiling with sugar; as, to *candy* fruits. **2.** To crystallize or congeal into sugar crystals. **3.** To make appear pleasant, as if covered with candy; to sweeten. — *v. i.* To become coated with sugar crystals; also, to crystallize, as preserved fruits.

can′dy·tuft′ (-tŭft′), *n.* Any of a genus (*Iberis*) of plants of the mustard family, orig. introduced from Candia (Crete), cultivated for their white, pink, or purple flowers.

cane (kān), *n.* [OF., fr. L. *canna*, fr. Gr. *kanna*, of Sem. origin.] **1.** Any hollow or pithy jointed stem, usually slender and more or less flexible. **2.** A walking stick; a staff; hence, a rod or stick used for flogging. **3.** *Bot.* **a** Rattan, esp. split rattan used for wickerwork, the seats of chairs, etc. **b** The stem of any one of various bamboolike grasses; also, any of the plants themselves, as the ***giant cane*** (*Arundinaria macrosperma*) of the southern U. S. **c** The sugar cane. **4.** *Hort.* One of the stems of certain small fruits, as of the raspberry. — *v. t.* **1.** To beat with a cane. **2.** To make or furnish with cane or rattan, as chairs.

cane′brake′ (kān′brāk′), *n.* A thicket of cane (def. 3 **b**).

ca·nel′la (kȧ·nĕl′ȧ), *n.* Also **ca·nel′la al′ba** (ăl′bȧ) *or* **canella bark.** [ML., dim. of L. *canna* a reed; — from the shape of the rolls of prepared bark.] The aromatic orange-colored inner bark of a tree (*Canella winteranda*) of southern Florida and the West Indies, used as a condiment and as a tonic.

can′er (kān′ẽr), *n.* One that canes something, as chairs.

ca·nes′cent (kȧ·nĕs′ĕnt), *adj.* [L. *canescens*, pres. part.] Growing white or whitish; specif., *Bot.*, having a fine grayish-white pubescence.

cane sugar. Sucrose, esp. from sugar cane. See SUGAR.

ca·nic′o·la fe′ver (kȧ·nĭk′ō·lȧ). [Leptospira *canicola*.] *Veter.* An acute, often fatal, gastroenteritis of dogs caused by a spirochete (*Leptospira canicola*); — called also *canine typhus.*

Ca·nic′u·la (kȧ·nĭk′ū·lȧ), *n.* [L., dim. of *canis* dog.] *Astron.* Sirius.

ca·nic′u·lar (-lẽr), *adj.* **1.** Pertaining to, or measured by, the rising of either Dog Star. **2.** Of or pertaining to the dog days (July–August).

ca′nine (kā′nīn; kȧ·nīn′; *or, esp. Brit.*, kăn′īn), *adj.* [L. *caninus*, fr. *canis* dog.] **1.** Of or pertaining to dogs or the family (Canidae) which includes the dogs, wolves, jackals, and foxes; having the nature or qualities of a dog; like a dog. **2.** *Anat. & Zool.* Of, pert. to, or designating the pointed tooth (**canine tooth**) next to the incisors, or one of like shape. See TOOTH, *Illust.* — *n.* **1.** A canine tooth. **2.** A dog.

canine typhus. = CANICOLA FEVER.

Ca′nis Ma′jor (kā′nĭs mā′jẽr); *genitive* CANIS MAJORIS (mȧ·jō′rĭs). [L., larger dog.] A constellation to the southeast of Orion, containing Sirius, the Dog Star; the Greater Dog.

Ca′nis Mi′nor (mī′nẽr); *genitive* CANIS MINORIS (mī·nō′rĭs). [L., lesser dog.] A constellation to the east of Orion, containing Procyon; the Lesser Dog.

can′is·ter (kăn′ĭs·tẽr), *n.* [L. *canistrum* a reed basket, fr. Gr. *kanastron*, fr. *kanna, kannē*, reed.] **1.** A small box or case for holding tea, coffee, etc. **2.** *Mil.* A kind of case shot for close-range artillery fire; — in full **canister shot.** **3.** A light perforated metal box containing material for absorbing or detoxicating poisons and irritants in the air. See GAS MASK, *Illust.*

can′ker (kăng′kẽr), *n.* [ONF. *cancre* and AS. *cancer*, both fr. L. *cancer* a cancer.] **1.** A corroding or sloughing ulcer; esp., a spreading gangrenous ulcer about the mouth. **2.** A cankerworm. **3.** *Obs.* The dog rose. **4.** That which corrodes, corrupts, or destroys. **5.** A lesion of the bark of a tree or shrub, causing decay. — *v. t. & i.* To affect or consume, or to be or become diseased, with canker; to eat away.

can′ker·ous (-ŭs), *adj.* **1.** Of the nature of canker or a canker; gangrenous. **2.** Corroding.

canker sore. A small painful ulceration, esp. of the mouth and lips.

can′ker·worm′ (kăng′kẽr·wûrm′), *n.* Any of various insect larvae injurious to plants; esp., *U. S.*, two species of measuring worms (see GEOMETRID) which injure fruit and shade trees.

can′na (kăn′ȧ), *n.; pl.* CANNAS (-ȧz). [L., a reed.] Any of a genus (*Canna*) of tropical herbs, type of the canna family (Cannaceae), having simple stems, large leaves, and a terminal raceme of irregular flowers; also, the flower.

can′na·bis (kăn′ȧ·bĭs), *n.* [L., hemp.] **a** The hemp (*Cannabis sativa*). **b** *Pharm.* The dried flowering spikes of pistillate plants of the hemp. See HEMP, 1 **c**.

canned (kănd), *adj.* **1.** Preserved in cans; tinned; as, *canned* goods. **2.** *Slang.* **a** Recorded for reproduction by mechanical means; as, *canned* music. **b** Intoxicated.

can′nel coal, *or* **can′nel** (kăn′ĕl; -'l), *n.* [Corrupt. fr. *candle coal.*] A fine coal, containing much volatile matter, that burns brightly.

can′ner (kăn′ẽr), *n.* One who cans fruit, meat, etc.

can′ner·y (-ĭ), *n.; pl.* -NERIES (-ĭz). A place where the business of canning fruit, meat, etc., is carried on.

can′ni·bal (kăn′ĭ·băl), *n.* [Sp. *canibal, caribal*, fr. Carib *calina, galibi*, Caribs.] A human being that eats human flesh; hence, any animal that devours its own kind. — **can′ni·bal**, *adj.*

can′ni·bal·ism (-ĭz'm), *n.* **1.** Act or practice of cannibals or a cannibal. **2.** Murderous cruelty. — **can′ni·bal·is′tic** (-ĭs′tĭk), *adj.* — **can′ni·bal·is′ti·cal·ly** (-tĭ·kăl·ĭ), *adv.*

can′ni·bal·ize (-īz), *v. t. & i.* To dismantle (a machine) for parts to be used as replacements in other machines.

can′ni·kin (kăn′ĭ·kĭn), *n.* [*can* + *-kin.*] A small can or drinking vessel.

can′ning (kăn′ĭng), *n.* The process or business of preserving foodstuffs in sealed containers.

can′non (kăn′ŭn), *n.; pl.* CANNONS (-ŭnz), collectively CANNON. [F. *canon*, fr. It., fr. L. *canna* reed, tube.] **1.** A piece of artillery; a gun; also, cannons collectively. **2.** [F. *canon*, prop., a hollow bit.] A smooth round horse bit; — called also *cannon*, or *canon, bit.* Cf. BIT, *Illust.* **3.** That part of a bell by which it is hung. **4.** The cannon bone; also, the part of the leg where it is situated. **5.** *Billiards.* A carom. — *v. i.* **a** To discharge cannon. **b** *Billiards.* To carom. — *v. t.* **a** To cannonade. **b** *Billiards.* To cause to carom; to carom into

can′non·ade′ (-ād′), *n.* [F. *canonnade*, fr. It. *cannonata.*] Act of discharging cannon for the purpose of destroying an army, or battering a town, ship, etc. — *v. t.* To attack with heavy artillery; to batter with cannon shot. — *v. i.* To discharge cannon.

cannon ball. Strictly, a round solid missile to be fired from a cannon, but often any missile for a cannon.

cannon bone. [F. *canon*, prop., a tube.] In hoofed quadrupeds, the bone supporting the leg from the knee or hock joint to the fetlock. See HORSE, *Illust.* (29, 42).

can′non·eer′ (kăn′ŭn·ēr′), *n.* [F. *canonnier.*] An artilleryman who serves the guns; a gunner. — **can′non·eer′ing**, *n.*

can′non·ry (kăn′ŭn·rĭ), *n.; pl.* CANNONRIES (-rĭz). **1.** Cannonading. **2.** Cannon, collectively; artillery.

cannon shot. **a** Shot from a cannon. **b** Range of a cannon.

can′not (kăn′[n]ŏt; kȧ·nŏt′). Compound form of *can not.*

can′nu·la (kăn′ū·lȧ), *n.; pl.* -NULAE (-lē). [L., a small reed, dim. of *canna* a reed, tube.] *Surg.* A small tube for insertion into a body cavity, as for drainage, or into ducts, vessels, etc.

can′nu·lar (-lẽr), **can′nu·late** (-lāt), *adj.* Tubular.

can′ny (kăn′ĭ), *adj.;* CAN′NI·ER (-ĭ·ẽr); CAN′NI·EST. [From CAN to know.] *Chiefly Scot.* **1.** Knowing; prudent; also, wary; cautious. **2.** Esp., cautious or shrewd in worldly affairs. **3.** Thrifty; frugal; — adopted into literary English as describing a quality characteristic of the Scots. **4.** Skillful; clever. **5.** In a superstitious sense, safe to deal with; of good omen; — esp. with a negative. **6.** Quiet; comfortable; snug; cozy. — *adv. Scot.* In a canny manner; cautiously; carefully; gently; quietly; — esp. in phrase *ca′ canny.* — **can′ni·ly**, *adv.* — **can′ni·ness**, *n.*

ca·noe′ (kȧ·no͞o′), *n.* [F., fr. Sp. *canoa*, of Arawakan and Cariban origin.] A form of small boat, long and narrow and sharp at both ends, usually propelled by paddles, with no rudder or sail. — *v. i.;* CA·NOED′ (-no͞od′); CA·NOE′ING. To paddle, sail in, or voyage in a canoe. — **ca·noe′ing**, *n.* — **ca·noe′ist**, *n.*

canoe birch. See BIRCH.

can′on (kăn′ŭn), *n.* [AS., rule, fr. L., fr. Gr. *kanōn* rule, rod.] **1.** An ecclesiastical decree, code, or constitution; specif., *R.C.Ch.*, a law, or rule of doctrine or discipline, enacted by a council and confirmed by the pope or sovereign; hence, ***the canon***, = CANON LAW. **2.** In general, any law, rule, or decree; esp., a principle accepted as true, fundamental, in conformity with good usage, or the like; as, the *canons* of art, of taste. **3.** A critical standard; a criterion. **4.** **a** *Bib.* The collection or list of books which are received as genuine and inspired Holy Scriptures. **b** Hence, a list of the works of a particular writer accepted as genuine. **5.** A list; a catalogue; *R.C.Ch.*, a catalogue of recognized saints. **6.** [*cap.*] *Liturgics.* Of the Mass, that part which begins after the Sanctus with the prayer "Te igitur." It contains the fixed rule according to which the "sacrifice" of the Mass is to be offered. **7.** *Music.* A composition in two or more voice parts, employing *imitation* (which see) in its strictest form. **8.** *Print.* The largest size of type (48 points) having a specific name. — **Syn.** See LAW.

can′on (kăn′ŭn), *n.* [ONF. *canoine*, fr. L. *canonicus*, fr. *canon* rule.] *Eccl.* A clergyman on the staff of a cathedral or certain other large churches.

ca′ñon (kăn′yŭn; *Sp.* kä·nyōn′). Var. of CANYON.

can′on bit (kăn′ŭn). = CANNON, a horse bit.

can′on·ess (kăn′ŭn·ĕs; -ĭs), *n.* *Eccl.* A woman living in a community under a rule but not under a perpetual vow.

ca·non′i·cal (kȧ·nŏn′ĭ·kăl), *adj.* Of, pert. to, or conforming to, a canon or canons. — **ca·non′i·cal·ly**, *adv.*

canonical hour. **a** *Eccl.* Any of certain stated times of the day (now seven: matins with lauds, prime, tierce, sext, nones, vespers, and complin) appointed for the offices of prayer and devotion. **b** In England, any of the hours from 8 A.M. to 3 P.M., before and after which marriage cannot be legally performed in any parish church.

ca·non′i·cals (kȧ·nŏn′ĭ·kălz), *n.pl.* The vestments prescribed by canon for a clergyman when officiating.

ca·non′i·cate (-kāt), *n.* Office of a canon; canonry.

can′on·ic′i·ty (kăn′ŭn·ĭs′ĭ·tĭ), *n.* Status, or quality warranting status, in a canon, esp. in the Biblical canon.

can′on·ist (kăn′ŭn·ĭst), *n.* A professor of, or one skilled in, canon law. — **can′on·is′tic** (-ĭs′tĭk), **can′on·is′ti·cal** (-tĭ·kăl), *adj.*

can′on·ize (-īz), *v. t.* **1.** *Eccl.* To declare (a deceased person) a saint; to put in the catalogue of saints. Cf. VENERABLE, 1; BEATIFICATION, 2. **2.** To sanction by ecclesiastical authority. **3.** To include in a canon, esp. the canon of Scripture. **4.** To glorify; to exalt. — **can′on·i·za′tion** (-ĭ·zā′shŭn; -ī·zā′-), *n.*

canon law. The body of ecclesiastical law by which a Christian church is governed; specif., the *Corpus Juris Canonici*, the body of ecclesiastical law by which the Roman Catholic Church was governed until 1918, or the new codification, *Codex Juris Canonici*, effective since May 19, 1918. — **canon lawyer.**

can′on·ry (kăn′ŭn·rĭ), *n.; pl.* -RIES (-rĭz). The benefice, dignity, or office of a canon; also, canons collectively.

can′on·ship, *n.* Canonry, esp. the office.

ca·no′pic jar *or* **vase** (kȧ·nō′pĭk). [L. *canopicus*, from *Canopus* city in ancient Egypt.] *Archaeol.* One of the four jars in which the Egyptians preserved the viscera of the deceased, usually for burial with the mummy.

Ca·no′pus (kȧ·nō′pŭs), *n.* [L., fr. Gr. *Kanōpos.*] *Astron.* Alpha (α) Argus, a star of the first magnitude in the constellation Argo, not visible north of 37° latitude.

can′o·py (kăn′ō·pĭ), *n.; pl.* -PIES (-pĭz). [F. *canapé* sofa, fr. It., fr. L., fr. Gr. *kōnōpeion* a bed with mosquito curtains, fr. *kōnōps* gnat.] **1.** A covering fixed over a bed, throne, shrine, or the like. **2.** Any overhanging shelter or shade; a covering. **3.** *Arch.* An ornamental rooflike structure; as, a *canopy* above a pulpit. **4.** *Aviation.* **a** The chief supporting surface of a parachute. **b** A sliding cockpit cover. — *v. t.;* -PIED (-pĭd); -PY·ING. To cover with or as with a canopy.

ca·no′rous (kȧ·nō′rŭs; 70), *adj.* [L. *canorus*, fr. *canor* melody, fr. *canere* to sing.] Melodious; euphoniously sonorous. — **ca·no′rous·ly**, *adv.* — **ca·no′rous·ness**, *n.*

canst (kănst), *2d person sing., present tense,* of CAN.

cant (kănt), *n.* [MD., fr. ONF. *cant* edge, angle.] **1. a** *Obs.* A corner; niche. **b** An external angle, as of a building. **2.** A sudden thrust producing a bias, or change of direction or position; also, the bias or turn so given. **3.** An oblique or slanting face or surface, as of a polygon, a buttress, a bank, etc. **4.** A slope or bevel; a tilt. — *v. t.* **1.** To give a cant, or oblique edge, to; to bevel. **2.** To incline; to set at an angle; to tip. **3.** To turn or throw off or out by tilting. **4.** To give a sudden turn or new direction to; to throw with a sudden jerk. — *v. i.* **1.** To lean; to tilt. **2.** To slant or slope. — *adj.* Having canted corners or sides; also, inclined from a perpendicular; sloping.

cant, *n.* [Prob. fr. ONF. *cant* (F. *chant*) singing.] **1.** An affected, singsong mode of speaking; a whine. **2.** The expressions peculiar to, and generally understood only by, members of a particular sect, class, or occupation; as: **a** The secret jargon of thieves, tramps, etc. **b** The special idiom of a profession or trade. **3.** A mode of talking used merely out of convention; esp., the insincere use of pious phraseology. — **Syn.** See DIALECT.

— *adj.* Having the quality or characteristics of cant; esp., suggestive of insincerity.

— *v. i.* **1.** To speak in a whining voice, or an affected singsong tone, as a beggar; hence, to beg. **2.** To talk with an affectation of piety or the like; to practice hypocrisy.

cant (kȧnt), *adj.* *Dial. Eng.* Lively; lusty; merry.

can't (kănt; kȧnt; 9). Contraction for CANNOT.

can·ta′bi·le (kän·tä′bē·lā), *adj.* [It., fr. *cantare* to sing.] *Music.* Suitable for singing; melodious and flowing.

Can′ta·brig′i·an (kăn′tȧ·brĭj′ĭ·ăn), *adj.* Of or pert. to Cambridge [in L. form *Cantabrigia*], England, or its university. — *n.* A native or resident of Cambridge; esp., a student or graduate of the University of Cambridge.

can′ta·le′ver, can′ta·li′ver. Vars. of CANTILEVER.

can′ta·loupe, can′ta·loup (kăn′tȧ·lōp *or, esp. Brit.,* -lōōp), *n.* [From F., fr. It.; — from the castle of *Cantalupo,* in Italy, where first grown in Europe.] **a** A variety (*Cucumis melo cantalupensis*) of muskmelon having a hard warty rind and reddish-orange flesh. **b** See MUSKMELON.

can·tan′ker·ous (kăn·tăng′kẽr·ŭs), *adj.* Exhibiting ill nature; perverse; contentious; cross-grained. — **can·tan′ker·ous·ly,** *adv.* — **can·tan′ker·ous·ness,** *n.*

can·ta′ta (kăn·tä′tȧ), *n.* [It., fr. *cantare* to sing.] A choral composition comprising choruses, solos, recitatives, interludes, etc., arranged in a somewhat dramatic manner and accompanied by organ, piano, or orchestra.

‖**can′ta·tri′ce** (kän′tä·trē′chā; *F.* käɴ′tȧ′trēs′), *n.; pl.* It. -TRICI (-trē′chē), F. -TRICES (-trēs′). [It. & F. (fr. It.).] A female professional singer; a chanteuse.

cant dog. A peavey.

can·teen′ (kăn·tēn′), *n.* [F. *cantine,* fr. It. *cantina* cellar, bottle case.] **1.** *Mil.* **a** A shop connected with a military post, etc., for supplying extra provisions, delicacies, liquors, etc., to the enlisted men. In the United States Army, the corresponding establishment is now called *post exchange.* **b** A chest containing a cooking kit used by officers. **2.** A small metal, wooden, leather, or plastic vessel or flask for water or other liquid, carried by soldiers, travelers, workmen, etc.

cant′er (kănt′ẽr), *n.* One who uses cant, as a beggar.

can′ter (kăn′tẽr), *n.* [Abbr. of *Canterbury.*] A gait resembling the gallop, but with moderate and easy bounds or leaps. — *v. t. & i.* To go, or make go, at a canter.

Can′ter·bur′y bell (kăn′tẽr·bĕr′ĭ; *esp. Brit.,* -bẽr·ĭ, -brĭ). Any of several campanulas (esp. *Campanula medium*) having handsome bell-shaped flowers.

can·thar′i·des (kăn·thăr′ĭ·dēz), *n. pl.* **a** Plural of CANTHARIS. **b** *Pharm.* A preparation of dried beetles, esp. the blister beetles, used externally as a rubefacient and vesicatory, and internally as a diuretic and stimulant.

can′tha·ris (kăn′thȧ·rĭs), *n.; pl.* CANTHARIDES (kăn·thăr′ĭ·dēz). [L.] See BLISTER BEETLE.

cant hook. *U. S.* A wooden lever having a movable iron hook near the end, and often a lipped iron ring round the tip. It is used for turning logs. Cf. PEAVEY, *Illust.*

can′thus (kăn′thŭs), *n.; pl.* -THI (-thī). [NL., fr. Gr. *kanthos.*] *Anat.* The corner on each side of the eye where the upper and under eyelids meet.

can′ti·cle (kăn′tĭ·k'l), *n.* [L. *canticulum,* dim. of *canticum* song, fr. *canere, cantum,* to sing.] A song or hymn; specif., one of ten songs of praise (not psalms), as the Magnificat, taken from the Bible.

Can′ti·cles (-k'lz), *n.* Also **Canticle of Canticles.** In the Douay Bible, the Song of Songs, or Song of Solomon (see BIBLE).

can′ti·le′ver (kăn′tĭ·lē′vẽr; -lĕv′ẽr), *n.* A projecting beam or member supported only at one end; specif., *Engin.,* either of the two beams or trusses, projecting from piers towards each other, which when joined, directly or by a suspended span, form a span of a **cantilever bridge.** See BRIDGE, *Illust.*

can′til·late (kăn′tĭ·lāt), *v. t.* [L. *cantillatus,* past part. of *cantillare* to sing low, dim. of *cantare.*] To chant or intone; to recite with musical tones (largely improvised) as in synagogues and other ritualistic churches. — **can′til·la′tion** (-lā′shŭn), *n.*

can·ti′na (kän·tē′nä), *n.* [Sp.] *Southwestern U. S.* **a** A saddlebag. **b** A saloon and provision store.

can′tle (kăn′t'l), *n.* [ONF. *cantel,* dim. of *cant* edge, corner.] **1.** A segment or slice, as a piece of land cut off or out. **2.** The upwardly projecting rear part of a saddle, opposite to the pommel.

can′to (kăn′tō), *n.; pl.* -TOS (-tōz). [It.] **1.** *Obs.* A song. **2.** One of the chief divisions of a long poem; a book.

can′ton (kăn′tŏn; kăn·tŏn′), *n.* [F., fr. Pr. *canton,* fr. same source as OF. *cant* edge, corner.] **1.** *Obs.* A division, part, or section of something. **2.** A small territorial division of a country; a district; specif.: **a** One of the states of Switzerland. **b** In France, a division of an arrondissement. **3.** A rectangular division occupying one fourth or less of a flag, usually in the upper corner near the staff and containing the national or other device. **4.** *Her.* A rectangular division of the shield, used in modern heraldry for a diminutive of the old quarter. Cf. ESCUTCHEON, *Illust.* — *v. t.* **1.** To divide into parts; esp., to divide into cantons or districts. **2.** To separate off or out by dividing or cutting. **3.** (*pron.* kăn·tŏn′; kăn′tŏn; *Brit.,* kăn·tōōn′) To allot quarters to, as to a body of troops; to quarter. — **can′ton·al** (kăn′tŏn·ăl), *adj.*

Can′ton crepe (kăn′tŏn; 2). See CREPE.

Can′ton·ese′ (kăn′tŏn·ēz′; -ēs′), *adj.* Of Canton, China, its inhabitants, or their dialect. — *n.* **1.** A native or natives of Canton. **2.** The dialect of Canton (see CHINESE, *n.,* 2), through which many Chinese loan words were adopted into English.

Can′ton flan′nel. See FLANNEL.

can·ton′ment (kăn·tŏn′mĕnt; kăn·tŏn′mĕnt; *or, esp. Brit.,* kăn·tōōn′mĕnt), *n.* [F. *cantonnement.*] *Mil.* **1.** The quartering of troops in temporary structures; also, a group of these structures. **2.** In India, a military post.

can′tor (kăn′tôr; -tẽr), *n.* [L., a singer, fr. *canere* to sing.] **1.** A singer; the leader of a church choir; a precentor. **2.** A soloist who sings liturgical music in the synagogue.

can′trip (kăn′trĭp), *n.* *Scot.* A charm; spell; trick.

‖**can′tus fir′mus** (kăn′tŭs fûr′mŭs). [ML.] Literally, fixed song; the plain chant or simple Gregorian melody prescribed as to form and use by ecclesiastical tradition.

cant′y (kănt′ĭ), *adj.* [From CANT, *adj.*] *Scot. & Dial. Eng.* Cheerful; sprightly.

Ca·nuck′ (kȧ·nŭk′), *n.* *Slang.* A Canadian: **a** *U. S.* Often, any Canadian. **b** *Canada.* A French Canadian.

can′u·la, can′u·lar, can′u·late. Vars. of CANNULA, CANNULAR, CANNULATE.

can′vas (kăn′vȧs), *n.* [ONF. (& F.) *canevas,* fr. L. *cannabis* hemp.] **1.** A heavy closely woven cloth of hemp or flax, used for tents, sails, etc.; also, a similar cloth of tow, jute, or cotton. **2.** A piece of canvas used for some particular purpose; as: **a** Sailcloth; also, a sail, or sails collectively. **b** A tent or a collection of tents; hence, the circus; circus life. **c** A surface prepared to receive painting, commonly painting in oil; hence, an oil painting. **3.** A coarse cloth so woven as to form regular meshes for working with the needle, as in tapestry or wool embroidery.

can′vas·back′ (-băk′), *n.; see* PLURAL, *Note,* 3. A North American wild duck (*Nyroca valisineria*), highly esteemed for its flesh.

can′vass (kăn′vȧs), *v. t.* [From CANVAS, *n.*] **1.** *Archaic.* To beat; to trounce; hence, to lash with criticism, invective, or the like. **2.** To examine in detail; to scrutinize, as votes at an election; to sift; discuss. **3.** To go through (a district) or go to (persons) to solicit orders, pledges, votes, etc. — *v. i.* To solicit or seek orders, votes, etc.; to solicit. — *n.* **1.** Examination, as in the way of discussion or debate; a scrutiny, as of votes. **2.** Act of canvassing for votes, orders, etc. — **can′vass·er,** *n.*

can′yon (kăn′yŭn), **ca′ñon** (kăn′yŭn; *Sp.* kä·nyōn′), *n.* [Sp. *cañon* tube, hollow.] A deep valley with high steep slopes, often with a stream flowing through it.

‖**can·zo′ne** (kän·tsō′nā), *n.; pl.* -ZONI (-nē). [It., a song, fr. L. *cantio,* fr. *canere* to sing.] A song or ballad; specif., a kind of Italian or Provençal lyric poem.

can′zo·net′ (kăn′zō·nĕt′), *n.* Any light and graceful little song.

caou′tchouc (kōō′chōōk; kou·chōōk′; *or, esp. Brit.,* kou′chōōk), *n.* [F., of Tupian origin.] Rubber; India rubber; specif., pure rubber.

cap (kăp), *n.* [AS. *cæppe,* fr. LL. *cappa.*] **1.** A covering for the head; esp.: **a** One of lace, muslin, etc., for women or infants. **b** One usually with a visor and without a brim, for men and boys. **c** One used as the mark of rank, office, or dignity. **d** A mortarboard. **2.** Anything resembling a cap in form, position, or use; as, a *cap* sealing a jar; a *cap* on an oil well; the *cap* (pileus) of a mushroom (see FUNGUS, *Illust.*). **3.** A percussion cap; also, a small piece of paper containing an explosive charge, used in toy pistols. **4.** Any of certain sizes of paper, about 14 × 17 inches; as, flat *cap;* foolscap or legal *cap* (U. S. 13 × 16 in.). **5.** A tread renewal of a pneumatic tire, called ***top cap*** when applied only to the top surface of the tread, and ***full cap*** when applied to the tread surface and tire shoulders as well. — *v. t.;* CAPPED (kăpt); CAP′PING. **1.** To cover with a cap or as with a cap; to cover the top or end of. **2. a** To match; to furnish an equal, a better, or an offset to; as, to *cap* a story. **b** To outdo or surpass; to excel. **3.** To form a cap to; to top; to crown. — ***cap the climax.*** To exceed the climax; reach the utmost limit in action or words.

ca′pa·bil′i·ty (kā′pȧ·bĭl′ĭ·tĭ), *n.; pl.* -TIES (-tĭz). **1.** Quality of being capable; capacity; esp., intellectual capacity. **2. a** Capacity of being used or developed. **b** A feature, condition, faculty, or the like, capable of development; — usually in *pl.*

ca′pa·ble (kā′pȧ·b'l), *adj.* [F., fr. LL., fr. L. *capere* to take, contain.] **1.** *Archaic.* Able to contain or hold. **2.** Having ability or fitness, physical or mental. **3. a** Of a nature to admit or allow; having qualities that suggest adjustment or adaptation; susceptible; as, *capable* of several interpretations. **b** Endowed with sufficient (good or evil) qualification; as, *capable* of sacrifice or of murder. **4.** *Obs.* Roomy or capacious; comprehensive. *Shak.* **5.** Having general ability; competent. — **Syn.** See ABLE. — **ca′pa·ble·ness,** *n.* — **ca′pa·bly** (-blĭ), *adv.*

ca·pa′cious (kȧ·pā′shŭs), *adj.* [L. *capax, -acis,* fr. *capere* to take.] Able to contain much; large; roomy; spacious; commodious. — **ca·pa′cious·ly,** *adv.* — **ca·pa′cious·ness,** *n.*

ca·pac′i·tance (kȧ·păs′ĭ·tăns), *n.* [From *capacity* reactance.] *Elec.* **a** That property of an isolated conductor or of a condenser which expresses its ability to keep the potential low for a given charge. **b** That property of a circuit or of a condenser which is exhibited by the force of flow of an alternating electric current; — opposed to *inductance.* **c** Specif., the ratio of the charge on a conductor to its potential, or the ratio of the charge on a positive plate of a condenser to the difference of potential between that of this plate and the corresponding negative plate. **d** A source of capacitance, as a condenser or an antenna functioning as one. — **ca·pac′i·tive** (-tĭv), *adj.*

ca·pac′i·tate (-tāt), *v. t.* To render capable; qualify.

ca·pac′i·tor (-tẽr), *n.* *Elec.* = CONDENSER, 2 **b.**

ca·pac′i·ty (kȧ·păs′ĭ·tĭ), *n.; pl.* -TIES (-tĭz). **1. a** Power of receiving, containing, or absorbing. **b** Extent of room or space; content; specif., volume; as, *capacity* for moisture; electric *capacity.* **c** The power of receiving and holding knowledge, etc. **d** Maximum output. **2.** Ability; as, *capacity* to pay. **3.** Capability, as of undergoing treatment. **4.** Outward condition; character; position; as, in the *capacity* of guide. **5.** *Elec.* **a** Capacitance. **b** The quantity of electricity that can be delivered under specified conditions, as from a battery at a given rate of discharge in ampere-hours. **c** Maximum power output, as from a generator. **6.** *Law.* Legal qualification, competency, power, or fitness.

cap′-à-pie′ (kăp′ȧ·pē′), *adv.* Often **cap-a-pie,** although not a Modern F. word. [OF. (*de*) *cap a pié* from head to foot, fr. L. *caput* head + *pes* foot.] From head to foot; at all points; as, armed *cap-a-pie.*

ca·par′i·son (kȧ·păr′ĭ·s'n; -z'n), *n.* [F. *caparaçon,* fr. Pr. *capa.* See CAPE garment.] **1.** An ornamental covering, or housing, for a horse;

trappings. **2.** The clothing or dress and ornaments of men and women; outfit. — *v. t.* To cover with caparisons; hence, to adorn with rich dress.

cape (kāp), *n.* [F., fr. Pr. *capa*, fr. LL. *cappa*.] A sleeveless garment, or part of a garment, hanging from the neck over the back, arms, and shoulders.

cape, *n.* [F. *cap*, fr. Pr. *cap* head, fr. L. *caput* head, point.] **1.** A point of land jutting out into water; a headland. Cf. PROMONTORY. **2.** [*usually cap.*] With *the.* Some particular cape, as Cape Horn, Cape Cod; esp., the Cape of Good Hope; hence, Cape of Good Hope Province, or, loosely, South Africa.

Cape, *adj.* Of or pertaining to the Cape of Good Hope, or to South Africa; as, the *Cape* buffalo (see BUFFALO, 1).

cap′e·lin (kăp′ĕ·lĭn), *n.* [F. *capelan, caplan, capelin*, lit., needy priest.] A small marine fish (*Mallotus villosus*) of the smelt family, used as food and as bait for cod.

Ca·pel′la (kȧ·pĕl′ȧ), *n.* [L., dim. of *caper* a goat.] A star of the first magnitude in Auriga; Alpha (α) Aurigae.

ca′per (kā′pẽr), *n.* [F. *câpre*, fr. It., fr. L., fr. Gr. *kapparis*.] **1.** Any of a genus (*Capparis*, esp. *C. spinosa*) of low prickly shrubs of the Mediterranean region, typifying a family (Capparidaceae, the caper family) distinguished from the related mustard family by the one-celled capsule. **2.** *pl.* The greenish flower buds and young berries of the caper, which are pickled and used in sauces, etc.

ca′per (kā′pẽr), *v. i.* [From CAPRIOLE.] To leap or jump about in a sprightly manner; to prance. — *n.* A frolicsome leap or spring; a skip; a jump, as in mirth or dancing. — **ca′per·er,** *n.*

cap′er·cail′lie, cap′er·cail′zie (kăp′ẽr·kāl′yĭ; -zĭ), *n.* [Gael. *capullcoille*.] The largest European grouse (*Tetrao urogallus*).

cape′skin′ (kāp′skĭn′), *n.* Any sheepskin tawed and dyed by dipping; esp. a glacé-finished leather from Cape (South African) sheepskin.

Ca·pe′tian (kȧ·pē′shăn), *adj.* Pert. to the French dynasty founded (A.D. 987) by Hugh Capet.

ca′pi·as (kā′pĭ·ăs; kăp′ĭ·ăs), *n.* [L., thou mayest take.] *Law.* A writ or process commanding the officer to take the body of the person named in it, that is, to arrest him.

cap′il·la′ceous (kăp′ĭ·lā′shŭs), *adj.* [L. *capillaceus* hairy, fr. *capillus* hair.] Threadlike; capillary.

cap′il·lar′i·ty (kăp′ĭ·lăr′ĭ·tĭ), *n.* **1.** Quality or state of being capillary. **2.** *Physics.* The action by which the surface of a liquid, where it is in contact with a solid (as in a capillary tube), is elevated or depressed; capillary attraction. Cf. MENISCUS, 3.

cap′il·lar′y (kăp′ĭ·lĕr′ĭ *or, esp. Brit.,* kȧ·pĭl′ȧ·rĭ), *adj.* [L. *capillaris*, fr. *capillus* hair.] **1.** Resembling a hair; very slender; specif., having a very small bore, as a tube (**capillary tube**) in which capillarity takes place; as, the *capillary* vessels of animals and plants. **2.** Relating to capillary tubes or vessels, or to the phenomena of surface tension; as, *capillary* action. — *n.; pl.* -IES (-ĭz). A capillary tube or vessel; specif., *Anat.*, a minute thin-walled vessel; esp., any of the smallest vessels of the blood-vascular system, forming networks throughout the body.

capillary attraction, capillary repulsion. The apparent attraction or repulsion caused by capillarity.

cap′i·tal (kăp′ĭ·tăl; -t′l), *adj.* [F., fr. L., fr. *caput* head.] **1.** Having reference to, or involving the forfeiture of, the head or life; punishable with death; as, a *capital* offense. **2.** Initial; — now only in phrase *capital letter.* **3.** Of primary importance; as, a *capital* error. **4.** Chief, in a political sense, as being the seat of government; as, a *capital* city. **5.** Of or relating to capital; as, *capital* stock, goods. **6.** Of first-rate quality; excellent. — **Syn.** Chief, principal, main, foremost. — *n.* **1.** A letter distinguished from the corresponding small (*lowercase*) letter of a font of type or style of writing by greater height and, usually, different form. *Small capitals* have the height of the body of lower-case letters. A capital is used as the initial letter of the first word of a sentence, a quotation, or a complete line of verse, or of such words as proper nouns and adjectives, titles of honor, etc. **2.** The capital city of a state or country. **3.** *Econ.* A stock of accumulated wealth; specif.: **a** The amount of property owned by an individual or corporation *at* a specified time, as distinct from the income received *during* a given period. **b** An aggregation of (economic) goods used to promote the production of other goods, instead of being valuable solely for immediate enjoyment. **4. a** = CAPITAL STOCK **b**. **b** *Accounting.* Net worth; excess of assets over liabilities. **5.** Capitalists, collectively; the capitalist class; as, relations between *capital* and labor. **6.** Anything that can be used to increase one's power or influence; as, to make *capital* out of a rival's mistakes.

cap′i·tal (kăp′ĭ·tăl; -t′l), *n.* [L. *capitellum*, dim. of *caput* head.] *Arch.* The uppermost member of a column, pilaster, etc., crowning the shaft and taking the weight of the entablature. See IONIC, ORDER, *Illusts.*

capital account. 1. An account of the owner's interest in a business. **2.** *Accounting.* An account of assets and liabilities, whose balancing item (profit and loss) shows either a surplus or a deficit at a given date. Cf. INCOME ACCOUNT.

capital expenditure. *Accounting.* Money spent or debts incurred for additions and betterments.

capital goods. Economic goods destined for use in production, as distinguished from *consumers' goods.*

cap′i·tal·ism (kăp′ĭ·tăl·ĭz′m; *Brit. also* kȧ·pĭt′ȧ·lĭz′m), *n.* **1.** The state of having capital; the position of a capitalist. **2.** An economic system in which capital and capitalists play the principal part; specif., one in which the ownership of land and natural wealth, the production, distribution, and exchange of goods, and the operation of the system itself, are effected by private enterprise and control under competitive conditions. Cf. SOCIALISM.

cap′i·tal·ist (kăp′ĭ·tăl·ĭst; *Brit. also* kȧ·pĭt′ȧ·lĭst), *n.* One who has capital; esp., a person who has or controls a large amount of accumulated wealth used in business. — **cap′i·tal·ist, cap′i·tal·is′tic** (-ĭs′tĭk), *adj.* — **cap′i·tal·is′ti·cal·ly** (-tĭ·kăl·ĭ), *adv.*

cap′i·tal·i·za′tion (kăp′ĭ·tăl·ĭ·zā′shŭn; -ī·zā′shŭn; *Brit. also* kȧ·pĭt′ȧ·lī-), *n.* **1.** Act or process of capitalizing. **2.** A sum or figure resulting from a process of capitalizing. **3.** *Accounting.* **a** The total permanent liabilities of a business, including outstanding stock. **b** The face value of such liabilities, esp. of stock not fully paid.

cap′i·tal·ize (kăp′ĭ·tăl·īz; *Brit. also* kȧ·pĭt′ȧ·līz), *v. t.* **1.** To convert into capital, or to use as capital; hence, to make use of for the sake of profit or advantage; as, to *capitalize* an opponent's mistakes. **2.** To compute the present value of (a periodical payment); to convert (an income, annuity, etc.) into a single payment or an equivalent capital sum. **3.** To furnish with capital; to provide capital for the operation of; as, to *capitalize* a business. **4.** To write, print, etc., with an initial capital, or in capital letters. — *v. i.* **1.** To accumulate capital. **2.** To profit (*by*); to take advantage (*of*); as, to *capitalize* on another's mistakes. **3.** To write, print, etc., with a capital letter.

capital levy. A levy on capital in addition to income tax and other taxes, in effect a general property tax.

cap′i·tal·ly (kăp′ĭ·tăl·ĭ), *adv.* In a capital manner; as: **a** Primarily; mainly. **b** Excellently; admirably.

capital ship. A warship of the first rank in size, armament, etc.; specif., one (excluding aircraft carriers) of over 10,000 tons displacement and mounting guns exceeding 8-inch caliber.

capital stock. *Accounting.* **a** The shares of a joint-stock corporation, considered as an aggregate. **b** The total face value of such shares, issued or authorized, whether fully paid or not; — often called simply *capital*, or, in the case of stock not fully paid in, *capitalization.*

cap′i·tate (kăp′ĭ·tāt), *adj.* [L. *capitatus*, fr. *caput* head.] Headlike in form; specif.: *Bot.* **a** Gathered into a head; as, *capitate* flowers. **b** Enlarged and globose; as, a *capitate* stigma.

cap′i·ta′tion (-tā′shŭn), *n.* [LL. *capitatio* a poll tax.] **1.** A direct uniform tax imposed on each head or person; poll tax. **2.** Any uniform per capita payment or fee.

Cap′i·tol (kăp′ĭ·tŏl; -t′l), *n.* [F. *capitole*, fr. L. *capitolium*, fr. *caput* head.] **1.** The temple of Jupiter at Rome on the Capitoline hill. **2.** The edifice at Washington in which the Congress of the United States holds its sessions; also, *U. S.* [*often not cap.*], the building in which a state legislature meets; a statehouse.

Cap′i·to·line (kăp′ĭ·tō·līn; kȧ·pĭt′ō·līn), *n.* The smallest of the seven hills of Rome. See SEVEN HILLS. — *adj.* Of or pert. to the Capitoline, the Capitol which anciently crowned it, or the gods whose cult centered there.

ca·pit′u·lar (kȧ·pĭt′ū·lẽr), *n.* [L. *capitulum* small head, chapter, dim. of *caput* head.] **a** *Eccl.* A member of a chapter. **b** = CAPITULARY, *n.*, 2. — *adj. Eccl.* Of or belonging to a chapter; capitulary; as, *capitular* estates.

ca·pit′u·lar′y (-lĕr′ĭ *or, esp. Brit.,* -lẽr·ĭ), *adj.* Of or relating to a chapter, esp. an ecclesiastical or masonic chapter. — *n.; pl.* -IES (-ĭz). **1.** A member of a chapter, esp. of an ecclesiastical or masonic chapter. **2.** An ordinance; chiefly *pl.*, a collection of ordinances; — because divided into chapters.

ca·pit′u·late (kȧ·pĭt′ū·lāt), *v. i.* [ML. *capitulatus*, past part. of *capitulare* to distinguish by chapters.] To surrender on conditions agreed upon; to make terms of surrender. — **Syn.** See YIELD.

ca·pit′u·la′tion (-lā′shŭn), *n.* **1.** A statement of the heads of a subject. **2.** *Hist.* Any of various conventions, made by the Turkish government, granting special privileges to foreign governments; hence, any such treaty. **3. a** The act or agreement of one who capitulates. **b** The instrument setting forth the terms of such an agreement.

ca·pit′u·lum (kȧ·pĭt′ū·lŭm), *n.; pl.* -LA (-lȧ). [L., a small head.] **1.** *Anat. & Zool.* A knoblike protuberance of any part, as at the end of a bone. **2.** *Bot.* An inflorescence consisting of a round or flat cluster of sessile flowers, as in the buttonbush. See INFLORESCENCE, *Illust.*

ca′pon (kā′pŏn), *n.* [AS. *capūn*, fr. L. *capo*.] **1.** A castrated cock, esp. when fattened for the table. **2.** *Archaic.* A eunuch.

ca′pon·ize (-īz), *v. t.* To castrate, as a cock.

cap′o·ral′ (kăp′ō·răl′), *n.* [F.] A coarse kind of tobacco.

ca·pote′ (kȧ·pōt′), *n.* [F., fr. *cape*.] A long cloak or overcoat, properly one with a hood.

cap′pa·ri·da′ceous (kăp′ȧ·rĭ·dā′shŭs), *adj.* [L. *capparis* caper.] *Bot.* Belonging to the caper family (Capparidaceae). See CAPER.

cap′per (kăp′ẽr), *n.* **1.** A worker or machine that caps or finishes caps. **2.** *Slang, U. S.* A decoy, as for gamblers.

cap′re·o·late (kăp′rē·ō·lāt; kȧ·prē′ō·lāt), *adj.* [L. *capreolus* tendril.] *Bot.* Having a tendril or tendrils.

ca·pric′cio (kä·prēt′chō), *n.; pl.* CAPRICCIOS (-chōz), CAPRICCI (-chē). [It.] **1.** A trick; also, a caprice; fancy. **2.** *Music.* An instrumental composition in a more or less free form, often of a whimsical style; a caprice.

ca·price′ (kȧ·prēs′), *n.* [F., fr. It. *capriccio*, fr. *capo* head + *riccio* hedgehog, fr. L. *ericius*.] **1.** An abrupt change in feeling, opinion, or action, proceeding from some whim or fancy; a fantastic notion. **2.** The mental disposition or state which produces or is subject to such changes; capriciousness. **3.** *Music.* A capriccio.

Syn. **Caprice, freak, whim, vagary, crotchet** mean an irrational or fanciful notion. **Caprice** emphasizes lack of apparent motivation and implies a certain willfulness or wantonness; **freak** suggests an impulsive, seemingly causeless, change of mind; **whim** implies a quaint, fantastic, capricious turn or inclination; **vagary** stresses the erratic, extravagant, or irresponsible character of the notion or fancy; **crotchet** implies a perversely heretical opinion, especially on some trivial point.

ca·pri′cious (kȧ·prĭsh′ŭs), *adj.* **1.** *Obs.* Fanciful. **2.** Governed or characterized by caprice; apt to change suddenly. — **Syn.** See INCONSTANT. — **Ant.** Steadfast. — **ca·pri′cious·ly,** *adv.* — **ca·pri′cious·ness,** *n.*

Cap′ri·corn (kăp′rĭ·kôrn), *n.* Also **Cap′ri·cor′nus** (-kôr′nŭs); *gen.* -NI (-nī). [L. *capricornus*, fr. *caper* goat + *cornu* horn.] *Astron.* **a** A southern zodiacal constellation between Sagittarius and Aquarius. **b** The tenth sign [♑] of the zodiac, into which the sun enters at the winter solstice, about December 22. See ZODIAC; TROPIC, *n.*, 1.

cap′ri·fi·ca′tion (kăp′rĭ·fĭ·kā′shŭn), *n.* [L. *caprificatio*, fr. *caprificus*. See CAPRIFIG.] Artificial pollination of certain figs by hanging in the trees fruits of the caprifig containing a wasp that carries the pollen to the edible figs.

cap′ri·fig′ (kăp′rĭ·fĭg′), *n.* [L. *caprificus*, fr. *caper* goat + *ficus* fig.] The wild fig (*Ficus carica sylvestris*) of southern Europe and Asia Minor; also, its fruit.

cap′ri·fo′li·a′ceous (-fō′lĭ·ā′shŭs), *adj.* [ML. *caprifolium*, fr. L. *caper* goat + *folium* leaf.] *Bot.* Belonging to the honeysuckle family (Caprifoliaceae). See HONEYSUCKLE.

cap′ri·ole (kăp′rĭ·ōl), *n.* [F., fr. It. *capriola*, fr. *capriolare* to caper.] **1.** A caper, as in dancing. **2.** *Manège.* A leap that a horse makes with all fours, upwards only, without advancing. — *v. i.* To perform a capriole.

cap·sa′i·cin (kăp·sā′ĭ·sĭn), *n.* [From CAPSICUM.] *Chem.* A colorless crystalline compound, $C_{18}H_{27}NO_3$, a powerful irritant, the pungent principle of cayenne pepper.

cap′si·cum (kăp′sĭ·kŭm), *n.* [NL., fr. L. *capsa* box, chest.] **1.** Any of a genus (*Capsicum*) of tropical herbs and shrubs of the nightshade family (Solanaceae), yielding dry, many-seeded berries known as *peppers*. See PEPPER, 3. **2.** *Pharm.* The dried ripe fruit of the species *C. frutescens*, used as a gastric and intestinal stimulant.

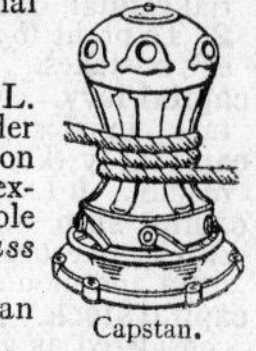
Capstan.

cap·size′ (kăp·sīz′), *v. t. & i.* To upset or overturn.

cap′stan (kăp′stăn), *n.* [F. *cabestan*, fr. Pr., fr. L. *capistrum*, fr. *capere* to hold.] A drum or cylinder revolving on an upright spindle, much used, esp. on shipboard, for moving or raising heavy weights or exerting great power by traction upon a rope or cable passing around the drum; — disting. from *windlass* and *winch*. Cf. DRUMHEAD, 3.

capstan bar. One of the levers for turning a capstan by hand.

cap′su·lar (kăp′sū·lẽr), *adj.* Of, pertaining to, or of the nature of a capsule; also, capsulate.

cap′su·late (-lāt), *adj.* Also **cap′su·lat′ed.** Enclosed in a capsule.

cap′sule (kăp′sūl), *n.* [F., fr. L. *capsula* a little box, fr. *capsa* case.] **1.** *Anat. & Zool.* **a** A membrane or saclike structure enclosing a part or organ. **b** Either of two layers or laminae of white matter in the cerebrum. **2.** *Bot.* Any closed receptacle containing spores or seeds; specif., in seed plants, a dry, dehiscent, usually many-seeded fruit composed of two or more carpels. See POPPY, *Illust.* **3.** *Pharm.* A small rounded container, often of gelatin, in which nauseous or acrid doses are enclosed to be swallowed. **4.** Brief but concise writing or discourse. — *adj.* Of a diminutive type or in a condensed or streamlined form; as, a *capsule* review, submarine, or education.

cap′tain (kăp′tĭn), *n.* [Through OF. & LL., fr. L. *caput* head.] **1.** A chief or headman; a leader. **2.** A person having authority over others acting in concert, as, in sports, the leader of a team. **3.** Abbr. *Capt.* **a** *Mil.* A commissioned officer ranking below a major and above a lieutenant. **b** *Naut.* The commanding officer, or master, of a vessel; — a title of courtesy. **c** *Nav.* A commissioned officer ranking above a commander and below a commodore. — *v. t.* To act as captain of; to lead. — **cap′tain·cy** (kăp′tĭn·sĭ), **cap′tain·ship,** *n.*

cap′tion (kăp′shŭn), *n.* [L. *captio*, fr. *capere* to take.] **1.** Act of taking or seizing; seizure. **2.** *Chiefly U. S.* The heading of a chapter, section, page, or article; also, a legend (def. 4) accompanying an illustration. **3.** The headline of an item in a newspaper. **4.** *Law.* That part of a legal instrument which shows where, when, and by what authority it was taken, found, or executed. **5.** *Motion Pictures.* A subtitle.

cap′tious (kăp′shŭs), *adj.* **1.** Apt to catch one; calculated to entangle subtly; insidious; as, *captious* questions. **2.** Apt to catch at faults; disposed to find fault; as, a *captious* critic. — **Syn.** See CRITICAL. — **cap′tious·ly,** *adv.* — **cap′tious·ness,** *n.*

cap′ti·vate (kăp′tĭ·vāt), *v. t.* [L. *captivatus*, past part. of *captivare* to capture, fr. *captivus* captive.] **1.** *Now Rare.* To capture; subdue. **2.** To acquire ascendancy over by art or attraction; to fascinate; charm. — **Syn.** See ATTRACT. — **Ant.** Repulse. — **cap′ti·va′tion** (-vā′shŭn), *n.* — **cap′ti·va′tor** (-vā′tẽr), *n.*

cap′tive (kăp′tĭv), *adj.* [L. *captivus*, fr. *capere* to take.] **1.** Made prisoner, esp. in war; held in bondage or in confinement; as, a *captive* bird; also, held in restraint; fastened; as, a *captive* balloon. **2.** Charmed; captivated. **3.** Of or pert. to bondage or confinement. **4.** Owned and operated by an industrial company or public utility for supplying its own needs, not for supplying the open market; — applied orig. to a coal mine. — *n.* **1.** One who is held in bondage, esp. by force, as by an enemy in war. **2.** One captivated, as by affection.

captive audience. An audience obliged to stay within hearing of a speech or demonstration, often to be subjected to propaganda.

cap·tiv′i·ty (kăp·tĭv′ĭ·tĭ), *n.; pl.* -TIES (-tĭz). State of being a captive.

cap′tor (kăp′tẽr; -tôr), *n.* One who captures.

cap′ture (kăp′tūr), *n.* [F., fr. L. *captura.*] **1.** Act of seizing by force or stratagem. **2.** A thing so taken; a prize. — *v. t.* To take captive; to seize by force or stratagem; also, to secure by effort, skill, or ingenuity in competition; as, to *capture* a prize. — **Syn.** See CATCH.

Cap′u·chin (kăp′ū·chĭn; kăp′ū·shēn′), *n.* [F., fr. It. *cappuccio* hood.] **1.** *Eccl.* A Franciscan monk of an austere branch. These monks wear a long pointed cowl (**ca·puche′** [*pron.* kȧ·po͞osh′; -po͞och′]). **2.** [*not cap.*] A garment for women, consisting of a cloak and hood. **3.** [*not cap.*] Any of a genus (*Cebus*) of South American monkeys, esp. *C. capucinus*, with the hair on its crown resembling a monk's cowl.

Cap′u·let (kăp′ū·lĕt), *n.* See ROMEO.

cap′y·ba′ra (kăp′ĭ·bä′rȧ), *n.* [Pg. *capybara*, Sp. *capibara*, of Tupian origin.] A large South American rodent (*Hydrochoerus capybara*), largely aquatic in habit. It is the largest existing rodent.

car (kär), *n.* [ONF. *carre*, fr. LL. *carra*, of Celt. origin.] **1.** A vehicle moved on wheels: **a** In general, carriage, cart, etc. **b** *Chiefly Poetic.* A chariot of war or of triumph. **c** Some particular vehicle so called, as a passenger automobile. **2.** A vehicle adapted to the rails of a railroad. **3.** The cage of an elevator or lift. **4.** That portion of an airship or balloon which carries the power plant, personnel, cargo, etc. **5.** A floating perforated box for keeping fish, etc., alive.

ca′ra·ba′o (kä′rä·bä′ō), *n.; pl.* -BAOS (-bä′ōz). [Sp., fr. Malay *karbau.*] *Phil. I.* A water buffalo (see BUFFALO).

car′a·bin (kăr′ȧ·bĭn), **car′a·bine** (-bīn). Vars. of CARBINE.

car′a·bi·neer′, car′a·bi·nier′ (-bĭ·nēr′), *n.* [F. *carabinier.*] A soldier, usually a cavalry soldier, armed with a carbine.

ca′ra·ca′ra (kä′rȧ·kä′rȧ; kȧ·rä′kȧ·rä′), *n.* [Sp. & Pg. *caracará*, of Tupian origin.] Any of certain large, mostly South American hawks of vulturelike habits, esp. the common species (*Polyborus plancus*) and the ***black caracara*** (*Ibycter ater*).

car′a·cole (kăr′ȧ·kōl), **car′a·col** (-kŏl), *n.* [F., appar. fr. a form of L. *conchylium* snail.] *Manège.* A half turn to right or left; loosely, any turn in a zigzag course, as in prancing. — *v. i.;* -COLED (-kōld), -COLLED (-kŏld); -COL′ING (-kōl′ĭng), -COL′LING (-kŏl′ĭng). *Manège.* To perform a caracole, or move in caracoles.

car′a·cul (kăr′ȧ·kŭl). Var. of KARAKUL.

ca·rafe′ (kȧ·răf′), *n.* [F.] A glass water bottle.

car′a·geen′ (kăr′ȧ·gēn′). Var. of CARRAGEEN.

car′a·mel (kăr′ȧ·mĕl), *n.* [F., fr. OF., fr. ML. *cannamellis* sugar cane.] **1.** Burnt sugar, used for coloring and flavoring. **2.** A kind of firm but plastic candy.

car′a·mel·ize (-īz), *v. t. & i.* Also **car′a·mel.** To turn into caramel.

ca·ran′goid (kȧ·răng′goid), *adj.* [From *Caranx*, type genus, fr. Sp. *caranga* + *-oid.*] Of, like, or pert. to a large family (Carangidae) of marine spiny-finned fishes, containing the pompanos, cavallas, etc., with narrow bodies and widely forked tails. — *n.* A carangoid fish.

car′a·pace (kăr′ȧ·pās), *n.* [F., fr. Sp. *carapacho.*] *Zool.* A bony or horny case or shield covering the back or part of the back of certain animals, as turtles and armadillos, and lobsters, crabs, and other crustaceans. See KING CRAB, *Illust.*

car′at (kăr′ăt), *n.* [F., through It. & Ar., fr. Gr. *keration* little horn, carob bean, carat.] Abbr. *car.* **1.** A unit of weight for precious stones. See WEIGHT, *Table* 2. **2.** A twenty-fourth part; — used to express the fineness of a gold alloy; as, 14 *carats* fine, i. e., being 14 parts gold and 10 alloy.

car′a·van (kăr′ȧ·văn; kăr′ȧ·văn′), *n.* [From F., fr. Per. *kārwān* a caravan (sense 1).] **1.** A company of travelers on a journey through desert or hostile regions, esp. in Asia or Africa; also, the vehicles in which such a company travel. Cf. SAFARI. **2.** A covered vehicle of various sorts; as: **a** *Eng.* Formerly, a large passenger vehicle. **b** A van. Cf. CONESTOGA WAGON.

car′a·van′sa·ry (kăr′ȧ·văn′sȧ·rĭ), *n.; pl.* -RIES (-rĭz). Also **car′a·van′se·rai** (-sĕ·rī; -rā). [From F., fr. Per. *kārwānsarāī*, fr. *kārwān* caravan + *sarāī* palace, inn.] **1.** A kind of inn, in the East, where caravans rest at night, being a large bare building surrounding a court. **2.** A large hotel or inn.

car′a·vel (kăr′ȧ·vĕl), *n.* Also **car′vel** (kär′vĕl), **car′a·velle.** [Through F., Pg., & LL., fr. Gr. *karabos* a kind of ship.] *Naut.* Any of several types of vessels, usually small sailing vessels; esp., in the 15th and 16th centuries, a small vessel with broad bows, high poop, and lateen sails.

car′a·way (kăr′ȧ·wā), *n.* [Through Sp. & Ar., fr. Gr. *karon.*] A biennial yellow-flowered aromatic herb (*Carum carvi*) of the carrot family, yielding aromatic, pungent seeds (**caraway seeds**), used in cookery, confectionery, and as a carminative.

car·bam′ate (kär·băm′āt; kär′bȧ·māt), *n.* A salt or ester of carbamic acid.

car·bam′ic (kär·băm′ĭk), *adj.* *Chem.* Pert. to or designating an acid, $NH_2.CO_2H$, occurring as a salt of ammonium in commercial ammonium carbonate.

car′ba·zole (kär′bȧ·zōl), *n.* [*carbon* + *az-* + *-ol.*] *Chem.* A crystalline, feebly basic compound, $C_{12}H_9N$, in anthracene. It is the parent of a number of dyes.

car′bide (kär′bīd; -bĭd), *n.* *Chem.* A binary compound of carbon; esp., calcium carbide (which see).

car′bine (kär′bīn; -bēn), *n.* [F. *carabine.*] A short light rifle or, formerly, musket, used esp. by cavalry. See RIFLE, *Illust.*

car′bi·neer′ (kär′bĭ·nēr′). Var. of CARABINEER.

car′bi·nol (kär′bĭ·nōl; -nŏl), *n.* *Chem.* Methanol, CH_3OH (in names of derivatives); also, by extension, any alcohol derived from it.

car′bo·hy′drate (kär′bō·hī′drāt), *n.* [*carbon* + *hydrate.*] *Chem.* Any of a group of neutral compounds composed of carbon, hydrogen, and oxygen, and including the sugars, starches, etc. Carbohydrates are formed by all green plants (see PHOTOSYNTHESIS) and constitute a major class of foods for animals (see FOOD, *n.*, 1).

car′bo·lat′ed (kär′bō·lāt′ĕd; -ĭd), *adj.* Impregnated with carbolic acid.

car·bol′ic (kär·bŏl′ĭk), *adj.* [L. *carbo* coal + *oleum* oil.] Pertaining to or designating a weak monoacid derived from coal tar and other sources and called also *phenol.*

car′bo·lize (kär′bō·līz), *v. t.* To mix or treat with carbolic acid.

car′bon (kär′bŏn), *n.* [F. *carbone*, fr. L. *carbo* coal.] **1.** *Chem.* An element occurring native as the diamond and as graphite, and forming a constituent of coal, petroleum, and asphalt, of limestone and other carbonates, and of all organic compounds. Symbol, *C*; at. no., 6; at. wt., 12.010. Carbon is also obtained artificially as lampblack, bone black, charcoal, coke, etc., in varying degrees of purity. It has a remarkable property of forming complex compounds, because of the ability of its atoms to unite into chains or rings. **2.** A piece of carbon paper; also, a carbon copy. **3.** *Elec.* A carbon rod used in an arc lamp; also, a plate of carbon used as one of the elements of a voltaic battery. — *adj.* Of, pert. to, resembling, or treated with carbon.

car′bo·na′ceous (kär′bō·nā′shŭs), *adj.* Pertaining to, containing, or composed of carbon.

car′bo·na′do (-nā′dō), *n.; pl.* -DOES or -DOS (-dōz). [From Sp., fr. L. *carbo* coal.] A broiled or grilled piece of meat or fish, scored before cooking. — *v. t.;* -DOED (-dōd); -DO·ING (-dō·ĭng). **1.** To make a carbonado of. **2.** To hack or slash.

car′bo·na′do (-nā′dō), *n.* [Pg., carbonated.] An opaque dark-colored diamond found in Brazil, used esp. for cutting and drilling hard materials.

‖**Car′bo·na′ri** (kär′bō·nä′rē), *n. pl.; sing.* (*rare*) -NARO (-rō). [It., charcoal burners.] A secret political association organized in Italy early in the 19th century to establish a republic.

car′bon·ate (kär′bŏn·āt), *n.* [F.] *Chem.* A salt or ester of carbonic acid; as, *carbonate* of lime (= CALCIUM CARBONATE); *carbonate* of soda (= SODIUM CARBONATE). — (-āt), *v. t.* **1.** To burn to carbon. **2.** *Chem.* **a** To convert into a carbonate. **b** To impregnate with carbonic acid (as, *carbonated* lime) or carbon dioxide (as, *carbonated* water). Cf. AERATE, *v. t.*, 1. — **car′bon·a′tion** (-ā′shŭn), *n.*

carbon bisulfide. Carbon disulfide.

carbon black. Specif., gas black.

carbon copy. A copy made with carbon paper; hence, an exact duplicate; a replica.

carbon dioxide. *Chem.* A heavy colorless gas, CO_2, extinguishing flame. Water charged with it becomes the soda water of the shops and the carbonated water of natural springs. Plants use it in photosynthesis, retaining the carbon for food material and giving out the oxygen.

carbon disulfide. A colorless inflammable liquid, CS_2, used as a solvent for rubber, etc., as an insecticide, etc.

car·bon′ic (kär·bŏn′ĭk), *adj.* *Chem.* **a** Of, pertaining to, or obtained from carbon. **b** Designating an acid (**carbonic acid,** H_2CO_3), existing only in solution and reacting with bases to form carbonates.

car·bon′ic–ac′id gas. Carbon dioxide.

car′bon·if′er·ous (kär′bŏn·ĭf′ẽr·ŭs), *adj.* [*carbon* + *-ferous.*] **1.** Producing or containing carbon or coal. **2.** [*cap.*] *Geol.* Of, pert. to, or designating the period of the Paleozoic era between the Devonian and the Permian, or the system of rocks formed during this period; — so called from the coal beds in the system. By some divided into the ***Lower Carboniferous*** or ***Mississippian*** and the ***Upper Carboniferous*** or ***Pennsylvanian*** (containing the *coal measures:* which see). — **Car′bon·if′er·ous,** *n.*

car′bon·ize (kär′bŏn·īz), *v. t.* **1.** To convert into a residue or carbon, as by fire; to char. **2.** To impregnate, cover, or combine with carbon. — **car′bon·i·za′tion** (-ĭ·zā′shŭn; -ī·zā′-), *n.*

carbon monoxide. *Chem.* A colorless odorless gas, CO, a product

of the incomplete combustion of carbon. It burns with a pale-blue flame, forming carbon dioxide. It is very poisonous.
carbon paper. a Thin paper coated with a preparation of lampblack, or of some color, used in making copies. Pressure on the back causes the color to be transferred to paper laid against it. b See CARBON PROCESS.
carbon process. *Photog.* A printing process depending on the effect of light on bichromated gelatin. Paper coated with a mixture of the gelatin and a pigment is called **carbon paper** *or* **carbon tissue.**
carbon tetrachloride. *Chem.* A colorless noninflammable liquid, CCl_4, of chloroformlike odor, used as a solvent and detergent, and as a fire extinguisher.
car′bon·yl (kär′bŏn·ĭl; -ēl), *n.* [*carbon* + *-yl.*] *Chem.* a The bivalent radical CO, occurring in aldehydes, ketones, organic acids, etc. b A compound of this radical with a metal; as, ***nickel carbonyl***, $Ni(CO)_4$. — **car′bon·yl′ic** (-ĭl′ĭk), *adj.*
Car′bo·run′dum (kär′bō·rŭn′dŭm), *n.* A trade-mark for certain abrasives.
car·box′yl (kär·bŏk′sĭl), *n.* [*carbon* + *oxygen* + *-yl.*] *Chem.* The univalent radical CO_2H, the characteristic group of most organic acids, as formic, acetic, benzoic acids, etc. — **car′box·yl′ic** (kär′bŏk·sĭl′ĭk), *adj.*
car′boy (kär′boi), *n.* [Per. *qarābah.*] A very large glass bottle enclosed in a box, or wickerwork, esp. for corrosives. Cf. DEMIJOHN.
car′bun·cle (kär′bŭng·k'l), *n.* [ONF., fr. L. *carbunculus,* dim. of *carbo* coal.] **1.** Formerly, any of several red precious stones, as the ruby; now, the garnet cut cabochon. **2.** a *Med.* A painful local inflammation of the subcutaneous tissue, larger and more serious than a boil. b A pimple or red spot, due to intemperance. **3.** A brown, redyellow in hue, of low saturation and low brilliance. See COLOR. — **car·bun′cu·lar** (kär·bŭng′kū·lẽr), *adj.*
car′bu·ret (kär′bū·rĕt), *n.* [From CARBON.] A carbide. — *v. t.;* -RET′ED or -RET′TED (-rĕt′ĕd; -ĭd); -RET′ING or -RET′TING. **1.** To combine chemically with carbon. **2.** To charge with volatile carbon compounds; as, to *carburet* air or gas by passing it through a light petroleum oil. — **car′bu·re′tion** (-rĕsh′ŭn), *n.*
car′bu·ret′ant (-rĕt′ănt), *n.* A carbureting agent.
car′bu·ret′or, car′bu·ret′tor (-rā′tẽr; -rĕt′ẽr), *n.* An apparatus in which air or gas is carbureted.
car′bu·rize (-rīz), *v. t.* a To combine or impregnate with carbon. b = CARBURET, *v. t.*, 2. — **car′bu·ri·za′tion** (-rĭ·zā′shŭn; -rī·zā′-), *n.*
car′ca·jou (kär′kȧ·jōō; -zhōō), *n.* [Can. F. corrupt. of an Indian name of the wolverine.] The wolverine; also, the Canada lynx, the cougar, or the badger of North America.
car′ca·net (kär′kȧ·nĕt), *n.* [Dim. fr. F., fr. ML. *carcannum.*] *Archaic.* An ornamental chain, necklace, collar, or, sometimes, headband, usually golden or jeweled.
car′cass (kär′kȧs), *n.; pl.* CARCASSES (-ĕz; -ĭz). Also **car′case** (-kȧs). [From F., fr. It. *carcassa.*] **1.** A dead body of a beast or (in contempt) of a man; esp., the dressed body (trunk) of an animal slaughtered for food. **2.** *Contemptuous.* The living body. **3.** The worthless or decaying remains of a great and once comely or vital thing; the shell or husk; as, a ship's *carcass.* **4.** The foundation structure of a pneumatic tire. See TIRE, *Illust.*
car·cin′o·gen (kär·sĭn′ō·jĕn; kär′sĭ·nō·jĕn), *n.* [Gr. *karkinos* cancer + *-gen.*] Any cancer-producing substance.
car′ci·no′ma (kär′sĭ·nō′mȧ), *n.; pl.* -NOMATA (-mȧ·tȧ), -NOMAS (-mȧz). [L., fr. Gr. *karkinōma* cancer, fr. *karkinos* crab. See -OMA.] A form of cancer consisting of a malignant growth originating in epithelial tissue. See CANCER, SARCOMA. Many varieties are distinguished. — **car′ci·nom′a·tous** (-nŏm′ȧ·tŭs; -nō′mȧ·tŭs), *adj.*
card (kärd), *n.* [F. *carte,* fr. L. *charta* paper, fr. Gr. *chartēs* a leaf of paper.] **1.** A playing card. **2.** *pl.* A game or games played with cards; card playing; — often construed as a singular. **3.** A person or thing that can be manipulated as a card; as, he is a safe *card* or a likely *card;* also, *Colloq.*, an eccentric; a droll fellow. **4.** A flat, stiff, usually rectangular, piece of paper or thin pasteboard, used for various purposes; as, a post *card,* Christmas *card,* visiting *card;* to receive *cards,* or invitations, for a wedding. **5.** Specif., a program of, or a form for keeping a record of, the items of races, games, regattas, etc.; hence, an attraction; as, this will be a good *card* for the fair. — *v. t.* **1.** To place or fasten on, or by means of, a card. **2.** To provide with a card. **3.** To enter or list on cards.
card, *n.* [F. *carde* teasel, card, fr. L. *cardus, carduus,* thistle.] **1.** An implement for raising a nap on cloth. **2.** An instrument or machine (**card′ing ma·chine′**) for disentangling and arranging the fibers of cotton, wool, flax, etc. — *v. t.* To cleanse and disentangle by a card or carding machine before spinning; as, to *card* wool. Carding disentangles and collects all the fibers, of whatever length, and thus differs from *combing,* in which only the longer fibers are collected while the short staple is combed away. — **card′er,** *n.*
car′da·mom (kär′dȧ·mŭm), *n.* Also **car′da·mum** (-mŭm), **car′da·mon** (-mŭn). [F. and L.; F., fr. L., fr. Gr. *kardamōmon.*] **1.** The aromatic capsular fruit of an East Indian herb (*Elettaria cardamomum*) of the ginger family, with seeds used as a condiment and in medicine. **2.** The plant.
card′board′ (kärd′bōrd′; 70), *n.* A stiff compact pasteboard of various qualities, for making cards, etc.
car′di·ac (kär′dĭ·ăk), **car·di′a·cal** (kär·dī′ȧ·kăl), *adj.* [Through F. and L., fr. Gr. *kardiakos,* fr. *kardia* heart.] *Anat.* **1.** Of, pert. to, or situated near the heart; as, *cardiac* murmur; *cardiac* muscles, nerves. **2.** Of, pert. to, or designating the part of the stomach into which the esophagus opens, or the whole stomach except the narrow pyloric end. — *n.* **1.** A medicine that excites stomach action. Cf. STOMACHIC, *n.* **2.** *Colloq.* A sufferer from heart disease.
car′di·al′gi·a (kär′dĭ·ăl′jĭ·ȧ), *n.* [NL., fr. Gr. *kardialgia,* fr. *kardia* heart + *algos* pain.] *Med.* A burning or gnawing pain, or feeling of distress, felt near the heart and usually a symptom of indigestion; heartburn.
car′di·gan (kär′dĭ·găn), *n., or* **cardigan jacket.** [After an earl of *Cardigan.*] A knitted worsted jacket.
car′di·nal (kär′dĭ·năl; -n'l), *adj.* [F. and L.; F., fr. L. *cardinalis,* fr. *cardo* hinge, turning point.] **1.** Of basic importance; main; chief; as, *cardinal* principles. **2.** Of or pertaining to a cardinal. **3.** Of the color cardinal red. — **Syn.** See ESSENTIAL. — *n.* **1.** *R.C.Ch.* One of the ecclesiastical princes who constitute the pope's council, or the college of cardinals, and who are appointed by the pope. **2.** *pl.* Short for CARDINAL NUMBERS, POINTS, etc. **3.** A woman's short hooded cloak, originally of scarlet cloth. **4.** Usually **cardinal red.** A color, yellowish-red in hue, of high saturation and low brilliance. See COLOR. **5.** = CARDINAL BIRD. — **car′di·nal·ly,** *adv.* — **car′di·nal·ship′,** *n.*
car′di·nal·ate (-āt), *n.* Office, rank, or dignity of a cardinal; also, the cardinals collectively.
cardinal bird. Any of several bright-colored songbirds of the genus *Richmondena,* esp. *R. cardinalis,* of the southern and middle United States, the male of which has bright-red plumage and bill; — called also **cardinal grosbeak.**
cardinal flower. The brilliant red flower of a North American herb (*Lobelia cardinalis*) of the lobelia family; also, the plant itself.
cardinal number *or* **numeral.** One of the numbers used in simple counting or in reply to the question, how many? — disting. from *ordinal number* (see ORDINAL, *adj.*, 1). See NUMBER, *Table.*
cardinal points. The four main points of the compass.
cardinal virtues. Prudence, justice, temperance, and fortitude, the four chief natural virtues. Some modern writers add the three "theological" virtues, faith, hope, and charity. Cf. DEADLY SINS.
car′di·o- (kär′dĭ·ō-), **car′di-** (kär′dĭ-). [Gr. *kardia* heart.] A combining form denoting *of* or *pertaining to the heart* (*and*); *cardiac;* as in **car′di·o-a·or′tic.**
car′di·o·gram′ (-grăm′), *n.* [*cardio-* + *-gram.*] The curve or tracing made by a cardiograph.
car′di·o·graph′ (-grȧf′; 9), *n.* [*cardio-* + *-graph.*] An instrument that registers graphically the duration and character of the heart's movements. — **car′di·o·graph′ic** (-grăf′ĭk), *adj.* — **car′di·og′ra·phy** (-ŏg′rȧ·fĭ), *n.*
car′di·ol′o·gy (kär′dĭ·ŏl′ō·jĭ), *n.* [*cardio-* + *-logy.*] The science that treats of the heart, its action, diseases, etc. — **car′di·ol′o·gist** (-jĭst), *n.*
car·di′tis (kär·dī′tĭs), *n.* [NL., fr. Gr. *kardia* heart + *-itis.*] Myocarditis. Cf. ENDOCARDITIS, PERICARDITIS.
card′sharp′ (kärd′shärp′), *n.* Also **card′sharp′er.** A professional swindler at cards. — **card′sharp′ing,** *n.*
car′du·a′ceous (kär′dū̇·ā′shŭs), *adj.* [L. *carduus* thistle.] Belonging to the aster or thistle family (Carduaceae). See ASTER, 1.
care (kâr), *n.* [AS. *caru, cearu.*] **1.** Mental suffering; grief. **2.** A burdensome sense of responsibility; heavy anxiety; also, a cause of anxiety. **3.** Painstaking or watchful attention; heed; caution. **4.** A caring, or liking; — with *of* or *for;* as, *care* for the public good. **5.** Charge, oversight, management, or custody; as, under a doctor's *care.* **6.** A person or thing that is an object of care.
Syn. **Care, concern, solicitude, anxiety, worry** mean a troubling and engrossing emotion or affair. **Care** implies oppression of the mind weighed down by responsibility or disquieted by apprehension; **concern** suggests less oppression than *care,* but a troubled state of mind because of one's interest, affection, or the like; **solicitude** implies profound concern and connotes either thoughtfulness for another's welfare or almost hovering attentiveness to one ill, in pain, or the like; **anxiety** stresses anguish of fear coupled with uncertainty or expectancy of misfortune; **worry** suggests more mental activity than anxiety, such as fretting or stewing over problems, persons, or situations that may or may not be a real cause of anxiety.
— *v. i.* **1.** To have, feel, or exercise care. **2.** To have a wish or inclination (to) or affection (for). **3.** To mind; to be concerned; to have objection; — in negative and conditional expressions; as, "Will you go?" — "I do not *care* if I do"; "Would you *care* if I were to decline?" — **car′er** (kâr′ẽr), *n.*
ca·reen′ (kȧ·rēn′), *v. t.* [From F., fr. It., fr. L. *carina* keel of a ship.] a To cause (a vessel) to lean over on one side; also, to clean, calk, or repair (a vessel in this position). b To cause to heel over, as a ship; to tip or incline, as a cart. — *v. i.* **1.** To heel over, as a ship under a breeze; hence, to lurch; to sway from side to side. **2.** To careen or renovate a ship; also, of a ship, to undergo such careening. — *n.* A careening; also, a careened position. — **ca·reen′er,** *n.*
ca·reer′ (kȧ·rēr′), *n.* [F. *carrière* highroad, racecourse, fr. It. *carriera,* fr. *carro* wagon.] **1.** A running; a course, esp. a swift one; hence, speed; full speed; — chiefly in phrases such as *in full career.* **2.** *Obs.* a A short gallop; a gambol or frisk. b A course, field, etc., as for racing. **3.** Course of a person's life, esp. in some particular pursuit. **4.** Notable or conspicuous progress or success in one's chosen calling; as, to make a *career* for oneself. **5.** A profession or other calling demanding special preparation and undertaken as a lifework; as, to follow diplomacy as a *career.*
— *v. i.* To move or run rapidly. — *v. t.* **1.** To cause to career, as a horse. **2.** To go over or across in a career. — **ca·reer′er,** *n.* — **ca·reer′ist,** *n.*
care′free′ (kâr′frē′), *adj.* Free from care; happy.
care′ful (kâr′fōōl; -f'l), *adj.* **1.** *Archaic.* a Full of care; anxious. b Fraught with care. **2.** Exercising or taking care; — often with *of, for,* or the infinitive. **3.** Marked by care; done or executed with care. — **care′ful·ly,** *adv.* — **care′ful·ness,** *n.*
Syn. **Careful, meticulous, scrupulous, punctilious, punctual** mean showing close attention to details of execution or performance. **Careful** usually implies painstaking efforts, thoroughness, cautiousness in avoiding errors, or the like; **meticulous** indicates either commendable extreme carefulness or finical caution about minutiae; **scrupulous** suggests a carefulness that adheres to what one's conscience tells one is right, true, exact, or the like; **punctilious** implies minute, often excessive, attention to the fine points of law, etiquette, morality, or the like; **punctual,** though formerly close to *punctilious,* now more often implies great carefulness in one's adherence to times appointed, as for engagements, in following a schedule, or the like.
care′less (-lĕs; -lĭs), *adj.* **1.** Free from care; untroubled. **2.** Without care; as: a Indifferent; as, *careless* of results. b Negligent; heedless; as, a *careless* housekeeper. **3.** Not receiving or exhibiting due care; as, *careless* work; a *careless* mistake. — **Syn.** Heedless, thoughtless, inadvertent. — **care′less·ly,** *adv.* — **care′less·ness,** *n.*
ca·ress′ (kȧ·rĕs′), *n.* [From F., fr. It., fr. L. *carus* dear.] An act of endearment; a tender or loving embrace, touch, etc. — *v. t.;* CA·RESSED′ (-rĕst′) or, *chiefly poetic,* CA·REST′; CA·RESS′ING. To touch, stroke, pat, etc., tenderly, lovingly, or softly; to bestow caresses upon; also, to affect as if a caress; as, echoes that *caress* the ear. — **ca·ress′er,** *n.* — **ca·ress′ing·ly,** *adv.* — **ca·res′sive** (kȧ·rĕs′ĭv), *adj.* — **ca·res′sive·ly,** *adv.*
Syn. **Caress, fondle, pet, cuddle** mean to manifest affection by touching or handling. **Caress** implies an expression of interest or affection, such as stroking or patting; **fondle** implies doting fondness shown by hugging, kissing, and the like; **pet,** in general, implies special attentions and indulgences, but, in current use, it often suggests flirtatious or

amorous fondling; **cuddle**, chiefly used in reference to a baby, suggests the action of mother or nurse in drawing it to her breast to keep it warm, happy, or quiet.

car'et (kăr'ĕt; kâr'-), *n.* [L. *caret* there is wanting.] A mark [∧] used by writers and proofreaders to indicate that something interlined above or inserted in the margin belongs in the place marked.

care'tak'er (kâr'tāk'ẽr), *n.* A person who takes charge and care of any place, thing, or other person.

care'worn' (-wōrn'; 70), *adj.* Showing effects of anxiety.

car'go (kär'gō), *n.; pl.* -GOES or -GOS (-gōz). [Sp., fr. *cargar* to load.] The lading or freight of a ship, aircraft, etc.; load; freight.

car'hop' (kär'hŏp'), *n.* A waiter or waitress of a drive-in restaurant who serves food and drinks to customers in their parked cars.

Car'ib (kăr'ĭb), *n.* [See CANNIBAL.] **1.** One of a Cariban tribe now found in Guiana, Venezuela, some of the Lesser Antilles, and on the Caribbean coast of Central America. **2.** Loosely, any Cariban Indian.

Car'ib·an (kăr'ĭ·băn), *adj.* Pertaining to or designating an important linguistic family of South American Indians found chiefly in Brazil, Colombia, Guiana, and Venezuela, and also in Central America and the Lesser Antilles. Cf. ARAWAKAN; see LANGUAGE, *Table.*

Car'ib·be'an (kăr'ĭ·bē'ăn; kă·rĭb'ē·ăn), *adj.* Of or pertaining to the Caribs, or the Caribbean Sea (see *Gaz.*). — *n.* A Carib.

‖**ca·ri'be** (kä·rē'bā; kăr'ĭ·bē), *n.* [Sp., lit., a cannibal.] A South American fish (genus *Serrasalmo*), small but very voracious, often attacking men and large animals that enter the water.

car'i·bou (kăr'ĭ·bōō), *n. sing. & pl.* [Can. F., of Algonquian origin.] A native North American reindeer found in Canada, Alaska, and Greenland. The larger forms, including the best-known species (*Rangifer caribou*), inhabit wooded localities.

car'i·ca·ture (kăr'ĭ·kȧ·tṳr; kăr'ĭ·kȧ·tṳr'), *n.* [F., fr. It. *caricatura*, fr. *caricare* to charge, overload, exaggerate.] **1.** Grotesque or ludicrous exaggeration; distortion by exaggeration of parts or characteristics. **2.** A picture, description, etc., characterized by burlesque exaggeration or distortion. **3.** A ludicrously poor imitation. — *v. t.* To make a caricature of. — **car'i·ca·tur·al** (-tṳr·ăl; -tṳr'ăl), *adj.* — **car'i·ca·tur·ist** (-ĭst), *n.*

Syn. **Caricature, burlesque, parody, travesty** mean a grotesque or bizarre imitation of a person or thing. **Caricature** implies ludicrous exaggeration or distortion of the peculiar features of a person, group, people, etc.; **burlesque** implies mimicry chiefly by treating a trifling subject in a mock-heroic vein or by giving a serious subject a frivolous or comic turn; **parody** implies the treatment of a ludicrous subject in the exact style of some serious and usually well-known composition or writer; **travesty** implies that the subject remains unchanged, but that the style is made extravagant or absurd.

car'i·es (kâr'ĭ·ēz; kâr'ēz), *n.* [L.] Decay of animal tissues; esp., ulceration and disintegration of bone; specif., *Dent.*, tooth decay.

car'il·lon (kăr'ĭ·lŏn; kȧ·rĭl'yŭn; *F.* kȧ'rē'yôN'), *n.* [F., a chime of bells, orig. of four bells.] **1.** A set of fixed bells sounded by striking with hammers operated either from a keyboard or mechanically. **2.** An organ stop imitating the sound of a carillon. **3.** A tune played on, or a peal from, a carillon. — (kăr'ĭ·lŏn; kȧ·rĭl'yŭn), *v. i.;* -LONNED (-lŏnd; -yŭnd); -LON'NING (-lŏn'ĭng; -yŭn·ĭng). To play a carillon. — **car'il·lon·neur'** (kăr'ĭ·lŏ·nûr'), *n.*

ca·ri'na (kȧ·rī'nȧ), *n.; pl.* -NAE (-nē). [L., keel.] *Biol.* A keellike part or structure. — **ca·ri'nal** (-năl), *adj.*

car'i·nate (kăr'ĭ·nāt), **car'i·nat'ed** (-nāt'ĕd; -ĭd), *adj.* [L. *carinatus*, fr. *carina* keel.] Keel-shaped.

car'i·ole, car'ri·ole (kăr'ĭ·ōl), *n.* [F., fr. It. *carriuola*, dim. of *carro.*] **1.** A small, light, one-horse carriage. Cf. CARRYALL, 1. **2.** A type of Canadian sleigh.

car'i·ous (kâr'ĭ·ŭs), *adj.* [L. *cariosus.*] Affected with caries. — **car'i·os'i·ty** (-ŏs'ĭ·tĭ), *n.* — **car'i·ous·ness**, *n.*

cark (kärk), *n.* [ME. *cark*, fr. northern form of F. *charge.*] Care; worry. — *v. t. & i. Archaic.* To make or be full of anxiety; worry. — **cark'ing**, *adj.* — **cark'ing·ly**, *adv.*

carl (kärl), *n.* [ON. *karl* a man.] **1.** *Archaic.* A man of the common people; specif., *Hist.*, a villein. **2.** *Scot.* A boor; a churl.

car'line (kär'lĭn; kẽr'lĭn), *n.* [ON. *kerling.* See CARL.] *Chiefly Scot.* A woman; esp., a hag, crone, or witch.

car'ling (kär'lĭng), *n.* One of the short timbers running lengthwise of a ship, between transverse deck beams.

Car'lism (kär'lĭz'm), *n.* **a** Adherence to Don Carlos of Spain or his successors, or formerly to Charles X of France. **b** Principles, plans, or claims of either group of adherents. — **Car'list** (-lĭst), *n.*

car'load' (kär'lōd'), *n.* **a** A load that fills a car. **b** The minimum number of tons required to ship at a rate (**carload rate**) lower than that quoted for small shipments of the same class. Abbr. *c.l.*

carload lot. *Com.* A shipment of freight meeting the official requirement for a minimum carload amount.

Car'lo·vin'gi·an (kär'lō·vĭn'jĭ·ăn), *adj.* Carolingian.

car'ma·gnole' (kär'mȧ·nyōl'; *F.* kȧr'mȧ'nyôl'), *n.* [F.] **1.** A metal-buttoned jacket with wide collar and lapels, worn originally in the south of France. **2.** The costume of the French Revolutionists, consisting of this jacket, wide black pantaloons, a red cap, and a scarlet or tricolored waistcoat. Cf. SANS-CULOTTE. **3.** A popular song and dance of the time of the first French Revolution. Cf. MARSEILLAISE, ÇA IRA. **4.** A soldier of the French Revolution.

Car'mel·ite (kär'mĕl·īt), *n.* A friar of a mendicant order founded on Mt. Carmel, in Syria, in the 12th century; also, a nun of the same order. — **Car'mel·ite**, *adj.*

car·min'a·tive (kär·mĭn'ȧ·tĭv; kär'mĭ·nā'tĭv; -nȧ·tĭv), *adj.* [L. *carminare* to card, hence, to cleanse, fr. *carmen* a card for wool.] Expelling gas from the alimentary canal; relieving colic, griping, etc. — *n.* A carminative agent.

car'mine (kär'mĭn; -mīn), *n.* [F. *carmin*, fr. ML. *carminium.*] **1.** A rich crimson or scarlet lake made from cochineal. **2.** A color, red in hue, of very high saturation and low brilliance. See COLOR.

car'nage (kär'nĭj), *n.* [F., fr. LL., fr. L. *caro, carnis*, flesh.] **1.** A collection of carcasses; flesh of the slain. **2.** [F., fr. It.] Great destruction of life, as in battle; slaughter.

car'nal (kär'năl; -n'l), *adj.* [L. *carnalis*, fr. *caro, carnis*, flesh.] **1.** Of the body or flesh; — opposed to *spiritual.* **2.** Of the body as the seat of appetites; specif., sexual. — **car·nal'i·ty** (kär·năl'ĭ·tĭ), *n.* — **car'nal·ly**, *adv.*

Syn. **Carnal, fleshly, sensual, animal** mean having or showing a connection with the body. **Carnal** once meant no more than this, but the word now is related to the body as the manifestation of man's lower nature and, as a result, is derogatory in its implications; **fleshly** implies a connection with the flesh, thought of as man's lower nature, but is not as condemnatory as *carnal;* **sensual** suggests habitual indulgence in sensations and desires having a physical origin and, commonly, implies bestiality; **animal** stresses a connection with man's physical as distinguished from his rational nature, and rarely implies a depreciatory intent.

car'nall·ite (kär'năl·īt), *n.* [After R. von *Carnall*, a Prussian.] A hydrous potassium-magnesium chloride, $KMgCl_3.6H_2O$, valuable as a source of potassium.

car·na'tion (kär·nā'shŭn), *n.* [F., the flesh tints in a painting, deriv. of L. *caro, carnis*, flesh.] **1.** Formerly, the color flesh; now (also **carnation red**), a color, bluish-red in hue, of high saturation and high brilliance. See COLOR. **2.** Any of many cultivated double-flowered varieties of the clove pink (see PINK, 1). The carnation is the State flower of Ohio.

car'na·u'ba (kär'nȧ·ōō'bȧ), *n.* [Pg., of Tupian origin.] The Brazilian wax palm (*Copernicia cerifera*). Its leaves yield **carnauba wax**, used in making candles, varnish, etc.

car·nel'ian (kär·nēl'yăn), *n.* [For *cornelian;* influenced by L. *carneus* fleshy, because of its color.] A reddish variety of chalcedony.

car'ni·val (kär'nĭ·văl), *n.* [F. and It.; F., fr. It. *carnevale*, fr. ML. *carne vale* O flesh, farewell!] **1.** The season or festival of merry-making before Lent. Cf. SHROVETIDE, MARDI GRAS. **2.** An amusement enterprise with merry-go-rounds, side shows, vaudeville, etc. **3.** Exuberant, often riotous, merrymaking.

car'ni·vore (kär'nĭ·vōr; 70), *n.* **1.** A flesh-eating animal; esp., *Zool.*, any of an order (**Car·niv'o·ra** [kär·nĭv'ō·rȧ]) of mammals, mostly flesh-eating, including the dogs, cats, bears, seals, etc. **2.** *Bot.* An insect-eating plant, as Venus's-flytrap. — **car·niv'o·ral** (kär·nĭv'ō·răl), *adj.*

car·niv'o·rous (kär·nĭv'ō·rŭs), *adj.* [L. *carnivorus*, fr. *caro, carnis*, flesh + *vorare* to devour.] **1.** Eating flesh; preying or feeding on animals; — opp. to *herbivorous.* **2.** *Bot.* Designating plants having specially modified leaves that trap insects and other small animal life, the decaying flesh of which supplies them with nitrogen. **3.** *Zool.* Of or pert. to the carnivores. — **car·niv'o·rous·ly**, *adv.* — **car·niv'o·rous·ness**, *n.*

car'no·tite (kär'nō·tīt), *n.* [After A. *Carnot*, a Frenchman.] A hydrous vanadate of uranium, potassium, etc. It is radioactive and has been used as a source of radium.

car'ob (kăr'ŏb), *n.* [F. *caroube*, fr. Ar. *kharrūbah.*] **1.** An evergreen tree (*Ceratonia siliqua*) of the senna family, of the Mediterranean region, bearing red racemose flowers; — called also *locust.* **2.** A pod of this tree, or its pulp, used esp. as fodder; — called also **carob bean.**

ca·roche' (kȧ·rōch'; -rōsh'), *n.* [MF. *carroche*, fr. It., deriv. of L. *carrus* wagon.] *Hist.* A kind of stately coach.

car'ol (kăr'ŭl), *n.* [OF. *carole*, fr. *caroler* to dance, prob. fr. L. *choraules* a flute player.] **1.** *Hist.* A round dance accompanied by song; also, the song. **2.** A song of joy; often, a joyful hymn; as, a Christmas *carol.* — *v. i. & t.;* -OLED (-ŭld) or -OLLED; -OL·ING or -OL·LING. **1.** To sing, esp. joyfully. **2.** To celebrate in song.

Car'o·line (kăr'ō·līn; -lĭn), *adj.* Of or pert. to Charles (ML. *Carolus*), as Charles the Great (Charlemagne), Charles I & II of England, or Charles II of Spain.

Car'o·lin'gi·an (-lĭn'jĭ·ăn), *adj.* [ML. *Carolus* Charles + *-ing*, a Germanic patronymic suffix.] Of or pertaining to the second Frankish dynasty of kings and emperors, ruling in France from Pepin the Short (751) to the death of Louis V (987) and in Germany to the death of Louis III, the Child (911); — so called either from Charles Martel, father of Pepin, or from Charlemagne. Cf. MEROVINGIAN. — **Car'o·lin'gi·an**, *n.*

Car'o·lin'i·an (kăr'ō·lĭn'ĭ·ăn), *adj.* **1.** Caroline. **2.** Of or pertaining to North or South Carolina. — *n.* A native or inhabitant of North or South Carolina.

car'om (kăr'ŭm), *n.* [F. *carambole.*] **1.** *Billiards.* A shot in which the cue ball strikes each of two object balls; a cannon. **2.** A similar shot in other games, as curling; hence, a striking and rebounding. — *v. i.* To make a carom.

car'o·tene (kăr'ō·tēn), **car'o·tin** (-tĭn), *n.* [From L. *carota* carrot.] A ruby-red crystalline hydrocarbon, $C_{40}H_{56}$, found in various plants and used as a pigment; by extension, any carotenoid hydrocarbon.

ca·rot'e·noid (kȧ·rŏt'ē·noid), *n.* [*carotene* + *-oid.*] *Biochem.* Any of an important group of yellow, orange, red, and purple pigments occurring in plant and animal fats and including the carotenes and related alcohols, ketones, ethers, etc. — **ca·rot'e·noid**, *adj.*

ca·rot'id (kȧ·rŏt'ĭd), *adj.* [Gr. *karōtides*, pl., fr. *karos* heavy sleep; — from the belief that the carotid arteries caused drowsiness.] *Anat.* Designating the chief artery or pair of arteries which pass up the neck and supply the head; hence, pertaining to or near such artery or arteries. — *n.* A carotid artery. — **ca·rot'id·al** (-ĭ·dăl), *adj.*

ca·rot'i·noid (-ĭ·noid), *n. & adj.* [*carotin* + *-oid.*] Var. of CAROTENOID.

ca·rous'al (kȧ·rouz'ăl; -'l), *n.* [From CAROUSE.] **1.** A jovial feast or festival; also, a drunken revel; a carouse. **2.** Erroneous for CAROUSEL **a.**

ca·rouse' (kȧ·rouz'), *n.* [From F., fr. G. *garaus* all out, in *garaus trinken* to empty the cup.] **1.** *Obs.* A draining of the cup in drinking; also, a drained cup; a toast. **2.** A drinking bout; a carousal. — *v. i. & t.* To drink deeply or freely; to take part in a carousal. — **ca·rous'er**, *n.*

car'ou·sel' (kăr'ōō·zĕl'; -sĕl'). Var. of CARROUSEL.

carp (kärp), *v. i.* [ON. *karpa* to boast, but influenced by L. *carpere* to pluck, calumniate.] To talk complainingly or censoriously; find fault; cavil. — **carp'er**, *n.*

carp, *n.;* see PLURAL, *Note*, 6. [OF. *carpe*, fr. Pr., fr. ML. *carpa.*] A soft-finned fresh-water edible fish (*Cyprinus carpio*, type of a family, Cyprinidae, the carp family, which includes also barbels, breams, chubs, daces, goldfishes, most fresh-water minnows, shiners, and tenches), inhabiting ponds and sluggish streams, sometimes living to a great age and weighing 40 lbs. or more; also, any of numerous fishes of the same family or any of certain fishes of other families.

-carp (-kärp). [Gr. *karpos.*] A combining form meaning *fruit*, as in endocarp, schizocarp, pleurocarp.

car'pal (kär'păl), *adj.* [From CARPUS.] *Anat.* Of or pertaining to the carpus, or wrist. — *n.* A carpal bone.

‖**car'pe di'em** (kär'pē dī'ĕm). [L.] Enjoy the day; hence, seize the present opportunity; — from Horace's Ode I. xi. 8, *carpe diem, quam minimum credula postero*, enjoy today, trust little to tomorrow.

car'pel (kär'pĕl), *n.* [NL. *carpellum,* fr. Gr. *karpos* fruit.] *Bot.* A one-celled ovule-bearing organ, or ovary, at the base of a pistil, the female sex organ in a flower, or one of the cells of a several-celled ovary. A carpel is a modified leaf. Cf. GYNOECIUM. — **car'pel·lar'y** (kär'pĕ·lĕr'ĭ *or, esp. Brit.,* -lẽr·ĭ), *adj.*

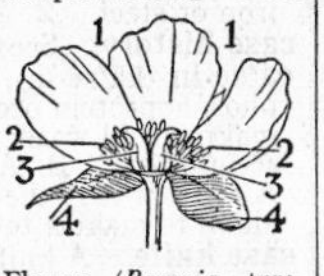

Flower (*Paeonia peregrina*), cut away. 1, 1 Petals; 2, 2 Stamens; 3, 3 Carpels; 4, 4 Sepals.

car'pel·late (kär'pĕ·lāt), *adj.* *Bot.* Having carpels.

car'pen·ter (kär'pĕn·tẽr), *n.* [From ONF., fr. LL., fr. L. *carpentum* wagon.] A workman who builds or repairs wooden structures, as houses or ships, or their structural parts. Cf. CABINETMAKER. — *v. i. & t.* To work or make as a carpenter. — **car'pen·ter·ing,** *n.* — **car'pen·try** (-trĭ), *n.*

carpenter bee. Any of various solitary bees (*Xylocopa* and allied genera) that gnaw galleries in sound timber.

car'pet (kär'pĕt; -pĭt), *n.* [OF. *carpite,* fr. ML. *carpeta, carpita,* woolly cloths, fr. L. *carpere* to pluck, to card (wool).] **1.** A heavy woven or felted fabric used as a floor covering; esp., such a fabric made in breadths to be sewed together and tacked to the floor. Cf. RUG. Of Oriental rugs, *rug* and *carpet* are used interchangeably. **2.** A carpetlike covering. — *v. t.* To cover with a carpet. — *adj.* Effeminate; esp., given to voluptuous ease; as, a **carpet knight.**

car'pet·bag' (-băg'), *n.* A satchel, esp. one made of carpet.

car'pet·bag'ger (-băg'ẽr), *n.* *Slang, U. S.* One who travels with a carpetbag; hence: **a** An itinerant wildcat banker of the West. **b** A Northerner who went to the South after the Civil War, esp. to make money by taking advantage of unsettled conditions.

carpet beetle *or* **bug.** A small beetle (*Anthrenus scrophulariae*) whose larva (*buffalo moth*) damages carpets and other woolen goods; — called also *buffalo bug.*

car'pet·ing, *n.* Cloth or materials for carpets; carpets.

car'pet·weed' (kär'pĕt·wēd'; kär'pĭt-), *n.* A North American weed (*Mollugo verticillata;* type of a family, Aizoaceae the carpetweed family) that forms a mat on the ground.

car'pi (kär'pī), *n., pl.* of CARPUS.

-car'pic (-kär'pĭk). Combining form equiv. to -CARPOUS.

carp'ing (kär'pĭng), *adj.* Faultfinding; captious. — **Syn.** See CRITICAL. — **carp'ing·ly,** *adv.*

car'po·go'ni·um (kär'pō·gō'nĭ·ŭm), *n.; pl.* -GONIA (-ȧ). [NL., fr. Gr. *karpos* fruit + root of Gr. *gignesthai* to be born.] *Bot.* **a** In red algae, the flask-shaped basal portion of the female reproductive organ (procarp) in which the egg is formed, and which develops into the sporocarp or cystocarp after fertilization. **b** An ascogonium. Cf. TRICHOGYNE. — **car'po·go'ni·al** (-ăl), *adj.*

car·pol'o·gy (kär·pŏl'ō·jĭ), *n.* [Gr. *karpos* fruit + *-logy.*] That branch of plant anatomy relating to structure of fruit and seeds. — **car·pol'o·gist** (-jĭst), *n.*

car·poph'a·gous (kär·pŏf'ȧ·gŭs), *adj.* [Gr. *karpophagos,* fr. *karpos* fruit + *phagein* to eat.] Feeding on fruits.

car'po·phore (kär'pō·fōr; 70), *n.* [Gr. *karpos* fruit + *-phore.*] *Bot.* **a** In fungi, the stalk of a sporocarp. **b** A slender prolongation of the floral axis which supports the carpels, as in the crane's-bill (*Geranium*).

car'port' (kär'pōrt'; 70), *n.* An open-sided roofed automobile shelter, usually formed by extension of the roof from the side of a building.

-car'pous (-kär'pŭs). [Gr. *karpos* fruit.] A combining form signifying *having* (such) *fruit* or (so many) *fruits,* as in *syncarpous, monocarpous.*

car'pus (kär'pŭs), *n.; pl.* CARPI (-pī). [NL., fr. Gr. *karpos* wrist.] The wrist; the bones of the wrist.

car'rack (kăr'ăk), *n.* Also **car'rick** (-ĭk). [Through OF. & Sp., fr. Ar. *qarāqir,* pl., fr. Gr. *kerkouros* a long-sterned Cypriote vessel.] *Hist.* A galleon.

car'ra·geen' (kăr'ȧ·gēn'), *n.* Also **car'ra·gheen'.** [From *Carragheen,* near Waterford, Ireland.] A dark-purple cartilaginous seaweed (*Chondrus crispus*) which, dried and bleached, is known as *Irish moss* and is used in making blancmange (also called *Irish moss*) and in pharmacy as a demulcent.

car'rel (kăr'ĕl), *n.* [Var. of CAROL in obs. sense of "monk's study."] A small alcove, as in a cloister or in a library, for individual study.

car'riage (kăr'ĭj), *n.* [ONF. *cariage,* fr. *carier* to cart. See CARRY.] **1.** Act of carrying; conveyance, esp. of goods. **2.** Manner of carrying one's body or self; bearing; formerly, also, behavior. **3.** Management; administration. **4.** (*also* kăr'ĭ·ĭj) Price or cost of carrying. **5.** A wheeled vehicle for persons, esp. one designed for comfort. **6.** A wheeled support carrying a burden; as, a gun *carriage.* **7.** A part, esp. of a machine, which moves and supports some other moving part. **8.** *Obs.* That which is carried; burden; load. — **Syn.** See BEARING.

car'rick bend (kăr'ĭk). See KNOT, *Illust.* (37, 38).

carrick bitts. *Naut.* The bitts supporting the windlass.

car'ried (kăr'ĭd), *past & past part.* of CARRY.

car'ri·er (kăr'ĭ·ẽr), *n.* **1.** A bearer; a messenger. **2.** A person, a company, or a corporation in the transportation business. **3.** Short for CARRIER PIGEON. **4.** A machine or device for carrying; a conveyer or container. **5.** A bearer and transmitter of disease germs; esp., a person who carries in his system germs of a disease to which he is immune. **6.** *Chem.* A catalyst by whose agency some element or group is transferred from one compound to another; as, iron is a *carrier* of oxygen. **7.** *Elec.* The wave, or current, or frequency transmitted in electrical communication. **8.** *Nav.* = AIRCRAFT CARRIER.

carrier pigeon. **1.** Orig. but now loosely, a pigeon used to carry messages; — now properly called *homing pigeon.* **2.** One of a fancy breed of large pigeons.

car'ri·ole (kăr'ĭ·ōl). Var. of CARIOLE.

car'ri·on (kăr'ĭ·ŭn), *n.* [ONF. *caroigne,* ultimately fr. L. *caries* decay.] The putrefying flesh of a carcass. — *adj.* Of, feeding on, or like carrion.

carrion crow. **a** The common European black crow (*Corvus corone*). **b** The black vulture (see VULTURE).

car'ritch (kăr'ĭch), *n.* *Chiefly Scot.* A catechism.

car'rom (kăr'ŭm). Var. of CAROM.

‖car'ro·ma'ta (kär'rō·mä'tä), *n.* [Sp. in Phil. I.] *Phil. I.* A light, two-wheeled, boxlike vehicle.

car'ron·ade' (kăr'ŭ·nād'), *n.* *Hist.* A short iron cannon.

car'rot (kăr'ŭt), *n.* [F. *carotte,* fr. L. *carota.*] A biennial plant (*Daucus carota sativa*) with a usually orange-colored, spindle-shaped edible root; also, the root, eaten as a vegetable. It is the type of a family (Ammiaceae, the carrot family) distinguished by alternate, mostly compound, often fragrant leaves, small flowers, and dry 2-carpellary fruits which split at maturity, and including the celery, parsley, and parsnip. Cf. WILD CARROT.

car'rot·y (-ĭ), *adj.* Like carrot roots in color, as hair.

car'rou·sel' (kăr'ōō·zĕl'; -sĕl'), *n.* Also **car'ou·sel'.** [F., fr. It. *carosello.*] **a** *Hist.* A tournament in which cavalrymen divided into troops execute evolutions, often with scenic shows, etc., added. **b** A merry-go-round.

car'ry (kăr'ĭ), *v. t.;* CAR'RIED (-ĭd); CAR'RY·ING. [ONF. *carier* (F. *charrier*), fr. *car* (F. *char*) car.] **1.** To move by vehicle, in the hands, etc.; to transport. **2.** Hence: **a** To transmit to another; as, to *carry* news. **b** To transfer from one place, thing, etc., to another; as, to *carry* war into Asia. **3.** To support; to sustain; as: **a** To have upon or about one's person; as, to *carry* a wound. **b** To bear the weight of; as, pillars *carry* the arch. **c** To support by confirming; as, a decision that *carries* another. **4.** To extend; continue; as, to *carry* the chimney through the roof. **5.** To drive; impel; as, ambition *carries* one far. **6.** To lead or bring along mentally or emotionally; as, to *carry* one's audience with one. **7.** To win; capture; as, to *carry* a citadel. **8.** To uphold through conflict, competition, etc.; as, to *carry* one's point; also, to succeed in; as, to *carry* an election. **9.** To hold or bear (the body, some part of it, or oneself); as, to *carry* one's head high; to comport; behave; as, to *carry* oneself proudly. **10.** To have as an attribute or the like; exhibit; imply; as, his tone *carried* conviction. **11.** To produce, as crops; to yield; to support, as cattle. **12.** *Com.* To bear the charges of having in stock, on one's books, in reserve, etc.; to hold for future sale, settlement, etc. **13.** *Colloq., So. U. S.* To escort. **14.** *Golf.* To cover (a distance) or pass (an object) at a single stroke. **15.** *Hunting.* To keep and follow, as the scent. **16.** *Mil.* To hold (a weapon or standard) in a certain prescribed way.

Syn. **Carry, bear, convey, transport** mean to move something from one place to another. **Carry** always implies a means by which something is moved, such as a wagon, a train, a ship, a personal agent, a pipe, or the like (as, trains *carrying* soldiers); **bear** is preferred when effort or the importance of that which is carried is suggested (as, to *bear* the wounded man to the house); **convey** is used of things that are moved continuously or in the mass or that pass through natural or artificial channels (as, a pipe to *convey* water; language *conveys* thought); **transport** stresses the movement of something to its destination (as, a vessel engaged in *transporting* troops).

— *v. i.* **1.** To act as a bearer. **2.** To have or exert power to propel, project, etc., something; as, her voice *carries* well. **3.** To hold the head, etc.; as, a horse *carries* well when he holds his head high.

— *n.; pl.* CARRIES (-ĭz). **1.** The range, as of a gun or projectile. **2.** *Golf.* The distance from the place where a ball is struck to where it first lands. **3.** *U. S. & Canada.* A portage between navigable waters. **4.** *Mil.* The position assumed at the order "carry arms," "carry sabers," etc.

car'ry·all' (-ôl'), *n.* [From *cariole.*] *U. S.* **1.** A light covered carriage for four or more persons. **2.** A passenger automobile having a closed body, equipped with two facing seats along the sides.

car'ry-o'ver, *n.* **1.** The part of a crop, stock, etc., remaining to be disposed of with a later crop or a fresher stock. **2.** *Bookkeeping.* The amount forwarded from one page to another.

carse (kärs; kẽrs), *n.* *Scot.* Low rich land, as along a river.

cart (kärt), *n.* [ME. *cart, carte,* fr. AS. *cræt.*] A light, small, usually two-wheeled vehicle; as: **a** A chariot. **b** A light open wagon for delivery, farm work, etc. **c** A small, open carriage. — *v. t. & i.* To convey or deliver (goods, etc.) in a cart. — **cart'er,** *n.*

cart'age (kär'tĭj), *n.* **1.** Act of carting. **2.** Price paid for carting.

carte (kärt), **‖quarte** (kȧrt), *n.* [F. *quarte,* prop., a fourth.] *Fencing.* A position in thrusting or parrying.

carte (kärt), *n.* [F. See 1st CARD.] **1.** *Scot.* A playing card; *pl.,* a game of cards. **2.** Menu; bill of fare; — used esp. in *à la carte.*

carte blanche (kärt' blänsh'; *F.* kȧrt'); *pl.* CARTES BLANCHES (kärts' blänsh'; *F.* kȧrt' blänsh'). [F., lit., white paper.] A blank paper, with a person's signature, etc., given to another with permission to superscribe what conditions he pleases; hence, full discretionary power.

car·tel' (kär·tĕl'; kär'tĕl), *n.* [F., fr. It. *cartello,* dim. fr. *carta,* fr. L. *charta.*] **1.** A letter of defiance or challenge, as to single combat. **2.** A written agreement between opposing nations. **3.** [G. *kartell.*] An association of private business organizations bound by contract to co-operate in regulating production and marketing of products, thus tending to restrict world markets and fix prices. **4.** [*often cap.*] In France and Belgium, a political bloc. — **Syn.** See MONOPOLY.

Car·te'sian (kär·tē'zhăn *or, esp. Brit.,* -tē'zĭ·ăn), *adj.* [From *Cartesius,* Latinized form of *Descartes.*] Of or pert. to the French philosopher René Descartes, or Cartesianism. — *n.* An adherent of Cartesianism.

Car·te'sian·ism (-ĭz'm), *n.* The philosophy of Descartes, the ideal of which was mathematical certitude in metaphysical demonstrations and which emphasized the distinction between thought and extension (mind and matter).

Car·thu'sian (kär·thū'zhăn *or, esp. Brit.,* -zĭ·ăn), *n.* [ML. *Cartusianus.*] A member of an austere religious order, founded in the mountainous region (Chartreuse), near Grenoble, France, by St. Bruno, in 1086. See CHARTREUSE, 1.

car'ti·lage (kär'tĭ·lĭj), *n.* [F., fr. L. *cartilago.*] *Anat.* **1.** A translucent elastic tissue which composes most of the skeleton of the embryos and very young of vertebrates, becoming for the most part converted into bone in the higher vertebrates. **2.** A part or structure composed of cartilage.

cartilage cells. See HYALINE CARTILAGE.

car'ti·lag'i·nous (-lăj'ĭ·nŭs), *adj.* **1.** Of, pert. to, or like cartilage. **2.** Having the skeleton composed mostly of cartilage; — of fishes.

Car'tist (kär'tĭst), *n.* [Sp. *cartista,* fr. *carta* paper, document. See CHART.] In Spain and Portugal, one who supports the constitution.

car'to·gram (kär'tō·grăm), *n.* [F. *cartogramme.* See 1st CARD; -GRAM.] A map using shades, curves, or the like, to show geographically statistics of various kinds.

car·tog'ra·phy (kär·tŏg'rȧ·fĭ), *n.* [See 1st CARD; -GRAPHY.] Art or business of drawing or making charts or maps. — **car·tog'ra·pher** (-fẽr), *n.* — **car'to·graph'ic** (kär'tō·grăf'ĭk), **car'to·graph'i·cal** (-ĭ·kăl), *adj.* — **car'to·graph'i·cal·ly,** *adv.*

car'ton (kär'tŏn), *n.* [F.] **1.** A light covered box of pasteboard or the like. **2.** A white disk or circle within the bull's-eye of a target; also, a shot which strikes this.

car·toon' (kär·tōōn'), *n.* [F. *carton,* fr. It., fr. L. *charta.*] **1.** An artist's full-size design or study, to be transferred or copied, as in making fresco paintings, stained-glass windows, etc. **2.** A large pictorial sketch; esp., a pictorial caricature. — **car·toon′**, *v. t. & i.* — **car·toon′ist**, *n.*

car·touche′, car·touch′ (kär·to͞osh′), *n.* [F. *cartouche*, fr. It. *cartoccio*, fr. *carta* paper.] **1.** A scroll-like design, esp. one used as an ornament. **2.** An oval or oblong figure, esp. one on an Egyptian monument, containing a sovereign's name. **3.** In some fireworks, the case containing the inflammable materials. **4.** *Mil.* A paper cartridge or a cartridge box.

car′tridge (kär′trĭj), *n.* [Formerly *cartrage*, corrupted fr. F. *cartouche*.] **1.** A case, capsule, shell, or bag of metal, pasteboard, or the like, containing the explosive charge and, in small arms and some cannon, the projectile to be fired. **2.** *Photog.* A roll of protected films for insertion in a camera.

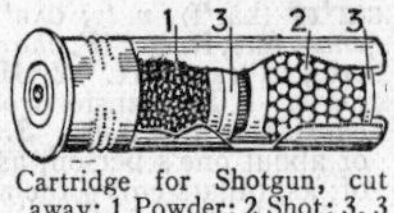

Cartridge for Shotgun, cut away: 1 Powder; 2 Shot; 3, 3 Wads.

car′tu·lar′y (kär′tū̇·lĕr′ĭ; -lẽr·ĭ). Var. of CHARTULARY.

cart wheel. 1. The wheel of a cart. **2.** *Slang.* A large coin, as the U. S. silver dollar. **3.** A sidewise handspring.

car′un·cle (kăr′ŭng·k'l; kȧ·rŭng′k'l), *n.* [L. *caruncula*, dim. of *caro* flesh.] **1.** A naked fleshy outgrowth, as the wattles and comb of certain birds. Cf. POULTRY, *Illust.* **2.** *Bot.* An outgrowth at or near the hilum of a seed. — **ca·run′cu·lar** (kȧ·rŭng′kū̇·lẽr), *adj.* — **ca·run′cu·late** (-lāt), **ca·run′cu·lat′ed** (-lāt′ĕd; -ĭd), *adj.* — **ca·run′cu·lous** (-lŭs), *adj.*

car′va·crol (kär′vȧ·krōl; -krŏl), *n.* [F. *carvi* caraway + L. *acer* (*acr-*) sharp + *-ol*.] *Chem.* A thick oil, $C_{10}H_{13}OH$, in various mints, used as an antiseptic and to relieve toothache.

carve (kärv), *v. t.* [AS. *ceorfan*.] **1.** To cut, esp. in an artistic manner; to shape by cutting. **2.** To make or get as if by cutting. **3.** To cut into pieces or slices, as meat at table. — *v. i.* **1.** To cut wood, marble, etc., artistically. **2.** To slice and apportion meat at table. — *n.* A carving stroke or cut. — **carv′er**, *n.*

car′vel (kär′vĕl). Var. of CARAVEL.

car′vel–built′, *adj.* *Shipbuilding.* Built with the planks meeting flush at the seams. Cf. CLINKER-BUILT.

carv′en (kär′vĕn), *adj.* Wrought by carving; carved.

carv′ing, *n.* Work of one who carves; carved work.

car′y·at′id (kăr′ĭ·ăt′ĭd), *n.*; *pl.* -IDS (-ĭdz), -IDES (-ĭ·dēz). [From L., fr. Gr. *Karyatides*, lit., priestesses in the temple of Diana at Caryae, in Laconia.] *Arch.* A draped female figure supporting an entablature. Cf. ATLANTES. — **car′y·at′i·dal** (-ĭ·dăl), **car′y·at′i·de′an** (-dē′ăn), **car′y·a·tid′ic** (-ȧ·tĭd′ĭk), *adj.*

car′y·o- (kăr′ĭ·ō-), **car′y-** (kăr′ĭ-). Vars. of KARYO-, KARY-.

car′y·o·phyl·la′ceous (-fĭ·lā′shŭs), *adj.* [Gr. *karyophyllon* clove tree, fr. *karyon* nut + *phyllon* leaf.] Belonging to the pink family (Caryophyllaceae). See 4th PINK, *n.*, 1.

car′y·op′sis (kăr′ĭ·ŏp′sĭs), *n.*; *pl.* -OPSES (-sēz), -OPSIDES (-sĭ·dēz). [NL., fr. *cary-* + *-opsis*.] *Bot.* A small, one-celled, dry, indehiscent fruit, with fruit and seed forming a single grain, as in wheat, barley, and other grasses.

‖**ca′sa** (kä′sä; *Pg.* kȧ′zȧ), *n.*; *pl.*, *Sp. & Pg.* CASAS (*Sp.*-säs; *Pg.*-zȧsh); *It.* CASE (kä′sā). [Sp., It., or Pg., fr. L. *casa* cabin.] A house.

ca·sa′ba (kȧ·sä′bȧ), *n.* Also **casaba melon.** [From *Kasaba*, near Smyrna, Asia Minor, whence the melon was introduced.] Any of several winter melons with a yellow rind. See WINTER MELON.

cas′ca·bel (kăs′kȧ·bĕl), *n.* [Sp., a little bell.] In certain muzzle-loading cannon, a projection behind the breech.

cas·cade′ (kăs·kād′), *n.* [F., fr. It. *cascata*, fr. *cascare* to fall.] **1.** A steep, usually small waterfall, often one of a series. **2.** Hence: **a** A kind of firework. **b** A fall of lace, net, etc., that takes a zigzag line. **c** A series, as of parts in an apparatus or of electric circuits, where a fluid, electricity, or the like, passes from one part, one circuit, etc., to another. — *v. i. & t.* To fall or pass in a cascade; to cause to fall or pass or to connect in this manner; as, to *cascade* electric circuits.

cas·car′a (kăs·kâr′ȧ; *Sp.* käs′kä·rä), *n.* [Sp. *cáscara* bark.] **1.** Usually **cas·car′a buck′thorn** (kăs·kâr′ȧ). A buckthorn (*Rhamnus purshiana*) of the Pacific coast of the United States; — called also *bearwood*. **2.** In full **cas·car′a sa·gra′da** (kăs·kâr′ȧ sȧ·grā′dȧ; *Sp.* käs′kä·rä sä·grä′thä). [Sp. *cáscara sagrada*, lit., sacred bark.] The dried bark of this tree, used as a laxative.

cas′ca·ril′la (kăs′kȧ·rĭl′ȧ), *n.* [Sp., a small thin bark, Peruvian bark, dim. of *cáscara* bark.] **a** Usually **cascarilla bark.** The aromatic bark of a Bahamian shrub (*Croton eluteria*) of the spurge family, used as a tonic and stomachic. **b** The shrub itself. See CROTON, 1.

case (kās), *n.* [OF. *cas*, fr. L. *casus*, fr. *cadere* to fall, happen.] **1.** A particular instance; a special or illustrative situation, occurrence, or the like. **2.** Actual condition, situation, or the like; existing facts; as, such being the *case*. **3.** A situation involving a problem; as, a *case* of conscience. **4.** One's present state of mind, health, or affairs; plight. **5.** An argument or set of arguments, esp. of convincing arguments; as, to make out a *case* against a bill. **6.** A person, esp. with reference to his character or tractableness. **7.** [L. *casus* a falling (from a perpendicular; cf. DECLENSION, 3).] *Gram.* One of the inflectional forms of a noun, pronoun, or adjective that indicate its sense relation to other words, as that of subject, object, attribute, etc.; also, this sense relation often indicated by word order. **8.** *Law.* A suit or action in law or equity. **9.** *Med.* **a** An instance of sickness or injury. **b** A patient. — **Syn.** See INSTANCE.

case, *n.* [ONF. *casse*, fr. L. *capsa* chest, fr. *capere* to hold.] **1.** A box, sheath, or covering. **2.** The contents of, or quantity in, such a box. **3.** A pair; couple; brace; as, a *case* of pistols. **4.** A casing; as, a window *case*. **5.** The cavity in the skull of the sperm whale containing spermaceti and a fine oil. **6.** *Print.* A shallow divided tray, for type. Cases are often arranged in pairs, the ***upper case*** containing capitals, accented and marked letters, etc., the ***lower case*** containing the small letters, figures etc. — *v. t.* To enclose in a case; cover with a case.

ca′se·ase (kā′sē·ās), *n.* [*casein* + *-ase*.] An enzyme formed by certain bacteria, used in ripening cheese.

ca′se·ate (-āt), *v. i.* [L. *caseatus* mixed with cheese, fr. *caseus* cheese.] *Med.* To undergo caseation.

ca′se·a′tion (-ā′shŭn), *n.* **1.** Conversion into cheese. **2.** *Med.* A process of degeneration in which the products of inflammation are converted into a cheesy substance.

ca′se·fy (kā′sē·fī), *v. t. & i.*; -FIED (-fīd); -FY′ING. [L. *caseus* cheese + *-fy*.] To make or become like cheese.

case′hard′en (kās′här′d'n), *v. t.* **1.** To harden the outer layer of, as iron or steel. **2.** To render callous.

case history. See HISTORY, 1 **b**.

ca′se·in (kā′sē·ĭn), *n.* [L. *caseus* cheese.] **1.** A white amorphous phosphoprotein occurring in the milk of various animals. It is used in making cold-water paint, glue, etc.; — called also **ca′se·in′o·gen** (kā′-sē·ĭn′ō·jĕn). **2.** A protein produced when milk is curdled by rennet. A form of it is the chief protein of cheese and is used combined with alkali to make a tough hornlike plastic; — called also ***paracasein.***

case knife. A knife carried, or such as is kept, in a sheath or case; a sheath knife; also, a table knife.

case law. *Law.* Law made by judicial decisions; judge-made law. See JUDGE-MADE; cf. CASE SYSTEM.

case′mate (kās′māt), *n.* [F., fr. It. *casamatta*.] A bombproof chamber in a fort or an armored enclosure in a ship of war in which cannon are mounted to be fired through embrasures.

case′ment (kās′mĕnt *or, esp. Brit.*, kāz′-), *n.* [OF. *encassement* frame.] **1.** A window sash that opens on hinges; hence, a window with such a sash or sashes. **2.** A casing. — **case′ment·ed**, *adj.*

ca′se·ose (kā′sē·ōs), *n.* [*casein* + *-ose*.] *Biochem.* A soluble product (proteose) formed in the gastric and pancreatic digestion of casein.

ca′se·ous (-ŭs), *adj.* [L. *caseus* cheese.] Cheesy.

ca·sern′, ca·serne′ (kȧ·zûrn′), *n.* [F. *caserne*.] *Mil.* A barrack in garrison towns, usually near the rampart.

case shot. A collection of small projectiles enclosed within a case, as a shrapnel or canister shot.

case system. The system of teaching law in which the instruction is chiefly on the basis of leading or selected cases as primary authorities instead of from textbooks.

case′work′ (kās′wûrk′), *n.* Thorough sociological study of the history and environment of a maladjusted individual or family for diagnosis and treatment. — **case′work′er**, *n.*

case′worm′ (kās′wûrm′), *n.* An insect larva that makes a case to protect itself, as a caddis worm. Cf. BAGWORM.

cash (kăsh), *n.* [F. or It.; F. *casse*, fr. It. *cassa* box, case, fr. L. *capsa*.] *Com.* **a** Money, esp. ready money. **b** Money or its equivalent paid promptly after purchasing. — **Syn.** Coin, specie, currency, money. — *v. t.* To pay, or to receive, cash for; as, to *cash* a check.

cash, *n. sing. & pl.* [Pg. *caixa*, fr. Tamil *kāsu*.] Any of various coins of small value in India, China, etc.; esp., a Chinese coin of copper alloy with a square hole in the center for stringing, — being replaced since 1919 by the coins (*cents*) of the yuan dollar.

ca·shaw′ (kȧ·shô′). *U. S.* Var. of CUSHAW.

cash′book′ (kăsh′bo͝ok′), *n.* *Bookkeeping.* A book in which record is kept of all cash receipts and disbursements.

ca·shew′ (kȧ·sho͞o′ *or, esp. when used attributively*, kăsh′o͞o), *n.* [F. *acajou*, Pg. *acaju*, of Tupian origin.] A tropical American tree (*Anacardium occidentale*) of the sumac family, naturalized in all warm countries, yielding gum and kidney-shaped fruit (**cash′ew nut**) edible when roasted.

cash·ier′ (kăsh·ēr′), *n.* [D. *kassier*, fr. F. *caissier*.] One who has charge of money; specif.: **a** One of the chief officers of a bank, responsible for moneys received and expended. **b** In a store, restaurant, etc., a person employed to collect and record customers' payments.

cash·ier′, *v. t.* [D. *kasseeren*, fr. F. *casser*, fr. L. *cassare* to annul and *quassare* to break.] **1.** To discharge; to dismiss with ignominy. **2.** To reject; discard.

cash·iers′ check (kăsh·ērz′). *Banking.* A check drawn by a bank upon its own funds, signed by the cashier.

cash′mere (kăsh′mēr; kăsh′mēr′), *n.* **1.** A shawl (**Cashmere shawl**) made of a fine wool found beneath the hair of the goats of Kashmir, Tibet, and the Himalayas; also, the wool. **2.** A soft twilled fabric, orig. made of this wool.

ca·shoo′ (kȧ·sho͞o′). Var. of CATECHU.

cash register. A device for recording the amount of cash received, usually having an automatic adding machine and a money drawer and exhibiting the amount of the sale.

cas′i·mere (kăs′ĭ·mēr), **cas′i·mire.** Vars. of CASSIMERE.

cas′ing (kās′ĭng), *n.* **1.** Something that incases, or material for incasing. **2.** An enclosing framework, esp. of a door or window. **3.** The shoe (def. 3) of a pneumatic tire. **4.** A cleaned intestine, as of cattle, hogs, or sheep, used as a container for sausage meat.

ca·si′no (kȧ·sē′nō), *n.*; *pl.* -NOS (-nōz), -NI (-nē). [It., dim. of *casa* house, fr. L. *casa* cottage.] **1.** In Italy, a country house; also, a summerhouse; hence, *Hist.*, a style of house imitating an Italian casino. **2.** A building or room used for dancing, gambling, etc. **3.** Var. of CASSINO.

cask (kåsk; 9), *n.* [Sp. *casco* potsherd, cask.] **1.** A barrel-shaped vessel made of staves, headings, and hoops, usually for liquids; — a generic term including *barrel, hogshead, pipe, butt, keg, tun*, etc. **2.** A cask and its contents; hence, the quantity contained in a cask.

cas′ket (kås′kĕt; -kĭt), *n.* [F. *cassette*, fr. It. *cassetta*, fr. *cassa*.] **1.** A small chest or box, as for jewels, etc. **2.** *Chiefly U.S.* A rectangular case or chest of wood or metal, often carved or decorated, to hold a corpse. Cf. COFFIN. — *v. t.* To put into a casket.

Cas′lon (kăz′lŏn), *n.* A style of type orig. designed by the English type founder William Caslon (1692–1766). See TYPE; cf. OLD STYLE.

casque (kăsk), *n.* [F., fr. Sp. *casco*. See CASK.] A piece of armor for the head; a helmet. See HELMET, *Illust.* (5). — **casqued** (kăskt), *adj.*

cas·sa′ba (kă·sä′bȧ). Var. of CASABA.

Cas·san′dra (kă·săn′drȧ), *n.* [L., fr. Gr. *Kassandra*.] *Gr. Antiq.* **1.** A daughter of Priam, King of Troy. Apollo gave her the gift of prophecy but afterwards, in anger, decreed that no one should believe her prophecies. **2.** Hence, any prophetess of evil who is not believed.

cas·sa′tion (kă·sā′shŭn), *n.* [F.] Act of annulling, canceling, or quashing; abrogation; as, Court of *Cassation*, the highest court of appeal in France.

cas·sa′va (kă·sä′vȧ), *n.* [Through F. or Sp., fr. Taino *casavi, cazavi*.] **1.** Any of several plants (genus *Manihot*) of the spurge family, grown in the tropics for their fleshy edible rootstocks, which yield a nutritious starch, esp. *M. utilissima*, the ***bitter cassava***, and *M. palmata aipi*, the ***sweet cassava.*** **2.** The starch from the rootstocks of the cassava; manioc.

cas′se·role (kăs′ĕ·rōl), *n.* [F., fr. Pr. *casola*, fr. *casa*.] **1.** A saucepan. **2.** *Chem.* A deep round porcelain dish with a handle, used for heating substances. **3.** *Cookery.* **a** A mold of boiled rice, mashed potato, or paste, baked and filled with vegetables or meat. **b** A vessel of earthenware, porcelain, etc., in which food may be baked and served. Food thus cooked and served is said to be ***en cas′se·role′*** (*F.* äɴ kàs′-rôl′). **c** Food cooked and served en casserole.

cas′sette′ (kä′sĕt′), *n.* [F., dim. of *casse* case.] *Photog.* A holder for a film or plate.

cas′si·a (kăsh′ĭ·*à*; kăs′ĭ·*à*; *in sense* 2, *generally* kăsh′*à*), *n.* [L., fr. Gr. *kassia*, *kasia*, fr. the Heb.] **1.** Any herb, shrub, or tree of the genus *Cassia* (see SENNA). The sweet pulp (**cassia pulp**) of the pods is a mild laxative. **2.** Originally, cassia bark; — now usually applied in commerce to any of the coarser varieties of cinnamon bark.

cas′sia bark (kăsh′*à*). Chinese cinnamon. See CINNAMON.

cas′si·mere (kăs′ĭ·mēr), *n.* [From an old form of *Kashmir.*] A medium-weight woolen cloth of soft texture.

cas·si′no (k*ă*·sē′nō), *n.* [It. *casino* a small house, gaming house. See CASINO.] A game at cards.

Cas′si·o·pe′ia (kăs′ĭ·ō·pē′y*à*), **Cas′si·e·pe′ia** (-*ĕ*·pē′y*à*), **Cas′si·o·pe′a** (-*à*), *n.* [L., fr. Gr. *Kassiopeia.*] **1.** Mother of Andromeda. **2.** [*gen.* CASSIOPEIAE (-yē).] A northern constellation between Andromeda and Cepheus.

Cas′si·o·pe′ia's Chair (-y*à*z). A group of stars in the constellation Cassiopeia, crudely resembling a chair.

cas·sit′er·ite (k*ă*·sĭt′ēr·īt), *n.* [Gr. *kassiteros* tin.] *Mineral.* Native tin dioxide, SnO_2; a dark-colored mineral, chief source of metallic tin. H., 6–7. Sp. gr., 6.8–7.1.

cas′sock (kăs′*ŭ*k), *n.* [F. *casaque*, fr. It. *casacca.*] **1.** *Eccl.* **a** A long close-fitting garment reaching to the feet, worn by the clergy of certain churches. **b** A shorter, light double-breasted jacket, worn under the Geneva gown. **2. a** The clerical, or priestly, office. **b** A clergyman; a priest.

cas′so·war′y (kăs′*ō*·wĕr′ĭ *or, esp. Brit.*, -wēr·ĭ), *n.; pl.* -WARIES (-ĭz). [Malay *kasuārī.*] Any of several large ratite birds (genus *Casuarius*) of Australia, etc., related to the emu.

cast (kȧst; 9), *v. t.;* CAST; CAST′ING. [ON. *kasta.*] **1.** To throw or fling with a quick motion and sudden release. Hence: **a** To deposit (a ballot); to give (a vote). **b** To deposit in a decisive, forcible, or violent manner; as, to *cast* a man into prison. **c** To direct or bestow, as a glance or one's affections. **2.** To throw off, out, or away; as, the horse *cast* a shoe; hence: **a** To shed or molt. **b** To bring forth; yield; esp., to bring forth prematurely. **3.** To overthrow; defeat. **4.** To compute; specif.: **a** *Obs.* To reckon; calculate. **b** To calculate astrologically; as, to *cast* a horoscope. **c** To perform (arithmetical operations); as, to *cast* accounts. **5.** To put into proper shape; to arrange, as in accordance with a plan; to distribute; divide. **6.** To throw up, as a rampart. **7.** To form (a plastic or liquid substance) into a particular shape, as by pouring it into a mold and letting it harden; to form by this process; as, to *cast* bullets. **8.** *Drama.* To allot (as the parts of a play among actors); to allot or assign the parts of (a play); also, to assign (an actor for a part). **9.** *Now Rare. Naut.* To veer or turn. **10.** *Print.* To stereotype or electrotype. — *v. i.* **1.** To throw; project; specif.: **a** To throw dice. **b** To throw forth a line in angling, esp. one with a fly. **2.** To vomit. **3.** *Obs.* **a** To consider; meditate. **b** To conjecture; to forecast. **4.** Formerly, to calculate; estimate; now, to add figures. **5.** *Hunting.* To make a cast; — of dogs. **6.** *Naut.* To turn or veer; also, to tack; to wear ship. — **Syn.** See THROW: DISCARD.

— *n.* [From CAST, *v.*] **1. a** Act of casting or throwing; a throw. **b** The distance to which a thing can be thrown. **c** Manner of casting or throwing. **2. a** A throw or stroke of fortune; hence, fortune; lot. **b** A throw of dice; also, the number thrown. **c** A throw of a fishing line, net, sounding lead, etc.; also, that which is so thrown. **3.** A turn; a change of direction or course; as: **a** A turn of the eye; hence, a look; glance. **b** A fixed turn, twist, or bent; esp., a slight strabismus; as, a *cast* in his left eye. **4.** An amount or quantity thrown; as, a *cast* of seed; specif., quantity or number produced; yield; as, a year's *cast* of lambs. **5.** Computation; reckoning; esp., addition; also, conjecture; forecast. **6. a** That which is formed in a mold or form; esp., a reproduction or copy, as of a work of art, in bronze or plaster, etc.; a casting. **b** Act of casting or founding; also, the quantity of metal cast at a single operation. **c** An impression or mold taken from a thing or person; a mold. **d** A rigid surgical dressing of plaster; plaster cast. **7.** Form into which anything or any work is thrown; arrangement. **8.** A tendency to any color; a tinge; a hue. **9. a** Form; appearance; as, a peculiar *cast* of countenance. **b** Kind; sort. **10.** Aid on one's way, as by a lift in a conveyance. **11.** That which is thrown out or off, shed, or ejected; as: **a** The skin of an insect. **b** The mass of undigested refuse thrown up from a hawk's or owl's stomach. **c** The excrement of an earthworm. **12.** *Angling.* **a** The flies or bait attached to the line at one time. **b** A place adapted to fishing. **13.** *Drama.* The assignment of parts in a play to the actors; the set of actors to whom the parts are assigned. **14.** *Falconry.* The number (a couple) of hawks let go at one time from the hand; hence, of other birds, a couple. **15.** *Hunting.* A scattering of the hounds in various directions to search for a lost scent. **16.** *Med.* A substance formed in cavities of various organs in diseased conditions and composed of effused plastic matter; as, renal *casts.*

Cas·ta′li·a (kăs·tā′lĭ·*à*; 58), *n.* Also **Cas′ta·ly, Cas′ta·lie** (kăs′t*à*·lĭ). A spring on Parnassus, sacred to Apollo and the Muses; hence, source of poetic inspiration. — **Cas·ta′li·an** (-tā′lĭ·*ă*n; -tāl′y*ă*n), *adj.*

cas′ta·net′ (kăs′t*à*·nĕt′; kăs′t*à*·nĕt), *n.* [Through F. & Sp., fr. L. *castanea* chestnut.] An instrument consisting of two small, concave, spoon-shaped shells of ivory or hard wood, fastened to the thumb and tapped together with the middle finger, used in accompaniment to music and dances.

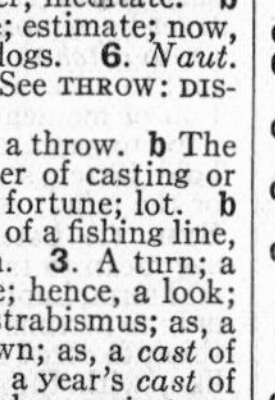

Castanets.

cast′a·way′ (kȧst′*à*·wā′), *adj.* **1.** Thrown away; cast off. **2.** Cast adrift; stranded; shipwrecked. — *n.* **1.** One who or that which is cast away or off, or rejected. **2.** One cast away at sea; a derelict or shipwrecked person.

caste (kȧst; 9), *n.* [Pg. *casta* race, prop., unmixed race, fr. L. *castus* pure.] **1.** One of the hereditary classes of social organization in India. Cf. BRAHMAN, KSHATRIYA, VAISYA, SUDRA. **2.** Hence: **a** A similar division or class of society in any community. **b** The principle or system of the division in India, or of social divisions in any community; also, the position conferred by the caste system or principle; as, to lose *caste.*

cas′tel·lan (kăs′t*ĕ*·l*ă*n), *n.* [ONF. *castelain*, fr. L. *castellanus* of a castle, in ML. governor of a castle, fr. L. *castellum* castle.] A governor or warden of a castle or fort; a chatelain. — **cas′tel·lan·ship′**, *n.*

cas′tel·lat′ed (-lāt′ĕd; -ĭd), *adj.* **1.** Built like a castle; having battlements, like a castle; as, a *castellated* mansion. **2.** Provided or dotted with castles.

cast′er (kȧs′tēr; 9), *n.* **1.** One who or that which casts (in any sense), as stones, type, accounts, cannon, etc. **2.** Also spelled **cas′tor.** **a** A vial, cruet, or the like, used to contain condiments at the table. See CRUET, *Illust.* **b** A stand to hold a set of cruets. **c** A wheel or set of wheels mounted in a swivel frame, used for supporting furniture, trucks, and various portable machines.

cas′ti·gate (kăs′tĭ·gāt), *v. t.* [L. *castigatus*, past part. of *castigare* to correct. See CHASTEN.] To punish, reprove, or criticize severely. — **Syn.** See PUNISH. — **cas′ti·ga′tor** (-gā′tēr), *n.*

cas′ti·ga′tion (-gā′sh*ŭ*n), *n.* Corrective punishment; now, severe punishment or reproof.

Cas′tile, *or* **cas′tile, soap** (kăs′tēl sōp′; 2). [From *Castile*, Spain.] **a** A fine, hard soap made from olive oil and caustic soda. **b** Any of certain soaps resembling this.

Cas·til′ian (kăs·tĭl′y*ă*n; -tĭl′ĭ·*ă*n), *n.* **1.** A native or inhabitant of Castile, in Spain. **2.** The standard Spanish, originally the dialect of Castile. See INDO-EUROPEAN LANGUAGES, *Table.* — *adj.* Of or pertaining to Castile, or its inhabitants, or Castilian (the language).

cast′ing, *n.* **1.** Act of one that casts. **2.** That which is cast in a mold; a metal object so cast. **3.** = CAST, *n.*, 11 **c**.

casting vote *or* **voice.** The deciding vote cast by a presiding officer in an assembly.

cast iron. A commercial variety of iron, containing more than 1.7 per cent carbon, poured molten into a mold so as to solidify in a desired shape. It is hard and brittle, but more easily fusible than steel. The ease and cheapness of its production, and its fluidity and fusibility, make it an excellent metal for casting. Cf. STEEL, INGOT IRON, WROUGHT IRON. — **cast′–i′ron** (*see Pron.*, § 2), *adj.*

cas′tle (kȧs′'l; 9), *n.* [AS. and ONF. *castel*, fr. L. *castellum*, dim. of *castrum* fortified place, castle.] **1.** A large fortified building or set of buildings, esp. that of a prince or nobleman. **2.** Anything resembling or likened to a castle; as: **a** A massive or imposing house. **b** A small wooden defensive tower, as on an elephant's back. **3.** *Chess.* A rook. — *v. t.;* CAS′TLED (-'ld); CAS′TLING (-lĭng). **1.** To put in or as in a castle. **2.** *Chess.* To move (the king) in castling. — *v. i. Chess.* To move the king two squares toward a castle and then (in the same move) the castle to the square next past the king; also, of the king, to move as above.

cas′tled (-'ld), *adj.* **1.** Having a castle. **2.** Built in castle style; castellated.

castle in the air, castle in Spain. A pleasant but purely visionary project; a day dream.

cast′off′ (kȧst′ôf′), *adj.* Cast or laid aside; cast away; discarded. — *n.* A castoff person or thing.

cas′tor (kȧs′tēr; 9), *n.* [L., the beaver, fr. Gr. *kastōr.*] **1.** *Rare.* A beaver. **2.** A creamy, bitter, orange-brown substance, with strong odor, consisting of the dried perineal glands and their secretion obtained from the beaver; castoreum, — used in medicine and by perfumers. **3.** A hat, esp. one of beaver fur; a beaver.

cas′tor (kȧs′tēr; 9), *n.* = CASTER, 2.

Cas′tor, *n.* **1.** *Gr. Myth.* See DIOSCURI. **2.** *Astron.* The more northern of the two bright stars in Gemini.

castor bean. **a** The seed of the castor-oil plant. **b** The plant itself. — **cas′tor–bean′**, *adj.*

cas·to′re·um (kăs·tō′rē·*ŭ*m; 70), *n.* [L., fr. Gr. *kastorion.*] The substance castor (see 1st CASTOR, 2).

castor oil. A yellowish or colorless viscous fixed oil, expressed or extracted from the seeds of the **cas′tor–oil′ plant**, a tropical African and Asiatic herb (*Ricinus communis*), of the spurge family, naturalized in all tropical countries. The oil is used as a lubricant, esp. for aircraft engines, in soap, as a cathartic, etc.

cas′tra·me·ta′tion (kăs′tr*à*·m*ĕ*·tā′sh*ŭ*n), *n.* [From F., fr. L. *castra* camp + *metari* to measure off.] The laying out of a military camp.

cas′trate (kăs′trāt), *v. t.* [L. *castratus*, past part. of *castrare* to castrate.] To deprive of the testicles; to geld; caponize; emasculate; also, by extension, to spay. — **cas·tra′tion** (kăs·trā′sh*ŭ*n), *n.*

cast steel. Steel which has been in a state of fusion, either in the making or afterward. — **cast′–steel′**, *adj.*

cas′u·al (kăzh′*ū*·*ă*l; kăz′-), *adj.* [F. and L.; F., fr. L. *casualis*, fr. *casus.* See 1st CASE.] **1.** Happening without design, and without being expected; coming by chance. **2.** Coming without regularity; occasional. **3.** *Obs.* Uncertain; precarious. **4.** Having the air of a chance or incidental occurrence; cursory; unconcerned. **5.** Appearing, present, or singled out by chance; as, a *casual* visitor. **6.** Without foresight, plan, or method; haphazard. **7.** *Brit.* Designating or pertaining to poor persons, vagrants, laborers, etc., who are not residents of the place where they receive public aid, or work, etc. **8.** Pertaining to, sustaining, or caused by accidents; as, a *casual* patient. **9.** Designed in open, easy, loose-fitting styles for comfort of wear, as for informal or sports events or for play or relaxation, as distinguished from dress wear. — **Syn.** See ACCIDENTAL: RANDOM. — *n.* **1.** A casual laborer, visitor, patient, pauper, etc.; drifter. **2.** A casual garment, hat, or shoe. **3.** *Mil.* An officer or soldier not attached to any unit and often without assignment, who is temporarily at a location. — **cas′u·al·ly**, *adv.* — **cas′u·al·ness**, *n.*

cas′u·al·ty (kăzh′*ū*·*ă*l·tĭ; kăz′-), *n.; pl.* -TIES (-tĭz). **1.** Chance; accident. **2.** An unfortunate occurrence; a mishap. **3.** Injury or death from accident; also, a person injured or killed by an accident; specif., *Mil. & Nav.:* **a** *pl.* Losses caused by death, wounds, etc. **b** A soldier unavailable for service because of death, wounds, etc.

cas′u·ist (kăzh′*ū*·ĭst; kăz′*ū*-), *n.* [F. *casuiste*, fr. L. *casus* fall, case.] One skilled in or given to casuistry.

cas′u·is′tic (-ĭs′tĭk), **cas′u·is′ti·cal** (-tĭ·k*ă*l), *adj.* Of or pert. to casuists or casuistry. — **cas′u·is′ti·cal·ly**, *adv.*

cas′u·ist·ry (kăzh′*ū*·ĭs·trĭ; kăz′*ū*-), *n.; pl.* -RIES (-trĭz). **1.** Science or doctrine of dealing with cases of conscience and of resolving questions of right or wrong in conduct. **2.** Sophistical, equivocal, or specious reasoning, esp. in regard to law or morals. Cf. SOPHISTRY.

‖**ca′sus** (kā′s*ŭ*s), *n.* [L., lit., a fall, falling.] An event; an occasion; a case.

‖**ca′sus bel′li** (bĕl′ī). [L.] An event or set of events which is a cause of war, or may be alleged to justify war.

cat (kăt), *n.* [AS. *cat*, *catt*, and ONF. *cat.*] **1. a** A carnivorous mammal (*Felis catus*) long domesticated and kept by man as a pet or for catching rats and mice. It appears to be of Egyptian or Eastern origin. **b** Any of the cat family (Felidae), which includes besides the domestic cat the lion, tiger, leopard, jaguar, cougar, wildcat, lynx, and cheetah. **2.** A person, as a spiteful woman, likened to a cat. **3. a** Short for CATFISH, CAT-O'-NINE-TAILS. **b** The fur or pelt of the cat. **4.** *Games.* **a** A Tipcat; also, the stick or the bat used in tipcat. **b** A game of ball, called, according to the number of batters, *one old cat, two old cat,* etc. **5.** *Naut.* **a** A strong tackle used to hoist an anchor to the cathead of a ship. **b** A catboat. **6.** *Swing Music.* A hepcat. — *v. t.;* CAT'TED; CAT'TING. **1.** *Naut.* To bring up to the cathead; as, to *cat* an anchor. **2.** To flog with a cat-o'-nine-tails. — *v. i. Slang, Eng.* To vomit.

cat'a- (kăt'ȧ-), **cat-, cath-.** [Gr. *kata-, kat-* (before vowels), *kath-* (before aspirates), fr. *kata* down.] A prefix denoting *down, downward, away, in accordance with, against, very, completely.* In English its separate force is often not felt, as in *cata*logue, *cate*chize, *cath*olic.

ca·tab'o·lism (kȧ·tăb'ō·lĭz'm), *n.* [*cata-* + Gr. *ballein* to throw.] *Biol. & Physiol.* Destructive metabolism; — opposed to *anabolism.* See METABOLISM. — **cat'a·bol'ic** (kăt'ȧ·bŏl'ĭk), *adj.* — **cat'a·bol'i·cal·ly** (-ĭ·kăl·ĭ), *adv.*

cat'a·chre'sis (kăt'ȧ·krē'sĭs), *n.; pl.* -SES (-sēz). [L., fr. Gr. *katachrēsis* misuse, fr. *kata* against + *chrēsthai* to use.] Misuse of words or abuse of terms: **a** *Rhet.* Use of one word for another that is the correct, or the preferable, word, as *aggravate* for *provoke,* or *infer* for *imply.* **b** *Philol.* The use of a word in an improper form through mistake as to its origin. — **cat'a·chres'tic** (-krĕs'tĭk; -krēs'tĭk), **cat'a·chres'ti·cal** (-tĭ·kăl), *adj.* — **cat'a·chres'ti·cal·ly,** *adv.*

cat'a·cli'nal (kăt'ȧ·klī'năl; -n'l), *adj.* [*cata-* + Gr. *klinein* to incline.] *Geol. & Phys. Geog.* Descending in the direction toward which strata dip; — opposed to *anaclinal.*

cat'a·clysm (kăt'ȧ·klĭz'm), *n.* [From L., fr. Gr. *kataklysmos,* fr. *kata* downward, against + *klyzein* to wash.] **1.** A flood; a deluge. **2.** *Geol.* Any violent change involving sudden and extensive alterations of the earth's surface; catastrophe. **3.** Any upheaval, esp. a social or political one. — **Syn.** See DISASTER. — **cat'a·clys'mal** (-klĭz'măl), **cat'a·clys'mic** (-mĭk), *adj.*

cat'a·comb (-kōm), *n.* [Through F. & It., fr. LL. *catacumba.*] *Chiefly pl.* A subterranean place of burial, esp. one consisting of galleries with recesses for tombs.

ca·tad'ro·mous (kȧ·tăd'rō·mŭs), *adj.* *Zool.* Living in fresh water and going to the sea to spawn, as the eel; — opp. to *anadromous.*

cat'a·falque (kăt'ȧ·fălk), *n.* [F., fr. It. *catafalco* scaffold.] **1.** A temporary structure sometimes used to hold the remains in funerals of eminent persons. **2.** A pall-covered coffin-shaped structure used at requiem masses celebrated after burial.

Cat'a·lan (kăt'ȧ·lăn; -lăn), *adj.* [Catalan *Català,* fem. *Catalana.*] Of or pertaining to Catalonia, Spain. — *n.* **a** A native or inhabitant of Catalonia. **b** The Romance language spoken in Catalonia, Valencia, and vicinity. See INDO-EUROPEAN LANGUAGES, *Table.*

cat'a·lase (kăt'ȧ·lās), *n.* [Cf. Gr. *katallassein* to exchange.] *Chem.* An enzyme capable of decomposing hydrogen peroxide into water and gaseous oxygen.

cat'a·lec'tic (-lĕk'tĭk), *adj.* [From LL., fr. Gr. *katalēktikos* incomplete, deriv. of *kata* down + *lēgein* to stop.] *Pros.* Lacking a syllable at the end; as, a *catalectic* verse.

cat'a·lep'sis (-lĕp'sĭs), *n.* [LL. & NL.] Catalepsy.

cat'a·lep'sy (kăt'ȧ·lĕp'sĭ), *n.* [Gr. *katalēpsis* a seizure, deriv. of *kata* down + *lambanein* to seize.] *Med. & Psychol.* A condition of peculiar muscular rigidity in which the body and limbs keep any position in which they are placed. — **cat'a·lep'tic** (-lĕp'tĭk), *adj. & n.*

cat'a·logue (kăt'ȧ·lŏg; 74), *n.* Also **cat'a·log.** [Through F. & LL., fr. Gr. *katalogos* list, fr. *kata* down + *legein* to pick out, count.] **1.** *Archaic.* A list; register; enumeration of items. **2. a** A list of names, titles, or articles arranged methodically, often in alphabetical order, and usually with descriptive details for each item, such as number and price for articles of merchandise. **b** A book or pamphlet containing such a list. **c** Specif., an official publication of a university or college giving regulations and announcements; — in British use called *calendar.* — *v. t. & i.;* CAT'A·LOGUED (-lŏgd); CAT'A·LOGU'ING (-lŏg'ĭng). To make a list or catalogue (of). — **cat'a·logu'er** (-lŏg'ẽr), **cat'a·log'er,** *n.* — **cat'a·logu'ist** (-lŏg'ĭst), **cat'a·log'ist,** *n.*

‖**ca'ta'logue' rai'son'né'** (kȧ'tȧ'lôg' rĕ'zô'nā'). [F.] A classified catalogue.

ca·tal'pa (kȧ·tăl'pȧ), *n.* [NL., fr. Creek *kutuhlpa.*] *Bot.* Any of a small genus (*Catalpa*) of American and Asiatic trees of the trumpet-creeper family, esp. the ornamental species *C. bignonioides* or *C. speciosa.*

ca·tal'y·sis (kȧ·tăl'ĭ·sĭs), *n.; pl.* -SES (-sēz). [NL., fr. Gr. *katalysis* dissolution, deriv. of *kata* wholly + *lyein* to loose.] *Physical Chem.* Acceleration of a reaction produced by a substance, called the **cat'a·lyst** (kăt'ȧ·lĭst), which may be recovered practically unchanged at the end of the reaction. Such acceleration is usually positive, but it may be negative when a substance, called an ***anticatalyst, or negative catalyst,*** retards a reaction. — **cat'a·lyt'ic** (kăt'ȧ·lĭt'ĭk), *adj. & n.*

cat'a·lyze (kăt'ȧ·līz), *v. t.* To subject to catalysis. — **cat'a·lyz'er** (-līz'ẽr), *n.*

cat'a·ma·ran' (kăt'ȧ·mȧ·răn'), *n.* [Tamil *kattumaram,* fr. *kattu* tie + *maram* tree.] **1.** A raft or float, consisting of logs or pieces of wood lashed together, and moved by paddles or sails. **2.** Any vessel with twin hulls side by side.

cat'a·me'ni·a (-mē'nĭ·ȧ), *n. pl.* [NL., fr. Gr. *ta katamēnia.*] *Physiol.* Menses. — **cat'a·me'ni·al** (-ăl), *adj.*

cat'a·mount (kăt'ȧ·mount), *n.* [*cat* + *a* for *of* + *mount.*] *U.S.* A catamountain; esp., the cougar or a lynx.

cat'a·moun'tain (-moun'tĭn), **cat'-o'-moun'tain** (kăt'ō-), *n.* Any of various wild animals of the cat family; esp.: **a** The European wildcat. **b** The leopard. **c** In America, the cougar or a lynx; catamount.

cat'a·pho·re'sis (-fō·rē'sĭs; -fŏr'ē·sĭs), *n.* [NL., fr. *cata-* + Gr. *phorēsis* a bearing.] *Physical Chemistry.* The movement of suspended particles through a fluid under the action of an applied electromotive force. — **cat'a·pho·ret'ic** (-fō·rĕt'ĭk), *adj.*

cat'a·pla'si·a (-plā'zhĭ·ȧ; -zĭ·ȧ), *n.; pl.* -SIAE (-ē). [NL., fr. *cata-* + *-plasia.*] *Biol.* Regressive change in cells or tissues; reversion to more primitive character.

cat'a·plasm (kăt'ȧ·plăz'm), *n.* *Med.* A poultice.

cat'a·pult (kăt'ȧ·pŭlt), *n.* [L. *catapulta,* fr. Gr. *katapeltēs,* fr. *kata* down + *pallein* to hurl.] **1.** An ancient engine, somewhat resembling a massive crossbow, for hurling missiles horizontally. Cf. BALLISTA. **2.** A slingshot. **3.** A device for launching an airplane from the deck of a ship. — *v. t.* To throw from or as from a catapult.

cat'a·ract (-răkt), *n.* [L. *cataracta* a waterfall, fr. Gr. *kataraktēs,* deriv. of *kata* down + *rhēgnynai* to break, or *arassein* to strike, smite.] **1.** A waterfall, esp. and usually, a large one. **2.** An overwhelming downpour, as of water; a deluge; a flood. **3.** *Med.* An opacity of the crystalline lens of the eye, or of its capsule, obstructing passage of the waves of light.

ca·tarrh' (kȧ·tär'), *n.* [From F., fr. L. *catarrhus,* fr. Gr. *katarrhoos* a running down, rheum, deriv. of *kata* down + *rhein* to flow.] *Med.* An inflammatory affection of any mucous membrane; as, *catarrh* of the stomach. In America, esp., a chronic inflammation of the membranes of the nose or air passages; in England, an acute influenza, resulting from a cold, and attended with cough. — **ca·tarrh'al** (-ăl), *adj.* — **ca·tarrh'ous** (-ŭs), *adj.*

ca·tas'ta·sis (kȧ·tăs'tȧ·sĭs), *n.; pl.* -SES (-sēz). [NL., fr. Gr. *katastasis,* fr. *kathistanai* to set in order, fr. *kata* down + *histanai* to place.] The height of the action of a play. Cf. PROTASIS, EPITASIS, CATASTROPHE.

ca·tas'tro·phe (-trō·fē), *n.* [Gr. *katastrophē,* deriv. of *kata* down + *strephein* to turn.] **1.** The final event in a drama, romance, etc., as a death in a tragedy or a marriage in a comedy. Cf. DENOUEMENT. **2.** An event overturning the order or system of things. **3.** A sudden calamity; a great misfortune. **4.** *Geol.* A violent and widely extended change in the surface of the earth; cataclysm. — **Syn.** See DISASTER. — **cat'a·stroph'ic** (kăt'ȧ·strŏf'ĭk), *adj.*

cat'a·to'ni·a (kăt'ȧ·tō'nĭ·ȧ), *n.* [NL., fr. *cata-* + Gr. *tonos* tension.] *Psychiatry.* A severe type of dementia praecox, characterized by negativism and incoherence and often by catalepsy, with alternate periods of stupor and activity. — **cat'a·ton'ic** (-tŏn'ĭk), *adj.*

Ca·taw'ba (kȧ·tô'bȧ), *n.; pl.* -BAS (-bȧz). **1.** A light-red variety of American grape. **2.** A light-colored and rich-flavored wine made from this grape.

cat'bird' (kăt'bûrd'), *n.* An American songbird (*Dumetella carolinensis*), dark-gray in color with black cap and reddish under tail coverts, — named from its call, like the mewing of a cat.

cat'boat' (-bōt'), *n.* *Naut.* A sailboat having a cat rig (see CAT RIG). It usually has a centerboard and is of light draft and broad beam.

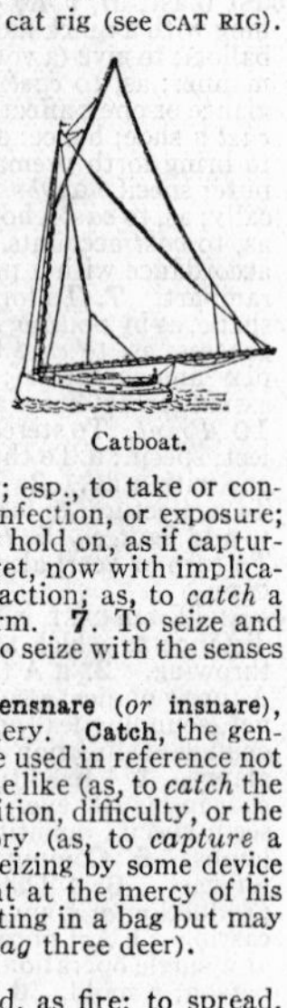
Catboat.

cat brier. Any of several species of smilax or greenbrier, including the common greenbrier (*Smilax rotundifolia*) and other prickly species.

cat'call' (kăt'kôl'), *n.* A sound like the cry of a cat, made to express disapproval, as at a theater, political gathering, etc. — **cat'call',** *v. i. & t.*

catch (kăch), *v. t.;* CAUGHT (kôt); CATCH'ING. [From ONF. deriv. of L. *captare,* v. intens. of *capere* to catch.] **1.** To capture or seize, as after pursuit; to take. **2.** Hence: **a** To ensnare or entangle. **b** To reach or get to, esp. in time; to overtake. **c** To come upon by surprise; to surprise; detect. **3.** To be seized or affected by; esp., to take or contract by sympathy, or by or as if by contagion, infection, or exposure; as, to *catch* the spirit of an occasion. **4.** To lay hold on, as if capturing; to seize, as with the hand. **5.** To take or get, now with implication of momentary possession or suddenness of action; as, to *catch* a nap; to *catch* a glimpse of. **6.** To please; charm. **7.** To seize and hold, fasten, secure, etc.; to seize securely. **8.** To seize with the senses or the mind; as, to *catch* what is said.

Syn. (1) **Catch, capture, trap, snare, entrap, ensnare** (*or* **insnare**), **bag** mean to take or seize by skill, craft, or trickery. **Catch,** the general term, implies pursuit or alertness and may be used in reference not only to persons but to things that are elusive or the like (as, to *catch* the thief; to *catch* fish); **capture** suggests more opposition, difficulty, or the like, with the result that success implies victory (as, to *capture* a stronghold); **trap, snare, entrap, ensnare** imply seizing by some device (literal or figurative) which holds the one caught at the mercy of his captor; **bag** usually implies a catching and a putting in a bag but may suggest only the first (as, to *bag* pheasants; to *bag* three deer). (2) See INCUR.

— *v. i.* **1.** To make captures. **2.** To take hold, as fire; to spread. **3.** To make a snatch or catch; to start forward in order to, or as if to, snatch; — now only with *at.* **4.** To be held or impeded by entanglement or obstruction; as, a kite *catches* in a tree. **5.** To take and retain hold; as, the bolt does not *catch.*

catch on. *Colloq.* **a** *Chiefly U.S.* To understand. **b** To please; to succeed; to gain favor. — ***catch up.*** **a** To interrupt or stop abruptly, as in captiously stopping a person speaking. **b** To overtake. **c** To gain or regain a position by or as by overtaking; — often with *on.*

— *n.* **1.** That which is caught or taken; as, a good *catch* of fish. **2.** That which catches; as: **a** A catching or ensnaring question. **b** Something designed to catch or arrest the attention, fancy, etc. **c** That by which anything is temporarily fastened; as, the *catch* of a gate. **d** *Mach.* A detent. **3.** Act or fact of catching; as: **a** Act of catching fish. **b** A momentary stoppage; as, a *catch* in the voice. **4.** One worth catching, esp. for husband or wife. **5.** A snatch, or small fragment; a scrap; as, *catches* of songs. **6.** *Agric.* The germination of a field crop, esp. to such an extent that replanting is unnecessary. **7.** *Games.* **a** The act of catching the ball. **b** A player who catches; a catcher. **c** A game which consists in throwing and catching a ball. **8.** *Music.* Orig., a round for three or more unaccompanied voices, written out as one continuous melody, each succeeding singer taking up a part in turn.

— *adj.* That catches, or is designed to catch, one's attention, liking, etc.; as, a *catch* phrase.

catch'all' (kăch'ôl'), *n.* A general receptacle for objects.

catch'er (-ẽr), *n.* One who or that which catches; specif., *Baseball,* the player who stands behind the batsman to catch the ball when pitched.

catch'ing, *adj.* **1.** That catches; specif., infectious; contagious. **2.** Alluring; catchy; as, a *catching* way.

catch'ment (kăch'mĕnt), *n.* **a** Act of catching. **b** That which catches; specif., a reservoir. **c** That which is caught.

catchment area *or* **basin.** The entire area from which drainage is received by a reservoir, river, or the like.

catch'pen'ny (kăch'pĕn'ĭ), *adj.* Devised to get small sums of money, as from the ignorant; as, *catchpenny* shows.

catch'pole', catch'poll' (-pōl'), *n.* [From an ONF. form of OF. *chacepol, chacipol,* taxgatherer.] A sheriff's officer or sergeant, esp. one who makes arrests for debt.

catch′up (kăch′ŭp; kĕch′ŭp), **cat′sup** (kăt′sŭp; kĕch′ŭp), **ketch′up** (kĕch′ŭp), *n.* [Malay *kĕcap* taste.] **a** A savory sauce made from the juice of mushrooms, walnuts, tomatoes, etc., stewed together. **b** *U. S.* A thick tomato sauce seasoned with vinegar, spices, and sugar.

catch′weight′ (kăch′wāt′), *n.* *Sport.* The weight of a contestant as he happens or chooses to be, instead of as fixed by agreement or rule.

catch′word′ (-wûrd′), *n.* **1.** *Print.* **a** The first word of any page of a book after the first page, inserted at the right-hand bottom corner of the preceding page. **b** Either of the words printed over the first and last columns of a page of a dictionary, encyclopedia, etc., being reprints of the headings of the first and last entries on the page. **2.** Among actors, the cue word. **3.** A word or phrase repeated until it becomes associated with a political party, etc.

catch′y (-ĭ), *adj.*; CATCH′I·ER (-ĭ·ẽr); CATCH′I·EST. **1.** Apt or tending to catch the fancy or attention; as, a *catchy* tune. **2.** Tending to catch or ensnare; as, a *catchy* question. **3.** Occurring in snatches; fitful; as, a *catchy* wind.

cat distemper. = FELINE ENTERITIS.

cate (kāt), *n.* [From earlier *acates*, prop., purchases, fr. ONF. *acat.*] Usually *pl.* Dainty or choice viands.

cat′e·che′sis (kăt′ē·kē′sĭs), *n.*; *pl.* -SES (-sēz). [LL., fr. Gr. *katēchēsis.*] Oral instruction, esp. of catechumens; catechizing. — **cat′e·chet′ic** (-kĕt′ĭk), **cat′e·chet′i·cal** (-ĭ·kăl), *adj.*

cat′e·chism (kăt′ē·kĭz′m), *n.* [See CATECHIZE.] **1.** *Obs.* Oral instruction; catechizing. **2.** A manual for catechizing, esp. for religious instruction. **3.** A set of formal questions put to candidates, etc.

cat′e·chist (-kĭst), *n.* Catechizer; teacher of catechumens.

cat′e·chis′tic (-kĭs′tĭk), **cat′e·chis′ti·cal** (-tĭ·kăl), *adj.* Of or pertaining to a catechist or a catechism.

cat′e·chize, cat′e·chise (kăt′ē·kīz), *v. t. & i.* [From LL., fr. Gr. *katēchizein*, fr. *katēchein* to resound, impress upon one by word of mouth, fr. *kata* wholly + *ēchein* to sound.] **1.** To instruct by asking questions, receiving answers, and offering explanations and corrections, esp. in regard to religious faith. **2.** To question systematically or fully. — **cat′e·chi·za′tion** (-kĭ·zā′shŭn; -kī·zā′-), *n.* — **cat′e·chiz′er** (-kīz′ẽr), *n.*

cat′e·chu (kăt′ē·chōō; -kū), *n.* Also **ca·shoo′** (kȧ·shōō′). [Malay *kāchū*, Kanarese *kāchu.*] Any of several dry, earthy, or resinlike astringent substances, obtained from certain tropical Asiatic plants; cutch; specif., ***Bengal catechu***, an extract from the heartwood of either of two East Indian acacias (*Acacia catechu* and *A. c. sundra*), used for dyeing, tanning, preserving fish nets, etc.; ***gambier***, from a Malayan woody vine (*Uncaria gambir*) of the madder family, used for chewing with the betel nut and for tanning and dyeing; ***Bombay catechu***, from the betel nut, used for tanning and dyeing.

cat′e·chu′men (-kū′mĕn), *n.* [F. and L.; F., fr. LL. *catechumenus*, fr. Gr. *katēchoumenos* instructed.] **1.** *Eccl.* One who is receiving rudimentary instruction in the doctrines of Christianity. **2.** One receiving rudimentary instruction in any set of principles, etc.

cat′e·gor′i·cal (-gŏr′ĭ·kăl), *adj.* **1. a** *Logic.* Absolute; unqualified. Cf. DISJUNCTIVE, 3; HYPOTHETICAL, 1. **b** Direct; explicit; as, *categorical* denial. **2.** Of or pertaining to, or in the form of, a category. — **cat′e·gor′i·cal·ly**, *adv.*

categorical imperative. Kant's famous principle: "Act only on that maxim whereby thou canst at the same time will that it should become a universal law."

cat′e·go′ry (kăt′ē·gō′rĭ *or, esp. Brit.*, -gẽr·ĭ), *n.*; *pl.* -RIES (-rĭz). [LL. *categoria*, fr. Gr. *katēgoria*, deriv. of *kata* down + root of *agoreuein* to harangue, assert.] **1.** *Logic.* An ultimate concept or form of thought; one of the primary fundamental conceptions to which all knowledge can be reduced. **2.** A class or division formed for the purposes of a given discussion or classification; as, species, genus, family, etc., are biological *categories* (see CLASSIFICATION, 2).

ca·te′na (kȧ·tē′nȧ), *n.*; *pl.* -NAE (-nē). [L., a chain.] A chain; a series; esp., a connected series.

cat′e·nar′y (kăt′ē·nẽr′ĭ *or, esp. Brit.*, kȧ·tē′nȧ·rĭ), *n.*; *pl.* -IES (-ĭz). [L. *catenarius*, fr. *catena* chain.] **1.** *Math.* The shape assumed by a perfectly flexible cord in equilibrium under given forces. The ***common catenary*** is exemplified in a chain or heavy cord hanging freely between two points of support. It has been applied in the construction of suspension bridges. **2.** A catenary curve. — **cat′e·nar′i·an** (kăt′ē·nâr′ĭ·ăn), *adj.* — **cat′e·nar′y**, *adj.*

cat′e·nate (kăt′ē·nāt), *v. t.* To connect in a series of links or ties; to link; concatenate. — **cat′e·na′tion** (-nā′shŭn), *n.*

ca′ter (kā′tẽr), *v. i.* [From AF. *acatour* buyer.] **1.** To provide a supply of food; act as caterer. **2.** To supply what is required or desired; — followed by *to* or *for*.

cat′er·an (kăt′ẽr·ăn), *n.* [Gael. *ceatharnach.*] An irregular soldier or marauder of the Scottish Highlands.

cat′er–cor′nered (kăt′ẽr·kôr′nẽrd; kā′tẽr-), **cat′er·cor′ner** (-nẽr), *adj.* [F. *quatre* four + E. *cornered.*] Set or located crosswise; diagonally placed; kitty-cornered; catty-cornered. — *adv.* Diagonally; crosswise.

ca′ter–cous′in (kā′tẽr·kŭz′'n), *n.* A first cousin; also, an intimate friend.

ca′ter·er (kā′tẽr·ẽr), *n.* [See CATER.] One who caters; one who provides provisions and service, esp. for entertainments at clubs, private houses, etc. — **ca′ter·ess** (-ĕs; -ĭs), *n.*

cat′er·pil′lar (kăt′ẽr·pĭl′ẽr), *n.* [ONF. *catepelose*, fr. L. *catta pilosa* hairy cat.] **1.** The long wormlike larva of a butterfly or moth; also, any of the similar larvae of certain other insects, as the sawflies. **2.** [*cap.*] A trade-mark for a tractor, made esp. for use on rough ground, that travels upon two endless metal belts. Cf. TANK, *Illust.*

cat′er·waul (kăt′ẽr·wôl), *v. i.* [*cat* + prob. E. *wawl*, *wrawl*, to cry, howl.] Of cats, to make a harsh cry at rutting time; hence, to make a harsh noise; also, to quarrel or wail like cats. — **cat′er·waul**, *n.*

cat′fac′ing (kăt′fās′ĭng), *n.* *Hort.* A disfiguration of peaches resulting from punctures of the fruit by various sucking insects.

cat′fall′ (kăt′fôl′), *n.* *Naut.* A rope or chain used in hoisting the anchor to the cathead.

cat′fish′ (-fĭsh′), *n.*; *pl.*, see FISH. Any of various fishes having catlike teeth, barbels about the mouth, etc.; esp., any of an order (Nematognathi) of scaleless teleost fishes including the common bullhead.

cat′gut′ (-gŭt′; *attrib. also* -gŭt), *n.* A tough cord made from the intestines of certain animals, esp. of sheep, used for strings of musical instruments, for sutures, etc. It is not known that the intestines of cats were ever so used.

cath-. Variant of CATA-.

ca·thar′sis (kȧ·thär′sĭs), *n.* [NL., fr. Gr. *katharsis.* See CATHARTIC.] **1.** *Med.* Purgation. **2.** *Aesthetics.* Purification or purgation of the emotions by art; — a term used by Aristotle in describing the effect of tragedy as "through pity and fear effecting a *catharsis* of these emotions." **3.** *Psychoanalysis.* Elimination of a complex by bringing it to consciousness and affording it expression.

ca·thar′tic (-tĭk), *adj.* [Gr. *kathartikos*, fr. *kathairein* to cleanse, fr. *katharos* pure.] Of or relating to catharsis; purgative; cleansing. — *n.* A cathartic medicine.

Ca·thay′ (kă·thā′), *n.* [ML. *Cataya*, of Tatar origin.] China; — so called formerly in western Europe.

cat′head′ (kăt′hĕd′), *n.* *Naut.* A projecting piece of timber or iron near the bow of a vessel, to which the anchor is hoisted and secured.

ca·the′dra (kȧ·thē′drȧ; kăth′ē·drȧ), *n.* [L., fr. Gr. *kathedra* seat.] The official throne of a bishop; hence, the episcopal see or dignity. By extension, the chair of a professor, teacher, or any person in high authority. Cf. EX CATHEDRA.

ca·the′dral (kȧ·thē′drăl), *adj.* **1.** Of, relating to, or containing the cathedra, or bishop's chair; as, a *cathedral* church. **2.** Emanating from the chair of office or authority, as of a pope or bishop; official; authoritative. **3.** Resembling aisles of a cathedral; as, *cathedral* walks beneath the elms. — *n.* Properly, the church which contains the cathedra; improperly, in nonepiscopal churches, any of various large or important churches.

cath′e·ter (kăth′ē·tẽr), *n.* [LL., fr. Gr. *kathetēr* a thing let down or put in, deriv. of *kata* down + *hienai* to send.] *Med.* Any of various instruments for passing along mucous canals to withdraw fluid from a cavity; esp., a tubular instrument to be introduced into the bladder through the urethra to draw off the urine.

cath′e·ter·ize (-īz), *v. t.* To introduce a catheter into.

ca·thex′is (kȧ·thĕk′sĭs), *n.* [NL., fr. Gr. *kathexis* retention.] *Psychoanalysis.* The concentration of desire upon some object or idea; also, the amount of desire so concentrated. — **ca·thec′tic** (kȧ·thĕk′tĭk), *adj.*

cath′ode (kăth′ōd), *n.* Also **kath′ode.** [Gr. *kathodos* descent, fr. *kata* down + *hodos* way.] *Physics & Chem.* The negative pole or electrode of an electrolytic cell, vacuum tube, etc. Cf. ANODE. — **ca·thod′ic** (kȧ·thŏd′ĭk), **ca·thod′i·cal** (-ĭ·kăl), *adj.*

cathode rays. *Physics.* Rays projected in the direction from cathode to anode in a vacuum tube in which an electric discharge takes place. They consist of electrons, moving at high speed in straight lines unless deflected by the action of a magnetic or electric field. By impinging on solids the cathode rays generate X rays. See ELECTRON, BETA RAY.

cath′o·lic (kăth′ō·lĭk; kăth′lĭk), *adj.* [F. *catholique*, fr. L., fr. Gr. *katholikos* universal, fr. *kath′ holou* in general, fr. *kata* down, concerning + *holos* whole.] **1.** Universal or general; affecting mankind as a whole, or affecting what is universal in human interest. **2.** Comprehensive in sympathies or understanding; liberal; as, a *catholic* taste. **3.** Of or pertaining to the church universal; specif., designating, or pertaining to, the ancient undivided Christian church or a church claiming historical continuity from it. After the Great Eastern Schism (1472) the Western Church officially assumed the designation *Catholic* and the Eastern Church the title of *Orthodox*. Since the Reformation, *Catholic* has been used in the following senses: [*cap.*] **a** = ROMAN CATHOLIC. **b** Pert. to or designating any of various churches claiming apostolic succession, as the churches of the Anglican Communion. **c** Designating the entire body of Christian believers, or that part of it which accepts the Apostles' Creed. — *n.* **1.** A person who belongs to the universal Christian church. **2.** [*cap.*] A member of a Catholic church, specif. of the Roman Catholic Church. — **ca·thol′i·cal·ly** (kȧ·thŏl′ĭ·kăl·ĭ), *adv.*

ca·thol′i·cism (kȧ·thŏl′ĭ·sĭz′m), *n.* **1.** Faith, practice, or system of the catholic church; adherence to the catholic church; catholicity. **2.** [*cap.*] Faith, practice, or system of a Catholic church, specif. of the Roman Catholic Church; Catholicity.

cath′o·lic′i·ty (kăth′ō·lĭs′ĭ·tĭ), *n.* **1.** State or quality of being catholic; liberality of sentiments. **2.** Catholicism (sense 1). **3.** [*cap.*] The faith or doctrine of a Catholic church, specifically of the Roman Catholic Church.

ca·thol′i·cize (kȧ·thŏl′ĭ·sīz), *v. t. & i.* To make, or become, catholic or [*cap.*] Catholic. — **ca·thol′i·ciz′er** (-sīz′ẽr), *n.*

ca·thol′i·con (-kŏn), *n.* [Gr. *katholikos*, neut. *katholikon*, universal.] A remedy for all diseases; a panacea.

cat′i′on (kăt′ī′ŏn), *n.* Also **kat′i′on.** [Gr. *kata* downward + *ion*, neut., going.] *Physical Chem.* A positive ion; — so called because in electrolysis it travels to the cathode. See ION.

cat′kin (kăt′kĭn), *n.* [*cat* + *-kin*; — from its resemblance to a cat's tail.] A scaly, usually drooping, inflorescence, as in the willow and birch; an ament.

cat′like′ (kăt′līk′), *adj.* Like a cat; stealthy.

cat nap. A very short light sleep.

cat′nip (kăt′nĭp), *n.* Also **cat′nep** (-nĕp), **cat′mint′** (-mĭnt′), *n.* [*cat* + *nip*, dial. form of *nep* catnip.] A strong-scented herb (*Nepeta cataria*) of the mint family, having whorls of small blue flowers in a terminal spike.

cat′–o′–moun′tain. Var. of CATAMOUNTAIN.

cat′–o′–nine′–tails′ (kăt′ō·nīn′tālz′), *n. sing. & pl.* An instrument consisting of knotted lines or cords (usually nine) fastened to a handle, used to flog offenders. Cf. CAT, *n.*, 3 a & *v. t.*, 2.

ca·top′trics (kȧ·tŏp′trĭks), *n.*; see -ICS. Also **ca·top′tric** (-trĭk). [Gr. *katoptrikos*, fr. *katoptron* mirror.] That part of optics which explains the properties and phenomena of reflected light, esp. light reflected from mirrors. Cf. DIOPTRICS. — **ca·top′tric, ca·top′tri·cal** (-trĭ·kăl), *adj.*

cat rig. *Naut.* A rig consisting of a single mast placed far forward and carrying a single large sail extended by a long boom. See CATBOAT, *Illust.* — **cat′rigged′** (kăt′rĭgd′), *adj.*

cat's cradle. A game played, esp. by children, with a string looped on the fingers so as to resemble a small cradle.

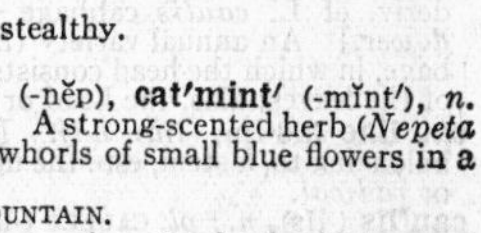

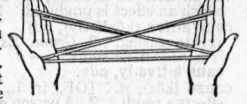

Cat's Cradle, first figure.

cat's′–eye′, *n.* *Mineral.* A gem exhibiting opalescent reflections from within like the eye of a cat, as a variety of chrysoberyl or of chalcedony.

cat's′–paw′, *n.* **1.** *Naut.* **a** A light air which ruffles the surface of the water in irregular patches during a calm. **b** A hitch in the bight of a rope so made as to form two eyes, into which a tackle may be hooked. See KNOT, *Illust.* (15). **2.** A person used by another as a tool.

cat′sup (kăt′sŭp; kĕch′ŭp). Var. of CATCHUP.

cat′tail′ (kăt′tāl′), *n.* **1. a** A tall marsh plant (*Typha latifolia*), family Typhaceae, with long flat leaves used for seating chairs, making mats, etc. In England it is called ***reed mace.*** **b** Any other species of *Typha.* **2.** A catkin or ament.

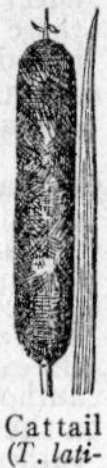

Cattail (*T. latifolia*) (⅟₁₂)

cat′ta·lo (kăt′ȧ·lō), *n.; pl.* -LOES or -LOS (-lōz). [*cattle* + *buffalo.*] A hybrid between the bison and domestic cattle, hardier than the latter.

cat′tle (kăt′'l), *n.* [ONF. *catel*, fr. L. *capitale*, neut. of *capitalis* chief, fr. *caput* head, capital, stock.] **1. a** Collectively, live animals held as property or raised for some use, now, commonly, including only domesticated, usually mature, bovine animals, as cows, bulls, and steers, but sometimes, esp. formerly, all domesticated quadrupeds, as sheep, goats, horses, mules, asses, and swine. Well-known breeds of beef cattle include *Aberdeen Angus, Durham, Galloway, Hereford, Shorthorn;* of dairy cattle, *Ayrshire, Brown Swiss, Dutch Belted, French Canadian, Guernsey, Holstein-Friesian, Jersey, Red Polled, Milking Shorthorn.* **b** Formerly, in *sing.*, a beast, ox, etc. **2.** By extension: **a** Such animals as vermin, insects, etc. **b** *Contemptuous.* Human beings.

cat′tle·man (-măn), *n.* A man who tends or raises cattle.

cat′ty (kăt′ĭ), *n.; pl.* CATTIES (-ĭz). [Malay *kātī.* See CADDY.] A weight of eastern Asia: **a** In East Indies, 1.36 lb. av.; in Philippine Islands, 1.39 lb. av.; in Japan, 1.32 lb. av. **b** In China, 16 liang or exactly 1⅓ lb. (604.8 grams). **c** In Siam, 1.32 lb. av., formerly 2.65 lb. av.

cat′ty, *adj.;* -TI·ER (-ĭ·ẽr); -TI·EST. **a** Of or relating to cats. **b** Like a cat; esp., slyly spiteful; malicious. — **cat′ti·ly,** *adv.* — **cat′ti·ness,** *n.*

cat′ty–cor′nered. Var. of CATER-CORNERED.

cat typhoid. = FELINE ENTERITIS.

cat′walk′ (kăt′wôk′), *n.* A narrow footway along a bridge or along the keel of a rigid airship.

cat whisker. *Radio.* A fine wire making contact with the crystal in a crystal detector.

Cau·ca′sian (kô·kā′zhăn; -shăn; -kăzh′ăn; -kăsh′ăn), *adj.* **1.** Of or pertaining to the Caucasus or its inhabitants. **2.** Belonging to or designating the native languages of the Caucasus region. **3.** Designating or pertaining to the division of mankind comprising the chief races of Europe, North Africa, and southwestern Asia, named the **Caucasian race** on the supposition that the people of the Caucasus were typical of the race; white. *Caucasian* should be distinguished from *Aryan.* — *n.* **1.** A member of one of various native peoples of the Caucasus. **2.** A member of the Caucasian race. — **Cau·cas′ic** (-kăs′ĭk), *adj.*

cau′cus (kô′kŭs), *n.* [Prob. of Algonquian origin.] **1.** A meeting of leaders of a party or group to decide on policies or candidates. **2.** In England, a system of party organization by committees. — *v. i.;* CAU′CUSED (-kŭst); CAU′CUS·ING. To hold, or meet in, a caucus or caucuses.

cau′dad (kô′dăd), *adv.* [L. *cauda* tail + *ad* to, toward.] *Zool.* Toward the tail or posterior end.

cau′dal (-dăl; -d'l), *adj.* [L. *cauda* tail.] Of, pert. to, or like a tail; near the tail. — **cau′dal·ly,** *adv.*

caudal anesthesia. Anesthesia induced by injection in the lower, or caudal, portion of the spinal canal.

cau′date (kô′dāt), *adj.* Also **cau′dat·ed** (-dāt·ĕd; -ĭd). [L. *cauda* tail.] Having a tail or a taillike appendage.

cau′dex (-dĕks), *n.; pl.* -DICES (-dĭ·sēz), -DEXES (-dĕk·sĕz; -sĭz). [L.] *Bot.* **a** The stem of a palm or of a tree fern. **b** The woody base of a perennial plant.

‖**cau·dil′lo** (kou·thē′lyō; -thē′yō), *n.* [Sp.] A military leader, often of irregular forces.

cau′dle (kô′d'l), *n.* [ONF. *caudel*, fr. L. *calidus* warm.] A kind of warm drink for sick persons; esp., a mixture of wine or ale with eggs, bread or gruel, sugar, and spices.

caught (kôt), *past & past part.* of CATCH.

caul (kôl), *n.* [F. *cale*, fr. *calotte.* See CALOTTE.] **a** The great omentum. See OMENTUM. **b** A part of the amnion, a membrane enveloping the fetus, which sometimes covers the head of the child at its birth.

cauld (kôld; käld; kôd). Dial. var. of COLD.

caul′dron (kôl′drŭn). Var. of CALDRON.

cau·les′cent (kô·lĕs′ĕnt; -'nt), *adj.* [L. *caulis* stalk, stem.] *Bot.* Having a leafy stem above ground.

cau′li·cle (kô′lĭ·k'l), *n.* [L. *cauliculus*, dim. of *caulis* stem.] *Bot.* A rudimentary stem, as of an embryo.

cau′li·flow′er (kô′lĭ·flou′ẽr), *n.* [From F. *chou-fleur* cauliflower, deriv. of L. *caulis* cabbage + *flos, floris,* flower; modified by E. *flower.*] An annual variety (*Brassica oleracea botrytis*) of the cabbage, in which the head consists of the thickened flower cluster instead of the leaves; also, the head or flower cluster. Cf. BROCCOLI.

cau′line (kô′lĭn; -līn), *adj.* [From CAULIS.] *Bot.* Growing on, or belonging to, a stem, esp. the upper portion of a stem; — opp. to *basal* or *radical.*

cau′lis (-lĭs), *n.; pl.* CAULES (-lēz). [L., a stem.] *Bot.* The stalk or stem of a plant.

caulk (kôk), **caulk′er.** Vars. of CALK, CALKER.

caus′a·ble (kôz′ȧ·b'l), *adj.* Capable of being caused.

caus′al (-ăl; -'l), *adj.* **a** Expressing a cause; causative; as, a *causal* clause. **b** Relating to a cause. **c** Implying or containing a cause or causes; of the nature of a cause. — *n. Gram.* A causative word or form. — **caus′al·ly,** *adv.*

cau·sal′i·ty (kô·zăl′ĭ·tĭ), *n.; pl.* -TIES (-tĭz). **1.** Causal quality or agency. **2.** The relation of cause and effect; also, the necessary connection of events through cause and effect.

‖**cau′sa si′ne qua non** (kô′zȧ sī′nē kwā nŏn′). [L.] Literally, cause without which not; hence, indispensable cause or condition.

cau·sa′tion (kô·zā′shŭn), *n.* **1.** Act of causing; also, act or agency by which an effect is produced. **2.** = CAUSALITY, 2.

caus′a·tive (kôz′ȧ·tĭv), *adj.* **1.** Effective or operating as a cause or agent; causing. **2.** *Gram.* Expressive of causation; as, *-en* in *darken* is a *causative* suffix. — *n. Gram.* A causative word or form. — **caus′a·tive·ly,** *adv.*

cause (kôz), *n.* [OF., fr. L. *causa.*] **1.** That which occasions or effects a result. **2.** A person or thing that is the occasion of an action or state; an agent that brings something about; reason; motive; as, *cause* for rejoicing. **3.** Any matter or question to be decided. **4.** The side of a question which is espoused, advocated, and upheld by a person or party. **5.** *Law.* A ground of action; also, a case.

Syn. Cause, determinant, antecedent, reason, occasion mean that which in whole or in part produces an effect. Cause applies to any circumstance, condition, event, etc., or to any combination thereof that necessarily brings about or contributes to a result; determinant applies to a cause or to one of the causes that fixes the nature of that which results, such as a product or an outcome (as, environment is an important *determinant* of character); antecedent applies to a person or thing that is responsible for a later person or thing, as by being one of the progenitors, precursors, etc.; reason applies to a traceable or explainable cause of a known effect (as, the *reason* for this situation); occasion applies to any person, situation, etc., that serves to bring about the effect of already existing causes.

— *v. t.* To be the cause of; to effect as an agent; to bring about. — **cause′less,** *adj.* — **caus′er** (kôz′ẽr), *n.*

‖**cause cé·lè′bre** (kōz′ sā′lĕ′br′). [F.] A celebrated (legal) case; usually, a criminal case which excites great public interest.

cau′se·rie′ (kō′zẽ·rē′; kō′zẽ·rē; *F.* kōz′rē′), *n.* [F., fr. *causer* to chat.] **a** Informal talk or discussion; a chat. **b** A short familiar article, as on a literary subject.

cause′way′ (kôz′wā′), *n.* [*causey* + *way.*] **1.** A raised way across wet ground. **2.** *Hist.* A highway or a paved way. — **cause′way′,** *v. t.*

cau′sey (kô′zĭ; -zĭ), *n.; pl.* -SEYS (-zĭz; -zĭz). [ONF. *caucie*, fr. LL. (*via*) *calciata*, fr. *calciare* to make a road.] **1.** = CAUSEWAY, 1. **2.** *Hist.* = CAUSEWAY, 2. **3.** *Now Dial.* A paved street or sidewalk. **4.** *Dial.* A street or area paved with cobblestones. — *v. t. Scot. & Dial.* To pave, esp. with small stones.

caus′tic (kôs′tĭk), *adj.* [Through F. and L., fr. Gr. *kaustikos*, fr. *kaiein* to burn.] **1.** Capable of destroying or eating away by chemical action; corrosive. **2.** Severe; satirical; sharp; as, a *caustic* remark. **3.** *Optics.* Pertaining to or designating the envelope of rays emanating from a point and reflected or refracted by a curved surface. The envelope is called a **caustic surface;** a plane section of it, a **caustic curve.** — *n.* **1.** A caustic substance. **2.** *Optics.* A caustic curve or surface. — **caus′ti·cal** (-tĭ·kăl), *adj.* — **caus′ti·cal·ly,** *adv.* — **caus·tic′i·ty** (kôs·tĭs′ĭ·tĭ), *n.*

caustic potash. Potassium hydroxide, KOH.

caustic soda. Sodium hydroxide, NaOH.

cau′ter·ize (kô′tẽr·īz), *v. t.* To sear with a cautery. — **cau′ter·i·za′tion** (-ĭ·zā′shŭn; -ī·zā′shŭn), *n.*

cau′ter·y (-ĭ), *n.; pl.* -TERIES (-ĭz). [L. *cauterium*, fr. Gr. *kautērion* a branding iron, fr. *kaiein* to burn.] **1.** A searing with a hot iron or a caustic; cauterization. **2.** The agent used in cauterizing.

cau′tion (kô′shŭn), *n.* [OF., a security, fr. L. *cautio*, fr. *cavere* to be on one's guard.] **1.** *Obs.* A precaution. **2.** A warning; a word, act, or the like, that conveys a warning. **3.** Prudence in regard to danger; wariness; cautiousness. **4.** *Colloq.* A person or thing so remarkable or unusual as to excite alarm, astonishment, etc. — *v. t.* To notify of danger or risk. — **Syn.** See WARN.

cau′tion·ar′y (-ẽr′ĭ *or, esp. Brit.,* -ẽr·ĭ), *adj.* Conveying, or of the nature of, a caution; warning.

cau′tious (kô′shŭs), *adj.* Attentive to examine probable effects and consequences of acts so as to avoid danger. — **cau′tious·ly,** *adv.* — **cau′tious·ness,** *n.*

Syn. Cautious, circumspect, wary, chary mean prudently attentive to dangers or risks. Cautious usually implies the promptings of fear for oneself or for others and the exercise of forethought so that risks may be avoided or minimized; circumspect usually suggests less fear, stressing rather a surveying of all possible consequences before making a decision, proceeding upon an action, etc.; wary emphasizes suspiciousness, alertness in watching for dangers or risks, or cunning in escaping them; chary implies excessive caution in giving, doing, saying, etc. — **Ant.** Adventurous.

cav′al·cade′ (kăv′ăl·kād′), *n.* [F., fr. It. *cavalcata*, fr. LL. *caballicare* to go on horseback, fr. L. *caballus* an inferior horse.] A procession of persons on horseback; hence, a procession of any sort; parade; pageant.

cav′a·le′ro (kăv′ȧ·lā′rō), **cav′a·lie′ro** (-lyā′rō), *n.* [Sp. *caballero.*] A cavalier; caballero.

cav′a·lier′ (kăv′ȧ·lēr′), *n.* [F., through It. & LL., fr. L. *caballus.* See CAVALCADE.] **1.** A mounted soldier; a knight. **2.** A gay, sprightly military man; a gallant. **3.** [*cap.*] One of the court party in England in the time of Charles I; a Royalist; — contrasted with *Roundhead.* — (kăv′ȧ·lēr′; 2), *adj.* **1.** Gay; easy; offhand. **2.** Supercilious; haughty; disdainful. **3.** [*cap.*] Of or relating to the Cavaliers. — **cav′a·lier′ly,** *adv. & adj.*

‖**ca·va·lier′,** *or* **ca′va·lie′re, ser·ven′te** (kä′vä·lyâr′, kä′vä·lyâ′rā, sâr·vĕn′tā). [It.] A lover of, or a gallant attentive to, a married lady; a cicisbeo.

ca·val′la (kȧ·văl′ȧ), *n.;* see PLURAL, *Note,* 6. Also **ca·val′ly** (-ĭ). [Pg. *cavalla*, Sp. *caballa.*] **a** The cero *Sierra cavalla.* **b** Any of various carangoid fishes (*Caranx* or related genera); esp., a marine food fish (*C. hippos*) of tropical American coasts.

cav′al·ry (kăv′ăl·rĭ), *n.; pl.* -RIES (-rĭz). [F. *cavalerie*, fr. It. *cavalleria.*] **1.** *Obs.* Horsemanship, esp. that of a knight. **2.** Horsemen, horses, etc., collectively. **3.** *Mil.* **a** That part of a military force which normally serves on horseback. **b** *U. S.* An arm of the regular army organized and equipped to carry out combat missions (as reconnaissance) requiring great mobility. — **cav′al·ry·man** (-măn), *n.*

cav′a·ti′na (kăv′ȧ·tē′nȧ; kä′vä·tē′nä), *n.* [It.] *Music.* Orig., a melody of simpler form than the aria; now, almost any kind of melodious composition.

cave (kāv), *n.* [OF., fr. L. *cava*, fr. *cavus* hollow.] **1.** A hollowed-out chamber in the earth; cavern. **2.** *Eng. Politics.* A secession, or a group of seceders, from a political party. — *v. t.* To make hollow. — *v. i. Colloq.* To cave in. — ***cave in.*** **1.** To fall, or to cause to fall, in or down. **2.** *Colloq.* To collapse; yield; give in.

ca′ve·at (kā′vē·ăt), *n.* [L. *caveat* let him beware.] **1.** *Law.* A notice given by an interested party to some officer not to do a certain act until the party is heard in opposition; as, a *caveat* entered to stop the proving of a will. **2.** A caution; warning; admonition.

‖**ca′ve·at emp′tor** (kā′vē·ăt ĕmp′tôr). [L.] *Law.* Let the purchaser beware (that is, he buys at his own risk).

‖**ca′ve ca′nem** (kā′vē kā′nĕm). [L.] Beware the dog.

cave′–in′ (kāv′ĭn′), *n.* A caving in or a section that has caved in.

cave man. 1. A **cave dweller,** one who dwells in a cave; esp., a man of the Stone Age. **2.** A man who acts with violence and passion.

cav′en·dish (kăv′ĕn·dĭsh), *n.* Leaf tobacco softened, sweetened, and pressed into plugs or cakes.

cav′ern (kăv′ẽrn), *n.* [OF. *caverne*, fr. L. *caverna*, fr. *cavus* hollow.]

A subterranean hollow; an underground chamber; a cave, esp. a large cave or one of indefinite extent. — *v. t.* **1.** To place in or as if in a cavern. **2.** To hollow out, or form by hollowing out.

cav′ern·ous (kăv′ẽr·nŭs), *adj.* **1.** Full of caverns; filled with cavities, cells, or interstices. **2.** Of the nature of or like a cavern; hollow. — **cav′ern·ous·ly**, *adv.*

ca·vet′to (kȧ·vĕt′ō; *It.* kä·vāt′tō), *n.; pl.* -VETTI (kȧ·vĕt′ĭ; *It.* kä·vāt′tē), -VETTOS (kȧ·vĕt′ōz). [It., fr. *cavo* hollow, fr. L. *cavus.*] A type of molding. See MOLDING, *Illust.*

cav′i·ar, cav′i·are (kăv′ĭ·är; kăv′yär), *n.* [F., fr. It., fr. Turk. *khāvyār.*] Prepared and salted roe of the sturgeon and certain other large fish, used as a relish.

ca′vie, ca′vy (kā′vĭ), *n.* *Scot.* A hencoop.

cav′il (kăv′ĭl; -′l), *v. i.; -*ILED or -ILLED (-ĭld; -′ld); -IL·ING or -IL·LING. [OF. *caviller*, fr. L. *cavillari* to practice jesting, to censure, fr. *cavilla* bantering jests, sophistry.] To raise captious and frivolous objections; carp. — *v. t.* To cavil at. — *n.* A captious or frivolous objection; quibble. — **cav′il·er, cav′il·ler**, *n.*

cav′il·ing, cav′il·ling, *adj.* Disposed to cavil or find fault. — **Syn.** See CRITICAL.

cav′i·ta′tion (kăv′ĭ·tā′shŭn), *n.* The formation of a cavity, as a hollow in a tuberculous lung, a partial vacuum in a fluid about a rapidly revolving propeller, or a gas-filled space in a liquid; also, the cavity itself.

cav′i·ty (kăv′ĭ·tĭ), *n.; pl.* -TIES (-tĭz). [L. *cavus* hollow.] A hollow place; a hollow; hole; pocket.

ca·vort′ (kȧ·vôrt′), *v. i.* *Colloq., U. S.* To prance; caper; — orig. of a horse or his rider.

ca′vy (kā′vĭ), *n.; pl.* CAVIES (-vĭz). [From *Cavia*, the generic name, of Cariban origin.] Any of several short-tailed, rough-haired rodents (family Caviidae), allied to the porcupines, including the guinea pig, agouti, and capybara; specif.: **a** The ***restless cavy*** (*Cavia porcellus*), the wild guinea pig of South America, from which the domestic varieties of guinea pig are supposed to be derived. **b** Any guinea pig.

caw (kô), *v. i. & n.* Croak, as (or of) a raven or crow.

cay (kē; kā), *n.* A low island or reef; = KEY. The spelling *cay* and pronunciation kē are the usual ones in the West Indies.

cay·enne′ (kī·ĕn′; kā·ĕn′), *n., or* **cay′enne pep′per** (kī′ĕn; kā′ĕn; 2). [From *Cayenne* (see *Gaz.*).] See PEPPER, *n.*, 3.

cay′man (kā′măn), *n.; pl.* -MANS (-mănz). [Sp. *caimán*, of Arawakan and Cariban origin.] Any of several tropical American alligators (genus *Caiman*) having the ventral armor composed of overlapping bony plates, each in two parts united by a suture.

Cay·u′ga (kā·ōō′gȧ; kā·yōō′gȧ), *n.; pl.* CAYUGA (-gȧ), CAYUGAS (-gȧz). An Indian of an Iroquoian tribe formerly inhabiting western New York, now living mostly in Ontario.

Cay′use (kī′ūs), *n.* **1.** An Indian of a western tribe, now restricted to a reservation in Oregon. **2.** *Western U. S.* [*not cap.*] A small hardy horse of western North America used by the American Indians and descended from stock introduced by the Spaniards.

C battery (sē). *Radio.* An electric battery connected in the grid circuit of an electron tube to control the amount of average plate current.

cease (sēs), *v. i.* [OF. *cesser*, fr. L. *cessare*, fr. *cedere, cessum*, to withdraw.] **1.** To come to an end. **2.** *Obs.* To become extinct; pass away. — *v. t.* To bring to an end; to discontinue or leave off; as, *Cease* firing! — **Syn.** See STOP. — *n.* Cessation; — *obs.*, exc. in *without cease.*

cease′less, *adj.* Without pause or stop; incessant.

ce′cal (sē′kăl), **ce′cum.** Vars. of CAECAL, CAECUM.

Ce·cro′pi·a moth (sē·krō′pĭ·ȧ). A large silkworm moth (*Samia cecropia*), the largest moth of the eastern United States.

Ce′crops (sē′krŏps), *n.* *Gr. Myth.* First king of Attica.

‖**ce′dant ar′ma to′gae** (sē′dănt är′mȧ tō′jē) [L.] Let arms yield to the toga, i. e., military to civil power; — motto of Wyoming.

ce′dar (sē′dẽr), *n.* [OF. *cedre*, fr. L. *cedrus*, fr. Gr. *kedros.*] **1.** Any of a large number of coniferous trees having fragrant durable wood; specif.: **a** Any tree of a genus (*Cedrus*) of the pine family, as the ***cedar of Lebanon*** (*C. libana*) and the deodar (see CONE, *Illust.*). **b** Any juniper (*Juniperus*), as the ***eastern red cedar*** (*J. virginiana*). **c** Any tree of the genus *Chamaecyparis*, as the ***white cedar*** (*C. thyoides*) of Atlantic coastal swamps of U. S. whose soft wood is used for shingles, boats, posts, etc. **d** Any tree of the genus *Thuja* (see ARBORVITAE), as the ***western red cedar*** (*T. plicata*) and the common arborvitae (*T. occidentalis*) sometimes called ***white cedar.*** **e** In full, ***Japan****, or* ***Japanese, cedar.*** See CRYPTOMERIA. **2.** Any of various tropical deciduous trees, chiefly of the mahogany family, as the mahogany and the toon.

ce′darn (sē′dẽrn), *adj.* *Poetic.* Of, or covered with, cedar or cedars

cedar waxwing. Also **ce′dar·bird′** (sē′dẽr·bûrd′), *n.* See WAXWING.

cede (sēd), *v. t.* [F. *céder*, fr. L. *cedere* to withdraw, yield.] To yield; grant; also, to assign; transfer.

ce·dil′la (sē·dĭl′ȧ), *n.* [Sp., dim. of *zeta*, Gr. name of *z*, because this letter was formerly written after the *c* to indicate the sibilant value.] A mark under the letter *c* [thus *ç*], to show it is to be sounded like *s*, as in *façade.*

ced′u·la (sĕd′ū·lȧ; *Sp.* thā′thōō·lä), *n.* [Sp. *cédula.* See SCHEDULE.] In Spanish countries, any of various certificates, etc.; esp., a personal registration tax certificate issued in the Philippines; also, the tax.

cee (sē), *n.* The letter C, c. — *adj.* C-shaped.

ce′i·ba, *n.* [Sp., of Arawakan origin.] **a** (sā′ē·bä; thā′ē-) The silk-cotton tree *Ceiba pentandra.* **b** (sā′ē·bä; sī′bȧ) Kapok.

ceil (sēl), *v. t.* [Prob. fr. F. *ciel* sky, canopy, fr. L. *caelum* sky, arched covering.] To furnish with a ceiling.

ceil′ing (sēl′ĭng), *n.* **1.** The overhead inside lining or finish, as of a room; hence, any overhanging surface looked at from below. **2. a** A maximum price, wage, salary, rent, fee, or the like, fixed by government authority as the upper legal limit, usually on the basis of the level prevailing on a certain date. **b** Any maximum; as, to approach the *ceiling* of gross yield of soybeans. **3.** *Meteorol. & Aeronautics.* **a** Height above ground from which prominent objects on the ground can be seen and identified; also, the height above the ground of the base of a layer of clouds when over half of the sky is obscured. *Ceiling unlimited* denotes a cloudless or nearly cloudless sky or a sky less than half obscured by clouds at levels lower than an arbitrary fixed altitude. **b** In full, ***absolute ceiling.*** The maximum altitude at which a given aircraft can maintain horizontal flight under standard air conditions. **c** In full, ***service ceiling.*** The altitude, under standard air conditions, at which a given airplane is unable to climb faster than a small specified rate (100 feet per minute in the U. S. and England). **d** The maximum altitude at which an individual is able to maintain satisfactory muscular co-ordination and mental efficiency without artificial aids, such as oxygen or a pressurized cabin.

ceil·om′e·ter (sēl·ŏm′ē·tẽr), *n.* [*ceiling* + *-meter.*] A photoelectric instrument for determining the height of the cloud ceiling above the earth. It indicates the angular elevation of a spot of light formed where a vertical beam of light (usually ultraviolet) meets the cloud, so that the height may be computed by triangulation.

cel′an·dine (sĕl′ăn·dīn), *n.* [OF. *celidoine*, fr. L., fr. Gr. *chelidonion*, fr. *chelidōn* the swallow.] **a** A yellow-flowered biennial herb (*Chelidonium majus*) of the poppy family; — called specif. ***great celandine.*** **b** The pilewort; — called specif. ***lesser celandine.***

Cel′a·nese (sĕl′ȧ·nēs; -nēz), *n.* A trade-mark applied to chemical, plastic, and textile products, including yarns and fabrics of cellulose acetate rayon.

-cele (-sēl). **a** [Gr. *kēlē.*] A combining form meaning *tumor, hernia*, as in varico*cele.* **b** Var. of -COELE.

cel′e·brant (sĕl′ē·brănt), *n.* One who celebrates a public religious rite; esp., the officiating priest at the Mass.

cel′e·brate (-brāt), *v. t.* [L. *celebratus*, past part. of *celebrare* to frequent, to celebrate, fr. *celeber* famous.] **1.** To perform publicly and with appropriate rites; solemnize. **2.** To honor or observe, as with solemn rites or ceremonies, by refraining from business, or by exuberant merrymaking. **3.** To proclaim; publish abroad. **4.** To extol; sound the praises of. — *v. i.* To observe or perform a religious ceremony (esp. Mass), a festival, holiday, or the like. — **Syn.** See KEEP. — **cel′e·bra′tion** (-brā′shŭn), *n.* — **cel′e·bra′tor** (-brā′tẽr), *n.*

cel′e·brat′ed (-brāt′ĕd; -ĭd), *adj.* Distinguished or famous in any way, esp. favorably; sometimes, notorious. — **Syn.** See FAMOUS.

ce·leb′ri·ty (sē·lĕb′rĭ·tĭ), *n.; pl.* -TIES (-tĭz). **1.** State of being celebrated; renown. **2.** A celebrated person.

ce·ler′i·ty (sē·lĕr′ĭ·tĭ), *n.* [F. *célérité*, fr. L. *celeritas*, fr. *celer* swift.] Rapidity of motion; speed; swiftness.

Syn. **Celerity, alacrity, legerity** mean quickness in movement or action **Celerity** implies speed in accomplishing work; **alacrity** stresses promptness in response, though swiftness in movement is usually implied; **legerity** implies nimbleness or ease as well as swiftness.

cel′er·y (sĕl′ẽr·ĭ), *n.* [F. *céleri*, fr. It. dial., fr. L. *selinum*, fr. Gr. *selinon* parsley.] A European plant (*Apium graveolens*) of the carrot family, the blanched leafstalks of a variety (*A. graveolens* var. *dulce*) of which are eaten raw and also cooked.

ce·les′ta (sē·lĕs′tȧ), *n.* [F. *célesta.*] A keyboard instrument giving its tones from steel plates struck by hammers.

ce·les′tial (sē·lĕs′chăl), *adj.* [OF. *celestiel*, fr. L. *caelestis*, fr. *caelum* heaven.] **1.** Of or pertaining to the sky or visible heavens; as, a *celestial* body. **2.** Of, pertaining to, or characteristic of, the spiritual heaven; heavenly; divine. **3.** [*usually cap.*] *Humorous.* Of or pertaining to the Chinese people or former Chinese Empire. — *n.* **1.** An inhabitant of heaven. **2.** [*usually cap.*] *Colloq.* A Chinese. —**-ly**, *adv.*

Celestial City. The heavenly Jerusalem. *Rev.* xxi.

Celestial Empire. The former Chinese Empire; — from the Chinese words *T′ien¹ Ch′ao²*, Heavenly Dynasty.

celestial equator. See EQUATOR, 2.

celestial globe. *Astron.* A globe on whose surface the celestial bodies are depicted.

celestial sphere. A sphere of indefinitely great radius, of which the apparent vault of the sky forms half.

cel′es·tite (sĕl′ĕs·tīt), **cel′es·tine** (-tĭn; -tīn), *n.* [L. *caelestis* of the sky.] *Mineral.* Native strontium sulfate, $SrSO_4$, commonly white, but occasionally a delicate blue.

ce′li·ac, coe′li·ac (sē′lĭ·ăk), *adj.* [L. *coeliacus*, fr. Gr. *koiliakos*, fr. *koilia* belly, fr. *koilos* hollow.] Pert. to the cavity of the abdomen.

celiac disease. *Med.* A chronic intestinal disease of young children, characterized by inability to absorb fats, distention of the intestines, wasting of the buttocks and groin, and inflammation of the mouth and tongue. It is often relieved by vitamins A and B or by ripe bananas and protein milk.

cel′i·ba·cy (sĕl′ĭ·bȧ·sĭ; sē·lĭb′ȧ·sĭ), *n.; pl.* -CIES (-sĭz). State of being unmarried; single life, esp. that of one bound by vows not to marry.

cel′i·bate (sĕl′ĭ·bāt), *n.* [L. *caelibatus*, fr. *caelebs* unmarried.] An unmarried person. — *adj.* Unmarried.

cell (sĕl), *n.* [OF. *celle*, fr. L. *cella.*] **1.** A very small and close apartment, as in a prison. **2.** A small compartment, hollow receptacle, cavity, or the like; as, the *cells* of a honeycomb; a *cell*, or calyculus enclosing a zooid in hydroids and corals; a *cell* in a plant ovary; an anther *cell*, or pollen sac. **3.** A small, often the smallest, unit devoted to organizing a radical or reform movement. **4.** *Biol.* A small, usually microscopic, mass of protoplasm bounded externally by a semipermeable membrane, usually including one or more nuclei and various nonliving products, and being capable, alone or interacting with other cells, of performing all the fundamental functions of life; the least structural aggregate of living matter capable of functioning as an independent unit. **5.** *Eccl.* A small religious house, a dependent of a monastery or convent. **6** *Elec.* A receptacle, as a cup or jar, containing electrodes and an electrolyte, either for generating electricity by chemical action, or for use in electrolysis.

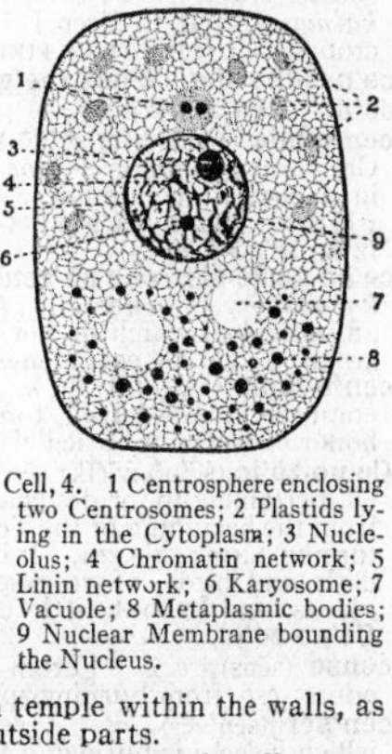

Cell, 4. 1 Centrosphere enclosing two Centrosomes; 2 Plastids lying in the Cytoplasm; 3 Nucleolus; 4 Chromatin network; 5 Linin network; 6 Karyosome; 7 Vacuole; 8 Metaplasmic bodies; 9 Nuclear Membrane bounding the Nucleus.

cel′la (sĕl′ȧ), *n.; pl.* -LAE (-ē). [L.] *Arch.* The part of an ancient Greek or Roman temple within the walls, as distinct from open porticoes and other outside parts.

cel′lar (sĕl′ẽr), *n.* [OF. *celier*, fr. L. *cellarium* pantry, fr. *cella* storeroom.] **1.** A room or set of rooms below the surface of the ground, usually under a building, used esp. for the keeping of provisions and other stores, or for refuge (as, a cyclone, or storm, *cellar*). **2.** Specif., a ***wine cellar***, a basement room or rooms for storing wines; hence, a stock of wines. — *v. t.* To place or store in a cellar.

cel′lar·age (-ĭj), *n.* **1.** Space in a cellar, as for storage. **2.** Charge for storage in a cellar.

cel′lar·er (sĕl′ẽr·ẽr), *n.* A steward of a monastery.
cel′lar·et′ (sĕl′ẽr·ĕt′), *n.* A cabinet or sideboard to hold a few bottles of wine or liquor.
cel′lo, ′cel′lo (chĕl′ō), *n.; pl.* -LOS (-ōz), -LI (-ē). A violoncello. — **cel′list, ′cel′list** (chĕl′ĭst), *n.*
cel·loi′din (sĕ·loi′dĭn), *n.* A purified form of pyroxylin obtained from collodion, used in microscopy, etc.
cel′lo·phane (sĕl′ō·fān), *n.* [*cell*ulose + *-phane*.] An elastic tissue made from viscose solidified in thin transparent sheets or strips, and usually having a moistureproof coating on both sides. — **cel′lo·phane,** *adj.*
cel′lu·lar (sĕl′ū·lẽr), *adj.* [F. or L.; F. *cellulaire*, fr. L. *cellula* a little cell.] Consisting of, characterized by, or pertaining to a cell or cells; as, *cellular* tissue.
cel′lule (sĕl′ūl), *n.* A small cell.
Cel′lu·loid (sĕl′ū·loid), *n.* A trade-mark for a substance, essentially of pyroxylin and camphor, and usually colorless or resembling ivory, used in making toilet articles, photographic film, etc.
cel′lu·lose (-lōs), *n.* [F.] *Chem.* An inert substance, the chief component of the solid framework (cell walls) of plants, used in paper, rayon, etc. It is a carbohydrate, $(C_6H_{10}O_5)_x$, convertible into glucose by hydrolysis.
cellulose acetate. *Chem.* Any of several compounds, insoluble in water, formed esp. by the action of acetic acid, anhydride of acetic acid, and sulfuric acid on cellulose, esp. cotton and wood, and used for making textile fibers, packaging sheets, photographic films, varnishes, etc.
cellulose nitrate. *Chem.* Any of several esters of nitric acid formed by the action of nitric acid on cellulose, as paper or linen or esp. cotton, and used for making explosives, plastics, rayon, varnishes, etc.
cel′lu·lo′sic (sĕl′ū·lō′sĭk), *adj.* Of, pertaining to, or containing cellulose. — *n.* Any plastic made from cellulose, as cellophane.
ce′lom (sē′lŏm). Var. of COELOM.
Cel′si·us (sĕl′sĭ·ŭs; -shĭ·ŭs), *n.* Also **Celsius thermometer.** See CENTIGRADE THERMOMETER. Abbr. *Cels., C.*
celt (sĕlt), *n.* [LL. *celtis* a chisel.] *Archaeol.* A primitive chisel or ax-shaped stone or metal implement.
Celt (sĕlt *or, esp. Brit.*, kĕlt), **Kelt** (kĕlt), *n.* [L. *Celta*, pl. *Celtae*, Gr. *Keltoi*.] **1.** An individual of any of various Celtic-speaking peoples, including the ancient Gauls and Britons and the modern Irish, Scots, Welsh, and Bretons. **2.** A member of a race of central and western Europe, described by the ancients as tall and blond.
Celt′ic (sĕl′tĭk; kĕl′tĭk), **Kelt′ic** (kĕl′tĭk), *adj.* Of or pertaining to the Celts or their language. — *n.* A group of Indo-European languages closely akin to the Italic, now found only in Brittany, Wales, Ireland, and the Scottish Highlands. It is divided into the Cymric and Goidelic branches, each of which in medieval times possessed a copious literature. See INDO-EUROPEAN LANGUAGES, *Table.*
Celtic cross. See CROSS, *Illust.* (7).
Celt′i·cism (sĕl′tĭ·sĭz′m; kĕl′tĭ-), *n.* A Celtic custom, expression, or idiom; also, attachment to Celtic customs.
cel′tuce (sĕl′tĭs; -tŭs), *n.* [*cel*ery + let*tuce*.] A vegetable that combines the flavors of lettuce and celery.
ce·ment′ (sē·mĕnt′; *the older* sĕm′ĕnt *is now little used*), *n.* [OF. *ciment*, fr. L. *caementum* a rough, unhewn stone, chips of marble, from which mortar was made.] **1. a** A substance used in a soft state to join stones in building, to cover floors, etc., and which afterwards becomes hard like stone; esp., such a substance made with lime, or a calcined mixture of clay and limestone. **b** Mortar made with such a substance. **2.** Any substance used for making bodies adhere to each other, as glue, paste, etc.; also, a plastic material for filling cavities. **3.** Bond of union; that which unites firmly. **4.** *Anat.* The bonelike substance which forms a layer covering the root and neck, and sometimes parts of the crown, of the teeth of mammals. **5.** *Metal.* The powder used in cementation. **6.** *Petrog.* The fine-grained groundmass or glass of a porphyry; residual uncrystallized material. — (sē·mĕnt′), *v. t.* **1.** To unite or stick by or as by cement. **2.** To overlay with cement. — *v. i.* To become cemented. — **ce·ment′er,** *n.*
ce′men·ta′tion (sē′mĕn·tā′shŭn; sĕm′ĕn-), *n.* **1.** Act or process of cementing; state of being cemented. **2.** *Metal.* Process of surrounding a solid, as iron or glass, with a powder, as of charcoal or sand, and heating the whole so that the solid is changed, as into steel or porcelain, by chemical combination with the powder.
ce·men′tum (sē·mĕn′tŭm), *n.* [NL.] *Anat.* Cement (def. 4).
cem′e·ter′y (sĕm′ē·tĕr′ĭ *or, esp. Brit.*, -trĭ), *n.; pl.* -TERIES (-ĭz). [LL. *coemeterium*, fr. Gr. *koimētērion* a sleeping chamber, burial place, fr. *koiman* to put to sleep.] A burial place or ground; graveyard; necropolis. Cf. POTTER'S FIELD.
ce′nes·the′si·a, ce′nes·the′sis, etc. Vars. of COENESTHESIA, etc.
ce′no-. Var. of COENO-.
cen′o·bite (sĕn′ō·bīt; sē′nō-), *n.* [LL. *coenobita*, fr. *coenobium*, fr. Gr. *koinos* common + *bios* life.] One of a religious order, dwelling in a convent community. Cf. ANCHORITE, HERMIT. — **cen′o·bit′ic** (-bĭt′ĭk), **cen′o·bit′i·cal** (-ĭ·kăl), *adj.* — **cen′o·bit·ism** (sĕn′ō·bīt·ĭz′m; sē′nō-), *n.*
ce′no·gen′e·sis, cae′no·gen′e·sis (sē′nō·jĕn′ē·sĭs; sĕn′ō-), *n.* [Gr. *kainos* new + *-genesis*.] *Biol.* The processes in the development of an individual which do not repeat the race history (phylogeny) of its group; — opp. to *palingenesis*. — **ce′no·ge·net′ic** (-jē·nĕt′ĭk), *adj.*
cen′o·taph (sĕn′ō·tăf; 9), *n.* [From L., fr. Gr. *kenotaphion*, fr. *kenos* empty + *taphos* burial, tomb.] An empty tomb or a monument in honor of a person buried elsewhere.
Ce′no·zo′ic (sē′nō·zō′ĭk; sĕn′ō-), *adj.* [Gr. *kainos* recent + *zōē* life.] Of, pertaining to, or designating an era of geological history extending from the beginning of the Tertiary to the present, or the group of rocks formed during this era. It is marked by a rapid evolution of the mammals and birds, of grasses, shrubs, and higher flowering plants, and by but little change in the invertebrates. — **Ce′no·zo′ic,** *n.*

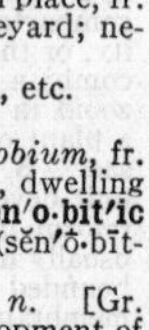
Censer.

cense (sĕns), *v. t.* [From INCENSE.] To perfume with odors, esp. from burning spices; to offer incense to.
cen′ser (sĕn′sẽr), *n.* A vessel for perfumes, esp. one in which incense is burned; a thurible.
cen′sor (sĕn′sẽr), *n.* [L., fr. *censere* to value, tax.] **1.** *Antiq.* One of two magistrates of Rome who took the census and became overseers of morals and conduct. **2.** One who acts as an overseer of morals and conduct; esp.: **a** An official empowered to examine written or printed matter, motion pictures, etc., in order to forbid publication if objectionable. **b** An official or a military officer charged in time of war with examining letters, printed matter, etc., in order to delete or suppress anything that might aid the enemy, injure discipline or morale, etc. **3.** A faultfinder; adverse critic. **4.** *Psychoanalysis.* The force or agency that excludes from consciousness unacceptable memories or complexes. — *v. t.* To subject to the action of a censor, or to censorship. — **cen·so′ri·al** (sĕn·sō′rĭ·ăl), *adj.*
cen·so′ri·ous (sĕn·sō′rĭ·ŭs; 70), *adj.* **1.** Addicted to censure; severe on others. **2.** Implying or expressing censure. — **Syn.** See CRITICAL. — **cen·so′ri·ous·ly,** *adv.* — **cen·so′ri·ous·ness,** *n.*
cen′sor·ship (sĕn′sẽr·shĭp), *n.* **1.** The office or power of a censor. **2.** The action of a censor. **3.** *Psychoanalysis.* The exclusion from consciousness of unacceptable memories or complexes, except in such transformations as occur in dreams.
cen′sur·a·ble (sĕn′shẽr·ȧ·b′l), *adj.* Deserving of, or subject to, censure; reprehensible; blamable. — **cen′sur·a·bil′i·ty** (-bĭl′ĭ·tĭ), *n.* — **cen′sur·a·bly** (-blĭ), *adv.*
cen′sure (sĕn′shẽr), *n.* [F., fr. L. *censura*, fr. *censere* to value, tax.] **1.** *Archaic.* Judgment; opinion; also, sentence; reprimand. **2.** Act of blaming, or condemning as wrong; hostile criticism. — *v. t.* **1.** *Obs.* To judge of. **2.** To find fault with or condemn as wrong; criticize adversely. — **Syn.** See CRITICIZE. — **cen′sur·er** (-shẽr·ẽr), *n.*
cen′sus (sĕn′sŭs), *n.* [L., fr. *censere*. See CENSOR.] **1.** *Rom. Hist.* A numbering of the people, and valuation of their estates, for taxation, etc. **2.** An official enumeration of the population of a country, city, or town, often with classified social and economic statistics.
cent (sĕnt), *n.* [F., hundred, fr. L. *centum*.] **1.** A hundred; — only in phrases, as *per cent* (see PER CENT). **2.** The 100th part of the unit in various monetary systems; also, a coin of this value; esp., in the United States, Canada, British colonies, China, etc., one 100th of a dollar, a coin of alloyed copper. The sign ¢, when used after a numeral (as, 1¢, 10¢), is read *cent* or *cents*. See MONEY, *Tables.* Abbr. *c.* or *ct.*, pl. *cts.*
cen′tal (sĕn′tăl; -t′l), *n.* [L. *centum* a hundred.] A weight of 100 pounds avoirdupois; — usually called *hundredweight* in U. S.
cen′tare′ (sĕn′târ′; *F.* säN′tȧr′). Var. of CENTIARE.
cen′taur (sĕn′tôr), *n.* [L. *Centaurus*, fr. Gr. *Kentauros*.] **1.** *Gr. Myth.* One of a race, half man and half horse, descendants of Ixion, dwelling in the mountains of Thessaly. **2.** [*cap.*] *Astron.* Centaurus.
Cen·tau′rus (sĕn·tô′rŭs), *n.; gen.* CENTAURI (-rī). [L.] A southern constellation between the Southern Cross and Hydra.
cen′tau·ry (sĕn′tô·rĭ), *n.; pl.* -TAURIES (-rĭz). [From L., fr. Gr. *kentaurion*, fr. the *centaur* Chiron.] Either of two Old World herbs (*Chlora perfoliata* and *Centaurium umbellatum*) of the gentian family, with medicinal properties reputedly discovered by the centaur Chiron.
cen·ta′vo (sĕn·tä′vō), *n.; pl.* -VOS (-vōz). **1.** [Amer. Sp., prop., hundredth.] A minor coin and money of account in the Philippine Islands and in Spanish American countries, one 100th of the monetary unit (usually the peso). See MONEY, *Tables.* **2.** [Pg.] In Portugal, one 100th of an escudo; in Brazil, one 100th of a cruzeiro.
cen′te·nar′i·an (sĕn′tē·nâr′ĭ·ăn), *adj.* One hundred years old; also, centenary. — *n.* A person 100 years old.
cen′te·nar′y (sĕn′tē·nĕr′ĭ; sĕn·tĕn′ȧ·rĭ; *or, esp. Brit.*, sĕn·tē′nȧ·rĭ, sĕn′tē·nȧ·rĭ), *adj.* [L. *centenarius*, fr. *centum* a hundred.] Of or pertaining to a period of 100 years; centennial. — *n.; pl.* -NARIES (-ĭz). A century; centennial.
cen·ten′ni·al (sĕn·tĕn′ĭ·ăl; 58), *adj.* [L. *centum* hundred + *annus* year.] **1.** Of or pertaining to a period of 100 years or its completion. **2.** Lasting, or aged, 100 years. — *n.* A 100th anniversary or its celebration. — **cen·ten′ni·al·ly,** *adv.*
Centennial State. Colorado; — a nickname, from the date (1876) of its admission to the Union.
cen′ter, cen′tre (sĕn′tẽr), *n.* [OF. *centre*, fr. L. *centrum*, fr. Gr. *kentron* sharp point, center of a circle.] **1.** That point lying equidistant or at the average distance from the exterior points of a figure, sphere, or other body, esp. of the earth. See CIRCLE, *Illust.* **2.** The point round which a body revolves or rotates; hence, a place considered as the middle of activity of some kind; as, a railroad *center*. **3.** The point toward which any force, feeling, or action tends or from which any force or influence takes its origin; as, a storm *center;* also, a point of equilibrium; as, *center* of gravity. **4.** A group of nerve cells having a common function; as, the motor *center*. **5.** *Linguistics.* See HEAD, 17. **6.** *Mach.* **a** One of the two tapered rods, whose ends are usually ground to 60° angles, upon which the work is supported, as in a lathe, and about or with which the work revolves. **b** The conical recess in the end of a shaft or other work, for receiving a center (sense **a**). **7.** *Mil.* **a** The portion of an army between the two wings. **b** That division of a target lying next outside the bull's-eye; also, a shot that strikes it. **8.** [*sometimes cap.*] *Politics.* In some legislative bodies of Europe, those members collectively who have seats in the center of the chamber between the conservatives and liberals; hence, persons of views intermediate between conservative and liberal. See LEFT; RIGHT. **9.** *Sports.* A player who occupies a more or less central position on a team. — *v. i.;* -TERED or -TRED (-tẽrd); -TER·ING (-tẽr·ĭng) or -TRING (-trĭng). To find a center or focus; to rest on or concentrate about a center. — *v. t.* **1.** To place or fix in or at the center. **2.** To collect to a point; concentrate. **3.** To furnish or mark with a center; specif., *Optics*, to adjust (a lens or mirror) so that the axes coincide.
center bit. A bit with a sharp center point for guidance, a scorer for marking the outline of the hole, and a lip for cutting away the wood inside the hole.
cen′ter·board′, cen′tre·board′ (sĕn′tẽr·bōrd′; 70), *n.* *Naut.* In some sailing vessels, a broad board or similar device, set in a casing amidships and pivoted at its forward lower corner, so that it may be lowered to provide a keel and thus prevent leeway or may be raised in shallow water. See SHARPIE, *Illust.*
center of gravity. *Mech.* That point in a body about which all the parts of the body exactly balance each other.
cen′ter·piece′, cen′tre·piece′ (sĕn′tẽr·pēs′), *n.* A piece put in the center of anything; specif., an ornament for the center, as of a table, ceiling, etc.; a central article, item, etc.
center punch. *Mach.* A punch for making holes in sheet metal, having a small conical tip to ensure correct location.
cen·tes′i·mal (sĕn·tĕs′ĭ·măl), *adj.* [L. *centesimus* hundredth.] Hundredth; pertaining to, or having divisions into, hundredths. — **cen·tes′i·mal·ly,** *adv.*
cen·tes′i·mo (-mō), *n.; pl.* -MI (-mē). [It.] The hundredth part of a lira. See MONEY, *Tables.*
cen·tes′i·mo, *n.; pl.* -MOS (-mōz). [Sp. *centésimo*.] In Panama, the hundredth part of a balboa; in Uruguay, the hundredth part of a peso.

cen′ti- (sĕn′tĭ-). [L. *centum.*] A combining form denoting: **a** *Hundred,* as in *centipede.* **b** *Hundredth part,* as in *centimeter.*
cen′ti·are′ (sĕn′tĭ·âr′; *F.* säN′tyȧr′), *n.* [F., fr. *centi-* + *are.*] See METRIC SYSTEM, *Table* 3.
cen′ti·grade (sĕn′tĭ·grād), *adj.* [F., fr. L. *centum* a hundred + *gradus* degree.] Consisting of a hundred degrees or divisions; specif., of or pertaining to the centigrade thermometer. Abbr. *C.*
centigrade thermometer. A thermometer on which the interval between the freezing point and boiling point of water is divided into one hundred parts or degrees, so that 0° C. corresponds to 32° F. and 100° C. to 212° F.; — called also ***Celsius thermometer,*** after Anders Celsius (1701–44), Swedish astronomer, who first described it (1742). See THERMOMETER, *Illust.;* cf. FAHRENHEIT.
cen′ti·gram, cen′ti·gramme (sĕn′tĭ·grăm), *n.* [F. *centigramme.*] See METRIC SYSTEM, *Table* 5.
cen′ti·li′ter, cen′ti·li′tre (-lē′tẽr), *n.* [F. *centilitre.*] See METRIC SYSTEM, *Table* 4.
cen′time (sän′tēm; *F.* säN′tēm′), *n.* [F.] The hundredth part of a franc in France, Belgium, and Switzerland; in Ethiopia, the hundredth part of a thaler; in Haiti, the hundredth part of a gourde. Abbr. *c.*
cen′ti·me′ter, cen′ti·me′tre (sĕn′tĭ·mē′tẽr; sän′tĭ-), *n.* [F. *centimètre.*] See METRIC SYSTEM, *Tables* 1, 2, & 6.
cen′ti·me′ter–gram′–sec′ond, cen′ti·me′tre–gram′–sec′ond, *adj. Physics.* Pertaining to or designating a system of units based upon the centimeter as the unit of length, the gram as the unit of mass, and the mean solar second as the unit of time. Abbr. *C.G.S.*
cen′ti·mo (sĕn′tĭ·mō), *n.; pl.* -MOS (-mōz). [Sp. *céntimo.*] The hundredth part of a bolivar, colon, guarani, or peseta.
cen′ti·pede (sĕn′tĭ·pēd), *n.* [L. *centipeda,* fr. *centum* a hundred + *pes, pedis,* foot.] Any of numerous myriapods with a long flattened body, and the anterior legs modified into poison fangs. See MYRIAPOD.
cen′ti·stere (sĕn′tĭ·stẽr; sän′tĭ-), *n.* [F. *centistère.*] One 100th of a stere. See METRIC SYSTEM, *Table* 6.
cent′ner (sĕnt′nẽr), *n.* [G., a hundredweight, fr. L. *centenarius* of a hundred.] **1.** A commercial hundredweight in several Continental systems, generally 50 kg. or 110.23 lb. avoirdupois. **2.** A weight (***metric centner***) of 100 kg. or 220.46 lb. **3.** The cental.
cen′to (sĕn′tō), *n.; pl.* CENTOS (-tōz). [L.] **1.** *Obs.* A patchwork. **2.** A literary composition formed of selections. **3.** Any work as a map, composed of incongruous parts.
centr-. = CENTRO-.
cen′tra (sĕn′trȧ), *n., pl.* of CENTRUM.
cen′tral (sĕn′trăl), *adj.* [L. *centralis.*] **1.** Relating to, situated in or near, or containing or constituting the center; equidistant or equally accessible from certain points; hence, basic; also, chief; dominant. **2.** *Anat. & Physiol.* Designating the part of the nervous system comprising, in vertebrates, the brain and spinal cord. See NERVOUS SYSTEM. **3.** *Phonet.* = MIXED, 7. — *n.* A telephone exchange; also, an operator handling calls at an exchange. — **cen′tral·ly,** *adv.*
‖**cen·tral′** (sĕn·träl′), *n.* [Amer. Sp.] *Sp. Am. & Phil. I.* A sugar mill which crushes cane for a wide territory.
cen′tral·ism (sĕn′trăl·ĭz′m), *n.* Centralization or the centralizing system, esp. in government. — **cen′tral·ist** (-ĭst), *n. & adj.*
cen·tral′i·ty (sĕn·trăl′ĭ·tĭ), *n.* Quality or state of being central; central situation or tendency.
cen′tral·ize (sĕn′trăl·īz), *v. t.* To bring to a central point; to bring into one system, or under one control. — **cen′tral·i·za′tion** (-ĭ·zā′shŭn; -ī·zā′-), *n.* — **cen′tral·iz′er** (-īz′ẽr), *n.*
Central Powers. Austria-Hungary and Germany and, sometimes, their allies, Bulgaria and Turkey; — so called during World War I.
Central standard time, Central time. See STANDARD TIME.
cen′tre (sĕn′tẽr). Var. of CENTER.
cen′tri- (sĕn′trĭ-). = CENTRO-, as in *centrifugal.*
cen′tric (sĕn′trĭk), *adj.* **1.** Placed in or at the center or middle; central. **2.** Of, pertaining to, or characterized by, a center; specif., *Physiol.,* of or pertaining to a nerve center. — **cen·tric′i·ty** (sĕn·trĭs′ĭ·tĭ), *n.*
cen′tri·cal (-trĭ·kăl), *adj.* Central; centric.
cen·trif′u·gal (sĕn·trĭf′ū·găl), *adj.* [*centri-* + L. *fugere* to flee.] Proceeding away from the center; developing outward; *Physiol.,* efferent; also, using, acting by, or separated by, centrifugal force; — opp. to *centripetal.* — *n.* A machine, as a blower or separator, acting by centrifugal force. — **cen·trif′u·gal·ly,** *adv.*
centrifugal force. That force which tends to impel a thing, or parts of a thing, outward from a center of rotation.
cen′tri·fuge (sĕn′trĭ·fūj), *n.* [F., adj.] A machine using centrifugal force for separating materials of different densities. — **cen′tri·fuge,** *v. t.* — **cen·trif′u·ga′tion** (sĕn·trĭf′ū·gā′shŭn), *n.*
cen·trip′e·tal (sĕn·trĭp′ē·tăl; -t'l), *adj.* [*centri-* + L. *petere* to move toward.] Proceeding or directed toward the center; developing inward; *Physiol.,* afferent; also, using or acting by centripetal force; — opp. to *centrifugal.* — **cen·trip′e·tal·ly,** *adv.*
centripetal force. That force which tends to impel a thing, or parts of a thing, inward toward a center of rotation.
cen′trist (sĕn′trĭst), *n.* [F. *centriste.*] *Politics.* A member of the center. See CENTER, *n.,* 8.
cen′tro- (sĕn′trō-), **centr-.** [Gr. *kentron.*] A combining form meaning *center,* as in **cen′tro·dor′sal, cen′tro·sym·met′ric, cen′tro·sym′me·try,** etc.
cen′tro·some (sĕn′trō·sōm), *n.* [*centro-* + 2d *-some.*] *Biol.* A minute protoplasmic body found in the cytoplasm, less often in the nucleus, of many animal and some plant cells, which takes an important part in mitosis. See CELL, *Illust.* — **cen′tro·som′ic** (-sŏm′ĭk), *adj.*
cen′tro·sphere′ (-sfẽr′), *n.* [*centro-* + *sphere.*] **1.** *Geol.* The central part of the earth. **2.** *Biol.* The central mass of an aster from which the rays extend and within which the centrosome lies when present. Cf. ASTER, 2; see CELL, *Illust.*
cen′trum (sĕn′trŭm), *n.; pl.* -TRUMS (-trŭmz), -TRA (-trȧ). [L.] **1.** A center. **2.** *Anat.* The body of a vertebra See VERTEBRA, *Illust.*
cen′tum lan′guag·es (kĕn′tŭm). See INDO-EUROPEAN LANGUAGES, *Table.*
cen′tu·ple (sĕn′tū·p'l), *adj.* [F., fr. L. *centuplus.*] Hundredfold. — *v. t.;* -TU·PLED (-p'ld); -TU·PLING (-plĭng). To increase a hundredfold.
cen·tu′pli·cate (sĕn·tū′plĭ·kāt), *v. t.* To centuple. — (-kăt), *adj. & n.* Hundredfold.
cen·tu′ri·al (-rĭ·ăl), *adj.* [See CENTURY.] Of or relating to a Roman century or to a hundred years.
cen·tu′ri·on (-rĭ·ŭn), *n.* [F. or L.; F., fr. L. *centurio,* fr. *centuria.*] A captain of a century in the Roman army.
cen′tu·ry (sĕn′tū·rĭ), *n.; pl.* -RIES (-rĭz). [L. *centuria,* fr. *centum* a hundred.] **1.** A sequence or group of a hundred. **2.** A period of 100 years (see MEASURE, *Table* 6); specif., one of the 100-year divisions of the Christian Era. **3.** *Rom. Hist.* **a** A division of the Roman army, prob. orig. of 100 men. **b** A civil division, formed for voting.
century plant. A Mexican fleshy-leaved agave (*Agave americana*) which flowers only once and then dies. See AGAVE, *Illust.*
ceorl (chĕôrl), *n.* [AS. See CHURL.] *O.Eng.Hist.* A freeman who was not a noble; a churl; a villein, — distinguished from a noble or a slave. — **ceorl′ish,** *adj.*
ceph′al·ad (sĕf′ăl·ăd), *adv.* [*cephal-* + L. *ad* to, toward.] *Zool.* Toward the head or anterior end of the body.
ce·phal′ic (sē·făl′ĭk), *adj.* [From L., fr. Gr. *kephalikos,* fr. *kephalē* head.] Of or pertaining to the head; directed toward, or situated near, on, or in the head.

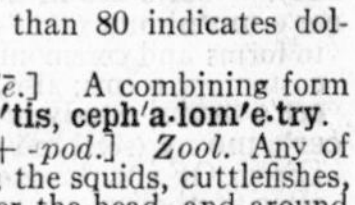
Cephalic Index. 1 Dolichocephalic Cranium; 2 Brachycephalic Cranium.

cephalic index. *Craniom.* A number obtained by dividing the maximum breadth of the cranium by its maximum length and multiplying by 100. A cephalic index of 80 or above indicates brachycephaly, one of less than 80 indicates dolichocephaly.
ceph′a·lo- (sĕf′ȧ·lō-), **cephal-.** [Gr. *kephalē.*] A combining form denoting *the head,* as in **ceph′a·late, ceph′a·li′tis, ceph′a·lom′e·try.**
ceph′a·lo·pod′ (sĕf′ȧ·lō·pŏd′), *n.* [*cephalo-* + *-pod.*] *Zool.* Any of a class (Cephalopoda) of mollusks, containing the squids, cuttlefishes, octopuses, etc., having a tubular siphon under the head, and around the front of the head a group of muscular arms, usually furnished with suckers. Most forms have a bag containing inklike fluid which they can eject from their siphons. — **ceph′a·lo·pod′,** *adj.* — **ceph′a·lop′o·dan** (-lŏp′ō·dăn), *adj. & n.*
ceph′a·lo·tho′rax (-thō′răks), *n.* In arachnids and higher crustaceans, the united head and thorax. See KING CRAB, *Illust.*
-ceph′a·lous (-sĕf′ȧ·lŭs). [Gr. *kephalē* head.] A combining form denoting *having a head of a* (specified) *type,* as in brachy*cephalous.*
Ce′pheus (sē′fūs; sē′fē·ŭs), *n.* [L., fr. Gr. *Kēpheus.*] **1.** *Gr. Myth.* Father of Andromeda. **2.** *gen.* CEPHEI (-fē·ī). A constellation between Cygnus and the North Pole.
cer-. = CERO-.
ce·ra′ceous (sē·rā′shŭs), *adj.* [L. *cera* wax.] Waxy.
ce·ram′al (sē·răm′ăl), *n.* [*ceramic* + *alloy.*] = CERMET.
ce·ram′ic (sē·răm′ĭk), *adj.* [Gr. *keramikos,* fr. *keramos* earthenware.] Of or pertaining to pottery or earthenware.
ce·ram′ics (-ĭks), *n.;* see -ICS. **1.** The art of making articles of baked clay, as pottery, tiles, etc.; — construed as a singular. **2.** Articles formed wholly or partly of clay and baked; — construed as a plural.
ce·ras′tes (sē·răs′tēz), *n.* [L., a horned serpent, fr. Gr. *kerastēs* horned, fr. *keras* horn.] A venomous viper (*Cerastes cornutus*) of the Near East, having a horny process over each eye; — called also *horned viper* or *sand viper* (see VIPER).
ce′rate (sē′rāt), *n.* [L. *ceratum,* neut. past part. of *cerare* to wax, fr. *cera* wax.] *Pharm.* An unctuous preparation for external use, consisting of wax (sometimes resin or spermaceti) mixed with oil, lard, and medicinal ingredients.
cer′a·to- (sĕr′ȧ·tō-), **cerat-.** [Gr. *keras, keratos.*] A combining form meaning *horn,* used in biology.
ce·rat′o·dus (sē·răt′ō·dŭs; sĕr′ȧ·tō′dŭs), *n.* [NL., fr. *cerat-* + Gr. *odous* tooth.] An Australian dipnoan food fish (*Neoceratodus forsteri*), about six feet long, known also as *salmon* and *barramunda.*
Cer′ber·us (sûr′bẽr·ŭs), *n.* [L., fr. Gr. *Kerberos.*] *Gr. & Rom. Myth.* A three-headed dog guarding the entrance to Hades. — **Cer·be′re·an** (sûr·bē′rē·ăn), *adj.*
cer·ca′ri·a (sûr·kā′rĭ·ȧ), *n.; pl.* -RIAE (-ē). [NL., from Gr. *kerkos* tail.] *Zool.* A larval stage of trematode worms, having the shape of a tadpole. — **cer·car′i·al** (-kâr′ĭ·ăl), *adj.*
cere (sẽr), *n.* [F. *cire,* fr. L. *cera* wax.] *Zool.* A soft swollen area, in which the nostrils open, in birds of prey and parrots.
cere, *v. t.* [F. *cirer,* fr. L. *cerare,* fr. *cera* wax.] To wrap in or as in a cerecloth; to wrap (a corpse).
ce′re·al (sẽr′ē·ăl), *adj.* [L. *Cerealis* pert. to Ceres, and hence, to agriculture.] Pertaining to grain or to the grasses which produce it. — *n.* **1.** Any grass yielding grain used for food, as wheat, rice, etc.; also, the grain so produced. **2.** A prepared foodstuff of grain.
cer′e·bel′lum (sĕr′ē·bĕl′ŭm), *n.; pl.* -LUMS (-ŭmz), -LA (-ȧ). [L., dim. of *cerebrum* brain.] *Anat.* A large dorsally projecting part of the hindbrain (which see), anterior to, above, and partly overlapping the medulla. It is concerned with co-ordinating the muscles and maintaining bodily equilibrium. See BRAIN, *Illust.* — **cer′e·bel′lar** (-ẽr), *adj.*
cer′e·bral (sĕr′ē·brăl; sē·rē′brăl), *adj.* [L. *cerebrum* brain.] **1.** Of or relating to the brain or the cerebrum. **2.** Appealing to intellectual appreciation; as, *cerebral* music.
cerebral palsy. *Med.* A disability due to damage of centers of the brain before or during birth resulting in imperfect control of the muscles and marked esp. by muscular in-co-ordination, spastic paralysis, and speech disturbances.
cer′e·brate (sĕr′ē·brāt), *v. i.* To exhibit or experience mental activity; hence, to think. — **cer′e·bra′tion** (-brā′shŭn), *n.*
cer′e·bro- (sĕr′ē·brō-), **cerebr-.** [L. *cerebrum.*] A combining form denoting *cerebrum* or *the brain,* also *cerebral* (*and*), as in **cer′e·broid, cer′e·brot′o·my, cer′e·bro·vis′cer·al** (see -OID, etc.).
cer′e·bro·spi′nal (-spī′năl; -n'l), *adj.* Of or pertaining to the brain and spinal cord; specif., designating that part of the nervous system comprising these with the cranial nerves and the spinal nerves which transmit sensory impulses to the voluntary muscles. See NERVOUS SYSTEM.
cerebrospinal meningitis. *Med.* An infectious, epidemic, febrile, bacterial disease producing headaches, vomiting, delirium, etc., often ending fatally; — called also ***cerebrospinal fever, spotted fever.***
cer′e·brum (sĕr′ē·brŭm; sē·rē′brŭm), *n.; pl.* -BRUMS (-brŭmz), -BRA (-brȧ). [L.] **1.** The brain; — now only figuratively. **2.** *Anat.* **a** *Chiefly Brit.* That part of the brain above and in front of the hindbrain. **b** The expanded anterior portion of the telencephalon, consisting of laterally paired, hollow, externally more or less convoluted lobes (the **cerebral hemispheres**) which are united medially by a large commissure (the corpus callosum) and which, in man and higher mammals, more or less completely overlie the midbrain and cerebellum. See BRAIN, 1. — **ce·re′bric** (sē·rē′brĭk; sē·rĕb′rĭk), *adj.*

cere′cloth′ (sēr′klŏth′; 74), *n.* [From *cered cloth.* See CERE, *v.*] Cloth treated with melted wax or gummy matter, used esp. for wrapping a corpse; cerement.

cere′ment (-mĕnt), *n.* [F. *cirement.*] Usually *pl.* A cerecloth; also, any shroud or wrapping for the dead.

cer′e·mo′ni·al (sĕr′ē·mō′nĭ·ăl; 58), *adj.* Relating to or of the nature of ceremonies or ceremony.

Syn. Ceremonial, ceremonious, formal, conventional mean marked by attention to details as prescribed. Ceremonial and ceremonious both imply strict attention to what is prescribed by the court, polite society, the ritual of a church, etc., but *ceremonial* applies only to things in themselves ceremonies or an essential part of them, and *ceremonious* to persons addicted to ceremonies and to acts attended by ceremony (as, *ceremonial* observance; a very *ceremonious* old man); formal applies both to things prescribed and to the behavior of those obedient, and carries a strong implication of set or established procedure or of stiffness and decorousness; conventional applies to persons or things in accord with the recognized and, frequently, artificial rules and often suggests lack of originality or independence.

— *n.* **1.** A system of rules and ceremonies, enjoined by law or established by custom; ritual. **2.** A ceremonial usage or formality; rite. — **cer′e·mo′ni·al·ism** (-ĭz′m), *n.* — **cer′e·mo′ni·al·ist** (-ĭst), *n.* & *adj.* — **cer′e·mo′ni·al·ly**, *adv.*

cer′e·mo′ni·ous (sĕr′ē·mō′nĭ·ŭs), *adj.* **1.** Ceremonial. **2.** Devoted to forms and ceremonies; punctilious. **3.** According to prescribed or customary forms; also, full of ceremony. — **Syn.** See CEREMONIAL. — **cer′e·mo′ni·ous·ly**, *adv.* — **cer′e·mo′ni·ous·ness**, *n.*

cer′e·mo′ny (sĕr′ē·mō′nĭ *or, esp. Brit.,* -mŭn·ĭ), *n.; pl.* -MONIES (-nĭz). [From OF., fr. L. *caerimonia.*] **1.** A formal act, or series of acts, often symbolical, prescribed by law, custom, or authority, in matters of religion, of state, etc. **2.** A conventional act of civility or etiquette. **3.** A mere outward form, or, loosely, anything done ceremoniously. **4.** Ceremonial observances collectively or as an established order; specif., the social behavior required by strict etiquette; formality.

Ce′res (sē′rēz), *n.* [L., Ceres, corn, grain.] **1.** *Rom. Relig.* Goddess of the growing vegetation, daughter of Ops and Saturn. She was identified with Demeter. **2.** *Astron.* The largest asteroid and the one first discovered (1801).

ce′re·us (sēr′ē·ŭs), *n.* [L., wax candle, fr. *cera* wax; — from the columnar shape of one species.] Any of certain cacti (of *Cereus* and related genera) of the western United States and tropical America, including forms with nocturnal flowers (see NIGHT-BLOOMING CEREUS).

ce′ri·a (sē′rĭ·ȧ), *n.* *Chem.* A white compound, CeO_2, one of the rare earths; cerium dioxide.

ce·rif′er·ous (sē·rĭf′ẽr·ŭs), *adj.* [L. *cera* wax + *-ferous.*] Producing wax.

ce·rise′ (sĕ·rēz′; -rēs′), *n.* [F., a cherry.] A cherrylike color; specif., a color, red in hue, of very high saturation and low brilliance. See COLOR. — **ce·rise′**, *adj.*

ce′rite (sēr′īt), *n.* [From CERIUM.] *Mineral.* A hydrous silicate of cerium and allied metals, generally brownish.

ce′ri·um (sē′rĭ·ŭm), *n.* [From the asteroid *Ceres.*] *Chem.* A metallic element, malleable and ductile, the most abundant of the rare-earth metals. Symbol, *Ce;* at. no., 58; at. wt., 140.13.

cerium metals. *Chem.* A group of related rare-earth metals: lanthanum, cerium, praseodymium, neodymium, illinium, and samarium.

cer′met′ (sûr′mĕt′), *n.* [*cer*amic + *met*al.] A strong alloy of a heat-resistant compound, as titanium carbide, and a metal, as nickel, used esp. for turbine blades; — called also *ceramal.*

cer′nu·ous (sûr′nū·ŭs), *adj.* [L. *cernuus* with the face turned toward the earth.] Inclining; nodding; pendulous.

ce′ro (sēr′ō), *n.; pl.* CERO (-ō) or CEROS (-ōz). See PLURAL, *Note.* [Corrupt. fr. Sp. *sierra* saw, sawfish, cero.] **a** A mackerellike food and game fish (*Sierra cavalla*) chiefly of the West Indies; — called also *cavalla* or *sierra.* **b** The pintado; — called specif. ***spotted cero.***

ce′ro- (sēr′ō-; sēr′ō-), **cer-.** [Gr. *kēros* wax.] A combining form denoting *presence of,* or *likeness to, wax,* as in **ce′ro·plas′tic**, relating to the art of modeling in wax.

ce·rot′ic (sē·rŏt′ĭk), *adj.* [L. *cerotum* a pomade, fr. Gr. *kērōton,* fr. *kēros* wax.] Relating to or designating a fatty acid (**cerotic acid**, $C_{26}H_{52}O_2$) occurring in beeswax.

ce′rous (sēr′ŭs), *adj.* [*cerium* + *-ous.*] *Chem.* Pertaining to, or containing, cerium in the trivalent state.

cer′tain (sûr′tĭn; -t′n), *adj.* [OF., fr. L. *certus* determined, orig. past part. of *cernere* to perceive, decide.] **1.** Fixed; settled. **2.** One or more specific (things or persons not further described); as, a *certain* town; *certain* persons. **3.** Sure or dependable; reliable; as, a *certain* remedy. **4.** Assured in mind; sure. **5.** **a** *Obs.* Thoroughly established, as a belief. **b** *Archaic.* Of a person, determined; steadfast. **6.** Not to be doubted or denied; indubitable. **7.** Destined; sure; — followed by an infinitive; as, it is *certain* to happen. — **Syn.** See SURE.

cer′tain·ly, *adv.* With certainty; surely.

cer′tain·ty (sûr′tĭn·tĭ; -t′n·tĭ), *n.; pl.* -TIES (-tĭz). [OF. *certaineté.*] **1.** Quality, state, or fact of being certain; certitude. **2.** A fact unquestionably established.

Syn. Certainty, certitude, assurance, conviction mean a state of being free from doubt. Certainty and certitude are distinguished only in very precise use, the former implying the existence of objective, unquestionable proofs, the latter, a faith or belief so strong that it resists all attack; assurance stresses sureness or confidence rather than certainty; conviction, though it may or may not imply previous doubt, usually implies that one is or has been convinced and is assured of the truth of something.

cer′tes (sûr′tēz; -tĭz; *rarely, in poetry,* sûrts), *adv.* [F.; prop. a pl. fem.] *Archaic.* Certainly; verily.

cer′ti·fi′a·ble (sûr′tĭ·fī′ȧ·b′l), *adj.* That may be certified.

cer·tif′i·cate (sẽr·tĭf′ĭ·kĭt), *n.* [F. *certificat,* fr. ML. *certificatus,* past part. of *certificare* to make certain.] **1.** A written testimony to the truth of any fact; a certification. **2.** A written declaration legally authenticated. **3.** *Educ.* A document certifying that one has met the requirements of a course or school. — (-kāt), *v. t.* **1.** To verify or attest by certificate. **2.** To furnish with, or authorize by, a certificate. — **cer·tif′i·ca·to′ry** (-kȧ·tō′rĭ *or, esp. Brit.,* -kā′tō·rĭ; -kȧ·tẽr·ĭ), *adj.*

certificate of indebtedness. A short-term negotiable evidence of indebtedness, esp. one issued by a government to meet current expenses.

certificate of stock. An instrument evidencing ownership of one or more shares of the capital stock of a corporation.

cer′ti·fi·ca′tion (sûr′tĭ·fĭ·kā′shŭn; sẽr·tĭf′ĭ·kā′shŭn), *n.* **1.** Act of certifying, or state of being certified; attestation. **2.** A certified statement; a certificate.

cer′ti·fied (sûr′tĭ·fīd), *adj.* Endorsed authoritatively.

certified check. *Banking, U. S.* A check certified to be good by the bank upon which it is drawn.

certified milk. Milk produced in dairies which operate under the rules and regulations of an authorized medical milk commission. Certified milk may be unpasteurized or pasteurized.

certified public accountant. *U. S.* An accountant who has met the requirements of a state law, has been given a state certificate, and is permitted to use the designation C.P.A. Cf. CHARTERED ACCOUNTANT.

cer′ti·fi′er (sûr′tĭ·fī′ẽr), *n.* One who certifies.

cer′ti·fy (-fī), *v. t.* [OF. *certifier,* fr. ML. *certificare,* fr. L. *certus* certain + *facere* to make.] **1.** To attest authoritatively; to verify. **2.** To testify to in writing. **3.** To assure; make certain. **4.** To endorse authoritatively as being of the standard quality, preparation, etc. **5.** *U. S.* Of a bank, to guarantee (a check) as good by so indicating on its face. **6.** In British medicolegal use, to declare insane. — **Syn.** See APPROVE.

cer′ti·o·ra′ri (sûr′shĭ·ō·rā′rī; -râr′ī), *n.* [From *certiorari* to be certified; — a term in the Latin form of the writ.] *Law.* A writ from a superior court to call up for review the records of an inferior court or a body acting in a quasi-judicial capacity.

cer′ti·tude (sûr′tĭ·tūd), *n.* Quality or state of being certain or of feeling certain. — **Syn.** See CERTAINTY.

ce·ru′le·an (sē·rōō′lē·ăn), *adj.* & *n.* [L. *caeruleus.*] Azure.

ce·ru′men (sē·rōō′mĕn), *n.* [NL., fr. L. *cera* wax.] The waxy secretion from the glands of the external ear; earwax. — **ce·ru′mi·nous** (-mĭ·nŭs), *adj.*

ce′ruse (sēr′ōōs; sē·rōōs′), *n.* [F. *céruse,* fr. L. *cerussa.*] **1.** White lead. **2.** A cosmetic containing white lead.

ce′rus·site (sēr′ŭ·sīt), *n.* [L. *cerussa* ceruse.] *Mineral.* Native lead carbonate, $PbCO_3$, occurring in colorless, transparent crystals, and also massive.

cer′vi·cal (sûr′vĭ·kăl; *Brit. also* sûr·vī′kăl), *adj.* [L. *cervix, -icis,* neck.] *Anat.* Of or pertaining to the neck; pert. to the cervix of an organ.

cer′vi·co- (sûr′vĭ·kō-), **cervic-.** A combining form denoting *cervical* (*and*), as in **cer′vi·co·dor′sal.**

cer′vine (sûr′vīn; -vĭn), *adj.* [L. *cervinus,* fr. *cervus* deer.] Deerlike; specif., *Zool.,* of or pertaining to the deer or the subfamily (Cervinae) to which most deer belong.

cer′vix (sûr′vĭks), *n.; pl.* CERVICES (sûr·vī′sēz), CERVIXES (sûr′vĭks·ĕz; -ĭz). [L.] *Anat. & Zool.* The neck, esp. the back part; a necklike or constricted portion of an organ or part, as of the uterus.

Ce·sar′e·an (sē·zâr′ē·ăn), **Ce·sar′i·an.** Var. of CAESAREAN.

ce·sar′e·vitch (sē·zär′ĕ·vĭch), *n.* [Russ. *tsesarevich.*] Formerly, the title of the eldest son of the tsar; later, the heir to the Russian throne. Cf. TSAREVITCH.

ce′si·um (sē′zĭ·ŭm), *n.* [NL., fr. L. *caesius* bluish-gray.] A soft silvery metallic element, the most electropositive of the elements. Symbol, *Cs;* at. no., 55; at. wt., 132.91.

ces′pi·tose (sĕs′pĭ·tōs), *adj.* [L. *caespes* turf.] Pertaining to or like turf; matted or tufted. — **ces′pi·tose·ly**, *adv.*

cess (sĕs), *n.* [For *sess,* contr. fr. ASSESS.] *Dial.* A tax; *Scot.,* a land tax.

cess, *n.* [Prob. contr. fr. *success.*] *Anglo-Irish.* Luck; — chiefly in the phrase *bad cess to,* bad luck to.

ces·sa′tion (sĕ·sā′shŭn), *n.* [F., fr. L. *cessatio,* fr. *cessare.* See CEASE.] A ceasing or discontinuance, as of action; a stop.

ces′sion (sĕsh′ŭn), *n.* [L. *cessio,* fr. *cedere* to give way.] **1.** A ceding or yielding, as of property or rights, to another. **2.** A portion of territory ceded.

cess′pit′ (sĕs′pĭt′), *n.* A pit to receive refuse matter, esp. from sinks and water closets.

cess′pool′ (-pōōl′), *n.* A cistern in a drain, to collect refuse matter, esp. from sinks and water closets.

‖**c′est-à-dire** (sĕ′-tȧ·dēr′). [F.] That is to say; namely.

‖**c′est au′tre chose** (sĕ′-tō′trĕ shōz′). [F.] That is different.

ces′tode (sĕs′tōd), *n.* [Gr. *kestos* girdle.] *Zool.* Any of a class (Cestoda) of internally parasitic flatworms (platyhelminths), including the tapeworms. — **ces′tode**, *adj.* — **ces′toid** (-toid), *adj.* & *n.*

‖**c′est plus qu′un crime, c′est une faute** (sĕ′ plü′ kŭN krēm′, sĕ′-tün′ fōt′). [F.] It is worse than a crime, it is a blunder; — said of the execution of the Duc d'Enghien in France (1804).

‖**c′est se·lon′** (sĕ′ slôN′). [F.] That depends.

ces′tus (sĕs′tŭs), *n.* [L., a girdle, fr. Gr. *kestos,* lit., stitched, embroidered.] *Gr. & Rom. Antiq.* A girdle, esp. that of Aphrodite (or Venus), which gave the wearer the power of exciting love.

ces′tus, *n.* [L. *caestus,* fr. *caedere* to strike.] *Rom. Antiq.* A covering for the hands of boxers, made of leather bands, and often loaded with lead or iron.

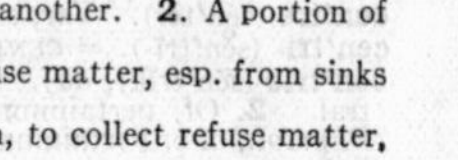

Cestus.

ce·su′ra, ce·su′ral. Vars. of CAESURA, CAESURAL.

ce·ta′cean (sē·tā′shăn), *adj.* [L. *cetus* whale, fr. Gr. *kētos.*] Of or pertaining to an order (Cetacea) of aquatic, mostly marine mammals, consisting of the whales, dolphins, porpoises, narwhals, grampuses, etc., having a large head, fishlike hairless body, and paddlelike forelimbs. — *n.* A cetacean animal. — **ce·ta′ceous** (-shŭs), *adj.*

ce′tane (sē′tān), *n.* [L. *cetus* whale.] *Chem.* A colorless oil, $C_{16}H_{34}$, of the methane series, found in petroleum

cetane number *or* **rating.** A measure of the ignition value of a diesel fuel oil. It is the percentage by volume of cetane in a mixture of cetane and a certain naphthalene derivative (1-methyl-naphthalene) which gives the same ignition lag as the oil being tested. The higher the cetane number the better the ignition value. Cf. OCTANE NUMBER.

‖**ce′te·ris pa′ri·bus** (sĕt′ĕ·rĭs păr′ĭ·bŭs). [L.] Other things (factors, etc.) being equal.

Ce′tus (sē′tŭs), *n.; gen.* CETI (-tī). [L., whale.] An equatorial constellation south of Pisces and Aries.

ce′vi·tam′ic ac′id (sē′vĭ·tăm′ĭk; -vī-). [*ce,* for the letter C + *vitam*in + *-ic.*] *Chem.* Vitamin C (see VITAMIN).

Cey·lon′ moss (sē·lŏn′). An East Indian red alga (*Gracilaria lichenoides*), one of the chief sources of agar-agar.

C.G.S. *Physics.* Abbr. of CENTIMETER-GRAM-SECOND.

Cha'blis' (shă'blē'; shăb'lē), *n.* [From *Chablis*, France.] A white Burgundy wine. See BURGUNDY.
cha'bouk, cha'buk (chä'bo͝ok), *n.* [Hind. *cābuk*, fr. Per.] In the Orient, a long whip, such as is used in flogging.
chac'ma (chăk'mȧ), *n.* [Hottentot.] A South African baboon (*Papio porcarius*).
‖**cha'cun' à son goût** (shȧ'kûɴ'-nȧ' sôɴ' go͞o'). [F.] Everyone to his taste.
chae'ta (kē'tȧ), *n.; pl.* -TAE (-tē). [NL., fr. Gr. *chaitē* hair.] A spine or bristle; a seta.
chae'to- (kē'tō-), **chaet-**. [Gr. *chaitē*.] A combining form meaning *hair, mane*, as in **chae·toph'o·rous**, *Zool.*, bearing bristles or setae.
chae'tog·nath (kē'tŏg·năth), *n.* [NL., fr. *chaeto-* + Gr. *gnathos* jaw.] Any of a class (Chaetognatha) of small, free-swimming marine worms, having movable curved chaetae on either side of the mouth.
chafe (chāf), *v. t.* [OF. *chaufer*, deriv. of L. *calefacere* to make warm, fr. *calere* to be warm + *facere* to make.] **1.** To warm; to heat; — now only in *chafing dish* (which see). **2.** To excite heat in by friction; as, to *chafe* one's hands. **3.** To rub so as to wear away or irritate; as, to *chafe* a cable; clothing that *chafes* one's skin. **4.** To excite anger in; to irritate. — *v. i.* **1.** To rub; to move, as one body on or against another, with friction. **2.** To be vexed or irritated. — *n.* **1.** Irritation; vexation. **2.** Friction; injury caused by friction.
chaf'er (chāf'ẽr), *n.* [AS. *ceafor.*] Any of various large beetles (family Scarabaeidae), as the June beetles, rose beetles, and esp. the cockchafer, feeding on leaves, flowers, etc.
chaff (chȧf; 9), *n.* [AS. *ceaf.*] **1.** The husks of grains and grasses separated from the seed by threshing, winnowing, etc. **2.** Anything light and worthless. **3.** *Bot.* The scales borne on the receptacle, subtending the florets in the heads of many composite plants. See COMPOSITE, *n.*, 2. — **chaff'y**, *adj.*
chaff, *v. t. & i.* To make fun of in a good-natured way; to banter; rally. — *n.* Light jesting talk; banter; raillery. — **chaff'er**, *n.*
chaf'fer (chăf'ẽr), *n.* [AS. *cēap* a bargain, price + *faru* a journey, hence, orig., a going to bargain, to market.] **1.** *Obs.* Traffic; buying and selling. **2.** Act of chaffering; bargaining. — *v. i.* **1.** To bargain or negotiate; to discuss terms. **2.** To bandy idle talk; to chatter. — *v. t. Obs.* **a** To buy or sell; trade in. **b** To exchange or bandy, as words. — **chaf'fer·er**, *n.*
chaf'finch (chăf'ĭnch), *n.* [AS. *ceaffinc.* See CHAFF; FINCH.] A European finch (*Fringilla coelebs*), the male of which has a reddish breast plumage and a cheerful song. It is often kept as a cage bird.
chaf'ing dish (chāf'ĭng). A kind of vessel for cooking at table, made on the principle of a double boiler.
Cha'gas' dis·ease' (chä'găs; shȧ'gȧs). [After Carlos *Chagas* (1879–1934), Brazilian physician.] *Med.* A form of trypanosomiasis that occurs esp. in Brazil.
cha·grin' (shȧ·grĭn' *or, esp. Brit.*, shȧ·grēn', shăg'rĭn), *n.* [F., fr. *chagraigner* to grieve, fr. OF. *graignier*, fr. *graim* sorrowful, sad.] Mental disquietude or distress caused by the humbling of pride, by failure, disappointment, etc.; mortification. — (shȧ·grĭn'; -grēn'), *v. t.;* CHA·GRINED' (-grĭnd'; -grēnd'); -GRIN'ING. To vex acutely by disappointing or the like; to mortify; — chiefly in the *passive*.
chain (chān), *n.* [OF. *chaeine* (F. *chaîne*), fr. L. *catena.*] **1.** A series of links or rings, usually of metal, connected, or fitted into one another, used for various purposes, as of support, of restraint, of ornament, of the transmission of mechanical power, etc. **2.** That which confines, fetters, or secures; a fetter; esp., *pl.*, bonds; fetters; hence, bondage. **3.** A series of things linked together; as, a *chain* of mountains; a *chain* of radio stations; a *chain* of events. **4.** A chainlike measuring instrument. The ***engineer's chain*** is 100 feet long; the ***Gunter's*** (*or* ***surveyor's***) ***chain***, 66 feet. See MEASURE, *Tables* 2 & 4. **5.** *Biol.* A series of organisms adhering together end to end. — *v. t.* **1.** To fasten, bind, or connect with a chain. **2.** To fetter; restrain. — **chain'less**, *adj.* — **chain'let**, *n.*
chain gang. A gang, esp. of convicts, chained together.
chain letter. A letter designed to pass from one to another of a series of recipients.
chain lightning. Lightning which appears to move very rapidly in a long angular, zigzag, or forked course.
chain mail. Flexible armor of interlinked metal rings. See MAIL, *Illust.*
chain measure. See MEASURE, *Table* 2.
chain pump. A pump consisting of an endless chain dipping below the water to be raised and running over a wheel by which it is moved.
chain'-re·act'ing pile. See PILE, *n.*, 5.
chain reaction. *Physics & Chem.* A reaction, either ordinary or nuclear, yielding energy or products which cause further reactions of the same kind, and so becoming self-sustaining, as in the fission, or splitting, of a uranium atom by a neutron, whereby more neutrons are released which cause further fissions, and so on.
chain reactor. *Physics & Chem.* = 2d PILE, *n.*, 5.
chain shot. *Mil.* A kind of shot consisting of two balls or half balls united by a short chain.
chain stitch. An ornamental stitch like the links of a chain, used in crocheting, sewing, and embroidery. See STITCH, *Illust.*
chain store. One of a number of retail stores under the same ownership, under a central management, selling uniform merchandise, and following a uniform policy.
chair (châr), *n.* [OF. *chaiere*, fr. L. *cathedra*, fr. Gr. *kathedra*, fr. *kata* down + root of *hezesthai* to sit.] **1.** A seat, usually movable, for one person. It usually has four legs and a back, and may have arms. **2.** An official seat of authority, state, or dignity; hence, the office, or place of authority, dignity, etc., or the dignity itself; specif., the office of a professor, judge, etc. **3.** A sedan chair. **4.** The presiding officer of an assembly; a chairman. **5.** Short for ELECTRIC CHAIR. — *v. t.* **1.** To place in a chair; esp., to install in a chair of office; to enthrone. **2.** *Eng.* To carry publicly in triumph on a chair or seat.
chair car. *U. S.* **a** A parlor car. **b** A railroad car having reclining chairs or chairs with high adjustable backs.
chair'man (châr'măn), *n.* **1.** The occupant of a chair of office or authority; specif., the presiding officer of a committee, meeting, or any organized body. **2.** One whose business it is to carry or wheel persons in a chair or sedan. — **chair'man·ship**, *n.* — **chair'wom'an** (-wo͝om'ăn), *n.*
chair rail. *Building.* A wooden molding on a wall around a room to protect the wall from being damaged by the backs of chairs.
chaise (shāz), *n.* [F., chair, chaise, or carriage, var. of *chaire* pulpit.] Any of various carriages; as: **a** A two-wheeled carriage for one or two persons, with a calash top, and the body hung on leather straps. It is usually drawn by one horse. **b** A similar four-wheeled pleasure carriage. **c** = POST CHAISE. **d** Loosely, any light carriage or pleasure cart.

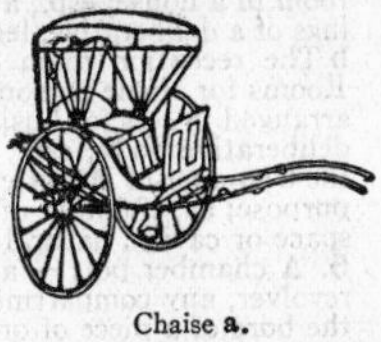
Chaise a.

chaise longue (shāz' lông'; *F.* shâz'); *pl. E.* CHAISE LONGUES (lôngz'), *F.* CHAISES LONGUES (shâz' lông'). [F., lit., long chair.] An elongated seat or couch, having usually a support for the back at one end only and often eight legs.
cha·la'za (kȧ·lā'zȧ), *n.; pl.* -ZAS (-zȧz), -ZAE (-zē). [NL., fr. Gr. *chalaza* hail.] *Embryol.* Either of a pair of spiral bands in the white of a bird's egg, extending from the ball of yolk and attached near each end of the egg to the lining membrane. See EGG, *Illust.*
chal·ced'o·ny (kăl·sĕd'ō·nĭ; kăl'sē·dō'nĭ; -dŭn·ĭ), *n.; pl.* -NIES (-nĭz). [L. *chalcedonius.*] *Mineral.* A translucent variety of quartz, commonly pale-blue or gray, with waxlike luster. Varieties of special or variegated color are known as *agate, carnelian, chrysoprase*, etc.
chal'cid fly (kăl'sĭd). [Gr. *chalkos* copper; — referring to their metallic colors.] A fly of any species of a very large group of hymenopterous insects, mostly very minute and in the larval state parasitic on the larvae or pupae of other insects. They benefit man by destroying many injurious insects. — **chal'cid**, *adj. & n.*
chal'co- (kăl'kō-). [Gr. *chalkos.*] A combining form meaning *copper, brass*, as in *chalcography.*
chal·cog'ra·phy (kăl·kŏg'rȧ·fĭ), *n.* [*chalco-* + *-graphy.*] Act or art of engraving on copper or brass, esp. for printing. — **chal·cog'ra·pher** (-fẽr), *n.* — **chal'co·graph'ic** (kăl'kō·grăf'ĭk), **chal'co·graph'i·cal** (-ĭ·kăl), *adj.* — **chal·cog'ra·phist** (kăl·kŏg'rȧ·fĭst), *n.*
chal'co·py'rite (kăl'kō·pī'rīt; -pĭr'īt), *n.* [*chalco-* + *pyrite;* — from its color.] A yellow copper-iron sulfide, $CuFeS_2$, an important ore of copper; copper pyrites.
Chal·da'ic (kăl·dā'ĭk), *adj. & n.* Chaldean.
Chal·de'an (-dē'ăn), *adj.* [L. *Chaldaeus*, fr. Gr. *Chaldaios.*] Of or pert. to Chaldea or its people; hence, of or pert. to astrology or magic. — *n.* **1.** One of an ancient Semitic tribe that became dominant in Babylonia. **2.** A person versed in Babylonian lore, esp. astrology; also, a soothsayer. **3.** The language of the Chaldeans.
Chal·dee' (kăl·dē'; kăl'dē), *adj. & n.* Chaldean; — used also, improperly, for Biblical Aramaic.
chal'dron (chôl'drŭn), *n.* [OF. *chauderon.* Same word as *caldron.*] A nearly obsolete English dry measure for coal, lime, etc., commonly equal to 32 bushels.
cha·let' (shă·lā'; shăl'ā; *F.* shȧ'lĕ'), *n.* Often, erroneously, **châ·let'**. [F.] **1.** A herdsman's hut or a cabin in the Swiss mountains; also, a small wooden house of the Alpine regions of Europe, esp. of Switzerland. **2.** A cottage or house in the style of a Swiss cottage.

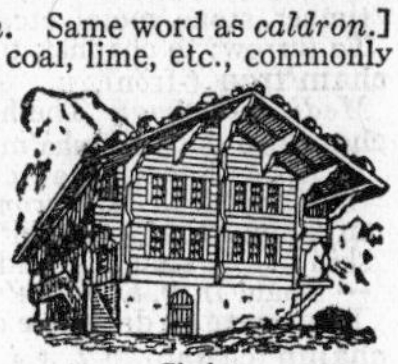
Chalet.

chal'ice (chăl'ĭs), *n.* [OF., fr. L. *calix* cup.] **1.** A drinking cup; goblet; esp., the cup used in the sacrament of the Lord's Supper; also, its contents. **2.** The cup-shaped interior of a flower.
chal'iced (-ĭst), *adj.* Having a cup-shaped blossom; — said of flowers.
chalk (chôk), *n.* [AS. *cealc*, fr. L. *calx, calcis*, stone, lime.] **1.** A soft limestone, white, gray, or buff in color, chiefly composed of the shells of foraminifers. **2.** Chalklike material, esp. that used in the form of crayons; also, a piece of such material. **3.** A score, reckoning, or account of credit given; hence, credit; tick. — *v. t.* **1.** To treat or mix with chalk; specif.: **a** To rub or mark with chalk. **b** To whiten with, or as with, chalk. **2.** To write, draw, sketch, or outline with chalk. **3.** To record in chalk (esp. an account); to score; to charge. — *adj.* Drawn in, on, or with chalk. — **chalk'y**, *adj.*
chalk'stone' (chôk'stōn'), *n. Med.* = TOPHUS.
chal'lenge (chăl'ĕnj; -ĭnj), *n.* [OF. *chalenge, chalonge*, claim, contest, fr. *chalengier, chalongier*, to claim, dispute, fr. L. *calumniari* to attack with false accusations.] **1.** An invitation to engage in a contest; specif., a summons to fight, as a duel; also, the message conveying the summons. **2.** Act of calling in question, or the state of being called in question; dispute; as, to bring one's title into *challenge.* **3.** *U. S.* An exception to a person as not legally qualified to vote. It must be made when the ballot is offered. **4.** *Immunol.* A test; specif., a test of immunity by exposure to virulent infective material after specific immunization. **5.** *Law.* A formal exception taken to a juror or jurors arrayed for the trial of a cause; also, a similar exception to a member of a court martial. A ***peremptory challenge*** is one of those allowed to be made in criminal cases without assigning any cause. **6.** *Mil.* Act of a sentry in questioning, examining, or demanding the countersign of anyone who appears near his post or attempts to pass the lines.
— *v. t.;* CHAL'LENGED (-ĕnjd; -ĭnjd); CHAL'LENG·ING (-ĕn·jĭng; -ĭn·jĭng). **1.** To claim as due; to lay claim to, as attention, respect, etc. **2.** To take exception to; to call in question; to dispute. **3.** To call or invite defiantly to a contest of any kind; to dare. **4.** To summon to a duel. **5.** *U. S.* To object to the reception of the vote of, as on the ground that the person is not qualified as a voter. **6.** *Law.* To object to or take formal exception to, as to a juror, or a member of a court. **7.** *Mil.* To question, and demand an identification or the countersign from (one who attempts to pass the lines). — *v. i.* **1.** To assert a right; to claim a place. **2.** Of a hound, to give tongue on finding the scent. **3.** To make a challenge. **4.** *Law.* To take exception; object. — **chal'lenge·a·ble**, *adj.* — **chal'leng·er** (-ĕn·jẽr; -ĭn·jẽr), *n.*
chal'lis (shăl'ĭ *or, esp. Brit.*, shăl'ĭs), *n.* Also **chal'lie, chal'ly** (shăl'ĭ). A very lightweight wool, or cotton and wool, fabric, usually printed.
chal'one (kăl'ōn), *n.* [Gr. *chalōn*, pres. part. of *chalaein* to slacken.] *Physiol.* An internal secretion which depresses activity. Cf. HORMONE.
cha·lyb'e·ate (kȧ·lĭb'ē·āt), *adj.* Impregnated with salts of iron; having a taste due to iron; as, *chalybeate* springs. — *n.* A chalybeate water, liquid, or medicine.
cham (kăm). Var. of KHAN.
cha·made' (shȧ·mäd'), *n.* [F., fr. Pg. *chamada*, fr. *chamar* to call, fr. L. *clamare.*] *Archaic. Mil.* A signal made for a parley by beat of drum or sound of trumpet.

cham′ber (chām′bẽr), *n.* [OF. *chambre*, fr. L. *camera* vault, in LL. chamber, fr. Gr. *kamara* anything with an arched covering.] **1.** A room in a house; esp., a bedroom. **2.** Hence: **a** A hall for the meetings of a deliberative, legislative, or judicial body; as, senate *chamber*. **b** The reception room of a great personage. **c** *pl. Chiefly Brit.* Rooms for single persons in a lodging house or tenement; also, rooms arranged in sets for business offices, etc. **3.** A legislative, judicial, or deliberative body; esp., a division of a parliament or legislature; as, the *Chamber* of Deputies; also, a voluntary council for some business purpose; as, *chamber* of commerce. **4.** A compartment; an enclosed space or cavity, natural or artificial; as, the *chamber* of a canal lock. **5.** A chamber pot; — a euphemism. **6.** *Firearms & Ordn.* **a** In a revolver, any compartment in the cartridge cylinder. **b** That part of the bore of a piece of ordnance which holds the charge. **7.** *Law.* A room where a lawyer or judge transacts business. — *v. t. & i.* To put in or reside in a chamber. — *adj.* Occurring or conducted in, pertaining to, or suitable for a chamber; as, *chamber* music. — **cham′bered** (-bẽrd), *adj.*

chamber concert. A concert of chamber music.

cham′ber·er (chām′bẽr·ẽr), *n.* **1.** *Obs.* A chambermaid; also, a valet. **2.** *Archaic.* A frequenter of ladies' chambers; a gallant.

cham′ber·lain (-lĭn), *n.* [OF. *chamberlenc* (F. *chambellan*), of Teut. origin.] **1.** *Archaic.* An attendant on a sovereign or lord in his bedchamber. **2.** In Europe, one of the high officers of a court. **3.** A steward, as in a nobleman's household. **4.** A treasurer or receiver of public money; as, city *chamberlain.*

cham′ber·maid′ (-mād′), *n.* A maidservant who has the care of chambers, making the beds, sweeping, etc.

chamber music. Vocal or instrumental music adapted to performance in a chamber, or small audience hall.

chamber of commerce. A board or association to promote the commercial interests of a locality.

chamber pot. A bedchamber vessel for urine.

cham′bray (shăm′brā), *n.* [From *Cambrai*, France.] A gingham woven with colored warp and white filling yarns.

cha·me′le·on (kȧ·mē′lē·ŭn; kȧ·mēl′yŭn), *n.* [From L., fr. Gr. *chamaileōn*, fr. *chamai* on the ground, dwarf + *leōn* lion.] **1.** Any of a group of lizards remarkable for the changes of color of the skin according to the mood of the animal or surrounding conditions. **2.** A person who is fickle or inconstant. — **cha·me′le·on′ic** (kȧ·mē′lē·ŏn′ĭk), *adj.*

cham′fer (chăm′fẽr), *n.* [F. *chanfrein*, fr. past part. of *chanfraindre*, fr. *chant* edge + OF. *fraindre* to break, fr. L. *frangere.*] The surface formed by cutting away the angle formed by two faces of a piece of timber, stone, metal, etc. Cf. SCARF JOINT, *Illust.* — *v. t.* **1.** *Carp.* To furrow; to channel; to flute. **2.** To make a chamfer on; to bevel.

cham′fron (-frŏn), *n.* Also **cham′frain** (-frĭn). [F. *chanfrein.*] *Medieval Armor.* The headpiece of a horse's armor.

cham′ois (shăm′ĭ; shȧ′mwä′), *n. sing. & pl.* [F., fr. LL. *camox.*] **1.** A small goatlike antelope (*Rupicapra rupicapra*) of Europe and the Caucasus. **2.** (*pron. usually* shăm′ĭ) Also **cham′my, sham′my, sha·moy′** (shȧ·moi′). A soft, pliant leather, prepared from the skin of the chamois, and also from the skin of the sheep, goat, etc. — (shăm′ĭ), *v. t.;* CHAM′OISED (shăm′ĭd); CHAM′OIS·ING (shăm′ĭ·ĭng). To prepare or dress like chamois.

champ (chămp), *v. t. & i.* To bite and chew with force and noise; as, to *champ* the bit. — **champ,** *n.*

cham′pac (chăm′păk; chŭm′pŭk), *n.* Also **cham′pak.** [Hind. *campak*, fr. Skr. *campaka.*] An East Indian tree (*Michelia champaca*) of the magnolia family, the yellow fragrant flowers of which yield **cham′pa·ca oil** (chăm′pȧ·kȧ; chŭm′-).

cham·pagne′ (shăm·pān′), *n.* [F. See CHAMPAIGN.] **1.** Properly, a white sparkling wine made in the old province of Champagne, France. **2.** Loosely, any wine of the same type made elsewhere.

cham·paign′ (shăm·pān′ *or, esp. Brit.*, chăm′pān), *n.* [OF. *champaigne*, fr. L. *campania.* See CAMPAIGN.] **1.** A stretch of flat open country. **2.** Country that is flat and open. **3.** *Obs.* A battlefield. — **cham·paign′,** *adj.*

cham′per·ty (chăm′pẽr·tĭ), *n.* [F. *champart* field rent, fr. ML. *campi pars*, fr. L. *campus* field + *pars* share.] *Law.* A proceeding by which a person having no legitimate concern in a suit bargains to aid in or carry on its prosecution or defense in consideration of his receiving, in the event of success, a share of the matter in suit. — **cham′per·tous** (-tŭs), *adj.*

cham·pi′gnon (shăm·pĭn′yŭn *or, esp. Brit.*, chăm-; *F.* shäɴ′pē′nyôɴ′), *n.* [F., ult. fr. L. *campania.* See CHAMPAIGN.] An edible fungus, esp. the common meadow mushroom (*Agaricus campestris*). See MUSHROOM, 1.

cham′pi·on (chăm′pĭ·ŭn; 58), *n.* [OF., fr. LL. *campio*, fr. L. *campus* (battle)field.] **1.** A combatant; a fighter; esp., one who acts or speaks in behalf of a person or a cause; a defender. **2.** Any person or thing receiving or winning first prize or place in competition. — *v. t.* **1.** *Obs.* To challenge; to defy. **2.** To attend or defend as champion; to protect. — **Syn.** See SUPPORT. — *adj.* Unexcelled; first-rate. — **cham′pi·on·ess,** *n.* — **cham′pi·on·less,** *adj.*

cham′pi·on·ship′, *n.* Act of championing, or state of being champion; advocacy; defense; leadership; supremacy.

Champs′ É′ly′sées′ (shäɴ′-zā′lē′zā′). [F.] Literally, Elysian fields; specif., an avenue in Paris celebrated for its beauty.

chance (chȧns; 9), *n.* [OF. *cheance*, fr. LL. *cadentia* a falling (esp. of dice, of fortune), fr. L. *cadere* to fall.] **1.** The happening of events; fortune; hap. **2.** Something that befalls as the result of unknown or unconsidered forces; a happening; often, *Archaic*, a mishap; mischance. **3.** That which happens to one; fortune; luck; lot. **4.** An opportunity; as, a *chance* to escape. **5.** In games of chance, any one of the contingencies on which a player takes a risk; as, number nine is my *chance;* hence, in general, a risk or gamble. **6.** A possibility of something happening; as, the *chances* are against him. **7.** A hypothetical agent regarded as determining what happens; fortune; fate; — often personified. **8.** *Sports.* Any opportunity to retire, or to assist in retiring, a player, as in baseball. — **Syn.** Accident, fortune, luck, hazard. — *v. i.;* CHANCED (chȧnst); CHANC′ING (chȧn′sĭng). To happen, come, or arrive without design or expectation. — **Syn.** See HAPPEN. — *v. t.* To take the chances of; to risk; as, to *chance* a fall. — *adj.* Happening by chance; casual.

chance′ful (-fo͝ol; -f'l), *adj.* **1.** *Archaic.* Dependent on chance; casual. **2.** Eventful.

chan′cel (chȧn′sĕl), *n.* [OF., fr. L. *cancelli* lattices, crossbars. The *chancel* was formerly enclosed with lattices or crossbars.] **1.** That part of a church reserved for the use of the clergy. **2.** All that part of a church which is east of the nave, including choir and sanctuary.

chan′cel·ler·y (chȧn′sĕ·lẽr·ĭ), *n.; pl.* -LERIES (-ĭz). **1.** The position, court, or department of a chancellor; hence, the office of the secretary or notary of a court. **2.** The building or room where a chancellor's office is. **3.** The office of an embassy, consulate, or the like.

chan′cel·lor (chȧn′sĕ·lẽr; 9), *n.* [OF. *chancelier*, fr. L. *cancellarius* chancellor, fr. *cancelli* lattices, which surrounded the seat of judgment.] **1.** A secretary, esp. an official one of a nobleman, prince, or king. **2.** Formerly, the chief minister of state in certain European states; also, the prime minister (Reichskanzler) in Germany. **3.** The chief secretary of an embassy. **4.** Elliptically: **a** The ***lord chancellor***, the chief chancery, or equity, judge in England. **b** Any of various other officials, as the chancellor of the exchequer. **5.** The head of some universities. **6.** *Law, U. S.* A judge in a court of chancery or equity in various states; specif., the presiding judge. — **chan′cel·lor·ship′,** *n.*

chancellor of the exchequer. A member of the British cabinet in charge of the public income and expenditure as the highest finance minister of the government.

chance′-med′ley (chȧns′mĕd′lĭ), *n.* [Prop., a mingled (OF. *medlée, meslée*, past part. fem.) chance.] **1.** *Law.* Accidental homicide, not entirely without fault of the killer, but without evil intent. **2.** Haphazard action.

chan′cer·y (chȧn′sẽr·ĭ), *n.; pl.* -CERIES (-ĭz). [OF. *chancellerie*, fr. *chancelier.* See CHANCELLOR.] **1.** In England, the court presided over by the lord chancellor, which was the highest court of judicature next to Parliament until under the Judicature Act of 1873 it became the Chancery Division of the High Court of Justice. **2.** In the United States, a court of equity. **3.** A court of record or office of public records. **4.** A chancellor's court or office, or the building or room where it is; a chancellery. **5.** Chancery proceedings, practice, or principles. **6.** *Wrestling.* Any hold that imprisons the head.
— ***in chancery.*** **1.** *Law.* In litigation in a court of chancery, as an estate. **2.** *Boxing.* Of the head of an antagonist, in a secure position under one's arm, so that one can pommel it. **3.** In a helpless position.

chan′cre (shăng′kẽr), *n.* [F.] *Med.* A venereal sore or ulcer; specif., the initial lesion of true syphilis, whether forming a distinct ulcer or not. — **chan′crous** (-krŭs), *adj.*

chan′croid (shăng′kroid), *n.* [*chancre* + *-oid.*] *Med.* A venereal sore resembling a chancre, but differing from it in being the starting point of a purely local process and never a systemic disease, and in being caused by a different microorganism; — called also *soft chancre.*

chanc′y (chȧn′sĭ; 9), *adj.;* CHANC′I·ER (-sĭ·ẽr); CHANC′I·EST. [From CHANCE, *n.*] **1.** *Scot.* Lucky; auspicious. **2.** *Colloq.* Uncertain; risky; hazardous.

chan′de·lier′ (shăn′dĕ·lēr′), *n.* [F., fr. OF. *chandelabre*, fr. L. *candelabrum.*] A candlestick, electric or gas fixture, or the like, having several branches and hanging from a ceiling. Cf. CANDELABRUM.

chan·delle′ (shăn·dĕl′; shăn′dĕl), *n.* [F., a candle, hence, a perpendicular support, a lob in tennis, a zoom.] *Aviation.* An abrupt climbing turn in which the airplane is carried upward at the expense of its stored kinetic energy. — *v. i.;* CHAN′DELLED′ (-dĕld′); CHAN·DELL′ING. To execute a chandelle.

chan′dler (chȧn′dlẽr), *n.* [OF. *chandelier*, fr. *chandoile* candle, fr. L. *candela.*] **1.** A maker or seller of candles. **2.** A dealer in groceries, provisions, small wares, etc.

chan′dler·y (-ĭ), *n.; pl.* CHANDLERIES (-ĭz). **1.** A place where candles, etc., are kept. **2.** The commodities sold by, or the business of, a chandler.

change (chānj), *v. t.;* CHANGED (chānjd); CHANG′ING (chān′jĭng). [OF. *changer*, fr. LL. *cambiare* to exchange, barter, of Celt. origin.] **1.** To alter by substituting something else for, or by giving up for something else; to put or take another or others in place of. **2.** To make different; to convert. **3.** To change the clothes or other coverings of; as, to *change* a bed. **4.** To give and take reciprocally; to exchange; as, to *change* places with another. **5.** To give, or receive, smaller denominations of money (*change*) or money of another currency for; as, to *change* a bill. — *v. i.* **1.** To be altered; to vary. **2.** Of the moon, to pass from one phase to another. **3.** *Colloq.* To change one's clothes. **4.** To make a change of place or circumstances; to shift; as: **a** To change vehicles, as railroad cars. **b** To effect an exchange.

Syn. **Change, alter, vary, modify** mean to make or become different. **Change** implies either an essential difference, sometimes amounting to a loss of identity, or the substitution of one thing for another; **alter** implies difference in some particular respect without suggesting loss of identity; **vary** implies a difference or differences due to shifting, diversification, growth, etc.; **modify** suggests a difference that limits or restricts: often, loosely, it implies the making of slight alterations.

change countenance. To change in color or expression of countenance, so as to show fright, surprise, chagrin, etc. — ***change face.*** **a** To change countenance. **b** To change front. — ***change front.*** Orig., *Mil.*, to face in another direction; now usually, to make a striking shift in argument or bearing.

— *n.* **1.** A substitution of one thing in the place of another. **2.** Any variation or alteration. **3.** Changefulness; fickleness. **4.** A place where merchants and others meet to transact business; an exchange. **5.** Of the moon, a passing from one monthly revolution to another; also, a passing from one phase to another. **6.** Change of key; modulation. **7.** That which makes a variety, or may be substituted. **8.** A fresh set of clothes to replace those in use; also, act of changing one's clothes. **9.** Money of lower denomination, or of one currency, exchanged for money of higher denomination, or of another currency. **10.** The amount returned when payment is tendered by a coin or note exceeding the sum due. **11.** *Bell Ringing.* Any order in which a set of bells is struck.

Syn. **Change, mutation, permutation, vicissitude** mean a variation or modification. **Change**, the inclusive word, may imply any variation whatsoever, whether affecting the thing essentially or superficially; **mutation** stresses lack of permanence and stability and regards change as inevitable; **permutation** implies transposition within a group or combination without variation of the constituent elements; **vicissitude** implies a change so great that it seems a reversal of what has been.

change′a·bil′i·ty (chān′jȧ·bĭl′ĭ·tĭ), *n.* Changeableness.

change′a·ble (chān′jȧ·b'l), *adj.* **1.** Capable of change; variable; inconstant. **2.** Appearing different, as in color, from different points of view, as certain fabrics. — **change′a·ble·ness,** *n.* — **change′a·bly** (-blĭ), *adv.*

change′ful (chānj′fo͝ol), *adj.* Full of change; uncertain. — **change′ful·ly,** *adv.* — **change′ful·ness,** *n.*

change′less (chānj′lĕs; -lĭs), *adj.* Unchanging; constant. — **change′less·ly,** *adv.* — **change′less·ness,** *n.*

change′ling (chānj′lĭng), *n.* [*change* + 1st *-ling.*] **1.** *Archaic.* One apt to change; a waverer; turncoat. **2.** One that is left or taken, often secretly, in the place of another; esp., a child secretly exchanged for another in infancy. **3.** *Archaic.* A simpleton; idiot.

change of life. *Physiol.* The menopause.

chang′er (chān′jẽr), *n.* **1.** One who or that which changes. **2.** *Obs.* A money-changer.

change ringing. *Bell Ringing.* The continual production, without repetition, of changes on bells.

chan′nel (chăn′ĕl; -′l), *n.* [OF. *chanel,* fr. L. *canalis.* See CANAL.] **1.** The bed where a natural stream of water runs. **2.** The deeper part of a river, harbor, strait, etc. **3.** A closed course or conduit through which anything flows, as a tube or a duct. **4.** That through which anything passes; passage. **5.** A long gutter, groove, or furrow. **6.** A rolled metal bar of |_____| section; — short for **channel bar, iron, rail, steel,** etc. **7.** *Geog.* A strait, or narrow sea, between two portions of land; as, the English *Channel.* **8.** [For CHAINWALE.] *Naut.* One of the flat ledges of heavy plank or metal bolted edgewise to the outside of a vessel, to increase the spread of the shrouds. **9.** *Radio & Television.* A narrow band of frequencies of sufficient width for transmission. — *v. t.;* CHAN′NELED (-ĕld; -′ld) or -NELLED; CHAN′NEL·ING or -NEL·LING. **1.** To form a channel in; to groove. **2.** To convey into or through a channel or channels.

chan′son (shăn′sŏn; *F.* shäɴ′sôɴ′), *n.; pl.* CHANSONS (-sŏnz; *F.* -sôɴ′). [F., fr. L. *cantio* song.] A song.

‖**chan′son′ de geste** (shäɴ′sôɴ′ dē zhĕst′). [F., song of heroic deeds.] Any Old French epic poem about events of early French history, as the *Chanson de Roland.*

chant (chånt; 9), *v. i.* [OF. *chanter,* fr. L. *cantare,* fr. *canere* to sing.] **1.** To sing; to warble. **2.** To utter or repeat a statement monotonously. **3.** *Music.* To sing a chant or as in a chant; to intone. — *v. t.* **1.** To sing. **2.** To celebrate in song. **3.** To talk or tell of monotonously. **4.** *Music.* To sing or recite after the manner of a chant; to intone.
— *n.* **1.** Song; singing. **2.** *Music.* A short and simple melody or phrase characterized by the reciting of an indefinite number of syllables to one tone, used in public worship. **3.** A composition chanted or arranged for chanting. **4.** Mode of singing or speaking in musical monotones.

chant′er (chån′tẽr), *n.* **1.** One who chants; a singer, esp. a cantor or a chorister. **2.** The chief singer or priest of a chantry. **3.** In a bagpipe, the pipe on which the melody is played. **4.** *Eng. Slang.* A tricky horse trader. — **chant′ress** (chån′trĕs; -trĭs), *n. fem.*

chan′te·relle′ (shăn′tē·rĕl′; chăn′tē·rĕl′), *n.* [F.] An edible mushroom (*Cantharellus cibarius*), rich yellow in color, with a pleasant aroma.

‖**chan′teuse′** (shäɴ′tûz′), *n.* [F.] A female singer; cantatrice.

chant′ey, chant′y (shån′tĭ; chån′tĭ; 9), *n.; pl.* -EYS, -IES (-tĭz). [F. *chantez,* imper. of *chanter* to sing.] *Naut.* A song sung by sailors in rhythm with their work.

chan′ti·cleer (chăn′tĭ·klēr), *n.* [From the name of the cock in "Reynard the Fox"; OF. *chanter* to sing, crow + *cler* clear.] A cock; — used chiefly as a proper name.

chan′try (chån′trĭ; 9), *n.; pl.* -TRIES (-trĭz). **1.** An endowment for chanting of masses and offering of prayers. **2.** A chapel or altar endowed for this purpose.

cha′os (kā′ŏs), *n.* [L., chaos (in senses 1 & 2), fr. Gr. *chaos.*] **1.** *Obs.* A chasm or abyss. **2.** The confused state of primordial matter before the creation of orderly forms; — sometimes personified [*cap.*], after the Greeks, as the most ancient of the gods. **3.** Any confused collection or state of things; complete disorder. — **Syn.** See ANARCHY.

cha·ot′ic (kā·ŏt′ĭk), *adj.* Also **cha·ot′i·cal** (-ĭ·kăl). In a state of chaos; completely confused. — **cha·ot′i·cal·ly,** *adv.*

chap (chăp; chåp), *n.* [From CHAPMAN.] **1.** *Dial.* A buyer; customer. **2.** *Colloq.* (*pron.* chăp) A fellow.

chap (chăp), *v. t. & i.;* CHAPPED (chăpt) or CHAPT; CHAP′PING. To open in slits or chinks; to split; to crack; to cause the skin of to crack or become rough. — *n.* **1.** A cleft or crack. **2.** *Scot.* A blow; rap; knock.

chap (chŏp; chăp), *n.* A jaw or the fleshy covering of a jaw; chop; — commonly in *pl.,* and used of animals.

‖**cha′pa·ra′jos** (chä′pä·rä′hōs), ‖**cha′pa·re′jos** (-rā′hōs), *n. pl.* [Mex. Sp.] Overalls of leather, usually open at the back, worn esp. by cowboys as a protection against thorns.

chap′ar·ral′ (chăp′ă·răl′), *n.* [Sp., fr. *chaparro* evergreen oak.] A thicket of dwarf evergreen oaks; hence, any dense thicket of stiff or thorny shrubs or dwarf trees.

chaparral cock *or, fem.,* **hen.** = ROAD RUNNER.

chaparral pea. A thorny Californian shrub (*Pickeringia montana*) forming thickets in tracts of chaparral.

chap′book′ (chăp′bŏŏk′), *n.* Any small book containing ballads, tracts, etc., such as were formerly carried about for sale by chapmen.

chape (chāp), *n.* [OF., fr. LL. *cappa.*] The metal mounting or trimming of a scabbard or sheath.

cha′peau′ (shă′pō′), *n.; pl.* -PEAUX (-pōz′; *F.* -pō′), -PEAUS (-pōz′). [F., fr. OF. *chapel* hat. See CHAPLET.] A hat.

chap′el (chăp′ĕl; -′l), *n.* [OF. *chapele,* fr. LL. *cappella,* orig., a short cloak (*cappa*); later, a reliquary, chapel (because the building where St. Martin's cloak was preserved came to be called *cappella*).] **1.** A subordinate place of worship, esp. of Christian worship; a sanctuary other than a parish or cathedral church. **2.** A room, recess, or cell in a cathedral or other church, containing an altar and separately dedicated. **3.** A choir of singers belonging to a chapel, as of a prince. **4.** A chapel service, as at a college or university. **5.** *Print.* Formerly, a printing office. **6.** *Brit.* A place of worship used by others, esp. Nonconformists, than members of an established church.

chap′er·on, chap′er·one (shăp′ẽr·ōn), *n.* [F. *chaperon.*] A person, esp. a matron, who accompanies one or more young unmarried women in public for propriety; hence, any mature person who is present for propriety at a social gathering of young persons. — *v. t.* To attend as a chaperon. — **chap′er·on′age** (-ōn′ĭj), *n.*

chap′fall′en (chŏp′fôl′ĕn; chăp′-), *adj.* Also **chop′fall′en** (chŏp′-). Having the lower chap, or jaw, drooping, as from weariness or humiliation.

chap′i·ter (chăp′ĭ·tẽr), *n.* *Arch.* A capital.

chap′lain (chăp′lĭn), *n.* [OF. *chapelain,* fr. ML., fr. *cappella.* See CHAPEL.] **1.** A clergyman who has a chapel. **2.** A clergyman officially attached to the army or navy, to some public institution, or to a family or court. **3.** A clergyman or layman chosen to conduct religious exercises for a society, etc. — **chap′lain·cy** (chăp′lĭn·sĭ), *n.* — **chap′lain·ship,** *n.*

chap′let (chăp′lĕt; -lĭt), *n.* [OF. *chapelet,* dim. fr. *chapel* hat, garland, dim. fr. LL. *cappa.* See CAP.] **1.** A garland or wreath to be worn on the head. **2.** A string of beads; a necklace. **3.** *Arch.* A small molding, carved into beads, pearls, etc. **4.** *R.C.Ch.* A third of a rosary, or 55 (sometimes 59) beads, used in praying; also, the prayers recited over this. — **chap′let·ed,** *adj.*

chap′man (chăp′măn), *n.; pl.* -MEN (-mĕn). [AS. *cēapman,* fr. *cēap* trade + *man* man.] **1.** *Archaic.* One who buys and sells; merchant; dealer. **2.** *Brit.* A peddler; hawker.

chaps (shăps; chăps), *n. pl.* *Colloq.* Short for CHAPARAJOS.

chap′ter (chăp′tẽr), *n.* [OF. *chapitre,* fr. L. *capitulum,* dim. of *caput* head.] **1.** A main division of a book, treatise, or the like. Abbr. *chap., ch.,* or *c.* **2.** A regular assembly of the canons of a cathedral or collegiate church, or of canonesses, monks, members of an order, etc. **3.** A body or community of those who hold a chapter, or an organized branch or body of some society or fraternity. **4.** *Brit.* A division of the acts of Parliament of a single session. Abbr. *c.* **5.** *R.C.Ch.* A short passage of Scripture between the last psalm and the hymn in lauds and the little hours. — *v. t.* To divide into, or arrange in, chapters, as a book.

chapter house. **1.** A house or room where a chapter meets. **2.** *U. S.* A meeting place or residence of a college fraternity.

‖**cha·que′ta** (chä·kā′tä), *n.* [Sp.] A jacket; specif., a heavy jacket of leather or cloth worn by cowboys.

char (chär). Var. of CHARE.

char, *n.; see* PLURAL, *Note,* 3. Also **charr.** [Gael. *ceara,* lit., blood-colored, fr. *cear* blood. From its red belly.] Any of a genus (*Salvelinus*) of trout having small scales. See TROUT, 1.

char (chär), *v. t. & i.;* CHARRED (chärd); CHAR′RING. **1.** To reduce to charcoal or carbon by burning; to burn. **2.** To burn slightly or partly; to scorch.

char′-à-banc′ (shăr′ȧ·băng′), **char′-à-banc′** (shăr′ȧ·băng′; -bäɴ′), *n.; pl.* CHARABANCS (-băngz′), CHAR-À-BANCS (-băngz′; -bäɴz′). [F. *char à bancs.*] A long open vehicle, typically an open motor coach, having several rows of seats extending across its width and facing forward.

char′ac·ter (kăr′ăk·tẽr; kăr′ĭk-; *before 1700, often* kȧ·răk′tẽr, *now dial. only*), *n.* [L., an instrument for marking, character, fr. Gr. *charaktēr,* fr. *charassein* to make sharp, to engrave.] **1.** A sign or token placed upon an object as an indication of some special fact, as ownership or origin; a mark, brand, or stamp. **2.** Hence: **a** A graphic symbol of any sort; esp., a graphic symbol employed in recording language, as a letter. **b** Writing; printing. **c** Style of writing or printing. **d** A private mode of writing; cipher. **3.** An attribute, quality, or property; esp., a distinguishing attribute. **4.** Quality, position, rank, or capacity; status; as, in his *character* as a son. **5.** The aggregate of distinctive qualities belonging to an individual or a race; the stamp of individuality impressed by nature, education, or habit; hence, *Colloq.,* particular kind or sort. **6.** The estimate put upon a person or thing; reputation; repute. **7.** Moral vigor or firmness, esp. as acquired through self-discipline. **8.** A description or detailed account of the qualities of a person; as, the "*Characters*" of Theophrastus. **9.** A written statement as to behavior, habits, competency, etc., given by an employer to an employee. **10.** A person regarded as characterized by notable traits; a personage; sometimes, *Colloq.,* an odd or eccentric person. **11.** One of the persons of a drama or novel. — **Syn.** See QUALITY: DISPOSITION: TYPE. — *v. t.* **1.** To engrave; inscribe; write. **2. a** *Archaic.* To represent; figure. **b** To characterize. — **char′acter·less,** *adj.*

char′ac·ter·is′tic (kăr′ăk·tẽr·ĭs′tĭk; kăr′ĭk-), *adj.* **1.** Pertaining to, or serving to constitute, the character; distinctive; typical. **2.** Serving as a character; serving to denote position in a scheme of classification. — *n.* A trait, quality, or property distinguishing an individual, group, or type. — **char′ac·ter·is′ti·cal** (-tĭ·kăl), *adj.* — **char′ac·ter·is′ti·cal·ly,** *adv.*

Syn. **Characteristic, individual, peculiar, distinctive** mean indicating a special quality or qualities. **Characteristic** applies to something that distinguishes and serves to identify a person or thing or group; **individual,** to something that distinguishes a person or thing from every other member of its class or kind; **peculiar,** to something, such as a quality, character, or emotion, which is the private and undisputed possession of an individual or group; **distinctive,** to something which marks an individual or group as apart from all others of its kind.

char′ac·ter·ize (kăr′ăk·tẽr·īz; kăr′ĭk-), *v. t.* **1.** To indicate or delineate the character of; to describe. **2.** To be a characteristic of; to distinguish as a trait. **3.** To give character to. — **char′ac·ter·i·za′tion** (-ĭ·zā′shŭn; -ī·zā′-), *n.*

char′ac·ter·y (kăr′ăk·tẽr·ĭ; kăr′ĭk-; *formerly also* kȧ·răk′tẽr·ĭ), *n.* Characters or symbols used to express thought.

cha·rade′ (shȧ·rād′ *or, esp. Brit.,* shȧ·räd′), *n.* [F.] A guessing game in which each syllable of a word to be found is represented by a tableau or by dramatic action.

char′coal′ (chär′kōl′), *n.* **1.** A dark or black porous form of carbon prepared from vegetable or animal substances, as by charring wood in a kiln from which air is excluded. **2.** *Fine Arts.* **a** A piece or pencil of fine charcoal used as a drawing implement. **b** A drawing made with such a pencil. — *v. t.* **1.** To mark, write, or draw with charcoal. **2.** To asphyxiate with charcoal fumes.

chard (chärd), *n.* [From F. *carde* chard, fr. Pr. *cardo.*] A variety of beet (*Beta vulgaris cicla*) with large leaves and succulent stalks, often cooked as a potherb; — often called *Swiss chard.*

chare (châr), **char** (chär), *n.* [AS. *cerr, cyrr,* turn, occasion, business.] A turn or occasional piece of work; a chore. — *v. i.;* CHARED (chârd) or CHARRED (chärd); CHAR′ING or CHAR′RING. To do odd jobs; to work as charwoman.

charge (chärj), *v. t.;* CHARGED (chärjd); CHARG′ING (chär′jĭng). [OF. *chargier,* deriv. of L. *carrus* wagon.] **1.** To lay or put a load on or in; to load. **2.** To place a charge, as of powder, within or upon. **3.** To task or load (*with*) mentally; to burden. **4.** To command, instruct, or exhort with authority. **5.** To accuse; to make a charge against. **6.** To impute or ascribe; to lay to one's charge. **7.** To bear down upon; to attack. **8.** To subject to a pecuniary charge or liability; to make liable for. **9.** To fix or demand as a price; also, to set a price on. **10.** To place something to the account of as a debt; to debit. **11.** *Elec.* To restore (the active materials in a battery) by the passage of a direct current through it in the opposite direction to that of discharge. **12.** *Her.* To assume as a bearing; as, he *charges* three roses or; to place a bearing on; as, he *charges* his shield with three roses or. **13.** *Mil.* To bring (a weapon) to a position fitted for attack; level. — **Syn.** See COMMAND. — *v. i.* **1.** To make a charge, or impetuous onset; to rush. **2.** To demand or set a price. **3.** To deliver a charge, as a bishop. **4.** To squat, with its head on its forepaws; — said of a dog. — *n.* [OF.] **1.** A load; a burden. **2.** The quantity, as of powder, electricity, ore, fuel, etc., which any apparatus, as a gun, battery, furnace, etc., is intended to receive and fitted to hold at one time. **3.** A duty or task laid upon a person; responsibility; obligation. **4.** An order; a command. **5.** An accusation of a wrong or offense; allegation. **6.** An address containing instruction or exhortation; as, the *charge* of a bishop to his clergy. **7.** A person or thing entrusted to the care of another. **8.** Pecuniary burden; expense. **9.** The price demanded for a thing or service. **10.** *Bookkeeping.* An entry or account of something due from one party to another. **11.** *Her.* A figure borne on the field; a bearing. **12.** *Law.* At the close of a trial, the statement made by the judge to the jury of the principles of law involved, etc. **13.** *Mil.* Act of rushing upon an enemy; an attack; also, signal for attack. — **Syn.** Price, expense, cost.

char′gé′, *n.* In full **char′gé′ d'af·faires′** (shär′zhā′ dă·fâr′; *F.* shȧr′-zhā′ dȧ′fâr′), *n.; pl.* CHARGÉS D'AFFAIRES (shär′zhāz′ dă·fâr′; *F.* shȧr′-zhā′ dȧ′fâr′). [F., charged with affairs.] **a** A temporary substitute for an ambassador or minister plenipotentiary. **b** A diplomatic representative of an inferior grade, accredited by the government of one state to the minister of foreign affairs of another.

charge′a·ble (chär′jȧ·b'l), *adj.* **1.** *Obs.* **a** Burdensome. **b** Weighty. **c** Responsible. **2.** That may be charged; as, a man *chargeable* with murder.

charge′ful (chärj′fo͝ol; -f'l), *adj.* *Obs.* Burdensome; expensive.

charg′er (chär′jẽr), *n.* *Archaic.* A large flat platter for carrying meat.

charg′er, *n.* One that charges; as: **a** A horse trained to charge; an officer's mount. **b** *Elec.* A device for charging storage batteries.

char′i·ly (châr′ĭ·lĭ), *adv.* In a chary manner; carefully.

char′i·ness (-ĭ·nĕs; -nĭs), *n.* **1.** Quality of being chary; caution. **2.** Carefully preserved state; integrity. *Shak.*

char′i·ot (chăr′ĭ·ŭt), *n.* [OF., fr. *char* car.] A wheeled vehicle; as: **a** Among the ancients, a two-wheeled vehicle for war, racing, processions, etc. **b** A light four-wheeled pleasure or state carriage. — *v. t. & i.* To drive or go in or as in a chariot.

char′i·ot·eer′ (chăr′ĭ·ŭt·ēr′), *n.* **1.** One who drives a chariot. **2.** [*cap.*] The constellation Auriga.

cha·ris′ma (kȧ·rĭz′mȧ), *n.* [Gr., gift.] A quality of extraordinary spiritual power attributed to a person or office capable of eliciting popular support in the direction of human affairs. — **char′is·mat′ic** (kăr′-ĭz·măt′ĭk), *adj.*

char′i·ta·ble (chăr′ĭ·tȧ·b'l), *adj.* [OF.] **1.** Liberal in benefactions to the poor; beneficent. **2.** Of or pertaining to, or springing from, charity; relating to almsgiving. **3.** Liberal in judging others; lenient. — **Syn.** Benevolent, humane, humanitarian, philanthropic. — **char′i·ta·ble·ness**, *n.* — **char′i·ta·bly** (-blĭ), *adv.*

char′i·ty (chăr′ĭ·tĭ), *n.; pl.* -TIES (-tĭz). [F. *charité*, fr. L. *caritas* dearness, love, fr. *carus* dear, loved.] **1.** Christian love; specif.: **a** *Now Rare.* Divine love for man. **b** Act of loving all men as brothers because they are sons of God. **2.** An act or feeling of affection or benevolence. **3.** Good will to the poor and the suffering; almsgiving; also, alms; hence, public provision for the relief of the poor. **4.** Lenience in judging men and their actions. **5.** An eleemosynary foundation or institution. — **Syn.** See MERCY.

cha′ri·va′ri (shä′rē·vä′rē; *also, U. S.*, shȧ·rĭv′ȧ·rē′, shĭv′ȧ·rē), *n.* [F.] A mock serenade of discordant noises, made with kettles, tin horns, etc.; a shivaree. Cf. CALLITHUMP. — **cha′ri·va′ri**, *v. t. & i.*

chark (chärk), *n.* *Obs. exc. Dial.* Charred wood or coal; charcoal; coke; cinder. — *v. t.* To burn to charcoal; to char.

char′kha (chŭr′kȧ), *n.* Also **char′ka**. [Hind. *carkhā* spinning wheel.] *India.* A domestic spinning wheel.

char′la·tan (shär′lȧ·tăn), *n.* [F., fr. It. *ciarlatano*, fr. *ciarratano* seller of papal indulgences.] A quack; a pretender to knowledge or ability. — **char′la·tan′ic** (-tăn′ĭk), *adj.*

char′la·tan·ism (-ĭz'm), **char′la·tan·ship′**, *n.* Charlatanry.

char′la·tan·ry (-rĭ), *n.; pl.* -RIES (-rĭz). Undue pretension to skill; quackery; also, an act or instance of quackery.

Charles's (chärl′zĭz), *or* **Charles′, Wain.** [*Charles* (i. e., *Charlemagne*) + *wain.*] The Big Dipper (see DIPPER, 2).

Charles′ton (chärlz′tŭn), *n.* [From *Charleston*, S. C.] A type of lively dance, in $\frac{4}{4}$ time.

Char′ley horse (chär′lĭ). *Colloq., U. S.* Stiffness from muscular strain in an arm or leg, as of a baseball player.

char′lock (chär′lŏk), *n.* [AS. *cerlic.*] A wild mustard (*Brassica kaber*), often troublesome in grainfields.

char′lotte (shär′lŏt), *n.* [F., fem. of *Charlot*, dim. of *Charles.*] A kind of pudding of fruit, gelatin, etc., enclosed in a mold of bread or cake.

char′lotte russe′ (shär′lŏt ro͞os′; *F.* shȧr′lôt′ rüs′). [F., lit., Russian charlotte.] A charlotte made with cake and a whipped-cream or custard-gelatin filling.

charm (chärm), *n.* [AS. *cirm, cyrm.* Cf. CHIRM.] *Obs.* Song or singing, as of birds or persons; melody.

charm, *n.* [OF. *charme*, fr. L. *carmen* song, verse, incantation.] **1.** Incantation; hence, any action, process, or thing believed to have magic power; a talisman or spell. **2.** Anything worn to avert ill or secure good fortune; amulet. **3.** A trait or quality that fascinates and allures, as if by a spell; hence, that which fascinates; any alluring quality; as, displaying all her *charms*. **4.** Any small decorative object, as a seal or a key, worn on a watch chain or the like. **Syn.** See FETISH. — *v. t.* **1.** To affect by or as by a charm or magic. **2.** To attract irresistibly; to delight exceedingly. **3.** To subdue or overcome by some secret power, or by that which gives pleasure. **4.** To endow with supernatural powers by charms; esp., to protect by or as if by charms; as, a *charmed* life. — **Syn.** See ATTRACT. — *v. i.* **1.** To use magic arts or occult power. **2.** To act as a charm; to please greatly.

charm′er, *n.* One who charms, or has power to charm.

charm′ing, *adj.* **1.** Making use of charms. **2.** Pleasing the mind or senses in a high degree. — **charm′ing·ly**, *adv.*

char′nel (chär′nĕl; -n'l), *n.* [OF., a charnel, as adj., carnal, fr. L. *carnalis.* See CARNAL.] **a** A burial place; a cemetery. **b** = CHARNEL HOUSE. — *adj.* Fit for, being, or suggestive of a charnel; sepulchral.

charnel house. A house, vault, or the like, often in connection with a church, where dead bodies or the bones of the dead are deposited.

Cha′ron (kā′rŏn; kâr′ŏn), *n.* [L., fr. Gr. *Charōn.*] **1.** *Gr. Myth.* The son of Erebus. He ferried the souls of the dead over the Styx. **2.** *Humorous.* A ferryman.

char′poy′ (chär′poi′), *n.* Also **char′pai′** (-pī′). [Hind. *cārpāī*, fr. Per., lit., four-footed.] *Anglo-Ind.* The common light bedstead or cot of India.

char′qui (chär′kē), *n.* [Sp. *charqui, charqué*, fr. Quechua *charqui* dried meat.] Jerked beef. See 2d JERK, *v. t.*

charr (chär). Var. of CHAR, fish.

chart (chärt), *n.* [F. *charte* charter, formerly also map, fr. L. *charta* sheet of paper.] **1.** A map; esp.: **a** A map for the use of navigators. **b** An outline map exhibiting, in geographical aspect, climatic variations, a plan of military operations, or the like. **2.** A sheet giving information in tabular form; also, (1) a graph, (2) a sheet of paper ruled and suitably graduated for use in a recording instrument. — *v. t.* To draw or exhibit in a chart; to map or graph.

char·ta′ceous (kär·tā′shŭs), *adj.* [L. *chartaceus.*] Resembling, or of the nature of, paper; papery.

char′ter (chär′tẽr), *n.* [OF. *chartre*, fr. L. *chartula* a little paper, dim. of *charta.* See CHART.] **1.** A written instrument executed in due form; as: **a** A deed. **b** A grant or guarantee of rights, franchises, or privileges, from the sovereign power of a state or country. Cf. MAGNA CHARTA. **c** Permission from the constituted authorities of an order, society, or fraternity, to form a lodge, branch, or chapter. **2.** A special privilege, immunity, or exemption. **3.** *Com.* Short for CHARTER PARTY. — *v. t.* **1.** To grant a charter to. **2.** To hire or let by charter party. **3.** To hire, esp. for exclusive use. — **Syn.** See HIRE. — **char′ter·age** (-ĭj), *n.* — **char′ter·er**, *n.*

char′tered ac·count′ant (chär′tẽrd). A member of an institute of chartered accountants in the British Empire. Abbr. *C. A.* Cf. CERTIFIED PUBLIC ACCOUNTANT.

charter party. *Com.* A mercantile lease of a vessel, or part of a vessel, to another person to be used by him in transportation for his own account.

Chart′ism (chär′tĭz'm), *n.* [F. *charte* charter.] *Eng. Hist.* The principles or practices of a body of political reformers (1837–48) whose platform for social reform was stated in a document called the ***National, or People's, Charter***; also, the movement itself. — **Chart′ist**, *n. & adj.*

char·tog′ra·pher (kär·tŏg′rȧ·fẽr), **char′to·graph′ic, char·tog′ra·phy**, etc. Vars. of CARTOGRAPHER, etc.

char·treuse′ (shär·tro͞oz′; *F.* shȧr′trûz′), *n.* [F.] **1.** (*pronounced* shȧr′trûz′) A Carthusian monastery; esp., ***La Grande Chartreuse***, chief house of the order until 1903, near Grenoble, France (see CARTHUSIAN). **2.** A liqueur, yellow, green, or white in color, made by Carthusian monks. **3.** The yellowish or yellowish-green color of this liqueur.

char′tu·lar′y (kär′tū·lĕr′ĭ *or, esp. Brit.*, -lẽr·ĭ), *n.; pl.* -IES (-ĭz). [ML. *chartularium*, fr. L. *chartula* a little paper.] A register of charters; esp., a book or books containing duplicates of all charters, title deeds, etc.

char′wom′an (chär′wo͝om′ăn), *n.* [See CHARE a chore.] A woman hired for odd jobs of domestic work, or for such work by the day.

char′y (châr′ĭ), *adj.;* CHAR′I·ER (-ĭ·ẽr); -I·EST. [AS. *cearig* careful, fr. *cearu, caru*, care.] **1.** *Rare.* **a** Treasured; dear. **b** Fastidious; also, reluctant. **2. a** Cautiously sparing; as, *chary* of bestowing praise. **b** Cautiously watchful; as, *chary* of one's own reputation. — **Syn.** See CAUTIOUS.

Cha·ryb′dis (kȧ·rĭb′dĭs), *n.* See SCYLLA.

chase (chās), *v. t.* [OF. *chacier*, deriv. of L. *captare* to strive to seize. See CATCH.] **1.** To pursue in order to seize, molest, make prize of, etc.; hence, to follow persistently, regularly, or sportively. **2.** Specif., to hunt; as, to *chase* the boar. **3.** To cause to depart or fly by threatening or molesting; put to flight. — **Syn.** See FOLLOW. — *v. i.* To pursue; also, *Colloq.*, to run speedily. — *n.* **1.** Act or practice of chasing; esp., with *the*, the hunting of game. **2.** That which is chased; esp., the quarry. **3.** *Eng.* An unenclosed preserve for game.

chase, *n.* [F. *châsse, chas*, fr. L. *capsa* box, case.] **1.** A prolonged hollow; furrow; as: **a** The part of a cannon from the trunnions to the mouth or the swell of the muzzle. **b** A groove; a trench. **2.** *Print.* A rectangular steel or iron frame into which pages or columns are fastened for printing or to make plates. — *v. t.* **1.** To groove or indent. **2.** [Contr. of ENCHASE.] To ornament (a surface of metal) by embossing, engraving, or the like. — **chas′er** (chās′ẽr), *n.*

chas′er (chās′ẽr), *n.* **1.** One who or that which chases; specif.: **a** A hunter. **b** A steeplechaser. **c** A small, speedy airplane used in repelling aircraft. **d** *Naut.* (1) A pursuing ship. (2) Also **chase gun.** A cannon at the bow or stern of an armed vessel used in pursuit. **2.** *Colloq., U. S.* A small drink, as of water, after strong liquor.

chasm (kăz'm), *n.* [L. *chasma*, fr. Gr. *chasma.*] **1.** A deep breach, as in the earth; an abyss; gorge. **2.** A hiatus; gap. — **chas′mal** (kăz′-măl), *adj.* — **chasm′y** (kăz′m·ĭ), *adj.*

chas·sé′ (shă·sā′ *or, esp. Brit.*, shă′sā; *often, colloq.*, să·shā′), *n.* [F.] A form of gliding dance step. — *v. i.;* CHAS·SÉD′ (-sād′); CHAS·SÉ′ING. To make a chassé.

chasse′pot′ (shȧs′pō′), *n.* [After A. A. *Chassepot*, French inventor.] A type of breech-loading, center-fire rifle.

chas′seur′ (shȧ′sûr′), *n.* [F.] **1.** A huntsman. **2.** One of a body of light troops, esp. in the French army, trained for rapid movements. **3.** A liveried attendant; footman.

chas′sis (shăs′ĭ; -ĭs), *n.; pl.* CHASSIS (shăs′ĭz). [F. *châssis.*] **1.** The under part of an automobile, consisting of the frame with the wheels and machinery. **2.** The framework supporting the body of an airplane. **3.** In coast-artillery gun mounts, the movable railway along which the top carriage and gun move. **4.** *Radio.* The frame on which are mounted the parts of a receiving set; also, the assemblage of parts thus mounted.

chaste (chāst), *adj.* [OF., fr. L. *castus* pure, chaste.] **1.** Innocent of unlawful sexual intercourse; virtuous. **2.** Unmarried; celibate. **3.** Pure in thought and act; modest. **4.** Pure and simple in design and expression; not ornate. — **chaste′ly**, *adv.* — **chaste′ness**, *n.*

Syn. Chaste, pure, modest, decent mean free from all taint of that which defiles. Chaste strictly implies a refraining from all acts, thoughts, etc., that are not virginal or in keeping with one's marriage vows; in current use, it also implies avoidance of anything that would debase or cheapen, as in style, etc.; pure differs from *chaste* in implying innocence and absence of temptation rather than control over one's impulses and actions; **modest** and **decent** are especially applied to behavior and dress as outward manifestations of inward chastity or purity.

chas'ten (chās''n), *v. t.* [OF. *chastier*, fr. L. *castigare* to punish, fr. *castus* pure + *agere* to drive.] **1.** To correct by punishment or by subjection to suffering, trial, etc. **2.** To purify or refine, by freeing from faults, excesses, etc. — **Syn.** See PUNISH. — **chas'ten·er**, *n.*

chas·tise' (chăs·tīz'), *v. t.* [See CHASTEN; -IZE.] **1.** To punish, as by whipping; to discipline, esp. with a lash, rod, or the like. **2.** *Archaic.* To chasten. — **Syn.** See PUNISH. — **chas'tise·ment** (chăs'tĭz·mĕnt; chăs·tīz'-), *n.* — **chas·tis'er** (chăs·tīz'ẽr), *n.*

chas'ti·ty (chăs'tĭ·tĭ), *n.* [OF. *chasteté.*] State or quality of being chaste; esp.: **a** Continence. **b** Virginity.

chas'u·ble (chăz'ū·b'l; chăs'-), *n.* [F., fr. LL. *casubla* a hooded garment.] *Eccl.* The outer vestment of the celebrant at Mass. See VESTMENT, *Illust.*

chat (chăt), *v. i.;* CHAT'TED; CHAT'TING. [From CHATTER.] To talk in a light, familiar manner; to converse informally. — *n.* **1.** Chatter; small talk. **2.** Light, familiar conversation; informal talk. **3.** Any of several oscine birds so called from their notes, esp. of the genus *Saxicola*, including the European *stonechat* and *whinchat* (see these terms), and in America the genus *Icteria*, including the ***yellow-breasted chat*** (*I. virens*) and the Pacific coast ***long-tailed chat*** (*I. v. longicauda*). Cf. WHEATEAR.

châ·teau' (shă·tō'; *F.* shä'tō'), *n.; pl.* -TEAUX (-tōz'; *F.* -tō'). [F., a castle.] **1.** A feudal castle in France. **2.** A large country house. — *adj.* [*cap.*] Designating any of several French wines made on wine-producing estates; as, **Châ'teau' La'fite'** (shä'tō' lȧ'fēt'), etc.

chat'e·lain (shăt'ĕ·lān; *F.* shä'tlăN'), *n.* [F. *châtelain.*] A castellan.

chat'e·laine (shăt'ĕ·lān; *F.* shä'tlĕn'), *n.* [F. *châtelaine.*] **1.** The wife of a chatelain; the mistress of a château. **2.** A broochlike clasp or hook from which a watch, purse, etc., is worn suspended.

cha·toy'ant (shȧ·toi'ănt; *F.* shȧ'twȧ'yäN'), *adj.* [F., pres. part., deriv. of *chat* cat.] Marked by a play of colors or lusters, as a cat's eye in the dark; as, *chatoyant* gems or silks. — **cha·toy'an·cy** (shȧ·toi'ăn·sĭ), *n.*

chat'tel (chăt''l), *n.* [OF. *chatel.* See CATTLE.] **1.** A slave; a bondman. **2.** *Law.* Any item of movable or immovable property except real estate, or the freehold, or the things which are parcel of it.

chattel mortgage. A mortgage on personal property.

chat'ter (chăt'ẽr), *v. i.* [Imitative.] **1.** To utter rapidly speechlike but inarticulate sounds, as some birds. **2.** To talk idly, incessantly, or with undue rapidity. **3.** To make a noise by rapid collisions, as the teeth. **4.** To vibrate rapidly in cutting, as a tool. — *v. t.* **1.** To utter rapidly, idly, or indistinctly. **2.** To cut (work) unevenly with a chattering tool. — *n.* Chattering sounds, talk, or noise.

chat'ter·box' (-bŏks'), *n.* An incessant chatterer; magpie.

chat'ter·er (-ẽr), *n.* **1.** One that chatters. **2.** Any of various passerine birds, as the waxwings.

chatter mark. **1.** One of the fine undulations formed on the surface of work by a chattering tool. **2.** *Geol.* One of a series of short curved cracks on a glaciated rock surface, transverse to the glacial striae.

chat'ty (chăt'ĭ), *adj.* Of the nature of, or given to, chat; talkative. — **chat'ti·ly**, *adv.* — **chat'ti·ness**, *n.*

chauf·feur' (shō·fûr'; shō'fẽr), *n.* [F., lit., stoker, fr. *chauffer* to heat.] One whose work is the operation of a motor vehicle.

chaul·moo'gra (chôl·mōō'grȧ), *n.* [Bengali *cā(u)lmugrā*, fr. *cā(u)l* rice + *mugrā* a fibrous plant.] An East Indian tree (*Taraktogenos kurzii*, family Flacourtiaceae) the seeds of which yield an acrid, clear oil (**chaulmoogra oil**) used in treating leprosy and certain skin diseases.

chaunt, chaunt'er, etc. Archaic vars. of CHANT, etc.

‖**chaus'sure'** (shō'sür'), *n.* [F.] Covering for the foot.

Chau·tau'qua (shȧ·tô'kwȧ), *n.* [From *Chautauqua* lake, town, and county, in western New York.] [*often not cap.*] An assembly for educational purposes, combining lectures, entertainments, etc., often held outdoors, modeled after summer schools established at Chautauqua, N. Y.

chau'vin·ism (shō'vĭn·ĭz'm), *n.* [F. *chauvinisme;* — from Nicolas *Chauvin* of Rochefort, a soldier of the First Republic and Empire, whose demonstrative patriotism and attachment to Napoleon came to be ridiculed by his comrades.] Vainglorious or exaggerated patriotism. Cf. JINGOISM. — **chau'vin·ist** (-ĭst), *n. & adj.* — **chau'vin·is'tic** (-ĭs'tĭk), *adj.* — **chau'vin·is'ti·cal·ly** (-tĭ·kăl·ĭ), *adv.*

chaw (chô), *v. t., v. i., & n.* *Now Vulgar.* Chew.

chay (shā), *n.* A corrupt. of CHAISE, mistaken as a plural.

chay (chā; chī), *n.* [Malayalam *cāyavēr.*] The root of an East Indian herb (*Oldenlandia umbellata*), yielding a red dye like madder; also, the plant.

cha·zan', chaz·zan' (kä·zän'; käz'ăn), *n.* Variants of HAZZAN.

cheap (chēp), *n.* [AS. *cēap* bargain, sale, price.] **1.** Market place; — now only in place names; as, *Cheap*side. **2.** *Now Rare.* **a** Bargain; purchase. **b** State of the market.

cheap, *adj.* [From *good cheap* a good purchase or bargain.] **1.** Bought or selling at, or charging, a low price or prices; inexpensive. **2.** Costing little effort or trouble to obtain. **3.** Worthless, or not worth much; hence, not prized or esteemed. **4.** Disconcerted; abashed; discomfited. **5.** Depreciated in value or purchasing power, as by the result of currency inflation; as, *cheap* dollars. **6.** *Finance.* Of money, obtainable at a low rate of interest. **7.** *Brit.* Specially reduced in price; as, *cheap* fare. — **Syn.** See CONTEMPTIBLE. — *adv.* Cheaply. — **cheap'ly**, *adv.* — **cheap'ness**, *n.*

cheap'en (chēp'ĕn), *v. t.* **1.** To bargain or chaffer for. **2.** To make cheap; to depreciate; to bring into contempt. — *v. i.* To become cheap. — **cheap'en·er**, *n.*

cheap'skate' (-skāt'), *n.* **1.** One who tends to choose the least expensive goods or pleasures. **2.** One who seeks to avoid his share of costs.

cheat (chēt), *n.* [From *escheat*, in sense of confiscation.] **1.** One who or that which deceives or defrauds; an impostor or imposture; specif.: **a** A swindler. **b** A thing made for show; a sham. **2.** *Bot.* Chess, the grass. **3.** *Law.* The obtaining of property from another by an intentional active distortion of the truth. — **Syn.** See IMPOSTURE. — *v. t.* **1.** To defraud by deceiving; swindle. **2.** To influence, or to bring about, by deceit or artifice; to trick. **3.** To foil. — *v. i.* To practice fraud or trickery, esp. in business, at cards, etc. — **cheat'er**, *n.* — **cheat'ing·ly**, *adv.*

Syn. **Cheat, cozen, defraud, swindle, overreach** mean to get something from another by dishonesty or trickery. **Cheat** suggests tricks which escape or are intended to escape observation; **cozen**, an archaic term, implies more artfulness or craft and, often, more allurements; **defraud** stresses depriving one of his rights and connotes, often, deliberate perversion of the truth; **swindle** implies gross cheating or defrauding, especially by imposture; **overreach**, getting the better of a person with whom one is dealing by cheating, defrauding, or swindling.

check (chĕk), *n.* [OF. *eschec, eschac*, through Ar., fr. Per. *shāh* king.] **1.** *Chess.* State of being in danger and under the necessity of being made safe in the next move; — of a player's king. **2.** *Now Dial.* A rebuke, or reprimand. **3.** A sudden interruption in progress; a rebuff or repulse. **4.** **a** A pattern in squares, like that of a checkerboard; also, a square in such a design. **b** A fabric having such a pattern. **5.** A person or thing that arrests or hinders action; a curb or restraint. **6.** Control or supervision to determine accuracy, efficiency, progress, etc.; tab; as, to keep *check* of employees. **7.** An examination, test, trial, comparison, etc., for the sake of controlling, verifying, etc. **8.** Anything which affords a standard, guide, or aid in verifying, testing, supervising, etc. **9.** One employed to check or control. **10.** A mark to indicate that something has been examined or compared. **11.** A ticket, certificate, or token by which a thing or person may be identified; also, a slip of paper showing the price of something; as, a dinner *check.* **12.** A crack or small chink, as in timber or steel. **13.** A rabbet, or rebate; a rabbet-shaped cutting. **14.** *Brit.* **cheque** (chĕk). *Banking.* A written order directing a bank or banker to pay money as therein stated. **15.** In certain games at cards, esp. gambling games, a counter, or token for money. **16.** *Ice Hockey.* A checking of an opposing play or player in any of various ways. **17.** *Phonet.* = STOP, *n.*, 12.

— *v. t.* **1.** *Chess.* To put (a king) in check. **2.** To bring to a sudden pause; to stop. **3.** To hold back; restrain. **4.** To keep a check upon; to control, test, verify, investigate, etc., by means of checks; — often with *up.* **5.** To mark, as an item, with a check; also, to mark with checks, or squares; to checker. **6.** To make checks or chinks in. **7.** To deposit for temporary safekeeping, receiving a check. **8.** *Agric.* To checkrow. **9.** *Ice Hockey.* To block the progress of (an opposing player or play), as by interposing the body or stick or by snatching away the puck. — **Syn.** See RESTRAIN. — *v. i.* **1.** At chess, to give check. **2.** *Archaic.* To make a sharp stop; wince. **3.** To correspond item for item, usually with an original. **4.** *U. S.* To draw a check. **5.** To crack; to crack in small checks. **6.** *Falconry.* To turn, when in pursuit of proper game, and fly after other and baser game; — with *at.* **7.** *Hunting.* Of dogs, to stop or pause, as on losing the scent. — *adj.* **1.** Serving to check; as, a *check* block, list, or experiment. **2.** Checkered; checked.

— **check'a·ble**, *adj.* — **check'er**, *n.*

check'book' (chĕk'bŏŏk'), *n.* A book of blank bank checks.

check'er, cheq'uer (chĕk'ẽr), *n.* [OF. *eschequier* a chessboard, fr. *eschec.*] **1.** *Obs.* A chessboard. **2.** A square or spot suggestive of those of a checkerboard; a pattern of such squares. **3.** [From the spotted fruit.] **a** Either of two European service trees (*Sorbus domestica* and *S. torminalis*); — called also **checker tree.** **b** *pl.* The fruit of either tree. **4.** A man in checkers or backgammon. — *v. t.* **1.** To mark with small squares like a checkerboard. **2.** To variegate or diversify; esp., to subject to frequent ups and downs; as, his career was *checkered.*

check'er·ber'ry (-bĕr'ĭ), *n.* **1.** The spicy, red, berrylike fruit of the American wintergreen (*Gaultheria procumbens*); also, the plant. **2.** Incorrectly, the partridgeberry.

check'er·bloom' (chĕk'ẽr·blōōm'), *n.* A wild mallow (*Sidalcea malvaeflora*) of the western United States.

check'er·board', cheq'uer·board' (-bōrd'; 70), *n.* A board with (usually) 64 squares of alternate colors, used for playing checkers.

check'ers (chĕk'ẽrz), *n.* Also **cheq'uers.** *U. S. & Dial. Eng.* A game played on a checkerboard by two persons, each having twelve men, or *checkers;* draughts.

check line. A checkrein.

check'mate' (chĕk'māt'), *interj.* [OF. *eschec mat* (F. *échec et mat*), fr. Ar. *al-shāh māt*, lit., the king is dead.] *Chess.* An exclamation by a player when he makes a move that puts the opponent's king in check from which there is no escape; — now commonly *mate.* — *n.* **1.** *Chess.* Act of checkmating; also, the position when a king is checkmated; a mate. **2.** A complete check; utter defeat. — *v. t.* **1.** *Chess.* To check (an opponent's king) so that escape is impossible; to mate. **2.** To defeat; frustrate.

check'rein' (chĕk'rān'), *n.* **1.** A short rein looped over a hook on the saddle of a harness to prevent a horse from lowering his head. Cf. OVERCHECK REIN; see HARNESS, *Illust.* **2.** A branch rein connecting the driving rein of one horse of a span or pair with the bit of the other horse.

check'row' (-rō'), *n.* One of a series of rows, as of corn, dividing land into squares between which a cultivator may be operated. — *v. t.* To plant in checkrows; to check.

Ched'dar cheese, *or* **Ched'dar** (chĕd'ẽr), *n.* A smooth-textured pressed cheese, orig. made at Cheddar, England, but now extensively elsewhere, esp. in the United States, where it is called *American cheese* and is the standard cheese.

cheek (chēk), *n.* [AS. *cēace, cēoce.*] **1.** The fleshy wall or side of the face below the eye and above, and to the side of, the mouth. **2.** Something suggestive of the human cheek in position or form. **3.** In general, side. **4.** *Colloq.* **a** Impudent or saucy talk or behavior. **b** Cool confidence; audacity. — *v. t.* *Colloq.* To address or face with cheek. — **Syn.** See TEMERITY.

cheek by jowl. With heads together; in close intimacy.

cheek'y (chēk'ĭ), *adj.;* CHEEK'I·ER (-ĭ·ẽr); -I·EST. **1.** *Colloq.* Brazen; impudent. **2.** Having well-developed cheeks, as a bulldog. — **cheek'i·ly**, *adv.* — **cheek'i·ness**, *n.*

cheep (chēp), *v. i. & t.* [Imitative.] To utter faint shrill sounds, as a young bird; chirp; peep. — *n.* Act or sound of cheeping. — **cheep'er**, *n.*

cheer (chēr), *n.* [OF. *chiere, chere*, face, fr. LL. *cara.*] **1.** *Archaic.* The countenance or its expression. **2.** Feeling; spirit; state of mind or heart; as, be of good *cheer.* **3.** Gaiety; mirth; animation. **4.** Provision or provisions for entertainment or feasting; esp., viands; food. **5.** That which cheers or gladdens; as, words of *cheer.* **6.** A shout or acclamation of joy, applause, favor, etc. — *v. t.* **1.** To raise the spirits of; to cause to become hopeful, comforted, or gladdened; esp., to enliven; to make rejoice. **2.** To urge on or encourage, now esp. by shouts or cheers; as, to *cheer* hounds. **3.** To salute or applaud with cheers. — *v. i.* **1.** *Obs.* To be in (such) spirits. **2.** To be or become cheerful. **3.** To utter cheers. — **cheer'er**, *n.*

cheer′ful (chēr′fo͝ol; -f'l), *adj.* Full of cheer; joyous; also, ungrudging; hearty. — **Syn.** See GLAD. — **cheer′ful·ly**, *adv.*
cheer′ful·ness, *n.* Quality or state of being cheerful.
cheer′i·o (chēr′ĭ·ō), **cheer′o** (-ō), *interj. Colloq.* Good cheer! Hello! Good-by! — used esp. as a farewell or a greeting. — **cheer′i·o, cheer′o**, *n.*
cheer′less (chēr′lĕs; -lĭs), *adj.* Without cheer; joyless. — **cheer′less·ly**, *adv.* — **cheer′less·ness**, *n.*
cheer′ly (-lĭ), *adv.* Cheerily; heartily.
cheer′y (-ĭ), *adj.;* -I·ER (-ĭ·ẽr); -I·EST. Cheerful; lively; gay; bright. — **cheer′i·ly**, *adv.* — **cheer′i·ness**, *n.*
cheese (chēz), *n.* [AS. *cēse, cȳse*, fr. L. *caseus.*] **1.** The consolidated curd of milk ripened by fermentation, used as food; also, a mass of this molded into a cake or other shape. **2.** Something like a cheese in shape or consistency.
cheese, *v. t. Slang.* To stop; leave off; — used esp. in exclamation *cheese it*, stop! look out! run!
cheese, *n.* [Prob. fr. Per. *chīz* thing.] *Slang.* The right thing; one that is first rate or of consequence.
cheese′cake′ (chēz′kāk′), *n.* **1.** A cake made by baking a mixture of sweet rennet curds, eggs, and sugar; also, a pie filling of similar texture. **2.** *Slang.* Photography or photographs displaying esp. female comeliness and shapeliness.
cheese′cloth′ (-klŏth′; 74), *n.* Coarse cotton gauze.
cheese′par′ing (-pâr′ĭng), *n.* **1.** Something as worthless as a paring of cheese rind. **2.** Miserly economizing. — **cheese′par′ing**, *adj.*
chees′y (chēz′ĭ), *adj.;* -I·ER (-ĭ·ẽr); -I·EST. Of, pert. to, or like cheese, esp. in consistency. — **chees′i·ness** (-ĭ·nĕs; -nĭs), *n.*
chee′tah (chē′tȧ), *n.* [*Hind. cītā.*] Any of a genus (*Acinonyx*) of Asiatic and African animals of the cat family, with only slightly retractile claws. They are about the size of a leopard, are very swift, and are trained to hunt.
chef (shĕf), *n.* [F.] A chief or head; specif., a head cook; hence, loosely, any cook.
‖**chef de cui′sine′** (shĕf′ dē kwē′zēn′). [F.] = CHEF, head cook.
chef′-d'oeu′vre (shĕ′dû′vr′), *n.; pl.* CHEFS- (shĕ′-). [F.] A masterpiece in art, literature, etc.
chei′ro- (kī′rō-), **chei·rog′ra·phy**, etc. Vars. of CHIRO-, etc.
Che′ka (chā′kä), *n.* [Russ., fr. *che* and *ka*, names of initial letters of the Russ. name.] A Soviet committee formerly operating as a secret police against counterrevolutionary movements. See GAY-PAY-OO, NKVD, MVD, MGB.
che′la (kē′lȧ), *n.; pl.* -LAE (-lē). [NL., fr. Gr. *chēlē* claw.] The pincerlike organ or claw borne by certain of the limbs of crustaceans and arachnids. See LOBSTER, *Illust.* — **che′late** (-lāt), *adj.* — **che·lif′er·ous** (kē·lĭf′ẽr·ŭs), *adj.* — **che′li·form** (kē′lĭ·fôrm; kĕl′ĭ-), *adj.*
che′la (chā′lä), *n.* [Hind. *celā*, fr. Skr. *ceṭaka.*] In India, a disciple or novice.
che·lo′ni·an (kē·lō′nĭ·ăn), *adj.* [Gr. *chelōnē* tortoise.] Of or relating to tortoises or turtles. — **che·lo′ni·an**, *n.*
chem′ic (kĕm′ĭk; *Brit. also* kĭm′ĭk), *adj. Archaic.* **a** Alchemic; hence, counterfeit; as, *chemic* gold. **b** Chemical. — *n. Obs.* A chemist.
chem′i·cal (kĕm′ĭ·kăl), *adj.* **1.** Of or pertaining to chemistry, or its forces, processes, etc. **2.** Acting, operated, or performed by the use of chemicals. — *n.* A substance obtained by a chemical process, or used for producing a chemical effect. — **chem′i·cal·ly**, *adv.*
chemical warfare. *Mil.* Warfare in which chemicals other than explosives are used, as poisonous gases, incendiary mixtures, etc.
‖**che·min′ de fer** (shē·măN′ dē fâr′; *colloq.* shmăNt′ fâr′). [F.] **1.** A railroad. **2.** A variety of baccarat.
che·mise′ (shē·mēz′; shē-), *n.* [F., fr. LL. *camisa, camisia*, shirt, thin dress.] A woman's shirtlike undergarment.
chem′i·sette′ (shĕm′ĭ·zĕt′), *n.* [F.] **1.** A woman's bodicelike, sleeveless undergarment. **2.** An ornamental detachable dress front or neckpiece.
chem′ism (kĕm′ĭz'm), *n.* Chemical activity or affinity.
chem′ist (kĕm′ĭst; *Brit. still occas.*, kĭm′ĭst), *n.* [Shortened from *alchemist.*] **1.** One versed in chemistry; formerly, an alchemist. **2.** *Brit.* A druggist. — **Syn.** See DRUGGIST.
chem′is·try (kĕm′ĭs·trĭ), *n.; pl.* -TRIES (-trĭz). **1.** The science that treats of the composition of substances, and of the transformations which they undergo. ***organic chemistry*** is the chemistry of the hydrocarbons and their derivatives (or, which is almost the same, of carbon compounds) whether found in organisms or not; ***inorganic chemistry*** treats of all other compounds and of the elements. Cf. BIOCHEMISTRY. **2.** Chemical composition, properties, or processes. **3.** Any process of combining, analyzing, etc., suggestive of a chemical process; as, the *chemistry* of a poet's imagination.
chem′o- (kĕm′ō-), **chem-.** [From CHEMICAL.] A combining form denoting *relation to chemical action* or *to chemicals*, as in:

chemasthenia	**chemoreflex**	**chemosynthesis**
chemokinesis	**chemoresistance**	**chemotaxis**
chemolysis	**chemosmosis**	**chemotropism**

chem′o·re·cep′tor (kĕm′ō·rē·sĕp′tẽr), *n.* Also **chem′o·cep′tor** (kĕm′ō·sĕp′tẽr). *Physiol.* A receptor for chemical stimuli, as a taste or smell receptor. — **chem′o·re·cep′tion** (-rē·sĕp′shŭn), *n.*
chem′o·ther′a·py (-thĕr′ȧ·pĭ), *n.* [*chemo-* + *therapy.*] Also **chem′o·ther′a·peu′tics** (-thĕr′ȧ·pū′tĭks). *Med.* The treatment of internal disease by chemical reagents that have a toxic effect upon the microorganism causing the disease, without seriously poisoning the patient. — **chem′o·ther′a·peu′tic** (-thĕr′ȧ·pū′tĭk), *adj.* — **chem′o·ther′a·pist** (-thĕr′ȧ·pĭst), *n.*
chem′ur·gy (kĕm′ûr·jĭ), *n.* [*chemistry* + *-urgy.*] That branch of applied chemistry devoted to industrial utilization of organic raw materials, esp. from farm products, as in the use of soybean oil for paints and varnishes and of Georgia pine for paper pulp. — **chem·ur′gic** (kĕm·ûr′jĭk), **chem·ur′gi·cal** (-jĭ·kăl), *adj.*
che·nille′ (shē·nēl′), *n.* [F., prop., a caterpillar.] A tufted cord, used for embroidery, fringes, etc.; also, a fabric made with a filling of this cord.
che′no·pod (kē′nō·pŏd; kĕn′ō-), *n.* Any plant of the goosefoot family (Chenopodiaceae). See GOOSEFOOT. — **che′no·po′di·a′ceous** (-pō′dĭ·ā′shŭs), *adj.*
cheque (chĕk), *n. Brit.* = CHECK, *n.*, 14.
cheq′uer (chĕk′ẽr), **cheq′uer·board′, cheq′uers.** Vars. of CHECKER, etc.

‖**cher′chez′ la femme** (shĕr′shā′ lȧ fȧm′). [F.] Look for the woman; — a phrase implying that a woman is at the bottom of the matter under discussion.
cher′ish (chĕr′ĭsh), *v. t.* [OF. *cherir*, fr. *cher* dear, fr. L. *carus.*] **1.** To hold dear; to treat with tenderness and affection; hence, to nurture with care. **2.** To harbor in the mind; cling to. — **Syn.** See APPRECIATE. — **Ant.** Neglect. — **cher′ish·er**, *n.* — **cher′ish·ing·ly**, *adv.*
Cher′o·kee′ (chĕr′ō·kē′ *or, esp. attributively*, chĕr′ō·kē′), *n.; pl.* -KEE, -KEES (-kēz′). An Indian of an Iroquoian tribe, now chiefly in Oklahoma; also, their language.
Cher′o·kee′ rose. A Chinese climbing rose (*Rosa laevigata*). Its white blossom is the State flower of Georgia.
che·root′ (shē·ro͞ot′), *n.* [Tamil *šuruṭṭu* cigar, roll.] A type of cigar, relatively long and narrow and having both ends square (instead of one end pointed).
cher′ry (chĕr′ĭ), *n.; pl.* -RIES (-ĭz). [ONF. *cherise* (F. *cerise*), deriv. of L. *cerasus* cherry tree, fr. Gr. *kerasos.* The French *s* was misunderstood in English as a plural ending (cf. PEA).] **1.** Any of several species of two closely related genera (*Prunus* and *Padus*) of trees of the peach family, bearing round drupes enclosing a smooth stone. Cultivated cherries have all originated from the wild ***sour cherry*** (*Prunus cerasus*) and the wild ***sweet cherry***, *or* ***mazzard*** (*Prunus avium*), the former yielding the sour cooking types (*amarelles* and *morellos*), the latter the sweet types (*geans* and *bigarreaus*). Other wild species include the European ***bird cherry***, *or* ***chokecherry*** (*Padus avium*), and the American ***black cherry*** (*Padus serotina*, a timber tree whose wood is used in cabinetwork, having black bark, hanging clusters of fragrant white flowers, and black, sour fruit), ***chokecherry*** (*Padus virginiana* of eastern U. S. or *Padus demissa* of western U. S.), and ***pin cherry*** (*Prunus pennsylvanica*). See CORYMB, ENDOCARP, *Illusts.* **2.** The fruit or wood of any of these trees. **3.** Also **cherry red.** A bright-red color; specif., a color, yellowish-red in hue, of very high saturation and medium brilliance. See COLOR. — **cher′ry**, *adj.* — **cher′ry-red′**, *adj.*
cherry stone. See CLAM, 1.
cher′so·nese (kûr′sō·nēz; -nēs), *n.* [L. *chersonesus*, ult. fr. Gr. *chersos* land + *nēsos* island.] A peninsula.
chert (chûrt), *n.* [E. dial.] An impure flintlike rock, usually dark in color. — **chert′y** (chûr′tĭ), *adj.*
cher′ub (chĕr′ŭb), *n.; pl.* CHERUBIM (-ū·bĭm; -o͞o·bĭm), CHERUBS (-ŭbz). In English, both **cher′u·bim**, the Hebrew plural, and **cher′u·bin** (-bĭn), a form appearing in the Vulgate, have been treated as singular, as plural, and as collective. [Heb. *kĕrūbh.*] **1.** A composite being, described in *Ezekiel* i and x. **2.** A representation of one of these beings; esp., the winged figure used in connection with the mercy seat of the Jewish ark and temple. *Ex.* xxv. 18, xxxvii. 7–9. **3.** One of an order of angels, usually ranked below the seraphim. **4.** An innocent-looking child or, by extension, adult, esp. a chubby, rosy one. **5.** A conventional representation of a cherub, the angel, or of a cherub, a child, esp. with wings. — **che·ru′bic** (chē·ro͞o′bĭk), *adj.* — **che·ru′bi·cal·ly** (-bĭ·kăl·ĭ), *adv.*
cher′vil (chûr′vĭl), *n.* [AS. *cerfille*, fr. L., fr. Gr. *chairephyllon*, fr. *chairein* to rejoice + *phyllon* leaf.] **a** An aromatic herb (*Anthriscus cerefolium*) of the carrot family, with divided leaves often used in soups and salads. **b** Any of several other related plants; as, the ***wild***, *or* ***cow, chervil*** (*A. vulgaris*).
cher·vo′nets (chĕr·vô′nĕts), *n.; pl.* CHERVONTSI (chĕr·vôn′tsē). [Russ., lit., ducat.] A currency unit of the U.S.S.R. based on gold but circulating in the form of unredeemable bank notes. It is equal to ten rubles. See MONEY, *Tables.*
Chesh′ire cat (chĕsh′ẽr; *less often*, -ĭr). In *Alice in Wonderland*, a grinning cat which gives Alice advice and then fades away.
Cheshire cheese. A hard cheese made chiefly in Cheshire, England.
chess (chĕs), *n.* [OF. *esches* (acc. pl. of *eschec*) check. See CHECK, *n.*] A game of pure skill played on a board (**chess′board′**) with sets of 16 pieces (**chess′men**, *sing.* CHESSMAN), the players moving alternately until the king of one is so attacked that he cannot escape.
chess, *n.; pl.* CHESS or CHESSES (-ĕz; -ĭz). One of the floor planks of a pontoon bridge.
chess (chĕs), *n. U. S.* **1.** Any of several brome grasses, esp. the wheat-field weed *Bromus secalinus.* **2.** = DARNEL.
chest (chĕst), *n.* [AS. *cest, cist*, fr. L. *cista*, fr. Gr. *kistē.*] **1.** A box with a lid, esp. for safekeeping of possessions. **2.** The treasury or coffer of a public institution; also, the fund so kept. **3.** The part of the body enclosed by the ribs and breastbone; thorax. See THORAX, *Illust.* **4.** A case for transporting tea, opium, etc.; also, the quantity in such a case. **5.** *Mach.* A tight receptacle for gas, steam, etc.
ches′ter·field (chĕs′tẽr·fēld), *n.* **1.** A tailored overcoat, orig. single-breasted, with concealed buttons; — after a 19th-cent. Earl of Chesterfield. **2.** A type of large overstuffed sofa.
Ches′ter White (chĕs′tẽr). One of a breed of large white swine said to have originated in Chester County, Pa.
chest′nut (chĕs′nŭt; chĕst′nŭt; -nŭt), *n.* [From *chesten nut*, fr. ME. *chesten, chasteine*, fr. OF. *chastaigne*, fr. L., fr. Gr. *kastanea, kastanon*, a chestnut.] **1.** The edible nut of any tree of a genus (*Castanea*) of the beech family; also, the tree bearing this nut or its wood. See CHINQUAPIN **a.** **2.** = HORSE CHESTNUT. **3.** Also **chestnut brown.** A brown color, red-yellow in hue, of low saturation and low brilliance. See COLOR. **4.** *Colloq.* An old joke or story. **5.** A chestnut-colored horse. — **chest′nut**, *adj.*
chet′nik (chĕt′nĭk; chĕt·nēk′), *n.; pl.* CHETNICI (chĕt·nē′tsē), CHETNIKS (chĕt′nĭks). [Serb. *četnik*, fr. *četa* troop, band.] A member of a secret Serbian home-defense band for resistance to oppressors by assassination, raiding, destruction of communications, and other guerrilla tactics. Members wear the emblem of skull and crossbones.
‖**che·val′ de ba′taille′** (shē·vȧl′ dē bȧ′tä′y′). [F.] A war horse; charger; hence, a favorite idea, argument, etc.
che·val′-de-frise′ (shē·vȧl′dē·frēz′), *n.; commonly in pl.* CHEVAUX-DE-FRISE (shē·vō′-). [F., fr. *cheval* horse + *Frise* Friesland, where first used.] **1.** *Mil.* A defense consisting of a timber or an iron barrel covered with projecting spikes and often strung with barbed wire. **2.** A protecting line as of spikes along a wall.

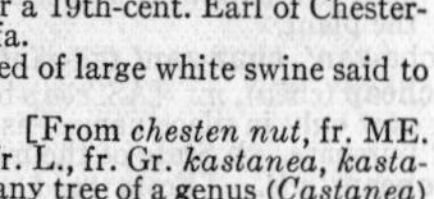

One form of Cheval-de-frise, 1.

che·val′ glass (shē·văl′). A full-length swinging mirror.
chev′a·lier′ (shĕv′ȧ·lēr′), *n.* [OF., fr. LL. *caballarius.* See CAVALIER.] **1.** *Archaic.* A knight. **2.** A member of certain orders of

knighthood or of merit, as the Legion of Honor. 3. *Hist.* a A French noble of the lowest rank. b A cadet of the French nobility. 4. A chivalrous man.

‖**che·ve·lure′** (shĕ·vlür′), *n.* [F.] 1. Head of hair; also, *Obs.*, a wig. 2. *Astron.* = COMA, 1.

Chev′i·ot (chĕv′ĭ·ŭt; chē′vĭ-; chĭv′ĭ-; *in sense* 2 *commonly* shĕv′ĭ·ŭt *in U. S.*), *n.* 1. One of a breed of hornless sheep originating in the Cheviot Hills. 2. [*often not cap.*] A napped, usually twilled, fabric, originally of Cheviot wool; also, a moderately heavy cotton fabric, used for shirts, waists, etc.

chev′ron (shĕv′rŭn), *n.* [F., rafter, chevron, fr. L. *capra* she-goat.] A distinguishing mark to indicate rank or service, consisting usually of stripes meeting at an angle on the coat or shirt sleeve.

chev′ro·tain (shĕv′rō·tān; -tĭn), *n.* [F., fr. *chevrot* kid, fawn, dim. of *chèvre* goat.] Any of several very small, hornless, deerlike ruminants (constituting the family Tragulidae) of tropical Asia and West Africa. They are among the smallest known ruminants.

chev′y (chĕv′ĭ), *n.; pl.* CHEVIES (-ĭz). *Eng.* 1. A cry used in hunting. 2. A hunt; chase. — *v. t. & i.;* CHEV′IED (-ĭd); CHEV′Y·ING. *Chiefly Dial., Eng.* 1. To chase; race; scamper. 2. *Usually* **chiv′y** (chĭv′ĭ) *or* **chiv′vy.** To torment or harass. — **Syn.** See BAIT.

chew (choo͞; chū), *v. t. & i.* [AS. *cēowan.*] 1. To bite and grind with the teeth; masticate. 2. To ruminate mentally. — *n.* Act of chewing; also, the thing chewed; a quid, as of tobacco. — **chew′er,** *n.*

chew′ing gum (choo͞′ĭng; chū′-). A preparation of chicle sweetened and flavored, chewed as a masticatory.

che·wink′ (chē·wĭngk′), *n.* The common towhee (*Pipilo erythrophthalmus*) of eastern North America.

Chey·enne′ (shī·ĕn′), *n. sing. & pl.; pl.* also CHEYENNES (-ĕnz′). One of a warlike Algonquian tribe of Indians formerly roving between the Arkansas and Missouri rivers.

chi (kī; kē; kē), *n.* [Gr.] The 22d letter (Χ, χ) of the Greek alphabet, transliterated by *ch.*

Chi·an′ti (kĭ·ăn′tĭ), *n.* [It.] Wine from the region of the Chianti Mountains, Tuscany, esp. a dry red variety; also, any wine of the same type made elsewhere.

chi·a′ro·scu′ro (kĭ·ä′rō·skū′rō), **chi·a′ro–o·scu′ro** (-ō·skū′rō), *n.; pl.* -ROS (-rōz). [It., clear dark.] 1. Style of pictorial art employing only light and shade, omitting the various colors; as, a sketch in *chiaroscuro.* 2. Arrangement of light and dark parts, as in a picture. — **chi·a′ro·scu′rist** (-skū′rĭst), *n.*

chi·as′ma (kī·ăz′mȧ), *n.; pl.* -MATA (-tȧ). Also **chi′asm** (kī′ăz′m). [NL., fr. Gr. deriv. of *chiazein* to mark with a *chi* (χ).] 1. *Anat.* An intersection, esp. of the optic nerves. 2. *Genetics.* A crosswise fusion, as of chromosomes. — **chi·as′mal** (-măl), **-mic** (-mĭk), *adj.*

chi·as′ma·typ′y (-tīp′ĭ), *n.* [Gr. *chiasma* two crossed lines + *typē* impression.] *Genetics.* The supposed spiral twisting of homologous chromosomes about each other during parasynapsis, with fusion and possible crossing over at the points of contact. — **chi·as′ma·type** (-tīp), *adj. & n.*

chiaus (chous; choush), *n.* [Turk. *chāwush.*] A Turkish messenger, sergeant, or the like.

Chib′cha (chĭb′chȧ), *n.* a An Indian of a Chibchan tribe formerly dwelling in central Colombia. b Any Chibchan Indian. c The language, now extinct, of the Chibchas.

Chib′chan (-chăn), *adj.* Pertaining to an American Indian linguistic family of South and Central America.

chi·bouk′, chi·bouque′ (chĭ·bo͝ok′; -bo͞ok′), *n.* [F. *chibouque,* fr. Turk. *chibūq.*] A Turkish tobacco pipe with a long (4 to 5 feet) stem of wood and a clay bowl.

chic (shēk; shĭk), *n.* [F.] *Colloq.* Striking but easy elegance in form or style. — *adj.;* CHIC′QUER (-ẽr); CHIC′QUEST. *Colloq.* Stylish; smart.

‖**chi′ca·lo′te** (chē′kä·lō′tā), *n.* [Sp., fr. Nahuatl *chicalotl.*] A white-flowered prickly poppy (*Argemone platyceras*) of Mexico and southwestern U. S.; also, the Mexican poppy. See PRICKLY POPPY.

chi·cane′ (shĭ·kān′; *now rarely* chĭ·kān′), *n.* [F., fr. *chicaner* to quibble.] 1. Chicanery. 2. *Bridge.* A hand without trumps. — **Syn.** See DECEPTION. — *v. i. & t.* To use or affect by chicanery.

chi·can′er·y (shĭ·kān′ẽr·ĭ), *n.; pl.* -ERIES (-ĭz). Trickery, esp. in legal proceedings; sharp practice; also, an instance of this. — **Syn.** See DECEPTION.

chick (chĭk), *n.* 1. A young chicken; also, a young bird. 2. A child.

chick′a·dee (chĭk′ȧ·dē), *n.* Any of several crestless titmice (genus *Penthestes*); specif., the ***black-capped chickadee*** (*P. atricapillus*), one of the tamest and most familiar North American birds.

chick′a·ree (-rē), *n.* See SQUIRREL, 1 a.

Chick′a·saw (chĭk′ȧ·sô), *n. sing. & pl.; pl.* also CHICKASAWS (-sôz). An Indian of a Muskhogean tribe, now citizens of Oklahoma.

chick′en (chĭk′ĕn; -ĭn), *n.* [AS. *cicen, cycen.*] 1. A young hen or cock. 2. A barnyard fowl or its flesh used as food. Cf. POULTRY, *Illust.* 3. The young of various other birds. 4. A young, youthful, or inexperienced person.

chicken breast. *Med.* = PIGEON BREAST.

chick′en·heart′ed (chĭk′ĕn·här′tĕd; -tĭd; chĭk′ĭn-; 2), *adj.* Timid; cowardly.

chicken pox. An acute contagious disease, chiefly of children, marked by eruptions on the skin; varicella.

chick′–pea′ (chĭk′pē′), *n.* [F. *chiche-pois,* fr. L. *cicer.*] An Asiatic herb (*Cicer arietinum*) of the pea family, bearing short pods with pealike seeds.

chick′weed′ (chĭk′wēd′), *n.* Any of several weeds (genera *Arenaria, Alsine* and *Cerastium,* family Alsinaceae, the chickweed family) bearing seeds and foliage relished by birds.

chic′le (chĭk′′l; chĭk′lē), *n., or* **chicle gum.** [Sp., fr. Nahuatl *chictli* chicle.] A gum obtained from the latex of the sapodilla. It is the chief ingredient of chewing gum.

chi′co (chē′kō), *n.; pl.* -COS (-kōz). [Sp. *chicalote.*] *Western U. S.* The common greasewood.

chic′o·ry (chĭk′ō·rĭ), *n.; pl.* -RIES (-rĭz). Also **chic′co·ry.** [F. *chicorée,* through ML. and L., fr. Gr. *kichora, kichoreia.*] a A European perennial (*Cichorium intybus*) common in U. S. as a weed, and cultivated for its roots and as a salad plant; — called also *succory.* It typifies a family (*Cichoriaceae,* the chicory family) of herbs or shrubs having milky juice and heads of narrow, flat flowers. b Its root, roasted for mixing with coffee.

chide (chīd), *v. i. & t.; past* CHID (chĭd), CHID′ED (chīd′ĕd; -ĭd); *past part.* CHID, CHID′DEN (chĭd′′n), CHID′ED; *pres. part.* CHID′ING (chīd′ĭng). [AS. *cīdan.*] To utter words of reproof; to scold. — **Syn.** See REPROVE. — **chid′er** (chīd′ẽr), *n.* — **chid′ing·ly,** *adv.*

chief (chēf), *n.* [OF. *chief, chef,* fr. L. *caput* head.] 1. The top; esp., *Her.,* the upper part of the shield, or the charge filling that space. See ESCUTCHEON, *Illust.* 2. The head or leader of any body or organization. 3. *Archaic.* Principal or most valuable part. — *adj.* 1. Highest in office or rank. 2. Most eminent, distinguished, influential, important, or the like. — **Syn.** Principal, leading, main, foremost. — *adv. Archaic.* Principally; mainly. — **chief′ly,** *adv.*

chief′tain (chēf′tĭn; -tĕn), *n.* [OF. *chevetain,* fr. LL. *capitanus.*] A chief, esp. of a band, tribe, or clan. — **chief′tain·cy** (-sĭ), *n.* — **chief′tain·ship,** *n.*

chield (chēld), **chiel** (chēl), *n.* [Var. of CHILD.] *Chiefly Scot.* a A youth. b A child.

chif·fon′ (shĭ·fŏn′; shĭf′ŏn), *n.* [F., lit., rag.] 1. Any ornamental addition, as a bunch of ribbon, on a woman's dress. 2. A sheer fabric, esp. of silk.

chif′fo·nier′ (shĭf′ō·nēr′), *n.* Also **chif′fon·nier′.** [F. *chiffonnier,* fr. *chiffon* rag.] A high, narrow chest of drawers, often with a mirror.

chig′ger (chĭg′ẽr), *n.* a = CHIGOE (flea). b The parasitic larva of certain mites; — called also *chigoe* and *jigger.*

chi′gnon (shēn′yŏn; *F.* shē′nyôN′), *n.* [F.] A knot of hair worn at the back or top of the head.

chig′oe (chĭg′ō), *n.; pl.* CHIGOES (-ōz). [F. *chique,* of Cariban origin.] a A flea (*Tunga penetrans*), common in tropical regions; — called also *chigger* and *jigger.* b = CHIGGER b.

Chi·hua′hua (chē·wä′wä), *n.* [From *Chihuahua,* state and city in Mexico.] A very small dog (average weight two to six pounds) of a kind native to Mexico and the southwestern United States, believed to antedate Aztec civilization.

chil′blain′ (chĭl′blān′), *n.* An inflammatory swelling or sore (blain) produced by exposure of the feet or hands to cold.

child (chīld), *n.; pl.* CHILDREN (chĭl′drĕn). [AS. *cild,* pl. *cildru.*] 1. a An unborn or newborn son or daughter; baby; infant; — now chiefly in phrases or compounds; as, **child′bear′ing, child′birth′.** b *Now Dial.* A female infant. 2. A young person of either sex, esp. between infancy and youth; hence, a childlike person. 3. A youth of noble birth; — usually in archaic spelling *childe.* 4. A son or a daughter; in *Law,* a legitimate offspring. 5. A descendant. 6. One like a child in discipleship, etc. — **child′less,** *adj.* — **child′less·ness,** *n.*

child′bed′ (-bĕd′), *n.* State of a woman bringing forth a child, or being in labor.

Chil′der·mas (chĭl′dẽr·mȧs), *n.* [AS. *cildamæsse,* lit., child Mass.] = HOLY INNOCENTS' DAY.

child′hood (chīld′ho͝od), *n.* State or time of being a child.

child′ing (chīl′dĭng), *adj.* Bearing children; pregnant; hence, fruitful.

child′ish, *adj.* [AS. *cildisc.*] 1. Of, like, or befitting a child. 2. Puerile; silly. — **Syn.** See CHILDLIKE. — **child′ish·ly,** *adv.* — **child′ish·ness,** *n.*

child′like′, *adj.* Of, characteristic of, or becoming to, a child; innocent, trustful, etc. — **child′like′ness,** *n.*

Syn. **Childlike, childish** mean having or showing the manner or disposition of a child. **Childlike** usually suggests those qualities of childhood worthy of emulation or of admiration, such as innocence or straightforwardness; **childish,** its less pleasing characteristics, such as peevishness or undeveloped mentality. The terms are applicable irrespective of age.

child′ly, *adj.* Childish; childlike.

child′ness, *n. Rare.* Childishness; childlikeness.

chil′dren (chĭl′drĕn), *n., pl.* of CHILD.

Chil′e salt′pe′ter (chĭl′ē). = SODIUM NITRATE.

chil′i (chĭl′ĭ), *n.; pl.* CHILIES (-ĭz). Also **chil′e** (-ē), **chil′li.** [Sp. *chili, chile,* fr. Nahuatl *chilli.*] 1. A pepper (*Capsicum frutescens*), or its fruit, a chief source of cayenne pepper. 2. *Southwest U. S.* A sauce seasoned with chilies; also, chili con carne. See PEPPER, 3; CAPSICUM, 2.

chil′i·ad (kĭl′ĭ·ăd), *n.* [Gr. *chilias, -ados,* fr. *chilioi* thousand.] 1. A thousand. 2. Period of a thousand years.

chil′i·arch (kĭl′ĭ·ärk), *n.* [Gr. *chiliarchēs, chiliarchos,* fr. *chilioi* a thousand + *archos* leader, fr. *archein* to lead.] *Greek Antiq.* The commander of a thousand men.

chil′i·asm (kĭl′ĭ·ăz′m), *n.* [Gr. *chiliasmos,* fr. *chilias.* See CHILIAD.] The belief in Christ's return to earth to reign during the millennium. — **chil′i·ast** (-ăst), *n.* — **chil′i·as′tic** (-ăs′tĭk), *adj.*

chil′i con car′ne (chĭl′ĭ kŏn kär′nē). [Sp. *chili* + *con* with + *carne* flesh.] A Mexican dish consisting of minced chilies of pungent red varieties and chopped meat, stewed together.

chil′i sauce (chĭl′ĭ). A spiced tomato sauce made with chilies.

chill (chĭl), *n.* [AS. *cele, cyle.*] 1. A sensation of cold attended with shivering. 2. A moderate but disagreeable degree of cold. 3. A check to enthusiasm or warmth of feeling. — *adj.* 1. Moderately cold; raw. 2. Numbed or shivering with cold. 3. Without warmth of feeling; cool. 4. Depressing; dispiriting. — *v. i.* 1. To cool. 2. To become surface-hardened by sudden cooling, as cast iron. — *v. t.* 1. To strike with a chill; make chilly. 2. To make cool, as in a refrigerator. 3. To check, as enthusiasm; dispirit. 4. To surface-harden (metal) by sudden cooling. — **chill′er,** *n.* — **chill′ing·ly,** *adv.* — **chill′ness,** *n.*

chill′y (chĭl′ĭ), *adj.;* -I·ER (-ĭ·ẽr); -I·EST. 1. Chilling; making cold, shivery, or dispirited. 2. Cold; without warmth. — **chill′i·ly,** *adv.* — **chill′i·ness,** *n.*

chi′lo- (kī′lō-), **chil-.** [Gr. *cheilos.*] A combining form meaning *lip,* as in **chi′lo·plas′ty, chi·lot′o·my** (see -PLASTY, -TOMY).

chi·mae′ra (kī·mēr′ȧ; kĭ-), *n.* [L.] 1. [*cap. & not cap.*] Var. of CHIMERA. 2. Any of a group (Holocephali), and esp. of a genus (*Chimaera*), of marine elasmobranch fishes related to the sharks, having a tapering or threadlike tail.

chim′ar (chĭm′ẽr). Var. of CHIMER, a robe.

chime (chīm), *n.* [OF. *chimble, cimble,* fr. L. *cymbalum.* See CYMBAL.] 1. An apparatus for chiming a bell or set of bells. 2. A set of bells musically tuned. 3. The music played on such a set of bells; — commonly in the *pl.* 4. Music or melody; harmony. — *v. i.* 1. To sound in harmonious accord. 2. To ring a set of bells so as to produce chimes. 3. To be in harmony; agree; — often with *with.* — *v. t.* 1. *Archaic.* To produce, as music, by chiming. 2. To make sound by striking; to ring or play. 3. To indicate (an hour of the day) with chimes. 4. To call, send, etc., by means of chimes. — **chim′er** (chīm′ẽr), *n.*

chime, chimb (chīm), *n.* [From stem of AS. *cimbing* joining, *cimbstān* base of a pillar.] The edge or rim of a cask.

chim'er (chĭm'ẽr; shĭm'ẽr), **chi·mere'** (chĭ·mēr'; shĭ·mēr'), *n.* [MF. *chamarre, samarre,* a loose gown, fr. Sp. *zamarra,* fr. Ar. *sammūr* the sable.] A loose robe; esp., one worn by some bishops of the Anglican Communion.

chi·me'ra, chi·mae'ra (kī·mēr'ȧ; kĭ-), *n.; pl.* -RAS (-ȧz). [L. *chimaera,* fr. Gr. *chimaira* chimera, she-goat.] **1.** [*cap.*] *Gr. Myth.* A she-monster represented as vomiting flames, and, usually, as having a lion's head, goat's body, and dragon's or serpent's tail. **2.** Any such imaginary monster. **3.** A frightful, vain, or foolish fancy. **4.** *Biol.* A mixture of tissues of different genetic constitution in the same part of an organism.

chi·mer'i·cal (-mĕr'ĭ·kăl), *adj.* Also **chi·mer'ic** (-ĭk). **1.** Merely imaginary; fanciful; fantastic. **2.** Inclined to entertain chimeras; visionary. — **Syn.** See IMAGINARY. — **chi·mer'i·cal·ly,** *adv.*

chim'ney (chĭm'nĭ), *n.; pl.* -NEYS (-nĭz). [OF. *cheminée,* fr. LL., fr. L. *caminus* furnace, fireplace, fr. Gr. *kaminos.*] **1.** *Now Chiefly Dial.* Fireplace or hearth. **2.** That part of a building which contains the smoke flues; esp., an upright flue of brick, stone, etc., usually extending above the roof. **3.** A tube, usually of glass, placed around a flame, as of a lamp. **4.** Smokestack, as of a locomotive or factory. **5.** Something resembling a chimney in form, use, etc.

chimney piece. A decorative construction, as a mantel, a piece of tapestry, or the like, over a fireplace.

chimney pot. A cylindrical pipe used at the top of a chimney to increase draft and carry off smoke.

chimney sweep. A person who cleans soot from chimneys.

chim'pan·zee' (chĭm'păn·zē'; chĭm·păn'zē), *n.* [Kongo dial. *ki(m)penzi, chi(m)penzi.*] An anthropoid ape (*Pan troglodytes*) of equatorial Africa, smaller and less ferocious than the gorilla.

chin (chĭn), *n.* [AS. *cin.*] The lower extremity of the face, below the mouth; often, the external surface below the lower jaw or between its branches. — *v. t.;* CHINNED (chĭnd); CHIN'NING. **1.** *Colloq.* To hold with the chin, as a fiddle. **2.** *Gymnastics.* To raise (oneself) when hanging by the hands until the chin is level with the hands. **3.** *Slang, U. S.* To talk to, esp. volubly. — *v. i.* To talk or converse, esp. volubly.

chi'na (chī'nȧ), *n.* [From *China.*] **a** Also **chi'na·ware'** (-wâr'). Porcelain ware, orig. that from the Far East. **b** Loosely, crockery.

China aster. See ASTER, 1.

chi'na bark (kī'nȧ; kē'nȧ). [Sp. *quina,* fr. Quechua *quina* bark.] **a** Cinchona. **b** Bark of a Brazilian shrub (*Cascarilla hexandra*).

chi'na·ber'ry (chī'nȧ·bĕr'ĭ), *n.* **a** A soapberry (*Sapindus saponaria*) of the southern United States and Mexico. **b** = CHINA TREE.

Chi'na·man (-măn), *n.* A native of China; a Chinese; — now superseded by *Chinese,* which is preferred except in derogatory uses.

China rose. **a** A Chinese shrub (*Rosa chinensis*). **b** See HIBISCUS.

Chi'na·town' (chī'nȧ·toun'), *n.* Chinese quarter of a city.

China tree. A handsome Asiatic tree (*Melia azedarach*) of the mahogany family, planted in America as a shade tree; — called also *chinaberry* or *pride of China* or *pride of India.*

chin'ca·pin (chĭng'kȧ·pĭn). Var. of CHINQUAPIN.

chinch (chĭnch), *n.* [Sp. *chinche,* fr. L. *cimex.*] Bedbug.

chinch bug. A small hemipterous insect (*Blissus leucopterus*), black and white when adult, very destructive to grass, wheat, corn, etc., esp. in dry seasons.

chin·chil'la (chĭn·chĭl'ȧ), *n.* [Sp.] **1.** A small South American rodent (*Chinchilla laniger*), having very soft pearly-gray fur; also, its fur or pelt. **2.** A long-napped, tufted woolen cloth.

chin'cough' (chĭn'kôf'), *n.* Whooping cough.

chine (chīn), *n.* [OF. *eschine,* of Teut. origin.] **1.** The backbone. **2.** A cut of meat or fish including the backbone or part of it and the surrounding flesh. **3.** A ridge; a crest. — *v. t.* To cut through the backbone of; to cut up.

chine. Var. of CHIME (of a cask).

Chi'nese' (chī'nēz'; -nēs'), *n.* **1.** *sing. & pl.* A native of China. **2.** The language of the Chinese. As written, its words have the same meaning throughout China. Their spoken sounds vary with the dialects, of which there are at least eight so different as to be mutually unintelligible. Mandarin, the dialect of the majority, spoken in north, west, and southwest China, is becoming in a purified form the national language, taught in all schools. Cf. CANTONESE, 2; MANDARIN, 2 b; PEKINGESE, 1 b. See LANGUAGE, *Table.* — **Chi'nese',** *adj.*

Chinese calendar. The calendar formerly used in China, in which the year consisted of twelve months of 29 or 30 days each, with an intercalary month added in every thirty. New Year's Day occurred (and is still popularly celebrated) on the first new moon after the sun entered the sign Aquarius, and hence was never earlier than January 21 or later than February 19. The Chinese era dated from 2697 B.C., when (according to tradition) the system of sixty-year cycles (***sexagenary cycles***) was established. Officially, the Gregorian calendar has been adopted in China and the year is now reckoned from the beginning of the Republic, in 1912; thus, 1948 was the 37th year of the Republic.

Chinese lantern. A collapsible lantern of thin, colored paper, esp. for decorative use; — called also *Japanese lantern.*

Chinese puzzle. An intricate or ingenious puzzle such as those made by the Chinese; hence, something intricate.

Chinese Wall. The famous defensive wall extending for 1,250 miles between Mongolia and China proper.

Chinese white. Zinc white, esp. a dense form of it.

Chinese windlass. = DIFFERENTIAL WINDLASS.

Ch'ing (chĭng), *n.* A Chinese dynasty. See MANCHU, *n.,* 1.

chink (chĭngk), *n.* A small cleft, rent, or fissure.

chink, *n.* [Imitative.] **1.** A short sharp sound, as of metal lightly struck. **2.** *Now Slang.* Coin. — *v. t. & i.* To make, or cause to make, a chink.

chin'ka·pin (chĭng'kȧ·pĭn). Var. of CHINQUAPIN.

Chi'no- (chī'nō-). = SINO-, as in **Chi'no-Jap'a·nese'.**

Chi·nook' (shĭ·no͝ok'; chĭ·no͝ok'; chĭ·no͝ok'), *n.* **1.** A Chinookan Indian. **2.** A lingua franca, comprising words from the language of Chinooks and other Indians and from English and French. Cf. BÊCHE-DE-MER, PIDGIN. **3.** [*not cap.*] **a** A warm, moist, southwest wind of the coast of Oregon and Washington. **b** A warm, dry, foehn-like wind that descends the Rocky Mountains.

Chi·nook'an (-ăn), *adj.* Pertaining to or designating a linguistic family of American Indians, on reservations in Washington and Oregon. — **Chi·nook'an,** *n.*

Chinook salmon. = QUINNAT SALMON.

Chinook State. Washington; — a nickname.

chin'qua·pin (chĭng'kȧ·pĭn), *n.* [Amer. Indian.] **a** A chestnut (*Castanea pumila*) of the U. S., or its sweet edible nut which is usually solitary in the bur; — called also *dwarf chestnut.* **b** A related tree (*Castanopsis chrysophylla*) of Calif. and Ore. or its edible nut.

chintz (chĭnts), *n.* [A pl. fr. Hind. *chīnt.*] Originally, painted or stained calico from India; now, printed cotton cloth, often glazed.

chip (chĭp), *n.* [See CHIP, *v.*] **1.** A small fragment, as of wood, chopped, cut, or broken off. **2.** Something suggestive of a chip, as having the qualities of that from which it is taken; — esp. of persons; as, ***a chip of*** (*or* ***off***) ***the old block,*** a child that resembles its father. **3.** Anything valueless or trivial; also, anything withered or without flavor. **4.** A piece of dried dung, used for fuel; as, buffalo *chips.* **5.** An act of chipping; also, a crack or the like caused by chipping. **6.** *Cookery.* A thin crisp morsel of food; as, potato *chips.* **7.** *Games.* One of the counters used in poker and other games. **8.** *Golf.* A chip shot. — *v. t.;* CHIPPED (chĭpt); CHIP'PING. [AS. *cippian.*] **1.** *Obs.* To pare (bread) by cutting off the crust. **2.** To cut or hew with an ax, chisel, or the like. **3.** To break or crack off a portion of, as of a piece of crockery. — *v. i.* **1.** To break off in small pieces, as crockery at the edges. **2.** *Golf.* To play a chip shot. — ***chip in.*** *Colloq.* To put in a chip or chips as one's share of a stake at cards.

chip'munk (chĭp'mŭngk), *n.* [From Amer. Indian name.] Any of numerous small striped American rodents (genera *Tamias* and *Eutamias*) of the squirrel family; — called often *ground squirrels* (see SQUIRREL, 1 **b**).

chipped beef (chĭpt). Smoked beef cut in paper-thin slices.

Chip'pen·dale (chĭp'ĕn·dāl), *adj.* Designating furniture made by or in the style of Thomas Chippendale (fl. 1750–75). It was graceful but often ornate, rococo ornamentation predominating.

chip'per (chĭp'ẽr), *n.* One who chips; a tool that chips.

chip'per, *adj.* *Colloq., U. S.* Lively and cheerful.

Chip'pe·wa (chĭp'ē·wä; -wā), **Chip'pe·way** (-wā). Vars. of OJIBWAY.

chip'ping spar'row. See SPARROW, 2.

chip shot. *Golf.* A short, usually lofted, shot played from just off the green largely by wrist movement.

chirk (chûrk), *v. i.* [ME. *chirken.*] *Obs. exc. Scot.* To make a strident, creaking, or squeaking noise, as a door, a frog, or a mouse. — ***chirk up.*** *Colloq.* To cheer (up).

chirm (chûrm), *n.* [AS. *cyrm.*] Noise; din, as of voices, insects, etc. — *v. i.* *Now Dial.* To make a chirm.

chi'ro- (kī'rō-). [Gr. *cheir.*] A combining form meaning *hand,* as in *chiro*graphy, *chiro*practic.

chi·rog'ra·phy (kī·rŏg'rȧ·fĭ), *n.* [*chiro-* + *-graphy.*] Art of writing or engrossing; handwriting. — **chi·rog'ra·pher** (-fẽr), *n.* — **chi'ro·graph'ic** (kī'rō·grăf'ĭk), **chi'ro·graph'i·cal** (-ĭ·kăl), *adj.*

chi'ro·man'cy (kī'rō·măn'sĭ), *n.* [*chiro-* + *-mancy.*] Divination by examination of the hand; palmistry. — **chi'ro·man'cer** (-sẽr), *n.*

Chi'ron (kī'rŏn), *n.* [L., fr. Gr. *Cheirōn.*] *Gr. Myth.* A centaur renowned for skill in medicine.

chi·rop'o·dy (kī·rŏp'ō·dĭ), *n.* [*chiro-* + Gr. *pous, podos,* foot.] Originally, the art of treating diseases of the hands and feet; now, the treatment of ailments of the feet. — **chi·rop'o·dist** (-dĭst), *n.*

chi'ro·prac'tic (kī'rō·prăk'tĭk), *n.* [*chiro-* + Gr. *praktikos* effective.] A system, or the practice, of adjusting the joints, esp. of the spine, by hand for the curing of disease.

chi'ro·prac'tor (kī'rō·prăk'tẽr), *n.* A practitioner of chiropractic.

chi·rop'ter (kī·rŏp'tẽr), *n.* [*chiro-* + Gr. *pteron* wing.] = BAT, the animal. — **chi·rop'ter·an** (-ăn), *adj. & n.*

chirp (chûrp), *v. i.* [Imitative.] **1.** To make a short sharp sound, as small birds or crickets. **2.** To speak in a way likened to the chirping of birds. — *v. t.* To utter by chirping. — **chirp,** *n.* — **chirp'er,** *n.*

chirr (chûr), *v. i.* To stridulate. — **chirr,** *n.*

chir'rup (chĭr'ŭp), *v. i. & t.* [See CHIRP.] To chirp, esp. repeatedly and with a lively effect. — **chir'rup,** *n.*

chi·rur'geon (kī·rûr'jŭn), *n.* [F. *chirurgien,* fr. Gr., fr. *cheir* hand + *ergon* work.] *Archaic.* A surgeon. — **chi·rur'ger·y** (-jẽr·ĭ), *n.* — **chi·rur'gic** (-jĭk), **chi·rur'gi·cal** (-jĭ·kăl), *adj.*

chis'el (chĭz''l), *n.* [ONF. *chisel,* fr. L. *caesus,* past part. of *caedere* to cut.] A metal tool with a cutting edge at the end of a blade, used in

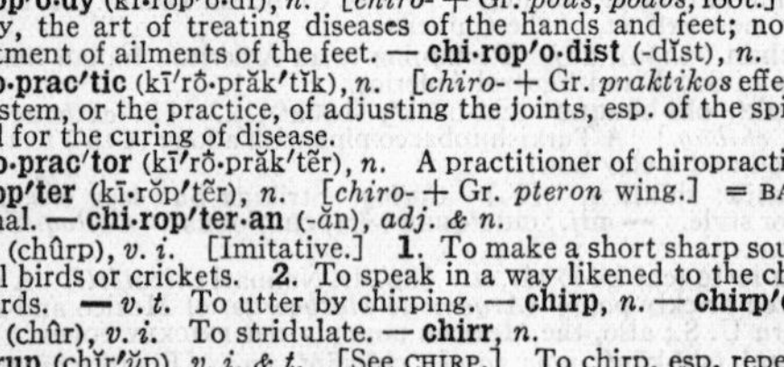

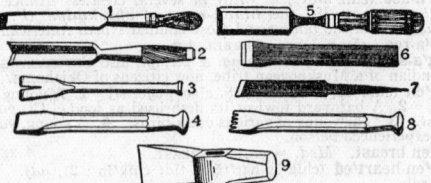

Chisels. 1 Socket Paring; 2 Corner; 3 Box; 4, 8 Stonecutter's; 5 Beveled Firmer; 6 Wire; 7 Turning; 9 Blacksmith's.

dressing, shaping, or working wood, stone, metal (see COLD CHISEL), etc. — *v. t. & i.;* CHIS'ELED (-'ld) or -ELLED; CHIS'EL·ING or -EL·LING. **1.** To cut or work with, or as with, a chisel. **2.** *Slang.* **a** To cheat. **b** To employ, or to obtain by, shrewd, sometimes unfair, practices. — **chis'el·er, chis'el·ler,** *n.*

chis'eled, chis'elled (-'ld), *adj.* **a** Cut or wrought with a chisel. **b** Appearing as if chiseled; clear-cut.

chi'-square' (kī'skwâr'), *n.* [From the name of the Gr. letter *X.*] The sum of the quotients obtained by dividing the square of the difference between the observed and theoretical values of a quantity by the theoretical value.

chit (chĭt), *n.* A child; also, a pert girl.

chit, *n.* [From *chitty,* fr. Hind. *citthi.*] A short letter or note; esp., a signed voucher of a small debt, as for food.

chit'chat' (chĭt'chăt'), *n.* [From CHAT.] Familiar or trifling conversation; small talk.

chi'tin (kī'tĭn), *n.* [F. *chitine,* fr. Gr. *chitōn.*] *Biochem.* A horny substance forming the harder part of the outer integument of insects, crustaceans, etc. — **chi'tin·ous** (-tĭ·nŭs), *adj.*

chi′ton (kī′tŏn), *n.* [Gr. *chitōn.*] **1.** *Gr. Antiq.* The garment commonly worn next to the skin by both sexes in classical times. **2.** A mollusk (genus *Chiton*) resembling the limpets in habits.
chit′ter (chĭt′ẽr), *v. i.* **1.** To twitter. **2.** *Scot. & Dial.* To shiver.
chit′ter·ling (-lĭng), *n.* Usually *pl.* The smaller intestines of swine, etc., esp. as fried or boiled.
chiv′al·ric (shĭv′ăl·rĭk; shĭ·văl′rĭk), *adj.* Pert. to chivalry; chivalrous.
chiv′al·rous (shĭv′ăl·rŭs), *adj.* [OF. *chevalerus, chevalereus,* fr. *chevalier.* See CHIVALRY.] **1.** *Obs.* Characteristic of, or like, a knight of feudal times, esp. in valor; valiant. **2.** Pertaining to chivalry or knight-errantry regarded as a system; as, *chivalrous* ideals. **3.** Of, pertaining to, or possessing the qualities of, the ideal knight of the age of chivalry; valorous and generous to foes; also, courteously attentive. — **Syn.** See CIVIL. — **-ly,** *adv.* — **-ness,** *n.*
chiv′al·ry (-rĭ), *n.* [OF. *chevalerie,* fr. *chevalier* knight, orig., horseman.] **1.** *Obs.* Mounted men-at-arms. **2.** *Archaic.* The rank, position, or characteristics of a feudal knight; esp., martial valor. **3.** A body of knights or illustrious mounted soldiers; hence, gallant and distinguished gentlemen. **4.** The dignity or system of knighthood; the spirit, usages, or manners of knighthood; the practice of knight-errantry. **5.** The qualifications or character of the ideal knight.
chive (chīv), *n.* [ONF. (F. *cive*), fr. L. *cepa, caepa,* onion.] A perennial plant (*Allium schoenoprasum*) allied to the onion. Its slender leaves are used to flavor soups, omelets, etc. Usually in *pl.*
chiv′y, chiv′vy (chĭv′ĭ). Var. of CHEVY.
chla′mys (klā′mĭs; klăm′ĭs), *n.; pl.* CHLAMYDES (klăm′ĭ·dēz), CHLAMYSES (klā′mĭs·ĕz; klăm′ĭs-; -ĭz). [L., fr. Gr. *chlamys.*] *Gr. Antiq.* A short oblong mantle fastened with a clasp in front or at the shoulder.
Chlo′ë (klō′ē), *n.* Also **Chlo′e.** See DAPHNIS AND CHLOË.
chlo′ral (klō′răl; klō·răl′), *n.* [*chlor*ine + *al*cohol.] **1.** *Chem.* A colorless oily liquid, CCl_3CHO, of a pungent odor and harsh taste, obtained by the action of chlorine upon alcohol. **2.** Loosely, **chloral hydrate,** $CCl_3CH(OH)_2$, a soporific.
chlo′ram·phen′i·col (klō′răm·fĕn′ĭ·kōl; -kŏl; 70), *n.* [*chlor-* + *am*id + *phen*ol + *ni*tr- + gly*col.*] An antibiotic isolated from a soil microorganism (*Streptomyces venezuelae*), also prepared synthetically, effective against certain diseases caused by bacteria, rickettsiae, and viruses.
chlo′rate (klō′rāt), *n.* *Chem.* A salt of chloric acid.
chlor′dan (klōr′dăn; 70), *n.* Also **chlor′dane** (-dān). [*chlor-* + *indan,* a compound derived from indene.] An odorless liquid insecticide (chemically an indene derivative, $C_{10}H_6Cl_8$).
chlo′ric (klō′rĭk; klŏr′ĭk), *adj.* [From CHLORINE.] *Chem.* Pert. to, or obtained from, chlorine; specif., pert. to or designating a monoacid (**chloric acid,** $HClO_3$) obtained from its salts (the chlorates).
chlo′ride (klō′rīd; -rĭd), *n.* Also **chlo′rid.** *Chem.* A compound of chlorine with another element or radical; as, **chloride of lime,** a nearly white powder made by passing chlorine gas over slaked lime and used as a bleach and disinfectant; — called also **chlorinated lime.**
chlo′rin·ate (klō′rĭ·nāt), *v. t.* To treat, or cause to combine, with chlorine; specif., to apply chlorine to (water or sewage) for sterilization. — **chlo′rin·a′tion** (-nā′shŭn), *n.* — **chlo′rin·a′tor** (-nā′tẽr), *n.*
chlo′rine (klō′rēn; -rĭn), *n.* Also **chlo′rin.** [Gr. *chlōros* light-green.] *Chem.* An element isolated as a heavy, greenish-yellow, irritating gas of suffocating odor. Symbol, *Cl;* at. no., 17; at. wt., 35.457. Chlorine is used as a bleach, a disinfectant, in water purification, etc.
chlo′rite (-rīt), *n.* [Gr. *chlōritis* (sc. *lithos* stone), fr. *chlōros* light-green.] Any of a group of monoclinic, usually green minerals, closely resembling the micas.
chlo′rite, *n.* [*chlor*ous + *-ite.*] A salt of chlorous acid.
chlo′ro- (klō′rō-), **chlor-.** [Gr. *chlōros.*] **1.** A combining form meaning *green.* **2.** *Chem.* A combining form denoting that *chlorine* is an ingredient in the substance named, as in *chloro*form.
chlo′ro·form (klō′rō·fôrm), *n.* [*chloro-,* 2 + *formy*l.] *Chem.* A colorless, volatile, heavy liquid, $CHCl_3$, of ethereal odor and sweetish taste, made usually by treating acetone or alcohol with bleaching powder. It is used as an anesthetic, counterirritant, and antiseptic. — *v. t.* To treat with chloroform, or to place under its influence, esp. so as to produce anesthesia.
Chlo′ro·my·ce′tin (klō′rō·mī·sē′tĭn; 70), *n.* A trade-mark applied to chloramphenicol.
chlo′ro·phyll, chlo′ro·phyl (-fĭl), *n.* [*chloro-,* 1 + *-phyll.*] The green coloring matter visible in leaves and present in all growing plants. Chlorophyll bodies (*chloroplasts*) under the stimulus of light are active in the manufacture of plant food, mainly starch, from carbon dioxide and water. Cf. PHOTOSYNTHESIS. — **chlo′ro·phyl′lose** (-fĭl′ōs), **chlo′ro·phyl′lous** (-ŭs), *adj.*
chlo′ro·pic′rin (klō′rō·pĭk′rĭn; -pī′krĭn), *n.* Also **chlor·pic′rin** (klōr-). [*chloro-,* 2 + *picric* + *-in.*] *Chem.* A heavy, colorless, pungent liquid, CCl_3NO_2, whose vapor causes vomiting.
chlo′ro·plast (klō′rō·plăst), *n.* [*chloro-,* 1 + *-plast.*] *Biol.* A plastid containing chlorophyll, developed only in cells exposed to the light. Chloroplasts are the seat of photosynthesis and starch formation. Cf. CHROMOPLAST.
chlo′ro·prene (klō′rō·prēn), *n.* [*chloro-* + iso*prene.*] *Chem.* A colorless liquid, C_4H_5Cl, made from acetylene and hydrochloric acid, used esp. in making neoprene.
chlo·ro′sis (klō·rō′sĭs), *n.* [NL., fr. Gr. *chlōros* light-green.] **1.** An anemic disease of young women, characterized by a greenish hue of the skin, menstrual disorders, etc.; greensickness. **2.** A diseased condition in plants, shown by the blanching of green parts.
chlo′rous (klō′rŭs), *adj.* [See CHLORINE.] *Chem.* Pert. to a strongly oxidizing monoacid (**chlorous acid,** $HClO_2$) known only in solution and in its salts, the chlorites.
chock (chŏk), *n.* **1.** A wedge or block to fill a space, to steady a cask, boat, wheel, or other body, or to prevent it from moving. **2.** *Naut.* A heavy casting of metal or wood, with two short horn-shaped arms curving inward, between which ropes or hawsers may pass for towing, mooring, etc. — *v. t.* To provide, stop, or make fast, with a chock or chocks. — *adv.* As close or tight as possible.

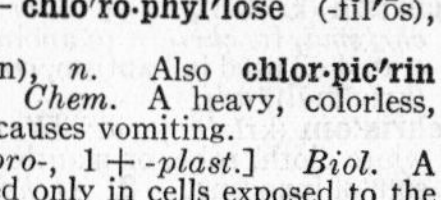
Chock, 2.

chock′a·block′ (chŏk′ȧ·blŏk′; 2), *adj.* **1.** *Naut.* Brought close together, as the two blocks of a tackle in hoisting. **2.** Hence, crowded.
chock′-full′, chuck′-full′, choke′-full′ (*see Pron.,* § 2), *adj.* Full to the extreme limit, to the brim, or the like.
choc′o·late (chŏk′ō·lĭt; chŏk′lĭt; 74), *n.* [Sp.; cf. Nahuatl *chocólatl.*] **1.** Ground roasted cacao beans; also, a beverage made from these ground-up beans. **2.** A small candy with a center, as of fondant, nougat, or nuts, and a coating of chocolate. **3.** Also **chocolate brown.** The color of chocolate; a brown, red-yellow in hue, of low saturation and low brilliance. — **choc′o·late,** *adj.*
chocolate tree. The cacao (def. 1), type of a family (Sterculiaceae, the **chocolate family**) of herbs, shrubs, and trees, natives of warm regions. See CACAO, *Illust.*
Choc′taw (chŏk′tô), *n.; pl.* CHOCTAW, -TAWS (-tôz). An Indian of one of the Muskhogean tribes, now in Oklahoma.
choice (chois), *n.* [OF. *chois,* fr. *choisir* to choose.] **1.** Act of choosing; selection. **2.** Power of choosing; option. **3.** That which is most excellent; the best part. **4.** A sufficient number and variety to choose among; also, a choice supply. **5.** A person or thing chosen. **6.** Care in selecting; discrimination. **7.** An alternative.
Syn. Choice, option, alternative, preference, selection, election mean the act or opportunity of choosing or the thing chosen. **Choice** usually implies the right or privilege of choosing freely; **option,** the power to choose, especially as granted by one (person, group, etc.) in whom the power is vested to another who is immediately affected by the choice; **alternative,** strictly, implies a choice between one thing and another when no other is possible; **preference** suggests the guidance of choice by one's judgment or predilections; **selection** implies a wide range of choice; **election** carries the implication of an end or purpose which requires exercise of judgment.
— *adj.* **1.** Worthy of being chosen; select. **2.** Selected with care; well-chosen. **3.** *Chiefly Dial.* **a** Of persons, exercising care in choosing; also, fastidious. **b** Preserving or using with care, as valuable; frugal. — **choice′ly,** *adv.* — **choice′ness,** *n.*
Syn. Choice, exquisite, elegant, rare, dainty, delicate mean having qualities that appeal to a fastidious taste. **Choice** stresses pre-eminence in quality or in kind; **exquisite** implies a perfection so fine and unobtrusive that it attracts only the most sensitive and fastidious; **elegant** implies a noble simplicity and restraint not incompatible with richness or grandeur; **rare** implies a superlative quality that gives distinction; **dainty** and **delicate** imply exquisiteness, *dainty* more often applying to that which is small, and *delicate* to that which is fine, subtle, or fragile.
choir (kwīr), *n.* Also **quire** (kwīr). [OF. *cuer* (F. *chœur*), fr. L. *chorus.* See CHORUS.] **1.** An organized company of singers, esp. in church service. **2.** Any organized company; specif.: **a** A company of dancers, or of dancers and singers. **b** A group or company organized for ensemble speaking. See CHORAL SPEAKING. **3.** A division of angels. **4.** *Arch.* That part of a church appropriated to the singers. — *v. t. & i.* To sing in chorus or concert, as a choir.
choir, *adj.* Of that class in a religious order devoted chiefly to the order's special work, as teaching or preaching; as, a *choir* brother; — contrasted with *lay.*
choir′boy′ (kwīr′boi′), *n.* A boy member of a choir.
choir loft. A gallery appropriated to a choir.
choir′mas′ter (-más′tẽr), *n.* The director of a choir.
choke (chōk), *v. t.* [ME. *choken, cheken,* fr. AS. *ācēocian* to suffocate.] **1.** To render unable to breathe, as by pressing the windpipe or by stopping the supply of air; to stifle; strangle; also, to smother. **2.** To check the growth, progress, or action of. **3.** To obstruct by filling up or clogging; also, to fill up. **4.** *Gas Engines.* To shut off the air intake of the carburetor of (a motor) to make the fuel mixture rich, as for starting. — *v. i.* **1.** To stifle; suffocate. **2.** To be obstructed; to stick. — *n.* **1.** Something that chokes. **2.** Act or sound of choking. **3.** A constriction, such as a narrowing towards the muzzle in the bore of a gun, etc. **4.** An obstructing piece in mechanism, to prevent passage of too much of anything, as the valve that permits the choking of a gasoline engine.
choke′ber′ry (-bĕr′ĭ; -bẽr·ĭ), *n.* The small berrylike astringent fruit of any shrub of the genus *Aronia* of the apple family; also, a shrub of this genus.
choke′bore′ (-bōr′; 70), *n.* **a** In a shotgun, a bore tapered toward the muzzle to retard scattering of the shot. **b** A shotgun with such a bore.
choke′cher′ry (-chĕr′ĭ), *n.* See CHERRY, *n.,* 1 & 2.
choke, *or* **chok′ing** (chōk′ĭng), **coil.** *Elec.* A reactor.
choke′damp′ (chōk′dămp′), *n.* *Mining.* A nonexplosive but suffocating gas or "damp" formed in mines and consisting essentially of carbon dioxide; — called also *blackdamp.* See DAMP, *n.,* 1.
choke′-full′. Var. of CHOCK-FULL.
chok′er (chōk′ẽr), *n.* **1.** One that chokes or puts to silence. **2.** *Chiefly Slang.* Something worn closely about the throat; as: **a** A wide cravat. **b** A very high collar. **c** A short necklace.
chol′e- (kŏl′ē-). = CHOLO-, as in **chol′e·cyst,** the gall bladder.
chol′er (kŏl′ẽr), *n.* [OF. *colere,* fr. L., fr. Gr. *cholera* cholera, prob. fr. *cholē* bile.] **1.** *Hist.* **a** The bile; — formerly supposed to be the cause of irascibility. See BILE; HUMOR, 2 **a.** **b** Biliousness. **2.** Irritation; anger.
chol′er·a (kŏl′ẽr·ȧ), *n.* [L., a bilious disease. See CHOLER.] **1.** *Obs. Med.* Choler, or bile. **2.** *Med. & Veter.* Any of certain diseases characteristically distinguished by vomiting, diarrhea, and general prostration; as, chicken *cholera;* hog *cholera;* specif., short for: **a Asiatic cholera,** a malignant, usually fatal disease originating in Asia but often epidemic elsewhere. **b chol′er·a in·fan′tum** (ĭn·făn′tŭm), a disease of infants, prevailing in summer. **c chol′er·a mor′bus** (môr′bŭs), acute gastroenteritis occurring in the hot months.
chol′er·ic (kŏl′ẽr·ĭk), *adj.* **1.** *Hist.* Characterized by choler or bile. **2.** *Obs.* **a** Producing biliousness. **b** Bilious. **c** Of hot or fiery nature. **3.** Hot-tempered; easily angered or irritated; also, angry; as, *choleric* words. — **Syn.** See IRASCIBLE.
cho·les′ter·ol (kō·lĕs′tẽr·ōl; -ŏl), *n.* [*chole-* + Gr. *stereos* stiff, solid.] *Biochem.* A white, fatty, crystalline alcohol, $C_{27}H_{45}OH + H_2O$, tasteless and odorless. It is found in bile, gallstones, egg yolk, and esp. nerve tissue.
cho′line (kō′lēn; kŏl′ēn; -ĭn), *n.* Also **cho′lin.** [Gr. *cholē* bile.] *Biochem.* A crystalline base, $C_5H_{15}NO_2$, widely distributed among animal and plant products. It is a member of the vitamin-B complex and is essential to the liver function.
chol′o- (kŏl′ō-), **chol-.** [Gr. *cholē, cholos.*] A combining form meaning *bile, gall,* as in **chol′o·lith,** a gallstone.
chon′drite (kŏn′drīt), *n.* *Mineral.* A meteoric stone characterized by the presence of small rounded grains or spherules.
chon′dro- (kŏn′drō-), **chondr-.** [Gr. *chondros* a grain, cartilage.] A combining form denoting *composed of,* or *having to do with, cartilage,* as in **chon·dro′ma,** a tumor composed of cartilage; **chon·drot′o·my** (see -TOMY).

chon'drule (kŏn'drōōl), *n.* *Mineral.* A peculiar rounded granule of cosmic origin found esp. embedded in many meteoric stones (*chondrites*).

choose (chōōz), *v. t.;* CHOSE (chōz); CHO'SEN (chō'z'n); CHOOS'ING. *Obs. past part.* CHOSE. [AS. *cēosan.*] **1.** To make choice of; to select. **2.** To think proper; to please; — with infinitive object. **3.** *Colloq.* To wish to have; desire; want. — *v. i.* **1.** To make a selection. **2.** To have choice; — *Obs.* exc. in *choose but* with a negative; as, he cannot *choose* but accept. — **choos'er** (chōōz'ẽr), *n.*

Syn. **Choose, select, elect, pick, cull, prefer** mean to fix upon one (or more) as one's choice. **Choose** implies a decision of the judgment and an actual taking or adoption; **select** implies a wide range and discrimination or care; **elect** stresses deliberate choice and, usually, the rejection of those not chosen; **pick** implies careful selection and **cull** implies a nice or fastidious choice; **prefer** implies a choice governed by what one favors.

chop (chŏp), *v. t.;* CHOPPED (chŏpt); CHOP'PING. **1.** To cut by striking, esp. repeatedly, with a sharp instrument; hence, to mince. **2.** *Cricket & Lawn Tennis.* To strike (a ball) down with a short, quick, cutting or slicing stroke. — *v. i.* **1.** To make a quick stroke, or repeated strokes, with an ax or other sharp instrument. **2.** To go, come, or make some movement, suddenly or violently, as in darting, pouncing, etc. — *n.* **1.** Act of chopping; a cutting stroke. **2.** A piece chopped off; a slice or small piece; specif., of meat, a small cut often including a rib; as, a lamb *chop.* **3.** A crack or cleft; a chap, as of the lips. **4.** Of waves, etc., a short, abrupt motion; also, a stretch of choppy sea. **5.** *Boxing.* A short, sharp blow from above.

chop, *v. t. Obs. exc. Dial.* To barter or truck; to exchange. — *v. i.* **1.** *Obs.* To barter; make an exchange. **2.** To turn with, or like, the wind; to veer. **3.** *Obs.* To bandy words; to answer back. — ***chop logic.*** To bandy logic; esp., to argue sophistically.

chop, *n.* **1.** A jaw; — commonly in *pl.* **2.** *pl.* The jaws with the space between them; chaps. **3.** *pl.* The mouth or entrance, as of a cannon, valley, or channel.

chop, *v. t.* **1.** *Obs.* To seize with the chops and eat; to snap. **2.** In reading or speaking, to cut off (one's words) sharply, so as to render utterance indistinct.

chop (chŏp), *n.* [Hind. *chāp* stamp, brand.] **1.** In India and China, a seal; an official stamp. **2.** In the India and China trade, a license rendered valid by a seal; a clearance; as, ***grand chop,*** a customs clearance. **3.** In the China trade, a mark on goods to indicate their nature, quality, etc.; hence, a particular kind, brand, or class of goods. **4.** *Anglo-Ind. & Colloq.* Quality, brand, rate, or the like.

chop'fall'en (chŏp'fôl'ĕn), *adj.* Chapfallen.

chop'house' (-hous'), *n.* An eating house where chops and the like are usually served as a specialty.

chop'house', *n. China.* A customhouse.

cho·pine' (chō·pēn'; chŏp'ĭn), *n.* Also **chop'in** (chŏp'ĭn). [Cf. OF. *chapin,* Sp. *chapín.*] = PATTEN.

chop'per (chŏp'ẽr), *n.* One who or that which chops.

chop'ping, *adj.* Large; strapping; — of children.

chop'py (chŏp'ĭ), *adj.;* CHOP'PI·ER (-ĭ·ẽr); CHOP'PI·EST. Full of cracks, or chaps.

chop'py, *adj.* [Cf. 1st CHOP, *n.,* 5.] Rough, with short, tumbling waves; — of the sea.

chop'py, *adj.* [From CHOP to barter.] Of the wind, repeatedly veering about; hence, changeable; variable.

chop'stick' (chŏp'stĭk'), *n.* [A pidgin-English translation of the Chinese name, which means hasteners, speedy ones.] One of two small sticks or slips of wood, ivory, etc., used, esp. by the Chinese, to convey food to the mouth.

chop stroke. *Lawn Tennis, etc.* A short, sharp, cutting or slicing stroke.

chop su'ey *or* **soo'y** (chŏp' sōō'ĭ). [From Cantonese pron. of Chin. (Pek.) *tsa²-sui⁴,* lit., miscellaneous pieces.] *U. S.* A mélange served in Chinese restaurants, consisting typically of bean sprouts, onions, mushrooms, etc., and sliced meats, fried and flavored with sesame oil.

cho·ra'gus (kō·rā'gŭs), *n.; pl.* -RAGI (-jī). [L., fr. Gr. *choragos, chorēgos,* fr. *choros* chorus + *agein* to lead.] **1.** *Gr. Antiq.* A chorus leader. **2.** The leader of a chorus, choir, or group. — **cho·rag'ic** (-răj'ĭk; -rā'jĭk), *adj.*

cho'ral (kō'răl; 70), *adj.* [F. *choral* or ML. *choralis.*] **1.** Of, pertaining to, or sung or recited by a choir or chorus. **2.** *Music.* Sung, or adapted to be sung, in chorus or harmony. — **cho'ral·ly,** *adv.*

cho·ral', cho·rale' (kō·răl'; kō·räl'), *n.* *Music.* A hymn tune; a simple sacred tune, sung in unison.

choral speaking. Artistic ensemble speaking and interpretation of works of poetry, prose, or drama by a group, called variously a ***speaking, speech, or verse-speaking choir,*** under the direction of a leader or conductor.

chord (kôrd), *n.* [L. *chorda.* See CORD.] **1.** A string of a musical instrument, as of a harp; hence, a particular emotion; as, to strike a responsive *chord.* **2.** *Aeronautics.* The line of a straightedge brought into contact with the lower surface of an airfoil section at two points. **3.** *Anat.* A cord, tendon, nerve, or filament. **4.** *Engin.* In a truss, one of the principal members, usually horizontal, braced by the web members. **5.** *Geom.* A straight line intersecting a curve; a secant; specif., the segment of the line between two points of its intersection with the curve. See CIRCLE, *Illust.* — **chord'al** (kôr'dăl; -d'l), *adj.*

chord (kôrd), *n.* [From ACCORD, *n.*] *Acoustics & Music.* A combination of tones which blend harmoniously when sounded together. — *v. i. Music.* To accord.

chor'date (kôr'dāt), *n.* [L. *chorda* cord.] One of a phylum (Chordata) of animals which at some stage of their development have a notochord, a dorsally situated central nervous system, and gill clefts. — *adj.* **a** Having a notochord. **b** Of or pertaining to a chordate.

chore (chōr; 70), *n.* [Same word as CHARE daywork.] *U. S.* A small or odd job; a chare; in the *pl.,* the regular or daily light work of a household or farm. — **Syn.** See TASK.

cho·re'a (kō·rē'ȧ), *n.* [NL., fr. Gr. *choreia* dance.] A nervous disorder, characterized by spasmodic twitchings; — called also *St. Vitus's dance.*

cho're·og'ra·phy (kō'rē·ŏg'rȧ·fĭ; kŏr'ē-), **cho·reg'ra·phy** (kō·rĕg'-), *n.* [Gr. *choreia* dance + *-graphy.*] **1.** The art of dancing, or of arranging dances, esp. ballets. **2.** Dancing, esp. ballet dancing, for the stage. — **cho're·og'ra·pher** (-fẽr), **cho·reg'ra·pher,** *n.* — **cho're·o·graph'ic** (-ō·grăf'ĭk), **cho're·graph'ic,** *adj.*

cho'ri·amb (kō'rĭ·ămb; kŏr'ĭ-), *n.* [L. *choriambus,* fr. Gr. *choriambos,* fr. *choreios* trochee + *iambos* iamb.] *Pros.* A foot consisting of a trochee and an iamb (-⏑⏑-).

cho'ric (kō'rĭk; kŏr'ĭk), *adj.* Of, pertaining to, or in the style of a chorus, esp. of a Greek tragedy; rarely, of a choir.

cho'ri·oid (kō'rĭ·oid; 70), *adj.* [Gr. *chorioeidēs.*] *Anat.* Pert. to or designating several delicate vascular membranes or structures; as, the **chorioid coat** *or* **membrane** between the sclerotic coat and retina of the eye (see EYE, *Illust.*). — *n.* The chorioid coat.

cho'ri·on (-ŏn), *n.* [NL., fr. Gr. *chorion.*] *Embryol.* A membrane enveloping the embryo of higher vertebrates (reptiles, birds, and mammals), lying external to and enclosing the amnion. Cf. PLACENTA.

cho'ri·pet'al·ous (kō'rĭ·pĕt'ăl·ŭs), *adj.* [NL., fr. Gr. *chōri, chōris,* asunder, apart.] *Bot.* Having the petals separate; polypetalous; — opp. to *gamopetalous.*

chor'is·ter (kŏr'ĭs·tẽr), *n.* **1.** A singer in a choir; specif., a choirboy. **2.** *U. S.* One who leads a church choir.

cho·rog'ra·phy (kō·rŏg'rȧ·fĭ), *n.* [From L., fr. Gr. *chōrographia,* fr. *chōros* place + *graphein* to describe.] **1.** Art of describing or mapping a region or district. **2.** A description or chart of a region; also, its physical conformation and features. — **cho·rog'ra·pher,** *n.* — **cho'ro·graph'ic** (kō'rō·grăf'ĭk), **cho'ro·graph'i·cal** (-ĭ·kăl), *adj.* — **cho'ro·graph'i·cal·ly,** *adv.*

cho'roid (kō'roid), *adj. & n.* [Gr. *choroeidēs.*] Chorioid.

chor'tle (chôr't'l), *v. t. & i.;* CHOR'TLED (-t'ld); CHOR'TLING (-tlĭng). [Appar. a blend of *chuckle* and *snort.*] To sing or chant exultantly; — a word coined by Lewis Carroll (Charles L. Dodgson). — **chor'tle,** *n.* — **chor'tler** (-tlẽr), *n.*

cho'rus (kō'rŭs; 70), *n.; pl.* CHORUSES (-ĕz; -ĭz). [L., a dance in a ring or with song, a chorus, a band of dancers and singers, fr. Gr. *choros.*] **1.** In Greek drama, a company of singers. **2.** In modern drama, a body of dancers and usually singers, who execute special numbers. **3.** The part of the drama sung or danced by the chorus. **4.** In the Elizabethan drama, a single character who speaks the prologue, epilogue, and at times comments on the course of events. **5.** The simultaneous singing of a number of persons; also, a part of a song recurring at intervals, as the refrain at the end of stanzas. **6.** The simultaneous utterance of speech, cries, etc., by a number of people or animals, as dogs in the chase; also, the sounds so uttered. **7.** *Music.* **a** A company of singers singing in concert. **b** A composition intended to be sung by a number of voices in concert. — *v. i. & t.* To sing in chorus; to exclaim simultaneously.

chose (chōz), *past tense & obs. past part.* of CHOOSE.

chose (shōz), *n.; pl.* CHOSES (shōz'ĕz; -ĭz). [F., fr. L. *causa* reason.] *Law.* A thing; a piece of personal property.

‖**chose ju'gée'** (shōz' zhü'zhā'). [F.] Literally, an adjudicated case; a matter that has been settled.

cho'sen (chō'z'n), *past part.* of CHOOSE. Specif.: *adj.* Selected from a number; picked out; choice; in *Theol.,* elect.

Chou (jō), *n.* A dynasty in China (1122–255 B.C.).

chough (chŭf), *n.* [ME. *choughe, kowe.*] Any bird of the Old World genus *Pyrrhocorax,* of the crow family (Corvidae), with red legs and glossy black plumage.

chouse (chous), *n.* [Turk. *chāwush* a messenger or interpreter, one of whom in 1609 is said to have cheated Turkish merchants in England.] *Obs.* **1.** A swindler; cheat. **2.** One easily cheated; gull; dupe. — *v. t. Colloq.* To cheat; trick.

chow (chou), *n.* [See CHOWCHOW.] **1.** *Slang.* Food; victuals. **2.** A profusely coated, lion-headed, straight-legged, compact and muscular dog of a breed believed to have originated in north China. Its tongue is blue-black.

chow (chou; chōō). Scot. & dial. var. of JOWL.

chow'chow' (chou'chou'), *adj.* [Pidgin Eng.] Mixed; miscellaneous. — *n.* **1.** Chopped mixed pickles in mustard sauce. **2.** A chow.

chow'der (chou'dẽr), *n.* [F. *chaudière* kettle, pot.] *Cookery.* A dish made of fresh fish or clams, pork, crackers, onions, etc., stewed together, often in milk; by extension, a similar dish in which a vegetable, as corn, replaces the fish. — **Syn.** See SOUP.

chow mein (chou' mān'). [Chin. (Pek.) *ch'ao³* to fry + *mien⁴* flour.] A thick stew of shredded chicken, mushrooms, celery, onions, etc., served with fried noodles.

chres·tom'a·thy (krĕs·tŏm'ȧ·thĭ), *n.; pl.* -THIES (-thĭz). [Gr. *chrēstomatheia,* fr. *chrēstos* useful + *mathein, manthanein,* to learn.] A selection of literary passages, esp. with notes, etc., to be used in learning a language.

chrism (krĭz'm), *n.* [AS. *crisma* or OF. *cresme;* both fr. LL., fr. Gr. *chrisma,* fr. *chriein* to anoint.] *Eastern & R. C. Churches.* Consecrated oil used in baptism, confirmation, ordination, etc. — **chris'mal** (krĭz'măl), *adj.*

chris'om (krĭz'ŭm), *n.* [Var. of CHRISM.] **1.** Chrism. **2.** *Hist.* A white cloth, robe, or mantle thrown over a child when baptized, as a sign of innocence. **3.** *Archaic.* A child in its chrisom; hence, a babe; an infant.

Christ (krīst), *n.* [L. *Christus,* fr. Gr. *Christos,* fr. *christos* anointed. See CHRISM.] **1.** The Messiah, whose coming was prophesied by the Jews. **2.** Jesus; — as fulfilling this prophecy. **3.** *Christian Science.* The divine manifestation of God, which comes to the flesh to destroy incarnate error. *Mary Baker Eddy.*

christ'cross' (krĭs'krŏs'; 74), *n.* Often written **criss'cross'** (krĭs'-). [Cf. CRISSCROSS.] **1.** **a** The mark of the cross (typically ✠), formerly put before the alphabet. **b** = MARK, *n.,* 8 **c.** **2.** *Dial. Eng.* The alphabet.

chris'ten (krĭs''n), *v. t.* [AS. *cristnian* to make a Christian, fr. *cristen* a Christian, fr. L. *christianus.*] **1.** To baptize; also, to name at baptism. **2.** To name; specif., to name (a ship) in a launching ceremony. **3.** *Colloq.* To use for the first time.

Chris'ten·dom (-dŭm), *n.* [AS. *cristendōm.*] **1.** *Obs.* Christianity. **2.** The whole body of Christians; the church. **3.** That portion of the world in which Christianity prevails, in distinction from heathen or Mohammedan lands.

chris'ten·ing (-ĭng), *n.* The ceremony of baptizing and naming a child, often followed by festivities.

Christ'hood (krīst'hŏŏd), *n.* State of being Christ.

Chris'tian (krĭs'chăn; krĭst'yăn), *adj.* **1.** Professing, or belonging to, Christianity. **2.** Of or pertaining to Christ or the religion based on Christ's teachings. **3.** Of or pertaining to a Christian or Christians. **4.** Representing Christianity; as, his most *Christian* majesty. **5.** Characteristic of Christian people; kindly. — *n.* **1.** One who believes, or professes or is assumed to believe, in Jesus Christ, and the truth as taught by him. **2.** **a** *Now Chiefly Dial.* A human being as distinguished from one of the lower animals. **b** *Colloq.* A decent, civilized, or presentable person. **3.** The hero of Bunyan's *Pilgrim's Progress.*

Christian Era. The era in use in all Christian countries, intended to commence with the birth of Christ. The date assigned originally as that of Christ's birth is now thought to be about four years too late.

Chris'ti·an'i·a (krĭs'chĭ·ăn'ĭ·ȧ; krĭs'tĭ-), *n.*, *or* **Christiania turn.** Also **Chris'ty** (krĭs'tĭ). [From *Christiania*, former name of Oslo, Norway.] *Skiing.* A Norwegian swinging turn accomplished by a moderate upward spring from a forward crouching position for unweighting and turning the skis, and an inward leaning with the legs and body to produce a skidding of the rear ends of the skis, which are driven in the desired direction by the impetus and centrifugal force.

Chris'tian·ism (krĭs'chăn·ĭz'm; krĭst'yăn-), *n.* The religious system, tenets, or practices of Christians.

Chris'ti·an'i·ty (krĭs'chĭ·ăn'ĭ·tĭ; -tĭ·ăn'ĭ·tĭ), *n.* **1.** The body of Christian believers; Christendom. **2.** The religion of Christians. **3.** State or fact of being a Christian; Christian character or spirit.

Chris'tian·ize (krĭs'chăn·īz; krĭst'yăn-), *v. t.* To make Christian; to convert to Christianity. — **Chris'tian·i·za'tion** (-ĭ·zā'shŭn; -ī·zā'-), *n.*

Christian name. The name given in baptism, as distinct from the family name; first name; given name.

Christian Science. A religion and system of healing disease of mind and body which teaches that all cause and effect is mental, and that sin, sickness, and death will be destroyed by a full understanding of the Divine Principle of Jesus' teaching and healing. The system was founded by Mary Baker Eddy in 1866, and bases its teaching on the Scriptures as understood by its adherents. The official name of the organization is *Church of Christ, Scientist.* — **Christian Scientist.**

Christ'less (krīst'lĕs; -lĭs), *adj.* Without Christ or faith in Christ; unchristian. — **Christ'less·ness,** *n.*

Christ'like' (-līk'), *adj.* Resembling Christ in character, spirit, actions, etc. — **Christ'like'ness,** *n.*

Christ'ly (-lĭ), *adj.* Of or pertaining to Christ; Christlike.

Christ'mas (krĭs'mȧs; krĭst'-), *n.* [*Christ* + *Mass.*] An annual church festival, kept on December 25 in memory of the birth of Christ, celebrated generally by special gifts, greetings, etc. — **Christmas Day.**

Christmas Eve. The evening before Christmas Day.

Christ'mas·tide' (-tīd'), *n.* [*Christmas* + *tide* time.] The festival season from Christmas Eve till after New Year's Day or, esp. in England, till Epiphany (Jan. 6).

Christmas tree. A tree, esp. an evergreen, usually decorated and illuminated, used in Christmas celebrations.

Christ's'-thorn' (krīsts'thôrn'), *n.* Any of several thorny shrubs (of the buckthorn family) of Palestine, esp. *Paliurus spina-christi* and the jujube *Zizyphus jujuba.* It is thought that one of these plants was used for Christ's crown of thorns.

Chris'ty (krĭs'tĭ), *n.* = CHRISTIANIA.

chrom-. = CHROMO-.

chro'ma (krō'mȧ), *n.* [Gr. *chrōma* color.] That quality of color which embraces hue and saturation together (see COLOR, 2). White, black, and grays have no chroma. — **Syn.** See COLOR.

chro'mate (krō'māt), *n.* A salt of chromic acid.

chro·mat'ic (krō·măt'ĭk), *adj.* [From L., fr. Gr. *chrōmatikos* suited for color (in music, chromatic), fr. *chrōma, chrōmatos,* color.] **1.** Of or pertaining to color or colors. **2.** *Music.* **a** Involving the use of tones foreign to a given mode or key; — applied to harmony utilizing freely the half-step interpolations in the diatonic scale. **b** Of, pert. to, or giving all tones of, the chromatic scale. — *n. Music.* In full **chromatic sign.** An accidental. — **chro·mat'i·cal·ly** (-ĭ·kăl·ĭ), *adv.*

chro·mat'ics (krō·măt'ĭks), *n.*; see -ICS. The branch of colorimetry which treats of hue and saturation. — **chro'ma·tist** (krō'mȧ·tĭst), *n.*

chromatic scale. *Music.* The diatonic scale with the five intermediate semitones.

chro'ma·tin (krō'mȧ·tĭn), *n.* [Gr. *chrōma, chrōmatos,* color.] *Biol.* A deeply staining protoplasmic material occurring in the nucleus of cells. Chromatin exists in small granules and is regarded as the physical basis of heredity. It consists largely of protein compounds of nucleic acid. See CELL, OVUM, *Illusts.*

chro'ma·tism (-tĭz'm), *n.* [Gr. *chrōmatismos* a coloring.] **1.** *Bot.* Abnormal coloration of the normally green parts of plants. **2.** *Optics.* See ABERRATION, *n.*, 4.

chro'ma·to- (krō'mȧ·tō-), **chromat-.** [Gr. *chrōma, chrōmatos,* color.] A combining form denoting: **a** *Color,* as in **chro'ma·to·pho'bi·a.** **b** *Chromatin,* as in *chromato*lysis. **c** *Pigment, pigmentation,* as in *chromato*phore.

chro'ma·tog'ra·phy (-tŏg'rȧ·fĭ), *n.* *Chem.* A separating of closely related compounds by allowing a solution of them to seep through an adsorbent so that the different compounds become adsorbed in separate colored layers comprising a **chro'ma·to·gram'** (krō'mȧ·tō·grăm').

chro'ma·tol'o·gy (-tŏl'ō·jĭ), *n.* [*chromato-* + *-logy.*] The science of, or a treatise on, colors.

chro'ma·tol'y·sis (-tŏl'ĭ·sĭs), *n.* [NL., fr. *chromato-* + *-lysis.*] *Med.* Solution and breaking up of chromatin.

chro'ma·to·phore' (krō'mȧ·tō·fōr'; 70), *n.* [*chromato-* + *-phore.*] **1.** *Zool.* A pigment cell, esp. one causing skin-color changes by varying its form or arrangement of pigment. **2.** *Bot.* A color plastid, as a chloroplast or chromoplast. — **chro'ma·to·phor'ic** (-fŏr'ĭk), *adj.*

chrome (krōm), *n.* [F., fr. Gr. *chrōma* color.] **1.** Chromium. **2.** *Dyeing.* Potassium (or sodium) dichromate. **3.** Short for CHROME YELLOW, CHROME STEEL, etc. — *v. t.* To treat with a compound of chromium, as in dyeing.

-chrome (-krōm). [Gr. *chrōma* color.] A combining form meaning: **a** *Color* or *colored,* as in poly*chrome.* **b** *Chromium,* as in ferro*chrome.* **c** *Coloring matter,* as in mono*chrome.*

chrome alum. *Chem.* Any alum in which chromium is the trivalent metal. Specif., a dark-violet salt, $KCr(SO_4)_2.12H_2O$, used in tanning and as a mordant in dyeing.

chrome red. Any of several pigments consisting of basic lead chromate.

chrome, *or* **chromium, steel.** An alloy steel containing chromium, commonly 0.5 to 2 per cent, and high in carbon. It is very strong and can be made extremely hard.

chrome yellow. A pigment consisting essentially of neutral lead chromate, $PbCrO_4$.

chro'mic (krō'mĭk), *adj.* *Chem.* **a** Of, pertaining to, or derived from, chromium; — said esp. of compounds in which this element is trivalent. **b** Designating an acid (**chromic acid,** H_2CrO_4), analogous to sulfuric acid, forming well-known salts, the *chromates.*

chro'mite (krō'mīt), *n.* *Mineral.* A mineral of the spinel group, composed of iron, chromium, and oxygen, $FeCr_2O_4$, valuable as a source of chromium.

chro'mi·um (krō'mĭ·ŭm), *n.* [NL. See CHROME.] A grayish-white metallic element, hard and brittle, and resistant to corrosion. Symbol, *Cr;* at. no., 24; at. wt., 52.01. Chromium is used in chrome steel and various alloys, and as a plating.

chro'mo- (krō'mō-), **chrom-.** [Gr. *chrōma* color.] A combining form denoting: **a** *Color,* as in *chromo*some. **b** *Chem.* A *colored compound* as distinguished from its colorless isomer. **c** *Pigment; pigmentation;* as in *chromo*gen. **d** *Chromium.*

chro'mo (-mō), *n.; pl.* -MOS (-mōz). A chromolithograph.

chro'mo·gen (krō'mō·jĕn), *n.* [*chromo-* + *-gen.*] **1.** *Biochem.* A substance which, as by contact with air, readily becomes a coloring matter. **2.** **a** A compound not itself a dye, but containing one or more color-forming groups and so capable of becoming a dye. **b** Any of several mordant dyes. — **chro'mo·gen'ic** (-jĕn'ĭk), *adj.*

chro'mo·lith'o·graph (-lĭth'ō·grăf; 9), *n.* A picture printed in colors from a series of stones prepared by the lithographic process. — **chro'mo·li·thog'ra·phy** (-lĭ·thŏg'rȧ·fĭ), *n.* — **chro'mo·li·thog'ra·pher** (*see* LITHOGRAPHER), *n.* — **chro'mo·lith'o·graph'ic** (-lĭth'ō·grăf'ĭk), *adj.*

chro'mo·pho'to·graph (-fō'tō·grăf; 9), *n.* A photograph in which the natural colors are reproduced. — **chro'mo·pho·tog'ra·phy** (-fō·tŏg'rȧ·fĭ), *n.* — **chro'mo·pho'to·graph'ic** (-fō'tō·grăf'ĭk), *adj.*

chro'mo·plasm (krō'mō·plăz'm), *n.* = CHROMATIN.

chro'mo·plast (-plăst), *n.* [*chromo-* + *-plast.*] *Biol.* A pigmented plastid; in botany, one containing red or yellow pigment (as disting. from *chloroplast,* containing green pigment). Chromoplasts give color to most flowers and fruits.

chro'mo·some (-sōm), *n.* [*chromo-* + 2d *-some.*] *Biol.* One of the small bodies, ordinarily definite in number in the cells of a given species, into which the chromatin of a cell nucleus resolves itself previous to the mitotic division of the cell. See MITOSIS, CHROMATIN, SEX CHROMOSOME.

chro'mo·sphere (krō'mō·sfēr), *n.* [*chromo-* + *sphere.*] *Astron.* A ruddy gaseous layer of incandescent hydrogen, helium, etc., surrounding the sun and between it and the corona (see CORONA, 3); also, a similar layer encircling a star. The solar chromosphere is visible at the time of a total eclipse. — **chro'mo·spher'ic** (-sfĕr'ĭk), *adj.*

chro'mous (krō'mŭs), *adj.* *Chem.* Of, pertaining to, or derived from chromium; — said esp. of compounds in which this element is bivalent.

chron'ic (krŏn'ĭk), *adj.* [F. *chronique,* fr. L., fr. Gr. *chronikos* concerning time, fr. *chronos* time.] **1.** Continuing for a long time; of a disease, of long duration; — opposed to *acute.* **2.** Hence, having long had an affliction or habit; confirmed; as, a *chronic* sufferer. **3.** Continuous; constant; as, *chronic* war. — **Syn.** See INVETERATE. — **chron'i·cal** (-ĭ·kăl), *adj.* *Rare.* — **chron'i·cal·ly,** *adv.*

chron'i·cle (krŏn'ĭ·k'l), *n.* [OF. *cronique,* fr. L., fr. Gr. *chronika,* neut. pl. of *chronikos.* See CHRONIC.] A historical account of events in the order of time; a history; esp., a simple chronological record. — *v. t.;* -I·CLED (-k'ld); -I·CLING (-klĭng). To record in a chronicle; to record. — **chron'i·cler** (-klēr), *n.*

Chron'i·cles (krŏn'ĭ·k'lz), *n. pl., construed as sing.* Either of two canonical books of the Old Testament. See BIBLE.

‖**chro'nique' scan'da'leuse'** (krō'nēk' skäɴ'dȧ'lûz'). [F.] A history or report that stresses scandalous details.

chron'o- (krŏn'ō-), **chron-.** [Gr. *chronos.*] A combining form denoting *time,* as in *chrono*meter.

chron'o·gram (-grăm), *n.* [*chrono-* + *-gram.*] **1.** An inscription, sentence, or phrase in which certain letters express a date or epoch. **2.** The record made by a chronograph. — **chron'o·gram·mat'ic** (-grȧ·măt'ĭk), *adj.*

chron'o·graph (-grăf; 9), *n.* [*chrono-* + *-graph.*] An instrument for measuring and recording time, velocity of projectiles, etc. — **chron'o·graph'ic** (-grăf'ĭk), *adj.*

chro·nol'o·ger (krō·nŏl'ō·jēr), *n.* A chronologist.

chron'o·log'ic (krŏn'ō·lŏj'ĭk), **chron'o·log'i·cal** (-ĭ·kăl), *adj.* Pertaining to chronology; containing an account of events in the order of time. — **chron'o·log'i·cal·ly,** *adv.*

chro·nol'o·gist (krō·nŏl'ō·jĭst), *n.* A person who investigates dates of events; one skilled in chronology.

chro·nol'o·gy (-jĭ), *n.; pl.* -GIES (-jĭz). [*chrono-* + *-logy.*] **1.** The science which treats of measuring time by regular divisions, and which assigns to events their proper dates. **2.** A chronological table, list, etc. **3.** Arrangement or relation as of events, in order of occurrence.

chro·nom'e·ter (krō·nŏm'ē·tēr), *n.* [*chrono-* + *-meter.*] An instrument for measuring time; a timepiece, esp. one intended to keep time with great accuracy. — **chron'o·met'ric** (krŏn'ō·mĕt'rĭk), **chron'o·met'ri·cal** (-rĭ·kăl), *adj.* — **chron'o·met'ri·cal·ly,** *adv.*

chro·nom'e·try (-trĭ), *n.* The art of measuring time; the measuring of time by periods or divisions.

chron'o·scope (krŏn'ō·skōp), *n.* [*chrono-* + *-scope.*] Any one of various instruments of precision for measuring minute intervals of time.

-chro·ous (-krō·ŭs). [Gr. *chrōs, chroos.*] An adjective suffix denoting *colored;* — chiefly in *Bot.,* as in iso*chroous.*

chrys'a·lid (krĭs'ȧ·lĭd), *n.* A chrysalis. — **chrys'a·lid,** *adj.*

chrys'a·lis (-lĭs), *n.; pl.* CHRYSALISES (-lĭs·ĕz; -ĭz), CHRYSALIDES (krĭ·săl'ĭ·dēz). [L. *chrysallis* gold-colored pupa of a butterfly, fr. Gr. *chrysallis,* fr. *chrysos* gold.] *Zool.* The pupa of insects (esp. of butterflies). See PUPA, *Illust.;* cf. COCOON.

chrys·an'the·mum (krĭs·ăn'thē·mŭm; krĭz-), *n.* [L., fr. Gr. *chrysanthemon,* fr. *chrysos* gold + *anthemon* flower.] An ornamental plant (genus *Chrysanthemum*) of the aster family; also, one of its large red, yellow, or white double flower heads of various shades and sizes. See POMPON, 2.

chrys'a·ro'bin (krĭs'ȧ·rō'bĭn), *n.* [Gr. *chrysos* gold + E. *araroba* Goa powder + *-in.*] *Chem.* A yellow crystalline compound, $C_{15}H_{12}O_3$, obtained from Goa powder and used in treating skin diseases.

Chry·se'is (krī·sē'ĭs), *n.* In the *Iliad,* daughter of a priest of Apollo, captured by the Greeks and given to Agamemnon, but later restored by him to avert a pestilence threatened by Apollo. Cf. BRISEIS.

chrys'el·e·phan'tine (krĭs'ĕl·ē·făn'tĭn; -tīn), *adj.* [Gr. *chryselephantinos,* fr. *chrysos* gold + *elephantinos* of ivory, fr. *elephas* ivory, elephant.] Composed of, or adorned with, gold and ivory, as certain ancient statues.

chrys'o·ber'yl (krĭs'ō·bĕr'ĭl), *n.* [From L., fr. Gr. *chrysobēryllos,* fr. *chrysos* gold + *bēryllos* beryl.] A yellowish mineral consisting of a compound of aluminum with a little iron, sometimes used as a gem.

chrys′o·lite (krĭs′ō·līt), *n.* [Through OF. & L., fr. Gr. *chrysolithos,* fr. *chrysos* gold + *lithos* stone.] *Mineral.* A magnesium iron silicate, $(Mg,Fe)_2SiO_4$, usually olive green. Transparent varieties are used as gems. — **chrys′o·lit′ic** (-lĭt′ĭk), *adj.*

chrys′o·prase (-prāz), *n.* [Through OF. & L., fr. Gr. *chrysoprasos,* fr. *chrysos* gold + *prason* leek.] *Mineral.* An apple-green variety of chalcedony. When brilliant it is valued as a gem.

chtho′ni·an, Chtho′ni·an (thō′nĭ·ăn), *adj.* [Gr. *chthonios* in or under the earth, fr. *chthōn, chthonos,* earth.] Designating, or relating to, gods or spirits of the underworld, esp. gods of the Greeks.

chub (chŭb), *n.;* see PLURAL, *Note,* 3. [ME. *chubbe.*] **1.** A European fresh-water fish (*Leuciscus cephalus*) of the carp family. **2.** In America: **a** Any of various fishes of the carp family, as the fallfish. **b** Any of several fishes of other families, as the tautog, largemouthed black bass, etc.

chub′by (chŭb′ĭ), *adj.;* -BI·ER (-ĭ·ẽr); -BI·EST. Like a chub; plump and round. — **chub′bi·ness** (-ĭ·nĕs; -nĭs), *n.*

chuck (chŭk), *v. i. & t.* [Imitative.] To cluck. — *n.* **1.** A cluck. **2.** A word of endearment.

chuck, *v. t.* **1.** To give a tap or pat. **2.** To toss or throw with a short action of the arm. — *n.* **1.** A slight blow or pat under the chin. **2.** A toss or jerk.

chuck, *n.* **1. a** A portion of a side of dressed beef (see BEEF, *Illust.*), including most of the neck, the parts about the shoulder blade, and those about the first three ribs. **b** The neck and shoulders of a carcass of dressed lamb or mutton, including three pairs of ribs. See LAMB, *Illust.* **2.** *Mach.* Any of various contrivances for holding work or a tool in a machine, esp. in a lathe. **3.** = CHOCK, 1.

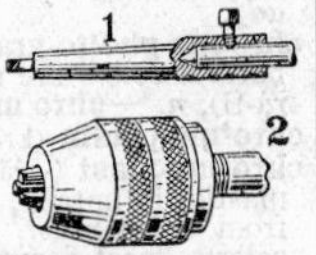
Chuck, 2. 1 With Setscrew; 2 Drill Chuck.

chuck′–full′. Var. of CHOCK-FULL.

chuck′le (chŭk′'l), *v. i.;* CHUCK′LED (-'ld); CHUCK′LING (-lĭng). [From 1st CHUCK.] To laugh in a quiet, hardly audible manner, as expressing inward satisfaction. — **chuck′le,** *n.* — **chuck′ler** (-lẽr), *n.*

chuck′le, *adj.* Clumsy; stupid.

chuck′le·head′ (-hĕd′), *n.* *Colloq.* A blockhead. — **chuck′le·head′ed** (-hĕd′ĕd; -ĭd; 2), *adj.* — **chuck′le·head′ed·ness,** *n.*

chuck′–will′s–wid′ow, *n.* A goatsucker (*Antrostomus carolinensis*) of the southern United States; — from its note.

chuck′y (chŭk′ĭ), *n.; pl.* -IES (-ĭz). *Scot. & Dial. Eng.* A little chick.

chud′dar (chŭd′ȧr), *n.* Also **chud′der** (-ẽr), **chud′dah** (-ȧ). [Hind. *cadar.*] *Anglo-Ind.* A square of cloth, worn as a mantle or shawl.

chuff (chŭf), *n.* A rustic; boor; churl. — **chuff′y,** *adj.*

chuff (chŭf; chōōf), **chuff′y,** *adj.* *Dial.* Fat; chubby.

chug (chŭg), *n.* Also **chug′–chug′.** A dull, explosive sound abruptly terminated, as of the exhaust of an engine. — *v. i.;* CHUGGED (chŭgd); CHUG′GING. *Colloq.* To move or go with chugs; — often with *along.*

chuk′ker (chŭk′ẽr), **chuk′kar** (-ȧr), *n.* [Hind. *cakkar, cakar,* fr. Skr. *cakra* a wheel.] A period of play at polo.

chum (chŭm), *n.* [From *chamber fellow.*] *Now Colloq.* A roommate, as in a college; also, an intimate friend. — *v. i.;* CHUMMED (chŭmd); CHUM′MING. *Colloq.* To occupy a room with another; to form or keep up intimacy.

chum (chŭm), *n.* [Origin obscure.] Chopped fish, or the like, thrown overboard to attract fish.

chum′my (chŭm′ĭ), *adj.;* -MI·ER (-ĭ·ẽr); -MI·EST. *Colloq.* Intimate; sociable. — **chum′mi·ly** (-ĭ·lĭ), *adv.*

chump (chŭmp), *n.* **1.** A short, thick, heavy piece of wood; a block. **2. a** *Colloq.* A blockhead; dolt. **b** *Slang.* Head. — ***off one's chump.*** *Slang, Eng.* Crazy.

chump, *v. t. & i.* To munch.

chunk (chŭngk), *n.* [Var. of CHUCK a portion.] **1.** *Colloq.* A short, thick fragment, as of wood. **2.** Figuratively, a fair quantity. **3.** *Colloq., U. S.* **a** A short, thickset person. **b** A strong, thickset horse.

chunk′y (-ĭ), *adj.;* CHUNK′I·ER (-ĭ·ẽr); CHUNK′I·EST. *Colloq.* Short and thick; thickset; also, lumpy.

church (chûrch), *n.* [AS. *circe,* fr. Gr. *kyriakon* the Lord's house, fr. *kyrios* master, lord, fr. *kyros* power.] **1.** A building for public worship, esp. Christian worship. **2.** Church service; divine worship. **3.** [*often cap.*] The organization of Christianity, as in a nation; esp., ecclesiastical power or government. **4.** The clerical profession. **5.** The collective body of Christians. **6.** A body of Christian believers having the same creed, rites, etc.; a denomination; as, the Presbyterian *Church.* **7.** Any body of worshipers; a religious society. — *v. t.* To bring or conduct to church to receive one of its rites, as baptism, the funeral rite, or a blessing after childbirth. — *adj.* Of, pertaining to, or connected with a church.

Church′es of Christ. See DISCIPLES OF CHRIST.

church′go′er (chûrch′gō′ẽr), *n.* One who goes to church, esp. habitually. — **church′go′ing,** *n. & adj.*

church′less (-lĕs; -lĭs), *adj.* **1.** Having no church, or no church affiliation or connection. **2.** Not sanctioned by the church.

church′ly, *adj.* [AS. *ciriclic.*] Pertaining to, or suitable for, church; ecclesiastical. — **church′li·ness,** *n.*

church′man (chûrch′măn), *n.* **1.** An ecclesiastic, clergyman, or priest. **2.** An adherent or devoted member of a church, esp. [*often cap.*] of an established church. — **church′man·ship,** *n.* — **church′wom′an** (-wŏŏm′ăn), *n.*

Church of Christ, Scientist. The official name of CHRISTIAN SCIENCE.

Church of England. The established episcopal church of England. It holds itself originally to have been the outcome of a merging of the early British church and the churches resulting from the Scoto-Irish and Italian missions of the 6th century, and to have been by law established, though not founded, at the time of the Reformation when the supremacy of the pope was repudiated and that of the sovereign asserted.

Church of the Brethren. See DUNKER.

Church Slavic. The ecclesiastical and literary language formed on the basis of a Bulgarian dialect by Cyril in the 9th century. It is the oldest and most primitive of the recorded Slavic tongues and is still used in the liturgy of the Eastern Church. Called also *Old Bulgarian.* See INDO-EUROPEAN LANGUAGES, *Table.*

church′ward′en (chûrch′wôr′d'n; 2), *n.* **1.** *Ch. of Eng.* A lay honorary parish official whose duties include the protection of the church building and property. **2.** *Prot. Episc. Ch.* A church officer whose duties relate chiefly to the management of the temporal affairs of the parish. **3.** *Colloq., Eng.* A clay tobacco pipe with a long stem.

churl (chûrl), *n.* [AS. *ceorl* a freeman of the lowest rank, man, husband.] **1.** A rustic; a peasant. **2.** A surly fellow; boor. **3.** A selfish miser; a niggard.

churl′ish (chûr′lĭsh), *adj.* **1.** *Obs. exc. Hist.* Of or pertaining to a churl or churls; rustic; mean. **2.** Like a churl; rough; surly; also, sordid; niggardly. **3.** Wanting pliancy; unmanageable; as, a *churlish* soil. — **Syn.** See BOORISH. — **Ant.** Courtly. — **-ly,** *adv.* — **-ness,** *n.*

churn (chûrn), *n.* [AS. *cyrin.*] A vessel in which milk or cream is stirred, beaten, or otherwise agitated in order to separate the oily globules from the other parts and thus to obtain butter. — *v. t.* **1.** To stir, beat, or agitate (milk or cream) in a churn, in order to make butter; to make (butter) by churning. **2.** To shake, stir, or agitate violently; to make, as foam, by thus doing. — *v. i.* **1.** To work a churn, as in making butter. **2.** To produce, or be in, violent agitation; as, the steamer's propeller *churns.* — **churn′er,** *n.* — **churn′ing,** *n.*

churr (chûr), *n.* [Cf. CHIRR.] A vibrant or whirring noise, as that made by the partridge. — **churr,** *v. i.*

chur′ri·gue·resque′ (chōōr′ĭ·gā·rĕsk′), *adj.* *Arch.* Pert. to the baroquelike style developed in Spain by José Churriguera (1650–1723).

chute (shōōt), *n.* [F., prop., a fall.] **1.** Of water, a fall; a quick descent, as in a river; a rapid. **2.** An inclined plane or trough down which various things may pass or slide to a lower level. **3.** Short for PARACHUTE. **4.** Descent; decline.

chut′ney (chŭt′nĭ), *n.; pl.* -NEYS (-nĭz). Also **chut′nee.** [Hind. *caṭnī.*] A hot-tasting or spicy condiment of fruit seasoned with chili, garlic, mustard, and vinegar.

chyle (kīl), *n.* [F. and L.; F., fr. L., fr. Gr. *chylos* juice, chyle, fr. *cheein* to pour.] *Physiol.* A modification of lymph which occurs in the lacteals (the lymphatics leading from the small intestine) and in the thoracic duct, from which it is poured into the veins. It contains globules of emulsified fat, derived from chyme contained in the small intestine. The chyle serves as the chief medium for the transfer of ingested fats to the blood. — **chy′lous** (kī′lŭs), *adj.*

chyme (kīm), *n.* [L. *chymus* chyle, fr. Gr. *chymos* juice, fr. *cheein* to pour.] *Physiol.* The semifluid mass of partly digested food expelled by the stomach into the duodenum. — **chy′mous** (kī′mŭs), *adj.*

chym′ic (kĭm′ĭk), **chym′is·try,** etc. Archaic vars. of CHEMIC, etc.

ci·bo′ri·um (sĭ·bō′rĭ·ŭm; 70), *n.; pl.* -RIA (-ȧ). [ML., fr. L. *ciborium* a cup, fr. Gr. *kibōrion* a seed vessel of the Egyptian bean.] **1.** *Arch.* A canopy, usually standing free and supported on four columns, covering the high altar; also, a similar canopy, used over a statue, etc. **2.** A vessel for Eucharistic wafers.

ci·ca′da (sĭ·kā′dȧ; -kä′dȧ), *n.; pl.* -DAS (-dȧz), -DAE (-dē). [L.] Any homopterous, stout-bodied insect of the family Cicadidae, with large transparent wings; — often called *locust;* esp., one of the type genus (*Cicada*), including the *seventeen-year locust* (which see). Certain cicadas are called also ***harvest flies,*** esp. the large American ***dog-day cicadas*** (genus *Tibicen*). Cicadas are noted for the prolonged shrill notes of the male, produced by vibrating membranes of special sound organs on the underside of the abdomen. Cf. GRASSHOPPER, KATYDID, LOCUST.

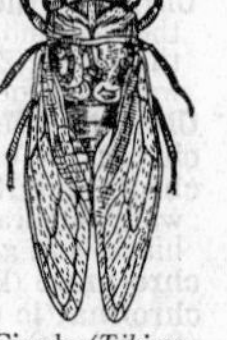
Cicada (*Tibicen pruinosa*). (⅔)

ci·ca′la (sĭ·kä′lȧ), *n.* [It., fr. L. *cicada.*] A cicada.

cic′a·tri′cle (sĭk′ȧ·trĭk′'l), *n.* [L. *cicatricula.*] **a** *Bot.* A cicatrix. **b** *Embryol.* The disc of protoplasm on the yolk of the egg of birds and reptiles. See EGG, *Illust.*

cic′a·trix (sĭk′ȧ·trĭks; sĭ·kā′trĭks), *n.; pl.* CICATRICES (sĭk′ȧ·trī′sēz). [L.] **1.** Also **cic′a·trice** (sĭk′ȧ·trĭs); *pl.* CICATRICES (-trĭs·ĕz; -ĭz). *Med.* The fibrous tissue which forms at the site of a wound and later contracts, forming the scar. **2.** A scar or scarlike mark, esp. one caused by the previous attachment of a part or organ; *Bot.,* the mark left on the stem after the fall of a leaf or bract; also, the hilum of a seed. — **cic′a·tri′cial** (sĭk′ȧ·trĭsh′ăl), *adj. Med.*

cic′a·trize (sĭk′ȧ·trīz), *v. t. & i.* *Med.* To heal with or by the formation of a cicatrix. — **cic′a·tri·za′tion** (-trĭ·zā′shŭn; -trī·zā′-), *n.*

cic′e·ly (sĭs′ĕ·lĭ), *n.; pl.* -LIES (-lĭz). [L. *seselis,* fr. Gr. *seseli, seselis.*] Any of several herbs (genera *Myrrhis, Osmorhiza,* etc.) of the carrot family, as the ***sweet cicely*** of Europe (*M. odorata*), with white flowers and aromatic root, and related American species (esp. *O. longistylis*).

ci′ce·ro′ne (chē′chĕ·rō′nā; sĭs′ĕ·rō′nē), *n.; pl.* -RONI (-nē), -RONES (-nēz). [It., fr. L. *Cicero,* the Roman orator.] A guide who conducts sight-seers.

Cic′e·ro′ni·an (sĭs′ĕ·rō′nĭ·ăn), *adj.* Of, pertaining to, or resembling Cicero or his style; hence, eloquent.

ci·cho′ri·a′ceous (sĭ·kō′rĭ·ā′shŭs), *adj.* [L. *cichoreum* chicory.] Belonging to the chicory family (Cichoriaceae). See CHICORY.

‖**ci·cis·be′o** (chē·chēz·bâ′ō; *E.* sĭ·sĭs′bē·ō), *n.; pl.* -BEI (-bâ′ē; -bē·ī). [It.] The gallant of a married woman; a cavalier servente.

Cid (sĭd; *Sp.* thēth), *n.* [Sp., fr. Ar. *sayyid* lord.] A title of Rodrigo (or Ruy) Díaz de Bivar, an 11th-century champion of Christianity, the hero of Corneille's *Cid* (1636).

-cid′al (-sīd′ăl; -'l; 2). [See -CIDE.] A suffix forming adjectives signifying *having power to kill,* as in bactericidal.

-cide (-sīd). **1.** [F., fr. L. *-cida,* fr. *caedere* to kill.] A suffix meaning *killer; destroyer;* as in fratricide. **2.** [L. *-cidium.*] A suffix meaning *a killing,* as in homicide.

ci′der (sī′dẽr), *n.* [OF. *sidre* (F. *cidre*), fr. LL., fr. Gr. *sikera* strong drink.] The expressed juice of apples, used for drinking and for making vinegar. Cider that has fermented is called ***hard cider*** and contains 2–8 per cent alcohol. Cf. APPLEJACK.

cider gum. See GUM, 5.

‖**ci′–de·vant′** (sē′dē·väN′), *adj.* [F., formerly.] Former.

ci·gar′ (sĭ·gär′), *n.* [Sp. *cigarro.*] A small roll of tobacco leaf, usually tapered at the ends, for smoking. Cigars are distinguished according to shape as *belvedere, corona, panatela, perfecto* (cf. also CHEROOT, STOGIE) and according to strength as *claro, colorado, maduro.*

cig′a·rette′ (sĭg′ȧ·rĕt′), *n.* Also **cig′a·ret′.** [F. *cigarette.*] A little roll of finely cut tobacco, enclosed usually in paper, for smoking.

cil′i·a (sĭl′ĭ·ȧ; 58), *n. pl.; sing.* CILIUM (-ŭm). [L. *cilium* eyelid.] **1.** *Anat.* The eyelashes. **2.** *Biol.* Hairlike processes, found on many cells, capable of a vibratory or lashing movement. **3.** *Bot.* Any minute marginal hairs forming a fringe.

cil′i·ar′y (-ẽr′ĭ *or, esp. Brit.,* -ẽr·ĭ), *adj.* **a** Of or pert. to cilia. **b** Pert. to certain structures of the eye. See EYE, *Illust.*

cil′i·ate (-āt), **cil′i·at′ed** (-āt′ĕd; -ĭd), *adj.* *Bot. & Zool.* Provided with cilia; as, a *ciliate* leaf; *ciliate* infusorians.

cil′ice (sĭl′ĭs), *n.* [F.] Haircloth; a hair shirt.

cil'i·o·late (sĭl'ĭ·ō·lāt), *adj. Biol. & Bot.* Minutely ciliate.

ci'mex (sī'mĕks), *n.; pl.* CIMICES (sĭm'ĭ·sēz). [L., a bug.] A bedbug (genus *Cimex*).

Cim·me'ri·an (sĭ·mēr'ĭ·ăn), *n.* One of a mythical people described by Homer as dwelling in a remote realm of mist and gloom. — *adj.* Shrouded in gloom or darkness.

cinch (sĭnch), *n.* [Sp. *cincha*, fr. L. *cingere* to gird.] *U. S.* **1.** A strong girth for a pack or saddle. **2.** *Colloq.* A tight grip. **3.** *Slang.* A sure or easy thing; a snap. — *v. t. U. S.* **1.** To put a cinch upon. **2.** *Slang.* To get a sure hold upon.

cinch, *n.* A game at cards.

cin·cho'na (sĭn·kō'nȧ), *n.* [NL., after the wife of Count *Chinchón*, viceroy of Peru in the 17th century.] A bitter bark from various Andean trees (genus *Cinchona*) of the madder family; also, any of these trees. The bark contains quinine, quinidine, and certain other white crystalline alkaloids, esp. **cin'cho·nine** (sĭn'kō·nēn; -nĭn) and **cin·chon'i·dine** (sĭn·kŏn'ĭ·dēn; -dĭn), $C_{19}H_{22}N_2O$, used as a specific in malaria, as an antipyretic, etc. See CALISAYA BARK, CHINA BARK. — **cin·chon'ic** (sĭn·kŏn'ĭk), *adj.*

cin'cho·nism (sĭn'kō·nĭz'm), *n. Med.* A condition produced by the excessive use of cinchona or its alkaloids, and marked by deafness, roaring in the ears, etc.

cinc'ture (sĭngk'tūr), *n.* [L. *cinctura*, fr. *cingere, cinctum*, to gird.] **1.** Act of girding or surrounding; also, an enclosure. **2.** That which surrounds, as a belt or a girdle. — *v. t.* To surround with or as with a cincture.

cin'der (sĭn'dẽr), *n.* [AS. *sinder* slag, dross.] **1.** The slag from a metal furnace; dross. **2.** A partly burned combustible; specif.: **a** A hot coal without flame. **b** A partly burned coal capable of further burning without flame. **c** *pl.* Ashes, esp. from soft coal. **3.** Slaggy lava from a volcano. — *v. t.* To burn or reduce to cinders. — **cin'der·y**, *adj.*

Cin'der·el'la (sĭn'dẽr·ĕl'ȧ), *n.* [Dim. fr. *cinder.*] The heroine of a popular tale, a household drudge who outshines her more favored sisters at a court ball, loses her glass slipper, and wins the prince.

cinder track. A running track surfaced with cinders.

cin'e- (sĭn'ē-). A combining form meaning *cinema*, as in **cin'e·cam'er·a**, a camera for taking motion pictures.

cin'e·ma (sĭn'ē·mȧ), *n.* [From *cinematograph.*] *Orig. Brit.* **1.** A motion picture; also, with *the*, motion pictures collectively. **2.** A motion-picture theater. — **cin'e·mat'ic** (-măt'ĭk), *adj.* — **cin'e·mat'i·cal·ly** (-ĭ·kăl·ĭ), *adv.*

cin'e·mat'o·graph (-măt'ō·grȧf; 9), *n.* [Gr. *kinēma, kinēmatos*, motion + *-graph.*] **1.** *Chiefly Brit.* A motion-picture projector. **2.** A camera for taking motion pictures. — *v. t. & i.* Also **cin'e·ma·tize** (sĭn'ē·mȧ·tīz). To photograph with a cinematograph. — **cin'e·ma·tog'ra·pher** (-mȧ·tŏg'rȧ·fẽr), *n.* — **cin'e·mat'o·graph'ic** (-măt'ō·grăf'ĭk), *adj.* — **cin'e·mat'o·graph'i·cal·ly** (-ĭ·kăl·ĭ), *adv.*

cin'e·ma·tog'ra·phy (-mȧ·tŏg'rȧ·fĭ), *n.* The producing of the illusion of motion with the aid of the motion picture.

cin'e·ole (sĭn'ē·ōl), *n.* Also **cin'e·ol** (-ōl; -ŏl). [From NL. *oleum cinae*, by transposition.] *Chem.* A liquid, $C_{10}H_{18}O$, of camphorlike odor, contained in many essential oils.

cin'e·ra'ri·a (sĭn'ē·râ'rĭ·ȧ; -rār'ĭ·ȧ), *n.* [NL., fr. L. *cinerarius* pert. to ashes, fr. *cinis* ashes; — from the ash-colored down on the leaves.] Any of several pot plants (all from *Senecio cruentus* of the Canary Islands) of the aster family, with heart-shaped leaves and daisylike flower heads.

cin'e·ra'ri·um (-ŭm), *n.; pl.* -RIA (-ȧ). [L.] A place to receive the ashes of the cremated dead. — **cin'er·ar'y** (sĭn'ẽr·ĕr'ĭ *or, esp. Brit.*, -ẽr·ĭ), *adj.*

cin'er·a'tor (sĭn'ẽr·ā'tẽr), *n.* A crematory; incinerator.

ci·ne're·ous (sĭ·nēr'ē·ŭs), **cin'er·i'tious** (sĭn'ẽr·ĭsh'ŭs), *adj.* [L. *cinereus; cineritius, cinericius.*] **a** Like, or of the nature of, ashes. **b** Ashen; ash-gray.

cin'gu·lum (sĭng'gū·lŭm), *n.; pl.* -LA (-lȧ). [L., a girdle.] A band or girdle; specif., *Zool.*, a band of color; any girdlelike structure. — **cin'gu·late** (-lāt), *adj.*

cin'na·bar (sĭn'ȧ·bär), *n.* [OF. *cenobre*, through L. and Gr., fr. Ar. *zinjafr*, fr. Per. *zinjifrah.*] **1.** Red mercuric sulfide, HgS, the only important ore of mercury. **2.** Artificial red mercuric sulfide, used principally as a pigment. **3.** The color vermilion.

cin·nam'ic (sĭ·năm'ĭk; sĭn'ȧ·mĭk), *adj. Chem.* **a** Pertaining to, or obtained from, cinnamon. **b** Designating an acid (**cinnamic acid**, $C_6H_5CH{:}CHCO_2H$), a white, crystalline, odorless compound found in oil of cinnamon, storax, etc.

cin'na·mon (sĭn'ȧ·mŭn), *n.* [F. and L.; F., fr. L., fr. Gr. *kinnamōmon, kinnamon*, fr. Heb. *qinnāmōn.*] **1.** The aromatic bark of any of several trees (genus *Cinnamomum*, esp. *C. zeylanicum* or *C. loureirii*) of the laurel family, used in powdered form as a spice; specif., that of *C. cassia* (***Chinese cinnamon***, or cassia bark). **2.** Any tree that yields this bark. **3.** A brown, yellowish red-yellow in hue, of medium saturation and medium brilliance. See COLOR.

cinnamon bear. See 2d BEAR, 1.

cinnamon stone. *Mineral.* Essonite, esp. when cinnamon color.

cin·quain' (sĭng·kān'), *n.* [F., fr. *cinq* five.] A group of five; specif., *Prosody*, a five-line stanza.

cinque (sĭngk), *n.* [F. *cinq*, fr. L. *quinque* five.] Five, esp. in dice or cards.

cin'que·cen'tist (chĭng'kwē·chĕn'tĭst), *n.* An Italian, esp. a poet or artist, of the 16th century.

cin'que·cen'to (-tō), *n.* [It., five hundred, abbr. for fifteen hundred, and hence the 16th century, i. e., 1501 to 1600.] The 16th century, esp. in Italian art and literature, including the Italian renaissance at its height.

cinque'foil' (sĭngk'foil'; săɴk'foil'), *n.* [*cinque* five + *foil.*] **1.** *Bot.* Any of several plants of a genus (*Potentilla*) of the rose family, having leaves of five divisions each. **2.** A decorative design likened to the leaf or flower of the cinquefoil, as, *Arch.*, an ornamental foliation having five cusps. See FOIL, *Illust.*

ci'on (sī'ŭn), *n.* [OF. See SCION.] A shoot of a plant consisting of one or more buds; a scion. See GRAFTAGE, *Illust.*; SCION, 1.

☞ Most American nurserymen and horticulturists use the spelling *cion.*

ci'pher (sī'fẽr), *n.* Also **cy'pher.** [OF. *cifre* zero, fr. Ar. *ṣifr* empty, cipher, zero.] **1.** *Math.* A character or symbol (written 0) denoting the absence of all magnitude or quantity; naught; zero. **2.** One that has no weight, worth, or influence; a nonentity. **3.** Any Arabic numeral. **4.** A method of secret writing that substitutes other characters for the letters intended, or transposes the letters after arranging them in blocks; also, a substitution alphabet so used. Cf. CODE, *n.*, 3. **5.** An interweaving of letters; a device; a monogram. — *v. i.* To use figures in a mathematical process; to do sums in arithmetic. — *v. t.* **1.** To express in, or put into, cipher. **2.** To compute arithmetically.

cir'ca (sûr'kȧ), *prep.* [L.] About; — with dates; as, *circa* 1740. Abbr. *c.* or *cir.* or *circ.*

Cir·cas'sian (sẽr·kăsh'ăn), *n.* **1.** An individual of a group of tribes of the Caucasus, of Caucasian race but not of Indo-European speech, noted for their physical beauty. **2.** An inhabitant of Circassia. — **Cir·cas'sian**, *adj.*

Cir'ce (sûr'sē), *n.* [L., fr. Gr. *Kirkē.*] In the *Odyssey*, an island sorceress who turned her victims by magic into beasts but was thwarted by Odysseus with the herb moly given him by Hermes. — **Cir·ce'an**, **Cir·cae'an** (sûr·sē'ăn), *adj.*

cir'ci·nate (sûr'sĭ·nāt), *adj.* [L. *circinatus*, past part., deriv. of Gr. *kirkinos* circle.] Ring-shaped; *Bot.*, rolled up on the axis with the apex as a center. — **cir'ci·nate·ly**, *adv.*

cir'cle (sûr'k'l), *n.* [OF. *cercle*, fr. L. *circulus*, dim. of *circus* circle.] **1.** A closed plane curve such that all of its points are equidistant from a point within, the *center*; a circumference; also, the plane surface bounded by such a curve. The area of a circle is the square of the radius multiplied by π (3.14159+). **2.** Something having in general a circular form, as a ring, halo, crown, sphere, orb, etc. **3.** The orbit or the period of revolution of a heavenly body. **4.** A series ending where it begins, and repeating itself. **5.** A set or series; a cycle; round. **6.** A company bound by a common tie; a coterie; a set. **7.** Circuit of action or influence; realm. **8.** In some European countries, a territorial subdivision, esp. of a province. **9.** A circle on the surface of a sphere; specif., ***great circle***, one whose plane passes through the center of the sphere (as the terrestrial sphere or the celestial sphere); often, a meridian of the terrestrial sphere along which latitude is measured; also, a parallel of latitude. **10.** *Astron.* An instrument of observation, the graduated limb of which consists of an entire circle. **11.** *Logic.* A form of reasoning in which the conclusion is unwarrantably assumed in the hypotheses; petitio principii. — *v. t.* **1.** To encompass by or as by a circle. **2.** To revolve around. — *v. i.* To move in a circle. — **cir'cler** (sûr'klẽr), *n.*

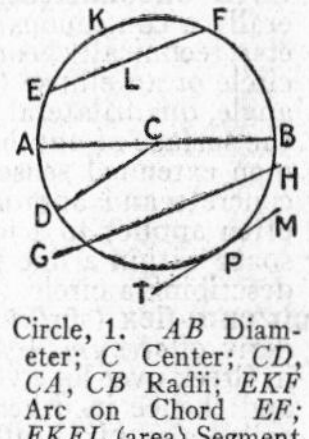

Circle, 1. *AB* Diameter; *C* Center; *CD*, *CA*, *CB* Radii; *EKF* Arc on Chord *EF*; *EKFL* (area) Segment on Chord *EF*; *ACD* (area) Sector; *GH* Secant; *TPM* Tangent at Point *P*; *EKFBPDAE* Circumference.

cir'clet (sûr'klĕt; -klĭt), *n.* A little circle; esp., an ornament, as a ring, bracelet, or headband.

cir'cuit (sûr'kĭt), *n.* [OF., fr. L. *circuitus*, deriv. of *circum* around + *ire* to go.] **1.** The circumference of any space; also, the space enclosed. **2.** Act of moving or revolving round, as in a circle or orbit; a circuitous route or journey. **3.** A regular or appointed journeying from place to place in the pursuit of one's calling, as of a judge or a preacher; also, the route or district covered in such journeying. **4.** A number of associated theaters in different centers at which productions are shown in turn. **5.** *Elec.* The complete path of an electric current, including, usually, the generating device. This complete path is called a ***closed circuit***, and when its continuity is broken, an ***open circuit***. **6.** *Radio.* A hookup. — **Syn.** See CIRCUMFERENCE. — *v. t. & i.* To go, travel, or move around; to compass; circulate.

circuit binding. A binding for books, having flexible projections, **circuit edges**, to protect the edges of the leaves.

circuit breaker. *Elec.* A device, other than a fuse, for interrupting a circuit under infrequent abnormal conditions.

cir·cu'i·tous (sẽr·kū'ĭ·tŭs), *adj.* Roundabout; indirect. — **cir·cu'i·tous·ly**, *adv.* — **cir·cu'i·tous·ness**, *n.*

circuit rider. *U. S.* A pioneer preacher assigned to a circuit, esp. on the frontier, necessitating travel on horseback.

cir·cu'i·ty (sẽr·kū'ĭ·tĭ), *n.; pl.* -TIES (-tĭz). Circuitousness.

cir'cu·lar (sûr'kū·lẽr), *adj.* [L. *circularis.*] **1.** In the form of, or bounded by, a circle. **2.** Moving in or describing a circle. **3.** Moving or happening in a cycle of repetition. **4.** Circuitous; roundabout. **5.** Addressed or pertaining to a circle, or to a number of persons; intended for circulation; as, a bank's *circular* note. — *n.* A circular letter or notice prepared, usually printed, in numbers for circulation. — **cir'cu·lar'i·ty** (-lăr'ĭ·tĭ), *n.; pl.* -TIES (-tĭz). — **cir'cu·lar·ly**, *adv.*

cir'cu·lar·ize (sûr'kū·lẽr·īz), *v. t.* **1.** To make circular. **2.** To send circulars to. **3.** To turn into a circular. — **cir'cu·lar·i·za'tion** (-ĭ·zā'shŭn; -ī·zā'-), *n.* — **cir'cu·lar·iz'er** (-īz'ẽr), *n.*

circular measure. See MEASURE, *Table* 7.

circular sailing. See SAILING.

circular saw. A thin steel disk with teeth on its periphery, used by revolving it upon a spindle. See SAW, *Illust.*

cir'cu·late (sûr'kū·lāt), *v. i.* **1.** To move or revolve in a circle or circuit, or to move round a course returning to the starting point, as the blood. **2.** To pass or go about from place to place, from person to person, etc.; specif., of books, periodicals, etc., to go into the hands of readers. **3.** *Math.* Of a decimal, to contain a group of figures which is repeated ad infinitum. — *v. t.* To cause to circulate. — **cir'cu·la'tor** (-lā'tẽr), *n.*

cir'cu·lat'ing dec'i·mal (-lāt'ĭng). **a** A decimal in which a group of figures recurs ad infinitum, as .354354354 . . . **b** Sometimes, = REPEATING DECIMAL.

cir'cu·la'tion (sûr'kū·lā'shŭn), *n.* **1.** A circulating. **2.** Act of passing from place to place or from person to person, or the extent to which this takes place; specif., the average total number of copies of a publication distributed per issue, or of books lent. **3.** The movement of the blood in the vessels of the body (cf. HEART, *Illust.*), or of the cytoplasm in plant cells. **4.** A currency. — **cir'cu·la'tive** (sûr'kū·lā'tĭv), *adj.* — **cir'cu·la·to'ry** (-lȧ·tō'rĭ *or, esp. Brit.*, -tẽr·ĭ), *adj.*

cir'cum- (sûr'kŭm-). [L. *circum* round about. See CIRCUS.] A prefix signifying: **a** *Around; about; on all sides;* — in nouns, verbs, adjectives, and their derivatives; as in:

circumambulate	**circumgyration**	**circumnavigate**
circumambulation	**circumgyratory**	**circumnavigation**
circumaviate	**circumjacent**	**circumnavigator**
circumfluent	**circumnavigable**	**circumrotation**

b *Surrounding; situated round; around;* as in:

circumanal	circuminsular	circumorbital
circumaxial	circumnuclear	circumpolar
circumbasal	circumocular	circumrenal
circumcolumnar	circumoral	circumvascular

c *Revolving about; surrounding;* as in:

circum-Jovial	circumlunar	circumsolar

cir′cum·am′bi·ent (sûr′kŭm·ăm′bĭ·ĕnt), *adj.* Surrounding; encompassing. — **cir′cum·am′bi·ence** (-ĕns), **cir′cum·am′bi·en·cy** (-ĕn·sĭ), *n.*

cir′cum·bend′i·bus (-bĕn′dĭ·bŭs), *n.* Circumlocution.

cir′cum·cise (sûr′kŭm·sīz), *v. t.* [L. *circumcisus*, past part. of *circumcidere*, fr. *circum-* + *caedere* to cut.] **1.** To cut off the prepuce of (males) or the internal labia of (females), specif. as a religious rite. **2.** To purify. — **cir′cum·cis′er** (-sīz′ẽr), *n.* — **cir′cum·ci′sion** (-sĭzh′ŭn), *n.*

cir·cum′fer·ence (sẽr·kŭm′fẽr·ĕns), *n.* [L. *circumferentia*, fr. *circum-* + *ferre* to bear.] The perimeter of a circle (see CIRCLE, *Illust.*); hence, in general, external boundary or surface of anything; periphery. — **cir·cum′fer·en′tial** (-ĕn′shăl), *adj.*

Syn. **Circumference, perimeter, periphery, circuit, compass** mean literally a continuous line enclosing an arc. **Circumference** and **perimeter**, technically geometrical terms, both apply to the line enclosing a circle or an ellipse (the second also to the set of lines enclosing a triangle, quadrilateral, or polygon) but both are loosely used to apply to the surface of anything thought of as spherical; **periphery**, in its common extended sense, applies to the edge, border, etc., of something concrete and approximately circular or spherical; **circuit** now more often applies to a journey around a periphery; **compass** refers to the space within a line such as might be covered by the leg of a compass describing a circle.

cir′cum·flex (sûr′kŭm·flĕks), *n.* [L. *circumflexus* a bending round, deriv. of *circum-* + *flectere* to bend.] A mark (^, ˜, later ~) orig. used in Greek over long vowels to indicate a compound (rising-falling) tone, and thence in other languages to mark length, contraction, etc.; — called also **circumflex accent.** — *adj.* **1.** Pert. to the circumflex. **2.** Bent or bending round; — of blood vessels. — *v. t.* **1.** To flex, or bend, round. **2.** To mark or pronounce with a circumflex. — **cir′cum·flex′ion** (-flĕk′shŭn), *n.*

cir·cum′flu·ous (sẽr·kŭm′flōō·ŭs), *adj.* [L. *circumfluus.*] **1.** Flowing round. **2.** Surrounded, as by water.

cir′cum·fuse′ (sûr′kŭm·fūz′), *v. t.* [L. *circumfusus*, past part., deriv. of *circum-* + *fundere* to pour.] To pour, spread, or diffuse round. — **cir′cum·fu′sion** (-fū′zhŭn), *n.*

cir′cum·lo·cu′tion (-lō·kū′shŭn), *n.* [L. *circumlocutio*, deriv. of *circum-* + *loqui* to speak.] Use of many words to express what might be expressed by few or one; roundabout expression; periphrasis. Cf. TAUTOLOGY. — **cir′cum·loc′u·to′ry** (-lŏk′ū·tō′rĭ *or, esp. Brit.*, -tẽr·ĭ), *adj.*

cir′cum·nu·ta′tion (-nū·tā′shŭn), *n.* The tendency of the growing portions of a plant to describe irregular curves or ellipses.

cir′cum·scis′sile (-sĭs′ĭl), *adj. Bot.* Bursting open along a line around the circumference. See PYXIDIUM.

cir′cum·scribe′ (-skrīb′), *v. t.* [L. *circumscribere, -scriptum*, fr. *circum-* + *scribere* to write, draw.] **1.** To draw a line round; to encircle. **2.** To limit, esp. narrowly. **3.** *Geom.* To draw, or be drawn, round so as to touch at as many points as possible. — **Syn.** See LIMIT. — **cir′cum·scrib′er** (-skrīb′ẽr), *n.*

cir′cum·scrip′tion (-skrĭp′shŭn), *n.* **1.** Act of circumscribing, or state of being circumscribed; limitation. **2.** *Archaic.* Definition or limitation of meaning. **3.** A thing that circumscribes; as: **a** The periphery of a body. **b** A surrounding or investing substance. **c** An inscription round anything, as a coin. **4.** A circumscribed space; a district. — **cir′cum·scrip′tive** (-tĭv), *adj.*

cir′cum·spect (sûr′kŭm·spĕkt), *adj.* [L. *circumspectus*, past part. of *circumspicere*, fr. *circum-* + *spicere, specere*, to look.] Attentive to all circumstances or consequences; discreet. — **Syn.** See CAUTIOUS. — **Ant.** Audacious. — **cir′cum·spect′ly**, *adv.* — **cir′cum·spect′ness**, *n.*

cir′cum·spec′tion (-spĕk′shŭn), *n.* **1.** Attention to all circumstances. **2.** Circumspect action or behavior. — **cir′cum·spec′tive** (-spĕk′tĭv), *adj.*

cir′cum·stance (sûr′kŭm·stăns *or, esp. Brit.*, -stăns), *n.* [From OF., fr. L. *circumstantia*, fr. *circumstans*, pres. part., deriv. of *circum-* + *stare* to stand.] **1.** A condition, fact, or event accompanying, or determining the occurrence of, another fact or event; specif.: **a** An essential condition of a fact or event; a primary qualification. **b** An accessory condition; a nonessential or casual detail. **2.** *pl.* Conditions environing and affecting a person or agent; as, as far as *circumstances* will allow; also, worldly estate. **3.** Only in *sing.* The sum of the essential conditions, or of the attendant facts, that bear upon the subject; as, the web of *circumstance.* **4.** The formality of any event; the carrying out of code, ceremonial, or convention. **5.** Copious or circumstantial detail, as in narration; circumstantiality. **6.** An event or incident in the general course of affairs. — **Syn.** See OCCURRENCE. — *v. t.*; -STANCED (-stănst; -stănst); -STANC′ING (-stăn′sĭng; -stăn-sĭng). **1.** To provide with or place in (particular) circumstances; — chiefly in past part.; as, poorly *circumstanced.* **2.** *Obs.* To garnish with detail. **3.** *Obs.* To govern by circumstance.

cir′cum·stan′tial (-stăn′shăl), *adj.* **1.** Consisting in, pertaining to, or dependent on, circumstances. **2.** Incidental; relating to, but not essential. **3.** Abounding with circumstances; detailed. — **cir′cum·stan′tial·ly**, *adv.*

Syn. **Circumstantial, minute, particular, detailed** mean dealing with a matter point by point. **Circumstantial** implies fullness and precision in mentioning; **minute** implies exhaustiveness or exactness in considering every detail; **particular** implies attentiveness to every feature or item; **detailed** comes close to *minute* but stresses abundance of detail.

circumstantial evidence. Evidence that tends to prove a fact in issue by proving circumstances which afford a basis for a reasonable inference of the occurrence of the fact.

cir′cum·stan′ti·al′i·ty (sûr′kŭm·stăn′shĭ·ăl′ĭ·tĭ), *n.* Quality of being circumstantial; minuteness of detail.

cir′cum·stan′ti·ate (-stăn′shĭ·āt), *v. t.* To support by circumstances; to exhibit with, or in, detail. — **cir′cum·stan′ti·a′tion** (-ā′shŭn), *n.*

cir′cum·val′late (-văl′āt), *adj.* [L. *circumvallatus*, past part., deriv. of *circum-* + *vallare* to wall, fr. *vallum* rampart.] Surrounded with a rampart; *Anat.*, surrounded by a ridge. — *v. t.* To surround with or as with a rampart, a wall, or a line of trenches. — **cir′cum·val·la′tion** (-vă·lā′shŭn), *n.*

cir′cum·vent′ (sûr′kŭm·vĕnt′), *v. t.* [L. *circumventus*, past part., deriv. of *circum-* + *venire* to come.] **1.** To surround, as by craft or stratagem; esp., to entrap. **2.** To gain advantage over by stratagem or deception. **3.** To go round. — **Syn.** See FRUSTRATE. — **cir′cum·vent′er, cir′cum·ven′tor** (-vĕn′tẽr), *n.* — **cir′cum·ven′tion** (-vĕn′shŭn), *n.*

cir′cum·vo·lu′tion (-vō·lū′shŭn), *n.* **1.** A turning or turn round a center or axis; rotation. **2.** A folding or fold of something about another thing **3.** A roundabout course; a sinuosity; specif., circumlocution.

cir′cum·volve′ (-vŏlv′), *v. t. & i.* [L. *circumvolvere, -volutum*, fr. *circum-* + *volvere* to roll.] To revolve.

cir′cus (sûr′kŭs), *n.* [L., circle, ring, circus (in sense 1).] **1.** *Rom. Antiq.* A level oblong space with tiers of seats on three sides, and divided lengthwise by a barrier, around which the track was laid out for chariot races, games, and public shows. **2.** A circular enclosure surrounded by tiers of seats and covered by a tent, for exhibition of feats of horsemanship, acrobatic performances, etc.; also, the company of performers, or the performance. **3.** *Obs.* Circle or ring. **4.** *Eng.* A circular area or open space at the intersection of streets; as, Piccadilly *Circus.* **5.** *Aeronautics.* = FLYING CIRCUS.

cirque (sûrk), *n.* [F.] **1.** *Archaic.* A circus. **2.** A circle or circlet. **3.** *Geol.* A steep-walled amphitheatric recess in a mountain; a corrie.

cir′rate (sĭr′āt), *adj.* [L. *cirratus* having ringlets, fr. *cirrus* a curl.] *Zool.* Bearing cirri (see CIRRUS, 3).

cir′rhi- (sĭr′ĭ-), **cir′rho-** (sĭr′ō-). Vars. of CIRRI-, CIRRO-.

cir·rho′sis (sĭ·rō′sĭs), *n.* [NL., fr. Gr. *kirrhos* orange-colored.] *Med.* Fibrosis with hardening caused by excessive formation of connective tissue followed by contraction; — esp. of the liver. — **cir·rhot′ic** (-rŏt′ĭk), *adj.*

cir′ri (sĭr′ī), *n., pl.* of CIRRUS.

cir′ri- (sĭr′ĭ-), **cir′ro-** (sĭr′ō-). [L. *cirrus* curl, ringlet.] Combining form for CIRRUS.

cir′ri·ped (sĭr′ĭ·pĕd), *n.* [L. *cirri-* + *-ped.*] Any of an order (Cirripedia) of degenerate marine crustaceans, free-swimming as larvae but permanently attached or parasitic as adults, including the barnacles. — **cir′ri·ped**, *adj.*

cir′ro-cu′mu·lus (sĭr′ō·kū′mū·lŭs), *n. Meteorol.* A cloud form of small, white, rounded masses at a high altitude, usually in regular groupings forming the *mackerel sky.* See CLOUD, *Illust.*

cir′rose (sĭr′ōs; sĭ·rōs′), *adj.* [See CIRRUS.] **a** Bearing a cirrus or cirri. **b** Like cirri; esp., like tufted or curly hair.

cir′ro-stra′tus (sĭr′ō·strā′tŭs), *n. Meteorol.* A fairly uniform layer of high stratus haze, darker than the cirrus. See CLOUD, *Illust.*

cir′rous (sĭr′ŭs), *adj.* **1.** Cirrose. **2.** Like cirrus clouds.

cir′rus (sĭr′ŭs), *n.; pl.* CIRRI (-ī). [L., lock, curl.] **1.** *Bot.* A tendril. **2.** *Meteorol.* A white filmy variety of cloud usually formed at altitudes of 20,000 to 40,000 feet, normally of ice crystals. See CLOUD, *Illust.* **3.** *Zool.* Any of various slender appendages; as: **a** An arm of a barnacle. See GASTROPOD, *Illust.* **b** A featherlike arm of a crinoid. **c** A barbel. **d** A tuft of hair on the legs and antennae of many insects.

cir′so- (sûr′sō-), **cirs-.** [Gr. *kirsos.*] = VARICO-, as in **cir′soid** (varicose), **cir·sot′o·my.**

cis- (sĭs-). [L. *cis* on this side.] A prefix denoting: **a** *On this side*, as in **cis·al′pine** (i. e., on the Roman side), **cis·mon′tane, cis′at·lan′tic.** **b** *Since; subsequent to;* — opposed to *pre-;* as in **cis′-E·liz′a·be′than.**

cis′co (sĭs′kō), *n.; pl.* -COES, -COS (-kōz). [Abbr. of Can. F. *ciscoette, ciscovet.*] Any of various whitefishes (genus *Leucichthys*), important food fishes of the Great Lakes region, as the ***mooneye cisco*** (*L. hoyi*) and the ***lake herring*** (esp. *L. artedi*), found from Lake Memphremagog to Lake Superior and northward.

cis′pa·dane′ (sĭs′pȧ·dān′; sĭs·pā′dān), *adj.* [*cis-* + L. *Padanus* pert. to the *Padus* or Po.] On the hither side of the river Po, usually with reference to Rome.

cist (sĭst), *n.* [L. *cista* box, fr. Gr. *kistē.*] *Rom. Antiq.* A box or chest, esp. for sacred utensils.

cist (sĭst; kĭst), **kist** (kĭst), *n.* [W., fr. L. *cista.*] *Archaeol.* A sepulchral stone chest or chamber.

cis·ta′ceous (sĭs·tā′shŭs), *adj.* [Gr. *kistos, kisthos*, rockrose.] Of or belonging to the rockrose family (Cistaceae). See ROCKROSE.

Cis·ter′cian (sĭs·tûr′shăn; -shĭ·ăn), *n.* A monk of the **Cistercian Order**, founded at Cîteaux (ML. *Cistercium*), France, in 1098. The **Cistercian Rule** is an extremely austere adaptation of that of the Benedictines. — **Cis·ter′cian**, *adj.*

cis′tern (sĭs′tẽrn), *n.* [OF. *cisterne*, fr. L., fr. *cista* box.] **1.** An artificial reservoir for storing water; esp., *U. S.*, a tank, often underground, for storing rain water. **2.** *Anat.* A fluid-containing sac or cavity in an organism.

cis·ter′na (sĭs·tûr′nȧ), *n.* [L., *cistern.*] *Anat.* A cistern; specif., one of the large subarachnoid spaces. — **cis·ter′nal** (-năl; -n′l), *adj.*

cistern barometer. See BAROMETER, 1.

cit′a·ble, cite′a·ble (sīt′ȧ·b′l), *adj.* That may be cited.

cit′a·del (sĭt′ȧ·dĕl; -d′l), *n.* [From F., fr. It. *cittadella*, dim. of *cittade* city, fr. L. *civitas.*] **1.** A fortress that commands a city; hence, a fortress; stronghold. **2.** In heavily armored war vessels, the protected central structure.

ci·ta′tion (sī·tā′shŭn; sĭ-), *n.* [OF., fr. L., fr. *citare* to cite.] **1.** An official summons to appear, as before a court. **2.** Act of citing a passage from a book; also, the passage; quotation. **3.** Enumeration; mention; specif., mention by way of eulogy, as in military orders or dispatches or in the conferring of an honorary academic degree. **4.** *Law.* A reference to decided cases, or books of authority. — **Syn.** See ENCOMIUM.

cite (sīt), *v. t.* [F. *citer*, fr. L. *citare*, fr. *citus* quick, past part. of *cire, ciēre*, to put in motion, excite.] **1.** To summon to appear, as before a court. **2.** To quote, as by way of authority or proof. **3.** To bring forward, as for illustration. **4.** *Mil.* To mention in a citation. — **Syn.** See SUMMON: ADDUCE.

cith′a·ra (sĭth′ȧ·rȧ), *n.* [L. See CITHER.] An ancient Greek musical instrument of the lyre class, having a wooden sound box.

cith′er (sĭth′ẽr), *n.* [F. *cithare*, fr. L., fr. Gr. *kithara.*] The cithara; loosely, the cittern.

cith′ern (-ẽrn). Var. of CITTERN.

cit′ied (sĭt′ĭd), *adj.* Occupied by a city or cities.

cit′i·fy (sĭt′ĭ·fī), *v. t.* To conform to city ways.

cit′i·zen (sĭt′ĭ·zĕn; -z′n), *n.* [OF. *citeain*, fr. *cité* city.] **1.** An inhabitant of a city or town; specif., *Hist.*, one enjoying its freedom and privileges as freeman or burgess. **2.** A member of a state; a person, native or naturalized, who owes allegiance to a government, and is entitled to protection from it; — opposed to *alien.* **3.** A civilian, as opposed to a soldier, policeman, etc. — **cit′i·zen·ess,** *n.* — **cit′i·zen·ship′,** *n.*

Syn. Citizen, subject, national here mean a person owing allegiance to and entitled to the protection of a sovereign state. All, in general, imply opposition to *alien.* The preferred term for any person, whether he lives in the implied country or not, is **citizen** when he owes allegiance to a state in which the sovereign power is retained by the people, and **subject** when that power is actually or theoretically retained by a personal sovereign, such as a monarch. **National,** more shifting in its meaning, usually refers to one living in a country other than the one in which he has or, sometimes, has had, the status of citizen or subject.

cit′i·zen·ry (sĭt′ĭ·zĕn·rĭ), *n.* The mass of citizens.

cit′ral (sĭt′răl), *n.* [*cit*ron + *al*dehyde.] *Chem.* An odoriferous liquid aldehyde, C_9H_{15}.CHO, found in oil of lemon, bay leaves, etc., used in making artificial perfumes.

cit′rate (sĭt′rāt; sī′trāt), *n.* A salt or ester of citric acid.

cit′ric (sĭt′rĭk), *adj.* [See CITRON.] *Chem.* Pertaining to or designating a triacid, **citric acid,** $C_3H_4OH.(CO_2H)_3$, extracted from lemons, currants, gooseberries, etc., and used in making artificial lemonade.

cit′ri·cul′ture (sĭt′rĭ·kŭl′tũr), *n.* [L. *citrus* citron tree + E. *culture.*] The cultivation of citrus fruits. — **cit′ri·cul′tur·ist** (-kŭl′tũr·ĭst), *n.*

cit′rin (sĭt′rĭn), *n.* [L. *citrus* citron tree (see CITRON) + *-in.*] Vitamin P. See VITAMIN.

cit′rine (sĭt′rĭn), *adj.* [OF. *citrin.*] Like a citron or lemon, esp. in color. — *n.* A semiprecious yellow stone like topaz but actually black quartz changed by heat.

cit′ron (sĭt′rŭn; *formerly* sĭt′ẽrn), *n.* [F., fr. It., fr. L. *citrus,* fr. Gr. *kedros* cedar, juniper.] **1. a** The fruit of a tree (*Citrus medica*), like the lemon in appearance and structure, but larger. **b** The tree bearing this fruit. **2.** The preserved rind of the citron, used in fruitcake and puddings. **3.** = CITRON MELON.

cit′ron·el′la (sĭt′rŭn·ĕl′ȧ), *n.* [NL. See CITRON.] A fragrant grass (*Cymbopogon nardus*) of southern Asia, which yields **citronella oil,** used in perfumery and as an insectifuge.

citron melon. One of a race of watermelons having a small fruit, the hard flesh of which is used like the citron.

cit′rus (sĭt′rŭs), *adj.* Also **cit′rous** (-rŭs). Pertaining to a genus (*Citrus*) of trees and shrubs of the rue family, often thorny, bearing large fruit with hard, usually thick peel, and pulpy flesh, as the citron, lemon, lime, orange, and grapefruit.

cit′tern (sĭt′ẽrn), **cith′ern** (sĭth′-), *n.* [See CITHER.] A medieval lutelike instrument played with a plectrum.

cit′y (sĭt′ĭ), *n.; pl.* CITIES (-ĭz). [OF. *cité,* fr. L. *civitas* citizenship, state, city, fr. *civis* citizen.] **1.** Any important town. **2.** *Brit.* A town traditionally entitled *city,* usually one that has been an episcopal see. **3.** *U. S.* A municipal corporation occupying a definite area and subject to the state from which it derives its powers. **4.** *Canada.* A municipality of the highest class. **5.** The inhabitants of a city collectively. **6.** *Antiq.* A city-state. — **cit′y–born′,** *adj.* — **cit′y–bred′,** *adj.* — **cit′y·folk′,** *n.*

— ***the City.*** The commercial center of Greater London.

cit′y–state′, *n.* A state in which the sovereignty is vested in the free citizens of an independent city and extends over the territories under its direct control, as ancient Athens.

civ′et (sĭv′ĕt; -ĭt), *n.* [F. *civette,* fr. It., fr. Ar. *zabād.*] **1.** A thick yellowish substance of strong musky odor, found in a pouch near the sexual organs of civet cats, and used as a perfume. **2.** A civet cat; also, its fur.

civet cat. A long-bodied, short-legged, catlike carnivorous animal (genera *Viverra, Civettictis*), native to Africa.

civ′ic (sĭv′ĭk), *adj.* [L. *civicus,* fr. *civis* citizen.] Relating to a citizen or a city or to citizenship or civil affairs.

civ′ics (sĭv′ĭks), *n.;* see -ICS. That department of political science dealing with rights of citizenship and duties of citizens.

civ′il (-ĭl), *adj.* [F., fr. L. *civilis,* fr. *civis* citizen.] **1.** Of, or made up of, citizens; pertaining to the whole body of citizens, or the state, or their interrelations; as, *civil* institutions or strife. **2.** Characteristic of or befitting a citizen or citizens; specif., courteous; urbane; often, ordinarily polite. **3.** Characteristic of or befitting a developed social community; civilized. **4.** Pertaining to civic or ordinary affairs, as distinguished from military, naval, or ecclesiastical; as, a *civil* marriage. **5.** Of or in accordance with Roman civil law or [*cap.*] modern Civil law. **6.** Recognized for purposes of ordinary life; — of divisions of time. **7.** *Law.* **a** Relating to the private rights of individuals in a community and to legal proceedings in connection with them; — disting. from *criminal* and *political.* **b** Legal; — disting. from *natural;* as, *civil* death.

Syn. Civil, polite, courteous, courtly, gallant, chivalrous mean observant of the forms required by good breeding. **Civil** suggests no more than that the requirements are fulfilled; **polite,** while sometimes suggesting a perfunctory attitude, commonly implies thoughtfulness and polished manners; **courteous** implies more considerate and dignified politeness; **courtly** implies more highbred, stately, and ceremonious politeness; **gallant** and **chivalrous** imply courteous attentiveness, especially to women, but *gallant* suggests spirited or ornate and florid expressions of courtesy and *chivalrous,* high-minded, disinterested, or self-sacrificing attentions.

civil death. *Law.* The change of status of a person equivalent in its legal consequences to natural death.

civil engineer. An engineer whose training or occupation is in **civil engineering,** the designing and construction of public works, as roads, harbors, irrigation. Abbr. *C. E.*

ci·vil′ian (sĭ·vĭl′yăn), *n.* **1.** *Law.* A student of, or a proficient in, civil or Civil law. **2.** One not professionally in the army or navy. — **ci·vil′ian,** *adj.*

Civilian Conservation Corps. An organization established by act of Congress in 1933 and recruited chiefly from unemployed youth, for carrying on public works involving forest conservation, building of parks, paths, and fire lanes, control of plant pests, and the like, on national and state domain. Liquidated by the 77th Congress (June 30, 1943). Abbr. *CCC*

ci·vil′i·ty (sĭ·vĭl′ĭ·tĭ), *n.; pl.* -TIES (-tĭz). **1.** *Archaic.* Polite education; hence, good breeding. **2.** Civil conduct; politeness; a polite act or expression.

civ′i·li·za′tion (sĭv′ĭ·lĭ·zā′shŭn; -lī·zā′-), *n.* [From CIVILIZE.] **1.** Advancement in social culture. **2.** A state of social culture characterized by relative progress in the arts, science, and statecraft. Cf. BARBARISM, SAVAGERY.

civ′i·lize (sĭv′ĭ·līz), *v. t.* To cause to come out of a savage or barbarous state; to instruct in the customs of civilization; educate; refine. — **civ′i·liz′a·ble** (-līz′ȧ·b′l), *adj.*

civil law. 1. *Roman Law.* The peculiar local law of Rome, as distinguished from the law for intercourse of Roman citizens with aliens. **2. a** In the Middle Ages, the Roman law as set forth (chiefly) in the Justinian Code, as disting. from the *canon law.* **b** In modern use, the body of private law developed from the Roman law in the states where the legal system is substantially Roman. In this sense usually written *Civil law.* — **civ′il–law′,** *adj.*

civil liberty. See LIBERTY, 4.

civ′il·ly (sĭv′ĭl·lĭ), *adv.* of CIVIL; specif., politely.

civil marriage. A marriage solemnized before a civil magistrate, as distinguished from one before a clergyman.

civil rights. Nonpolitical rights of a citizen; specif., *U. S.,* rights secured by the 13th and 14th Amendments to the Constitution, and by certain acts of Congress abolishing the civil incidents of involuntary servitude.

civil servant. *Brit.* A member of the civil service.

civil service. All branches of the public service which are not military, naval, legislative, or judicial.

civil war. A war between different sections or parties of the same country or nation; as, the American *Civil War,* or ***War between the States*** (1861–65); the English *Civil War,* or ***Great Rebellion*** (1642–49).

civ′ism (sĭv′ĭz′m), *n.* Good citizenship; orig., devotion to the Revolutionary order in France (1789–99).

clab′ber (klăb′ẽr; klȧb′-), *n.* [Ir. & Gael. *clābar.*] Curdled milk; bonnyclabber. — *v. t. & i.* To curdle.

clach′an (klȧk′ăn), *n.* [Gael.] *Scot. & Ir.* A hamlet.

clack (klăk), *v. i.* **1.** To let the tongue run; to chatter. **2.** To make a clack. **3.** To cackle or cluck, as a hen. — *v. t.* To utter tattlingly; blab. — *n.* **1.** Loud, continual, empty chatter; prattle. **2. a** A sharp, abrupt noise made by the striking together of objects. **b** Anything that causes such a noise, as a clapper. **3.** *Derogatory.* The tongue. — **clack′er,** *n.*

clack valve. *Mach.* A valve, esp. one hinged at one edge, which, when raised from its seat, falls with a clack.

clad (klăd), *past & past part.* of CLOTHE.

clad′o·phyll (klăd′ō·fĭl), *n.* [Gr. *klados* a sprout + *-phyll.*] *Bot.* A branch, assuming the form of and closely resembling an ordinary foliage leaf, often bearing other leaves or flowers on the surface or margin. See PHYLLOCLADE.

claim (klām), *v. t.* [OF. *clamer* (3d sing. pres. il *claime*), fr. L. *clamare* to cry out, call.] **1.** To ask for, or seek to obtain, by virtue of authority, right, or supposed right; to demand as due. **2.** To assert as a fact, right, or relation which ought to be acknowledged; as, to *claim* the championship. **3.** To call for; require; as, the subject *claims* our attention. — **Syn.** See DEMAND.

— *n.* **1.** A demand for something due or supposed to be due; as, a *claim* for damages; an insurance *claim;* a *claim* under a workmen's compensation law. **2.** A title to any debt, privilege, or other thing in possession of another; also, a title to anything which another should concede to, or confer on, the claimant. **3.** That which one claims; specif., an area claimed by a settler or prospector and marked by staking. — **claim′a·ble,** *adj.* — **claim′ant** (-ănt), *n.* — **claim′er,** *n.*

claim′ing race. A horse race in which horses are entered subject to claim of the right to purchase for a certain price (not less than twice the value of the race to the winner) by anyone registered for racing and starting a horse at that meeting.

claim jumper. One who illegally takes possession of another's mining claim.

clair·voy′ance (klâr·voi′ăns; *the F. pron.,* klĕr′vwȧ′yäNs′, *is still used by some, esp. in England*), *n.* [F.] **1.** The power of discerning objects not present to the senses but regarded as having objective reality. **2.** Preternaturally clear or acute perception, esp. of what is not ordinarily discernible; perspicacity. — **Syn.** See DISCERNMENT.

clair·voy′ant (klâr·voi′ănt), *adj.* [F.] Of or having clairvoyance. — *n.* One held to have the power of clairvoyance.

clam (klăm), *n.* Clammy or viscid matter; clamminess.

clam (klăm), *n.* [AS. *clamm* a bandage, bond.] A clamp; — usually *pl.*

clam (klăm), *n.* [From *clamshell,* fr. CLAM a clamp.] **1.** Any of various bivalve mollusks, esp. of certain edible kinds, specif. the common thick-shelled ***round,*** *or* ***hard,*** *or* ***hard-shelled, clam*** (*Venus mercenaria*), called also ***quahog,*** and the common thin-shelled ***long,*** *or* ***soft,*** *or* ***soft-shelled, clam*** (*Mya arenaria*) having long siphons. A small quahog is known as a ***cherry stone*** (***clam***); the young of the quahog when large enough to be eaten raw is called ***littleneck*** (***clam***). **2.** The soft part of any of these mollusks used raw or cooked for food; — usually *pl.* **3.** *Colloq., U. S.* A very reticent person. — *v. i.;* CLAMMED (klămd); CLAM′MING. To dig clams.

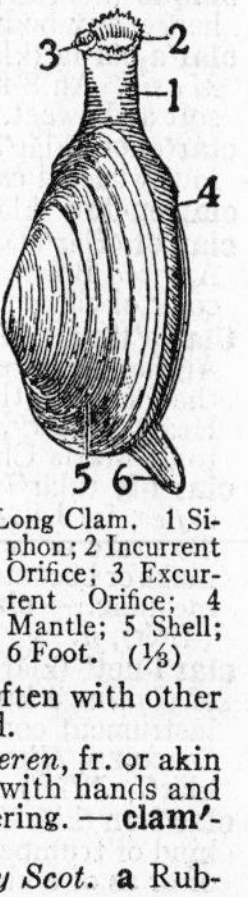

Long Clam. 1 Siphon; 2 Incurrent Orifice; 3 Excurrent Orifice; 4 Mantle; 5 Shell; 6 Foot. (⅓)

cla′mant (klā′mănt), *adj.* [L. *clamans,* pres. part. of *clamare* to call.] **1.** Clamorous. **2.** *Scot.* Demanding notice.

clam′a·to′ri·al (klăm′ȧ·tō′rĭ·ăl), *adj.* [L. *clamator* a bawler.] Belonging to a large suborder (Clamatores) of passerine birds, with little power of singing, as the tyrant flycatcher.

clam′bake′ (klăm′bāk′), *n.* *U. S.* The baking of clams, esp. on hot stones with a covering of seaweed, often with other food; also, a gathering at which clams are thus cooked.

clam′ber (klăm′bẽr), *v. i. & t.* [ME. *clambren, clameren,* fr. or akin to CLIMB.] To climb crawlingly or by catching hold with hands and feet, or, of plants, by tendrils. — *n.* Act of clambering. — **clam′ber·er,** *n.*

clam·jam′fry (klăm·jăm′frĭ; klȧm·jȧm′-), *n.* *Chiefly Scot.* **a** Rubbish. **b** Rabble; canaille.

clam′my (klăm′ĭ), *adj.;* CLAM′MI·ER (-ĭ·ẽr); -MI·EST. Damp, soft, sticky, and (usually) cool. — **clam′mi·ness,** *n.*

clam′or, clam′our (klăm′ẽr), *n.* [From OF., fr. L. *clamor,* fr. *clamare* to cry out.] **1.** A great outcry or loud shouting. **2.** A continued violent expression of discontent; popular outcry. 3. Any loud and continued noise, as of animals, musical instruments, a storm, etc. — *v. i.* To make a clamor. — *v. t.* To disturb or drive, or to utter, with clamor. — **clam′or·er, clam′our·er,** *n.*

clam′or, clam′our (klăm′ẽr), *v. t.* To silence. *Shak.*

clam′or·ous (-ŭs), *adj.* Full of, or of the nature of, clamor; noisy. — **Syn.** See VOCIFEROUS. — **Ant.** Taciturn. — **clam′or·ous·ly,** *adv.* — **clam′or·ous·ness,** *n.*

clamp (klămp), *n.* [LG. or D. *klamp.*] 1. A device that holds fast, binds things together, or wedges adjacent parts against other members of a unit. 2. Any of various instruments or appliances having parts brought together esp. by a screw or screws, for holding or compressing anything. — *v. t.* To fasten with, or place in, a clamp.

clamp, *v. i.* To tread heavily or clumsily; to clump. — **clamp,** *n.*

clam′shell′ buck′et (klăm′shĕl′). A dredging or loading bucket hinged like a clamshell.

clan (klăn), *n.* [Gael. *clann* offspring, descendants.] 1. A social group comprising a number of households the heads of which claim descent from a common ancestor, — esp. with reference to the Scottish Highlands. Cf. SEPT, 1. 2. A clique; a set. 3. *Sociol.* An exogamous division of a tribe, descended from a common ancestor, tracing descent in one line only, and constituting the chief unit of tribal society; a sib.

clan·des′tine (klăn·dĕs′tĭn), *adj.* [F. or L.; F., fr. L. *clandestinus,* fr. *clam* secretly.] Conducted with secrecy by design, usually for an evil or illicit purpose; as, *clandestine* meetings; a *clandestine* correspondence. — **Syn.** See SECRET. — **clan·des′tine·ly,** *adv.* — **clan·des′tine·ness,** *n.*

clang (klăng), *v. i.* [L. *clangere* to cry, peal.] To give out, or cry with, a clang. — *v. t.* To strike together with a clang. — *n.* 1. A loud, ringing sound, as of metallic objects struck together. 2. The cry of cranes or geese.

clang′or, clang′our (klăng′ẽr; klăng′gẽr), *n.* [L. *clangor,* fr. *clangere.*] Sharp, harsh, ringing sound; a clang. — *v. i.* To make a clangor. — **clang′or·ous,** *adj.*

clank (klăngk), *n.* A sharp, brief, ringing sound, duller than *clang,* made by collision of sonorous bodies. — *v. i. & t.* To make a clank; to sound or move with a clank.

clan′nish (klăn′ĭsh), *adj.* Of a clan; disposed to associate only with one's clique; actuated by the traditions, habits, etc., of a clan. — **clan′nish·ly,** *adv.* — **clan′nish·ness,** *n.*

clans′man (klănz′măn), *n.* One of a clan.

clap (klăp), *v. i.;* CLAPPED (klăpt) or CLAPT; CLAP′PING. [ME. *clappen,* prob. fr. AS.; cf. AS. *clæppan* to throb.] 1. To make a clack, or clatter; to come together with a clap. 2. To strike the hands together in applause. — *v. t.* 1. To strike vigorously or resoundingly; to bring together or to, with a clap. 2. **a** To strike (the hands) together, as an expression of applause, encouragement, etc. **b** To applaud by striking the hands together. **c** To strike or slap with the hand by way of approbation or encouragement. 3. To put, place, apply, set, thrust, etc., vigorously and effectually; as, to *clap* on more sail. 4. *Archaic.* To make or contrive hastily. — *n.* 1. *Archaic.* A clapper, as of a bell. 2. A loud noise made by or as by the sudden impact of hard surfaces; esp., a peal, as of thunder. 3. *Dial.* A sudden stroke of fortune, usually bad. 4. A hard slap with the hand. 5. The explosive sound made by striking the hands together, or the act of thus doing, esp. to express applause.

clap (klăp), *n.* [OF. *clapoir.*] Gonorrhea.

clap′board (klăb′ẽrd; klăb′ōrd; klăp′bōrd), *n.* 1. *Eng.* A size of board for making staves and wainscoting. 2. *U. S.* A narrow board, thicker at one edge, for weatherboarding frame buildings. — *v. t. U. S.* To cover with clapboards.

clap′per (klăp′ẽr), *n.* 1. That which makes a clapping noise; as: **a** The tongue of a bell. See BELL, *Illust.* **b** *Colloq.* The tongue. **c** One of a pair of flat sticks, bones, etc., held between a person's fingers and clapped, as by a Negro minstrel; — often called *bones.* 2. A person who claps, or applauds.

clap′per·claw′ (klăp′ẽr·klô′; *dial. also* klăp′ẽr·klō′, -klä′), *v. t. Archaic & Dial.* 1. To claw with the hand and nails. 2. To revile; to scold. — **clap′per·claw′er,** *n.*

clap′trap′ (klăp′trăp′), *n.* A trick, device, or expression to gain applause; hence, pretentious language, specious argument, insincere sentiment, etc., designed to gain applause.

claque (klăk; klȧk), *n.* [F.] A body of paid applauders at a play; hence, any body of truckling applauders.

clar′a·bel′la (klăr′ȧ·bĕl′ȧ), *n.* [NL., fr. L. *clarus* clear + *bellus* fine.] *Music.* An 8-foot organ stop with open wooden pipes. The tone is soft and sweet. See STOP, *n.*

clar′ence (klăr′ĕns), *n.* [From *Clarence,* Eng. dukedom.] A closed four-wheeled carriage, seating four inside.

clar′en·don (klăr′ĕn·dŭn), *n. Print.* A style of type. See TYPE.

clar′et (klăr′ĕt), *n.* [From OF. dim. of *cler* clear, fr. L. *clarus.*] 1. Any red Bordeaux or other red table wine. 2. Also **claret red.** The color of claret; a purplish red. 3. *Slang.* Blood. — **clar′et,** *adj.*

Cla·re′tian (klă·rē′shăn), *adj. R.C.Ch.* Of or pertaining to Blessed Anthony Claret or the Claretians. — *n. R.C.Ch.* A member of the Congregation of the Missionary Sons of the Immaculate Heart of Mary, founded in 1849 by Blessed Anthony Claret (Antonio María Claret y Clara, 1807–70).

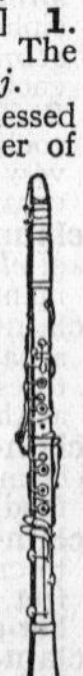
Clarinet.

clar′i·fy (klăr′ĭ·fī), *v. t. & i.;* -FIED (-fīd); -FY′ING. [OF. *clarifier,* fr. LL. *clarificare,* fr. *clarus* clear + *facere* to make.] To make or become pure and clear; as, to *clarify* a liquid; to make or become more readily understandable; as, to *clarify* one's meaning. — **clar′i·fi·ca′tion** (-fĭ·kā′shŭn), *n.* — **clar′i·fi′er** (-fī′ẽr), *n.*

clar′i·net′ (klăr′ĭ·nĕt′; klăr′ĭ·nĕt, -nĭt), *n.* [F. *clarinette,* dim. of *clarine* a kind of bell, fr. L. *clarus.*] *Music.* A wood-wind instrument consisting of a bellmouthed tube with a single reed. See REED, *Illust.* — **clar′i·net′ist, clar′i·net′tist** (klăr′ĭ·nĕt′ĭst; klăr′ĭ·nĕt′ĭst), *n.*

clar′i·on (klăr′ĭ·ŭn), *n.* [OF. *claron,* fr. L. *clarus* clear.] 1. A kind of trumpet with clear, shrill tones. 2. *Poetic.* The sound of or as of a clarion. — *adj.* Loud and clear.

clar′i·o·net′ (klăr′ĭ·ō·nĕt′; klăr′ĭ·ō·nĕt; klăr′ĭ·nĕt). Var. of CLARINET.

clar′i·ty (klăr′ĭ·tĭ), *n.* [F. and L.; F. *clarté, clarité,* fr. L. *claritas.*] Clearness; lucidity.

clark′i·a (klär′kĭ·ȧ), *n.* [NL., after William Clark, Am. explorer.] A showy annual herb (genus *Clarkia*) of the evening-primrose family, of the Pacific slope of North America, esp. *C. pulchella* and *C. elegans,* which have large red or purple flowers.

cla′ro (klä′rō), *adj.* [Sp.] Light-colored and, generally, mild; — of cigars. Cf. COLORADO, MADURO. — *n.* A claro cigar.

clar′y (klâr′ĭ), *n.; pl.* CLARIES (-ĭz). Also **clary sage.** [F. *sclarée,* fr. ML. *sclarea.*] **a** A mint (*Salvia sclarea*) of southern Europe. **b** A related ornamental species (*S. horminum*).

clash (klăsh), *v. i.* [Imitative.] 1. To make a clash. 2. To collide; also, to conflict; as, interests that *clash.* — *v. t.* 1. To produce, as a sound, by a collision. 2. To strike with a clash. — *n.* 1. A loud, usually metallic, noise resulting from collision. 2. Collision or hostile meeting; also, opposition; conflict.

clasp (klȧsp; 9), *v. t.;* CLASPED (klȧspt) or CLASPT; CLASP′ING. [ME. *claspen, clapsen.*] 1. To fasten together with or as with a clasp. 2. To cling or entwine about; loosely, to surround; enwrap; specif., to embrace. 3. To seize with or in the hand. — *n.* 1. Any of various forms of catch or hook. 2. An embrace; a grasp. 3. *Mil.* **a** A bar across the suspension ribbon of a service medal inscribed with the name of the action (***battle clasp***) or of the campaign or area (***service clasp***) for which it was awarded. On a service ribbon, a star is worn instead of a battle clasp. See STAR, *n.,* 6. **b** An addition to a service ribbon to indicate a subsequent award of the basic medal.

clasp knife. A jackknife with a blade folding into the handle, esp. one with a catch to hold the blade open.

class (klȧs; 9), *n.* [F. *classe,* fr. L. *classis* class, collection, fleet.] 1. A group of individuals ranked together as possessing common characteristics or as having the same status; as, the educated *class.* 2. The system of thus dividing society; caste; social rank, esp. high rank; as, the feeling of *class;* hence, ***the classes,*** the upper classes. 3. **a** A body of students meeting regularly to study the same subject or to attend lectures or recitations. **b** An assembling or the period of assembling of such a body. **c** A body of students whose year of graduation is the same. 4. A group of persons, things, qualities, etc., having common characteristics; set; kind. 5. A division, grouping, or distinction based on grade or quality; as, to travel first *class.* 6. *Slang.* Superior quality; style. 7. *Bot. & Zool.* A comprehensive group of animals or plants, forming a category ranking above an order and below a phylum. See CLASSIFICATION, 2. 8. *Mil.* A group of conscripts designated as made up of men born in a given year; as, the *class* of 1920. — *v. t.* 1. To classify. 2. To place in a class. — *v. i.* To be classified or classed. — **class′a·ble,** *adj.* — **class′er,** *n.*

class consciousness. Consciousness pervading a social class of its solidarity. — **class′–con′scious,** *adj.*

class day. In American colleges and schools, a day during commencement on which members of the senior class present the class poem, history, oration, etc.

clas′sic (klăs′ĭk), *adj.* [F. or L.; F. *classique,* fr. L. *classicus* relating to the classes of the Roman people, and esp. to the first class; hence, of the first rank.] 1. Of or relating to the first class or rank, esp. in literature or art; standard. 2. Of or pertaining to a coherent system embodying principles and methods accepted as authoritative in application to arts, science, and literature; specif., of or pert. to the ancient Greeks and Romans or their culture, esp. their authors, artists, etc., or places made famous by their deeds or writings. 3. Noted because of literary or historical associations; as, *classic* Oxford. 4. Classical (senses 3 & 6). 5. Of fashions, characterized by simple tailored lines, correct for a variety of places and occasions, and basically in fashion year after year. — *n.* 1. A work, esp. in literature or art, of the highest class and of acknowledged excellence, or its author. 2. A classicist. 3. A classic fashion. — ***the classics.*** Greek and Latin works or authors.

clas′si·cal (klăs′ĭ·kăl), *adj.* 1. Classic (senses 1 & 2). 2. Versed in, or devoted to, the classics. 3. Characteristic of or pertaining to classicism; esp., conforming to the models or rules of the ancient Greek and Roman classics; — contrasted with *romantic.* 4. Concerned with, and giving instruction in, the humanities, the fine arts, and the broad aspects of science; as, a *classical* course. 5. Taught as soundly authoritative and standard, in distinction from radical or revolutionary in theory as growing out of recent experimentation and discovery; as, *classical* economics. 6. *Music.* **a** Appealing to critical interest or developed taste; conforming to an established form, as the sonata. **b** Of or pert. to the school of composers characterized by classicism.

clas′si·cal·ism (-ĭz′m), *n.* Classicism. — **clas′si·cal·ist** (-ĭst), *n.*

clas′si·cal′i·ty (klăs′ĭ·kăl′ĭ·tĭ), *n.* 1. Quality of being classical, as in literary style. 2. Classical scholarship.

clas′si·cal·ly, *adv.* of CLASSIC, CLASSICAL.

classical Sanskrit. See SANSKRIT.

clas′si·cism (klăs′ĭ·sĭz′m), *n.* 1. Classic principles in literature or art; conformity to, or practice of, classical style; in criticism, the principles and characteristics of a literature or art established as a formal standard, originally those of Greek and Roman literature and art, embodying lucidity, simplicity, dignity, and correctness of style; likewise, in music, formal beauty or the qualities of clearness, symmetry, finish, and repose. As contrasted with *romanticism,* classicism typifies pure taste, sobriety, and proportion, and, in a less favorable sense, the restraints of conventional formality. 2. A classical idiom or expression.

clas′si·cist (-sĭst), *n.* 1. An advocate or follower of classicism. 2. One learned in the classics.

clas′si·cize (-sīz), *v. t. & i.* To make classic; affect classic style.

clas′si·fi′a·ble (-fī′ȧ·b′l), *adj.* That may be classified.

clas′si·fi·ca′tion (-fĭ·kā′shŭn), *n.* 1. Act or result of classifying; systematic arrangement in classes. 2. *Biol.* Systematic arrangement of animals and plants in groups or categories based upon some definite scheme, now usually that of natural relationships. The common categories are, in order, *phylum* (or, in botany, *division*), *class, order, family, genus, species, variety.*

clas′si·fi·ca′to·ry (klăs′ĭ·fĭ·kā′tō·rĭ; klă·sĭf′ĭ·kȧ·tō′rĭ), *adj.* Pertaining to or involving classification; taxonomic.

clas′si·fied (klăs′ĭ·fīd), *adj.* Forbidden to be disclosed outside a specified ring of secrecy for reasons of national security.

clas′si·fy (klăs′ĭ·fī), *v. t.;* -FIED (-fīd); -FY′ING. [L. *classis* class + *-fy.*] To group or segregate in classes which have systematic relations. — **Syn.** See ASSORT. — **clas′si·fi′er** (-fī′ẽr), *n.*

clas′sis (klăs′ĭs), *n.; pl.* CLASSES (-ēz). [L. See CLASS.] *Eccl.* In Dutch and German Reformed churches, a governing body consisting of the ministers and representative elders of a district; also, the district.

class′mate′ (klȧs′māt′), *n.* One belonging to the same class with another, as at school or college.

class meaning. *Linguistics.* The meaning or meanings of a form class; as, "they" has the *class meanings* of substantives and plurals.
class′room′ (klȧs′ro͞om′), *n.* A room in a school or college building for class recitations, lectures, etc.
class′y (klȧs′ĭ), *adj.* *Slang.* Of superior quality; stylish.
clas′tic (klăs′tĭk), *adj.* [Gr. *klastos* broken, fr. *klan* to break.] **1.** Capable of being taken apart, as to show internal structure; — applied to anatomical models. **2.** Made up of fragments of pre-existing rocks.
clat′ter (klăt′ẽr), *v. i.* [AS. *clatrung* a rattle.] **1.** To make, or to move with, a clatter. **2.** To chatter; prattle. — *v. t.* To cause to clatter or rattle. — *n.* **1.** A rattling noise, esp. of hard bodies colliding. **2.** Commotion; disturbance. **3.** Babble; chatter. — **clat′ter·er,** *n.*
claught (klôĸt; kläĸt), *past* of CLEEK.
clause (klôz), *n.* [OF., fr. ML. *clausa*, equiv. to L. *clausula* clause, prop., close of a rhetorical period, fr. *claudere* to shut, end.] **1.** A separate portion of a discourse or writing; a distinct article in a formal document. **2.** *Gram.* A word group formed by subject and predicate but constituting a member of a complex or compound sentence instead of ranking as a completed sentence. Clauses are distinguished as *principal* when they carry the main predication, and *subordinate* when they enter into the sentence structure with the force of a part of speech, either noun, adjective, or adverb. — **claus′al** (klôz′ăl; -′l), *adj.*
claus′tral (klôs′trăl), *adj.* [ML. *claustralis.*] Cloistral.
claus′tro·pho′bi·a (klôs′trō·fō′bĭ·ȧ), *n.* [NL., fr. L. *claustrum* a confined place + *-phobia.*] *Med.* Morbid dread of being in closed rooms or narrow spaces. Cf. AGORAPHOBIA. — **claus′tro·pho′bic** (-fō′bĭk; -fŏb′ĭk), *adj.*
cla′vate (klā′vāt), *adj.* [L. *clava* club.] Club-shaped.
clave (klāv). See CLEAVE.
cla′ver (klā′vẽr; klăv′ẽr), *n. & v.* *Scot.* Chatter; gossip.
clav′i·chord (klăv′ĭ·kôrd), *n.* [ML. *clavichordium*, fr. L. *clavis* key + *chorda* string.] A keyboard instrument, precursor of the piano, having horizontal strings struck by small brass pins operated by the keys. Cf. HARPSICHORD.
clav′i·cle (-k′l), *n.* [From F., fr. L. *clavicula*, dim. of *clavis* key.] *Anat.* A bone of the pectoral arch, joined to the breastbone and the shoulder blade, and called in man *collarbone.* See THORAX, *Illust.* — **cla·vic′u·lar** (klȧ·vĭk′ū·lẽr), *adj.*
clav′i·corn (-kôrn), *adj.* [L. *clava* club + *cornu* horn.] Belonging to a large superfamily (Clavicornia) of beetles having the antennae usually club-shaped. — **clav′i·corn,** *n.* — **clav′i·cor′nate** (-kôr′nāt), *adj.*
cla′vi·er (klā′vĭ·ẽr; klăv′ĭ·ẽr; klȧ·vẹr′), *n.* [F., fr. L. *clavis* key.] **1.** The keyboard of an organ, pianoforte, or harmonium. **2.** [G. *klavier*, fr. F.] A keyboard stringed instrument.
clav′i·form (klăv′ĭ·fôrm), *adj.* Club-shaped; clavate.
claw (klô), *n.* [AS. *clawu*, *clēa.*] **1.** A sharp nail on the finger or toe of an animal, esp. when slender and curved. **2. a** Any similar sharp curved process, esp. one at the end of a limb, as on the legs of insects, etc. **b** A limb ending in such a process. **3.** One of the pincerlike organs terminating certain limbs of some crustaceans (as the lobster), scorpions, etc. **4.** Anything resembling the claw of an animal, as the forked end of a hammer, or, *pl.*, human fingers. **5.** A scratch from or as from a claw. — *v. t. & i.* To tear, scratch, scrape, seize, dig, make, or the like, with or as with claws or nails.
claw hammer. **1.** A hammer with a forked end (claw) for drawing nails. See HAMMER, *Illust.* **2.** = SWALLOW-TAILED COAT.
claw hatchet. A hatchet with one end of the head cleft. See HATCHET, *Illust.*
clay (klā), *n.* [AS. *clǣg.*] **1.** An earthy material, plastic when moist but hard when baked or fired. Pure white clay is known as *kaolin* (which see). Clay mixtures are baked to make brick, tile, earthenware, etc. Cf. MARL. **2.** Loosely, earth; mire; mud. **3.** Earth in general, as representing the elementary particles of the human body; hence, the human body. — **clay′ey** (-ĭ), *adj.* — **clay′ish,** *adj.*
clay′more′ (-mōr′), *n.* [Gael. *claidheamh* sword + *mōr* great, large.] A large two-edged sword used formerly by the Scottish Highlanders; also, inaccurately, their basket-hilted broadsword.

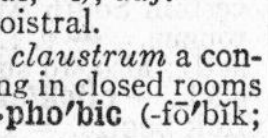
Clay Pigeon.

clay pigeon. A saucer of baked clay or other material to be thrown with a scaling motion from the trap, for a target in trapshooting.
clay·to′ni·a (klā·tō′nĭ·ȧ), *n.* [NL., after John *Clayton* (1693–1773), Am. botanist.] Any of a genus (*Claytonia*) of mainly North American succulent herbs of the purslane family. See SPRING BEAUTY.
-cle. [F. or L.; F., fr. L. *-culus, -cula, -culum.*] A noun suffix forming diminutives, as in fasci*cle.* See -CULE.
clean (klēn), *adj.* [AS. *clǣne.*] **1.** Free from whatever sullies or defiles; pure; unsoiled. **2.** Specif.: **a** Of precious stones, having no interior flaws. **b** Of printers' proofs, having few or no corrections; of copy, legible. **3.** Free from moral defilement. **4.** *Bible.* Free or freed from ceremonial defilement; also, of food or of animals, not defiling; fit to eat. **5.** That makes clean, or free from defilement, imperfection, etc. **6.** Free from obstructions or imperfections. **7.** *Obs.* Free from errors; correct. **8.** Of a ship: **a** Having the bottom not fouled. **b** Having an empty hold. **9.** Well-proportioned; trim; as, *clean* limbs. **10.** Clever; dexterous; as, a *clean* trick. **11.** Habitually clean; cleanly; as, a *clean* animal. — *adv.* **1.** So as to be free from dirt, rubbish, or obstructions; cleanly. **2.** Quite; thoroughly; also, skillfully. — *v. t.* To render clean; to cleanse. — *v. i.* To undergo or perform the process of cleaning, as a room; — often with *up.*
Syn. **Clean, cleanse** mean to remove soil or dirt from something. **Clean** may imply washing, sweeping, or clearing away; **cleanse** often implies the use of gasoline, ether, or the like, as to remove dirt or stains from clothes, or the use of purgatives to remove foul matter from the bowels, but it more often suggests a purification of any sort. — **Ant.** Dirty.
clean′a·ble (klēn′ȧ·b′l), *adj.* Capable of being cleaned.
clean′-cut′ (*see Pron.*, § 2), *adj.* Cut so that the surface or edge is smooth and even; hence, sharply defined or outlined.
clean′er (klēn′ẽr), *n.* One that cleans; specif., a device for cleaning or a preparation for use in cleaning.
clean′hand′ed (-hăn′dĕd; -dĭd; 2), *adj.* Having clean hands; innocent of wrongdoing.
clean′-limbed′ (-lĭmd′; 2), *adj.* With well-proportioned limbs or parts likened to limbs; trim.
clean′ly (klĕn′lĭ), *adj.*; CLEAN′LI·ER (-lĭ·ẽr); -LI·EST. **1.** Careful to keep clean. **2.** Habitually kept clean. — **clean′li·ly** (-lĭ·lĭ), *adv.* — **clean′li·ness,** *n.*
clean′ly (klēn′lĭ), *adv.* In a clean manner or degree.
clean′ness (klēn′nĕs; -nĭs), *n.* Clean quality or condition.
cleanse (klĕnz), *v. t.* [AS. *clǣnsian*, fr. *clǣne* clean.] To render clean. — **Syn.** See CLEAN. — **cleans′er,** *n.*
clear (klẹr), *adj.* [OF. *cler*, fr. L. *clarus* clear, bright, loud, renowned.] **1.** Bright or luminous; light; hence, unclouded, as by passion; serene; also (formerly), brilliant; illustrious. **2.** Clean; free from blotch or blemish, muddiness, turbidity, etc. **3.** Easily or distinctly heard; audible. **4.** Distinct; plain; as, a *clear* outline; of thought, lucid. **5.** Able to see or perceive distinctly; as, a *clear* intellect. **6.** Free from doubt; certain; sure. **7.** Free from guile, guilt, or strain; innocent. **8.** Free from burden, limitation, etc.; as: **a** Free from charges, etc.; net; as, *clear* profit. **b** Free from qualification; absolute; entire. **c** Free from contact with anything that encumbers; quit; rid; as, the cables are *clear.* **d** Free from impediment or obstruction; open. **e** Free from knots or other defects; as, *clear* lumber. **f** Freed, or emptied, of burden, contents, or cargo, as a ship. **g** Free from debt. **h** Of space or time, without deduction or diminution; as, the walk is five feet *clear* from side to side. **i** Having certain bones removed, as certain cuts of meat.
Syn. (1) **Clear, transparent, translucent, pellucid, limpid** mean capable of being seen through. **Clear** implies freedom from cloudiness, haziness, muddiness, or the like; **transparent,** so very clear that objects or, by extension, motives, etc., can be seen through it; **translucent,** admitting the free passage of light yet not so clear as to be transparent; **pellucid,** crystallike clearness; **limpid,** the soft clearness of or as of pure water.
(2) **Clear, perspicuous, lucid** mean quickly and easily understood. **Clear** implies freedom from ambiguity, obscurity, etc.; **perspicuous,** a quality of style that is simple and elegant as well as clear; **lucid,** a clearness that depends mainly on logical qualities such as order and arrangement.
(3) See EVIDENT.
— *adv.* In a clear manner; clearly.
— *v. t.* **1.** To make clear, as by illumination; to free from turbidness, muddiness, cloudiness, etc. **2.** To make clear mentally; enlighten. **3.** To free from impurities; cleanse. **4.** To free from imputation of guilt, blame, or the like; to vindicate. **5.** To open for passage, action, use, etc.; as, to *clear* land; hence: **a** To empty or disburden; as, to *clear* a ship of her cargo. **b** In general, to free or rid; as, to *clear* an equation of fractions. **6.** To disentangle; to get clear; as, to *clear* a hawser. **7.** To free from obligation; as: **a** To settle, as a debt, or to free from debt. **b** To free (a ship or cargo) by payment of duties, harbor dues, etc. **8.** To render (the eyes or sight) clear or keen. **9.** To make (the voice) clear; to rid, as the throat, of anything. **10.** To take or move away and thus leave a place clear; as, to *clear* the snow from the walk. **11.** To leap or pass by, over, or around; as, to *clear* a hedge. **12.** *Banking.* To pass (a check, etc.) through the clearinghouse; loosely, to get the cash for. **13.** *Commerce.* To gain without deduction; to net. — *v. i.* **1.** To become clear or bright. **2.** *Banking.* To make exchanges of checks, bills, etc., and settle balances, as in a clearinghouse. **3.** *Naut. & Com.* To conform to port regulations by payment of duties, etc., so as to obtain permission to leave port (***clear out*** or ***outwards***) or to discharge cargo (***clear in*** or ***inwards***).
— *n.* **1.** A clear space or part. **2.** Clearance; unobstructed space; also (chiefly in phrase ***in the clear***), minimum distance between bounding parts or surfaces, as of an opening; interior width.
clear′a·ble (klẹr′ȧ·b′l), *adj.* Capable of being cleared.
clear′ance (-ăns), *n.* **1.** Act of clearing. **2.** The distance by which one thing clears another, or the clear space between them. **3.** *Banking.* Settlement of debts or claims; passage of checks, etc., through the clearinghouse. **4.** *Naut. & Com.* Act of clearing a ship at the customhouse; also, the certificate or papers (**clearance papers**) showing that the ship has cleared.
clear′-cut′ (*see Pron.*, § 2), *adj.* Having a sharp distinct outline; sharply defined; concise and distinct. — **Syn.** See INCISIVE.
clear′er (klẹr′ẽr), *n.* One who or that which clears.
clear′-eyed′, *adj.* Having clear eyes; also, perspicuous.
clear′head′ed (klẹr′hĕd′ĕd; -ĭd; 2), *adj.* Having a clear understanding. — **clear′head′ed·ness,** *n.*
clear′ing (klẹr′ĭng), *n.* **1.** Act or process of making or becoming clear. **2.** A tract of land cleared of wood. **3.** *Banking.* **a** A method adopted by banks and bankers for making an exchange of checks, etc., held by each against the others, and settling differences of accounts; also, the machinery or procedure established under this method. **b** *pl.* The amount of the balances so adjusted.
clear′ing·house′ (-hous′), *n.* **1.** *Banking.* An institution or establishment for carrying on the business of clearing. **2.** Any agency for classifying and distributing; as, a *clearinghouse* for news.
clear′ly, *adv.* In a clear manner.
clear′ness (klẹr′nĕs; -nĭs), *n.* Clear quality or state.
clear′-sight′ed, *adj.* Seeing with clearness; discerning. — **clear′-sight′ed·ly,** *adv.* — **clear′-sight′ed·ness,** *n.*
clear′starch′ (klẹr′stärch′), *v. t. & i.* To starch.
clear′sto′ry (-stō′rĭ). Var. of CLERESTORY.
clear′wing′ (-wĭng′), *n.* A moth (esp. of the families Aegeriidae or Sphingidae) having the wings largely transparent and devoid of scales.

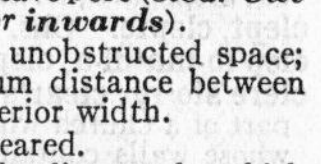
Cleat, 1.

cleat (klēt), *n.* [AS. *clēat.*] **1.** A wedge-shaped piece fastened to something to act as a support, check, etc., as for a rope on the spar of a ship; hence, a device having two arms, used to secure a line or rope by belaying it or passing it through a hole, or the like. **2.** A strip fastened across something to give strength, furnish a grip, etc. — *v. t.* To secure to, or by, a cleat.
cleav′a·ble (klēv′ȧ·b′l), *adj.* That may be cleft or divided.
cleav′age (-ĭj), *n.* **1.** A cleaving, or splitting; state of being cleft; division. **2.** *Biol.* Cell division; specif., *Embryol.*, the series of mitotic divisions of the egg which results in the formation of the blastomeres and changes the single-celled egg into a multicellular embryo; segmentation; also, any mitotic division belonging to that series.
cleave (klēv), *v. i.*; *past* CLEAVED (klēvd); *past part.* CLEAVED; *pres. part.* CLEAV′ING. Archaic pasts CLAVE (klāv), CLOVE (klōv). [AS. *cleofian, clifian.*] To adhere closely; to stick; cling. — **Syn.** See STICK.
cleave, *v. t.*; *past* CLEFT (klĕft), CLEAVED, CLOVE; *past part.* CLEFT, CLEAVED, CLO′VEN (klō′vĕn); *pres. part.* CLEAV′ING. Archaic past CLAVE; poetic past part. CLOVE. [AS. *clēofan.*] **1.** To part, divide, or pierce by force, as with a cutting blow; to split; to cut. **2.** To sep-

arate as if by cutting. — *v. i.* **1.** To split; crack; separate, as parts of bodies. **2.** To make one's way by or as by cutting. — **Syn.** See TEAR.

cleav'er (klēv'ẽr), *n.* One that cleaves; esp., a butcher's instrument for cutting animal bodies into joints or pieces.

cleav'ers (-ẽrz), *n. sing. & pl.* Also **cliv'ers** (klĭv'-). Any of several plants (genus *Galium*, esp. *G. aparine*) of the madder family, having the stems covered with curved prickles.

cleek (klēk), *v. t.;* CLAUGHT (klôKt; kläKt), CLEEKED (klēkt); CLEEKED; CLEEK'ING. [ME. *cleken, clechen.*] *Chiefly Scot.* **1.** To seize; clutch. **2.** To hook (a fish). **3.** To link (together); marry. — *n.* **1.** A hook. **2.** *Golf.* An iron club with a straight narrow face and a long shaft.

clef (klĕf), *n.* [F., fr. L. *clavis* key.] A character used in musical notation to determine the pitches to be represented by the lines and spaces of the staff. The clefs are three in number, called the ***C clef***, the ***F***, *or* ***bass***, ***clef***, and the ***G***, ***treble***, *or* ***violin***, ***clef***, and are corruptions or modifications of these letters. They indicate that the absolute pitch belonging to the lines upon which they are placed is respectively that of middle C, the F next below, and the G next above. See PITCH.

cleft (klĕft), *n.* [ME. *clift.*] **1.** A space or opening made by splitting; a crack; fissure. **2.** Any opening or hollow like a crack; as, a *cleft* in one's chin.

cleft, *past & past part.* of CLEAVE, to split. Specif.: *part. adj.* **1.** Divided; split; often, partly divided or split; as, a *cleft* stick. **2.** *Bot.* Divided slightly more than halfway to the midrib, with narrow sinuses; — of leaves. See LOBATION, *Illust.*

cleft palate. Congenital fissure of the roof of the mouth.

cleis·tog'a·my (klīs·tŏg'ȧ·mĭ), *n.* [Gr. *kleistos* closed + *-gamy.*] *Bot.* The self-pollination or self-pollinating nature of closed flowers, as violets, which develop small flowers additional to the ordinary flowers. — **cleis'to·gam'ic** (klīs'tō·găm'ĭk), **cleis·tog'a·mous** (klīs·tŏg'ȧ·mŭs), *adj.*

clem'a·tis (klĕm'ȧ·tĭs; *Brit. also* klē·mā'tĭs), *n.* [L., fr. Gr. *klēmatis,* fr. *klēma* twig.] A vine or herb (genus *Clematis,* or allied genera *Atragene* and *Viorna*) of the crowfoot family, having three leaflets and white or purple flowers. Climbing species are also called *virgin's-bower* (as *C. virginiana* of the United States).

clem'en·cy (klĕm'ĕn·sĭ), *n.; pl.* -CIES (-sĭz). [L. *clementia,* fr. *clemens* mild, calm.] **1.** Disposition to be merciful; leniency; also, an act of leniency or mercy. **2.** Mildness of the elements; as, the *clemency* of the season. — **Syn.** See MERCY. — **Ant.** Harshness.

clem'ent (klĕm'ĕnt), *adj.* Inclined to be merciful; lenient; also, of weather, mild. — **clem'ent·ly,** *adv.*

clench (klĕnch), *v. t.* [See CLINCH.] **1.** = CLINCH, *v. t.,* 1. **2.** To set closely together; interlock; as, to *clench* the teeth, the fist. **3.** To hold or grasp firmly. — *n.* The act of clenching; a thing that clenches.

clepe (klēp), *v. t.* [AS. *cleopian, clipian.*] *Obs.* **1.** To call, or summon; to bid; also, to call upon or to. **2.** *Archaic.* To call, or name; — esp. in past part. *y-cleped, y-clept.*

clep'sy·dra (klĕp'sĭ·drȧ), *n.; pl.* -DRAS (-drȧz), -DRAE (-drē). [L., fr. Gr. *klepsydra,* fr. *kleptein* to steal + *hydōr* water.] A water clock.

clept, clepte. Obs. past tense of CLEPE.

clep'to·ma'ni·a, clep'to·ma'ni·ac. Vars. of KLEPTOMANIA, etc.

clere'sto'ry, clear'sto'ry (klēr'stō'rĭ), *n.; pl.* -STORIES (-rĭz). That part of a church which rises clear of the roofs of the other parts, and whose walls contain windows for lighting the interior (see GOTHIC, *Illust.*); hence, a similar construction in a building, railroad car, etc.

cler'gy (klûr'jĭ), *n.* [OF. *clergie,* confused with OF. *clergié,* both fr. LL. *clericus* priest.] In the Christian church, the body of men ordained to the service of God; ministry.

cler'gy·man (-măn), *n.* A member of the clergy.

cler'ic (klĕr'ĭk), *n.* [LL. *clericus.* See CLERK.] **1.** A clergyman. **2.** One who has received the ecclesiastical tonsure; a clerk. — *adj.* Clerical.

cler'i·cal (-ĭ·kăl), *adj.* [LL. *clericalis.*] **1.** Of, pertaining to, or characteristic of, the clergy, or a clergyman. **2.** Of or relating to a clerk (def. 4) or office worker; consisting of clerks. — *n.* **1.** A clergyman. **2.** [*cap.*] One of a party, esp. in politics, seeking to further ecclesiastical power in a nation. — **cler'i·cal·ly,** *adv.*

cler'i·cal·ism (-ĭz'm), *n.* Clerical principles, policies, or practices; also, adherence to these. — **cler'i·cal·ist** (-ĭst), *n.*

cler'i·hew (klĕr'ĭ·hū), *n.* [After Edmund *Clerihew* Bentley (1875–), English writer, its originator.] A humorous pseudo-biographical quatrain having lines of unequal length rhyming aabb.

cler'i·sy (klĕr'ĭ·sĭ), *n.* [ML. *clericia.*] The literati.

clerk (klûrk; *Brit. usually* klärk, *also heard in Amer. dial., as in Kentucky*), *n.* [From OF. *clerc,* or fr. AS. *clerc, cleric,* clerk, priest, both fr. LL., fr. Gr. *klērikos* of the clergy, fr. *klēros* lot, allotment, clergy.] **1. a** *Now Chiefly Hist.* A clergyman. **b** *R.C.Ch.* = CLERIC, 2. **2.** A layman who performs some minor ecclesiastical office. **3.** *Archaic & Hist.* A person who can read, or read and write; a scholar. **4.** One employed to keep records or accounts, or to have charge of correspondence, etc. **5.** *U. S.* An assistant in a shop; a salesman or saleswoman, esp. in a retail store. — *v. i.* To act or work as a clerk.

clerk'ly (-lĭ), *adj.;* -LI·ER (-lĭ·ẽr); -LI·EST. Of, pertaining to, or characteristic of a clerk; esp., *Archaic,* learned; scholarly. — *adv.* In a clerkly manner. — **clerk'li·ness,** *n.*

clerk'ship, *n.* State, quality, office, or business of a clerk.

cleve'ite (klēv'īt; klā'vĕ·īt), *n.* [After P. T. *Cleve* (1840–1905), Sw. chemist.] A crystallized variety of uraninite from Norway, rich in helium, and radioactive.

clev'er (klĕv'ẽr), *adj.* **1.** Possessing quickness of intellect, skill, etc.; skillful; talented. **2.** Showing skill; as, a *clever* trick. **3.** *Now Chiefly Dial.* Having fitness; satisfactory. **4.** *Colloq., U. S.* Good-natured. — **clev'er·ish,** *adj.* — **clev'er·ly,** *adv.* — **clev'er·ness,** *n.*

Syn. (1) See INTELLIGENT.

(2) **Clever, adroit, cunning, ingenious** mean having or showing great practical intelligence, especially in contriving. **Clever** usually stresses mental quickness and resourcefulness but, sometimes, a very great aptitude; **adroit** usually suggests more shrewdness or astuteness than *clever* and often implies the skillful or crafty use of expedients to gain one's ends in spite of difficulties; **cunning,** as here compared, implies great skill in constructing or creating; **ingenious,** in inventing or discovering a way of accomplishing something.

clev'is (klĕv'ĭs), *n.* A device, usually a U-shaped piece of metal with the ends perforated to receive a pin, used on the end of the tongue of a wagon, etc., to attach it to a draft chain, whiffletree, etc., or, in bridge construction, to fasten the end of a rod to another part. See PLOW, *Illust.*

clew, clue (klōō; 114), *n.* [AS. *cleowen, cliwen.*] **1.** A ball of thread, yarn, or cord; in legend, a ball of thread used in guiding one's way out of a labyrinth. **2.** An indication which guides one in solving anything of a doubtful or intricate nature. In this sense, *clue* is now the usual spelling. **3.** *Naut.* **a** A lower corner of a square sail, or the after lower corner of a fore-and-aft sail. **b** A loop and thimbles at the corner of a sail. Cf. CRINGLE. **c** *pl.* A combination of lines by which a hammock is suspended. — *v. t.;* CLEWED or CLUED (klōōd); CLEW'ING or CLU'ING. **1.** To roll into a ball. **2.** To point out by or as by a clew; — with *out.* **3.** To track as by a clew. **4.** *Naut.* To haul (a sail) by means of lines (**clew lines**), up to a yard or mast; — with *up.*

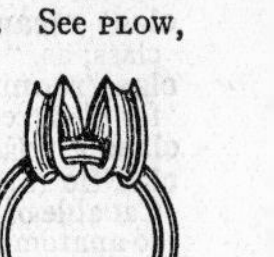

Iron Ring Clew, 3 b.

cli·ché' (klē·shā'; *F.* klē'shā'), *n.; pl.* CLICHÉS (-shāz'; *F.* -shā'). [F., fr. *clicher* to stereotype.] **1.** A stereotype plate or similar reproduction. **2.** A trite phrase; a hackneyed expression.

click (klĭk), *n.* [Imitative.] **1.** A slight sharp noise, such as is made by the cocking of a pistol. **2.** *Mach.* A detent. See RATCHET WHEEL, *Illust.* **3.** *Phonet.* Any of a class of sounds occurring especially in certain South African languages, formed by smacking or clicking the tongue. — *v. i.* **1.** To make a click. **2.** *Slang.* To fit or agree exactly; also, to succeed in performance. — *v. t.* To cause to make a click. — **click'er,** *n.*

click beetle. = ELATER, 3 **a.**

cli'ent (klī'ĕnt), *n.* [F. and L.; F., fr. L. *cliens, -entis,* client, dependent, fr. the root of *cluere* to be named.] **1.** *Rom. Hist.* One of a class of dependents attached to the patrician families. **2.** A dependent; one under the protection of another. **3.** One who employs the services of any professional man, as a lawyer; also, loosely, a patron of any shop, etc. — **cli·en'tal** (klī·ĕn'tăl; klī'ĕn-), *adj.*

cli'ent·age (klī'ĕn·tĭj), *n.* A body of clients; clientele.

cli'en·tele' (klī'ĕn·tĕl'; *F.* klē'äN'tĕl'), *n.* [F. and L.; F. *clientèle,* fr. L. *clientela,* fr. *cliens.*] **1.** A body of clients; clients collectively. **2.** A body of clients, as of a lawyer or doctor. **3.** A body of customers or patrons, as of a shop, hotel, etc.

cliff (klĭf), *n.* [AS. *clif.*] A high steep face of rock.

cliff dweller. One of those American Indians whose dwellings have been discovered in recesses in the walls of canyons in the southwestern United States and northern Mexico. They were ancestors of the Pueblo Indians. — **cliff dwelling.**

cli·mac'ter·ic (klī·măk'tẽr·ĭk; klī'măk·tẽr'ĭk), *adj.* [From L., fr. Gr. *klimaktēr* round of a ladder, fr. *klimax* ladder.] Relating to, or constituting, a climacteric; critical. — *n.* **1.** A period or point in human life (as the menopause) in which some great change in the constitution, health, or fortune takes place or is supposed likely to occur; as, ***the climacteric*** *or* ***grand climacteric,*** one's 63d year. **2.** Any critical period. — **cli'mac·ter'i·cal** (klī'măk·tẽr'ĭ·kăl), *adj. & n.*

cli·mac'tic (klī·măk'tĭk), *adj.* Also **cli·mac'ti·cal** (-tĭ·kăl). Of or pertaining to a climax.

cli'mate (klī'mĭt), *n.* [OF. *climat,* fr. L. *clima, -atis,* fr. Gr. *klima, -atos,* slope, supposed slope of the earth, region, fr. *klinein* to slope.] **1.** Average condition of the weather at a place, over a period of years, as shown by temperature, wind velocity, rains, etc. **2.** The trend of fundamental concepts and attitudes pervading a community, nation, or era; as, intellectual *climate.* — **cli·mat'ic** (klī·măt'ĭk), *adj.*

cli'ma·tol'o·gy (klī'mȧ·tŏl'ō·jĭ), *n.* The science which treats of climates and their phenomena. — **cli'ma·to·log'ic** (-tō·lŏj'ĭk), **cli'ma·to·log'i·cal** (-ĭ·kăl), *adj.* — **cli'ma·tol'o·gist** (klī'mȧ·tŏl'ō·jĭst), *n.*

cli'max (klī'măks), *n.* [L., fr. Gr. *klimax* ladder, staircase, fr. *klinein* to lean.] **1.** *Rhet.* A figure in which a number of propositions are so arranged that each succeeding one rises above its predecessor in force. **2.** Popularly, the highest member of a rhetorical climax. **3.** Hence, the highest point; culmination; acme. **4.** The relatively stable community achieved by a population of plants or animals culminating from successful adjustment to an environment. See COMMUNITY. — **Syn.** See SUMMIT. — *v. t. & i.* To come or bring to a climax.

climb (klīm), *v. i. & t.* [AS. *climban.*] **1.** To ascend, or, with *down,* to descend, as by grasping or clinging or by a hold or footing, esp. by use of the hands and feet. **2.** To ascend or rise to a higher point. **3.** To slope upward. **4.** *Bot.* To ascend in growth by twining about a support, or by tendrils, etc. — **Syn.** See ASCEND. — ***climb down.*** *Colloq.* To retreat or withdraw, as from a position previously taken. — *n.* Act of climbing; ascent by climbing; a place where climbing is necessary. — **climb'a·ble** (-ȧ·b'l), *adj.* — **climb'er** (-ẽr), *n.*

climb'ing bit'ter·sweet' (klīm'ĭng). See BITTERSWEET, 2.

climbing fish. See ANABAS.

climbing iron. A steel framework with spikes, to be affixed to one's boots for climbing poles, trees, etc.; crampon.

clime (klīm), *n.* [L. *clima.* See CLIMATE.] *Poetic.* Climate; also, a region, often with reference to its climate.

clin-. = CLINO-.

cli·nan'thi·um (klĭ·năn'thĭ·ŭm), *n.; pl.* -THIA (-ȧ). [NL., fr. Gr. *klinē* bed + *anthos* flower.] *Bot.* The dilated receptacle of an inflorescence, as in the head of a composite plant.

clinch (klĭnch), *v. t.* [AS. *clencan* (in comp.) to hold fast, clinch.] **1.** To fasten or fix securely, as with nails; to turn over the point of (something driven through an object), so that it will hold fast; to fasten (anything) in this way. **2.** To make conclusive; to confirm. — *v. i.* **1.** To clinch a nail, bolt, etc. **2.** *Chiefly Boxing.* To seize or grasp one another, or another, firmly; to grapple. — *n.* **1.** Act or process of clinching, as a nail; a grip; grasp. **2.** A fastening in which a nail or bolt is clinched; also, the clinched part of the nail or bolt, or a clinched nail or bolt. **3.** *Now Rare.* A pun. **4.** *Boxing.* A position in which the contestants hold each other around the body with one or both arms.

clinch'er (klĭn'chẽr), *n.* One that clinches; as: **a** A nail adapted for clinching. **b** A tool for clinching nails. **c** *Colloq.* That which ends a dispute; a decisive argument. **d** In full, **clincher tire.** A tire having flanged beads on each side of its inner periphery which fit into the turned-over edges of the wheel rim.

cline (klīn), *n.* [From Gr. *klinein* to slope.] *Biol.* A character gradient within a taxonomic group usually associated with a corresponding environmental gradient; also, a group exhibiting such a gradient.

cling (klĭng), *v. i.;* CLUNG (klŭng); CLING'ING. [AS. *clingan* to adhere, shrink, shrivel.] **1.** To stick together in a stiff mass, as liquid in freezing; — now with *together.* **2.** To adhere closely, as a wet garment; to stick or hold fast, as by twining round or embracing. **3.** To be or

keep near, as if adhering. **4.** To stick in one's thought, memory, etc. — **Syn.** See STICK. — *n. Rare.* Act of clinging; clasp. — **cling′er,** *n.*
cling′ing, *adj.* That clings. — **cling′ing·ly,** *adv.*
cling′stone′ (klĭng′stōn′), *n.* A stone which in certain varieties of peach, plum, cherry, etc., adheres closely to the flesh; hence, any peach having such a stone. Cf. FREESTONE.
clin′ic (klĭn′ĭk), *adj.* Clinical. — *n.* **1.** *Med.* **a** Instruction of a class by treatment of patients in the presence of the pupils. **b** Gathering of students at a clinical lecture. **c** An institution connected with a hospital or medical school, for treatment of outpatients. **2.** A similar organization in which special problems are studied by concrete examples and expert advice or treatment given; as, a vocational *clinic.*
clin′i·cal (-ĭ·kăl), *adj.* [L. *clinicus,* fr. Gr., fr. *klinē* bed.] **1.** Of or pertaining to a sickbed or deathbed. **2.** *Med.* **a** Of, pertaining to, or by means of a clinic. **b** Occupied with investigation of disease in the living subject by observation, as distinguished from controlled experiment. **c** *Eccl.* Administered or made on a sickbed or deathbed; as, *clinical* baptism. — **clin′i·cal·ly,** *adv.*
cli·ni′cian (klĭ·nĭsh′ăn), *n.* One versed in clinical medicine or surgery; also, an expert in social-work clinics.
clink (klĭngk), *v. i. & t.* To make a slight, sharp, tinkling sound; to jingle. — **clink,** *n.*
clink, *n. Colloq.* A prison or prison cell; — prob. from the name of a noted prison in Southwark, London.
clink′er (klĭngk′ẽr), *n.* [D. *klinker,* fr. *klinken* to clink.] **1.** A kind of brick. **2.** A brick whose surface has become vitrified; also, a mass of bricks run together, as by heat. **3.** Stony matter fused together, as in a furnace. — *v. i.* To make clinkers in burning, as slaggy coal.
clink′er–built′, *adj.* Having the external planks (of a ship) or plates (of a boiler) put on so that one edge of each overlaps the edge of the plank or plate next it like clapboards on a house; lapstreak. Cf. CARVEL-BUILT.
clink′stone′ (klĭngk′stōn′), *n. Petrog.* = PHONOLITE.
cli′no- (klī′nō-), **clin-.** [Gr. *klinein.*] A combining form meaning *to incline,* as in *clino*meter.
cli·nom′e·ter (klī·nŏm′ē·tẽr), *n.* Any of various instruments for measuring angles of elevation or inclination. — **cli′no·met′ric** (klī′nō·mĕt′rĭk), **cli′no·met′ri·cal** (-rĭ·kăl), *adj.*
clin′quant (klĭng′kănt), *adj.* [MF.] Glittering, as with gold; dressed in, or overlaid with, tinsel. — *n.* [F.] Imitation gold leaf; tinsel.
clin·to′ni·a (klĭn·tō′nĭ·ȧ), *n.* [NL., after De Witt *Clinton,* Am. statesman.] Any of a genus (*Clintonia*) of the lily-of-the-valley family, as ***yellow clintonia*** (*C. borealis*) with yellow flowers and blue beadlike fruits.
Cli′o (klī′ō), *n. Gr. Myth.* The Muse of history.
clip (klĭp), *v. t. & i.;* CLIPPED (klĭpt) or CLIPT; CLIP′PING. [AS. *clyppan* to embrace, clasp.] **1.** *Archaic & Dial.* To embrace; hug. **2.** To clutch; to hold in a tight grip. **3.** *Amer. Football.* To throw the body, illegally, from behind across the leg or legs (below the knees) of a player who is not carrying the ball. — *n.* **1.** *Obs.* An embrace. **2.** That which clips, or clasps; a device for clasping and holding tightly; esp., a device for holding together papers, letters, etc. **3.** *Firearms.* A device to hold cartridges for charging the magazine of some rifles; also, the number of cartridges so held.
clip, *v. t.* [ON. *klippa.*] **1.** To cut, cut off, or snip, as with shears. **2.** Specif.: **a** To trim the hair of. **b** To shear (sheep); to cut off (fleece). **3.** To curtail; to cut short. **4.** *Colloq.* To deal (one) a clip, esp. a quick punch. — *v. i.* **1.** To clip or cut anything, as the hair. **2.** *Archaic.* To fly swiftly. **3.** *Colloq.* To move or run swiftly. **4.** To make clippings from newspapers, etc. — *n.* **1.** *pl. Chiefly Scot.* Shears. **2.** That which is clipped; a clipping, as from cloth; specif., the product of a single shearing of sheep; also, a season's crop of wool. **3.** An act of clipping; a shearing. **4.** *Colloq.* A sharp blow. **5.** A rapid gait or pace; as, going at a good *clip.*
clip′per (klĭp′ẽr), *n.* **1.** One who clips, or cuts, as a shearer of sheep. **2.** *Often pl.* A clipping or cutting instrument, as for clipping hair. **3.** [Cf. *clip* to move swiftly, and, for meaning, *cutter* vessel.] One that clips, moves swiftly, or runs or scuds along; as: **a** A fast horse. **b** A coasting sled. **c** *Slang.* A person or thing of striking excellence. **d** *Naut.* A fast sailing vessel with fine lines, an overhanging bow, tall raking masts, and a large sail area.
clip′ping (klĭp′ĭng), *n.* **1.** Act of one that clips. **2.** That which is clipped off or out of something.
clip′ping, *adj.* **1.** That clips, or cuts, as with shears; that clips, or moves swiftly. **2.** *Slang.* First-rate.
clique (klēk; klĭk), *n.* [F., fr. OF. *cliquer* to make a noise, fr. D. *klikken.*] **1.** A small and exclusive set or coterie of persons. **2.** The system of cliques; cliquishness. — *v. i.;* CLIQUED (klēkt; klĭkt); CLI′QUING (klē′kĭng; klĭk′ĭng). *Colloq.* To associate in a clique. —
cli′quish (klē′kĭsh; klĭk′ĭsh), *adj.* — **cli′quish·ly,** *adv.* — **-ness,** *n.*
cli′quy, cli′quey (klē′kĭ; klĭk′ĭ), *adj.* Forming, or given to forming, cliques.
clish′ma·cla′ver (klĭsh′mȧ·klā′vẽr), *n. & v. Dial.* Gossip.
cli′to·ris (klī′tō·rĭs; klĭt′ō·rĭs), *n.* [NL., fr. Gr. *kleitoris,* fr. *kleiein* to shut up.] *Anat.* A small organ at the upper part of the vulva, homologous to the penis in the male.
cliv′ers (klĭv′ẽrz). Var. of CLEAVERS.
clo·a′ca (klō·ā′kȧ), *n.; pl.* -CAE (-sē). [L.] **1.** A sewer. **2.** A privy or water closet. **3.** A channel for moral filth or corruption. **4.** *Zool.* The common chamber into which the intestinal, urinary, and generative canals discharge in birds, reptiles, amphibians, and many fishes. — **clo·a′cal** (-kăl), *adj.*
cloak (klōk), *n.* [OF. *cloke, cloque,* cloak (from the bell-like shape), bell.] **1.** A loose outer garment. **2.** That which conceals; a blind; disguise; mask. — *v. t.* **1.** To cover with or as with a cloak. **2.** To hide or conceal. — **Syn.** See DISGUISE.
clob′ber (klŏb′ẽr), *v. t.* [Perh. modification of Scot. dial. *clabber* to spatter.] *Slang.* **a** To pound or beat mercilessly; to knock down. **b** To defeat overwhelmingly.
cloche (klōsh; *F.* klôsh), *n.* [F., prop., bell.] A bell-shaped article; as: **a** A close-fitting helmet-shaped hat for women. **b** *Hort.* A bell jar to protect a plant.
clock (klŏk), *n.* [MD. *clocke,* fr. OF. *cloque, cloche,* bell, or ML. *clocca.*] **1.** A device for measuring or indicating time, esp. one not a watch. **2.** *Colloq.* An indicator, dial, or registering device attached to a mechanism to measure its functioning or record its output. — *v. t. Colloq.* To time (one), as in a race; also, to register with a mechanical recording device.
☞ *What o'clock? it is nine o'clock,* etc., are contracted from *what of the clock? it is nine of the clock,* etc.
clock (klŏk), *n.* An ornamental figure on the side of a stocking.
clock′wise′ (-wīz′), *adv.* In the direction in which the hands of a clock rotate, as viewed from in front. Cf. RIGHT-HANDED, DEXTROROTATORY, COUNTERCLOCKWISE. — **clock′wise′,** *adj.*
clock′work′ (-wûrk′), *n.* The machinery of a clock; hence, machinery containing a train of wheels of small size, as in mechanical toys. — *adj.* Automatic; regular.
clod (klŏd), *n.* [ME. *clodde,* later form of *clot.* See CLOT.] **1.** A lump or mass, esp. of earth. **2.** Soil; earth. **3.** That which is earthy and of little value, as the body in comparison with the soul. **4.** A stupid fellow; dolt. **5.** A part of the shoulder of a beef. See BEEF, *Illust.* — **clod′dish,** *adj.* — **clod′dish·ness,** *n.* — **clod′dy,** *adj.*
clod′hop′per (-hŏp′ẽr), *n.* **1.** Plowman; rustic. **2.** *pl.* Heavy shoes such as are worn by plowmen.
clod′hop′ping, *adj.* Boorish; rude.
clod′pate′ (-pāt′), *n.* A blockhead; a dolt.
clod′poll′ (-pōl′), **clod′pole′** (-pōl′), *n.* A clodpate.
clog (klŏg), *n.* [ME. *clogge* stump, block.] **1.** *Now Dial.* A short thick piece of wood. **2.** A weight attached to a man or an animal to hinder motion. **3.** A kind of stout clumsy shoe, having a thick, usually wooden, sole, now chiefly used as a cheap form of working shoe or in a light form for clog dancing. **4.** That which hinders or impedes motion; hence, any encumbrance. **5.** Short for CLOG DANCE. — *v. t.;* CLOGGED (klŏgd); CLOG′GING. **1.** To encumber; hence, to hamper; impede. **2.** To obstruct; choke up. — *v. i.* **1.** To become clogged, as with extraneous matter. **2.** To unite in a mass. **3.** To perform a clog dance. — **Syn.** See HAMPER. — **clog′gy,** *adj.*
clog dance. A dance wherein the performer wears clogs and beats out a clattering rhythm upon the floor, platform, or stage. — **clog dancer.** — **clog dancing.**
cloi′son·né′ (kloi′zŏ·nā′; *F.* klwȧ′zô′nā′), *adj.* [F., partitioned.] Inlaid between partitions; — said of a surface decoration set in enamel between bent wire fillets secured to the base. — *n.* Cloisonné enamel.
clois′ter (klois′tẽr), *n.* [OF. *cloistre,* fr. L. *claustrum,* pl. *claustra,* bar, bolt, bounds, fr. *claudere, clausum,* to close.] **1.** A monastic establishment; a monastery or convent; also, monastic life. **2.** A covered passage on the side of a court, usually having one side walled, and the other an open arcade or colonnade.
Syn. **Cloister, convent, monastery, nunnery, abbey, priory** mean a house of a religious community. **Cloister** and **convent** are general terms, but *cloister* implies seclusion from the world and *convent* community of living; a **monastery** is, properly, a cloister for monks, and **nunnery** (now archaic), for nuns. *Convent,* in a narrow sense, is now more often used than *nunnery; monastery* may be used of the house of any cloistered community. A monastery or nunnery governed by an abbot or abbess is an **abbey;** one governed by a prior or prioress is a **priory.**
— *v. t.* **1.** To confine in or as in a cloister; to seclude from the world. **2.** To surround with a cloister.
clois′tered (-tẽrd), *adj.* Sequestered; recluse.
clois′tral (-trăl), *adj.* Of, relating to, or like a cloister.
clois′tress (-trĕs; -trĭs), *n.* A nun.
cloke (klōk). Var. of CLOAK.
clone (klōn), **clon** (klōn; klŏn), *n.* [Gr. *klōn* a twig or slip.] *Biol.* The aggregate of individual organisms descended by asexual reproduction from a single sexually produced individual; — used specif. of animals that reproduce parthenogenetically (as aphids) or by budding (as hydras) or of plant varieties propagated by vegetative means (as cuttings).
clo′nus (klō′nŭs), *n.* Also **clo′nos** (-nŏs). [NL., fr. Gr. *klonos* violent motion.] *Physiol. & Med.* A forced series of alternating contractions and partial relaxations of the same muscle. Clinically, it is a sign of nerve lesions. — **clon′ic** (klŏn′ĭk), *adj.* — **clo·nic′i·ty** (klō·nĭs′ĭ·tĭ), *n.*
cloot (klōōt; *Scot.* klüt), *n. Chiefly Scot.* **1.** One of the divisions of a cleft hoof; also, the whole hoof. **2.** [*cap.*] The Devil; Clootie; — usually in "auld *Cloots.*"
cloot′ie (klōōt′ĭ; *Scot.* klüt′ĭ), *n. Scot. & N. of Eng.* **a** A little hoof. **b** [*cap.*] The Devil.
close (klōs), *adj.* [OF. *clos,* fr. L. *clausus,* past part. of *claudere* to close.] **1.** Shut fast; closed. **2.** Shut in; enclosed; also, enclosing. **3.** Confined or confining strictly. **4.** Secluded; secret; hidden. **5.** Disposed to keep secrets; secretive. **6.** Narrow; confined. **7.** Oppressive; stifling; — said of the air, weather, etc. **8.** Tightfisted; stingy. **9.** Closed to open or public competition or admission; restricted as to membership, etc. **10.** Dense; compact; also, viscous; tenacious. **11.** Fitting tightly or exactly; as, a *close* bonnet; next to the surface on which it grows or rests; short. **12.** Adhering strictly to a standard or original; exact; as, a *close* translation. **13.** Intimate; familiar; as, *close* friends; hence, in accord emotionally; as, in *close* communion. **14.** Near in space, time, or thought. **15.** Strict; rigorous; as, *close* questioning. **16.** Concise; compactly expressed. **17.** Accurate; precise. **18.** Nearly equal; almost evenly balanced. **19.** *Finance.* Difficult to obtain; as, money is *close.* **20.** *Phonet.* Of a vowel, uttered with some part of the tongue close to the palate (*ē* of *eve; ōō* of *boot*).
Syn. (1) Also *adv.* **Close, near, nigh** mean not far away, as in place, time, or relationship. **Close** suggests so slight a difference that contact, coincidence, or the like, are almost, if not actually, implied; **near** carries a much less explicit suggestion of contiguousness, coincidence, or the like, but, nevertheless, implies an approach to them; **nigh,** now archaic or dialectal, comes very close to *near.*
(2) **Close, dense, compact, thick** mean massed tightly together. **Close** applies to texture, weave, or something comparable where parts or particles come into contact (as, to write a *close* hand); **dense** implies compression of parts or elements so great as to be almost impenetrable (as, a *dense* forest); **compact** suggests a firm union or consolidation of parts within a small compass (as, a *compact* arrangement); **thick,** a condensation or concentration and an abundance of parts or units (as, *thick* hair).
(3) See STINGY.
— *adv.* In a close position or manner.
close (klōz), *v. t.* [ME. *closen,* fr. stem *clos-* of OF. *clore* to close.] **1.** To stop, or fill up, as an opening; to shut. **2.** To enclose; encompass; confine. **3.** To bring to an end or period. **4.** To unite; consolidate; make close. — *v. i.* **1.** To come together or shut; to unite or coalesce, as parts separated. **2.** To come close or near; hence, to grap-

ple; to engage at close quarters. **3.** To end or terminate. **4.** To agree (*on, upon, with*). — *n.* Conclusion; end.

Syn. **Close, end, conclude, finish, complete, terminate** mean to bring or come to a stopping point or a limit. **Close** refers to a thing that was in some sense *open* (as, to *close* an account); **end** conveys a stronger idea of finality and refers to a progress or development that has been carried through (as, to *end* one's life); **conclude**, more formal than *end*, applies to transactions, proceedings, etc., that have a formal ending (as, to *conclude* a speech with a peroration); **finish** implies that what one set out to do has been done (as, to *finish* a piece of work); **complete** implies a removal of all deficiencies (as, to *complete* one's education in Europe); **terminate** implies the setting of a limit in time or space (as, hostilities *terminated* at sundown).

close (klōs), *n.* [OF. *clos* enclosure.] **1.** An enclosed place, as land about a cathedral. **2.** *Scot. & Local Eng.* A passage from a street to a court and the houses within, or to the common stair of a tenement.

close corporation (klōs). *Finance. Colloq.* A corporation the stock of which is held by very few persons.

closed chain (klōzd). *Chem.* An arrangement of atoms represented in formulas or models as a ring (see RING, 11); — opp. to *open chain.*

closed shop. An establishment in which the employer by agreement hires and retains in employment only union members in good standing, except that, by some agreements, when union members are unavailable, the employer may hire nonunion workers provided they apply for union membership or obtain work permits before beginning work.

closed syllable. *Phonet.* A syllable ending in a consonant.

close′fist′ed (klōs′fĭs′tĕd; -tĭd; 2), *adj.* Stingy; niggardly. — **close′-fist′ed·ly,** *adv.* — **close′fist′ed·ness,** *n.*

close′–hauled′ (-hôld′; 2), *adj.* Having the sails set so as to sail as nearly against the wind as the vessel will go.

close′ly (klōs′lĭ), *adv.* In a close manner.

close′mouthed′ (klōs′mouthd′; -moutht′; 2), *adj.* Cautious in speaking; uncommunicative; also, secretive.

close′ness (klōs′nĕs; -nĭs), *n.* State or quality of being close.

clos′er (klōz′ẽr), *n.* One who or that which closes.

clos′et (klŏz′ĕt; -ĭt), *n.* [OF., little enclosure, dim. of *clos.*] **1.** A small room for privacy. **2.** A monarch's private chamber for counsel or devotions. **3.** A small room or recess for household utensils, clothing, etc. **4.** A water closet. — *v. t.* **1.** To shut up in or as in a closet. **2.** To take into a closet for an interview. — *adj.* **1.** Secret; private. **2.** Working in, or fitted for use or enjoyment only in, the closet, as the place of seclusion, study, or thought; as, *closet* drama, suited primarily for reading rather than production.

close′–up′ (klōs′ŭp′), *n.* **1. a** *Motion Pictures.* A picture of a character or a portion of a scene taken with the camera moved closer than for the main part of the picture. **b** Hence, any photograph taken at close range. **2.** A close or intimate view or examination of anything.

clo′sure (klō′zhẽr), *n.* [OF., fr. L. *clausura,* fr. *claudere* to shut.] **1.** *Obs.* Enclosure. **2.** Act of closing or shutting. **3.** A conclusion; an end. **4.** That which closes or shuts. **5.** *Parl. Practice.* A method of ending debate and securing an immediate vote upon a measure before a legislative body; cloture. It is done by adoption of a motion that "the question be now put." Cf. PREVIOUS QUESTION. — *v. t. & i.* *Parl. Practice.* To subject to, or make use of, a closure.

clot (klŏt), *n.* [AS. *clott, clot.*] A mass; esp., a soft, slimy concretion, as of blood. — *v. i. & t.;* CLOT′TED; CLOT′TING. To coagulate, or thicken, as soft or fluid matter by evaporation; to become a clot.

cloth (klôth; 74), *n.; pl.* CLOTHS (klôthz *or, esp. in sense "kinds of cloth,"* klôths), except in the sense of garments, when it is CLOTHES (klōthz; *colloq.* klōz). [AS. *clāth.*] **1.** A pliable fabric woven, felted, or knitted from any filament; commonly, fabric of woven cotton, woolen, silk, rayon, or linen fiber, used for garments, etc.; also, a piece of such fabric. **2.** *Obs.* **a** Clothing. **b** A garment. **3.** A tablecloth. **4.** The distinctive dress of any profession, esp. of the clergy; hence, ***the cloth,*** the clergy. **5.** *Naut.* Canvas; sails collectively. **6.** *Theater.* A drop curtain. — **cloth,** *adj.*

clothe (klōth), *v. t.;* CLOTHED (klōthd) or CLAD (klăd); CLOTH′ING (klōth′ĭng). **1.** To put garments on; dress. **2.** To provide with clothes. **3.** To cover as with a garment.

clothes (klōthz; *formerly, and still colloq.,* klōz), *n. pl.* [Pl. of CLOTH.] **1.** Covering for the human body; clothing. **2.** Bedclothes. — **Syn.** Clothing, dress, apparel, attire, raiment.

☞ COMBINATIONS are:

clothesbasket **clothesbrush** **clothesline**

clothes′horse′ (-hôrs′), *n.* A frame on which to hang clothes, as for drying.

clothes′pin′ (-pĭn′), *n.* A forked piece of wood, or a small spring clamp, used for fastening clothes on a line.

clothes′press′ (-prĕs′), *n.* A receptacle for clothes, as a chest or wardrobe.

cloth′ier (klōth′yẽr; 58), *n.* One who makes or sells cloths or clothing.

cloth′ing (klōth′ĭng), *n.* Garments in general; clothes; dress; also, a covering.

Clo′tho (klō′thō), *n.* [L., fr. Gr. *Klōthō,* lit., the spinner.] *Gr. Myth.* One of the Fates. See FATE, *n.,* 4.

clo′ture (klō′tūr; *F.* klō′tür′), *n.* [F. *clôture.*] *Parl. Practice.* Closure. — **clo′ture,** *v. t. & i.*

cloud (kloud), *n.* [AS. *clūd* rock, hillock.] **1.** A visible mass of fog or haze suspended at a height in the air. See CIRRUS, CUMULUS, NIMBUS, STRATUS. **2.** In general, a visible mass of particles in the air or in a gas; as, a *cloud* of smoke or of dust. **3.** A great crowd or multitude. **4.** That which has a dark, lowering, or threatening aspect. **5.** A dark or opaque vein or spot, as in marble; hence, a blemish or defect. — *v. t.* **1.** To overspread with a cloud or clouds. **2.** To darken or obscure; hence, to render gloomy or sullen. **3.** To blacken; sully; — esp. used of reputation. — *v. i.* To grow cloudy. — **cloud′less,** *adj.*

cloud′ber′ry (-bĕr′ĭ; -bẽr·ĭ), *n.* A raspberry (*Rubus chamaemorus*) of north temperate regions.

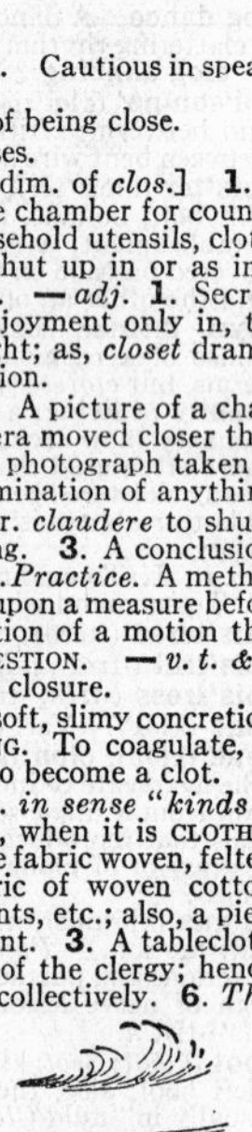

1 2 3 4 5 6 7 8 9 10

Clouds. 1 Cirrus (Ci); 2 Cirro-stratus (Cs); 3 Cirro-cumulus (Cc); 4 Alto-stratus (As); 5 Alto-cumulus (Ac); 6 Strato-cumulus (Sc); 7 Nimbo-stratus (Ns); 8 Cumulus (Cu); 9 Cumulo-nimbus (Cn); 10 Stratus (St).

cloud′burst′ (kloud′bûrst′), *n.* A sudden copious rainfall.

cloud chamber. A vessel containing saturated water vapor whose sudden expansion reveals the passage of an ionizing particle by a trail of visible droplets.

cloud′land′ (-lănd′), *n.* The realm of visionary hypothesis or uncertain speculation; also, realm of poetic imagination.

cloud′let (kloud′lĕt; -lĭt), *n.* A little cloud.

cloud′y (-ĭ), *adj.;* CLOUD′I·ER (-ĭ·ẽr); -I·EST. [From CLOUD, *n.*] **1.** Consisting of, or pertaining to, a cloud or clouds; cloudlike. **2.** Overcast with clouds; clouded. **3.** Clouded, as by gloom or anxiety. **4.** Confused; obscure. — **cloud′i·ly,** *adv.* — **cloud′i·ness,** *n.*

clout (klout), *n.* [AS. *clūt* a little cloth, piece of metal.] **1.** *Archaic & Dial.* A patch of cloth, leather, etc.; shred; rag. **2.** *Now Dial.* Swaddling clothes; — chiefly in *pl.* **3.** Also **clout nail.** A type of nail. See NAIL, *Illust.* **4.** *Colloq.* A blow, as with the hand. **5.** *Archery.* A white target placed at 160–240 yards; also, a hit in the clout. **6.** *Slang, Baseball.* A long hard hit. — *v. t.* **1.** To bandage, patch, or mend. **2.** *Colloq. & Dial.* To give a blow to; to strike.

clove (klōv), *n.* [AS. *clufu.*] One of the small bulbs developed in the axils of the scales of a large bulb, as in garlic.

clove, *n.* [OF. *clou* nail, *clou de girofle* a clove, lit. nail of clove, fr. L. *clavus* nail.] The dried flower bud of a tropical tree (*Eugenia aromatica*) of the myrtle family, used as a spice; also, the tree. The oil obtained from cloves is used in perfumery manufacture and in medicine.

clove (klōv), **clo′ven** (klō′vĕn). See CLEAVE.

clove hitch. A type of knot. See KNOT, *Illust.* (23).

cloven foot *or* **hoof.** Figuratively, the sign of devilish character, Satan being often represented as cloven-footed.

clo′ven–foot′ed (klō′vĕn·fo͝ot′ĕd; -ĭd; 2), *adj.* Having the foot divided or cleft into two or more parts, as the ox and sheep.

clo′ver (klō′vẽr), *n.* [AS. *clāfre, clǣfre.*] **1.** Any of a genus (*Trifolium*) of low herbs of the pea family, with trifoliolate leaves and flowers in dense heads, including many valuable forage and bee plants, as ***white clover*** (*T. repens*), a common ingredient of lawn and pasture grass-seed mixtures; ***red clover*** (*T. pratense*), the State flower of Vermont; ***hop clover,*** any yellow-flowered species (esp. *T. agrarium* and *T. procumbens*); ***alsike clover,*** *or* ***alsike*** (*T. hybridum*) with pinkish flowers; ***crimson clover*** (*T. incarnatum*). See also SHAMROCK. **2.** Any of several other plants of the same family; as, ***sweet clover*** (any species of *Melilotus,* grown for hay, pasture, and soil improvement); ***bush clover*** (*Lespedeza*), esp. *L. striata,* also called ***Japan clover***; ***prairie clover*** (*Petalostemon*); ***spotted clover*** (*Medicago*). — ***in clover.*** In prosperity or comfort.

clo′ver–leaf′ (klō′vẽr·lēf′), *adj.* Of or resembling a clover leaf.

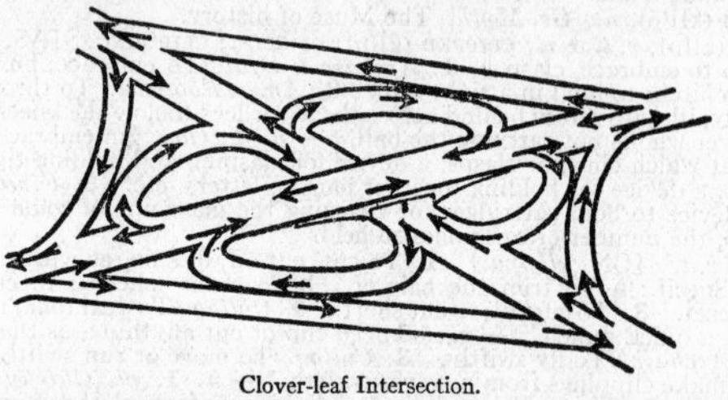

Clover-leaf Intersection.

clown (kloun), *n.* **1.** A rustic; churl. **2.** An ill-bred person; a boor. **3.** A fool or buffoon in a play, circus, etc. — *v. i.* To act as a clown.

clown′ish, *adj.* Of, like, or characteristic of a clown. — **Syn.** See BOORISH. — **Ant.** Urbane. — **clown′ish·ly,** *adv.* — **clown′ish·ness,** *n.*

cloy (kloi), *v. t.* [From OF. *encloer,* fr. L. *inclavare,* fr. *clavus* a nail.] To satisfy or fill to capacity or to excess, as the appetite. — *v. i.* To cause surfeit. — **Syn.** See SATIATE. — **cloy′ing·ly,** *adv.*

club (klŭb), *n.* [ON. *klubba.*] **1.** A heavy staff of wood, usually tapering; a cudgel. **2.** Hence: **a** A weapon of wood or metal, for delivering rough blows; a war club. **b** A stick, mallet, or bat used in various games with a ball, as in golf, hockey, etc. See GOLF, *Illust.* **c** Short for INDIAN CLUB. **3.** An association of persons for some common object, esp. one jointly supported and meeting periodically. **4.** A building or room occupied by a club. **5.** *Cards.* [Trans. of Sp. *basto* or It. *bastone.*] Any card or, *pl.,* the suit of cards having a figure like the trefoil or clover leaf. **6.** *Naut.* A light or small spar, as one used to extend the spread of a gaff-topsail beyond the gaff.
— *v. t.;* CLUBBED (klŭbd); CLUB′BING. **1.** To beat with or as with a club. **2.** To gather or combine into a clublike mass or body. **3.** To unite for a common end, or contribute to a common stock; as, to *club* efforts or resources. **4.** To raise or defray by a proportional assessment. **5.** *Mil.* To turn (a musket, rifle, etc.) butt uppermost, so as to use as a club. — *v. i.* **1.** To form a club; to combine or unite. **2.** To pay a proportionate share of a common charge or expense.
— *adj.* Pertaining to, like, or suggestive of a club (sense 3).

club′ba·ble, club′a·ble (klŭb′ȧ·b'l), *adj.* *Colloq.* Suitable for membership in a club; sociable.

club′by (klŭb′ĭ), *adj.* Sociable; companionable.

club car. A parlor car with movable chairs and, usually, with magazines, writing desk, etc.

club chair *or* **sofa.** A thickly upholstered easy chair or sofa, with rather low back, solid sides and arms, and ball-shaped legs.

club′foot′ (klŭb′fo͝ot′), *n.* *Med.* **1.** (*pl.* CLUBFEET.) A foot misshapen and twisted out of position from birth. **2.** This deformity, technically called *talipes.* — **club′foot′ed** (-fo͝ot′ĕd; -ĭd; 2), *adj.*

club grass. = CATTAIL, 1 **a.**

club′haul′ (-hôl′), *v. t.* *Naut.* To put (a vessel) on the other tack, when in danger of going into irons, by dropping the lee anchor as the vessel's head comes to the wind and hauling on a hawser from the lee quarter to the anchor until the vessel pays off on the other tack.

club moss. Any plant of the genus *Lycopodium* (family Lycopodiaceae, the club-moss family); — from the club-shaped strobiles in which the sporangia are usually borne. See LYCOPOD, GROUND PINE **b.**

club steak. A small beefsteak cut from the tip of the loin.

club topsail. A gaff-topsail having its foot bent on a club (def. 6). See SLOOP, *Illust.*

cluck (klŭk), *v. i.* [Imitative.] To make a cluck. — *v. t.* To call with, or as with, a cluck. — *n.* A hen's call to her chicks.

clue (klōō; 114), *n.* & *v.* Clew. See CLEW.

clum′ber span′iel (klŭm′bẽr). [From an estate of the Duke of Newcastle.] See SPANIEL.

clump (klŭmp), *n.* [MLG. *klumpe, klompe.*] **1.** An unshaped mass or heap; a lump. **2.** A cluster, as of trees; a thicket. **3.** A heavy tramping sound. **4.** *Bacteriol.* A mass of bacteria in a quiescent condition. See AGGLUTINATION, 3. — *v. i.* **1.** To tread clumsily. **2.** *Bacteriol.* To form clumps. — *v. t.* **1.** To arrange in a clump; cluster. **2.** To cause to form clumps. — **clump′ish, clump′y,** *adj.*

clum′sy (klŭm′zĭ), *adj.;* -SI·ER (-zĭ·ẽr); -SI·EST. [ME. *clumsed* benumbed.] **1.** Without skill or grace; awkward; as, *clumsy* fingers; a *clumsy* dancer. **2.** Ill-made, misshapen, or inappropriate; as, *clumsy* shoes; a *clumsy* excuse. — **Syn.** See AWKWARD. — **Ant.** Dexterous. — **clum′si·ly,** *adv.* — **clum′si·ness,** *n.*

clung (klŭng), *past & past part.* of CLING.

clu′pe·id (klōō′pē·ĭd), *n.* [L. *clupea* a small river fish + *-id.*] *Zool.* One of a large family (Clupeidae) of soft-finned teleost fishes, including the herrings, sardines, shads, etc. — **clu′pe·id,** *adj.*

clu′pe·oid (-oid), *adj.* *Zool.* Pert. to or like the typical herrings (family Clupeidae). — *n.* A clupeoid fish.

clus′ter (klŭs′tẽr), *n.* [AS. *cluster, clyster.*] A number of similar things growing together, or of things or persons collected together; a bunch; a group. See OAK-LEAF CLUSTER. — *v. i. & t.* To grow, gather, or unite in a cluster or clusters. — **clus′ter·y,** *adj.*

clutch (klŭch), *v. t. & i.* [AS. *clyccean.*] To seize, clasp, or grip with the hand, hands, or claws; hence, to grasp avidly; as, to *clutch* power. — **Syn.** See TAKE. — *n.* **1.** Usually in *pl.* A claw, talon, or hand in the act of grasping firmly; hence, control or power. **2.** A grip as with the fingers or claws; seizure; grasp. **3.** Any device for gripping an object, as a coupling for connecting two working parts, such as shafts or a shaft and a pulley, permitting either to be thrown at will into or out of gear with the other by moving a lever; also, a lever operating such a device. **4.** A critical juncture; a pinch; — used originally of sports (he is a good batter in the *clutch*).

clutch, *n.* A nest of eggs or a brood of chicks. — *v. t.* To hatch.

clut′ter (klŭt′ẽr), *n.* **1.** A confused collection; hence, crowded confusion; disorder; as, the room is in a *clutter.* **2.** Clatter; confused noise. — *v. t.* To throw into disorder; to disarrange; — often with *up.* — *v. i.* To run together in disorder; also, to bustle; clatter.

Clydes′dale′ (klīdz′dāl′), *n.* A heavy draft horse of a breed originally from Clydesdale, Scotland.

Clydesdale terrier. A small terrier of a breed resulting from selective breeding of the Skye terrier.

clyp′e·ate (klĭp′ē·āt), **clyp′e·at′ed** (-āt′ĕd; -ĭd), *adj.* [Deriv. of L. *clypeus* shield.] *Biol.* **a** Shaped like a round shield; scutate. **b** *Zool.* Furnished with a clypeus.

clyp′e·i·form′ (-ĭ·fôrm′), *adj.* Shield-shaped; clypeate.

clyp′e·us (klĭp′ē·ŭs), *n.; pl.* CLYPEI (-ī). [L., a round shield.] *Zool.* A plate or shield on the anterior median part of an insect's head. — **clyp′e·al** (-ăl), *adj.*

clys′ter (klĭs′tẽr), *n.* [F. or L.; F. *clystère,* fr. L., fr. Gr. *klystēr,* fr. *klyzein* to wash off or out.] *Med.* An enema.

Cly′tem·nes′tra, Cly′taem·nes′tra (klī′tĕm·nĕs′trȧ), *n.* Half sister of Helen and wife of Agamemnon. With Aegisthus, her paramour, she effects Agamemnon's assassination. She is slain by Orestes.

co-. [See COM-.] A form of the prefix *com-,* signifying in general *with, together, in conjunction, jointly.* It is used: **1.** With verbs; as, *co*operate; *co*exist; etc. **2.** With participles, adjectives, and adverbs, with the sense of *in* or *to the same degree, amount,* etc.; as, *co*extensive. **3. a** With nouns in general, often importing rights or liabilities which are *joint* or *in common;* as, *co*education. **b** With nouns of agency, office, or occupation, meaning *fellow;* as, *co*author. **4.** With adjectives and adverbs, expressing a sense of joint action or state; as, *co*educational, *co*educationally. **5. a** In mathematics, to indicate the *corresponding function of the complement* of an arc or angle, as in *co*sine, *co*tangent, etc. **b** In astronomy, to indicate the *complement* of the declination, latitude, etc., that is, the difference between 90° and the declination, latitude, etc., as in *co*declination.

coach (kōch), *n.* [F. *coche,* fr. G., fr. Hung. *kocsi,* fr. *Kocs,* village in Hungary.] **1.** A large carriage, now usually one having four wheels and a closed body with doors in the sides, and an elevated seat in front for the driver. **2. a** An enclosed, two-door, single-compartment automobile. **b** In full, ***motor coach.*** An automotive omnibus. **3.** One who coaches; as: **a** A private tutor who assists students in their studies. **b** An instructor in athletics, debating, etc. **4.** *Railroads.* An ordinary passenger car, as distinguished from a drawing-room car, sleeping car, etc.; — often called ***day coach.*** — *v. t.* **1.** To convey in, seat in, or provide with, a coach. **2.** To prepare for public examination, or for an athletic or other contest, by private instruction; to train. **3.** *Baseball.* To direct the movements of (a player, esp. a base runner). — *v. i.* **1.** To instruct as, or receive instruction from, a coach. **2.** *Baseball.* To direct the movements of a player, esp. a base runner.

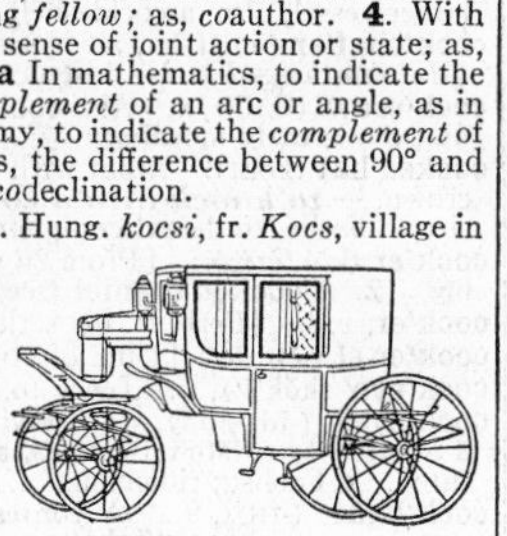

Coach, 1.

coach dog. = DALMATIAN, 2.

coach′er (kōch′ẽr), *n.* **1.** *Obs.* A coachman. **2.** A coach horse. **3.** One who coaches, as in baseball.

coach horse. A horse used or adapted for drawing a coach.

coach′man (-măn), *n.* **1.** A man whose business is to drive a coach or carriage. **2.** *Angling.* An artificial fly with white wings, peacock herl body, brown hackle, and gold tag. — **coach′man·ship,** *n.*

co·act′ (kō·ăkt′), *v. t. & i.* [*co-* + *act,* v.] To do, or act, together. — **co·ac′tive** (-ăk′tĭv), *adj.* — **co·ac′tor** (-tẽr), *n.*

co·ac′tion (kō·ăk′shŭn), *n.* **1.** Action in concert. **2.** *Ecol.* The interaction of organisms; the reciprocal effects of living beings; as, the *coaction* of fox, rabbit, and sapling.

co·ac′tion (kō·ăk′shŭn), *n.* [L. *coactio.*] Force; compulsion; coercion. — **co·ac′tive** (-tĭv), *adj.*

co′ad·ju′tor (kō′ă·jōō′tẽr; kō·ăj′ōō·tẽr), *n.* [From OF., fr. L. *coadjutor.* See CO-; AID.] **1.** An assistant. **2.** A bishop assisting a bishop in charge of a diocese. — **co′ad·ju′tress** (-trĕs; -trĭs), *n.* — **co′ad·ju′trix** (-trĭks), *n. fem.; pl.* -TRICES (kō·ăj′ōō·trī′sēz; kō′ă·jōō′trĭ·sēz).

co·ad′u·nate (kō·ăd′ū·nāt), *adj.* [LL. *coadunatus,* past part. of *coadunare.*] United; esp., *Zool. & Bot.,* grown together· combined into one. — **co·ad′u·na′tion** (-nā′shŭn), *n.*

co·ag′u·la·ble (kō·ăg′ū·lȧ·b′l), *adj.* Capable of being coagulated. — **co·ag′u·la·bil′i·ty** (-bĭl′ĭ·tĭ), *n.*

co·ag′u·lant (-lănt), *n.* [L. *coagulans,* pres. part.] That which produces coagulation.

co·ag′u·late (-lāt), *v. t. & i.* [L. *coagulatus,* past part. of *coagulare* to coagulate, deriv. of *cogere* to drive together.] **1.** To curdle; clot; congeal; as, rennet *coagulates* milk. **2.** To form into a compact or dense mass; solidify. — (-lāt), *adj.* *Rare.* Coagulated.

co·ag′u·la′tion (-lā′shŭn), *n.* The act or state of becoming viscous, jellylike, or solid, or of uniting into a coherent mass; esp., the change from a liquid to a thickened curdlike state by chemical reaction; as, the *coagulation* of blood. — **co·ag′u·la′tive** (-ăg′ū·lā′tĭv), *adj.* — **co·ag′u·la′tor** (-lā′tẽr), *n.*

co·ag′u·lin (kō·ăg′ū·lĭn), *n.* = PRECIPITIN.

co·ag′u·lum (-lŭm), *n.; pl.* -LA (-lȧ). [L.] **1.** *Obs.* A coagulant. **2.** A coagulated mass or substance.

coal (kōl), *n.* [AS. *col.*] **1.** A piece of glowing carbon or charred wood or the like; an ember. **2.** = CHARCOAL, 1. **3. a** A black, or brownish black, solid, combustible substance formed by the partial decomposition of vegetable matter without free access of air, under the influence of moisture, pressure, and temperature. A complete series can be traced from the cellulose of wood through *lignite* (brown coal) and *bituminous coal* (soft coal) to *anthracite* (hard coal) or, as a final product, to graphite. Cf. CANNEL COAL, CHARCOAL, COB COAL, COKE. Coal is found in beds or veins, and is mined for use as fuel, etc. **b** *pl. Eng.* A quantity, or pieces, of this substance broken up for burning; as, a ton of *coals.*

☞ COMBINATIONS and PHRASES are:

coalbag	**coal heaver**	**coal mining**
coalbin	**coal hod**	**coal scuttle**
coaldealer	**coal mine**	**coalyard**

— ***to haul, drag, rake,*** etc., ***over the coals.*** To criticize, censure, or reprimand severely; to call to account.
— *v. t.* **1.** To burn to charcoal; to char. **2.** To supply with coal. — *v. i.* To take in coal.

coal′er (-ẽr), *n.* Anything wholly or chiefly employed in transporting or supplying coal, as a railroad or vessel.

co′a·lesce′ (kō′ȧ·lĕs′), *v. i.;* -LESCED′ (-lĕst′); -LESC′ING (-lĕs′ĭng). [L. *coalescere, coalitum,* fr. *co-* + *alescere* to grow.] **1.** To grow together into one body. **2.** To combine into one body or community; as, vapors or parties *coalesce.* — **Syn.** See MIX. — **co′a·les′cence** (-lĕs′ĕns; -′ns), *n.* — **co′a·les′cent,** *adj.*

coal′fish′ (kōl′fĭsh′), *n.; pl.,* see FISH. [From its dark back.] **1.** See POLLACK. **2.** The beshow.

coal gas. Gas made from coal; specif.: **a** Gas thrown off by burning coal, as in a furnace. **b** Gas made by distilling bituminous coal, used for lighting and heating.

coal′ing sta′tion. A port at which vessels may coal.

co′a·li′tion (kō′ȧ·lĭsh′ŭn), *n.* [ML. *coalitio.*] **1.** Act of coalescing; union. **2.** A combination or union; specif., a temporary alliance for joint action; — often attributively; as, a *coalition* cabinet. — **co′a·li′tion·ist,** *n.*

coal measures. *Geol.* Beds of coal with the associated rocks; specif. [*caps.*], a series of the Carboniferous system including most of the world's workable coal beds.

coal oil. Petroleum, or oil refined from it; esp., kerosene.

coal′sack′ (kōl′săk′), *n.* *Astron.* Any of the very black spaces in the Milky Way; esp. [*cap.*], the large space near the Southern Cross.

coal tar. Tar obtained by the distillation of bituminous coal, and used as a raw material for making various explosives, dyes, medicines, etc.

coam′ing (kōm′ĭng), *n.* **1.** A raised frame as around a hatchway or skylight to keep out water. **2.** *Naut.* One of the raised pieces of wood or iron around a hatchway, skylight, etc., to prevent water from running below.

co·arc′tate (kō·ärk′tāt), *adj.* [L. *coarctatus,* past part., deriv. of *co-* + *arctare* to press together.] *Biol.* Pressed together; closely connected; specif., *Zool.,* having the abdomen separated from the thorax by a constriction only.

coarse (kōrs; 70), *adj.* [From the noun COURSE; cf. *of course* in the common manner of proceeding, common, and hence, plain, rude, rough, gross.] **1.** Common; of inferior quality or appearance; mean; hence, as applied to metals, unrefined. **2. a** Composed of large parts or particles; — opposed to *fine.* **b** Harsh, rough, or rude, as opposed to *delicate* or *dainty.* **3.** Unrefined; vulgar; gross. — **coarse′ly,** *adv.* — **coarse′ness,** *n.*

Syn. **Coarse, vulgar, gross, obscene, ribald** mean offensive to one of good taste or morals. **Coarse** implies roughness, rudeness, or crudeness of spirit, behavior, words, etc.; **vulgar,** as here compared, is more condemnatory than *coarse,* often implying extreme offensiveness to good taste or decency; **gross** implies a pronounced coarseness, sometimes a bestiality unworthy of man; **obscene** stresses a loathsome indecency or nastiness; **ribald,** a vulgarity that provokes laughter from those not easily offended.

coars′en (kōr′s'n), *v. t. & i.* To make or turn coarse.

coast (kōst), *n.* [OF. *coste* rib, hill, coast, fr. L. *costa* rib, side.] **1.** The seashore, or land near it. Cf. HINTERLAND. **2.** *Obs.* The frontier; border. **3.** A slope suited to coasting; also, act of coasting. See COAST, *v. i.,* 2. — *v. i.* **1.** To move by the side or in a roundabout way; to pass (*by, along,* etc.); esp., to sail by or near the shore. **2.** [Cf. OF. *coste* hill, hillside.] *U. S. & Canada.* To slide downhill upon snow or ice, as on a sled; hence, to ride or glide by the force of gravity, as on a bicycle without pedaling or in an automobile out of gear. — *v. t.* **1.** *Obs.* To move or keep near; to skirt. **2.** To sail by or near; to follow the coast line of. — **coast′al** (kōs′tăl), *adj.*

coast artillery. *Mil.* **a** Artillery designed to defend a coast line. **b** [*caps.*] The arm of the service charged with the care and use of the coast defenses.

coast′er (kōs′tẽr), *n.* **1.** One that coasts; esp., a vessel sailing along a coast, or engaged in trade between coastal ports. **2.** A round low tray, often on wheels, for making a decanter "coast" the circuit of the dinner table; also, a shallow container, or a plate or mat, to protect a surface, esp. of a table, as from moisture from drinking vessels. **3.** A sled used in coasting. **4.** = CRADLE, *n.,* 2 **b.**

coaster brake. A brake in a freewheel of a bicycle, operated by reverse pressure on the pedals.

coast guard. **1.** *Eng.* A body of men originally employed along the coast to prevent smuggling, and now drilled as a naval reserve. **2.** Any military or naval force employed in guarding a coast line. **3.** [*caps.*] The organization in charge of the lifesaving stations along the coasts of the United States. **4.** A member of any of these bodies.

coast′ing trade. Trade along a coast.

coast′ward (kōst′wẽrd), **coast′wards** (-wẽrdz), *adv.* Toward the coast. — **coast′ward,** *adj.*

coast′wise′ (-wīz′), **coast′ways′** (-wāz′), *adv.* By way of, or along, the coast. — **coast′wise′,** *adj.*

coat (kōt), *n.* [OF. *cote, cotte,* of Teut. origin.] **1.** An outer garment fitting the upper part of the body; esp., such a garment worn by men; also, an overcoat. **2.** *Now Dial.* A petticoat; a skirt; — usually in *pl.* **3.** External growth on animals, like a garment, as of fur, skin, wool, or feathers. **4.** A layer of any substance covering another. — *v. t.* **1.** To cover with a coat. **2.** To cover with a finishing, protecting, or enclosing layer of any substance. — **coat′less,** *adj.*

coat card. A card bearing a coated figure; the king, queen, or knave of playing cards. Cf. COURT CARD, FACE CARD.

co·a′ti (kō·ä′tē), *n.; pl.* COATIS (-tēz). [Sp. & Pg., of Tupian origin.] A mammal (genus *Nasua*) of tropical America, allied to the raccoon, but with a longer body and tail and a long flexible snout.

coat′ing (kōt′ĭng), *n.* **1.** A coat. **2.** Cloth for coats.

coat of arms. [After F. *cotte d'armes,* a light garment worn over the armor in the 15th and 16th centuries, often charged with the heraldic bearings of the wearer.] *Her.* **a** The bearings of any person, taken together. **b** A tabard or surcoat embroidered with armorial bearings.

coat of mail; *pl.* COATS OF MAIL. A defensive garment of metal scales or chain mail (see 2d MAIL, 1). Cf. HAUBERK.

co·au′thor (kō·ô′thẽr), *n.* A joint or associate author.

coax (kōks), *v. t.* [From older *cokes* a fool, a person easily imposed upon.] **1.** *Obs.* To make a fool of; to dupe. **2.** *Obs.* To blandish, fondle, or pet. **3.** To influence or urge by gentle courtesy, flattering, or fondling. **4.** To succeed in gaining by soft words, flattery, etc. — **Syn.** Wheedle, cajole. — **coax′er,** *n.* — **coax′ing·ly,** *adv.*

co·ax′i·al (kō·ăk′sĭ·ăl), **co·ax′al** (-ăk′săl), *adj. Math.* Having coincident axes, as ellipses and hyperbolas.

coaxial cable. *Elec.* A cable consisting of a tube of conducting material surrounding a central conductor held in place by insulators, the whole assembly being covered with insulation. It is used to transmit telegraph, telephone, and television signals.

cob (kŏb), *n.* [ME. *cob, cobbe.*] **1.** *Dial. Eng.* A large man; also, a leader or chief. **2.** A male swan. Cf. CYGNET, 3d PEN. **3.** A lump or piece of anything, as of coal, ore, or stone. **4.** A short-legged, stocky horse; esp., in America, one having an artificially high stylish leg movement. **5.** = CORNCOB.

co′balt (kō′bôlt; -bŏlt), *n.* [G. *kobalt,* fr. *kobold* goblin, fr. MHG. *kobolt.*] A tough, lustrous, silver-white, somewhat magnetic metal related to, and occurring with, iron and nickel. Symbol, *Co;* at. no., 27; at. wt., 58.94. — **co·bal′tic** (kō·bôl′tĭk), *adj.* — **co·bal′tous** (-tŭs), *adj.*

co·bal′tite (kō·bôl′tīt; kō′bôlt·īt), **co′balt·ine** (kō′bôl·tēn; -tĭn), *n. Mineral.* A grayish to silver-white cobalt sulfarsenide, CoAsS, used in making smalt.

cob′ble (kŏb′'l), *n.* [From COB, 3.] **1.** A cobblestone. **2.** *pl.* Cob coal. — *v. t.* To pave with cobblestones.

cob′ble, *v. t.;* COB′BLED (-'ld); COB′BLING (-lĭng). To make or mend coarsely; to patch.

cob′bler (kŏb′lẽr), *n.* **1.** A mender of shoes. **2.** A clumsy workman; a botcher. **3.** *U. S.* A drink made of wine, sugar, orange or lemon, etc., and pounded ice. **4.** *U. S.* A deep-dish fruit pie with a thick upper crust.

cob′ble·stone′ (kŏb′'l·stōn′), *n.* A naturally rounded stone larger than a pebble, esp. one from six inches to a foot in diameter.

cob coal. Coal in rounded lumps from the size of an egg to that of a football.

co′ble (kō′b'l; kŏb′'l), *n.* [Bret. *caubal,* fr. L. *caupulus.*] *Scot.* A flat-bottomed rowboat.

cob′nut′ (kŏb′nŭt′), *n.* A filbertlike fruit yielded by a variety (*Corylus avellana grandis*) of the hazel; also, the plant bearing this fruit.

co′bra (kō′brȧ), *n.* [Pg. *cobra de capello* serpent of the hood.] **a** Any of several very venomous Asiatic and African snakes (genus *Naja*) which, when excited, expand the skin of the neck into a broad hood by a movement of the ribs, as the large and very venomous ***king cobra*** (*N. hannah*) found from India to southern China. The typical species (*N. tripudians*), to which the name **co′bra de ca·pel′lo** (dē kȧ·pĕl′ō) [*pl.* COBRAS DE CAPELLO (-brȧz)] is usually restricted, is very variable in color and is especially abundant in India, where it causes many deaths. **b** Also ***tree cobra.*** = MAMBA.

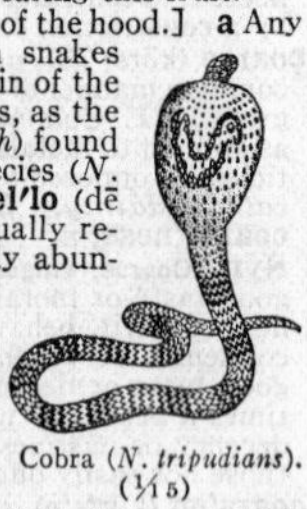

Cobra (*N. tripudians*). (1/15)

cob′web′ (kŏb′wĕb′), *n.* [ME. *coppeweb,* fr. *coppe* spider + *web.*] **1.** The network spread by a spider. **2.** A single thread spun by a spider or by an insect larva. **3.** Anything likened to a spider web as being flimsy, entangling, etc. — *v. t.;* -WEBBED′ (-wĕbd′); -WEB′BING. To cover with cobwebs. — **cob′web′ber·y** (-wĕb′ẽr·ĭ), *n.* — **cob′web′by,** *adj.*

co′ca (kō′kȧ), *n.* [Sp., fr. Quechua *coca, cuca.*] **1.** Any of several South American shrubs (genus *Erythroxylon,* esp. *E. coca;* family Erythroxylaceae) with leaves resembling those of tea. The leaves are chewed by natives to impart endurance. **2.** *Pharm.* The dried leaves of the shrub *E. coca,* yielding cocaine.

co·caine′ (kō·kān′; kō′kān; *more formally,* kō′kȧ·ēn; -ĭn), *n.* Also **co·cain′.** A bitter crystalline alkaloid, $C_{17}H_{21}NO_4$, obtained from coca leaves, and used as a narcotic.

co·cain′ism (kō·kān′ĭz'm; kō·kā′ĭn-), *n. Med.* A morbid condition produced by excessive use of cocaine.

co·cain′ize (-īz), *v. t.* To treat or anesthetize with cocaine. — **co·cain′i·za′tion** (-ĭ·zā′shŭn; -ī·zā′-), *n.*

coc′cus (kŏk′ŭs), *n.; pl.* COCCI (-sī). [NL., fr. Gr. *kokkos* a grain, seed.] **1.** *Bot.* **a** One of the separable carpels of a schizocarp, as that of the mallow. **b** In certain hepatics, a spore mother cell. **2.** *Bacteriol.* A spherical bacterium. See BACTERIA. — **coc′coid** (kŏk′oid), *adj.*

-coc′cus (-kŏk′ŭs). *Coccus* used in forming names in bacteriology, as in strepto*coccus.* Corresponding adjectives end in **-coc′cal** (-ăl), **-coc′cic** (-sĭk), or **-coc′coid** (-oid).

coc′cyx (kŏk′sĭks), *n.; pl.* COCCYGES (kŏk·sī′jēz). [L., cuckoo, fr. Gr. *kokkyx, kokkygos,* cuckoo, coccyx; — from the resemblance to the beak of a cuckoo.] *Anat.* In man and certain apes, the end of the vertebral column beyond the sacrum. — **coc·cyg′e·al** (kŏk·sĭj′ē·ăl), *adj.*

Co′chin (kō′chĭn; kŏch′ĭn), *n.* Also **Cochin China.** A large domestic fowl of an Asiatic breed, having thick plumage, small wings and tail, and densely feathered legs and feet. Varieties are white, black, buff, and partridge.

coch′i·neal′ (kŏch′ĭ·nēl′; kŏch′ĭ·nēl), *n.* [F. *cochenille,* fr. Sp. *cochinilla* cochineal, orig., wood louse, dim. of *cochina* sow.] A dyestuff consisting of the dried bodies of females of a scale insect (*Dactylopius coccus,* syn. *Coccus cacti*) native to Mexico, Central America, etc., and found on several cacti, esp. the **cochineal cactus, fig,** *or* **plant** (*Nopalea coccinellifera*). It is used as a reddish or purple coloring, esp. for foods, and as the source of carmine.

coch′le·a (kŏk′lē·ȧ), *n.; pl.* -LEAE (-ē). [L., snail, snail shell, fr. Gr. *kochlias* snail, fr. *kochlos* shellfish with a spiral shell.] *Anat.* A division of the labyrinth of the ear, in shape like the coil of a snail shell. See EAR, *Illust.* — **coch′le·ar** (-ẽr), *adj.*

coch′le·ate (-āt), **coch′le·at′ed** (-āt′ĕd; -ĭd), *adj.* [L. *cochleatus* spiral or screw-formed. See COCHLEA.] Having the form of a snail shell.

cock (kŏk), *n.* [AS. *cocc.*] **1.** The male of the common barnyard fowl (see POULTRY, *Illust.*); also, the male of other birds, esp. of gallinaceous birds. **2.** A cock's crow, esp. in early morning; cockcrow. **3.** A weathercock. **4.** A chief person; leader. **5.** A faucet, tap, valve, or the like. **6.** The hammer in the lock of a firearm; also, the cocked position of the hammer. Cf. HALF COCK. **7.** Act of cocking; also, the tilt so given; as, the *cock* of the eyes. **8.** *Curling.* The tee.

cock, *v. i.* [ME. *cocken,* prob. fr. *cock* the bird.] **1.** To strut; swagger. **2.** To turn or stick up, as the ear. **3.** To cock the hammer of a firearm. — *v. t.* **1.** To set erect; to tip up or to one side; as, to *cock* one's head. **2.** To turn (the eye) obliquely and partially close its lid, as an expression of derision. **3.** To draw the hammer of (a firearm) back and set it for firing; also, to set (the trigger) for firing.

cock, *n.* [Dan. *kok.*] A small conical pile of hay, or of dung, turf, etc. — *v. t.* To put into cocks, as hay.

cock, *n.* [OF. *coque,* fr. MD. *cogghe.*] *Obs.* A cockboat.

cock·ade′ (kŏk·ād′), *n.* [F. *cocarde,* fr. OF. *cocard* vain, fr. *coq* cock.] A rosette, knot, or similar device, worn upon the hat as a badge. — **cock·ad′ed** (-ād′ĕd; -ĭd), *adj.*

cock′-a-hoop′ (kŏk′ȧ·hōōp′), *adj.* Boastful; elated.

Cock·aigne′ (kŏk·ān′), *n.* [OF. *pais de cocaigne,* land of cake.] An imaginary country of idleness and luxury.

cock′a·leek′ie (kŏk′ȧ·lēk′ĭ), *n. Scot.* A soup made of cock or other fowl boiled with leeks.

cock′a·lo′rum (kŏk′ȧ·lō′rŭm), *n.* A little cock; a bantam; hence, a self-important man, esp. a small man.

cock′-and-bull′ sto′ry. An extravagant, incredible story.

cock′a·teel′, cock′a·tiel′ (kŏk′ȧ·tēl′), *n.* [D. *kaketielje* (*Oxf. E. D.*), ult. fr. source of E. *cockatoo.*] A small Australian parrot (*Leptolophus hollandicus*).

cock′a·too′ (kŏk′ȧ·tōō′ *or, esp. attrib.,* kŏk′ȧ·tōō′), *n.* [D. *kaketoe,* fr. Malay *kakatuwa.*] Any of various brilliant-colored parrots (family Kakatoidae, esp. genus *Kakatoë*), chiefly of the Australian region, many of which have handsome crests. Cf. PARROT, 1.

cock′a·trice (kŏk′ȧ·trĭs *or, esp. Brit.,* -trīs), *n.* [OF. *cocatris,* corrupt. (after *coq* cock) fr. LL. *calcare* to tread, follow. The word was confused in F. with F. dial. & OF. *cocodrille* crocodile.] **1.** A fabulous serpent with deadly glance, said to be hatched by a reptile from a cock's egg. Cf. BASILISK. **2.** *Bib.* A venomous serpent not identified.

cock′boat′ (kŏk′bōt′), *n.* A small boat, esp. one used as a tender to a larger vessel; also, a cockleshell.

cock′chaf′er (-chăf′ẽr), *n.* [See CHAFER the beetle.] A large chafer (*Melolontha vulgaris*) destructive to vegetation, esp. in France.

cock′crow′ (-krō′), *n.* Also **cock′crow′ing.** The time at which cocks first crow; early morning.

cocked hat (kŏkt). A hat with large stiff flaps turned up to a peaked crown. — ***to knock into a cocked hat.*** *Slang.* To knock out of shape; hence, to defeat completely; ruin.

cock′er (kŏk′ẽr), *n.* [From 2d COCK.] **1.** A man given to cockfighting. **2.** A **cocker spaniel** (see SPANIEL).

cock′er, *v. t.* [Perh. fr. COCK the bird.] To pamper.

cock′er·el (-ĕl), *n.* [Dim. of COCK.] A young domestic cock.

cock′eye′ (kŏk′ī′), *n.* [*cock* to turn up + *eye.*] A squinting eye.

cock′eyed′ (-īd′), *adj.* **1.** Having a cockeye or cockeyes. **2.** *Slang.* **a** Slanted or twisted awry; as, knocked *cockeyed.* **b** Slightly intoxicated. **c** Foolish; ridiculous.

cock′fight′ (-fīt′), *n.* A contest of gamecocks usually heeled with metal spurs. — **cock′fight′ing,** *n. & adj.*

cock′horse′ (-hôrs′), *n.* A child's rocking horse.

cock′i·ness (-ĭ·nĕs; -nĭs), *n.* The quality of being cocky.

cock′le (kŏk′'l), *n.* [AS. *coccel.*] **a** = DARNEL. **b** = CORN COCKLE. **c** Any of several other plants growing in grainfields, as the cocklebur, corn poppy (see POPPY), etc.

cock′le, *n.* [OF. *cokille, coquille,* shell, fr. L., fr. Gr. *konchylion.*] **1.** Any of certain bivalve mollusks (*Cardium* or allied genera), esp. the common edible European species (*C. edule*). The shell has convex radially ribbed valves. **2.** =COCKLESHELL, 1. **3.** = COCKLESHELL, 2. **4.** *U. S.* A confection of flour and sugar.

cock′le, *n. & v.* Pucker; wrinkle.

cock′le·boat′ (-bōt′), *n.* A cockboat.

cock′le·bur′ (-bûr′), *n.* Any bur-bearing plant of a genus (*Xanthium*) of the ragweed family; also, the common burdock (*Arctium lappa*).

cock′le·shell′ (-shĕl′), *n.* **1.** One of the shells or valves of a cockle; loosely, also, a scallop shell, etc. **2.** A light, and often flimsy, boat; also, a cockboat.

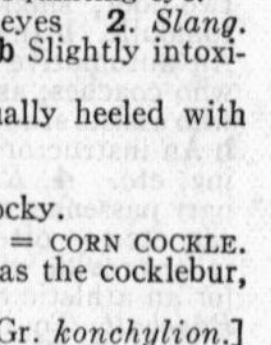

Cockleshell. (1/2)

cock′les of the heart (kŏk′'lz). A phrase (in which *cockles* is of uncertain meaning) denoting the depths of the heart; as, to delight, rejoice, cheer, warm, etc., *the cockles of one's heart.*

cock′loft′ (kŏk′lŏft′; 74), *n.* An upper loft or attic.

cock′ney (kŏk′nĭ), *n.; pl.* -NEYS (-nĭz). [ME. *cokenay, cokeney,* prob. fr. a dial. form of OF. ult. fr. *coquin* rogue, rascal.] **1.** *Obs.* A spoilt child; an effeminate person; sometimes, a squeamish or affected woman. **2.** [*often cap.*] A native of London, esp. of its East End, talking with a characteristic dialect; also, this dialect or twang. — *adj.* Of, relating to, or like cockneys. — **cock′ney·dom**, *n.* — **cock′ney·ish**, *adj.* — **cock′ney·ism**, *n.*

cock′ney·ese′ (kŏk′nĭ·ēz′; -ēs′), *n.* Cockney dialect.

cock′ney·fy (kŏk′nĭ·fī), *v. t.;* -FIED (-fīd); -FY′ING. [*cockney* + *-fy.*] *Colloq.* To make cockney or cockneylike.

cock′pit′ (kŏk′pĭt′), *n.* **1.** A pit for cockfights; hence, a region noted for many conflicts. **2.** *Obs.* The pit of a theater. **3.** *Aeronautics.* In airplanes, a space in the fuselage for the seating of pilots, passengers, etc. See AIRPLANE, *Illust.* **4.** *Naut.* **a** An apartment of the old sailing war vessel, forming quarters for junior officers, and occupied by the wounded in an engagement. **b** In small vessels, a space lower than the rest of the deck, giving access to the cabin.

cock′roach′ (-rōch′), *n.* [Sp. *cucaracha.*] Any of a family (Blattidae, order Orthoptera) of insects, many species of which are troublesome pests in houses and ships, esp. in warm climates. See CROTON BUG.

cocks′comb′ (kŏks′kōm′), *n.* **1.** A coxcomb. **2.** A garden plant (genus *Celosia*) of the amaranth family, cultivated for its showy red, purplish, or yellow flowers.

cock′shut′ (kŏk′shŭt′), *n.* *Obs. exc. Dial.* Evening twilight.

cock′shy′ (-shī′), *n.* A throw or shy at an object set up as a mark; also, a mark or target so made or taken.

cock′spur′ (-spûr′), *n.* **1.** A cock's spur. **2.** A species of hawthorn (*Crataegus crus-galli*) having long thorns.

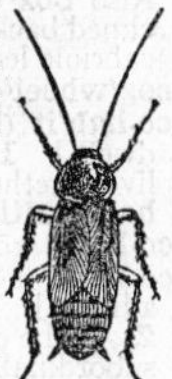

Cockroach (*Blatta orientalis*). (½)

cock′sure′ (-sho͝or′; 2), *adj.* **1.** *Obs.* Perfectly safe. **2.** Wholly trustworthy; of certain issue. **3.** Quite certain; now, often, presumingly certain. — **Syn.** See SURE. — **cock′sure′ness**, *n.*

cock′swain (kŏk′s'n; kŏk′swān). Var. of COXSWAIN.

cock′tail′ (kŏk′tāl′), *n.* **1. a** A horse with its tail docked like a cock's tail. **b** *Stock Breeding.* A horse not of wholly pure breed. **c** A person passing for a gentleman, but underbred. **2.** An iced drink of spirituous liquor well mixed with flavoring ingredients. **3.** An appetizer of raw oysters, clams, etc., served with a sauce (**cocktail sauce**) of catchup, lime juice, and a peppery seasoning; also, an appetizer of chilled cut fruits, or tomato juice, etc.

cock′up′ (kŏk′ŭp′), *n.* **1.** A turnup at the point of anything. **2.** A hat or cap turned up in front.

cock′y (-ĭ), *adj.;* -I·ER; -I·EST. *Colloq.* Pert; conceited.

cock′y·ol′ly, *or* **cock′y·ol′y, bird** (kŏk′ĭ·ŏl′ĭ). A pet name for any small bird.

co′co (kō′kō), *n.; pl.* COCOS (-kōz). Also, less correctly, **co′coa**. [Pg. & Sp. *coco*, fr. L. *coccum* kernel, stone (of fruit), fr. Gr. *kokkos.*] The coconut palm or tree; also, its fruit, the coconut. — *adj.* Made from the fibrous husk of the coconut; as, *coco* matting.

co′coa (kō′kō), *n.* [Sp., fr. *cacao*, after *coco.*] **1.** Cacao. **2. a** Chocolate (sense 1) deprived of a portion of its fat and pulverized. **b** The beverage prepared by cooking this powder in boiling water or milk. **3.** A brown, red-yellow in hue, of medium saturation and low brilliance. See COLOR.

cocoa beans, cocoa butter. See CACAO, 2.

co·con′scious·ness (kō·kŏn′shŭs·nĕs; -nĭs), *n.* [See CO-.] *Psychol.* Secondary consciousness, made up of mental processes outside the main stream of consciousness. — **co·con′scious**, *adj.* — **-ly**, *adv.*

co′co·nut′ (kō′kō·nŭt′), *n.* Also **co′coa·nut′**. **a** The fruit of the coconut palm, a most important economic product of the tropics. Its dried meat yields **coconut oil**. Cf. COPRA. **b** The tree. — **co′co·nut′, co′coa·nut′**, *adj.*

coconut palm *or* **tree**. A tall pinnate-leaved palm (*Cocos nucifera*) found throughout the tropics. Its leaves furnish thatch and a straw used in weaving hats, etc.; a matting is made from the fibrous husk of its fruit. See COIR.

co·coon′ (kŏ·ko͞on′), *n.* [F. *cocon*, fr. Pr. *coucoun*, fr. *coco* shell.] *Zool.* **a** The envelope, often largely of silk, which the larvae of many insects form about themselves and in which they pass the pupa stage. Silkworm cocoons are the source of silk. Cf. CHRYSALIS; PUPA, *Illust.* **b** Any of various other protective coverings produced by animals.

coco palm. The coconut palm or tree.

co′cotte′ (kô′kôt′), *n.* [F.] A young woman of loose morals; a strumpet.

coc′o·zel′le (kŏk′ō·zĕl′ē), *n.* A form of summer squash resembling the zucchini but often having light-green or yellowish stripes or mottling.

Co·cy′tus (kō·sī′tŭs), *n.* [L., fr. Gr. *Kōkytos*, lit., a wailing.] *Gr. Myth.* A river tributary to the Acheron in Hades.

cod (kŏd), *n.* [AS. *codd.*] **1.** *Obs.* A bag. **2.** *Dial.* A husk; pod.

cod, *n.* [ON. *koddi.*] *Scot. & Dial.* Pillow; cushion.

cod, *n.;* see PLURAL, *Note*, 6. [Origin uncert.] **a** A soft-finned gadoid fish (*Gadus morrhua*), one of the most important food fishes, found esp. on the Newfoundland Banks (***bank cod***) and along the New England coast (***shore***, *or* ***native, cod***) and off Norway. A closely allied species, the ***Alaska cod*** (*G. macrocephalus*) inhabits the North Pacific. Cf. SCROD. **b** Any fish of the family (Gadidae) containing the cod, including the haddock, pollack, and tomcod.

co′da (kō′dȧ), *n.; pl.* CODAS (-dȧz). [It., tail, fr. L. *cauda.*] **1.** *Music.* A concluding passage, the function of which is to bring a composition or division to a proper close. **2.** *Prosody.* = TAIL, *n.*, 11.

cod′dle (kŏd′'l), *v. t.;* COD′DLED (-'ld); COD′DLING (-lĭng). **1.** To cook slowly and gently, as eggs or fruit, in water just below the boiling point. **2.** To treat with tenderness; to pamper. — **cod′dler** (-lẽr), *n.*

code (kōd), *n.* [F., fr. L. *codex, caudex*, stem of a tree, board smeared with wax to write on; hence, a book, a writing.] **1.** Any systematic body of law, esp. one given statutory force; a digest. **2.** Any system of principles or rules; as, a *code* of ethics. **3.** A system of signals for communication by telegraph, flags, etc. (see SEMAPHORE, *Illust.*); also, a system of words or other symbols arbitrarily used to represent words; as, a secret *code*. Cf. CIPHER, 4. — *v. t. Colloq.* To put in, or into the form or symbols of, a code; as, to *code* laws.

code′ball′ (kōd′bôl′), *n.* [After Dr. Wm. E. *Code* of Chicago, the inventor.] A game in which a pair or two pairs of players play an inflated ball six inches in diameter entirely with the feet, either against the six surfaces of a standard handball court or on a golflike course into fourteen inverted metal bowls.

co′dec·li·na′tion (kō′dĕk·lĭ·nā′shŭn), *n.* *Astron.* The complement of the declination; — called *polar distance.* See CO-, 5 **b**.

co′de·fend′ant (kō′dē·fĕn′dănt), *n.* A joint defendant.

co′de·ine (kō′dē·ēn; -ĭn), **co′de·in** (-ĭn), *n.* [Gr. *kōdeia* poppy head.] *Chem.* A crystalline alkaloid, $C_{18}H_{21}NO_3.H_2O$, associated in opium with morphine and similar to the latter, but feebler in its action.

co′dex (kō′dĕks), *n.; pl.* CODICES (kō′dĭ·sēz; kŏd′ĭ-). [L.] **1.** *Archaic.* A code. **2.** A manuscript book, as of the Scriptures or the classics.

Co′dex Ju′ris Ca·no′ni·ci (jo͞o′rĭs kȧ·nŏn′ĭ·sī). [L.] *R.C.Ch.* See CANON LAW.

cod′fish′ (kŏd′fĭsh′), *n.; pl.*, see FISH. The cod.

codg′er (kŏj′ẽr), *n.* *Colloq.* A strange fellow, esp. one old, cranky, or uncouth.

cod′i·cil (kŏd′ĭ·sĭl), *n.* [L. *codicillus*, dim. of *codex* code.] **1.** *Law.* An instrument made subsequently to a will and modifying it in some respects. **2.** An added provision; appendix. — **cod′i·cil′la·ry** (-sĭl′ȧ·rĭ), *adj.*

cod′i·fy (kŏd′ĭ·fī; kō′dĭ-), *v. t.;* -FIED (-fīd); -FY′ING. [*code* + *-fy.*] To reduce to a code, as laws; to systematize; classify. — **cod′i·fi·ca′tion** (-fĭ·kā′shŭn), *n.* — **cod′i·fi′er** (-fī′ẽr), *n.*

cod′ling (kŏd′lĭng), *n.;* see PLURAL, *Note*, 3. [Dim. of *cod* the fish.] **a** A young cod. Cf. SCROD. **b** = HAKE, 2.

cod′ling (-lĭng), **cod′lin** (-lĭn), *n.* [From F. *cœur de lion* heart of lion, influenced by *coddle* to stew, bake.] **1.** A small immature apple. **2.** A variety of apple elongated in shape, having a number of horticultural forms.

codling, *or* **codlin, moth.** A small moth (*Carpocapsa pomonella*) which in the larval state lives in apples, pears, and quinces, often doing great damage.

cod′–liv′er oil. An oil obtained from the liver of the codfish and allied fishes and used in medicine.

cod′piece′ (kŏd′pēs′), *n.* [*cod* a bag + *piece.*] A flap or bag, often ornamented, concealing an opening in the front of men's breeches, a fashion of the 15th and 16th centuries.

co′ed′, *or* **co′–ed′** (kō′ĕd′), *n.* *U. S.* A female student in a coeducational institution, esp. a college or university.

co′ed′u·ca′tion (kō′ĕd′ū·kā′shŭn), *n.* Joint education; esp., the education of students of both sexes at the same institution. — **co′ed′u·ca′tion·al** (-ăl; -'l), *adj.* — **co′ed′u·ca′tion·al·ism** (-ĭz'm), *n.* — **co′ed′u·ca′tion·al·ly**, *adv.*

co′ef·fi′cient (kō′ĕ·fĭsh′ĕnt; kō′ĭ-), *n.* **1.** A joint agent. **2.** *Math.* Any numeral or literal symbol placed before another symbol or combination of symbols as a multiplier. **3.** *Physics.* A number expressing the amount of some change or effect under certain conditions as to temperature, length, volume, etc.; as, the *coefficient* of expansion, friction, etc.

-coele (-sēl). Also **-cele**. [Gr. *koilia* cavity of the body.] A combining form denoting *cavity, ventricle*, or *chamber of the body*, as in neuro*coele*.

coe·len′ter·ate (sē·lĕn′tẽr·āt), *n.* [Gr. *koilos* hollow + *enteron* an intestine.] Any member of a phylum (Coelenterata) of invertebrate animals, including the corals, sea anemones, jellyfishes, and hydroids. — **coe·len′ter·ate**, *adj.*

coe·len′ter·on (-ŏn), *n.; pl.* -TERA (-ȧ). [NL.] *Zool.* The internal cavity of coelenterates.

coe′li·ac (sē′lĭ·ăk). Var. of CELIAC.

coe′lom (sē′lŏm), **coe′lome** (-lōm), *n.* [Gr. *koilōma* a hollow, fr. *koilos* hollow.] *Zool.* The body cavity of most metazoans above the sponges and coelenterates.

coe′nes·the′sis (sē′nĕs·thē′sĭs; sĕn′ĕs-), *n.* Also **coe′nes·the′si·a** (-zhĭ·ȧ; -zhȧ; -sĭ·ȧ). [NL., fr. Gr. *koinos* common + *aisthēsis* sensation.] *Psychol.* The undifferentiated complex of organic sensation by which one is aware of the body and bodily condition.

coe′no- (sē′nō-; sĕn′ō-), **coen-**. [Gr. *koinos.*] A combining form meaning *common*, as in *coeno*cyte, *coen*esthesis.

coe′no·bite (-bīt), **coe′no·bit′ic** (-bĭt′ĭk), etc. Vars. of CENOBITE, etc.

coe′no·cyte (-sīt), *n.* [*coeno-* + *-cyte.*] *Biol.* An organism, as in some algae and fungi, composed of a number of united protoplasts forming a single large cell.

coe·nu′rus (sē·nū′rŭs), *n.* [NL., fr. *coen-* + Gr. *oura* tail.] A larval tapeworm consisting of many infective scolices contained in a simple cyst; esp., the larva of a tapeworm (*Multiceps multiceps*), which causes gid in sheep.

co·en′zyme (kō·ĕn′zīm), *n.* [*co-* + *enzyme.*] *Biochem.* A substance necessary for the activity of an enzyme.

co·e′qual (kō·ē′kwăl), *adj.* Being on an equality, as in rank, age, or extent. — *n.* One coequal with another. — **co′e·qual′i·ty** (kō′ē·kwŏl′ĭ·tĭ), *n.* — **co·e′qual·ly**, *adv.*

co·erce′ (kō·ûrs′), *v. t.;* CO·ERCED′ (-ûrst′); CO·ERC′ING (-ûr′sĭng). [L. *coercere*, fr. *co-* + *arcere* to shut up, press together.] **1.** To restrain by force, esp. by law or authority; to repress; curb. **2.** To compel to any action. **3.** To enforce; as, to *coerce* obedience. — **Syn.** See FORCE.

co·er′ci·ble (kō·ûr′sĭ·b'l), *adj.* Capable of being coerced.

co·er′cion (-shŭn), *n.* The act, process, or power of coercing. — **co·er′cion·ar′y** (-ẽr′ĭ; -ẽr·ĭ), *adj.* — **co·er′cion·ist**, *n.*

co·er′cive (-sĭv), *adj.* Serving or intended to coerce. — **co·er′cive·ly**, *adv.* — **co·er′cive·ness**, *n.*

co′es·sen′tial (kō′ĕ·sĕn′shăl), *adj.* Having one essence or being. — **co′es·sen′ti·al′i·ty** (-shĭ·ăl′ĭ·tĭ), *n.*

co′e·ta′ne·ous (kō′ē·tā′nē·ŭs), *adj.* [LL. *coaetaneus*, fr. *co-* + *aetas* age.] Of the same age or duration; contemporary. — **co′e·ta′ne·ous·ly**, *adv.* — **co′e·ta′ne·ous·ness**, *n.*

co′e·ter′nal (-tûr′năl; -n'l), *adj.* Equally or jointly eternal. — **co′e·ter′nal·ly**, *adv.* — **co′e·ter′ni·ty** (-nĭ·tĭ), *n.*

co·e′val (kō·ē′văl), *adj.* [LL. *coaevus*, fr. *co-* + *aevum* age.] Of the same age or duration. — **Syn.** See CONTEMPORARY. — *n.* A contemporary. — **co·e′val·ly**, *adv.*

co′ex·ec′u·tor (kō′ĕg·zĕk′ū·tẽr; *see* EXECUTOR), *n.* A joint executor. — **co′ex·ec′u·trix** (-trĭks), *n. fem.*

co′ex·ist′ (kō′ĕg·zĭst′), *v. i.* To exist together or at the same time. — **co′ex·ist′ence** (-zĭs′tĕns), *n.* — **co′ex·ist′ent**, *adj.*

co′ex·tend′ (kō′ĕks·tĕnd′), *v. t. & i.* To extend through the same space or time with another. — **co′ex·ten′sion** (-tĕn′shŭn), *n.* — **co′ex·ten′sive** (-sĭv), *adj.* — **co′ex·ten′sive·ly**, *adv.*

coff (kŏf), *v. t.;* COFT (kŏft); COFF′ING. *Scot.* To buy.

cof′fee (kŏf′ĭ; 74), *n.* [It. *caffè*, fr. Turk. *qahveh*, fr. Ar. *qahwah* wine, coffee.] **1.** A drink made by infusion or decoction from the roasted and ground or pounded seeds of a shrub or small tree (*Coffea arabica, C. liberica, C. robusta*, or other species of *Coffea*) of the madder family. **2.** The green or roasted seeds (**coffee beans**) obtained from the berrylike fruit of this plant; also, the plant. **3.** A brown, like the color of coffee.

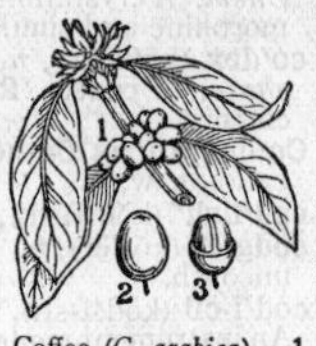

Coffee (*C. arabica*). 1 Flowering and Fruiting Branch (½); 2, 3 Fruit (⅓): 3 with Pericarp partly removed to show Seeds.

cof′fee·house′ (-hous′), *n.* A house of entertainment where coffee and refreshments are supplied.

coffee nut. The Kentucky coffee tree; also, its fruit.

cof′fee·pot′ (kŏf′ĭ·pŏt′), *n.* A covered pot in which coffee is prepared, or from which it is served.

cof′fee·room′ (-ro͞om′), *n.* Also **coffee shop.** A room or shop where coffee and light refreshments are served.

coffee table. Any very low living-room table customarily placed in front of a sofa to accommodate a coffee service, etc., while serving.

coffee tree. **1.** The plant which yields coffee beans. See COFFEE, 1. **2.** = KENTUCKY COFFEE TREE. **3.** = CASCARA, 1.

cof′fer (kŏf′ẽr), *n.* [OF. *cofre, coffre*, fr. L. *cophinus* basket, fr. Gr. *kophinos.*] **1.** A casket, chest, or trunk, esp. one for valuables. **2.** Treasure or funds; — usually in the *pl.* **3.** The chamber of a canal lock. **4.** A cofferdam. **5.** An ornamental recessed panel in the ceiling of a vault, dome, etc.; a caisson. — *v. t.* **1.** To put into a coffer. **2.** To make with coffers, or recessed panels.

cof′fer·dam′ (-dăm′), *n.* **1.** A watertight enclosure from which the water is pumped to expose the bottom (of a river, etc.) and permit work to be done there; also, a caisson (def. 2 **a**). **2.** A watertight structure on the side of a ship, for making repairs below the water line.

cof′fin (kŏf′ĭn; 74), *n.* [OF. *cofin* basket, receptacle, fr. L. *cophinus.*] **1.** A chest or case for a corpse; — now often in trade use in the United States restricted to a wedge-shaped receptacle or to one with a bulge near one end. Cf. CASKET, 2; SARCOPHAGUS. **2.** *Veter.* The hollow crust or hoof of a horse's foot. — *v. t.* To enclose in or as in a coffin.

coffin bone. The foot bone of the horse and allied animals, enclosed within the hoof.

coffin corner. *Amer. Football.* One of the corners formed by a goal line and a side line, into which a punt is often aimed so that it may go out of bounds close to the defenders' goal line.

cof′fle (kŏf′'l), *n.* [Ar. *qāfilah* caravan.] A train of men or beasts fastened together; esp., a slave caravan.

coft (kŏft), *past* of COFF.

cog (kŏg), *v. t.;* COGGED (kŏgd); COG′GING. **1.** To cheat, orig. and esp. at casting dice; hence, to wheedle. **2.** To obtrude or thrust in by deception; as, to *cog* in a word; also, to palm off. — *v. i. Now Rare.* To deceive. — *n.* A deception; a falsehood. — ***cog a die*** *or* ***the dice.*** To cheat in throwing dice.

cog, *n.* [ME. *cogge*, of Scand. origin.] **1.** A tooth on the rim of a wheel; hence, a gear tooth. **2.** A person functioning as part of a process or organization.

cog, *n.* *Carp.* A tenon or projection on a timber, received into a notch or mortise in another timber to secure the two together. See SCARF JOINT, *Illust.* — *v. t. & i.* *Carp.* To connect by means of a cog.

co′gen·cy (kō′jĕn·sĭ), *n.* Quality or state of being cogent.

co′gent (-jĕnt), *adj.* [L. *cogens*, pres. part. of *cogere* to drive together, force, fr. *co-* + *agere* to drive.] Compelling or constraining; esp., appealing forcibly to the mind or reason; convincing. — **Syn.** See VALID. — **co′gent·ly,** *adv.*

cog′i·ta·ble (kŏj′ĭ·tȧ·b'l), *adj.* Thinkable.

cog′i·tate (-tāt), *v. t. & i.* [L. *cogitatus*, past part. of *cogitare* to reflect upon, fr. *co-* + *agitare* to drive, agitate, meditate upon.] To think over; ponder; plan. — **Syn.** See THINK.

cog′i·ta′tion (-tā′shŭn), *n.* **1.** Act or faculty of thinking or reflecting; meditation. **2.** A thought, idea, etc.

cog′i·ta′tive (kŏj′ĭ·tā′tĭv), *adj.* **1.** Possessing the power of thinking or meditating. **2.** Given to thought; meditative. — **cog′i·ta′tive·ly,** *adv.* — **cog′i·ta′tive·ness,** *n.*

cog′i·ta′tor (kŏj′ĭ·tā′tẽr), *n.* One who cogitates.

‖**co′gi·to er′go sum** (kŏj′ĭ·tō ûr′gō sŭm). [L.] I think, therefore I exist; — the postulate which Descartes made the first step in his philosophy.

co′gnac (kō′nyăk; kŏn′yăk), *n.* [F.] A superior French brandy made from wine produced at or near Cognac, on the Charente, France; loosely, any French brandy.

cog′nate (kŏg′nāt), *adj.* [L. *cognatus*, fr. *co-* + *gnatus, natus*, past part. of *nasci*, anciently *gnasci*, to be born.] **1.** Allied by blood, esp. on the mother's side. Cf. AGNATE. **2. a** Having a common parent language; as, English and German are *cognate* languages. **b** Of words, having in common the same original word or root (*father*, G. *vater*, L. *pater*). **3.** Of the same or similar nature. — *n.* **1.** One who is related to another by blood, esp. on the mother's side. **2.** A cognate word or language.

cog·na′tion (kŏg·nā′shŭn), *n.* Cognate relationship.

cog·ni′tion (-nĭsh′ŭn), *n.* [L. *cognitio*, fr. *cognoscere, cognitum*, to become acquainted with, know, fr. *co-* + *noscere, gnoscere*, to get a knowledge of.] **1.** *Obs.* Act or faculty of knowing. **2.** The process of knowing; knowledge or the capacity for it; also, a product of this process, as a perception or notion. — **cog·ni′tion·al,** *adj.* — **cog′ni·tive** (kŏg′nĭ·tĭv), *adj.*

cog′ni·za·ble (kŏg′nĭ·zȧ·b'l; kŏn′-; kŏg·nīz′-), *adj.* **1.** Capable of being known. **2.** Capable of being judicially heard and determined. — **cog′ni·za·bly** (-blĭ), *adv.*

cog′ni·zance (kŏg′nĭ·zăns *or, esp. Law,* kŏn′ĭ·zăns), *n.* [OF. *conoissance*, fr. *conoistre*, fr. L. *cognoscere* to know.] **1.** Apprehension by the understanding; hence, heed; notice. **2.** The range of what may be known by observation. **3.** A distinguishing mark or badge, as a heraldic bearing, etc. **4.** *Law.* **a** Jurisdiction, or the power given by law to hear and decide controversies. **b** The judicial hearing of a matter.

cog′ni·zant (-zănt), *adj.* Having cognizance (of). — **Syn.** See AWARE.

cog′nize (kŏg′nīz), *v. t.* To know or perceive; to recognize.

cog·no′men (kŏg·nō′mĕn), *n.; pl.* -NOMENS (-mĕnz), -NOMINA (-nŏm′ĭ·nȧ). [L., fr. *co-* + (*g*)*nomen* name.] **1.** The family name, the third of the usual three names (*praenomen, nomen, cognomen*) of a person among the ancient Romans. See AGNOMEN. **2.** A surname. **3.** Loosely, a name; a nickname. — **cog·nom′i·nal** (-nŏm′ĭ·năl; -nō′mĭ·năl; -n'l), *adj.*

‖**co·gno·scen′te** (kō·nyō·shĕn′tā), *n.; pl.* -TI (-tē). [It.] A connoisseur.

cog·nos′ci·ble (kŏg·nŏs′ĭ·b'l), *adj.* Cognizable. — *n.* A cognizable thing. — **cog·nos′ci·bil′i·ty** (-bĭl′ĭ·tĭ), *n.*

co′gon (kō′gōn; kō·gōn′), *n.* [Sp. *cogón*, fr. Tag., Visayan, & Bikol *cógon.*] Either of two tall coarse grasses (*Imperata cylindrica koenigii* and *I. exaltata*) of the Philippine Islands and adjacent countries, used for thatching.

Cogs′well chair (kŏgz′wĕl; -wĕl). [After the name of the inventor.] Also **Cox′well chair** (kŏks′-). An upholstered easy chair with inclined back, often an undivided back and seat cushion, thin arms, and cabriole legs.

cog′wheel′ (kŏg′hwēl′), *n.* A wheel with cogs or teeth.

co·hab′it (kō·hăb′ĭt), *v. i.* [LL. *cohabitare*, fr. *co-* + *habitare* to dwell.] **1.** *Archaic.* To dwell or abide in company. **2.** To dwell or live together as husband and wife. — **co·hab′it·ant** (-ĭ·tănt), *n.* — **co·hab′i·ta′tion** (-ĭ·tā′shŭn), *n.*

co·heir′ (kō·âr′), *n.* A joint heir. — **co·heir′ess,** *n. fem.*

co·here′ (kō·hēr′), *v. i.* [L. *cohaerere, cohaesum*, fr. *co-* + *haerere* to adhere.] **1.** To stick together; to hold fast, as parts of the same mass. **2.** To be connected by some common principle or relationship, as by subordination to one purpose or idea; to be logically consistent. — **Syn.** See STICK.

co·her′ence (-hēr′ĕns), *n.* **1.** A sticking together; cohesion. **2.** Connection or congruity arising from some common principle or relationship; consistency. **3.** *Rhet.* Connectedness of thought such that parts of a discourse are clearly interrelated.

co·her′en·cy (-ĕn·sĭ), *n.* Quality of being coherent.

co·her′ent (-ĕnt), *adj.* **1.** Sticking together; cohesive; cleaving. **2.** Composed of interdependent or related parts; consistent. **3.** Logically consistent. — **co·her′ent·ly,** *adv.*

co·her′er (-ẽr), *n.* **1.** One that coheres. **2.** *Radio.* A detector in which an imperfectly conducting contact between conductors loosely resting against each other is improved in conductance by the passage of high-frequency current.

co·he′sion (kō·hē′zhŭn), *n.* **1.** Act or state of cohering; a cleaving together. **2.** *Physics.* Molecular attraction by which the particles of a body are united throughout the mass, whether like or unlike; — distinguished from *adhesion.*

co·he′sive (-sĭv), *adj.* **1.** Causing to cohere. **2.** Cohering, or sticking together. — **co·he′sive·ly,** *adv.* — **co·he′sive·ness,** *n.*

co′hort (kō′hôrt), *n.* [L. *cohors*, prop., an enclosure.] **1.** In the Roman army, one of the ten divisions of a legion. **2.** A company or band, esp. of warriors.

co′hosh (kō′hŏsh; kō·hŏsh′), *n.* [Of Algonquian origin.] Any of several related American medicinal plants, as the ***black cohosh*** (*Cimicifuga racemosa*), the ***blue cohosh*** (*Caulophyllum thalictroides*), and the baneberry.

coif (koif), *n.* [OF. *coife, coiffe*, fr. LL. *cofea, cuphia.*] A close-fitting cap; as: **a** A hoodlike cap worn by nuns under a veil. **b** *Hist.* A soldier's defensive skullcap, worn under the hood of mail. **c** A white cap formerly worn by English lawyers, esp. serjeants-at-law; a biggin; hence, the order or rank of a serjeant-at-law. — *v. t.;* COIFED (koift); COIF′ING. To cover or invest with or as with a coif.

coif (kwäf), *n. & v. t.* Short for COIFFURE.

‖**coif·feur′** (kwȧ′fûr′), *n. masc.; fem.* ‖**coif·feuse′** (kwȧ′fûz′). [F.] A hairdresser.

coif·fure′ (kwä·fūr′), *n.* [F.] A headdress, or manner of dressing the hair. Cf. HAIRDO. — *v. t.;* -FURED′ (-fūrd′); -FUR′ING (-fūr′ĭng). To dress in a coiffure.

coign, coigne (koin), *n.* Vars. of COIN, QUOIN, a corner, wedge, etc.; — chiefly used in **coign of vantage**, a position advantageous for action or observation.

coil (koil), *v. t. & i.* [OF. *coillir* to collect, fr. L. *colligere*, fr. *col-* + *legere* to gather.] To wind cylindrically or spirally. — *n.* **1.** A series of rings, or a spiral, of cable, rope, or the like, when coiled; also, a single ring of such a series. **2.** A series of connected pipes in rows, layers, or windings, as in steam-heating or water-heating apparatus. **3.** *Elec.* A spiral of wire, or an instrument composed of such a spiral and its accessories. Cf. INDUCTION COIL.

coil, *n.* *Archaic.* A tumult; also, trouble.

coil spring. See SPRING, *Illust.*

coil stamps. Postage stamps issued in coils, with perforation either horizontally or vertically.

coin (koin), *n.* [F., fr. L. *cuneus* wedge.] **1.** A corner, cornerstone, or wedge; a quoin; coign. **2.** A piece of metal marked and issued by governmental authority to be used as money; also, such pieces collectively. — **Syn.** Money, currency, specie. — *v. t.* **1.** To make (coins) by stamping; convert (metal) into coins; mint. **2.** To make; fabricate; invent; as, to *coin* a word or a phrase. — *v. i.* To make coins; mint. — **coin′a·ble,** *adj.* — **coin′er,** *n.*

coin′age (-ĭj), *n.* Act of coining; something coined; coins.

co′in·cide′ (kō′ĭn·sīd′), *v. i.* [ML. *coincidere*, fr. *co-* + *incidere* to fall on, fr. *in* + *cadere* to fall.] **1.** To occupy the same place in space or the same period of time. **2.** To correspond exactly; to agree; as, our aims *coincide.* — **Syn.** See AGREE.

co·in′ci·dence (kō·ĭn′sĭ·dĕns), *n.* **1.** Condition, fact, or instance of coinciding; correspondence. **2.** A group of concurrent events or circumstances, or one of them, remarkable from lack of apparent causal connection.

co·in′ci·dent (-dĕnt), *adj.* Having coincidence; concurrent; consonant. — **Syn.** See CONTEMPORARY. — **co·in′ci·dent·ly,** *adv.*

co·in′ci·den′tal (-dĕn′tăl; -t'l), *adj.* Of the nature of a coincidence; happening, acting, etc., coincidently. — **co·in′ci·den′tal·ly,** *adv.*

co′in·her′it·ance (kō′ĭn·hĕr′ĭ·tăns), *n.* Joint inheritance.

co′in·sure′ (kō′ĭn·sho͝or′), *v. t. & i.* To insure jointly with another or others. — **co′in·sur′ance** (-sho͝or′ăns), *n.*

coir (koir), *n.* [Tamil *kayiṟu* rope.] A stiff elastic fiber extracted from the outer husk of the coconut, used for making matting.

cois′trel (kois′trĕl), **cois′tril** (-trĭl), *n.* *Archaic.* **a** A lad serving a knight as a groom. **b** A menial; varlet.

co·i′tion (kō·ĭsh′ŭn), *n.* [L. *coitio.*] Sexual intercourse.

co′i·tus (kō′ĭ·tŭs), *n.* [L.] Coition.

coke (kōk), *n.* **a** The residue obtained when coal is subjected to destructive distillation. It is used as fuel. **b** A similar residue left when petroleum, shale oil, etc., are distilled to dryness. — *v. t. & i.* To change into coke.

col (kŏl; *F.* kôl), *n.* [F., neck, fr. L. *collum* neck.] A pass between adjacent peaks in a mountain chain.

col-. An assimilated form of COM- (which see).

col-. = COLO- (which see), as in **co·lal′gi·a** (kō·lăl′jĭ·*ȧ*), **co·lec′to·my** (-lĕk′tō·mĭ) (see -ALGIA, -ECTOMY).

co′la (kō′l*ȧ*). [NL.] Var. of KOLA.

co′la, *n., pl.* of COLON.

col′an·der (kŭl′ăn·dẽr; kŏl′-), *n.* A bowl-shaped sieve or strainer usually with handles and a base.

co·lat′i·tude (kō·lăt′ĭ·tūd), *n. Astron.* See co-, 5 b.

col·can′non (kŏl·kăn′ŭn; kôl′kăn·ŭn), *n.* [Ir. *cāl ceannain*, fr. *cāl* cabbage + *ceannan* white-headed.] *Ir. & Scot.* Potatoes, cabbage, etc., boiled and mashed together.

col′chi·cine (kŏl′chĭ·sēn; -sĭn; kŏl′kĭ-), *n. Chem.* A poisonous alkaloid, $C_{22}H_{25}NO_6$, extracted from the corms or seeds of a small crocuslike herb (*Colchicum autumnale*), used esp. as a plant hormone in plant breeding and genetics.

col′chi·cum (kŏl′chĭ·kŭm; kŏl′kĭ-), *n.* [L., a plant with a poisonous root.] **1.** Any of a genus (*Colchicum*) of Old World bulbous herbs of the bunchflower family. **2.** The dried corm or ripe seeds of a colchicum (*C. autumnale*), used esp. in treating gout and rheumatism.

col′co·thar (kŏl′kō·thẽr), *n.* [ML. *colcothar*, fr. Ar. *qulquṭār*, fr. Gr. *chalkanthos*.] A reddish-brown oxide of iron left as a residue when ferrous sulfate is heated, — used to polish glass, and as a pigment.

cold (kōld), *adj.* [AS. *cald, ceald.*] **1.** Decidedly below the normal temperature; specif.: **a** Gelid; frigid. **b** Not warm; as, a *cold* bath. **2.** Unemotional; not easily moved to love, enthusiasm, etc. **3.** Chilling; discouraging; dispiriting; as, *cold* comfort; also, unenlivening. **4.** Suffering from lack of heat; as, he is *cold* and hungry. **5.** Not colored by prejudice, personal feeling, etc. **6.** Waged by political and economic strategy, propaganda, and other measures short of armed conflict; as, a *cold* war. **7.** Of a color, bluish or greenish in tone; as, a *cold* gray. **8.** *Slang.* **a** Fast or secure; sure. **b** Dead; also, unconscious. **9.** *Sports.* **a** Faint; — said of a scent. **b** Distant from anything concealed; — said of one seeking it. — **Syn.** Chilly, freezing, icy, frigid. — **Ant.** Hot. — *n.* **1.** A condition of low temperature. **2.** A sensation of being chilly or chilled. **3.** A disordered bodily condition, esp. of the respiratory tract, caused by exposure; a catarrh; coryza. **4.** Cold weather; frost. — **cold′ly,** *adv.* — **cold′ness,** *n.*

cold′-blood′ed (kōld′blŭd′ĕd; -ĭd; 2), *adj.* **1.** Having cold blood; specif., having a variable body temperature not internally regulated but approximating that of the environment, as fish, amphibians, and reptiles; — opp. to *warm-blooded.* **2.** Sensitive to cold. **3.** Insensitive; unfeeling; — opp. to *hot-blooded.* **4.** Done or considered with unnatural lack of feeling; as, a *cold-blooded* murder. — **cold′-blood′ed·ly,** *adv.* — **cold′-blood′ed·ness,** *n.*

cold chisel. A chisel made of tool steel of a strength and temper suitable for chipping or cutting cold metal. — **cold′-chis′el,** *v. t. & i.*

cold cream. A cooling and soothing ointment for the skin.

cold frame. A glass-covered frame, without artificial heat, used to protect plants and seedlings.

cold rubber. A synthetic rubber highly resistant to wear, made at a low temperature (41° F. or lower), used especially for tire treads.

cold sore. A vesicular eruption appearing about the mouth as the result of a cold, or in the course of a fever.

cold war. See COLD, *adj.*, 6.

cole (kōl), *n.* [AS. *cāl, cāwl*, or fr. ON. *kāl*, both fr. L. *caulis* stem, cabbage stalk, cabbage.] Any of various species of a genus (*Brassica*) of the mustard family, including the cabbage; esp., rape (*B. napus*).

cole′man·ite (kōl′măn·īt), *n.* [After W. T. *Coleman* of San Francisco.] A hydrous calcium borate, occurring massive and in brilliant colorless or white monoclinic crystals.

co′le·op′ter·on (kō′lē·ŏp′tẽr·ŏn; kŏl′ē-), *n.; pl.* -TERA (-*ȧ*). [NL.] A coleopterous insect.

co′le·op′ter·ous (-ŭs), *adj.* [Gr. *koleopteros*, fr. *koleos* sheath + *pteron* wing.] Belonging to an order (Coleoptera) of insects, comprising the beetles and weevils, having the anterior pair of wings (elytra) hard and horny, and serving as coverings for the posterior membranous pair. — **co′le·op′ter·al** (-*ă*l), *adj.* — **co′le·op′ter·an** (-ăn), *adj. & n.*

co′le·o·rhi′za (kō′lē·ō·rī′z*ȧ*; kŏl′ē·ō-), *n.; pl.* -ZAE (-zē). [NL., fr. Gr. *koleos* sheath + *rhiza* root.] *Bot.* The sheath investing the radicle in some plants, through which the roots burst.

cole′slaw′ (kōl′slô′), *n.* [D. *kool sla* cabbage salad.] A salad made of sliced or chopped raw cabbage.

co′le·us (kō′lē·ŭs), *n.; pl.* COLEUSES (-ĕz; -ĭz). [NL., fr. Gr. *koleos* a sheath; — referring to the way the stamens are united.] Any of a genus (*Coleus*, esp. *C. blumei*) of showy foliage herbs of the mint family.

cole′wort′ (kōl′wûrt′), *n.* **1.** Cole. **2.** Any variety of cabbage in which the leaves do not form a compact head.

col′ic (kŏl′ĭk), *n.* [F. *colique*, fr. L. *colicus* sick with the colic, deriv. of Gr. *kolon* the colon.] A paroxysmal abdominal pain due to spasm, obstruction, or distention of any of the hollow viscera. — **col′ick·y** (-ĭk·ĭ), *adj.*

col′ic, *adj.* Of or pertaining to the colon or colic.

col′ic·root′ (-rōōt′), *n.* **1.** Either of two bitter American herbs (*Aletris farinosa* and *A. aurea*) of the lily family, with basal leaves and racemose white or yellow flowers. **2.** Any of several other plants reputed to cure colic, as a wild yam (*Dioscorea paniculata*).

col′ic·weed′ (-wēd′), *n.* **a** Dutchman's-breeches. **b** Squirrel corn. **c** A small yellow-flowered herb (*Corydalis flavula*) of eastern N. Am.

col′in (kŏl′ĭn), *n.* [Sp. *colín*, fr. Nahuatl *çolin.*] **1.** = BOBWHITE. **2.** A bird of related species.

col′i·se′um (kŏl′ĭ·sē′ŭm), *n.* [NL.] **1.** [*cap.*] Colosseum (sense 1). **2.** A large structure for public entertainments or sporting events.

co·li′tis (kō·lī′tĭs), *n.* [NL., fr. 2d *col-* + *-itis.*] Inflammation of the large intestine, esp. of its mucous membrane.

col·lab′o·rate (kŏ·lăb′ō·rāt), *v. i.* [L. *collaborare* to labor together, fr. *col-* + *laborare* to labor.] **1.** To work or act jointly, esp. to share in literary, scientific, or other intellectual production. **2.** To cooperate voluntarily as a nation with another or other nations in international political or economic adjustment. **3.** To willingly comply with, co-operate with, or assist enemy forces occupying one's country; — usually with an implication of traitorous dealing in distinction from passive acquiescence; also, sometimes, to give to an enemy nation aid of nonmilitary kind, as by radio propaganda in enemy service. — **col·lab′o·ra′tion** (-rā′shŭn), *n.* — **col·lab′o·ra′tive** (-lăb′ō·rā′tĭv; -r*ȧ*·tĭv), *adj.* — **col·lab′o·ra′tor** (-rā′tẽr), *n.*

col·lab′o·ra′tion·ist (kŏ·lăb′ō·rā′shŭn·ĭst), *n.* One who collaborates (in sense 3). Hence, **col·lab′o·ra′tion·ism** (-ĭz′m), *n.*

col·lage′ (kŏ·läzh′; *F.* kô′läzh′), *n.* [F., gluing, pasting. See PROTOCOL.] **1.** *Art.* An agglomeration of fragments such as matchboxes, bus tickets, playing cards, pasted together and transposed, often with relating lines or color dabs, into an artistic composition of incongruous effect. It is a type of abstraction (def. 6). **2.** Any mounted composite of usually odd borderless prints, photographs, or cutouts.

col′la·gen (kŏl′*ȧ*·jĕn), *n.* [Gr. *kolla* glue + *-gen.*] A gelatinlike protein occurring in vertebrates, the chief constituent of the fibrils of connective tissue and of the bones.

col·lapse′ (kŏ·lăps′), *v. i.* [L. *collapsus*, past part. of *collabi* to collapse, fr. *col-* + *labi* to fall.] **1.** To break down or go to pieces suddenly, esp. by the falling in of sides; to cave in. **2.** Hence: **a** To be made so that the parts fall or fold together into compact form, as for transportation, as some crates, boats, etc. **b** To break down or fail abruptly and utterly, as health, plans, negotiations. **c** To suffer a physical collapse. — *v. t.* To cause to collapse. — *n.* An instance of collapsing; esp., of persons, a physical breakdown. — **col·laps′i·ble** (-lăp′sĭ·b'l), *adj.* — **col·laps′i·bil′i·ty** (-bĭl′ĭ·tĭ), *n.*

col′lar (kŏl′ẽr), *n.* [OF. *colier* necklace, collar, fr. L. *collum* neck.] **1.** Something worn about the neck; as: **a** A fabric band or turnover piece forming a part or an accessory of a shirt, blouse, or coat. **b** A band, chain, necklace, or the like worn as an ornament or badge, or for identification, etc. **2.** Something like a collar in shape or use; as: **a** A part of the harness of draft animals, fitted over the shoulders and bearing the stress of drawing. **b** *Mach.* A ring or round flange used to limit motion, hold something in place, etc. **c** *Zool.* Any of various collarlike structures or markings. — *v. t.* **1.** To put a collar on. **2.** To seize by the collar. **3.** *Colloq.* To get control of.

col′lar·bone′ (-bōn′), *n.* The clavicle. See THORAX, *Illust.*

col′lards (-ẽrdz), *n. pl.* [Corrupt. fr. *colewort.*] A variety of kale.

col·late′ (kŏ·lāt′), *v. t.* [See COLLATION.] **1.** To compare critically, as texts. **2.** To examine (a set of sheets or a book) to verify the order and number of signatures, pages, plates, etc. **3.** *Eccl.* To admit and institute (a cleric) to a benefice; — with *to.* — **Syn.** See COMPARE.

col·lat′er·al (kŏ·lăt′ẽr·*ă*l), *adj.* [ML. *collateralis*, fr. *col-* + L. *lateralis* lateral.] **1.** Accompanying or related, but secondary or subordinate; auxiliary; contributory; as, *collateral* issues. **2.** Accompanying one another as co-ordinates; specif.: **a** Parallel; side by side; as, *collateral* fibers. **b** Concomitant; coincident; as, *collateral* events. **c** Corresponding in rank, value, function, etc.; as, proofs *collateral* to those offered. **3.** Belonging to the same ancestral stock but not in a direct line of descent; — opp. to *lineal.* See CONSANGUINITY, *Illust.* **4.** *Com. & Law.* Designating, or pert. to, an obligation or security attached to another to secure its performance; hence, secured or guaranteed by additional security; as, a *collateral* loan. — *n.* One who or that which is collateral; specif.: **a** A collateral relative. **b** That which is used as collateral security. — **col·lat′er·al·ly,** *adv.*

col·la′tion (kŏ·lā′shŭn), *n.* [OF. *collacion*, deriv. of L. *collatus* (as past part. of *conferre*), fr. *col-* + *latum* (as supine of *ferre* to bear).] **1.** A gathering together for conference or to listen to reading, a sermon, etc., esp. of monks at the close of the day. **2.** Act or result of collating, as in determining a text. **3.** A light meal or repast; esp., one allowed on fast days in place of lunch or supper. **4.** *Eccl.* Bestowal of a living or other preferment upon a clergyman; specif., *Ch. of Eng.*, the bestowal of a living when the bishop is the patron.

col·la′tor (-tẽr), *n.* [L.] One who collates or makes a collation.

col′league (kŏl′ēg), *n.* [F. *collègue*, fr. L. *collega*, fr. *col-* + root of *legare* to send or choose as deputy.] An associate in a profession or a civil or ecclesiastical office or employment. — **col′league·ship,** *n.*

col′lect (kŏl′ĕkt), *n.* [From OF., fr. ML. *collecta*, L. *collecta* a collection in money, assemblage, fr. *colligere* to collect.] The opening prayer, or prayers, varying with the day, said before the Epistle in the Mass or in the Anglican Communion service.

col·lect′ (kŏ·lĕkt′), *v. t.* [From OF. *collecter* and fr. L. *collectus*, past part. of *colligere* to bind together, fr. *col-* + *legere* to gather.] **1.** To gather into one body or place; assemble. **2.** To infer; gather (def. 7). **3.** To regain command of (oneself, one's powers). **4.** **a** To demand and obtain payment of. **b** To obtain, as contributions, from many persons. **5.** To gather (specimens), as for study or ornament. — *v. i.* **1.** To assemble; also, to accumulate. **2.** To collect money, specimens, etc. — **Syn.** See GATHER. — *adj. & adv.* To be paid for by the recipient; as, a *collect* telegram. — **col·lect′i·ble, col·lect′a·ble,** *adj.*

col′lec·ta′ne·a (kŏl′ĕk·tā′nē·*ȧ*), *n. pl.* [Neut. pl. fr. L. *collectaneus* collected.] Collected writings; a collection of excerpts. Cf. ANA.

col·lect′ed (kŏ·lĕk′tĕd; -tĭd), *adj.* Self-possessed; calm. — **Syn.** See COOL. — **col·lect′ed·ly,** *adv.* — **col·lect′ed·ness,** *n.*

col·lec′tion (kŏ·lĕk′shŭn), *n.* **1.** Act or process of collecting. **2.** That which is collected; an assemblage; an accumulation.

col·lec′tive (-tĭv), *adj.* **1.** Formed by collecting; gathered into a mass; as, the *collective* wisdom of the ages. **2.** Characteristic of or relating to a group as an aggregate of individuals; as, the *collective* interests of a community; also, common to or characteristic of the individuals forming such an aggregate or group; as, *collective* behavior. **3.** Having plurality of origin or authority; as, a *collective* petition. **4.** Denoting a whole composed of individuals as, "man" understood in a *collective* sense; sometimes, denoting a number of individuals comprising a whole. — *n.* **1.** A collective body or whole. **2.** A collectivistic organization; specif., a **collective farm**, in communistic countries, a farm made up of several holdings and worked on a co-operative basis, with machinery collectively owned, under partial or complete state control. **3.** *Gram.* = COLLECTIVE NOUN. — **col·lec′tive·ly,** *adv.*

collective bargaining. Negotiation for the settlement of hours, wages, etc., between an employer and an organized body of workers.

collective fruit. A fruit derived from the more or less fused ovaries of several flowers, as the pineapple, etc.; — opp. to *simple fruit.*

collective noun. *Gram.* A noun naming a collection or aggregate of individuals by a singular form (as *assembly, army, jury*). It takes a singular verb when the group is thought of as a unit, and a plural verb when the component individuals are in mind.

col·lec′tiv·ism (kŏ·lĕk′tĭv·ĭz′m), *n.* A politico-economic system of organization characterized by collective control over production and distribution, for example, government ownership of wealth, as in communism, or control by a party under state supervision, as in fascism. — **col·lec′tiv·ist** (-ĭst), *n.* — **col·lec′tiv·is′tic** (-ĭs′tĭk), *adj.*

col′lec·tiv′i·ty (kŏl′ĕk·tĭv′ĭ·tĭ), *n.* **1.** Quality or state of being collective. **2.** A collective whole; specif., the people as a body.

col·lec′tiv·ize (kŏ·lĕk′tĭv·īz), *v. t.* To organize under collectivistic control. — **col·lec′tiv·i·za′tion** (-tĭ·vĭ·zā′shŭn; -vī·zā′-), *n.*

col·lec'tor (kŏ-lĕk'tēr) *n.* **1.** One who collects; esp., one deputed to collect moneys; as, a tax *collector*. **2.** Something that collects; specif., a device maintaining contact between the moving and stationary parts of an electric circuit. — **col·lec'tor·ship** *n.*

col'leen (kŏl'ēn; kŏ-lēn'), *n.* [Ir. *cailín*.] *Irish.* Girl.

col'lege (kŏl'ĕj; -ĭj), *n.* [OF., fr. L. *collegium* a society, fr. *collega* colleague. See COLLEAGUE.] **1.** A body of persons having common interests or corporate functions; as, the electoral *college*; the *college* of cardinals; specif., a body of clergy living in common on a foundation. **2.** A society of scholars incorporated for study or instruction, esp. in the higher branches of knowledge; a university or one of its schools; an educational institution concerned chiefly with a four-year course of general studies leading to a bachelor's degree; also, a building or group of buildings used for such study. **3.** A company or assemblage. **4.** *Eng. Slang.* A prison. **5.** A course of study. **6.** An institution for special or professional instruction; as, a medical *college*.

college ice. = SUNDAE.

col'leg·er (kŏl'ĕj·ēr; -ĭj·ēr), *n.* A collegian.

col·le'gi·al (kŏ-lē'jĭ·ăl), *adj.* Collegiate.

col·le'gi·an (-jĭ·ăn; -jăn), *n.* A member of a college; a college student or graduate.

col·le'gi·ate (kŏ-lē'jĭ·ĭt; -jĭt), *adj.* **1.** Of the nature of, or constituted as, a college or body of colleagues. **2.** Of, pertaining to, or characteristic of collegians.

collegiate church. a A church which, though not a cathedral, or bishop's church, has a *college*, or chapter of canons (and, in the Church of England, a dean), as Westminster Abbey. **b** In Scotland, a church which regularly has two or more ministers of equal rank. **c** In the U. S., a church or an association of churches possessing common revenues administered under the joint pastorate of several ministers.

col·len'chy·ma (kŏ-lĕng'kĭ·mà), *n.* [NL., fr. Gr. *kolla* glue + *parenchyma*.] *Bot.* A tissue of living cells, usually elongated, with walls variously thickened, esp. at the angles, but capable of further growth. See HYPODERMA, 1; cf. SCLERENCHYMA.

col'let (kŏl'ĕt; -ĭt), *n.* [F., dim. fr. *col* neck, fr. L. *collum*.] **1.** A metal band, ring, or the like; esp., *Horol.*, a small collar pierced to receive the inner end of a balance spring. **2.** A circle or flange in which a precious stone is set. — *v. t.* To furnish or surround with a collet.

col·lide' (kŏ-līd'), *v. i.* [L. *collidere, collisum*, fr. *col-* + *laedere* to strike.] To strike or dash against each other; to come into collision; clash.

col'lie (kŏl'ĭ), *n.* A large dog of a breed originating in Scotland, used for generations in herding sheep. The variety with a rough thick coat is commoner than the smooth-coated variety.

col'lied (-ĭd), *adj.* Blackened; grimy.

col'lier (kŏl'yēr; 58), *n.* **1.** A worker or dealer in coal; esp., a coal miner. **2.** A vessel for transporting coal.

col'lier·y (-ĭ), *n.; pl.* -IES (-ĭz). A place where coal is dug: a coal mine and associated works.

col'lie·shang'ie (kŏl'ĭ·shăng'ĭ), *n. Scot.* A quarrel.

col'li·gate (kŏl'ĭ·gāt), *v. t.* [L. *colligatus*, past part. of *colligare* to collect, fr. *col-* + *ligare* to bind.] **1.** To bind together; unite. **2.** *Logic.* To bring together (isolated facts), as for generalization. — **col'li·ga'tion** (-gā'shŭn), *n.*

col'li·mate (kŏl'ĭ·māt), *v. t.* [Prob. a false reading (*collimare*) for L. *collineare* to direct in a straight line, fr. *col-* + *linea* line.] *Physics & Astron.* To render parallel, as rays of light; to adjust the line of sight of (a transit, level, etc.). — **col'li·ma'tion** (-mā'shŭn), *n.*

col'li·ma'tor (-mā'tēr), *n. Optics.* **a** A tube with a convex lens or achromatic objective and, at the focus of the latter, an arrangement of cross hairs, used in collimating certain instruments, esp. a transit. **b** A tube having at one end a convex lens, and at its principal focus a slit, used for producing a beam of parallel rays, as in the spectroscope; also, a lens so used.

col·lin'e·ar (kŏ-lĭn'ē·ēr), *adj.* [See 1st COL-; LINEAR.] Lying in the same straight line. — **col·lin'e·ar·ly**, *adv.*

col·lin'si·a (kŏ-lĭn'sĭ·à), *n.* [NL., after Zaccheus *Collins* (1764–1831), Am. botanist.] *Bot.* Any of a genus (*Collinsia*) of biennial or annual herbs of the figwort family, of the United States having irregular whorled flowers.

col·li'sion (kŏ-lĭzh'ŭn), *n.* [LL. *collisio*, fr. *collidere.* See COLLIDE.] Act or instance of colliding; clash.

col'lo·cate (kŏl'ŏ·kāt), *v. t.* [L. *collocatus*, past part. of *collocare.* See COUCH.] To place side by side or in a definite order; to arrange.

col'lo·ca'tion (-kā'shŭn), *n.* Act or instance of collocating; esp., an arrangement, as of words.

col·lo'di·on (kŏ-lō'dĭ·ŭn), *n.* [Gr. *kollōdēs* like glue, fr. *kolla* glue + *eidos* form.] *Chem.* A viscous solution of pyroxylin, as in alcohol and ether, or in acetone, used as a coating for wounds, for photographic films, etc.

col·logue' (kŏ-lōg'), *v. i.* **1.** *Dial.* To intrigue; conspire. **2.** *Colloq.* To talk or confer secretly.

col'loid (kŏl'oid), *n.* [Gr. *kolla* glue + *-oid*.] **1.** Any substance in a certain state of fine division, the colloidal state, in which the particles range in diameter from about 0.2 to about .005 micron. Mixed with certain media colloids form so-called colloidal solutions, colloidal systems, or sols, of which an aqueous starch solution is a typical example. Opposed to *crystalloid*. **2.** *Med.* A gelatinous or mucinous substance found in some morbid conditions. — *adj.* Colloidal.

col·loi'dal (kŏ-loi'dăl; -d'l), *adj.* Of, pertaining to, or of the nature of, a colloid or colloids; as, *colloidal* gold.

col'lop (kŏl'ŭp), *n.* [ME. *coloppe, colhoppe*, an egg fried in grease.] A small portion or slice, esp. of meat.

col·lo'qui·al (kŏ-lō'kwĭ·ăl), *adj.* Pertaining to, or used in, conversation, esp. familiar conversation; acceptable and correct in ordinary conversation, friendly letters, or informal speeches, but unsuited to formal speech or writing; hence, informal. — **col·lo'qui·al·ly**, *adv.* — **col·lo'qui·al·ness**, *n.*

col·lo'qui·al·ism (-ĭz'm), *n.* Colloquial style or quality; also, a colloquial expression.

col'lo·quy (kŏl'ŏ·kwĭ), *n.; pl.* -QUIES (-kwĭz). [L. *colloquium*, fr. *colloqui* to converse, fr. *col-* + *loqui* to speak.] Mutual discourse; esp., a somewhat formal conference. — **col'lo·quist** (-kwĭst), *n.*

col'lo·type (kŏl'ŏ·tīp), *n.* [Gr. *kolla* glue + *-type*.] A print made by the photogelatin process; also, the process itself; — so called esp. in England. — **col'lo·type**, *v. t.* — **col'lo·typ'ic** (-tĭp'ĭk), *adj.* — **col'lo·typ'y** (kŏl'ŏ·tīp'ĭ), *n.*

col·lude' (kŏ-lūd'), *v. i.* [L. *colludere, -lusum*, fr. *col-* + *ludere* to play.] To have secretly a joint part in an action; to conspire; connive. — **col·lud'er** (kŏ-lūd'ēr), *n.*

col·lu'sion (-lū'zhŭn), *n.* A secret agreement and co-operation for a fraudulent or a deceitful purpose; deceit; fraud. — **col·lu'sive** (-sĭv), *adj.* — **col·lu'sive·ly**, *adv.* — **col·lu'sive·ness**, *n.*

col'ly (kŏl'ĭ), *v. t.; -*LIED (-ĭd); -LY·ING. [See COAL.] *Dial.* To smut. — *n. Dial.* Grime or soot.

col·lyr'i·um (kŏ-lĭr'ĭ·ŭm), *n.; pl.* -LYRIA (-à), -IUMS (-ŭmz). [L., fr. Gr. *kollyrion* poultice, eye salve.] A medicated application for the eyes, usually an eyewater.

co'lo- (kō'lŏ-; kŏl'ŏ-), **col-**. [Gr. *kolon*.] A combining form denoting the *colon*, as in **co·lec'to·my**, **co·los'to·my**, **co·lot'o·my** (see -ECTOMY, -STOMY, -TOMY).

col'o·cynth (kŏl'ŏ·sĭnth), *n.* [From L., fr. Gr. *kolokynthis*.] A Mediterranean and African herbaceous vine (*Citrullus colocynthis*) allied to the watermelon; also, its fruit, from which is prepared a powerful cathartic.

co·logne' (kŏ-lōn'), *n.* [F. *Cologne*, a city in Germany, fr. L. *Colonia Agrippina*.] A toilet water bearing the trade-mark Eau de Cologne; — called also **Cologne water.**

co'lon (kō'lŏn), *n.; pl.* COLONS (-lŏnz), COLA (-là). [L., fr. Gr. *kolon*.] That part of the large intestine which extends from the caecum to the rectum. It includes the sigmoid flexure.

co'lon, *n.* [L., a portion of a poem, fr. Gr. *kōlon* limb, member, clause of a sentence.] **1.** The character [:] used in writing and printing (1) after a formal introduction and before an explanation, example, restatement, quotation, etc.; (2) after the salutation of a business letter (Dear Sir:); (3) between the clauses of a compound sentence, esp. when they are in antithesis or not connected by a conjunction. **2.** *pl.* COLA (kō'là). *Pros.* A section of a rhythmical period, composed of a group of from two to not more than six feet, formed into a rhythmic unit by a principal accent.

co·lon' (kŏ-lōn'), *n.; pl.* COLONS (-lōnz'), COLONES (-lō'nās). [Amer. Sp. *colón*.] The monetary unit of Costa Rica and of El Salvador. See MONEY, *Tables*.

colo'nel (kûr'nĕl; -n'l), *n.* [F., fr. It. *colonnello*, fr. *colonna* column (of soldiers), fr. L. *columna*.] *Mil.* A commissioned officer ranking above a lieutenant colonel and below a brigadier general. His normal command is a regiment. Abbr. *Col.* — **colo'nel·cy** (-sĭ), *n.* — **colo'nel·ship**, *n.*

co·lo'ni·al (kŏ-lō'nĭ·ăl), *adj.* Of, pertaining to, or living in a colony or colonies; specif., *American Hist.*, the thirteen colonies which formed the United States of America. — *n.* A citizen or inhabitant of a colony.

co·lon'ic (kŏ-lŏn'ĭk), *adj.* Of or pertaining to the colon.

col'o·nist (kŏl'ŏ·nĭst), *n.* A member or inhabitant of a colony; one engaged in the founding of a colony.

col'o·nize (kŏl'ŏ·nīz), *v. t.* **1.** To plant or establish a colony or colonies in. **2.** To gather, settle, or establish in a colony. — *v. i.* To make or establish a colony or colonies. — **col'o·ni·za'tion** (-nĭ·zā'shŭn; -nī·zā'-), *n.* — **col'o·ni·za'tion·ist**, *n.* — **col'o·niz'er** (-nīz'ēr), *n.*

col'on·nade' (kŏl'ŏ·nād'), *n.* [F., fr. It., fr. *colonna* column.] *Arch.* A series or range of columns at regular intervals, usually carrying an architrave. — **col'on·nad'ed** (-nād'ĕd; -ĭd), *adj.*

col'o·ny (kŏl'ŏ·nĭ), *n.; pl.* -NIES (-nĭz). [OF. and L.; OF., fr. L. *colonia*, fr. *colonus* farmer, fr. *colere* to cultivate, dwell.] **1.** A company of people transplanted from their mother country to another land but remaining subject to the parent state. **2.** A number of persons living more or less in isolation. **3.** The district colonized; settlement; also, any distant territory dependent on a ruling power. **4.** *Bacteriol.* A circumscribed mass of microorganisms, growing in or upon a solid or semisolid medium. **5.** *Biol.* A collection of organisms of the same kind living in close association. Cf. SOCIAL, *adj.*, 11.

col'o·phon (kŏl'ŏ·fŏn), *n.* [LL., fr. Gr. *kolophōn* finishing stroke, summit.] **1.** An inscription placed at the end of a book or manuscript, often with a scribe's name, the place and date of the work, etc. **2.** An emblem, usually a device assumed by the publishing house, placed on the title page or at the end of a book.

col'o·pho'ny (kŏl'ŏ·fō'nĭ; kŏ-lŏf'ŏ·nĭ), *n.* [From Gr., fr. *Kolophōnios* of Colophon in Ionia.] Rosin.

col'o·quin'ti·da (kŏl'ŏ·kwĭn'tĭ·dà), *n.* Colocynth.

col'or, col'our (kŭl'ēr), *n.* [OF. *color, colour*, fr. L. *color*.] **1.** A quality of visible phenomena, distinct from form and from light and shade, such as the red of blood; also, a variety of this quality; a hue. **2.** A sensation evoked as a response to the stimulation of the eye and its attached nervous mechanisms by radiant energy of certain wave lengths and intensities. All colors are divisible into two classes: *achromatic colors*, as reds, greens, purples, browns, and pinks; *achromatic colors*, including black, white, and the series of grays intermediate between black and white, which differ from each other only in the degree of resemblance to white or difference from black. *Brilliance* is the attribute which measures this variation among the grays. Dark grays have *low*, median gray *medium*, and light grays *high*, brilliance. Chromatic, as well as achromatic, colors differ from each other in brilliance. Chromatic colors differ from each other also in hue and saturation. Thus, any color can be specified in terms of these three attributes, hue, saturation, and brilliance. *Hue* is that attribute in respect to which colors may be described as red, yellow, green, or blue, or as intermediate between two of these, as red-yellow denotes a hue equally resembling red and yellow. *Saturation* is that attribute in respect to which colors may be differentiated as being higher or lower in degree of vividness of hue; that is, as differing in degree from gray. Thus, emerald is a color, yellow-green in hue, of medium saturation and medium brilliance. Certain standard analyses showing sets of *primary colors* that is, colors in terms of which all other colors may be described or from which all other colors may be evoked by mixture, differ from the above; as, the *physiological*, or *fundamental*, *primaries* are red, green, and blue; the *psychological primaries* are red, yellow, green, blue, black, and white; in painting, red, blue, and yellow are the primaries. **3.** Specif., a chromatic color. **4.** Complexion; specif.: **a** A healthful or ruddy complexion. **b** A blush. **c** The hue or complexion of men not classed as white; esp., the complexion of Negroes. **5.** Coloring matter; a pigment or dye. **6.** *pl.* A dis-

White
Brilliance
Tints
Blue
Saturation
Red
Median gray
Green
Yellow
Hue
Shades
Black

Color Solid.

tinguishing colored badge, device, ribbon, or dress (as the cap and jacket of a jockey). **7.** Chiefly in *pl.* A national flag, ensign, etc., flown by a ship, or the flag of a body of infantry, artillery, or engineers; hence, ***the colors***, military service; as, to join *the colors.* **8.** *pl.* **a** Hostile standard or foe. *Shak.* **b** Side espoused, advocated, etc.; as, to stick to one's *colors.* **9. a** Outward show; semblance; guise; as, his argument has the *color* of reason. **b** Pretext; show of reason; justification; as, the circumstances lend *color* to his argument. **c** Kind; species; as, cattle of this *color.* **10.** Vividness, picturesqueness, and piquancy, esp. in written or spoken composition; specif., an effect of reality and lifelikeness given by use of concrete words, graphic descriptions, peculiarities of speech, etc.; as, stories with local *color.* **11.** *Acoustics.* Tone color; timbre. **12.** *Art.* The tone, scheme, or harmony of colors in painting; coloration in producing effects; also, an effect of coloration produced by chiaroscuro, as in an engraving. **13.** *Law.* An appearance or semblance of a right, authority, office or the like. **14.** *Mining.* A small particle of gold left in a pan after washing. **15.** *pl. U.S.Navy.* A salute to the flag at 8 A.M. and sunset, at hoisting and lowering it.

Syn. **Color** (*or* **colour**), **chroma, hue, shade, tint, tinge** mean a property of a thing visible only in light. **Color** is the general term but is specifically applicable to the property of things seen as red, yellow, blue, purple, etc., as distinct from the property of things seen as white, gray, or black. Scientists prefer **chroma** in this specific sense. **Hue** usually implies some modification of chroma, or color; **shade,** degree of color; **tint,** a light or delicate touching with color; **tinge,** an interfusion or stain of color.

— *v. t.* [OF. *colorer.*] **1.** To change the color of; to dye, tint, paint, or stain. **2.** To give color to; to imbue with color. **3.** To give a specious appearance to, to misrepresent, esp. by glossing, excusing, or admitting prejudice. **—** *v. i.* To acquire or change color.

col′or·a·ble, col′our·a·ble (kŭl′ẽr·ȧ·b'l), *adj.* **1.** Capable of being colored. **2.** Seemingly valid or genuine; plausible; also, feigned; counterfeit. — **Syn.** See PLAUSIBLE. — **col′or·a·bil′i·ty, col′our·a·bil′i·ty** (-bĭl′ĭ·tĭ), *n.* — **col′or·a·ble·ness, col′our·a·ble·ness,** *n.* — **col′or·a·bly, col′our·a·bly** (-blĭ), *adv.*

col′o·ra′do (kŏl′ō·rä′dō), *adj.* [Sp., red.] **1.** *Southwestern U.S.* Reddish; — used in proper names, as of rivers. **2.** Medium in color and strength; — said of cigars. Cf. CLARO, MADURO.

col′or·a′tion, col′our·a′tion (kŭl′ẽr·ā′shŭn), *n.* **1.** Act or art of coloring; state of being colored. **2.** Use or combination of colors; color pattern; distinctive color.

col′o·ra·tu′ra (kŭl′ẽr·ȧ·tū′rȧ· kō′lō·rä·tōō′rä), *n.* [It.] Also **col′or·a·ture** (kŭl′ẽr·ȧ·tūr; kŏl′ō·rȧ-). Florid ornaments in vocal music, as runs, trills, etc.; also, music characterized by such effects. — **col′o·ra·tu′ra,** *adj.*

coloratura soprano. A high soprano voice of clearness and flexibility; also, the singer having such a voice.

col′or–blind′, col′our–blind′ (kŭl′ẽr·blīnd′), *adj.* Affected with **color blindness,** or total or partial inability to recognize or distinguish chromatic colors. Partial color blindness (*dichromatism*) is the usual form.

col′or·cast′ (-kȧst′; 9), *n.* [*color* + broad*cast.*] *Television.* A broadcast in color. — **col′or·cast′,** *v. t. & i.*

col′ored, col′oured (kŭl′ẽrd), *adj.* **1.** Having color. **2.** Of some other race than the Caucasian, or white; esp., Negro. **3.** Prejudiced; partial; — of a statement or opinion.

col′or·er, col′our·er (kŭl′ẽr·ẽr), *n.* One who colors.

col′or·ful, col′our·ful (kŭl′ẽr·fōōl; -f'l), *adj.* Full of color; esp.: **a** Abounding in startling contrasts; full of variety. **b** Full of literary color. — **col′or·ful·ly, col′our·ful·ly,** *adv.* — **-ful·ness,** *n.*

col′or·if′ic (kŭl′ẽr·ĭf′ĭk; kŏl′ō·rĭf′-), *adj.* [L. *color* color + *facere* to make.] Giving color; loosely, pert. to color.

col′or·im′e·ter (kŭl′ẽr·ĭm′ē·tẽr), *n.* [*color* + *-meter.*] An instrument for determining and specifying colors or measuring intensity of color.

col′or·im′e·try (-trĭ), *n.* Measurement or analysis by means of a colorimeter. — **col′or·i·met′ric** (-ĭ·mĕt′rĭk), **col′or·i·met′ri·cal** (-rĭ·kăl), *adj.* — **col′or·i·met′ri·cal·ly,** *adv.*

col′or·ing, col′our·ing (kŭl′ẽr·ĭng), *n.* **1.** Act of applying colors; also, that which produces color. **2.** Change of appearance, as by adding color. **3.** The effect of applying colors; ornamentation or work in color. **4.** Complexion; coloration.

col′or·ist, col′our·ist (-ĭst), *n.* A colorer; esp., an artist skilled in the use of colors. — **col′or·is′tic, col′our·is′tic** (-ĭs′tĭk), *adj.*

col′or·less, col′our·less, *adj.* Lacking color; specif.: **a** Pallid; blanched. **b** Lacking variety, animation, spontaneity, etc.

color phase. *Zool.* One of two or more types of coloration of the fur, plumage, etc., assumed by certain animals, as according to season, age, etc. Cf. FOX.

color point. See ESCUTCHEON, *Illust.*

co·los′sal (kō·lŏs′ăl; -'l), *adj.* **1.** Of the size of a colossus; huge; tremendous. **2.** *Colloq.* Incredible or astonishing; as, *colossal* stupidity. — **Syn.** See ENORMOUS. — **co·los′sal·ly,** *adv.*

Col′os·se′um (kŏl′ō·sē′ŭm), *n.* [Neut., fr. L. *colosseus* gigantic, fr. *colossus.*] **1.** An amphitheater built by Vespasian and Titus about A.D. 80, in great part still standing southeast of the Forum in Rome; — applied also to any Roman amphitheater. **2.** [*not cap.*] = COLISEUM, 2.

Co·los′sians (kō·lŏsh′ănz), *n. pl., construed as sing.* The Epistle to the Colossians, or Christians of Colossae. See BIBLE.

co·los′sus (kō·lŏs′ŭs), *n.; pl.* -SI (-ī), -SUSES (-ŭs·ĕz; -ĭz). [L., fr. Gr. *kolossos.*] **1.** A statue of gigantic size; as, the **Colossus of Rhodes,** a statue of Apollo, about 120 feet high, made by Chares about 280 B.C. **2.** Anything of gigantic size.

co·los′trum (-lŏs′trŭm), *n.* [L., beestings.] The first milk secreted by a female mammal, up to a few days after delivery of offspring. Cf. BEESTINGS.

col′our, col′our·a·ble, etc. Vars. of COLOR, COLORABLE, etc.

-colous. [L. *colere* to inhabit.] A combining form denoting *inhabiting, growing* or *living in, on,* or *among,* as in arenicolous.

col′por′tage (kŏl′pōr′tĭj; *F.* kôl′pôr′tȧzh′), *n.* [F.] A colporteur's work.

col′por′teur (kŏl′pōr′tẽr; kôl′pôr′tûr′), *n.* [F., fr. *colporter* to peddle (after *col* neck), fr. OF. *comporter* to carry around, endure.] A hawker or distributor, esp. of religious tracts and books.

colt (kōlt), *n.* [AS. *colt.*] **1.** The young of the horse, ass, zebra, etc.; a foal; sometimes distinctively, a male foal, as distinguished from a *filly.* **2.** One like a colt in youth, inexperience, etc. — **colt′ish,** *adj.*

col′ter (kōl′tẽr), *n.* Also **coul′ter.** [AS. *culter* and OF. *coltre,* both fr. L. *culter* plowshare, knife.] A cutter on a plow to cut the turf.

colts′foot′ (kōlts′fōōt′), *n.; pl.* -FOOTS (-fōōts′). A medicinal herb (*Tussilago farfara*) of the aster family.

col′u·brine (kŏl′ū·brīn; -brĭn), *adj.* [L. *colubrinus,* fr. *coluber* serpent.] **1.** Of or characteristic of a snake. **2.** Of or pertaining to a subfamily (Colubrinae), a family (Colubridae), or a suborder (formerly Colubrina) of nonpoisonous snakes, including the familiar harmless snakes of North America and Europe.

co·lu′go (kō·lōō′gō), *n.* = FLYING LEMUR.

col′um·ba′ri·um (kŏl′ŭm·bā′rĭ·ŭm), *n.; pl.* -BARIA (-ȧ). [L., fr. *columba* dove.] **1.** A vault with niches for cinerary urns. **2.** *pl.* The niches in such a vault.

col′um·bar′y (kŏl′ŭm·bẽr′ĭ), *n.; pl.* -IES (-ĭz). [See COLUMBARIUM.] A dovecot; a pigeon house.

Co·lum′bi·a (kō·lŭm′bĭ·ȧ), *n.* America; the United States; — a poetical appellation in honor of Columbus.

Co·lum′bi·an (-ăn), *adj.* [From COLUMBIA.] Of or pertaining to Columbia or Christopher Columbus.

Co·lum′bi·an, *n.* A size of type (16 points). See TYPE.

col′um·bine (kŏl′ŭm·bīn), *n.* [F. and ML.; F. *colombine,* fr. ML., fr. L. *columbinus* dovelike, fr. *columba* dove.] Any of a genus (*Aquilegia,* esp. *A. canadensis* and *A. coerulea*) of plants of the crowfoot family, having irregular, showy flowers. *A. vulgaris* is the source of the garden varieties. *A. coerulea* is the State flower of Colorado.

col′um·bine (-bīn; -bĭn), *adj.* [L. *columbinus.*] Of or pertaining to a dove; dovelike; dove-colored.

Col′um·bine (-bīn), *n.* [It. *Colombina.*] The saucy, adroit sweetheart of Harlequin in old Italian popular comedy, in pantomime, etc.

co·lum′bite (kō·lŭm′bīt), *n.* [See COLUMBIUM.] *Mineral.* A native black compound of iron and columbium, $Fe(CbO_3)_2$, often containing manganese, and grading into tantalite.

co·lum′bi·um (-bĭ·ŭm), *n.* [NL., fr. *Columbia.*] *Chem.* A steel-gray, lustrous metallic element; niobium. Symbol, *Cb* (or *Nb*); at. no., 41; at. wt., 92.91.

Co·lum′bus Day (kō·lŭm′bŭs). The 12th day of October, on which day in 1492 Columbus discovered America; Discovery Day. It is a legal holiday in most states.

col′u·mel′la (kŏl′ū·mĕl′ȧ), *n.; pl.* -LAE (-ē). [L., dim. of *columen* column.] Any of several columnlike formations in animals, plants, etc. — **col′u·mel′lar** (-ẽr), *adj.*

col′umn (kŏl′ŭm), *n.* [OF. & L.; OF. *colomne,* fr. L. *columna.*] **1.** *Arch.* A kind of supporting pillar, esp. one consisting of shaft (usually round), base, and capital. See ORDER, BASE, *Illusts.* **2.** Anything resembling a column in form, position, or function; as, a *column* of smoke; the spinal *column.* **3.** A formation of soldiers, ships, etc., placed one behind another. **4.** *Math.* A perpendicular line of figures or other symbols. **5.** *Print.* One of two or more upright sections separated by a rule or a blank space; hence, in newspapers, such a column carrying under a permanent title a daily feature article, usually of a humorous or gossipy character, written by a special writer, or **col′um·nist** (kŏl′ŭm·nĭst; *dial. or humorous,* kŏl′yŭm·ĭst; *by some,* kŏl′ŭm·ĭst). — **co·lum′nar** (kō·lŭm′nẽr), *adj.* — **col′umned** (kŏl′ŭmd), *adj.*

co·lum′ni·a′tion (kō·lŭm′nĭ·ā′shŭn), *n.* The employment, or system of arrangement, of columns in a structure.

co·lure′ (kō·lūr′; kō′lūr), *n.; pl.* COLURES (-lūrz′; -lūrz). [LL. *coluri,* pl., fr. Gr. *hai kolouroi* (sc. *grammai* lines) the colures, fr. *kolos* docked + *oura* tail; — because in ordinary latitudes a part is always beneath the horizon.] Either of two circles of the celestial sphere intersecting at the poles, one passing through the equinoctial points, and the other at right angles to it.

col′za (kŏl′zȧ), *n.* [F., fr. D. *koolzaad,* prop., cabbage seed.] Cole or its seed; esp., rapeseed, the source of a fine oil, **colza oil** (= RAPE OIL).

com-. [From L. *cum* with.] A prefix meaning *with, together, very.*

co′ma (kō′mȧ), *n.; pl.* COMAS (-mȧz). [NL., fr. Gr. *kōma* lethargy.] A state of profound insensibility, caused by disease, injury, or poison.

co′ma, *n.; pl.* COMAE (-mē). [L., hair, fr. Gr. *komē.*] **1.** *Astron.* A nebulous mass surrounding the nucleus of a comet, and with it constituting the comet's head. **2.** A blur of light from and partly around an image produced by a lens, caused by lateral spherical aberration. **3.** *Bot.* A tuft or bunch, as of branches or hairs. — **co′mal** (-măl), *adj.*

Co′ma Ber′e·ni′ces (bẽr′ē·nī′sēz); *gen.* COMAE BERENICES (kō′mē). [L.] A constellation north of Virgo and between Boötes and Leo.

Co·man′che (kō·măn′chē), *n.; pl.* -CHES (-chēz). An Indian of a Shoshonean tribe, now in Oklahoma.

Co·man′che·an (-ăn), *adj.* [From *Comanche,* town and county, Texas.] *Geol.* See CRETACEOUS, 2. — **Co·man′che·an,** *n.*

co·mate′ (kō·māt′; 2), *n.* [*co-* + *mate.*] A companion.

co′mate (kō′māt), *adj.* [L. *comatus.*] Hairy; comose.

com′a·tose (kŏm′ȧ·tōs; -tōz; kō′mȧ-), *adj.* Relating to or like coma; in a coma; lethargic. — **com′a·tose·ly,** *adv.*

co·mat′u·la (kō·măt′ū·lȧ), *n.; pl.* -LAE (-lē). [NL.] = COMATULID.

co·mat′u·lid (kō·măt′ū·lĭd), *n.* [From NL. *Comatulidae,* family name, fr. L. *comatulus* having hair neatly curled.] A free-swimming stalkless crinoid; a feather star.

comb (kōm), *n.* [AS. *camb.*] **1.** A toothed instrument for adjusting, cleaning, or confining the hair, or for adornment. **2.** A currycomb. **3.** The fleshy crest or caruncle on the head of the domestic fowl and certain other gallinaceous birds. See POULTRY, *Illust.* (1). **4.** A thing resembling a cock's comb, as the curling crest of a wave. **5.** Any of various toothed instruments; esp., one for separating and cleansing wool, flax, hair, etc. Cf. 2d CARD, *v. t.* **6.** A honeycomb, or similar mass of cells. **—** *v. t.* **1.** To disentangle, cleanse, or adjust, with or as with a comb. Cf. 2d CARD, *v. t.* **2.** To search systematically or thoroughly. **—** *v. i. Naut.* To roll over or break, as waves.

comb, combe (kōōm; kōm). Vars. of COOMB.

com·bat′ (kŏm·băt′; kŏm′băt; kŭm′băt), *v. i.;* COM·BAT′ED, COM·BAT′TED; -BAT′ING, -BAT′TING. [F. *combattre.* See COM-; BATTER to beat.] To fight or struggle, as with an enemy. **—** *v. t.* To fight with; contend against. — **Syn.** See OPPOSE. — **com·bat′a·ble** (-ȧ·b'l), *adj.*

☞ Although stress on the final syllable of the verb *combat* in American pronunciation calls for doubling of the final *t* before an ending that begins with a vowel, as *combatted, combatting* (see § 2, page 1145), forms with the single *t* predominate in inflection and derivatives.

com′bat (kŏm′băt; kŭm′-), *n.* [F.] Fighting or a fight; struggle for supremacy, revenge, etc.; specif.: **a** *Mil.* A battle. **b** A fight between two contestants; a duel. **—** *adj.* Used or for use in actual fighting.

com′bat·ant (kŏm′bȧ·tănt; kŏm·băt′'nt; kŭm′bȧ·tănt), *adj.* Combating; ready to combat; also, *Mil.*, taking part in, or prepared to take part in, active fighting. — **com′bat·ant**, *n.*

combat car. *U. S. Army.* An armed motor vehicle of track or wheeled type, designed for combat; often, specif., a tank.

com·bat′ive (kŏm·băt′ĭv; kŏm′bȧ·tĭv; kŭm′-), *adj.* Disposed to fight; pugnacious. — **com·bat′ive·ly**, *adv.* — **com·bat′ive·ness**, *n.*

combat team. *Mil. & Nav.* A tactical nonorganic grouping of forces capable of operating independently.

comb′er (kōm′ẽr), *n.* **1.** One who or that which combs; a worker or machine that combs wool, flax, etc. **2.** A long curling wave rolling in from the ocean; a beachcomber.

com′bi·na′tion (kŏm′bĭ·nā′shŭn), *n.* **1.** Act or process of combining, or state of being combined. **2.** A union or aggregate made by combining persons or things together so as to effect a purpose; as (*U. S.*), a **combination in restraint of trade**, any agreement, conspiracy, and organization to monopolize any part of interstate or foreign commerce. **3.** The series of letters or numbers in given succession chosen in setting the mechanism of a lock (**combination lock**) operated by a dial; also, the mechanism operating, or moved by, the series. **4.** Any of certain one-piece undergarments covering the waist and thighs. **5.** *Chem.* Act or process of uniting to form a chemical compound; also, the compound. **6.** *Math.* Any of the different sets into which a number of individuals, as letters, may be grouped without regard to the order of arrangement within the group. Cf. PERMUTATION, 2. — **com′bi·na′tion·al** (-ăl; -′l), *adj.*

com′bi·na′tive (kŏm′bĭ·nā′tĭv; kŏm·bīn′ȧ·tĭv), *adj.* Tending or able to effect combination; marked by, pertaining to, or resulting from, combination.

com·bine′ (kŏm·bīn′), *v. t. & i.* [LL. *combinare, combinatum*, fr. *com-* + *binus*, pl. *bini*, two and two, double.] To unite or join; to bring into or form a union. — **Syn.** See JOIN. — **com·bin′a·ble** (-bīn′ȧ·b′l), *adj.* — **com·bin′er** (-bīn′ẽr), *n.*

com′bine (kŏm′bīn; kŏm·bīn′), *n.* **1.** Combination; esp., *Colloq., U. S.*, a combination of persons or organizations, as for commercial or political advantage. **2.** (*pron.* kŏm′bīn) A machine which harvests, threshes, and cleans grain while moving over the field.

comb′ings (kōm′ĭngz), *n. pl.* Loose hairs, etc., removed by a comb.

com·bin′ing form (kŏm·bīn′ĭng). A word or a word element (a formation on a Greek or Latin stem, or an English word used without change) used with another word or element to form a compound, as in *phono*graph, grapho*phone*, trade-*mark*, crack*brained*. Combining forms have concrete sense and co-ordinating or modifying function (as in *medico*legal, *auto*mobile), as contrasted with *prefixes* and *suffixes*, which have abstract sense and derivative, formative, or inflectional function (as in *il*legal, dead*ly*).

com·bust′ (kŏm·bŭst′), *adj.* [OF., fr. L. *combustus*, past part. of *comburere* to burn up.] *Astrol.* Obscured by nearness to the sun; — of a planet or star.

com·bus′ti·ble (-bŭs′tĭ·b′l), *adj.* [F.] Capable of combustion; inflammable; also, easily excited; irascible. — *n.* A combustible thing. — **com·bus′ti·bil′i·ty** (-bĭl′ĭ·tĭ), *n.* — **com·bus′ti·ble·ness**, *n.* — **com·bus′ti·bly** (-blĭ), *adv.*

com·bus′tion (-bŭs′chŭn), *n.* **1.** Act or instance of burning. **2.** Any chemical process, commonly the union of substances with oxygen, accompanied by the evolution of light and heat; hence, slower oxidation, as in the animal body. **3.** Violent agitation; tumult. — **com·bus′tive** (-tĭv), *adj.*

com·bus′tor (-tẽr), *n.* [*combust*, v. (*archaic*) + *-or*.] In a jet engine, the chamber in which combustion occurs.

come (kŭm; 4), *v. i.*; CAME (kām); COME; COM′ING (kŭm′ĭng). [AS. *cuman*.] **1.** To move hitherward; approach; as, he is *coming*; — opposed to *go*. **2.** To appear or arrive, as on a scene of action, in a course of events, or the like; as, he *came* to the rescue. **3.** To arrive at or reach the point of being, becoming, getting, amounting, etc. **4.** To take place or have its place in a series, sequence, calendar, scale of values, or the like. **5.** To issue as by birth, emanation, development, etc.; as, to *come* of good stock. **6.** To be obtainable or obtained; to be attainable or attained; as, the garments *come* in three sizes. **7.** To extend or reach, esp. in space; — often figurative; as, the dress *came* to her knees. **8.** To be favorably moved; to yield. — *v. t. Colloq.* To act, practice, perform, or play.

come about. **a** To come to pass, as in due course. **b** To change. *Shak.* **c** *Naut.* Of a sailing craft, to change direction while still heading to the wind. — ***come back.*** **a** *Colloq.* To regain a former condition or position from which one has declined or been removed. **b** *Slang.* To retort. — ***come out.*** **a** To emerge; to be seen, known, etc. **b** To be presented in society. **c** To be issued or published. — ***come round*** (*or* ***around***). **a** *Colloq.* To recover; also, to regain consciousness. **b** To change, as the wind or as a person in his opinion. — ***come to.*** **a** To recover, as from a swoon. **b** *Naut.* To luff; to bring the ship's head nearer the wind; to anchor or stop in a certain point.

come′back′ (kŭm′băk′), *n.* **1.** *Colloq.* A coming back, or return to a former condition or position. **2.** *Slang.* A retort.

co·me′di·an (kō·mē′dĭ·ăn), *n.* [F. *comédien*.] **1.** An actor in comedy; also, a writer of comedy. **2.** An amusing person.

co·me′di·enne′ (kō·mē′dĭ·ĕn′; *F.* kō′mā′dyĕn′), *n. fem.*; *pl.* -DIENNES (-dĭ·ĕnz′; *F.* -dyĕn′). [F. *comédienne*, fem. of *comédien*.] An actress who plays comedy.

com′e·do (kŏm′ē·dō), *n.*; *pl.* -DONES (-dō′nēz), -DOS (-dōz). [L., a glutton. See COMESTIBLE.] *Med.* = BLACKHEAD, 2.

come′down′ (kŭm′doun′), *n.* A downfall, esp. in rank or dignity.

com′e·dy (kŏm′ē·dĭ), *n.*; *pl.* -DIES (-dĭz). [OF. *comedie*, fr. L., fr. Gr. *kōmōidia*, fr. *kōmos* a festal procession, an ode sung at it + *aeidein* to sing.] **1.** A drama of light and amusing rather than serious character and typically having a happy ending; also, the dramatic quality characteristic of comedies. **2.** Theory or art of composing or of acting comedies. **3.** An event, situation, or the like, providing amusement or matter suitable for comedy. **4.** A literary work treating its subject matter in one or more ways characteristic of comedy; — used chiefly in titles or in literary criticism; as, Dante's Divine *Comedy*.

come′ly (kŭm′lĭ), *adj.*; -LI·ER (-lĭ·ẽr); -LI·EST. [AS. *cȳmlīc*, fr. *cȳme* beautiful + *-līc*. See LIKE, *adj.*] **1.** Pleasing or agreeable to the sight. **2.** *Archaic.* Becoming; decent. — **Syn.** See BEAUTIFUL. — **come′li·ness**, *n.*

com′er (kŭm′ẽr), *n.* **1.** One who comes or arrives. **2.** *Colloq.* One making rapid progress or showing promise, as of future success.

co·mes′ti·ble (kō·mĕs′tĭ·b′l), *adj.* [F., fr. L. *comesus, comestus*, past part. of *comedere* to eat, fr. *com-* + *edere* to eat.] Eatable. — *n.* Food; — usually in *pl.*

com′et (kŏm′ĕt; -ĭt), *n.* [From L., fr. Gr. *komētēs* comet, prop., long-haired, deriv. of *komē* hair.] A luminous heavenly body, generally irregular in form, often having a long nebulous train, or tail, and following an orbit about the sun. Symbol, ☄. — **com′et·ar′y** (kŏm′ē·tĕr′ĭ *or, esp. Brit.*, -tẽr·ĭ), *adj.* — **co·met′ic** (kō·mĕt′ĭk), *adj.*

co·meth′er (kō·mĕth′ẽr), *n.* [Dial. pron. of *come hither*, in calling cows.] *Ir.* **1.** Matter; affair. **2.** Friendly association. — ***put the***, *or* ***one's, comether on.*** To exercise persuasion or charm upon.

come·up′pance (kŭm·ŭp′ăns), *n.* *Colloq., U. S.* A deserved rebuke or chastisement; deserts.

com′fit (kŭm′fĭt; kŏm′-), *n.* [OF. *confit*, prop. a past part., fr. *confire* to preserve, fr. L. *conficere* to prepare, fr. *con-* + *facere* to make.] A fruit, root, or seed preserved with sugar and dried. Cf. SWEETMEAT. — *v. t. Obs.* To make into a comfit; to preserve.

com′fort (kŭm′fẽrt), *v. t.* [OF. *conforter*, fr. LL. *confortare* to strengthen much, fr. *con-* + *fortis* strong.] **1.** To assist; to aid; — now only in legal use. **2.** To impart strength and hope to; now, usually, to relieve of mental distress; console.

Syn. **Comfort, console, solace** mean to give help to a person in sorrow or pain. **Comfort**, the homely, intimate term, implies the imparting of cheer, hope, and strength as well as, in some degree, the lessening of pain; **console** emphasizes the alleviation of grief or the mitigation of the sense of loss rather than distinct relief; **solace** suggests a lift of spirits that may mean relief from loneliness, dullness, etc., as well as from grief or pain.

— *n.* **1.** Strengthening aid; — now only in the legal phrase *aid and comfort* (see TREASON, *n.*, 2). **2.** Solace; consolation in trouble. **3.** State or feeling of having relief, cheer, or consolation; freedom from pain or trouble. **4.** That which gives or brings comfort.

com′fort·a·ble (kŭm′fẽrt·ȧ·b′l), *adj.* **1.** Affording comfort; esp., consoling. **2.** *Colloq.* Fairly adequate; sufficient; as, a *comfortable* income, fortune. **3.** In a state of comfort; as: **a** *Obs.* Cheerful. **b** In a state of content; at ease. **4.** Marked by, or giving an appearance of, comfort; easy and undisturbed. — *n. U. S.* A stuffed or quilted cover for a bed; a puff. — **com′fort·a·ble·ness**, *n* — **com′fort·a·bly**, *adv.*

Syn. **Comfortable, cozy** (*or* **cosy**), **snug, easy, restful, reposeful** mean enjoying or providing conditions that make for content or security. **Comfortable** applies to things (sometimes, persons) that encourage serenity, well-being, complacency, or the like; **cozy** suggests comfortableness derived from warmth, shelter, ease, friendliness; **snug** suggests the state of mind of one who has as much room, or responsibility, or freedom, or money, or the like, as is essential to one's well-being, but no more; **easy** implies relief from all that makes for discomfort or hardship; **restful** and **reposeful** usually apply to that which contributes to or induces a mood of relaxation and comfort.

com′fort·er (-ẽr), *n.* **1.** One that gives comfort. **2.** [*cap.*] *Bib. & Theol.* The Holy Spirit. **3.** *U. S.* A comfortable. **4.** A long, narrow, knitted woolen scarf or muffler. **5.** *Brit.* = PACIFIER, 2.

com′fort·ing (kŭm′fẽrt·ĭng), *adj.* Consoling; cheering.

com′fort·less, *adj.* Having or affording no comfort. — **Syn.** Forlorn, desolate, cheerless, inconsolable.

com′frey (kŭm′frĭ), *n.*; *pl.* -FREYS (-frĭz). [OF. *confirie*.] Any of a genus (*Symphytum*) of plants of the borage family.

com′ic (kŏm′ĭk), *adj.* [L. *comicus*, fr. Gr. *kōmikos*.] **1.** Relating to comedy, as distinct from tragedy. **2.** Designed to excite mirth. — **Syn.** See LAUGHABLE. — *n.* **1.** That element in art or nature which provokes mirth. **2.** A strip (**comic strip**) of consecutive drawings in panels, usually presenting humorous situations or adventures; — also called *the funnies*; also, a book or other collection of such drawings. **3.** A motion picture presenting broad comedy.

com′i·cal (-ĭ·kăl), *adj.* **1.** *Obs.* Relating to or befitting comedy; hence, of style, etc., trivial; not elevated. **2.** Causing mirth or laughter. — **Syn.** See LAUGHABLE. — **com′i·cal·ly**, *adv.* — **com′i·cal′i·ty** (-kăl′ĭ·tĭ), *n.* — **com′i·cal·ness**, *n.*

Com′in·form′ (kŏm′ĭn·fôrm′), *n.* [*Com*munist *Inform*ation Bureau.] An international organization of Communist party representatives formed in Sept., 1947, with headquarters first at Belgrade, later at other places, for spreading and strengthening communism throughout the world in the struggle against capitalist influence; dissolved April, 1956.

com′ing (kŭm′ĭng), *adj.* **1.** Approaching. **2.** *Colloq.* Gaining importance or distinction; as, a *coming* man. — *n.* **1.** Approach; arrival. **2.** Advent; esp. [*usually cap.*], the Second Advent of Christ.

Com′in·tern′ (kŏm′ĭn·tûrn′), *n.* [*Com*munist *Intern*ational.] See INTERNATIONAL, *n.*, 2 **c**.

co·mi′ti·a (kō·mĭsh′ĭ·ȧ), *n. pl.* [L.] *Rom. Antiq.* An assembly of the people to act on matters submitted to them by duly authorized officials. — **co·mi′tial** (-mĭsh′ăl), *adj.*

com′i·ty (kŏm′ĭ·tĭ), *n.*; *pl.* -TIES (-tĭz). [L. *comitas*, fr. *comis* courteous, kind.] Courtesy; friendly civility.

comity of nations *or* **states.** The courtesy by which nations recognize, and give effect within their own territory to, the institutions or laws of another nation; also, the group of nations observing such a code.

com′ma (kŏm′ȧ), *n.* [L., part of a sentence, fr. Gr. *komma* clause, fr. *koptein* to cut off.] **1.** A point [,] used in writing and printing to indicate separation of words, phrases, or clauses from others not closely connected in the structure of the sentence. **2.** Hence, a slight separation or pause.

comma bacillus. The bacterium (*Vibrio comma*) which causes Asiatic cholera. Cf. BACILLUS, 2.

com·mand′ (kŏ·mȧnd′; 9), *v. t.* [OF. *comander*, deriv. of L. *com-* + *mandare* to commit to, to command.] **1.** To direct authoritatively; to order. **2.** To have at command or have command over; specif.: **a** To have at bidding or at disposal; as, you may *command* my services. **b** To secure authoritatively as (one's) right or due; as, the best goods *command* the best price. **c** To dominate in situation; as, the hill *commands* the road. **3.** *Obs.* To give order for; require. — *v. i.* **1.** To have or to exercise direct authority; to govern; also, to be commander. **2.** To dominate or overlook, as from a superior position.

Syn. **Command, order, bid, enjoin, direct, instruct, charge** mean to issue orders. **Command** and **order** imply authority, *command* suggesting its official exercise, and *order*, often, its peremptory or arbitrary exercise; **bid** (archaic or colloquial) usually also suggests peremptoriness; **enjoin, direct,** and **instruct** are less imperative but all connote expectation of obedience, *enjoin* implying authority and pressing admonition, *direct* and *instruct*, official or business relations, the former being more mandatory, the latter, more formal; **charge** adds to *enjoin* the implication of imposing as a duty or task.

— *n.* **1.** Act of commanding; bidding. **2.** An order given. **3.** Faculty or power of commanding; as: **a** Authority to command, esp. by military or naval rank. **b** Power to dominate or overlook by means of position; also, scope of vision; survey. **c** Control; mastery; as, to have *command* over one's temper. **4.** *Mil. & Naval.* **a** A body of troops under a commander. **b** A position in which one commands, as a military post. **c** A military order. — **Syn.** See POWER.

com′man·dant′ (kŏm′ăn·dănt′; -dänt′), *n.* [F., orig. pres. part.] A commander; commanding officer.

command car. *U. S. Army.* A motor vehicle, usually armed and armored and equipped with radio, for use of the commander of a unit, esp. a four-seated car with six speeds forward and four-wheel drive.

com′man·deer′ (kŏm′ăn·dēr′), *v. t.* [D. *kommandeeren*, lit., to command.] To compel to perform military service; to seize for military purposes; hence, *Colloq.*, to take forcible possession of.

com·mand′er (kŏ·mȧn′dẽr; 9), *n.* **1.** One who commands; hence, a chief or leader. **2.** In medieval military orders, the chief officer of a commandery; hence, in certain secret orders, a similar officer. **3.** *Mil.* The chief officer of an army or a subdivision of it. **4.** *Nav.* A commissioned officer ranking above a lieutenant commander and below a captain. Abbr. *Comdr.* — **com·mand′er·ship,** *n.*

commander in chief; *pl.* COMMANDERS IN CHIEF. **a** The officer or official holding supreme command of the military or naval forces of a nation. In the United States the president is commander in chief of the army and navy. **b** Loosely, the highest commanding officer in an area, of a detached force, or the like.

com·mand′er·y (kŏ·mȧn′dẽr·ĭ), *n.; pl.* -IES (-ĭz). The jurisdiction of a commander. Specif.: **a** A district or a manor under a commander of an order of knights; hence, a pension or benefice attached to a commandership of an order of knighthood. **b** *U. S.* An assembly or lodge in certain secret orders. **c** A district under the administration of a military commander.

com·mand′ing, *adj.* That commands, orders, dominates, etc. — **com·mand′ing·ly,** *adv.*

com·mand′ment (kŏ·mȧnd′mĕnt), *n.* Act of commanding, power of command, or what is commanded; specif., *Bib.*, one of the Ten Commandments.

com·man′do (kŏ·mȧn′dō), *n.; pl.* -DOS, -DOES (-dōz). [D., fr. Pg. *commando.*] **1.** In South Africa, a military body or command; also, a raid. **2.** Orig., in the British Army, a small band of specially trained amphibious shock troops engaged in hit-and-run raids into enemy country; hence, commonly, a member of any specialized raiders' organization.

com·meas′ure (kŏ·mĕzh′ẽr), *v. t.* To be commensurate with; to equal. — **com·meas′ur·a·ble,** *adj.*

‖**comme il faut** (kô′·mēl fō′). [F.] As it should be; proper.

com·mem′o·rate (kŏ·mĕm′ō·rāt), *v. t.* [L. *commemoratus*, past part., deriv. of *com-* + *memorare* to mention, fr. *memor* mindful.] To call to remembrance or serve as a memorial of. — **Syn.** See KEEP. — **com·mem′o·ra′tor** (-rā′tẽr), *n.*

com·mem′o·ra′tion (-rā′shŭn), *n.* Act of commemorating; celebration. — **com·mem′o·ra′tion·al,** *adj.*

com·mem′o·ra′tive (kŏ·mĕm′ō·rā′tĭv; -rȧ·tĭv), *adj.* Tending or intended to commemorate. — *n.* Anything commemorative. — **com·mem′o·ra′tive·ly,** *adv.*

com·mence′ (kŏ·mĕns′), *v. i.;* -MENCED′ (-mĕnst′); -MENC′ING (-mĕn′sĭng). [OF. *comencer*, deriv. of L. *com-* + *initiare* to begin.] **1.** To start; begin. **2.** To begin to be or to act as; as, he *commenced* actor at an early age. **3.** *Eng.* To take a degree at a university. — *v. t.* To enter upon; begin. — **Syn.** See BEGIN. — **Ant.** Conclude. — **com·menc′er** (-mĕn′sẽr), *n.*

com·mence′ment (-mĕnt), *n.* **1.** Act, fact, or time of commencing. **2.** *Educ.* The day when, or the ceremonies at which, degrees are conferred; also, the period of festivities at this time.

com·mend′ (kŏ·mĕnd′), *v. t.* [L. *commendare*, fr. *com-* + *mandare* to entrust, commit.] **1.** To commit, entrust, or give in charge for care. **2.** To recommend as worthy of confidence or regard. **3.** To mention with approbation; to praise. **4.** *Archaic.* To mention by way of courtesy. — **Syn.** Recommend, applaud, compliment. — **Ant.** Censure. — **com·mend′a·ble,** *adj.* — **com·mend′a·bly,** *adv.*

com·men′dam (kŏ·mĕn′dăm), *n.* [ML. *dare in commendam* to give into trust.] *Eccl.* **a** The custody or holding of a benefice by one to whom it has been commended, or given in charge. A living so held was said to be held *in commendam.* **b** The benefice so held.

com′men·da′tion (kŏm′ĕn·dā′shŭn), *n.* **1.** Act of commending; also, that which commends. **2.** Chiefly *pl. Archaic.* A message of affection or respect; greeting.

com·mend′a·to′ry (kŏ·mĕn′dȧ·tō′rĭ *or, esp. Brit.,* -tẽr·ĭ), *adj.* **1.** Of or serving for commendation; laudatory. **2.** *Eccl.* Holding or held in commendam.

com·men′sal (kŏ·mĕn′săl), *n.* [F., fr. ML. *commensalis*, fr. L. *com-* + *mensa* table.] **1.** One who eats at the same table with others; a messmate. **2.** *Biol.* An organism, not truly parasitic, which lives in, with, or on, another. — *adj.* Having the character of a commensal; also, pertaining to or designating those who habitually eat together. — **com·men′sal·ism** (-ĭz′m), *n.* — **com′men·sal′i·ty** (kŏm′ĕn·săl′ĭ·tĭ), *n.* — **com·men′sal·ly,** *adv.*

com·men′su·ra·ble (kŏ·mĕn′shŏŏ·rȧ·b′l), *adj.* [From LL., fr. *com-* + *mensurabilis* measurable.] **1.** Capable of being exactly measured by the same number, quantity, or measure. **2.** Suitably or duly proportioned. — **Syn.** See PROPORTIONAL. — **com·men′su·ra·bil′i·ty** (-bĭl′ĭ·tĭ), *n.* — **com·men′su·ra·bly** (-blĭ), *adv.*

com·men′su·rate (-rĭt), *adj.* [LL. *commensuratus* equal. See COM-; MENSURATION.] **1.** Equal in measure or extent; also, proportionate; corresponding. **2.** Commensurable; reducible to a common measure. — **Syn.** See PROPORTIONAL. — **com·men′su·rate·ly,** *adv.* — **com·men′su·ra′tion** (-rā′shŭn), *n.*

com′ment (kŏm′ĕnt), *n.* [OF.] **1.** A note or observation intended to explain, illustrate, or criticize the meaning of a writing, book, etc.; annotation. **2.** A remark or criticism.

com′ment (kŏm′ĕnt; *now rarely* kŏ·mĕnt′), *v. i. & t.* [F. *commenter*, fr. L. *commentari* to meditate upon, explain, v. intens. of *comminisci*, *commentus*, to reflect upon, invent.] To make or write comments (on).

com′men·tar′y (kŏm′ĕn·tĕr′ĭ *or, esp. Brit.,* -tẽr·ĭ), *n.; pl.* -IES (-ĭz). A series of comments or memoranda. Specif.: **a** A brief account of transactions or events written as if for a memorandum. **b** A book of expositions on a part of the Scriptures. **c** A thing serving for exposition or illustration; comment. — **com′men·tar′i·al** (-târ′ĭ·ăl), *adj.*

com′men·ta′tor (-tā′tẽr), *n.* [L.] **1.** One who writes a commentary or comments; annotator. **2.** *Radio.* One employed to broadcast summaries of current events or daily news, often with personal comments, or firsthand narration.

com′merce (kŏm′ûrs; -ẽrs), *n.* [F., fr. L. *commercium*, fr. *com-* + *merx, mercis*, merchandise.] **1.** Business intercourse; esp., the exchange or buying and selling of commodities on a large scale between different places; extended trade. **2.** Social intercourse. **3.** Mental or spiritual intercourse or communion. **4.** Sexual intercourse. — **Syn.** See BUSINESS.

com·merce′ (kŏ·mûrs′), *v. i.;* COM·MERCED′ (-mûrst′); COM·MERC′ING (-mûr′sĭng). **1.** *Obs.* To trade. **2.** To hold personal intercourse; to commune.

com·mer′cial (kŏ·mûr′shăl), *adj.* **1.** Of or pertaining to commerce; mercantile; as, *commercial* houses; a *commercial* treaty. **2.** Having financial profit as the primary aim; as, a *commercial* drama. **3. a** Produced or producible in large quantities for commerce. **b** Paid for by an advertiser; — of a radio broadcast or program. — *n.* **1.** A commercial broadcast or program. **2.** *Eng.* Short for COMMERCIAL TRAVELER. — **com·mer′cial·ly,** *adv.*

com·mer′cial·ism (kŏ·mûr′shăl·ĭz′m), *n.* Commercial spirit or method; mercantilism; also, a practice characteristic of commercial affairs. — **com·mer′cial·ist** (-ĭst), *n.* — **com·mer′cial·is′tic** (-ĭs′tĭk), *adj.*

com·mer′cial·ize (-īz), *v. t.* To render commercial; esp., to make profitable in a business way. — **com·mer′cial·i·za′tion** (-ĭ·zā′shŭn; -ī·zā′-), *n.*

commercial paper. *Banking.* Short-term negotiable instruments arising out of commercial transactions.

commercial traveler. A traveling representative of a manufacturing or mercantile house who solicits orders.

com′mie (kŏm′ĭ), *n.; pl.* COMMIES (-ĭz). [*often cap.*] A Communist party member or agent or a fellow traveler.

com′mi·na′tion (kŏm′ĭ·nā′shŭn), *n.* [F., fr. L. *comminatio*, fr. *comminari* to threaten, fr. *com-* + *minari* to threaten.] A threat or threatening; denunciation. — **com·min′a·to′ry** (kŏ·mĭn′ȧ·tō′rĭ; -tẽr·ĭ; kŏm′ĭ·nȧ-), *adj.*

com·min′gle (kŏ·mĭng′g′l), *v. t. & i.* To mingle. — **Syn.** See MIX.

com′mi·nute (kŏm′ĭ·nūt), *v. t.* [L. *comminutus*, past part., deriv. of *com-* + *minuere* to lessen.] To reduce to fine powder; pulverize; triturate. — **com′mi·nu′tion** (-nū′shŭn), *n.*

com·mis′er·ate (kŏ·mĭz′ẽr·āt), *v. t.* [L. *commiseratus*, past part., deriv. of *com-* + *miserari* to pity.] To feel or express sorrow or compassion for. — *v. i.* To condole or sympathize.

com·mis′er·a′tion (-ā′shŭn), *n.* Sorrow, or an expression of condolence, for the wants or distresses of another. — **Syn.** See PITY. — **com·mis′er·a′tive** (kŏ·mĭz′ẽr·ā′tĭv; -ȧ·tĭv), *adj.* — **-ly,** *adv.*

com′mis·sar′ (kŏm′ĭ·sär′), *n.* [F. *commissaire.*] A commissary; specif., a commissioner; in recent use [through Russ. *komissar*], esp., one of the ***People's Commissars***, or heads of the commissariats in the Union of Soviet Socialist Republics.

com′mis·sar′i·al (kŏm′ĭ·sâr′ĭ·ăl), *adj.* Of or pertaining to a commissary.

com′mis·sar′i·at (-sâr′ĭ·ăt), *n.* [F., a body of commissaries.] **1.** *Mil.* The organized system by which armies are supplied with food and daily necessaries; also, the body of officers charged with such service. **2.** A body of commissars; the office of commissar or of a commissar; in recent use [Russ. *komissariat*], esp., any of the departments of government within the U.S.S.R. **3.** Food supply.

com′mis·sar′y (kŏm′ĭ·sĕr′ĭ *or, esp. Brit.,* -sẽr·ĭ), *n.; pl.* -IES (-ĭz). [ML. *commissarius*, fr. L. *commissus*, past part. of *committere.* See COMMIT.] **1.** One to whom is committed some charge or office by a superior power. **2.** A department or store supplying equipment and provisions, as in a lumber camp. **3.** [F. *commissaire.*] In the French police, a superior officer under the mayor or the prefect of police. **4.** [Russ. *komissar.*] In Soviet Russia, a commissar. **5.** *Ch. of Eng.* An officer who represents a bishop, as in a distant part of the diocese. **6.** *Mil.* Formerly, an officer of the commissariat. — **com′mis·sar′y·ship,** *n.*

com·mis′sion (kŏ·mĭsh′ŭn), *n.* [F., fr. L. *commissio.* See COMMIT.] **1.** A formal written warrant or authority, granting certain powers and authorizing the performance of certain duties. **2.** Authorization or command made by or as if by such a warrant. **3.** Authority given to act for, or in behalf and in place of, another; also, a thing to be done by one as agent for another. **4.** A body of commissioners. **5.** The condition of being empowered by, or subject to, instructions or authority given, as by a warrant; — used esp. in the phrase ***in commission.*** **6.** Act of committing, doing, or performing; also, the thing committed or done. **7.** *Com.* The allowance made to a factor or agent for transacting business for another. **8.** *Mil. & Nav.* A certificate conferring military or naval rank and authority; also, the rank and command so conferred. Cf. WARRANT, *n.*, 3 **d.** — ***put, place,*** etc., ***a vessel in*** *or* ***into commission.*** *Naut.* To equip and man a vessel and send it out on service after it has been laid up. — ***put, place,*** etc., ***a vessel out of commission.*** *Naut.* To detach the officers and crew of a vessel and retire it from active service.
— *v. t.* **1.** To give a commission to; to appoint and authorize. **2.** *Naut.* To put in commission; — said of a ship.

com·mis′sion·aire′ (kŏ·mĭsh′ŭn·âr′), *n.* [F. *commissionnaire.*] **1.** One entrusted with a small commission; esp., an attendant, doorkeeper, or the like, in a public office, hotel, etc. **2.** One of a corps of pensioned soldiers, as in England, employed as doorkeepers, messengers, etc.

com·mis′sioned of′fi·cer (kŏ·mĭsh′ŭnd). *Mil. & Nav.* An officer who holds rank by virtue of a commission.

com·mis′sion·er (kŏ·mĭsh′ŭn·ẽr), *n.* **1.** A person who has received a warrant or commission to perform some office; a member of a commission. **2.** An officer having charge of some department or bureau of the public service; as, *commissioner* of education. — **com·mis′sion·er·ship′,** *n.*

commission merchant. One who buys or sells another's goods for a commission (def. 7).

commission plan. A method of municipal government in which legislative, executive, and administrative powers are in a small elective commission, each commissioner being directly in charge of one municipal department.

com′mis·sure (kŏm′ĭ·shŏŏr), *n.* [F., fr. L. *commissura* a joining together.] A joint, seam, or closure; the place where two bodies or parts meet and unite; juncture. — **com·mis′su·ral** (kŏ·mĭsh′ŏŏ·răl; kŏm′ĭ·sū′răl), *adj.*

com·mit′ (kŏ·mĭt′), *v. t.;* -MIT′TED; -MIT′TING. [L. *committere, -missum,* to connect, commit, fr. *com-* + *mittere* to send.] **1.** To give in trust; entrust; consign. **2.** Specif.: **a** To consign (for preservation); — chiefly in phrases; as, to *commit to memory, paper, print, writing,* etc. **b** To consign (for safekeeping or disposal), as by storing or by burial. **c** To consign to a place of detention, as a jail or an institution for the insane. **3.** To do; perpetrate, as a crime. **4.** To pledge; to bind; as, to *commit* oneself to a certain course. **5.** *Parl. Practice.* To refer, as to a committee, to be considered and reported. — **com·mit′ta·ble** (kŏ·mĭt′ȧ·b'l), *adj.*

Syn. **Commit, entrust** (*or* **intrust**), **confide, consign, relegate** mean to assign, as for custody or safekeeping. **Commit,** the widest term, always implies a transfer or delivery, as to a superior power, another person's charge, a place of custody; **entrust** is to commit with trust and confidence; **confide** is to entrust with reliance or assurance; **consign** usually suggests a transfer that removes a thing (or a person) from one's control; **relegate** implies a consigning to a particular class, position, or sphere, usually with the implication of getting rid of.

com·mit′ment (kŏ·mĭt′mĕnt), *n.* **1.** Act of committing; state of being committed; consignment, esp. of a person to prison. **2.** Act of doing or performing something; commission. **3.** A promise or pledge to do something. **4.** *Law.* A warrant for imprisonment; a mittimus. **5.** *Parl. Practice.* Act of referring a matter to a committee. **6.** *Stock Exch., U. S.* The purchase or sale of, or agreement to buy or sell, a security, usually on margin.

com·mit′tal (-ăl; -'l), *n.* Commitment; consignment.

com·mit′tee (kŏ·mĭt′ĭ), *n.* **1.** (*Brit. pron. now* kŏm′ĭ·tē′) A person to whom some trust or charge is committed. **2.** A body of persons appointed or elected to take action upon some matter or business, as by a court or legislature.

com·mit′tee·man (-măn), **com·mit′tee·wom′an** (-wo͝om′ăn), *n.* A member of a committee.

committee of the whole [**house**]. A committee, embracing all the members present, into which a deliberative body resolves itself for purposes of discussion under rules differing from those governing the general proceedings.

com·mix′ (kŏ·mĭks′), *v. t. & i.*; see MIX. To mix; blend.

com·mix′ture (-tūr), *n.* [L. *commixtura.*] Mixture.

com·mode′ (kŏ·mōd′), *n.* [F., fr. *commode* convenient, fr. L. *commodus,* fr. *com-* + *modus* measure, mode.] **1.** A lady's high ornamental cap in style about 1670–1730. **2.** *Furniture.* **a** A chest of drawers. **b** A stool or box to hold a chamber pot. **c** A movable sink or washstand, with cupboard underneath.

com·mo′di·ous (kŏ·mō′dĭ·ŭs), *adj.* **1.** Adapted to wants; serviceable. **2.** Spacious and comfortable, as a house. — **Syn.** Spacious, ample, capacious. — **com·mo′di·ous·ly,** *adv.* — **com·mo′di·ous·ness,** *n.*

com·mod′i·ty (-mŏd′ĭ·tĭ), *n.*; *pl.* -TIES (-tĭz). **1.** Quality or state of being commodious; also, that which is commodious; convenience; — now only in *Law.* **2.** That which affords convenience or profit, esp. in commerce, including everything movable that is bought and sold (goods, wares, merchandise, produce of land, etc.). **3.** An element of wealth; an economic good.

commodity dollar. A unit of a proposed form of currency (**commodity money**) whose gold value is arbitrarily determined by an index number obtained from the statistics covering the market prices of many basic commodities, and whose nominal gold content is periodically restated as the index number reflects changes in commodity prices.

com′mo·dore′ (kŏm′ō·dōr′; *form. also* kŏm′ō·dōr′; 70), *n.* [Earlier *commandore,* fr. F. *commandeur.* F. *commodore* is fr. E.] **1.** *Naval.* **a** In the British Navy, a captain commanding a squadron or a division of a fleet. The title is temporary and the grade is not recognized. **b** In the United States Navy, 1862–1899 and 1943 ff., an officer commanding a squadron, division, ship of the first class, naval station, etc., having a rank above a captain and below a rear admiral. **2.** *Naut.* **a** The senior captain of a line of ships. **b** The president or chief officer of a yacht club or the like.

com′mon (kŏm′ŭn), *adj.* [OF. *comun, commun,* fr. L. *communis.*] **1.** Belonging or pertaining to the community at large; public. **2.** Habitual or notorious; as, a *common* thief. **3.** Shared similarly by two or more individuals or species or by all the members of a group or kind. **4.** Of ordinary occurrence or appearance; familiar. **5.** General or prevalent; as, *common* knowledge. **6.** Hence: **a** Of the usual type. **b** Below the ordinary standards; second-rate. **c** *Colloq.* Of manners, language, etc., without refinement. **7.** Designating the more familiar type of anything; as, *common* salt. **8.** *Gram.* **a** Of case (**common case**), not inflected and so capable of being used as subject or object (as, *dog bites dog*). **b** Of gender (**common gender**), not definitely either masculine or feminine (as, *parent, child*). **c** Of number (**common number**), not definitely singular or plural (as, *any, alms*). **d** Of a noun or name (esp. **common noun**), naming any of a class of beings or things and, in specific use, capable of taking a limiting modifier; — opp. to *proper* (def. 11 **a**). See NOUN. **9.** *Math.* Belonging equally to two or more quantities; as, *common* denominator, divisor, multiple.

Syn. (1) See RECIPROCAL.

(2) **Common, ordinary, familiar, popular, vulgar** mean generally seen, known, used, thought, or the like. **Common** implies usual, everyday character or quality or frequency of occurrence, occasionally connoting inferiority; **ordinary** stresses accordance with the regular order or run of things; **familiar** stresses the fact of being generally known and easily recognized; **popular** and **vulgar** (as here compared) imply commonness as a result of acceptance of or prevalence among the masses of people.

— *n.* **1.** The people; community; — now only in pl. (= COMMONS, 1). **2.** Land held in common, as by a community. **3.** That which is general or usual; as, out of the *common.* **4.** *Law.* The right of taking a profit in the land of another, in common either with the owner or with other persons, as in **common of pasture,** the right to pasture animals on another's land, **common of piscary** (see PISCARY, 1).

com′mon·a·ble (kŏm′ŭn·ȧ·b'l), *adj.* **1.** Held in common. **2.** Allowed to pasture on public commons.

com′mon·age (-ĭj), *n.* **1.** The right of pasturing on a common; also, condition of being held in common, or that which is so held. **2.** The commonalty.

com′mon·al·ty (-ăl·tĭ), *n.*; *pl.* -TIES (-tĭz). **1.** Also **com′mon·al′i·ty** (-ăl′ĭ·tĭ), *n.* The common people; the commons. **2.** The general membership of a body corporate.

common carrier. A public transportation business, line, or system, or the person or company owning it.

common council. In some forms of municipal government, the representative (legislative) body, or its lower branch. See ALDERMAN, 2 **b.** — **common councilman.**

common denominator. A common multiple, usually the least, of the denominators of a number of fractions.

common divisor *or* **factor.** A number or quantity that divides two or more numbers or quantities without remainder.

com′mon·er (kŏm′ŭn·ẽr), *n.* **1.** A citizen; specif. [*cap.*], a member of the Court of Common Council of the City of London. **2.** One of the common people; one having no rank of nobility. **3.** In some English colleges, as Oxford, a student who is not dependent on a foundation for support. See PENSIONER, 3. **4.** Formerly, a member of the House of Commons.

common fraction. See FRACTION.

common law. **a** The general and ordinary law of a country or community. **b** The unwritten law (esp. of England) that receives its binding force from immemorial usage and universal reception; hence, any similarly developed system of jurisprudence. — **com′mon–law′,** *adj.*

com′mon–law′ mar′riage. *Law.* An agreement between a man and a woman to enter into the marriage relation without ecclesiastical or civil ceremony. In many jurisdictions it is not recognized.

com′mon·ly, *adv.* In a manner or degree that is common.

common measure *or* **time.** *Music.* Any duple or quadruple measure, especially $\frac{4}{4}$.

common multiple. *Math.* A multiple of each of two or more numbers, quantities, or expressions. The ***lowest*** (*or* ***least***) ***common multiple*** of several integers or polynomials is exactly divisible by each of them; — abbr. *L.C.M.*

com′mon·ness, *n.* Quality of being common.

com′mon·place′ (kŏm′ŭn·plās′; 2), *n.* **1.** A passage noted for ready reference; also, formerly, a collection of such passages. **2.** Anything common, ordinary, or trite; esp., a trite or customary remark. — **Syn.** Platitude, truism. — *adj.* Common; ordinary; trite. — **com′mon·place′ness,** *n.*

com′mons (kŏm′ŭnz), *n. pl.* **1.** The mass of the people, as disting. from the nobility; the commonalty. **2.** [*cap.*] Usually with *the,* the House of Commons. **3.** Provisions for a common table, as in colleges; hence, rations. **4.** Quarters, now usually a dining hall, esp. in a college.

common school. *U. S.* A public elementary school.

common sense. Sound, ordinary sense; good judgment. — **Syn.** See SENSE.

common stock. Ordinary capital stock not sharing the privileges of preferred stock. Cf. PREFERRED STOCK.

common time. = COMMON MEASURE.

com′mon·weal′ (kŏm′ŭn·wēl′), *n., or* **com′mon weal′.** **a** The general welfare. **b** *Archaic.* A commonwealth.

com′mon·wealth′ (-wĕlth′), *n.* **1.** *Now Rare.* The general welfare; commonweal. **2.** The body of people constituting a state or politically organized community; as, the British *Commonwealth* of Nations; hence, a state; as, the *Commonwealth* of Australia. **3.** [*cap.*] **a** *Eng. Hist.* The English state (1649–1660) as organized under Oliver Cromwell, his son Richard, and Parliament, to the Restoration. **b** *U. S.* Any of the individual states of the U. S. Massachusetts, Pennsylvania, Virginia, and Kentucky are officially called commonwealth. **c** *or* **Commonwealth of Nations.** Short for BRITISH COMMONWEALTH OF NATIONS.

com·mo′tion (kŏ·mō′shŭn), *n.* **1.** Disturbed or violent motion; agitation. **2.** A disturbance; a popular uprising.

com·move′ (kŏ·mo͞ov′), *v. t.* [From OF., fr. L. *commovere, -motum,* fr. *com-* + *movere* to move.] **1.** To disturb; agitate; unsettle. **2.** *Obs.* To urge or incite.

com′mu·nal (kŏm′ū·năl; kŏ·mū′năl; -n'l), *adj.* **1.** Of or pertaining to a commune or a society characterized by communes; hence, characteristic of a simple social life; as, *communal* poetry. **2.** Of or belonging to the common people. **3.** Owned in common; participated in jointly by a whole community. — **com′mu·nal·ly,** *adv.*

com′mu·nal·ism (kŏm′ū·năl·ĭz'm; kŏ·mū′-), *n.* **1.** A system in which communes or other small political units have large powers. **2.** Communism (sense 1). — **com′mu·nal·ist** (-ĭst), *n.* — **-is′tic** (-ĭs′tĭk), *adj.*

com′mu·nal·ize (-īz), *v. t.* To render communal. — **com′mu·nal·i·za′tion** (-ĭ·zā′shŭn; -ī·zā′-), *n.* — **com′mu·nal·iz′er** (-īz′ẽr), *n.*

Com′mu·nard (kŏm′ū·närd), *n.* [F.] One who supported or participated in the Commune of Paris in 1871.

com·mune′ (kŏ·mūn′; *in verse often* kŏm′ūn), *v. i.* [OF. *communer* to put in common.] **1.** To confer together; now, to converse intimately. **2.** *Eccl.* To receive Communion. — (kŏm′ūn), *n.* Communion; intercourse.

com′mune (kŏm′ūn), *n.* [F., fr. L. *communia,* neut. pl.] **1.** The commonalty; the common people; hence, *Hist.,* any of various bodies treated as a unit at law, as the peasantry sharing the common rights and property in a village community. **2.** The smallest administrative district in France; also, the inhabitants, or the government, of such a district; also, a similar district elsewhere, as in Belgium or Italy. **3.** In ethnology, etc., the typical society of a primitive class, tribe, etc.

Commune of Paris, the; *or* **the Commune.** *Fr. Hist.* **a** The government established in Paris (1792–94) by representatives chosen by the communes. **b** The insurrectionary government which took possession of Paris from March 18 to May 28, 1871.

com·mu′ni·ca·ble (kŏ·mū′nĭ·kȧ·b'l), *adj.* [F.] **1.** Capable of communicating or of being communicated or imparted; as, *communicable* knowledge, diseases. **2.** *Archaic.* Communicative. — **com·mu′ni·ca·bil′i·ty** (-bĭl′ĭ·tĭ), **com·mu′ni·ca·ble·ness,** *n.* — **com·mu′ni·ca·bly** (-blĭ), *adv.*

com·mu′ni·cant (-kănt), *n.* **1.** One who partakes of, or is entitled to partake of, Communion; a church member. **2.** One who communicates. — *adj.* Communicating.

com·mu′ni·cate (-kāt), *v. t.* [L. *communicatus,* past part. of *communicare* to communicate, fr. *communis* common.] **1.** To impart; convey; as, to *communicate* a disease. **2.** To make known; as, to *communicate* a secret. — *v. i.* **1.** To partake of the Lord's Supper. **2.** To hold or afford communication; to converse; also, to be connected; join; as, rooms that *communicate.* — **com·mu′ni·ca′tor** (-kā′tẽr), *n.*

Syn. **Communicate, impart** mean to convey information, a quality, or the like. **Communicate** stresses making common to all that which is given usually by or to one; **impart** stresses sharing with another or others what is primarily one's own.

com·mu′ni·ca′tion (-kā′shŭn), *n.* **1.** Act or fact of communicating. **2.** Intercourse by words, letters, or messages; interchange of thoughts or opinions. **3.** That which is communicated; a verbal or written message. **4.** Act, power, or means of communicating or passing from place to place; specif.: *pl.* **a** A system, as of telephone, telegraph, etc., for communicating. **b** A system of routes for moving troops, supplies, etc., in military operations.

com·mu′ni·ca′tive (kŏ·mū′nĭ·kā′tĭv; -kȧ·tĭv), *adj.* **1.** Inclined to communicate; talkative. **2.** Of or relating to communication. — **com·mu′ni·ca′tive·ly,** *adv.* — **com·mu′ni·ca′tive·ness,** *n.*

com·mun′ion (kŏ·mūn′yŭn), *n.* **1.** Act of sharing; community of condition or relation; participation. **2.** Mutual intercourse; esp., intimate intercourse. **3.** A body of Christians having one common faith and discipline; as, the Anglican *Communion.* **4.** [*cap.*] The sacrament of the Eucharist; also, the service (**communion service** or, in Anglican churches, **Holy Communion**) or the part of the Mass in which the consecrated elements are partaken of.

com·mu′ni·qué′ (kŏ·mū′nĭ·kā′ *or, esp. Brit.,* kŏ·mū′nĭ·kā), *n.; pl.* -QUÉS (-kāz′; -kāz). [F.] A communication or piece of information given out officially.

com′mu·nism (kŏm′ū·nĭz′m), *n.* [F. *communisme.*] **1.** Any system of social organization in which goods are held in common; as, Brook Farm was an experiment in *communism.* **2.** A doctrine and program based upon revolutionary Marxian socialism as developed by N. Lenin and the Bolshevik party, which interprets history as a relentless class war eventually to result everywhere in the victory of the proletariat and establishment of the dictatorship of the proletariat, and which calls for regulation of all social, economic, and cultural activities through the agency of a single authoritarian party as the leader of the proletariat in all countries so as to achieve its ultimate objectives, a classless society and establishment of a world union of socialist soviet republics. Cf. COMMUNIST PARTY, DIALECTICAL MATERIALISM.

com′mu·nist (-nĭst), *adj.* **1.** Of or pertaining to communism or communists. **2.** [*cap.*] Of or belonging to the Communist party. — *n.* **1.** One who believes in communism. **2.** [*cap.*] A member of the Communist party in any country. **3.** *Hist.* [*cap.*] A Communard. — **Syn.** See SOCIALIST.

com′mu·nis′tic (-nĭs′tĭk), *adj.* **1.** Of or pertaining to communism or communists. **2.** Tending toward or influenced by communism. **3.** *Hist.* Of or pertaining to or supporting the Commune of Paris (1871). — **com′mu·nis′ti·cal·ly** (-tĭ·kăl·ĭ), *adv.*

Communist party. **1.** The sole Soviet party organized as the Bolshevik party by N. Lenin for leadership of the proletariat in its struggle to victory, which has controlled the U.S.S.R. and striven to promote communism throughout the world. **2.** Any national political party adhering to communism and accepting the leadership of the Soviet party.

com·mu′ni·ty (kŏ·mū′nĭ·tĭ), *n.; pl.* -TIES (-tĭz). **1.** A body of people having common organization or interests or living in the same place under the same laws; hence, an assemblage of animals or plants living in a common home under similar conditions. **2.** Society at large; the people in general; restrictedly, the people of a particular region, or the region itself. **3.** Joint ownership or participation; as, a *community* of goods; *community* of interests. **4.** Common character; likeness. **5.** *Ecol.* An aggregate of organisms with mutual relations; — applied to any unit of undetermined rank, or as a synonym for a more specific group.

community chest. *U. S. & Can.* A general fund, accumulated from individual subscriptions, to defray the demands on a community for charity and social welfare.

com′mu·nize (kŏm′ū·nīz), *v. t.* **1.** To subject to common property rights; to make common. **2.** To bring into accord with communism. — **com′mu·ni·za′tion** (-nĭ·zā′shŭn; -nī·zā′-), *n.*

com·mut′a·ble (kŏ·mūt′ȧ·b′l), *adj.* Capable of being commuted. — **com·mut′a·bil′i·ty** (-bĭl′ĭ·tĭ), *n.*

com′mu·tate (kŏm′ū·tāt), *v. t. Elec.* To turn or direct (a current), esp. so as to form a current continuous as to direction. Cf. COMMUTATOR.

com′mu·ta′tion (kŏm′ū·tā′shŭn), *n.* **1.** A substitution, as of a lesser thing for a greater; specif., the substitution of one form of payment for another. **2.** That which is given or paid in substitution. **3.** *Colloq., U. S.* The act of traveling regularly on a commutation ticket. **4.** *Law.* Change of a penalty to a lesser punishment by the pardoning power. — **com·mu′ta·tive** (kŏ·mū′tȧ·tĭv; kŏm′ū·tā′tĭv), *adj.*

commutation ticket. A ticket for transportation, as by a railroad company, at a reduced rate for a certain number of trips, or for daily trips, between specified places. Cf. SEASON TICKET.

com′mu·ta′tor (kŏm′ū·tā′tẽr), *n. Elec.* **a** A device for reversing the direction of an electric current. **b** An attachment for the armature of a dynamo for commutating or rectifying the induced currents in the armature conductors, or in a motor for conveying the current to the conductors. See DYNAMO, *Illust.*

com·mute′ (kŏ·mūt′), *v. t.* [L. *commutare, -mutatum,* fr. *com-* + *mutare* to change.] **1.** To exchange, interchange, or substitute. **2.** To substitute for (one exaction or due, as a payment, penalty, etc.) another that is lighter or less; as, to *commute* a death sentence to life imprisonment. **3.** To pay in a lump sum instead of part by part; as, to *commute* an annuity into a capital sum. **4.** *Elec.* To commutate. — *v. i.* **1.** To give compensation; as, allowed to *commute* for penances; also, to serve as a substitute. **2.** To travel by use of a commutation ticket, esp. daily to and from a city. — **com·mut′er** (-mūt′ẽr), *n.*

co′mose (kō′mōs), *adj.* [L. *comosus* hairy, fr. *coma* hair.] *Bot.* Bearing a coma, or tuft of soft hairs; comate.

com·pact′ (kŏm·păkt′; 2), *adj.* [L. *compactus,* past part. of *compingere* to join, fr. *com-* + *pangere* to fix.] **1.** Composed or made; — with *of.* **2.** Closely united or packed; closely knit; solid; dense; also, lying in a narrow compass or arranged so as to economize space; close. **3.** Brief; pithy; not diffuse. — **Syn.** See CLOSE. — *v. t.* **1.** To press closely together; consolidate. **2.** To form by connecting firmly. — **com·pact′ly,** *adv.* — **com·pact′ness,** *n.*

com′pact (kŏm′păkt), *n.* A small vanity case for the purse, containing face powder, and often (***double compact***) rouge.

com′pact (kŏm′păkt; *form. also* kŏm·păkt′), *n.* [L. *compactum,* fr. *compacisci,* past part. *compactus,* to make an agreement with.] An agreement between parties.

com·pan′ion (kŏm·păn′yŭn), *n.* [OF. *compagnon,* deriv. of L. *com-* + *panis* bread.] **1.** An associate; comrade. **2.** *Obs.* A fellow; — in contempt. **3.** One of a pair or set of like things. **4.** A person employed to live or travel with another and act in the capacity of a friend. — *v. t.* To accompany. — **com·pan′ion·less,** *adj.*

com·pan′ion, *n.* [D. *kompanje,* fr. OF. *compagne.*] *Naut.* **a** The hood or covering at the top of a companionway; — called also **companion hatch** *or* **head.** **b** A companionway.

com·pan′ion·a·ble (-ȧ·b′l), *adj.* Fitted to be a companion; agreeable; sociable. — **com·pan′ion·a·bil′i·ty** (-bĭl′ĭ·tĭ), **com·pan′ion·a·ble·ness,** *n.* — **com·pan′ion·a·bly,** *adv.*

com·pan′ion·ate (-ăt), *adj.* Shared in as by companions.

companionate marriage. A proposed form of marriage, in which legalized birth control would be practiced, the divorce of childless couples by mutual consent permitted, and neither party would have any claim on the other.

com·pan′ion·ship, *n.* Fellowship; association.

com·pan′ion·way′ (kŏm·păn′yŭn·wā′), *n. Naut.* **a** A set of steps leading from the deck to a cabin or saloon below. **b** The space occupied by these steps.

com′pa·ny (kŭm′pȧ·nĭ), *n.; pl.* -NIES (-nĭz). For construction with sing. or pl. vb., see COLLECTIVE NOUN. [OF. *compagnie,* fr. *compagne* company, fr. (assumed) VL. *compania.* See 1st COMPANION.] **1.** Fellowship; society; friendly intercourse; also, companions; associates. **2.** An assemblage of persons; band; retinue. **3.** An association of persons for a joint purpose, esp. for carrying on a business. **4.** Those members of a partnership firm whose names do not appear in the firm name; as, John Doe and *Company.* Abbr. *Co.* **5.** A band of musical or dramatic performers. **6.** *Colloq.* Guests or visitors. **7.** Society; specif., a social gathering. **8.** *Mil.* **a** A body of soldiers. **b** Specif., a unit, esp. of infantry, consisting basically of a headquarters and two or more platoons. It is the normal command of a captain. **9.** *Naut.* The crew of a ship, including the officers. — **Syn.** Party, band, troop. — *adj.* Of or pert. to company or a company; as, *company* manners; *company* stores; also, concerned or dealing with companies; as, *company* law. — *v. t. & i.;* -NIED (-nĭd); -NY·ING. *Archaic.* To accompany or go with; to associate.

company union. An association of employees of a single firm for advancing their common interests, in the United States specifically one that is without union affiliation and is dominated by the employer.

com′pa·ra·ble (kŏm′pȧ·rȧ·b′l), *adj.* Capable of being compared; worthy of comparison. — **com′pa·ra·ble·ness, com′pa·ra·bil′i·ty** (-bĭl′ĭ·tĭ), *n.* — **com′pa·ra·bly,** *adv.*

com·par′a·tive (kŏm·păr′ȧ·tĭv), *adj.* **1.** Of or pertaining to comparison. **2.** Studied systematically by comparison of phenomena; as, *comparative* literature. **3.** Relative; not absolute. **4.** Comparable to, but not quite, the thing itself; as, *comparative* comfort. **5.** *Gram.* Of an adjective or adverb, expressing an increased (or, with *less,* a diminished) degree or amount of the quality, manner, etc., denoted by the simple form. See COMPARISON, 2. Abbr. *comp.* or *compar.* — *n. Gram.* The comparative degree or form. — **com·par′a·tive·ly,** *adv.*

com′pa·ra′tor (kŏm′pȧ·rā′tẽr; kŏm·păr′ȧ·tẽr), *n.* [L., a comparer.] An instrument for comparing anything with a like thing or with a standard measure.

com·pare′ (kŏm·pâr′), *v. t.* [F. *comparer,* fr. L. *comparare.* See COMPEER.] **1.** To represent as similar; to liken. **2.** To examine the character or qualities of, for the purpose of discovering their resemblances or differences. **3.** *Gram.* To modify according to the degrees of comparison; to state the positive, comparative, and superlative forms of. See COMPARISON, 2. — *v. i.* **1.** To be like or equal; to admit, or be worthy of, comparison. **2.** To vie; to assume a likeness or equality.

☞ One object is compared *with* another when set side by side with it in order to show their relative value or excellence; *to* another when it is formally represented as like it; as, Pope *compares* Homer *with* Vergil; he *compares* Homer *to* the Nile in boundless flow of riches.

Syn. **Compare, contrast, collate** mean to set side by side in order to show likenesses and differences. **Compare** implies as its aim the showing of relative values or excellences by bringing out characteristic qualities, whether similar or divergent; **contrast** implies as its aim an emphasis upon the differences; **collate** implies minute and critical examination in order to note points of agreement or divergence.

— *n.* Comparison; as, beyond *compare.*

com·par′i·son (kŏm·păr′ĭ·sŭn; -s′n), *n.* **1.** Act of comparing, or state of being compared; a relative estimate; also, state, quality, or relation admitting of being compared; as, points of *comparison.* **2.** *Gram.* The modification, by inflection or otherwise, of an adjective or adverb to denote degrees of quality, quantity, or relation. The three degrees of comparison are: *positive,* the simple form of the adjective or adverb; *comparative* (used in comparing two things), expressing a higher degree or increased amount of what is denoted by the simple form; *superlative* (used in comparing more than two things but sometimes, colloquially, only two things), expressing the highest degree or amount of what is denoted by the simple form.

☞ Most adjectives of one syllable, those of two syllables ending in *-er, -le, -ow,* or *-y,* and the most familiar of those having two syllables with stress on the second, usually form the comparative and superlative by adding *-er* and *-est* (slow, slower, slowest; dirty, dirtier, dirtiest; remote, remoter, remotest). Other adjectives, esp. those belonging to literary diction, and most adverbs, usually form the comparative and superlative by using *more* and *most* before the positive (beautiful, more beautiful, most beautiful). Some adjectives and adverbs have irregular forms of comparison (good, better, best; well, better, best). Inverted comparison, expressing decrease or diminution of what is denoted by the positive, is often made by use of *less* and *least* before the positive (beautiful, less beautiful, least beautiful).

3. *Rhet.* A figure by which one person or thing is compared to another.

com·part′ (kŏm·pärt′), *v. t.* [OF. or L.; OF. *compartir,* fr. L. *compartiri,* fr. *com-* + *partiri* to share.] To mark out into parts, specif., *Arch.,* in accordance with a plan.

‖**com·par′ti·men′to** (kŏm·pär′tē·mān′tō), *n.; pl.* -MENTI (-tē). [Ital.] One of the 18 divisions or departments in which the 90 provinces of modern Italy are usually grouped.

com·part′ment (kŏm·pärt′mĕnt), *n.* [F. *compartiment,* fr. It. *compartimento.*] One of the parts into which an enclosed space is divided; a separate division or section.

com′pass (kŭm′pȧs), *n.* [OF. *compas,* fr. *compasser* to go round, deriv. of L. *com-* + *passus* a step, pace.] **1.** The enclosing limit, boundary, or circumference of any area. **2.** An enclosed space; area; hence, limits; reach, sweep, or capacity. **3.** *Archaic.* A circuit; circuitous course. **4.** An instrument for describing circles, transferring measurements, etc., consisting, in its simple form, of two pointed branches, or legs, joined at the top by a pivot; — called also *compasses, pair of compasses,* or *dividers.* **5.** A device for determining directions by means of a magnetic needle or group of needles swinging on a free pivot and pointing to the magnetic north; — called specif. ***mariner's compass.*** See GYROCOMPASS; cf. VARIATION, *Illust.* **6.** *Music.* The range of tones within the capacity of a voice or instrument. — **Syn.** See CIRCUMFERENCE. — *adj.* Circular; curved; specif., semicircular. — *v. t.* [OF. *compasser* to arrange, regulate, ponder.] **1.** To devise or contrive (a purpose); to plot. **2.** To make the circuit of. **3.** To enclose on all sides; to surround. **4.** To reach; hence, to bring about; to accomplish. **5.** *Obs.* To curve. — **Syn.** See REACH. — **com′pass·a·ble,** *adj.*

compass card. The circular card of a mariner's compass (see COMPASS, 5), on which are marked the 32 points of direction and the 360 degrees of the circle.

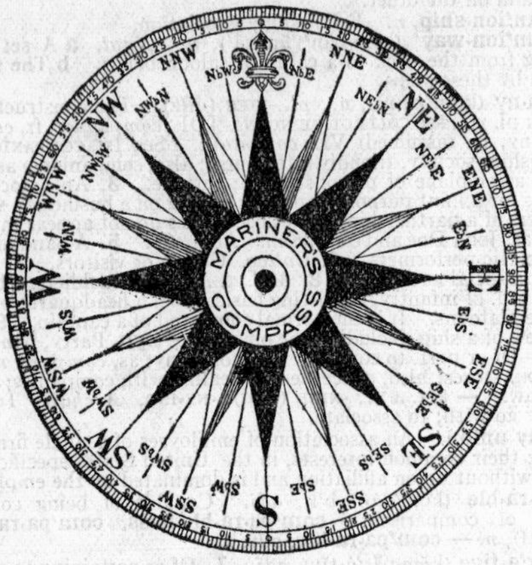

Compass Card.

com·pas′sion (kŏm·păsh′ŭn), *n.* [OF., fr. LL. *compassio*, fr. *compati* to have compassion, fr. *com-* + *pati* to bear, suffer.] Sorrow or pity excited by the distress or misfortunes of another; sympathy. — **Syn.** See PITY.

com·pas′sion·ate (-ĭt), *adj.* **1.** Disposed to pity; sympathetic. **2.** *Obs.* Inviting pity; pitiable. — **Syn.** Sympathetic, tender, responsive. — (-āt), *v. t.* To pity. — **com·pas′sion·ate·ly,** *adv.* — **com·pas′sion·ate·ness,** *n.*

compass plant. Any plant (as the rosinweed *Silphium laciniatum*) whose leaves or branches are so disposed on the axis as to indicate the cardinal points of the compass.

com·pat′i·bil′i·ty (kŏm·păt′ĭ·bĭl′ĭ·tĭ), *n.* Quality or power of being compatible; as, a *compatibility* of tempers.

com·pat′i·ble (kŏm·păt′ĭ·b'l), *adj.* [F., deriv. of L. *compati*. See COMPASSION.] **1.** Capable of coexisting in harmony; — usually followed by *with*. **2.** *Television.* Designating or pert. to a system in which color broadcasts may be received in black and white on receivers not specially equipped for color reception. — **Syn.** See CONSONANT. — **com·pat′i·ble·ness,** *n.* — **com·pat′i·bly,** *adv.*

com·pa′tri·ot (kŏm·pā′trĭ·ŭt; -păt′rĭ·ŭt), *n.* [F. *compatriote*, fr. LL. *compatriota*, fr. *com-* + *patriota* a native.] A fellow countryman. — *adj.* Of the same country.

com·peer′ (kŏm·pēr′; kŏm′pēr), *n.* [From F., fr. L. *compar*, fr. *com-* + *par* equal.] An equal; a peer; also, a companion. — (kŏm·pēr′) *v. t. Obs.* To be equal with; to match.

com·pel′ (kŏm·pĕl′), *v. t.*; -PELLED′ (-pĕld′); -PEL′LING. [From OF., fr. L. *compellere, -pulsum*, to drive together, compel, fr. *com-* + *pellere* to drive.] **1.** To drive or urge with force; to constrain. **2.** To take by force; to exact or extort. **3.** To drive together or gather in a crowd. **4.** To force to yield; to overpower. — **Syn.** See FORCE. — **com·pel′la·ble,** *adj.* — **com·pel′ler,** *n.*

com′pel·la′tion (kŏm′pĕ·lā′shŭn), *n.* [L. *compellatio*, fr. *compellare* to accost.] Act of addressing or calling upon; style of salutation; an appellation.

com·pel′lent (kŏm·pĕl′ĕnt), *adj.* Compelling; forceful.

com′pend (kŏm′pĕnd), *n.* A compendium.

com·pen′di·ous (kŏm·pĕn′dĭ·ŭs), *adj.* [L. *compendiosus*.] Containing the substance in a small compass; abridged; summarized; — esp. of literary work. — **Syn.** See CONCISE. — **com·pen′di·ous·ly,** *adv.* — **com·pen′di·ous·ness,** *n.*

com·pen′di·um (-ŭm), *n.*; *pl.* -DIUMS (-ŭmz), -DIA (-ȧ). [L., that which is weighed, saved, or shortened, a short way, fr. *compendere* to weigh, fr. *com-* + *pendere* to weigh.] A brief summary of the main heads, main principles, or substance, of a larger work or system.

Syn. **Compendium, syllabus, digest, survey, sketch, précis, aperçu** mean a treatment of a subject in brief compass but, unlike the words discriminated at ABRIDGMENT, do not stress condensation from a previous work, though some of them sometimes imply this. **Compendium** designates a work which gathers together and presents most briefly all the details essential to a comprehensive knowledge of a subject; **syllabus** applies to one which gives the material necessary for a view of the whole (as a course, a series of lectures) and an understanding of its drift or pattern; **digest,** to a body of legal information, or the like, gathered from many sources and arranged for ready reference; **survey,** to any brief but comprehensive treatment of a field of knowledge; **sketch** suggests a similar treatment, but slighter and more tentative; **précis,** sometimes used as equal to *abstract* (see ABRIDGMENT), more often applies to a brief, clean-cut statement of essential facts or points; **aperçu** applies to a sketch that ignores details, giving only a quick impression of the whole.

com·pen′sa·ble (kŏm·pĕn′sȧ·b'l), *adj.* [F.] That is to be compensated or entitles to compensation.

com′pen·sate (kŏm′pĕn·sāt; -pĕn·sāt; *form.* kŏm·pĕn′sāt), *v. t.* [L. *compensatus*, past part. of *compensare*, prop., to weigh several things with one another, fr. *compendere* to weigh.] **1.** To be equivalent to; to make up for. **2.** To make equal return to; to remunerate; to requite suitably. **3.** To stabilize in purchasing power by varying the gold content to counteract change in price level; as, a *compensated* dollar. **4.** *Mech.* To provide with means of counteracting variation; to counteract (the variation or varying parts). — *v. i.* To supply an equivalent or a return; to make amends; — usually with *for*.

Syn. (1) **Compensate, countervail, balance, offset** mean to make up for that which is excessive, deficient, harmful, helpful, etc., in another. **Compensate** implies a making amends for or supplying a recompense for whatever has been suffered or lost through another; **countervail** suggests the counteraction of a bad or harmful influence or of damage suffered through it; **balance** implies the harmonious adjustment of two or more things that are contrary or opposed so that no one outweighs the other or others or can exert a harmful influence; **offset** implies the neutralization of one thing's good or evil effect by something that exerts a contrary effect. (2) See PAY.

com′pen·sat′ing gear (kŏm′pĕn·sāt′ĭng; kŏm′pĕn-). *Mach.* Differential gear.

com′pen·sa′tion (kŏm′pĕn·sā′shŭn; kŏm′pĕn-), *n.* **1.** Act or principle of compensating; also, an instance of this. **2.** That which compensates for loss or privation; recompense. **3.** *Biol. & Med.* Correction of an organic inferiority or loss, by hypertrophy or increased functioning of another organ or unimpaired parts of the same organ. **4.** *Optics.* **a** Adjustment of the retardation of one light ray with respect to that of another. **b** = COMPENSATOR, 3. **5.** *Psychol.* The act or result of seeking a substitute for something unacceptable or unattainable. — **com′pen·sa′tion·al,** *adj.*

com′pen·sa′tive (kŏm′pĕn·sā′tĭv; kŏm′pĕn-; kŏm·pĕn′sȧ·tĭv), *adj.* Affording compensation. — **com′pen·sa′tive,** *n.*

com′pen·sa′tor (kŏm′pĕn·sā′tẽr; kŏm′pĕn-), *n.* **1.** One who or that which compensates. **2.** *Elec.* A transformer in which the primary and secondary are combined as a single coil. **3.** *Optics.* A plate or combination of prisms for equalizing the retardation of two light rays.

com·pen′sa·to′ry (kŏm·pĕn′sȧ·tō′rĭ *or, esp. Brit.,* kŏm·pĕn′sȧ·tẽr·ĭ *or* kŏm′pĕn·sā′tẽr·ĭ), *adj.* Serving for or to give compensation; making amends; making up for loss.

com·pete′ (kŏm·pēt′), *v. i.* [F. and L.; F. *compéter*, fr. L. *competere*, *-petitum*, to compete for, fr. *com-* + *petere* to seek.] To contend emulously; to contend in rivalry, as for a prize or in business.

com′pe·tence (kŏm′pē·tĕns), *n.* **1.** Means sufficient for the necessaries of life; sufficiency without excess. **2.** Quality of being competent; fitness; ability.

com′pe·ten·cy (-tĕn·sĭ), *n.* Competence.

com′pe·tent (-tĕnt), *adj.* [F. and L.; F. *compétent*, fr. L. *competens*, pres. part. of *competere*. See COMPETE.] **1.** Answering to all requirements; adequate; capable; fit. **2.** *Chiefly Legal.* Rightfully belonging; appertaining; — followed by *to*. **3.** *Law.* Legally qualified or capable. — **Syn.** See ABLE (**Ant.** incompetent) : SUFFICIENT. — **com′pe·tent·ly,** *adv.*

com′pe·ti′tion (kŏm′pē·tĭsh′ŭn), *n.* **1.** Act of competing; emulous contest; rivalry. **2.** A contest between rivals; a match. **3.** *Com. & Econ.* The effort of two or more parties, acting independently, to secure the custom of a third party by offering most favorable terms. — **com·pet′i·to′ry** (kŏm·pĕt′ĭ·tō′rĭ *or, esp. Brit.,* -tẽr·ĭ), *adj.*

com·pet′i·tive (kŏm·pĕt′ĭ·tĭv), *adj.* Of or pertaining to competition; based on, used in, or resulting from competition. — **com·pet′i·tive·ly,** *adv.* — **com·pet′i·tive·ness,** *n.*

com·pet′i·tor (-tẽr), *n.* **1.** One who competes; as, *competitors* in a race; a rival. **2.** Specif., one who is engaged in selling (or buying) goods or services in the same market as another. — **com·pet′i·tress** (-trĕs; -trĭs), *n.*

com′pi·la′tion (kŏm′pĭ·lā′shŭn *or, esp. Brit.,* kŏm′pī-), *n.* **1.** Act or process of compiling. **2.** That which is compiled; esp., a book composed of materials gathered from other books or documents.

com·pile′ (kŏm·pīl′), *v. t.* [OF. *compiler*, fr. L. *compilare* to gather together, plunder.] **1.** To collect (literary materials) into a volume. **2.** To compose out of materials from other documents. — **com·pil′er** (-pīl′ẽr), *n.*

com·pla′cence (kŏm·plā′sĕns; -s'ns), *n.* Also **com·pla′cen·cy** (-sĕn·sĭ; -s'n·sĭ). **1.** Contentment; satisfaction; esp., self-satisfaction. **2.** A source of gratification. **3.** *Now Rare.* Good nature; affability; complaisance.

com·pla′cent (-sĕnt; -s'nt), *adj.* [L. *complacens* very pleasing, pres. part. of *complacere*, fr. *com-* + *placere* to please.] **1.** Satisfied; esp., self-satisfied. **2.** Feeling or showing complaisance. — **com·pla′cent·ly,** *adv.*

com·plain′ (kŏm·plān′), *v. i.* [OF. *complaindre*, fr. LL., fr. *com-* + L. *plangere* to strike, beat the breast in grief, lament.] **1.** To give utterance to grief, pain, discontent, etc. **2.** To make a formal accusation or charge. — **com·plain′er,** *n.* — **com·plain′ing·ly,** *adv.*

com·plain′ant (-ănt), *n.* *Law.* The party who makes the complaint in an action or proceeding; plaintiff.

com·plaint′ (kŏm·plānt′), *n.* [OF. *complainte*.] **1.** Expression of grief, pain, or resentment. **2.** That concerning which one complains. **3.** An ailment· sickness. **4.** *Law.* A formal allegation against a party. — **Syn.** Disease, ailment, distemper.

com·plai′sance (kŏm·plā′zăns; -săns; kŏm′plā·zăns′), *n.* [F.] Disposition to please or oblige; affability.

com·plai′sant (kŏm·plā′zănt; -sănt; kŏm′plā·zănt′), *adj.* [F., pres. part. of *complaire* to acquiesce as a favor, fr. L. *complacere*. See COMPLACENT.] Disposed to please; affable; obliging. — **Syn.** See AMIABLE.

com·plect′ (kŏm·plĕkt′), *v. t.* [L. *complecti*. See COMPLEX, *adj.*] To plait together; interweave.

com·plect′ed (-plĕk′tĕd; -tĭd), *adj.* *Dial., U.S.* Complexioned; — usually in compounds; as, dark-*complected*.

com′ple·ment (kŏm′plē·mĕnt), *n.* [F. or L.; F., fr. L. *complementum*. See COMPLETE.] **1.** That which fills up or completes; as: **a** The quantity or number required to fill a thing or make it complete. **b** That which is required to supply a deficiency; one of two mutually completing parts. **2.** Full quantity, number, or amount; a complete set. **3.** *Gram.* Any added word or words by which a predication is made complete (they made Saul *king*). **4.** *Immunol.* The thermolabile substance in serum and protoplasm which, in combination with immune bodies, causes the destruction of bacteria, foreign blood corpuscles, etc. **5.** *Math.* The amount of angle or arc by which a given angle or arc falls short of 90°. Cf. SUPPLEMENT, *n.*, 3. **6.** *Music.* The interval required with a given interval to complete the octave. **7.** *Naut.* The whole force or personnel of a vessel. — (-mĕnt) *v. t.* **1.** To supply a lack. **2.** *Obs.* To compliment. — *v. i. Obs.* To compliment.

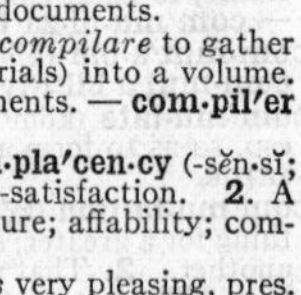

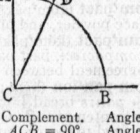

Complement. Angle *ACB* = 90°. Angle *ACD* and arc *AD* are the complements respectively of angle *DCB* and arc *DB*, and vice versa.

com′ple·men′tal (-mĕn′tăl; -t'l), *adj.* **1.** Of the nature of, or pert. to, a complement. **2.** *Obs.* **a** Accomplished. **b** Ceremonious; complimentary. — **com′ple·men′tal·ly,** *adv.*

com′ple·men′ta·ry (-tȧ·rĭ), *adj.* **1.** Serving to fill out or complete.

2. Mutually supplying each other's lack. 3. Designating or pertaining to either of a pair of contrasting colors which, when mixed in proper proportions, give a neutral color, or gray.

complementary angles *or* **arcs.** *Math.* Two angles or arcs whose sum is a right angle or quadrant.

complement fixation. *Immunol.* The binding or fixation of complement, specif. to the compound formed by the union of an antigen and antibody, as in certain tests for syphilis and gonorrhea.

com·plete′ (kŏm·plēt′; 2), *adj.* [L. *completus*, past part. of *complere* to fill up, fr. *com-* + *plere* to fill.] 1. Filled up; with no part lacking. 2. Brought to an end; concluded. 3. *Archaic.* Perfectly equipped or skilled. 4. Fully realized; thorough; as, *complete* combustion. 5. *Bot.* Of a flower, having all the parts belonging to it or to the typical form; — opp. to *incomplete*. — **Syn.** See FULL. — (kŏm·plēt′), *v. t.* To bring to entirety or perfection; to finish. — **Syn.** See CLOSE. — **com·plete′ly,** *adv.* — **com·plete′ness,** *n.* — **com·ple′tive** (-plē′tĭv), *adj.*

com·ple′tion (-plē′shŭn), *n.* 1. Act or process of making complete. 2. State of being complete; fulfillment.

com·plex′ (kŏm·plĕks′; kŏm′plĕks; 2), *adj.* [L. *complexus*, past part. of *complecti* to entwine around, comprise, fr. *com-* + *plectere* to twist.] 1. Composed of two or more parts; not simple; as, a *complex* being; a *complex* sentence (see SENTENCE). 2. *Gram.* Of a word: (1) Consisting of a base and one or more bound forms (*unmanly*). (2) Consisting of two or more bound forms (*conceive*). 3. Complicated; intricate. — **com·plex′ly,** *adv.* — **com·plex′ness,** *n.*

Syn. Complex, complicated, intricate, involved, knotty mean marked by confusingly interrelated parts or elements. Complex suggests not so much a fault as a necessary quality that makes for difficulty; complicated suggests great difficulty in understanding, solving, or explaining; intricate implies such interlacing of parts that it is almost impossible to follow; involved implies extreme complication and disorder; knotty not only implies complication but also entanglements which make for increased difficulty in solution.

com′plex (kŏm′plĕks), *n.* 1. A whole made up of complicated or interrelated parts. 2. *Psychol.* **a** A system of desires and memories which in disguised form exerts a dominating influence upon the personality; as, an ***inferiority complex,*** a morbid sense of one's own inferiority, shown by undue timidity or, sometimes, undue aggressiveness; ***superiority complex,*** an exaggerated conviction of one's own superiority; ***Oedipus complex,*** a complex involving an early and primary attachment to the parent of opposite sex, with hostility to the other (often restricted to its appearance in males); ***Electra complex,*** the Oedipus complex in females (so called because of Electra's love for her father). **b** Loosely, an exaggerated fear of or interest in some subject or situation; as, the communist *complex*.

com′plex frac′tion. See FRACTION.

com·plex′ion (kŏm·plĕk′shŭn), *n.* [OF., fr. L. *complexio*. See COMPLEX, *adj.*] 1. *Obs. exc. Hist.* The combination in a certain proportion of the qualities *hot, cold, moist, dry,* supposed in medieval times to determine the nature of a body, plant, etc. 2. Constitution or habit of body or mind; temperament; nature; — now chiefly fig.; as, the *complexion* of contemporary thought. 3. The hue or appearance of the skin, esp. of the face. 4. General appearance or aspect; as, the threatening *complexion* of the sky. — **Syn.** See DISPOSITION.

com·plex′ioned (-shŭnd), *adj.* Of a certain complexion; — chiefly in combination; as, dark-*complexioned*.

com·plex′i·ty (kŏm·plĕk′sĭ·tĭ), *n.; pl.* -TIES (-tĭz). 1. State of being complex; intricacy. 2. Anything complex; a complication.

com·pli′a·ble (kŏm·plī′ȧ·b'l), *adj.* Compliant. — **com·pli′a·ble·ness,** *n.* — **com·pli′a·bly,** *adv.*

com·pli′ance (-ăns), *n.* Also **com·pli′an·cy** (-ăn·sĭ). 1. Act or practice of complying; yielding, as to a desire, demand, or proposal. 2. A disposition to yield to others.

com·pli′ant (-ănt), *adj.* Complying or wont to comply; complaisant; submissive. — **com·pli′ant·ly,** *adv.*

com′pli·ca·cy (kŏm′plĭ·kȧ·sĭ), *n.; pl.* -CIES (-sĭz). State or quality of being complicated; a complicated thing.

com′pli·cate (-kāt), *adj.* [L. *complicatus*, past part. of *complicare* to fold together, fr. *com-* + *plicare*.] 1. *Archaic.* Complex; complicated. 2. **a** *Bot.* Folded lengthwise. **b** *Zool.* Folded longitudinally one or more times; — said of insects' wings. — (-kāt), *v. t. & i.* To fold or twist together; to make or become complex or difficult.

com′pli·cat′ed (-kāt′ĕd; -ĭd), *adj.* Consisting of parts intricately combined; difficult of separation, analysis, solution, etc. — **Syn.** See COMPLEX. — **com′pli·cat′ed·ly,** *adv.* — **com′pli·cat′ed·ness,** *n.*

com′pli·ca′tion (-kā′shŭn), *n.* 1. Act or process of complicating, or state of being complicated; intricate or confused relation of parts. 2. A situation or a detail of a character entering into and complicating the main thread of a plot. 3. *Med.* A disease or condition coexistent with and modifying a primary disease.

com′plice (kŏm′plĭs), *n.* [F., fr. LL. *complex, -plicis*, confederate.] *Archaic.* An associate or accomplice.

com·plic′i·ty (kŏm·plĭs′ĭ·tĭ), *n.; pl.* -TIES (-tĭz). 1. State of being an accomplice; participation. 2. Complexity.

com′pli·ment (kŏm′plĭ·mĕnt), *n.* [F., through It. & Sp., fr. L. *complere* to fill up.] 1. A ceremonious expression of approbation, civility, or admiration; a flattering speech or attention. 2. A ceremonious greeting; — usually *pl.* 3. *Archaic & Dial.* A complimentary gift; a gratuity. — (-mĕnt), *v. t.* [F. *complimenter*.] 1. To make or pay a compliment to. 2. To present or bestow upon (a person) by way of civility or compliment.

com′pli·men′ta·ry (-mĕn′tȧ·rĭ), *adj.* 1. Expressive of regard; of the nature of, or containing, a compliment. 2. Presented free by way of compliment; as, a *complimentary* ticket. 3. Given to, or using, compliment. — **com′pli·men′ta·ri·ly,** *adv.*

com′plin (kŏm′plĭn), **com′pline** (-plĭn; -plīn), *n.* [OF. *complie* and LL. *completa* the religious exercise which closes the service of the day.] [*often cap.*] *Eccl.* The seventh and last of the canonical hours; the last liturgical prayer of the day, said after nightfall.

com′plot (kŏm′plŏt), *n.* [F.] A plotting together.

com·plot′ (kŏm·plŏt′), *v. t. & i.*; see PLOT. To plot together. — **com·plot′ter,** *n.*

com·ply′ (kŏm·plī′), *v. i.*; -PLIED′ (-plīd′); -PLY′ING. [It. *complire*, fr. Sp. *complir*.] 1. *Obs.* To be ceremoniously courteous. 2. To yield; acquiesce; consent; act in accordance; — usually followed by *with*. — **com·pli′er** (kŏm·plī′ẽr), *n.*

com′po (kŏm′pō), *n.; pl.* -POS (-pōz). Short for COMPOSITION; as: **a** A mortar made of sand and cement. **b** A composition for billiard balls.

com·po′nent (kŏm·pō′nĕnt), *adj.* [L. *componens*, pres. part. of *componere*. See COMPOUND, *v.*] Serving, or helping, to constitute; constituent. — *n.* 1. A constituent part; an ingredient. 2. *Mech.* One of the parts into which a vector, or tensor quantity, as force, momentum, velocity, may be resolved. Cf. COMPOSITION OF FORCES. — **Syn.** See ELEMENT.

com·port′ (kŏm·pōrt′; 70), *v. t.* [F. and L.; F. *comporter*, fr. L. *comportare* to bring together, fr. *com-* + *portare* to carry.] To carry; to conduct; — with a reflexive pronoun. — *v. i.* To agree, accord, or suit (*with*). — **Syn.** See BEHAVE: AGREE. — *n. Obs.* Behavior; deportment.

com·port′ance (-pōr′tăns), *n. Obs.* Behavior; comport.

com·port′ment (-pōrt′mĕnt), *n.* Behavior; bearing.

com′pos (kŏm′pŏs), *adj.* = COMPOS MENTIS.

com·pose′ (kŏm·pōz′), *v. t.* [F. *composer*, fr. *com-* + *poser* to place.] 1. To form by putting together; to make up; to fashion. 2. To form the substance of, or part of the substance of; to constitute; in the *passive*, to be made up (of); as, *composed* of many ingredients. 3. To design and execute, or to put together, in a fashion involving adaptation of forms of expression to ideas or to laws of harmony and proportion; as, to *compose* a sentence, a sonata, a picture. 4. To dispose in proper form; to put in proper state or condition; to adjust, regulate, or arrange. 5. To free from agitation or disturbance; to calm; quiet. 6. *Print.* To arrange (type) for printing; to set (type). — *v. i.* To practice composition, as of literary or musical work, or in printing.

com·posed′ (kŏm·pōzd′), *adj.* 1. *Obs.* Put together well or with art. 2. Free from agitation; calm. — **Syn.** See COOL. — **com·pos′ed·ly** (-pōz′ĕd·lĭ), *adv.* — **com·pos′ed·ness,** *n.*

com·pos′er (kŏm·pōz′ẽr), *n.* One who or that which composes; specif., an author; esp., a writer of music.

com·pos′ing stick (kŏm·pōz′ĭng). *Print.* A tray, usually of metal, which the compositor holds, usually in his left hand, and in which he arranges the type in words and lines.

com·pos′ite (kŏm·pŏz′ĭt; *Brit. now usually* kŏm′pō·zĭt), *adj.* [L. *compositus*, past part. of *componere*. See COMPOUND, *v.*] 1. Made up of distinct parts or elements; compounded. 2. [*cap.*] *Arch.* Belonging to a modification of the Corinthian order, combining angular Ionic volutes with the acanthus ornamentation of the Corinthian. Cf. ORDER, *Illust.* 3. *Bot.* Belonging to, or having the characteristics of, a composite. 4. *Math.* Of numbers, being a product of two or more integers each greater than 1; — opposed to *prime*. — *n.* 1. A composite thing; a composition, combination, or compound. 2. *Bot.* Any of an immense natural group (Compositae) of herbs, shrubs, and trees, embracing the most highly developed families in the vegetable kingdom, and characterized by having the small flowers borne in dense involucrate heads resembling single flowers, as in the daisy, dandelion, aster, ragweed, and wormwood. 3. *Math.* A composite number. — **com·pos′ite·ly,** *adv.*

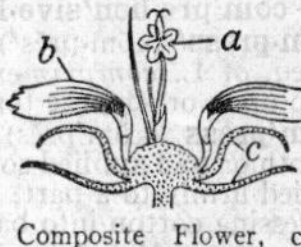

Composite Flower, cut away. *a* Disk Floret; *b* Ray Floret; *c* Bracts.

com′po·si′tion (kŏm′pō·zĭsh′ŭn), *n.* 1. Act of composing; esp., arranging of words to form sentences, paragraphs, verses, etc.; the art or practice of writing. 2. Manner of being composed, as to style or elements; as, a picture excelling in *composition*; also, constitution, formerly of the body, now esp. of the mind; — of persons. 3. State or quality of being put together, or composed; conjunction; combination. 4. That which is composed or has been composed; as: **a** A mutual agreement. **b** A mass or body formed by combining two or more elements or ingredients; as, a *composition* of several acids. 5. A literary, musical, or artistic product; — often used of an essay done as an educational exercise. 6. *Fine Arts.* The art or practice of so combining the parts of a work of art as to produce a harmonious whole. 7. *Print.* The setting up of type.

composition of forces. *Mech.* The finding of a single force (*resultant*) which shall be equal in effect to two or more given ones (*components*).

com·pos′i·tor (kŏm·pŏz′ĭ·tẽr), *n.* One who composes; esp., *Print.*, one who sets type. — **com·pos′i·to′ri·al** (-tō′rĭ·ăl; 70), *adj.*

com′pos men′tis (kŏm′pŏs mĕn′tĭs). [L.] *Law.* Sane in mind; being of sound mind, memory, and understanding.

com′post (kŏm′pōst; *Brit.* -pŏst *or* -pōst), *n.* [OF., fr. L. *compositus*, past part. See COMPOSITE.] 1. A composition or compound. 2. A mixture for fertilizing or renovating land; esp., a fertilizing mixture composed of peat, leaf mold, manure, lime, etc., mingled and decomposed.

com·po′sure (kŏm·pō′zhẽr), *n.* 1. *Obs.* Composition. 2. A settled state; calmness; repose. — **Syn.** See EQUANIMITY.

com′po·ta′tion (kŏm′pō·tā′shŭn), *n.* [L. *compotatio*, fr. *com-* + *potare* to drink.] A drinking or tippling together.

com′po·ta′tor (kŏm′pō·tā′tẽr), *n.* [LL.] One who drinks with another. — **com·po′ta·to′ry** (kŏm·pō′tȧ·tō′rĭ), *adj.*

com′pote (kŏm′pōt; *F.* kôɴ′pôt′), *n.* [F., fr. OF. *composte*.] 1. A dish of fruits cooked in sirup. 2. A bowl-shaped dish of glass, porcelain, or metal, usually with a base and stem, sometimes with a cover, from which compotes, fruits, or nuts are served.

com′pound (kŏm′pound), *n.* [Malay *kampuṅ*.] In the East Indies, India, China, etc., an enclosure containing a house, outbuildings, etc.; esp., one occupied by foreigners.

com·pound′ (kŏm·pound′), *v. t.* [From OF., fr. L. *componere, -positum*, fr. *com-* + *ponere* to put.] 1. To put together, as elements or parts, to form a whole; to combine; unite. 2. To settle amicably; to compromise, as the settlement of an obligation. 3. To increase by geometric progression or by an increment that itself increases; as, to *compound* interest quarterly. 4. *Obs.* To compose; to constitute. 5. *Law.* To forbear prosecution of (an offense) for a consideration. 6. *Elec.* To wind the field magnets of (a dynamo) so that it will be excited by both a shunt and a series current. — *v. i.* To effect a composition; to agree; to settle by a compromise. — **com·pound′a·ble,** *adj.* — **com·pound′er,** *n.* — ***compound a felony.*** To accept a consideration for forbearing to prosecute, such compounding being an offense.

com′pound (kŏm′pound; kŏm·pound′; 2), *adj.* 1. Composed of, or produced by the union of, several elements or parts; composite; as, a *compound* sentence (see SENTENCE). 2. *Bot.* Having like parts united into a common whole; — opp. to *simple*; as, ***compound flower*** (see ANTHODIUM); ***compound fruit*** (= COLLECTIVE FRUIT); ***compound leaf,*** one having two or more blades on one stalk, as a pinnate leaf (see LEAF, *Illust.*); ***compound ovary,*** one of more than one carpel. 3. *Gram.* Formed by the aggregation of otherwise independent elements; as, a *compound* word. 4. *Zool.* Composed of several joined individuals, or elemental, esp. similar, parts; as, a *compound* eye; most corals are *compound* animals.

com'pound (kŏm'pound), *n.* 1. That which is formed by the union or mixture of elements or parts; a compound substance. 2. *Chem.* A distinct substance formed by a union of two or more ingredients in definite proportions by weight. 3. *Gram.* **a** A word made up of two or more distinct words, either in solid or hyphened form (*doorkeeper, jack-in-the-pulpit*). **b** A phrase serving as a name or single part of speech (*postal card, glass snake, sacrifice hit; in spite of*). **c** A word having one or more affixes (*superimpose, childhood, unwillingly*); — called also *derivative.*

com'pound–com'plex sen'tence. See SENTENCE.

compound engine. *Mach.* An engine, esp. a steam engine, in which the working fluid is expanded successively in stages so as to minimize losses, as from cylinder condensation.

compound fraction. See FRACTION.

compound interest. See INTEREST, *n.*, 4.

compound number. *Math.* A number involving different denominations, or more than one unit (3 yd. 2 ft. 5 in.).

com'pra·dor' (kŏm'prȧ·dôr'), **com'pra·dore'** (-dōr'; 70), *n.; pl.* -DORS (-dôrz') or -DORES (-dōrz'). [Pg. *comprador* a buyer.] A native agent and factotum employed by a foreign establishment, as commercial houses, consulates, etc., in China, to have charge of its native employees, etc.

com'pre·hend' (kŏm'prē·hĕnd'), *v. t.* [L. *comprehendere, -hensum,* fr. *com-* + *prehendere* to grasp.] 1. To grasp the meaning of; to understand. 2. To contain; to embrace; to include. — *v. i.* To understand. — **Syn.** See UNDERSTAND: INCLUDE. — **com'pre·hend'i·ble,** *adj.*

com'pre·hen'si·ble (-hĕn'sĭ·b'l), *adj.* Capable of being comprehended; intelligible; conceivable. — **com'pre·hen'si·bil'i·ty** (-bĭl'ĭ·tĭ), *n.* — **com'pre·hen'si·bly** (-blĭ), *adv.*

com'pre·hen'sion (kŏm'prē·hĕn'shŭn), *n.* 1. Act of comprehending, or comprising; inclusion. 2. Comprehensiveness; inclusiveness. 3. The capacity of the mind for understanding; apperceptive knowledge. 4. *Logic.* = INTENSION, 6.

com'pre·hen'sive (-sĭv), *adj.* 1. Including much; inclusive. 2. Having the power to comprehend many things; of wide mental grasp. — **com'pre·hen'sive·ly,** *adv.* — **com'pre·hen'sive·ness,** *n.*

com·press' (kŏm·prĕs'), *v. t.* [OF. *compresser,* fr. LL. *compressare,* freq. of L. *comprimere* to compress, fr. *com-* + *premere* to press.] To press or squeeze together; to condense. — **Syn.** See CONTRACT.

com'press (kŏm'prĕs), *n.* [F. *compresse.*] 1. *Med.* A folded cloth or pad applied so as to press upon a part; also, a folded cloth applied firmly to a part, as to allay inflammation. 2. A press for compressing cotton into bales, etc.

com·pressed' (kŏm·prĕst'; 2), *adj.* 1. Pressed together. 2. Flattened; esp., *Bot.*, flattened laterally, as petioles. 3. *Zool.* Narrow from side to side, and deep in a dorsoventral direction, as the body of many fishes.

com·press'i·ble (kŏm·prĕs'ĭ·b'l), *adj.* Capable of being compressed. — **com·press'i·bil'i·ty** (-bĭl'ĭ·tĭ), *n.*

com·pres'sion (kŏm·prĕsh'ŭn), *n.* 1. Act of compressing, or state of being compressed. 2. *Engin. & Thermodyn.* **a** Act of compressing the remaining working fluid, as steam, in an engine cylinder after exhaust and before admission. **b** Act of compressing the working fluid in a heat-engine cycle after admission and before the working stroke, esp. in a cycle of operations for an internal-combustion engine.

com·pres'sive (-prĕs'ĭv), *adj.* Tending to compress; as, a *compressive* force. — **com·pres'sive·ly,** *adv.*

com·pres'sor (kŏm·prĕs'ẽr), *n.* [L.] One that serves to compress; as: **a** *Anat.* A muscle that compresses certain parts. **b** *Mach.* A machine for compressing something, as air for motive power. **c** *Surg.* An instrument for compressing an artery or other part.

com·pres'sure (kŏm·prĕsh'ẽr), *n.* Compression.

com·prise', com·prize' (-prīz'), *v. t.* [F. *compris,* past part. of *comprendre,* fr. L. *comprehendere.* See COMPREHEND.] 1. To comprehend or include. 2. To consist or be made up of. — **com·pris'a·ble, com·priz'a·ble** (-prīz'ȧ·b'l), *adj.*

com'pro·mise (kŏm'prō·mīz), *n.* [F. *compromis,* fr. L. *compromissum* a mutual promise to abide by a decision, deriv. of *com-* + *promittere* to promise.] 1. A settlement by arbitration or by consent reached by mutual concessions. 2. A committal to something derogatory, hazardous, or objectionable; a prejudicial concession; a surrender; as, a *compromise* of character. 3. The result or embodiment of concession or adjustment; hence, *Colloq.*, a thing intermediate between, or blending qualities of, two different things. — *v. t.* 1. *Obs.* To bind by mutual agreement. 2. To adjust and settle by mutual concessions; to settle by compromise. 3. To endanger the life or reputation of, by some act which cannot be recalled; to expose to discredit or mischief. — *v. i.* To come to agreement by concession. — **com'pro·mis'er** (-mīz'ẽr), *n.*

compt (kount), **compt'a·ble,** etc. Vars. of COUNT, etc.

‖**compte ren'du'** (kônt' räN'dü'). [F.] **a** A report, as of proceedings in an investigation. **b** *Com.* Account rendered.

Comp·tom'e·ter (kŏmp·tŏm'ē·tẽr), *n.* A trade-mark applied to a kind of calculating machine.

comp·trol'ler (kŏn·trōl'ẽr), *n.* [Orig. an erron. spelling of *controller.*] A controller (def. 1). — **comp·trol'ler·ship,** *n.*

com·pul'sion (kŏm·pŭl'shŭn), *n.* [F., fr. LL. *compulsio.* See COMPEL.] 1. Act of compelling, or state of being compelled; subjection to force. 2. *Psychopathol.* An impulse or feeling of being irresistibly driven toward the performance of some irrational action.

com·pul'sive (-sĭv), *adj.* Compelling. — **com·pul'sive·ly,** *adv.*

com·pul'so·ry (-sō·rĭ), *adj.* 1. Obligatory; enforced. 2. Coercive. — **com·pul'so·ri·ly,** *adv.* — **com·pul'so·ri·ness,** *n.*

com·punc'tion (kŏm·pŭngk'shŭn), *n.* [OF., fr. LL. *compunctio,* fr. *compungere, -punctum,* to prick, fr. *com-* + *pungere* to prick, sting.] Poignant uneasiness proceeding from a sense of guilt; remorse; now, often, a transient feeling of regret for some slight wrong. — **Syn.** See PENITENCE: QUALM. — **com·punc'tious** (-shŭs), *adj.*

com'pur·ga'tion (kŏm'pûr·gā'shŭn), *n.* [LL. *compurgatio,* fr. *compurgare* to purify wholly.] *Law.* The clearing of an accused person by the oaths of persons (**com'pur·ga'tors** [kŏm'pûr·gā'tẽrz]) who swear to his veracity or innocence, — abolished in England in 1833.

com·put'a·ble (kŏm·pūt'ȧ·b'l; kŏm'pū·tȧ·b'l), *adj.* Capable of being computed. — **com·put'a·bil'i·ty** (-bĭl'ĭ·tĭ), *n.*

com'pu·ta'tion (kŏm'pū·tā'shŭn), *n.* 1. Act or process of computing; calculation. 2. A system of reckoning. 3. The result of computing; amount computed.

com·pute' (kŏm·pūt'), *v. t. & i.* [L. *computare.* See COUNT, *v.*] To determine by calculation; to reckon. — **Syn.** See CALCULATE. — *n.* Computation. — **com·put'er** (-pūt'ẽr), *n.* — **com·put'ist** (-pūt'ĭst; kŏm'pū·tĭst), *n.*

com'rade (kŏm'răd; -rĭd; *also* kŏm'răd, kŭm'rĭd), *n.* [F. *camarade,* fr. Sp. *camarada* a chamber fellow, fr. L. *camera.* See CHAMBER.] 1. A mate; companion; associate; — orig. applied to one who shared the same room or (of soldiers) tent. 2. [*often cap.*] A fellow member of a trade union or of a communistic society. — **com'rade·ship,** *n.*

Com'ti·an (kŏm'tĭ·ăn; kôN'-), *adj.* Of or pert. to Auguste Comte (1798–1857) or his doctrines. See POSITIVISM.

Comt'ism (kŏm'tĭz'm; kôNt'ĭz'm), *n.* Positivism. — **Comt'ist,** *n. & adj.*

con (kŏn), *v. t.;* CONNED (kŏnd); CON'NING. [Orig. same as *can* am able, perh. also confused somewhat with ME. *cunnen* to try, AS. *cunnian.*] To study; to commit to memory; to regard studiously.

con, *adv.* [Abbr. fr. L. *contra* against.] Against; in opposition; on the negative side; — opposed to *pro.* — *n.* An opposing argument, vote, voter, etc.

con, *n. & v. Naut.* Var. of CONN.

con, *adj.* Slang or cant abbr. for *confidence;* as, a *con* game; a *con* man. — *v. t.* To deceive; swindle.

con, *n. Eng.* A rap or knock, as with the knuckles.

con-. = COM- (before consonants except *b, h, l, m, p, r, w*).

‖**con a·mo're** (kŏn ä·mō'rā). [It.] 1. With love; with devotion or zest; as, to undertake or do something *con amore.* 2. *Music.* Tenderly; — a direction.

co·na'tion (kō·nā'shŭn), *n.* [L. *conatio.*] *Philos.* The power or act of striving, with or without a conscious goal. — **con'a·tive** (kŏn'ȧ·tĭv; kō'nȧ-), *adj.*

co·na'tus (kō·nā'tŭs), *n. sing. & pl.* [L., fr. *conari* to attempt.] 1. Striving; inclination; conation. 2. A natural tendency, impulse, or effort.

‖**con bri'o** (kŏn brē'ō). [It.] With spirit; — a direction.

con·cat'e·nate (kŏn·kăt'ē·nāt), *adj.* [L. *concatenatus,* past part. of *concatenare* to concatenate, deriv. of *con-* + *catena* chain.] Linked together; forming a chain or series, as certain unicellular organisms. — *v. t.* To link together; to unite in a series or chain; to catenate.

con·cat'e·na'tion (-nā'shŭn), *n.* 1. Union in a linked series. 2. A series of links united; a series or order of things depending on each other, as if linked; a chain.

con'cave (kŏn'kāv), *n.* [OF.] A concave line or surface.

con'cave (kŏn'kāv; kŏn·kāv'; kŏng'kāv; 2), *adj.* [F., fr. L. *concavus,* fr. *con-* + *cavus* hollow.] 1. *Obs.* Hollow; void. 2. Hollow and curved or rounded; vaulted; — said of the interior of a curved surface or line, and opp. to *convex.* See LENS, *Illust.* — **con'cave·ly,** *adv.* — **con'cave·ness,** *n.*

con·cav'i·ty (kŏn·kăv'ĭ·tĭ), *n.; pl.* -TIES (-tĭz). Quality or state of being concave; a concave line or surface; hollow.

con·ca'vo–con'cave (kŏn·kā'vō·kŏn'kāv; -kŏn·kāv'; -kŏng'kāv), *adj.* Concave or hollow on both sides; double concave. See LENS, *Illust.*

con·ca'vo–con'vex (-kŏn'vĕks; -kŏn·vĕks'), *adj.* 1. Concave on one side and convex on the other, as an eggshell or a lens. See LENS, *Illust.* 2. Specif., in optics, having the concave side of smaller radius of curvature than the convex side.

con·ceal' (kŏn·sēl'), *v. t.* [OF. *conceler* (3d sing. pres. *conceile*), fr. L. *concelare,* fr. *con-* + *celare* to hide.] To hide or withdraw from observation; to withhold knowledge of. — **Syn.** See HIDE. — **Ant.** Reveal. — **con·ceal'a·ble,** *adj.* — **con·ceal'ment,** *n.*

con·cede' (-sēd'), *v. t.* [F. or L.; F., fr. L. *concedere, concessum,* fr. *con-* + *cedere* to yield.] 1. To yield or suffer to pass; to surrender. 2. To admit to be true; to acknowledge. 3. To grant, as a right or privilege. — *v. i.* To yield or make concession. — **Syn.** See GRANT. — **Ant.** Deny. — **con·ced'er** (-sēd'ẽr), *n.*

con·ceit' (kŏn·sēt'), *n.* [ME. *conseyte, conceyte, conceipt.*] 1. *Archaic.* **a** Conception or concept; a thought. **b** Personal judgment; opinion. **c** Favorable opinion; — now esp. in ***out of conceit with,*** dissatisfied with. 2. An overweening idea of oneself; vanity. 3. A quaint, artificial, or affected notion, or a witty thought or turn of expression. 4. Imagination; active fancy. 5. *Obs.* A fancy article. — *v. t.* 1. *Obs.* To conceive; think. 2. *Archaic.* To imagine; suppose. 3. *Now Dial.* To conceive well of; to take a fancy to.

con·ceit'ed (-ĕd; -ĭd), *adj.* 1. *Obs.* Intelligent; clever. 2. Entertaining a flattering opinion of oneself. 3. *Obs. exc. Dial.* Whimsical; fanciful. — **con·ceit'ed·ly,** *adv.* — **con·ceit'ed·ness,** *n.*

con·ceiv'a·ble (kŏn·sēv'ȧ·b'l), *adj.* Capable of being conceived, imagined, or understood. — **con·ceiv'a·bil'i·ty** (-bĭl'ĭ·tĭ), **con·ceiv'a·ble·ness,** *n.* — **con·ceiv'a·bly** (-blĭ), *adv.*

con·ceive' (kŏn·sēv'), *v. t.* [OF. *conceivre, conceveir,* fr. L. *concipere, -ceptum,* to take, conceive, fr. *con-* + *capere* to take.] 1. To become pregnant with (a child or young). 2. To take into one's mind; to devise, form a conception of, or imagine. 3. To apprehend by reason or imagination; to understand. 4. To think; suppose. — **Syn.** See THINK. — *v. i.* 1. To become pregnant. 2. To have a conception, idea, or opinion; to think. — **con·ceiv'er** (-sēv'ẽr), *n.*

con·cent' (kŏn·sĕnt'), *n.* [L. *concentus,* deriv. of *con-* + *canere* to sing.] *Archaic.* Concert of voices; hence, concord; harmony. — *v. t. & i. Obs.* To harmonize.

con·cen'ter, con·cen'tre (kŏn·sĕn'tẽr), *v. t. & i.* To draw or direct to a common center; to concentrate.

con'cen·trate (kŏn'sĕn·trāt), *v. t. & i.* [*con-* + L. *centrum* center.] 1. To bring or come to, or direct toward, a common center; to gather into one body, mass, or force; as, to *concentrate* rays to a focus; to *concentrate* attention. 2. To increase in strength by removing diluting or admixed material; as, to *concentrate* ores by washing; a *concentrated* food. — **Syn.** Consolidate, compact. — *n.* That which has been concentrated, as an ore. — **con'cen·tra'tor** (-trā'tẽr), *n.*

con'cen·trat'ed lye (-trāt'ĕd; -ĭd). See LYE, 1.

con'cen·tra'tion (-trā'shŭn), *n.* 1. Act of concentrating, or state of being concentrated; as, a *concentration* of all available forces. 2. A concentrated mass or thing. 3. Close mental application or exclusive attention. 4. Of a solution, the relative content in dissolved material; strength. — **Syn.** See ATTENTION.

concentration camp. 1. A military camp in which troops are temporarily concentrated. 2. A detention camp in which prisoners of war, political prisoners, foreign nationals, refugees, and the like, are confined.

con′cen·tra′tive (kŏn′sĕn·trā′tĭv; kŏn·sĕn′trȧ·tĭv), *adj.* Tending to concentrate. — **con′cen·tra′tive·ness,** *n.*

con·cen′tric (kŏn·sĕn′trĭk), **con·cen′tri·cal** (-trĭ·kăl), *adj.* Having a common center, as circles or spheres one within another; — opp. to *eccentric.* — **con·cen′tri·cal·ly,** *adv.* — **con′cen·tric′i·ty** (kŏn′sĕn·trĭs′ĭ·tĭ), *n.*

con′cept (kŏn′sĕpt), *n.* [L. *conceptus,* fr. *concipere* to conceive.] **1.** A thought; an opinion. **2.** *Philos.* A mental image of a thing formed by generalization from particulars; also, an idea of what a thing in general should be. — **Syn.** See IDEA.

con·cep′ta·cle (kŏn·sĕp′tȧ·k'l), *n.* [L. *conceptaculum,* fr. *concipere* to receive. See CONCEIVE.] *Bot.* In many thallophytes, an external cavity containing reproductive cells.

con·cep′tion (kŏn·sĕp′shŭn), *n.* **1.** A conceiving or being conceived; hence, beginning; also, that which is conceived. **2.** Specif.: **a** The power of the mind to form ideas or to devise schemes or designs, as for works of art. **b** The exercise of this power. **c** Something, as a work of art, that results from exercise of this power. **3.** *Philos.* = CONCEPT, 2. — **Syn.** See IDEA. — **con·cep′tion·al,** *adj.* — **con·cep′tive** (-tĭv), *adj.*

con·cep′tu·al (-tū̇·ăl), *adj.* [See CONCEPT.] Of or pertaining to conception or concepts. — **con·cep′tu·al·ly,** *adv.*

con·cep′tu·al·ism (kŏn·sĕp′tū̇·ăl·ĭz'm), *n.* *Philos.* A theory, intermediate between realism and nominalism, that universals exist in the mind as subjects of discourse or as predicates which may be properly affirmed of reality. — **con·cep′tu·al·ist** (-ĭst), *n.* — **con·cep′tu·al·is′tic** (-ĭs′tĭk), *adj.*

con·cern′ (kŏn·sûrn′), *v. t.* [F. and ML.; F., fr. ML. *concernere* to regard, LL. *concernere* to mix together, fr. *con-* + *cernere* to separate, sift, perceive, see.] **1.** To relate or belong to; to affect the interest of. **2.** To implicate, or involve; — now only in the passive. **3.** To engage by feeling or sentiment; to interest. — *v. i. Obs.* To be important. — *n.* **1.** That which relates or belongs to one; business; affair. **2.** That which affects the welfare or happiness; interest. **3.** Interest in, or care for, any person or thing; regard; solicitude; anxiety; as, to show *concern* for an invalid. **4.** A business organization. **5.** *Colloq.* A contrivance or thing slightingly regarded. — **Syn.** See CARE.

con·cerned′ (-sûrnd′), *adj.* Disturbed; anxious; worried; as, to be *concerned* for (or about) one's safety or health.

con·cern′ing, *prep.* Pertaining to; regarding.

con·cern′ment (kŏn·sûrn′mĕnt), *n.* **1.** *Archaic.* That in which one is concerned; affair. **2.** Relation; bearing; as, a matter of general *concernment.* **3.** Importance; consequence. **4.** Concern; participation; as, one's *concernment* with (or in) some matter. **5.** Solicitude; anxiety.

con·cert′ (kŏn·sûrt′), *v. t. & i.* [F. *concerter,* fr. It. *concertare,* fr. L. *concertare* to contend, fr. *con-* + *certare* to strive.] **1.** To plan together; to settle by agreement; to agree. **2.** To plan; devise.

con′cert (kŏn′sûrt), *n.* [F.] **1.** Agreement in a design or plan; harmony; simultaneous action. **2.** Musical harmony; concord. **3.** A musical performance of some length by several voices or instruments or both. — *adj.* Adapted to use in concerts; as, *concert* music; *concert* pitch (see PITCH, *n.,* 6 **b**).

con·cert′ed (kŏn·sûr′tĕd; -tĭd), *adj.* **1.** Mutually contrived; agreed on; as, *concerted* schemes. **2.** *Music.* Arranged in parts for several voices or instruments. — **con·cert′ed·ly,** *adv.*

con′cer·ti′na (kŏn′sĕr·tē′nȧ), *n.* A small musical instrument on the principle of the accordion.

con′cert·mas′ter (kŏn′sûrt·mȧs′tẽr), *n.* Concertmeister.

con′cert·meis′ter (kŏn′sûrt·mīs′tẽr; kŏn·tsĕrt′-), *n.* [G., now *konzertmeister.*] *Music.* The first violinist or leader of the strings in an orchestra; the subleader of the orchestra.

con·cer′to (kŏn·chĕr′tō; kŏn·sûr′-), *n.; pl.* -TOS (-tōz). [It.] *Music.* A composition (usually in symphonic form with three movements) in which one instrument (or two or three) stands out in bold relief against the orchestra.

con·ces′sion (kŏn·sĕsh′ŭn), *n.* [F. or L.; F., fr. L. *concessio.* See CONCEDE.] **1.** Act of conceding or yielding. **2.** The admitting of a point claimed in argument. **3.** A thing yielded; an acknowledgment. **4.** A grant by a government of land or property or of a right to use land or property for some specified purpose. **5.** *U. S.* A grant or lease of a portion of premises for some specific use; as, a *concession* to sell peanuts at a baseball park. **6.** A tract of land granted to a foreign power, within which it has extraterritorial rights and enjoys local self-government.

con·ces′sion·aire′ (-âr′), *n.* [F. *concessionnaire.*] The beneficiary of a concession (esp., *U. S.,* in sense 5).

con·ces′sion·ar′y (kŏn·sĕsh′ŭn·ĕr′ĭ *or, esp. Brit.,* -ẽr·ĭ), *adj.* Of or pert. to a concession. — *n.; pl.* -ARIES (-ĭz). A concessionaire.

con·ces′sive (kŏn·sĕs′ĭv), *adj.* **1.** Of the nature of, or making for, concession. **2.** *Gram.* Expressive of concession; as, a *concessive* clause or conjunction (let justice be done, *though* the heavens fall).

conch (kŏngk; *also* kŏnch), *n.; pl.* CONCHS (kŏngks), CONCHES (kŏn′chĕz; -chĭz). [L. *concha,* fr. Gr. *konchē.*] **1. a** Any of various large spiral univalve marine shells of several genera (esp. *Strombus, Cassis,* and their allies). Conchs are often converted into a kind of horn. **b** The animal in such a shell. **2.** In art, the shell used by Triton as a trumpet.

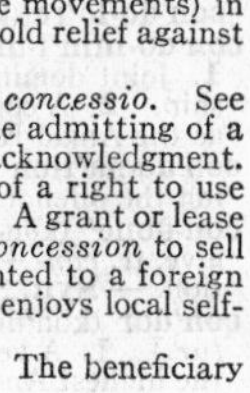

Conch (*S. pugilis*). (⅓)

‖**con′cha** (kŏng′kȧ), *n.; pl.* -CHAE (-kē). [L. See CONCH.] **1.** *Anat.* Any of various structures shaped like a shell; esp., the largest and deepest concavity of the external ear; also, the entire external ear. See EAR, *Illust.* **2.** *Arch.* The plain semidome of an apse; sometimes, the entire apse.

con·chif′er·ous (kŏng·kĭf′ẽr·ŭs), *adj.* Shell-bearing.

con·chi′o·lin (-kī′ō·lĭn), *n.* [L. *concha* shell + *-ole* + *-in.*] *Biochem.* An albuminoid forming the organic basis of mollusk shells, esp. mother-of-pearl.

con·choi′dal (kŏng·koi′dăl; -d'l), *adj.* [Gr. *konchē* shell + *eidos* form.] *Mineral.* Having elevations or depressions in form like one half of a bivalve shell.

con·chol′o·gy (kŏng·kŏl′ō·jĭ), *n.* [Gr. *konchē* shell + *-logy.*] The branch of zoology which deals with shells or mollusks. — **con′cho·log′i·cal** (kŏng′kō·lŏj′ĭ·kăl), *adj.* — **con·chol′o·gist** (kŏng·kŏl′ō·jĭst), *n.*

con′ci·erge (kŏn′sĭ·ĕrzh; *F.* kôɴ′syĕrzh′), *n.* [F.] A doorkeeper, male or female; formerly, also, a warden.

con·cil′i·a·ble (kŏn·sĭl′ĭ·ȧ·b'l), *adj.* Capable of being conciliated or reconciled.

con·cil′i·ar (-ẽr), *adj.* Of or pertaining to, or issued by, a council.

con·cil′i·ate (kŏn·sĭl′ĭ·āt), *v. t.* [L. *conciliatus,* past part. of *conciliare* to draw together, unite, fr. *concilium* council.] **1.** To gain (good will or favor, etc.) by pleasing acts. **2.** To cause to agree; make compatible. **3.** To win over; to gain the good will of; to make friendly. — **Syn.** See PACIFY. — **Ant.** Antagonize. — **con·cil′i·a′tion** (-ā′shŭn), *n.* — **con·cil′i·a′tive** (-ā′tĭv; -ȧ·tĭv), *adj.* — **con·cil′i·a′tor** (-ā′tẽr), *n.*

con·cil′i·a·to′ry (kŏn·sĭl′ĭ·ȧ·tō′rĭ *or, esp. Brit.,* -tẽr·ĭ), *adj.* Tending to conciliate; propitiating. — **con·cil′i·a·to′ri·ly** (-tō′rĭ·lĭ; -tẽr·ĭ·lĭ), *adv.* — **con·cil′i·a·to′ri·ness,** *n.*

con·cin′ni·ty (kŏn·sĭn′ĭ·tĭ), *n.; pl.* -TIES (-tĭz). [L. *concinnitas,* fr. *concinnus* skillfully put together, harmonious.] Internal harmony or fitness; mutual adaptation of parts; elegance; — used esp. of style.

con·cise′ (kŏn·sīs′), *adj.* [L. *concisus* cut off, short, past part. of *concidere* to cut in pieces, fr. *con-* + *caedere* to cut.] Expressing much in a few words; condensed; brief. — **con·cise′ly,** *adv.* — **con·cise′ness,** *n.*

Syn. **Concise, terse, succinct, laconic, summary, pithy, compendious** mean very brief in statement or expression. **Concise** suggests the removal of all that is superfluous or elaborative; **terse** implies conciseness that is pointed and elegant; **succinct** implies compression into the smallest possible space; **laconic** implies such succinctness as to seem curt, brusque, mystifying, etc.; **summary** implies the bare outlines without details; **pithy** adds to *terse* or *succinct* the implication of richness of substance or meaning; **compendious** implies a concise, summary style weighted with matter. — **Ant.** Redundant.

con·ci′sion (-sĭzh′ŭn), *n.* **1.** A cutting off or up; a division; a schism. **2.** Conciseness; succinctness.

con′clave (kŏn′klāv; kŏng′klāv), *n.* [F., fr. L. *conclave* a room that may be locked up, fr. *con-* + *clavis* key.] **1.** *Obs.* A private room. **2.** *Eccl.* The set of apartments within which, since 1274, the cardinals of the Roman Catholic Church are continuously secluded while choosing a pope. **3.** The meeting of cardinals shut up in the conclave for the election of a pope; hence, the body of cardinals. **4.** A private meeting or secret assembly.

con′clav·ist (-klāv·ĭst), *n.* One of the two ecclesiastics allowed to attend a cardinal in the conclave.

con·clude′ (kŏn·klōōd′; 114), *v. t.* [L. *concludere, -clusum,* fr. *con-* + *claudere* to shut.] **1.** *Obs.* To shut up; enclose; also, to restrain. **2.** To bring to an end. **3.** To reach as an end of reasoning; to close, as an argument, by inferring. **4.** To judge; to decide; as, he *concluded* that he would wait. **5.** To bring about as a result; to effect; as, to *conclude* a bargain or a peace. — *v. i.* **1.** To come to a termination; to end. **2.** To form a final judgment; to reach a decision or agreement. — **Syn.** See CLOSE (**Ant.** commence): INFER. — **con·clud′er** (-klōōd′ẽr), *n.*

con·clu′sion (kŏn·klōō′zhŭn; 114), *n.* **1.** The last part of anything; end. **2.** An inference; a reasoned judgment; as, to form *conclusions* from experience. **3.** The last summing up of a discourse. **4.** Final decision; outcome. **5.** Act of concluding; arrangement, as of an armistice. **6.** *Law.* The closing portion of a pleading. **7.** *Logic.* The inferred proposition of a syllogism; the necessary consequence of two or more related propositions taken as premises.

con·clu′sive (-sĭv), *adj.* Belonging to a close or termination; specif., putting an end to debate or question; decisive; final. — **con·clu′sive·ly,** *adv.* — **con·clu′sive·ness,** *n.*

Syn. **Conclusive, decisive, determinative, definitive** mean bringing something to an end. **Conclusive** applies to reasoning or its proofs that put an end to all debate or questioning; **decisive** applies more generally, including acts, events, etc., that put an end to doubt, controversy, competition, vacillation, or the like; **determinative** adds to *decisive* the implication of giving a fixed course, direction, or the like; **definitive** applies to that which is put forth as not tentative, not provisional, not unsettled, etc., but as final and permanent.

con·coct′ (kŏn·kŏkt′; kŏn-), *v. t.* [L. *concoctus,* past part. of *concoquere* to cook together, digest, fr. *con-* + *coquere* to cook.] **1.** *Obs.* To digest. **2.** *Obs.* To prepare, perfect, or refine chemically by heat. **3.** To prepare from crude materials; to prepare by combining different ingredients. **4.** Hence, to compose, devise, or make up; as, to *concoct* a story, excuse, plan, or intrigue. — **con·coct′er,** *n.*

con·coc′tion (-kŏk′shŭn), *n.* Act of concocting; also, that which is concocted. — **con·coc′tive** (-tĭv), *adj.*

con·com′i·tance (kŏn·kŏm′ĭ·tăns), *n.* Also **con·com′i·tan·cy** (-tăn·sĭ). **1.** State of accompanying; accompaniment; as, the *concomitance* of dire poverty and great wealth. **2.** Fact or instance of being concomitant.

con·com′i·tant (-tănt), *adj.* [L. *concomitans,* pres. part. of *concomitari* to accompany, fr. *con-* + *comitari* to accompany, fr. *comes* companion.] Accompanying; conjoined; attending; as, *concomitant* circumstances. — **Syn.** See CONTEMPORARY. — *n.* That which accompanies. — **con·com′i·tant·ly,** *adv.*

con′cord (kŏn′kôrd; kŏng′-), *n.* [OF. *concorde,* fr. L. *concordia,* fr. *concors* agreeing, fr. *con-* + *cor, cordis,* heart.] **1.** A state of agreement; harmony. **2.** Agreement by stipulation, covenant, or treaty. **3.** *Gram.* Agreement between words in their inflection to mark grammatical connection (*this hat, these hats*). **4.** [Perhaps influenced by 2d *chord.*] *Music.* **a** An agreeable combination of tones simultaneously heard; harmony. **b** Consonance.

Con′cord (kŏn′kôrd; kŏng′kẽrd), *n.* [From *Concord,* Mass.] *Hort.* A leading American variety of grape. It has large, bluish-black, sweet-flavored fruit.

con·cord′ance (kŏn·kôr′dăns; kŏn-), *n.* **1.** Agreement; accordance; an accord. **2.** An alphabetical index of the principal words in a book, or in the works of an author, with their contexts.

con·cord′ant (-dănt), *adj.* Agreeing; correspondent; harmonious; consonant. — **con·cord′ant·ly,** *adv.*

con·cor′dat (kŏn·kôr′dăt), *n.* [F., fr. ML. *concordatum,* prop. past part. neut. of *concordare* to agree, bring into union.] **1.** A compact or covenant. **2.** An agreement made between the pope and a sovereign or government for the regulation of ecclesiastical matters.

con·cor′po·rate (kŏn·kôr′pō·rāt), *v. t. & i.* [L. *concorporatus,* past part.] *Archaic.* To unite in one body; incorporate. — (-rāt), *adj.* *Archaic.* United in one body.

con′course (kŏn′kōrs; kŏng′-; 70), *n.* [F. *concours,* fr. L. *concursus,* fr. *concurrere* to run together.] **1.** A flocking together, as of

people; any moving, flowing, or running together. **2.** An assemblage; gathering. **3.** An open space where several roads or paths meet, as in a park; an open space or hall where crowds may gather.
con·cres′cence (kŏn·krĕs′ĕns; -′ns), *n.* [L. *concrescentia.*] *Biol.* A growing together, esp. of parts originally separate.
con′crete (kŏn′krēt; kŏn·krēt′; 2), *adj.* [L. *concretus,* past part. of *concrescere* to grow together, fr. *con-* + *crescere* to grow.] **1.** United in growth; compounded or coalesced; solid. **2. a** Naming a thing, or a class of things, as opposed to naming a quality or attribute; thus, "man" is a *concrete* term but "human" is abstract. **b** Having a specific application; particular; as, a *concrete* term or number; — opp. to *abstract* or *general.* **3.** Of the nature of, or characterized by, immediate experience; belonging to actual things or events; real; not abstract or ideal; also, dealing with what is concrete; not abstract or general; as, *concrete* ideas. **4.** Pertaining to or made of concrete. — **Syn.** See SPECIAL. — **Ant.** Abstract. — **con′crete·ly** (see *adj.*), *adv.* — **con′crete·ness,** *n.*
con′crete (kŏn′krēt *or, esp. in senses* 1 & 3, kŏn·krēt′), *n.* **1.** A concrete form or object; also, with *the,* that which is concrete. **2.** A mass formed by concretion or coalescence of separate particles of matter in one body. **3.** An artificial building material made by mixing cement and sand with gravel, broken stone, or other aggregate, and sufficient water to cause the cement to set and bind the entire mass.
con·crete′ (kŏn·krēt′), *v. t. & i.* **1.** To form or unite into a solid mass; to solidify. **2.** (*pron.* kŏn′krēt; kŏn·krēt′) To cover with, set in, or form of concrete.
con·cre′tion (kŏn·krē′shŭn), *n.* **1.** Act or process of concreting, or state of being concreted. **2.** A concreted mass; specif.: **a** *Med.* A hard inorganic body formed in a body cavity or organic tissue, as in the bladder or kidney; a calculus; stone. **b** *Geol.* A mass of mineral matter, generally in rock of a composition different from its own, produced by deposition from aqueous solution in the rock. — **con·cre′tion·ar′y** (-ĕr′ĭ *or, esp. Brit.,* -ĕr·ĭ), *adj.*
con·cu′bi·nage (kŏn·kū′bĭ·nĭj), *n.* [F.] The cohabiting of a man with a concubine; state of being a concubine. Concubinage is recognized in many systems of primitive law, as that of the ancient Hebrews.
con·cu′bi·nar′y (-nĕr′ĭ *or, esp. Brit.,* -nĕr·ĭ), *adj.* Relating to, living in, or sprung from concubinage. — *n.; pl.* -NARIES (-ĭz). One who lives in concubinage.
con′cu·bine (kŏng′kū·bīn), *n.* [OF., fr. L. *concubina,* fr. *con-* + *cubare* to lie down.] Among some peoples, a woman who, though not legally a wife, lives with a man and has a recognized position in his household.
con·cu′pis·cent (kŏn·kū′pĭ·sĕnt; -s′nt), *adj.* [L. *concupiscens,* pres. part. of *concupiscere,* deriv. of *con-* + *cupere* to desire.] Ardently desirous; specif., having sexual lust; lustful. — **con·cu′pis·cence** (-sĕns; -s′ns), *n.*
con·cu′pis·ci·ble (kŏn·kū′pĭ·sĭ·b′l), *adj.* *Now Rare.* That is most desirable; also, lustful.
con·cur′ (kŏn·kûr′), *v. i.;* CON·CURRED′ (-kûrd′); CON·CUR′RING. [L. *concurrere* to run together, agree, fr. *con-* + *currere* to run.] **1.** *Obs.* To run together; meet. **2.** To happen together; to coincide. **3.** To act jointly; to combine. **4.** To unite or agree (in nature or opinion); to accord; correspond. — **Syn.** See AGREE. — **Ant.** Dissent.
con·cur′rence (-kûr′ĕns), *n.* **1.** Act of concurring; a coming together. **2.** Agreement or union in action. **3.** A meeting of minds; agreement. **4.** Competition; rivalry; — now a Gallicism. **5.** *Geom.* The meeting of lines, surfaces, etc.; esp., a point common to three or more lines. **6.** *Law.* A common right; coincidence of equal powers.
con·cur′ren·cy (-ĕn·sĭ), *n.* Concurrence.
con·cur′rent (-ĕnt), *adj.* **1.** Running together; existing or happening at the same time; as, *concurrent* forces. **2.** Meeting in, or directed to, the same point; as, *concurrent* lines. **3.** Acting in conjunction; cooperating. **4.** *Law.* Joint and equal in authority or jurisdiction. — **Syn.** See CONTEMPORARY. — *n.* **1.** A joint or contributory cause. **2.** A rival; opponent. — **con·cur′rent·ly,** *adv.*
con·cus′sion (kŏn·kŭsh′ŭn), *n.* [L. *concussio,* fr. *concutere, -cussum,* to shake violently, fr. *con-* + *quatere* to shake.] **1.** A shaking or agitation; a shock caused by collision of bodies. **2.** *Med.* A condition of lowered functional activity, without visible structural change, produced in an organ by a shock, as by a fall or blow; as, a *concussion* of the brain. — **con·cus′sion·al** (-ăl; -′l), *adj.* — **con·cus′sive** (-kŭs′ĭv), *adj.*
con·demn′ (kŏn·dĕm′), *v. t.* [OF. *condemner,* fr. L. *condemnare,* fr. *con-* + *damnare* to condemn.] **1.** To pronounce to be wrong; to disapprove of. **2.** To declare the guilt of; to pronounce guilty; to convict of guilt; as, his words *condemn* him. **3.** To pronounce a judicial sentence against; to sentence to punishment; to doom. **4.** *Obs.* To amerce or fine. **5.** To adjudge or pronounce to be unfit for use or service; as, to *condemn* meat; to *condemn* a building as unsafe. **6.** To pronounce incurable. **7.** *Law.* To pronounce to be taken for public use, under the right of eminent domain. — **Syn.** See CRITICIZE. — **con·dem′na·ble** (-dĕm′nȧ·b′l), *adj.* — **con·demn′er** (-dĕm′ẽr), *n.*
con′dem·na′tion (kŏn′dĕm·nā′shŭn), *n.* **1.** Act of condemning; censure; reprobation. **2.** Act of judicially condemning, or adjudging guilty. **3.** State or fact of being condemned. **4.** The ground or reason of condemning. — **con·dem′na·to′ry** (kŏn·dĕm′nȧ·tō′rĭ *or, esp. Brit.,* -tẽr·ĭ), *adj.*
con·den′sa·ble (kŏn·dĕn′sȧ·b′l), *adj.* Capable of being condensed. — **con·den′sa·bil′i·ty** (-bĭl′ĭ·tĭ), *n.*
con·den′sate (-sāt), *n.* [L. *condensatus,* past part.] *Physics, Chem., etc.* A product of condensation.
con′den·sa′tion (kŏn′dĕn·sā′shŭn), *n.* **1.** Act or process of condensing; state of being condensed; also, a product of condensing. **2.** *Chem.* A reaction involving union between atoms in the same or different molecules to form a new compound of greater complexity and, frequently, greater molecular weight or density. **3.** *Physics.* Act or process of reducing from one form to another and denser form, as steam to water.
con·dense′ (kŏn·dĕns′), *v. t. & i.* [F. *condenser,* fr. L. *condensare,* fr. *con-* + *densare* to make dense, fr. *densus* dense.] **1.** To make or become more compact; to compress; as, to *condense* a story; also, to intensify; concentrate. **2.** *Chem. & Physics.* To subject to condensation. — **Syn.** See CONTRACT.
con·densed′ (-dĕnst′), *adj.* **1.** That has been subjected to condensation. **2.** *Printing.* Of type, having a narrower face than normal type of the same series. See TYPE.
condensed milk. Milk concentrated by evaporation with the addition of sugar. Cf. EVAPORATED MILK.
con·dens′er (kŏn·dĕn′sẽr), *n.* **1.** One that condenses. **2.** Specif.: **a** An instrument for compressing air or gases. **b** *Elec.* An instrument for holding or storing an electric charge; — called also *capacitor.* **c** A lens or mirror used to concentrate light upon an object. **d** Any apparatus for condensing gases or vapors to a liquid or solid state.
con·den′si·ble. Less correct form of CONDENSABLE.
con′de·scend′ (kŏn′dē·sĕnd′), *v. i.* [OF. *condescendre,* fr. LL. *condescendere,* fr. *con-* + *descendere.* See DESCEND.] **1.** To stoop or descend to an attitude less formal or stately; specif.: **a** To waive the privilege of rank or dignity. **b** To bestow courtesies with some air of superiority; to act in a patronizing manner. **2.** *Obs.* To concede; to assent. — **Syn.** See STOOP.
con′de·scend′ence (-sĕn′dĕns; -d′ns), *n.* **1.** Condescension. **2.** *Scot.* A specification of particulars.
con′de·scend′ing, *adj.* Showing condescension; patronizing. — **con′de·scend′ing·ly,** *adv.*
con′de·scen′sion (-sĕn′shŭn), *n.* Act or instance of condescending.
con·dign′ (kŏn·dīn′; 2), *adj.* [F. *condigne,* fr. L. *condignus* very worthy, fr. *con-* + *dignus* worthy.] **1.** *Obs.* Worthy; suitable. **2.** Deserved; adequate; fit; — now only of punishment and often implying severity. — **con·dign′ly,** *adv.*
con′di·ment (kŏn′dĭ·mĕnt), *n.* [F., fr. L. *condimentum,* fr. *condire* to pickle, season.] Something, usually a pungent substance, as pepper, to give relish to food; seasoning.
con′dis·ci′ple (kŏn′dĭ·sī′p′l), *n.* [L. *condiscipulus.* See DISCIPLE.] A fellow disciple or student; a schoolfellow.
con·di′tion (kŏn·dĭsh′ŭn), *n.* [OF. *condicion,* fr. L. *conditio* agreement, condition.] **1.** Something established or agreed upon as a requisite to the doing or taking effect of something else; a stipulation or provision; hence, an agreement determining one or more such prerequisites. **2.** That which exists as an occasion of something else; a prerequisite. **3.** That which limits or modifies the existence or character of something; a qualification. **4.** A mode or state of being; as, matter in a gaseous *condition;* specif.: **a** Social estate; rank; position. **b** *Archaic.* Mental or moral nature, character, or disposition. **c** Proper condition, as for work; state of being fit. **5.** *Archaic.* A characteristic or trait (of a person or object). **6.** *Educ.* The requirement made of a student who is conditioned. **7.** *Gram.* A conditional clause. **8.** *Law.* A provision in a contract, will, etc., providing that a modification of an interest in property shall depend upon an uncertain event, which may or may not exist or happen; also, the event itself. **9.** *Logic.* A proposition either necessary to or sufficient for the truth of another. — **Syn.** See STATE.
— *v. i.* To make conditions or terms; to stipulate. — *v. t.* **1.** To stipulate; to bargain for. **2.** To limit by, or subject to, conditions. **3.** To put into proper, or the desired, condition; as, to *condition* a horse for a race; to *condition* the air of a room (see AIR CONDITIONING). **4.** *Educ.* To require (a student) to pass a new examination or show a certain degree of proficiency in a specified study, as a condition of remaining in the class or institution. **5.** *Psychol.* To attach to a new stimulus or a new response; also, to produce a new attachment of stimulus and response in (an individual). — **con·di′tion·er,** *n.*
con·di′tion·al (kŏn·dĭsh′ŭn·ăl; -′l), *adj.* **1.** Containing, implying, subject to, or depending on a condition or conditions; not absolute; made or granted on certain terms; as, a *conditional* promise. **2.** *Gram. & Logic.* Expressing, containing, or implying a supposition or condition; as, a *conditional* clause, sentence, or proposition. — **con·di′tion·al′i·ty** (-ăl′ĭ·tĭ), *n.* — **con·di′tion·al·ly,** *adv.*
con·di′tioned (kŏn·dĭsh′ŭnd), *adj.* **1.** Conditional. **2.** Brought or put into good condition. Cf. CONDITION, *v. t.,* 3.
con·dole′ (kŏn·dōl′), *v. i.* [LL. *condolere,* fr. L. *con-* + *dolere* to feel pain, grieve.] To grieve; now only, to grieve in sympathy; to express such grief; commiserate. — *v. t. Archaic.* To grieve in sympathy over or with. — **con·dole′ment** (-mĕnt), *n.* — **con·dol′er** (kŏn·dōl′ẽr), *n.*
con·do′lence (kŏn·dō′lĕns; kŏn′dō·lĕns), *n.* Expression of sympathy with another in sorrow. — **Syn.** See PITY.
‖**con do·lo′re** (kōn dō·lō′rā). [It.] With grief; sorrowfully.
con′do·min′i·um (kŏn′dō·mĭn′ĭ·ŭm), *n.* [NL. See CON-; DOMINIUM.] **1.** Joint dominion or sovereignty; specif., *Roman Law,* joint ownership. **2.** A country or region jointly governed by two or more powers, as the Anglo-Egyptian Sudan.
con′do·na′tion (-nā′shŭn), *n.* Tacit forgiveness of an offense by treating the offender as if it had not been committed.
con·done′ (kŏn·dōn′), *v. t.* [L. *condonare, -donatum,* to remit, forgive, fr. *con-* + *donare* to give.] To pardon; to overlook in condonation. — **Syn.** See EXCUSE. — **con·don′er** (-dōn′ẽr), *n.*
con′dor (kŏn′dẽr; -dôr), *n.* [Sp. *cóndor,* fr. Quechua *condor, cuntur.*] **1.** A very large American vulture (*Vultur gryphus*), found in the highest Andes. It has the head and neck bare, with a white neck ruff. **2.** (*Sp. pron.* kōn′dôr) *Sp. pl.* CONDORES (kōn·dō′rās). A gold coin of Chile (10 pesos), Colombia (10 pesos), and Ecuador (25 sucres), bearing a condor for its device.
‖**con·dot·tie′re** (kōn·dōt·tyâ′rā), *n.; pl.* -TIERI (-rē). [It., captain.] **1.** From the 14th to the 16th century, a captain of a roving band of mercenaries; also, any member of such a band. Cf. FREE COMPANION, FREE LANCE. **2.** Hence, an adventurer.
con·duce′ (kŏn·dūs′), *v. i.;* -DUCED′ (-dūst′); -DUC′ING (-dūs′ĭng). [L. *conducere* to bring together, conduce, fr. *con-* + *ducere* to lead.] To lead or tend, esp. with reference to a desirable result; contribute; — with *to* or *toward.* — **con·duc′er** (-dūs′ẽr), *n.* — **con·duc′i·ble** (-ĭ·b′l), *adj.* — **con·duc′i·ble·ness,** *n.* — **con·duc′i·bly** (-blĭ), *adv.*
Syn. **Conduce, contribute, redound** mean to lead to an end. **Conduce** implies a tendency to further an end; **contribute** suggests taking an effective part in furthering an end; **redound** implies leading to an unforeseen end by the flowing back of an action's consequences.
con·du′cive (-dū′sĭv), *adj.* That conduces; helpful; contributive. — **con·du′cive·ness,** *n.*
con′duct (kŏn′dŭkt), *n.* [L. *conductus,* fr. *conducere, conductum.* See CONDUCE.] **1.** Act or method of leading; guidance. **2.** Act or manner of carrying on, as a business; management; direction. **3.** Manner of conducting oneself; one's actions in general; behavior. **4.** *Obs.* Convoy; escort; also, a guide.
con·duct′ (kŏn·dŭkt′), *v. t.* **1.** To lead; guide; escort. **2.** To have the direction of; manage; carry on. **3.** To serve as a channel or medium for; convey; transmit, as heat. **4.** To behave (oneself). **5.** To direct (an orchestra, etc.) as leader; also, to direct the performing or execution of, as a symphony. — *v. i.* **1.** To be, or show, the way; to lead, as a road or passage. **2.** To act as a conductor, as of heat or electricity. **3.** *Music.* To act as a conductor. **4.** *Now Rare.* To behave. —

con·duct′i·bil′i·ty (kŏn·dŭk′tĭ·bĭl′ĭ·tĭ), *n.* — **con·duct′i·ble** (-dŭk′-tĭ·b'l), *adj.*

Syn. (1) See ACCOMPANY.
(2) **Conduct, manage, control, direct** mean to lead or guide through the exercise of skill or authority. **Conduct**, except when the idea of leading is obscured, implies responsibility for the acts and achievements of a group; **manage** specifically implies handling or manipulating in order to bring about a response to one's wishes; **control** implies a regulating or restraining in order to keep within bounds; **direct** implies the aim of keeping persons or things involved straight, well organized, or properly administered.
(3) See BEHAVE.

con·duct′ance (-dŭk′tăns), *n.* [*conduct*, v. + *-ance*.] Capacity or fitness for, or power or property of, conducting, or transmitting; — in *Elec.*, the reciprocal of *resistance*.

con·duc′tion (-dŭk′shŭn), *n.* **1.** Act of conducting or conveying, as water through a pipe. **2.** *Physics.* Transmission through or by means of a conductor; also, conductivity; — distinguished, in the case of heat, from *convection* and *radiation*. **3.** *Physiol.* The transmission of excitation through living tissue, esp. in a nerve.

con·duc′tive (kŏn·dŭk′tĭv), *adj.* Possessing conductivity.

con′duc·tiv′i·ty (kŏn′dŭk·tĭv′ĭ·tĭ), *n.; pl.* -TIES (-tĭz). **1.** Quality or power of conducting, or transmitting, as heat, electricity, etc. **2.** *Elec.* The conductance of a cubic centimeter of any material; — the reciprocal of *resistivity*.

con·duc′tor (kŏn·dŭk′tẽr), *n.* One who or that which conducts; specif.: **a** A guide, esp. of a party of travelers. **b** One in charge of a public conveyance, as a streetcar, or, *U. S.*, a railroad train. **c** A lightning rod. **d** *Music.* One who directs an orchestra, chorus, or the like. **e** *Physics & Elec.* A substance or body capable of transmitting electricity, heat, etc.; — opp. to *nonconductor*. Cf. INSULATOR. — **con·duc′tor·ship**, *n.* — **con·duc′tress** (-trĕs; -trĭs), *n.*

con′duit (kŏn′dwĭt; -do͝o·ĭt; -dū·ĭt; -dĭt), *n.* [OF., fr. L. *conductus*. See CONDUCT, *n.*] **1.** An artificial or natural channel for conveying water or fluid, as a pipe, aqueduct, or canal. **2.** *Archaic.* A fountain. **3.** A tube or trough for receiving and protecting electric wires or cables, as for telephones, railways, etc.

con·du′pli·cate (kŏn·dū′plĭ·kĭt), *adj.* *Bot.* Folded lengthwise; — of leaves or petals in the bud.

con′dyle (kŏn′dĭl), *n.* [F., fr. L. *condylus* knuckle, joint, fr. Gr. *kondylos*.] A prominence, usually one of a pair, at the end of a bone serving to articulate with an adjoining bone. See RODENT, *Illust.* — **con′dy·lar** (-dĭ·lẽr), *adj.* — **con′dy·loid** (-loid), *adj.*

con′dy·lo′ma (kŏn′dĭ·lō′mȧ), *n.; pl.* -LOMATA (-tȧ). [NL., fr. Gr. *kondylōma*, fr. *kondylos* knuckle.] *Med.* A wartlike new growth on the skin or adjoining mucous membrane, usually near the anus and genital organs. — **con′dy·lom′a·tous** (-lŏm′ȧ·tŭs; -lō′mȧ·tŭs), *adj.*

cone (kōn), *n.* [F. or L.; F. *cône*, fr. L. *conus*, fr. Gr. *kōnos*.] **1.** *Bot.* **a** In trees of the pine family and in cycads, a mass of ovule-bearing or pollen-bearing scales; a strobile. **b** Any of several conelike flower or fruit clusters, as in the hop. **2.** *Geom.* **a** A solid generated by rotating a right triangle about one of its legs; — called specif. ***right circular cone***. **b** A solid figure whose bottom is a circle and whose sides taper evenly up to a point, or apex. Cf. FRUSTUM, *Illust.* **c** A conical surface; any surface traced by a moving right line passing through a fixed vertex. **3.** A cone-shaped structure, formation, or the like; specif.: **a** A crisp, edible shell for ice cream. **b** *Mach.* A conical or conoidal piece or part, as the inner race for ball bearings, or a kind of pulley. — *v. t.* To render cone-shaped; to bevel like the circular segment of a cone.

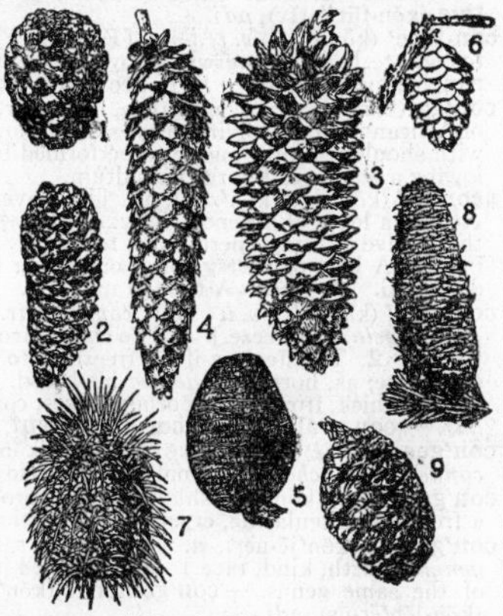

Cones, 1. (All reduced.) 1 Stone Pine (*Pinus pinea*); 2 Cluster Pine (*P. pinaster*); 3 Big-cone Pine (*P. coulteri*); 4 Sugar Pine (*P. lambertiana*); 5 Deodar (*Cedrus deodara*); 6 Red Spruce (*Picea rubens*); 7 Santa Lucia Fir (*Abies venusta*); 8 Nordmann's Fir (*A. nordmanniana*); 9 Giant Sequoia (*Sequoiadendron giganteum*).

cone′flow′er (-flou′ẽr), *n.* = RUDBECKIA.

cone′nose′ (-nōz′), *n.* Any of certain large insects of a genus (*Conorhinus*, esp. *C. sanguisugus*) often found in houses, esp. in the southern and western United States. Cf. KISSING BUG.

Con′es·to′ga wagon (kŏn′ĕs·tō′gȧ). A type of broad-wheeled covered wagon for traveling in soft soil and on prairies; — from Conestoga, Pa., where manufactured.

co′ney (kō′nĭ; kŭn′ĭ), *n.; pl.* CONEYS (-nĭz; -ĭz). Var. of CONY.

con′fab (kŏn′făb; kŏn·făb′), *n. & v. i.* Colloq. short form of CONFABULATION, CONFABULATE.

con·fab′u·late (kŏn·făb′ū·lāt), *v. i.* [L. *confabulatus*, past part., deriv. of *con-* + *fabulari* to speak, fr. *fabula*.] To converse familiarly; chat. — **con·fab′u·la′tion** (-lā′shŭn), *n.*

con′fect (kŏn′fĕkt), *n.* *Obs.* A comfit; a confection.

con·fect′ (kŏn·fĕkt′), *v. t.* [L. *confectus*, past part. of *conficere* to prepare. See COMFIT.] To prepare or make up by compounding; specif.: **a** To preserve or pickle; to make a confection of. **b** To construct; make.

con·fec′tion (kŏn·fĕk′shŭn), *n.* **1.** Act or process of confecting. **2.** Something confected; specif.: **a** A prepared dish or dainty; esp., a sweet, as jam, a fancy dessert, a bonbon, etc. **b** A product of fine workmanship; — a Gallicism used in the trade, esp. of articles of apparel. **c** A pharmaceutical preparation; esp., one compounded with sugar, sirup, or honey. — **con·fec′tion**, *v. t.*

con·fec′tion·ar′y (-ĕr′ĭ *or, esp. Brit.*, -ẽr·ĭ), *n.; pl.* -IES (-ĭz). *Now Rare.* **1.** A confectioner. **2.** = CONFECTIONERY, 2. **3.** A sweetmeat; a confection. — **con·fec′tion·ar′y**, *adj.*

con·fec′tion·er (kŏn·fĕk′shŭn·ẽr), *n.* A manufacturer of or dealer in confections, candies, etc.

con·fec′tion·er′y (-ĕr′ĭ *or, esp. Brit.*, -ẽr·ĭ), *n.; pl.* -ERIES (-ĭz). **1.** Sweetmeats, in general; confections; candies. **2.** The confectioner's art, business, or place of business.

con·fed′er·a·cy (kŏn·fĕd′ẽr·ȧ·sĭ), *n.; pl.* -CIES (-sĭz). **1.** A league or compact for mutual support or common action; alliance. **2.** A combination of persons for unlawful purposes; a combine. **3.** The body formed by persons, states, etc., united by a league. **4.** [*cap.*] In full, *Confederate States of America*. The eleven southern states that seceded from the United States, in 1860 and 1861.

con·fed′er·ate (-ĭt), *adj.* [LL. *confoederatus*, past part. of *confoederare* to join by a league, fr. *con-* + *foederare* to establish by treaty or league, fr. *foedus* league, compact.] **1.** United in a league; confederated. **2.** [*cap.*] Of or pertaining to the Confederacy, its army, flag, etc. — *n.* **1.** One united with others in a confederacy or a confederation; an ally; also, in a bad sense, an accomplice. **2.** [*cap.*] An adherent of the Confederacy. — (-āt), *v. t. & i.* To unite or become united in a league, confederacy, or conspiracy.

con·fed′er·a′tion (kŏn·fĕd′ẽr·ā′shŭn), *n.* **1.** Act of confederating, or state of being confederated; a league; alliance. **2.** A confederacy; esp., a body of independent states more or less permanently united for joint action. **3.** [*cap.*] With *the.* The union of the American colonies (1781–89) under a compact called ***Articles of Confederation***.

con·fed′er·a′tive (kŏn·fĕd′ẽr·ā′tĭv; -ȧ·tĭv), *adj.* Of or pertaining to a confederation or confederates.

con·fer′ (kŏn·fûr′), *v. t.;* -FERRED′ (-fûrd′); -FER′RING. [L. *conferre* to bring together, fr. *con-* + *ferre* to bear.] **1.** To compare; — now only in the imperative. Abbr. *cf.* **2.** To grant; bestow. — **Syn.** See GIVE. — *v. i.* To converse; consult; compare views; hold conference. — **con′fer·ee′, con′fer·ree′** (kŏn′fẽr·ē′), *n.* — **con·fer′ment**, *n.* — **con·fer′ra·ble**, *adj.* — **con·fer′rer**, *n.*

con′fer·ence (kŏn′fẽr·ĕns), *n.* **1.** Formal consultation or discussion; interchange of views; also, a meeting therefor. **2.** Specif., a meeting of the two branches of a legislature, by their committees, to adjust differences. **3.** Conferment, as of a degree. **4.** *Eccl.* **a** [*cap.*] *Methodist & Mennonite Churches.* A stated meeting of preachers and others, invested with authority to take cognizance of ecclesiastical matters. **b** A voluntary association of Congregational churches of a district; also, a district containing such churches. **5.** *U. S.* An association of athletic teams. — **con′fer·en′tial** (-ĕn′shăl), *adj.*

con·fer′va (kŏn·fûr′vȧ), *n.; pl.* -VAE (-vē), -VAS (-vȧz). [L., a kind of water plant.] Any of a genus (*Tribonema*) of algae; formerly, any of the threadlike greenish algae forming scums in ponds. — **con·fer′void** (-void), *adj. & n.*

con·fess′ (kŏn·fĕs′), *v. t.;* -FESSED′ (-fĕst′) or -FEST′; -FESS′ING. [OF. *confesser*, fr. LL., fr. L. *confiteri* to confess, fr. *con-* + *fateri* to confess.] **1.** To acknowledge or own, as a fault or debt. **2.** *Eccl.* **a** To make known or acknowledge (one's sins), esp. to a priest in order to receive absolution. **b** To hear (a penitent) confessing; — of a priest. **3.** To admit or concede. **4.** To acknowledge faith in; to profess or avow adhesion to; as, to *confess* Christ before men. **5.** *Now Poetical.* To give evidence of; make manifest. — *v. i.* To make confession of one's faults, faith, etc.; esp., to make or hear a confession of sins. — **Syn.** See ACKNOWLEDGE. — **con·fess′er**, *n.*

con·fess′ed·ly (kŏn·fĕs′ĕd·lĭ; -ĭd·lĭ), *adv.* By confession; admittedly.

con·fes′sion (kŏn·fĕsh′ŭn), *n.* **1.** Act of confessing; esp., the act of disclosing one's sins to a priest to obtain sacramental absolution. **2.** A statement, esp. a written statement, of something confessed. **3.** Public or open profession of faith. **4.** *Eccl.* **a** A form, as for use in public worship, for the general acknowledgment of sinfulness. **b** A formal statement of doctrinal belief, ordinarily intended for public avowal, as by an individual, a congregation, a synod, or a church; a creed, catechism, etc.; — also called **confession of faith**. **c** A church or body of Christians having a particular confession of faith; a communion. **5.** *Eccl. Arch.* The tomb of a martyr or confessor; also, an altar, crypt, shrine, or church associated with such a tomb. — **con·fes′sion·al** (-ăl; -'l), *adj.* — **con·fes′sion·ar′y** (-ĕr′ĭ *or, esp. Brit.*, -ẽr·ĭ), *adj.*

con·fes′sion·al (-ăl; -'l), *n.* **1.** The recess, seat, or enclosed place where a priest sits to hear confessions. **2.** Act or practice of confessing to a priest.

con·fes′sor (kŏn·fĕs′ẽr; *formerly & still by some, esp. in church use,* kŏn′fĕssor), *n.* One who confesses; specif.: **a** One who professes or gives heroic evidence of his faith in Christ; as, Saint Edward the *Confessor*. **b** A priest who hears confessions and is authorized to grant absolution.

con·fet′ti (kŏn·fĕt′ĭ), *n. pl.* [It., lit., bonbons, confections.] Disks or pieces of paper, thrown broadcast, as at festivals.

con′fi·dant′, *n. masc.*, **con′fi·dante′**, *fem.* (kŏn′fĭ·dănt′; kŏn′fĭ·dănt′). [F.] One to whom secrets are confided; often, a confidential friend.

con·fide′ (kŏn·fīd′), *v. i.* [L. *confidere*, fr. *con-* + *fidere* to trust.] **1.** To put or have faith (*in*); to trust. **2.** *Colloq.* To entrust a secret, esp. a secret trouble or difficulty; — followed by *in*. — *v. t.* **1.** To tell or impart confidentially. **2.** To entrust; commit; — with *to*. **Syn.** See COMMIT. — **con·fid′er** (-fīd′ẽr), *n.*

con′fi·dence (kŏn′fĭ·dĕns), *n.* **1.** State of one who confides; trust; reliance. **2.** Self-confidence. **3.** State of feeling sure; assurance. **4.** That in which faith is put or reliance had. **5.** Reliance upon another's secrecy and fidelity; as, to tell in *confidence*. **6.** Hence, a communication made in confidence.

Syn. **Confidence, assurance, self-possession, aplomb** mean a state of mind free from diffidence, doubt, or misgivings. **Confidence** stresses faith in oneself and in one's powers but it does not, usually, imply conceit; **assurance** carries a far stronger implication of certainty and, sometimes, of arrogance; **self-possession** implies the ease and coolness arising from command over one's powers; **aplomb** describes the behavior or bearing of one whose assurance is conspicuously, but not necessarily disagreeably, manifest. — **Ant.** Diffidence.

confidence game, trick (or the like). Any swindling operation in which advantage is taken of confidence reposed by the victim in the swindler (**confidence man**).

con′fi·dent (kŏn′fĭ·dĕnt), *adj.* **1.** Confiding; trustful. *Shak.* **2.** Having confidence; esp., self-reliant, full of assurance, or, sometimes, presumptuous. — *n.* A confidant. — **con′fi·dent·ly**, *adv.*

con′fi·den′tial (-dĕn′shăl), *adj.* **1.** Communicated in confidence; secret; hence, private; as, a *confidential* file (of documents). **2.** Indicating close intimacy or communication in confidence; as, a *confidential* tone. **3.** Enjoying, or treated with, confidence; as, a *confidential* clerk. — **con′fi·den′tial·ly**, *adv.* — **con′fi·den′tial·ness**, *n.*

con·fid′ing (kŏn·fīd′ĭng), *adj.* **1.** That confides; trustful. **2.** *Obs.* Reliable; trustworthy. — **con·fid′ing·ly,** *adv.*

con·fig′u·ra′tion (kŏn·fĭg′ū·rā′shŭn), *n.* [LL. *configuratio,* fr. *configurare* to form from or after.] **1.** Relative disposition of parts; the figure, contour, or pattern produced by such disposition. **2.** *Psychol.* A Gestalt. — **Syn.** See FORM. — **con·fig′u·ra′tion·al** (-ăl; -'l), *adj.* — **con·fig′u·ra′tion·al·ly,** *adv.* — **con·fig′u·ra′tive** (-fĭg′ū·rā′tĭv; -rȧ·tĭv), *adj.*

con·fig′u·ra′tion·ism (-ĭz'm), *n.* Gestalt psychology.

con′fine (kŏn′fīn; *in senses* 3 & 4, kŏn·fīn′), *n.* [F. *confins,* pl., fr. L., fr. *confinis* bordering, fr. *con-* + *finis* end, border.] **1.** A boundary; also, frontier; — now usually *pl.* **2.** *Archaic.* Region; — usually in the *pl.* **3.** *Poetic.* Confinement. **4.** *Obs.* Prison.

con·fine′ (kŏn·fīn′), *v. i.* [F. *confiner.*] To border; to lie contiguous. — *v. t.* **1.** To restrain within limits; as, to *confine* oneself to facts. **2.** To shut up; imprison. **3.** To restrain from going out; to keep within doors; as, the cold has *confined* him all week. — **Syn.** See LIMIT. — **con·fin′a·ble** (-fīn′ȧ·b'l), **con·fine′a·ble,** *adj.* — **con·fin′er** (-fīn′ẽr), *n.*

con·fined′ (-fīnd′), *adj.* In childbed; in parturition.

con·fine′ment (kŏn·fīn′mĕnt), *n.* [F.] A confining or being confined; specif., restraint within doors by sickness, esp. that attending childbirth; accouchement.

con·firm′ (kŏn·fûrm′), *v. t.* [OF. *confermer,* fr. L. *confirmare,* fr. *con-* + *firmare* to make firm, fr. *firmus* firm.] **1.** To make firm or firmer; establish; strengthen, as in a habit, in faith, etc. **2.** To render valid by formal assent; ratify. **3.** *Eccl.* To administer confirmation to. **4.** To give new assurance of the truth of; verify; corroborate. — **con·firm′a·ble,** *adj.* — **con·firm′a·tive** (-fûr′mȧ·tĭv), *adj.* — **con·firm′er** (-fûr′mẽr), *n.*

Syn. **Confirm, corroborate, substantiate, verify, authenticate, validate** mean to attest to the truth or validity of something. **Confirm** implies the resolving of all doubts, as by an authoritative statement; **corroborate,** the strengthening of testimony or of evidence by that of others; **substantiate** implies the offering of evidence that sustains or nearly sustains the contention; **verify** implies the established correspondence of actual facts or details to those given; **authenticate** and **validate** imply evidence from those in a position to know whether a thing is genuine, valid, or the like.

con′fir·ma′tion (kŏn′fẽr·mā′shŭn), *n.* **1.** Act of confirming, establishing, ratifying. **2. a** Corroboration; verification; as, the report lacks *confirmation.* **b** That which confirms; proof. **3.** *Eccl.* A rite supplemental to baptism, administered usually to those who have reached years of discretion, and conferring upon them the fullness of the privileges gained through baptism. See SACRAMENT, 1.

con·firm′a·to′ry (kŏn·fûr′mȧ·tō′rĭ *or, esp. Brit.,* -tẽr·ĭ), *adj.* Serving to confirm; corroborative.

con·firmed′ (kŏn·fûrmd′), *adj.* **1.** Established; settled; esp., inveterate; chronic. **2.** *Eccl.* Having received the rite of confirmation. — **Syn.** See INVETERATE. — **con·firm′ed·ly** (-fûr′mĕd·lĭ; -mĭd·lĭ), *adv.* — **con·firm′ed·ness,** *n.*

con·fis′ca·ble (kŏn·fĭs′kȧ·b'l), *adj.* Liable to confiscation.

con′fis·cate (kŏn′fĭs·kāt; kŏn·fĭs′-), *adj.* [L. *confiscatus,* past part. of *confiscare* to confiscate, prop., to lay up in a chest, fr. *con-* + *fiscus* basket, treasury.] **1.** Confiscated; forfeited. **2.** Deprived of property by confiscation. — *v. t.* **1.** To seize as forfeited to the public treasury; to appropriate for public use. **2.** To seize by or as if by authority. — **Syn.** See ARROGATE. — **con′fis·ca′tor** (kŏn′fĭs·kā′tẽr), *n.*

con′fis·ca′tion (kŏn′fĭs·kā′shŭn), *n.* Act of confiscating, or state of being confiscated; properly, the seizure of private property to the public use as being forfeited.

con·fis′ca·to′ry (kŏn·fĭs′kȧ·tō′rĭ *or, esp. Brit.,* kŏn·fĭs′kȧ·tẽr·ĭ, kŏn′fĭs·kā′tẽr·ĭ), *adj.* Effecting, or of the nature of, confiscation; characterized by confiscations.

con·fit′e·or (kŏn·fĭt′ē·ôr), *n.* [L., I confess. See CONFESS.] A prayer in which confession of sinfulness is made.

con′fi·ture (kŏn′fĭ·tūr), *n.* [F.] A confection; a comfit.

con·fla′grant (kŏn·flā′grănt), *adj.* [L. *conflagrans,* pres. part. of *conflagrare,* fr. *con-* + *flagrare* to blaze.] Burning; blazing.

con′fla·gra′tion (kŏn′flȧ·grā′shŭn), *n.* [L. *conflagratio,* fr. *conflagrare* to burn.] A raging destructive fire.

con·fla′tion (kŏn·flā′shŭn), *n.* [LL. *conflatio,* fr. L. *conflare* to blow together, fr. *con-* + *flare* to blow.] A combining or fusing together, as of two variant readings of a text; a fusion.

con·flict′ (kŏn·flĭkt′), *v. i.* [L. *conflictus,* past part. of *confligere* to conflict, fr. *con-* + *fligere* to strike.] **1.** *Archaic.* To contend; battle. **2.** To clash; to be incompatible or at variance; as, opinions that *conflict; conflicting* laws. — **con·flic′tion** (-flĭk′shŭn), *n.*

con′flict (kŏn′flĭkt), *n.* **1.** A strife for mastery; hostile encounter; a fight; battle; esp., a prolonged struggle. **2.** Clash or divergence of opinions, interests, etc.; esp., a mental or moral struggle occasioned by incompatible desires, aims, etc. **3.** A dashing together, as of waves. — **Syn.** See DISCORD.

con′flu·ence (kŏn′flōō·ĕns; 114), *n.* **1.** The meeting or junction of two or more streams; also, the place of meeting. **2.** The stream or body formed by such a junction. **3.** A flocking together in one place; hence, a crowd; a concourse.

con′flu·ent (-ĕnt), *adj.* [L. *confluens, -entis,* pres. part. of *confluere, -fluxum,* fr. *con-* + *fluere* to flow.] **1.** Flowing or coming together to form one, as streams. **2.** *Med.* Running or run together, as pimples or pustules; characterized by such pimples or pustules. — *n.* [L. *confluens.*] One of confluent streams; loosely, a tributary.

con′flux (kŏn′flŭks), *n.* Confluence.

con·fo′cal (kŏn·fō′kăl), *adj.* *Math.* Having the same foci.

con·form′ (kŏn·fôrm′), *v. t.* & *i.* [OF. *conformer,* fr. L. *conformare, -formatum,* fr. *con-* + *formare* to form, fr. *forma* form.] To make or be like; to bring into, or be or act in, harmony or agreement. — **Syn.** See ADAPT; AGREE. — **con·form′er,** *n.*

con·form′, *adj.* [F. *conforme,* fr. LL. *conformis,* fr. *con-* + *forma* form.] *Now Rare.* Conformable.

con·form′a·ble (-fôr′mȧ·b'l), *adj.* **1.** That conforms; being like or in agreement, harmony, etc.; — usually followed by *to.* **2.** Submissive; compliant; obedient. **3.** *Geol.* Following in unbroken sequence; — said of strata formed under the same general conditions. — **con·form′a·bil′i·ty** (-bĭl′ĭ·tĭ), **con·form′a·ble·ness,** *n.* — **con·form′a·bly** (-blĭ), *adv.*

con·form′ance (-măns), *n.* Act of conforming; conformity.

con′for·ma′tion (kŏn′fôr·mā′shŭn; -fŏr·mā′shŭn), *n.* **1.** Act of conforming or producing conformity; adaptation. **2.** Formation or fashioning of anything by the symmetrical arrangement of its parts. **3.** Structure; form; specif., the form or outline of an animal or of a dressed carcass. — **Syn.** See FORM.

con·form′ist (kŏn·fôr′mĭst), *n.* One who conforms; esp., *Eng.,* one who conforms to the Established Church. Cf. NONCONFORMIST.

con·form′i·ty (-mĭ·tĭ), *n.; pl.* -TIES (-tĭz). **1.** State or quality of being in agreement, harmony, etc.; congruity. **2.** A point of agreement, similarity, etc.; as, to note *conformities* in style. **3.** Act of one who conforms; as, her well-bred *conformities.* **4.** Religious compliance; esp., *Eng.,* compliance with Established Church usages.

con·found′ (kŏn·found′; kŏn-), *v. t.* [OF. *confondre,* fr. L. *confundere, -fusum,* to pour together, fr. *con-* + *fundere* to pour.] **1.** *Archaic.* **a** To bring to ruin or naught; destroy; rout. **b** To put to shame; abash; discomfit. **2.** (*pron.* kŏn·found′; kŏn′found′) To damn; — used in the imperative as a mild imprecation. **3.** To throw into confusion; perplex; dismay. **4.** To mix up in the mind; to fail to distinguish clearly; to confuse. **5.** *Obs.* **a** To confute. **b** To waste; spend. — **Syn.** See PUZZLE. — **con·found′er,** *n.*

con·found′ed (-foun′dĕd; -dĭd), *adj.* **1.** Confused; perplexed. **2.** Damned; hence, odious; detestable. — **con·found′ed·ly,** *adv.*

con′fra·ter′ni·ty (kŏn′frȧ·tûr′nĭ·tĭ), *n.; pl.* -TIES (-tĭz). [From F., fr. ML. *confraternitas.* See FRATERNITY.] A society or body of men united for some purpose, esp. religious or charitable, or in some profession; brotherhood.

con′frere (kŏn′frâr; *F.* kôɴ′frâr′), *n.* [F. *confrère.*] A fellow member of a brotherhood or society; also, a colleague; a fellow worker, as in a profession.

con·front′ (kŏn·frŭnt′), *v. t.* [F. *confronter* to confront, fr. ML. *confrontare,* fr. L. *con-* + *frons* forehead, front.] **1.** To face, esp. hostilely. **2.** To bring face to face; cause to face or meet; as, to *confront* a person with his accuser; to *confront* one with proofs. **3.** To set side by side for comparison. — **con′fron·ta′tion** (kŏn′frŭn·tā′shŭn), *n.* — **con·front′er,** *n.* — **con·front′ment,** *n.*

Con·fu′cian·ism (kŏn·fū′shăn·ĭz'm), *n.* The ethics of Confucius and his disciples. Filial piety, benevolence, justice, propriety, intelligence, and fidelity are cardinal virtues. — **Con·fu′cian·ist** (-ĭst), *n.* & *adj.*

con·fuse′ (kŏn·fūz′), *v. t.* [F. *confus* confused, fr. L. *confusus,* past part. of *confundere.* See CONFOUND.] **1.** *Obs.* To bring to ruin or naught. **2.** To perplex; disconcert. **3.** To mix or blend so that things cannot be distinguished; jumble together; as, to *confuse* verse with poetry; a *confused* report; *confused* noises. — **Syn.** Muddle, bemuddle, addle, fuddle, befuddle. — **con·fus′ed·ly** (-fūz′ĕd·lĭ; -fūzd′lĭ), *adv.* — **con·fus′ed·ness,** *n.* — **con·fus′ing·ly** (-fūz′ĭng·lĭ), *adv.*

con·fu′sion (kŏn·fū′zhŭn), *n.* Act of confusing; state or quality of being confused; specif.: **a** A state of great disorder. **b** A deranged mental condition. — **con·fu′sion·al** (-ăl; -'l), *adj.*

con′fu·ta′tion (kŏn′fū·tā′shŭn), *n.* **1.** Act or process of confuting; refutation. **2.** That which confutes, as an argument. — **con·fut′a·tive** (kŏn·fūt′ȧ·tĭv), *adj.*

con·fute′ (kŏn·fūt′), *v. t.* & *i.* [F. or L.; F. *confuter,* fr. L. *confutare* to confute.] **1.** To overwhelm by argument; to refute. **2.** To bring to naught; to confound. — **Syn.** See DISPROVE. — **con·fut′er** (-fūt′ẽr), *n.*

con′ga (kŏng′gȧ; *Sp.* kōng′gä), *n.* [Sp., fr. *Congo.*] A Cuban dance of African origin involving three steps followed by a bumping together with shoulders, hips, and legs, performed by groups in double file following a leader with large bass drum.

‖**con′gé′** (kôɴ′zhā′; kŏn′zhā), *n.* [F., leave, fr. OF. *congié,* fr. L. *commeatus* a leave of absence, deriv. of *com-* + *meare* to go.] **1. a** Authoritative or formal permission to depart. **b** Ceremonious leave-taking. **c** A bow or curtsy, orig. on taking leave. **2.** Unceremonious dismissal. **3.** *Arch.* A type of molding. See MOLDING, *Illust.*

con·geal′ (kŏn·jēl′), *v. t.* [OF. *congeler,* fr. L. *congelare, -gelatum,* fr. *con-* + *gelare* to freeze.] **1.** To change from a fluid to a solid by cold; freeze. **2.** To affect as if by freezing; to make thick, curdled, etc.; coagulate; as, horror *congealed* his blood. — *v. i.* To become hard, stiff, or thick, from cold or other causes; coagulate. — **con·geal′a·ble,** *adj.* — **con·geal′er,** *n.* — **con·geal′ment,** *n.*

con′gee (kŏn′jē), *n.* = CONGÉ, 1. — (kŏn·jē′), *v. i.* [OF. *congier, congeer.*] *Archaic.* To make a congé; to take one's leave.

con′ge·la′tion (kŏn′jĕ·lā′shŭn), *n.* The process or result of congealing; a freezing, coagulating, crystallizing, or the like.

con′ge·ner (kŏn′jē·nẽr), *n.* [L., of the same kind, fr. *con-* + *genus, generis,* birth, kind, race.] **a** One allied in nature or action. **b** One of the same genus. — **con′ge·ner′ic** (kŏn′jē·nĕr′ĭk), **con·gen′er·ous** (kŏn·jĕn′ẽr·ŭs), *adj.*

con·gen′ial (kŏn·jēn′yăl; -jē′nĭ·ăl), *adj.* [See CON-; GENIAL.] **1.** Kindred in spirit, tastes, interests, etc.; as, *congenial* persons. **2.** In accord with one's nature, temperament, needs, etc.; compatible; suitable; as, *congenial* occupations; a soil *congenial* to roses. — **Syn.** See CONSONANT. — **con·ge′ni·al′i·ty** (-jē′nĭ·ăl′ĭ·tĭ; -jēn′yăl′ĭ·tĭ), *n.* — **con·gen′ial·ly,** *adv.*

con·gen′i·tal (-jĕn′ĭ·tăl; -t'l), *adj.* [L. *congenitus.* See CON-; GENITAL.] **1.** Existing at, or dating from, birth; constitutional. **2.** Specif., acquired during development in the uterus; — distinguished from *hereditary* (transmitted by the germ plasm); as, *congenital* deformity. — **Syn.** See INNATE. — *n.* One with a congenital disease or defect. — **con·gen′i·tal·ly,** *adv.*

con′ger eel, *or* **con′ger** (kŏng′gẽr), *n.* [OF. *congre,* fr. L. *conger, congrus,* fr. Gr. *gongros.*] A large, marine, entirely scaleless eel (*Conger conger*), sometimes becoming eight feet long. It is an important food fish. See EEL.

con·ge′ri·es (kŏn·jē′rĭ·ēz; -jēr′ēz), *n. sing.* & *pl.* [L., fr. *congerere.* See CONGEST.] A collection of particles, parts, or bodies into one mass; heap; aggregation; as, a *congeries* of ballads.

con·gest′ (kŏn·jĕst′), *v. t.* [L. *congestus,* past part. of *congerere* to bring together, fr. *con-* + *gerere.*] **1.** *Obs.* To gather into a mass. **2.** To cause an overfullness of the blood vessels of (an organ or part). **3.** To block, obstruct, or affect by an overaccumulation of anything or by overcrowding; as, traffic was *congested.* — *v. i.* To become congested. — **con·ges′tion** (-jĕs′chŭn), *n.* — **con·ges′tive** (-jĕs′tĭv), *adj.*

con′gi·us (kŏn′jĭ·ŭs), *n.; pl.* CONGII (-jĭ·ī). [L.] **1.** In ancient Rome, a liquid measure, about three quarts. **2.** *Pharm.* A gallon. Abbr. *cong.* or *C.*

con·glo′bate (kŏn·glō′bāt; kŏng′glō·bāt), *adj.* [L. *conglobatus,* past part. of *conglobare* to conglobate.] Collected into, or forming, a rounded mass or ball. — *v. t.* & *i.* Also **con·globe′** (kŏn·glōb′). To make or become conglobate. — **con′glo·ba′tion** (kŏn′glō·bā′shŭn), *n.*

con·glom′er·ate (kŏn·glŏm′ẽr·ĭt), *adj.* [L. *conglomeratus,* past part.

of *conglomerare* to roll together, fr. *con-* + *glomerare* to wind into a ball.] **1.** Gathered into a ball or a mass; closely clustered; as, *conglomerate* fruit; also, consisting of parts collected from various sources; as, a *conglomerate* language. **2.** *Geol.* Conglomeratic. — *n.* **1.** Something conglomerate; an accumulation; mass; as, a *conglomerate* of florets. **2.** *Geol.* A rock composed of rounded fragments, varying from small pebbles to large boulders, in a cement of hardened clay, or the like. — (-āt), *v. t. & i.* To gather or form into a ball, a compact mass, etc. — **con·glom′er·a′tion** (-ā′shŭn), *n.* — **con·glom′er·at′ic** (-ăt′ĭk), **con·glom′er·it′ic** (-ĭt′ĭk), *adj.*

con·glu′ti·nate (kŏn·glōō′tĭ·nāt), *adj.* [L. *conglutinatus*, past part. of *conglutinare* to glue, fr. *con-* + *glutinare* to glue, fr. *gluten* glue.] Glued together. — *v. t. & i.* To unite by or as if by some glutinous or tenacious substance. — **con·glu′ti·na′tion** (-nā′shŭn), *n.*

Con′go dye *or* **col′or** (kŏng′gō). Any of a group of direct azo dyes, most of which are derivatives of benzidine.

Congo red. A Congo dye used in dyeing cotton and wool red, and as an indicator, either in solution or on test paper (**Congo paper**), being turned blue by acids. Cf. LITMUS.

congo snake *or* **eel.** Either of two eellike amphibians (genus *Amphiuma*) of the southeastern United States, esp. one (*A. means*) that is bluish-black, with two pairs of very short limbs, each ending in two or three toes.

con′gou (kŏng′gōō), **con′go** (-gō), *n.* [Chin. (Pek.) *kung*[1]*-fu*[1] labor.] A black tea (see TEA, 1 **b**) from China.

con·grat′u·lant (kŏn·grăt′ū·lănt), *adj.* Congratulating; congratulatory. — *n.* A congratulator.

con·grat′u·late (-lāt), *v. t.* [L. *congratulatus*, past part. of *congratulari* to wish joy abundantly, fr. *con-* + *gratulari* to wish joy, fr. *gratus* pleasing.] **1.** To address with expressions of happiness in another's joy, success, etc.; to wish joy to; felicitate. **2.** *Obs.* **a** To express sympathetic pleasure at. **b** To salute; to greet. — **Syn.** See FELICITATE. — **con·grat′u·la′tor** (-lā′tẽr), *n.*

con·grat′u·la′tion (-lā′shŭn), *n.* Act of congratulating; also, *pl.*, congratulatory words or speeches; felicitations.

con·grat′u·la·to′ry (kŏn·grăt′ū·là·tō′rĭ *or, esp. Brit.*, -tẽr·ĭ, -lā′tẽr·ĭ), *adj.* Expressing or conveying congratulations.

con′gre·gate (kŏng′grē·gāt), *adj.* [L. *congregatus*, past part. of *congregare* to congregate, fr. *con-* + *gregare* to collect, fr. *grex* flock.] Collected; assembled; also, collective. — (-gāt), *v. t. & i.* To collect into a crowd or mass; to assemble. — **Syn.** See GATHER. — **con′gre·ga′tor** (-gā′tẽr), *n.*

con′gre·ga′tion (kŏng′grē·gā′shŭn), *n.* **1.** Act of congregating; state of being congregated; also, a collection or mass of separate things. **2.** An assembly of persons, esp. one gathered for religious worship and instruction. **3.** *Bib.* The whole body of the Jewish people. **4.** *New Eng. Hist.* In the colonies in which the Congregational Church was established, the whole body of people of a settlement, town, or parish having its particular place of worship. Cf. SOCIETY, 6. **5.** *R.C.Ch.* **a** An order of religious under a common rule, either with or without vows. **b** A permanent body or committee of cardinals to which is entrusted some department of church business; as, the *Congregation* of Propaganda, which has charge of missions.

con′gre·ga′tion·al (-ăl; -′l), *adj.* **1.** Of, pertaining to, or of the nature of a congregation. **2.** [*cap.*] Belonging to Congregationalism, or to Congregationalists.

Con′gre·ga′tion·al·ism (-ĭz′m), *n.* **1.** Church organization which vests all ecclesiastical power in the assembled brotherhood of each local church. **2.** [*cap.*] Faith and polity of a body of evangelical Trinitarian churches which recognize the brotherhood of each church as independent in ecclesiastical matters but which are united in fellowship and action. — **Con′gre·ga′tion·al·ist** (-ĭst), *n. & adj.*

con′gre·ga′tive (kŏng′grē·gā′tĭv), *adj.* Tending to congregate. — **con′gre·ga′tive·ness**, *n.*

con′gress (kŏng′grĕs; -grĭs), *n.* [L. *congressus*, fr. *congredi*, past part. *-gressus*, to go or come together, fr. *con-* + *gradi* to go, fr. *gradus* step.] **1.** A meeting; encounter. **2.** Intercourse; esp., sexual intercourse. **3.** A gathering or assembly; esp., a formal assembly, as of princes, deputies, representatives, or envoys. **4.** The body of senators and representatives of a nation, esp. of a republic, constituting its chief legislative body. The Congress of the United States is a bicameral body, the two houses of which are the Senate and the House of Representatives. The united body of senators and representatives for any term of two years for which the whole body of representatives is chosen is called *one Congress.* **5.** [*cap.*] The lower house of the Spanish Cortes.

congress boot. A high shoe having the top adjusted to it by an elastic gusset.

con·gres′sion·al (kŏn·grĕsh′ŭn·ăl; -′l), *adj.* Of or pertaining to a congress, esp. [*cap.*] the Congress of the United States. — **con·gres′sion·al·ist** (-ĭst), *n.*

Congressional medal. = MEDAL OF HONOR.

con′gress·man (kŏng′grĕs·măn; -grĭs·măn), *n.* A member of the Congress of the United States, esp. of the House of Representatives. — **con′gress·wom′an** (-wŏŏm′ăn), *n.*

con′gru·ent (kŏng′grŏŏ·ĕnt), *adj.* [L. *congruens*, pres. part.] **1.** Possessing congruity; congruous. **2.** *Geom.* Superposable so as to be coincident throughout; as, *congruent* plane figures. — **con′gru·ence** (-ĕns), **con′gru·en·cy** (-ĕn·sĭ), *n.* — **con′gru·ent·ly**, *adv.*

con·gru′i·ty (kŏn·grōō′ĭ·tĭ), *n.*; *pl.* -TIES (-tĭz). **1.** State or quality of being congruous; agreement, harmony, or correspondence between things. **2.** A point of agreement, correspondence, etc. **3.** *Geom.* Exact coincidence throughout; — said of figures.

con′gru·ous (kŏng′grŏŏ·ŭs), *adj.* [L. *congruus*, fr. *congruere* to come together, agree.] **1.** Suitable or concordant in nature or qualities; correspondent; in harmony; consistent. **2.** Accordant to what is proper, reasonable, or right; hence, suitable, fitting, or the like. **3.** *Geom.* = CONGRUENT, 2. — **Syn.** See CONSONANT. — **con′gru·ous·ly**, *adv.* — **con′gru·ous·ness**, *n.*

con′ic (kŏn′ĭk), *adj.* [F. or L.; F. *conique*, fr. NL., fr. Gr. *kōnikos.* See CONE.] Of, pertaining to, in the form of, or like a cone. — *n. Math.* A conic section. — **con′i·cal** (-ĭ·kăl), *adj.* — **con′i·cal·ly**, *adv.*

con′ics (-ĭks), *n.*; see -ICS. *Math.* The theory of conic sections.

conic section. *Math.* A curve formed by the intersection of a plane and a right circular cone (see CONE, 2 **a**). According to the angle of intersection the curve is a *circle, ellipse, parabola,* or *hyperbola.*

conic sections. That branch of geometry which treats of the parabola, ellipse, and hyperbola.

co·nid′i·o·phore′ (kō·nĭd′ĭ·ō·fōr′; 70), *n.* [*conidium* + *-phore.*] *Bot.* In certain fungi, a specialized hyphal branch which produces successive conidia by abstriction.

co·nid′i·um (kō·nĭd′ĭ·ŭm), *n.*; *pl.* -IA (-à). [NL., fr. Gr. *konis* dust.] *Bot.* An asexual spore produced by abstriction from the tip of a conidiophore. — **co·nid′i·al** (-ăl), *also* **co·nid′i·an** (-ăn), *adj.*

co′ni·fer (kō′nĭ·fẽr; kŏn′ĭ·fẽr), *n.* [L., cone-bearing. See CONE; -FEROUS.] Any of an order (Pinales) of trees and shrubs, mostly evergreens, including those of the pine family (Pinaceae), bearing true cones, and those of the yew family (Taxaceae), having a berrylike fruit. See CONE, *Illust.*; EVERGREEN, *n.*, 1.

co·nif′er·ous (kō·nĭf′ẽr·ŭs), *adj.* **a** Bearing cones, as the pine and cypress. **b** Of or pertaining to conifers.

co′ni·ine (kō′nĭ·ēn; -ĭn; kō′nēn), *n.* Also **co′nine** (-nēn; -nĭn), **co′nin** (-nĭn). [See CONIUM.] *Chem.* A poisonous liquid alkaloid, $C_8H_{17}N$, with a peculiar odor, found in the poison hemlock *Conium maculatum* (see HEMLOCK, 1).

co·ni′um (kō·nī′ŭm; kō′nĭ·ŭm), *n.* [L., hemlock, fr. Gr. *kōneion.*] Any of a genus (*Conium*) of poisonous herbs of the carrot family. Cf. HEMLOCK, 1.

con·jec′tur·al (kŏn·jĕk′tṳr·ăl), *adj.* **1.** Of, pertaining to, or of the nature of, conjecture; as, *conjectural* emendations. **2.** Given to conjectures. — **con·jec′tur·al·ly**, *adv.*

con·jec′ture (-tṳr), *n.* [F. or L.; F., fr. L. *conjectura*, fr. *conjicere*, *-jectum*, to throw together, infer, conjecture, fr. *con-* + *jacere* to throw.] **1.** *Obs.* **a** Divination; prognostication. **b** Supposition. *Shak.* **2.** Inference from defective or presumptive evidence; as, opinions based on *conjecture;* also, a guess, theory, etc., based on such evidence; surmise. — *v. t.* To reach by conjecture; to form conjectures about. — *v. i.* To form conjectures. — **con·jec′tur·a·ble** (-tṳr·à·b′l), *adj.* — **con·jec′tur·a·bly** (-blĭ), *adv.* — **con·jec′tur·er**, *n.*

Syn. **Conjecture, surmise, guess** mean to draw inferences from slight evidence. **Conjecture** implies formation of an opinion or judgment upon insufficient evidence; **surmise** implies even slighter evidence and some support from imagination or suspicion; **guess** stresses a hitting upon a conclusion either at random or from very uncertain evidence.

con·join′ (kŏn·join′), *v. t. & i.* [OF. *conjoindre*, fr. L. *conjungere*, *-junctum*, fr. *con-* + *jungere* to join.] To join together as in action or purpose; unite; combine.

con·joint′ (kŏn·joint′; kŏn′joint; 2), *adj.* [F.] **1.** United; conjoined. **2.** Pertaining to, made up of, or carried on by, two or more in combination; joint. — **con·joint′ly**, *adv.*

con′ju·gal (kŏn′jŏŏ·găl), *adj.* [F. or L.; F., fr. L. *conjugalis*, fr. *conjux* husband, wife, consort, fr. *conjungere* to unite, marry.] Pertaining to marriage, the married state, or matrimonial relations. — **Syn.** See MATRIMONIAL. — **con′ju·gal′i·ty** (-găl′ĭ·tĭ), *n.* — **con′ju·gal·ly**, *adv.*

con′ju·gate (-gāt), *adj.* [L. *conjugatus*, past part. of *conjugare* to unite, fr. *con-* + *jugare* to join, yoke, marry, fr. *jugum* yoke.] **1.** Yoked or united, esp. in pairs or in marriage; coupled. **2.** *Bot.* Bijugate. **3.** *Gram.* Of the same derivation and hence usually of kindred signification; — of words (as, *just, justice, justly*). **4.** *Math.* Presenting themselves simultaneously and being interchangeable in the enunciation of properties, as two quantities, points, lines, axes, curves, etc. — *n.* **1.** A conjugate word. **2.** A conjugate axis, diameter, number, etc. — (-gāt), *v. t. & i.* **1.** To make conjugate; specif., to unite sexually or in marriage. **2.** *Biol.* To fuse or unite in conjugation. **3.** *Gram.* To inflect (a verb), or give in order the forms of its several voices, moods, tenses, numbers, and persons. — **con′ju·ga′tor** (-gā′tẽr), *n.*

con′ju·ga′tion (-gā′shŭn), *n.* **1.** Act of conjugating; state of being conjugated; union; conjunction. **2.** **a** *Biol.* The fusion of two similar gametes or two unicellular organisms, as in the lower thallophytes, by a process analogous to fertilization among higher organisms. **b** *Zool.* Temporary union with exchange of nuclear material, the usual sexual process among ciliate protozoans. **3.** *Gram.* **a** A schematic arrangement of the inflectional forms of a verb. **b** A class of verbs having the same type of inflectional forms; as, the strong or the weak *conjugation.* — **con′ju·ga′tion·al** (-ăl; -′l), *adj.* — **con′ju·ga′tion·al·ly**, *adv.* — **con′ju·ga′tive** (kŏn′jŏŏ·gā′tĭv), *adj.*

con·junct′ (kŏn·jŭngkt′; kŏn′jŭngkt; 2), *adj.* [L. *conjunctus*, past part. See CONJOIN.] United; conjoined; joint. — **con·junct′ly**, *adv.*

con·junc′tion (kŏn·jŭngk′shŭn), *n.* **1.** Act of conjoining, or state of being conjoined; union; association; combination; also, an instance of such union. **2.** Concurrence, as of events. **3.** *Astrol. & Astron.* The meeting or passing of two or more celestial bodies in the same degree of the zodiac. **4.** *Gram.* A connective having the special function of joining together sentences, clauses, phrases, or words, and classifiable as *co-ordinating* (*and, but, or*) or *subordinating* (*though, if, as, since*). Abbr. *conj.* — **con·junc′tion·al**, *adj.* — **con·junc′tion·al·ly**, *adv.*

con′junc·ti′va (kŏn′jŭngk·tī′và), *n.*; *pl.* -TIVAS (-vàz), -TIVAE (-vē). [NL., fr. LL. *conjunctivus* connective.] The mucous membrane which lines the inner surface of the eyelid and covers the fore part of the eyeball. See EYE, *Illust.* — **con′junc·ti′val** (-văl), *adj.*

con·junc′tive (kŏn·jŭngk′tĭv), *adj.* **1.** Connective. **2.** Done or existing in conjunction. **3.** *Gram.* **a** Of the nature of a conjunction. **b** Designating a conjunction, such as *and*, which both joins words, phrases, etc., in a co-ordinate construction and expresses a unity of their ideas. — *n.* A conjunctive word, phrase, etc.; specif., a conjunctive, or copulative, conjunction. — **con·junc′tive·ly**, *adv.*

con·junc′ti·vi′tis (kŏn·jŭngk′tĭ·vī′tĭs), *n.* [NL., fr. *conjunctiva* + *-itis.*] Inflammation of the conjunctiva.

con·junc′ture (kŏn·jŭngk′tṳr), *n.* **1.** *Obs.* A joining together. **2.** A combination of events or circumstances; a crisis produced by such combination; a juncture.

con′ju·ra′tion (kŏn′jŏŏ·rā′shŭn), *n.* **1.** Act of conjuring; incantation; now usually, practice of magic. **2.** An expression or trick used in conjuring. **3.** *Archaic.* Solemn entreaty or appeal, as to God.

con·jure′ (*see each def.*), *v. i.* [OF. *conjurer*, fr. L. *conjurare* to swear together, conspire, fr. *con-* + *jurare* to swear.] **1.** (kŏn·jŏŏr′) *Obs.* To conspire. **2.** (kŭn′jẽr; kŏn′-) **a** To summon a devil, spirit, etc., by an invocation or incantation. **b** To practice magic, now usually legerdemain; juggle. — *v. t.* **1.** (kŏn·jŏŏr′) *Obs.* To charge or call on solemnly. **2.** (kŭn′jẽr; kŏn′-) To summon by invocation or incantation. **3.** (kŏn·jŏŏr′) To implore or beseech with earnestness or solemnity. **4.** (kŭn′jẽr) To affect or effect by or as if by conjuring; to make come or go, evoke, etc., as if by magic; as, his imagination *conjured* up a scene of horror.

con′jure man or **woman** (kŭn′jẽr; kŏn′-). *Colloq., Southern U. S. & West Indies.* A practitioner of magic; a witch doctor or witch.

con′jur·er, con′jur·or (kŭn′jẽr·ẽr; *in sense* 2 kŏn·jo͝or′ẽr), *n.* **1.** One who practices magic arts; also, a practitioner of legerdemain; magician; juggler. **2.** One who implores or charges solemnly.

conn (kŏn), *v. t. & i.* To steer or direct the steering of, as a vessel. — *n.* Act or station of one who conns.

con′nate (kŏn′āt), *adj.* [LL. *connatus,* past part. of *connasci* to be born together. See COGNATE.] **1.** Congenital; inborn. **2.** Agreeing in nature; cognate. **3.** Born or originated together; — of two or more innate qualities, etc. **4.** *Biol.* Congenitally united; firmly united. — **con′nate·ly,** *adv.* — **con′nate·ness,** *n.* — **con·na′tion** (kŏ·nā′shŭn), *n.*

con·nat′u·ral (kŏ·năt′ū·răl), *adj.* **1.** Connected by nature, united in nature; inborn; natural. **2.** Of the same nature; allied; cognate. — **con·nat′u·ral·ly,** *adv.*

con·nect′ (kŏ·nĕkt′), *v. t.* [L. *connectere, -nexum,* fr. *con-* + *nectere* to bind.] **1.** To join, or fasten together, as by something intervening; specif.: **a** To unite or link together as in an electrical circuit. **b** To join or unite by a means of communication, as by telephone. **2.** To attach by personal associations; as, to *connect* oneself with a new business. **3.** To associate in thought. — **Syn.** See JOIN. — *v. i.* **1.** To join; unite; to be closely associated. **2.** *U. S.* To meet or make connections, as for the transference of passengers. — **con·nec′tor, con·nect′er** (-nĕk′tẽr), *n.*

con·nect′ed·ly, *adv.* In a connected manner; coherently.

con·nect′ing rod. *Mach.* A rod or bar jointed to, and connecting, two or more moving parts.

con·nec′tion, con·nex′ion (kŏ·nĕk′shŭn), *n.* [L. *connexio.*] The spelling *connection* arose by analogy with such words as *collection,* etc. *Connexion* is now rare in the U. S. but frequent in England. **1.** Act of connecting; state or quality of being connected; union; alliance; relationship. **2.** Specif.: **a** Causal or logical relationship. **b** Logical sequence, as of ideas; coherence. **c** Contextual relations or associations; context. **3.** A relation of personal intimacy; specif.: **a** Sexual relation. **b** Relationship by family ties. **c** Relation in a practical way; a having to do with anything. **4.** A thing that connects; bond; link. **5.** A person connected by some tie, as by blood, marriage, friendship, etc.; also, *pl.,* such relatives, friends, or associates, collectively; often, kin. **6.** A body of persons connected by some common interest; specif. (spelled *connexion*), a religious sect or denomination; as, the Wesleyan *connexion.* **7.** The act, event, or means of communication or of continuation of a journey; as, a telephone *connection;* to make *connections* at Boston. — **con·nec′tion·al, con·nex′ion·al,** *adj.*

con·nec′tive (-nĕk′tĭv), *adj.* Connecting or tending to connect. — *n.* That which connects; specif.: **a** *Bot.* The tissue connecting the two lobes of an anther. **b** *Gram.* A word or element that connects words, clauses, or sentences; esp., a conjunction, relative pronoun, or preposition. — **con·nec′tive·ly,** *adv.* — **con′nec·tiv′i·ty** (kŏn′ĕk·tĭv′ĭ·tĭ), *n.*

conn′ing tow′er (kŏn′ĭng). *Nav.* **a** An armored pilothouse, as on a battleship, with slits for observation purposes. **b** A raised structure on the deck of a submarine used as an observation post and as an entrance to the vessel.

con·nip′tion (kŏ·nĭp′shŭn), *n., or, in full,* **conniption fit.** *Colloq., U. S.* A fit of anger, hysteria, etc.; tantrum.

con·niv′ance (kŏ·nīv′ăns), *n.* Formerly **con·niv′ence** (-ĕns). **1.** Act of conniving; passive consent or co-operation. **2.** *Law.* Corrupt or guilty assent to wrongdoing, not involving actual participation in it, but knowledge of and failure to oppose it.

con·nive′ (kŏ·nīv′), *v. i.* [F. or L.; F. *conniver,* fr. L. *connivere* to shut the eyes, connive.] **1.** To feign ignorance, now esp. of something which duty calls on one to oppose; — usually with *at.* **2.** To co-operate (*with*) secretly, or to have a secret understanding (*with*). — **con·niv′er** (-nīv′ẽr), *n.*

con′nois·seur′ (kŏn′ĭ·sûr′; -sūr′), *n.* [F. (obs. spelling), fr. OF., fr. L. *cognoscere* to become acquainted with. See COGNITION.] One aesthetically versed in any subject; esp., one competent to act as a critical judge of an art, or in a matter of taste.

con′no·ta′tion (kŏn′ō·tā′shŭn), *n.* **1.** The suggestive significance of a word apart from its explicit and recognized meaning. **2.** *Logic.* = INTENSION, 6. — **Syn.** See under DENOTE.

con·not′a·tive (kŏ·nōt′ȧ·tĭv; kŏn′ō·tā′tĭv), *adj.* Connoting or tending to connote; pertaining to connotation. — **con·not′a·tive·ly,** *adv.*

con·note′ (kŏ·nōt′), *v. t.* [ML. *connotare,* fr. *con-* + *notare* to note.] To suggest, indicate, or mean along with, or in addition to, the explicit and recognized meaning. — **Syn.** See DENOTE.

con·nu′bi·al (kŏ·nū′bĭ·ăl), *adj.* [L. *connubialis,* fr. *connubium* marriage, fr. *con-* + *nubere* to marry.] Of or pertaining to marriage, or the marriage state; conjugal. — **Syn.** See MATRIMONIAL. — **con·nu′bi·al′i·ty** (-ăl′ĭ·tĭ), *n.* — **con·nu′bi·al·ly,** *adv.*

co′noid (kō′noid), **co·noi′dal** (kō·noi′dăl; -d′l), *adj.* [Gr. *kōnoeidēs* conical, fr. *kōnos* cone + *eidos* form.] Cone-shaped. — **co′noid,** *n.*

con′quer (kŏng′kẽr), *v. t.* [OF. *conquerre,* fr. L. *conquaerere* to seek or search for, bring together, LL., to conquer, fr. *con-* + *quaerere* to seek.] **1.** To gain or acquire by force of arms; to subjugate; also, to overcome by force of arms; to vanquish. **2.** To gain or win by overcoming obstacles or opposition. **3.** To overcome by mental or moral power; to surmount. — *v. i.* To gain the victory; to be victorious; win. — **con′quer·a·ble,** *adj.*

Syn. Conquer, vanquish, defeat, beat, lick, subdue, subjugate, reduce, overcome, surmount, overthrow, rout mean to get the better of by force or strategy. Conquer implies mastery of someone or something; vanquish implies a complete overpowering or discomfiture of someone; defeat does not imply the finality of *vanquish* but otherwise equals it; beat is colloquial for *defeat* and, sometimes, for *vanquish;* lick implies a humiliating beating; subdue implies a defeating and suppression; subjugate implies a complete subjection; reduce implies a forcing to capitulate or surrender; overcome and surmount imply an overpowering or, in the case of *surmount,* an exceeding, in power, skill, or the like; overthrow and rout imply not only defeat but disaster, *overthrow* suggesting destruction and *rout,* complete dispersion.

con′quer·or (-ẽr), *n.* One who conquers; victor. — ***the Conqueror.*** A surname given to William, Duke of Normandy, who won the battle of Hastings, in 1066, and became William I of England.

con′quest (kŏng′kwĕst; kŏn′-), *n.* [OF., fr. past part. of *conquierre, conquerre.* See CONQUER.] **1.** Act or process of conquering. **2.** That which is conquered; as: **a** Territory appropriated in war. **b** A person whose favor or hand has been won. — **Syn.** See VICTORY. — ***the (Norman) Conquest.*** *Eng. Hist.* Subjugation of England by William of Normandy in 1066.

con·quis′ta·dor (kŏn·kwĭs′tȧ·dôr; *Sp.* kōng·kēs′tä·thôr′), *n.; pl.* -DORS (-dôrz), -DORES (-dōrz; *Sp.* -thō′rās). [Sp., fr. *conquistar* to conquer.] A conqueror; specif., any one of the leaders in the Spanish conquest of America, esp. of Mexico and Peru, in the 16th century.

con·san′guine (kŏn·săng′gwĭn), *adj.* Consanguineous.

con′san·guin′e·ous (kŏn′săng·gwĭn′ē·ŭs), *adj.* [L. *consanguineus,* fr. *con-* + *sanguis* blood.] Of the same blood; descended from the same ancestor.

con′san·guin′i·ty (kŏn′săng·gwĭn′ĭ·tĭ), *n.* **1.** Blood relationship; descent from a common ancestor; — disting. from *affinity* (def. 1). The degrees of lineal consanguinity are reckoned as one degree for each person in the line of descent, exclusive of him from whom the computation begins. **2.** Any close relation or connection; affinity.

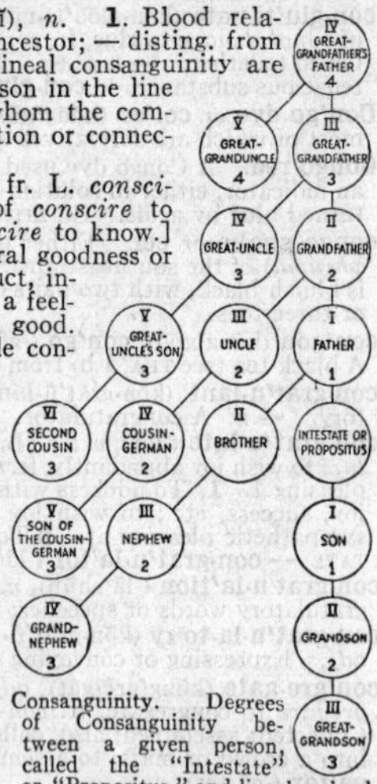

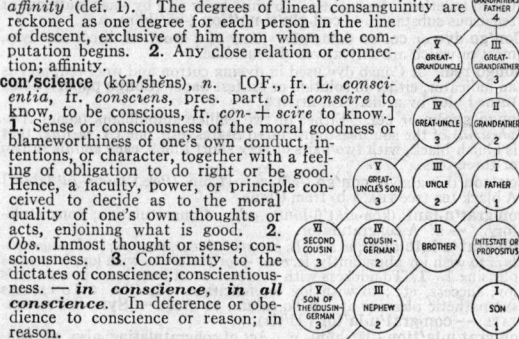

Consanguinity. Degrees of Consanguinity between a given person, called the "Intestate" or "Propositus," and lineal and collateral relations are shown according to the common-law and canon-law computation (Arabic numerals) and the civil-law computation (Roman numerals), lineal relations being represented by the disks vertically connected, collateral relations by those at the side.

con′science (kŏn′shĕns), *n.* [OF., fr. L. *conscientia,* fr. *consciens,* pres. part. of *conscire* to know, to be conscious, fr. *con-* + *scire* to know.] **1.** Sense or consciousness of the moral goodness or blameworthiness of one's own conduct, intentions, or character, together with a feeling of obligation to do right or be good. Hence, a faculty, power, or principle conceived to decide as to the moral quality of one's own thoughts or acts, enjoining what is good. **2.** *Obs.* Inmost thought or sense; consciousness. **3.** Conformity to the dictates of conscience; conscientiousness. — ***in conscience, in all conscience.*** In deference or obedience to conscience or reason; in reason.

conscience clause. A clause in a general law exempting persons whose religious scruples forbid compliance therewith, as from taking judicial oaths, service, etc.

con′science·less, *adj.* Having no conscience; unprincipled.

conscience money. Money paid to relieve the conscience by rendering or restoring, usually anonymously, what has been wrongfully acquired or withheld.

con′sci·en′tious (kŏn′shĭ·ĕn′shŭs), *adj.* Influenced by, governed by, or conformed to, a strict regard to the dictates of conscience. — **Syn.** See UPRIGHT. — **con′sci·en′tious·ly,** *adv.* — **con′sci·en′tious·ness,** *n.*

conscientious objector. One who, for conscience' sake, objects to warfare or to military service.

con′scion·a·ble (kŏn′shŭn·ȧ·b'l), *adj.* *Now Rare.* Accordant with good conscience; just. — **con′scion·a·bly** (-blĭ), *adv.*

con′scious (kŏn′shŭs), *adj.* [L. *conscius,* fr. *con-* + *scire* to know.] **1.** Sharing another's knowledge or awareness of something; — now only figuratively; as, these *conscious* stones. **2.** Aware or sensible (of an inward state or outward fact). **3.** Possessed with a sense of guilt. **4.** Involving consciousness of something; as, *conscious* guilt. **5.** Self-conscious. **6.** Mentally awake or active. **7.** Wrought or working with critical awareness; intentional; as, *conscious* artistry or artists. — **Syn.** See AWARE. — **con′scious·ly,** *adv.*

con′scious·ness (-nĕs; -nĭs), *n.* **1.** Awareness, esp. of something within oneself; state or fact of being conscious in regard to something. **2.** *Philos.* That state of being characterized by sensation, emotion, thought, etc.; mind in the broadest sense. **3.** The totality of conscious states, as of an individual. See STREAM OF CONSCIOUSNESS. **4.** The normal state of conscious life. **5.** The upper level of mental life, as contrasted with unconscious processes. See COCONSCIOUSNESS, SUBCONSCIOUS.

con′script (kŏn′skrĭpt), *adj.* [L. *conscriptus,* past part. of *conscribere* to write together, enroll, fr. *con-* + *scribere* to write.] **1.** Enrolled or chosen. **2.** Enlisted by compulsion; formed by compulsory enrollment; as, *conscript* soldiers, armies, or labor. — *n.* One compulsorily enrolled to serve, esp. as a soldier or sailor or in a set job under a dictatorial regime.

con·script′ (kŏn·skrĭpt′), *v. t.* To enroll by compulsion for military or naval service or for service imposed through arbitrary power; to draft.

con′script fa′thers. (Rarely in *sing.*) **a** *Roman Hist.* The senators of ancient Rome. **b** The senators of medieval Venice. **c** Allusively, the legislators of any political unit.

con·scrip′tion (kŏn·skrĭp′shŭn), *n.* A compulsory enrollment of men, esp. for military or naval service; a draft; also, a forced contribution of money imposed by a government in time of war.

con′se·crate (kŏn′sē·krāt), *adj.* [L. *consecratus,* past part. of *consecrare* to consecrate, fr. *con-* + *sacrare* to consecrate, fr. stem of *sacer* sacred.] Consecrated; hallowed. — *v. t.* **1.** To make, or declare, sacred or holy; to set apart or devote to the service or worship of God. Cf. DESECRATE. **2.** To dedicate or devote to some particular purpose; as, a life *consecrated* to art. **3.** To render sacred; hallow; sanctify. — **Syn.** See DEVOTE. — **con′se·cra′tor** (-krā′tẽr), *n.* — **con′se·cra·to′ry** (-krȧ·tō′rĭ *or, esp. Brit.,* -krā′tẽr·ĭ), *adj.*

con′se·cra′tion (-krā′shŭn), *n.* Act or ceremony of consecrating; state of being consecrated; dedication.

con′se·cu′tion (-kū′shŭn), *n.* [L. *consecutio.* See CONSEQUENT.] **1.** Logical sequence; chain of reasoning. **2.** Succession; series; sequence, as of events.

con·sec′u·tive (kŏn·sĕk′ū·tĭv), *adj.* [See CONSEQUENT.] **1.** Succeeding one another in a regular order, series, or sequence; without interval or break; successive. **2.** Proceeding by successive interrelated stages of thought. **3.** *Gram.* Expressing consequence; as, a *consecutive* clause. **4.** *Music.* Having a parallel sequence; as, *consecutive* fifths. — **con·sec′u·tive·ly,** *adv.* — **con·sec′u·tive·ness,** *n.*

Syn. Consecutive, successive mean following one after the other. Consecutive, however, stresses immediacy in following and close connection in time, space, or logic between the units; successive may be applied to things which follow each other, regardless of length of interval between; as, four *consecutive* days; three *successive* leap years.

con·sen′su·al (kŏn·sĕn′shŏŏ·ăl; -shŏŏ·ăl), *adj.* [See CONSENSUS.] **1.** *Law.* Existing or made by mere mutual consent without further act or writing; as, a *consensual* contract. **2.** *Physiol.* Designating involuntary movement accompanying, or correlative with, voluntary movement. — **con·sen′su·al·ly**, *adv.*

con·sen′sus (-sĕn′sŭs), *n.; pl.* CONSENSUSES (-ĕz; -ĭz). [L. See CONSENT.] Agreement in matters of opinion, testimony, etc.; accord; also, loosely, the convergent trend, as of opinion.

☞ The expression *consensus of opinion*, although objected to by some, is now generally accepted as in good use.

con·sent′ (kŏn·sĕnt′), *v. i.* [OF. *consentir*, fr. L. *consentire*, *-sensum*, to feel together, agree, fr. *con-* + *sentire* to feel.] **1.** *Archaic.* To agree; to accord; concur. "Saul was *consenting* unto his death" (*Acts* viii. 1). **2.** To give assent or approval; as, to *consent* to his daughter's marriage. — **Syn.** See ASSENT. — *n.* **1.** Voluntary accordance with, or concurrence in, what is done or proposed by another; acquiescence; approval. **2.** *Archaic.* Correspondence in parts, qualities, or operations; agreement. **3.** *Archaic.* Agreement as to action or opinion; accord. — **con·sent′er**, *n.*

con′sen·ta′ne·ous (kŏn′sĕn·tā′nē·ŭs), *adj.* [L. *consentaneus.*] **1.** Agreeing; suitable. **2.** Done with one consent; unanimous. — **con′sen·ta′ne·ous·ly**, *adv.* — **con′sen·ta′ne·ous·ness**, *n.*

con·sen′tient (kŏn·sĕn′shĕnt; -shĭ·ĕnt), *adj.* Agreeing; concurrent; esp., united in opinion; unanimous. — **con·sen′tience** (-shĕns; -shĭ·ĕns), *n.*

con′se·quence (kŏn′sē·kwĕns *or, esp. Brit.*, -kwĕns), *n.* **1.** That which follows something on which it depends; a natural or necessary result; — contrasted with mere *sequence.* **2.** *Logic.* = INFERENCE, 2. **3.** Chain of causes and effects; consecution. **4.** Act of following something else as a result; relation of an effect to its cause. **5.** Importance with respect to what comes after; value; moment; hence, importance, as in rank, social position, etc. **6.** Assumed importance; consequentiality. — **Syn.** See EFFECT; IMPORTANCE.

con′se·quent (-kwĕnt; -kwĕnt), *adj.* [OF., fr. L. *consequens*, *-entis*, pres. part. of *consequi* to follow, fr. *con-* + *sequi* to follow.] **1.** Following as a result or effect. **2.** Observing or marked by consecutiveness, or logical sequence; logically consistent. **3.** *Logic.* Following by necessary inference. — *n.* **1.** A consequence; outcome. **2.** A thing or circumstance which follows another, as in time or order, without any causal connection being implied. **3.** *Logic.* = INFERENCE, 2. **4.** *Math.* The second term of a ratio, as the term *b* in the ratio *a:b*, the first, *a*, being the *antecedent.*

con′se·quen′tial (-kwĕn′shăl), *adj.* **1.** Of the nature of, or following as, a consequence, result, or logical inference. **2.** *Now Rare.* Of consequence; important. **3.** Assuming or showing self-importance. — **con′se·quen′ti·al′i·ty** (-shĭ·ăl′ĭ·tĭ), *n.* — **con′se·quen′tial·ly**, *adv.* — **con·se·quen′tial·ness**, *n.*

con′se·quent·ly (kŏn′sē·kwĕnt·lĭ *or, esp. Brit.*, -kwĕnt·lĭ), *adv.* By consequence; by logical sequence.

con·serv′a·ble (kŏn·sûr′vȧ·b'l), *adj.* That can be conserved.

con·serv′an·cy (-văn·sĭ), *n.* Conservation; esp., official conservation, as of trees, rivers, or public health.

con′ser·va′tion (kŏn′sẽr·vā′shŭn), *n.* **1.** A conserving, preserving, guarding, or protecting; a keeping in a safe or entire state; preservation. **2.** Official maintenance and supervision, as of natural resources. **3.** A division, as of a forest, under such care. — **con′ser·va′tion·al**, (-ăl; -'l), *adj.*

con′ser·va′tion·ist (-ĭst), *n.* One who advocates conservation, esp. of a state's or nation's forests or natural resources.

conservation of energy. *Physics.* The principle that the total amount of energy in an isolated system remains unchanged while internal changes of any kind occur.

conservation of mass *or* **matter.** *Physics & Chem.* The principle that the total mass of any material system is neither increased nor diminished by reactions between the parts.

con·serv′a·tism (kŏn·sûr′vȧ·tĭz'm), *n.* [For *conservativism.*] **1.** Conservative principles; the disposition and tendency to preserve what is established; opposition to change. **2.** [*cap.*] The principles and practice of the Conservative party in England; Toryism.

con·serv′a·tive (-tĭv), *adj.* **1.** Conserving; preservative. **2.** Disposed to maintain existing institutions or views; opposed to change. **3.** Within safe bounds; moderate; as, a *conservative* estimate; also, adhering to sound principles; believed to involve little risk; as, a *conservative* investment. **4.** [*cap.*] Designating, pertaining to, or characteristic of, a political party which favors the conservation of existing institutions and forms of government. — *n.* **1.** A conservative agent or principle; preservative. **2.** A conservative person. **3.** [*cap.*] A member of the Conservative party. — **con·serv′a·tive·ly**, *adv.* — **con·serv′a·tive·ness**, *n.*

con·ser′va·toire′ (kŏn·sûr′vȧ·twär′; -sûr′vȧ·twär), *n.* [F.] = CONSERVATORY, 3.

con′ser·va′tor (kŏn′sẽr·vā′tẽr; kŏn·sûr′vȧ·tẽr), *n.* **1.** One who preserves from injury or violation; a protector. **2.** Any of various officials charged with the duty of protecting something. **3.** A person, official, or institution designated, as by a court, to take over and protect the interests of an incompetent, as a minor child, an insane person, a convict, etc.

con·serv′a·to′ry (kŏn·sûr′vȧ·tō′rĭ *or, esp. Brit.*, -tẽr·ĭ), *adj.* Conserving; preservative. — *n.; pl.* -RIES (-rĭz). **1.** *Obs.* A place for preservation or safekeeping of things. **2.** A glasshouse or greenhouse for growing or displaying plants. **3.** A place of instruction in any special branch, esp. music and the arts; a conservatoire.

con·serve′ (kŏn·sûrv′; kŏn′sûrv), *n.* [OF., fr. *conserver.*] **1.** A sweetmeat prepared and conserved with sugar; a confection. **2.** *pl.* Preserves, as of fruit.

con·serve′ (kŏn·sûrv′), *v. t.* [OF. *conserver*, fr. L. *conservare*, fr. *con-* + *servare* to guard.] **1.** To keep in a safe or sound state; to preserve. **2.** To prepare with sugar, etc., for the purpose of preservation, as fruits, etc.; to make a conserve of. — **con·serv′er** (-sûr′vẽr), *n.*

con·sid′er (kŏn·sĭd′ẽr), *v. t.* [OF. *considerer*, fr. L. *considerare*, *-sideratum.*] **1.** *Archaic.* To look at attentively; to examine. **2.** To think on with care; to ponder; to study. **3.** *Obs.* To estimate; calculate. **4.** To have regard for in a practical way; to treat with consideration; to regard highly; esteem. **5.** To view as in a certain relation; to judge; as, to *consider* a man unfit; also, to think; believe. **6.** To give thought to with a view to purchasing, accepting, or adopting. — *v. i.* To reflect; deliberate.

Syn. **Consider, study, contemplate, weigh, revolve** mean to fix one's mind on something so as to know it or to solve a problem involved in it. **Consider** often implies little more than applying one's mind as from one point of view or in thinking it over; **study** implies great concentration and more attention to details and minutiae; **contemplate** implies the focusing of attention and a dwelling upon an experience, an idea, etc.; **weigh** implies an attempt to get at the truth as by balancing counterclaims, conflicting evidence, etc.; **revolve** implies turning over mentally a question, a problem, a plan, etc., so that all sides are taken into account.

con·sid′er·a·ble (kŏn·sĭd′ẽr·ȧ·b'l), *adj.* **1.** Worthy of consideration; of importance. **2.** Rather large in extent, and, *Colloq., U.S.*, in amount. — *n.* **1.** *Obs.* A thing to be considered. **2.** *Colloq., U.S.* A considerable amount, degree, extent, etc. — **con·sid′er·a·bly** (-blĭ), *adv.*

con·sid′er·ance (-ăns), *n.* *Obs.* Consideration.

con·sid′er·ate (-ĭt), *adj.* **1.** Marked by or given to careful consideration; circumspect. **2.** Observant of the rights and feelings of others; showing thoughtful kindness. — **Syn.** See THOUGHTFUL. — **con·sid′er·ate·ly**, *adv.* — **con·sid′er·ate·ness**, *n.*

con·sid′er·a′tion (-ā′shŭn), *n.* **1.** Act or process of considering; careful thought; deliberation. **2.** Thoughtful or sympathetic regard or notice. **3.** That which is, or should be, considered as a ground of opinion or action. **4.** A result of considering; a matured opinion; reflection. **5.** Attentive respect; appreciative regard. **6.** Claim to notice; importance. **7.** A recompense, as for a service; a fee or compensation; specif., *Law*, that which is regarded as the equivalent or return given or suffered by one for the act or promise of another.

con·sid′ered (kŏn·sĭd′ẽrd), *adj.* **a** Matured by extended deliberative thought. **b** Regarded with respect or esteem.

con·sid′er·ing, *prep.* In view of; taking into account.

con·sign′ (kŏn·sīn′), *v. t.* [F. *consigner*, fr. L. *consignare*, *-signatum*, to seal or sign, fr. *con-* + *signare*, fr. *signum* mark.] **1.** *Obs.* To mark or dedicate with the sign of the cross. **2.** To give, transfer, or deliver, formally. **3.** To give in charge; commit; entrust. **4.** To assign; to devote; as, to *consign* a room to one's use. **5.** *Com.* To send or address (by bill of lading or otherwise) to an agent to be cared for or sold. — *v. i.* *Obs.* To yield consent; to subscribe. — **Syn.** See COMMIT. — **con·sign′a·ble**, *adj.* — **con′sig·na′tion** (kŏn′sĭg·nā′shŭn), *n.*

con′sign·ee′ (kŏn′sī·nē′; -sĭ·nē′), *n.* [*consign* + *-ee.*] One to whom something is consigned or shipped.

con·sign′ment (kŏn·sīn′mĕnt), *n.* Act of one who consigns anything; also, that which is consigned; — chiefly with reference to goods consigned to an agent.

con·sign′or (kŏn·sīn′ẽr; kŏn′sī·nôr′; kŏn′sĭ-), *n.* Also **con·sign′er** (kŏn·sīn′ẽr). One who consigns something.

con·sist′ (kŏn·sĭst′), *v. i.* [F. or L.; F. *consister*, fr. L. *consistere* to stand still, fr. *con-* + *sistere* to cause to stand, fr. *stare* to stand.] **1.** *Archaic.* To hold together; to be supported and maintained. **2.** To reside or inhere (*in*), as the cause, substance, or essential nature; as, ancient Greek religion did not *consist* in myth. **3.** To be composed or made up (*of*). **4.** **a** *Archaic.* To exist or be capable of existing (*with*). **b** To be consistent or harmonious (*with*). — (kŏn′sĭst), *n.* *Cant.* Make-up; composition, as by classes or grades.

con·sist′ence (-sĭs′tĕns), *n.* Consistency.

con·sist′en·cy (-tĕn·sĭ), *n.; pl.* -ENCIES (-sĭz). **1.** Condition of adhering together, as the parts of a body; firmness; coherence. **2.** *Obs.* A solid substance or body. **3.** A degree of firmness, density, viscosity, or the like. **4.** Firmness of constitution or character; persistency. **5.** Agreement or harmony of parts; congruity; correspondence; specif., harmony of conduct with profession; also, uniformity, as of practice.

con·sist′ent (-tĕnt), *adj.* **1.** Possessing firmness or coherence; solid. **2.** Having agreement with itself or with something else; accordant; congruous. **3.** Living or acting conformably to one's own belief or professions. — **Syn.** See CONSONANT. — **con·sist′ent·ly**, *adv.*

con·sis′to·ry (kŏn·sĭs′tō·rĭ; kŏn′sĭs·tẽr·ĭ), *n.; pl.* -RIES (-rĭz). [From ONF., fr. L. *consistorium* a place of assembly, fr. *consistere.* See CONSIST.] **1.** A place of assembly; esp., a council chamber; hence, any solemn council. **2.** A church tribunal; specif.: **a** *R.C.Ch.* The papal senate or a session of it. **b** *Ch. of Eng.* A diocesan court presided over by the bishop's chancellor or commissary and dealing only with spiritual and ecclesiastical matters. **c** In the Dutch and other Reformed churches, the lowest court, composed of the minister (or ministers), the elders, and sometimes, esp. in U. S., the deacons, of a congregation. **3.** *Freemasonry.* The organization that confers the degrees of the Scottish Rite from the 19th to the 32d, inclusive. — **con′sis·to′ri·al** (kŏn′sĭs·tō′rĭ·ăl; 70), *adj.*

con·so′ci·ate (kŏn·sō′shĭ·āt), *adj.* [L. *consociatus*, past part. of *consociare* to associate, unite, fr. *con-* + *sociare* to join, unite. See SOCIAL.] Consociated; associate. — *n.* An associate. — (-āt), *v. t. & i.* To associate together. — **con·so′ci·a′tion** (-sĭ·ā′shŭn; -shĭ·ā′shŭn), *n.*

con′sol (kŏn′sŏl; kŏn·sŏl′), *n., sing.* of CONSOLS.

con′so·la′tion (kŏn′sō·lā′shŭn), *n.* Act or instance of consoling, or state of being consoled; comfort; also, one that consoles. — **con·sol′a·to′ry** (kŏn·sŏl′ȧ·tō′rĭ *or, esp. Brit.*, -tẽr·ĭ), *adj.*

consolation game, match, race, etc. A game, match, etc., open only to losers in early stages of a contest.

con·sole′ (kŏn·sōl′), *v. t. & i.* [F. *consoler*, fr. L. *consolari*, past part. *-atus*, fr. *con-* + *solari* to console.] To soothe in distress or depression; to comfort. — **Syn.** See COMFORT. — **con·sol′a·ble** (-sōl′ȧ·b'l), *adj.* — **con·sol′er** (-ẽr), *n.*

con′sole (kŏn′sōl), *n.* [F., a bracket.] **1.** *Arch.* A bracketlike member used to support a cornice, etc., or for ornament, as on the keystone of an arch. Cf. CORBEL. **2.** *Furniture.* A console table. **3.** *Music.* The part of an organ which contains the keyboards, pedals, etc., and from which the instrument is played. **4.** A cabinet for a radio or television set or a record player.

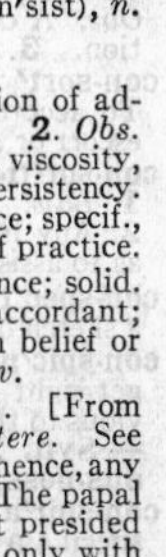
Console, 1.

con′sole ta′ble. A table whose top is carried, at least in part, by one or more consoles.

con·sol′i·date (kŏn·sŏl′ĭ·dāt), *adj.* [L. *consolidatus*, past part. of *consolidare* to make firm, fr. *con-* + *solidare* to make firm, fr. *solidus* solid.] Consolidated. — *v. t. & i.* **1.** To unite or press into a compact mass; also, to make firm; strengthen; as, to *consolidate* one's political power. **2.** To combine into a single whole; as, to *consolidate* two armies. **3.** *Mil.* To organize and strengthen (a position recently captured). — **con·sol′i·da′tor** (-dā′tẽr), *n.*

con·sol′i·da′tion (-dā′shŭn), *n.* **1.** Act or process of consolidating, or state of being consolidated. **2.** *Finance.* The merger of two or more corporations. See MERGER.

con·sol'ing (kŏn·sōl'ĭng), *adj.* That consoles, soothes, or comforts. — **con·sol'ing·ly,** *adv.*

con'sols (kŏn'sŏlz; kŏn·sŏlz'), *n. pl.* [Contr. of *consol*idated (annuities).] British funded government securities.

con'som·mé' (kŏn'sŏ·mā'; *F.* kôɴ'sô'mā'), *n.* [F., lit., consumed (of the meat).] A clear soup made usually from a combination of veal or chicken and other meats. — **Syn.** See SOUP.

con'so·nance (kŏn'sō·năns), *n.* Also **con'so·nan·cy** (-năn·sĭ). **1.** Agreement or congruity; as, *consonance* of opinions. **2.** Correspondence or agreement of sounds, as in words; assonance. **3.** *Music.* **a** Loosely, a pleasing combination of tones. **b** A combination of tones giving a sense of repose, that is, not requiring resolution; — opp. to *dissonance.* **4.** *Physics.* Sympathetic vibration; resonance.

con'so·nant (-nănt), *adj.* [OF., fr. L. *consonans, -antis,* pres. part. of *consonare* to sound at the same time, agree, fr. *con-* + *sonare* to sound.] **1.** Having agreement; consistent; according. **2.** Having like sounds; as, *consonant* syllables. **3.** Consonantal. **4.** *Music.* **a** Agreeable in sound. **b** Not requiring resolution; — opp. to *dissonant.* **5.** *Physics.* Pertaining to or exhibiting consonance; resonant.

Syn. **Consonant, consistent, compatible, congruous, congenial, sympathetic** mean in agreement with one another or agreeable one to the other. **Consonant** basically implies absence of discord that shows harmony or conformity between two things; **consistent** implies such agreement between details of the same thing or between related things that they will not be in conflict; **compatible** implies a capacity for going or existing together without disagreement, discord, or the like; **congruous,** more positive than *compatible,* suggests a fitness or appropriateness to each other so that the effect is pleasing or agreeable; **congenial** most often suggests a fitness of persons to the taste of each other, or of one thing to a person's taste, that pleasure or satisfaction follows, but occasionally it is used of things that are satisfyingly congruous; **sympathetic** suggests qualities in a person or thing that make it in agreement with a person's likings, taste, or habits.

— *n.* A speech sound articulated by narrowing the breath channel enough to cause audible friction (e.g., *f* in *fee*), or by blocking some part of the channel other than the nose completely (e.g., *g* in *go*) or partially (e.g., *l* in *lie*); also, a letter representing such a sound. Distinguished from *vowel.*

con'so·nan'tal (-năn'tăl; -t'l), *adj.* Of the nature of a consonant; pertaining to, or marked by, a consonant.

con'so·nant·ism (kŏn'sō·năn·tĭz'm), *n.* The consonant system of a language or dialect.

con'so·nant·ly, *adv.* In consonance; in accord.

con'sort (kŏn'sôrt; *orig. accented* con·sort'), *n.* [F., fr. L. *consors, -sortis,* fr. *con-* + *sors* lot, fate, share.] A partner, companion, or colleague; specif.: **a** A wife or husband; spouse. **b** The wife (***queen consort***) of a reigning king, or the husband (***prince consort***) of a queen regnant. **c** *Naut.* A ship keeping company with another.

con'sort, *n.* [Cf. OF. *consorte* a company, fr. L. *consortium.*] **1.** *Obs.* A company; group. **2.** *Obs.* Concurrence or accord; association. **3.** *Hist.* [Confused with *concert.*] Harmony of sounds.

con·sort' (kŏn·sôrt'), *v. i.* **1.** To keep company; to associate. **2.** To accord; harmonize. — *v. t.* **1.** To unite or join. **2.** *Obs.* To escort or attend; accompany.

con·sor'ti·um (kŏn·sôr'shĭ·ŭm), *n.; pl.* -TIA (-shĭ·ȧ). [L., fellowship.] **1.** *Law.* Fellowship; partnership; union; esp., marital association. **2.** Any international business or banking agreement or combination, as to assist another nation.

con·spec'tus (kŏn·spĕk'tŭs), *n.* [L.] A general mental survey; esp., a sketch or outline of a subject; a synopsis. — **Syn.** See ABRIDGMENT.

con·spic'u·ous (-spĭk'ū·ŭs), *adj.* [L. *conspicuus,* fr. *conspicere* to get sight of, perceive, fr. *con-* + *spicere, specere,* to look.] **1.** Obvious to the eye or mind; manifest. **2.** Attracting attention; striking. — **Syn.** See NOTICEABLE. — **con·spic'u·ous·ly,** *adv.* — **con·spic'u·ous·ness,** *n.*

con·spir'a·cy (kŏn·spĭr'ȧ·sĭ), *n.; pl.* -CIES (-sĭz). Act of conspiring; specif.: **a** Combination (of persons) for an evil purpose; a plot. **b** Combination or union (of persons or things) for a single purpose or end; harmonious action. **c** *Law.* An agreement, manifesting itself in words or deeds, by which two or more persons confederate to do an unlawful act, or to use unlawful means to do an act which is lawful. — **Syn.** See PLOT.

con·spir'a·tor (-tēr), *n.* One who conspires; a plotter. — **con·spir'a·tress** (-trĕs; -trĭs), *n.*

con·spir'a·to'ri·al (-tō'rĭ·ăl), *adj.* Of or characteristic of conspiracy.

con·spire' (kŏn·spīr'), *v. i. & t.* [OF. *conspirer,* fr. L. *conspirare* to blow together, harmonize, agree, plot, fr. *con-* + *spirare* to breathe, blow.] **1.** To make an agreement, esp. in secret, to do some unlawful deed; to plot together. **2.** To concur or work to one end; act in harmony; co-operate. — **con·spir'er** (-spīr'ēr), *n.*

con'sta·ble (kŭn'stȧ·b'l; kŏn'-), *n.* [OF. *conestable,* fr. LL. *comes stabuli,* orig., count of the stable, equerry, fr. *comes* count (L. companion) + L. *stabulum* stable.] **1.** A high officer in the monarchial and princely establishments of the Middle Ages; as, the ***constable of France,*** highest officer of the crown and commander in chief of the army; the ***(lord high) constable of England,*** commander in chief of the forces. **2.** The keeper of a royal castle or of a fortified town. **3.** Any of various officers having power as conservators of the public peace, and bound to execute the warrants of judicial officers, as a policeman or a member of a constabulary. — **con'sta·ble·ship',** *n.*

con·stab'u·lar'y (kŏn·stăb'ū·lĕr'ĭ *or, esp. Brit.,* -lēr·ĭ), *adj.* Of or pertaining to a constable; consisting of constables. — *n.; pl.* -IES (-ĭz). **1.** The body of constables in any town, district, or country. **2.** An armed police force of the civil government of a country organized on military lines. — **con·stab'u·lar** (-lēr), *adj.*

con'stan·cy (kŏn'stăn·sĭ), *n.* **1.** Steadfastness or firmness of mind; fidelity. **2.** Freedom from change; stability.

con'stant (-stănt), *adj.* [OF., fr. L. *constans, -antis,* pres. part. of *constare* to stand firm, be consistent, fr. *con-* + *stare* to stand.] **1.** Firm or steadfast; resolute; also, faithful. **2.** Fixed or invariable; uniform. **3.** Continually recurring; regular. **4.** *Obs.* Confident; positive. — **Syn.** See FAITHFUL; CONTINUAL. — **Ant.** Fitful. — *n.* **1.** Anything invariable or not subject to change. **2.** *Math.* A magnitude that is supposed not to change its value in a certain discussion or stage of investigation; — opp. to *variable.* — **con'stant·ly,** *adv.*

con'stel·late (kŏn'stĕ·lāt), *v. i. & t.* To shine with united radiance; to unite in one luster, as stars.

con'stel·la'tion (-lā'shŭn), *n.* [OF. *constellacion,* fr. LL. *constellatio.* See STELLATE.] **1.** *Astrol.* Configuration of the stars, esp. at one's birth (cf. HOROSCOPE); hence, *Obs.,* character as determined by one's stars. **2.** **a** Any one of a number of arbitrary groups of fixed stars. About ninety constellations are now recognized by astronomers. **b** A division of the stellar heavens including such a group. — **con·stel'la·to'ry** (kŏn·stĕl'ȧ·tō'rĭ *or, esp. Brit.,* -tēr·ĭ), *adj.*

con'ster·nate (kŏn'stēr·nāt), *v. t.* To fill with consternation.

con'ster·na'tion (-nā'shŭn), *n.* [F. or L.; F., fr. L. *consternatio,* fr. *consternare* to overcome, *consternere* to prostrate, fr. *con-* + *sternere* to spread out.] Amazed terror that confounds the faculties; dismay. — **Syn.** See FEAR.

con'sti·pate (kŏn'stĭ·pāt), *v. t.* [L. *constipatus,* past part. of *constipare* to press together.] **1.** *Now Rare.* To cram together; to condense. **2.** *Med.* To render costive; to cause constipation in. — **con'sti·pat'ed** (-pāt'ĕd; -ĭd), *adj.*

con'sti·pa'tion (-pā'shŭn), *n.* **1.** *Obs.* Compression; condensation. **2.** A state of the bowels in which the evacuations are infrequent and difficult; costiveness.

con·stit'u·en·cy (kŏn·stĭt'ū·ĕn·sĭ), *n.; pl.* -CIES (-sĭz). A body of constituents, as the voters in a representative district; also, the district represented.

con·stit'u·ent (-ĕnt), *adj.* [F. or L.; F. *constituant,* fr. L. *constituens, -entis,* pres. part.] **1.** Serving to form, compose, or make up; component. **2.** Having power to elect or appoint; as, a *constituent* body. **3.** Having power to form or revise a constitution; as, a *constituent* assembly. — *n.* **1.** A component; element. **2.** One who aids, as an elector, in the establishment of the rights of another as his representative in a legislative body; broadly, any resident of a district represented. **3.** *Ling.* One of two or more forms (morphemes, phrases, clauses) entering into a morphological or syntactical construction. Constituents are classified as *immediate* and *ultimate;* thus, *he write-s review-s* is a clause with two immediate constituents (*he* and *writes reviews*) and five ultimate constituents. — **Syn.** See ELEMENT.

con'sti·tute (kŏn'stĭ·tūt), *v. t.* [L. *constitutus,* past part. of *constituere* to constitute, fr. *con-* + *statuere* to place.] **1.** To station in a given situation; now, to appoint or ordain to an office or function. **2.** To set up; establish; specif.: **a** To enact, as a law. **b** To found, as a social or political institution. **3.** To make up as the constituent element or elements; as, vivacity *constitutes* her greatest charm; fifty-two cards *constitute* a pack.

con'sti·tu'tion (kŏn'stĭ·tū'shŭn), *n.* **1.** Act or process of constituting; esp., act of enacting, establishing, or appointing. **2.** *Hist.* An authoritative or established law or custom. **3.** The aggregate of the physical and vital powers of an individual; also, temperament or disposition. **4.** Natural structure or texture. **5.** The mode of organization of a social group. **6.** The fundamental organic law or principles of government of a nation, state, society, or other organized body of men, embodied in written documents, or implied in institutions and customs; also, a written instrument embodying such organic law.

con'sti·tu'tion·al (-ăl; -'l), *adj.* **1.** Belonging to, or inherent in, the constitution, or structure of body or mind; as, a *constitutional* infirmity. **2.** Pertaining to the composition of anything; essential. **3.** Of or pert. to the constitution of a state; as, *constitutional* law; specif.: **a** In accordance with, or authorized by, a constitution. **b** Regulated by, dependent on, or secured by, a constitution; as, *constitutional* rights. **4.** Loyal to, or supporting, the constitution. **5.** For the benefit of one's constitution, or health. — *n. Colloq.* A walk or other exercise taken for one's health.

con'sti·tu'tion·al·ism (-ĭz'm), *n.* Adherence to, or government according to, constitutional principles; also, a constitutional system of government.

con'sti·tu'tion·al·ist (-ĭst), *n.* An adherent of some particular constitution, or an advocate or student of, or a writer on, constitutionalism or constitutions.

con'sti·tu'tion·al'i·ty (-ăl'ĭ·tĭ), *n.; pl.* -TIES (-tĭz). Quality or state of being constitutional; esp., accordance with the governmental constitution.

con'sti·tu'tion·al·ly, *adv.* **1.** **a** In accordance with one's constitution; naturally; as, he was *constitutionally* timid. **b** In structure, composition, or constitution. **2.** In accordance with the constitution, or fundamental law; legally.

Constitution State. Connecticut; — a nickname.

con'sti·tu'tive (kŏn'stĭ·tū'tĭv; kŏn·stĭt'ū·tĭv), *adj.* **1.** Having power to enact, establish, or create. **2.** Constituting or helping to constitute; constituent; essential. — **con'sti·tu'tive·ly,** *adv.*

con·strain' (kŏn·strān'), *v. t.* [OF. *constraindre,* fr. L. *constringere,* fr. *con-* + *stringere* to draw tight.] **1.** To compel; force. **2.** To force or produce in an unnatural or strained manner; as, a *constrained* smile. **3.** To secure by bonds; to confine. **4.** To bring into narrow compass; also, to clasp tightly. **5.** To hold back by force; to restrain. — **Syn.** See FORCE. — **con·strain'a·ble,** *adj.* — **con·strain'ed·ly** (-strān'ĕd·lĭ; -ĭd·lĭ), *adv.* — **con·strain'er,** *n.*

con·straint' (-strānt'), *n.* [OF. *constreinte.*] **1.** Act of constraining, or state of being constrained; compulsion; also, restraint. **2.** Repression; hence, embarrassment or unnaturalness of manner.

con·strict' (kŏn·strĭkt'), *v. t.* [L. *constrictus,* past part. of *constringere.* See CONSTRAIN.] To draw together; to bind. — **Syn.** See CONTRACT.

con·stric'tion (-strĭk'shŭn), *n.* A constricting, or state of being constricted; tightness; also, anything that constricts; a constricted part.

con·stric'tive (-tĭv), *adj.* Of, pertaining to, or marked by constriction; tending to constrict.

con·stric'tor (-tēr), *n.* [NL.] **1.** That which constricts. **2.** *Anat.* A muscle which contracts a cavity or orifice, or compresses an organ. **3.** *Zool.* A snake that kills its prey by crushing it with its coils, as the anaconda, boa constrictor, and python.

con·stringe' (kŏn·strĭnj'), *v. t.* [L. *constringere.* See CONSTRAIN.] To draw together; contract; constrict; astringe.

con·strin'gent (-strĭn'jĕnt), *adj.* Causing constriction; astringent. — **con·strin'gen·cy** (-jĕn·sĭ), *n.*

con·stru'a·ble (kŏn·stro͞o'ȧ·b'l), *adj.* That may be construed. — **con·stru'a·bil'i·ty** (-bĭl'ĭ·tĭ), *n.*

con·struct' (kŏn·strŭkt'), *v. t.* [L. *constructus,* past part. of *construere* to construct, fr. *con-* + *struere* to pile up, set in order.] **1.** To put together the parts of (something); to build. **2.** To set in order mentally; to arrange. — **con·struct'er, con·struc'tor** (-strŭk'tēr), *n.*

con'struct (kŏn'strŭkt), *n.* Something constructed; specif., *Psychol.,* an intellectual synthesis; as every sense perception is a *construct.*

con·struc′tion (kŏn·strŭk′shŭn), *n.* **1.** Process, art, or manner of constructing; act of devising and forming; also, a thing constructed; structure. **2.** Act or result of construing, interpreting, or explaining a declaration or fact; interpretation. **3.** *Art.* Any nonrepresentational creation fashioned in the manner of sculptural, architectural, or mathematical models. **4.** *Gram.* Arrangement and connection of words in a sentence; syntactical arrangement. **5.** *Ling.* The meaningful arrangement of two or more morphemes. A *morphological construction* consists of a free form and a bound form (*play-ed*) or only of bound forms (*re-ceive*); a *syntactic construction* consists entirely of free forms (*he is out*). — **con·struc′tion·al** (-ăl; -′l), *adj.*

con·struc′tion·ist (-ĭst), *n.* A person who puts a certain construction or interpretation on some instrument, such as the United States Constitution; as, a strict *constructionist.*

con·struc′tive (-tĭv), *adj.* **1.** Constructing or given to construction. **2.** Of or resembling construction; also, as opposed to *destructive,* helpful toward construction; as, *constructive* criticism. **3.** Derived from, or depending on, construction or interpretation; — often applied in law to an act or condition assumed from other acts or conditions; as, a *constructive* fraud. — **con·struc′tive·ly,** *adv.* — **con·struc′tive·ness,** *n.*

con·struc′tiv·ism (-tĭv·ĭz′m), *n.* A Russian radical movement in painting, architecture, and engineering, applying scientific technique to art and characterized by counter reliefs, highly abstract conceptions, and bold structural projects.

con·strue′ (kŏn·strōō′; kŏn′strōō), *v. t.* [L. *construere.* See CONSTRUCT.] **1.** To apply the rules of syntax to (a sentence or clause) so as to exhibit the structure or discover the sense; also, to translate, esp. orally. **2.** To put a construction upon; to explain the sense of; interpret. — *v. i.* To analyze syntax, esp. in connection with translating; also, to admit of being construed. — **con·stru′er** (kŏn·strōō′ẽr; kŏn′strōō·ẽr), *n.*

con′strue (kŏn′strōō), *n.* An act of construing.

con′sub·stan′tial (kŏn′sŭb·stăn′shăl), *adj.* [LL. *consubstantialis.*] Of the same kind or nature; having the same substance or essence. — **con′sub·stan′ti·al′i·ty** (-shĭ·ăl′ĭ·tĭ), *n.* — **con′sub·stan′tial·ly,** *adv.*

con′sub·stan′ti·ate (-shĭ·āt), *v. t.* [ML. *consubstantiatus,* past part. of *consubstantiare.*] To regard as, or make to be, united in one common substance or nature. — *v. i.* **a** To adhere to the doctrine of consubstantiation. **b** To become united in substance.

con′sub·stan′ti·a′tion (-ā′shŭn), *n.* *Theol.* The actual substantial presence and combination of the body of Christ with the Eucharistic bread and wine; — disting. from *transubstantiation* and *impanation.*

con′sue·tude (kŏn′swē·tūd), *n.* [OF., fr. L. *consuetudo.* See CUSTOM.] Custom; habit; social usage.

con′sue·tu′di·nar′y (-tū′dĭ·nĕr′ĭ; -nẽr·ĭ), *adj.* Customary.

con′sul (kŏn′sŭl), *n.* [L.] **1.** *Rom. Hist.* Either of the two joint chief magistrates of the republic. **2.** *Fr. Hist.* One of the three chief magistrates of the republic from 1799 to 1804. **3.** An official appointed by a government to reside in some foreign country, to care for the commercial interests of the citizens of the appointing government. — **con′su·lar** (kŏn′sū·lẽr), *adj.* — **con′sul·ship,** *n.*

con′su·late (kŏn′sū·lāt), *n.* [L. *consulatus.*] **1.** Consular government or term of office. **2.** The premises occupied by a consul. **3.** [*cap.*] [F. *Consulat.*] *Fr. Hist.* The consular government (Nov. 9, 1799, to May 18, 1804).

con·sult′ (kŏn·sŭlt′), *v. i.* [L. *consultare,* fr. *consulere* to consult.] To seek the advice of another; to confer. — *v. t.* **1.** *Obs.* To take counsel to bring about; devise. **2.** To ask advice of; to refer to. **3.** To have regard to, in judging or acting; to consider. — **con·sult′a·ble,** *adj.* — **con·sult′er,** *n.*

con′sult (kŏn′sŭlt; kŏn·sŭlt′), *n.* *Rare.* A consultation.

con·sult′ant (kŏn·sŭl′tănt), *n.* **1.** One who consults another. **2.** One who gives professional advice or services, as a consulting physician.

con′sul·ta′tion (kŏn′sŭl·tā′shŭn), *n.* Act of consulting or conferring; a council or conference.

con·sult′a·tive (kŏn·sŭl′tȧ·tĭv), *adj.* Pert. to consultation; having the privilege or right of conference; advisory.

con·sult′a·to′ry (-tō′rĭ *or, esp. Brit.,* -tẽr·ĭ), *adj.* Advisory.

con·sult′ing, *adj.* Designating one called in conference for professional advice; as, a *consulting* physician, engineer.

con·sul′tive (kŏn·sŭl′tĭv), *adj.* Consultative.

con·sum′a·ble (kŏn·sūm′ȧ·b′l), *adj.* Capable of being consumed. — *n.* A thing that may be consumed.

con·sume′ (kŏn·sūm′), *v. t.* [OF. *consumer,* fr. L. *consumere* to take wholly, consume, fr. *con-* + *sumere* to take, fr. *sub* + *emere* to buy.] **1.** To destroy, as by fire. **2.** To spend wastefully; hence, to use up; expend. **3.** To eat or drink up (food); devour. **4.** To engage the attention or energy of; to engross; as, *consumed* with curiosity. — *v. i.* To waste or burn away; to perish.

con·sum′ed·ly (-sūm′ĕd·lĭ; -ĭd·lĭ), *adv.* Excessively.

con·sum′er (-sūm′ẽr), *n.* **1.** One who consumes. **2.** *Econ.* One who uses (economic) goods, and so diminishes or destroys their utilities; — opposed to *producer.*

con·sum′ers′ goods. *Econ.* Economic goods that directly satisfy human wants or desires, such as food, clothes, etc.; — dist. from *producers' goods* and *capital goods.*

con·sum′mate (kŏn·sŭm′ĭt), *adj.* [L. *consummatus,* past part. of *consummare* to accomplish, sum up, fr. *con-* + *summa* sum.] Consummated; carried to the utmost extent or degree; perfect. — **con·sum′mate·ly,** *adv.*

con′sum·mate (kŏn′sŭ·māt), *v. t. & i.* **1.** To bring to completion; to complete; achieve. **2.** *Obs.* To perfect. **3.** To complete by intercourse; — said of marriage. — **con′sum·ma′tion** (-mā′shŭn), *n.* — **con′sum·ma′tive** (kŏn′sŭ·mā′tĭv), *adj.* — **con′sum·ma′tor** (-mā′tẽr), *n.*

con·sump′tion (kŏn·sŭmp′shŭn), *n.* [L. *consumptio,* fr. *consumere.* See CONSUME.] **1.** Act or process of consuming; waste; destruction; also, the using up of anything, as food, heat, or time. **2.** *Econ.* The use of (economic) goods, resulting in the diminution or destruction of their utilities; — opposed to *production.* **3.** *Med.* A progressive wasting away of the body, esp. from pulmonary tuberculosis; hence, pulmonary tuberculosis (see TUBERCULOSIS).

con·sump′tive (-tĭv), *adj.* **1.** Destructive; wasteful. **2.** *Med.* Pert. to, of the nature of, affected with, or inclined to pulmonary tuberculosis. — *n.* A person affected with pulmonary tuberculosis. — **con·sump′tive·ly,** *adv.* — **con·sump′tive·ness,** *n.*

con′tact (kŏn′tăkt), *n.* [F. or L.; F., fr. L. *contactus,* fr. *contingere, -tactum,* to touch on all sides. See CONTINGENT.] **1.** A touching or meeting of bodies. **2.** A coming or being in touch physically or mentally; — followed by *with.* **3.** *Elec.* The junction of two conductors through which a current passes; also, a special part made for such a junction or connection. — *v. t. & i.* **1.** To come or bring into contact; to enter or be in contact with; to touch. **2.** *Colloq. U. S.* To get into communication with (a person or agency). — *interj.* Contact has been made; the ignition switch has been closed; — addressed by an aircraft pilot to his mechanic.

contact flying. Navigation of an aircraft by means of direct observation of landmarks; — opposed to *instrument flying.* — **contact flight.**

contact lens. A very thin plastic lens fitted to the eyeball.

contact print. *Photog.* A print made with the negative in contact with the sensitive paper, plate, or film.

con·ta′gion (kŏn·tā′jŭn), *n.* [F. and L.; F., fr. L. *contagio.* See CONTACT.] **1. a** The transmission of a disease by direct or indirect contact. **b** A contagious disease. **c** A medium to transmit disease, as a virus. **2.** Hence: **a** Poison. **b** Contagious influence, as of miasmata. **3.** Communication of any influence to the mind or heart; as, the *contagion* of enthusiasm.

con·ta′gious (-jŭs), *adj.* [From OF., fr. LL. *contagiosus.*] **1.** Communicable by contact; catching; as, *contagious* diseases. **2.** Conveying contagion; charged with disease germs. **3.** Spreading from one to another. — **con·ta′gious·ly,** *adv.* — **con·ta′gious·ness,** *n.*

contagious disease. A type of infectious disease (which see) caused by receiving living germs directly from a person afflicted with the disease, or by contact with a secretion of his or with some object he has touched. Many infectious diseases are not contagious, some special method of transmission or inoculation of the germs being required.

con·ta′gi·um (kŏn·tā′jĭ·ŭm), *n.; pl.* -GIA (-jĭ·ȧ). [L.] *Med.* Contagious matter.

con·tain′ (kŏn·tān′), *v. t.* [OF. *contenir,* fr. L. *continere, -tentum,* fr. *con-* + *tenere* to hold.] **1.** To hold within fixed limits; include. **2.** To have capacity for; to hold. **3.** To restrain; to check. **4.** *Arith. & Alg.* To be a multiple of, or to be divisible by, generally without a remainder. **5.** *Mil. & Nav.* To retain (the enemy) within a given area, as by attacking or threatening. — *v. i. Rare.* To restrain oneself. — **con·tain′a·ble,** *adj.*

Syn. **Contain, hold, accommodate** mean to have or be able to have within so much, so many, or the like. **Contain** and **hold** are often used interchangeably but careful writers prefer *contain* when the actual number, amount, substance, etc., is indicated, and *hold* when the capacity of a vessel, a box, or the like, is in mind (as, this bottle *contains* milk or *holds* one quart); **accommodate** stresses holding without crowding or inconvenience.

con·tain′er (-ẽr), *n.* **1.** One that contains. **2.** A box, carton, crate, etc., used for holding goods.

con·ta′ki·on. Var. of KONTAKION.

con·tam′i·nate (kŏn·tăm′ĭ·nāt), *v. t.* [L. *contaminatus,* past part. of *contaminare* to bring into contact, contaminate, fr. *contamen* contagion, fr. *con-* + root of *tangere* to touch.] **1.** To soil, stain, or corrupt by contact; to pollute. **2.** To render (water otherwise satisfactory) unfit for a specified use, as by the introduction of bacteria, sewage, etc.

Syn. **Contaminate, taint, pollute, defile** mean to make impure or unclean. **Contaminate** suggests contact as the cause or source of danger; **taint,** the influence of something that causes corruption and decay; **pollute,** the loss of purity and cleanness through contamination; **defile,** the befouling of that which ought to be clean, pure, or held sacred.

— (-nāt), *adj.* *Archaic.* Contaminated. — **con·tam′i·na′tive** (-nā′tĭv), *adj.* — **con·tam′i·na′tor** (-nā′tẽr), *n.*

con·tam′i·na′tion (-nā′shŭn), *n.* A contaminating, or state of being contaminated; also, that which contaminates; an impurity.

con·tan′go (kŏn·tăng′gō), *n.; pl.* -GOES (-gōz). *London Stock Exch.* Premium or interest paid by a buyer to the seller to be allowed to defer payment until a future settlement.

conte (kônt), *n.; pl.* CONTES (kônts; *F.* kônt). [F.] A short story; formerly, esp., a tale of adventure or of marvels.

con·temn′ (kŏn·tĕm′), *v. t.* [OF. *contemner,* fr. L. *contemnere, -temptum,* fr. *con-* + *temnere* to slight, despise.] To view or treat with contempt; to despise; scorn. — **Syn.** See DESPISE. — **con·temn′er** (-tĕm′ẽr; -tĕm′nẽr), **con·tem′nor** (-tĕm′nẽr), *n.*

con·tem′pla·ble (-tĕm′plȧ·b′l), *adj.* Capable of being contemplated.

con′tem·plate (kŏn′tĕm·plāt; *by some,* kŏn·tĕm′plāt), *v. t.* [L. *contemplatus,* past part. of *contemplari* to contemplate, fr. *con-* + *templum* temple.] **1.** To view or consider with continued attention; to meditate on. **2.** To have in view as contingent or probable, or as an end or intention; to purpose or intend. — **Syn.** See CONSIDER. — *v. i.* To consider or think studiously; to ponder; meditate. — **con′tem·pla′tor** (kŏn′tĕm·plā′tẽr), *n.*

con′tem·pla′tion (kŏn′tĕm·plā′shŭn), *n.* **1.** Meditation on spiritual things. **2.** Act of considering with attention; musing; study. **3.** Intention; expectation.

con·tem′pla·tive (kŏn·tĕm′plȧ·tĭv; kŏn′tĕm·plā′tĭv), *adj.* Marked by, or of the nature of, contemplation; specif., devoted to prayer and meditation; as, the *contemplative* life. — *n.* A contemplative monk, nun, or the like. — **con·tem′pla·tive·ly,** *adv.* — **con·tem′pla·tive·ness,** *n.*

con·tem′po·ra′ne·ous (kŏn·tĕm′pō·rā′nē·ŭs), *adj.* [L. *contemporaneus,* fr. *con-* + *tempus* time.] Contemporary. — **Syn.** See CONTEMPORARY. — **con·tem′po·ra′ne·ous·ly,** *adv.* — **-ous·ness,** *n.*

con·tem′po·rar′y (-tĕm′pō·rĕr′ĭ *or, esp. Brit.,* -rẽr·ĭ), *adj.* [*con-* + L. *temporarius* belonging to time, fr. *tempus* time.] **1.** Living, occurring, or existing at the same period of time; contemporaneous. **2.** Of the same age; coeval.

Syn. **Contemporary, contemporaneous, coeval, synchronous, simultaneous, coincident, concomitant, concurrent** mean existing or occurring at the same time. **Contemporary** (applied chiefly to persons, their works, etc.) and **contemporaneous** (to events) may refer to any time or any duration; **coeval** usually implies contemporaneousness for a very long time and at a more or less remote period; **synchronous** implies exact correspondence in time; **simultaneous** implies correspondence in instant of time; **coincident** applies to events happening at practically the same time; **concomitant** often implies coincidence, but tends to stress attendance or association; **concurrent** implies synchronousness but also parallelism or agreement.

— *n.; pl.* -IES (-ĭz). **1.** One who lives at the same time with another. **2.** One of the same, or nearly the same, age as another; a coeval.

con·tem′po·rize (-rīz), *v. t. & i.* To make or be contemporary.

con·tempt′ (kŏn·tĕmpt′; 89), *n.* [OF. or L.; OF., fr. L. *contemptus,* fr. *contemnere.* See CONTEMN.] **1.** Act of contemning; the feeling with which one regards that which is esteemed mean, vile, or worthless; scorn. **2.** State of being despised; disgrace. **3.** *Law.* Willful disobedience to, or open disrespect of, a court of justice or a legislative body.

con·tempt'i·ble (kŏn·tĕmp'tĭ·b'l), *adj.* **1.** Worthy of contempt; despicable. **2.** *Obs.* Scornful; contemptuous. — **con·tempt'i·bil'i·ty** (-bĭl'ĭ·tĭ), **con·tempt'i·ble·ness**, *n.* — **con·tempt'i·bly**, *adv.*

Syn. **Contemptible, despicable, pitiable, sorry, scurvy, cheap, beggarly** mean arousing or deserving scorn. **Contemptible** implies a quality provoking scorn, such as insignificance, meanness, etc.; **despicable** and **pitiable** stress a person's attitude, *despicable* usually connoting indignant disapprobation and *pitiable*, the inspiring of pity mixed with contempt; **sorry** usually implies pitiable inadequacy, wretchedness, or sordidness; **scurvy** adds to *despicable* the implication of disgust; **cheap** and **beggarly** imply that a person or thing has been made contemptible by falling far below a standard of worthiness in *cheap* or of adequacy in *beggarly.*

con·temp'tu·ous (-tĕmp'tū·ŭs), *adj.* Expressing contempt or disdain. — **con·temp'tu·ous·ly**, *adv.* — **con·temp'tu·ous·ness**, *n.*

con·tend' (kŏn·tĕnd'), *v. i.* [OF. or L.; OF. *contendre*, fr. L. *contendere, -tentum*, fr. *con-* + *tendere* to stretch.] To strive in opposition or rivalry; to compete; vie. — *v. t.* To maintain or assert; argue. — **con·tend'er**, *n.*

con'tent (kŏn'tĕnt; *formerly, and still by some, esp. in sense* 1, kŏn·tĕnt'), *n.; pl.* CONTENTS. [L. *contentum*, past part. neut. of *continere* to contain. See CONTAIN.] **1.** *Usually pl.* That which is contained; as, the *contents* of a cask. **2.** *pl.* The topics or matter treated in a document or the like **3.** The sum and substance; the gist, as of a discourse; hence, essential meaning. **4.** Power of containing; capacity; hence, extent; size. **5.** Quantity of space or matter within certain limits. **6.** *sing. only.* The matter dealt with by, or presented in, a field of study; as, the *content* of sociology is inexhaustible. **7.** The amount (of specified material) contained; as, the sulfur *content* of a sample of coal.

con·tent' (kŏn·tĕnt'), *adj.* [OF., fr. L. *contentus*, past part. of *continere* to hold together, restrain. See CONTAIN.] **1.** Having the desires limited to that which one has; satisfied. **2.** Assenting; agreeing. — *v. t.* To make content; to appease the desires of. — **Syn.** See SATISFY. — *n.* **1.** State of being content; contentment. **2.** *Obs.* That which contents; a means of contentment. **3.** *Brit. House of Lords.* An expression of assent; an affirmative vote.

con·tent'ed (kŏn·tĕn'tĕd; -tĭd), *adj.* Content; satisfied. — **con·tent'ed·ly**, *adv.* — **con·tent'ed·ness**, *n.*

con·ten'tion (-tĕn'shŭn), *n.* **1.** Act or instance of contending; strife; esp., altercation or controversy. **2.** A point maintained in an argument. — **Syn.** See DISCORD.

con·ten'tious (-tĕn'shŭs), *adj.* **1.** Given to contention; quarrelsome. **2.** Involving, or characterized by, contention. — **Syn.** See BELLIGERENT. — **con·ten'tious·ly**, *adv.* — **con·ten'tious·ness**, *n.*

con·tent'ment (kŏn·tĕnt'mĕnt), *n.* **1.** *Archaic.* Act or process of making content. **2.** Contentedness.

con·ter'mi·nous (kŏn·tûr'mĭ·nŭs; kŏn-), *adj.* Also **con·ter'mi·nal** (-năl; -n'l). Having the same bounds or limits; coterminous. — **con·ter'mi·nous·ly**, *adv.*

con·test' (kŏn·tĕst'), *v. t.* [F. *contester*, fr. L. *contestari* to call to witness, fr. *con-* + *testari* to be a witness, fr. *testis* witness.] **1.** To make a subject of dispute, contention, or litigation; to contend for or about; also, to call in question the validity of; as, to *contest* an election. **2.** To struggle to gain or hold; as, to *contest* every inch of ground. — *v. i.* To contend; strive; vie; — followed by *with* or *against.* — **con·test'a·ble**, *adj.* — **con·test'er**, *n.*

con'test (kŏn'tĕst), *n.* Earnest struggle for superiority, victory, defense, etc.; competition; strife or argument; also, an encounter of such nature, as in arms.

con·test'ant (kŏn·tĕs'tănt), *n.* [F.] One contesting or competing; specif., one who contests an award or decision; as, a *contestant* of election returns.

con'tes·ta'tion (kŏn'tĕs·tā'shŭn), *n.* Act or instance of contesting; contention; controversy; competition.

con'text (kŏn'tĕkst), *n.* [L. *contextus*, fr. *contexere* to weave, join together, fr. *con-* + *texere* to weave.] The part of a discourse in which a word or passage occurs and which helps to explain the meaning of the word or passage.

con·tex'tu·al (kŏn·tĕks'tū·ăl), *adj.* Of, pertaining to, or derived from the context. — **con·tex'tu·al·ly**, *adv.*

con·tex'ture (kŏn·tĕks'tūr), *n.* [F.] **1.** A weaving together; also, structure, composition, etc., marked by interweaving of parts; texture. **2.** Something so fabricated; fabric.

con'ti·gu'i·ty (kŏn'tĭ·gū'ĭ·tĭ), *n.* **1.** State of being contiguous; proximity. **2.** A continuous mass or series.

con·tig'u·ous (kŏn·tĭg'ū·ŭs), *adj.* [L. *contiguus.*] In actual contact; touching; also, near, though not in contact; adjoining. — **Syn.** See ADJACENT. — **con·tig'u·ous·ly**, *adv.* — **con·tig'u·ous·ness**, *n.*

con'ti·nence (kŏn'tĭ·nĕns), *n.* Also **con'ti·nen·cy** (-nĕn·sĭ). Self-restraint, esp. in refraining from sexual intercourse.

con'ti·nent (-nĕnt), *adj.* [OF., fr. L. *continens, -entis*, prop., pres. part. of *continere* to hold together, to repress.] **1.** Exercising restraint as to the indulgence of desires or passions; specif., exercising continence sexually; esp., chaste. **2.** *Obs.* **a** Restrictive. **b** Receptive; retentive. — *n.* **1.** *Archaic.* That which contains or holds within limits. **2.** A continuous extent of land; mainland; — now chiefly in ***the Continent***, the mainland of Europe. **3.** One of the grand divisions of land on the globe, usually regarded as seven: North America, South America, Europe, Asia, Africa, Australia, and Antarctica.

con'ti·nen'tal (-nĕn'tăl; -t'l), *adj.* **1.** Of, pertaining to, or characteristic of a continent or [*cap.*] the Continent. **2.** [*cap.*] Of or pertaining to the confederated colonies at the time of the American Revolution. — *n.* **1.** One belonging to a continent or [*cap.*] the Continent. **2.** [*cap.*] A soldier in the Continental army. **3.** *Colloq., U.S.* The least bit; — from the low value of Continental currency.

Continental Celtic. See GAULISH.

continental code, continental Morse code. *Teleg.* See MORSE CODE.

continental shelf. *Phys. Geog.* A submarine plain bordering nearly every continent and descending in a sharp slope (**continental slope**) to the ocean depths.

con'ti·nent·ly (kŏn'tĭ·nĕnt·lĭ), *adv.* In a continent manner.

con·tin'gence (kŏn·tĭn'jĕns), *n.* Contact; a touching.

con·tin'gen·cy (-jĕn·sĭ), *n.; pl.* -CIES (-sĭz). **1.** Quality or state of being contingent. **2.** A possible or not unlikely event or condition. **3.** An adjunct or accessory; an incidental expense, or the like. **4.** *Philos.* The fact of existing as an individual human being in time, dependent on others for existence, menaced by death, dependent on oneself for the course and quality of existence. — **Syn.** See JUNCTURE.

con·tin'gent (-jĕnt), *adj.* [F. or L.; F., fr. L. *contingens, -entis*, pres. part. of *contingere* to touch on all sides, happen, fr. *con-* + *tangere* to touch.] **1.** Liable, but not certain, to occur; possible. **2.** Coming from or subject to unforeseen conditions; chance; as, a *contingent* result of a war. **3.** Dependent; conditional; — with *on* or *upon*; as, an agreement *contingent* upon certain concessions. **4.** *Accounting.* Dependent on something that may or may not occur; as, *contingent* assets. **5.** *Logic.* Depending upon some condition or upon the truth of something else. — **Syn.** See ACCIDENTAL. — *n.* **1.** A contingent event; accident. **2.** A share, proportion, or allotment. **3.** A quota or a representative group; as, the American *contingent* at the Olympic games; a *contingent* of troops for foreign service. — **con·tin'gent·ly**, *adv.*

con·tin'u·al (kŏn·tĭn'ū·ăl), *adj.* **1.** Characterized by continuity; continuous; as, a *continual* din. **2.** Occurring in steady, rapid, but not unbroken, succession; as, *continual* gibes. — **con·tin'u·al·ly**, *adv.*

Syn. **Continual, continuous, constant, incessant, perpetual, perennial** mean existing or recurring over a long period of time. **Continual** implies a close and very prolonged succession or recurrence; **continuous** implies an uninterrupted flow of events, parts, or the like, and may suggest space as well as time; **constant** implies uniform, steady, or persistent occurrence or recurrence; **incessant** implies ceaseless or uninterrupted activity; **perpetual** implies unfailing repetition or lasting duration; **perennial** implies existence over an indeterminate number of years, but, in current use, often also connotes constant renewal.

con·tin'u·ance (-ăns), *n.* [OF.] **1.** A continuing in a state or course; duration. **2.** Uninterrupted succession; continuation. **3.** A sequel. **4.** *Law.* Adjournment of proceedings to a specified day. — **Syn.** See CONTINUATION.

con·tin'u·ant (-ănt), *n.* [L. *continuans*, pres. part.] **1.** That which continues or has continued existence. **2.** *Phonet.* A consonant sound which may be prolonged during one breath, as that of *f, v*, etc.; — opp. to *stop* (def. 12).

con·tin'u·ate (-āt), *adj.* *Obs.* Uninterrupted; continued.

con·tin'u·a'tion (-ā'shŭn), *n.* **1.** State of being continued, extended, prolonged, etc. **2.** Act of continuing; esp., a resumption, as of a story. **3.** That which continues, as an extension, a supplement, an installment of a novel, etc. — **con·tin'u·a'tive** (kŏn·tĭn'ū·ā'tĭv; -ȧ·tĭv), *adj.*

Syn. **Continuation, continuance, continuity** mean something which continues or is being continued. **Continuation** suggests prolongation or resumption; **continuance**, duration, perseverance, or stay; **continuity**, uninterrupted or unbroken connection, sequence, or extent.

con·tin'u·a'tor (kŏn·tĭn'ū·ā'tẽr), *n.* A continuer of a work.

con·tin'ue (kŏn·tĭn'ū), *v. i.* [OF. *continuer*, fr. L. *continuare, -tinuatum*, to connect, continue, fr. *continuus.* See CONTINUOUS.] **1.** To remain in a given place or condition; abide; stay. **2.** To endure; last. **3.** To persevere; persist. **4.** To resume a story, speech, etc. — *v. t.* **1.** To extend in duration; persist in. **2.** To carry onward; extend. **3.** To resume, as a discourse. **4.** Of a legal proceeding, to keep on the calendar or undecided. **5.** To suffer to remain; retain; as, *continued* in office. — **con·tin'u·a·ble** (-ū·ȧ·b'l), *adj.* — **con·tin'u·er** (-ū·ẽr), *n.*

Syn. **Continue, last, endure, abide, persist** mean to exist indefinitely. **Continue** refers to a process and stresses its lack of end rather than its duration; **last**, when unqualified, stresses length of existence passing that which is normal or expected; **endure** adds the implication of resistance, especially to destructive forces or agencies; **abide** implies stability and constancy, especially as opposed to mutability and impermanence; **persist** adds the implication of outlasting the appointed or normal time.

con·tin'ued frac'tion (-ūd). See FRACTION.

con'ti·nu'i·ty (kŏn'tĭ·nū'ĭ·tĭ), *n.; pl.* -TIES (-tĭz). **1.** Quality or state of being continuous. **2.** Something that has or gives continuousness or sequence. **3.** *Motion Pictures.* A scenario. **4.** *Radio.* Prepared copy from which the spoken part of a program is presented. — **Syn.** See CONTINUATION.

con·tin'u·ous (kŏn·tĭn'ū·ŭs), *adj.* [L. *continuus*, fr. *continere* to hold together.] Having continuity of parts; without cessation or interruption; continued. — **Syn.** See CONTINUAL. — **con·tin'u·ous·ly**, *adv.* — **con·tin'u·ous·ness**, *n.*

con·tin'u·um (-ŭm), *n.; pl.* CONTINUA (-ȧ). [L., neut. of *continuus* continuous.] **1.** That which is continuous and selfsame; that of which no distinction of content can be affirmed except by reference to something else; as, a space-time *continuum* (see FOURTH DIMENSION). **2.** Anything continuous in which a fundamental common character is discernible; as, the *continuum* of consciousness. Cf. STREAM OF CONSCIOUSNESS.

con'to (kŏn'tō), *n.; pl.* CONTOS (-tōz). [Pg.] Literally, a million; hence, formerly, a million reis; in Brazil, 1000 cruzeiros, in Portugal, 1000 escudos.

con·tort' (kŏn·tôrt'), *v. t.* [L. *contortus*, past part. of *contorquere* to twist, fr. *con-* + *torquere* to twist.] To twist together or upon itself; bend into curves; writhe. — **Syn.** See DEFORM. — **con·tor'tion** (-tôr'shŭn), *n.* — **con·tor'tive** (-tĭv), *adj.*

con·tor'tion·ist (kŏn·tôr'shŭn·ĭst), *n.* One who contorts; esp., an acrobat who assumes unnatural postures.

con'tour (kŏn'to͝or; kŏn·to͝or'), *n.* [F., fr. It. *contorno*, fr. *contornare* to compass about, fr. L. *con-* + *tornare* to turn.] **1.** The outline of a figure, body, mass, etc.; the line or lines representing such an outline; as, the *contours* of a statue or of a coast. **2.** = CONTOUR LINE. — **Syn.** See OUTLINE. — *adj.* Following the contour lines, or running furrows or ridges along the contour lines, for retardation of erosion by rain water; as, *contour* plowing; *contour* farming. — *v. t.* **1.** To make in contour; to draw, or lay down, the contour of. **2.** To construct, as a road, in conformity to a contour.

contour line. A line, as on a map or chart, connecting the points on a land surface that have the same elevation.

contour map. A map showing the configuration of a surface by means of contour lines representing regular intervals of elevation (**contour intervals**), as one for every twenty feet.

con'tra- (kŏn'trȧ-). [L.] A prefix meaning *against, contrary, in opposition*, etc., as in *contra*distinction.

con'tra·band (kŏn'trȧ·bănd), *n.* [From F., fr. It. *contrabbando*, fr. *contra* against + *bando* proclamation.] **1.** Illegal or prohibited commerce. **2.** Goods or merchandise the importation or exportation of which is forbidden; also, smuggled goods. **3.** In full, **contraband of**

war. That which, according to international law, cannot be supplied to one belligerent except at the risk of seizure and condemnation by the other. 4. Hence, *U. S.*, a Negro slave who escaped to, or was brought within, the Union lines during the Civil War. — **con'tra·band**, *adj.*

con'tra·band'ist (kŏn'trȧ·băn'dĭst), *n.* One engaged in contraband commerce; a smuggler.

con'tra·bass' (-bās'), *adj.* *Music.* Having a range below normal bass. — *n.* A contrabass instrument or voice; specif., the largest instrument of the viol class, sounding an octave below the normal bass instrument. — **con'tra·bass'ist** (-bās'ĭst; -băs'ĭst), *n.*

‖**con'tra bo'nos mo'res** (kŏn'trȧ bō'nōs mō'rēz). [L.] Against good morals; harmful to the moral welfare of society.

con'tra·cep'tion (kŏn'trȧ·sĕp'shŭn), *n.* [*contra-* + *-ception* as in *inception*.] Prevention of conception or impregnation. — **con'tra·cep'tive** (-tĭv), *adj. & n.*

con'tra·clock'wise' (-klŏk'wīz'), *adj. & adv.* = COUNTERCLOCKWISE.

con'tract (kŏn'trăkt), *n.* [OF. (F. *contrat*), fr. L. *contractus* a contract, fr. *contrahere* to contract.] 1. An agreement, esp. one legally enforceable, between two or more persons to do or forbear something; a bargain; covenant. 2. Hence: **a** The written evidence of such an agreement. **b** The branch of law concerned with such contracts. 3. The formal agreement of marriage or of betrothal. 4. *Bridge.* **a** The number of tricks named by the highest bidder. **b** = CONTRACT BRIDGE.

con·tract' (kŏn·trăkt'; *in sense* 1, *often* kŏn'trăkt), *v. t.* [F. and L.; chiefly fr. L. *contractus*, past part. of *contrahere* to draw together, fr. *con-* + *trahere* to draw.] 1. To establish or undertake by contract. 2. *Now Rare.* To betroth. 3. To bring on; incur; acquire. 4. To draw together; reduce in length, compass, etc.; shorten; narrow; shrink. 5. To wrinkle or knit (the brow). 6. *Gram.* To shorten by omitting one or more letters or sounds, or by reducing two or more vowels or syllables to one. See CONTRACTION, 3. — *v. i.* 1. To make a contract. 2. To become contracted. — **con·tract'i·ble** (kŏn·trăk'tĭ·b'l), *adj.* — **con·tract'i·bil'i·ty** (-bĭl'ĭ·tĭ), **con·tract'i·ble·ness**, *n.*

Syn. (1) See INCUR.

(2) **Contract, shrink, condense, compress, constrict, deflate** mean to decrease in bulk, volume, or content. **Contract** implies a drawing together of sides or particles with a reduction in compass or a temporary compacting of the mass; **shrink** implies a contracting (literal or figurative) so as to fall short of its original length, bulk, or volume; **condense** implies a reduction of something homogeneous to greater compactness without material loss of content; **compress** differs from *condense* in implying squeezing something formless or diffused into definite shape and small compass; **constrict** implies a tightening that decreases diameter; **deflate**, a shrinkage by exhaustion of gas, air, etc.

con'tract bridge (kŏn'trăkt). A variety of auction bridge in which the declarer's side can score toward game only the number of tricks named in the contract, any additional tricks being scored in the honor column, and slams receiving a bonus only when bid.

con·trac'tile (kŏn·trăk'tĭl), *adj.* Having the power or property of contracting; contractive. — **con'trac·til'i·ty** (kŏn'trăk·tĭl'ĭ·tĭ), *n.*

con·trac'tion (-shŭn), *n.* 1. Act or process of contracting; state of being contracted. 2. Specif.: **a** Limitation or reduction, as of credit. **b** Shortening and thickening of a muscle fiber or of a muscle when in action. 3. An abbreviation formed by contracting a word or phrase; — usually restricted to the omission of medial letters (as, *can't* for *cannot*, *Dr.* for *doctor*, *shd* for *should*).

con·trac'tive (-tĭv), *adj.* Tending to produce contraction; also, contractile. — **con·trac'tive·ness**, *n.*

con·trac'tor (kŏn·trăk'tẽr *or, esp. U. S.*, kŏn'trăk·tẽr), *n.* [LL.] 1. One who contracts or is party to a contract; specif., one who contracts to perform work, or supply articles on a large scale, at a certain price or rate. 2. That which contracts, shortens, or narrows, as a muscle.

con·trac'tu·al (kŏn·trăk'tū·ăl), *adj.* Of, pertaining to, or of the nature of a contract.

con·trac'ture (kŏn·trăk'tūr), *n.* [F. or L.; F. *contracture*, fr. L. *contractura* a drawing together.] *Med.* A state of permanent contraction of the muscles.

con'tra·dance' (kŏn'trȧ·dȧns'). Var. of CONTREDANSE.

con'tra·dict' (kŏn'trȧ·dĭkt'), *v. t.* [L. *contradictus*, past part. of *contradicere* to speak against, fr. *contra* + *dicere* to speak.] 1. To assert the contrary of; to deny the truth of; gainsay. 2. *Obs.* To resist; oppose. 3. To be contrary to; go counter to; confute; as, the results of the experiment *contradicted* his theory. — **Syn.** See DENY. — *v. i.* To oppose in words; gainsay. — **con'tra·dict'a·ble**, *adj.* — **con'tra·dict'er, con'tra·dic'tor** (-dĭk'tẽr), *n.*

con'tra·dic'tion (-dĭk'shŭn), *n.* 1. An assertion of the contrary. 2. Status or fact of contradicting each other; logical incompatibility; as, a *contradiction* in terms. 3. Something involving such conflict, inconsistency, etc. Cf. PARADOX.

con'tra·dic'tious (-shŭs), *adj.* Contradictory.

con'tra·dic'tive (-tĭv), *adj.* Contradictory.

con'tra·dic'to·ry (-dĭk'tō·rĭ), *adj.* 1. Tending to contradict; of the nature of, given to, or involving contradiction. 2. *Logic.* Having the nature of a contradictory. — **Syn.** See OPPOSITE. — *n. Logic.* **a** A proposition so related to another that if either is true the other must be false. **b** A term which is the exact negative of another (as, *white* and *not white*). Cf. CONTRARY, *n.*, 3. — **con'tra·dic'to·ri·ly**, *adv.* — **con'tra·dic'to·ri·ness**, *n.*

con'tra·dis·tinc'tion (-dĭs·tĭngk'shŭn), *n.* Distinction by contrast; — chiefly in the phrase ***in contradistinction to.*** — **con'tra·dis·tinc'tive** (-tĭv), *adj.* — **con'tra·dis·tinc'tive·ly**, *adv.*

con'tra·dis·tin'guish (-dĭs·tĭng'gwĭsh), *v. t.* To distinguish by a contrast of opposite qualities.

con'tra·in'di·cate (-ĭn'dĭ·kāt), *v. t.* *Med.* To point to as an improper or harmful remedy or treatment. — **con'tra·in'di·ca'tion** (-kā'shŭn), *n.*

con·tral'to (kŏn·trăl'tō), *n.; pl.* -TOS (-tōz), -TI (-tē). [It., fr. *contra* + *alto* alto.] **a** Originally, the part sung by the highest male or lowest female voices; now, that of the lowest female voice, having a range of about two octaves from f upward. See PITCH, *Illust.* **b** A contralto voice or singer. — **con·tral'to**, *adj.*

con'tra·oc'tave (kŏn'trȧ·ŏk'tāv), *n.* See PITCH, *Illust.*

con'tra·po·si'tion (kŏn'trȧ·pō·zĭsh'ŭn), *n.* Opposition.

con'tra·prop' (kŏn'trȧ·prŏp'), *n.* [*contra* + *propeller.*] *Aeronautics.* A device comprising a pair of propellers on concentric shafts, turning in opposite directions.

con·trap'tion (kŏn·trăp'shŭn), *n.* *Colloq.* Contrivance; gadget.

con'tra·pun'tal (kŏn'trȧ·pŭn'tăl; -t'l), *adj.* [It. *contrappunto* counterpoint.] *Music.* **a** Of, or according to the rules of, counterpoint. **b** Polyphonic. — **con'tra·pun'tal·ly**, *adv.*

con'tra·pun'tist (kŏn'trȧ·pŭn'tĭst), *n.* One skilled in counterpoint.

con'tra·ri'e·ty (kŏn'trȧ·rī'ĕ·tĭ), *n.; pl.* -TIES (-tĭz). 1. State or quality of being contrary; variance. 2. Something contrary to something else; an inconsistency.

con·trar'i·ous (kŏn·trâr'ĭ·ŭs), *adj.* *Archaic.* Contrary.

con'tra·ri·wise' (kŏn'trẽr·ĭ·wīz'; kŏn'trȧ·rĭ-; *see* CONTRARY), *adv.* 1. On the contrary; on the other hand. 2. Conversely; vice versa. 3. Contrarily; perversely.

con'tra·ry (kŏn'trẽr·ĭ *or, esp. Brit.*, kŏn'trȧ·rĭ; *see note below*), *adj.* [OF. *contrarie*, fr. L. *contrarius*, fr. *contra* against.] 1. Opposed; diametrically different. 2. That is opposite in position, nature, direction, etc. 3. Unfavorable; adverse; — now only of wind, weather, etc. 4. Counter; as, *contrary* to law. 5. Given to opposition; captious. 6. *Logic.* Having the nature of a contrary. — *n.; pl.* -RIES (-rĭz). 1. The opposite; a proposition, condition, etc., incompatible with another. 2. One of two contrary things. 3. *Logic.* **a** A proposition so related to another that, though both may be false, they cannot both be true. **b** Either of a pair of terms that cannot both be affirmed of the same subject (as, *black* and *white*). Cf. CONTRADICTORY, *n.* — *adv.* Contrarily; contrariwise; counter. — **con'tra·ri·ly** (kŏn'trẽr·ĭ·lĭ; *emphatic also* kŏn·trâr'ĭ·lĭ), *adv.* — **con'tra·ri·ness** (-ĭ·nĕs; -nĭs), *n.*

☞ The accent was orig. *con·tra'ry*, but *con'tra·ry* has existed side by side with it since Chaucer's time and now prevails in cultivated usage, while con·tra'ry (used esp. in sense 5) is almost exclusively dial., colloq., or playful. The accent on the first syllable also prevails in those derivatives the accentuation of which naturally follows that of the adj., as *con'tra·ri·ly*, *con'tra·ri·wise'*, etc.

Syn. (1) See OPPOSITE.

(2) **Contrary, perverse, restive, balky, froward, wayward** mean given to opposing wishes, commands, conditions, and the like. **Contrary** implies a temperamental unwillingness to accept dictation or advice; **perverse** implies obstinacy or wrongheadedness or, in current use, sexual maladjustment; **restive**, as here compared, suggests great intractability or unruliness; **balky** suggests a stopping short and obstinately refusing to go further; **froward** suggests a proneness to disobedience that compliance even with reasonable requests is impossible; **wayward** suggests a perverseness that makes a person go his own way, however capricious or depraved it may be.

— ***by contraries.*** By way of opposition; contrary to expectation. — ***on the contrary.*** In opposition; on the other hand. — ***to the contrary.*** To an opposite effect or intent.

con·trast' (kŏn·trȧst'), *v. i.* [F. *contraster*, fr. It., fr. LL., fr. L. *contra* + *stare* to stand.] To exhibit noticeable differences when compared or set side by side. — *v. t.* To place, arrange, etc., so as to set off or to bring out differences. — **Syn.** See COMPARE. — (kŏn'trȧst), *n.* 1. Act or process of contrasting; state of being contrasted. 2. A person or thing that exhibits differences when contrasted. 3. *Fine Arts.* Diversity of adjacent parts in color, emotion, tone, etc. — **contrast'a·ble**, *adj.*

con'tra·val·la'tion (kŏn'trȧ·vă·lā'shŭn), *n.* [See CONTRA-; VALLATION.] *Fort.* A series of works confronting the walls of an invested place, erected by the besiegers to isolate the defenders and safeguard themselves against sallies.

con'tra·vene' (-vēn'), *v. t.* [F. or L.; F., fr. LL. *contravenire*, fr. *contra-* + *venire* to come.] 1. To go or act contrary to; to infringe; as, to *contravene* a law. 2. To oppose; contradict. — **Syn.** See DENY. — **Ant.** Uphold. — **con'tra·ven'er** (-vēn'ẽr), *n.*

con'tra·ven'tion (-vĕn'shŭn), *n.* Act of contravening; transgression; violation.

‖**con'tre·danse'** (kôɴ'trĕ·däɴs'), *n.* [F., fr. E. COUNTRY-DANCE.] A country-dance.

con'tre·temps' (kôɴ'trĕ·täɴ'), *n.; pl.* -TEMPS (-täɴz'; *F.* -täɴ'). [F., fr. *contre* (L. *contra*) + *temps* time, fr. L. *tempus*.] An inopportune and embarrassing occurrence, often one causing a hitch in one's plans or procedure.

con·trib'ute (kŏn·trĭb'ūt), *v. t.* [L. *contributus*, past part. of *contribuere* to bring together, add, fr. *con-* + *tribuere* to grant.] 1. To give or supply in common with others. 2. To supply (an article) for publication. — *v. i.* To give or furnish something, as to a common stock or for a common purpose. — **Syn.** See CONDUCE. — **con·trib'ut·a·ble** (-ū·tȧ·b'l), *adj.* — **con·trib'u·tor** (-ū·tẽr), *n.*

con'tri·bu'tion (kŏn'trĭ·bū'shŭn), *n.* 1. A levy or tax, esp. an extraordinary one; an impost. 2. Act of contributing; also, the sum or thing contributed. 3. A writing for publication, esp. in a periodical. — **con·trib'u·tive** (kŏn·trĭb'ū·tĭv), *adj.* — **con·trib'u·tive·ly**, *adv.* — **con·trib'u·tive·ness**, *n.*

con·trib'u·to'ry (kŏn·trĭb'ū·tō'rĭ *or, esp. Brit.*, -tẽr·ĭ), *adj.* 1. Contributing, as to a common fund or enterprise. 2. Of the nature of, or forming, a contribution; serving as a contribution; esp., aiding in affecting an end or result; as, *contributory* causes. — **Syn.** Subservient, auxiliary. — *n.; pl.* -RIES (-rĭz). One who contributes; a contributor; also, a contributing factor.

con'trite (kŏn'trīt; *often, in poetry*, kŏn·trīt'), *adj.* [OF. *contrit*, fr. L. *contritus* bruised, past part. of *conterere* to grind, bruise, fr. *con-* + *terere* to rub, grind.] 1. Broken down with sorrow for sin; humbly and thoroughly penitent. 2. Proceeding from sincere repentance; as, *contrite* sighs. — **con'trite·ly**, *adv.* — **con'trite·ness**, *n.*

con·tri'tion (kŏn·trĭsh'ŭn), *n.* Sincere repentance. Cf. ATTRITION. — **Syn.** See PENITENCE.

con·triv'ance (kŏn·trīv'ăns), *n.* 1. Act or power of contriving; also, the way in which something is contrived, designed, or adapted. 2. A thing contrived or used in contriving; an invention; esp., a mechanical device or appliance.

con·trive' (kŏn·trīv'), *v. t.* [OF. *controver*, fr. LL. *contropare* to compare, appar. of Teut. origin.] 1. To devise; plan; as, to *contrive* means of meeting. 2. To fabricate as a work of art or ingenuity; design; invent; as, to *contrive* a new type of airship. 3. To bring about or effect, as by ingenuity or stratagem; to manage; as, to *contrive* to keep cool. — *v. i.* To make devices; to form schemes or designs. — **con·triv'a·ble** (-trīv'ȧ·b'l), *adj.* — **con·triv'er** (-ẽr), *n.*

con·trol' (kŏn·trōl'), *v. t.;* -TROLLED' (-trōld'); -TROL'LING. [F. *contrôler*, fr. *contrôle* counter register, deriv. of *contre* + *rôle* roll, catalogue.] 1. To check or regulate, as payments; to keep within limits, as speed. 2. To test or verify (a statement or experiment) by counter or parallel evidence or experiment. 3. To exercise directing, guiding, or restraining power over. — **Syn.** See CONDUCT. — *n.* 1. Power or authority to control. 2. Reserve or restraint. 3. Anything affording a standard of comparison or means of verification; a check. Cf. CONTROL EXPERIMENT. 4. The apparatus used to control a mechanism or machine in operation, as an aircraft or motorboat; also, any of the mechanisms of such an apparatus. **5**. In vehicle racing, a part of the course not reckoned in the timing; specif., a station where an airplane may stop a limited time for minor repairs. **6**. *Spiritualism.* A personality or spirit believed to actuate the utterances or performances of the medium. — **Syn.** See POWER. — **con·trol'la·ble**, *adj.* — **con·trol'ment**, *n.*

control experiment. An experiment to check the results of other experiments, as by maintaining identical conditions, except for one varied factor, whose causal significance can thus be inferred.

con·trol'ler (kŏn·trōl'ẽr), *n.* **1**. An officer appointed to check expenditures; comptroller. **2**. A governor, director, or the like. **3**. A mechanical or electrical device for controlling power, speed, pressure, etc. — **con·trol'ler·ship**, *n.*

con'tro·ver'sial (kŏn'trŏ·vûr'shăl; -sĭ·ăl), *adj.* Subject to, relating to, or of the nature of controversy; polemical; disputatious. — **con'tro·ver'sial·ist**, *n.* — **con'tro·ver'sial·ly**, *adv.*

con'tro·ver'sy (kŏn'trŏ·vûr'sĭ), *n.; pl.* -SIES (-sĭz). [L. *controversia*, fr. *controversus* turned against, disputed, fr. *contro-* (= *contra*) + *versus*, past part. See VERSION.] A discussion of a controverted matter or controversial issue; dispute; debate; sometimes, quarrel; strife.

con'tro·vert (kŏn'trŏ·vûrt; kŏn'trŏ·vûrt'; 2), *v. t.* To oppose with arguments; deny; contradict; as, to *controvert* a statement; also, to contest; oppose; as, *controverted* doctrines. — **Syn.** See DISPROVE. — **con'tro·vert'er**, *n.* — **con'tro·vert'i·ble**, *adj.*

con'tu·ma'cious (kŏn'tū·mā'shŭs), *adj.* Perverse in resisting authority; stubbornly disobedient. — **Syn.** Rebellious, insubordinate. — **con'tu·ma'cious·ly**, *adv.* — **con'tu·ma'cious·ness**, *n.*

con'tu·ma·cy (kŏn'tū·mȧ·sĭ; kŏn·tū'-), *n.; pl.* -CIES (-sĭz). [L. *contumacia*, fr. *contumax*, *-acis*, insolent.] Contumacious spirit or action; defiance of authority.

con'tu·me'ly (kŏn'tū·mē'lĭ; kŏn·tū'mĕ·lĭ), *n.; pl.* -LIES (-lĭz). [OF. *contumelie*, fr. L. *contumelia*.] Contemptuous or arrogant language or treatment; scornful insolence; also, an instance of this; an insult. — **con'tu·me'li·ous** (kŏn'tū·mē'lĭ·ŭs; 58), *adj.* — **con'tu·me'li·ous·ly**, *adv.* — **con'tu·me'li·ous·ness**, *n.*

con·tuse' (kŏn·tūz'), *v. t.* [L. *contusus*, past part. of *contundere* to beat, crush, fr. *con-* + *tundere* to beat.] To injure (flesh, skin, etc.) without laceration; to bruise.

con·tu'sion (-tū'zhŭn), *n.* A contusing; also, a bruise.

co·nun'drum (kō·nŭn'drŭm), *n.* [Origin unknown.] **1**. A kind of riddle, based upon some fanciful or fantastic resemblance between things quite unlike, forming a puzzling question, of which the answer is a pun or involves a pun. **2**. An unanswerable or purely speculative question. — **Syn.** See MYSTERY.

con'va·lesce' (kŏn'vȧ·lĕs'), *v. i.*; -LESCED' (-lĕst'); -LESC'ING (-lĕs'ĭng). [L. *convalescere*, fr. *con-* + *valescere* to grow strong, fr. *valere* to be strong.] To gather strength after sickness; to recover health gradually. Cf. RECUPERATE.

con'va·les'cence (-lĕs'ĕns; -'ns), *n.* The process or period of convalescing. — **con'va·les'cent** (-ĕnt; -'nt), *adj. & n.*

con'val·lar'i·a'ceous (kŏn'vă·lâr'ĭ·ā'shŭs), *adj.* [L. *convallis* a valley.] Belonging to the lily-of-the-valley family (Convallariaceae).

con·vec'tion (kŏn·vĕk'shŭn), *n.* [LL. *convectio*, fr. *convehere* to bring together, fr. *con-* + *vehere* to carry.] A conveying; specif., *Physics*, transference of heat or electricity by moving masses of matter, as by currents in gases and liquids caused by differences in density, or by electrically charged particles across a spark gap. — **con·vec'tion·al**, *adj.* — **con·vec'tive** (-vĕk'tĭv), *adj.* — **con·vec'tive·ly**, *adv.*

‖**con've·nance'** (kôɴv'näɴs'; *often Angl.*, kŏn'vĕ·näns' *or* kŏn'vĕ·näns, *with pl.* -năn'sĕz; -sĭz), *n.* [F., fitness.] **1**. Conventional usage; *pl.*, the conventionalities. **2**. Convenience; suitability. Cf. MARIAGE DE CONVENANCE.

con·vene' (kŏn·vēn'), *v. i.* [F. *convenir*, fr. L. *convenire*, fr. *con-* + *venire* to come.] To come together in a body; to assemble. — *v. t.* **1**. To cause to assemble; convoke. **2**. To summon before a tribunal. — **Syn.** See SUMMON. — **Ant.** Adjourn. — **con·ven'er** (-vēn'ẽr), *n.*

con·ven'ience (-vēn'yĕns), *or, now less commonly*, **con·ven'ien·cy** (-yĕn·sĭ), *n.* **1**. Quality of being convenient; fitness; suitability. **2**. Personal comfort; ease; hence, any labor-saving or comfort-giving appliance, fixture, etc. **3**. A convenient time; opportunity.

con·ven'ient (-yĕnt), *adj.* [L. *conveniens*, *-entis*, suitable, pres. part. of *convenire*. See CONVENE.] **1**. *Obs.* Fit; appropriate; proper. **2**. Suited to one's personal ease or comfort or to one's easy performance of some act or function. **3**. *Colloq.* Near at hand; easy of access. — **con·ven'ient·ly**, *adv.*

con'vent (kŏn'vĕnt *or, esp. Brit.*, -vĕnt), *n.* [L. *conventus* a meeting, ML. also, a convent. See CONVENE.] A community of recluses devoted to a religious life under a superior; also, their establishment, as a monastery or nunnery; — now usually restricted to a community of nuns, or a nunnery. — **Syn.** See CLOISTER.

con·vent' (kŏn·vĕnt'), *v. t. & i.* *Obs.* To convene.

con·ven'ti·cle (-vĕn'tĭ·k'l), *n.* [L. *conventiculum*, dim. of *conventus*.] **1**. *Obs.* An assembly. **2**. An assembly for religious worship; esp., a secret or illicit meeting for worship in forms other than those of the established church, as, formerly in England, by nonconformists, or dissenters. **3**. A meetinghouse. — **con·ven'ti·cler** (-klẽr), *n.*

con·ven'tion (kŏn·vĕn'shŭn), *n.* **1**. Act of convening. **2**. A body of delegates, representatives, members, or the like, periodically convened for a common purpose. **3**. Agreement or an agreement; contract; covenant; specif.: **a** An international agreement, now usually less formal than a treaty. **b** An agreement between opposing military commanders with respect to military operations. **4**. General agreement as the basis of any custom, usage, or the like; hence, custom; fixed usage; conventionality; as, slaves to *convention*. **5**. A rule, practice, form, etc., which has its sanction in custom or usages; as, the *conventions* of the novel; social *conventions*.

con·ven'tion·al (-ăl; -'l), *adj.* **1**. Of, pertaining to, or of the nature of, convention or a convention. **2**. Formed by agreement or compact; stipulated; contractual; — opposed in law to *legal* and *judicial*. **3**. Growing out of, depending on, or sanctioned by, custom or usage; as, *conventional* full dress. **4**. Lacking spontaneity, originality, or individuality; formal. **5**. Conventionalized; as, the *conventional* design of the shamrock. — **Syn.** See CEREMONIAL. — **con·ven'tion·al·ism** (-ăl·ĭz'm), *n.* — **con·ven'tion·al·ist** (-ĭst), *n.* — **con·ven'tion·al·ly**, *adv.*

con·ven'tion·al'i·ty (-ăl'ĭ·tĭ), *n.; pl.* -TIES (-tĭz). **1**. State or quality of being conventional; specif., adherence to social formalities or usages. **2**. A conventional usage, practice, or rule; a convention.

con·ven'tion·al·ize (kŏn·vĕn'shŭn·ăl·īz), *v. t.* To make conventional; specif., to design, draw, etc., so as to show typical rather than individual lines or features. — **-i·za'tion** (-ĭ·zā'shŭn; -ī·zā'-), *n.*

con·ven'tu·al (kŏn·vĕn'tū·ăl), *adj.* Of, pertaining to, or characteristic of a convent. — *n.* **1**. A member of a convent. **2**. [*cap.*] One of a branch of the Franciscan order or of the Carmelite order following a mitigated rule.

con·verge' (-vûrj'), *v. i.*; -VERGED' (-vûrjd'); -VERG'ING (-vûr'jĭng). [LL. *convergere*, fr. *con-* + *vergere* to turn, incline.] To tend to one point; to incline and approach nearer together; — opposed to *diverge*. — *v. t.* To cause to converge.

con·ver'gence (-vûr'jĕns), *n.* **1**. Also **con·ver'gen·cy** (-jĕn·sĭ). Act or state of converging; also, a degree or point of convergence; — opposed to *divergence*. **2**. Tendency to grow alike; development of similarities in form, habits, etc. — **con·ver'gent**, *adj.*

con·vers'a·ble (kŏn·vûr'sȧ·b'l), *adj.* **1**. Affable; approachable. **2**. Pert. to, or suitable for, converse or social intercourse; as, a *conversable* evening or mood. — **con·vers'a·ble·ness**, *n.*

con'ver·sance (kŏn'vẽr·săns; -s'ns; *see adj.*), *n.* Also **con'ver·san·cy** (-săn·sĭ). Conversant quality, state, or practice; familiarity; intimacy of knowledge.

con'ver·sant (kŏn'vẽr·sănt; -s'nt; *formerly, and still by some*, kŏn·vûr'sănt), *adj.* [OF., fr. L. *conversans*, pres. part. of *conversari* to associate with.] **1**. *Now Rare.* Wont to dwell. **2**. Intimately acquainted; familiar. **3**. Familiar by use or study; versed; — usually followed by *with*. — **con'ver·sant·ly**, *adv.*

con'ver·sa'tion (kŏn'vẽr·sā'shŭn), *n.* [OF. *conversacion*, *-tion*, fr. L. *conversatio*. See CONVERSE, *v.*] **1**. *Archaic.* **a** An abiding. **b** Manner of living; conduct. **2**. Social interchange; intercourse. **3**. Sexual intercourse. **4**. Oral and, usually, informal or friendly interchange of views, sentiments, etc.; talk or a talk. **5**. Conversance resulting from experience, study, etc. **6**. In modern diplomacy, an informal discussion between representatives of two or more governments regarding policy, treaties, etc. — **con'ver·sa'tion·al**, *adj.* — **-al·ly**, *adv.*

con'ver·sa'tion·al·ist (-ăl·ĭst), *n.* Also **con'ver·sa'tion·ist**. One who converses much or excels in conversation.

‖**con'ver·sa·zi·o'ne** (kŏn'vâr·sä·tsyō'nā; kŏn'vẽr·săt'sĭ·ō'nē; -săt'sĭ·ō'nē), *n.; pl.* -ZIONI (kŏn'vâr·sä·tsyō'nē), -ZIONES (kŏn'vẽr·săt'sĭ·ō'nēz; -săt'sĭ·ō'nēz). [It.] A social gathering for conversation about art, literature, science, etc.

con·verse' (kŏn·vûrs'), *v. i.* [OF. *converser*, fr. L. *conversari* to associate with, fr. *conversare* to turn often, fr. *convertere*. See CONVERT.] **1**. *Archaic.* To hold intercourse; to have conversation or conversance. **2**. To interchange thoughts and opinions in speech; to talk. — **Syn.** See SPEAK. — **con·vers'er** (-vûr'sẽr), *n.*

con'verse (kŏn'vûrs), *n.* **1**. Intercourse; communion. **2**. Familiar discourse; conversation.

con'verse (kŏn'vûrs; 2), *adj.* [L. *conversus*, past part. See CONVERT.] Turned about; reversed in order or relation; as, a *converse* proposition. — (kŏn'vûrs), *n.* **1**. In general, that which is related to something else in a way that is converse; loosely, the opposite or reverse. **2**. *Logic.* A proposition obtained by conversion. See CONVERSION, 4. — **con·verse'ly** (kŏn·vûrs'lĭ; kŏn-), *adv.*

con·ver'sion (kŏn·vûr'shŭn; -zhŭn), *n.* **1**. Act of converting, or state of being converted. **2**. A spiritual and moral change attending a change of belief with conviction; specif., the experience associated with and involving a definite and decisive adoption of religion, esp. a Christian religion. **3**. *Law.* **a** An appropriation of, and dealing with, the property of another as if it were one's own, without right. **b** *Equity.* The exchange of property of one nature to property of another nature, as of real to personal. **4**. *Logic.* Act of interchanging the terms of a proposition, as by putting the subject in the place of the predicate, or vice versa. **5**. *Math.* A change or reduction of the form of a proposition or expression; esp., the reduction by multiplication from a fractional to an integral form. — **con·ver'sion·al**, *adj.* — **con·ver'sion·ar'y** (-ẽr'ĭ *or, esp. Brit.*, -ẽr·ĭ), *adj.*

con·vert' (kŏn·vûrt'), *v. t.* [OF. *convertir*, fr. L. *convertere*, *-versum*, fr. *con-* + *vertere* to turn.] **1**. *Obs.* To turn. **2**. To turn from one belief or course to another. **3**. To cause spiritual conversion of or in. **4**. To transmute; transform; esp., in manufacturing, to change the chemical nature of; as, to *convert* starch into sugar. **5**. To divert; to apply to a different use, specif., *Law*, to an improper or dishonest use. **6**. To exchange for an equivalent; as, to *convert* goods into money. **7**. *Finance.* To change (one form of security, obligation, or the like) into an equivalent of a different nature. **8**. *Law.* To subject (property) to conversion (def. 3 **b**). **9**. To alter (a proposition) by conversion (def. 4). — **Syn.** See TRANSFORM. — *v. i.* To be converted.

con'vert (kŏn'vûrt), *n.* A converted person; esp., one who experiences or undergoes religious conversion.

Syn. **Convert**, **proselyte** mean one who has embraced another creed, opinion, etc., than that which he previously accepted. **Convert** is used in a good sense implying a sincere and voluntary change; **proselyte** now implies one who has been won over to a belief previously rejected.

con·vert'er, **con·ver'tor** (kŏn·vûr'tẽr), *n.* **1**. One who converts or makes converts. **2**. A merchant who buys unfinished fabrics, etc., and has them dyed, bleached, etc. **3**. An apparatus for converting; specif.: **a** *Steel Mfg.* Short for BESSEMER CONVERTER. **b** *Elec.* A device employing mechanical rotation for transforming electrical energy. **c** *Television.* An auxiliary device for adapting a receiver to receive channels for which it was not originally designed.

con·vert'i·ble (kŏn·vûr'tĭ·b'l), *adj.* Capable of being converted, as by being transposed, by being transformed from one type to another, or by being exchanged for an equivalent. — *n.* A convertible thing. — **con·vert'i·bil'i·ty** (-bĭl'ĭ·tĭ), *n.* — **con·vert'i·ble·ness**, *n.* — **con·vert'i·bly**, *adv.*

con·vert'i·plane' (kŏn·vûr'tĭ·plān'), *n.* [*convert* + *plane*.] An aircraft that takes off and lands like a helicopter but flies like a conventional plane.

con'vert·ite (kŏn'vẽr·tīt), *n.* A convert.

con'vex (kŏn'vĕks; kŏn·vĕks'; 2), *adj.* [F. *convexe*, fr. L. *convexus* vaulted, arched, convex, concave, fr. *convehere* to bring together.] Curved or rounded as the exterior of a spherical or circular form viewed from without; — opposite of *concave*. See LENS, *Illust.* — (kŏn'vĕks; *form. often* kŏn·vĕks'), *n.* A convex body, surface, part, lens, etc. — **con'vex·ly**, *adv.*

con·vex'i·ty (kŏn·vĕk'sĭ·tĭ), *n.; pl.* -TIES (-tĭz). Convex curvature; also, a convex surface, curve, or part.

con·vex'o- (kŏn·vĕk'sō-). A combining form denoting *convexly*, *convex and*, as in: **con·vex'o-con'cave**, convex on one side and concave on the other; **con·vex'o-con'vex**; **con·vex'o-plane'**.

con·vey' (kŏn·vā'), *v. t.* [OF. *conveier* (ONF.), *convoier*, to escort, convoy, deriv. of L. *con-* + *via* way.] **1.** To bear from one place to another; carry; transport. **2.** To carry away, esp. secretly; hence, euphemistically, to steal; to plagiarize. **3.** To serve as a medium or conduit for. **4.** To impart, as by language. **5.** To transfer to another, esp., *Law*, to transfer (real estate) or pass (a title) by a sealed writing. **6.** *Obs.* To conduct secretly or craftily. — **Syn.** See CARRY. — **con·vey′a·ble**, *adj.*

con·vey′ance (kŏn·vā′ăns), *n.* **1.** Act of conveying. **2.** Means or way of conveying; esp., a vehicle. **3.** An instrument or deed conveying the title to property.

con·vey′anc·ing (-ăn·sĭng), *n.* *Law.* The act or business of drawing deeds, leases, etc., for transferring the title to property. — **con·vey′anc·er** (-ăn·sẽr), *n.*

con·vey′er, con·vey′or (-ẽr), *n.* One that conveys; specif.: **a** A person who transfers property. **b** A mechanical apparatus for carrying material from one point to another, as by an endless belt, chain of receptacles, or the like.

con·vict′ (kŏn·vĭkt′), *part. adj.* [L. *convictus*, past part. See CONVINCE.] *Archaic.* Convicted. — *v. t.* **1.** To prove or find guilty. **2.** *Archaic.* To convince (one), esp. of one's own wrongdoing or error.

con′vict (kŏn′vĭkt), *n.* **1.** One convicted of, and under sentence for, a crime. **2.** In popular use, a person serving a prison sentence, usually for a long term.

con·vic′tion (kŏn·vĭk′shŭn), *n.* **1.** A convicting; the condition of being convicted, as of a felony. **2.** Act of convincing someone. **3. a** State of being convinced, esp. of sin. **b** A strong persuasion or belief; as, to live up to one's *convictions.* — **Syn.** See CERTAINTY; OPINION. — **con·vic′tion·al**, *adj.*

con·vic′tive (-vĭk′tĭv), *adj.* Convincing.

con·vince′ (kŏn·vĭns′), *v. t.*; -VINCED′ (-vĭnst′); -VINC′ING (-vĭn′sĭng). [L. *convincere, -victum*, to refute, prove, fr. *con-* + *vincere* to conquer.] **1.** *Obs.* To overpower; overcome. **2.** To bring by argument to belief beyond doubt; satisfy by proof. **3.** *Obs.* **a** To convict. **b** To demonstrate or show (as existing or as of a certain character). **c** To disprove. — **con·vince′ment**, *n.* — **con·vinc′er** (-vĭn′sẽr), *n.* — **con·vin′ci·ble** (-vĭn′sĭ·b'l), *adj.*

con·vinc′ing (-vĭn′sĭng), *adj.* Satisfying or assuring by argument or proof. — **Syn.** See VALID. — **con·vinc′ing·ly**, *adv.* — **con·vinc′ing·ness**, *n.*

con·viv′i·al (-vĭv′ĭ·ăl; -yăl), *adj.* [L. *convivialis*, fr. *convivium* a feast, fr. *con-* + *vivere* to live.] Of, characterized by, or given to eating and drinking in jovial fellowship; jovial; festive; gay. — **con·viv′i·al′i·ty** (-ăl′ĭ·tĭ), *n.* — **con·viv′i·al·ly**, *adv.*

con′vo·ca′tion (kŏn′vō·kā′shŭn), *n.* [See CONVOKE.] **1.** Act of convoking. **2.** An assembly of persons convoked. **3.** *Ch. of Eng.* An assembly of clergy by their representatives, to consult on ecclesiastical affairs. **4.** *Prot. Epis. Ch.* **a** A meeting of a voluntary organization of the clergy and some of the laity of a section of a diocese, to promote interest in diocesan missions, etc.; hence, the organization, or the territorial division represented. **b** The annual meeting of the bishop, clergy, and lay delegates of a missionary jurisdiction. **5.** *Universities.* **a** In some English universities, an advisory or elective body composed of graduates; also, an assembly of this body. **b** In some U. S. and Canadian universities, an assembly at which degrees are conferred; commencement. — **con′vo·ca′tion·al**, *adj.*

con′vo·ca′tor (kŏn′vō·kā′tẽr), *n.* [ML.] One who convokes an assembly; also, a member of a convocation.

con·voke′ (kŏn·vōk′), *v. t.* [F. *convoquer*, fr. L. *convocare*, fr. *con-* + *vocare* to call.] To call together; to summon to meet; assemble by summons. — **Syn.** See SUMMON. — **con·vok′er** (-vōk′ẽr), *n.*

con′vo·lute (kŏn′vō·lūt), *v. t. & i.* [L. *convolutus*, past part. of *convolvere*. See CONVOLVE.] **1.** To twist around; contort. **2.** To make convolute. — *adj.* Rolled or wound together, one part upon another, as leaves in a bud. — **con′vo·lute·ly**, *adv.*

con′vo·lu′tion (-lū′shŭn), *n.* **1.** Convoluted state or formation. **2.** One of the windings, folds, coils, whorls, etc., in something convoluted; specif., one of the irregular ridges on the surface of the brain of man and some animals; a gyrus. See BRAIN, *Illust.*

con·volve′ (kŏn·vŏlv′), *v. t.* [L. *convolvere, -volutum*, fr. *con-* + *volvere* to roll.] To roll together; convolute.

con·vol′vu·la′ceous (-vŏl′vū·lā′shŭs), *adj.* Belonging to the morning-glory family (Convolvulaceae). See MORNING-GLORY **b**.

con·vol′vu·lus (-vŏl′vū·lŭs), *n.*; *pl.* -LUSES (-ĕz; -ĭz), -LI (-lī). [L., bindweed, fr. *convolvere* to roll around; — from its twining stems.] Any of a genus (*Convolvulus*) of erect, trailing, or twining herbs and shrubs (typifying the family Convolvulaceae) including species popularly called *bindweed* or sometimes *morning-glory*. See MORNING-GLORY **b**.

con·voy′ (kŏn·voi′; kŏn-), *v. t.* [OF. *convoier*. See CONVEY.] **1.** *Archaic.* To accompany; guide; conduct. **2.** To accompany for protection, by sea or land; escort. — **Syn.** See ACCOMPANY.

con′voy (kŏn′voi), *n.* [F. *convoi*.] **1.** Act of convoying; state of being convoyed. **2.** One that convoys another; an escort. **3.** *Obs.* Means or medium of conducting or conveying. **4.** A convoyed vessel, fleet, train, party, etc.

con·vulse′ (kŏn·vŭls′), *v. t.* [L. *convulsus*, past part. of *convellere* to tear up, shake, fr. *con-* + *vellere* to pluck, pull.] To shake or agitate violently; esp., to shake with or as if with irregular spasms, as in excessive laughter, or in agony from grief or pain. — **Syn.** See SHAKE.

con·vul′sion (-vŭl′shŭn), *n.* **1.** (Usually in *pl.*) A violent and involuntary contraction or series of contractions of the muscles; spasm. **2.** A violent disturbance, as an earthquake or social upheaval.

con·vul′sion·ar′y (-ẽr′ĭ; -ẽr·ĭ), *adj.* Of, pertaining to, or characteristic of convulsion or convulsionaries. — *n.*; *pl.* -IES (-ĭz). One who has convulsions, esp. as a result of religious mania or ecstasy.

con·vul′sive (kŏn·vŭl′sĭv), *adj.* Of the nature of a convulsion; attended with, or characterized by, convulsions. — **Syn.** See FITFUL. — **con·vul′sive·ly**, *adv.* — **con·vul′sive·ness**, *n.*

co′ny, co′ney (kō′nĭ; *formerly, and still by some*, kŭn′ĭ), *n.*; *pl.* -NIES, -NEYS (-nĭz). [OF. *conil*, fr. L. *cuniculus* rabbit, cony.] **1. a** A rabbit, esp. the European rabbit (*Oryctolagus cuniculus*); also, rabbit skin or fur. **b** = DAMAN; — the *cony* of the Bible. **c** A pika. **2.** *Archaic.* A simpleton; a dupe.

coo (kōō), *v. i.*; COOED (kōōd); COO′ING. [Imitative.] **1.** To make the low sound characteristic of doves, or a sound like it. **2.** To converse amorously; — usually in *bill and coo*. — *v. t.* To utter, express, or effect with a coo or coos. — *n.* The sound made in cooing.

coo′ee, coo′ey (kōō′ĭ; -ē), *n.* A peculiar hailing cry of Australian aborigines, used also by Australian colonists. — *v. i.* To call out *cooee*.

coof (kōōf; kŭf), *n.* *Dial.* A blockhead.

cook (kŏŏk), *n.* [AS. *cōc*, fr. L. *cocus, coquus*, fr. *coquere, coctum*, to cook.] One who prepares food for eating. — *v. t.* **1.** To prepare (food) by boiling, roasting, baking, etc. **2.** To subject to the action of heat or fire, as in curing tobacco. **3.** *Colloq.* To concoct; hence, to tamper with; doctor; — often with *up*. **4.** *Slang.* To ruin; spoil; — esp. in ***to cook one's goose***, to ruin or undo a person or his plans. — *v. i.* **1.** To do the work of a cook. **2.** To undergo cooking. — **cook′er**, *n.*

cook (kōōk; kŏŏk), *v. i.* *Chiefly Scot.* To crouch down.

cook′book′ (kŏŏk′bŏŏk′), *n.* *Chiefly U. S.* A book of directions and recipes for cooking.

cook′er·y (kŏŏk′ẽr·ĭ), *n.*; *pl.* -ERIES (-ĭz). Art, process, work, or place of cooking.

cook′y, cook′ie (kŏŏk′ĭ), *n.*; *pl.* -IES (-ĭz). [D. *koekje*, dim. of *koek* cake.] *U. S.* A small, flat, dry, usually sweetened cake of various kinds. Cf. BISCUIT, 1.

cool (kōōl), *adj.* [AS. *cōl*.] **1.** Moderately cold; lacking in warmth. **2.** Not retaining or admitting heat; as, a *cool* dress. **3.** Not ardent or passionate; hence, exercising self-control; calm; self-possessed. **4.** Manifesting coldness or dislike; as, a *cool* greeting. **5.** Calmly impudent; inconsiderately audacious; as, a *cool* stare. **6.** Stated or estimated without exaggeration; as, to inherit a *cool* million. **7.** Of colors, producing a sense of coolness; specif., of a hue near green or blue; — opp. to *warm*.

Syn. **Cool, composed, collected, unruffled, imperturbable, nonchalant** mean actually or apparently free from agitation or excitement. **Cool** specifically implies dispassionateness, calmness, deliberation, appearance, or the like; **composed** implies this freedom as the sign of a decorous, sedate temper or of self-discipline; **collected** implies a concentration of mind or spirit that eliminates distractions; **unruffled** implies coolness, placidity, and often poise in the midst of excitement; **imperturbable** implies such coolness or assurance that one is beyond agitation; **nonchalant** implies casualness of manner, the sign but not the result of unconcern.

— *n.* **1.** A cool time, place, etc. **2.** Coolness. — *v. i. & t.* **1.** To become or make cool. **2.** To calm; allay. — **cool′ly** (kōōl′lĭ), *adv.* — **cool′ness**, *n.*

cool′ant (kōōl′ănt), *n.* [See COOL, *adj.*; -ANT **b**.] A cooling agent.

cool′er (kōōl′ẽr), *n.* That which cools; as: **a** A vessel used to cool liquids. **b** A refrigerator. **c** A refrigerant. **d** *Slang.* A prison; esp., a cell for violent prisoners.

coo′lie, coo′ly (kōō′lĭ), *n.*; *pl.* -LIES (-lĭz). [Hind. *qūlī, qulī*.] In India, China, etc., a native unskilled laborer or porter; elsewhere, a cheap laborer from the Orient.

cool′ish (kōōl′ĭsh), *adj.* Somewhat cool.

coom, coomb (kōōm), *n.* **1.** *Scot. & Dial. Eng.* Soot; smut. **2.** Refuse grease, esp. from vehicle axles.

coomb, combe, comb (kōōm; kōm), *n.* [AS. *cumb*.] **a** *Eng.* A narrow ravinelike valley. **b** *Dial. Eng. & Scot.* A hollow in the side of a hill or mountain.

coon (kōōn), *n.* A raccoon.

coon′can (kōōn′kăn), *n.* A game at cards.

coon′tie (kōōn′tĭ), *n.* [Seminole *kunti* coontie flour.] Any of several tropical American woody plants (genus *Zamia*, family Cycadaceae) whose roots and stems yield arrowroot.

coop (kōōp; 85), *n.* **1.** A cage or small enclosure, as for poultry. **2.** A place of confinement; specif., *Slang*, a jail. — *v. t.* To confine in, or as in, a coop; — esp. with *up* or *in*.

coop′er (-ẽr), *n.* A maker or repairer of barrels or casks. — *v. t. & i.* To work as a cooper (on).

coop′er·age (-ĭj), *n.* Work done by a cooper or the pay for it; also, a place for coopers' work.

co–op′er·ate (kō·ŏp′ẽr·āt), *v. i.* Also **co·öp′er·ate, co·op′er·ate.** [LL. *cooperatus*, past part. of *cooperari* to co-operate, fr. *co-* + *operari* to work.] **1.** To act or operate jointly with another or others. **2.** To join in economic co-operation. — **-a′tor** (-ā′tẽr), *n.*

co–op′er·a′tion (-ā′shŭn), *n.* Also **co·öp′er·a′tion, co·op′er·a′tion.** **1.** A co-operating. **2.** *Econ.* Collective action, as in industry, for mutual profit or common benefit. — **-a′tion·ist**, *n.*

co–op′er·a′tive (kō·ŏp′ẽr·ā′tĭv; -ȧ·tĭv), *adj.* Also **co·öp′er·a′tive, co·op′er·a′tive.** **1.** Co-operating; pertaining to or characterized by co-operation. **2.** Pertaining to or designating any association for buying and selling to the better advantage of its members or participants by elimination of middlemen's profits. — *n.* A co-operative business, society, etc. — **-tive·ly**, *adv.* — **-tive·ness**, *n.*

coop′er·y (kōōp′ẽr·ĭ; 85), *n.* = COOPERAGE.

co–opt′ (kō·ŏpt′), *v. t.* Also **co·öpt′.** [L. *cooptare*, fr. *co-* + *optare* to choose.] To choose or elect (a person) as a fellow member or a colleague; — esp. of the joint action, as of a board. — **co′–op·ta′tion, co′öp-** (kō′ŏp·tā′shŭn), *n.* — **co–op′ta·tive, co·öp′-** (kō·ŏp′tȧ·tĭv), *adj.*

co–or′di·nate (kō·ôr′dĭ·nāt), *adj.* Also **co·ör′di·nate, co·or′di·nate.** [*co-* + L. *ordinatus*, past part. of *ordinare* to regulate.] **1.** Equal in rank or order; of the same rank or order; not subordinate; specif., *Gram.*, designating members of like rank in a compound sentence; as, *co-ordinate* clauses. **2.** Of, pert. to, or involving co-ordination or co-ordinates; co-ordinative; specif., *Gram.*, joining word groups or words of the same rank; as, a *co-ordinate* conjunction. **3.** Having separate colleges for men and women. — (-nāt), *v. t. & i.* **1.** To make or become co-ordinate. **2.** To bring into common action, condition, etc. — (-nāt), *n.* **1.** One that is co-ordinate. **2.** *Math.* Any of a number of magnitudes that determine position, as of points, planes, etc. — **-nate·ly**, *adv.* — **-nate·ness**, *n.* — **-na′tor** (-nā′tẽr), *n.*

co–or′di·na′tion (-nā′shŭn), *n.* Also **co·ör′di·na′tion, co·or′di·na′tion.** Act of co-ordinating; state of being co-ordinate; harmonious adjustment or functioning.

co–or′di·na′tive (kō·ôr′dĭ·nā′tĭv; -nȧ·tĭv), *adj.* Also **co·ör′di·na′tive, co·or′di·na′tive.** Co-ordinating; co-ordinate.

coot (kōōt), *n.* **1.** Any of a genus (*Fulica*) of ducklike birds of the rail family (Rallidae), esp. *F. atra* (the ***bald coot***) of Europe and *F. americana* of North America. They are stupid, slow in flight, and are not classed as game birds. **2.** Any North American scoter (see SCOTER). **3.** *Colloq.* A stupid fellow; simpleton.

coot′ie (kōōt′ĭ), *n.* *Slang.* A body louse (see LOUSE, 1).

cop (kŏp), *n.* [AS. *cop, copp*, top.] **1.** *Dial.* Top; crest. **2.** A conical mass of yarn wound on a spindle. **3.** A tube or quill upon which silk is wound.

cop (kŏp), *v. t.*; COPPED (kŏpt); COP′PING. [Prob. fr. OF. *caper* to seize, fr. L. *capere*.] *Slang.* **a** To catch; capture. **b** To steal.

cop (kŏp), *n.* *Slang.* A policeman.

co′pa·cet′ic (kō′pȧ·sĕt′ĭk), *adj.* *Slang, U. S.* Capital; snappy; prime.

co·pai′ba (kō·pā′bȧ; -pī′bȧ), *n.* [Sp. & Pg., of Tupian origin.] A stimulant and diuretic oleoresin obtained from certain South American trees (genus *Copaifera*) of the senna family.

co′pal (kō′păl; -pål), *n.* [Sp., fr. Nahuatl *copalli.*] A resin from various tropical trees, used in varnishes, lacquers, etc.

co′palm′ (kō′päm′), *n.* See GUM, *n.*, 5 **a** (2).

co·par′ce·nar′y (kō·pär′sē·nĕr′ĭ *or, esp. Brit.*, -nĕr·ĭ), *n.; pl.* -NARIES (-ĭz). **1.** Also **co·par′ce·ny** (-nĭ). *Law.* Joint heirship. **2.** Copartnership; joint ownership.

co·par′ce·ner (kō·pär′sē·nẽr), *n.* *Law.* A joint heir.

co·part′ner (kō·pärt′nẽr), *n.* One of those jointly sharing; one of equal partners. — **co·part′ner·ship,** *n.*

cope (kōp), *n.* [ML. *capa, cappa.*] **1.** *Eccl.* A long enveloping capelike vestment. See VESTMENT, *Illust.* **2.** A copelike covering; as: **a** A vault; canopy; esp., the arch of the sky. **b** Hence, vertex; height. **c** Coping. — *v. t.* To cover or furnish with a cope or coping.

cope, *v. i.* [OF. *couper, colper*, to strike, fr. *coup, colp*, blow.] **1.** *Obs.* To strike; fight. **2.** To struggle or contend, now usually on equal terms or with some success; — followed by *with*. **3.** *Archaic.* To meet (*with*); have to do (*with*). — *v. t.* **1.** *Archaic.* To meet; encounter. **2.** *Obs.* To requite.

cope, *v. t.* [F. *coper, couper*, to cut off.] To notch; hence, *Arch.*, to shape, as the end of a beam to fit a coping or to conform to the shape of a supporting member.

co′peck (kō′pĕk). Var. of KOPECK.

cope′mate′ (kōp′māt′), **copes′mate′** (kōps′-), *n.* *Obs.* **a** An antagonist. **b** A partner; comrade; associate.

co′pen·ha′gen blue (kō′pĕn·hā′gĕn). A color, blue in hue, of low saturation and low brilliance. Cf. COLOR.

co′pe·pod (kō′pē·pŏd), *n.* [Gr. *kōpē* an oar + *-pod.*] One of a large subclass (Copepoda) of usually minute, fresh-water and salt-water crustaceans. — **co′pe·pod,** *adj.*

Co·per′ni·can (kō·pûr′nĭ·kăn), *adj.* Of or pertaining to Copernicus (see *Biog.*), who held that the earth rotates daily on its axis and that the planets revolve in orbits round the sun. Hence, **Copernican system.** Cf. PTOLEMAIC SYSTEM.

cope′stone′ (kōp′stōn′), *n.* A stone forming a coping; hence, figuratively, crown; finishing touch.

cop′i·er (kŏp′ĭ·ẽr), *n.* A transcriber; a copyist.

cop′ing (kōp′ĭng), *n.* The covering course of a wall, often with a sloping top.

cop′ing saw (kōp′ĭng). [See 3d COPE.] A small-sized type of scroll saw.

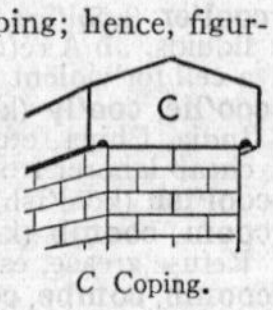

C Coping.

co′pi·ous (kō′pĭ·ŭs), *adj.* [L. *copiosus*, fr. *copia* abundance.] **1.** *Obs.* Abounding (*in*). **2.** Full of thought, matter, or the like; also, wordy, diffuse, or profuse. **3.** Plentiful; abundant. — **Syn.** See PLENTIFUL. — **Ant.** Meager. — **co′pi·ous·ly,** *adv.* — **co′pi·ous·ness,** *n.*

co·pol′y·mer·ize (kō·pŏl′ĭ·mẽr·īz; kō′pō·lĭm′ẽr·īz), *v. t. & i.* [See CO-, 1.] *Chem.* To polymerize together; — said of two or more polymerizing substances which together form complex molecules of a product, called a **co·pol′y·mer** (kō·pŏl′ĭ·mẽr). Copolymers differ in properties from the polymers formed by the components singly and from mixtures of such polymers. Copolymerization is important in the preparation of plastics and synthetic rubber. — **co·pol′y·mer·i·za′tion** (kō-pŏl′ĭ·mẽr·ĭ·zā′shŭn; kō′pō·lĭm′ẽr-; -ī·zā′shŭn), *n.*

cop′per (kŏp′ẽr), *n.* [AS. *caper, copor*, fr. L. *cuprum*, fr. *Cyprus*, anciently renowned for its copper mines.] **1.** A common metal, reddish in color, ductile, malleable, and very tenacious, and one of the best conductors of heat and electricity. Symbol, *Cu;* at. no., 29; at. wt., 63.54; sp. gr., 8.92. **2.** Something made of copper; as: **a** A copper (or bronze) coin. **b** A large boiler, as for laundry or for cooking (now usually made of iron). **3.** The color of copper. — *v. t.* **1.** To cover, coat, or sheathe with copper. **2.** *U. S.* To bet against; — orig. used in faro. — **cop′per,** *adj.*

cop′per (kŏp′ẽr), *n.* [See COP, *v.*] *Slang.* A policeman.

cop′per·as (kŏp′ẽr·ȧs), *n.* [OF. *couperose.*] Green vitriol (see VITRIOL).

cop′per·head′ (kŏp′ẽr·hĕd′), *n.* **1.** A poisonous snake (*Agkistrodon mokasen*) allied to the rattlesnake, but quicker and without rattles, found in the eastern U. S. See MOCCASIN, 2. **2.** [*cap.*] *U. S.* A person in the Northern States who sympathized with the South during the Civil War; — a nickname. — **cop′per·head′ism** (-ĭz′m), *n.*

cop′per·plate′ (kŏp′ẽr·plāt′), *n.* **a** A plate of copper on which a design or writing is engraved. **b** An impression taken from such a plate. **c** Engraving or printing from such a plate.

copper pyrites. Chalcopyrite.

cop′per·smith′ (kŏp′ẽr·smĭth′), *n.* A worker in copper.

cop′per·y (-ĭ), *adj.* Mixed with, containing, or like copper.

cop′pice (kŏp′ĭs), *n.* [OF. *copeiz*, fr. *coper, couper*, to cut.] A thicket or grove of small trees. See COPSE.

cop′ra (kŏp′rȧ; kō′prȧ), *n.* Also **cop′rah, cop′pra,** and **cop′per·ah** (kŏp′ẽr·ȧ). [Pg. *copra*, fr. Malayalam *koppara*, fr. Hind. *khoprā.*] Dried coconut meat, yielding coconut oil.

cop′ro- (kŏp′rō-), **copr-.** [Gr. *kopros.*] A combining form meaning *dung, excrement*, as in **cop·re′mi·a, cop·rae′mi·a** (kŏp·rē′mĭ·ȧ), intoxication from products absorbed into the blood from feces; **cop′ro·lite** (kŏp′rō·līt), fossil dung; **cop·roph′a·gous** (kŏp·rŏf′ȧ·gŭs), feeding on dung.

copse (kŏps), *n.* A shortened form of COPPICE.

Copt (kŏpt), *n.* [NL. *Coptus.*] An Egyptian of the native race descended from the ancient Egyptians; esp., a member of the **Cop′tic Church,** the ancient Christian church of Egypt, now surviving mainly among fellahin.

Cop′tic (kŏp′tĭk), *adj.* [Ar. *Qufṭ, Qibṭ*, the Copts, fr. Coptic *Gyptios, Kyptaios*, Egyptian, fr. Gr. *Aigyptios.*] Of or pertaining to the Copts or Coptic. — *n.* The Hamitic language derived from ancient Egyptian, now used only as the liturgical language of the Coptic Church. See LANGUAGE, *Table.*

cop′u·la (kŏp′ū·lȧ), *n.; pl.* -LAS (-lȧz), *rarely* -LAE (-lē). [L., bond.] **1.** That which connects; a link. **2.** Also **copulative verb.** *Gram.* A link verb; as, the verb *be*, which has little meaning of its own, is sometimes called "the *copula.*" **3.** *Logic.* The relation or connecting link between the subject and predicate of a proposition.

cop′u·late (kŏp′ū·lāt), *v. i.* To unite in sexual intercourse.

cop′u·la′tion (kŏp′ū·lā′shŭn), *n.* **1.** Act of coupling or joining; union; conjunction. **2.** Sexual union; coition.

cop′u·la′tive (kŏp′ū·lā′tĭv; -lȧ·tĭv), *adj.* **1.** Serving to connect or join. **2.** *Gram.* **a** Joining words in co-ordinate construction and expressing a uniting of their ideas; as, a *copulative* conjunction (*and, neither . . . nor*). **b** Of the nature of a copula; as, *seem* is a *copulative* verb. — *n.* A copulative word. — **cop′u·la′tive·ly,** *adv.*

cop′y (kŏp′ĭ), *n.; pl.* -IES (-ĭz). [OF. *copie*, fr. L. *copia* abundance, number, ML. also, a transcript, fr. *co-* + *opia*, fr. *ops* wealth.] **1.** An imitation or reproduction of an original work. **2.** An individual one of a number of books, engravings, or the like, reproducing the same composition or work. **3.** That which is to be imitated or reproduced; a pattern or example, esp. of penmanship. **4.** Manuscript or other matter (typewritten, printed, or the like) to be put in type; hence, reading matter. — **Syn.** See REPRODUCTION. — *v. t. & i.;* COP′IED (-ĭd); COP′Y·ING. **1.** To make a copy or copies of; to reproduce. **2.** To imitate; to follow, as in manners or life.

Syn. **Copy, imitate, mimic, ape, mock** mean to make something resembling an existent thing. **Copy** implies duplication of an original and as close resemblance as is possible; **imitate** stresses following something as a pattern or model, as in emulation or simulation; **mimic** implies close copying, as of a person's voice or mannerisms, sometimes for sport, sometimes for lifelike representation; **ape** is colloquial for *imitate* or *mimic;* **mock** adds to *mimic* the clear implication of a derisive intent.

cop′y·book′ (-bŏŏk′), *n.* **a** A book containing copies, as of correspondence. **b** A book in which copies, esp. of penmanship, are written or printed for learners to imitate.

cop′y·cat′ (-kăt′), *n. & v.* *Colloq.* Mimic.

copy desk. In newspaper offices, the desk at which news stories are revised and headlines are affixed.

cop′y·hold′ (-hōld′), *n.* *Law.* In England and Ireland, the holding of land by right of being recorded as holder in the court of the manor.

cop′y·hold′er (-hōl′dẽr), *n.* **1.** *Eng. Law.* One holding land in copyhold. **2.** A device for holding copy, esp. for a typesetter. **3.** One who reads copy for a proofreader.

cop′y·ist (-ĭst), *n.* A transcriber; also, an imitator.

cop′y·right′ (-rīt′), *n.* The exclusive right to reproduce, publish, and sell the matter and form of a literary or artistic work. In U. S. and Britain, copyright rests upon statutory provisions. Cf. PATENT, *n.*, 2; ROYALTY, 6 **b.** — *v. t.* To secure a copyright on. — *adj.* Secured by copyright. — **cop′y·right′a·ble,** *adj.* — **cop′y·right′er,** *n.*

coque′li·cot′ (kōk′lē·kō′), *n.* [F.] **a** The corn poppy (*Papaver rhoeas*). See POPPY. **b** = POPPY RED.

co·quet′ (kō·kĕt′), *adj.* [F.] Coquettish. — *n.* *Now Rare.* A male flirt. — *v. t. & i.;* CO·QUET′TED; CO·QUET′TING. Also **co·quette′.** [See COQUETTE.] To flirt; to play the coquette; hence, to play or dally (with). — **Syn.** See TRIFLE.

co′quet·ry (kō′kĕ·trĭ; kō′kĭ-; kō·kĕt′rĭ), *n.; pl.* -RIES (-trĭz). **1.** The conduct or art of a coquette; flirtation. **2.** Dallying or trifling attention or consideration.

co·quette′ (kō·kĕt′), *n.* [F., fr. *coquet, coquette*, coquettish, orig., cocklike, strutting, fr. *coq* a cock.] A woman who endeavors without affection to attract men's amorous attention, esp. by playful arts; a flirt. — **co·quet′tish,** *adj.* — **co·quet′tish·ly,** *adv.* — **co·quet′tish·ness,** *n.*

co·quil′la nut (kō·kēl′yȧ; -kē′yȧ). [Pg. *coquilho* or Sp. *coquillo*, dim. of *coco* a coconut.] The fruit or nut of a piassava palm (*Attalea funifera*) of Brazil. The hard brown shell is much used, like vegetable ivory, by turners.

co·qui′na (kō·kē′nȧ), *n.* [Sp., shellfish.] A soft, whitish natural limestone, of broken shells and corals cemented together, used in the southern U. S. for building, etc.

cor-. An assimilated form of COM-, as in *cor*rode.

cor′a·ci′i·form (kŏr′ȧ·sī′ĭ·fôrm), *adj.* [Gr. *korax* crow, raven + *-form.*] Of or relating to an order (Coraciiformes) of arboreal nonpasserine birds comprising the rollers, kingfishers, hornbills, hoopoes, motmots, and allies.

cor′a·cle (kŏr′ȧ·k'l), *n.* [W. *corwgl, cwrwgl*, fr. *corwg, cwrwg*, any round body, carcass.] *Brit.* A small boat made by covering a wicker frame with hide, cloth, or the like, used by the ancient Britons; now, a boat made of broad hoops covered with horsehide or tarpaulin.

cor′a·coid (-koid), *adj.* [Gr. *korakoeidēs*, fr. *korax* crow + *eidos* form.] *Anat. & Zool.* Designating a process or cartilage bone of many vertebrates which extends from the scapula to or toward the sternum. — *n.* The coracoid process or bone.

cor′al (kŏr′ăl), *n.* [OF. *coral*, fr. L. *corallum, coralium*, fr. Gr. *korallion.*] **1. a** The calcareous or hornlike skeleton of various anthozoans and a few hydrozoans (the millepores); also, the entire animal, a compound polyp, which produces this skeleton. **b** A particular species of this animal, as the ***red coral*** (*Corallium nobile*) and ***white coral*** (*Amphihelia oculata*) of the Mediterranean. **c** The skeletons of these animals solidified into a stony mass, of which many tropical islands, reefs, and atolls are formed. **2.** A piece of coral, esp. of red coral. **3.** The ovaries of a lobster. **4.** = CORAL RED. **5.** A child's teething ring or toy, made of coral. — *adj.* **a** Of, pert. to, or like coral; as, *coral* reefs, limestone. **b** Coral-red.

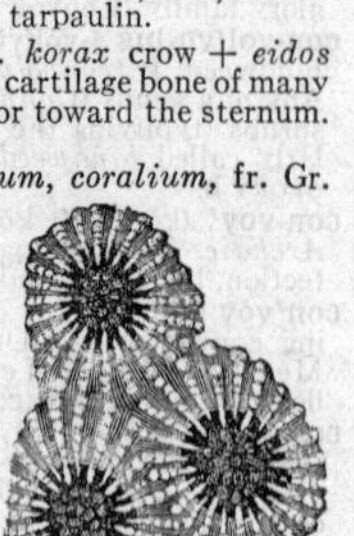
One kind of Coral (*Orbicella annularis*).

coralli-. [L. *corallum.*] A combining form meaning *coral*, as in **cor′al·lif′er·ous,** producing coral.

cor′al·line (kŏr′ă·lĭn; -līn), *adj.* Of or like coral.

cor′al·loid (-loid), **cor′al·loi′dal** (-loi′dăl; -d'l), *adj.* Like coral.

coral red. A color, yellowish-red in hue, of high saturation and medium brilliance. See COLOR. — **cor′al-red′,** *adj.*

coral snake. **1.** Any of several venomous, chiefly tropical New World snakes (genus *Micrurus*) brilliantly banded in red, black, and yellow or white, including two species (*M. fulvius* and *M. euryxanthus*) that extend their range into the southern U. S. **2.** Any of several harmless snakes resembling the coral snakes.

‖**co′ram po′pu·lo** (kō′răm pŏp′ū·lō). [L.] Publicly; in public.

co·ran′to (kō·răn′tō; -rän′tō), *n.* = COURANTE.

cor′ban (kôr′băn; kôr·bän′), *n.* [Heb. *qorbān.*] *Jewish Antiq.* An offering devoted to God. *Mark* vii. 11.

cor'beil (kôr'bĕl), *n.* [F. *corbeille*, fr. LL. *corbicula* a little basket.] *Arch.* A sculptured basket of flowers, fruit, etc.

cor'bel (kôr'bĕl; -bĕl), *n.* [OF., prop., raven, dim. of *corp*, fr. L. *corvus* raven.] **1.** *Arch.* A projection from the face of a wall, supporting a weight. **2.** A short timber placed lengthwise under a girder to afford a bearing. — *v. t.*; -BELED (-bĕld) or -BELLED; -BEL·ING or -BEL·LING. To furnish with a corbel.

cor'bel·ing, cor'bel·ling, *n.* Corbel work or the construction of corbels; a series of corbels.

cor'bie (kôr'bĭ), *n.*; *pl.* -BIES (-bĭz). Also **corbie crow.** [See CORBEL.] *Chiefly Scot.* A raven or crow.

corbie gable. A gable having corbiesteps.

cor'bie·step' (-stĕp'), *n.* *Arch.* One of the steps in which a gable wall is often finished in place of a slope.

cord (kôrd), *n.* [OF. *corde*, fr. L. *chorda* catgut, chord, cord, fr. Gr. *chordē*.] **1.** A string, or small rope; also, such string as a material. **2.** A hangman's rope. **3.** Any moral influence by which persons are held or drawn, as if by a cord. **4.** A cubic measure used esp. for wood cut for fuel; also, the quantity of wood in such a measure. In U. S. now legally a pile 8 ft. long, 4 ft. high, and 4 ft. wide (128 cu. ft.). A one-foot length of such a pile is a **cord foot** (16 cu. ft.). See MEASURE, *Table* 5. **5.** A cordlike rib on a textile fabric; also, a ribbed fabric, esp. corduroy; in *pl.*, trousers of corduroy. **6.** *Anat.* A structure likened to a cord, esp. a tendon or a nerve. **7.** *Elec.* A small flexible insulated cable (def. 4 **b**) with a plug at one or both ends, used to connect a lamp, toaster, etc., with a socket. — *v. t.* **1.** To furnish, bind, or connect with a cord or cords. **2.** To arrange or pile up (wood, etc.) in cords. — **cord'er,** *n.*

cord'age (kôr'dĭj), *n.* **1.** Ropes or cords, collectively; esp., the ropes in the rigging of a ship. **2.** The number of cords, as of wood, on a given area.

cor'date (kôr'dāt), *adj.* [L. *cor*, *cordis*, heart.] Heart-shaped; cordiform; as, a *cordate* leaf. See LEAF, *Illust.* — **cor'date·ly,** *adv.*

cord'ed (kôr'dĕd; -dĭd), *adj.* **1.** Bound with cords. **2.** Striped or ribbed with cords; twilled; as, a *corded* cloth.

Cor·de'lia (kôr·dēl'yȧ; -dē'lĭ·ȧ), *n.* See KING LEAR.

Cor'de·lier' (kôr'dĕ·lēr'; -lyā'), *n.* [F., fr. *cordelle* small cord, dim. fr. *corde* string, rope. See CORD.] **1.** *Eccl. Hist.* A Franciscan. **2.** *Fr. Hist.* A member of a French political club of the time of the first Revolution. It met in an old Cordelier convent in Paris.

cor'dial (kôr'jăl; kôrd'yăl; *or, esp. Brit.*, -dĭ·ăl), *adj.* [ML. *cordialis*, fr. L. *cor*, *cordis*, heart.] **1.** *Obs.* Of or belonging to the heart; vital. **2.** Tending to revive, cheer, or invigorate. **3.** Hearty; sincere. — **Syn.** See GRACIOUS. — *n.* **1.** Any stimulating preparation, as a medicine. **2.** *Com.* An aromatized and sweetened spirit, used as a beverage; a liqueur. — **cor'dial·ly,** *adv.* — **cor'dial·ness,** *n.*

cor·dial'i·ty (kôr·jăl'ĭ·tĭ; kôr'dĭ·ăl'-), *n.*; *pl.* -TIES (-tĭz). Cordial quality; warmth of regard; heartiness.

cor'di·form (kôr'dĭ·fôrm), *adj.* [L. *cor*, *cordis*, heart + *-form*.] Heart-shaped; cordate.

cor'dil·le'ra (kôr'dĭl·yâr'ȧ; kôr·dĭl'ĕr·ȧ), *n.* [Sp., lit., little rope or string.] A mountain range or system, orig. one of the Andes; sometimes, the main mountain axis of a continent. — **cor'dil·le'ran** (-ăn), *adj.*

cord'ite (kôr'dīt), *n.* [From CORD, *n.*] A smokeless powder composed of nitroglycerin, guncotton, and mineral jelly. The ingredients are mixed into a paste with acetone, and pressed out into cords which are dried and cut into lengths.

cor'do·ba (kôr'dō·bȧ; *Sp.* kôr'thō·vä; 17), *n.*; *pl.* CORDOBAS (-bȧz; -väs). [Sp. *córdoba*, after the explorer Francisco F. de *Córdoba*.] The monetary unit of Nicaragua, originally established as equal to the U. S. gold dollar. See MONEY, *Tables.*

cor'don (kôr'dŏn), *n.* [F., fr. *corde* cord.] **1.** An ornamental cord, used esp. on costumes. **2.** A line or circle of persons around any person or place; as, a *cordon* of police; specif., ***sanitary cordon***, a line of guards stationed to isolate an infected district. **3.** A cord or ribbon worn as a badge or decoration. **4.** *Arch.* A stringcourse.

Cor'do·van (kôr'dō·văn), *adj.* Of or pertaining to Cordova (Spanish, Córdoba), Spain; hence [*not cap.*], made of the leather manufactured at Cordova. — *n.* [*not cap.*] A soft, fine-grained, colored leather, orig. made at Cordova, Spain.

cor'du·roy (kôr'dŭ·roi; -dū·roi; kôr'dŭ·roi'; -dū·roi'), *n.* [Prob. for F. *corde du roi* king's cord.] **1.** A coarse durable cotton fabric, having a piled surface, like that of velvet, raised in cords, ridges, or ribs. **2.** *pl.* Trousers or breeches of this material. — *adj.* **1.** Made of corduroy, as a jacket. **2.** Designating a road (**corduroy road**), bridge, etc., formed of logs laid side by side transversely, as across a swampy place. — *v. t.* To form (a road) of logs laid side by side transversely.

cord'wain (kôrd'wān), *n.* [OF. *cordoan*, fr. Sp. *cordobán*.] *Archaic.* Cordovan leather.

cord'wain·er (-ĕr), *n.* **1.** *Archaic.* A worker in cordovan leather. **2.** A shoemaker. — **cord'wain·er·y** (-ĕr·ĭ), *n.*

cord'wood' (-wŏŏd'), *n.* **a** Wood piled up or sold in cords. **b** Standing timber of size and quality fit only for burning as fuel.

core (kōr; 70), *n.* [ME., prob. fr. L. *cor* heart.] **1.** The central portion in certain fruits, esp. of the apple family. **2.** The central part of anything. **3.** A portion removed from the interior of a mass, as from rock by boring. **4.** The heart of timber; hence, a lumber center or base, usually of soft wood, on which veneers are glued. **5.** The central strand around which others are twisted in some kinds of rope. **6.** The gist, essence, or central meaning; the inmost part. **7.** *Elec.* **a** The conducting wire with its insulation; — said of cables. **b** A bar of iron, a bundle of iron wires, or the like, used to concentrate and intensify an induced magnetic field, as in a transformer, induction coil, or armature. See MAGNETO, *Illust.* **8.** *Founding.* The portion of a mold which shapes the inside of a hollow casting. — *v. t.* To take out the core of.

core, *n.* [F. *corps*.] *Chiefly Scot.* A company, as of curlers.

co're·la'tion (kō'rē·lā'shŭn), *n.* Correlation. — **co·rel'a·tive** (kō·rĕl'ȧ·tĭv), *adj.* — **co·rel'a·tive·ly,** *adv.*

co're·li'gion·ist (kō'rē·lĭj'ŭn·ĭst), *n.* One of the same religion.

co're·op'sis (kō'rē·ŏp'sĭs; kôr'ē-), *n.* [NL., fr. Gr. *koris* bug + *-opsis*; — in allusion to the achene.] Any of a genus (*Coreopsis*) of herbs of the aster family, including several garden species having heads with yellow or crimson rays; also, the flower; — called also *calliopsis*.

cor'er (kōr'ĕr), *n.* An instrument for coring fruit.

co're·spond'ent (kō'rē·spŏn'dĕnt), *n.* In a suit for divorce on the grounds of adultery, the person named as guilty of adultery with the defendant. — **co're·spond'en·cy** (-dĕn·sĭ), *n.*

corf (kôrf), *n.*; *pl.* CORVES (kôrvz). [MD., basket.] Formerly, a basket (of any kind); now, specif., *Brit.*, a truck used for conveying ore, coal, etc., to the pit mouth.

cor'gi (kôr'gĭ), *n.* = WELSH CORGI.

co'ri·a'ceous (kō'rĭ·ā'shŭs; kôr'ĭ-; 70), *adj.* [LL. *coriaceus*, fr. *corium* leather.] Leatherlike; tough.

co'ri·an'der (-ăn'dĕr), *n.* [F. *coriandre*, fr. L., fr. Gr. *koriandron*.] An Old World herb (*Coriandrum sativum*) of the carrot family, with aromatic fruits (**coriander seeds**) used as a stomachic and carminative, and for seasoning.

Co·rin'thi·an (kō·rĭn'thĭ·ăn), *adj.* **1.** Of or pertaining to Corinth. **2.** *Arch.* Of, pertaining to, or designating, the lightest and most ornate of the three Greek orders, characterized esp. by its bell-shaped capital enveloped with acanthus leaves. See ORDER, ACANTHUS, *Illusts.* **3.** In allusion: **a** To Corinthian morals: given to luxurious dissipation. **b** To Corinthian art: gracefully ornate. — *n.* **1.** A native or resident of Corinth. **2. a** *Obs.* A gay, licentious fellow. **b** A fashionable man about town; esp., a sportsman.

Co·rin'thi·ans (-ănz), *n. pl.*, *construed as sing.* Either of two Epistles to the Corinthians, in the New Testament. See BIBLE.

Cor'i·o'lis force (kôr'ĭ·ō'lĭs). [After G. G. *Coriolis* (1792–1842), French civil engineer.] *Physics.* A deflecting force acting on a body in motion, as a projectile, airplane, or hurricane, due to the earth's rotation, diverting horizontal motions to the right in the northern hemisphere and to the left in the southern hemisphere.

co'ri·um (kō'rĭ·ŭm; 70), *n.*; *pl.* -RIA (-ȧ). [L., leather.] The derma, or deeper vascular and sensitive layer of the skin; the corresponding layer of the mucous membranes.

cork (kôrk), *n.* [Sp. Ar. al*corque*.] **1.** The elastic, tough, cortical tissue of the **cork oak** (*Quercus suber*), useful for stoppers for bottles, life preservers, etc. **2.** A piece of cork, or any of various objects made of it. **3.** A stopper for a bottle, cask, etc., esp. one cut out of cork. **4.** *Angling.* A float; a bob. **5.** *Bot.* A tissue in the stems of most woody plants, making up the greater part of the bark. — *v. t.* **1.** To furnish or fit with cork or a cork. **2.** To stop with or as with a cork; hence, to restrain. **3.** To blacken with burnt cork.

cork'age (kôr'kĭj), *n.* A charge made by innkeepers, etc., for every bottle of wine, etc., uncorked and served.

cork'er (kôr'kĕr), *n.* **1.** A worker or machine that corks. **2.** *Slang.* A conclusive argument, statement, or fact; a clincher; also, a person or thing of superior quality, ability, etc.

cork'screw' (kôrk'skrōō'), *n.* An instrument with a spiral device for drawing corks from bottles. — *v. t. & i.* *Colloq.* To proceed or cause to proceed in a winding way. — *adj.* Having the shape of a corkscrew; spiral.

cork'wood' (-wŏŏd'), *n.* Any of several trees having light or corky wood, as: **a** Esp., a small tree (*Leitneria floridana*), the sole species of its genus, which constitutes the family Leitneriaceae or the order Leitneriales. **b** = BALSA, 1.

cork'y (kôr'kĭ), *adj.*; CORK'I·ER (-kĭ·ĕr); CORK'I·EST. Of the nature of, or like, cork. — **cork'i·ness,** *n.*

corm (kôrm), *n.* [Gr. *kormos* trunk of a tree (with the boughs cut off), fr. *keirein* to shear.] *Bot.* A short, bulblike, underground, upright stem, invested with a few thin membranes or scale leaves, as in the crocus and gladiolus. Cf. BULB, TUBER.

cor'mo·rant (kôr'mō·rănt), *n.* [OF. *cormareng*.] **1.** Any of a genus (*Phalacrocorax*) of dark-colored, voracious sea birds having a long neck, webbed feet, wedge-shaped tail, hooked beak, and a patch of bare, often brightly colored, distensible skin under the mouth. In the Far East some species are used for catching fish, a band being placed about the bird's throat so that it cannot swallow the fish. **2.** A greedy or gluttonous person. — *adj.* Ravenous; voracious.

corn (kôrn), *n.* [AS.] **1.** *Now Dial.* A small, hard particle; a grain. **2.** Any small, hard seed; esp., the seed of any one of the cereal grasses. **3.** Collectively, the seeds of any of the cereal grasses used for food; grain. *Corn* is often specifically used for the important cereal crop of a given region; thus, in England it refers to wheat, in Scotland and Ireland to oats, and in the United States, Canada, and Australia to Indian corn, or maize. **4.** Any plant which produces such seed. **5.** *Colloq.* = CORN WHISKY. **6.** *Skiing.* Granular snow. **7.** *Slang.* Corny music, playing, jokes, etc. — *v. t.* **1.** To preserve and season with salt in grains; now, specif., to salt slightly in brine and preservatives; as, to *corn* beef. **2.** To form into grains; to granulate, as gunpowder. **3.** To feed with corn or grain.

corn, *n.* [OF., fr. L. *cornu* horn.] A horny hardening of the epidermis at some point, esp. on the toes, produced by friction or pressure.

cor·na'ceous (kôr·nā'shŭs), *adj.* [L. *cornus* cornel + *-aceous*.] Belonging to the dogwood family (Cornaceae). See DOGWOOD.

corn borer. In full, ***European corn borer.*** The larva of a European moth (*Pyrausta nubilalis*), now a serious pest in U. S., boring in the ears and stems of Indian corn.

corn bread. Bread made from corn; specif., *U. S.*, bread made of Indian meal baked in a shallow pan.

corn'cake' (kôrn'kāk'; 2), *n.* *U. S.* Johnnycake.

corn'cob' (-kŏb'), *n.* *U. S.* **1.** The chaffy axis on which the kernels of Indian corn are arranged in rows. **2.** A **corncob pipe**, a tobacco pipe with the bowl made from a corncob.

corn cockle. An annual hairy weed (*Agrostemma githago*), of the pink family. It has bright-red flowers, and is common in grainfields.

corn crake. The land rail (see RAIL).

cor'ne·a (kôr'nē·ȧ), *n.*; *pl.* -NEAS (-ȧz). [Fem. sing., fr. L. *corneus* horny, fr. *cornu* horn.] The transparent part of the coat of the eyeball, which covers the iris and pupil and admits light. See EYE, *Illust.* — **cor'ne·al** (-ăl), *adj.*

cor'nel (kôr'nĕl), *n.* [Prob. fr. MLG. *kornelle*, fr. OF. *corneille*, fr. L. *cornicula*, fr. *cornus*.] **a** Any plant of the genus *Cornus* and related genera, esp. the red dogwood and flowering dogwood (see DOGWOOD). **b** Either of two red-berried herbs, *Chamaepericlymenum canadense*, with whorled leaves and white floral bracts (called also *bunchberry*), and *C. suecica*, with opposite leaves and purple bracts.

cor·nel'ian (kôr·nēl'yăn; kôr-), *n.* [OF. *corneline* (F. *cornaline*), fr. *corneole*.] *Mineral.* Carnelian.

cor'ne·ous (kôr'nē·ŭs), *adj.* [L. *corneus*.] Horny.

cor'ner (kôr'nĕr), *n.* [OF. *corniere*, fr. ML., fr. L. *cornu* horn, end, point.] **1.** The point or place where two converging lines, sides, or edges meet; angle. **2.** A position from which escape by retreat is impossible. **3.** An out-of-the-way place; a nook. **4.** An edge or extremity; hence, any quarter or part; esp., a quarter of the earth. **5.** A piece designed to form, occupy, mark, protect, or adorn a corner of

anything. 6. *Com. & Exchanges.* The state of things produced by a person or persons who buy up the whole or the available part of any stock or species of property, thus compelling those who need such stock or property to buy of them at their own price; as, a *corner* in wheat or in cotton. — **Syn.** See MONOPOLY.
— *v. t.* 1. To provide with corners. 2. To put or set in a corner. 3. To drive into a corner or into a position of difficulty. 4. *Com. & Exchanges.* To get command of (a stock, etc.), so as to be able to put one's own price on it. — *v. i. U. S.* To form, have, or come to, a corner.
— *adj.* 1. Situated at a corner. 2. Used or fitted for use in a corner.
cor′ner·stone′ (kôr′nẽr·stōn′), *n.* 1. A stone forming a part of a corner or angle in a wall; esp., such a stone laid at the formal inauguration of the erection of a building. 2. Hence, something of fundamental importance.
cor′ner·wise′ (-wīz′), **cor′ner·ways′** (-wāz′), *adv.* With the corner in front; so as to form a corner; diagonally.
cor′net (kôr′nĕt; -nĭt; *now often* kôr·nĕt′ *in the U. S., esp. in sense* 1), *n.* [F., dim. fr. OF. *corn* horn, fr. L. *cornu.*] 1. *Music.* A brass-wind instrument, like the trumpet, with cupped mouthpiece and three valves moved by small pistons or sliding rods. 2. Something shaped like a horn, as a piece of paper twisted into the form of a cone.
cor′net, *n.* [F. *cornette,* dim.] 1. The large white headdress of members of a certain Roman Catholic sisterhood (Sisters of Charity). 2. *Mil.* Formerly: **a** A troop of cavalry. **b** The grade of commissioned officer in a British cavalry troop, who carried the standard. 3. *Naut.* A pennant used in signaling.
cor′net-à-pis′tons (kôr′nĕt·ȧ·pĭs′tŭnz; kôr·nĕt′-; *F.* kôr′nĕ′ȧ·pēs′-tôN′), *n.; pl.* CORNETS-À-PISTONS (kôr′nĕts-; kôr·nĕts′-; *F.* kôr′nĕ′-zȧ·pēs′tôN′). [F.] *Music.* A cornet.
cor′net·cy (kôr′nĕt·sĭ), *n.* Commission or rank of a cornet.
cor·net′tist (kôr·nĕt′ĭst), **cor′net·ist** (kôr′nĕt·ĭst; -nĭ·tĭst), *n.* A performer on the cornet.
corn flour. Cornstarch. *Chiefly Brit.*
corn′flow′er (kôrn′flou′ẽr), *n.* 1. = CORN COCKLE. 2. = BLUEBOTTLE, 1 **a**.
cor′nice (kôr′nĭs), *n.* [F. *cornice, corniche,* fr. It. *cornice,* fr. L. *coronis,* fr. Gr. *korōnis.*] 1. *Arch.* The horizontal member (typically molded and projecting) which crowns a composition, as a façade; hence, the top course or courses of the wall when treated as a crowning member. See ORDER, *Illust.* 2. In upholstery, etc., a decorative band, as to conceal the rings by which a curtain is hung. — *v. t.;* -NICED (-nĭst); -NIC·ING (-nĭs·ĭng). To crown with or as with a cornice.
Cor′nish (kôr′nĭsh), *adj.* Of or pertaining to Cornwall, Cornishmen, or Cornish. — *n.* The Celtic dialect which survived in Cornwall until late in the 18th century. See INDO-EUROPEAN LANGUAGES, *Table.* — **Cor′nish·man** (-măn), *n.*
corn law. A law regulating trade in corn; *pl.*, the series of laws dating back to 1436 and in force in Great Britain till 1846, regulating the export and import of corn.
corn pone. *Southern U. S.* Corn bread, esp. when made without milk or eggs.
corn sirup. See GLUCOSE, 2.
corn′starch′ (kôrn′stärch′; 2), *n. U. S.* Starch made from Indian corn; esp., a white flour used for puddings, etc.
corn sugar. Dextrose made from maize. See DEXTROSE.
cor′nu (kôr′nū), *n.; pl.* CORNUA (-nū·ȧ). [L.] A horn; — applied in anatomy to any of various horn-shaped structures.
cor′nu·co′pi·a (kôr′nū·kō′pĭ·ȧ; 58), *n.; pl.* -PIAS (-ȧz). [L. *cornu copiae* horn of plenty.] 1. The horn of Amalthaea, or horn of plenty, an emblem of abundance. 2. An abundance. 3. A receptacle shaped like a horn or cone.
cor′nus (kôr′nŭs), *n.* [L., cornel.] A cornel.
cor·nute′ (kôr·nūt′), *v. t. Archaic.* To cuckold.
cor·nu′to (kôr·nū′tō), *n.; pl.* -TOS (-tōz). [It., fr. L. *cornutus* horned.] *Obs.* A cuckold.
corn whisky *or, Colloq.,* **corn liquor.** Whisky distilled from mash consisting largely of maize.
corn′y (kôr′nĭ), *adj.;* CORN′I·ER (-nĭ·ẽr); CORN′I·EST. 1. Of or pert. to, or producing or abounding in corn (esp. sense 3). 2. Tiresomely trite, outworn, and countrified, or ridiculously naïve; as, a *corny* joke. 3. *Swing Music.* Affecting, or rendered in, a banal, bland, or unsophisticated style, so as to elicit sentimental feelings; — contrasted with *hot.*
corn′y, *adj.* Pertaining to or having corns on the feet.
cor′o·dy, cor′ro·dy (kŏr′ō·dĭ), *n.; pl.* -DIES (-dĭz). [ML. *corrodium, corredium, conredium,* provision.] *Old Eng. Law.* An allowance of provisions for maintenance.
co·rol′la (kō·rŏl′ȧ), *n.* [L., dim. of *corona* crown.] *Bot.* The petals of a flower, collectively; the inner perianth, or floral envelope surrounding the sporophylls, — disting. from the *calyx.* Cf. GAMOPETALOUS.
cor′ol·lar′y (kŏr′ŏ·lẽr′ĭ *or, esp. Brit.,* kō·rŏl′ȧ·rĭ), *n.; pl.* -IES (-ĭz). [L. *corollarium* corollary, gift, fr. *corolla.* See COROLLA.] 1. A deduction, consequence, or additional inference, from a proved proposition. 2. Something that naturally follows; a result. — *adj.* Of the nature of a corollary; consequential.
cor′ol·late (kŏr′ŏ·lāt), **cor′ol·lat′ed** (-lāt′ĕd; -ĭd), *adj. Bot.* Having a corolla.
co·ro′na (kō·rō′nȧ), *n.; pl.* -NAS (-nȧz), -NAE (-nē). [L., crown.] 1. *Anat.* A crownlike structure, esp. the upper part of a tooth or the skull. 2. *Arch.* The projecting part of a classic cornice. 3. *Astron. & Meteorol.* **a** A luminous envelope surrounding the sun, beyond the chromosphere. It is seen only during a total eclipse. **b** A circle, usually colored, often seen around a luminous body, as the sun or moon. It is due to diffraction produced by suspended droplets. 4. *Bot.* An appendage on the inner side of the corolla in certain flowers, as in the daffodil, jonquil, milkweeds, etc. 5. *Elec.* The discharge of electricity which appears on the surface of a conductor under high voltage. 6. *Zool.* See ROTIFER. 7. A long cigar with sides straight to the unsealed end and roundly blunted at the sealed end. See CIGAR.

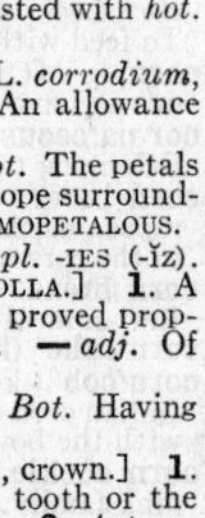

a Corona of Jonquil.

Co·ro′na Aus·tra′lis (kō·rō′nȧ ôs·trā′lĭs); *gen.* CORONAE AUSTRALIS (-nē). [L., southern crown.] A southern constellation adjoining Sagittarius on the south; the Southern Crown.
Co·ro′na Bo′re·a′lis (bō′rē·ā′lĭs· -ăl′ĭs); *gen.* CORONAE BOREALIS (-nē). [L., northern crown.] A northern constellation between Hercules and Boötes; the Northern Crown.
cor′o·nach (kŏr′ō·năĸ), *n.* [Ir. *corānach,* fr. *comh-* with + *rānach* a roaring.] *Scot. & Ir.* A lamentation for the dead; a dirge, whether sung or played, as on the bagpipes.
co·ro′na·graph (kō·rō′nȧ·grȧf; 9), *n.* [*corona* + *-graph.*] An instrument for observing the solar corona in full sunlight.
cor′o·nal (kŏr′ō·năl; -n'l), *n.* A circlet for the head; a crown or coronet.
co·ro′nal (kō·rō′năl; kŏr′ō·năl; -n'l), *adj.* 1. Of or pertaining to a crown or corona. 2. *Anat.* Lying in the direction of the coronal suture. — **co·ro′nal·ly,** *adv.*
coronal suture. *Anat.* A suture extending across the skull between the parietal and frontal bones.
cor′o·nar′y (kŏr′ō·nẽr′ĭ *or, esp. Brit.,* -nẽr·ĭ), *adj.* 1. Of or pertaining to, or of the nature of, a crown. 2. *Anat.* Like, or situated like, a crown; specif., of, designating, or pert. to either of two arteries (right and left) which arise from the aorta and supply the tissues of the heart itself; as, a *coronary* artery; *coronary* thrombosis.
cor′o·na′tion (-nā′shŭn), *n.* Act or ceremony of investing a sovereign or his consort with the royal crown.
cor′o·ner (kŏr′ō·nẽr), *n.* [OF. *corone* crown, fr. L. *corona.*] A public officer whose principal duty is to inquire by an inquest held in the presence of a jury (**coroner's jury**) into the cause of any death which appears to be due to unnatural causes. — **cor′o·ner·ship′,** *n.*
cor′o·net (-nĕt; -nĕt′; -nĭt), *n.* [OF. *coronete,* dim. of *corone* crown.] 1. A small crown, esp. one marking a rank lower than sovereignty. 2. An ornamental fillet or wreath worn round the temples. 3. The lower part of a horse's pastern where the horn terminates in skin. See HORSE, *Illust.* (32, 46). — **cor′o·net′ed, cor′o·net′ted,** *adj.*
cor′po·ra (kôr′pō·rȧ), *n., pl.* of CORPUS.
cor′po·ral (-răl), *n.* Also **cor′po·ra′le** (-rā′lē). [ML. *corporale.* See CORPORAL, *adj.*] *Eccl.* A linen cloth used in the Eucharist.
cor′po·ral, *adj.* [OF., fr. L. *corporalis,* fr. *corpus* body.] 1. Belonging or relating to the body; bodily. 2. Hence, personal. 3. *Archaic.* Corporeal. — **Syn.** See BODILY. — **cor′po·ral·ly,** *adv.*
cor′po·ral, *n.* [F. *caporal,* also *corporal,* fr. It., fr. L. *caput* head.] Abbr. *cpl., corp.* 1. *Mil.* The lowest noncommissioned officer, next below sergeant and above private, first class; as of 1948 in the U. S. Army, equal in grade to the former sergeant (4th grade). 2. *Brit. Navy.* A petty officer assistant to the master-at-arms. — **-ship′,** *n.*
cor′po·ral′i·ty (kôr′pō·răl′ĭ·tĭ), *n.; pl.* -TIES (-tĭz). State or quality of being or having a body; corporeality.
corporal punishment. *Law.* Punishment applied to the body of the offender, including the death penalty, whipping, and imprisonment.
cor′po·ral's guard (kôr′pō·rălz). A small detachment such as a corporal commands; hence, a small group.
cor′po·rate (kôr′pō·rĭt), *adj.* [L. *corporatus,* past part. of *corporare* to shape into a body, fr. *corpus* body.] 1. Combined into one body; united. 2. Formed into a body by legal enactment; incorporated; as, a *corporate* town. 3. Belonging to a corporation or incorporated body; as, *corporate* property. 4. = CORPORATIVE, 2. — **cor′po·rate·ly,** *adv.*
cor′po·ra′tion (-rā′shŭn), *n.* 1. A body of associated persons; specif. [*cap.*], a body of municipal authorities; as, the *Corporation* of the City of London. 2. *Law.* An entity recognized by law as constituted by one or more persons and as having various rights and duties together with the capacity of succession; a juristic person constituted by one or more natural persons; as, a municipal *corporation;* a business *corporation.* 3. *Colloq.* The abdomen or belly, esp. when protuberant. 4. See CORPORATIVE, 2.
cor′po·ra′tive (kôr′pō·rā′tĭv; -rȧ·tĭv), *adj.* 1. Pert. to, or consisting of, a corporation. 2. Centering supreme authority in one corporate body made up of representatives of key corporations (employer-employee bodies) exercising regimentation severally in industry, business, banking, and labor; as, the *corporative* state of Italian fascism.
cor′po·ra′tor (kôr′pō·rā′tẽr), *n.* A member of a corporation.
cor·po′re·al (kôr·pō′rē·ăl; 70), *adj.* [L. *corporeus,* fr. *corpus* body.] 1. Of the nature of, consisting of, or pertaining to, matter; material; physical. 2. Corporal; bodily; as, man's *corporeal* frame. 3. Tangible or palpable; as, a *corporeal* hereditament. — **Syn.** See MATERIAL; BODILY. — **cor·po′re·al′i·ty** (-ăl′ĭ·tĭ), *n.* — **cor·po′re·al·ly,** *adv.* — **cor·po′re·al·ness,** *n.*
cor′po·re′i·ty (kôr′pō·rē′ĭ·tĭ), *n.* State or quality of having or being a body; physical nature.
cor′po·sant (kôr′pō·zănt), *n.* [It. or Pg. *corpo santo* holy body, or L. *corpus sancti* body of a saint.] = ST. ELMO'S FIRE.
corps (kōr; *as pl.,* kōrz; 70), *n. sing. & pl.* [F., fr. L. *corpus* body.] 1. (*originally,* kôrs) A corpse (in any sense); — *corps* being an earlier spelling. 2. A body of persons organized or under common direction; esp., an organized subdivision of the military establishment; as, the Marine *Corps;* specif., a large unit of an army, comprising two divisions and auxiliary troops. Cf. ARMY, 1 **b**; INSIGNIA, *Illust.* 3. In some European countries, a students' social society with a rigid code of honor.
corps area. *Mil.* In the United States, a territorial division of states based on the military population, for purposes of administration, training, and tactical control.
‖**corps de bal′let′** (kôr′ dẽ bȧ′lĕ′). [F.] A company of ballet dancers.
corpse (kôrps; *rarely* kôrs), *n.* Orig., **corps** (*at first pron'd* kôrs). [ME. *cors, corps,* body, fr. OF. *cors* (later spelled *corps*), fr. L. *corpus.*] 1. *Obs.* A human or animal body, whether living or dead. 2. A dead body, esp. of a human being; hence, anything defunct.
corps′man (kōr′măn), *n.; pl.* -MEN (-mĕn). *U. S. Navy.* An enlisted man trained to give first aid and apprentice medical treatment.
cor′pu·lence (kôr′pū·lĕns), **cor′pu·len·cy** (-lĕn·sĭ), *n.* [F.] Bodily bulk; esp., excessive fatness; fleshiness.
cor′pu·lent (-lĕnt), *adj.* [F., fr. L. *corpulentus,* fr. *corpus* body.] Bulky; very fat. — **Syn.** Fat, obese, portly, fleshy. — **-lent·ly,** *adv.*
cor′pus (kôr′pŭs), *n.; pl.* CORPORA (-pō·rȧ). [L.] 1. The body of a man or animal, esp. when dead; — now chiefly humorous. 2. *Anat.* A comparatively solid and homogeneous structure forming a part of an organ, esp. of the brain. 3. A general collection of writings; the whole literature of a subject. 4. The main body; esp., the principal of a fund or estate, as opposed to interest, etc.
‖**cor′pus cal·lo′sum** (kă·lō′sŭm); *pl.* CORPORA CALLOSA (-sȧ). [NL., callous body.] *Anat.* The great band of commissural fibers uniting the cerebral hemispheres in man and in the higher mammals. See BRAIN, *Illust.*
Cor′pus Chris′ti (krĭs′tĭ; -tī). [L., body of Christ.] *R.C.Ch.* A festival in honor of the Eucharist, observed on the Thursday after Trinity Sunday.
cor′pus·cle (kôr′pŭs·'l), *n.* [L. *corpusculum,* dim. of *corpus* body.]

1. A minute particle. **2.** *Anat.* A protoplasmic cell, esp. one of those that float free in blood, lymph, and pus. The corpuscles of the blood of vertebrates are colored (***red corpuscles or erythrocytes***) or colorless (***white corpuscles or leucocytes***). The red corpuscles contain hemoglobin, and carry the oxygen from the lungs to the various parts of the body. The white corpuscles are nucleated amoeboid cells found not only in the blood but also in lymph and in the bodily tissues and constitute the chief cellular elements in pus. Certain white corpuscles (***phagocytes***) show special activity in ingesting and destroying waste and harmful material, bacteria, etc., in the blood or tissues of the body. — **cor·pus′cu·lar** (kôr·pŭs′kū·lẽr), *adj.*

cor·pus′cule (kôr·pŭs′kūl), *n.* A corpuscle.

cor′pus de·lic′ti (kôr′pŭs dē·lĭk′tī). [L., the body of the crime.] *Law.* The basic facts necessary to the commission of a crime, as, in murder, the actual death of the person alleged to have been murdered; — often used erroneously to designate the body of the victim.

cor′pus ju′ris (jōō′rĭs). [L.] A body of law; a comprehensive collection of the law of a country or jurisdiction.

Cor′pus Ju′ris Ca·no′ni·ci (kȧ·nŏn′ĭ·sī). [L.] *R.C.Ch.* See CANON LAW.

Cor′pus Ju′ris Ci·vi′lis (sĭ·vī′lĭs). [L.] The body of the Civil or Roman law, promulgated under Justinian's authority, A.D. 528–534, and the basis of the actual law in most of continental Europe.

‖**cor′pus lu′te·um** (lū′tē·ŭm); *pl.* CORPORA LUTEA (-ȧ). [NL., luteous body.] **1.** *Anat.* The reddish-yellow mass of endocrine tissue that forms from a ruptured Graafian follicle in the mammalian ovary. **2.** *Pharm.* A preparation of the corpus luteum of the hog or cow, used in ovarian dysfunction.

‖**cor′pus stri·a′tum** (strī·ā′tŭm); *pl.* CORPORA STRIATA (-tȧ). [NL., striate body.] *Anat.* Either of a pair of large nuclei of the brain situated beneath and external to the anterior cornua of the lateral ventricles and forming part of their floor.

cor·rade′ (kŏ·rād′), *v. t. & i.* [L. *corradere, -rasum,* fr. *cor-* + *radere* to rub.] **1.** *Obs.* To scrape. **2.** *Geol.* To wear away, as by running water or glaciers. — **cor·ra′sion** (kŏ·rā′zhŭn), *n.*

cor·ral′ (kŏ·răl′; kō·răl′), *n.* [Sp., a yard, a yard for cattle, fr. *corro* ring, fr. L. *currere* to run.] A pen or enclosure for confining or capturing animals; also, an enclosure for defense and security. Cf. KRAAL, STOCKADE. — (kŏ·răl′), *v. t.;* -RALLED′ (-răld′); -RAL′LING. **1.** To confine in or as in a corral. **2.** To arrange (wagons) so as to form a corral. **3.** *Colloq., U.S.* To get and keep hold of; to capture.

cor·rect′ (kŏ·rĕkt′), *v. t.* [See CORRECT, *adj.*] **1.** To make or set right; rectify. **2. a** To indicate for amendment the errors or faults of; as, to *correct* proofs, tests. **b** To reprove for faults; chastise. **3.** To counteract by the agency of opposite qualities or tendencies; neutralize. **4.** To alter or adjust so as to bring to a required condition; as, to *correct* a lens for spherical aberration.

Syn. (1) **Correct, rectify, emend, remedy, redress, amend, reform, revise** mean to make right that which is wrong. **Correct** implies attention to errors, faults, or defects in form, behavior, method, etc.; **rectify,** to that which requires straightening out because not right, just, properly controlled, etc.; **emend** specifically implies correction of a text or manuscript; **remedy,** correction of that which makes a person or thing, such as the body politic, unsound or abnormal; **redress,** the rectification of inequities and, usually, their reparation; **amend, reform,** and **revise,** an improvement by corrective changes, *amend* often implying slight and *reform* drastic changes, while *revise* (applied generally to that which is written) connotes a detailed search for imperfections.
(2) See PUNISH.

— *adj.* [L. *correctus,* past part. of *corrigere* to make straight, correct, fr. *cor-* + *regere* to lead straight.] **1.** Conforming to an approved or conventional standard; proper; as, *correct* manners, costume, grammar. **2.** Conforming to fact or truth; of reasoning, in accordance with logical principles; of statements or opinions, according with known facts; of a copy, free from errors. — **cor·rect′ly,** *adv.* — **cor·rect′ness,** *n.*

Syn. Correct, accurate, exact, precise, nice, right mean conforming to fact, standard, or truth. **Correct** usually implies freedom from fault or error as judged by some standard; **accurate** implies, more positively, fidelity to fact or truth attained by the exercise of care; **exact** stresses strict accordance with fact, standard, or truth; **precise** stresses sharpness of definition or delimitation; **nice,** as here compared, stresses great precision and delicacy, as in adjustment, discrimination, etc.; **right** comes close to *correct* but throws more emphasis upon conformity to fact, truth, or a standard than on freedom from error or fault.

cor·rec′tion (kŏ·rĕk′shŭn), *n.* **1.** Act of correcting; amendment; rectification; also, reproof; punishment; chastisement. **2.** Neutralization of noxious qualities; as, *correction* of acidity in the stomach. **3.** That which is substituted in the place of what is wrong; an emendation. **4.** A quantity applied by way of correcting; as, the index *correction* of a sextant. — **cor·rec′tion·al** (-ăl; -′l), *adj.*

cor·rect′i·tude (kŏ·rĕk′tĭ·tūd), *n.* [From *correct* on the analogy of *rectitude.*] Correctness; esp., propriety.

cor·rec′tive (kŏ·rĕk′tĭv), *adj.* Having the power or property of correcting, or restoring to a normal condition. — *n.* A corrective agent. — **cor·rec′tive·ly,** *adv.*

cor·rec′tor (-tẽr), *n.* [L.] One that corrects.

cor′re·late (kŏr′ĕ·lāt), *n.* [See RELATE, CORRELATION.] Either of two related things, esp. things so connected that one directly implies the other. — (kŏr′ĕ·lāt; kŏr′ĕ·lāt′), *v. i.* To have reciprocal relations; to be correlative. — *v. t.* **1.** To connect systematically; as, to *correlate* English and history in the schools. **2.** To establish a mutual or reciprocal relation of or between; as, to *correlate* mental states with corresponding brain processes. — (kŏr′ĕ·lāt), *adj.* Correlated.

cor′re·la′tion (-lā′shŭn), *n.* [NL. *correlatio,* fr. L. *cor-* + *relatio.*] The act or process of correlating; mutual relation; esp., *Biol.,* reciprocal relation in the occurrence of different structures, processes, etc., in organisms.

cor·rel′a·tive (kŏ·rĕl′ȧ·tĭv), *adj.* **1.** Having, indicating, or involving, a reciprocal relation; mutually related. **2.** *Gram.* Having a mutual relation; corresponding and regularly used together; as, "either" and "or" are *correlative* conjunctions. — *n.* A correlate; as: **a** *Biol.* A correlated characteristic structure, etc. **b** *Gram.* Either of two correlative words or expressions. **c** *Physics.* A correlative force. — **cor·rel′a·tive·ly,** *adv.* — **cor·rel′a·tiv′i·ty** (-tĭv′ĭ·tĭ), *n.*

cor′re·spond′ (kŏr′ē·spŏnd′), *v. i.* [F. or ML.; F. *correspondre,* fr. ML. *correspondere.*] **1.** To answer (to something else) in fitness, character, function, amount, etc.; to suit, agree, fit, or match. **2.** To have communication, esp. by letters. — **Syn.** See AGREE.

cor′re·spond′ence (-spŏn′dĕns), *n.* **1.** Also **cor′re·spond′en·cy** (-dĕn·sĭ). Act or state of corresponding; relation or agreement of things to each other or of one thing to another. **2.** Intercourse between persons by letters. **3.** The letters which pass between correspondents.

correspondence school. A school that teaches by correspondence, the instruction being based on instruction sheets and papers written by the student in answer to their questions or requirements.

cor′re·spond′ent (kŏr′ē·spŏn′dĕnt), *adj.* Answering (to something) in fitness or adaptation; conformable; corresponding. — *n.* **1.** Something that corresponds; a correlative. **2.** One with whom intercourse is carried on by letter. **3.** A person employed to contribute news regularly from a particular place. **4.** *Com.* One who has regular commercial relations with another, esp. with a firm at a distance. — **cor′re·spond′ent·ly,** *adv.*

cor′re·spond′ing, *adj.* **1.** Answering; correspondent; as, *corresponding* parts. **2.** Carrying on intercourse by letters. — **cor′re·spond′ing·ly,** *adv.*

cor′re·spon′sive (-spŏn′sĭv), *adj.* Mutually responsive.

‖**cor·ri′da** (kôr·rē′thä), *n.* [Sp.] A bullfight.

cor′ri·dor (kŏr′ĭ·dôr; -dẽr), *n.* [F., fr. Pr. *corredor,* fr. *correr* to run, fr. L. *currere.*] **1.** A passageway, usually covered; esp., one, as in a hotel, into which rooms, etc., open. **2.** [*often cap.*] *Polit. Geog.* A narrow strip of land across territory previously foreign, joining a country to its seaport; as, the Polish *Corridor* (which see, in *Gaz.*).

cor′rie (kŏr′ĭ), *n.* [Gael. *coire* caldron.] A circular hollow in the side of a hill or mountain; a cirque.

Cor′rie·dale (kŏr′ĭ·dāl), *n.* A rather large sheep of a dual-purpose breed developed in New Zealand.

cor′ri·gen′dum (kŏr′ĭ·jĕn′dŭm), *n.; pl.* -GENDA (-dȧ). [L.] A fault or error to be corrected, as in a manuscript or a printed work; *pl.,* a list of such errors with corrections.

cor′ri·gi·ble (kŏr′ĭ·jĭ·b'l), *adj.* [Through F. & L., fr. L. *corrigere* to correct.] **1.** Capable of being set right, amended, or reformed. **2.** Submissive to correction. — **cor′ri·gi·bil′i·ty** (-bĭl′ĭ·tĭ), *n.* — **cor′ri·gi·bly** (-blĭ), *adv.*

cor·ri′val (kŏ·rī′văl), *n.* [F., fr. L. *corrivalis.*] A rival; competitor. — *adj.* Having rivaling claims; rival.

cor·rob′o·rant (kŏ·rŏb′ō·rȧnt), *adj.* Corroborating; strengthening; of medicines, invigorating. — *n.* A tonic.

cor·rob′o·rate (-rāt), *adj. Archaic.* Corroborated. — (-rāt), *v. t.* [L. *corroboratus,* past part. of *corroborare* to corroborate, fr. *cor-* + *roborare* to strengthen, fr. *robur* strength.] To make more certain; to confirm; establish. — **Syn.** See CONFIRM. — **cor·rob′o·ra′tor** (-rā′tẽr), *n.*

cor·rob′o·ra′tion (-rā′shŭn), *n.* Act of corroborating; a strengthening or confirming; also, that which corroborates.

cor·rob′o·ra′tive (kŏ·rŏb′ō·rā′tĭv; -rȧ·tĭv), *adj.* Tending to corroborate; specif., confirmatory. — *n.* A corroborant. — **cor·rob′o·ra′tive·ly,** *adv.*

cor·rob′o·ra·to′ry (kŏ·rŏb′ō·rȧ·tō′rĭ *or, esp. Brit.,* -tẽr·ĭ), *adj.* Corroborative.

cor·rob′o·ree (kŏ·rŏb′ō·rē), *n.* Also **cor·rob′bo·ree, cor·rob′o·ri,** etc. [Native name.] *Australia.* **a** A nocturnal festivity, including symbolic dances, with which the Australian aborigines celebrate important tribal events. **b** A festivity; also, tumult; uproar.

cor·rode′ (kŏ·rōd′), *v. t.* [F. *corroder,* fr. L. *corrodere, -rosum,* fr. *cor-* + *rodere* to gnaw.] **1.** To eat away by degrees, as if by gnawing; to wear away gradually, as by the action of strong acid, caustic alkali, or other chemical; also, formerly, to erode. **2.** To consume; to impair; as, *corroding* cares. — *v. i.* To undergo corrosion. — **cor·rod′i·ble** (-rōd′ĭ·b'l), *adj.*

cor′ro·dy (kŏr′ō·dĭ). Var. of CORODY.

cor·ro′sion (kŏ·rō′zhŭn), *n.* **1.** Action or effect of corroding, or of corrosive agents. **2.** A product of such action or agents.

cor·ro′sive (-sĭv), *adj.* **1.** Eating away; corroding, as an acid. **2.** Having the quality of fretting or vexing. — *n.* A substance which corrodes. — **cor·ro′sive·ly,** *adv.* — **cor·ro′sive·ness,** *n.*

corrosive sublimate. *Chem.* = MERCURY CHLORIDE.

cor′ru·gate (kŏr′ū·gāt; kŏr′ōō-), *adj.* [L. *corrugatus,* past part. of *corrugare,* fr. *cor-* + *rugare* to wrinkle.] Wrinkled; furrowed; corrugated. — (-gāt), *v. t. & i.* To form or shape into wrinkles or folds, or alternate ridges and grooves. — **cor′ru·gat′ed** (-gāt′ĕd; -ĭd), *adj.*

cor′ru·gat′ed i′ron. Sheet iron or sheet steel, usually galvanized, shaped into straight, parallel, regular, and equally curved ridges and hollows.

cor′ru·ga′tion (kŏr′ū·gā′shŭn; kŏr′ōō-), *n.* Act of corrugating; also, a wrinkle or groove of a corrugated surface.

cor·rupt′ (kŏ·rŭpt′), *adj.* [OF., fr. L. *corruptus,* past part. of *corrumpere* to corrupt, fr. *cor-* + *rumpere* to break.] **1.** *Now Rare.* Changed from a sound to a putrid state; tainted. **2.** Changed from a state of uprightness, correctness, truth, etc., to a bad state; depraved. — **Syn.** See VICIOUS. — *v. t.* To make corrupt; as: **a** To make putrid; to taint. **b** To change from good to bad; to debase. **c** To draw aside from rectitude and duty; to pervert. **d** To falsify, as a text. — **Syn.** See DEBASE. — *v. i.* To become corrupt; as: **a** To become putrid or tainted. **b** To become debased; to lose virtue. — **cor·rupt′ly,** *adv.* — **cor·rupt′ness,** *n.*

cor·rupt′er, cor·rup′tor (kŏ·rŭp′tẽr), *n.* One that corrupts.

cor·rupt′i·ble (-rŭp′tĭ·b'l), *adj.* Capable of being corrupted; liable to corruption. — *n.* Something corruptible; specif., the human body. (1 *Cor.* xv. 53.) — **cor·rupt′i·bil′i·ty** (-bĭl′ĭ·tĭ), **cor·rupt′i·ble·ness,** *n.* — **cor·rupt′i·bly** (-blĭ), *adv.*

cor·rup′tion (kŏ·rŭp′shŭn), *n.* **1.** A corrupting, or state of being corrupt; as: **a** Decay. **b** Depravity; impurity. **c** Bribery. **2.** An instance of making or becoming corrupt; perversion. **3.** An agency or influence that corrupts.

cor·rup′tion·ist (-ĭst), *n.* One who practices or defends corruption, esp. in politics.

corruption of blood. *Law.* The taint or impurity of blood of a person which at common law was held to result from attainder of treason or felony, so that the attainted person's estate escheated at once and he was disabled from retaining any estate, rank, or title, and from inheriting and transmitting any estate.

cor·rup′tive (kŏ·rŭp′tĭv), *adj.* Producing corruption.

cor·sage′ (kôr·säzh′; kôr′sĭj), *n.* [F. See CORSET.] **1.** The waist or bodice of a woman's dress. **2.** A bouquet made up to be worn, orig. at the waist.

cor'sair (kôr'sâr), *n.* [F. *corsaire*, fr. It., fr. ML. *cursarius*, fr. L. *cursus* a running, course.] **1.** A privateer, esp. of the Turks or Saracens; hence, a pirate. **2.** The vessel of a privateer or a pirate.

corse (kôrs), *n.* [OF. *cors* (F. *corps*). See CORPSE.] *Chiefly Poetic.* A corpse; a dead body.

corse'let, cors'let (kôrs'lĕt; -lĭt), *n.* [F., dim. of OF. *cors* body. See CORSE.] **1.** Armor for the body. **2.** Usually **cor'se·let'** (*pron.* kôr'sĕ·lĕt'). A woman's one-piece supporting undergarment made up of a bra with shoulder straps combined with a girdle or corset, usually opening at the side with a slide fastener or hooks, with garters attached.

cor'set (kôr'sĕt; -sĭt), *n.* [OF., dim. of *cors* (F. *corps*) body.] **1.** In the Middle Ages, a close-fitting outer garment. **2.** Often *pl.* A woman's close-fitting, boned, supporting undergarment, typically hooked and laced and extending from above or beneath the bust or from the waist to below the hips, usually having garters attached. See 2d STAY, *n.*, 2. — *v. t.* To dress in or fit with a corset.

corset cover. A woman's underwaist covering the top of a corset.

cor·tege' (kôr·tēzh'; -tāzh'), *n.* Also ‖**cor'tège'** (kôr'tĕzh'). [F. *cortège*, fr. It. *corteggio*, fr. *corte* court.] **a** A train of attendants; a retinue. **b** A procession.

Cor'tes (kôr'tĕz; -tĭz; *Sp.* kôr'tās), *n.* [Sp. & Pg., pl. of *corte* court.] The national legislature of Spain or of Portugal.

cor'tex (kôr'tĕks), *n.; pl.* CORTICES (-tĭ·sēz). [L., bark.] **1.** *Bot.* **a** In higher plants, a tissue of the stem or root external to the vascular tissues and internal to the corky or outermost tissues. **b** Loosely, all of the tissues external to the wood; the bark. **c** In lower plants, an outer or investing layer or tissue, as in certain lichens, seaweeds, and fungi. **2.** *Anat.* The outer or superficial part of an organ, as the kidney; esp., the outer layer of gray matter of the cerebrum and cerebellum.

cor'ti·cal (-tĭ·kăl), *adj.* **a** Of, pertaining to, or consisting of cortex, esp. the cortex of the brain or kidneys. **b** Resulting from the action or condition of the cerebral cortex, or involving it; as, *cortical* blindness. — **cor'ti·cal·ly,** *adv.*

cor'ti·cate (kôr'tĭ·kāt), **cor'ti·cat'ed** (-kāt'ĕd; -ĭd), *adj.* [L. *corticatus.*] Covered with bark or with a cortex.

cor'ti·cose (kôr'tĭ·kōs), **cor'ti·cous** (-kŭs), *adj. Bot.* Corticate.

cor'tin (kôr'tĭn), *n.* [*cortex* + *-in.*] *Biochem.* The hormone produced by the cortex of the suprarenal gland.

cor'ti·sone (kôr'tĭ·sōn), *n.* [dehydro*corticos*ter*one*, a chemical.] *Biochem.* A compound isolated from the cortex of the adrenal gland, also produced synthetically, effective in treating rheumatoid arthritis.

co·run'dum (kō·rŭn'dŭm), *n.* [Tamil *kurundam*, fr. Skr. *kuruvinda* ruby.] *Mineral.* Native alumina, or aluminum oxide, Al_2O_3, the hardest mineral except the diamond. H., 9. Sp. gr., 3.95–4.10. Corundum is an excellent abrasive, esp. for materials of high tensile strength, as steel. Pure, transparent or translucent corundum is prized as a gem, called according to its color *sapphire* (blue), *ruby* (red) and by other names (see SAPPHIRE, 1 **b**).

co·rus'cant (kō·rŭs'kănt), *adj.* Coruscating.

cor'us·cate (kŏr'ŭs·kāt; kō·rŭs'kāt), *v. i.* [L. *coruscare* to flash.] To glitter or gleam in flashes. — **Syn.** See FLASH.

cor'us·ca'tion (kŏr'ŭs·kā'shŭn), *n.* A coruscating; a sudden flash or play of light or (fig.) of intellectual brilliancy.

‖**cor'vée'** (kôr'vā'), *n.* [F., fr. ML. *corrogata*, fr. L. *corrogare* to entreat together, fr. *cor-* + *rogare* to ask.] **1.** *Feudal Law.* Unpaid labor due from a vassal to his lord. **2.** *Econ.* Unpaid or but partly paid labor exacted by public authorities, esp. for highways, etc.

corves (kôrvz), *n., pl.* of CORF.

cor·vette' (kôr·vĕt'), **cor'vet** (kôr'vĕt), *n.* [F. *corvette*, prob. fr. MD. *corf* a kind of ship.] **1.** *Naut.* A war vessel ranking in the old sailing navies next below a frigate, and having usually only one tier of guns. **2.** *Brit. & Canadian navies.* A highly maneuverable escort vessel, smaller than a destroyer, armed with antisubmarine and antiaircraft guns, and only lightly armored.

cor'vine (kôr'vīn; -vĭn), *adj.* [L. *corvinus*, fr. *corvus* raven.] Of or pertaining to the crow; crowlike.

Cor'vus (-vŭs), *n.; gen.* CORVI (-vī). [L., raven.] A small constellation adjoining Virgo on the south.

Cor'y·bant (kŏr'ĭ·bănt), *n.; pl.* -BANTES (-băn'tēz), -BANTS (-bănts). [F. *Corybante*, fr. L. *Corybas*, fr. Gr. *Korybas.*] *Gr. Relig.* One of the mythical attendants of Cybele, supposed to accompany her with wild dances and music while she wandered by torchlight over the mountains. — **Cor'y·ban'tine** (-băn'tĭn; -tīn), **Cor'y·ban'tian** (-shăn), *adj.*

Cor'y·ban'tic (-băn'tĭk), *adj.* Of the Corybantes; also, [*l.c.*] frenzied.

co·ryd'a·lis (kō·rĭd'ȧ·lĭs), *n.* [NL., fr. Gr. *korydallis* a crested lark, fr. *korys* helmet.] *Bot.* An herb of a large genus (*Corydalis*) of the fumitory family, with racemose irregular flowers.

Cor'y·don (kŏr'ĭ·dŏn), *n.* [L., fr. Gr. *Korydōn.*] *Poetic.* A shepherd in Theocritus's *Idyls* and Vergil's *Eclogues;* — used in modern pastorals as a name for a young rustic swain.

cor'ymb (kŏr'ĭmb; -ĭm), *n.* [L. *corymbus* cluster of flowers, fr. Gr. *korymbos.*] *Bot.* A simple racemose inflorescence, in which the outer pedicels are longer than those nearer the axis, as in the cherry, many mustards, etc. See INFLORESCENCE, *Illust.* (2); CYME **b.** — **co·rym'bose** (kō·rĭm'bōs), **co·rym'bous** (-bŭs), *adj.* — **co·rym'bose·ly,** *adv.*

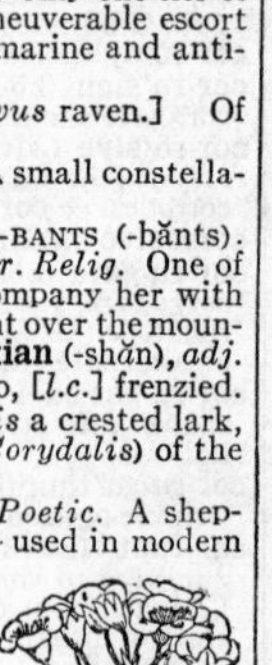

Corymb of Cherry. 1 Peduncle; 2, 2 Pedicels; 3, 3 Bracts.

cor'y·phae'us (kŏr'ĭ·fē'ŭs), *n.; pl.* -PHAEI (-ī). [L., fr. Gr. *koryphaios* leader of the chorus, fr. *koryphē* head, top.] The leader of the chorus, esp. in the Greek drama.

co'ry·phee' (kō'rē·fā'; 70), *n.* [F. *coryphée.*] A leading ballet dancer, formerly a man; hence, a female ballet dancer, esp. a leader.

co·ry'za (kō·rī'zȧ), *n.* [NL., fr. Gr. *koryza* catarrh.] *Med.* Nasal catarrh; cold in the head. Cf. COLD, *n.*, 3.

cose (kōz). Var. of COZE.

co·se'cant (kō·sē'kănt), *n.* [For *co. secans*, abbr. of NL. *complementi secans.*] *Trig.* The secant of the complement of an arc or angle. Abbr. *cosec* or *csc* (no period).

co'sey (kō'zĭ). Var. of COZY, *adj. & n.*

cosh'er (kŏsh'ẽr), *v. t.* To pet; pamper; cosset.

co'sie (kō'zĭ), *adj.* Var. of COSY.

co·sig'na·to'ry (kō·sĭg'nȧ·tō'rĭ *or, esp. Brit.*, -tẽr·ĭ), *adj.* Signing jointly or in common. — *n.; pl.* -RIES (-rĭz). One of the joint signers of a document, as a treaty.

co'sine (kō'sīn), *n.* [For *co. sinus*, abbr. of NL. *complementi sinus.*] *Trig.* The sine of the complement of an arc or angle. Abbr. *cos*

Cos lettuce (kŏs). = ROMAINE.

cos·met'ic (kŏz·mĕt'ĭk), *adj.* [Gr. *kosmētikos* skilled in decorating, fr. *kosmos* order, ornament.] **1.** Pertaining to or making for beauty, esp. of the complexion; beautifying or intended for beautifying; as, *cosmetic* salves, treatments. **2.** Protecting or cleansing the skin, hair, or nails. — *n.* Any preparation (except soap) to be applied to the surface of the human body for lending attractiveness, for theatrical make-up, or for cleansing or conditioning the skin, hair, nails, etc.

cos'me·tol'o·gy (kŏz'mē·tŏl'ō·jĭ), *n.* The art or practice of giving cosmetic treatments. — **cos'me·tol'o·gist** (-jĭst), *n.*

cos'mic (kŏz'mĭk), *adj.* [Gr. *kosmikos* of the world, fr. *kosmos.*] **1.** Pert. to the cosmos; expansively vast and grandiose. **2.** Harmonious; orderly. — **cos'mi·cal** (-mĭ·kăl), *adj.* — **cos'mi·cal·ly,** *adv.*

cosmic dust. *Astron.* Fine particles, probably of meteoric matter, constantly falling upon the earth from space.

cosmic ray. Any of the rays of extremely high penetrating power produced, it is thought, beyond the earth's atmosphere by transmutations of atoms continually taking place through interstellar space. They bombard the earth and are responsible for some of the ionization of the earth's atmosphere.

cos'mo- (kŏz'mō-), **cosm-.** [Gr. *kosmos.*] A combining form meaning *world*, as in *cosmo*logy.

cos·mog'o·ny (kŏz·mŏg'ō·nĭ), *n.; pl.* -NIES (-nĭz). [Gr. *kosmogonia*, fr. *kosmos* the world + root of *gignesthai* to be born.] The creation and origination of the world or universe, or a theory regarding such creation. Cf. YUGA. — **cos·mog'o·nal** (-năl; -n'l), **cos'mo·gon'ic** (kŏz'mō·gŏn'ĭk), **cos'mo·gon'i·cal** (-ĭ·kăl), *adj.* — **cos·mog'o·nist** (kŏz·mŏg'ō·nĭst), *n.*

cos·mog'ra·phy (kŏz·mŏg'rȧ·fĭ), *n.; pl.* -PHIES (-fĭz). [Gr. *kosmographia*, fr. *kosmos* the world + *graphein* to write.] A general description of the world or of the universe; also, the science that treats of the constitution of the whole order of nature. — **cos·mog'ra·pher** (-fẽr), *n.* — **cos'mo·graph'ic** (kŏz'mō·grăf'ĭk), **-i·cal** (-ĭ·kăl), *adj.*

cos·mol'o·gy (kŏz·mŏl'ō·jĭ), *n.* [*cosmo-* + *-logy.*] That branch of metaphysics which treats of the character of the universe as an orderly system, or cosmos. — **cos'mo·log'ic** (kŏz'mō·lŏj'ĭk), **cos'mo·log'i·cal** (-ĭ·kăl), *adj.* — **cos·mol'o·gist** (kŏz·mŏl'ō·jĭst), *n.*

cos·mop'o·lis (kŏz·mŏp'ō·lĭs), *n.* A cosmopolitan city.

cos'mo·pol'i·tan (kŏz'mō·pŏl'ĭ·tăn), *adj.* [See COSMOPOLITE.] **1.** Belonging to all the world; not local. **2.** At home in any country; without local national attachments or prejudices. **3.** Characteristic of a cosmopolite; as, *cosmopolitan* traits. **4.** Composed of elements gathered from all or various parts of the world; as, a *cosmopolitan* population. **5.** *Nat. Hist.* Found in most parts of the world, as the bats. — *n.* A cosmopolite. — **cos'mo·pol'i·tan·ism** (-ĭz'm), *n.*

cos·mop'o·lite (kŏz·mŏp'ō·līt), *n.* [Gr. *kosmopolitēs*, fr. *kosmos* world + *politēs* citizen, fr. *polis* city.] **1.** A cosmopolitan person. **2.** A plant or animal found in most parts of the world. — **cos·mop'o·lit·ism** (-lĭt·ĭz'm), *n.*

cos'mos (kŏz'mŏs *or, esp. in sense* 4, -mŭs), *n.* [NL., fr. Gr. *kosmos* order, harmony, the world.] **1.** The universe conceived as an orderly and harmonious system. **2.** Hence, order; harmony. **3.** Any self-inclusive system characterized by order and harmony. **4.** *Bot.* A tall garden herb of a genus (*Cosmos*) of the aster family, having fall-blooming flowers with yellow or red disks and rays of various colors.

cos'mo·tron (kŏz'mō·trŏn), *n.* [*cosmo-* (fr. *cosmic ray*) + *-tron* as in elec*tron.*] A proton accelerator similar to the bevatron.

coss. Variant of KOS.

Cos'sack (kŏs'ăk; -ăk), *n.* [Russ. *kozak, kazak.*] One of a warlike, pastoral people of the Russian steppes, skillful as horsemen, and used as cavalry troops.

cos'set (kŏs'ĕt; -ĭt), *n.* A pet lamb; a pet. — *v. t.* To treat as a pet; to fondle; pamper; cosher.

cost (kŏst; 74), *n.* [OF. (F. *coût*). See COST, *v.*] **1.** The amount or equivalent paid, given, or charged, or engaged to be paid or given, for anything; charge; price; hence, whatever, as labor, self-denial, etc., is requisite to secure benefit. **2.** Loss of any kind; detriment. **3.** The outlay of money, time, labor, etc. **4.** *pl. Law.* In a general sense, expenses incurred in litigation; as: **a** Those payable to the attorney or counsel by his client, esp. when fixed by law; — commonly called *fees.* **b** Those given by the law or the court to the prevailing party against the losing party. — **Syn.** Price, expense, charge. — *v. i. & t.;* COST; COST'ING. [OF. *coster, couster*, fr. L. *constare* to stand at, cost, fr. *con-* + *stare* to stand.] **1.** To require to be given, expended, or laid out therefor, as in barter, purchase, etc.; to be of the price of. **2.** To require or cause to be borne or suffered. **3.** To estimate or figure on the cost of; as, to *cost* leather.

cos'ta (kŏs'tȧ), *n.; pl.* -TAE (-tē). [L.] **a** *Anat.* A rib. **b** A part likened to a rib, as the vein (esp. midrib) of a leaf, or the anterior vein of an insect's wing. — **cos'tal** (-tăl; -t'l), *adj.* — **cos'tate** (-tāt), *adj.*

cost accounting. *Accounting.* Any system of accounts which reveals the cost elements incident to production; also, the keeping of such accounts. — **cost accountant.**

cos'tard (kŏs'tẽrd), *n.* **1.** A large English variety of apple. **2.** The head; — used contemptuously or humorously.

cos'ter (kŏs'tẽr), *n. & v.* Short for COSTERMONGER.

cos'ter·mon'ger (-mŭng'gẽr), *n.* [*costard* + *monger.*] *Chiefly Brit.* A hawker of fruit or vegetables from a street stand, barrow, or cart. — **cos'ter·mon'ger,** *v. i.*

cos'tive (kŏs'tĭv), *adj.* [OF. *costivé*, past part., fr. L. *constipare.* See CONSTIPATE.] **1.** Constipated; also, causing constipation. **2.** *Obs.* Reserved; slow or stiff in expression or action. **3.** Niggardly. — **cos'tive·ly,** *adv.* — **cos'tive·ness,** *n.*

cost'ly (kŏst'lĭ; 74), *adj.;* -LI·ER (-lĭ·ẽr); -LI·EST. **1.** Of great cost; expensive. **2.** Gorgeous; sumptuous. **3.** *Archaic.* Extravagant. — **cost'li·ness** (-lĭ·nĕs; -nĭs), *n.*

Syn. Costly, expensive, dear, valuable, precious, invaluable, priceless mean having a high value or valuation, especially in terms of money. **Costly** applies to that which costs much and usually implies sumptuousness, rarity, or the like; **expensive** applies to that which is high priced, often also implying a price beyond the thing's value or the buyer's means; **dear** commonly suggests a high, often exorbitant, price but it usually implies a relation to other factors than the intrinsic worth of a thing; **valuable** as often suggests worth measured in usefulness, etc., as in the price it would bring in a sale; **precious,** still applied to things which because of rarity, etc., have great monetary value, is also applied to things whose worth cannot be calculated; **invaluable** and **priceless** literally imply inestimable worth, but are now, especially *priceless*, often used hyperbolically.

cost′mar′y (kŏst′mâr′ĭ), *n.* [L. *costum* an Oriental plant + *Maria* Mary.] A tansy-scented herb (*Chrysanthemum majus*) of the aster family, used as a potherb.

cos′to- (kŏs′tō-), **cost-**. [L. *costa* rib.] *Anat., Surg., Zool.* A combining form denoting: **a** *A rib* or *costa;* — in nouns, as in **cos·tec′to·my, cos·tot′o·my** (see -ECTOMY, -TOMY). **b** *Costal* (*and*); — in adjectives, as in **cos′to·scap′u·lar**, costal and scapular.

cos′trel (kŏs′trĕl), *n.* [OF. *costerel*, dim. fr. *costier*, fr. L. *costa* rib, side.] *Now Dial.* A bottle of leather, earthenware, or wood, having ears by which it may be hung up.

cos′tume (kŏs′tūm *or, esp. Brit., and formerly,* kŏs·tūm′), *n.* [F., fr. It., custom, dress, fr. L. *consuetudo* custom.] **1.** Dress in general, including ornaments and the style of wearing the hair; esp., the distinctive style of dress of a people, class, locality, or period. **2.** A suit or dress characteristic of a particular class of person, period, or locality, worn at fancy balls, etc. **3.** A suit or dress; clothes, esp. of a woman. — *adj.* **1.** Characterized by the use of costume (def. 2); as, a *costume* play, party. **2.** Suitable to a particular costume; as, *costume* jewelry. — (kŏs·tūm′), *v. t.* To provide with, or put on, a costume.

cos·tum′er (kŏs·tūm′ẽr; kŏs′tūm·ẽr), *n.* Also **cos·tum′i·er** (kŏs·tūm′ĭ·ẽr; *F.* kôs′tü′myā′), *n.* One who makes or deals in costumes, as for theaters, fancy balls, etc.

co′sy (kō′zĭ), *adj.;* CO′SI·ER (-zĭ·ẽr); CO′SI·EST. Also **co′sey, co′sie.** Cozy. — **co′si·ly,** *adv.* — **co′si·ness,** *n.*

co′sy. Var. of COZY, *n.*

cot (kŏt), *n.* [AS. *cot, cote,* cottage.] **1.** A small house. **2.** A cote. **3.** A cover or sheath; as, a *cot* for a sore finger.

cot, *n.* [Hind. *khāṭ*, fr. Skr. *khaṭvā.*] A small bed, often of canvas stretched on a frame.

co·tan′gent (kō·tăn′jĕnt), *n.* [For *co. tangens,* abbr. of NL. *complementi tangens.*] *Trig.* The tangent of the complement of an arc or angle. Abbr. *cot* (no period). — **co′tan·gen′tial** (kō′tăn·jĕn′shăl), *adj.*

cote (kōt), *n.* [See COT a small house.] **1.** *Now Dial.* A cottage or hut. **2.** (*pron.* kōt, *or, esp. in compounds, as* dovecote, -kŏt) A shed or coop for small domestic animals, as sheep or doves.

cote, *v. t.* *Obs.* To pass by; to outstrip.

co·tem′po·ra′ne·ous (kō·tĕm′pō·rā′nē·ŭs), **co·tem′po·rar′y,** etc. Vars. of CONTEMPORANEOUS, etc.

co·ten′ant (kō·tĕn′ănt), *n.* A tenant in common; joint tenant. — **co·ten′an·cy** (-ăn·sĭ), *n.* — **co·ten′ure** (-ūr), *n.*

co′te·rie (kō′tē·rĭ; -rē; *F.* kô′trē′), *n.* [F.] A group of persons who meet familiarly, as for social purposes. Cf. CLIQUE.

co·ter′mi·nous (kō·tûr′mĭ·nŭs), *adj.* Conterminous.

co·thur′nus (kō·thûr′nŭs), *n.; pl.* -NI (-nī). [L., fr. Gr. *kothornos.*] **a** Also **co′thurn** (kō′thûrn; kō·thûrn′). A high, thick-soled, laced boot, worn by actors in Greek and Roman tragic drama; a buskin. **b** Hence, the dignified, somewhat stilted spirit of ancient tragedy.

co·tid′al (kō·tīd′ăl; -'l), *adj.* Marking equality of tides or coincidence in the time of high tides; as, *cotidal* lines.

co·til′lion (kō·tĭl′yŭn), *n.* Also **co·til′lon** (kō·tĭl′yŭn; *F.* kô′tē′yôɴ′). [F. *cotillon,* orig. petticoat, fr. OF. *cote* coat.] **1.** Orig., a ballroom dance for couples, resembling the quadrille; now, *Chiefly U. S.,* at formal balls, an elaborate dance, executed under the leadership of one couple, marked by the giving of favors and frequent changing of partners; a german. **2.** Music for this dance.

co·to′ne·as′ter (kō·tō′nē·ăs′tẽr), *n.* [NL., fr. L. *cotonea* quince + (prob.) 2d *-aster.*] Any of a genus (*Cotoneaster*) of Old World flowering shrubs of the apple family (Malaceae).

cot′quean (kŏt′kwēn), *n.* [*cot* cottage + *quean.*] *Archaic.* **a** A coarse, masculine woman. **b** A man who busies himself with affairs properly feminine.

Cots′wold (kŏts′wōld; -wŭld), *n.* A sheep of a large, long-wooled English breed; — from the Cotswold hills, England.

cot′ta (kŏt′ȧ), *n.* [ML. See COAT.] *Eccl.* A surplice; specif., a short vestment worn by choristers.

cot′tage (kŏt′ĭj), *n.* [ME. *cotage,* fr. AF. *cotage,* fr. OF. *cote* hut.] A small house; any modest country or suburban dwelling.

cottage cheese. The drained curd of soured milk, seasoned and sometimes pressed.

cottage pudding. A simple pudding consisting of a piece of plain cake covered with a sweet sauce.

cot′tag·er (kŏt′ĭj·ẽr), *n.* One who lives in a cottage.

cot′ter, cot′tar (kŏt′ẽr), *n.* [ML. *cotarius, coterius.*] **1.** A cottager; a cottier. **2. a** In Scotland, a peasant occupying a small holding. **b** An Irish cottier.

cot′ter (kŏt′ẽr), *n.* **a** A piece of wood or metal, commonly tapering or wedge-shaped, used to fasten together parts of a structure; a key (def. 3). **b** A cotter pin.

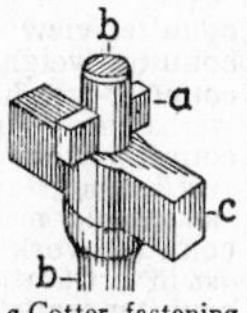

a Cotter, fastening together parts *b* and *c.*

cotter pin. *Mach.* A split metal pin, the ends of which are bent after insertion through a slot or hole. See BOLT, *Illust.*

cot′ti·er (kŏt′ĭ·ẽr), *n.* [OF. *cotier,* fr. *cote* cot.] **1.** In Great Britain and Ireland, a peasant cottager. **2.** *Archaic. Ir.* A tenant on a small farm under the rack-rent system.

cot′ton (kŏt′'n), *n.* [OF. *coton,* fr. Sp. *cotón,* fr. Ar. *quṭn, quṭun,* cotton.] **1.** A soft, white, fibrous substance composed of the hairs clothing the seeds of an erect, freely branching tropical plant (**cotton plant**) of the genus *Gossypium,* of the mallow family. Most of the cotton grown in the U. S. is of one of two types: ***upland cotton,*** with a short staple, and ***Egyptian cotton,*** with a long silky staple. The ***sea-island cotton,*** with unusually long silky fiber, formerly grown along the southeast coast of U. S., is now chiefly grown in the West Indies. **2.** The cotton plant; also, the crop. **3.** Fabric made of cotton. **4.** Thread spun from cotton. **5.** Any downy cottonlike substance produced by various plants, as the silk-cotton tree and the cottonwood. — *v. i.* **1.** *Obs.* To succeed; to develop well. **2.** To agree; also, *Colloq.,* to make friends; fraternize. **3.** *Colloq.* To take to; to become attached by personal liking.

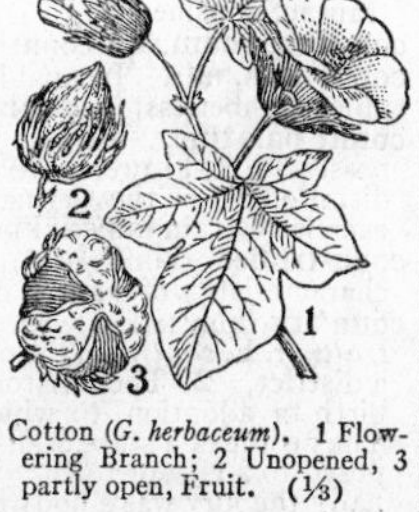

Cotton (*G. herbaceum*). 1 Flowering Branch; 2 Unopened, 3 partly open, Fruit. (⅓)

cotton belt. An area of the southern United States especially devoted to the raising of cotton.

cotton flannel. Canton flannel. See FLANNEL, 2.

cotton gin. A machine to separate the seeds from cotton.

cotton grass. Any sedge of the genus *Eriophorum.*

cotton gum. See GUM, 5 **a.**

cot′ton·mouth′ (kŏt′'n·mouth′), *n.* See MOCCASIN, 2.

cotton seed, *or, usually collectively,* **cot′ton·seed′** (-sēd′), *n.* The seed of the cotton plant, yielding a fixed semidrying oil (**cottonseed oil**) used in cooking, soapmaking, etc., and a meal (**cottonseed meal**) used as a feed and fertilizer.

cotton stainer. A red bug (*Dysdercus suturellus*) which stains the fibers of growing cotton.

Cotton State. Alabama; — a nickname.

cot′ton·tail′ (kŏt′'n·tāl′), *n.* Any of several small sandy-brown American rabbits (genus *Sylvilagus*) with white-tufted tail, esp. the ***wood rabbit*** (*S. transitionalis*) of the eastern United States.

cot′ton·weed′ (-wēd′), *n.* Cudweed.

cot′ton·wood′ (-wo͝od′), *n.* Any of several poplars (esp. *Populus deltoides*), with a cottony coma investing the seeds; also, the wood of these trees.

cotton wool. Raw cotton.

cot′ton·y (kŏt′'n·ĭ), *adj.* **1.** Covered with hairs, like cotton; downy. **2.** Of or pertaining to cotton; soft.

cot′y·le′don (kŏt′ĭ·lē′dŭn), *n.* [L., navelwort, fr. Gr. *kotylēdōn* a cup-shaped hollow, fr. *kotylē* anything hollow.] *Bot.* The first leaf, or one of the first pair or whorl of leaves, developed in seed plants. Cf. DICOTYLEDON; MONOCOTYLEDON; see PLUMULE, EMBRYO, *Illusts.* — **cot′y·le′don·al** (-lē′dŭn·ăl; -lĕd′ŭn·ăl; -'l), *adj.* — **cot′y·le′don·ar′y** (-ẽr′ĭ *or, esp. Brit.,* -ẽr·ĭ), *adj.* — **cot′y·le′don·ous** (-ŭs), *adj.*

couch (kouch), *v. t.* [OF. *coucher* to lay down, put to bed, fr. L. *collocare* to lay, put, fr. *col-* + *locare* to place.] **1.** To lay upon a bed or other resting place. **2.** *Archaic.* To deposit in a bed or layer. **3.** To overlay; embroider. **4.** *Obs.* To conceal; hide. **5.** To lower; to bring down; as, advancing with spears *couched.* **6.** To put into language; to express. **7.** *Surg.* Formerly, to treat (a cataract) by turning down the opaque lens of the eye. — *v. i.* **1.** To lie down or recline, as on a bed. **2.** To hide; lurk. **3.** To lie or be situated. — **Syn.** See LURK. — *n.* **1.** A bed or structure for repose or sleep; often, specif., a lounge or sofa. **2.** The burrow of an otter; also, *Obs.,* the den of a beast. — **couch′er,** *n.*

couch′ant (kouch′ănt), *adj.* Lying down; specif., *Her.,* lying down with the head raised.

couch grass (kouch; ko͞och). [Var. of QUITCH GRASS.] Any of various grasses having creeping rhizomes by which they spread rapidly; specif., the European grass *Agropyron repens,* naturalized in North America as a weed, called also *quick, quitch, twitch,* or *witch grass.*

Cou′é′ism (ko͞o′ā′ĭz'm), *n.* A system of psychotherapy, introduced by Émile Coué (1857–1926), based upon autosuggestion of health.

cou′gar (ko͞o′gẽr; -gär), *n.;* see PLURAL, *Note,* 3. [F. *couguar* (Buffon), fr. a misspelling of the Tupi name.] A large quadruped (*Felis concolor*) of the cat family, tawny-brown in color without spots, found from Canada to Patagonia; — called also *puma, panther, catamount,* and *mountain lion.*

cough (kŏf; 74), *v. i.* [ME. *coughen, coghen, couwen.*] To expel air from the lungs suddenly with an explosive noise made by the opening of the glottis. — *v. t.* **1.** To expel by coughing. **2.** *Slang.* To pay; deliver; — often with *up.* — *n.* **1.** Frequent repetition of coughing, being a symptom of disease. **2.** An act or sound of coughing. — **cough′er,** *n.*

could (ko͝od; 4), *past* of CAN. [AS. *cūthe.* The *l* was inserted under the influence of *should, would.*] Was, should be, or would be, able; — used as an auxiliary.

cou′lee (ko͞o′lĭ), *n.* Also ‖**cou′lée′** (ko͞o′lā′). [F. *coulée,* fr. *couler* to flow.] **1.** *Geol.* A solidified stream of lava. **2.** *Western U. S.* A steep-walled, trenchlike valley.

‖**cou′leur′ de rose** (ko͞o′lûr′ dē rōz′). [F.] Color of rose; hence, chiefly figurative, rose-colored; roseate.

cou·lisse′ (ko͞o·lēs′), *n.* [F., fr. *couler* to glide.] **1.** A piece of timber having a groove in which something glides, as an upright of a sluice. **2.** A side scene of the stage in a theater, or the space between the side scenes.

‖**cou′loir′** (ko͞o′lwär′), *n.* [F.] **1.** A gorge on a mountainside, esp. in the Swiss Alps. **2.** A dredging machine.

cou·lomb′ (ko͞o·lŏm′), *n.* [After Charles A. de *Coulomb,* French physicist.] *Physics.* A measure of the amount of an electric charge conveyed by an electric current of one ampere in one second.

coul′ter (kōl′tẽr). Var. of COLTER.

cou′ma·rin (ko͞o′mȧ·rĭn), *n.* [F. *coumarine,* fr. *coumarou* the tonka-bean tree.] *Chem.* A white crystalline compound, $C_9H_6O_2$, of vanillalike odor, found esp. in the tonka bean, and used in flavoring and perfumery.

cou′ma·rone (ko͞o′mȧ·rōn), *n.* [*coumarin* + *-one.*] *Chem.* A compound, C_8H_6O, found in coal tar, also prepared synthetically. It polymerizes to form **coumarone resins** used in varnishes, printing inks, adhesives, etc.

coun′cil (koun′sĭl; -s'l), *n.* [OF. *cuncile, concile,* fr. L. *concilium,* prob. fr. *con-* + *calare* to call.] **1.** An assembly summoned for consultation, advice, etc. **2.** *Eccl.* An assembly of ecclesiastics convened to consider matters of doctrine, discipline, law, or morals. **3.** In the New Testament, an assembly or meeting of the authorities, esp. of the Sanhedrin. **4.** A body of men elected or appointed to constitute a more or less permanent advisory or legislative body; as, a governor's *council.* Cf. COMMON COUNCIL, PRIVY COUNCIL. **5.** A governing body consisting of voting delegates from local labor unions united in a federation. **6.** The deliberation in a council.

coun′cil·man (koun′sĭl·măn), *n.; pl.* -MEN (-mĕn). A member of a council, esp. of the common council of a city.

coun′ci·lor, coun′cil·lor (koun′sĭ·lẽr), *n.* A member of a council. — **coun′ci·lor·ship′, coun′cil·lor·ship′,** *n.*

coun′sel (koun′sĕl), *n.* [OF. *cunseil, conseil,* fr. L. *consilium,* fr. root of *consulere* to consult.] **1.** Advice, esp. that given as the result of consultation. **2.** Mutual advising; deliberation together. **3.** *Archaic.* The exercise of deliberate judgment; prudence. **4.** Deliberate purpose; design. **5.** *Obs.* A secret opinion or purpose; a private matter. 6. *Law.* One who gives advice, esp. in legal matters; one professionally engaged to conduct a cause in court; also, collectively, the legal advocates united in the management of a case. — **Syn.** See ADVICE: LAWYER. — *v. t.;* -SELED (-sĕld) or -SELLED; -SEL·ING or -SEL·LING. **1.** To give advice to; to advise. **2.** To recommend, as an act or course. — **Syn.** See under ADVICE. — *v. i.* To take or give counsel; to advise.

coun′se·lor, coun′sel·lor (koun′sĕ·lẽr), *n.* **1.** An adviser. **2.** One whose profession is to give advice in law, and manage causes for clients in court; a counsel. — **Syn.** See LAWYER. — **coun′se·lor·ship′, coun′sel·lor·ship′,** *n.*

count (kount), *v. t.* [OF. *cunter, conter,* later *compter,* fr. L. *computare* to reckon, compute, fr. *com-* + *putare* to reckon, think.] **1.** To tell or name one by one, or by groups, to ascertain the whole number of units in a collection; to number. **2.** To esteem; account; judge. **3.** To name the numerals in regular succession up to and including (a specified numeral). **4.** *Archaic.* To ascribe or impute. **5.** To take into account; to include in reckoning. — *v. i.* **1.** To name articles or numerals one by one or by groups. **2.** *Obs.* To take account or note; — with *of.* **3.** To reckon; rely; depend; — with *on* or *upon.* **4.** To be accounted; to possess value. — **Syn.** See RELY. — *n.* **1.** The act of numbering; also, the number ascertained by counting. **2.** A reckoning; accounting. **3.** *Archaic.* Regard, notice, or value; account. **4.** *Law.* A particular allegation or charge in a declaration or indictment, separately stating the cause of action or prosecution.

count, *n.* [OF. *conte* (F. *comte*), fr. L. *comes, comitis,* associate, companion.] A nobleman on the continent of Europe, corresponding in rank to an English earl.

count′a·ble (koun′tȧ·b'l), *adj.* Capable of being counted.

coun′te·nance (koun′tē·năns), *n.* [OF. *contenance* demeanor, fr. L. *continentia* continence, ML., also, demeanor, fr. L. *continere* to hold together, repress, contain.] **1.** *Obs.* Bearing or conduct. **2.** The expression of the face, esp. as indicative of mental composure. **3.** The face; visage. **4.** Approving bearing or facial aspect; hence, favor; aid. — **Syn.** See FACE: FAVOR. — *v. t.;* -NANCED (-nănst); -NANC·ING (-năn·sĭng). To give countenance to; favor. — **coun′te·nanc·er** (-năn·sẽr), *n.*

count′er (koun′tẽr), *n.* [OF. *contouer, comptouer,* fr. ML. *computatorium,* prop., computing place, fr. L. *computare.* See COUNT, *v.*] **1.** A device, as a piece of metal, ivory, etc., used in reckoning, and in games, etc. **2.** A token coin of base metal; hence, a coin. **3.** A table or board on which money is counted and over which business is transacted, goods are handled, etc.

count′er (koun′tẽr), *n.* One that counts; a computer.

coun′ter (koun′tẽr), *adv.* [F. *contre,* fr. L. *contra* against.] **1.** In the wrong way; contrary to the right course. **2.** Contrary; in opposition; — used chiefly with *run* or *go.* — *adj.* Contrary; opposite. — **Syn.** See ADVERSE. — *n.* **1.** The opposite or contrary. **2.** The act of giving a blow when receiving or parrying one, as in boxing; also, the blow so given. **3.** *Fencing.* A circular parry in which the blade follows that of the opponent. **4.** *Naut.* That portion of a vessel's stern from the water line to the extreme outward swell. **5.** *Shoe Mfg.* A stiffener of leather or fiber to give form to a boot or shoe upper around the heel. See SHOE, *Illust.* **6.** *Type Founding.* The depression between lines in the face of a type. See TYPE, *Illust.* — *v. t. & i.* To go, act, move, speak, fight, or the like, counter to; to oppose.

coun′ter- (koun′tẽr-). A combining form of *counter,* adv., denoting: **a** In combination with a verb, action which is: (1) *opposite* or *contrary,* (2) *reciprocal,* (3) *retaliatory,* or (4) *complementary,* to the action of the verb. **b** In combination with nouns or adjectives, *opposition, reversal, reciprocality,* etc.

☞ The meanings of the following may be inferred from the definitions of the root words:

counteraccusation	**countermanifesto**	**counterstatement**
counterattraction	**countermove**	**counterstratagem**
counterblast	**counteroffer**	**counterstroke**
countercharge	**counterpropaganda**	**countersuggestion**
countercurrent	**counterproposal**	**countersuit**
counterdeclaration	**counterproposition**	**countertendency**
counterdemonstration	**counterreform**	**counterthreat**
counterespionage	**counterresolution**	**counterthrust**

coun′ter·act′ (koun′tẽr·ăkt′), *v. t.* To act in opposition to; to frustrate by contrary action or influence; to neutralize. — **coun′ter·ac′tion** (-ăk′shŭn), *n.* — **coun′ter·ac′tive** (-ăk′tĭv), *adj.* — **Syn.** See ADVERSE.

coun′ter·at·tack′ (koun′tẽr·ă·tăk′), *n.* An attack made to counter an enemy's attack. — **coun′ter·at·tack′,** *v. t. & i.*

coun′ter·bal′ance (-băl′ăns), *n.* **1.** A weight that balances another; a counterweight. **2.** Influence or power which balances or offsets contrary influence or power.

coun′ter·bal′ance (-băl′ăns), *v. t. & i.;* see BALANCE. To oppose with an equal weight or power; to counterweigh.

coun′ter·change′ (-chānj′), *v. t.;* see CHANGE. **1.** To cause to change places; to shift. **2.** To checker; diversify.

coun′ter·claim′ (koun′tẽr·klām′), *n.* An opposing claim.

coun′ter·claim′ (-klām′), *v.t. & i.* To present or demand as a counterclaim. — **coun′ter·claim′ant** (-ănt), *n.*

coun′ter·clock′wise′ (-klŏk′wīz′), *adv.* In the direction opposite to that in which the hands of a clock rotate, as viewed from in front. Cf. LEFT-HANDED, 5 **a**; LEVOROTATORY; CLOCKWISE. — **coun′ter·clock′-wise′,** *adj.*

coun′ter·feit (koun′tẽr·fĭt; *Brit. also* -fēt), *adj.* [OF. *contrefet, contrefait,* past part. of *contrefaire* to counterfeit, fr. *contre* (L. *contra*) + *faire* to make, fr. L. *facere.*] Made in imitation of something else with a view to defraud; hence, spurious. — *n.* **1.** That which is made in imitation of something, with a view to deceive; a forgery. **2.** *Archaic.* A likeness; a portrait; a copy. **3.** *Obs.* An impostor. — **Syn.** See IMPOSTURE. — *v. t.* To imitate, esp. for deceiving; to forge. — *v. i.* **1.** To dissemble; to pretend. **2.** To make counterfeits, especially of money. — **Syn.** See ASSUME. — **coun′ter·feit′er** (-fĭt′ẽr; -fēt′ẽr), *n.*

coun′ter·foil (koun′tẽr·foil′), *n.* [*counter-* + *foil* a leaf.] The part of a writing (as the stub of a bank check) in which are noted particulars of the issued item; a stub (def. 3).

coun′ter·in·tel′li·gence (koun′tẽr·ĭn·tĕl′ĭ·jĕns), *n.* *Mil.* Organized activity or activities collectively of an intelligence service designed to block the enemy's sources of information by concealment, camouflage, codes and ciphers, censorship, and other measures, and to deceive the enemy by ruses and misinformation, and the like.

coun′ter·ir′ri·tant (-ĭr′ĭ·tănt), *n.* *Med.* An irritant to produce a blister, a pustular eruption, or the like, to relieve an existing irritation elsewhere; — also used figuratively. — **coun′ter·ir′ri·tant,** *adj.*

count′er·jump′er (koun′tẽr·jŭmp′ẽr), *n.* *Colloq.* A salesman in a shop or store; — used contemptuously.

count′er·man (-măn), *n.* One who tends a counter.

coun′ter·mand′ (koun′tẽr·månd′; koun′tẽr·månd; 2), *v. t.* [From F., fr. *contre* (L. *contra*) + *mander* to command, fr. L. *mandare.*] **1.** To revoke (a former command). **2.** To recall or order back by a superseding contrary order. — **coun′ter·mand** (koun′tẽr·månd; 2), *n.*

coun′ter·march′ (koun′tẽr·märch′), *n.* **1.** A marching back. **2.** *Mil.* A movement of a body of troops by which it reverses its direction of march.

coun′ter·march′ (koun′tẽr·märch′; koun′tẽr·märch′; 2), *v. i. & t.* *Mil.* To march back; also, to execute a countermarch.

coun′ter·mine′ (koun′tẽr·mīn′), *n.* **1.** *Mil.* An underground gallery to intercept and destroy an enemy mine. **2.** A stratagem for defeating a stratagem or attack. **3.** A floating or submerged mine or any device used to explode prematurely mines previously laid by the enemy. — **coun′ter·mine′** (-mīn′), *v. i. & t.*

coun′ter·of·fen′sive (koun′tẽr·ŏ·fĕn′sĭv), *n.* *Mil.* An offensive operation undertaken by a force which has hitherto been engaged in warding off attack. Cf. COUNTERATTACK.

coun′ter·pane′ (-pān′; -pĭn), *n.* [Corrupt. fr. *counterpoint* coverlet.] An outer covering for a bed; bedspread.

coun′ter·part′ (-pärt′), *n.* **1.** A part or thing corresponding to another; also, *Obs.,* a copy. **2.** A thing that serves to complete or complement something else. **3.** A person who closely resembles another.

coun′ter·plot′ (-plŏt′), *n.* A plot opposed to a plot.

coun′ter·plot′ (koun′tẽr·plŏt′; koun′tẽr·plŏt′; 2), *v. t. & i.;* -PLOT′TED; -PLOT′TING. To oppose (a plot) by plotting.

coun′ter·point′ (koun′tẽr·point′), *n.* [F. *contrepoint.* Cf. CONTRAPUNTAL.] *Music.* **a** A melody added to a given melody as accompaniment. **b** The art of plural melody, that is, of melody not single, but moving attended by one or more related but independent melodies.

coun′ter·poise′ (-poiz′), *n.* [ONF. *countrepeis,* OF. *contrepois.*] **1.** A counterweight; counterbalance. **2.** An equivalent power or force acting in opposition. **3.** A state of balance; equilibrium. — *v. t. & i.* To counterbalance; counterweigh.

coun′ter·ref′or·ma′tion (-rĕf′ẽr·mā′shŭn), *n.* An opposing reformation; specif. [*cap.*] (usually written **Counter Reformation**), the reformatory movement in the Roman Catholic Church which followed the Reformation.

coun′ter·rev′o·lu′tion (-rĕv′ō·lū′shŭn), *n.* A revolution opposed to a former one. — **coun′ter·rev′o·lu′tion·ar′y** (-ẽr′ĭ *or, esp. Brit.,* -ẽr·ĭ), *adj. & n.* — **coun′ter·rev′o·lu′tion·ist,** *n.*

coun′ter·scarp′ (koun′tẽr·skärp′), *n.* [F. *contrescarpe.*] *Fort.* The exterior slope or wall of the ditch. Cf. SCARP.

coun′ter·shaft′ (-shȧft′), *n.* *Mach.* An intermediate shaft which receives motion from a main shaft and transmits it to a working part.

coun′ter·sign′ (-sīn′), *n.* [OF. *contresigne.*] **1.** The signature of a person to a writing already signed by another, to attest its authenticity. **2.** A sign used in reply to another; specif., *Mil.,* a secret signal, which must be given by one wishing to pass a guard. Cf. PAROLE, 3.

coun′ter·sign′ (koun′tẽr·sīn′; koun′tẽr·sīn′), *v. t.* To sign on the opposite side of (an instrument or writing); hence, to sign in addition to the signature of another, in order to attest the authenticity of that signature.

coun′ter·sig′na·ture (koun′tẽr·sĭg′nȧ·tūr), *n.* The signature made by one who countersigns anything.

coun′ter·sink′ (koun′tẽr·sĭngk′; koun′tẽr·sĭngk′), *v. t.;* see SINK. **1.** To chamfer or form a flaring depression around the top of (a hole in wood, metal, etc.), for receiving the head of a screw, bolt, etc. **2.** To sink, as a screw, even with or below the surface. — (koun′tẽr·sĭngk′), *n.* A countersunk hole; also, a tool for countersinking a hole.

coun′ter·ten′or (koun′tẽr·tĕn′ẽr), *n.* *Music.* **a** One of the middle parts in music, between the tenor and the soprano. **b** A man's falsetto voice singing such a part; a male alto.

coun′ter·type′ (-tīp′), *n.* **1.** An opposite type; an antitype. **2.** A corresponding or parallel type.

coun′ter·vail′ (koun′tẽr·vāl′), *v. t.* [From OF., fr. *contre* (L. *contra*) + *valoir* to avail, fr. L. *valere* to be strong, avail.] **1.** To furnish an equivalent to or for; compensate. **2.** *Obs.* To counterbalance. **3.** To thwart by opposing force; to avail against. — **Syn.** See COMPENSATE.

coun′ter·view′ (koun′tẽr·vū′), *n.* *Obs.* Confrontation.

coun′ter·weigh′ (-wā′), *v. t. & i.* To counterbalance.

coun′ter·weight′ (koun′tẽr·wāt′), *n.* An equivalent weight; a counterbalance. Cf. GYROSCOPE, *Illust.* — *v. t.* To counterweigh.

coun′ter·word′ (koun′tẽr·wûrd′), *n.* A word taken up popularly and used in a greater and greater variety of situations and with vaguer and vaguer meaning (as *awful, fierce*).

coun′ter·work′ (-wûrk′), *n.* Any work done counter to another work, as in fortifications.

coun′ter·work′ (-wûrk′), *v. t. & i.* To work in opposition.

count′ess (koun′tĕs; -tĭs), *n.* [OF. *contesse* (F. *comtesse*).] The wife or widow of an earl in the British peerage, or of a count in the Continental nobility; also, a lady possessed of the same dignity in her own right.

count′ing·house′ (kount′ĭng·hous′), *n.* The building, room, or office in which a merchant, trader, or manufacturer keeps his books and transacts business.

counting room. A countinghouse.

count′less, *adj.* Incapable of being counted or estimated; innumerable; numberless; incalculable.

count palatine. **a** *Eng.* Formerly, the proprietor of a county who possessed royal prerogatives within his county. **b** Orig., a high judicial officer of the German emperors; later, one granted the right to exercise certain imperial powers in his own domains.

coun′tri·fied (kŭn′trĭ·fīd), *adj.* Also **coun′try·fied.** Having the characteristics of a rustic or of rural life; rustic.

coun′try (kŭn′trĭ), *n.; pl.* -TRIES (-trĭz). [OF. *contrée,* fr. LL. *contrata,* fr. L. *contra* on the opposite side.] **1.** A region or tract of land; a district. **2.** The territory of a nation. **3.** The land of a person's birth or adoption, to which he owes his allegiance; fatherland. **4.** The people of a state or district; the nation. **5.** Rural regions, as opposed to a city or town. **6.** *Law.* A jury; — so called because originally the jury was a body of men chosen from the country or neighbor hood, a jury trial being called ***trial by the country***, and the litigants being said to ***put themselves upon the, or their, country***. — *adj.* **1.** *Now Dial.* Pertaining, or peculiar, to one's own country; native. **2.** Rural; rustic. **3.** Churlish; rude.

☞ COMBINATIONS are: **coun′try–bred′**, **coun′try·folk′**, **coun′try-peo′ple**, **coun′try–style′**.

coun′try–dance′, *n.* A native English dance in which the partners are arranged in two lines so as to face each other; a contredanse.

coun′try·man (kŭn′trĭ·măn), *n.* **1.** An inhabitant or native of a country; also, a compatriot. **2.** A rustic. — **coun′try·wom′an** (-wo͝om′ăn), *n.*

coun′try·seat′ (kŭn′trĭ·sēt′; 2), *n.* A dwelling or estate of some pretensions in the country.

coun′try·side′ (-sīd′; 2), *n.* A rural area or its people; also, rural areas (as of a country) collectively.

coun′ty (koun′tĭ), *n.; pl.* -TIES (-tĭz). [OF. *cunté, conté* (F. *comté*), fr. L. *comitatus.* See COUNT nobleman.] **1.** *Obs. exc. Hist.* An earldom. **2.** In Great Britain and Northern Ireland, one of the territorial divisions constituting the chief units for administrative, judicial, and political purposes. Cf. SHIRE. **3.** *Chiefly Eng.* The inhabitants of such a territorial division. **4.** In the United States, the largest division for local government in all states except Louisiana, where the corresponding division is the *parish.* **5.** One of the larger administrative divisions in various British dominions.

☞ Abbreviation (for senses 2, 4, 5) *Co.*

count′y (koun′tĭ), *n.* *Obs.* Count (the title).

county palatine. The territory of a count palatine.

county town *or* (*U. S.*) **seat.** A town (sometimes, one of the towns) which is the seat of county administration.

coup (kōp; ko͞op), *v. i. & t.* [See COPE to contend.] *Dial.* **1.** To upset; also, to tip. **2.** To drink off; to drain.

coup (ko͞o), *n.; pl.* COUPS (ko͞oz; *F.* ko͞o). [F., deriv. of L. *colaphus* a cuff, fr. Gr. *kolaphos.*] Literally, a blow; hence, a brilliant sudden stroke or stratagem.

‖**coup de grâce** (ko͞o′ dẽ gräs′). [F.] A merciful blow; the death blow with which an executioner ended the sufferings of the condemned; hence, a decisive, finishing stroke.

‖**coup de main** (măN′). [F.] *Chiefly Mil.* A sudden and unexpected movement or attack.

‖**coup de maî′tre** (mâ′tr′). [F.] A master stroke.

‖**coup de so′leil′** (sô′lā′y′). [F.] *Med.* Sunstroke.

‖**coup d'es′sai′** (dĕ′sĕ′). [F.] An experiment; trial.

‖**coup d'é′tat′** (dā′tà′). [F.] *Politics.* A sudden decisive exercise of force whereby the existing government is subverted; an unexpected stroke of policy.

‖**coup de thé′â′tre** (dẽ tā′ä′tr′). [F.] A sudden and sensational turn in a play; hence, any theatrical act.

coup d'oeil (dû′y′). [F.] A brief survey, as at one glance.

cou′pé′ (ko͞o′pā′; *often colloquially Anglicized* ko͞op), *n.* [F., fr. *coupé,* past part., cut.] **1.** A four-wheeled closed carriage for two persons inside, with an outside seat for the driver. **2.** A two-door automobile having an enclosed body of one compartment, usually seating two to five persons.

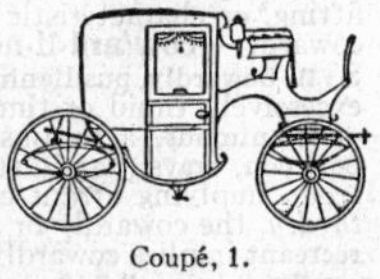

Coupé, 1.

cou′ple (kŭp′′l), *n.* [OF., fr. L. *copula* a bond, band, fr. *co-* + *apere, aptum,* to join.] **1.** That which links two things together; a bond or tie; a coupler. **2. a** Two of the same kind connected together; a pair; brace. **b** *Colloq.* Approximately two; a few. **3.** A male and female associated together; esp., a man and woman married, betrothed, or partners at a dance. **4.** *Elec.* = VOLTAIC COUPLE. **5.** *Mech.* A pair of equal parallel forces, acting in opposite directions and tending to produce rotation. — *v. t.;* COU′PLED (kŭp′′ld); COU′PLING (-lĭng). **1.** To link or tie. **2.** *Colloq.* To marry. — *v. i.* **1.** To copulate; to pair. **2.** To come together, forming a pair.

cou′pled (kŭp′′ld), *adj.* **1.** United in a couple; paired; joined. **2.** Designating the coupling (see COUPLING, 2) of an animal; — chiefly in compounds; as, a short-*coupled* horse.

cou′ple·ment (kŭp′′l·mĕnt), *n.* [OF.] *Now Rare.* Union.

cou′pler (kŭp′lẽr), *n.* **1.** One who or that which couples, as a link, ring, or shackle, to connect cars; a drawbar. **2.** A contrivance in an organ by which two or more keys or keyboards are made to act together.

cou′plet (kŭp′lĕt; -lĭt), *n.* [F., dim. of *couple.*] **1.** A pair of verses; esp., two successive verses rhyming with each other. **2.** *Rare.* Two taken together; a pair or couple.

cou′pling (kŭp′lĭng), *n.* **1.** Act of bringing or coming together; connection. **2.** The joining of, or the part of the body joining, the hindquarters and forequarters of a dog, horse, etc. **3.** *Elec.* Means of electric connection of two electric circuits by having a part common to both. See DYNAMO, *Illust.* **4.** *Mach.* A device or contrivance that serves to couple or connect the ends of adjacent parts or objects.

cou′pon (ko͞o′pŏn *or, esp. Brit.,* ko͞o′pông; *in U. S. often* kū′pŏn), *n.* [F., fr. *couper* to cut.] **1.** *Com.* A certificate of interest due, designed to be cut off and presented for payment when interest is due. **2.** A section, as of a ticket or certificate, showing the holder to be entitled to some service or right (as to purchase certain goods). **3.** A certificate given with a purchase of goods and redeemable in merchandise or cash. **4.** A part of a printed advertisement designed to be cut off for use as an order blank.

cour′age (kûr′ĭj), *n.* [OF. *corage, curage,* fr. *cuer* (F. *cœur*), fr. L. *cor* heart.] **1.** *Obs.* Mind, spirit, temper, or disposition. **2.** That quality of mind which enables one to meet danger and difficulties with firmness; valor.

Syn. **Courage, mettle, spirit, resolution, tenacity** mean a human quality which keeps one going in the face of opposition or danger. **Courage** stresses firmness of mind or purpose and the casting aside of fear; **mettle** suggests an ingrained capacity for meeting stress or strain; **spirit,** though suggesting less vitality than *mettle,* implies an ability to hold one's own or to keep up one's morale indefinitely; **resolution,** like *courage,* implies firmness of mind and purpose, but it stresses determination to achieve one's ends; **tenacity** adds to *resolution* the implications of stubborn persistence and unwillingness to acknowledge defeat.

cou·ra′geous (kŭ·rā′jŭs), *adj.* Possessing, or characterized by, courage. — **Syn.** Brave, valiant, dauntless, intrepid. — **cou·ra′geous·ly,** *adv.* — **cou·ra′geous·ness,** *n.*

cou·rante′ (ko͞o·rȧnt′; *F.* ko͞o′räNt′), *n.* Also **cou·rant′.** [F. *courante,* fr. *courant,* pres. part.] A former dance with quick running steps; also, the music for this dance.

‖**cou′reur′ de bois** (ko͞o′rûr′ dẽ bwä′); *pl.* COUREURS DE BOIS (ko͞o′rûr′). [F.] One of the French or half-breed trappers of western North America, esp. of Canada.

cour′i·er (ko͝or′ĭ·ẽr; kûr′-), *n.* [F. *courrier,* fr. It. *corriere* (after L. *currere* to run).] **1.** A special messenger. **2.** An attendant on travelers, who arranges for their convenience at inns and on the way.

cour′lan (ko͞or′lăn; *F.* ko͞or′läN′), *n.* [F.] Either of two tropical American long-billed, raillike birds (genus *Aramus,* family Aramidae). The species (*A. pictus,* syn. *giganteus*) of Florida, Central America, and the West Indies is commonly called *limpkin.*

course (kōrs; 70), *n.* [From F. *cours* (OF. *cors, curs*), fr. L. *cursus,* and fr. F. *course,* fr. It. *corsa,* fr. *correre* to run; both fr. L. *currere, cursum,* to run.] **1.** The act of moving from one point to another; progress; passage; also, direction of progress. **2.** *Hist.* A single charge of opposing knights in a tourney. **3.** The ground or path traversed; track; way; specif.: **a** A racecourse. **b** Golf links. **c** A watercourse. **4.** That part of a meal served at one time, with its accompaniments. **5.** One of a series of layers, as of cement in road making or of shingles on a roof. **6.** A series or succession of acts or practices; as, a *course* of conduct. **7.** Progress considered with regard to time; as, in the *course* of a year. **8.** Customary sequence of events. **9.** Method of procedure; conduct; behavior. **10.** *Aeronautics.* The direction of flight of an aircraft, measured as a clockwise angle from north. **11.** *Arch.* A continuous level range of brick or masonry throughout the face or faces of a building. **12.** *Educ.* **a** An entire series of studies usually leading to a degree. **b** A unit of instruction consisting of recitations, lectures, or the like, in a particular subject; also, the subject matter of such a unit. **13.** *Naut.* **a** The lowest sail on any square-rigged mast of a vessel. **b** A point of the compass. — ***of course.*** As was to be expected; naturally.

— *v. t.* **1.** To run, hunt, or chase after; to pursue; as, to *course* hares. **2.** To cause to chase after game; as, to *course* hounds. **3.** To run through or over. — *v. i.* **1.** To take or follow a course. **2.** To run as in a tournament or in hunting. **3.** To move with speed; race.

cours′er (kōr′sẽr; 70), *n.* [From COURSE, *v.*] One who courses or hunts; also, a dog for coursing.

cours′er, *n.* [OF. *corsier* (F. *coursier*).] *Poetic.* A swift or spirited horse; a war horse or racer; a charger.

cours′er, *n.* [L. *cursorius* pert. to running.] Any of a small group of birds related to the plovers, of Africa and southern Asia, remarkable for their speed in running.

cours′ing (kōr′sĭng), *n.* **1.** The act of one who courses. **2.** The pursuit of running game with dogs that follow by sight instead of by scent.

court (kōrt; 70), *n.* [OF. *court, cort,* fr. L. *cohors, cors,* gen. *cohortis, cortis,* enclosure, court, crowd.] **1.** An uncovered area partly or wholly enclosed by buildings or by walls and grating. **2.** A building, or group of buildings, enclosed in a courtyard; hence, a manorial house; — now only in some proper names. **3.** An open space like a short street. **4.** A space, primarily quadrangular, for playing one of various games with a ball, as lawn tennis, rackets, basketball, handball, etc. **5.** A courtlike section or area of a museum or exhibition. **6.** The residence of a sovereign, prince, or the like; palace. **7.** The collective body of persons composing the retinue of a sovereign or person high in authority; also, a sovereign and his officials as a political body. **8.** Any formal assembling of the retinue of a sovereign. **9.** Attention directed to a person in power; homage; courtship. **10.** *Law.* **a** The place where justice is administered. **b** The persons duly assembled under authority of law for the administration of justice. **c** A tribunal established for the administration of justice. **d** The session of a judicial assembly. **11.** A body of directors, managers, or the like, qualified to superintend the general affairs of an organization.

— *v. t.* **1.** To endeavor to gain the favor of by attention or flattery. **2.** To endeavor to gain the affections of; to woo. **3.** To attempt to gain; to solicit. **4.** To allure; attract. — **Syn.** See INVITE. — *v. i.* To make love; to woo.

— *adj.* Suitable to the court of a sovereign.

court′–bar′on, *n.* *Eng. Law.* The court, usually that of a manor, in which a lord exercised his private jurisdiction.

court card. A corrupted form of COAT CARD.

cour′te·ous (kûr′tē·ŭs), *adj.* [OF. *curteis, corteis* (F. *courtois*). See COURT.] Of courtlike manners; civil; polite. — **Syn.** See CIVIL. — **Ant.** Discourteous. — **cour′te·ous·ly,** *adv.* — **cour′te·ous·ness,** *n.*

cour′te·san, cour′te·zan (kōr′tē·zăn; kûr′-; *Brit. usually* kōr′tē·zăn′), *n.* [F. *courtisane,* fr. *courtisan* courtier, fr. It. *cortigiano.* See COURT.] A court mistress; a loose woman; a prostitute.

cour′te·sy (kûr′tĕ·sĭ; kōr′tĕ·sĭ; 70), *n.; pl.* -SIES (-sĭz). [OF. *curteisie, cortoisie.* See COURTEOUS.] **1.** Courtly politeness. **2. a** A favor performed with politeness. **b** An expression of respect. **3.** Favor or indulgence, as distinguished from right; as, a title given one by *courtesy.* **4.** A curtsy.

court hand. The hand, or manner of writing, formerly used in charters, deeds, and other legal documents.

court′house′ (kōrt′hous′; 70), *n.* **1.** A building in which established courts of law are held. **2.** *Local, U. S.* A county town.

cour′ti·er (kōr′tĭ·ẽr; kōrt′yẽr; 70), *n.* **1.** One who is in attendance at the court of a prince. **2.** One who practices courtierlike flattery.

court′ly (kōrt′lĭ), *adj.;* -LI·ER (-lĭ·ẽr); -LI·EST. **1.** Of a quality befitting the court; elegant; polite; also, insincerely flattering. **2.** Favoring the policy or party of the court. — **Syn.** See CIVIL. — *adv.* In the manner of courts; politely. — **court′li·ness** (-lĭ·nĕs; -nĭs), *n.*

court′–mar′tial (kōrt′mär′shăl; 2; 70), *n.; pl.* COURTS-MARTIAL. A court consisting of military or naval officers, for the trial of one belonging to the army or navy, or of offenses against military or naval law. — *v. t.;* -TIALED (-shăld) or -TIALLED; -TIAL·ING or -TIAL·LING. To subject to trial by a court-martial.

court plaster. Sticking plaster of silk or other fabric coated commonly with a mixture of isinglass and glycerin.

court′room′ (kōrt′ro͞om′), *n.* A room in which a court of law is held.

court′ship (-shĭp), *n.* **1.** The act of courting, or wooing. **2.** *Obs.* Courtliness.

court tennis. See TENNIS, 1.

court′yard′ (kōrt′yärd′), *n.* A court or enclosure attached to a house, castle, or palace.

cous′in (kŭz′′n), *n.* [OF. *cosin, cusin, cousin,* fr. L. *consobrinus* the child of a mother's sister, cousin, fr. *con-* + *sobrinus* a cousin by the mother's side, fr. *soror* sister.] **1.** *Obs.* A person collaterally related more remotely than a brother or sister; also, *Law,* any of the next of kin, except parent or child. **2.** Specif.: A son or daughter of one's uncle or aunt (called more fully ***own, first, or full, cousin,*** or ***cousin-german***); also, a relative descended the same number of steps by a different line from a common ancestor. The children of first cousins are ***second cousins*** to each other. The child of one's first cousin is properly called ***first cousin once removed,*** but often popularly ***second cousin.*** See CONSANGUINITY, *Illust.* **3.** One akin to, or of the same kind as, another. **4.** A title used by a sovereign in addressing a nobleman of his own country or another sovereign. — **cous'in·hood,** *n.* — **cous'in·ly,** *adj. & adv.* — **cous'in·ship,** *n.*

cous'in-ger'man (kŭz''n·jûr'măn), *n.; pl.* COUSINS-GERMAN. [F. *cousin germain.* See GERMAN, *adj.*] A first cousin. See COUSIN, *n.,* 2.

‖**cou'teau'** (kōō'tō'), *n.; pl.* -TEAUX (*F.* -tō'). [F.] A knife; esp., a large knife; also, loosely, a two-edged dagger.

‖**coûte que coûte** (kōōt' kẽ kōōt'). [F.] Cost what it may.

couth (kōōth). *Obs. past & past part.* of CAN; specif., *part. adj.* Known; familiar; noted. Cf. UNCOUTH.

couth'ie (kōōth'ĭ), *adj. Now Dial.* Kindly; agreeable.

‖**cou'tu'rier'** (kōō'tü'ryā'; *Angl.* kōō·tōōr'ĭ·ēr), *n., prop. masc.,* ‖**cou'tu'rière'** (kōō'tü'ryâr'; *Angl.* kōō·tōōr'ĭ·ēr), *fem.* [F.] A dressmaker; modiste.

cou·vade' (kōō·väd'), *n.* [F., fr. *couver* to hatch.] A primitive custom in accordance with which when a child is born the father takes to his bed, cares for the child, or submits himself to fasting and purification.

co·va'lence (kō·vā'lĕns), **co·va'len·cy** (-lĕn·sĭ), *n. Chem.* The number of pairs of electrons an atom can share with its neighbors. — **co·va'lent** (-lĕnt), *adj.*

cove (kōv), *n.* [AS. *cofa* a room.] **1.** A small sheltered inlet, creek, or bay; also, a sheltered nook. **2.** *Chiefly Dial.* **a** A strip of prairie extending into woodland. **b** A small valley in the side of a mountain. **3.** *Arch.* **a** A concave molding. **b** A member whose section is a concave curve; — used esp. with regard to an inner roof or ceiling, as around a skylight. — *v. t. & i. Arch.* To arch over.

cove, *n.* [A Gypsy word, *covo* that man, *covi* that woman.] *Slang.* A chap or fellow; also, queer fellow; codger.

cov'e·nant (kŭv'ĕ·nănt), *n.* [OF., fr. *covenir* to agree, fr. L. *convenire.* See CONVENE.] **1.** An agreement between persons or parties. **2.** A solemn compact between members of a church to maintain its faith, discipline, etc. **3.** [*cap.*] *Hist.* Any of several agreements for the defense of Presbyterianism, made by Scottish Presbyterians, esp. one called the ***National Covenant*** (1638) made against episcopacy, and one called ***The Solemn League and Covenant*** (1643) agreed to by the Scottish and English parliaments. **4.** [*cap.*] **The Covenant of the League of Nations,** being the first part (containing 26 articles) of the Treaty of Versailles (1919). **5.** *Law.* **a** An undertaking or promise of legal validity. **b** The common-law form of action to recover damages for breach of such a contract. **6.** *Theol.* The promises of God as revealed in the Scriptures.
— *v. i.* To agree (*with*); to enter into a formal agreement. — **Syn.** Engage, contract, promise, pledge. — *v. t.* To promise by covenant.

cov'e·nan·tee' (kŭv'ĕ·năn·tē'), *n.* The person to whom the promise of a covenant is made.

cov'e·nant·er (kŭv'ĕ·năn·tẽr; *Scot.* kŭv'ĕ·năn'tẽr), *n.* **1.** One who makes a covenant. **2.** [*cap.*] *Eccl. Hist.* An adherent of the Scottish National Covenant of 1638.

cov'e·nan·tor (kŭv'ĕ·năn·tẽr), *n.* The party to a covenant who is bound to perform the obligation expressed in it.

Cov'en·try (kŏv'ĕn·trĭ; *Brit. usually* kŭv'-), *n.* **1.** A town in Warwickshire, England. **2.** A state of ostracism or exclusion from social intercourse; — used esp. in the phrase ***to send to Coventry,*** to refuse to associate with.

cov'er (kŭv'ẽr), *v. t.* [OF. *covrir,* fr. L. *cooperire,* fr. *co-* + *operire* to cover.] **1.** To place a covering over. **2.** To envelop; to clothe. **3.** To invest (oneself *with* something); as, he *covered* himself with glory. **4.** To spread over. **5. a** To copulate with (a female); as, a horse *covers* a mare. **b** To brood or sit on; incubate, as eggs. **6.** To place one's money or stake upon or in equal jeopardy with (the money or stake of one's opponent) in a wager. **7.** To bring or hold within range, as of a revolver. **8.** To shelter, as from evil or danger; to protect. **9.** To hide from sight; to conceal. **10.** To remove from remembrance; to remit. **11.** To comprehend, include, or embrace. **12.** To be sufficient for; to compensate. **13.** To pass over (a distance); as, the train *covered* ten miles. **14.** To have as one's territory, field of activity, or the like; as, a salesman who *covers* Ohio. **15.** *Journalism.* To report the proceedings, news, etc., of (an event, meeting, or the like). **16.** *Mil.* To stand, or march, directly behind (another man or unit).
— *n.* **1.** Anything placed about or over, or naturally overlying, another thing; as: **a** A lid. **b** A binding or case for a book. **c** An envelope or wrapping. **2.** Shelter; protection. **3.** Anything which veils or conceals; a screen. **4.** [After F. *couvert.*] A tablecloth and other table fittings, esp. for one person at a meal. **5.** *Hunting.* Covert (def. 2). **6.** *Philately.* An envelope that has passed through the mail and bears postal markings of philatelic interest. **7.** *Roofing.* That portion of a slate, tile, or shingle which is hidden by the overlap of the course above. Cf. LAP, *n.,* 4.

cov'er·age (-ĭj), *n.* **1.** Act or fact of covering or including; condition of being covered; also, an aggregate of items covered. **2.** *Advertising.* The portion of a group or a community reached by a particular advertising medium. **3.** *Finance.* The amount, as of gold, available to meet liabilities; as, a 40 per cent gold *coverage* of paper currency. **4.** *Insurance.* The aggregate of risks covered by the terms of a contract of insurance.

cover charge. A charge made by a restaurant for service, in addition to the charge for food.

cover crop. *Agric.* A crop, as rye or clover, planted, esp. in orchards, to protect the soil in winter.

cov'ered wag'on (kŭv'ẽrd). *U. S.* A large long wagon with an arched cover. See CONESTOGA WAGON.

cov'er·er (kŭv'ẽr·ẽr), *n.* One who or that which covers.

cov'er·ing (kŭv'ẽr·ĭng), *n.* Anything that covers or conceals, as a roof, a screen, a wrapper, etc.

cov'er·let (-lĕt; -lĭt), *n.* Also **cov'er·lid** (-lĭd). [ME. *coverlyte,* fr. OF. *covrir* to cover + *lit* bed, fr. L. *lectus* bed.] An outer covering of a bed; bedspread; counterpane.

cov'er-point', *n.* In cricket and lacrosse, one of the playing positions, or the player in this position.

co'versed sine (kō'vûrst). The versed sine of the complement of an arc or angle. Abbr. *covers* (no period).

cov'ert (kŭv'ẽrt), *adj.* [OF., past part. of *covrir.* See COVER, *v.*] **1.** Covered over; sheltered; as, a *covert* nook; private; hidden; secret. **2.** *Law.* Under cover, authority, or protection (of her husband); — said of a married woman. — **Syn.** See SECRET. — **Ant.** Overt. — *n.* **1.** A covering; esp., a place that covers and protects; a shelter. **2.** A thicket affording cover for game. **3.** Also **covert cloth.** A cloth of wool, or wool and silk or rayon, sometimes waterproof, made in mixtures of colors. **4.** [Cf. F. *couverte.*] *Zool.* One of the special feathers covering the bases of the quills of the wings and tail of a bird. See BIRD, POULTRY, *Illusts.* — **cov'ert·ly,** *adv.*

cov'er·ture (kŭv'ẽr·tūr), *n.* **1.** A covering; specif.: **a** Shelter; defense. **b** Hiding or disguise. **2.** *Law.* The status of a woman during marriage.

cov'et (kŭv'ĕt; -ĭt), *v. t. & i.* [OF. *coveitier,* deriv. of L. *cupiditas* desire, fr. *cupere* to desire.] To desire; to long for, esp. something belonging to another person. — **Syn.** See DESIRE. — **cov'et·a·ble,** *adj.* — **cov'et·er,** *n.*

cov'et·ous (kŭv'ĕ·tŭs), *adj.* [OF. *coveitos.*] **1.** *Archaic.* Eager (to obtain). **2.** Inordinately desirous, esp. of something belonging to another person. — **cov'et·ous·ly,** *adv.* — **cov'et·ous·ness,** *n.*

Syn. **Covetous, greedy, acquisitive, grasping, avaricious** mean having a strong desire for possessions; **covetous** always implies inordinateness of desire, often for that which belongs to another; **greedy** stresses absence of restraint in desire, but it is a derogatory term only when the thing longed for is evil in itself or leads to evil; **acquisitive** implies not only eagerness to possess but the capacity for acquiring and retaining that which is desired; **grasping** adds to *covetous* the implication of selfishness and often suggests the use of wrongful or unfair means; **avaricious** implies acquisitiveness, especially of money, and exceeding stinginess.

cov'ey (kŭv'ĭ), *n.; pl.* -EYS (-ĭz). [OF. *covée,* fr. *cover* to brood on, fr. L. *cubare* to lie down.] **1.** A brood or hatch of birds; a small flock; — of partridge, quail, etc. **2.** A company; a bevy.

cow (kou), *n.; pl.* COWS (kouz); *old pl., now chiefly poetic,* KINE (kīn). [AS. *cū.*] The mature female of any bovine animal, or of any animal the male of which is called *bull,* as the elephant, moose, elk, whale, sea lion, etc.

cow (kou; kō), *v. Chiefly Scot.* To poll; lop off.

cow (kou), *v. t.* [ON. *kūga.*] To depress with fear; to daunt; overawe. — **Syn.** Intimidate, browbeat.

cow'age (kou'ĭj). Var. of COWHAGE.

cow'ard (kou'ẽrd), *adj.* [OF. *couard* coward, cowardly, prop., with tail between the legs, fr. *coe* (F. *queue*) tail, fr. L. *coda, cauda.*] **1.** Destitute of courage; cowardly. **2.** Proceeding from, or expressive of, cowardice. — *n.* A person who lacks courage.

cow'ard·ice (kou'ẽr·dĭs), *n.* Want of courage; ignoble timidity.

cow'ard·ly (kou'ẽrd·lĭ), *adj.* **1.** Wanting courage; not brave. **2.** Befitting, or characteristic of, a coward. — *adv.* In the manner of a coward. — **cow'ard·li·ness** (-lĭ·nĕs; -nĭs), *n.*

Syn. **Cowardly, pusillanimous, poltroon, craven, dastardly, recreant** mean excessively timid or timorous. **Cowardly** implies a weak or ignoble, **pusillanimous,** a mean-spirited and contemptible, lack of courage; **poltroon, craven,** and **dastardly** are extremely opprobrious terms, *poltroon* implying arrant cowardice, *craven,* abject pusillanimity, *dastardly,* the cowardly or skulking commission of an outrageous crime; **recreant** implies cowardly submission, especially under a threat.

cow'bane' (kou'bān'), *n.* Any of several poisonous plants of the carrot family, esp. species of *Cicuta* (see HEMLOCK, 1), as *C. virosa* of England and *C. maculata* (called specif. ***spotted cowbane*** or ***spotted hemlock***) of the U. S.

cow'bell' (-bĕl'), *n.* **1.** A bell hung about the neck of a cow to indicate her whereabouts. **2.** See CAMPION.

cow'ber'ry (-bĕr'ĭ; -bẽr·ĭ), *n.* The berry of any of several pasture shrubs; also, any of these shrubs; specif.: **a** A low evergreen shrub (*Vaccinium vitis-idaea*) with white flowers and dark-red acid berries. **b** A purple-flowered herb (*Comarum palustre*) of the rose family. **c** *U. S.* = PARTRIDGEBERRY **a.**

cow'bird' (-bûrd'), *n.* Also **cow blackbird, cow bunting.** A small North American blackbird (*Molothrus ater*).

cow'boy' (-boi'), *n.* A cattle herder, esp. of the western U. S.

cow'catch'er (kou'kăch'ẽr), *n. U. S.* A strong inclined frame in front of a locomotive for throwing off cattle or other obstructions; a pilot.

cow'er (kou'ẽr), *v. i.* [ME. *couren.*] To crouch or shrink quivering, as from cold or fear; to quail. — **Syn.** See FAWN.

cow'fish' (kou'fĭsh'), *n.; pl.,* see FISH. **1. a** Any of various small cetaceans, as the grampus and species of porpoises and dolphins. **b** A sirenian, as the manatee. **2.** Any of various trunkfishes with hornlike projections over the eyes.

cow'hage, cow'age (kou'ĭj), *n.* Also **cow'itch** (kou'ĭch). [Hind. *kāvāc,* fr. Skr. *kapikacchu.*] A tropical woody vine (*Mucuna,* syn. *Stizolobium, pruritum*) of the pea family, having pods covered with barbed hairs which cause intolerable itching.

cow'herd' (kou'hûrd'), *n.* One who tends cows.

cow'hide' (-hīd'), *n.* **1.** The hide of a cow, or leather from it. **2.** A coarse whip made of rawhide or braided leather. — *v. t.* To flog with a cowhide. — **cow'hid'ing** (-hīd'ĭng), *n.*

cowl (koul), *n.* [AS. *cuhle, cugle, cugele,* fr. L. *cucullа, cucullus,* hood.] **1. a** A monk's hood. **b** A similar covering for the head; a hood. **2.** An elaborate chimney pot to improve drafts. **3. a** In an automobile, the top portion of the front part of the body forward of the front doors, to which are attached the windshield and instrument board. Cf. HOOD, 5. **b** Cowling. — *v. t.* **1.** To garb with a cowl; to make monkish. **2.** To cover with, or as with, a cowl.

cowled (kould *or, as in poetry,* kou'lĕd), *adj.* **1.** Wearing a cowl; hooded. **2.** *Bot. & Zool.* Hooded; hood-shaped.

cow'lick' (kou'lĭk'), *n.* A tuft of hair turned up or awry (usually over the forehead), as if licked by a cow.

cowl'ing (koul'ĭng), *n. Aeronautics.* A removable metal covering which houses the engine and, sometimes, also a portion of the fuselage or of the nacelle. See AIRPLANE, *Illust.*

cowl'staff' (koul'stăf'), *n.* [*cowl* a vessel + *staff.*] *Dial.* A staff on which a vessel is borne between two persons.

cow'man (kou'măn), *n.* A cattle owner; also, a workman who rears and tends cattle.

co–work′er (kō·wûr′kẽr), *n.* One who works with another.
cow′pea′ (kou′pē′), *n.* **1.** A sprawling herb (*Vigna sinensis*) of the pea family, more nearly related to the bean than to the pea, widely cultivated in southern U. S. for forage and green manure. **2.** The seed of this plant, used often for food.
Cow′per's gland (kou′pẽrz; kōō′pẽrz; *the name was originally pronounced* kōō′pẽr). [After the discoverer, William *Cowper*, Eng. surgeon.] Either of two small glands discharging into the male urethra.
cow pony. A horse used in herding cattle. *Western U. S.*
cow′pox′ (kou′pŏks′), *n. Med.* A pustular eruptive disease of the cow, which, when communicated to the human system, as by vaccination, protects from the smallpox; vaccinia. Cf. VACCINE.
cow′punch′er (-pŭn′chẽr), *n. Colloq., U. S.* A cowboy.
cow′rie, cow′ry (kou′rĭ), *n.; pl.* COWRIES (-rĭz). [Hind. *kaurī.*] The shell of a marine gastropod (genus *Cypraea*), used as money in Africa and some Asiatic countries.
cow′slip (kou′slĭp), *n.* [AS. *cūslyppe.*] **1.** In Great Britain, a primrose (*Primula veris*) with yellow flowers appearing in early spring. **2.** *U. S.* = MARSH MARIGOLD. **3.** = SHOOTING STAR, 2. **4.** Usually ***Virginia cowslip.*** A smooth erect herb (*Mertensia virginica*, of the borage family) of eastern North America, having entire leaves and showy blue flowers, pink in bud.
cox (kŏks), *n.; pl.* COXES (kŏk′sĕz; -sĭz). *Colloq.* Short for COXSWAIN. — *v. i. & t.* To act as coxswain (to).
cox′a (kŏk′sȧ), *n.; pl.* COXAE (-sē). [L., hip, angle.] *Anat.* The hip or hip joint.
cox·al′gi·a (kŏk·săl′jĭ·ȧ), *n.* Also **cox′al′gy** (kŏk′săl′jĭ). [NL., fr. *coxa* + *-algia.*] *Med.* Pain in the hip. — **cox·al′gic** (kŏk·săl′jĭk), *adj.*
cox′comb′ (kŏks′kōm′), *n.* [Corrupt. of *cock's comb.*] **1.** A strip of red cloth, notched like the comb of a cock, which licensed jesters formerly wore in their caps; also, the jester's cap with a coxcomb. **2.** *Humorous.* The top of the head, or the head itself. **3.** A conceited, silly man; a fop. **4.** *Bot.* A cockscomb. — **cox′comb′ry** (kŏks′kōm′rĭ), *n.*
cox·comb′i·cal (kŏks·kōm′ĭ·kăl; -kŏm′-), *adj.* Also, *Rare*, **cox·com′i·cal** (-kŏm′ĭ·kăl), *adj.* Like a coxcomb; foppish; vain.
cox′swain, cock′swain (kŏk′s'n; kŏk′swān), *n.* [*cock* cockboat + *swain.*] The steersman of a ship's boat, a racing shell, or the like.
Cox′well chair (kŏks′wĕl; -wĕl). = COGSWELL CHAIR.
coy (koi), *adj.* [OF. *coi*, fr. *quei*, deriv. of L. *quietus* quiet.] **1.** *Obs.* Disdainful. **2.** Shrinking modestly or coquettishly from familiarity; shy; — usually applied to women. — **Syn.** See SHY. — **Ant.** Pert. — *v. t. Obs.* **1.** To soothe. **2.** To caress; to stroke. — *v. i. Archaic.* To behave with coyness. — **coy′ly**, *adv.* — **coy′ness**, *n.*
coy′ote (kī′ōt; kī·ō′tē), *n.* See PLURAL, *Note*, 3. [Amer. Sp., fr. Nahuatl *coyotl.*] A small wolf (*Canis latrans*) of western North America; the prairie wolf. See WOLF, 1 **a**.
Coyote State. South Dakota; — a nickname.
co′yo·til′lo (kō′yō·tēl′yō; kī′ō-), *n.* [Mex. Sp. dim. See COYOTE.] A poisonous shrub (*Karwinskia humboldtiana*, of the buckthorn family) of southwestern U. S. and Mexico.
coy′pu (koi′pōō), *n.* [Sp. *coipu*, fr. Araucan *coypu.*] **1.** A South American aquatic rodent (*Myocastor coypus*) with webbed hind feet; the nutria. **2.** The fur of this rodent; — usually called *nutria.*
coz (kŭz), *n. Colloq.* Short for COUSIN.
coze (kōz), *v. i.* To have a friendly chat. — *n.* A friendly chat.
coz′en (kŭz′'n), *v. t. & i.* [F. *cousiner*, fr. *cousin*, hence, lit., to deceive through pretext of relationship.] To cheat; to defraud, usually in a petty way. — **Syn.** See CHEAT. — **coz′en·er**, *n.*
coz′en·age (-ĭj), *n.* **1.** The art or practice of cozening; fraud. **2.** An act of deceit or fraud.
co′zy, co′sy (kō′zĭ), *adj.;* CO′ZI·ER, CO′SI·ER (-zĭ·ẽr); CO′ZI·EST, CO′SI·EST. Also **co′zey, co′sey, co′zie, co′sie.** [Scot. *cozie, cosie.*] **1.** Snug; comfortable. **2.** [See COZE.] *Eng.* Chatty; talkative. — **Syn.** See COMFORTABLE. — **co′zi·ly**, *adv.* — **co′zi·ness**, *n.*
co′zy, co′sy, co′sey, *n.* A padded covering for a teapot or other vessel to keep the contents hot.
C Q (sē′ kū′). *Radio.* The general call used at the beginning of radiograms of general information, safety notices, etc.
craal (kräl). Var. of KRAAL.
crab (krăb), *n.* [AS. *crabba.*] **1. a** Any of numerous marine or land crustaceans, constituting the suborder Brachyura (order Decapoda), distinguished by the short, broad, and usually flattened carapace, the small abdomen, which is curled up beneath the body and fits into a depression under the thorax, and the short antennae. Common crabs include: the ***swimming crabs***, as the ***blue crab*** (genus *Callinectes*) of the Atlantic and Gulf coasts of U. S. and the ***lady crab*** (*Ovalipes ocellatus* of U. S. Atlantic coast and *Portunus puber* of England); ***rock crabs*** (esp. *Cancer irroratus* and *C. borealis* of northeastern coasts of North America); the edible ***green, or shore, crab*** (*Carcinides maenas*) of Europe and America; the edible ***stone crab*** (*Menippe mercenaria*) of southern coast of U. S.; ***beach, or sand, crabs***, which live in holes on sandy seashores, including the ***sprite, or white crab*** (*Ocypode*, esp. *O. arenaria* of America) and the ***fiddler, or calling, crab*** (*Uca*, esp. *U. minax* of New England); the very small ***pea crabs*** (*Pinnotheres*, esp. *P. pisum* of Europe) living as commensals in bivalves; the ***spider crabs*** (of the superfamily Oxyrrhyncha) including the Japanese ***giant crab*** (*Macrocheira kampferi*) measuring about one foot across the shell but sometimes more than 10 feet across with legs extended; the ***land crabs*** of warm coasts and islands, including many large edible species, as *Gecarcinus ruricola* of the West Indies. In the U. S., local usage distinguishes between ***hard-shelled, or hard-shell, crab***, one which has not recently shed its shell, and ***soft-shelled, or soft-shell, crab***, which has recently shed its hard shell and has a new soft shell, the principal commercial soft-shelled crab being the blue crab *Callinectes sapidus* common from Texas to Delaware. **b** Any of various other crustaceans resembling true crabs in the more or less reduced condition of the abdomen, esp. members of the group Anomura, including the *hermit crab* and *purse crab* (see these terms). Cf. KING CRAB. **2.** [*cap.*] *Astron.* The zodiacal sign and constellation Cancer, between Gemini and Leo. **3.** *Mach.* Any of various machines for raising heavy weights, orig. a machine with claws. — ***to catch a crab.*** *Rowing.* A phrase used of a rower upset or partly unseated, either when he fails to raise the oar clear of the water on the recovery, or when he misses the water altogether in making a stroke. — *v. i.;* CRABBED (krăbd); CRAB′BING. To hunt for or catch crabs.

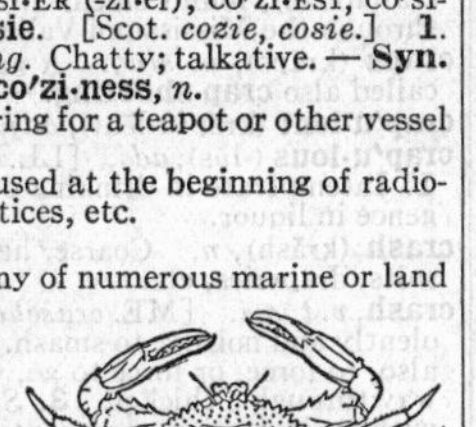

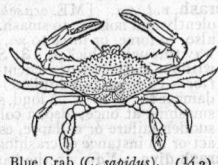

Blue Crab (*C. sapidus*). (1/2)

crab, *n.* [Perh. fr. 1st CRAB.] **1.** A crab apple. **2.** A sour or crabbed, ill-tempered person. — *adj.* Sour.
crab, *v. t. & i.* [MD. *crabben.*] **1.** Of hawks, to scratch or claw; to fight. **2.** *Colloq.* To find fault with. **3.** To head (an airplane) by means of the rudder into a cross wind to counteract drift. — *n.* Apparent sidewise motion of an airplane headed into a cross wind.
crab apple. Also **crab**, *n.* **1.** A small wild sour apple. **2.** An apple of a cultivated variety having small, acid fruit.
crab′bed (krăb′ĕd; -ĭd), *adj.* [From CRAB the animal.] **1.** Characterized by, or manifesting, a peevish, morose, or sour temper; cross. **2.** Obscure or intricate; difficult; as, a *crabbed* author. **3.** Cramped; irregular; as, *crabbed* handwriting. — **Syn.** See SULLEN. — **crab′bed·ly**, *adv.* — **crab′bed·ness**, *n.*
crab′ber (krăb′ẽr), *n.* One whose occupation is catching crabs; also, a kind of boat used in crab fishing.
crab′ber, *n.* One who carps or complains.
crab′by (-ĭ), *adj.* Crabbed; cross; ill-natured.
crab grass. A grass (esp. *Digitaria sanguinalis*) with creeping or decumbent stems which root freely at the nodes.
crab′stick′ (krăb′stĭk′), *n.* **1.** A stick, cane, or cudgel, of crab-tree wood. **2.** A crabbed, ill-natured person.
crab tree. A crab-apple tree.
crack (krăk), *v. i.* [AS. *cracian.*] **1.** To make a sharp, sudden sound in or as in breaking. **2. a** *Now Dial.* To brag; to boast. **b** *Scot. & N. of Eng.* To chat; to gossip. **3.** To fail in sound; become discordant or harsh; to break; as, his voice *cracked.* **4.** To break, with or without separation into parts. **5.** *Slang.* To fail; to break down. — *v. t.* **1.** To break or burst, as something brittle or hollow, with a sharp or explosive sound. **2.** Hence: **a** To rend or burst, as with grief or pain. **b** To open and drink; as, to *crack* a bottle of wine. **c** To damage irreparably, as a reputation. **3.** To utter smartly and strikingly, as a joke. **4. a** *Slang.* To hit; slap. **b** To cause to make a sharp noise; as, to *crack* a whip. **5.** To cause to crack, as the voice. **6.** To subject (petroleum) to cracking. **7.** *Colloq.* To cry up; to extol; to praise; — usually with *up.* — ***to crack a crib.*** *Thieves' Slang.* To break into a house, store, etc. — ***crack down.*** *Slang, U. S.* To inflict a sudden punitive or retributive blow, often designed to coerce into obedience. — ***crack up.*** *Slang.* To collapse or crash from strain, collision, faulty landing, etc., as an airplane; to cause (an airplane) to so crack up; hence, to collapse, break down, go to pieces. — *n.* **1.** A sharp, sudden sound, as of anything burst or broken. **2.** Hence: **a** *Colloq.* A shot as with a rifle. **b** *Colloq.* The time a crack lasts; an instant. **c** *Colloq.* A sharp resounding blow. **d** *Slang.* An experimental attempt; a try. **e** *Slang.* A gibing retort; a quip. **3. a** *Archaic & Dial.* A boast; boasting. **b** *Colloq.* A thing or person fit to be boasted of; a racer, athlete, vessel, etc., of superior excellence. **c** *Scot. & Dial. Eng.* Talk; gossip. **4.** A break or breaking; as: **a** A chink; crevice. **b** Rupture; flaw. **c** The breaking or broken tone of the voice, as when changed at puberty. **d** Mental flaw; partial insanity. **5.** *Thieves' Slang.* A burglar; also, burglary.
— *adv.* With a crack or cracking sound.
— *adj.* Of superior excellence; as, a *crack* ship.
crack′a·jack′ (krăk′ȧ·jăk′), *adj. Slang.* Of striking ability or excellence. — **crack′a·jack′**, *n. Slang.*
crack′brain′ (-brān′), *n.* A crackbrained or crazy person.
crack′brained′ (-brānd′; 2), *adj.* Crazy; reasonless.
crack′down′ (-doun′), *n.* Act or instance of cracking down. *Slang, U. S.*
cracked (krăkt), *adj.* **a** Broken; fractured. **b** *Colloq.* Crackbrained. **c** Of the voice, marked by discordant notes.
crack′er (krăk′ẽr), *n.* **1.** One who or that which cracks. **2.** Formerly, a boaster; a braggart. **3.** A firecracker. **4.** A round paper favor holder containing an explosive which discharges when the ends are pulled; — called also **cracker bonbon.** **5.** The snapping part at the end of a whiplash; a snapper. **6.** *U. S.* One of the lower class of the white population of the southern United States, esp. of Georgia and Florida, inhabiting the backwoods; — a nickname. **7.** A dry, usually thin biscuit, often hard or crisp. Cf. BISCUIT, 1.
crack′er·jack′ (-jăk′). Var. of CRACKAJACK.
Cracker State. Georgia; — a nickname.
crack′ing (krăk′ĭng), *n.* A process in which the complex hydrocarbons composing petroleum or other similar oils are broken up by heat and, usually, pressure into lighter hydrocarbons of simpler molecular formulas. Cracking is used in producing commercial gasoline, and in enriching illuminating gas.
crack′le (krăk′'l), *v. i.;* CRACK′LED (-'ld); CRACK′LING (-lĭng). [Dim. of *crack.*] To make small, sharp, sudden and repeated noises. — *v. t.* To crack or break with slight crushing rapidly repeated. — *n.* **1.** The noise of slight and frequent cracks; a crackling. **2.** *Fine Arts.* A peculiar cracked surface (the same as "craze," but made deliberately) common in much Oriental porcelain; also, ware (**crack′le·ware′** [-wâr′]) having such a surface.
crack′ling (-lĭng), *n.* **1.** The making of small, sharp cracks or reports. **2.** The crisp rind of roasted pork. **3.** Usually *pl. Dial.* The crisp residue of fat, esp. hogs' fat, after the lard or fat has been removed; also, corn bread containing it.
crack′ly (-lĭ), *adj.* Inclined to crackle; crisp and brittle.
crack′nel (-nĕl; -n'l), *n.* [F. *craquelin*, fr. D. *krakeling.*] **1.** A hard, brittle kind of biscuit. **2.** Crackling (sense 3).
crack′pot′ (krăk′pŏt′), *n.* A crackbrain. — **crack′pot′**, *adj.*
cracks′man (krăks′măn), *n. Slang.* A housebreaker or burglar; one who cracks safes.
crack′–up′ (krăk′ŭp′), *n.* Act or instance of cracking up, as of an airplane.
-cra·cy (-krȧ·sĭ). [Gr. *kratos* strength, rule.] A combining form meaning *a* (specified) *type of government, sway, ruling power*, or *authority*, as in autocracy, plutocracy, etc.
cra′dle (krā′d'l), *n.* [AS. *cradel, cradol.*] **1.** A bed or cot for a baby, usually on rockers or pivots; hence, place of origin or nurture. **2.** A support suggestive of a baby's cradle; as: **a** A supporting or protecting framework of bars, rods, etc. **b** A low frame on casters, used by mechanics to support themselves while working under an automobile; a coaster. **3.** *Aeronautics.* A support for a rigid airship or a semirigid airship during construction. **4.** *Agric.* A kind of attachment of fin-

gerlike rods to a scythe; also, a scythe (**cradle scythe**) with such an attachment. **5.** *Mining.* A rocking device used in washing out auriferous earth by hand; — called also *rocker.* **6.** *Naut.* A framework of timbers, or iron frames, used to support, lift, or carry ships or other vessels, heavy guns, etc.
— *v. t.;* CRA'DLED (-d'ld); CRA'DLING (-dlĭng). **1.** To place, lay to rest, or rock, in or as in a cradle. **2.** To nurse or train in infancy. **3.** To mow with a cradle scythe, as grain. **4.** To place, raise, support, or transport on a cradle. **5.** *Mining.* To wash in a cradle. — *v. i.* **1.** To lie or lodge as in a cradle. **2.** To mow grain with a cradle scythe.
cra'dle-song' (krā'd'l-sŏng'; 74), *n.* = BERCEUSE.
craft (kráft; 9), *n.* [AS. *cræft* strength, skill, cunning.] **1.** Art or skill; hence, an occupation requiring this; a manual art; a trade, business, or profession. **2.** Those engaged in any trade, taken collectively; a guild. **3.** Cunning, art, or skill, in a bad sense; guile. **4.** *Aeronautics.* An aircraft, or aircraft collectively. **5.** *Naut.* A vessel; vessels of any kind. — **Syn.** See ART.
crafts'man (kráfts'măn), *n.; pl.* -MEN (-mĕn). [*craft's* + *man.*] **1.** One who practices some trade or manual occupation; an artisan. **2.** A person, as a writer or artist, skilled in the mechanics of his craft. — **crafts'man·ship,** *n.*
craft union. *Labor.* A union whose members are all of one trade or calling; — called also *horizontal union.* Cf. INDUSTRIAL UNION.
craft'y (kráf'tĭ), *adj.;* CRAFT'I·ER (-tĭ·ĕr); CRAFT'I·EST. **1.** *Archaic.* Skillful; ingenious. **2.** Skillful at deceiving others; cunning; wily. — **Syn.** See SLY. — **craft'i·ly,** *adv.* — **craft'i·ness,** *n.*
crag (krăg), *n.* [Of Celt. origin.] A steep, rugged rock; a rough, broken cliff or projecting rock. — **crag'ged** (krăg'ĕd; -ĭd), *adj.* — **crag'gi·ness,** *n.* — **crag'gy** (-ĭ), *adj.*
crag (krăg; *dial.* kràg), *n. Now Dial.* The neck or throat.
crags'man (krăgz'măn), *n.; pl.* -MEN (-mĕn). One accustomed to, or expert in, climbing crags or cliffs.
crake (krāk), *n.* See PLURAL, *Note,* 3. Any of various rails, esp. the land rail (or ***corn crake***) and other short-billed kinds (as the sora and other species of *Porzana*). See RAIL.
cram (krăm), *v. t.;* CRAMMED (krămd); CRAM'MING. [AS. *crammian.*] **1.** To press, force, or drive, esp. in filling, or in thrusting one thing into another; to stuff. **2.** To fill with or as with food to satiety. **3.** *Slang.* To fill the mind of (a person), as with false stories. **4.** *Colloq.* To put (a person) hastily through a course of study as in preparation for examination. — *v. i.* **1.** To eat greedily; stuff. **2.** *Colloq.* To cram a subject, as for examination. — (krăm; kràm), *n.* **1.** *Colloq.* A crammed or overcrowded state. **2.** *Colloq.* Act of cramming, as for examination; also, the information so acquired. — **cram'mer,** *n.*
cram'bo (krăm'bō), *n.* **1.** A game in which one person or group gives a word, to which another finds a rhyme. **2.** *Derogatory.* A word rhyming with another.
cram'oi·sy, cram'oi·sie (krăm'oi·zĭ; -ĕ·zĭ), *adj.* [F. *cramoisi,* ult. fr. Ar. *qirmiz* kermes. See CRIMSON.] *Archaic.* Crimson. — *n. Archaic.* Crimson cloth.
cramp (krămp), *n.* [OF. *crampe,* fr. MD. *crampe, cramp.*] *Med.* **a** Spasmodic and painful involuntary contraction of a muscle or muscles. **b** A paralysis of certain muscles due to excessive use; as, writer's *cramp.* **c** Sharp abdominal pains; — usually in *pl.*
cramp, *n.* [MD. *crampe, cramp,* cramp iron, spasm.] **1.** A device, usually of iron bent at the ends, used to hold together blocks of stone, timbers, etc. **2.** A clamp. **3.** A restraining or restricting force, influence, etc.; a restraint. — *v. t.* **1.** To cause to have a cramp. **2.** To compress; to restrain from free action. **3.** To turn (the front wheels of a vehicle) sharply out of line with the rear wheels, as in making a turn. **4.** To fasten or hold with or as with a cramp. — *adj.* **1.** Knotty; difficult. **2.** Contracted; confined.
cramp'fish' (-fĭsh'), *n.; pl.,* see FISH. See 1st RAY.
cram'pon (krăm'pŏn), *n.* Also **cram·poon'** (krăm·po͞on'). [F. *crampon,* of Teut. origin.] **1.** A form of hooked clutch or dog for raising stones, lumber, blocks of ice, etc.; — usually in *pl.* **2.** A climbing iron; — usually in *pl.*

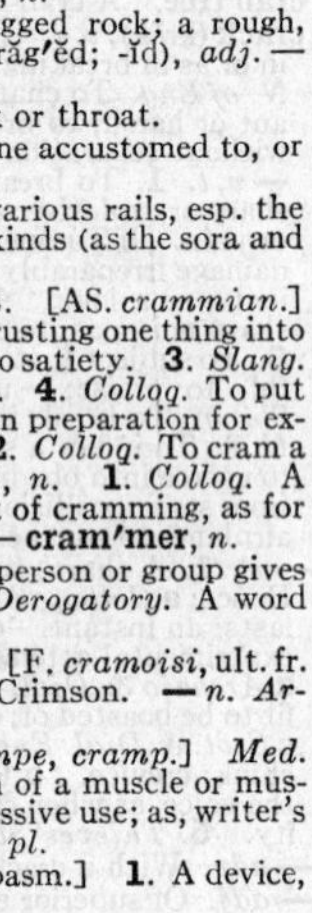
Crampon, 1.

cran'ber'ry (krăn'bĕr'ĭ; -bĕr·ĭ), *n.* [LG. *kranbere.* See CRANE; BERRY.] **1.** The bright-red, acid berry of a plant (genus *Vaccinium*) of the heath family; also, the plant. The European cranberry (*V. palustris*) is known in U. S. as the ***small cranberry***, to distinguish it from *V. macrocarpus,* the ***large cranberry*** or *crowberry.* Cranberries are grown in low, periodically flooded areas, called **cranberry bogs. 2.** Any of various plants, or their berries, resembling the true cranberry; as: **a** The cranberry tree or ***bush cranberry***, a North American and European tree or shrub (*Viburnum trilobum*) of the honeysuckle family. See GUELDER-ROSE. **b** The ***mountain cranberry***, a dwarf variety (*Vaccinium vitis-idaea minus*) of the cowberry.
crane (krān), *n.* See PLURAL, *Note,* 3. [AS. *cran.*] **1.** A bird (family Gruidae, order Gruiformes), of a group of tall wading birds superficially resembling the herons, but structurally more nearly related to the rails; as, the ***sandhill crane*** (*Grus canadensis tabida*) of eastern and central North America. **2.** *U. S.* Also ***blue crane.*** The great blue heron (see HERON). **3.** A machine for raising, shifting, and lowering heavy weights, commonly by means of a projecting swinging arm. **4.** Any arm which swings about a vertical axis at one end, used for supporting a weight. — *v. t. & i.* **1.** To raise or lift by or as by a crane. **2.** To stretch (the neck) as a crane does. **3.** In hunting, to stop at an obstacle and look over it before leaping; hence, to hesitate.
crane fly. Any of numerous long-legged, slender, two-winged flies (family Tipulidae), which resemble large mosquitoes, but do not bite.
crane's'-bill', cranes'bill' (krānz'bĭl'), *n.* See GERANIUM, 1.
cra'ni·al (krā'nĭ·ăl), *adj.* Of or pertaining to the skull. — **cra'ni·al·ly,** *adv.*
cra'ni·ate (-āt), *adj. Zool.* Having a skull or cranium, as the mammals, birds, reptiles, amphibians, and fishes (*Craniata*). — *n.* A cranite animal.
cra'ni·o- (krā'nĭ·ō-). [Gr. *kranion* skull.] A combining form denoting: **a** *The cranium,* as in *craniology.* **b** *Cranial and,* as in **cra'ni·o·fa'cial** (-fā'shăl), of or pert. to the cranium and the face.
cra'ni·ol'o·gy (krā'nĭ·ŏl'ō·jĭ), *n.* [*cranio-* + *-logy.*] The science dealing with variations in size, shape, and proportions of the cranium, esp. with the variations characterizing the different races of men. Cf. CRANIOMETRY. — **cra'ni·o·log'i·cal** (-ō·lŏj'ĭ·kăl), *adj.* — **cra'ni·o·log'i·cal·ly,** *adv.* — **cra·ni·ol'o·gist** (-ŏl'ō·jĭst), *n.*
cra'ni·om'e·ter (-ŏm'ē·tĕr), *n.* [*cranio-* + *-meter.*] An instrument for measuring skulls.
cra'ni·om'e·try (-ŏm'ē·trĭ), *n.* The science of measuring the skull, esp. for determining the dimensions and proportions characterizing race, sex, and developmental stages. Cf. CEPHALIC INDEX, FACIAL ANGLE, GNATHIC INDEX. — **cra'ni·o·met'ric** (-ō·mĕt'rĭk), *adj.* — **cra'ni·o·met'ri·cal** (-rĭ·kăl), *adj.* — **cra'ni·o·met'ri·cal·ly,** *adv.* — **cra'ni·om'e·trist** (-ŏm'ē·trĭst), *n.*
cra'ni·um (krā'nĭ·ŭm), *n.; pl.* CRANIUMS (-ŭmz), CRANIA (-ȧ). [ML., fr. Gr. *kranion.*] *Anat.* **a** The skull of a vertebrate. **b** Specif., the part of the skull enclosing the brain; brainpan.
crank (krăngk), *n.* [AS. *cranc.*] **1.** *Mach.* An arm keyed at right angles to the end of a shaft, by which motion is imparted to or received from it. **2.** *Obs.* Any bend, turn, or winding. **3.** A twist or turn in speech; also, anything fantastic in action, manner, etc. **4.** A caprice; whim; crotchet; also, *Colloq.,* a crotchety person. — *v. t.* **1.** To bend into the shape of a crank. **2.** To furnish or fasten with a crank. **3.** To move or operate by a crank; specif., to start the engine of (an automobile, etc.) by use of a crank. — *v. i.* **1.** To wind and turn; to zigzag. **2.** To turn a crank.

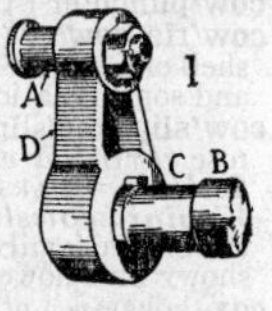

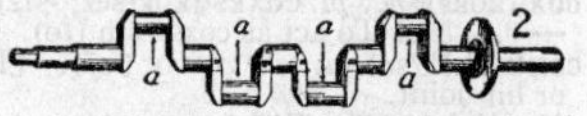

1 Single Overhung Crank. *A* Crankpin; *B* Crankshaft; *C* Journal; *D* Web. 2 Crankshaft with four Double Cranks. *a, a, a, a* Crankpins.

crank, *adj.* [Partly fr. D. *krank* sick, weak.] **1.** Out of gear; loose; shaky. **2.** [D. *krengen* to careen.] *Naut.* Of a vessel, easily inclined by any external force, as of the wind on the sails.
crank, *adj. Dial. & U. S.* Full of spirit; sprightly; hence, aggressively confident; cocky.
crank'case' (krăngk'kās'), *n.* The case or covering of the crankshaft of an engine, as in an automobile.
cran'kle (krăng'k'l), *n. & v.* Bend; turn.
crank'pin' (krăngk'pĭn'), *n.* Also **crank pin.** *Mach.* The cylindrical piece which forms the handle of a crank, or to which the connecting rod is attached. See CRANK, *Illust.*
crank'shaft' (-shaft'; 9), *n.* A shaft turning, or driven by, a crank. See CRANK, *Illust.*
crank'y (krăngk'ĭ), *adj.;* CRANK'I·ER (-ĭ·ĕr); CRANK'I·EST. **1.** Out of gear or order; shaky. **2.** Irritable; also, eccentric; crotchety. **3.** *Naut.* Liable to heel; crank. — **Syn.** See IRASCIBLE. — **crank'i·ly,** *adv.* — **crank'i·ness,** *n.*
cran'nied (krăn'ĭd), *adj.* Having crannies, or chinks.
cran'nog (krăn'ŏg), *n.* Erroneously also **cran'noge** (-ŏj). [Ir. *crannog,* Gael. *crannag.*] *Scot. & Ir. Antiq.* An island refuge, in a lake or bog. Cf. LAKE DWELLING.
cran'ny (krăn'ĭ), *n.; pl.* -NIES (-ĭz). [F. *cran, cren,* notch.] A small, narrow cleft; a crevice, as in a wall.
cran'reuch (krăn'rŭĸ), *n. Scot.* Hoarfrost.
crape (krāp), *n.* [F. *crêpe,* fr. OF. *crespe* curled, crisped, fr. L. *crispus.*] **1.** Crepe (def. 1). **2.** Black crepe used for a special purpose, as to show mourning; also, a piece of this material. See CREPE, 2. — *v. t. Obs.* To crimp (the hair).
crape myrtle. An ornamental flowering East Indian shrub (*Lagerstroemia indica*) commonly cultivated in the southern U. S.
crap'pie (krăp'ĭ; krŏp'ĭ), *n.; pl.* CRAPPIES (-ĭz), sometimes CRAPPIE. A North American fresh-water fish (*Pomoxis annularis,* family Centrarchidae), found chiefly in the Great Lakes region and southward through the Mississippi Valley.
craps (krăps), *n. sing.* A gambling game played with two dice; — called also **crap shooting.** — **crap'shoot'er** (krăp'sho͞ot'ĕr), *n.*
crap'u·lent (krăp'ū·lĕnt), *adj.* Crapulous. — **crap'u·lence** (-lĕns), *n.*
crap'u·lous (-lŭs), *adj.* [LL. *crapulosus,* fr. L. *crapula* intoxication.] **1.** Intemperate in drinking or eating. **2.** Sick from excessive indulgence in liquor.
crash (krăsh), *n.* Coarse, heavy linen fabric, as for towels, summer suits, draperies, etc.
crash, *v. t. & i.* [ME. *craschen,* of imitative origin.] **1.** To break violently and noisily; to smash. **2.** To cause to crash, or sound noisily; also, to force, or force to go, with a crashing noise; as, to *crash* one's way through a thicket. **3.** *Slang, U. S.* To intrude upon by entering without invitation or credentials; as, to *crash* a dance. **4.** *Aeronautics.* To bring (an airplane) down in such a manner that the craft is damaged. — *n.* **1.** A loud, sudden, confused sound, as of many things smashing at once; also, a collision, or the shock of a collision. **2.** A sudden failure or collapse, esp. of a business. **3.** *Aeronautics.* The act or an instance of crashing. — **crash'er,** *n.*
crash dive. *Nav.* In the handling of submarines, a dive made in the least possible time.
cra'sis (krā'sĭs), *n.; pl.* -SES (-sēz). [NL., fr. Gr. *krasis* a mixing, combination.] Constitution; temperament.
crass (krăs), *adj.* [L. *crassus* thick, fat, gross.] **1.** *Now Rare.* Gross; coarse. **2.** Very stupid; unrefined. — **Syn.** See STUPID. — **crass'ly,** *adv.* — **crass'ness,** *n.*
cras'si·tude (krăs'ĭ·tūd), *n.* Grossness.
cras'su·la'ceous (krăs'ū·lā'shŭs), *adj.* [From NL. *Crassula,* type genus, dim. fr. L. *crassus* thick.] *Bot.* Belonging to the orpine family (Crassulaceae). See ORPINE.
-crat (-krăt). [F. *-crate* (after Gr. *-kratēs*).] A combining form meaning *a partisan* or *member of a class* or *type of government,* as in demo*crat,* pluto*crat.*
cratch (krăch; *dial. also* kràch, krăch), *n.* [OF. *creche,* of Teut. origin.] **1.** *Now Dial.* A crib or rack, esp. for fodder. **2.** *Archaic.* The manger at Bethlehem. Cf. CRÈCHE.
crate (krāt), *n.* [L. *cratis* hurdle.] **1.** A large wicker basket or hamper. **2.** A container, as for fruits, with open spaces to provide ventilation. — *v. t.* To pack in a crate. — **crat'er** (krāt'ĕr), *n.*
cra'ter (krā'tĕr), *n.* [L., fr. Gr. *kratēr,* fr. *kerannynai* to mix.] **1.** *Class. Antiq.* A jar or vase typically with large round body, wide mouth, small handles, and a base; — in this sense usually spelled ***kra'ter.*** Cf. AMPHORA, AMPULLA. **2.** *Geol.* The bowl-shaped depression around the mouth of a volcano or a geyser. **3.** *Mil.* A hole formed by the explosion of a mine or the like.

craunch (krănch; krônch), *v.t., v.i., & n.* Crunch.

cra·vat′ (krȧ·văt′), *n.* [F. *cravate*, fr *Cravate* a Croatian.] A necktie.

crave (krāv), *v.t.* [AS. *crafian.*] **1.** To ask earnestly; to beg, esp. as a favor. **2.** To long for; hence, to require; to need. — *v.i.* To desire strongly. — **Syn.** See DESIRE. — **crav′er** (krāv′ẽr), *n.*

cra′ven (krā′vĕn), *adj.* [OF. *cravant*, fr. L. *crepans*, pres. part. of *crepare* to break, crack.] Afraid; cowardly; also, *Obs.*, defeated. — **Syn.** See COWARDLY. — *n.* A confessed coward. — *v.t.* To make cowardly. — **cra′ven·ly**, *adv.* — **cra′ven·ness**, *n.*

Cra′ven·ette′ (krā′vĕn·ĕt′), *n.* A trade-mark for cloth (or sometimes leather) made waterproof by special chemical processes.

crav′ing (krāv′ĭng), *n.* Desire (for something); esp., an abnormal or excessive desire, as for a food or drug.

craw (krô), *n.* [ME. *crawe.*] **a** The crop of a bird or insect. See CROP, 1. **b** The stomach of an animal.

craw′fish′ (krô′fĭsh′), *n.; pl.*, see FISH. [See CRAYFISH.] A crayfish. — *v.i. Colloq., U.S.* To retreat from a position; to back out.

crawl (krôl), *v.i.* [ON. *krafla* to paw, scrabble with the hands.] **1.** To move slowly by drawing the body along the ground, as a worm; to creep (def. 1). **2.** To move or advance feebly, slowly, or timorously. **3.** Of plants, to creep (def. 3). **4.** To be swarming with a number of crawling things; also, to have a sensation as of insects creeping over the body. — **Syn.** See CREEP. — *n.* **1.** Act or motion of crawling; slow motion, like that of a creeping animal. **2.** *Swimming.* A racing stroke in which the swimmer, lying flat in the water with face submerged except for breathing intervals, propels himself by overarm strokes and a thrashing movement with the legs. — **crawl′er**, *n.* — **crawl′ing·ly**, *adv.*

crawl, *n.* [D. *kraal.*] An enclosure in shallow waters, used to confine or hold turtles, sponges, etc.

crawl′y (krôl′ĭ), *adj. Colloq.* Creepy.

cray′fish′ (krā′fĭsh′), **craw′fish′** (krô′-), *n.; pl.*, see FISH. [OF. *crevice* (F. *écrevisse*), of Teut. origin.] **1.** Any of numerous fresh-water crustaceans (family Astacidae), like the lobster, but much smaller. **2.** Also ***sea crayfish.*** See LOBSTER, 1.

cray′on (krā′ŏn), *n.* [F., fr. *craie* chalk, fr. L. *creta.*] **1.** A small rounded stick of chalk, graphite, or the like, for drawing, writing, or coloring. **2.** A drawing made with a crayon or crayons. — *v.t.* To draw or sketch with crayons.

craze (krāz), *v.t. & i.* [ME. *crasen* to break, fr. Scand.] **1.** *Obs.* To break; shatter. **2.** *Archaic.* To weaken or destroy, as health. **3.** To become or render insane. **4.** *Pottery.* To produce minute cracks on the surface or glaze of. Cf. CRACKLE, *n.*, 2. — *n.* **1.** *Obs.* A break; flaw. **2.** A transient infatuation, as for a new fashion; a mania. **3.** *Ceramics.* A crack in glaze or enamel. See CRACKLE, *n.*, 2. — **Syn.** See FASHION.

cra′zy (krā′zĭ), *adj.*; CRA′ZI·ER (-zĭ·ẽr); CRA′ZI·EST. **1.** Full of cracks or flaws; unsound. **2.** Insane; demented. **3.** *Colloq.* Distracted with eager desire, excitement, etc. — **cra′zi·ly**, *adv.* — **cra′zi·ness**, *n.*

crazy bone. = FUNNY BONE.

crazy quilt. A quilt with a covering made of pieces of cloth of various sizes, shapes, and colors sewed together; a patchwork quilt.

cra′zy·weed′ (krā′zĭ·wēd′), *n.* The locoweed.

creak (krēk), *v.i.* [ME. *creken* to croak.] To make a prolonged sharp grating or squeaking sound. — *v.t.* To cause to creak. — *n.* The sound produced by creaking. — **creak′i·ly**, *adv.* — **creak′i·ness**, *n.* — **creak′y**, *adj.*

cream (krēm), *n.* [OF. *cresme* (F. *crème*), fr. LL. *chrisma* chrism. See CHRISM.] **1.** The rich, oily, yellowish part of milk. **2.** Hence: **a** A fancy dish or confection prepared from cream, etc., or so as to resemble cream. **b** A creamlike emulsion or cosmetic. **c** A sirupy liqueur. Cf. CRÈME. **d** Creamed purée or stock; — with *of*; as, *cream* of celery soup. **3.** The choicest part of a thing. **4.** The color of cream; a color, reddish-yellow in hue, of low saturation and very high brilliance. See COLOR. — *adj.* **1.** Of, like, or for cream. **2.** Of the color cream. — *v.i.* To form or become covered with cream; to froth. — *v.t.* **1.** To draw off as cream; hence, to take the choicest part of. **2.** To skim the cream from, as milk. **3.** To furnish with or as with cream. **4.** To beat, as butter and sugar, till it is of a light creamy consistency.

cream cheese. An unripened cheese, similar to Neufchâtel, made from whole sweet milk enriched with cream.

cream′cups′ (krēm′kŭps′), *n. sing. & pl.* Any of several California annuals (esp. *Platystemon californicus*) of the poppy family.

cream′er (krēm′ẽr), *n.* **1.** A small pitcher or other vessel for holding cream. **2.** = SEPARATOR **a.**

cream′er·y (-ĭ), *n.; pl.* -ERIES (-ĭz). An establishment where butter and cheese are made or where milk and cream are sold or prepared for market.

cream of tartar. *Chem.* Purified tartar, a white crystalline substance, with a gritty, acid taste, used as an ingredient of baking powder, and as a cathartic, diuretic, and refrigerant. See 1st TARTAR, 1.

cream′y (krēm′ĭ), *adj.*; CREAM′I·ER (-ĭ·ẽr); CREAM′I·EST. Full of, or containing, cream; resembling cream. — **cream′i·ly**, *adv.* — **cream′i·ness**, *n.*

crease (krēs), *n.* [From *creast*, var. of CREST.] **1.** A line or mark made by folding any pliable substance; hence, a similar mark, however produced. **2.** *Cricket.* Any one of the lines marked on the ground at each end of the pitch to indicate the position of batsman (***popping crease***) or bowler (***bowling crease***); also, the space at either end between the popping and bowling creases. **3.** *Ice Hockey.* A rectangular area, bounded by lines in front of the goal cage, which attacking players are forbidden to enter except subject to certain special rules. — *v.t. & i.* To make a crease in or on; to wrinkle. — **creas′er** (krēs′ẽr), *n.* — **creas′y** (-ĭ), *adj.*

crease. Var. of CREESE.

cre·ate′ (krē·āt′), *adj.* [L. *creatus*, past part. of *creare* to create.] *Archaic.* Created. — *v.t.* **1.** To bring into being; to cause to exist. **2.** Hence: **a** To invest with a new form, office, or character; to constitute. **b** To produce, form, or bring to pass, by influence over others; as, to *create* a favorable opinion. **3.** To produce as a work of thought or imagination, esp. as a work of art. — **Syn.** See INVENT.

cre′a·tine (krē′ȧ·tēn; -tĭn), *n.* Also **cre′a·tin.** [Gr. *kreas* flesh.] *Biochem.* A white, crystalline, nitrogenous substance, $C_4H_9N_3O_2$, found in the muscles of vertebrates and in the brain, blood, etc.

cre·a′tion (krē·ā′shŭn), *n.* **1.** Act of creating, or fact of being created; specif., the act of causing to exist, or fact of being brought into existence, by divine power; esp., the act of bringing this world into existence out of nothing. **2.** Act of investing with a new character, title, or the like. **3.** The presentation of a new conception in an artistic embodiment. **4.** Something which is created. — **cre·a′tion·al** (-ăl; -′l), *adj.*

cre·a′tive (krē·ā′tĭv), *adj.* **1.** Having the power or quality of creating. **2.** Productive; — followed by *of.* — **-ly**, *adv.* — **-ness**, *n.*

cre·a′tor (-tẽr), *n.* One that creates, produces, or constitutes; specif. [*cap.*], the Supreme Being.

crea′tur·al (krē′tūr·ăl), *adj.* Of, pertaining to, or of the nature of a creature or creatures.

crea′ture (krē′tūr), *n.* [OF., fr. LL. *creatura.*] **1.** Anything created; anything not self-existent; esp.: **a** A living created being; an animal or a human being. **b** *Rural, U.S.* A domestic animal such as the horse or ox. **c** Something, as food or drink, that promotes the comfort of human beings. **d** (*pron.* krē′tẽr *or* krā′tẽr) *Dial. & Humorous.* Intoxicating liquor, esp. whisky. **2.** A servile dependent; a tool.

creature comfort. A thing, as food, which gives comfort.

crèche (krāsh; krĕsh), *n.* [F.] **1.** A day nursery. **2.** A foundling hospital. **3.** A representation of the stable at Bethlehem, with the infant Jesus surrounded by Mary, Joseph, the cattle, shepherds, and Magi. Cf. CRATCH.

cre′dence (krē′dĕns; -d′ns), *n.* [OF. *credence*, fr. ML. *credentia*, fr. L. *credens, -entis*, pres. part. of *credere* to trust, believe.] **1.** Belief; mental acceptance; credit. **2.** Source or warrant of confidence or credit; — now only in *letters of credence.* **3.** [F. *crédence*, fr. It. *credenza.* Orig., a table used for tasting to guard against poison.] A kind of Renaissance sideboard, used chiefly for valuable plate. **4.** *Eccl.* A small table beside the communion table, on which the bread and wine rest before being consecrated. — **Syn.** See BELIEF.

cre·den′da (krē·dĕn′dȧ), *n. pl.; sing.* CREDENDUM (-dŭm). [L., fr. *credere* to believe.] *Theol.* Doctrines to be believed; articles of faith; — disting. from *agenda.*

cre′dent (krē′dĕnt; -d′nt), *adj.* **1.** Giving credence; confiding. **2.** Having credit or repute; credible.

cre·den′tial (krē·dĕn′shăl), *adj.* Giving a title or claim to credit or confidence; accrediting; as, *credential* letters. — *n.* That which gives a title to credit or confidence; specif., *pl.*, accrediting testimonials.

cre·den′za (krē·dĕn′zȧ), *n.* [It.] **1.** = CREDENCE, 3. **2.** A sideboard, buffet, or bookcase patterned after the credence of the Renaissance, esp. one without legs whose base rests flat on the floor.

cred′i·ble (krĕd′ĭ·b′l), *adj.* Capable of being credited; worthy of belief; also, *Archaic*, exc. in "credible witness," entitled to confidence; trustworthy; reliable. — **Syn.** See PLAUSIBLE. — **cred′i·bil′i·ty** (-bĭl′ĭ·tĭ), *n.* — **cred′i·ble·ness**, *n.* — **cred′i·bly** (krĕd′ĭ·blĭ), *adv.*

cred′it (krĕd′ĭt), *n.* [F. *crédit*, fr. It. *credito*, fr. L. *creditus* (past part. of *credere* to trust), *creditum* a loan.] **1.** Reliance on the truth or reality of something; belief; faith. **2.** Quality of being believed or of being worthy of belief; trustworthiness. **3.** Reputation; now, favorable reputation. **4.** A source of honor; as, a *credit* to one's family. **5.** The balance in a person's favor in an account, as in a bank. **6.** Time given for payment for lands or goods sold on trust. **7.** A printed or spoken acknowledgment of the authorship, source, or ownership of material used in a publication, or in a play, motion picture, or radio program. **8.** *Accounting.* Opp. to *debit.* **a** A record of the reduction of a debt, as by entry on the right-hand side of an account. **b** Any one, or the sum, of the items on the right-hand side of an account, recording payments or other values received. **c** The right-hand side of an account, where such items are recorded. The abbreviation *Cr.* (for *creditor*) is written at the top of this side. **9.** *Com.* Trust given or received; expectation of future payment for property transferred; as, to buy goods on *credit.* **10.** *Educ.* Official certification of the completion of a course of study; also, a unit of academic work for which such acknowledgment is made. — **Syn.** See BELIEF; INFLUENCE.
— *v.t.* **1.** To confide in the truth of; to believe. **2.** To bring into credit; esp., *Archaic*, to bring honor upon. **3.** To give credit for; to attribute or ascribe *to* or *with.* **4.** *Bookkeeping.* To enter upon the right-hand (credit) side of an account; to give credit for. **5.** *Com.* To give credit to. **6.** *Educ.* To give a credit or credits to; — followed by *with.* — **Syn.** See ASCRIBE.

cred′it·a·ble (-ȧ·b′l), *adj.* Sufficiently good to bring esteem; deserving of praise. — **cred′it·a·bil′i·ty** (-bĭl′ĭ·tĭ), *n.* — **cred′it·a·bly** (-blĭ), *adv.*

credit line. A line, note, or name accompanying a news despatch, a published article, illustration, reproduction of a photograph or drawing, or the like, giving acknowledgment of the source.

cred′i·tor (krĕd′ĭ·tẽr), *n.* One who gives credit in business matters; hence, one to whom money is due; — correlative of *debtor.* Cf. CREDIT, *n.*, 8 **c.**

cre′do (krē′dō; krā′dō), *n.; pl.* CREDOS (-dōz). [L., I believe. See CREED.] A creed; a set of professed opinions; specif. [*cap.*], the Nicene Creed said or sung as a part of the Mass.

cre·du′li·ty (krē·dū′lĭ·tĭ), *n.; pl.* CREDULITIES (-tĭz). Belief or readiness of belief, esp. on slight evidence.

cred′u·lous (krĕd′ū·lŭs), *adj.* [L. *credulus*, fr. *credere* to believe.] **1.** Inclined to believe, esp. on slight evidence. **2.** Based upon, or proceeding from, credulity. — **-ly**, *adv.* — **-ness**, *n.*

Cree (krē), *n.; pl.* CREE, CREES (krēz). An Indian of an Algonquian tribe formerly of Manitoba and Saskatchewan.

creed (krēd), *n.* [AS. *crēda*, fr. L. *credo* I believe, at the beginning of the Apostles' and Nicene Creeds.] **1.** *Eccl.* A brief, authoritative formula of religious belief; specif., the Apostles', the Nicene, or the Athanasian Creed. ***The Creed*** usually means the Apostles' Creed. **2. a** Any formula or confession of religious faith. **b** A summary of principles or opinions professed or adhered to, in science, politics, etc.

creek (krēk; *dial. or colloq.* krĭk), *n.* [ME. *creke, crike*, fr. ON. *kriki.*] **1.** A small inlet or bay, narrower and extending farther inland than a cove. **2.** Hence, *Chiefly U.S.*, a stream of water smaller than a river and larger than a brook. Cf. BAYOU. **3.** *Dial.* A narrow or winding passage.

Creek (krēk), *n.* An Indian of a confederacy of tribes, mostly of Muskhogean stock, formerly occupying most of Alabama and Georgia, and parts of northern Florida.

creel (krēl), *n.* [OF. *creil.*] **1.** A wickerwork basket, as for fish. **2.** *Spinning.* A bar or set of bars with skewers for holding paying-off bobbins.

creep (krēp), *v.i.*; CREPT (krĕpt); CREEP′ING. [AS. *crēopan.*] **1.** To move along with the body prone and close to the ground or other surface, as a worm or reptile; to crawl; to move slowly on hands and knees. **2.** To move or advance slowly, timidly, or stealthily. **3.** *Bot.* To run or spread along or beneath the surface of the ground, commonly rooting at intervals, or to climb by means of aerial rootlets, tendrils, etc. **4.** To have a sensation as of insects creeping on the skin. **5.** To slip or become slightly displaced; specif., of metal rails, to shift longitudinally under traffic.

Syn. Creep, crawl mean to move across the ground or floor in a prone or crouching position. **Creep,** however, is used more often of quadrupeds or of human beings who move on all fours, often stealthily; **crawl,** of serpents, snakes, worms, and, sometimes, human beings who move by drawing the body along the ground or a surface. Figuratively, both imply intolerable slowness, but *creep* usually suggests insidious methods, and *crawl,* abjectness, cringing, and the like.

— *n.* **1.** A movement of or like creeping. **2.** A distressing sensation, like that occasioned by the creeping of insects; a feeling of apprehension or horror; — often *colloq.* in *pl., the creeps* or *the cold creeps.*

creep′er (krēp′ẽr), *n.* **1.** One that creeps, as an insect or reptile. **2.** A creeping plant; as, the Virginia *creeper* and trumpet *creeper* (see these terms). Cf. VINE. **3.** Any of various birds which creep about on trees, bushes, etc., searching for insects; as, the ***tree creepers*** (family Certhiidae) including the common European species (*Certhia familiaris*), its North American variety, the ***brown creeper*** (*C. f. americana*), and the ***wall creeper*** (*Tichodroma muraria*) of southern Asia, Europe and North Africa, and the ***honey creepers*** (family Coerebidae) of tropical America. **4.** Any of various tools, implements, etc.; as: **a** A grapnel. **b** = CLIMBING IRON. **c** A fixture with iron points worn on a shoe to prevent slipping. **d** Any device for causing material to move steadily from one part of a machine to another. **e** *Skiing.* A canvas strip with flaps, attachable to the bottom of the ski to prevent slipping backward in uphill climbing.

creep′ie (krēp′ĭ; krĭp′ĭ), *n.* *Dial.* A three-legged stool.

creeping eruption. A severe spreading dermatitis due to larval hookworms, of species not normally parasitic in man, penetrating the skin and wandering in the tissues immediately beneath it.

creep′y (krēp′ĭ), *adj.;* CREEP′I·ER (-ĭ·ẽr); CREEP′I·EST. **1.** Marked by creeping, or slow motion. **2.** Having or producing a sensation as if insects are creeping on the skin, or a feeling of nervous fear; crawly. — **creep′i·ness,** *n.*

creese (krēs), *n.* Also **kris** (krēs). [Malay *kris.*] A dagger used by the Malays, having a serpentine blade.

creesh (krēsh), *n. & v. t.* [OF. *creisse, cresse,* n.] *Scot.* Grease.

cre′mate (krē′māt; krē·māt′), *v. t.* [L. *crematus,* past part. of *cremare* to burn.] To burn; incinerate; as, to *cremate* a corpse. — **cre·ma′tion** (krē·mā′shŭn), *n.*

cre′ma·tor (krē′mā·tẽr; krē·mā′-), *n.* [LL.] **a** One who cremates corpses. **b** A crematory. **c** An incinerator for rubbish.

cre′ma·to′ry (krē′mȧ·tō′rĭ; krĕm′ȧ-; *or, esp. Brit.,* krĕm′ȧ·tẽr·ĭ), *n.; pl.* CREMATORIES (-rĭz). Also **crem′a·to′ri·um** (krĕm′ȧ·tō′rĭ·ŭm; krē′mȧ-); *pl.* CREMATORIUMS (-ŭmz); CREMATORIA (-ȧ). [NL. *crematorium.*] A furnace for cremating. — *adj.* Of, relating to, or employed in cremation.

‖**crème** (krâm), *n.* [F.] Cream; — used esp. in names of creamed dishes; also, a sirupy liqueur; as, **crème de menthe** (dē mäɴt′), flavored with mint, and **crème de ca′ca′o′** (kȧ′kȧ′ō′), flavored with the essential oil of the kola nut.

‖**crème de la crème** (dē lȧ krâm′). [F.] Cream of the cream; the very choicest.

Cre·mo′na (krē·mō′nȧ), *n.* A violin made in Cremona, Italy, in the 16th, 17th, and 18th centuries, esp. a Stradivarius or a Guarnerius or an Amati (see these terms).

cre′nate (krē′nāt), *adj.* [NL. *crenatus,* fr. *crena* a notch.] Having the margin cut into rounded scallops, as a leaf. — **cre′nate·ly,** *adv.* — **cre′nat·ed** (-nāt·ĕd; -ĭd), *adj.*

cre·na′tion (krē·nā′shŭn), *n.* **a** A crenate formation; a rounded projection, as on the edge of a leaf. **b** State or quality of being crenate.

cren′a·ture (krĕn′ȧ·tūr; krē′nȧ-), *n.* A crenation; also, sometimes, a notch or indentation, as between crenations.

cren′el (krĕn′ĕl), **cre·nelle′** (krē·nĕl′), *n.* [OF. *crenel,* fr. dim. of VL. *crena* a notch.] One of the openings alternating with the merlons in a battlement. See BARTIZAN, BATTLEMENT, *Illusts.* — *v. t.;* CREN′ELED (-ĕld) or -ELLED; CREN′EL·ING or -EL·LING. To crenelate.

cren′el·ate, cren′el·late (krĕn′ĕ·lāt), *v. t.* [F. *créneler* to indent. See CRENEL.] To furnish with battlements. — *adj.* Crenelated.

cren′el·at′ed, cren′el·lat′ed (-lāt′ĕd; -ĭd), *adj.* Having battlements.

cren′el·a′tion, cren′el·la′tion (-lā′shŭn), *n.* Act of crenelating, or state of being crenelated; hence, crenelated work.

cren′u·late (krĕn′ū·lāt), *adj.* [From *crenula,* dim. of *crena* notch.] Minutely crenate, as certain leaves.

cren′u·lat′ed (-lāt′ĕd; -ĭd), *adj.* Crenulate.

cren′u·la′tion (-lā′shŭn), *n.* **a** A minute crenation. **b** The state of being minutely crenate or scalloped.

cre′ole (krē′ōl), *n.* [F. *créole,* fr. Sp. *criollo,* fr. Pg. *crioulo,* fr. *criar* to bring up, fr. L. *creare* to produce.] **1.** [*usually cap.*] A person of French or Spanish descent born and reared in a colonial or remote region, esp. a tropical region. **2.** [*usually cap.*] *U. S.* **a** A white person descended from the French or Spanish settlers of Louisiana and the Gulf States, and preserving their characteristic speech and culture. **b** The French patois spoken in Louisiana. **3.** A Negro born in America; — more properly, **creole Negro. 4.** A person of mixed Creole and Negro blood speaking a dialect of French and Spanish; a half-breed.

— *adj.* **1.** [*usually cap.*] Designating or relating to a Creole or Creoles; of Creole blood and culture. **2.** Designating or relating to a creole or creoles; as, a *creole* Negro or dialect.

cre′o·sol (krē′ō·sōl; -sŏl), *n.* [*creosote* + *-ol,* 2.] *Chem.* A colorless aromatic liquid, $C_8H_{10}O_2$, resembling carbolic acid, obtained from guaiacum (gum) and from the tar made from beech.

cre′o·sote (krē′ō·sōt), *n.* [Gr. *kreas,* gen. *kreōs,* flesh + *sōzein* to preserve.] **1.** An oily antiseptic liquid, obtained by the distillation of wood tar, esp. that of beechwood. It is a complex mixture of various phenols and their ethers, and is used in the preservation of wood, (smoked) meat, etc. **2.** A similar substance made from coal tar. — *v. t.* To impregnate with creosote, as timber.

creosote bush. A desert shrub (*Covillea mexicana*), of the bean-caper family, found in the southwestern U. S.

crepe (krāp), **crêpe** (krāp), *n.* [F. *crêpe.*] **1.** A thin crinkled fabric of silk, wool, cotton, or rayon; as, **crepe de Chine** (dē shēn′), a fairly sheer silk crepe, and the soft but heavier silk ***Canton crepe.*** **2.** Black crepe used for mourning; also, a piece of such fabric; — in this sense usually *crape.* **3.** = CREPE PAPER. **4.** = CREPE RUBBER.

crepe, *or* **crêpe, myrtle.** = CRAPE MYRTLE.

crepe paper. Paper made to resemble crepe, as by crowding the wet sheet on a roll. — **crepe′-pa′per,** *adj.*

crepe rubber. Crude rubber in crinkled sheets, prepared by passing the coagulated latex through powerful rollers; also, synthetic rubber of similar form, used esp. for the soles of shoes.

crepe su·zette′ (krāp′ sōō·zĕt′); *pl.* CREPES SUZETTE (krāp′). A French pancake folded in quarters or rolled and heated in a sauce of butter, sugar, orange or lemon juice and grated rind, and a liqueur, with added cognac, curaçao, or rum usually set ablaze for serving.

crep′i·tant (krĕp′ĭ·tănt), *adj.* Having or making a crackling sound.

crep′i·tate (krĕp′ĭ·tāt), *v. i.* [L. *crepitare* to crackle, v. intens. of *crepare* to crack.] To make a series of crackling sounds; to crackle. — **crep′i·ta′tion** (-tā′shŭn), *n.*

crept (krĕpt), *past & past part.* of CREEP.

cre·pus′cle (krē·pŭs′'l), *n.* Also **cre·pus′cule** (krē·pŭs′kūl *or, Brit.,* krĕp′ŭs·kūl), **cre·pus′cu·lum** (krē·pŭs′kū·lŭm). [L. *crepusculum,* fr. *creper* dusky.] Twilight.

cre·pus′cu·lar (-kū·lẽr), *adj.* **1.** Of, pert. to, or like twilight; dim. **2.** Active in the twilight, as certain birds and insects.

cre·scen′do (krĕ·shĕn′dō; -sĕn′dō), *n.; pl.* -DOS (-dōz). [It., fr. *crescere* to increase.] *Music.* A gradual increase in volume of sound; also, a passage so rendered. — *adj. & adv.* *Music.* Increasing; — a direction to increase gradually the volume of tone, usually indicated by the abbreviation *cresc.* or the sign <. The opposite of *diminuendo* or *decrescendo.*

cres′cent (krĕs′ĕnt; -′nt; *or, Brit.,* krĕz′-), *n.* [OF. *creissant,* fr. L. *crescere* to increase.] **1.** The increasing moon; the moon in her first quarter, or its figure, defined by a concave and a convex edge. **2.** The emblem of the former Turkish Empire, adopted after the taking of Constantinople (1453); hence, the Turkish power, and, by extension, Mohammedanism as a political force. **3.** Any crescent-shaped object. — *adj.* **1.** Increasing. **2.** Shaped like the moon in her first quarter.

‖**cre′sci·te et mul′ti·pli·ca′mi·ni** (krĕs′ĭ·tē ĕt mŭl′tĭ·plĭ·kăm′ĭ·nī). [L.] Increase and multiply; — motto of Maryland.

‖**cre′scit e·un′do** (krĕs′ĭt ē·ŭn′dō). [L.] It grows as it goes; — motto of New Mexico.

cres′cive (krĕs′ĭv), *adj.* Increasing; growing.

cre′sol (krē′sōl; -sŏl), *n.* [From CREOSOTE.] *Chem.* Any of three isomeric substances, $CH_3C_6H_4OH$, resembling phenol. They are obtained from coal tar and wood tar as liquids or solids, and are disinfectant.

cress (krĕs), *n.* [AS. *cresse, cerse.*] Any of numerous plants of the mustard family (Brassicaceae), the moderately pungent leaves of which are used in salads and garnishings; as, the ***water cress*** (*Roripa nasturtium-aquaticum*), a white-flowered perennial growing in clear running water, the yellow-flowered ***marsh cress*** (*R. palustris*), and the ***bitter cresses*** (genus *Cardamine*), ***rock cresses*** (*Arabis*) and ***winter cresses*** (*Barbarea*).

cres′set (krĕs′ĕt; -ĭt), *n.* [OF.] An iron holder for an illuminant, as burning oil or pitchy wood, mounted as a torch, or hung as a lantern.

Cres′si·da (krĕs′ĭ·dȧ), *n.* In medieval legend, a Trojan girl, proverbial for her infidelity to her lover Troilus.

crest (krĕst), *n.* [OF. *creste,* fr. L. *crista.*] **1.** A tuft or process on the head of a bird or animal, as the comb of a cock. **2.** The plume of feathers, or other decoration, worn on a helmet, as by a knight; hence, a helmet. **3.** Something suggesting a crest, esp. as being the head, crown, or top; specif.: **a** A peak; esp., the top line of a mountain or hill. **b** The ridge or top of a wave. **4.** *Arch.* The ornamental ridging of a roof, canopy, etc. **5.** *Her.* A bearing set, not upon the shield but on the helm, and used separately as an ornament for plate, liveries, etc. — *v. t.* **1.** To furnish with, or surmount as, a crest; to top; crown. **2.** To reach the crest of, as a wave. — *v. i.* To form or rise to a crest; — of waves.

crest′ed (krĕs′tĕd; -tĭd), *adj.* Having a crest.

crested flycatcher. See FLYCATCHER.

crest′fall′en (krĕst′fôl′ĕn), *adj.* With drooping crest or hanging head; hence, dispirited; dejected; cowed. — **crest′fall′en·ly,** *adv.* — **crest′fall′en·ness,** *n.*

crest′less (krĕst′lĕs; -lĭs), *adj.* Without a crest.

cre·syl′ic (krē·sĭl′ĭk), *adj.* [*cresol* + *-yl* + *-ic.*] *Chem.* Pertaining to, or derived from, cresol, creosote, etc.

cre·ta′ceous (krē·tā′shŭs), *adj.* [L. *cretaceus,* fr. *creta* chalk.] **1.** Of the nature of, or abounding in, chalk. **2.** [*cap.*] *Geol.* Of, pert. to, or designating the latest period of the Mesozoic era, following the Jurassic, or the system of rocks formed in this period. By some divided into the ***Lower Cretaceous,* or *Comanchean,*** and the ***Upper Cretaceous.*** It is marked by chalk and coal deposits. — **Cre·ta′ceous,** *n.*

cre′tin (krē′tĭn *or, esp. Brit.,* krĕt′ĭn), *n.* [F. *crétin,* fr. a dial. form meaning prop. Christian, hence human being, fr. L. *christianus.*] One afflicted with cretinism.

cre′tin·ism (krē′tĭn·ĭz′m *or, esp. Brit.,* krĕt′ĭn-), *n.* A congenital morbid condition, characterized by deformity, with goiter or virtual absence of the thyroid gland, and, commonly, idiocy.

cre·tonne′ (krē·tŏn′; krē′tŏn; *Brit. usually* krĕt′ŏn), *n.* [F., fr. *Creton,* village in Normandy.] A strong unglazed printed cotton cloth.

cre·vasse′ (krĕ·văs′), *n.* [F.] **1.** A deep crevice or fissure, esp. in a glacier. **2.** *U. S.* A breach in a levee. — *v. t.;* CRE·VASSED′ (-văst′); CRE·VASS′ING. To open or fissure with crevasses.

crev′ice (krĕv′ĭs), *n.* [OF. *crevace,* fr. *crever* to break, fr. L. *crepare* to crack, break.] A narrow opening resulting from a split or crack; a fissure. — **crev′iced** (-ĭst), *adj.*

crew (krōō), *past* of CROW (sense 1).

crew (krōō; 114), *n.* [OF. *creüe* growth, increase, fr. *creistre* to grow.] **1.** *Archaic.* Any band or force of armed men. **2.** A company or assemblage. **3.** A set; gang; — often derogatorily. **4.** The body of men manning or trained to man a machine, gun, racing shell, or the like, or employed under one officer or foreman. **5.** The company of seamen who man a ship or boat; — legally including officers and master unless context shows the contrary.

crew′el (krōō′ĕl; -ĭl), *n.* Worsted yarn, slackly twisted, used for embroidery and fancy work. — **crew′el·work′** (-wûrk′), *n.*

crib (krĭb), *n.* [AS. *cribb.*] **1.** A manger for feeding animals. **2.** A stall for oxen or other cattle. **3.** A hut; also, a small narrow room. **4.** An osier or wickerwork basket; a crate. **5.** A bin or a building for storing grain, salt, etc., usually of open or slat construction. **6.** A small bedstead with high sides, for a child. **7.** Any of various devices of cratelike construction, as a frame of beams built as a retaining wall.

8. A small theft; a plagiarism; hence, a translation, etc., to aid a student in reciting. 9. In cribbage, cards discarded for the dealer to use in scoring.
— *v. t.;* CRIBBED (krĭbd); CRIB′BING. 1. To confine, or cage; hence, to cramp. 2. To provide with, or put in, a crib or cribs. 3. *Colloq.* To steal; to plagiarize. — *v. i.* 1. *Colloq.* To steal; plagiarize; also, to use a crib, as in translating. 2. To crib-bite. — **crib′ber**, *n.*

crib′bage (krĭb′ĭj), *n.* [From CRIB, *v. t.*, 3.] A game of cards in which the chief object is to form counting combinations, the dealer having an extra set of players' discards, the *crib.* The score is usually kept by moving pegs on a special board (**cribbage board**).

crib biting. Also **crib′bing** (krĭb′ĭng), *n.* A vice of horses, in which they grasp the manger with the incisor teeth, arch the neck, and swallow large quantities of air. — **crib′-bite′**, *v. i.*

crick (krĭk), *n.* A painful spasmodic affection of the muscles, as of the neck or back. — *v. t.* To turn so as to cause a crick.

crick′et (krĭk′ĕt; -ĭt), *n.* [OF. *criquet*, fr. MD. *crīkel.*] A leaping orthopterous insect (family Gryllidae, esp. genus *Gryllus*) noted for the chirping notes produced by the male by rubbing together specially modified parts of the forewings.

crick′et, *n.* [OF. *criquet* goal stake in the game of bowls, fr. MD. *cricke* stick, staff.] 1. An outdoor game played with bats, ball, wickets, etc., usually between sides of eleven players each. 2. *Colloq.* Fair, sportsmanlike conduct or procedure. — *v. i.* To play cricket. — **crick′et·er**, *n.*

crick′et, *n.* A low wooden footstool.

cri′coid (krī′koid), *adj.* [Gr. *krikos* ring + *-oid.*] *Anat.* Designating, or pertaining to, a cartilage of the larynx with which the arytenoid cartilages articulate.

cri′er (krī′ẽr), *n.* A person who cries; esp., one who proclaims orders of a court. Cf. TOWN CRIER.

crime (krīm), *n.* [OF., fr. L. *crimen* accusation, fault, crime.] 1. An act or omission forbidden by law and punishable upon conviction, including public offenses often classified as treason, felony, and misdemeanor. 2. Gross violation of human law, in distinction from a misdemeanor; hence, any aggravated offense against morality. 3. Criminal activity. — **Syn.** See OFFENSE.

crim′i·nal (krĭm′ĭ·năl; -n'l), *adj.* 1. Involving, or of the nature of, a crime. 2. Relating to crime or its punishment; as, *criminal* law; — disting. from *civil.* 3. Guilty of crime. — *n.* One who has committed a crime; a felon. — **crim′i·nal·ly**, *adv.*

criminal conversation. Unlawful intercourse with a married woman; adultery. Abbr. *crim. con.*

crim′i·nal′i·ty (krĭm′ĭ·năl′ĭ·tĭ), *n.* Quality of being criminal.

crim′i·nate (krĭm′ĭ·nāt), *v. t.* [L. *criminatus*, past part. of *criminare* to criminate. See CRIME.] 1. To accuse of crime; also, to incriminate. 2. To represent (a thing) as criminal; to censure strongly. — **crim′i·na′tion** (-nā′shŭn), *n.* — **crim′i·na′tive** (krĭm′ĭ·nā′tĭv), **crim′i·na·to′ry** (-nȧ·tō′rĭ *or, esp. Brit.*, -tẽr·ĭ), *adj.*

crim′i·nol′o·gy (-nŏl′ō·jĭ), *n.* [L. *crimen, criminis*, crime + *-logy.*] The scientific study of crime as a social phenomenon, of criminals, and of penal treatment. — **crim′i·no·log′ic** (-nō·lŏj′ĭk), **crim′i·no·log′i·cal** (-ĭ·kăl), *adj.* — **crim′i·nol′o·gist** (-nŏl′ō·jĭst), *n.*

crim′mer (krĭm′ẽr). Var. of KRIMMER.

crimp (krĭmp), *v. t.* [D. & LG. *krimpen.*] 1. To fold or plait in small regular undulations; to give a wavy appearance to. 2. To gash, as the flesh of a fish, so as to cause the muscles to contract. 3. To fold the edge of (a cartridge case) inward so as to confine the charge. 4. To form (leather) into the required shape, as in making boot uppers. 5. *Slang, U. S.* To put a crimp (def. 4) in. — *n.* 1. Act or product of crimping, as of wood from too rapid drying; also, a small undulation or wrinkle or a series of them; specif., the curl in wool fiber. 2. A device for crimping. 3. Hair which has been crimped; — usually *pl.* 4. *Slang, U. S.* An interfering element that inhibits or cramps; as, to put a *crimp* in one's style.

crimp, *n.* One whose business is to lure, entrap, or force men into shipping as sailors against their will, or, formerly, into enlisting in military or sea service. — *v. t.* To entrap, in the role of a crimp.

crimp′er, *n.* A worker or device that crimps.

crimp′y (krĭmp′ĭ), *adj.;* -I·ER (-ĭ·ẽr); -I·EST. Having a crimped appearance, frizzly.

crim′son (krĭm′z'n), *n.* [Sp. *cremesín*, ult. fr. Ar. *qirmiz* kermes, fr. Skr. *kṛmi* worm, insect.] Any of several colors, ranging in hue from red to bluish-red, of high saturation and low brilliance. See COLOR. — *adj.* Of the color crimson; hence, sanguinary; bloody. — *v. t. & i.* To make or become crimson.

cringe (krĭnj), *v. i.;* CRINGED (krĭnjd); CRING′ING (krĭn′jĭng). [ME. *crengen*, fr. the root of AS. *cringan, crincan*, to yield, fall.] 1. To draw in or contract one's muscles involuntarily; to shrink. 2. To bend or crouch in fear or with base humility; to wince; hence, to fawn. — **Syn.** See FAWN. — **cringe**, *n.* — **cring′er** (krĭn′jẽr), *n.*

crin′gle (krĭng′g'l), *n.* [LG. *kringel*, fr. *kring* a ring.] *Naut.* An iron or rope thimble or grommet at the edge or corner of a sail, for making it fast; also, in light sails, an eyelet worked in the sail itself. Cf. CLEW, GROMMET, *Illusts.*

cri′nite (krī′nīt), *adj.* [L. *crinitus*, past part. of *crinire* to provide or cover with hair, fr. *crinis* hair.] 1. Having hair or a hairlike tail. 2. *Bot. & Zool.* Covered or provided with hairy growths.

cri′nite (krī′nīt; krĭn′īt), *n.* A fossil crinoid.

crin′kle (krĭng′k'l), *v. i. & t.;* CRIN′KLED (-k'ld); CRIN′KLING (-klĭng). 1. To turn or wind in many short bends or turns; also, to wrinkle; ripple. 2. To rustle, as stiff cloth. 3. To bend over without breaking clear off, as barley. — *n.* A winding or wrinkle. — **crin′kly** (-klĭ), *adj.*

crin′kle·root′ (-rōōt′), *n.* See TOOTHWORT **b**.

crin′kum-cran′kum (krĭng′kŭm-krăng′kŭm), *n.* *Colloq.* Something full of twists and turns; a twist; a whimsey.

cri′noid (krī′noid; krĭn′oid), *adj.* [Gr. *krinoeidēs* like a lily, fr. *krinon* lily. See -OID.] Lily-shaped; hence, of or pertaining to a large class (Crinoidea) of echinoderms, mostly attached by the part opposite the mouth and having typically a more or less cup-shaped body with five or more featherlike arms (cirri). — *n.* A crinoid echinoderm. See COMATULID, FEATHER STAR, SEA LILY, STONE LILY.

crin′o·line (krĭn′ō·lĭn; -lēn), *n.* [F., fr. L. *crinis* hair + *linum* thread, linen.] 1. A stiff cloth, originally made of horsehair and linen thread, used for stiffening and as lining. 2. A lady's skirt of any stiff material; also, a hoop skirt.

cri′o·sphinx (krī′ō·sfĭngks), *n.* [Gr. *krios* ram + *sphinx* sphinx.] A ram-headed sphinx. See SPHINX, 3.

crip′ple (krĭp′'l), *n.* [AS. *crypel.*] 1. A lame or partly disabled person or animal. 2. *Local, U. S.* Bog; swamp. — *adj.* Lame; disabled. — *v. t.;* CRIP′PLED (-'ld); CRIP′PLING (-lĭng). 1. To deprive of the use of a limb, esp. of a leg; to lame. 2. To deprive of strength, activity, or capability for service. — **Syn.** See WEAKEN. — **crip′pler** (-lẽr), *n.*

cri′sis (krī′sĭs), *n.; pl.* CRISES (-sēz). [L., fr. Gr. *krisis*, fr. *krinein* to separate.] 1. *Med.* That change in a disease which indicates whether the result is to be recovery or death. 2. The decisive moment; turning point. 3. A crucial time; specif., the culminating point of a period of business prosperity, following which a period of liquidation ensues. — **Syn.** See JUNCTURE.

crisp (krĭsp), *adj.* [AS., fr. L. *crispus* quivering, curly.] 1. Curly; in curls or ringlets. 2. Roughened into small curls, frets, waves, or folds. 3. Brittle; friable; short, as pastry. 4. Sharp, clean-cut, and clear; as, *crisp* outlines. 5. Lively; sparkling, as repartee. 6. Firm and fresh, as lettuce. 7. Inducing briskness; bracing. — **Syn.** See FRAGILE: INCISIVE. — *n.* That which is crisp or brittle. — *v. t. & i.* 1. To form into curls or ringlets; ripple. 2. To make or become crisp. — **crisp′ly**, *adv.* — **crisp′ness**, *n.*

cris·pa′tion (krĭs·pā′shŭn), *n.* 1. A curling, or state of being curled. 2. A slight spasmodic contraction; shudder.

crisp′er (krĭs′pẽr), *n.* One that crisps; esp., a curling iron.

crisp′y (-pĭ), *adj.;* CRISP′I·ER (-pĭ·ẽr); CRISP′I·EST. 1. Formed into short, close ringlets. 2. Brittle; short.

criss′cross′ (krĭs′krŏs′; 74), *n.* [For earlier *Christcross.*] 1. A christcross (def. 1). 2. A pattern of crossed lines, or something forming such a pattern. 3. Ticktacktoe (the game). — *v. t.* To mark or cover with cross lines; also, to traverse crisscross. — *v. i.* To go or pass crisscross. — *adj.* Disposed in crossing lines; crossed; marked by crossings. — *adv.* In a way to cross something else; also, at cross purposes; awry.

cris′tate (krĭs′tāt), **cris′tat·ed** (-tāt·ĕd; -ĭd), *adj.* [L. *cristatus*, fr. *crista* crest.] Having a crest; crested.

cri·te′ri·on (krī·tẽr′ĭ·ŭn), *n.; pl.* -RIA (-ȧ), sometimes -RIONS (-ŭnz). [Gr. *kritērion* a means for judging, fr. *kritēs* judge, fr. *krinein* to separate.] A standard of judging; a rule or test by which anything is tried in forming a correct judgment respecting it. — **Syn.** See STANDARD.

crit′ic (krĭt′ĭk), *n.* [F. and L.; F. *critique*, fr. L. *criticus*, fr. Gr. *kritikos*, prop., able to discuss, fr. *krinein* to judge, discern.] 1. One who expresses a reasoned opinion on any matter, involving a judgment of its value, truth, or righteousness or an appreciation of its beauty or technique. 2. One given to harsh or captious judgment; a caviler or carper. 3. One skilled in judging the merits of literary or artistic works. 4. Formerly: **a** Criticism. **b** A critique.

crit′i·cal (krĭt′ĭ·kăl), *adj.* 1. Inclined to criticize, esp. unfavorably; captious; censorious. 2. Exercising, or involving, careful judgment; exact; nicely judicious. 3. Pertaining to or indicating or constituting a crisis or turning point; decisive; as, the *critical* stage of a fever. 4. Of doubtful issue; attended with risk; as, a *critical* situation. 5. Of the nature of, or pertaining to, criticism or critics; as, *critical* traditions. 6. *Physics, Math., etc.* Marking a transition point at which some character or property suffers a finite change; as, *critical* point, temperature. 7. Indispensable in tipping the balance toward success but so scarce as to require controlled distribution and exploitation of new sources; — chiefly of raw material and labor. — **crit′i·cal·ly**, *adv.* — **crit′i·cal·ness**, *n.*

Syn. (1) **Critical, hypercritical, faultfinding, captious, caviling** (*or* **caviling**), **carping, censorious** mean exhibiting the spirit of one who notices faults or defects. In precise use, **critical** implies an effort to see a thing clearly and truly in order to judge it fairly; in less precise but acceptable use, *critical* implies harshness in judging. In the latter sense, **hypercritical** is often preferred. **Faultfinding**, a colloquial term, usually implies querulousness or an exacting temperament; **captious** implies a readiness to detect trivial faults or to take exceptions on slight grounds; **caviling** stresses the act or habit of raising picayune objections; **carping** implies an ill-natured or perverse picking of flaws; **censorious** implies a disposition to be severely critical and condemnatory of that which one criticizes.
(2) See ACUTE.

critical angle. 1. *Optics.* The least angle of incidence at which total reflection takes place. 2. The angle of attack at which the flow about an airfoil changes abruptly, with like changes in the lift and drag.

critical point. *Physics.* The point at which the gaseous and liquid conditions of a substance merge into each other.

critical temperature. *Physical Chem.* The temperature above which a fluid cannot exist as a liquid or as a vapor and hence cannot be liquefied by pressure alone (for water, 365° C.; for hydrogen, –242° C.).

crit′ic·as′ter (krĭt′ĭk·ăs′tẽr), *n.* [See 2d -ASTER.] An inferior or contemptible critic. — **crit′ic·as′try** (-trĭ), *n.*

crit′i·cism (krĭt′ĭ·sĭz'm), *n.* 1. The act of criticizing, esp. unfavorably; censure; also, a critical observation, judgment, or review. 2. The art of judging with knowledge and propriety the beauties and faults of works of art or literature; hence, similar consideration of moral or logical values.

crit′i·cize, crit′i·cise (-sīz), *v. i.* To express criticism. — *v. t.* To examine and judge as a critic; to express a criticism of; also, to find fault with. — **crit′i·ciz′a·ble** (-sīz′ȧ·b'l), *adj.* — **crit′i·ciz′er** (-sīz′ẽr), *n.*

Syn. Criticize, reprehend, blame, censure, reprobate, condemn, denounce mean to find fault with openly, often publicly. **Criticize**, only in its extended sense, implies faultfinding; **reprehend**, in current use, implies both criticism and severe rebuking; **blame** fundamentally implies speaking in dispraise of a person or thing and often suggests the attitude of one who accuses or reprehends; **censure** carries a stronger suggestion of authority or competence and of reprimanding than *blame;* **reprobate** implies strong disapproval and, usually, vigorous censure; **condemn** sometimes suggests a definitive judgment, sometimes a wholly unfavorable or merciless judgment; **denounce** adds to *condemn* the implication of a public declaration.

cri·tique′ (krĭ·tēk′), *n.* [F.] 1. A critical estimate of a work of literature or art. 2. The art of criticism. 3. A critical discussion of the execution of a problem, military training exercise, or the like.

croak (krōk), *v. i.* [From the root of AS. *crācettan* to croak.] 1. To make a low, hoarse noise in the throat, as a frog or crow. 2. To grumble; to forebode evil. 3. *Slang.* To die. — *v. t.* 1. To utter in a low, hoarse voice; to forebode. 2. *Slang.* To kill. — *n.* A hoarse harsh cry, as of a frog. — **croak′y**, *adj.*

croak′er (-ẽr), *n.* 1. An animal that croaks, as a frog. 2. Any of various fishes that produce croaking or grunting noises. **3.** A grumbler or foreboder of evil.

Cro′at (krō′ăt), *n.* A native of Croatia (see *Gaz.*); esp., one of the native Slavic-speaking race, or their language.

Cro·a′tian (krō·ā′shăn), *adj.* Of or pertaining to Croatia. — *n.* A Croat; also, the Croatian language, linguistically identical with Serbian, but written in Roman characters. See INDO-EUROPEAN LANGUAGE, *Table.*

cro·chet′ (krō·shā′ *or, Brit.,* krō′shā, -shĭ), *n.* [F., small hook.] A type of knitting done with a long hooked needle (**crochet needle**). — *v. t. & i.;* -CHETED (-shād′); -CHET′ING (-shā′ĭng). To knit with a crochet needle or hook. — **cro·chet′er** (-shā′ẽr), *n.* — **cro·chet′ing** (krō·shā′ĭng; *Brit.* krō′shā·ĭng, -shĭ·ĭng), *n.*

cro·cid′o·lite (krō·sĭd′ō·līt), *n.* [Gr. *krokis, -idos,* nap on cloth + *-lite.*] A lavender-blue or bluish-green mineral of the amphibole group, usually fibrous. See TIGEREYE.

crock (krŏk), *n.* [AS. *croc, crocca.*] Any piece of crockery, as a jar, esp. of coarse earthenware.

crock, *n.* **1.** *Scot. & Dial. Eng.* An old or barren ewe. **2.** *Colloq.* A person physically worn or broken down. — *v. t. & i.* To impair, or become impaired, as in vigor, usefulness, or efficiency.

crock, *n.* *Now Dial.* Soot; smut; also, coloring matter which rubs off from cloth. — *v. t. & i.* To soil with, or give off, crock. — **crock′y,** *adj.*

crock′er·y (-ẽr·ĭ), *n.* Earthenware; crocks collectively.

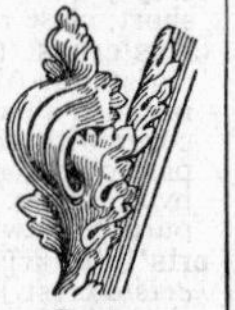

Crocket.

crock′et (krŏk′ĕt; -ĭt), *n.* [ONF. *croquet* (OF. *crochet*).] *Arch.* An ornament, often resembling curved foliage, on the sloping edge of a gable, spire, etc.

croc′o·dile (krŏk′ō·dīl), *n.* [L. *crocodilus,* fr. Gr. *krokodilos* lizard, crocodile.] Any of a genus (*Crocodilus*) of large, thick-skinned, long-tailed, aquatic reptiles of tropical, chiefly fresh, waters; loosely, any crocodilian. See ALLIGATOR, MUGGER.

crocodile bird. An African ploverlike bird which alights upon the crocodile and devours its insect parasites.

crocodile tears. False or affected tears; — from the fiction that crocodiles weep in sympathy for their prey.

croc′o·dil′i·an (krŏk′ō·dĭl′ĭ·ăn), *adj.* **a** Like a crocodile. **b** Belonging to an order (Crocodilia) of reptiles including the crocodiles, gavials, alligators, and related extinct forms. — **croc′o·dil′i·an,** *n.*

cro′co·ite (krō′kō·īt), **cro·co′i·site** (krō·kō′ĭ·sīt), *n.* [Gr. *krokos* saffron.] *Mineral.* Native lead chromate, $PbCrO_4$; — called also *red lead ore.*

cro′cus (krō′kŭs), *n.; pl.* -CUSES (-ĕz; -ĭz), -CI (krō′sī). [L., fr. Gr. *krokos* saffron.] **1.** *Bot.* **a** Any of a large genus (*Crocus*) of bulbous herbs of the iris family, having solitary long-tubed flowers arising with grasslike leaves from a fibrous-coated corm. See SAFFRON, 1. **b** A bulb or flower of this plant. **2.** = SAFFRON YELLOW. **3.** *Old Chem.* A metallic oxide, esp. colcothar.

Croe′sus (krē′sŭs), *n.* A king of Lydia in the 6th century B.C., having vast wealth; hence, any very rich man.

croft (krŏft; 74), *n.* [AS.] *Brit.* **a** A small enclosed field. **b** A small agricultural holding worked by a tenant.

croft′er (krŏf′tẽr), *n.* *Brit.* One who rents and tills a croft.

Croix de Feu (krwäd′fû′). [F., lit., fiery cross.] A French fascist organization headed by Col. François de la Rocque, which was disbanded in 1936 and reorganized as the French Social party.

‖**Croix de guerre** (krwä′ dē gâr′; *Fr.* krwäd′gâr′). [F., war cross.] *Mil., French.* A decoration awarded for gallant action in war.

Cro-Ma′gnon (krō·măn′yŏn), *adj.* Belonging to a race of tall, erect men remains of whom have been found in the Cro-Magnon cave in Dordogne, France, and who are regarded as of the same species (*Homo sapiens*) as modern man. See MAN, *Illust.*

crom′lech (krŏm′lĕk; -lĕk), *n.* [W., fr. *crom* bent, concave + *llech* a flat stone.] *Archaeol.* **a** = DOLMEN. **b** A circle of monoliths, usually enclosing a dolmen or mound.

crone (krōn), *n.* [OF. and D.; D. *kronje, karonje,* old ewe, hag, fr. ONF. *carogne* carrion.] A withered old woman.

Cro′nus (krō′nŭs), *n.* [L., fr. Gr. *Kronos.*] *Gr. Myth.* A Titan, son of Uranus, who dethroned his father and was in turn dethroned by his son Zeus. See SATURN.

cro′ny (krō′nĭ), *n.; pl.* -NIES (-nĭz). An intimate companion.

crood (kro͝od), *v. i.* [Imitative.] *Scot.* To coo.

crook (kro͝ok), *n.* [ME. *crok,* fr. ON. *krōkr* hook, bend.] **1.** Any implement having a bent or hooked form; as: **a** A hook; esp., a pothook. **b** A shepherd's staff; also, a crosier. **2.** Act of crooking, or state of being crooked. **3.** A bend, turn, or curve. **4.** Any hooked or curved appendage, part, or contrivance; specif., a crooked piece of timber; a knee. **5.** *Colloq.* A swindler, sharper, cheat, or the like. — *v. t. & i.* To turn from a straight line; bend.

crook′back′ (-băk′), *n.* A crooked back; hence, a hunchback. — **crook′backed′** (-băkt′), *adj.*

crook′ed (kro͝ok′ĕd; -ĭd), *adj.* **1.** (*pron.* kro͝okt) Having a crook or curved part; as, a *crooked* stick. **2.** Characterized by a crook or curve; bent; twisted. **3.** Not straightforward; deviating from rectitude. **4.** False; dishonest; fraudulent. — **crook′ed·ly,** *adv.* — **crook′ed·ness,** *n.*

Syn. **Crooked, devious, oblique** mean not straight or straightforward. **Crooked** literally implies curves, turns, or bends, and, figuratively, fraudulence, cheating, graft, etc.; **devious** implies departure from the direct, appointed course and, hence, wandering or errancy; **oblique** implies departure from a perpendicular or horizontal direction and, so, indirection or lack of perfect straightforwardness.

Crookes tube (kro͝oks). [After Sir Wm. *Crookes,* Eng. physicist.] *Physics.* A vacuum tube in which the rarefaction is carried to that high degree, known as the **Crookes vacuum,** in which molecular actions have free play.

crook′neck′ (kro͝ok′nĕk′), *n.* Any of several varieties of squash with tapering, recurved necks. See 1st SQUASH.

croon (kro͞on), *v. i. & t.* [MD. *cronen* (D. *kreunen*).] **1.** *Scot. & N. of Eng.* To bellow; boom. **2.** To hum or sing in a low voice; specif., to sing popular sentimental songs with exaggerated pathos. — *n.* The sound made in crooning. — **croon′er,** *n.*

crop (krŏp), *n.* [AS. *crop, cropp,* craw, top, bunch, ear of corn.] **1.** A pouchlike enlargement of the gullet of many birds and insects, serving as a receptacle for the food and for its preliminary maceration; craw. Cf. GIZZARD, PROVENTRICULUS. **2.** The stock or handle of a whip; specif., a riding whip with a short straight stock and a loop (for opening gates). **3.** Of grain or fruit, that which is cropped, cut, or gathered from a single field, or of a single kind, or in a single season or part of a season; harvest; hence, the yield of anything during one season; as, the ice *crop.* **4.** An entire tanned cowhide. **5.** [From the *v.*] Act or product of cropping; specif.: **a** Hair cut short; the style of wearing the hair so cut. **b** An earmark on an animal, made by cropping. — *v. t.;* CROPPED (krŏpt) or, rarely, CROPT; CROP′PING. **1.** To cut off the tops or tips of; to bite or snip off; to pluck or reap. **2.** To cut off short; specif., to clip the ears or, sometimes, hair, etc., of. — *v. i.* **1.** To yield a crop or crops. **2.** To appear, as from concealment; to manifest itself unexpectedly; as, a few errors *crop* up.

crop′-eared′ (-ērd′; 2), *adj.* **1.** Having the ears cropped. **2.** Having the hair cropped, so that the ears are prominent.

crop′per (krŏp′ẽr), *n.* **1.** One that crops. **2.** One who raises crops; esp., one who cultivates another's farm, receiving as wages a share of the crop. See SHARECROPPER.

crop′per, *n.* *Colloq.* A severe fall, as from a horse; hence, a failure or collapse; as, to come, fall, or get a *cropper.*

cro·quet′ (krō·kā′; *Brit. usually* krō′kā, -kĭ), *n.* [Prob. a northern dial. form of F. *crochet,* prop., a hooked stick used in playing a game. See CROCKET.] **1.** A game in which the players try with mallets to drive wooden balls through a series of hoops set on the turf. **2.** Act of croqueting. — *v. t. & i.;* CRO·QUETED′ (-kād′; -kăd, -kĭd); CRO·QUET′ING (-kā′ĭng; -kā·ĭng, -kĭ·ĭng). To play from or with (a ball) after putting one's own in contact with it.

cro·quette′ (krō·kĕt′), *n.* [F., fr. *croquer* to crunch.] A ball made of minced meat, fowl, rice, or the like, coated with egg and bread crumbs and fried in deep fat.

cro′qui·gnole (krō′kĭ·nōl; -kĭn·yōl), *n.* [F., fillip, cracknel.] Also **croquignole wave.** A style of permanent wave in which the hair is wound on metal rods from the ends of the hair toward the scalp.

crore (krōr; 70), *n.* [Hind. *karor,* fr. Skr. *koṭi* end, top.] *Anglo-Ind.* Ten million; specif., ten million rupees (written Rs. 1,00,00,000), or 100 lacs.

cro′sier, cro′zier (krō′zhẽr), *n.* [OF. *crocier, crossier,* staff bearer, fr. *croce, crosse,* pastoral staff.] The staff of a bishop, abbot, or abbess, resembling a shepherd's crook and borne as a symbol of a pastoral office. See VESTMENT, *Illust.*

cross (krŏs; 74), *n.* [ME. *crois,* fr. OF. *crois;* ME. *cros,* fr. AS. *cros:* both fr. L. *crux.*] **1.** A structure, typically an upright supporting a horizontal beam, anciently used in the execution of malefactors; specif. [*usually cap.*], with *the,* that on which Jesus Christ was crucified. **2. a** A device or emblem shaped like this structure. **b** A monument or other structure in the form of a cross, or surmounted by a cross. **3.** A cruciform badge, ornament, etc., as a standard surmounted by a crucifix carried in religious processions. **4.** The crusaders' symbol; hence, ***to take the cross,*** to take the crusader's vows. **5.** A representation of the cross as the symbol of Christ's death; hence, the chosen symbol of Christianity; also, the Christian religion or, specif., the gospel of redemption through the death of Christ. **6.** Any figure or mark formed by the intersection of two straight lines, specif. one made as a mark of signature. **7.** A common heraldic bearing representing the Christian emblem or some variation of it. **8.** The intersection of two lines or ways. **9.** A thwarting; altercation. **10.** Affliction or trial regarded as a test of Christian patience or virtue. **11.** A mixing of breeds, races, or the like; also, the product of such intermixture; a crossbreed; a hybrid. **12.** [*cap.*] *Astron.* **a** The Northern Cross. **b** The Southern Cross. — *v. t.* **1.** To make the sign of the cross upon or over. **2.** To cancel by marking crosses on or over. **3.** To put or lay across or athwart; also, to lie or pass across; to intersect. **4.** To pass or extend from one side to the other of; to traverse. **5.** To carry or take across, as an army. **6.** To meet and pass. **7.** *Archaic.* To confront. *Shak.* **8.** To thwart; obstruct. **9.** To draw or write something, as a line, across; as, to *cross* one's t's; to mark with cross lines. **10.** To cause (animals or plants of different races or kinds) to interbreed; to hybridize, cross-pollinate, or the like. — *v. i.* **1.** To lie or be athwart. **2.** To move or pass, or to extend, from one side to the other, or from place to place; — often with *over.* **3.** To meet and pass, as letters. **4.** To interbreed; to hybridize. — ***cross over.*** *Biol.* To pass over from one homologous chromosome to another in an interchange of chromatin material; — of a gene or factor.

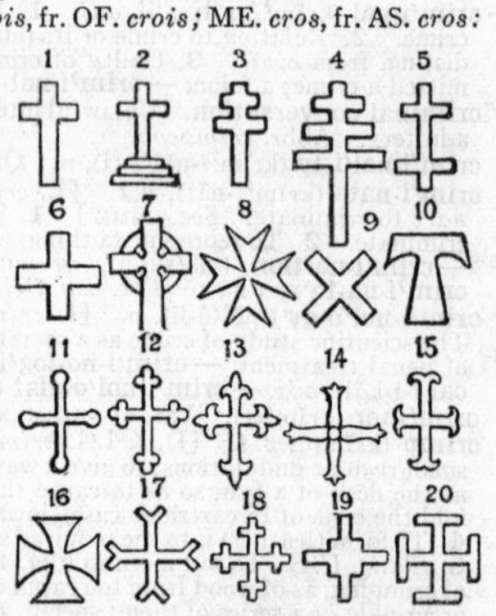

Cross. 1 Latin; 2 Calvary; 3 Patriarchal or Archiepiscopal; 4 Papal; 5 Lorraine; 6 Greek; 7 Celtic; 8 Maltese; 9 St. Andrew's; 10 Tau; 11 Pommée; 12 Botonée; 13 Pattée; 14 Avellan; 15 Moline; 16 Formée; 17 Fourchée; 18 Crosslet; 19 Quadrate; 20 Potent (Jerusalem). See also ANKH, SWASTIKA, *Illusts.*

— *adj.* **1.** Not parallel; lying, falling, or passing athwart; transverse; crossed; as, a *cross* street; *cross* keys. **2.** Contrary or adverse; opposite or counter; also, mutually opposed or contradictory. **3.** Ill-humored. **4.** Involving mutual interchange or relation; reciprocal. **5.** Crossbred; hybrid. — **Syn.** See IRASCIBLE. — **cross′ly,** *adv.* — **cross′ness,** *n.*

cross-. A combining form of *cross* in various senses as noun, adjective, and adverb, esp. *of* or *having a cross, crossed, transverse, counter, across, athwart,* as in:

crossarm	cross-feed, *n. & v.*	crossline
crossband	crossflow	crosspath
crossbeam	cross-handed	crossrow
cross-bearer	cross index	crosstie
cross-bias, *n. & v.*	cross-index, *v.*	cross-town, *adj.*
crossbones	cross-legged	crosswalk
crosscurrent	crosslight	crossway

cross′bar′ (krŏs′bär′), *n.* A transverse piece or stripe. — *v. t.;* see BAR. To provide or mark with transverse stripes.

cross′bill′ (-bĭl′), *n.* Any of a genus (*Loxia*) of finches having mandibles strongly curved and crossing each other.

cross′bow′ (krŏs′bō′), *n.* A medieval weapon for discharging quarrels, stones, etc., formed of a bow set crosswise on a stock. See ARBALEST; cf. LONGBOW. — **cross′bow′man** (-măn), *n.*

cross′bred′ (-brĕd′; 2), *adj.* & *n.* Hybrid; mongrel.

cross′breed′ (-brēd′), *v. t.* & *i.*; -BRED′ (-brĕd′); -BREED′ING. To hybridize; specif., to breed between two varieties or breeds of the same species. — *n.* A breed or an individual produced by crossbreeding; a hybrid. Cf. HYBRID.

cross bun. A bun or cake marked with a cross, commonly eaten on Good Friday; — called also ***hot cross bun.***

cross′-coun′try, *adj.* Across fields; not by roads; as, a *cross-country* race.

cross′cut′ (krŏs′kŭt′), *adj.* **1.** Made or used for crosscutting; as, a **crosscut saw. 2.** Cut transversely, esp. across the grain. — *n.* **1.** A direct path oblique to the main road; a short cut. **2.** A mine working driven at right angles to an adit, drift, vein, etc. — *v. t.* & *i.*; CROSS′CUT′; -CUT′TING. To cut, drive, saw, etc., transversely, as across the grain of wood.

crosse (krŏs; 74), *n.* [F., crosier, hooked stick.] A lacrosse racket.

cross′-ex·am′ine (*see Pron.*, § 2), *v. t.* & *i.* *Law.* To examine or question, esp. as a check to a previous examination. — **cross′-ex·am′i·na′tion,** *n.* — **cross′-ex·am′in·er,** *n.*

cross′-eye′, *n.* See STRABISMUS. — **cross′-eyed′,** *adj.*

cross′-fer′ti·li·za′tion, *n.* **1.** Fertilization by cross-pollination. **2.** *Zool.* The fertilization of the eggs of a hermaphroditic animal by spermatozoa of another individual. — **cross′-fer′ti·lize,** *v. t.* & *i*

cross fire. In combat, firing from two or more points so that the lines of fire cross; hence, any like form of attack; as, a *cross fire* of questions.

cross′-grained′ (krŏs′grānd′; 2), *adj.* **1.** Having the grain or fibers running transversely or irregularly. **2.** Perverse; intractable.

cross hair. One of the fine threads in the focus of the eyepiece of optical instruments, used to define the line of sight with accuracy.

cross′hatch′ (krŏs′hăch′), *v. t.* & *i.* To mark with series of parallel lines that cross, esp. obliquely; as, to *crosshatch* parts of a map.

cross′head′ (-hĕd′), *n.* *Mach.* A beam or bar across the head or end of a rod, etc., or a block attached to it.

cross′-im·mu′ni·ty, *n.* Immunity toward one of a pair of antigens following immunization toward the other. It has been used to assess relationship of certain antigens. — **cross′-im′mu·ni·za′tion,** *n.*

cross′ing (krŏs′ĭng), *n.* **1.** Act of one that crosses, as in traversing, opposing, crossbreeding; also, an instance of it. **2.** A point of intersection, as of roads, railroad tracks, etc. See GRADE CROSSING. **3.** A place where a street, stream, etc., is crossed.

cross′let (krŏs′lĕt; -lĭt), *n.* A small cross, esp. as a heraldic bearing. See CROSS, *Illust.* (18).

cross′line′ (krŏs′līn′), *adj.* *Biol.* Of or pertaining to the offspring resulting from the crossbreeding of two pure lines.

cross′o′ver (krŏs′ō′vẽr), *n.* **1.** A crossing from one side, level, track, etc., to another or the place where such crossing is made; also, a passageway, or the like, for effecting such a crossing. **2.** *Biol.* A crossing over; also, a character so inherited. See *cross over,* under CROSS, *v.*

cross′piece′ (krŏs′pēs′), *n.* A piece placed across another.

cross′-pol′li·na′tion, *n.* *Bot.* The deposition of pollen from one flower on the stigma of another, as by wind or insects, or artificially to produce new varieties (see HYBRID). Cf. SELF-POLLINATED. — **cross′-pol′li·nate,** *v. t.* & *i.*

cross′-pur′pose, *n.* A counter or opposing purpose. — ***at cross purposes.*** Acting contrary to another person without intending to do so.

cross′-ques′tion, *v. t.* **1.** To cross-examine. **2.** To subject to close questioning. — *n.* A question asked in cross-examining.

cross reference. A reference made from one part of a book, index, etc., to another part. — **cross′-re·fer′,** *v. t.* & *i.*

cross′road′ (krŏs′rōd′), *n.* **1.** A road that crosses a main road or runs across country between main roads. **2.** Often *pl.* but construable as *sing.* or *pl.* **a** The place of intersection of two or more roads. **b** The meeting place of the scattered inhabitants of a countryside.

cross′ruff′ (-rŭf′), *n.* *Whist, Bridge, etc.* The play in which partners trump different suits, led to each other for that purpose. — **cross′ruff′,** *v. i.*

cross section. 1. A cutting or section, or a piece of something cut off, at right angles to an axis. **2.** A composite representation typifying the constituents of a thing in their relations; as, a *cross section* of the people. **3.** *Physics.* The probability that a certain reaction will occur when a nucleus or particle is subjected to bombardment.

cross′-stitch′, *n.* A form of stitch, or a kind of needlework, in which the stitches are diagonal and in pairs crossing to form x's. See STITCH, *Illust.* — **cross′-stitch′,** *v. t.* & *i.*

cross′trees′ (krŏs′trēz′), *n. pl.* *Naut.* Two horizontal pieces of timber or metal supported by trestletrees at the head of a lower mast, which spread the upper shrouds to support an upper mast.

cross′wise′ (-wīz′), *adv.* Also **cross′ways′** (-wāz′). **1.** In the form or figure of a cross. **2.** So as to cross something; across. **3.** In a way contrary to what is right or to what is purposed; perversely.

cross′word′ puz′zle (-wûrd′). A word-guessing puzzle arranged in a diagram in which the words, when correctly supplied, cross each other vertically and horizontally, so that most letters appear in two words.

crotch (krŏch), *n.* [F. *croche* a hook, fr. *croc.*] **1.** A pole or stake with forked top, used as a prop. **2.** The angle formed by the parting of two legs or branches; a fork; bifurcation; as, the *crotch* of the human body or of a tree. — **crotched** (krŏcht), *adj.*

crotch′et (krŏch′ĕt; -ĭt), *n.* [OF. *crochet,* fr. *croc* hook.] **1.** A small hook or hooklike instrument or process; specif., *Obs.*, a brooch. **2. a** A perverse fancy; a whimsey. **b** A fanciful contrivance. **3.** *Music.* See NOTE, *n.*, 11. — **Syn.** See CAPRICE.

crotch′et·y (krŏch′ĕ·tĭ; -ĭ·tĭ), *adj.* **1.** Given to, or full of, crotchets; subject to whims or perverse fancies. **2.** Of the nature of a crotchet or whimsey. — **crotch′et·i·ness** (-tĭ·nĕs; -nĭs), *n.*

cro′ton (krō′t'n), *n.* [NL., fr. Gr. *krotōn* a tick (which the seeds resemble).] **1.** Any of a genus (*Croton*) of herbs and shrubs of the spurge family, esp. one of a species (*C. eluteria*) of the Bahamas yielding cascarilla bark or of an East Indian species (*C. tiglium*) yielding **croton oil,** a viscid, acrid fixed oil used as a drastic cathartic, a vesicant, and a pustulant. **2.** Any plant of an allied genus (*Codiaeum*) cultivated as a garden shrub for its handsomely colored foliage.

Cro′ton bug (krō′t'n). [From the *Croton* water of New York City (by aqueduct from Croton River).] A small, active, winged cockroach (*Blatella germanica*) common round hot-water pipes.

crouch (krouch), *v. i.* [OF. *crochir,* fr. *croc* hook.] **1.** To stoop or cower with the limbs close to the body, as an animal waiting for prey, or in fear. **2.** To bend servilely; cringe. — *v. t.* To bow, or bend, low.

croup (kro͞op), *n.* [OF. *croupe.*] The posterior part of the back of a quadruped, esp. of the horse; rump; crupper. See HORSE, *Illust.* (19).

croup, *n.* [Scot.] Any affection of the larynx or trachea marked by a hoarse, ringing cough and difficult breathing. — **croup′ous** (kro͞op′ŭs), *adj.* — **croup′y** (-ĭ), *adj.*

crou′pi·er (kro͞o′pĭ·ẽr; *F.* kro͞o′pyā′), *n.* [F., prop., one who sits on the croup, and hence, in the second place.] **1.** One who presides at a gaming table and collects and, usually, pays the stakes. **2.** One who at a public dinner party sits at the lower end of the table as assistant chairman.

crouse (kro͞os), *adj.* [MD. *cruus.*] *Dial.* Cocky; brisk.

crou·ton′ (kro͞o·tôN′; -tŏn′), *n.* [F. *croûton,* fr. *croûte* a crust.] *Cookery.* A small piece of bread toasted or fried crisp, used in soups, in garnishing, etc.

crow (krō), *v. i.*; CREW (kro͞o), *now only in sense* 1, or CROWED (krōd); CROWED; CROW′ING. [AS. *crāwan.*] **1.** To make the loud shrill sound characteristic of a cock. **2.** To utter a sound expressive of pleasure. **3.** To exult; brag. — **Syn.** See BOAST. — *n.* The cry of the cock.

crow, *n.* [AS. *crāwe* a crow (in sense 1).] **1.** Any of various large, usually entirely glossy black, oscine birds (of *Corvus* and allied genera); specif., the American species (*C. brachyrhynchos*), which is gregarious and feeds on grains, and the common European species (*C. corone*), called also ***carrion crow.*** Other species include the *rook* and *raven* (see these terms), the ***hooded crow*** (*C. cornix*) of Europe, the related ***house crow*** (*C. splendens*) of India, a well-known scavenger, and the fish-eating ***fish crow*** (*C. ossifragus*) of the U. S. Atlantic coast. The crows typify a family (Corvidae, the crow family) which includes also the choughs, jays, and magpies. **2.** A bar of iron with a beak, crook, or claw, for use as a lever or pry; esp., a crowbar. **3.** [*cap.*] The constellation Corvus. — ***as the crow flies.*** In a direct line.

crow′bar′ (-bär′), *n.* A bar of iron or steel, usually wedge-shaped at the working end, used as a pry or lever, etc.

crow′ber′ry (-bĕr′ĭ; -bẽr·ĭ), *n.* **1.** A heathlike undershrub (*Empetrum nigrum;* family Empetraceae, the crowberry family) of arctic and alpine regions; also, its black, insipid berry. **2.** *U. S.* See CRANBERRY, 1.

crowd (kroud), *n.* [W. *crwth.*] An ancient Celtic musical instrument. See *Illust.*

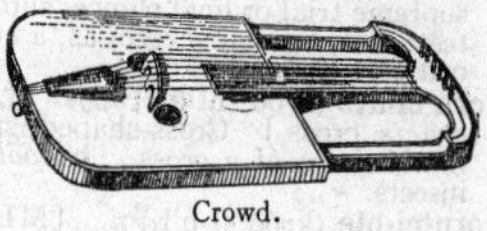

Crowd.

crowd (kroud), *v. i.* [AS. *crūdan.*] **1.** To press or drive on; — orig. of a ship. **2.** To press forward; to force oneself or itself. **3.** To press together in numbers; to throng. — *v. t.* **1.** To shove or push. **2.** To press, force, or thrust, as into a much smaller space or time; cram. **3.** To fill or occupy to excess or obstruction. **4.** *Colloq.* To put pressure upon; urge; specif., to dun. — ***crowd (on) sail*** *or* ***canvas.*** *Naut.* To carry an extraordinary amount of sail to accelerate the speed. — *n.* **1.** A large number of persons collected into a close body without order; a throng. **2.** A great number of persons; esp., the populace. **3.** A set; a clique.

Syn. Crowd, throng, press, crush, mob, rout, horde mean a closely assembled multitude. Crowd implies a pressing together and, often, in current use, a loss of individuality in the unit; throng carries a stronger implication of movement and pushing; press (now archaic) suggests a concentrated mass through which one cannot easily move; crush suggests so great compactness as to make for discomfort; mob, often an intensive for *crowd,* strictly applies to a crowd or throng of rabble bent on destruction; rout and horde apply especially to a disorderly or tumultuous crowd or throng.

crow′dy, crow′die (kro͞o′dĭ; kro͝od′ĭ), *n.* *Scot. & Dial. Eng.* A thick gruel of oatmeal and water, milk, etc.

crow′foot′ (krō′fo͝ot′), *n.*; *pl.*, *except sense* 1, -FEET (-fēt′). **1.** [*pl.* -FOOTS (-fo͝ots′).] Any of a genus (*Ranunculus*) of herbs having simple or variously lobed leaves, mostly yellow five-sepaled flowers, and flattened achenes borne in a spike; — called also *buttercup, goldcup,* or *kingcup.* Common species include *R. bulbosus* (the ***meadow crowfoot***), *R. acris* (the ***tall buttercup***), and *R. aconitifolius* (the ***garden buttercup***). The genus typifies a family (Ranunculaceae, the crowfoot family), which includes also the aconitum, anemone, clematis, delphinium, and peony. **2.** *Elec.* A zinc electrode in a gravity cell, shaped like a crow's foot. **3.** *Naut.* A number of divergent small cords rove through a long block. **4.** = CROW'S-FOOT, in various senses.

crow′hop′ (krō′hŏp′), *n.* A short hop; *Western U. S.*, a rigid posture taken by a horse while bucking.

crow′keep′er (-kēp′ẽr), *n.* *Obs. exc. Dial.* A scarecrow.

crown (kroun), *n.* [OF. *corone, corune,* fr. L. *corona* crown, wreath, fr. Gr. *korōnē* anything curved, crown.] **1.** A garland or fillet about the head, esp. as a reward of victory or mark of honor; hence, any reward. **2.** A royal or imperial headdress or cap of sovereignty. **3.** Imperial or regal power. **4.** [*often cap.*] One entitled to wear a crown; — with *the.* **5.** The topmost part of the skull or head; the top part of a hat or other headgear. **6.** Anything which imparts beauty, splendor, honor, or finish; also, the highest state or quality of anything. **7.** Any of several coins (orig., one bearing a crown), esp. a British silver coin worth five shillings. For related coins of other countries, see ÉCU, KORUNA, KRONA, KRONE, KROON. **8.** A representation of a crown as a heraldic bearing, a watermark, hallmark, etc. **9.** Anything like a crown, as in being crown-shaped, as bearing a representation of a crown, or as being the summit. **10.** Short for CROWN LENS, CROWN GLASS, CROWN SAW. **11.** *Anat. & Zool.* **a** *Anat.* The part of a tooth above the gum; also, the top of a tooth; also, *Dent.*, the artificial substitute for the top of a tooth. See TOOTH, *Illust.* **b** The crest, as of a bird. See BIRD, *Illust.* **12.** *Bot.* **a** An appendage on the summit of a seed; a corona. **b** The junction of stem and root in a seed plant. See ROOT, *Illust.* **c** The head of foliage, as in a tree. **13.** *Naut.* The thick arching end of an anchor where the arms are joined to it. See ANCHOR, *Illust.* — *v. t.* **1.** To place a crown upon; to cover, decorate, or invest with a crown; hence, to enthrone. **2.** To bestow something upon as a mark of honor, dignity, or recompense; to adorn. **3.** To top, cap, or surmount, as with a crown. **4.** To form or furnish the topmost part of; to complete; perfect; also, to form the supreme adornment of. **5.** To cause to round upward; to make convex. **6.** *Checkers.* To make a king of (a man), as by placing another man on it. — **crown′er,** *n.*

crown antler. See ANTLER, *Illust.*

crown colony. A colony of the British Commonwealth in which the crown retains certain control of legislation. Crown colonies range in organization from those administered by a governor alone (as St. Helena) to those over which the crown retains only a veto on legislation (as Jamaica).

crown′er (kroun′ẽr; krōōn′ẽr), *n. Obs.* A coroner.

crown′et (kroun′ĕt; -ĭt), *n. Obs.* A coronet.

crown glass (kroun). **1.** Window glass blown and whirled into a disk, with a knot left by the worker's rod. **2.** Optical alkali-lime glass, having a low dispersion relative to the index of refraction. Cf. FLINT GLASS.

crown land. a Land belonging to the crown, to the revenues of which the reigning sovereign is entitled. **b** In some parts of the British Empire, public lands.

crown′land′ (kroun′lănd′), *n.* Formerly, in Austria-Hungary, one of the largest administrative divisions of the monarchy.

crown lens. The convex lens of an achromatic lens, made of crown glass (see ACHROMATIC, *Illust.*).

crown′piece′ (kroun′pēs′), *n.* A part forming the crown or top of anything.

crown prince. The heir apparent to a crown or throne.

crown princess. The wife of a crown prince; also, a female heir apparent.

crown saw. A cylindrical rotary saw.

crown′work′ (kroun′wûrk′), *n. Dentistry.* The application of artificial crowns to teeth; also, a piece of such work.

crow's′-foot′ (krōz′fŏŏt′), *n.; pl.* CROW'S-FEET (-fēt′). **1.** Anything having the form of a crow's foot; specif.: **a** One of the small wrinkles at the outer corners of the eyes; — usually *pl.* **b** A contrivance of two pieces fastened together crosswise to support a post. **2.** = CROWFOOT, in various senses. **3.** *Aeronautics.* A system of diverging short ropes for distributing the pull of a single rope.

crow's′-nest′, *n.* **1.** *Naut.* A partly enclosed platform high on a mast for a lookout. Cf. TOP, *n.*, 14. **2.** Any similar lookout on land.

cro′zier (krō′zhẽr). Var. of CROSIER.

cru′ces (krōō′sēz), *n., pl.* of CRUX.

cru′cial (krōō′shăl), *adj.* [F., fr. L. *crux, crucis*, cross.] **1.** Having the form of a cross; cruciform. **2.** Of the nature of, or relating to, a supreme trial or final choice; supremely critical; decisive; as, a *crucial* test; also, trying; severe; as, a *crucial* period. — **Syn.** See ACUTE. — **cru′cial·ly**, *adv.*

cru′ci·ate (krōō′shĭ·āt), *adj.* [L. *cruciatus*, past part., deriv. of *crux, crucis*, cross.] Cross-shaped; specif.: **a** *Bot.* Having leaves or petals in the form of a cross. **b** *Zool.* Crossing; — of the wings of some insects.

cru′ci·ble (krōō′sĭ·b'l), *n.* [ML. *crucibulum* earthen pot, a hanging lamp, fr. L. *crux, crucis*, cross.] **1.** A pot of some very refractory substance, as clay, graphite, porcelain, or a relatively infusible metal, used for melting and calcining substances which require a high degree of heat, as metal, ores, etc. **2.** A hollow at the bottom of a furnace, for melted metal. **3.** A severe trial or test.

crucible steel. A superior cast steel made by melting crude steel or by fusing iron, carbon and flux in crucibles.

cru′ci·fer (krōō′sĭ·fẽr), *n.* [LL. See CRUX; -FEROUS.] **1.** *Eccl.* One who carries a cross, as at the head of a procession. **2.** *Bot.* Any plant of the mustard family (Brassicaceae, syn. Cruciferae).

cru′ci·fix (krōō′sĭ·fĭks), *n.* [OF. or L.; OF. *crucefix*, fr. L. *crucifixus*, fr. *crux, crucis*, cross + *figere, fixum*, to fix.] A representation of Christ on the cross; also, loosely, the cross, as a Christian emblem.

cru′ci·fix′ion (-fĭk′shŭn), *n.* **1.** A crucifying; specif. [*cap.*], the execution of Christ on the cross; also, a representation of it in art. Cf. CALVARY, 2. **2.** Intense suffering; painful trial.

cru′ci·form (krōō′sĭ·fôrm), *adj.* [L. *crux, crucis*, cross + *-form.*] Cross-shaped; cruciate. — **cru′ci·form′ly**, *adv.*

cru′ci·fy (krōō′sĭ·fī), *v. t.;* -FIED (-fīd); -FY′ING. [OF. *crucifier*, deriv. of L. *crux, crucis*, cross + *figere* to fix.] **1.** To put to death by nailing or binding the hands and feet to a cross of execution. **2.** To subdue completely; to mortify; as, to *crucify* the flesh. **3.** To torture; torment; treat cruelly.

crud (krŭd; *dial. also* krōōd, krōōd). See CURD, *v.*

crude (krōōd), *adj.* [L. *crudus* raw.] **1.** In a natural state; not cooked or prepared by heat; raw; also, not refined. **2.** Unripe; immature. **3.** Wanting finish, grace, tact, taste, or other quality characteristic of maturity or culture; rude. **4.** Unglossed by alleviating disguise; bald. — **Syn.** See RUDE. — *n.* A crude substance; specif., petroleum as extracted from the ground; crude oil. — **crude′ly**, *adv.* — **crude′ness**, *n.*

cru′di·ty (krōō′dĭ·tĭ), *n.; pl.* -TIES (-tĭz). **1.** Quality of being crude. **2.** That which is crude.

cru′el (krōō′ĕl; -ĭl), *adj.;* CRU′EL·ER (-ẽr); CRU′EL·EST. [OF., fr. L. *crudelis*, fr. *crudus* raw.] **1.** Disposed to give pain to others; inhuman; merciless. **2.** Causing, or fitted to cause, pain or grief. — **Syn.** See FIERCE. — **cru′el·ly**, *adv.* — **cru′el·ness**, *n.*

cru′el·ty (-ĕl·tĭ), *n.; pl.* -TIES (-tĭz). **1.** Quality of being cruel. **2.** A cruel and barbarous deed; inhuman treatment.

cru′et (krōō′ĕt; -ĭt), *n.* [AF., dim. of OF. *crue, cruie.*] A vial or small glass bottle for vinegar, oil, etc., for the table; a caster.

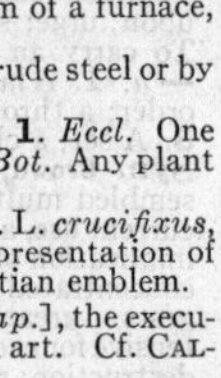
Cruet.

cruise (krōōz), *v. i.* [D. *kruisen* to zigzag, cruise, fr. *kruis* cross, fr. L. *crux.*] **1.** To sail about touching at a series of ports, making for no set destination. **2.** To make a similar trip on or over land, as in an airplane. **3.** To go wandering about; as, a taxicab *cruising* for fares. **4.** *Forestry.* To inspect forest land in order to estimate its yield of lumber. — *v. t.* To cruise over or about. — *n.* A cruising voyage or journey.

cruis′er (krōōz′ẽr), *n.* **1.** A vessel, vehicle, or the like, that cruises. **2.** A man-of-war less heavily armed and armored than a battleship, having superior speed. **3.** A powerboat equipped with cabin, plumbing, and all arrangements necessary for living aboard; — called also *cabin cruiser.* **4.** = SQUAD CAR. **5.** *Forestry.* Also *timber cruiser.* A timber estimator. See CRUISE, *v. i.*, 4.

crul′ler (krŭl′ẽr), *n.* A friedcake made of a rich egg batter, cut in strips or twists, and fried brown in deep fat.

crumb (krŭm), *n.* Also, commonly till 19th century, **crum.** [AS. *crūma.*] **1.** A small fragment or piece, esp. of bread, cake, or the like. **2.** A bit; as, *crumbs* of learning, information, comfort. **3.** The soft part of bread; — disting. from *crust.* — *v. t. & i.* **1.** To break into crumbs, as bread. **2.** *Cookery.* To cover, thicken, or dress with crumbs. **3.** *Colloq.* To remove crumbs from; as, to *crumb* a table after a meal.

crum′ble (krŭm′b'l), *v. t. & i.;* CRUM′BLED (-b'ld); CRUM′BLING (-blĭng). [Freq. of *crumb*, v. t.] To break into small pieces; hence, to fall to decay. — **Syn.** See DECAY. — *n.* Crumbling substance.

crum′bly (-blĭ), *adj.;* -BLI·ER (-blĭ·ẽr); -BLI·EST. Easily crumbled; friable. — **crum′bli·ness** (-blĭ·nĕs; -nĭs), *n.*

crum′mie, crum′my (krŭm′ĭ; krŏŏm′ĭ), *n. Scot. & N. of Eng.* A cow, esp. one with crumpled horns.

crump (krŭmp; krŏŏmp), *v. t. & i.* To crunch.

crump, *adj. Dial.* Brittle or friable; crisp.

crum′pet (krŭm′pĕt; -pĭt), *n.* [Dial. also *crampit*, ME. *crompid cake* wafer.] A flat soft leavened cake made of batter cooked on a griddle or spider.

crum′ple (krŭm′p'l), *v. t.;* CRUM′PLED (-p'ld); CRUM′PLING (-plĭng). [AS. *crump* crooked, bent, *gecrympan* to crimp, curl.] To draw or press into wrinkles or folds; crush together. — *v. i.* **1.** To contract irregularly. **2.** *Colloq.* To collapse. — *n.* A wrinkle or crease made by crumpling.

crum′pled (-p'ld), *adj.* Bent, as in a spiral curve.

crunch (krŭnch), *v. i. & t.* **1.** To chew with a crushing or grinding noise; to craunch. **2.** To grind or press with a noise of crushing; as, to *crunch* through snow. — *n.* The act of crunching; a sound made by crunching.

cru′or (krōō′ôr), *n.* [L., blood.] *Physiol.* The clotted portion of coagulated blood; gore.

crup′per (krŭp′ẽr; krŏŏp′ẽr), *n.* [OF. *cropiere*, fr. *crope, croupe.*] **1.** A leather loop passing under a horse's tail and buckled to the saddle or harness. See HARNESS, *Illust.* **2.** The rump of a horse; croup; also, *Humorous*, the buttocks.

cru′ral (krŏŏr′ăl), *adj.* [L. *cruralis*, fr. *crus, cruris*, leg.] *Anat.* **a** Of or pert. to the thigh or leg. **b** Specif., femoral.

crus (krŭs), *n.; pl.* CRURA (krōō′rȧ). [L., the leg.] *Anat. & Zool.* **1.** That part of the hind limb between the femur and the tarsus; the shank. **2.** Any of various parts likened to a leg, or (in plural) to a pair of legs, as the peduncles of the cerebrum (‖**cru′ra ce′re·bri** [sĕr′ē·brī]).

cru·sade′ (krōō·sād′), *n.* [From Sp. *cruzada*, with ending fr. F. *croisade*, fr. a verb signifying to mark with the cross, fr. L. *crux* cross.] **1.** [*often cap.*] Any of the seven (some reckon nine) military expeditions undertaken by Christian powers, in the 11th, 12th, and 13th centuries, to recover the Holy Land from the Moslems. **2.** Any hostile expedition under papal sanction. **3.** Any remedial enterprise undertaken with zeal and enthusiasm. — *v. i.* To engage in a crusade. — **cru·sad′er** (-sād′ẽr), *n.*

cru·sa′do (-sā′dō), *n.; pl.* -DOES or -DOS (-dōz). [Pg. *cruzado*, prop., marked with a cross.] An old Portuguese coin of gold or silver, of various values.

cruse (krōōs; krōōz), *n.* A jar or cup, for water, oil, etc.

crush (krŭsh), *v. t.* [OF. *cruisir, croissir*, of Teut. origin.] **1.** To compress or bruise between two hard bodies; to squeeze or force by pressure so as to destroy the natural condition, shape, or integrity of the parts. **2.** To reduce to fine particles by pounding or grinding. **3.** To suppress as if by pressure or weight. **4.** To force out or extract by pressure. **5.** To drink, as a bottle of wine or pot of ale. **6.** To flatten out the grain of, as leather, by pressing. — *v. i.* To be or become crushed. — *n.* **1.** Act of crushing; violent compression. **2.** A crowd which produces uncomfortable pressure. **3.** *Colloq.* A reception, or the like, overcrowded by guests. **4.** *Slang, U. S.* An intense, often sudden infatuation; also, the object of such infatuation. — **Syn.** See CROWD. — **crush′er**, *n.*

crust (krŭst), *n.* [OF. and L.; OF. *croste, crouste*, fr. L. *crusta.*] **1** The hardened exterior part of bread, in distinction from crumb; also, a piece of this or of any bread grown dry or hard. **2.** The cover or case of a pie. **3.** A hard outer shell; an incrustation. **4.** A hardened surface layer of earth, snow, etc. **5.** An incrustation on the interior surface of wine bottles; beeswing. **6.** *Geol.* The exterior relatively cool part of the globe. **7.** *Med.* A hard mass of dried secretions, blood, or pus. — *v. t. & i.* **1.** To cover with, or become covered with, an incrustation. **2.** To form or gather into a crust.

crus·ta′cean (krŭs·tā′shăn), *n.* [NL. *crustaceus*, fr. L. *crusta* the hard surface of a body, rind, shell.] *Zool.* Any of a large class (Crustacea) of arthropods, principally aquatic, including the lobsters, shrimps, crabs, wood lice, water fleas, barnacles, etc., commonly covered with a horny shell. — **crus·ta′cean**, *adj.*

crus·ta′ceous (-shŭs), *adj.* **1.** Pertaining to, or of the nature of, crust, or shell; having a crustlike shell or scab. **2.** *Zool.* Crustacean.

crust′y (krŭs′tĭ), *adj.;* CRUST′I·ER (-tĭ·ẽr); -I·EST. **1.** Having the nature of crust; pertaining to a hard covering. **2.** Having a harsh exterior, or a curt, rough manner. — **Syn.** See BLUFF. — **crust′i·ly**, *adv.* — **crust′i·ness**, *n.*

crutch (krŭch), *n.* [AS. *crycc.*] **1.** A staff with a crosspiece at the top to support the lame or infirm in walking; hence, a prop or support. **2.** A forked leg rest constituting the pommel of a sidesaddle. **3.** The crotch of a human being. **4.** Anything resembling a crutch in shape or use; as, *Naut.*, a forked support for a fore-and-aft boom when its sail is stowed. — *v. t.* To support on crutches; to prop up.

crux (krŭks), *n.; pl.* CRUXES (krŭk′sĕz; -sĭz), CRUCES (krōō′sēz). [L., cross, torture.] **1.** A cross, as in heraldry; specif. [*cap., gen.* CRUCIS (krōō′sĭs)], *Astron.*, the Southern Cross. **2.** Anything very puzzling or difficult to explain. **3.** A crucial or critical point.

‖**crux an·sa′ta** (ăn·sā′tȧ). [L.] The ankh (which see).

cru·zei′ro (krōō·zā′rō; *Pg.* -zā′ē·rōō), *n.* [Pg., fr. *cruz* cross.] The monetary unit of Brazil, replacing (1942) the milreis. 1000 cruzeiros equal a conto. See MONEY, *Tables.*

cry (krī), *v. i.;* CRIED (krīd); CRY′ING. [OF. *crier*, fr. L. *quiritare* to raise a plaintive cry, scream.] **1.** To make a loud call or cry, as in prayer, pain, anger, etc.; to shout. **2.** To lament audibly; to weep. **3.** Of an animal, to utter its characteristic call. — *v. t.* **1.** To beg for; implore; — now chiefly in *to cry quarter.* **2.** To utter loudly; shout; proclaim; also, to advertise by outcry, as goods for sale. — ***cry down.*** To decry; to depreciate. — ***cry quarter.*** To ask for quarter in combat. — ***cry quits.*** To declare oneself clear or even with another, as for past injuries.
— *n.; pl.* CRIES (krīz). **1.** A loud, vehement utterance or call; also, *Obs.*, clamor; outcry. **2.** An entreaty; appeal. **3.** A loud calling out of words, as for proclamation, etc. **4.** A watchword or battle cry. **5.**

Common report; fame. **6.** The utterance of the general opinion, feeling, or desire; the public voice. **7.** A fit of weeping. **8.** A sound or call characteristic of an animal. **9.** The giving voice of hounds in chase; hence, a pack of hounds. — ***a far cry.*** A great distance. — ***in full cry.*** In full pursuit, as hounds following a scent. — ***(all) the cry.*** The fashion; the latest thing.

cry'ing (krī'ĭng), *adj.* That cries; hence, calling for notice; as, a *crying* need; notorious; heinous; as, a *crying* evil.

cry'mo·ther'a·py (krī'mō·thĕr'ȧ·pĭ), *n.* [Gr. *krymos* frost + *-therapy.*] Therapeutic use of cold.

cry'o- (krī'ō-). [Gr. *kryos* icy cold.] A combining form meaning *cold, freezing,* as in: **cry·om'e·ter**, a thermometer for measuring low temperatures; **cry·os'co·py**, determination of the freezing points of liquids.

cry'o·gen (krī'ō·jĕn), *n.* [*cryo-* + *-gen.*] A refrigerant.

cry'o·gen'ic (krī'ō·jĕn'ĭk), *adj.* Of or pert. to **cry·og'e·ny** (krī·ŏj'ē·nĭ), the science of refrigeration, esp. with reference to methods for producing very low temperatures.

cry'o·lite (krī'ō·līt), *n.* [*cryo-* + *-lite;* — from its icy appearance.] *Mineral.* A sodium-aluminum fluoride, Na_3AlF_6, found in Greenland, usually in white cleavable masses, used in making soda, aluminum, etc.

crypt (krĭpt), *n.* [L. *crypta,* fr. Gr. *kryptē,* fr. *kryptos* hidden, fr. *kryptein* to hide.] **1.** A vault wholly or partly underground, as under the floor of a church. **2.** *Anat.* A simple gland or glandular cavity; a follicle.

crypt'a·nal'y·sis (krĭpt'ȧ·năl'ĭ·sĭs), *n.* Decipherment of cryptograms. — **crypt·an'a·lyst** (krĭpt·ăn'ȧ·lĭst), *n.*

cryp'tic (krĭp'tĭk), *adj.* Also **cryp'ti·cal** (-tĭ·kăl). **1.** Hidden; secret; occult; as, nature's *cryptic* ways. **2.** Loosely, enigmatic; mysterious; as, a *cryptic* comment. — **Syn.** See OBSCURE. — **cryp'ti·cal·ly**, *adv.*

cryp'to- (krĭp'tō-), **crypt-.** [Gr. *kryptos.*] A combining form meaning *hidden, covered, secret,* as in **cryp'to·gen'ic**, *Med.*, of obscure origin, as certain diseases.

cryp'to·clas'tic (-klăs'tĭk), *adj.* *Petrog.* Made up of very minute fragmental particles with microscopic grains.

cryp'to·gam (krĭp'tō·găm), *n.* [F. *cryptogame,* fr. *crypto-* + Gr. *gamos* marriage.] *Bot.* A plant which does not produce flowers or seeds, as ferns, mosses, algae, etc.; — opp. to *spermatophyte.* — **cryp'to·gam'ic** (-găm'ĭk), **cryp·tog'a·mous** (krĭp·tŏg'ȧ·mŭs), *adj.*

cryp'to·gram (-grăm), *n.* [*crypto-* + *-gram.*] A writing in cipher or secret arrangement of letters or words; also, a symbolic figure or representation having a hidden significance. — **cryp'to·gram'mic** (-grăm'ĭk), *adj.*

cryp'to·graph (-grăf; 9), *n.* A cryptogram.

cryp·tog'ra·phy (krĭp·tŏg'rȧ·fĭ), *n.* Act or art of writing in secret characters; also, secret characters, or cipher. — **cryp·tog'ra·pher** (-fẽr), **cryp·tog'ra·phist** (-fĭst), *n.* — **cryp'to·graph'ic** (krĭp'tō·grăf'ĭk), **cryp'to·graph'i·cal** (-ĭ·kăl), *adj.* — **cryp'to·graph'i·cal·ly**, *adv.*

cryp'to·me'ri·a (krĭp'tō·mē'rĭ·ȧ), *n.* [NL. See CRYPTO-; -MERE. Alluding to the concealment of the seeds of the cones within bracts.] An evergreen tree (genus *Cryptomeria*) of the pine family. The only known species (*C. japonica*), the *Japan cedar*, is a valuable timber tree of Japan.

cryp'to·phyte (krĭp'tō·fīt), *n.* *Bot.* A cryptogam.

crys'tal (krĭs'tăl; -t'l), *n.* [OF. *cristal,* fr. L. *crystallum* crystal, ice, fr. Gr. *krystallos,* fr. *kryos* icy cold, frost.] **1.** Quartz that is transparent or nearly so; also, a piece of this material, as one cut for ornament or for use in magic. **2.** Anything resembling crystal, as clear water, etc. **3.** A body formed by a chemical element or compound solidifying so that it is bounded by plane surfaces symmetrically arranged, which are the external expression of a definite internal structure; as, quartz *crystals;* snow *crystals.* **4.** Glass of superior brilliancy, made into articles for the table, etc.; flint glass; also, such glassware. **5.** The glass over a watch dial. **6.** *Radio.* = QUARTZ PLATE. — *adj.* **1.** Consisting of, or like, crystal; clear; transparent. **2.** *Radio.* Of, relating to, or using, a crystal; as, a *crystal* set; *crystal* detector.

crystal detector. *Radio.* A detector which operates by means of the rectifying action of the surface of contact between certain crystals and a metallic electrode.

crystal gazing. Gazing at a crystal to evoke the images of crystal vision (which see), conceived as a method of divination. — **crys'tal-gaz'er**, *n.*

crys'tal·lif'er·ous (krĭs'tă·lĭf'ẽr·ŭs), **crys'tal·lig'er·ous** (-lĭj'ẽr·ŭs), *adj.* [L. *crystallum* crystal + *-ferous, -gerous.*] Producing or containing crystals.

crys'tal·line (krĭs'tăl·ĭn; -īn; *poet.* krĭs·tăl'ĭn, -īn), *adj.* **1.** Consisting or made of crystal. **2.** Resembling crystal; transparent. **3.** Of the nature of a crystal or crystals.

crystalline lens. The lens of the eye in vertebrates.

crys'tal·lite (krĭs'tăl·īt), *n.* [See CRYSTAL.] *Mineral.* A minute mineral form like those in glassy volcanic rocks, not having a definite crystalline outline but marking the first step in crystallization. — **crys'tal·lit'ic** (-ĭt'ĭk), *adj.*

crys'tal·li·za'tion (-ĭ·zā'shŭn; -ī·zā'-), *n.* Act or process of crystallizing; also, a form of body resulting from this. Cf. WATER OF CRYSTALLIZATION.

crys'tal·lize (krĭs'tăl·īz), *v. t. & i.* **1.** To form or cause to form crystals or assume crystalline character. **2.** To assume or cause to assume a fixed and definite form; as, his plans *crystallized.* — **crys'tal·liz'a·ble** (krĭs'tă·līz'ȧ·b'l), *adj.*

crys'tal·lo- (krĭs'tăl·ō-), **crystall-.** [Gr. *krystallos.*] A combining form meaning *crystal.*

crys'tal·lo·graph'ic (-grăf'ĭk), **crys'tal·lo·graph'i·cal** (-ĭ·kăl), *adj.* Pertaining to or dealing with crystallography or crystals. — **crys'tal·lo·graph'i·cal·ly**, *adv.*

crys'tal·log'ra·phy (krĭs'tă·lŏg'rȧ·fĭ), *n.* [*crystallo-* + *-graphy.*] The science of crystallization, treating of the system of forms among crystals, their structure, etc. — **crys'tal·log'ra·pher** (-fẽr), *n.*

crys'tal·loid (krĭs'tăl·oid), *adj.* [*crystall-* + *-oid.*] Crystallike; of the nature of a crystalloid. — *n.* *Chem.* A substance which forms a true solution and is capable of being crystallized; — opposed to *colloid.* — **crys'tal·loi'dal** (krĭs'tă·loi'dăl; -d'l), *adj.*

crys'tal·lose (-ōs), *n.* The sodium salt of saccharin, intensely sweet like saccharin but more soluble; saccharin soluble.

crystal set. *Radio.* A receiving set having a crystal detector but no electron tubes.

crystal vision. Visual images aroused by gazing upon a crystal or crystallike surface in which the objects seem to be seen; also, the faculty of seeing such images.

cten'o- (tĕn'ō-; tē'nō-), **cten-.** [Gr. *kteis, ktenos,* comb.] A combining form denoting, in zoology, a *ctenoid plate, scale,* etc.

cte'noid (tē'noid; tĕn'oid), *adj.* [*cten-* + *-oid.*] *Zool.* Having a comblike margin.

cte·noph'o·ran (tē·nŏf'ō·răn), *adj.* Belonging or pertaining to a ctenophore (animal). — **cte·noph'o·ran**, *n.*

cten'o·phore (tĕn'ō·fōr; tē'nō-; 70), *n.* [*cteno-* + *-phore.*] **a** One of a phylum (Ctenophora) of marine jellyfishlike animals that show decided biradial symmetry and swim by means of eight meridional bands of transverse comblike plates. **b** One of the meridional bands of a ctenophore.

cub (kŭb), *n.* **1.** The young of the fox, bear, wolf, lion, tiger, etc., and sometimes of the whale or shark. **2.** Jocosely or in contempt, a boy or girl; esp., an awkward, ill-mannered boy. **3.** Also **cub reporter.** *Colloq.* An inexperienced and, usually, young newspaper reporter. **4.** A member of a division of the Boy Scouts for boys 8 through 10 (in the British organization, 8 to 11) years old; — in Brit. use *wolf cub.*

cu'ba·ture (kū'bȧ·tůr), *n.* [L. *cubus* cube.] **a** Determination of cubic contents. **b** Cubic content; volume.

cub'by·hole' (kŭb'ĭ·hōl'), *n.* A snug or confined place.

cube (kūb), *n.* [F., fr. L. *cubus,* fr. Gr. *kybos* a cube, a cubical die.] **1.** *Geom.* The regular solid of six equal square sides. **2.** *Math.* The third power; the product got by taking a number or quantity three times as a factor; as, $2 \times 2 \times 2 = 8$, the *cube* of 2. — *v. t.* **1.** To raise to the third power; to form the cube of. **2.** To form into a cube or cubes; as, to *cube* ice; to *cube* sugar. Cf. DICE, *v. t.*, 2.

cu'be (kū'bā), *n.* [Sp. *quibey,* of Cariban origin.] Any of several tropical American plants furnishing rotenone, used esp. in insecticides.

cu'beb (kū'bĕb), *n.* [F. *cubèbe,* fr. ML., fr. Ar. *kabābah.*] *Pharm.* The dried, unripe berry of a tropical shrub (*Piper cubeba*) of the pepper family, which is crushed and smoked in cigarettes for catarrh.

cube root. *Math.* A number or quantity whose cube is the given number or quantity; as, 3 is the *cube root* of 27.

cu'bic (kū'bĭk), *adj.* **1.** Having the form of a cube; cubical. **2.** Three-dimensional; esp., with a unit of length, denoting the volume of a cube whose edge is that unit; as, a *cubic* inch, foot, yard, etc. See MEASURE, *Table* 5; METRIC SYSTEM, *Table* 6. Abbr. *c.* or *cu.* **3.** *Crystallog.* = ISOMETRIC, 2. **4.** *Math.* Of third degree, order, or power.

cu'bi·cal (-bĭ·kăl), *adj.* Cubic; esp., cube-shaped. — **cu'bi·cal·ly**, *adv.* — **cu'bi·cal·ness**, *n.*

cu'bi·cle (kū'bĭ·k'l), *n.* [L. *cubiculum,* fr. *cubare* to lie down.] A sleeping place, esp. one partitioned off from a dormitory; hence, any small partitioned space, as an individual compartment for study in a library.

cubic measure. See MEASURE, *Table* 5.

cu'bi·form (kū'bĭ·fôrm), *adj.* Of the form of a cube.

cub'ism (kūb'ĭz'm), *n.* *Art.* A phase of postimpressionism which stresses abstract form at the expense of other pictorial elements, aiming, largely by use of intersecting, often transparent cubes, cones, and other geometric solids, to produce a specific aesthetic sensation rather than a representation of nature. — **cub'ist** (-ĭst), *n. & adj.*

cu'bit (kū'bĭt), *n.* [L. *cubitum* elbow, cubit.] A measure of length, orig. the length of the forearm, from the elbow to the end of the middle finger; in English measure, 18 inches (45.72 cm.).

cu'boid (kū'boid), *adj.* Approximately cubic in shape; specif., *Anat.*, designating the outermost of the distal row of tarsal bones of many of the higher vertebrates. — *n.* **a** *Math.* A rectangular parallelepiped. **b** *Anat.* The cuboid bone. — **cu·boi'dal** (kū·boi'dăl; -d'l), *adj.*

cuck'ing stool (kŭk'ĭng). A type of chair formerly used for punishing scolds, dishonest tradesmen, etc., by fastening them in it to be pelted, and sometimes ducked. Cf. DUCKING STOOL.

cuck'old (kŭk'ŭld), *n.* [OF. *cucuault, couquiol,* fr. *cucu* cuckoo.] A man whose wife is unfaithful. — *v. t.* To make a cuckold of (a husband). — **cuck'old·ly**, *adj.* — **cuck'old·ry**, *n.*

cuck'oo (kŏŏk'ōō; kōō'kōō), *n.* [ME. *cuccu, cukkow,* imitative.] **1.** A European bird (*Cuculus canorus*), famed for its habit of laying its eggs in the nests of other birds for them to hatch. **2.** Any bird of the same family (Cuculidae, the cuckoo family), including the North American ***black-billed cuckoo*** (*Coccyzus erythropthalmus*) and ***yellow-billed cuckoo*** (*C. americanus*), which usually incubate their own eggs, and the ani and road runner (see these terms). **3.** The call of the cuckoo. **4.** *Slang, U.S.* A cuckoo person. — *v. i.;* CUCK'OOED (-ōōd); CUCK'OO·ING. To utter the call of the cuckoo, or a sound like it. — *adj.* *Slang, U.S.* Stupidly silly; crazy.

cuck'oo·flow'er (-flou'ẽr), *n.* **a** A bitter cress (*Cardamine pratensis*), of Europe and America; — called also *lady's-smock.* **b** = RAGGED ROBIN.

cuck'oo·pint' (-pīnt'), *n.* A European arum (*Arum maculatum*) with erect spathe and short purple spadix.

cuckoo spit. Also **cuckoo spittle.** **a** A frothy secretion found upon plants, exuded by the young of spittle insects; — called also *toad spittle* and *frog spit.* **b** = SPITTLE INSECT.

cu·cu'li·form (kū·kū'lĭ·fôrm), *adj.* [L. *cuculus* cuckoo + *-form.*] *Zool.* Like, or belonging to, the cuckoos or the order (Cuculiformes) of birds including the cuckoos.

cu'cul·late (kū'kŭ·lāt; kū·kŭl'āt), *adj.* Also **cu'cul·lat'ed** (-lāt'ĕd, -ĭd; -āt·ĕd, -ĭd). [LL. *cucullatus,* fr. L. *cucullus* cap.] Hooded; hood-shaped, as certain leaves.

cu'cum·ber (kū'kŭm·bẽr), *n.* [L. and OF.; OF. *cocombre,* fr. Pr. *cogombre,* fr. L. *cucumis, -meris.*] **1.** The long, succulent fruit of a vine (*Cucumis sativus*) of the gourd family, cultivated as a garden vegetable, which is usually eaten uncooked as a salad. The young fruit are much used for pickles. **2.** The vine itself.

cucumber tree. See MAGNOLIA.

cu·cu'mi·form (kū·kū'mĭ·fôrm), *adj.* [L. *cucumis* cucumber + *-form.*] Having the form of a cucumber.

cu·cur'bit (kū·kûr'bĭt), *n.* In sense 1 also **cu·cur'bite.** [F. *cucurbite,* fr. L. *cucurbita* a gourd.] **1.** *Archaic, Chem.* A vessel or flask for distillation used with or forming part of an alembic. Cf. ALEMBIC *Illust.* **2.** A plant of the gourd family.

cu·cur'bi·ta'ceous (-bĭ·tā'shŭs), *adj.* Belonging to the gourd family (Cucurbitaceae). See GOURD.

cud (kŭd), *n.* [AS. *cudu, cwudu.*] **1.** That portion of food which is brought up into the mouth by ruminating animals from their first stomach, to be chewed a second time. **2.** *Slang.* A quid.

cud′dle (kŭd′'l), *v. t. & i.;* CUD′DLED (-'ld); CUD′DLING (-lĭng). To hold or lie close for warmth or comfort or in affection; to snuggle; nestle. — **Syn.** See CARESS. — *n.* A close embrace; act of nestling. — **cud′dle·some** (-sŭm), *adj.* — **cud′dly** (kŭd′lĭ), *adj.*
cud′dy (kŭd′ĭ), *n.; pl.* CUDDIES (-ĭz). **1.** *Naut.* A small cabin; also, the galley or pantry of a small vessel. **2.** Any small room or closet.
cud′dy (kŭd′ĭ; kŏŏd′ĭ), *n.* *Scot.* A donkey; also, blockhead.
cudg′el (kŭj′ĕl), *n.* [AS. *cycgel.*] A short heavy club. — ***to take up the cudgels.*** To engage in a contest. — *v. t.;* CUDG′ELED (-ĕld) or CUDG′ELLED; CUDG′EL·ING or CUDG′EL·LING. To beat with a cudgel. — ***cudgel one's brains.*** To harass one's wits for ideas.
cud′weed′ (kŭd′wēd′), *n.* Any of certain plants (*Gnaphalium* and related genera of the aster family) with silky or cottony herbage.
cue (kū), *n.* [Prob. fr. F. *queue* end, tail. See CUE a queue.] **1.** The last word of a speech, or the end of an action, in a play, as indicating the time for the next person to speak or act. **2.** A hint; intimation. **3.** The part one has to perform in or as in a play. **4.** Humor; temper of mind.
cue, *n.* [F. *queue.*] **1.** = QUEUE. **2.** A straight tapering rod tipped with leather used to impel the balls in billiards and other games. — *v. t.* To braid; to twist.
cue ball. *Billiards & Pool.* The ball which a player strikes with his cue. Cf. OBJECT BALL.
cuff (kŭf), *n.* [ME. *coffe, cuffe.*] **1.** An ornamental band covering the wrist, as a wide stiffened band worn either attached to the shirt sleeve or separate. **2.** A band resembling a turned-back hem, finishing a trouser leg.
cuff, *v. t.* [Late ME. *cuffe.*] To strike with or as with the flat of the hand; to buffet. — *n.* A slap.
Cu′fic (kū′fĭk). Var. of KUFIC.
‖**cui bo′no** (kī bō′nō; kwī). [L.] Who benefits by it? Also, inaccurately, of what use is it?
cuif (kŏŏf; kûf). Var. of COOF. *Scot. & N. of Eng.*
cui·rass′ (kwē·răs′), *n.* [F. *cuirasse,* deriv. of L. *coriaceus* of leather, fr. *corium* leather, hide.] **1.** A piece of armor, orig. of leather, covering the body; also, the breastplate of such a piece. **2.** *Zool.* A bony protective structure, resembling armor, as on the armadillo. — *v. t.* To cover or armor with or as with a cuirass.
cui′ras·sier′ (kwē′ră·sēr′), *n.* [F.] A mounted soldier wearing a cuirass.
cui·sine′ (kwē·zēn′), *n.* [F., fr. L. *coquina* kitchen.] The kitchen or cooking department; also, style of cooking or the food prepared.
cuisse (kwĭs), **cuish** (kwĭsh; *formerly* kwĭs), *n.* [From pl. of OF. *cuissel,* fr. *cuisse* thigh, fr. L. *coxa* hip.] A piece of defensive armor for the thighs; in *pl.,* CUISSES (kwĭs′ĕz; -ĭz), defensive plate armor for the thighs. See ARMOR, *Illust.*
cuit′tle (küt′'l), **cui′tle** (kü′t'l), *v.* *Scot.* To coax; tickle.
culch (kŭlch). Var. of CULTCH.
cul′–de–sac′ (kōōl′dē·săk′; kŭl′-; F. küd′săk′), *n.; pl.* CUL-DE-SACS (kōōl′dē·săks′; kŭl′-), F. CULS-DE-SAC (küd′săk′). [F., lit., bottom of a bag.] A passage or place with only one outlet, as a blind alley.
-cule (-kūl). [F. or L.; F. *-cule,* fr. L. *-culus, -cula, -culum.*] A suffix forming noun diminutives, as in mole*cule,* animal*cule,* etc. See -CLE.
cu′let (kū′lĕt; -lĭt), *n.* [OF., dim. of *cul* bottom, breech, fr. L. *culus.*] *Jewelry.* The small flat facet parallel to the table, at the bottom of a brilliant. See BRILLIANT, *Illust.*
cu′lex (kū′lĕks), *n.* [L., a gnat.] A mosquito of a genus (*Culex*) that includes the common house mosquito of Europe and North America. Cf. AËDES, ANOPHELES.
cu′li·nar′y (kū′lĭ·nĕr′ĭ; kŭl′ĭ-; *esp. Brit.,* -nĕr·ĭ), *adj.* [L. *culinarius,* fr. *culina* kitchen.] Of or relating to the kitchen or cookery.
cull (kŭl), *n.* *Slang & Dial.* A dupe; a gull; a cully.
cull (kŭl), *v. t.* [OF. *cuillir, coillir.* See COIL, *v.*] **1.** To separate or pick out; to choose and gather. **2.** To identify and remove culls from (a flock, herd, etc.). — **Syn.** See CHOOSE. — *n.* Something selected, esp. as inferior or worthless, to be removed.
cul′len·der (kŭl′ĕn·dẽr; kŭl′ĭn-). Var. of COLANDER.
cul′let (kŭl′ĕt; -ĭt), *n.* [F. COLLET, prop. a little neck, applied to the bits of glass at the neck of a bottle detached from the iron in blowing the glass.] *Glass Mfg.* Broken or refuse glass, a certain amount of which is necessary in the batch.
cul′lion (kŭl′yŭn), *n.* [F. *couillon* testicle, *couillon* base fellow.] *Archaic.* A mean or base fellow.
cul′lis (kŭl′ĭs), *n.* [F. *coulisse* groove, gutter. See COULISSE]. *Arch.* A gutter in a roof.
cul′ly (kŭl′ĭ), *n.; pl.* -LIES (-ĭz). *Now Rare.* A dupe; a gull. — *v. t.* *Obs.* To trick or cheat.
culm (kŭlm), *n.* **1.** Coal dust or coal slack. **2.** *Geol.* Also **culm measures.** A Lower Carboniferous formation in which marine fossil-bearing beds alternate with those containing plant remains.
culm, *n.* [L. *culmus* stalk.] *Bot.* The jointed stem of a grass. See VAGINATE, *Illust.* — *v. i.* *Bot.* To form or grow into a culm.
cul·mif′er·ous (kŭl·mĭf′ẽr·ŭs), *adj.* *Geol.* Containing or abounding in culm.
cul′mi·nant (kŭl′mĭ·nănt), *adj.* Culminating.
cul′mi·nate (-nāt), *v. i.* [ML. *culminatus,* past part. of *culminare* to culminate, fr. *culmen, -inis,* top.] **1.** *Astron.* To reach its highest altitude; also, to be directly overhead. **2.** To reach the highest point, as of rank, etc.; to reach a climax; to attain full development.
cul′mi·na′tion (-nā′shŭn), *n.* Act of culminating; also, culminating position; apex; consummation. — **Syn.** See SUMMIT.
cu·lottes′ (kū·lŏts′), *n. pl.* [F., breeches.] A woman's garment giving the appearance of a skirt, but divided and seamed like trousers.
cul′pa·ble (kŭl′pȧ·b'l), *adj.* [OF. *coupable, culpable,* fr. L. *culpabilis,* fr. *culpare* to blame, fr. *culpa* fault.] Deserving censure or blame. — **Syn.** See BLAMEWORTHY. — **cul′pa·bil′i·ty** (-bĭl′ĭ·tĭ), **cul′pa·ble·ness,** *n.* — **cul′pa·bly** (-blĭ), *adv.*
cul′prit (kŭl′prĭt), *n.* [From AF. *cul.* (abbr. of *culpable* guilty) + *prit, prist,* ready (i. e., to prove it), fr. LL. *praestus.*] **1.** One accused of, or arraigned for, a crime, as in court. **2.** One guilty of a crime or a fault.
cult (kŭlt), *n.* [F. and L.; F. *culte,* fr. L. *cultus* care, culture, fr. *colere* to cultivate.] **1.** A system of worship of a deity; as, the *cult* of Apollo. **2.** Hence: **a** The rites of a religion. **b** Great devotion to some person, idea, or thing, esp. such devotion viewed as an intellectual fad. **c** A sect.
cultch, culch (kŭlch), *n.* **1.** Rubbish. **2.** Any material, as oyster shells, laid down on oyster grounds to furnish points of attachment for the spat.
cul′ti·gen (kŭl′tĭ·jĕn), *n.* [*culti*vate + *-gen.*] A plant race or form, as the cabbage, which has arisen or is known only in cultivation; also, a cultural variety.
cult′ist (kŭl′tĭst), *n.* A devotee or practitioner of a cult.
cul′ti·va·ble (kŭl′tĭ·vȧ·b'l), *adj.* [F.] Capable of being cultivated. — **cul′ti·va·bil′i·ty** (-bĭl′ĭ·tĭ), *n.*
cul′ti·var (kŭl′tĭ·vär; -vẽr), *n.* *Biol.* A cultural variety.
cul′ti·vate (kŭl′tĭ·vāt), *v. t.* [ML. *cultivatus,* past part. of *cultivare* to cultivate, fr. *cultivus* cultivated, fr. L. *cultus,* past part. of *colere* to till, cultivate.] **1.** To prepare, or to prepare and use, for the raising of crops; to till; specif., to loosen or break up the soil about (growing plants), as in order to kill weeds. **2.** To raise, or foster the growth of, by tillage; to produce by culture. **3.** To civilize; refine. **4.** To devote time and thought to; hence, to foster; cherish. **5.** To seek the society of; to court intimacy with. — **cul′ti·vat′a·ble** (-vāt′ȧ·b'l), *adj.*
cul′ti·vat′ed (-vāt′ĕd; -ĭd), *adj.* Cultured; refined in manners, taste, thought, etc.
cul′ti·va′tion (-vā′shŭn), *n.* **1.** Art or act of cultivating; specif.: **a** Tillage. **b** Assiduous devotion (to a branch of learning, or the like) or development (of the mind, tastes, etc.). **2.** Culture; refinement.
cul′ti·va′tor (kŭl′tĭ·vā′tẽr), *n.* **1.** One who cultivates something, as the soil, an art, the mind. **2.** *Agric.* An implement used to loosen the soil while crops are growing.

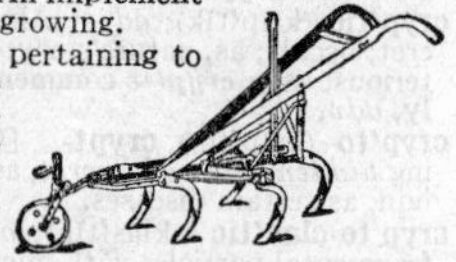
Cultivator, 2.

cul′tur·al (kŭl′tūr·ăl), *adj.* **1.** Of or pertaining to culture or a culture; conducive to culture; as, *cultural* studies. **2.** Produced by breeding; as, a *cultural* variety.
cul′ture (kŭl′tūr), *n.* [F., fr. L. *cultura,* fr. *colere* to till, cultivate.] **1.** Cultivation; tillage. **2.** Act of developing by education, discipline, training, etc. **3.** The cultivation or rearing of a particular product or crop; as, oyster *culture.* **4.** The enlightenment and refinement of taste acquired by intellectual and aesthetic training. **5.** A particular stage of advancement in civilization or the characteristic features of such a stage or state; as, primitive or Greek *culture.* **6.** *Biol.* Cultivation of microorganisms, as bacteria, or of tissues, fungi, etc., in prepared nutrient media (**culture media**); also, an instance or product of such cultivation. — *v. t.* **1.** To cultivate. **2.** *Biol.* **a** To grow (microorganisms, tissues, etc.) in a prepared medium. **b** To start a culture from; as, to *culture* soil; also, to make a culture of; as, *cultured* milk.
cul′tured (-tūrd), *adj.* **1.** Under culture; cultivated. **2.** Characterized by culture (sense 4).
cul′tus (kŭl′tŭs), *n.* [L.] Cult.
cul′ver (kŭl′vẽr), *n.* [AS. *culfre.*] A dove; a pigeon.
cul′ver·in (-ĭn), *n.* [F. *coulevrine,* fr. *couleuvre* adder, fr. L. *colubra.*] A firearm, orig. a rude sort of musket, later (16th and 17th centuries) a long cannon.
cul′vert (kŭl′vẽrt), *n.* A transverse drain under a road, canal, etc.; an arched drain or sewer; also, a conduit.
cum′ber (kŭm′bẽr), *v. t.* [ME. *combren, cumbren.* See ENCUMBER.] **1.** *Obs.* To trouble; perplex. **2.** To hinder or embarrass by interference or by being in the way. **3.** To rest upon as a troublesome or useless load; to burden. — *n.* **1.** That which cumbers. **2.** Hindrance; encumbrance. — **cum′ber·er,** *n.*
cum′ber·some (-sŭm), *adj.* **1.** *Obs. exc. Dial.* Burdensome. **2.** Cumbrous; clumsy. — **Syn.** See HEAVY. — **cum′ber·some·ly,** *adv.* — **cum′ber·some·ness,** *n.*
cum′brance (kŭm′brăns), *n.* Encumbrance; trouble.
cum′brous (-brŭs), *adj.* **1.** *Obs.* Giving trouble; vexatious. **2.** Unwieldy; burdensome. — **Syn.** See HEAVY. — **cum′brous·ly,** *adv.* — **cum′brous·ness,** *n.*
‖**cum gra′no sa′lis** (kŭm grā′nō sā′lĭs). [L.] With a grain of salt.
cum′in (kŭm′ĭn), *n.* Also **cum′min.** [AS. *cymen* (fr. L.) and OF. *cumin,* fr. L. *cuminum,* fr. Gr. *kyminon.*] A dwarf plant (*Cuminum cyminum*), of the carrot family, native to Egypt and Syria, cultivated for its aromatic seeds.
‖**cum lau′de** (kŭm lô′dē; kōōm lou′dĕ). [L.] With praise; — used esp. in diplomas to indicate that the recipient has done work of a higher grade than ordinary. Three such grades of work are often indicated by the phrases ***mag′na cum lau′de*** (măg′nȧ; mäg′nä) [L. *magna* great], ***in·sig′ne cum lau′de*** (ĭn·sĭg′nē; -nĕ) [L. *insigne* notable], ***sum′ma cum lau′de*** (sŭm′ȧ; sōōm′mä) [L. *summa* highest].
cum′mer (kŭm′ẽr), *n.* [F. *commère.*] *Chiefly Scot.* **a** A godmother. **b** A female friend. **c** A woman or girl.
cum′mer·bund′ (kŭm′ẽr·bŭnd′), *n.* [Hind.-Per. *kamarband,* fr. Ar.-Per. *kamar* loins + Per. *band* band, bandage.] *India.* A sash or band worn round the waist.
cum′quat (kŭm′kwŏt). Var. of KUMQUAT.
cum′shaw (kŭm′shô), *n.* [Amoy *kam sia,* Chin. (Pek.) *kan³ hsieh⁴,* grateful thanks; — a phrase used by beggars.] A present; a tip.
cu′mu·late (kū′mū·lāt), *v. t. & i.* [L. *cumulatus,* past part. of *cumulare* to heap up, fr. *cumulus* a heap.] To heap together; to accumulate.
cu′mu·la′tion (-lā′shŭn), *n.* A cumulating; also, a heap.
cu′mu·la′tive (kū′mū·lā′tĭv; -lȧ·tĭv), *adj.* **1.** Formed, or becoming larger, by successive additions. **2.** Subject to cumulation; that is to be, or that may be, added. **3.** *Finance.* Designating a dividend, interest, etc., which if not paid or received when due is added to what is to be paid in the future. **4.** *Law.* Tending to prove the same point to which other evidence has been offered; — said of evidence. — **cu′mu·la′tive·ly,** *adv.*
cu′mu·lo–cir′rus (kū′mū·lō·sĭr′ŭs), *n.* A small cumulus cloud at a high altitude, white and delicate like the cirrus. Cf. CLOUD, *Illust.*
cu′mu·lo–nim′bus, *n.* A mountainous cloudy mass of condensed vapor discharging showers of rain, snow, sleet, etc. See CLOUD, *Illust.*
cu′mu·lo–stra′tus, *n.* A cumulus whose base extends horizontally as a stratus cloud. Cf. CLOUD, *Illust.*
cu′mu·lous (kū′mū·lŭs), *adj.* Like cumulus clouds.
cu′mu·lus (-lŭs), *n.; pl.* -LI (-lī). [L., a heap.] **1.** A heap; accumulation. **2.** A massy cloud form with a flat base and rounded outlines piled up like a mountain. See CLOUD, *Illust.*

cunc·ta′tion (kŭngk·tā′shŭn), *n.* [L. *cunctatio*, fr. *cunctari* to delay.] Delay. — **cunc′ta·tive** (kŭngk′tȧ·tĭv), *adj.*

cunc·ta′tor (-tẽr), *n.* [L.] One who delays.

cu′ne·ate (kū′nē·āt), *adj.* Also **cu′ne·at′ed** (-āt′ĕd; -ĭd). [L. *cuneatus.*] Wedge-shaped; as, a *cuneate* leaf. See LEAF, *Illust.* (12). — **cu′ne·ate·ly**, *adv.*

cu′ne·at′ic (-ăt′ĭk), *adj.* Cuneiform.

cu·ne′i·form (kū·nē′ĭ·fôrm; kū′nē·ĭ·fôrm′), *adj.* Also **cu′ni·form** (kū′nĭ·fôrm). [L. *cuneus* a wedge + *-form.*] Wedge-shaped; — applied esp. to the wedge-shaped characters of ancient inscriptions of Assyria, Babylonia, Persia, etc. — *n.* Cuneiform characters or writing.

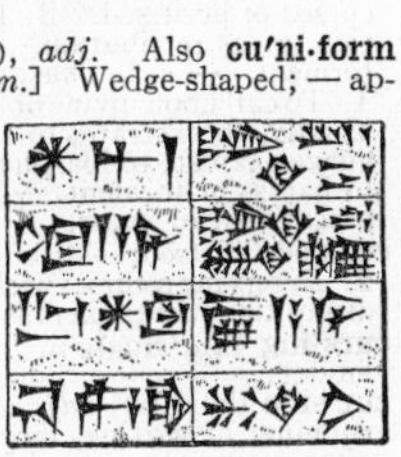

Cuneiform.

cun′ner (kŭn′ẽr), *n.* *Zool.* Either of two species of fishes related to the wrasses, one (*Crenilabrus melops*) of England, and one (*Tautogolabrus adspersus*) abundant on the New England shore.

cun′ning (kŭn′ĭng), *adj.* [Prop. pres. part., fr. AS. *cunnan* to know, be able.] **1.** Wrought with, or exhibiting, skill. **2.** Crafty, sly, or artful. **3.** Keen; clever. **4.** *U. S.* Prettily or piquantly interesting. — **Syn.** See CLEVER: SLY. — *n.* **1.** *Archaic.* Skill; dexterity. **2.** The faculty or act of using stratagem; craft. — **Syn.** See ART. — **cun′ning·ly**, *adv.* — **cun′ning·ness**, *n.*

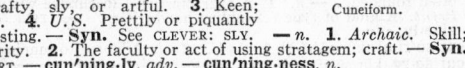

cup (kŭp), *n.* [AS. *cuppe*, fr. LL. *cuppa* cup, fr. L. *cupa* tub, cask.] **1.** A small open bowl-shaped vessel to hold liquids. **2.** The containing part of a drinking vessel that has a stem and a foot. **3.** A drinking vessel and its contents; a cupful. **4.** The wine of the Communion. **5.** That which is to be received, whether to enjoy or endure; a portion. **6.** *pl.* Repeated potations; excessive indulgence in intoxicating drinks. **7.** A beverage of liquor, sweetened and flavored with various fruits, herbs, etc.; as, claret *cup.* **8.** A thing resembling a cup (sense 1) in shape or use. **9.** *Bot.* A cup-shaped organ or part of a plant. **10.** *Golf.* The metal case inside the hole; also, the hole. **11.** *Med. & Surg.* A cupping glass or other utensil for producing the vacuum in cupping. **12.** *Sporting.* An ornamental cup or other vessel offered as a prize. — ***in one's cups.*** Drunk; formerly, drinking. — *v. t.;* CUPPED (kŭpt); CUP′PING. **1.** *Med.* To subject to cupping. See CUPPING. **2.** To receive, take, or place in or as in a cup.

cup barometer. See BAROMETER, 1.

cup′bear′er (kŭp′bâr′ẽr), *n.* One whose office it is to fill and hand the cups in which drink is served.

cup′board (kŭb′ẽrd), *n.* [*cup* + *board.*] A closet with shelves to receive dishes, food, etc.; hence, any small closet.

cup′cake′ (kŭp′kāk′), *n.* A cake baked in a cup or similar mold.

cu′pel (kū′pĕl; kū·pĕl′), *n.* [F. and L.; F. *coupelle* (ML. *cupella*), dim. of *coupe* cup (L. *cuppa* cup). See CUP.] A small, shallow, porous cup, used in assaying to separate precious metals from lead, etc. — *v. t.;* -PELED (-pĕld) or -PELLED′ (-pĕld′); -PEL·ING or -PEL′LING. To refine by means of a cupel. — **cu′pel·er** (kū′pĕl·ẽr), **cu·pel′ler** (kū-pĕl′ẽr), *n.*

cu′pel·la′tion (kū′pĕ·lā′shŭn), *n.* Refinement of gold or silver, etc., in a cupel by exposure to high temperature in a blast of air, by which lead, copper, tin, etc., are oxidized and sink into the porous cupel.

cup′ful (kŭp′fo͝ol), *n.; pl.* -FULS (-fo͝olz). As much as a cup will hold; in cookery, a half pint.

Cu′pid (kū′pĭd), *n.* [L. *Cupido*, lit., desire.] **1.** *Rom. Myth.* The god of love, son of Venus. See EROS, PSYCHE. **2.** [*not cap.*] A representation of Cupid as a naked, winged boy with bow and arrow.

cu·pid′i·ty (kū·pĭd′ĭ·tĭ), *n.* [F. *cupidité*, fr. L. *cupiditas*, fr. *cupidus* longing, fr. *cupere* to long for, desire.] Inordinate desire, esp. for wealth; avarice; greed.

Cu′pid's bow (kū′pĭdz). The classical form of bow (see 2d BOW, *Illust.*); also, a line resembling it, esp. as seen in shapely lips.

cu′po·la (kū′pō·lȧ), *n.* [It., fr. L. *cupula* little tub, small vault, fr. *cupa* tub.] **1.** *Arch.* A roof or ceiling having a rounded form. **2.** Loosely, a small structure built on top of a roof or building for a lookout, to complete a design, etc. **3.** A furnace resembling a blast furnace but smaller, used for melting metals, as in foundries and steelworks.

cupped (kŭpt), *adj.* Formed like a cup; cup-shaped.

cup′ping (kŭp′ĭng), *n.* *Med.* The operation of drawing blood to or from the surface of the body by forming a partial vacuum over a certain spot. — **cup′per** (-ẽr), *n.*

cu′pre·ous (kū′prē·ŭs), *adj.* [L. *cupreus*, fr. *cuprum* copper.] Containing copper, or resembling copper; coppery.

cupri-. A combining form of *cuprum*, as in **cu·prif′er·ous** (see -FEROUS), used in chemistry for CUPRIC.

cu′pric (kū′prĭk), *adj.* [From CUPRUM.] *Chem.* Of, pertaining to, or containing, copper when bivalent.

cu′prite (kū′prīt), *n.* *Mineral.* Cuprous oxide, or red copper oxide, Cu_2O, an important ore of copper.

cu′pro- (kū′prō-), **cupr-.** [L. *cuprum* copper.] A combining form denoting *composed of copper and*, as in **cu′pro·man′ga·nese**, a copper alloy with about 30 per cent of manganese.

cu′prous (kū′prŭs), *adj.* *Chem.* Of, pertaining to, or containing, copper when univalent.

cu′prum (kū′prŭm), *n.* [L.] Copper.

cu′pu·late (kū′pū·lāt), *adj.* Also **cu′pu·lar** (-lẽr). Shaped like a cupule; having, or bearing, a cupule.

cu′pule (kū′pūl), *n.* [L. *cupula*, dim. of *cupa* tub, (late) cup.] *Bot.* A cup-shaped involucre in which the bracts are indurated and coherent, esp. characteristic of the oak.

cur (kûr), *n.* **1.** A mongrel or inferior dog. **2.** A worthless snarling fellow; — used in contempt.

cur′a·ble (kūr′ȧ·b′l), *adj.* Capable of being cured. — **cur′a·bil′i·ty** (-bĭl′ĭ·tĭ), **cur′a·ble·ness**, *n.* — **cur′a·bly**, *adv.*

cu′ra·çao′ (kū′rȧ·sō′), *n.; pl.* -ÇAOS (-sōz′). Also **cu′ra·çoa′.** [From *Curaçao*, island of the Netherlands Antilles.] A liqueur made from dried peel of a kind of orange grown in Curaçao.

cu′ra·cy (kū′rȧ·sĭ), *n.; pl.* -CIES (-sĭz). The office or employment of a curate.

cur′agh (kŭr′ȧᴋ; *-ȧ*). Var. of CURRACH.

cu·ra′re, cu·ra′ri (kū·rä′rē), *n.* Also **cu·ra′ra** (-rȧ). [Pg. or Sp., of Tupian origin.] The dried aqueous extract of a vine (*Strychnos toxifera;* family Loganiaceae), used as an arrow poison by South American Indians, and in medicine as an antispasmodic; also, the vine. See STRYCHNOS.

cu′ra·rize (kū′rȧ·rīz; kū·rä′rīz), *v. t.* To bring under the influence of curare. — **cu′ra·ri·za′tion** (-rĭ·zā′shŭn; -rī·zā′-), *n.*

cu′ras·sow (kū′rȧ·sō; kū·răs′ō), *n.* [From the island of *Curaçao.*] Any of several large arboreal birds (genus *Crax*, family Cracidae) of South and Central America, related to the domestic fowls.

cu′rate (kū′rāt; -rĭt), *n.* [ML. *curatus*, prop., one who is charged with the care (L. *cura*) of souls.] Orig., any clergyman; now, an assistant or deputy of a rector or vicar.

cur′a·tive (kūr′ȧ·tĭv), *adj.* Relating to, or used in, the cure of diseases. — *n.* A remedy.

cu·ra′tor (kū·rā′tẽr; *in sense* 1 *also* kū′rȧ·tẽr), *n.* [F. *curateur*, or L. *curator*, fr. *curare* to take care of, fr. *cura* care.] **1.** *Law.* A guardian appointed for minors or others past the age of puberty (generally fourteen years for males, and twelve for females). **2.** A person having the care of anything; an overseer, keeper, or custodian, as of a museum, etc. — **cu′ra·to′ri·al** (kū′rȧ·tō′rĭ·ăl), *adj.* — **cu·ra′tor·ship**, *n.*

curb (kûrb), *n.* [F. *courbe* curve, curved piece of wood or iron, fr. *courbe* crooked, curved, fr. L. *curvus.*] **1.** A chain or strap attached to the upper part of the branches of a bit, used for restraint by drawing against the lower jaw of the horse. See BIT, *Illust.* **2.** That which restrains or subdues; a check. **3.** An enclosing frame, border, or edging. **4.** A raised edge or margin, or a wall, casing, or the like, to strengthen or confine something. **5.** Also, esp. *Brit.*, **kerb** (kûrb). A vertical member along the edge of a street to form part of a gutter. **6.** *Stock Exch.* A market conducted after the closing hours of a near-by exchange, or one trading in securities not listed on the exchange. Originally such trading was done on the street or sidewalk, but is now usually done in a building; — called also ***curb***, or ***outside, market.*** Cf. OVER-THE-COUNTER.
— *v. t.* **1.** To guide and manage, or restrain, as with a curb. **2.** [From CURB, *n.*] To furnish with a curb. — **Syn.** See RESTRAIN.

curb bit. A stiff bit having branches by which a leverage is obtained upon the jaws of a horse. See BIT, *Illust.*

curb′ing (kûr′bĭng), *n.* Structural material forming a curb.

curb roof. A roof having a double slope. Cf. GAMBREL ROOF, MANSARD ROOF.

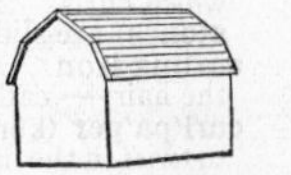

Curb Roof.

curb′stone′ (kûrb′stōn′), *n.* Also **kerb′stone′.** A stone set along a margin as a limit and protection.

curch (kûrch), *n.* *Scot.* A kerchief.

cur·cu′li·o (kûr·kū′lĭ·ō), *n.; pl.* -LIOS (-ōz). [L., a grain weevil.] Any snout beetle, esp. one which injures fruit, as the ***plum curculio*** (*Conotrachelus nenuphar*).

cur′cu·ma (kûr′kū·mȧ), *n.* [NL., fr. Ar. *kurkum.*] *Bot.* A plant of a genus (*Curcuma*) of Old World tropical herbs of the ginger family. The roots of some species yield arrowroot. One species (*C. longa*) is the turmeric.

curd (kûrd), *n.* [ME. *curd, crud, crod.*] The coagulated or thickened part of milk, as distinguished from the whey, or watery part. — *v. t. & i.* Also, *Dial. & Poetic*, **crud** (krŭd; *dial. also* kro͞od, kro͝od); CRUD′DED; CRUD′DING. To coagulate or thicken; to curdle.

cur′dle (kûr′d′l), *v. t. & i.;* CUR′DLED (-d′ld); CUR′DLING (-dlĭng). To change into curd; coagulate; thicken.

cure (kūr; 114), *n.* [OF., care, fr. L. *cura* care, medical attendance, cure.] **1.** Spiritual charge; care of souls; hence, a curacy. **2.** A method of medical treatment. **3.** Act of healing, or state of being healed. **4.** Means of the removal of disease or evil; a remedy. **5.** Process or method of curing, as of fish, pork, etc. — *v. t.* **1.** To heal; to restore to health, soundness, or sanity. **2.** To subdue or remove by remedial means; remedy; heal. **3.** To prepare for keeping or use; to preserve, as by drying, salting, etc.; as, to *cure* fish. **4.** To alter industrially, as to vulcanize (rubber) or to treat (synthetic resins) with heat or chemicals to make infusible. — *v. i.* **1.** To restore health; to effect a cure. **2.** To be or become cured; as, the hay is *curing* in the sun. — **cure′less**, *adj.* — **cur′er** (kūr′ẽr), *n.*

Syn. **Cure, heal, remedy** mean to rectify an unhealthy condition. **Cure** and **heal** were at first interchangeable but in current use are seldom so, *cure* implying restoration to health after disease, and *heal* restoration to soundness after a wound or lesion; **remedy** suggests correction or relief of a morbid condition. Figuratively, the same distinctions hold.

cu·ré′ (kū·rā′; *F.* kü′rā′), *n.* [F.] A parish priest.

cure′–all′, *n.* A remedy for all diseases or ills; panacea.

cu·ret′tage (kū·rĕt′ĭj; kū′rĕ·täzh′), *n.* [F.] *Surg.* Scraping or cleaning by means of a curette.

cu·rette′ (kū·rĕt′), *n.* [F., fr. *curer* to cleanse.] *Surg.* A scoop for removing foreign bodies, growths, etc., from the walls of a cavity. — *v. t.* *Surg.* To scrape with a curette.

cur′few (kûr′fū), *n.* [OF. *cuevrefu, covrefeu*, fr. *covrir* to cover + *feu* fire, fr. L. *focus* hearth.] A regulation directing that fires be covered or extinguished at a fixed hour in the evening, when a bell was rung, in force in the Middle Ages; also, the ringing of the bell, or the bell itself; hence, the ringing of a bell or some other signal, as for children to retire from the streets.

‖**cu′ri·a** (kū′rĭ·ȧ), *n.; pl.* CURIAE (-ē). [L., in sense 1, in ML., court.] **1.** *Rom. Antiq.* **a** A political subdivision of a tribe in early Rome. **b** The place of assembly of one of these divisions. **c** The senate house. **2.** Formerly, in England, any court held in the king's name. **3.** [*cap.*] In full, **Cu′ri·a Ro·ma′na** (rō·mā′nȧ). The body of congregations, tribunals, and offices through which the pope governs the Roman Catholic Church. — **cu′ri·al** (kū′rĭ·ăl), *adj.*

cu′rie (kū′rē; kū·rē′), *n.* [After Mme. Marie *Curie*, chemist.] *Physical Chem.* Formerly, a unit of mass of radium emanation, being the amount in equilibrium with one gram of radium; now, a unit quantity of any radioactive species in which 3.7×10^{10} disintegrations occur per second.

Cu·rie's′ law (kū·rēz′). [After Pierre *Curie*, French chemist.] *Physical Chem.* The law that the magnetic susceptibility of a paramagnetic substance is inversely proportional to the absolute temperature. The proportionality constant is known as the **Cu·rie′ con′stant** (kū·rē′). This law ceases to be valid at a point (**Cu·rie′ point**) below which the substance ceases to be paramagnetic.

cu′ri·o (kū′rĭ·ō), *n.; pl.* CURIOS (-ōz). [Abbr. of *curiosity.*] Any article of virtu.

cu′ri·os′i·ty (kū′rĭ·ŏs′ĭ·tĭ), *n.; pl.* -TIES (-tĭz). **1.** *Obs.* Careful attention; fastidiousness. **2.** Disposition to inquire into anything, often implying meddlesomeness. **3.** That which is curious, or fitted to excite attention; — now chiefly of an article valued for rarity or strangeness.

cu′ri·ous (kū′rĭ·ŭs), *adj.* [OF. *curios, curius,* fr. L. *curiosus* careful, inquisitive, fr. *cura* care.] **1.** *Obs.* Taking pains; markedly careful. **2.** Exhibiting care or nicety; — now restricted to actions, inquiries, etc., but formerly of anything regarded as exquisite or choice, as food, clothing, etc. **3.** Careful or anxious to learn; also, habitually inquisitive; prying. **4.** Exciting attention or inquiry; strange; rare. **5.** *Colloq.* Extraordinary or eccentric; odd. — **cu′ri·ous·ly,** *adv.* — **cu′ri·ous·ness,** *n.*

Syn. **Curious, inquisitive, prying** mean interested in ascertaining facts or conditions. **Curious** may or may not suggest obtrusiveness, but it always implies eagerness to learn; **inquisitive** implies habitual, impertinent curiosity and, usually, the asking of many questions about something secret or unrevealed; **prying** stresses a busy meddling and officiousness. — **Ant.** Incurious.

cu′ri·um (kū′rĭ·ŭm), *n.* [NL., fr. the *Curies* (Pierre and Marie) + *-ium.*] *Chem.* A metallic element artificially produced by bombardment of plutonium with high-energy helium nuclei. Symbol, *Cm;* at. no., 96.

curl (kûrl), *v. t. & i.* [ME. *curlen, crullen,* fr. *crul* curly.] **1.** To twist or form into ringlets, as the hair. **2.** *Obs.* To deck with or as if with curls. **3.** To form into a curved shape; to coil. — *n.* **1.** A lock of hair that curves spirally; ringlet. **2.** A spiral or winding form, as of smoke; a coil. **3.** Action of curling, or state of being curled. **4.** *Plant Pathol.* Any abnormal curling of leaves.

curl′er (kûr′lẽr), *n.* **1.** One who or that which curls. **2.** A player at the game called *curling.*

cur′lew (kûr′lū), *n.* See PLURAL, *Note,* 3. [OF. *corlieu, courlis* (F. *courlieu*).] Any of a number of large, brownish birds (family Scolopacidae, genera *Numenius* and *Phaeopus*) having long legs and a long, slender, downwardly curved bill. North American species include *N. americanus, P. hudsonicus,* and *P. borealis.*

curl′i·cue (kûr′lĭ·kū), *n.* Also **curl′y·cue.** Something fancifully curled or spiral, as a flourish in writing.

curl′ing (kûr′lĭng), *n.* **1.** Act or state of that which curls. **2.** A game in which stones (**curling stones**) are slid along ice toward a mark.

Curling Stone.

curling iron. An instrument for curling or waving the hair; — called also **curling irons** *or* **tongs.**

curl′pa′per (kûrl′pā′pẽr), *n.* A strip of soft paper to twist in the hair to impart a curl; — chiefly in *pl.*

curl′y (kûr′lĭ), *adj.;* CURL′I·ER (-lĭ·ẽr); -I·EST. **1.** Curling or tending to curl; having curls. **2.** Of the grain of lumber, having fibers that undulate without crossing; also, having such grain; as, *curly* maple. — **curl′i·ly,** *adv.* — **curl′i·ness,** *n.*

cur·mudg′eon (kẽr·mŭj′ŭn), *n.* An avaricious, grasping fellow; niggard; churl; also, a cross, ill-natured, cantankerous man. — **cur·mudg′eon·ly,** *adj.*

curn (kŭrn), *n.* *Scot.* A grain; a corn; a small number.

curr (kûr), *v. i.* To make a murmuring sound, as doves.

cur′rach, cur′ragh (kŭr′ȧκ; -ȧ), *n.* Also **cur′agh.** [Ir. & Gael. *curach.*] *Ir. & Scot.* A coracle.

cur′ra·jong, cur′ri·jong. Vars. of KURRAJONG.

cur′rant (kûr′ănt), *n.* [F. raisins de *Corinthe,* raisins of Corinth, currants (in sense 1), fr. *Corinth* in Greece, whence, probably, the raisins were first imported, the *Ribes* fruit receiving the name from its resemblance to these raisins.] **1.** A small seedless raisin, grown chiefly in the Levant. **2.** The acid berry of several species of a genus (*Ribes*) of shrubs of the gooseberry family, used chiefly for jelly and jam; also, the plant which bears this fruit.

cur′ren·cy (kûr′ĕn·sĭ; 117), *n.; pl.* -CIES (-sĭz). **1.** State of being current; general acceptance or reception; circulation, as of bank notes. **2.** That which is in circulation as a medium of exchange, including coin, government notes, and bank notes.

cur′rent (-ĕnt), *adj.* [OF. *corant, curant,* pres. part. of *corre* to run, fr. L. *currere.*] **1.** Passing from person to person, or from hand to hand; circulating; as, a *current* coin. **2.** In general use or knowledge; prevalent; also, generally accepted; in vogue. **3.** Now passing, as time, or belonging to the present time or season; as, the *current* month. **4.** Open or running, as a business account. — **Syn.** See PREVAILING. — *n.* **1.** A flowing or passing; onward motion; hence, a stream, esp. the swiftest part of it. **2.** General course; movement or tendency. **3.** *Elec.* A movement of electricity analogous to the flow of a stream of water; also, the rate of such movement. See ALTERNATING CURRENT, DIRECT CURRENT. — **Syn.** See TENDENCY. — **cur′rent·ly,** *adv.* — **cur′rent·ness,** *n.*

current density. *Elec.* See DENSITY, 3 **b.**

‖**cur·ren′te ca′la·mo** (kŭ·rĕn′tē kăl′ȧ·mō). [L.] With a running pen; hence, of writing, offhand; careless.

cur′ri·cle (kûr′ĭ·k′l), *n.* [L. *curriculum* a race course, chariot.] A two-wheeled chaise drawn by two horses abreast.

cur·ric′u·lum (kŭ·rĭk′ū·lŭm), *n.; pl.* -LUMS (-lŭmz), -LA (-lȧ). [L., a running, racecourse, fr. *currere* to run.] **a** A course of study, as in a college. **b** The whole body of courses offered in an educational institution, or by a department thereof; — the usual sense. — **cur·ric′u·lar** (-lẽr), *adj.*

‖**cur·ri′cu·lum vi′tae** (kŭ·rĭk′ū·lŭm vī′tē). [L.] **a** Course of (one's) life; career. **b** A short statement of the leading incidents in one's career and of one's qualifications, as prepared by an applicant for a position.

cur′ri·er (kûr′ĭ·ẽr; 117), *n.* [OF. *corier,* fr. L. *coriarius,* fr. *corium* leather.] One who curries and dresses leather after it is tanned; also, one who curries a horse.

cur′ri·er·y (-ĭ), *n.* The trade of a currier of leather, or the place where currying is done.

cur′rish (kûr′ĭsh), *adj.* Pertaining to, or like, a cur; snarling; also, base; ignoble. — **cur′rish·ly,** *adv.*

cur′ry (kûr′ĭ; 117), *v. t.;* CUR′RIED (-ĭd); CUR′RY·ING. [OF. *conreer, correer,* to prepare, furnish, curry (a horse), fr. *cor-* + *roi, rei,* arrangement, order.] **1.** To dress the hair or coat of (a horse, ox, etc.) with a currycomb. **2.** To dress or prepare (leather) by scraping, cleansing, stuffing, beating, smoothing, and coloring. **3.** To beat or bruise; to drub. — ***curry favor.*** To seek to gain favor, as by flattery.

cur′ry, *n.; pl.* CURRIES (-ĭz). Also **cur′rie.** [Tamil *kari.*] *Cookery.* **a** Also **curry powder.** A highly spiced condiment introduced from India. **b** A stew cooked with curry. — *v. t.;* CUR′RIED (kûr′ĭd); CUR′RY·ING. To flavor or cook with curry.

cur′ry·comb′ (-kōm′), *n.* A metal-toothed comb for currying horses. — **cur′ry·comb′,** *v. t.*

curse (kûrs), *n.* [AS. *curs.*] **1.** A prayer or invocation for harm or injury to come upon one; an imprecation; oath. **2.** That which is cursed or accursed. **3.** Evil that comes as if in response to imprecation, or as retribution. **4.** The cause of great harm or misfortune; torment. — *v. t.;* CURSED (kûrst) or CURST; CURS′ING. [AS. *cursian.*] **1.** To call upon divine or supernatural power to send injury upon; now, usually, to execrate; to swear at. **2.** To use profanely insolent language against; to blaspheme. **3.** To bring great evil upon; to afflict; to harass or torment. — **Syn.** See EXECRATE. — *v. i.* To utter imprecations; to swear.

curs′ed (kûr′sĕd; -sĭd; kûrst), *adj.* **1.** Being under a curse; damned. **2.** Deserving a curse; wicked; hateful. **3.** *Chiefly Dial.* Of a vicious disposition; cantankerous; — usually *curst.* — **-ly,** *adv.* — **-ness,** *n.*

curs′ing (kûr′sĭng), *n.* Act of one who curses. — **Syn.** See BLASPHEMY.

cur′sive (kûr′sĭv), *adj.* [ML. *cursivus.* See COURSE.] Coursing; running; of writing, flowing; formed with strokes joined and angles often rounded. — *n.* **1.** A character used in cursive writing. **2.** *Print.* A kind of type resembling handwriting. See TYPE. — **cur′sive·ly,** *adv.*

cur·so′ri·al (kûr·sō′rĭ·ăl; 70), *adj.* *Zool.* Adapted to running.

cur′so·ry (kûr′sō·rĭ), *adj.* [L. *cursorius,* fr. *cursor* a runner.] Rapidly, often superficially, performed; passing hurriedly over or through something which invites exhaustive treatment. — **Syn.** See SUPERFICIAL. — **cur′so·ri·ly,** *adv.* — **cur′so·ri·ness,** *n.*

curst (kûrst), *past & past part.* of CURSE. Hence: *adj.* Cursed.

curt (kûrt), *adj.* [L. *curtus.*] **1.** Short; as, limbs crooked and *curt.* **2.** Short in language; brief; esp., rudely concise. — **Syn.** See BLUFF. — **curt′ly,** *adv.* — **curt′ness,** *n.*

cur·tail′ (kûr·tāl′; *formerly* kûr′tāl), *v. t.* [From CURTAL, *adj.;* by popular etym. assoc. with *tail.*] To cut off the end, or any part, of; hence, to shorten or lessen. — **Syn.** See SHORTEN. — **cur·tail′er,** *n.* — **cur·tail′ment,** *n.*

cur′tain (kûr′tĭn; -t'n), *n.* [OF. *curtine, cortine,* fr. LL. *cortina* curtain.] **1.** A hanging screen, usually admitting of being drawn back or up at pleasure; esp., drapery of cloth or lace at a window. **2.** *Arch.* That part of a wall between two pavilions, towers, etc. **3.** *Fort.* That part of a bastioned front connecting two neighboring bastions. See BASTION, *Illust.* **4.** *Theater.* **a** The descent of a curtain at the end of a scene, act, or play. **b** The final situation or line of a scene, act, or play. **5.** Anything that acts as a barrier or obstacle by protecting, hiding, or separating; as, a security *curtain.* — *v. t.* To furnish with curtains.

curtain call. A call to return to the stage, at the end of a scene, act, or play, to acknowledge plaudits.

curtain lecture. A censorious lecture by a wife to her husband within the bed curtains, or in bed.

curtain raiser. *Theat.* A short piece, usually of one scene with few characters, used to open a performance.

cur′tal (kûr′tăl; -t'l), *adj.* *Obs.* **1.** Having a docked tail; hence, curtailed. **2.** Wearing a short frock; as, a *curtal* friar. — *n.* *Obs.* An animal with a docked tail.

cur′tal (kûr′tăl; -t'l), *or* **cur′tle** (-t'l), **ax.** *Archaic corrupt.* Cutlass.

cur′ti·lage (kûr′tĭ·lĭj), *n.* [From OF., fr. *cortil, courtil,* courtyard, fr. stem of L. *cors* court.] A yard within the fence surrounding a house.

curt′sy, curt′sey (kûrt′sĭ), *n.; pl.* -SIES, -SEYS (-sĭz). A variant of COURTESY, now chiefly: An act of civility, respect, or reverence, made esp. by women, consisting of a slight inclination of the body, with bending of the knees. — *v. t. & i.;* -SIED, -SEYED (-sĭd); -SY·ING, -SEY·ING. To make a curtsy (to); — now only of women.

cu′rule (kū′rōōl), *adj.* [L. *curulis.*] **1.** Designating a form of seat, like a campstool with curved legs, appropriated in ancient Rome to the use of the highest dignitaries. **2.** Privileged to sit in a curule chair; hence, of highest rank.

cur·va′ceous (kûr·vā′shŭs), *adj.* Also **cur·va′cious** (-shŭs). [*curve* + *-aceous, -acious.*] Having a well-proportioned feminine figure marked by pronounced curves.

cur′va·ture (kûr′vȧ·tūr), *n.* Act of curving, or state of being curved; a curving or bending; esp., abnormal curving; as, *curvature* of the spine.

curve (kûrv), *adj.* [L. *curvus* bent, curved.] Curved. — *n.* [See CURVE, *adj.,* CURB.] **1.** A bending without angles; a flexure. **2.** Something curved, as a line, a curved ruler, etc. **3.** *Usually in pl.* A curving line outlining any of the rounded prominences characteristic of the female figure. **4.** *Baseball.* A ball so thrown that its course is a curve different from that ordinarily caused by the force of gravity acting on a projectile; also, the deflection from the ordinary course. **5.** *Math.* Analytically, a line or lines that may be precisely defined by an equation or equations. Geometrically, a curve is the intersection of two surfaces, or the path of a moving point, or the envelope of a moving line. — *v. t. & i.* To bend; to crook; to swerve from a plane projectile path. — **curv′ed·ness** (kûr′vĕd·nĕs; -vĭd-; -nĭs), *n.*

Syn. **Curve, bend, turn, twist** mean to swerve or cause to swerve from a straight line. **Curve** implies that the line followed is, or resembles, the arc of a circle or ellipse; **bend** applies to that which is normally straight but that yields to efforts to curve or change its direction; **turn** is often used in place of *bend* but is required in certain idiomatic phrases (as, to *turn* one's ankle); **twist** implies the influence of an irresistible force in bending, often suggesting a wrenching.

cur′vet (kûr′vĕt), *n.* [Earlier *corvetto,* fr. It. *corvetta,* dim. fr. L. *curvus,* adj.] A certain prancing leap of a horse.

cur·vet′ (kûr·vĕt′; kûr′vĕt), *v. i.;* CUR·VET′TED or CUR′VET·ED; -VET′TING or -VET·ING. **a** To make a curvet; to leap. **b** To frisk; frolic.

cur′vi- (kûr′vĭ-). [L. *curvus.*] A combining form meaning *curved, bent,* as in *curvi*linear; — esp. in *Bot. & Zool.*

cur′vi·lin′e·ar (kûr′vĭ·lĭn′ē·ẽr), **cur′vi·lin′e·al** (-ăl), *adj.* Consisting of, or bounded by, curved lines; as, a *curvilinear* angle.

cu′sec (kū′sĕk), *n.* [*cubic* + *second.*] A cubic foot per second.

Cush (kŭsh), *n.* *Bib.* The eldest son of Ham; also, the "land of Cush," usually identified as Ethiopia.

cush′at (kŭsh′ăt; kŏŏsh′ăt), *n.* [AS. *cusceote.*] The ringdove or wood pigeon of Europe.

cu·shaw′ (kŭ·shô′), *n.* Also, *U. S.,* **ca·shaw′** (kȧ·shô′). A crookneck winter variety of the squash *Cucurbita moschata.* See 1st SQUASH.

cush′ion (kŏŏsh′ŭn; -ĭn), *n.* [OF. *cossin, coissin,* deriv. of L. *culcita* cushion.] **1.** A soft pillow or pad to rest on or against. **2.** Something made or shaped like a cushion, as a small pillow used in lacemaking. **3.** Something serving as a pad, shock absorber, etc.; as: **a** The elastic lining on the rim of the inner part of a billiard table. **b** A strip of soft resilient rubber between the breaker and carcass of a pneumatic tire. See TIRE, *Illust.* **c** *Mach.* An elastic medium, as of air or steam, for reducing shock. — *v. t.* **1.** To seat or place on or as if on a cushion. **2.** To furnish with cushions. **3.** To conceal, as if under a cushion. **4.** *Mach.* To check gradually so as to minimize shock; as, to *cushion* a piston by leaving some steam in the cylinder after exhaust.

Cush·it′ic (kŭsh·ĭt′ĭk), *n.* The Hamitic language of ancient Cush. See LANGUAGE, *Table.*

cusk (kŭsk), *n.; pl.* CUSK or CUSKS (kŭsks). **a** A large edible marine fish (*Brosmius brosme*), allied to the cod. **b** The burbot (*Lota maculosa*).

cusp (kŭsp), *n.* [L. *cuspis, -idis,* point, pointed end.] **1.** A pointed end; apex; peak; esp., a pointed end, part, or projection formed by converging curves; as, the *cusps* of a crescent or of a tooth's crown. **2.** *Arch.* A triangular projection from the intrados of an arch, or from an inner curve of tracery. Cf. FOIL, *Illust.* — **cusp′al** (kŭs′păl), *adj.*

cus′pate (kŭs′pāt), **cus′pat·ed** (-pāt·ĕd; -ĭd), *adj.* Also **cusped** (kŭspt). Having a cusp or cusps; cusp-shaped.

cus′pid (kŭs′pĭd), *n.* [See CUSP.] *Anat.* A canine tooth.

cus′pi·date (kŭs′pĭ·dāt), **cus′pi·dat′ed** (-dāt′ĕd; -ĭd), *adj.* [L. *cuspidatus* pointed.] Having a cusp or cusps; terminating in a point; as, a *cuspidate* leaf. — **cus′pi·da′tion** (-dā′shŭn), *n.*

cus′pi·dor (kŭs′pĭ·dôr), *n.* [Pg. *cuspideira,* fr. *cuspir* to spit, fr. L. *conspuere.*] A spittoon.

cuss (kŭs), *n.* [From CURSE.] *Colloq.* **1.** A curse. **2.** A queer fellow, animal, or thing; — often humorously. — *v. t. & i. Colloq.* To curse.

cuss′ed (kŭs′ĕd; -ĭd), *adj. Colloq.* Cursed. — **cuss′ed·ly,** *adv.*

cuss′ed·ness (-nĕs; -nĭs), *n.* Perversity; obstinacy.

cus′tard (kŭs′tẽrd), *n.* [From (assumed) OF. *coustarde,* fr. Pr. deriv. of L. *crusta.*] A cooked sweetened mixture of milk and eggs.

custard apple. **1.** Any of a family (Annonaceae, the custard-apple family) of trees and shrubs having alternate leaves, flowers with three sepals and six petals, and fleshy fruit; esp.: **a** A small West Indian tree (*Annona reticulata*); also, its fruit. **b** The sweetsop (*Annona squamosa*). **2.** The North American papaw *Asimina triloba.*

cus·to′di·al (kŭs·tō′dĭ·ăl), *adj.* Relating to guardianship.

cus·to′di·an (kŭs·tō′dĭ·ăn), *n.* One who has custody, as of a public building; a keeper. — **cus·to′di·an·ship′,** *n.*

cus′to·dy (kŭs′tō·dĭ), *n.; pl.* -DIES (-dĭz). [L. *custodia,* fr. *custos* guard.] **1.** A keeping or guarding; also, the state of being guarded or watched. **2.** Judicial or penal safekeeping; specif., as to persons, imprisonment.

cus′tom (kŭs′tŭm), *n.* [OF. *custume, costume,* fr. L. *consuetudo, -dinis,* fr. *consuescere* to accustom, deriv. of *con-* + *suere* to be accustomed.] **1.** A habitual or usual course of action; usage or practice. **2.** The whole body of usages or practices which regulate social life; generally accepted conventions. **3.** *Law.* Long-established practice considered as unwritten law. **4.** Money, services, etc., rendered by a feudal tenant to his lord as due; also, the obligation to give or the right to receive this. **5.** *pl.* Duties, tolls, or imposts imposed on imports or (now rarely) exports. **6.** Habitual buying of goods; frequent patronage; also, customers, collectively. — **Syn.** See HABIT. — *adj.* **1.** Made or done to order; as, *custom* clothes. **2.** Manufacturing, or dealing in, things made to order; as, a *custom* tailor.

cus′tom·a·ble (-ȧ·b'l), *adj.* Subject to customs; dutiable.

cus′tom·ar′y (-ẽr′ĭ *or, esp. Brit.,* -ẽr·ĭ), *adj.* **1.** Agreeing with, or established by, custom; established by common usage; habitual. **2.** *Law.* **a** Liable or subject to, or holding by payment of, customs or dues; as, *customary* tenure. **b** Holding, or held by, or owing its validity as law to, custom; as, *customary* service. — **Syn.** See USUAL. — **cus′tom·ar′i·ly** (-ẽr′ĭ·lĭ; *emphat. also* -âr′ĭ·lĭ), *adv.* — **cus′tom·ar′i·ness,** *n.*

cus′tom·er (kŭs′tŭm·ẽr), *n.* [A doublet of *customary,* adj.] **1.** One who gives his custom to a particular store or business house; a patron. **2.** *Colloq.* A strange or unusual person; chap; as, a queer *customer;* a hard *customer* to deal with.

cus′tom·house′ (-hous′), *n.* The building where customs and duties are paid, and where vessels are entered or cleared.

‖**cus′tos** (kŭs′tŏs), *n.; pl.* CUSTODES (kŭs·tō′dēz). [L., guard, keeper.] Custodian.

‖**cus′tos mo′rum** (mō′rŭm). [L.] Guardian of morals; censor.

cut (kŭt), *n.* [Origin obscure.] One of several pieces, as of straw, paper, or wood, used in drawing lots.

cut (kŭt), *v. t.;* CUT; CUT′TING. [ME. *cutten, kitten, ketten.*] **1.** To penetrate so as to cleave or gash; as, the scissors *cut* wire. **2.** To sever, gash, incise, divide into parts, etc., with or as with an edged instrument; as, to *cut* bread. **3.** Specif.: **a** To carve. **b** To fell; hew. **c** To mow; reap. **d** To trim; pare. **4.** To make less by or as if by removing a part; to reduce, shorten, dilute, or the like; as, to *cut* prices; to *cut* liquor. **5.** To form, shape, or adorn by cutting; as, to *cut* a diamond or a garment. **6.** To intersect; cross, as lines. **7. a** To strike sharply, as with a whip. **b** To wound the sensibilities of; as, sarcasm *cuts* him to the quick. **8.** *Colloq.* **a** To refuse to recognize (an acquaintance). **b** To absent oneself from (a class). **c** To perform; execute; hence, ***cut a caper, figure,*** etc., to be conspicuous. **9.** To divide or separate (a deck of cards) by removing cards from the top; also, to draw (a card) from a deck. **10.** *Sports.* To strike (a ball) with a bat, racket, or the like, or with a driven or bowled ball, so as to deflect it or, usually, to put a spin upon it.

— *v. i.* **1.** To do the work of cleaving, gashing, severing, etc.; as, the knife *cuts* well. **2.** To admit of incision or severance; as, cheese *cuts* easily. **3.** To use a cutting instrument. **4.** To pierce the gum in growing; — said of teeth. **5.** To move, pass, or go quickly, by a short route, or as by breaking one's way; as, to *cut* across a field. **6.** To perform the operation of cutting something or to produce the effect of cutting a person or thing; as, to *cut* in playing tennis; remarks that *cut;* to *cut* for a deal.

cut a tooth** or **one's teeth. To have a tooth, or teeth, cut its way through the gum. — ***cut back.*** **a** To shorten by cutting off the end or ends; as, to *cut back* a plant. **b** To interrupt the sequence of a plot by introducing events prior to those last presented. **c** To reduce as in rate, amount, or number; as, to *cut back* production. **d** *Amer. Football.* To change direction suddenly to a course more or less diagonally opposite. — ***cut in.*** **a** To interrupt; interpose. **b** To enter from one side into a moving line of traffic. **c** *Colloq.* To interrupt a dancing couple and take one of them for one's partner. — ***cut off.*** **a** To put or bring to an end, esp. prematurely. **b** To interrupt; also, to intercept. **c** To disinherit. — ***cut out.*** **a** To fit as if by design or natural intention; — usually in the passive; as, he is not *cut out* to do heavy work. **b** To scheme; contrive; prepare; as, to *cut out* a place for oneself. **c** To step in and take the place of; supplant. **d** To debar. **e** To move, esp. sharply or without warning, to one side or the other out of a moving line, as of traffic. **f** *Colloq.* To eliminate; hence, *Slang,* to stop doing, using, etc.

— *adj.* **1.** That has been subjected to the action of cutting; specif.: **a** Formed, shaped, or adorned by cutting; as, *cut* glass. **b** Castrated. **c** Reduced, as prices. **2.** *Slang.* Tipsy; drunk. **3.** *Bot.* Incised; — said of foliage or floral leaves.

— *n.* **1.** A cleft; gash; slit; slash. **2.** A notch, passage, or channel made by excavation, or worn by natural action. **3.** A straight or easy passage or course; as, a short *cut.* **4.** Manner in which a thing is cut or formed; shape; style; fashion. **5.** An action or expression that hurts the feelings; esp., a slight. **6.** Act or the result of cutting; specif.: **a** A stroke or blow with a knife edge, whiplash, etc.; the injury thus inflicted. **b** A reduction; an elimination; also, a lowering; as, a *cut* in salary. **c** An absence, as from class. **d** In sports, the cutting of a ball; also, the resulting spin. **7.** A severed part or portion; a division or segment; specif., in butchering, often, a part of an animal, whether severed from the body or not, which forms a natural or customary segment. **8.** An engraved block or plate for printing; the impression from such an engraving; as, a book illustrated with fine *cuts.*

cu·ta′ne·ous (kū·tā′nē·ŭs), *adj.* [ML. *cutaneus,* fr. L. *cutis* skin.] Of or pertaining to the skin; existing on, or affecting, the skin.

cut′a·way′ (kŭt′ȧ·wā′), *adj.* Having a part cut away; as, a *cutaway* illustration.

cut′a·way′, *n.* In full, **cutaway coat.** A coat with skirts tapering from front waistline to tails.

cut′back′ (kŭt′băk′), *n.* Act or result of cutting back; specif.: **a** A plant that has been cut back. **b** An interruption in the sequence of a plot introducing events prior to those last presented. **c** A reduction as in rate, amount, or number.

cutch (kŭch), *n.* Catechu.

cut·cher′ry (kŭ·chẽr′ĭ), **cutch′er·y** (kŭch′ẽr·ĭ; *the first pron. is used in northern India, the second at Madras. Oxf. E. D.*), *n.* [Hind. *kacahrī.*] *India.* A place for judicial or administrative business, as a courthouse, an office, or the like.

cute (kūt), *adj.* [From ACUTE.] *Colloq.* **1.** Clever; shrewd. **2.** Attractive by reason of daintiness or picturesqueness, as a child. — **cute′ly,** *adv.* — **cute′ness,** *n.*

cut glass. Glass shaped or ornamented by cutting or grinding, and polishing. Flint glass is generally used.

cut′–grass′, *n.* Any grass (esp. genus *Leersia*) having the edges of the leaf blade beset with minute hooked prickles.

cu′ti·cle (kū′tĭ·k'l), *n.* [L. *cuticula,* dim. of *cutis* skin.] **1.** A skin or membrane; in the higher animals and man, the epidermis. **2.** Dead or hardened skin such as that around the base and sides of a fingernail or toenail. **3.** *Bot.* A very thin detachable skin covering a plant. — **cu·tic′u·lar** (kū·tĭk′ū·lẽr), *adj.*

cu′tin (kū′tĭn), *n.* [L. *cutis* skin, outside.] *Biochem.* A mixture of waxes, fatty acids, soaps, etc., that forms the chief ingredient of the cuticle of many plants.

cu′tis (kū′tĭs), *n.* Also ‖**cu′tis ve′ra** (vē′rȧ). [L.] *Anat.* The corium, or deeper layer of the skin.

cut′lass (kŭt′lȧs), *n.* Also **cut′las.** [F. *coutelas,* fr. Pr., fr. L. *cultellus* small knife, fr. *culter* knife.] A short, heavy, curving sword, formerly used by sailors on war vessels.

cut′ler (kŭt′lẽr), *n.* [F. *coutelier,* fr. LL., fr. L. *cultellus.* See CUTLASS.] One who makes, deals in, or repairs, cutlery.

cut′ler·y (-ĭ), *n.* **1.** The business of a cutler. **2.** Edged or cutting instruments, as razors, knives, etc.; esp., implements for use in cutting food.

cut′let (kŭt′lĕt; -lĭt), *n.* [F. *côtelette,* prop., little rib, dim. of *côte* rib, fr. L. *costa.*] A small piece of meat, as of veal, cut from the leg or ribs, for broiling or frying; also, a croquette shaped like a cutlet.

cut′off′ (kŭt′ôf′), *n.* **1.** A passage, road, etc., providing a short cut. **2.** *Engin.* The act of shutting off the working fluid, as steam, from an engine cylinder; also, the point at which this occurs or the mechanism for effecting it. **3.** *Phys. Geog.* A channel formed by a river breaking through the neck of an oxbow; also, the water thus cut off.

cut′out′ (-out′), *n.* **1.** A design or shape of or on paper, cardboard, wood, etc., prepared by or for cutting out. **2.** *Elec.* A device, as a switch or circuit breaker, for interrupting or closing a connection. **3.** A valve in the exhaust pipe of an internal-combustion engine through which the exhaust gases may pass directly into the air.

cut′o′ver (-ō′vẽr), *adj.* That has had most of its salable timber cut; as, *cutover* land.

cut′purse′ (-pûrs′), *n.* Originally, a thief who cuts purses from girdles; hence, a pickpocket.

cut′–rate′, *adj. U. S.* That offers goods at reduced prices.

cut′ter (kŭt′ẽr), *n.* **1.** One who or that which cuts. **2.** A one-horse sleigh. **3.** *Naut.* **a** A broad square-sterned boat for carrying stores and passengers, used by ships of war. **b** A fore-and-aft-rigged vessel with one mast and a jib and forestaysail. Cf. SLOOP. **c** *U. S.* A small armed vessel in the coast guard, formerly known as ***revenue cutter.***

cut′throat′ (kŭt′thrōt′), *n.* One who cuts throats; a murderer; an assassin. — *adj.* **1.** Murderous; hence, destructive; ruinous. **2.** Designating a game, as of cards, played by three, each playing for himself.

cut′ting (kŭt′ĭng), *n.* **1.** Act of a person or thing that cuts. **2.** Something cut, cut off, or cut out; specif., *Hort.,* any section of a plant, used for propagation, esp., a stem cutting. — *adj.* **1.** Adapted to cut. **2.** Chilling; piercing; as, a *cutting* wind. **3.** Severe; sarcastic; as, a *cutting* remark, criticism. — **Syn.** See INCISIVE. — **cut′ting·ly,** *adv.*

cut′tle·fish′ (kŭt′'l·fĭsh′), *n.; pl.,* see FISH. Also **cut′tle** (kŭt′'l). [AS. *cudele.*] A ten-armed marine mollusk (subclass Dibranchia and class Cephalopoda) differing from a squid in having a calcified internal shell, **cut′tle·bone′** (kŭt′'l·bōn′), used for polishing powder, bird food, etc.

cut′ty (kŭt′ĭ; ko͝ot′ĭ), *adj. Scot. & Dial.* Short. — (kŭt′ĭ), *n.; pl.* -TIES (-ĭz). Something short, as a spoon or pipe.

cut′ty stool (kŭt′ĭ). *Scot.* **a** A low stool. **b** A seat in old Scottish churches where offenders, esp. against chastity, sat for public rebuke.

cut′wa′ter (kŭt′wô′tẽr; -wŏt′ẽr), *n.* The fore part of a ship's stem.

cut′work′ (-wûrk′), *n.* Openwork embroidery, esp. that in which some of the fabric is cut away.

cut′worm′ (-wûrm′), *n.* A caterpillar which at night eats off young plants of cabbage, corn, etc., usually at the ground. The common cutworms are larvae of various genera (esp. *Agrotis*) of noctuid moths.

-cy (-sĭ). [L. *-cia, -tia;* Gr. *-kia, -keia, -tia, -teia.*] A noun suffix signifying *state, quality, office, rank,* occurring chiefly in the compound suffixes *-acy, -ancy, -ency, -cracy, -mancy* (which see).

cy′an·am′ide (sī′ăn·ăm′ĭd, -īd; sī·ăn′ȧ·mīd, -mĭd), *n.* Also **cy′an·am′id.** [See CYANIC; AMIDE.] **1.** *Chem.* A crystalline compound, $CN.NH_2$, obtained by the action of ammonia gas on ***cyanogen chloride,*** CNCl, and by other methods. **2.** *Com.* Short for CALCIUM CYANAMIDE.

cy′a·nate (sī′ȧ·nāt), *n.* A salt or ester of cyanic acid.

cy·an′ic (sī·ăn′ĭk), *adj.* [Gr. *kyanos* a dark-blue substance.] **1.** Pert. to or containing cyanogen. **2.** Blue; specif., *Bot.,* having a blue tinge; — of flowers, opposed to *xanthic.*

cyanic acid. *Chem.* A strong acid, HOCN, obtained by heating cyanuric acid.

cy′a·nide (sī′ȧ·nīd; -nĭd), *n.* Also **cy′a·nid.** A compound of cyanogen with an element or radical; specif., potassium cyanide (or **cyanide of potassium**), KCN, and sodium cyanide (or **cyanide of sodium**), NaCN. — *v. t.* To treat with a cyanide.

cyanide process. *Metal.* A method of extracting gold and silver from ores by treatment with a dilute solution of sodium cyanide or potassium cyanide.

cy′a·nite (sī′ȧ·nīt), *n.* [See CYANIC.] An aluminum silicate, Al_2SiO_5, occurring commonly in blue thin-bladed triclinic crystals and crystalline aggregates.

cy′a·no- (sī′ȧ·nō-), **cyan-.** [See CYANIC.] A combining form meaning *dark-blue;* specif., *Chem.,* denoting the presence of the cyanogen group.

cy·an′o·gen (sī·ăn′ō·jĕn), *n.* [*cyano-* + *-gen.*] **1.** A univalent radical, CN, composed of carbon and nitrogen, present in hydrocyanic acid and the cyanides. **2.** A colorless, inflammable, poisonous gas, $(CN)_2$.

cy′a·no′sis (sī′ȧ·nō′sĭs), *n.* [NL. See CYANIC.] Also **cy′a·nop′a·thy** (-nŏp′ȧ·thĭ). A morbid condition in which the surface of the body becomes blue because of insufficient aeration of the blood. — **cy′a·not′ic** (-nŏt′ĭk), *adj.*

cy·an′o·type (sī·ăn′ō·tīp), *n.* [*cyano-* + *-type.*] A blueprint.

cy′a·nu′ric (sī′ȧ·nū′rĭk), *adj.* [*cyan-* + *uric.*] Pertaining to or designating a white, crystalline acid, **cyanuric acid,** $C_3N_3(OH)_3$.

Cyb′e·le (sĭb′ĕ·lē), *n.* [L., fr. Gr. *Kybelē.*] The great nature goddess of the ancient peoples of Anatolia. See CORYBANT.

cy′ber·net′ics (sī′bẽr·nĕt′ĭks), *n.;* see -ICS. [From Gr. *kybernētēs* steersman, governor.] Comparative study of the control system formed by the nervous system and brain and mechanical-electrical communication systems, such as computing machines. — **cy′ber·net′ic** (-ĭk), *adj.* — **cy′ber·net′i·cist** (-ĭ·sĭst), *n.*

cy′cad (sī′kăd), *n.* [From *Cycas,* type genus.] A fernlike tropical evergreen plant (family Cycadaceae) often cultivated in greenhouses.

cy′cas (sī′kăs), *n.* Any of a genus (*Cycas*) of tropical gymnospermous plants (family Cycadaceae) intermediate in appearance between tree ferns and palms. — **cyc′a·da′ceous** (sĭk′ȧ·dā′shŭs; sī′kȧ-), *adj.*

cyc′la·men (sĭk′lȧ·mĕn), *n.; pl.* CYCLAMENS (-mĕnz). [NL., fr. Gr. *kyklaminos, kyklamis.*] Any of a genus (*Cyclamen*) of plants of the primrose family, having white or pink flowers with reflexed petals.

cy′cle (sī′k'l), *n.* [F. and L.; F., fr. LL. *cyclus,* fr. Gr. *kyklos* ring or circle, cycle.] **1.** An interval or space of time in which is completed one round of events or phenomena that recur regularly and in the same sequence; as, the *cycle* of seasons. **2.** Hence: **a** A complete course of operations, returning to the original state; circle; round; circuit. **b** An age; a long period of time. **3.** An orbit in the heavens. **4. a** The complete series of poems and romances which have narrated the exploits of a hero and his followers and built up a body of legend about him as a center; as, the Arthurian *cycle.* **b** A group of poems or songs on the same theme. **5.** A bicycle, tricycle, or other similar vehicle. **6.** *Biol.* A series of changes regarded as leading back to its starting point. **7.** *Bot.* A verticil. **8.** *Chem.* = RING, *n.,* 11. **9.** *Elec.* One period of an alternating electric current. — *v. i.* **1.** To pass through a cycle; to recur in cycles. **2.** To ride a cycle. — **cy′cler** (-klẽr), *n.*

cy′clic (sī′klĭk; sĭk′lĭk), *adj.* **1.** Of or pertaining to a cycle; moving or recurring in cycles; of the nature of a cycle. **2.** *Chem.* Of, pertaining to, or characterized by a ring or closed-chain formation. — **cy′cli·cal** (sī′klĭ·kăl; sĭk′lĭ-), *adj.*

cy′clist (sī′klĭst), *n.* One who rides a cycle.

cy′clo- (sī′klō-; sĭk′lō-), **cycl-.** [Gr. *kyklos* a circle.] A combining form denoting: **a** *Circular, of a circle* or *wheel,* as in *cyclo*rama. **b** *Chem. A cyclic compound of a* (specified) *type.*

cy′clo·hex′ane (-hĕk′sān), *n.* [*cyclo-* + *hexane.*] *Chem.* A saturated cyclic hydrocarbon, C_6H_{12}, regarded as consisting of six methylene groups. It is found in petroleum.

cy′cloid (sī′kloid), *n.* [Gr. *kykloeidēs* circular, fr. *kyklos* circle + *eidos* form.] A curve traced by a point on a circle rolling in a plane along a line in the plane. — *adj.* Circular; arranged in circles. — **cy·cloi′dal** (sī·kloi′dăl; -d'l), *adj.*

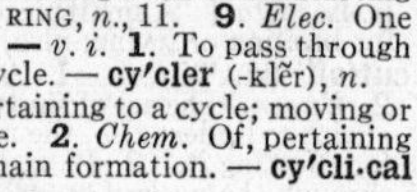

Cycloid.

cy·clom′e·ter (sī·klŏm′ē·tẽr), *n.* [*cyclo-* + *-meter.*] **1.** An instrument to measure arcs of circles. **2.** A contrivance for recording the revolutions of a wheel, as of a bicycle, and the distance traversed; odometer. Cf. SPEEDOMETER.

cy′clone (sī′klōn), *n.* [Irreg. fr. Gr. *kyklos* circle. See CYCLE.] **1. a** A wind blowing circularly, esp. in a storm. **b** Popularly, a tornado. **2.** *Meteorol.* A storm 50 to 900 miles in diameter, moving 20 to 30 miles an hour, with winds (often violent in the tropics) and much rain. The winds rotate at 90 to 130 miles an hour in a counterclockwise direction (in the northern hemisphere) around a calm center of low atmospheric pressure; a hurricane; a typhoon. Cf. HURRICANE, TYPHOON. — **cy·clon′ic** (sī·klŏn′ĭk), **-i·cal** (-ĭ·kăl), *adj.* — **cy·clon′i·cal·ly,** *adv.*

Cy′clo·pe′an (sī′klō·pē′ăn; sī·klō′pē·ăn), *adj.* [L. *Cyclopeus.* See CYCLOPS.] Pertaining to, or characteristic of, the Cyclopes; huge.

cy′clo·pe′di·a, cy′clo·pae′di·a (sī′klō·pē′dĭ·ȧ), *n.* [NL., for earlier *encyclopedia,* fr. Gr. *kyklos* circle + *paideia* the bringing up of a child, education, deriv. of *pais* child.] An encyclopedia.

cy′clo·pe′dic, cy′clo·pae′dic (-pē′dĭk; -pĕd′ĭk), *adj.* Encyclopedic; hence, of great range, extent, or amount; as, *cyclopedic* knowledge. — **cy′clo·pe′di·cal·ly** (-pē′dĭ·kăl·ĭ; -pĕd′ĭ·kăl·ĭ), *adv.*

cy′clo·pe′dist, cy′clo·pae′dist (-pē′dĭst), *n.* A maker of, or writer for, a cyclopedia.

cy′clo·pro′pane (sī′klō·prō′pān; sĭk′lō-), *n.* [*cyclo-* + *propane.*] *Chem.* A saturated cyclic gaseous hydrocarbon, C_3H_6, used esp. as an anesthetic.

Cy′clops (sī′klŏps), *n.; pl.* CYCLOPES (sī·klō′pēz). [L., fr. Gr. *Kyklōps,* lit., round-eyed.] *Gr. Myth.* One of a race of giants having one eye in the middle of the forehead, fabled to inhabit Sicily, and, in later tradition, said to assist in the workshops of Hephaestus (Vulcan), under Mt. Etna. According to Homer they were shepherds.

cy′clo·ra′ma (sī′klō·rä′mȧ; -răm′ȧ), *n.* [*cyclo-* + Gr. *horama* sight, spectacle.] A large pictorial representation encircling the spectator and often having real objects as a foreground. — **cy′clo·ram′ic** (-răm′ĭk), *adj.*

cy·clos′to·mate (sī·klŏs′tō·māt), *adj.* Also **cy′clo·stom′a·tous** (sī′klō·stŏm′ȧ·tŭs; -stō′mȧ·tŭs; sĭk′lō-). *Zool.* **a** Having a circular mouth. **b** Cyclostome.

cy′clo·stome (sī′klō·stōm; sĭk′lō-), *adj.* [*cyclo-* + Gr. *stoma, -atos,* mouth.] Of or pertaining to the lowest class (Cyclostomata) of craniate vertebrates, comprising the lampreys and hagfishes, with eellike bodies and large sucking mouths. — *n.* A cyclostome animal.

cy′clo·thy′mi·a (-thī′mĭ·ȧ), *n.* [NL., fr. *cyclo-* + Gr. *thymos* spirit.] *Psychiatry.* A temperament characterized by alternation of lively and depressed moods; — opposed to *schizothymia.* — **cy′clo·thy′mic** (-mĭk), *adj. & n.*

cy′clo·tron (sī′klō·trŏn; sĭk′lō-), *n.* [NL., fr. Gr. *kyklos* circle, cycle (because particles move in circles) + *-tron* as in elec*tron.*] *Physics.* An apparatus for imparting high speeds to electrified particles by electromagnetic and electrostatic means, used esp. for bombarding the nuclei of atoms to produce transmutations and artificial radioactivity.

cyg′net (sĭg′nĕt; -nĭt), *n.* [Dim. of F. *cygne* swan, fr. L., fr. Gr. *kyknos.*] A young swan. Cf. 1st COB, 2; 3d PEN.

Cyg′nus (sĭg′nŭs), *n.; genitive* CYGNI (-nī). [L., a swan.] A northern constellation between Lyra and Pegasus, in the Milky Way.

cyl′in·der (sĭl′ĭn·dẽr), *n.* [F. *cylindre,* fr. L., fr. Gr. *kylindros,* fr. *kylindein* to roll.] **1.** *Geom.* **a** The surface traced by one side of a rectangle rotated round the parallel side as axis. **b** The volume generated by a rectangle so rotated. **c** The surface traced by any straight line, called *generatrix* or *element,* moving parallel to a fixed straight line. **d** The space bounded by any such surface and two parallel planes cutting the elements. A plane section perpendicular to any element is a ***right section;*** the bounded volume is a ***right cylinder;*** if a right section be a circle the cylinder is ***right-circular;*** any curve that the generatrix constantly meets is a ***directrix.*** **2.** Any body of cylindrical form; as: **a** The turning chambered breech of a revolver. **b** The barrel of a pump or of various farm implements; as, a threshing-machine *cylinder.* **c** A cylindrical vessel or container. **d** *Archaeol.* A cylindrical stone seal, engraved in intaglio to be impressed by a rolling motion; also, a cylindrical clay object inscribed with cuneiform inscriptions. **e** *Mach.* The piston chamber in an engine. **f** *Print.* (1) On a flat-bed press, the revolving platen which produces the impression. (2) On a rotary press, any of various parts designed to receive the impression, carry the printing plates, etc.

cy·lin′dri·cal (sĭ·lĭn′drĭ·kăl), *adj.* Also **cy·lin′dric** (-drĭk). Relating to, or having the form or properties of, a cylinder. — **cy·lin′dri·cal′i·ty** (-kăl′ĭ·tĭ), *n.* — **cy·lin′dri·cal·ly,** *adv.*

cyl′in·droid (sĭl′ĭn·droid), *n.* [Gr. *kylindros* cylinder + *-oid.*] *Math.* A cylinder with elliptic right sections.

cy′ma (sī′mȧ), *n.; pl.* CYMAE (-mē). [NL., fr. Gr. *kyma.* See CYME.] *Arch.* A member or molding of the cornice having a wavelike profile. The ‖**cy′ma rec′ta** (rĕk′tȧ) is hollow and the ‖**cy′ma re·ver′sa** (rē·vûr′sȧ) swelling in the projecting part. See MOLDING, *Illust.* (11, 12).

cy·mar′ (sĭ·mär′), *n.* [F. *simarre.*] A loose robe or garment worn by women.

cy·ma′ti·um (sĭ·mā′shĭ·ŭm), **cy·ma′ti·on** (-ŏn), *n.; pl.* -TIA (-ȧ). [L. *cymatium,* fr. Gr. *kymation,* dim. of *kyma* wave.] A capping or crowning molding in classic architecture; also, a cyma.

cym′bal (sĭm′băl), *n.* [From AS. *cymbal* and OF. *cymbale,* both fr. L. *cymbalum,* fr. Gr. *kymbalon,* fr. *kymbē, kymbos,* hollow vessel.] *Music.* One of a pair of brass half globes or concave plates, clashed together to produce a sharp ringing sound. — **cym′bal·er** (-ẽr), **cym′bal·eer′** (-ēr′), **cym′bal·ist** (-ĭst), *n.*

cyme (sīm), *n.* [L. *cyma* cabbage sprout, fr. Gr. *kyma,* prop., anything swollen, hence also, cyma, wave.] *Bot.* **a** Any form of inflorescence in which the main and secondary axes always terminate in a single flower. **b** Strictly, any flower cluster of this type containing several or many flowers, as in the pink and phlox. They may always be distinguished from corymbs by the opening of the central flower first, the others expanding in order toward the periphery. See INFLORESCENCE, *Illust.* (9).

cy′mene (sī′mēn), *n.* [Gr. *kyminon* cumin.] *Chem.* Any of three isomeric hydrocarbons, $CH_3.C_6H_4.C_3H_7$, distinguished as *orthocymene, metacymene,* and *paracymene,* all methyl isopropyl derivatives of benzene. ***Paracymene,*** or ordinary cymene, is a colorless liquid of pleasant odor, obtained from oil of cumin, oil of wild thyme, etc.

cy′mo·gene (sī′mō·jēn), *n.* [See CYMENE; -GEN.] An inflammable gaseous petroleum product used for producing low temperatures.

cy′mo·graph (-grăf), *n.* [*cyma* + *-graph.*] **a** A device for making tracings of the contour of profiles, moldings, etc **b** Var. of KYMOGRAPH. — **cy′mo·graph′ic** (-grăf′ĭk), *adj.*

cy′mo·phane (-fān), *n.* [Gr. *kyma* wave + *-phane.*] *Mineral.* Chrysoberyl, esp. an opalescent variety.

cy′mo·scope (-skōp), *n.* *Elec.* Any device for detecting the presence of electric waves.

cy′mose (sī′mōs; sī·mōs′), *adj.* [L. *cymosus* full of shoots. See CYME.] *Bot.* Of the nature of, or derived from, a cyme; bearing, or pert. to, a cyme; as, *cymose* inflorescence. See INFLORESCENCE, *Illust.*

Cym′ric (sĭm′rĭk; kĭm′rĭk), **Kym′ric** (kĭm′-), *adj.* [W. *Cymru* Wales.] Of, pert. to, or designating the Celtic population of Wales or their speech, or peoples speaking Celtic of the same branch as Welsh; Brythonic. — *n.* The Welsh language. See INDO-EUROPEAN LANGUAGES, *Table.*

Cym′ry (kĭm′rĭ), **Kym′ry,** *n.; pl.* -RY, -RIES (-rĭz). [W., pl.] The Welsh, collectively.

cyn′ic (sĭn′ĭk), *n.* [See CYNICAL.] **1.** [*cap.*] *Philos.* One of a Greek school of philosophers who taught that virtue is the only good, and that its essence lies in self-control and independence. Later Cynics were violent critics of social customs and current philosophies. **2.** Hence, a faultfinding, captious critic; a misanthrope; specif., one who believes that human conduct is motivated wholly by self-interest. — **cyn′ic,** *adj.*

cyn′i·cal (sĭn′ĭ·kăl), *adj.* [L. *cynicus* of the sect of Cynics, fr. Gr. *kynikos*, prop., doglike, fr. *kyōn, kynos*, dog.] **1.** Faultfinding; captious; currish. **2.** Having the attitude or temper of a cynic; contemptuously distrustful of human nature and motives. — **cyn′i·cal·ly,** *adv.* — **cyn′i·cal·ness,** *n.*

Syn. Cynical, misanthropic, pessimistic, misogynic mean deeply distrustful. **Cynical** implies a sneering disbelief in sincerity and rectitude; **misanthropic**, a rooted distrust of one's fellows and aversion to their society; **pessimistic**, a distrustful and gloomy view of things in general; **misogynic**, a deep-seated distrust of and aversion to women.

cyn′i·cism (sĭn′ĭ·sĭz′m), *n.* **1.** [*cap.*] The doctrine of the Cynics. **2.** Characteristic temper or views of a cynic; also, an instance or expression of such temper or views.

cy′no·sure (sī′nō·shōōr; sĭn′ō-; -zhōōr), *n.* [F. and L.; F., fr. L. *Cynosura* the constellation Cynosure, fr. Gr. *kynosoura* dog's tail, fr. *kyōn, kynos*, dog + *oura* tail.] **1.** [*cap.*] The northern constellation Ursa Minor; also, the North Star. **2.** Anything to which attention is strongly turned; a center of attraction; as, she is the *cynosure* of all eyes this evening.

Cyn′thi·a (sĭn′thĭ·ȧ), *n.* Artemis; hence, the moon personified.

cy′per·a′ceous (sī′pẽr·ā′shŭs; sĭp′ẽr-), *adj.* [Gr. *kypeiros* sedge.] Belonging to the sedge family (Cyperaceae). See SEDGE.

cy′pher (sī′fẽr). Var. of CIPHER.

cy′ pres′ (sē′ prā′). Also **cy′pres′,** *adv.* [OF. *si pres* so nearly (as may be).] *Law.* As nearly as possible in conformity to the intention of the testator or settlor; as, to construe a will *cy pres.*

cy′press (sī′prĕs; -prĭs), *n.* Also **cy′prus** (-prŭs). [ME. *cipres*, fr. OF. *Cipre, Cypre,* Cyprus.] *Hist.* A fabric originally made in or near Cyprus; as: **1.** A rich heavy satin. **2.** A fine, usually black, lawn or silk gauze.

cy′press, *n.* [OF. *cipres, cypres*, fr. L., fr. Gr. *kyparissos.*] **1.** Any of a genus (*Cupressus*) of mostly evergreen trees with symmetrical habit. **2.** Any of several evergreen trees of allied genera, as some cedars (genus *Chamaecyparis*) of the western United States, and the ***bald cypress***, either of two large swamp trees (*Taxodium distichum* and *T. ascendens*) of the southern United States, whose hard red wood is much used for shingles. **3.** The wood of any of these trees, which is valuable in carpentry and building.

cypress vine. A tropical American garden plant (*Quamoclit pennata*) with red or white tubular flowers and finely dissected leaves.

Cyp′ri·an (sĭp′rĭ·ăn), *adj.* [L. *Cyprius*, fr. Gr. *Kyprios*, fr. *Kypros.*] Of or pert. to Cyprus (reputed birthplace of Aphrodite), the people of Cyprus, or their language; also (in allusion to Aphrodite worship), licentious. — *n.* **1.** One of the people of Cyprus. **2.** A prostitute.

cy·pri′nid (sĭ·prī′nĭd; sĭp′rĭ·nĭd), *n. & adj.* Cyprinoid.

cy·prin′o·dont (sĭ·prĭn′ō·dŏnt; sĭ·prī′nō-), *n.* [Gr. *kyprinos* a kind of carp + *-odont.*] Any of a large family (Cyprinodontidae) of small, oviparous, soft-finned fishes, including the killifishes and related minnows.

cyp′ri·noid (sĭp′rĭ·noid; sĭ·prī′noid), *adj.* [Gr. *kyprinos* a kind of carp + *-oid.*] Of, belonging to, or like the carp family (Cyprinidae). See CARP. — **cyp′ri·noid,** *n.*

Cyp′ri·ote (sĭp′rĭ·ōt), **Cyp′ri·ot** (-ŏt), *adj.* [F. *Cypriot, Chypriot.*] Of or pertaining to Cyprus; Cyprian. — *n.* An inhabitant of Cyprus; a Cyprian.

cyp′ri·pe′di·um (sĭp′rĭ·pē′dĭ·ŭm), *n.; pl.* CYPRIPEDIA (-dĭ·ȧ). [NL., lady's-slipper, fr. Gr. *Kypris* Venus + *podion* slipper, little foot.] A plant or flower of a genus (*Cypripedium*) of leafy-stemmed orchids, with large drooping flowers, usually showily colored or marked, the lip forming a large inflated sac or pouch. See LADY'S-SLIPPER.

cy′prus (sī′prŭs). Var. of 1st CYPRESS.

cyp′se·la (sĭp′sē·lȧ), *n.; pl.* -LAE (-lē). [NL., fr. Gr. *kypselē* hollow vessel.] An achene with two carpels and an adherent calyx tube, as in plants of the aster family.

Cy·ril′lic (sĭ·rĭl′ĭk), *adj.* Pertaining to or designating the old Slavic alphabet ascribed to Cyril, 9th-century missionary to the Slavs. In its present form the Cyrillic alphabet is the alphabet of Russia, Bulgaria, and Serbia.

cyst (sĭst), *n.* [NL. *cystis*, fr. Gr. *kystis* bladder, sac.] **1.** *Med.* A pouch or sac without an opening, provided with a distinct membrane and containing fluid or semifluid morbid matter, abnormally developed in one of the natural cavities or in the substance of an organ. **2.** *Biol.* Any of various cystlike structures; as: **a** The resting spore in certain algae. See RESTING, *adj.* **b** An air vesicle in rockweeds. **c** A capsule about certain cells, as bacteria in a resting-spore stage. **d** A sac secreted about themselves by certain protozoans as in estivation or before spore formation.

-cyst (-sĭst). [See CYST.] A suffix meaning *bladder, bag, pouch.*

cyst-, cys′ti- (sĭs′tĭ-). = CYSTO-.

cyst′ic (sĭs′tĭk), *adj.* **1.** Of, like, pertaining to, or containing a cyst. **2.** *Anat.* Of or pertaining to the gall bladder or the urinary bladder. **3.** *Zool.* Contained in a cyst; encysted.

cys′ti·cer′cus (sĭs′tĭ·sûr′kŭs), *n.; pl.* -CERCI (-sûr′sī). [NL., fr. *cysti-* + Gr. *kerkos* tail.] *Zool.* = BLADDER WORM.

cys′tine (sĭs′tēn; -tĭn), *n.* Also **cys′tin.** [Gr. *kystis* bladder.] *Biochem.* A white crystalline acid, $C_6H_{12}N_2O_4S_2$, formed as a product of the splitting of proteins. It is essential in the diets of animals.

cys′to- (sĭs′tō-), **cyst-.** [Gr. *kystis* bladder.] A combining form denoting *likeness to* or *connection with a bladder* or *cyst*, esp. the urinary bladder, as in **cys·tec′to·my, cys·ti′tis, cys·tol′o·gy, cys′to·scope, cys·tos′to·my, cys·tot′o·my** (see -ECTOMY, -ITIS, -LOGY, -SCOPE, -STOMY, -TOMY).

cys′to·carp (sĭs′tō·kärp), *n.* [*cysto-* + *-carp.*] In red algae, a sporocarp. — **cys′to·car′pic** (-kär′pĭk), *adj.*

cys′to·cele (-sēl), *n.* [*cysto-* + *-cele.*] *Med.* Hernia of a bladder, specif. of the urinary bladder; vesical hernia.

cyst′oid (sĭs′toid), *adj.* Bladderlike. — *n.* A cystoid formation.

cy·tas′ter (sī·tăs′tẽr; sĭt′ăs′tẽr), *n.* *Biol.* = ASTER, 2.

-cyte (-sīt). [See CYTO-.] A suffix meaning *hollow vessel*, used to denote a *cell*, as in leucocyte.

Cyth′er·e′a (sĭth′ẽr·ē′ȧ), *n.* [L., fr. Gr. *Kythereia.*] Aphrodite; hence, Venus. — **Cyth′er·e′an** (-ăn), *adj.*

cy′to- (sī′tō-), **cyt-.** [Gr. *kytos.*] A combining form meaning *hollow vessel*, denoting *connection with, relation to*, or *derivation from, a cell, cells*, or *cytoplasm*, as in **cy′to·gen′e·sis, cy′to·tax′is, cy·tot′ro·pism** (see -GENESIS, -TAXIS, -TROPISM).

cy′to·chrome (sī′tō·krōm), *n.* [*cyto-* + *-chrome.*] *Biochem.* Any of a series of iron-containing pigments comprising the **cytochrome system** which plays a major role in intracellular oxidations.

cy′to·ge·net′ics (-jē·nĕt′ĭks), *n.;* see -ICS. [*cyto-* + *genetics.*] The branch of biology which deals with the structural basis of heredity and variation. Cf. CYTOLOGY, GENETICS. — **cy′to·ge·net′ic** (-ĭk), **-i·cal** (-ĭ·kăl), *adj.* — **-i·cal·ly,** *adv.* — **cy′to·ge·net′i·cist** (-ĭ·sĭst), *n.*

cy′to·ki·ne′sis (-kĭ·nē′sĭs; -kī-), *n.* [NL., fr. *cyto-* + Gr. *kinēsis* motion.] *Biol.* The changes affecting the cytoplasm of a cell involved in mitosis, meiosis, and fertilization. See KARYOKINESIS.

cy·tol′o·gy (sī·tŏl′ō·jĭ), *n.; pl.* -GIES (-jĭz). [*cyto-* + *-logy.*] **1.** The branch of biology treating of the structure, functions, etc., of cells. **2.** The structure, organic processes, etc., of cells. — **cy′to·log′i·cal** (sī′tō·lŏj′ĭ·kăl), *adj.* — **cy·tol′o·gist** (sī·tŏl′ō·jĭst), *n.*

cy·tol′y·sin (sī·tŏl′ĭ·sĭn), *n.* A substance producing cytolysis.

cy·tol′y·sis (-sĭs), *n.* [NL., fr. *cyto-* + *-lysis.*] *Physiol.* The dissolution or disintegration of cells.

cy·toph′a·gy (sī·tŏf′ȧ·jĭ), *n.* [*cyto-* + *-phagy.*] *Biol.* The absorption or ingestion of cells; phagocytosis. — **cy·toph′a·gous** (-gŭs), *adj.*

cy′to·plasm (sī′tō·plăz′m), *n.* [*cyto-* + *-plasm.*] The protoplasm of the cell exclusive of the nucleus. Cf. KARYOPLASM; see CELL, OVUM, *Illusts.* — **cy′to·plas′mic** (-plăz′mĭk), *adj.*

cy′to·plast (-plăst), *n.* Cytoplasmic contents of the cell. — **cy′to·plas′tic** (-plăs′tĭk), *adj.*

czar (zär), **czar′e·vitch** (zär′ĕ·vĭch), etc. Vars. of TSAR, TSAREVITCH.

Czech (chĕk; chĕᴋ), *n.* **1.** An individual of the most westerly branch of the Slavs (Bohemians, Moravians, and Silesians). **2.** The Czechoslovak language; specif., the language of the Czechs. See CZECHOSLOVAK. — **Czech, Czech′ic** (-ĭk), **Czech′ish** (-ĭsh), *adj.*

Czech′o·slo′vak, Czech′o–Slo′vak (chĕk′ō·slō′văk; -slō·văk′; chĕᴋ′ō-), *n.* **1.** One of the Czechs or Slovaks of Czechoslovakia. **2.** The Slavic language of the Czechoslovaks. It employs a Latin alphabet. See INDO-EUROPEAN LANGUAGES, *Table.* — *adj.* Of or pertaining to Czechoslovaks, their nation, or their language. — **Czech′o·slo·va′ki·an, Czech′o–Slo·va′ki·an** (-slō·vä′kĭ·ăn; -slō·văk′ĭ·ăn), *adj. & n.*

D

D, d (dē), *n.; pl.* D's, D's, Ds, DS (dēz). **1.** The fourth letter of the English alphabet. D comes from Latin D, which came from Greek Δ (delta), which in turn was derived from the Phoenician. **2.** The sound of this letter. In modern English, D usually represents the voiced alveolar stop. See *Pron.*, § 25. **3.** [*cap.*] (1) In Roman numerals, 500. (2) In the form D̅, 500,000 or, sometimes, 5,000. **4.** *Music.* **a** The second tone in the model major scale (that of C), or the fourth of its relative minor scale (that of A minor). **b** A key or string producing this tone. See PITCH, *Illust.* **5.** As a *symbol*, the fourth in order or class.

D (dē), *adj.* *Chem.* [*cap.* or *small cap.*] Similar in configuration to *d*-glyceraldehyde; as, D-glucose, the D family.

dab (dăb), *v. t. & i.;* DABBED (dăbd); DAB′BING. **1.** To strike or hit with a sudden motion; to peck. **2.** To strike or touch gently, as with a soft or moist substance; also, to apply by striking in that way; hence, to strike or pat with a dabber. — *n.* **1.** A blow; variously: **a** A gentle blow, as with the hand or a soft substance. **b** A sudden hit; a peck. **2.** A flattish mass of anything soft or moist. **3.** *Chiefly Dial.* A small portion.

dab, *n.* Any flatfish; specif., any of several flounders, esp. one (*Limanda limanda*) of Europe, and the ***sand dab L. ferruginea, or rusty dab***, of America.

dab, *n.* *Colloq.* A skillful hand; an expert.

dab′ber (dăb′ẽr), *n.* One who or that which dabs; as: **a** A worker who removes or puts on by dabbing. **b** A pad used by etchers, engravers, etc., to apply ink, color, etc., evenly.

dab′ble (dăb′'l), *v. t.;* DAB′BLED (-'ld); DAB′BLING (-lĭng). [Freq. of dab, or fr. D. *dabbelen.*] To wet by splashing or by little dips or strokes; to sprinkle. — *v. i.* **1.** To play in water, as with the hands. **2.** To work in a slight or superficial manner; as, to *dabble* in politics.

dab′bler (dăb′lẽr), *n.* One who dabbles; a dilettante. — **Syn.** See AMATEUR.

dab′chick′ (dăb′chĭk′), *n.* The little grebe (*Podiceps ruficollis*) of Europe, or the pied-billed grebe (*Podilymbus podiceps*) of America.

dab′ster (-stẽr), *n.* **1.** *Dial.* An expert; an adept. **2.** *Colloq.* A dabbler at anything; an unskilled hand.

‖da ca′po (dä kä′pō). [It., from (the) head or beginning.] *Music.* From the beginning; a direction to return to the beginning and repeat; — indicated by the letters *D.C.*

‖d'ac′cord′ (dȧ′kôr′). [F.] In accord; in tune; agreed.

dace (dās), *n.; pl.* DACE (dās), DACES (dās′ĕz; -ĭz). [ME. *darce*, fr. OF. *dars.*] **a** A small European fish (*Leuciscus leuciscus*) of the carp family. **b** Any of many small North American fresh-water fishes of the carp family (esp. genus *Rhinichthys*).

dachs′hund′ (däks′hōōnt′; *often* dăks′hōōnd′, dăsh′hŭnd′, dăsh′ŭnd), *n.* [G., fr. *dachs* badger + *hund* dog.] A small hound of a breed originating in Germany, having very short legs in comparison with its length and ranging in weight between 15 and 22 lbs. It is used in tracking badgers, foxes, etc.

dack′er (dăk′ẽr; *Scot.* dāk′ẽr), *v. i. & n.* *Dial.* Saunter; also, wrangle.

da·coit′ (dȧ·koit′), *n.* [Hind. *ḍakait.*] One of a class of murderous robbers, in India and Burma, who act in gangs.

da·coit′y (-ĭ), *n.; pl.* -IES (-ĭz). [Hind. *ḍakaitī.*] Robbery by dacoits.

dac′tyl (dăk′tĭl), *n.* [L. *dactylus,* fr. Gr. *daktylos* finger, dactyl.] *Pros.* A poetical foot of three syllables (– ⏑ ⏑), one long followed by two short, or, in accentual verse, one accented followed by two unaccented (L. *flūmĭnă,* E. *mer′-ci·ful*). — **dac·tyl′ic** (dăk·tĭl′ĭk), *adj. & n.*

-dac·tyl′i·a (-dăk·tĭl′ĭ·*à*), **-dac′-ty·ly** (-dăk′tĭ·lĭ). [Gr. *daktylos* finger.] A combining form denoting *a* (specified) *condition as to the digits,* as in brachy*dactyly.*

dac′ty·lo- (dăk′tĭ·lō-), **dactyl-.** [Gr. *daktylos.*] A combining form meaning *finger, toe, digit,* as in **dac′ty·li′tis** (see -ITIS).

dac′ty·lol′o·gy (dăk′tĭ·lŏl′ō·jĭ), *n.* [*dactylo-* + *-logy.*] Art of communicating ideas by signs made with the fingers, as in the manual alphabets of deaf-mutes.

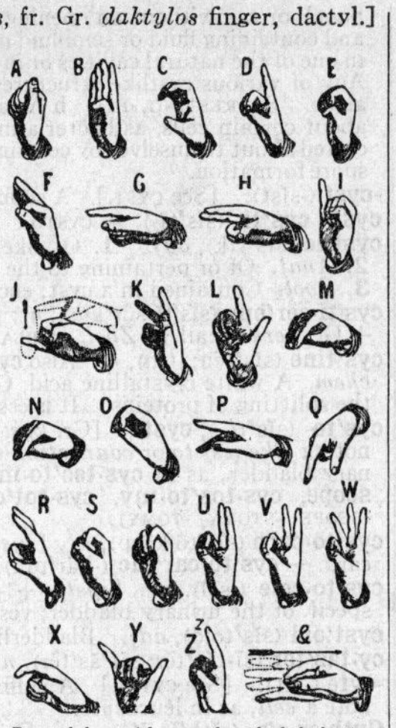

Dactylology (the one-hand alphabet).

dad (dăd), *n.* Father; — used familiarly, or by children.

dad (dăd; däd), **daud** (dôd; däd), *v. & n. Scot.* Thump.

dad′dle (dăd′'l). Var. of DIDDLE, to cheat.

dad′dy (dăd′ĭ), *n.; pl.* -DIES (-ĭz). Dad; — used familiarly.

daddy longlegs. A popular name (given on account of their long slender legs) of: **a** A crane fly. **b** A harvestman.

da′do (dā′dō; *occas.* dä′-), *n.; pl.* DADOES (-dōz). [It., die, cube, pedestal, fr. L. *datus* given.] **1.** *Arch.* That part of a pedestal included between the base and the surbase. **2.** In interior decoration, the lower part of the wall of an apartment when specially decorated.

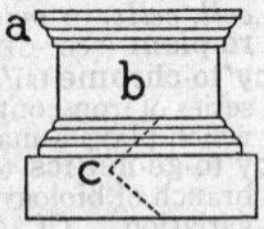

a Surbase; *b* Dado; *c* Base.

dae′dal (dē′dăl; -d'l), *adj.* [L. *daedalus,* fr. Gr. *daidalos.*] **1.** Cunningly or ingeniously formed or working; skillful. **2.** *Poetic.* Varied; variegated; rich.

Daed′a·lus (dĕd′*à*·lŭs; *or, esp. Brit.,* dē′d*à*-), *n.* [L., fr. Gr. *Daidalos,* lit., the cunning worker.] *Gr. Myth.* The builder of the Cretan labyrinth, in which he and his son Icarus were later imprisoned. They escaped by means of wings made from feathers; but Icarus flew too near the sun, the wax of his wings melted, and he was drowned in the sea thenceforth called Icarian. — **Dae·da′li·an** (dē·dā′lĭ·ăn; -dāl′yăn), **Dae·da′le·an** (-dā′lē·ăn), *adj.*

dae′mon (dē′mŏn), *n.; pl.* DAEMONS (-mŏnz), DAEMONES (dē′mō·nēz). [L., fr. Gr. *daimōn.*] **1.** *Gr. Relig.* A tutelary deity or spirit. **2.** Var. of DEMON. — **dae·mon′ic** (dē·mŏn′ĭk), *adj.*

daff (dȧf), *v. i. Scot.* To act or talk sportively; to toy.

daff, *v. t.* **1.** *Obs.* To doff. **2.** To thrust aside; — used esp. in the phrase *to daff the world aside.*

daff′ing (-ĭng), *n. Scot. & N. of Eng.* Fooling; folly.

daf′fo·dil (dăf′ō·dĭl), *n.* [D. *de affodil* the affodil (asphodel), fr. OF. *afrodille,* fr. L. *asphodelus.*] A species of narcissus (*Narcissus pseudo-narcissus*) with large yellow single or double flowers.

daf′fo·dil′ly (dăf′ō·dĭl′ĭ), *n.; pl.* -LIES (-ĭz). Also **daf′fy·down·dil′ly** (dăf′ĭ·doun·dĭl′ĭ), **daf′fa·dil′ly** (dăf′*à*-), **daf′fa·down·dil′ly.** Dial. & poetic var. of DAFFODIL.

daff′y (dȧf′ĭ), *adj.;* DAFF′I·ER (-ĭ·ẽr); DAFF′I·EST. *Chiefly Colloq., U. S.* Crazy; imbecile; daft.

daft (dȧft; 9), *adj.* [ME. *dafte, defte,* stupid, meek.] **1.** Foolish; idiotic; also, crazy; insane. **2.** *Scot.* Giddy; gay. — **daft′ly,** *adv.* — **daft′ness,** *n.*

dag (dăg), *n.* [ME. *dagge.*] A loose hanging end or shred; specif., *Australia,* a daglock.

Da′gan (dä′gän), *n. Babylon. Relig.* God of the earth.

dag′ger (dăg′ẽr), *n.* [F. *dague,* fr. Pr. *daga,* ML. *daggarius.*] **1.** A short weapon used for stabbing. **2.** Anything shaped like, or suggesting, a dagger. **3.** *Print.* A mark of reference [†]. See DOUBLE DAGGER.

dag′gle (dăg′'l), *v. t. & i.;* DAG′GLED (-'ld); DAG′GLING (-lĭng). To clog with mud or mire; also, to draggle.

dag′lock′ (dăg′lŏk′), *n.* A dirty or clotted lock, as of wool on a sheep or hair on a dog.

Da′go (dā′gō), *n.; pl.* DAGOS or DAGOES (-gōz). [Sp. *Diego,* a common proper name.] [*also not cap.*] *U. S. & Can.* A person of Spanish, Portuguese, or, now most commonly, Italian, birth or descent; — used chiefly in contempt.

Da′gon (dā′gŏn), *n.* [L., fr. Gr., fr. Heb. *Dāgōn,* prop., little fish.] *Bib.* The principal deity of the Philistines, originally a fish-god, but later a god of agriculture.

da·guerre′o·type (d*à*·gĕr′ō·tīp; -ē·ō·tīp), *n.* [From L. J. M. *Daguerre,* French inventor + *-type.*] An early variety of photograph, produced on a silver plate or on a copper plate covered with silver; also, the process of producing such pictures. — *v. t.* To produce or represent by the daguerreotype process. — **da·guerre′o·typ′er** (-tīp′ẽr), *n.* — **da·guerre′o·typ′ist** (-ĭst), *n.* — **da·guerre′o·typ′y** (-ĭ), *n.*

da′ha·be′ah (dä′h*à*·bē′*à*), *n.* Also **da′ha·bee′yah** (-bē′y*à*), **da′ha·bi′ah** (-bē′*à*), **da′ha·bi′yeh** (-yĕ). [Ar. *dhahabīyah.*] A long light-draft houseboat, lateen-rigged, and now often propelled wholly or partly by engines, used on the Nile. Cf. LATEEN SAIL, *Illust.*

dahl′ia (däl′y*à*; dăl′y*à*; dāl′y*à*), *n.* [NL., after A. *Dahl,* Swedish botanist.] *Bot.* Any of a genus (*Dahlia*) of Mexican and Central American tuberous-rooted herbs of the aster family, having large showy flowers of bright red and other colors; also, a flower or tuber of such a plant.

dai′ker (dā′kẽr). Var. of DACKER. *Scot.*

Dail Eir′eann (dôl âr′ĭn; *Ir.* thôl), or, in shortened form, **Dail.** [Ir. *dāil* assembly + *Ēireann,* gen. of *Ēire* Ireland.] The lower house, or Chamber of Deputies, of the legislature (*Oireachtas*) of the Republic of Ireland. See SEANAD EIREANN.

dai′ly (dā′lĭ), *adj.* Happening, belonging to, done, or issued each day, or each weekday. — *n.; pl.* DAILIES (-lĭz). A daily newspaper. — *adv.* Every day; day by day.

Syn. **Daily, diurnal, quotidian** mean of each or every day. **Daily** (used in opposition to *nightly*) implies reference to the ordinary concerns of the day or daytime and **diurnal** (used sometimes in opposition to *nocturnal*) is chiefly in astronomical or poetic use; **quotidian** emphasizes the quality of daily recurrence.

dai′men (dā′mĭn; *dial.* dĕm′ĭn), *adj. Scot. & Ir.* Occasional.

dai′mio (dī′myō), *n.; pl.* DAIMIO (-myō) or -MIOS (-myōz). Also **dai′-myo.** [Jap., fr. Chin., lit., great name.] A feudal baron of Japan under the old regime (1600–1867).

dai′mon (dī′mōn), *n.* [Gr. *daimōn.*] Daemon; — a transliteration of the Greek. — **dai·mon′ic** (dī·mŏn′ĭk), *adj.*

dain′ty (dān′tĭ), *adj.;* DAIN′TI·ER (-tĭ·ẽr); DAIN′TI·EST. [From DAINTY, *n.*] **1.** Delicious to the palate; toothsome. **2.** Of a delicate beauty or charm. **3.** Having or showing delicate taste; fastidious; often, overnice; finical. — **Syn.** See CHOICE: NICE. — *n.; pl.* -TIES (-tĭz). [OF. *daintié, deintié,* delicacy, orig., dignity, honor, fr. L. *dignitas,* fr. *dignus* worthy.] Anything that arouses favor or excites pleasure; now, a delicacy. — **dain′ti·ly,** *adv.* — **dain′ti·ness,** *n.*

dair′y (dâr′ĭ), *n.; pl.* -IES (-ĭz). [ME. *deierie,* fr. *deie, daie,* maid, fr. AS. *dǣge.*] **1.** The place, room, or house where milk is kept and converted into butter or cheese. **2.** The business of producing milk, butter, and cheese. **3.** Hence, a dairy farm; also, the cows of a farm. **4.** An establishment for the sale or distribution of milk or milk products. — **dair′y·maid′,** *n.* — **dair′y·man** (-măn), *n.*

dairy cattle. Cattle of breeds adapted and raised especially for milk production.

dair′y·ing, *n.* Business of conducting a dairy.

da′is (dā′ĭs; dās), *n.; pl.* DAISES (dā′ĭs·ĕz; dās′ĕz; -ĭz). [OF. *deis* table, fr. L. *discus* a quoit, dish, LL., table. See DISH.] A platform above the floor of a hall or large room, to give prominence to those occupying it.

dai′sied (dā′zĭd), *adj.* Full of, or adorned with, daisies.

dai′sy (dā′zĭ), *n.; pl.* -SIES (-zĭz). [AS. *dæges-ēage* day's eye, daisy.] **1.** A low scapose European herb (*Bellis perennis*) of the aster family, having heads with small white or pink rays and yellow disks. In the United States it is called ***English daisy.*** **2.** A rather tall leafy-stemmed related plant (*Chrysanthemum leucanthemum*), having larger heads with long white rays. It is called also ***oxeye daisy.*** See SHASTA DAISY; cf. MICHAELMAS DAISY. **3.** **a** *Slang.* A first-rate person or thing. **b** *U. S.* Also **daisy ham.** A boned and smoked piece of pork off the shoulder.

daisy stitch. = RAILWAY STITCH.

dak, dawk (dôk; däk), *n.* [Hind. *ḍāk.*] *India.* Transport by relays of men and horses; hence, post; mail.

da′ker hen (dā′kẽr). = LAND RAIL (see RAIL).

Da′kin's so·lu′tion (dā′kĭnz). [After Henry D. *Dakin,* Eng.-Am. chemist.] *Pharm.* An antiseptic solution, a faintly alkaline 0.5 per cent solution of sodium hypochlorite (NaOCl) in water, used in World War I for the treatment of wounds.

da·koit′ (d*à*·koit′), **da·koit′y.** Vars. of DACOIT, DACOITY.

Da·ko′ta (d*à*·kō′t*à*), *n.* See SIOUX. — **Da·ko′ta,** *adj.*

Da·lai′ La′ma (dä·lī′ lä′m*à*). [Mongolian *dalai* ocean.] The Grand Lama, head of the Lamaist monks. See LAMAISM.

dale (dāl), *n.* [AS. *dæl.*] *Poet. & Dial.* A vale or valley.

dales′man (dālz′măn), *n.* One living in a dale, esp. among the valleys in the north of England. Hence, **dales′folk′** (-fōk′), **dales′peo′ple** (-pē′p'l), **dales′wom′an** (-wo͝om′ăn), *n.*

dalles (dălz), *n. pl.* [F. *dalle* trough.] The nearly vertical walls of a canyon or gorge; dells.

dal′li·ance (dăl′ĭ·ăns; 58), *n.* Act of dallying; trifling; esp., amorous or wanton play; fondling.

dal′ly (dăl′ĭ), *v. i.;* DAL′LIED (-ĭd); DAL′LY·ING. [OF. *dalier.*] **1.** To act playfully; to sport; esp., to play amorously; to wanton. **2.** To trifle, play, or be light (with a person or matter). **3.** To waste time; to delay; dawdle; dillydally. — **Syn.** See TRIFLE: DELAY. — **dal′li·er** (-ĭ·ẽr), *n.*

Dal·ma′tian (dăl·mā′shăn), *adj.* Of or relating to Dalmatia. — *n.* **1.** One of the Slavic-speaking people inhabiting Dalmatia. **2.** Also **Dalmatian dog.** A large, short-haired, spotted dog of a breed supposed to have originated in Dalmatia; — called often *coach dog.*

dal·mat′ic (-măt′ĭk), *n.* [F. *dalmatique,* fr. L. *dalmatica* (*vestis*).] **1.** In the Western Church, an outer vestment worn by a deacon or by certain prelates, esp. bishops. See VESTMENT, *Illust.* **2.** A similar robe worn on state occasions, as that worn by English kings at their coronation.

‖**dal se′gno** (däl sā′nyō). [It.] *Music.* From the sign; — a direction to go back to the sign 𝄋 and repeat from there.

Dal′ton·ism (dôl′t'n·ĭz'm), *n.* Congenital red-green blindness; — so named from its discoverer, John Dalton.

dam (dăm), *n.* [MD. *dam, damm.*] **1.** A barrier to prevent the flow of water; esp., a bank or wall across a watercourse. **2.** A body of water confined by a dam. — *v. t.;* DAMMED (dămd); DAM′MING. To provide with a dam; to restrain the flow of by, or as by, a dam.

dam, *n.* [See DAME.] A female parent; — used esp. of quadrupeds.

dam′age (dăm′ĭj), *n.* [OF., deriv. of L. *damnum* damage.] **1.** Loss due to injury; injury to person, property, or reputation; hurt; harm. **2.** *pl. Law.* The estimated reparation in money for injury sustained. — *v. t.;* DAM′AGED (-ĭjd); DAM′AG·ING (-ĭj·ĭng). To occasion damage to; to impair. — **Syn.** See INJURE. — *v. i.* To become damaged. — **dam′age·a·ble,** *adj.* — **dam′ag·ing·ly,** *adv.*

dam′an (dăm′ăn), *n.* [Ar. *damān Isrā'īl* the sheep of Israel.] A small, herbivorous, hoofed mammal (*Procavia syriaca*) of Palestine, Syria, etc., the "cony" of the Old Testament.

Dam′a·scene (dăm′*à*·sēn; dăm′*à*·sēn′), *adj.* [L. *Damascenus* of Damascus, fr. *Damascus.*] **1.** Of or relating to Damascus. **2.** [*not cap.*] Of or pertaining to damask or the art of damascening; as, *damascene* work. — *n.* **1.** A native or inhabitant of Damascus. **2.** [*not cap.*] Damascene work.

dam′a·scene′ (dăm′*à*·sēn′; dăm′*à*·sēn), *v. t.* [See DAMASK STEEL.] To decorate, as iron, steel, etc., with a peculiar marking or "water" produced in the manufacture.

Da·mas′cus blade, steel, sword (d*à*·măs′kŭs). See DAMASK STEEL.

dam′ask (dăm′*à*sk), *n.* [It. *damasco,* fr. L. *Damascus,* the city.] **1.** A reversible figured fabric of linen, silk, wool, etc.; esp., a linen fabric of this kind used for tablecloths. **2.** Damask steel; also, the peculiar markings of such steel. **3.** A color, red in hue, of medium saturation and medium brilliance. See COLOR. — *adj.* **1.** Pertaining to, originating at, or brought from, Damascus. **2.** Made of, or provided with, damask. **3.** Made of, or resembling, damask steel. **4.** Of the color damask. — *v. t.* **1.** To damascene. **2.** To weave or adorn with the ornamentation characteristic of damask.

dam'a·skeen' (dăm'ȧ·skēn'), *v. t.* To damascene.

damask rose. A large, hardy, and very fragrant pink rose (*Rosa damascena*) of Asia Minor.

damask, *or* **Damascus, steel.** Steel of the kind orig. made at Damascus, ornamented with wavy lines, formerly valued for sword blades (**Damascus blade, Damascus sword**); also, any steel marked with similar wavy patterns.

dame (dām), *n.* [OF., fr. L. *domina* mistress, lady, fem. of *dominus* master, lord.] **1.** A woman of station or authority; specif.: **a** *Archaic & Dial.* The mistress of a household. **b** *Hist.* The wife or daughter of a lord; a lady. **c** The mistress of a school. **2.** A title equivalent to *Lady, Madam, Mistress, Miss,* used as a form of address. **3.** A matron or an elderly woman. **4.** [*cap.*] A title of the Order of the British Empire, corresponding to *Knight,* conferred on women for services rendered to the Empire.

dam'mar (dăm'ẽr), *n.* Also **dam'mer** (-ẽr). [Malay *damar.*] **1.** A resin derived from various evergreen trees (genus *Agathis*) of the pine family, in Australia, New Zealand, and the East Indies, used mostly for making colorless varnish. **2.** Any of certain similar resins from various East Indian trees (genera *Hopea, Shorea,* etc.).

damn (dăm), *v. t.;* DAMNED (dămd); DAMN'ING (dăm'ĭng; dăm'nĭng; *in sense* 5, dăm'ĭng *only*). [OF. *damner, dampner,* fr. L. *damnare, damnatum,* to condemn, fr. *damnum* damage, penalty.] **1.** *Archaic.* To adjudge (a person) guilty; also, to doom. **2.** *Theol.* To doom to everlasting punishment. **3.** To condemn as invalid, illegal, immoral, or wicked; in modern usage, to denounce as being a failure; esp., to pronounce adverse judgment upon (a work of art or literature). **4.** To bring ruin upon; to be the ruin of. **5.** To swear at, using "damn." — **Syn.** See EXECRATE. — *v. i.* To curse; swear. — *n.* Utterance of "damn" as an oath.

dam'na·ble (dăm'nȧ·b'l), *adj.* **1.** Deserving to be condemned. **2.** Worthy of imprecation; detestable. — **dam'na·ble·ness,** *n.* — **dam'na·bly** (-blĭ), *adv.*

‖**dam'nant quod non in·tel'li·gunt** (dăm'nănt kwŏd nŏn ĭn·tĕl'ĭ·gŭnt). [L.] They condemn what they do not understand.

dam·na'tion (dăm·nā'shŭn), *n.* **1.** Act of damning, or state of being damned. **2.** A sin deserving of, or exposing one to, everlasting punishment. **3.** *Theol.* Condemnation to everlasting punishment, or the punishment itself.

dam'na·to'ry (dăm'nȧ·tō'rĭ *or, esp. Brit.,* -tẽr·ĭ), *adj.* Expressing, imposing, or causing condemnation; condemnatory.

damned (dămd; *poet. or rhetorical,* dăm'nĕd; -nĭd), *adj.* **1.** Doomed; specif., doomed to eternal punishment; as, *damned* souls. **2.** Deserving of condemnation.

damn'ing (dăm'ĭng; dăm'nĭng), *adj.* Incurring or bringing damnation. — **damn'ing·ly,** *adv.*

Dam'o·cles (dăm'ō·klēz), *n.* [L., fr. Gr. *Damoklēs.*] A flatterer whom Dionysius of Syracuse rebuked for his constant praises of the happiness of kings by seating him at a royal banquet beneath a sword hung by a single hair.

dam'oi·selle' (dăm'ĭ·zĕl'), **dam'o·sel** (dăm'ō·zĕl), **dam'o·zel,** etc. *Archaic.* Vars. of DAMSEL.

Da'mon (dā'mŭn), *n.* [L., fr. Gr. *Damōn.*] A Sicilian whose friend Pythias was condemned to death by Dionysius of Syracuse. Pythias was allowed time to arrange his affairs when Damon pledged his life for his friend's return. Pythias returned, and Dionysius pardoned him.

damp (dămp), *n.* [MLG. & MD., vapor.] **1.** A noxious exhalation, gas, or vapor. *Obs.* except specif., *Mining,* a gas occurring esp. in coal mines; as, choke*damp,* fire*damp* (see these terms). **2.** Moisture; humidity. **3.** Dejection; depression. — *adj.* **1.** *Archaic.* Dejected; depressed. **2.** Slightly wet; moist. — **Syn.** See WET. — *v. t.* **1.** To affect with or as with a noxious exhalation; to choke; stifle. **2.** To depress or deject; to check or restrain, as action or vigor. **3.** To render damp; to moisten. **4.** *Acoustics, Music, etc.* To check the vibration of, as a string. **5.** *Physics & Elec.* To diminish progressively in amplitude; — said of oscillations, waves, etc. — ***damp off.*** *Plant Pathol.* To undergo damping-off.

damp'en (dămp'ĕn), *v. t. & i.* **1.** To depress or deaden; to damp. **2.** To make or become damp. — **damp'en·er,** *n.*

damp'er (-ẽr), *n.* **1.** One who or that which damps; as: **a** A valve or plate in the flue of a furnace, etc., used to regulate the draft. **b** A contrivance, as the felt-covered pieces in a piano, or the mute of a horn, to deaden vibrations. **2.** *Elec.* **a** A device, as a nonmagnetic conductor or a vane, for diminishing the oscillation of a suspended magnetic needle or freely moving coil. **b** A copper piece around, or embedded in, each of the pole pieces of a synchronous machine, or between them, to decrease hunting.

damp'ing–off', *n. Plant Pathol.* A diseased condition of seedlings or cuttings caused by certain parasitic fungi which invade the plant tissues near the ground, producing rotting.

damp'ish, *adj.* Somewhat damp. — **damp'ish·ness,** *n.*

damp'ly, *adv.* In a damp manner.

damp'ness, *n.* Quality or state of being damp.

dam'sel (dăm'zĕl), *n.* Also, *Poetic and Archaic,* **dam'o·zel** (-ō·zĕl). [OF. *damoisele, dameisele,* gentlewoman, dim. fr. L. *domina, dominus.*] **1.** *Archaic.* A young maid of gentle birth. **2.** A girl; maiden.

dam'son (dăm'zŭn; -z'n), *n.* [ME. *damasin* the Damascus plum.] A small dark-purple plum (*Prunus institia*), orig. from Asia Minor; also, the tree producing this fruit.

damson plum. Orig., the damson; now, in England, a sweeter variety of the damson.

Dan (dăn), *n.* [OF. *danz, dan,* master, fr. L. *dominus.* See DAME.] *Archaic.* A title of honor equivalent to *Master,* or *Sir;* as, *Dan* Cupid; *Dan* Chaucer.

Dan (dăn), *n.* [Heb. *Dān.*] *Bib.* See JACOB. — ***from Dan to Beersheba.*** From limit to limit, Dan (home of the tribe of Dan) and Beersheba being formerly the northern and southern limits of Palestine.

Dan'a·ë (dăn'ā·ē), *n.* [L., fr. Gr. *Danaē.*] *Class. Myth.* The mother of Perseus by Zeus, who visited her as a golden shower in her prison tower.

Da·na'i·des (dȧ·nā'ĭ·dēz), *n. pl.; sing.* DANAÏD (dăn'ā·ĭd). *Gr. Myth.* The fifty daughters of **Dan'a·üs** (dăn'ā·ŭs), all but one (Hypermnestra) of whom slew their husbands at their father's command. The forty-nine were doomed forever to draw water with a sieve in Hades.

dance (dȧns; 9), *v. i.;* DANCED (dȧnst); DANC'ING (dȧn'sĭng). [OF. *dancier, danser.*] **1.** To perform, either alone or with others, a rhythmic and patterned succession of movements, commonly to music. **2.** To move nimbly or merrily. — *v. t.* **1.** To perform or take part in, as a dancer. **2.** To cause to dance. **3.** To cause to be in a specified condition by dancing. — *n.* **1.** A measured leaping or stepping, in unison with music. **2.** A round or turn of dancing; also, a social meeting for the purpose of dancing, as a ball. **3.** *Music.* A kind of music by which dancing is regulated, as the waltz. — **danc'er** (dȧn'sẽr), *n.* — **danc'ing** (-sĭng), *n.*

dan'de·li'on (dăn'dē·lī'ŭn), *n.* [F. *dent de lion* lion's tooth, fr. L. *dens* tooth + *leo* lion.] A well-known yellow-flowered plant (*Taraxacum officinale*), of the chicory family, abundant as a weed.

dan'der (dăn'dẽr; *Scot.* dȧn'-), *v. i. Scot.* To saunter.

dan'der (dăn'dẽr), *n. Colloq.* Anger; temper.

Dan'die Din'mont ter'ri·er (dăn'dĭ dĭn'mŏnt; -mŭnt). A courageous terrier with short legs, long body, pendulous ears, and rough coat, of a breed originating along the English-Scottish border.

dan'di·fy (dăn'dĭ·fī), *v. t.;* -FIED (-fīd); -FY'ING. To dress like a dandy or fop. — **dan'di·fi·ca'tion** (-fĭ·kā'shŭn), *n.*

dan'dle (dăn'd'l), *v. t.;* DAN'DLED (-d'ld); DAN'DLING (-dlĭng). [It. *dondolare.*] **1.** To move up and down on one's knee or in one's arms in affectionate play, as an infant. **2.** To fondle; pamper. — **dan'dler** (-dlẽr), *n.*

dan'druff (dăn'drŭf), *n.* Also **dan'driff** (-drĭf). A scurf that forms on the scalp and comes off in small white or grayish scales. — **dan'druff·y** (-ĭ), *adj.*

dan'dy (dăn'dĭ), *n.* Also **dandy fever.** = DENGUE.

dan'dy, *n.; pl.* -DIES (-dĭz). **1.** One who gives undue attention to dress; a fop. **2.** *Slang.* Anything excellent of its kind. **3.** *Naut.* A yawl; also, its after sail; mizzen; jigger. — **dan'dy·ish,** *adj.* — **dan'dy·ism,** *n.*

dandy roll *or* **roller.** *Paper Mfg.* A roller which impresses the watermark.

Dane (dān), *n.* [Dan. *Daner,* pl., ON. *Danir,* LL. *Dani.*] **1.** A native or inhabitant of Denmark, or person of Danish descent. **2.** = GREAT DANE.

Dane'geld' (dān'gĕld'), **Dane'gelt'** (-gĕlt'), *n. Eng. Hist.* An annual tax probably imposed originally to buy off Danish invaders but continued later as a land tax.

Dane'law' (dān'lô'), *n.* Also erron. **Da'ne·la'ga** (dä'nĕ·lä'gȧ), **Dane'lagh'** (dān'lô'). [AS. *Dena lagu.*] *Hist.* The Danish law anciently in force in the northeastern part of England held by the Danes; also, that part of England.

dan'ger (dān'jẽr), *n.* [OF. *danger, dangier,* deriv. of L. *dominium* lordship.] **1.** *Archaic.* Authority; jurisdiction; hence, reach or range, as of a missile. **2.** Exposure or liability to injury, loss, pain, or other evil. **3.** A case or cause of danger. — **Syn.** Peril, jeopardy, hazard, risk.

dan'ger·ous (dān'jẽr·ŭs), *adj.* Attended with danger; perilous. — **dan'ger·ous·ly,** *adv.* — **dan'ger·ous·ness,** *n.*

Syn. **Dangerous, hazardous, precarious, perilous, jeopardous, risky** mean attended by possibilities of harm or other evils. **Dangerous** applies to that which should be avoided or dealt with most carefully; **hazardous** implies so many chances of evil that the thing so described is exceedingly dangerous; **precarious,** which strictly means neither *dangerous* nor *hazardous,* but *uncertain* or *insecure,* is comparable only when it suggests both of these ideas (as, a *precarious* hold); **perilous** strongly implies the immediacy of a threatened evil; **jeopardous** (now infrequently used) implies that the chances of good are about equal to those of evil; **risky** comes close to *perilous* in suggesting high possibility of harm, but is often applied to that which is done with a knowledge of perils and risks.

dan'gle (dăng'g'l), *v. i.;* DAN'GLED (-g'ld); DAN'GLING (-glĭng). [Of Scand. origin.] **1.** To hang loosely with a swinging or jerking motion. **2.** To be a hanger-on or dependent. — *v. t.* To cause to dangle; to swing. — *n.* A dangling; anything that dangles. — **dan'gler** (-glẽr), *n.*

Dan'iel (dăn'yĕl), *n.* [Heb. *Dānī'ēl, Dānīyāl.*] *Bib.* **a** A Hebrew prophet. **b** A book of the Old Testament. See BIBLE.

Dan'ish (dān'ĭsh), *adj.* Of or relating to the Danes or their language or country. — *n.* The Scandinavian language of the Danes. See INDO-EUROPEAN LANGUAGES, *Table.*

Danish pastry. A rich pastry made of dough raised with yeast, the shortening being mixed as in puff paste.

Dan'ite (dăn'īt), *n.* A descendant of Dan. *Judges* xiii. 2.

dank (dăngk), *adj.* Damp; wet; esp., disagreeably moist. — **Syn.** See WET. — **dank'ly,** *adv.* — **dank'ness,** *n.*

dan'seuse' (däɴ'sûz'), *n.; pl.* -SEUSES (*F.* -sûz'; *E.* -sûz'ĕz; -ĭz). [F., fr. *danser* to dance.] A woman ballet dancer.

Dan'te·an (dăn'tē·ăn; dăn·tē'ăn), *adj.* Of or pertaining to the poet Dante or his writings; Dantesque (which see). — *n.* A student or admirer of Dante.

Dan·tesque' (dăn·tĕsk'), *adj.* Like Dante or his work, esp. the *Inferno,* as being movingly graphic, austerely intense, and rich in allegorical significance.

dap (dăp), *v. i.;* DAPPED (dăpt); DAP'PING. **1.** *Angling.* To drop, or fish by dropping, the bait gently on the water. **2.** To dip quickly into water, as a bird. **3.** To rebound; skip, as a stone over water. — *v. t.* To bounce or skip.

Daph'ne (dăf'nē), *n.* [L., fr. Gr. *Daphnē,* fr. *daphnē* laurel.] **1.** *Gr. Myth.* A nymph, pursued by Apollo, from whom she escaped by being transformed into a laurel tree. **2.** [*not cap.*] The laurel *Laurus nobilis.* **3.** [*not cap.*] *Bot.* Any of a genus (*Daphne*) of Eurasian shrubs of the mezereon family, having fragrant flowers with a colored calyx resembling a corolla.

Daph'nis (-nĭs), *n.* [L., fr. Gr.] *Gr. Myth.* A Sicilian shepherd, son of Hermes and inventor of bucolic poetry.

Daph'nis and Chlo'ë (klō'ē). A pair of unsophisticated lovers in a Greek pastoral romance of the 4th or 5th century A.D.

dap'per (dăp'ẽr), *adj.* [MD., agile, energetic.] Little and active; spruce; trim. — **Syn.** Fashionable, stylish, modish.

dap'ple (dăp''l), *n.* [ON. *depill* a spot, a dot, fr. *dapi* a pool.] **1.** Dappled state or appearance; spotting. **2.** A dappled animal, as a horse. — *v. t.;* DAP′PLED (-'ld); DAP′PLING (-lĭng). To variegate with spots. — *adj.* Dappled.

dap′pled (dăp″'ld), *adj.* Marked with small spots, esp. of gray; as, a *dappled* horse; a *dappled* fawn.

dar′bies (där′bĭz), *n.* *Slang.* Manacles; handcuffs.

Dar′by and Joan (där′bĭ ănd jōn; jō·ăn′). A married couple, esp. an elderly couple, who live in conjugal felicity.

Dar′dan (där′dăn), *adj.* & *n.* Also **Dar·da′ni·an** (där·dā′nĭ·ăn). [L. *Dardanus, Dardanius.*] Trojan.

dare (dâr), *v. i.;* DARED (dârd) or DURST (dûrst); DARED; DAR′ING (dâr′ĭng). [AS. *ic dear* I dare, imp. *dorste*, inf. *durran.*] To have sufficient courage for any purpose; not to be afraid; to venture. — *v. t.* **1.** To have courage for; to venture to do, meet, etc. **2.** To meet defiantly; also, to challenge (one) to a (specified) action as a proof of his courage or ability.

☞ The present *dare* is an original past form, so that the 3d sing. is *dare*, now usually replaced by *dares.*

— *n.* **1.** Act of daring; challenge. **2.** *Rare.* Daring.

dare (dâr; *dial.* där, dȧr), *v. t.* [AS. *darian.*] *Now Dial.* **1.** To terrify; daunt. **2.** To daze; to dazzle and fascinate.

dare′dev′il (dâr′dĕv″'l), *n.* A recklessly bold fellow. — *adj.* Ostentatiously or recklessly daring. — **Syn.** See ADVENTUROUS. — **dare′dev′il·try** (-trĭ), **dare′dev′il·ry** (-rĭ), *n.*

dar′er (dâr′ẽr), *n.* One who dares or defies.

darg, dargue (därg), *n.* *Scot.* A day's work.

dar′ic (dăr′ĭk), *n.* [Gr. *dareikos*, of Per. origin.] A gold coin of ancient Persia, worth about $5.50.

dar′ing (dâr′ĭng), *n.* Venturesome boldness. — *adj.* Fearlessly bold. — **Syn.** See ADVENTUROUS. — **dar′ing·ly**, *adv.* — **dar′ing·ness**, *n.*

dark (därk), *adj.* [AS. *deorc.*] **1.** Destitute, or partly destitute, of light; not receiving, reflecting, or transmitting light; also, not light-colored. **2.** Destitute of moral or spiritual light; wicked. **3.** Gloomy; dismal. **4.** Not clear to the understanding. **5.** Destitute of knowledge and culture; ignorant. **6.** Reticent; secretive. **7.** Not known to the public; — chiefly in *dark horse.* **8.** Of colors, of low or very low brilliance.

Syn. (1) **Dark, dim, dusky, obscure, murky, gloomy** mean partly or wholly destitute of light. **Dark**, the general term, may imply lack of illumination literally or figuratively; **dim** suggests just so much darkness that things cannot be seen clearly or distinctly; **dusky** suggests grayness and a close approach to darkness; **obscure** suggests a darkening by covering, concealing, or the like (as, *obscure* stars); **murky** originally implied and still implies intense darkness in which things are not even faintly visible, but it now often implies a heavy darkness such as that caused by smoke-laden fog; **gloomy** implies causes that interfere seriously with the radiation of light, such as dense clouds. — **Ant.** Light.

(2) See OBSCURE.

— *n.* **1.** Absence of light; darkness; night; nightfall. **2.** Dark color or shade, as in a painting. **3.** The condition of being secret or obscure; often, underhand secrecy; also, ignorance; as, to be in the *dark* about one's intentions.

— *v. i.* & *t.* *Archaic.* To darken; obscure.

Dark Ages (ā′jĕz; -jĭz). See MIDDLE AGE **b**.

Dark Continent. Africa, as being formerly little known.

dark′en (där′kĕn), *v. i.* To grow dark; to become obscure. — *v. t.* **1.** To make dark or black; to obscure. **2.** To render dim; blind. **3.** To cloud; perplex. **4.** To make foul; sully. **5.** To cast a gloom upon; as, to *darken* mirth. **6.** To make of darker color. — **dark′en·er**, *n.*

dark horse. **a** In racing, a horse whose capabilities and chances of success are not known; hence, an unknown or little-known competitor that unexpectedly wins. **b** Hence, *Political Cant*, a candidate unexpectedly nominated.

dark′ish, *adj.* Somewhat dark; dusky. — **dark′ish·ness**, *n.*

dark lantern. A lantern with a single opening, which may be closed to conceal the light.

dar′kle (där′k'l), *v. i.;* DAR′KLED (-k'ld); DAR′KLING (-klĭng). [From DARKLING.] To lurk or loom in the dark; also, to grow dark; to become clouded or gloomy.

dark′ling (därk′lĭng), *adv.* [*dark* + 2d *-ling.*] In the dark. — *adj.* Being or occurring in darkness; dark.

dark′ly, *adv.* In a dark manner.

dark′ness (därk′nĕs; -nĭs), *n.* State or quality of being dark.

dark′room′ (-rōōm′; 85), *n.* *Photog.* A room protected from actinic rays, for handling sensitive plates, etc.

dark′some (-sŭm), *adj.* *Chiefly Poetic.* Dark or darkish.

dark star. *Astron.* A star so feebly luminous as to be invisible, or one entirely nonluminous.

dar′ling (där′lĭng), *n.* [AS. *dēorling*, fr. *dēore* dear + 1st *-ling.*] One dearly beloved. — *adj.* Dearly beloved.

darn (därn), *v. t.* & *i.* [Formerly also *dern*, fr. dialects of northern France.] To mend with interlacing stitches. — *n.* Act or result of darning; place darned. See STITCH, *Illust.*

dar′nel (där′nĕl; -n'l), *n.* [ME., fr. dial. F. *darnelle.*] An annual grass (*Lolium temulentum*) with awned lemmas, often found as a weed in fields of grain.

darn′ing nee′dle. **a** A long, strong needle used in darning. **b** Any species of dragonfly. See DRAGONFLY, *Illust.*

dart (därt), *n.* [OF.] **1.** A short lance; a javelin; hence, any sharp-pointed missile weapon, as an arrow. **2.** **a** Anything that pierces or wounds like a dart. **b** A representation of a dart. See EGG AND DART. **3.** Act of moving like a dart; a quick movement. **4.** *Dressmaking.* A short tapering seam made in fitting a garment to the figure. — *v. t.* & *i.* **1.** To throw with a sudden effort, as a dart. **2.** To shoot out or emit suddenly or rapidly. **3.** To move like a dart; to start and run fast.

dart′er (där′tẽr), *n.* One who or that which darts; as: **a** = SNAKEBIRD. **b** Any of many small American fresh-water fishes closely related to the perches.

dar′tle (där′t'l), *v. t.* & *i.;* DAR′TLED (-t'ld); DAR′TLING (-tlĭng). To dart repeatedly; — frequentative of *dart.*

darts (därts), *n. pl., construed as sing.* A game in which small metal-pointed, feathered darts are thrown at a flat-surfaced upright target (**dart′board′**).

Dar·win′i·an (där·wĭn′ĭ·ăn), *adj.* Of or relating to the naturalist Charles R. Darwin, his theories or followers. — *n.* An advocate of Darwinism.

Darwinian theory. *Biol.* Darwinism.

Dar′win·ism (där′wĭn·ĭz'm), *n.* The theory of the origin and perpetuation of new species of animals and plants by a process of natural selection and survival of the fittest, propounded by Charles Robert Darwin in 1858. See NATURAL SELECTION. — **Dar′win·ist** (-ĭst), *n.* & *adj.* — **Dar′win·is′tic** (-ĭs′tĭk), *adj.* — **Dar′win·ite** (där′wĭn·īt), *n.*

dash (dăsh), *v. t.* [ME. *daschen.*] **1.** To shatter; crush; to strike violently. **2.** To knock, throw, hurl, or thrust (something) *away* or *out*, or *against, upon*, or *into* something else, with violence or suddenness. **3.** To splotch or bespatter; hence, to throw on roughly, in the manner of a splashing fluid; as, to *dash* color on a canvas. **4.** To ruin; frustrate. **5.** To put to shame; also, to abash; depress. **6.** To qualify, or adulterate, by throwing in something of a different quality; as, to *dash* wine with water. **7.** To form, write, or sketch rapidly or carelessly. — *v. i.* To advance violently; to rush.

— *n.* **1.** A violent blow or stroke. **2.** A stroke or line made as with a pen. **3.** The striking or breaking of a liquid in violent motion; also, the sound of dashing. **4.** A sudden discouraging setback. **5.** A small quantity or portion dashed into or upon anything; a slight admixture. **6.** A display; as, to cut a *dash.* **7.** Energy in style or action; animation. **8.** A sudden onset or rush. **9.** **a** A churn dasher. **b** A dashboard. **10.** *Punctuation.* A mark [—] used in printing and writing, singly and in pairs, to interrupt a sentence or to set off parts of it. **11.** *Racing.* A short swift race. **12.** *Telegraphy.* A long click on a telegraph sounder, forming a letter or part of a letter, as in the Morse code. Cf. DOT, *n.*, 5.

dash′board′ (dăsh′bōrd′; 70), *n.* **1.** A screen, on the fore part of a vehicle, to intercept water, mud, or snow; splashboard. **2.** In automobiles, airplanes, etc., a partition facing the operator and directly below the windshield; — called also *instrument board.*

dash′er (-ẽr), *n.* **1.** *Colloq.* One who dashes; specif., a dashing person. **2.** That which dashes or agitates; as, the *dasher* of a churn. **3.** *U. S.* = DASHBOARD, 1.

dash′ing, *adj.* **1.** Characterized by dash, or energy; spirited. **2.** Inclined to make a display; showy. — **dash′ing·ly**, *adv.*

dash′y (dăsh′ĭ), *adj.;* DASH′I·ER (-ĭ·ẽr); DASH′I·EST. Characterized by dash or dashes; esp., showy; dashing.

das′tard (dăs′tẽrd), *n.* [ME., dullard, coward.] A mean or arrant coward; a poltroon; one who sneakingly does malicious acts. — *adj.* Dastardly.

das′tard·ly (-lĭ), *adj.* Characteristic of a dastard; meanly cowardly. — **Syn.** See COWARDLY. — **das′tard·li·ness** (-lĭ·nĕs; -nĭs), *n.*

das′y·ure (dăs′ĭ·ūr), *n.* [Gr. *dasys* thick, shaggy + *oura* tail.] Any of a genus (*Dasyurus*) of arboreal, carnivorous, marsupial mammals (suborder Polyprotodontia) of the Australian region, like the martens in habits.

da′ta (dā′tȧ; dä′tȧ), *n., pl.* of DATUM. A group of facts or statistics; — often used with a sing. verb; as, this *data* has been furnished by the Mayor's office.

da′ta·ry (dā′tȧ·rĭ), *n.;* *pl.* -RIES (-rĭz). [ML. *dataria.*] *R.C.Ch.* A curial office or officer charged with investigating the fitness of candidates for papal benefices.

date (dāt), *n.* [OF. (F. *datte*), fr. L. *dactylus*, fr. Gr. *daktylos.*] **1.** The fruit of a palm (*Phoenix dactylifera*), constituting a staple food of northern Africa and western Asia, and also imported into other countries. **2.** The tall tree (**date palm**), with pinnate leaves and clusters of dioecious flowers, which yields this fruit. See PALM, *Illust.*

date (dāt), *n.* [OF., fr. ML. *data*, fr. L. *datus*, past part. of *dare* to give.] **1.** That statement affixed to a writing, coin, etc., which specifies the time, and often the place, of making. **2.** The point of time at which a transaction or event takes place. **3.** Time of lasting of anything; duration; also, the period of time to which anything belongs, esp. historically; as, sculptures of an early *date.* **4.** A point or period of time to which anything is referred as present, as to usage, style, knowledge, etc.; — chiefly in: ***out of date***, obsolete or behind the times; ***up, or down, to date***, up to the modern or present standard or style. **5.** *Colloq.* An appointment for a specified time. — *v. t.* **1.** To note the time of writing or executing; as, to *date* a letter. **2.** To ascertain, estimate, or give the date of. **3.** *Colloq.* To make an appointment with. — *v. i.* **1.** To reckon chronologically. **2.** To be dated; to bear date; — usually with *from.* **3.** To belong to a given period; — usually with *from.* — **dat′er** (dāt′ẽr), *n.*

date′less (dāt′lĕs; -lĭs), *adj.* Without date; as: **a** Undated. **b** Having no fixed term; endless. **c** So old as not to be assignable to any date; immemorial. **d** Of lasting interest.

date line. **1.** A line relating to a date or dates, as the line where the date of issue appears in a newspaper. **2.** A hypothetical line approximately along the meridian 180° from Greenwich, fixed by international agreement as the place where each calendar day *first* begins. Thus, any given day, say Monday, begins at midnight on the *date line*, and following the midnight line begins continuously farther westward, in New Zealand, Australia, etc. A vessel crossing the date line to the westward sets the date forward by one day, as from Sunday to Monday; if the line is crossed in going eastward, the date is set back.

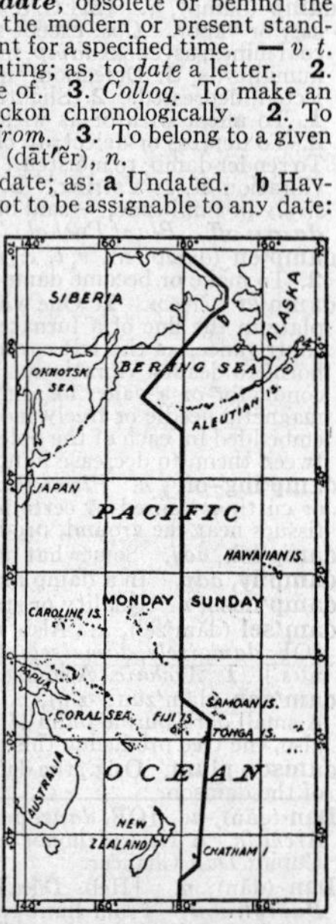

Date Line (heavy line).

da′tive (dā′tĭv), *adj.* [F. or L.; F. *datif*, fr. L. *dativus* appropriate to giving, fr. *dare* to give.] **1.** *Gram.* Designating or pertaining to the case, in most Indo-European languages, that characteristically indicates a person or thing as the one to whose advantage or disadvantage the expressed action, condition, or feeling is directed. In modern English the old dative is recognizable in indirect objects immediately following the verb (they picked *him* a choice gift), but in other positions a prepositional phrase (esp. with *to, for*, or *on*) is substituted. **2.** *Law.* **a** In one's gift; capable of being disposed of at will and pleasure, as an office. **b** Removable, as distinguished from *perpetual;* — said of an officer. **c** Given or appointed.

— *n. Gram.* The dative case, or a form in that case. Abbr. *dat.* —
da·ti′val (dā·tī′văl), *adj.* — **da′tive·ly,** *adv.*
‖**da′to, dat′to** (dä′tō), *n.; pl.* -TOS (-tōz; *E.* -tōz). [Tag. & Sp.] **1.** In Malay countries, the headman of a barrio or tribe. **2.** *Philippine Islands.* The chief of a (Moslem) Moro tribe.
da′tum (dā′tŭm; dä′tŭm), *n.; pl.* DATA (-tȧ). [L.] **1.** Something given or admitted, as a fact on which an inference is based. **2.** Something, actual or assumed, used as a basis of reckoning; — in phrases; as: **datum line, datum plane** *or* **level, datum point.**
da·tu′ra (dȧ·tū′rȧ), *n.* [NL., fr. Hind. *dhatūrā*, fr. Skr. *dhattūra*.] *Bot.* A plant of a genus (*Datura*) of ill-smelling herbs, shrubs, or trees of the nightshade family (Solanaceae), including the jimson weed (*D. stramonium*); also, a flower of such a plant.
daub (dôb), *v. t.* [OF. *dauber* to plaster, fr. L. *dealbare* to whitewash, plaster, fr. *de* + *albare* to whiten, fr. *albus* white.] **1.** To cover, coat, or smear with soft, adhesive matter, as plaster, mud, etc. **2.** To paint in a coarse or unskillful manner. — *v. i.* **1.** To do daubing; to apply plaster, paint, or the like, coarsely and unskillfully. **2.** *Obs. exc. Dial.* To put on a specious or false exterior. — *n.* **1.** Material, as plaster, used to daub walls, etc. **2.** Anything daubed on; a smear. **3.** An act or case of daubing. **4.** *Paint.* A picture unskillfully executed. — **daub′er,** *n.* — **daub′er·y** (dôb′ẽr·ĭ), **daub′ry** (dôb′rĭ), *n.* — **daub′y,** *adj.*
daud (dôd; däd). Var. of DAD, to thump.
daugh′ter (dô′tẽr), *n.; pl.* -TERS (-tẽrz); *obs. pl.* -TREN (-trĕn; -trĭn). [AS. *dohtor, dohter.*] **1.** A human female considered with reference to her parents (abbr. *dau.*); a female child; also, a female descendant; in figurative use, a girl or woman of a given country, religion, etc. **2.** *Archaic.* A maiden. **3.** Anything (regarded as feminine) considered with reference to its source. — *adj.* **1.** Having the nature or relationship of a daughter. **2.** *Biol.* Without reference to sex, having the relation of offspring of the first generation; as, a *daughter* cell.
daugh′ter–in–law′, *n.; pl.* DAUGHTERS-IN-LAW. The wife of one's son.
daugh′ter·ly (dô′tẽr·lĭ), *adj.* Befitting a daughter; filial.
dauk (dôk). Var. of DAK.
daunt (dônt; dänt), *v. t.* [OF. *danter, donter*, fr. L. *domitare*, v. intens. of *domare* to tame.] To subdue the courage of; to intimidate. — **Syn.** See DISMAY.
daunt′less (dônt′lĕs; -lĭs; dänt′-), *adj.* Undaunted; bold; fearless; intrepid; valiant. — **daunt′less·ly,** *adv.* — **daunt′less·ness,** *n.*
dau′phin (dô′fĭn), *n.* [F., prop., a dolphin. See DOLPHIN.] *Fr. Hist.* From 1349 to 1830, the title of the eldest son of the king of France.
dau′phin·ess (-ĕs; -ĭs), *n.* Also **dau′phine** (-fēn). The title of the wife of the dauphin.
daut, dawt (dôt; dät), *v. t. Scot.* To caress.
daut′ie, dawt′ie (dôt′ĭ; dät′ĭ), *n. Scot.* A darling.
dav′en·port (dăv′ĕn·pōrt; 70), *n.* [From the name of some maker.] **1.** A kind of small writing desk. **2.** A large upholstered sofa, often convertible into a bed.
Da′vid (dā′vĭd), *n.* [Heb. *Dāwid, Dāwīd.*] *Bib.* The youngest son of Jesse of Bethlehem. He slew Goliath with his sling, and charmed Saul with his harping; but, incurring Saul's ill will, he was driven into outlawry. After Saul's death David reigned over Israel about forty years.
dav′it (dăv′ĭt; dā′vĭt), *n.* [OF. *daviot, daviet*, davit, fr. the proper name *David.*] *Naut.* A form of crane for hoisting boats, anchor, cargo, etc.

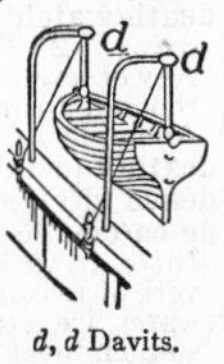

d, d Davits.

Da′vy Jones (dā′vĭ jōnz′). The spirit of the sea; sea devil.
Da′vy Jones's lock′er (jōn′zĭz). The ocean, or bottom of the ocean; hence, ***gone, sent,*** etc., ***to Davy Jones's locker,*** drowned, sunk, etc., and buried in the sea.
Da′vy lamp (dā′vĭ). See SAFETY LAMP.
daw (dô), *n.* [ME. *dawe.*] **1.** A jackdaw. **2.** *Archaic.* A simpleton.
daw (dô), *n. & v. i. Chiefly Scot.* Dawn.
daw′dle (dô′d'l), *v. i. & t.;* DAW′DLED (-d'ld); DAW′DLING (-dlĭng). To waste (time) in idle lingering or sluggish semblance of activity; to trifle; dally. — **Syn.** See DELAY. — **daw′dler** (-dlẽr), *n.*
dawk (dôk). Var. of DAK.
dawn (dôn), *v. i.* **1.** To begin to grow light in the morning. **2.** To begin to appear, expand, develop, or give promise. **3.** To begin to be perceived or understood; as, this fact has just *dawned* upon me. — *n.* **1.** The break of day. **2.** First appearance; beginning.
dawt (dôt). Var. of DAUT.
day (dā), *n.* [AS. *dæg.*] **1.** The time of light, or interval between one night and the next. **2.** The period of the earth's revolution on its axis. **3.** The mean solar day, used in ordinary reckoning of time (see MEAN TIME), and usually beginning at mean midnight: its hours are usually numbered in two series, each from 1 to 12, but sometimes in a single series from 1 to 24. See MEASURE, *Table* 6. **4.** A specified day or date; as, one's wedding *day;* without *day* (= SINE DIE). **5.** With reference to contests, the conflict or contention of the day; as, to win, or lose, the *day.* **6.** A specified time or period; age; time. **7.** Those hours allotted by usage or law for work; as, an eight-hour *day.* **8.** *Astron.* The time required by a celestial body in turning once on its axis; as, the moon's *day* (27 solar days).
day bed. Orig., a type of chaise longue; now, a couch with low head and foot pieces.
day′book′ (dā′bŏŏk′), *n.* A book in which transactions of the day are recorded; specif.: **a** A diary. **b** *Bookkeeping.* A book of original entry in which are recorded the debits and credits, or accounts of the day, in their order.
day′break′ (-brāk′), *n.* Dawn, or the time at which dawn comes.
day coach. See COACH, *n.,* 4.
day′dream′ (dā′drēm′), *n.* A reverie filled with pleasing, often illusory, visions or anticipations. — *v. i.* To indulge in daydreams. — **day′dream′er,** *n.*
day laborer. One who works by the day or for daily wages, esp. as an unskilled laborer.
day letter *or* **lettergram.** See LETTERGRAM.
day′light′ (dā′līt′), *n.* **1.** The light of day. **2.** Full knowledge or understanding of what has been obscure.
daylight saving. The saving or utilizing of daylight by moving ahead all timepieces (generally one hour), usually in the spring, and then setting them back to standard time, usually in the fall.
day lily. 1. Any plant of a genus (*Hemerocallis*, esp. *H. fulva* and *H. flava*) of the lily family, with long narrow basal leaves and showy yellow or tawny flowers in small clusters on naked scapes. **2.** Any plant of a related genus (*Hosta*) bearing racemose white or violet flowers. **3.** The flower of any of these plants.
day nursery. A nursery that takes care of children, as of working mothers, in the daytime.
Day of Atonement. Yom Kippur. See JEWISH HOLIDAYS.
days′man (dāz′măn), *n.* [From *day* in the sense of *day fixed for trial.*] *Archaic.* Arbiter; mediator.
days of grace. The days (usually three) allowed in some places for payment of a note or bill after it becomes due.
day′spring′ (dā′sprĭng′), *n.* The beginning of day; dawn.
day′star′ (-stär′), *n.* **1.** The morning star. **2.** *Poetic.* The sun.
day′time′ (-tīm′), *n.* Time during which there is daylight. — **day′-time′,** *adj.*
daze (dāz), *v. t.* [ME. *dasen.*] To stupefy with excess of light, a blow, fear, grief, etc.; stun; dazzle. — *n.* State of being dazed. — **daz′ed·ly** (dāz′ĕd·lĭ; dāz′ĭd-), *adv.*
daz′zle (dăz′'l), *v. i.* [Freq. of DAZE.] **1.** To be overpowered or dazed by light. **2.** To excite admiration by brilliancy. — *v. t.* **1.** To confuse the vision of by excess of light, moving lights, etc. **2.** To bewilder or surprise with brilliancy or display of any kind. — *n.* Act of dazzling; that which dazzles. — **daz′zling·ly** (dăz′lĭng·lĭ), *adv.*
D day (dē′ dā′). **1.** [From *D* for (undesignated) *day.*] *Mil.* The day set for launching a specific tactical operation; thus, June 6, 1944, was *D day* on the Normandy beaches. Hence, D + 11, the eleventh day after D day. **2.** The day of demobilization.
DDT (dē′dē′tē′). [From *d*ichloro-*d*iphenyl-*t*richloro-ethane.] A colorless, odorless, water-insoluble, crystalline insecticide, $C_{14}H_9Cl_5$, used esp. against body lice, house flies, mosquitoes, and agricultural pests.
DE (dē′ē′). *U.S. Navy.* Short for *destroyer escort* vessel, smaller than a destroyer but faster than a submarine and heavily gunned and equipped with depth charges and, usually, torpedo tubes.
de-. [L. *de* from, down, away; also fr. F. *dé-*, going back to L. *de-*, or (through OF. *des-*) to L. *dis-*. See DIS-.] A prefix denoting: **1.** *Down,* as in *de*pose, put down, *de*pend, hang down. **2.** *Separation; off; away,* as in *de*sist, stand off, *de*legate, send away; also, *out of,* as in *de*train. **3.** *Intensification; completely,* as in *de*relict, abandoned utterly, *de*nude, make quite nude. **4.** *Reversing* or *undoing* of an action, or *depriving* or *ridding* of, or *freeing* from, as in *de*form, *de*gum.
dea′con (dē′k'n; -k'n), *n.* [AS. *diacon*, fr. LL., fr. Gr. *diakonos* servant, minister.] In Christian churches, a cleric or a layman who assists a priest or minister, his duties varying in different communions; also, a cleric in orders next below a priest. — *v. t. U.S.* **a** To read aloud each verse of, as a psalm, before singing it. **b** To pack, as fruit, with the best on top; hence, to adulterate, doctor, or the like. — **dea′con·ry,** *n.* — **dea′con·ship,** *n.*
dea′con·ess (-ĕs; -ĭs), *n.* A woman chosen or assigned to assist in church work.
dead (dĕd), *adj.* [AS. *dēad.*] **1.** Deprived of life; — opp. to *alive* and *living.* **2.** Manifesting or marked by absence of sensation, consciousness, etc.; as, a *dead* faint. **3.** Being without feeling, spirit, vitality, etc.; as, *dead* to pity. **4.** *Colloq.* Very tired. **5.** Devoid of motion or action; stagnant; as, *dead* air. **6.** Completely ineffective or ineffectual; as, a *dead* law. **7.** Lacking in elasticity or resilience; as, a *dead* ball. **8.** Extinct; extinguished; disused; obsolete. **9.** Dull; tame; quiet; as, a *dead* social season. **10.** Deprived or devoid of significance; as, a *dead* custom. **11.** Unproductive; unprofitable; as, *dead* capital. **12.** Barren; sterile; as, *dead* soil. **13.** Having no outlet; as, a *dead* hole. **14.** Lacking fire, glow, luster, color, tang, etc. **15.** Being as certain, complete, irrelievable, etc., as death; as, a *dead* shot; absolute; as, a *dead* loss; unvarying; as, a *dead* level; unrelieved; unalleviated; as, a *dead* weight. **16.** *Elec.* Not electrically connected to a source of voltage; not electrically charged. **17.** *Law.* Being in the state of civil death; cut off from the rights of a citizen. **18.** *Print.* Having been used, or not to be used; — said of type ready to be distributed, of plates and type ready to be melted, or the like. **19.** *Sports.* Out of play (permanently or temporarily).
Syn. **Dead, defunct, deceased, departed, late, lifeless, inanimate** mean devoid of life. **Dead** literally applies to that deprived of life in its ordinary sense, but it is figuratively used of that which is destitute of life in any sense of the word; **defunct** differs little from *dead* except in being literally applied to persons in grandiose or slightly humorous language and, figuratively, to something that by failure or dissolution has ceased to function or operate; **deceased, departed,** and **late** always apply to persons who have died, usually recently, *deceased* being largely in legal or journalistic use, *departed* in religious use, and *late* being referred to a person who preceded the present one in a relation or status; **lifeless** and **inanimate** characteristically apply to that which never has had life but both, especially *lifeless,* may equal *dead* in its literal and figurative use. — **Ant.** Alive.
— *n.* **1.** One who is dead; — now commonly used collectively; as, the *dead* and the living. **2.** The most quiet or deathlike time; as, the *dead* of winter.
— *adv.* **1.** Absolutely; utterly; as, *dead* ripe; *dead* tired. **2.** With sudden and entire, or almost entire, stoppage of motion or action; as, he stopped *dead.* **3.** Directly; exactly; as, they ran *dead* away from us.
dead′beat′ (dĕd′bēt′), *adj. Physics.* Making a beat without recoil; giving indications by a single beat or excursion.
dead′–beat′, *adj. Colloq.* Completely tired out.
dead beat. *Slang.* A sponge; a beat (sense 6).
dead center. *Mach.* **a** In a crank and connecting rod, either of the two positions at the ends of a stroke when the crank and rod are in the same straight line. **b** A center that does not revolve, as in a machine tool. Cf. LIVE CENTER. — **dead′–cen′ter,** *adj.*

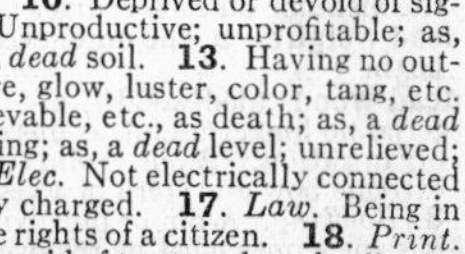

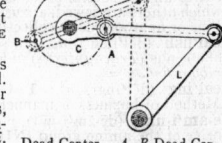

Dead Center. *A, B* Dead Centers; *C* Crank; *L* Lever.

dead′en (dĕd′'n), *v. t.* **1.** To make as dead; impair in vigor, force, etc.; dull. **2.** Hence: **a** To lessen the velocity or momentum of. **b** To make lusterless, vapid, spiritless, etc. **c** To render impervious to sound, as a wall. — *v. i.* To become dead; to lose life, force, etc. — **dead′en·er** (-ẽr), *n.*
dead′en·ing, *n.* Material used to soundproof walls or floors, to remove gloss or luster, etc.

dead'eye' (dĕd'ī'), *n.* *Naut.* A wooden block, encircled by a rope or an iron band, and pierced with holes to receive the lanyard, used esp. to set up shrouds and stays.
dead'fall' (-fôl'), *n.* A trap made so that a log or other weight falls upon the animal and kills or disables it. Cf. DOWNFALL, 2.
dead hand. Mortmain.
dead'head' (dĕd'hĕd'), *n.* A person who receives free tickets for theaters, public conveyances, etc. — *v. t. & i.* To treat or behave as a deadhead.
dead heat. A heat or course in which the contestants reach the goal at the same instant, so that neither wins.
dead letter. **a** That which has lost its force or authority, yet has not been formally abolished; as, that law has become a *dead letter.* **b** An uncalled-for or undeliverable letter which after a fixed time is sent to a department of the general post office (the **dead-letter office**) to be opened, and either returned to the writer or destroyed.
dead'light' (dĕd'līt'), *n.* **1.** *Naut.* **a** A strong shutter to fit ports or cabin windows and keep out water. **b** A piece of heavy glass in a deck or ship's side to admit light. **2.** A skylight made so as not to open.
dead line. **a** *Mil.* A line drawn around a prison, to cross which involves for a prisoner the liability of being instantly shot. **b** Hence, a fixed limit, beyond which disaster is imminent. **c** Usually **dead'line'** (dĕd'līn'). The hour at which the printing forms of a newspaper are locked, after which no copy can be inserted; hence, the time set as a limit for completion of any operation.
dead load. An inert, inactive load, such as, in structures (as a bridge, car, building, engine), is due to the weight of the members, the supported structure, and permanent attachments.
dead'lock' (dĕd'lŏk'), *n.* A stoppage produced by counteraction; a state of inaction or indecision resulting from the opposition of equally powerful persons or factions. — *v. t. & i.* To bring or come to a deadlock.
dead'ly (dĕd'lĭ), *adj.;* -LI·ER (-lĭ·ẽr); -LI·EST. **1.** Likely to cause death; capable of causing death; as, a *deadly* disease. **2.** Causing death; as, a *deadly* blow. **3.** Implacable; desperately hostile; as, *deadly* enemies. **4.** Like death; deathly; as, *deadly* pallor. **5.** *Colloq.* Very great; excessive.
Syn. **Deadly, mortal, fatal, lethal** mean causing or capable of causing death. **Deadly** applies to anything that is certain or extremely likely to cause death; **mortal** usually implies that death has occurred; **fatal** stresses inevitability and applies to that which will result in, or has actually resulted in, death or destruction; **lethal** applies only to that which by its very nature is bound to cause death or which exists for the purpose of destroying life.
— *adv.* **1.** *Archaic.* Mortally; fatally. **2.** Deathly; as, *deadly* pale. **3.** Extremely; excessively; as, *deadly* dull. — **dead'li·ness** (-lĭ·nĕs; -nĭs), *n.*
deadly nightshade. = BELLADONNA, 1.
deadly sins. Also **seven deadly sins.** The seven capital sins, pride, covetousness, lust, anger, gluttony, envy, and sloth, considered as fatal to spiritual progress. Cf. CARDINAL VIRTUES.
dead'ness (dĕd'nĕs; -nĭs), *n.* State of being dead.
dead pan. *Slang.* An expressionless, immobile face. — **dead'-pan'**, *adj. & v. i.*
dead point. = DEAD CENTER.
dead reckoning. *Naut.* Method of finding the place of a ship without aid of celestial observations, from a record of the courses sailed and the distance on each course.
dead weight. **a** The unrelieved weight of anything inert. **b** = DEAD LOAD.
dead'wood' (dĕd'wŏŏd'), *n.* **1.** Wood dead on the tree; hence, material no longer useful, as unsalable stock or inefficient members of an organization. **2.** *pl.* Solid timbers, usually horizontal, built in at the extreme bow and stern of a vessel when too narrow to permit framing. **3.** *Bowling.* A pin or pins lying on the alley or in the gutters, which in some games must be removed before the next ball is rolled.
deaf (dĕf; *dial. & archaic* dēf), *adj.* [AS. *dēaf.*] **1.** Wanting, or deprived of, the sense of hearing, either wholly or in part. **2.** Unwilling to hear or listen; determinedly inattentive. — **deaf'ly**, *adv.* — **deaf'ness**, *n.*
deaf'-and-dumb' al'pha·bet. The alphabet used in dactylology (which see).
deaf'en (-ĕn; -'n), *v. t.* **1.** To make deaf. **2.** To drown out, as a sound. **3.** To make soundproof; deaden. — **deaf'en·ing·ly**, *adv.*
deaf'-mute', *n.* A deaf person who cannot, or has not been taught to, speak. — **deaf'-mute'**, *adj.*
deal (dēl), *n.* [AS. *dǣl.*] **1.** A portion; hence, an indefinite amount. **2.** *Colloq.* A good or great deal.
deal (dēl), *v. t.;* DEALT (dĕlt); DEAL'ING. [AS. *dǣlan.*] **1.** To give in portions or as one's portion; to distribute; apportion. **2.** To bestow; deliver, as blows. **3.** To distribute (cards) to the players, as at the beginning of a game; to give (a particular card) in distributing. — **Syn.** See DISTRIBUTE. — *v. i.* **1.** To make distribution, esp. of cards. **2.** To have to do; variously, to be occupied or concerned, or to have intercourse or business relations. **3.** To conduct oneself; behave; as, to *deal* justly with all. **4.** To contend; to struggle in order to check, correct, etc. **5.** To do a distributing or retailing business; as, to *deal* in silks. — *n.* **1.** Act of dealing; also, *Card Playing*, a hand. **2.** *Colloq.* **a** A bargain. **b** Treatment or method of treatment, with regard esp. to justice; as, a square *deal.* **c** A particular policy of administration, esp. of economic or politico-economic affairs. **d** A clandestine and mutually advantageous arrangement, as in business or politics. **3.** Apportionment. — **deal'er**, *n.*
deal, *n.* [MD. or MLG. *dele.*] **1.** A board, now always of fir or pine, cut to any of several specified sizes. Thus, ***standard deals***, from which others are sawed, are usually 3 by 9 inches and 12 feet long. **2.** Pine or fir wood; deals collectively. — **deal**, *adj.*
deal'fish' (dēl'fĭsh'), *n.; pl.*, see FISH. [From *deal* a plank.] Any of a genus (*Trachypterus*) of long, thin, deep-sea fishes; — called also *ribbonfish.*
deal'ing (dēl'ĭng), *n.* **1.** Usually *pl.* Intercourse; traffic. **2.** Method of business or manner of conduct.
de·am'i·nate (dē·ăm'ĭ·nāt), *v. t.* [See DE-; AMINO-.] *Chem.* To deprive of the amino group (NH_2). — **de·am'i·na'tion** (-nā'shŭn), *n.*
de·am'i·nize (-nīz), *v. t.* *Chem.* = DEAMINATE. — **de·am'i·ni·za'tion** (-nĭ·zā'shŭn; -nī·zā'-), *n.*
dean (dēn), *n.* [OF. *deien* (F. *doyen*), fr. LL. *decanus* chief of ten, fr. *decem* ten.] **1.** *Eccl.* In a collegiate or cathedral church, the head of the chapter. **2.** *Educ.* **a** *Eng.* A university officer supervising undergraduates. **b** *U. S.* A university or college administrative officer, under the president, supervising a school, a faculty, a class or a sex of students. **3.** The chief or senior of a company or body of men, as of a diplomatic corps; — a courtesy title. — **dean'ship**, *n.*
dean'er·y (-ẽr·ĭ), *n.; pl.* -IES (-ĭz). Office, jurisdiction, or official residence of a dean.
dear, dere (dēr), *adj.* [AS. *dēor.*] *Archaic.* Hard; severe.
dear (dēr), *adj.* [AS. *dēore.*] **1.** *Obs.* Glorious; honorable. **2.** Highly valued or esteemed; loved; beloved; cherished; as, a *dear* friend; — in forms of address, an expression of politeness; as, *Dear Sir.* **3.** **a** Costly; expensive. **b** High; — of prices, etc. **4.** Heartfelt; earnest; as, his *dearest* wish. — **Syn.** See COSTLY. — *adv.* Dearly. — *n.* A dear one; darling. — **dear'ly**, *adv.* — **dear'ness**, *n.*
dearth (dûrth), *n.* [ME. *derthe.*] **1.** *Obs.* Dearness; costliness. **2.** Scarcity which renders dear; specif., famine. **3.** Lack of sufficiency; as, a *dearth* of news.
death (dĕth), *n.* [AS. *dēath.*] **1.** Act or fact of dying. **2.** Cause or occasion of loss of life; *Obs.*, a pestilence. **3.** Anything so dreadful as to seem like death. **4.** [*cap.*] The destroyer of life, conventionally represented as a skeleton with a scythe. **5.** State of being dead. **6.** Cessation or privation, as of function, existence, capacity for development, etc.; extinction. **7.** The being deprived of rights and privileges as a citizen or a member of society; civil death. **8.** Murder; bloodshed. **9.** *Christian Science.* An illusion, the lie of life in matter; the unreal and untrue; opposite of Life. *Mary Baker Eddy.*
death adder. See ADDER.
death'bed' (dĕth'bĕd'), *n.* The bed in which a person dies; the closing hours of life of one who dies in bed.
death'blow' (dĕth'blō'), *n.* A mortal or crushing blow.
death camass. A common plant (*Zygadenus venenosus*) of the bunchflower family, of the western United States, the bulb of which is poisonous to stock.
death cup. A very poisonous mushroom (*Amanita phalloides*); also, a cup-shaped part at its base.
death duty. *Law.* A tax or duty imposed on the transfer of property to an heir at the owner's death.
death'ful (dĕth'fŏŏl; -f'l), *adj.* Deadly; murderous; deathly.
death'less (-lĕs; -lĭs), *adj.* Not subject to death; immortal. — **death'less·ly**, *adv.* — **death'less·ness**, *n.*
death'like' (-līk'), *adj.* Deathly.
death'ly (-lĭ), *adj.* [AS. *dēathlīc.*] **1.** Deadly; fatal. **2.** Like death. **3.** *Poetic.* Of death. — *adv.* In a deathlike manner or degree.
death mask. A cast taken from the face of a dead person.
death rate. The number of deaths per hundred or per thousand persons in a given group within a given time.
death rattle. A rattling or gurgling sound produced by air passing through mucus in the throat of a dying person.
death ray. A supposititious ray that destroys life at great distances.
death's'-head' (dĕths'hĕd'), *n.* A skull, emblem of death.
deaths'man (-măn), *n.* *Archaic.* Executioner.
death warrant. **a** *Law.* A warrant to carry out a death sentence. **b** That which ends expectation, joy, etc.
death'watch' (dĕth'wŏch'), *n.* **1.** A vigil kept with the dead or the dying. **2.** The guard set over a criminal before his execution. **3.** Any of several small insects which make a ticking sound superstitiously thought to presage death; esp., any of certain small beetles (family Anobiidae).
death'y (dĕth'ĭ), *adj. & adv.* *Rare.* Deathly.
deave (dēv), *v. t.* *Dial.* To deafen; bewilder.
de·ba'cle (dē·bä'k'l; -băk''l), *n.* Also ‖**dé'bâ'cle** (dā'bä'kl'). [F. *débâcle*, fr. *débâcler*, earlier *desbacler*, to free, appar. fr. *dé-*, *des-* + a verb of LG. origin.] **1.** A breaking up of ice in a stream, or the rush of water, ice, etc., that follows. **2.** **a** A violent disruption; rout. **b** A sudden breakdown; collapse.
de·bar' (dē·bär'), *v. t.;* -BARRED' (-bärd'); -BAR'RING. [F. *débarrer.*] To cut off from entrance, as if by a bar; preclude; — usually with *from.* — **Syn.** See EXCLUDE. — **de·bar'ment**, *n.*
de·bark' (dē·bärk'), *v. t. & i.* [F. *débarquer*, fr. *dé-* (fr. L. *dis-*) + *barque.*] To disembark. — **de'bar·ka'tion** (dē'bär·kā'shŭn), *n.*
de·base' (dē·bās'), *v. t.* [*de-* + *base.*] To reduce from a higher to a lower state or grade, as in dignity, quality, purity, value, etc. — **de·base'ment**, *n.* — **de·bas'er** (-bās'ẽr), *n.*
Syn. (1) **Debase, vitiate, deprave, corrupt, debauch, pervert** mean to cause a person or thing to deteriorate in quality or character. **Debase** implies a loss of position, worth, value, or dignity; **vitiate**, a destruction of purity, validity, or effectiveness by allowing entrance of a fault, defect, or the like; **deprave** now implies moral deterioration by evil thoughts, evil influences, and the like; **corrupt**, applied to persons and to things, implies loss of soundness, purity, integrity, or the like, through forces that break down, pollute, or destroy; **debauch** implies a depraving, especially through sensual indulgences; **pervert** implies a twisting or distorting of something (or someone) from what is (to be), is truly, or should be.
(2) See ABASE.
de·bate' (dē·bāt'), *v. i.* [OF. *debatre.* See DE-; BATTER.] **1.** *Archaic.* To engage in strife or combat. **2.** To dispute; hence, to discuss or examine a question by considering arguments on both sides. **3.** To participate in a debate. — *v. t.* **1.** To contend for; esp., to strive to maintain or controvert (a proposition) by argument. **2.** To engage in a debate about. **3.** To consider the arguments for or against in one's own mind. — **Syn.** See DISCUSS. — *n.* **1.** A debating; discussion; controversy. **2.** A regulated discussion of a given proposition between two matched sides as a test of forensic ability. — **de·bat'a·ble** (-bāt'ȧ·b'l), *adj.* — **de·bat'er** (-bāt'ẽr), *n.*
de·bauch' (dē·bôch'), *v. t.* [F. *débaucher*, fr. OF. *desbochier* to leave work, be idle.] **1.** *Obs.* To lead away or seduce, as from an allegiance; to disaffect. **2.** To lead away from virtue or excellence; corrupt. — **Syn.** See DEBASE. — *v. i.* To indulge excessively in sensual pleasures, esp. eating and drinking. — *n.* An act or occasion of debauchery; also, debauchery. — **de·bauch'ed·ly** (-ĕd·lĭ; 30), *adv.* — **de·bauch'er**, *n.* — **de·bauch'ment**, *n.*
deb'au·chee' (dĕb'ô·shē'; -chē'), *n.* [F. *débauché.*] One given to sensual excesses; esp., a libertine.
de·bauch'er·y (dē·bôch'ẽr·ĭ), *n.; pl.* -ERIES (-ĭz). **1.** Excessive indulgence of the appetites; sensuality; *pl.*, orgies; carousals. **2.** Seduction from virtue, duty, etc.

de·ben′ture (dē·bĕn′tūr), *n.* [L. *debentur* (they) are due.] A writing or certificate issued as an evidence of debt; specif., any of various instruments (often called **debenture bonds**) issued by corporations as evidences of debt, sometimes secured by a mortgage or other charge upon property, and sometimes no more than an unsecured promissory note of the issuing corporation.

de·bil′i·tate (dē·bĭl′ĭ·tāt), *v. t.* [L. *debilitatus*, past part. of *debilitare* to debilitate, fr. *debilis*.] To impair the strength of; to enfeeble. — **Syn.** See WEAKEN. — **de·bil′i·tat′ed** (-tāt′ĕd; -ĭd), *adj.* — **de·bil′i·ta′tion** (-tā′shŭn), *n.*

de·bil′i·ty (-tĭ), *n.; pl.* -TIES (-tĭz). [L. *debilitas*, fr. *debilis* weak.] Weakness; infirmity.

deb′it (dĕb′ĭt), *n.* [L. *debitum* what is due, debt, fr. *debere* to owe.] *Accounting.* Opp. to *credit.* **a** A record of an indebtedness, as by entry on the left-hand side of an account. **b** Any one, or the sum, of the items on the left-hand side of an account, recording indebtedness. **c** The left-hand side of an account, where such items are recorded. The abbreviation *Dr.* (for *debtor*) is written at the top of this side. — *v. t.* To enter upon the left-hand side of an account; to charge.

deb′i·tor (dĕb′ĭ·tẽr), *n.* *Obs.* A debtor.

deb′o·nair′, deb′o·naire′ (dĕb′ō·nâr′), *adj.* Also **deb′on·naire′.** [OF. *de bon aire*, prop., of good kind or race (F. *débonnaire* debonair).] **1.** *Obs.* Good or gentle in disposition. **2.** Affable and courteous; graceful and gay. — **deb′o·nair′ly**, *adv.* — **deb′o·nair′ness**, *n.*

‖**de bonne grâce** (dē bôn′ gräs′). [F.] With good grace; willingly.

Deb′o·rah (dĕb′ō·rȧ), *n.* [Heb.] *Bib.* A Hebrew prophetess who helped free the Israelites and celebrated the victory in a famous song of triumph. *Judges* iv, v.

de·bouch′ (dē·bo͞osh′), *v. i.* [F. *déboucher*, fr. *dé-* (fr. L. *dis-*) + *bouche* opening, fr. L. *bucca* cheek.] **1.** *Mil.* To march out from a confined spot, as a defile, into open ground. **2.** To emerge; issue. — *v. t.* To cause to debouch. — *n.* Usually ‖**dé′bou′ché′** (dā′bo͞o′shā′). [F.] An outlet in works for debouching of troops; hence, an exit; an outlet, as for goods. — **de·bouch′ment**, *n*

dé·bride′ (dā·brēd′), *v. t.* [F. *débrider.*] To cleanse by débridement.

‖**dé′bri′de·ment′** (dā′brēd′mäɴ′), *n.* [F.] The surgical removal of lacerated, macerated, or contaminated tissue.

de·bris′ (dĕ·brē′; dĕb′rē), **dé·bris′** (dā·brē′ *or, esp. Brit.*, dā′brē, dĕb′rē), *n.* [F. *débris*, fr. OF. *debrisier* to break.] **1.** Rubbish, esp. such as results from destruction; ruins. **2.** *Geol.* Any accumulation of fragments of rock; detritus.

debt (dĕt), *n.* [OF. *dette*, deriv. of L. *debitus* owed, past part. of *debere* to owe, prop., to have on loan, fr. *de* + *habere* to have.] **1.** That which is due from one person to another; thing owed; obligation; liability. **2.** A sin; trespass. **3.** State of owing; as, to be in *debt.* **4.** That portion of the capital of a company represented by obligations secured by the property of the company.

debt′or (dĕt′ẽr), *n.* One who owes a debt; — correlative of *creditor.* See DEBIT **c**.

de·bunk′ (dē·bŭngk′), *v. t.* To divest of bunk, esp. of legendary fabrications; to expose the sham pretensions of. — **de·bunk′er**, *n.*

de′but (dā′bū; dā·bū′ *or, esp. Brit.*, dā′bo͞o, dĕb′o͞o), *n.* [F. *début*, fr. *débuter* to make one's first appearance, begin.] Entrance upon a career or profession; specif.: **a** A first public appearance, as of an actor. **b** Formal entrance into society.

deb′u·tante′ (dĕb′ū·tänt′), *n. fem.;* **deb′u·tant′** (dĕb′ū·tänt′; dĕb′ū·tănt), *masc.* [F. *débutante, débutant*, pres. part. See DEBUT.] One making a debut (esp. sense **b**).

dec′a- (dĕk′ȧ-), **dec-**. [Gr. *deka.*] A prefix meaning *ten.*

dec′ade (dĕk′ād *or, esp. Brit.*, -ăd; dĕ·kād′; 2), *n.* [F. *décade*, fr. L. *decas, -adis*, fr. Gr. *dekas*, fr. *deka* ten.] A group of ten; esp., a period of ten years.

de·ca′dence (dē·kā′dĕns; dĕk′ȧ·dĕns), *n.* Also **de·ca′den·cy** (-dĕn·sĭ). [ML. *decadentia*, fr. L. *de* + *cadere* to fall.] Deterioration; decline; esp., a period of retrogression in art or letters. — **Syn.** See DETERIORATION.

de·ca′dent (-dĕnt), *adj.* Characterized by decadence; also, of or characteristic of decadents. — *n.* **1.** A decadent person or thing. **2.** One of a school of French writers of the late 19th century, including Baudelaire, Verlaine, and Mallarmé, who cultivated the abnormal, artificial, and neurotic in subject; — now called *symbolist.*

dec′a·gon (dĕk′ȧ·gŏn; -gŭn), *n. & adj.* [ML. *decagonum.* See DECA-; POLYGON.] *Geom.* A polygon, esp. a plane polygon, of ten angles and ten sides. — **de·cag′o·nal** (dē·kăg′ō·năl; -n′l), *adj.*

dec′a·gram, dec′a·gramme (-grăm), *n.* [F. *décagramme.*] See METRIC SYSTEM, *Table* 5.

dec′a·he′dron (-hē′drŏn), *n.; pl.* -DRONS (-drŏnz), -DRA (-drȧ). Also, less correctly, **dec′a·e′dron** (-ē′drŏn). [NL., fr. *deca-* + Gr. *hedra* base.] A polyhedron of ten faces. — **dec′a·he′dral** (-drăl), *adj.*

de′cal (dē′kăl; dē·kăl′; dĕk′ăl), *n.* [By shortening.] = DECALCOMANIA.

de·cal′ci·fy (dē·kăl′sĭ·fī), *v. t.* To deprive of calcareous matter. — **de·cal′ci·fi·ca′tion** (-fĭ·kā′shŭn), *n.* — **de·cal′ci·fi′er** (-kăl′sĭ·fī′ẽr), *n.*

de·cal′co·ma′ni·a (dē·kăl′kō·mā′nĭ·ȧ), *n.* [F. *décalcomanie.*] **1.** A process of transferring pictures and designs from specially prepared paper to china, glass, etc. **2.** A picture or design to be so transferred.

de′ca·les′cence (dē′kȧ·lĕs′ĕns; -′ns), *n.* [L. *decalescens, -entis*, pres. part. of *decalescere* to grow warm.] *Physics.* Sudden absorption of heat when metals in process of heating pass certain temperatures.

dec′a·li′ter, dec′a·li′tre (dĕk′ȧ·lē′tẽr), *n.* [F. *décalitre.*] See METRIC SYSTEM, *Table* 4.

Dec′a·logue (dĕk′ȧ·lŏg; 74), *n.* Also **Dec′a·log.** [F. *décalogue*, fr. LL., fr. Gr. *dekalogos*, fr. *deka* ten + *logos* speech.] [*sometimes not cap.*] *Bib.* The Ten Commandments.

De·cam′er·on (dē·kăm′ẽr·ŏn), *n.* [It. *Decamerone*, fr. Gr. *deka* ten + *hēmera* day.] An Italian collection of 100 tales (1353) by Boccaccio.

de·cam′er·ous (dē·kăm′ẽr·ŭs), *adj.* [*deca-* + *-merous.*] Having ten parts or divisions; specif., *Bot.*, having the parts in tens; — said of a flower and usually written *10-merous.*

dec′a·me′ter, dec′a·me′tre (dĕk′ȧ·mē′tẽr), *n.* [F. *décamètre.*] See METRIC SYSTEM, *Tables* 1 & 2.

de·camp′ (dē·kămp′), *v. i.* [F. *décamper*, fr. *dé-* (fr. L. *dis*) + *camp* camp.] **1.** To break up a camp, esp. secretly. **2.** To depart suddenly; run away. — **Syn.** Escape; flee; abscond. — **de·camp′ment**, *n.*

dec′ane (dĕk′ān), *n.* [See DECA-.] *Chem.* Any of several isomeric liquid hydrocarbons, $C_{10}H_{22}$, of the methane series.

de·cant′ (dē·kănt′), *v. t.* [F. *décanter*, fr. ML. *decanthare* to pour off, fr. *de* + *-canthus* in the sense of the lip of a vessel.] To pour off gently, as liquor, so as not to roil it; also, to pour from one vessel into another. — **de′can·ta′tion** (dē′kăn·tā′shŭn), *n.*

de·cant′er (dē·kăn′tẽr), *n.* A vessel used to decant liquors, or for receiving decanted liquors.

Decanter.

de·cap′i·tate (dē·kăp′ĭ·tāt), *v. t.* [ML. *decapitatus*, past part. of *decapitare*, fr. L. *de* + *caput* head.] To behead. — **de·cap′i·ta′tion** (-tā′shŭn), *n.* — **de·cap′i·ta′tor** (-tā′tẽr), *n.*

dec′a·pod (dĕk′ȧ·pŏd), *n.* [*deca-* + *-pod.*] One of an order (Decapoda) of the largest, most highly organized crustaceans, including the shrimps, lobsters, crabs, etc. The decapods have five pairs of legs upon the thorax, and stalked eyes. — **dec′a·pod**, *adj.*

de·car′bon·ate (dē·kär′bŏn·āt), *v. t.* To deprive of carbon dioxide or carbonic acid. — **de·car′bon·a′tor** (-ā′tẽr), *n.*

de·car′bon·ize (-īz), *v. t. & i.* To remove carbon (from). — **de·car′bon·i·za′tion** (-ĭ·zā′shŭn; -ī·zā′-), *n.* — **de·car′bon·iz′er** (-īz′ẽr), *n.*

de′car·box′yl·ate (dē′kär·bŏk′sĭ·lāt), *v. t.* *Chem.* To deprive of carboxyl (CO_2H). — **de′car·box′yl·a′tion** (-lā′shŭn), *n.*

de·car′bu·rize (dē·kär′bū·rīz), *v. t. & i.* To decarbonize. — **de·car′bu·ri·za′tion** (-rĭ·zā′shŭn; -rī·zā′-), *n.*

dec′are (dĕk′âr; dĕk·âr′), *n.* [F. *décare.*] A metric measure of surface equal to 10 ares, or 0.2471 acre.

dec′a·stere (dĕk′ȧ·stēr), *n.* [F. *décastère.*] See METRIC SYSTEM, *Table* 6.

dec′a·syl·lab′ic (dĕk′ȧ·sĭ·lăb′ĭk), *adj.* Having ten syllables. — *n.* Also **dec′a·syl′la·ble** (-sĭl′ȧ·b′l). A decasyllabic verse.

de·cath′lon (dē·kăth′lŏn), *n.* [See DECA-; PENTATHLON.] *Athletics.* A composite contest consisting of ten events on the track and field, esp. in the modern Olympic games.

de·cay′ (dē·kā′), *v. i.* [ONF. *decaïr*, deriv. of L. *de* + *cadere* to fall.] **1.** To pass gradually from a sound or prosperous state to one of imperfection, adversity, or dissolution; waste away. **2.** To decrease in numbers, volume, or intensity, or in health, strength, or vigor. **3.** To rot; decompose. **4.** To undergo decay. See DECAY, *n.*, 5. — *v. t.* To cause to decay.

Syn. Decay, decompose, rot, putrefy, spoil, disintegrate, crumble mean to undergo or, in some cases, to cause to undergo, destructive dissolution. Decay implies change from a state of soundness or perfection; decompose stresses a breaking down, but when applied to animal or vegetable matter, a corruption; rot is a clear substitute for *decompose* in this latter sense and often suggests foulness; putrefy implies the rotting of animal matter and its offensiveness to sight and smell; spoil is colloquial for decomposition of foods; disintegrate implies a breaking down or apart so that the cohesiveness of parts or particles is destroyed; crumble implies disintegration of, or as if of, a substance that breaks into fine particles.

— *n.* **1.** Gradual decline or deterioration. **2.** Ruin; dilapidation. **3.** A disease, esp. phthisis. **4.** Decrease in numbers, volume, or intensity. **5.** *Physics.* Spontaneous disintegration of a radioactive substance.

de·cease′ (dē·sēs′), *n.* [OF. *deces*, fr. L. *decessus* departure, death, fr. *decedere* to depart, die, fr. *de* + *cedere* to withdraw.] Death. — *v. i.* To die.

de·ceased′ (dē·sēst′), *adj.* Dead. — **Syn.** See DEAD. — ***the deceased.*** The dead person.

de·ce′dent (dē·sē′dĕnt), *n.* [L. *decedens*, pres. part.] A deceased person; — in U. S. chiefly as a law term.

de·ceit′ (dē·sēt′), *n.* [OF. *deceite*, fr. past part. of *deceveir.* See DECEIVE.] **1.** A deceiving; an attempt to deceive; deception. **2.** A disposition to deceive; deceitfulness. — **Syn.** See IMPOSTURE.

de·ceit′ful (-fo͝ol; -f′l), *adj.* Full of, or marked by, deceit; deceptive; misleading; tricky; fraudulent. — **Syn.** See DISHONEST. — **de·ceit′ful·ly**, *adv.* — **de·ceit′ful·ness**, *n.*

de·ceive′ (dē·sēv′), *v. t.* [OF. *deceivre, deceveir*, fr. L. *decipere* to catch, deceive, fr. *de* + *capere* to take, catch.] **1.** To mislead; delude; cheat. **2.** *Archaic.* To beguile; while away. — *v. i.* To use or practice deceit. — **de·ceiv′a·ble** (-sēv′ȧ·b′l), *adj.* — **de·ceiv′a·bly** (-blĭ), *adv.* — **de·ceiv′er**, *n.* — **de·ceiv′ing·ly**, *adv.*

Syn. Deceive, mislead, delude, beguile mean to lead astray or frustrate, usually by underhandedness. Deceive implies the imposing of an idea or belief that contributes to a person's bewilderment or helplessness or makes him further the agent's end; mislead stresses a being led astray usually, though not invariably, by deliberately deceiving; delude and beguile stress the reactions of one deceived or misled, *delude* implying an inability to distinguish between the true and false, and *beguile*, a readiness to be imposed upon by the allurements of the one who deceives.

de·cel′er·ate (dē·sĕl′ẽr·āt), *v. t. & i.* [*de-* + *accelerate.*] To retard; to slow down; to move with decreasing speed. Cf. ACCELERATION. — **de·cel′er·a′tion** (-ā′shŭn), *n.* — **de·cel′er·a′tor** (-ā′tẽr), *n.*

De·cem′ber (dē·sĕm′bẽr), *n.* [OF. *decembre*, fr. L. *December*, fr. *decem* ten; — this being the tenth month among the early Romans.] The twelfth and last month of the year, having 31 days. Abbr. *Dec.*

De·cem′brist (dē·sĕm′brĭst), *n.* *Russian Hist.* One who conspired for constitutional government against the Emperor Nicholas on his accession in December, 1825.

de·cem′vir (dē·sĕm′vẽr), *n.; pl.* -VIRS (-vẽrz), -VIRI (-vĭ·rī). [L., fr. *decemviri*, pl., fr. *decem* ten + *vir* a man.] **1.** One of a body of ten magistrates in ancient Rome. **2.** A member of any body of ten men in authority. — **de·cem′vi·ral** (-vĭ·răl), *adj.* — **de·cem′vi·rate** (-rāt), *n.*

de·cen′a·ry, de·cen′na·ry (dē·sĕn′ȧ·rĭ), *adj.* [ML. *decennarius*, fr. *decena, decenna*, a tithing.] *Eng. Hist.* Of or pertaining to a tithing. — *n.; pl.* -RIES (-rĭz). A tithing.

de′cen·cy (dē′sĕn·sĭ; -s′n·sĭ), *n.; pl.* -CIES (-sĭz). **1.** Quality or state of being decent; propriety; seemliness; hence, modest or decorous behavior or words. **2.** That which is proper or becoming; — chiefly in *pl.* — **Syn.** See DECORUM.

de·cen′na·ry (dē·sĕn′ȧ·rĭ), *n.; pl.* -RIES (-rĭz). [L. *decennis* of ten years.] Period of ten years. — *adj.* Decennial.

de·cen′na·ry. Var. of DECENARY.

de·cen′ni·al (dē·sĕn′ĭ·ăl; 58), *adj.* Consisting of or happening every ten years; as, a *decennial* period; *decennial* games. — *n.* A tenth anniversary. — **de·cen′ni·al·ly**, *adv.*

de·cen′ni·um (-ŭm), *n.; pl.* -NIUMS (-ŭmz), -NIA (-ȧ). [L., fr. *decennis* of ten years, fr. *decem* ten + *annus* year.] A period of ten years.

de'cent (dē'sĕnt; -s'nt), *adj.* [F. or L.; F. *décent*, fr. L. *decens, decentis*, pres. part. of *decere* to be fitting.] **1.** *Archaic.* Appropriate; suitably elegant. **2.** Conforming to standards of what is fitting; proper; seemly. **3.** Free from immodesty or obscenity. **4.** Moderate, but sufficient; hence, fairly good. — **Syn.** See CHASTE. — **de'cent·ly**, *adv.* — **de'cent·ness**, *n.*

de·cen'ter, de·cen'tre (dē·sĕn'tẽr), *v. t.*; see CENTER. To place out of center; to render or make eccentric.

de·cen'tral·ize (-trăl·īz), *v. t.* To deprive of centralization; esp., to divide and distribute (what has been centralized, united, or concentrated), as the administration of public affairs. — **de·cen'tral·i·za'tion** (-ĭ·zā'shŭn; -ī·zā'-), *n.*

de·cep'tion (dē·sĕp'shŭn), *n.* [F. *déception*, fr. LL. *deceptio*, fr. *decipere, deceptum*. See DECEIVE.] **1.** Act of deceiving; fact or state of being deceived. **2.** That which deceives or is meant to deceive; fraud.

Syn. (1) **Deception, fraud, double-dealing, subterfuge, trickery, chicane, chicanery** mean the act, practice, or means of one who deliberately deceives. **Deception** may or may not imply blameworthiness, for it may suggest cheating or, merely, tricking; **fraud** always implies guilt, often criminality, in act or practice; **double-dealing** usually suggests an act, etc., contrary to one's professed attitude; **subterfuge** suggests an act or practice as the means of deceiving another and of gaining one's end; **trickery**, usually a collective term, implies acts and practices intended to dupe or befool others; **chicane** and **chicanery** imply petty or paltry trickery, especially in legal proceedings.
(2) See IMPOSTURE.

de·cep'tive (-tĭv), *adj.* That may or can deceive. — **de·cep'tive·ly**, *adv.* — **de·cep'tive·ness**, *n.*

de·cern' (dē·sûrn'), *v. t.* [L. *decernere*. See DECREE.] **1.** To distinguish clearly; discern. **2.** *Scots Law.* To decree; adjudge. — *v. i.* To distinguish; specif., to discern clearly.

dec'i- (dĕs'ĭ-). [F. *déci-*, fr. L. *decimus*.] A combining form denoting *tenth;* specif., in the metric system *a tenth of a* (specified) *unit*, as in *deci*gram.

dec'i·are (dĕs'ĭ·âr), *n.* [F. *déciare*.] A metric measure of surface equal to 1/10 are, 10 sq. meters, or 11.96 sq. yd.

dec'i·bel (dĕs'ĭ·bĕl), *n.* [*deci-* + *bel*.] The usual unit for measuring the relative loudness of sounds, being approximately the smallest degree of difference of loudness ordinarily detectable by the human ear, the range of which includes about 130 decibels. Ordinary speech is about 60 decibels greater than sounds that are just at the level of audibility. More technically, *bels* and *decibels* are used as units for the logarithmic expression of ratios of power, voltage, or current, in wire or radio communication. A **bel** is ten decibels. The number of bels difference between two amounts of power is the logarithm to the base ten of the ratio of one amount to another. Abbr. *db.*

de·cide' (dē·sīd'), *v. t.* [F. *décider*, fr. L. *decīdere*, fr. *de* + *caedere* to cut, cut off.] **1.** To terminate by giving the victory or rendering judgment; determine; settle. **2.** To bring to a decision. — *v. i.* To come to a conclusion; to give decision. — **de·cid'a·ble** (-sīd'ȧ·b'l), *adj.*

Syn. **Decide, determine, settle, rule, resolve** mean to come to or to force a conclusion. **Decide** implies the cutting off of doubt, wavering, debate, etc.; **determine** adds the implication of fixing something definitely or unalterably (as, to *decide* to give a dinner; to *determine* the guests to be invited); **settle** implies a conclusion reached by some superior power which ends all dispute, indecision, or the like; **rule** implies a determination by authority, especially by authority of a court; **resolve** implies a clear decision to do or refrain from doing something.

de·cid'ed (dē·sīd'ĕd; -ĭd), *adj.* **1.** Unquestionable; clear-cut. **2.** Free from doubt or wavering; determined. — **de·cid'ed·ly**, *adv.* — **de·cid'ed·ness**, *n.*

de·cid'u·a (dē·sĭd'ū·ȧ), *n.* [NL., fr. L. *deciduus*. See DECIDUOUS.] The portion of the mucous membrane lining the uterus which undergoes special modifications in preparation for and during pregnancy and is cast off at parturition. — **de·cid'u·al** (-ăl), *adj.*

de·cid'u·ous (-ŭs), *adj.* [L. *deciduus*, fr. *decĭdere* to fall off, fr. *de* + *cadere* to fall.] **1.** Falling off at maturity, or at certain seasons, as the antlers of deer, or some leaves; — opposed to *persistent*. Cf. CADUCOUS, FUGACIOUS. **2.** Having leaves of this type; — opp. to *evergreen*. **3.** Ephemeral. — **de·cid'u·ous·ness**, *n.*

dec'i·gram, dec'i·gramme (dĕs'ĭ·grăm), *n.* [F. *décigramme*.] See METRIC SYSTEM, *Table* 5.

dec'ile (dĕs'ĭl), *n.* [F. *décil*, fr. L. *decem* ten.] *Statistics.* Any of the values of an attribute which separate the entire frequency distribution into ten groups of equal frequency. See *frequency distribution*, under FREQUENCY. — *adj.* Designating or pertaining to a decile or division into deciles.

dec'i·li'ter, dec'i·li'tre (dĕs'ĭ·lē'tẽr), *n.* [F. *décilitre*.] See METRIC SYSTEM, *Table* 4.

de·cil'lion (dē·sĭl'yŭn), *n.* & *adj.* [L. *decem* ten + the ending of *million*.] See NUMERATION, *Table*. — **de·cil'lionth** (-yŭnth), *adj.* & *n.*

dec'i·mal (dĕs'ĭ·măl), *adj.* [From ML. & F., fr. L. *decimus* tenth, fr. *decem* ten.] Numbered or proceeding by tens, each unit being ten times the unit next smaller. — *n.* A decimal fraction. See NUMBER, *Table;* CIRCULATING DECIMAL; REPEATING DECIMAL. — **dec'i·mal·ly**, *adv.*

dec'i·mal·ize (-īz), *v. t.* To reduce to a decimal system; as, to *decimalize* the currency. — **dec'i·mal·i·za'tion** (-ĭ·zā'shŭn; -ī·zā'-), *n.*

dec'i·mate (dĕs'ĭ·māt), *v. t.* [L. *decimatus*, past part. of *decimare* to decimate (in senses 1 & 2), fr. *decimus* tenth.] **1.** To take the tenth part of. **2.** To select by lot and punish with death every tenth man of. **3.** To destroy a large part of. — **dec'i·ma'tion** (-mā'shŭn), *n.* — **dec'i·ma'tor** (-mā'tẽr), *n.*

dec'i·me'ter, dec'i·me'tre (dĕs'ĭ·mē'tẽr), *n.* [F. *décimètre*.] See METRIC SYSTEM, *Tables* 1, 2, & 6.

de·ci'pher (dē·sī'fẽr), *v. t.* [*de-* + *cipher*.] **1.** To translate from secret characters into intelligible terms; decode. **2.** *Obs.* To depict. **3.** To find out the meaning of; make out, as words partly obliterated. — **de·ci'pher·a·ble**, *adj.* — **de·ci'pher·ment**, *n.*

de·ci'sion (dē·sĭzh'ŭn), *n.* [F. *décision*, fr. L. *decisio*. See DECIDE.] **1.** A settling or terminating, as of a controversy, by giving judgment on the matter; also, a conclusion arrived at after consideration. **2.** A report of a conclusion, esp. of a judicial determination of a question. **3.** The quality of being decided; promptness or firmness in deciding.

de·ci'sive (dē·sī'sĭv), *adj.* **1.** Having the power or quality of deciding, or terminating, a controversy, contest, etc.; as, *decisive* proofs. **2.** Marked by decision; showing decision. — **Syn.** See CONCLUSIVE. — **de·ci'sive·ly**, *adv.* — **de·ci'sive·ness**, *n.*

dec'i·stere (dĕs'ĭ·stẽr), *n.* [F. *décistère*.] See METRIC SYSTEM, *Table* 6.

deck (dĕk), *n.* [D. *dek*. See DECK, *v.*] **1.** A floorlike platform of a ship. **2.** A flat space likened to a ship's deck, as a horizontal main surface on an airplane. **3.** A pack of playing cards. — *v. t.* [D. *dekken* to cover.] **1.** To cover; overspread. **2.** To dress, esp. elegantly; array; adorn; — often with *out*. **3.** To furnish with a deck, as a vessel. — **Syn.** See ADORN.

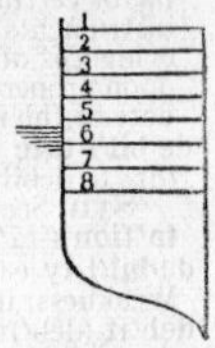

Decks of a typical Merchant Ship, amidships. 1 Bridge Deck; 2 Boat Deck; 3 Promenade Deck; 4 Shelter, Weather, or Superstructure Deck; 5 Upper, or Freeboard, Deck; 6 Main, or 2d, Deck; 7 Lower, or 3d, Deck; 8 Orlop, or 4th, Deck.

deck'er (-ẽr), *n.* Something, as a vessel, having a deck or decks; as, a single-*decker*.

deck hand. A common sailor.

deck'house' (dĕk'hous'), *n.* *Naut.* A house, cabin, or saloon erected on the upper deck.

deck'le (dĕk''l), *n.* Also **deck'el**. [G. *deckel* cover, lid.] *Paper Mfg.* **a** A separate thin wooden frame used to form the border of a hand mold. **b** A curb on either side of the apron to confine the flowing pulp and so determine the width of the paper. **c** In full **deckle edge.** The rough edge of paper left by the deckle, or one imitating this. — **deck'le–edged'** (-ĕjd'; 2), *adj.*

de·claim' (dē·klām'), *v. i.* & *t.* [L. *declamare*, fr. *de* + *clamare* to cry out.] To speak or deliver rhetorically; harangue. — **de·claim'er**, *n.* — **dec'la·ma'tion** (dĕk'lȧ·mā'shŭn), *n.*

de·clam'a·to'ry (dē·klăm'ȧ·tō'rĭ *or, esp. Brit.*, -tẽr·ĭ), *adj.* Suited for or characterized by declaiming; oratorical; bombastic.

de·clar'ant (dē·klâr'ănt), *n.* **1.** One who makes a declaration. **2.** *Law, U. S.* An alien who has declared his intention of becoming a citizen of the United States by signing his first papers in the process of naturalization.

dec'la·ra'tion (dĕk'lȧ·rā'shŭn), *n.* **1.** Act of declaring; announcement; assertion. **2.** That which is declared, or the instrument containing it. **3.** *Cards.* **a** In bezique and other games, an announcement during the play of points scored by a player. **b** *Bridge.* A bid; specif., the winning bid. **4.** *Law.* **a** The first pleading in an action, consisting of the plaintiff's statement of his cause of complaint and demand for relief. **b** A solemn statement made by witnesses, etc., instead of the oath, and subjecting them to perjury for its violation.

de·clar'a·tive (dē·klăr'ȧ·tĭv), **de·clar'a·to'ry** (-tō'rĭ *or, esp. Brit.*, -tẽr·ĭ), *adj.* Making declaration, pronouncement, or assertion.

de·clare' (dē·klâr'), *v. t.* [OF. *declarer*, fr. L. *declarare*, fr. *de* + *clarare* to make clear, *clarus* clear, bright.] **1.** To make known explicitly; proclaim; announce. **2.** To manifest; show. **3.** To assert openly; affirm. **4.** To make full statement of (goods, etc., subject to taxes, duties, etc.) as being in one's possession or ownership. **5.** *Cards.* To make a declaration of, as points in bezique; also, to make (a certain suit) trumps, as at bridge. — *v. i.* To make a declaration; to proclaim oneself. — **de·clar'er** (-klâr'ẽr), *n.*

Syn. (1) **Declare, announce, publish, proclaim, promulgate** mean to make known openly or publicly. **Declare** implies explicitness and, usually, formality in making known; **announce** implies declaration, especially for the first time, of something of interest or that has created speculation; **publish** implies a making public, now commonly through the medium of print; **proclaim** implies a publishing clearly, authoritatively, and in an impressive manner; **promulgate** implies the proclaiming of a dogma, doctrine, or law.
(2) See ASSERT.

de·clen'sion (dē·klĕn'shŭn), *n.* [Perh. a fusion of L. *declinatio, -onis*, inflection, and *descensio, -onis*, a descending.] **1.** Descent; slope. **2.** A decline; deterioration. **3.** Inflection of nouns, adjectives, etc., according to a definite sequence of their case forms; also, the inflectional class of a word declined by cases. — **de·clen'sion·al** (-ăl; -'l), *adj.*

dec'li·na'tion (dĕk'lĭ·nā'shŭn), *n.* **1.** Act of deviating; swerving. **2.** Decay; decline. **3.** A bending downward; inclination. **4.** A refusal, esp. a polite one. **5.** The angle which the magnetic needle makes with the geographical meridian. See VARIATION, *Illust.* **6.** Angular distance north or south from the celestial equator. Cf. CODECLINATION. — **de·clin'a·to'ry** (dē·klīn'ȧ·tō'rĭ *or, esp. Brit.*, -tẽr·ĭ), *adj.*

de·clin'a·ture (dē·klīn'ȧ·tūr), *n.* A declination.

de·cline' (dē·klīn'), *v. i.* [OF. *decliner*, fr. L. *declinare* to turn aside, inflect (a part of speech), avoid, fr. *de* + *clinare* to incline.] **1.** To turn or bend aside; deviate; stray. **2.** To draw towards a close, decay, or extinction; wane; fail. **3.** To bend or lean downward; slope, sink, or hang down; hence, to stoop (to). **4.** To fail to accept; refuse. — *v. t.* **1.** To cause to decline. **2.** To put or turn aside; refuse; reject; esp., to refuse politely. **3.** To inflect (a noun or adjective).

Syn. **Decline, refuse, reject, repudiate, spurn** mean to turn away by not accepting, receiving, or considering. **Decline**, as the most courteous term, applies especially to invitations, offers of help, etc.; **refuse** suggests more positiveness and, even, ungraciousness, and often implies the denial of something asked for; **reject** implies a peremptory refusal as by discarding; **repudiate** implies a casting off or disowning, especially as untrue, unauthorized, or the like; **spurn** stresses contempt or disdain in rejection or repudiation.

— *n.* **1.** A falling off; a diminution or decay; also, the period when a thing is declining. **2.** A declivity; descending slope. **3.** *Med.* **a** A gradual wasting away of the physical and mental faculties. **b** Any wasting disease, esp. pulmonary tuberculosis. **4.** *Plant Pathol.* Any progressively deleterious disease or condition of plants. — **Syn.** See DETERIORATION. — **de·clin'a·ble** (-klīn'ȧ·b'l), *adj.* — **de·clin'er** (-ẽr), *n.*

dec'li·nom'e·ter (dĕk'lĭ·nŏm'ē·tẽr), *n.* [L. *declinare* to decline + *-meter*.] An instrument to register declinations.

de·cliv'i·tous (dē·klĭv'ĭ·tŭs), *adj.* Moderately steep.

de·cliv'i·ty (-tĭ), *n.*; *pl.* -TIES (-tĭz). [L. *declivitas*, fr. *declivis* sloping, downhill, fr. *de* + *clivus* slope, hill.] **1.** Deviation from the horizontal; gradual descent; slope. **2.** A descending slope, as of a hill; — opp. to *acclivity*.

de·coct' (dē·kŏkt'), *v. t.* [L. *decoctus*, past part. of *decoquere* to boil down, fr. *de* + *coquere* to cook, boil.] To prepare by boiling; steep in hot water.

de·coc'tion (-kŏk'shŭn), *n.* A decocting; also, an extract obtained by decocting.

de·code' (dē·kōd'), *v. t.* & *i.* [*de-* + *code*.] To convert from code into ordinary language; decipher.

de'co·here' (dē'kō·hẽr'), *v. t.* & *i.* [See DE-, 4.] *Elec.* To restore or return to the normal condition; — said of a coherer affected by an electric wave. — **de'co·her'ence** (-hẽr'ĕns), *n.* — **de'co·her'er**, *n.*

de'co·he'sion (-hē'zhŭn), *n.* *Elec.* Decoherence.

de·col′late (dē·kŏl′āt), *v. t.* [L. *decollatus*, past part. of *decollare* to behead, fr. *de* + *collum* neck.] To sever from the neck; behead. — **de′col·la′tion** (dē′kŏ·lā′shŭn), *n.* — **de′col·la′tor** (dē′kŏ·lā′tēr), *n.*

dé′col′le·tage′ (dā′kŏl′ĕ·täzh′; *F.* dā′kôl′täzh′), *n.* [F.] The upper part of a décolleté dress, bodice, etc.; also, décolleté costume.

dé′col′le·té′ (dā′kŏl′ĕ·tā′; *F.* dā′kôl′tā′), *adj.* [F., past part. of *décolleter* to bare the neck and shoulders.] **1.** Leaving the neck and shoulders uncovered. **2.** Wearing a low-necked gown.

de·col′or, de·col′our (dē·kŭl′ēr), *v. t.* [F. *décolorer*.] To decolorize.

de·col′or·ant (-ănt), *adj.* Capable of removing color; bleaching. — *n.* A decolorant substance.

de·col′or·ize, de·col′our·ize (-īz), *v. t.* To deprive of color. — **de·col′or·i·za′tion** (-ĭ·zā′shŭn; -ī·zā′-), *n.* — **de·col′or·iz′er** (-īz′ēr), *n.*

de′com·pose′ (dē′kŏm·pōz′), *v. t.* & *i.* [F. *décomposer.* See COMPOSE.] **1.** To separate or resolve into constituent parts or elements, or into simpler compounds. **2.** To bring to or undergo disintegration; decay; rot. — **Syn.** See DECAY. — **de′com·pos′a·ble** (-pōz′ȧ·b'l), *adj.* — **de′com·po·si′tion** (dē′kŏm·pŏ·zĭsh′ŭn), *n.*

de′com·pound′ (dē′kŏm·pound′), *adj.* **1.** Compounded of what is already compounded; compounded again. **2.** *Bot.* Having divisions that are compound; — said of leaves. — *v. t.* **1.** To compound with a compound. **2.** To reduce to constituent parts; decompose.

de′com·press′ (dē′kŏm·prĕs′), *v. t.* To release from pressure or compression. — **de′com·pres′sion** (-prĕsh′ŭn), *n.*

de′con·tam′i·nate (dē′kŏn·tăm′ĭ·nāt), *v. t.* To free of contamination; specif., to rid of poison gas. — **de′con·tam′i·na′tion** (-nā′shŭn), *n.*

de′con·trol′ (-trōl′), *v. t.* & *i.* To remove control (of); as, to *decontrol* the price of butter. — **de′con·trol′**, *n.*

dé′cor′ (dā′kôr′), *n.* [F.] That which serves to decorate; ornamental placing of accessories, esp. in home and stage decoration.

dec′o·rate (dĕk′ŏ·rāt), *v. t.* [L. *decoratus*, past part. of *decorare*, fr. *decus* ornament.] **1.** To improve by addition of something beautiful or becoming; to adorn; also, to make striking, often incongruous, additions to; to garnish. **2.** To award a decoration of honor to. — *v. i.* To set forth decorations. — **Syn.** See ADORN. — **dec′o·ra′tor** (-rā′tēr), *n.*

Dec′o·rat′ed style (-rāt′ĕd; -ĭd). *Arch.* English Gothic of the middle period (14th century), characterized by geometrical tracery and floral decoration.

dec′o·ra′tion (dĕk′ŏ·rā′shŭn), *n.* **1.** Act of decorating. **2.** An embellishment; ornament. **3.** A badge of honor, as a medal or cross; specif., *U. S.*, a military award for personal heroism or gallantry, as distinguished from a service medal (which see), usually of a distinctive shape other than round.

Decoration Day. Memorial Day.

dec′o·ra′tive (dĕk′ŏ·rā′tĭv; -rȧ·tĭv), *adj.* Tending to decorate; ornamental. — **dec′o·ra′tive·ly**, *adv.* — **dec′o·ra′tive·ness**, *n.*

dec′o·rous (dĕk′ŏ·rŭs; dē·kō′rŭs), *adj.* [L. *decōrus*, fr. *decor* comeliness, beauty.] Suitable to a character, or to the time, place, and occasion; becoming; proper; seemly. — **dec′o·rous·ly**, *adv.* — **dec′o·rous·ness**, *n.*

de·cor′ti·cate (dē·kôr′tĭ·kāt), *v. t.* [L. *decorticatus*, past part., deriv. of *de* + *cortex* bark.] To divest of the bark, husk, or coating; to husk; peel; hull. — **de·cor′ti·ca′tion** (-kā′shŭn), *n.* — **de·cor′ti·ca′tor** (-kā′tēr), *n.*

de·co′rum (dē·kō′rŭm; 70), *n.*; *pl.* -RUMS (-rŭmz), -RA (-rȧ). [L., prop. neut. of *decōrus*. See DECOROUS.] **1.** Observance of the proprieties, now esp. in conduct; conformity to accepted standards; as, social *decorum*. **2.** The code of good form; the proprieties. **3.** Decorousness; orderliness; seemliness; as, to disturb the *decorum* of a meeting.

Syn. **Decorum, decency, propriety, dignity, etiquette** mean a code of rules respecting what is right, fitting, honorable, etc., in conduct or behavior or the character derived from observing it. **Decorum** suggests rigidity or formality in code or behavior; **decency** (now rare in this sense) suggests fitness of one to another, as, in a person, of profession and condition in life or, in a thing, of its character in relation to its end; **propriety** suggests a standard of what is proper or correct, as in conduct or in diction, and, often, implies extreme formality in observance; **dignity**, though less clearly implying a code, does suggest a character based upon obedience to what one's class, one's profession, etc., regards as elevated, noble, or the like; **etiquette** is now the usual word for the code governing manners and conduct, especially in society, and for the conventional observance of these rules.

de·coy′ (dē·koi′), *n.* [D. *kooi* cage, enclosure for trapping wild fowl, fr. L. *cavea* cage.] **1.** A place into which wild fowl, esp. ducks, are enticed for capture. **2.** Hence: **a** Anything intended to lead into a trap or snare; a lure; bait; specif., an imitation fowl used by sportsmen to lure wild fowl, esp. ducks, within gunshot. **b** A person employed to inveigle another into a position where he may be trapped, robbed, or the like. — *v. t.* & *i.* To lure or be lured by a decoy. — **Syn.** See LURE. — **de·coy′er** (-ēr), *n.*

de·crease′ (dē·krēs′; dē-; 2), *v. i.* & *t.* [OF. *decreistre, descreistre*, fr. L. *decrescere*, fr. *de* + *crescere* to grow.] To grow or cause to grow less; to diminish gradually in size, degree, number, etc. — **de·creas′ing·ly** (-krēs′ĭng·lĭ), *adv.*

Syn. **Decrease, lessen, diminish, reduce, abate, dwindle** mean to make or grow less. **Decrease** strictly suggests progressive decline, as in size, amount, numbers, etc.; **lessen** suggests decline at any rate; **diminish** emphasizes a perceptible loss, as in numbers or amount, and implies its subtraction from the total; **reduce** implies a bringing down or lowering; **abate** implies a bringing down or lowering of something excessive as in force, intensity, or amount; **dwindle**, like *decrease*, implies progressive lessening but is more often applied to things growing visibly smaller and smaller. — **Ant.** Increase.

de′crease (dē′krēs; dē·krēs′; dē-), *n.* **1.** A decreasing; a diminution. **2.** Amount of diminution.

de·cree′ (dē·krē′), *n.* [OF. *decré, decret*, fr. L. *decretum*, neut. of *decretus*, past part. of *decernere* to decide, fr. *de* + *cernere* to decide.] **1.** An authoritative order or decision deciding what is, or is to be, done; edict. **2.** [*often cap.* & *pl.*] A collection of church law; as, the *Decree* of Gratian. **3.** *Theol.* An eternal purpose of God foreordaining some event or condition. — *v. t.*; DE·CREED′ (-krēd′); DE·CREE′ING. To command; to appoint by decree; ordain.

dec′re·ment (dĕk′rē·mĕnt), *n.* **1.** Decrease; diminution; waste; loss. **2.** Quantity lost by gradual diminution or waste; — opp. to *increment*. **3.** *Math.* The quantity by which a variable is decreased.

de·crep′it (dē·krĕp′ĭt), *adj.* [L. *decrepitus*.] Broken down with age; worn out. — **Syn.** See WEAK. — **de·crep′it·ly**, *adv.*

de·crep′i·tate (dē·krĕp′ĭ·tāt), *v. t.* To roast or calcine so as to cause crackling. — *v. i.* To crackle, as salt when heated. — **de·crep′i·ta′tion** (-tā′shŭn), *n.*

de·crep′i·tude (-tūd), *n.* State of being decrepit.

de′cre·scen′do (dā′krē·shĕn′dō; dē′krē·sĕn′dō), *adj.* [It.] *Music.* Gradually diminishing in volume; diminuendo; — a direction, usually indicated by the abbr. *decresc.* or by the sign ⟩. The opposite of *crescendo*. — *n.* A decrescendo passage or its rendering.

de·cres′cent (dē·krĕs′ĕnt; -'nt), *adj.* [L. *decrescens*, pres. part. of *decrescere*. See DECREASE.] Decreasing; waning. — **de·cres′cence** (-ĕns; -'ns), *n.*

de·cre′tal (dē·krē′tăl; -t'l), *adj.* [LL. *decretalis*, fr. *decretum*. See DECREE.] Pertaining to, or containing, a decree. — *n.* A decree; specif.: **a** A papal epistle replying to some question concerning general ecclesiastical law. **b** Usually in *pl.* The collection of such decrees forming the second part of the old body of canon law.

de·cre′tist (-tĭst), *n.* One versed in canon law.

de·cre′tive (-tĭv), *adj.* Having the force of a decree; decretory. — **de·cre′tive·ly**, *adv.*

dec′re·to′ry (dĕk′rē·tō′rĭ *or, esp. Brit.,* dē·krē′tēr·ĭ), *adj.* Of the nature of, or fixed by, a decree.

de·cri′al (dē·krī′ăl), *n.* A decrying; a clamorous censure.

de·cry′ (dē·krī′), *v. t.*; -CRIED′ (-krīd′); -CRY′ING. [F. *décrier*, fr. OF. *descrier*, fr. *des-* (fr. L. *dis-*) + *crier* to cry.] **1.** To depreciate officially or publicly. **2.** To censure freely; clamor against. — **de·cri′er** (-krī′ēr), *n.*

Syn. **Decry, depreciate, disparage, derogate from, detract from, belittle, minimize** mean to express one's low opinion of something. **Decry** implies open condemnation with intent to discredit; **depreciate** implies the ascription of smaller worth than is generally believed; **disparage** implies depreciation by subtle methods, such as slighting or invidious reference; **derogate from** and **detract from** stress a taking away to the injury of reputation or value, but *detract from* only may have a personal subject as well as an impersonal one; **belittle** and **minimize** both imply depreciation, but *belittle* usually suggests a contemptuous attitude.

dec′u·man (dĕk′ū·măn), *adj.* [L. *decumanus* of the tenth, fr. *decem* ten.] Every tenth in order, thought of as largest in its series; as, a *decuman* wave.

de·cum′bent (dē·kŭm′bĕnt), *adj.* [L. *decumbens, -entis*, pres. part. of *decumbere*, fr. *de* + *cumbere* (only in comp.), *cubare* to lie down.] Recumbent; specif., *Bot.*, lying on the ground, but with ascending apex or extremity; — of stems or shoots. — **de·cum′ben·cy** (-bĕn·sĭ), **de·cum′bence** (-bĕns), *n.*

dec′u·ple (dĕk′ū·p'l; dē·kū′p'l), *adj.* [F. *décuple*, fr. L. *decuplus*, fr. *decem* ten.] **a** Tenfold. **b** Taken by tens. — *n.* A number ten times repeated. — *v. t.* To make tenfold.

de·cu′ri·on (dē·kū′rĭ·ŏn), *n.* [L. *decurio, -onis*, fr. *decuria* a squad of ten, fr. *decem* ten.] *Rom. Hist.* **a** A head or representative of a decury. **b** A municipal or colonial senator.

de·cur′rent (dē·kûr′ĕnt), *adj.* [L. *decurrens, -entis*, pres. part. of *decurrere* to run down, fr. *de* + *currere* to run.] Running or flowing downward; specif., *Bot.*, extending downward; — said of a leaf whose base extends down. — **de·cur′rent·ly**, *adv.*

dec′u·ry (dĕk′ū·rĭ), *n.*; *pl.* -RIES (-rĭz). [L. *decuria*, fr. *decem* ten.] *Rom. Hist.* A division or company of ten, or later of any number; a division, class, etc., as of judges.

de·cus′sate (dē·kŭs′āt; dĕk′ŭs-), *v. t.* & *i.* [L. *decussatus*, past part. of *decussare* to cross like an X, fr. *decussis* the number ten, which the Romans represented by X.] To cross or cut in the form of an X; intersect. — (dē·kŭs′āt), *adj.* **a** Decussated. **b** *Bot.* Arranged in pairs each at right angles to the next pair above or below; as, *decussate* leaves or branches. — **de·cus′sate·ly**, *adv.* — **de′cus·sa′tion** (dē′kŭ·sā′shŭn; dĕk′ŭ-), *n.*

‖**de·dans′** (dē·däN′), *n.* [F.] A gallery at the service end of a tennis court, for spectators; hence, the spectators.

ded′i·cate (dĕd′ĭ·kāt), *adj.* [L. *dedicatus*, past part. of *dedicare* to affirm, fr. *de* + *dicare* to declare, dedicate.] Dedicated. — (-kāt), *v. t.* **1.** To devote to the service or worship of a divine being, or to sacred uses. **2.** To set apart to a definite use or service. **3.** To inscribe by way of compliment, as a book. — **Syn.** See DEVOTE. — **ded′i·ca′tor** (-kā′tēr), *n.*

ded′i·ca′tion (-kā′shŭn), *n.* **1.** Act or rite of dedicating to a sacred use; also, a setting aside for any particular purpose. **2.** A name, and, often, a message, prefixed to a book or artistic production, expressing affection for a friend or cause. — **ded′i·ca′tive** (dĕd′ĭ·kā′tĭv; -kȧ·tĭv), *adj.* — **ded′i·ca·to′ry** (dĕd′ĭ·kȧ·tō′rĭ *or, esp. Brit.,* dĕd′ĭ·kā′tō·rĭ, dĕd′ĭ·kȧ·tēr·ĭ), *adj.*

de·duce′ (dē·dūs′), *v. t.*; -DUCED′ (-dūst′); -DUC′ING (-dūs′ĭng). [L. *deducere*, fr. *de* + *ducere* to lead, draw.] **1.** To trace the course of; as, to *deduce* one's descent. **2.** To derive by reasoning; specif., *Logic*, to infer by deduction. Cf. INDUCE. — **Syn.** See INFER. — **de·duc′i·ble** (-dūs′ĭ·b'l), *adj.*

de·duct′ (dē·dŭkt′), *v. t.* [L. *deductus*, past part. of *deducere* to deduct. See DEDUCE.] **1.** To take away in numbering or estimating; to subtract. **2.** To deduce; — now only in sense of *to draw as a conclusion from reasoning*. — **de·duct′i·ble**, *adj.*

de·duc′tion (-dŭk′shŭn), *n.* **1.** Act of deducting, or taking away; subtraction. **2.** That which is deducted; the part taken away. **3. a** A deducing. **b** *Logic.* Reasoning from the general to the particular, or from the universal to the individual, or, specif., from given premises to their necessary conclusion; also, the conclusion so reached. Cf. INDUCTION. — **de·duc′tive** (-tĭv), *adj.* — **de·duc′tive·ly**, *adv.*

dee (dē), *n.* *Physics.* One of the hollow D-shaped semicylindrical copper electrodes in the cyclotron.

deed (dēd), *n.* [AS. *dǣd*.] **1.** That which is done; act; thing done. **2.** Illustrious act; exploit; feat. **3.** Performance; doing, esp. as contrasted with words. **4.** *Law.* A sealed instrument in writing, duly executed and delivered, containing some transfer, bargain, or contract, as in conveyance of real estate. — **Syn.** See ACTION. — ***in deed.*** In fact; in truth; verily. See INDEED. — *v. t.* To convey or transfer by deed. — **deed′less**, *adj.*

deem (dēm), *v. t.* & *i.* [AS. *dēman* to judge, condemn.] To have an opinion; to think; judge; suppose.

deem′ster (dēm′stēr), *n.* *Isle of Man.* A judge.

deep (dēp), *adj.* [AS. *dēop*.] **1.** Extending far, or comparatively far, below the surface. **2.** Extending far back from the front or outer part. **3.** Extending far laterally; wide. **4.** Lying or situated far down or back. **5.** Coming from, or reaching to, a place far down, back, or within. **6.** Hard to comprehend; profound; obscure. **7.** Solemn; serious; grave. **8.** Wise; sagacious; also, tricky. **9.** Immersed; absorbed; involved. **10.** Very great; intense; extreme. **11.** Of colors, rich; vivid and dark. **12.** Of low tone; not high or sharp. **13.** *Physiol.* Subcutaneous.

Syn. (1) **Deep, profound, abysmal** mean having great extension downward or, sometimes, backward or inward: as used literally, the words follow a climactic order, **deep** being the general and less definite term, **profound** adding the implication of exceeding depth, and **abysmal**, immeasurable depth. Figuratively, therefore, *deep* applies to that which demands or gives penetration (as, *deep* plots; *deep* knowledge), *profound* to that which takes one very far below the surface (as, a *profound* thinker; a *profound* idea) and *abysmal* to that which in extent or degree cannot be calculated (as, *abysmal* ignorance).
(2) See BROAD.

— ***to go off*** (*or, go off at, go in at,* etc.) ***the deep end.*** To plunge into deep water; hence, *Colloq.*: **a** *U.S.* To enter rashly upon a course. **b** *Brit.* To become very excited.

— *n.* **1.** That which is deep, as deep water or body of water. **2.** Hence, the ocean, the firmament, the extent of space or time, chaos, etc. **3.** The middle, or most intense, part; as, the *deep* of winter. **4.** *Naut.* Any of the fathom points on a sounding, or lead, line not designated by "marks." See SOUNDING LINE, *Illust.*

— *adv.* [AS. *dēope.*] **1.** To a great depth; profoundly. **2.** Far on (in time); late; as, *deep* in the night. — **deep′ly,** *adv.* — **deep′ness,** *n.*

deep′en (dēp′ĕn), *v. t. & i.* To make or become deep or deeper.

Deep′freeze′ (dēp′frēz′), *n.* A trade-mark applied to a freezer for the quick-freezing and storage of food.

deep′–laid′ (dēp′lād′; 2), *adj.* Laid deeply; formed with cunning and sagacity; as, *deep-laid* plans.

deep′–root′ed (*see Pron.,* § 2), *adj.* Having deep roots; deeply embedded or implanted. — **Syn.** See INVETERATE.

deep′–sea′ (dēp′sē′), *adj.* Of or pertaining to the deeper parts of the sea; as, *deep-sea* soundings.

deep′–seat′ed (*see Pron.,* § 2), *adj.* Settled deeply; not easily removed. — **Syn.** See INVETERATE.

deer (dēr), *n. sing. & pl.* [AS. *dēor, dīor,* beast.] **1.** *Obs.* Any animal; esp., a wild animal. **2.** Any of a family (Cervidae) of ruminant mammals, distinguished chiefly by the peculiar type of horns, called *antlers,* borne by the males and shed and renewed annually. In popular language, the term often excludes the large species of the family, as the elk, moose, and caribou. See 2d BUCK, 1; DOE; VENISON; BLACK-TAILED DEER; FALLOW DEER; MULE DEER; RED DEER; ROE DEER; VIRGINIA DEER; MUSK DEER.

deer′hound′ (-hound′), *n.* A large hound of a breed originating in Scotland, and formerly much used in hunting deer. It has a rough, blue-gray coat, a beard and silky mustache, and a long tail.

deer lick. A lick to which deer resort.

deer′skin′ (dēr′skĭn′), *n.* The skin of a deer, or leather made from it; also, a garment of such leather.

deer′stalk′ing (-stôk′ĭng), *n.* The hunting of deer on foot, by stealing upon them unawares. — **deer′stalk′er,** *n.*

de·face′ (dē·fās′), *v. t.;* DE·FACED′ (-fāst′); DE·FAC′ING (-fās′ĭng). [OF. *desfacier,* fr. L. *dis-* + *facies* face.] To destroy or mar the face or appearance of; to disfigure. — **de·face′a·ble,** *adj.* — **de·face′ment,** *n.* — **de·fac′er,** *n.*

Syn. **Deface, disfigure, disfeature** mean to mar the appearance of. **Deface** implies superficial injuries, such as the removal or the intrusion of a detail or details; **disfigure** suggests deeper injuries but such as impair in beauty or attractiveness; **disfeature** suggests the marring, as by distortion, deformation, etc., of anything known for its beauty of outline, contour, or the like.

‖**de fac′to** (dē făk′tō). [L.] Actually; in fact; in reality; — distinguished from *de jure,* and often used attributively.

de·fal′cate (dē·făl′kāt; dē′făl·kāt), *v. t.* [ML. *defalcatus,* past part. of *defalcare* to deduct, orig., to cut off with a sickle, fr. L. *de* + *falx, falcis,* a sickle.] *Now Rare.* To take away or deduct a part of. — *v. i.* To commit defalcation; to embezzle. — **de′fal·ca′tor** (dē′făl-kā′tẽr; dĕf′ăl-), *n.*

de′fal·ca′tion (dē′făl·kā′shŭn; dĕf′ăl-), *n.* **1.** *Now Rare.* Reduction; abatement. **2.** A misappropriation of money by one who has it in trust; also, the sum abstracted; embezzlement.

def′a·ma′tion (dĕf′ȧ·mā′shŭn; dē′fȧ-), *n.* Act of defaming another; calumny; aspersion. — **de·fam′a·to′ry** (dē·făm′ȧ·tō′rĭ *or, esp. Brit.,* -tẽr·ĭ), *adj.*

de·fame′ (dē·fām′), *v. t.* [OF. *diffamer,* fr. L. *diffamare,* fr. *dis-* (here confused with *de*) + *fama* a report.] **1.** *Archaic.* To harm or destroy the good fame of. **2.** To cast aspersion on the good name or reputation of; to slander; calumniate. **3.** *Rare.* To charge; accuse. — **Syn.** See MALIGN. — **de·fam′er** (-fām′ẽr), *n.*

de·fault′ (dē·fôlt′), *n.* [OF. *defaute,* deriv. of L. *de* + *fallere* to deceive, fail.] **1.** Failure to do what is required by duty or law; neglect. **2.** *Archaic.* A fault; offense; also, a mistake or error. **3.** A failure to pay financial debts. **4.** *Law.* In practice, the failure of a defendant or plaintiff to appear at the required time to defend or prosecute an action or proceeding. **5.** *Sports.* Failure to compete in or to finish an appointed contest. — ***in default of.*** In case of failure or lack of.

— *v. i.* **1.** To fail in fulfilling a contract, agreement, or duty, esp. a financial obligation. **2.** To fail to appear in court; to let a case go by default. **3.** To fail to engage in or to finish a contest, esp. an athletic contest; also, *Sports,* to forfeit the contest by such failure. — *v. t.* **1.** To fail to perform or pay. **2.** To fail to contest, as a race; also, *Sports,* to forfeit by such failure.

de·fault′er (dē·fôl′tẽr), *n.* One who makes or commits a default; specif.: **a** One who fails to appear in court when summoned. **b** An embezzler. **c** One who fails to pay his debts. **d** *Brit.* A soldier guilty of a military offense.

de·fea′sance (dē·fē′zăns; -z′ns), *n.* [OF. *defesance,* fr. *defesant, desfesant,* pres. part. of *desfaire* to undo.] *Law.* **1.** A rendering null or void. **2.** A condition the fulfillment of which avoids an instrument.

de·fea′si·ble (dē·fē′zĭ·b'l), *adj.* Capable of being annulled or undone. — **de·fea′si·ble·ness, de·fea′si·bil′i·ty** (-bĭl′ĭ·tĭ), *n.*

de·feat′ (dē·fēt′), *v. t.* [OF. *desfait,* past part. of *desfaire* to undo, deriv. of L. *dis-* + *facere* to do.] **1.** *Obs.* To undo; destroy; disfigure. **2.** To render null and void, as a title; to deprive, as of an estate; to frustrate, as hope. **3.** To overcome or vanquish. — **Syn.** See CONQUER. — *n.* **1.** *Obs.* An undoing; destruction. **2.** Frustration by prevention of success; as, the *defeat* of a plan. **3.** An overthrow, as of an army in battle; loss of a contest.

de·feat′ism (-ĭz′m), *n.* The policy or practice of admitting defeat of one's own country, party, etc., on the ground that the continuation of a contest is impossible or inadvisable. — **de·feat′ist** (-ĭst), *n. & adj.*

de·fea′ture (dē·fē′tūr), *n.* [OF. *desfaiture* a killing, prop., an undoing.] **1.** *Obs.* Defeat. **2.** *Archaic.* Disfigurement.

def′e·cate (dĕf′ē·kāt), *v. t.* [L. *defaecatus,* past part. of *defaecare,* fr. *de* + *faex, faecis,* dregs, lees.] To clear from impurities; to clarify; refine. — *v. i.* **1.** To cast off impurities; to become pure. **2.** To void excrement. — **def′e·ca′tion** (-kā′shŭn), *n.* — **def′e·ca′tor** (-kā′tẽr), *n.*

de·fect′ (dē·fĕkt′; dē′fĕkt), *n.* [L. *defectus,* fr. *deficere, defectum,* to desert, fail, be wanting, fr. *de* + *facere* to make, do.] **1.** Want of something necessary for completeness; deficiency. **2.** Imperfection; blemish; fault. — **Syn.** See BLEMISH.

de·fec′tion (dē·fĕk′shŭn), *n.* **1.** Failing; failure. **2.** Conscious breach of allegiance or duty; desertion.

de·fec′tive (-tĭv), *adj.* **1.** Incomplete; deficient; faulty. **2.** *Gram.* Lacking one or more of the usual forms of declension or conjugation, as in **defective verb** (*ought, may, can, must*). **3.** *Psychol.* Markedly subnormal in intelligence. — *n.* **1.** A person or thing that is defective, as a person subnormal in intelligence. **2.** *Gram.* A defective word. — **de·fec′tive·ly,** *adv.* — **de·fec′tive·ness,** *n.*

defective year. See JEWISH CALENDAR.

de·fence′ (dē·fĕns′), *n.* Defense; — the British spelling.

de·fend′ (dē·fĕnd′), *v. t.* [OF. *defendre,* fr. L. *defendere,* fr. *de* + *fendere* (only in comp.) to strike.] **1.** To repel danger or harm from; to protect; to maintain against force or argument. **2.** Of a lawyer, to act on behalf of (an accused person). **3.** *Law.* To oppose or resist, as a claim at law; to contest, as a suit. **4.** *Now Rare.* To prohibit; forbid. — *v. i.* To make a defense. — **de·fend′er,** *n.*

Syn. (1) **Defend, protect, shield, guard, safeguard** mean to secure from danger or against attack. **Defend** implies the aim to ward off that which threatens or to repel that which attacks; **protect** implies something (literally or figuratively a covering) that serves as a bar to the admission or impact of that which may injure or destroy; **shield** suggests protective intervention in imminent danger, in actual attack, or the like; **guard** implies a standing watch over and commonly implies use of men; **safeguard,** on the other hand, implies protective measures where merely potential danger exists.
(2) See MAINTAIN.

de·fend′ant (-fĕn′dănt), *adj.* **1.** Defending. **2.** *Obs.* Defensive. — *n.* *Law.* A person required to make answer in an action or suit; — opposed to *plaintiff.*

de·fen′es·tra′tion (dē·fĕn′ĕs·trā′shŭn), *n.* [L. *de* + *fenestra* window.] A throwing out of a person or thing through a window.

de·fense′, de·fence′ (dē·fĕns′), *n.* [OF. *defense, defens,* fr. L. *defensa, defensum,* fr. past part. of *defendere.* See DEFEND.] **1.** Resistance to or protection from attack. **2.** Argument in support or in justification, as of one's action. **3.** A means of warding off attack, danger, etc. **4.** The art of self-protection, esp. fencing and boxing; in sports, the guarding of oneself or of one's goal against attack. **5.** *Law.* The defendant's denial, answer, or plea. — **de·fense′less, de·fence′less,** *adj.* — **-less·ly,** *adv.* — **-less·ness,** *n.*

defense mechanism *or* **reaction.** **1.** A defensive reaction by an organism, as against disease germs. **2.** *Psychol.* A mode of behavior, or a belief, adopted by a person to conceal the true condition pertaining to himself or his beliefs.

de·fen′si·ble (dē·fĕn′sĭ·b'l), *adj.* Capable of being defended. — **de·fen′si·bil′i·ty** (-bĭl′ĭ·tĭ), **de·fen′si·ble·ness,** *n.* — **de·fen′si·bly,** *adv.*

de·fen′sive (-sĭv), *adj.* **1.** Serving to defend or protect. **2.** Devoted to resisting or preventing aggression or attack; — opposed to *offensive.* **3.** In a posture of defending. — *n.* That which defends; a defensive position. — **de·fen′sive·ly,** *adv.* — **de·fen′sive·ness,** *n.*

de·fer′ (dē·fûr′), *v. t. & i.;* DE·FERRED′ (-fûrd′); DE·FER′RING. [OF. *differer.* See DIFFER.] To put off; postpone; delay.

Syn. **Defer, postpone, intermit, suspend, stay** mean to delay an action, activity, or proceeding. **Defer** suggests little more than to put off to a later time, but it may imply a delay in fulfillment or attainment occasioned by conditions beyond one's control; **postpone** ordinarily implies an intentional deferring; **intermit** implies a stopping for a time either for relief or as a break in a course or proceeding; **suspend** also implies a temporary stoppage but adds the implication of waiting until someone or some condition is satisfied; **stay** suggests the interposition of some obstacle that either stops or suspends progress.

de·fer′, *v. t. & i.* [F. *déférer* to pay deference, yield, bring before a judge, fr. L. *deferre* to bring down, fr. *de* + *ferre* to bear.] To yield or submit to the opinion or wishes of another, or to authority. — **Syn.** See YIELD.

def′er·ence (dĕf′ẽr·ĕns), *n.* Act of deferring; courteous or complaisant regard for another's wishes. — **Syn.** See HONOR.

def′er·ent (dĕf′ẽr·ĕnt), *adj.* Deferential.

def′er·ent, *adj.* [L. *deferens,* pres. part. of *deferre.* See DEFER to yield.] **1.** Serving to carry down or out, as a conduit. **2.** *Anat.* Of or pertaining to the vas deferens; as, the *deferent* arteries.

def′er·en′tial (-ĕn′shăl), *adj.* Expressing, or given to, deference; respectful. — **def′er·en′tial·ly,** *adv.*

de·fer′ment (dē·fûr′mĕnt), *n.* Delay; postponement.

de·fer′ra·ble (dē·fûr′ȧ·b'l), *adj.* Also **de·fer′a·ble.** That can be deferred; eligible for deferment, or such as renders one eligible for deferment, esp. under the Selective Service System. — *n.* One eligible for deferment.

de·ferred′ (dē·fûrd′), *adj.* Delayed, as a right that does not begin or vest till a future time; withheld for or until a stated time; as, *deferred* annuity; *deferred* assets or liabilities.

de·fer′rer (dē·fûr′ẽr), *n.* One who defers, or puts off.

de·fi′ance (dē·fī′ăns), *n.* **1.** Act of defying; a challenge. **2.** Disposition to resist; contempt of opposition.

de·fi′ant (-ănt), *adj.* [F. *défiant,* pres. part. of *défier.* See DEFY.] Full of defiance; bold; insolent. — **de·fi′ant·ly,** *adv.* — **de·fi′ant·ness,** *n.*

de·fi′cience (dē·fĭsh′ĕns), *n.* *Now Rare.* Deficiency.

de·fi′cien·cy (-ĕn·sĭ), *n.; pl.* -CIES (-sĭz). **1.** State or quality of being deficient. **2.** A shortage; deficit.

deficiency disease. *Med.* A disease, as scurvy, caused by a diet lacking in certain elements (cf. VITAMIN).

deficiency judgment. *Law.* A judgment for the balance of a debt after the security has been realized and the proceeds applied to payment.
de·fi′cient (dē·fĭsh′ĕnt), *adj.* [L. *deficiens, -entis,* pres. part. of *deficere* to be wanting. See DEFECT.] Lacking in some quality necessary for completeness; defective. — *n.* One that is deficient. — **-ly,** *adv.*
def′i·cit (dĕf′ĭ·sĭt), *n.* [Lit., it is wanting, 3d pers. pres. indic. of L. *deficere.*] Deficiency in amount, as of income.
‖**de fi′de** (dē fī′dē). [L.] Literally, of the faith; specif., *R.C.Ch.,* designating a revealed truth taught by the Church.
de·fi′er (dē·fī′ēr), *n.* One who defies.
def′i·lade′ (dĕf′ĭ·lād′), *v. t. & i.* *Fort.* To arrange (fortifications) so as to protect the lines from frontal or enfilading fire and the interior of the works from plunging or reverse fire. — *n. Mil.* Act or process of defilading.
de·file′ (dē·fīl′), *v. t.* [Influenced by *foul* and by *file* to foul, but orig. fr. OF. *defouler* to trample, crush, fr. *de-* + *fouler* to trample.] **1.** To make filthy; to befoul. **2.** *Archaic.* To ravish; to violate. **3.** To make ceremonially unclean; to pollute. **4.** To tarnish, as reputation; to dishonor. — **Syn.** See CONTAMINATE. — **de·file′ment,** *n.* — **de·fil′er** (-fīl′ēr), *n.*
de·file′, *v. t. & i.* [F. *défiler,* fr. *dé-* (fr. L. *de*) + *file* a row or line.] To march off in a line, file by file; to file off.
de·file′ (dē·fīl′; dē′fīl), *n.* Any narrow passage or gorge.
de·fine′ (dē·fīn′), *v. t.* [OF. *definer, definir,* fr. L. *definire* to limit, define, fr. *de* + *finire* to limit, end, fr. *finis* limit.] **1.** To mark the limits or boundaries of; to make distinct or fix in outline or character. **2.** To describe, expound, or interpret; to explain; hence, to determine the precise signification of; to discover and set forth the meaning of, as a word. **3.** To set apart in a class by identifying marks; to distinguish. — **de·fin′a·ble** (-fīn′ȧ·b′l), *adj.* — **de·fin′er** (-fīn′ēr), *n.*
def′i·nite (dĕf′ĭ·nĭt), *adj.* [L. *definitus,* past part. of *definire.* See DEFINE.] **1.** Having distinct or certain limits; limited; fixed. **2.** Clear and unmistakable in meaning; precise in detail; explicit. **3.** Limiting; determining; as, the *definite* article. — **Syn.** See EXPLICIT. — **Ant.** Indefinite. — **def′i·nite·ly,** *adv.* — **def′i·nite·ness,** *n.*
definite article. *Gram.* The article *the,* which is used to designate a particular person or thing.
def′i·ni′tion (dĕf′ĭ·nĭsh′ŭn), *n.* **1.** Explanation of the meaning or meanings of a word; also, a formulation of such meaning or meanings; as, dictionary *definitions.* **2.** Act or power of making definite and clear or of bringing into sharp relief. **3.** Distinctness or clarity of detail or outline, as in a picture. **4.** *Radio & Television.* The degree of precision with which a receiver reproduces sound or images.
de·fin′i·tive (dē·fĭn′ĭ·tĭv), *adj.* **1.** Serving to decide something; conclusive. **2.** Serving to define precisely; distinguishing. **3.** *Biol.* Complete; fully developed. — **Syn.** See CONCLUSIVE. — **Ant.** Tentative, provisional. — *n. Gram.* A word used to define or limit the meaning of a common noun. The definite article, and some pronouns, as *this, any, other, some, all, none,* are *definitives.* — **de·fin′i·tive·ly,** *adv.* — **de·fin′i·tive·ness,** *n.*
de·fin′i·tude (-tūd), *n.* Precision; definiteness.
def′la·grate (dĕf′lȧ·grāt; dē′flȧ-), *v. t. & i.* [L. *deflagratus,* past part. of *deflagrare* to burn up, fr. *de* + *flagrare* to burn.] *Chem.* To burn with sudden and sparkling combustion; to burn or vaporize suddenly. — **def′la·gra′tion** (-grā′shŭn), *n.*
de·flate′ (dē·flāt′), *v. t. & i.* [*de-* + L. *flare, flatum,* to blow.] To reduce from an inflated state by release of the distending air or gas; to collapse. — **Syn.** See CONTRACT. — **de·fla′tor** (-flā′tēr), *n.*
de·fla′tion (dē·flā′shŭn), *n.* **1.** A deflating; state of being deflated. **2.** Disproportionate and relatively sharp and sudden decrease in the quantity of money or credit, or both, relative to the amount of goods available for purchase. Deflation produces a fall in the general price level. — **de·fla′tion·ar′y** (-ĕr′ĭ *or, esp. Brit.,* -ēr·ĭ), *adj.* — **de·fla′tion·ist,** *n. & adj.*
deflationary spiral. See SPIRAL, *n.,* 5.
de·flect′ (dē·flĕkt′), *v. t. & i.* [L. *deflectere, deflexum,* fr. *de* + *flectere* to bend or turn.] To turn aside; deviate.
de·flec′tion, de·flex′ion (dē·flĕk′shŭn), *n.* For spelling, see the note at CONNECTION. **1.** A turning, or state of being turned, aside; a turning from a straight line or given course; a bending, esp. downward; deviation. **2.** *Optics.* Formerly, diffraction. **3.** *Physics.* The deviation from zero of the moving system of a galvanometer or other instrument. — **de·flec′tive** (-flĕk′tĭv), *adj.* — **de·flec′tor** (-tēr), *n.*
def′lo·ra′tion (dĕf′lō·rā′shŭn; dē′flō-), *n.* [LL. *defloratio.*] A deflowering.
de·flow′er (dē·flou′ēr), *v. t.* [OF. *desflorer,* fr. LL. *deflorare,* fr. L. *de* + *flos, floris,* flower.] **1.** To deprive of virginity; to violate; ravish. **2.** To ravage; despoil. **3.** To deprive or strip of flowers.
de·flux′ion (dē·flŭk′shŭn), *n.* [LL. *defluxio.*] *Med.* A flowing down of fluid matter, as a catarrhal discharge.
de·fo′li·ate (dē·fō′lĭ·āt), *v. t. & i.* [ML. *defoliatus,* past part. of *defoliare,* fr. L. *de* + *folium* leaf.] To strip or become stripped of leaves. — **de·fo′li·a′tion** (-ā′shŭn), *n.*
de·force′ (dē·fōrs′; 70), *v. t.*; -FORCED′ (-fōrst′); -FORC′ING (-fōr′sĭng). [AF. *deforcer,* OF. *deforcier,* fr. *de-, des-* (fr. L. *dis-*) + *forcier* to force.] *Law.* To keep by force from the rightful owner, as lands; also, to keep (a person) out of possession by force. — **de·force′ment,** *n.*
de·for′ciant (dē·fōr′shănt; 70), *n. Law.* One who deforces the owner.
de·for′est (dē·fŏr′ĕst; -ĭst), *v. t.* To clear of forests. — **de·for′est·a′tion** (-ĕs·tā′shŭn; -ĭs-), *n.* — **de·for′est·er,** *n.*
de·form′ (dē·fôrm′), *adj.* [L. *deformis.*] *Archaic.* Misshapen.
de·form′, *v. t.* [F. *déformer,* fr. L. *deformare,* fr. *de* + *formare* to form, shape, fr. *forma.*] **1.** To spoil the form of; disfigure. **2.** To deprive of comeliness, grace, or perfection. **3.** To cause to have a new form. **4.** *Mech.* To change the shape of (a body) by the action of forces or stresses. — *v. i.* To become disfigured; to lose its form. — **de·form′a·bil′i·ty** (-fôr′mȧ·bĭl′ĭ·tĭ), *n.* — **de·form′a·ble,** *adj.*
Syn. **Deform, distort, contort, warp, gnarl** mean to mar the appearance or nature of as if by twisting. **Deform** carries a slighter implication of twisting than any of these at times, but the suggestion of pulling out of shape is usually present; **distort** and **contort** clearly imply a twisting or wresting from that which is natural, normal, or true, but *contort* suggests a more involved twisting and, usually, a more grotesque or painful effect than *distort;* **warp,** which literally suggests a drying and shrinking out of shape, figuratively applies to that which has been given a bias, a wrong slant, an abnormal direction, or the like; **gnarl,** used both literally and figuratively, suggests contortions induced by old age, weather, heavy work, misfortune, etc.
de′for·ma′tion (dē′fôr·mā′shŭn; dĕf′ŏr-), *n.* **1.** Act of deforming, or state of being deformed; disfiguration. **2.** Change for the worse. **3.** Alteration of form or shape; also, the product of such alteration.
de·formed′ (dē·fôrmd′), *adj.* Distorted in form; misshapen. — **de·form′ed·ly** (-fôr′mĕd·lĭ; 30), *adv.* — **de·form′ed·ness,** *n.*
de·form′i·ty (-fôr′mĭ·tĭ), *n.; pl.* -TIES (-tĭz). **1.** State of being deformed; disfigurement. **2.** Depravity; ugliness; also, a moral or aesthetic flaw or defect. **3.** A deformed person or thing.
de·fraud′ (dē·frôd′), *v. t.* [L. *defraudare,* fr. *de* + *fraudare* to cheat, fr. *fraus, fraudis,* fraud.] To deprive of some right, interest, or property, by deceit. — **Syn.** See CHEAT. — **de′frau·da′tion** (dē′frô·dā′shŭn), *n.* — **de·fraud′er,** *n.*
de·fray′ (dē·frā′), *v. t.* [F. *défrayer,* fr. *dé-* (fr. L. *de*) + *frais,* pl., expense.] **1.** To pay, or to provide for the payment of. **2.** *Archaic.* To bear the expenses of. — **de·fray′a·ble,** *adj.* — **de·fray′al,** *n.* — **de·fray′er,** *n.* — **de·fray′ment,** *n.*
de·frock′ (dē·frŏk′), *v. t.* To unfrock.
de·frost′ (dē·frŏst′), *v. t.* To free from frost.
de·frost′er (-frŏs′tēr), *n.* A device for freeing or keeping free from frost or ice; specif., one for a windshield.
deft (dĕft), *adj.* [ME. *defte.* See DAFT.] Characterized by dexterity; quick and neat in action; skillful. — **Syn.** See DEXTEROUS. — **Ant.** Awkward. — **deft′ly,** *adv.* — **deft′ness,** *n.*
de·funct′ (dē·fŭngkt′), *adj.* [L. *defunctus,* past part. of *defungi* to acquit oneself of, finish, depart, die, fr. *de* + *fungi* to perform.] Dead; deceased. — **Syn.** See DEAD. — *n. Rare.* A dead person.
de·fy′ (dē·fī′), *v. t.*; -FIED′ (-fīd′); -FY′ING. [OF. *desfier* (F. *défier*), deriv. of L. *dis-* + *fidus* faithful.] **1.** *Archaic.* To challenge to combat. **2.** To challenge to perform an action proposed as impossible; to dare. **3.** To set at nought; as, to *defy* public opinion; also, to resist attempts at; as, to *defy* description. — *n.; pl.* DEFIES (-fīz′). [F. *défi,* fr. the v.] *Slang.* A challenge; defiance.
‖**dé′ga′gé′** (dā′gȧ′zhā′), *adj.* [F., past part. of *dégager* to disengage.] Free; at ease; unconstrained.
de·gas′ (dē·găs′), *v. t.*; DE·GASSED′ (-găst′); DE·GAS′SING (-găs′ĭng). To free from gas.
de Gaull′ist (dē gōl′ĭst). A follower of Charles de Gaulle: during World War II, one of the Fighting French (which see); in postwar France, a member of Rassemblement du Peuple Français, de Gaulle's rightist party (formed April, 1947). — **de Gaull′ism** (-ĭz′m).
de·gauss′ (dē·gous′; -gôs′), *v. t.* [*de* + *gauss,* unit of magnetic induction, after Karl F. *Gauss,* German mathematician.] To equip (a steel ship) with a web of insulated cable girdling the ship's hull and carrying an electric current that creates a magnetic field equal but opposite to the earth's magnetic field, thus demagnetizing the field and rendering the ship no longer liable to deflect the needle in the detonating device of a magnetic mine.
de·gen′er·a·cy (dē·jĕn′ēr·ȧ·sĭ), *n.* Act of becoming, or state of being, degenerate; deterioration.
de·gen′er·ate (-ĭt), *adj.* [L. *degeneratus,* past part. of *degenerare* to degenerate, fr. *degener* base, degenerate, fr. *de* + *genus* race, kind.] **1.** Having sunk to a state below that normal to a type or thing; having declined markedly, as in virtue or courage, from one's ancestors, predecessors, or former self; degraded. **2.** *Biol.* Characterized by degeneration. — **Syn.** See VICIOUS. — *n.* One having the characteristics of degeneration, esp. by birth. — (-āt), *v. i.* **1.** To pass from a higher to a lower type or condition; to become depraved; to deteriorate. **2.** *Biol.* To undergo progressive deterioration; to become of a lower type. — **de·gen′er·ate·ly,** *adv.* — **de·gen′er·ate·ness,** *n.*
de′gen·er·a′tion (dē′jĕn·ēr·ā′shŭn), *n.* **1.** A growing or becoming worse; degeneracy; deterioration. **2.** *Biol.* A progressive deterioration, as a return to a less highly organized condition in the evolution of a group of animals or plants. **3.** *Med.* Deterioration of a tissue or an organ in which its vitality is diminished. — **Syn.** See DETERIORATION. — **de·gen′er·a′tive** (dē·jĕn′ēr·ā′tĭv; -ȧ·tĭv), *adj.*
de·glu′ti·nate (dē·glōō′tĭ·nāt), *v. t.* [L. *deglutinatus,* past part. of *deglutinare,* fr. *de* + *glutinare* to glue.] To extract gluten from, as wheat flour. — **de·glu′ti·na′tion** (-nā′shŭn), *n.*
de′glu·ti′tion (dē′glōō·tĭsh′ŭn; dĕg′lū-), *n.* [F. *déglutition,* fr. L. *deglutitio,* fr. *deglutire* to swallow down.] Act or process of swallowing food.
deg′ra·da′tion (dĕg′rȧ·dā′shŭn), *n.* **1.** Act or process of degrading. **2.** Reduction in rank, condition, etc.; debasement; disgrace. **3.** Degeneration; deterioration. **4.** *Phys.Geog.* A wearing down by erosion.
de·grade′ (dē·grād′), *v. t.* [OF. *degrader,* fr. LL. *degradare,* fr. L. *de* + *gradus* step, degree.] **1.** To reduce from a higher to a lower rank or degree; to deprive of office or dignity. **2.** To lower the physical, moral, or intellectual character of; to debase; to corrupt. **3.** To bring into disrepute or disfavor; to depreciate. **4.** *Geol.* To wear down by erosion. — **Syn.** See ABASE. — **Ant.** Uplift.
de·grad′ed (dē·grăd′ĕd; -ĭd), *adj.* Debased; degenerate. — **de·grad′ed·ly,** *adv.* — **de·grad′ed·ness,** *n.*
de·grad′ing (-ĭng), *adj.* That degrades; debasing.
de·gree′ (dē·grē′), *n.* [OF. *degre,* deriv. of LL. *degradare.* See DEGRADE.] **1.** A step, stair, or rung; now, a steplike member of a series; a tier, bank, rank, or the like. **2.** A step or station in any series; as, to advance by *degrees.* **3.** A grade of social advancement; relative station in life. **4.** A remove in the line of descent; as, a relation in the third *degree.* See CONSANGUINITY, *Illust.* **5.** Relative quantity or intensity; as, *degrees* of heat and cold. **6.** A position or space on the earth or in the heavens as measured by degrees (sense 10 **b**) of latitude or longitude. **7.** A division, space, or interval marked on a mathematical or other instrument, as on a thermometer. Symbol ° (as, 32° F.). **8.** *Educ.* A grade or rank to which scholars are admitted by a college or university, in recognition of their attainments; as, the *degree* of bachelor of arts. **9.** *Gram.* One of the three grades — positive, comparative, superlative — in the comparison of an adjective or adverb. **10.** *Math.* **a** *Alg.* Rank as defined by the sum of exponents; as, a^2b^3c is a term of the sixth *degree.* **b** *Trig., etc.* A 360th part of the circumference of a circle, or of a round angle. See MEASURE, *Tables* 7, 8, & 9; cf. COMPASS CARD, *Illust.* Symbol ° (as, an angle of 90°). **11.** *Music.* **a** A line or space of the staff. **b** The interval between any adjacent diatonic tones.
— ***by degrees.*** Step by step; gradually. — ***to a degree.*** To a considerable extent; also, in a measure; somewhat.
de·gree′-day′, *n.; pl.* DEGREE-DAYS. A unit representing one degree of declination from a given point (as 65°) in the mean outdoor temperature for one day, often used in measuring fuel requirements of buildings.

de·gum′ (dē·gŭm′), *v. t.*; DE·GUMMED′ (-gŭmd′); DE·GUM′MING. To free from gum or gummy substance.

de·gust′ (dē·gŭst′), *v. t. & i.* Also **de·gus′tate** (-gŭs′tāt). [L. *degustare*, fr. *de* + *gustus* taste.] *Rare.* To taste; to savor. — **de′gus·ta′tion** (dē′gŭs·tā′shŭn; dĕg′ŭs-), *n.*

‖**de gus′ti·bus non est dis′pu·tan′dum** (dē gŭs′tĭ·bŭs nŏn ĕst dĭs′pū·tăn′dŭm). [L.] There is no disputing about tastes.

de·hisce′ (dē·hĭs′), *v. i. & t.*; DE·HISCED′ (-hĭst′); DE·HISC′ING (-hĭs′ĭng). [L. *dehiscere*, fr. *de* + *hiscere* to gape.] To gape; to discharge by dehiscence.

de·his′cence (-hĭs′ĕns; -′ns), *n.* A bursting open; as: **a** *Biol.* The opening of an organ along a definite line to discharge its contents. **b** *Bot.* The bursting open of a capsule, pod, or silique at maturity. — **de·his′cent**, *adj.*

de·horn′ (dē·hôrn′), *v. t.* To deprive of horns.

de·hort′ (dē·hôrt′), *v. t.* [L. *dehortari*, fr. *de* + *hortari* to urge.] *Now Rare.* To urge to abstain or refrain; to dissuade. — **de′hor·ta′tion** (dē′hôr·tā′shŭn), *n.* — **de·hor′ta·tive** (dē·hôr′tȧ·tĭv), *adj. & n.* — **de·hor′ta·to′ry** (-tō′rĭ *or, esp. Brit.*, -tēr·ĭ), *adj. & n.* — **de·hort′er**, *n.*

de·hu′man·ize (dē·hū′măn·īz), *v. t.* To divest of human qualities, human interests, etc. — **de·hu′man·i·za′tion** (-ĭ·zā′shŭn; -ī·zā′-), *n.*

de′hu·mid′i·fy (dē′hū·mĭd′ĭ·fī), *v. t.*; -FIED (-fīd); -FY′ING. To free from moisture, as the atmosphere. — **de′hu·mid′i·fi′er** (-fī′ēr), *n.*

de·hy′drate (dē·hī′drāt), *v. t. & i.* To deprive of, or to lose, water; esp., to render or to become free or relatively free from water, as in the drying of foods to preserve them or to reduce their weight and bulk. — **de′hy·dra′tion** (dē′hī·drā′shŭn), *n.*

de·hyp′no·tize (dē·hĭp′nō·tīz), *v. t.* To arouse from the hypnotic state.

De′ia·ni′ra (dē′yȧ·nī′rȧ), *n.* [L., fr. Gr. *Dēianeira.*] *Gr. Myth.* The wife of Hercules. See NESSUS.

de·ice′ (dē·īs′), *v. t.* *Aviation.* To keep free or rid of accumulations of ice by means of a **de·ic′er** (-īs′ēr), variously (1) a mixture of alcohol and glycerin or a pump for spraying this mixture on windshield and side windows, (2) a slinger ring (which see), (3) a mechanism consisting of hollow tubes, or boots, overlying leading edges of wing and tail surfaces, which are alternately inflated and deflated for cracking ice formations.

de′i·cide (dē′ĭ·sīd), *n.* [LL. *deicida* a deicide (in sense 1), fr. *deus* god + *caedere* to cut, kill.] **1.** The killer or destroyer of a god; esp., one concerned in putting Christ to death. **2.** Act of killing a divine being.

de·if′ic (dē·ĭf′ĭk), *adj.* [F. and L.; F. *déifique*, fr. L. *deificus*, fr. *deus* god + *facere* to make.] Deifying.

de′i·form (dē′ĭ·fôrm), *adj.* [ML. *deiformis.*] Godlike.

de′i·fy (-fī), *v. t.*; -FIED (-fīd); -FY′ING. [OF. *deifier*, fr. LL. *deificare*, fr. L. *deificus*. See DEIFIC.] **1.** To make a god of; to enroll among the deities. **2.** To treat as an object of supreme regard. — **de′i·fi·ca′tion** (-fĭ·kā′shŭn), *n.*

deign (dān), *v. i.* [OF. *deignier*, fr. L. *dignare, dignari*, fr. *dignus* worthy.] To think worthy or in keeping with one's dignity; to condescend. — *v. t.* **1.** *Obs.* To condescend to receive or accept. **2.** To condescend to give; as, to *deign* no reply. — **Syn.** See STOOP.

‖**De′i gra′ti·a** (dē′ī grā′shĭ·ȧ). [L.] By the grace of God.

deil (dēl), *n.* *Scot.* Devil.

Deir′dre (dẹr′drē; -drȧ; dâr′-), *n.* [OIr. *Derdriu* the raging one.] Heroine of an old Irish legend.

de′ism (dē′ĭz′m), *n.* [L. *deus* god.] Belief in a personal God as creator of the world and final judge of men, but as remaining in the interval completely beyond the range of human experience. — **de′ist** (-ĭst), *n.* — **Syn.** See ATHEIST. — **de·is′tic** (dē·ĭs′tĭk), **de·is′ti·cal** (-tĭ·kăl), *adj.* — **de·is′ti·cal·ly**, *adv.*

de′i·ty (dē′ĭ·tĭ), *n.*; *pl.* -TIES (-tĭz). [OF. *deite* (F. *déité*), fr. LL. *deitas*, fr. L. *deus* god.] **1.** Divine nature or rank; divinity. **2.** A god or goddess.

de·ject′ (dē·jĕkt′), *adj.* [L. *dejectus*, past part. of *dejicere* to throw down, fr. *de* + *jacere* to throw.] *Archaic.* Dejected. — *v. t.* **1.** *Archaic.* To cast down. **2.** To cast down the spirits of; to dishearten.

de·jec′ta (dē·jĕk′tȧ), *n. pl.* [NL., neut. pl. fr. L. *dejectus*, past part.] Excrements; as, the *dejecta* of the sick.

de·ject′ed (dē·jĕk′tĕd; -tĭd), *adj.* Low-spirited; depressed. — **de·ject′ed·ly**, *adv.* — **de·ject′ed·ness**, *n.*

de·jec′tion (dē·jĕk′shŭn), *n.* **1.** Lowness of spirits; depression. **2.** *Physiol.* **a** Discharge of excrement. **b** Feces; excrement. — **Syn.** See SADNESS. — **Ant.** Exhilaration.

dé′jeu′né′ (dā′zhû′nā′), **de·jeune′** (dē·jōōn′), *n.* [OF. *desjeün.*] Breakfast.

‖**dé′jeu′ner′** (dā′zhû′nā′; *E.* dā′zhĕ·nā), *n.* [F. *déjeuner* breakfast, as a verb, to breakfast, fr. OF. *desjeuner.*] A breakfast; sometimes, also, a lunch or collation.

‖**de ju′re** (dē jōō′rē). [L.] *Law.* By right; by a lawful title; — distinguished from *de facto.*

dek′a- (dĕk′ȧ-). *Metric System.* Var. of DECA-, as in **dek′a·gram**, **dek′a·li′ter**, **dek′a·me′ter**, **dek′a·stere**, etc.

de·laine′ (dē·lān′), *n.* [Short for *muslin delaine*, fr. F. *de laine* of wool.] A light woolen, or woolen and cotton, dress fabric.

de·lam′i·nate (dē·lăm′ĭ·nāt), *v. i.* To split into layers. — **de·lam′i·na′tion** (-nā′shŭn), *n.*

de·late′ (dē·lāt′), *v. t.* [L. *delatus*, used as past part. of *deferre*. See DEFER to yield.] **1.** *Chiefly Scot.* To inform against; to accuse. **2.** To spread abroad; to make public. — **de·la′tion** (-lā′shŭn), *n.* — **de·la′tor** (-tēr), *n.*

Del′a·ware (dĕl′ȧ·wâr), *n.* [After Lord *De La Warr.*] **1.** An American grape, with small, sweet-flavored, reddish berries. **2.** An Indian of an Algonquian tribe (now mostly in Oklahoma), formerly of the Delaware Valley.

de·lay′ (dē·lā′), *v. t.* [OF. *delaier.*] **1.** To put off; defer. **2.** To stop, detain, or hinder, for a time. — *v. i.* To move slowly; stop for a time; linger.

Syn. (1) **Delay, retard, slow, slacken, detain** mean to make late or behind in movement or progress. **Delay** implies the operation, usually the interference, of something that keeps back from completion or arrival; **retard** applies to motion, movement, or progress and suggests some cause of reducing its speed; **slow** (usually followed by *up* or *down*) and **slacken** also imply a reduction in speed, *slow* often suggesting deliberate intention, and *slacken* an easing or letting up; **detain** implies a holding up so as to delay someone, as in reaching a place, in doing something, etc. — **Ant.** Expedite.

(2) **Delay, procrastinate, lag, loiter, dawdle, dally** mean to move or act slowly so as to hinder progress or accomplishment. **Delay** usually carries an implication of putting off, as one's departure, one's beginning of an action or activity, or the like; **procrastinate** implies blameworthy or inexcusable delay, such as that caused by laziness, indifference, or hesitation; **lag** implies failure to maintain a speed or pace either as set by others or as necessary to the accomplishment of an end; **loiter** and **dawdle** imply delay while in progress, often when one is walking, but *dawdle* more clearly implies a wasting of time; **dally** suggests dawdling, usually by trifling, pottering, or the like. — **Ant.** Hasten.

— *n.* The act of delaying; also, state or instance of being delayed; detention.

— **de·lay′er** (dē·lā′ēr), *n.*

de′le (dē′lē), *imperative sing.* of L. *delere*, to destroy. *Print.* Erase; remove; — a direction usually expressed by a form of delta, thus: δ. — *v. t. & i.*; DE′LED (dē′lēd); DE′LE·ING. *Print.* To erase; delete.

de·lec′ta·ble (dē·lĕk′tȧ·b'l), *adj.* [OF., fr. L. *delectabilis*, fr. *delectare* to delight.] Highly pleasing; delightful. — **de·lec′ta·ble·ness**, *n.* — **de·lec′ta·bly** (-blĭ), *adv.*

de·lec′tate (-tāt), *v. t.* [L. *delectatus*, past part. of *delectare*. See DELIGHT.] To delight.

de′lec·ta′tion (dē′lĕk·tā′shŭn), *n.* Delight; now, enjoyment; diversion. — **Syn.** See PLEASURE.

del′e·ga·cy (dĕl′ē·gȧ·sĭ), *n.*; *pl.* -CIES (-sĭz). Act of delegating, or state of being delegated; deputed power.

de·le′gal·ize (dē·lē′găl·īz), *v. t.* To remove the status of statutory authorization from (something).

del′e·gate (dĕl′ē·gāt), *n.* [L. *delegatus*, past part. of *delegare* to delegate, fr. *de* + *legare* to send with a commission, depute.] One sent and empowered to act for another; a deputy; a representative; specif.: **a** *U. S.* A representative of a territory in the House of Representatives, having the right to debate but not to vote. **b** A member of the lower or popular branch (***House of Delegates***) of the legislature of Maryland, Virginia, or West Virginia.

— (-gāt), *v. t.* **1.** To send as one's representative; commission; depute. **2.** To entrust to the care or management of another; commit. **3.** *Civil Law.* To assign (a debtor of oneself) to a creditor as a debtor in place of oneself.

del′e·ga′tion (-gā′shŭn), *n.* **1.** Act of delegating; a deputing. **2.** One or more persons commissioned to represent others, as in a convention; a deputation.

‖**de·len′da est Car·tha′go** (dē·lĕn′dȧ ĕst kär·thā′gō). [L.] Carthage must be destroyed.

de·lete′ (dē·lēt′), *v. t. & i.* [L. *deletus*, past part. of *delere* to destroy.] To erase; dele. — **Syn.** See ERASE.

del′e·te′ri·ous (dĕl′ē·tēr′ĭ·ŭs), *adj.* [ML. *deleterius*, fr. Gr. *dēlētērios*, fr. *dēleisthai* to hurt, damage.] Hurtful; noxious. — **Syn.** See PERNICIOUS. — **del′e·te′ri·ous·ly**, *adv.* — **del′e·te′ri·ous·ness**, *n.*

de·le′tion (dē·lē′shŭn), *n.* [L. *deletio*, fr. *delere.* See DELETE.] Act of deleting; also, a deleted passage.

delft′ware′ (dĕlft′wâr′), *n.* Also **delft** (dĕlft), **delf** (dĕlf). Pottery made in Delft in Holland; esp.: **a** Brown pottery covered with an opaque, decorated white glaze. **b** In England, popularly, common glazed pottery for table use, etc.

de·lib′er·ate (dē·lĭb′ēr·ĭt), *adj.* [L. *deliberatus*, past part. of *deliberare* to deliberate, fr. *de* + *librare* to weigh.] **1.** Done with deliberation; formed, arrived at, or determined upon as a result of careful thought. **2.** Given to weighing facts and arguments; careful in considering. **3.** Slow in action; unhurried. — **Syn.** See VOLUNTARY. — **Ant.** Impulsive. — (-āt), *v. t.* To weigh in the mind; to consider maturely. — *v. i.* To take counsel; to think long and carefully. — **Syn.** See THINK. — **de·lib′er·ate·ly**, *adv.* — **de·lib′er·ate·ness**, *n.*

de·lib′er·a′tion (dē·lĭb′ēr·ā′shŭn), *n.* **1.** A deliberating, or a weighing and examining reasons for and against a choice or measure. **2.** Quality or state of being deliberate; deliberateness. — **de·lib′er·a′tive** (-lĭb′ēr·ā′tĭv; -ȧ·tĭv), *adj.* — **de·lib′er·a′tive·ly**, *adv.* — **de·lib′er·a′tive·ness**, *n.*

de·lib′er·a′tor (dē·lĭb′ēr·ā′tēr), *n.* [L.] One who deliberates.

del′i·ca·cy (dĕl′ĭ·kȧ·sĭ), *n.*; *pl.* -CIES (-sĭz). **1.** *Obs.* Pleasure; gratification; luxuriousness. **2.** A luxury; a dainty; as, *delicacies* of the table. **3.** Nicety or fineness of form or constitution; slender shapeliness; also, frailty or weakness. **4.** Nicety of touch; as, the *delicacy* of the painter's stroke; also, quality or state of requiring delicate management; as, the *delicacy* of a diplomatic situation. **5.** Critical niceness; sensitiveness. **6.** Nice sensibility in feeling and conduct; also, excessive fastidiousness.

del′i·cate (-kĭt), *adj.* [F. and L.; F. *délicat*, fr. L. *delicatus* pleasing the senses, voluptuous, soft and tender.] **1.** *Obs.* Self-indulgent; luxury-loving. **2.** Satisfying or pleasing because of its fine quality, flavor, odor, or the like. **3.** Finely made or formed; exquisite in workmanship, structure, etc.; hence, fragile; easily injured. **4.** Characterized by, or endowed with, nice appreciation or discrimination; exquisitely sensitive; hence: **a** Fastidious. **b** Scrupulous; considerate. **5.** Capable of registering to a minute degree; as, a *delicate* balance. **6.** Requiring nicety and skill in technique; critical; as, a *delicate* operation; also, marked by ingenuity. — **Syn.** See CHOICE. — **Ant.** Gross. — *n.* One that is delicate; as: **a** *Obs.* A luxurious person. **b** *Obs.* A delight, esp. of the senses; a luxury. **c** A dainty; a delicacy. — **del′i·cate·ly**, *adv.* — **del′i·cate·ness**, *n.*

del′i·ca·tes′sen (dĕl′ĭ·kȧ·tĕs′ĕn), *n. pl.* [G.] Prepared foods, such as cooked meats, preserves, relishes, etc.; also, a store where such foods are sold.

de·li′cious (dē·lĭsh′ŭs), *adj.* [OF. *delicieus*, fr. LL. *deliciosus*, fr. *deliciae* delight, fr. *delicere* to allure.] Affording exquisite pleasure; delightful. — **de·li′cious·ly**, *adv.* — **de·li′cious·ness**, *n.*

De·li′cious, *n.* *Hort.* An American variety of light-red apple of high quality and aromatic flavor.

de·lict′ (dē·lĭkt′), *n.* [L. *delictum* fault.] *Law.* An offense against law; — chiefly in Civil and Scots law.

de·light′ (dē·līt′), *n.* [OF. *delit*, fr. *deliter* to delight. See DELIGHT, *v.*] **1.** A high degree of gratification of mind or sense; extreme satisfaction. **2.** Anything that gives great pleasure. **3.** Power of affording pleasurable emotion. — **Syn.** See PLEASURE. — *v. t.* [OF. *deliter*, *deleitier*, fr. L. *delectare* to delight, deriv. of *de* + *lacere* to entice.] To give joy or satisfaction to; to please. — *v. i.* **1.** To take great pleasure; to be greatly pleased. **2.** To give keen enjoyment. — **de·light′er**, *n.*

de·light′ed (-ĕd; -ĭd), *adj.* **1.** *Obs.* Delightful. **2.** Highly pleased; gratified; joyous. — **de·light′ed·ly**, *adv.* — **de·light′ed·ness**, *n.*

de·light′ful (-fōōl; -f'l), *adj.* Highly pleasing. — **de·light′ful·ly**, *adv.* — **de·light′ful·ness**, *n.*

de·light'some (dē·līt'sŭm), *adj.* Very pleasing; delightful. — **de·light'some·ly,** *adv.* — **de·light'some·ness,** *n.*

De·li'lah (dē·lī'lȧ), *n.* [Heb. *Delīlāh,* lit., delicate.] The mistress of Samson, who betrayed him (*Judges* xvi); hence, a harlot.

de·lim'it (dē·lĭm'ĭt), *v. t.* [F. *délimiter,* fr. L. *delimitare.*] To fix the limits of; to bound.

de·lim'i·tate (dē·lĭm'ĭ·tāt), *v. t.* To delimit. — **de·lim'i·ta'tion** (-tā'shŭn), *n.* — **de·lim'i·ta'tive** (-tā'tĭv), *adj.*

de·lin'e·ate (dē·lĭn'ē·āt), *v. t.* [L. *delineatus,* past part. of *delineare* to delineate, fr. *de* + *lineare* to draw, fr. *linea* line.] **1.** To represent by sketch, design, or diagram; to portray; hence, to represent accurately. **2.** To convey clearly through the medium of words; to describe.

de·lin'e·a'tion (-ā'shŭn), *n.* **1.** A representing, portraying, or describing, as by lines, sketches, etc. **2.** A sketch or description in words. — **de·lin'e·a'tive** (-lĭn'ē·ā'tĭv), *adj.*

de·lin'e·a'tor (dē·lĭn'ē·ā'tēr), *n.* **1.** One who or that which delineates; a sketcher. **2.** *Tailoring.* A pattern adjustable to varying sizes.

‖**de·li'ne·a'vit** (dē·lĭn'ē·ā'vĭt). [L.] He, or she, drew (it).

de·lin'quen·cy (dē·lĭng'kwĕn·sĭ), *n.; pl.* -CIES (-sĭz). Failure, omission, or violation, of duty; fault; misdeed.

de·lin'quent (-kwĕnt), *adj.* [L. *delinquens, -entis,* pres. part. of *delinquere* to fail, do wrong, fr. *de* + *linquere* to leave.] Failing in duty; offending by neglect or violation of duty or of law. — *n.* A delinquent person; as, juvenile *delinquents.* — **de·lin'quent·ly,** *adv.*

del'i·quesce' (dĕl'ĭ·kwĕs'), *v. i.;* -QUESCED' (-kwĕst'); -QUESC'ING (-kwĕs'ĭng). [L. *deliquescere* to melt, dissolve, fr. *de* + *liquescere* to become fluid, fr. *liquere* to be fluid.] **1.** To melt away; esp., to dissolve gradually and become liquid by attracting and absorbing moisture from the air. **2.** *Bot.* To ramify into fine divisions, as the veins of a leaf. — **del'i·ques'cence** (-kwĕs'ĕns; -'ns), *n.* — **del'i·ques'cent,** *adj.*

del'i·ra'tion (dĕl'ĭ·rā'shŭn), *n.* [L. *deliratio.*] Aberration of mind; delirium; irrational action or speech.

de·lir'i·ous (dē·lĭr'ĭ·ŭs), *adj.* Having a delirium; raving; frenzied. — **de·lir'i·ous·ly,** *adv.* — **de·lir'i·ous·ness,** *n.*

de·lir'i·um (-ŭm), *n.; pl.* -IUMS (-ŭmz), -IA (-ȧ). [L., fr. *delirare* to rave, prop., to go out of the furrow in plowing, fr. *de* + *lira* furrow.] **1.** A more or less temporary state of mental disturbance, characterized by confusion, disordered speech, and often hallucinations. **2.** Frenzied excitement or wild enthusiasm.

de·lir'i·um tre'mens (trē'mĕnz). [L., trembling delirium.] A violent delirium, induced by excessive and prolonged use of alcoholic liquors.

de·liv'er (dē·lĭv'ēr), *v. t.* [OF. *delivrer,* fr. LL. *deliberare* to liberate, give over, fr. L. *de* + *liberare* to set free.] **1.** To set free from restraint; to release; also, to rescue from evil actual or feared. **2.** To give or transfer; to commit; to surrender; to resign. **3.** To disburden of, or as of, young; to relieve (of) in parturition; — used only in the passive. **4.** To disburden (oneself), as of words; to give forth in words; to utter; hence, to communicate; impart. **5.** To give or put forth in action or exercise; to discharge; as, to *deliver* a blow. — **Syn.** See RESCUE. — *adj. Archaic.* Nimble; sprightly. — **de·liv'er·a·ble,** *adj.* — **de·liv'er·er,** *n.*

de·liv'er·ance (-ăns), *n.* **1.** Act of delivering, or state of being delivered. **2.** Anything delivered or communicated, as a publicly expressed opinion or decision.

de·liv'er·y (dē·lĭv'ēr·ĭ), *n.; pl.* -ERIES (-ĭz). **1.** A delivering; release; liberation. **2.** Surrender; transfer of a thing. **3.** Parturition. **4.** Utterance; manner of speaking or singing. **5.** Act or manner of sending forth, discharging, or throwing, as in pitching a ball. **6.** That which is delivered. **7.** *Com.* The transportation of a purchase to the purchaser. **8.** *Law.* The act of putting property into the legal possession of another.

dell (dĕl), *n.* [AS.] **1.** A small, retired valley or vale. **2.** *pl.* Dalles.

de·lo'cal·ize (dē·lō'kăl·īz), *v. t.* To remove from its place or locality. — **de·lo'cal·i·za'tion** (-ĭ·zā'shŭn; -ī·zā'-), *n.*

de·louse' (dē·lous'; -louz'), *v. t.* To remove lice from.

Del'phi·an (dĕl'fĭ·ăn; 58), *adj.* Also **Del'phic** (-fĭk). [L. *Delphi,* fr. Gr. *Delphoi.*] Of or relating to Delphi in ancient Greece or to the famous oracle located there.

del'phi·nine (dĕl'fĭ·nēn; -nĭn), *n.* Also **del'phi·nin.** *Chem.* A poisonous crystalline alkaloid obtained from various larkspurs (genus *Delphinium*) and used in an ointment to relieve neuralgia.

del·phin'i·um (dĕl·fĭn'ĭ·ŭm; 58), *n.* [NL., fr. Gr. *delphinion* larkspur, fr. *delphis, -inos,* a dolphin; — so named from the shape of the nectary.] Any of a genus (*Delphinium*) of perennial or annual herbs of the crowfoot family, of the North Temperate Zone, having irregular, showy, chiefly blue flowers; a larkspur.

Del·phi'nus (dĕl·fī'nŭs), *n.; gen.* -NI (-nī). [L., a dolphin.] A northern constellation nearly west of Pegasus.

Del·sarte' (dĕl·särt'), *n., or* **Delsarte system.** A system of calisthenics; — from François Delsarte (1811–71), a French teacher.

del'ta (dĕl'tȧ), *n.* [Gr.] **1.** The fourth letter (Δ, δ) of the Greek alphabet, corresponding to the English *d.* **2.** Anything having the shape of the capital Δ. Specif.: **a** The alluvial tract of land at the mouth of the Nile. **b** An alluvial deposit at the mouth of any river. — **del·ta'ic** (dĕl·tā'ĭk), *adj.*

del'toid (-toid), *adj.* [Gr. *deltoeidēs* delta-shaped, fr. *delta* (Δ) + *eidos* form.] Shaped like a capital delta (Δ); triangular; as, a *deltoid* leaf. See LEAF, *Illust.* (13). — *n. Anat.* A large triangular muscle covering the shoulder joint and serving to raise the arm laterally.

de·lude' (dē·lūd'), *v. t.* [L. *deludere, delusum,* fr. *de* + *ludere* to play, mock.] **1.** To lead from truth or into error; to mislead. **2.** *Obs.* To frustrate or disappoint. **3.** *Obs.* To evade; elude. — **Syn.** See DECEIVE. — **de·lud'er** (-lūd'ēr), *n.* — **de·lud'ing·ly,** *adv.*

del'uge (dĕl'ūj), *n.* [OF., fr. L. *diluvium,* fr. *diluere* to wash away, fr. *di-* (= *dis-*) + *luere* to wash.] **1.** An overflowing of the land by water; a flood. **2.** An irresistible rush of anything in overwhelming numbers, quantity, or volume. — *v. t.;* DEL'UGED (-ūjd); DEL'UG·ING (-ū·jĭng). **1.** To inundate; flood. **2.** To overwhelm as with a deluge. — ***the Deluge.*** The great flood in the days of Noah (*Gen.* vii).

de·lu'sion (dē·lū'zhŭn), *n.* **1.** Act of deluding, or state of being deluded; esp., a misleading of the mind. **2.** False belief; a fixed misconception; as, to cling to a *delusion.* **3.** *Psychiatry.* A false belief regarding the self, common in paranoia and dementia praecox; as, *delusions* of grandeur, or of persecution. — **de·lu'sion·al,** *adj.*

Syn. Delusion, illusion, hallucination, mirage mean something which one accepts as true or real but which is actually false or unreal. Delusion implies deception, commonly self-deception, and, usually, a disordered state of mind; illusion implies an ascription of truth or reality to that which only seems to be true or real; hallucination implies the perception of objects or conditions which have no basis in reality but are the result of disordered nerves or mental derangement; mirage, literally an optical illusion, in its extended sense applies to a dream, a hope, or the like, which one accepts as true, not realizing it is an illusion.

de·lu'sive (dē·lū'sĭv), *adj.* Apt or fitted to delude; deceptive. — **de·lu'sive·ly,** *adv.* — **de·lu'sive·ness,** *n.*

de·lu'so·ry (-sō·rĭ), *adj.* Delusive.

de luxe (dē lo͝oks'; lŭks'; *F.* dē lüks'). [F., lit., of luxury.] Specially elegant; sumptuous; as, a *de luxe* edition of a book.

delve (dĕlv), *v. t.* [AS. *delfan* to dig.] **1.** *Now Chiefly Dial.* To dig. **2.** *Archaic & Dial.* **a** To make, as a hole, by digging. **b** To exhume. — *v. i.* To dig or labor with a spade, or as with a spade; to seek laboriously (in books, etc.) for information. — *n. Rare.* A pit; den; cave. — **delv'er** (dĕl'vēr), *n.*

de·mag'net·ize (dē·măg'nĕ·tīz; -nĭ·tīz), *v. t.* To deprive of magnetic properties. See MAGNETIZE. — **de·mag'net·i·za'tion** (-tĭ·zā'shŭn; -tī·zā'-), *n.* — **de·mag'net·iz'er** (-tīz'ēr), *n.*

dem'a·gog'ic (dĕm'ȧ·gŏj'ĭk; -gŏg'ĭk), **dem'a·gog'i·cal** (-ĭ·kăl), *adj.* Of, relating to, or like, a demagogue; factious. — **dem'a·gog'i·cal·ly,** *adv.*

dem'a·gog·ism (dĕm'ȧ·gŏg·ĭz'm), *n.* The principles or practices of demagogues; demagogic character.

dem'a·gogue (dĕm'ȧ·gŏg; 74), *n.* Also **dem'a·gog.** [Gr. *dēmagōgos,* fr. *dēmos* the people + *agōgos* leading, fr. *agein* to lead.] **1.** *Chiefly Hist.* A popular leader or orator. **2.** A speaker who seeks to make capital of social discontent and gain political influence. — **dem'a·gog'uer·y** (-gŏg'ēr·ĭ; -gŏg'rĭ), *n.*

dem'a·gog'y (-gŏj'ĭ; -gō·jĭ; -gŏg'ĭ), *n.* Demagogism.

‖**de mal en pis** (dē măl' äN' pē'). [F.] From bad to worse.

de·mand' (dē·mȧnd'; 9), *v. t.* [OF. *demander,* fr. LL. *demandare* to demand, summon, fr. L. *demandare* to give in charge, entrust, fr. *de* + *mandare* to commit to one's charge, command.] **1.** To ask or call for with authority; to claim as due. **2.** To inquire authoritatively; to ask, esp. in a peremptory manner. **3.** To require; to be in need of; as, the case *demands* care. **4.** To summon; to require to appear. — *v. i.* To make a demand; to inquire.

Syn. Demand, claim, require, exact mean to call for something as due or as necessary. Demand strongly implies peremptoriness and insistency and, often, when the subject names a person, the right to make a request which shall be regarded as a command; claim implies the delivery or concession of something due one as one's own, one's right, or the like; require in precise English suggests such imperativeness as arises from inner necessity, the compulsion of law or regulation, or the exigencies of the situation; exact not only implies demanding but getting what one demands.

— *n.* **1.** Act of demanding; a peremptory urging of a claim. **2.** That which is demanded, esp. by right, or as due. **3.** Earnest inquiry; a query. **4.** An expressed desire for ownership or use, as of a commodity; as, an increased *demand* for labor. **5.** *Econ.* **a** Desire to purchase a commodity, accompanied by means of payment. **b** The quantity of an article demanded at a given price. Cf. SUPPLY, *n.,* **4.** — ***on,*** or formerly ***at, demand.*** *Finance.* Upon presentation and request for payment.

— **de·mand'a·ble,** *adj.* — **de·mand'er,** *n.*

de·mand'ant (dē·măn'dănt), *n.* The plaintiff in a real action.

demand bill *or* **draft.** *Finance.* A bill payable at sight.

demand deposit. *Banking.* A deposit which may be withdrawn without notice.

demand loan. A call loan. See CALL LOAN.

demand note. A note payable on demand.

de·man'toid (dē·măn'toid), *n.* [G. *demant* diamond + *-oid.*] A green variety of andradite used as a gem.

de·mar'cate (dē·mär'kāt; dē'mär-), *v. t.* [A back formation from the n., fr. F. *démarcation,* fr. Sp. *demarcación,* fr. *de-* (fr. L. *de*) + *marcar* to mark.] To mark by bounds; delimit; hence, to separate; discriminate. — **de'mar·ca'tion** (dē'mär·kā'shŭn), *n.*

‖**dé'marche'** (dā'mȧrsh'), *n.* [F.] A course of action, esp. one involving a change of policy, as in diplomacy.

de'ma·te'ri·al·ize (dē'mȧ·tēr'ĭ·ăl·īz), *v. t. & i.* To deprive, or become deprived, of material qualities; to lose material form. — **de'ma·te'ri·al·i·za'tion** (-ĭ·zā'shŭn; -ī·zā'-), *n.*

deme (dēm), *n.* [Gr. *dēmos* deme.] *Gr. Hist.* One of the hundred townships into which Cleisthenes divided Attica (about 508 B.C.).

de·mean' (dē·mēn'), *v. t.* [*de-* + *mean,* adj.] To debase; to lower; to degrade; — usually reflexive. — **Syn.** See ABASE.

de·mean', *v. t.* [OF. *demener* to conduct, manage, fr. *de-* (fr. L. *de*) + *mener* to lead, conduct, fr. L. *minare* to drive animals, fr. *minari* to threaten.] **1.** *Obs.* To manage; to conduct. **2.** To behave or comport (oneself). — **Syn.** See BEHAVE.

de·mean'or, de·mean'our (-ēr), *n.* [For *demeanure,* fr. *demean* to manage.] Outward bearing or behavior. — **Syn.** See BEARING.

de·ment' (dē·mĕnt'), *v. t.* [L. *dementare,* fr. *demens.* See DEMENTIA.] To deprive of reason.

de·ment'ed (dē·mĕn'tĕd; -tĭd), *adj.* Insane; mad. — **de·ment'ed·ly,** *adv.* — **de·ment'ed·ness,** *n.*

de·men'ti·a (dē·mĕn'shĭ·ȧ; -shȧ), *n.* [L., fr. *demens, dementis,* mad, fr. *de* + *mens* mind.] Insanity; in psychiatry, any condition of deteriorated mentality. — **Syn.** See INSANITY.

de·men'ti·a prae'cox (prē'kŏks). [L. *praecox* early ripe, precocious.] A form of insanity, developing usually in late adolescence, and characterized by loss of interest in people and things and incoherence of thought and action.

de·mer'it (dē·mĕr'ĭt; dē-), *n.* [From OF. *demerite* ill desert (fr. L. *dis-* + *mérite* merit), and from L. *demerere, demeritum,* to deserve well (fr. *de* + *merere* to deserve).] **1.** *Obs.* Merit; desert. **2.** That which deserves blame; fault. **3.** *Educ.* In full **demerit mark.** A mark denoting a fault or offense, esp. in conduct.

de·mesne' (dē·mān'; -mēn'), *n.* [AF. (with silent *s*), for OF. *demeine,* fr. L. *dominicus.* See DOMAIN.] **1.** *Law.* Possession (of land) as one's own. **2.** *Law.* Formerly, an estate or land of which the owner is in possession; now, a lord's chief manor place. **3.** Region in general; hence, realm or province, esp. of activity; domain.

De·me'ter (dē·mē'tēr), *n.* [L., fr. Gr. *Dēmētēr.*] *Gr. Relig.* Goddess of the fruitful soil, of agriculture, and of the fruitfulness of mankind, and guardian of marriage, — identified by the Romans with *Ceres*.

de′mi (dē′mī), *n., pl.* of DEMOS.

dem′i- (dĕm′ĭ-; *the accent is variable in the compounds*). [F. *demi-*, fr. L. *dimidius* half, fr. *di-* (= *dis-*) + *medius* middle.] A prefix signifying *half*, and hence, often, *below the standard or normal in size, quality*, etc.

dem′i·bas′tion (dĕm′ĭ·băs′chŭn), *n.* [F.] *Fort.* A half bastion, consisting of one face and one flank.

dem′i·god′ (dĕm′ĭ·gŏd′; *cf.* GOD), *n.* A divine or semidivine being, as the offspring of a deity and a mortal; a godling; hero (def. 1 **b**). — **dem′i·god′dess**, *n.*

dem′i·john (-jŏn), *n.* [F. *dame-jeanne*, i. e., Lady Jane.] A large narrow-necked bottle of glass or stoneware, enclosed in wickerwork. It holds from 1 to 10 gallons. Cf. CARBOY.

de·mil′i·ta·rize (dē·mĭl′ĭ·tȧ·rīz), *v. t.* *Mil.* To do away with the military organization of; as, to *demilitarize* a frontier. — **de·mil′i·ta·ri·za′tion** (-rĭ·zā′shŭn; -rī·zā′-), *n.*

dem′i·lune′ (dĕm′ĭ·lūn′), *n.* [F.] *Fort.* A work, orig. crescent-shaped, to defend the entrance to a fort.

dem′i·mon·daine′ (dĕm′ĭ·mŏn·dān′), *n.* [F.] A woman of the demimonde.

dem′i·monde (dĕm′ĭ·mŏnd; -mŏnd′; dē·mē′mōnd′), *n.* [F., fr. *demi-* + *monde* world, fr. L. *mundus*.] Women of doubtful reputation; courtesans; hence, the class of society to which such women belong.

dem′i·pique′ (dĕm′ĭ·pēk′), *adj.* [*demi-* + *peak*, confused with F. *pique* pike.] Having a peak of about half the height of that of an older style of saddle; — said of an 18th-century war saddle. — *n.* A demipique saddle.

dem′i·re·lief′ (-rē·lēf′), *n.* Also **dem′i·re·lie′vo** (-rē·lē′vō), **dem′i·ri·lie′vo**. *Sculpture.* Half relief. See RELIEF.

dem′i·rep′ (dĕm′ĭ·rĕp′), *n.* [Contr. fr. *demi-reputation*.] *Slang.* A woman of doubtful repute; an adventuress.

de·mise′ (dē·mīz′), *n.* [F. *démettre*, past part. *démis, démise*, to put away, dismiss, fr. L. *demittere* to send away, fr. *de* + *mittere* to send.] **1.** *Law.* The conveyance of an estate, chiefly by lease. **2.** Transfer of the crown or sovereignty to a successor, as by death or abdication. **3.** The decease of a royal or princely person; hence, grandiloquently, decease; death. — *v. t. & i.* **1.** *Law.* To convey, as an estate; esp., to lease. **2.** To transmit by succession or inheritance. — **de·mis′a·ble** (-mīz′ȧ·b'l), *adj.*

dem′i·sem′i·qua′ver (dĕm′ĭ·sĕm′ĭ·kwā′vẽr), *n.* *Music.* See NOTE, *n.*, 11.

de·mis′sion (dē·mĭsh′ŭn), *n.* [F. *démission*, fr. L. *demissio*.] Act of demitting; relinquishment; abdication.

de·mit′ (dē·mĭt′), *v. t. & i.*; DE·MIT′TED (-ĕd; -ĭd); DE·MIT′TING. [F. *démettre*. See DEMISE.] **1.** *Archaic.* To dismiss. **2.** *Chiefly Scot.* To resign.

dem′i·tasse′ (dĕm′ĭ·tăs′; -täs′; *F.* dē·mē′täs′), *n.* [F., fr. *demi-* + *tasse* cup.] A small cup for, or of, black coffee.

dem′i·urge (dĕm′ĭ·ûrj), *n.* Also **dem′i·ur′gos** (-ûr′gŏs) and **dem′i·ur′gus** (-gŭs); L. *pl.* DEMIURGI (-jī). [Gr. *dēmiourgos* a worker for the people, a workman, esp. the maker of the world, the Creator, fr. *dēmios* belonging to the people (fr. *dēmos* the people) + *-ergos* worker.] **1.** In some of the Peloponnesian states of ancient Greece, a magistrate. **2.** [*cap.*] *Philos.* In Platonic philosophy, the subordinate god who created the world. **3.** In some Gnostic systems, an inferior, not absolutely intelligent, deity, the creator of the world, identified by some with the creator God of the Old Testament, and distinguished from the supreme God. — **dem′i·ur′geous** (-ûr′jŭs), *adj.* — **dem′i·ur′gic** (-jĭk), **dem′i·ur′gi·cal** (-jĭ·kăl), *adj.*

dem′i·volt′ (-vōlt′), *n.* Also **dem′i·volte′**. [F. *demi-volte*.] *Manège.* A half vault with the forelegs raised.

de·mo′bi·lize (dē·mō′bĭ·līz), *v. t.* *Mil.* To disband, as troops. — **de·mo′bi·li·za′tion** (-mō′bĭ·lĭ·zā′shŭn; -lī·zā′shŭn; -mŏb′ĭ-), *n.*

de·moc′ra·cy (dē·mŏk′rȧ·sĭ), *n.; pl.* -CIES (-sĭz). [F. *démocratie*, fr. ML., fr. Gr. *dēmokratia*, fr. *dēmos* the people + *kratein* to rule, *kratos* authority.] **1.** Government by the people; government in which the supreme power is retained by the people and exercised either directly (***absolute, or pure, democracy***), or indirectly (***representative democracy***) through a system of representation. **2.** A community or state so governed. **3.** [*cap.*] *U. S.* The principles and policy of the Democratic party; also, that party, or its members. **4.** Belief in or practice of social equality; absence of snobbery.

dem′o·crat (dĕm′ō·krăt), *n.* **1.** An adherent of democracy; hence, one who practices social equality. **2.** [*cap.*] *U. S.* A member of the Democratic party.

dem′o·crat′ic (dĕm′ō·krăt′ĭk), *adj.* Also **dem′o·crat′i·cal** (-ĭ·kăl). **1.** Pertaining to democracy; based upon the principles of democracy. **2.** Of or characteristic of, or befitting, the common people; as, *democratic* art. **3.** Favoring social equality; not snobbish or socially exclusive. **4.** Designating or pertaining to a political party called *democratic*. — **dem′o·crat′i·cal·ly**, *adv.*

Democratic party. *U. S. Politics.* One of the two great political parties since 1828 in the United States.

de·moc′ra·tize (dē·mŏk′rȧ·tīz), *v. t. & i.* To render, or to become, democratic. — **de·moc′ra·ti·za′tion** (-tĭ·zā′shŭn; -tī·zā′-), *n.*

‖**dé′mo′dé′** (dā′mō′dā′), *adj.* [F.] Passed out of fashion; out of date.

De′mo·gor′gon (dē′mō·gôr′gŭn; dĕm′ō-), *n.* *Myth.* A mysterious, terrible, and evil divinity, commanding the spirits of the lower world, and appearing in medieval literature as a demon of magic or as a primordial creative power.

de·mog′ra·phy (dē·mŏg′rȧ·fĭ), *n.* [Gr. *dēmos* the people + *-graphy*.] The statistical study of populations, as to births, marriages, mortality, health, etc. — **de·mog′ra·pher** (-fẽr), *n.* — **de′mo·graph′ic** (dē′mō·grăf′ĭk), *adj.* — **de′mo·graph′i·cal** (-ĭ·kăl), *adj.* — **de′mo·graph′i·cal·ly**, *adv.* — **de·mog′ra·phist** (dē·mŏg′rȧ·fĭst), *n.*

dem′oi·selle′ (dĕm′wä·zĕl′; *F.* dē·mwȧ′zĕl′), *n.* [F. See DAMSEL.] **1.** A young lady; a damsel. **2.** A small crane (*Anthropoides virgo*), found in Asia, North Africa, and southeast Europe. **3.** Any of numerous slender-bodied dragonflies (*Agrion, Calopteryx*, and allied genera).

de·mol′ish (dē·mŏl′ĭsh), *v. t.* [F. *démolir*, fr. L. *demoliri*, past part. *demolitus*, fr. *de* + *moliri* to construct, fr. *moles* a huge mass or structure.] To throw or pull down; raze; hence, to ruin; destroy. — **de·mol′ish·er**, *n.* — **de·mol′ish·ment**, *n.*

dem′o·li′tion (dĕm′ō·lĭsh′ŭn; dē′mō-), *n.* Act of demolishing; destruction. — **dem′o·li′tion·ist**, *n.*

de′mon (dē′mŭn), *n.* [F. and L.; F. *démon*, fr. L. *daemon* spirit, evil spirit, fr. Gr. *daimōn* a divinity.] **1.** A tutelary divinity; a daemon. **2.** [L. *daemonium*, fr. Gr. *daimonion*, neut. of *daimonios* of a divinity, fr. *daimōn*.] An evil spirit; a devil. **3.** A person of great energy or skill.

demon-. = DEMONO-.

de·mon′e·tize (dē·mŏn′ē·tīz; dē·mŭn′-), *v. t.* To deprive (a coin or paper money) of standard value as money; to abandon use of (a metal) as money. — **de·mon′e·ti·za′tion** (-tĭ·zā′shŭn; -tī·zā′-), *n.*

de·mo′ni·ac (dē·mō′nĭ·ăk), **de′mo·ni′a·cal** (dē′mō·nī′ȧ·kăl), *adj.* [LL. *daemoniacus*.] **1.** Influenced or produced by a demon. **2.** Devilish; demonic. — **de′mo·ni′a·cal·ly**, *adv.*

de·mo′ni·ac, *n.* One supposedly possessed by an evil spirit.

de·mon′ic (dē·mŏn′ĭk), *adj.* Also **de·mo′ni·an** (dē·mō′nĭ·ăn). [LL. *daemonicus*.] Of, pert. to, or of the nature of a demon or demons.

de′mon·ism (dē′mŭn·ĭz'm), *n.* Belief in demons; also, demonology. — **de′mon·ist** (-ĭst), *n.*

de′mon·ize (-īz), *v. t.* **1.** To convert into a demon; to infuse demonic fury into. **2.** To control by a demon.

de′mon·o- (dē′mŭn·ō-), **de′mon-**. [Gr. *daimōn, daimonos*, daemon, demon.] A combining form meaning *demon*, as in **de′mon·oc′ra·cy, de′mon·o·man′cy, de′mon·o·pho′bi·a** (see -CRACY, -MANCY, -PHOBIA).

de′mon·ol′a·ter (dē′mŭn·ŏl′ȧ·tẽr), *n.* A demon worshiper.

de′mon·ol′a·try (-trĭ), *n.* [*demono-* + *-latry*.] Worship of ghosts, spirits, and demonic powers.

de′mon·ol′o·gy (-ŏl′ō·jĭ), *n.* [*demono-* + *-logy*.] The branch of learning concerned with demons, or the description of popular beliefs in demons; also, belief in or theory of demons. — **de′mon·ol′o·gist** (-jĭst), *n.*

de·mon′stra·ble (dē·mŏn′strȧ·b'l; dĕm′ŭn-), *adj.* **1.** Capable of being demonstrated. **2.** *Obs.* Apparent; evident. — **de·mon′stra·bil′i·ty** (-bĭl′ĭ·tĭ), *n.* — **de·mon′stra·bly** (-blĭ), *adv.*

de·mon′strant (dē·mŏn′strănt), *n.* One making or participating in a public demonstration.

dem′on·strate (dĕm′ŭn·strāt), *v. t.* [L. *demonstratus*, past part. of *demonstrare* to demonstrate, fr. *de* + *monstrare* to show.] **1.** *Obs.* To point out; portray. **2.** To prove by reasoning, as by deduction; to establish as true. **3.** To explain or illustrate, as in teaching, by use of examples, etc. **4.** To show or prove publicly. — **Syn.** See SHOW. — *v. i.* To make an outward or public display, as of feelings, of military force, etc.; also, to teach by use of examples, experiments, etc.

dem′on·stra′tion (-strā′shŭn), *n.* **1.** An outward expression or display, as of feelings; a manifestation; specif., a public display by a crowd, as of sympathy or antagonism. **2.** Act, process, or means of demonstrating; proof; also, a proof. **3.** A public showing and emphasizing of the salient merits, utility, efficiency, etc., of an article or product. **4.** *Logic.* A demonstrating; proof. **5.** *Math.* A course of reasoning showing that a certain result is a consequence of assumed premises. **6.** *Mil.* An exhibition of force, or a movement indicating an attack, as to show readiness for war if necessary. — **dem′on·stra′tion·al**, *adj.* — **dem′on·stra′tion·ist**, *n.*

de·mon′stra·tive (dē·mŏn′strȧ·tĭv), *adj.* **1.** Making evident; exhibiting conclusively. **2.** *Gram.* Serving to designate or point out the person or thing referred to or intended; as, a *demonstrative* adjective or pronoun (see PRONOUN). **3.** Given to displaying feeling; often, effusive. — *n.* *Gram.* A word, as a demonstrative pronoun, having a demonstrative function. — **de·mon′stra·tive·ly**, *adv.* — **de·mon′stra·tive·ness**, *n.*

dem′on·stra′tor (dĕm′ŭn·strā′tẽr), *n.* One who makes a demonstration; one who or that which demonstrates; specif., a teacher or assistant whose duty it is to demonstrate experiments, dissections, or the like.

de·mor′al·ize (dē·mŏr′ăl·īz), *v. t.* [F. *démoraliser*.] **1.** To corrupt in morals; to pervert. **2.** To render untrustworthy in discipline, spirit, or the like. **3.** To cast into disorder. — **de·mor′al·i·za′tion** (-ĭ·zā′shŭn; -ī·zā′-), *n.* — **de·mor′al·iz′er** (-īz′ẽr), *n.*

‖**de mor′tu·is nil ni′si bo′num** (dē môr′tū·ĭs nĭl nī′sī bō′nŭm). [L.] Of the dead (say) nothing but good.

de′mos (dē′mŏs), *n.; pl.* DEMI (-mī). [L., fr. Gr. *dēmos*.] **1.** A deme. **2.** The commons or commonalty of an ancient Greek state; hence, the common people; the populace.

de·mote′ (dē·mōt′), *v. t.* [*de-* + *mote* as in *promote*.] To reduce to a lower grade, as in school or in the army; — opposed to *promote*. — **de·mo′tion** (-mō′shŭn), *n.*

de·mot′ic (dē·mŏt′ĭk), *adj.* [Gr. *dēmotikos*, fr. *dēmos* the people.] **1.** Of or pertaining to the people; popular. **2.** *Egypt. Archaeol.* Designating a simplified form of the hieratic character, used for books, deeds, etc.

de·mot′ics (-ĭks), *n.*; see -ICS. Sociology in its broadest sense; — used in library cataloguing.

de·mount′ (dē·mount′), *v. t.* To remove from a mounted position; as, to *demount* a rim, an airplane motor. — **de·mount′a·ble**, *adj.*

demp′ster (dĕmp′stẽr; 89), *n.* A deemster.

de·mul′cent (dē·mŭl′sĕnt; -s'nt), *adj.* [L. *demulcens*, pres. part. of *demulcere*.] Softening; mollifying; soothing. — *n.* *Med.* A substance capable of soothing an inflamed or abraded mucous membrane or protecting it from irritation.

de·mur′ (dē·mûr′), *v. i.*; DE·MURRED′ (-mûrd′); DE·MUR′RING. [OF. *demurer, demorer*, to linger, stay, fr. L. *demorari*, fr. *de* + *morari* to delay, stay.] **1.** To delay; hesitate. **2.** To scruple or object; to take exception. **3.** *Law.* To interpose a demurrer. — *n.* **1.** Pause; delay. **2.** Objection; scruple. **3.** *Obs., Law.* A demurrer. — **Syn.** See QUALM.

de·mure′ (dē·mūr′), *adj.* [OF. *meür* mature, ripe, fr. L. *maturus*.] **1.** Of sober or serious mien; staid; grave. **2.** Affectedly modest, decorous, or serious; prim. — **de·mure′ly**, *adv.* — **de·mure′ness**, *n.*

de·mur′rage (dē·mûr′ĭj), *n.* The detention of a vessel, a freight car, etc., by the freighter beyond the time allowed for loading, unloading, etc.; also, the payment made for such detention.

de·mur′ral (dē·mûr′ăl), *n.* Demur; delay.

de·mur′rer (dē·mûr′ẽr), *n.* One who demurs.

de·mur′rer, *n.* [OF. inf. *demorer*, used as a noun. See DEMUR, *v.*] **1.** *Law.* A pleading which, assuming the truth of the matter alleged by the opposite party, sets up that it is insufficient in law, or that there is some other defect on the face of the pleadings constituting a legal reason why the opposing party should not be allowed to proceed further. Cf. PLEA, *n.*, 4 **a**. **2.** An objection, or demur.

de·my′ (dē·mī′), *n.; pl.* DEMIES (-mīz′). [See DEMI-.] **1.** A scholar on the foundation at Magdalen College, Oxford. **2.** Any of certain sizes of paper, about 16 × 21 inches.

den (dĕn), *n.* [AS. *denn.*] **1.** The lair of a wild beast, esp. of a beast of prey; hence, a cavern as a place of concealment. **2.** A squalid place of resort; a haunt. **3.** A quiet, snug, private retreat, as a room set apart for reading. — *v. t. & i.* To live in or as in a den.

de·nar′i·us (dē·nâr′ĭ·ŭs), *n.; pl.* -NARII (-ĭ·ī). [L., orig. equiv. to ten asses, fr. *deni* ten by ten.] **1.** A Roman coin, originally of silver, later much debased. It was the penny of the New Testament. **2.** A Roman gold coin of the same weight as the silver denarius.

Denarius of Julius Caesar, 44 B.C.

den′a·ry (dĕn′ȧ·rĭ; dē′nȧ·rĭ), *adj.* [L. *denarius.*] Containing ten; tenfold; based on or proceeding by tens.

de·na′tion·al·ize (dē·năsh′ŭn·ăl·īz), *v. t.* To divest or deprive of national character or rights. — **de·na′tion·al·i·za′tion** (-ĭ·zā′shŭn; -ī·zā′-), *n.*

de·nat′u·ral·ize (dē·năt′ṳ·răl·īz), *v. t.* **1.** To render unnatural; to alienate from its true or proper nature. **2.** To deprive of the rights and duties of a natural subject or citizen. — **de·nat′u·ral·i·za′tion** (-ĭ·zā′shŭn; -ī·zā′-), *n.*

de·na′tur·ant (dē·nā′tṳr·ănt), *n.* A denaturing agent.

de·na′ture (-tṳr), *v. t.* To deprive of natural qualities; to change the nature of; specif.: **a** To render unfit for some purpose, as eating or drinking, without impairing usefulness for other purposes, as alcohol. **b** To so modify (a protein), as by heat, acid, or alkali, that it no longer has all its original properties. — **de·na′tur·a′tion** (-tṳr·ā′shŭn), *n.*

de·na′tur·ize (-tṳr·īz), *v. t.* To denature. — **de·na′tur·i·za′tion** (-ĭ·zā′shŭn; -ī·zā′-), *n.* — **de·na′tur·iz′er** (-īz′ẽr), *n.*

de·na′zi·fy (dē·nä′tsē·fī; -năt′sē·fī), *v. t.* To rid of Nazism and its influence. — **de·na′zi·fi·ca′tion** (-fĭ·kā′shŭn), *n.*

den′dri·form (dĕn′drĭ·fôrm), *adj.* [*dendr-* + *-form.*] Resembling a tree in structure.

den′drite (dĕn′drīt), *n.* [Gr. *dendritēs* of a tree, fr. *dendron* a tree.] **1.** *Min.* A branching treelike figure produced on or in a mineral by a foreign mineral, as in the moss agate; also, the mineral so marked. **2.** *Anat. & Physiol.* Any of the branching, tapering processes of a nerve cell which, as a rule, conduct impulses toward the cell body. Cf. AXON. — **den·drit′ic** (dĕn·drĭt′ĭk), **den·drit′i·cal** (-ĭ·kăl), *adj.*

den′dro- (dĕn′drō-), **dendr-.** [Gr. *dendron.*] A combining form meaning *tree,* as in **den·drol′a·try, den′dro·phile.**

den′dro·chro·nol′o·gy (-krō·nŏl′ō·jĭ), *n.* [*dendro-* + *chronology.*] The determination of dates of events and intervals of time in former periods by comparative study of the sequence of rings of growth in trees and aged wood. — **den′dro·chron′o·log′i·cal** (-krŏn′ō·lŏj′ĭ·kăl), *adj.* — **den′dro·chro·nol′o·gist** (-krō·nŏl′ō·jĭst), *n.*

den′droid (dĕn′droid), *adj.* [Gr. *dendroeidēs* treelike, fr. *dendron* tree + *eidos* form.] Also **den·droi′dal** (dĕn·droi′dăl; -d'l). Resembling a tree in form; arborescent.

den·drol′o·gy (dĕn·drŏl′ō·jĭ), *n.* [*dendro-* + *-logy.*] The study of trees. — **den′dro·log′ic** (dĕn′drō·lŏj′ĭk), **den′dro·log′i·cal** (-ĭ·kăl), **den·drol′o·gous** (dĕn·drŏl′ō·gŭs), *adj.* — **den·drol′o·gist** (-jĭst), *n.*

den′dron (dĕn′drŏn), *n.* = DENDRITE, 2.

-den′dron (-dĕn′drŏn). [Gr. *dendron.*] *Bot. & Zool.* A combining form meaning *tree, treelike formation.*

dene (dēn), *n. Eng.* A sandy tract by the sea.

Den′eb (dĕn′ĕb), *n.* [Ar. *dhanab aldajājah* the tail of the hen.] A star of the first magnitude in Cygnus.

den′e·ga′tion (dĕn′ē·gā′shŭn), *n.* [L. *denegatio,* fr. *denegare* to deny.] Denial.

den′gue (dĕng′gā; -gē), *n.* [West Indian Sp.] *Med.* A specific epidemic disease, chiefly tropical, attended with fever, eruptions, and severe pains; — called also *breakbone fever; dandy* (*fever*). See AËDES.

de·ni′a·ble (dē·nī′ȧ·b'l), *adj.* That may be denied.

de·ni′al (dē·nī′ăl), *n.* **1.** Refusal to grant; rejection of a request; — the contrary of *compliance.* **2.** Refusal to admit the truth of a statement, charge, etc.; assertion of the untruth of a thing stated; — the contrary of *affirmation.* **3.** Refusal to acknowledge; disavowal. **4.** A restriction or limitation upon one's normal activity or desires; — the contrary of *indulgence.*

de·nic′o·tin·ize (dē·nĭk′ō·tĭn·īz), *v. t.* To deprive (tobacco) of part of its nicotine, as by washing in water.

de·ni′er (dē·nī′ẽr), *n.* One who denies.

de·nier′, *n.* [F., fr. L. *denarius.*] **1.** (dē·nēr′; *F.* dē·nyā′) A minor coin of France and western Europe, orig. of silver, and current from the 8th to the 19th century. **2.** (dĕn′yẽr) A unit expressing the fineness of silk, rayon, or nylon yarns in terms of weights in grams per 9000 meters of length; thus, 100-*denier* yarn is finer than 150-*denier* yarn.

den′i·grate (dĕn′ĭ·grāt), *v. t.* [L. *denigrare,* fr. *de* + *nigrare* to blacken, fr. *niger* black.] To blacken; hence, to sully; to defame. — **den′i·gra′tion** (-grā′shŭn), *n.* — **den′i·gra′tor** (-grā′tẽr), *n.*

den′im (dĕn′ĭm), *n.* [F. *serge de Nîmes* serge of Nîmes, France.] A coarse cotton drilling used for overalls, carpeting, etc.; also, a finer variety used for cushions, etc.

de·ni′trate (dē·nī′trāt), *v. t.* To remove nitric acid, nitrates, the nitro group, or nitrogen oxides, from. — **de′ni·tra′tion** (dē′nī·trā′shŭn), *n.*

de·ni′tri·fy (dē·nī′trĭ·fī), *v. t.* [*de-* + *nitro*gen + *-fy.*] To deprive of, or free from, nitrogen or its compounds; also, to convert (nitrates) by reduction into lower compounds. — **de·ni′tri·fi·ca′tion** (-fĭ·kā′shŭn), *n.*

den′i·zen (dĕn′ĭ·zĕn; -z'n), *n.* [OF. *denzein,* prop., one living within (a city or country), fr. *denz* within, fr. L. *de intus,* prop., from within.] **1.** An inhabitant. **2.** One admitted to residence in a foreign country; esp., an alien admitted to the rights of citizenship; a naturalized citizen. **3.** One naturalized in any society, fellowship, or region; — often applied to a word, animal, or plant. — *v. t.* **1.** To make (one) a denizen. **2.** To provide with denizens.

de·nom′i·nate (dē·nŏm′ĭ·nāt), *adj.* [L. *denominatus,* past part. of *denominare* to name, fr. *de* + *nominare* to call by name.] Having a specific name or denomination; thus, *7 feet* is a *denominate* quantity, while *7* is a mere abstract quantity or number. — (-nāt), *v. t.* To give a name to; to entitle; name; call.

de·nom′i·na′tion (-nā′shŭn), *n.* **1.** Act of denominating, or naming. **2.** A name, designation, or title; esp., a general name; a category. **3.** A class, or society of individuals, called by the same name; a sect. **4.** One of a series of related units or values denoted by special names; as, the *denominations* of United States money ($1, $2, $5, etc.). — **de·nom′i·na′tion·al** (-ăl; -'l), *adj.* — **de·nom′i·na′tion·al·ism,** *n.* — **de·nom′i·na′tion·al·ist,** *n.* — **de·nom′i·na′tion·al·ly,** *adv.*

de·nom′i·na′tive (dē·nŏm′ĭ·nā′tĭv; -nȧ·tĭv), *adj.* **1.** Conferring a denomination, or name. **2.** *Gram.* Derived from a substantive or an adjective. — *n. Gram.* A denominative word. — **de·nom′i·na′tive·ly,** *adv.*

de·nom′i·na′tor (dē·nŏm′ĭ·nā′tẽr), *n.* **1.** One that denominates; hence, the origin or source of a name. **2.** *Arith. & Alg.* The part of a fraction below the line. In simple fractions it states into how many equal parts the unit is supposed to be divided.

de′no·ta′tion (dē′nō·tā′shŭn), *n.* **1.** The marking off or separation of anything. **2.** A sign, indication, or token; a name or designation. **3.** Meaning or signification. **4.** *Logic.* = EXTENSION, 4. — **Syn.** See under DENOTE.

de·no′ta·tive (dē·nō′tȧ·tĭv), *adj.* Having power to denote. — **de·no′ta·tive·ly,** *adv.* — **de·no′ta·tive·ness,** *n.*

de·note′ (dē·nōt′), *v. t.* [F. *dénoter,* fr. L. *denotare,* fr. *de* + *notare* to mark, fr. *nota* mark, sign.] **1.** To mark out plainly; to indicate; point out. **2.** To signify by way of definition; to mean. **3.** *Logic.* To name; to signify by way of denotation. — **de·not′a·ble** (-nōt′ȧ·b'l), *adj.* — **de·note′ment,** *n.*

Syn. **Denote, connote,** when used of terms, together equal *mean.* Taken singly, **denote** implies all that strictly belongs to the definition of the word, **connote** all of the ideas that are suggested by the term; thus, "home" *denotes* the place where one lives with one's family, but it usually *connotes* comfort, intimacy, and privacy. The same implications distinguish **denotation** and **connotation.**

de·noue′ment (dā·nōō′mäɴ; dā′nōō·mäɴ′), *n.* [F. *dénouement,* fr. *dénouer* untie, fr. *dé-* + *nouer* to tie, fr. L. *nodare,* fr. *nodus* knot.] **1.** The final revelation or occurrence which clarifies the nature and outcome of a plot; also, the passage in which it occurs. Cf. CATASTROPHE, 1. **2.** The issue, outcome, or solution of a complex situation.

de·nounce′ (dē·nouns′), *v. t.;* DE·NOUNCED′ (-nounst′); DE·NOUNC′ING (-noun′sĭng). [OF. *denoncer,* fr. L. *denuntiare, denunciare,* fr. *de* + *nunciare, nuntiare,* to announce, fr. *nuntius* messenger, message.] **1.** *Archaic.* To proclaim (esp. an evil); of things, to portend. **2.** To threaten by some outward sign or expression. **3.** To inform against; accuse. **4.** To invoke censure upon; stigmatize. **5.** To give notice of the termination of (a treaty, armistice, or the like). — **Syn.** See CRITICIZE. — **de·nounce′ment,** *n.* — **de·nounc′er** (-noun′sẽr), *n.*

‖**de no′vo** (dē nō′vō). [L.] Anew; afresh.

dense (dĕns), *adj.* [F., fr. L. *densus.*] **1.** Having its parts massed or crowded together; close; compact. **2.** Of ignorance, stupidity, or the like, impenetrable; crass; hence, of persons, stupid. **3.** *Photog.* Relatively opaque; as, a *dense* negative. — **Syn.** See CLOSE: STUPID. — **dense′ly,** *adv.* — **dense′ness,** *n.*

den·sim′e·ter (dĕn·sĭm′ē·tẽr), *n.* [L. *densus* dense + *-meter.*] *Phys. Chem.* An instrument for measuring densities. — **den′si·met′ric** (dĕn′sĭ·mĕt′rĭk), *adj.* — **den′si·met′ri·cal·ly** (-rĭ·kăl·ĭ), *adv.*

den′si·tom′e·ter (dĕn′sĭ·tŏm′ē·tẽr), *n.* [*density* + *meter.*] **a** A densimeter. **b** An instrument for measuring photographic density.

den′si·ty (dĕn′sĭ·tĭ), *n.; pl.* -TIES (-tĭz). **1.** Quality or state of being dense; specif., the quantity of anything per unit of volume or area; as, the ***density of population,*** the average number of persons per unit of area (usually per sq. mi.). **2.** Stupidity. **3.** *Elec.* **a** Of a static charge, the quantity of electricity per unit area, or per unit volume. **b** Short for ***current density,*** the current flowing through unit cross-section area of a conductor. **4.** *Physics.* The ratio of the mass of a homogeneous portion of matter to its volume. Abbr. *d* or *D*

dent (dĕnt), *n.* [Var. of DINT.] A slight depression, or hollow, like that made by a blow or by pressure; indentation. — *v. t.* To make a dent upon; to indent. — *v. i.* To become indented.

dent, *n.* [F., fr. L. *dens, dentis,* tooth.] A toothlike notch, as of a card, a gear wheel, in a lock, etc.

dent-. = DENTI-, as in **den·tal′gi·a** (dĕn·tăl′jĭ·ȧ).

den′tal (dĕn′tăl; -t'l), *adj.* [L. *dens, dentis,* tooth.] **1.** Of or pertaining to the teeth or dentistry. **2.** *Phonet.* Formed with the tip of the tongue against or near the upper front teeth (Eng. *th,* French *t, d*) or, less exactly, the upper alveolar ridge (Eng. *t, d, s, z*). The English consonants usually or sometimes classed as dental are *th, th, t, d, n, l, r, s, z, sh, zh, ch, j.* — *n.* A dental consonant.

den′tate (-tāt), *adj.* [L. *dentatus.*] *Bot. & Zool.* Having a toothed margin; specif., *Bot.,* having regular sharp-pointed marginal teeth directed outward; as, a *dentate* leaf. Cf. SERRATE.

den·ta′tion (dĕn·tā′shŭn), *n.* State or quality of being dentate; also, an angular toothlike projection.

den′ti- (dĕn′tĭ-). [L. *dens, dentis,* tooth.] A combining form meaning: **a** *Tooth,* as in *denti*form. **b** *Dental and,* as in **den′ti·lin′gual,** pronounced with the tongue against the teeth.

den′ti·cle (dĕn′tĭ·k'l), *n.* [L. *denticulus,* dim.] A small tooth or projection.

den·tic′u·late (dĕn·tĭk′ṳ·lāt), *adj.* Also **den·tic′u·lat′ed** (-lāt′ĕd; -ĭd). Having very small toothlike projections; specif., *Arch.,* cut into dentils. — **den·tic′u·late·ly,** *adv.*

den·tic′u·la′tion (-lā′shŭn), *n.* State of being denticulate; also, a diminutive tooth or toothlike projection.

den′ti·form (dĕn′tĭ·fôrm), *adj.* [*denti-* + *-form.*] Having the form of a tooth or of teeth; tooth-shaped.

den′ti·frice (-frĭs), *n.* [F., fr. L. *dentifricium,* fr. *dens, dentis,* tooth + *fricare* to rub.] A powder, paste, or liquid used in cleaning the teeth.

den′til (dĕn′tĭl), *n.* [MF. *dentille.*] *Arch., Furniture, etc.* A small rectangular block in a series projecting like teeth, as under a cornice.

den′ti·la′bi·al (dĕn′tĭ·lā′bĭ·ăl), *adj. & n.* Labiodental.

den′tine (dĕn′tēn; -tĭn), **den′tin** (-tĭn), *n.* [L. *dens, dentis,* tooth.] *Anat.* A calcareous material which composes the main part of a tooth; ivory.

den′tist (dĕn′tĭst), *n.* [F. *dentiste,* fr. L. *dens, dentis,* tooth.] One whose profession it is to treat the teeth and to make and insert artificial teeth.

den′tist·ry (dĕn′tĭs·trĭ), *n.* Art or profession of a dentist.

den·ti′tion (dĕn·tĭsh′ŭn), *n.* [L. *dentitio,* fr. *dentire* to cut teeth.] **1.** The development of teeth; teething. **2.** The number, kind, and arrangement of teeth of an animal.

den′to- (dĕn′tō-). **a** = DENTI-, as in **den′to·lin′gual. b** *Dental and,* as in **den′to·sur′gi·cal,** pertaining to, or used in, dentistry and surgery.

den′ture (dĕn′tṳr), *n.* [F., fr. L. *dens, dentis,* tooth.] A set of teeth; specif., *Dentistry,* a set of artificial teeth.

den′u·date (dĕn′ṳ·dāt; dē·nū′dāt), *v. t.* To denude.

de·nude' (dê·nūd'), *v. t.* [L. *denudare*, fr. *de* + *nudare* to make bare, fr. *nudus* naked.] To divest of covering; strip; specif., *Geol.*, to lay bare, as by erosion. — **den'u·da'tion** (dĕn'ū̇·dā'shŭn; dē'nū-), *n.* — **de·nud'er** (dê·nūd'ẽr), *n.*

de·nun'ci·ate (dê·nŭn'shî·āt; -sĭ·āt), *v. t. & i.* [L. *denuntiatus, -ciatus*, past part. See DENOUNCE.] To denounce.

de·nun'ci·a'tion (dê·nŭn'sĭ·ā'shŭn; -shĭ-), *n.* **1.** A denouncing; specif.: **a** *Obs.* Proclamation. **b** Announcement or warning of impending evil. **c** Act of stigmatizing; arraignment. **d** Formal denouncing of a treaty. **2.** That by which anything is denounced; a threat of evil; a public menace. — **de·nun'ci·a'tive** (-nŭn'shî·ā'tĭv; -sĭ·ā'tĭv; -ȧ·tĭv), *adj.* — **de·nun'ci·a'tive·ly**, *adv.*

de·nun'ci·a'tor (-nŭn'shî·ā'tẽr; -sĭ·ā'tẽr), *n.* One who denounces.

de·nun'ci·a·to·ry (-ȧ·tō'rĭ or, *esp. Brit.*, -tẽr·ĭ), *adj.* Pert. to, or characterized by, denunciation; accusing; threatening.

de·ny' (dê·nī'), *v. t.;* DE·NIED' (-nīd'); DE·NY'ING. [OF. *denier, deneier*, fr. L. *denegare*, fr. *de* + *negare* to deny.] **1.** To declare not to be true; contradict. **2.** To refuse to grant, gratify, or yield to; as, to *deny* a request. **3.** To disclaim connection with or responsibility for; to disavow. **4.** *Archaic.* To refuse (to do, or accept, something); decline. **5.** To refuse access to (one called on); to represent as "not at home"; as, she *denied* herself to callers. **6.** To reject as a false conception; as, to *deny* man's free will.

deny oneself. To practice self-denial.

Syn. Deny, gainsay, contradict, negative, traverse, impugn, contravene mean to declare untrue or to go counter to the truth. Deny commonly implies a refusal to accept a statement as true; gainsay implies a disputing the truth of what has been said or the integrity of the person saying it; contradict implies an open or flat denial by suggesting the statement's (or the speaker's, etc.) running counter to the truth; negative, a milder term, implies refusal to assent; traverse, chiefly a legal term, implies a formal denial of truth; impugn stresses an attack upon the truth of a statement or of a person making it; contravene stresses a running into conflict between what has been said or taught (and, in law, done) and things as they are. — **Ant.** Concede.

de'o·dand (dē'ō̇·dănd), *n.* [From ML., fr. L. *Deo dandum* to be given to God.] *Eng. Law.* A thing which, because it had been the immediate cause of the death of a person, was given to God, that is, forfeited to the crown for pious uses.

de'o·dar (dē'ō̇·där), *n.* [Hind. *deodār*, fr. Skr. *devadāru*, prop., timber of the gods.] An East Indian species of cedar (*Cedrus deodara*), valued for its size, beauty, and timber. See CONE, *Illust.;* CEDAR, 1 **a**.

de·o'dor·ant (dê·ō'dẽr·ănt), *adj.* Destroying or masking offensive odors. — *n.* Anything deodorant. It may or may not be an antiseptic or disinfectant.

de·o'dor·ize (-īz), *v. t.* To deprive of odor, esp. offensive odor. — **de·o'dor·i·za'tion** (-ĭ·zā'shŭn; -ī·zā'-), *n.* — **de·o'dor·iz'er** (-īz'ẽr), *n.*

‖**De'o fa·ven'te** (dē'ō̇ fȧ·vĕn'tê). [L.] With God's favor.

‖**De'o gra'ti·as** (grā'shî·ăs). [L.] Thanks to God.

de·on·tol'o·gy (dē'ŏn·tŏl'ō̇·jĭ), *n.* [Gr. *deon, deontos*, necessity, obligation (neut. part. of *dei* it is necessary) + *-logy*.] The science or theory of duty or moral obligation; the ethics of duty. — **de·on'to·log'i·cal** (dê·ŏn'tō̇·lŏj'ĭ·kăl), *adj.* — **de·on·tol'o·gist** (dē'ŏn·tŏl'ō̇·jĭst), *n.*

‖**De'o vo·len'te** (dē'ō̇ vō̇·lĕn'tê). [L.] God willing. Abbr. *D.V.*

de·ox'i·dize (dê·ŏk'sĭ·dīz), *v. t.* To deprive of oxygen; to reduce from the state of an oxide. — **de·ox'i·di·za'tion** (-dĭ·zā'shŭn; -dī·zā'-), *n.* — **de·ox'i·diz'er** (-dīz'ẽr), *n.*

de·ox'y·gen·ate (dê·ŏk'sĭ·jĕn·āt), *v. t.* Also **de·ox'y·gen·ize** (-īz). *Chem.* To deprive of oxygen, esp. free oxygen; as, *deoxygenated* water, sewage, or blood. — **de·ox'y·gen·a'tion** (-ā'shŭn), **de·ox'y·gen·i·za'tion** (-ĭ·zā'shŭn; -ī·zā'-), *n.*

de·paint' (dê·pānt'), *v. t.* *Now Rare.* To depict; paint.

de·part' (dê·pärt'), *v. i.* [OF. *departir* to divide, *soi departir* to separate oneself, depart, fr. *de-* (fr. L. *de*) + *partir* to part, depart, fr. L. *partire.* See PART, *v.*] **1.** To go forth or away; to leave; — opposed to *arrive.* **2.** To turn aside; to desist or deviate; — with *from.* **3.** To pass away; to die. — **Syn.** See GO; SWERVE. — *v. t.* *Archaic.* To leave; to depart from; as, to *depart* this life (that is, to die). — *n.* *Archaic.* Departure; hence, death.

de·part'ed (dê·pär'tĕd; -tĭd), *adj.* Bygone; also, deceased. — **Syn.** See DEAD.

de·part'ment (dê·pärt'mĕnt), *n.* **1.** *Rare.* A part or subdivision. **2.** A distinct sphere; province. **3.** A division or branch of governmental administration, national or municipal. **4.** Also ‖**dé'par'te·ment'** (dā'pȧr'tä·mäN'). In France, one of the ninety divisions made for purposes of local government. **5.** A division of a business concern; as, the accounting *department.* **6.** *Educ.* A division within a college or school, giving instruction in a branch of the arts and sciences; as, the physics *department.* **7.** *Mil.* A territorial subdivision made for the administration and training of military units. Abbr. *dept.* — **de'-part·men'tal** (dē'pärt·mĕn'tăl; -t'l), *adj.*

department store. A store keeping a great variety of goods arranged in several departments.

de·par'ture (dê·pär'tụ̇r), *n.* **1.** A departing, or going away; hence, a setting out, as on a journey. **2.** *Archaic.* Death; decease. **3.** Deviation or abandonment, as of a course of action. **4.** *Navig.* **a** The distance due east or west made by a ship in its course. **b** A ship's position in latitude and longitude at the beginning of a voyage, as a point from which to begin the dead reckoning.

de·pas'ture (dê·pȧs'tụ̇r), *v. t. & i.* To pasture; graze.

de·pend' (dê·pĕnd'), *v. i.* [OF. *dependre*, fr. L. *dependēre*, confused with *pendēre* to hang, v. t., fr. *de* + *pendēre, pendĕre*, to hang.] **1.** To hang down. **2.** To be contingent; — with *on;* as, his trip *depends* on his father's consent. **3.** To be conditioned; to be based, as through subjection or relatedness; as, the sciences *depend* on one another. **4.** To be pending, or undecided. **5.** To trust; to rely. **6.** To be dependent, esp. for support; — with *on* or *upon.* — **Syn.** See RELY.

de·pend'a·ble (dê·pĕn'dȧ·b'l), *adj.* Worthy of being depended on; trustworthy; reliable. — **de·pend'a·bil'i·ty** (-bĭl'ĭ·tĭ), **de·pend'a·ble·ness**, *n.* — **de·pend'a·bly**, *adv.*

de·pend'ance (dê·pĕn'dăns), **de·pend'an·cy**, **de·pend'ant.** Vars. of DEPENDENCE, etc.

de·pend'ence (dê·pĕn'dĕns), *n.* **1.** State of being influenced and determined by, or of being conditional upon, something else. **2.** State of depending, or being subject; esp., subjection to the direction or disposal of another. **3.** Reliance; trust. **4.** That on which one depends or relies.

de·pend'en·cy (-dĕn·sĭ), *n.; pl.* -CIES (-sĭz). **1.** State of being depend-

ent; dependence. **2.** That which depends; that which is attached to something else as its consequence, subordinate, annex, etc. **3.** A territory or state subject to the dominion of another, esp. a distinct and more or less remote province; as, Puerto Rico is a *dependency* of the United States.

de·pend'ent (-dĕnt), *adj.* **1.** Hanging down. **2.** Relying on, or subject to, something else for support. **3.** *Gram.* Subordinate; as, a *dependent* clause.

de·pend'ent, *n.* **1.** That which depends; a dependency. **2.** One who is sustained by another, or who relies on another for support or favor.

de·peo'ple (dê·pē'p'l), *v. t.;* see PEOPLE. To depopulate.

de·pict' (dê·pĭkt'), *v. t.* [L. *depictus*, past part. of *depingere* to depict, fr. *de-* + *pingere* to paint.] **1.** To represent by a picture; to portray. **2.** To portray in words; to describe. — **de·pic'tion** (-pĭk'-shŭn), *n.*

de·pic'ture (-pĭk'tụ̇r), *v. t.* To depict; also, to imagine.

dep'i·late (dĕp'ĭ·lāt), *v. t.* [L. *depilatus*, past part. of *depilare*, fr. *de* + *pilare* to deprive of hair.] To strip of hair. — **dep'i·la'tion** (-lā'shŭn), *n.* — **dep'i·la'tor** (-lā'tẽr), *n.*

de·pil'a·to·ry (dê·pĭl'ȧ·tō'rĭ or, *esp. Brit.*, -tẽr·ĭ), *adj.* Having the quality or power of depilating. — *n.* An agent used to remove hair or wool.

de·plete' (dê·plēt'), *v. t.* [L. *depletus*, past part. of *deplere* to empty out, fr. *de-* + *plere* to fill.] **1.** *Med.* To empty or unload, as the vessels of the human system by bloodletting or by purgation. **2.** To reduce by destroying or consuming; as, to *deplete* one's strength; to exhaust, as a country of its strength or resources. — **de·ple'tive** (-plē'tĭv), *adj. & n.* — **de·ple'to·ry** (-tō̇·rĭ), *adj.*

Syn. Deplete, drain, exhaust, impoverish, bankrupt mean to deprive of something essential to a thing's existence or potency. Deplete implies a reduction in numbers, quantity, etc., to a dangerous point; drain implies a gradual withdrawal and ultimate deprivation of that which is a necessity to a thing's existence; exhaust stresses an emptying or evacuation rather than a disastrous depletion; impoverish suggests a deprivation of something as essential to a thing as money is to a human being; bankrupt suggests such impoverishment as to be in danger of immediate collapse.

de·ple'tion (dê·plē'shŭn), *n.* **1.** Act of depleting, or state of being depleted. **2.** *Accounting.* Impairment of capital.

de·plor'a·ble (dê·plōr'ȧ·b'l; 70), *adj.* Lamentable; hence, sad; grievous; wretched. — **de·plor'a·bly** (-blĭ), *adv.*

de·plore' (dê·plōr'; 70), *v. t.* [F. *déplorer*, fr. L. *deplorare*, fr. *de* + *plorare* to cry out, lament.] To feel or express deep grief for; to sorrow over.

Syn. Deplore, lament, bewail, bemoan mean to grieve for or over something. Deplore implies keen regret, especially for that worth keeping; lament implies mourning, now especially in utterance, for something past and gone; bewail and bemoan imply poignant sorrow finding an outlet in words or cries, bewail commonly suggesting loudness, and bemoan lugubriousness.

de·ploy' (dê·ploi'), *v. t. & i.* [F. *déployer*.] *Mil. & Nav.* To extend the front and reduce the depth (of); as, to *deploy* a column of troops. — **de·ploy'ment**, *n.*

de·plume' (dê·plōōm'; 114), *v. t.* [From F. or ML., fr. L. *de* + *plumare* to cover with feathers, fr. *pluma* feather.] To pluck off the feathers of; hence, to strip of possessions, honors, etc. — **de'plu·ma'tion** (dē'plōō·mā'shŭn), *n.*

de·po'lar·ize (dê·pō'lẽr·īz), *v. t.* *Optics.* To deprive of polarity; to reduce to an unpolarized condition. — **de·po'lar·i·za'tion** (-ĭ·zā'-shŭn; -ī·zā'-), *n.* — **de·po'lar·iz'er** (-īz'ẽr), *n.*

de·pone' (dê·pōn'), *v. t. & i.* [L. *deponere, depositum*, to put down, in ML., to assert under oath, fr. *de* + *ponere* to put.] To assert under oath; to testify.

de·po'nent (-pō'nĕnt), *adj.* [L. *deponens, -entis*, pres. part.] *Gram.* Having the form of the passive or middle voice with an active meaning, as certain Latin and Greek verbs. — *n.* **1.** One who gives evidence, esp. in writing. **2.** *Gr. & Lat. Gram.* A deponent verb.

de·pop'u·late (dê·pŏp'ū̇·lāt), *adj. Archaic.* Depopulated.

de·pop'u·late (-lāt), *v. t.* [L. *depopulatus*, past part., deriv. of *de* + *populari* to ravage, fr. *populus* people.] **1.** *Obs.* To ravage. **2.** To deprive of inhabitants, as by war or pestilence. — **de·pop'u·la'tion** (-lā'shŭn), *n.* — **de·pop'u·la'tor** (-lā'tẽr), *n.*

de·port' (dê·pōrt'; 70), *v. t.* [F. *déporter* to behave; also, to transport (fr. L. *deportare* to carry away, fr. *de* + *portare* to carry).] **1.** To carry, conduct, or behave (oneself). **2.** To send into banishment; to exile. — **Syn.** See BEHAVE; BANISH. — *n. Obs.* Bearing; deportment.

de'por·ta'tion (dē'pōr·tā'shŭn; 70), *n.* **1.** Act of deporting; banishment. **2.** In modern law, the removal, from a country, of an alien not lawfully there or considered inimical to the public welfare.

de'por·tee' (dē'pōr·tē'), *n.* [F. *déporté* deported criminal.] A deported person, or one under sentence of deportation.

de·port'ment (dê·pōrt'mĕnt; 70), *n.* Manner of deporting oneself; behavior; conduct. — **Syn.** See BEARING.

de·pos'al (dê·pōz'ăl; -'l), *n.* Act of deposing from office.

de·pose' (dê·pōz'), *v. t.* [OF. *deposer*, in sense of L. *deponere* to put down, but fr. *de-* (fr. L. *de*) + *poser* to place.] **1.** To remove from a throne or other high station; deprive of office. **2.** To say under oath; testify, esp. by an affidavit. — *v. i.* To bear witness; testify. — **de·pos'a·ble** (-pōz'ȧ·b'l), *adj.*

de·pos'it (dê·pŏz'ĭt), *v. t.* [L. *depositus*, past part. of *deponere.* See DEPONE.] **1.** To lodge for safekeeping or as a pledge; to entrust; esp., to put on deposit in a bank. **2.** To lay down; to place; to put; to let fall (as sediment). — *v. i.* **1.** To be precipitated; to settle. **2.** To make a deposit. — *n.* **1.** State of being deposited in trust or safekeeping. **2.** That which is entrusted to the care of another; esp.: **a** Money lodged with a bank or banker, subject to order. **b** Anything given as a pledge or security. **3.** A depository. **4.** That which is deposited, or laid or thrown down. **5.** *Geol. & Mining.* A natural occurrence or accumulation of mineral material, as iron ore, oil, or gas.

de·pos'i·tar'y (-ĭ·tĕr'ĭ or, *esp. Brit.*, -tẽr·ĭ), *n.; pl.* -IES (-ĭz). **1.** The one receiving a deposit. **2.** A storehouse; a depository.

dep'o·si'tion (dĕp'ō̇·zĭsh'ŭn; dē'pō̇-), *n.* **1.** Act of deposing, as a sovereign. **2.** An opinion, example, or statement, laid down or asserted; testimony. **3.** Act or process of depositing. **4.** That which is deposited; sediment. **5.** *Law.* A testifying or testimony under oath, esp. in writing.

de·pos'i·tor (dê·pŏz'ĭ·tẽr), *n.* One who makes a deposit, esp. of money in a bank.

de·pos'i·to'ry (dē·pŏz'ĭ·tō'rĭ *or, esp. Brit.,* -tẽr·ĭ), *n.; pl.* -RIES (-rĭz). **1.** A place where anything is deposited, as for safekeeping or for sale. **2.** Depositary (sense 1).

de'pot (dē'pō *or, esp. mil. and Brit.,* dĕp'ō), *n.* [F. *dépôt,* fr. OF. *depost,* fr. L. *depositum* a deposit.] **1.** A place of deposit for goods; a storehouse. **2.** *U. S.* A railroad station. **3.** *Mil.* **a** A storage point for supplies. **b** A station where recruits are assembled and trained.

dep'ra·va'tion (dĕp'rȧ·vā'shŭn; dē'prȧ-), *n.* Act of depraving, or state of being depraved; corruption; depravity.

de·prave' (dē·prāv'), *v. t.* [OF. *depraver* to pervert, fr. L. *depravare, depravatum,* fr. *de* + *pravus* crooked, perverse, wicked.] **1.** To make bad; vitiate; corrupt. **2.** *Obs.* To speak ill of; to malign. — **Syn.** See DEBASE.

de·praved' (-prāvd'), *adj.* Characterized by corruption; esp., perverted; evil. — **de·prav'er** (-prāv'ẽr), *n.*

de·prav'i·ty (-prăv'ĭ·tĭ), *n.; pl.* -TIES (-tĭz). **1.** State of being depraved; corruption. **2.** A corrupt act or practice.

dep're·cate (dĕp'rē·kāt), *v. t.* [L. *deprecatus,* past part. of *deprecari* to avert by prayer, deprecate, fr. *de* + *precari* to pray.] **1.** To seek to avert, as by prayer. **2.** To express disapproval of. — **dep're·cat'ing·ly** (-kāt'ĭng·lĭ), *adv.* — **dep're·ca'tion** (-kā'shŭn), *n.*

dep're·ca'tive (-kā'tĭv), *adj.* Deprecatory. — **dep're·ca'tive·ly,** *adv.*

dep're·ca·to'ry (dĕp'rē·kȧ·tō'rĭ *or, esp. Brit.,* dĕp'rē·kā'tẽr·ĭ), *adj.* Serving to deprecate; hence, apologetic. — **dep're·ca·to'ri·ly,** *adv.* — **dep're·ca·to'ri·ness,** *n.*

de·pre'ci·a·ble (dē·prē'shĭ·ȧ·b'l), *adj.* That can or may be depreciated in valuation.

de·pre'ci·ate (dē·prē'shĭ·āt; 103), *v. t. & i.* [L. *depretiatus,* past part. of *depretiare* to depreciate, fr. *de* + *pretiare* to prize, fr. *pretium* price.] To lessen in price or estimated value; also, to undervalue; disparage; belittle. — **Syn.** See DECRY. — **Ant.** Appreciate.

de·pre'ci·a'tion (-shĭ·ā'shŭn; -sĭ·ā'shŭn), *n.* A decrease in value; specif.: **a** Of money, a reduction or loss in exchange value or purchasing power. **b** A lowering in estimation; disparagement. **c** *Accounting.* Decline in value of an asset due to such causes as wear or obsolescence.

de·pre'ci·a'tive (dē·prē'shĭ·ā'tĭv; -ȧ·tĭv), *adj.* Depreciatory. — **de·pre'ci·a'tive·ly,** *adv.*

de·pre'ci·a'tor (-ā'tẽr), *n.* [L.] One who depreciates.

de·pre'ci·a·to'ry (-ȧ·tō'rĭ *or, esp. Brit.,* -ā'tẽr·ĭ, -ȧ·tẽr·ĭ), *adj.* Tending to depreciate or disparage.

dep're·date (dĕp'rē·dāt), *v. t. & i.* [L. *depraedatus,* past part. of *depraedari,* fr. *de* + *praedari* to plunder, fr. *praeda* plunder, prey.] To plunder; to despoil. — **dep're·da'tor** (-dā'tẽr), *n.* — **dep're·da'to·ry** (-dā'tō·rĭ; dē·prĕd'ȧ·tō'rĭ *or, esp. Brit.,* -tẽr·ĭ), *adj.*

dep're·da'tion (-dā'shŭn), *n.* Act of despoiling; a ravaging.

de·press' (dē·prĕs'), *v. t.* [OF. *depresser,* fr. L. *depressus,* past part. of *deprimere,* fr. *de* + *premere* to press.] **1.** *Obs.* To suppress. **2.** To press down; to let fall; lower. **3.** To lessen the activity, force, etc., of; to make dull, as trade. **4.** To lower the pitch of, as the voice. **5.** To lessen in value or price; depreciate. **6.** To sadden. — **de·press'ing,** *adj.* — **de·press'ing·ly,** *adv.*

Syn. Depress, weigh down (*or* weigh on *or* upon), oppress mean to load a person or thing so heavily that he or it sinks under the weight. Depress now chiefly implies a lowering of spirits, of activity, or the like, by mental or physical causes; weigh down (*or* weigh on *or* weigh upon) stresses the imposition of difficulty or burden on a person or thing; oppress stresses the burden which is borne and its effect, such as a harassing or a subjection to misery.

de·pres'sant (dē·prĕs'ănt; -'nt), *adj.* Lowering functional or vital activity. — *n.* A depressant drug or other agent.

de·pressed' (dē·prĕst'), *adj.* **1.** Pressed down; hence, dejected; dispirited. **2.** Underprivileged. **3.** *Bot.* Vertically flattened; concave on the upper surface. **4.** *Zool.* Having the vertical diameter, as of the body, shorter than the horizontal.

depressed classes. The lowest Indian caste; the untouchables. *Brit.*

de·pres'sion (dē·prĕsh'ŭn), *n.* **1.** Act of depressing, or state of being depressed. **2.** A place or part that is depressed; a hollow. **3.** Dejection, as of mind. **4.** Reduction in amount, quality, or force; as, a phase of the business cycle marked by industrial and commercial stagnation, scarcity of goods and money, low prices, and mass unemployment. **5.** *Astron.* Angular distance of a celestial object below the horizon; negative altitude. **6.** *Med.* Lowering of vitality or functional activity. **7.** *Meteorol.* A low. **8.** *Psychopathol.* An abnormal state of inactivity and unpleasant emotion, as in manic-depressive insanity. **9.** *Surv.* The angular distance of an object beneath the horizontal plane that passes through the observer. — **Syn.** See SADNESS.

de·pres'sive (-prĕs'ĭv), *adj.* Tending to depress; characterized by depression. — **de·pres'sive·ly,** *adv.*

de·pres'so·mo'tor (dē·prĕs'ō·mō'tẽr; 2), *adj. Physiol.* Inhibiting movement, or motor response. — *n.* Any depressomotor agent, as bromides, etc.

de·pres'sor (dē·prĕs'ẽr), *n.* [NL.] **1.** One that depresses. **2.** *Anat.* A muscle that depresses or draws down a part. **3.** *Physiol.* A nerve (**depressor nerve**) that decreases the activity or tone of an organ. Cf. PRESSOR. **4.** *Surg.* An appliance for keeping a part, as the tongue, out of the way during an operation.

de·priv'al (dē·prīv'ăl), *n.* Act of depriving; deprivation.

dep'ri·va'tion (dĕp'rĭ·vā'shŭn), *n.* Act of depriving, dispossessing, or bereaving; specif., act of deposing; also, privation; loss.

de·prive' (dē·prīv'), *v. t.* [OF. *depriver,* fr. L. *de* + *privare* to bereave, deprive.] **1.** To dispossess; bereave; to hinder from possessing; debar. **2.** *Obs.* To put an end to; destroy. — **de·priv'a·ble** (-prīv'ȧ·b'l), *adj.*

‖**de pro·fun'dis** (dē prō·fŭn'dĭs). [L.] Out of the depths; — used of a cry from the depths of misery.

‖**de pro'pri·o mo'tu** (prō'prĭ·ō mō'tū). [L.] Of one's, or its, own motion; spontaneously.

dep'side (dĕp'sīd; -sĭd), *n.* Also **dep'sid.** [Gr. *depsein* to tan + *-ide.*] *Chem.* Any of a class of tanninlike condensation products of aromatic hydroxy acids.

depth (dĕpth), *n.* [From DEEP.] **1.** That which is deep; specif., the watery deep. **2.** An abyss. **3. a** Perpendicular measurement downward from the surface; as, the *depth* of a river. **b** Direct linear measurement from the point of view, as backward from the front. **4.** The midmost part, esp. of something that must be penetrated; also, the mid-time of a dark or cold season; as, the *depth* of night. **5.** Quality of being deep; deepness; hence, profoundness. **6. a** Lowness of pitch; as, *depth* of sound. **b** Degree of saturation and brilliance; — said of colors.

depth charge. An explosive projectile to be used against targets under water, especially submarines; — called also, erroneously, **depth bomb.**

dep'u·rate (dĕp'ū·rāt; dē·pū'-), *v. t. & i.* [ML. *depuratus,* past part. of *depurare* to purify, fr. L. *de* + *purare* to purify, fr. *purus* clean, pure.] To free or become free from impurities. — **dep'u·ra'tion** (dĕp'ū·rā'shŭn), *n.* — **dep'u·ra'tive** (dĕp'ū·rā'tĭv; dē·pū'rȧ·tĭv), *adj. & n.* — **dep'u·ra'tor** (-rā'tẽr), *n.*

dep'u·ta'tion (dĕp'ū·tā'shŭn), *n.* **1.** Appointment, as of a deputy; delegation. **2.** A person or persons deputed to act in one's behalf; a delegation. **3.** *Obs.* An appointment as gamekeeper, — often used as a way of giving hunting privileges.

de·pute' (dē·pūt'), *v. t.* [F. *députer,* fr. L. *deputare* to esteem, consider, in LL., to allot, fr. *de* + *putare* to reckon, think.] **1.** To appoint as deputy or agent; to delegate. **2.** To assign as to a deputy.

dep'u·tize (dĕp'ū·tīz), *v. t. & i.* To appoint, or to act, as deputy.

dep'u·ty (-tĭ), *n.; pl.* -TIES (-tĭz). [F. *député,* prop. past part.] **1.** One appointed to act for another; a substitute. **2.** A member of a legislative chamber known as the Chamber of Deputies. — **Syn.** See AGENT.

de·rac'i·nate (dē·răs'ĭ·nāt), *v. t.* [F. *déraciner,* fr. *dé-* (fr. L. *dis-*) + *racine* root, fr. L. *radix, radicis,* root.] To pluck up by the roots; extirpate. — **de·rac'i·na'tion** (-nā'shŭn), *n.*

de·raign' (dē·rān'), *v. t.* [OF. *deraisnier* to allege, plead, fr. *de-* (fr. L. *de*) + *raisnier* to speak, reason, deriv. of L. *ratio* reason.] *Now Rare. Law.* To prove or vindicate, esp. by wager of battle. — ***deraign battle, combat,*** etc. To battle; to array for battle.

de·rail' (dē·rāl'), *v. t.* [F. *dérailler,* fr. *dé-* (see DE-, 4) + *rail* rail, fr. E.] To cause to run off the rails. — **de·rail'ment,** *n.*

de·range' (dē·rānj'), *v. t.;* see RANGE. [F. *déranger,* fr. *dé-* (fr. L. *dis-*) + *ranger* to range.] **1.** To disorder; disarrange. **2.** To disturb in action or function, as a part or organ, or the whole of a machine or organism. **3.** To render insane.

de·ranged' (dē·rānjd'), *adj.* Disordered; insane.

de·range'ment (-rānj'mĕnt), *n.* Disarrangement; confusion; esp., mental disorder; insanity.

de·ray' (dē·rā'), *n.* [OF. *desrei,* fr. *des-* (fr. L. *dis-*) + *rei* order.] *Archaic.* Disorder; esp., disorderly merriment.

Der'by (dûr'bĭ *or, esp. for sense* 1, dûr'bĭ; *in England usually* där'bĭ), *n.* **1.** (*pron.* där'bĭ) A race for three-year-old horses, instituted in 1780 by the earl of Derby, and run annually at Epsom (near London) over a course 1½ miles and 29 yards long. **2.** (*pron.* dûr'bĭ *or* där'bĭ) A race or contest of similar prominence of its kind; as, the Kentucky *Derby.* **3.** [*not cap.*] A race or contest open to all comers; as, a trout *derby;* bicycle *derby.* **4.** (*pron.* dûr'bĭ; *Brit.* där'bĭ) [*not cap.*] A stiff felt hat with a dome-shaped crown; a bowler. **5.** [*not cap.*] *pl.* Handcuffs; darbies.

dere (dēr). Var. of DEAR, hard.

‖**de rè'gle** (dē rā'gl'). [F.] According to proper form.

der'e·lict (dĕr'ĕ·lĭkt), *adj.* [L. *derelictus,* past part. of *derelinquere* to abandon, fr. *de* + *relinquere* to leave.] **1.** Given up by the owner; abandoned. **2.** *Chiefly U. S.* Unfaithful; neglectful. — *n.* **1.** A vessel abandoned on the high seas and constituting a menace to navigation. **2.** *Law.* **a** A thing voluntarily abandoned. **b** A tract of land left dry by water receding from its former bed. **3.** A person abandoned, or outside the pale of respectable society; a "human wreck." **4.** *U. S.* One guilty of neglect of duty.

der'e·lic'tion (-lĭk'shŭn), *n.* **1.** Abandonment; an utter forsaking. **2.** State of being abandoned. **3.** A failure in duty; shortcoming. **4.** *Law.* A retiring of a body of water, so that land above high-water mark is gained.

de·ride' (dē·rīd'), *v. t.* [L. *deridere, derisum,* fr. *de* + *ridere* to laugh.] To laugh at with contempt; to mock. — **Syn.** See RIDICULE. — **de·rid'er** (-rīd'ẽr), *n.* — **de·rid'ing·ly,** *adv.*

‖**de ri'gueur'** (dē rē'gûr'). [F.] According to strict etiquette; obligatory for good form.

de·ris'i·ble (dē·rĭz'ĭ·b'l), *adj.* Worthy of derision or scorn.

de·ri'sion (dē·rĭzh'ŭn), *n.* **1.** Act of deriding, or state of being derided. **2.** An object of derision or scorn.

de·ri'sive (dē·rī'sĭv), *adj.* Expressing, serving for, or characterized by derision. — **de·ri'sive·ly,** *adv.* — **de·ri'sive·ness,** *n.*

de·ri'so·ry (dē·rī'sō·rĭ), *adj.* Derisive.

de·riv'a·ble (dē·rīv'ȧ·b'l), *adj.* That can be derived.

der'i·va'tion (dĕr'ĭ·vā'shŭn), *n.* **1.** Act or process of deriving or drawing from a source; transmission. **2.** That from which a thing is derived; origin. **3.** *Math.* The operation of deducing one function from another according to some fixed law. **4.** *Philol.* The development of a word from its more original or radical elements; also, the tracing or a statement of this process. — **der'i·va'tion·al,** *adj.*

de·riv'a·tive (dē·rĭv'ȧ·tĭv), *adj.* Derived, transmitted, or educed; hence, not radical, original, or fundamental. — *n.* **1.** Anything obtained or deduced from another. **2.** *Chem.* A substance so related to another substance by modification or partial substitution as to be regarded as derived from it, even when not obtainable from it in practice; thus, the amino compounds are *derivatives* of ammonia. **3.** *Gram.* **a** A word derived from another by any process of word development, as by adding a prefix or suffix. **b** = COMPOUND, *n.,* 3 **c.** — **de·riv'a·tive·ly,** *adv.*

de·rive' (dē·rīv'), *v. t.* [OF. *deriver,* fr. L. *derivare,* fr. *de* + *rivus* stream, brook.] **1.** To gather by inference; deduce. **2.** *Obs.* To cause to come; bring down (*upon*). **3.** To receive, as from a source or origin; — followed by *from;* as, a custom *derived* from paganism. **4.** To trace the origin, descent, or derivation of. **5.** *Chem.* To obtain by actual or theoretical substitution from another substance. — *v. i.* To take origin; to proceed; to be deduced. — **Syn.** See SPRING. — **de·riv'er** (-rīv'ẽr), *n.*

-derm (-dûrm). [Gr. *derma, -atos,* skin, fr. *derein* to flay.] A suffix signifying *skin, integument, covering,* as in blasto*derm,* ecto*derm.*

der'ma (dûr'mȧ), *n.* [NL. See -DERM.] *Anat. & Zool.* The sensitive layer of the skin beneath the epidermis. — **der'mal** (-măl), *adj.*

der'ma·to- (dûr'mȧ·tō-), **dermat-.** [See -DERM.] A combining form meaning *skin, hide,* as in **der'ma·ti'tis** (see -ITIS).

der·mat'o·gen (dẽr·măt'ō·jĕn; dûr'mȧ·tō·jĕn), *n.* [*dermato-* + *-gen.*] *Bot.* The thin external layer of primary meristem covering the growing points, esp. of roots, and giving rise to the epidermis.

der'ma·tol'o·gy (dûr'mȧ·tŏl'ō·jĭ), *n.* [*dermato-* + *-logy.*] The science which treats of the skin, its structure, functions, and diseases. —

der'ma·to·log'i·cal (dûr'mȧ·tō·lŏj'ĭ·kăl), adj. — **der'ma·tol'o·gist** (-tŏl'ṓ·jĭst), n.

der'ma·to·phyte' (dûr'mȧ·tō·fīt'), n. [dermato- + -phyte.] Med. Any fungus parasitic upon the skin of man or animals, as one (Trichophyton schoenleinii) causing favus. — **der'ma·to·phyt'ic** (-fĭt'ĭk), adj. — **der'ma·to·phy·to'sis** (-fī·tō'sĭs), n.

der'mis (dûr'mĭs), n. [NL. See -DERM.] Anat. The derma. — **der'mic** (-mĭk), adj.

der'mo- (dûr'mṓ-), derm-. = DERMATO-.

der'ni·er (dûr'nĭ·ẽr; F. dẽr'nyā'), adj. [F., fr. OF. derrenier, fr. derrain, fr. L. de + retro back, backward.] Last; final.

‖**der'nier' cri** (dẽr'nyā' krē'). [F.] Literally, latest cry; the latest word; also, the newest fashion.

‖**der'nier' res·sort'** (rĕ·sôr'). [F.] Last resort or expedient.

der'o·gate (dĕr'ṓ·gāt), adj. [L. derogatus, past part. of derogare to derogate, fr. de + rogare to ask, to ask the people about a law.] Rare. Derogated. — (-gāt), v. t. 1. Obs. To lessen; detract from; disparage. 2. Archaic. To take away (from) so as to cause injury or impairment. — v. i. 1. To take away; to detract; — usually with from. 2. To act beneath one's position or character. — **Syn.** See DECRY. — **der'o·gate·ly**, adv. Rare. — **der'o·ga'tion** (-gā'shŭn), n.

de·rog'a·tive (dḗ·rŏg'ȧ·tĭv), adj. Tending to derogate; derogatory; disparaging. — **de·rog'a·tive·ly**, adv.

de·rog'a·to·ry (-tō'rĭ or, esp. Brit., -tẽr·ĭ), adj. 1. Disparaging; detracting. 2. Expressive of derogation, esp. of low estimation or disdain; — of a word or usage. — **de·rog'a·to·ri·ly**, adv. — **-ri·ness**, n.

der'rick (dĕr'ĭk), n. [From a hangman named Derrick, early 17th century.] 1. Any of various hoisting apparatus employing a tackle rigged at the end of a spar or beam. 2. The framework or tower over a deep drill hole, as an oil well, for supporting the tackle for boring or hoisting or lowering.

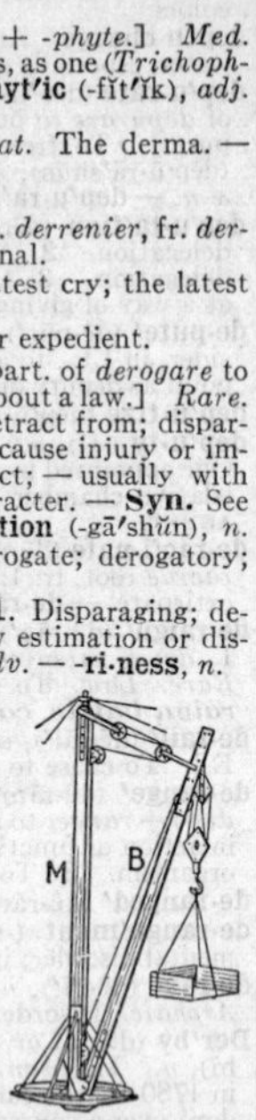

der'ring–do' (dĕr'ĭng·dōō'), n. Daring action; — used as an (erroneous) archaism.

der'rin·ger (dĕr'ĭn·jẽr), n. [After Henry Deringer, Amer. inventor.] A short-barreled pocket pistol of large caliber.

der'ris (dĕr'ĭs), n. [NL., fr. Gr. derris a leather covering.] A plant or root of an Old World genus (Derris), of the pea family, several East Indian species of which yield toxic products, esp. rotenone, used as fish or arrow poisons or as insecticides.

der'ry (dĕr'ĭ), n. A meaningless refrain word in old songs; — sometimes **der'ry–down'** (-doun'); hence, a ballad.

Derrick, 1. M Mast; B Boom.

der'vish (dûr'vĭsh), n. [Turk. dervīsh, fr. Per. darvīsh beggar.] A member of any of various Moslem orders taking vows of poverty and austerity, and living in monasteries or wandering as friars.

des'cant (dĕs'kănt), n. [OF. and L.; OF. deschant, fr. ML. discantus, fr. L. dis- + cantus singing, melody, fr. canere to sing.] 1. Music. **a** Originally, a melody or counterpoint sung above the plain song of the tenor. **b** The art of composing or singing part music; also, the music so composed or sung. **c** The soprano or treble. 2. A song or strain of melody. 3. A discourse or comment on a theme, like variations on a musical air; also, a dissertation.

des·cant' (dĕs·kănt'), v. i. 1. Music. **a** To sing or play a descant. **b** To sing. 2. To discourse at length.

de·scend' (dḗ·sĕnd'), v. i. [OF. descendre, fr. L. descendere, descensum, fr. de + scandere to climb.] 1. To pass from a higher to a lower place; hence, to proceed in any series from a higher or more distant to a lower or nearer point; — opposed to ascend. 2. To pass in discourse from the more general or important to the particular or less important. 3. To come down, as from a source, original, or stock; also, to fall or pass by inheritance. 4. To make an attack, or incursion, esp. suddenly and violently. 5. To come down in the social, mental, or moral scale. 6. Astron. To move toward the south; also, to approach the horizon. — v. t. To come down or along. — **de·scend'i·ble** (-sĕn'dĭ·b'l), also **de·scend'a·ble** (-dȧ·b'l), adj.

de·scend'ant (dḗ·sĕn'dȧnt), adj. Descendent. — n. One who descends, as offspring, however remotely; — opposed to ancestor.

de·scend'ent (-dĕnt), adj. 1. Descending. 2. Proceeding from an ancestor or source.

de·scen'sion (dḗ·sĕn'shŭn), n. Now Rare. Descent.

de·scent' (dḗ·sĕnt'), n. [OF. descente, fr. descendre.] 1. Act of descending; change from higher to lower. 2. Derivation, as from an ancestor; lineage; pedigree. Cf. CONSANGUINITY, Illust. 3. A degree in the scale of genealogy; generation. 4. A downward step in station, virtue, value, etc.; decline. 5. Inclination downward; slope; hence, a descending way, as a stairway. 6. Incursion; sudden attack; onslaught. 7. Law. Transmission of an estate by inheritance.

de·scribe' (dḗ·skrīb'), v. t. [L. describere, descriptum, fr. de + scribere to write.] 1. To represent by words; to give an account of. 2. To trace or traverse the outline of; as, to describe a circle. 3. By confusion, for DESCRY. — **Syn.** Relate, recount, narrate. — **de·scrib'a·ble** (-skrīb'ȧ·b'l), adj. — **de·scrib'er** (-ẽr), n.

de·scrip'tion (dḗ·skrĭp'shŭn), n. 1. Discourse, or an example of it, designed to give a mental image of a scene, person, emotional situation, etc. 2. The characterizing features of a class; also, a class, sort, or type. 3. The tracing or traversing of a course. — **Syn.** See TYPE.

de·scrip'tive (-tĭv), adj. 1. Serving to describe; characterized by description; as, a descriptive science, or branch of a science, that is, one which recounts, characterizes, or classifies the material of the science. 2. Gram. **a** Of an adjunct, expressing quality, kind, or condition; as, a descriptive adjective (red rose). **b** Specif., of an adjective clause, conveying a qualification or statement that is simply additional or parenthetic and not essential to the definiteness of the meaning of the antecedent (the older boys, who work, eat before the others); — opp. to restrictive. — **de·scrip'tive·ly**, adv. — **de·scrip'tive·ness**, n.

descriptive geometry. That branch of geometry which provides a graphic solution of a three-dimensional problem by means of projections upon two mutually perpendicular auxiliary planes.

de·scry' (dḗ·skrī'), v. t.; DE·SCRIED' (-skrīd'); DE·SCRY'ING. [ME., fr. OF. descrier to proclaim, decry.] 1. To spy out or discover by the eye, as objects distant or obscure; hence, to discern or discover by observation or investigation; detect. 2. Obs. To reveal.

Des'de·mo'na (dĕz'dḗ·mō'nȧ), n. See OTHELLO.

des'e·crate (dĕs'ḗ·krāt), v. t. [de- + -secrate (as in consecrate).] To vio-

late the sanctity of; to profane. Cf. CONSECRATE. — **des'e·crat'er** (-krāt'ẽr), **des'e·cra'tor** (-krā'tẽr), n.

des'e·cra'tion (dĕs'ḗ·krā'shŭn), n. Act or instance of desecrating; profanation. — **Syn.** See PROFANATION.

de·seg're·gate (dḗ·sĕg'rḗ·gāt), v. t. & i. [de- + segregate.] To free (itself) of any law, provision, or practice requiring isolation of the members of a particular race in separate units, esp. in military service or in education. — **de'seg·re·ga'tion** (dḗ'sĕg·rḗ·gā'shŭn), n.

de·sen'si·tize (dḗ·sĕn'sĭ·tīz), v. t. [de- + sensitize.] To render insensitive; specif.: **a** Physiol. To render insensitive to, or cause to become nonreactive to, the action of a serum, antitoxin, etc. **b** Photog. To render insensitive to light. **c** Psychiatry. To render immune to a morbid emotional domination; to free from a neurotic state. — **de·sen'si·ti·za'tion** (-tĭ·zȧ'shŭn; -tī·zā'-), n. — **de·sen'si·tiz'er** (-tīz'ẽr), n.

de·sert' (dḗ·zûrt'), n. [OF. deserte, fr. deservir to merit. See DESERVE.] 1. Worthiness of reward or punishment; merit or demerit. 2. That which is deserved; due reward or punishment. 3. Excellence; worth; also, a worthy deed.

des'ert (dĕz'ẽrt), n. [OF., fr. LL. desertum, fr. L. desertus solitary, desert, past part. of deserere to desert, fr. de + serere to join together.] 1. A deserted region; a region left unoccupied. 2. An arid region lacking moisture to support vegetation. — adj. 1. (pron. dḗ·zûrt') Archaic. Forsaken. 2. Of or pertaining to a desert; waste; barren.

de·sert' (dḗ·zûrt'), v. t. 1. To leave in the lurch; to abandon; also, to fail (one) at need; as, his courage deserted him. 2. Mil. & Nav. To abandon (the service) without leave. — **Syn.** See ABANDON. — v. i. To abandon a service, esp. the military or naval service, without leave. — **de·sert'er**, n.

de·ser'tion (dḗ·zûr'shŭn), n. 1. Act of deserting; abandonment of a service, a party, a wife, or any post of duty. 2. State of being forsaken; desolation.

de·serve' (dḗ·zûrv'), v. t. & i. [OF. deservir to merit, fr. L. deservire to serve zealously, fr. de + servire to serve.] To earn; to be worthy of (either good or evil); to merit. — **de·serv'er**, n.

de·served' (dḗ·zûrvd'), adj. Such as one deserves. — **de·serv'ed·ly** (-zûr'vĕd·lĭ; -vĭd·lĭ), adv. — **de·serv'ed·ness**, n.

de·serv'ing (-zûr'vĭng), n. Desert; merit. — adj. Meritorious; worthy. — **de·serv'ing·ly**, adv. — **de·serv'ing·ness**, n.

des'ha·bille' (dĕz'ȧ·bēl'), n. Dishabille.

des'ic·cant (dĕs'ĭ·kănt), adj. Drying. — n. A drying agent.

des'ic·cate (-kāt), v. t. & i. [L. desiccatus, past part. of desiccare to dry up, fr. de + siccare to dry, fr. siccus dry.] To dry up; to preserve by drying, as fish, fruit, or eggs. — **des'ic·ca'tion** (-kā'shŭn), n. — **des'ic·ca'tive** (dĕs'ĭ·kā'tĭv; dḗ·sĭk'ȧ·tĭv), adj. & n. — **des'ic·ca'tor** (dĕs'ĭ·kā'tẽr), n.

de·sid'er·a'ta (dḗ·sĭd'ẽr·ā'tȧ), n., pl. of DESIDERATUM.

de·sid'er·ate (dḗ·sĭd'ẽr·āt; dḗ·zĭd'-), v. t. [L. desideratus, past part. of desiderare to desire, miss.] To regard as a desideratum. — **de·sid'er·a'tive** (dḗ·sĭd'ẽr·ā'tĭv; dḗ·zĭd'-; -ȧ·tĭv), adj. & n.

de·sid'er·a'tum (-ā'tŭm), n.; pl. -ATA (-tȧ). [L.] Anything desired as essential or needed.

de·sign' (dḗ·zīn'), v. t. [F. désigner, fr. L. designare, fr. de + signare to mark, mark out, fr. signum mark, sign.] 1. To designate; as: **a** Archaic. To indicate, as by a mark or name. **b** To appoint or assign, as to an office or a given use. 2. To assign, or set apart, as for a purpose; also, to intend; to mean; as, designed for one's good. 3. To plan mentally; to outline; to scheme; — distinguished from execute. 4. To fashion according to a plan; specif.: **a** Obs. To picture. **b** To sketch as a pattern or model. **c** To execute as a whole. — v. i. To conceive or execute a scheme or plan.
— n. [F. dessein, fr. It. disegno, fr. disegnare to design, fr. L. designare.] 1. A plan; scheme. 2. Purpose in view; aim; intention. 3. A secret, usually underhanded, scheme; plot; also, deliberate scheming. 4. Art. **a** A sketch of something to be executed; a delineation; plan. **b** The arrangement of details which make up a work of art. — **Syn.** See PLAN; INTENTION.

des'ig·nate (dĕz'ĭg·nāt; dĕs'-), adj. [L. designatus, past part. of designare.] Designated. — (-nāt), v. t. 1. To mark out and make known; to indicate; show; specify. 2. To name; characterize. 3. To indicate or set apart for a purpose. — **des'ig·na'tor** (-nā'tẽr), n.

des'ig·na'tion (-nā'shŭn), n. 1. Act of designating; indication. 2. Appointment for a specific purpose. 3. A distinguishing mark, or title; appellation. — **des'ig·na'tive** (dĕz'ĭg·nā'tĭv; dĕs'-), adj.

de·signed' (dḗ·zīnd'), adj. Done by design or purposely. — **de·sign'ed·ly** (-zīn'ĕd·lĭ; -ĭd·lĭ), adv.

des'ig·nee' (dĕz'ĭg·nē'), n. One who is designated.

de·sign'er (dḗ·zīn'ẽr), n. 1. One who designs, or plans; also, a plotter; schemer. 2. Fine Arts. One who produces original works of art.

de·sign'ing, n. Act or art of making designs; also, act of marking out, appointing, planning, plotting, etc. — adj. **a** Planning; foreseeing. **b** Intriguing; artful; scheming. — **de·sign'ing·ly**, adv.

de·sign'ment (-mĕnt), n. Obs. Plan; purpose.

de·sir'a·ble (dḗ·zīr'ȧ·b'l), adj. Worthy of desire, longing, or choice; pleasing; agreeable. — **de·sir'a·bil'i·ty** (-bĭl'ĭ·tĭ), n. — **de·sir'a·ble·ness**, n. — **de·sir'a·bly** (-blĭ), adv.

de·sire' (dḗ·zīr'), v. t. [OF. desirer, fr. L. desiderare.] 1. To long for; covet. 2. To express a wish for or to. — v. i. To have or feel desire.
Syn. Desire, wish, want, crave, covet mean to long for. Desire usually stresses ardor, but sometimes striving; wish, especially in poetic language, connotes longing for the unattainable, but is sometimes used as less formal than desire; want, long regarded as colloquial and not to be used in place of wish unless need or lack was also implied, is now frequently used in place of wish when a less formal term is desired (as, the senator does not want [or wish] renomination); crave often definitely implies the impulsion of physical or mental appetite or need; covet implies eager or inordinate longing often, but far from invariably for something that belongs to another.
— n. 1. A longing; a craving. 2. An expressed wish; a request. 3. Anything desired.

de·sir'ous (dḗ·zīr'ŭs), adj. 1. Impelled or governed by desire; covetous. 2. Dial. Desirable; delectable.

de·sist' (dḗ·zĭst'), v. i. [OF. desister, fr. L. desistere, fr. de + sistere to stand, stop, fr. stare to stand.] To cease to proceed or act; to stop. — **Syn.** See STOP. — **de·sist'ance** (-ȧns), n.

desk (dĕsk), n. [ML. desca, fr. It. desco desk, table, fr. L. discus disk, LL., table.] 1. A table, frame, or case with a sloping or a flat top, for the use of writers, readers, etc. **2.** A reading table or lectern to support the book from which the liturgical service is read; also (esp. in the United States), a pulpit; hence, the clerical profession.

des'man (dĕz'măn), *n.; pl.* -MANS (-mănz). [Sw., musk.] A molelike, aquatic, insectivorous mammal (*Desmana moschata*) of Russia.

des'mid (dĕz'mĭd), *n.* Also **des·mid'i·an** (dĕz·mĭd'ĭ·ăn). [Dim. fr. Gr. *desmos* chain.] *Bot.* Any of a family (Desmidiaceae) of microscopic unicellular fresh-water algae.

des'moid (dĕz'moid), *adj.* [Gr. *desmos* chain + *-oid.*] Ligamentous; fibroid. — *n.* A dense connective-tissue tumor.

Des Moines squash (dĕ moin'). = ACORN SQUASH.

des'o·late (dĕs'ō·lĭt), *adj.* [L. *desolatus*, past part. of *desolare* to leave alone, forsake, fr. *de* + *solare* to make lonely, fr. *solus* alone.] **1.** Destitute, or deprived, of inhabitants; deserted; hence, gloomy. **2.** Laid waste; in a ruinous condition; as, *desolate* altars. **3.** Left alone; forsaken; lonely. — **Syn.** See ALONE. — (-lāt), *v. t.* To make desolate; as: **a** To deprive of inhabitants. **b** To lay waste; ravage. **c** To forsake. **d** To make wretched. — **des'o·late·ly**, *adv.* — **des'o·late·ness**, *n.* — **des'o·lat'er** (-lāt'ẽr), **des'o·la'tor** (-lā'tẽr), *n.*

des'o·la'tion (-lā'shŭn), *n.* **1.** Act of desolating, or laying waste; ruin; also, solitariness; gloominess. **2.** Hence, a place or country wasted and forsaken. **3.** Grief; woe. **4.** Loss of companionship; loneliness.

de·spair' (dē·spâr'), *v. i.* [OF. *desperer* (3d sing. pres. *il despeire*), fr. L. *desperare*, fr. *de* + *sperare* to hope.] To be hopeless; to give up hope. — *v. t. Archaic.* To despair of. — *n.* **1.** Loss of hope; hopelessness. **2.** That which is despaired of, or which causes despair.

de·spair'ing, *adj.* Feeling or expressing despair. — **Syn.** See DESPONDENT. — **de·spair'ing·ly**, *adv.* — **de·spair'ing·ness**, *n.*

des·patch', des·patch'er. Vars. of DISPATCH, etc.

des'per·a'do (dĕs'pẽr·ā'dō; -ä'dō), *n.; pl.* -DOES or -DOS (-dōz). [OSp., past part.] A desperate criminal or lawbreaker.

des'per·ate (dĕs'pẽr·ĭt), *adj.* [L. *desperatus*, past part. of *desperare.* See DESPAIR.] **1.** *Archaic.* Without hope; in despair. **2.** Beyond or almost beyond hope; causing despair. **3.** Proceeding from, or directed by, despair; rash; reckless; frantic. **4.** Extreme; often, outrageous. — **Syn.** See DESPONDENT. — **-ly**, *adv.* — **-ness**, *n.*

des'per·a'tion (-ā'shŭn), *n.* **1.** *Rare.* Act of despairing; a giving up of hope. **2.** A state of despair or hopelessness leading to recklessness.

des'pi·ca·ble (dĕs'pĭ·kȧ·b'l; *formerly, and still occas.*, dĕs·pĭk'ȧ·b'l), *adj.* [LL. *despicabilis*, fr. *despicari* to despise.] Fit or deserving to be despised; contemptible. — **Syn.** See CONTEMPTIBLE. — **des'pi·ca·ble·ness**, *n.* — **des'pi·ca·bly** (-blĭ), *adv.*

de·spight', de·spight'ful, etc. Obs. vars. of DESPITE, etc.

de·spise' (dē·spīz'), *v. t.* [OF. *despis-*, in some forms of *despire* to despise, fr. L. *despicere, despectum*, to despise, fr. *de* + *spicere, specere*, to look.] To look down upon with disfavor or contempt; to contemn. — **de·spis'er** (-spīz'ẽr), *n.*

Syn. Despise, contemn, scorn, disdain, scout mean to regard a person or thing as beneath one's notice. **Despise** may imply any emotional reaction from strong distaste to loathing; **contemn** implies even a harsher judgment than despise; **scorn** implies quick, indignant, or profound contempt; **disdain** implies an arrogant aversion to what is, or seems to be, base; **scout** implies a derisive refusal to consider a person or thing of any value, efficacy, or the like.

de·spite' (dē·spīt'), *n.* [OF. *despit*, fr. L. *despectus* contempt, fr. *despicere.* See DESPISE.] **1.** *Archaic.* Scorn; contempt; also, malice; spite. **2.** Act of insult, malice, hatred, or defiance; highhanded abuse or injury. — ***in despite of.*** In defiance of; in spite of. — *v. t.* **1.** *Archaic.* To despise. **2.** *Obs.* To vex; enrage. — *prep.* In spite of; notwithstanding.

de·spite'ful (-fo͝ol; -f'l), *adj.* Full of despite; insulting. — **de·spite'ful·ly**, *adv.* — **de·spite'ful·ness**, *n.*

des·pit'e·ous (dĕs·pĭt'ē·ŭs), *adj.* Feeling or showing despite; malicious. — **des·pit'e·ous·ly**, *adv.*

de·spoil' (dē·spoil'), *v. t.* [OF. *despoillier*, fr. L. *despoliare, despoliatum*, fr. *de* + *spoliare* to strip, rob, fr. *spolium* spoil.] To strip of belongings, or the like; pillage. — **Syn.** See RAVAGE. — **de·spoil'er**, *n.* — **de·spoil'ment**, *n.*

de·spo'li·a'tion (dē·spō'lĭ·ā'shŭn), *n.* Spoliation; pillage.

de·spond' (dē·spŏnd'), *v. i.* [L. *despondere* to promise away, give up, lose (courage), fr. *de* + *spondere* to promise solemnly.] To become discouraged or disheartened. — *n. Rare.* Despondency.

de·spond'ence (dē·spŏn'dĕns), *n.* Despondency.

de·spond'en·cy (-dĕn·sĭ), *n.* State of being despondent; loss of hope and cessation of effort; dejection of mind.

de·spond'ent (-dĕnt), *adj.* [L. *despondens*, pres. part.] Marked by, or given to, despondency. — **de·spond'ent·ly**, *adv.*

Syn. Despondent, despairing, desperate, hopeless mean having lost all or nearly all hope. **Despondent** implies deep dejection arising out of a loss of hope and a conviction of the uselessness of further efforts; **despairing** implies the passing of all hope and, often, accompanying despondency; **desperate** implies despair, but not the cessation of effort, for it often applies to struggles in the face of defeat or frustration; **hopeless** suggests despair and the cessation of effort, often implying acceptance or resignation.

de·spond'ing, *adj.* Despondent. — **de·spond'ing·ly**, *adv.*

des'pot (dĕs'pŏt), *n.* [OF., fr. Gr. *despotēs* master, lord.] **1.** A title signifying "master" or "lord," formerly applied to: **a** The Byzantine emperor and princes. **b** Bishops and patriarchs of the Greek Church. **c** Hereditary princes, nobles, or military leaders in the Italian cities, esp. of the 14th and 15th centuries. **2.** An absolute ruler; autocrat; now, usually, a tyrant.

des·pot'ic (dĕs·pŏt'ĭk), *adj.* Also **des·pot'i·cal** (-ĭ·kăl). Having the character of, or pertaining to, a despot; tyrannical; arbitrary. — **des·pot'i·cal·ly**, *adv.*

des'pot·ism (dĕs'pŏt·ĭz'm), *n.* **1.** The power, spirit, or principles of a despot; tyranny. **2.** A government directed by a despot.

des'qua·mate (dĕs'kwȧ·māt; dē·skwā'māt), *v. i.* [L. *desquamatus*, past part. of *desquamare* to scale off, fr. *de* + *squama* scale.] *Med.* To peel off in scales. — **des'qua·ma'tion** (dĕs'kwȧ·mā'shŭn), *n.*

des·sert' (dĭ·zûrt'; *the dialectal* dĕz'ẽrt *is still common*), *n.* [F., fr. *desservir* to remove from table, clear the table, fr. *des-* (fr. L. *dis-*) + *servir* to serve.] **a** *U. S.* A course of fruit, pastry, pudding, ice cream, or the like, served at the close of a meal. **b** *Eng.* Fruits served after pudding, cake, etc. — **des·sert'**, *adj.*

des·sert'spoon' (-spo͞on'), *n.* A spoon used in eating dessert. It is intermediate in size between a teaspoon and a tablespoon. — **des·sert'spoon·ful'** (-fo͝ol'), *n.*

des'sia·tine (dĕs'yȧ·tēn), *n.* [Russ. *desyatina.*] A Russian measure of surface equal to 2.7 acres.

de·ster'i·lize (dē·stĕr'ĭ·līz), *v. t.* To release from sterilization and return to useful service, as gold from an insulated condition in the treasury to use as a basis for issuance of additional currency certificates. — **de·ster'i·li·za'tion** (-lĭ·zā'shŭn; -lī·zā'-), *n.*

des'ti·na'tion (dĕs'tĭ·nā'shŭn), *n.* **1.** Act of destining, or appointing. **2.** Purpose for which anything is destined. **3.** The place set for the end of a journey, or to which something is sent.

des'tine (dĕs'tĭn), *v. t.* [OF. *destiner*, fr. L. *destinare.*] **1.** To decree beforehand, as by divine will; to predetermine; often, *passive*, to be fated; as, a plan *destined* to fail. **2.** To ordain, appoint, design; to designate; specif., *passive*, to be bound or directed; as, a vessel *destined* for London.

des'ti·ny (dĕs'tĭ·nĭ), *n.; pl.* -NIES (-nĭz). [OF. *destinee*, fr. *destiner.*] **1.** That to which any person or thing is destined. **2.** The predetermined course of events often conceived as a resistless power or agency; fate. **3.** [*cap.*] The goddess of destiny; *pl.*, the three Fates. — **Syn.** See FATE.

des'ti·tute (dĕs'tĭ·tūt), *adj.* [L. *destitutus*, past part. of *destituere* to set away, leave alone, forsake, fr. *de* + *statuere* to set.] **1.** *Obs.* Abandoned; forsaken. **2.** Bereft or not in possession (of something necessary or desirable); lacking. **3.** Not possessing the necessaries of life; in condition of extreme want.

des'ti·tu'tion (-tū'shŭn), *n.* State of being destitute; extreme poverty. — **Syn.** See POVERTY.

des'tri·er (dĕs'trĭ·ẽr; dĕs·trēr'), *n.* [AF. *destrer*, OF. *destrier*, fr. L. *dextra* right hand.] *Archaic.* A war horse.

de·stroy' (dē·stroi'), *v. t.* [OF. *destruire*, deriv. of L. *destruere, -structum*, fr. *de* + *struere* to pile up, build.] **1.** To ruin the structure, organic existence, or condition of; to demolish. **2.** To bring to naught by putting out of existence; to kill; to abolish; to nullify.

de·stroy'er (-ẽr), *n.* **1.** One who destroys, ruins, kills, or desolates. **2.** *Nav.* A small, speedy war vessel, armed with guns, torpedoes, and, usually, depth charges.

destroyer escort. See DE, in *Vocab.*

de·struct'i·ble (dē·strŭk'tĭ·b'l), *adj.* Capable of being destroyed. — **de·struct'i·bil'i·ty** (-bĭl'ĭ·tĭ), *n.*

de·struc'tion (dē·strŭk'shŭn), *n.* **1.** Act of destroying; demolition; ruin. **2.** Condition of being destroyed. **3.** A destroying agency.

de·struc'tion·ist, *n.* **1.** One who delights in destroying. **2.** An advocate of destroying existing institutions.

de·struc'tive (dē·strŭk'tĭv), *adj.* **1.** Causing destruction; ruinous. **2.** Designed or tending to destroy. — **de·struc'tive·ly**, *adv.* — **de·struc'tive·ness**, *n.*

destructive distillation. The process of decomposing a substance (as wood, coal, bone) in a closed vessel by means of heat, and collecting the volatile products evolved.

de'struc·tiv'i·ty (dē'strŭk·tĭv'ĭ·tĭ), *n.* Destructiveness.

de·struc'tor (dē·strŭk'tẽr), *n.* [LL., fr. *destruere.* See DESTROY.] A furnace for burning refuse.

des'ue·tude (dĕs'wē·tūd *or, esp. Brit.*, dē'swē-), *n.* [L. *desuetudo*, fr. *desuescere* to grow out of use, fr. *de* + *suescere* to become accustomed.] State of disuse.

de·sul'fur (dē·sŭl'fẽr), *v. t.* To desulfurize.

de·sul'fu·rize (dē·sŭl'fū·rīz; -fẽr·īz), *v. t.* Also **de·sul'fu·rate** (-fū·rāt). To remove sulfur from. — **de·sul'fu·ri·za'tion** (-rĭ·zā'shŭn; -ĭ·zā'shŭn; -rī·zā'shŭn; -ī·zā'-), *n.* — **de·sul'fu·riz'er** (-rīz'ẽr; -īz'ẽr), *n.*

de·sul'phur, de·sul'phu·rize, etc. Vars. of DESULFUR, etc.

des'ul·to'ry (dĕs'ŭl·tō'rĭ *or, esp. Brit.*, -tẽr·ĭ), *adj.* [L. *desultorius*, fr. *desultor* a leaper, fr. *desilire, desultum*, to leap down, fr. *de* + *salire* to leap.] **1.** Jumping, or passing, from one thing or subject to another, without order or rational connection; aimless; as, *desultory* reading. **2.** Out of course; by the way; as a digression; as, a *desultory* remark. — **Syn.** See RANDOM. — **des'ul·to'ri·ly** (-rĭ·lĭ; *emphatic also* -tō'rĭ·lĭ), *adv.* — **des'ul·to'ri·ness** (-rĭ·nĕs; -nĭs), *n.*

de·tach' (dē·tăch'), *v. t.* [F. *détacher.*] To part; to separate or disunite; disengage. — **Ant.** Attach. — **de·tach'a·bil'i·ty** (-ȧ·bĭl'ĭ·tĭ), *n.* — **de·tach'a·ble**, *adj.* — **de·tach'er**, *n.*

de·tached' (dē·tăcht'), *adj.* Separate; unconnected; also, aloof. — **Syn.** See INDIFFERENT.

de·tach'ment (dē·tăch'mĕnt), *n.* **1.** Act of detaching; separation. **2.** Dispatch of a body of troops or part of a fleet from the main body on special service; also, the portion so dispatched. **3.** Isolation; aloofness; specif., indifference to worldly concerns or partisan opinion.

de·tail' (dē·tāl'; dē'tāl), *n.* [F. *détail*, fr. *détailler* to cut in pieces, tell in detail, fr. *dé-* (fr. L. *de*) + *tailler* to cut.] **1.** A narrative which relates minute points; also, itemizing; as, to go into *detail.* **2.** A small part; an item. **3.** *Arch. & Mach.* **a** A minor part, as, in a building, the cornice, caps of the buttresses, capitals of the columns, etc., or (called ***larger details***) a porch, a gable, etc. **b** In full, **detail drawing**, a separate drawing of a small part of a machine, structure, etc. **4.** *Mil.* Selection for some special service; also, the person or body of persons selected. — **Syn.** See ITEM. — ***in detail.*** Item by item; circumstantially. — (dē·tāl'), *v. t.* **1.** To relate in particulars; to report minutely and distinctly. **2.** *Chiefly Mil.* To tell off or appoint for a particular service, as an officer or a squad of soldiers.

de·tailed' (dē·tāld'; dē'tāld), *adj.* Circumstantially told, drawn, or the like; full of details. — **Syn.** See CIRCUMSTANTIAL.

de·tain' (dē·tān'), *v. t.* [OF. *detenir*, fr. L. *detinere, detentum*, fr. *de* + *tenere* to hold.] **1.** To hold or keep as in custody. **2.** To keep back; to withhold, as that which is due. **3.** To restrain, esp. from proceeding; to delay. — **Syn.** See KEEP; DELAY. — **de·tain'er**, *n.* — **de·tain'ment**, *n.*

de·tain'er (-ẽr), *n.* [OF. *detenir*, inf. used as a n.] *Law.* **a** A keeping in one's possession, esp. of what is another's. **b** A writ authorizing the keeper of a prison to continue to keep a person in custody.

de·tect' (dē·tĕkt'), *v. t.* [L. *detectus*, past part. of *detegere* to uncover, detect, fr. *de* + *tegere* to cover.] **1.** *Now Rare.* To uncover; reveal. **2.** To discover the character or action of. **3.** To discover the existence, presence, or fact of (something hidden or obscure). **4.** *Radio.* To rectify, as in a detector. — **de·tect'a·ble, de·tect'i·ble**, *adj.*

de·tec'ta·phone (dē·tĕk'tȧ·fōn), *n.* A telephonic apparatus with an attached microphone transmitter, used esp. for listening secretly.

de·tec'tion (dē·tĕk'shŭn), *n.* **1.** Act of detecting; discovery. **2.** *Radio.* **a** Rectification, as in a detector. **b** Conversion of a modulated wave or current into the original signal wave or current.

de·tec'tive (dē·tĕk'tĭv), *adj.* Fitted for, employed for, or concerned with, detection. — *n.* One who detects; specif., one employed in detecting lawbreakers.

de·tec'tor (dē·tĕk'tẽr), *n.* [LL., a revealer.] **1.** One who detects. **2.** One that detects; as: **a** An indicator showing the depth of the water in a boiler. **b** *Elec.* (1) A galvanometer for indicating the direction of a current. (2) Any device for detecting the presence of electric waves. **c** *Radio.* A device for rectifying high-frequency electric current, as to vibrate a telephone-receiver diaphragm which of itself will not respond to such high frequencies.

de·tent' (dē·tĕnt'; dē'tĕnt), *n.* [F. *détente,* fr. *détendre* to unbend, relax, fr. *dé-* (fr. L. *dis-*) + *tendre* to stretch, fr. L. *tendere.*] *Mech.* That which locks or unlocks a movement; a catch, pawl, dog, or click. See JACK, *Illust.*

‖**dé'tente'** (dā'täɴt'), *n.* [F.] A relaxing, as of strained relations between nations.

de·ten'tion (dē·tĕn'shŭn), *n.* **1.** Act of detaining; a keeping back; also, a holding back of an action or progress. **2.** State of being detained; forced delay.

‖**dé'te·nu'** (dāt'nü'), *n. masc.,* ‖**dé'te·nue'** (-nü'), *fem.* [F.] A detained person; a prisoner.

de·ter' (dē·tûr'), *v. t.;* DE·TERRED' (-tûrd'); DE·TER'RING. [L. *deterrere,* fr. *de* + *terrere* to frighten, terrify.] To turn aside or discourage through fear; hence, to prevent from action by fear of consequences. — **de·ter'ment,** *n.*

de·terge' (dē·tûrj'), *v. t.;* DE·TERGED' (-tûrjd'); DE·TERG'ING (-tûr'jĭng). [F. or L.; F. *déterger,* fr. L. *detergere, detersum,* fr. *de* + *tergere* to wipe off.] To cleanse; to purge away, as foul matter.

de·ter'gence (dē·tûr'jĕns), *n.* Detergency.

de·ter'gen·cy (-jĕn·sĭ), *n.* Cleansing quality or power.

de·ter'gent (-jĕnt), *adj.* Cleansing; purging. — *n.* A cleansing agent, as water, soap, or a soluble or liquid preparation ("soapless soap"), usually synthetic, that resembles soap in the ability to emulsify oils and hold dirt in suspension.

de·te'ri·o·rate (dē·tēr'ĭ·ō·rāt), *v. t. & i.* [LL. *deterioratus,* past part. of *deteriorare* to deteriorate, fr. *deterior* worse.] To make or grow worse; to impair; degenerate. — **de·te'ri·o·ra'tion** (-rā'shŭn), *n.*

Syn. Deterioration, degeneration, decadence, decline mean the falling from a higher to a lower level as in quality, character, or the like. Deterioration implies impairment, as of vigor, usefulness, or the like; degeneration stresses retrogression physically, intellectually, or often morally; decadence presupposes a former reaching of the peak of development and implies a turn downward with a consequent loss in vitality, or the like; decline differs from *decadence* in suggesting more momentum, more obvious evidences of deterioration, and less hope of revivification.

de·te'ri·o·ra'tive (-rā'tĭv), *adj.* Tending to deteriorate; deteriorating.

de·ter'mi·na·ble (dē·tûr'mĭ·nȧ·b'l), *adj.* **1.** Capable of being determined or definitely ascertained. **2.** Terminable.

de·ter'mi·nant (-nănt), *n.* That which serves to determine. — **Syn.** See CAUSE.

de·ter'mi·nate (-nāt), *adj.* [L. *determinatus,* past part. See DETERMINE.] **1.** Having defined limits; definite. **2.** Determined by resolving or deciding; decided. **3.** Resolute; resolved. **4.** *Bot.* Cymose. — **de·ter'mi·nate·ly,** *adv.* — **de·ter'mi·nate·ness,** *n.*

de·ter'mi·na'tion (dē·tûr'mĭ·nā'shŭn), *n.* **1.** *Archaic.* Termination; limit. **2.** Judicial decision; settlement, as of a controversy. **3.** Act of coming to a decision; also, conclusion. **4.** A determining of bounds; a fixing of the extent, position, or character of anything. **5.** Act, process, or result of any accurate measurement, as of length, volume, etc. **6.** Direction or tendency to a certain end; impulsion. **7.** The mental quality, habit, or power of deciding definitely and firmly; decision of character. **8.** *Logic.* **a** The act of defining a concept by giving its essential constituents. **b** The addition of a differentia to a concept, thus limiting its extent; — the opposite of *generalization.*

de·ter'mi·na'tive (dē·tûr'mĭ·nā'tĭv; -nȧ·tĭv), *adj.* Having power or tendency to determine. — **Syn.** See CONCLUSIVE. — *n.* **1.** One that serves to determine. **2.** In some languages, a spoken element attached to a word to determine its meaning more definitely. — **de·ter'mi·na'tive·ly,** *adv.* — **de·ter'mi·na'tive·ness,** *n.*

de·ter'mine (dē·tûr'mĭn), *v. t.* [OF. *determiner,* fr. L. *determinare, determinatum,* fr. *de* + *terminare* to limit, fr. *terminus* limit.] **1.** To set bounds or limits to; to limit in extent, scope, etc. **2.** To bring to a close; to terminate. **3.** To fix conclusively or authoritatively; to decide. **4.** To come to a decision concerning, as the result of investigation, reasoning, etc.; to settle. **5.** To regulate; as, demand *determines* the price. **6.** To obtain definite and firsthand knowledge of as to character, location, quantity, or the like. **7.** To give a definite direction, impetus, or bias to; to impel. — *v. i.* **1.** *Now Chiefly Law.* To come to an end; to end. **2.** To come to a decision; to decide; to resolve. — **Syn.** See DECIDE; DISCOVER. — **de·ter'min·er** (-mĭn·ẽr), *n.*

de·ter'mined (-mĭnd), *adj.* Decided; resolute. — **de·ter'mined·ly** (-mĭnd·lĭ; -mĭn·ĕd·lĭ; -ĭd·lĭ), *adv.* — **de·ter'mined·ness,** *n.*

de·ter'min·ism (-mĭn·ĭz'm), *n.* Any doctrine that acts of the will, social changes, etc., result from determining causes. Cf. NECESSITARIANISM. — **de·ter'min·ist** (-ĭst), *n. & adj.* — **de·ter'min·is'tic** (-ĭs'tĭk), *adj.*

de·ter'rent (dē·tûr'ĕnt; dē·tĕr'-), *adj.* Serving to deter. — *n.* That which deters. — **de·ter'rence** (-ĕns), *n.*

de·ter'sive (dē·tûr'sĭv), *adj. & n.* Detergent.

de·test' (dē·tĕst'), *v. t.* [F. *détester,* fr. L. *detestari* to curse while calling a deity to witness, execrate, detest, fr. *de* + *testari* to be a witness, fr. *testis* a witness.] To hate intensely; to abominate. — **Syn.** See HATE. — **de·test'er,** *n.*

de·test'a·ble (-tĕs'tȧ·b'l), *adj.* Arousing intense antipathy or dislike; abominable. — **Syn.** See HATEFUL. — **de·test'a·bil'i·ty** (-bĭl'ĭ·tĭ), **de·test'a·ble·ness,** *n.* — **de·test'a·bly,** *adv.*

de'tes·ta'tion (dē'tĕs·tā'shŭn; dĕt'ĕs-), *n.* **1.** Intense antipathy or dislike; abhorrence. **2.** That which is detested.

de·throne' (dē·thrōn'), *v. t.* To remove from a throne; to depose. — **de·throne'ment,** *n.* — **de·thron'er** (-thrōn'ẽr), *n.*

det'i·nue (dĕt'ĭ·nū), *n.* [OF. *detenue* detention, fr. *detenir* to detain.] Detention of something due; also, *Law,* a common-law form of action, or the writ used, for the recovery of a personal chattel (or its value) wrongfully detained.

det'o·nate (dĕt'ō·nāt; dē'tō-), *v. i. & t.* [L. *detonare,* v. i., to thunder down, fr. *de* + *tonare* to thunder.] To explode with sudden violence. — **det'o·na'tion** (-nā'shŭn), *n.* — **det'o·na'tor** (-nā'tẽr), *n.*

de'tour (dē'tōōr; dē·tōōr'), **dé·tour'** (dā·tōōr'), *n.* [F. *détour,* fr. *détourner* to turn aside, fr. *dé-* (fr. L. *dis-*) + *tourner* to turn.] A turning; a deviation from a direct course; specif., a roundabout way temporarily replacing part of a route. — *v. i.* To go by a detour.

de·tox'i·cate (dē·tŏk'sĭ·kāt), *v. t.* [*de-* + L. *toxicum* poison.] To remove the poison or effect of poison from.

de·tract' (dē·trăkt'), *v. t.* [F. *détracter,* fr. L. *detractus,* past part. of *detrahere* to detract, fr. *de* + *trahere* to draw.] **1.** To withdraw; subtract. **2.** *Now Rare.* To take credit or reputation from; disparage. **3.** To distract. — *v. i.* To take away a part or something, esp. from one's credit; to lessen reputation. — **Syn.** See DECRY. — **de·trac'tor** (-trăk'tẽr), *n.* — **de·trac'tress,** *n.*

de·trac'tion (dē·trăk'shŭn), *n.* Act of taking away from the reputation or good name of another, esp. by calumny or slander. — **de·trac'tive** (-tĭv), *adj.* — **de·trac'tive·ly,** *adv.* — **de·trac'to·ry** (-tō·rĭ), *adj.*

de·train' (dē·trān'), *v. i. & t.* To leave, or to cause to leave, a railroad train. — **de·train'ment,** *n.*

det'ri·ment (dĕt'rĭ·mĕnt), *n.* [L. *detrimentum,* fr. *deterere, detritum,* to rub away, fr. *de* + *terere* to rub.] Injury or damage, or that which causes it; mischief; hurt.

det'ri·men'tal (-mĕn'tăl), *adj.* Causing detriment; hurtful. — **Syn.** See PERNICIOUS. — **Ant.** Beneficial. — **det'ri·men'tal·ly,** *adv.*

de·tri'tion (dē·trĭsh'ŭn), *n.* A wearing off or away.

de·tri'tus (dē·trī'tŭs), *n.* [L., a rubbing away.] **1.** *Geol.* Any loose material that results directly from rock disintegration; debris. **2.** That which remains after disintegration or wearing away. — **de·tri'tal** (-tăl; -t'l), *adj.*

‖**de trop** (dē trō'). [F.] Too much or too many; superfluous; — esp. of a person when in the way.

de·trude' (dē·trōōd'), *v. t.* [L. *detrudere, detrusum,* fr. *de* + *trudere* to thrust, push.] To thrust or force down, out, or away. — **de·tru'sion** (-trōō'zhŭn), *n.*

de·trun'cate (dē·trŭng'kāt), *v. t.* [L. *detruncatus,* past part., deriv. of *de* + *truncare* to maim, cut off.] To shorten by cutting; lop off. — **de'trun·ca'tion** (dē'trŭng·kā'shŭn), *n.*

Deu·ca'li·on and Pyr'rha (dū·kā'lĭ·ŏn, pĭr'ȧ). [L. *Deucalion,* fr. Gr. *Deukaliōn*; L. & Gr. *Pyrrha.*] *Gr. Myth.* A king and queen of Thessaly, the only human pair that survived a great deluge sent by Zeus. They floated in a ship for nine days, came to rest on a mountain, and, in obedience to an oracle, cast behind them stones, from which sprang men and women. Cf. NOAH.

deuce (dūs), *n.* [F. *deux* two, fr. OF. *deus,* fr. L. *duos,* acc. of *duo* two.] **1.** The side of a die bearing two pips; a cast in which two aces turn up; also, a card with two spots. **2.** A tied score at three points for each side in a game of lawn tennis. **3.** [Prob. fr. *deuce,* two at dice, as lowest throw.] A plague; bad luck; the devil; — an oath. — *v. t.* To bring the score of (a game or a set) to deuce.

deu'ced (dū'sĕd; -sĭd; dūst), *adj.* Plaguy; — used in mild imprecations. — **deu'ced,** *adv.* — **deu'ced·ly,** *adv.*

‖**de'us ex ma'chi·na** (dē'ŭs ĕks măk'ĭ·nȧ). [L.] Literally, a god from a machine; hence, any person or thing artificially introduced, as in a story, to solve a difficulty.

De'us Mi'se·re·a'tur (mĭz'ē·rē·ā'tẽr). [L.] (May) God be merciful; — used as title for the 67th psalm.

‖**De'us vult** (vŭlt'). [L.] God wills (it); — rallying cry of the First Crusade.

deu·te'ri·um (dū·tēr'ĭ·ŭm), *n.* [NL. See DEUTERO-.] *Chem.* The hydrogen isotope of mass number 2. Symbol, H^2 or D See *heavy water,* under WATER.

deuterium oxide. *Chem.* Heavy water, D_2O, composed of deuterium and oxygen.

deu'ter·o- (dū'tẽr·ō-), **deuter-.** [Gr. *deuteros.*] A combining form meaning *second, secondary,* as in **deu'ter·ag'o·nist** (-ăg'ō·nĭst), an actor in ancient Greek drama taking parts of secondary importance. Cf. PROTAGONIST.

deu'ter·o·ca·non'i·cal (-kȧ·nŏn'ĭ·kăl), *adj.* [*deutero-* + *canonical.*] Belonging to a second, or later, canon, or list of genuine Scriptural books; — used esp. by Roman Catholics of those books called *Apocrypha* by Protestants and of certain parts of the New Testament.

deu'ter·og'a·my (dū'tẽr·ŏg'ȧ·mĭ), *n.* [Gr. *deuterogamia,* fr. *deuteros* second + *gamos* marriage.] Marriage after the death of the first spouse. Cf. MONOGAMY. — **deu'ter·og'a·mist** (-mĭst), *n.*

deu'ter·on (dū'tẽr·ŏn), *n.* [From Gr. *deuteros* second.] *Chem.* The nucleus of the deuterium atom (D or H^2), assumed to consist of one proton and one neutron; — called also **deu'ton** (dū'tŏn).

Deu'ter·on'o·my (dū'tẽr·ŏn'ō·mĭ), *n.* [LL. *Deuteronomium,* fr. Gr. *Deuteronomion,* fr. *deuteros* second + *nomos* law.] Fifth book of the Bible. It contains a repetition of the law of Moses. See BIBLE.

deu'to- (dū'tō-), **deut-.** A shortened form of DEUTERO-, as in **deu'to·plasm** (-plăz'm), the food matter in the cytoplasm of an egg.

Deut'sche mark (doi'chĕ märk'). The monetary unit of Western Germany which replaced the reichsmark June, 1948. See MONEY, *Tables.*

deut'zi·a (dūt'sĭ·ȧ; doit'sĭ·ȧ), *n.* [NL., after Jan *Deutz* of Holland.] Any of a genus (*Deutzia*) of bushy, ornamental, usually white-flowered shrubs of the hydrangea family, originally of Asia and Central America.

de'va (dā'vȧ), *n.* [Skr.] *Hinduism & Buddhism.* A divine being, angel, or deity, as Indra.

de·val'u·ate (dē·văl'ū·āt), *v. t.* [See DE-.] To diminish the value of; specif., *Finance,* to fix the value of a currency at a low level to which an emergency has driven it. — **de·val'u·a'tion** (-ā'shŭn), *n.*

De'va·na'ga·ri (dā'vȧ·nä'gȧ·rē), *n.* [Skr. *devanāgarī.*] The alphabet usually employed in writing Sanskrit.

dev'as·tate (dĕv'ăs·tāt), *v. t.* [L. *devastatus,* past part. of *devastare* to devastate, fr. *de* + *vastare* to lay waste, fr. *vastus* waste.] To lay waste; ravage. — **Syn.** See RAVAGE. — **dev'as·tat'ing·ly** (-tāt'ĭng·lĭ), *adv.* — **dev'as·ta'tor** (-tā'tẽr), *n.*

dev'as·ta'tion (-tā'shŭn), *n.* Act of devastating, or state of being devastated; a laying waste; desolation.

dev'el (dĕv''l), *v. & n. Scot.* (To deal) a stunning blow.

de·vel'op (dē·vĕl'ŭp), *v. t.* Also **de·vel'ope.** [F. *développer,* fr. *dé-* (fr. L. *dis-*), after *envelopper.* See ENVELOP.] **1.** To lay open by degrees or in detail; to disclose; reveal. **2.** To unfold more completely; to evolve the possibilities of; to make active (something latent); advance; further; to promote the growth of. **3.** To unfold gradually, as a flower from a bud; to form or expand by a process of growth. **4.** To make more available or usable; as, to *develop* water power. **5.** *Math.* To express in expanded form, as in a series. **6.** *Music.* To elaborate by the unfolding of a musical idea, by the working out of rhythmic, melodic, or harmonic changes in the theme, etc. **7.** *Photog.* To subject to the action of chemical agents to bring out the latent image on a sensitized surface; also, to render visible in this way. — *v. i.* **1.** To go through a process of natural evolution or growth; to evolve. **2.** To become gradually visible or manifest. **3.** To become apparent; come to light. — **Syn.** Mature, ripen. — **de·vel′op·a·ble,** *adj.*

de·vel′op·er (dē·vĕl′ŭp·ẽr), *n.* One that develops; specif., a chemical reagent used in developing photographs.

de·vel′op·ment (-mĕnt), *n.* Also **de·vel′ope·ment.** The act, process, or result of developing, or state of being developed. — **de·vel′op·men′tal** (-mĕn′tăl), **de·vel′op·men′ta·ry** (-tȧ·rĭ), *adj.*

de·vest′ (dē·vĕst′), *v. t.* [OF. *devester, desvestir,* deriv. of L. *dis-* + *vestire* to dress.] Divest.

De′vi (dā′vē), *n.* [Skr. *Devī,* prop., goddess.] *Hinduism.* Any female divinity; esp., the consort of Siva and daughter of Himavat (the Himalaya Mountains).

de′vi·ant (dē′vĭ·ănt), *n.* = DEVIATE.

de′vi·ate (dē′vĭ·āt), *v. i.* [LL. *deviare* to deviate, fr. *de* + *viare* to go, travel, fr. *via* way.] To turn aside from a course; to stray, as from a standard, a topic. — *v. t.* To cause to deviate. — **Syn.** See SWERVE. — (-āt), *n.* An individual who differs considerably from the average. — (-āt), *adj.* Characterized by or given to considerable departure from the norms of behavior in a given society. — **de′vi·a′tor** (-ā′tẽr), *n.*

de′vi·a′tion (-ā′shŭn), *n.* Act or instance of deviating; a turning aside.

de·vice′ (dē·vīs′), *n.* [From OF. *devis* division, plan, wish, difference; confused with ME. *devise,* fr. OF. *devise,* with similar meanings. Both F. words fr. *deviser.* See DEVISE, *v.*] **1.** That which is devised, or formed by design; as: **a** A scheme; often, a scheme to deceive; a stratagem. **b** A mechanical contrivance or appliance. **2.** An emblematic design, used esp. as a heraldic bearing; also, a motto. **3.** Anything fancifully designed, as a masque, or show. **4.** *Archaic.* The act or power of devising; invention. **5.** Will; desire; — now only *pl.;* as, left to his own *devices.*

dev′il (dĕv′'l), *n.* [AS. *dēofol, dēoful,* fr. LL. *diabolus,* fr. Gr. *diabolos* the devil, the slanderer, fr. *diaballein* to calumniate, orig., to throw across, fr. *dia* across + *ballein* to throw.] **1.** [*cap. or not cap.*] In Jewish and Christian theology, the personal supreme spirit of evil and unrighteousness. **2.** A lesser evil or malignant spirit; a demon. **3.** A malignantly wicked person; a human fiend. **4.** Used, with *the,* as an oath. **5.** Jocosely or familiarly, a person of superabundant energy, recklessness, etc. **6.** = PRINTER'S DEVIL. **7.** A wretched fellow; as, poor *devil!* **8.** *Mach.* Any of various machines, as one for tearing or shredding something, as paper stock. **9.** *India.* A dust storm. **10.** *Christian Science.* Evil; a lie; error; neither corporeality nor mind; the opposite of Truth; a belief in sin, sickness, and death; animal magnetism or hypnotism. *Mary Baker Eddy.* — *v. t.;* -ILED (-'ld) or -ILLED; -IL·ING (-'l·ĭng) or -IL·LING. **1.** *Colloq.* To tease; annoy; haze. **2.** In cooking, to grill with pepper and hot condiments; to season highly; as, to *devil* eggs. **3.** To treat in a machine called a devil (sense 8); as, to *devil* rags.

dev′iled *or* **dev′illed** (dĕv′'ld), *adj.* Chopped fine and highly seasoned, usually after being cooked; as, *deviled* ham.

dev′il·fish′ (dĕv′'l·fĭsh′), *n.; pl.,* see FISH. **1.** Any of several gigantic viviparous rays (genus *Manta* and allied genera, family Mobulidae), found in warm seas. **2.** An octopus or other large cephalopod.

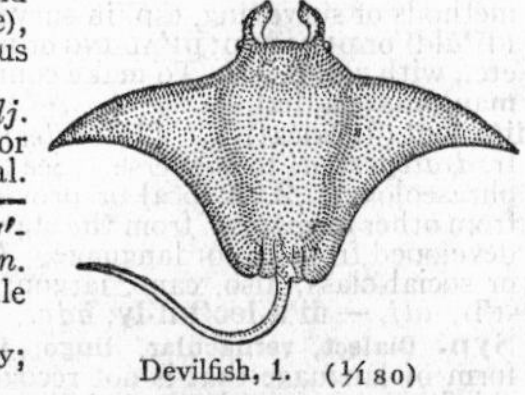

Devilfish, 1. (1/80)

dev′il·ish (dĕv′'l·ĭsh; dĕv′lĭsh), *adj.* **1.** Resembling, characteristic of, or pertaining to, the Devil; diabolical. **2.** *Colloq.* Extreme; excessive. — *adv. Colloq.* Excessively. — **dev′il·ish·ly,** *adv.* — **dev′il·ish·ness,** *n.*

dev′il·kin (dĕv′'l·kĭn), *n.* A little devil; an imp.

dev′il·ment (-mĕnt), *n.* Devilry; reckless mischief.

dev′il·ry (-rĭ), *n.; pl.* -RIES (-rĭz). **1.** Satanic magic; diabolical art. **2.** Wickedness; malignant cruelty. **3.** Reckless conduct; mischief.

dev′il's ad′vo·cate (dĕv′'lz). [ML. *advocatus diaboli.*] **a** *R.C.Ch.* An official appointed to point out defects in the evidence upon which a plea for beatification or canonization rests. **b** Hence, a champion of the worse cause for the sake of argument.

dev′il's–darn′ing–nee′dle, *n.* A dragonfly. See DRAGONFLY, *Illust.*

devil's tattoo. A drumming with the fingers or feet.

dev′il·try (dĕv′'l·trĭ), *n.; pl.* -TRIES (-trĭz). Devilry.

dev′il·wood′ (-wŏŏd′), *n.* A small tree (*Osmanthus americanus*) of the olive family, of the southern United States.

de′vi·ous (dē′vĭ·ŭs), *adj.* [L. *devius,* fr. *de* + *via* way.] **1.** Out of a straight line; winding; as, a *devious* path. **2.** Deviating from the right or common course; going astray; erring. — **Syn.** See CROOKED. — **de′vi·ous·ly,** *adv.* — **de′vi·ous·ness,** *n.*

de·vis′al (-ăl; -'l), *n.* A devising.

de·vise′ (dē·vīz′), *v. t. & i.* [OF. *deviser* to distribute, regulate, fr. L. *divisus* divided, distributed, past part. of *dividere* to divide.] **1.** *Obs.* To divide; distribute. **2.** To form in the mind by new combinations of ideas, etc.; to invent; contrive. **3.** *Archaic.* To plan for. **4.** *Law.* To give by will; — now esp. of real estate. **5.** *Obs.* To divine; guess. — *n.* **1.** Act of disposing of property by will; also, a will or clause of a will making such a gift or disposal. **2.** Property devised. — **de·vis′a·ble** (dē·vīz′ȧ·b'l), *adj.* — **de·vis′er** (-vīz′ẽr), *n.*

dev′i·see′ (dĕv′ĭ·zē′; dē·vīz′ē′), *n. Law.* One to whom a devise is made.

de·vi′sor (dē·vī′zẽr; -zôr), *n.* One who devises property.

de·vi′tal·ize (dē·vī′tăl·īz), *v. t.* To deprive of life or vitality. — **de·vi′tal·i·za′tion** (-ĭ·zā′shŭn; -ī·zā′-), *n.*

de·vit′ri·fy (dē·vĭt′rĭ·fī), *v. t.;* -FIED (-fīd); -FY′ING. To deprive of glasslike luster and transparency; to change from a vitreous to a crystalline condition. — **de·vit′ri·fi·ca′tion** (-fĭ·kā′shŭn), *n.*

de·vo′cal·ize (dē·vō′kăl·īz), *v. t. Phonet.* To deprive of sonant, or vocal, quality. — **de·vo′cal·i·za′tion** (-ĭ·zā′shŭn; -ī·zā′-), *n.*

de·void′ (dē·void′), *adj.* [OF. *desvuidier, desvoidier,* to empty out. See DE-; VOID.] Destitute; not in possession; — with *of;* as, *devoid* of sense or of pride.

de·voir′ (dĕ·vwär′; dĕv′wär), *n.* [F., fr. L. *debere* to owe. See DUE.] Duty; hence, due act of civility or respect; — now in *pl.*

dev′o·lu′tion (dĕv′ō·lū′shŭn), *n.* **1.** Transference from one person to another; a devolving upon a successor. **2.** *Biol.* Retrograde development; degeneration.

de·volve′ (dē·vŏlv′), *v. t. & i.* [L. *devolvere, devolutum,* to roll down, fr. *de* + *volvere* to roll.] **1.** To roll onward or downward. **2.** To transfer from one person to another; to hand down; to pass by transmission or succession.

Dev′on (dĕv′ŭn), *n.* An animal of a small, active, hardy breed of cattle originating in Devon, England.

De·vo′ni·an (dē·vō′nĭ·ăn; 58), *adj.* **1.** Of or pertaining to Devonshire (or Devon) in England. **2.** *Geol.* Of, pertaining to, or designating the period of the Paleozoic era between the Silurian and the Carboniferous, or the system of rocks formed during this period. It is marked esp. by the development of aquatic vertebrates and is sometimes called the "age of fishes." — **De·vo′ni·an,** *n.*

de·vote′ (dē·vōt′), *v. t.* [L. *devotus,* past part. of *devovere,* fr. *de* + *vovere* to vow.] **1.** To appropriate by vow; to dedicate by a solemn act; to consecrate; also, to consign over; to doom. **2.** To give up wholly; to direct the attention of wholly or chiefly; as, to *devote* oneself to science. — *adj. Archaic.* Devoted. — **de·vote′ment,** *n.*

Syn. Devote, dedicate, consecrate, hallow mean to set apart for a particular use or end. Devote, which originally implied a vow, now suggests motives as impelling as a vow; dedicate implies solemn and exclusive devotion to a sacred or serious use; consecrate is even stronger than *dedicate,* for it also implies investing with a solemn and sacred character; hallow, a native word, is often used in place of *consecrate,* but it often implies the ascription of intrinsic holiness.

de·vot′ed (-vōt′ĕd; -ĭd), *adj.* **1.** Consecrated to a purpose; devout. **2.** Dedicated; vowed; also, doomed. — **Syn.** Affectionate, fond, loving. — **de·vot′ed·ly,** *adv.* — **de·vot′ed·ness,** *n.*

dev′o·tee′ (dĕv′ō·tē′), *n.* One zealously devoted; an ardent adherent, partisan, or the like; a votary; specif., one devoted to religious ceremonies; also, a religious fanatic.

de·vo′tion (dē·vō′shŭn), *n.* **1.** State or quality of being devoted; ardent affection; zealous attachment; specif., religious fervor; piety. **2.** An act evincing devotedness. **3.** *pl.* Prayers or supplications, esp. as designed for private worship; as, a book of *devotions.* **4.** Act of devoting; dedication. — **Syn.** See FIDELITY. — **de·vo′tion·al,** *adj.* — **de·vo′tion·al·ly,** *adv.*

de·vour′ (dē·vour′), *v. t.* [OF. *devorer,* fr. L. *devorare,* fr. *de* + *vorare* to eat greedily.] **1.** To eat up greedily or ravenously. **2.** To seize upon and destroy, or appropriate greedily or wantonly; to waste; annihilate. **3.** To prey upon; as, to be *devoured* by fear. **4.** To take in eagerly by the senses or mind; as, to *devour* a book. — **de·vour′er,** *n.* — **de·vour′ing·ly,** *adv.*

de·vout′ (dē·vout′), *adj.* [OF. *devot,* fr. L. *devotus* devoted, past part. See DEVOTE.] **1.** Devoted to religion or to religious duties or exercises; pious; religious. **2.** Expressing devotion or piety. **3.** Warmly devoted; sincere. — **de·vout′ly,** *adv.* — **de·vout′ness,** *n.*

Syn. Devout, pious, religious, pietistic, sanctimonious here mean showing fervor and reverence in religious observances. Devout stresses a mental attitude that leads to frequent, though not necessarily outwardly evident, prayer or worship; pious, the faithful performance of one's religious duties; religious may, and usually does, imply devoutness and piety, but it emphasizes faith in a God or gods and adherence to a way of life in keeping with that faith; pietistic basically implies an insistence upon the emotional as opposed to the intellectual aspects of religion; sanctimonious has lost its implications of holiness and now implies pretensions to or the appearance of piety or holiness.

dew (dū; 114), *n.* [AS. *dēaw.*] **1.** Moisture condensed upon the surfaces of cool bodies, esp. at night. **2.** Figuratively, anything that falls lightly and in a refreshing manner. **3.** An emblem of dawn, or of morning freshness, purity, or vigor; as, the *dew* of one's youth. **4.** Any moisture that exudes or appears in small drops, as tears, sweat, etc. — *v. t.* To wet with or as with dew; to bedew.

de·wan′ (dē·wän′; dē·wôn′), *n.* Also **di·wan′** (dē-). [Ar. & Per. *dīwān.* See DIVAN.] *India.* A chief officer or steward, such as a minister of finance, the chief native officer of certain government departments, etc.

Dew′ar ves′sel (dū′ẽr). [After Sir James *Dewar* (1842–1923), Scottish chemist.] A double-walled glass vessel for holding liquid air, etc., having the walls silvered and the space between them exhausted so as to prevent transmission of heat; — called also **Dewar bulb, Dewar flask, Dewar tube,** etc.

dew′ber′ry (dū′bĕr′ĭ; -bẽr·ĭ), *n.* The fruit of certain brambles or blackberries (genus *Rubus*); also, any plant bearing this fruit.

dew′claw′ (-klô′), *n.* A vestigial digit on the foot of a quadruped, or a claw or hoof terminating such a digit, as the inner digit of a dog's forefoot.

dew′drop′ (-drŏp′), *n.* A drop of dew.

dew′lap′ (-lăp′), *n.* **1.** The pendulous fold of skin under the neck of certain animals, orig. of the ox tribe, but now also of other animals, esp. dogs (see DOG, *Illust.*); also, the wattles under the neck of certain birds. **2.** A flaccid fold of fat or flesh on the human throat. — **dew′lapped′** (-lăpt′), *adj.*

dew point. The temperature at which a vapor begins to deposit as liquid.

dew′y (dū′ĭ), *adj.;* -I·ER (-ĭ·ẽr); -I·EST. Having, affected by, or resembling dew. — **dew′i·ness,** *n.*

dex′ter (dĕk′stẽr), *adj.* [L.] **1.** Pertaining to, or situated on, the right hand. **2.** *Her.* Designating the side of a shield, or escutcheon, at the right of the person wearing it. See ESCUTCHEON, *Illust.* **3.** Appearing, or observed, on the right side; hence, auspicious; fortunate.

dex·ter′i·ty (dĕks·tẽr′ĭ·tĭ), *n.* **1.** Quickness, skill, and ease in using the hands; deftness. **2.** Mental quickness or readiness; adroitness.

dex′ter·ous (dĕk′stẽr·ŭs), **dex′trous** (dĕks′trŭs), *adj.* Characterized by or manifesting dexterity; skillful; expert. — **dex′ter·ous·ly, dex′trous·ly,** *adv.* — **dex′ter·ous·ness, dex′trous·ness,** *n.*

Syn. Dexterous, adroit, deft, feat mean ready and skilled in physical or, sometimes, mental movement. Dexterous implies expertness with consequent facility and agility in manipulation or movement; adroit basically implies dexterity but tends to stress resourcefulness or artfulness; deft emphasizes lightness, neatness, and sureness of touch or handling; feat, a bookish word, adds the connotation of grace or beauty of movement. — **Ant.** Clumsy.

dex′tral (dĕks′trăl), *adj.* **1.** Being on the right side; turned or turning to the right; — opp. to *sinistral.* **2.** Right-handed. **3.** Favorable; auspicious; — of omens. **4.** *Conchol.* Having the whorls turning from the left toward the right as viewed with the apex toward the observer or having the aperture open toward the observer to the right of the axis when held with the spire uppermost; as, the shells of most univalves are *dextral;* — opposed to *sinistral.* — **dex·tral′i·ty** (dĕks·trăl′ĭ·tĭ), *n.* — **dex′tral·ly,** *adv.*

dex'trin (dĕks'trĭn), *n.* Also **dex'trine** (-trĭn; -trēn). [F. *dextrine.* See DEXTROROTATORY.] A soluble gummy carbohydrate formed by the decomposition of starch by heat, acids, or enzymes. It is used for sizing, as an adhesive, etc.

dex'tro- (dĕks'trō-). [L. *dexter* right.] A combining form meaning: **a** *Of, pertaining to,* or *toward the right.* **b** *Chem.* *Dextrorotatory,* as in *dextro*glucose (= DEXTROSE). Abbr. *d* - (no period).

dex'tro (dĕks'trō), *adj.* *Chem.* = DEXTRO- **b**. Abbr. *d* (no period).

dex'tro·glu'cose (dĕks'trō·glōō'kōs), *n.* See DEXTROSE.

dex'tro·gy'rate (-jī'rāt), **dex'tro·gy'rous** (-rŭs), *adj.* Dextrorotatory.

dex'tro·ro·ta'tion (-rō·tā'shŭn), *n.* *Physics & Chem.* Right-handed or clockwise rotation, esp. of the plane of polarization of light.

dex'tro·ro'ta·to'ry (-rō'tȧ·tō'rĭ *or, esp. Brit.,* -tĕr·ĭ), *adj.* [*dextro-* + *rotatory.*] Turning toward the right, or clockwise; esp., turning the plane of polarized light to the right; as, *dextrorotatory* crystals; — opp. to *levorotatory.*

dex'trorse (dĕks'trôrs; dĕks·trôrs'), *adj.* [L. *dextrorsum* toward the right side, fr. *dexter* right + *versus, vorsus,* past part., turned.] **1.** *Bot.* Twining spirally upward around an axis from left to right; — left to right being interpreted by some botanists as giving a clockwise twining and by others a counterclockwise twining, depending on the point of view: (1) clockwise, as in the hop (*Humulus*), when the point of view is above or within the spiral; (2) counterclockwise, as in the morning-glory (*Ipomoea*), when the point of view is outside the spiral, in which case a ring of the spiral is observed as passing upward from left to right between the observer and the axis. Cf. SINISTRORSE. **2.** *Conchol.* Dextral. — **dex'trorse·ly**, *adv.*

dex'trose (dĕks'trōs), *n.* *Chem.* A crystalline dextrorotatory sugar, $C_6H_{12}O_6$, occurring in many plants and in the animal organism; — called also *grape sugar, dextroglucose,* or D-*glucose* (see GLUCOSE). It is obtained, with levulose, by inversion of sucrose but is chiefly made from starch by action of heat and acids. Cf. INVERT SUGAR, CORN SUGAR.

dex'trous (dĕks'trŭs), **dex'trous·ly**, etc. Vars. of DEXTEROUS, etc.

dey (dā), *n.* [F., fr. Turk. *dāi,* orig., maternal uncle.] *Hist.* **a** The governor of Algiers before 1830. **b** A ruler or pasha of Tunis or Tripoli.

dhar'ma (där'mȧ; *Skr.* dŭr'mȧ), *n.* [Skr., law.] **1.** *Hinduism & Buddhism.* Religious law or conformity to it; practice of religion; virtue. **2.** [*cap.*] *Hindu Myth.* An ancient sage whose numerous progeny are personifications of virtues and religious rites.

dhar'na (dŭr'nä), *n.* Also **dhur'na**. [Hind. *dharnā.*] *India.* An appeal for justice, by fasting even to death while seated at the door of the wronger.

dhole (dōl), *n.*; see PLURAL, *Note,* 3. A wild dog (*Cuon dukhunensis*) of India, that hunts, in packs, tigers and other large wild animals.

dhoo'ly (dōō'lĭ). Var. of DOOLY.

dho'ti (dō'tē), **dhoo'ti** (dōō'tē), *n.* [Hind. *dhotī.*] The long loincloth worn by Hindu men; also, a fabric for this use.

dhow (dou), *n.* An Arab lateen-rigged vessel with, usually, a long overhang forward, a high poop, and an open waist. See LATEEN SAIL, *Illust.*

di- (dī-). [Gr. *dis* twice.] A prefix signifying *twofold, double, twice;* specif., *Chem.,* denoting *two* atoms, radicals, groups, etc.

di-. A prefix denoting *separation* or *reversal* (= 1st DIS-).

di'a- (dī'ȧ-), **di-.** [Gr. *dia* through, orig., dividing into two parts.] A prefix denoting *through;* also, *between, apart, across.*

di'a·base (dī'ȧ·bās), *n.* [F., fr. Gr. *diabasis* a crossing over, passage.] *Petrog.* **a** Formerly, diorite. **b** *Eng.* An altered basalt. **c** *U.S.* A partly crystalline rock of the composition of gabbro, but with an ophitic texture. — **di'a·ba'sic** (-bā'sĭk), *adj.*

di'a·be'tes (dī'ȧ·bē'tēz; *colloq.* -tĭs), *n.* [NL., fr. Gr. *diabētēs,* fr. *diabainein* to pass through.] A disease attended with a persistent, excessive discharge of urine; specif., ‖***di'a·be'tes mel·li'tus*** (dī'ȧ·bē'tēz mĕ·lī'tŭs), or ***sugar diabetes,*** a grave form in which the body is unable to utilize properly the carbohydrates in the diet due to failure in the secretion of insulin by the pancreas. It is marked by sugar in the urine, excessive thirst and hunger, and progressive emaciation. — **di'a·bet'ic** (-bĕt'ĭk; -bē'tĭk), *adj. & n.*

di·a'ble·rie (dĭ·ä'blĕ·rĭ; *F.* dyȧ'blĕ·rē'), **di·ab'ler·y** (dĭ·ăb'lĕr·ĭ), *n.* [F. *diablerie,* fr. *diable* devil.] **1.** Devilry; sorcery; black magic. **2.** Demon lore. **3.** Excessive or extravagant spiritedness.

di'a·bol'ic (dī'ȧ·bŏl'ĭk), **di'a·bol'i·cal** (-ĭ·kăl), *adj.* [F. *diabolique,* fr. LL., fr. Gr. *diabolikos* devilish. See DEVIL.] **1.** Of or pertaining to the Devil or devils. **2.** Devilish; demoniacal; fiendish. — **di'a·bol'i·cal·ly**, *adv.* — **di'a·bol'i·cal·ness**, *n.*

di·ab'o·lism (dī·ăb'ō·lĭz'm), *n.* **1.** Commerce with the Devil; demonic possession; devilishness, or an instance of it. **2.** Worship of devils; Satanism. **3.** The character, nature, or condition of a devil. — **di·ab'o·list** (-lĭst), *n.* — **di·ab'o·lize** (-līz), *v. t.*

di'a·caus'tic (dī'ȧ·kôs'tĭk), *adj.* *Optics.* Designating, or pertaining to, a caustic curve or surface caused by refraction. See CAUSTIC, *adj.,* 3. — *n.* A diacaustic curve or surface.

di·ach'y·lon (dī·ăk'ĭ·lŏn), **di·ach'y·lum** (-lŭm), *n.* [NL., fr. Gr. *diachylos* very juicy, fr. *dia* thoroughly + *chylos* juice.] An adhesive plaster made of litharge and olive oil (or olive oil and lard).

di·ac'id (dī·ăs'ĭd), *adj.* [1st *di-* + *acid.*] *Chem.* **a** Able to react with two molecules of a monoacid, or one of a diacid, to form a salt or ester; — of bases and alcohols. **b** Having two hydrogen atoms replaceable by basic atoms or radicals; — of acids and acid salts. — *n.* An acid having two acid hydrogen atoms, as sulfuric acid or oxalic acid.

di·ac'o·nal (dī·ăk'ō·năl; -n'l), *adj.* [ML. *diaconalis.* See DEACON.] Of or pertaining to a deacon.

di·ac'o·nate (-nāt), *n.* The office of a deacon; also, a body or board of deacons.

di'a·crit'ic (dī'ȧ·krĭt'ĭk), *adj.* [Gr. *diakritikos,* fr. *diakrinein* to distinguish, fr. *dia-* + *krinein* to separate.] **1.** Diacritical. **2.** *Med.* Diagnostic. — *n.* A diacritical mark, point, or symptom.

di'a·crit'i·cal (-ĭ·kăl), *adj.* Serving to separate or distinguish; — said of a mark, point, or sign attached to a letter to distinguish it in form or sound. — **di'a·crit'i·cal·ly**, *adv.*

di'ac·tin'ic (dī'ăk·tĭn'ĭk), *adj.* *Physics.* Capable of transmitting the chemical or actinic rays of light. — **di·ac'tin·ism** (dī·ăk'tĭn·ĭz'm), *n.*

di'a·del'phous (dī'ȧ·dĕl'fŭs), *adj.* [Gr. *di-* (= *dis*) twice + *adelphos* brother.] *Bot.* United by the filaments into two bundles or fascicles, as in Dutchman's-breeches (genus *Dicentra*) and most plants of the pea family; — said of stamens.

di'a·dem (dī'ȧ·dĕm), *n.* [OF. *diademe,* fr. L., fr. Gr. *diadēma,* fr. *diadein* to bind round, fr. *dia* through, across + *dein* to bind.] **1.** A crown; specif., an ornamental headband, worn by Eastern monarchs. **2.** Regal power or dignity. — *v. t.* To adorn with a diadem; crown.

di·aer'e·sis, di·er'e·sis (dī·ĕr'ĕ·sĭs *or, esp. Brit.,* dī·ēr'ĕ·sĭs), *n.; pl.* -SES (-sēz). [LL. *diaeresis,* fr. Gr. *diairesis,* fr. *diairein* to divide, fr. *dia-* + *hairein* to take.] **1.** The resolution of one syllable into two, esp. by separating the vowel elements of a diphthong. **2.** A mark, [¨], placed over a vowel to indicate its pronunciation in a separate syllable, as in *Chloë.* **3.** *Pros.* A break caused by the coincidence of the end of a foot with the end of the word. Sign #. — **di'ae·ret'ic, di'e·ret'ic** (dī'ĕ·rĕt'ĭk), *adj.*

di'ag·nose' (dī'ăg·nōs'; -nōz'), *v. t. & i.* To make a diagnosis (of).

di'ag·no'sis (-nō'sĭs), *n.; pl.* -NOSES (-sēz). [NL., fr. Gr. *diagnōsis,* fr. *diagignōskein* to distinguish, fr. *dia* + *gignōskein* to know.] **1.** The art or act of recognizing disease from its symptoms; also, the decision reached. **2.** Scientific determination; critical scrutiny or its resulting judgment. — **di'ag·nos'tic** (-nŏs'tĭk), *adj.* — **di'ag·nos'ti·cal·ly** (-tĭ·kăl·ĭ), *adv.*

di'ag·nos'tic (dī'ăg·nŏs'tĭk), *n.* [Gr. *diagnōstikos* able to distinguish.] **1.** A diagnostic mark or symptom. **2.** Also **di'ag·nos'tics** (-tĭks); see -ICS. Art of diagnosing.

di'ag·nos'ti·cate (-nŏs'tĭ·kāt), *v. t. & i.* To diagnose.

di'ag·nos·ti'cian (-nŏs·tĭsh'ăn), *n.* One who makes diagnoses; esp., an expert in making diagnoses.

di·ag'o·nal (dī·ăg'ō·năl; -n'l), *adj.* [L. *diagonalis,* fr. Gr. *diagōnios* from angle to angle, fr. *dia-* + *gōnia* an angle.] **1.** *Geom.* Joining two nonadjacent vertices of a rectilinear or polyhedral figure; running across from corner to corner. **2.** Having an oblique direction or extension. **3.** Having diagonal parts, markings, or weave. — *n.* **1.** A diagonal straight line or plane. **2.** A diagonal direction, row, or arrangement or a part of a structure placed diagonally. **3.** In full **diagonal cloth.** A plain twilled fabric with diagonal stripes, ridges, or welts. — **di·ag'o·nal·ly**, *adv.*

di'a·gram (dī'ȧ·grăm), *n.* [F. or L.; F. *diagramme,* fr. L., fr. Gr. *diagramma,* fr. *diagraphein* to mark out by lines, fr. *dia-* + *graphein* to draw.] **1.** A line drawing as for scientific purposes. **2.** An explanatory graphic design, as a chart or graph. — *v. t.;* DI'A·GRAMED (-grămd) or DI'A·GRAMMED; DI'A·GRAM'ING or DI'A·GRAM'MING. To represent by, or put into the form of, a diagram. — **di'a·gram·mat'ic** (-grȧ·măt'ĭk), **di'a·gram·mat'i·cal** (-ĭ·kăl), *adj.* — **-i·cal·ly**, *adv.*

di'a·graph (-gräf), *n.* [Gr. *diagraphein* to draw.] A drawing instrument combining a protractor and scale.

di'a·ki·ne'sis (dī'ȧ·kĭ·nē'sĭs; -kī-), *n.* [NL., fr. *dia-* + Gr. *kinēsis* motion.] *Biol.* A stage in meiosis during which the chromosomes as double or quadruple rods lie close to or on the nuclear membrane.

di'al (dī'ăl), *n.* [ML. *dialis* daily, fr. L. *dies* day.] **1.** An instrument for showing the time of day from the shadow of a style or gnomon; esp., a sundial. **2.** A large-faced watch or clock operated by a spring or by springs. **3.** The graduated face of a timepiece. **4.** A graduated plate or face with a pointer for indicating something, as steam pressure. **5.** A lettered or numbered plate for establishing connections as by radio or telephone. **6.** *Surv.* A compass used in certain methods of surveying, esp. in surveying mines. — *v. t. & i.;* DI'ALED (dī'ăld) or DI'ALLED; DI'AL·ING or DI'AL·LING. **1.** To measure, survey, etc., with a dial. **2.** To make connections with by means of a dial; to manipulate a dial.

di'a·lect (dī'ȧ·lĕkt), *n.* [F. *dialecte,* fr. L. *dialectus,* fr. Gr. *dialektos,* fr. *dialegesthai* to converse. See DIALOGUE.] **1.** Language; tongue; phraseology. **2.** A local or provincial form of a language, differing from other forms, esp. from the standard or literary form. **3.** A branch developed from a root language. **4.** The customary speech of a rank or social class; also, cant; jargon. — **di'a·lect, di'a·lec'tal** (-lĕk'tăl; -t'l), *adj.* — **di'a·lec'tal·ly**, *adv.*

Syn. **Dialect, vernacular, lingo, jargon, cant, argot, slang** mean a form of language that is not recognized as standard. **Dialect** applies chiefly to a form of language persisting in a locality or among a group, and marked by peculiarities in vocabulary, pronunciation, usage, etc.; **vernacular** applies to the form of language spoken by the people in contrast to that employed by learned or literary men; **lingo** is a term of contempt for any language which is not easily or readily understood; **jargon** is a term for the technical or esoteric language used by a profession, a class, a cult, or the like; **cant** is a term for a peculiar language adopted by a class, such as preachers, sports writers, etc.; **argot** is a term for the peculiar language of a clique, a set, or other closely knit group; **slang** is used more often to designate a class of recently coined terms than a language made up of them but, in either case, it suggests an appeal to popular fancy and a nonacceptance by authorities.

dialect atlas. = LINGUISTIC ATLAS.

dialect geography. The study of local variations of speech with the aid of a linguistic atlas; — called also *linguistic geography.*

di'a·lec'tic (dī'ȧ·lĕk'tĭk), *n.* [OF. *dialetique,* fr. L., fr. Gr. *dialektikē* (sc. *technē*).] **1.** Also **di'a·lec'tics** (-tĭks); see -ICS. That branch of logic which teaches the art of disputation and of discriminating truth from error; esp., the art of reasoning about matters of opinion. **2.** Disputation or debate conducted in conformity with the laws of logic.

di'a·lec'tic (-tĭk), **di'a·lec'ti·cal** (-tĭ·kăl), *adj.* **1.** Pertaining to dialectics. **2.** Dialectal. — **di'a·lec'ti·cal·ly**, *adv.*

dialectical materialism. The theory of reality affirming continuous transformation of matter and dynamic interconnectedness of things and concepts, and implying social transformation through socialism toward a classless society, which was advanced by Karl Marx and Friedrich Engels and adopted as the official Soviet philosophy.

di'a·lec·ti'cian (dī'ȧ·lĕk·tĭsh'ăn), *n.* **1.** One versed in dialectics. **2.** One who studies dialects.

di'a·lec'ti·cism (-lĕk'tĭ·sĭz'm), *n.* **1.** The practice of dialectics. **2.** The nature or characteristics of dialect; dialectal influence; also, a dialectal expression.

di'a·lec'tics (-tĭks), *n.;* see -ICS. Dialectic (sense 1).

di'al·ing, di'al·ling (dī'ăl·ĭng), *n.* **1.** Art of constructing dials; science treating of measuring time by dials. **2.** A method of surveying, esp. in mines. **3.** Act of one who dials.

di'al·lage (dī'ȧ·lĭj), *n.* [F., fr. Gr. *diallagē* change; — alluding to its dissimilar planes of fracture.] *Mineral.* A dark-green or bronze-colored laminated pyroxene, common in certain igneous rocks. H., 4. Sp. gr., 3.2–3.35.

di·al'o·gist (dī·ăl'ō·jĭst), *n.* **1.** One who participates in a dialogue. **2.** A writer of dialogues. — **di'a·lo·gis'tic** (dī'ȧ·lō·jĭs'tĭk), *adj.*

di'a·logue (dī'ȧ·lŏg; 74), *n.* Also **di'a·log.** [OF. *dialoge,* fr. L., fr.

Gr. *dialogos*, fr. *dialegesthai* to converse, fr. *dia-* + *legein* to speak.] **1.** A written composition representing two or more persons as conversing or reasoning. **2.** A colloquy between two or more. **3.** The conversational element, as in literary or dramatic composition. — *v. i. & t.* To take part or express in dialogue. — **di′a·logu′er** (-lŏg′ẽr), *n.*

di·al′y·sis (dī·ăl′ĭ·sĭs), *n.; pl.* DIALYSES (-sēz). [L., separation, fr. Gr. *dialysis*, deriv. of *dia* through + *lyein* to loose.] **1.** Dissolution; separation. **2.** *Chem.* The separation of colloids from substances in true solution (crystalloids), by means of their unequal diffusion through certain membranes. — **di′a·lyt′ic** (dī′ȧ·lĭt′ĭk), *adj.* — **di′a·lyt′i·cal·ly** (-ĭ·kăl·ĭ), *adv.*

di′a·lyze (dī′ȧ·līz), *v. t.* *Chem.* To separate, prepare, or obtain by dialysis; to pass through a suitable membrane; to subject to dialysis. — **di′a·lyz′er** (-līz′ẽr), *n.*

di′a·mag·net′ic (dī′ȧ·măg·nĕt′ĭk), *adj.* *Physics.* Possessing, or pertaining to, the magnetic properties of bodies or substances, as bismuth, whose permeability is less than that of a vacuum. Cf. FERROMAGNETIC, PARAMAGNETIC. — *n.* A diamagnetic substance. — **di′a·mag·net′i·cal·ly** (-ĭ·kăl·ĭ), *adv.* — **di′a·mag′net·ism** (-măg′nĕ·tĭz′m), *n.*

di·am′e·ter (dī·ăm′ē·tẽr), *n.* [OF. *diametre*, fr. L., fr. Gr. *diametros*, fr. *dia-* + *metron* measure.] Abbr. *diam.* or *dia.* **1.** *Geom.* Any chord passing through the center of a figure or body. See CIRCLE, *Illust.* **2.** The length of a straight line through the center of an object; thickness. — **di·am′e·tral** (-trăl), *adj.*

di′a·met′ric (dī′ȧ·mĕt′rĭk), **di′a·met′ri·cal** (-rĭ·kăl), *adj.* **1.** Of, pertaining to, or of the nature of a diameter. **2.** As remote as possible; directly adverse. — **di′a·met′ri·cal·ly**, *adv.*

di′a·mond (dī′ȧ·mŭnd), *n.* [OF. *diamant*, fr. ML. *diamas, -antis*, corrupt. fr. L. *adamas* steel, diamond, fr. Gr. *adamas*.] **1.** Native crystallized carbon, highly valued, when transparent and free from flaws, as a precious stone; also, a piece of this material. H., 10. Sp. gr. of crystals, 3.52. Diamond is the hardest substance known. **2.** A plane figure formed by four equal straight lines bounding two acute and two obtuse angles; a lozenge. **3.** A tool holding a diamond, for cutting glass. **4.** *Baseball.* The infield; loosely, the playing field. **5.** *Cards.* A red lozenge stamped on a card; a card, or (in *pl.*) the suit, so marked. **6.** *Print.* A size of type (4½ points). See TYPE. — *v. t.* To deck with diamonds.

di′a·mond·back′ (-băk′), *adj.* Also **di′a·mond–backed′** (-băkt′). Having marks like diamonds or lozenges on the back; as, a *diamondback* rattlesnake (see RATTLESNAKE); *diamondback* terrapin (see TERRAPIN).

Diamond State. Delaware; — a nickname alluding to its small size.

Di·an′a (dī·ăn′ȧ), *n.* [L.] **1.** *Roman Relig.* Goddess of the wood and helper of women in childbirth. She was later identified with the Greek Artemis and represented as a huntress and worshiped as a moongoddess. **2.** The moon.

di·an′drous (dī·ăn′drŭs), *adj.* Having two stamens.

di′a·no·et′ic (dī′ȧ·nō·ĕt′ĭk), *adj.* [Gr. *dianoētikos*, fr. *dia-* + *noein* to revolve in the mind.] Of or pertaining to reasoning, esp. discursive reasoning. — **di′a·no·et′ic**, *n.*

di·an′thus (dī·ăn′thŭs), *n.* [NL., fr. Gr. *Zeus*, gen. *Dios*, Zeus + *anthos* flower.] Any of a genus (*Dianthus*) of plants of the pink family, including the pinks and carnations.

di′a·pa′son (dī′ȧ·pā′zŭn; -z′n; -pā′sŭn; -s′n), *n.* [L., fr. Gr. *diapasōn*, fr. *dia* through + *pasōn*, gen. pl. of *pas* all.] *Music.* **a** A part in music sounding the consonance of the octave; concord. **b** The entire compass of tones. **c** A standard of pitch. See PITCH. **d** A tuning fork. **e** One of two sonorously toned organ stops covering the entire compass of the instrument and sounding pitches in unison with, or an octave higher or lower than, the notes played. The ***open diapason*** is of metal pipes; the ***stopped diapason*** is of wooden pipes and has a powerful flute tone.

di′a·per (dī′ȧ·pẽr), *n.* [OF. *diapre, diaspre*, sort of figured cloth, fr. ML. *diasprus*.] **1.** A fabric, now usually white linen or cotton, woven in a pattern formed by the continuous repetition of a simple unit of design; also, such a pattern (**diaper pattern**). **2.** A piece of diaper used as a towel, or esp., as an infant's breechcloth. — *v. t.* To furnish with or as with a diaper, esp. a diaper pattern.

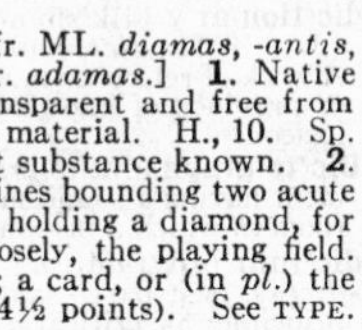
One style of Diaper Pattern.

di′a·pha·ne′i·ty (-fȧ·nē′ĭ·tĭ), *n.* Diaphanous quality.

di·aph′a·nous (dī·ăf′ȧ·nŭs), *adj.* [ML. *diaphanus*, fr. Gr. *diaphanēs*, deriv. of *dia-* + *phainein* to show.] So delicate or fine in texture as to be transparent or translucent. — **di·aph′a·nous·ly**, *adv.* — **di·aph′a·nous·ness**, *n.*

di′a·pho·re′sis (dī′ȧ·fō·rē′sĭs), *n.* [LL., fr. Gr. *diaphorēsis*, fr. *dia-* + *phorein* to carry.] *Med.* Perspiration, esp. profuse perspiration artificially induced.

di′a·pho·ret′ic (-rĕt′ĭk), *adj.* Having power to increase perspiration. — *n.* A diaphoretic agent.

di′a·phragm (dī′ȧ·frăm), *n.* [LL. *diaphragma*, fr. Gr. *diaphragma*, fr. *diaphragnynai* to fence by a partition wall, fr. *dia-* + *phragnynai*, *phrassein*, to fence.] **1.** A partition composed of muscles and sinews; specif., the partition separating the cavity of the chest from that of the abdomen. **2.** A dividing membrane, or thin partition. **3.** Hence: **a** A partition in a tube or pipe. **b** A porous partition, often cup-shaped, for separating solutions, as in a voltaic cell. **c** A vibrating disk or membrane, as in a telephone or phonograph. **d** *Optics.* A device as a perforated plate, to limit the aperture of a lens or optical system. — *v. t.* To fit or supply a diaphragm to. — **di′a·phrag·mat′ic** (-frăg·măt′ĭk), *adj.* — **di′a·phrag·mat′i·cal·ly** (-ĭ·kăl·ĭ), *adv.*

di·aph′y·sis (dī·ăf′ĭ·sĭs), *n.; pl.* -SES (-sēz). [NL., fr. Gr. *diaphysis* a growing through, fr. *dia-* + *phyein* to bring forth.] *Anat.* The shaft of a long bone, — the part first ossified. Cf. EPIPHYSIS. — **di′a·phys′i·al** (dī′ȧ·fĭz′ĭ·ăl), *adj.*

di′a·poph′y·sis (dī′ȧ·pŏf′ĭ·sĭs), *n.; pl.* -SES (-sēz). [NL. See DIA-; APOPHYSIS.] *Anat. & Zool.* The transverse process of a vertebra (see VERTEBRA); — when there are two or more pairs of transverse processes, used of the dorsal pair. — **di′ap·o·phys′i·al** (dī′ăp·ō·fĭz′ĭ·ăl), *adj.*

di′arch·y (dī′är·kĭ), *n.* **1.** Government vested in two supreme rulers. **2.** = DYARCHY. — **di·ar′chi·al** (dī·är′kĭ·ăl), **di·ar′chic** (-är′kĭk), *adj.*

di′a·rist (dī′ȧ·rĭst), *n.* One who keeps or writes a diary.

di′ar·rhe′a, di′ar·rhoe′a (dī′ȧ·rē′ȧ), *n.* [LL. *diarrhoea*, fr. Gr. *diarrhoia*, deriv. of *dia-* + *rhein* to flow.] A morbidly profuse discharge from the intestines. — **di′ar·rhe′al, di′ar·rhoe′al** (-ăl), **di′ar·rhe′ic, di′ar·rhoe′ic** (-ĭk), **di′ar·rhet′ic, di′ar·rhoet′ic** (-rĕt′ĭk), *adj.*

di′ar·thro′sis (dī′är·thrō′sĭs), *n.* [NL., fr. Gr. *diarthrōsis*, deriv. of *dia-* + *arthroun* to fasten by a joint, fr. *arthron* joint.] A form of articulation which admits of free movement. — **di′ar·thro′di·al** (-dĭ·ăl), *adj.*

di′a·ry (dī′ȧ·rĭ), *n.; pl.* -RIES (-rĭz). [L. *diarium*, fr. *dies* day.] A daily record, esp. of personal experiences or observations; also, a book for keeping such a record.

Di·as′po·ra (dī·ăs′pō·rȧ), *n.* [Gr. *diaspora* a scattering, fr. *dia* through, asunder + *speirein* to sow.] Literally, "Dispersion"; — applied collectively: **a** To those Jews scattered through the Old World after the Exile. **b** To Jewish Christians of the apostolic age living among the heathen.

di′a·spore (dī′ȧ·spōr; 70), *n.* *Mineral.* An aluminum hydroxide, $HAlO_2$.

di′a·stase (-stās), *n.* [F., fr. Gr. *diastasis* separation, deriv. of *dia-* + *histanai* to set.] *Biochem.* **a** = AMYLASE. **b** Any of the amylases found in plants or seeds; specif., the amylase of malt. **c** Any enzyme.

di′a·stat′ic (-stăt′ĭk), *adj.* Pertaining to, or having the properties of, diastase; converting starch into sugar.

di·as′ter (dī·ăs′tẽr), *n.* [*di-* + 1st *-aster*.] A stage in mitosis when the chromosomes, having split and separated, group themselves near the poles of the spindle. — **di·as′tral** (-trăl), *adj.*

di·as′to·le (dī·ăs′tō·lē), *n.* [LL., fr. Gr. *diastolē*, deriv. of *dia-* + *stellein* to set.] **1.** The rhythmical expansion or dilatation of the cavities of the heart, during which they fill with blood; — correlative to *systole*. **2.** *Pros.* A lengthening of a short quantity or syllable. — **di′as·tol′ic** (dī′ăs·tŏl′ĭk), *adj.*

di·as′tro·phism (dī·ăs′trō·fĭz′m), *n.* [Gr. *diastrophē* distortion, fr. *dia* through, thoroughly + *strephein* to turn.] *Geol.* The process or processes by which the earth's crust is deformed, producing continents, ocean basins, mountains, etc.; also, the results of these processes. See EPEIROGENY. — **di′a·stroph′ic** (dī′ȧ·strŏf′ĭk), *adj.*

di′a·tes′sa·ron (dī′ȧ·tĕs′ȧ·rŏn), *n.* [L., fr. Gr. *diatessarōn* the interval of a fourth.] **1.** *Anc. Music.* The interval of a fourth. **2.** *Bible Hist.* A combination of the four Gospels into a single consecutive narrative.

di′a·ther′man·cy (-thûr′măn·sĭ), *n.* [Gr. *diathermainein* to warm through.] *Physics.* The property of transmitting infrared radiation.

di′a·ther′ma·nous (-mȧ·nŭs), *adj.* Diathermic; — opposed to *athermanous*.

di′a·ther′mic (-thûr′mĭk), *adj.* [*dia-* + Gr. *thermē* heat.] **1.** Affording a free passage to heat rays. **2.** Of or pertaining to diathermy.

di′a·ther′my (dī′ȧ·thûr′mĭ), *n.* Also **di′a·ther′mi·a** (-thûr′mĭ·ȧ). The therapeutic heating of tissues beneath the skin by means of high-frequency electrical oscillations; also, the apparatus used. — **di′a·ther′mize** (-thûr′mīz), *v. t.*

di·ath′e·sis (dī·ăth′ē·sĭs), *n.* [NL., fr. Gr. *diathesis*, deriv. of *dia-* + *tithenai* to place.] Bodily condition or constitution predisposing to a disease. — **di′a·thet′ic** (dī′ȧ·thĕt′ĭk), *adj.*

di′a·tom (dī′ȧ·tŏm; -tōm), *n.* [Gr. *diatomos* cut in two.] Any of a class (Bacillarieae) of microscopic unicellular or colonial algae, the silicified skeletons of which form kieselguhr.

di′a·to·ma′ceous (-tō·mā′shŭs), *adj.* Pertaining to, consisting of, or abounding in, diatoms or their siliceous remains, as **diatomaceous earth**, or kieselguhr (which see).

di′a·tom′ic (dī′ȧ·tŏm′ĭk), *adj.* *Chem.* **a** Consisting of two atoms; having two atoms in the molecule. **b** Bivalent. **c** Having two replaceable atoms or radicals.

di·at′o·mite (dī·ăt′ō·mīt), *n.* Diatomaceous earth.

di′a·ton′ic (dī′ȧ·tŏn′ĭk), *adj.* [From L., fr. Gr. *diatonikos, diatonos*, deriv. of *dia-* + *teinein* to stretch.] **a** *Gr. Music.* Comprising two steps and a half step; — distinguished from *chromatic* and *enharmonic*. **b** *Modern Music.* Pertaining to or designating a standard major or minor scale of eight tones to the octave. Cf. CHROMATIC; see PITCH. — **di′a·ton′i·cal·ly** (-ĭ·kăl·ĭ), *adv.*

di′a·tribe (dī′ȧ·trīb), *n.* [F., fr. L. *diatriba* a learned discussion, fr. Gr. *diatribē*, prop., a wearing away of time, deriv. of *dia-* + *tribein* to rub.] A prolonged discussion; esp., a bitter or abusive harangue.

di·at′ro·pism (dī·ăt′rō·pĭz′m), *n.* [*dia-* + *-tropism*.] Tropistic tendency of certain plant organs to place themselves transversely to the line of action of a stimulus. — **di′a·trop′ic** (dī′ȧ·trŏp′ĭk), *adj.*

di′a·zine (dī′ȧ·zēn; dī·ăz′ēn; -ĭn), *n.* Also **di′a·zin.** [*di-* + *az-* + *-ine*.] Any of three parent compounds, $C_4H_4N_2$, containing a ring of four carbon and two nitrogen atoms.

di·az′o- (dī·ăz′ō-; dī·ā′zō-). [*di-* + *azo-*.] *Chem.* A combining form denoting the *presence* of a group *of two nitrogen atoms*, N_2, in direct union with *one* hydrocarbon radical and, usually, with some other group or an atom. Diazo compounds in which the N_2 group forms part of a cation are called **di′a·zo′ni·um com′pounds** (dī′ȧ·zō′nĭ·ŭm). — **di·az′o** (dī·ăz′ō; -ā′zō), *adj.* — **di·az′o·tize** (dī·ăz′ō·tīz), *v. t.*

di′a·zole (dī′ȧ·zōl; dī·ăz′ōl), *n.* [*di-* + *az-* + L. *oleum* oil.] A parent compound containing a ring of three carbon and two nitrogen atoms, or a derivative of it.

dib (dĭb), *v. i.;* DIBBED (dĭbd); DIB′BING. **1.** To dip. **2.** *Angling.* To let the bait bob and dip lightly.

di·bas′ic (dī·bās′ĭk), *adj.* *Chem.* **a** Having two hydrogen atoms replaceable by basic atoms or radicals; — of acids. **b** Containing two atoms of a univalent metal. — **di′ba·sic′i·ty** (dī′bȧ·sĭs′ĭ·tĭ), *n.*

dib′ber (dĭb′ẽr), *n.* A dibble.

dib′ble (dĭb′'l), *n.* A pointed implement used to make holes in the ground for plants or seeds; a small narrow trowel. — *v. t.;* DIB′BLED (-'ld); DIB′BLING (-lĭng). To plant, or to make holes in (soil), with or as with a dibble.

dib′ble, *v. i.* **1.** To dib. **2.** To dabble.

dib′buk (dĭb′ŭk; dĭ·bōōk′), *n.* [Heb. *dibbuq*, fr. *dabaq* to cling, cleave.] *Jewish Folklore.* **a** An evil spirit possessing a man. **b** The soul of a dead person, residing in another's body and acting through it.

di·bran′chi·ate (dī·brăng′kĭ·āt), *adj.* [See 1st DI-; BRANCHIA.] Of or pertaining to a group (Dibranchia) of cephalopod mollusks, including the squids and octopuses, having eight or ten cephalic arms, and an apparatus for emitting an inky fluid. — *n.* A dibranchiate mollusk.

di′cast (dī′kăst; dĭk′ăst), *n.* [Gr. *dikastēs*, fr. *dikazein* to judge, fr. *dikē* right, judgment, justice.] *Gr. Antiq.* A judge; usually, a member of the highest court of the Athenian democracy. — **di·cas′tic** (dī·kăs′tĭk), *adj.*

dice (dīs), *n.; pl.* of DIE. Small cubes marked on their faces with spots from one to six, used in gaming or in determining by chance; also, the casting of, or gaming with, dice. — *v. t.*; DICED (dīst); DIC'ING (dīs'-ĭng). **1.** To lose, waste, etc., by playing at dice. **2.** To cut into small cubes. **3.** To mark with a dicelike pattern; checker. — *v. i.* To play games with dice. — **dic'er** (dīs'ẽr), *n.*

di·cen'tra (dī·sĕn'trȧ), *n.* [NL., fr. *di-* + Gr. *kentron* spur.] Any of a genus (*Dicentra*) of North American and Asiatic herbs of the fumitory family, with dissected leaves and irregular flowers; specif., the bleeding heart.

di·cha'si·um (dī·kā'zhĭ·ŭm; -zĭ·ŭm), *n.*; *pl.* -SIA (-ȧ). [NL., fr. Gr. *dichasis* division, fr. *dicha* in two, fr. *dis* twice.] *Bot.* A cymose inflorescence which produces two main axes, as in a dichotomous cyme. Cf. MONOCHASIUM, POLYCHASIUM. — **di·cha'si·al** (-ăl), *adj.*

di·chlo'ride (dī·klō'rīd; -rĭd), *n.* Also **di·chlo'rid.** A compound containing two atoms of chlorine with an element or radical.

di'cho- (dī'kō-), **dich-.** [Gr. *dicha.*] A combining form meaning *in two, asunder*, as in **di'cho·car'pous** (see -CARPOUS).

di·chog'a·my (dī·kŏg'ȧ·mĭ), *n.* [*dicho-* + *-gamy.*] *Bot.* Maturing of stamens and pistils at different periods, insuring cross-pollination; — opp. to *homogamy.* — **di·chog'a·mous** (-mŭs), **di'cho·gam'ic** (dī'kō·găm'ĭk), *adj.*

di·chot'o·mize (dī·kŏt'ō·mīz), *v. t. & i.* To make a dichotomy (of); to exhibit a dichotomy (of). — **di·chot'o·mist** (-mĭst), *n.* — **di·chot'o·mi·za'tion** (-mĭ·zā'shŭn; -mī·zā'-), *n.*

di·chot'o·my (-mĭ), *n.*; *pl.* -MIES (-mĭz). [Gr. *dichotomia*, fr. *dicha* in two, asunder + *temnein* to cut.] **1.** Division into two subordinate parts; hence, a cutting in two; a division. **2.** *Astron.* That phase of the moon or planet whose path is within the orbit of the earth in which just half its disk appears illuminated. **3.** *Biol.* A forking or bifurcation, esp. repeated bifurcation, as of the stem of a plant. **4.** *Bot.* A system of branching in which the main axis forks repeatedly into two branches, forming a helicoid axis when the corresponding member of each pair is suppressed or a scorpioid axis when alternate members of adjacent pairs are suppressed. See SYMPODIUM, *Illust.* **5.** *Logic.* Division of a class into two subclasses, esp. two opposed by contradiction, as *white* and *not white.* — **di·chot'o·mous** (-mŭs), **di'cho·tom'ic** (dī'kō·tŏm'ĭk), *adj.*

di·chro'ic (dī·krō'ĭk), *adj.* Also **di'chro·it'ic** (dī'krō·ĭt'ĭk). [See DICHROISM.] **1.** Having the property of dichroism. **2.** Dichromatic.

di'chro·ism (dī'krō·ĭz'm), *n.* [Gr. *dichroos* two-colored, fr. *di-* (= *dis*) twice + *chroa* color.] **1.** *Cryst.* The property of presenting different colors in two different directions, by transmitted light. **2.** *Physics.* The property of some bodies of differing in color with the thickness of the transmitting layer, or, in liquids, with the degree of concentration of the solution. **3.** Dichromatism.

di'chro·ite (-īt), *n.* *Mineral.* Iolite.

di·chro'mate (dī·krō'māt; dī'krō-), *n.* See DICHROMIC ACID.

di'chro·mat'ic (dī'krō·măt'ĭk), *adj.* **1.** Having or exhibiting two colors. **2.** Of, pertaining to, or affected by dichromatism. **3.** *Biol.* Having two color varieties or phases, independently of age or sex, as certain birds and insects.

di·chro'ma·tism (dī·krō'mȧ·tĭz'm), *n.* **1.** State, condition, or property of being dichromatic. **2.** *Psychol.* The condition of seeing, or being able to see, only two of the fundamental colors, or two colors and their combinations. See COLOR-BLIND, *adj.*

di·chro'mic (dī·krō'mĭk), *adj.* *Chem.* Containing two atoms, or equivalents, of chromium.

dichromic acid. An acid, $H_2Cr_2O_7$, forming a series of stable salts called *dichromates* or *bichromates.*

di·chro'o·scope (dī·krō'ō·skōp), **di'chro·scope** (dī'krō·skōp), *n.* [*di-* + Gr. *chroa* color + *-scope.*] An apparatus for examining dichroism. — **di'chro·scop'ic** (dī'krō·skŏp'ĭk), *adj.*

dick (dĭk), *n.* *Slang, U. S.* A detective.

dick·cis'sel (dĭk·sĭs'ĕl), *n.* The black-throated bunting (*Spiza americana*), a migratory bird of the central U. S.

dick'ens (dĭk'ĕnz; -ĭnz), *n. & interj.* The devil; the deuce; — a euphemism.

Dick·en'si·an (dĭk·ĕn'zĭ·ăn), *adj.* Having or exhibiting qualities of Dickens's novels, as, esp., kindly humor and pathos in the portrayal of odd characters from humble life.

dick'er (dĭk'ẽr), *n.* [From L. *decuria* a division consisting of ten, fr. *decem* ten.] *Com.* Originally, ten, as of hides or skins; now, any of various numbers or quantities, esp. twelve.

dick'er, *v. i. & t.* *U. S.* To barter; haggle; make a dicker. — *n.* *U. S.* A bartering; exchange; also, loosely, an agreement.

dick'ey, dick'y (dĭk'ĭ), *n.*; *pl.* -EYS, -IES (-ĭz). [From *Dick*, a familiar name.] **1.** Any of various articles of clothing, as a false shirt front or a woman's partial blouse consisting of a front, and often also a back panel, worn with suit, sweater, or dress. **2.** One of various animals, as a donkey or a small bird. **3.** In a vehicle: **a** A seat for the driver; — called also **dickey box.** **b** A seat at the back; a rumble.

Dick test (dĭk). [After George F. *Dick* (b. 1881) and Gladys H. *Dick* (b. 1881), Am. physicians.] *Med.* A test to determine susceptibility to scarlet fever, made by injecting scarlet fever toxin into the skin.

di'cli·nous (dī'klĭ·nŭs; dī·klī'nŭs), *adj.* [*di-* + Gr. *klinē* bed.] *Bot.* Having the androecium and gynoecium in separate flowers. — **di'cli·nism** (dī'klĭ·nĭz'm), *n.*

di'cot (dī'kŏt), **di·cot'yl** (dī·kŏt'ĭl), *n.* *Bot.* A dicotyledon.

di·cot'y·le'don (dī·kŏt'ĭ·lē'dŭn), *n.* [*di-* + *cotyledon.*] *Bot.* A plant having two cotyledons, or seed leaves; a member of one (Dicotyledones) of the two subclasses of angiospermous plants, including all that produce two cotyledons, such as most deciduous trees, and most herbs and shrubs. — **di·cot'y·le'don·ous** (-lē'dŭn·ŭs; -lĕd'ŭn·ŭs), *adj.*

di·cou'ma·rin (dī·ko͞o'mȧ·rĭn), *n.* [*di-* + *coumarin.*] A crystalline compound, $C_{19}H_{12}O_6$, that prolongs the coagulation time of blood. It is extracted from spoiled sweet clover or synthesized.

di·crot'ic (dī·krŏt'ĭk), *adj.* [*di-* + Gr. *krotein* to beat.] *Physiol.* Indicating or pertaining to the second expansion of the artery, which occurs during the diastole of the heart; as, a *dicrotic* wave or pulse. — **di'cro·tism** (dī'krō·tĭz'm; dĭk'rō-), *n.*

dic'ta (dĭk'tȧ), *n.*, *pl.* of DICTUM.

Dic'ta·phone (dĭk'tȧ·fōn), *n.* A trade-mark for a phonographic instrument combining a recorder and reproducer, for use in dictating letters and other matter.

dic'tate (dĭk'tāt; dĭk·tāt'), *v. t.* [L. *dictatus*, past part. of *dictare*, freq. of *dicere* to say.] **1.** To tell or utter so that another may write down. **2.** To say, utter, or communicate authoritatively; to deliver (a command); to impose; require; as, to *dictate* terms. — *v. i.* **1.** To dictate a letter or the like. **2.** To give or impose orders.

dic'tate (dĭk'tāt), *n.* An authoritative direction, rule, etc.; a command; as, the *dictates* of conscience.

dic·ta'tion (dĭk·tā'shŭn), *n.* **1.** Act of dictating something to be written down. **2.** Authoritative utterance or arbitrary command. **3.** That which is dictated. — **dic·ta'tion·al** (-ăl; -'l), *adj.*

dic·ta'tor (dĭk·tā'tẽr; dĭk'tāt·ẽr), *n.* [L.] One who dictates; specif., one who exercises supreme authority in a state. — **dic·ta'tor·ship,** *n.* — **dic·ta'tress** (dĭk·tā'trĕs; -trĭs), *n.*

dic'ta·to'ri·al (dĭk'tȧ·tō'rĭ·ăl), *adj.* Pertaining or suited to a dictator; absolute; imperious. — **dic'ta·to'ri·al·ly,** *adv.* — **dic'ta·to'ri·al·ness,** *n.*

Syn. Dictatorial, magisterial, dogmatic, doctrinaire, oracular mean imposing or tending to impose one's will or opinions on others. Dictatorial stresses autocratic, highhanded methods and, often, an imperious manner; magisterial stresses excessive display of powers, such as those of magistrate or schoolmaster, in controlling or in forcing acceptance of one's opinions; dogmatic implies the attitude of one who lays down principles as true and beyond dispute; doctrinaire implies a disposition to be guided by abstract theories in framing laws or in making decisions affecting others; oracular implies the manner of one who delivers his opinions in cryptic phrases or with pompous dogmatism.

dic'tion (dĭk'shŭn), *n.* [F. or L.; F., fr. L. *dictio* saying, word; akin to L. *dicere, dictum*, to say.] **1.** Choice of words to express ideas; mode of expression in language. **2.** Art or manner of speaking or singing, esp. in public; enunciation, vocal expression, etc.

dic'tion·ar'y (dĭk'shŭn·ĕr'ĭ *or, esp. Brit.*, -ẽr·ĭ, -rĭ; 3), *n.*; *pl.* -ARIES (-ĭz). [ML. *dictionarium* or *dictionarius* (sc. *liber*). See DICTION.] A work of reference in which the words of a language or of any system or province of knowledge are entered alphabetically and defined; a lexicon.

Dic'to·graph (dĭk'tō·grăf; 9), *n.* A trade-mark for a telephonic instrument having a sound-magnifying device that transmits sounds from a room in which a person is stationed or concealed.

dic'tum (dĭk'tŭm), *n.*; *pl.* -TA (-tȧ), -TUMS (-tŭmz). [L., neuter of *dictus*, past part., said.] **1.** An authoritative statement; dogmatic principle; as, critical *dicta*; also, current saying; as, a mere *dictum.* **2.** *Law.* A judicial opinion on a point other than the precise issue involved in a case.

did (dĭd), *past tense of* DO.

Did'a·che (dĭd'ȧ·kē), *n.* [Gr. *didachē* teaching.] A Christian manual of the 2d century by an unknown author (called **Did'a·chist** [-kĭst] *or* **Did'a·chog'ra·pher** [-kŏg'rȧ·fẽr]).

di·dac'tic (dī·dăk'tĭk; dĭ-), **di·dac'ti·cal** (-tĭ·kăl), *adj.* [Gr. *didaktikos*, fr. *didaskein* to teach.] Fitted or intended to teach; preceptive; instructive. — **di·dac'ti·cal·ly,** *adv.* — **di·dac'ti·cism** (-tĭ·sĭz'm), *n.*

di·dac'tics (-tĭks), *n.*; see -ICS. Pedagogy; art of teaching; systematic instruction.

di'dap'per (dī'dăp'ẽr), *n.* A dabchick or other small grebe.

did'dle (dĭd''l), *v. i. & t.*; DID'DLED (-'ld); DID'DLING (-lĭng). *Colloq.* To move jerkily up and down, or back and forth; to jiggle.

did'dle, *v. t. & i.* *Colloq.* **1.** To swindle; hoax. **2.** To waste (time) in trifling; potter. — **did'dler** (dĭd'lẽr), *n.*

Di'do (dī'dō), *n.*; *pl.* (in sense 2) DIDOES, *sometimes* DIDOS (-dōz). [L., fr. Gr. *Didō.*] **1.** A Tyrian princess, queen of Carthage and its reputed founder. In Vergil's *Aeneid*, she entertains Aeneas after his flight from Troy, falls in love with him, and on his desertion stabs herself. **2.** [*not cap.*] *U. S.* A trick; antic; caper.

didst (dĭdst), *2d pers. sing. past* of DO.

di·dym'i·um (dī·dĭm'ĭ·ŭm; dĭ-), *n.* Also **di'dym** (dĭ'dĭm). [NL., fr. Gr. *didymos* twin.] *Chem.* A rare metal usually associated with lanthanum. Formerly supposed to be an element, it has been separated into the elements *neodymium* and *praseodymium.*

did'y·mous (dĭd'ĭ·mŭs), *adj.* [Gr. *didymos* twofold, twin.] *Bot. & Zool.* Growing in pairs; twin or twofold.

die (dī), *v. i.*; DIED (dīd); DY'ING (dī'ĭng). [ME. *dien, deyen*, fr. ON. *deyja.*] **1.** To cease to live; become dead; decease. **2.** To suffer the pains of, or as if of death. **3.** To become extinct; also, to vanish; pass; fade. **4.** To suffer spiritual death. **5.** To grow faint; sink. **6.** To languish; hence, to long intensely. **7.** To cease from or as if from functioning; stop. **8.** To become indifferent or as if dead to; as, to *die* unto sin.

die (dī), *n.*; *pl.* in senses 1, 2, and (rarely) 3, DICE (dīs); in 4, 5, DIES (dīz). [OF. *de*, fr. L. *datus* given, thrown, past part. of *dare* to give, throw.] **1.** One of the small cubes used in gaming. **2.** A small cube; as, to cut potatoes into *dice.* **3.** That which is, or might be, determined by a throw of the die; chance. **4.** *Arch.* The dado of a pedestal. See DADO, *Illust.* **5.** *Mach.* Any of various tools used to shape or impress an object or material; as: **a** One of a pair (also, the pair) of cutting or shaping tools which operate by being pressed or driven toward one other, the smaller tool, or one that enters the larger, being called a *punch*, the larger a *matrix* or *die.* **b** A hollow, internally threaded screw-cutting tool, as for forming screw threads on bolts, etc. **c** A cutter to cut out blanks. **d** A perforated block, as of hard metal, used in making wire by drawing or extrusion. — *v. t.*; DIED (dīd); DIE'ING. To cut or shape with a die.

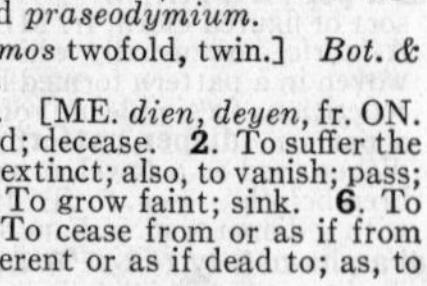

Die, 5 b (four pieces of a Tap-and-Die Set). 1 Adjustable round split Die; 2 Diestock; 3 Tap; 4 Tap Wrench.

die'back' (dī'băk'), *n.* *Plant Pathol.* A condition in woody plants in which the ends of branches die, often progressively backward, due to disease, insect injury, or winter injury.

di·e'cious, di·e'cious·ly. Vars. of DIOECIOUS, DIOECIOUSLY.

die'-hard' (dī'härd'), *n.* Also **die'hard'.** An irreconcilable opponent of a winning measure, usually a conservative.

di'e·lec'tric (dī'ē·lĕk'trĭk), *n.* [*dia-* + *electric.*] *Elec.* A nonconducting material. — **di'e·lec'tric, di'e·lec'tri·cal** (-trĭ·kăl), *adj.* — **di'e·lec'tri·cal·ly,** *adv.*

di'en·ceph'a·lon (dī'ĕn·sĕf'ȧ·lŏn), *n.* See FOREBRAIN.

di·er'e·sis. Var. of DIAERESIS.

‖**di'es** (dī'ēz), *n. sing. & pl.* [L.] Day.

die'sel en'gine (dē'zĕl), *or* **die'sel,** *n.* [After Rudolf *Diesel* (1858–1913), the inventor.] An internal-combustion engine in which air is compressed to a temperature sufficiently high to ignite fuel injected directly into the cylinder. Its operations constitute the **diesel cycle:**

compression of air; injection and ignition of fuel during the beginning of the power stroke and expansion of gases during the rest of the stroke; expulsion of gases; intake of air. Diesel engines may be of four-stroke cycle or two-stroke cycle.

‖**di′es faus′tus** (dī′ēz fôs′tŭs). [L.] A day of favorable omen.

‖**di′es in·faus′tus** (ĭn·fôs′tŭs). [L.] A day of unfavorable omen.

die′sink′er (dī′sĭngk′ẽr), *n.* One who makes cutting and shaping dies. — **die′sink′ing**, *n.*

‖**Di′es I′rae** (dī′ēz ī′rē). [L., day of wrath.] A Latin hymn on the Day of Judgment, sung in requiem masses.

di′e·sis (dī′ĕ·sĭs), *n.; pl.* -SES (-sēz). [L., fr. Gr. *diesis*, deriv. of *dia-* + *hienai* to let go, send.] = DOUBLE DAGGER.

‖**di′es non** (dī′ēz nŏn). [L.] *Law.* A day on which the business of courts cannot be lawfully carried on.

die′stock′ (dī′stŏk′), *n.* A stock to hold screw-cutting dies. See DIE, *Illust.*

di′et (dī′ĕt), *n.* [OF. *diete*, fr. L. *diaeta*, fr. Gr. *diaita* manner of living.] **1.** Habitual course of living or, esp., feeding; hence, food and drink regularly provided or consumed; fare. **2.** Prescribed allowance of food with reference to a particular state of health; regimen prescribed. — *v. t. & i.* To cause to eat and drink, or to eat and drink, esp. sparingly or by prescribed rules. — **di′et·er**, *n.*

di′et, *n.* [ML. *dieta* day's journey, assembly (whence F. *diète*), fr. L. *dies* day.] **1.** *Scot.* A day set for a meeting, appearance, etc.; also, a session or sitting. **2.** A formal public assembly; used specif. [*often cap.*] as the English name for various national or local legislative assemblies.

di′e·tar′y (dī′ĕ·tĕr′ĭ *or, esp. Brit.,* -tẽr·ĭ), *n.; pl.* -TARIES (-ĭz). A rule of, or a treatise on, diet; also, a fixed allowance of food. — **di′e·tar′y**, *adj.*

dietary laws. *Jewish Relig.* Laws observed by orthodox Jews relating to the fitness of certain foods for eating, and the prohibition of certain combinations of foods.

di′e·tet′ic (dī′ĕ·tĕt′ĭk), *adj.* Also **di′e·tet′i·cal** (-ĭ·kăl). Of or pertaining to diet. — **di′e·tet′i·cal·ly**, *adv.*

di′e·tet′ics (-ĭks), *n.;* see -ICS. The science and art dealing with the application of principles of nutrition to the feeding of individuals or groups.

di·eth′yl·stil·bes′trol, di·eth′yl·stil·boes′trol (dī·ĕth′ĭl·stĭl·bĕs′trōl; -trŏl), *n.* [*di-* + *ethyl* + *stilbestrol.*] *Biochem.* A colorless crystalline synthetic compound, $C_{18}H_{20}O_2$, used as a potent estrogen; — called also *stilbestrol.*

di′e·ti′tian, di′e·ti′cian (dī′ĕ·tĭsh′ăn), *n.* [*diet* + *physician.*] One versed in or practicing dietetics.

‖**Dieu a′vec′ nous** (dyû′ à′vĕk′ nōō′). [F.] God with us.

‖**Dieu dé′fend′ le droit** (dā′fäN′ lẽ drwä′). [F.] God defends the right.

‖**Dieu et mon droit** (ā môN drwä′). [F.] God and my right; — motto in British royal arms.

‖**Dieu vous garde** (vōō′ gàrd′). [F.] God keep you; — formerly a salutation.

dif′fer (dĭf′ẽr), *v. i.* [OF. *differer*, fr. L. *differre* to carry apart, postpone, be different, fr. *dis-* + *ferre* to bear, carry.] **1.** To be or stand apart because of unlikeness; to be distinguished; — followed by *from.* **2.** To be of unlike or opposite opinion; to disagree; — with *from* or *with.* **3.** To have a difference or quarrel; — followed by *with.*

dif′fer·ence (dĭf′ẽr·ĕns), *n.* **1.** State, quality, or measure of being different; variation; dissimilarity; also, an instance of such dissimilarity. **2.** Distinction, as in treatment; discrimination. **3.** Disagreement in opinion; dissension; hence, cause of dissension; matter in controversy. **4.** *Now Rare.* Mark of distinction; characteristic quality. **5.** *Logic.* A differentia. **6.** *Math.* The magnitude or quantity by which one magnitude or quantity differs from another of the same kind. — **Syn.** See DISSIMILARITY. — *v. t.* To cause to differ; to make a difference in; differentiate; discriminate.

dif′fer·ent (-ĕnt), *adj.* **1.** Of various or contrary nature, form, or quality; partly or totally unlike; dissimilar; — usually followed by *from*, but also by *to*, esp. colloquially in England, and by *than.* The constructions with *to* and *than* have long literary usage to support them, but are considered incorrect by some. **2.** Distinct; separate; not the same; other; as, five *different* churches. **3.** Out of the ordinary; unusual; as, she is *different.*

Syn. **Different, diverse, divergent, disparate, various** mean not identical or alike in kind or character. **Different** may imply distinctness or separateness of, or contrast or contrariness between, the individuals; **diverse** implies both distinctness and contrast; **divergent** implies a movement away from each other and unlikelihood of ultimate meeting, combination, reconciliation, or the like; **disparate** goes further than *divergent* in implying incongruity or incompatibility; **various** stresses the number of sorts or of kinds.

dif′fer·en′ti·a (dĭf′ẽr·ĕn′shĭ·ȧ), *n.; pl.* -TIAE (-ē). [L., difference.] *Logic.* That property or mark distinguishing a species from other species of the same genus.

dif′fer·en′ti·a·ble (-shĭ·ȧ·b′l), *adj.* That may be differentiated.

dif′fer·en′tial (-shăl), *adj.* **1.** Relating to, indicating, or exhibiting a difference or differences; as, *differential* characteristics. **2.** Creating, constituting, or making a difference; as, a *differential* wage. **3.** Having different effects; as, *differential* erosion; producing effects, esp. mechanical effects, by means of differences, different parts, etc.; as, a *differential* gear. **4.** Pertaining to, resulting from, or involving, a differential, differentials, a differential mechanism, etc. — *n.* Something differential; specif.: **a** A difference between the rates, as on railroads, over two routes to the same point. The lower rate is called a **differential rate.** **b** *Elec.* One of two coils of conducting wire producing contrary polar action. **c** *Mach.* = DIFFERENTIAL GEAR. **d** *Math.* An infinitesimal or arbitrarily small change assigned to a variable. — **dif′fer·en′tial·ly**, *adv.*

differential calculus. *Math.* See CALCULUS, 2 **b.**

differential coefficient *or* **quotient.** *Math.* The limit of the ratio of the corresponding changes of function and argument, as the latter change approaches 0.

differential equation. *Math.* An equation with one or more differential coefficients.

differential gear *or* **gearing.** An arrangement of gears in an epicyclic train that connects two shafts or axles in the same line, divides the driving force equally between them, and permits one shaft to revolve faster than the other. Cf. EPICYCLIC TRAIN, *Illust.*

differential windlass. A windlass whose barrel has two parts of different diameters; — called also *Chinese windlass.* See WINDLASS, *Illust.*

dif′fer·en′ti·ate (dĭf′ẽr·ĕn′shĭ·āt), *v. t.* **1.** To distinguish by a specific difference; develop differential characteristics or forms in. **2.** To ascertain or express the specific difference of; discriminate. **3.** *Math.* To form the differential, or differential coefficient, of; as, to *differentiate* an expression or equation. — *v. i.* To acquire a distinct character; to become differentiated. — **dif′fer·en′ti·a′tion** (-ā′shŭn), *n.*

dif′fer·ent·ly (dĭf′ẽr·ĕnt·lĭ), *adv.* In a different manner.

dif′fi·cile′ (dĭf′ĭ·sēl′; *form.* dĭ·fĭs′ĭl), *adj.* [F., fr. L. *difficilis.*] Difficult; hard to do, manage, or deal with.

dif′fi·cult (dĭf′ĭ·kŭlt; -kŭlt), *adj.* [From DIFFICULTY.] **1.** Hard to do, make, or carry out; not easy. **2.** Involving difficulties in dealing with, understanding, reaching, etc.; as, a *difficult* child, book, or summit. — **Syn.** See HARD. — **Ant.** Simple. — **dif′fi·cult·ly**, *adv.*

dif′fi·cul·ty (-kŭl·tĭ; -kŭl·tĭ), *n.; pl.* -TIES (-tĭz). [L. *difficultas*, fr. *difficilis* difficult, fr. *dis-* + *facilis* easy.] **1.** Quality or state of being difficult. **2.** A thing that is difficult. **3.** Show of reluctance; demur. **4.** Embarrassment of affairs.

Syn. **Difficulty, hardship, rigor, vicissitude** mean something not to be overcome without effort or endurance. **Difficulty** applies to any situation, condition, experience, or task almost beyond one's ability to suffer, surmount, or solve, yet requiring skill, perseverance, and patience; **hardship** stresses suffering, toil, privation, or the like, and does not necessarily imply any effort to overcome, or any patience in enduring; **rigor**, as here considered, applies to a hardship imposed upon one, as by an austere religion, a tyrannical government, a severely trying climate, or the like; **vicissitude**, as here considered, applies to a difficulty or hardship incident to one's life or one's career, and, often, beyond one's powers of control.

dif′fi·dence (dĭf′ĭ·dĕns), *n.* State or quality of being diffident.

dif′fi·dent (-dĕnt), *adj.* [L. *diffidens, -entis*, pres. part. of *diffidere*, fr. *dis-* + *fidere* to trust.] **1.** *Archaic.* Wanting confidence; distrustful. **2.** Wanting confidence in oneself; unduly timid. — **Syn.** See SHY. — **Ant.** Confident. — **dif′fi·dent·ly**, *adv.*

dif·fract′ (dĭ·frăkt′), *v. t.* [L. *diffractus*, past part. of *diffringere* to break in pieces, fr. *dis-* + *frangere* to break.] To cause to undergo diffraction. — **dif·frac′tive** (-frăk′tĭv), *adj.* — **dif·frac′tive·ly**, *adv.* — **dif·frac′tive·ness**, *n.*

dif·frac′tion (-frăk′shŭn), *n.* *Physics.* A modification which light undergoes, as in passing by the edges of opaque bodies or through narrow slits, in which the rays appear to be deflected, producing fringes of parallel light and dark or colored bands; also, the analogous phenomenon observed in the case of sound, electricity, etc.

diffraction grating. *Optics.* = GRATING, 2.

dif·fuse′ (dĭ·fūs′), *adj.* [F. *diffus*, fr. L. See DIFFUSE, *v.*] Poured widespread; spread out; hence, copious; verbose; prolix. — **Syn.** See WORDY. — **dif·fuse′ly**, *adv.* — **dif·fuse′ness**, *n.*

dif·fuse′ (-fūz′), *v. t. & i.* [F. or L.; F. *diffuser*, fr. L. *diffusus*, past part. of *diffundere* to pour out, fr. *dis-* + *fundere* to pour.] **1.** To pour out so as to spread in all directions; hence, to spread throughout, widely, wastefully, etc. **2.** To perplex. *Shak.* **3.** *Physics.* To subject to or undergo diffusion.

dif·fus′er (-fūz′ẽr), **dif·fu′sor** (-fū′zẽr), *n.* **1.** One that diffuses. **2.** Specif.: *Aeronautics.* A device whose function is to reduce the velocity and increase the static pressure of a fluid passing through a system.

dif·fus′i·ble (-fūz′ĭ·b′l), *adj.* Capable of diffusing, or of being diffused. — **dif·fus′i·bil′i·ty** (-bĭl′ĭ·tĭ), *n.*

dif·fu′sion (dĭ·fū′zhŭn), *n.* **1.** Act of diffusing, or state of being diffused. **2.** Diffuseness; prolixity; — said of speech or writing. **3.** *Physics & Chem.* **a** A spontaneous process of equalization of physical states, as of temperature by heat conduction or of gases when one gas is liberated in another. **b** The reflection of light by a rough reflecting surface or transmission of light through a translucent material.

dif·fu′sive (-sĭv), *adj.* Tending to diffuse; marked by diffusion. — **dif·fu′sive·ly**, *adv.* — **dif·fu′sive·ness**, *n.*

dig (dĭg), *v. t.;* DUG (dŭg) or DIGGED (dĭgd); DIG′GING. [ME. *diggen*, fr. F. *diguer* to excavate, prick, of LG. origin.] **1.** To turn up, or delve in (earth), with a spade or a hoe; pierce, open, or loosen, with or as with a spade. **2.** To bring to the surface or get by digging; to exhume; as, to *dig* potatoes; hence, to unearth; — often with *out* or *up;* as, to *dig* up facts. **3.** To form, as a ditch, by removing earth; excavate. **4.** To thrust; prod. — *v. i.* **1.** To dig anything; delve. **2.** *Colloq.* To drudge; specif., *U. S.*, to study ploddingly. — *n. Colloq.* **a** A thrust; a poke. **b** A verbal thrust. **c** A plodding student.

di·gam′ma (dī·găm′ȧ), *n.* [Gr., fr. *di-* (= *dis*) twice + *gamma* the letter Γ; — from resemblance to two *gammas* one above the other.] A letter (Ϝ, *Ϝ*) of the original Greek alphabet, afterwards disused, in sound approximating English W. — **di·gam′mat·ed** (-āt·ĕd; -ĭd), *adj.*

dig′a·my (dĭg′ȧ·mĭ), *n.* [LL. *digamia*, fr. Gr. *digamia* a second marriage.] Being twice married legally; deuterogamy. Cf. BIGAMY, MONOGAMY. — **dig′a·mous** (-mŭs), *adj.*

di·gas′tric (dī·găs′trĭk), *adj.* [*di-* + Gr. *gastēr* belly.] *Anat.* Fleshy at each end and having a tendon in the middle; — of a muscle, esp. one of the depressors of the lower jaw.

di·gen′e·sis (-jĕn′ĕ·sĭs), *n.* [*di-* + *-genesis.*] *Biol.* Successive reproduction by sexual and asexual methods. — **di′ge·net′ic** (dī′jĕ·nĕt′ĭk), *adj.*

di′gest (dī′jĕst), *n.* [L. *digestum*, pl. *digesta*, neut., fr. *digestus*, past part. See DIGEST, *v.*] **1.** A body of information that is classified and arranged under proper heads or titles, often in condensed form. **2.** **a** Compilation of legal rules, statutes, or decisions systematically arranged. **b** The Pandects. **3.** The product resulting from the action of an enzyme on a substrate; as, a tryptic *digest* of casein. — **Syn.** See COMPENDIUM.

di·gest′ (dĭ·jĕst′; dī-), *v. t.* [L. *digestus*, past part. of *digerere* to separate, arrange, dissolve, digest, fr. *di-* (= *dis-*) + *gerere* to bear, carry, wear.] **1.** To distribute or arrange methodically; to classify; specif., to codify. **2.** To think over and arrange methodically in the mind. **3.** To convert (food) into absorbable form. **4.** To appropriate or assimilate mentally. **5.** To bear patiently; to tolerate; brook. **6.** *Chem.* To soften by heat and moisture; to heat or warm (a liquid, or a solid in contact with liquid). — *v. i.* **1.** To digest food. **2.** To undergo digestion.

di·gest′ant (dĭ·jĕs′tănt), *n. & adj.* Digestive.

di·gest′er (dĭ·jĕs′tẽr; dī-), *n.* **1.** One who makes a digest. **2.** A thing that aids digestion. **3.** A strong closed vessel in which substances may be heated under pressure, usually with a liquid, in order to decompose or soften them, or to extract a soluble ingredient.

di·gest′i·ble (dĭ·jĕs′tĭ·b′l; dī-), *adj.* Capable of being digested. — **di·gest′i·bil′i·ty** (-bĭl′ĭ·tĭ), *n.* — **di·gest′i·bly**, *adv.*

di·ges′tion (dĭ·jĕs′chŭn), *n.* The process or power of digesting, esp. food by dissolving and breaking it down chemically through the action of secretions containing enzymes, as the saliva, and the gastric, pancreatic, and intestinal juices in the alimentary canal of higher animals. In lower animals, digestion occurs in simpler organs. True digestion occurs also in insectivorous plants, as the pitcher plant, which obtain much of their nitrogenous food from the bodies of entrapped insects.

di·ges′tive (-tĭv), *adj.* Pertaining to digestion; having the power to cause or promote digestion. — **di·ges′tive**, *n.*

dig′ger (dĭg′ẽr), *n.* **1.** One who or that which digs; also, a tool for digging. **2.** [*cap.*] A North American Indian of a tribe of low culture who dig roots for food.

dig′ging (dĭg′ĭng), *n.* **1.** Act of one that digs. **2.** *pl.* The materials excavated. **3. a** A place of excavating. **b** *pl.* (often construed as singular). A place where ore, metals, or precious stones are got by digging. **4.** *pl. Colloq.* Lodgings.

dight (dīt), *v. t.;* DIGHT or DIGHT′ED; DIGHT′ING. [AS. *dihtan* to dictate, command, dispose, fr. L. *dictare* to say often, dictate, order.] **1.** *Archaic.* To equip; to dress. **2.** *Dial.* To wipe clean or dry.

dig′it (dĭj′ĭt), *n.* [L. *digitus* finger, toe.] **1.** *Now Humorous.* A finger. **2.** A finger's breadth (0.75 in.). **3.** Any of the figures 1 to 9 inclusive and, usually, the symbol 0. **4.** *Zool.* A finger or toe.

dig′it·al (dĭj′ĭ·tăl; -t′l), *adj.* Of the fingers or digits; digitate. — *n.* **1.** *Humorous.* A finger. **2.** An organ key. — **dig′it·al·ly**, *adv.*

digital computer. A type of calculating machine that operates with numbers expressed directly as digits in the decimal or some other system.

dig′i·tal′in (dĭj′ĭ·tăl′ĭn; -tā′lĭn), *n. Chem.* A white crystalline glucoside, $C_{35}H_{56}O_{14}$, found in digitalis seeds.

dig′i·tal′is (dĭj′ĭ·tăl′ĭs; -tā′lĭs), *n.* [NL., fr. L. *digitalis* pertaining to a finger; — so named from its finger-shaped corolla.] **1.** Any of a genus (*Digitalis*) of Eurasian herbs of the figwort family, having showy bell-shaped flowers. See FOXGLOVE, *Illust.* **2.** *Pharm.* The dried leaf of the common foxglove, containing several important glucosides and serving as a powerful cardiac stimulant and a diuretic. — **dig′i·tal·ize** (dĭj′ĭ·tăl·īz), *v. t.*

dig′i·tal·ism (dĭj′ĭ·tăl·ĭz′m), *n. Med.* The bodily condition produced by excessive use of digitalis.

dig′i·tate (-tāt), *adj.* **1.** Having fingers or digits. **2.** Resembling a finger or fingers; *Bot.*, having divisions like fingers, as various leaves. — **dig′i·tat′ed** (-tāt′ĕd; -ĭd), *adj.* — **dig′i·tate·ly**, *adv.* — **dig′i·ta′tion** (-tā′shŭn), *n.*

dig′i·ti·form′ (dĭj′ĭ·tĭ·fôrm′), *adj.* Finger-shaped.

dig′i·ti·grade′ (-grād′), *adj.* [L. *digitus* finger, toe + *gradi* to walk.] Walking on the digits; — of animals (as the horse and cow) in which the digits only bear on the ground, the posterior part of the foot being raised. Cf. PLANTIGRADE. — *n.* A digitigrade animal.

di′glot (dī′glŏt), *adj.* [Gr. *diglōttos* speaking two languages, fr. *di-* (= *dis*) twice + *glōtta, glōssa*, tongue. See GLOTTIS.] Bilingual. — *n.* A diglot edition, as of a book.

dig′ni·fied (dĭg′nĭ·fīd), *adj.* Marked by dignity; stately. — **dig′ni·fied′ly** (-fīd′lĭ; -fī′ĕd·lĭ, -fī′ĭd·lĭ), *adv.*

dig′ni·fy (-fī), *v. t.;* -FIED (-fīd); -FY′ING. [OF. *dignifier*, fr. ML. *dignificare*, fr. L. *dignus* worthy + *-ficare* to make.] **1.** To invest with dignity; to give distinction to. **2.** To invest with a pretentious name or appearance.

dig′ni·tar′y (dĭg′nĭ·tĕr′ĭ *or, esp. Brit.*, -tẽr·ĭ), *n.; pl.* -IES (-ĭz). One in a position of dignity or honor, esp. in the church. — **dig′ni·tar′y**, *adj.*

dig′ni·ty (-tĭ), *n.; pl.* -TIES (-tĭz). [OF. *digneté, dignité*, fr. L. *dignitas*, fr. *dignus* worthy.] **1.** Elevation of character; intrinsic worth; excellence. **2.** Quality of being esteemed; degree of estimation; as, the *dignity* of one's profession. **3.** Elevated rank; high office or position; hence, rank; degree. **4. a** A dignitary. **b** Persons of rank collectively; as, to exile the *dignity* of the nation. **5.** Nobleness or formal reserve of manner, aspect, or style; stateliness. — **Syn.** See DECORUM.

di′graph (dī′grăf; 9), *n.* [*di-* + Gr. *graphē* a writing.] A group of two letters representing a single speech sound (*ea* in *head; th* in *bath*); also, incorrectly, a ligature. — **di·graph′ic** (dī·grăf′ĭk), *adj.*

di·gress′ (dĭ·grĕs′; dī-), *v. i.* [L. *digressus*, past part. of *digredi* to deviate, fr. *di-* (= *dis-*) + *gradi* to step, walk.] To turn aside; to deviate, esp. from the main subject in writing or speaking. — **Syn.** See SWERVE.

di·gres′sion (-grĕsh′ŭn), *n.* **1.** A digressing; deviation. **2.** In discourse, departure from a subject or its main course of treatment. — **di·gres′sion·al** (-ăl; -′l), *adj.*

di·gres′sive (-grĕs′ĭv), *adj.* Digressing, or of the nature of digression. — **di·gres′sive·ly**, *adv.* — **di·gres′sive·ness**, *n.*

di·he′dral (dī·hē′drăl), *adj.* [*di-* + Gr. *hedra* a seat, base.] **1.** Having, or formed by, two plane faces. **2.** *Aeronautics.* **a** Having wings whose upper surfaces make a dihedral angle, usually less than 180°. **b** Of wing pairs, inclined at a dihedral angle to each other. — *n.* **1.** *Math.* The figure formed by two intersecting planes. **2.** *Aeronautics.* The angle of inclination of the right and left main supporting surfaces of an airplane, upward or downward from a horizontal transverse line.

di·hy′dro·ta·chys′ter·ol (dī·hī′drō·tă·kĭs′tẽr·ōl; -ŏl), *n.* [*di-* + *hydro-* + *tachy-* + *sterol.*] *Biochem.* A crystalline sterol, $C_{28}H_{45}OH$, obtained by irradiating a derivative of ergosterol. It has vitamin D activity.

dik′–dik′ (dĭk′dĭk′), *n.* [*dig-dig*, native name in Ethiopia.] A small antelope (genera *Madoqua, Rhynchotragus*), about the size of a hare.

dike (dīk), *n.* Also **dyke** (dīk). [AS. *dīc.*] **1.** A ditch. **2.** A bank of earth thrown up from a ditch; hence, a causeway. **3.** A bank thrown up to form a barrier; esp., a levee. **4.** *Geol.* A tabular body of igneous rock that has been injected while molten into a fissure, often resisting erosion and standing like a wall. — *v. t.* To surround or protect with a dike; also, to drain by a dike. — **dik′er** (dīk′ẽr), *n.*

di·lac′er·ate (dĭ·lăs′ẽr·āt; dī-), *v. t.* [L. *dilaceratus* torn apart.] To tear to pieces. — **di·lac′er·a′tion** (-ā′shŭn), *n.*

di·lan′tin (dī·lăn′tĭn), *n.* [*diphenyl* + hy*dantoin* a sweetish compound in beet juice.] A synthetic drug, $C_{15}H_{11}N_2NaO_2$, used in the treatment of epilepsy; — called also **dilantin sodium.**

di·lap′i·date (dĭ·lăp′ĭ·dāt), *v. t.* [L. *dilapidare* to scatter like stones, fr. *di-* (= *dis-*) + *lapidare* to throw stones, fr. *lapis* a stone.] To bring (a building) into a condition of decay or partial ruin by neglect or misuse; hence, to squander. — *v. i.* To fall into disrepair or partial ruin. — **di·lap′i·da′tion** (-dā′shŭn), *n.*

di·lap′i·dat′ed, *adj.* Falling or fallen into partial ruin or decay.

di·lat′ant (dī·lāt′ănt; dĭ-), *adj.* Having the property of increasing in volume when changed in shape, owing to wider spacing of the particles. — **di·lat′an·cy** (-ăn·sĭ), *n.*

di·lat′ate (dī·lāt′āt; dĭ′lȧ·tāt), *adj.* [L. *dilatatus*, past part. of *dilatare* to dilate.] Widened in some part; dilated.

dil′a·ta′tion (dĭl′ȧ·tā′shŭn; dī′lȧ-), *n.* **1.** A dilating; state of being dilated; *Med.*, enlargement, as of the cavities of the heart. **2.** A dilated part.

di·late′ (dī·lāt′; dĭ-), *v. t.* [OF. *dilater*, fr. L. *dilatare*, fr. *di-* (= *dis-*) + *latus* wide. See LATITUDE.] **1.** *Now Rare.* To enlarge upon; to tell in detail. **2.** To distend; to enlarge or extend in bulk or size. — *v. i.* **1.** To enlarge or expatiate; — with *on* or *upon.* **2.** To expand. — **Syn.** See EXPAND. — **di·lat′a·bil′i·ty** (-lāt′ȧ·bĭl′ĭ·tĭ), *n.* — **di·lat′a·ble** (-lāt′ȧ·b′l), *adj.* — **di·lat′er** (-lāt′ẽr), **di·la′tor** (-lā′tẽr), *n.*

di·la′tion (dī·lā′shŭn; dĭ-), *n.* Dilatation; act of dilating.

di·la′tive (-tĭv), *adj.* Causing dilation; tending to dilate.

dil′a·to′ry (dĭl′ȧ·tō′rĭ *or, esp. Brit.*, -tẽr·ĭ), *adj.* [LL. *dilatorius*, fr. *dilator* a delayer, fr. *dilatus*, used as past part. of *differre* to defer, delay. See DIFFER.] **1.** Having the nature or intent of causing delay; tending to delay. **2.** Characterized by, or given to, procrastination; tardy; slow. — **dil′a·to′ri·ly**, *adv.* — **dil′a·to′ri·ness**, *n.*

di·lem′ma (dĭ·lĕm′ȧ; dī-), *n.* [LL., fr. Gr. *dilēmma*, fr. *di-* (= *dis*) twice + *lēmma* assumption.] **1.** An argument presenting an antagonist with two or more alternatives (or "horns"), but equally conclusive against him, whichever he chooses. **2.** A situation involving choice between equally unsatisfactory alternatives. — **Syn.** See PREDICAMENT.

dil′et·tan′te (dĭl′ĕ·tăn′tē; -tänt′; -tănt′), *n.; pl.* DILETTANTI (-tăn′tē), DILETTANTES (-tăn′tēz; -tänts′; -tănts′). [It., prop. pres. part. of *dilettare* to take delight in.] A lover of the fine arts; esp., one who follows an art or a branch of knowledge desultorily or superficially, or as a pastime. — **Syn.** See AMATEUR. — *adj.* Of or characteristic of a dilettante. — **dil′et·tant′ism** (-tăn′tĭz′m; -tän′tĭz′m), **dil′et·tan′te·ism** (-tăn′tē·ĭz′m), *n.*

dil′i·gence (dĭl′ĭ·jĕns; *F.* dē′lē′zhäɴs′), *n.* [F.] A public stagecoach; also, its passengers.

dil′i·gence (dĭl′ĭ·jĕns), *n.* **1.** Quality of being diligent. **2.** Persevering application; assiduity.

dil′i·gent (-jĕnt), *adj.* [OF., fr. L. *diligens*, pres. part. of *diligere, dilectum*, to esteem highly, fr. *di-* (= *dis-*) + *legere* to choose.] **1.** Perseveringly attentive; assiduous; industrious. **2.** Prosecuted with careful attention; painstaking. — **Syn.** See BUSY. — **dil′i·gent·ly**, *adv.*

dill (dĭl), *n.* [AS. *dile.*] A European herb (*Anethum graveolens*) of the carrot family, the anise of Scripture, whose seeds are carminative and stimulant, and are used in cookery and in flavoring pickles (**dill pickles**).

dil′ly·dal′ly (dĭl′ĭ·dăl′ĭ), *v. i.;* see DALLY. To loiter or trifle; dally; dawdle; vacillate.

dil′u·ent (dĭl′ū·ĕnt), *adj.* [L. *diluens*, pres. part. See DILUTE.] Diluting; also, dissolving; solvent. — *n.* A diluting agent.

di·lute′ (dĭ·lūt′; dī-), *v. t.* [L. *dilutus*, past part. of *diluere* to wash away, dilute, fr. *di-* (= *dis-*) + *luere* to wash.] To make thinner or more liquid by admixture, esp. with water; to diminish the strength, flavor, or brilliancy of, by thinning; hence, to attenuate. — *adj.* Diluted; weak. — **di·lute′ness**, *n.*

di·lu′tion (dĭ·lū′shŭn; dī-), *n.* Act of diluting, or state of being diluted; also, that which is diluted.

di·lu′vi·al (dĭ·lū′vĭ·ăl; dī-), **di·lu′vi·an** (-ăn), *adj.* [L. *diluvium* deluge.] Of, pertaining to, or effected by, a flood or deluge, esp. that of Genesis vii.

dim (dĭm), *adj.;* DIM′MER (-ẽr); DIM′MEST. [AS. *dim, dimme.*] **1.** Not bright or distinct; hence: **a** Not clearly visible; indistinct. **b** Dull, or without luster; — of color. **c** Faint; — of sound. **d** Tarnished. **2.** Of obscure vision; hence, dull of apprehension; obtuse. — **Syn.** See DARK. — *v. t. & i.;* DIMMED (dĭmd); DIM′MING. **1.** To render or become dim. **2.** To deprive of or lose distinct vision. — ***dim out.*** To obscure in dimness, as by limiting illumination to mere slits of light, to blue lights, to lights shaded from above, etc.

dime (dīm), *n.* [OF., fr. L. *decima*, fr. *decimus* tenth, fr. *decem* ten.] *U. S. & Canada.* A silver coin worth 1/10 dollar. See MONEY, *Tables.*

dime novel. Orig., a novel, usually sensational, sold for a dime; hence, any cheap, lurid novel. Cf. DREADFUL, *n.;* 2d SHOCKER.

di·men′sion (dĭ·mĕn′shŭn), *n.* [F., fr. L. *dimensio*, fr. past part. of *dimetiri* to measure out, fr. *di-* (= *dis-*) + *metiri* to measure.] **1.** Measure in a single line, as length, breadth, height, thickness, or circumference; also, usually *pl.*, measure in length, breadth, and thickness. **2.** The quality of extension; magnitude; hence, scope; importance; as, a project of large *dimensions.* **3.** *Math.* A literal factor, as numbered in characterizing a term; thus, a^2b^2c is a term of five *dimensions.* — **di·men′sion·al** (-ăl; -′l), *adj.*

dim′er·ous (dĭm′ẽr·ŭs), *adj.* [*di-* + Gr. *meros* part.] **a** *Biol.* Having the tarsi two-jointed. **b** *Bot.* Having two members in each whorl; — of flowers. Often written *2-merous.* — **dim′er·ism** (-ĭz′m), *n.*

dim′e·ter (dĭm′ē·tẽr), *n.* [LL., fr. Gr. *dimetros*, fr. *di-* (= *dis*) twice + *metron* measure.] *Pros.* A verse consisting of two metrical feet or of two dipodies.

di·mid′i·ate (dĭ·mĭd′ĭ·āt; dī-), *v. t.* [L. *dimidiatus*, past part. of *dimidiare* to halve, fr. *dimidius* half.] To halve or reduce to the half. — *adj.* Halved.

di·min′ish (dĭ·mĭn′ĭsh), *v. t.* [From earlier *diminue* (fr. L. *diminuere* to lessen), and from *minish.*] **1.** To make less; lessen. **2.** To lessen the authority or dignity of; to degrade; abase. **3.** *Arch.* To cause to taper. **4.** *Music.* To make smaller by a half step; to make (an interval) less than perfect or minor; as, a *diminished* fifth; a *diminished* seventh. — *v. i.* To become less; dwindle; taper. — **Syn.** See DECREASE. — **di·min′ish·a·ble**, *adj.* — **di·min′ish·ing·ly**, *adv.*

di·min′ish·ing re·turn′. The observed fact that increase of labor or capital applied beyond a certain point causes a less than proportionate increase in production.

di·min′u·en′do (dĭ·mĭn′ū·ĕn′dō; *It.* dē·mē·nwĕn′dō), *adj. & adv.* [It.] *Music.* With gradually diminishing volume; decrescendo; — a direction noted by *Dim.*, or *Dimin.*, or the sign >. The opposite of *crescendo.* — *n.; pl.* -DOS (-dōz). Diminution in volume, force, etc.; *Music*, a diminuendo passage or effect.

dim′i·nu′tion (dĭm′ĭ·nū′shŭn), *n.* [L. *diminutio.*] Act of diminishing, or process of being diminished; decrease.

di·min′u·tive (dĭ·mĭn′ū·tĭv), *adj.* [OF. *diminutif*, fr. L. *diminutivus, deminutivus.*] **1.** Expressing diminution, as a suffix. **2.** Below the average size; very small. — **Syn.** See SMALL. — *n.* **1.** A derivative denoting something small or young of the kind, or with verbs a petty form of the action. In English, the chief suffixes which form diminutives are *-cule, -el, -et, -ette, -ie, -in, -kin, -let, -ling, -ock, -ule, -y.* **2.** A diminutive form or variety. — **di·min′u·tive·ly,** *adv.* — **di·min′u·tive·ness,** *n.*

dim′is·so′ry (dĭm′ĭ·sō′rĭ *or, esp. Brit.,* -sẽr·ĭ; dĭ·mĭs′ō·rĭ), *adj.* [LL. *dimissorius.*] Dismissing; granting leave to depart, esp. to another diocese.

dim′i·ty (dĭm′ĭ·tĭ), *n.; pl.* -TIES (-tĭz). [It. *dimiti,* pl. of *dimito,* fr. Gr. *dimitos* of double thread, dimity, fr. *di-* (= *dis*) twice + *mitos* warp thread.] A fine, thin, corded cotton fabric, often figured.

dim′ly (dĭm′lĭ), *ad.* In a dim or obscure manner.

dim′mer (dĭm′ẽr), *n.* A device for causing an incandescent lamp to burn or shine less brightly.

dim′ness (-nĕs; -nĭs), *n.* Quality or state of being dim.

di·mor′phic (dī·môr′fĭk), **di·mor′phous** (-fŭs), *adj.* [*di-* + *-morphic, -morphous.*] Characterized by dimorphism.

di·mor′phism (-fĭz′m), *n.* **1.** *Biol.* Difference of form, color, or structure between members of the same species; in *Bot.,* specif., the occurrence of two distinct forms of leaves, flowers, or other organs upon the same plant, or upon other plants of the same species; in *Zool.,* strictly, unusual differences such as having two forms of the same sex or two color phases (dichromatism). **2.** *Cryst.* Crystallization in two independent forms of the same chemical compound.

dim′-out′ (dĭm′out′), *n.* Act of dimming out; condition of being dimmed out. See *dim out,* under DIM, *v.;* cf. BLACKOUT.

dim′ple (dĭm′p'l), *n.* [ME. *dympull.*] A slight natural depression or indentation in the surface of some part of the body, esp. on the cheek or chin. — *v. i. & t.;* DIM′PLED (-p'ld); DIM′PLING (-plĭng). To form, or mark with, dimples. — **dim′ply** (-plĭ), *adj.*

dim′wit′ (dĭm′wĭt′), *n. Slang.* A stupid or mentally slow person.

din (dĭn), *n.* [AS. *dyn, dyne.*] Loud noise; esp., a welter of confused and discordant sounds; deafening uproar; clangor. — *v. t.;* DINNED (dĭnd); DIN′NING. **1.** To strike or stun with a din. **2.** To impress by insistent repetition. — *v. i.* To make a din.

di·nar′ (dē·när′), *n.* [Ar. *dīnār,* fr. Gr., fr. L. *denarius.*] **1.** The chief gold coin of the Moslems, first struck in the 7th century. **2.** A coin unit of Yugoslavia (about $0.02). **3.** The gold monetary unit of Iraq (= £1), divided into 1000 fils; — officially known as the *Iraqi dinar.* **4.** A minor coin value of Iran, the hundredth part of a rial.

din′dle (dĭn′d'l; dĭn′'l), *v. i. & t.;* DIN′DLED (-d'ld; -'ld); DIN′DLING (-dlĭng; -lĭng). *Chiefly Scot.* To ring; vibrate; tingle. — *n.* Thrill; tingling.

dine (dīn), *v. i.* [OF. *disner* (F. *dîner*), deriv. of L. *dis-* + *jejunare* to fast, fr. *jejunus* fasting.] To take dinner. — *v. t.* To entertain at dinner. — *n. Obs. exc. Scot.* Dinner; also, noon.

din′er (dīn′ẽr), *n.* **1.** One who dines. **2.** A railroad dining car or any restaurant resembling this.

di·ner′ic (dī·nĕr′ĭk), *adj.* [1st *di-* + Gr. *nēros* liquid.] *Physics.* Being, or pertaining to, the interface between two liquids, as oil and water, in the same vessel.

di·ne′ro (dē·nā′rō), *n.; pl.* -ROS (-rōz). Formerly, a silver coin of Peru equal to 1/10 peso or 1/10 sol.

di·nette′ (dī·nĕt′; dĭ-), *n.* **1.** *U.S.* An alcove used for a dining room, as in a small apartment. **2.** *Brit.* A hot luncheon.

ding (dĭng), *v. i. & t.* **1.** To sound, as a bell; to ring. **2.** *Colloq.* To talk or impress with vehemence or reiteration.

ding′dong′ (dĭng′dŏng′), *n.* The sound as of repeated strokes on a metallic body, such as a bell. — *adj. Colloq.* Marked by a series of blows; hence, vigorously contested; as, a *dingdong* race.

din′ghy, din′gy, din′gey (dĭng′gĭ), *n.; pls.* DINGHIES, DINGIES, DINGEYS (-gĭz). [Beng. *dingi.*] **1.** A kind of East Indian rowing boat. **2.** A man-of-war's small boat. **3.** A light rowboat or skiff, often a tender.

din′gle (dĭng′g'l), *n.* A small, narrow, wooded valley.

din′go (dĭng′gō), *n.; pl.* DINGOES (-gōz). [Native name.] A wild dog (*Canis dingo*) of Australia, supposed to have been introduced by man at a very early period.

din′gy (dĭn′jĭ), *adj.;* DIN′GI·ER (-jĭ·ẽr); DIN′GI·EST. Dark-colored; grimy; smoky. — **din′gi·ly,** *adv.* — **din′gi·ness,** *n.*

din′ing room, hall, car (dīn′ĭng), etc. A room, hall (as in a school), railroad car, etc., where dinner and other meals are eaten.

di·ni′tro- (dī·nī′trō-). [*di-* + *nitro-.*] *Chem.* A combining form denoting *the presence of two nitro* (NO_2) *groups,* esp. replacing hydrogen, as in **di·ni′tro·ben′zene,** any of three isomeric compounds, $C_6H_4(NO_2)_2$, formed by the action of concentrated nitric acid on benzene or on nitrobenzene. The meta variety of dinitrobenzene is used as a dye intermediate.

dink (dĭngk), *adj.* [Origin uncert.] *Scot.* Trim; neat. — *v. t. Scot.* To deck.

dink′ey (dĭngk′ĭ), *n. Colloq.* A small locomotive for hauling freight, shunting cars, etc.

din′ner (dĭn′ẽr), *n.* [OF. *disner* (F. *dîner*), inf. used as n.] The principal meal of the day, eaten about midday or in the evening; also, a formal feast in honor of some person or event.

dinner coat *or* **jacket.** = TUXEDO.

din′nle (dĭn′'l). Var. of DINDLE.

di·noc′er·as (dī·nŏs′ẽr·ăs), *n.* [NL., fr. Gr. *deinos* terrible + *keras* horn.] A huge extinct herbivorous hoofed animal having three pairs of bony protuberances on the skull.

di′no·saur (dī′nō·sôr), *n.* [Gr. *deinos* terrible + *sauros* lizard.] Any of a group (Dinosauria) of extinct reptiles varying in length from

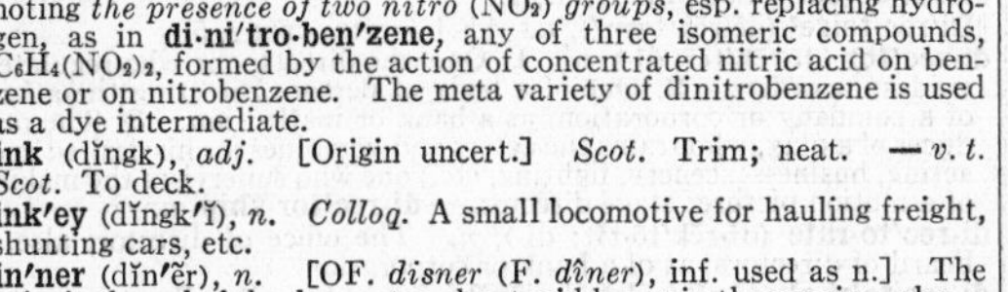

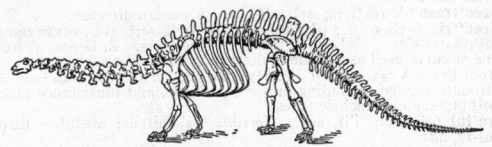

Skeleton of a Dinosaur (*Brontosaurus*) restored. (1/200)

2 to 90 feet and having limbs adapted for progressing on land and a long tapering tail. See DIPLODOCUS. — **di′no·sau′ri·an** (-sô′rĭ·ăn), *adj. & n.*

di′no·there (-thēr), *n.* [Gr. *deinos* terrible + *therion* wild beast.] An animal of a genus (*Dinotherium*) of extinct proboscidean mammals, notable for a pair of tusks directed downward from the apex of the lower jaw.

dint (dĭnt), *n.* [AS. *dynt.*] **1.** A blow; a stroke. **2.** Force; — esp. in *by dint of.* **3.** A dent. — *v. t.* To make a dint in; also, to imprint, as a dent.

di·oc′e·san (dī·ŏs′ē·săn; -zăn), *adj.* Of or governing a diocese. — *n.* One in charge of a diocese.

di′o·cese (dī′ō·sēs *or, esp. Brit.,* -sĭs), *n.* [OF. *diocise,* fr. L., fr. Gr. *dioikēsis* housekeeping, province, diocese, deriv. of *dia* through + *oikein* to manage a household, fr. *oikos* a house.] *Eccl.* The district in which a bishop has authority.

di′ode (dī′ōd), *n.* [2d *di-* + 2d *-ode.*] A vacuum tube with a cold anode and a heated cathode, serving as a rectifier.

di·oe′cious (dī·ē′shŭs), *adj.* [*di-* + Gr. *oikos* house.] *Biol.* Having the male reproductive organs in one individual, the female in another; — often, of ferns, **di·oi′cous** (-oi′kŭs). — **di·oe′cious·ly,** *adv.*

Di′o·me′des (dī′ō·mē′dēz), **Di′o·med** (dī′ō·mĕd), *n.* [L. *Diomedes,* fr. Gr. *Diomēdēs.*] *Gr. Myth.* One of the Greek warriors before Troy, who helped Odysseus steal the horses of Rhesus and the Palladium.

Di′o·ny′si·a (dī′ō·nĭsh′ĭ·ȧ; -nĭs′ĭ·ȧ; -nĭz′ĭ·ȧ), *n. pl.* [L., fr. Gr. *Dionysia.*] *Gr. Relig.* Any of the festivals of Dionysus, specif. those of Attica in connection with which Greek drama developed. Cf. BACCHANALIA.

Di′o·nys′i·ac (-nĭs′ĭ·ăk; -nĭz′ĭ·ăk), *adj.* [L. *Dionysiacus,* fr. Gr. *Dionysiakos.*] Of or pertaining to Dionysus or the Dionysia; Bacchic.

Di′o·ny′sian (-nĭsh′ăn; -nĭs′ĭ·ăn; -nĭz′ĭ·ăn), *adj.* **1.** Of or characteristic of Dionysius, as the elder or the younger Dionysius, cruel tyrants of Syracuse. **2.** Dionysiac.

Di′o·ny′sus (dī′ō·nī′sŭs), **Di′o·ny′sos** (-sŏs), *n.* [L., fr. Gr. *Dionysos.*] *Gr. Relig.* An Olympian god, giver of the grape and its wine, and as such worshiped with orgiastic rites; — called also *Bacchus.* In early art he is figured as bearded, later as youthful and somewhat effeminate; the thyrsus, ivy, and the vine are his commonest attributes.

di·op′side (dī·ŏp′sīd; -sĭd), *n.* [*di-* + Gr. *opsis* a sight.] *Mineral.* A variety of pyroxene with little or no aluminum.

di·op′tase (-tās), *n.* [*di-* (= *dia-*) + Gr. *optazein* to see.] *Mineral.* A hydrous copper silicate found in emerald-green crystals, also massive. H., 5. Sp. gr., 3.47.

di·op′ter (-tẽr), *n.* [See DIOPTRIC.] Also **di·op′tre** (-tẽr). *Optics.* A unit used to express the power of a lens. It is equal to the reciprocal of the focal length in meters. — **di·op′tral** (-trăl), *adj.*

di′op·tom′e·ter (dī′ŏp·tŏm′ē·tẽr), *n.* [*di-* + *optic* + *-meter.*] An instrument used in measuring the accommodation and refraction of the eye.

di·op′tric (dī·ŏp′trĭk), **di·op′tri·cal** (-trĭ·kăl), *adj.* [Gr. *dioptrikos* belonging to the use of the *dioptra,* fr. *di-* (= *dia*) through + the root of *opsomai* I shall see.] **1.** Of or pertaining to dioptrics; refractive; as, a *dioptric* telescope. **2.** Of or pertaining to a diopter or the metric system of numbering optical glasses. — **di·op′tri·cal·ly,** *adv.*

di·op′trics (-trĭks), *n.;* see -ICS. Optics treating of the refraction of light, esp. by lenses. Cf. CATOPTRICS.

di′o·ra′ma (dī′ō·rä′mȧ; -răm′ȧ), *n.* [Gr. *di-* (= *dia*) through + *horama* that which is seen, a sight.] **1.** A mode of scenic representation in which a painting (partly translucent) is seen from a distance through an opening. **2.** A small scenic representation employing diminutive three-dimensional figures in an illuminated setting.

di′o·rite (dī′ō·rīt), *n.* [F., fr. Gr. *diorizein* to distinguish.] A granular, crystalline, igneous rock, commonly of acid plagioclase and hornblende. — **di′o·rit′ic** (-rĭt′ĭk), *adj.*

Di′os·cu′ri (dī′ŏs·kū′rī), *n. pl.* [Gr. *Dioskouroi,* fr. *Zeus,* gen. *Dios,* Zeus + *kouros, koros,* boy, son.] *Class. Myth.* The twins Castor and Pollux, the former mortal, the latter immortal, who were reunited after Castor's death by Zeus's decree that they live in the upper and lower worlds on alternate days. In another version they become the constellation Gemini.

di·os′mose (dī·ŏs′mōs; -ŏz′mōs), *n. & v. t.,* **di′os·mo′sis** (dī′ŏs·mō′sĭs; dī′ŏz-), *n.,* etc. = OSMOSE, OSMOSIS, etc.

di·ox′ide (dī·ŏk′sīd; -sĭd), *n.* Also **di·ox′id.** [*di-* + *oxide.*] An oxide having two atoms of oxygen in the molecule.

dip (dĭp), *v. t.;* DIPPED (dĭpt) or DIPT; DIP′PING. [AS. *dyppan.*] **1.** To plunge or immerse partly or for a time, as into liquid so as to moisten, color, coat, etc. **2.** *Poetic.* To wet, as if by immersing. **3.** To procure or take out with, or as if with, an implement that scoops; as, to *dip* water from a boiler. **4.** To lower by bending; to lower and raise quickly, as a flag. **5.** To make (a candle) by repeated dipping of a wick in fat or wax. **6.** To immerse in a dye, in slip, in a plating or galvanizing solution, etc. **7.** To immerse (as a sheep or hog) in a solution that kills bacteria or other parasites. **8.** *U. S.* To rub (snuff) on the gums.

— *v. i.* **1.** To immerse oneself in a liquid and quickly emerge. **2.** To drop down, or out of sight, esp. with suddenness. **3.** To reach down with, or as with, a ladle or scoop, esp. to withdraw a part of the contents of something. **4.** To enter slightly or cursorily; specif., to read superficially. **5.** To incline downward; to slope; specif., *Geol.,* to incline from the plane of the horizon. **6.** *Aeronautics.* To drop suddenly before climbing.

— *n.* **1.** Action of dipping or plunging into water or the like. **2.** Inclination downward; pitch; also, a depression. **3.** A thing made or obtained by or used in dipping; as, a tallow *dip;* also, a portion dipped. **4.** Any liquid into which objects may be dipped, as for cleansing, coloring, lacquering, etc. **5.** *Aeronautics.* A sudden drop followed by a climb. **6.** *Geol.* The angle which a stratum or similar feature makes with a horizontal plane. **7.** *Gymnastics.* An exercise on the parallel bars consisting in letting oneself sink until chin is level with the bars, and then raising oneself by straightening the arms. **8.** *Magnetism.* The angle formed with the horizon by a dipping needle (which see).

di′phase′ (dī′fāz′), *adj.* Also **di′phas′ic** (-fāz′ĭk). *Elec.* Carrying, producing, or operated by two alternating currents differing in phase by 90°.

di·phen′yl (dī·fĕn′ĭl; -fē′nĭl), *n. Chem.* = BIPHENYL.

di·phen′yl·a·mine′ (dī·fĕn′ĭl·ȧ·mēn′; -ăm′ĭn; dī·fē′nĭl-), *n.* Also **di·phen′yl·am′in.** [*diphenyl* + *amine.*] *Chem.* An aromatic crystalline compound, $(C_6H_5)_2NH$, obtained by heating aniline with aniline hydrochloride ($C_6H_5NH_2.HCl$), and used in making dyes and explosives and as a test for nitric acid.

di·phos′gene (dī·fŏz′jēn), *n.* [*di-* + *phosgene.*] *Chem.* A liquid compound $ClCO_2CCl_3$, used as a lethal gas in World War I.

diph·the′ri·a (dĭf·thēr′ĭ·*à*), *n.* [NL., fr. F. *diphthérie*, fr. Gr. *diphthera* leather (hence taken in the sense of *membrane*).] A febrile, infectious and contagious disease in which the air passages become coated with a membrane formed by a fibrous inflammatory exudation. It is caused by the ***Klebs-Löffler bacillus*** (*Corynebacterium diphtheriae*). — **diph·the′ri·al** (-ăl), *adj.*

diph′the·rit′ic (dĭf′thē·rĭt′ĭk), **diph·ther′ic** (dĭf·thĕr′ĭk), *adj.* Pertaining to diphtheria; having characteristics like those of diphtheria, esp. the membranous exudation; as, a *diphtheritic* sore throat.

diph′thong (dĭf′thŏng; 74), *n.* [F. *diphthongue*, fr. LL., fr. Gr. *diphthongos*, fr. *di-* (= *dis*) twice + *phthongos* voice, sound.] *Phonet.* **1.** A speech sound changing continuously from one vowel to another in the same syllable, often distinguished as ***proper***, *or* ***full, diphthong*** (*oi* in *oil*, *ou* in *out*, or *ī* in *ice*) and ***imperfect***, *or* ***partial, diphthong*** (as English ō = pure ō + o͞o). **2.** Loosely, one of the ligatures *æ*, *œ*, which were diphthongs in classical Latin. **3.** An inseparable consonant combination, as *ch* (*t* + *sh*), *j* (*d* + *zh*); — called also ***consonantal diphthong***. — **diph·thon′gal** (dĭf·thŏng′găl; -thŏng′ăl), *adj.* — **diph·thong′ic** (-thŏng′gĭk; -ĭk), *adj.*

diph′thong·ize (dĭf′thŏng·gīz; -īz), *v. t. & i.* To change (a simple vowel) into a diphthong. — **diph′thong·i·za′tion** (-gĭ·zā′shŭn; -gī·zā′-), *n.*

di·phyl′lous (dī·fĭl′ŭs), *adj.* *Bot.* Having two leaves.

di′plex (dī′plĕks), *adj.* [*di-* + *-plex* as in du*plex*.] *Radio.* Pertaining to simultaneous transmission or reception of two independent signals.

dip′lo- (dĭp′lō-), **dipl-.** [Gr. *diploos*.] A combining form meaning *double*, used to signify *two, twice, double, twin*, as in **dip′lo·car′di·ac**, having the heart completely divided.

dip′lo·coc′cus (dĭp′lō·kŏk′ŭs), *n.; pl.* -cocci (-kŏk′sī). [NL., fr. *diplo-* + Gr. *kokkos* grain, seed.] *Bacteriol.* Any of a genus (*Diplococcus*) of Gram-positive, elongated, capsulate bacteria occurring in pairs or chains and parasitic, including the pneumococcus (*D. pneumoniae*) which causes lobar pneumonia. Cf. streptococcus. — **dip′lo·coc′cal** (-kŏk′ăl), **dip′lo·coc′cic** (-kŏk′sĭk), *adj.*

di·plod′o·cus (dĭ·plŏd′ō·kŭs), *n.* [NL., fr. *diplo-* + Gr. *dokos* a bearing beam.] *Paleontol.* Any of a genus (*Diplodocus*) of gigantic herbivorous dinosaurs from the Upper Jurassic of Colorado and Wyoming.

dip′loid (dĭp′loid), *adj.* [*dipl-* + *-oid.*] Double or twofold; specif., *Biol.*, having the basic chromosome number twice the number in normal gametes. Cf. haploid. — **dip′loid**, *n.* — **dip·loi′dic** (dĭp·loi′dĭk), *adj.*

di·plo′ma (dĭ·plō′m*à*), *n.; pl.* -mas (-m*à*z), *rarely* -mata (-m*à*·t*à*). [L., fr. Gr. *diplōma*, fr. *diploun* to double, fr. *diploos* twofold.] **1.** A writing conferring some privilege, honor, or power. **2.** A historical or state document, such as a charter. **3.** *Educ.* A document bearing record of graduation from, or of a degree conferred by, an educational institution. — *v. t.*; -maed (-m*à*d); -ma·ing. To furnish with a diploma.

di·plo′ma·cy (dĭ·plō′m*à*·sĭ), *n.; pl.* -cies (-sĭz). [F. *diplomatie*. See diploma.] **1.** Art and practice of conducting negotiations between nations, as in arranging treaties. **2.** Artful management in securing advantages without arousing hostility; address or tact.

dip′lo·mat (dĭp′lō·măt), *n.* One employed or skilled in international diplomacy; one having tact or address.

dip′lo·mat′ic (-măt′ĭk), *adj.* **1.** Of international diplomacy; relating to the foreign ministers at a court or capital, called the **diplomatic body** *or* **corps. 2.** Characterized by or skilled in diplomacy; tactful. — **Syn.** See suave. — **dip′lo·mat′i·cal·ly** (-ĭ·kăl·ĭ), *adv.*

dip′lo·mat′ics (-ĭks), *n.;* see -ics. **1.** Diplomacy. **2.** The branch of paleography which deals with ancient official documents, diplomas, charters, and bulls.

di·plo′ma·tist (dĭ·plō′m*à*·tĭst), *n.* **1.** A diplomat. **2.** One who is tactful or artful in meeting situations.

di·plo′pi·a (dĭ·plō′pĭ·*à*), *n.; pl.* -pias (-*à*z). [NL., fr. *dipl-* + *-opia.*] Double vision of a single object, esp., *Med.*, when constituting a disorder of sight. — **di·plop′ic** (-plŏp′ĭk), *adj.*

di·plo′sis (dĭ·plō′sĭs), *n.* [NL., fr. Gr. *diplōsis* a doubling.] *Biol.* The increasing of the chromosome number by the fusion of two haploid sets in the union of cells. Cf. haplosis.

dip′no·an (dĭp′nō·ăn), *adj.* [Gr. *dipnoos* with two breathing apertures, fr. *di-* (= *dis*) twice + *pnoē* breath.] *Zool.* Of or pertaining to a group (Dipnoi) of fishes which have pulmonary circulation, and both gills and lungs. — *n.* A dipnoan fish.

dip′o·dy (dĭp′ō·dĭ), *n.; pl.* -dies (-dĭz). [Gr. *dipodia*, fr. *dipous* two-footed, fr. *di-* (= *dis*) twice + *pous, podos*, foot.] *Pros.* A verse having two feet; a dimeter.

di′pole′ (dī′pōl′), *n.* *Physical Chem.* Any object that is oppositely charged at two points or poles.

dip′per (dĭp′ẽr), *n.* **1.** A worker who dips; a vessel or apparatus for dipping, esp. a ladle. **2.** [*cap.*] **a** The seven principal stars (***Big***, *or* ***Great, Dipper***) in the constellation of Ursa Major. See Ursa Major, *Illust.* **b** The seven principal stars (***Little Dipper***) in Ursa Minor, the North Star forming the outer end of the handle. See Ursa Minor, *Illust.* **3.** *Zool.* Any of several diving birds, as the dabchicks, the bufflehead, and the water ouzels.

dip′ping, *or* **dip, nee′dle.** A magnetic needle so suspended that it can be used to measure the magnetic dip.

dip′so·ma′ni·a (dĭp′sō·mā′nĭ·*à*), *n.* [NL., fr. Gr. *dipsa* thirst + *mania.*] A morbid and uncontrollable craving for alcohol. — **dip′so·ma·ni′a·cal** (-m*à*·nī′*à*·kăl), *adj.*

dip′so·ma′ni·ac (-ăk), *n.* One affected with dipsomania.

dip′ter·al (dĭp′tẽr·ăl), *adj.* *Arch.* Having a double peristyle; having a double row of columns all around.

dip′ter·on (-ŏn), *n.* [Gr., neut.] A dipterous insect.

dip′ter·ous (-ŭs), *adj.* [NL. *dipterus*, fr. Gr. *dipteros* with two wings, fr. *di-* (= *dis*) twice + *pteron* feather, wing.] **a** *Bot. & Zool.* Having two wings or winglike appendages. **b** *Zool.* Belonging to an order (Diptera) of insects comprising the true or winged flies (as the housefly), the mosquitoes, gnats, etc., all, with the exception of wingless parasitic forms, having two wings and a posterior pair of small club-shaped organs (halteres). — **dip′ter·al** (-ăl), *adj.* — **dip′ter·an** (-ăn), *adj. & n.*

dip′tych (dĭp′tĭk), *n.* [LL. *diptycha*, pl., fr. Gr. *diptychos* folded, doubled, fr. *di-* (= *dis*) twice + *ptyssein* to fold, double up.] **1.** *Rom. Antiq.* A two-leaved hinged writing tablet protecting the writing by folding together; hence, any similar tablet. **2.** A picture or series of pictures, as an altarpiece, painted on two hinged tablets. Cf. triptych.

dir′dum (dĭr′dŭm; dûr′-), *n.* *Chiefly Scot.* Uproar; tumult; also, a scolding; blame; punishment.

dire (dīr), *adj.;* dir′er (dīr′ẽr); dir′est. [L. *dirus.*] **1.** Extremely evil or terrible. **2.** Fatal; also, ill-boding. **3.** Extreme; overpowering. — **dire′ly**, *adv.* — **dire′ness**, *n.*

di·rect′ (dĭ·rĕkt′; dī-), *v. t.* [L. *directus*, past part. See direct, *adj.*] **1.** Orig., to send in writing, as a message; hence, to address explicitly, as a speech. **2.** To mark with name and residence of one to whom a thing is sent; to superscribe. **3.** To cause (a person or thing) to turn, move, point, or follow a course; as, to *direct* one's attention to certain faults. **4.** To point out to (one) the right way or road. **5.** To regulate the activities or course of; specif., to govern or control; to give guidance to. **6.** To give an order or instruction to, esp. authoritatively; as, the judge *directs* the jury in matters of law; also, to ask for or order with authority; as, the judge *directed* a verdict for the defendant. — *v. i.* To give direction. — **Syn.** See conduct; command. — (*see Pron.*, § 2), *adj.* [OF., fr. L. *directus*. See dress.] **1.** Proceeding from one point to another in time or space without deviation or interruption; not crooked, refracted, or circuitous. **2.** Straightforward; going straight to the point. **3.** Immediate; making contact or effected without an intermediary; hence, not deputed; personal. **4.** In the line of descent; lineal, not collateral. **5.** *Astron.* In the direction of the general planetary motion, or from west to east; not retrograde; hence, counterclockwise. **6.** *Dyeing.* Not requiring the aid of a mordant; substantive. **7.** *Elec.* Flowing in one direction only; as, *direct* current. **8.** *Gram.* Given or quoted in the exact words of a speaker, as in ***direct discourse*** (He said, "I can do it"), ***direct question*** (He asked me, "What is your opinion?"). **9.** *Polit. Science.* Pertaining to, or effected immediately by, action of the people through their votes instead of through one or more representatives; as, *direct* legislation. — (dĭ·rĕkt′; dī-), *adv.* In a direct manner; directly; straight. — **di·rect′ness**, *n.*

Syn. Direct, immediate as applied to relations mean uninterrupted. However, direct suggests unbroken connection or a bearing straight upon the object; immediate, the absence of any intervening medium or influence; as, a *direct* tax; an *immediate* inference.

direct action. Action directed toward an immediate end; specif., action on the part of labor, designed to attain its purpose by means of strikes, sabotage, or other coercive acts; violence in social reform.

direct current. *Elec.* An electric current flowing in one direction only. Abbr. *D.C.* or *d.c.*

di·rec′tion (dĭ·rĕk′shŭn; dī-), *n.* **1.** Act of directing; guidance; management. **2.** That which is imposed by directing; command; also, authoritative instruction. **3.** The address placed upon something to be delivered; superscription. **4.** The line or course upon which anything is moving or is aimed to move, or to which anything is pointing; as, to sail in a southerly *direction;* also, the line of tendency; a trend. **5.** *Drama.* Work of the director of a play, motion picture, etc., involving selection of the effects to be produced and the means adopted for producing these effects. **6.** *Music.* In a score, a phrase or sign indicating the appropriate tempo, mood, intensity, etc.

di·rec′tion·al (-ăl; -′l), *adj.* **1.** Of direction in space. **2.** *Radio.* Suitable for detecting the direction from which signals come or for sending out signals in one direction only.

direction finder. A radio receiving device for determining the direction of incoming radio waves, commonly a coil antenna rotating freely on a vertical axis. — **direction finding.**

direction indicator. *Aeronautics.* A compass helping a pilot to fly a predetermined course by direct reading and comparison of two indicators, one of which, the reference index, is set for the desired heading, while the other shows the actual heading. When the two indicators point alike the aircraft is flying the desired course.

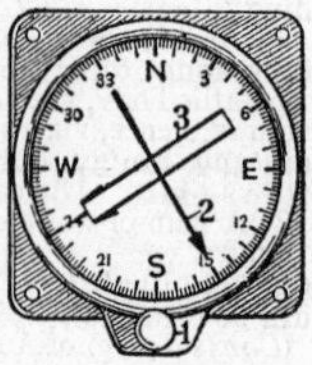

Direction Indicator. 1 Index Setting Knob; 2 Pointer; 3 Index.

di·rec′tive (dĭ·rĕk′tĭv; dī-), *adj.* **1.** Serving or qualified to direct. **2.** Amenable to direction. **3.** Serving to point direction. — *n.* A general instruction as to procedure, esp. a military communication setting a policy or specific order, or an order by a federal, state, or business executive.

direct lighting. See lighting, *n.*, 3.

di·rect′ly (dĭ·rĕkt′lĭ; dī-), *adv.* **1.** In a direct manner; without anything intervening. **2.** Straightway; at once. — *conj. Chiefly Colloq.* Immediately after; as soon as.

direct object. See object, *n.*, 4.

‖**Di′rec′toire′** (dē′rĕk′twȧr′), *n.* [F.] = directory, 5.

di·rec′tor (dĭ·rĕk′tẽr; dī-), *n.* **1.** One who directs; one who regulates, guides, or orders. **2.** One of a body of persons directing the affairs of a company or corporation, as a bank or institution. **3.** The producer of a play, who trains the actors and combines for his desired ends acting, business, scenery, lighting, etc.; one who supervises the making of a motion picture; stage director. — **di·rec′tor·ship**, *n.*

di·rec′to·rate (dĭ·rĕk′tō·rĭt; dī-), *n.* The office of director; also, a board of directors, as of a bank or corporation.

di·rec′to′ri·al (dĭ·rĕk′tō′rĭ·ăl; dī′rĕk-; 70), *adj.* Of a director.

di·rec′to·ry (dĭ·rĕk′tō·rĭ; dī-), *adj.* Serving to direct; directive. — *n.; pl.* -ries (-rĭz). [ML. *directorium.*] **1.** That which directs; esp., a collection or body of directions. **2.** A book containing the names and residences of the inhabitants of any place or of those engaged in a particular profession, business, or the like. **3.** A body of directors. **4.** *Eccl.* A book of directions for the conduct of worship. **5.** *Fr. Hist.* [*cap.*] [F. *Directoire.*] The body of five men which held the executive power, under the constitution of 1795, from 1795 to 1799 in the First Republic.

di·rec′tress (dĭ·rĕk′trĕs; -trĭs; dī-), *n.* A woman director.

di·rec′trix (-trĭks), *n.; pl.* directrixes (-trĭk·sĕz; -sĭz), directrices (dī′rĕk·trī′sēz). [NL.] **1.** *Rare.* A directress. **2.** *Geom.* A fixed line or curve used as a guide in describing a curve or surface.

direct tax. A tax exacted directly from the person who is to bear the ultimate burden, including property, income, and inheritance taxes, poll taxes, and franchise taxes.

dire′ful (dīr′fo͝ol; -f′l), *adj.* Terrible; calamitous; woeful. — **dire′ful·ly**, *adv.*

dirge (dûrj), *n.* [Contr. of L. *dirige* direct thou (imper. of *dirigere*), beginning the opening antiphon in Latin.] **1.** *R.C.Ch.* The Office for the Dead; also, a psalm sung for a departed soul, or a requiem mass. **2.** A lyrical or musical composition expressive of grief, as to accompany funeral or memorial rites.

dirge′ful (-fo͝ol; -f′l), *adj.* Funereal; mourning.

dir′i·gi·ble (dĭr′ĭ·jĭ·b'l), *adj.* [L. *dirigere* to direct.] That may be steered. — *n.* A lighter-than-air aircraft that is engine-driven and steerable. See AIRSHIP. — **dir′i·gi·bil′i·ty** (-bĭl′ĭ·tĭ), *n.*

‖**di′ri·go** (dĭr′ĭ·gō). [L.] I direct or guide; — motto of Maine.

dir′i·ment (dĭr′ĭ·mĕnt), *adj.* [L. *dirimens*, pres. part. of *dirimere* to interrupt, destroy.] *Law.* Absolutely nullifying; — chiefly in **diriment impediment**, an impediment, such as an existing marriage, that nullifies marriage ab initio.

dirk (dûrk), *n.* A dagger. — *v. t.* To stab with a dirk.

dirl (dĭrl; dûrl), *v. t. & i.* *Scot.* To pierce; vibrate; tingle.

dirn′dl (dûrn′d'l), *n.* [G., dim. fr. *dirne* girl, lass.] **a** A type of dress with close-fitting bodice and full skirt gathered at the waist, imitative of Alpine peasant costume. **b** Also **dirndl skirt**. A full skirt gathered to a tight waistband.

dirt (dûrt), *n.* [ME. *drit*, fr. ON. *drit* excrement.] **1.** Any foul substance, as excrement, mud, dust, etc. **2.** Loose or packed soil. **3.** Quality of being foul, esp. in a moral sense; uncleanness in action; obscenity; also, slanderous gossip. **4.** *Mining.* Alluvial earth, gravel, or other foreign matter.

dirt′y (dûr′tĭ), *adj.*; DIRT′I·ER (-tĭ·ĕr); DIRT′I·EST. **1.** Defiled with dirt; serving to defile. **2.** Base; sordid; despicable. **3.** Smutty. **4.** Foggy; gusty; stormy. **5.** Sullied; clouded; muddied; — of color. — **dirt′i·ly**, *adv.* — **dirt′i·ness**, *n.*

Syn. Dirty, filthy, foul, nasty, squalid mean conspicuously unclean or impure. Dirty emphasizes the fact, rather than an emotional reaction; filthy adds the suggestion of offensiveness and, usually, of dirt that besmears or clutters up; foul implies a revolting offensiveness and an accumulation of that which is rotten, putrid, or stinking; nasty, once equal to *foul*, now applies to that which is repugnant to one who likes cleanliness, sweetness, freshness, etc.; squalid implies both extreme dirtiness and extreme slovenliness or neglect. All these terms also imply obscenity: *dirty* suggests despicableness, *filthy* and *foul* its disgusting ugliness, *nasty* its extreme unpleasantness, and *squalid* its base sordidness.

— *v. t.*; DIRT′IED (dûr′tĭd); DIRT′Y·ING. **a** To foul; to soil. **b** To tarnish or sully, as reputation, etc. — *v. i.* To become soiled or dirty.

Dis (dĭs), *n.* [L.] *Rom. Relig.* God of the underworld, identical with the Greek Pluto; also, his realm.

dis- (dĭs-; *in a few words, as* discern, disease, dĭz-). [L. *dis-*, sometimes through OF. *des-* (see DE-). As a living prefix in English, *dis-* is the invariable form.] A prefix denoting: **1.** *Separation* or *parting from*, as in *dis*miss, *dis*tribute, *dis*suade. **2.** *Reversal, undoing, depriving*, or *negation*; — used at will to form: **a** Verbs (with their verbals and corresponding nouns and adjectives of action), denoting either (1) *reversal of an action*, as in *dis*own, *dis*join; or (2) *undoing* or *depriving of a character, quality, rank*, or the like, as in *dis*able; or (3) *expulsion from*, or *depriving of, possession*, as in *dis*bar, *dis*frock. **b** Nouns, denoting the *opposite of*, or *absence of, something*, as in *dis*union, *dis*affection. **c** Adjectives, denoting the *absence* or *contrary of a quality*, as in *dis*honest.

☞ Where the simple word contains the idea of separation, reversal, or negation, *dis-* sometimes operates as a simple intensive, as in *dis*annul.

dis-. [See 1st DI-.] A prefix meaning *twice, double*.

dis′a·bil′i·ty (dĭs′ȧ·bĭl′ĭ·tĭ), *n.*; *pl.* -TIES (-tĭz). **1.** State of being disabled; absence of competent physical, intellectual, or moral power, fitness, or the like; also, an instance of such lack. **2.** Legal incapacity, incompetency, or disqualification.

dis·a′ble (dĭs·ā′b'l), *v. t.*; -A′BLED (-b'ld); -A′BLING (-blĭng). **1.** To render unable or incapable; to deprive of the force, vigor, or power of action; to cripple. **2.** *Law.* To render legally incapable; to disqualify. — **Syn.** See WEAKEN. — **dis·a′ble·ment**, *n.*

dis·a′bled (-b'ld), *adj.* Incapable; incapacitated.

dis·a·buse′ (dĭs′ȧ·būz′), *v. t.* To undeceive; to set right.

di·sac′cha·ride (dī·săk′ȧ·rīd; -rĭd), *n.* Also **di·sac′cha·rid** (-rĭd). [*di-* + *saccharide*.] *Chem.* Any of a group of sugars which yield on hydrolysis two monosaccharide molecules. Common disaccharides are sucrose, lactose, and maltose.

dis′ac·cord′ (dĭs′ă·kôrd′), *v. i.* [OF. *desaccorder*.] To refuse assent; to disagree. — *n.* Disagreement.

dis′ac·cus′tom (dĭs′ă·kŭs′tŭm), *v. t.* To free from a habit; to wean.

dis′ad·van′tage (dĭs′ăd·văn′tĭj; 9), *n.* **1.** Deprivation of advantage; unfavorable or prejudicial condition or circumstance; handicap. **2.** Loss or damage to reputation, credit, finances, etc.; detriment. — *v. t.*; -TAGED (-tĭjd); -TAG·ING (-tĭj·ĭng). To injure the interest of.

dis·ad′van·ta′geous (dĭs·ăd′văn·tā′jŭs), *adj.* Attended with disadvantage; unfavorable to success. — **dis·ad′van·ta′geous·ly**, *adv.* — **dis·ad′van·ta′geous·ness**, *n.*

dis′af·fect′ (dĭs′ă·fĕkt′), *v. t.* To alienate in feeling or allegiance, esp. from those in authority; fill with discontent. — **Syn.** See ESTRANGE. — **dis′af·fect′ed** (-fĕk′tĕd; -tĭd), *adj.*

dis′af·fec′tion (-fĕk′shŭn), *n.* State of being disaffected; alienation or want of good will; disloyalty.

dis′af·firm′ (dĭs′ă·fûrm′), *v. t.* **1.** To assert the contrary of; to contradict; deny. **2.** *Law.* To refuse to confirm; to annul or reverse, as a judicial decision. — **dis′af·firm′ance** (-fûr′măns), *n.* — **dis′af·fir·ma′tion** (-ăf·ĕr·mā′shŭn), *n.*

dis′af·for′est (-fŏr′ĕst; -ĭst), *v. t.* [ML. *disafforestare*.] **1.** *Eng. Law.* To reduce from the privileges of a forest to the state of ordinary land. **2.** To deforest. — **dis′af·for′es·ta′tion** (-ĕs·tā′shŭn), *n.* — **dis′af·for′est·ment**, *n.*

dis′a·gree′ (dĭs′ȧ·grē′), *v. i.* **1.** To fail to agree; to differ; to be at variance; — often followed by *with*. **2.** To differ in opinion; also, to quarrel. **3.** To be unsuitable; as, tropic heat *disagrees* with him.

dis′a·gree′a·ble (-ȧ·b'l), *adj.* **1.** Exciting repugnance; offensive. **2.** Not disposed to be agreeable; ill-tempered; also, causing discomfort. — **dis′a·gree′a·ble·ness**, *n.* — **dis′a·gree′a·bly** (-blĭ), *adv.*

dis′a·gree′ment (-mĕnt), *n.* **1.** Act of disagreeing. **2.** State of being at variance.

‖**dis a′li·ter vi′sum** (dĭs ăl′ĭ·tĕr vī′sŭm). [L.] The gods decreed otherwise.

dis′al·low′ (dĭs′ă·lou′), *v. t.* To refuse to allow.

dis′al·low′ance (-ăns), *n.* Act of disallowing; rejection.

dis′an·nul′ (dĭs′ă·nŭl′), *v. t.*; see ANNUL. To annul completely. — **dis′an·nul′ment**, *n.*

dis′a·noint′ (dĭs′ȧ·noint′), *v. t.* To void the consecration of.

dis′ap·pear′ (dĭs′ă·pēr′), *v. i.* **1.** To cease to appear or to be perceived; to vanish. **2.** To cease to be; to be lost.

dis′ap·pear′ance (-ăns), *n.* A disappearing; a vanishing.

dis′ap·point′ (dĭs′ă·point′), *v. t.* [OF. *desapointier*, fr. *des-* (fr. L. *dis-*) + *apointier* to appoint.] To defeat of expectation or hope; to fail to come up to the expectation of; as, one is *disappointed of* a thing not obtained, *disappointed in* a thing obtained.

dis′ap·point′ed (-poin′tĕd; -tĭd), *adj.* **1.** Balked, as of an expectation or hope. **2.** *Obs.* Not adequately appointed, equipped, or prepared. *Shak.*

dis′ap·point′ment (dĭs′ă·point′mĕnt), *n.* **1.** Act or instance of disappointing, or state or emotion of being disappointed. **2.** One who or that which disappoints.

dis′ap·pro·ba′tion (dĭs′ăp·rō·bā′shŭn), *n.* Act of disapproving, or state of being disapproved; condemnation.

dis′ap·prov′al (-ă·prōōv′ăl), *n.* Disapprobation; censure.

dis′ap·prove′ (-ă·prōōv′), *v. t.* **1.** To pass unfavorable judgment upon; to condemn; to regard as wrong. **2.** To refuse approbation to; to decline to sanction. — *v. i.* To feel or express disapprobation (*of*). — **dis′ap·prov′ing·ly** (-prōōv′ĭng·lĭ), *adv.*

dis·arm′ (dĭs·ärm′), *v. t.* [OF. *desarmer*, fr. *des-* (fr. L. *dis-*) + *armer* to arm.] **1.** To deprive of arms or weapons. **2.** To deprive of means or disposition to harm or be hostile; to render harmless. — *v. i.* To abandon or reduce materially the military establishment.

dis·ar′ma·ment (-är′mȧ·mĕnt), *n.* The reduction of a military establishment to a minimum set by some authority.

dis·arm′ing, *adj.* Allaying irritation or anger.

Syn. Disarming, ingratiating, insinuating mean winning or attempting to win another's favor or interest. Disarming implies irritation in the person to be won, and some quality, such as candor or innocence, in the person who wins; ingratiating carries a stronger implication of design than *disarming*, sometimes suggesting a sedulous, sometimes a servile, attempt to win favor; insinuating implies suave, subtle, and often artful means of winning confidence.

dis′ar·range′ (dĭs′ă·rānj′), *v. t.*; see ARRANGE. To disturb the due arrangement of. — **dis′ar·range′ment**, *n.*

dis′ar·ray′ (-ă·rā′), *v. t.* **1.** To throw into disorder; to break the array of. **2.** To unrobe. — *n.* **1.** Disorder. **2.** Disorderly, usually incomplete, attire; dishabille.

dis′ar·tic′u·late (-är·tĭk′ū·lāt), *v. t. & i.* To disjoint; to separate joint from joint. — **dis′ar·tic′u·la′tion** (-lā′shŭn), *n.*

dis′as·sem′ble (-ă·sĕm′b'l), *v. t.* To take apart; as, to *disassemble* a watch or a motor.

dis′as·sem′bly (-blĭ), *n.* State or condition of being disassembled; also, a disassembling.

dis′as·so′ci·ate (-ă·sō′shĭ·āt), *v. t.* To disconnect from association; dissociate.

dis·as′ter (dĭ·zȧs′tĕr; 9), *n.* [F. *désastre*, fr. *dés-* (fr. L. *dis-*) + *astre* star, fr. L. *astrum*.] **1.** *Obs.* A baleful aspect of a planet or star. **2.** Sudden and extraordinary misfortune; a calamity.

Syn. Disaster, calamity, catastrophe, cataclysm mean an event or situation regarded as a terrible misfortune. Disaster implies an unforeseen mischance bringing with it destruction of life or property or the ruin of projects, careers, etc.; calamity implies a grievous misfortune, usually public yet affecting many persons and, often, causing widespread distress; catastrophe (properly a denouement) applies generally to a disastrous conclusion; cataclysm, literally, applies to a deluge or convulsion; figuratively, to any event or situation that effects an upheaval or complete reversal.

dis·as′trous (dĭ·zȧs′trŭs), *adj.* **1.** Full of unpropitious stellar influences; unpropitious. **2.** Attended with disaster; calamitous. — **dis·as′trous·ly**, *adv.*

dis′a·vow′ (dĭs′ȧ·vou′), *v. t.* [OF. *desavouer*, fr. *des-* (fr. L. *dis-*) + *avouer* to avow.] To refuse to own or acknowledge; to deny responsibility for; to disclaim.

dis′a·vow′al (-ăl), *n.* A disavowing; repudiation.

dis·band′ (dĭs·bănd′), *v. t.* [MF. *desbander*.] **1.** To break up the organization of; as, to *disband* an army. **2.** To disunite the parts of; dissolve. — *v. i.* To break ranks, as troops; to scatter. — **dis·band′ment**, *n.*

dis·bar′ (dĭs·bär′), *v. t.*; see BAR. *Law.* To expel from the bar; to deprive (an attorney, etc.) of his status and privileges as such. — **dis·bar′ment**, *n.*

dis′be·lief′ (dĭs′bē·lēf′), *n.* Act of disbelieving; mental rejection of a statement as untrue. — **Syn.** See UNBELIEF.

dis′be·lieve′ (-lēv′), *v. t. & i.* To reject belief in; not to believe. — **dis′be·liev′er** (-lēv′ĕr), *n.*

dis·bos′om (dĭs·bōōz′ŭm; -bōō′zŭm), *v. t.* To confess.

dis·bow′el (dĭs·bou′ĕl), *v. t.* To disembowel.

dis·branch′ (dĭs·brȧnch′), *v. t.* To tear off, as a branch.

dis·bur′den (-bûr′d'n), *v. t.* **1.** To rid of a burden; to disencumber; hence, to relieve, esp. of something oppressive. **2.** To put off (a burden or load); to unload. — *v. i.* To relieve oneself of a burden. — **dis·bur′den·ment**, *n.*

dis·burse′ (dĭs·bûrs′), *v. t.* [OF. *desbourser*, fr. *des-* (fr. L. *dis-*) + *bourse* purse.] To pay out; to expend. — **dis·burs′a·ble** (-bûr′sȧ·b'l), *adj.* — **dis·burs′er**, *n.*

dis·burse′ment (-mĕnt), *n.* Act of disbursing; also, that which is disbursed; funds paid out.

disc (dĭsk), *n.* Disk; — preferred spelling in some senses. See DISK.

disc, *v. t.*; DISCED (dĭskt); DISC′ING (dĭs′kĭng). To disk.

dis·calced′ (dĭs·kălst′), *adj.* Unshod; barefooted.

dis′cant (dĭs′kănt, *n.*; dĭs·kănt′, *v.*). Var. of DESCANT.

dis·card′ (dĭs·kärd′; dĭs′kärd), *v. t.* **1.** *Card Playing.* **a** To reject from the hand (a card or cards). **b** To play (a card, not a trump, of a different suit from the card led). **2.** To cast off as useless or as no longer of service; to reject. — *v. i.* *Card Playing.* To throw off or trash a card.

Syn. Discard, cast, shed, slough, scrap, junk mean to get rid of as of no use or service. Discard implies the getting rid of that which has become an annoyance, an interference, or the like; cast, especially with *off, away*, and *out*, now implies a rejection or repudiation; shed implies a throwing off of something such as old leaves, old habits, discarded beliefs, etc.; slough implies a shedding, literally, of its skin by a reptile, and figuratively, of a bad habit or the like; scrap and junk imply throwing away as refuse or rubbish, *scrap* often implying the breaking up into parts.

dis′card (dĭs′kärd), *n.* **1.** A discarding; also, the card or cards discarded. **2.** Something discarded; a castoff.

dis·case′ (dĭs·kās′), *v. t.* To remove the case or sheath of.

dis·cept′ (dĭ·sĕpt′), *v. i.* [L. *disceptare.*] To debate; also, to disagree. — **dis′cep·ta′tion** (dĭs′ĕp·tā′shŭn), *n.*

dis·cern′ (dĭ·zûrn′; dĭ·sûrn′), *v. t.* [OF. *discerner*, fr. L. *discernere*, *-cretum*, fr. *dis-* + *cernere* to distinguish.] **1.** To make out as with the eye or by the mind; to see; to understand; to detect. **2.** To identify as separate and distinct; to discriminate. — *v. i.* To see or understand the difference; to make distinction. — **Syn.** Perceive, observe, descry. — **dis·cern′er**, *n.* — **dis·cern′i·ble** (-zûr′nĭ·b'l; -sûr′nĭ·b'l), *adj.* — **dis·cern′i·ble·ness**, *n.* — **dis·cern′i·bly** (-blĭ), *adv.*

dis·cern′ing, *adj.* Discriminating. — **dis·cern′ing·ly**, *adv.*

dis·cern′ment (-mĕnt), *n.* Act or faculty of discerning; quickness and accuracy in discriminating.

Syn. **Discernment, discrimination, perception, penetration, insight, acumen, divination, clairvoyance** here mean a power to see what is not evident to the average mind. **Discernment** stresses accuracy, as in reading character, motives, etc.; **discrimination** stresses the power to distinguish or to select the excellent, the true; **perception** implies quick discernment and delicate feeling; **penetration** implies a searching mind that goes beyond the reach of the senses; **insight** suggests depth of discernment and understanding sympathy; **acumen** implies characteristic penetration combined with keen judgment; **divination** implies instinctive insight; **clairvoyance** implies preternaturally clear or acute perception.

dis·cerp′ti·ble (dĭ·sûrp′tĭ·b'l), *adj.* That can be rent asunder; separable; divisible. — **dis·cerp′ti·bil′i·ty** (-bĭl′ĭ·tĭ), *n.*

dis·charge′ (dĭs·chärj′), *v. t.;* see CHARGE. [OF. *deschargier.* See DIS-, 2; CHARGE.] **1.** To relieve of a charge, load, or burden; as: **a** To unload (a ship, etc.). **b** To absolve; to free (one) from that which oppresses, as an obligation. **c** To let go the charge of; to fire (a gun, bow, etc.). **2.** To release or set free; as: **a** To remove or let go; to clear out; as, to *discharge* a cargo. **b** To shoot; to fire (a bullet, arrow, etc.). **c** To set at liberty. **d** To emit; to pour forth. **3.** To dismiss; to throw off; as: **a** To send away from service or employment. **b** To get rid of as a debt or duty by paying or performing. **c** To dismiss by satisfying (one) or giving satisfaction for. **d** To set aside; to dismiss legally. **4.** *Arch.* **a** To receive and distribute, as the weight of a wall above an opening. **b** To relieve, as an opening or the lintel spanning an opening, from the weight of the wall. **5.** *Dyeing & Calico Printing.* To bleach out or to remove, as by a chemical process. — *v. i.* To deliver a load, charge, or burden; to unload; also, to go off, as a gun; to run, as a dye; to emit or give vent to fluid or other contents. — **Syn.** See FREE: PERFORM.

— (dĭs·chärj′; dĭs′chärj), *n.* **1.** Act of discharging; unloading. **2.** Act of relieving of something which oppresses one, as an obligation, accusation, penalty; release. **3.** The state or fact of being discharged; acquittal; exoneration. **4.** That which discharges or releases, as from imprisonment, an obligation, or a liability; also, a certification of release or payment; as, to produce his *discharge* as evidence. **5.** Legal release from confinement; liberation. **6.** Firing off; letting off; as, a *discharge* of arrows. **7.** A flowing or issuing out; also, a rate of flow or that which flows. **8.** Act of getting rid of an obligation or liability, as by the payment of a debt or the performance of a duty. **9. a** Release or dismissal from an office, employment, etc. **b** Release from military or naval service, as at the end of an enlistment period; as, an honorable *discharge.* Cf. RUPTURED DUCK, *Illust.* **10.** *Elec.* The equalization of a difference of electric potential between two points. — **dis·charge′a·ble**, *adj.* — **dis·charg′er** (dĭs·chär′jẽr), *n.*

dis·ci′ple (dĭ·sī′p'l), *n.* [OF., fr. L. *discipulus*, fr. *discere* to learn.] One who receives instruction from another; specif.: **a** A professed follower of Christ in his lifetime, esp. one of the twelve apostles or one of the seventy (seventy-two in the Vulgate). *Luke* x. 1. **b** An adherent of a school, as in art or philosophy. — **Syn.** See SCHOLAR: FOLLOWER. — ***the disciples, or the twelve disciples.*** The twelve selected companions of Jesus; — called also the *apostles.* See APOSTLE. — **dis·ci′ple·ship**, *n.*

Disciples of Christ. A Christian denomination founded in Pennsylvania in 1810 by Thomas and Alexander Campbell (hence its members are also called *Campbellites*). It rejects human creeds and sectarian names, holds the Bible alone to be the rule of faith and practice, celebrates the Lord's Supper every Sunday, and baptizes believers by immersion only. It is congregational in church government. Following a separation in 1906, the conservative element became a separate denomination, *Churches of Christ.*

dis′ci·pli′nal (dĭs′ĭ·plī′năl; -n'l; dĭs′ĭ·plĭn·ăl; -'l), *adj.* Of or relating to discipline; of the nature of discipline.

dis′ci·pli·nar′i·an (dĭs′ĭ·plĭ·nâr′ĭ·ăn), *adj.* Of or pertaining to discipline. — *n.* One who disciplines; one who enforces order.

dis′ci·pli·nar′y (dĭs′ĭ·plĭ·nĕr′ĭ *or, esp. Brit.*, -nẽr·ĭ), *adj.* Of or relating to discipline or disciplinarians; corrective.

dis′ci·pline (dĭs′ĭ·plĭn), *n.* [OF., fr. L. *disciplina*, fr. *discipulus.*] **1.** *Obs.* Instruction. **2.** A branch of knowledge involving research. **3.** Training which corrects, molds, strengthens, or perfects. **4.** Punishment; chastisement. **5.** Control gained by enforcing obedience or order, as in a school or army; hence, orderly conduct; as, troops noted for their *discipline.* **6.** Rule or system of rules affecting conduct or action; esp., *Eccl.*, practical rules, as disting. from dogmatic formulations. — *v. t.* **1.** To develop by instruction and exercise; to train in self-control or obedience to given standards. **2.** To chasten; punish. **3.** To train; drill. — **Syn.** See TEACH: PUNISH. — **dis′ci·plin·a·ble** (-plĭn·ȧ·b'l), *adj.* — **dis′ci·plin·er**, *n.*

disc jockey. One who conducts and announces a radio program of musical recordings, often with interspersed nonmusical comments.

dis·claim′ (dĭs·klām′), *v. i.* [AF. *desclamer.* See DIS-; CLAIM.] **1.** *Law.* To renounce or repudiate a legal claim; to make a disclaimer. **2.** *Obs.* To disavow all part or share (*in*). — *v. t.* **1.** *Law.* To renounce a legal claim to. **2.** To deny or disavow any connection with or responsibility for; to repudiate.

dis·claim′er (-ẽr), *n.* [AF. *desclamer*, inf. used as n.] Act of disclaiming; a denial or disavowal of claim.

dis′cla·ma′tion (dĭs′klȧ·mā′shŭn), *n.* Disavowal; disclaimer.

dis·close′ (dĭs·klōz′), *v. t.* [From pres. stem of OF. *desclore*, fr. L. *disclaudere.*] **1.** *Obs.* To open. **2.** To uncover and expose to view; also, to hatch. **3.** To make known; to reveal. — **Syn.** See REVEAL. — *n. Obs.* Disclosure. — **dis·clos′er** (-klōz′ẽr), *n.*

dis·clo′sure (-klō′zhẽr), *n.* **1.** Act of disclosing; exposure. **2.** That which is disclosed, revealed, or divulged.

dis·cob′o·lus (dĭs·kŏb′ō·lŭs), *n.* [L., fr. Gr. *diskobolos*, fr. *diskos* discus + *ballein* to throw.] A discus thrower.

dis·cog′ra·phy (dĭs·kŏg′rȧ·fĭ), *n.* [*disc* + *-graphy.*] **1.** A descriptive, classified catalogue or listing of phonograph records, usually including dates and names of performers. **2.** The history or description of recorded music.

dis′coid (dĭs′koid), *adj.* [Gr. *diskoeidēs*, fr. *diskos* a round plate, quoit + *eidos* form.] **1.** Like a disk or discus; flat and circular. **2.** *Bot.* In composite plants, having a tubular instead of a ligulate corolla, as the florets in the center of a daisy. — *n.* Anything having the form of a discus or disk. — **dis·coi′dal** (dĭs·koi′dăl; -d'l), *adj.*

dis·col′or, dis·col′our (dĭs·kŭl′ẽr), *v. t. & i.* [OF. *descolorer*, fr. L. *dis-* + *colorare* to color.] To change to a different color; to stain.

dis·col′or·a′tion, dis·col′our·a′tion (-ā′shŭn), *n.* **1.** Act of discoloring, or state of being discolored. **2.** A stain.

dis·col′or·ment, dis·col′our·ment (-kŭl′ẽr·mĕnt), *n.* Discoloration.

dis·com′fit (dĭs·kŭm′fĭt), *v. t.* [OF. *desconfit*, past part. of *desconfire*, fr. L. *dis-* + *conficere* to make ready.] **1.** To scatter in fight; to put to rout. **2.** To frustrate the plans of; to balk. — **Syn.** See EMBARRASS. — *n. Obs.* Rout; discomfiture.

dis·com′fi·ture (-fĭ·tŭr), *n.* Act of discomfiting, or state of being discomfited; rout; overthrow; frustration.

dis·com′fort (-kŭm′fẽrt), *v. t.* [OF. *desconforter*, fr. *des-* (fr. L. *dis-*) + *conforter* to comfort.] **1.** *Archaic.* To discourage; deject. **2.** To disturb the comfort of; to make uneasy. — *n.* **1.** Want of comfort; uneasiness, mental or physical; distress. **2.** That which causes distress.

dis·com′fort·a·ble (-ȧ·b'l), *adj.* **1.** *Now Rare.* Causing mental discomfort. **2.** Uncomfortable.

dis′com·mend′ (dĭs′kŏ·mĕnd′), *v. t.* **1.** To disapprove. **2.** To expose to censure or ill favor. — **dis′com·mend′a·ble** (-mĕn′dȧ·b'l), *adj.*

dis′com·men·da′tion (dĭs′kŏm·ĕn·dā′shŭn), *n.* Blame.

dis′com·mode′ (dĭs′kŏ·mōd′), *v. t.* To incommode.

dis′com·mod′i·ty (-mŏd′ĭ·tĭ), *n.; pl.* -ITIES (-tĭz). **1.** Disadvantageousness; inconvenience. **2.** Disadvantage; *Econ.*, any substance or action that possesses disutility, that is, anything that it is desired to avoid or get rid of; — the opposite of *commodity.*

dis·com′mon (dĭs·kŏm′ŭn), *v. t.* **1.** *Eng. Univ.* To forbid (a tradesman) to deal with undergraduates. **2.** *Law.* **a** To deprive of the right of common, as of pasture. **b** To deprive of commonable quality, as lands.

dis′com·pose′ (dĭs′kŏm·pōz′), *v. t.* **1.** To destroy the composure of; to agitate. **2.** To disturb the order of; to disarrange.

Syn. **Discompose, disquiet, disturb, perturb, agitate, upset, fluster, flurry** mean to destroy one's capacity for collected thought or prompt action. **Discompose** usually implies greater emotional stress than *disconcert* or *discomfit* and actual loss of self-control or self-confidence; **disquiet** suggests the loss of one's sense of security or peace of mind; **disturb** implies interference with one's mental processes that is caused by worry, perplexity, interruption, etc.; **perturb** implies deep disturbance and unsettlement of mind; **agitate** implies a loss of calmness and obvious signs of nervous or emotional excitement; **upset**, like *agitate* in many ways, suggests disappointment, distress, or sorrow; **fluster** suggests bewildered agitation caused by sudden and unexpected demands, commands, etc.; **flurry** suggests excitement, commotion, and confusion induced by great haste or alarm.

dis′com·po′sure (-pō′zhẽr), *n.* State of being discomposed; disorder; agitation; perturbation.

dis′con·cert′ (dĭs′kŏn·sûrt′), *v. t.* To throw into confusion; to upset; discompose. — **Syn.** See EMBARRASS. — **dis′con·cert′ing·ly**, *adv.* — **dis′con·cer′tion** (-sûr′shŭn), *n.*

dis′con·cert′ed (-sûr′tĕd; -tĭd), *adj.* Disturbed; perturbed. — **dis′con·cert′ed·ly**, *adv.* — **dis′con·cert′ed·ness**, *n.*

dis′con·form′i·ty (-fôr′mĭ·tĭ), *n.* Want of conformity.

dis′con·nect′ (dĭs′kŏ·nĕkt′), *v. t.* To undo or dissolve the union or connection of; to disunite; break up.

dis′con·nect′ed (-nĕk′tĕd; -tĭd), *adj.* Disjoined; not connected; hence, incoherent; disjointed. — **dis′con·nect′ed·ly**, *adv.* — **-ness**, *n.*

dis′con·nec′tion, dis′con·nex′ion (-nĕk′shŭn), *n.* Act of disconnecting, or state of being disconnected; separation.

dis′con·sid′er (-kŏn·sĭd′ẽr), *v. t.* To bring into disrepute.

dis·con′so·late (dĭs·kŏn′sō·lĭt), *adj.* [ML. *disconsolatus*, fr. L. *dis-* + *consolatus*, past part. of *consolari* to console. See CONSOLE, *v.*] **1.** Destitute of consolation; deeply dejected; sad. **2.** Inspiring dejection; cheerless. — **dis·con′so·late·ly**, *adv.* — **-ness**, *n.*

dis′con′so·la′tion (-lā′shŭn), *n.* State of being disconsolate.

dis′con·tent′ (dĭs′kŏn·tĕnt′), *adj.* Not content; discontented; dissatisfied. — *n.* Want of content; dissatisfaction. — *v. t.* To dissatisfy; displease.

dis′con·tent′ed (-tĕn′tĕd; -tĭd), *adj.* Dissatisfied; uneasy in mind. Cf. MALCONTENT. — **dis′con·tent′ed·ly**, *adv.* — **-ness**, *n.*

dis′con·tent′ment (-tĕnt′mĕnt), *n.* Discontent.

dis′con·tin′u·ance (dĭs′kŏn·tĭn′ū·ăns), *n.* **1.** Lack of continued connection; interruption. **2.** *Law.* In practice, the termination of an action by the failure of the plaintiff to properly continue it or by the entry of a discontinuing order on his motion.

dis′con·tin′u·a′tion (-ā′shŭn), *n.* Discontinuance.

dis′con·tin′ue (dĭs′kŏn·tĭn′ū), *v. t. & i.* **1.** To interrupt the continuance of; to stop; to give up. **2.** *Law.* To abandon or terminate by a discontinuance. — **Syn.** See STOP. — **dis′con·tin′u·er** (-ū·ẽr), *n.*

dis′con·ti·nu′i·ty (dĭs′kŏn·tĭ·nū′ĭ·tĭ), *n.* **1.** Lack of continuity or cohesion. **2.** A break in continuity; a gap.

dis′con·tin′u·ous (dĭs′kŏn·tĭn′ū·ŭs), *adj.* Not continuous; broken off; also, lacking sequence or coherence; as, a *discontinuous* series. — **dis′con·tin′u·ous·ly**, *adv.* — **dis′con·tin′u·ous·ness**, *n.*

dis′cord (dĭs′kôrd), *n.* [OF. *discord*, earlier *descort*, fr. *descorder.* See DISCORD, *v. i.*] **1.** Lack of concord or agreement; disagreement; hence, dissension; conflict. **2.** *Music.* **a** Want of concord or harmony. **b** A combination of musical sounds which strikes the ear harshly. **c** Dissonance. **3.** A harsh sound; esp., noise of conflict; din.

Syn. **Discord, strife, conflict, contention, dissension, variance** mean action or state manifesting lack of harmony. **Discord** also implies quarreling, factiousness, antagonism, dissonance, or the like; **strife** implies a struggle for superiority rather than the incongruity or incompatibility of the persons or things involved; **conflict** usually stresses the process, its ups and downs, the uncertainty of its outcome, etc., but, in a weakened sense, implies an irreconcilability, as of duties; **contention** now chiefly applies to strife that manifests itself in quarreling, disputing, controversy, and the like; **dissension** implies strife or discord between persons or parties, but stresses a breach or division into factions;

variance implies a clash between persons or things owing to a difference in opinion, nature, or the like.

dis·cord′ (dĭs·kôrd′), *v. i.* [OF. *descorder*, fr. L. *discordare*, fr. *discors, -cordis*, discordant, fr. *dis-* + *cor, cordis*, heart.] To disagree; to jar; clash.

dis·cord′ance (-kôr′dăns), **dis·cord′an·cy** (-dăn·sĭ), *n.* **1.** State or instance of being discordant; disagreement. **2.** Discord of sounds.

dis·cord′ant (dĭs·kôr′dănt), *adj.* **1.** Disagreeing; quarrelsome; not harmonious. **2.** *Music.* Not in harmony or concord; harsh; jarring. — **dis·cord′ant·ly**, *adv.*

dis′count (dĭs′kount; dĭs·kount′), *v. t.* [OF. *desconter, descompter*, to deduct, deriv. of L. *dis-* + *computare* to count. See COUNT, *v.*] **1.** To deduct from an account, debt, charge, or the like. **2.** To lend money upon, deducting the discount or allowance for interest. **3.** To depreciate, as by leaving out of account; to disregard. **4.** To make allowance for exaggeration in (a tale, etc.); as, to *discount* his story. **5.** To take in advance at less than the full value of; as, to *discount* one's enjoyment of a book by reading its advance reviews. — *v. i.* To lend, or make practice of lending, money, deducting the interest in advance; as, the banks *discount* for 60 or 90 days. — (dĭs′kount), *n.* **1.** The act of discounting; esp.: **a** A deduction made from a gross sum. **b** A deduction made for interest, in advancing money upon, or purchasing, a bill or note not due. See BANK DISCOUNT. Abbr. *disc.* **2.** The rate of interest (**discount rate**) charged in discounting. — **dis′count·a·ble**, *adj.* — **dis′count·er**, *n.*

— ***at a discount.*** Below par, or below the nominal value; hence, out of favor; poorly or lightly esteemed.

dis·coun′te·nance (dĭs·koun′tē·năns), *v. t.;* see COUNTENANCE. [MF. *descontenancer.*] **1.** To put out of countenance; to abash; disconcert. **2.** To refuse to look with favor upon; to discourage by disapproval. — *n. Rare.* Disapprobation.

dis·cour′age (dĭs·kûr′ĭj; 117), *v. t.;* -AGED (-ĭjd); -AG·ING (-ĭj·ĭng). [OF. *descoragier.*] **1.** To lessen the courage of; to dishearten. **2.** To seek to check by disfavoring; also, to cause (one) to weaken in an intention; to deter. — **dis·cour′ag·er** (-ĭj·ẽr), *n.*

dis·cour′age·ment (-mĕnt), *n.* **1.** Act of discouraging, or state of being discouraged; depression. **2.** That which discourages; a deterrent.

dis·cour′ag·ing (-ĭj·ĭng), *adj.* Depressing; dispiriting. — **dis·cour′ag·ing·ly**, *adv.*

dis·course′ (dĭs·kōrs′; dĭs′kōrs; 70), *n.* [F. *discours*, fr. L. *discursus*, fr. *discurrere, discursum*, to run to and fro, discourse, fr. *dis-* + *currere* to run.] **1.** Act, power, or faculty of thinking consecutively and logically; reasoning power. **2.** *Archaic.* Coherent reflection or thought. **3.** Conversation; also, art or manner of conversing. **4.** Formal or orderly communication of thought in speech or writing; also, an extended treatment of a subject in a speech, writing, oration, or the like. — (dĭs·kōrs′), *v. i.* To express oneself in discourse, esp. oral discourse; to talk. — *v. t.* **1.** *Archaic.* To narrate; tell; discuss. **2.** *Poetic.* To utter or give forth. — **dis·cours′er** (dĭs·kōr′sẽr), *n.*

dis·cour′te·ous (dĭs·kûr′tē·ŭs), *adj.* Uncivil; rude. — **dis·cour′te·ous·ly**, *adv.* — **dis·cour′te·ous·ness**, *n.*

dis·cour′te·sy (-kûr′tē·sĭ), *n.; pl.* -SIES (-sĭz). Incivility; also, a rude act.

dis·cov′er (dĭs·kŭv′ẽr), *v. t.* [OF. *descovrir, descouvrir*, fr. LL. *discooperire.* See DIS-; COVER.] **1.** *Now Rare.* To reveal; to disclose; also, to betray. **2.** *Archaic.* To make a display of; to exhibit; also, to disclose unwittingly, esp. by actions; to manifest. **3.** To obtain for the first time sight or knowledge of, as of a thing existing already, but not perceived or known. — **dis·cov′er·a·ble**, *adj.* — **dis·cov′er·er**, *n.*

Syn. (1) See REVEAL.
(2) **Discover, ascertain, determine, unearth, learn** mean to find out something not previously known to one. **Discover** presupposes exploration, investigation, accident, or the like, but it always implies previous existence of that now known; **ascertain** presupposes one's awareness of ignorance or uncertainty and implies effort to find the facts or the truth; **determine** emphasizes the intent to establish the facts, often in order to settle a dispute; **unearth** figuratively implies bringing to light knowledge which has been forgotten, hidden, or the like; **learn**, as here compared, implies discovery of that which entails little effort.
(3) See INVENT.

dis·cov′ert (-ẽrt), *adj.* [OF. *descovert* uncovered.] *Law.* Not covert or under coverture.

dis·cov′er·y (dĭs·kŭv′ẽr·ĭ), *n.; pl.* -ERIES (-ĭz). **1.** Act of discovering. **2.** That which is discovered.

Discovery Day. = COLUMBUS DAY.

dis′cre·ate′ (dĭs′krē·āt′), *v. t.* To annihilate; to reduce to chaos. — **dis′cre·a′tion** (-ā′shŭn), *n.*

dis·cred′it (dĭs·krĕd′ĭt), *v. t.* [*dis-* + *credit*, v., after F. *discréditer.*] **1.** To refuse to accept as true; to disbelieve. **2.** To destroy confidence or trust in. **3.** To bring into discredit; to disgrace. — *n.* **1.** Loss of credit or reputation; disesteem. **2.** Lack of belief or confidence; disbelief; doubt. **3.** Lack of commercial credit.

dis·cred′it·a·ble (-ȧ·b'l), *adj.* Not creditable; disgraceful; disreputable. — **dis·cred′it·a·bly** (-blĭ), *adv.*

dis·creet′ (dĭs·krēt′), *adj.* [OF. *discret*, fr. L. *discretus*, past part. of *discernere.* See DISCERN.] Possessed of or showing discernment or good judgment in conduct and esp. in speech; prudent; circumspect. — **Ant.** Indiscreet. — **dis·creet′ly**, *adv.* — **dis·creet′ness**, *n.*

dis·crep′ance (dĭs·krĕp′ăns; *sometimes* dĭs′krē·păns), *n. Now Rare.* Discrepancy.

dis·crep′an·cy (-ăn·sĭ; *occas.* dĭs′krē·păn·sĭ), *n.; pl.* -CIES (-sĭz). State or quality of being discrepant; also, an instance of this; variance.

dis·crep′ant (dĭs·krĕp′ănt; *sometimes* dĭs′krē·pănt), *adj.* [OF., fr. L. *discrepans, -antis*, pres. part. of *discrepare* to sound discordantly, fr. *dis-* + *crepare* to rattle, creak.] Discordant; at variance; disagreeing; different; as, *discrepant* versions.

dis·crete′ (dĭs·krēt′; dĭs′krēt; 2), *adj.* [L. *discretus.* See DISCREET.] **1.** Separate; individually distinct. **2.** Composed of distinct parts or discontinuous elements. — **dis·crete′ly**, *adv.* — **dis·crete′ness**, *n.*

dis·cre′tion (dĭs·krĕsh′ŭn), *n.* **1.** Disjunction; discontinuity. **2.** *Now Rare.* Act or faculty of discerning; discernment. **3.** Power of free decision; individual judgment; undirected choice. **4.** Quality of being discreet; prudence; hence, cautious reserve, esp. in speech. — **dis·cre′tion·al** (-ăl; -'l), *adj.* — **dis·cre′tion·al·ly**, *adv.* — **dis·cre′tion·ar′y** (-ẽr′ĭ *or, esp. Brit.*, -ẽr·ĭ), *adj.* — ***at discretion.*** At will; according to one's judgment.

dis·crim′i·nate (dĭs·krĭm′ĭ·nĭt), *adj.* [L. *discriminatus*, past part. of *discriminare* to divide, deriv. of *discernere* to discern.] **1.** Distinguished by certain tokens; distinct. **2.** Marked by discrimination; carefully distinguishing. — (-nāt), *v. t.* **1.** *Now Rare.* To serve to distinguish; to differentiate. **2.** To separate (like things) one from another in comprehension or use by discerning the minute differences; as, to *discriminate* synonyms. — *v. i.* **1.** To make a distinction; to distinguish accurately. **2.** To make a difference in treatment or favor (of one as compared with others). — **dis·crim′i·nate·ly**, *adv.*

dis·crim′i·nat′ing (-nāt′ĭng), *adj.* That discriminates. — **dis·crim′i·nat′ing·ly**, *adv.*

dis·crim′i·na′tion (dĭs·krĭm′ĭ·nā′shŭn), *n.* **1.** Act of discriminating, or state of being discriminated. **2.** That which discriminates; a mark of distinction. **3.** The quality of being discriminating; faculty of nicely distinguishing. **4.** A distinction, as in treatment; esp., an unfair or injurious distinction. — **Syn.** See DISCERNMENT.

dis·crim′i·na′tive (-krĭm′ĭ·nā′tĭv; -nȧ·tĭv), *adj.* **1.** Marking a difference; distinguishing. **2.** Observing distinctions; discriminating. — **dis·crim′i·na′tive·ly**, *adv.*

dis·crim′i·na·to′ry (-nȧ·tō′rĭ *or, esp. Brit.*, -tẽr·ĭ), *adj.* Discriminative; showing favoritism.

dis·crown′ (dĭs·kroun′), *v. t.* To deprive of a crown.

dis·cur′sive (dĭs·kûr′sĭv), *adj.* Passing from one subject to another; roving; digressive. — **dis·cur′sive·ly**, *adv.* — **dis·cur′sive·ness**, *n.*

dis′cus (dĭs′kŭs), *n.; pl.* DISCUSES (-ĕz; -ĭz), DISCI (dĭs′ī). [L. See DISK.] A heavy, circular plate to be thrown or hurled as a trial of strength and skill; a sort of quoit; also, the exercise or game of throwing the discus.

dis·cuss′ (dĭs·kŭs′), *v. t.* [L. *discussus*, past part. of *discutere* to strike asunder, LL. to discuss, examine, fr. *dis-* + *quatere* to strike.] **1.** *Obs. exc. Med.* To drive away; to dispel. **2.** To investigate, as that which is uncertain; esp.: **a** To argue by presenting the various sides of, as a question; debate. **b** To discourse about; as, to *discuss* one's friends. **3.** *Obs.* To explain; declare. **4.** *Colloq.* To consume appreciatively (food or drink).

Syn. Discuss, argue, debate, dispute mean to discourse about so as to reach conclusions or to convince. **Discuss** also implies a sifting or examining, especially by presenting considerations pro and con; **argue**, the adducing of evidence or reasons in support of one's position; **debate** implies formal or public argument between opposing parties or, less often, deliberation with oneself; **dispute** (archaic in the sense of *discuss*) now implies contentious or heated argument.

dis·cus′sion (dĭs·kŭsh′ŭn), *n.* Consideration of a question in open debate; argument for the sake of arriving at truth or clearing up difficulties.

dis·dain′ (dĭs·dān′), *v. t.* [OF. *desdeignier*, fr. L. *dedignari* to scorn. See DEIGN.] **1.** To think unworthy; to deem unsuitable. **2.** To reject as unworthy of oneself, or as not deserving one's notice; to scorn to accept, perform, recognize, etc. — **Syn.** See DESPISE. — *n.* [OF. *desdain, desdeign*, fr. the verb.] A feeling of contempt and aversion for that which is regarded as beneath one; scorn.

dis·dain′ful (-fo͝ol; -f'l), *adj.* Full of, or expressing, disdain; scornful; contemptuous. — **Syn.** See PROUD. — **dis·dain′ful·ly**, *adv.* — **dis·dain′ful·ness**, *n.*

dis·ease′ (dĭ·zēz′), *n.* [OF. *desaise*, fr. *des-* (fr. L. *dis-*) + *aise* ease.] **1.** *Archaic.* Lack of ease; discomfort. **2.** A condition in which bodily health is impaired; sickness; illness; also, a malady; an ailment. **3.** An affection, usually caused by microorganisms, impairing the quality of certain products; as, the *diseases* of wine. — *v. t.* To afflict with disease; to derange. — **dis·eased′** (dĭ·zēzd′), *adj.*

dis′em·bark′ (dĭs′ĕm·bärk′), *v. i. & t.* To remove to shore from on board a vessel; to land; debark. — **dis·em′bar·ka′tion** (dĭs·ĕm′bär·kā′shŭn), *n.* — **dis′em·bark′ment**, *n.*

dis′em·bar′rass (dĭs′ĕm·băr′ăs), *v. t.* To free from something that impedes or embarrasses; to clear; disentangle. — **Syn.** See EXTRICATE.

dis′em·bod′y (-ĕm·bŏd′ĭ), *v. t.;* see EMBODY. To divest of the body or corporeal existence; as, *disembodied* spirits. — **dis′em·bod′i·ment** (-ĭ·mĕnt), *n.*

dis′em·bogue′ (-bōg′), *v. i. & t.* [Sp. *desembocar*, fr. *des-* (fr. L. *dis-*) + *embocar* to put into the mouth, fr. *en* (fr. L. *in*) + *boca* mouth, fr. L. *bucca* cheek.] To pass through the mouth of a stream into a sea; to discharge contents; to emerge. — **dis′em·bogue′ment**, *n.*

dis′em·bos′om (dĭs′ĕm·bo͝oz′ŭm; -bo͞o′zŭm), *v. t.* To separate from the bosom; to reveal. — *v. i.* To reveal oneself; to unbosom.

dis′em·bow′el (-bou′ĕl), *v. t.;* see EMBOWEL. To take or let out the bowels of; to eviscerate. — **dis′em·bow′el·ment**, *n.*

dis′en·a′ble (dĭs′ĕn·ā′b'l), *v. t.;* see ENABLE. To render legally incapable; to disable; disqualify.

dis′en·chant′ (-ĕn·chȧnt′; 9), *v. t.* To free from enchantment. — **dis′en·chant′er**, *n.* — **dis′en·chant′ment**, *n.*

dis′en·cum′ber (-ĕn·kŭm′bẽr), *v. t.* To free from encumbrance. — **Syn.** See EXTRICATE. — **Ant.** Burden, impede.

dis′en·dow′ (-ĕn·dou′), *v. t.* To strip of endowment. — **dis′en·dow′er**, *n.* — **dis′en·dow′ment**, *n.*

dis′en·fran′chise (-frăn′chīz), *v. t.* To disfranchise. — **dis′en·fran′chise·ment** (-chĭz·mĕnt), *n.*

dis′en·gage′ (-ĕn·gāj′), *v. t.;* see ENGAGE. To release from that with which anything is engaged, engrossed, or involved; to detach. — *v. i.* To release or detach oneself; to get free.

dis′en·gage′ment (-mĕnt), *n.* **1.** Act of disengaging, or setting free, or state of being disengaged. **2.** Freedom from engrossing ties, occupation, etc.; ease.

dis′en·tail′ (-ĕn·tāl′), *v. t. Law.* To free from entail.

dis′en·tan′gle (-tăng′g'l), *v. t. & i.;* see TANGLE. To free or become free from entanglement; straighten out. — **Syn.** See EXTRICATE. — **dis′en·tan′gle·ment**, *n.*

dis′en·throne′ (dĭs′ĕn·thrōn′), *v. t.* To dethrone; depose. — **dis′en·throne′ment**, *n.*

dis′en·ti′tle (-tī′t'l), *v. t.* To deprive of title or claim.

dis′en·tomb′ (-to͞om′), *v. t.* To take out from a tomb; to disinter. — **dis′en·tomb′ment**, *n.*

dis′en·train′ (-trān′), *v. t. & i. Mil.* To detrain.

dis′en·trance′ (-trȧns′), *v. t.;* see ENTRANCE, *v. t.* To awaken from a trance or enchantment.

dis′en·twine′ (-twīn′), *v. t. & i.* To untwine; disentangle.

dis′es·tab′lish (dĭs′ĕs·tăb′lĭsh), *v. t.* To deprive of an established position, privilege, etc.; specif., to deprive (a church) of its official connection with and support by the state. — **dis′es·tab′lish·ment**, *n.*

dis′es·teem′ (dĭs′ĕs·tēm′), *v. t.* To regard with contempt; to slight. — *n.* Disfavor; disrepute.

dis·fa′vor, dis·fa′vour (dĭs·fā′vẽr), *n.* **1.** Act of not favoring; withdrawal of favor; displeasure; disapproval; dislike; as, to incur the *disfavor* of a friend; to look upon a movement with *disfavor;* also, an unkindness; a disobliging act. **2.** State or fact of not being favored or in favor; as: **a** Absence of esteem; disrepute; disregard. **b** Condition of being deprived of favor or under displeasure; as, to be in *disfavor* at court. **c** Absence or loss of that which favors one's reputation, cause, finances, etc.; detriment. **3.** *Obs.* Homeliness; ill favor. — *v. t.* To withhold or withdraw favor from; regard with disesteem.

dis·fea′ture (dĭs·fē′tũr), *v. t.* To mar the appearance of. — **Syn.** See DEFACE.

dis·fig′u·ra′tion (-fĭg′ū·rā′shŭn), *n.* Disfigurement.

dis·fig′ure (-fĭg′ūr; *see* FIGURE), *v. t.* [OF. *desfigurer*, fr. L. *dis-* + *figurare*, fr. *figura* figure.] To mar the figure of; to render less complete or beautiful in appearance or character. — **Syn.** See DEFACE. — **dis·fig′ure·ment**, *n.* — **dis·fig′ur·er** (-ūr·ẽr), *n.*

dis·for′est (-fŏr′ĕst; -ĭst), *v. t.* To disafforest; also, to deforest. — **dis·for′est·a′tion** (-fŏr′ĕs·tā′shŭn; -fŏr′ĭs-), *n.*

dis·fran′chise (dĭs·frăn′chīz), *v. t.* To deprive of a franchise or chartered right; to dispossess of the rights of a citizen or of a privilege, as of voting, holding office, etc. — **dis·fran′chise·ment** (-chĭz·mĕnt), *n.*

dis·frock′ (dĭs·frŏk′), *v. t.* To unfrock.

dis·fur′nish (-fûr′nĭsh), *v. t.* To deprive of that (furniture, equipments, etc.) with which anything is furnished; to strip; divest. — **dis·fur′nish·ment**, *n.*

dis·gorge′ (dĭs·gôrj′), *v. t. & i.;* see GORGE. [OF. *desgorger*, fr. *des-* (fr. L. *dis-*) + *gorge* gorge.] To discharge by the throat and mouth; to vomit; hence, to discharge violently, confusedly, or as a result of force.

dis·grace′ (dĭs·grās′), *n.* [F. *disgrâce*, fr. It. *disgrazia*, fr. *dis-* (fr. L. *dis-*) + *grazia* grace, fr. L. *gratia.*] **1.** Condition of being out of favor. **2.** State of being dishonored; shame. **3.** That which brings dishonor; cause of shame.

Syn. **Disgrace, dishonor, disrepute, shame, infamy, ignominy, opprobrium, obloquy, odium, scandal** mean the condition or cause of suffering disesteem, reproach, or censure. **Disgrace** implies a loss of favor or esteem once enjoyed and, sometimes, severe humiliation; **dishonor** often equals *disgrace* but may imply loss of self-respect or self-esteem; **disrepute** stresses loss of one's good name or the attribution of a bad name or reputation; **shame** stresses a particularly humiliating disgrace or disrepute often suffered because of another; **infamy** stresses both notoriety and shame; **ignominy** stresses disgrace or its cause that makes one an object of contempt; **opprobrium** adds to *disgrace* the implication of being severely reproached or condemned, **obloquy** that of being abused or vilified; **odium** applies to the disgrace or opprobrium attached to being an object of widespread hatred; **scandal**, as here compared, comes close to *shame* but always implies that the disgrace and humiliation must be borne by others.

— *v. t.;* see GRACE. **1.** To put (another) to shame or out of favor; to dishonor. **2.** To bring reproach or shame to; reflect discredit upon. — **dis·grac′er** (-grās′ẽr), *n.*

dis·grace′ful (-fōōl; -f'l), *adj.* Bringing or involving disgrace; shameful. — **dis·grace′ful·ly**, *adv.* — **dis·grace′ful·ness**, *n.*

dis·grun′tle (dĭs·grŭn′t'l), *v. t.;* -GRUN′TLED (-t'ld); -GRUN′TLING (-tlĭng). [*dis-* + obs. & dial. *gruntle* to grunt, complain, freq. of *grunt.*] To put in bad humor; to arouse peevish dissatisfaction in.

dis·guise′ (dĭs·gīz′), *v. t.* [OF. *desguiser*, fr. *des-* (fr. L. *dis-*) + *guise* guise.] **1.** To change the dress or appearance of, so as to conceal one's identity or counterfeit another's. **2.** To hide or obscure the true nature or character of, by altering appearance or distinguishing quality.

Syn. **Disguise, cloak, mask, dissemble** mean to assume an appearance that hides one's identity, feeling, or the like. **Disguise** basically implies a change of costume, but in extended use it may imply any change, as in manner, words, etc., that serves to cover up something one wishes to conceal; **cloak** suggests a disguise that, like a heavy, enveloping cloak, hides something (often an evil design) completely; **mask**, a disguise like a face mask, that prevents recognition of a thing's true character, nature, presence, or the like (as, icy patches *masked* with snow); **dissemble** stresses simulation for the purpose of deceiving as well as disguising (as to *dissemble* his disappointment).

— *n.* **1.** Apparel assumed to conceal one's identity; hence, anything used to conceal one's identity; specif., a player's or masker's costume, etc. **2.** Any outward form which, intentionally or not, misrepresents the true nature or identity of a person or thing.

— **dis·guis′ed·ly** (-gīz′ĕd·lĭ; -ĭd·lĭ), *adv.* — **dis·guis′er** (-ẽr), *n.*

dis·gust′ (dĭs·gŭst′), *v. t.* [MF. *desgouster*, fr. *des-* (fr. L. *dis-*) + *goust* taste, fr. L. *gustus.*] **1.** To nauseate; hence, to provoke (one) to loathing or aversion; to be offensive to. **2.** To cause or arouse effective aversion in. — *n.* Aversion to that which excites nausea or squeamishness or deeply offends the sensibilities.

dis·gust′ed (-gŭs′tĕd; -tĭd), *adj.* Affected by disgust. — **dis·gust′ed·ly**, *adv.* — **dis·gust′ed·ness**, *n.*

dis·gust′ful (-gŭst′fōōl; -f'l), *adj.* Provoking disgust; nauseating. — **dis·gust′ful·ly**, *adv.*

dis·gust′ing, *adj.* Causing disgust; revolting. — **dis·gust′ing·ly**, *adv.*

dish (dĭsh), *n.* [AS. *disc* plate, fr. L. *discus*, fr. Gr. *diskos* quoit, platter, fr. *dikein* to throw.] **1.** A vessel, as a platter, used for serving food at the table. **2.** Something resembling a dish in form, as a cup, a shallow concave vessel, or a natural hollow. **3.** The food served in a dish; hence, any particular food; as, a cold *dish.* **4.** The contents or capacity of a dish; a dishful. **5.** State of being concave, or like a dish, or the degree of such concavity; as, the *dish* of a wheel. — *v. t.* **1.** To put into a dish or dishes, as food for serving. **2.** To make concave, like a dish. **3.** To make (a hole) like a dish; to countersink (a hole). **4.** *Slang.* To frustrate; cheat.

dis′ha·bille′ (dĭs′ȧ·bēl′), **des′ha·bille′** (dĕz′ȧ·bēl′), *n.* [F. *déshabillé*, prop., undressed.] A loose negligee; also, the state of being dressed in a loose or careless style.

dis·hal′low (dĭs·hăl′ō), *v. t.* To violate; profane.

dis·har·mo′ni·ous (dĭs′här·mō′nĭ·ŭs), *adj.* Unharmonious.

dis·har′mo·nize (dĭs·här′mō·nīz), *v. t. & i.* To put, or to be, out of harmony. — **dis·har′mo·nism** (-nĭz'm), *n.*

dis·har′mo·ny (-nĭ), *n.; pl.* -NIES (-nĭz). Discord.

dish′cloth′ (dĭsh′klŏth′; 74), *n.* A cloth for washing dishes.

dish′clout′ (-klout′), *n.* A dishcloth.

dis·heart′en (dĭs·här′t'n), *v. t.* To discourage; to deject. — **dis·heart′en·ing·ly**, *adv.* — **dis·heart′en·ment** (dĭs·här′t'n·mĕnt), *n.*

dished (dĭsht), *adj.* Concave; as, a *dished* face or hoof; of wheels, nearer together at the bottom than at the top.

dis·helm′ (dĭs·hĕlm′), *v. t. & i.* To deprive of, or to remove, the helmet.

dis·her′it (dĭs·hĕr′ĭt), *v. t.* To disinherit.

di·shev′el (dĭ·shĕv′ĕl; -'l), *v. t.;* DI·SHEV′ELED (-ĕld; -'ld) or DI·SHEV′ELLED; DI·SHEV′EL·ING or DI·SHEV′EL·LING. [OF. *descheveler*, deriv. of L. *dis-* + *capillus* the hair of the head.] To loosen or let hang, as hair and the like; to let fall in disorder; hence, to ruffle. — **di·shev′el·ment**, *n.*

dish gravy. = GRAVY, 2.

dis·hon′est (dĭs·ŏn′ĕst; -ĭst), *adj.* **1.** Characterized by fraud; knavish; fraudulent. **2.** Lacking honesty or integrity; not trustworthy. — **dis·hon′est·ly**, *adv.*

Syn. **Dishonest, deceitful, mendacious, lying, untruthful** mean unworthy of trust or belief. **Dishonest** may imply a willful perversion of truth or a stealing, cheating, or defrauding; **deceitful** usually implies the intent to mislead and, therefore, commonly suggests a false or specious appearance, double-dealing, or the like; **mendacious** differs little from **lying** except in being used more often to suggest the habit or character of telling lies, the latter usually referring to an act or instance; **untruthful** is often used as a less brutal term than *mendacious* or *lying*, especially in application to accounts, descriptions, and the like.

dis·hon′es·ty (-ĕs·tĭ; -ĭs·tĭ), *n.* **1.** Lack of honesty, probity, or integrity. **2.** A dishonest act; a fraud.

dis·hon′or, dis·hon′our (dĭs·ŏn′ẽr), *n.* [OF. *deshonor, deshonur*, fr. L. *dis-* + *honor.*] **1.** The reverse of honor; as: **a** Disgrace; shame. **b** The state of one who has fallen from favor. **c** An insult. **2.** A source of disgrace; a dishonorable action or person. **3.** *Law.* The nonpayment or nonacceptance of commercial paper by the party on whom it is drawn. — **Syn.** See DISGRACE. — *v. t.* **1.** To deprive of honor; to disgrace. **2.** To refuse to accept or pay (a draft, check, etc.). — **dis·hon′or·er, dis·hon′our·er** (-ẽr), *n.*

dis·hon′or·a·ble, dis·hon′our·a·ble (-ȧ·b'l), *adj.* **1.** Lacking honor; not honorable; disgraceful. **2.** Lacking honors or esteem. — **dis·hon′or·a·ble·ness, dis·hon′our·a·ble·ness**, *n.* — **dis·hon′or·a·bly, dis·hon′our·a·bly** (-blĭ), *adv.*

dish′rag′ (dĭsh′răg′), *n.* A dishcloth.

dish′wa′ter (-wô′tẽr; -wŏt′ẽr), *n.* Water in which dishes have been or are to be washed; hence, refuse water.

dis′il·lu′sion (dĭs′ĭ·lū′zhŭn), *v. t.* Also **dis′il·lu′sion·ize** (-īz). To free from illusion; disenchant. — **dis′il·lu′sion**, *n.* — **dis′il·lu′sion·ment**, *n.*

dis′il·lu′sive (-lū′sĭv), *adj.* Tending to disillusion.

dis·in′cli·na′tion (dĭs·ĭn′klĭ·nā′shŭn), *n.* State or quality of being disinclined; want of inclination; slight aversion.

dis′in·cline′ (dĭs′ĭn·klīn′), *v. t.* To turn away the inclination of; to make averse. — *v. i.* To be unwilling or not inclined (to do something).

dis′in·clined′ (-klīnd′), *adj.* Unwilling; averse.

Syn. **Disinclined, hesitant, reluctant, loath, averse** mean having neither the will nor the desire to do that which is indicated. **Disinclined** implies lack of taste or inclination, or actual disapproval of a thing suggested; **hesitant**, a holding back through fear, irresolution, disinclination, or the like; **reluctant**, hesitancy and unwillingness; **loath**, hesitancy because not in accord with one's opinions, predilections, or the like; **averse** (followed by *to* or *from*), because distasteful or repugnant.

dis′in·fect′ (-fĕkt′), *v. t.* To free from infection, esp. by destroying disease germs. — **dis′in·fec′tor** (-fĕk′tẽr), *n.*

dis′in·fect′ant (-fĕk′tănt), *n.* An agent that frees from infection; usually, a chemical agent which destroys disease germs or other harmful microorganisms (but not, ordinarily, bacterial spores); — commonly used of substances applied to inanimate objects.

dis′in·fec′tion (-fĕk′shŭn), *n.* Act or process of disinfecting.

dis′in·fest′ (-fĕst′), *v. t.* To free from infesting insects, rodents, etc. — **dis·in′fes·ta′tion** (dĭs·ĭn′fĕs·tā′shŭn), *n.*

dis′in·gen′u·ous (dĭs′ĭn·jĕn′ū·ŭs), *adj.* Not ingenuous; not frank and candid; also, meanly or unworthily artful; deceivingly simple. — **dis′in·gen′u·ous·ly**, *adv.* — **dis′in·gen′u·ous·ness**, *n.*

dis′in·her′it (-hĕr′ĭt), *v. t.* To cut off from, or deprive of, an inheritance. — **dis′in·her′it·ance** (-ĭ·tăns), *n.*

dis′in·hume′ (dĭs′ĭn·hūm′), *v. t.* To disinter.

dis·in′te·grate (dĭs·ĭn′tē·grāt), *v. t. & i.* [L. *dis-* + *integratus*, past part. of *integrare* to renew, fr. *integer* entire.] To separate or decompose into fragments; to break up; hence, to destroy the wholeness, unity, or identity of. — **Syn.** See DECAY. — **dis·in′te·gra′tion** (-grā′shŭn), *n.* — **dis·in′te·gra′tor** (-grā′tẽr), *n.*

dis′in·ter′ (dĭs′ĭn·tûr′), *v. t.;* see INTER. **1.** To take out of the grave or tomb; to exhume; to dig up. **2.** To bring from obscurity into view. — **dis′in·ter′ment**, *n.*

dis·in′ter·est·ed (dĭs·ĭn′tẽr·ĕs·tĕd; -ĭs·tĭd), *adj.* **1.** Lacking or revealing lack of interest; uninterested. *Now Rare.* **2.** Not influenced by regard to personal advantage. — **Syn.** See INDIFFERENT. — **dis·in′ter·est·ed·ly**, *adv.* — **dis·in′ter·est·ed·ness**, *n.*

dis·jas′ked, dis·jas′kit (-jăs′kĭt), *adj.* *Scot.* Jaded; decayed.

dis·ject′ (dĭs·jĕkt′), *v. t.* [L. *disjicere, disjectum*, to throw asunder, fr. *dis-* + *jacere* to throw.] To separate by force; tear apart; scatter violently.

‖**dis·jec′ta mem′bra** (dĭs·jĕk′tȧ mĕm′brȧ). [L.] Scattered parts; disjointed quotations.

dis·join′ (dĭs·join′), *v. t. & i.* [OF. *desjoindre*, fr. L. *disjungere*, fr. *dis-* + *jungere* to join.] To dissolve or undo the joining of; to disunite; separate; detach.

dis·joint′ (-joint′), *adj.* [OF. *desjoint*, past part. of *desjoindre*. See DISJOIN.] *Obs.* Disjointed. — *v. t. & i.* **1.** To break up into divisions; to disturb or undo the connections, order, or coherence of. **2.** To separate at the joints; to divide into fragments.

dis·joint′ed (-join′tĕd; -tĭd), *adj.* Separated as at the joint; disconnected; hence, incoherent; as, *disjointed* phrases. — **dis·joint′ed·ly**, *adv.* — **dis·joint′ed·ness**, *n.*

dis·junct′ (dĭs·jŭngkt′), *adj.* [L. *disjunctus*, past part. of *disjungere*. See DISJOIN.] Disconnected; disjoined.

dis·junc′tion (-jŭngk′shŭn), *n.* Act of disjoining, or state of being disjoined; disunion; separation.

dis·junc′tive (-tĭv), *adj.* **1.** Tending to disjoin; involving disjunction. **2.** *Gram.* Joining words in co-ordinate construction and expressing an alternative between their ideas, as in **disjunctive conjunction** (*either ... or*), **disjunctive adverb** (*else, otherwise,* or *else*). **3.** *Logic.* Expressing alternatives, esp. mutually exclusive alternatives. Cf. CATEGORICAL, 1 **a.** — *n.* **1.** *Gram.* A disjunctive conjunction. **2.** *Logic.* A disjunctive proposition. — **dis·junc′tive·ly,** *adv.*

dis·june′ (dĭs·jo͞on′), *n. Scot.* Breakfast.

disk (dĭsk), *n.* Also **disc.** [L. *discus.* See DISH.] **1.** A discus. **2.** A flat circular plate; as, a *disk* of metal; also, something resembling a plate; specif. (usually **disc**), a phonograph record. **3.** *Bot.* In composites (family Carduaceae), the central portion of the head, composed of tubular flowers. See COMPOSITE, *n.*, 2. **4.** Usually **disc.** *Zool.* Any of various structures likened to a disk.

disk (dĭsk), *v. t.* **1.** To cut or form into a disk or disks. **2.** To cultivate with a disk harrow. **3.** To record on a phonograph disc.

disk harrow. A form of harrow in which the earth is broken up by disks arranged at an angle with the line of draft. See HARROW, *Illust.*

disk jockey. Variant of DISC JOCKEY.

disk wheel. A wheel, as on an automobile, presenting a solid surface, either convex or concave, from hub to rim.

dis·like′ (dĭs·līk′), *v. t.* To feel antipathy or aversion to; disrelish; disapprove. — (dĭs·līk′; *with contrasting stress,* dĭs′līk), *n.* Aversion or distaste; an aversion. — **dis·lik′a·ble** (dĭs·līk′ȧ·b'l), *adj.*

dis·limn′ (dĭs·lĭm′), *v. t. & i.;* see LIMN. *Poet.* To efface, or to fade.

dis′lo·cate (dĭs′lō·kāt; dĭs·lō′kāt), *v. t.* [ML. *dislocatus,* past part. of *dislocare,* fr. L. *dis-* + *locare* to place, fr. *locus* place.] **1.** To displace; esp., to remove (a bone) from its normal connections with a neighboring bone; to disjoint. **2.** To disarrange, as affairs or plans. — **dis′lo·ca′tion** (dĭs′lō·kā′shŭn), *n.*

dis·lodge′ (dĭs·lŏj′), *v. t. & i.;* see LODGE. To drive from a lodge or place of rest; hence, to drive out from hiding or defense. — **dis·lodg′-ment** (-lŏj′mĕnt), *n.*

dis·loy′al (-loi′ăl), *adj.* [OF. *desloial.*] Not loyal; false where allegiance is due. — **Syn.** See FAITHLESS. — **dis·loy′al·ly,** *adv.*

dis·loy′al·ty (-tĭ), *n.* **1.** Lack of loyalty; violation of allegiance. **2.** A disloyal act or thought.

dis′mal (dĭz′măl), *n.* [ME. *dismale* evil days, fr. OF. *dis mal,* fr. L. *dies mali.*] **1.** A dismal person, state, or thing; specif., *pl., Colloq.,* the blues; low spirits; — with *the;* also, gloomy circumstances. **2.** *Southern U.S.* A swamp. — *adj.* **1.** *Obs.* Unlucky; ill-omened; sinister; fatal. **2.** Woeful; dreadful; horrifying. **3.** Gloomy to the eye or ear; cheerless. — **dis′mal·ly,** *adv.* — **dis′mal·ness,** *n.*

dis·man′tle (dĭs·măn′t'l), *v. t.;* see MANTLE. **1.** To strip of dress or covering; to divest. **2.** To strip of furniture and equipment; as, to *dismantle* a house; specif., to strip of guns or defenses; as, to *dismantle* a fort. — **dis·man′tle·ment,** *n.*

dis·mast′ (dĭs·mȧst′), *v. t.* To deprive of a mast.

dis·may′ (dĭs·mā′), *v. t.* [ME. *dismaien, desmaien,* for OF. *esmaier,* fr. L. *ex* out + a root of Teut. origin; cf. OHG. *magan* to be strong or able.] To disable with alarm; depress the spirits or courage of; daunt.

Syn. **Dismay, appall, horrify, daunt** mean to unnerve and arrest in action. **Dismay** implies loss of power to proceed because one is balked by terror or great perplexity; **appall** implies an overwhelming and paralyzing dread or terror or, in current use, a sense of impotence when one is confronted by that which confounds yet which one is unable to alter; **horrify** strictly implies a shuddering revulsion from that which is ghastly or hideously offensive, but is now often used in a weakened sense; **daunt** presupposes an attempt to do something requiring courage and therefore implies a stoppage by that which cows or subdues.

— *n.* Sudden loss of spirit through fear; disabling terror; consternation. — **Syn.** See FEAR.

dis·mem′ber (-mĕm′bẽr), *v. t.* [OF. *desmembrer,* fr. L. *dis-* + *membrum* limb.] To tear limb from limb; to disjoin the limbs of; hence, to tear or cut in pieces; mangle. — **dis·mem′ber·ment,** *n.*

dis·miss′ (dĭs·mĭs′), *v. t.* [L. *dis-* + *missus,* past part. of *mittere* to send.] **1.** To send away; to cause or permit to go. **2.** To send or remove from office, service, or employment; discharge. **3.** To put away; esp., to put out of mind; to cease to consider. **4.** *Law.* To put (an action or party) out of consideration; to refuse to hear further; — said of the court. — **Syn.** See EJECT.

dis·miss′al (-ăl; -'l), *n.* Act of dismissing, or state or fact of being dismissed; — now more usual than **dis·mis′sion** (dĭs·mĭsh′ŭn).

dis·mount′ (dĭs·mount′), *v. i.* **1.** *Poetic.* To come down; descend. **2.** To alight from a horse, camel, motorcycle, or the like. — *v. t.* **1.** To throw or remove from the carriage or mount; — said esp. of artillery. **2.** To remove from a setting, as a jewel. **3.** To unhorse; also, *Mil.,* to deprive of horses, as cavalry. **4.** *Mech.* To take apart (a machine); disassemble. — *n.* Act, process, or method of dismounting.

dis·na′ture (-nā′tūr), *v. t. & i.* To make or become unnatural.

dis′o·be′di·ence (dĭs′ō·bē′dĭ·ĕns; 58), *n.* Neglect or refusal to obey; violation of a command or prohibition.

dis′o·be′di·ent (-ĕnt), *adj.* Neglecting or refusing to obey; refractory. — **dis′o·be′di·ent·ly,** *adv.*

dis′o·bey′ (dĭs′ō·bā′), *v. t. & i.* [OF. *desobeir,* fr. L. *dis-* + *obedire* to obey.] To refuse or neglect to obey.

dis′o·blige′ (dĭs′ō·blīj′), *v. t.;* see OBLIGE. **1.** To refuse to oblige; to be unaccommodating to; hence, to offend; affront. **2.** To cause inconvenience to; to incommode. — **dis′o·blig′ing** (-blīj′ĭng), *adj.*

dis·or′der (dĭs·ôr′dẽr), *n.* **1.** Lack of order; confusion; disarray. **2.** Neglect of order or system; irregularity. **3.** Breach of public order; tumult. **4.** Sickness; ailment. — *v. t.* **1.** To disarrange; to confuse. **2.** To disturb the natural functions of (body or mind); to derange.

dis·or′dered (-dẽrd), *adj.* Thrown into disorder; deranged; affected with disorder or disease; specif., morbid; crazed.

dis·or′der·ly (-dẽr·lĭ), *adj.* **1.** Not in order; disarranged. **2.** Unruly; turbulent; as, *disorderly* people. **3.** *Law.* Offensive to good morals and public decency. **disorderly conduct** is a petty offense. **disorderly houses** include common brothels, common gaming houses, etc. A **disorderly person** is one guilty of any one of various acts (against the public peace, order, morals, or safety) declared by statute to be offenses. — *adv.* In a disorderly manner; irregularly; confusedly. — **dis·or′der·li·ness,** *n.*

dis·or′gan·i·za′tion (dĭs·ôr′găn·ĭ·zā′shŭn; -ī·zā′shŭn), *n.* Act of disorganizing, or state of being disorganized.

dis·or′gan·ize (dĭs·ôr′găn·īz), *v. t.* To destroy the organic structure or regular system of; to throw into disorder; to disarrange. — **dis·or′gan·iz′er** (-īz′ẽr), *n.*

dis·o′ri·ent (dĭs·ō′rĭ·ĕnt), *v. t.* [*dis-* + *orient.*] **1.** *Rare.* To cause to face or turn away from the east. **2.** To cause to lose one's bearings; to confuse, as in one's sense of what is right or proper. **3.** To cause to depart from the normal or proper position, adjustment, arrangement, or relationship. **4.** *Psychiatry.* To cause loss of appreciation of place and time or of one's own identity, as in certain diseases.

dis·o′ri·en·tate′ (-ō′rĭ·ĕn·tāt′; -ō′rĭ·ĕn′tāt), *v. t.* To disorient. — **dis·o′ri·en·ta′tion** (-ō′rĭ·ĕn·tā′shŭn), *n.*

dis·own′ (dĭs·ōn′), *v. t.* To refuse to acknowledge as belonging to oneself; to repudiate; disclaim; disavow.

dis·par′age (dĭs·păr′ĭj), *v. t.;* -AGED (-ĭjd); -AG·ING (-ĭj·ĭng). [OF. *desparagier* to marry unequally, fr. *des-* (fr. L. *dis-*) + *parage* extraction, lineage, fr. *per* peer.] To lower in rank or estimation by actions or words; hence, to speak slightingly of; to depreciate. — **Syn.** See DECRY. — **dis·par′ag·er** (-ĭj·ẽr), *n.*

dis·par′age·ment (-mĕnt), *n.* **1.** Diminution of esteem or standing; disgrace. **2.** Act of disparaging; depreciation.

dis·par′ag·ing (-ĭj·ĭng), *adj.* That disparages; as, a *disparaging* remark. — **dis·par′ag·ing·ly,** *adv.*

dis′pa·rate (dĭs′pȧ·răt), *adj.* [L. *disparatus,* past part. of *disparare* to part, fr. *dis-* + *parare* to prepare.] Unequal; dissimilar; distinct in respect to quality or ultimate character. — **Syn.** See DIFFERENT. — **dis′pa·rate·ly,** *adv.* — **dis′pa·rate·ness,** *n.*

dis·par′i·ty (dĭs·păr′ĭ·tĭ), *n.; pl.* -TIES (-tĭz). Inequality; difference in age, rank, or condition; also, difference in character or kind.

dis·part′ (dĭs·pärt′), *v. t. & i.* [OF. *despartir,* fr. L. *dispartire.*] To part asunder; separate.

dis·part′, *n. Gun.* A piece of metal placed on the muzzle, or near the trunnions, on the top of a piece of ordnance, to make the line of sight parallel to the axis of the bore; — called also **dispart sight.**

dis·part′ment (-mĕnt), *n.* A parting or division.

dis·pas′sion·ate (dĭs·păsh′ŭn·ĭt), *adj.* Free from passion; not carried away by feeling; calm; impartial. — **Syn.** See FAIR. — **dis·pas′sion·ate·ly,** *adv.* — **dis·pas′sion·ate·ness,** *n.*

dis·patch′ (dĭs·păch′), *v. t.* [Sp. *despachar.*] **1.** To send off or away, esp. on official business; as, to *dispatch* a messenger. **2.** To put to death. **3.** To dispose of speedily, as business; to execute quickly. — *v. i. Archaic.* To hasten; to finish up a matter of business. — **Syn.** See KILL. — *n.* **1.** A dispatching; as: **a** The sending of a message or messenger. **b** Dismissal or discharge; esp., official discharge. **c** Act of putting to death; killing. **d** Prompt disposal; quick riddance; esp., the speedy finishing up of a business; hence, diligence; haste. **2.** A message, esp. an important official message, sent with speed; also, an item of news sent in by a reporter to a newspaper. **3.** An agency for sending goods promptly to their destination. — **Syn.** See HASTE. — **dis·patch′er** (-ẽr), *n.*

dispatch boat. A vessel for conveying dispatches.

dis·pel′ (dĭs·pĕl′), *v. t.;* -PELLED′ (-pĕld′); -PEL′LING. [L. *dispellere,* fr. *dis-* + *pellere* to push, drive.] To drive away by scattering; to clear away; dissipate. — **Syn.** See SCATTER.

dis·pend′ (dĭs·pĕnd′), *v. t.* [OF. *despendre,* fr. L. *dispendere.* See DISPENSE, *v.*] *Archaic.* To spend; squander.

dis·pen′sa·ble (dĭs·pĕn′sȧ·b'l), *adj.* **1.** *Eccl.* Admitting dispensation. **2.** Capable of being dispensed or administered. **3.** Capable of being dispensed with; hence, not binding. — **dis·pen′sa·bil′i·ty** (-bĭl′ĭ·tĭ), **dis·pen′sa·ble·ness,** *n.*

dis·pen′sa·ry (-rĭ), *n.; pl.* -RIES (-rĭz). A place where medicines are prepared and dispensed, esp. free or at low cost to the poor.

dis′pen·sa′tion (dĭs′pĕn·sā′shŭn), *n.* **1.** Act of dispensing, or dealing out; esp., *Theol.,* the distribution of good and evil by God to man. **2.** That which is dispensed, dealt out, or appointed. **3.** A specific arrangement; a provision; as, a happy *dispensation* of nature. **4.** A release from performance or obligation; remission; esp., *R.C.Ch.,* exemption from an ecclesiastical law, an impediment, or a vow; as, a marriage *dispensation.* **5.** *Theol.* A system of principles, promises, and rules ordained and administered; as, the Christian *dispensation.* — **dis′pen·sa′tion·al** (-ăl; -'l), *adj.*

dis′pen·sa′tor (dĭs′pĕn·sā′tẽr), *n.* One who dispenses.

dis·pen′sa·to′ry (dĭs·pĕn′sȧ·tō′rĭ *or, esp. Brit.,* -tẽr·ĭ), *n.; pl.* -TORIES (-rĭz). **1.** A book containing a systematic description of drugs used in medicine. **2.** A dispensary.

dis·pense′ (dĭs·pĕns′), *n. Obs.* Dispensation.

dis·pense′, *v. t.* [OF. *dispenser,* fr. L. *dispensare,* intens. of *dispendere* to weigh out, dispense, fr. *dis-* + *pendere* to weigh.] **1.** To deal out in portions; to distribute. **2.** To apply, as laws; to administer. **3.** To exempt; excuse; absolve. **4.** To put up (a prescription or medicine). — **Syn.** See DISTRIBUTE. — *v. i.* **1.** *Rare.* To make up; to compensate. **2.** To grant dispensation. — ***dispense with.*** **a** To give up, release, or do without, as services, attention, etc. **b** To arrange with for a dispensation. — **dis·pens′er** (-pĕn′sẽr), *n.*

dis·peo′ple (dĭs·pē′p'l), *v. t.;* -PEO′PLED (-p'ld); -PEO′PLING (-plĭng). [OF. *despeupler.*] To depopulate.

dis·per′sal (dĭs·pûr′săl; -s'l), *n.* Act or result of dispersing or scattering; dispersion, distribution.

dis·perse′ (dĭs·pûrs′), *v. t.* [L. *dispersus,* past part. of *dispergere* to disperse, fr. *dis-* + *spargere* to strew.] **1.** To cause to break apart and go different ways; to scatter. **2.** To cause to become widely separated; to distribute. **3.** To spread or distribute from a fixed or constant source; to disseminate; specif.: **a** *Physics.* To subject to dispersion. **b** *Physical Chem.* To distribute, as colloidal particles, in some other substance (the **dispersion medium**). **4.** To dissipate or dispel, as a vapor. — *v. i.* **1.** To separate; to go or move into different parts; hence, to be dissipated; to vanish. **2.** To share one's abundance with others. — **Syn.** See SCATTER. — **dis·pers′ed·ly** (-pûr′sĕd·lĭ; -sĭd·lĭ), *adv.* — **dis·pers′er** (-pûr′sẽr), *n.* — **dis·pers′i·ble** (-sĭ·b'l), *adj.*

dis·per′sion (dĭs·pûr′shŭn; -zhŭn), *n.* **1.** Act of dispersing, or state of being dispersed. **2.** *Physics.* The separation of complex light, as by a prism, into its different colored rays; also, the analogous phenomenon in the case of electric waves, etc. **3.** *Physical Chem.* A dispersed substance; also, the system composed of dispersed substance and dispersion medium.

dis·per′sive (-pûr′sĭv), *adj.* Tending to disperse.

dis·pers′oid (dĭs·pûr′soid), *n.* [*disperse* + *-oid.*] *Chem.* A substance dispersed in colloidal form; a colloid.

dis·pir′it (dĭs·pĭr′ĭt), *v. t.* To deprive of cheerful spirits; to depress; dishearten. — **dis·pir′it·ed,** *adj.* — **dis·pir′it·ed·ly,** *adv.* — **dis·pir′it·ed·ness,** *n.*

dis·pit′e·ous (dĭs·pĭt′ē·ŭs), *adj.* Full of despite; pitiless.
dis·place′ (dĭs·plās′), *v. t.* **1.** To remove from the usual or proper place. **2.** To crowd out; to take the place of. **3.** To remove from a state, office, or the like; discharge. **4.** To expel from one's habitation temporarily or permanently, as by devastation of war or conquerors' compulsion. **5.** *Obs.* To banish, as hunger. — **Syn.** See REPLACE.
dis·placed′ per′son (-plāst′). A person expelled or deported from his country of nationality or of habitual residence by one of the nazi, fascist, or quisling regimes as a prisoner of war or for forced labor or because of race, nationality, religion, or political opinions. Abbr. *DP* or *D.P.*
dis·place′ment (dĭs·plās′mĕnt), *n.* **1.** Act of displacing, or state of being displaced. **2.** The volume or weight of a fluid, as water, displaced by a floating body, as by a ship, the weight of the displaced fluid being equal to that of the displacing body. **3.** The difference between the initial position of a body and any later position; specif., a geological fault. See FAULT, 5, *Illust.*
dis·plant′ (dĭs·plȧnt′; 9), *v. t.* *Obs.* To displace; dislodge.
dis·play′ (dĭs·plā′), *v. t.* [OF. *despleier*, fr. L. *displicare* to scatter, unfold, fr. *dis-* + *plicare* to fold.] **1.** To unfold; to spread out or wide. **2.** To spread before the view; to show. **3.** *Print.* To make conspicuous, as by use of large or prominent type. — **Syn.** See SHOW. — *n.* **1.** An opening or unfolding; exhibition. **2.** Ostentatious show; parade. **3.** *Print.* Varying arrangement of lines, as by use of different styles of type faces; also, matter thus printed.
dis·please′ (dĭs·plēz′), *v. t.* To incur the disapproval of, esp. disapproval accompanied by aversion or dislike; to be offensive to. — *v. i.* To give displeasure or offense.
dis·pleas′ure (-plĕzh′ẽr), *n.* **1.** The feeling of one who is displeased. **2.** Discomfort; trouble. **3.** That which displeases; offense; injury. — *v. t. Archaic.* To displease.
dis·plode′ (dĭs·plōd′), *v. t. & i.* [L. *displodere.*] *Obs.* To explode.
dis·plume′ (dĭs·plōōm′; 114), *v. t.* To strip of plumes; to dishonor.
dis·pone′ (dĭs·pōn′), *v. t. & i.* [L. *disponere.* See DISPOSITION.] *Obs. exc. Scot.* To dispose; to arrange.
dis·port′ (dĭs·pōrt′; 70), *n.* [OF. *desport*, fr. *desporter*, v.] Play, sport, or diversion. — *v. t.* [OF. *desporter*, fr. *des-* (fr. L. *dis-*) + *porter* to carry; orig., to carry away from work.] To divert or amuse; to make merry. — *v. i.* To indulge in gaiety; esp., to wanton or frolic.
dis·pos′a·ble (dĭs·pōz′ȧ·b'l), *adj.* Subject to disposal; not assigned to any special use.
dis·pos′al (-ăl; -'l), *n.* **1.** A disposing; arrangement. **2.** Management; administration; dispensation; as, divine *disposal.* **3.** Transference of anything into new hands, a new place, etc.; bestowal. **4.** Power or authority to dispose of; — esp. in the phrase *at the disposal of.*
dis·pose′ (dĭs·pōz′), *v. t.* [OF. *disposer*, fr. *dis-* + *poser* to place.] **1.** To distribute and put in place; to arrange. **2.** To regulate; adjust; settle. **3.** To deal out; to assign to a use; to employ; to dispose of. **4.** To incline the mind of; to incline. — *v. i.* **1.** To arrange or settle matters finally. **2.** *Obs.* To bargain; to make terms. — **Syn.** See INCLINE. — ***dispose of.*** **a** To determine the fate, condition, employment, etc., of. **b** To get rid of; to put out of the way. **c** To part with; relinquish; bargain away. — *n.* **1.** *Obs.* Act of disposing; management; also, power or right of disposal. **2.** *Archaic.* Disposition; also, demeanor. — **dis·pos′er** (-pōz′ẽr), *n.*
dis′po·si′tion (dĭs′pō·zĭsh′ŭn), *n.* [OF., fr. L. *dispositio*, fr. *disponere* to dispose, fr. *dis-* + *ponere* to place.] **1.** Act or power of disposing, or state of being disposed; disposal; as: **a** Management; often, specif., divine dispensation. **b** The getting rid, or making over, of anything; relinquishment; also, the power of making such disposition; control. **c** The ordering or arranging of anything, or the state of being arranged, esp. systematically; as, the *disposition* of draperies; the *disposition* of troops. **2.** Natural tendency to any action or state; aptitude. **3.** Natural or prevailing temper of mind; also, mood; humor.
Syn. **Disposition, temperament, temper, complexion, character, personality, individuality** mean the dominant quality or qualities which mark a person or group. **Disposition** implies the predominating bent of one's mind or spirit; **temperament** implies the sum total of characteristics that are innate or inherent and the result of one's physical or nervous organization; **temper** now implies the qualities, largely acquired through experience, that determine the way a person, a people, an age, or the like, meets situations or difficulties; **complexion**, now archaic, comes close to *temperament;* **character** applies to the aggregate of qualities, especially moral qualities, which must be taken into account in any ethical judgment of a person; **personality** applies to an aggregate of qualities which distinguish one as a person; **individuality** implies a personality that distinguishes one from all others.
dis′pos·sess′ (dĭs′pŏ·zĕs′), *v. t.* To put out of possession, esp. of land. — **dis′pos·ses′sion** (-zĕsh′ŭn), *n.* — **dis′pos·ses′sor** (-zĕs′ẽr), *n.*
dis·po′sure (dĭs·pō′zhẽr), *n.* Disposal or disposition.
dis·praise′ (dĭs·prāz′), *v. t.* To notice with disapprobation or censure; to disparage; depreciate. — *n.* Censure; disparagement. — **dis·prais′er**, *n.* — **dis·prais′ing·ly**, *adv.*
dis·pread′, dis·spread′ (dĭs·prĕd′), *v. t. & i.* To spread abroad, or different ways; to expand.
dis·prize′ (dĭs·prīz′), *v. t.* To fail to prize; undervalue.
dis·proof′ (dĭs·prōōf′), *n.* A proving to be other than is maintained; confutation; refutation.
dis′pro·por′tion (dĭs′prō·pōr′shŭn), *n.* [F.] Lack of proportion; lack of symmetry or of due relation; disparity. — *v. t.* To violate symmetry in; to mismatch. — **dis′pro·por′tion·al** (-ăl; -'l), *adj.*
dis′pro·por′tion·ate (-ĭt), *adj.* Not proportioned; unsymmetrical; out of proportion. — **dis′pro·por′tion·ate·ly**, *adv.* — **-ate·ness**, *n.*
dis·prove′ (dĭs·prōōv′; 2), *v. t.* [OF. *desprover.*] To prove false; refute. — **dis·prov′a·ble** (-prōōv′ȧ·b'l), *adj.*
Syn. **Disprove, refute, confute, rebut, controvert** mean to show or attempt to show the untruth of. **Disprove** implies the success of an argument in showing the falsity or invalidity of another's argument; **refute** stresses the method more than the effect of argument in disproof; **confute** implies a reducing to silence of opponents by disproving their arguments utterly or by refuting them brilliantly; **rebut** even more than *refute* suggests a formal method in use by those who would disprove; **controvert** implies both a contradiction of one's opponent's arguments and an attempt to refute them.
dis′pu·ta·ble (dĭs′pū·tȧ·b'l; dĭs·pūt′ȧ·b'l), *adj.* Subject to dispute; debatable. — **dis′pu·ta·bil′i·ty** (-bĭl′ĭ·tĭ), *n.* — **dis′pu·ta·bly** (-blĭ), *adv.*
dis′pu·tant (dĭs′pū·tănt), *adj.* Disputing; engaged in controversy. — *n.* One who disputes.
dis′pu·ta′tion (-tā′shŭn), *n.* **1.** Act of disputing; controversy; debate. **2.** *Obs.* Conversation; discussion.
dis′pu·ta′tious (-shŭs), *adj.* Inclined to dispute. — **dis′pu·ta′tious·ly**, *adv.* — **dis′pu·ta′tious·ness**, *n.*
dis·put′a·tive (dĭs·pūt′ȧ·tĭv), *adj.* Disputatious.
dis·pute′ (dĭs·pūt′), *v. i.* [OF. *desputer, disputer*, fr. L. *disputare, -tatum*, fr. *dis-* + *putare* to reckon, think.] To contend in argument; to debate; often, to argue irritably; wrangle. — *v. t.* **1.** To make a subject of disputation; to argue pro and con. **2.** To oppose by argument or assertion; to deny the truth or validity of. **3.** To contend about; contest. — **Syn.** See DISCUSS. — *n.* **1.** Verbal controversy; controversial discussion; also, a quarrel. **2.** *Obs.* Armed or physical combat; a contest. — **dis·put′er** (-pūt′ẽr), *n.*
dis·qual′i·fi·ca′tion (dĭs·kwŏl′ĭ·fĭ·kā′shŭn), *n.* Act of disqualifying, or state of being disqualified; disability; also, that which disqualifies or incapacitates.
dis·qual′i·fy (-kwŏl′ĭ·fī), *v. t.;* -FIED (-fīd); -FY′ING. **1.** To deprive of the qualities necessary for any purpose; to render unfit. **2.** To deprive of some power or privilege, as by positive restriction; to disable legally. **3.** *Sports.* To debar from further participation or competition because of an infringement of the rules or of official rulings.
dis·qui′et (-kwī′ĕt), *v. t.* To render unquiet; to deprive of peace, rest, or tranquillity; to make uneasy. — **Syn.** See DISCOMPOSE. — *adj. Rare.* Disquieted; uneasy. — *n.* Want of quiet; uneasiness.
dis·qui′et·ing, *adj.* Causing disquiet. — **dis·qui′et·ing·ly**, *adv.*
dis·qui′et·ly, *adv.* In a disquiet manner; uneasily.
dis·qui′e·tude (dĭs·kwī′ĕ·tūd), *n.* Want of quiet; disquiet.
dis′qui·si′tion (dĭs′kwĭ·zĭsh′ŭn), *n.* [L. *disquisitio*, fr. *disquirere* to inquire diligently, fr. *dis-* + *quaerere* to seek.] A formal inquiry or discussion; elaborate essay.
dis·rate′ (dĭs·rāt′), *v. t.* To reduce in rating, rank, or class.
dis′re·gard′ (dĭs′rē·gärd′), *v. t.* Not to regard; to pay no heed to; hence, to slight as unworthy of regard. — **Syn.** See NEGLECT. — *n.* A disregarding, or state of being disregarded; esp., intentional neglect.
dis′re·gard′ful (-fōōl; -f'l), *adj.* Neglectful; heedless.
dis·rel′ish (dĭs·rĕl′ĭsh), *n.* Want of relish; distaste. — *v. t.* Not to relish; to regard as offensive.
dis′re·mem′ber (dĭs′rē·mĕm′bẽr), *v. t.* *Dial. & Colloq.* To forget.
dis′re·pair′ (-rē·pâr′), *n.* State of being in need of repair.
dis·rep′u·ta·ble (dĭs·rĕp′ū·tȧ·b'l), *adj.* Not reputable; of bad repute. — **dis·rep′u·ta·bil′i·ty** (-bĭl′ĭ·tĭ), **dis·rep′u·ta·ble·ness**, *n.* — **dis·rep′u·ta·bly** (-blĭ), *adv.*
dis·rep′u·ta′tion (-tā′shŭn), *n.* Disrepute.
dis′re·pute′ (dĭs′rē·pūt′), *n.* Loss or want of reputation; ill character; low estimation; dishonor. — **Syn.** See DISGRACE.
dis′re·spect′ (-rē·spĕkt′), *n.* Want of respect; incivility; discourtesy. — *v. t.* To show disrespect to.
dis′re·spect′a·ble (-spĕk′tȧ·b'l), *adj.* Not having or deserving respect. — **dis′re·spect′a·bil′i·ty** (-bĭl′ĭ·tĭ), *n.*
dis′re·spect′ful (-spĕkt′fōōl; -f'l), *adj.* Wanting in respect; uncivil. — **dis′re·spect′ful·ly**, *adv.* — **dis′re·spect′ful·ness**, *n.*
dis·robe′ (dĭs·rōb′), *v. t. & i.* To undress. — **dis·robe′ment**, *n.*
dis·root′ (dĭs·rōōt′), *v. t.* To uproot; hence, to dislodge.
dis·rupt′ (dĭs·rŭpt′), *adj.* [L. *disruptus, diruptus*, past part. of *disrumpere, dirumpere*, to break asunder, fr. *dis-* + *rumpere* to break, burst.] Broken asunder; disrupted. — *v. t. & i.* To break asunder. — **dis·rupt′er, dis·rup′tor** (-rŭp′tẽr), *n.*
dis·rup′tion (-rŭp′shŭn), *n.* Act of rending asunder, or state of being rent asunder; breach.
dis·rup′tive (-tĭv), *adj.* Causing, or tending to cause, disruption. — **dis·rup′tive·ly**, *adv.*
dis′sat·is·fac′tion (dĭs′săt·ĭs·făk′shŭn), *n.* State of being dissatisfied, unsatisfied, or discontented; discontent.
dis′sat·is·fac′to·ry (-tō·rĭ), *adj.* Causing dissatisfaction.
dis·sat′is·fy (dĭs·săt′ĭs·fī), *v. t.;* -FIED (-fīd); -FY′ING. To render unsatisfied; to displease.
dis·seat′ (dĭs·sēt′), *v. t.* To unseat.
dis·sect′ (dĭ·sĕkt′), *v. t.* [L. *dissectus*, past part. of *dissecare*, fr. *dis-* + *secare* to cut.] **1.** To divide into separate parts, as an animal or a plant, for examination; to anatomize. **2.** To analyze, esp. critically. — **Syn.** See ANALYZE. — **dis·sec′tor** (-sĕk′tẽr), *n.*
dis·sect′ed (-sĕk′tĕd; -tĭd), *adj.* Cut into several parts; specif.: **a** *Bot.* Cut deeply into many fine lobes or divisions; as, a *dissected* leaf. **b** *Phys. Geog.* Divided into ridges by valleys or gorges; as, a *dissected* plateau.
dis·sec′tion (-sĕk′shŭn), *n.* **1.** Act of dissecting. **2.** Anything dissected; esp., an anatomical specimen so prepared.
dis·seize′, dis·seise′ (dĭs·sēz′), *v. t.* [OF. *dessaisir*, fr. *des-* (fr. L. *dis-*) + *saisir* to seize, put in possession.] *Law.* To dispossess or oust wrongfully.
dis′sei·zee′, dis′sei·see′ (dĭs′sē·zē′; dĭs·sēz′ē′), *n.* *Law.* A person disseized; — correlative to *disseizor.*
dis·sei′zin, dis·sei′sin (dĭs·sē′zĭn), *n.* [OF. *dessaisine.*] *Law.* Act of disseizing, or state of being disseized.
dis·sei′zor, dis·sei′sor (-zẽr; -zôr), *n.* *Law.* One who disseizes another; — correlative to *disseizee.*
dis·sem′blance (dĭ·sĕm′blăns), *n.* [OF. *dessemblance.*] Lack of resemblance; unlikeness; difference.
dis·sem′blance, *n.* Act of dissembling; dissimulation.
dis·sem′ble (dĭ·sĕm′b'l), *v. t.;* -SEM′BLED (-b'ld); -SEM′BLING (-blĭng). [From earlier *dissimule* to dissimulate (fr. OF. *dissimuler*, fr. L. *dissimulare*).] **1.** To hide under a false semblance; to feign; disguise. **2.** To make pretense of; simulate. **3.** To pass as if unnoticed; as, to *dissemble* wrongs. — **Syn.** See DISGUISE. — *v. i.* To conceal the real fact, motives, or feeling by a pretense. — **dis·sem′bler** (-blẽr), *n.*
dis·sem′i·nate (dĭ·sĕm′ĭ·nāt), *v. t. & i.* [L. *disseminatus*, past part. of *disseminare* to disseminate, fr. *dis-* + *seminare* to sow, fr. *semen* seed.] To sow broadcast or as seed; to spread abroad. — **dis·sem′i·na′tion** (-nā′shŭn), *n.* — **dis·sem′i·na′tive** (-nā′tĭv), *adj.* — **dis·sem′i·na′tor** (-nā′tẽr), *n.*
dis·sen′sion (dĭ·sĕn′shŭn), *n.* Disagreement in opinion; esp., partisan and contentious division; discord. — **Syn.** See DISCORD.
dis·sent′ (dĭ·sĕnt′), *v. i.* [F. or L.; F. *dissentir*, fr. L. *dissentire, dissensum*, fr. *dis-* + *sentire* to feel, think.] **1.** To differ in opinion; to disagree. **2.** *Eccl.* To differ from an established church in regard to doctrines, rites, or government. — *n.* **1.** Act of dissenting; disagree-

ment. **2.** *Eccl.* Separation from an established church, esp. that of England; nonconformity.

dis·sent'er (dĭ·sĕn'tēr), *n.* One who dissents; specif., one who separates from an established church; esp. [*often cap.*], in England, a Protestant (formerly also a Roman Catholic) who disputes the authority of the Church of England; nonconformist.

dis·sen'tient (dĭ·sĕn'shĕnt), *adj.* Declaring dissent; dissenting. — *n.* One who dissents. — **dis·sen'tience** (-shĕns), *n.*

dis·sent'ing (dĭ·sĕn'tĭng), *adj.* Expressing disagreement; as, without a *dissenting* voice. — **dis·sent'ing·ly**, *adv.*

dis·sen'tious (-sĕn'shŭs), *adj.* Quarrelsome; factious.

dis·sep'i·ment (dĭ·sĕp'ĭ·mĕnt), *n.* [L. *dissaepimentum*, fr. *dissaepire*, fr. *dis-* + *saepire* to hedge in, enclose.] A separating tissue; a partition; a septum.

dis·sert' (dĭ·sûrt'), *v. i. & t.* [L. *dissertus*, past part. of *disserere*, fr. *dis-* + *serere* to join.] To discourse; discuss.

dis'ser·tate (dĭs'ēr·tāt), *v. i.* [L. *dissertatus*, past part. of *dissertare* to discuss, freq. fr. *disserere*.] To give a dissertation; discourse. — **dis'ser·ta'tor** (-tā'tēr), *n.*

dis'ser·ta'tion (dĭs'ēr·tā'shŭn), *n.* An extended treatment of a subject, esp. in writing; essay; thesis.

dis·serve' (dĭs·sûrv'), *v. t.* To serve ill; to damage.

dis·serv'ice (-sûr'vĭs), *n.* Ill service; injury; harm.

dis·sev'er (dĭ·sĕv'ēr), *v. t. & i.* To sever thoroughly; disunite. — **dis·sev'er·ance** (-ăns), *n.* — **dis·sev'er·ment**, *n.*

dis'si·dence (dĭs'ĭ·dĕns), *n.* Disagreement; dissent.

dis'si·dent (-dĕnt), *adj.* [L. *dissidens, -entis*, pres. part. of *dissidere* to sit apart, disagree, fr. *dis-* + *sedere* to sit.] Not agreeing; different. — *n.* One who dissents; a dissenter.

dis·sil'i·ent (dĭ·sĭl'ĭ·ĕnt), *adj.* [L. *dissiliens, -entis*, pres. part. of *dissilire* to leap asunder, fr. *dis-* + *salire* to leap.] Starting asunder; springing apart; specif., *Bot.*, bursting open or dehiscing violently, as the ripe capsules of the balsam. — **dis·sil'i·en·cy** (-ĕn·sĭ), *n.*

dis·sim'i·lar (dĭ·sĭm'ĭ·lēr; dĭs·sĭm'-), *adj.* Not similar; unlike. — **dis·sim'i·lar'i·ty** (-lăr'ĭ·tĭ), *n.*

Syn. **Dissimilarity, unlikeness, difference, divergence, distinction** mean a (or the) lack of correspondence between two or more things. **Dissimilarity** and **unlikeness**, the general terms, are distinguishable only in very precise use, *dissimilarity* being preferred when the contrast between the things is obvious and *unlikeness* when they are of the same species or sort; **difference** suggests notice of a quality or feature which marks each thing as apart from the others; **divergence** applies to a difference between things (often persons) having the same origin, the same end, or the like, and making for their cleavage; **distinction** implies a want of resemblance in detail, especially in some minute or not obvious detail apparent only through study, analysis, or the like.

dis·sim'i·late (dĭ·sĭm'ĭ·lāt), *v. t. & i.* To make or become dissimilar; to cause to undergo, or to undergo, dissimilation.

dis·sim'i·la'tion (dĭ·sĭm'ĭ·lā'shŭn), *n.* A making or becoming dissimilar; specif., *Phonet.*, development of dissimilarity between two identical sounds near each other in a word (as Lat. peregrinus, vulgar Lat. pelegrinus).

dis'si·mil'i·tude (dĭs'ĭ·mĭl'ĭ·tūd; dĭs'sĭ-), *n.* Lack of resemblance; unlikeness.

dis·sim'u·late (dĭ·sĭm'ū·lāt), *v. t. & i.* [L. *dissimulatus*, past part. of *dissimulare*.] To dissemble; feign; pretend. — **dis·sim'u·la'tion** (-lā'shŭn), *n.* — **dis·sim'u·la'tive** (-lā'tĭv), *adj.* — **dis·sim'u·la'tor** (-lā'tēr), *n.*

dis'si·pate (dĭs'ĭ·pāt), *v. t.* [L. *dissipatus*, past part. of *dissipare*, fr. *dis-* + *sipare, supare*, to throw.] **1.** To scatter; to break up and drive off; disperse; dispel; dissolve. **2.** To scatter aimlessly or foolishly; as, to *dissipate* one's energies. **3.** To squander. — *v. i.* **1.** To separate into parts and disappear; to waste away; vanish. **2.** To be wasteful or dissolute in the pursuit of pleasure. — **Syn.** See SCATTER. — **dis'si·pat'er** (-pāt'ēr), **dis'si·pa'tor** (-pā'tēr), *n.*

dis'si·pat'ed (-pāt'ĕd; -ĭd), *adj.* **1.** Scattered; esp., wasted. **2.** Wasteful in pursuit of pleasure; dissolute. — **dis'si·pat'ed·ly**, *adv.* — **dis'si·pat'ed·ness**, *n.*

dis'si·pa'tion (-pā'shŭn), *n.* **1.** Act of dissipating, or state of being dissipated; dispersion; diffusion; also, wasteful expenditure. **2.** Diversion; usually, idle, wasteful, or harmful diversion. **3.** A dissolute course of life; dissoluteness. — **dis'si·pa'tive** (dĭs'ĭ·pā'tĭv), *adj.*

dis·so'ci·a·ble (dĭ·sō'shĭ·ȧ·b'l; -sō'shȧ·b'l), *adj.* **1.** Not well associated; incongruous. **2.** (*pron.* dĭ·sō'shȧ·b'l) Unsociable. **3.** Separable.

dis·so'cial (-sō'shăl), *adj.* Unfriendly to society; unsocial.

dis·so'ci·ate (-shĭ·āt), *v. t. & i.* [L. *dissociatus*, past part. of *dissociare*, fr. *dis-* + *sociare* to associate, fr. *socius* companion.] **1.** To separate from union; disunite; disassociate. **2.** To subject to, or undergo, dissociation.

dis·so'ci·a'tion (-sĭ·ā'shŭn; -shĭ·ā'shŭn), *n.* **1.** Act of dissociating or state of being dissociated; disunion. **2.** *Chem.* Process by which a chemical combination breaks up into simpler constituents; — said esp. of the action of heat or other energy on gases, and of solvents upon dissolved substances. **3.** *Psychol.* **a** The separation of an idea or desire from the main stream of consciousness and making it coconscious. **b** The splitting of the personality into disunited parts. — **dis·so'ci·a'tive** (-sō'shĭ·ā'tĭv; -ȧ·tĭv), *adj.*

dis·sol'u·ble (dĭ·sŏl'ū·b'l; dĭs'ō·lū·b'l), *adj.* Capable of being dissolved. — **dis·sol'u·bil'i·ty** (dĭ·sŏl'ū·bĭl'ĭ·tĭ), *n.*

dis'so·lute (dĭs'ō·lūt), *adj.* [L. *dissolutus*, past part. of *dissolvere* to loosen, dissolve.] Loosed from restraint; esp., loose in morals and conduct; debauched. — **dis'so·lute·ly**, *adv.* — **dis'so·lute·ness**, *n.*

dis'so·lu'tion (-lū'shŭn), *n.* **1.** Act or process of dissolving or breaking up; specif.: **a** Separation into component parts; disintegration. **b** Termination or destruction by breaking down or disrupting; ruin. **c** The extinction of life; death. **d** The dispersion of an assembly by terminating its sessions. **e** The breaking up of a partnership. **2.** *Finance.* The final liquidation of a business. — **dis'so·lu·tive** (dĭs'ō·lū·tĭv), *adj.*

dis·solv'a·ble (dĭ·zŏl'vȧ·b'l), *adj.* Capable of being dissolved.

dis·solve' (dĭ·zŏlv'), *v. t.* [L. *dissolvere, -solutum*, fr. *dis-* + *solvere* to loose, free.] **1.** To separate into component parts; to disintegrate; esp., to destroy. **2.** To disconnect; disunite. **3.** To cause to pass into solution; as, to *dissolve* sugar in water; hence, figuratively, to merge entirely; to melt. **4.** To solve; clear up. **5.** To bring to an end by dispersal, as an assembly. **6.** *Law.* To annul; rescind; as, to *dissolve* an injunction. — *v. i.* **1.** To waste away; to be dissipated; to be decomposed. **2.** To pass into solution; also, *Obs.*, to become melted or liquefied; hence, to merge; to be converted. **3.** To fade away; to lose power. **4.** *Motion Pictures.* To appear or fade gradually and be replaced by a different scene. — **Syn.** See ADJOURN. — *n.* *Motion Pictures.* A view that dissolves into a different view. — **dis·solv'er**, *n.*

dis·sol'vent (dĭ·zŏl'vĕnt), *adj.* Having power to dissolve other substances. — *n.* A solvent.

dis'so·nance (dĭs'ō·năns), *n.* Also **dis'so·nan·cy** (-năn·sĭ). **1.** A mingling of discordant sounds; discord. **2.** *Music.* **a** The sounding together of tones so out of harmonic relation as to give beats. **b** An unrestful chord, needing a consonance to follow for completeness. **3.** Want of agreement, incongruity.

dis'so·nant (dĭs'ō·nănt), *adj.* [F. or L.; L. *dissonans, -antis*, pres. part. of *dissonare* to disagree in sound, be discordant, fr. *dis-* + *sonare* to sound.] **1.** Marked by dissonance; discordant. **2.** Disagreeing; incongruous. — **dis'so·nant·ly**, *adv.*

dis·suade' (dĭ·swād'), *v. t.* [F. or L.; F. *dissuader*, fr. L. *dissuadere, -suasum*, fr. *dis-* + *suadere* to advise.] **1.** To advise or exhort against (a course); to advise (a person against some course). **2.** To divert by persuasion; to turn from a purpose. — **dis·suad'er** (-swād'ēr), *n.*

dis·sua'sion (dĭ·swā'zhŭn), *n.* Act of dissuading.

dis·sua'sive (-sĭv), *adj.* Tending to dissuade. — **dis·sua'sive·ly**, *adv.* — **dis·sua'sive·ness**, *n.*

dis·syl'la·ble (dĭ·sĭl'ȧ·b'l; dĭs'sĭl'-), *n.* [F. *dissyllabe*, fr. L., adj., fr. Gr. *disyllabos*, fr. *di-* (= *dis*) twice + *syllabē* syllable.] A word of two syllables, as *pa·per*. — **dis'syl·lab'ic** (dĭs'ĭ·lăb'ĭk; dĭs'sĭ-), *adj.*

dis·sym'me·try (dĭs·sĭm'ē·trĭ), *n.*; *pl.* -TRIES (-trĭz). Absence or defect of symmetry. — **dis'sym·met'ric** (dĭs'sĭ·mĕt'rĭk), **dis'sym·met'ri·cal** (-rĭ·kăl), *adj.* — **dis'sym·met'ri·cal·ly**, *adv.*

dis'taff (dĭs'tȧf; 9), *n.*; *pl.* DISTAFFS (-tȧfs), rarely DISTAVES (-tȧvz). [AS. *distæf*.] **1.** The staff for holding the flax, tow, or wool, in spinning. **2.** Woman's work, authority, or domain; also, a woman or women collectively; — used also attributively; as, the *distaff* side, the female branch of a family.

dis·tain' (dĭs·tān'), *v. t.* [OF. *desteindre* to take away color, fr. L. *dis-* + *tingere* to color.] *Archaic.* To discolor; tarnish.

dis'tal (dĭs'tăl; -t'l), *adj.* [From DISTANT.] Remote from the point of attachment or origin; — opposed to *proximal*.

dis'tance (dĭs'tăns), *n.* **1.** *Obs.* Discord; quarrel. **2.** The space between two objects; measure of separation in place; hence, length or interval of time. **3.** Quality or condition of being distant, or spatially remote. **4.** Remoteness in any scale, as in allusion, interest, etc. **5.** Representation of distance or spatial separation, as in a painting. **6.** A distant point or region; as, fading in the *distance*. **7.** *Music.* The interval between two notes; as, the *distance* of a fourth. **8.** *Racing.* A limit specially marked, as by a flag, in the last part of a racecourse which a horse in a heat race must reach by the time the winner crosses the finish line or be disqualified for later heats. — *v. t.*; -TANCED (-tănst); -TANC·ING (-tăn·sĭng). **1.** To place or keep at a distance. **2.** To cause to appear remote. **3.** To outstrip; leave far behind; to surpass greatly. **4.** *Racing.* To beat by a distance. See DISTANCE, *n.*, 8.

dis'tant (-tănt), *adj.* [OF., fr. L. *distans, -antis*, pres. part. of *distare* to stand apart, be distant, fr. *dis-* + *stare* to stand.] **1.** Separated; at a distance; away. **2.** Far separated; not near, in a spatial or any other scale; remote. **3.** Different in kind; esp., repugnant. **4.** Reserved or repelling in manner; not cordial. **5.** At, from, or into a distance; as, *distant* neighbors, voyages. — **dis'tant·ly**, *adv.*

Syn. **Distant, far, faraway, far-off, remote, removed** mean not close or near, as in space, time, or relationship. **Distant** stresses separation and so implies an obvious interval, whether short or long and whether made explicit in the context or not; **far**, more often suggesting a space interval, usually implies a relatively long distance away from one; **faraway** and **far-off** not only mean extremely far but are usually preferred when distance in time is indicated; **remote** suggests a far removal from one's point of view, one's time, one's location, and the like; **removed**, commonly used in the predicate, carries a stronger implication of removal than *remote* and implies a contrast not only in space or time but in character or quality.

dis·taste' (dĭs·tāst'), *v. t.* **1.** To dislike the taste of; hence, to feel aversion to. **2.** To offend; displease. — *n.* **1.** Dislike of food or drink; disrelish. **2.** Aversion; dislike.

dis·taste'ful (-fōōl; -f'l), *adj.* **1.** Unpleasant to the taste; nauseous. **2.** Offensive; disagreeable. — **Syn.** See REPUGNANT. — **dis·taste'ful·ly**, *adv.* — **dis·taste'ful·ness**, *n.*

dis·tem'per (dĭs·tĕm'pēr), *n.* [From DISTEMPER to derange.] **1.** An undue or unnatural temper, as showing loss of balance; disaffection; bad temper. **2.** A morbid state of the animal system; malady; — chiefly applied to various infectious diseases of animals, esp. a contagious, often fatal, disease of young dogs. **3.** By extension, civil or political disorder; tumult. — *v. t.* [OF. *destemprer* to disorder, fr. L. *dis-* + *temperare* to mingle properly.] **1.** To derange the bodily, mental, or spiritual functions of; unsettle. **2.** To disturb; ruffle; to make ill-humored.

dis·tem'per, *v. t.* [OF. *destemprer, destremper*, to mix, soak, fr. L. *distemperare* to dissolve, dilute, fr. *dis-*, intens. + *temperare* to mingle in due proportion.] **1.** *Archaic.* To dilute, soak, steep, or the like. **2.** *Paint.* **a** To mix (colors) in the way of distemper. **b** To paint in distemper. — *n.* A process of painting in which the pigments are mixed, or tempered, with an emulsion of egg yolk, with size, or with white of egg as a vehicle, usually for mural decoration; also, the paint used in this process, or a painting done in it.

dis·tem'per·a·ture (dĭs·tĕm'pēr·ȧ·tūr), *n.* A disordered condition; distemper; mental or bodily derangement.

dis·tend' (dĭs·tĕnd'), *v. t. & i.* [L. *distendere, -tentum, -tensum*, fr. *dis-* + *tendere* to stretch.] **1.** To extend; to stretch. **2.** To stretch out or extend in all directions; to enlarge; to swell. — **Syn.** See EXPAND. — **Ant.** Constrict.

dis·ten'si·ble (-tĕn'sĭ·b'l), *adj.* That may be distended. — **dis·ten'si·bil'i·ty** (-bĭl'ĭ·tĭ), *n.*

dis·tent' (-tĕnt'), *adj.* [L. *distentus*.] Distended.

dis·ten'tion (-tĕn'shŭn), *n.* Also **dis·ten'sion**. Act of distending, or state of being distended.

dis'tich (dĭs'tĭk), *n.*; *pl.* -TICHS (-tĭks). [L. *distichon*, fr. Gr. *distichon*, fr. *di-* (= *dis*) twice + *stichos* row, verse.] *Pros.* A strophic group of two lines.

dis'tich·ous (dĭs'tĭ·kŭs), *adj.* [Gr. *distichos*.] *Nat. Hist.* Disposed in two vertical rows. — **dis'tich·ous·ly**, *adv.*

dis·till′, dis·til′ (dĭs·tĭl′), *v. i.*; -TILLED′ (-tĭld′); -TILL′ING. [OF. *distiller*, fr. L. *distillare*, fr. *de* + *stillare* to drop, fr. *stilla* drop.] To drop; trickle. — *v. t.* **1.** To let fall in drops; to let fall (drops). **2.** To obtain by, or as if by, distillation; as, to *distill* brandy from wine; to *distill* a philosophy from one's experience. **3.** To subject to, or transform by, distillation. — **dis·till′a·ble** (-*à*·b'l), *adj.*

dis′til·late (dĭs′tĭ·lāt; dĭs·tĭl′ât), *n.* *Chem.* A condensed product of distillation; as, the *distillate* from molasses.

dis′til·la′tion (dĭs′tĭ·lā′shŭn), *n.* **1.** Act, fact, or process of distilling. **2.** The process of driving off gas or vapor from liquids or solids, as by heat, in a retort or still, and condensing products therefrom; also, the purification of substances by this operation; rectification. **3.** Hence, the abstract or essence of anything.

dis·till′er (dĭs·tĭl′ẽr), *n.* One who or that which distills.

dis·till′er·y (-ĭ), *n.*; *pl.* -ERIES (-ĭz). The works where distilling, esp. of alcoholic liquors, is carried on.

dis·till′ment, dis·til′ment (dĭs·tĭl′mĕnt), *n.* Distillation.

dis·tinct′ (dĭs·tĭngkt′), *adj.* [OF., fr. L. *distinctus*, past part. of *distinguere*. See DISTINGUISH.] **1.** *Obs.* Distinguished; marked out. **2.** Distinguished by nature or station; not the same; individual; as, a herd is composed of *distinct* animals; unlike others; distinctive. **3.** That may be clearly seen; clear. **4.** *Poetic.* Marked; variegated. — **Syn.** See EVIDENT.

dis·tinc′tion (-tĭngk′shŭn), *n.* **1.** *Obs.* Separation into parts; division; also, a section. **2.** Act of distinguishing a difference or differences; discrimination; as, hairsplitting *distinctions.* **3.** The object or result of distinguishing; a difference. **4.** State or quality of being distinguishable or distinct. **5.** A distinguishing quality or mark. **6.** Act of giving special recognition; also, the mark or indication of such recognition; the state of being so distinguished; eminence. — **Syn.** See DISSIMILARITY.

dis·tinc′tive (-tĭv), *adj.* **1.** Marking or expressing distinction; distinguishing. **2.** *Phonet.* Capable of differentiating meaning; — applied to a speech sound. Cf. NONDISTINCTIVE. — **Syn.** See CHARACTERISTIC. — **dis·tinc′tive·ly**, *adv.* — **dis·tinc′tive·ness**, *n.*

dis·tinct′ly (dĭs·tĭngkt′lĭ), *adv.* With distinctness; clearly.

dis·tinct′ness, *n.* Quality or state of being distinct.

dis·tin′gué (dĭs·tăng′gā; dĭs′tăng·gā′; *F.* dēs′tăN′gā′), *adj.*; *fem.* -GUÉE (-gā; -gā′). [F.] Distinguished; of superior bearing.

dis·tin′guish (dĭs·tĭng′gwĭsh), *v. t.* [F. *distinguer*, fr. L. *distinguere*, *-tinctum*, fr. *dis-* + *stinguere* (in comp.) to prick.] **1.** To recognize or discriminate (one thing from or among others) by marks, signs, etc. **2.** To perceive clearly; to discern, esp. by physical sense. **3.** To separate into kinds, classes, or categories; as, to *distinguish* sounds into high and low. **4.** To set apart from others by visible marks; also, to characterize. **5.** To make eminent; to confer distinction upon. — *v. i.* To make distinctions; to exercise discrimination. — **dis·tin′guish·a·ble**, *adj.* — **dis·tin′guish·a·bly**, *adv.*

dis·tin′guished (-gwĭsht), *adj.* Marked; notable. — **Syn.** See FAMOUS. — **Ant.** Commonplace.

Distinguished Conduct Medal. *Mil., Brit.* A decoration awarded for distinguished conduct in the field. Abbr. *D.C.M.*

Distinguished Flying Cross. **1.** *Mil., U.S.* A decoration awarded for heroism or extraordinary achievement while participating in an aerial flight. Abbr. *D.F.C.* **2.** *Mil., Brit.* A decoration awarded for acts of gallantry when flying in operations against an enemy. Abbr. *D.F.C.*

Distinguished Service Cross. **1.** *U. S. Army.* A decoration awarded for extraordinary heroism during operations against an armed enemy. Abbr. *D.S.C.* **2.** *Mil., Brit.* A decoration awarded for distinguished service against the enemy. Abbr. *D.S.C.*

Distinguished Service Medal. **1.** *Mil., U.S.* A decoration awarded for exceptionally meritorious service to the government in a wartime duty of great responsibility. Abbr. *D.S.M.* **2.** *Mil., Brit.* A decoration awarded for distinguished conduct in war. Abbr. *D.S.M.*

Distinguished Service Order. *Mil., Brit.* A decoration awarded for especial services in action. Abbr. *D.S.O.*

dis·tin′guish·ing, *adj.* Distinctive; characteristic.

dis·tort′ (dĭs·tôrt′), *v. t.* [L. *distortus*, past part. of *distorquere* to twist, distort, fr. *dis-* + *torquere* to twist.] **1.** To twist out of regular shape; to twist physically. **2.** To twist aside mentally or morally. **3.** To wrest from the true meaning; to pervert. — **Syn.** See DEFORM. — **dis·tort′er**, *n.*

dis·tort′ed (-tôr′tĕd; -tĭd), *adj.* Twisted. — **dis·tort′ed·ly**, *adv.* — **dis·tort′ed·ness**, *n.*

dis·tor′tion (-tôr′shŭn), *n.* A distorting; a twisting motion or twisted or misshapen condition. — **dis·tor′tion·al** (-ăl; -'l), *adj.*

dis·tract′ (dĭs·trăkt′), *adj.* [L. *distractus*, past part. of *distrahere* to draw asunder, fr. *dis-* + *trahere* to draw.] *Archaic.* Distraught; hence, insane. — *v. t.* **1.** To draw (the sight, mind, or attention) to a different object or in different directions; to divert. **2.** To agitate by conflicting passions or by a variety of motives or cares; to confuse. **3.** To craze; madden. — **Syn.** See PUZZLE. — **dis·tract′ed** (-trăk′tĕd; -tĭd), *adj.* — **dis·tract′ed·ly**, *adv.* — **dis·tract′i·ble** (-tĭ·b'l), *adj.*

dis·trac′tion (dĭs·trăk′shŭn), *n.* **1.** A distracting, or state of being distracted; perplexity; confusion; disorder. **2.** Agitation from violent emotions; hence, mental derangement; madness. **3.** That which diverts attention; a diversion. — **dis·trac′tive** (-tĭv), *adj.*

dis·train′ (dĭs·trān′), *v. t.* [OF. *destreindre* to oppress, force, fr. L. *distringere*, *-trictum*, to draw asunder, molest, fr. *di-* (= *dis-*) + *stringere* to press together.] *Law.* **a** To coerce or punish by levying a distress; later, to levy a distress upon (a person). **b** To seize as a pledge or, later, indemnification. — *v. i.* To levy a distress. — **dis·train′a·ble**, *adj.* — **dis·train′ment**, *n.* — **dis·train′or** (dĭs·trān′ẽr; dĭs′trā·nôr′), **dis·train′er** (dĭs·trān′ẽr), *n.*

dis·traint′ (dĭs·trānt′), *n.* *Law.* Act of distraining.

dis·trait′ (dĭs·trā′; *F.* dēs′trĕ′), *adj.* [F.] Absent-minded; inattentive because of anxiety, pain, or apprehension.

dis·traught′ (dĭs·trôt′), *adj.* [An alteration of *distract.*] Distracted; beset with mental conflict; also, crazed.

dis·tress′ (dĭs·trĕs′), *n.* [OF. *destrece*, fr. L. *districtus*, past part. See DISTRAIN.] **1.** Oppressed or distressed state; suffering. **2.** That which occasions suffering; affliction. **3.** A state of danger or necessity; as, a ship in *distress.* **4.** *Law.* **a** Seizure and detention of the goods of another as security to obtain satisfaction of a claim, as for rent, taxes, or an injury, by sale of the goods seized. **b** That which is seized to procure satisfaction.

Syn. **Distress, suffering, misery, agony** mean the state of being in great trouble. **Distress** is more general than the others, being applicable not only to persons but to things as they affect persons, but it always suggests being under great stress or strain from any cause and in need of relief; **suffering,** usually applied to human beings, implies conscious endurance of pain or distress and, often, its acceptance as a trial of merit; **misery** stresses the unhappy or wretched conditions attending sickness, poverty, etc., and often connotes sordidness, abjectness, or the like; **agony** suggests pain of body or mind so intense that one is involved in a struggle to bear it.

— *v. t.* **1.** To put to straits; hence, to afflict; to harass. **2.** To compel by or as by inflicting pain. **3.** *Law.* To levy a distress upon; to distrain.

dis·tress′ful (-fo͝ol; -f'l), *adj.* Full of distress; causing or indicating distress. — **dis·tress′ful·ly**, *adv.*

dis·tress′ing, *adj.* Causing distress. — **dis·tress′ing·ly**, *adv.*

dis·trib′ute (dĭs·trĭb′ūt), *v. t.* [L. *distributus*, past part. of *distribuere* to distribute, fr. *dis-* + *tribuere* to allot.] **1.** To divide among several or many; to deal out; allot. **2.** *Archaic.* To dispense or administer, as justice. **3.** To spread out so as to cover a surface; as, to *distribute* fertilizer. **4.** To divide or separate, as into classes; to classify. **5.** *Logic.* To use (a term) so as to convey information about every member of the class which it names; thus, the proposition "All men are mortal" *distributes* the term "man" but does not *distribute* "mortal." **6.** *Print.* To separate (type matter that has been used) and return the pieces to their compartments in the case. — **dis·trib′ut·a·ble** (-ū·t*à*·b'l), *adj.* — **dis·trib′ut·er** (-ū·tẽr), *n.*

Syn. **Distribute, dispense, divide, deal, dole** mean to give as his share to many or to each. **Distribute** implies the separation or spreading out of units, parts, amounts, etc., in apportioning or assigning; **dispense** suggests the giving of a carefully weighed or measured portion to each of a group; **divide** implies a separation for the purposes of dispensing or sharing; **deal,** in current use, implies the delivery of a suitable portion to each of a group; **dole** (often with *out*) strictly implies a dispensing of alms to the needy, but in extended use it implies scantiness and niggardliness in distributing or in giving periodically.

dis′tri·bu′tion (dĭs′trĭ·bū′shŭn), *n.* **1.** Act of distributing; apportionment. **2.** The mode or manner in which things are distributed. **3.** Arrangement into parts; classification. **4.** That which is distributed.

dis·trib′u·tive (dĭs·trĭb′ū·tĭv), *adj.* **1.** Tending or serving to divide. **2.** *Gram.* Expressing separation among or into individuals or individual groups; as, "each," "either," and "every" may be used as *distributive* adjectives. **3.** *Logic.* Taken in its full extension; — said of a term. — *n.* A distributive term. — **dis·trib′u·tive·ly**, *adv.* — **dis·trib′u·tive·ness**, *n.*

dis·trib′u·tor (-tẽr), *n.* [L.] **1.** One who or that which distributes. **2.** An agent or agency for marketing goods. **3.** *Motor Engines.* An apparatus for directing the secondary current from the induction coil to the various spark plugs of a multicylinder engine in their proper firing order.

dis′trict (dĭs′trĭkt), *n.* [F., fr. ML. *districtus* district, fr. L. *districtus*, past part. of *distringere*. See DISTRAIN.] **1.** A defined portion of a state, city, etc., made for administrative, electoral, or other purposes. **2.** Loosely, any portion of territory; region; tract. — *v. t.* To divide into districts.

district attorney. *U. S.* The prosecuting officer of a given district. Abbr. *D.A.*

dis·trust′ (dĭs·trŭst′), *v. t.* To feel no trust or confidence in; to mistrust. — *n.* Lack or absence of trust; suspicion.

dis·trust′ful (-fo͝ol; -f'l), *adj.* Not confident; lacking confidence or trust. — **dis·trust′ful·ly**, *adv.* — **dis·trust′ful·ness**, *n.*

dis·turb′ (dĭs·tûrb′), *v. t.* [OF. *destorber*, *desturber*, fr. L. *disturbare*, *-turbatum*, fr. *dis-* + *turbare* to disturb, trouble.] **1.** To throw into disorder or confusion; to agitate. **2.** To agitate the mind of; to disquiet. **3.** To interfere with; to interrupt. **4.** To damage by shaking, jarring, etc. **5.** To put to inconvenience; as, don't *disturb* yourself. — **Syn.** See DISCOMPOSE. — **dis·turb′er**, *n.*

dis·turb′ance (dĭs·tûr′b*ă*ns), *n.* **1.** A disturbing, as of peace or quiet, or of a regular procedure. **2.** Confusion of the mind; agitation. **3.** Violent agitation in the body politic; public commotion.

di·sul′fide (dī·sŭl′fīd; -fĭd), *n.* Also **di·sul′fid, di·sul′phide, di·sul′phid.** *Inorg. Chem.* A compound containing two atoms of sulfur combined with an element or radical.

dis·un′ion (dĭs·ūn′yŭn), *n.* **1.** The termination of union; separation; disjunction. **2.** Breach of concord; dissension.

dis·un′ion·ist (-ĭst), *n.* One who favors disunion; specif., in U. S. history, a secessionist. — **dis·un′ion·ism** (-ĭz'm), *n.*

dis′u·nite′ (dĭs′ū·nīt′), *v. t.* **1.** To destroy the unity of; to divide, disjoin, or separate. **2.** To alienate in spirit. — *v. i.* To part; to fall asunder.

dis·use′ (dĭs·ūs′), *n.* Cessation of use, practice, or exercise.

dis·use′ (dĭs·ūz′), *v. t.* To cease to use.

dis′u·til′i·ty (dĭs′ū·tĭl′ĭ·tĭ), *n.* *Econ.* Quality of causing inconvenience, discomfort, or pain; — opposite of *utility.*

dis·val′ue (dĭs·văl′ū), *v. t.* To undervalue; depreciate.

dis·yoke′ (dĭs·yōk′), *v. t.* To unyoke.

dit (dĭt), *v. t.*; DIT′TED; DIT′TING. [AS. *dyttan.*] *Dial.* To obstruct.

‖**di′tat De′us** (dī′tăt dē′ŭs). [L.] God enriches; — motto of Arizona.

ditch (dĭch), *n.* [AS. *dīc.* See DIKE.] A trench dug in the earth, as for drainage or irrigation. — *v. t.* **1.** To dig a ditch or ditches in, as for drainage. **2.** *U. S.* To throw into a ditch; as, the engine was *ditched.* **3.** To land (a landplane) on water. **4.** *Slang, U. S.* To abandon; cast off. — **ditch′er**, *n.*

di′the·ism (dī′thē·ĭz'm), *n.* [*di-* + *theism.*] Belief in the existence of two gods or of two original principles, one good and one evil. — **di′the·ist** (-ĭst), *n.* — **di′the·is′tic** (-ĭs′tĭk), *adj.*

dith′er (dĭth′ẽr), *n.* **1.** *Chiefly Dial.* A trembling; shaking; quivering. **2.** *Colloq.* A distracted or unbalanced state of overexcitement. — *v. i.* & *t.* To be or put in a dither; also, *Dial.*, to tremble; quake.

di′thi·on′ic (dī′thĭ·ŏn′ĭk; dĭth′ĭ-), *adj.* [*di-* + *thionic.*] *Chem.* Pert. to or designating an acid (**dithionic acid,** $H_2S_2O_6$) known only in solution and in the form of salts.

di·thi′o·nite (dī·thī′ō·nīt), *n.* [*di-* + *thion-* (fr. Gr. *theion* brimstone, sulfur) + *-ite.*] *Chem.* = HYPOSULFITE **b.**

di·thi′o·nous (-nŭs), *adj.* *Chem.* = HYPOSULFUROUS.

dith′y·ramb (dĭth′ĭ·rămb; -răm), *n.* [From L., fr. Gr. *dithyrambos* a kind of lyric poetry in honor of Dionysus.] **1.** A kind of lyric poetry in honor of Dionysus. **2.** A poem in a wild irregular strain. — **dith′y·ram′bic** (-răm′bĭk), *adj.*

dit′ta·ny (dĭt′ȧ·nĭ), *n.; pl.* -NIES (-nĭz). [OF. *ditan, dictam,* fr. L., fr. Gr. *diktamnon, -nos,* a plant abundant on Mount *Dicte* in Crete.] *Bot.* Any of various herbs; as: **a** A mint (*Origanum dictamnus*), native to Crete, having drooping spikes of pink flowers. **b** The fraxinella. **c** *U.S.* A small aromatic herb (*Cunila origanoides*) of the mint family.

dit′tied (dĭt′ĭd), *adj.* Set, sung, or composed as a ditty.

dit′to (dĭt′ō), *n.; pl.* DITTOS (-ōz). [It. *detto, ditto,* fr. L. *dictum* dictum.] The aforesaid thing; the same (as before); — often abbreviated to *do.*, or represented by two "turned commas" ("), or small marks (**ditto marks**). It is used in bills, accounts, tables of names, etc., to save repetition. — *adv.* As before, or aforesaid; in the same manner, place, or division of time; as, I will act *ditto.*

dit′ty (dĭt′ĭ), *n.; pl.* -TIES (-ĭz). [OF. *dité, ditié,* fr. L. *dictatum,* past part. neut. of *dictare* to compose. See DICTATE, *v.*] A song; a lay; a little poem intended to be sung; — now esp., any short song of simple character.

ditty bag. Also **ditty box.** A sailor's small bag or box to hold thread, needles, tape, etc.

di′u·re′sis (dī′ū·rē′sĭs), *n.* [NL. See DIURETIC.] *Med.* Free or excessive excretion of urine.

di′u·ret′ic (-rĕt′ĭk), *adj.* Also **di′u·ret′i·cal** (-ĭ·kăl). [LL. *diureticus,* fr. Gr. *diourētikos,* deriv. of *dia* through + *ourein* to make water, fr. *ouron* urine.] *Med.* Tending to increase the secretion and discharge of urine. — *n.* A medicine with diuretic properties.

di·ur′nal (dī·ûr′năl; -n'l), *adj.* [L. *diurnalis,* fr. *diurnus,* fr. *dies* day.] **1.** Daily; recurring every day. **2.** Relating to the daytime; — opposed to *nocturnal.* — **Syn.** See DAILY. — *n.* **1.** *Archaic.* A daybook; a journal; diary. **2.** *Archaic.* A newspaper. — **di·ur′nal·ly,** *adv.*

diurnal arc. See ARC, 2.

di′va (dē′vȧ), *n.; pl.* DIVAS (-vȧz), DIVE (-vā). [It., prop. fem. of *divo* divine, fr. L. *divus.*] A prima donna.

di′va·gate (dī′vȧ·gāt), *v. i.* [L. *divagari,* fr. *di-* (= *dis-*) + *vagari* to stroll about.] To wander about; to stray; hence, to digress. — **di′va·ga′tion** (-gā′shŭn), *n.*

di·va′lent (dī·vā′lĕnt; dĭv′ȧ·lĕnt), *adj.* [*di-* + L. *valens.*] *Chem.* Bivalent. — **di·va′lence** (-lĕns), *n.*

di′van (dī′văn *or, esp. in senses* 1, 2, & 5, dĭ·văn′), *n.* [Turk. *divān,* fr. Per. *dīwān* a book of many leaves, a senate, council.] **1.** In Turkey and other Oriental countries: A council of state; a royal court. **2.** A hall where a council is held; a large reception room. **3.** A large low couch with no back or ends; loosely, any couchlike piece of furniture. **4.** A coffee and smoking saloon. **5.** *Persia.* A collection of poems written by one author.

di·var′i·cate (dī·văr′ĭ·kāt; dĭ-), *v. i.* [L. *divaricatus,* past part. of *divaricare* to stretch apart, fr. *di-* (= *dis-*) + *varicare* to straddle.] To part into two branches; to fork. — (-kāt), *adj.* Diverging; spreading asunder. — **di·var′i·cate·ly,** *adv.* — **di·var′i·ca′tor** (-kā′tẽr), *n.*

di·var′i·ca′tion (-kā′shŭn), *n.* **1.** A stretching apart; a straddling. **2.** A separation into two parts or branches. **3.** A disagreement or difference in opinion.

dive (dīv), *v. i.;* DIVED (dīvd); DIV′ING (dīv′ĭng). *Colloq. past, chiefly U.S.,* DOVE (dōv). [AS. *dȳfan* to sink, v. t., *dūfan,* v. i.] **1.** To plunge into water head foremost. **2.** Specif., to submerge, as a submarine. **3.** To penetrate with the body or with the hand into any substance or recess; — usually implying haste or suddenness. **4.** To plunge deeply into any subject, business, etc. **5.** *Aviation.* To descend in a dive. **6.** *Fancy Diving.* To execute a dive. — *n.* **1.** Act of one who dives. **2.** *U.S.* A place of low resort. **3.** *Aviation.* A steep descent, in which the air speed attained is greater than the maximum speed in horizontal flight. **4.** *Fancy Diving.* A plunge into water executed by a person in a particular or set manner.

dive bomber. A type of bombing plane designed and equipped to discharge a bomb aimed by pointing the nose of the plane at the target in a steep dive to within a short distance of the objective. Cf. STUKA. — **dive′-bomb′,** *v. t. & i.*

div′er (dīv′ẽr), *n.* **1.** One who or that which dives. **2.** *Zool.* A loon; also, any of various other birds skillful in diving, as grebes (hell-divers), auks, penguins, etc.

di·verge′ (dī·vûrj′; dĭ-), *v. i.;* -VERGED′ (-vûrjd′); -VERG′ING (-vûr′jĭng). [NL. *divergere,* fr. L. *di-* (= *dis-*) + *vergere* to bend, incline.] **1.** To extend from a common point in different directions; to deviate (as from a given direction); — opposed to *converge.* **2.** To differ from a typical form; to vary from normal. — **Syn.** See SWERVE.

di·ver′gence (-vûr′jĕns), *n.* **1.** A receding from each other in moving from a common center; — the opposite of *convergence.* **2.** Disagreement; deviation from a standard. — **Syn.** See DISSIMILARITY.

di·ver′gen·cy (-jĕn·sĭ), *n.; pl.* -CIES (-sĭz). Divergence.

di·ver′gent (-jĕnt), *adj.* **1.** That diverges; — opposed to *convergent.* **2.** Relating to, or characterized by, divergence or disagreement. — **Syn.** See DIFFERENT. — **di·ver′gent·ly,** *adv.*

di′vers (dī′vẽrz), *adj.* [OF., fr. L. *diversus* turned in different directions, different. See DIVERT.] **1.** *Archaic.* Different in kind; diverse. **2.** Several; sundry.

di·verse′ (dī·vûrs′; dī′vûrs; dĭ·vûrs′), *adj.* [Same word as DIVERS.] **1.** Different; unlike; distinct; separate. **2.** Capable of various forms; multiform. — **Syn.** See DIFFERENT. — **Ant.** Identical. — **di·verse′ly,** *adv.* — **di·verse′ness,** *n.*

di·ver′si·fied (dī·vûr′sĭ·fīd; dĭ-), *adj.* Variegated; as, *diversified* farming; also, distributed, as investments, among different types of securities.

di·ver′si·form (-fôrm), *adj.* [L. *diversus* different + *-form.*] Of a different form; of varied forms.

di·ver′si·fy (-fī), *v. t.;* -FIED (-fīd); -FY′ING. [ML. *diversificare,* fr. L. *diversus* diverse + *-ficare* (in comp.).] **1.** To make diverse, or various, in form or quality; to give variety to; to variegate. **2.** To distribute (investments) among different kinds of securities, or the like. — **di·ver′si·fi·ca′tion** (-fĭ·kā′shŭn), *n.* — **di·ver′si·fi′er** (-fī′ẽr), *n.*

di·ver′sion (dĭ·vûr′shŭn; -zhŭn; dī-), *n.* **1.** Act of turning (anything) aside from its course, or (a person) from an occupation or purpose. **2.** That which diverts; that which relaxes and amuses; sport; pastime. **3.** *Mil.* An attack or feint that draws the attention and force of the enemy from the point of the principal operation.

di·ver′sion·ar′y (-ẽr′ĭ *or, esp. Brit.,* -ẽr·ĭ), *adj.* Of the nature of a diversion, specif., a military diversion, or feint intended to draw the enemy's forces away from the point of principal attack.

di·ver′si·ty (dī·vûr′sĭ·tĭ; dĭ-), *n.; pl.* -TIES (-tĭz). **1.** A state or an instance of difference; unlikeness. **2.** Multiformity; variety; as, *diversity* of opinion.

di·vert′ (dī·vûrt′; dĭ-), *v. t.* [OF. *divertir,* fr. L. *divertere, -versum,* to go different ways, turn aside, fr. *di-* (= *dis-*) + *vertere* to turn.] **1.** To turn aside (from or to); to deflect. **2.** To turn away from any business or study; to amuse; to entertain. — **Syn.** See AMUSE. — **di·vert′er,** *n.*

di′ver·tic′u·lum (dī′vẽr·tĭk′ū·lŭm), *n.; pl.* -ULA (-lȧ). [L., a bypath.] *Anat.* A blind tube or sac branching off from a cavity or canal; a caecum. — **di′ver·tic′u·lar** (-lẽr), *adj.*

di·vert′ing (dī·vûr′tĭng; dĭ-), *adj.* Amusing; entertaining; distracting. — **di·vert′ing·ly,** *adv.*

‖**di′ver′tisse′ment′** (dē′vĕr′tēs′mäN′), *n.* [F.] **1.** An entertainment; diversion; amusement. **2. a** A short ballet, or other entertainment, between the acts of a play. **b** A light, diverting piece of music.

Di′ves (dī′vēz), *n.* [L., rich.] The rich man in the parable of "the rich man and Lazarus" (*Luke* xvi. 19–31); hence, a rich man.

di·vest′ (dī·vĕst′; dĭ-), *v. t.* [From *devest,* after ML. *divestire, disvestire.* See DEVEST.] **1.** To unclothe; to strip, as of clothes, arms, or equipage. **2.** To dispossess; as, to *divest* one of his rights.

di·vest′i·ture (-vĕs′tĭ·tūr), *n.* Also **di·ves′ture** (-vĕs′tūr). Act of divesting or state of being divested.

di·vest′ment (dī·vĕst′mĕnt; dĭ-), *n.* Divestiture.

di·vid′a·ble (dĭ·vīd′ȧ·b'l), *adj.* Divisible.

di·vide′ (dĭ·vīd′), *v. t.* [L. *dividere, divisum,* fr. *di-* (= *dis-*) + a root akin to L. *vidua* widow.] **1.** To part asunder (a whole); to sever. **2.** To cause to be separate; to keep apart by a partition, or by an imaginary line or limit. **3.** To make partition of among a number; to apportion. **4.** To make hostile; to set at variance. **5.** To separate into classes or parts; to classify. **6.** *Math.* To subject to mathematical division. **7.** *Mech.* To mark divisions on; to graduate; as, to *divide* a sextant. — **Syn.** See SEPARATE: DISTRIBUTE. — *v. i.* **1.** To be separated; to part; to branch. **2.** To have a share; to partake. **3.** *Colloq.* To deal out something in portions or equal shares. **4.** To vote, as in the British Parliament, by separating into two parties, that is, the "ayes" dividing from the "noes." — *n.* **1.** *Colloq.* A division or distribution. **2.** A dividing ridge between two areas of drainage; a watershed.

di·vid′ed (dĭ·vīd′ĕd; -ĭd), *adj.* **1.** Parted; disunited. **2.** *Bot.* Cut into distinct parts by incisions extending to the base or to the midrib; — said of a leaf. See LOBATION, *Illust.* (4).

‖**di′vi·de et im′pe·ra** (dĭv′ĭ·dē ĕt ĭm′pĕ·rȧ). [L.] Divide and rule; — an ancient political maxim.

div′i·dend (dĭv′ĭ·dĕnd), *n.* [L. *dividendum* thing to be divided.] **1.** *Math.* The number or quantity that is to be divided by another (called the *divisor*). See QUOTIENT; REMAINDER, 5. **2.** A sum or quantity to be divided and distributed; also, the share of a sum divided that falls to each individual; — applied to the profits as apportioned among shareholders, and to assets as apportioned among creditors; as, the *dividend* of a bank, or of a bankrupt estate. **3.** *Insurance.* A share of surplus allocated to a policyholder in a participating insurance policy; — in England often called *bonus.*

di·vid′er (dĭ·vīd′ẽr), *n.* **1.** One who or that which divides. **2.** Usually *pl.* An instrument for dividing lines, etc. See COMPASS, *n.,* 4.

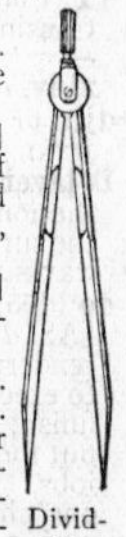
Dividers.

div′i-div′i (dĭv′ĭ-dĭv′ĭ), *n.* [Sp. *dividivi,* fr. native name.] **a** A small tree of tropical America (*Caesalpinia coriaria*) of the senna family; also, its astringent pods, yielding tannic and gallic acid. **b** A tree of a related species (*C. tinctoria*); also, its pods.

di·vid′u·al (dĭ·vĭd′ū·ăl), *adj.* [L. *dividuus* divisible, divided.] **1. a** Separate; distinct. **b** Divisible. **2.** Shared or participated in. — **di·vid′u·al·ly,** *adv.*

div′i·na′tion (dĭv′ĭ·nā′shŭn), *n.* [OF., fr. L. *divinatio,* fr. *divinare, -natum,* to foresee, foretell, fr. *divinus* divine.] **1.** The act or practice of foreseeing or foretelling future events or discovering hidden knowledge. **2.** Augury; omen; also, prediction. **3.** Exercise of intuition; also, an intuitive perception. — **Syn.** See DISCERNMENT. — **di·vin′a·to′ry** (dĭ·vĭn′ȧ·tō′rĭ *or, esp. Brit.,* -tẽr·ĭ), *adj.*

di·vine′ (dĭ·vīn′), *adj.* [OF. *divin, devin,* fr. L. *divinus,* fr. *divus* belonging to a deity.] **1.** Of or pertaining to God. **2.** Appropriated to God, or celebrating his praise; religious; holy. **3.** Pertaining to, or proceeding from a deity. **4.** Godlike; heavenly; supremely admirable. — *n.* A priest; clergyman; also, a theologian. — *v. t.* **1.** To perceive through sympathy, or intuition; to detect; to conjecture. **2.** *Obs.* To foretell; presage; portend. — **Syn.** See FORESEE. — *v. i.* **1.** To use or practice, or to foretell by, divination; to prophesy. **2.** To have or feel a presage or foreboding. **3.** To conjecture or guess. — **di·vine′ly,** *adv.* — **di·vine′ness,** *n.*

di·vin′er (dĭ·vīn′ẽr), *n.* [OF. *devineor.*] One who divines.

div′ing (dīv′ĭng), *adj.* That dives or is used for diving.

diving bell. A hollow inverted vessel in which men may work under water, respiration being provided by compressed air at the top, or by fresh air pumped in through a tube.

di·vin′ing rod *or* **stick** (dĭ·vīn′ĭng). A rod, commonly of witch hazel, with forked branches, used professedly as an aid in discovering water or metals under ground; a dowser. Cf. DOODLEBUG.

di·vin′i·ty (dĭ·vĭn′ĭ·tĭ), *n.; pl.* -TIES (-tĭz). **1.** State or quality of being divine; deity; godhead. **2.** A deity; a god; specif. [*cap.*], usually with *the,* the Deity; God. **3.** A celestial being, inferior to God, but superior to man. **4.** Divine attribute; supernatural power or virtue. **5.** The science of divine things; theology.

di·vis′i·ble (dĭ·vĭz′ĭ·b'l), *adj.* Capable of being divided or separated. — **di·vis′i·bil′i·ty** (-bĭl′ĭ·tĭ), *n.* — **di·vis′i·ble·ness,** *n.* — **di·vis′i·bly** (-blĭ), *adv.*

di·vi′sion (dĭ·vĭzh′ŭn), *n.* **1.** Act or process of dividing, or state of being divided; separation; distribution. **2.** That which divides or keeps apart; partition. **3.** The portion separated by the dividing. **4.** Disunion; dissension; discord. **5.** *Obs.* Distinction; contrast. **6.** Separation of the members of a deliberative body, esp. of the Houses of Parliament, to ascertain the vote. **7.** *Biol.* A group of organisms forming a part of some larger group. See CLASSIFICATION, 2. **8.** *Math.* The process of, or rule for, finding how many times one number or quantity is contained in another. The sign ÷ (**division sign** *or* **mark**) placed between numerical expressions indicates that the preceding quantity is to be divided by the following quantity. **9.** *Mil.* The elementary organic unit of the combined arms, the normal command of a major general. In the U. S. Army, the division consists of a headquarters, two infantry brigades, one light-artillery brigade, and certain auxiliary troops. Cf. CORPS, 2. **11.** *Nav.* One of the groups, usually of four vessels, into which a fleet or large squadron is divided. — **Syn.** See PART. — **di·vi′sion·al** (dĭ·vĭzh′ŭn·ăl; -'l), *adj.*

di·vi′sion·ism (-ĭz'm), *n.* *Painting.* A method of painting in which the colors are separated into their component hues and these, in pure color, laid side by side upon the canvas in order to be recomposed in the eye of the observer, the purpose being to produce an effect of greater vibration and luminosity. See IMPRESSIONISM, POINTILLISM.

di·vi′sive (dĭ·vī′sĭv), *adj.* **1.** Indicating division; making distinctions. **2.** Creating dissension or discord.

di·vi′sor (-zẽr), *n.* *Math.* The number or quantity by which another (the *dividend*) is divided. See QUOTIENT; REMAINDER, 5; COMMON DIVISOR.

di·vorce′ (dĭ·vōrs′; 70), *n.* [OF., fr. L. *divortium*, fr. *divortere, divertere.* See DIVERT.] **1.** *Law.* A legal dissolution of the marriage relation. **2.** Disunion; separation.

di·vorce′, *v. t.*; -VORCED′ (-vōrst′); -VORC′ING (-vōr′sĭng). **1.** To put away by divorce. **2.** To disunite; sunder; sever. — **Syn.** See SEPARATE. — **di·vorc′er** (-vōr′sẽr), *n.*

di·vor′cé′ (dĭ·vōr′sā′; 70), *n. masc.*, **di·vor′cée′** (-sā′), *fem.* [F.] A divorcee.

di·vor′cee′ (-sē′), *n.* A person divorced.

di·vorce′ment (dĭ·vōrs′mĕnt), *n.* Divorce; separation.

div′ot (dĭv′ŭt), *n.* **1.** *Scot.* A thin oblong turf. **2.** *Golf.* A piece of turf cut out in making a stroke.

di·vul′gate (dĭ·vŭl′gāt), *v. t.* [L. *divulgatus*, past part. of *divulgare.* See DIVULGE.] To divulge; disclose. — **di·vul′gat·er** (-gāt·ẽr), *n.* — **div′ul·ga′tion** (dĭv′ŭl·gā′shŭn), *n.*

di·vulge′ (dĭ·vŭlj′), *v. t.*; -VULGED′ (-vŭljd′); -VULG′ING (-vŭl′jĭng). [L. *divulgare*, fr. *di-* (= *dis-*) + *vulgare* to spread among the people, fr. *vulgus* the common people.] **1.** *Rare.* To indicate publicly; proclaim. **2.** To make public; reveal; disclose. — **Syn.** See REVEAL. — **di·vulge′ment**, *n.* — **di·vulg′er** (-vŭl′jẽr), *n.*

di·vul′gence (-vŭl′jĕns), *n.* Act of divulging; disclosure.

di·vul′sion (dĭ·vŭl′shŭn), *n.* [F. or L.; F., fr. L. *divulsio*, fr. *divulsus*, past part. of *divellere* to rend.] A tearing apart; a rending asunder. — **di·vul′sive** (-sĭv), *adj.*

di·wan′ (dē·wän′; dē·wôn′). Var. of DEWAN.

Dix′ie (dĭk′sĭ), *n.*, *or* **Dixie Land.** [Prob. fr. *dix, dixie*, a $10 note, widely current in Louisiana before the Civil War, with a large F. *dix* (ten) in the center of the reverse.] **a** A collective designation of the Southern States of the United States. **b** A song composed in 1859 by D. D. Emmett, which became a popular Confederate war song and later a national favorite.

dix′it (dĭk′sĭt), *n.* [L., he has said. See DICTION.] One's (unsupported) statement or affirmation. Cf. IPSE DIXIT.

diz′en (dĭz′'n; dī′z'n), *v. t.* [MD. *disen*, fr. MLG. *dise* bunch of flax on a distaff.] To dress gaudily; bedizen.

diz′zy (dĭz′ĭ), *adj.*; DIZ′ZI·ER (-ĭ·ẽr); DIZ′ZI·EST. [AS. *dysig* foolish.] **1.** *Colloq.* Foolish; stupid. **2.** Mentally confused or unsteady. **3.** Causing, tending to cause, or characterized by giddiness or vertigo. — *v. t.*; DIZ′ZIED (-ĭd); DIZ′ZY·ING. To make dizzy or giddy. — **diz′zi·ly**, *adv.* — **diz′zi·ness**, *n.*

djin *or* **djinn** (jĭn), **djin·nee′** (jĭ·nē′), **djin·ni′**. Vars. of JIN, JINNEE, JINNI.

D layer (dē). *Radio.* The lowest of the layers commonly present in the ionosphere. It occurs at varying heights, 25 to 50 miles above the surface of the earth. In it occurs absorption of the energy of radio waves which are reflected by higher layers.

do (do͞o; 4), *v. t. & auxiliary*; DID (dĭd); DONE (dŭn); DO′ING (do͞o′ĭng). [AS. *dōn.*] **1.** To bring about; to produce, as an effect or result; to render; to pay; as, to *do* one reverence. **2.** To perform, as an action; to execute; transact; administer. **3.** To bring to an end by action; to finish; — used in the past participle; as, I have *done* fighting. **4.** To put forth; to exert; as, to *do* one's best. **5.** To work at; as, to *do* odd jobs. **6.** To treat or deal with in any way; as, to *do* the dishes; to *do* one's hair. **7.** To traverse, as distance; as, the car *does* twenty miles on a gallon. **8.** *Colloq.* **a** To trick; to cheat. **b** To serve; to suit. **9.** As an auxiliary verb followed by an infinitive without *to*, to form a periphrastic present and past indicative, and imperative; as, I *did* say so, and I *do* say so now. **10.** As a substitute verb, to save repetition of a principal verb or a verb and its object; as, "I chose my wife as she *did* her wedding gown." — *v. i.* **1.** To act or behave; to conduct oneself. **2.** To fare; to prosper; as, wheat is *doing* well. **3.** To act; to work; to achieve; as, "Let us *do* or die." **4.** To suffice; to avail; to answer the purpose. **5.** *Colloq.* To care or provide; specif., to cook meals and keep rooms in order; — with *for.*

do away. *Obs.* To get rid of. — ***do away with.*** **a** To throw away; to get rid of. **b** To kill; to destroy. — ***do for.*** To put an end to; to ruin; hence, to kill. — ***do in.*** *Slang.* **a** To thrash. **b** To overcome; to kill. — ***do up.*** **a** To clean and prepare for wearing; to launder; also, to set to rights or renovate, as a dwelling. **b** To collect and wrap up, esp. into a bundle; to bind up (one's hair).

— (do͞o), *n.* **1.** *Dial.* Ado; stir. **2.** *Now Rare.* Deed; duty. **3.** *Colloq., Eng.* A cheat; a swindle.

do (dō), *n.* *Music.* The first of the syllables used in solmization; — applied to the first tone of the diatonic scale.

do′a·ble (do͞o′ȧ·b'l), *adj.* Capable of being done.

do′-all′ (do͞o′ôl′), *n.* General manager; factotum.

dob′ber (dŏb′ẽr), *n.* *Local, U. S.* A float to a fishing line.

dob′bin (dŏb′ĭn), *n.* [For *Robin, Robert.*] A farm horse; a gentle family horse; sometimes, an old nag.

dob′by (-ĭ), *n.*; *pl.* -BIES (-ĭz). *Dial.* A spirit like a brownie, but often malicious.

Do·bell's′ so·lu′tion (dō·bĕlz′). [After H. B. *Dobell* (1828–1917), Eng. physician.] *Pharm.* An aqueous solution of carbolic acid, borax, sodium bicarbonate, and glycerin, used as a spray in diseases of the nose and throat.

Do′ber·man pin′scher (dō′bẽr·măn pĭn′shẽr; *G.* dō′bẽr·män). Also **Do·ber·man.** A short-haired medium-sized dog of a breed of German origin.

do′bla (dō′blä), *n.* [Sp.] An old Spanish gold coin.

do·blon′ (dō·blōn′; *Sp.* -vlōn′; 17), *n.*; *pl.* DOBLONES (*Sp.* dō·vlō′nās; 17). [Sp. *doblón.*] A former gold coin of Spain and Spanish America. Cf. DOUBLOON.

do′bra (dō′brȧ), *n.* [Pg.] Any of various former Portuguese coins; specif., a gold coin, the double of the johannes.

dob′son (dŏb′s'n), *n.* The hellgrammite.

do′by (dō′bĭ), *n.* *Colloq., U. S.* Short for ADOBE.

do·cent′ (dō·sĕnt′; *G.* -tsĕnt′), *n.* [G. *docent, dozent*, fr. L. *docens*, pres. part.] Orig., short for PRIVATDOCENT; now, a teacher or lecturer. — **do·cent′ship**, *n.*

doch′-an-dor′rach, -dor′roch, *or* **-dor′ris,** etc. (dŏκ′ăn·dŏr′ăκ, -ŭκ, -ĭs), *n.* A stirrup cup.

doc′ile (dŏs′ĭl; *Brit.* dō′sīl, dŏs′īl), *adj.* [F., fr. L. *docilis*, fr. *docere* to teach.] Disposed to be taught; tractable; as, a *docile* child. — **Syn.** See OBEDIENT. — **doc′ile·ly**, *adv.* — **do·cil′i·ty** (dō·sĭl′ĭ·tĭ), *n.*

dock (dŏk), *n.* [AS. *docce.*] **a** One of a genus (*Rumex*) of plants of the buckwheat family. Most docks are troublesome weeds having long taproots. **b** Any of various other weedy plants, as the coltsfoot and the burdocks.

dock, *n.* The solid part of an animal's tail, as distinguished from the hair; the part of a tail left after clipping or cutting. — *v. t.* **1.** To cut off, as the end; to clip. **2.** To shorten; to deduct from, as wages.

dock, *n.* [MLG. & MD. *docke* (D. *dok*).] **1.** An artificial basin for the reception of vessels, with gates to keep in or shut out the water. See DRY DOCK, FLOATING DOCK. **2. a** The slip or waterway extending between two piers for the reception of ships. **b** *Colloq.* A landing pier for boats; a wharf. — *v. t.* To haul or guide (a ship) into a dock, as for repairing, cleaning, or loading. — *v. i.* To come or go into dock.

dock, *n.* [Flem. *dok, docke*, cage, enclosure.] The place in court where a prisoner stands or sits.

dock′age (dŏk′ĭj), *n.* Curtailment; deduction.

dock′age, *n.* *Naut.* **a** A charge made for the use of a dock. **b** Docking facilities. **c** The docking of vessels.

dock′er (-ẽr), *n.* One who or that which docks.

dock′er, *n.* One connected with docks, or wharves; specif., a dock laborer; a longshoreman.

dock′et (dŏk′ĕt; -ĭt), *n.* [Origin obscure.] **1.** *Law.* An abridged entry of a proceeding in an action, or a register of such entries. In the United States the record containing the list of causes to be tried is called the ***trial docket.*** **2.** *U. S.* A list or calendar of business matters to be acted on in any assembly. **3.** A bill tied to goods, containing some direction; a label; a ticket. — *v. t.* **1.** To inscribe with a docket; to ticket. **2.** *Law.* To enter in a docket book or list.

dock′mack·ie (dŏk′măk·ĭ), *n.* A North American shrub (*Viburnum acerifolium*), of the honeysuckle family, with white flowers succeeded by red berries.

dock′yard′ (dŏk′yärd′), *n.* A yard or storage place for naval stores or timber for shipbuilding, with facilities for building or repairing ships; in England, a navy yard.

doc′tor (dŏk′tẽr), *n.* [OF. *doctour*, fr. L. *doctor* teacher, fr. *docere* to teach.] **1.** *Archaic.* A teacher; a learned man. **2.** An advanced academic title; hence, one on whom this title has been conferred by a university or college. A doctor's degree may be merely honorary. Abbr. *Dr.* **3.** One duly licensed to practice medicine; a physician; a surgeon. Abbr. *Dr.* **4.** A wizard or medicine man in a savage tribe. **5.** *Obs. Slang.* A loaded die. **6.** *Angling.* Any of several brightly colored artificial flies. **7.** *Mech. & Mach.* Any mechanical contrivance for remedying a difficulty, esp. a makeshift one used in emergency. — *v. t.* **1.** *Colloq.* To treat as a physician does; to apply remedies to. **2.** *Colloq.* To tamper with and arrange to suit one's own purposes. — *v. i.* **1.** *Colloq.* To practice medicine. **2.** *Colloq.* To take medicine or medical treatment. — **doc′tor·al** (-ăl), *adj.* — **doc′tor·ship**, *n.*

doc′tor·ate (-ĭt), *n.* Degree, title, or rank of doctor.

Doc′tors' Com′mons (dŏk′tẽrz). The common dining hall and later the buildings of the College of Doctors of Civil Law, in London, in which were the ecclesiastical and admiralty courts and offices having jurisdiction of marriage licenses, divorces, registration of wills, etc.

doc′tress (dŏk′trĕs; -trĭs), *n.* *Now Rare.* A female doctor.

doc′tri·naire′ (dŏk′trĭ·nâr′), *n.* [F.] One who would apply a political or economic system based on abstract doctrines or theories, without enough regard for practical difficulties. — *adj.* Of or relating to a doctrinaire; also, dogmatic about the practical applicability of one's own theories. — **Syn.** See DICTATORIAL. — **doc′tri·nair′ism** (-nâr′ĭz'm), *n.*

doc′tri·nal (dŏk′trĭ·năl; -n'l; *Brit. also* dŏk·trī′năl), *adj.* Pertaining to, or containing, doctrine or something taught and to be believed. — **doc′tri·nal·ly**, *adv.*

doc′trine (dŏk′trĭn), *n.* [OF., fr. L. *doctrina*, fr. *doctor.* See DOCTOR.] **1.** *Archaic.* Teaching; instruction. **2.** That which is taught; a principle, or body of principles, in any branch of knowledge; tenet; dogma; principle of faith.

Syn. Doctrine, dogma, tenet mean a principle accepted as authoritative. **Doctrine** implies acceptance of a principle as taught by a body of believers or of adherents to a philosophy, a school, or the like; **dogma** implies a doctrine that is laid down as true and beyond dispute; **tenet** stresses acceptance and belief rather than teaching and applies to a principle that is held or adhered to.

doc′u·ment (dŏk′ū·mĕnt), *n.* [OF., fr. L. *documentum*, fr. *docere* to teach.] **1.** *Obs.* An example or warning; also, evidence; proof. **2.** An original or official paper relied upon as the basis, proof, or support of anything else; — in its broadest sense including any writing, book, or other instrument conveying information. — (-mĕnt), *v. t.* **1.** *Obs.* To teach; to instruct. **2.** To furnish documentary evidence of. **3.** To furnish with documents. **4.** To equip with exact references to authoritative information as proof of statements made; as, to *document* a book. — **doc′u·men′tal** (-mĕn′tăl; -t'l), *adj.*

doc′u·men′ta·ry (-mĕn′tȧ·rĭ), *adj.* **1.** Consisting of, or of the nature of, documents; contained or certified in writing. **2.** Recording or depicting in artistic form a factual and authoritative presentation, as of an event or a social or cultural phenomenon; as, a *documentary* journalist or film. — *n.* A documentary film.

doc′u·men·ta′tion (-mĕn·tā′shŭn), *n.* The provision of documents, copies, etc., in substantiation; also, documentary evidence, as in a treatise; use of historical documents, or conformity to the historical or objective facts.

dod′der (dŏd′ẽr), *n.* Any plant of a genus (*Cuscuta*, family Cuscutaceae) of leafless parasites with yellow or whitish threadlike stems.

dod′der (dŏd′ẽr), *v. i.* To shake; totter; potter.

dod′dered (-ẽrd), *adj.* Deprived of branches through age or decay, as an oak; hence, shattered; infirm.

dod′der·ing, *adj.* Senile; foolish; inane.

do′dec·a- (dō′dĕk·ȧ-), **dodec-.** [Gr. *dōdeka.*] A prefix meaning *twelve*, as in *dodeca*hedron.

do·dec′a·gon (dō·dĕk′ȧ·gŏn; -gŭn), *n.* [Gr. *dōdekagōnon*, fr. *dōdeka* + *gōnia* angle.] A polygon of twelve angles and therefore twelve sides. — **do′de·cag′o·nal** (dō′dĕ·kăg′ō·năl; -n'l), *adj.*

do′dec·a·he′dron (dō′dĕk·ȧ·hē′drŭn), *n.; pl.* -HEDRONS (-drŭnz), -HEDRA (-drȧ). [Gr. *dōdekaedron*, fr. *dōdeka* twelve + *hedra* seat, base.] *Geom. & Cryst.* A solid having twelve plane faces. In the ***regular dodecahedron*** these faces are twelve equal regular pentagons. — **do′dec·a·he′dral** (-drăl), *adj.*

dodge (dŏj), *v. i. & t.;* DODGED (dŏjd); DODG′ING (dŏj′ĭng). [Origin uncert.] **1.** To start suddenly aside, as to avoid a blow; to evade by a sudden shift of position. **2.** To evade a duty by low craft; to practice mean shifts. — *n.* Act of evading by some skillful movement; hence, an artful device to evade, deceive, or cheat; a cunning trick.

dodg′er (dŏj′ĕr), *n.* **1.** One who dodges or evades; esp., one who uses tricky devices. **2.** *U. S. & Australasia.* A small handbill. **3.** A cake made of Indian meal.

do′do (dō′dō), *n.; pl.* DODOES or DODOS (-dōz). [Pg. *doudo*, prop., silly.] A large, heavy, flightless bird (*Didus ineptus*), now extinct, related to the pigeons, but larger than a turkey, formerly found in Mauritius.

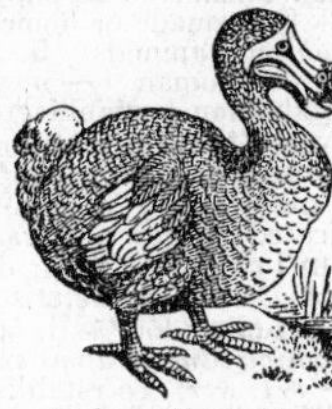

Dodo. (About 1/20)

Do′do·nae′an, Do′do·ne′an (dō′dō·nē′ăn), *adj.* Of or pertaining to the oracle of Zeus at ancient Dodona, in Epirus. Its responses were interpreted from the rustling of oak leaves.

doe (dō), *n.* [AS. *dā*.] The female of almost any species of deer, antelope, hare, or other animal whose male is called a *buck;* — not properly applied to the female of the elk or moose (called *cow*) or red deer (which see).

do′er (dōō′ĕr), *n.* One who does; an agent.

does (dŭz; 4), *3d pers. sing. pres.* of DO.

doe′skin′ (dō′skĭn′), *n.* The skin of the doe, or leather made of it; hence, a firm woolen cloth with a smooth, soft surface like a doe's skin, for men's wear. — **doe′-skin′**, *adj.*

doff (dŏf; 73), *v. t.* [*do* + *off*.] To put off, as dress; to remove or lift (the headgear); hence, to put or thrust away; to rid oneself of.

dog (dŏg; 74), *n.* [AS. *docga*.] **1.** A carnivorous domesticated mammal (*Canis familiaris*), type of the family Canidae. Cf. HOUND. **2.** A male dog. **3.** A mean worthless fellow; a wretch. **4.** *Colloq.* **a** A rascally fellow. **b** Ostentatious style or affected dignity. **5.** Short for DOGFISH, PRAIRIE DOG, etc. **6.** [*cap.*] *Astron.* Either of the constellations Canis Major (***Greater Dog***) or Canis Minor (***Lesser Dog***). **7.** *Mech.* Any of various devices for holding, gripping, or fastening something, as one consisting of a spike or bar of metal with a ring, hook, claw, or lug at the end. Cf. CRAMPON, *Illust.* **8.** A firedog; an andiron. **9.** *Meteorol.* A sundog, fogdog, etc. — *v. t.;* DOGGED (dŏgd); DOG′GING (dŏg′ĭng). To hunt or track like a hound; to worry as if by dogs. — *adv.* Extremely; utterly; — used in combinations; as, **dog′-cheap′, dog′-poor′, dog′-sick′, dog′-tired′, dog′-wea′ry.**

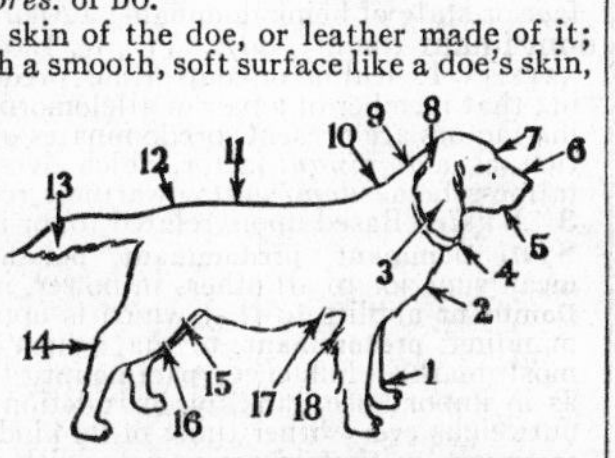

Dog, 1. 1 Pastern; 2 Chest; 3 Leather; 4 Dewlap; 5 Flews; 6 Muzzle; 7 Stop; 8 Occiput; 9 Crest; 10 Withers; 11 Loin; 12 Rump; 13 Feather; 14 Hock; 15 Stifle; 16 Knee; 17 Brisket; 18 Elbow.

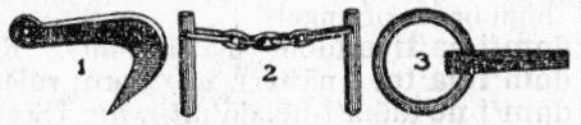

Dogs, 7, used in logging. 1 Regular form; 2 Chain Rafting Dog; 3 Ring Dog.

dog ape. A baboon, or allied ape.

dog′bane′ (dŏg′bān′), *n.* Any plant (genus *Apocynum*) typifying a family (Apocynaceae, the dogbane family) of chiefly tropical, mostly poisonous plants with milky juice and often showy flowers. The oleander and periwinkle are cultivated species.

dog′ber′ry (-bĕr′ĭ; -bĕr·ĭ), *n.* **1.** The fruit of the dogwood *Cornus sanguinea*. **2.** Any of several other plants, or their fruits; as: **a** *United States.* (1) The chokeberry. (2) The yellow clintonia. See CLINTONIA. **b** *Local, Eng.* The guelder-rose, dog rose, or bearberry.

dog′cart′ (-kärt′), *n.* **1.** A cart drawn by a dog or dogs. **2.** A light one-horse carriage, commonly two-wheeled and high, with two transverse seats set back to back.

dog′-day′ ci·ca′da. See CICADA.

dog days. A period of from four to six weeks between early July and early September; popularly, the sultry, close part of the summer. Cf. CANICULAR.

doge (dōj), *n.* [It., fr. L. *dux, ducis*, leader.] The chief magistrate in the former republics of Venice (697–1797) and Genoa (1339–1797 and 1802–05). — **doge′dom** (-dŭm), *n.* — **doge′ship**, *n.*

dog′-ear′, *n. & v.* = DOG'S-EAR. — **dog′-eared′**, *adj.*

dog fennel. a = MAYWEED. **b** = HEATH ASTER.

dog′fight′ (dŏg′fīt′), *n.* A fight as between dogs; a melee; specif., in aerial warfare, a free-for-all engagement involving several planes in daring maneuvers at close quarters. — **dog′fight′**, *v. i. & t.*

dog′fish′ (dŏg′fĭsh′), *n.; pl.*, see FISH. Any of various small sharks, esp. the ***spiny, or piked, dogfish*** (*Squalus acanthias* or *S. suckleyi*) of the North Atlantic or California coasts, and the ***smooth dogfish*** (*Cynias canis, Mustelus mustelus*, etc.) of North Atlantic and southern European waters.

dog fox. A male fox.

dog′ged (dŏg′ĕd; -ĭd), *adj.* Stubbornly determined; tenacious. — **Syn.** See OBSTINATE. — **dog′ged·ly**, *adv.* — **dog′ged·ness**, *n.*

dog′ger (dŏg′ĕr), *n.* A broad-bowed, two-masted, ketchlike fishing vessel, used in the North Sea.

dog′ger·el (dŏg′ĕr·ĕl), *adj.* Also **dog′grel** (dŏg′rĕl). Low in style and irregular in measure; undignified; trivial; as, *doggerel* rhymes. — *n.* A sort of loose or irregular verse, esp. burlesque or comic.

dog′ger·y (dŏg′ĕr·ĭ), *n.; pl.* DOGGERIES (-ĭz). **1.** Doglike behavior. **2.** Dogs collectively; rabble; canaille.

dog′gish (dŏg′ĭsh), *adj.* **1.** Like a dog; esp., currish; snapping. **2.** Stylish in a showy way. — **dog′gish·ly**, *adv.* — **dog′gish·ness**, *n.*

dog′go (dŏg′ō), *adv. Slang.* In hiding; — in ***to lie doggo.***

dog′gy (dŏg′ĭ), *adj.;* DOG′GI·ER (-ĭ·ĕr); DOG′GI·EST. **1.** Doglike; doggish. **2.** *Colloq.* Pretentiously fashionable; stylish.

dog′gy, dog′gie (dŏg′ĭ), *n.; pl.* DOGGIES (-ĭz). A small dog.

dog′house′ (dŏg′hous′), *n.* **1.** A dog's kennel. **2.** *Colloq.* An ignominious state of repudiation or disfavor; — esp. in *in the doghouse.*

do′gie, do′gy (dō′gĭ), *n.; pl.* DOGIES (-gĭz). *Western U.S.* A motherless calf in a range herd; — a cowboy term.

dog in the manger. *Colloq.* One who follows a secretive or underhand policy, esp. to prevent others from enjoying something he does not himself want; — from a fable of Aesop.

dog Latin. Barbarous Latin; a jargon imitating Latin.

dog′-leg′ged (dŏg′lĕg′ĕd; -ĭd; -lĕgd′), *adj.* Also **dog′leg′** (-lĕg′). Crooked or bent like a dog's hind leg.

dog′ma (dŏg′mȧ; 74), *n.; pl.* DOGMAS (-mȧz), DOGMATA (-mȧ·tȧ). [L., fr. Gr. *dogma*, pl. *dogmata*, fr. *dokein* to think.] **1.** That which is held as an opinion; esp., a definite tenet; also, a code of such tenets. **2.** A doctrine or body of doctrines of theology and religion formally stated and authoritatively proclaimed by a church or sect. — **Syn.** See DOCTRINE.

dog·mat′ic (dŏg·măt′ĭk), *adj.* Also **dog·mat′i·cal** (-ĭ·kăl). **1.** Of or pertaining to dogma. **2.** Characterized by, or given to the use of, dogmatism; asserting a matter of opinion as if it were fact; hence, positive in manner or utterance. — **Syn.** See DICTATORIAL. — **dog·mat′i·cal·ly**, *adv.* — **dog·mat′i·cal·ness**, *n.*

dog·mat′ics (-ĭks), *n.;* see -ICS. The science treating of religious, esp. Christian, doctrines; doctrinal theology.

dog′ma·tism (dŏg′mȧ·tĭz′m), *n.* Positiveness in assertion in matters of opinion; derogatorily, such positiveness when unwarranted or arrogant. See SKEPTICISM, 1.

dog′ma·tist (-tĭst), *n.* One who dogmatizes.

dog′ma·tize (-tīz), *v. i. & t.* [ML. *dogmatizare* to lay down an opinion, fr. Gr. *dogmatizein*, fr. *dogma*.] To speak or write in a dogmatic way. — **dog′ma·ti·za′tion** (-tĭ·zā′shŭn; -tī·zā′-), *n.* — **dog′ma·tiz′er** (-tīz′ĕr), *n.*

do′-good′er (dōō′good′ĕr; 2), *n.* An earnest, usually impractical-minded humanitarian bent on promoting welfare work or reform; — commonly with a derogatory implication of naïveté or blundering ineffectualness. — **do′-good′** (2), *v. i.* — **do′-good′ism** (-ĭz′m), *n.*

dog rose. A common European wild rose (*Rosa canina*) having stout hooked prickles and light-pink single flowers.

dog's′-ear′ (dŏgz′ēr′), *n.* The corner of a leaf in a book, turned down like the ear of a dog. — *v. t.* To make a dog's-ear or dog's-ears in. — **dog's′-eared′** (-ērd′), *adj.*

dog's letter. The letter *r*, esp. when trilled.

dog's′-tail′, *n., or* **dog's-tail grass. a** Any grass of a genus (*Cynosurus*) of grasses having spikelike panicles. **b** The yard grass (*Eleusine indica*).

Dog Star. Sirius; also, sometimes, Procyon.

dog's′-tongue′, *n.* = HOUND'S-TONGUE.

dog tent. *Mil. Slang.* A shelter tent.

dog′tooth′ (dŏg′tōōth′), *n.; pl.* -TEETH (-tēth′). **1.** Also **dog tooth.** A canine tooth. **2.** *Arch.* An ornament common in early English Gothic, usually of four leaves radiating from a raised point at the center.

dog′tooth′ vi′o·let. Also **dog's′-tooth′ vi′o·let. a** A European bulbous herb (*Erythronium denscanis*) of the lily family, with two mottled basal leaves and a solitary nodding purple flower appearing in early spring. **b** Any of several related American species, esp. one (*E. americanum*) with yellow flowers, and one (*E. albidium*) with white flowers, often called *adder's-tongue.*

dog′trot′ (dŏg′trŏt′), *n.* A gentle trot, like that of a dog.

dog′vane′ (-vān′), *n. Naut.* A small vane carried on the weather rail to indicate the direction of the wind.

dog′watch′ (-wŏch′), *n.* A watch of two hours on shipboard. There are two, from 4 to 6 and from 6 to 8 P.M.

dog whelk. Any of certain thick-shelled marine snails, esp. of the genus *Alectrion* or family Alectrionidae. See GASTROPOD, *Illust.*

dog′wood′ (dŏg′wood′), *n.* Any tree or shrub of the genera *Cornus* and *Cynoxylon*, of the family Cornaceae (the dogwood family), including the ***red dogwood*** (*Cornus sanguinea*), the ***flowering dogwood*** (*Cornus florida;* the State flower of Virginia and North Carolina), the ***red osier dogwood*** (*Cornus stolonifera*), etc. Cf. CORNEL **a.**

do′gy (dō′gĭ). Var. of DOGIE.

doiled (doild), *adj. Dial.* Stupid; confused; dazed.

doi′ly (doi′lĭ), *n.; pl.* -LIES (-lĭz). [From the name of a London draper.] **1.** A small napkin. **2.** A small ornamental piece of linen or lace, for a table.

do′ing (dōō′ĭng), *n.* Usually *pl.* Anything done; deed; action.

doit (doit), *n.* [D. *duit*.] A former Dutch coin, equal to about ½ farthing; hence, a bit; a trifle.

doit′ed (doit′ĕd; -ĭt), *adj. Scot.* Turned to dotage; senile.

‖**dol′ce** (dōl′chā), *adj.* [It., fr. L. *dulcis* sweet, soft.] Soft; sweet; specif., *Music*, soft and smooth in execution.

‖**dol′ce**, *n.; pl.* DOLCI (-chē). [It., sweet, soft.] *Music.* A very soft flute organ stop of either 8-foot or 4-foot pitch. See STOP, *n.*

‖**dol′ce far nien′te** (fär nyĕn′tā). [It.] Literally, it is pleasant to do nothing; hence, delightful idleness.

dol′drums (dŏl′drŭmz), *n. pl.* **1.** Dullness; state of listlessness or boredom. **2.** A part of the ocean near the equator, abounding in calms, squalls, and light, baffling winds.

dole (dōl), *n.* [AS. *dāl* portion, same word as *dǣl*. See DEAL.] **1.** *Archaic.* One's part, lot, or destiny. **2.** A distribution, esp. of food or money; also, that which is so distributed; esp., a ration for the needy; alms. **3.** Payment out of public moneys made, beginning in 1918, by the British government to unemployed workers; hence, any government grant to the unemployed. — *v. t.* To deal out in small portions; distribute in the form of a dole. — **Syn.** See DISTRIBUTE.

dole, *n.* [OF. *dol, deol*, fr. L. *dolere* to suffer.] *Archaic.* Grief.

dole′ful (-fool; -f'l), *adj.* Full of grief; expressing or exciting sorrow. — **dole′ful·ly**, *adv.* — **dole′ful·ness**, *n.*

dol′er·ite (dŏl′ĕr·īt), *n.* [Gr. *doleros* deceptive; — because easily confounded with *diorite.*] *Petrog.* **a** Any coarse basalt. **b** *Eng.* Diabase. **c** *U. S.* Loosely, any dark igneous rock whose constituents are not determinable megascopically. — **dol′er·it′ic** (-ĭt′ĭk), *adj.*

dole′some (dōl′sŭm), *adj.* Doleful; dismal; gloomy.

dol′i·cho·ce·phal′ic (dŏl′ĭ·kō·sĕ·făl′ĭk), **dol′i·cho·ceph′a·lous** (-sĕf′ȧ·lŭs), *adj.* [Gr. *dolichos* long + *kephalē* head.] *Craniom.* Long-headed; having a cephalic index of less than 80. See CEPHALIC INDEX. — **dol'i·cho·ceph'a·lism** (dŏl'ĭ·kō·sĕf'ȧ·lĭz'm), *n.* — **dol'i·cho·ceph'a·ly** (-sĕf'ȧ·lĭ), *n.*

doll (dŏl), *n.* [For *Dorothy*, the proper name.] **1.** A child's puppet; a toy baby for a child. **2.** A pretty but empty-headed person, esp. a woman. — *v. i. & t. Slang, U. S.* To array (oneself) in fine, or one's best, attire; — with *up*. — **doll'ish**, *adj.* — **doll'ish·ly**, *adv.* — **doll'ish·ness**, *n.*

dol'lar (dŏl'ẽr), *n.* [LG. & D. *daler*, fr. G. *thaler* (now *taler*), for *Joachimst(h)aler*, i. e., a piece of money first coined, 1519, in the valley (G. *thal, tal*) of St. *Joachim*, in Bohemia.] **1.** Orig. the German taler; hence, any of various similar large coins, as: **a** Either of two silver coins issued by the British government for use in the Far East: (1) The ***Straits dollar***, used in Malaya and the Straits Settlements, no longer legal currency after 1948. (2) The ***Hong Kong****, or* ***British, dollar****,* used in Hong Kong. **b** The ***Maria Theresa****, or* ***Levant, dollar*** *or* ***thaler***, a silver coin originally minted in Austria bearing the image of Maria Theresa and the date, 1780, of first minting. It was issued for trade purposes and is still used as currency in some parts of the Near East, esp. in the interior regions. **c** A silver coin of Canada. **d** Any of three U. S. coins: (1) The ***silver dollar***, first issued in 1794 and since 1837 weighing 412.5 grains of silver .900 fine. Prior to 1873 it was the U. S. monetary unit. (2) A silver coin of 420 grains, called the ***trade dollar***, not coined since 1885. (3) The ***gold dollar*** of 25.8 grains .900 fine, minted 1849–1890. **2.** A paper currency note of the value of a dollar, used in several countries, as the U. S., Canada, Federation of Malaya, and Ethiopia. **3.** The monetary unit in various countries, as the U. S. (see STANDARD DOLLAR), Canada, Ethiopia, Federation of Malaya, Liberia, British Honduras, and Hong Kong. See MONEY, *Tables*. **4.** The value of a dollar; one hundred cents. Symbol, $ or $, usually placed before the sum; also, often in large sums, written without ciphers, as $16.4 billion. **5.** See PESO. **6.** = YUAN.

dollar diplomacy. Diplomacy used to promote the financial or commercial interests of a country abroad.

dol'lar·fish' (dŏl'ẽr·fĭsh'), *n.; pl.*, see FISH. A small, spiny-finned, smooth-scaled marine fish (*Poronotus triacanthus*, family Stromateidae) with a laterally compressed body; — called also *butterfish*.

dol'lop (dŏl'ŭp), *n.* A lump; a large hunk.

doll'y (dŏl'ĭ), *n.; pl.* DOLLIES (-ĭz). **1.** A child's name for a doll. **2.** *Dial. Eng.* A wooden instrument used to beat or stir clothes in the process of washing. **3.** A small wheeled truck for moving heavy beams, columns, etc. **4.** *Mach.* A heavy bar with a cupped head for holding against the made head of a rivet while the other end is being headed. **5.** *Mining.* A contrivance, turning on a vertical axis by a handle or winch, for stirring ore to be washed. **6.** *Motion Pictures.* A wheeled platform on which a camera is mounted, for ready movement about a set. **7.** *Railroads.* A compact narrow-gauge locomotive for moving construction trains, switching, etc.

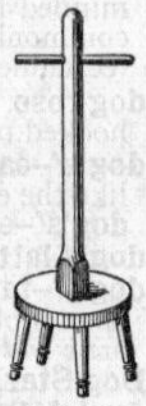
Dolly, 2.

Doll'y Var'den (vär'd'n). **1.** In Dickens's *Barnaby Rudge*, a beautiful, lively, and brightly dressed girl. **2. a** A style of dress made with a pointed bodice and a skirt of bright, flowered material draped over a skirt of plain color. **b** A large hat for women, having one side bent down and trimmed with many flowers.

Dolly Varden trout. See TROUT.

dol'man (dŏl'măn), *n.; pl.* -MANS (-mănz). [F. *doliman, dolman*, through G. & Hung., fr. Turk. *dōlāmān*.] A woman's cloak with capelike pieces instead of sleeves.

dolman sleeve. A sleeve cut to fit a very large armhole and give a capelike outline to a garment.

dol'men (dŏl'mĕn), *n.* [F.] *Archaeol.* A monument consisting of several megaliths arranged so as to form a chamber, usually regarded as a tomb. Cf. CROMLECH.

dol'o·mite (dŏl'ō·mīt), *n.* [After D. de *Dolomieu*, French geologist.] **a** *Mineral.* A calcium magnesium carbonate of varying proportions, $(Ca,Mg)CO_3$. It includes much of the common white marble. **b** *Petrog.* A limestone or marble rich in magnesium carbonate.

do'lor, do'lour (dō'lẽr; dŏl'ẽr), *n.* [OF. *dolor*, fr. L. *dolor*, fr. *dolere* to suffer.] *Poetic.* Grief; distress; anguish.

dol'or·ous (dŏl'ẽr·ŭs; dō'lẽr-), *adj.* **1.** Painful; grievous. **2.** Sorrowful; doleful. — **dol'or·ous·ly**, *adv.* — **dol'or·ous·ness**, *n.*

dol'phin (dŏl'fĭn), *n.* [OF. *daulphin, daufin* (F. *dauphin* dolphin, dauphin), fr. L. *delphinus* dolphin, fr. Gr. *delphis*.] **1.** Any of various cetaceans (genus *Delphinus* and allies, family Delphinidae) having the snout produced into a beak. The common dolphin (*D. delphis*) becomes about seven feet long. The ***bottle-nosed dolphin*** (*Tursiops truncatus*), called also *bottlenose* and popularly *porpoise*, is the best-known American species. **2.** Either of two active pelagic spiny-finned fishes (genus *Coryphaena*, family Coryphaenidae) noted for their brilliant colors when taken out of the water. **3.** [*cap.*] *Astron.* The Delphinus. **4.** A mooring spar or buoy.

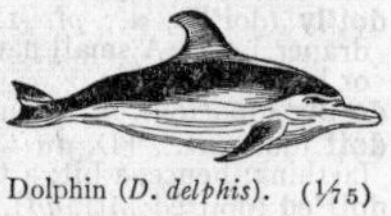
Dolphin (*D. delphis*). (1/75)

dolphin striker. *Naut.* A vertical spar under the end of the bowsprit, to extend and support the martingale, or a stay supporting the jib boom; — called also *martingale*.

dolt (dōlt), *n.* A heavy stupid fellow. — **dolt'ish**, *adj.* — **dolt'ish·ly**, *adv.* — **dolt'ish·ness**, *n.*

dom (dŏm; *Pg.* dōN, thōN), *n.* [Pg.] **1.** A title used in addressing ecclesiastics; — now used only by Benedictines and a few monastic orders. **2.** In Portugal and Brazil, a title given to certain members of the higher classes, prefixed to the Christian name.

-dom (-dŭm). [AS. *-dōm*; from same root as *doom* judgment.] A suffix forming nouns with the meanings: **a** *Dignity, office, dominion, realm*, or *jurisdiction* (of); as in king*dom*, Christen*dom*. **b** *State, condition*, or *fact of being*, esp. with adjectives, as in free*dom*, state of being free. **c** In a secondary sense, *a total of those having the given office, occupation, interest, character*, or *state*, as in official*dom*.

do·main' (dō·mān'), *n.* [F. *domaine*, fr. L. *dominium*, fr. *dominus* master, owner.] **1.** An estate held in possession; landed estate. **2.** The territory over which dominion is exerted; hence, sphere of action, thought, influence, etc.

dome (dōm), *n.* [L. *domus* a house.] **1.** *Chiefly Poet.* A building; a mansion. **2.** *Arch.* [F. *dôme*, through Pr., fr. LL. *doma* a roof, house, fr. Gr. *dōma*.] A large hemispherical roof structure; a cupola, esp. a large one. **3.** Any erection or natural formation resembling the dome or cupola of a building. **4.** *Cryst.* A form composed of planes parallel to a lateral axis which meet above in a horizontal edge, like a roof. If the planes are parallel to the longer lateral axis, it is called a ***macrodome***; if parallel to the shorter, a ***brachydome***. See PRISM, 3. — *v. t.* To cover with or as if with a dome; to shape like a dome. — *v. i.* To swell outward like a dome.

Do'mei' (dō'mā'), *n.* In full **Do'mei' Tsu'shin'–sha'** (tsōō'shĕn'-shä'). [Jap. *domei* federation.] The official Japanese Federated News Agency.

domes'day' (dōōmz'dā'; dŏmz'dā'), *n.* A day of judgment. A var. of DOOMSDAY, now chiefly used in **Domesday Book**, the record of a great survey of the lands of England, made, 1085–86, by order of William the Conqueror.

do·mes'tic (dō·mĕs'tĭk), *adj.* [F. and L.; F. *domestique*, fr. L. *domesticus*, fr. *domus* house.] **1.** Of or pertaining to the household or family; as, *domestic* duties. **2.** Of or pertaining to, or made in, a nation considered as one's own country; internal; as, *domestic* trade. **3.** Homemade or home-grown; native. **4.** Domesticated; tame; as, *domestic* animals. **5.** Devoted to home duties or pleasures; as, a *domestic* woman. — *n.* **1.** A house servant. **2.** *pl.* Articles of home production or manufacture. — **do·mes'ti·cal·ly** (-tĭ·kăl·ĭ), *adv.*

do·mes'ti·cate (-tĭ·kāt), *v. t. & i.* To make or become domestic. — **do·mes'ti·ca'tion** (-kā'shŭn), *n.*

do'mes·tic'i·ty (dō'mĕs·tĭs'ĭ·tĭ), *n.* State of being domestic or domesticated; domestic character.

dom'i·cal (dōm'ĭ·kăl; dŏm'-), *adj.* Relating to, or shaped like, a dome; also, characterized by domes.

dom'i·cile (dŏm'ĭ·sĭl; 56), *n.* Also **dom'i·cil**. [F. *domicile*, fr. L. *domicilium*, fr. *domus* house.] A place of residence; a dwelling place. — *v. t. & i.* To establish in a domicile; to settle or dwell. — **dom'i·cil'i·ar'y** (-sĭl'ĭ·ĕr'ĭ *or, esp. Brit.*, -sĭl'yȧ·rĭ), *adj.*

dom'i·cil'i·ar (-sĭl'ĭ·ẽr), *n.* A member of a minor order of canons.

dom'i·cil'i·ate (-āt), *v. t. & i.* To domicile.

dom'i·nance (dŏm'ĭ·năns), *n.* Also **dom'i·nan·cy** (-năn·sĭ). The fact or state of being dominant; authority.

dom'i·nant (-nănt), *adj.* [F., fr. L. *dominans, -antis*. See DOMINATE.] **1.** Ruling or controlling; predominant. **2.** *Biol.* Designating that member of a pair of allelomorphs which, when both contrasting factors are present, predominates over the other in its manifestation; as, a *dominant* factor, which gives rise to a *dominant* character; tallness being *dominant*, dwarfness recessive. See MENDEL'S LAW. **3.** *Music.* Based upon, related to, or in the key of, the dominant.

Syn. **Dominant, predominant, paramount, preponderant, sovereign** mean superior to all others in power, influence, position, or the like. **Dominant** applies to that which is uppermost as in ruling or commanding; **predominant**, to that which for the time being exerts the most marked influence; **paramount**, to that which has supremacy as in importance, rank, or jurisdiction; **preponderant**, to that which outweighs every other thing of its kind in power, influence, or force; **sovereign**, to that in comparison with which every other thing of its kind is subordinate, inferior, or of lower value.

— *n. Music.* The fifth note of the scale; — from its harmonic importance.

dom'i·nate (-nāt), *v. t. & i.* [L. *dominatus*, past part. of *dominari* to dominate, fr. *dominus* master, lord.] To predominate over; rule; control.

dom'i·na'tion (-nā'shŭn), *n.* **1.** Act of dominating; exercise of power in ruling; sovereignty; often, arbitrary or insolent sway. **2.** *pl.* A high order of angels.

dom'i·na'tive (dŏm'ĭ·nā'tĭv), *adj.* Ruling; imperious.

dom'i·na'tor (-nā'tẽr), *n.* Lord; ruler; ruling power.

dom'i·ne (dŏm'ĭ·nē; dō'mĭ-), *n.* [See DOMINIE.] *Obs.* Lord; master; — used as a title of respect.

‖**do'mi·ne, di'ri·ge nos** (dŏm'ĭ·nē, dĭr'ĭ·jē nōs). [L.] Lord, direct us; — motto of the City of London.

dom'i·neer' (dŏm'ĭ·nēr'), *v. i. & t.* [D. *domineren*, fr. F. *dominer*, fr. L. *dominari*. See DOMINATE.] To rule with insolence or arbitrary sway; to be overbearing.

dom'i·neer'ing (dŏm'ĭ·nēr'ĭng), *adj.* That domineers; tyrannical. — **Syn.** See MASTERFUL. — **Ant.** Subservient. — **dom'i·neer'ing·ly**, *adv.* — **dom'i·neer'ing·ness**, *n.*

do·min'i·cal (dō·mĭn'ĭ·kăl), *adj.* [ML. *dominicalis*, fr. L. *dominicus* of a master or lord, fr. *dominus* master, lord.] **1.** Of or pertaining to Jesus Christ as Lord. **2.** Designating, or pertaining to, the Lord's day, or Sunday.

dominical letter. In church calendars, that letter of the first seven in the alphabet which designates the first Sunday of any given year, and consequently all Sundays of that year; as, for 1938, B; 1939, A; 1940 (leap year), G & F.

Do·min'i·can (dō·mĭn'ĭ·kăn), *adj.* [ML. *Dominicanus*, fr. *Dominicus, Dominic*.] Of or pertaining to St. Dominic (Domingo de Guzmán, 1170–1221), or the religious communities named from him. — *n.* One of an order of mendicant preaching friars, founded by St. Dominic in 1215.

dom'i·nie (dŏm'ĭ·nĭ; *in sense* 2 *usually* dō'mĭ·nĭ), *n.* [L. *domine*, vocative of *dominus* master.] **1.** *Scot.* A schoolmaster. **2.** *U. S.* Properly, a pastor of the Reformed Dutch Church; hence, *Colloq.*, any minister.

do·min'ion (dō·mĭn'yŭn), *n.* [MF., fr. ML. *dominio*, equiv. to L. *dominium*.] **1.** Supreme authority; sovereignty. **2.** Territory governed. **3.** [*usually cap.*] One of the self-governing units (exclusive of Great Britain and the republics of India and Pakistan) included in the British Commonwealth of Nations. **4.** *pl.* = DOMINATION, 2. — **Syn.** See POWER.

Dominion Day. In Canada, a legal holiday, July 1st, anniversary of the proclamation of the Dominion in 1867.

Dom'i·nique' (dŏm'ĭ·nēk'), *n.* [F., Dominica.] An American breed of domestic fowls with rose combs, yellow legs, and barred plumage; — called also **Dom'i·nick** (dŏm'ĭ·nĭk).

do·min'i·um (dō·mĭn'ĭ·ŭm), *n.* [L. See DOMAIN.] *Law.* Ownership; control; authority.

dom'i·no (dŏm'ĭ·nō), *n.; pl.* -NOES, -NOS (-nōz). [F., fr. L. *dominus* master. The *domino* was orig. a hood worn by the canons of a cathedral.] **1.** A masquerade costume, consisting of a robe with a hood, and a light half mask. **2.** A kind of mask; esp., a half mask. **3.** A person wearing a domino. **4.** *pl.* A game played with flat, oblong pieces, or men, dotted after the manner of dice; — used with a singular verb. Also, *sing.*, one of these pieces.

‖**Do'mi·nus vo·bis'cum** (dŏm'ĭ·nŭs vō·bĭs'kŭm). [L.] The Lord (be) with you; — a liturgical phrase addressed by the priest to the people in celebrating the Mass.

don (dŏn; *Sp.* dōn, tħōn), *n.* [Sp., fr. L. *dominus* master.] **1.** [*cap.*] Sir; Mr.; — a title in Spain. **2.** A Spanish nobleman or gentleman. **3.** A grand personage; esp., *Colloq.*, a head, tutor, or fellow in a college of Oxford or Cambridge.

don (dŏn), *v. t.;* DONNED (dŏnd); DON'NING. [*do* + *on;* — opposed to *doff.*] To put on, or dress in, as a garment.

‖**Do'ña** (dō'nyä; thō'-), *n.* [Sp. See DON, DUENNA.] **a** Lady; madam; — a Spanish title of respect prefixed to the Christian name of a lady. **b** [*not cap.*] A Spanish lady.

‖**Do'na** (dō'nȧ; thō'-), *n.* [Pg.] **a** A Portuguese title of courtesy corresp. to Sp. *Doña.* **b** [*not cap.*] A Portuguese lady.

Do'nar (dō'när), *n.* [OHG.] *Teut. Relig.* A Germanic deity, the god of thunder.

do'nate (dō'nāt *or, esp. Brit.,* dō·nāt'), *v. t. & i.* [L. *donatus,* past part. of *donare* to donate, fr. *donum* gift, fr. *dare* to give.] *Chiefly U. S.* To make a donation (of); to bestow; present. — **Syn.** See GIVE.

do·na'tion (dō·nā'shŭn), *n.* **1.** Act of giving. **2.** A gift.

Don'a·tism (dŏn'ȧ·tĭz'm), *n.* *Eccl. Hist.* The doctrines or beliefs peculiar to the Donatists.

Don'a·tist (-tĭst), *n.* *Eccl. Hist.* A member of a rigoristic party among the Christians of North Africa which went into schism (311–431) under Donatus.

don'a·tive (dŏn'ȧ·tĭv; dō'nȧ-), *n.* [L. *donativum.*] Gift; present.

done (dŭn), *past part.* of DO.

do'nee' (dō'nē'), *n.* The recipient of a gift.

Don'go·la kid *or* **leath'er** (dŏng'gō·lȧ). [See DONGOLA, *Gaz.*] A leather made by the **Dongola process,** a process of tanning goatskin, calfskin, or sheepskin, so that it resembles kid.

don'jon (dŭn'jŭn; dŏn'jŭn), *n.* [See DUNGEON.] A massive chief tower in ancient castles.

Don Ju'an (dŏn jōō'ăn; *Sp.* dōn hwän'). **1.** In Spanish tradition, a profligate nobleman of Seville who kills the father of a lady whom he has sought to seduce. **2.** An irresistible lover and seducer of women.

don'key (dŏng'kĭ; *form.* dŭng'kĭ), *n.; pl.* -KEYS (-kĭz). **1.** The ass. **2.** A stupid or obstinate fellow; an ass.

donkey engine. A small, usually portable, auxiliary engine.

don'na (dŏn'ȧ; *It.* dôn'nä), *n.; pl.* DONNE (*It.* dôn'nā). [It., fr. L. *domina.* See DAME.] A lady; madam; — title given a lady in Italy.

don'nered (dŏn'ẽrd), *adj.* *Chiefly Scot.* Stupefied.

don'nish (dŏn'ĭsh), *adj.* Pertaining to, or thought to resemble, a university don; pedantic. — **don'nish·ness,** *n.*

Don'ny·brook Fair (dŏn'ĭ·brŏŏk). An annual fair, noted for debauchery and fighting, formerly held at Donnybrook, Ireland; hence, any riotous occasion.

do'nor (dō'nẽr *or, esp. in Law,* dō'nôr, *and in contrast with* donee *often* dō'nôr'), *n.* [OF. *doneor,* fr. L. *donator,* fr. *donare* to give.] **1.** One who gives, donates, or presents; a giver. **2.** *Biol. & Med.* One furnishing blood (for transfusion) or tissue (for transplantation) to another. — **do'nor·ship,** *n.*

Don Quix'ote (dŏn kwĭk'sŏt; *Sp.* dōn kē·hō'tā). [Sp.] The title and hero of a Spanish romance (1605 and 1615), written by Cervantes to ridicule the books of chivalry. Don Quixote is a country gentleman who, crazed by his reading of the books of chivalry, rides forth to defend the oppressed and right wrongs.

don'sie (dŏn'sĭ), *adj.* *Dial.* Perverse; unlucky; ailing.

don't (dōnt; 4). Colloquial contraction of *do not;* — sometimes loosely used for *does not.*

don'zel (dŏn'zĕl), *n.* [It. *donzello.*] *Archaic.* A young squire; a page.

doo'dle (dōō'd'l), *n.* An aimless, more or less automatic scribble, outline, design, or improvised sketch traced while one is mentally occupied with something else. — *v. i.* To draw or trace a doodle or doodles. — *v. t.* To mark or overspread with doodles. — **doo'dler** (-dlẽr), *n.*

doo'dle, *n.* = 2d DOODLEBUG, 2.

doo'dle·bug' (dōō'd'l·bŭg'), *n.* Any unscientific device with which it is claimed that minerals may be located. Cf. DIVINING ROD.

doo'dle·bug', *n.* **1.** *U. S.* The larva of an ant lion; loosely, any of several other insects. **2.** Also **doo'dle.** = ROBOT BOMB.

doo'ly, doo'lie (dōō'lĭ), *n.; pl.* -LIES (-lĭz). Also **doo'lee, doo'ley, doo'li.** [Hind. *ḍolī.*] *East Indies.* A kind of litter borne on men's shoulders.

doom (dōōm), *n.* [AS. *dōm.*] **1.** *Hist.* A statute, law, or decree. **2.** A judgment or sentence. **3.** Specif., the Last Judgment (see JUDGMENT), as in *crack of doom* and *day of doom.* **4.** Destiny or fate; esp., unhappy destiny; hence, ruin; death. — **Syn.** See FATE. — *v. t.* **1.** To pronounce sentence or judgment on. **2.** To destine; to fix the fate of. **3.** To decree; ordain.

dooms (dōōmz), *adv.* *Chiefly Scot.* Very.

dooms'day' (dōōmz'dā'), *n.* [AS. *dōmes dæg.*] **1.** The day of the final judgment. **2.** A day of judgment, sentence, or condemnation.

Doomsday Book. = DOMESDAY BOOK.

door (dōr; 70), *n.* [AS. *dor, duru.*] **1.** The movable frame or barrier, usually turning on hinges or sliding, by which an entranceway is closed and opened; also, a similar part of a piece of furniture, as in a bookcase. **2.** A doorway. **3.** Passage; means of access.

☞ COMBINATIONS are:

doorkeeper	**doorpost**	**doorstep**
doorplate	**doorsill**	**doorway**

door'nail' (dōr'nāl'; 70), *n.* A large-headed nail; — chiefly in phrases, such as "as dead as a *doornail.*"

door'yard' (-yärd'), *n.* *U. S.* The yard about a house door.

dope (dōp), *n.* [D. *doop* a dipping, sauce, fr. *doopen* to dip.] **1.** Any thick liquid or pasty preparation, as of opium for medicinal purposes, of grease, etc. **2.** *Slang.* Any preparation, as of opium, used to stupefy; an opiate; also, a user of opiates. **3.** *Racing Slang.* Any preparation, as of opium, given to horses to stimulate them temporarily. **4.** Absorbent material, as sawdust, used in certain manufacturing processes, as in making dynamite. **5.** Any of various liquid preparations applied to, or introduced into, a substance or a liquid to increase its efficiency; specif.: **a** The material applied to the cloth surfaces on airplanes to strengthen and, by shrinking, to tighten those surfaces, and to act as a filler to ensure their being airtight. **b** The material applied to the rubberized fabric on airships to make it more gastight. **6.** *Slang, U. S.* Information; esp., confidential information. — *v. t.* **1.** To treat or affect with dope. **2.** *Slang.* To judge, guess, or predict the result of, as by the aid of special information. — **dop'er** (dōp'ẽr), *n.*

dope fiend. *Slang.* A drug addict.

dop'ey (dōp'ĭ), *adj.;* DOP'I·ER (dōp'ĭ·ẽr); DOP'I·EST. *Slang.* Affected by "dope"; esp., sluggish or dull as if doped.

‖**Dop'pel·gäng'er** (dôp'ĕl·gĕng'ẽr), *n.* = DOUBLEGANGER.

dor (dôr), *n.* *Obs.* A trick or joke.

dor'bee'tle (dôr'bē't'l), *n.* Also **dor, dor bug.** A common European dung beetle (*Geotrupes stercorarius*); also, the cockchafer or other beetle flying with a buzzing noise.

Dor'cas (dôr'kȧs), *n.* A Christian female disciple who made coats and garments for the poor. *Acts* ix. 36–41. Church sewing societies are often called **Dorcas Societies.**

Do'ri·an (dō'rĭ·ăn), *adj.* [L. *Dorius,* fr. Gr. *Dōrios.*] Doric. — *n.* One of a race which about the 12th century B.C. invaded Greece and settled in Doris, Laconia, etc.

Dor'ic (dŏr'ĭk), *adj.* **1.** Pertaining to Doris, in ancient Greece, or to the Dorians. **2.** *Arch.* Of, pertaining to, or designating the oldest and simplest of the Greek orders, or a modified Roman form of it. See ORDER, *Illust.* — *n.* The Doric dialect of Greek. See GREEK, *n.,* 4.

Dor'king (dôr'kĭng), *n.* [From *Dorking,* Surrey, Eng.] A large domestic fowl of an English breed.

dorm (dôrm), *n.* *Colloq.* A dormitory.

dor'man·cy (dôr'măn·sĭ), *n.* Dormant state.

dor'mant (-mănt), *adj.* [OF., pres. part. of *dormir* to sleep, fr. L. *dormire.*] **1.** Sleeping; appearing in a state of suspended animation; hence, inactive; quiescent; also, not disclosed, asserted, or insisted on. **2.** *Her.* In a sleeping posture; as, a lion *dormant.* **3.** *Bot.* Resting or nonvegetative; — applied to buds or other parts of a plant in winter, or to the plant. — **Syn.** See LATENT.

dor'mer (dôr'mẽr), *n.,* *or* **dormer window.** *Arch.* A window vertical in a roof; also, the houselike structure containing it. — **dor'mer-win'dowed,** *adj.*

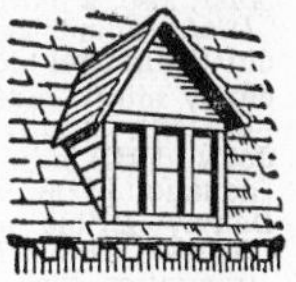
Dormer Window.

dor'mi·ent (dôr'mĭ·ĕnt), *adj.* [L. *dormiens, -entis,* pres. part of *dormire* to sleep.] Dormant; sleeping.

dor'mi·to'ry (dôr'mĭ·tō'rĭ *or, esp. Brit.* -tẽr·ĭ, -trĭ), *n.; pl.* -RIES (-rĭz). [L. *dormitorium,* fr. *dormitorius* of or for sleeping, fr. *dormire* to sleep.] A room, apartment, or building containing sleeping accommodations.

dor'mouse' (dôr'mous'), *n.; pl.* -MICE (-mīs'). Any of a family (Muscardinidae) of Old World rodents resembling small squirrels.

dor'my, dor'mie (dôr'mĭ), *adj.* *Golf.* Up, or ahead, as many holes as remain to be played; — said of a player or side.

dor'nick (dôr'nĭk), *n.* [Origin uncert.] *U. S.* A stone or boulder; specif., a boulder of iron ore found in limonite mines.

do·ron'i·cum (dō·rŏn'ĭ·kŭm), *n.* [NL., fr. Ar. *durūnaj, darūnaj.*] Any of a genus (*Doronicum*) of Eurasian plants of the thistle family (*Carduaceae*); — called also *leopard's-bane.* Several commonly cultivated species have showy yellow daisylike flowers.

dorp (dôrp), *n.* [D. See THORP.] A hamlet.

dorr (dôr), **dorr'bee'tle.** Vars. of DOR, DORBEETLE.

dor'sal (dôr'săl; -s'l), *adj.* [F., fr. L. *dorsualis,* fr. *dorsum* back.] **1.** Pertaining to, or situated near or on, the back, or dorsum, of an animal or of one of its parts; — opp. to *ventral.* **2.** *Bot.* Designating the surface turned away from the axis, as the underside of a leaf. — **dor'sal·ly,** *adv.*

dor'sal (dôr'săl; -s'l), *n.* [ML. *dorsale.*] An ornamental cloth hung at the back of a throne, altar, etc.

Dor'set Horn (dôr'sĕt; -sĭt). [From *Dorsetshire,* England.] A sheep of an English breed having very large horns, close-textured fleece, and wool of medium length.

dor'si- (dôr'sĭ-). [L. *dorsum* back.] A combining form meaning: **a** *Of* or *on the back,* as in **dor'si·col'umn, dor'si·com'mis·sure, dor·sif'er·ous, dor'si·spi'nal. b** = DORSO-.

dor'si·ven'tral (-vĕn'trăl), *adj.* [*dorsi-* + *ventral.*] **a** *Bot.* Having distinct dorsal and ventral surfaces, as most foliage leaves. **b** *Zool.* Dorsoventral.

dor'so- (dôr'sō-). [See DORSI-.] A combining form denoting *dorsal, dorsally, dorsal and,* as in **dor'so·cen'tral, dor'so·lat'er·al.**

dor'so·ven'tral (-vĕn'trăl), *adj.* [*dorso-* + *ventral.*] **a** *Zool.* Extending from the dorsal toward the ventral side; as, the *dorsoventral* axis. **b** *Bot.* Dorsiventral. — **dor'so·ven'tral·ly,** *adv.*

dor'sum (dôr'sŭm), *n.; pl.* DORSA (-sȧ). [L.] The back.

dort'y (dôr'tĭ), *adj.* *Dial.* Sulky; saucy; haughty.

do'ry (dō'rĭ; 70), *n.; pl.* DORIES (-rĭz). [Cen. Amer. Indian *dóri, dúri* dugout.] A flat-bottomed boat with flaring sides.

do'ry, *n.* [From its color, F. *dorée,* lit., gilded.] The John Dory (*Zeus faber*) or other allied fish.

dos'-à-dos' (dō'-zȧ·dō'; *in square dancing, commonly* dō'sē·dō'), *adv.* [F.] Back to back. — *n.; pl.* -DOS (-dōz'). A sofa, open carriage, or the like, so constructed that the occupants sit back to back.

dos'age (dōs'ĭj), *n.* **1.** Administration of medicine in doses; also, the amount of medicine or medicinal agent in a dose. **2.** The process of adding some ingredient, as to wine, to give flavor, character, or strength.

dose (dōs), *n.* [F., fr. ML., fr. Gr. *dosis* a giving, dose, fr. *didonai* to give.] **1.** The measured quantity of a medicine to be taken at one time or in a given period of time. **2.** A definite quantity of anything regarded as having a beneficial influence. **3.** Anything nauseous that one is obliged to take. **4.** An ingredient added to wine in dosage. — *v. t.;* DOSED (dōst); DOS'ING (dōs'ĭng). **1.** To give a dose or doses to; also, to give out in doses, as medicine. **2.** To treat by dosage, as champagne. — *v. i.* To take medicine. — **dos'er** (dōs'ẽr), *n.*

do·sim'e·ter (dō·sĭm'ē·tẽr), *n.* [ML. *dosis* dose + *-meter.*] An apparatus for measuring doses. — **do·sim'e·try** (-trĭ), *n.*

doss (dŏs), *n.* *Slang.* A bed or place to sleep; sleep.

dos'sal (dŏs'ăl), **dos'sel** (-ĕl), *n.* A dorsal or a dosser.

dos'ser (dŏs'ẽr), *n.* [OF. *dossier,* fr. *dos* back, fr. L. *dorsum* back.] **1.** A basket to be carried on a person's back or, in pairs, by a beast of burden. Cf. PANNIER. **2.** A cloth or tapestry for the back, esp. of a throne or chair.

doss house (dŏs). *Slang.* A cheap low-class lodginghouse.

dos'si·er (dŏs'ĭ·ā; -ĭ·ẽr; *F.* dô'syā'), *n.* [F.] A bundle of papers containing a detailed report or detailed information.

dos'sil (dŏs'ĭl), *n.* [OF. *dosil, duisil,* spigot, deriv. of L. *ducere* to conduct.] A pledget or compress of lint, as for a wound.

dost (dŭst; 4). *Archaic 2d pers. sing. indic. pres.* of DO.

dot (dŏt; *F.* dôt), *n.* [F., fr. L. *dos, dotis,* dowry.] *Civil Law.* A woman's marriage portion, or dowry, the income of which belongs to the husband during coverture. — **do'tal** (dō'tăl; -t'l), *adj.*

dot (dŏt), *n.* [AS. *dott.*] **1.** A small point made with a pointed instrument. **2.** A speck; also, a small, usually round, figure. **3.** *Colloq.* A precise point, as in time. **4.** *Music.* **a** A point placed after a note or rest to indicate increase in its length, by one half if one, or by three quarters if two. **b** A point placed over a note to indicate staccato. **5.** A short click on a telegraph sounder, forming a letter or part of a letter, as in the Morse code. Cf. DASH, *n.*, 12. — *v. t.;* DOT'TED; DOT'TING. **1.** To mark with or as with dots. **2.** To scatter or disperse like dots. — *v. i.* To make a dot or dots. — **dot'ter,** *n.*

dot'age (dōt'ĭj), *n.* [From DOTE, *v.*] **1.** Feeble-mindedness, esp. in old age; senility. **2.** Excessive fondness; doting.

do'tard (dō'tẽrd), *n.* A foolish old person; one whose mind is impaired by age.

dote (dōt), *v. i.* [ME. *doten, dotien.*] **1.** To be weak-minded, esp. from age. **2.** To be foolishly fond; to love to excess; — with *on* or *upon.* — **dot'er** (dōt'ẽr), *n.*

doth (dŭth; 4). *Archaic 3d pers. sing. pres.* of DO.

dot'ing (dōt'ĭng), *adj.* **1.** That dotes; senile; also, excessively fond. **2.** Decaying from age, as trees. — **dot'ing,** *n.* — **dot'ing·ly,** *adv.* — **dot'ing·ness,** *n.*

dot'ted swiss (dŏt'ĕd; -ĭd). A light muslin fabric ornamented with raised dots.

dot'ter·el (dŏt'ẽr·ĕl), **dot'trel** (-rĕl), *n.;* see PLURAL, *Note,* 3. [From DOTE, *v.*] **1.** A European and Asiatic plover (*Eudromias morinellus*); also, a plover of certain related species in other countries. **2.** *Dial.* A dupe; gull.

dot'tle, dot'tel (dŏt''l), *n.* Tobacco ash caked in the bowl of a pipe.

dot'ty (dŏt'ĭ), *adj.* [From DOT a point.] **1.** Dotted. **2.** *Colloq.* Unsteady in gait; hence, feeble; also, half-witted; crazy.

dot'y (dōt'ĭ), *adj.* Discolored by doting, as timbers.

‖**douane** (dwȧn), *n.* [F.] A customhouse.

Dou'ay' Bi'ble *or* **Ver'sion** (dōō'ā'; dōō'ā'; *in England usually* dou'ĭ). [From *Douay,* or *Douai,* a town in France.] An English translation (pub., New Testament, 1582; Old Testament, 1609–10) from the Latin Vulgate, for Roman Catholics. Abbr. *D.V.* See BIBLE.

dou'ble (dŭb''l), *adj.* [OF., fr. L. *duplus,* lit., twofold.] **1.** Twofold; made or being twice as great, as large, as much, as many, as strong, etc. **2.** Being in pairs; coupled. **3.** Being twofold in character, relation, structure, etc.; dual; not single; as, a *double* use; also, having two parts; as, a *double* boiler. **4.** Equivocal; deceitful; insincere. **5.** Folded; doubled. **6.** *Bot.* Having the floral leaves increased beyond the natural number, usually by cultivation. **7.** *Music.* Duple.
— *n.* **1.** Twice as much; twice the number, quantity, value, etc. **2.** A counterpart of another; duplicate. **3.** That which is doubled; fold. **4.** A turn or circuit in escaping; hence, trick; shift. **5.** One prepared to substitute for an actor, singer, etc.; understudy. **6.** *Astron.* A double star. **7.** *Baseball.* A hit on which a batter reaches second base. **8.** *Bridge.* A doubling of a bid or a hand justifying it. **9.** *Eccl.* One of a rank or class of church feasts. **10.** *pl. Games.* A game between two pairs of players. **11.** A combined bet placed upon two different contests, with especially high odds because of the greater risk, as in horse racing and greyhound racing. **12.** *Motion Pictures.* An anonymous actor or actress who takes the place of a principal, as for an athletic feat.
— *v. t.;* DOU'BLED (dŭb''ld); DOU'BLING (-lĭng). **1.** To make double as in size, number, or strength. **2.** To make of two thicknesses or folds; specif., to clench. **3.** To be the double of. **4.** To make a double, or circuit, of; also, to avoid by a double; elude. **5.** *Bridge.* To increase the trick point value of, or the trick penalty of, as the bid of an adversary. **6.** *Naut.* To pass or sail round; as, to *double* the cape. — *v. i.* **1.** To be or become double or doubled. **2.** To make a double, or return circuit. **3.** To serve or act as a double, for a double purpose, etc. **4.** To double something, as a bid.
— *adv.* Doubly; in a pair; two together.
— **dou'ble·ness,** *n.* — **dou'bler** (dŭb'lẽr), *n.*

double bar. See BAR, *n.*, 13.

double bass. *Music.* Contrabass. — **dou'ble–bass',** *adj.*

double bassoon. A large bassoon an octave lower in pitch than the common bassoon.

double boiler. A cooking utensil consisting of two vessels fitting into each other, the contents of the upper being cooked by boiling water in the lower.

dou'ble–breast'ed (*see Pron.*, § 2), *adj.* Lapping over the breast and having two rows of buttons; as, a *double-breasted* coat.

double cross. *Slang.* **a** The act or an instance of winning, or of doing one's best to win (a fight or a match), after engaging to lose. **b** A betraying, cheating, or the like, of an associate. — **dou'ble–cross',** *v. t.* — **dou'ble–cross'er,** *n.*

double dagger. *Print.* A mark of reference [‡], next in order after the dagger [†]; a diesis.

dou'ble–deal'ing, *n.* Duplicity. — **Syn.** See DECEPTION. — **dou'ble–deal'er,** *n.*

dou'ble–deck'er, *n.* A ship, bus, pier, etc., having two decks, floors, etc.

‖**dou'ble–en'ten'dre** (dōō'bl'·äN'täN'dr'), *n.* [F. *double* double + *entendre* to mean (the inf. used substantively). The usual French form is *double entente* ambiguity.] A word or expression admitting of two interpretations, one often indelicate.

double entry. A method of bookkeeping in which every transaction is recorded in two parts, in one place as a debit to one account and in another place as a credit to another account.

dou'ble–faced' (dŭb''l·fāst'; 2), *adj.* Hypocritical.

double first. *Eng. Univ.* The distinction of obtaining a first-class honors degree in two different subjects.

dou'ble·gang'er (dŭb''l·găng'ẽr), *n.* [G. *doppelgänger,* fr. *doppel* double + *gänger* walker.] A wraith of one alive.

dou'ble–head'er, *n.* *U.S. & Can.* **1.** A train with two engines at the front. **2.** Two games, as of baseball, between the same teams on the same day; also, two games between two different pairs of teams on the same occasion.

double image. *Surrealism.* A representation of an object which is at the same time without deformation a representation of a different object.

dou'ble–mind'ed, *adj.* Vacillating; also, deceitful.

double possessive. See POSSESSIVE, *n.*, **a.**

dou'ble–quick', *adj.* *Mil.* In marching, performed in the fastest time, or step, next to a run. — *n.* = DOUBLE TIME. — *v. t. & i.* To move, or cause to move, in double-quick time.

dou'ble–reed', *adj.* Designating a group of wind instruments having a mouthpiece of two reeds bound together, as the oboe.

dou'ble–rip'per, *n.* A long sled, made of two sleds connected by a board; — called also **dou'ble–run'ner.** Cf. BOBSLED.

double salt. *Chem.* **a** A salt, as Rochelle salt, yielding two different cations or anions. **b** A salt regarded as a molecular combination of two distinct salts.

double star. Two stars very near to each other and generally seen as separate only by means of a telescope. Such stars may be only optically near each other, that is, in nearly the same line of sight, or they may be physically connected (see BINARY STAR).

double stem. *Skiing.* A position for slowing down assumed by spreading the rear ends of the skis with pressure on the heels, and bringing the points close together.

dou'blet (dŭb'lĕt; -lĭt), *n.* [F., dim. of *double* double.] **1.** A close-fitting, often elaborate, jacket worn by men of Western Europe in the Renaissance. **2.** One of a pair; also, a pair. **3.** *pl.* Two thrown dice each of which has the same number of spots on the face lying uppermost. **4.** *Philol.* One of two words in the same language derived from the same original, as *guard* and *ward.*

dou'ble–take', *n.* A delayed reaction to the importance or meaning of something that at first escaped notice.

double talk. Talk or writing that to all appearances is earnest and meaningful but is actually a mixture of sense and gibberish.

double time. *Mil.* The quickest step in marching next to a run. In the U. S. Army it is 180 steps, of 36 inches each, to the minute.

dou'ble–tongue', *v. i.* To play staccato or similar notes, as on the flute, with vibrations of the tongue.

dou'ble·tree' (dŭb''l·trē'; -trĭ), *n.* The crosspiece of a vehicle, plow, or the like, to which the singletrees are attached.

double wing back formation. See WING BACK FORMATION.

dou·bloon' (dŭb·lōōn'), *n.* [F. or Sp.; F. *doublon,* fr. Sp. *doblón,* fr. *doble* double.] A former Spanish gold coin orig. equal to 16 dollars.

‖**dou'blure'** (dōō'blür'), *n.* [F.] Lining of a book cover, esp. one of tooled leather, painted vellum, or brocade.

dou'bly (dŭb'lĭ), *adv.* **1.** Twice. **2.** Deceitfully; as, to deal *doubly.* **3.** In a twofold manner; — used esp. in botany; as, *doubly* crenate, having crenations which are themselves crenate.

doubt (dout), *v. i.* [OF. *duter, douter,* to doubt, fear, fr. L. *dubitare.*] To waver in opinion; hesitate in belief; be undecided. — *v. t.* **1.** To question or hold questionable; be inclined not to believe; distrust. **2.** To be apprehensive of; fear; also, to suspect. — *n.* **1.** Unsettled state of opinion concerning the reality or the truth of something; lack of certainty. **2.** State of being uncertain, unsettled, etc.; as, the result is in *doubt.* **3.** *Obs.* Suspicion; dread. **4.** Difficulty expressed or urged for solution; point unsettled. — **Syn.** See UNCERTAINTY. — **doubt'a·ble** (dout'ȧ·b'l), *adj.* — **doubt'er** (-ẽr), *n.*

doubt'ful (-fōōl; -f'l), *adj.* **1.** Admitting of doubt; not obvious, clear, or certain. **2.** Of questionable character; dubious; equivocal. **3.** Not settled in opinion; undetermined. **4.** Being uncertain, as of an issue or event. — **doubt'ful·ly,** *adv.* — **doubt'ful·ness,** *n.*

Syn. **Doubtful, dubious, problematical, questionable** mean not affording one certainty of its (or his) worth, soundness, or the like. **Doubtful** is usually as positive as to impute worthlessness, dishonesty, or the like, to the person or thing in question; **dubious** stresses suspicion, mistrust, or hesitation in accepting, believing, choosing, or the like; **problematical** is especially applicable to something the existence, meaning, realization, etc., of which is so uncertain that the probabilities balance one another; **questionable** may imply little more than the existence of doubt concerning the thing so qualified. In its commonest use *questionable* is euphemistically employed in guarded statements where one does not wish to assert what he believes to be true (as, *questionable* dealings; a *questionable* character).

doubt'less, *adj.* Free from doubt. — *adv.* Undoubtedly; also, presumably. — **doubt'less·ly,** *adv.* — **doubt'less·ness,** *n.*

douce (dōōs), *adj.* [F. *doux,* masc., *douce,* fem., sweet, fr. L. *dulcis* sweet.] *Dial.* Genial; *Scot.*, sober; sedate.

‖**dou'ceur'** (dōō'sûr'), *n.* [F., fr. *doux* sweet.] **1.** Gentleness of manner; amiability. **2.** Honorarium; tip; often, a bribe.

douche (dōōsh), *n.* [F., fr. It. *doccia,* deriv. of L. *ducere* to lead.] **1.** A jet of water or vapor, directed upon or into a part of the body; also, a bath taken by such means. **2.** A douching instrument. — *v. t. & i.* To give or take a douche.

dough (dō), *n.* [ME. *dogh, dow, dagh,* fr. AS. *dāg.*] **1.** A soft mass of moistened flour or meal, thick enough to knead or roll, as in making bread; — disting. from *batter.* **2.** Anything of doughlike consistency. **3.** *Slang.* Money; cash.

dough'boy' (dō'boi'), *n.* *Colloq.* **a** A flour dumpling. **b** *U.S.* An infantryman.

dough'nut' (-nŭt'), *n.* A friedcake, specif. one of yeast-leavened dough.

dought (dout). *Scot.* Past of DOW, to be able.

dough'ty (dou'tĭ), *adj.;* DOUGH'TI·ER (-tĭ·ẽr); DOUGH'TI·EST. [AS. *dohtig.*] *Now Humorous.* Able; strong; valiant. — **dough'ti·ly,** *adv.* — **dough'ti·ness,** *n.*

dough'y (dō'ĭ), *adj.;* DOUGH'I·ER (-ĭ·ẽr); DOUGH'I·EST. Like dough; pasty.

Doug'las fir (dŭg'lȧs). Also **Douglas spruce, pine,** *or* **hemlock.** [After David *Douglas,* Scot. botanist in America.] A pinaceous timber tree of great size (*Pseudotsuga taxifolia*) of the western United States; — called also *red fir, Oregon pine.*

Dou'kho·bors. Var. of DUKHOBORS.

dou'ma (dōō'mä). Var. of DUMA.

dour (dōōr; dour), *adj.* [L. *durus.*] **1.** *Chiefly Scot.* Inflexible; stern; severe. **2.** Sour or sullen in aspect.

dou'ra, dou'rah (dōō'rȧ). Vars. of DURRA.

douse (dous), *v. t.* **1.** *Naut.* To lower in haste, as a sail; to stow. **2.** *Colloq.* **a** To take off; doff. **b** To extinguish. **3.** [Perh. a different word.] To duck; immerse; drench. — *v. i.* To be or become doused. — *n. Dial.* **a** A blow; stroke. **b** A drenching. — **dous'er** (dous'ẽr), *n.*

dou'ze·pers' (dōō'zē·pârz'), *n. pl.; sing.* DOU'ZE·PER' (-pâr'). [F. *les douze pairs* (OF. *per*).] A body of twelve peers or companions in French romance and history; esp., twelve paladins, or guards of honor, in Carolingian romances.

dove (dŭv), *n.* [ME. *dove, duve, douve.*] **1.** A pigeon; — applied specif. to many of the smaller species, as the *turtledove, mourning* *dove*, etc. **2.** One regarded as pure and gentle. **3.** The emblem of the Holy Spirit; sometimes [*cap.*], the Holy Spirit.

dove (dōv). Colloq. past tense of DIVE.

dove′cot′ (dŭv′kŏt′), **dove′cote′** (-kōt′; -kŏt′), *n.* A small, compartmented, raised house or box for domestic pigeons.

dove′kie (dŭv′kĭ), *n.* Also **dove′key.** [Dim. of DOVE.] **a** The black guillemot (*Cepphus grylle*). **b** A small short-billed auk (*Alle alle*) of arctic regions; — called also *rotche* or *little auk.*

Do′ver's pow′der (dō′vẽrz). [After Thomas *Dover* (1660–1742), Eng. physician.] An anodyne diaphoretic powder of ipecac and opium, now compounded in the United States with lactose, in England with potassium sulfate.

dove′tail′ (dŭv′tāl′), *n.* Anything shaped like a dove's tail; specif., a flaring tenon, tongue, or machine part so shaped. — *v. t. & i.* **1.** *Carp.* **a** To cut to a dovetail. **b** To join by dovetails. **2.** To fit in or connect strongly, or nicely.

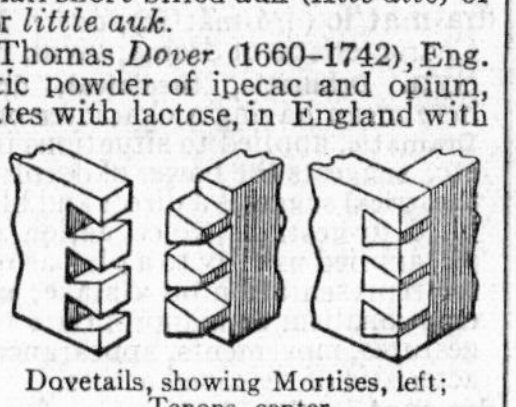

Dovetails, showing Mortises, left; Tenons, center.

dow (dou; dō), *v. i.* [AS. *dugan.*] *Scot.* To be able; also, to prosper.

dow′a·ger (dou′ȧ·jẽr), *n.* [OF. *douagiere*, fr. *douage* dower. See DOWER.] **1.** *Eng. Law.* A widow enjoying some property coming from her deceased husband. **2.** An elderly woman of dignity.

dow′dy (dou′dĭ), *adj.*; -DI·ER (-dĭ·ẽr); -DI·EST. [ME. *doude* a slovenly woman.] Not neatly, smartly, or becomingly dressed. — *n.*; *pl.* -DIES (-dĭz). **1.** A dowdy woman. **2.** A deep-dish fruit pie. — **dow′di·ly**, *adv.* — **dow′di·ness**, *n.* — **dow′dy·ish**, *adj.*

dow′el (dou′ĕl), *n.* Also **dowel pin.** A pin, fitting into a hole in an abutting piece to prevent motion or slipping. — *v. t.*; DOW′ELED (-ĕld) or DOW′ELLED; DOW′EL·ING or DOW′EL·LING. To fasten by, or furnish with, dowels.

dow′er (dou′ẽr), *n.* [OF. *douaire*, fr. ML. *dotarium*, fr. L. *dos* dower.] **1.** That portion of, or interest in, the real estate of a deceased husband which the law gives for life to his widow. **2.** Dowry. **3.** Endowment. — *v. t.* To supply with a dower; endow.

dow′itch·er (dou′ĭch·ẽr), *n.*; see PLURAL, *Note*, 3. [Of Iroquoian origin.] A long-billed snipe (*Limnodromus griseus*) intermediate between true snipes (genus *Capella*) and sandpipers.

down (doun), *n.* [AS. *dūn.*] **1.** A hill; esp., a hillock of sand thrown up by wind on or near the shore; — usually in *pl.* **2.** A tract of open upland; — usually in *pl.* **3.** [*cap.*] A sheep of any breed originating in the Downs of southern England, esp. one of the Southdown breed. — ***the Downs.*** **a** Treeless chalk uplands along the south coast of England. **b** A North Sea roadstead, near Deal.

down, *n.* [ON. *dúnn.*] **1.** A covering of soft fluffy feathers, as on young birds or under the ordinary feathers of adult birds; also, one of these feathers. **2.** Something downlike, as a soft hairy outgrowth on the face or on a plant; pubescence.

down, *adv.* [For older *adown*, fr. AS. *adūn*, *adūne*, *of dūne*, prop., from or off the hill.] **1.** Toward or in a lower position; below. **2.** Toward or upon the ground, floor, bottom, etc. **3.** To the full extent or capacity; as, to load *down*; to get *down* to work. **4.** From a past time; as, handed *down.* **5.** In a direction considered the opposite of *up.* **6.** To the metropolis, the country, the south, etc.; as, trains going *down.* **7.** From a greater to a less bulk, amount, etc. **8.** In cash or on the spot; as, to pay *down.* — *adj.* **1.** Downward; descending; going down. **2.** Gone, come, put, pulled, cut, paid, etc., down. **3.** Low, as in spirits or condition. **4.** *Football.* Of the ball, not in play because either: (1) Its holder cries "down," (2) its progress is wholly stopped, or (3) the officials stop the play for any reason. **5.** *Games.* Behind an opponent in the scoring or count, as of holes in golf; as, to be one *down.* — *prep.* Down through, along, toward, in, or upon. — *v. t. & i.* To go or come or cause to go or come down. — *n.* **1.** A descent; hence, a reverse. **2.** *Colloq.* A grudge; a dislike. **3.** *Football.* The termination by the referee of an attempt to advance the ball; also, the attempt or its duration.

down′beat′ (doun′bēt′), *n.* The downward stroke of the conductor's baton marking the principally accented note of a measure; also, this note.

down′-bow′ (doun′bō′), *n.* *Music.* In playing a bowed instrument, a stroke toward the point of the bow; — indicated by the sign ⊓. Cf. UP-BOW.

down′cast′ (doun′kȧst′; 9), *adj.* Cast down; esp., dejected.

down′fall′ (doun′fôl′), *n.* **1.** A fall, esp. a sudden or heavy fall, as of rain. **2.** A sudden descent as from rank, prosperity, or reputation; ruin. **3.** A trap in which a falling object holds or injures the prey. Cf. DEADFALL. — **down′fall′en** (-fôl′ĕn), *adj.*

down′grade′ (-grād′), *n.* A downward grade or slope; hence, a descent toward an inferior state. — *v. t.* To lower in status, rank, grade, etc.

down′haul′ (-hôl′), *n.* *Naut.* A rope to haul down, or to assist in hauling down, a sail; as, a staysail *downhaul.*

down′heart′ed (-här′tĕd; -tĭd; 2), *adj.* Dejected. — **down′heart′ed·ly**, *adv.* — **down′heart′ed·ness**, *n.*

down′hill′ (doun′hĭl′), *adv.* Towards the bottom of a hill. — (*see Pron.*, § 2), *adj.* Sloping downhill.

down′pour′ (doun′pōr′; 70), *n.* A pouring rain.

down′right′ (doun′rīt′; doun′rīt′), *adv.* **1.** *Now Rare.* Straight down. **2.** In plain terms; without ceremony. **3.** Thoroughly.

down′right′ (doun′rīt′), *adj.* **1.** *Archaic.* Directed vertically downwards. **2.** Unceremonious; blunt. **3.** Absolute; thorough; as, a *downright* lie. — **down′right′ly**, *adv.* — **down′right′ness**, *n.*

down′stage′ (doun′stāj′), *adv.* Toward or at the front of the stage. Cf. UPSTAGE. — *adj.* Of or pertaining to the front of the stage; hence, *Colloq.*, friendly.

down′stairs′ (-stârz′; 2), *adv.* Also **down′stair′** (-stâr′). Down the stairs; on or to a lower floor. — (-stârz′; 2), *adj.* Below stairs; as, a *downstairs* room.

down′stairs′ (doun′stârz′), *n.* The lower floor or floors of a house.

down′stream′ (doun′strēm′), *adv.* Down the stream. — (doun′strēm′; 2), *adj.* In the direction of flow of a stream.

down′town′ (doun′toun′), *adv.* To, toward, or in the business center of a town. — **down′town′** (doun′toun′; 2), *adj.*

down′trend′ (-trĕnd′), *n.* An incipient downward swing.

down′trod′den (doun′trŏd′′n; 2), *adj.* Also, esp. formerly, **down′trod′** (-trŏd′). Trampled down; oppressed.

down′ward (doun′wẽrd), **down′wards** (-wẽrdz), *adv.* **1.** From a higher to a lower place, condition, etc. **2.** From the past; from an ancestor or predecessor.

down′ward, *adj.* **1.** Moving or extending downward. **2.** Descending from a head, origin, or source. **3.** Tending to a lower state; dejected. — **down′ward·ly**, *adv.* — **down′ward·ness**, *n.*

down′y (doun′ĭ), *adj.*; -I·ER (-ĭ·ẽr); -I·EST. **1.** Having, or covered with, down, or with pubescence or soft hairs. **2.** Made of, or resembling, down; hence, soft; quiet. — **down′i·ness**, *n.*

dow′ry (dou′rĭ), *n.*; *pl.* -RIES (-rĭz). [Contr. from *dowery*, fr. OF. *douaire.* See DOWER.] **1.** A widow's dower. **2.** The money, goods, or estate which a woman brings to her husband in marriage; dot. **3.** A gift of property by a man to or for his bride; dower. **4.** Gift of nature; talent.

dow′sa·bel (dou′sȧ·bĕl), *n.* *Obs.* A sweetheart.

dowse (dous), **dows′er** (dous′ẽr). Vars. of DOUSE, DOUSER.

dowse (douz), *v. i.* To use the divining rod, as in search of water, ore, etc. — **dows′er** (douz′ẽr), *n.*

dox·ol′o·gy (dŏks·ŏl′ō·jĭ), *n.*; *pl.* -GIES (-jĭz). [ML. *doxologia*, fr. Gr. *doxologia*, fr. *doxologos*, deriv. of *doxa* opinion, glory, praise + *legein* to speak.] One of certain hymns or chants of praise to God; specif.: **a** The Gloria in Excelsis; — called the ***greater doxology.*** **b** The Gloria Patri; — called the ***lesser doxology.*** **c** A stanza beginning "Praise God from whom all blessings flow." — **dox′o·log′i·cal** (dŏk′sō·lŏj′ĭ·kăl), *adj.*

dox′y (dŏk′sĭ), *n.*; *pl.* DOXIES (-sĭz). *Slang.* A loose wench; harlot.

dox′y, *n.* [See ORTHODOXY, HETERODOXY, etc.] Opinion; doctrine; an ism; esp., religious opinion.

‖**doy′en′** (dwȧ′yăN′; *E.* dwä′yĕn, doi′yĕn), *n. masc.* [F. See DEAN.] A dean; the senior member of a body or group. — ‖**doy′enne′** (dwȧ′yĕn′), *n. fem.*

doy′ley, doy′ly (doi′lĭ). Vars. of DOILY.

doze (dōz), *v. i.* [Of Scand. origin.] To slumber; sleep lightly; be drowsy or dull. — *v. t.* To pass or spend in drowsiness. — *n.* A light sleep. — **doz′er** (dōz′ẽr), *n.*

doz′en (dŭz′′n), *n.*; *pl.* DOZEN (before another noun, and usually following a numeral), DOZENS (-′nz). [OF. *doseine*, fr. *douze* twelve, fr. L. *duodecim*, fr. *duo* two + *decem* ten.] A group, set, or collection of twelve. Abbr. *doz.* (sing. & pl.). — **doz′enth** (-′nth), *adj.*

doz′en (dōz′′n), *v. t.* *Chiefly Scot.* To stun; stupefy.

doz′y (dōz′ĭ), *adj.*; -I·ER (-ĭ·ẽr); -I·EST. Drowsy.

DP *or* **D.P.** (dē′pē′); *pl.* DPs, DP's, D.P.'s (-pēz′). Displaced person.

drab (drăb), *n.* [Origin obscure.] **1.** A slatternly woman. **2.** A loose woman; a prostitute. — *v. i.*; DRABBED (drăbd); DRAB′BING. To associate with drabs.

drab, *n.* [F. *drap* cloth, fr. LL. *drappus.*] **1.** A thick woolen fabric of dull brownish-yellow color. **2.** A brown, red-yellow in hue, of low saturation and medium brilliance. See COLOR. — *adj.*; DRAB′BER; DRAB′BEST. **1.** Of the color drab. **2.** Dull; monotonous. — **drab′ly**, *adv.* — **drab′ness**, *n.*

drab′bet (drăb′ĕt; -ĭt), *n.* [From DRAB cloth.] *Eng.* A coarse drab linen fabric, or duck, used for smock frocks, etc.

drab′ble (drăb′′l), *v. t.*; -BLED (-′ld); -BLING (-lĭng). To draggle.

dra·cae′na (drȧ·sē′nȧ), *n.* [NL., fr. Gr. *drakaina* she-dragon.] Also **dracaena palm.** Any of a genus (*Dracaena*) or of an allied genus (*Cordyline*) of shrubs or trees of the lily family, natives of the Old World tropics.

drachm (drăm), *n.* [See DRAM, DRACHMA.] **1.** A drachma. **2.** A dram.

drach′ma (drăk′mȧ), *n.*; *pl.* -MAS (-mȧz), -MAE (-mē), or -MAI (-mī). [L., fr. Gr. *drachmē.* See DRAM.] **1. a** A small ancient Greek weight of various values. **b** Any of several modern weights; esp., a dram. **2.** An ancient Greek silver coin, weighing one drachma. **3.** The monetary unit of modern Greece. It was stabilized in 1928 at $0.013 but stabilization was suspended in 1932. See MONEY, *Tables.*

Dra′co (drā′kō), *n.*; *genitive* DRACONIS (drā·kō′nĭs). [L. See DRAGON.] A northern circumpolar constellation within which is the north pole of the ecliptic.

Dra·co′ni·an (drā·kō′nĭ·ăn), *adj.* Of or pertaining to Draco, an Athenian archon, or the rigorous code of laws said to have been framed about 621 B.C. by him; hence, barbarously severe; harsh. — **Dra·co′ni·an·ism** (-ĭz′m), *n.*

dra·con′ic (drā·kŏn′ĭk), **dra·co′ni·an** (-kō′nĭ·ăn), *adj.* [L. *draco*, *-onis*, dragon. See DRAGON.] Of, relating to, or like a dragon.

Dra·con′ic, Dra·con′i·cal (-ĭ·kăl), *adj.* Draconian.

draff (drăf), *n.* Refuse; swill. — **draff′y** (-ĭ), *adj.*

draft, draught (drȧft; 9), *n.* [AS. *dragan* to draw.]

☞ Unless otherwise indicated, *draft* is the usual spelling. **1.** Act of drawing; also, the thing or the quantity drawn. **2.** Act of drawing loads, as by beasts of burden; also, formerly, a load. **3.** A delineating or representing; also, a drawing, map, plan, etc.; esp., a tentative sketch or outline. **4.** (Usually *draught.*) Act of drawing a net; also, the quantity of fish taken. **5.** (Usually *draught.*) A drinking or inhaling; also, the liquor, smoke, etc., taken in; hence, a drink; a dose. **6.** (Usually *draught.*) A drawing from a cask or keg on order; as, beer on *draught.* **7. a** A current, esp. of air. **b** Any contrivance for regulating the draft in a fireplace, stove, furnace, etc. **8.** An order from one person or party to another, directing the payment of money. **9.** A heavy demand; a strain. **10.** The detaching or selecting of certain individuals from a mass, esp. of men for compulsory military service; also, the group or a body so selected. **11.** *pl.* = DRAUGHTS. **12.** *Com.* An allowance granted for loss in weight. **13.** *Hydraul.* The area of an opening for discharge of water. **14.** *Masonry.* A narrow border, or stonecutter's guide, along the edge or across the face of a stone. **15.** *Mech.* Angle or taper; specif., the taper given to a pattern or die to enable the work to be easily withdrawn. **16.** *Naut.* The depth of water a ship draws, esp. when laden. — *v. t.* **1.** To make a draft or draught of, from, upon, etc. **2.** To draw by selection for a particular purpose, as men for military service. **3.** To draw away or off. — *adj.* **1.** Used for, or adapted to, drawing loads; as, a *draft* horse. **2.** (Usually *draught.*) On draught; also, drawn; as, *draught* beer; — disting. from *bottled.* **3.** Drafted. — **draft·ee′** (drȧf′tē′), *n.* — **draft′er, draught′er**, *n.*

draft horse. A horse for drawing loads, esp. heavy loads, as disting. from a saddle horse or carriage horse.

drafts′man, draughts′man (drȧfts′măn), *n.* **1.** One who draws pleadings or other writings. **2.** One who draws plans and sketches, as of machinery or structures. — **drafts′man·ship, draughts′man·ship**, *n.*

draft′y, draught′y (drȧf′tĭ), *adj.*; -I·ER (-tĭ·ẽr); -I·EST. Pertaining to, or exposed to, a draft, or current of air. — **draft′i·ly, draught′i·ly**, *adv.* — **draft′i·ness, draught′i·ness**, *n.*

drag (drăg), *v. t.;* DRAGGED (drăgd); DRAG′GING. [ME. *draggen,* fr. ON. *draga,* or perh. dial. fr. AS. *dragan.*] **1.** To draw slowly or heavily, esp. along the ground or other surface; haul. **2.** To draw along, as something burdensome; hence, to pass slowly, painfully, or tediously; as, to *drag* out one's life. **3.** To dredge or search with or as with a drag, grapnel, etc. **4.** To catch with a dragnet or trawl. — *v. i.* **1.** To be drawn along on the ground; trail. **2.** To fish, or search, with a drag. **3.** To lag behind. **4.** To move, pass, or proceed tediously; to be tiresomely protracted. — **Syn.** See PULL. — *n.* **1.** Act of dragging. **2.** Anything dragged; as: **a** A heavy harrow for breaking up ground. **b** A device for dragging under water, esp. along the bottom, as a grapnel, a dredger, etc. **3.** A sledge for conveying heavy bodies. **4.** A heavy coach with seats on top. **5.** Anything used to drag a body with, as a dragrope of a gun. **6.** Anything that retards; a clog. **7.** A dragging movement, as of the feet in walking. **8.** *Slang.* Influence; "pull"; special favor. **9.** *Aeronautics.* The component parallel to the relative wind of the total force on an airfoil or aircraft due to the air through which it moves. **10.** *Hunting.* **a** The scent trail. **b** Something drawn over the ground to leave a scented trail.

‖**dra′gée′** (drȧ′zhā′), *n.* [F.] **1.** A sugar-coated fruit or nut. **2.** A sweetmeat containing a portion of medicine at its center.

drag′gle (drăg′'l), *v. t.;* -GLED (-'ld); -GLING (-lĭng). [Freq. of *drag.*] To wet and soil by dragging, as on wet grass; drabble. — *v. i.* **1.** To be or become draggled. **2.** To straggle.

drag′gle-tail′ (-tāl′), *n.* **1.** A slattern who allows her gown to trail in the mire. **2.** Skirts that draggle.

drag′line′ (drăg′līn′), *n.* A dragrope; a guide rope.

drag link. A link joining the cranks of two shafts.

drag′net′ (drăg′nĕt′), *n.* A net to be dragged as in fishing or in clearing out small game; hence, a network of measures for pursuit, as of criminals.

drag′o·man (drăg′ō·măn), *n.; pl.* -MANS (-mănz), -MEN (-mĕn). [Through F. & It., fr. MGr. *dragomanos,* fr. Ar. *tarjumān.*] An interpreter; — so called in the Near East and Iran.

drag′on (drăg′ŭn), *n.* [OF., fr. L. *draco, -onis,* fr. Gr. *drakōn.*] **1.** *Now Rare.* A huge serpent. **2.** A fabulous animal, generally a monstrous winged scaly serpent, lizard, or saurian. **3.** A fierce or very strict person, esp. a woman; a duenna. **4.** Any of several plants of the arum family popularly associated with dragons, as the European ***green dragon*** (*Dracunculus vulgaris*) and the American ***green dragon*** (*Arisaema dracontium*). **5.** A word used in the Authorized Version to translate several Hebrew forms, some of which are translated by *jackal* or *serpent* in the Revised Version. **6.** Formerly, a short musket carried hooked to a soldier's belt; also, a soldier (dragoon) carrying such a musket. **7.** An armored tractor. **8.** Also ***flying dragon.*** Any of a genus (*Draco*) of small arboreal lizards of the East Indies and southern Asia. Some of the hind ribs, on each side, are prolonged and covered with weblike skin, aiding them in leaping from tree to tree. **9.** [*cap.*] *Astron.* The constellation Draco.

drag′on·et (drăg′ŭn·ĕt; -ĭt), *n.* [OF.] **1.** A little dragon. **2.** A small gobylike British marine fish (*Callionymus draco*); also, any fish of the same genus or family (Callionymidae).

drag′on·fly′ (drăg′ŭn·flī′), *n.* Any of an order (Odonata) of large harmless insects that feed on flies, gnats, and mosquitoes; — popularly known also as *darning needle.*

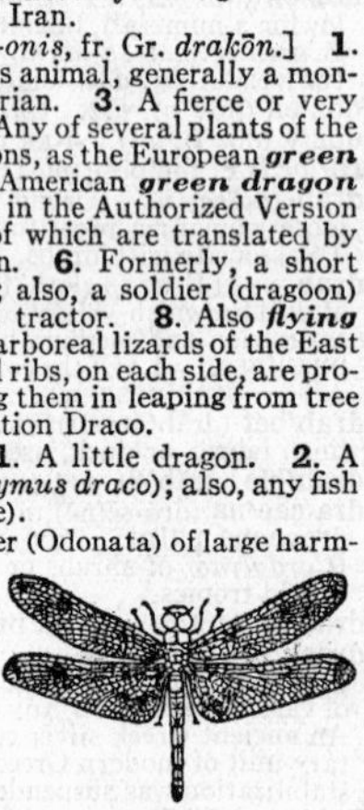

Dragonfly (*Diplax elisa*). (½)

drag′on·head′ (-hĕd′), *n.* Any of either of two genera (*Dracocephalum* and *Moldavica,* esp. *M. parviflora*) of mints.

drag′on·nade′ (drăg′ō·nād′), *n.* [F., fr. *dragon* dragoon.] Usually *pl.* **1.** The persecution of French Protestants under Louis XIV, esp. by dragoons. **2.** A devastating incursion.

drag′on's blood (drăg′ŭnz). Any of several resinous, mostly dark-red, substances derived from various trees, esp. that from the fruit of a Malayan palm (*Calamus draco*).

dragon's head, *or, chiefly in sense* 1, **drag′on's-head′,** *n.* **1.** *Bot.* = DRAGONHEAD. **2.** *Astron.* The ascending node of the moon or a planet. Symbol ☊.

dragon's tail. *Astron.* The descending node of the moon or a planet. Symbol ☋.

dragon tree. A tree (*Dracaena draco*) of the lily family, of the Canary Islands, yielding a variety of dragon's blood.

dra·goon′ (drȧ·gōōn′), *n.* [F. *dragon* dragon, dragoon. See DRAGON.] **1.** *Obs.* An ancient musket, or dragon. **2.** Formerly, a mounted infantryman; now, a cavalryman, usually heavily equipped. — *v. t.* To harass by or as if by dragoons; to subject to military persecution; also, to compel (to a certain course of action) as if by the use of dragoons.

drag′rope′ (drăg′rōp′), *n.* A rope that drags or is used for dragging; as: **a** A rope attached to an artillery carriage and used in dragging it or locking its wheels. **b** The rope dropped from an aerostat for use as a variable ballast, as a brake, or as a mooring line.

drag sail *or* **sheet.** A sea anchor made usually from a sail.

drain (drān), *v. t.* [AS. *drēhnigean, drēahnian.*] **1.** To draw off by degrees; to draw off utterly; exhaust; as, to *drain* pus. **2.** To make gradually dry or empty; hence, to empty of wealth, resources, etc. **3.** To filter. — **Syn.** See DEPLETE. — *v. i.* **1.** To flow off gradually. **2.** To become emptied by flowing or dripping of moisture. **3.** To empty its waters; as, the Middle Western States *drain* into the Gulf of Mexico. — *n.* **1.** Act of draining. **2.** A means of drainage, as a channel, trench, sewer, or sink. — **drain′er,** *n.* — **drain′pipe′** (-pīp′), *n.*

drain′age (drān′ĭj), *n.* **1.** Act, process, or mode of draining; also, that drained off. **2.** A drain; a device for draining; also, a system of drains. **3.** Area or district drained; as, the *drainage* of the Po.

drake (drāk), *n.* [AS. *draca* dragon, fr. L. *draco.* See DRAGON.] **1.** *Archaic.* A dragon. **2.** A small piece of artillery of the 17th and 18th century. **3.** In full **drake fly.** A May fly, sometimes used in angling.

drake, *n.* The male of members of the duck family, as the merganser, the swan, the goose.

dram (drăm), *n.* [OF. *drame,* fr. L. *drachma* drachm, drachma, fr. Gr. *drachmē,* prop., a handful, fr. *drassesthai* to grasp.] **1.** Abbr. *dr.* (sing. & pl.). **a** A weight. See WEIGHT, *Tables* 1 & 3. **b** A fluid dram. See MEASURE, *Table* 12. **2.** A small drink or draft, esp. of spirit. **3.** A mite; a bit. — *v. i. & t.;* DRAMMED (drămd); DRAM′MING. To drink drams; to ply with drams.

dra′ma (drä′mȧ; drăm′ȧ), *n.* [LL., fr. Gr. *drama,* fr. *dran* to do, act.] **1.** A composition in prose or verse portraying life or character by means of dialogue and action and designed for theatrical performance; a play. A ***closet drama*** is a play suited primarily for reading rather than for stage production. **2.** Dramatic art, literature, or affairs. **3.** A series of real events having dramatic unity and interest.

Dram′a·mine (drăm′ȧ·mēn; -mĭn), *n.* A trade-mark applied to a synthetic drug (chemically, a theophylline derivative), used especially for the relief of motion sickness.

dra·mat′ic (drȧ·măt′ĭk), *adj.* **1.** Of or pertaining to the drama. **2.** Characteristic of drama; vivid; moving.

Syn. **Dramatic, theatrical, dramaturgic, melodramatic, histrionic** here mean having a character or effect like that of some acted plays. **Dramatic,** applied to situations in real life, or in literature to speeches, etc., suggests the power of deeply stirring the imagination or emotions; **theatrical** suggests a direct and blatant appeal to the emotions or, as applied to gestures, voice, action, etc., a marked artificiality; **dramaturgic,** applied usually to a play as read or acted, suggests a decided fitness for representation on a stage; **melodramatic** suggests an exaggerated emotionalism or inappropriate theatricalism; **histrionic,** as applied to gestures, movements, appearance, etc., suggests likeness to those characteristic of seasoned actors.

dra·mat′i·cal (-ĭ·kăl), *adj.* Dramatic. — **dra·mat′i·cal·ly,** *adv.*

dra·mat′ics (-ĭks), *n. sing. & pl.;* see -ICS. Dramatic writings or performances, esp. of amateurs.

dram′a·tis per·so′nae (drăm′ȧ·tĭs pẽr·sō′nē). [L.] The characters or actors in a drama.

dram′a·tist (drăm′ȧ·tĭst), *n.* A playwright.

dram′a·tize (-tīz), *v. t.* **1.** To relate in the form of the drama; make into a drama. **2.** To give the character of a dramatic presentation to, as to one's acts; to make a dramatic scene of. — **dram′a·ti·za′tion** (-tĭ·zā′shŭn; -tī·zā′-), *n.* — **dram′a·tiz′er** (-tīz′ẽr), *n.*

dram′a·tur′gy (drăm′ȧ·tûr′jĭ), *n.* [F. & G. *dramaturgie,* fr. Gr. *dramatourgia* dramatic composition.] Art of dramatic composition and theatrical representation. — **dram′a·tur′gic** (-tûr′jĭk), **dram′a·tur′gi·cal** (-jĭ·kăl), *adj.* — **Syn.** See DRAMATIC. — **dram′a·tur′gi·cal·ly,** *adv.* — **dram′a·tur′gist** (-jĭst), *n.*

dram′mock (drăm′ŭk), *n.* Also **dram′mach** (-ŭĸ). *Dial.* A mixture of meal and water.

dram′shop′ (drăm′shŏp′), *n.* A barroom.

drank (drăngk), *past* of DRINK.

drape (drāp), *v. t.* [F. *draper,* fr. *drap* cloth.] **1.** To cover or adorn with or as with drapery. **2.** To arrange in decorative folds; to hang. — *v. i.* To design or arrange drapery. — *n.* A hanging or curtain of drapery. — **drap′er** (drāp′ẽr), *n.*

drap′er (drāp′ẽr), *n.* [AF. (OF. *drapier*).] Formerly, a maker of cloth; now, a dealer in cloths or dry goods.

dra′per·y (drā′pẽr·ĭ), *n.; pl.* DRAPERIES (-ĭz). **1.** Cloth; woolen stuffs. **2.** A draper's occupation and, formerly, shop. **3.** A textile fabric used for decorative purposes, esp. when hung loosely; also, hangings, as of a room or bed. **4.** The disposition of such draperies or their representation in art. — **dra′per·ied** (-ĭd), *adj.*

dras′tic (drăs′tĭk), *adj.* [Gr. *drastikos,* fr. *dran* to do, act.] Acting rapidly, violently, or harshly; extreme in effect; rigorous; as, *drastic* measures. — **dras′ti·cal·ly** (-tĭ·kăl·ĭ), *adv.*

D ration (dē). *U.S. Army.* An emergency ration consisting of three four-ounce bars of concentrated food, including chocolate and skim milk, each furnishing 600 calories and containing vitamin B_1.

draught (dráft; 9), **draughts′man,** etc. Vars. of DRAFT, etc.

draughts (dráfts), *n. Brit.* The game of checkers.

drave (drāv). Archaic & dial. past of DRIVE.

Dra·vid′i·an (drȧ·vĭd′ĭ·ăn), *n.* **1.** An individual of an ancient race in India, numerous in the south. **2.** The group of related languages of the Dravidians, including Tamil, Telugu, etc. — **Dra·vid′i·an,** *adj.*

draw (drô), *v. t.;* DREW (drōō); DRAWN (drôn); DRAW′ING. [AS. *dragan.*] **1.** To pull or use force upon so as to cause to follow or to come down, up, out, off, etc., as desired; as, to *draw* a cart. **2.** To cause to come, go, or move; as, to *draw* one aside; hence, to bring about or bring on; as, to *draw* troubles upon one. **3.** To attract; entice; allure; as, to *draw* a crowd. **4.** To inhale; also, to utter or produce by an inhalation; as, to *draw* a sigh. **5.** To require (a specified depth, as of water) for floating; — said of a vessel. **6.** To accumulate or gain. **7.** To bring forth or out by design or chance; as, to *draw* no reply. **8.** To remove the contents of, as by sucking, eviscerating, steeping, etc.; as, to *draw* a fowl or tea. **9.** To leave (a contest) undecided; to tie. **10.** To pucker, wrinkle, lengthen, etc., as if by pulling; also, to protract. **11.** To produce by tracing a pen or pencil over a surface; also, to delineate; hence, to produce or represent as if by drawing. **12.** To write in due form; as, to *draw* a deed. **13.** To formulate; as, to *draw* comparisons. **14.** To withdraw; as, to *draw* money from the bank. **15.** *Billiards.* To strike (the cue ball) below the center so as to give it a backward rotation which causes it to take a backward direction on striking another ball. **16.** *Cards.* To take (cards) from a dealer or from a stock. **17.** *Cricket.* To play (a short-length ball directed at the leg stump) with an inclined bat so as to deflect the ball between the legs and the wicket. **18.** *Curling.* To throw up (the stone) gently. **19.** *Mech.* To stretch, spread, or shape (metal) by passing through dies, by hammering, etc.; specif., to make a metal rod into (wire) by pulling it through a series of holes of diminishing size. — **Syn.** See PULL.

— *v. i.* **1.** To draw or move oneself; as, to *draw* near. **2.** To attract patrons, spectators, etc.; as, the play still *draws.* **3.** To draw something, usually understood; as, to *draw* on an assailant; the ship *draws* deep; the boy *draws* well. **4.** To stretch or to contract; esp., to shrink. **5.** To be drawn; to admit of being drawn; specif., of tea, to infuse. **6.** To make a draft or written demand for payment of money deposited or due; hence, to make a demand; serve as a drain. **7.** To produce or admit of a draft, or current, as a chimney. **8.** Of a hound, to track game by the scent; also, to approach the game cautiously after pointing. **9.** To be effective as an irritant or blistering agent, as a poultice. **10.** To come out even; play a drawn match.

— *n.* **1.** Act, process, or result of drawing; state of being drawn; specif., a drawn battle, game, etc. **2.** That which is drawn, or is subject to drawing; as: **a** An amount drawn. **b** A lot or chance drawn. **c** The movable part of a drawbridge. **3.** That which draws; an attraction. **4. a** In draw poker, the deal to improve the hands after players have discarded. **b** *Colloq.* = DRAW POKER (see POKER).

draw′back′ (drô′băk′), *n.* **1.** A loss of advantage, value, profit, etc.; also, a hindrance; objectionable feature; handicap. **2.** Money remitted after being collected; esp., duties or customs remitted by the government on the exportation of that on which they were levied.

draw′bar′ (drô′bär′), *n.* *Railroads.* A coupler.

draw′bore′ (-bōr′; 70), *n.* *Joinery.* A kind of bore for a mortise pin, designed to draw the tenon and thus make the joint tighter.

draw′bridge′ (-brĭj′), *n.* A bridge made to be drawn up, down, or aside, in order to admit or hinder passage. See BASCULE BRIDGE.

draw′ee′ (drô′ē′), *n.* The person on whom an order or bill of exchange is drawn; — correlative of *drawer.*

draw′er (drô′ẽr; drôr; *see def.* 2), *n.* **1.** One who or that which draws; as: **a** One who draws liquor. **b** A draftsman. **c** One who draws an order or bill of exchange; — correlative of *drawee.* Also, the maker of a promissory note. **2.** That which is drawn; as: **a** (*pron.* drôr) A sliding box or receptacle in a table, desk, etc. **b** *pl.* (*pron.* drôrz) An undergarment worn on the lower body and the legs.

draw′ing (drô′ĭng), *n.* **1.** Act of drawing. **2.** A small portion of tea for steeping. **3.** A picture, sketch, etc., made by drawing; also, the art of making such sketches.

drawing account. An account showing cash paid or available to a partner or employee, as for expenses; esp., one showing advances to a salesman.

drawing card. Anything, as a feature or performer, that attracts a great deal of attention or esp. patronage.

drawing room. [From *withdrawing room.*] **1.** A room for the reception or entertainment of company. **2.** The company assembled in such a room; also, a reception. **3.** *Railways.* A private compartment having a double-berth section, a lounge, and sometimes toilet facilities.

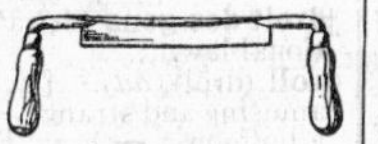

Drawknife.

draw′knife′ (drô′nīf′), *n.* Also **drawing knife.** A woodworker's tool having a blade with a handle at each end, used to shave off surfaces by drawing it toward one.

drawl (drôl), *v. t. & i.* [Prob. fr. *draw.*] To utter or speak in a slow, lengthened tone. — *n.* A drawling utterance. — **drawl′er,** *n.* — **drawl′ing·ly,** *adv.*

drawn (drôn), *past part.* of DRAW.

drawn butter. A sauce of melted butter, often thickened.

drawn work. Ornamentation, esp. of linens, by drawing parallel threads and uniting the cross threads to form a pattern.

draw′plate′ (drô′plāt′), *n.* A die plate for drawing wires.

draw poker. See POKER.

draw′shave′ (-shāv′), *n.* A drawknife.

draw′tube′ (-tūb′), *n.* A sliding or telescopic tube, as that supporting the eyepiece and objective of a microscope.

dray (drā), *n.* [AS. *dræge* a dragnet, *dragan* to drag.] A strong, low cart or wagon, without permanent sides, used for carrying heavy loads. — *v. t. & i.* To carry on or drive a dray.

dray′age (drā′ĭj), *n.* Work or cost of draying.

dray′man (drā′măn), *n.* One whose work is draying.

dread (drĕd), *v. t. & i.* [AS. *drǣdan,* in comp.] **1.** To fear greatly; to have terror or apprehension (of). **2.** *Archaic.* To stand in awe of. — *n.* **1.** Great fear, esp. of impending evil. **2.** Reverential fear; awe. **3.** An object of fear or awe. — **Syn.** See FEAR. — *adj.* **1.** Exciting great fear; dreaded. **2.** Inspiring with awe; venerable.

dread′ful (-fo͝ol; -f'l), *adj.* **1.** Inspiring fear or awe. **2.** Distressing; shocking; very distasteful. — **Syn.** See FEARFUL. — *n.* A morbidly sensational story or periodical; as, a penny *dreadful.* Cf. 2d SHOCKER, DIME NOVEL. — **dread′ful·ly,** *adv.* — **dread′ful·ness,** *n.*

dread′nought′, dread′naught′ (drĕd′nôt′), *n.* **1.** A fearless person. **2.** A warm garment made of very thick cloth; also, the cloth. **3. a** [*cap.*] A British battleship of 17,000 tons, completed 1906–07, having an armament of ten 12-inch guns, and twenty-four 12-pound quick-fire guns. **b** Hence [*not cap.*], any battleship having its main armament entirely of big guns all of one caliber. Since the Dreadnought was built, the size of battleships and the caliber of the heaviest guns have greatly increased. The term *superdreadnought* is popularly applied to these greater battleships.

dream (drēm), *n.* [ME. *dream, dreme.*] **1.** A series of thoughts, images, or emotions occurring during sleep; any seeming of reality occurring to one sleeping. **2.** A state of mind of one who is abstracted or lost in imaginary visions; reverie; daydreaming. **3.** An imaginary vision or a reality suggestive of such a vision. — *v. i.;* DREAMED (drēmd; 25) or DREAMT (drĕmt; 89); DREAM′ING. **1.** To have a dream or dreams. **2.** To indulge in daydreams. **3.** To conceive as possible or probable; — with *of.* — *v. t.* **1.** To have a dream of; dream of. **2.** To spend or pass in dreaming; — with *away, out,* etc.

dream up. *Colloq.* To invent, devise, or concoct, esp. in an outburst of artistic improvisation or an unbridled flight of fancy.

— **dream′er,** *n.* — **dream′ful,** *adj.* — **dream′ing·ly,** *adv.* — **dream′less,** *adj.* — **dream′like′** (-līk′), *adj.*

dream′land′ (drēm′lănd′), *n.* An unreal delightful country such as is sometimes pictured in dreams; fairyland.

dream world. Dreamland; a world of illusions.

dream′y (-ĭ), *adj.;* DREAM′I·ER (-ĭ·ẽr); DREAM′I·EST. **1.** Abounding in dreams or given to dreaming; causing dreams. **2.** Like, or characteristic of, a dream; soothing; languid; as, *dreamy* music. — **dream′i·ly,** *adv.* — **dream′i·ness,** *n.*

drear (drēr), *adj.* Melancholy; gloomy; doleful.

drear′y (drēr′ĭ), *adj.;* DREAR′I·ER (-ĭ·ẽr); DREAR′I·EST. [AS. *drēorig* sad, bloody.] **1.** *Now Rare.* Sad; doleful. **2.** Exciting cheerless sensations, feelings, or associations; dismal; gloomy. — **drear′i·ly,** *adv.* — **drear′i·ness,** *n.* — **drear′i·some,** *adj.*

dredge (drĕj), *n.* [From the root of DRAW, DRAG.] **1.** An oblong iron frame, with a bag net attached, dragged over the sea bottom, used esp. for gathering shellfish. **2.** A dredging machine; also, a boat used in dredging. — *v. t. & i.;* DREDGED (drĕjd); DREDG′ING. To catch, gather, excavate, search, etc., with or as with a dredge. — **dredg′er** (drĕj′ẽr), *n.*

dredge, *v. t.* To sprinkle with flour or the like; also, to sift or sprinkle as flour. — **dredg′er,** *n.*

dredg′ing ma·chine′. A machine for scooping up or removing earth, as in excavating, deepening channels, etc.

dree (drē), *v. t.* [AS. *drēogan.*] *Chiefly Scot.* To undergo; suffer. — *adj.* Also **dreegh** (drēк). Tedious.

dreg (drĕg), *n.; pl.* DREGS (drĕgz). [ON. *dregg.*] **1.** (Usually *pl.*) Corrupt matter in a liquid, or precipitated from it; lees; grounds; sediment; hence, the most worthless part of anything. **2.** A remnant; residue.

‖**Drei′bund′** (drī′bo͝ont′), *n.* [G., fr. *drei* three + *bund* league.] A triple alliance; specif., the alliance of Germany, Austria-Hungary, and Italy, formed in 1882, ended by Italy's entry, on the side of the Allies, into World War I in 1915.

drench (drĕnch), *v. t.* [AS. *drencan* to give to drink, to drench.] **1.** To cause to drink; esp., to dose by force; hence, to purge violently by physic; to scour. **2.** To wet thoroughly; soak; saturate. — **Syn.** See SOAK. — *n.* **1.** A drink; a draft; esp., a forced dose or a purgative potion. **2.** Act of drenching. **3.** Something that drenches; esp., a solution for soaking. — **drench′er,** *n.*

dress (drĕs), *v. t.;* DRESSED (drĕst) or DREST; DRESS′ING. [OF. *dresser, drecier,* to arrange, deriv. of L. *dirigere* to direct, fr. *dis-* + *regere* to rule.] **1.** To address with severity; rebuke; — now *Colloq.,* with *down* or *off.* **2.** To prepare for display; array; adorn. **3.** To clothe; esp., to clothe in formal attire. **4.** To make ready; to prepare for use. **5.** To do up (hair) attractively. **6.** To trim, embellish, etc., as by polishing, arranging, or garnishing. **7.** To cultivate, till, prune, or weed. **8.** To treat with remedies, bandages, etc., as a wound. **9.** To arrange in exact line, as soldiers; align. — *v. i.* **1.** To dress oneself, esp. in formal clothes. **2.** *Mil.* To arrange oneself in due position in a line of soldiers; — the word of command to form alignment in ranks.

dress ship. *Naut.* To hoist the national colors and run lines of signal flags and other bunting from point to point; specif., *U. S. Navy,* to hoist an ensign of the largest size at the flagstaff, and ensigns at each masthead. — ***dress up*** *or* ***out.*** To dress formally or showily.

— *n.* **1.** Clothes; apparel; attire; raiment; as, full *dress.* **2.** A lady's gown. **3.** Guise; form.

— *adj.* **1.** Pertaining to or used for a dress or dresses; as, *dress* goods. **2.** Pertaining to or suitable for a ceremonial or formal occasion; as, *dress* clothes, uniform; also, requiring or permitting formal dress.

dres·sage′ (drĕ·säzh′; *F.* drĕ′sȧzh′), *n.* [F.] *Manège.* Guidance of a mount through a set of maneuvers without perceptible use of the hands, reins, legs, etc.

dress circle. A circle or section of seats, often a balcony, as in a theater, where dress clothes are, or were formerly, worn.

dress′er (drĕs′ẽr), *n.* One who or that which dresses.

dress′er, *n.* [F. *dressoir.*] **1.** A table or bench on which meat and other things are dressed. **2.** A cupboard to hold dishes and cooking utensils. **3.** A chest of drawers or bureau, with a mirror.

dress′ing, *n.* **1.** Act of dressing. **2.** That which is used to dress anything; specif.: **a** Dress; raiment. **b** Manure, crushed stone, etc., spread over land, as a field or road. **3.** Castigation; a beating or scolding; — often with *down.* **4.** *Cookery.* A sauce or condiment to add to certain dishes, as a salad; also, the seasoned mixture, as of bread, spices, etc., often used to stuff poultry or roasts. **5.** *Surg.* An application to a sore or wound.

dressing gown. A loose robe worn while dressing or lounging.

dressing sack. A loose jacket worn while dressing.

dressing station. *Mil.* A medical establishment for administering early assistance to the wounded in battle.

dressing table. **1.** A low table or stand with a mirror for use by a person making a toilet; — called also *vanity* or *vanity table.* **2.** A table on which something is dressed.

dress′mak′er (drĕs′māk′ẽr), *n.* One, esp. a woman, who makes dresses or similar articles of clothing. — *adj.* Of women's clothes, having certain feminine effects associated with the dressmaker's art; — contrasted with *tailor-made.*

dress′mak′ing (drĕs′māk′ĭng), *n.* Art, process, or occupation of making dresses.

dress parade. *Mil.* A formal parade in dress uniform of troops in a camp, cantonment, or the like.

dress rehearsal. A rehearsal of a play in costume and with properties, usually the final rehearsal before performance.

dress′y (drĕs′ĭ), *adj.;* DRESS′I·ER (-ĭ·ẽr); DRESS′I·EST. **1.** Showy in dress. **2.** *Colloq.* Of garments, ornaments, etc., stylish; smart. — **dress′i·ness,** *n.*

drew (dro͞o), *past* of DRAW.

drib′ble (drĭb′'l), *v. i.;* DRIB′BLED (-'ld); DRIB′BLING (-lĭng). [Freq. of DRIB.] **1.** To fall in, or as in, drops; to trickle. **2.** To slaver; drivel. **3.** In various games, to dribble the ball. — *v. t.* **1.** To let fall in drops or driblets. **2.** In various games, to propel (the ball) by successive slight taps, kicks, or the like, keeping it always in control. — *n.* **1.** A small trickling stream; a driblet. **2.** *Colloq.* A drizzling shower. **3.** An act of dribbling a ball. — **drib′bler** (-lẽr), *n.*

drib′let, drib′blet (drĭb′lĕt; -lĭt), *n.* A small piece; a small quantity; a falling drop.

driech, driegh (drēк). Vars. of DREE.

dri′er (drī′ẽr), **dri′est,** *compar. & superl.* of DRY, *adj.*

dri′er, dry′er (drī′ẽr), *n.* **1.** One who or that which dries. **2.** A substance dissolved in paints, varnishes, etc., to make them dry more quickly. **3.** *In this sense usually* **dry′er.** A device for drying, esp. by heat or forced ventilation.

drift (drĭft), *n.* [ME.; akin to E. DRIVE.] **1.** Act of driving; propulsion; also, controlling influence; as, inspired by the *drift* of public opinion. **2.** State of being driven; act or motion of drifting. **3.** The course on which anything is driven. **4.** Tendency of an act, argument, or the like; purport; also, import or meaning. **5.** That which is driven, forced, or urged along; as: **a** Anything driven at random. **b** A driving storm or cloud, as of snow or dust. **6.** A mass of matter, as of snow or sand, that has been piled together in a heap by the wind. **7.** A tool used for ramming down or driving anything. **8.** *Aeronautics.* **a** The lateral velocity of an aircraft, due to air currents, etc. **b** Also **drift angle.** The angular deviation from a set course due to cross currents of wind. **9.** *Civil Engin.* A small tunnel driven to connect two larger shafts or to guide excavation. **10.** *Geol.* Rock material deposited in one place after having been moved from another; as, river *drift.* **11.** *Mining.* A mine passageway driven on, or parallel to, the course of a vein or rock stratum. **12.** *Naut.* The deviation of a ship from its set course caused by currents; rarely, leeway. **13.** *Phys. Geog.* One of the slower movements of oceanic circulation; as, the easterly *drift* of the North Pacific. — **Syn.** See TENDENCY. — *v. i. & t.* **1.** To float or be driven along by or as by a current of water or air. **2.** To pile up in heaps by the force of wind. — **drift′er,** *n.*

drift′age (drĭf′tĭj), *n.* **1.** The process of drifting; also, deviation due to drifting. **2.** Anything that drifts.

drift′wood′ (drĭft′wo͝od′), *n.* Wood drifted by water; figuratively, that which is drifting or floating as on water.

drift'y (drĭf'tĭ), *adj.;* DRIFT'I·ER (-tĭ·ẽr); DRIFT'I·EST. Full of drifts; also, tending to form drifts, as snow.

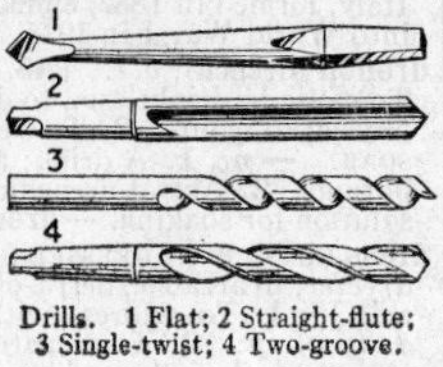

Drills. 1 Flat; 2 Straight-flute; 3 Single-twist; 4 Two-groove.

drill (drĭl), *n.* [See DRILL to bore.] **1.** An instrument for boring holes in hard substances. **2.** Act or exercise of training soldiers in the military art, as in the manual of arms. **3.** Hence, any exercise, physical or mental, enforced with regularity and by constant repetition. **4.** Manner or style of drilling. **5.** A marine snail (*Urosalpinx cinerea*) very destructive to oysters. — *v. t. & i.* [D. *drillen* to bore, drill (soldiers).] **1.** To pierce or bore with or as with a drill; to perforate. **2.** To train in the military art. **3.** To instruct thoroughly in any art or branch of knowledge; to discipline. — **Syn.** See PRACTICE.

drill, *n.* [See MANDRILL.] A West African baboon (*Papio leucophaeus*). It is smaller than the mandrill.

drill, *v. t.* **1.** To sow, as seeds, by dribbling them along a furrow. **2.** To sow (ground) in drills. — *n. Agric.* **a** An implement for planting seeds, usually by making holes or furrows into which it drops them. **b** A light furrow into which seed is sown. **c** A row of seed sown in a furrow.

drill, *n.* [From earlier *drilling*, fr. G. *drillich*, fr. L. *trilix* having three threads.] A heavy fabric of linen or cotton, having a diagonal weave.

drill chuck. See CHUCK, *Illust.* (2).

drill'er (drĭl'ẽr), *n.* One who or that which drills, or bores holes, trains persons, sows seed, etc.

drill'ing (drĭl'ĭng), *n.* Drill, the fabric.

drill'ing, *n.* Act of one that drills.

drill'mas'ter (drĭl'màs'tẽr), *n.* One who teaches drill or by drilling; esp., one who teaches or oversees military drill.

drill press. A metal-drilling machine the drill of which is pressed to the metal by hand or by power.

drill'stock' (drĭl'stŏk'), *n. Mach.* A frame or head for holding a drill spindle or a drill.

dri'ly (drī'lĭ). Var. of DRYLY.

drink (drĭngk), *v. t.; past* DRANK (drăngk), formerly also DRUNK (drŭngk); *past part.* DRUNK, DRUNK'EN; *pres. part.* DRINK'ING. *Drunken* is now rarely used except as a verbal adj. in sense of intoxicated. [AS. *drincan.*] **1.** To swallow (a liquid); to imbibe. **2.** To take in (a liquid), in any manner; to absorb. **3.** To take in; to receive through the senses; to inhale, hear, see, etc. **4.** To drink a toast to; as, to *drink* the President. — *v. i.* **1.** To swallow anything liquid; to imbibe; to receive something as if in satisfaction of thirst. **2.** To drink intoxicating liquors, as convivially; hence, to take alcoholic liquors to excess; to tipple. **3.** To drink a toast; as, to *drink* to your good health. — *n.* **1.** Liquid to be swallowed; a beverage. **2.** Intoxicating liquor. **3.** Excessive indulgence in intoxicating liquor. **4.** A potion; a draft.

drink'a·ble (drĭngk'à·b'l), *adj.* Capable of being drunk; suitable for drink. — *n.* A beverage; — usually in *pl.*

drink'er (drĭngk'ẽr), *n.* One who drinks; esp., one who drinks intoxicating liquors to excess; a drunkard.

drip (drĭp), *v. t.;* DRIPPED (drĭpt) or DRIPT; DRIP'PING. [AS. *dryppan.*] To let fall in drops. — *v. i.* **1.** To let fall drops of moisture or liquid. **2.** To fall in, or as in, drops. — *n.* **1.** A falling in drops; also, that which drips; dripping. **2.** *Arch.* That part of a cornice, sill course, etc., which projects to throw off rain water; also, an overlapping metal strip for the same purpose.

drip'ping, *n.* **1.** A letting fall drop by drop. **2.** Often *pl.* That which drips; specif., fat and juice dripped from roasting meat; esp., such fat used as shortening, etc.

dripping, *or* **drip, pan.** A pan for catching drippings.

drip'stone' (drĭp'stōn'), *n.* **1.** *Arch.* A stone drip. **2.** Calcium carbonate, $CaCO_3$, in the form of stalactites or stalagmites.

drive (drīv), *v. t.; past* DROVE (drōv), formerly also DRAVE (drāv); *past part.* DRIV'EN (drĭv'ĕn); *pres. part.* DRIV'ING (drīv'ĭng). [AS. *drīfan.*] **1.** To impel away from, or along before, the impelling force; to push or urge forward. **2.** To clear, by forcing away, or rousing from covert, what is contained; esp., to search (a district) for game. **3.** To urge on and direct the motions or course of, as the beasts which draw a vehicle or the vehicle drawn; as, to *drive* a team; hence, also, to convey in a vehicle. **4.** To carry along or keep in motion; as, to *drive* machinery by steam power. **5.** To carry on or carry through energetically; as, to *drive* a bargain. **6.** To force; to constrain, as by necessity, persuasion, etc. **7.** To urge to effort or work; as, the slaves were *driven* too much. **8.** To force (a passage into or through) by pressing, digging, etc.; as, to *drive* a well. **9.** *Sports.* **a** In baseball, cricket, etc., to propel (the ball) swiftly, as by a hard or direct stroke or forcible throw. **b** *Golf.* To hit (the ball) from the tee. Cf. DRIVER **c**. — **Syn.** See MOVE: RIDE. — *v. i.* **1.** To rush and press with violence. **2.** To be forced along; to be driven. **3.** To go by a vehicle whose course is under one's direction. **4.** To press forward; to aim or tend to a point, as in discourse or argument. **5.** *Sports.* To drive the ball, bowl, etc.

— *n.* **1.** Act of driving; esp., a trip in a carriage or automobile. **2.** A road prepared for driving, esp. for leisure driving, as in a park; also, a driveway. **3.** The driving together of animals for capture, killing, branding, etc. **4.** A concerted effort put forth as in the execution of some plan; as, a *drive* to raise funds. **5.** *Trade Slang.* An offering of goods or stocks at a low price, as in attempting to depress prices. **6.** Violent motion; esp., hurried dispatch of business. **7.** *Automobile Vehicles.* The apparatus by means of which the propulsion of a vehicle is directed. **8.** *Logging.* A mass of logs floating down a river. **9.** *Mach.* The means for giving motion to a machine or machine part; as, a belt *drive.* **10.** *Sports.* The act, or the manner, of driving the ball; the stroke or blow.

— *adj.* Used in or for driving; as, a *drive* shaft (see SHAFT).

drive'–in', *adj.* Built for the accommodation of patrons' automobiles from which the occupants may watch, purchase, etc. — *n.* A drive-in motion-picture theater, refreshment stand, bank, etc.

driv'el (drĭv''l), *v. i.;* -ELED (-'ld) or -ELLED; -EL·ING or -EL·LING. [AS. *dreflian.*] **1.** To slaver. **2.** To flow from the mouth like spittle. **3.** To be silly in manner of speech. — *v. t.* **1.** To make flow, or let flow, from the mouth. **2.** To utter in an infantile or imbecile fashion. — *n.* **1.** Slaver; saliva flowing from the mouth. **2.** Foolish talk; twaddle. — **driv'el·er, driv'el·ler** (-'l·ẽr), *n.*

driv'en (drĭv'ĕn), *past part. & part. adj.* of DRIVE.

driv'er (drīv'ẽr), *n.* One who or that which drives, urges, or impels anything onward; as: **a** A coachman, chauffeur, etc. **b** A mallet, hammer, or the like. **c** *Golf.* A wooden club with a nearly straight face, used in playing the ball from the tee. See GOLF, *Illust.* **d** *Mech. & Mach.* A piece for imparting motion to another piece, either directly or indirectly.

driver ant. Any of certain African stinging ants (genera *Dorylus* and *Anomma*, subfamily Dorylinae) which move in vast armies; — called also *army ant* (see FORAGING ANT).

drive'way' (drīv'wā'), *n.* A passage along which vehicles or animals may be driven.

driv'ing (drīv'ĭng), *adj.* Having great force of impulse; as, a *driving* storm; also, communicating force; impelling; as, a *driving* shaft; a *driving* wheel of a locomotive. — **driv'ing·ly,** *adv.*

driving iron. See GOLF, *Illust.*

driz'zle (drĭz''l), *v. i. & t.;* DRIZ'ZLED (-'ld); DRIZ'ZLING (-lĭng). [Prob. freq. of ME. *dresen* to fall, fr. AS. *drēosan.*] To rain in very small drops; to sprinkle. — *n.* A fine mistlike rain. — **driz'zly** (-lĭ), *adj.*

drogue (drōg), *n. Aeronautics & Naut.* A sea anchor.

droit (droit; *F.* drwȧ), *n.* [F.] *Law.* A right; also, that to which one has a right; *pl.*, dues; duties.

‖**droit des gens** (drwȧ' dā zhäɴ'). [F.] The law of nations; international law.

droll (drōl), *adj.* [F. *drôle.*] Queer, and fitted to provoke laughter; amusing and strange. — **Syn.** See LAUGHABLE. — *n.* A wag; a jester; a buffoon. — *v. i.* To jest or make sport; to play the buffoon.

droll'er·y (drōl'ẽr·ĭ), *n.; pl.* -ERIES (-ĭz). **1.** Something that is droll; as: **a** *Obs.* A comic picture. **b** A comic entertainment; also, a puppet. **c** A droll story; jest. **2.** Jesting; buffoonery. **3.** Quality of being droll; humor.

-drome (-drōm). [Gr. *dromos* a running, fr. the root of *dramein* to run.] A suffix denoting *a running, running course*, as in hippo*drome*, air*drome*.

drom'e·dar'y (drŏm'ĕ·dẽr'ĭ; drŭm'-, *or, esp. Brit.,* drŭm'ĕ·dẽr·ĭ; drŏm'-), *n.; pl.* -IES (-ĭz). [OF. *dromedaire*, fr. LL. *dromedarius* (sc. *camelus*), fr. L. *dromas* a dromedary, fr. Gr. *dromas* running.] Orig., a camel of unusual speed, trained esp. for riding; now, more often, the Arabian or one-humped camel (*Camelus dromedarius*).

drom'ond (drŏm'ŭnd; drŭm'-), **drom'on** (-ŭn), *n.* [OF. *dromont*, fr. L. *dromo*, fr. Gr. *dromōn* light vessel.] In the Middle Ages, a large fast-sailing galley or cutter.

-dromous. [See -DROME.] A suffix meaning *running*, as in anad*romous*, catad*romous*.

drone (drōn), *n.* [AS. *drān.*] **1.** The male of bees, esp. of the honeybee. It has no sting and gathers no honey. **2.** One who lives on the labors of others; a sluggard. **3.** A pilotless airplane, vessel, or other craft remote-controlled by radio, as for target purposes or ammunition-laden for blasting enemy defenses.

drone, *v. i. & t.* To make or sound with a low, dull, monotonous, murmuring sound; hence, to speak monotonously. — *n.* **1.** A bagpipe or similar instrument; also, one of the largest pipes in a bagpipe. **2.** One who speaks monotonously, as with a drawl. **3.** A humming sound; as, the *drone* of bees or of a motor. **4.** *Music.* A monotonous bass; a deep sustained monotone.

drool (drōōl), *v. i.* [Contr. fr. DRIVEL.] *Dial. Eng. & U.S.* To drivel. — *n. Slang, U.S.* Drivel; esp., foolish talk.

droop (drōōp), *v. i.* [ON. *drūpa.*] **1.** To hang bending downward, as from exhaustion, hunger, etc. **2.** To grow dispirited or depressed; to languish. **3.** To proceed toward a close. — *v. t.* To let droop or sink. — *n.* A drooping. — **droop'ing·ly,** *adv.* — **droop'y,** *adj.*

drop (drŏp), *n.* [AS. *dropa.*] **1.** The quantity of fluid which falls in one spherical mass; a liquid globule; sometimes, specif., a minim (see MEASURE, *Table* 12). **2.** A minute quantity, esp. of a liquid. **3.** A modicum of drink. **4.** That which resembles, or hangs like, a liquid drop, as an earring, a sugarplum, etc.; hence: **a** *pl.* Any medicine the dose of which is measured by drops. **b** A small droplike candy; as, lemon *drops.* **5.** Sudden fall or descent. **6.** The depth to which or the distance through which one drops. **7.** Whatever is arranged to drop, hang, or fall from an elevated position; also, a contrivance for lowering something; as: **a** A trap door; also, the gallows. **b** A drop press or drop hammer. **c** A slot in which something is to be dropped. **8.** *Football.* Short for DROP KICK. **9.** *Naut.* The distance from the head to the foot of a course. **10.** *Theater.* A drop curtain.

— *v. t.;* DROPPED (drŏpt) or DROPT; DROP'PING. **1.** To pour or let fall in drops; also, to cover with drops. **2.** To let fall; release. **3.** Hence: **a** To communicate by a suggestion; as, to *drop* a hint. **b** To give birth to; as, to *drop* a lamb. **c** To send (a letter) as by dropping it in the letter box; as, please *drop* me a line. **4.** To let go; dismiss; as, to *drop* a subject. **5.** To fell or bring down; as, to *drop* one's man. **6.** To lower, as a curtain. **7.** *Cookery.* To cook by poaching; as, *dropped* eggs. **8.** *Football.* **a** To drop-kick (a ball). **b** To score (a goal) by drop-kicking. **9.** *Naut.* To leave behind; outdistance. — *v. i.* **1.** To fall in drops; also, drip. **2. a** To descend; as, ripe fruit *drops.* **b** To pass from one condition into another less active, desirable, etc.; as, he *dropped* asleep. **3.** To be depressed; to fall; as, the market is *dropping.* **4.** To fall dead. **5.** To come unexpectedly; as, my friend *dropped* in for a visit. **6.** To come to an end; to cease. **7. a** To move easily down a river; as, the barges *drop* down on the ebb tide. **b** To fall behind. **8.** To be born; also, to let young fall in giving birth; — said of animals.

drop curtain. *Theater.* A curtain which is lowered instead of drawn.

drop'–forge' (drŏp'fōrj'; -fôrj'; 70), *v. t.;* see FORGE. To forge between dies by a drop hammer. — **drop'–forg'er** (-fôr'jẽr; -fōr'jẽr), *n.* — **drop forging.**

drop hammer. *Mach.* A power hammer for forging, shaping metal, etc., having a weight which is raised and then released to drop on the metal resting on an anvil or die.

drop kick. *Football.* A kick given to the ball as it rebounds after having been dropped from the hands; also, the resulting flight of a ball or the distance covered. — **drop'–kick',** *v. t. & i.* — **drop'–kick'er,** *n.*

drop leaf. A table leaf hinged to the side or end of a table and folded down when not in use. — **drop'–leaf',** *adj.*

drop'let (drŏp'lĕt; -lĭt), *n.* A minute drop.

drop letter. *U.S.* A letter to be delivered from the office where posted.

drop′light′ (drŏp′līt′), *n.* An attachment to a lighting fixture for bringing the light down nearer to a table or desk.

drop′per (drŏp′ẽr), *n.* One who or that which drops.

drop′ping (drŏp′ĭng), *n.* **1.** Act of causing to drop or of letting drop. **2.** That which falls in drops, as rain, melting wax, or (now *pl.*) the dung of animals.

drop press. *Mach.* = DROP HAMMER.

drop shot. Soft shot made by the process of dropping the molten shot metal from a height.

drop′si·cal (drŏp′sĭ·kăl), *adj.* **1.** Diseased with dropsy. **2.** Of or pertaining to dropsy. — **drop′si·cal·ly,** *adv.*

drop′sy (drŏp′sĭ), *n.* [OF. *idropisie,* fr. L. *hydropisis,* fr. Gr. *hydrōps* dropsy, fr. *hydōr* water.] *Med. & Veter.* = EDEMA. — **drop′sied** (-sĭd), *adj.*

drop′wort′ (drŏp′wûrt′), *n.* **a** A Eurasian herb (*Filipendula hexapetala*) of the rose family, with panicles of white or reddish flowers. **b** Any of a genus (*Oenanthe*) of plants of the carrot family.

drosh′ky (drŏsh′kĭ), **dros′ky** (drŏs′kĭ), *n.; pl.* -KIES (-kĭz). [Russ. *drozhki.*] A low, four-wheeled, open carriage used in Russia, consisting of a kind of long bench on which the passengers ride as on a saddle. By extension, any of certain forms of two-wheeled or four-wheeled public carriages used in Russia and other European countries.

Dro·soph′i·la (drō·sŏf′ĭ·lȧ), *n.* [NL., fr. Gr. *drosos* dew, liquid + *philos* loving.] *Zool.* **a** A genus containing the common fruit fly (*D. melanogaster*), used extensively in breeding experiments to study inheritance of characters and the mechanism of heredity. It is the type genus of a family, **Dros′o·phil′i·dae** (drŏs′ō·fĭl′ĭ·dē). **b** [*not cap.; pl.* -LAE (-lē).] Any fly of this genus.

dross (drŏs; 74), *n.* [AS. *drōs* filth, lees.] **1.** The scum thrown off from molten ore or metal. **2.** Waste matter; refuse. — **dross′y** (-ĭ), *adj.*

drought (drout), *n.* Also **drouth** (drouth). [AS. *drūgath,* fr. *drūgian* to dry.] **1.** Dryness; want of rain. **2.** A dry spell, esp. when protracted. **3.** *Dial.* Thirst. — **drought′y, drouth′y,** *adj.*

drouk (drōōk), *v. t.; past & past part.* DROUKED (drōōkt), DROUK′IT (drōōk′ĭt), DROUK′ET; *pres. part.* DROUK′ING, DROUK′AN (-ăn). *Scot.* To soak; drench; hence, overwhelm.

drove (drōv), *n.* [AS. *drāf,* fr. *drīfan* to drive.] **1.** A collection of cattle driven or collected for driving. **2.** Any collection of animals; also, a crowd of people moving in one direction. **3.** *Stonecutting.* **a** Also **drove chisel.** A stonecutter's chisel used in smoothing the finished stone. **b** The grooved surface of stone finished by the drove chisel; — called also **drove work.**
— *v. t. & i.;* DROVED (drōvd); DROV′ING. **1.** To drive, as cattle or sheep; to follow the occupation of a drover. **2.** To finish, as stone, with a drove chisel.

drove, *past of* DRIVE.

dro′ver (drō′vẽr), *n.* One who drives sheep, pigs, or other domestic animals, to market; hence, a dealer in cattle.

drown (droun), *v. i.* [ME. *drunen, drounen,* prob. of Scand. origin.] To be suffocated in water or other liquid. — *v. t.* **1.** To submerge in water. **2.** To deprive of life by immersion in water or other liquid. **3.** To overpower; overcome; — esp. of sound.

drowse (drouz), *v. i. & t.* [AS. *drūsian, drūsan,* to sink, become inactive.] To be or make heavy with sleepiness; also, to pass (time) as in drowsing. — *n.* A doze.

drow′si·head (drou′zĭ·hĕd), *n.* Also **drow′si·hood** (-hōōd). *Archaic.* Drowsiness.

drow′sy (-zĭ), *adj.;* DROW′SI·ER (-zĭ·ẽr); DROW′SI·EST. [See DROWSE, *v.*] **1.** Inclined to drowse. **2.** Disposing to sleep; lulling. — **drow′si·ly,** *adv.* — **drow′si·ness,** *n.*

drub (drŭb), *v. t.;* DRUBBED (drŭbd); DRUB′BING. **1.** To beat with a stick; cudgel; belabor. **2.** To stamp (the feet). — *v. i.* To tap or stamp; to drum. — *n.* A blow with a cudgel; a thump. — **drub′ber** (-ẽr), *n.*

drub′bing (drŭb′ĭng), *n.* A beating; a thrashing.

drudge (drŭj), *v. i.;* DRUDGED (drŭjd); DRUDG′ING. To perform menial work; hence, to toil at any difficult and monotonous task. — *n.* One who drudges; a hack. — **drudg′er** (drŭj′ẽr), *n.*

drudg′er·y (drŭj′ẽr·ĭ), *n.; pl.* -IES (-ĭz). Act of drudging; ignoble or wearisome toil. — **Syn.** See WORK.

drug (drŭg), *n.* [OF. *drogue.*] **1.** Any substance used as a medicine, or in making medicines; also, formerly, any stuff used in dyeing or in chemical operations. **2.** An article of slow sale, or in no demand; as, a *drug* on (or in) the market. **3.** A narcotic substance or preparation. — *v. t.;* DRUGGED (drŭgd); DRUG′GING. To affect with drugs; esp., to stupefy by a narcotic drug.

drug′get (drŭg′ĕt; -ĭt), *n.* [F. *droguet.*] **1. a** Formerly, a woolen or mixed stuff for clothing. **b** A coarse cloth used as a lining or covering for carpets or furniture. **c** A rug having a cotton warp and a wool filling. **2.** Anything made of drugget.

drug′gist (-ĭst), *n.* One who deals in drugs; a pharmacist.
Syn. **Druggist, pharmacist, pharmaceutist, apothecary, chemist** mean one who deals in medicinal drugs. **Druggist** now commonly designates the owner or operator of a store or wholesale house selling drugs or medicinal preparations: it is loosely applied instead of the precise terms, **pharmacist** and **pharmaceutist,** to one skilled in compounding drugs and in dispensing medicines prescribed by a physician; **apothecary,** in early English use, was distinguished from *druggist,* the latter then designating a dealer in "crude drugs" or herbs, roots, and other ingredients of medicines, and the former, one who compounded these ingredients, thus making medicines, and was used until recently in the United States for a practitioner of pharmacy; **chemist** is, in England, the popular or commercial equivalent of *druggist.*

drug′less (drŭg′lĕs; -lĭs), *adj.* Not using drugs; as, *drugless* treatment of a disease.

drug′store′ (drŭg′stōr′), *n.* A pharmacy; a retail shop where drugs and various small articles are sold.

dru′id (drōō′ĭd), *n.* [F. *druide,* fr. L. *druides, druidae,* pl., of Celt. origin.] [*often cap.*] A member of a religious order in ancient Gaul, Britain, and Ireland. In the Irish and Welsh sagas, and later Christian legends, the druids appear as conjurers and not as priests and philosophers. — **dru′id·ess** (-ĕs; -ĭs), *n.* — **dru·id′ic** (drōō·ĭd′ĭk), **dru·id′i·cal** (-ĭ·kăl), *adj.*

dru′id·ism (-ĭz′m), *n.* The system of religion, philosophy, and instruction of the druids.

drum (drŭm), *n.* [Gael. & Ir. *druim* ridge.] **1.** *Scot. & Ir.* A long narrow hill or ridge. **2.** *Geol.* = DRUMLIN.

drum, *n.* **1.** A musical instrument, commonly consisting of a hollow cylinder with a skin or vellum head stretched over each end or (cf. KETTLEDRUM) of a hemispherical metal shell with a single head, which is beaten with a stick or pair of sticks in playing. **2.** The sound of this instrument; also, any similar sound. **3.** Something resembling a drum in shape; as: **a** A cylindrical machine or mechanical device or part, as the winding part of a capstan. **b** The body of a banjo or similar instrument. **c** A cylindrical box, tub, case, or the like, as for packing or storing goods. **d** A cylindrical magazine in certain automatic firearms. **4.** *Hist.* A noisy assembly of fashionable people at a private house. **5.** *Anat.* The tympanum of the ear; often, in common usage, the tympanic membrane. **6.** = DRUMFISH.

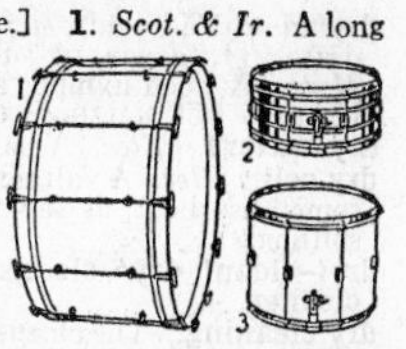

1 Bass Drum; 2 Orchestra Snare Drum; 3 Parade, or Street, Snare Drum.

— *v. i.;* DRUMMED (drŭmd); DRUM′MING. **1.** To beat or play on a drum. **2.** To beat with a rapid succession of strokes; also, to sound rhythmically. — *v. t.* **1.** To assemble by, or as by, beat of drum. **2.** To expel ignominiously, with beat of drum; — with *out, down,* etc. **3.** To drive or force by reiteration. **4.** To strike or thump as in beating a drum.

drum′ble (drŭm′b'l; drōōm′b'l; -'l), *v. i.;* DRUM′BLED (-b'ld; -'ld); DRUM′BLING (-blĭng; -lĭng). *Obs. exc. Dial.* To be sluggish or lazy.

drum′fire′ (drŭm′fīr′), *n.* The discharge of weapons along a front, so continuous as to sound like a drum.

drum′fish′ (-fĭsh′), *n.; pl.,* see FISH. Any of various sciaenoid fishes that make a drumming noise, esp. the common drumfish (*Pogonias cromis*) of the Atlantic coast, the ***red drumfish,* or *red drum*** (*Sciaenops ocellata*), a large edible species of the Atlantic coast, and the ***fresh-water drumfish*** (*Aplodinotus grunniens*) of the Great Lakes and Mississippi Valley.

drum′head′ (-hĕd′), *n.* **1.** The parchment or skin stretched over either end of a drum. **2.** The tympanic membrane, or eardrum. **3.** The top of a capstan which is pierced with sockets for levers used in turning it. See CAPSTAN, *Illust.*

drumhead court–martial. *Mil.* A summary court-martial to try offenses on the battlefield or the line of march. It is sometimes held around a drumhead as table.

drum′lin (drŭm′lĭn), *n.* [Gael. *druim* the ridge of a hill.] *Geol.* An elongate or oval hill of glacial drift.

drum′ly (drŭm′lĭ; drōōm′-), *adj. Scot.* Turbid; muddy; also, troubled.

drum major. The marching leader of a band or drum corps.

drum majorette. A female drum major.

drum′mer (drŭm′ẽr), *n.* **1.** One who beats the drum, as in a band. **2.** *Chiefly U. S.* A commercial traveler.

drum′mock (drŭm′ŭk). Var. of DRAMMOCK.

Drum′mond light (drŭm′ŭnd). [After T. *Drummond,* Scottish engineer.] **a** = LIMELIGHT, 1. **b** A type of heliostat.

drum′stick′ (drŭm′stĭk′), *n.* **1.** A stick for beating a drum. **2.** The joint of a fowl's leg between the thigh and tarsus.

drunk (drŭngk), *past part. & former past tense* of DRINK. Specif.: *adj.* **1.** Intoxicated with or as with strong drink. **2.** *Obs.* Drenched with moisture or liquid.
Syn. **Drunk, drunken, intoxicated, inebriated, tipsy, tight** mean under the influence of liquor. **Drunk** and **drunken** are the plain-spoken, direct, and inclusive terms, *drunk* being commonly used predicatively and *drunken,* attributively; **intoxicated** is thought of as a less offensive term and is often, though not correctly, applied to one who is slightly drunk; **inebriated** adds to *drunk* implications of exhilaration or undue excitement; **tipsy,** a degree of intoxication that deprives one of muscular control; **tight,** a slang term, implies obvious signs of intoxication without loss of muscular control. — **Ant.** Sober.
— *n. Slang.* A drunken condition; spree; also, a drunken person.

drunk′ard (-ẽrd), *n.* [*drunk* + *-ard.*] A toper; sot.

drunk′en (-ĕn), *past part.* of DRINK; specif.: *adj.* **1.** Intoxicated; drunk. **2.** Saturated with moisture; drenched. **3.** Pertaining to, proceeding from, or characterized by intoxication. — **Syn.** See DRUNK. — **drunk′en·ly,** *adv.* — **drunk′en·ness,** *n.*

dru·pa′ceous (drōō·pā′shŭs), *adj. Bot.* Pertaining to, or of the nature of, drupes; bearing drupes.

drupe (drōōp), *n.* [F. or L.; F., fr. L. *drupa, druppa,* an overripe olive, fr. Gr. *dryppa.*] *Bot.* A fruit consisting of a pulpy, leathery, or fibrous epicarp, and a hard endocarp (the stone) enclosing a single seed, as in the plum, cherry, apricot, peach, etc. See ENDOCARP, *Illust.*

drupe′let (-lĕt; -lĭt), *n. Bot.* A small drupe, as one of the pulpy grains of the blackberry.

Druse (drōōz), *n.* [Ar. *Durūz,* pl.] One of a people and religious sect dwelling chiefly in the Lebanon mountains of Syria. Their religion is an outgrowth of Mohammedanism. — **Dru′se·an** (drōō′zē·ăn), **Dru′si·an** (-zĭ·ăn), *adj.*

dry (drī), *adj.;* DRI′ER (drī′ẽr); DRI′EST. [AS. *dryge.*] **1.** Free from moisture; not wet or moist. **2.** Designating, pertaining to, or characterized by, absence, avoidance, dissipation, etc., of moisture; as: **a** Dried; dried up; as, a *dry* brook. **b** Not in or under water; as, *dry* land. **c** Exhausted in its supply of water, fluid, or sustenance; as, a *dry* fountain pen. **d** Of animals, not giving milk. **e** Thirsty; needing drink. **f** Of the eyes, not shedding tears. **g** Of war, death, injuries, or the like: without bloodshed. **h** Without butter, milk, or the like; — said of bread or toast. **i** Of commodities, solid, as opposed to liquid. **3.** Lacking tenderness, sympathy, or spiritual emotion; hence: **a** Severe; grave. **b** Sharp; shrewd. **c** Barren; jejune; plain; as, a *dry* speech. **4.** Lacking sweetness; — said esp. of wines. **5.** Lacking smooth or liquid quality of sound; as, a *dry* cough. **6.** *Colloq., U. S.* Marked by, concerned with, or advocating laws prohibiting the manufacture, sale, etc., of intoxicating liquor. **7.** *Mil.* Orig., without live ammunition; hence, simulated or rehearsed for practice only; as, a *dry* run over a target.
Syn. **Dry, arid** mean devoid of moisture. But **dry** may suggest absence of moisture in any degree from deficiency to exhaustion, and as a normal or abnormal condition; **arid** always implies abnormality, suggesting such an extreme of dryness that literally it (usually land or region) cannot produce or support life. This is the basic difference between the two words in their many figurative senses. — **Ant.** Wet.
— *v. t. & i.;* DRIED (drīd); DRY′ING. To make or become dry.
— *n.; pl.* DRYS (drīz). *Colloq., U. S.* A prohibitionist.

dry'ad (drī'ăd; -ăd), *n.; pl.* DRY'ADS (-ădz; -ădz), DRY'A·DES (drī'ȧ·dēz). [L. *dryas,* pl. *-ades,* fr. Gr. *dryas,* fr. *drys* oak, tree.] *Gr. Myth.* A wood nymph; a nymph whose life is bound up with that of her tree. Cf. NAIAD. — **dry·ad'ic** (drī·ăd'ĭk), *adj.*
dry battery. *Elec.* A battery of dry cells.
dry cell. *Elec.* A voltaic cell whose contents are treated by the use of some absorbent, as sawdust, gelatin, etc., so as to ensure their not spilling.
dry'-clean', dry'-cleanse', *v. t.* To subject to dry cleaning. — **dry cleaner.**
dry cleaning. The cleansing of textiles with solvents other than water, as benzine.
dry dock. A dock from which the water may be shut or pumped out, used in constructing or repairing ships. See FLOATING DOCK; cf. GRAVING DOCK.
dry'-dock', *v. t. & i.* To place in, or to enter, a dry dock, as a vessel for repairs.
dry'er (drī'ẽr), **dry'est.** Var. of DRIER, DRIEST.
dry farming. *Agric.* Production of crops without irrigation in regions of little rainfall, chiefly by tillage methods conserving soil moisture and by the use of drought-enduring crops. — **dry farm.** — **dry farmer.** — **dry'-farm',** *v. t. & i.*
dry goods. *Com., Chiefly U. S.* Textile fabrics, — in distinction from hardware, jewelry, groceries, etc.
Dry Ice. A trade-mark for solidified carbon dioxide used as a substitute for ice.
dry'ing, *adj.* **1.** Adapted or tending to exhaust moisture; as, a *drying* wind. **2.** Having the quality of rapidly becoming dry, as certain oils.
dry kiln. An artificially heated chamber for drying and seasoning cut lumber.
dry law. A law intended to enforce prohibition.
dry'ly, dri'ly (drī'lĭ), *adv.* In a dry manner.
dry measure. A system of measures of volume for dry articles. See MEASURE, *Table* 10.
dry'ness (drī'nĕs; -nĭs), *n.* State or quality of being dry.
dry nurse. **1.** A nurse who attends and feeds a child by hand. Cf. WET NURSE. **2.** *Colloq.* One who aids or instructs another. — **dry'-nurse',** *v. t.*
dry point. *Fine Arts.* An engraving made with a needle instead of a burin, and engraved without acid; also, the needle used.
dry rot. *Plant Pathol.* **1. a** A decay of seasoned timber caused by any of several fungi; also, any of these fungi. **b** Any of various fungous diseases of fruits and vegetables. **2.** Figuratively, deterioration or disintegration, esp. as due to lack of new blood or progressive ideas.
dry'-salt', *v. t.* To cure by drying and salting, as food.
dry'salt'er (drī'sôl'tẽr), *n. Eng.* A dealer in crude dry chemicals, dyes, salted food products, etc.
dry'salt'er·y (-ĭ), *n. Eng.* The articles kept by a drysalter; also, the business of a drysalter.
dry'-shod', *adj.* Having dry shoes; not wetting the shoes.
dry wash. A washing cleaned and dried, but not ironed.
du'ad (dū'ăd), *n.* [See DYAD.] A union of two; a pair; a set or group of two.
du'al (dū'ăl), *adj.* [L. *dualis,* fr. *duo* two.] **1.** Pertaining to two; — contrasted with *singular* and *plural;* as, *dual* number. **2.** Twofold; double. **3.** To be shared by two agents; as, an airplane with *dual* control. — *n. Gram.* The dual number, as in Greek; also, a word in that form. — **du·al'i·ty** (dū·ăl'ĭ·tĭ), *n.*
du'al·ism (-ĭz'm), *n.* **1.** State of being dual, or twofold; any system which is founded on a double principle, or a twofold distinction. **2.** *Philos.* Any theory which considers the ultimate nature of the universe to be twofold, as mind and matter; — contrasted with *monism* and *pluralism.* **3.** *Theol.* **a** The doctrine that the universe is under the dominion of two opposing principles, a good and an evil. **b** A view of man as constituted of two original and independent elements, as matter and spirit. — **du'al·ist** (-ĭst), *n.* — **du'al·is'tic** (-ĭs'tĭk), *adj.*
du'al-pur'pose, *adj.* **1.** Designed or used for two purposes. **2.** *Agric.* Of twofold function; — applied esp. to animals or breeds which are qualified to serve in two capacities.
dub (dŭb), *v. t.;* DUBBED (dŭbd); DUB'BING. [AS. *dubbian* to dub a knight.] **1.** To confer knighthood upon. **2.** To invest with any dignity or new character; to call; name. **3.** To strike, rub, or dress smooth, as a timber.
dub, *v. t. & i.* To thrust or make a thrust; to poke. — *n.* **1.** A drumbeat. **2.** *Rare.* A thump.
dub (dŭb), *n.* [Origin obscure.] *Colloq.* A bungling, unskillful person.
dub (dŭb; dōōb), *n. Chiefly Scot.* A pool or puddle.
dub (dŭb), *v. t.* [Short for *double.*] To provide (a film) with a new sound track; to blend auxiliary music, sound effects, etc., into (a radio or television broadcast); to add (sound effects) to a film, or to radio or television production.
dub'bing (dŭb'ĭng), *n.* **1.** Act of dubbing. **2.** A dressing of flour and water used by weavers; also, a mixture of oil and tallow for dressing leather. **3.** The materials tied to a fishhook in making an artificial fly.
du·bi'e·ty (dū·bī'ĕ·tĭ), **du'bi·os'i·ty** (dū'bĭ·ŏs'ĭ·tĭ), *n.; pl.* -TIES (-tĭz). Doubtfulness or an instance of it; dubiousness. — **Syn.** See UNCERTAINTY.
du'bi·ous (dū'bĭ·ŭs), *adj.* [L. *dubiosus,* fr. *dubium* doubt, fr. *duo* two.] **1.** Occasioning doubt; not clear and straightforward; equivocal; as, a *dubious* answer. **2.** Doubtful, or not settled in opinion. **3.** Of uncertain event or issue; as, in *dubious* battle. **4.** Of questionable character; as, a *dubious* transaction. — **Syn.** See DOUBTFUL. — **du'bi·ous·ly,** *adv.* — **du'bi·ous·ness,** *n.*
du'bi·ta·ble (-bĭ·tȧ·b'l), *adj.* Liable to be doubted; uncertain.
du'bi·ta'tion (-tā'shŭn), *n.* [F., fr. L. *dubitatio.*] Doubt.
du'bi·ta'tive (dū'bĭ·tā'tĭv), *adj.* [LL. *dubitativus.*] **a** Tending or given to doubt; doubtful. **b** Expressing doubt; as, a *dubitative* conjunction. — **du'bi·ta'tive·ly,** *adv.*
du'cal (dū'kăl), *adj.* [F., fr. L. *ducalis* of a leader.] Of or pertaining to a duke or dukedom. — **du'cal·ly,** *adv.*
duc'at (dŭk'ăt), *n.* [OF., fr. It., fr. MGr. *doukas,* fr. L. *dux* leader.] A gold coin of several countries of Europe, first coined about 1150 and worth about $2.25. In recent years, in Austria, Czechoslovakia, etc., a coin of about the same value has been issued for trade purposes.
‖**du'ce** (dōō'chā), *n.* [It.] Leader; chief; specif., *il Du'ce* (ēl), the head of the Fascisti.
duch'ess (dŭch'ĕs; -ĭs), *n.* [OF. *duchesse,* fr. *duc* duke.] The wife or widow of a duke; also, a woman who has the sovereignty of a duchy in her own right.
duch'y (-ĭ), *n.; pl.* -IES (-ĭz). [OF. *duché,* fr. LL. *ducatus* duchy, fr. L. *dux* leader.] The territory of a duke; a dukedom.
duck (dŭk), *n.* [D. *doek* cloth, canvas.] **1.** A linen or cotton fabric, finer and lighter than canvas, but similar to it. **2.** *pl. Colloq.* Light clothes, esp. trousers, of duck.
duck, *n.* [AS. *dūce.*] **1.** Any of various swimming birds (family Anatidae), having short neck and legs, and a somewhat depressed body. See BILL, *Illust.* The ***sea ducks,*** which chiefly frequent salt water, constitute a subfamily (Fuligulinae, the duck family). See CANVASBACK, SCAUP DUCK, SCOTER, SURF DUCK, etc. **2.** A female duck as distinguished from a male, or drake. **3.** *Colloq.* A pet; a darling.
duck, *n. U. S. Army.* A 2½-ton six-wheel-drive truck and barge combined, equipped with a propeller and capable of locomotion on land or water, for ferrying, lighter service, or landing troops. Officially *DUKW* or *dukw*
duck, *v. t. & i.* [ME. *duken, douken,* to dive.] **1.** To thrust or plunge under water or other liquid and suddenly withdraw. **2.** To bow; to bob down. **3.** *Colloq.* To avoid, as a blow, by bobbing one's head; hence, to move off quickly to avoid danger or observation; also, to evade. — *n.* Act of ducking; a quick plunge, nod, etc.
duck and drake, *or* **ducks and drakes.** The sport of throwing flat stones or shells so that they will skim or bound along the surface of the water; hence: ***play,*** *or* ***play at, ducks and drakes with,*** *or* ***make ducks and drakes of,*** to throw away heedlessly or squander.
duck'bill' (dŭk'bĭl'), *n.* A small aquatic mammal (*Ornithorhynchus anatinus*) of Australia and Tasmania, having a bill resembling that of a duck; the platypus.
duck'board' (-bōrd'; 70), *n.* A walk made of boards or slabs on supports above a wet surface.
duck'er (dŭk'ẽr), *n.* One who ducks.
duck'er, *n.* One who raises ducks; also, a hunter of ducks.
duck'-foot'ed, *adj. Poultry.* Having the hind toe more or less forwardly directed; — said of domestic fowls.
duck'ing stool. A stool on which common scolds, disorderly women, etc., were formerly tied and plunged into water as a punishment. Cf. CUCKING STOOL.
duck'ling (dŭk'lĭng), *n.* A young or little duck.
duck'pin' (-pĭn'), *n. Tenpins.* **a** A form of pin 9⅜ inches high and from 3½ to 4⁷⁄₁₆ inches in diameter. **b** *pl.* Tenpins played with such pins and with balls not more than 5 in. in diameter.
duck soup. Something easy to do and, often, remunerative.
duck'weed' (dŭk'wēd'), *n.* Any plant of a family (Lemnaceae) of small, free-floating aquatics, eaten by ducks.
duct (dŭkt), *n.* [L. *ductus* a leading, conduit, fr. *ducere, ductum,* to lead.] **1.** Any tube or canal by which a fluid or other substance is conveyed. **2.** *Anat.* A tube or vessel; — usually applied to those that carry off the secretion of a gland. **3.** *Elec.* A pipe or tubular runway for electric power, telephone, etc., cables. — **duct'less,** *adj.*
duc'tile (dŭk'tĭl; 56), *adj.* [F., fr. L. *ductilis,* fr. *ducere* to lead.] **1.** Capable of being drawn out or hammered thin; — said esp. of metals, as gold. **2.** Easily led or drawn. — **Syn.** See PLASTIC. — **duc·til'i·ty** (dŭk·tĭl'ĭ·tĭ), *n.*
duct'less gland (dŭkt'lĕs; -lĭs). *Anat.* Any of certain glands which have no efferent duct for their secretion, but pour it into the lymph or into blood circulating through them, as the suprarenals, the thyroid, and pituitary glands.
dud (dŭd), *n.* **1.** *Colloq.* A garment; usually in *pl.,* clothes. **2.** *pl. Colloq.* Things in general; "traps"; belongings. **3.** A bomb or shell that fails to explode. **4.** A person or thing that proves a flat failure.
dud'die, dud'dy (dŭd'ĭ), *adj. Scot.* Ragged; tattered.
dude (dūd), *n.* **1.** *U. S.* A dandy; a fop. **2.** *Slang, Western U. S.* An Eastern or city-bred person. — **dud'ish** (dūd'ĭsh), *adj.*
du·deen' (dōō·dēn'; thōō-), *n.* [Ir. *dūidīn,* dim. of *dūd* pipe.] *Orig. Ir.* A short tobacco pipe.
dude ranch. *U. S.* A ranch operated for entertainment of tourists.
dudg'eon (dŭj'ŭn), *n. Obs.* A dagger having a handle of a certain wood; also, a handle of this same wood.
dudg'eon, *n.* Aggrieved or angered feeling. — **Syn.** See OFFENSE.
due (dū; 114), *adj.* [OF. *deü,* past part. of *devoir* to owe, fr. L. *debere.*] **1.** Owed or owing as a debt. **2.** Becoming, fit, or appropriate; as, *due* respect; a *due* penalty. **3.** Capable of satisfying an obligation; adequate; sufficient; as, in *due* time; also, regular; lawful; as, *due* process of law. **4.** Owing or attributable (*to* something); as, death *due* to pneumonia. Prepositional *due to,* meaning "because of" and introducing an adverbial modifier, though objected to by some, is in common and reputable use; as, he failed *due to* faulty training. **5.** *Finance.* Having reached the date at which payment is required; payable; — said esp. of a note. **6.** Appointed or required to arrive (at a given time). — *n.* **1.** That which is due or owed. **2.** Usually *pl.* A legal charge, fee, toll, tribute, or the like. — *adv.* **1.** *Archaic.* Duly (in various senses). **2.** Directly; as, he went *due* east.
due bill. *Com.* A written acknowledgment of a debt, not made payable to order like a promissory note.
du'el (dū'ĕl), *n.* [F., fr. It. *duello* or ML. *duellum,* fr. L. *duellum* (old form of *bellum*) war.] **1.** A combat between two persons, fought with deadly weapons by agreement, usually under formal conditions and in the presence of witnesses (*seconds*) on each side. **2.** Any contest between two antagonists. — *v. i. & t.;* DU'ELED (-ĕld) or DU'ELLED; DU'EL·ING or DU'EL·LING. To fight or kill in a duel. — **du'el·er, du'el·ler,** *n.* — **du'el·ist, du'el·list,** *n.*
du·el'lo (dōō·ĕl'ō), *n.; pl.* -LOS (-ōz). [It.] **1.** Dueling; also, the code of the duel. **2.** *Obs.* A duel.
du·en'na (dū·ĕn'ȧ), *n.; pl.* DUENNAS (-ȧz). [Sp. *dueña,* fr. L. *domina.* See DAME.] **1.** An elderly lady in charge over the younger ladies in a Spanish or a Portuguese family. **2.** Hence, a governess; a chaperon.
du·et' (dū·ĕt'), *n.* [It. *duetto,* dim. of *duo* a duet, fr. It. & L. *duo* two.] *Music.* A composition for two performers.
duff (dŭf), *n.* [ME. *dogh.* See DOUGH.] A pudding, esp. a stiff flour pudding boiled in a bag; as, plum *duff.*
duff, *n.* **1.** *Scot. & U. S.* The partly decayed vegetable matter on the forest floor. **2.** Fine coal; slack.
duf'fel (dŭf'ĕl), *n.* [D., fr. *Duffel,* a town near Antwerp, Belgium.] **1.** A kind of coarse woolen cloth having a thick nap. **2.** *Colloq., U. S.* Supplies, as for camping; kit. — *adj.* **1.** Made of duffel. **2.** Made to carry duffel, or personal equipment.

duff'er (dŭf'ẽr), *n.* *Chiefly Slang.* **1.** A peddler or hawker, esp. of cheap, flashy articles. **2.** A person incompetent or clumsy, as at a game.
duf'fle. Var. of DUFFEL.
dug (dŭg), *past & past part.* of DIG.
dug, *n.* A teat.
du'gong (do͞o'gŏng), *n.* [From Malay *duyun*, Jav. *duyun*, with erroneous *g* for *y*.] An aquatic herbivorous mammal (*Dugong dugon*), allied to the manatee, but with a bilobate tail; a sea cow.
dug'out (dŭg'out'), *n.* **1.** *Orig. U.S.* A canoe or boat made by hollowing out a large log. **2.** A shelter dug out of a hillside; specif., a cave, the side of a trench, etc., often roofed with logs and sod, for storage, protection, etc. **3.** *Baseball.* A low shelter containing a players' bench and facing upon the diamond.
‖**du haut en bas** (dü ō'-täN' bä'). [F.] Literally, from above downward; from top to bottom; hence, condescendingly.
dui'ker (dī'kẽr), **dui'ker·bok'** (-bŏk'), *n.* Also **dui'ker·buck'** (-bŭk'). [D. *duiker* diver + *bok* a buck, lit., diver buck; — from its habit of diving suddenly into the bush.] Any of certain small African antelopes (genus *Cephalophus*).
duke (dūk; 114), *n.* [OF. *duc, ducs, dux*, fr. L. *dux, ducis*, leader, commander, fr. *ducere* to lead.] **1.** In some European countries, a sovereign prince, ruler of a duchy. **2.** In Great Britain and certain other European countries, a nobleman of the highest hereditary rank after that of prince.
duke'dom (-dŭm), *n.* A duchy; also, the title or dignity of a duke.
Du'kho·bors (do͞o'kō·bôrz), **Du·kho·bor'tsy** (*Russ.* do͞o·ĸŭ·bôr'tsĭ), *n. pl.* [Russ. *dukhobortsy* spirit wrestlers, fr. *dukh* spirit + *bortsy* wrestlers.] A Russian religious sect, dating from 1785. In 1898, because of persecution, thousands of these sectaries migrated to Canada.
‖**dul'ce et de·co'rum est pro pa'tri·a mo'ri** (dŭl'sē ĕt dē·kō'rŭm ĕst prō pā'trĭ·ȧ mō'rī; păt'rĭ·ȧ). [L.] It is sweet and seemly to die for one's country.
dul'cet (dŭl'sĕt; -sĭt), *adj.* [OF. *doucet*, dim. of *douz* sweet, fr. L. *dulcis*.] **1.** *Archaic.* Sweet to the taste. **2.** Sweet to the ear; melodious; also, soothing or agreeable. — *n. Music.* An organ stop like the dulciana, but an octave higher.
dul'ci·an'a (dŭl'sĭ·ăn'ȧ), *n.* [NL., fr. L. *dulcis* sweet.] *Music.* A labial organ stop having metal pipes and a tone of soft, sweet, stringlike quality.
dul'ci·fy (dŭl'sĭ·fī), *v. t.;* -FIED (-fīd); -FY'ING. [L. *dulcis* sweet + *-fy*.] **1.** *Obs.* To sweeten. **2.** To mollify; to render agreeable. — **dul'ci·fi·ca'tion** (-fĭ·kā'shŭn), *n.*
dul'ci·mer (dŭl'sĭ·mẽr), *n.* [OF. *doulcemer, doulcemele*, fr. L. *dulcis* sweet + *melos* song, fr. Gr. *melos*.] *Music.* **1.** An instrument having wires stretched over a trapezoidal soundboard, played with two light hammers. **2.** A kind of bagpipe. *Daniel* iii. 10.
Dul·cin'e·a (dŭl·sĭn'ē·ȧ; dŭl'sĭ·nē'ȧ), *n.* [Sp.] A mistress; a sweetheart; — from Don Quixote's ladylove in Cervantes' novel.
du·li'a (dū·lī'ȧ), *n.* [ML., fr. Gr. *douleia* servitude, fr. *doulos* slave.] *R.C.Ch.* Veneration of the angels and saints; — distinguished from *latria*. Cf. HYPERDULIA.
dull (dŭl), *adj.* [ME. *dul*.] **1.** Stupid; doltish. **2.** Slow in perception or sensibility; hence, unfeeling; insensible; as, the *dull* clods. **3.** Slow in action or motion; hence, listless; inert. **4.** Without zest; depressed. **5.** Not keen or sharp; blunt. **6. a** Lacking brilliance of light; dim; as, a *dull* fire. **b** Lacking luster; as, a *dull* mirror. **c** Of low saturation and low brilliance; as, a *dull* green. **d** Not clear and ringing; — of sound. **7.** Tedious; melancholy; as, a *dull* story. **8.** Cloudy; overcast; as, a *dull* day. **9.** Sluggish; — of trade.
Syn. (1) See STUPID.
(2) **Dull, blunt, obtuse** mean not sharp or keen. **Dull** applies literally to an edge or point which has lost its sharpness through use, or figuratively to that which lacks or has lost that which gives keenness, zest, pungency, or the like (as, a *dull* knife; a *dull* book); **blunt** applies literally to an edge or point that is through use, nature, or intention, not sharp or keen, or figuratively to that like perception, emotion, etc., which lacks sharpness or keenness (as, the *blunt* edge of a knife; *blunt* in feeling); **obtuse** applies literally to the shape of something whose point is the end of an angle broader than a right angle, and figuratively to that which is inordinately blunt in perception, in sensibility, or the like (as, an *obtuse* apex; an *obtuse* audience).
— *v. t. & i.* To make or become dull.
dull'ard (dŭl'ẽrd), *n.* [*dull* + *-ard*.] A stupid person.
dull'ish (dŭl'ĭsh), *adj.* Somewhat dull.
dull'ness, dul'ness (-nĕs; -nĭs), *n.* Quality or state of being dull.
dul'ly (dŭl'lĭ), *adv.* In a dull manner.
dulse (dŭls), *n.* [Gael. *duileasg*.] Any of several coarse red seaweeds (chiefly *Rhodymenia palmata*, family Rhodymeniaceae) used as food in Scotland, Iceland, and other, principally northern, countries.
du'ly (dū'lĭ), *adv.* In a due manner, time, or degree.
du'ma (do͞o'mä), *n.* [Russ. *duma*, of Teut. origin.] In Russia, a council; specif. [*cap.*], the Council of State, or Russian parliament, created by imperial ukase in 1905, and overthrown by the Bolshevist revolution (1917).
dumb (dŭm), *adj.* [AS.] **1.** Destitute of the power of speech; speechless. **2.** Not willing to speak; mute; silent. **3.** [Partly fr. G. *dumm*, in Pa.] *Colloq., U.S.* Dull; stupid. **4.** Not having the usual accompaniments of speech and sound; as, *dumb* show. **5.** Lacking in something usual or normal; specif., *Eng.*, lacking masts and sails, and depending on outside power; as, a *dumb* barge. — **Syn.** See STUPID. — **dumb'ly**, *adv.*
dumb ague. Intermittent fever with no well-defined "chill."
dumb'bell' (dŭm'bĕl'), *n.* **1.** A weight, consisting of two spheres connected by a short bar, used for calisthenic exercise. **2.** *Slang, U.S.* A stupid person.
dumb'ness (-nĕs; -nĭs), *n.* Quality or state of being dumb.
dumb show. a Formerly, a part of a dramatic representation, shown in pantomime. **b** Signs and gestures without words; as, to tell in *dumb show*. — **dumb'-show'** (*see Pron.*, § 2), *adj.*
dumb'-wait'er, *n.* **a** A portable serving table or stand. **b** A lift on which dishes, food, etc., are passed from one room or story of a house to another.
dum'dum (dŭm'dŭm), *n.*, *or* **dumdum bullet.** [From *Dum-Dum*, India.] *Mil.* A kind of expanding manstopping bullet.
dum'found', dumb'found' (dŭm'found'), *v. t. & i.* Also **dum'-found'er, dumb'found'er.** [*dumb* + con*found*.] To strike dumb, as with astonishment; to amaze. — **Syn.** See PUZZLE.

dum'my (dŭm'ĭ), *n.; pl.* -MIES (-ĭz). **1.** One who is dumb; hence, one who is habitually silent; also, a dolt. **2.** One posing or represented as acting for himself, but in reality acting for another. **3.** A copy of something, to be used as a substitute; a sham, as a lay figure on which clothing is exhibited by dealers. **4.** *Cards.* In various games, as bridge, an exposed hand played by one of the players in addition to his own hand; also, a player who lays his cards face up on the table to be so played by his partner. **5.** *Printing.* A pattern volume, often with blank pages, made in advance of an edition for demonstration purposes. — *adj.* **1.** Silent; mute. **2.** Fictitious or sham. **3.** Apparently acting for oneself, but really for another. **4.** Having the appearance of a (specified) thing but lacking capacity to function; as, *dummy* hinges. **5.** *Card Playing.* Played with a dummy; as, *dummy* whist.
dump (dŭmp), *n.* [MD. *domp* haze.] **1.** A dull, gloomy state of the mind; low spirits; — usually in the phrase *in the dumps*. **2.** *Archaic.* A melancholy tune; by extension, any tune.
dump, *n.* *Chiefly Eng.* A thick, ill-shaped lump or hunk of anything; specif., a lead counter used by boys in games.
dump, *v. t.* **1.** *Chiefly U.S.* To let fall in a mass; hence, to unload, as from a cart by tilting it; as, to *dump* coal, etc. **2.** *Com.* To sell in quantity at a very low price or practically regardless of the price; specif., to sell (surplus goods) abroad at less than the market price at home. — *v. i.* **1.** To drop down. **2.** *Chiefly U.S.* To deposit something in a heap or unshaped mass, as from a cart. **3.** *Com.* To dump goods. — *n.* **1.** *Chiefly U.S.* A place for dumping anything; also, that which is dumped. **2.** *Slang, U.S.* A shabby or dirty house; a place fit only for refuse. **3.** *Mil.* A place for the temporary storage of a division's supplies in the field; as, an ammunition *dump*. — **dump'er,** *n.*
dump'ish, *adj.* Dull; stupid; sad; moping; melancholy. — **dump'-ish·ly,** *adv.* — **dump'ish·ness,** *n.*
dump'ling (dŭmp'lĭng), *n.* [*dump* an ill-shaped piece + 1st *-ling*.] **1.** A small light mass of baking-powder-biscuit dough cooked either by boiling, as with a soup or stew, or by steaming or baking, esp. when it contains fruit. **2.** *Colloq.* A short, fat, dumpy person or animal.
dumps (dŭmps), *n. pl.* See 1st DUMP, 1.
dump'y (dŭmp'ĭ), *adj.;* DUMP'I·ER (-ĭ·ẽr); DUMP'I·EST. Sullen or discontented; in the dumps.
dump'y, *adj.* Short and thick; of proportionately low stature. — **dump'i·ly,** *adv.* — **dump'i·ness,** *n.*
dumpy level. *Surv.* A level having a short telescope, usually an inverting one, rigidly fixed to a table capable only of rotatory movement in a horizontal plane.
‖**dum spi'ro, spe'ro** (dŭm spī'rō, spē'rō). [L.] While I breathe, I hope; — a motto of South Carolina. Cf. ANIMIS OPIBUSQUE PARATI.
dun (dŭn), *v. t. & i.;* DUNNED (dŭnd); DUN'NING. To ask or beset, as a debtor, for payment; to urge importunately. — *n.* One who duns; also, an urgent request for payment.
dun, *adj.* [AS. *dunn*.] Dingy or dull grayish-brown. — *n.* **1.** Any of several colors varying from red to yellow in hue, of low or very low saturation and brilliance. See COLOR. **2.** A May fly. **3.** *Angling.* **a** Any winged insect as it emerges from the nymphal state. **b** Any artificial fly tied to imitate such an insect.
Dun'can Phyfe (dŭng'kăn fīf'). Designating furniture designed or like that designed by Duncan Phyfe, a New York City cabinetmaker (1768–1854).
dunce (dŭns), *n.* [From Joannes *Duns* Scotus (d. 1308), called the *Subtle Doctor*. Orig. in the phrase "a *Duns* man."] **1.** *Obs.* A sophist; hence, a pedant. **2.** A dull-witted person.
dunch (dŭnsh; do͝onsh), *n.* *Dial.* A short solid blow or shove.
dun'der·head' (dŭn'dẽr·hĕd'), *n.* Also **dun'der·pate'** (-pāt'). A dunce; blockhead. — **dun'der·head'ed,** *adj.*
dune (dūn), *n.* [F., of D. origin.] A hill or ridge of sand piled up by the wind.
dun fly. *Angling.* Any of various artificial flies, tied in imitation of certain flies in the nymphal stage.
dung (dŭng), *n.* [AS.] Manure; excrement. — *v. t.* To fertilize or dress with dung. — **dung'y** (-ĭ), *adj.*
dung (dŭng; do͝ong), *adj.* *Scot.* Exhausted.
dun'ga·ree' (dŭng'gȧ·rē'), *n.* Also **dun'ga·ri'** (-rē'). [Hind. *dūgrī*.] **1.** A coarse kind of East Indian cotton fabric worn by the poorer classes, and also used for tents, sails, etc. **2.** *pl.* Trousers, overalls, or working clothes of dungaree.
dung beetle. Any of numerous beetles, as the tumblebugs, dorbeetles, etc., that feed upon and breed in dung.
dun'geon (dŭn'jŭn), *n.* [OF. *donjon*, of Teut. origin.] **1.** A donjon. **2.** A close dark prison or vault, commonly underground.
dung'hill' (dŭng'hĭl'), *n.* **1.** A heap of dung. **2.** Any mean situation, condition, or thing; a vile abode. — **dung'hill',** *adj.*
dun'ie·was'sal (do͞on'ĭ·wŏs'ăl), *n.* [Gael. *duine* man + *uasal* noble.] *Scot.* A gentleman, esp. one of secondary rank.
dunk (dŭngk), *v. t. & i.* [G. *tunken*.] To dip (bread, or the like) into coffee, tea, etc., while eating. — **dunk'er,** *n.*
Dunk'er (dŭngk'ẽr), *n.* Also **Dunk'ard** (-ẽrd). [G. *tunker*, fr. *tunken* to dip.] A member of the Church of the Brethren or any of several related denominations practicing trine immersion and refusing oaths and military service.
Dun'kirk (dŭn'kûrk; dŭn·kûrk'), *n.* A desperate evacuation under bombardment of remnants of a defeated army; — after the retreat of the British from Dunkirk in June, 1940. See *Gaz.* — *v. i. & t.* To execute or force to execute a Dunkirk.
dun'lin (dŭn'lĭn), *n.;* see PLURAL, *Note*, 3. [*dun* brown + *-ling*.] A sandpiper (*Pelidna alpina*).
dun'nage (dŭn'ĭj), *n.* *Naut.* **1.** Loose material used around a cargo to prevent damage. **2.** Baggage or personal effects.
dunn'ite (dŭn'īt), *n.* [After Col. B. W. *Dunn* (1860–1936), Amer. soldier.] An explosive consisting chiefly of ammonium picrate.
dunt (dŭnt; do͝ont), *n.* [Var. of DINT.] *Scot. & Dial.* A dull-sounding blow; a wound or bruise from such a blow. — *v. t. & i.* *Chiefly Scot.* To strike or bruise with a dunt.
du'o (do͞o'ō), *n.; pl.* DUOS (-ōz), DUI (-ē). [It.] *Music.* A duet, esp. an instrumental duet.
du'o- (dū'ō-). [L. *duo*, or (irregularly) Gr. *duo* two.] A combining form meaning *two*.
du'o·de·cil'lion (-dē·sĭl'yŭn), *n.* See NUMERATION, *Table*.
du'o·dec'i·mal (-dĕs'ĭ·măl), *adj.* [L. *duodecim* twelve. See DOZEN.] Pertaining to twelve or twelfths; proceeding in computation by twelves.

Cf. DECIMAL. — *n.* 1. A twelfth part. 2. *pl. Arith.* A system of numbers whose denominations rise in a scale of twelves.

du′o·dec′i·mo (dū′ō·dĕs′ĭ·mō), *n.; pl.* -MOS (-mōz). [L. *in duodecimo* in twelfth.] A size of a book, or of its pages, resulting from folding each sheet into twelve leaves, measuring about 5¼ × 8⅛ inches; also, a book of such size; — called colloquially *twelvemo*, often written 12mo or 12°. — *adj.* Having twelve leaves to a sheet.

du′o·de′nal (-dē′n′l; dū·ŏd′′n·′l), *adj.* Of or pert. to the duodenum.

du′o·den′a·ry (dū′ō·dĕn′ȧ·rĭ; -dē′nȧ·rĭ; dū·ŏd′′n·ĕr′ĭ), *adj.* [L. *duodenarius*, fr. *duodeni* twelve each.] Containing twelve; twelvefold; increasing by twelves; having the radix twelve.

du′o·de′no- (dū′ō·dē′nō-; dū·ŏd′′n·ō-), **duoden-**. A combining form of *duodenum*, used to indicate *connection with*, or *relation to, the duodenum*, as in **du′o·de·ni′tis, du′o·de·nos′to·my, du′o·de·not′o·my** (see -ITIS, -STOMY, -TOMY).

du′o·de′num (dū′ō·dē′nŭm; dū·ŏd′′n·ŭm), *n.; pl.* -NA (-nȧ; -ȧ). [ML., fr. *duodeni* twelve each; from its length, about twelve fingers' breadth.] *Anat.* The first part of the small intestine leading from the stomach to the jejunum.

du′o·logue (dū′ō·lŏg; 74), *n.* [*duo-* + *-logue* as in mono*logue*.] Dialogue confined to two persons.

‖**duo′mo** (dwô′mō), *n.; pl.* -MI (-mē). [It.] In Italy, a cathedral.

du′o·tone (dū′ō·tōn), *adj.* Also **du′o·toned** (-tōnd). Having or yielding two tones or colors.

dup (dŭp), *v. t.* [Contr. fr. *do up*, that is, to lift up the latch.] *Obs. exc. Dial.* To open.

dupe (dūp), *n.* [F., earlier *duppe*, fr. L. *upupa* hoopoe.] One who has been or is easily deceived. — *v. t.* To delude; deceive; gull. — **dup′a·ble** (dūp′ȧ·b′l), *adj.* — **dup′er** (-ẽr), *n.*

Syn. Dupe, gull, trick, hoax mean to delude one by underhanded means. Dupe suggests unwariness in the person deluded and the acceptance of what is false as true, of counterfeit as genuine, or the like; gull, great credulousness in the victim or a disposition to be imposed upon; trick, an intent to delude on the part of the agent by means of a ruse, fraud, or the like, but it does not always imply a base end; hoax, a tricking with the aim of proving how gullible a person or persons can be when a skillful imposture is presented to them.

dup′er·y (dūp′ẽr·ĭ), *n.; pl.* -ERIES (-ĭz). Act or practice of duping; state of one who is duped.

du·pla′tion (dū·plā′shŭn), *n.* Doubling.

du′ple (dū′p′l), *adj.* [L. *duplus*. See DOUBLE.] 1. a Twofold. b Taken by twos. 2. So constructed rhythmically that there are two beats or some multiple of two to the measure; as, *duple* time.

du′plex (dū′plĕks), *adj.* [L., fr. *duo* two + the root of *plicare* to fold.] 1. Double; twofold. 2. *Mach.* Having two parts that operate at the same time or in the same way, where the simpler form has but one; as, a *duplex* lathe; a *duplex* drill. — **du·plex′i·ty** (dū·plĕk′sĭ·tĭ), *n.*

duplex apartment. In an apartment house, a suite that includes rooms on two floors.

duplex house. *U. S.* A two-family house.

duplex telegraphy. A system of telegraphy for sending two messages over the same wire simultaneously; — now restricted to sending of messages in opposite directions.

du′pli·cate (dū′plĭ·kāt), *adj.* [L. *duplicatus*, past part. of *duplicare* to double, fr. *duplex*. See DUPLEX.] 1. a Double; twofold. b That is a duplicate. 2. Designating a game, as at whist, in playing which the cards are kept as dealt and played again by other players, allowing a comparison of scores. — *n.* 1. That which exactly resembles or corresponds to something else; hence, a copy; counterpart. 2. *Card Playing.* Duplicate whist, bridge, etc. — **Syn.** See REPRODUCTION. — (-kāt), *v. t.* 1. To double; to fold; to render double. 2. To make a duplicate, copy, or transcript of.

du′pli·ca′tion (-kā′shŭn), *n.* 1. Act of duplicating, or state of being duplicated; esp., a doubling; a fold. 2. A duplicate; counterpart. — **du′pli·ca′tive** (dū′plĭ·kā′tĭv), *adj.*

du′pli·ca′tor (dū′plĭ·kā′tẽr), *n.* [LL., a doubler.] A copying machine, as a device for duplicating typewriting.

du·plic′i·ty (dū·plĭs′ĭ·tĭ), *n.; pl.* -TIES (-tĭz). [F. *duplicité*, fr. LL. *duplicitas*, fr. *duplex*. See DUPLEX.] Deception by pretending to entertain one set of feelings and acting under the influence of another; double-dealing.

du′ra (dū′rȧ), *n.* = DURA MATER. — **du′ral** (-răl), *adj.*

du′ra·ble (dū′rȧ·b′l), *adj.* [OF., fr. L. *durabilis*, fr. *durare* to last. See DURE, *v.*] Able to endure; lasting; enduring; not wearing out. — **Syn.** See LASTING. — **du′ra·bil′i·ty** (-bĭl′ĭ·tĭ), **du′ra·ble·ness**, *n.* — **du′ra·bly** (-blĭ), *adv.*

Du·ral′u·min (dū·răl′ū·mĭn), *n.* A trade-mark for an alloy of aluminum, light but comparable in strength and hardness to soft steel.

du′ra ma′ter (dū′rȧ mā′tẽr), *n.* [ML., lit., hard mother.] *Anat.* The tough, fibrous membrane which envelops the brain and spinal cord external to the arachnoid and pia mater.

du·ra′men (dū·rā′mĕn), *n.* [L., hardness, a hardened, i. e., ligneous, vine branch, fr. *durare* to harden.] *Bot.* The hard tough heartwood of a dicotyledonous tree.

dur′ance (dūr′ăns), *n.* [OF., duration.] 1. *Archaic.* Continuance; duration. 2. Imprisonment; duress.

‖**du·ran′te vi′ta** (dū·răn′tē vī′tȧ). [L.] During life.

du·ra′tion (dū·rā′shŭn), *n.* [OF. See DURE, *v.*] 1. Continuance in time. 2. The time within which a thing persists or lasts.

dur′bar (dûr′bär), *n.* [Hind. *darbār*, fr. Per. *darbār* house, court, hall of audience, fr. *dar* door, gate + *bār* court, assembly.] *India.* a An audience hall. b The court of a native prince; a state levee. c A formal reception of native princes, given by the governor general.

dure (dūr), *adj.* [L. *durus*.] *Archaic.* Hard; severe.

dure, *v. i. & t.* [OF. *durer*, fr. L. *durare*, prob. fr. L. *durus* hard.] *Archaic & Dial.* To endure; to last.

du′ress (dū′rĕs; dū·rĕs′), *n.* [OF. *duresse* hardship, severity, fr. L. *duritia, durities*, fr. *durus* hard.] Imprisonment; also, constraint; compulsion.

Dur′ham (dûr′ăm), *n.* An animal of a breed of short-horned beef cattle, originating in Durham, England.

du′ri·an (dōō′rĭ·ăn), **du′ri·on** (-ŏn), *n.* [Malay *durian*, fr. *duri* thorn.] The large oval edible fruit of a tree (*Durio zibethinus*) of the chocolate family, of the East Indies, having a hard prickly rind and soft pulp of fine flavor but offensive smell; also, the tree.

dur′ing (dūr′ĭng), *prep.* In the time of; throughout the course of; as, *during* life.

dur′mast (dûr′măst), *n.* A European oak (*Quercus sessiliflora*), having valuable dark, heavy, tough, elastic wood.

du′ro (dōō′rō), *n.; pl.* -ROS (-rōz). [Sp., short for *peso duro* hard peso.] A Spanish and Spanish American peso or dollar.

Du′roc–Jer′sey (dū′rŏk·jûr′zĭ), *n.* An animal of an American breed of short-headed red swine.

dur′ra (dōōr′ȧ), *n.* [Ar. *dhurah*.] A variety of a grain-yielding sorghum, widely grown for food, etc., in southern Asia and northern Africa.

durst (dûrst), *past* of DARE.

du′rum wheat (dū′rŭm). Also **du′rum**. See WHEAT.

dusk (dŭsk), *adj.* [ME. *dosc, deosc*, fr. AS. *dox*.] Tending to darkness; moderately dark; dusky. — *v. i. & t.* To grow or appear dusk; to darken. — *n.* 1. The darker part of twilight or of dawn. Cf. TWILIGHT. 2. Quality of being, or that which is, dusk; gloom; duskness. — **dusk′ish**, *adj.*

dusk′en (dŭs′kĕn), *v. t. & i.* To make, or grow, dusk.

dusk′y (dŭs′kĭ), *adj.;* DUSK′I·ER (-kĭ·ẽr); DUSK′I·EST. 1. Somewhat dark; blackish. 2. Gloomy; sad. — **dusk′i·ly**, *adv.* — **dusk′i·ness**, *n.*

Syn. (1) See DARK.

(2) Dusky, swarthy, tawny mean dark and dull. Dusky applies to what is somewhat dark yet not black and void of light or color; swarthy and tawny apply to darkness or dullness of hue or color only, *swarthy*, to a shade verging on blackness, *tawny*, to a yellowish-brown or tan color.

dust (dŭst), *n.* [AS. *dūst*.] 1. Fine dry pulverized particles of earth; hence, fine powder of any kind; as, bone *dust*. 2. The earthy remains of bodies once alive; esp., the human corpse. 3. The earth; the ground. 4. A cloud of dust; hence, turmoil. 5. *Rare.* A single particle, as of earth. 6. Something worthless; also, a low or mean condition; humiliation. 7. *Brit.* Sweepings or other refuse ready for collection. 8. Gold dust; hence, *Slang*, cash. — *v. t.* 1. To make dusty; to soil with dust. 2. To free from dust; to brush dust from. 3. To sprinkle with dust, powder, or the like. 4. To strew or sprinkle as dust or in the form of dust. — *v. i.* 1. To cover oneself with dust, as a bird. 2. To remove dust, as from furniture. — **dust′less**, *adj.*

dust′bin′ (dŭst′bĭn′), *n.* A receptacle for dust, ashes, etc.

dust bowl. A region that suffers from prolonged droughts and dust storms; specif., *U. S.* [*often caps.*], the region along the western border of the Great Plains.

dust′er (dŭs′tẽr), *n.* 1. One who or that which dusts. 2. A light overgarment to protect clothing from dust. 3. A device for sprinkling dust; as, a pepper *duster*.

dust′man′ (dŭst′măn′; -măn), *n.* 1. *Brit.* One whose employment is to remove dirt and refuse. 2. *Folklore.* The genius of sleep, whose coming is marked by one's winking or rubbing the eyes as if to remove dust; a sandman.

dust′pan′ (dŭst′păn′), *n.* A shovellike utensil for receiving and conveying away dust swept from the floor.

dust shot. The smallest size of shot, .04 inch in diameter.

dust storm. *Meteorol.* A violent dust-laden whirlwind moving across an arid region. The air is very hot, excessively dry, and attended by high electrical tension.

dust′y (dŭs′tĭ), *adj.;* DUST′I·ER (-tĭ·ẽr); DUST′I·EST. 1. Filled, abounding, or covered with dust. 2. Like, or of the nature of, dust. — **dust′i·ly**, *adv.* — **dust′i·ness**, *n.*

dusty miller. *Angling.* A type of artificial salmon fly. Cf. FLY, *Illust.*

Dutch (dŭch), *adj.* [MD. *dutsch, duutsc*, Hollandish, Germanic (D. *duitsch* German).] 1. *Now Local or Slang.* German; Germanic. 2. Of or pertaining to the Netherlands, or its inhabitants. 3. Characteristic of the Dutch. — *n.* 1. The language of the Netherlands Dutch, of which there are various dialects. See LOW GERMAN, INDO-EUROPEAN LANGUAGES, *Table.* 2. Collective *pl.* With *the*. The people of the Netherlands. 3. See PENNSYLVANIA DUTCH. — ***in Dutch.*** *Slang, U. S.* In disfavor or disgrace.

Dutch Belted. An animal of medium-sized breed of dairy cattle, black with a broad band of white around the body.

Dutch cheese. A small, round, hard cheese, made from skim milk; also, cottage cheese.

Dutch courage. *Colloq.* Courage due to intoxicants.

Dutch door. A door divided horizontally, so that the lower part can be shut while the upper remains open.

Dutch elm disease. A disease of elms caused by a fungus (*Graphium ulmi*), and characterized by yellowing of the foliage, defoliation, and death of the tree.

Dutch foil, leaf, *or* **gold.** Tombac rolled or beaten into thin sheets, used in Holland to ornament toys and paper.

Dutch′man (dŭch′măn), *n.* 1. A person of any of the Dutch (German) peoples. *Obs.*, exc. in local, careless, or slang usage. 2. A native of the Netherlands. 3. *Naut.* A Dutch vessel.

Dutch′man's–breech′es (dŭch′mănz·brĭch′ĕz; -ĭz), *n. sing. & pl.* A delicate spring-flowering herb (*Dicentra cucullaria*) of the fumitory family, of the eastern United States, having cream-white double-spurred flowers.

Dutch′man's–pipe′, *n.* A vine (*Aristolochia macrophylla*) of the birthwort family, with large leaves, and early summer flowers having the tube of the calyx curved like the bowl of a pipe.

Dutch metal. Tombac, esp. in the form of foil.

Dutch oven. a A tin screen for roasting before an open fire. b *U. S.* A shallow iron kettle for baking, with a rimmed cover to hold burning coals. c A brick oven in which cooking is done by the preheated walls after the fire has been let out.

Dutch treat. *Colloq.* A treat in which each person treats himself, or pays his own way.

Dutch uncle. *Colloq.* One who admonishes or reprimands with great severity and directness; a severe mentor.

du′te·ous (dū′tē·ŭs), *adj.* Fulfilling duty; dutiful; obedient. — **du′te·ous·ly**, *adv.* — **du′te·ous·ness**, *n.*

du′ti·a·ble (dū′tĭ·ȧ·b′l), *adj.* Subject to a duty, as imports.

du′ti·ful (-tĭ·fōōl; -f′l), *adj.* 1. Performing, or ready to perform, duties; obedient. 2. Controlled by, or proceeding from, a sense of duty; as, *dutiful* affection. — **du′ti·ful·ly**, *adv.* — **du′ti·ful·ness**, *n.*

du′ty (dū′tĭ; 114), *n.; pl.* DUTIES (-tĭz). [AF. *dueté*. See DUE.] 1. Conduct due to parents and superiors, as shown in obedience or submission; respect. 2. That which is required by one's station or occupation; any assigned service or business; as, the *duties* of a soldier. 3. That which a person is bound by moral obligation to do, or not to do;

also, the moral obligation itself. **4.** Any payment, service, or other render imposed and recoverable by law or custom, esp. one payable to the government. **5.** *Agric.* The quantity of irrigation water required to mature a given area of a given crop, expressed in acre-inches or acre-feet per acre; — called **duty of water.** **6.** *Mach.* Generally, work done by a given machine, etc., under given conditions. — **Syn.** See OBLIGATION: FUNCTION: TASK.

du·um′vir (dū·ŭm′vẽr), *n.; pl.* -VIRS (-vẽrz), -VIRI (-vĭ·rī). [L.] *Rom. Antiq.* Either member of a commission or board of two men.

du·um′vi·rate (-vĭ·răt), *n.* Union of two men in the same office; also, the government of two men thus associated.

du′ve·tyn (do͞o′vĕ·tēn), *n.* Also **du′ve·tine, du′ve·tyne.** [F. *duvet* down.] A soft fabric with a fine velvety nap, made of wool mixed with spun silk, or cotton, or both.

dwalm, dwam (dwäm; dwȧm), *n. & v. i.* *Dial.* Swoon.

dwarf (dwôrf), *n.* [AS. *dweorg, dweorh.*] **1.** An animal or plant much below the normal size of its species or kind; specif., a diminutive human being. **2.** *Astron.* In full, **dwarf star.** One of a class of stars of great density and relatively small mass whose average luminosity is about 1/100 that of the sun. Certain dwarfs of high temperature and extremely great density are known as ***white dwarfs.*** — *v. t.* To hinder from growing to natural size; to stunt; hence, to diminish in size, scope, power, etc. — *v. i.* To become dwarfed; to become small. — *adj.* Of less than the usual or normal size; stunted; puny. — **dwarf′ness,** *n.*

dwarf alder. A small American buckthorn (*Rhamnus alnifolia*) with alderlike leaves.

dwarf chestnut. = CHINQUAPIN **a.**

dwarf cornel. Either of two red-berried herbs of the dogwood family (*Chamaepericlymenum canadense* and *C. suecica*).

dwarf′ish (dwôr′fĭsh), *adj.* Like a dwarf; very small; pygmy. — **dwarf′ish·ly,** *adv.* — **dwarf′ish·ness,** *n.*

dwarf mallow. A prostrate European plant (*Malva rotundifolia*) of the mallow family, having roundish leaves and small flat fruits.

dwell (dwĕl), *v. i.;* DWELT (dwĕlt) or sometimes DWELLED (dwĕld); DWELL′ING. [AS. *dwellan* to mislead, hinder, tarry.] **1.** To delay; to tarry. **2.** To abide; remain; linger. **3.** To abide as a resident; to live in a place; reside. — **dwell′er** (-ẽr), *n.*

dwell′ing, *n.* Abode; residence.

dwin′dle (dwĭn′d'l), *v. i.;* DWIN′DLED (-d'ld); DWIN′DLING (-dlĭng). [AS. *dwīnan* to languish.] To diminish; to become less; to waste or consume away. — *v. t.* To make less; to bring low. — **Syn.** See DECREASE.

dwine (dwīn), *v. i.* *Archaic exc. Dial.* To waste away.

DX (dē′ĕks′). *Radio.* Distant; distance; — used to designate long-distance transmission.

dy′ad (dī′ăd), *n.* [LL. *dyas, dyadis,* the number two, fr. Gr. *dyas.*] **1.** Two units treated as one; a couple; a pair. **2.** *Biol.* One of the groups of two chromosomes formed by the division of a tetrad (which see); also, in morphology, a secondary unit formed of an aggregate of monads. — *adj.* Consisting of two; dyadic. — **dy·ad′ic** (dī·ăd′ĭk), *adj.*

Dy′ak (dī′ăk), *n.* One of the aborigines of Borneo, a group of tribes of Malayan speech.

dy′arch·y (dī′är·kĭ), *n.* [Gr. *dyo* two + *-archy.*] A dual form of government that obtained from 1919 to 1937 in each of the nine major provinces of India. — **dy·ar′chic** (dī·är′kĭk), **dy·ar′chi·cal,** *adj.*

dyb′buk (dĭb′ŭk). Var. of DIBBUK.

dye (dī), *n.* [AS. *dēag, dēah.*] **1.** Color produced by dyeing. **2.** A material used for dyeing; dyestuff. — *v. t.;* DYED (dīd); DYE′ING. **1.** To stain; to color, esp. by impregnating the substance with a coloring agent. **2.** To impart (a given color) by dyeing. — *v. i.* To take or impart color in dyeing. — ***dye in the wool.*** To imbue thoroughly. — **dy′er** (dī′ẽr), *n.*

dye′ing (dī′ĭng), *n.* Process or art of fixing coloring matters permanently and uniformly in the fibers of wool, cotton, etc.

dy′er's-broom′ (dī′ẽrz-bro͞om′), *n.* = WOODWAXEN.

dy′er's-weed′ (dī′ẽrz-wēd′), *n.* Any of several dye-yielding plants, as the woodwaxen.

dye′stuff′ (dī′stŭf′), *n.* A material used for dyeing; a dye.

dye′weed′ (-wēd′), *n.* **a** The woodwaxen. **b** A small American weedy herb (*Eclipta alba*) of the aster family.

dye′wood′ (-wo͝od′), *n.* Any wood, such as logwood, fustic, etc., from which coloring matter is extracted for dyeing.

dy′ing (dī′ĭng), *adj.* **1.** In the act of dying; mortal; perishable. **2.** Of or pertaining to dying or death.

dyke (dīk). Var. of DIKE.

dy′na- (dī′nȧ-; dĭn′ȧ-), **dyn-.** [See DYNAMIC.] A combining form meaning *power.*

dy·nam′e·ter (dī·năm′ē·tẽr; dĭ-), *n.* [*dyna-* + *-meter.* Cf. DYNAMOMETER.] *Optics.* An instrument for determining the magnifying power of telescopes.

dy·nam′ic (dī·năm′ĭk; dĭ-), *adj.* Also **dy·nam′i·cal** (-ĭ·kăl). [Gr. *dynamikos* powerful, fr. *dynamis* power, fr. *dynasthai* to be able.] **1.** *Physics.* **a** Of or pertaining to physical forces or energy; as, the *dynamic* theory of heat. **b** Of or pertaining to dynamics; active; — opposed to *static.* **2.** Belonging to, or characterized by, energy; forceful. **3.** Pertaining to change or process (regarded as manifestation of energy or agency). — **dy·nam′i·cal·ly,** *adv.*

dy·nam′ics (-ĭks), *n.;* see -ICS. **1.** That branch of mechanics treating of the motion of bodies (*kinematics*) and the action of forces in producing or changing their motion (*kinetics*). **2.** The moving moral, as well as physical, forces of any kind, or the laws relating to them.

dy′na·mism (dī′nȧ·mĭz'm; dĭn′ȧ-), *n.* *Philos.* Any theory which views the universe as essentially constituted by forces; as, the theory that energy is the ultimate physical reality is an example of *dynamism.* — **dy′na·mist** (-mĭst), *n.* — **dy′na·mis′tic** (-mĭs′tĭk), *adj.*

dy′na·mite (dī′nȧ·mīt; *now seldom* dĭn′ȧ-), *n.* [Gr. *dynamis* power.] An explosive made of nitroglycerin absorbed in a porous material. It was invented by Alfred Nobel in 1866. — ***v. t.*** To shatter with dynamite.

dy′na·mit′er (-mīt′ẽr), *n.* Also **dy′na·mit′ist** (-mīt′ĭst). One who uses dynamite, esp. for the anarchistic or other lawless destruction of life or property.

dy′na·mo (dī′nȧ·mō), *n.; pl.* -MOS (-mōz). [Short for *dynamoelectric machine.*] *Elec.* A machine for converting mechanical energy into electrical energy, esp. into direct-current electricity, by magnetoelectric induction. A dynamo may also be used as a motor. Cf. GENERATOR.

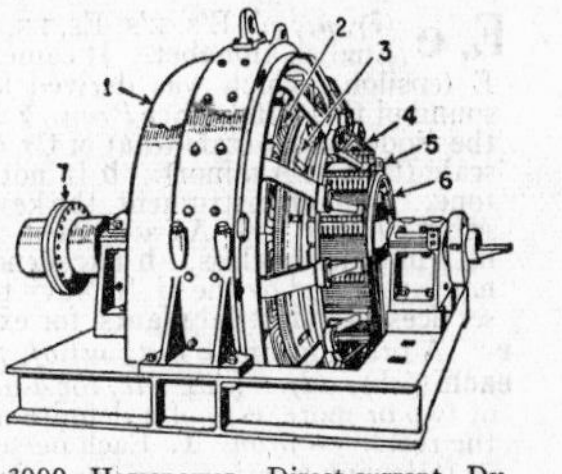

3000 Horsepower, Direct-current Dynamo. 1 Frame; 2 Field; 3 Armature; 4 Brush Rigging; 5 Brushes; 6 Commutator; 7 Coupling.

dy′na·mo- (dī′nȧ·mō-; dĭn′ȧ-). [See DYNAMIC.] A combining form meaning *power.*

dy′na·mo·e·lec′tric (-ē·lĕk′trĭk), *adj.* Also **dy′na·mo·e·lec′tri·cal** (-trĭ·kăl). Pertaining to the conversion, by induction, of mechanical energy into electrical energy, or of electrical energy into mechanical.

dy′na·mom′e·ter (dī′nȧ·mŏm′ē·tẽr; dĭn′ȧ-), *n.* [F. *dynamomètre.*] An apparatus for measuring power, esp. muscular effort of men or animals, or the power developed by a motor, or that required to operate machinery.

dy′na·mom′e·try (-trĭ), *n.; pl.* -TRIES (-trĭz). Art or process of measuring forces doing work. — **dy′na·mo·met′ric** (-mō·mĕt′rĭk), **dy′na·mo·met′ri·cal** (-rĭ·kăl), *adj.*

dy′na·mo′tor (dī′nȧ·mō′tẽr; dĭn′ȧ-), *n.* *Elec.* A special form of motor generator combining the motor and generator in a single machine.

dy′nast (dī′năst; -năst; *esp. Brit.,* dĭn′ăst), *n.* [L. *dynastes,* fr. Gr. *dynastēs,* fr. *dynasthai* to be able.] A ruler; prince.

dy′nas·ty (dī′năs·tĭ *or, esp. Brit.,* dĭn′ăs-), *n.; pl.* -TIES (-tĭz). A race or succession of kings, of the same line or family; the continued lordship of a race of rulers. — **dy·nas′tic** (dī·năs′tĭk; dĭ-), **dy·nas′ti·cal** (-tĭ·kăl), *adj.* — **dy·nas′ti·cal·ly,** *adv.*

dy′na·tron (dī′nȧ·trŏn; dĭn′ȧ-), *n.* [NL., fr. *dyna-* + electr*on.*] *Elec.* A multielectrode vacuum tube in which the secondary emission of electrons from the plate results in a decrease in the plate current as the plate voltage increases. The dynatron is often used in radio as an oscillator.

dyne (dīn), *n.* [F., fr. Gr. *dynamis* power.] *Physics.* The unit of force in the C.G.S. system of physical units. It is such a force that under its influence a body whose mass is one gram would experience an acceleration of one centimeter per second per second.

dys- (dĭs-). [Gr. *dys-* hard, ill.] A prefix used to signify *ill, bad, hard, difficult,* and the like.

dys·cra′si·a (dĭs·krā′zhĭ·ȧ; -zhȧ), *n.* [ML., fr. Gr. *dyskrasia,* fr. *dys-* bad + *krasis* mixture, fr. *kerannynai* to mix.] *Med.* An ill habit or state of the constitution.

dys′en·ter′y (dĭs′ĕn·tẽr′ĭ *or, esp. Brit.,* -trĭ), *n.* [OF. *dissenterie,* fr. L., fr. Gr. *dysenteria,* fr. *dys-* + *enteron,* pl. *entera,* intestines.] *Med.* A disease attended with inflammation of the large intestine, griping pains, constant desire to evacuate the bowels, and the discharge of mucus and blood. — **dys′en·ter′ic** (dĭs′ĕn·tẽr′ĭk), *adj.*

dys·func′tion (dĭs·fŭngk′shŭn), *n.* [*dys-* + *function.*] *Med.* Impaired functioning, as of an organ of the body.

dys·gen′ic (-jĕn′ĭk), *adj.* [*dys-* + *-genic.*] *Eugenics & Biol.* Detrimental to the hereditary qualities of a stock, as of man; biologically defective. Cf. EUGENIC.

dys·gen′ics (-jĕn′ĭks), *n.;* see -ICS. The study of racial degeneration. Cf. EUGENICS.

dys′lo·gis′tic (dĭs′lō·jĭs′tĭk), *adj.* [*dys-* + eu*logistic.*] Unfavorable. Cf. EULOGISTIC. — **dys′lo·gis′ti·cal·ly** (-tĭ·kăl·ĭ), *adv.*

dys·met′ri·a (dĭs·mĕt′rĭ·ȧ), *n.* [NL., fr. *dys-* + Gr. *metron* measure + *-ia.*] *Psychiatry.* Impaired ability to estimate distance in muscular action.

dys′pa·thy (dĭs′pȧ·thĭ), *n.* [*dys-* + sym*pathy.*] *Rare.* Antipathy; lack of sympathy.

dys·pep′sia (dĭs·pĕp′shȧ; -sĭ·ȧ), *n.* [L., fr. Gr. *dyspepsia,* fr. *dys-* hard + *peptein, pessein,* to cook, digest.] *Med.* Difficult or deranged digestion; indigestion.

dys·pep′sy (-pĕp′sĭ), *n.* *Now Chiefly Dial.* Dyspepsia.

dys·pep′tic (-tĭk), **dys·pep′ti·cal** (-tĭ·kăl), *adj.* Pertaining to or having dyspepsia. — **dys·pep′ti·cal·ly,** *adv.*

dys·pep′tic, *n.* A person having dyspepsia.

dys·pha′gi·a (dĭs·fā′jĭ·ȧ), *n.* [NL., fr. *dys-* + *-phagia.*] Difficulty in swallowing. — **dys·phag′ic** (-făj′ĭk), *adj.*

dys·pha′si·a (-zhĭ·ȧ; -zhȧ), *n.* [NL., fr. *dys-* + *-phasia.*] Imperfection in, or loss of, the power to use or to understand language, caused by injury to or disease of the brain. Cf. APHASIA.

dys·pho′ni·a (dĭs·fō′nĭ·ȧ), *n.* [NL., fr. Gr. *dysphōnia,* fr. *dys-* hard + *phōnē* sound, voice.] Difficulty in pronouncing vocal sounds. — **dys·phon′ic** (-fŏn′ĭk), *adj.*

dys·pho′ri·a (-fō′rĭ·ȧ), *n.* [NL., fr. Gr., fr. *dysphoros* hard to bear.] *Psychol.* A sense of ill-being and dissatisfaction.

dysp·ne′a, dysp·noe′a (dĭsp·nē′ȧ), *n.* [L. *dyspnoea,* fr. Gr. *dyspnoia,* fr. *dyspnoos* short of breath, fr. *dys-* hard + *pnoē, pnoiē,* breathing.] *Med.* Difficult or labored respiration. Cf. EUPNEA, HYPERPNEA. — **dysp·ne′al, dysp·noe′al** (-ăl), **dysp·ne′ic, dysp·noe′ic** (-ĭk), **dysp·no′ic** (-nō′ĭk), *adj.*

dys·pro′si·um (dĭs·prō′shĭ·ŭm; -sĭ·ŭm), *n.* [NL., fr. Gr. *dysprositos* hard to get at.] *Chem.* An element of the rare-earth group, the most magnetic substance known. Symbol, *Dy;* at. no., 66; at. wt., 162.46.

dys′tro·phy (dĭs′trō·fĭ), *n.* Also **dys·tro′phi·a** (dĭs·trō′fĭ·ȧ). [NL. *dystrophia.*] *Med. & Biol.* Imperfect or faulty nutrition. — **dys·troph′ic** (dĭs·trŏf′ĭk), *adj.*

dys·u′ri·a (dĭs·ū′rĭ·ȧ), *n.* [LL., fr. Gr. *dysouria,* fr. *dys* + *ouron* urine.] *Med.* Difficult discharge of urine.

E

E, e (ē), *n.; pl.* E's, e's, Es, es, ees (ēz). **1.** The fifth letter of the English alphabet. It came through the Latin from the Greek E (epsilon), which was derived from a Phoenician letter. **2.** The sound of this letter. See *Pron.*, § 26. **3.** *Music.* **a** The third tone of the model major scale (that of C), or the fifth tone of its relative minor scale (that of A minor). **b** In notation, any symbol representing this tone. **c** On an instrument, the key or string producing this tone. See PITCH, *Illust.* **4.** As a *symbol*, used to denote or indicate: **a** The fifth in order or class. **b** Excellence — specif. when displayed on pennants awarded by the U. S. Navy to ships and crews, and by the armed services to industrial plants, for exceptional performance.

e-. A prefix meaning *out, out of, from,* etc. See EX-.

each (ēch), *adj.* [AS. *ǣlc*, for *ā-gelīc* ever alike.] Every (individual of two or more, esp. of a definite number) considered separately from the rest. — *pron.* **1.** Each person. **2.** All, considered one by one; — following a series. — *adv.* To or for each; apiece. Abbr. *ea.*

each other. A phrase used as a reciprocal pronoun in oblique cases; as, we saw *each other's* faces.

ea'ger (ē'gẽr), *adj.* [OF. *aigre*, fr. L. *acer* sharp, sour, spirited, zealous.] **1.** *Archaic.* Sharp; keen. **2.** Spirited; sharply contested, as a fight. **3.** Ardent to pursue, perform, or obtain; keenly desirous. — **ea'ger·ly**, *adv.* — **ea'ger·ness**, *n.*

Syn. **Eager, avid, keen, anxious, athirst** mean actuated by urgent desire. **Eager** implies ardor and, often, enthusiasm and, less often, impatience; **avid** adds to *eager* the implication of greed or unbounded desire; **keen** suggests intensity of interest and quick responsiveness in action; **anxious** emphasizes fear lest one's desires be frustrated or one's hopes not realized; **athirst** stresses yearning more vividly than the others but it seldom connotes readiness for action. — **Ant.** Listless.

ea'ger (ē'gẽr; ā'gẽr). Var. of EAGRE.

eager beaver. One who is overzealous, overdiligent, and feverishly impatient to perform not only his part but to volunteer for more.

ea'gle (ē'g'l), *n.* [OF. *egle, aigle*, fr. L. *aquila.*] **1.** Any of various large diurnal birds of prey of the falcon family (Falconidae), noted for their strength, size, graceful figure, keenness of vision, and powers of flight. The typical eagles constitute a genus (*Aquila*) in which the legs are feathered to the toes. Well-known species include: the large powerful ***golden eagle*** (*Aquila chrysaëtos*) of the Northern Hemisphere, of which the American race (*A. c. canadensis*) is now rare; the ***imperial eagle*** (*A. heliaca*) of Europe; the common North American eagle, ***bald eagle*** (*Haliaeetus leucocephalus*), having white feathers covering the head and neck after it is several years old; the allied flesh-eating ***sea eagle***, esp. the northern European ***white-tailed sea eagle*** (*Haliaeetus albicilla*); the large double-crested ***harpy eagle*** (*Harpia harpyja*) of tropical America. **2.** The seal or standard of any nation having an eagle as emblem, as the United States, or France under the Bonapartes. **3.** A gold coin of the United States, of the value of ten dollars; — from the eagle on the reverse. **4.** [*cap.*] The constellation Aquila. **5.** *Golf.* A score of two strokes less than par on any hole but a par-three hole. Cf. BIRDIE.

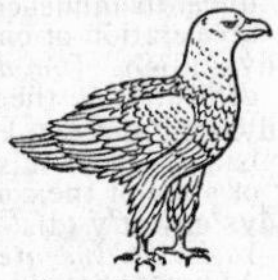
Eagle (*Haliaeetus leucocephalus*).

ea'gle·stone' (-stōn'), *n.* *Mineral.* A concretionary nodule of clay ironstone, about the size of a walnut. Ancients believed that eagles took these stones to their nest to facilitate egg-laying.

ea'glet (ē'glĕt; -glĭt), *n.* [F. *aiglette.*] A young eagle.

ea'gre (ē'gẽr; ā'gẽr), *n.* A bore; a tidal flood, or flow.

eal'der·man, eal'dor·man. Obs. exc. hist. forms of ALDERMAN.

ean'ling (ēn'lĭng), *n.* *Obs.* A yeanling.

ear (ēr), *n.* [AS. *ēare.*] **1.** The organ of hearing. In man and the other mammals the ear consists of three parts: the external ear, which includes the *pinna* and external auditory meatus, or opening; the middle ear, drum, or *tympanum;* and the internal ear, or *labyrinth.* The middle ear is a cavity connected by the *Eustachian tube* with the pharynx, separated from the external auditory meatus by the *tympanic membrane,* and containing a chain of three small bones, named *malleus, incus,* and *stapes,* which connect this membrane with the internal ear. **2.** The external ear of man and most mammals. **3.** The sense or act of hearing; also, a refined or acute sense of hearing; as, a nice *ear* for music. **4.** Attention, esp. favorable attention; hearing; audience. **5.** That which resembles in shape or position the ear of an animal, as one of a pair of tufts of feathers on the head of a bird, a projecting lug on a vase or jar, etc.

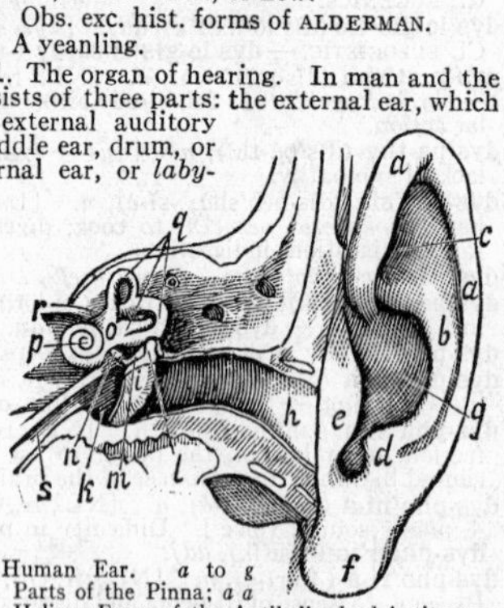

Human Ear. *a* to *g* Parts of the Pinna; *a a* Helix; *c* Fossa of the Antihelix, *b*; *d* Antitragus; *e* Tragus; *f* Lobule or Lobe; *g* Concha; *h* Auditory Canal; *i* Tympanic Membrane; *k* Tympanum; *l* Malleus; *m* Incus; *n* Stapes; *o* Vestibule; *p* Cochlea; *q* three Semicircular Canals; *r* Auditory Nerve; *s* Eustachian Tube.

ear (ēr), *n.* [AS. *ēar.*] The fruiting spike of any cereal (as Indian corn, wheat, rye, etc.), including the kernels or grains. — *v. i.* To put forth ears; to form ears.

ear'ache' (ēr'āk'), *n.* Ache or pain in the ear.

ear'drop' (-drŏp'), *n.* A pendant for the ear.

ear'drum' (-drŭm'), *n.* Tympanic membrane of the ear.

eared (ērd), *adj.* Having ears; esp., having external ears; as, the **eared seal**, a seal (family Otariidae) with small but well-developed ears.

ear'ing (ēr'ĭng), *n.* [From 1st EAR.] *Naut.* A line used to fasten the upper corners of a sail to the yard or gaff.

earl (ûrl), *n.* [AS. *eorl* man, noble.] In Great Britain and Ireland, a nobleman ranking below a marquis and above a viscount. The rank of earl corresponds to that of the *count* of the continent of Europe. Hence, the wife of an earl is still called *countess.* — **earl'ship**, *n.*

earl'dom (-dŭm), *n.* The jurisdiction, territorial possessions, title, or dignity of an earl.

earl marshal. The head of the Heralds' College in England. The office is now hereditary in the line of the dukes of Norfolk. The earl marshal attends the sovereign at the opening and closing of parliament, arranges the order of state processions, etc.

ear'ly (ûr'lĭ), *adv.; -LI·ER* (-lĭ·ẽr); *-LI·EST.* [AS. *ǣrlīce*, fr. *ǣr* sooner + *-līce* -ly.] **1.** At or in a time or position near the beginning of a period, epoch, season, series, etc. **2.** In good season; betimes. — *adj.* **1.** Coming or occurring in advance of the usual or appointed time; in good season. **2.** Coming near the beginning of a period, series, etc.; specif.: **a** Occurring in, or belonging to, remote past time; ancient. **b** Near in the future; as, reply at an *early* date. — **ear'li·ness** (-lĭ·nĕs; -nĭs), *n.*

ear'mark' (ēr'märk'), *n.* A mark of identification on the ear; hence, any mark of identification. — *v. t.* To place an earmark on; to mark in a distinctive way.

earn (ûrn), *v. t.* [AS. *earnian.*] **1.** To merit or deserve, as by labor or service. **2.** To acquire by labor, service, or performance; as, to *earn* a good living. — **Syn.** See GET. — **earn'er**, *n.*

earn, *v. i. & t.* [See YEARN.] *Obs.* To yearn; grieve.

ear'nest (ûr'nĕst; -nĭst), *n.* [AS. *eornost, eornest.*] An aroused and intent mental state; as, to be in *earnest.* — *adj.* **1.** Characterized by, or proceeding from, an intense and serious state of mind; not flippant. **2.** Of important nature; not trivial. — **Syn.** See SERIOUS. — **ear'nest·ly**, *adv.* — **ear'nest·ness**, *n.*

ear'nest, *n.* [Appar. fr. OF. *erres*, pl., fr. L. *arra, arrha, arrhabo*, fr. Gr. *arrhabōn*, fr. Heb. *'ērābōn.*] **1.** *Law.* Something of value given by a buyer to a seller, to bind the bargain. **2.** A token of what is to come; pledge.

earnest money. Money paid as earnest (sense 1).

earn'ing (ûr'nĭng), *n.* [AS. *earnung.*] Act or process of earning, or what is earned; esp., *pl.*, wages.

ear'phone' (ēr'fōn'), *n.* *Colloq.* A headphone.

ear'ring' (ēr'rĭng'), *n.* Orig., an ornament consisting of a ring through the pierced lobe of the ear, with or without a pendant; now, usually, an ornament screwed to the ear.

ear shell. An abalone. See ABALONE, *Illust.*

ear'shot' (ēr'shŏt'), *n.* Also **ear'reach'** (-rēch'). The range within which the unaided voice may be heard.

ear stone. An otolith.

earth (ûrth), *n.* [AS. *eorthe.*] **1.** The softer part of land, in distinction from rock; soil. **2.** The world as the dwelling place of man, in distinction from heaven and hell. **3.** The land; land areas, as distinguished from the sea or air. **4.** *Now Poetic.* A part of the ground; a country. **5.** The planet which we inhabit, the fifth in order of size and third in order of distance from the sun. Astronomical symbol, ⊕. It has a diameter of 7918 miles, a period of 365.26 days, and a mean distance of 92,900,000 miles from the sun. See PLANET, *Table.* **6.** The people on this planet. **7.** The lair of a burrowing animal. **8. a** The mortal body. **b** Worldly things, as opposed to spiritual things. **9.** *Chem.* Any of several difficultly reducible metallic oxides, as alumina, zirconia, yttria, formerly classed as elements. See RARE EARTH. **10.** *Elec.* = GROUND, *n.*, 10.

Syn. **Earth, world, universe** here mean the entire area in which man thinks of himself as living. **Earth**, in this sense, usually refers to the sphere or globe which astronomers call the earth, but is sometimes thought of as opposed to unastronomical regions of heaven and hell; **world**, a far less definite term, may apply to that illimitable area which, to man's limited senses, includes the earth and other planets and all the space surrounding it and all the bodies contained in it, but it is often used as equal to *earth;* **universe**, in its most precise sense, denotes the entire system of created things (or of physical phenomena) regarded as a unit both in its organization and operation.

— *v. t. & i.* **1.** *Obs. exc. Dial.* To inter; bury. **2.** To hide, or drive to hiding, in the earth. **3.** *Elec. & Radio.* To ground.

earth'born' (-bôrn'), *adj.* **1.** Born on or of the earth; human; mortal. **2.** Relating to, or caused by, earthly objects.

earth'-bound', *adj.* Bound by earth or earthly interests.

earth'en (ûr'thĕn), *adj.* Made of earth; also, earthly.

earth'en·ware' (-wâr'), *n.* Vessels, ornaments, or the like, made of fired clay, esp. the coarser kinds.

earth'light' (ûrth'līt'), *n.* *Astron.* Earthshine.

earth'ling (-lĭng), *n.* An inhabitant of the earth.

earth'ly (ûrth'lĭ), *adj.* [AS. *eorthlīc.*] **1.** Of, like, or pertaining to the earth; esp., belonging to this world, or to man's existence on the earth; worldly. **2.** Possible; conceivable; as, no *earthly* use. — **earth'li·ness** (-lĭ·nĕs; -nĭs), *n.*

Syn. **Earthly, terrestrial, mundane, worldly** mean belonging to or characteristic of earth. **Earthly** is used chiefly in opposition to *heavenly* (as, *earthly* love); **terrestrial**, in opposition to *celestial* (as, the *terrestrial* globe); **mundane** and **worldly** both imply a relation to the world thought of as the concerns and activities of men, *mundane* implying opposition to *eternal* (as, *mundane* interests) and *worldly* to *spiritual* (as, a *worldly* character). — **Ant.** Heavenly.

earth'nut' (-nŭt'), *n.* Any of various roots, tubers, or subterranean pods, such as the peanut; specif., the hognut or pignut; also, any plant producing such a root or tuber.

earth'pea' (-pē'), *n.* A vine (*Amphicarpa comosa*) of the pea family, which ripens its pods underground like the peanut.

earth'quake' (-kwāk'), *n.* A trembling of a portion of the earth, caused by faulting of the rocks or by volcanic shocks.

earth'shine' (ûrth'shīn'), *n.* *Astron.* Sunlight which the earth reflects, and which faintly illumines the darker part of the moon near the time of new moon.

earth'star' (-stär'), *n.* A fungus (genus *Geaster*), the outer layer of which splits into the shape of a star.

earth'ward (-wẽrd), **earth'wards** (-wẽrdz), *adv.* Toward the earth. — **earth'ward**, *adj.*

earth'work' (-wûrk'), *n.* *Engin.* The operations connected with excavations and embankments of earth in construction work; also, an embankment or construction made of earth, specif. one constructed for military purposes.

earth'worm' (ûrth'wûrm'), *n.* **1.** Any of numerous oligochaetous worms (*Lumbricus* and allied genera) found in damp soil. **2.** A mean, sordid person.

earth'y (ûr'thĭ), *adj.;* EARTH'I·ER (-thĭ·ẽr); EARTH'I·EST. **1.** Consisting of, or resembling, earth. **2.** Of or pertaining to the earth; terrestrial; esp., worldly. **3.** Gross; low.

ear trumpet. A trumpet-shaped instrument for collecting and intensifying sounds to aid a person of defective hearing.

ear'wax' (ēr'wăks'), *n. Physiol.* Cerumen.

ear'wig' (-wĭg'), *n.* [AS. *ēarwicga,* fr. *ēare* ear + *wicga* beetle, worm.] **1.** Any of a family (Forficulidae) of harmless insects having slender many-jointed antennae, and a pair of large forcepslike appendages at the end of the body; — so called from the mistaken belief that they crept into the human ear. **2.** *U.S.* Also, any of a genus (*Geophilus*) of small centipedes. — *v. t.;* -WIGGED' (-wĭgd'); -WIG'-GING. To annoy, or attempt to influence, by private talk.

ease (ēz), *n.* [OF. *aise* elbowroom, comfort, fr. L. *adjacens* neighborhood, environs.] **1.** State of being comfortable; freedom from pain, trouble, or annoyance; quiet. **2.** Freedom from constraint, formality, embarrassment, etc.; naturalness; as, *ease* of address. **3.** Freedom from difficulty or effort; as, *ease* in writing or composing. — *v. t. & i.* [OF. *aaisier,* fr. *aise.*] **1.** To free from anything that pains, disquiets, or oppresses; to relieve. **2.** To render less painful; to alleviate. **3.** To lessen the pressure or tension of, as by slackening, lifting, or shifting. **4.** To make less difficult; to facilitate. **5.** *Naut.* To put the helm of (a ship) alee, or to regulate the sail of, so as to meet a wave bow on. — ***ease the helm or rudder.*** *Naut.* To let the tiller come back a little after having been put hard over.

ease'ful (ēz'fo͝ol; -f'l), *adj.* Full of ease; restful.

ea'sel (ē'z'l), *n.* [D. *ezel* ass, donkey, hence, easel, fr. L. *asinus* ass.] A frame to hold a canvas upright for the painter's convenience, or to hold a picture or the like for exhibition.

ease'ment (ēz'mĕnt), *n.* **1.** Act of easing, or relieving, as from pain or discomfort; that which gives ease or relief. **2.** *Law.* An acquired privilege or right of use or enjoyment which one person may have in the land of another.

eas'i·er (ēz'ĭ·ẽr), **eas'i·est,** *adj., compar. & superl.* of EASY.

eas'i·ly (ēz'ĭ·lĭ), *adv.* In any easy manner.

eas'i·ness (-ĭ·nĕs; -nĭs), *n.* State or condition of being easy.

east (ēst), *n.* [AS. *ēast, ēastan,* adv.] **1.** The direction of sunrise; accurately, that point on the sensible horizon (see HORIZON, *n.,* 3) where the center of the sun is seen to rise at the equinox; the direction toward the right hand of one facing north. Abbr. *E.* See COMPASS CARD, *Illust.* **2.** [*cap.*] Regions or countries lying to the east, collectively; specif.: **a** The countries of Asia and of the Asiatic archipelagoes; the Orient; — so called as being east of Europe. **b** *U.S. Hist. & Geog.* Formerly, the part of the United States east of the Allegheny Mountains, esp. the New England States; now, often, the region east of the Mississippi River, esp. that north of Maryland and the Ohio River. — *adj.* **1.** Toward or at the east; also, from the east; as, the *east* wind. **2.** *Eccl.* Toward or in the direction of the altar as situated with respect to the nave. — *adv.* Eastward.

east by north. *Navig. & Surv.* One point, or 11° 15', north of due east; N. 78° 45' E. Abbr. *E b* (or *by*) *N.* See COMPASS CARD, *Illust.*

east by south. *Navig. & Surv.* One point, or 11° 15', south of due east; S. 78° 45' E. Abbr. *E b* (or *by*) *S.* See COMPASS CARD, *Illust.*

East'er (ēs'tẽr), *n.* [AS. *ēastre,* pl. *ēastron,* fr. name of old Teut. goddess of spring, AS. *Ēastre.*] An annual church celebration commemorating Christ's resurrection. Easter is the first Sunday after the first full moon that falls on or next after the vernal equinox (March 21 in the Gregorian calendar); if the full moon happens on Sunday, Easter is celebrated one week later. Easter Sunday cannot be earlier than March 22 or later than April 25; dates of all other movable church feasts depend on that of Easter.

The Easter dates for the years 1945–1964 are:

Year	Ash Wednesday	Easter	Year	Ash Wednesday	Easter
1945	Feb. 14	Apr. 1	1955	Feb. 23	Apr. 10
1946	Mar. 6	Apr. 21	1956	Feb. 15	Apr. 1
1947	Feb. 19	Apr. 6	1957	Mar. 6	Apr. 21
1948	Feb. 11	Mar. 28	1958	Feb. 19	Apr. 6
1949	Mar. 2	Apr. 17	1959	Feb. 11	Mar. 29
1950	Feb. 22	Apr. 9	1960	Mar. 2	Apr. 17
1951	Feb. 7	Mar. 25	1961	Feb. 15	Apr. 2
1952	Feb. 27	Apr. 13	1962	Mar. 7	Apr. 22
1953	Feb. 18	Apr. 5	1963	Feb. 27	Apr. 14
1954	Mar. 3	Apr. 18	1964	Feb. 12	Mar. 29

Easter egg. An egg or, now often, a candy or other imitation of an egg, given as a present at Easter.

east'er·ling (ēs'tẽr·lĭng), *n. Hist.* A native of a country or region eastward of another.

east'er·ly, *adj. & adv.* Situated, directed, or moving toward the east; also, of winds, blowing from the east.

Easter Monday. See HOLIDAY, 3.

east'ern (ēs'tẽrn), *adj.* **1.** [*cap.*] Belonging to, or characteristic of, the East; Oriental. **2.** East or easterly; as, an *eastern* wind or voyage. — **east'ern·most** (-mōst), *adj.*

Eastern Church. Orig., the Church in the Eastern Roman Empire; now, any body of Christians following an Eastern rite (Armenian, Byzantine, Chaldean, Coptic, Maronite, Syrian) as distinguished from the Roman rite.

east'ern·er (ēs'tẽr·nẽr), *n.* A native or inhabitant of the east, esp. [*cap.*] of the eastern United States.

Eastern Question. Orig., the problem of international politics arising from the instability of the Mohammedan power of Turkey and its relations with the other nations of Europe; later, other problems of the Near East.

Eastern standard time, Eastern time. See STANDARD TIME.

East'er·tide' (ēs'tẽr·tīd'), *n., or* **Easter time.** The period from Easter to Ascension Day (40 days), or, sometimes, to Whitsunday (50 days) or to Trinity Sunday (57 days).

east'ing (ēs'tĭng), *n.* **1.** *Navig.* Departure in an easterly direction. See DEPARTURE, 4 **a.** **2.** Easterly direction.

east'-north'east', *n., adj., & adv. Navig.* Two points, or 22° 30', north of due east; N. 67° 30' E. Abbr. *ENE.* See COMPASS CARD, *Illust.*

east'-south'east', *n., adj., & adv. Navig.* Two points, or 22° 30', south of due east; S. 67° 30' E. Abbr. *ESE.* See COMPASS CARD, *Illust.*

east'ward (ēst'wẽrd), **east'wards** (-wẽrdz), *adv.* Toward the east; in the direction of east from some point or place.

east'ward, *adj.* Moving, bearing, or looking toward the east. — *n.* The east.

east'ward·ly (-lĭ), *adv. & adj.* Toward the east, or, of winds, from the east.

eas'y (ēz'ĭ), *adj.;* EAS'I·ER (-ĭ·ẽr); EAS'I·EST. [OF. *aisié,* prop. past part. of *aisier.*] **1.** At ease; free from trouble, pain, care, worry, constraint, etc. **2.** Causing or attended with little difficulty or discomfort. **3.** Supportable with ease; not burdensome; of garments or fittings, not unduly tight. **4.** Of persons, moods, etc.: **a** Not harsh or exacting; lenient. **b** Not difficult to influence; tractable. **5. a** Giving ease, freedom from care, or comfort. **b** Given to ease or to idleness. **6.** Moderate; unhurried. **7.** *Card Playing.* Evenly divided between opposing sides; as, *easy* aces. **8.** *Finance.* Designating a money market in which funds are plentiful and interest rates low. Cf. TIGHT, *adj.,* 11.

Syn. (1) See COMFORTABLE.

(2) **Easy, facile, simple, light, effortless, smooth** mean not demanding or involving much effort or difficulty. **Easy,** however, is applicable not only to persons and things that impose tasks but to the activities required by such tasks; **facile,** once a close synonym of *easy,* now more often applies to that which comes, moves, works, etc., seemingly without effort or at call, and often connotes, in derogatory use, undue haste, shallowness, or the like; **simple,** as here compared, stresses ease in understanding because lacking in intricacy; **light** stresses freedom from exactions that make heavy demands on one; **effortless** stresses the appearance of ease but, usually, the attainment of mastery, artistry, etc.; **smooth** stresses the absence or removal of all difficulties or hardships, as from a course or career. — **Ant.** Hard.

eas'y·go'ing (-gō'ĭng; 2), *adj.* Having a comfortable gait; hence, taking life easily. — **eas'y·go'ing·ness,** *n.*

eat (ēt), *v. t.; past* ATE (āt; *Brit. commonly* ĕt), *Archaic* EAT (ĕt; ēt); *past part.* EAT'EN (ēt''n), *Archaic* EAT (ĕt; ēt); *pres. part.* EAT'ING. [AS. *etan.*] **1.** To take in through the mouth as food; ordinarily, to chew and swallow, as solid food. **2.** To devour or consume; to destroy, use up, or waste, as by eating; hence, to ravage. **3.** To consume gradually; to waste or wear away; to corrode. **4.** To gnaw, perforate, or bore into. — *v. i.* **1.** To take food or a meal. **2.** To wear or waste away, as by corrosion, rusting, etc. — ***eat crow*** (krō). To accept what one has fought against. — ***eat humble pie.*** To be submissive, esp. when compelled to retract something or to retreat from a position. See HUMBLE PIE. — ***eat one's words.*** To retract what one has said.

eat'a·ble (ēt'ȧ·b'l), *adj.* Capable of being, or fit to be, eaten. — *n.* Something eatable; esp., *pl.,* things to eat.

eat'er (ēt'ẽr), *n.* One who or that which eats.

eath (ēth; ēth), *adj. & adv. Scot.* Easy; easily.

‖**eau** (ō), *n.; pl.* EAUX (ō). [F., fr. L. *aqua.*] Water.

Eau de Co·logne' (dē kō·lōn'). A trade-mark for a perfumed liquid, composed of alcohol and certain aromatic oils, used as a toilet water. See COLOGNE.

‖**eau de vie** (ō' d'vē'; ōd'vē'). [F., lit., water of life.] Any spirit distilled from wine, esp. brandy.

eaves (ēvz), *n. pl.; sing.* EAVE. Historically, EAVES is a singular, but it is now taken as a plural, and an assumed singular EAVE has been formed. [AS. *efes* eaves, brim, brink.] The projecting lower edges of a roof, overhanging the walls of a building.

eaves'drop' (ēvz'drŏp'), *formerly* **eaves'drip'** (-drĭp'), *n.* Also **eave'-drop'** (ēv'-). Water which falls in drops from the eaves of a house; also, the ground on which the water falls from the eaves.

eaves'drop', *v. i.;* -DROPPED' (-drŏpt'); -DROP'PING. To stand under eaves, as to listen; hence, to listen secretly. — **eaves'drop'per** (-drŏp'ẽr), *n.* — **eaves'drop'ping,** *n.*

ebb (ĕb), *n.* [AS. *ebba.*] **1.** Reflux, or flowing back, of the tide toward the sea; — opposed to *flood.* **2.** State or time of passing away; decline; decay. — *v. i.* **1.** To recede from its flood, as the tide toward the ocean; — opposed to *flow.* **2.** To fall back from a better to a worse state; to decline. — **Syn.** See ABATE. — **Ant.** Flow.

ebb tide. The tide while ebbing or at ebb. See TIDE.

E'-boat' (ē'bōt'), *n.* [For enemy boat.] *Brit.* See MOTOR TORPEDO BOAT.

eb'on (ĕb'ŭn), *n. Now Poetic.* Ebony. — *adj.* Consisting of, or like, ebony; of color, black; dark.

eb'on·ite (-īt), *n.* [*ebony* + *-ite.*] A black variety of hard rubber, used for combs and buttons, and for insulating material in electric apparatus.

eb'on·ize (-īz), *v. t.* To make black, or stain black.

eb'on·y (-ĭ), *n.; pl.* EBONIES (-ĭz). [L. *ebenus,* fr. Gr. *ebenos,* fr. Egypt. *hebni.*] Any tree (genus *Diospyros*) typifying a family (Ebonaceae, the ebony family) of trees of tropical Asia and Africa, yielding a hard, heavy, durable wood; also, the wood of any of these trees. The most highly prized ebony is black and takes a high polish. — *adj.* **a** Made of ebony. **b** Resembling ebony, esp. in color; black.

e·brac'te·ate (ē·brăk'tē·āt), *adj.* Also **e·brac'te·at'ed** (-āt'ĕd; -ĭd). *Bot.* Without bracts.

e·bul'li·ence (ē·bŭl'ĭ·ĕns; -yĕns; 58), **e·bul'li·en·cy** (-ĭ·ĕn·sĭ; -yĕn·sĭ), *n.* A boiling up or over; overflow; esp., exhilaration of spirits.

e·bul'li·ent (-ĭ·ĕnt; -yĕnt), *adj.* [L. *ebulliens, -entis,* pres. part. of *ebullire* to boil up, fr. *e* out + *bullire* to boil.] Boiling up, or causing such action; hence, manifesting exhilaration or excitement, as of feeling; effervescent. — **e·bul'li·ent·ly,** *adv.*

eb'ul·li'tion (ĕb'ŭ·lĭsh'ŭn), *n.* Act, process, or state of boiling or bubbling up; hence, agitation or excitement.

e'bur·na'tion (ē'bẽr·nā'shŭn; ĕb'ẽr-), *n.* [L. *eburnus* of ivory, fr. *ebur* ivory.] *Med.* A diseased condition in which bone or cartilage becomes hard like ivory.

é'car·té' (ā'kär·tā'; *Brit.* ā·kär'tā; *F.* ā'kȧr'tā'), *n.* [F.] A game at cards for two persons.

‖**ec'ce** (ĕk'sē; ĕk'ā), *interj.* [L.] Lo; behold.

‖**ec′ce ho′mo** (ĕk′sē hō′mō; ĕk′ā). [L.] Behold the man; — Latin version of the words used by Pilate in presenting Christ, wearing the crown of thorns, to the Jews (*John* xix. 5).

ec·cen′tric (ĕk·sĕn′trĭk; ĭk-), *adj.* [F. and ML.; F. *excentrique*, fr. ML., fr. Gr. *ekkentros*, fr. *ek* out of + *kentron* center.] **1.** Not having the same center; — opposed to *concentric*. **2.** Deviating from the center, or from the line of a circle; as, an *eccentric* or elliptical orbit. **3.** Deviating from stated methods, usual practice, or established forms or laws; irregular; odd; as, *eccentric* conduct. — **Syn.** See STRANGE. — *n.* **1.** A circle not having the same center as another contained in some measure within it. **2.** One who or that which is eccentric, unusual, or odd. **3.** *Mach.* A device consisting of a disk through which a shaft is keyed eccentrically, and a circular strap which works freely round the rim of the disk for communicating its motion to one end of a rod, the other end of which is constrained to move in a straight line so as to produce reciprocating motion. Its effective radius or throw, called its *eccentricity*, is the distance between the disk center and the center of the shaft with which it revolves. — **ec·cen′tri·cal** (-trĭ·kăl), *adj.* — **ec·cen′tri·cal·ly**, *adv.*

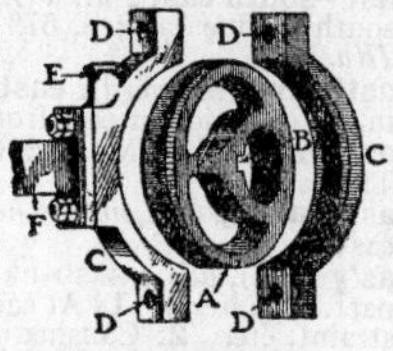

One form of Eccentric, 3. *A* Eccentric Disk with material cut out to save weight; *B* Hole for Crankshaft; *C C* Eccentric Strap; *D D* Bolt Holes for uniting the Strap; *E* Lubricator; *F* Eccentric Rod.

ec′cen·tric′i·ty (ĕk′sĕn·trĭs′ĭ·tĭ; ĕk′sĕn-), *n.; pl.* -TIES (-tĭz). **1.** State or degree of being eccentric; as, the *eccentricity* of a planet's orbit. **2.** Deviation from customary conduct; oddity. **3.** *Mach.* See ECCENTRIC, *n.*, 3. **4.** *Math.* The ratio of the distances from any point of a conic to a focus and the corresponding directrix.

Syn. **Eccentricity, idiosyncrasy** mean a singular trait, trick, or habit. **Eccentricity** stresses divergence from the usual or customary; **idiosyncrasy**, the following of one's peculiar temperament or bent; the former often suggests mental aberration, the latter, strong individuality and independence of action.

ec·cle′si·a (ĕ·klē′zhĭ·ȧ; -zĭ·ȧ; ĭ-), *n.; pl.* -SIAE (-ē). [L., fr. Gr. *ekklēsia*.] **1.** In ancient Greek states, a political assembly of the citizens. **2.** A church, either the body of members or building.

Ec·cle′si·as′tes (ĕ·klē′zĭ·ăs′tēz; ĭ-), *n.* [L., fr. Gr. *ekklēsiastēs* a preacher.] A book of the Bible, containing maxims for the cultivation of wisdom. See BIBLE. Abbr. *Eccles.*

ec·cle′si·as′tic (-ăs′tĭk), *adj.* [F. and L.; F. *ecclésiastique*, fr. L., fr. Gr. *ekklēsiastikos*, fr. *ekklēsia* an assembly of citizens called out by the crier, also, the church, deriv. of *ek* out + *kalein* to call.] Ecclesiastical. — *n.* A clergyman; priest.

ec·cle′si·as′ti·cal (-tĭ·kăl), *adj.* Of or relating to the church or its organization or government; not secular; — distinguished from *temporal* (see 2d TEMPORAL, 3). — **ec·cle′si·as′ti·cal·ly**, *adv.*

ec·cle′si·as′ti·cism (-tĭ·sĭz′m), *n.* Ecclesiastical principles, forms, or practices; also, attachment to these.

Ec·cle′si·as′ti·cus (ĕ·klē′zĭ·ăs′tĭ·kŭs; ĭ-), *n.* [L.] A book of proverbs of the Old Testament in the Douay Version or of the Apocrypha. See BIBLE. Abbr. *Ecclus.*

ec·cle′si·ol′a·try (ĕ·klē′zĭ·ŏl′ȧ·trĭ; ĭ-), *n.* [Gr. *ekklēsia* church + *-latry*.] Literally, worship of the church; hence, excessive devotion to the church. — **ec·cle′si·ol′a·ter** (-tẽr), *n.*

ec·cle′si·ol′o·gy (-ŏl′ō·jĭ), *n.* [Gr. *ekklēsia* church + *-logy*.] The science or study of ecclesiastical art and antiquities, esp. with reference to the adornment of churches. — **ec·cle′si·o·log′ic** (-ō·lŏj′ĭk), **ec·cle′si·o·log′i·cal** (-ĭ·kăl), *adj.*

ec·dys′i·ast (ĕk·dĭz′ĭ·ăst), *n.* [From *ecdysis*.] *Chiefly Humorous.* A strip-teaser; — coined by H. L. Mencken.

ec′dy·sis (ĕk′dĭ·sĭs), *n.; pl.* -SES (-sēz). [NL., fr. Gr. *ekdysis* a getting out.] *Zool.* Act of shedding an outer cuticular layer, as in the case of insects, crustaceans, etc.

eche (ēch), *v. t. & i.* [ME. *echen*, fr. AS. *ēcan*. See EKE.] *Obs.* To increase; augment; also, to eke (*out*).

ech′e·lon (ĕsh′ĕ·lŏn; *F.* āsh′lôɴ′), *n.* [F. *échelon*, fr. *échelle* ladder, fr. L. *scala*.] **1.** *Mil.* An arrangement of troops with units drawn up in parallel lines, but each somewhat to the left or right of the one in the rear, like a series of steps; also, one of the divisions. **2.** *Nav.* An arrangement of the vessels of a fleet in a line of bearing at an angle to the way the ships head. **3.** *Mil. Aviation.* Arrangement of aircraft in a formation in which each flies at a certain elevation above and a certain distance behind and to right or left of the plane ahead. **4.** *Mil.* One of the fractions of a command arranged in order from combat front to rear, for example in a combat division, the command, reconnaissance, striking, support, and service *echelons*; also, either a forward or rear subdivision of a unit's headquarters. **5.** A fraction or subdivision of any arrangement consisting of a series of steps, as one of the grades of command in an army, one of the levels of authority in an organization, one of the ordered steps in an operation or process. — *adj.* Of, pert. to, or of the form of an echelon. — (ĕsh′ĕ·lŏn), *v. t. & i. Mil.* To place, arrange, or take position, in echelon.

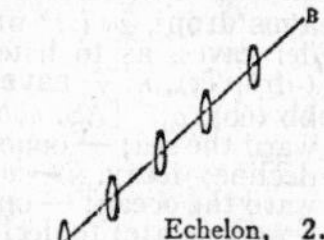

Echelon, 2. *AB* Line of Bearing.

e·chid′na (ē·kĭd′nȧ), *n.* [L., a viper, adder, fr. Gr. *echidna*.] A mammal (*Tachyglossus aculeatus*, order Monotremata) found in Australia, Tasmania, and New Guinea. It is somewhat larger than a hedgehog, with spines on the upper part of the body, a long and tapering snout, and a toothless mouth. It feeds largely on ants.

ech′i·nate (ĕk′ĭ·nāt), *adj.* Also **ech′i·nat′ed** (-nāt′ĕd; -ĭd). Set with prickles; prickly, like a hedgehog.

e·chi′no·derm (ē·kī′nō·dûrm; ĕk′ĭ·nō·dûrm′), *n.* [Gr. *echinos* urchin + *-derm*.] A marine animal of a phylum (Echinodermata) consisting of the starfishes, sea urchins, and their allies.

e·chi′noid (ē·kī′noid; ĕk′ĭ·noid), *n.* [See ECHINUS; -OID.] *Zool.* = SEA URCHIN. — **e·chi′noid**, *adj.*

e·chi′nus (ē·kī′nŭs), *n.; pl.* ECHINI (-nī). [L., hedgehog, sea urchin, fr. Gr. *echinos*.] **1.** A sea urchin. **2.** *Arch.* The rounded molding supporting the abacus of the capital in the Greek Doric order; hence, a similar member in other orders.

ech′o (ĕk′ō), *n.; pl.* ECHOES (-ōz). [L., fr. Gr. *ēchō* echo, sound.] **1.** The repetition of a sound caused by reflection of sound waves; hence, the sound due to such reflection and distinguished from it. **2.** [*cap.*] The personification of this phenomenon or its cause; esp., *Gr. Myth.*, a nymph who pined away for love of Narcissus until nothing was left of her but her voice. **3.** Response, esp. as implying sympathetic appreciation. **4.** Any repetition, as of the style, sentiments, etc., of another person; also, one who imitates or repeats another's words, ideas, or acts. **5.** *Bridge, Whist, etc.* The play of a conventional card, in response to a partner's lead, to convey information. — *v. t.;* ECH′OED (ĕk′ōd); ECH′O·ING (-ō·ĭng). **1.** To send back or repeat (a sound). **2.** To repeat or imitate, as words. — *v. i.* To give an echo.

e·cho′ic (ē·kō′ĭk), *adj.* **1.** Of the nature of an echo. **2.** *Philol.* Formed in imitation of some natural sound; imitative; onomatopoeic.

ech′o·la′li·a (ĕk′ō·lā′lĭ·ȧ), *n.* [NL., fr. *echo* + Gr. *lalia*, talking, chat.] *Psychol.* A habit of repeating what is said by other people, as if echoing them. — **ech′o·lal′ic** (-lăl′ĭk), *adj.*

é·clair′ (ā·klâr′), *n.* [F.] A small oblong shell of baked paste filled with flavored cream, and glazed or frosted.

‖**é′clair′cisse′ment′** (ā′klâr′sēs′mäɴ′), *n.* [F., fr. *éclaircir* to explain.] A clarification; enlightenment.

ec·lamp′si·a (ĕk·lămp′sĭ·ȧ), *n.* [NL., fr. Gr. *eklampsis* a shining forth, deriv. of *ek* out + *lampein* to shine.] A sudden attack of convulsions, esp. during pregnancy or parturition.

é·clat′ (ā·klä′), *n.* [F., fragment, explosion, splendor.] **1.** Notoriety; also, a scandal. **2.** Brilliancy of achievement greeted with acclaim. **3.** Demonstration of approval; acclaim.

ec·lec′tic (ĕk·lĕk′tĭk), *adj.* [Gr. *eklektikos*, fr. *eklegein* to pick out, choose out.] **1.** Selecting; choosing, as doctrines or methods, from various sources, systems, etc. **2.** Pertaining to or manifesting eclecticism. **3.** Containing, or made up, of what is chosen or selected; as, an *eclectic* magazine. — *n.* An eclectic philosopher, physician, or painter. — **ec·lec′ti·cal·ly** (-tĭ·kăl·ĭ), *adv.*

ec·lec′ti·cism (-tĭ·sĭz′m), *n.* Method or practice of selecting what seems best from various systems, esp. in forming religious or philosophical doctrine; also, the chosen body of doctrines, methods, etc.

e·clipse′ (ē·klĭps′), *n.* [OF., fr. L. *eclipsis*, fr. Gr. *ekleipsis*, prop., forsaking, deriv. of *ek* out + *leipein* to leave.] **1.** *Astron.* The obscuration of light from one celestial body by another. Thus, a ***solar eclipse*** is caused by the moon's passing between sun and earth; a ***lunar eclipse***, by the moon's entering the earth's shadow. **2.** A dimming, darkening, or obscuring; esp., a temporary obscuring of luster or brilliancy; as, the *eclipse* of one's powers. — *v. t.* **1.** To cause an eclipse of; to darken or hide. **2.** To obscure or extinguish the beauty, luster, honor, etc., of; to cloud; sully.

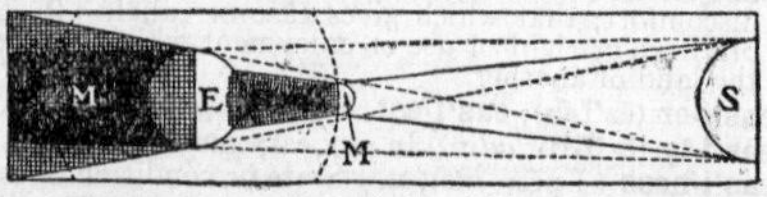

Diagram of Eclipses, showing positions of the Sun *S*, Earth *E*, and Moon, *M* in a Solar, and M^1 in a Lunar, Eclipse.

e·clip′tic (ē·klĭp′tĭk), *n.* [From F. or L. See ECLIPTIC, *adj.*] **1.** *Astron.* That great circle of the celestial sphere which is the apparent path of the sun, or of the earth as seen from the sun; the plane of the earth's orbit extended to meet the celestial sphere, and inclined to the celestial equator at an angle of about 23° 27′. **2.** A great circle drawn on a terrestrial globe, making an angle of about 23° 27′ with the equator, and used for illustrating and solving astronomical problems.

e·clip′tic (-tĭk), **e·clip′ti·cal** (-tĭ·kăl), *adj.* [F. or L.; F. *écliptique*, fr. L. *eclipticus* of an eclipse, fr. Gr. *ekleiptikos*.] Pertaining to the ecliptic or eclipses.

ec′logue (ĕk′lŏg; 74), *n.* [F. and L.; F. *églogue*, fr. L. *ecloga*, fr. Gr. *eklogē* a selection, choice extracts, fr. *eklegein* to pick out.] A poem in which shepherds are introduced conversing; a bucolic; an idyl.

e·col′o·gy (ē·kŏl′ō·jĭ), *n.* Also **oe·col′o·gy.** [Gr. *oikos* house + *-logy*.] Biology dealing with the mutual relations between organisms and their environment; bionomics. — **ec′o·log′ic, oec′o·log′ic** (ĕk′ō·lŏj′ĭk; ē′kō-), **-log′i·cal** (-ĭ·kăl), *adj.* — **-log′i·cal·ly**, *adv.* — **e·col′o·gist, oe·col′o·gist** (ē·kŏl′ō·jĭst), *n.*

e′co·nom′ic (ē′kō·nŏm′ĭk; ĕk′ō-), *adj.* [F. or L.; F. *économique*, fr. L. *oeconomicus* orderly, methodical, fr. Gr. *oikonomikos* economical. See ECONOMY.] **1.** Of or pertaining to the management of one's private business; hence, *Now Rare*, thrifty. **2.** Of or pert. to the management of the affairs of a government or community with reference to its source of income, its expenditures, the development of its natural resources, etc.; as, our country's *economic* policy; hence, of or pert. to economics; as, *economic* theory. **3.** Of or pert. to the satisfaction of man's needs; utilitarian; as, *economic* botany.

e′co·nom′i·cal (-ĭ·kăl), *adj.* **1.** *Archaic.* Domestic. **2.** Managing or managed without waste; frugal; thrifty; provident. **3.** Economic. — **Syn.** See SPARING. — **e′co·nom′i·cal·ly**, *adv.*

e′co·nom′ics (ē′kō·nŏm′ĭks; ĕk′ō-), *n.;* see -ICS. The science that investigates the conditions and laws affecting the production, distribution, and consumption of wealth, or the material means of satisfying human desires; political economy.

e·con′o·mist (ē·kŏn′ō·mĭst), *n.* **1.** A manager of affairs; esp., a frugal or thrifty one. **2.** One conversant with economics.

e·con′o·mize (-mīz), *v. t.* To manage with economy; to use economically or to the best advantage. — *v. i.* To be sparing in expenditure; to be frugal. — **e·con′o·miz′er** (-mīz′ẽr), *n.*

e·con′o·my (-mĭ), *n.; pl.* -MIES (-mĭz). [F. or L.; F. *économie*, fr. L. *oeconomia* household management, fr. Gr. *oikonomia*, fr. *oikonomos* a steward, fr. *oikos* house + a derivative of *nemein* to manage.] **1.** The management or regulation of domestic or household affairs with special regard for costs; hence, management of the affairs of a community, estate, or establishment, and directly concerned with its maintenance or productiveness. **2.** Thrifty administration; often, retrenchment in expenditure; strict husbanding of resources. **3.** An economizing act, move, or means; also, the disposition to economize. **4.** The management or ordering of parts, functions, etc., in an organic or organized system; organization; also, a system or body so managed or ordered. **5.** An economic stage in man's development or history; also, the economic system characterizing such a stage; as, a slave *economy*; a barter *economy*. **6.** *Theol.* **a** The Creator's plan; the design of Providence. **b** A special dispensation suited to the needs of a nation or period; as, the Mosaic *economy*.

e′co·spe′cies (ē′kō·spē′shĭz [ĕk′ō-] *or, esp. in the pl.*, -shēz), *n. sing. & pl.* [Gr. *oikos* house + *species*.] A biological group comprising organisms fully fertile among themselves but only weakly fertile with members of allied groups; — more or less equivalent to a taxonomic species. — **e′co·spe·cif′ic** (-spē·sĭf′ĭk), *adj.* — **-i·cal·ly**, *adv.*

e'co·tone (ē'kō·tōn; ĕk'ō-), *n.* [Gr. *oikos* house + *tone.*] *Ecology.* A transition area between two adjacent communities, as forest and grassland, and as such usually exhibiting competition between species common to both. — **e'co·ton'al** (-tōn'ăl), *adj.*

e'co·type (-tīp), *n.* *Biol.* A subdivision of an ecospecies that maintains its identity through isolation and environmental selection; — more or less equivalent to a taxonomic subspecies. — **e'co·typ'ic** (-tĭp'ĭk), *adj.* — **-i·cal·ly**, *adv.*

‖**é'cra'seur'** (ā'krȧ'zûr'), *n.* [F., fr. *écraser* to crush.] *Surg.* An instrument used, esp. in removing certain tumors, to lessen danger of hemorrhage. It severs by the gradual tightening of a chain or wire loop.

ec'ru (ĕk'rōō; ā'krōō; ȧ·krōō'), *adj.* [F. *écru*, fr. *cru* raw, fr. L. *crudus.*] Having the beige color of unbleached cloth. — *n.* Ecru cloth; also, its characteristic beige color.

ec'sta·sy (ĕk'stȧ·sĭ), *n.; pl.* ECSTASIES (-sĭz). [OF. *extasie*, fr. LL., fr. Gr. *ekstasis*, fr. *existanai* to put out of place, derange, fr. *ex* (= *ek* out) + *histanai* to set, stand.] **1.** State of being beside oneself; state of being beyond all reason and self-control, as when obsessed by a powerful emotion. **2.** A state of overmastering feeling, esp. joy; rapture. **3.** A mystic, prophetic, or poetic trance.

Syn. **Ecstasy, rapture, transport** mean intense exaltation of mind and feelings. **Ecstasy**, in strictest use, implies a trancelike state in which the mind is fixed on what it contemplates or conceives; **rapture**, etymologically a seizing, in earlier use implied a lifting of the mind or soul by divine power, so that it might see things beyond the range of human vision; **transport** implies a carrying out of oneself by any violent emotion. All of these terms now, in looser use, usually imply any overmastering emotion, particularly that of joy or bliss.

— *v. t.;* EC'STA·SIED (-sĭd); EC'STA·SY·ING. To fill with ecstasy.

ec·stat'ic (ĕk·stăt'ĭk), *adj.* Pertaining to, causing, or caused by, ecstasy; of the nature, or in a state, of ecstasy. — *n.* **1.** One subject to ecstasy. **2.** *pl.* Ecstatic expressions. — **ec·stat'i·cal** (-ĭ·kăl), *adj.* — **ec·stat'i·cal·ly**, *adv.*

ec'to- (ĕk'tō-), **ect-**. [Gr. *ektos* outside.] A combining form denoting *without, outside, external*, as in **ec'to·cor'ne·a, ec'to·cra'ni·al**.

ec'to·derm (-dûrm), *n.* [*ecto-* + *-derm.*] The investing cellular membrane of a multicellular animal, including any tissue derived from the epiblast. — **ec'to·der'mal** (-dûr'măl), **-der'mic** (-mĭk), *adj.*

ec'to·en'zyme (-ĕn'zīm; -zĭm), *n.* Also **ec'to·en'zym** (-zĭm). [*ecto-* + *enzyme.*] *Biochem.* An enzyme acting outside the cell.

ec'to·gen'ic (ĕk'tō·jĕn'ĭk), **ec·tog'e·nous** (ĕk·tŏj'ē·nŭs), *adj.* *Bacteriol.* Capable of development apart from the host; — used of certain pathogenic bacteria.

ec'to·mere (ĕk'tō·mēr), *n.* [*ecto-* + *-mere.*] *Embryol.* A blastomere forming ectoderm. — **ec'to·mer'ic** (-mĕr'ĭk), *adj.*

ec'to·mor'phic (ĕk'tō·môr'fĭk), *adj.* [*ecto-* + *-morphic.*] *Anthropol.* Characterized by predominance of the structures developed from the ectodermal layer of the embryo, that is, the skin, nerves, sense organs, and brain; hence, of the light or asthenic type of body build. Cf. ENDOMORPHIC, MESOMORPHIC. — **ec'to·mor'phy** (ĕk'tō·môr'fĭ), *n.* — **ec'to·morph** (-môrf), *n.*

-ec'to·my (-ĕk'tō·mĭ). [Gr. *ektomē* excision. See EX-, 2; -TOMY.] A combining form denoting *surgical removal*, as in appendectomy.

ec'to·par'a·site (ĕk'tō·păr'ȧ·sīt), *n.* Any parasite which lives on the exterior of animals; — opp. to *endoparasite.*

ec'to·plasm (ĕk'tō·plăz'm), *n.* [*ecto-* + *-plasm* as in proto*plasm.*] **1.** *Biol.* An external or cortical modified layer of protoplasm in a cell; — opposed to *endoplasm.* **2.** *Spiritualism.* The emanation from a medium which apparently produces motion in objects at a distance without physical contact. — **ec'to·plas'mic** (-plăz'mĭk), *adj.*

ec'to·sarc (ĕk'tō·särk), *n.* [*ecto-* + Gr. *sarx, sarkos*, flesh.] *Biol.* Ectoplasm in some unicellular organisms, as the amoeba.

ec'type (ĕk'tīp), *n.* [Gr. *ektypos* cameo, fr. *ek* out + *typos* stamp, figure.] A copy from an original; a reproduction of an archetype or prototype. — **ec'ty·pal** (ĕk'tĭ·păl), *adj.*

‖**é'cu'** (ā'kü'), *n.; pl.* ÉCUS (*F.* ā'kü'). [F., fr. L. *scutum* shield.] **1.** The small shield carried by a mounted soldier of the 14th and 15th centuries. **2.** Any of several French gold and silver coins, esp. the silver crown of the 17th–18th cent., or the current five-franc piece.

ec'u·men'i·cal, oec'u·men'i·cal (ĕk'ū·mĕn'ĭ·kăl *or, esp. Brit.,* ē'kū-), *adj.* Also **ec'u·men'ic, oec'u·men'ic** (-mĕn'ĭk). [LL. *oecumenicus*, fr. Gr. *oikoumenikos*, fr. *oikoumenē* (sc. *gē*) the inhabited world, fr. *oikein* to inhabit, fr. *oikos* house, dwelling.] General; world-wide in extent, influence, etc. An **ecumenical council** represents the entire church. — **-i·cal·ly**, *adv.*

ec'ze·ma (ĕk'sē·mȧ; ĕg'zē-; ĭg·zē'-), *n.* [NL., fr. Gr. *ekzema*, fr. *ek* out + *zein* to boil.] An inflammatory disease of the skin, characterized by redness, itching, and formation of scales or crusts. — **ec·zem'a·tous** (ĕk·zĕm'ȧ·tŭs; ĕk·sĕm'-; ĕg·zĕm'-; ĭg·zĕm'-), *adj.*

-ed (*pron., when a separate syllable* -ĕd; -ĭd; 30; *when combined with a preceding sonant, pron.* -d, *as in* spelled, *with a preceding surd, pron.* -t, *as in* dropped). [AS. *-ede, -ode, -ade.*] The ending of the past tense of regular, or weak, verbs. Some verbs (chiefly regular) ending in a surd consonant (except *t*) are often spelled with *-t* for *-ed* in past tense and past participle.

-ed. [AS. *-ed, -ad, -od.*] A suffix forming: **a** The past participle of regular, or weak, verbs (see 1st -ED). **b** Analogous forms from participles and adjectives ending in *-ate*, as in foliat*ed*. **c** Adjectives from nouns, having the sense of *possessed of, provided* or *furnished with, characterized by*, as in money*ed;* also, *having the characteristics of*, as in bigot*ed*.

e·da'cious (ē·dā'shŭs), *adj.* [L. *edax, edacis*, fr. *edere* to eat.] Voracious; devouring. — **e·dac'i·ty** (ē·dăs'ĭ·tĭ), *n.*

E'dam (ē'dăm; ē'dăm), *n., or* **Edam cheese.** A Dutch pressed cheese of yellow color, made in balls usually colored dark red outside; — from Edam, near Amsterdam.

e·daph'ic (ē·dăf'ĭk), *adj.* [Gr. *edaphos* soil.] Pertaining to or influenced by soil, rather than climatic, conditions; hence, indigenous.

Ed'da (ĕd'ȧ), *n.; pl.* EDDAS (-ȧz). [ON.] Either of two works in the Old Norse, or Icelandic, language: **a** The ***Elder,*** *or* ***Poetic, Edda***, a collection of mythological and heroic songs, dating probably from between the 10th and the 13th centuries. **b** The ***Younger,*** *or* ***Prose, Edda***, on Norse mythology, language, and poetics, by Snorri Sturluson (1178–1241). — **Ed·da'ic** (ĕ·dā'ĭk), **Ed'dic** (ĕd'ĭk), *adj.*

ed'do (ĕd'ō), *n.; pl.* EDDOES (-ōz). [Prob. of W. Afr. origin.] The taro or its root; also, the edible root or stem of any of several related plants.

ed'dy (ĕd'ĭ), *n.; pl.* EDDIES (-ĭz). [ME. *ydy*, prob. fr. ON. *itha.*] **1.** A current of air or water running contrary to the main current; esp., one moving circularly; a small whirlpool. **2.** Any similar current, as of dust or, figuratively, of thought, argument, affairs, etc. — *v. t. & i.;* ED'DIED (-ĭd); ED'DY·ING. To move as an eddy, or as in an eddy.

e'del·weiss (ā'dĕl·vīs), *n.* [G., fr. *edel* noble + *weiss* white.] A small perennial herb (*Leontopodium alpinum*) of the aster family, growing high in the Alps.

e·de'ma (ē·dē'mȧ), *n.; pl.* EDEMATA (-mȧ·tȧ). [NL., fr. Gr. *oidēma* a swelling, tumor, fr. *oidein* to swell.] Abnormal accumulation of serous fluid in the interfibrillar spaces of connective tissue or in the serous cavities, as the peritoneal or pleural cavities; dropsy. — **e·dem'a·tous** (ē·dĕm'ȧ·tŭs), **e·dem'a·tose** (-tōs), *adj.*

E'den (ē'd'n), *n.* [LL., fr. Heb. *'ēden* delight, a place of pleasure, Eden.] In the Bible, the garden where Adam and Eve first dwelt; Paradise; hence, a paradise.

e·den'tate (ē·dĕn'tāt), *adj.* [L. *edentatus* rendered toothless, fr. *e* out + *dens, dentis*, tooth.] *Biol.* **a** Destitute of teeth. **b** Belonging to the edentates. — *n.* One of a group (Edentata) of placental mammals, a few toothless, including sloths, armadillos, and many anteaters.

edge (ĕj), *n.* [AS. *ecg.*] **1.** The thin cutting side of the blade of an instrument. **2.** The brink or extreme verge, as of a cliff. **3.** Sharpness; hence, penetrating power. **4.** Any sharp terminating border, or the part adjacent; a line where something else begins; as, the *edge* of a book or of a stream. — **Syn.** See BORDER. — ***on edge.*** Eager, impatient, or anxious; also, nervous. — *v. t. & i.;* EDGED (ĕjd); EDG'ING (ĕj'ĭng). **1.** To furnish with an edge. **2.** To move by little and little or as by pressing forward edgewise. **3.** *Skiing.* To incline (a ski) sidewise so that the edge cuts into the surface of the snow.

edge'bone' (ĕj'bōn'). Corruption of AITCHBONE.

edge tool. A tool with a sharp cutting edge, as a chisel.

edge'ways' (ĕj'wāz'), **edge'wise'** (-wīz'), *adv.* With the edge toward or foremost; on, by, or with, the edge.

edg'ing (ĕj'ĭng), *n.* That which forms an edge or border.

edg'y (ĕj'ĭ), *adj.* **1.** Having an edge; sharp in line, as a sculpture. **2.** Being on edge; also, snappish.

edh (ĕth), *n.* Also **eth** (ĕth). An Anglo-Saxon letter formed with a stroke across the simple *d* (ð, cap. Đ) and answering in general to the modern *th.* ð and þ (see THORN, 4) were used interchangeably to represent the dental spirant *th*, originally voiceless (as in English *thin*), but presumably voiced (as in English *then*) when occurring between voiced sounds.

ed'i·ble (ĕd'ĭ·b'l), *adj.* [LL. *edibilis*, fr. *edere* to eat.] Fit to be eaten as food; eatable; esculent. — *n.* Anything edible. — **ed'i·ble·ness, ed'i·bil'i·ty** (-bĭl'ĭ·tĭ), *n.*

e'dict (ē'dĭkt), *n.* [L. *edictum*, fr. *edicere, edictum*, to declare, proclaim, fr. *e* out + *dicere* to say.] A public notice issued by official authority; proclamation of a command, law, or rule of conduct by sovereign power or competent authority; decree. — **e·dic'tal** (ē·dĭk'tăl; -t'l), *adj.*

ed'i·fice (ĕd'ĭ·fĭs), *n.* [F. *édifice*, fr. L. *aedificium.* See EDIFY.] A building; a structure; esp., a large or massive building, such as a palace or a church. — **ed'i·fi'cial** (-fĭsh'ăl), *adj.*

ed'i·fy (-fī), *v. t.;* -FIED (-fīd); -FY'ING. [OF. *edifier*, fr. L. *aedificare*, fr. *aedes* a building, house, orig., a fireplace + *-ficare* to make.] **1.** *Archaic.* To build; to construct; hence, to organize; establish. **2.** To instruct and improve, esp. by good example; to profit morally or spiritually. — **ed'i·fi·ca'tion** (-fĭ·kā'shŭn), *n.* — **ed'i·fi·ca'to·ry** (ĕd'ĭ·fĭ·kā'tō·rĭ; ē·dĭf'ĭ·kȧ·tō'rĭ), *adj.* — **ed'i·fi'er** (ĕd'ĭ·fī'ēr), *n.*

e'dile (ē'dīl). Var. of AEDILE.

ed'it (ĕd'ĭt), *v. t.* [L. *editus*, past part. of *edere* to give out, publish, fr. *e* out + *dare* to give.] **1.** To revise and prepare as for publication; as, to *edit* a manuscript; also, to prepare an edition of; as, to *edit* Poe's works. **2.** To direct the editorial policies of; as, to *edit* a newspaper.

e·di'tion (ē·dĭsh'ŭn), *n.* Abbr. *ed.* **1.** The form in which a literary work is published; as, a single-volume *edition.* **2.** The whole number of copies of a work published at one time; as, the first *edition* of a work; — disting. from *impression.* **3.** One of the several issues of a newspaper for a single day.

‖**e·di'ti·o prin'ceps** (ē·dĭsh'ĭ·ō prĭn'sĕps). [L.] First edition.

ed'i·tor (ĕd'ĭ·tēr), *n.* [L.] Abbr. *ed.* **1.** One who edits, as a text, book, magazine, etc. **2. a** One who directs the policies and contributions of a newspaper, magazine, book of reference, etc.; as, a dictionary *editor.* **b** One who has supervision of a special department of a newspaper, magazine, book of reference, etc.; as, a financial *editor.* **3.** One who writes editorials. — **ed'i·tor·ship'**, *n.*

ed'i·to'ri·al (-tō'rĭ·ăl; 70), *adj.* Of or relating to an editor; as, *editorial* office; also, written or sanctioned by an editor; as, *editorial* policy. — *n.* An article in a newspaper or magazine giving the editor's views or those of the person or persons in control of the paper; a leader. — **ed'i·to'ri·al·ly**, *adv.*

E'dom·ite (ē'dŭm·īt), *n.* One of the descendants of Esau, or **E'dom** (ē'dŭm), brother of Jacob. — **E'dom·it'ish** (-īt'ĭsh), *adj.*

ed'u·ca·ble (ĕd'ū·kȧ·b'l), *adj.* Capable of being educated.

ed'u·cate (ĕd'ū·kāt), *v. t.* [L. *educatus*, past part. of *educare* to bring up a child, educate, fr. *educere.* See EDUCE.] To develop and cultivate mentally or morally; fit for a calling by systematic instruction; teach; also, to train, discipline, or form; as, to *educate* the taste. — **Syn.** See TEACH.

ed'u·cat'ed (-kāt'ĕd; -ĭd), *adj.* **1.** Having an education complete according to an accepted standard. **2.** Trained to a semblance of intelligence; as, *educated* dogs. **3.** Giving evidence of education, training, or cultivation; as, *educated* diction.

ed'u·ca'tion (-kā'shŭn), *n.* **1.** Act or process of educating; discipline of mind or character through study or instruction; also, a stage of such a process or the training in it; as, to receive a college *education.* **2.** A science dealing with the principles and practice of teaching and learning. — **ed'u·ca'tion·al** (-ăl; -'l), *adj.* — **ed'u·ca'tion·al·ist, ed'u·ca'tion·ist**, *n.*

ed'u·ca'tive (ĕd'ū·kā'tĭv), *adj.* Tending to educate; educating.

ed'u·ca'tor (-tēr), *n.* [L.] One who educates; a teacher.

ed'u·ca·to'ry (-kȧ·tō'rĭ *or, esp. Brit.,* -kā'tēr·ĭ), *adj.* Educative.

e·duce' (ē·dūs'), *v. t.;* E·DUCED' (-dūst'); E·DUC'ING (-dūs'ĭng). [L. *educere* to lead forth, fr. *e* out + *ducere* to lead.] To draw forth, as something latent; bring out; elicit. — **e·duc'i·ble** (-ĭ·b'l), *adj.* — **e·duc'tion** (-dŭk'shŭn), *n.*

Syn. **Educe, evoke, elicit, extract, extort** mean to draw out something hidden, latent, reserved, or the like. **Educe** implies the drawing out of a person or thing something potential or latent; **evoke**, originally to call forth by incantation, now implies a powerful stimulus that arouses an emotion, a passion, or an interest; **elicit** usually implies pains, trouble, or skill in drawing forth information, affection, etc.; **extract**, both in literal and figurative use, implies pressure, suction, or the like, in bringing out something; **extort**, a wringing or wresting, especially from one reluctant or resisting.

e′duct (ē′dŭkt), *n.* [L. *eductum*, fr. *educere*.] **1.** That which is educed. **2.** *Chem.* A substance separated from material in which it already existed; — distinguished from *product*.

e·duc′tive (ē·dŭk′tĭv), *adj.* Tending to draw out; extractive.

e·dul′co·rate (ē·dŭl′kō·rāt), *v. t.* [ML. *edulcoratus*, past part., fr. *e* out + *dulcorare* to sweeten, fr. *dulcor* sweetness, fr. *dulcis* sweet.] **1.** To sweeten. **2.** *Chem.* To free from acids, salts, or other soluble substances, by washing; purify. — **e·dul′co·ra′tion** (-rā′shŭn), *n.* — **e·dul′co·ra′tive** (-rā′tĭv), *adj.*

-ee (-ē). [Formed on the F. past-participle ending *-é*, masc.] A suffix used to indicate the object of an action, the one *to whom* an act *is done* or *on whom* a right *is conferred*, as in assignee, grantee.

eel (ēl), *n.*; see PLURAL, *Note*, 3. [AS. *ǣl*.] **1.** Any of an order (Apodes) of voracious, snakelike teleost fishes having a smooth, slimy skin and no pelvic fins. See CONGER EEL, ELVER, MORAY. **2.** Any of various other elongate fishes, as the electric eel (which see). **3.** An eelworm. — **eel′y** (ēl′ĭ), *adj.*

eel′grass′ (ēl′gràs′), *n.* *U.S.* A submerged marine plant (*Zostera marina*), typifying a family (Zosteraceae, the eelgrass family), with very long narrow leaves, abundant along the North Atlantic coast.

eel′pout′ (-pout′), *n.*; see PLURAL, *Note*, 6. [AS. *ǣlepūte*.] **1.** Any of a family (Zoarcidae) of marine blennylike fishes. **2.** See BURBOT.

eel′worm′ (-wûrm′), *n.* Any of various small roundworms (class Nematoda). One kind is found in vinegar, sour paste, etc. (*vinegar eel*), and others cause plant diseases.

e′en (ēn), *adv.* A contraction of EVEN.

-eer (-ēr). [F. *-ier*, fr. L. *-arius*.] A noun suffix denoting agency, *one who deals in* or *is concerned with*, *one who conducts, manages*, or *produces, professionally*, as in charioteer, cannoneer, and (formed from English nouns) auctioneer, sonneteer, often with a derogatory implication in the English formation. See -IER.

e′er (âr; ār; 6), *adv.* Ever; — a contraction.

ee′rie, ee′ry (ē′rĭ; ēr′ĭ), *adj.* [Scot., fr. AS. *earh* timid.] **1.** Affected with fear, as of ghosts; frightened; timid. **2.** Serving to inspire fear, as of ghosts; weird; uncanny. — **Syn.** See WEIRD. — **ee′ri·ly**, *adv.* — **ee′ri·ness**, *n.*

ef·face′ (ĕ·fās′; ĭ-), *v. t.*; EF·FACED′ (-fāst′); EF·FAC′ING (-fās′ĭng). [F. *effacer*, fr. *es-* (fr. L. *ex*) + *face* face; prop., to destroy the face or form.] To make indistinct or to obliterate by rubbing out, striking out, etc., as an inscription or impression; erase. — **Syn.** See ERASE. — **ef·face′a·ble**, *adj.* — **ef·face′ment**, *n.* — **ef·fac′er** (-fās′ẽr), *n.*

ef·fect′ (ĕ·fĕkt′; ĭ-), *n.* [OF., fr. L. *effectus*, fr. *efficere*, *effectum*, to effect, fr. *ex* + *facere* to make.] **1.** That which is produced by an agent or cause; immediate result. **2. a** Purport; intent; — in phrase *to that* (or *this*) *effect*. **b** Fulfillment or accomplishment; — in phrases *to carry into effect*, *to bring to effect*. **c** Reality; fact; — in phrase *in effect*. **d** The producing or the object of producing a particular impression; effectiveness; — chiefly in phrase *for effect*. **3.** *pl.* Goods; possessions. **4.** State or fact of being operative or enforced; as, the law goes into *effect* soon.

Syn. **Effect, consequence, result, event, issue, outcome** mean a condition, occurrence, or the like, traceable to a cause. **Effect** applies only to those factors in a complex situation that may be definitely attributed to the operation of a cause; **consequence** implies a looser or remoter connection with a cause than *effect* does; **result**, in very precise use, applies to the effect that terminates the operation of a cause and is often, therefore, the last in a series of effects traceable to a given cause (thus, the *effect* of a blow on the head is concussion of the brain; its *consequence*, shattered health; its *result*, retirement from business). When the result cannot be foreseen or is affected by conditions beyond human control, it is often called **event**; when it means an exit from or solution of difficulties, etc., it is called **issue**; when it is visible, tangible, or the like, it is called **outcome**.

ef·fect′, *v. t.* **1.** To bring to pass; execute; accomplish. **2.** To produce; make. — **Syn.** See PERFORM. — **ef·fect′er**, *n.* — **ef·fect′i·ble**, *adj.*

ef·fec′tive (ĕ·fĕk′tĭv; ĭ-), *adj.* **1.** Producing a decided, decisive, or desired effect; as, *effective* measures. **2.** Impressive; striking; as, an *effective* speech. **3.** Being in effect; operative, as a law. **4.** Ready for service or action; — of warships, soldiers, etc.

Syn. **Effective, effectual, efficient, efficacious** mean producing or capable of producing a result. **Effective** emphasizes the actual production of an effect when in use, exercise, force, or the like; **effectual** suggests the accomplishment of a result or the fulfillment of an intention and looks backward rather than forward; **efficient**, applied especially but not invariably to persons, suggests having given proof of power or skill in producing results; **efficacious** implies possession of a quality or virtue that gives a thing (rarely a person) the power to become effective.

— *n.* One equipped, fit, and ready for active service; esp., a soldier fit for duty. — **ef·fec′tive·ly**, *adv.* — **ef·fec′tive·ness**, *n.*

ef·fec′tor (-tẽr), *n.* [L.] *Physiol.* An organ of response, as a muscle or gland.

ef·fec′tu·al (-tū·ăl), *adj.* Producing, or powerful enough to produce, the intended effect; adequate. — **Syn.** See EFFECTIVE. — **ef·fec′tu·al·ly**, *adv.*

ef·fec′tu·ate (-āt), *v. t.* [After F. *effectuer*. See EFFECT, *n.* & *v.*] To effect. — **ef·fec′tu·a′tion** (-ā′shŭn), *n.*

ef·fem′i·na·cy (ĕ·fĕm′ĭ·nȧ·sĭ; ĭ-), *n.*; *pl.* EFFEMINACIES (-sĭz). Quality of being effeminate.

ef·fem′i·nate (-nĭt), *adj.* [L. *effeminatus*, past part. of *effeminare* to make a woman of, fr. *ex* out + *femina* a woman.] Having marked womanlike traits of character; wanting in manly strength or force; esp., marked by weakness, softness, and love of ease; as, an *effeminate* civilization. — **Syn.** See FEMALE. — **Ant.** Virile. — (-nāt), *v. t.* & *i.* To make or become effeminate.

ef·fen′di (ĕ·fĕn′dĭ), *n.*; *pl.* EFFENDIS (-dĭz). [Turk. *efendi*, deriv. of Gr. *authentēs* a chief.] Master; sir; — a Turkish title of respect.

ef′fer·ent (ĕf′ẽr·ĕnt), *adj.* [L. *efferens*, *-entis*, pres. part., deriv. of *ex* out + *ferre* to bear.] Bearing away, or discharging, as certain blood vessels; conveyed outward, as a nerve impulse; — opposed to *afferent*. — **ef′fer·ent**, *n.*

ef′fer·vesce′ (ĕf′ẽr·vĕs′), *v. i.*; -VESCED′ (-vĕst′); -VESC′ING (-vĕs′ĭng). [L. *effervescere*, fr. *ex* + *fervescere* to begin boiling, fr. *fervere* to boil.] **1.** To bubble, hiss, and foam, as carbonated water. **2.** To show liveliness or exhilaration; to be boisterous. — **ef′fer·ves′cence** (-vĕs′ĕns; -′ns), **ef′fer·ves′cen·cy** (-ĕn·sĭ; -′n·sĭ), *n.* — **ef′fer·ves′cent**, *adj.*

ef·fete′ (ĕ·fēt′; ĭ-), *adj.* [L. *effetus* that has brought forth, exhausted, fr. *ex* + *fetus* that has brought forth. See FETUS.] **1.** Exhausted of fertility; no longer capable of producing young, as an animal, fruit, or the earth. **2.** Worn out with age; exhausted of energy; spent. — **ef·fete′ness**, *n.*

ef′fi·ca′cious (ĕf′ĭ·kā′shŭs), *adj.* [L. *efficax*, *-acis*, fr. *efficere*. See EFFECT, *n.*] Having the power to produce intended effect; also, manifesting such power; as, *efficacious* medicines. — **Syn.** See EFFECTIVE. — **ef′fi·ca′cious·ly**, *adv.* — **ef′fi·ca′cious·ness**, *n.*

ef′fi·ca·cy (ĕf′ĭ·kȧ·sĭ), *n.*; *pl.* -CACIES (-sĭz). Power to produce effects; — used of things; as, the *efficacy* of prayer, of medicine.

ef·fi′cien·cy (ĕ·fĭsh′ĕn·sĭ; -′n·sĭ; ĭ-), *n.*; *pl.* -CIES (-sĭz). **1.** Quality or degree of being efficient; efficient operation. **2.** Effective operation as measured by a comparison of production with cost in energy, time, money, etc.

ef·fi′cient (-ĕnt; -′nt), *adj.* [F., fr. L. *efficiens*, *-entis*, pres. part. of *efficere*. See EFFECT, *n.*] **1.** Immediately effecting; as, the *efficient* cause; hence, effective in causing or producing; as, *efficient* action. **2.** Highly capable or productive; effective in operation; as, *efficient* workers. — **Syn.** See EFFECTIVE. — **ef·fi′cient·ly**, *adv.*

‖**ef·fi′gi·es** (ĕ·fĭj′ĭ·ēz), *n.* [L.] An effigy.

ef′fi·gy (ĕf′ĭ·jĭ), *n.*; *pl.* -GIES (-jĭz). [F. or L.; F. *effigie*, fr. L. *effigies*, fr. *effingere* to form, fr. *ex* + *fingere* to form.] An image or representation, esp. of a person; often, a crude image or figure representing one who is the object of odium; as, to burn or hang (one) in *effigy*. — **ef·fi′gi·al** (ĕ·fĭj′ĭ·ăl), *adj.*

ef′flo·resce′ (ĕf′lō·rĕs′), *v. i.*; -RESCED′ (-rĕst′); -RESC′ING (-rĕs′ĭng). [L. *efflorescere* to bloom, fr. *ex* + *florescere*, incho., fr. *florere* to blossom.] **1. a** *Obs.* To blossom forth; flower. **b** To burst forth or become manifest as if flowering. **2.** *Chem.* **a** To change on the surface, or throughout, to a powder from loss of water of crystallization. **b** To form, or become covered with, a powdery crust.

ef′flo·res′cence (-rĕs′ĕns; -′ns), *n.* Also **ef′flo·res′cen·cy** (-ĕn·sĭ; -′n·sĭ). [F. *efflorescence*.] **1.** Act, process, period, or result of efflorescing; hence, a coming to a head; a fullness of manifestation, as of power or beauty. **2.** *Med.* A redness of the skin; eruption. — **ef′flo·res′cent**, *adj.*

ef′flu·ence (ĕf′lū·ĕns), *n.* [L. *effluens*, *-entis*, pres. part. of *effluere* to flow out, fr. *ex* + *fluere* to flow.] Outflow; emanation; issue. — **ef′flu·ent**, *adj.* & *n.*

ef·flu′vi·um (ĕ·flōō′vĭ·ŭm), *n.*; *pl.* -VIA (-ȧ), -VIUMS (-ŭmz). [L., a flowing out, fr. *effluere*. See EFFLUENCE.] **1.** *Physics.* A hypothetical imponderable medium to the efflux of which from electrified bodies, magnets, etc., their powers of attraction and repulsion were formerly ascribed. **2.** An invisible emanation; esp., a noxious exhalation. — **ef·flu′vi·al** (-ăl), *adj.*

ef′flux (ĕf′lŭks), *n.*; *pl.* EFFLUXES (-lŭk·sĕz; -sĭz). [See EFFLUENCE, FLUX.] Effusion; outflow; also, an emanation, effluvium, etc.

ef′fort (ĕf′ẽrt; -ôrt), *n.* [F., fr. OF. *esfort*, deriv. of L. *ex* out + *fortis* strong.] **1.** Exertion of power, physical or mental. **2.** A product of exertion; as, a literary *effort*. **3.** *Mech.* Effective force, as disting. from the passive resistance called into action by such a force.

Syn. **Effort, exertion, pains, trouble** mean the active use of energy in producing a desired result. **Effort** may suggest a single action or continued activity involving toiling or straining to achieve one's end; **exertion** may mean either a laborious effort or the active, vigorous exercise of any power of mind or body; **pains** implies toilsome or solicitous effort; **trouble** implies effort that inconveniences or incommodes. — **Ant.** Ease.

ef′fort·less, *adj.* Showing little or no effort; easy; smooth. — **Syn.** See EASY. — **ef′fort·less·ly**, *adv.*

ef·fron′ter·y (ĕ·frŭn′tẽr·ĭ), *n.*; *pl.* -TERIES (-ĭz). [F. *effronterie*, deriv. of LL. *effrons*, *-ontis*, barefaced, shameless.] Impudence; presumptuousness; shameless boldness. — **Syn.** See TEMERITY.

ef·fulge′ (ĕ·fŭlj′), *v. t.* & *i.*; -FULGED′ (-fŭljd′); -FULG′ING (-fŭl′jĭng). [L. *effulgere*, fr. *ex* + *fulgere* to shine.] To shine; radiate.

ef·ful′gent (ĕ·fŭl′jĕnt), *adj.* Diffusing a flood of resplendent light; radiant. — **ef·ful′gence** (-jĕns), *n.* — **ef·ful′gent·ly**, *adv.*

ef·fuse′ (ĕ·fūs′), *adj.* [L. *effusus*, past part. of *effundere* to pour out, fr. *ex* + *fundere* to pour.] **1.** *Archaic.* Poured out freely; overflowing. **2.** *Bot.* **a** Diffuse. **b** Spread out flat without definite form. **3.** *Zool.* Having the lips separated by a gap; — said of certain shells.

ef·fuse′ (ĕ·fūz′), *v. t.* To pour out or forth; hence, diffuse; disseminate. — *v. i.* **1.** To emanate; issue. **2.** *Physics.* To flow out through an aperture; — of gases passing through an opening too small to permit the fluid to move as a mass.

ef·fu′sion (ĕ·fū′zhŭn; ĭ-), *n.* **1.** Act of effusing. **2.** That which is effused; a gushing or unrestrained utterance. **3.** *Med.* Escape of a fluid from its vessels, as by rupture.

ef·fu′sive (-sĭv), *adj.* **1.** Pouring out or forth. **2.** Unduly demonstrative; gushing. **3.** *Geol.* Formed by solidification of magma at the surface; volcanic; extrusive. Cf. INTRUSIVE. — **ef·fu′sive·ly**, *adv.* — **ef·fu′sive·ness**, *n.*

eft (ĕft), *n.* [AS. *efete* lizard.] A newt.

eft, *adv.* [AS.] *Archaic.* Again; afterwards.

eft·soons′ (ĕft·sōōnz′), *adv.* Also **eft·soon′** (-sōōn′). [ME. *eftsone*, *eftsones*, fr. AS. *eft* + *sōna* soon.] *Archaic.* **a** Again; also, soon afterwards. **b** Often.

e·gad′ (ē·găd′), *interj.* By God; — a minced oath.

e′gal, e′gall (ē′găl), *adj.* [F. *égal*.] *Obs.* Equal.

e·gal′i·tar′i·an (ē·găl′ĭ·târ′ĭ·ăn), *adj.* [F. *égalitaire*.] Equalitarian. — **e·gal′i·tar′i·an**, *n.* — **e·gal′i·tar′i·an·ism** (-ĭz′m), *n.*

‖**é′ga′li′té′** (ā′gȧ′lē′tā′), *n.* [F.] Equality.

E·ge′ri·a (ē·jēr′ĭ·ȧ), *n.* [L., fr. Gr. *Ēgeria*.] A woman adviser; — from Egeria, a nymph, reputed adviser to the second legendary king of Rome, Numa Pompilius.

e·gest′ (ē·jĕst′), *v. t.* [L. *egestus*, past part. of *egerere* to carry out, discharge, fr. *e* out + *gerere* to carry.] To excrete, as from intestines, lungs, or skin. — **e·ges′tion** (-jĕs′chŭn), *n.* — **e·ges′tive** (-tĭv), *adj.*

e·ges′ta (ē·jĕs′tȧ), *n. pl.* [NL., neut. pl. fr. past part. of L. *egerere*. See EGEST.] That which is egested; — opposed to *ingesta*. Cf. EXCRETA.

egg (ĕg), *v. t.*; EGGED (ĕgd); EGG′ING. [ON. *eggja*, fr. *egg* edge.] To urge (on).

egg (ĕg), *n.* [ON.] **1.** **a** The reproductive body produced by birds and many reptiles, from which, after a period of incubation or development, the young hatches out; esp., in common usage, that of the domestic hen. **b** Also **egg cell.** *Biol.* An ovum. See FERTILIZATION, 2. **2.** Something egglike in form or function. **3.** *Slang.* Fellow; chap; as, a good (or bad) *egg.* **4.** *Slang.* **a** A performance or a joke that falls flat. **b** An aerial bomb. **c** An underwater mine.

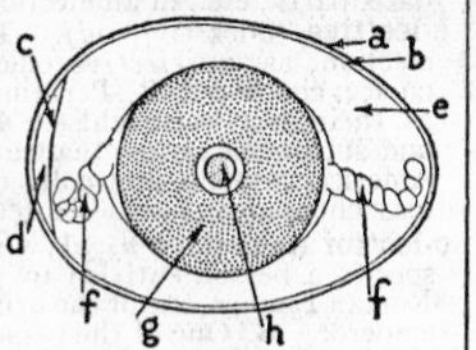

Diagrammatic Section of Hen's Egg: *a* Shell; *b, c* Inner Lining of Shell, enclosing Air Space, *d; e* Albumen or White; *f, f* Chalazas; *g* Yolk; *h* Cicatricle.

egg, *v. t.* **1.** To cover or mix with eggs, as for cooking. **2.** *Colloq.* To pelt with eggs.
egg and dart *or* **anchor** *or* **tongue.** *Arch., Furniture, etc.* An egg-shaped ornament, alternating with another in the form of a dart or an anchor or a tongue. — **egg′–and–dart′,** *adj.*
egg′er (ĕg′ẽr), *n.* Any of various moths (family Lasiocampidae) whose larvae feed on the foliage of trees.
egg′head′ (ĕg′hĕd′), *n. Slang.* An intellectual; a highbrow; — usually used disparagingly.
egg′nog′ (ĕg′nŏg′), *n.* [*egg* + *nog* ale.] A drink of eggs beaten up with sugar, milk, and, sometimes, an alcoholic liquor.
egg′plant′ (-plȧnt′; 9), *n.* **a** A widely cultivated herb (*Solanum melongena*), allied to the potato. **b** The large smooth ovoid fruit of this plant, used as a vegetable.
e′gis (ē′jĭs). Var. of AEGIS.
eg′lan·tine (ĕg′lăn·tīn), *n.* Also, *Archaic,* **eg′la·tere′** (ĕg′lȧ·tēr′). [F. *églantine,* fr. OF. *aiglent, aiglentier.*] **a** The sweetbrier. **b** The honeysuckle *Lonicera periclymenum;* — also known as *woodbine* and *twisted eglantine.*
e′go (ē′gō; ĕg′ō), *n.; pl.* EGOS (ē′gōz; ĕg′ōz). [L., lit., I.] **1.** [*often cap.*] *Philos.* **a** *Schol.* The entire man considered as union of soul and body. **b** The conscious and permanent subject of all experience. **c** *Psychol.* The self, whether considered as an organization or system of mental states, or as the consciousness of the individual's distinction from other selves. **2.** *Colloq.* Egotistic nature. **3.** *Psychoanalysis.* The self-assertive and self-preserving tendency.
e′go·cen′tric (ē′gō·sĕn′trĭk; ĕg′ō-), *adj.* [*ego* + *centric.*] **1.** Regarding everything in its relation to oneself; self-centered. **2.** *Philos.* Centering in the ego, or self; viewed from one's own mind as a center; — said esp. of the world as known. — *n.* An egocentric person. — **e′go·cen·tric′i·ty** (-sĕn·trĭs′ĭ·tĭ), *n.* — **e′go·cen′trism** (-sĕn′trĭz′m), *n.*
ego ideal. Positive standards, ideals, goals, and ambitions that a person has assimilated by introjection from parents or parent figures.
e′go·ism (ē′gō·ĭz′m; ĕg′ō-), *n.* [F. *égoïsme,* fr. L. *ego* I.] **1.** Excessive love and thought of self; an egocentric attitude. **2.** Egotism. **3.** *Ethics.* The doctrine that individual self-interest is the valid end of all action or the motive of all conscious action.
e′go·ist (-ĭst), *n.* [F. *égoïste.* See EGOISM.] **1.** One given overmuch to egoism. **2.** A believer in egoism. — **e′go·is′tic** (-ĭs′tĭk), **e′go·is′ti·cal** (-tĭ·kăl), *adj.* — **e′go·is′ti·cal·ly,** *adv.*
e′go·tism (-tĭz′m), *n.* [L. *ego* I + *-tism* for *-ism.*] The frequent use of the word *I;* the practice of referring overmuch to oneself; conceit; also, loosely, egoism.
e′go·tist (-tĭst), *n.* One addicted to egotism. — **e′go·tis′tic** (-tĭs′tĭk), **e′go·tis′ti·cal** (-tĭ·kăl), *adj.* — **e′go·tis′ti·cal·ly,** *adv.*
e·gre′gious (ē·grē′jŭs; -jĭ·ŭs), *adj.* [L. *egregius,* lit., apart from the herd, i. e., distinguished, fr. *e* out + *grex, gregis,* herd.] **1.** *Now Rare.* Prominent; eminent. **2.** Conspicuous for bad quality; flagrant. — **e·gre′gious·ly,** *adv.* — **e·gre′gious·ness,** *n.*
e′gress (ē′grĕs), *n.* [L. *egressus,* fr. *egredi* to go out, fr. *e* out + *gradi* to go.] **1.** Act or right of going out or leaving; emergence. **2.** *Astron.* The emergence of a heavenly body from eclipse, occultation, or transit. **3.** A place or means of exit; an outlet.
e·gress′ (ē·grĕs′), *v. i.* To go out; issue forth.
e·gres′sion (ē·grĕsh′ŭn), *n.* Egress; emergence.
e′gret (ē′grĕt; ē·grĕt′; ĕg′rĕt), *n.;* see PLURAL, *Note,* 3. [F. *aigrette* egret, tuft of feathers.] **1.** Any of several herons which, during the breeding season, bear long plumes (aigrettes). **2.** An aigrette.
E·gyp′tian (ē·jĭp′shăn), *adj. & n.* from EGYPT, *Gaz.;* also, *Obs.,* GYPSY.
Egyptian cotton. See COTTON, 1.
E′gyp·tol′o·gy (ē′jĭp·tŏl′ō·jĭ), *n.* [Gr. *Aigyptos* Egypt + *-logy.*] The science or study of Egyptian antiquities. — **E·gyp′to·log′i·cal** (ē·jĭp′tō·lŏj′ĭ·kăl), *adj.* — **E′gyp·tol′o·gist** (ē′jĭp·tŏl′ō·jĭst), *n.*
ei′der (ī′dẽr), *n.;* see PLURAL, *Note,* 3. Also **eider duck.** [Icel. *æthr.*] Any of several large sea ducks (genus *Somateria* and allied genera) of northern Europe, Asia, and America. The female lines her nest with very soft down (**eider down**) plucked from her body.
ei·do′lon (ī·dō′lŏn), *n.; pl.* EIDOLA (-lȧ). [NL., fr. Gr. *eidōlon* image. See IDOL.] An image; phantom.
eight (āt), *n.* [AS. *eahta.*] **1.** See NUMBER, *Table.* **2.** Something having as an essential feature eight units or members, as a playing card with eight pips. — **eight,** *adj.*
eight ball. **1.** *Pool.* A black ball numbered "8." **2.** *Radio.* A round microphone equally receptive from all directions.
— ***behind the eight ball.*** In a highly disadvantageous position or baffling situation; — because, in one variety of pool, the cue ball is in a disadvantageous position when the eight ball is between it and an object ball, a player being forbidden to shoot directly at, or pocket, the eight ball until his other object balls have been pocketed. *Slang, U. S.*
eight′een′ (ā′tēn′; 2), *n. & adj.* [AS. *eahtatȳne, -tēne.*] See NUMBER, *Table.* — **eight′eenth′** (-tēnth′; 2), *n. & adj.*
eight′een′mo′ (ā′tēn′mō′), *n. & adj.* = OCTODECIMO.
eight′fold′ (āt′fōld′; 2), *adj. & adv.* See -FOLD.
eighth (ātth), *n.* [AS. *eahtotha.*] **1.** See NUMBER, *Table.* **2.** *Music.* An octave. — **eighth,** *adj.*
eighth note. *Music.* See NOTE, *n.,* 11.
eight′y (ā′tĭ), *n. & adj.* [AS. *eahtatig.*] See NUMBER, *Table.* — **eight′i·eth** (ā′tĭ·ĕth; -ĭth), *n. & adj.*
eight′y·fold′ (-fōld′; 2), *adj. & adv.* See -FOLD.
ei′kon (ī′kŏn). Var. of ICON.
eild (ēld). Scot. var. of ELD, age, old age.
‖**Ein′ fes′te Burg ist un′ser Gott** (īn fĕs′tĕ bo͝ork′ ĭst o͝on′zẽr gôt′). [G.] A mighty fortress is our God; — title and first line of a hymn by Martin Luther.
ein′korn′ (īn′kôrn′), *n.* [G.] See WHEAT.
Ein′stein e·qua′tion (īn′stīn). See MASS-ENERGY EQUATION.
Ein·stein′i·an (īn·stīn′ĭ·ăn), *adj.* Of or pertaining to Albert Einstein, German-Swiss physicist, or the theory of relativity (**Ein′stein the′o·ry** [īn′stīn]) developed by him. See RELATIVITY.
eis·tedd′fod (ĕs·tĕth′vŏd), *n.; pl.* EISTEDDFODS (-vŏdz), EISTEDDFODAU (ĕs′tĕth·vŏd′ī). [W., session, fr. *eistedd* to sit.] An annual congress of bards and literati of Wales, in its present form a 19th-century revival. — **eis′tedd·fod′ic** (ĕs′tĕth·vŏd′ĭk), *adj.*
ei′ther (ē′thẽr; ī′thẽr), *adj.* [AS. *ǣgther, ǣghwæther,* each.] **1.** Each of two; the one and the other; as, danger on *either* side. **2.** One or the other (of alternatives); as, take *either* road. — *pron.* One of two; the one or the other. — *conj.* A disjunctive correlative used before two or more co-ordinate words, phrases, or clauses which are joined by *or;* as, the assertion must be *either* true or false. — *adv.* Any more so or any more truly; — following and emphasizing the latter or last of two or more choices, esp. in negative expressions; as, not wise or handsome *either.*
e·jac′u·late (ē·jăk′ū·lāt), *v. t.* [L. *ejaculatus,* past part. of *ejaculari* to throw out, fr. *e* out + *jaculari* to throw, fr. *jaculum* dart, fr. *jacere* to throw.] **1.** To eject (fluids from the body). **2.** To throw out, as an exclamation; to utter briefly or suddenly as by impulse; as, to *ejaculate* a prayer. — **e·jac′u·la′tive** (-lā′tĭv; -lȧ·tĭv), *adj.* — **e·jac′u·la′tor** (-lā′tẽr), *n.*
e·jac′u·la′tion (-lā′shŭn), *n.* An ejaculating; an ejaculated utterance, as a short, sudden exclamation.
e·jac′u·la·to′ry (ē·jăk′ū·lȧ·tō′rĭ *or, esp. Brit.,* -tẽr·ĭ), *adj.* **1.** Ejaculating; specif., *Physiol.,* related to, or concerned in, ejaculation; as, *ejaculatory* vessels. **2.** Of the nature of an ejaculation; as, an *ejaculatory* prayer.
e·ject′ (ē·jĕkt′), *v. t.* [L. *ejectus,* past part. of *eicere,* fr. *e* out + *jacere* to throw.] **1.** To throw forth or out; to thrust or drive out; expel; as, to *eject* a person from a room. **2.** *Law.* To dispossess; as, to *eject* tenants. — **e·jec′tion** (-jĕk′shŭn), *n.* — **e·jec′tive** (-tĭv), *adj.* — **e·jec′tor** (-tẽr), *n.*
Syn. **Eject, expel, oust, evict, dismiss** mean to force something or someone out. **Eject** carries an especially strong implication of throwing out from within, and often specifically implies actions so far apart as emitting, discharging, disgorging, etc.; **expel** implies usually a voluntary ejection as from school, an organization, or the like; **oust** implies ejection by removal, dispossession, or the like, by power of the law, by compulsion of necessity, or the like; **evict,** in legal use to recover property to which one has a clear or proved right or claim, has come to mean to turn out of house or home, as a tenant who has fallen behind in payments; **dismiss** implies a getting rid of something such as a petition, a grudge, a duty, an employee, by taking measures to ensure its or his no longer confronting one.
e′ject (ē′jĕkt), *n. Old Psychol.* A mental state, percept, etc., viewed apart from a person's mind, as though projected from it.
e·jec′ta (ē·jĕk′tȧ), *n. pl.* [L., neut. pl. of *ejectus* cast out. See EJECT.] Matter ejected, as from a volcano.
e·ject′ment (ē·jĕkt′mĕnt), *n.* **1.** An ejecting; dispossession; ejection. **2.** *Law.* A mixed action for the recovery of possession of real property and damages and costs.
e′ka- (ē′kȧ-; ā′kȧ-). [Skr. *eka* one.] *Chem.* A combining form prefixed to the name of a known element to designate provisionally a predicted element which should stand next in order in the same family of the periodic system.
eke (ēk), *v. t.* [AS. *ēcan, ȳcan.*] **1.** *Archaic.* To increase; enlarge. **2.** Commonly **eke out.** **a** To supplement; make additions to; as, to *eke* out small wages by doing odd jobs. **b** To make (a living) or support (existence) in scanty fashion or bit by bit.
eke (ēk), *adv. & conj.* [AS. *ēac.*] *Archaic.* Also.
el (ĕl), *n.; pl.* ELS (ĕlz). **1.** The letter L, l. **2.** *Colloq.* = ELEVATED RAILROAD. — **el,** *adj.*
e·lab′o·rate (ē·lăb′ō·rĭt), *adj.* [L. *elaboratus,* past part. of *elaborare* to work out, fr. *e* out + *laborare* to labor, fr. *labor* labor.] Wrought out with great care; studied; painstaking; as, *elaborate* preparations. — (-rāt), *v. t.* **1.** To produce with labor. **2.** To work out in detail; to perfect, embellish, or develop by labor, care, or the like. — *v. i.* To work, write, or speak in detail or with embellishments; as, to *elaborate* upon a theme. — **e·lab′o·rate·ly,** *adv.* — **e·lab′o·rate·ness,** *n.* — **e·lab′o·ra′tion** (-rā′shŭn), *n.* — **e·lab′o·ra′tive** (ē·lăb′ō·rā′tĭv; -rȧ·tĭv), *adj.* — **e·lab′o·ra′tor** (-rā′tẽr), *n.*
el′ae·op′tene (ĕl′ē·ŏp′tēn), *n.* Also **el′ae·op′ten** (-tĕn). [Gr. *elaion* olive oil, oil + *ptēnos* winged, fleeting.] *Chem.* The portion of natural essential oils which does not solidify; — distinguished from *stearoptene.*
E·laine′ (ē·lān′), *n.* Any of several ladies in the Arthurian legends; esp., "the lily maid of Astolat," whose story is the subject of one of Tennyson's *Idylls of the King.*
‖**é′lan′** (ā′läɴ′), *n.* [F., fr. *élancer* to dart.] Ardor; eagerness for action; spirit.
e′land (ē′lănd), *n.;* see PLURAL, *Note,* 6. [D., elk.] Either of two large oxlike African antelopes (genus *Taurotragus*).
‖**é′lan′ vi′tal′** (ā′läɴ′ vē′tȧl′). [F.] The vital force or impulse of life; according to Bergson, the creative principle immanent in all organisms and responsible for evolution.
e·lapse′ (ē·lăps′), *v. i.* [L. *elapsus,* past part. of *elabi* to glide away, fr. *e* out + *labi* to fall, slide.] To slip or glide away; to pass, as time.
e·las′mo·branch (ē·lăs′mō·brăngk; ē·lăz′-), *adj.* [Gr. *elasmos* a metal plate + L. *branchia* a gill.] Of or pertaining to a class of fishes (Elasmobranchii) characterized by lamellate gills, and comprising the sharks, the rays, extinct allies of these fishes, and the chimaeras. — *n.* An elasmobranch fish.
e·las′tic (ē·lăs′tĭk), *adj.* [NL. *elasticus,* fr. Gr. *elastikos,* fr. *elaunein* to drive.] **1.** Springing back; springy; of solids, capable of recovering size and shape after deformation; of gases, indefinitely expansive. **2.** Of persons, temperaments, etc., able to recover quickly from depression, fatigue, etc. **3.** Capable of being readily stretched or expanded without essential alteration; as, an *elastic* rubber band; an *elastic* meaning of a word. — **e·las′ti·cal·ly** (-tĭ·kăl·ĭ), *adv.*
Syn. **Elastic, resilient, springy, flexible, supple** mean able to endure strain or distortion. **Elastic** and **resilient** are both in technical and in popular use, *elastic* implying the property of resisting deformation up to a certain point, and *resilient* the ability to recover shape quickly after the deforming force has been removed; **springy,** a wholly popular

term, implies both the ease with which a thing yields to pressure or strain and the quickness of its return; **flexible** applies to anything which can be bent or turned without breaking (though not necessarily resilient); **supple**, to anything that can be bent, twisted, or folded without any signs of injury. In extended use, *elastic* implies ease in stretching or expanding; *resilient*, a tendency to rebound quickly in health, spirits, etc.; *springy*, youth, freshness, and buoyancy; *flexible*, adaptability or tractability; *supple*, a flexibility of temperament that lends itself to the needs of a situation. — **Ant.** Rigid.

e·las′tic (ē·lăs′tĭk), *n.* **1.** Fabric made elastic by rubber woven into it; also, a cord, band, or garter made from such fabric. **2.** Rubber specially prepared in cords, strings, or bands, so as to be very elastic; also, something made from such rubber.

e·las′tic′i·ty (ē·lăs′tĭs′ĭ·tĭ; ē′lăs-), *n.* Quality or state of being elastic; springiness; resilience. Popularly, a body is said to possess great elasticity when it is easily deformed and is quick in recovering. Scientifically, elasticity is that property of a body which causes it to resist deformation and thereby to recover its original shape and size when the deforming forces are removed.

e·las′tin (ē·lăs′tĭn), *n.* [*elastic* + *-in*.] *Biochem.* An albuminoid forming the chief constituent of elastic fibers.

e·las′to·mer (ē·lăs′tō·mẽr), *n.* [*elastic* + *-o* + Gr. *meros* part.] *Chem.* An elastic, rubberlike substance, as natural or synthetic rubber.

e·late′ (ē·lāt′), *adj.* [L. *elatus*, fr. *e* out + *latus* (used as past part. of *ferre* to bear).] Lifted up or elevated, esp. in spirits; elated. — *v. t.* To exalt the spirit of; to elevate or flush with success. — **e·lat′er** (-lāt′ẽr), *n.* — **e·la′tion** (-lā′shŭn), *n.*

e·lat′ed (ē·lāt′ĕd; -ĭd), *adj.* Exalted in spirit. — **e·lat′ed·ly**, *adv.*

el′a·ter (ĕl′ȧ·tẽr), *n.* [NL., fr. Gr. *elatēr* driver, fr. *elaunein* to drive.] **1.** *Obs.* Elasticity. **2.** *Bot.* A filament or filamentous appendage for dispersing spores, as in the capsule of a liverwort. **3.** *Zool.* **a** Any of a family (Elateridae) of long tapering beetles which jump with a snap or click when laid on the back or held by the abdomen; — called also *snapping beetle* and *click beetle*. **b** One of the caudal springing organs of the springtails. — **e·lat′er·id** (ē·lăt′ẽr·ĭd), *n. & adj.*

e·lat′er·in (ē·lăt′ẽr·ĭn), *n.* *Chem.* A white, crystalline, slightly bitter substance, the active principle of elaterium.

e·lat′er·ite (-īt), *n.* *Mineral.* A dark-brown elastic mineral resin, occurring in soft flexible masses.

el′a·te′ri·um (ĕl′ȧ·tẽr′ĭ·ŭm), *n.* [L., fr. Gr. *elatērion*, neut. of *elatērios* driving.] *Pharm.* A purgative obtained from the juice of a Mediterranean plant (*Ecballium elaterium*) of the gourd family.

E layer. *Radio.* A layer in the ionosphere which reflects radio waves. It occurs at varying heights, 50 to 90 miles above the earth's surface.

el′bow (ĕl′bō), *n.* [AS. *elboga*, *elnboga*; cf. AS. *eln* ell (orig., forearm) and *boga* a bending.] **1.** The joint of the arm; the outer curve of a bent arm. **2.** A corresponding joint in the anterior limb of an animal. See DOG, *Illust.* **3.** Any bend like that of the elbow. — *v. t. & i.* To push, lift, or force, with or as with the elbows; to jostle or make one's way by jostling.

el′bow·room′ (-rōōm′), *n.* Room to extend the elbows on each side; hence, ample room for motion or action; free scope.

eld (ĕld), *n.* [AS. *yldu*, *yldo*, *eldo*, old age, fr. *ald*, *eald*, old.] **1.** *Dial.* Age, esp. old age. **2.** *Archaic.* Old times; antiquity.

eld′er (ĕl′dẽr), *adj.* [AS. *yldra*, *eldra*, *ieldra*, compar. of *eald* old.] **1.** Older; of the greater age or of earlier birth. **2.** Earlier; former; of or pertaining to former time. **3.** Belonging to a more mature time or age; later in life. **4.** Prior or superior, in rank, office, validity, etc.; senior; as, an *elder* title. — *n.* **1.** One who lived at an earlier period; esp., an ancestor. **2. a** One who is older; a senior. **b** An aged person. **3.** A person who, on account of his age, occupies the office of ruler or judge; hence, one of certain officers, in various churches, given special functions or authority consistent with their age, experience, or dignity; specif., in Presbyterian churches, either a ***teaching elder***, or minister, or a ***ruling elder***, one of the laymen who share with the ministers the government of the church. **4.** In the Mormon Church, a person ordained to the higher order of priesthood. — **eld′er·ship**, *n.*

el′der (ĕl′dẽr), *n.* [AS. *ellen*, *ellern*.] **a** Any of a genus (*Sambucus*) of shrubs or trees of the honeysuckle family, bearing flat clusters of small white or pink flowers, and black or red berrylike drupes. **b** *Eng.* The European alder (*Alnus vulgaris*).

el′der·ber′ry (-bĕr′ĭ), *n.* **a** The berrylike drupe of the elder. Those of some species are often made into wine. **b** The shrub or tree itself.

eld′er·ly (ĕl′dẽr·lĭ), *adj.* Somewhat old; advanced beyond middle age; also, of or pertaining to later life.

elder statesmen. **a** In Japan, an informal body (*genro*) of confidential advisers of the emperor, consisting of the more distinguished statesmen and nobles who are retired from active public life. It was practically discontinued after 1922. **b** Any similar class of persons.

eld′est (ĕl′dĕst; -dĭst), *adj.* Oldest.

eldest, *or* **elder, hand.** *Cards.* Player on the dealer's left.

el′ding (ĕl′dĭng), *n.* [ON.] *Chiefly Scot.* Fuel.

El Do·ra′do (ĕl dō·rä′dō); *pl.* EL DORADOS (-dōz). Also **El′do·ra′do**, *n.* [Sp., lit., the gilded.] **1.** A legendary rich king of a South American tribe or his imaginary kingdom, abounding in gold. **2.** Any place of fabulous richness.

el′dritch (ĕl′drĭch), *adj.* *Orig. Scot.* Weird; eerie.

El′e·at′ic (ĕl′ē·ăt′ĭk), *adj.* [L. *Eleaticus*, from *Elea* (or *Velia*) in Italy.] Of, pertaining to, or designating a school of Greek philosophers, of the 6th century B.C., who taught the unity of being and the unreality of motion or change. — **El′e·at′ic**, *n.* — **El′e·at′i·cism** (-ĭ·sĭz′m), *n.*

el′e·cam·pane′ (ĕl′ē·kăm·pān′), *n.* [ML. *enula campana*, lit., field inula, fr. L. *inula* elecampane.] **1.** A coarse herb (*Inula helenium*) of the aster family, with yellow-rayed flowers. **2.** A sweetmeat made from the root of the plant.

e·lect′ (ē·lĕkt′), *adj.* [L. *electus*, past part. of *eligere* to elect, fr. *e* out + *legere* to choose.] **1.** Chosen; select. **2.** Elected to an office but not yet inducted into it; as, the mayor-*elect*. **3.** *Theol.* Chosen by divine election; set apart to eternal life. — *n.* One who is elect; hence, ***the elect***, the body of those set apart as elect or select. — *v. t. & i.* **1.** To choose. **2.** To select or take for an office by vote. — **Syn.** See CHOOSE.

e·lec′tion (ē·lĕk′shŭn), *n.* **1.** Act of electing. **2.** The process of filling an office by vote, esp. of the electorate. **3.** *Theol.* Divine choice; esp., as one of the "five points" of Calvinism, predestination of individuals as objects of mercy and salvation; also, those elected. — **Syn.** See CHOICE.

e·lec′tion·eer′ (-ēr′), *v. i.* To work for, or in the interest of, a candidate, party, etc., in an election. — **e·lec′tion·eer′er** (-ẽr), *n.*

e·lec′tive (ē·lĕk′tĭv), *adj.* **1.** Appointed, bestowed, or passing, by election; as, an *elective* office. **2.** Having or exerting a power of choice; choosing. **3.** Pertaining to, or consisting in, choice; electoral; as, their *elective* franchise. **4.** Tending to combine with, or act upon, one substance rather than another; as, *elective* affinity. — *n.* In American schools and colleges, a subject or course which a student may choose for study. — **e·lec′tive·ly**, *adv.* — **e·lec′tive·ness**, *n.*

e·lec′tor (ē·lĕk′tẽr), *n.* **1.** One who elects, or has the right of choice; specif., a person entitled to vote. **2.** [*usually cap.*] In the Holy Roman Empire, one of the princes entitled to take part in choosing the emperor. **3.** One of the persons chosen, by vote of the people, to the **electoral college**, whose function is to elect the president and vice-president of the United States.

e·lec′tor·al (-ăl), *adj.* Pertaining to or consisting of electors; as, the *electoral* college. See ELECTOR.

e·lec′tor·ate (-ĭt), *n.* **1.** The territory, jurisdiction, or dignity of a German elector. **2.** The body of persons entitled to vote in an election. **3.** An electoral district.

E·lec′tra (ē·lĕk′trȧ), *n.* See ORESTES.

Electra complex. See COMPLEX, *n.*, 2.

e·lec′tress (ē·lĕk′trĕs; -trĭs), *n.* **1.** [*usually cap.*] The wife or widow of an elector (sense 2). **2.** A female voter.

e·lec′tric (ē·lĕk′trĭk), **e·lec′tri·cal** (-trĭ·kăl), *adj.* [NL. *electricus* electric, produced from amber (by friction), fr. L. *electrum* amber, fr. Gr. *ēlektron*.] **1.** Pertaining to electricity; consisting of, containing, producing, derived from, or produced or operated by, electricity. **2.** Electrifying; thrilling; as, *electric* eloquence.

e·lec′tric, *n.* **1.** *Physics.* A nonconductor of electricity, as amber, glass, resin, etc., used to excite or store electricity. **2.** *Colloq.* An electric car or trolley. — **e·lec′tri·cal·ly**, *adv.*

e·lec′tri·cal tran·scrip′tion (-trĭ·kăl). *Radio.* **a** Broadcasting from a phonograph record by means of apparatus which causes the impulses given by the record to be impressed upon transmitted radio waves. **b** A phonograph record designed for use in radio broadcasting.

electric cable. See CABLE, 4 **b**.

electric chair. A chair used in executing the death penalty by electrocution; hence, the penalty itself.

electric eel. An eel-shaped fish (*Electrophorus electricus*), of the Orinoco and Amazon basins, constituting a family (Electrophoridae), having special organs by which it can communicate severe electric shocks.

electric eye. A photoelectric cell.

e·lec′tri′cian (ē·lĕk′trĭsh′ăn; ĕl′ĕk-), *n.* One who designs, makes, or repairs electric instruments, machinery, etc., or sets up electric installations.

e·lec′tric′i·ty (ē·lĕk′trĭs′ĭ·tĭ; ĕl′ĕk-), *n.* **1.** The property of certain substances, as amber and glass, when activated by friction, to attract; also, their state when so activated. **2.** One of the fundamental quantities in nature, consisting of elementary particles, electrons and protons. Electricity is characterized especially by the fact that it gives rise to a field of force possessing potential energy and that, when moving in a stream (an electric current), it gives rise to a magnetic field of force with which kinetic energy is associated. The elementary particles of electricity, the electron and the proton, are opposites electrically. Electricity of which the elementary unit is the electron is called ***negative electricity***; electricity of which the elementary unit is the proton is called ***positive electricity***. If a substance has on its surface more protons than electrons it is said to be charged with positive electricity. The quantity of an electric charge may be measured, the practical unit being the coulomb. The term ***statical electricity*** applies properly to the electricity of stationary charges, however produced; the term ***dynamical electricity***, to moving charges, which give rise to the phenomena of the electric current, whether generated by friction, by induction, by means of a voltaic battery or dynamo, or in any other way. The electric current is of practical importance as a means of transferring energy to a distance and for the transformation of energy, as in the electric furnace, the electric light, in electrolysis, etc. **3.** The science which treats of the phenomena and laws of electricity.

electric organ. A musical instrument that uses electrical devices instead of wind to produce tones similar in quality to those produced by a pipe organ.

electric ray. See 1st RAY.

electric thermometer. See THERMOMETER.

e·lec′tri·fy (ē·lĕk′trĭ·fī), *v. t.*; -FIED (-fīd); -FY′ING. [*electric* + *-fy*.] **1.** To communicate electricity to; to charge with electricity. **2. a** To give an electric shock to. **b** To excite suddenly and violently; to thrill. **3.** To equip, as a railroad, for use of electric power. — **e·lec′tri·fi·ca′tion** (-fĭ·kā′shŭn), *n.* — **e·lec′tri·fi′er** (-fī′ẽr), *n.*

e·lec′trize (-trīz), *v. t. & i.* To electrify. — **e·lec′tri·za′tion** (-trĭ·zā′shŭn; -trī·zā′-), *n.* — **e·lec′triz·er** (-trīz·ẽr), *n.*

e·lec′tro (ē·lĕk′trō), *n.*; *pl.* ELECTROS (-trōz). Short for ELECTROTYPE, ELECTROPLATE.

e·lec′tro- (ē·lĕk′trō-). [Gr. *ēlektron* amber.] A combining form denoting: **a** *Electric, electric and, electricity, electricity and*, as in *electro*lysis, *electro*cute. **b** *Electrolytic*, as in *electro*analysis.

e·lec′tro·a·nal′y·sis (-ȧ·năl′ĭ·sĭs), *n.* *Chem.* Analysis by electrolytic methods.

e·lec′tro·car′di·o·gram′ (-kär′dĭ·ō·grăm′), *n.* *Med.* A graphic record of the heart's action, made by an electrocardiograph.

e·lec′tro·car′di·o·graph′ (-kär′dĭ·ō·grȧf′; 9), *n.* [*electro-* + *cardio-* + *-graph*.] *Med.* An instrument for recording the changes of electrical potential occurring during the heartbeat. It is valuable in diagnosing irregularities of heart action. — **e·lec′tro·car′di·og′ra·phy** (-ŏg′rȧ·fĭ), *n.*

e·lec′tro·chem′is·try (-kĕm′ĭs·trĭ), *n.* The science of the relation of electricity to chemical changes. — **e·lec′tro·chem′i·cal** (-ĭ·kăl), *adj.* — **e·lec′tro·chem′ist** (-ĭst), *n.*

e·lec′tro·cute (ē·lĕk′trō·kūt), *v. t.* [*electro-* + *-cute* as in *execute*.] To execute (a criminal) by electricity; hence, to kill by an electric shock. — **e·lec′tro·cu′tion** (-kū′shŭn), *n.*

e·lec′trode (ē·lĕk′trōd), *n.* [*electro-* + 2d *-ode*.] *Elec.* Either terminal of an electric source; esp., either conductor by which the current enters and leaves an electrolyte.

e·lec′tro·de·pos′it (ē·lĕk′trō·dē·pŏz′ĭt), *n.* A deposit made by electrical action. — *v. t.* To deposit (nickel, copper, rubber, etc.) electrically. — **e·lec′tro·dep′o·si′tion** (-dĕp′ō·zĭsh′ŭn; -dē′pō-), *n.*

e·lec′tro·dy·nam′ics (ē·lĕk′trō·dī·năm′ĭks; -dĭ-), *n.*; see -ICS. The phenomena of electricity in motion; also, the science treating of the action of electric currents on themselves and on one another, and of the interaction of currents and magnets. — **e·lec′tro·dy·nam′ic** (-ĭk), **e·lec′tro·dy·nam′i·cal** (-ĭ·kăl), *adj.*

e·lec′tro·dy′na·mom′e·ter (-dī′nȧ·mŏm′ē·tẽr; -dĭn′ȧ-), *n.* An instrument which measures current by indicating the strength of the forces between a current flowing in fixed coils and one flowing in movable coils.

e·lec′tro·en·ceph′a·lo·graph′ (-ĕn·sĕf′ȧ·lō·grăf′; 9), *n.* [*electro-* + *encephalo-* + *-graph.*] *Med.* An apparatus for detecting and recording brain waves. The tracing made by it is called an **e·lec′tro·en·ceph′a·lo·gram′** (-grăm′). — **e·lec′tro·en·ceph′a·log′ra·phy** (-lŏg′rȧ·fĭ), *n.* — **e·lec′tro·en·ceph′a·lo·graph′ic** (-lō·grăf′ĭk), *adj.*

e·lec′tro·graph (ē·lĕk′trō·grăf; 9), *n.* [*electro-* + *-graph.*] **a** A record or tracing made by the action of electricity, as by an electrometer. **b** An electrically controlled apparatus used to trace designs for etching. **c** An instrument for the electric transmission of pictures, maps, etc. **d** An image made by X rays. **e** A cinematograph using the arc light. — **e·lec′tro·graph′ic** (-grăf′ĭk), *adj.* — **e·lec′trog′ra·phy** (ē·lĕk′trŏg′rȧ·fĭ), *n.*

e·lec′tro·ki·net′ics (ē·lĕk′trō·kĭ·nĕt′ĭks; -kī-), *n.*; see -ICS. The branch of electrodynamics which treats of the laws of distribution of electric current. — **e·lec′tro·ki·net′ic** (-ĭk), *adj.*

e·lec′tro·lier′ (ē·lĕk′trō·lēr′), *n.* [*electro-* + *-lier* as in chande*lier*.] A support for electric lamps, esp. one like a chandelier.

e·lec′trol′y·sis (ē·lĕk′trŏl′ĭ·sĭs; ĕl′ĕk-), *n.* [*electro-* + *-lysis.*] Chemical decomposition by the action of the electric current; also, subjection to this process.

e·lec′tro·lyte (ē·lĕk′trō·līt), *n.* [*electro-* + Gr. *lytos* dissoluble.] *Physics & Chem.* **a** A substance in which the conduction of electricity is accompanied by chemical decomposition; — called also **electrolytic conductor**. **b** Any substance which, when dissolved in a suitable liquid, or when fused, becomes an electrolyte (sense **a**).

e·lec′tro·lyt′ic (-lĭt′ĭk), *adj.* Also **e·lec′tro·lyt′i·cal** (-ĭ·kăl). Pertaining to or deposited by electrolysis; made by electrolysis; pertaining to or containing an electrolyte. — **e·lec′tro·lyt′i·cal·ly**, *adv.*

e·lec′tro·lyze (ē·lĕk′trō·līz), *v. t.* To subject to electrolysis. — **e·lec′tro·ly·za′tion** (-lĭ·zā′shŭn; -lī·zā′-), *n.* — **e·lec′tro·lyz′er** (-līz′ẽr), *n.*

e·lec′tro·mag′net (ē·lĕk′trō·măg′nĕt; -nĭt), *n.* A core of magnetic material, in practice always soft iron, surrounded by a coil of wire through which an electric current is passed to magnetize the core.

e·lec′tro·mag·net′ic (-măg·nĕt′ĭk), **e·lec′tro·mag·net′i·cal** (-ĭ·kăl), *adj.* Of, pertaining to, or produced by electromagnetism. — **e·lec′tro·mag·net′i·cal·ly**, *adv.*

electromagnetic induction. See INDUCTION, 4.

electromagnetic wave. *Physics.* A wave produced by the oscillation of an electric charge, as a light wave and a radio wave.

e·lec′tro·mag′net·ism (ē·lĕk′trō·măg′nĕ·tĭz′m; -nĭ·tĭz′m), *n.* **1.** Magnetism developed by a current of electricity. **2.** The branch of science treating of the physical relations between electricity and magnetism as shown by development of magnetism by the electric current, the effect of magnets upon currents, etc. — **e·lec′tro·mag′net·ist** (-măg′nĕ·tĭst; -nĭ·tĭst), *n.*

e·lec′tro·met′al·lur′gy (-mĕt′′l·ûr′jĭ; -mĕ·tăl′ẽr·jĭ), *n.* That department of metallurgy employing the electric current, either for electrolytic deposition or as a source of heat in smelting, refining, etc. — **e·lec′tro·met′al·lur′gi·cal** (-mĕt′′l·ûr′jĭ·kăl), *adj.* — **e·lec′tro·met′al·lur′gist** (-mĕt′′l·ûr′jĭst; -mĕ·tăl′ẽr·jĭst), *n.*

e·lec′trom′e·ter (ē·lĕk′trŏm′ē·tẽr; ĕl′ĕk-), *n.* [*electro-* + *-meter.*] *Elec.* An instrument for measuring the difference of potential between two points, as of a conductor.

e·lec′tro·mo′tion (ē·lĕk′trō·mō′shŭn), *n.* Motion of or produced by electricity.

e·lec′tro·mo′tive (-mō′tĭv), *adj.* Pertaining to electromotion; producing, or tending to produce, an electric current; causing electrical action or effects.

electromotive force. That which moves, or tends to move, electricity; the amount of energy derived from an electrical source per unit quantity of electricity passing through the source (cell, generator). Abbr. *e.m.f.*

e·lec′tro·mo′tor (ē·lĕk′trō·mō′tẽr), *n.* **1.** A mover or exciter of electricity; an apparatus for generating a current of electricity. **2.** An electric motor.

e·lec′tron (ē·lĕk′trŏn), *n.* [NL., fr. Gr. *ēlektron.* See ELECTRIC.] *Physics & Chem.* A very light particle associated with the elementary charge of negative electricity. Each electron has a charge of 4.80×10^{-10} C.G.S. electrostatic units. Its mass is approximately 1/1845 that of the proton. Electrons are constituents of atoms. See ATOM. They constitute cathode rays and beta rays, and are emitted by hot bodies. — **e·lec′tron′ic** (ē·lĕk′trŏn′ĭk; ĕl′ĕk-), *adj.*

e·lec′tro·neg′a·tive (ē·lĕk′trō·nĕg′ȧ·tĭv), *adj.* = NEGATIVE, *adj.*, 4. — *n.* An electronegative substance.

electron gun. *Television.* In a cathode-ray tube, the electron-emitting cathode and its surrounding assembly for concentrating, controlling, and focusing, by means of an electrostatic or an electromagnetic field, the stream of electrons to a spot of desired size.

e·lec′tron′ics (ē·lĕk′trŏn′ĭks; ĕl′ĕk-), *n.*; see -ICS. That branch of physics which treats of the emission, behavior, and effects of electrons, esp. in vacuum tubes, photoelectric cells, and the like.

electron microscope. An optical instrument using a beam of electrons focused by means of a surrounding electrostatic or magnetic field (an **electron lens**) to produce an enlarged image of a minute object on a fluorescent screen or photographic plate.

electron optics. A branch of electronics dealing with those properties of beams of electrons that are analogous to the properties of rays of light in image formation.

electron tube. *Elec.* A form of vacuum tube consisting of a heated cathode, of an anode, or plate, and of a third electrode, or grid, for controlling the current flowing between the other two electrodes. It is used for the detection of radio waves, for amplification of currents, generation of alternating currents of a very great frequency range, and, since it transmits current in one direction only, as a rectifier of alternating currents. Called also *radio tube, vacuum tube* or *valve*, etc.

electron volt. *Physics.* The amount of energy gained by an electron in passing from a point of low potential to a point one volt higher in potential.

e·lec′trop′a·thy (ē·lĕk′trŏp′ȧ·thĭ; ĕl′ĕk-), *n.* Electrotherapeutics. — **e·lec′tro·path′ic** (ē·lĕk′trō·păth′ĭk), *adj.*

e·lec′tro·pho·re′sis (ē·lĕk′trō·fō·rē′sĭs), *n.* [NL., fr. *electro-* + Gr. *phorēsis* a being borne.] = CATAPHORESIS.

e·lec′troph′o·rus (ē·lĕk′trŏf′ō·rŭs; ĕl′ĕk-), *n.*; *pl.* -TROPHORI (-rī). [NL., fr. *electro-* + Gr. *-phoros*, fr. *pherein* to bear.] *Physics.* An instrument for the production of electric charges by induction. It consists of a disk of resin, shellac, ebonite, or the like, and a metal plate.

e·lec′tro·plate′ (ē·lĕk′trō·plāt′), *v. t.* To plate or cover with a coating by electrical means, especially with metal by electrolysis. Nonconductors, such as wax recording disks, may be electroplated by first coating them with graphite or other conductor. Electroplating from a colloidal solution, as of rubber, is usually called *electrodeposition.* — *n.* Something electroplated. — **e·lec′tro·plat′er** (-plāt′ẽr), *n.* — **e·lec′tro·plat′ing**, *n.*

e·lec′tro·pos′i·tive (ē·lĕk′trō·pŏz′ĭ·tĭv), *adj.* = POSITIVE, *adj.*, 7. — *n.* An electropositive substance.

e·lec′tro·scope (ē·lĕk′trō·skōp), *n.* *Physics.* An instrument for detecting the presence of an electric charge on a body, or for determining whether the charge is positive or negative. — **e·lec′tro·scop′ic** (-skŏp′ĭk), *adj.*

e·lec′tro·stat′ic in·duc′tion (ē·lĕk′trō·stăt′ĭk). See INDUCTION, 4.

e·lec′tro·stat′ics (-stăt′ĭks), *n.*; see -ICS. The science which deals with statical electricity. — **e·lec′tro·stat′ic** (-ĭk), *adj.*

e·lec′tro·ther′a·peu′tics (ē·lĕk′trō·thĕr′ȧ·pū′tĭks), *n.*; see -ICS. *Med.* Use or science of electricity as a curative agent. — **e·lec′tro·ther′a·peu′tic** (-tĭk), **e·lec′tro·ther′a·peu′ti·cal** (-tĭ·kăl), *adj.* — **e·lec′tro·ther′a·peu′tist** (-tĭst), *n.*

e·lec′tro·ther′a·py (-thĕr′ȧ·pĭ), *n.* *Med.* Electrotherapeutics. — **e·lec′tro·ther′a·pist** (-pĭst), *n.*

e·lec′trot′o·nus (ē·lĕk′trŏt′ō·nŭs; ĕl′ĕk-), *n.* [NL., fr. *electro-* + Gr. *tonos* tension.] *Physiol.* The modified condition of a nerve when a constant current of electricity passes through any part of it. — **e·lec′tro·ton′ic** (ē·lĕk′trō·tŏn′ĭk), *adj.*

e·lec′tro·type (ē·lĕk′trō·tīp), *n.* **1.** A facsimile plate, esp. for use in printing, made by electroplating a wax impression. **2. a** A print made from such a plate. **b** Electrotypy. — *v. t. & i.* To make facsimile plates (of) by electrotypy. — **e·lec′tro·typ′er** (-tīp′ẽr), *n.* — **e·lec′tro·typ′ing**, *n.*

e·lec′tro·typ′y (-tīp′ĭ), *n.* The process of producing electrotype plates. — **e·lec′tro·typ′ic** (-tĭp′ĭk), *adj.* — **e·lec′tro·typ′ist** (-tīp′ĭst), *n.*

e·lec′tro·va′lence (-vā′lĕns), **e·lec′tro·va′len·cy** (-lĕn·sĭ), *n.* [*electro-* + *valence, valency.*] *Physical Chem.* The number of electrons which an atom must gain or lose to acquire the same stable grouping of electrons as found in the atom of the nearest related inert gas; — called also *polar valence.* — **e·lec′tro·va′lent** (-lĕnt), *adj.*

e·lec′trum (ē·lĕk′trŭm), *n.* [L., fr. Gr. *ēlektron.* See ELECTRIC.] A natural pale-yellow alloy of gold and silver.

e·lec′tu·ar′y (-tū·ĕr′ĭ *or, esp. Brit.*, -ẽr·ĭ), *n.*; *pl.* -IES (-ĭz). [ML. (& LL.) *electuarium*, fr. Gr. *ekleikton*, fr. *ekleichein* to lick up, fr. *ek* out + *leichein* to lick.] *Pharm.* A medicine incorporated with honey or sirup so as to form a pasty mass.

el′ee·mos′y·nar′y (ĕl′ē·mŏs′ĭ·nĕr′ĭ; ĕl′ē·ē-; -mŏz′-; *or, esp. Brit.*, -nẽr·ĭ), *adj.* [ML. *eleemosynarius*, fr. L. *eleemosyna* alms. See ALMS.] **1.** Relating or devoted to charity or alms. **2.** Given in charity or alms. **3.** Supported by charity.

el′e·gance (ĕl′ē·găns), *n.* **1.** Refined gracefulness, or propriety expressing fastidious taste; esp., richness and refinement combined. **2.** An elegant expression.

el′e·gan·cy (-găn·sĭ), *n.*; *pl.* -CIES (-sĭz). Elegance.

el′e·gant (-gănt), *adj.* [F. *élégant*, fr. L. *elegans, -antis.*] **1.** Correctly fine in dress and person. **2.** Characterized by, or having, elegance. **3.** Fastidiously tasteful. **4.** In vulgar use, excellent; fine. — **Syn.** See CHOICE. — **el′e·gant·ly**, *adv.*

el′e·gi′ac (ĕl′ē·jī′ăk; -ăk; ē·lē′jĭ·ăk), *adj.* **1.** Of, belonging to, or written in, elegiacs; writing, or having written, elegiacs. **2.** Plaintive; expressing sorrow or lamentation. **3.** Used in or suited to elegies. — *n.* **1.** A pentameter verse, anciently scanned as follows: -⌣⌣|-⌣⌣|--|⌣⌣-|⌣⌣-. It was used not only for elegies but for martial, gnomic, and lyric themes. **2.** *pl.* A poem or poems in such verse. — **el′e·gi′a·cal** (ĕl′ē·jī′ȧ·kăl), *adj.*

el′e·gist (ĕl′ē·jĭst), *n.* A composer of elegies.

e·le′git (ē·lē′jĭt), *n.* [L., he has chosen, fr. *eligere* to choose.] *Law.* A writ of execution by which a defendant's goods are appraised and delivered to the plaintiff, to be held till the debt is paid.

el′e·gize (ĕl′ē·jīz), *v. t. & i.* To lament or celebrate in elegy.

el′e·gy (-jĭ), *n.*; *pl.* -GIES (-jĭz). [F. *élégie*, fr. L. *elegia*, fr. Gr. *elegeia*, fr. *elegeios* elegiac, fr. *elegos* a song of mourning.] **1.** *Hist.* Any poem in elegiac meter. **2. a** A lyrical poem, often a lament, esp. of unrequited love. **b** Now, chiefly, a poem of lamentation for the dead.

el′e·ment (ĕl′ē·mĕnt), *n.* [OF., fr. L. *elementum.*] **1.** One of the simple substances or principles (fire, air, water, and earth) formerly believed to compose the physical universe. **2.** Hence: **a** One of the four elements in its natural form or occurrence; as, the watery *element*, that is, water. **b** *pl.* Conditions of weather viewed as activities of the elements, now usually implying severe weather. **c** One of the four elements viewed as a natural habitat; as, water is the *element* of fishes; hence, the state or sphere suited to any person or thing. **3.** One of the constituent parts, principles, or traits of anything. **4.** Hence: *pl.* **a** The simplest principles of any system in philosophy, science, or art; rudiments. **b** Any outline regarded as containing the fundamental features of a thing. **5.** *Chem.* Any one of a limited number (96 or more) of distinct varieties of matter which, singly or in combination, compose substances of all kinds. Elements are not the ultimate constituents of matter. See ATOM.

CHEMICAL ELEMENTS

WITH INTERNATIONAL ATOMIC WEIGHTS, 1952. (O = 16.)

	Symbol	At. no.	At. wt.		Symbol	At. no.	At. wt.
Actinium	Ac	89	227	Bismuth	Bi	83	209.00
Aluminum	Al	13	26.98	Boron	B	5	10.82
Americium	Am	95	[243]*	Bromine	Br	35	79.916
Antimony	Sb	51	121.76	Cadmium	Cd	48	112.41
Argon	A	18	39.944	Calcium	Ca	20	40.08
Arsenic	As	33	74.91	Californium	Cf	98	[246]*
Astatine	At	85	[210]*	Carbon	C	6	12.010
Barium	Ba	56	137.36	Cerium	Ce	58	140.13
Berkelium	Bk	97	[245]*	Cesium	Cs	55	132.91
Beryllium	Be	4	9.013	Chlorine	Cl	17	35.457

	Sym-bol	At. no.	At. wt.		Sym-bol	At. no.	At. wt.
Chromium	Cr	24	52.01	Phosphorus	P	15	30.975
Cobalt	Co	27	58.94	Platinum	Pt	78	195.23
Copper	Cu	29	63.54	Plutonium	Pu	94	[242]*
Curium	Cm	96	[243]*	Polonium	Po	84	210
Dysprosium	Dy	66	162.46	Potassium	K	19	39.100
Erbium	Er	68	167.2	Praseodymium	Pr	59	140.92
Europium	Eu	63	152.0	Promethium	Pm	61	[145]*
Fluorine	F	9	19.00	Protactinium	Pa	91	231
Francium	Fr	87	[223]*	Radium	Ra	88	226.05
Gadolinium	Gd	64	156.9	Radon	Rn	86	222
Gallium	Ga	31	69.72	Rhenium	Re	75	186.31
Germanium	Ge	32	72.60	Rhodium	Rh	45	102.91
Gold	Au	79	197.2	Rubidium	Rb	37	85.48
Hafnium	Hf	72	178.6	Ruthenium	Ru	44	101.7
Helium	He	2	4.003	Samarium	Sm	62	150.43
Holmium	Ho	67	164.94	Scandium	Sc	21	44.96
Hydrogen	H	1	1.0080	Selenium	Se	34	78.96
Indium	In	49	114.76	Silicon	Si	14	28.09
Iodine	I	53	126.91	Silver	Ag	47	107.880
Iridium	Ir	77	193.1	Sodium	Na	11	22.997
Iron	Fe	26	55.85	Strontium	Sr	38	87.63
Krypton	Kr	36	83.80	Sulfur	S	16	32.066
Lanthanum	La	57	138.92	Tantalum	Ta	73	180.88
Lead	Pb	82	207.21	Technetium	Tc	43	[99]*
Lithium	Li	3	6.940	Tellurium	Te	52	127.61
Lutetium	Lu	71	174.99	Terbium	Tb	65	159.2
Magnesium	Mg	12	24.32	Thallium	Tl	81	204.39
Manganese	Mn	25	54.93	Thorium	Th	90	232.12
Mercury	Hg	80	200.61	Thulium	Tm	69	169.4
Molybdenum	Mo	42	95.95	Tin	Sn	50	118.70
Neodymium	Nd	60	144.27	Titanium	Ti	22	47.90
Neon	Ne	10	20.183	Tungsten	W	74	183.92
Neptunium	Np	93	[237]*	Uranium	U	92	238.07
Nickel	Ni	28	58.69	Vanadium	V	23	50.95
Niobium	Nb	41	92.91	Xenon	Xe	54	131.3
Nitrogen	N	7	14.008	Ytterbium	Yb	70	173.04
Osmium	Os	76	190.2	Yttrium	Y	39	88.92
Oxygen	O	8	16.0000	Zinc	Zn	30	65.38
Palladium	Pd	46	106.7	Zirconium	Zr	40	91.22

* Mass number of isotope of longest known half life.

6. *pl. Eccl.* The bread and wine used in the Eucharist. **7.** *Elec.* **a** Either of the pieces constituting a voltaic couple. **b** The positive and negative electrodes of a voltaic couple assembled complete. **c** The active part of an electrical device; as, the rotating *element* of a watt-hour meter. **8.** *Kinematics.* Either of the components of a pair. See PAIR, *n.*, 8. **9.** *Math.* An infinitesimal part of any magnitude of the same nature as the entire magnitude. **10.** *Mil.* **a** One of the subdivisions of a unit or other command, such as a file, squad, or company. **b** A flight formation of two or three planes flying as a unit.

Syn. **Element, component, constituent, ingredient, factor** mean one of the substances, principles, or the like, which make up a compound or complex thing. **Element** (except in its specific sense in science) is the comprehensive term applicable to material and immaterial things and often (always in its scientific sense) connotes irreducible simplicity; **component** and **constituent** are often used to designate any of the substances (whether elements or compounds), or any of the principles or qualities, which enter into the make-up of a complex product, *component*, however, stressing its separate identity or distinguishable character, *constituent* its essential and formative character; **ingredient** is applicable to any of the substances or materials which when combined form a particular mixture such as a medicine, an alloy, etc.; **factor**, to any constituent or element that enables a substance, a system, or the like, to perform a certain kind of work or to accomplish a definite result.

el′e·men′tal (ĕl′ē·mĕn′tăl; -t'l), *adj.* **1.** Of, pertaining to, or like the elements (see ELEMENT, 1, 2) or one of them; hence: **a** Simple; pure; primal; as, *elemental* fire. **b** Ruling or animating the elements or an element; as, an *elemental* spirit. **c** Pertaining to the powers or phenomena of physical nature in general; as, *elemental* worship. **2.** *Chem.* Elementary; uncombined. **3.** Pertaining to rudiments; elementary. **4.** Forming a constituent part. — **el′e·men′tal·ly**, *adv.*

el′e·men′ta·ry (-tȧ·rĭ), *adj.* **1.** = ELEMENTAL, *adj.*, 1. **2.** Pertaining to, or treating of, the elements or first principles of anything; rudimentary. **3.** *Chem.* Of or pertaining to an element; consisting of a single element; simple; uncombined; as, an *elementary* substance. **4.** *Educ.* Pert. to or concerned with the teaching of basic subjects; as, *elementary* education; *elementary* school, one above the kindergarten and below the secondary school (in the United States commonly embracing either 6 or 8 grades). — **-ri·ly** (-rĭ·lĭ), *adv.* — **-ri·ness**, *n.*

elementary particle. *Physics.* Any of the ultimate constituents of matter, considered as infinitely small charged or uncharged bodies. Commonly accepted elementary particles are: (1) electron (2) proton (3) neutron (4) positron (5) meson (6) neutrino.

el′e·mi (ĕl′ē·mĭ), *n.* [Sp. *elemí*, fr. Ar. *al-lāmi.*] A fragrant oleoresin obtained from various tropical trees, used in making varnishes, and medicinally in ointments.

‖**e·len′chus** (ē·lĕng′kŭs), *n.*; *pl.* ELENCHI (-kī). [L., fr. Gr. *elenchos.*] *Logic.* A refutation cast in syllogistic form.

e·lenc′tic (ē·lĕngk′tĭk), *adj.* [Gr. *elenktikos.*] *Logic.* Serving to refute.

el′e·phant (ĕl′ē·fănt), *n.* [OF. *olifant* (F. *éléphant*), fr. L., fr. Gr. *elephas, -antos*, ivory, elephant.] Any of certain thickset, mostly huge, nearly hairless four-footed mammals (family Elephantidae, esp. genera *Elephas* and *Loxodonta*), having a prolonged muscular proboscis, or *trunk*, and two incisors in the upper jaw developed, esp. in the male, into long tusks, which furnish ivory.

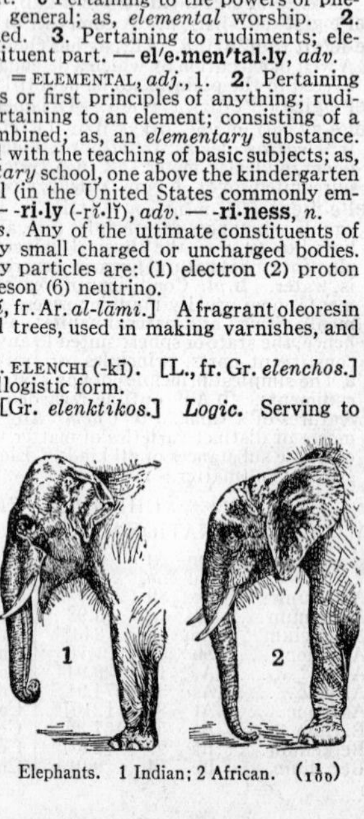

Elephants. 1 Indian; 2 African. (1/100)

el′e·phan·ti′a·sis (ĕl′ē·făn·tī′ȧ·sĭs), *n.* [L., fr. Gr. *elephantiasis*, fr. *elephas* elephant.] A disease in which the skin becomes thick, hard, and fissured like an elephant's hide, and the part affected is enormously enlarged because of inflammation and obstruction of the lymphatics. The most severe form is endemic in the tropics and is caused by infestation with a parasitic worm (*Wuchereria bancrofti*).

el′e·phan′tine (-făn′tĭn; -tīn), *adj.* Like the elephant; hence, huge; ponderous; ungainly.

el′e·phant's-ear′ (ĕl′ē·fănts·ēr′), *n.* *Bot.* **a** The begonia. **b** The taro; — so called by florists.

el′e·phant's-foot′, *n.* A South African vine (*Testudinaria elephantipes*) of the yam family, with a massive rootstock covered with a fissured bark.

El′eu·sin′i·an mys′ter·ies (ĕl′ū·sĭn′ĭ·ăn). Religious mysteries at Eleusis, in ancient Attica, in worship of Demeter and Persephone.

el′e·vate (ĕl′ē·vāt), *adj.* [L. *elevatus*, past part. of *elevare*, fr. *e* out + *levare* to lift up.] *Now Poetic.* Elevated. — *v. t.* **1.** To lift up; to raise. **2.** To raise in rank or station; to exalt; ennoble. **3.** To raise (the voice) in loudness or pitch. **4.** To raise the spirits of; to elate. — **Syn.** See LIFT. — **Ant.** Lower.

el′e·vat′ed (-vāt′ĕd; -ĭd), *adj.* **1.** Lifted up; raised; hence, exalted; also, elated. **2.** On a high moral or intellectual plane. — *n.* *Colloq.* An elevated railroad.

elevated railroad *or* **railway.** A railroad or railway raised, as on trestlework, above the ground level, usually in cities and so as to permit traffic or passage underneath.

el′e·va′tion (-vā′shŭn), *n.* **1.** Act of elevating; the raising of anything from a lower place, condition, or quality to a higher. **2.** Condition or quality of being elevated; height. **3.** An elevated place or station. **4.** *Astron.* Altitude. **5.** *Drawing.* A geometrical projection on a plane perpendicular to the horizon. **6.** *Geog., etc.* Altitude; height above the level of the sea. **7.** *R.C.Ch.* [*cap.*, with *the.*] That part of the Mass in which the priest raises the just-consecrated Eucharistic elements for the people to adore. There are two Elevations, one of the Host, the other of the chalice. — **Syn.** See HEIGHT.

‖**é′lé′va′tion′** (ā′lā′vä′syôɴ′), *n.* [F.] A ballet dancer's leap and illusory suspension in the air.

el′e·va′tor (ĕl′ē·vā′tẽr), *n.* [LL.] **1.** One that raises or lifts up anything; as: **a** An endless belt or chain conveyer with scoops or buckets for raising material. **b** A cage or platform and its hoisting machinery in a building, mine, etc., for conveying persons or goods to or from different levels; — called in England a *lift.* **c** A building for elevating, storing, discharging, and sometimes processing grain. **2.** *Aeronautics.* A movable auxiliary airfoil, usually attached to the tail plane, the function of which is to cause the craft to rotate about its lateral axis. See AIRPLANE, *Illust.*

e·lev′en (ē·lĕv′ĕn), *n.* [AS. *endleofan, endlufon.*] **1.** See NUMBER, *Table.* **2.** Something having as an essential feature eleven units or numbers; as, a football *eleven.* — **e·lev′en**, *adj.* — **e·lev′enth** (-ĕnth), *n. & adj.*

e·lev′en·fold′ (-fōld′; 2), *adj. & adv.* See -FOLD.

elf (ĕlf), *n.*; *pl.* ELVES (ĕlvz). [AS. *ælf, ylf.*] **1.** A mythological being, commonly a sprite, often frail and diminutive, and including pixies, mermaids and mermen, nixes, dwarfs, incubi, and succubi. **2.** An elflike human being; esp., a dainty or mischievous child. — **elf′ish**, *adj.* — **elf′ish·ly**, *adv.* — **elf′ish·ness**, *n.*

elf′in (ĕl′fĭn), *adj.* **1.** Pertaining to elves; produced or ruled by elves. **2.** Resembling elves or an elf. — *n.* An elf.

elf′lock′ (ĕlf′lŏk′), *n.* Hair matted, as if by elves.

E′li (ē′lī), *n.* [Heb. *'Ēlī.*] *Bib.* A high priest of Israel, in whose care Samuel was trained.

e·lic′it (ē·lĭs′ĭt), *v. t.* [L. *elicitus*, past part. of *elicere* to elicit, fr. *e* out + *lacere* to entice.] **1.** To draw out or forth; to educe; as, to *elicit* truth by discussion. **2.** To draw or entice forth; to evoke; as, to *elicit* a reply. — **Syn.** See EDUCE. — **e·lic′i·ta′tion** (-ĭ·tā′shŭn), *n.* — **e·lic′i·tor** (ē·lĭs′ĭ·tẽr), *n.*

e·lide′ (ē·līd′), *v. t.* [L. *elidere* to strike out or off, fr. *e* + *laedere* to hurt by striking.] **1.** *Scots Law.* To nullify or annul. **2.** To omit from consideration; to ignore. **3.** To cut off or omit in pronunciation, as a vowel or a syllable, usually the final one. — **e·lid′i·ble** (ē·līd′ĭ·b'l), *adj.*

el′i·gi·bil′i·ty (ĕl′ĭ·jĭ·bĭl′ĭ·tĭ), *n.*; *pl.* -TIES (-tĭz). Quality or state of being eligible; fitness; qualification.

el′i·gi·ble (ĕl′ĭ·jĭ·b'l), *adj.* [F. *éligible*, fr. L. *eligere.* See ELECT.] Fitted or qualified to be chosen; legally or morally suitable; as, an *eligible* candidate. — *n.* One who is eligible. — **el′i·gi·bly** (-blĭ), *adv.*

eligible paper. *U. S. Banking.* Notes and bills designated as proper for discount, or rediscount, by Federal reserve banks.

E·li′jah (ē·lī′jȧ), *n.* [Heb. *Ēlīyāh.*] *Bib.* A great Hebrew prophet of the 9th century B.C. See 1 & 2 *Kings.*

e·lim′i·nate (ē·lĭm′ĭ·nāt), *v. t.* [L. *eliminatus*, past part. of *eliminare*, fr. *e* out + *limen* threshold.] **1.** To remove and get rid of; expel; exclude. **2.** To set aside as unimportant; to leave out of consideration; to ignore. **3.** *Alg.* To cause to disappear by combining two or more equations; as, to *eliminate* an unknown quantity. **4.** *Physiol.* To expel from the system; to excrete. — **Syn.** See EXCLUDE. — **e·lim′i·na′tion** (-nā′shŭn), *n.* — **e·lim′i·na′tive** (-nā′tĭv; -nȧ·tĭv), *adj.* — **e·lim′i·na′tor** (-nā′tẽr), *n.*

E·li′sha (ē·lī′shȧ), *n.* [Heb. *Elīshā'.*] *Bib.* A Hebrew prophet, disciple and successor of Elijah.

e·li′sion (ē·lĭzh′ŭn), *n.* [L. *elisio*, fr. *elidere, elisum*, to strike out. See ELIDE.] A cutting off, esp. of a vowel, for the sake of meter or euphony, as, in poetry, the dropping or partial pronunciation of a final vowel before an initial vowel or *h* in the next word. Cf. SYNCOPE.

e·lite′ (ā·lēt′), *n.* [F. *élite*, fr. *élire* to choose, fr. L. *eligere.* See ELECT.] **1.** The choice or select part; esp., a group or body considered or treated as socially superior. **2.** A 10-point typewriter type, having a spacing of twelve (standard) or ten (special) letters per inch.

Elite Guard. The Schutzstaffel, or a member of it.

e·lix′ir (ē·lĭk′sẽr), *n.* [ML., fr. Ar. *al-iksīr*, fr. Gr. *xērion* a medicinal powder, fr. *xēros* dry.] **1.** *Alchemy.* A substance for transmuting metals into gold; also, one for prolonging life indefinitely; as, the *elixir* of life; hence, a cure-all; panacea. **2.** *Pharm.* A tincture or medicine composed of various substances held in solution by alcohol in some form. **3.** The refined spirit; quintessence.

E·liz′a·be′than (ē·lĭz′ȧ·bē′thăn; ē·lĭz′ȧ·bĕth′ăn), *adj.* Pertaining to or characteristic of Queen Elizabeth or her times. — *n.* An individual, esp. a playwright or poet, of Elizabethan England.

elk (ĕlk), *n. sing. & pl.* [ON. *elgr.*] **1. a** In Europe, the largest existing deer (*Alces alces*) of Europe and Asia, having broad palmate antlers. The male is called a *bull*, the female a *cow*. **b** In America, the wapiti. **2.** A light, very flexible, tanned calf or horsehide leather.

elk′hound′ (ĕlk′hound′), *n.* A large strong dog of a breed originating in Norway, where it is a farm dog often used as a draft animal and sometimes to herd reindeer; — called also ***Norwegian elkhound.***

ell (ĕl), *n.* [AS. *eln.*] A measure, chiefly for cloth, now little used. It varies between the English ell of 45 inches and the old Dutch or Flemish ell of 27 inches.

ell, *n.* An extension or addition to a house built at right angles to the length of a main building. See L, *n.*, 4 **a.**

el·lipse′ (ĕ·lĭps′; ĭ-), *n.* [Back formation, ult. fr. Gr. *elleipsis* defect.] *Geom.* A plane curve, the path of a point the sum of whose distances from two fixed points (the foci) is constant; a conic section, the closed intersection of a plane with a right circular cone.

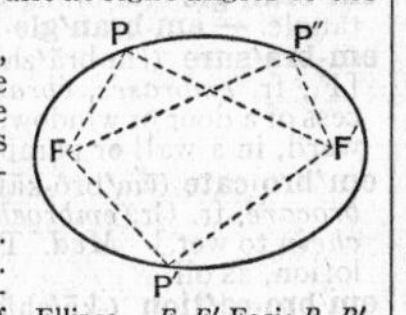

Ellipse. *F, F′* Foci; *P, P′, P″* any Point on the Curve; *FP* + *PF′* = *FP″* + *P″F′* = *FP′* + *P′F′*.

el·lip′sis (ĕ·lĭp′sĭs; ĭ-), *n.; pl.* -LIPSES (-sēz). [L., fr. Gr. *elleipsis* a leaving, defect, fr. *elleipein* to leave in, fall short, fr. *en* in + *leipein* to leave.] **1.** *Gram.* Omission of one or more words, obviously understood, but necessary to make the expression grammatically complete ("virtues I admire," instead of "virtues *which* I admire"). **2.** *Print.* A mark or marks, as . . . or ***, showing omissions.

el·lips′oid (ĕ·lĭp′soid; ĭ-), *n.* [*ellipse* + *-oid.*] *Geom.* A surface all plane sections of which are ellipses or circles; also, the corresponding solid. — **el·lips′oid, el′lip·soi′dal** (ĕl′ĭp·soi′dăl; -d'l), *adj.*

el·lip′tic (-lĭp′tĭk), **el·lip′ti·cal** (-tĭ·kăl), *adj.* **1.** Of, pertaining to, or shaped like an ellipse. See LEAF, *Illust.* (4). **2.** Relating to or characterized by ellipsis; having a part omitted. — **-ti·cal·ly,** *adv.*

el′lip·tic′i·ty (ĕl′ĭp·tĭs′ĭ·tĭ), *n.* Deviation of an ellipse or a spheroid (as the earth) from the form of a circle or a sphere.

elliptic spring. See SPRING, *Illust.*

elm (ĕlm), *n.* [AS.] Any of a genus (*Ulmus*) of large graceful trees (family Ulmaceae, the elm family) with alternate stipulate leaves and small apetalous perfect or unisexual flowers (see SAMARA, *Illust.*); also, the wood of any of these trees. The American elm (*U. americana*) and the English elm (*U. campestris*) are planted for shade. See SLIPPERY ELM, WYCH-ELM.

elm bark beetle. Any bark beetle injurious to elm trees, esp. a European beetle (*Scolytus multistriata*, family Scolytidae) now established in New England.

elm beetle. Any of several beetles that feed on the leaves of the elm, esp. the imported **elm leaf beetle** (*Galerucella luteola*), a yellowish-brown beetle with indistinct dark stripes.

elm blight. = DUTCH ELM DISEASE.

el′o·cu′tion (ĕl′ō·kū′shŭn), *n.* [L. *elocutio*, fr. *eloqui*. See ELOQUENT.] **1.** Style or manner of speaking or reading in public. **2.** The art of oratorical public speaking. — **el′o·cu′tion·ar′y** (-ĕr′ĭ *or, esp. Brit.*, -ẽr·ĭ), *adj.* — **el′o·cu′tion·ist,** *n.*

E·lo′him (ĕ·lō′hĭm), *n. pl.* [Heb. *ĕlōhīm*, pl.] God, or gods; — a term used in the Hebrew Scriptures.

El′o·his′tic (ĕl′ō·hĭs′tĭk), *adj.* Characterized by the use of *Elohim* as a name of God; — said of certain parts of the Old Testament, esp. of the Hexateuch. Cf. YAHWISTIC.

e·loign′ (ē·loin′), *v. t.* Also **e·loin′.** [F. *éloigner*, fr. OF. *esloignier*, fr. *es-* (fr. L. *ex*) + *loin* far, far off, fr. L. *longe*, fr. *longus* long.] **1.** To remove afar off; — now only reflexively. **2.** *Law.* To convey to a distance, or to conceal, as goods liable to distress. — **e·loign′er, e·loin′er,** *n.* — **e·loign′ment, e·loin′ment,** *n.*

e·lon′gate (ē·lŏng′gāt *or, esp. Brit.*, ē′lŏng·gāt; 74), *v. t. & i.* [LL. *elongatus*, past part. of *elongare* to prolong, remove, fr. *e* + *longus* long, *longe* far off.] To lengthen; to stretch out. — **Syn.** See EXTEND. — (-gāt), *adj.* Elongated.

e·lon′ga′tion (-gā′shŭn), *n.* **1.** A lengthening, or state of being lengthened; extension. **2.** That which lengthens out; continuation.

e·lope′ (ē·lōp′), *v. i.* [AF. *aloper.*] **1.** To run away from one's spouse or home with a lover; — orig. of a married woman only, now also of an unmarried woman (usually intending to be married to her companion in flight), and, by extension, of the man in either case. **2.** To abscond; slip away. — **e·lope′ment,** *n.* — **e·lop′er** (-lōp′ẽr), *n.*

el′o·quence (ĕl′ō·kwĕns), *n.* Discourse characterized by force and persuasiveness; also, the art, action, or power of using such discourse.

el′o·quent (-kwĕnt), *adj.* [F. *éloquent*, fr. L. *eloquens, -entis*, pres. part. of *eloqui* to declaim, fr. *e* out + *loqui* to speak.] **1.** Expressing oneself, or expressed, with moving force and fluency. **2.** Vividly or movingly expressive or revealing. — **el′o·quent·ly,** *adv.*

else (ĕls), *adj.* [AS. *elles*, gen. sing. of an adj. signifying *other.*] Other; esp.: **a** Additional to, or accompanying. **b** Taking the place of, or different from (what is mentioned or implied); as, what *else* can he do but this? — *pron. Obs.* Some or any other thing. — *adv.* In a different manner, place, time, or respect; as, to go somewhere *else.* — *conj.* If the facts were different; if not; otherwise.

else′where (ĕls′hwâr; 2), *adv.* In or to another place.

e·lu′ci·date (ē·lū′sĭ·dāt), *v. t.* [LL. *elucidatus*, past part. of *elucidare*, fr. *e* + *lucidus* full of light, clear.] To make lucid or manifest or intelligible. — **Syn.** See EXPLAIN. — **e·lu′ci·da′tion** (-dā′shŭn), *n.* — **e·lu′ci·da′tive** (-dā′tĭv), *adj.* — **e·lu′ci·da′tor** (-dā′tẽr), *n.*

e·lude′ (ē·lūd′), *v. t.* [L. *eludere, elusum*, fr. *e* + *ludere* to play.] **1.** To avoid adroitly, as by artifice; evade. **2.** To escape the notice of. — **Syn.** See ESCAPE.

E·lul′ (ĕ·lōōl′), *n.* [Heb. *Elūl.*] See JEWISH CALENDAR.

e·lu′sion (ē·lū′zhŭn), *n.* [ML. *elusio.* See ELUDE.] Act of eluding; adroit escape, as by artifice; evasion.

e·lu′sive (-sĭv), *adj.* Baffling; evasive. — **-ly,** *adv.* — **-ness,** *n.*

e·lu′so·ry (-sō·rĭ), *adj.* Elusive.

e·lu′tri·ate (ē·lū′trĭ·āt), *v. t.* [L. *elutriatus*, past part. of *elutriare.*] To purify by washing and straining or decanting. — **e·lu′tri·a′tion** (-ā′shŭn), *n.*

e·lu′vi·al (ē·lū′vĭ·ăl), *adj.* **a** Of or pertaining to eluvium. **b** Of or pertaining to eluviation or its products.

e·lu′vi·a′tion (-ā′shŭn), *n.* The movement of dissolved or suspended soil materials from one place to another within the soil when rainfall exceeds evaporation. Cf. ILLUVIATION. — **e·lu′vi·ate** (ē·lū′vĭ·āt), *v. i.*

e·lu′vi·um (ē·lū′vĭ·ŭm), *n.* Rock debris or soil originating in situ by weathering and disintegration of rock. Cf. ALLUVIUM.

el′ver (ĕl′vẽr), *n.* A young eel.

elves (ĕlvz), *n., pl.* of ELF.

elv′ish (ĕl′vĭsh), *adj.* Elfish; hence, mischievous.

E·ly′sian (ē·lĭzh′ăn; ē·lĭz′ĭ·ăn; -yăn), *adj.* **a** Of or like Elysium; as, *Elysian* fields. **b** Blissful; delightful.

E·ly′si·um (ē·lĭzh′ĭ·ŭm; ē·lĭz′ĭ·ŭm; -yŭm), *n.* [L., fr. Gr. *Ēlysion* (*pedion*) Elysian field.] **1.** *Class. Myth.* The place where the good dwelt after death, located in the Western Ocean or in the lower world. **2.** Abode or state of ideal delight and happiness; paradise.

el′y·troid (ĕl′ĭ·troid), *adj.* *Zool.* Resembling an elytrum.

el′y·trum (-trŭm), **el′y·tron** (-trŏn), *n.; pl.* ELYTRA (-trȧ). [NL., fr. Gr. *elytron*, fr. *elyein* to roll round.] *Zool.* One of the anterior pair of wings in coleopterous and some other insects, protecting the posterior pair; a wing cover. See BEETLE, *Illust.*

El′ze·vir (ĕl′zē·vẽr; -vẽr), *adj.* **a** Designating, or pertaining to, books or editions printed and published by the Elzevir family at Amsterdam, Leiden, etc., from about 1583 to 1680. **b** Designating a style of type introduced by them. See TYPE, *n.*, 9.

em (ĕm), *n.; pl.* EMS (ĕmz). [Name of the letter *m*, L. *em.*] **1.** The letter M, m. **2.** *Print.* **a** The portion of a line formerly occupied by the letter m, then a square type, used as a unit of measure for printed matter. **b** An em pica, approximately 1/6 of an inch, — commonly used as a standard of measurement, esp. of column width. — **em,** *adj.*

em-. = 1st EN-; — used before *b, p,* or *m*, as in *em*broil.

e·ma′ci·ate (ē·mā′shĭ·āt), *v. t.* [L. *emaciatus*, past part. of *emaciare* to make lean, fr. *e* + *maciare* to make lean, fr. *macies* leanness.] To cause to lose flesh so as to become very thin. — **e·ma′ci·a′tion** (-sĭ·ā′shŭn; -shĭ·ā′shŭn), *n.*

em′a·nate (ĕm′ȧ·nāt), *v. i.* [L. *emanare, -natum*, to emanate, fr. *e* out + *manare* to flow.] To issue forth from a source; as, fragrance *emanates* from flowers. — **Syn.** See SPRING.

em′a·na′tion (-nā′shŭn), *n.* **1.** Act of emanating. **2.** That which emanates; efflux. **3.** *Chem.* A gaseous substance produced by a radioactive transformation; as, radium *emanation.* — **em′a·na′tive** (ĕm′ȧ·nā′tĭv), *adj.*

e·man′ci·pate (ē·măn′sĭ·pāt), *v. t.* [L. *emancipatus*, past part. of *emancipare*, fr. *e* out + *mancipare* to transfer ownership in, fr. *manceps* purchaser, fr. *manus* hand + *capere* to take.] **1.** *Law.* **a** *Rom. Law.* To free or release (a child) from paternal power. **b** To set free from paternal power; — used chiefly in Civil-law systems. **2.** To set free; to liberate; specif., to free from bondage, as a slave, or a country. — **Syn.** See FREE.

e·man′ci·pa′tion (-pā′shŭn), *n.* Act or process of setting or making free; liberation, specif. of slaves.

e·man′ci·pa′tor (ē·măn′sĭ·pā′tẽr), *n.* [LL.] One who emancipates.

e·mar′gi·nate (ē·mär′jĭ·nāt), **e·mar′gi·nat′ed** (-nāt′ĕd; -ĭd), *adj.* Having the margin notched, as a leaf, the tail of a bird, etc.

e·mas′cu·late (ē·măs′kū·lāt), *v. t.* [L. *emasculare*, fr. *e* out + *masculus* male.] **1.** To castrate; geld. **2.** To deprive of masculine vigor or spirit; to weaken. — **Syn.** See UNNERVE. — (-lāt), *adj.* Deprived of virility or vigor. — **e·mas′cu·la′tion** (-lā′shŭn), *n.* — **e·mas′cu·la′tor** (-lā′tẽr), *n.* — **e·mas′cu·la·to′ry** (-lȧ·tō′rĭ; -tẽr·ĭ), *adj.*

em·balm′ (ĕm·bäm′), *v. t.* [OF. *embaumer*, fr. *en-* (L. *in*) + *baume* balm. See EM-; BALM.] **1.** To treat (a dead body) with preparations, as with certain aromatic oils, to preserve it from decay. **2.** *Poetic.* To perfume. **3.** To preserve from decay or oblivion as if with balm. — **em·balm′er,** *n.* — **em·balm′ment,** *n.*

em·bank′ (ĕm·băngk′), *v. t.* To confine or protect by throwing up a bank, as of earth; to place embankments on.

em·bank′ment (-mĕnt), *n.* **1.** Act of embanking. **2.** A raised structure of earth, gravel, etc., as to hold back water.

em·bar′ (ĕm·bär′), *v. t.;* see BAR. [F. *embarrer.*] **1.** To bar or shut in, as with bars. **2.** To stop; to block up.

em′bar·ca′tion (ĕm′bär·kā′shŭn). Var. of EMBARKATION.

em·bar′go (ĕm·bär′gō), *n.; pl.* -GOES (-gōz). [Sp., fr. *embargar* to embargo, fr. *em-* (L. *in*) + *barra* bar.] **1.** An edict of a government prohibiting the departure or entry of ships of commerce at its ports. **2.** Any prohibition imposed by law upon commerce. **3.** A stoppage or impediment; prohibition. **4.** An order issued by a common carrier or public regulatory agency, prohibiting the acceptance of freight, as because of traffic congestion. — *v. t.* To lay or put an embargo on.

em·bark′ (ĕm·bärk′), *v. t. & i.* [F. *embarquer*, fr. *en-* + *barque* bark.] **1.** To put or go on shipboard for a voyage. **2.** To engage, enlist, or invest (as persons, money, etc.) in any enterprise; as, he *embarked* his fortune in trade. — **em·bark′ment,** *n.*

em′bar·ka′tion (ĕm′bär·kā′shŭn), *n.* Act or process of embarking; as, the *embarkation* of troops.

em·bar′rass (ĕm·băr′ȧs), *v. t.* [F. *embarrasser*, through It. or Sp., fr. LL. *in* + *barra* bar.] **1.** To hinder from liberty of movement; to impede. **2.** To confuse; perplex; also, to disconcert. **3.** To render intricate; to complicate. **4.** To involve in difficulties concerning money matters.

Syn. **Embarrass, discomfit, abash, disconcert, rattle** mean to balk by confusing or confounding. **Embarrass** implies some influence that impedes thought, speech, or action, and may be used with reference not only to persons but to the things they plan or desire to do; **discomfit,** literally to put to rout, now implies a frustrating accompanied by confusion, and not, as in loose use, a making uncomfortable; **abash** usually presupposes self-confidence and implies a sudden check upon that mood by some influence that awakens shyness, a conviction of inferiority, or the like; **disconcert** may be used in reference to actions, plans, or persons, for it always implies an upsetting and, in the case of persons, a loss of equanimity or assurance; **rattle,** a colloquial term, stresses the agitation accompanying a disconcerting and therefore implies the disorganization of one's mental processes. — **Ant.** Relieve; facilitate.

em·bar′rass·ing, *adj.* Serving or tending to embarrass. — **em·bar′rass·ing·ly,** *adv.*

em·bar′rass·ment (-mĕnt), *n.* **1.** State of being embarrassed. **2.** That which embarrasses.

em·bas′sa·dor (ĕm·băs′ȧ·dẽr). Var. of AMBASSADOR.

em′bas·sage (ĕm′bȧ·sĭj), *n.* *Archaic.* Embassy.

em′bas·sy (ĕm′bȧ·sĭ), *n.; pl.* -SIES (-sĭz). [OF. *ambassée*, fr. It., fr. Pr. *ambaisada*, fr. Goth. *andbahti* service, of Celt. origin.] **1.** The function, business, or position of an ambassador; also, the dispatch of ambassadors. **2.** The person or persons sent as ambassadors or envoys. **3.** The residence or office of an ambassador.

em·bat′tle (ĕm·băt′'l), *v. t.;* see BATTLE. [OF. *embataillier*, fr. *en-* (L. *in*) + *bataille* battle.] To arrange in order of battle; to array for battle; also, to fortify.

em·bat'tle (ĕm·băt''l), *v. t.* To furnish with battlements.
em·bay' (ĕm·bā'), *v. t.* To shut in, or shelter, as in a bay.
em·bay'ment (-mĕnt), *n.* Formation of a bay; also, a bay or a baylike conformation.
em·bed' (ĕm·bĕd'), *v. t.; see* BED. To set solidly as in a bed; to lay in surrounding matter; to bed.
em·bel'lish (ĕm·bĕl'ĭsh), *v. t.* [OF. *embellir*, fr. *en-* (L. *in*) + *bel*, *beau*, beautiful.] **1.** To make beautiful or elegant as by ornaments; to ornament, beautify. **2.** To enhance the interest of (an account) with fanciful, esp. fictitious, particulars. — **Syn.** See ADORN.
em·bel'lish·ment (-mĕnt), *n.* **1.** An embellishing; ornamentation. **2.** That which adds beauty or elegance.
em'ber (ĕm'bẽr), *n.* [AS. *ǣmerge*.] A glowing fragment of coal, coke, wood, or the like, from a fire; esp., such a coal smoldering in ashes; *pl.*, smoldering remains of a fire.
em'ber, *adj.* [AS. *ymbren*, *ymbryne*, prop., running around, fr. *ymbe* around + *ryne* a running, fr. *rinnan* to run.] *R.C. & Anglican Ch.* Designating, or pertaining to, days (**Ember days**) set apart for fasting and prayer in each of the four seasons of the year. The weeks in which these days fall are called **Ember weeks.**
em·bez'zle (ĕm·bĕz''l), *v. t.;* EM·BEZ'ZLED (-'ld); EM·BEZ'ZLING (-lĭng). [OF. *embesillier*.] **1.** *Obs.* To make away with; to steal. **2.** *Obs.* To squander; dissipate. **3.** To appropriate fraudulently to one's own use, as property entrusted to one's care. — **em·bez'zle·ment,** *n.* — **em·bez'zler** (-lẽr), *n.*
em·bit'ter (ĕm·bĭt'ẽr), *v. t.* To make bitter or more bitter; to intensify ill feeling in or among. — **em·bit'ter·ment** (-mĕnt), *n.*
em·blaze' (ĕm·blāz'), *v. t.* [*em-* + *blaze* to make public.] **1.** *Obs.* To set forth in, or adorn with, heraldic devices; to emblazon. **2.** To adorn sumptuously; to embellish.
em·blaze', *v. t.* To illuminate, as by fire; also, to kindle.
em·bla'zon (ĕm·blā'z'n), *v. t.* **1.** To inscribe or adorn with heraldic bearings, devices, etc. **2.** To deck or picture in bright colors; also, to celebrate; extol. — **em·bla'zon·er,** *n.* — **em·bla'zon·ment,** *n.* — **em·bla'zon·ry,** *n.*
em'blem (ĕm'blĕm; -blĕm; -blĭm), *n.* [L. *emblema*, *-atis*, inlaid work, that which is put in or on, fr. Gr. *emblēma*, deriv. of *en* in + *ballein* to throw.] **1.** *Obs.* Inlaid or mosaic work. **2.** A picture accompanied with a motto, a set of verses, or the like, intended as a moral lesson. **3.** A visible sign of an idea; an object, or the figure of an object, symbolizing and suggesting another object, or an idea; as, a scepter is the *emblem* of sovereignty. **4.** Any device, symbol, design, or figure used as an identifying mark, as a publisher's colophon.
— *v. t.;* EM'BLEMED (ĕm'blĕmd; -blĕmd; -blĭmd); EM'BLEM·ING. To represent by or as by an emblem; to image.
em'blem·at'ic (ĕm'blĕ·măt'ĭk), **em'blem·at'i·cal** (-ĭ·kăl), *adj.* Pertaining to, containing, or consisting in an emblem; symbolic; as, a crown is *emblematic* of royalty. — **em'blem·at'i·cal·ly,** *adv.* — **em'blem·at'i·cal·ness,** *n.*
em·blem'a·tize (ĕm·blĕm'ȧ·tīz), *v. t.* To represent by or as by an emblem.
em'ble·ment (ĕm'blē·mĕnt), *n.* [OF. *emblaement*, fr. *emblaer* to sow a field with grain.] *Law.* The growing crop or vegetable growth, or profits of a crop; — usually in the *pl.*
em·bod'i·ment (ĕm·bŏd'ĭ·mĕnt), *n.* **1.** Act of embodying, or state of being embodied. **2.** That in which a soul, idea, or the like, is embodied; incarnation; as, he is the *embodiment* of courage.
em·bod'y (ĕm·bŏd'ĭ), *v. t.;* -BOD'IED (-ĭd); -BOD'Y·ING. **1.** To give a body to (a spirit); to incarnate. **2.** To render concrete by expression in perceptible form; as, to *embody* ideals in a treaty. **3.** To cause to become a body or part of a body; to incorporate; as, to *embody* a treaty in a law.
em·bold'en (-bōl'dĕn; -d'n), *v. t.* To make bold or brave.
em·bol'ic (ĕm·bŏl'ĭk), *adj.* [See EMBOLUS, EMBOLISM.] **1.** *Med.* Of or pertaining to an embolus or embolism. **2.** *Embryol.* Pushing or growing in; — applied to the typical form of invagination (which see).
em'bo·lism (ĕm'bō·lĭz'm), *n.* [LL. *embolismus*, fr. Gr. *embolismos*, fr. *emballein* to throw or put in, insert.] **1.** Intercalation; insertion of days, months, or years, in an account of time, for regularity; also, the time intercalated. **2.** *Med.* The lodgment of an embolus in a tube or canal too small to permit its passage; also, loosely, an embolus. — **em'bo·lis'mic** (-lĭz'mĭk), *adj.*
em'bo·lus (-lŭs), *n.; pl.* -LI (-lī). [L., fr. Gr. *embolos* wedge, stopper, fr. *emballein.* See EMBLEM.] Any foreign or abnormal particle circulating in the blood, as a bubble of air, a blood clot, etc.
‖**em'bon'point'** (äN'bôN'pwăN'), *n.* [F., fr. *en bon point* in good condition.] Plumpness of person; stoutness.
em·bos'om (ĕm·bo͝oz'ŭm; -bo͞o'zŭm), *v. t.* **1.** To take into, or place in, the bosom; to cherish; foster. **2.** To enclose; to shelter closely.
em·boss' (ĕm·bŏs'; 74), *v. t.* [OF. *embocer.*] **1.** To raise the surface of into bosses or protuberances; esp., to ornament with raised work. **2.** To raise in relief from a surface, as an ornament, a head on a coin, type on a letterhead, etc. **3.** Hence, to adorn or embellish. — **em·boss'er,** *n.* — **em·boss'ment,** *n.*
em·boss', *v. t.;* EM·BOSSED' (-bŏst') or EM·BOST'; EM·BOSS'ING. *Obs.* To exhaust (a hunted animal) by the chase; also, to make to foam at the mouth.
em'bou·chure' (ŏm'bo͞o·sho͞or'; äN'bo͞o'shür'), *n.* [F., fr. *emboucher* to put to the mouth, fr. *en-* (L. *in*) + *bouche* mouth.] **1.** The mouth of a river; also, expansion of a river valley into a plain. **2. a** The mouthpiece of a musical instrument. **b** The shaping of lips, tongue, etc., in producing a musical tone, esp. on a wind instrument.
em·bow' (ĕm·bō'), *v. t.* **1.** *Obs.* To bend into a bow. **2.** To vault; to form into an arch. — **em·bow'ment,** *n.*
em·bowed' (-bōd'), *adj.* Curved; arched; vaulted.
em·bow'el (ĕm·bou'ĕl), *v. t.;* -ELED (-ĕld) or -ELLED; -EL·ING or -EL·LING. **1.** To disembowel. **2.** *Obs.* To hide in the inward parts; to embed.
em·bow'er (-bou'ẽr), *v. t. & i.* To lodge in a bower.
em·brace' (ĕm·brās'), *v. t.;* -BRACED' (-brāst'); -BRAC'ING (-brās'ĭng). [OF. *embracer*, ult. fr. L. *in* + L. *brachium* arm.] **1.** To clasp in the arms; hence, to cherish; love. **2.** To encircle; enclose. **3.** *Archaic.* To take in hand; to undertake. **4.** To receive readily; to welcome; to avail oneself of; as, to *embrace* an opportunity. **5.** To take up; to adopt; as, to *embrace* a soldier's life. **6.** To include as parts of a whole; to comprehend; to take in. — *v. i.* To participate in an embrace. — **Syn.** See ADOPT; INCLUDE. — *n.* A close encircling with the arms; a clasp. — **em·brace'ment,** *n.* — **em·brac'er** (-brās'ẽr), *n.*

em·brace' (ĕm·brās'), *v. t.* *Law.* To attempt or act so as to influence corruptly, as a jury. — **em·brac'er,** *n.*
em·brace'or (-ẽr), *n.* [OF. *embraseor* one who fires, instigator, fr. *embraser* to set fire to.] *Law.* One guilty of embracery.
em·brac'er·y (ĕm·brās'ẽr·ĭ), *n.* *Law.* Act of one who attempts or acts so as to influence a court, jury, etc., corruptly, by promises, entreaties, money, etc.
em·branch'ment (ĕm·brȧnch'mĕnt), *n.* A branching off or out; a branch; a ramification.
em·bran'gle (ĕm·brăng'g'l), *v. t.* [*em-* + *brangle.*] To confuse; entangle. — **em·bran'gle·ment** (-mĕnt), *n.*
em·bra'sure (ĕm·brā'zhẽr; *in sense* 2 *also* ĕm'brȧ·zho͞or'; 118), *n.* [F., fr. *embraser*, *ébraser*, to widen an opening.] **1.** *Arch.* A recess of a door or window. **2.** *Fort.* An opening, with sides flaring outward, in a wall or parapet, through which cannon are fired.
em'bro·cate (ĕm'brō·kāt), *v. t.* [ML. *embrocatus*, past part. of *embrocare*, fr. Gr. *embrochē* lotion, fomentation, deriv. of *en* in + *brechein* to wet.] *Med.* To moisten and rub (a part of the body) with a lotion, as oil.
em'bro·ca'tion (-kā'shŭn), *n.* *Med.* Act of embrocating, or the liquid or lotion used.
em·broi'der (ĕm·broi'dẽr), *v. t. & i.* [See EM-; BROIDER.] **1.** To ornament with needlework; also, to form by needlework; as, to *embroider* a flower. **2.** To embellish; ornament; hence, to exaggerate. — **em·broi'der·er,** *n.*
em·broi'der·y (-ĭ), *n.; pl.* -DERIES (-ĭz). **1.** The art or process of embroidering, or ornamenting cloths, leather, etc., with needlework; also, needlework used in embroidering. **2.** Elaboration in details, as of a story; inclusion of interesting or picturesque matters to improve a narrative.
em·broil' (ĕm·broil'), *v. t.* [F. *embrouiller.* See EM-; BROIL a brawl.] **1.** To confuse or stir up by discord; to distract. **2.** To implicate in confusion; to entangle in difficulties. — **em·broil'ment,** *n.*
em·brown' (ĕm·broun'), *v. t.* To darken; esp., to tan.
em·brue' (ĕm·bro͞o'), **em·brute'.** Vars. of IMBRUE, etc.
em'bry·ec'to·my (ĕm'brĭ·ĕk'tō·mĭ), *n.* [See -ECTOMY.] Surgical removal of an embryo.
em'bry·o (ĕm'brĭ·ō), *n.; pl.* EMBRYOS (-ōz). [Gr. *embryon*, fr. *en* in + *bryein* to swell, teem.] **1.** Orig., *Biol.*, a young organism in the early stages of development, as before hatching from the egg. In mammals, *embryo* is applied only to early stages passed within the mother's body; later the young is called a *fetus.* Cf. FETUS, LARVA, OVUM. **2.** Hence, a beginning or undeveloped stage of anything. **3.** *Bot.* In seed plants, the young sporophyte. — *adj.* Incipient; embryonic; as, an *embryo* bud.

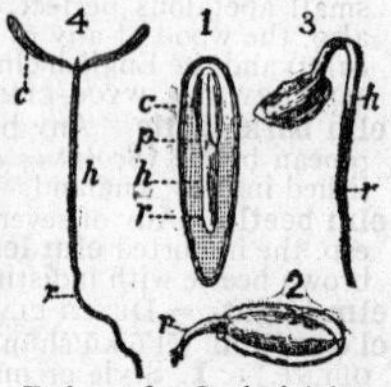

Embryo, 3. Seed of Arborvitae (*Thuja*), 1 showing Embryo; 2 sprouting; 3, 4 further advanced. *c* Cotyledon; *p* Plumule; *h* Hypocotyl; *r* Radicle.

em'bry·o- (ĕm'brĭ·ō-), **embry-.** [See EMBRYO.] A combining form used for *embryo*, *embryonic*, as in *embryo*geny, *embryo*logy.
em'bry·og'e·ny (-ŏj'ē·nĭ), **em'bry·o·gen'e·sis** (-ō·jĕn'ē·sĭs), *n.* [*embryo-* + *-geny.*] *Biol.* The formation and development of the embryo. — **em'bry·o·gen'ic** (-ō·jĕn'ĭk), *adj.*
em'bry·ol'o·gy (-ŏl'ō·jĭ), *n.* [*embryo-* + *-logy.*] *Biol.* The department of biology which relates to embryogeny in animals and plants. — **em'bry·o·log'ic** (-ō·lŏj'ĭk), **em'bry·o·log'i·cal** (-ĭ·kăl), *adj.* — **em'bry·ol'o·gist** (-ŏl'ō·jĭst), *n.*
em'bry·on (ĕm'brĭ·ŏn), *n.* = EMBRYO. — **em'bry·o·nal** (-ō·năl; -n'l), *adj.*
em'bry·on'ic (-ŏn'ĭk), *adj.* Of or pertaining to an embryo; incipient and rudimentary.
embryo sac. *Bot.* A large thin-walled cell within the nucellus of the ovule, in which the egg, becoming after fertilization an embryo, is developed.
em'cee' (ĕm'sē'), *n.* [For the initial letters *M.C.*] Master of ceremonies. — *v. t. & i.;* EM'CEED' (-sēd'); EM'CEE'ING. To conduct or act as master of ceremonies.
eme (ēm), *n.* [AS. *ēam.*] *Dial.* Uncle; also, friend; crony.
e·meer' (ē·mēr'), **e·meer'ate.** Vars. of EMIR, EMIRATE.
e·mend' (ē·mĕnd'), *v. t.* [L. *emendare.* See AMEND.] To free from faults or defects; specif., to make corrections in (a literary work). — **Syn.** See CORRECT. — **e·mend'a·ble,** *adj.*
e'men·dan'dum (ē'mĕn·dăn'dŭm; ĕm'ĕn-), *n.; pl.* EMENDANDA (-dȧ). [L., fr. *emendare* to emend.] = CORRIGENDUM.
e'men·date (ē'mĕn·dāt), *v. t.* To emend (a text). — **e'men·da'tor** (ē'mĕn·dā'tẽr; ĕm'ĕn-), *n.*
e'men·da'tion (ē'mĕn·dā'shŭn; ĕm'ĕn-), *n.* **1.** Act of emending; correction. **2.** Critical alteration or correction, as of a literary text; also, a correction. — **e·mend'a·to'ry** (ē·mĕn'dȧ·tō'rĭ *or, esp. Brit.,* -tẽr·ĭ), *adj.*
em'er·ald (ĕm'ẽr·ăld), *n.* [OF. *esmeraude*, *esmeralde*, fr. VL. *smaraldus*, for L. *smaragdus*, fr. Gr. *smaragdos.*] **1. a** A rich green variety of beryl, prized as a precious stone. **b** In full ***Oriental emerald.*** Green sapphire (see SAPPHIRE, 1 **b**). **2.** A color, yellow-green in hue, of medium saturation and medium brilliance, the color of the emerald. See COLOR. **3.** *Print.* A size of type intermediate between minion and nonpareil. Cf. TYPE, 9. — *adj.* Of the color of the emerald.
Emerald Isle. Ireland; — so called from its verdure.
e·merge' (ē·mûrj'), *v. i.;* E·MERGED' (-mûrjd'); E·MERG'ING (-mûr'jĭng). [L. *emergere*, *emersum*, fr. *e* out + *mergere* to dip.] **1.** To rise from or as from an enveloping fluid; to come out into view; as, the sun *emerges* from eclipse. **2.** To issue from an obscure or inferior condition into well-being; as, to *emerge* from poverty, slavery.
e·mer'gence (ē·mûr'jĕns), *n.* **1.** Act or instance of emerging. **2.** *Bot.* Any of various outgrowths from the tissue below the epidermis, as a prickle on a rose.
e·mer'gen·cy (-jĕn·sĭ), *n.; pl.* -CIES (-sĭz). **1.** *Now Rare.* = EMERGENCE, 1. **2.** An unforeseen combination of circumstances which calls for immediate action; also, less properly, exigency. — **Syn.** See JUNCTURE.
e·mer'gent (-jĕnt), *adj.* **1.** Emerging out of a fluid or anything that covers; issuing forth; rising into notice. **2.** Arising unexpectedly;

calling for prompt action; urgent. **3.** *Philos. & Biol.* Appearing as something novel or unpredictable in the course of an evolution.

e·mer'i·tus (ē·mĕr'ĭ·tŭs), *adj.* [L., past part. of *emerere, emereri,* to obtain by service, serve out one's term, fr. *e* out + *merere, mereri,* to merit.] Retired, as for age, with a title corresponding to that held in active service. — *n.; pl.* -TI (-tī). An emeritus clergyman, professor, etc.

e·mersed' (ē·mûrst'), *adj.* [L. *emersus,* past part. See EMERGE.] Standing out of, or rising above, a surface, as of water.

e·mer'sion (ē·mûr'shŭn), *n.* Act of emerging; emergence.

em'er·y (ĕm'ēr·ĭ), *n.* [F. *émeri,* fr. It., fr. Gr. *smiris, smēris.*] A dark granular variety of corundum, used esp. for grinding.

e·met'ic (ē·mĕt'ĭk), *adj.* [L. *emeticus,* fr. Gr. *emetikos,* fr. *emein* to vomit.] *Med.* Causing vomiting. — *n.* An agent which causes vomiting.

em'e·tine (ĕm'ē·tēn; -tĭn), *n.* Also **em'e·tin.** [See EMETIC.] *Chem.* A crystalline alkaloid, $C_{29}H_{40}N_2O_4$, extracted from ipecac root. It is used as an emetic and expectorant.

e'meu (ē'mū). Var. of EMU.

‖**é'meute'** (ā'mût'; *E.* ē·mūt'), *n.* [F.] A seditious tumult; an outbreak.

-e'mi·a, -ae'mi·a (-ē'mĭ·ȧ). [NL., fr. Gr. *-aimia,* fr. *haima* blood.] A suffix denoting *a* (specified) *condition of the blood,* used esp. in naming diseases, as in py*emia.*

em'i·grant (ĕm'ĭ·grănt; -grănt), *adj.* Departing from a country to settle permanently elsewhere. — *n.* One who emigrates.

Syn. **Emigrant, immigrant** mean a person who leaves his country to settle in another. Both refer to the same person, **emigrant** as leaving his country, and **immigrant** as settling in another country.

em'i·grate (-grāt), *v. i.* [L. *emigratus,* past part. of *emigrare* to remove, fr. *e* out + *migrare* to migrate.] To leave a place of abode, esp. a country, for life or residence in another.

em'i·gra'tion (-grā'shŭn), *n.* **1.** Departure from a place of abode for life or residence elsewhere. **2.** A body of emigrants; emigrants collectively.

‖**é'mi'gré'** (ā'mē'grā'), *n.; pl.* ÉMIGRÉS (*F.* -grā'). [F.] An emigrant; specif.: **a** One of the Royalist fugitives from France at the time of the French Revolution. **b** A fugitive from Soviet Russia.

em'i·nence (ĕm'ĭ·nĕns), *n.* **1.** An elevated condition among men, either in rank, office, or celebrity; high rank. **2.** That which is eminent or lofty; a high ground or place. **3.** [*cap.*] A title of honor; — in the Roman Catholic Church applied exclusively to a cardinal.

em'i·nen·cy (-nĕn·sĭ), *n.; pl.* EMINENCIES (-sĭz). Eminence.

em'i·nent (-nĕnt), *adj.* [L. *eminens, -entis,* pres. part. of *eminere* to stand out, be prominent.] **1.** High; lofty. **2.** Distinguished as being above others, whether by birth, high station, merit, talent, or virtue. **3.** Standing out clearly; evident; notable. — **Syn.** See FAMOUS. — **em'i·nent·ly,** *adv.*

eminent domain. *Law.* That superior dominion of the sovereign power over property within the state which authorizes it to appropriate all or any part thereof to a necessary public use, reasonable compensation being made.

e·mir', e·meer' (ĕ·mēr'), *n.* [Ar. *amīr* commander.] **a** An Arabian military commander, chieftain, or ruler. **b** A title given to descendants of Mohammed through his daughter Fatima. **c** A Turkish title of dignity. — **e·mir'ate** (-āt), *n.*

em'is·sar'y (ĕm'ĭ·sĕr'ĭ *or, esp. Brit.,* -sĕr·ĭ), *n.; pl.* -IES (-ĭz). [L. *emissarius,* fr. *emittere, emissum,* to send out. See EMIT.] An agent employed to further certain interests or to gain information; esp., a secret agent. — *adj.* Pertaining to, or acting as, an emissary.

e·mis'sion (ē·mĭsh'ŭn), *n.* **1.** Act of emitting; emanation. **2.** That which is emitted; discharge. **3.** A putting in circulation; issuing; as, the *emission* of paper money; also, *Obs.,* publication. **4.** *Elec.* Flow of electrons out of the heated filament or cathode of an electron tube. — **e·mis'sive** (-mĭs'ĭv), *adj.* — **em'is·siv'i·ty** (ĕm'ĭ·sĭv'ĭ·tĭ), *n.*

e·mit' (ē·mĭt'), *v. t.;* E·MIT'TED; E·MIT'TING. [L. *emittere* to send out, fr. *e* out + *mittere* to send.] **1.** To send forth; to throw off; as, fire *emits* heat and smoke. **2.** To print and circulate, as bank notes; also, *Obs.,* to publish. **3.** To give utterance to; voice. — **e·mit'ter,** *n.*

em·men'a·gogue (ĕ·mĕn'ȧ·gŏg; ĕ·mē'nȧ-; 74), *n.* [Gr. *emmēna,* n. pl., menses (fr. *en* in + *mēn* month) + *-agogue.*] *Med.* Any agent that promotes the menstrual discharge.

em'mer (ĕm'ēr), *n.* See WHEAT.

em'met (ĕm'ĕt; -ĭt), *n.* [See ANT.] *Archaic.* An ant.

e·mol'li·ent (ē·mŏl'ĭ·ĕnt; -yĕnt; 58), *adj.* [L. *emolliens, -entis,* pres. part., deriv. of *e* out + *mollire* to soften, fr. *mollis* soft.] Softening; soothing to the skin or mucous membrane. — *n. Med.* A softening or soothing application.

e·mol'u·ment (ē·mŏl'ū·mĕnt), *n.* [L. *emolumentum* exertion, profit.] Profit from office, employment, or labor; fees or salary. — **Syn.** See WAGE.

e·mo'tion (ē·mō'shŭn), *n.* [F. *émotion,* fr. L. *emovere, emotum,* fr. *e* out + *movere* to move.] **1.** *Obs.* An agitation; strong feeling; any disturbance. **2.** A departure from the normal calm state of an organism of such nature as to include strong feeling, an impulse toward open action, and certain internal physical reactions; any one of the states designated as fear, anger, disgust, grief, joy, surprise, yearning, etc. — **Syn.** See FEELING.

e·mo'tion·al (-ăl; -'l), *adj.* **1.** Pertaining to emotion; prone to emotion; as, an *emotional* person or nature. **2.** Appealing to, or arousing, emotion. — **e·mo'tion·al·ly,** *adv.*

e·mo'tion·al·ism (-ĭz'm), *n.* Cultivation of an emotional state of mind; tendency to regard things emotionally.

e·mo'tion·al·ist (-ĭst), *n.* **1.** One who is excessively emotional, or who endeavors to arouse emotions. **2.** One who uses emotional effects in art, or bases theory or practice in art, ethics, or the like on emotional phenomena.

e·mo'tion·al'i·ty (-ăl'ĭ·tĭ), *n.* Quality or state of being emotional.

e·mo'tive (ē·mō'tĭv), *adj.* Attended by, or having the character of, emotion; expressing emotion. — **e·mo'tive·ly,** *adv.* — **e·mo'tive·ness, e'mo·tiv'i·ty** (ē'mō·tĭv'ĭ·tĭ), *n.*

em·pale' (ĕm·pāl'). Var. of IMPALE.

em·pan'el (ĕm·păn'ĕl; -'l), *v. t.;* EM·PAN'ELED (-ĕld; -'ld) or EM·PAN'ELLED; EM·PAN'EL·ING or EM·PAN'EL·LING. To impanel, esp. a jury.

em'pa·thy (ĕm'pȧ·thĭ), *n.* [Gr. *empatheia,* fr. *en-* in + *pathos* suffering.] Imaginative projection of one's own consciousness into another being. — **em·path'ic** (ĕm·păth'ĭk), *adj.*

‖**em'pen'nage'** (äN'pĕ'nȧzh'), *n.* [F.] Tail of an aircraft. See TAIL, *n.,* 9; AIRPLANE, *Illust.*

em'per·or (ĕm'pēr·ēr), *n.* [OF. *empereor,* fr. L. *imperator,* fr. *imperare* to command, fr. *in* in + *parare* to order.] The sovereign or supreme monarch of an empire. — **em'per·or·ship',** *n.*

em'per·y (ĕm'pēr·ĭ), *n.; pl.* EMPERIES (-ĭz). [ME. *emperie,* fr. OF., fr. *emperer* to command, fr. L. *imperare.*] Absolute dominion; sovereignty; empire; also, imperial domain.

em'pha·sis (ĕm'fȧ·sĭs), *n.; pl.* EMPHASES (-sēz). [L., fr. Gr. *emphasis* significance, fr. *emphainein* to indicate, fr. *en* in + *phainein* to show.] **1.** A special impressiveness of expression or weight of thought; stress. **2.** Insistence upon a particular object as of preeminent value or importance. **3.** *Rhet.* In reading or speaking, a prominence of utterance given to one or more words or syllables.

em'pha·size (-sīz), *v. t.* To give emphasis to; to stress.

em·phat'ic (ĕm·făt'ĭk), *adj.* [Gr. *emphatikos.*] **1.** Uttered with emphasis. **2.** Employing, or given to, emphatic speech or decisive action. **3.** Attracting special attention; striking. — **em·phat'i·cal·ly** (-ĭ·kăl·ĭ), *adv.*

em'phy·se'ma (ĕm'fĭ·sē'mȧ), *n.* [NL., fr. Gr. *emphysēma* inflation, deriv. of *en* in + *physan* to blow.] **a** *Med.* A swelling produced by gas in any body tissue. **b** *Veter.* Heaves. — **em'phy·sem'a·tous** (-sĕm'ȧ·tŭs; -sē'mȧ·tŭs), *adj.*

em'pire (ĕm'pīr; *formerly also* -pĭr), *n.* [OF., also *empirie, emperie,* fr. L. *imperium* sovereignty, empire.] **1.** A group of nations or states under a single sovereign power; as, the *empire* of Alexander. **2.** A state characterized by having great extent of territories and variety of peoples united under one rule, or by having *emperor* as the title of its ruler. **3.** Imperial sovereignty or rule; dominion. **4.** A domain under imperial rule. — ***the Empire.*** **a** The first French Empire (1804–15). **b** The Holy Roman Empire. **c** The British Empire.

Em'pire (ĕm'pīr; *with ref. to French fashions, etc., also* ŏm'pĭr), *adj.* **1.** Of or pertaining to an empire, esp. to the first French Empire (1804–15); as, *Empire* fashions. **2.** Designating a style of furniture developed under Napoleon I (1804–15), having long curving lines, some carving, and ornamentation in brass and ivory.

Empire Day. See HOLIDAY, 3.

Empire gown. A gown with a short waist, short puffed sleeves, and long flowing skirt, fashionable at the time of the first French Empire.

Empire State. New York; — a nickname.

em·pir'ic (ĕm·pĭr'ĭk), *n.* [L. *empiricus,* fr. Gr. *empeirikos* experienced, equiv. to *empeiros,* fr. *en* in + *peira* experiment.] **1.** One who follows an empirical method; one who relies upon practical experience. **2.** A quack; charlatan.

em·pir'i·cal (-ĭ·kăl), *adj.* Also **em·pir'ic.** **1.** Depending on experience or observation alone, without due regard to science and theory; as, *empirical* remedies. **2.** Pertaining to, or founded upon, experiment or experience; as, *empirical* knowledge. — **em·pir'i·cal·ly,** *adv.*

empirical formula. See FORMULA, 4.

em·pir'i·cism (-ĭ·sĭz'm), *n.* **1.** Empirical method or practice; as: **a** Pursuit of knowledge by observation and experiment. **b** A practice of medicine founded on mere experience, without the aid of science. **c** Quackery. **2.** The philosophical theory attributing the origin of all knowledge to experience; — applied esp. to British philosophy from Locke to Hume. — **em·pir'i·cist** (-sĭst), *n. & adj.*

em·place'ment (ĕm·plās'mĕnt), *n.* **1.** Assignment to a definite place; localization. **2.** *Fort.* **a** The space in a fortification assigned to a gun or group of guns. **b** The gun platform, parapet, and accessories.

em·ploy' (ĕm·ploi'), *v. t.* [F. *employer,* fr. L. *implicare* to infold, involve, engage, fr. *in* + *plicare* to fold.] **1.** To make use of; to use. **2.** To make use of the services of. **3.** To occupy; devote; as, to *employ* time in study.

Syn. (1) See USE.

(2) **Employ, hire** here mean to engage for work. **Employ,** however, stresses the use of a person's services; **hire,** the act of engaging a person's services for compensation.

— *n.* Employment; state of being employed, esp. in rendering service for wages; as, to be in one's *employ.*

em·ploy'a·ble (-ȧ·b'l), *adj.* See -ABLE **a.**

em·ploy'ee (ĕm·ploi'ē; ĕm'ploi·ē'; 2), **em·ploy'é** (ĕm·ploi'ē *or, esp. Brit.,* ŏm·ploi'ā; *F.* äN'plwȧ'yā'), **em·ploy'e** (ĕm·ploi'ē), *n.; pl.* EMPLOYEES (-ēz; -ēz'), EMPLOYÉS (-ēz), EMPLOYES (-ēz). [F. *employé,* past part. of *employer.*] One who works for wages or salary in the service of an employer; — disting. from *official* or *officer.*

em·ploy'er (ĕm·ploi'ēr), *n.* One who employs another.

em·ploy'ment (-mĕnt), *n.* **1.** Act of employing, or state of being employed; as, to seek *employment.* **2.** That which engages or occupies time or attention; also, an occupation, profession, or trade. — **Syn.** See WORK.

em·poi'son (ĕm·poi'z'n), *v. t.* [F. *empoisonner.*] **1.** *Obs.* To poison. **2.** To corrupt; taint.

em·po'ri·um (ĕm·pō'rĭ·ŭm), *n.; pl.* -RIUMS (-ŭmz), -RIA (-ȧ). [L., fr. Gr. *emporion,* fr. *emporios* of commerce, fr. *emporos* traveler, trader, fr. *en* in + *poros* way, path.] **1.** A place of trade; a market place; esp., a commercial center. **2.** A store carrying a diversity of articles.

em·pow'er (ĕm·pou'ēr), *v. t.* To give authority to; to authorize. — **Syn.** See ENABLE.

em'press (ĕm'prĕs; -prĭs), *n.* [OF. *emperesse.*] The consort of an emperor, or a female sovereign of an empire; hence, a sovereign mistress.

‖**em'presse'ment'** (äN'prĕs'mäN'), *n.* [F., fr. *s'empresser* to hasten.] Demonstrative warmth or cordiality.

em·prise', em·prize' (ĕm·prīz'), *n.* [OF. *emprise,* fr. past part. of *emprendre* to undertake, deriv. of L. *in* + *prehendere* to take.] *Archaic.* **a** Enterprise; adventure. **b** Venturesome nature; boldness.

emp'ti·ly (ĕmp'tĭ·lĭ), *adv.* In an empty manner.

emp'ti·ness (ĕmp'tĭ·nĕs; -nĭs), *n.* Quality or state of being empty, esp. in senses 1 and 4.

emp'ty (ĕmp'tĭ), *adj.;* EMP'TI·ER (-tĭ·ēr); EMP'TI·EST. [AS. *æmetig* empty, idle, fr. *æmetta* quiet, leisure, rest.] **1.** Containing nothing; not filled. **2.** Vacant; unoccupied. **3.** Having nothing to carry; unburdened. **4.** Destitute of reality or substance; hollow; vain; destitute of effect, sincerity, or sense. **5.** Destitute or devoid *of* (formerly also with *in* and *from*). **6.** *Colloq.* Hungry.

Syn. (1) **Empty, vacant, blank, void, vacuous** mean lacking that which it may hold. That is **empty** which has nothing in it; that is **vacant** which is without an occupant, such as an incumbent, a tenant, an inmate; that is **blank** (usually a surface) which is free from writing or marks of any kind or has vacant spaces left to be filled in; that is **void**

which is absolutely empty so far as senses can discover; that is **vacuous** which is void or encloses a vacuum. — **Ant.** Full.
(2) See VAIN.
— *v. t. & i.;* EMP′TIED (-tĭd); EMP′TY·ING. **1.** To make or become empty or vacant; also, to transfer by dumping out of a receptacle until all its contents are gone; as, to *empty* grain from a sack into a bin. **2.** To discharge itself; as, the river *empties* into the ocean.
— *n.; pl.* EMPTIES (-tĭz). An empty container, car, or the like.
em·pur′ple (ĕm·pûr′p'l), *v. t.* To tinge or color purple.
em′py·e′ma (ĕm′pĭ·ē′mȧ), *n.; pl.* -EMATA (-ē′mȧ·tȧ; -ĕm′ȧ·tȧ). [NL., fr. Gr. *empyēma*, fr. *empyein* to suppurate, fr. *en* in + *pyon* pus.] *Med.* An accumulation of pus, usually in the pleural cavity. — **em′py·e′mic** (-ē′mĭk; -ĕm′ĭk), *adj.*
em·pyr′e·al (ĕm·pĭr′ē·ăl; ĕm′pĭ·rē′ăl; ĕm′pī-), *adj.* [LL. *empyrius*, *empyreus*, fr. Gr. *empyrios*, *empyros*, in fire, fiery, fr. *en* in + *pyr* fire.] **1.** Of or pertaining to the empyrean; celestial; sublime. **2.** Composed of a pure or sublimated fire.
em′py·re′an (ĕm′pĭ·rē′ăn; ĕm′pī-), *n.* **1.** The highest heaven, anciently thought to be of fire or light; hence, among modern Christian poets, the uppermost or essential paradise. **2.** The firmament; the heavens. — *adj.* Empyreal.
e′mu, e′meu (ē′mū), *n.* [Prob. fr. Pg. *ema* crane, ostrich.] An Australian ratite bird (either *Dromiceius novae-hollandiae* of central eastern Australia or *D. irroratus* of west Australia). Next to the ostrich, to which they are closely related, the emus are the largest existing birds.
em′u·late (ĕm′ū·lāt), *adj.* [L. *aemulatus*, past part. of *aemulari.*] *Obs.* Emulous. — (-lāt), *v. t.* To strive to equal or excel (another); to rival. — **em′u·la′tor** (-lā′tẽr), *n.*
em′u·la′tion (-lā′shŭn), *n.* **1.** Ambition or endeavor to equal or excel; rivalry. **2.** *Obs.* Ambitious or envious rivalry. — **em′u·la′tive** (ĕm′ū·lā′tĭv), *adj.* — **em′u·la′tive·ly**, *adv.*
em′u·lous (ĕm′ū·lŭs), *adj.* [L. *aemulus.*] **1.** Ambitious to equal another; also, characterized by, or due to, emulation. **2.** *Obs.* Jealously rivaling. — **em′u·lous·ly**, *adv.* — **em′u·lous·ness**, *n.*
e·mul′si·fy (ē·mŭl′sĭ·fī), *v. t.; -*FIED (-fīd); -FY′ING. To convert into, or treat with, an emulsion. — **e·mul′si·fi·ca′tion** (-fĭ·kā′shŭn), *n.* — **e·mul′si·fi′er** (-fī′ẽr), *n.*
e·mul′sion (ē·mŭl′shŭn), *n.* [NL. *emulsio*, fr. L. *emulgere*, *emulsum*, to milk out, fr. *e* out + *mulgere* to milk.] Any of various milky liquids; as: **a** *Pharm.* An oily mass in suspension in a watery liquid, used esp. to render a medicine more pleasant; as, *emulsion* of cod-liver oil. **b** *Photog.* A suspension of sensitive silver salt in a viscous medium, used for coating plates, films, etc. **c** *Physical Chem.* A dispersion of fine particles or globules of a liquid in a liquid. — **e·mul′sive** (-sĭv), *adj.*
e·mul′soid (-soid), *n.* A lyophilic sol, as a gelatin solution.
e·munc′to·ry (ē·mŭngk′tō·rĭ), *n.; pl.* -RIES (-rĭz). [LL. *emunctorium* a pair of snuffers, fr. *emungere*, *emunctum*, to blow the nose, hence, to cleanse.] Any organ or part of the body (as the kidneys, skin, etc.) which serves to carry off waste. — *adj.* Excretory.
en (ĕn), *n.* [Name of the letter *n*, L. *en.*] **1.** The letter N, n. **2.** *Print.* Half of the width of an em. See EM.
en- (ĕn-). [F., fr. L. *in.*] A prefix signifying *in*, *into*, forming verbs: **1.** From nouns, *en-* having the sense of *put into* or *upon*, *cover with*, *wrap up in.* **2.** From nouns or adjectives, *en-* having the sense of *make*, *make into*, or *make like.* **3.** From other verbs, mostly transitive, *en-* adding sometimes a sense of *in*, but oftener a mere intensive force.
en-. [Gr. *en.*] A prefix meaning *in.*
-en (-ĕn *or* -'n). [AS. *-an.*] A suffix formerly used to form the plural of many nouns, as in ey*en*, ox*en*.
-en (-ĕn *or* -'n, *according to the preceding consonant:* see each word). [AS.] The past participle ending of many strong verbs, as in brok*en*, ridd*en*, fall*en*.
-en. [AS.] An adjective suffix meaning *made of*, added chiefly to nouns denoting material, as in gold*en*, lead*en*, wood*en*.
-en. [AS. *-nian.*] A suffix meaning *to make*, *to render* (of a given character or quality), as in quick*en*, whit*en*.
en·a′ble (ĕn·ā′b'l), *v. t.;* EN·A′BLED (-b'ld); EN·A′BLING (-blĭng). **1.** To make able; to give (one) strength or authority sufficient for the purpose. **2.** To make practicable or easy; as, steam and electricity *enable* rapid transit.
Syn. **Enable, empower** mean to make one able to do something. **Enable** implies provision of the means or opportunity for doing; **empower**, granting of power or delegation of authority to do.
en·act′ (ĕn·ăkt′), *v. t.* **1.** To make into a law, as by legislative act; to decree. **2.** To act the part of; to play.
en·ac′tive (ĕn·ăk′tĭv), *adj.* Having power to enact; enacting.
en·act′ment (-ăkt′mĕnt), *n.* **1.** Act of enacting, or state of being enacted. **2.** That which is enacted; a law.
en·am′el (ĕn·ăm′ĕl), *n.* [From ENAMEL, *v.*] **1.** A vitreous composition, usually opaque, for coating the surface of metal, glass, or pottery, for ornament, protection, or as a basis for decoration. Cf. GLAZE, *n.*, 1 **b.** **2.** Any glossy surface resembling enamel. **3.** A paint which flows out to a smooth coat when applied, and, usually, dries with a glossy appearance. **4.** That which is enameled; enameled ware. **5.** A cosmetic intended to produce a glossy appearance. **6.** *Anat. & Zool.* The hard calcareous outer layer of the teeth. — *v. t.;* -ELED (-ĕld) *or* -ELLED; -EL·ING *or* -EL·LING. [AF. *enameler*, *enamayller*, fr. *en-* + *amayl*, OF. *esmail*, enamel.] **1.** To inlay or cover with enamel. **2.** To variegate with colors as if with enamel; also, *Obs.*, to adorn. **3.** To form a glossy surface like enamel upon; as, to *enamel* leather. — **en·am′el·er, en·am′el·ler, en·am′el·ist, en·am′el·list,** *n.*
en·am′or, en·am′our (ĕn·ăm′ẽr), *v. t.* [OF. *enamourer*, fr. *en-* (fr. L. *in*) + *amour* love, fr. L. *amor.*] To inflame with love; to charm; captivate.
en·am′ored, en·am′oured (-ẽrd), *adj.* Fondly in love; charmed; fascinated.
Syn. **Enamored, infatuated** mean passionately in love. **Enamored** usually connotes complete absorption in the passion, and **infatuated**, blind folly and unreasoning ardor.
‖**en ar′rière′** (äN·nȧ′ryâr′). [F.] In or to the rear; in arrears.
en′ar·thro′sis (ĕn′är·thrō′sĭs), *n.* [NL., fr. Gr. *enarthrōsis*, fr. *enarthros* jointed, fr. *en* in + *arthron* joint.] *Anat.* A ball-and-socket joint, as the hip joint.
‖**en a′vant′** (äN·nȧ′väN′). [F.] Forward; into the future; as a command, forward.
en bloc′ (ĕn blŏk′; *F.* äN blôk′). [F.] In a lump; as a whole.
en·cae′ni·a (ĕn·sē′nĭ·ȧ; -nyȧ; 58), *n. pl.* [L., fr. Gr. *enkainia* a feast of dedication, fr. *en* in + *kainos* new.] A festival commemorative of the founding of a city or the consecration of a church; also [*cap.*], at Oxford University, the annual ceremony in June including commemoration with recital of poems and essays and conferring of degrees.
en·cage′ (ĕn·kāj′), *v. t.* To put in a cage; to cage.
en·camp′ (ĕn·kămp′), *v. i.* To form and occupy a camp. — *v. t.* To form into a camp; to place in a camp.
en·camp′ment (-mĕnt), *n.* **1.** Act of encamping, or state of being encamped. **2.** A camp.
en·car′nal·ize (ĕn·kär′năl·īz), *v. t.* To incarnate.
en·case′ (ĕn·kās′), *v. t.* To incase.
en·caus′tic (ĕn·kôs′tĭk), *adj.* [L. *encausticus*, fr. Gr. *enkaustikos*, deriv. of *en* in + *kaiein* to burn.] *Fine Arts.* Prepared by means of heat; burned in or done by burning in. — *n.* Encaustic painting.
encaustic painting. *Fine Arts.* Painting by means of wax with which colors are combined, and which is afterwards fused with hot irons, thus fixing the colors.
-ence (-ĕns). [F. and L.; F., fr. L. *-entia.*] A noun suffix signifying *action*, *state*, *quality*, or *degree*, as in exist*ence*, etc. See -ANCE.
‖**en′ceinte′** (äN′săNt′; äN·sănt′), *adj.* [F., fr. LL. *incincta*, fr. L. *in* not + *cinctus*, past part. of *cingere* to gird about.] Pregnant; with child.
‖**en′ceinte′**, *n.* [F., fr. *enceindre* to gird about, surround, fr. L. *incingere*, fr. *in* (intens.) + *cingere* to gird.] *Fort.* The enclosing line of works of a fortress.
encephal-. = ENCEPHALO- (which see), as in **en·ceph′a·lal′gi·a, en·ceph′a·las·the′ni·a.** See -ALGIA, ASTHENIA.
en′ce·phal′ic (ĕn′sē·făl′ĭk), *adj.* *Anat.* **a** Pert. to the encephalon. **b** Situated in the cranial cavity.
en·ceph′a·li′tis (ĕn·sĕf′ȧ·lī′tĭs), *n.* [NL., fr. *encephal-* + *-itis.*] Inflammation of the brain. — **en·ceph′a·lit′ic** (-lĭt′ĭk), *adj.*
‖**en·ce′pha·li′tis le·thar′gi·ca** (ĕn·sĕf′ȧ·lī′tĭs lē·thär′jĭ·kȧ). [NL.] *Med.* = SLEEPING SICKNESS, 2.
en·ceph′a·lo- (ĕn·sĕf′ȧ·lō-), **encephal-.** [Gr. *enkephalos.*] A combining form meaning *the brain*, as in **en·ceph′a·lot′o·my** (see -TOMY).
en·ceph′a·lo·gram′ (-grăm′), *n.* *Med.* = ENCEPHALOGRAPH **a.**
en·ceph′a·lo·graph′ (-grȧf′; 9), *n.* [*encephalo-* + photo*graph.*] *Med.* **a** An X-ray photograph of the brain. **b** = ELECTROENCEPHALOGRAPH. — **en·ceph′a·log′ra·phy** (-lŏg′rȧ·fĭ), *n.*
en·ceph′a·lo′ma (-lō′mȧ), *n.; pl.* -LOMATA (-lō′mȧ·tȧ), -LOMAS (-lō′mȧz). *Med.* A tumor of the brain.
en·ceph′a·lo·my′e·li′tis (-lō·mī′ĕ·lī′tĭs), *n.* *Veter.* An epizootic, usually insect-transmitted, virus disease of horses, marked by fever and central nervous symptoms, occurring esp. in summer. Two forms occur in the United States, a severe eastern and a milder western form due to distinct viruses either of which may produce a type of sleeping sickness in man.
en·ceph′a·lon (ĕn·sĕf′ȧ·lŏn), *n.; pl.* ENCEPHALA (-lȧ). [NL., fr. Gr. *enkephalos*, fr. *en* in + *kephalē* head.] *Anat.* The brain.
en·chain′ (ĕn·chān′), *v. t.* [F. *enchaîner.*] **1.** To bind with, or hold in, chains; to fetter. **2.** To attract and hold, as the attention or emotions. — **en·chain′ment**, *n.*
en·chant′ (ĕn·chȧnt′), *v. t.* [OF. *enchanter*, fr. L. *incantare*, fr. *in* in, against + *cantare* to sing.] **1.** To act on by charms or sorcery; esp., to lay under a spell. **2.** *Obs.* Hence, to delude. **3.** To delight in a high degree; to charm. — **Syn.** See ATTRACT.
en·chant′er (ĕn·chȧn′tẽr), *n.* One who enchants; esp., a sorcerer.
en·chant′ing (-tĭng), *adj.* Charming; fascinating. — **-ly**, *adv.*
en·chant′ment (ĕn·chȧnt′mĕnt), *n.* **1.** An enchanting, or state of being enchanted. **2.** That which enchants or charms.
en·chant′ress (ĕn·chȧn′trĕs; -trĭs), *n.* A sorceress; also, a woman of bewitching charms.
en·chase′ (ĕn·chās′), *v. t.* [F. *enchâsser*, fr. *en-* (fr. L. *in*) + *châsse* frame, case, fr. L. *capsa* box, case.] **1.** To incase or enclose in a border; to surround with an ornamental casing, as a gem with gold. **2.** To ornament by embossing, inlaying, or engraving; also, to cut, carve, or engrave (a design, figure, etc.) on a surface.
en′chi·rid′i·on (ĕn′kī·rĭd′ĭ·ŏn; ĕn′kĭ-), *n.* [LL., fr. Gr. *encheiridion*, fr. *en* in + *cheir* hand.] A handbook; a manual.
en′chon·dro′ma (ĕn′kŏn·drō′mȧ), *n.; pl.* -DROMATA (-mȧ·tȧ), -DROMAS (-mȧz). [NL., fr. Gr. *en* in + *chondr-* + *-oma.*] *Med.* A tumor consisting of cartilaginous tissue. — **en′chon·drom′a·tous** (-drŏm′ȧ·tŭs; -drō′mȧ·tŭs), *adj.*
en·cho′ri·al (ĕn·kō′rĭ·ăl), **en·chor′ic** (-kŏr′ĭk), *adj.* [Gr. *enchōrios* domestic, native, fr. *en* in + *chōra* place, country.] Belonging to, or used in, a country; native; domestic; — used esp. of demotic writing. See DEMOTIC, 2.
en·ci′na (ĕn·sē′nȧ), *n.* [Sp.] **a** The California live oak (*Quercus agrifolia*). **b** The common live oak (*Q. virginiana*). — **en·ci′nal** (-năl; -n'l), *adj.*
en·cir′cle (ĕn·sûr′k'l), *v. t.;* see CIRCLE. **1.** To form a circle about; to surround. **2.** To pass completely around. — **en·cir′cle·ment**, *n.*
‖**en clair** (äN klâr′). [F.] In actual words, as opposed to code; — used esp. of diplomatic messages sent by telegraph.
en·clasp′ (ĕn·klȧsp′; 9), *v. t.* To clasp within.
en′clave (ĕn′klāv; *F.* äN′klȧv′), *n.* [F.] A tract or territory enclosed within foreign territory. See EXCLAVE.
en·clit′ic (ĕn·klĭt′ĭk), *adj.* [LL. *encliticus*, fr. Gr. *enklitikos*, fr. *enklinein* to incline, fr. *en* in + *klinein* to bend.] *Gram.* Leaning or dependent (with reference to accent); — used of a word which, losing its own accent, is attached in pronunciation to a preceding word, as *thee* in prithee, *not* in cannot. — *n.* An enclitic word or particle.
en·close′ (ĕn·klōz′), **in·close′** (ĭn-), *v. t.* [*en-* + *close*, after OF. *enclos*, past part. of *enclore* to enclose.] **1.** To shut up or in. **2.** To surround; encompass; hem in.
en·clo′sure (ĕn·klō′zhẽr), **in·clo′sure** (ĭn-), *n.* **1.** Act of enclosing; state of being enclosed. **2.** That which is enclosed, or placed within something. **3.** That which encloses, as a fence.
en·co′mi·ast (ĕn·kō′mĭ·ăst), *n.* [Gr. *enkōmiastēs.* See ENCOMIUM.] One who praises; a panegyrist. — **en·co′mi·as′tic** (-ăs′tĭk), **en·co′mi·as′ti·cal** (-tĭ·kăl), *adj.*
en·co′mi·um (ĕn·kō′mĭ·ŭm; 58), *n.; pl.* -MIUMS (-ŭmz), -MIA (-ȧ). [L., fr. Gr. *enkōmion*, fr. *en* in + *kōmos* a revel.] Warm or high praise; panegyric.
Syn. **Encomium, eulogy, panegyric, tribute, citation** mean a formal expression of praise. **Encomium** implies enthusiasm or warmth in prais-

ing a person or thing; **eulogy**, a studied speech or writing extolling the virtues and the services of a person (especially at a funeral); **panegyric**, an elaborate, often poetic, compliment; **tribute** implies deep praise as conveyed not only through writing or speaking but by any significant act or the like; **citation** applies to the formal praise which accompanies the mention of a person such as in a military order or in awarding an honorary degree.

en·com′pass (ĕn·kŭm′pȧs), *v. t.* **1.** To encircle; surround. **2.** To enclose; to contain. **3.** *Obs.* To outwit. — **en·com′pass·ment**, *n.*

en′core (äng′kōr; än′-; 70), *interj.* [F.] An exclamation meaning once more! again! — used by the audience at plays, concerts, etc.

en′core, *n.* The demand for repetition or reappearance made by an audience, as by applause; also, the further appearance or performance.

en′core, *v. t.* To call for a repetition of or by; as, to *encore* a song or a singer.

en·coun′ter (ĕn·koun′tẽr), *v. t. & i.* [OF. *encontrer*, fr. L. *in* in + *contra* against.] **1.** To meet in opposition or with hostile intent; to engage in conflict. **2.** To meet; to come face to face with. — *n.* **1.** A meeting with hostile purpose; hence, a combat; battle. **2.** A meeting face to face; interview. **3.** *Obs.* Behavior on meeting; address.

Syn. **Encounter, skirmish, brush** mean a minor battle. An **encounter** is a hostile meeting, often unexpected; a **skirmish**, a slight and desultory *encounter*, as between light detachments; a **brush**, a short but brisk *skirmish*.

en·cour′age (ĕn·kûr′ĭj; 117), *v. t.*; -AGED (-ĭjd); -AG·ING (-ĭj·ĭng). [F. *encourager*, fr. *en-* (fr. L. *in*) + *courage* courage.] **1.** To inspire with courage, spirit, or hope; to animate; hearten; cheer on or up. **2.** To give help or patronage to, as an industry; to foster.

en·cour′age·ment (-mĕnt), *n.* **1.** Act of encouraging, or state of being encouraged. **2.** That which encourages.

en·cour′ag·ing (-ĭj·ĭng), *adj.* Giving hope; inspiriting; favoring. — **en·cour′ag·ing·ly**, *adv.*

en·crim′son (ĕn·krĭm′z′n), *v. t.* To make or dye crimson.

en′cri·nite (ĕn′krĭ·nīt), *n.* [Gr. *en* in + *krinon* a lily.] *Paleontol.* A fossil crinoid; sometimes, any crinoid.

en·croach′ (ĕn·krōch′), *v. i.* [OF. *encrochier* to seize, fr. *en-* (fr. L. *in*) + *croc* hook.] **1.** To enter by gradual steps or by stealth into the possessions or rights of another; to trespass; intrude. **2.** To advance beyond desirable or normal limits. — **Syn.** See TRESPASS. — **en·croach′er**, *n.* — **en·croach′ment**, *n.*

en·crust′ (ĕn·krŭst′), *v. t.* To incrust.

en·cum′ber (ĕn·kŭm′bẽr), *v. t.* [OF. *encombrer* to obstruct, fr. *combre* abatis, of Celt. origin.] **1.** To impede the motion or action of, as with a burden. **2.** To render awkward, obstructive, or disagreeable, by superfluous parts or the like. **3.** To place a burden upon; esp., to load with debts, or other legal claims.

en·cum′brance (-brăns), *n.* **1.** That which encumbers; a burden that impedes action. **2.** A dependent person, esp. a child. **3.** *Law.* A claim or lien upon an estate.

-en·cy (-ĕn·sĭ). [L. *-entia.*] A noun suffix signifying *quality* or *state*, as in expedi*ency*. See -ANCE.

en·cyc′lic (ĕn·sĭk′lĭk; -sī′klĭk), *adj. & n.* Encyclical.

en·cyc′li·cal (-sĭk′lĭ·kăl; -sī′klĭ-), *adj.* [LL. *encyclicus*, for *encyclius*, fr. Gr. *enkyklios*, fr. *en* in + *kyklos* circle.] Sent to many persons or places; general; as, an *encyclical* letter. — *n.* An encyclical letter; specif., a papal letter addressed to the bishops of the world.

en·cy′clo·pe′di·a, en·cy′clo·pae′di·a (ĕn·sī′klō·pē′dĭ·ȧ), *n.* [NL., fr. Gr. *enkyklopaideia*, for *enkyklios paideia*, instruction in the circle of arts and sciences. See CYCLOPEDIA.] **1.** A summary of knowledge, or of a branch of knowledge. **2.** A work in which the various branches or fields of learning are treated in separate articles. **3.** [*cap.*] The work of the Encyclopedists.

en·cy′clo·pe′dic, en·cy′clo·pae′dic (-pē′dĭk; -pĕd′ĭk), *adj.* Also **en·cy′clo·pe′di·cal, en·cy′clo·pae′di·cal** (-pē′dĭ·kăl; -pĕd′ĭ-). Pertaining to, or of the nature of, an encyclopedia; embracing a wide range of subjects.

en·cy′clo·pe′dism, en·cy′clo·pae′dism (-pē′dĭz′m), *n.* **1.** Possession of the whole range of knowledge. **2.** [*cap.*] The writings, views, and influence of the Encyclopedists.

en·cy′clo·pe′dist, en·cy′clo·pae′dist (-dĭst), *n.* The compiler of an encyclopedia. — ***the Encyclopedists.*** The writers of the great French Encyclopedia (1751–72), edited by Diderot and d'Alembert, embodying the enlightened thought of the period.

en·cyst′ (ĕn·sĭst′), *v. t. & i.* To enclose or become enclosed in a cyst or capsule. — **en·cyst′ment**, *n.*

end (ĕnd), *n.* [ME. & AS. *ende.*] **1.** A limit or boundary; esp., a limiting region or part. **2.** Death; destruction. **3.** The extremity or conclusion of any event or series of events. **4.** The extreme or last point or part; extremity; tip. **5.** The object aimed at in any effort; purpose. **6.** Conclusion; issue; consequence; also, ultimate state. **7.** That which is left; a remnant; as, odds and *ends*. **8.** *Games.* A player stationed on the end of a line or team, as in football.

Syn. (1) **End, termination, ending, terminus** mean the point or line beyond which a thing does not or cannot go. **End**, the ordinary and inclusive term, implies the final limit not only in time, space, or magnitude, but in extent of influence, range of possibility, etc.; **termination** and **ending** apply to the end in time or, less often, in space, of something having a set term or predetermined limits, or being complete, finished, futile, or the like; **terminus** applies to the end commonly, but not invariably, in space to which a person or thing moves or progresses. — **Ant.** Beginning.

(2) See INTENTION.

— *v. t. & i.* **1.** To bring or come to an end. **2.** To die or put to death. **3.** To form or be at the end of. — **Syn.** See CLOSE. — **Ant.** Begin.

end, *v. t.* *Now Dial.* To put (corn, hay, etc.) into a barn, stack, etc.

end-. = ENDO-.

en·dam′age (ĕn·dăm′ĭj), *v. t.*; see DAMAGE. To harm.

en′da·moe′ba (ĕn′dȧ·mē′bȧ), *n.*; *pl.* ENDAMOEBAE (-bē), ENDAMOEBAS (-bȧz). Also **en′da·me′ba**, *n.*; *pl.* ENDAMEBAS (-bȧz), ENDAMEBAE (-bē). [Gr. *endon* within + *amoeba.*] An organism (genus *Endamoeba*) one species of which is parasitic in the intestines and liver of higher animals and man, where it produces amoebic dysentery and liver abscesses.

en·dan′ger (ĕn·dān′jẽr), *v. t.* To bring into danger or peril.

end′brain′ (ĕnd′brān′), *n.* See FOREBRAIN.

en·dear′ (ĕn·dēr′), *v. t.* **1.** *Obs.* **a** To make higher in cost or estimation. **b** To hold in affection or love. **2.** To cause to become an object of affection. — **en·dear′ing·ly**, *adv.*

en·dear′ment (-mĕnt), *n.* Act of endearing; also, that which manifests affection; a caress.

en·deav′or, en·deav′our (ĕn·dĕv′ẽr), *v. t.* [ME. *endever, endevor*, fr. *en-* + *dever, devor*, duty, fr. OF. *deveir.*] *Archaic.* To strive to achieve or reach; to try. — *v. i.* To work for a certain end. — **Syn.** See ATTEMPT. — *n.* An exertion toward attainment of an object; attempt. — **en·deav′or·er, en·deav′our·er** (-ẽr), *n.*

en·dem′ic (ĕn·dĕm′ĭk), *adj.* Also **en·dem′i·cal** (-ĭ·kăl). [Gr. *endēmos, endēmios*, fr. *en* in + *dēmos* the people.] **1.** Native to a particular people or country; not introduced or naturalized. **2.** *Biol.* Confined to, or indigenous in, a certain region; as, an *endemic* animal or plant; — opposed to *exotic*. **3.** *Med.* Peculiar to a district, or class of persons; as, an *endemic* disease. — **Syn.** See NATIVE. — *n.* An endemic disease. — **en·dem′i·cal·ly**, *adv.*

end′er (ĕn′dẽr), *n.* One who or that which ends.

en·der′mic (ĕn·dûr′mĭk), *adj.* [Gr. *en* in + *derma* skin.] *Med.* Acting through the skin, or by direct application to the skin; as, *endermic* medication.

‖**en dés′ha′bil′lé′** (äɴ dā′zȧ′bē′yā′). [F.] In dishabille.

end′ing (ĕn′dĭng), *n.* [AS. *endung.*] **1.** Termination; conclusion; also, death. **2.** *Gram.* One or more letters, sounds, or syllables added to a word base, esp. in inflection. — **Syn.** See END. — **Ant.** Beginning.

en′dive (ĕn′dĭv; -dīv; än′dēv; *F.* äɴ′dēv′), *n.* [F., fr. a deriv. of L. *intybum, intibus*, endive.] **1.** An annual or biennial herb (*Cichorium endivia*) related to chicory. Its curled leaves are used for salads. **2.** A variety of chicory having leaves that are blanched and used raw as a salad; — called also ***French endive.***

end′less (ĕnd′lĕs; -lĭs), *adj.* **1.** Having no end; of time, eternal; of space, infinite. **2.** Continuous; united at the ends; as, an *endless* belt. — **Syn.** Interminable, everlasting, unceasing. — **end′less·ly**, *adv.* — **end′less·ness**, *n.*

end′long′ (-lông′), *adv.* **1.** Lengthwise. **2.** On end.

end man. The last man in a row; specif., the man at either end of the line of performers in a minstrel show.

end′most (-mōst), *adj.* Farthest; remotest; at the very end.

en′do- (ĕn′dō-), **end-.** [Gr. *endon.*] Combining form meaning *within.*

en′do·blast (-blăst), *n.* [*endo-* + *-blast.*] *Biol.* Hypoblast. — **en′do·blas′tic** (-blăs′tĭk), *adj.*

en′do·car′di·al (-kär′dĭ·ăl), *adj.* Also **en′do·car′di·ac** (-ăk). [*endo-* + Gr. *kardia* the heart.] *Anat.* Situated within the heart; of or pert. to the endocardium.

en′do·car·di′tis (-kär·dī′tĭs), *n.* [NL. See -ITIS.] *Med.* Inflammation of the thin serous membrane (**en′do·car′di·um** [-kär′dĭ·ŭm]) lining the cavities of the heart. Cf. MYOCARDITIS. — **en′do·car·dit′ic** (-dĭt′ĭk), *adj.*

en′do·carp (ĕn′dō·kärp), *n.* *Bot.* The inner layer of the pericarp, as the stone of a cherry or other drupe, enclosing the single seed.

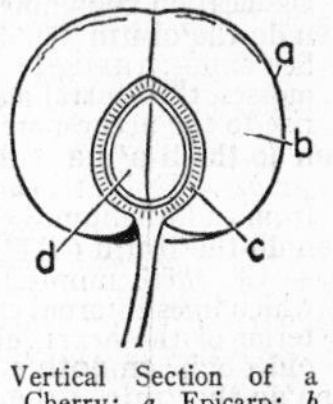

Vertical Section of a Cherry: *a* Epicarp; *b* Mesocarp (Sarcocarp); *c* Endocarp, or Stone; *d* Seed. *a*, *b*, and *c* together form the Pericarp.

en′do·cen′tric (-sĕn′trĭk), *adj.* *Ling.* Having the same grammatical function as one of its component parts; thus, the phrase *little Mary* in "little Mary won the prize" is *endocentric*; — opp. to *exocentric.*

en′do·crine (ĕn′dō·krīn; -krĭn; -krēn), **en′do·crin** (-krĭn), *n.* *Physiol.* **a** Any internal secretion. **b** An endocrine gland. — **en′do·cri′nal** (-krī′năl; -n'l), **en·doc′ri·nous** (ĕn·dŏk′rĭ·nŭs), *adj.*

en′do·crine, *adj.* [*endo-* + Gr. *krinein* to separate.] *Physiol.* **a** Secreting internally; — applied esp. to glands (**endocrine glands**), as the thyroid and pituitary, whose secretions (autacoids, or hormones) pass directly into the blood or lymph. Opp. to *exocrine.* **b** Relating to an autacoid or the gland producing it.

en′do·cri·nol′o·gy (-krĭ·nŏl′ō·jĭ; -krī-), *n.* The science or study of the internal secretions and endocrine glands. — **en′do·cri·nol′o·gist** (-jĭst), *n.*

en′do·derm (ĕn′dō·dûrm), *n.* [*endo-* + *-derm.*] *Zool.* The epithelium lining the greater part of the digestive tract; the tissue derived from the hypoblast of the embryo. When *endoderm* is applied to embryonic structures it is strictly synonymous with *hypoblast.* — **en′do·der′mal** (-dûr′măl), **en′do·der′mic** (-mĭk), *adj.*

en′do·der′mis (-dûr′mĭs), *n.* [NL. See ENDODERM.] *Bot.* A single layer of living cells, usually with thickened radial walls, occurring inside the cortex and surrounding the vascular tissues of many plants, esp. in the roots.

en′do·en′zyme (ĕn′dō·ĕn′zīm; -zĭm), *n.* Also **en′do·en′zym** (-zĭm). [*endo-* + *enzyme.*] *Biochem.* An enzyme which acts within the cell; an intracellular enzyme.

en·dog′a·my (ĕn·dŏg′ȧ·mĭ), *n.* [*endo-* + *-gamy.*] Marriage within the tribe, caste, or social group; inbreeding. Cf. EXOGAMY. — **en′do·gam′ic** (ĕn′dō·găm′ĭk), **en·dog′a·mous** (ĕn·dŏg′ȧ·mŭs), *adj.*

en′do·gen (ĕn′dō·jĕn), *n.* *Bot.* A monocotyledon.

en·dog′e·nous (ĕn·dŏj′ē·nŭs), *adj.* **1.** Produced from within; originating from or due to internal causes; autogenous; — disting. from *exogenous.* **2.** *Biol.* Growing from or on the inside; developing within the cell wall, as certain spores. **3.** *Physiol. & Biochem.* Designating or pertaining to the metabolism of the nitrogenous substances of cells and tissues, the catabolic products excreted being relatively constant in the normal organism. — **en·dog′e·nous·ly**, *adv.*

en·dog′e·ny (-nĭ), *n.* [*endo-* + *-geny.*] *Biol.* Growth from within; endogenous cell formation.

en′do·lymph (ĕn′dō·lĭmf), *n.* [*endo-* + *lymph.*] *Anat.* The watery fluid in the membranous labyrinth of the ear.

en′do·morph (-môrf), *n.* [*endo-* + *-morph.*] **1.** *Mineral.* A crystal of one species enclosed in one of another. Cf. PERIMORPH. **2.** *Anthropol.* A person having the endomorphic type of body build.

en′do·mor′phic (-môr′fĭk), *adj.* **1.** *Mineral.* **a** Of or pertaining to an endomorph. **b** Of, pert. to, or produced by, endomorphism. **2.** *Anthropol.* Characterized by predominance of the structures developed from the endodermal layer of the embryo, that is, the internal organs; hence, of the pyknic type of body build. Cf. ECTOMORPHIC, MESOMORPHIC. — **en′do·mor′phy** (ĕn′dō·môr′fĭ), *n.*

en′do·mor′phism (-môr′fĭz′m), *n.* *Petrog.* Any change produced in an intrusive rock by reaction with the wall rock.

en′do·par′a·site (-păr′ȧ·sīt), *n.* *Zool.* Any parasite which lives in the internal organs of an animal, as tapeworms; — opp. to *ectoparasite.*

en′do·phyte (ĕn′dō·fīt), *n.* [*endo-* + *-phyte.*] *Bot.* A plant which grows within another plant. Cf. ENTOPHYTE.

en′do·plasm (-plăz′m), *n.* [*endo-* + *-plasm.*] *Biol.* The inner or central portion of the cytoplasm in a cell; — opposed to *ectoplasm.* — **en′do·plas′mic** (-plăz′mĭk), *adj.*

end organ. *Physiol.* A specialized structure, of sensory or motor function, composed of peripheral nerve ends and accessory parts.

en·dorse′ (ĕn·dôrs′), *v. t.* [OF. *endosser,* fr. *en-* (fr. L. *in*) + *dos* back, fr. L. *dorsum.*] **1. a** To write on the back of; specif., to sign one's name as payee on the back of (a check) in order to obtain the cash or credit represented on the face of the document. **b** Loosely, to inscribe (one's signature) on a check, bill, etc. **c** To make over to another party (the value represented in a check, bill, note, or the like) by inscribing one's name on the document. **d** To acknowledge receipt of (a sum specified) by one's signature. **2.** To give one's name or support to; to sanction. — **Syn.** See APPROVE. — **en·dors′a·ble** (-dôr′sȧ·b′l), *adj.* — **en′dor·see′** (ĕn′dôr·sē′), *n.* — **en·dors′er** (ĕn·dôr′sẽr), *n.*

en·dorse′ment (-mĕnt), *n.* **1.** Act of writing on the back of a note, bill, or other written instrument. **2.** That which is written on the back of a note, bill, or other paper; a writing on a negotiable instrument, by which the property therein is assigned and transferred. **3.** Sanction or approval; as, the *endorsement* of an opinion. **4.** *Insurance.* A provision added to an insurance contract whereby the scope of its coverage is restricted or enlarged.

en′do·sarc (ĕn′dō·särk), *n.* [*endo-* + Gr. *sarx, sarkos,* flesh.] Endoplasm, as in the amoeba.

en′do·scope (-skōp), *n.* *Med.* An instrument for examining the interior of a hollow organ, as of the rectum, the urethra, and the bladder. — **en·dos′co·py** (ĕn·dŏs′kō·pĭ), *n.*

en′do·skel′e·ton (-skĕl′ĕ·tŭn; -t′n), *n.* *Anat. & Zool.* An internal skeleton or supporting framework in an animal. — **en′do·skel′e·tal** (-tăl; -t′l), *adj.*

en′dos·mo′sis (ĕn′dŏs·mō′sĭs; ĕn′dŏz-), *n.* [NL.] See OSMOSIS. — **en′dos·mo′sic** (-mō′sĭk), **en′dos·mot′ic** (-mŏt′ĭk), *adj.*

en′do·sperm (ĕn′dō·spûrm), *n.* *Bot.* The nutritive tissue formed within the embryo sac in seed plants. See SEED, *Illust.*

en′do·spore (-spōr; 70), *n.* **a** *Bot.* = ENDOSPORIUM. **b** *Bacteriol.* An asexual spore developed within the cell. — **en·dos′po·rous** (ĕn·dŏs′pō·rŭs; ĕn′dō·spō′rŭs), *adj.*

en′do·spo′ri·um (-spō′rĭ·ŭm; 70), *n.; pl.* -RIA (-ȧ). [NL.] *Bot.* The inner layer or coating of the spore wall.

en·dos′te·um (ĕn·dŏs′tē·ŭm), *n.; pl.* -TEA (-ȧ). [NL., fr. *end-* + Gr. *osteon* a bone.] *Anat.* The layer of vascular connective tissue lining the medullary cavities of bone.

en′dos·to′sis (ĕn′dŏs·tō′sĭs), *n.* [NL., fr. *end-* + *ostosis.*] *Anat.* Ossification beginning in the substance of a cartilage.

en′do·the′ci·um (ĕn′dō·thē′shĭ·ŭm; -sĭ·ŭm), *n.; pl.* -CIA (-ȧ). [NL. See ENDO-; THECA.] *Bot.* **a** The inner lining of an anther cell. **b** In mosses, the central mass of cells within the young sporogonium, giving rise to the archespore.

en′do·the′li·o′ma (-thē′lĭ·ō′mȧ), *n.; pl.* -OMATA (-ō′mȧ·tȧ), -OMAS (-mȧz). [NL., fr. *endothelium* + *-oma.*] *Med.* A tumor developing from endothelium.

en′do·the′li·um (-thē′lĭ·ŭm), *n.; pl.* ENDOTHELIA (-ȧ). [NL., fr. *endo-* + Gr. *thēlē* nipple.] *Anat.* An epithelium of mesoblastic origin which lines internal cavities of the body, as the serous cavities, the interior of the heart, etc. — **en′do·the′li·al** (-ăl), *adj.* — **en′do·the′li·oid** (-oid), **en·doth′e·loid** (ĕn·dŏth′ĕ·loid), *adj.*

en′do·ther′mic (-thûr′mĭk), **en′do·ther′mal** (-măl), *adj.* *Chem.* Designating or pertaining to a reaction which occurs with absorption of heat; — opposed to *exothermic.*

en′do·tox′in (ĕn′dō·tŏk′sĭn), *n.* [*endo-* + *toxin.*] Any of a class of poisonous substances present in certain bacteria (as the typhoid bacillus), retained within the cell until its disintegration. Cf. EXOTOXIN. — **en′do·tox′ic** (-sĭk), *adj.*

en·dow′ (ĕn·dou′), *v. t.* [OF. *endouer,* fr. *en-* (fr. L. *in*) + *douer* to endow, fr. L. *dotare.*] **1.** *Archaic.* To furnish with a dower. **2.** To furnish with money or its equivalent, as a permanent fund for support. **3.** To enrich with anything of the nature of a gift, as a quality or faculty.

en·dow′ment (-mĕnt), *n.* **1.** Act of endowing. **2.** That which is bestowed or settled on a person or an institution. **3.** Gift of nature; talents. **4.** *Insurance.* Insurance (**endowment insurance**) providing for payment of a stated amount to designated beneficiaries if the insured should die within a stipulated time or to the insured himself if he survives to the end of such time.

end paper. A once-folded sheet of paper, one leaf of which is pasted flat against the inside of a front or back cover of a book and the other pasted at the base to the first or last page to form an extra flyleaf.

en·due′ (ĕn·dū′), *v. t.* [From OF. *enduire* to lead into (fr. L. *ducere*) and *enduire* to put on (fr. L. *inducere* and L. *induere*); — confused with E. *endow.*] **1.** To invest; clothe. **2.** To endow. **3.** To provide with some quality or power; as, *endued* with heavenly grace.

en·dur′a·ble (ĕn·dūr′ȧ·b′l), *adj.* Capable of being endured.

en·dur′ance (-ăns), *n.* **1.** State or capability of lasting; continuance. **2.** Act of suffering; a continuing or the power of continuing under pain or hardship without being overcome. **3.** *Rare.* A hardship.

en·dure′ (-dūr′; 114), *v. i.* [OF. *endurer,* fr. L. *indurare* to harden, fr. *in* + *durare* to harden, fr. *durus* hard.] **1.** To continue in the same state without perishing; to last. **2.** To remain firm, as under suffering; to suffer patiently; to bear up. — **Syn.** See CONTINUE. — *v. t.* **1.** To remain firm under; to sustain; undergo. **2.** To bear with patience, as pain or misfortune. **3.** To tolerate; to put up with. **4.** *Archaic.* To be compatible with; to allow. — **Syn.** See BEAR.

en·dur′ing (-dūr′ĭng), *adj.* Lasting; durable; long-suffering. — **en·dur′ing·ly,** *adv.* — **en·dur′ing·ness,** *n.*

end′ways′ (ĕnd′wāz′), *adv.* **1.** On end; erectly. **2.** With the end forward. **3.** Lengthwise.

end′wise′ (-wīz′), *adv.* Endways. See -WAYS.

En·dym′i·on (ĕn·dĭm′ĭ·ŏn), *n.* [L., fr. Gr. *Endymiōn.*] *Gr. Myth.* A youth loved by Selene, by whom he was thrown into a sleep that he might be unconscious of her caresses.

-ene (-ēn). *Chem.* A suffix used in forming the names of certain hydrocarbons, as in benz*ene.* Specif., it is used to indicate the *presence of one double bond.*

-ene (-ēn). A termination in many commercial or popular names of substances.

‖**en ef′fet′** (äN·nĕ′fĕ′). [F.] In effect; really; in fact.

en′e·ma (ĕn′ĕ·mȧ), *n.; pl.* ENEMAS (-mȧz). [LL., fr. Gr. *enema,* fr. *enienai* to send in.] *Med.* A liquid injected into the rectum as a medicine or purge; also, the apparatus used.

en′e·my (ĕn′ĕ·mĭ), *n.; pl.* -MIES (-mĭz). [OF. *enemi,* fr. L. *inimicus,* fr. *in-* (negative) + *amicus* friend.] **1.** One hostile to another; one who seeks the overthrow or failure of that to which he is opposed. **2.** A military foe; also, a hostile force, ship, or the like. **3.** In general, anything that injures one. — ***the enemy.*** The Devil; Satan.

Syn. **Enemy, foe** mean a person or group that manifests hostility. **Enemy** stresses antagonism whether it shows itself in hatred or intense dislike or in a destructive attitude or action; **foe** stresses active warfare but is now used chiefly in figurative language.

— *adj.* **1.** *Obs.* Hostile; inimical. **2.** Of or pertaining to a hostile force or nation.

en′er·ge′sis (ĕn′ẽr·jē′sĭs), *n.* [NL., fr. Gr. *energein* to be in activity.] *Plant Physiol.* The chemical process or series of processes within the plant cell by which energy is made available through catabolic changes.

en′er·get′ic (-jĕt′ĭk), *adj.* Also **en′er·get′i·cal** (-ĭ·kăl). [Gr. *energētikos.* See ENERGY.] **1.** Exhibiting energy; forcible; as, *energetic* measures. **2.** Having energy or energies; active. — **Syn.** See VIGOROUS. — **Ant.** Lethargic. — **en′er·get′i·cal·ly,** *adv.*

en′er·get′ics (-jĕt′ĭks), *n.;* see -ICS. Science of the conditions and laws governing manifestation of energy.

en′er·gize (ĕn′ẽr·jīz), *v. i.* To put forth energy; to act. — *v. t.* To impart energy to; to make vigorous. — **en′er·giz′er** (-jīz′ẽr), *n.*

en′er·gu′men (ĕn′ẽr·gū′mĕn), *n.* [LL. *energumenos,* fr. Gr. *energoumenos* possessed by an evil spirit.] One possessed by an evil spirit; a demoniac.

en′er·gy (ĕn′ẽr·jĭ), *n.; pl.* -GIES (-jĭz). [LL. *energia,* fr. Gr. *energeia,* fr. *energos* active, fr. *en* in + *ergon* work.] **1.** Strength of expression; force of utterance. **2. a** Internal or inherent power; capacity of acting. **b** *pl.* Such powers, esp. when in exercise; activities. **3.** Power efficiently and forcibly exerted. **4.** *Physics.* Capacity for performing work. — **Syn.** See POWER. — **Ant.** Inertia.

en′er·vate (ĕn′ẽr·vāt; *formerly, & still occas.,* ē·nûr′vāt), *v. t.* [L. *enervatus,* past part. of *enervare,* fr. *enervis* nerveless, weak, fr. *e* out + *nervus* sinew.] **1.** To deprive of nerve, force, or strength. **2.** To lessen the mental or moral vigor of. — **Syn.** See UNNERVE. — (ē·nûr′vāt), *adj.* Weak; feeble. — **en′er·va′tion** (ĕn′ẽr·vā′shŭn), *n.* — **en′er·va′tor** (ĕn′ẽr·vā′tẽr), *n.*

en·face′ (ĕn·fās′), *v. t.;* see FACE. To write or print on the face of (a draft, bill, etc.). — **en·face′ment,** *n.*

‖**en fa·mille′** (äN fȧ′mē′y′). [F.] In or with (one's) family; at home.

‖**en′fant′ gâ′té′** (äN′fäN′ gȧ′tā′). [F.] A spoiled child.

‖**en′fant′ per′du′** (pĕr′dü′). [F.] Literally, a lost child; hence, a soldier sent to a very dangerous advanced post; *pl.,* a forlorn hope.

‖**en′fant′ ter′ri′ble** (tĕ′rē′bl′). [F.] A child whose inopportune remarks cause embarrassment.

‖**en′fant′ trou′vé′** (trōō′vā′). [F.] A foundling.

en·fee′ble (ĕn·fē′b′l), *v. t.;* EN·FEE′BLED (-b′ld); EN·FEE′BLING (-blĭng). [OF. *enfeblir, enfeiblir.*] To make feeble. — **Syn.** See WEAKEN. — **en·fee′ble·ment** (-mĕnt), *n.*

en·feoff′ (ĕn·fĕf′; -fēf′), *v. t.* [AF. *enfeoffer,* OF. *enfieffer.*] **1.** *Law.* To invest with a fief or fee. **2.** To give in vassalage. — **en·feoff′ment** (-mĕnt), *n.*

‖**en fête** (äN fât′). [F.] In festal dress; making a holiday showing.

en·fet′ter (ĕn·fĕt′ẽr), *v. t.* To bind in fetters; enchain.

En′field ri′fle (ĕn′fēld). [From *Enfield,* in Middlesex, Eng.] **a** A muzzle-loading rifled musket of .577-inch caliber, generally used in the British Army from 1852 to 1866 and largely by United States troops in the Civil War. **b** A .303-caliber magazine rifle of bolt type used by the British. **c** Sometimes, the United States rifle, caliber .30, model 1917, used during World War I; — so called because based upon the British Enfield rifle. See RIFLE, *Illust.*

en′fi·lade′ (ĕn′fĭ·lād′), *n.* [F., fr. *enfiler* to thread, rake with shot, fr. *en-* (fr. L. *in*) + *fil* thread, fr. L. *filum.*] *Mil.* A condition permitting the delivery of a raking fire at an objective, as a trench, line of troops, etc. — *v. t.* *Mil.* To rake, or be in a position to rake, with gunfire in the direction of the length of, as a trench.

‖**en′fin′** (äN′făN′), *adv.* [F.] In fine; briefly; in a word.

en′fleu′rage′ (äN′flû′rȧzh′), *n.* [F., fr. *en-* (fr. L. *in*) + *fleur* flower.] A process of extracting perfumes by exposing absorbents, as fixed oils, to the exhalations of flowers.

en·fold′ (ĕn·fōld′), *v. t.* To infold.

en·force′ (ĕn·fōrs′; 70), *v. t.;* see FORCE. [OF. *enforcier* to strengthen, force.] **1.** To give force to. **2.** To urge with energy. **3.** To use force upon; to assail forcibly. **4.** To force; compel. **5.** To make or gain by force. **6.** To put in force; to execute with vigor; as, to *enforce* the laws. — **en·force′a·ble,** *adj.* — **en·force′ment,** *n.* — **en·forc′er** (-fōr′sẽr), *n.*

Syn. **Enforce, implement** mean to put into effect or operation. **Enforce** is used chiefly in reference to laws or statutes and implies the exercise of executive or police power; **implement,** in current use, suggests reference to bills or acts which have been passed, policies which have been adopted, and the like, and implies the performance of such actions as will definitely put them into effect or ensure their being put into operation.

en·fran′chise (ĕn·frăn′chīz), *v. t.* [OF. *enfranchir,* fr. *en-* + *franc* free.] **1.** To set free; to liberate from slavery. **2.** To endow with a franchise; to admit to citizenship. — **en·fran′chise·ment** (-chĭz·mĕnt), *n.*

en·gage′ (ĕn·gāj′), *v. t.;* EN·GAGED′ (-gājd′); EN·GAG′ING (-gāj′ĭng). [F. *engager,* fr. *en-* (fr. L. *in*) + *gage* pledge, pawn.] **1.** *Obs.* To offer or place as security for a debt or the like. **2.** To put under pledge; to pledge. **3.** To entangle; to involve. **4.** To employ the attention and efforts of; to occupy; engross. **5.** To gain over; to win and attach. **6.** To bring to conflict; also, to join or interlock (weapons). **7.** To pledge in marriage; to betroth. **8.** To secure or bespeak the services of (a person); to hire; also, to secure or bespeak (service, aid, or the like); as, to *engage* a stateroom. **9.** *Mach.* To interlock with; as, the teeth of one gear wheel *engage* those of another. — *v. i.* **1.** To promise or pledge oneself. **2.** To embark in a business; to involve oneself. **3.** To enter into conflict; to join battle. **4.** *Mach.* To be in gear; to interlock and interact. — **Syn.** Promise, pledge, covenant.

en·gaged′ (ĕn·gājd′), *adj.* **1.** Occupied; employed. **2.** Pledged; promised, esp. in marriage. **3.** Involved; esp., involved in a hostile encounter. **4.** *Arch.* Partly embedded or bonded in, as a column in a wall. **5.** *Mach.* Being in gear; meshed.

en·gage′ment (ĕn·gāj′mĕnt), *n.* **1.** Act of engaging or state of being engaged; specif., betrothal. **2.** That which engages, as occupation, obligation, promise, etc. **3.** Specif.: **a** A promise to be present at a specified time and place. **b** Employment, esp. for a stated time. **4.** *pl. Com.* Pecuniary obligations. **5.** *Mach.* State of being in gear. **6.** *Mil.* Hostile encounter. — **Syn.** See BATTLE.

en·gag′ing (-gāj′ĭng), *adj.* Tending to draw the attention or affections; attractive. — **en·gag′ing·ly**, *adv.*

‖**en gar′çon** (äN gȧr′sôN′). [F.] As or like a bachelor.

‖**en garde** (gȧrd′). [F.] On guard.

en·gar′land (ĕn·gär′lănd), *v. t.* To encircle with a garland.

en·gen′der (ĕn·jĕn′dẽr), *v. t.* [OF. *engendrer*, fr. L. *ingenerare*, fr. *in* + *generare* to beget.] **1.** To beget. **2.** To cause to develop; to bring forth; produce; as, angry words *engender* strife. — **Syn.** Breed, generate, procreate, propagate. — *v. i.* To assume form; to come into being.

en′gine (ĕn′jĭn; *dial. or humorous*, -jīn), *n.* [OF. *engin* skill, machine, engine, fr. L. *ingenium* natural capacity, invention, fr. *in* in + the root of *gignere* to produce.] **1.** *Archaic.* Anything used to effect a purpose; any agent, means, or method. **2.** Any mechanical tool; also, machinery; esp., an instrument or machine of war or torture. **3.** *Mach.* Any machine by which physical power is applied to produce a physical effect, as one for converting heat into a more directly usable form, as torque on a crankshaft. **4.** Specif., a railroad locomotive.

en′gi·neer′ (ĕn′jĭ·nēr′), *n.* **1.** A designer or constructor of engines. **2.** *Mil. & Naval.* One of a corps of men who perform engineering work, as in building forts, bridges, etc. **3.** One versed in, or who follows as a calling, any branch of engineering. **4.** One who operates an engine. **5.** *Colloq.* One who skillfully manages or carries through some enterprise.

en′gi·neer′, *v. t.* **1.** To lay out, construct, or manage as an engineer. **2.** To guide the course of; to manage; as, to *engineer* a bill through Congress. — **Syn.** See GUIDE.

en′gi·neer′ing, *n.* **1.** Originally, the art of managing engines. **2.** Applied science concerned with utilizing inorganic products of earth, properties of matter, sources of power in nature, and physical forces for supplying human needs in the form of structures, machines, manufactured products, precision instruments, industrial organization, the means of lighting, heating, refrigeration, communication, transportation, sanitation, and public safety, and other productive work. **3.** Maneuvering; contriving.

en′gi·neer′s′ chain (ĕn′jĭ·nērz′). See CHAIN, *n.*, 4.

en′gine·ry (ĕn′jĭn·rĭ), *n.* Engines or machines in general, esp. instruments of war.

en′gi·nous (ĕn′jĭ·nŭs; ĕn·jē′-), *adj.* [OF. *engignos.*] *Obs.* Ingenious; crafty.

en·gird′ (ĕn·gûrd′), *v. t.*; see GIRD. To gird; encompass.

Eng′land·er (ĭng′glăn·dẽr), *n.* A native of England.

Eng′lish (ĭng′glĭsh), *adj.* [AS. *Englisc*, fr. *Engle*, *Angle*, Engles, Angles, whence also AS. *Engla land* the land of the Angles, *England*.] **1.** Of, pertaining to, or characteristic of England or its inhabitants or citizens. **2.** Of or belonging to the English language. — *n.* **1.** Collectively, the people of England. **2.** The language of the English, and of the people of the United States and most of the British colonies. It is commonly divided by periods into ***Anglo-Saxon, or Old English*** (about 450–1100), ***Middle English*** (about 1100–1500), and ***Modern English*** (from about 1500). See INDO-EUROPEAN LANGUAGES, *Table*. **3.** The English pronunciation, vocabulary, syntax, style, etc., of a locality, or a person; as, American *English*. **4.** An English translation or rendering, as of a foreign word. **5.** [*sometimes not cap.*] *U. S. Billiards, etc.* A spinning or rotary motion round the vertical axis given to a ball by striking it to the right or left of its center. **6.** *Print.* A size of type (14 points). See TYPE, *n.* — *v. t.* **1.** To translate into English. **2.** [*sometimes not cap.*] *U. S. Billiards.* To impart English to (a ball).

English daisy. The daisy *Bellis perennis.* See DAISY, 1.

English horn. *Music.* A double-reed wood-wind instrument similar to the oboe but a fifth lower in pitch.

Eng′lish·ism (ĭng′glĭsh·ĭz′m), *n.* **1.** A quality, characteristic, or mode of procedure peculiar to the English. **2.** A form of expression peculiar to English as spoken in England. **3.** Attachment to that which is English.

English ivy. See IVY.

Eng′lish·man (ĭng′glĭsh·măn), *n.* A native or a citizen of England. — **Eng′lish·wom′an** (-wo͝om′ăn), *n.*

Eng′lish·man's tie (-mănz). See KNOT, *Illust.* (36).

English Pale. See PALE, *n.*, 4.

English Revolution. See REVOLUTION, 5.

Eng′lish·ry (ĭng′glĭsh·rĭ), *n.* **1.** State or fact of being of English birth. **2.** *Hist.* People of English descent, esp. in Ireland.

English setter. See SETTER.

English sparrow. See SPARROW, 1.

English toy spaniel. See SPANIEL.

English wintergreen. See WINTERGREEN.

English yew. See YEW, *n.*, 1.

en·glut′ (ĕn·glŭt′), *v. t.*; see GLUT. [F. *engloutir*, fr. LL. *ingluttire*. See 1st EN-; GLUT to swallow.] To swallow or gulp down.

en·gorge′ (ĕn·gôrj′), *v. t. & i.*; see GORGE. [F. *engorger* to cram, in OF. also to devour, gorge. See GORGE, *n.*] To gorge; glut; devour; specif., *Med.*, to fill or congest, as a vein with blood. — **en·gorge′ment**, *n.*

en·graft′ (ĕn·grȧft′; 9), *v. t.* To insert, as a scion of one tree in another for propagation; to graft.

en·grail′ (ĕn·grāl′), *v. t.* [F. *engrêler.*] To ornament, esp. with a pattern indented on the edge.

en·grain′ (ĕn·grān′), *v. t.* [ME. *engreynen* to dye scarlet, fr. OF. *en graine*, fr. *graine* seed, kermes; now confused with E. *grain* texture.] **1.** *Archaic.* To dye in grain, or of a fast color. **2.** To incorporate with the grain or texture; to infuse deeply; — chiefly in *past part.* The spelling of the finite forms of the verb is *engrain*, but in the past part. and part. adj. the spelling *ingrained* is now commoner. — **Syn.** See INFUSE.

en′gram (ĕn′grăm), *n.* **1.** *Biol.* A permanent impression left on protoplasm as the result of a stimulus. **2.** *Psychol.* A lasting trace left in an organism by psychic experience.

en·grave′ (ĕn·grāv′), *v. t.* [*en-* + *grave* to carve, after OF. *engraver.*] **1.** To impress deeply; to infix, as if with a graver. **2.** To carve figures, letters, or devices upon. **3.** To form by incisions upon wood, stone, metal, or the like, esp. for printing; also, to print by means of a plate so formed. — **en·grav′er** (-grāv′ẽr), *n.*

en·grav′ing (-grāv′ĭng), *n.* **1.** The act or art of producing upon hard material incised or (by extension) raised patterns, characters, lines, etc., esp. on metal or wood. **2.** That which is engraved; an engraved plate or block. **3.** An impression from an engraved plate or block; a print.

en·gross′ (ĕn·grōs′), *v. t.* [From F. *en-* (fr. L. *in*) + *gros* gross, *grosse*, n., an engrossed document, writing in large letters, and fr. OF. *engroissier* to make thick, or gross.] **1.** To copy or write in a large hand; to write a fair copy of, as of a statute. **2.** To buy quantities of (commodities), so as to control the market and so make a monopoly profit. **3.** Hence, to concentrate in one's possession; to take the whole of. — **en·gross′er** (-ẽr), *n.*

en·grossed′ (-grōst′), *adj.* Monopolized; absorbed; fully occupied. — **Syn.** See INTENT.

en·gross′ing (-grōs′ĭng), *adj.* Monopolizing; absorbing. — **en·gross′ing·ly**, *adv.*

en·gross′ment (-mĕnt), *n.* **1.** Act of engrossing, in writing or by purchase; also, that which has been engrossed. **2.** State of being engrossed, or absorbed.

en·gulf′ (ĕn·gŭlf′), *v. t.* To swallow up as in a gulf; to plunge into or as if into a gulf.

en·hance′ (ĕn·hȧns′; 9), *v. t. & i.*; EN·HANCED′ (-hȧnst′); EN·HANC′ING (-hȧn′sĭng). [AF. *enhauncer*, *enhaucer*, for OF. *enhalcier*, fr. VL. *in* + *altiare*, fr. L. *altus* high.] To advance, augment, or elevate; to make or become greater, as in value or desirability. — **Syn.** See INTENSIFY. — **en·hance′ment**, *n.*

en′har·mon′ic (ĕn′här·mŏn′ĭk), *adj.* [LL. *enharmonicus*, fr. Gr. *enarmonikos*, *enarmonios*, fitting, accordant, fr. *en* in + *harmonia* harmony.] *Music.* **a** Pertaining to a change of notes to the eye where a keyed instrument can mark no difference to the ear, as the substitution of A♭ for G♯; as, an *enharmonic* interval. **b** Pertaining to a scale of perfect intonation which recognizes all the notes and intervals that result from the exact tuning of diatonic scales and their transposition into other keys; as, the *enharmonic* scale. — **en′har·mon′i·cal·ly** (-ĭ·kăl·ĭ), *adv.*

e·nig′ma (ē·nĭg′mȧ), *n.*; *pl.* -MAS (-mȧz). [L. *aenigma*, fr. Gr. *ainigma*, fr. *ainissesthai* to speak darkly, fr. *ainos* tale, fable.] **1.** An obscure saying; a riddle. **2.** Anything inexplicable; also, an inscrutable person. — **Syn.** See MYSTERY.

e′nig·mat′ic (ē′nĭg·măt′ĭk; ĕn′ĭg-), **e′nig·mat′i·cal** (-ĭ·kăl), *adj.* Relating to, or resembling, an enigma; inexplicable; puzzling. — **Syn.** See OBSCURE. — **e′nig·mat′i·cal·ly**, *adv.*

en·isle′ (ĕn·īl′), *v. t.*; -ISLED (-īld′); -ISL′ING (-īl′ĭng). To place apart, as on an island; also, to make an island of.

en·jamb′ment, en·jambe′ment (ĕn·jămb′mĕnt; ĕn·jăm′-; *F.* äN′zhäNb′mäN′), *n.* [F. *enjambement*, fr. *enjamber* to stride, encroach.] *Pros.* The running over of a sentence from one line into another, so that closely related words fall in different lines.

en·join′ (ĕn·join′), *v. t.* [OF. *enjoindre*, fr. L. *injungere* to join into, charge, fr. *in* + *jungere* to join.] **1.** To command; to admonish or direct with authority. **2.** To forbid; prohibit. — **Syn.** See COMMAND. — **en·join′er** (-ẽr), *n.*

en·joy′ (ĕn·joi′), *v. t.* [OF. *enjoir* to enjoy, fr. *en-* (fr. L. *in*) + *joir* to enjoy, fr. L. *gaudere.*] **1.** To have satisfaction in experiencing, possessing, etc. **2.** To have possession or use of; to have the benefit of. — **en·joy′a·ble** (-ȧ·b'l), *adj.* — **en·joy′a·ble·ness**, *n.* — **en·joy′a·bly** (-blĭ), *adv.*

en·joy′ment (-mĕnt), *n.* **1.** Action or state of enjoying anything; possession and use. **2.** Something which is enjoyed. — **Syn.** See PLEASURE.

en·kin′dle (ĕn·kĭn′d'l), *v. t. & i.*; see KINDLE. To kindle. — **en·kin′dler** (-dlẽr), *n.*

en·lace′ (ĕn·lās′), *v. t.*; see LACE. [OF. *enlacer.*] **1.** To lace; to encircle or enfold. **2.** To entangle; to entwine. **3.** To cover as with lace. — **en·lace′ment**, *n.*

en·large′ (ĕn·lärj′), *v. t. & i.*; -LARGED′ (-lärjd′); -LARG′ING (-lär′jĭng). [OF. *enlargier*, fr. *en-* (fr. L. *in*) + *large* wide.] To make or grow larger; to increase in size, capacity, or extent; extend; expand; also, to elaborate; expatiate; as, to *enlarge* upon a theme. — **Syn.** See INCREASE. — **en·larg′er** (-lär′jẽr), *n.*

en·large′ment (-mĕnt), *n.* **1.** Act or instance of enlarging, or state of being enlarged; also, that which is enlarged. **2.** *Photog.* A print larger than the negative, made by projecting through a lens an image of the negative upon a photographic printing surface.

en·light′en (ĕn·līt′'n), *v. t.* **1.** *Archaic.* To supply with light. **2.** To shed the light of truth and knowledge upon; to free from ignorance, error, etc.; inform. **3.** To supply with spiritual light; to give insight to. — **en·light′en·er** (-'n·ẽr), *n.*

en·light′en·ment (-mĕnt), *n.* **1.** Act or means of enlightening; state of being enlightened. **2.** [*cap.*, with *the.*] A philosophic movement of the 18th century, characterized by a lively questioning of authority, much theorizing in the sphere of politics, and emphasis on empirical method in science.

en·list′ (ĕn·lĭst′), *v. t.* **1.** To engage for military or naval service, usually for a definite period of time. **2.** To list, as in a class or category. **3.** To secure the support or aid of; as, to *enlist* one in a cause. — *v. i.* To enroll and bind oneself for military or naval service, usually for a definite period of time. — **en·list′ment**, *n.*

en·list′ed man (-lĭs′tĕd; -tĭd). In the United States service, a private, seaman, or marine, or noncommissioned officer, as distinguished from a warrant or commissioned officer, the latter two not being technically *enlisted*.

en·liv′en (ĕn·lĭv′ĕn), *v. t.* [*en-* + *live*, adj., or *life*, n.] To give life, action, vigor, spirit, or vivacity to; animate. — **Syn.** See QUICKEN. — **en·liv′en·er** (-ẽr), *n.*

en masse (ĕn măs′; *F.* äN mȧs′). [F.] In mass; in a body.

en·mesh′ (ĕn·mĕsh′), *v. t.* To entangle in or as in meshes.

en′mi·ty (ĕn′mĭ·tĭ), *n.*; *pl.* -TIES (-tĭz). [OF. *enemistié*. See ENEMY.] Ill will on one side or on both; hatred; esp., mutual antagonism.

Syn. **Enmity, hostility, antipathy, antagonism, animosity, rancor, animus** mean intense dislike or ill will. **Enmity** suggests positive hatred which may be open or concealed or dormant; **hostility** suggests active and, often, open enmity showing itself in warfare, in attacks, and the like; **antipathy** and **antagonism** imply a constitutional basis for one's hatred or dislike, *antipathy* suggesting repugnance, and *antagonism* a mood which stresses a clash of temperaments and easily breaks into hostility; **animosity** and **rancor** suggest intense anger or bitterness that threaten to kindle hostilities; **animus** adds to *animosity* the implication of violent prejudice or ill will. — **Ant.** Amity.

en'ne·ad (ĕn'ē·ăd), *n.* [Gr. *enneas, -ados*, fr. *ennea* nine.] A group of nine, esp. [*cap.*], *Egypt. Relig.*, of nine gods.

en·no'ble (ĕ·nō'b'l; ĕn·nō'-), *v. t.;* EN·NO'BLED (-b'ld); EN·NO'BLING (-blĭng). **1.** To make noble; to elevate. **2.** To raise to the nobility. — **en·no'ble·ment,** *n.* — **en·no'bler** (-blẽr), *n.*

en'nui (än'wē; *F.* äN'nwē'), *n.; pl.* ENNUIS (än'wēz; *F.* äN'nwē'). [F. See ANNOY.] A feeling of weariness and dissatisfaction; tedium; boredom.

‖**en'nuy'é'** (äN'nwē'yā'), *adj. masc.*, ‖**en'nuy'ée'** (-yā'), *fem.* [F., past part. of *ennuyer.*] Affected with ennui. — *n.* One affected with ennui.

E'noch (ē'nŭk), *n.* [Gr. *Enōch*, fr. Heb. *Ḥanōkh.*] *Bib.* **a** A patriarch who "walked with God." See *Gen.* v. 24. **b** A son of Cain.

e·norm' (ē·nôrm'), *adj.* [F. *énorme.*] *Archaic.* Enormous.

e·nor'mi·ty (ē·nôr'mĭ·tĭ), *n.; pl.* -TIES (-tĭz). [F. *énormité*, fr. L. *enormitas*, fr. *enormis* enormous. See ENORMOUS.] State or quality of being enormous; esp., exceeding wickedness; also, an outrageous act or offense.

e·nor'mous (ē·nôr'mŭs), *adj.* [L. *enormis*, fr. *e* out + *norma* rule.] **1.** Greatly exceeding the norm, rule, or measure; inordinate; hence, atrocious; outrageous; as, *enormous* offenses. **2.** Greatly exceeding the usual size, number, or degree; huge; immense. — **e·nor'mous·ly,** *adv.* — **e·nor'mous·ness,** *n.*

Syn. **Enormous, immense, huge, vast, gigantic, colossal, mammoth** mean exceedingly large or big. **Enormous** suggests an exceeding of all bounds not only in size or amount but in degree; **immense** implies a size, an extent, an amount, or a degree greatly exceeding ordinary measurements or standards, without, however, suggesting abnormality or monstrousness; **huge** usually suggests immensity of bulk; **vast** usually suggests immensity of extent; **gigantic** implies comparison, literally or figuratively, with the size, prowess, or activities of a giant; **colossal** suggests stupendousness or incredibility in something that is large or big; **mammoth** suggests not only the hugeness but the ponderousness characteristic of the mammoth, an extinct and enormous elephant.

e·nough' (ē·nŭf'), *adj.* [AS. *genōh, genōg*, adj. & adv.] Satisfying desire; giving content; sufficient; ample. — **Syn.** See SUFFICIENT. — *adv.* **1.** In a degree or quantity that satisfies; sufficiently. **2.** Hence: **a** Fully; quite; as, ready *enough* to go. **b** Tolerably; as, she sings well *enough.* — *n.* A sufficiency. — *interj.* Short for *it is enough.*

e·nounce' (ē·nouns'), *v. t.;* E·NOUNCED' (-nounst'); E·NOUNC'ING (-noun'sĭng). [F. *énoncer*, fr. L. *enuntiare*, fr. *e* out + *nuntiare* to announce, fr. *nuntius* messenger.] **1.** To set forth, as a proposition or argument; state formally or publicly. **2.** To utter; enunciate; pronounce.

e·now' (ē·nou'; *archaic* -nō'), *adj. & adv. Archaic.* Enough.

‖**en pas'sant'** (äN pä'säN'). [F.] In passing; in the course of any procedure; — said specif., *Chess*, of the taking of an adverse pawn, which has just made a first move of two squares, by a pawn already so advanced as to threaten the first of these squares. The pawn which takes *en passant* is advanced to the threatened square.

en'phy·tot'ic (ĕn'fī·tŏt'ĭk), *adj.* [2d *en-* + Gr. *phyton* a plant.] *Bot.* Occurring regularly among the plants of a district, as certain fungous diseases. Cf. ENDEMIC, EPIPHYTOTIC.

en·plane' (ĕn·plān'), *v. i.* To board an airplane.

‖**en plein air** (äN plĕ'·nâr'). [F.] In the open air.

‖**en plein jour** (pläN' zhōōr'). [F.] In open day; hence, without concealment.

‖**en prise** (prēz'). [F.] *Chess.* Exposed to capture.

‖**en queue** (kû'). [F.] Literally, as a tail; hence, behind; in pursuit; also, in a line.

en·quire' (ĕn·kwīr'), **en·quir'y,** etc. Vars. of INQUIRE, etc.

en·rage' (ĕn·rāj'), *v. t. & i.;* see RAGE. [F. *enrager* to be enraged.] To fill with rage; madden.

‖**en rap'port'** (äN rȧ'pôr'). [F.] In or into close or harmonious relations.

en·rapt' (ĕn·răpt'), *adj.* Rapt; enraptured.

en·rap'ture (-răp'tūr), *v. t.* To transport or delight beyond measure; to throw into ecstasy.

en·rav'ish (ĕn·răv'ĭsh), *v. t.* To enrapture.

en·reg'is·ter (-rĕj'ĭs·tẽr), *v. t.* To register; enroll.

‖**en rè'gle** (äN râ'gl'). [F.] According to rule; in due form.

‖**en re·vanche'** (äNr'vänsh'). [F.] In return or compensation.

en·rich' (ĕn·rĭch'), *v. t.* [OF. *enrichir.*] **1.** To make rich or richer. **2.** To ornament; adorn. **3.** To fertilize (soil). **4.** To improve (a food) in nutritive value by addition in processing of vitamins and minerals. — **en·rich'er,** *n.* — **en·rich'ment,** *n.*

en·robe' (ĕn·rōb'), *v. t.* To invest or adorn with a robe.

en·roll', en·rol' (ĕn·rōl'), *v. t.;* EN·ROLLED' (-rōld'); EN·ROLL'ING. [OF. *enroller* (F. *enrôler*).] **1.** To insert in a roll, list, or catalogue; hence, to record; also, reflexively, to enlist. **2.** To engross (a document). **3.** To roll, coil, or wrap up. — **en·roll'er,** *n.* — **en·roll'ment, en·rol'ment,** *n.*

en·root' (ĕn·rōōt'), *v. t.* To fix by the root; implant deep.

en route (än rōōt'; *F.* äN). [F.] On or along the way.

‖**ens** (ĕnz), *n.; pl.* ENTIA (ĕn'shĭ·ȧ). [ML. *ens, entis*, a thing.] *Philos.* Being, in the most abstract sense, as having existence without or within the mind.

en·sam'ple (ĕn·sȧm'p'l; 9), *n.* [OF. *ensample*, for *essample.* See EXAMPLE.] *Archaic.* An example; a pattern.

en·san'guine (ĕn·săng'gwĭn), *v. t.* To make bloody.

en·sconce' (ĕn·skŏns'), *v. t.;* EN·SCONCED' (-skŏnst'); EN·SCONC'ING (-skŏn'sĭng). [*en-* + *sconce* a fortification.] **1.** To shelter or hide. **2.** To settle comfortably or snugly.

en·sem'ble (än·sŏm'b'l; än'sŏm'b'l; *F.* äN'säN'bl'), *adv.* [F.] All at once; together. — *n.* **1.** A whole; all the parts together or the total effect produced by them. **2.** Specif.: **a** *Music.* The united performance of all voices and instruments rendering concerted music. **b** A complete costume, the pieces of which match or harmonize.

‖**en'se pe'tit pla'ci·dam sub li'ber·ta'te qui·e'tem** (ĕn'sē pē'tĭt plăs'ĭ·dăm sŭb lĭb'ẽr·tā'tē kwī·ē'tĕm). [L.] With the sword she seeks calm repose under liberty; — motto of Massachusetts.

en·sep'ul·cher, en·sep'ul·chre (ĕn·sĕp'ŭl·kẽr), *v. t.* To entomb.

en·shrine' (ĕn·shrīn'), *v. t.* To enclose in, or as in, a shrine; hence, to cherish as sacred. — **en·shrine'ment** (-mĕnt), *n.*

en·shroud' (ĕn·shroud'), *v. t.* To put in or as in a shroud.

en'si·form (ĕn'sĭ·fôrm), *adj.* [L. *ensis* sword + *-form.*] Sword-shaped, as a leaf. See LEAF, *Illust.* (5).

en'sign (ĕn'sīn; *also, esp. in sense* 4, ĕn'sĭn), *n.* [OF. *enseigne*, fr. L. *insignia*, pl. neut. of *insignis* distinguished, fr. *in* + *signum* mark, sign.] **1.** A flag; a banner; esp., the national flag, or a banner indicating nationality. **2.** *Obs.* A signal. **3.** Sign; badge of office, rank, or power. **4.** (*Army and navy pron. usually* ĕn'sĭn) *Mil. & Nav.* **a** In the British Army previous to 1871, a commissioned officer serving as standard-bearer. **b** The lowest commissioned officer in the United States Navy, ranking below a lieutenant, junior grade. — **en'sign·cy, en'sign·ship,** *n.*

en'si·lage (ĕn'sĭ·lĭj), *n.* [F.] The process of preserving fodder in a silo; also, fodder thus preserved.

en·sile' (ĕn·sīl'; ĕn'sīl), *v. t.* [F. *ensiler*, fr. *en-* (fr. L. *in*) + *silo*, fr. Sp. *silo.*] To store (fodder) in a silo.

en·slave' (ĕn·slāv'), *v. t.* To make a slave or slaves of. — **en·slave'ment,** *n.* — **en·slav'er** (-slāv'ẽr), *n.*

en·snare' (ĕn·snâr'), *v. t.* To snare; entrap. — **Syn.** See CATCH.

en·sor'cell, en·sor'cel (ĕn·sôr'sĕl), *v. t.* [OF. *ensorceler.* See SORCERY.] To bewitch; enchant.

en·soul', in·soul' (ĕn·sōl', ĭn-), *v. t.* To endue or imbue with a soul; animate; also, to receive or put in the soul.

en·sphere' (ĕn·sfēr'), *v. t.* To place in a sphere; encircle.

en·sue' (ĕn·sū'; 114), *v. t.* [OF. *ensuivre*, past part. *enseu*, deriv. of L. *insequi*, fr. *in* + *sequi* to follow.] To follow; pursue; seek after. — *v. i.* To follow; to come afterwards or as a consequence; as, silence *ensued.* — **Syn.** See FOLLOW. — **en·su'ing·ly** (-sū'ĭng·lĭ), *adv.*

‖**en suite** (äN swēt'). [F.] In a succession, series, or set; connected with one another; as, rooms *en suite.*

en·sure' (ĕn·shōōr'; 84), *v. t.* [AF. *enseurer.*] **1.** *Now Rare.* **a** To give assurance to. **b** To insure. **2.** To make sure or certain; guarantee; as, to *ensure* the rule of the majority.

Syn. **Ensure, insure, assure, secure** mean to make a person or thing sure. **Ensure** always implies a making certain and inevitable (as, this treatment will *ensure* his recovery); **insure,** really a variant of *ensure*, is not restricted to this sense, for its technical meaning (to indemnify against loss) has affected its more general use so that it sometimes implies a making secure or protected (as, to take measures to *insure* plants against freezing); **assure** is the preferred word when it takes a personal object and implies a making sure by removing all doubt or suspense (as, to *assure* one that he cannot fail); **secure** implies the performance of an act or the like that assures one of safety or protection against contingencies (as, he needs a good income to *secure* him against poverty in his old age).

en·swathe', in·swathe' (ĕn·swāth', ĭn-), *v. t.* To swathe; envelop. — **en·swathe'ment** (-mĕnt), *n.*

ent-. = ENTO-.

-ent (-ĕnt). [F. and L.; F. *-ent*, fr. L. *-entem.*] A suffix forming adjectives and nouns of agency. See -ANT.

en·tab'la·ture (ĕn·tăb'lȧ·tūr), *n.* [MF., fr. It. *intavolatura* ceiling, fr. *in* + *tavola* board, tablet, fr. L. *tabula.*] *Arch.* The upper section of a wall or story, generally supported on columns or pilasters. In classical orders it consists of architrave, frieze, and cornice. See ORDER, *Illust.*

en·ta'ble·ment (ĕn·tā'b'l·mĕnt), *n.* [F., fr. L. *tabulamentum* boarding.] **1.** Entablature. **2.** The platform or platforms supporting a statue and above the dado.

en·tail' (ĕn·tāl'), *v. t.* **1.** *Law.* To settle, as lands, inalienably on a person and his descendants. **2.** To impose or involve as a necessary accompaniment or result; as, the work *entails* expense. — *n.* An entailing or an entailed estate; also, the rule by which the descent is fixed. — **en·tail'ment,** *n.*

en'ta·moe'ba (ĕn'tȧ·mē'bȧ), *n.; pl.* -BAE (-bē), -BAS (-bȧz). Also **en'ta·me'ba.** [NL.] An endamoeba. — **en'ta·moe'bic, en'ta·me'bic** (-bĭk), *adj.*

en·tan'gle (ĕn·tăng'g'l), *v. t.;* see TANGLE. **1.** To make tangled, complicated, or confused. **2.** To involve in a tangle. — **en·tan'gle·ment,** *n.* — **en·tan'gler** (-glẽr), *n.*

en·tel'e·chy (ĕn·tĕl'ē·kĭ), *n.; pl.* -CHIES (-kĭz). [L. *entelechia*, fr. Gr. *entelecheia*, fr. *en telei echein* to be complete.] *Philos.* **a** The realization of that which a thing is by virtue of its form; actual, as contrasted with mere potential, existence. **b** Among vitalists, the nonmechanical agency responsible for the phenomena of life and growth.

en·tel'lus (ĕn·tĕl'ŭs), *n.* [NL.] An East Indian long-tailed monkey (*Presbytis entellus*).

en'tente' (äN'täNt'), *n.* [F.] Understanding; an agreement, based on conventions or declarations; also, the parties to such an understanding or agreement.

en'tente' cor'diale' (kôr'dyȧl'). Cordial understanding; specif. [*caps.*], an agreement between France and Great Britain (1904), later (1907) expanded into the ***Triple Entente*** by the inclusion of Russia.

en'ter (ĕn'tẽr), *v. i.* [OF. *entrer*, fr. L. *intrare.*] **1.** To go or come in to a place or condition; make or effect an entrance. **2.** To make a beginning; start; as, to *enter* upon a career or into society. **3.** To go (into) as a part, party, or participant; to take part or form a part; as, to *enter* into a discussion; tin *enters* into the composition of pewter. **4.** *Law.* To go in (upon lands) as owner; to take possession. — *v. t.* **1.** To come or go into. **2.** To make a beginning or start in; take up. **3.** To cause to go, or to be received (into); to effect the penetration, insertion, admission, etc., of; as, to *enter* a boy in college. **4.** To inscribe; enroll; record. **5.** To train in the rudiments or first steps. **6.** To join as a member; also, to become a participant in. **7.** To make report of (a vessel or her cargo) at the customhouse. **8.** *Law.* To place in regular form before the court.

Syn. **Enter, penetrate, pierce, probe** mean to make way into something. **Enter,** the most general and least explicit of these words, may imply either going in or forcing a way in, but without a context it offers no clear clue; **penetrate** carries a strong implication of an impelling force or of a compelling power that makes for entrance; **pierce** adds to *penetrate* a clear implication of running through with or as if with a sharp-pointed instrument; **probe** more clearly implies an investigating or exploring something beyond the surface by, or more often, as if by, a surgeon's probe, a long narrow instrument used in examining cavities, hidden wounds, etc.

en′ter- (ĕn′tẽr-). = ENTERO-, as in **en′ter·al′gi·a, en′ter·ec′to·my, en′ter·i′tis** (see -ALGIA, -ECTOMY, -ITIS).
en·ter′ic (ĕn·tĕr′ĭk), *adj.* [Gr. *enterikos.*] Of or pertaining to the enteron, or alimentary canal; intestinal.
enteric fever. Typhoid fever.
en′ter·o- (ĕn′tẽr·ō-), **en′ter-.** [Gr. *enteron.*] A combining form meaning *intestine*, as in **en′ter·ol′o·gy, en′ter·os′to·my, en′ter·ot′o·my** (see -LOGY, -STOMY, -TOMY).
en′ter·on (ĕn′tẽr·ŏn), *n.* [NL., fr. Gr. *enteron* an intestine.] The alimentary, or enteric, canal or cavity.
en′ter·prise (ĕn′tẽr·prīz), *n.* [OF. *entreprise*, fr. *entreprendre* to undertake, fr. *entre* between (fr. L. *inter*) + *prendre* to take.] **1.** An undertaking, esp. one which involves activity, courage, energy, or the like; an important or daring project; a venture. **2.** The character or disposition that leads one to attempt the difficult, the untried, etc.
en′ter·pris′er (-prīz′ẽr), *n.* One who undertakes enterprises; specif., an entrepreneur (which see).
en′ter·pris′ing (-prīz′ĭng), *adj.* Given to or characterized by enterprise. — **en′ter·pris′ing·ly,** *adv.*
en′ter·tain′ (ĕn′tẽr·tān′), *v. t.* [OF. *entretenir*, fr. *entre* between (fr. L. *inter*) + *tenir* to hold, fr. L. *tenere.*] **1.** *Now Rare.* **a** To maintain; keep up. **b** To retain, as in service. **c** To give reception to; to receive. **2.** To receive and provide for, esp. in one's home; have as guests. **3.** To receive into or keep in the mind; to consider or dwell upon; as, to *entertain* an idea; also, to harbor; cherish, as a grudge. **4.** To engage the attention of agreeably; amuse; divert. — *v. i.* To provide entertainment, esp. for guests. — **Syn.** See AMUSE. — **en′ter·tain′er,** *n.*
en′ter·tain′ing, *adj.* Affording entertainment; diverting. — **en′ter·tain′ing·ly,** *adv.* — **en′ter·tain′ing·ness,** *n.*
en′ter·tain′ment (-mĕnt), *n.* **1.** Act of entertaining. **2.** *Obs.* State or cost of being entertained, esp. in service; maintenance. **3.** Hospitable provision for a guest. **4.** That which entertains; specif., a performance intended to entertain, amuse, divert, etc.
en·thal′py (ĕn·thăl′pĭ; ĕn′thăl·pĭ), *n.* [Gr. *enthalpein* to warm in.] *Physics.* The sum of the internal and external energies of a fluid system; thermodynamic potential at constant pressure.
en·thet′ic (ĕn·thĕt′ĭk), *adj.* [Gr. *enthetikos* fit to insert.] *Med.* Caused by an implanted morbific virus.
en·thrall′, en·thral′ (ĕn·thrôl′), *v. t.*; -THRALLED′ (-thrôld′); -THRALL′ING. To hold in or reduce to thralldom; hence, to hold spellbound; captivate. — **en·thrall′er,** *n.* — **en·thrall′ing·ly,** *adv.* — **en·thrall′ment, en·thral′ment,** *n.*
en·throne′ (ĕn·thrōn′), *v. t.* To seat on a throne; hence: **a** To invest with sovereignty. **b** To install (a bishop) in his see. — **en·throne′ment,** *n.*
en·thron′ize (ĕn·thrōn′īz), *v. t.* To enthrone, esp. a bishop. — **en·thron′i·za′tion** (-ĭ·zā′shŭn; -ī·zā′-), *n.*
en·thuse′ (ĕn·thūz′), *v. t. & i. Colloq.* To make, or become, enthusiastic.
en·thu′si·asm (ĕn·thū′zĭ·ăz′m; 114), *n.* [Gr. *enthousiasmos*, fr. *enthousiazein* to be inspired or possessed by the god, fr. *entheos*, *enthous*, inspired. See 2d EN-; THEISM.] **1.** *Hist.* Divine inspiration or possession. **2.** *Archaic.* Ecstasy; transport. **3.** Ardent zeal or interest; fervor. **4.** An instance, or an object or cause, of such interest. — **Syn.** See INSPIRATION; PASSION.
en·thu′si·ast (-ăst), *n.* One actuated by enthusiasm.
en·thu′si·as′tic (-ăs′tĭk), *adj.* Also **-ti·cal** (-tĭ·kăl). Filled with, or characterized by, enthusiasm; ardent. — **en·thu′si·as′ti·cal·ly,** *adv.*
en′thy·meme (ĕn′thĭ·mēm), *n.* [L. *enthymema*, fr. Gr. *enthymēma*, fr. *enthymeisthai* to keep in mind, consider, fr. *en* in + *thymos* mind.] *Logic.* An argument in which one of the propositions, usually a premise, is understood but not stated.
en·tice′ (ĕn·tīs′), *v. t.*; -TICED′ (-tīst′); -TIC′ING (-tīs′ĭng). [OF. *enticier*, fr. L. *in* + *titio* firebrand.] To draw on by exciting hope or desire; allure; attract; often, in a bad sense, to tempt; seduce. — **Syn.** See LURE. — **en·tice′ment,** *n.* — **en·tic′er** (-tīs′ẽr), *n.* — **en·tic′ing·ly,** *adv.*
en·tire′ (ĕn·tīr′), *adj.* [OF. *entier*, fr. L. *integer* untouched, entire.] **1.** Complete in all parts; undiminished; unimpaired; whole. **2.** *Chiefly Bot.* Consisting of one piece; undivided; specif., of a leaf, having the margin continuous; not incised, dentate, serrate, etc. **3.** Without mixture or alloy; unqualified. **4.** Not gelded; — of male animals. — **Syn.** See WHOLE; PERFECT. — *n.* **1.** Entirely; the whole. **2.** *Brewing, Eng.* Porter. — **en·tire′ly,** *adv.* — **en·tire′ness,** *n.*
en·tire′ty (ĕn·tīr′tĭ; ĕn·tī′rĕ·tĭ), *n.*; *pl.* -TIES (-tĭz). Entireness; completeness; also, that which is entire; sum total.
en·ti′tle (ĕn·tī′t'l), *v. t.*; -TI′TLED (-t'ld); -TI′TLING (-tlĭng). [AF. *entitler*, OF. *entituler*, fr. LL. *intitulare.*] **1.** To give a title to; hence, to dignify by an honorary designation; style; call. **2.** To give a right, legal title, or claim to; to qualify (one) for; as, his knowledge *entitles* him to speak.
en′ti·ty (ĕn′tĭ·tĭ), *n.*; *pl.* -TIES (-tĭz). [ML. *entitas*, fr. *ens*, *entis*, thing, fr. L. *ens*, pres. part. of *esse* to be.] A being; esp., a thing which has reality and distinctness of being either in fact or for thought; as, to view the state as an *entity*.
en′to- (ĕn′tō-), **ent-.** [Gr. *entos* within.] A combining form signifying *within*, *inner*, as in **en′to·cra′ni·al, ent·op′tic, ent·o′tic.**
en′to·blast (ĕn′tō·blăst), *n. Biol.* **a** The endoderm. **b** A blastomere forming endoderm. — **en′to·blas′tic** (-blăs′tĭk), *adj.*
en′to·derm (-dûrm), *n.* Endoderm. — **en′to·der′mal** (-dûr′măl), **en′to·der′mic** (-mĭk), *adj.*
en·toil′ (ĕn·toil′), *v. t.* To take with toils; to ensnare.
en·tomb′ (ĕn·tōōm′), *v. t.* [F. *entomber.*] To deposit in a tomb; bury; also, to serve as a tomb for. — **en·tomb′ment** (-mĕnt), *n.*
en′to·mo- (ĕn′tō·mō-). [Gr. *entomon.*] A combining form meaning *insect*, as in **en′to·moph′a·gous,** insectivorous.
en′to·mol′o·gize (ĕn′tō·mŏl′ō·jīz), *v. i.*; EN′TO·MOL′O·GIZED (-jīzd); EN′TO·MOL′O·GIZ′ING (-jīz′ĭng). To study entomology; to collect insects for study.
en′to·mol′o·gy (ĕn′tō·mŏl′ō·jĭ), *n.*; *pl.* -GIES (-jĭz). [Gr. *entomon* insect (so called because nearly cut in two, fr. *entomos* cut in, fr. *en* in + *temnein* to cut) + *-logy.*] Zoology that treats of insects; also, a treatise on this subject. — **en′to·mo·log′ic** (-mō·lŏj′ĭk), **en′to·mo·log′i·cal** (-ĭ·kăl), *adj.* — **en′to·mo·log′i·cal·ly,** *adv.* — **en′to·mol′o·gist** (-mŏl′ō·jĭst), *n.*
en′to·mos′tra·can (-mŏs′trȧ·kăn), *adj.* [NL., fr. *entomo-* + Gr. *ostrakon* shell.] *Zool.* Belonging to a primary division of crustaceans including the branchiopods, copepods, cirripeds, etc., which are of comparatively simple organization and usually of small, often minute, size. — *n.* An entomostracan crustacean.
en′to·phyte (ĕn′tō·fīt), *n.* [*ento-* + *-phyte.*] A plant living within an animal or another plant. Cf. ENDOPHYTE. — **en′to·phyt′ic** (-fĭt′ĭk), *adj.*
en′tou·rage′ (än′tōō·räzh′; *F.* äN′tōō′räzh′), *n.* [F.] Surroundings; specif., one's attendants or associates.
en·tr′acte′ (än·trăkt′; *F.* äN′trȧkt′), *n.* [F.] *Theater.* **a** The interval between two acts. **b** A dance, piece of music, or interlude performed between two acts.
en′trails (ĕn′trĕlz; ĕn′trālz), *n. pl.* [OF. *entrailles*, fr. LL. *intralia*, fr. *intranea*, fr. L. *interaneum* intestine, fr. *interaneus* inward, fr. *inter* within.] Internal parts; specif., bowels; guts; viscera.
en·train′ (ĕn·trān′), *v. t. & i.* To put or go aboard a train.
en·train′, *v. t.* [F. *entraîner.*] To draw along in its train; specif., *Chem.*, to carry along or over (esp. mechanically), as in precipitation or distillation.
en′trance (ĕn′trăns), *n.* [OF., fr. *entrer* to enter. See ENTER.] **1.** Act of entering; entry; ingress; figuratively, induction, debut, or the like. **2.** A door, gate, or way at which one enters. **3.** Power or permission to enter; admittance. **4.** The point at which a performer enters or begins, as in a play.
en·trance′ (ĕn·trȧns′; 9), *v. t.*; EN·TRANCED′ (-trȧnst′); EN·TRANC′ING (-trȧn′sĭng). To put into a trance or ecstasy; to carry away with delight, wonder, or rapture. — **en·trance′ment,** *n.* — **en·tranc′ing·ly,** *adv.*
en′trant (ĕn′trănt), *n.* [F., pres. part.] One who enters.
en·trap′ (ĕn·trăp′), *v. t.*; see TRAP. [OF. *entraper*, *entrapper.*] To catch in or as in a trap; ensnare. — **Syn.** See CATCH.
en·treas′ure (ĕn·trĕzh′ẽr), *v. t.* To store in a treasury.
en·treat′ (ĕn·trēt′), *v. t.* [OF. *entraiter* to treat of, fr. *en-* (fr. L. *in*) + *traiter* to treat.] **1.** *Archaic.* To treat; deal with. **2.** To ask earnestly; petition with urgency. **3.** *Obs.* To prevail upon by solicitation. — *v. i.* To make an entreaty; plead. — **Syn.** See BEG. — **en·treat′ing·ly,** *adv.* — **en·treat′ment,** *n.*
en·treat′y (ĕn·trēt′ĭ), *n.*; *pl.* ENTREATIES (-ĭz). Earnest petition or solicitation. — **Syn.** Request, supplication.
‖**en′tre·chat′** (äN′trĕ·shȧ′), *n.* [F.] A leap during which a dancer repeatedly strikes the heels together or crosses the legs while in the air.
en·tree, en′trée (än′trā; *F.* äN′trā′), *n.* [F. *entrée.*] **1.** Entrance; freedom to enter; access. **2.** A dish served between the chief courses, or, in English usage, before the roast; hence, a meat dish not classed as a roast, or a meat substitute, esp. one served as the chief course.
en′tre·mets (än′trĕ·mā; *F.* äN′trĕ·mĕ′), *n.*; *pl.* -METS (-māz; *F.* -mā′). [F., fr. *entre* between + *mets* a dish, mess. See MESS, *n.*] A side dish or dainty.
en·trench′ (ĕn·trĕnch′), **in·trench′** (ĭn-), *v. i.* To invade; encroach; trespass. — *v. t.* **1.** To surround with a trench or trenches. **2.** To establish in a position of power or settled habit rendering dislodgment extremely difficult. — **Syn.** See TRESPASS. — **en·trench′ment,** *n.*
‖**en′tre nous** (äN′trĕ nōō′). [F.] Between us; hence, in confidence.
en′tre·pôt (än′trĕ·pō; *F.* äN′trĕ·pō′), *n.* [F.] A warehouse.
en′tre·pre·neur′ (än′trĕ·prĕ·nûr′; *F.* äN′trĕ-), *n.* [F. See ENTERPRISE.] One who assumes the risk and management of business; enterpriser; undertaker. — **en′tre·pre·neur′ship,** *n.*
en′tre·sol (ĕn′tẽr·sŏl; *F.* äN′trĕ·sôl′), *n.* [F.] = MEZZANINE.
en′tro·py (ĕn′trō·pĭ), *n.* [From Gr. *tropē* a turning, change, after *energy.*] A mathematical factor which is a measure of the unavailable energy in a thermodynamic system.
en·trust′ (ĕn·trŭst′), **in·trust′** (ĭn-), *v. t.* To confer a trust upon; esp., to deliver to (another) something in trust, or to surrender (something) to another with confidence regarding his care, use, or disposal of it; as, to *entrust* a servant with one's goods, or to *entrust* one's goods to a servant. — **Syn.** See COMMIT.
en′try (ĕn′trĭ), *n.*; *pl.* ENTRIES (-trĭz). [OF. *entree*, fr. *entrer* to enter. See ENTER.] **1.** Entrance; esp., ingress. **2.** Also **en′try·way′** (-wā′). An entrance, as a passage, vestibule, or hallway. **3.** Act of entering into a record, list, etc.; also, the item entered. **4.** The exhibition or depositing by a ship's officer of the papers required by law, at the customhouse, to procure license to land goods. **5.** One entered or enrolled for a contest, race, etc. **6.** *Law.* The actual taking possession of lands or tenements, by entering or setting foot on them.
en·twine′ (ĕn·twīn′), *v. t. & i.* To twine together or round.
en·twist′ (ĕn·twĭst′), *v. t.* To entwine.
e·nu′cle·ate (ē·nū′klē·āt), *v. t.* [L. *enucleatus*, past part. of *enucleare* to enucleate, fr. *e* out + *nucleus* kernel.] **1.** To bring or peel out, as a kernel, from husks or shell; hence, to explain. **2.** *Biol.* To deprive of a nucleus. **3.** *Surg.* To remove without cutting into (as a tumor, the eyeball, etc.). — (-āt), *adj.* Enucleated. — **e·nu′cle·a′tion** (-ā′shŭn), *n.* — **e·nu′cle·a′tor** (-ā′tẽr), *n.*
e·nu′mer·ate (ē·nū′mẽr·āt), *v. t.* [L. *enumeratus*, past part. of *enumerare* to enumerate, fr. *e* out + *numerare* to count.] To count over, or tell off one after another; to number; count; to name over. — **e·nu′mer·a′tion** (-ā′shŭn), *n.* — **e·nu′mer·a′tive** (-ā′tĭv; -ȧ·tĭv), *adj.* — **e·nu′mer·a′tor** (-ā′tẽr), *n.*
e·nun′ci·a·ble (ē·nŭn′shĭ·ȧ·b'l; -sĭ·ȧ·b'l), *adj.* Capable of being enunciated. — **e·nun′ci·a·bil′i·ty** (-bĭl′ĭ·tĭ), *n.*
e·nun′ci·ate (-shĭ·āt; -sĭ·āt), *v. t. & i.* [L. *enuntiatus*, *-ciatus*, past part. of *enuntiare*, *-ciare*. See ENOUNCE.] **1.** To state formally or definitively; also, to announce; proclaim; declare. **2.** To pronounce with distinctness of articulation. — **e·nun′ci·a′tion** (-sĭ·ā′shŭn; -shĭ·ā′shŭn), *n.* — **e·nun′ci·a′tive** (ē·nŭn′shĭ·ā′tĭv; -ȧ·tĭv; -sĭ-), *adj.* — **e·nun′ci·a′tive·ly,** *adv.* — **e·nun′ci·a′tor** (-ā′tẽr), *n.* — **e·nun′ci·a·to′ry** (-ȧ·tō′rĭ *or*, *esp. Brit.*, -tẽr·ĭ), *adj.*
en·ure′ (ĕn·ūr′). Var. of INURE.
en′u·re′sis (ĕn′ū·rē′sĭs), *n.* [NL., fr. Gr. *enourein* to urinate in.] Incontinence of urine. — **en′u·ret′ic** (-rĕt′ĭk), *adj.*
en·vel′op (ĕn·vĕl′ŭp), *v. t.* [OF. *enveloper*, fr. *envoloper*, fr. *en-* (fr. L. *in*) + a stem of uncert., perh. Celt., origin.] **1.** To put a covering about; to wrap up or in. **2.** *Mil.* To surround. — **en·vel′op·er,** *n.* — **en·vel′op·ment,** *n.*
en′ve·lope (ĕn′vĕ·lōp; ŏn′-), *n.* Also **en·vel′op** (ĕn·vĕl′ŭp). [F. *enveloppe.*] **1.** That which envelops; a wrapper. **2.** A piece of folded, gummed paper to enclose a letter. **3.** *Aeronautics.* **a** The outer covering of an aerostat. **b** In a balloon or airship, the bag which contains the gas. **4.** *Astron.* A distinct vaporous mass surrounding the nucleus of a comet on the side toward the sun and appearing like a bow

or parabola. **5.** *Biol.* Any enclosing membrane, shell, etc.; integument. **6.** *Bot.* Any surrounding leaves, cover, or integument. **7.** *Geom.* The locus of the intersections of consecutive elements of a family of curves or surfaces.

en·ven′om (ĕn·vĕn′ŭm), *v. t.* [OF. *envenimer*.] To taint or impregnate with venom; hence, to embitter.

en′vi·a·ble (ĕn′vĭ·*à*·b′l), *adj.* Such as to excite envy or a desire to have or be like; covetable. — **en′vi·a·bly** (-blĭ), *adv.*

en′vi·er (ĕn′vĭ·ẽr), *n.* One who envies.

en′vi·ous (-ŭs), *adj.* [OF. *envieus*, fr. L. *invidiosus*, fr. *invidia*. See ENVY.] **1.** Feeling or exhibiting envy; actuated by, or proceeding from, envy. **2.** *Obs.* **a** Emulous. **b** Malignant; spiteful. — **en′vi·ous·ly**, *adv.* — **en′vi·ous·ness**, *n.*

Syn. **Envious, jealous** mean grudging another's possession of something desirable. **Envious** implies a grudging of that which one covets inordinately; **jealous,** a grudging of that which one regards as peculiarly one's own.

en·vi′ron (ĕn·vī′rŭn), *v. t.* [OF. *environner*, fr. *environ* about, fr. *en-* (fr. L. *in*) + *viron* circuit.] To form a ring around; surround, encompass, or encircle.

en·vi′ron·ment (-mĕnt), *n.* **1.** Act of environing; state of being environed. **2.** That which environs; surroundings; specif., the aggregate of all the external conditions and influences affecting the life and development of an organism, etc., human behavior, society, etc. — **en·vi′ron·men′tal** (-mĕn′tăl; -t′l), *adj.* — **en·vi′ron·men′tal·ly**, *adv.*

en·vi′rons (ĕn·vī′rŭnz; ĕn′vĭ·rŭnz), *n. pl.* [F.] The suburbs or districts round about a place; hence, surroundings.

en·vis′age (ĕn·vĭz′ĭj; -vĭs′ĭj), *v. t.*; EN·VIS′AGED (-ĭjd); EN·VIS′AG·ING (-ĭj·ĭng). [F. *envisager*.] **1.** To confront; face. **2.** To view with the mind's eye; visualize. — **Syn.** See THINK.

en·vi′sion (ĕn·vĭzh′ŭn), *v. t.* To have a mental picture of (something to be). — **Syn.** See THINK.

‖**en′voi′** (äN′vwá′), *n.* [F.] = 1st ENVOY.

en′voy (ĕn′voi; än′-), *n.* [OF. *envoy* (F. *envoi*), fr. *envoier, enveier*, to send, fr. L. *in* + *via* way.] A postscript to a poem, essay, or book; specif., a short stanza appended to a ballade and some other metrical forms.

en′voy, *n.* [F. *envoyé* envoy, fr. *envoyer* to send.] One dispatched upon a mission; a messenger; esp., a person deputed to represent one sovereign or government in its intercourse with another; specif., a diplomatic agent ranking between an ambassador and a minister and having as his full title **envoy extraordinary and minister plenipotentiary.**

en′vy (ĕn′vĭ), *n.; pl.* ENVIES (-vĭz). [OF. *envie*, fr. L. *invidia*, fr. *invidus* envious.] **1.** *Obs.* **a** Spite. **b** Odium. **2.** Chagrin or discontent at the excellence or good fortune (of another); resentful begrudging. **3.** An object of envious notice or feeling. **4.** Longing; desire. — *v. t.*; EN′VIED (-vĭd); EN′VY·ING. **1.** To feel envy at or toward; be envious of. **2.** To feel envy on account of; begrudge. **3.** To long after; covet. — *v. i.* To feel or show envy; — used esp. with *at*. — **en′vy·ing·ly**, *adv.*

en·wind′ (ĕn·wīnd′). Var. of INWIND.

en·womb′ (ĕn·wo͞om′), *v. t.* To bury or contain, as in a womb.

en·wrap′ (ĕn·răp′), *v. t.*; see WRAP. To infold; hence, to involve, immerse, or engross.

en·wreathe′ (ĕn·rēth′), *v. t.* To wreathe in or envelop.

en′zo·ot′ic (ĕn′zō·ŏt′ĭk), *adj.* [Gr. *en* in + *zōion* an animal.] Afflicting animals. — *n.* An enzootic disease.

en′zyme (ĕn′zīm; -zĭm), **en′zym** (-zĭm), *n.* [MGr. *enzymos* leavened, fr. Gr. *en* in + *zymē* leaven.] Any of a class of complex organic substances, as amylase, pepsin, etc., that accelerate (catalyze) specific chemical transformations, as in the digestion of foods, in plants and animals. Cf. -ASE. — **en′zy·mat′ic** (ĕn′zī·măt′ĭk; ĕn′zĭ-), **en·zy′mic** (ĕn·zī′mĭk; -zĭm′ĭk), *adj.*

e′o- (ē′ō-). [Gr. *ēōs*.] A combining form meaning *dawn, daybreak*, used, as in paleontology and geology, to indicate *connection with*, or *relation to, an early period of time.*

E′o·an·thro′pus (-ăn·thrō′pŭs; -ăn′thrō·pŭs), *n.* [NL., fr. *eo-* + Gr. *anthrōpos* man.] Genus to which Piltdown man was assigned.

E′o·cene (ē′ō·sēn), *adj.* [*eo-* + Gr. *kainos* recent.] *Geol.* Of, pert. to, or designating the earliest period of the Tertiary division of the Cenozoic era, or the system of rocks formed during this period.

E′o·cene, *n.* The Eocene epoch or series.

e′o·hip′pus (ē′ō·hĭp′ŭs), *n.* [NL., fr. *eo-* + Gr. *hippos* horse.] Any of a genus (*Eohippus*) of small primitive four-toed horses from the lower Eocene of the western U. S.

E·o′li·an, E·ol′ic, e·o′ni·an. Vars. of AEOLIAN, etc.

e′o·lith′ic (ē′ō·lĭth′ĭk), *adj.* [*eo-* + *lithic*.] *Archaeol.* Pertaining to or designating the earliest assumed stage (**Eolithic period**) of human culture, represented by the use of a type (**e′o·lith** [ē′ō·lĭth]) of rude stone implements.

e′on (ē′ŏn), *n.* Var. of AEON; specif., *Geol.*, any of the grand divisions of geological time.

‖**e′o no′mi·ne** (ē′ō nŏm′ĭ·nē). [L.] By or under that name.

E′os (ē′ŏs), *n.* [L., fr. Gr. *Ēōs*.] *Gr. Myth.* The goddess of dawn, corresponding to Aurora.

e′o·sin (ē′ō·sĭn), *n.* Also **e′o·sine** (-sĭn; -sēn). [Gr. *ēōs* dawn.] *Chem.* **a** A dye, $C_{20}H_8Br_4O_5$, obtained by the action of bromine on fluorescein; also, the brownish-red sodium or potassium salt. It is used in making pink lakes and red ink, as a rose dye, and in microscopy as a stain. **b** Any of several similar dyes. — **e′o·sin′ic** (-sĭn′ĭk), *adj.*

e′o·sin′o·phile (ē′ō·sĭn′ō·fīl; -fĭl), **e′o·sin′o·phil** (-fĭl), *adj.* [*eosin* + *-phile, -phil*.] *Biol.* Staining readily with eosin; specif., *Anat.*, designating a form of leucocyte containing in the cytoplasm numerous coarse granules that stain with eosin. — **e′o·sin′o·phil′ic** (-fĭl′ĭk), *adj.*

-eous. [L. *-eus*, as in *ligneus* ligneous.] A suffix forming adjectives, meaning *of the nature of*, or *like*, as in *aqueous*.

E′o·zo′ic (ē′ō·zō′ĭk), *adj. & n.* [*eo-* + Gr. *zōion* animal + *-ic*.] *Geol.* **a** Pre-Cambrian. **b** Proterozoic, or Algonkian.

ep-. = EPI-, as in **ep·ax′i·al**, above, or on the dorsal side of, an axis.

e′pact (ē′păkt), *n.* [F. *épacte*, fr. LL., fr. Gr. *epaktos* added, fr. *epagein* to bring.] In chronology, the period added to harmonize the lunar with the solar calendar.

ep′arch (ĕp′ärk), *n.* [Gr. *eparchos*, fr. *epi* over + *archos* chief.] **1.** In ancient Greece, the prefect of a province. **2.** *Eccl.* A metropolitan.

ep′arch·y (ĕp′är·kĭ), *n.; pl.* -ARCHIES (-kĭz). **1.** A province, prefecture, or territory under the jurisdiction of an eparch; esp., one of the larger divisions of a nomarchy. **2.** *Eastern Church.* A diocese or archdiocese. — **ep·ar′chi·al** (ĕp·är′kĭ·ăl), *adj.*

ep′au·let, ep′au·lette (ĕp′ŏ·lĕt), *n.* [F. *épaulette*, dim. of *épaule* shoulder, fr. L. *spatula*. See SPATULA.] A shoulder ornament, consisting usually of a fringed pad attached by a strap, now worn chiefly on military uniforms on certain occasions.

‖**é′pée′** (ā′pā′), *n.* [F.] Sword; specif., a weapon with a sharp-pointed blade and without a cutting edge, much used in fencing and dueling.

é′pée′ist (-ĭst), *n.* [See -IST.] One expert in épée play.

e·pei′ro·gen′e·sis (ē·pī′rō·jĕn′ē·sĭs), *n.* Epeirogeny. — **e·pei′ro·ge·net′ic** (-jē·nĕt′ĭk), *adj.*

ep′ei·rog′e·ny (ĕp′ī·rŏj′ē·nĭ), *n.* Also **ep′i·rog′e·ny.** [Gr. *ēpeiros* mainland + *-geny*.] *Geol.* The deformation of the earth's crust by which such features as continents, ocean basins, and greater plateaus are produced. See DIASTROPHISM. — **e·pei′ro·gen′ic, e·pi′ro·gen′ic** (ē·pī′rō·jĕn′ĭk), *adj.*

ep′en·ceph′a·lon (ĕp′ĕn·sĕf′*à*·lŏn), *n.* [NL., fr. Gr. *epi* upon, near + *enkephalos* brain.] *Anat.* The cerebellar division of the brain. — **ep′en·ce·phal′ic** (-sĕ·făl′ĭk), *adj.*

ep·en′the·sis (ĕp·ĕn′thē·sĭs), *n.; pl.* EPENTHESES (-sēz). [LL., fr. Gr. *epenthesis*, fr. *epi* + *entithenai* to put or set in.] Insertion of a sound in the body of a word (*b* in *nimble* from ME. *nimel*). — **ep′en·thet′ic** (ĕp′ĕn·thĕt′ĭk), *adj.*

e·pergne′ (ē·pûrn′; ā·pĕrn′), *n.* [F. *épargne* a sparing or saving.] A centerpiece for table decoration, usually consisting of several grouped dishes or receptacles.

ep·ex′e·ge′sis (ĕp·ĕk′sē·jē′sĭs), *n.* [NL., fr. Gr. *epexēgēsis* a detailed narrative, deriv. of *epi* + *exēgeisthai* to lead, point out. See EXEGESIS.] Additional explanation or explanatory matter. — **ep·ex′e·get′ic** (-jĕt′ĭk), **ep·ex′e·get′i·cal** (-ĭ·kăl), *adj.* — **ep·ex′e·get′i·cal·ly**, *adv.*

e′phah, e′pha (ē′f*à*), *n.* [Heb. *ēphāh*.] A Hebrew dry measure equal to a little more than a bushel.

e·phe′bus (ē·fē′bŭs), **e·phe′bos** (-bŏs), *n.; pl.* -BI (-bī), -BOI (-boi). [L. *ephebus*, fr. Gr. *ephēbos*, fr. *epi* upon, to + *hēbē* youth, puberty.] *Gr. Hist.* A youth entering manhood or just enrolled as a citizen. — **e·phe′bic** (-bĭk), *adj.*

e·phed′rine (ē·fĕd′rĭn; *by chemists generally* ĕf′ē·drēn; -drĭn), *n.* Also **e·phed′rin.** [L. *ephedra* horsetail, fr. Gr.] *Pharm.* A crystalline alkaloid, $C_{10}H_{15}NO$, occurring in certain plants (genus *Ephedra*, family Gnetaceae), used esp. for colds, in oil solutions applied to the mucous membranes in the head.

e·phem′er·a (ē·fĕm′ẽr·*à*), *n.; pl.* -AE (-ē), -AS (-*à*z). [NL., fr. Gr. *ephēmeron* a dayfly, fr. *ephēmeros* daily, lasting but a day, fr. *epi* over + *hēmera* day.] **1.** A May fly or ephemerid. **2.** An ephemeral thing.

e·phem′er·al (-ăl), *adj.* Beginning and ending in a day; hence, short-lived. — **Syn.** See TRANSIENT. — *n.* An ephemeral thing. — **e·phem′er·al·ly**, *adv.*

e·phem′er·id (-ĭd), *n.* *Zool.* A May fly; any of an order (Ephemerida) of slender delicate insects with membranous wings. Their adult life is only a few hours or days, though the larval stages often last from one to three years.

e·phem′er·is (-ĭs), *n.; pl.* EPHEMERIDES (ĕf′ē·mĕr′ĭ·dēz). [L., a diary, fr. Gr. *ephēmeris*, also, a calendar, fr. *ephēmeros*. See EPHEMERA.] **1.** *Obs.* A diary; journal. **2.** A calendar or almanac; specif.: **a** An astronomical almanac. **b** Any tabular statement of the assigned places of a celestial body for regular intervals.

e·phem′er·on (-ŏn), *n.; pl.* -ERA (-*à*), -ERONS (-ŏnz). [NL. See EPHEMERA.] An ephemerid; an ephemeral.

E·phe′sians (ē·fē′zhănz; -zĭ·ănz), *n. pl., construed as sing. Bib.* The Epistle to the Ephesians, in the New Testament. See BIBLE.

eph′od (ĕf′ŏd; ē′fŏd), *n.* [Heb. *ēphōdh*, fr. *āphadh* to gird on.] *Jewish Antiq.* An official garment for the high priest.

eph′or (ĕf′ôr; -ẽr), *n.; pl.* EPHORS (-ôrz; -ẽrz), EPHORI (ĕf′ō·rī). [L. *ephorus*, fr. Gr. *ephoros*, fr. *ephoran* to oversee, fr. *epi* + *horan* to see.] A magistrate in various ancient Dorian states; esp., one of a body of five Spartan magistrates.

E′phra·im (ē′frā·ĭm; ē′frĭ·ŭm), *n.* [Heb. *Ephrayim*.] *Bib.* **1.** See JACOB. **2.** The Kingdom of Israel.

ep′i- (ĕp′ĭ-), **ep-.** Before aspirated words, **eph-.** [Gr. *epi* on, upon, to.] A prefix meaning *upon, beside, among, on the outside, above, over, anterior.*

ep′i·blast (-blăst), *n.* [*epi-* + *-blast*.] The outer layer of the blastoderm. — **ep′i·blas′tic** (-blăs′tĭk), *adj.*

e·pib′o·ly (ē·pĭb′ō·lĭ), *n.* [Gr. *epibolē* a throwing upon, deriv. of *epi* upon + *ballein* to throw.] *Embryol.* The growing of one part around another. — **ep′i·bol′ic** (ĕp′ĭ·bŏl′ĭk), *adj.*

ep′ic (ĕp′ĭk), *adj.* [L. *epicus*, fr. Gr. *epikos*, fr. *epos* speech, tale, song.] **1.** Designating, pertaining to, or characteristic of, a kind of narrative poetry dealing with heroic action and written in elevated style. **2.** Heroic in scale or mold; as, *epic* actions. — *n.* **1.** An epic poem; also, an epiclike theme or work of art. **2.** [*cap.*] = OLD IONIC. See GREEK, *n.*, 4. — **ep′i·cal** (-ĭ·kăl), *adj.* — **ep′i·cal·ly**, *adv.*

ep′i·ca′lyx (ĕp′ĭ·kā′lĭks; -kăl′ĭks), *n.* [NL., fr. *epi-* + *calyx*.] *Bot.* An involucre resembling an exterior calyx. See FLOWER, *Illust.*

ep′i·car′di·um (-kär′dĭ·ŭm), *n.; pl.* -DIA (-*à*). [NL., fr. *epi-* + Gr. *kardia* heart.] The visceral part of the pericardium which closely invests the heart. — **ep′i·car′di·al** (-ăl), **ep′i·car′di·ac** (-ăk), *adj.*

ep′i·carp (ĕp′ĭ·kärp), *n.* [*epi-* + *-carp*.] *Bot.* The outermost layer of the pericarp of a fruit. See ENDOCARP, *Illust.*

ep′i·ce′di·um (-sē′dĭ·ŭm; -sē·dī′ŭm), *n.; pl.* EPICEDIA (-*à*). [L., fr. Gr. *epikēdeion*, fr. *epikēdeios* funereal, fr. *epi* + *kēdos* sorrow.] A dirge; elegy.

ep′i·cene (ĕp′ĭ·sēn), *adj.* [L. *epicoenus*, fr. Gr. *epikoinos*, fr. *epi* + *koinos* common.] **1.** Common to both sexes; specif., *Gram.*, having but one form to indicate either sex, the qualifiers showing the gender. **2.** Having characteristics of, or adapted to, both sexes. **3.** Neither one thing nor the other; sometimes, effeminate. — *n.* One who is epicene. — **ep′i·cen·ism** (-sēn·ĭz′m), *n.*

ep′i·cen′ter, ep′i·cen′tre (ĕp′ĭ·sĕn′tẽr), *n.* The earth's surface directly above the focus of an earthquake; hence, any focal point. — **ep′i·cen′tral** (-sĕn′trăl), *adj.*

ep′i·cen′trum (-sĕn′trŭm), *n.; pl.* -TRA (-tr*à*). [NL.] An epicenter.

ep′i·cot′yl (-kŏt′ĭl), *n.* [*epi-* + *cotyl*edon.] *Bot.* The upper portion of the axis of an embryo or seedling, above the cotyledons. Cf. HYPOCOTYL.

ep′i·crit′ic (ĕp′ĭ·krĭt′ĭk), *adj.* [Gr. *epikritikos* determinative.] *Physiol. & Psychol.* Designating or pert. to a type of cutaneous reception or receptor capable of delicate sensory discrimination. Cf. PROTOPATHIC.

ep′i·cure (ĕp′ĭ·kūr), *n.* [L. *Epicurus*, Greek philosopher regarded (erroneously) as teaching a doctrine of refined voluptuousness.] Formerly, a luxurious sensualist, esp. in matters of food and drink; now, one who displays fastidiousness in his tastes or enjoyments; a connoisseur.

Syn. **Epicure, gourmet, gourmand, glutton, bon vivant** mean one who takes pleasure in eating and drinking. **Epicure** implies fastidiousness of taste and, sometimes, voluptuousness; **gourmet** implies being a connoisseur in viands, wines, and the like, and the fastidious enjoyment of them; **gourmand** suggests a hearty interest in good food and drink rather than, as **glutton**, the habit of greedy and voracious eating and drinking; **bon vivant** adds to *gourmand* a strong connotation of spirited enjoyment of the pleasures of the table, especially in the company of others.

Ep′i·cu·re′an (-kū·rē′ăn), *adj.* **1.** Pertaining to Epicurus, or to his philosophy, which taught that pleasure is the end of all morality and that genuine pleasure is derived from a life of prudence, honor, and justice. **2.** [*not cap.*] Characteristic of, or adapted to, the tastes of epicures. — **Syn.** See SENSUOUS. — *n.* **1.** A follower of Epicurus. **2.** [*not cap.*] An epicure; esp., a sensualist. — **Ep′i·cu·re′an·ism** (-ĭz′m), *n.*

ep′i·cur·ism (ĕp′ĭ·kūr·ĭz′m; *sense* 1 *gen.* ĕp′ĭ·kū′rĭz′m), *n.* **1.** [*cap.*] Epicureanism. **2.** Epicurean habits or tastes.

ep′i·cy′cle (ĕp′ĭ·sī′k′l), *n.* [LL. *epicyclus*, fr. Gr. *epikyklos*.] **1.** A small circle, esp. one in which a planet moves, the center of which is carried upon the circumference of a large circle. **2.** *Geom.* The circle generating an epicycloid or hypocycloid. — **ep′i·cy′clic** (-sī′klĭk; -sĭk′lĭk), **ep′i·cy′cli·cal** (-sī′klĭ·kăl; -sĭk′lĭ·kăl), *adj.*

ep′i·cy′clic train. A train of spur or bevel wheels, belt pulleys, or the like, having one or more of these constrained to move bodily around the circumference of another, which may be fixed or moving. This device permits an unusual velocity ratio without undue complexity of parts.

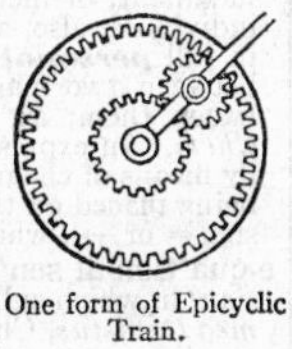

One form of Epicyclic Train.

ep′i·cy′cloid (ĕp′ĭ·sī′kloid), *n.* *Geom.* A curve traced by a point of a circle that rolls on the outside of a fixed circle. Cf. HYPOCYCLOID. — **ep′i·cy·cloi′dal** (-sī·kloi′dăl; -d′l), *adj.*

ep′i·cy·cloi′dal wheel. Any wheel of an epicyclic train.

ep′i·dem′ic (ĕp′ĭ·dĕm′ĭk), *adj.* Also **ep′i·dem′i·cal** (-ĭ·kăl). [ML. *epidemia*, fr. Gr. *epidēmia*, fr. *epidēmios*, fr. *epi* in + *dēmos* people.] Common to, or affecting at the same time, many in a community; — of diseases. — *n.* An unarrested spread of something epidemic, as a disease. — **ep′i·dem′i·cal·ly**, *adv.* — **ep′i·de·mic′i·ty** (-dē·mĭs′ĭ·tĭ), *n.*

ep′i·de′mi·ol′o·gy (ĕp′ĭ·dē′mĭ·ŏl′ō·jĭ; -dĕm′ĭ-), *n.* Medical science treating of epidemics. — **ep′i·de′mi·ol′o·gist** (-jĭst), *n.*

ep′i·der′mal (ĕp′ĭ·dûr′măl), *adj.* Also **ep′i·der′mic** (-mĭk). Of, relating to, or arising from the epidermis.

ep′i·der′mis (-dûr′mĭs), *n.* [LL., fr. Gr. *epidermis*, fr. *epi* over + *derma* skin.] **1.** The outer epithelial layer of an animal's skin; in vertebrates, the nonsensitive and nonvascular layer over the derma; specif., in the higher animals and man, the cuticle. **2.** Any of various other integuments; esp., the outer covering of the shells of many mollusks. **3.** The thin layer of cells forming the external integument in seed plants and ferns.

ep′i·der′moid (ĕp′ĭ·dûr′moid), **ep′i·der·moi′dal** (-dûr·moi′dăl; -d′l), *adj.* Of the nature of or resembling epidermis.

ep′i·did′y·mis (-dĭd′ĭ·mĭs), *n.*; *pl.* -DIDYMIDES (-dĭ·dĭm′ĭ·dēz). [NL., fr. Gr. *epididymis*, fr. *epi* upon + *didymos* testicle.] An elongated mass at the back of the testicle, composed chiefly of the greatly convoluted efferent tubes of that organ. — **ep′i·did′y·mal** (-măl), *adj.*

ep′i·dote (ĕp′ĭ·dōt), *n.* [F. *épidote*, fr. Gr. *epididonai* to give besides; from the enlargement of the base in some crystal forms.] A yellowish-green mineral, occurring massive or in grains, columns, or monoclinic crystals, sometimes used as a gem. — **ep′i·dot′ic** (-dŏt′ĭk), *adj.*

ep′i·fo′cal (-fō′kăl), *adj.* Over the focus of an earthquake; as, *epifocal* district. Cf. EPICENTER.

ep′i·gas′tric (-găs′trĭk), *adj.* [Gr. *epigastrios* over the belly, fr. *epi* upon + *gastēr* belly.] Lying over the stomach; pertaining to the anterior walls of the abdomen.

ep′i·gas′tri·um (-găs′trĭ·ŭm), *n.* [NL., fr. Gr. *epigastrion*.] The epigastric region.

ep′i·ge′al (-jē′ăl), **ep′i·ge′an** (-ăn), *adj.* **1.** *Bot.* Epigeous. **2.** *Zool.* Living near the ground, as certain insects.

ep′i·gene (ĕp′ĭ·jēn), *adj.* [Gr. *epigenēs* growing after or late, fr. *epi* upon, after + *gignesthai* to be born, grow.] *Geol.* Formed, originating, or taking place, on the surface of the earth; — opposed to *hypogene*; as, *epigene* rocks.

ep′i·gen′e·sis (-jĕn′ĕ·sĭs), *n.* **1.** The theory of generation holding that the germ or embryo is created entirely new. Cf. PREFORMATION. **2.** *Geol.* Change in the mineral character of a rock owing to outside influences. Cf. METAMORPHISM. **3.** *Med.* Occurrence of secondary symptoms. — **ep′i·ge·net′ic** (-jē·nĕt′ĭk), *adj.*

e·pig′e·nous (ē·pĭj′ē·nŭs), *adj.* *Bot.* Growing upon the surface of a leaf or other organ. Cf. HYPOGENOUS.

ep′i·ge′ous (ĕp′ĭ·jē′ŭs), *adj.* [Gr. *epigeios* of the earth.] *Bot.* **a** Growing upon or above the ground. **b** Borne above ground after germination; — of cotyledons. Cf. HYPOGEOUS.

ep′i·glot′tis (-glŏt′ĭs), *n.* [NL., fr. Gr. *epiglōttis*, fr. *epi* upon + *glōtta*, *glōssa*, tongue.] *Anat. & Zool.* A thin plate of yellow elastic cartilage in front of the glottis, which folds back over and protects the glottis in swallowing.

ep′i·gram (ĕp′ĭ·grăm), *n.* [L. *epigramma*, fr. Gr. *epigramma* inscription, epigram, deriv. of *epi* upon + *graphein* to write.] **1.** A short poem treating concisely, pointedly, often satirically, a single thought or event, and now usually ending with a witticism. **2.** A bright or witty thought tersely and ingeniously expressed; also, such expression. — **ep′i·gram·mat′ic** (-gră·măt′ĭk), **ep′i·gram·mat′i·cal** (-ĭ·kăl), *adj.* — **ep′i·gram·mat′i·cal·ly**, *adv.* — **ep′i·gram′ma·tism** (-grăm′ȧ·tĭz′m), *n.* — **ep′i·gram′ma·tist** (-tĭst), *n.*

ep′i·gram′ma·tize (ĕp′ĭ·grăm′ȧ·tīz), *v. t.* To make an epigram of; express epigrammatically. — *v. i.* To write epigrams.

ep′i·graph (ĕp′ĭ·grȧf; 9), *n.* [Gr. *epigraphē*. See EPIGRAM.] **1.** An inscription on a building, a statue, etc. **2.** A pertinent motto at the beginning of a book, chapter, etc.

ep′i·graph′ic (-grăf′ĭk), *adj.* Also **ep′i·graph′i·cal** (-ĭ·kăl). Of or pertaining to epigraphs or epigraphy. — **ep′i·graph′i·cal·ly**, *adv.*

e·pig′ra·phy (ē·pĭg′rȧ·fĭ), *n.* **a** Epigraphs or inscriptions collectively. **b** The study or science of inscriptions; esp., the deciphering and interpretation of ancient inscriptions. — **e·pig′ra·pher** (-fẽr), **e·pig′ra·phist** (-fĭst), *n.*

e·pig′y·nous (ē·pĭj′ĭ·nŭs), *adj.* [*epi-* + Gr. *gynē* woman.] *Bot.* Adnate to the surface of the ovary as if inserted upon the top of it; — said of stamens, petals, etc., of flowers whose parts are of this type. — **e·pig′y·ny** (-nĭ), *n.*

ep′i·lep′sy (ĕp′ĭ·lĕp′sĭ), *n.* [LL. *epilepsia*, fr. Gr. *epilēpsia* a seizure, deriv. of *epi* upon, besides + *lambanein* to take.] *Med.* A chronic nervous disease, characterized by fits, occurring at intervals, and attended by convulsive motions of the muscles and loss of consciousness.

ep′i·lep′tic (-lĕp′tĭk), *adj.* Pertaining to, having, or of the nature of epilepsy. — *n.* One having epilepsy. — **ep′i·lep′ti·cal·ly** (-tĭ·kăl·ĭ), *adv.*

ep′i·lep′toid (-lĕp′toid), *adj.* *Med.* Resembling epilepsy.

ep′i·logue (ĕp′ĭ·lŏg; 74), *n.* Also **ep′i·log.** [F. *épilogue*, fr. L. *epilogus*, fr. Gr. *epilogos* conclusion, deriv. of *epi* upon, besides + *legein* to say.] **1.** A speech, short poem, or the like, addressed to the spectators, and spoken after the conclusion of a play; also, the speaker or speakers of this. **2.** A concluding section, as of a novel, serving to complete the plan of the work.

Ep′i·me′theus (ĕp′ĭ·mē′thūs; -thē·ŭs), *n.* [L., fr. Gr. *Epimētheus*.] *Gr. Myth.* Brother of Prometheus and husband of Pandora.

ep′i·nas′ty (ĕp′ĭ·năs′tĭ), *n.* [*epi-* + Gr. *nastos* pressed close.] *Plant Physiol.* That state in which the more vigorous growth of the upper surface of an organ, as in an unfolding leaf, causes a downward curvature. Cf. HYPONASTY. — **ep′i·nas′tic** (-năs′tĭk), *adj.*

ep′i·neph′rine (-nĕf′rĭn; -rēn), *n.* Also **ep′i·neph′rin.** [*epi-* + Gr. *nephros* kidney.] Adrenaline.

ep′i·neu′ri·um (-nū′rĭ·ŭm), *n.* [NL., fr. *epi-* + Gr. *neuron* a nerve.] The external connective-tissue sheath of a nerve trunk. — **ep′i·neu′ri·al** (-ăl), *adj.*

E·piph′a·ny (ē·pĭf′ȧ·nĭ), *n.*; *pl.* -NIES (-nĭz). [OF. *epiphanie*, fr. LL., fr. LGr. *epiphania*, Gr. *epiphaneia* appearance, deriv. of *epi* to + *phainein* to show.] **1.** A feast celebrated January 6, commemorating the coming of the Magi as being the first manifestation of Christ to the Gentiles. Cf. TWELFTH-NIGHT, TWELFTHTIDE. **2.** [*not cap.*] A manifestation, esp. of divinity.

ep′i·phe·nom′e·non (ĕp′ĭ·fē·nŏm′ē·nŏn; -nŭn), *n.*; *pl.* -NOMENA (-nȧ). [NL.] An attendant phenomenon appearing with something else and referred to that as its cause.

e·piph′y·sis (ē·pĭf′ĭ·sĭs), *n.*; *pl.* -YSES (-sēz). [NL., fr. Gr. *epiphysis* deriv. of *epi* upon + *phyein* to grow.] A part or process of a bone, which ossifies separately and subsequently becomes ankylosed to the main part of the bone. Cf. DIAPHYSIS. — **ep′i·phys′e·al** (ĕp′ĭ·fĭz′ē·ăl; ē·pĭf′ĭ·sē′ăl), **ep′i·phys′i·al** (ĕp′ĭ·fĭz′ĭ·ăl), *adj.*

ep′i·phyte (ĕp′ĭ·fīt), *n.* [*epi-* + *-phyte*.] *Bot.* A plant, as many mosses, lichens, and orchids, which grows upon other plants but is not parasitic, deriving the moisture for its development chiefly from the air; an air plant; — contrasted with *geophyte* and *hydrophyte*. — **ep′i·phyt′ic** (-fĭt′ĭk), **ep′i·phyt′i·cal** (-ĭ·kăl), *adj.*

ep′i·phy·tot′ic (-fī·tŏt′ĭk), *adj.* [*epi-* + Gr. *phyton* plant + *-otic* as in *epizootic*.] Common among plants, as certain fungous diseases. Cf. ENPHYTOTIC.

ep′i·rog′e·ny, e·pi′ro·gen′ic. Vars. of EPEIROGENY, etc.

e·pis′co·pa·cy (ē·pĭs′kō·pȧ·sĭ), *n.* **1.** Government of the church by a hierarchy in which bishops are the highest in rank. **2.** The state, rank, or length of tenure of a bishop; also, the body of bishops; the episcopate.

e·pis′co·pal (-păl), *adj.* [F. *épiscopal*, fr. ML. (& LL.) *episcopalis*, fr. *episcopus*. See BISHOP.] **1.** Of or pertaining to bishops; governed by bishops. **2.** [*cap.*] Of or pertaining to the Protestant Episcopal Church, or to any church of the Anglican Communion; — preferred to *Episcopalian*. — *n.* *Obs. exc. Colloq.* An Episcopalian. — **e·pis′co·pal·ly, E·pis′co·pal·ly**, *adv.*

e·pis′co·pa′li·an (-pā′lĭ·ăn; -pāl′yăn; 58), *adj.* **1.** Pertaining to episcopal government or churches. **2.** [*cap.*] = EPISCOPAL, 2. — *n.* **1.** One who belongs to an episcopal church, or adheres to episcopal church government. **2.** [*cap.*] A member of the Protestant Episcopal Church. — **E·pis′co·pa′li·an·ism** (-ĭz′m), *n.*

e·pis′co·pal·ism (ē·pĭs′kō·păl·ĭz′m), *n.* *Eccl.* The theory that in church government supreme authority resides in a body of bishops, and not in any individual, such as the pope. This theory was rejected by the Roman Catholic Church at the Vatican Council (1869–70).

e·pis′co·pate (-pāt), *n.* **a** A bishopric. **b** Also **e·pis′co·pa·ture** (-pȧ·tūr). The collective body of bishops. **c** The period of a bishop's office.

ep′i·sode (ĕp′ĭ·sōd), *n.* [Gr. *epeisodion*, prop. neut. of *epeisodios* coming in besides, fr. *epi* on, besides + *eisodos* a coming in, fr. *eis* into + *hodos* way.] **1.** *Gr. Drama.* The part of a tragedy between two choric songs. **2.** A separate but not unrelated incident introduced in narration, for variety or artistic effect; also, a similar digression in a musical composition. **3.** A set of events that stand out or apart from others as of particular moment. — **Syn.** See OCCURRENCE. — **ep′i·sod′ic** (-sŏd′ĭk), **ep′i·sod′i·cal** (-ĭ·kăl), *adj.* — **ep′i·sod′i·cal·ly**, *adv.*

ep′i·spas′tic (ĕp′ĭ·spăs′tĭk), *adj.* [Gr. *epispastikos*, fr. *epispan* to draw to, attract, fr. *epi* upon, to + *span* to draw.] *Med.* Causing a blister or producing a serous discharge by exciting inflammation. — *n.* A blistering agent; a vesicant.

ep′i·stax′is (-stăk′sĭs), *n.* [NL., fr. *epi-* + Gr. *stazein* to drop.] *Med.* Bleeding at the nose; nosebleed.

e·pis′te·mol′o·gy (ē·pĭs′tē·mŏl′ō·jĭ), *n.* [Gr. *epistēmē* knowledge + *-logy*.] The theory or science of the method and grounds of knowledge, esp. with reference to its limits and validity. — **e·pis′te·mo·log′i·cal** (-mō·lŏj′ĭ·kăl), *adj.* — **e·pis′te·mo·log′i·cal·ly**, *adv.*

ep′i·ster′num (ĕp′ĭ·stûr′nŭm), *n.*; *pl.* -NA (-nȧ). [NL., fr. *epi-* + *sternum*.] **1.** *Zool.* The interclavicle. **2.** *Anat.* In man and many mammals, the anterior part of the sternum; the manubrium. — **ep′i·ster′nal** (-năl), *adj. & n.*

e·pis′tle (ē·pĭs′'l), *n.* [OF. *epistle*, *epistre*, fr. L. *epistola* (whence also AS. *epistole*), fr. Gr. *epistolē*, fr. *epistellein* to send to, fr. *epi* upon, to + *stellein* to send.] **1.** A letter to a person; esp., a formal, didactic, or elegant letter. **2.** [*cap.*] **a** One of the Apostolic letters in the New Testament. **b** A selection, usually from one of the Epistles, appointed to be read between the collect and the Gospel in various liturgies, at the right side (**epistle side**) of the altar.

e·pis'tler (ē·pĭs'lẽr; -tlẽr), *n.* **1.** A writer of epistles, or of an Epistle of the New Testament. **2.** The ecclesiastic who reads the Epistle at the Communion service.

e·pis'to·lar'y (ē·pĭs'tō·lĕr'ĭ *or, esp. Brit.*, -lẽr·ĭ), *adj.* **1.** Pertaining or suitable to letters. **2.** Contained in or carried on by letters.

ep'i·style (ĕp'ĭ·stīl), *n.* [L. *epistylium*, fr. Gr. *epistylion*, fr. *epi* upon + *stylos* column.] *Arch.* = ARCHITRAVE **a**.

ep'i·taph (ĕp'ĭ·tȧf; 9), *n.* [OF. and L.; OF. *epitaphe*, fr. L. *epitaphium* a funeral oration, fr. Gr. *epitaphios*, orig. an adj., at a tomb, fr. *epi* upon + *taphos* tomb.] An inscription on or at a tomb in memory of the one buried there; also, a brief statement worded as if to be inscribed on a monument. — **ep'i·taph'ic** (-tăf'ĭk), *adj.*

e·pit'a·sis (ē·pĭt'ȧ·sĭs), *n.* [NL., fr. Gr. *epitasis* a stretching, deriv. of *epi* upon + *teinein* to stretch.] Part of a play developing the main action and leading to the catastrophe. Cf. CATASTASIS, PROTASIS.

ep'i·tha·la'mi·on (ĕp'ĭ·thȧ·lā'mĭ·ŏn), *n.; pl.* -MIA (-ȧ). [NL. & Gr.] An epithalamium.

ep'i·tha·la'mi·um (-ŭm), *n.; pl.* -MIUMS (-ŭmz), -MIA (-ȧ). [L., fr. Gr. *epithalamios*, fr. *epi* upon, at + *thalamos* bridechamber.] A nuptial song or poem in honor of the bride and bridegroom.

ep'i·the'li·al (-thē'lĭ·ăl), *adj.* Of or pert. to epithelium.

ep'i·the'li·oid (-thē'lĭ·oid), *adj.* Like epithelium.

ep'i·the'li·o'ma (-ō'mȧ), *n.; pl.* -OMATA (-tȧ), -OMAS (-mȧz). [NL., fr. *epithelium* + *-oma.*] *Med.* A malignant growth of epithelial cells; an epithelial cancer. — **ep'i·the'li·om'a·tous** (-ŏm'ȧ·tŭs; -ō'mȧ·tŭs), *adj.*

ep'i·the'li·um (-thē'lĭ·ŭm), *n.; pl.* -LIUMS (-ŭmz), -LIA (-ȧ). [NL., fr. *epi-* + Gr. *thēlē* nipple.] *Anat. & Biol.* A cellular, membranelike tissue covering a free surface or lining a cavity, and consisting of one or more layers of cells with little intercellular substance.

ep'i·thet (ĕp'ĭ·thĕt), *n.* [L. *epitheton*, fr. Gr. *epitheton*, fr. *epithetos* added, deriv. of *epi* upon, to + *tithenai* to put.] **1.** A descriptive adjective, noun, or phrase, often complimentary, accompanying or occurring in place of the name of a person or thing (Alfred *the Great*, *Stonewall* Jackson, *rosy-fingered* dawn, *man's faithful friend*). **2.** An uncomplimentary name or nickname, or a contemptuous term, used invectively. **3.** *Biol.* The part of a taxonomic name designating a species or lesser division of a genus; thus, in *Rosa chinensis longifolia*, *chinensis* is the specific epithet, *longifolia* a varietal epithet.

ep'i·thet'ic (-thĕt'ĭk), **ep'i·thet'i·cal** (-ĭ·kăl), *adj.* **a** Of the nature of, or relating to, an epithet. **b** Abounding with epithets.

e·pit'o·me (ē·pĭt'ō·mē), *n.; pl.* -OMES (-mēz). [L., fr. Gr. *epitomē* incision, also, an abridgment, deriv. of *epi* upon + *temnein* to cut.] **1.** A brief statement of the contents of a topic or a work; abstract. **2.** A part which represents typically a whole. — **Syn.** See ABRIDGMENT.

e·pit'o·mize (-mīz), *v. t.* To abridge; summarize.

ep'i·zo'on (ĕp'ĭ·zō'ŏn), *n.; pl.* -ZOA (-ȧ). [NL., fr. *epi-* + *zoon.*] *Zool.* An external parasite or commensal.

ep'i·zo·ot'ic (-zō·ŏt'ĭk), *adj.* [F. *épizootique.*] Affecting many animals (of one kind) at the same time; epidemic. — *n.* Also **ep'i·zo'o·ty** (-zō'ō·tĭ). An epizootic disease.

‖**e plu'ri·bus u'num** (ē plōō'rĭ·bŭs ū'nŭm; plŏŏr'ĭ·bŭs). [L.] One out of many; one composed of many; — motto of the United States.

ep'och (ĕp'ŏk; ē'pŏk), *n.* [ML. *epocha*, fr. Gr. *epochē* stop, epoch, fr. *epechein* to hold on, check, fr. *epi* upon + *echein* to hold.] **1.** Any event or time of an event marking the beginning of a relatively new development; as, Chaucer's poetry marks an *epoch* in English literature. **2.** A period of time characterized by a distinctive development or by a memorable series of events; as, the *epoch* of maritime discovery. **3.** *Astron.* An instant of time or a date selected as a point of reference. **4.** *Geol.* One of the divisions of geologic time; as, the Niagara *epoch* of the Silurian period. — **Syn.** See PERIOD. — **ep'och·al** (ĕp'ŏk·ăl), *adj.* — **ep'och·al·ly**, *adv.*

ep'ode (ĕp'ōd), *n.* [L. *epodos*, fr. Gr. *epōidos*, adj., singing to, sung or said after, deriv. of *epi* upon, to + *āidein* to sing.] *Pros.* **a** A species of lyric poem in which a longer verse is followed by a shorter one; as, the *epodes* of Horace. **b** The part of a choral or a Pindaric ode which follows the strophe and antistrophe.

ep'o·nym (ĕp'ō·nĭm), *n.* [Gr. *epōnymos*, fr. *epi* upon, to + *onoma*, *onyma*, name.] **1.** The person from whom a family, race, city, or nation is supposed to have taken its name; as, Hellen is the *eponym* of the Hellenes. **2.** One whose name is so prominently connected with anything as to be a figurative designation for it. — **ep'o·nym'ic** (-nĭm'ĭk), *adj.* — **ep·on'y·mous** (ĕp·ŏn'ĭ·mŭs), *adj.*

ep·on'y·my (ĕp·ŏn'ĭ·mĭ), *n.* Derivation of the name of a race, tribe, etc., from an eponym.

ep'o·pee' (ĕp'ō·pē'; ĕp'ō·pē'), *n.* Also **ep'o·poe'ia** (ĕp'ō·pē'yȧ). [F. *épopée*, fr. Gr. *epopoiia*, fr. *epos* song + *poiein* to make.] Epic poetry; also, an epic poem.

ep'os (ĕp'ŏs), *n.* [L., fr. Gr. *epos.*] Epic poetry; also, an epic poem.

ep'si·lon (ĕp'sĭ·lŏn *or, esp. Brit.*, ĕp·sī'lŏn), *n.* [Gr. *e psilon* a mere *e.*] The fifth letter (Ε, ε) of the Greek alphabet, corresponding to the English short *e* (ĕ).

Ep'som salts *or* **salt** (ĕp'sŭm). [From *Epsom*, Eng.] A bitter colorless or white crystalline salt (magnesium sulfate heptahydrate, $MgSO_4.7H_2O$), having cathartic qualities.

eq'ua·ble (ĕk'wȧ·b'l; ē'kwȧ-), *adj.* [L. *aequabilis*, fr. *aequare* to make level or equal, fr. *aequus* even, equal.] **1.** Uniform; not varying or changing; as, an *equable* style. **2.** Even; tranquil; as, an *equable* temper. — **Syn.** See STEADY. — **eq'ua·bil'i·ty** (-bĭl'ĭ·tĭ), **eq'ua·ble·ness**, *n.* — **eq'ua·bly** (-blĭ), *adv.*

e'qual (ē'kwăl), *adj.* [L. *aequalis*, fr. *aequus* even, equal.] **1.** Exactly the same in measure, quantity, number, or degree; like in value, quality, status, or position. **2.** *Archaic.* Characterized by justice; fair. **3.** *Obs.* Uniform; equable. **4.** Level. **5.** Evenly balanced or proportioned. **6.** Having competent power, abilities, or means. — **Syn.** See SAME. — **Ant.** Unequal. — *n.* One having the same or a similar age, rank, station, talents, strength, etc.; also, an equal quantity or number. — *v. t.;* E'QUALED (ē'kwăld) *or* E'QUALLED; E'QUALING *or* E'QUAL·LING. **1.** *Archaic.* To make equal or equal to. **2.** To be or become equal to; to match. **3.** To recompense fully.

e'qual–a're·a, *adj.* Designating or pertaining to a map projection of a global surface having in all parts correct representation of area (square mileage). Its central regions are shown in true shape, its outer regions distorted, but with all areas of the same scale. The Mollweide and sinusoidal projections are equal-area projections.

e·qual'i·tar'i·an (ē·kwŏl'ĭ·târ'ĭ·ăn), *adj.* Asserting or promoting the view that men are equal, esp. politically or socially. — *n.* One who holds equalitarian views. — **e·qual'i·tar'i·an·ism** (-ĭz'm), *n.*

e·qual'i·ty (ē·kwŏl'ĭ·tĭ), *n.; pl.* EQUALITIES (-tĭz). Character or condition of being equal.

Equality State. Wyoming; — a nickname alluding to the fact that it was the first state in the United States to grant woman suffrage.

e'qual·ize (ē'kwăl·īz), *v. t.* **1.** To make equal. **2.** To make uniform or constant. — **e'qual·i·za'tion** (-ĭ·zā'shŭn; -ī·zā'shŭn), *n.*

e'qual·iz'er (-īz'ẽr), *n.* **1.** One that equalizes. **2.** *Elec.* A conductor of low resistance joining points of equal potential in the armature winding of an electrical machine.

e'qual·ly (ē'kwăl·ĭ), *adv.* In an equal manner or degree.

e'qua·nim'i·ty (ē'kwȧ·nĭm'ĭ·tĭ; ĕk'wȧ-), *n.* [L. *aequanimitas*, fr. *aequanimis*, fr. *aequus* equal + *animus* mind.] Evenness of mind; calm temper; composure.

Syn. Equanimity, composure, sang-froid, phlegm mean self-possession or lack of perturbation. **Equanimity** suggests a habit of mind that repels all that disturbs, or that is liable to disturbance only under great strain; **composure** commonly implies the conquest of emotional or mental agitation but it may imply temperamental freedom from it; **sang-froid** implies great coolness and steadiness, especially under strain; **phlegm** implies more insensitiveness than any of the other terms and often suggests apathy rather than discipline or self-control.

e·quate' (ē·kwāt'), *v. t.* [L. *aequatus*, past part. of *aequare* to make equal, fr. *aequus* level, equal.] **1.** To make equal, or to represent or express as equal. **2.** To make such a correction in as will reduce to a common standard.

e·qua'tion (ē·kwā'zhŭn; -shŭn), *n.* **1.** Act or process of making, or state of being, equal; equilibrium. **2.** Variation as in observation, judgment, or method, occasioned by the personal peculiarities of an individual; also, a correction or allowance made for such variation; — in full ***personal equation.*** **3.** *Math.* An expression of equality between two magnitudes or operations, the sign = being placed between them; as, a binomial *equation;* a quadratic *equation.* **4.** *Chem.* An expression representing a chemical reaction quantitatively by means of chemical symbols, the formulas of the reacting substances being placed on the left, and those of the products on the right, of the sign = or →, which should be read "give," not "equal to."

e·qua'tion·al sen'tence (-ăl). *Gram.* A sentence, as in Latin and Russian, in which subject and predicate are not linked by a verb (L. *spes mea Christus*, Christ [is] my hope); — called also *nominal sentence.*

e·qua'tor (ē·kwā'tẽr), *n.* [LL. *aequator* one who equalizes.] **1.** *Geog.* An imaginary great circle on the earth's surface, everywhere equally distant from the two poles, dividing the earth's surface into the Northern and Southern Hemispheres. **2.** *Astron.* The great circle (***celestial equator***) in which the plane of the earth's equator intersects the celestial sphere; — so called because, when the sun is crossing it, day and night are everywhere of equal length. **3.** Any circle dividing the surface of a body into two equal and symmetrical parts, in the manner of the equator of a sphere.

e'qua·to'ri·al (ē'kwȧ·tō'rĭ·ăl; 70), *adj.* **a** Of or pertaining to the equator or an equator. **b** Resembling conditions at the equator, esp. in climate; as, *equatorial* heat. — *n.* *Astron.* A telescope so mounted as to have two axes of motion at right angles, one of them (the polar axis) parallel to the earth's axis.

eq'uer·ry (ĕk'wẽr·ĭ; ē·kwĕr'ĭ), *n.; pl.* -RIES (-ĭz). [F. *écurie* stable, fr. OF. *escurie*, confused with OF. *escuier* squire. The Eng. word has been influenced by L. *equus* horse.] **1.** An officer of princes or nobles, charged with the care of their horses. In England equerries are officers of the royal household. **2.** A personal attendant upon one of the members of the British royal household.

e·ques'tri·an (ē·kwĕs'trĭ·ăn), *adj.* [L. *equester*, fr. *eques* horseman, fr. the stem of *equus* horse.] **1.** Of or pertaining to horses, horsemen, or horsemanship. **2.** Being or riding on horseback; mounted. **3.** Of, pert. to, or composed of knights. — *n.* One who rides on horseback.

e·ques'tri·enne' (ē·kwĕs'trĭ·ĕn'), *n.* [*equestrian* + F. fem. suffix *-enne.*] A female equestrian; a horsewoman.

e'qui- (ē'kwĭ-). [L. *aequus* equal.] A prefix, meaning *having equal, equally*, as in *equi*librium, *equi*distant.

e'qui·an'gu·lar (-ăng'gū·lẽr), *adj.* Having equal angles.

e'qui·dis'tance (-dĭs'tăns), *n.* Equal distance.

e'qui·dis'tant (-tănt), *adj.* Equally distant. — **e'qui·dis'tant·ly**, *adv.*

e'qui·lat'er·al (ē'kwĭ·lăt'ẽr·ăl), *adj.* [LL. *aequilateralis*, fr. *aequus* equal + *latus*, *lateris*, side.] Having all sides equal. — *n.* A side exactly corresponding, or equal, to others; also, a figure of equal sides. See TRIANGLE, *Illust.* — **e'qui·lat'er·al·ly**, *adv.*

e·quil'i·brant (ē·kwĭl'ĭ·brănt), *n.* *Physics.* Any force or system of forces which is capable of balancing a given force or system of forces.

e'qui·li'brate (ē'kwĭ·lī'brāt; ē·kwĭl'ĭ·brāt), *v. t.* [LL. *aequilibratus* in equilibrium, fr. *aequus* equal + *libra* balance.] **1.** To balance, as two scales. **2.** To be balanced with; to counterbalance. — **e'qui·li·bra'tion** (ē'kwĭ·lī·brā'shŭn; ē·kwĭl'ĭ-), *n.* — **e'qui·li'bra·tor** (-lī'brā·tẽr), *n.*

e·quil'i·brist (ē·kwĭl'ĭ·brĭst), *n.* [F. *équilibriste.*] One who balances himself in unnatural positions and hazardous movements, as in ropedancing. — **e·quil'i·bris'tic** (-brĭs'tĭk), *adj.*

e'qui·lib'ri·um (ē'kwĭ·lĭb'rĭ·ŭm), *n.; pl.* -UMS (-ŭmz), -A (-ȧ). [L. *aequilibrium*, fr. *aequilibris* in equilibrium, level, fr. *aequus* equal + *libra* balance.] **1.** *Phys. Science.* A state of balance between opposing forces or actions, either *static*, as in the case of a body acted on by forces whose resultant is zero, or *dynamic*, as in a reversible chemical reaction when the velocities in both directions are equal. **2.** A state of balance, or even adjustment, between opposing influences, interests, etc.

e'quine (ē'kwīn), *adj.* [L. *equinus*, fr. *equus* horse.] Of, pertaining to, or like a horse. — *n.* A horse.

e'qui·noc'tial (ē'kwĭ·nŏk'shăl; ĕk'wĭ-), *adj.* **1.** Pertaining to an equinox, or to a state or the time of equal day and night. **2.** Pertaining to the regions or climate of the equinoctial line or equator; in or near that line. **3.** Pertaining to the time when the sun passes the equinoctial points; as, an *equinoctial* storm, that is, one happening at or near the time of the equinox. — *n.* **1.** The equinoctial circle. **2.** An equinoctial storm.

equinoctial circle *or* **line.** The celestial equator. See EQUATOR, 2.

e'qui·nox (ē'kwĭ·nŏks; ĕk'wĭ-), *n.* [F. or L.; F. *équinoxe*, fr. L. *aequinoctium*, fr. *aequus* equal + *nox, noctis*, night.] **1.** The time when the sun's center crosses the equator and day and night are everywhere of equal length, that is, about March 21 (***vernal equinox***) or September 23 (***autumnal equinox***). **2.** Either of the two points (**equinoctial points**) where the celestial equator intersects the ecliptic.

e·quip' (ē·kwĭp'), *v. t.;* E·QUIPPED' (-kwĭpt'); E·QUIP'PING. [F. *équiper* to supply.] **1.** To furnish for service; to fit out, as troops. **2.** To dress; array. — **Syn.** See FURNISH.

eq'ui·page (ĕk'wĭ·pĭj), *n.* **1.** Furniture or outfit, as for a vessel, an army, etc. **2.** A set of small articles for table service, for personal use, etc.; also, a case to hold such articles. **3.** A carriage of state or of pleasure, with horses, liveried servants, etc.; a carriage.

e·quip'ment (ē·kwĭp'mĕnt), *n.* **1.** Act of equipping; state or manner of being equipped. **2.** Articles comprised in an outfit, as furnishings or apparatus; equipage. **3.** The mental or temperamental traits and resources which equip a person; as, the *equipment* of an educated man. **4.** *Railroads.* Cars and locomotives; rolling stock, as contrasted with the roadbed and stations.

e'qui·poise (ē'kwĭ·poiz; ĕk'wĭ-), *n.* **1.** Equality of weight; hence, equilibrium or balance. **2.** Counterpoise.

e'qui·pol'lence (ē'kwĭ·pŏl'ĕns), **e'qui·pol'len·cy** (-ĕn·sĭ), *n.* Equality of power, force, or signification.

e'qui·pol'lent (-ĕnt), *adj.* [F. *équipollent*, fr. L. *aequipollens*, fr. *aequus* equal + *pollens, -entis*, pres. part. of *pollere* to be strong, able.] **1.** Equal in force, validity, or effectiveness. **2.** Equivalent as regards signification or result. — *n.* An equivalent.

e'qui·pon'der·ance (-pŏn'dẽr·ăns), **e'qui·pon'der·an·cy** (-ăn·sĭ), *n.* Equality of weight; equipoise.

e'qui·pon'der·ant (-ănt), *adj.* Evenly balanced.

e'qui·pon'der·ate (-āt), *v. i. & t.* [ML. *aequiponderare*, fr. L. *aequus* equal + *ponderare* to weigh.] To be or make equal in weight; to counterbalance.

e'qui·po·ten'tial (-pō·tĕn'shăl), *adj.* **1.** Having equal power, potentiality, or capability. **2.** *Physics.* Having the same potential.

eq'ui·se'tum (ĕk'wĭ·sē'tŭm), *n.; pl.* EQUISETUMS (-tŭmz), EQUISETA (-tȧ). [L. *equisaetum, -setum*, the horsetail, fr. *equus* horse + *saeta, seta*, bristle.] *Bot.* = HORSETAIL, 2 **a**.

eq'ui·ta·ble (ĕk'wĭ·tȧ·b'l), *adj.* **1.** Possessing or exhibiting equity; just. **2.** *Law.* That can be sustained in a court of equity; existing or valid in equity as distinguished from law. — **Syn.** See FAIR. — **eq'ui·ta·ble·ness**, *n.* — **eq'ui·ta·bly** (-blĭ), *adv.*

eq'ui·tant (-tănt), *adj.* [L. *equitans, -antis*, pres. part. of *equitare* to ride, fr. *eques* horseman.] *Bot.* Overlapping each other; — said of leaves whose bases overlap the leaves within or above them, as in the iris.

eq'ui·ta'tion (-tā'shŭn), *n.* [L. *equitatio.*] Act or art of riding on horseback; horsemanship.

eq'ui·tes (ĕk'wĭ·tēz), *n. pl.* [L., pl. of *eques* horseman.] *Rom. Hist.* Members of a military order serving as cavalry and having special privileges and emoluments.

eq'ui·ty (ĕk'wĭ·tĭ), *n.; pl.* -TIES (-tĭz). [OF. *equité*, fr. L. *aequitas*, fr. *aequus* even, equal.] **1.** State or quality of being equal or fair; fairness in dealing. **2.** That which is equitable or fair. **3.** *Law.* **a** The system of law which originated in the extraordinary justice formerly administered by the king's chancellor and was later developed into a body of rules supplementary to or aiding the common and statute law. The term has come to designate the formal system of legal and procedural rules and doctrines according to which justice is administered within certain limits of jurisdiction. **b** An equitable claim or right. **4.** Hence, any body of legal doctrines and rules similarly developed to enlarge, supplement, or override a system of law which has become too narrow and rigid in its scope. **5.** *Collog.* The amount or value of a property or properties above the total of liens or charges.

equity capital. = VENTURE CAPITAL.

e·quiv'a·lence (ē·kwĭv'ȧ·lĕns), **e·quiv'a·len·cy** (-lĕn·sĭ), *n.* **1.** State of being equivalent; equality of worth, meaning, or force. **2.** *Chem.* **a** Equality of valence. **b** = VALENCE.

e·quiv'a·lent (-lĕnt), *adj.* [LL. *aequivalens, -entis*, pres. part., deriv. of *aequus* equal + *valere* to be strong, be worth.] **1.** *Obs.* Equal in force or authority. **2.** Alike in significance. **3.** Equal in value, esp. for exchange. **4.** Virtually or in effect identical; tantamount; as, his remark was *equivalent* to an insult. **5.** *Chem.* Having the same combining or reacting value; as, *equivalent* quantities of two elements. **6.** *Geom.* Equal in measure but not admitting of superposition; — applied to magnitudes; as, a square may be *equivalent* to a triangle. — **Syn.** See SAME. — *n.* Something equivalent. — **e·quiv'a·lent·ly**, *adv.*

e·quiv'o·cal (ē·kwĭv'ō·kăl), *adj.* [LL. *aequivocus*, fr. *aequus* equal + *vocare* to call.] **1.** Having two or more significations; ambiguous; as, *equivocal* words. **2.** Uncertain as an indication or sign; doubtful. **3.** Questionable or suspicious as regards genuineness or reputation. — **Syn.** See OBSCURE. — **e·quiv'o·cal·ly**, *adv.*

e·quiv'o·cate (-kāt), *v. i.* [ML. *aequivocatus*, past part. of *aequivocare*, fr. LL. *aequivocus*. See EQUIVOCAL.] To use equivocal language, esp. with intent to deceive; hence, to prevaricate; to lie. — **Syn.** See LIE. — **e·quiv'o·ca'tion** (-kā'shŭn), *n.* — **e·quiv'o·ca'tor** (-kā'tẽr), *n.*

eq'ui·voque, eq'ui·voke (ĕk'wĭ·vōk; ē'kwĭ-), *n.* [LL. *aequivocus* equivocal.] **1.** An ambiguous term; also, a pun; punning. **2.** Double meaning; ambiguity.

-er (-ẽr). [AS. *-ere.*] A suffix forming: **a** Nouns from other nouns, with the sense of *one who has to do with*, esp. as a matter of trade, profession, etc.; as, tinner, one whose occupation is with tin. **b** Nouns denoting: (1) *Things* or *actions related to* (the meaning of the root word), as in facer. (2) *One of a size, capacity, value,* or *date* (specified by a number), as in fiver, six-pounder. **c** Nouns from nouns or adjectives of place, denoting *resident of, one living in*, as in islander, Londoner, New Zealander. **d** Nouns from verbs, denoting the *agent*, esp. a person (orig. a male), machine, or implement, as in maker, player.

-er. [AS. *-ra*, in adjectives; *-or*, in adverbs.] A suffix forming the comparative degree of adjectives and adverbs; as, warmer.

-er. [AF. *-er*, OF. *-ier*, fr. L. *-arius, -arium.*] A suffix forming nouns denoting a *person (-arius)* or *thing (-arium) connected with*, as in carpenter, usher, grocer.

e'ra (ē'rȧ; ẹr'ȧ), *n.* [LL. *aera* an era, in L. the items of an account, counters, pl. of *aes, aeris*, brass, money.] **1.** A chronological order or system computed from a given date as basis; as, the Christian *Era.* **2.** A fixed point of time from which a series of years is reckoned. **3.** A period of time reckoned from some particular date. **4.** A signal stage of history; epoch. **5.** One of the major divisions of geologic time; as, the Paleozoic *era.* — **Syn.** See PERIOD.

e·ra'di·ate (ē·rā'dĭ·āt), *v. i. & t.* To shoot forth, as rays of light; to radiate. — **e·ra'di·a'tion** (-ā'shŭn), *n.*

e·rad'i·ca·ble (ē·răd'ĭ·kȧ·b'l), *adj.* That can be eradicated.

e·rad'i·cate (-kāt), *v. t.* [L. *eradicatus*, past part. of *eradicare* to eradicate, fr. *e* out + *radix, radicis*, root.] To pluck up by the roots; hence, to extirpate. — **Syn.** See EXTERMINATE. — **e·rad'i·ca'tion** (-kā'shŭn), *n.* — **e·rad'i·ca'tive** (-kā'tĭv; -kȧ·tĭv), *adj. & n.* — **e·rad'i·ca'tor** (-kā'tẽr), *n.*

e·rase' (ē·rās'; *esp. Brit.*, -rāz'), *v. t.* [L. *erasus*, past part. of *eradere* to erase, fr. *e* out + *radere* to scrape.] To rub or scrape out, as letters or characters written, engraved, or painted; to efface; expunge. — **e·ras'a·ble** (-rās'ȧ·b'l; -rāz'ȧ·b'l), *adj.*

Syn. **Erase, expunge, cancel, efface, obliterate, blot out, delete** mean to strike out something. **Erase** implies action such as or like rubbing or scraping out; **expunge** now implies so thoroughgoing an erasure that the thing affected is wiped out; **cancel** implies some action, such as marking, rescinding, or neutralizing, that makes a thing no longer useful or effective; **efface** implies removal of every sign of a thing's identity or of its existence; **obliterate** and **blot out** both imply a smearing with or as if with ink that removes all traces of a thing's existence; **delete** now suggests a marking, an obliteration, etc., that means the elimination of the thing.

e·ras'er (ē·rās'ẽr; -rāz'ẽr), *n.* One that erases; specif., a sharp instrument or a piece of rubber or cloth used to erase marks made with ink, pencil, chalk, or the like.

E·ras'tian (ē·răs'chăn; -tĭ·ăn; 58), *adj.* Of or pertaining to Thomas Erastus, a Swiss physician and Zwinglian theologian (1524–83), or his doctrines; hence, designating or advocating the doctrine of state supremacy in ecclesiastical affairs, ascribed to Erastus. — **E·ras'tian**, *n.* **E·ras'tian·ism** (-ĭz'm), *n.*

e·ra'sure (ē·rā'zhẽr; -shẽr), *n.* Act or instance of erasing.

Er'a·to (ĕr'ȧ·tō), *n.* [L., fr. Gr. *Eratō*, fr. *erasthai* to love.] *Class. Myth.* Muse of lyric and amatory poetry.

er'bi·um (ûr'bĭ·ŭm), *n.* [NL., fr. Ytt*erby*, in Sweden.] *Chem.* A metallic element, one of the rare-earth metals. Symbol, *Er;* at. no., 68; at. wt., 167.2.

ere (âr; 6), *prep.* [AS. *ǣr*, prep., adv., & conj., prop. adv. in the comparative.] Before. — ***ere long.*** Before long; soon. — ***ere now.*** Formerly; heretofore. — *conj.* **1.** Before. **2.** Sooner than; rather than.

Er'e·bus (ĕr'ē·bŭs), *n.* [L., fr. Gr. *Erebos.*] *Gr. Myth.* The gloomy space through which souls passed to Hades.

Er'ech·the'um (ĕr'ĕk·thē'ŭm), **Er'ech·thei'on** (-thī'ŏn), *n.* [Gr. *Erechtheion.*] A temple on the Acropolis in Athens, built (5th century B.C.) reputedly by King Erechtheus. It is the best preserved and most perfect example of Ionic architecture, and is famous especially for its caryatids.

e·rect' (ē·rĕkt'), *adj.* [L. *erectus*, past part. of *erigere* to erect, fr. *e* out + *regere* to lead straight.] **1.** Upright; not leaning or prone; specif., *Bot.*, not spreading or decumbent; as, an *erect* stem. **2.** Directed upward; uplifted. **3.** *Obs.* Watchful; alert. — *v. t.* **1.** To raise, as a building; to build. **2.** *Obs.* To raise in rank or esteem; exalt. **3.** To set upright; rear; as, to *erect* a flagstaff. **4.** *Archaic.* To set up or establish; to found. **5.** To cause to stand up or out from the body. **6.** *Geom.* To draw or construct (a perpendicular or figure) upon a given base. **7.** *Mach.* To put together in position for use; to set up. — **e·rect'er**, *n.* — **e·rect'ly**, *adv.* — **e·rect'ness**, *n.*

e·rec'tile (ē·rĕk'tĭl; 56), *adj.* Susceptible of being erected. — **e'rec·til'i·ty** (ē'rĕk·tĭl'ĭ·tĭ; ĕr'ĕk-), *n.*

e·rec'tion (ē·rĕk'shŭn), *n.* **1.** Act of erecting; also, state of being erected; a raising, building, founding, etc. **2.** The assembling and connection of the different parts of a machine or structure. **3.** *Physiol.* State of a part which has become hard and swollen by the accumulation of blood in the erectile tissue.

e·rec'tor (-tẽr), *n.* One who or that which erects.

ere'long' (âr'lŏng'; 74), *adv.* Before long; soon.

er'e·mite (ĕr'ē·mīt), *n.* [LL. *eremita.* See HERMIT.] A hermit; a religious recluse or solitary. — **er'e·mit'ic** (-mĭt'ĭk), **er'e·mit'i·cal** (-ĭ·kăl), **er'e·mit'ish** (ĕr'ē·mīt'ĭsh), *adj.*

ere'now' (âr'nou'), *adv.* Ere now; heretofore.

e·rep'sin (ē·rĕp'sĭn), *n.* [From L. *eripere* to take away, set free, after *pepsin.*] *Biochem.* An enzyme of the intestinal juice, capable of decomposing proteoses and peptones, but not native proteins (except casein).

er'e·thism (ĕr'ē·thĭz'm), *n.* [Gr. *erethismos* irritation, fr. *erethizein* to stir, rouse.] *Physiol.* Excessive irritability, as of a muscle.

ere'while' (âr'hwīl'), *adv.* Also **ere'whiles'** (-hwīlz'). *Archaic.* Some time ago; a little while before; heretofore.

erg (ûrg), *n.* [Gr. *ergon* work.] *Physics.* A unit of energy or work, being the work done by one dyne acting through a distance of one centimeter. Abbr. *e.*

‖**er'go** (ûr'gō), *conj. & adv.* [L.] Therefore; hence.

er'gon (ûr'gŏn), *n.* [NL., fr. Gr. *ergon* work.] *Physics.* **a** Work, measured in terms of the quantity of heat to which it is equivalent. **b** = ERG.

er·gos'ter·ol (ẽr·gŏs'tẽr·ōl; -ŏl), *n.* [*ergot* + *sterol.*] *Biochem.* A sterol first prepared from ergot, but now obtained from yeast and other sources, and held to be the principle in foods and in the body which, when exposed to ultraviolet radiation, prevents or cures rickets.

er'got (ûr'gŏt), *n.* [F., fr. OF. *argot*, lit., a spur.] *Plant Pathol.* **1.** A fungous disease of rye, other cereals, and wild grasses, in which the grains are replaced by dark-colored growths; also, the fungus causing this disease. **2.** One of the dark growths produced in the disease. **3.** The dried sclerotial bodies of the fungus, constituting a valuable drug, which contracts the unstriped muscle fibers, and is used to control hemorrhage and to contract the uterus, esp. during or after labor.

er'got·ism (-ĭz'm), *n.* *Med.* A diseased condition of man or animals, produced by eating grain or grasses infected with ergot fungus, or from chronic excessive use of the drug.

er'i·ca'ceous (ĕr'ĭ·kā'shŭs), *adj.* [From L. *erice* heath, fr. Gr. *ereikē.*] *Bot.* Belonging to the heath family (Ericaceae). See HEATH.

er'i·coid (ĕr'ĭ·koid), *adj.* Like the heath (genus *Erica*).

E'rie (ẹr'ĭ), *n.* See IROQUOIAN.

e·rig′er·on (ē·rĭj′ẽr·ŏn), *n.* [L., groundsel, fr. Gr. *ērigerōn*, fr. *ēri* early + *gerōn* old man; — from the hoary pubescence of many species.] *Bot.* Any of a genus (*Erigeron*) of herbs of the aster family, having white-rayed flower heads resembling those of the aster.

Er′in (ĕr′ĭn; ē̤r′ĭn), *n.* [OIr. *Ériu*, dat. *Érinn*, Ir. *Éire*, Ireland.] *Poetic.* Ireland.

e·rin′go (ē·rĭng′gō). Var. of ERYNGO.

E·rin′ys (ē·rĭn′ĭs; ē·rī′nĭs; ĕ-), *n.; pl.* ERINYES (-rĭn′ĭ·ēz). [L., fr. Gr. *Erinys.*] *Gr. Relig.* One of three avenging spirits, snaky-haired women who pursued evildoers and inflicted madness.

E′ris (ē′rĭs; ĕr′ĭs), *n. Gr. Myth.* Goddess of discord.

er·is′tic (ĕr·ĭs′tĭk), *adj.* Also **er·is′ti·cal** (-tĭ·kăl). [Gr. *eristikos*, fr. *erizein* to strive, fr. *eris* strife.] Pertaining to, suitable for, or given to disputation.

erl′king′ (ûrl′kĭng′; ĕrl′-), *n.* [G. *erlkönig*, fr. Dan. *elle(r)konge*, *elve(r)konge*, fr. *elv* elf.] *Scandinavian & German Folklore.* King of the elves, who works mischief and ruin, esp. to children.

er′mine (ûr′mĭn), *n.*; see PLURAL, *Note*, 6. [OF.] **1.** Any of several species of weasels (genus *Mustela*) of the northern parts of both hemispheres, which assume a pure-white coat in winter, except for the end of the tail, which remains jet black; also, the fur of these animals when white. See STOAT. **2.** The office or functions of a judge, whose state robe, lined with ermine, is emblematic of purity and honor.

er′mined (ûr′mĭnd), *adj.* Clothed or adorned with ermine.

erne, ern (ûrn), *n.* [AS. *earn* eagle.] A sea eagle (esp. *Haliaeetus albicilla*). See EAGLE, 1.

e·rode′ (ē·rōd′), *v. t.* [L. *erodere*, *erosum*, fr. *e* out + *rodere* to gnaw.] To eat into or away; to destroy by slow disintegration; specif., *Geol. & Phys. Geog.*, to wear away, as land by the action of water; also, to produce or form by erosion; as, glaciers *erode* U-shaped valleys. — *v. i.* To be eroded or worn away.

e·rog′e·nous (ē·rŏj′ē·nŭs), *adj.* Also **er′o·gen′ic** (ĕr′ō·jĕn′ĭk). [Gr. *eros* love + *-genous.*] *Psychol.* Productive of erotic desire.

E′ros (ē̤r′ŏs; ĕr′ŏs), *n.* [L., fr. Gr. *erōs* love, *Erōs* Eros.] *Gr. Relig.* The god of love, usually represented as the son of Aphrodite equivalent to the Roman god Cupid.

e·rose′ (ē·rōs′), *adj.* [L. *erosus*, past part. See ERODE.] **1.** Irregular or uneven as if eaten or worn away. **2.** *Bot.* Having the margin irregularly notched as if gnawed.

e·ro′sion (ē·rō′zhŭn), *n.* Act of eroding, or state of being eroded.

e·ro′sive (ē·rō′sĭv), *adj.* Tending to erode.

e·rot′ic (ē·rŏt′ĭk; ĕ-), *adj.* [Gr. *erōtikos*. See EROS.] **1.** Of, relating to, or treating of sexual love; amatory. **2.** Strongly affected by sexual desire; as, an *erotic* person. — *n.* An erotic person. — **e·rot′i·cal** (-ĭ·kăl), *adj.* — **e·rot′i·cal·ly**, *adv.*

e·rot′i·cism (-ĭ·sĭz′m), *n.* **1.** Erotic character or sentiment. **2.** *Psychoanalysis.* = EROTISM, 2.

er′o·tism (ĕr′ō·tĭz′m), *n.* **1.** Sexual desire. **2.** *Psychoanalysis.* The love life in any or all of its physical or psychical manifestations.

err (ûr), *v. i.* [OF. *errer*, fr. L. *errare.*] To fall into error; to go astray; esp., to do wrong; to sin.

er′rand (ĕr′ănd), *n.* [AS. *ǣrende.*] **1.** A journey for a purpose entrusted; now, esp., a short trip to discharge the business of another. **2.** A special business entrusted to a messenger.

er′rant (ĕr′ănt; *formerly also* ăr′ănt), *adj.* [F., pres. part. fr. OF. *errer* to travel, fr. L. *iter* journey.] **1.** Wandering, or given to wandering, in search of adventure or on missions of chivalry; as, knights-*errant.* **2.** Deviating from the true or correct; erring. **3.** *Obs.* Arrant. — **er′rant·ly**, *adv.*

er′rant·ry (ĕr′ănt·rĭ), *n.* Errant character, condition, or deed; hence, conduct characteristic of knights-errant.

‖**er·ra′re hu·ma′num est** (ĕ·rā′rē hū·mā′nŭm ĕst). [L.] To err is human.

er·ra′ta (ĕ·rā′tȧ), *n., pl.* of ERRATUM.

er·rat′ic (ĕ·răt′ĭk), *adj.* [L. *erraticus*, fr. *errare* to wander.] **1.** Having no certain course; wandering; — formerly applied to the planets. **2.** Deviating from a wise or common course in opinion or conduct; eccentric; queer. **3.** *Geol.* Transported, as masses of rock or gravel, from their original resting places, esp. by ice. — **Syn.** See STRANGE. — **er·rat′i·cal·ly** (-ĭ·kăl·ĭ), *adv.*

er·ra′tum (ĕ·rā′tŭm), *n.; pl.* ERRATA (-tȧ). [L., past part. neut. of *errare* to err.] A printer's or writer's error in a publication; *pl.*, such errors or a list of them with corrections.

err′ing (ûr′ĭng; ĕr′-), *adj.* That errs. — **err′ing·ly**, *adv.*

er·ro′ne·ous (ĕ·rō′nē·ŭs; 58), *adj.* [L. *erroneus.*] **1.** *Archaic.* Wandering; straying. **2.** Containing error; incorrect. — **er·ro′ne·ous·ly**, *adv.* — **er·ro′ne·ous·ness**, *n.*

er′ror (ĕr′ẽr), *n.* [OF. & L., fr. L. *errare* to err.] **1.** Belief in what is untrue, the state of holding such belief, or an instance of it. **2.** A moral offense; sin. **3.** An act involving a departure from truth or accuracy; a mistake. **4.** *Baseball.* A fault of a player of the side in the field, which prolongs the time at bat of the batsman, or prolongs the life of a base runner, or allows a base runner to advance one or more bases when perfect play would have ensured his being put out. Passed balls and wild pitches are not scored as errors. **5.** *Christian Science.* The contradiction of Truth; a belief without understanding; that which seemeth to be and is not. *Mary Baker Eddy.* **6.** *Math.* The difference between an observed or calculated value, generally of a physical quantity, and the true value.

Syn. **Error, mistake, blunder, slip, lapse** mean a departure from what is true, right, or proper. **Error** is the most comprehensive term: it may imply carelessness or intention but it may suggest an inaccuracy where accuracy is impossible; **mistake** implies misconception, misunderstanding, inadvertence, or the like, and is seldom a harsh term; **blunder** commonly implies ignorance or stupidity and, usually, blameworthiness; **slip** carries a stronger implication of inadvertence or accident especially in a trivial mistake; **lapse** implies forgetfulness, weakness, or inattention.

er·satz′ (ĕr·zäts′), *n.* [G.] Replacement; substitution. — *adj.* Substitute; as, *ersatz* coffee.

Erse (ûrs), *n.* [A var. of *Irish.*] Scottish Gaelic; less properly, Irish Gaelic; Irish. — **Erse**, *adj.*

erst (ûrst), *adv.* [AS. *ǣrest*, superl. of *ǣr*. See ERE.] **1.** *Obs.* First; in the first place. **2.** *Archaic.* Previously; formerly; erstwhile. — *adj. Archaic.* First; former.

erst′while′ (ûrst′hwīl′; ûrst′hwīl′), *adv.* Also, *Rare*, **erst′whiles′** (-hwīlz′; -hwīlz′). *Archaic.* At a time past; formerly; heretofore. — **erst′while′** (*see Pron.*, § 2), *adj.*

er′u·bes′cent (ĕr′ōō·bĕs′ĕnt; -′nt), *adj.* [L. *erubescens*, pres. part. See RUBESCENT.] Red, or reddish; blushing. — **er′u·bes′cence** (-ĕns; -′ns), *n.*

e·ruct′ (ē·rŭkt′), *v. t. & i.* Also **e·ruc′tate** (ē·rŭk′tāt). [L. *eructare*, fr. *e* out + *ructare* to belch.] To eject, as wind, from the stomach; to belch; hence, to emit, as fumes. — **e′ruc·ta′tion** (ē′rŭk·tā′shŭn; ĕr′ŭk-), *n.* — **e·ruc′ta·tive** (ē·rŭk′tȧ·tĭv), *adj.*

er′u·dite (ĕr′ōō·dīt; ĕr′ū-), *adj.* [L. *eruditus*, past part. of *erudire* to free from rudeness, polish, instruct, fr. *e* out + *rudis* rude.] Characterized by wide knowledge of a bookish kind; learned. — **er′u·dite·ly**, *adv.* — **er′u·dite·ness**, *n.*

er′u·dit′i·cal (-dĭt′ĭ·kăl), *adj. Rare.* Erudite.

er′u·di′tion (-dĭsh′ŭn), *n.* Learning, esp. in literature, history, or criticism; scholarship. — **er′u·di′tion·al** (-ăl; -′l), *adj.*

e·rupt′ (ē·rŭpt′), *v. i.* [See ERUPTION.] **1.** To burst or break out, as ashes from a volcano. **2.** To break out in eruption, as a geyser. — *v. t.* To cause to erupt; to eject, as lava.

e·rup′tion (ē·rŭp′shŭn), *n.* [L. *eruptio*, fr. *erumpere*, *eruptum*, to break out, fr. *e* out + *rumpere* to break.] **1.** Act of breaking out or bursting forth, esp. of confined elements; as, *eruptions* of fire, lava, etc.; esp.: **a** *Now Rare.* A sudden hostile movement of armed men from one country to another. **b** A violent commotion; outbreak. **2.** *Med.* The breaking out of a rash, as on the skin; also, the rash itself. — **e·rup′tive** (-tĭv), *adj.*

-ery. [ME. *-erie*, fr. OF. *-erie*, fr. *-ier* (fr. L. *-arius*) + *-ie* (fr. L. *-ia*).] A noun suffix signifying: **a** *Qualities collectively, character, behavior, conduct*, or the like, as in fool*ery*, snobb*ery*, etc. **b** *Act, art, trade, occupation*, or the like, as in arch*ery*. **c** Place (where something is done or is kept, or grows, gathers), as in bak*ery*, rook*ery*. **d** *Collection* or *aggregate*, as in fin*ery*.

e·ryn′go (ē·rĭng′gō), *n.* [Gr. *ēryngos.*] *Obs.* Candied sea-holly root, formerly regarded as an aphrodisiac.

er′y·sip′e·las (ĕr′ĭ·sĭp′ĕ·lăs; ĭr′ĭ-), *n.* [L., fr. Gr. *erysipelas.*] *Med.* An acute febrile disease associated with intense local inflammation of the skin and subcutaneous tissue, caused by a hemolytic streptococcus. — **er′y·si·pel′a·tous** (-sĭ·pĕl′ȧ·tŭs), *adj.*

er′y·the′ma (ĕr′ĭ·thē′mȧ), *n.* [NL., fr. Gr. *erythēma*, fr. *erythainein* to redden, fr. *erythros* red.] *Med.* Abnormal redness of the skin due to capillary congestion, as in inflammation. — **er′y·them′a·tous** (-thĕm′ȧ·tŭs; -thē′mȧ·tŭs), **er′y·the·mat′ic** (-thē·măt′ĭk), **er′y·the′mic** (-thē′mĭk), *adj.*

e·ryth′rism (ē·rĭth′rĭz′m; ĕ·rĭth′-), *n.* [Gr. *erythros* red.] Excessive redness, esp. in the plumage of birds or hair of mammals. — **er′y·thris′mal** (ĕr′ĭ·thrĭz′măl), *adj.* — **er′y·thris′tic** (-thrĭs′tĭk), *adj.*

e·ryth′rite (-rīt), *n.* [Gr. *erythros* red.] **1.** Erythritol. **2.** *Mineral.* A hydrous, usually rose-red, cobalt arsenate, $Co_3(AsO_4)_2.8H_2O$, found esp. in monoclinic crystals.

e·ryth′ri·tol (-rĭ·tōl; -tŏl), *n.* *Chem.* A colorless, sweet, crystalline compound, $CH_2OH(CHOH)_2CH_2OH$, extracted from certain lichens and algae.

e·ryth′ro- (ē·rĭth′rō-; ĕ·rĭth′rō-), **erythr-.** [Gr. *erythros.*] A combining form meaning *red*, as in *erythro*cyte.

e·ryth′ro-. Comb. form for *erythrocyte*, as in *erythro*blast.

e·ryth′ro·blast (-blăst), *n.* [2d *erythro-* + *-blast.*] *Anat. & Med.* A nucleated cell or corpuscle of the type from which red blood corpuscles are developed. — **e·ryth′ro·blas′tic** (-blăs′tĭk), *adj.*

e·ryth′ro·cyte (-sīt), *n.* [1st *erythro-* + *-cyte.*] A red blood corpuscle. See CORPUSCLE. — **e·ryth′ro·cyt′ic** (-sĭt′ĭk), *adj.*

e·ryth′ro·cy·tom′e·ter (-sī·tŏm′ē·tẽr), *n.* [*erythrocyte* + *-meter.*] An instrument for counting red blood corpuscles.

e·ryth′ro·poi·e′sis (-poi·ē′sĭs), *n.* [2d *erythro-* + Gr. *poiēsis* a making.] The production of red blood cells (erythrocytes) from the bone marrow. — **-poi·et′ic** (-poi·ĕt′ĭk), *adj.*

E′sau (ē′sô), *n.* [L., fr. Gr. *Ēsau*, fr. Heb. *'Ēsāw.*] *Bib.* The elder son of Isaac and Rebekah. He sold his birthright to his brother Jacob. *Gen.* xxvii.

es′ca·drille′ (ĕs′kȧ·drĭl′; *F.* ĕs′kȧ′drē′y′), *n.* [F., dim. of *escadre* squadron, with suff. after Sp. *escuadrilla.*] **1.** *Naval.* A squadron of war vessels, usually eight. **2.** *Mil.* In European air commands, esp. in the French army, a unit containing, usually, six airplanes.

es′ca·lade′ (ĕs′kȧ·lād′), *n.* [F., fr. It. *scalata*, fr. *scalare* to scale, fr. *scala* ladder, fr. L. *scala.*] An attack on a fortified place, in which ladders are used. — *v. t.* To mount and pass or enter by ladders; to scale.

Es′ca·la′tor (ĕs′kȧ·lā′tẽr), *n.* A trade-mark for a stairway or incline arranged like an endless belt so that the steps or treads ascend or descend continuously.

es′ca·la′tor (ĕs′kȧ·lā′tẽr), *n.* A means for effecting increases and decreases or advancements and ascents; as, a cost-of-living *escalator;* the social *escalator;* — also used attributively; as, an *escalator* amendment.

escalator clause. A clause in a contract providing for the upward or downward adjustment of certain items, to cover specified contingencies.

es·cal′op, es·cal′lop (ĕs·kŏl′ŭp; ĕs·kăl′-), *n.* [OF. *escalope* shell. See SCALLOP.] The scallop or its shell.

es·cap′a·ble (ĕs·kāp′ȧ·b'l; ĭs-), *adj.* See -ABLE **b.**

es′ca·pade′ (ĕs′kȧ·pād′; ĕs′kȧ·păd), *n.* [F.] **1.** Act of escaping from control. **2.** A prankish adventure; prank.

es·cape′ (ĕs·kāp′; ĭs-), *v. i.* [ONF. *escaper* (OF. *eschaper*), deriv. of L. *ex* out of + *cappa* cape.] **1.** To get away, as by flight. **2.** To avoid a threatened ill; to miss imminent pain, punishment, or misfortune. **3.** To issue from confinement or enclosure of any sort; as, gas *escaping* from a pipe. **4.** *Bot.* To run wild from cultivation. See ESCAPE, *n.*, 4. — *v. t.* **1.** To get, or be, out of the way of (a person or thing one wishes to avoid); to succeed in averting (pain, punishment, or misfortune); to avoid. **2.** To fail of (notice) or to fail of being noticed or recalled by (a person). **3.** To issue from, or be uttered by (one), involuntarily.

Syn. **Escape, avoid, evade, elude, shun, eschew** mean to get away or keep away from that which threatens. **Escape** usually implies a threat to one's liberty or well-being, but it does not always imply a running away or an effort to miss (as, to *escape* suspicion, infection, a blow by dodging); **avoid** carries a stronger implication of averting by keeping clear of persons or places known to be a source of danger (thus, one may *avoid* all known sources of contagion yet not *escape* infection); **evade** implies adroitness, ingenuity, etc., in escaping or avoiding; **elude** implies a slippery or baffling quality in the person or thing that escapes; **shun** comes close to *avoid* but it carries a strong implication of repug-

nance, abhorrence, or the like; **eschew**, once nearly equal to *avoid*, now implies avoidance for a moral or prudential reason.
— *n.* **1.** Act of escaping, or fact of having escaped; evasion of injury or any evil; also, the means of escape. **2.** Leakage or outflow, as of steam. **3.** Mental relief from reality or routine; as, literature of *escape*. **4.** *Bot.* A plant which has run wild from cultivation. **— *adj.*** **1.** Of a nature to provide escape from reality; as, *escape* literature. **2.** Providing a basis for evasion of a major claim or responsibility; as, an *escape* clause. — **es·cap′er** (ĕs·kāp′ẽr; ĭs-), *n.*
escape mechanism. *Psychol.* A mode of behavior or thinking adopted to evade unpleasant facts or responsibilities.
es·cape′ment (ĕs·kāp′mĕnt; ĭs-), *n.* **1.** *Rare.* Act of escaping; escape; also, way of escape; vent. **2.** A contrivance in a timepiece which controls the motion of the train of wheelwork and through which the energy of the weight or mainspring is delivered to the pendulum or balance; — so called because it allows a tooth to escape from a pallet at regular intervals. **3.** In typewriters, the mechanism which controls movement of the carriage.

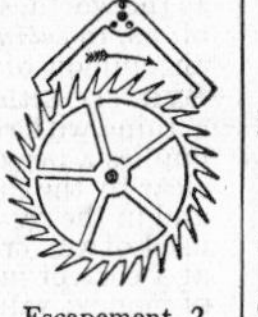
Escapement, 2 (Deadbeat form).

es·cap′ism (ĕs·kāp′ĭz′m; ĭs-), *n.* Habitual diversion of the mind to purely imaginative activity or entertainment to escape from reality or routine. — **es·cap′ist** (-ĭst), *adj. & n.*
es′ca·role (ĕs′kȧ·rōl; 70), *n.* [F.] = ENDIVE, 1.
es·carp′ (ĕs·kärp′), *n.* [F. *escarpe*, fr. It. *scarpa.*] A scarp. **— *v. t.*** *Mil.* To make into, or furnish with, a scarp, or steep slope.
es·carp′ment (-mĕnt), *n.* **1.** A long, high, steep face of rock; a long cliff. **2.** *Mil.* Ground about a fortified place, cut away steeply to prevent hostile approach.
-esce (-ĕs). [L. *-escere.*] A suffix forming inchoative, or inceptive, verbs, as in convale*sce*, efferve*sce*.
-es′cence (-ĕs′ĕns; -′ns). [L. *-escentia.*] A suffix of abstract nouns corresponding to adjectives in -ESCENT, as in convale*scence*, deliqu*escence*, adol*escence*.
-es′cent (-ĕs′ĕnt; -′nt). [L. *-escens*, *-escentis*, the pres. part. ending of Latin inchoative verbs.] An adjective suffix denoting *beginning, beginning to be, slightly*, as in adol*escent* (cf. ADULT).
esch′a·lot (ĕsh′ȧ·lŏt; ĕsh′ȧ·lŏt′), *n.* Shallot.
es′char (ĕs′kär; -kẽr), *n.* [F. and L.; F. *eschare*, fr. L. *eschara.* See SCAR.] *Med.* A dry slough, crust, or scab.
es′char. Var. of ESKER.
es′cha·rot′ic (ĕs′kȧ·rŏt′ĭk), *adj. & n.* [LL. *escharoticus*, fr. Gr. *escharōtikos.*] *Med.* Caustic.
es′cha·tol′o·gy (ĕs′kȧ·tŏl′ō·jĭ), *n.* [Gr. *eschatos* the furthest, last + *-logy.*] *Theol.* The doctrine of the last or final things, as death, resurrection, immortality, judgment. — **es′cha·to·log′i·cal** (-tō·lŏj′ĭ·kăl; ĕs′kăt·ō-), *adj.* — **es′cha·tol′o·gist** (-tŏl′ō·jĭst), *n.*
es·cheat′ (ĕs·chēt′), *n.* [OF. *eschete, escheoite*, fr. *escheoir*, deriv. of L. *ex* out + *cadere* to fall.] *Law.* **1.** In the English feudal law, the reversion of lands to the lord of the fee upon the failure of heirs capable of inheriting under the original grant. **2.** Reversion of land to the crown, or to the state in the United States, by failure of persons legally entitled to hold the same. **3.** Escheated property; also, escheatage. **— *v. i.*** *Law.* To revert, lapse, or pass by escheat. **— *v. t.*** To cause to escheat. — **es·cheat′a·ble** (-ȧ·b′l), *adj.*
es·cheat′age (-ĭj), *n.* Right of taking by escheat.
es·chew′ (ĕs·chōō′; -chū′; 114), *v. t.* [OF. *eschiuver, eschiver*, to shun, avoid, of Teut. origin.] To abstain from or shun as something wrong or distasteful. — **Syn.** See ESCAPE. — **es·chew′al** (-ăl), *n.*
es′cort (ĕs′kôrt), *n.* [F. *escorte*, fr. It. *scorta* a guard or guide, fr. *scorgere* to discern, lead, deriv. of L. *ex* out, quite + *corrigere* to correct.] **1.** A body of persons (orig. armed soldiers) or an individual accompanying another or others for protection or as a mark of honor or courtesy. **2.** A protective screen of warships or fighter planes, or a single ship or plane, attending upon one or more vulnerable craft for fending off enemy attack.
es·cort′ (ĕs·kôrt′), *v. t.* To accompany as escort. — **Syn.** See ACCOMPANY.
escort carrier. *Nav.* A small auxiliary aircraft carrier of about 4000 tons or a converted cargo hull or tanker with flight and hangar decks built on. In United States Navy classed as ***CVE***; in navy slang, *jeep.*
escort fighter. An offensive fighter plane of great fuel capacity for escorting heavy bombers on raids.
es′cri·toire′ (ĕs′krĭ·twär′; ĕs′krĭ·twär), *n.* [OF., fr. LL. *scriptorium.* See SCRIPTORIUM.] A writing table or desk.
es′crow′ (ĕs′krō′; ĕs′krō′), *n.* [OF. *escroe, escroue*, a roll of writings, bond. See SCROLL.] *Law.* A deed, bond, or other written engagement, delivered to a third person, to be delivered by him to the grantee only upon the performance or fulfillment of some condition. The deposit of the escrow places it beyond the control of the grantor; but no title passes until the fulfillment of the condition.
es·cu′do (ĕs·kōō′dō; *Sp.* ās·kōō′thō), *n.; pl.* -DOS (-dōz; *Sp.* -thōs). [Sp. & Pg., lit., shield, fr. L. *scutum.*] **1.** Any of several former gold or silver coins of Spanish countries. **2.** (ĕs·kōō′dō; *Pg.* ĕsh·kōō′thōō) The gold monetary unit of Portugal, containing 100 centavos; also, an alloy coin of this value. See MONEY, *Tables.*
es′cu·lent (ĕs′kū·lĕnt), *adj. & n.* [L. *esculentus*, fr. *esca* food, fr. *edere* to eat.] Eatable; edible.
es·cutch′eon (ĕs·kŭch′ŭn), *n.* [ONF. *escuchon* (OF. *escuçon*), deriv. of L. *scutum* shield.] **1.** The surface, usually shield-shaped, on which armorial bearings are displayed. The ground of the escutcheon is called the *field* and its tincture is mentioned first in blazoning. The upper part is the *chief*, the lower part the *base*, and the sides *dexter* and *sinister*, respectively on the right and left of the wearer of the shield. **2.** *Arch. & Carp.* A shield to protect wood, or for ornament, as the metal shield around a keyhole. **3.** *Naut.* The part of a vessel's stern on which her name is displayed.

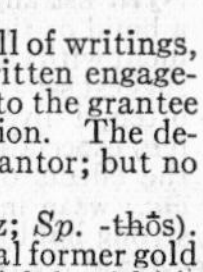

Escutcheon, 1. *A* Dexter Chief Point; *B* Middle Chief Point; *C* Sinister Chief Point; *D* Honor, or Color, Point; *E* Fess, or Heart, Point; *F* Nombril or Navel; *G* Dexter Base Point; *H* Middle Base Point; *I* Sinister Base Point.

Es′dras (ĕz′drăs; -drȧs), *n.* [Gr., Ezra.] **a** *Douay Bib.* Ezra. His name is also given to the book of Nehemiah. **b** One of two books of the Apocrypha. See BIBLE.
-ese (-ēz; -ēs). [OF. *-eis*, fr. L. *-ensis.*] An adjective and noun suffix signifying: **a** *Of, pertaining to,* or *originating in* (a certain place or country). **b** *Native, inhabitant,* or *language* (of a certain place or country); as, Japan*ese*. **c** *Peculiar literary style* or *diction* (of a certain person or type of publication); as, journal*ese*.
es′er·ine (ĕs′ẽr·ēn; -ĭn), *n.* Also **es′er·in.** [F. *ésérine*, fr. Tshi *aser*, prop. *ase*, bean.] = PHYSOSTIGMINE.
es′ker (ĕs′kẽr), *n.* Also **es′kar** (-kär; -kẽr). [Ir. *eiscir* a ridge.] *Geol.* A narrow ridge or mound of gravelly and sandy drift, deposited by a subglacial stream.
Es′ki·mau′an, Es′ki·mo′an (ĕs′kĭ·mō′ăn), *adj.* Of or pert. to the Eskimos, or designating the linguistic family comprising the Eskimos and the Aleuts.
Es′ki·mo (ĕs′kĭ·mō), *n.; pl.* -MOS (-mōz) or -MO (-mō). [Dan., fr. name applied by the Algonquians to the tribes north of them.] **1.** A member of a race whose main habitat is the arctic coasts of America and who are characterized by short to medium stature, yellow complexion, straight eyes, and prominent cheekbones. **2.** The language of the Eskimos.
Eskimo dog. A dog of a broad-chested, powerful breed native to Greenland and Labrador, having an outer coat of long, usually grayish hair, and an under coat of soft wool, used by the Eskimos to draw sledges and for hunting.
es′ne (ĕz′nĕ), *n.* [AS.] Among the Anglo-Saxons, a domestic slave of a certain class.
e′so·phag′e·al, oe′so·phag′e·al (ē′sō·făj′ē·ăl; ē·sŏf′ȧ·jē′ăl), *adj.* Of or pertaining to the esophagus.
e·soph′a·gus, oe·soph′a·gus (ē·sŏf′ȧ·gŭs), *n.; pl.* -GI (-jī). [NL., fr. Gr. *oisophagos*, perh. fr. root of *oisō* I shall carry + *phagein* to eat.] *Anat. & Zool.* The tube that leads from the pharynx to the stomach; the gullet. In man it is about nine inches long, and passes down the neck between the trachea and the spinal column. See RUMINANT, *Illust.*
es′o·ter′ic (ĕs′ō·tẽr′ĭk), *adj.* [Gr. *esōterikos*, fr. *esōteros* inner.] **1.** Designed for, and understood by, the specially initiated alone; abstruse; also, belonging to the circle initiated in such teachings. **2.** Withheld from open avowal; private; as, an *esoteric* purpose.
es·pal′ier (ĕs·păl′yẽr), *n.* [F., deriv. of It. *spalla* shoulder.] *Hort.* **a** A railing or trellis on which fruit trees or shrubs are trained flat. **b** A plant or row of plants so trained. **— *v. t.*** To train on or as an espalier; to furnish with an espalier.
es·par′to (ĕs·pär′tō), *n., or* **esparto grass.** [Sp.] Either of two Spanish and Algerian grasses (*Stipa tenacissima* and *Lygeum spartum*), of which cordage, shoes, baskets, paper, etc., are made.
es·pe′cial (ĕs·pĕsh′ăl; ĭs-), *adj.* [OF., fr. L. *specialis*, fr. *species.* See SPECIES.] **1.** Not general; special. **2.** Distinguished among others of the same class as exceptional in degree. — **Syn.** See SPECIAL. — **es·pe′cial·ly,** *adv.*
es′per·ance (ĕs′pẽr·ăns), *n.* [F. *espérance*, fr. L. *sperans*, pres. part. of *sperare.*] *Archaic.* Hope; expectation.
Es′pe·ran′to (ĕs′pĕ·rän′tō; -răn′tō), *n.* An artificial language devised by Dr. L. Zamenhof, a Russian, who adopted the pseudonym "Dr. Esperanto" (1887). The vocabulary is based on words common to the chief European languages, and sounds peculiar to any one language are eliminated. Cf. VOLAPÜK. — **Es′pe·ran′tism** (-tĭz′m), *n.* — **Es′pe·ran′tist** (-tĭst), *n. & adj.*
es·pi′al (ĕs·pī′ăl), *n.* **1.** Act of spying; observation. **2.** *Obs.* A spy; a scout. **3.** Discovery; notice.
‖**es′piè′gle** (ĕs′pyĕ′gl′), *adj.* [F.] Roguish; frolicsome.
‖**es′piè′gle·rie′** (ĕs′pyĕ′glĕ·rē′), *n.* [F.] Literally, a roguish trick; hence, roguishness; frolicsomeness.
es′pi·o·nage (ĕs′pĭ·ō·nĭj; ĕs′pĭ·ō·näzh′; ĕs′pĭ·ō·näj′; ĕs·pē′ō·nĭj; ĕs·pī′ō·nĭj), *n.* [F. *espionnage*, fr. *espionner* to spy, fr. *espion* spy, fr. It. *spione*, aug. of *spia* spy.] The practice of spying on others, or the employment of spies.
es′pla·nade′ (ĕs′plȧ·nād′; -näd′), *n.* [F., fr. It. *spianata*, fr. *spianare* to level, fr. L. *explanare.* See EXPLAIN.] A clear level space, esp. one along a shore used for public walks or drives.
es·pous′al (ĕs·pouz′ăl; -′l), *n.* [OF. *espousailles*, pl., fr. L. *sponsalia*, fr. *sponsalis* of espousal, fr. *sponsus.* See ESPOUSE.] **1.** Act of espousing; marriage ceremony; a wedding; or, esp., in later times, a betrothal ceremony. **2.** Act of espousing, or taking up as a supporter; adoption.
es·pouse′ (ĕs·pouz′), *v. t.* [OF. *espouser*, fr. L. *sponsare* to betroth, fr. *sponsus* betrothed, past part. of *spondere* to promise solemnly.] **1.** To take a spouse; to marry. **2.** *Obs.* To betroth. **3.** To make one's own; to take up the cause of; embrace. — **Syn.** See ADOPT. — **es·pous′er** (-pouz′ẽr), *n.*
‖**es′prit′** (ĕs′prē′; ĕs′prē), *n.* [F. See SPIRIT.] Spirit; cleverness accompanied with vivacity; sprightly wit.
‖**es′prit′ de corps** (dĕ kôr′). [F.] The common spirit pervading the members of a group. It implies enthusiasm, devotion, and jealous regard for the honor of the group.
es·py′ (ĕs·pī′), *v. t.*; ES·PIED′ (-pīd′); ES·PY′ING. [OF. *espier*, of Teut. origin.] To catch sight of; descry.
-esque (-ĕsk). [F., fr. It. *-esco.*] A suffix of adjectives and nouns, mostly from French and Italian, denoting *in the manner* or *style of; like;* as in arab*esque* (original meaning, after the manner of the Arabs). It is often added to the names of poets or artists, as in Dant*esque*.
Es′qui·line (ĕs′kwĭ·līn), *n.* [L. *Esquilinus*, adj.] One of the seven hills of Rome. See SEVEN HILLS. — **Es′qui·line,** *adj.*
Es′qui·mau (ĕs′kĭ·mō), *n.; pl.* -MAUX (-mō; -mōz). [F.] Var. of ESKIMO.
es·quire′ (ĕs·kwīr′; ĭs-), *n.* [OF. *esquier, escuier*, fr. L. *scutarius* shield-bearer, fr. *scutum* shield.] **1.** Orig., a shield-bearer; esp., in chivalry, a candidate for knighthood as attendant on a knight. **2.** A man of the English rank of gentry next below a knight. **3.** *Archaic.* A rural landed proprietor; a squire. **4.** [*cap.*] A title of courtesy (usually abbr. to *Esq.*), now written after the surname with no title, such as *Mr.* or *Doctor*, prefixed. **5.** A gentleman publicly escorting a lady. **— *v. t.*** **1.** To raise to the rank of, or attend as, esquire. **2.** To address as Esquire.
ess (ĕs), *n.; pl.* ESSES (ĕs′ĕz; -ĭz). **1.** The letter S, s. **2.** Anything having the shape of the letter S.
-ess (-ĕs; -ĭs; 30). [OF. *-esse*, fr. LL. *-issa*, fr. Gr. *-issa.*] A suffix used to form feminine nouns, as in patron*ess*.
es·say′ (ĕ·sā′), *v. t.* [OF. *essayer, assaier*, fr. L. *exagium* a weighing, balance, fr. *ex* out + *agere* to drive, do.] **1.** To test or try out; specif., to assay (metals). **2.** To make an effort to perform; attempt; try. — **Syn.** See ATTEMPT. — **es·say′er** (-ẽr), *n.*

es'say (ĕs'ā; *formerly, & still often in sense* 1, ĕ·sā'), *n.* [OF. *essai.*] **1.** An effort to do something; attempt; trial. **2.** A literary composition, analytical or interpretative, dealing with its subject from a more or less limited or personal standpoint. **3.** *Archaic.* A trial specimen or attempt. **4.** *Philately.* A trial design or proof of a postage stamp, for which a die has been made but not accepted.

es'say·ist (ĕs'ā·ĭst), *n.* One who essays or writes essays.

‖**es'se** (ĕs'ē), *n.* [L., to be.] Existence; actual being.

es'sence (ĕs'ĕns; -'ns), *n.* [F., fr. L. *essentia,* formed as if fr. a pres. part. of *esse* to be.] **1.** *Philos.* That in being which underlies all outward manifestations and is permanent and unchangeable; substance. **2.** Substance; primarily, a necessary constituent; element; secondarily, metaphysical substance; substance as distinguished from and as supporting attributes. **3.** Ultimate or intrinsic nature; prime character; as, to fathom the *essence* of poetry. **4.** Something that exists; an entity. **5.** A substance distilled or otherwise extracted from a plant, drug, etc., and believed to possess its virtues in concentrated form; also, an alcoholic solution of such a substance, esp. of an oil. **6.** Perfume, or the volatile matter constituting perfume.

Es·sene' (ĕ·sēn'; ĕs'ēn), *n.* [L. *Esseni,* pl., fr. Gr. *Essēnoi.*] A member of a severely ascetic brotherhood among the Jews of Palestine from the 2d century B.C. to the 2d century A.D. — **Es·se'ni·an** (ĕ·sē'nĭ·ǎn; 58), **Es·sen'ic** (sĕn'ĭk), *adj.*

es·sen'tial (ĕ·sĕn'shǎl; ĭ-), *adj.* [See ESSENCE.] **1.** Being such in essence, or by reason of its substance or intrinsic nature; absolute; as, what is *essential* poetry? **2.** Ideally perfect or complete; as, *essential* bliss. **3.** Important in the highest degree; indispensable; as, *essential* foods. **4.** Having the nature of, or containing, an essence (see ESSENCE, *n.,* 4 & 5). Thus an **essential oil** is one of the volatile oils found in plants and imparting odor and, often, other characteristic properties. **5.** *Logic.* Pertaining to the essence; necessary; inherent; as, an *essential* property of matter.

Syn. Essential, fundamental, vital, cardinal mean so important as to be indispensable. Essential implies a belonging to the very nature or essence of a thing and, therefore, incapable of removal without destroying the thing itself or its character, efficacy, or the like; fundamental applies to that upon which everything else in a system, institution, or the like, is built up or by which the whole is supported, or from which each addition is derived and without which, therefore, the entire construction would collapse; vital applies to something as necessary to a thing's continued vigor, efficiency, etc., as food, drink, and health are to living things; cardinal applies to something comparable to a hinge, on which everything turns or depends.

— *n.* Something essential, inherent, intrinsic, or indispensable. — **es·sen'ti·al'i·ty** (-shĭ·ăl'ĭ·tĭ), *n.* — **es·sen'tial·ly,** *adv.* — **es·sen'tial·ness,** *n.*

‖**es'se quam vi·de'ri** (ĕs'ē kwăm vĭ·dē'rī). [L.] To be rather than to seem; — motto of North Carolina.

es'so·nite (ĕs'ō·nīt), *n.* [Gr. *hēssōn* inferior (in hardness to true hyacinth).] *Mineral.* A yellow to brown variety of grossularite; — called also *cinnamon stone.*

-est (-ĕst; -ĭst; 30). [AS. -*ost,* -*est.*] A suffix forming the superlative of adjectives and adverbs; as, dear*est,* late*st.*

es·tab'lish (ĕs·tăb'lĭsh; ĭs-), *v. t.* [OF. *establir,* fr. L. *stabilire,* fr. *stabilis* firm, stable.] **1.** To make stable or firm; to fix immovably or firmly; settle. **2.** To appoint, enact, or ordain, for permanence, as officers, laws, etc. **3.** To found; institute, as a colony, a state, etc. **4.** To set on a firm basis; to gain full recognition or acceptance of; as, to *establish* a reputation or a claim. **5.** To set up or place (oneself), as in business, a favorable condition, etc. **6.** To make a national or state institution of (a church). **7.** *Cards.* To gain such control of (a suit) that one can win every remaining trick. — **es·tab'lish·er** (-ẽr), *n.*

es·tab'lished church (-lĭsht). A church supported by the civil authority, as [*caps.*], in England, the Church of England.

es·tab'lish·ment (ĕs·tăb'lĭsh·mĕnt; ĭs-), *n.* **1.** Act of establishing, or state or fact of being established. **2.** Settled position in life, as in business or, formerly, by marriage; also, regular means of support; income. **3.** That which is established; as: **a** A settled arrangement or order, esp. a law or code of laws. **b** A form of government; esp., an established church; hence, the *Establishment,* the Church of England, or the (Presbyterian) Church of Scotland. **c** A permanent civil, military, or commercial organization. **d** Permanent place of residence or business; hence, such a place with its grounds, furnishings, staff, etc.

es'ta·fette' (ĕs'tå·fĕt'), *n.* [F.] A mounted courier.

‖**es'ta'mi'net'** (ĕs'tȧ'mē'nĕ'), *n.* [F.] A small café.

es·tate' (ĕs·tāt'; ĭs-), *n.* [OF. *estat,* fr. L. *status,* fr. *stare* to stand.] **1.** State or condition of being; as, to come to man's *estate.* **2.** *Archaic.* Social standing or rank, esp. of a high order; also, pomp; state. **3.** A social or political class or rank; specif., one of the great classes (called **estates of the realm**) vested with distinct political powers. Generally in feudal Europe and later, esp. in France, the **three estates** were the clergy, nobles, and commons. Cf. FOURTH ESTATE. **4.** A person's property in lands and tenements or, in the aggregate, loosely, fortune; possessions. **5.** A landed property; as, a country *estate.* **6.** *Law.* The degree, quality, nature, and extent of one's interest in, or ownership of, land or other tenements. — *v. t. Archaic.* To establish in, or endow with, an estate.

Es·tates—**Gen'er·al,** *n.* = STATES-GENERAL, 1.

es·teem' (ĕs·tēm'; ĭs-), *v. t.* [OF. *estimer,* fr. L. *aestimare* to value, estimate.] **1.** To set a value on; appraise; to regard as; as, to *esteem* learning vain. **2.** To appreciate the worth of; to hold in high regard; prize; as, to *esteem* learning or learned men. **3.** *Obs.* To form an opinion or judgment of. — **Syn.** See REGARD. — *n.* **1.** *Archaic.* **a** Worth; standing; rank. **b** An estimate; appraisal. **2.** High estimation; great regard.

es'ter (ĕs'tẽr), *n.* [G., fr. *äther* ether + *säure* acid.] *Chem.* A compound which may be regarded as formed by replacement of the acid hydrogen of an acid by a hydrocarbon radical. When the radical is not specified, *ethyl* is often understood; as, acetic *ester,* or ethyl acetate.

es'ter·ase (-ās), *n.* [ester + -ase.] *Biochem.* Any of a class of enzymes that accelerate the hydrolysis of esters.

es·ter'i·fy (ĕs·tĕr'ĭ·fī), *v. t. & i.;* -FIED (-fīd); -FY'ING. *Chem.* To convert or be converted into an ester.

Es'ther (ĕs'tẽr), *n.* [L., fr. Heb. *Estēr.*] **1.** The Jewish heroine of the Old Testament book of this name. **2.** A book of the Old Testament; also, a book of the Protestant Apocrypha. See BIBLE.

es·the'si·a, aes·the'si·a (ĕs·thē'zhĭ·å; -zhå; -zĭ·å), *n.* [NL., fr. Gr. *aisthēsis* sensation.] Sensibility; capacity for sensation. Cf. ANESTHESIA.

es·the'si·om'e·ter, aes·the'si·om'e·ter (ĕs·thē'zĭ·ŏm'ē·tẽr; -sĭ-), *n.* [*esthesio*- (fr. Gr. *aisthēsis* sensation) + *-meter.*] An instrument for determining the distance by which two points, pressed against the skin, must be separated in order that they may be felt as separate.

es·the'sis, aes·the'sis (ĕs·thē'sĭs), *n.* [See ESTHESIA.] Sensation; esp., rudimentary sensation.

es'thete, es·thet'ic, etc. Vars. of AESTHETE, AESTHETIC, etc.

es'ti·ma·ble (ĕs'tĭ·må·b'l), *adj.* **1.** Capable of being estimated. **2.** *Archaic.* Valuable. **3.** Worthy of esteem; deserving regard. — **es'ti·ma·ble·ness,** *n.* — **es'ti·ma·bly** (-blĭ), *adv.*

es'ti·mate (ĕs'tĭ·māt), *v. t.* [L. *aestimatus,* past part. of *aestimare.* See ESTEEM.] **1.** To fix, esp. roughly, or to calculate approximately, as the worth, size, or cost; also, to fix or calculate the worth, size, etc., of; as, to *estimate* the value of a gem or a printing job. **2.** To form an opinion of; gauge; judge. — *v. i.* To make an estimate.

Syn. (1) Estimate, appraise, evaluate, value, rate, assess mean to judge a thing with respect to its worth. Estimate, the comprehensive term, implies a personal judgment the significance of which can only be made clear by the context; appraise strictly implies an intent to fix definitely and in the capacity of an expert the monetary worth of a thing, but is used of any critical judgment; evaluate suggests an attempt to arrive at a correct judgment of something's worth in other terms than those of money; value equals *appraise* in its strict sense without, however, implying expert opinion; rate adds to *estimate* the implication of fixing in a scale of values; assess, literally to value for the purposes of taxation, implies, in extended use, a critical appraisal for the purpose of understanding, interpreting, etc.
(2) See CALCULATE.

— (-mát), *n.* A result of estimating; specif.: **a** A judgment or opinion based on thought or research. **b** A rough or approximate calculation. **c** A statement of the amount for which certain work will be done by one who undertakes to do it. — **es'ti·ma'tive** (-mā'tĭv; -mȧ·tĭv), *adj.* — **es'ti·ma'tor** (-mā'tẽr), *n.*

es'ti·ma'tion (-mā'shŭn), *n.* **1.** Act of estimating. **2.** An estimate. **3.** Judgment; opinion. **4.** Esteem; respect; honor.

e·stip'u·late (ē·stĭp'ū·lāt), *adj. Bot.* Exstipulate.

es'ti·val, aes'ti·val (ĕs'tĭ·vǎl; ĕs·tī'vǎl: *in this and the following words aes- is pronounced ēs- by many, esp. in England*), *adj.* [F. *estival,* fr. L. *aestivalis,* fr. *aestivus,* fr. *aestus* heat, *aestas* summer.] Of or belonging to the summer; as, *estival* flowers.

es'ti·vate, aes'ti·vate (ĕs'tĭ·vāt), *v. i.* **1.** To spend the summer. **2.** *Zool.* To pass the summer in a torpor. Cf. HIBERNATE. — **es'ti·va'tor, aes'ti·va'tor** (-vā'tẽr), *n.*

es'ti·va'tion, aes'ti·va'tion (-vā'shŭn), *n.* **1.** State of animals, as certain snails, that estivate. **2.** *Bot.* The arrangement of floral parts in a bud.

Es·to'ni·an (ĕs·tō'nĭ·ǎn; 58), *n.* **1.** A member of a Caucasian people dwelling chiefly in Estonia, formerly a Russian province, now a republic in the Soviet Union. **2.** The language of the Estonians, highly inflected, and related to the Finnish and the Lapp. See LANGUAGE, *Table.* — *adj.* Of or pertaining to Estonia, the Estonians, or their language.

es·top' (ĕs·tŏp'), *v. t.;* ES·TOPPED' (-tŏpt'); ES·TOP'PING. [From AF. *estopper* and OF. *estoper, estouper,* fr. L. *stuppa* tow.] **1.** To plug up; bar; stop up. **2.** *Law.* To impede or bar by estoppel. **3.** To prevent; prohibit. — **es·top'page** (-ĭj), *n.*

‖**es'to per·pe'tu·a** (ĕs'tō pẽr·pĕt'ū·ȧ). [L.] May she (it) endure forever; — motto of Idaho.

es·top'pel (ĕs·tŏp'ĕl), *n.* [OF. *estoupail* bung.] An estopping; esp., *Law,* a bar to one's alleging or denying a fact because of one's own previous action, by which the contrary has been admitted, implied, or determined.

es·to'vers (ĕs·tō'vẽrz), *n. pl.* [OF. *estoveir, estovoir,* prop. an infin. meaning to be necessary.] *Law.* Necessary supplies; esp.: **a** Wood allowed a tenant for fuel, repairs, etc. **b** Alimony allowed to a woman who has obtained a divorce.

es'tra·di'ol (ĕs'trȧ·dī'ōl; -ŏl), *n.* [oestrus + di- + -ol.] *Biochem.* A crystalline estrogenic substance, obtained from the ovary, etc.

es·trange' (ĕs·trānj'; ĭs-), *v. t.;* ES·TRANGED' (-trānjd'); ES·TRANG'ING (-trǎn'jĭng). [OF. *estrangier* to remove, fr. *extraneus* strange. See STRANGE.] **1.** To take away or keep at a distance; as, to *estrange* oneself from social life. **2.** To divert from its original use; to alienate. **3.** To cause to become alienated; to separate by enmity or indifference. — **es·trange'ment,** *n.* — **es·trang'er** (-trǎn'jẽr), *n.*

Syn. Estrange, alienate, disaffect, wean mean to cause one to break a bond or tie. Estrange always further implies separation or divorcement with consequent indifference or hostility; alienate may or may not suggest separation but it always implies loss of affection or interest and, often, a diversion of that affection or interest to another; disaffect refers especially to groups from whom loyalty is expected and stresses the effects of alienation without separation, as in unrest, rebellion, etc.; wean implies separation from someone or something that has a strong hold upon one.

es·tray' (ĕs·trā'; ĭs-), *n.* [AF. See STRAY.] **1.** *Law.* Any valuable animal, not wild, found wandering from its owner. **2.** Anything out of its normal place. — *v. i.* To stray.

es·treat' (ĕs·trēt'), *n.* [OF. *estraite,* fr. past part. of *estraire* to extract, fr. L. *extrahere.* See EXTRACT.] *Law.* A true copy, duplicate, or extract of an original record, esp. of amercements or penalties. — *v. t.* **1.** *Law.* To extract from the records of a court so as to enforce or prosecute. **2.** To take by way of a levy, fine, etc.

es'trin (ĕs'trĭn). Var. of OESTRIN.

es'tri·ol (ĕs'trĭ·ōl; -ŏl; ēs·trī'-), *n.* [See OESTRUS; -OL, 1.] A crystalline estrogenic phenol alcohol, $C_{18}H_{24}O_3$; theelol. *Estriol* is now the preferred term.

es'tro·gen (ĕs'trō·jĕn), *n.* [See OESTRUS; -GEN.] *Biochem.* Any oestrus-promoting substance, as the hormone estrone.

es'tro·gen'ic (ĕs'trō·jĕn'ĭk), *adj. Biochem.* Promoting oestrus; of or pertaining to an estrogen or estrogens.

es'trone (ĕs'trōn), *n.* [See OESTRUS; -ONE.] *Biochem.* A female hormone, $C_{18}H_{22}O_2$, that stimulates changes characteristic of oestrus and induces growth of the female genital organs; — called also *oestrin, theelin.*

es'tru·al (ĕs'trōō·ǎl), **es'trum** (ĕs'trŭm), **es'trus** (-trŭs), etc. Vars. of OESTRUAL, OESTRUM, OESTRUS, etc.

es'tu·ar'y (ĕs'tū·ĕr'ĭ or, esp. Brit., -ẽr·ĭ), *n.; pl.* -IES (-ĭz). [L. *aestuarium,* fr. *aestus* swell of the sea, tide.] A passage where the tide meets the river current; esp., an arm of the sea at the lower end of a river; a firth. — **es'tu·ar'i·al** (ĕs'tū̇·âr'ĭ·ăl), **es'tu·a·rine** (ĕs'tū̇·ȧ·rīn; -rĭn), *adj.*

e·su'ri·ent (ē·sū'rĭ·ĕnt), *adj.* [L. *esuriens*, pres. part. of *esurire*, fr. *edere* to eat.] Inclined to eat; hungry; greedy. — **e·su'ri·ence** (-ĕns), **e·su'ri·en·cy** (-ĕn·sĭ), *n.* — **e·su'ri·ent·ly**, *adv.*

-et (-ĕt; -ĭt; 30). [OF. *-et, -ete* (F. *-et, -ette*).] A noun suffix, occurring in diminutives from French; as, isl*et*, bill*et*. The diminutive force is often lost, esp. when the primitive is not in English; as, hatch*et*, pock*et*.

e'ta (ē'tȧ; ā'tȧ), *n.* [Gr. *ēta*.] The seventh letter (Η, η) of the Greek alphabet, a long, open vowel pronounced like Eng. *a* in *ale*.

et'a·mine (ĕt'ȧ·mēn), *n.* [F. *étamine*.] A light, loosely woven cotton or worsted fabric, used for dresses.

‖**é'tape'** (ā'tȧp'), *n.* [F., fr. OF. *estaple*.] **1.** A public storehouse. **2.** Supplies issued to troops on the march; also, a halting place, esp. for troops on the march; also, a day's march.

et cet'er·a (ĕt sĕt'ēr·ȧ; sĕt'rȧ). Also **et caet'er·a**. [L. *et* and + *cetera* other things.] And others (of the like kind); and the rest; and so on; and so forth; — sometimes written as one word; usually abbreviated to *etc.* or *&c.*

etch (ĕch), *v. t.* [D. *etsen*, fr. G. *ätzen* to feed, corrode, etch, fr. MHG. *etzen*, causative of *ezzen* to eat.] To produce, as designs, on metal, glass, etc., by lines eaten in by a corrosive; also, to etch such designs in, as a plate. — *v. i.* To practice etching. — **etch'er**, *n.*

etch'ing (ĕch'ĭng), *n.* **1.** The act of an etcher. **2.** The art of producing pictures or designs by means of etched plates. **3.** The design produced on, or the impression taken in ink from, an etched plate.

E·te'o·cles (ē·tē'ō·klēz), *n.* [L., fr. Gr. *Eteoklēs*.] See SEVEN AGAINST THEBES.

e·ter'nal (ē·tûr'năl; -n'l), *adj.* [OF. (F. *éternel*), fr. L. *aeternalis*, fr. *aeternus*. See ETERNE.] **1.** Of infinite duration; everlasting; — opposite of *temporal*. **2.** Continued unintermittedly; perpetual. **3.** Valid or existing at all times; immutable. **4.** Timeless. **5.** Confounded; also, constantly and tiresomely used, repeated, etc.; as, his *eternal* complaints. — *n.* **1.** [*cap.* with *the*] God. **2.** *pl.* Eternal things. — **e·ter'nal·ly**, *adv.* — **e·ter'nal·ness**, *n.*

Eternal City, the. Rome.

e·terne' (ē·tûrn'), *adj.* [OF., fr. L. *aeternus*, for *aeviternus*, fr. *aevum* age.] *Archaic.* Eternal.

e·ter'ni·ty (ē·tûr'nĭ·tĭ), *n.; pl.* -TIES (-tĭz). [OF. *eternité*, fr. L. *aeternitas*, fr. *aeternus*.] **1.** Infinite duration; eternal existence. **2.** The state after death; esp., immortality. **3.** An endless or immeasurable time.

e·ter'nize (ē·tûr'nīz; *also, esp. formerly*, ē'tēr-), *v. t.* **1.** To make eternal; also, to prolong indefinitely. **2.** To make forever famous; to immortalize. — **e·ter'ni·za'tion** (ē·tûr'nĭ·zā'shŭn; -nī·zā'-), *n.*

e·te'sian (ē·tē'zhăn; -zĭ·ăn), *adj.* [L. *etesiae*, pl., periodic winds, fr. Gr. *etēsiai*, fr. *etos* year.] [*often cap.*] Periodical; annual; — applied to certain Mediterranean winds.

eth (ĕth). Var. of EDH.

-eth (-ĕth; -ĭth; 30). [AS. *-eth, -ath, -th*.] *Archaic.* The Middle English ending of the present indicative third person singular; as, know*eth*, think*eth*.

-eth. A suffix of ordinal numbers. See NUMBER, *Table*.

eth'ane (ĕth'ān), *n.* [From ETHER.] *Chem.* A gaseous hydrocarbon, CH_3CH_3, occurring in natural gas and (in small amounts) in coal gas. It burns with a pale flame.

eth'a·nol (ĕth'ȧ·nōl; -nŏl), *n.* [*ethane* + *-ol*, 1.] *Chem.* Ethyl alcohol. See ALCOHOL.

e'ther (ē'thẽr), *n.* [L. *aether*, fr. Gr. *aithēr*.] **1.** Also **ae'ther** (ē'-). The upper regions of space or the rarefied element supposed to fill them. **2.** *Chem.* **a** A volatile, inflammable liquid, $(C_2H_5)_2O$, of a characteristic aromatic odor, obtained by the distillation of alcohol with sulfuric acid. It is used as a solvent and anesthetic; — called specif. ***ethyl ether***. **b** Any of a class of compounds of which ordinary ether is the type. **3.** *Physics.* A medium postulated in the undulatory theory of light as permeating all space, and as transmitting transverse waves.

e·the're·al (ē·thē̆r'ē·ăl), *adj.* **1.** Of, pertaining to, or characteristic of ether, esp. the upper regions; hence, celestial, spiritlike, airy, tenuous, etc.; — often implying delicacy or spirituality. **2.** *Chem.* Pertaining to, containing, or resembling ether or an ether; as, an *ethereal* solution. — **e·the're·al'i·ty** (-ăl'ĭ·tĭ), *n.* — **e·the're·al·ly**, *adv.* — **e·the're·al·ness**, *n.* — **e·the're·ous** (-ŭs), *adj.*

e·the're·al·ize (-īz), *v. t.* To render ethereal.

e·ther'i·fy (ē·thĕr'ĭ·fī; ē'thẽr-), *v. t.;* -I·FIED (-fīd); -I·FY'ING. To convert into ether or an ether. — **e·ther'i·fi·ca'tion** (-fĭ·kā'shŭn), *n.*

e'ther·ize (ē'thẽr·īz), *v. t.* **1.** To etherify. **2.** To treat or anesthetize with ether, as by inhalation. — **e'ther·i·za'tion** (-ĭ·zā'shŭn; -ī·zā'-), *n.* — **e'ther·iz'er** (-īz'ẽr), *n.*

eth'ic (ĕth'ĭk), *n.* [F. *éthique*, fr. L. *ethica*. See ETHICAL.] Ethics; also, an ethical system. — *adj.* Moral.

eth'i·cal (-ĭ·kăl), *adj.* [L. *ethicus*, fr. Gr. *ēthikos*, fr. *ēthos* custom, usage, character.] **1.** Of or relating to moral action, motive, or character; also, treating of morals, morality, or ethics. **2.** Conforming to professional standards of conduct. — **Syn.** See MORAL. — **eth'i·cal'i·ty** (-kăl'ĭ·tĭ), *n.* — **eth'i·cal·ly**, *adv.* — **eth'i·cal·ness**, *n.*

eth'i·cize (ĕth'ĭ·sīz), *v. t.* To make ethical; to consider as an ethical being or in ethical relations.

eth'ics (ĕth'ĭks), *n.; see* -ICS. **1.** A treatise on morals. **2.** The science of moral values and duties; the study of ideal human character, actions, and ends. **3.** Moral principles, quality, or practice.

E'thi·op (ē'thĭ·ŏp; 58), **E'thi·ope** (-ōp), *n.* & *adj.* [L. *Aethiops*, fr. Gr. *Aithiops*, appar. fr. *aithein* to burn + *ōps* face.] Ethiopian.

E'thi·o'pi·an (-ō'pĭ·ăn; 58), *adj.* Of or pertaining to Ethiopia (see *Gaz.*), or the Ethiopians, or the Ethiopian race. — *n.* **1.** A native of Ethiopia, esp. of the modern kingdom (Abyssinia). **2.** *Ethnol.* A member of one of the former five divisions of mankind, the **Ethiopian race**, which includes the Negro and Negrito peoples of Africa. **3.** A Negro; a blackamoor.

E'thi·op'ic (-ŏp'ĭk; -ō'pĭk), *adj.* **1.** Ethiopian. **2.** Designating, or relating to, the language of the Semitic conquerors of Abyssinia. — *n.* The Ethiopic language. See LANGUAGE, *Table*.

eth'moid (ĕth'moid), *adj.* [Gr. *ēthmoeidēs* like a sieve, fr. *ēthmos* sieve + *eidos* form.] Designating one or more bones forming part of the walls and septum of the nasal cavity. — *n.* An ethmoid bone. — **eth·moi'dal** (ĕth·moi'dăl; -d'l), *adj.*

eth'narch (ĕth'närk), *n.* [Gr. *ethnarchēs*, fr. *ethnos* nation + *archos*.] The governor of a province or people.

eth'narch·y (-när·kĭ), *n.; pl.* -NARCHIES (-kĭz). The dominion of an ethnarch, or his office or rank.

eth'nic (ĕth'nĭk), *adj.* Also **eth'ni·cal** (-nĭ·kăl). [L. *ethnicus*, fr. Gr. *ethnikos*, fr. *ethnos* nation, (eccles.) *ta ethnē* the nations, heathens, gentiles.] **1.** Neither Jewish nor Christian; pagan. **2.** Of, pertaining to, or designating races or groups of races discriminated on the basis of common traits, customs, etc.; ethnological; as, the *ethnic* divisions of mankind. — **eth'ni·cal·ly**, *adv.*

eth'no- (ĕth'nō-), **ethn-**. [Gr. *ethnos* nation.] A combining form meaning *race, peoples*, as in **eth'no·cen'tric**, **eth·noc'ra·cy** (see -CENTRIC, -CRACY).

eth·nog'e·ny (ĕth·nŏj'ē·nĭ), *n.* [*ethno-* + *-geny*.] The genesis of races or the branch of ethnology treating of this.

eth·nog'ra·phy (ĕth·nŏg'rȧ·fĭ), *n.* [*ethno-* + *-graphy*.] Descriptive anthropology; sometimes, loosely, ethnology. — **eth·nog'ra·pher** (-fẽr), *n.* — **eth'no·graph'ic** (ĕth'nō·grăf'ĭk), **eth'no·graph'i·cal** (-ĭ·kăl), *adj.* — **eth'no·graph'i·cal·ly**, *adv.*

eth·nol'o·gy (ĕth·nŏl'ō·jĭ), *n.* [*ethno-* + *-logy*.] The science that treats of the division of mankind into races, their origin, distribution, relations, and peculiarities. — **eth'no·log'ic** (ĕth'nō·lŏj'ĭk), **eth'no·log'i·cal** (-ĭ·kăl), *adj.* — **eth'no·log'i·cal·ly**, *adv.* — **eth·nol'o·gist** (ĕth·nŏl'ō·jĭst), *n.*

e'thos (ē'thŏs), *n.* [L., fr. Gr. *ēthos* character.] **1.** The moral, ideal, or universal element in a work of art as distinguished from that which is emotional in its appeal or subjective. Cf. PATHOS. **2.** The distinguishing character or tone of a racial, religious, social, or other group.

eth'yl (ĕth'ĭl), *n.* [*ether* + *-yl*.] **1.** A univalent hydrocarbon radical, C_2H_5 or CH_3CH_2. **2.** [*cap.*] A trade-mark for an antiknock compound used in motor fuel. The active antiknock constituent of the compound is lead.

ethyl acetate. *Chem.* A colorless liquid, $CH_3CO_2C_2H_5$, of agreeable odor, made by the interaction of ethyl alcohol, sodium acetate, and sulfuric acid. It is used in flavoring, in organic synthesis, as a solvent, etc.

ethyl alcohol. Ordinary alcohol. See ALCOHOL.

eth'yl·ate (ĕth'ĭ·lāt), *v. t.* To treat, as alcohol, so as to cause the introduction of one or more ethyl groups (C_2H_5). — **eth'yl·a'tion** (-lā'shŭn), *n.*

eth'yl·ene (ĕth'ĭ·lēn), *n.* [From ETHYL.] *Chem.* A colorless, gaseous, unsaturated hydrocarbon, C_2H_4 or $CH_2{:}CH_2$, forming an ingredient of coal gas, and obtained in other ways, as by the action of concentrated sulfuric acid on alcohol. It forms an explosive mixture with air.

ethylene glycol. *Chem.* = GLYCOL **a**.

ethyl ether. See ETHER, 2 **a**.

e·thyl'ic (ē·thĭl'ĭk), *adj.* Pertaining to, derived from, or containing ethyl; as, an *ethylic* ester.

e'ti·o·late (ē'tĭ·ō·lāt), *v. t.* & *i.* [F. *étioler*, fr. *éteule*, fr. L. *stupula*, *stipula*, stubble.] To blanch, as by exclusion of sunlight; to bleach; — esp. of plants. — **e'ti·o·la'tion** (-lā'shŭn), *n.*

e'ti·ol'o·gy, ae'ti·ol'o·gy (ē'tĭ·ŏl'ō·jĭ), *n.* [LL. *aetiologia*, fr. Gr. *aitiologia*, fr. *aitia* cause + *logos* description.] **1.** The science, doctrine, or demonstration of causes; esp., the investigation of the causes of any disease. **2.** The assignment of a cause or reason; as, the *etiology* of a custom. — **e'ti·o·log'i·cal, ae'ti·o·log'i·cal** (-ō·lŏj'ĭ·kăl), *adj.* — **-log'i·cal·ly**, *adv.* — **-ol'o·gist** (-ŏl'ō·jĭst), *n.*

et'i·quette (ĕt'ĭ·kĕt *or, esp. Brit.*, ĕt'ĭ·kĕt'), *n.* [F. *étiquette*. See TICKET.] The forms required by good breeding, social conventions, or prescribed by authority, to be observed in social or official life; the rules of decorum. — **Syn.** See DECORUM.

et'na (ĕt'nȧ), *n.* [From Mt. *Etna*.] A vessel for heating liquids, consisting of a cup fixed in a saucer of alcohol.

E·to'ni·an (ē·tō'nĭ·ăn; 58), *n.* A student or former student of Eton College, England. — **E·to'ni·an**, *adj.*

E'ton jack'et *or* **coat** (ē't'n). A short jacket, open at the front, and cut square at the hips, of a pattern originally worn by students at Eton College. The student's jacket is worn with a large stiff turnover collar (**Eton collar**).

E·tru'ri·an (ē·trōōr'ĭ·ăn), *n.* & *adj.* Etruscan.

E·trus'can (ē·trŭs'kăn), *adj.* [L. *Etruscus*.] Of or pertaining to ancient Etruria, its inhabitants, art, language, or civilization. — *n.* A native of Etruria; also, the language (of unknown affinities) of the Etruscans.

-ette (-ĕt). [F. *-ette*, fem. of *-et*.] A diminutive suffix found in nouns of recent borrowing from the French (cigar*ette*, statu*ette*), often with loss of the diminutive force. The suffix is also added to English words to form diminutives (as wagon*ette*), feminine nouns (as farmer*ette*), and trade names of imitation materials (as satin*ette*).

et'tle (ĕt''l), *n.* [ON. *ætla*.] *Scot.* An endeavor; intent.

‖**et tu, Bru'te!** (ĕt tū, brōō'tē). [L.] Thou also, Brutus; — words attributed to Julius Caesar when he saw his friend Brutus among his assassins. Hence, a charge of treachery against one's intimate friend.

é'tude (ā'tūd; ā·tūd'), *n.* [F. See STUDY.] A study; specif., *Music*, a piece for practice of some special point of technique; also, an instrumental composition built upon a single technical motive but played for its artistic value.

e·tui' (ā·twē'; ē·twē'; ĕt'wē), **e·twee'** (ē·twē'; ĕt'wē), *n.* [F. *étui*.] A case for small articles, esp. toilet articles.

et'y·mol'o·gist (ĕt'ĭ·mŏl'ō·jĭst), *n.* One versed in etymology.

et'y·mol'o·gize (-jīz), *v. t.* & *i.* To seek or formulate an etymology for; to study or formulate etymologies.

et'y·mol'o·gy (ĕt'ĭ·mŏl'ō·jĭ), *n.; pl.* -GIES (-jĭz). [F. *étymologie*, fr. L., fr. Gr. *etymologia*. See ETYMON; -LOGY.] **1.** The origin or derivation of a word as shown by its analysis into elements, by pointing out the root or primitive upon which it is based, or by referring it to an earlier form in its parent language; also, an account setting forth such origin or derivation. **2.** The branch of philology concerned with etymologies. — **et'y·mo·log'i·cal** (-mō·lŏj'ĭ·kăl), *adj.* — **et'y·mo·log'i·cal·ly**, *adv.*

et'y·mon (ĕt'ĭ·mŏn), *n.; pl.* -MONS (-mŏnz), ETYMA (-mȧ). [L., fr. Gr. *etymon* the literal sense of a word according to its origin, an etymon, fr. *etymos* true, real.] A primitive or root word.

Et'zel (ĕt'sĕl), *n.* [G.] In German legend, a character, esp. a wise king, representing the historical Attila.

eu- (ū-). [Gr. *eu* well, orig. neut. of *eys* good.] A prefix meaning *good, advantageous;* — the opposite of *dys-*.

eu·caine′ (ū·kān′), *n.* [*eu-* + cocaine.] Either of two synthetic alkaloids derived from piperidine, *α-eucaine*, $C_{19}H_{27}NO_4$, or *β-eucaine*, $C_{15}H_{21}NO_2$. The hydrochlorides have been used as local anesthetics.
eu′ca·lypt (ū′kȧ·lĭpt), *n.* A eucalyptus. — **eu′ca·lyp′tic** (-lĭp′tĭk), *adj.*
eu′ca·lyp′tole (ū′kȧ·lĭp′tōl), **eu′ca·lyp′tol** (-tōl; -tŏl), *n.* [*eucalyptus* + L. *ol*eum oil.] Cineole.
eu′ca·lyp′tus (-lĭp′tŭs), *n.; pl.* EUCALYPTI (-tī), EUCALYPTUSES (-tŭs-ĕz; -ĭz). [NL., fr. *eu-* + Gr. *kalyptos* covered, alluding to the covering of the buds.] Any of a genus (*Eucalyptus*) of Australasian trees (rarely shrubs) of the myrtle family, most of which are important timber trees and some of which secrete resinous gums, whence the alternative name *gum tree* or *gum* (as, *blue gum, gray gum*, etc.; see GUM, *n.*, 5 **a** (3)). An essential oil (**eucalyptus oil**) is derived from the leaves of any of numerous species of *Eucalyptus*.
eu′cha·ris (ū′kȧ·rĭs), *n.* [NL., fr. LL. *eucharis* agreeable, fr. Gr. *eucharis*.] Any of a small genus (*Eucharis*) of South American herbs of the amaryllis family, bearing white bell-shaped flowers.
Eu′cha·rist (ū′kȧ·rĭst), *n.* [OF. *eucariste*, fr. LL. *eucharistia*, fr. Gr. *eucharistia*, deriv. of *eu* + *charizesthai* to show favor, fr. *charis* favor, thanks.] **1.** The sacrament of the Lord's Supper; hence: **a** Any of various Christian rites in which bread and wine are consecrated and distributed at the Communion. **b** The consecrated elements of bread and wine. **2.** *Christian Science.* Spiritual communion with the one God. *Mary Baker Eddy.* — **Eu′cha·ris′tic** (-rĭs′tĭk), **Eu′cha·ris′ti·cal** (-tĭ·kăl), *adj.*
eu′chre (ū′kẽr), *n.* **a** A card game played with a reduced pack and having for its *right bower*, or highest card, the knave of trumps and for its *left bower*, or next highest card, the other knave of the same color. See FIVE HUNDRED. **b** The defeat of the trump-making side by winning three tricks. — *v. t.;* EU′CHRED (-kẽrd); EU′CHRING (-krĭng). To cause the euchre of; hence, *Slang*, to defeat in any scheme.
eu·chro′ma·tin (ū·krō′mȧ·tĭn), *n.* [*eu-* + *chromatin*.] *Biol.* Weakly staining chromatin regarded as largely made up of genes. Cf. HETEROCHROMATIN. — **eu′chro·mat′ic** (ū′krō·măt′ĭk), *adj.*
eu·chro′mo·some (ū·krō′mō·sōm), *n.* *Biol.* A somatic chromosome; — opposed to *heterochromosome.*
eu′clase (ū′klās), *n.* [*eu-* + Gr. *klasis* a breaking.] A brittle silicate of beryllium and aluminum, $HBeAlSiO_5$, occurring in yellow, green, or blue prismatic crystals.
Eu′clid (ū′klĭd), *n.* A Greek geometer of about 300 B.C.; also, his treatise on geometry (Euclid's *Elements*), and, hence, the principles of Euclidean geometry in general.
Eu·clid′e·an (ū·klĭd′ē·ăn; 58), **Eu·clid′i·an** (-ĭ·ăn), *adj.* Of or pert. to Euclid or the geometry of Euclid; esp., *Geom.*, adopting Euclid's assumptions with respect to space.
eu·dae′mon (ū·dē′mŏn), *n.* Also **eu·de′mon.** [*eu-* + Gr. *daimōn* one's daemon.] A good spirit; a daemon.
eu′dae·mo′ni·a (ū′dē·mō′nĭ·ȧ), *n.* [Gr. *eudaimonia.*] Well-being; happiness; esp., in Aristotle's use, felicity resulting from life of activity in accordance with reason. — **eu′dae·mon′ic** (-mŏn′ĭk), **eu′dae·mon′i·cal** (-ĭ·kăl), *adj.*
eu·dae′mon·ism (ū·dē′mŏn·ĭz′m), *n.* [Gr. *eudaimonismos* a thinking happy, fr. *eudaimōn* blessed with a good genius, happy. See EU-; DEMON.] That system of ethics which defines and enforces moral obligation by its relation to happiness or personal well-being. Cf. HEDONISM. — **eu·dae′mon·ist** (-ĭst), *n.* — **eu·dae′mon·is′tic** (-ĭs′tĭk), **eu·dae′mon·is′ti·cal** (-tĭ·kăl), *adj.* — **eu·dae′mon·is′ti·cal·ly**, *adv.*
eu′di·om′e·ter (ū′dĭ·ŏm′ē·tẽr), *n.* [Gr. *eudia* fair, clear weather, fr. *eudios* fine, clear + *-meter.*] An instrument, usually a finely graduated and calibrated tube, for the volumetric measurement and analysis of gases; — formerly used to determine the purity of the air. — **eu′di·o·met′ric** (-ō·mĕt′rĭk), **eu′di·o·met′ri·cal** (-rĭ·kăl), *adj.* — **eu′di·o·met′ri·cal·ly**, *adv.* — **eu′di·om′e·try** (-ŏm′ē·trĭ), *n.*
eu·gen′ic (ū·jĕn′ĭk), **eu·gen′i·cal** (-ĭ·kăl), *adj.* [Gr. *eugenēs* well-born.] Pertaining to eugenics or to the production of good offspring; also, born of sound or fit parents. Cf. DYSGENIC. — **-i·cal·ly**, *adv.*
eu·gen′ics (-ĭks), *n.;* see -ICS. The science which deals with influences that improve inborn or hereditary qualities of a race or breed, esp. of the human race. — **eu·gen′i·cist** (ū·jĕn′ĭ·sĭst), **eu′ge·nist** (ū′jē·nĭst), *n.*
eu′ge·nol (ū′jē·nōl; -nŏl), *n.* [*Eugen*ia, the genus to which the clove belongs + *-ol.*] A colorless aromatic liquid, $C_{10}H_{12}O_2$, found in oil of cloves, and in some other oils.
eu·he′mer·ism (ū·hē′mẽr·ĭz′m; ū·hĕm′ẽr-), *n.* [L. *Euhemerus*, fr. Gr. *Euēmeros*, a Sicilian philosopher, about 300 B.C.] The theory, held by Euhemerus, that the gods of mythology were but deified mortals; hence, interpretation of myths as traditional accounts of historical personages and events. — **eu·he′mer·ist** (-ĭst), *n.* — **eu·he′mer·is′tic** (-ĭs′tĭk), *adj.* — **-ti·cal·ly**, *adv.* — **eu·he′mer·ize** (-īz), *v. t.*
eu·lo′gi·a (ū·lō′jĭ·ȧ), *n.* [LL., fr. Gr. *eulogia.* See EULOGY.] Bread blessed but not consecrated, and distributed in small pieces to the congregation at the end of Mass.
eu′lo·gist (ū′lō·jĭst), *n.* One who eulogizes; a panegyrist.
eu′lo·gis′tic (-jĭs′tĭk), **eu′lo·gis′ti·cal** (-tĭ·kăl), *adj.* Of, pertaining to, or characterized by eulogy; laudatory. Cf. DYSLOGISTIC. — **eu′lo·gis′ti·cal·ly**, *adv.*
eu·lo′gi·um (ū·lō′jĭ·ŭm), *n.; pl.* EULOGIUMS (-ŭmz), EULOGIA (-ȧ). A eulogy.
eu′lo·gize (ū′lō·jīz), *v. t.* To speak or write in high praise of; extol. — **Syn.** Extol, acclaim, praise, laud. — **eu′lo·giz′er** (-jīz′ẽr), *n.*
eu′lo·gy (-jĭ), *n.; pl.* -GIES (-jĭz). [Gr. *eulogia*, fr. *eu* well + *legein* to speak.] A discourse, esp. a set oration, in commendation of someone or something, as of the character and services of a deceased person; also, high praise; laudation. — **Syn.** See ENCOMIUM.
Eu·men′i·des (ū·mĕn′ĭ·dēz), *n. pl.* [L., fr. Gr. *Eumenides*, lit., gracious ones.] The Erinyes; — a euphemistic name.
eu′nuch (ū′nŭk), *n.* [L. *eunuchus*, fr. Gr. *eunouchos*, prop., guarding the couch, fr. *eunē* couch + *echein* to keep.] A castrated male person, originally one in charge of a harem or employed in a palace as a chamberlain.
eu·on′y·mus (ū·ŏn′ĭ·mŭs), *n.* Evonymus.
eu′pa·to′ri·um (ū′pȧ·tō′rĭ·ŭm; 70), *n.* [NL., fr. Gr. *eupatorion* hemp agrimony, fr. *Eupator*, king of Pontus.] Any of a genus (*Eupatorium*) of herbs of the aster family, that includes boneset, joe-pye weed, etc.; esp., any cultivated variety, as the mistflower (*E. coelestinum*).
eu·pat′rid (ū·păt′rĭd; ū′pȧ·trĭd), *n.* [Gr. *eupatridēs*, fr. *eu* well + *patēr* father.] [*also cap.*] One of the Eupatridae. — **eu′pa·trid**, *adj.*
eu·pat′ri·dae (ū·păt′rĭ·dē), *n. pl.* [Gr. *eupatridai*, pl. of *eupatridēs.*] [*often cap.*] The hereditary aristocrats of ancient Athens and other states of Greece, who in early times exclusively made and administered the law.
eu·pep′sia (ū·pĕp′shȧ; -sĭ·ȧ; 103), *n.* [NL., fr. Gr. *eupepsia.* See EU-; DYSPEPSIA.] Good digestion.
eu·pep′tic (ū·pĕp′tĭk), *adj.* Of, produced by, or having good digestion.
eu′phe·mism (ū′fē·mĭz′m), *n.* [Gr. *euphēmismos*, fr. *euphēmizein* to use words of a good omen, fr. *eu* well + *phanai* to speak.] The substitution of an inoffensive or mild expression for one that may offend or suggest something unpleasant; also, the expression so substituted, as "passing away" for "dying." — **eu′phe·mist** (-mĭst), *n.* — **eu′phe·mis′tic** (-mĭs′tĭk), **eu′phe·mis′ti·cal** (-tĭ·kăl), *adj.* — **eu′phe·mis′ti·cal·ly**, *adv.*
eu′phe·mize (-mīz), *v. t. & i.* To express by a euphemism; to make use of euphemisms. — **eu′phe·miz′er** (-mīz′ẽr), *n.*
eu·phon′ic (ū·fŏn′ĭk), **eu·phon′i·cal** (-ĭ·kăl), *adj.* Of or pertaining to euphony; in accordance with the laws of euphony. — **eu·phon′i·cal·ly**, *adv.* — **eu·phon′i·cal·ness**, *n.*
eu·pho′ni·ous (ū·fō′nĭ·ŭs), *adj.* Pleasing in sound; smooth-sounding. — **eu·pho′ni·ous·ly**, *adv.* — **eu·pho′ni·ous·ness**, *n.*
eu·pho′ni·um (ū·fō′nĭ·ŭm), *n.* [NL. See EUPHONY.] A band instrument, similar to the baritone, but with a larger bore, giving a broader, mellower tone.
eu′pho·nize (ū′fō·nīz), *v. t.* To make euphonious.
eu′pho·ny (-nĭ), *n.; pl.* -NIES (-nĭz). [LL. *euphonia*, fr. Gr. *euphōnia*, fr. *euphōnos* sweet-voiced, fr. *eu* well + *phōnē* sound, voice.] **1.** Pleasing or sweet sound; the acoustic effect produced by words so formed and combined as to please the ear; — opposed to *cacophony*. **2.** *Phonet.* Tendency to greater ease of pronunciation, resulting in combinative changes, probably due to increased speed of utterance and economy of effort rather than to a striving after a pleasing effect, as once supposed.
eu·phor′bi·a (ū·fôr′bĭ·ȧ), *n.; pl.* EUPHORBIAS (-ȧz). [NL., fr. L. *euphorbea* an African plant, fr. Gr. *euphorbion;* — after *Euphorbus*, a Greek physician.] Any of the spurges, or cactuslike plants, constituting a large genus (*Euphorbia*) chiefly of South African arid regions.
eu·phor′bi·a′ceous (-ā′shŭs), *adj.* Belonging to the spurge family (Euphorbiaceae). See SPURGE.
eu·pho′ri·a (ū·fō′rĭ·ȧ; 70), *n.* [NL., fr. Gr., fr. *eu* well + *pherein* to bear.] *Psychol.* A sense of well-being and buoyancy. — **eu·phor′ic** (-fŏr′ĭk), *adj. & n.*
eu′phra·sy (ū′frȧ·sĭ), *n.* [ML. *euphrasia*, fr. Gr. *euphrasia* delight, deriv. of *eu* well + *phrēn* heart, mind.] The eyebright *Euphrasia officinalis.*
Eu·phros′y·ne (ū·frŏs′ĭ·nē; -frŏz′ĭ·nē), *n.* [L., fr. Gr. *Euphrosynē.*] *Gr. Myth.* One of the Graces. See GRACE, *n.*, 11.
eu′phu·ism (ū′fū·ĭz′m), *n.* **1.** The affected style of conversation and writing fashionable in the Elizabethan age, and marked by antithesis, alliteration, farfetched similes, and other signs of an effort after elegance; — from ***Euphues***, a prose work by John Lyly. **2.** Artificial elegance of language; high-flown diction. — **eu′phu·ist** (-ĭst), *n.* — **eu′phu·is′tic** (-ĭs′tĭk), **eu′phu·is′ti·cal** (-tĭ·kăl), *adj.* — **eu′phu·is′ti·cal·ly**, *adv.*
eu·plas′tic (ū·plăs′tĭk), *adj.* [*eu-* + *-plastic.*] *Physiol.* Having the capacity of becoming organized readily; adapted to the formation of tissue. — *n.* A euplastic substance.
eup·ne′a, eup·noe′a (ūp·nē′ȧ), *n.* [NL., fr. Gr. *eupnoia* easy breathing, fr. *eu* well + *pnein* to breathe.] *Physiol.* Normal respiration. Cf. DYSPNEA, HYPERPNEA.
Eur·a′sian (ū·rā′zhăn; -shăn), *adj.* Of or pertaining to Europe and Asia as a whole (*Eurasia*) or the Eurasians. — *n.* A person of mixed European and Asiatic (especially Indian) descent.
eu·re′ka (ū·rē′kȧ), *interj.* [Gr. *heurēka.*] "I have found (it)"; — the exclamation attributed to Archimedes upon discovering a method of determining the purity of gold and now expressing triumph over a discovery. It is the motto of the State of California.
eu·rhyth′mic (ū·rĭth′mĭk; -rĭth′mĭk), **eu·rhyth′my, etc.** Vars. of EURYTHMIC, etc.
Eu·roc′ly·don (ū·rŏk′lĭ·dŏn), *n.* [NL., fr. Gr. *euroklydōn* (*Acts* xxvii. 14).] A tempestuous northeast wind of the Mediterranean.
Eu·ro′pa (ū·rō′pȧ), *n.* [L., fr. Gr. *Eurōpē.*] *Gr. Myth.* A Phoenician princess, whom Zeus, in the form of a white bull, carried off, swimming with her to Crete, where she became mother of Minos, Rhadamanthus, and Sarpedon.
Eu′ro·pe′an (ū′rō·pē′ăn; *Brit. also* yôr′ō-), *adj.* Of or pert. to Europe or its inhabitants. — *n.* A native or inhabitant of Europe; loosely, a person of European descent.
European corn borer. See CORN BORER.
Eu′ro·pe′an·ize (ū′rō·pē′ăn·īz), *v. t.* To cause to become like Europeans or habituated to European usages.
European plan. In hotels, a plan by which lodging and service only are engaged by guests, and meals are taken at their option; — contrasted with *American plan.*
European Recovery Program. = MARSHALL PLAN. Abbr. *ERP*
eu·ro′pi·um (ū·rō′pĭ·ŭm), *n.* [NL., fr. *Europe.*] *Chem.* A metallic element, one of the rare-earth metals, discovered spectroscopically in 1896. Symbol, *Eu*; at. no., 63; at. wt., 152.0.
Eu′rus (ū′rŭs), *n.* [L., fr. Gr. *Euros.*] The southeast wind.
eu′ry- (ū′rĭ-). [Gr. *eurys.*] A combining form meaning *wide, broad*, as in **eu′ry·ce·phal′ic, eu′ryg·nath′ic, eu′ry·prog′na·thous.**
Eu·ryd′i·ce (ū·rĭd′ĭ·sē), *n.* See ORPHEUS.
eu·ryp′ter·id (ū·rĭp′tẽr·ĭd), *n.* [*eury-* + Gr. *pteron* wing.] Any of an order (Eurypterida) of aquatic, exclusively Paleozoic arthropods, related to the arachnids and especially to the king crabs. Individuals of one genus (*Pterygotus*) sometimes exceeded six feet in length and are the largest known arthropods. — **eu·ryp′ter·id**, *adj.*
eu·ryth′mics, eu·rhyth′mics (ū·rĭth′mĭks; -rĭth′mĭks), *n.;* see -ICS. The art of harmonious and expressive bodily movement, esp. as based on musical patterns, usually improvised, as an aid to better rhythmic response on the part of students of music and of the dance.
eu·ryth′my, eu·rhyth′my (ū·rĭth′mĭ; -rĭth′mĭ), *n.* [L. *eurythmia*, fr. Gr. *eurythmia*, fr. *eu* well + *rhythmos* rhythm, measure, symmetry.] Harmonious proportion or movement. — **eu·ryth′mic, eu·rhyth′mic** (-mĭk), **eu·ryth′mi·cal** (-mĭ·kăl), *adj.*
eu′sol (ū′sōl; -sŏl), *n.* [*eu-* + *sol*ution.] An antiseptic solution containing 0.5 per cent of hypochlorous acid.
Eu·sta′chi·an tube (ū·stā′kĭ·ăn). [After Bartolommeo *Eustachio*, It. physician (d. 1574).] A tube connecting the middle ear with the

nasopharynx and equalizing air pressure on both sides of the tympanic membrane. See EAR, *n.*, 1.

eu·tec′tic (ū·tĕk′tĭk), *adj.* [Gr. *eutēktos* easily melted, fr. *eu* well + *tēkein* to melt.] Of maximum fusibility; — of an alloy or solution having the lowest melting point possible with its components; hence, designating or pertaining to such an alloy or solution or its melting or freezing point. — *n.* A eutectic alloy or solution.

eu·tec′toid (ū·tĕk′toid), *adj.* [*eutectic* + *-oid.*] Like a eutectic. — *n.* A eutectoid alloy, esp. pearlite.

Eu·ter′pe (ū·tûr′pē), *n.* [L., fr. Gr. *Euterpē.*] The Muse of music. See MUSE, *n.*, 1.

eu′tha·na′si·a (ū′thȧ·nā′zhĭ·ȧ; -zhȧ; -zĭ·ȧ), *n.* [NL., fr. Gr. *euthanasia*, fr. *eu* well + *thanatos* death.] Act or practice of painlessly putting to death persons suffering from incurable and distressing disease.

eu·then′ics (ū·thĕn′ĭks), *n.*; see -ICS. [Gr. *euthēnein* to thrive.] The science having to do with the betterment of living conditions to secure more efficient human beings.

eux′e·nite (ūk′sē·nīt), *n.* [Gr. *euxenos* hospitable; — so named because it contains a number of rare elements.] A brownish-black mineral with a metallic luster, containing columbium, titanium, yttrium, erbium, cerium, and uranium. H., 6.5. Sp. gr., 4.7–5.0.

e·vac′u·ant (ē·văk′ū·ănt), *adj.* *Med.* Emetic, diuretic, or cathartic. — *n.* An evacuant agent.

e·vac′u·ate (-āt), *v. t.* [L. *evacuatus*, past part. of *evacuare* to empty, nullify, fr. *e* out + *vacuus* empty.] **1.** To empty of contents or content. **2.** To discharge, as excrement; void. **3. a** To remove (troops, wounded, civilians, etc.), as from a military position or zone. **b** To withdraw from military occupation of (a fort or region). **c** To vacate (premises). — *v. i.* To withdraw, as from a town in danger of attack. — **e·vac′u·a′tor** (-ā′tẽr), *n.*

e·vac′u·a′tion (-ā′shŭn), *n.* **1.** Act of evacuating; specif.: **a** *Mil.* Withdrawal of troops from a town, fortress, etc., or of a population from a city or territory. **b** *Med.* Voidance of matter by the natural passages of the body, by an artificial opening, or by cathartics, venesection, etc. **2.** That which is evacuated or discharged.

e·vac′u·ee′ (ē·văk′ū·ē′), *n.* One withdrawn from one's dwelling or home district in an evacuation; specif., one removed by public authorities because of the danger of bombing or military action.

e·vade′ (ē·vād′), *v. i.* [F. *évader*, fr. L. *evadere, evasum*, fr. *e* out + *vadere* to go, walk.] **1.** *Now Rare.* To escape; slip away. **2.** To use trickery or sophistry in avoidance or escape; practice evasion. — *v. t.* **1.** To get away from or avoid by dexterity, subterfuge, or ingenuity. **2.** To be too elusive for; baffle; as, words that *evade* definition. — **Syn.** See ESCAPE. — **e·vad′a·ble** (-vād′ȧ·b'l), **e·vad′i·ble** (-ĭ·b'l), *adj.* — **e·vad′er** (-vād′ẽr), *n.*

e·vag′i·nate (ē·văj′ĭ·nāt), *v. t. & i.* [L. *evaginatus*, past part., unsheathed, fr. *e* out + *vagina* sheath.] To turn inside out; to protrude, or cause to protrude, by eversion of an inner surface. — **e·vag′i·na′tion** (-nā′shŭn), *n.*

e·val′u·ate (ē·văl′ū·āt), *v. t.* [F. *évaluer.*] To ascertain the value or amount of; to appraise; specif., *Math.*, to express numerically. — **Syn.** See ESTIMATE. — **e·val′u·a′tion** (-ā′shŭn), *n.*

ev′a·nesce′ (ĕv′ȧ·nĕs′ *or, esp. Brit.*, ē′vȧ-), *v. i.*; EV′A·NESCED′ (-nĕst′); EV′A·NESC′ING (-nĕs′ĭng). [L. *evanescere*, fr. *e* out + *vanescere* to vanish, fr. *vanus* empty, vain.] To dissipate like vapor; vanish. — **ev′a·nes′cence** (-nĕs′ĕns; -'ns), *n.*

ev′a·nes′cent (-nĕs′ĕnt; -'nt), *adj.* Tending to evanesce; fleeting. — **Syn.** See TRANSIENT. — **ev′a·nes′cent·ly**, *adv.*

e·van′gel (ē·văn′jĕl), *n.* [OF. *evangile*, fr. LL. *evangelium*, fr. Gr. *euangelion* glad tidings, fr. *eu* well + *angellein* to bear a message.] **1.** The message or news of man's redemption through Christ; hence [*cap.*], any one of the four Gospels. **2.** Good news; glad tidings.

e·van′gel, *n.* An evangelist.

e′van·gel′i·cal (ē′văn·jĕl′ĭ·kăl; ĕv′ăn-), *adj.* Also **e′van·gel′ic** (-ĭk). **1.** Contained in, or relating to, the four Gospels. **2.** Belonging to, contained in, agreeable to, or in the spirit of, the gospel, or teachings of the New Testament. **3.** Pertaining to or designating any school of Protestants which holds that the essence of the gospel consists mainly in its doctrines of man's sinful condition and need of salvation, the revelation of God's grace in Christ, the necessity of spiritual renovation, and participation in the experience of redemption through faith; — applied esp. to the Low Church party in the Anglican Church, various Lutheran churches in Prussia, and in the United States to churches called *orthodox*, as disting. from Unitarians, Universalists, etc. — *n.* One belonging to an evangelical church. — **e′van·gel′i·cal·ism** (-ĭz'm), *n.* — **e′van·gel′i·cal·ly**, *adv.*

e·van′ge·lism (ē·văn′jĕ·lĭz'm), *n.* Preaching or promulgation of the gospel, esp. in revival services.

e·van′ge·list (-lĭst), *n.* **1.** [*cap.*] A writer of any of the four Gospels; Matthew, Mark, Luke, or John. **2.** A preacher of the gospel; specif.: **a** A traveling missionary. **b** An evangelizer. **c** A revivalist. **3.** *Mormon Ch.* A patriarch.

e·van′ge·lis′tic (-lĭs′tĭk), *adj.* **1.** Of or pertaining to evangelists. **2.** Evangelical. **3.** Evangelizing. — **e·van′ge·lis′ti·cal·ly** (-tĭ·kăl·ĭ), *adv.*

e·van′ge·lize (ē·văn′jĕ·līz), *v. t.* To instruct in the gospel; to convert to Christianity. — **e·van′ge·li·za′tion** (-lĭ·zā′shŭn; -lī·zā′-), *n.* — **e·van′ge·liz′er** (-līz′ẽr), *n.*

e·van′ish (ē·văn′ĭsh), *v. i.* To vanish completely; die.

e·vap′o·ra·ble (ē·văp′ō·rȧ·b'l), *adj.* Capable of being evaporated. — **e·vap′o·ra·bil′i·ty** (-bĭl′ĭ·tĭ), *n.*

e·vap′o·rate (ē·văp′ō·rāt), *v. i.* [L. *evaporatus*, past part. of *evaporare*, fr. *e* out + *vapor* steam or vapor.] **1.** To pass off in vapor, as a fluid; to escape as vapor or in the manner of vapor. **2.** To give forth vapor. — *v. t.* **1.** To convert into vapor; to draw off in vapor or fumes. **2.** To expel moisture from, as by heat, until dry or concentrated; as, to *evaporate* fruit or milk. — **e·vap′o·ra′tion** (-rā′shŭn), *n.* — **e·vap′o·ra′tive** (-rā′tĭv; -rȧ·tĭv), *adj.* — **e·vap′o·ra′tor** (-rā′tẽr), *n.*

e·vap′o·rat′ed milk (-rāt′ĕd; -ĭd). Milk concentrated by evaporation, without the addition of sugar, to one half or less of its bulk and usually containing a specified amount of milk fat and milk solids. Cf. CONDENSED MILK.

e·vap′o·rim′e·ter (ē·văp′ō·rĭm′ē·tẽr), **e·vap′o·rom′e·ter** (-rŏm′ē·tẽr), *n.* [L. *evaporare* to evaporate + *-meter.*] An instrument for measuring the rate of the evaporating power of the air.

e·va′sion (ē·vā′zhŭn), *n.* Act of evading; esp., an evading of the truth or the point at issue when arguing or being questioned; also, a means of evading, as a subterfuge or equivocal statement.

e·va′sive (-sĭv), *adj.* Tending to evade; not straightforward or frank. — **e·va′sive·ly**, *adv.* — **e·va′sive·ness**, *n.*

eve (ēv), *n.* [See EVEN, *n.*] **1.** *Poetic.* Evening. **2.** The evening, or the day, before a feast, as Christmas. **3.** The period immediately preceding some important event.

Eve (ēv), *n.* [AS. *Ēfe*, fr. LL. *Eva, Heva*, fr. Heb. *Ḥawwāh.*] *Bib.* The wife of Adam and the mother of mankind.

e·vec′tion (ē·vĕk′shŭn), *n.* [L. *evectio* a going up, fr. *evehere* to carry out, fr. *e* out + *vehere* to carry.] *Astron.* An inequality of the moon's motion in its orbit, due to the attraction of the sun. — **e·vec′tion·al**, *adj.*

e′ven (ē′vĕn), *n.* [AS. *ǣfen, ēfen.*] *Now Poetic & Dial.* Evening; eve.

e′ven, *adj.* [AS. *efen, efn.*] **1.** Without elevation or depression; level. **2.** Free from inequality, irregularity, or fluctuation; uniform; as, *even* rhythm; also, equable; as, an *even* temper. **3.** Hence: **a** Equitable; fair; as, an *even* bargain. **b** Straightforward; plain; direct. *Shak.* **c** Equal in quality or station. **4.** Equal in size, number, or quantity; as, *even* shares. **5.** In the same plane, or in line; parallel; as, snow *even* with the eaves. **6.** Equal in respect to owing each other or the other nothing; square; esp., revenged, as for an insult. **7.** Not odd; divisible by two; — of numbers. **8.** Exact; precise; as, an *even* mile, dozen. — **Syn.** See LEVEL: STEADY. — ***of even date.*** Of the same date. — *adv.* [AS. *efne.*] **1.** *Obs.* In an even manner; evenly. **2.** In or to such (indicated) degree or kind; specif.: **a** Precisely; as, it is *even* so. **b** Fully; quite. **c** Of time: just; but just; as, *even* now, he was here. **3.** As an intensive particle: **a** *Archaic.* Emphasizing identity; as, I honor him, *even* every word he utters. **b** Serving to indicate what might not be expected; as, admired, *even* by his enemies. **c** Emphasizing a comparative; yet; still; as, he did *even* better. — *v. t. & i.* **1.** To make, be, or become even; level. **2.** To equal or make equal; specif.: **a** To make quits. **b** *Now Dial.* To liken; compare. — **e′ven·er**, *n.* — **e′ven·ly**, *adv.* — **e′ven·ness**, *n.*

e′ven·fall′ (ē′vĕn·fôl′), *n.* Dusk; nightfall.

e′ven·hand′ed (-hăn′dĕd; -dĭd; 2), *adj.* Fair or impartial.

even if. Notwithstanding; although.

eve′ning (ēv′nĭng), *n.* [AS. *ǣfnung*, fr. *ǣfnian* to grow towards evening, fr. *ǣfen* evening.] **1.** The latter part and close of the day and early part of darkness or night; specif.: **a** Locally in England and the southern states of the United States, the period from noon to and including sunset and twilight. **b** The period from sunset or from the evening meal to ordinary bedtime. **2.** The latter portion, as of life, strength, or glory. **3.** The period of an evening's entertainment. — **eve′ning**, *adj.*

evening primrose. Any of a genus (*Oenothera*, esp. *O. biennis*), typifying a family (Onagraceae, the evening-primrose family), of plants, mostly with yellow nocturnal flowers; also, any of several plants of related genera.

evening star. The bright planet of early evening in the western sky; — called also *Vesper* and *Hesperus.* Venus is most conspicuous as evening star. See MORNING STAR.

e′ven·song′ (ē′vĕn·sŏng′; 74), *n.* [AS. *ǣfensang.*] [*often cap.*] *Eccl.* **a** Vespers. **b** The Anglican service of evening prayer.

e·vent′ (ē·vĕnt′), *n.* [OF., fr. L. *eventus*, fr. *evenire* to happen, come out, fr. *e* out + *venire* to come.] **1.** The fact of taking place or occurring; occurrence; as, in the *event* of his death, his wife will inherit his fortune. **2.** That which comes, arrives, or happens; any incident, esp. a noteworthy one. **3.** Consequence; issue; conclusion. **4.** Any of the contests in a series or program of sports. **5.** *Philos.* That which occupies a restricted portion of four-dimensional space time; thus, from this point of view, one's body from sunrise to sunset is an *event.* — **Syn.** See OCCURRENCE: EFFECT.

e·vent′ful (-fo͝ol; -f'l), *adj.* Full of events; also, momentous. — **e·vent′ful·ly**, *adv.* — **e·vent′ful·ness**, *n.*

e′ven·tide′ (ē′vĕn·tīd′), *n.* *Archaic & Poet.* Evening.

e·ven′tu·al (ē·vĕn′tū·ăl), *adj.* **1.** Belonging to, or determined by, the outcome or issue; final; ultimate; as, *eventual* success. **2.** Dependent on events; contingent. — **Syn.** See LAST. — **e·ven′tu·al·ly**, *adv.*

e·ven′tu·al′i·ty (-ăl′ĭ·tĭ), *n.*; *pl.* -TIES (-tĭz). An outcome; esp., a contingent outcome; as, to be prepared for all *eventualities.*

e·ven′tu·ate (ē·vĕn′tū·āt), *v. i.* To come out finally; result.

ev′er (ĕv′ẽr), *adv.* [AS. *ǣfre.*] **1.** At all times; always. **2.** At any time; as, he is seldom if *ever* a visitor. **3.** In any case; at all.

☞ *Ever*, as used in many idiomatic phrases and constructions with more or less modified sense, often constitutes no more than an intensive or emphatic particle. Thus ***ever and anon, for ever and ever, for ever and a day***, etc., indicate indefinite repetition or continuation. In ***or ever*** (see under 1st OR), ***before ever, ever so***, etc., *ever* has chiefly an intensive force.

ev′er·glade (-glād), *n.* A swamp or inundated tract of low land. — ***the Everglades.*** A great tract of this nature in Florida.

ev′er·green′ (-grēn′), *adj.* *Bot.* Remaining verdant, as coniferous trees and many tropical plants. Cf. DECIDUOUS. — *n.* **1.** An evergreen plant. The word *evergreen* is often used loosely as a synonym of *conifer;* but some conifers, as the larch, are deciduous, and many evergreens, as the laurel, are not conifers. Cf. CONE, *Illust.* **2.** *pl.* Twigs and branches of evergreen plants used for decoration.

Evergreen State. Washington; — a nickname.

ev′er·last′ing (ĕv′ẽr·lȧs′tĭng), *adj.* **1.** Lasting or enduring forever; eternal. **2.** Continuing long or indefinitely; perpetual; hence, tedious from repetition. **3.** Wearing indefinitely; durable. — *n.* **1.** Eternity. **2.** [*cap.*] God; — with *the.* **3.** Any of several plants, chiefly of the aster family, whose flowers may be dried without loss of form or color. **4.** One of certain long-wearing fabrics. **5.** A card game which continues until one player has all the cards. — **ev′er·last′ing·ly**, *adv.* — **ev′er·last′ing·ness**, *n.*

ev′er·more′ (ĕv′ẽr·mōr′; ĕv′ẽr·mōr; 2; 70), *adv.* Forever; at all times; — often used substantively, with *for;* as, he will regret it for *evermore.*

e·ver′si·ble (ē·vûr′sĭ·b'l), *adj.* Capable of being everted.

e·ver′sion (-shŭn), *n.* An everting; state of being everted.

e·vert′ (ē·vûrt′), *v. t.* [L. *evertere, eversum*, fr. *e* + *vertere* to turn.] To turn outward, or inside out, as an intestine.

e·ver′tor (ē·vûr′tẽr), *n.* *Anat.* A muscle which rotates a part outward.

ev′er·y (ĕv′ẽr·ĭ; ĕv′rĭ), *adj.* [AS. *ǣfre* ever + *ǣlc* each.] **1.** Each (individual or part), without exception; as, his *every* word. **2.** *Obs.* All, taken severally. **3.** Each within a possible range; as, given *every* opportunity. **4.** Complete; entire; as, to have *every* confidence in him.

ev′er·y·bod′y (-bŏd′ĭ; -bŭd·ĭ), *pron.* Every person.

ev′er·y·day′ (ĕv′ẽr·ĭ·dā′; ĕv′rĭ-; -dā′), *adj.* Used or fit for, or coming, every day; usual; routine; as, *everyday* affairs; also, suitable for ordinary days; as, his *everyday* clothes.

ev′er·y·one′ (ĕv′ẽr·ĭ·wŭn′; ĕv′rĭ·wŭn; -wŭn), *pron.* This one, that one, and the other ones, so that all are included; as, *everyone* has his peculiar foible.

every one. **1.** Everyone. **2.** Each separate and distinct person or thing without exception; — often with *of.*

ev′er·y·thing′ (-thĭng′), *pron.* Every object, fact, etc., whatever; all that pertains to the subject considered. — **ev′er·y·thing′**, *n.*

ev′er·y·where′ (-hwâr′), *adv.* In or to every place.

e·vict′ (ē·vĭkt′), *v. t.* [L. *evictus*, past part. of *evincere* to overcome completely, recover one's property by judicial decision, to prove. See EVINCE.] *Law.* To put out (a person) or to recover (property) by legal process, or by virtue of a paramount right or claim; to eject. — **Syn.** See EJECT. — **e·vic′tion** (ē·vĭk′shŭn), *n.* — **e·vic′tor** (-tẽr), *n.*

ev′i·dence (ĕv′ĭ·dĕns), *n.* **1.** Clearness. **2.** An outward sign; indication; also, that which furnishes any mode of proof. **3.** One who bears witness; as, state's *evidence.* **4.** *Law.* That which is legally submitted to a competent tribunal as a means of ascertaining the truth of any alleged matter of fact under investigation before it; — distinguished from *proof*, the effect of evidence, and from *testimony*, that form of evidence which is orally given. — ***in evidence.*** In a situation to be readily seen. — *v. t.;* EV′I·DENCED (-dĕnst); EV′I·DENC·ING (-dĕn·sĭng). To render evident or clear; evince; attest. — **Syn.** See SHOW.

ev′i·dent (-dĕnt), *adj.* [OF., fr. L. *evidens, -entis*, fr. *e* out + *videns*, pres. part. of *videre* to see.] Clear to the vision and understanding. — **ev′i·dent·ly**, *adv.*

Syn. Evident, manifest, patent, distinct, obvious, apparent, plain, clear mean readily perceived or apprehended. **Evident** implies existence of visible signs which serve as indications of a person's state of mind, the imminence of an event, or the like; **manifest** implies a display so evident that seemingly no inference is involved; **patent** usually applies to that which is not imperceptible or obscure, such as a cause, an effect, or an imperfection, but so evident to a person knowing the material, the subject, etc., that it can be pointed out; **distinct** implies such sharpness of outline or of definition that the thing requires no effort of eyes to see, of ears to hear, or of mind to apprehend or comprehend; **obvious** implies such ease in discovering or accounting for that it often connotes conspicuousness or little need for perspicacity in the observer; **apparent** implies more conscious inference than does *evident*, its close synonym; **plain** and **clear** imply unmistakability, *plain* because of lack of intricacy or complexity, *clear* because of an absence of that which confuses the mind or obscures the issues.

ev′i·den′tial (ĕv′ĭ·dĕn′shăl), *adj.* Of the nature of, relating to, or affording evidence; also, relying on evidence.

e′vil (ē′v'l; -vĭl), *adj.* [AS. *yfel.*] **1.** Injurious; mischievous. **2.** Morally corrupt; wicked. **3.** Producing or threatening sorrow, distress, or calamity; unpropitious; calamitous. **4.** Arising from bad character, actual or imputed. — **Syn.** See BAD. — ***the Evil One.*** The Devil; Satan. — *n.* **1.** Anything impairing happiness or welfare or depriving of good. **2.** Moral badness. **3.** King's evil. — *adv.* In an evil manner. — **e′vil·do′er** (-dōō′ẽr), *n.* — **e′vil–do′ing**, *n.* — **e′vil·ly**, *adv.* — **e′vil·ness**, *n.*

evil eye. An eye supposed to be capable of inflicting blight or injury.

e′vil–mind′ed (-mīn′dĕd; -dĭd; 2), *adj.* Having an evil disposition or evil intentions.

e·vince′ (ē·vĭns′), *v. t.;* E·VINCED′ (-vĭnst′); E·VINC′ING (-vĭn′sĭng). [L. *evincere* to vanquish completely, prevail, fr. *e* out, quite + *vincere* to vanquish.] **1.** *Obs.* To subdue. *Milton.* **2.** To make evident or manifest. **3.** To exhibit or display, as a quality or trait. — **Syn.** See SHOW. — **e·vin′ci·ble** (-vĭn′sĭ·b'l), *adj.*

e·vin′cive (ē·vĭn′sĭv), *adj.* Tending to prove.

e·vis′cer·ate (ē·vĭs′ẽr·āt), *v. t.* [L. *evisceratus*, past part. of *eviscerare* to eviscerate, fr. *e* out + *viscera* the bowels.] To disembowel; hence, to deprive of force, as an argument; to devitalize. — **e·vis′cer·a′tion** (-ā′shŭn), *n.*

ev′i·ta·ble (ĕv′ĭ·tȧ·b'l), *adj.* [L. *evitabilis.*] Avoidable.

e·vite′ (ē·vīt′), *v. t.* [L. *evitare.*] *Archaic.* To shun.

ev′o·ca·ble (ĕv′ō·kȧ·b'l), *adj.* That may be called forth.

ev′o·ca′tion (-kā′shŭn), *n.* [L. *evocatio*, fr. *evocare.* See EVOKE.] **1.** Act of calling forth, as from seclusion or the grave, or of summoning a spirit by incantation. **2.** *Law.* The evoking, or summoning, of a cause from an inferior court by a superior court.

e·voc′a·tive (ē·vŏk′ȧ·tĭv; ē·vō′kȧ·tĭv), *adj.* Tending or serving to evoke.

ev′o·ca′tor (ĕv′ō·kā′tẽr), *n.* One who calls forth; esp., one who summons spirits.

e·voke′ (ē·vōk′), *v. t.* [F. *évoquer*, fr. L. *evocare*, fr. *e* out + *vocare* to call, fr. *vox, vocis*, voice.] To summon forth, as from seclusion. — **Syn.** See EDUCE.

ev′o·lute (ĕv′ō·lūt; *Brit.* ē′vō-, ĕv′ō-), *n.* [L. *evolutus* unrolled, past part. of *evolvere.* See EVOLVE.] *Geom.* The locus of the center of curvature, or the envelope of the normals, of a related curve called the *involute.* See INVOLUTE.

ev′o·lu′tion (ĕv′ō·lū′shŭn; *Brit.* ē′vō-, ĕv′ō-), *n.* [L. *evolutio* an unrolling. See EVOLVE.] **1.** An unfolding; a process of opening out what is contained or implied in something; a development, esp., as leading to a definite end; as, the *evolution* of the tragedy. **2.** A movement forming one of a series of motions, as of a machine; hence, an intricate form, as if produced by such a series; as, the *evolutions* of an arabesque pattern. **3.** A process of disengaging, so as to expose or free, as of gas from limestone. **4.** *Biol.* The development of a race, species, or other group; phylogeny; broadly, the process by which, through a series of changes, any living organism or group of organisms has acquired the morphological and physiological characters which distinguish it; hence, the theory that the various types of animals and plants have their origin in other pre-existing types, the distinguishable differences being due to modifications in successive generations. See LAMARCKISM; DARWINISM; NATURAL SELECTION. **5.** A thing evolved. **6.** *Math.* The extraction of roots; — the inverse of *involution.* **7.** *Mil. & Nav.* Any movement of troops or vessels designed to effect a new arrangement by passing from one formation to another. **8.** *Philos.* Any process which exhibits a direction of change; esp., the process of the whole universe, conceived as a progression of interrelated phenomena. — **ev′o·lu′tion·al** (-ăl; -'l), *adj.* — **ev′o·lu′tion·al·ly**, *adv.*

ev′o·lu′tion·ar′y (-ĕr′ĭ *or, esp. Brit.,* -ẽr·ĭ), *adj.* **1. a** Pertaining to evolution. **b** Pertaining to evolutions, or maneuvers. **2.** Of or pertaining to formative and disintegrative forces which determine the genetic composition of populations; as, *evolutionary* statics and dynamics.

ev′o·lu′tion·ist (-ĭst), *n.* One who holds a doctrine of evolution.

e·volve′ (ē·vŏlv′), *v. t.* [L. *evolvere, evolutum*, fr. *e* out + *volvere* to roll.] **1.** To exhibit or produce by evolution; derive; deduce. **2.** To disengage or emit, as gases. — *v. i.* To become open, disclosed, or developed; to pass through a process of evolution. — **e·volve′ment** (-mĕnt), *n.*

ev·on′y·mus (ĕv·ŏn′ĭ·mŭs), *n.* [NL., fr. L., fr. Gr. *euonymos*, lit., of good name.] Any of a large genus (*Evonymus*, family Celastraceae) of evergreen shrubs or vines having bright-colored fruit with arillate seeds, as the wahoo.

e·vul′sion (ē·vŭl′shŭn), *n.* [L. *evulsio*, fr. *evellere, evulsum*, to pluck out.] Act of plucking out; a rooting out.

ev′zone (ĕv′zōn), *n.; pl.* EVZONES (-zōnz). [NGr. *euzōnoi* light infantry, fr. Gr. *euzōnos* active, lit., well-girdled.] In the Greek army, a member of a select infantry corps recruited from the mountain regions.

ewe (ū; *dial.* yō), *n.* [AS. *eowu, ewe.*] The female of the sheep.

ewe lamb. Figuratively, a poor person's one prized possession; also, an only child.

ewe′–neck′, *n.* A thin sheeplike neck, having an insufficient or concave arch, as in horses. — **ewe′–necked′** (-nĕkt′), *adj.*

ew′er (ū′ẽr), *n.* [AF., for OF. *eviere, aiguiere*, fr. L. *aquarium*, fr. *aqua* water.] A type of widemouthed jug.

ex (ĕks), *prep.* [L.] Out of; without; — in commercial phrases; as: **a** *Finance.* Without the right to have; as, *ex* dividend, *ex* coupon. **b** *Com.* Free of charges precedent to removal from the specified place, purchaser to provide transportation; as, *ex* dock; *ex* ship.

ex (ĕks), *n.; pl.* EXES (ĕk′sĕz; -sĭz). The letter X, x.

ex-. [L. *ex* out of, from.] A prefix denoting: **a** *Out of*, as in *ex*hale. **b** *Off, from*, as in *ex*scind. **c** *Beyond*, as in *ex*ceed. **d** *Away from, out of*, as in *ex*patriate. **e** *Without, not*, as in *ex*caudate. **f** *Thoroughly, completely*, as in *ex*asperate. **g** *Formerly but not now;* — as hyphened to names implying office or condition, as in *ex*-president.

ex-. See EXO-.

ex·ac′er·bate (ĕg·zăs′ẽr·bāt; ĕks·ăs′-), *v. t.* [L. *exacerbatus*, past part. of *exacerbare*, fr. *ex* out (intens.) + *acerbare* to irritate.] To render more violent or bitter, as a disease or anger; to irritate. — **ex·ac′er·ba′tion** (-bā′shŭn), *n.*

ex·act′ (ĕg·zăkt′; ĭg-), *adj.* [L. *exactus* precise, past part. of *exigere* to drive out, demand, enforce, finish, determine, measure, fr. *ex* out + *agere* to drive.] **1.** Strict; rigorous; as, *exact* laws. **2.** Marked by accuracy and thoroughness; precise and full; as, *exact* knowledge. **3.** Marked by agreement with a standard or the truth; correct; as, an *exact* copy. **4.** Capable of great nicety or precision; as, the *exact* sciences. — **Syn.** See CORRECT.

ex·act′, *v. t.* **1.** To demand or require authoritatively or peremptorily; to compel to yield or furnish; hence, to wrest, as a fee when none is due. **2.** To call for; to require as becoming or fit. — **Syn.** See DEMAND. — **ex·act′a·ble**, *adj.* — **ex·ac′tor, ex·act′er**, *n.*

ex·act′ing, *adj.* Tryingly or unremittingly severe in making demands. — **Syn.** See ONEROUS. — **ex·act′ing·ly**, *adv.* — **ex·act′ing·ness**, *n.*

ex·ac′tion (ĕg·zăk′shŭn; ĭg-), *n.* **1.** Act or process of exacting; hence, extortion. **2.** That which is exacted.

ex·act′i·tude (-zăk′tĭ·tūd), *n.* The quality of being exact; exactness.

ex·act′ly (-zăkt′lĭ), *adv.* **1.** In an exact manner; precisely; accurately. **2.** Quite so; as you say.

ex·act′ness (-nĕs; -nĭs), *n.* Exactitude.

exact science. A mathematical science, or a science on a quantitative basis.

‖ex ae′quo et bo′no (ĕks ē′kwō ĕt bō′nō). [L.] According to what is just and good.

ex·ag′ger·ate (ĕg·zăj′ẽr·āt; ĭg-), *v. t.* [L. *exaggeratus*, past part. of *exaggerare* to heap up, fr. *ex* out + *aggerare* to heap up, fr. *agger* heap.] **1.** To enlarge beyond bounds or the truth; to overstate the truth concerning. **2.** To enlarge or increase beyond the normal. — *v. i.* To misrepresent by overstating. — **ex·ag′ger·at′ed·ly** (-āt′ĕd·lĭ; -ĭd·lĭ), *adv.* — **ex·ag′ger·a′tor** (-ā′tẽr), *n.*

ex·ag′ger·a′tion (-ā′shŭn), *n.* Act of exaggerating, or state of being exaggerated; overstatement.

ex·ag′ger·a′tive (ĕg·zăj′ẽr·ā′tĭv; -ȧ·tĭv; ĭg-), *adj.* Tending to exaggerate; given to or involving exaggeration.

ex·ag′ger·a·to′ry (-ȧ·tō′rĭ *or, esp. Brit.,* -tẽr·ĭ), *adj.* Exaggerative.

ex·alt′ (ĕg·zôlt′; ĭg-), *v. t.* [OF. *exalter*, fr. L. *exaltare*, fr. *ex* out (intens.) + *altus* high.] **1.** To raise high; to lift up. **2.** To elevate in rank, dignity, power, wealth, character, or the like; to dignify; promote. **3.** To magnify; extol; glorify. **4.** To lift up with joy, pride, or success; to elate. **5.** To intensify or heighten, as a color or the imagination. — **Syn.** Magnify, aggrandize. — **Ant.** Abase. — **ex·alt′er**, *n.*

ex′al·ta′tion (ĕg′zôl·tā′shŭn), *n.* **1.** An exalting; state of being exalted. **2.** Abnormal intensification of a mental state or of the power of an organ or function; esp., abnormal sense of personal well-being, power, or importance.

ex·alt′ed (ĕg·zôl′tĕd; -tĭd; ĭg-), *adj.* Raised to a state of exaltation; elevated; sublime. — **ex·alt′ed·ly**, *adv.* — **ex·alt′ed·ness**, *n.*

ex·am′ (ĕg·zăm′; ĭg-), *n.* Colloq. contr. of EXAMINATION.

ex·a′men (ĕg·zā′mĕn), *n.* [L., tongue of a balance, examination, for *exagmen* or *exagmen*, fr. *ex* + *agere*, L. *exigere* to weigh accurately. See EXACT.] *Eccl.* Examination.

ex·am′i·nant (ĕg·zăm′ĭ·nănt), *n.* One who examines.

ex·am′i·na′tion (ĕg·zăm′ĭ·nā′shŭn; ĭg-), *n.* **1.** Act of examining, or state of being examined; a search or investigation. **2.** A testing of knowledge or qualification, or the questions or answers made in such test. — **ex·am′i·na′tion·al** (-ăl; -'l), *adj.*

ex·am′ine (ĕg·zăm′ĭn; ĭg-), *v. t.* [OF. *examiner*, fr. L. *examinare*, *examinatum*, fr. *examen.* See EXAMEN.] **1.** To test by an appropriate method; to subject to inquiry or inspection; to investigate; scrutinize. **2.** To interrogate closely, as in a judicial proceeding; to try or test by question, as a witness or student. — **Syn.** See SCRUTINIZE. — **ex·am′in·a·ble**, *adj.* — **ex·am′i·na·to′ri·al** (-ĭ·nȧ·tō′rĭ·ăl), *adj.* — **ex·am′i·nee′** (-ĭ·nē′), *n.* — **ex·am′in·er** (-ĭn·ẽr), *n.*

ex·am′ple (ĕg·zăm′p'l; ĭg-; 9), *n.* [For *ensample*, fr. OF. *example*, *essample*, fr. L. *exemplum*, orig., what is taken out of a larger quantity, as a *sample*, fr. *eximere* to take out. See EXEMPT.] **1.** One or a portion taken to show the character or quality of all; a sample. **2.** That which is to be followed or imitated; a pattern. **3.** A precedent, model, or parallel case. **4.** A warning case, esp. a punishment inflicted to serve as a warning. **5.** An instance illustrating a rule or precept, as a problem to be solved. Abbr. *ex.* — **Syn.** See INSTANCE: MODEL. — *v. t.*; EX·AM'PLED (-p'ld); EX·AM'PLING (-plĭng). To set an example for; to match; parallel; — chiefly passive.

ex·an'i·mate (ĕg·zăn'ĭ·māt), *adj.* [L. *exanimatus*, past part. of *exanimare* to deprive of life or spirit, fr. *ex* out + *anima* air, breath, life, spirit.] Lifeless; spiritless.

‖**ex a'ni·mo** (ĕks ăn'ĭ·mō). [L.] From the heart; sincerely.

ex'an·the'ma (ĕk'săn·thē'mȧ), *n.*; *pl.* -THEMATA (-thĕm'ȧ·tȧ; -thē'mȧ·tȧ), -THEMAS (-thē'mȧz). [LL., fr. Gr. *exanthēma*, fr. *exanthein* to burst forth as flowers, break out as ulcers, fr. *ek*, *ex*, out + *anthein* to bloom, fr. *anthos* flower.] *Med.* Any eruptive disease or its symptomatic eruption, esp. when febrile, as measles, smallpox, and scarlatina. — **ex·an'the·mat'ic** (ĕks·ăn'thē·măt'ĭk; ĕg·zăn'-), **ex'an·them'a·tous** (ĕk'săn·thĕm'ȧ·tŭs), *adj.*

ex'arch (ĕk'särk), *n.* [LL. *exarchus*, fr. Gr. *exarchos* a commander, fr. *ek*, *ex*, out + *archein* to rule.] **1.** A viceroy of a Byzantine emperor. **2.** *Eastern Ch.* A deputy of a patriarch, usually a bishop. — **ex'arch·ate** (ĕk'sär·kāt; ĕks·är'kāt), *n.*

ex·as'per·ate (ĕg·zăs'pĕr·āt; ĭg-), *v. t.* [L. *exasperatus*, past part. of *exasperare*, fr. *ex* out (intens.) + *asperare* to make rough, fr. *asper* rough.] **1.** To arouse to keen or bitter vexation; to inflame the anger of. **2.** To make grievous, or more grievous or malignant; as, to *exasperate* enmity or disease. — **Syn.** See IRRITATE. — **Ant.** Mollify. — **ex·as'per·at'er** (-āt'ẽr), *n.* — **ex·as'per·at'ing·ly**, *adv.*

ex·as'per·a'tion (-ā'shŭn), *n.* Act of exasperating or state of being exasperated; keen anger.

Ex·cal'i·bur (ĕks·kăl'ĭ·bẽr), *n.* [OF. *Escalibor*, fr. ML. *Caliburnus*, of Celt. origin.] Either of two swords of King Arthur, one unfixed from a stone, the other received from Vivian.

ex ca·the'dra (ĕks kȧ·thē'drȧ; kăth'ē·drȧ). [L., from the chair.] By virtue of or in the exercise of one's office; with authority. — **ex'-ca·the'dra**, *adj.*

ex·cau'date (ĕks·kô'dāt), *adj.* Tailless.

ex'ca·vate (ĕks'kȧ·vāt), *v. t.* [L. *excavatus*, past part. of *excavare* to excavate, fr. *ex* out + *cavare* to make hollow, fr. *cavus* hollow.] **1.** To hollow out; to form a cavity or hole in. **2.** To form by hollowing, as a tunnel. **3.** To dig out and remove, as earth. **4.** To expose to view by digging away superposed material.

ex'ca·va'tion (-vā'shŭn), *n.* Act or process of excavating; a cavity formed by cutting, digging, or scooping.

ex'ca·va'tor (ĕks'kȧ·vā'tẽr), *n.* One who or that which excavates, as a steam shovel.

ex·ceed' (ĕk·sēd'; ĭk-), *v. t.* [OF. *exceder*, fr. L. *excedere*, *excessum*, to go beyond, fr. *ex* out + *cedere* to go.] **1.** To go or be beyond the limit or measure of; as, to *exceed* one's authority. **2.** To be greater than or superior to; to surpass. — *v. i.* To be more or greater than others.

Syn. **Exceed, surpass, transcend, excel, outdo, outstrip** mean to go or be beyond a limit, measure, or degree. **Exceed** implies overpassing any limit, such as one set by authority, or determined by an earlier performance, attainment, or the like; **surpass** is preferred to *exceed* when the idea of superiority is implied in passing a limit; **transcend** implies great measure in exceeding or surpassing; **excel** implies pre-eminence in accomplishment or attainment, especially when no standard of comparison is indicated; **outdo** and **outstrip** (more colloquial than *excel* or *surpass*) are often preferred, *outdo* when the breaking of a previous record is to be inferred, and *outstrip* when one wishes to suggest successful competition in efforts to surpass.

ex·ceed'ing, *adj.* Extraordinary. — *adv. Archaic.* Extremely. — **ex·ceed'ing·ly**, *adv.*

ex·cel' (ĕk·sĕl'; ĭk-), *v. t. & i.*; EX·CELLED' (-sĕld'); EX·CEL'LING. [L. *excellere*, *excelsum*, fr. *ex* out + *cellere* (in comp.) to rise, project.] To go beyond or surpass in good qualities or deeds; to outdo. — **Syn.** See EXCEED.

ex'cel·lence (ĕk'sĕ·lĕns), *n.* **1.** Quality of being excellent; exalted merit. **2.** An excellent quality; a virtue. **3.** [*usually cap.*] Excellency (sense 2).

ex'cel·len·cy (-lĕn·sĭ), *n.*; *pl.* -CIES (-sĭz). **1.** Excellence (senses 1 & 2). **2.** [*usually cap.*] A title of honor given to certain high dignitaries, as viceroys and ambassadors, and constitutionally belonging to the governors of New Hampshire and Massachusetts.

ex'cel·lent (-lĕnt), *adj.* [OF., fr. L. *excellens*, *-entis*, pres. part. of *excellere*.] **1.** *Archaic.* Excelling; superior. **2.** Extremely good of its kind; first-class; hence, of great worth; eminently good. — **ex'cel·lent·ly**, *adv.*

ex·cel'si·or (ĕk·sĕl'sĭ·ôr; -ẽr), *adj.* [L., compar. of *excelsus* elevated, lofty, past part. of *excellere*. See EXCEL.] Still higher; ever upward; — motto of New York state. — (-ẽr), *n.* **1.** A material of curled shreds of wood used for stuffing upholstery, for packing, etc. **2.** *Print.* A size of type (3 points). See TYPE.

ex·cept' (ĕk·sĕpt'; ĭk-), *v. t.* [F. *excepter*, fr. L. *exceptare*, fr. *exceptus*, past part. of *excipere* to take or draw out, except, fr. *ex* out + *capere* to take.] To take or leave out (anything) from a number or a whole; to omit; bar. — *v. i.* To take exception. — *conj. Archaic.* Unless. — *prep.* **1.** With exclusion, rejection, or exception of. **2.** Otherwise or other than; as, take no orders *except* from me. Abbr. *exc.*

ex·cept'ing, *prep.* Except; with the exception that. — *conj. Archaic.* Except.

ex·cep'tion (ĕk·sĕp'shŭn; ĭk-), *n.* **1.** Act of excepting; exclusion. **2.** That which is excepted; as, every rule has its *exceptions*. **3.** Objection; something taken as objectionable; hence, cavil; complaint; as, to be beyond *exception*. **4.** *Law.* An objection, oral or written, taken, in the course of an action or proceeding, as to bail, to the decision or a ruling of a judge, or to something in his charge to a jury.

ex·cep'tion·a·ble (-ȧ·b'l), *adj.* Liable to exception. — **Syn.** See EXCEPTIONAL. — **ex·cep'tion·a·bly** (-blĭ), *adv.*

ex·cep'tion·al (-ăl; -'l), *adj.* Forming an exception; uncommon; hence, superior. — **ex·cep'tion·al·ly**, *adv.*

Syn. **Exceptional, exceptionable.** That is **exceptional** which is an exception, or out of the ordinary; that is **exceptionable** to which exception may be taken, and which is therefore objectionable.

ex·cep'tive (ĕk·sĕp'tĭv; ĭk-), *adj.* Pertaining to, containing, or constituting exception; also, captious.

ex·cerpt' (ĕk·sûrpt'), *v. t.* [L. *excerptus*, past part. of *excerpere*, fr. *ex* out + *carpere* to pick.] To select, as a literary passage; to extract; quote. — **ex·cerp'tion** (-sûrp'shŭn), *n.*

ex'cerpt (ĕk'sûrpt; ĕk·sûrpt'; ĭk-), *n.* An extract; a passage selected or copied from a book or record.

ex·cess' (ĕk·sĕs'; ĭk-), *n.* [OF. *exces*, fr. L. *excessus* a going out, loss of self-possession, fr. *excedere*. See EXCEED.] **1.** State or fact of going beyond limits, esp. beyond sufficiency, necessity, or duty; also, that which exceeds what is usual, proper, just, or specified; as, *excess* of grief. **2.** Intemperance. **3.** The amount or degree by which one thing or number exceeds another; remainder. — (ĕk·sĕs'; ĭk-; ĕk'sĕs; 2), *adj.* More than or above the usual or specified amount.

ex·ces'sive (ĕk·sĕs'ĭv; ĭk-), *adj.* Characterized by, or exhibiting, excess. — **ex·ces'sive·ly**, *adv.*

Syn. **Excessive, immoderate, inordinate, extravagant, exorbitant, extreme** mean going beyond or above a set or a normal limit. **Excessive** implies an amount, quantity, extent, or the like, too great to be just, reasonable, endurable, etc.; **immoderate** usually implies lack of restraint or of measure; **inordinate** implies an exceeding of bounds or limits prescribed by authority or dictated by good judgment; **extravagant** adds to *excessive* or *immoderate* the implication of indifference to restraints imposed by truth, prudence, fairness, etc.; **exorbitant** implies departure from that which is the usual amount or degree; **extreme** implies exceeding the range of possibility but the term is often hyperbolical in actual use. — **Ant.** Deficient.

ex·change' (ĕks·chānj'; ĭks-), *n.* [OF. *eschange*, fr. *eschangier* to exchange, deriv. of L. *ex* out + *cambiare* to change. See CHANGE.] **1.** Act of giving or taking one thing in return for another as an equivalent; trade; specif., barter. **2.** Act of substituting one thing for another, as of grief for joy; also, act of giving and receiving or losing and taking reciprocally; interchange; as, an *exchange* of civilities. **3.** The thing given or received in return; esp., a publication exchanged for another. **4.** A place where things or services are exchanged; specif.: **a** The place where merchants, brokers, bankers, etc., meet to do business; as, a cotton *exchange*. Abbr. *exch.* **b** A headquarters or central office or place of business (of a designated sort); as, a telephone *exchange*. **5.** *Com.* **a** The process of settling accounts between parties remote from each other, without using money, by exchanging orders or drafts, called *bills of exchange*. **b** A bill of exchange. **c** The amount paid for the collection of a draft, bill of exchange, check, etc., drawn in one place upon another. **d** (1) Interchange or conversion of the money of two countries, or of current and uncurrent money, with allowance for difference in value. (2) Short for ***rate of exchange***, that is, the price or sum per unit at which the currency of one country is exchanged for currency of another country, or uncurrent money for current money. (3) The amount of the difference in value between two currencies, or between values at two places. **e** *pl.* In a clearinghouse, the items (drafts, checks, etc.) which are presented for settlement by mutual interchange of credits and debits and payment of balances.
— *v. t.*; EX·CHANGED' (-chānjd'); EX·CHANG'ING (-chān'jĭng). **1.** To part with, give, or transfer to another for an equivalent; specif., to obtain or to supply something else in place of (goods returned). **2.** To part with for a substitute, as a palace for a cell. **3.** To give and receive or lose and take reciprocally, as things of the same kind; to barter; swap. — *v. i.* To make an exchange, or to pass in exchange. — **ex·change'a·bil'i·ty** (-chān'jȧ·bĭl'ĭ·tĭ), *n.* — **ex·change'a·ble** (-chān'jȧ·b'l), *adj.*

exchange rate. *Com.* See EXCHANGE, *n.*, 5 **d** (2).

ex·cheq'uer (ĕks·chĕk'ẽr; ĕks'chĕk·ẽr), *n.* [ME. *escheker*, prop., a chessboard, fr. OF. *eschequier*. See CHECKER.] **1.** [*cap.*] *Eng. Hist.* Originally, an office of state charged with the management of the royal revenue; then, a court, the ***Court of Exchequer***, having jurisdiction in revenue matters, later merged in the King's Bench Division of the High Court of Justice. **2.** [*often cap.*] *Great Britain.* The department of state charged with the receipt and care of the national revenue; hence, the national banking account. **3.** A treasury; esp., a national or royal treasury. **4.** One's financial resources; funds.

ex·cide' (ĕk·sīd'), *v. t.* [L. *excidere*.] To cut out.

ex·cip'i·ent (ĕk·sĭp'ĭ·ĕnt; 58), *n.* [L. *excipiens*, *-entis*, pres. part. of *excipere*. See EXCEPT.] *Pharm.* An inert substance used to give preparations a suitable form or consistency.

ex'cise (ĕk'sīz; ĕk'sĭs; ĕk·sīz'; ĕk·sĭs'), *n.* [Prob. fr. MD. *excijs*, *accijs*, fr. OF. *acceis*, *accens*, deriv. of L. *ad* to + *census* tax.] A duty or impost levied upon the manufacture, sale, or consumption of commodities within the country, or, in the form of exactions for license, for permission to practice or conduct certain sports, trades, occupations, etc. — *v. t.* To impose excise upon or force to pay excise. — **ex·cis'a·ble** (ĕk·sīz'ȧ·b'l; ĭk-), *adj.*

ex·cise' (ĕk·sīz'), *v. t.* [L. *excisus*, past part. of *excidere* to cut.] To cut out, as a tumor; to remove as by cutting out; to erase; expunge; extirpate. — **ex·cis'a·ble** (-sīz'ȧ·b'l), *adj.* — **ex·ci'sion** (-sĭzh'ŭn), *n.*

ex'cise·man (ĕk'sīz·măn; ĕk'sĭs-; ĕk·sīz'-; ĕk·sĭs'-), *n. Brit.* An officer who inspects and rates articles liable to excise duty.

ex·cit'a·bil'i·ty (ĕk·sīt'ȧ·bĭl'ĭ·tĭ; ĭk-), *n.* Quality of being readily excitable; specif., *Physiol.*, the capacity to be excited (by stimuli).

ex·cit'a·ble (ĕk·sīt'ȧ·b'l; ĭk-), *adj.* Capable of being excited; susceptible of stimulation. — **ex·cit'a·ble·ness**, *n.*

ex·cit'ant (ĕk·sīt'ănt; ĭk-; ĕk'sĭ·tănt), *adj. & n.* Stimulant.

ex'ci·ta'tion (ĕk'sĭ·tā'shŭn), *n.* Act of exciting, or state of being excited; excitement.

ex·cit'a·tive (ĕk·sīt'ȧ·tĭv), *adj.* Tending or able to excite.

ex·cit'a·to'ry (ĕk·sīt'ȧ·tō'rĭ *or, esp. Brit.*, -tẽr·ĭ; ĭk-), *adj.* Tending to excite; containing, or marked by, excitement.

ex·cite' (ĕk·sīt'; ĭk-), *v. t.* [OF. *exciter*, fr. L. *excitare*, fr. *ex* out + *citare* to move rapidly, rouse.] **1.** To call to activity in any way; to rouse to feeling. **2.** *Elec.* To energize (an electromagnet); to produce a magnetic field in, as a dynamo. **3.** *Physiol.* To arouse, or to increase the activity of, as a living organism or any of its parts or tissues; to stimulate. — **Syn.** See PROVOKE.

ex·cit'ed (-sīt'ĕd; -ĭd), *adj.* **1.** Roused to activity; aroused emotionally. **2.** *Physics & Chem.* Pert. to or designating the state of an atom in which one or more electrons have been ejected from their normal orbits to orbits farther away from the nucleus. — **ex·cit'ed·ly**, *adv.*

ex·cite'ment (-sīt'mĕnt), *n.* **1.** Act of exciting, or state of being excited; agitation. **2.** That which excites or rouses.

ex·cit'er (-sīt'ẽr), *n.* **1.** One who or that which excites. **2.** *Elec.* A dynamo or battery which supplies the electric current used to produce the magnetic field in another dynamo or motor.

ex·cit′ing (-sīt′ĭng), *adj.* Producing excitement. — **ex·cit′ing·ly,** *adv.*
ex·ci′to- (ĕk·sī′tō-; ĭk-). [L. *excitare* to excite.] A combining form denoting *exciting* or *stimulating*, esp. to reflex action, as in **ex·ci′to·mo′tor, ex·ci′to·mo′to·ry,** *adj.*
ex·ci′tor (ĕk·sī′tẽr; -tôr; ĭk-), *n.* An exciter; *Physiol.*, an afferent nerve increasing activity in the part which it supplies.
ex·claim′ (ĕks·klām′; ĭks-), *v. i. & t.* [L. *exclamare, exclamatum,* fr. *ex* + *clamare* to cry out.] To cry out, or speak, in strong or sudden emotion; to speak or utter loudly or vehemently, as in protest. — **ex·claim′er** (-ẽr), *n.*
ex′cla·ma′tion (ĕks′klȧ·mā′shŭn), *n.* **1.** Act of exclaiming; a sharp utterance of strong feeling. **2.** *Gram.* A word of outcry; an interjection. **3.** = EXCLAMATION POINT.
exclamation point or **mark.** The mark [!] used in writing and printing to indicate forceful utterance or strong feeling.
ex·clam′a·to′ry (ĕks·klăm′ȧ·tō′rĭ *or, esp. Brit.*, -tẽr·ĭ; ĭks-), *adj.* Containing, expressing, using, or pertaining to, exclamation.
ex′clave (ĕks′klāv), *n.* [From *enclave,* with *ex-* for *en-.*] A portion of a country which is separated from the main part and surrounded by politically alien territory. The same territory is an *enclave* in respect to the surrounding country and an *exclave* with respect to the country to which it is politically attached.
ex·clo′sure (ĕks·klō′zhẽr; ĭks-), *n.* [From *ex-*, after *enclosure.*] A space fenced with an artificial barrier proof against livestock, rodents, insects, etc.
ex·clude′ (ĕks·klōōd′; ĭks-), *v. t.* [L. *excludere, exclusum,* fr. *ex* out + *claudere* to shut.] **1.** To hinder from entrance; to refuse participation, enjoyment, consideration, or inclusion, to. **2.** To eject; expel. — **ex·clud′a·ble** (-klōōd′ȧ·b'l), *adj.* — **ex·clud′er** (-ẽr), *n.*
Syn. Exclude, debar, eliminate, suspend mean to prevent from becoming or remaining a constituent, a member, or the like. Exclude strictly implies keeping out what is already outside and may be used in reference to persons and things; debar implies a barrier (literal or figurative) which is effectual in excluding (chiefly persons) from enjoying certain privileges, powers, etc., open to others; eliminate implies the getting rid of or removal of what is already within; suspend implies the elimination of a person from a school or other organization usually as a penalty and, often, for the time being. — **Ant.** Include; admit.
ex·clu′sion (-klōō′zhŭn), *n.* **1.** Act or instance of excluding; state of being excluded; rejection. **2.** *Physiol.* Act of expelling.
ex·clu′sion·ist (-ĭst), *n.* One who would exclude another from some right or privilege. — **ex·clu′sion·ism** (-ĭz'm), *n.*
exclusion principle. *Physics.* The principle that no two electrons of an atomic system will be exactly equivalent.
ex·clu′sive (-sĭv), *adj.* **1.** Excluding or having power to exclude; limiting or limited to possession, control, or use by a single individual, organization, etc. **2.** Excluding or inclined to exclude others, esp. outsiders; sometimes, snobbishly aloof. **3.** Admitting of only a socially restricted patronage; hence, stylish. **4.** Single; sole; also, singly devoted; undivided. **5.** Not taking into the account; as, *exclusive* of fees. Abbr. *excl.* — **ex·clu′sive·ly,** *adv.* — **ex·clu′sive·ness,** *n.*
ex·cog′i·tate (ĕks·kŏj′ĭ·tāt), *v. t.* [L. *excogitatus,* past part. of *excogitare.* See EX-; COGITATE.] To think out; to devise; contrive. — **ex·cog′i·ta′tion** (-tā′shŭn), *n.* — **ex·cog′i·ta′tive,** *adj.*
ex′com·mu′ni·ca·ble (ĕks′kŏ·mū′nĭ·kȧ·b'l), *adj.* Liable to or deserving excommunication.
ex′com·mu′ni·cate (-kāt), *adj.* [LL. *excommunicatus,* past part. of *excommunicare* to excommunicate. See EX-; COMMUNICATE.] Excommunicated. — *n.* One excommunicated. — (-kāt), *v. t.* To cut off, or shut out, from communion with the church, by an ecclesiastical sentence. — **ex′com·mu′ni·ca′tor** (-kā′tẽr), *n.*
ex′com·mu′ni·ca′tion (-kā′shŭn), *n.* An ecclesiastical censure whereby one is, for the time, cast out of the communion of the church.
ex′com·mu′ni·ca′tive (-mū′nĭ·kā′tĭv; -kȧ·tĭv), *adj.* Tending toward, decreeing, or favoring, excommunication.
ex′com·mu′ni·ca·to′ry (-kȧ·tō′rĭ *or, esp. Brit.*, -tẽr·ĭ), *adj.* Pertaining to, causing, or declaring, excommunication.
ex·co′ri·ate (ĕks·kō′rĭ·āt), *v. t.* [LL. *excoriare,* fr. *ex* out + *corium* hide.] **1.** To strip or wear off the skin of; to flay; chafe; gall. **2.** To censure scathingly. — **ex·co′ri·a′tion** (-ā′shŭn), *n.*
ex′cre·ment (ĕks′krē·mĕnt), *n.* [L. *excrementum,* fr. *excernere.* See EXCRETE.] Waste matter discharged from the body, esp. from the alimentary canal; fecal matter. — **ex′cre·men′tal** (-mĕn′tăl; -t'l), **ex′cre·men·ti′tious** (-mĕn·tĭsh′ŭs), *adj.*
ex·cres′cence (ĕks·krĕs′ĕns; -'ns; ĭks-), *n.; pl.* -CENCES (-ĕn·sĕz; -sĭz). **1.** Abnormal growth or increase. **2.** A normal appendage or development, as hair. **3.** An abnormal outgrowth, as a wart.
ex·cres′cen·cy (-ĕn·sĭ; -'n·sĭ), *n.; pl.* -CIES (-sĭz). State of being excrescent; esp., abnormal protrusion or growth.
ex·cres′cent (-ĕnt; -'nt), *adj.* [L. *excrescens, -entis,* pres. part. of *excrescere, excretum,* to grow out, fr. *ex* out + *crescere* to grow.] **1.** Forming an abnormal, excessive, or useless outgrowth; superfluous. **2.** Of a sound in a word, growing out of the action of speech organs in forming neighboring sounds, as *d* in *alder* (AS. *alr*).
ex·cre′ta (ĕks·krē′tȧ), *n. pl.* [NL., fr. L. pl. of *excretum.* See EXCRETE.] Excretions; — sometimes including also feces.
ex·crete′ (ĕks·krēt′), *v. t.* [L. *excretus,* past part. of *excernere* to sift out, discharge, fr. *ex* out + *cernere* to sift.] To separate and eliminate or discharge (waste or harmful material) from the blood or tissues, or from the active protoplasm in plants.
ex·cre′tion (-krē′shŭn), *n.* **1.** Act or process of excreting. **2.** That which is excreted; useless, superfluous, or harmful material (esp. urine and sweat) eliminated from the body, differing from an ordinary *secretion* in not being produced to perform a useful function.
ex′cre·to′ry (ĕks′krē·tō′rĭ; ĕks·krē′tō·rĭ), *adj.* Pertaining to, or serving for, excretion. — *n.* An excretory organ.
ex·cru′ci·ate (ĕks·krōō′shĭ·āt; ĭks-), *v. t.* [L. *excruciatus,* past part. of *excruciare* to excruciate, fr. *ex* out + *cruciare* to crucify.] To inflict agonizing pain upon; to torture; rack.
ex·cru′ci·at′ing (-āt′ĭng), *adj.* Torturing; so intense as to be painful or distressing. — **ex·cru′ci·at′ing·ly,** *adv.*
ex·cru′ci·a′tion (-shĭ·ā′shŭn; -sĭ·ā′shŭn), *n.* Act of inflicting agonizing pain, or state of being thus afflicted; torture.
ex′cul·pate (ĕks′kŭl·pāt; ĕks·kŭl′-), *v. t.* [L. *ex* out + *culpatus,* past part. of *culpare* to find fault with, blame, fr. *culpa* fault.] To clear from alleged fault or guilt. — **ex·cul′pa·ble** (ĕks·kŭl′pȧ·b'l), *adj.* — **ex′cul·pa′tion** (ĕks′kŭl·pā′shŭn), *n.*
Syn. Exculpate, absolve, exonerate, acquit, vindicate mean to free from a charge or burden. Exculpate implies a clearing from blame, especially in a matter of small importance; absolve implies a release either from an obligation that binds the conscience or from the consequences of disobeying the law, especially the moral law; exonerate implies relief, often in a moral sense, from what is regarded as a load or burden; acquit implies a decision in one's favor with reference to a specific charge; vindicate may have reference to things, as well as to persons, that have been subjected to attack, suspicion, etc., and implies the clearing through proof of the injustice or unfairness of such criticism or blame. — **Ant.** Inculpate.
ex·cul′pa·to′ry (ĕks·kŭl′pȧ·tō′rĭ *or, esp. Brit.*, -tẽr·ĭ), *adj.* Clearing, or tending to clear, from alleged fault or guilt.
ex·cur′rent (ĕks·kŭr′ĕnt), *adj.* [L. *excurrens,* pres. part. of *excurrere, excursum,* to run out, fr. *ex* out + *currere* to run.] **1.** Flowing outward. **2.** *Bot.* **a** Having the axis prolonged, forming an undivided main stem, as conifers. **b** Projecting beyond the apex, as the midrib of a sharp-pointed leaf. **3.** *Zool.* Characterized by a current which flows outward; as, an *excurrent* orifice. Cf. CLAM, *Illust.*
ex·cur′sion (ĕks·kûr′zhŭn; -shŭn; ĭks-), *n.* [L. *excursio.* See EXCURRENT.] **1.** A going forth; an expedition. **2.** A journey chiefly for recreation; a pleasure trip. **3.** Deviation from a definite path; hence, a digression. **4.** *Mech.* A movement outward, or from a mean position or axis; also, the distance traversed; amplitude.
ex·cur′sion·ist (-ĭst), *n.* One who goes on an excursion.
ex·cur′sive (ĕks·kûr′sĭv), *adj.* Of the nature of a digression; also, prone to make excursions; digressive. — **ex·cur′sive·ly,** *adv.* — **ex·cur′sive·ness,** *n.*
ex·cur′sus (-sŭs), *n.; pl.* EXCURSUSES (-ĕz; -ĭz), or, now less usual, EXCURSUS. [L., fr. *excurrere, excursum.* See EXCURRENT.] An appendix or a digression containing extended exposition of some point.
ex·cus′a·to′ry (ĕks·kūz′ȧ·tō′rĭ *or, esp. Brit.*, -tẽr·ĭ; ĭks-), *adj.* Apologetic.
ex·cuse′ (ĕks·kūz′; ĭks-), *v. t.* [OF. *escuser, excuser,* fr. L. *excusare,* fr. *ex* out + *causa* cause.] **1.** To make apology for; to endeavor to remove blame from (a person) or the blame of (a fault); to seek to extenuate. **2.** To seek or obtain exemption or release for, esp. oneself. **3.** To accept an excuse for, or to regard as excusable; to forgive; to pardon; as, to say "*excuse* me" to a stranger. **4.** To grant exemption or release to (a person as from an obligation) or from (an obligation, exaction, etc.). **5.** To serve as excuse for; to free from imputation of fault; to exculpate; justify. — **ex·cus′a·ble** (-kūz′ȧ·b'l), *adj.* — **ex·cus′a·bly** (-blĭ), *adv.*
Syn. Excuse, condone, pardon, forgive mean not to exact punishment or redress for (an offense) or from (an offender). Both excuse and condone imply an overlooking either without censure or adequate punishment, *excuse* applying to faults, omissions, neglects, and *condone* to grave offenses such as a breach of the moral code; pardon strictly implies the freeing from the penalty due for an offense; forgive implies the giving up not only of any claim to requital or retribution but also of any resentment or desire for revenge.
ex·cuse′ (ĕks·kūs′; ĭks-), *n.* **1.** Act of excusing. **2.** That which is offered as a reason for being excused; an apology. **3.** That which excuses; that which extenuates or justifies a fault. — **Syn.** See APOLOGY.
ex′e·cra·ble (ĕk′sē·krȧ·b'l), *adj.* **1.** Deserving to be execrated; detestable. **2.** Very bad. — **ex′e·cra·bly** (-blĭ), *adv.*
ex′e·crate (-krāt), *v. t.* [L. *execratus, exsecratus,* past part. of *execrare, exsecrare,* to execrate, fr. *ex* out + *sacrare* to consecrate, declare accursed, fr. the stem of *sacer* sacred.] To imprecate evil upon; to curse; hence, to detest utterly; to abhor. — *v. i.* To curse. — **ex′e·cra′tive** (-krā′tĭv), *adj.* — **ex′e·cra′tor** (-krā′tẽr), *n.*
Syn. Execrate, curse, damn, ban, anathematize, objurgate mean to denounce violently. Execrate implies intense loathing and, usually, a fury of passion; curse, damn, and ban once implied an opposition to *bless,* but now *curse* and *damn* imply angry denunciation by blasphemous oaths or profane imprecations, and *ban* only, in literary use, retains its earlier sense; anathematize implies solemn denunciation of an evil, an injustice, or the like; objurgate implies less fury and passion than *execrate,* yet often suggests the denunciations of an extremist or savage critic.
ex′e·cra′tion (-krā′shŭn), *n.* **1.** Act of execrating; also, a curse uttered. **2.** That which is execrated; a detested thing. — **ex′e·cra·to′ry** (-krȧ·tō′rĭ; -krā′tō·rĭ), *adj.*
ex·ec′u·tant (ĕg·zĕk′ū·tănt; ĭg-; ĕk·sĕk′-; ĭk-), *n.* One who executes, or performs; esp., one skilled in technique, as of an art.
ex′e·cute (ĕk′sē·kūt), *v. t.* [OF. *executer,* fr. ML. *executare,* fr. L. *executus, exsecutus,* past part. of *exsequi* to follow to the end, pursue, fr. *ex* out + *sequi* to follow.] **1.** To follow out or through to the end, as a purpose; to complete; effect; perform. **2.** To give effect to; to do what is provided or required by, as a writ. **3.** To put to death in conformity to a legal sentence. **4.** To produce by art in accordance with a design, plan, or the like; as, a statue *executed* in bronze; to perform, as a piece of music, either on an instrument or with the voice. **5.** To perform what is required to give validity to (a deed, will, etc.) as by signing, sealing, delivering. — **ex′e·cut′a·ble** (ĕk′sē·kūt′ȧ·b'l; ĕg·zĕk′ū·tȧ-; ĭg-), *adj.* — **ex′e·cut′er** (ĕk′sē·kūt′ẽr), *n.*
Syn. (1) See PERFORM.
(2) Execute, administer mean to effect the will of another (a people, a legislature, etc.). Idiom, much more than meaning, determines their use. Execute implies enforcing the directions of a law, a will, etc.; administer implies management, as of the affairs of a state, a government, an estate, or the like; as, the president is sworn to *execute* the laws of this country, but he often finds difficulty in *administering* affairs to the satisfaction of all.
(3) See KILL.
ex′e·cu′tion (-kū′shŭn), *n.* **1.** Act or process of executing; achievement. **2.** Capital punishment. **3.** Act or mode of performing a work of art or of performing on an instrument. **4.** Effective, esp. destructive, action; as, the broadside did great *execution.* **5.** *Law.* A judicial writ by which an officer is empowered to carry a judgment into effect.
ex′e·cu′tion·er (-ẽr), *n.* One who puts to death legally.
ex·ec′u·tive (ĕg·zĕk′ū·tĭv; ĭg-; ĕk·sĕk′-; ĭk-), *adj.* **1.** Designed or fitted for, or pertaining to, execution; as, *executive* talent. **2.** Qualified for, concerned with, or pertaining to, the execution of the laws or the conduct of affairs; as, *executive* power; *executive* officer, department, etc. — *n.* **1.** The executive branch of a government; also, the person or persons who constitute the executive magistracy of a state. **2.** Hence, any person or body charged with administrative or executive work.

ex·ec′u·tor (ĕg·zĕk′ū·tẽr; ĭg-; ĕk·sĕk′-; ĭk-; *see sense* 1), *n.* [AF. *executour*, fr. L.] **1.** (*pron.* ĕk′sē·kū′tẽr) One who executes something. **2.** The person appointed by a testator to execute his will. — **ex·ec′u·to′ri·al** (-tō′rĭ·ăl), *adj.* — **ex·ec′u·trix** (-trĭks), *n. fem.*

ex·ec′u·to′ry (-tō′rĭ; -tẽr·ĭ; 3), *adj.* **1.** Executive. **2.** *Law.* Designed, or of such a nature as, to be executed in time to come, or to take effect on a future contingency; as, an *executory* devise.

ex′e·ge′sis (ĕk′sē·jē′sĭs), *n.; pl.* -GESES (-sēz). [NL., fr. Gr. *exēgēsis*, fr. *exēgeisthai* to interpret, fr. *ex* out + *hēgeisthai* to guide.] Exposition; esp., a critical explanation of a portion of Scripture. Cf. HERMENEUTICS.

ex′e·gete (ĕk′sē·jēt), *n.* One skilled in exegesis.

ex′e·get′ic (ĕk′sē·jĕt′ĭk), **ex′e·get′i·cal** (-ĭ·kăl), *adj.* [Gr. *exēgētikos.*] Pert. to exegesis; expository. — **ex′e·get′i·cal·ly**, *adv.*

ex′e·get′ics (-ĭks), *n.; see* -ICS. The science of exegesis.

ex·em′plar (ĕg·zĕm′plẽr; ĭg-; -plär), *n.* [From L. *exemplar* (fr. *exemplaris*, adj.), and fr. OF. *exemplaire*, *essemplaire*, fr. L. *exemplarium*, fr. *exemplum.* See EXAMPLE.] **1.** One who or that which serves as a model or pattern; esp., an ideal model; archetype. **2.** An instance or example; a type or specimen. — **Syn.** See MODEL.

ex·em′pla·ry (ĕg·zĕm′plȧ·rĭ; ĭg-; ĕg′zĕm·plẽr′ĭ; -plẽr·ĭ), *adj.* **1.** Serving as a pattern; deserving imitation. **2.** Serving as a warning; monitory; as, **exemplary damages**, *Law*, damages given in excess of actual loss, in order to punish. **3.** Serving as a type, instance, or illustration. — **ex·em′pla·ri·ly**, *adv.* — **ex·em′pla·ri·ness**, *n.*

ex·em′pli·fi·ca′tion (ĕg·zĕm′plĭ·fĭ·kā′shŭn; ĭg-), *n.* **1.** Act of exemplifying; a showing or illustrating by example. **2.** A case in point. **3.** *Law.* An exemplified copy.

ex·em′pli·fy (-zĕm′plĭ·fī), *v. t.;* -FIED (-fīd); -FY′ING. [L. *exemplum* example + *-fy.*] **1.** To illustrate by example; to serve as an example of. **2.** To make an attested copy or transcript of, under seal. — **ex·em′pli·fi·ca′tive** (-fĭ·kā′tĭv), *adj.*

‖**ex·em′pli gra′ti·a** (ĕg·zĕm′plī grā′shĭ·ȧ). [L.] For the sake of example; for example or instance. Abbr. *e.g.*

ex·empt′ (ĕg·zĕmpt′; ĭg-), *adj.* [OF., fr. L. *exemptus*, past part. of *eximere* to take out, remove, free, fr. *ex* out + *emere* to buy, take.] **1.** *Now Rare.* Cut off; set apart. **2.** Free, or released, from some liability. — *n.* One exempted or freed from duty or from a levy. — *v. t.* **1.** *Obs.* To set apart. **2.** To release from some liability to which others are subject; to except or excuse, as from jury duty. — **ex·empt′i·ble** (-zĕmp′tĭ·b′l), *adj.*

ex·emp′tion (-zĕmp′shŭn), *n.* Act of exempting, or state of being exempt; immunity.

ex·en′ter·ate (ĕks·ĕn′tẽr·āt), *v. t.* [L. *exenteratus*, past part., deriv. of Gr. *ex* out + *enteron* intestine.] **1.** *Rare.* To eviscerate. **2.** *Surg.* To remove (an organ), as the eyeball. — **ex·en′ter·a′tion** (-ā′shŭn), *n.*

ex′e·qua′tur (ĕk′sē·kwā′tẽr), *n.* [L., 3d pers. sing. pres. subj. of *exequi*, *exsequi*, to perform, execute.] A written authorization of a consular officer, by the government to which he is accredited.

ex′e·quy (ĕk′sē·kwĭ), *n.; pl.* -QUIES (-kwĭz). [From OF., fr. L. *exequiae*, *exsequiae*, a funeral procession, fr. *exsequi* to follow out.] Usually *pl.* A funeral rite; obsequies.

ex′er·cise (ĕk′sẽr·sīz), *n.* [OF. *exercice*, fr. L. *exercitium*, fr. *exercere*, *exercitum*, to drive on, keep busy, fr. *ex* out + *arcere* to shut up, enclose.] **1.** Act of exercising; a setting in action or practicing; use; habitual activity; occupation. **2.** Exertion for the sake of training or improvement, whether physical, intellectual, or moral; specif., bodily exertion for keeping the organs and functions healthy. **3.** That done or prescribed to be done for training or improvement; as, a musical *exercise*. **4.** *pl.* A program as of songs, speeches, etc.; as, the graduation *exercises*. **5.** Performance, as of a ceremony. — *v. t.* **1.** To set in action; to bring to bear or employ actively, as the power of choice. **2.** To exert repeatedly; to busy; train; — used reflexively and in passive; as, *exercised* in godliness. **3.** To exert or practice for the sake of training or improvement, as the wits or the limbs; to subject to discipline. **4.** To occupy the attention and effort of; to tax, esp. vexatiously; to harass; vex. **5.** To put in practice, as justice or patience; to discharge, wield, or exert, as authority or influence. — *v. i.* To drill; to take exercise. — **Syn.** See PRACTICE. — **ex′er·cis′a·ble** (-sīz′ȧ·b′l), *adj.*

ex′er·cis′er (-sīz′ẽr), *n.* **1.** One who takes or gives exercise. **2.** An apparatus for use in physical exercise.

ex·er′ci·ta′tion (ĕg·zûr′sĭ·tā′shŭn), *n.* [OF., fr. L. *exercitatio*, deriv. of *exercere* to exercise.] Exercise; practice or training; also, a mode or result of exercise, as an essay.

ex·ergue′ (ĕg·zûrg′; ĕk′sûrg), *n.* [F., fr. ML. *exergum*, fr. Gr. *ex* out + *ergon* work, i. e., accessory work.] The segment beneath the base line of the subject engraved on a coin or medal, often with the date, place, mint mark, etc.

ex·ert′ (ĕg·zûrt′; ĭg-), *v. t.* [L. *exertus*, *exsertus*, past part. of *exerere*, *exserere*, to thrust out, fr. *ex* out + *serere* to join together.] **1.** *Obs.* To thrust forth; reveal. **2.** To put forth, as strength, ability, or any active faculty; to put in vigorous action. — **ex·er′tive** (-zûr′tĭv), *adj.*

ex·er′tion (-zûr′shŭn), *n.* Act of exerting; exercise of any power of faculty; an effort, esp. a laborious or perceptible effort; as, *exertion* or strength. — **Syn.** See EFFORT.

ex′e·unt (ĕk′sē·ŭnt; -ŭnt). [L., 3d pers. pl. pres. of *exire* to go out. See EXIT.] They go out, or retire from the scene; — a stage direction.

‖**ex′e·unt om′nes** (ŏm′nēz). [L.] All go out or retire.

ex·fo′li·ate (ĕks·fō′lĭ·āt), *v. t. & i.* [LL. *exfoliatus*, past part. of *exfoliare* to strip of leaves, fr. *ex* out, from + *folium* leaf.] To cast or come off in scales, laminae, or splinters; to scale or flake off, as skin, bone, mineral, bark. — **ex·fo′li·a′tion** (-ā′shŭn), *n.*

ex·fo′li·a′tive (-ā′tĭv), *adj.* Causing exfoliation.

ex·hal′ant (ĕks·hāl′ănt; ĕg·zăl′-), *adj.* Having the quality of exhaling or evaporating; emissive; as, the *exhalant* siphon of a clam. — *n.* An exhaling duct.

ex′ha·la′tion (ĕks′hȧ·lā′shŭn; ĕk′sȧ-; ĕg′zȧ-), *n.* **1.** An exhaling, as of steam or vapor; evaporation; expiration; as, an *exhalation* of breath. **2.** That which is exhaled; effluvium; emanation.

ex·hale′ (ĕks·hāl′; ĕg·zāl′), *v. t.* [OF. *exhaler*, fr. L. *exhalare*, fr. *ex* out + *halare* to breathe.] **1.** To breathe out; hence, to give forth (gaseous matter), as a plant; to emit, as vapor. **2.** To cause to be emitted in vapor; as, the sun *exhales* the surface moisture. — *v. i.* **1.** To rise or be given off as vapor. **2.** To emit breath or vapor.

ex·haust′ (ĕg·zôst′; ĭg-), *v. t.* [L. *exhaustus*, past part. of *exhaurire*, fr. *ex* out + *haurire*, *haustum*, to draw, esp. water.] **1.** To draw or let out wholly, as the air from a bell jar. **2.** To use or expand wholly, or to the end of supply, as one's patience or resources. **3.** To tire out or fatigue extremely. **4.** To empty by drawing or letting out the contents, as a well or a treasury. **5.** To bring out or develop completely, as a subject. **6.** To deprive completely of removable ingredients or of its strength or virtue; as, to *exhaust* a drug with successive solvents or molasses by crystallization. — **Syn.** See DEPLETE: TIRE. — *n.* **1.** *Engin.* The escape of the working fluid, as steam, from an engine cylinder at the end of the working stroke. **2.** Generation or induction of air currents by creating a partial vacuum; also, an apparatus for such a purpose, as to carry away dust in a flour mill. **3.** Material exhausted, as from an internal-combustion engine; also, *Colloq.*, the pipe through which it is passed. — **ex·haust′er**, *n.* — **ex·haust′i·bil′i·ty** (-zôs′tĭ·bĭl′ĭ·tĭ), *n.* — **ex·haust′i·ble** (-zôs′tĭ·b′l), *adj.*

ex·haus′tion (-zôs′chŭn), *n.* Act or process of exhausting, or state of being exhausted; fatigue; depletion.

ex·haus′tive (-zôs′tĭv), *adj.* Serving or tending to exhaust; hence, thorough; testing all possibilities. — **ex·haus′tive·ly**, *adv.* — **ex·haus′tive·ness**, *n.*

ex·haust′less, *adj.* Not to be exhausted; inexhaustible. — **ex·haust′less·ly**, *adv.* — **ex·haust′less·ness**, *n.*

ex·hib′it (ĕg·zĭb′ĭt; ĭg-), *v. t.* [L. *exhibitus*, past part. of *exhibere* to hold forth, tender, exhibit, fr. *ex* out + *habere* to have.] **1.** To present to view; to show, esp. publicly for purposes of competition or demonstration; to display. **2.** To reveal by signs, as fear. **3.** *Law.* To submit to a court or public officer; to present officially or in legal form to a court. **4.** *Med.* To administer as a remedy. — *v. i.* To display anything for inspection. — **Syn.** See SHOW. — *n.* **1.** Act of showing; display. **2.** Something exhibited; specif., an article, or articles, displayed in an exhibition. **3.** *Law.* A document or material object produced and identified in court or before an examiner for use as evidence. — **ex·hib′i·tor**, **ex·hib′it·er** (-zĭb′ĭ·tẽr), *n.*

ex′hi·bi′tion (ĕk′sĭ·bĭsh′ŭn), *n.* **1.** Act or instance of exhibiting. **2.** That which is exhibited. **3.** Any public display, as of works of art, manufacture, commerce, or of feats of skill. **4.** *Brit.* A sum given to a student from the funds of the college; a scholarship; hence, **ex′hi·bi′tion·er**, a recipient of this.

ex′hi·bi′tion·ism (-ĭz′m), *n.* **1.** *Psychol.* Morbid disposition to display that which modesty conceals, whether physical or mental. **2.** Proneness to self-complacent display or parade to attract attention to oneself. — **ex′hi·bi′tion·ist** (-ĭst), *n.*

ex·hib′i·tive (ĕg·zĭb′ĭ·tĭv; ĭg-), *adj.* Having the function of exhibiting; — often with *of.*

ex·hib′i·to′ry (-tō′rĭ *or, esp. Brit.*, -tẽr·ĭ), *adj.* Pertaining to or calling for exhibition.

ex·hil′a·rant (ĕg·zĭl′ȧ·rănt; ĭg-), *adj.* Exhilarating. — *n.* That which exhilarates.

ex·hil′a·rate (-rāt), *v. t.* [L. *exhilaratus*, past part. of *exhilarare* to gladden, fr. *ex* out + *hilarare* to make merry, fr. *hilaris* merry.] To make merry; to give spirit or vivacity to; to animate; enliven; cheer. — **ex·hil′a·rat′ing** (-rāt′ĭng), *adj.*

ex·hil′a·ra′tion (-rā′shŭn), *n.* Act of exhilarating, or state of being exhilarated.

ex·hil′a·ra′tive (ĕg·zĭl′ȧ·rā′tĭv; -rȧ·tĭv; ĭg-), *adj.* Also **ex·hil′a·ra·to′ry** (-rȧ·tō′rĭ; -tẽr·ĭ). Producing exhilaration.

ex·hort′ (ĕg·zôrt′; ĭg-), *v. t. & i.* [OF. *exhorter*, fr. L. *exhortari*, fr. *ex* out + *hortari* to incite, encourage.] To incite by words or advice; to advise or warn earnestly. — **ex·hort′er**, *n.*

ex′hor·ta′tion (ĕg′zôr·tā′shŭn; ĕk′sôr-), *n.* **1.** Act or instance of exhorting. **2.** Language intended to incite and encourage.

ex·hor′ta·tive (ĕg·zôr′tȧ·tĭv; ĭg-), **ex·hor′ta·to′ry** (-tō′rĭ *or, esp. Brit.*, -tẽr·ĭ), *adj.* Of exhortation; intended to exhort.

ex·hume′ (ĕks·hūm′; ĕg·zūm′; ĭg-), *v. t.* [F. *exhumer*, fr. ML. *exhumare*, fr. L. *ex* out + *humus* ground.] To dig out of the ground; to disinter. — **ex′hu·ma′tion** (ĕks′hū·mā′shŭn; ĕks′ū-), *n.*

ex′i·gen·cy (ĕk′sĭ·jĕn·sĭ), *n.; pl.* -CIES (-sĭz). Also **ex′i·gence** (ĕk′sĭ·jĕns). **1.** State or quality of being exigent; urgent want; a case demanding action or remedy. **2.** Such need as belongs to the occasion; requirements. — **Syn.** See NEED: JUNCTURE.

ex′i·gent (-jĕnt), *adj.* [L. *exigens*, *-entis*, pres. part. of *exigere* to drive out, exact. See EXACT.] **1.** Requiring immediate aid or action; critical. **2.** Requiring much; as, this *exigent* life.

ex′i·gi·ble (-jĭ·b′l), *adj.* That may be exacted; chargeable.

ex·ig′u·ous (ĕg·zĭg′ū·ŭs; ĭg-; ĕks·ĭg′-; ĭks-), *adj.* [L. *exiguus.*] Scanty in amount; diminutive. — **Syn.** See MEAGER. — **ex′i·gu′i·ty** (ĕk′sĭ·gū′ĭ·tĭ), *n.* — **ex·ig′u·ous·ness**, *n.*

ex′ile (ĕk′sīl; ĕg′zīl), *n.* [OF. *exil*, *essil*, fr. L. *exilium*, *exsilium.*] **1.** Forced, or sometimes voluntary, removal from one's native country; banishment. **2.** A person expelled, or who separates himself, from his country. — ***the Exile.*** The Babylonian captivity. See BABYLON, 3. — *v. t.* To banish or expel from one's own country or home. — **Syn.** See BANISH. — **ex·il′ic** (ĕg·zĭl′ĭk; ĕks·ĭl′-), *adj.*

ex·im′i·ous (ĕg·zĭm′ĭ·ŭs), *adj.* [L. *eximius* taken out, i. e., select, fr. *eximere* to take out. See EXEMPT.] *Now Rare.* Choice; excellent.

ex·ist′ (ĕg·zĭst′; ĭg-), *v. i.* [L. *existere*, *exsistere*, to emerge, appear, exist, fr. *ex* out + *sistere* to cause to stand, fr. *stare* to stand.] **1.** To have actual or real being, whether material or spiritual. **2.** To have being in any specified condition or place; as, salt *exists* in solution. **3.** To continue to be; to live.

ex·ist′ence (-zĭs′tĕns), *n.* **1.** The fact or state of existing; specif., sentient being; continuance in life. **2.** Continued or repeated manifestation; actual occurrence; as, the *existence* of a state of war. **3.** A mode of being. **4.** A specific being or entity. — **ex′is·ten′tial** (ĕg′zĭs·tĕn′shăl; ĕk′sĭs-), *adj.*

ex·ist′ent (-tĕnt), *adj.* Having being.

ex′is·ten′tial·ism (ĕg′zĭs·tĕn′shăl·ĭz′m; ĕk′sĭs-), *n.* [From Ger. & Dan. adjs. of *Existenz* & *Eksistens* (philos. sense) + *-ism.*] **1.** *Philos.* An introspective humanism or theory of man which expresses the individual's intense awareness of his contingency and freedom; a theory which states that the existence of the individual precedes his essence. Specif.: **a** ***philosophical existentialism***, a theory which stresses the individual's responsibility for making himself what he is. **b** ***Christian existentialism***, a theory which stresses the subjective aspects of the human person considered as a creature of God. **2.** *Lit.* The theory or practice which aims to give readers a sense of an individual's passionate awareness of personal contingency and freedom. — **ex′is·ten′tial**, *adj.* — **ex′is·ten′tial·ist** (-ĭst), *n. & adj.*

ex′it (ĕk′sĭt; ĕg′zĭt). [L., 3d pers. sing. pres. of *exire* to go out. See ISSUE.] He (or she) goes off stage; as, *exit* Leah; — a stage direction.

ex′it (ĕk′sĭt; ĕg′zĭt), *n.* [From 1st *exit*, or fr. L. *exitus* a going out.] **1.** The departure of a player from the stage. **2.** Any departure; death. **3.** A way of departure; egress.

‖**ex li′bris** (ĕks lī′brĭs). [L. *ex* from + *libris* books.] A bookplate, often with *ex libris* (from the library of) before the owner's name.

‖**ex ni′hi·lo ni′hil fit** (nī′hĭ·lō nī′hĭl fĭt). [L.] From (or out of) nothing, nothing is made (or comes).

ex′o- (ĕk′sō-), **ex-.** [Gr. *exō*.] A prefix signifying *out of, outside, outer layer*, as in *exo*gamy, *exo*toxin.

ex′o·carp (-kärp), *n.* [*exo-* + *-carp*.] *Bot.* Epicarp.

ex′o·cen′tric (-sĕn′trĭk), *adj. Ling.* Not having the same grammatical function as one of its component parts; thus, the phrase *in the barn* in "they played in the barn" is *exocentric*; — opp. to *endocentric*.

ex′o·crine (ĕk′sō·krīn; -krĭn; -krēn), *adj.* [*exo-* + Gr. *krinein* to separate.] *Physiol.* Secreting externally; — of glands that discharge their secretion through a duct. Opp. to *endocrine*.

ex′o·don′ti·a (-dŏn′shĭ·ȧ), *n.* [NL., fr. 2d *ex-* + Gr. *odōn, odontos*, tooth + *-ia*.] The branch of dentistry dealing with the extraction of teeth. — **ex′o·don′tist** (-tĭst), *n.*

ex′o·dus (ĕk′sō·dŭs), *n.* [LL., fr. Gr. *exodos* a going out, fr. *ex* out + *hodos* way.] **1.** A going out; specif. (***the Exodus***), the journey of the Israelites from Egypt under Moses. **2.** [*cap.*] The second book of the Pentateuch. See BIBLE.

ex′o·en′zyme (-ĕn′zīm; -zĭm), *n.* = ECTOENZYME.

ex of·fi′ci·o (ĕks ŏ·fĭsh′ĭ·ō). [L.] By virtue or because of an office.

ex·og′a·my (ĕks·ŏg′ȧ·mĭ), *n.* [*exo-* + *-gamy*.] **1.** Marriage outside of the same kinship group, clan, or sib, as required by custom; outbreeding. Cf. ENDOGAMY. **2.** *Biol.* Conjugation between gametes of different ancestry, as in certain protozoans. — **ex′o·gam′ic** (ĕk′sō·găm′ĭk), *adj.* — **ex·og′a·mous** (ĕks·ŏg′ȧ·mŭs), *adj.*

ex′o·gen (ĕk′sō·jĕn), *n. Bot.* A dicotyledon.

ex·og′e·nous (ĕks·ŏj′ē·nŭs), *adj.* [*exo-* + *-genous*.] **1.** Produced from without; originating from or due to external causes; as, *exogenous* delusions; — distinguished from *endogenous*. **2.** *Biol.* Growing from or on the outside, or by addition to the exterior. **3.** *Physiol. & Biochem.* Pertaining to or designating the metabolism of nitrogenous substances obtained from food, the catabolic products excreted being proportionate to the protein ingested in the diet. — **-nous·ly**, *adv.*

ex·on′er·ate (ĕg·zŏn′ẽr·āt; ĭg-), *v. t.* [L. *exoneratus*, past part. of *exonerare* to free from a burden, fr. *ex* out, from + *onerare* to load, fr. *onus* load.] **1.** To relieve, as of a charge; to clear, as from accusation. **2.** To free from blame; to exculpate. — **Syn.** See EXCULPATE. — **ex·on′er·a′tion** (-ā′shŭn), *n.* — **ex·on′er·a′tive** (-ā′tĭv; -ȧ·tĭv), *adj.*

ex′oph·thal′mic (ĕk′sŏf·thăl′mĭk), *adj.* Exhibiting, or accompanied by, exophthalmos; as, *exophthalmic* goiter (see GOITER).

ex′oph·thal′mos (-mŏs), **ex′oph·thal′mus** (-mŭs), *n.* [NL., fr. Gr. *exophthalmos* with prominent eyes, fr. *ex* out + *ophthalmos* the eye.] *Med.* Abnormal protrusion of the eyeball.

ex′o·ra·ble (ĕk′sō·rȧ·b'l), *adj.* [L. *exorabilis*.] Responsive to entreaty. — **ex′o·ra·bil′i·ty** (-bĭl′ĭ·tĭ), *n.*

ex·or′bi·tance (ĕg·zôr′bĭ·tăns; ĭg-), *n.; pl.* -TANCES (-tăn·sĕz; -sĭz). **1.** Gross deviation from rule, right, or propriety. **2.** Tendency or disposition to be exorbitant; greed.

ex·or′bi·tan·cy (-tăn·sĭ), *n.; pl.* -TANCIES (-sĭz). The quality or condition of being exorbitant; exorbitance.

ex·or′bi·tant (-tănt), *adj.* [L. *exorbitans, -antis*, pres. part. of *exorbitare* to go out of the track, fr. *ex* out + *orbita* track.] **1.** Going beyond the established limits of right or propriety; excessive. **2.** *Law.* Not within the orbit, or scope, of the law. — **Syn.** See EXCESSIVE. — **Ant.** Just. — **ex·or′bi·tant·ly**, *adv.*

ex′or·cise, ex′or·cize (ĕk′sôr·sīz), *v. t.* [F. *exorciser*, fr. LL. *exorcizare*, fr. Gr. *exorkizein*, fr. *ex* out + *horkizein* to bind by an oath, fr. *horkos* oath.] To expel or drive off (an evil spirit) by adjuration, esp. by use of a holy name; to deliver (a person, place, etc.) from an evil spirit. — **ex′or·cis′er, ex′or·ciz′er** (-sīz′ẽr), *n.*

ex′or·cism (-sĭz'm), *n.* Act or process of exorcising; conjuration of evil spirits; also, a formula used in exorcising. — **ex′or·cist** (-sĭst), *n.*

ex·or′di·um (ĕg·zôr′dĭ·ŭm; ĕk·sôr′-), *n.; pl.* -DIUMS (-ŭmz), -DIA (-ȧ). [L., fr. *exordiri* to begin a web, begin, fr. *ex* out + *ordiri* to begin a web, begin.] A beginning; an introduction, esp. of an oration. Cf. PERORATION. — **ex·or′di·al** (-ăl), *adj.*

ex′o·skel′e·ton (ĕk′sō·skĕl′ē·tŭn; -t'n), *n. Zool.* A hard supporting or protective structure developed on or secreted by the outside of the body, as the shell of a crustacean. Cf. ENDOSKELETON.

ex′os·mo′sis (ĕk′sŏs·mō′sĭs; ĕk′sŏz-), *n.* Also **ex′os·mose** (ĕk′sŏs·mōs; ĕk′sŏz-). [NL.] See OSMOSIS. — **ex′os·mot′ic** (-mŏt′ĭk), **ex·os′mic** (ĕks·ŏs′mĭk; -ŏz′mĭk), *adj.*

ex′os·to′sis (ĕk′sŏs·tō′sĭs), *n.; pl.* -SES (-sēz). [NL., fr. Gr. *exostōsis*, fr. *ex* out + *osteon* bone.] A spur or bony outgrowth from a bone or the root of a tooth.

ex′o·ter′ic (ĕk′sō·tĕr′ĭk), *adj.* [LL. *exotericus*, fr. Gr. *exōterikos*, fr. *exō* outside.] **1.** External; exterior. **2.** Suitable to be imparted to the public; hence, readily comprehensible. Cf. ESOTERIC.

ex′o·ther′mic (-thûr′mĭk), *adj.* [*exo-* + *thermic*.] Characterized by, or formed with, evolution of heat; — opp. to *endothermic*.

ex·ot′ic (ĕks·ŏt′ĭk; ĕg·zŏt′-), *adj.* [L. *exoticus*, fr. Gr. *exōtikos*, fr. *exō* outside.] Introduced from a foreign country; extraneous; foreign; also, strikingly unusual, as in color, design, etc.; excitingly strange. — *n.* An exotic thing, as a plant or a word.

ex′o·tox′in (ĕk′sō·tŏk′sĭn), *n. Biochem.* A toxin excreted by a microorganism; a true toxin. Cf. ENDOTOXIN. — **ex′o·tox′ic** (-sĭk), *adj.*

ex·pand′ (ĕks·pănd′; ĭks-), *v. t.* [L. *expandere, expansum*, fr. *ex* out + *pandere* to spread out, open.] **1.** To open wide; to spread out; to diffuse. **2.** To make to occupy more space; to dilate; to distend; to enlarge. **3.** To work out or develop in full detail, as an argument or an equation. — *v. i.* To spread apart; distend; enlarge; swell. — **ex·pand′a·ble**, *adj.* — **ex·pand′er**, *n.*

Syn. **Expand, amplify, swell, distend, inflate, dilate** mean to increase in size, bulk, or volume. **Expand**, the most comprehensive term, may be used whether the increase comes from within or without or in any way, such as unfolding or spreading; **amplify** implies extension of that which is inadequate, as by filling out with details or by magnifying in volume; **swell** implies expansion, sometimes abnormal expansion, beyond a thing's original circumference or normal limits; **distend** implies swelling caused by pressure from within forcing extension outward; **inflate** implies distention by artificial means, as literally by the introduction of gas or air; **dilate** implies expansion in diameter and suggests a widening of something circular. — **Ant.** Contract.

ex·panse′ (ĕks·păns′; ĭks-), *n.* [L. *expansum*. See EXPAND.] That which is expanded or its extent; a wide extent of space.

ex·pan′si·ble (-păn′sĭ·b'l), *adj.* Capable of being expanded.

ex·pan′sile (-sĭl; 56), *adj.* Capable of, pertaining to, or characteristic of expansion; as, *expansile* movements.

ex·pan′sion (ĕks·păn′shŭn; ĭks-), *n.* **1.** Act or process of expanding, or state of being expanded; dilatation. **2.** That which is expanded; extended surface; an expanded part. **3.** Extent of expansion; also, pure space. **4.** *Engin.* The increasing in volume of the working fluid, as steam, in an engine cylinder after cutoff, or, in an internal-combustion engine, after explosion. **5.** *Math.* The developed result of an indicated operation; as, the *expansion* of $(a + b)^2$ is $a^2 + 2ab + b^2$.

ex·pan′sion·ism (-ĭz'm), *n.* Advocacy of expansion, as of a nation's territory or currency. — **ex·pan′sion·ist** (-ĭst), *n. & adj.*

ex·pan′sive (ĕks·păn′sĭv; ĭks-), *adj.* **1.** Having a capacity or tendency to expand; diffusive; also, wide-extending. **2.** Of persons, feelings, etc., unrestrained; liberal; comprehensive, esp. in sympathies. **3.** Working by expansion. **4.** *Psychiatry.* Characterized by exaggerated sense of well-being and by delusions of greatness. — **ex·pan′sive·ly**, *adv.* — **ex·pan′sive·ness**, *n.*

ex par′te (ĕks pär′tē). [L. See EX-; PART.] Upon, from, or in the interest of, one side only.

ex·pa′ti·ate (ĕks·pā′shĭ·āt), *v. i.* [L. *expatiatus, exspatiatus*, past part. of *expatiari, exspatiari*, to expatiate, fr. *ex* out + *spatiari* to walk about, fr. *spatium* space.] **1.** *Rare.* To range at large, or without restraint. **2.** To enlarge in discourse or writing; to talk freely and at length. — **ex·pa′ti·a′tion** (-ā′shŭn), *n.*

ex·pa′tri·ate (ĕks·pā′trĭ·āt), *adj.* [ML. *expatriatus*, past part. of *expatriare*, fr. L. *ex* out + *patria* fatherland, fr. *pater* father.] Exiled; expatriated. — *n.* An exile; a person who withdraws from his own country to live in another country. — (-āt), *v. t.* To banish; to make an exile of. — *v. i.* To withdraw from one's native country and become a citizen of another country. — **ex·pa′tri·a′tion** (-ā′shŭn), *n.*

ex·pect′ (ĕks·pĕkt′; ĭks-), *v. t.* [L. *expectare, exspectare, -tatum*, to look out for, await, expect, fr. *ex* out + *spectare* to look at.] **1.** *Archaic.* To wait for; to await. **2. a** To look for (mentally); to look forward to; to look for with some confidence. **b** To look for as due; to consider (one) in duty bound; as, he was *expected* to do his duty. — *v. i.* **1.** *Archaic.* To wait; stay. **2.** To look forward; to look with expectation.

Syn. **Expect, hope, look** mean to await some event, occurrence, or the like. **Expect** usually implies a high degree of certainty and also involves the idea of making preparation, of envisioning, or the like; **hope** implies entertainment of the idea that one may expect what one desires or longs for and, though it seldom implies certitude, it often connotes confidence or assurance; as, to *hope* to succeed; to *hope* for success; **look**, the colloquial term, suggests a counting upon or a degree of expectancy rather than confidence or certainty; as, to *look* for a profit; to *look* to profit by the venture.

ex·pect′ance (ĕks·pĕk′tăns; ĭks-), *n.* Expectancy.

ex·pect′an·cy (-tăn·sĭ), *n.* **1.** The quality or state of expecting; expectation. **2.** State of being expected or a subject of expectation. **3.** That which is expected; the object of expectation or hope. **4.** That which is to be expected on the basis of statistical probability; as, ***life expectancy***, = EXPECTATION OF LIFE.

ex·pect′ant (-tănt), *adj.* Expecting; waiting; having expectations. — *n.* One who expects; a candidate for a position. — **ex·pect′ant·ly**, *adv.*

ex′pec·ta′tion (ĕks′pĕk·tā′shŭn), *n.* **1.** Act or state of expecting. **2.** Prospect of the future; anticipation, esp. of benefits. **3.** That which is expected or looked for. **4.** State of being expected; as, benefits in *expectation*.

expectation of life. The duration of the life of an individual or group after any specified age to be expected from the averages shown in mortality tables.

ex·pect′a·tive (ĕks·pĕk′tȧ·tĭv; ĭks-), *adj.* Pertaining to, or constituting, an object of expectation; contingent.

ex·pec′to·rant (ĕks·pĕk′tō·rănt), *adj. Med.* Tending to facilitate expectoration, discharges of mucus, etc. — *n.* An expectorant medicine.

ex·pec′to·rate (-rāt), *v. t. & i.* [L. *expectorare* to drive from the breast, fr. *ex* out + *pectus, pectoris*, breast.] To discharge, as phlegm, by coughing, hawking, and spitting; to spit.

ex·pec′to·ra′tion (-rā′shŭn), *n.* Act of expectorating, or that which is expectorated; saliva; spit.

ex·pe′di·ence (ĕks·pē′dĭ·ĕns; 58), *n.* Expediency.

ex·pe′di·en·cy (-ĕn·sĭ), *n.* **1.** Quality or condition of being expedient; fitness. **2.** Cultivation of, or adherence to, expedient means and methods; esp., subordination of moral principle for the sake of facilitating an end or purpose.

ex·pe′di·ent (-ĕnt), *adj.* [OF., fr. L. *expediens, -entis*, pres. part. of *expedire* to be expedient, release, extricate. See EXPEDITE.] **1.** Apt and suitable to the end in view; as, an *expedient* solution; hence, advantageous. **2.** Conducive to special advantage rather than to what is universally right; also, of persons, guided by expediency.

Syn. **Expedient, politic, advisable** mean dictated by practical wisdom, as an action, a course, or a method. **Expedient** implies the accrual of definite and, often, immediate advantages and is now, more often than formerly, used with a derogatory implication; **politic** stresses judiciousness and tactical value but sometimes, like *expedient*, implies a material motive; **advisable** is now often preferred by those who wish to avoid the unpleasant implications of *expedient* or *politic*.

— *n.* **1.** That which is expedient; suitable means to accomplish an end. **2.** Means devised in an exigency; shift. — **Syn.** See RESOURCE.

— **ex·pe′di·en′tial** (-ĕn′shăl), *adj.* — **ex·pe′di·ent·ly**, *adv.*

ex′pe·dite (ĕks′pē·dīt), *v. t.* [L. *expeditus*, past part. of *expedire* to free one caught by the foot, extricate, make ready, fr. *ex* out + *pes, pedis*, foot.] **1.** To accelerate the process or progress of; to facilitate. **2.** To execute or carry through with dispatch. **3.** To dispatch; to issue officially. — *adj.* Free of impediment or obstacles; hence: **a** Free; light; easy. **b** Quick; prompt. **c** Handy; convenient. — **ex′pe·dit′er** (-dīt′ẽr), *n.*

ex′pe·di′tion (-dĭsh′ŭn), *n.* **1.** Act of expediting, state of being expedited, or quality of being expedite; efficient promptness. **2.** A sending forth or setting forth for some object. **3.** A journey for a specific purpose; as, a military or exploring *expedition*; also, the body of persons making such an excursion. — **Syn.** See HASTE.

ex′pe·di′tion·ar′y (-ĕr′ĭ *or, esp. Brit.*, -ẽr·ĭ), *adj.* Of, pert. to, or constituting an expedition; as, a military *expeditionary* force.

ex′pe·di′tious (-dĭsh′ŭs), *adj.* Possessed of, or characterized by, efficiency and rapidity in action; quick; speedy; as, an *expeditious* march. — **Syn.** See FAST. — **ex′pe·di′tious·ly**, *adv.* — **ex′pe·di′tious·ness**, *n.*
ex·pel′ (ĕks·pĕl′; ĭks-), *v. t.*; EX·PELLED′ (-pĕld′); EX·PEL′LING. [L. *expellere, expulsum*, fr. *ex* out + *pellere* to drive.] **1.** To drive or force out; to eject. **2.** To cut off from membership in or the privileges of an institution or society; as, to *expel* a student from college. — **Syn.** See EJECT. — **ex·pel′la·ble**, *adj.*
ex·pel′lant (-pĕl′ănt), *adj.* Also **ex·pel′lent** (-ĕnt). Tending or serving to expel. — *n.* An expellant medicine.
ex·pend′ (ĕks·pĕnd′; ĭks-), *v. t.* [L. *expendere, expensum*, to weigh out, pay out, fr. *ex* out + *pendere* to weigh.] To consume by use in any way; to use up; to spend.
ex·pend′a·ble (-pĕn′dȧ·b'l), *adj.* Capable of being expended; specif., *Mil.*, normally used up or consumed in service; hence, left in the path of the enemy and sacrificed, according to plan, in order to gain time, esp. in a delaying action. — *n. Usually pl.* Item of equipment, armament, or the like, unit or member of personnel, etc., treated as expendable. — **ex·pend′a·bil′i·ty** (-bĭl′ĭ·tĭ), *n.*
ex·pend′i·ture (-pĕn′dĭ·tūr), *n.* **1.** A laying out of money; disbursement. **2.** That which is expended.
ex·pense′ (ĕks·pĕns′; ĭks-), *n.* [AF. (OF. *espense*), fr. ML. *expensa*, fr. L. *expensus*, past part. of *expendere*. See EXPEND.] **1.** *Archaic.* Act of expending; disbursement; hence, a using up; loss. **2.** That which is expended; outlay; hence, the burden of expenditure; as, the *expenses* of war. **3.** A source or cause of expenditure; as, children are an *expense*.
ex·pen′sive (-pĕn′sĭv), *adj.* Occasioning expense; costly. — **Syn.** See COSTLY. — **Ant.** Inexpensive. — **ex·pen′sive·ly**, *adv.* — **ex·pen′sive·ness**, *n.*
ex·pe′ri·ence (ĕks·pēr′ĭ·ĕns; ĭks-), *n.* [OF., fr. L. *experientia*, fr. *experiens, -entis*, pres. part. of *experiri, expertus*, to try, fr. *ex* out + the root of *peritus* experienced.] **1.** The actual living through an event or events; actual enjoyment or suffering; hence, the effect upon the judgment or feelings produced by personal and direct impressions; as, to know by *experience*. **2.** State, extent, or duration of being engaged in a particular study or work, or in affairs; as, business *experience*. **3.** Knowledge, skill, or technique resulting from experience. **4. a** The sum total of the conscious events which compose an individual life. **b** Observed facts and events in contrast with what is supplied by thought; as, knowledge originates in *experience*. **5.** One thing or all things experienced; as, a recent *experience*; never in my *experience*. — *v. t.*; -ENCED (-ĕnst); -ENC·ING (-ĕn·sĭng). To have experience of or learn by experience; to undergo. — ***experience religion.*** To undergo conversion.
ex·pe′ri·enced (ĕks·pēr′ĭ·ĕnst; ĭks-), *adj.* Having experience; made skillful or wise by means of trials, use, or observation.
experience table. *Life Insurance.* A mortality table based upon the experience of statisticians as to insured lives.
ex·pe′ri·en′tial (-ĕn′shăl), *adj.* Derived from, based on, or pert. to, experience; empirical. — **ex·pe′ri·en′tial·ly**, *adv.*
ex·per′i·ment (ĕks·pĕr′ĭ·mĕnt; ĭks-), *n.* [OF., fr. L. *experimentum*, fr. *experiri* to try. See EXPERIENCE.] **1.** A trial made to confirm or disprove something doubtful; an operation undertaken to discover some unknown principle or effect, or to test some suggested truth, or to demonstrate some known truth; as, a laboratory *experiment*. **2.** The conducting of tests. — (-mĕnt), *v. i.* To make experiment. — **ex·per′i·ment·er** (-mĕn·tẽr), *n.*
ex·per′i·men′tal (-mĕn′tăl; -t'l), *adj.* **1.** Relating to, or based on, experience, esp. personal experience, as distinct from theory. **2.** Of the nature of experiment; founded on experiment; as, *experimental* science; given to, or skilled in, experiment. — **ex·per′i·men′tal·ly**, *adv.*
ex·per′i·men·ta′tion (-mĕn·tā′shŭn), *n.* Act of experimenting; practice by experiment.
experiment station. An institution for scientific research in such fields as engineering, mining, biology, or esp., agriculture, where experiments are tried, studies of practical value made, and information disseminated.
ex·pert′ (ĕks·pûrt′; ĕks′pûrt; 2), *adj.* [OF., fr. L. *expertus*, past part. of *experiri* to try. See EXPERIENCE.] Taught by use, practice, or experience; skillful; as, an *expert* surgeon. — **Syn.** See PROFICIENT. — **Ant.** Amateurish. — **ex·pert′ly**, *adv.* — **ex·pert′ness**, *n.*
ex′pert (ĕks′pûrt), *n.* [F.] An expert or experienced person; hence, one who has special skill or knowledge in a subject; a specialist.
ex′pi·a·ble (ĕks′pĭ·ȧ·b'l), *adj.* Capable of being expiated or atoned for.
ex′pi·ate (-āt), *v. t.* [L. *expiatus*, past part. of *expiare* to expiate, fr. *ex* out + *piare* to seek to appease, purify with sacred rites, fr. *pius* pious.] To make complete satisfaction for; atone for; as, to *expiate* sin. — **ex′pi·a′tor** (-ā′tẽr), *n.*
ex′pi·a′tion (-ā′shŭn), *n.* **1.** Act of expiating. **2.** The means of atonement.
ex′pi·a·to′ry (ĕks′pĭ·ȧ·tō′rĭ *or, esp. Brit.*, ĕks′pĭ·ā′tẽr·ĭ, -ȧ·tẽr·ĭ), *adj.* Having power, or intended, to make expiation; atoning.
ex′pi·ra′tion (ĕk′spĭ·rā′shŭn), *n.* **1.** Act of expiring; as: **a** Act or process of emitting air from the lungs. **b** *Obs.* Emission of volatile matter; exhalation. **2.** A coming to a close; end; also, death. **3.** That which is expired; matter breathed forth; that which is produced by breathing out, as a sound.
ex·pir′a·to′ry (ĕk·spīr′ȧ·tō′rĭ *or, esp. Brit.*, -tẽr·ĭ), *adj.* Pertaining to, or employed in, the expiration or emission of air from the lungs.
ex·pire′ (ĕk·spīr′; ĭk-), *v. t.* [F. *expirer*, fr. L. *expirare, exspirare, -atum*, fr. *ex* out + *spirare* to breathe.] **1.** To breathe out; to emit from the lungs; — opposed to *inspire*. **2.** *Obs.* To emit or exhale, as an odor. — *v. i.* **1.** To emit the breath. **2.** To emit the last breath; to die. **3.** To cease; terminate. — **ex·pir′er** (-spīr′ẽr), *n.*
ex·pi′ry (ĕk·spī′rĭ; ĕk′spĭ·rĭ), *n.*; *pl.* -RIES (-rĭz). **1.** *Archaic.* Death. **2.** A coming to an end; termination.
ex·plain′ (ĕks·plān′; ĭks-), *v. t.* [L. *explanare* to flatten, explain, fr. *ex* out + *planare* to make level or plain, fr. *planus* plain.] To make plain; to expound. — *v. i.* To give an explanation. — **ex·plain′a·ble** (-ȧ·b'l), *adj.*
Syn. **Explain, expound, explicate, elucidate, interpret** mean to make something clear to the mind. **Explain** implies a making plain or intelligible; **expound** implies a careful, often elaborate explanation; **explicate** adds the idea of a developed or detailed analysis; **elucidate** stresses the throwing of light upon, as by luminous exposition or illustration; **interpret** adds to all these the use of imagination, sympathy, etc., in going below the surface of that which is to be explained.
ex′pla·na′tion (ĕks′plȧ·nā′shŭn), *n.* **1.** Act or process of explaining. **2.** That which explains. **3.** The interpretation; sense. **4.** A mutual exposition of terms, meaning, or motives, with a view to reconcile differences.
ex·plan′a·tive (ĕks·plăn′ȧ·tĭv; ĭks-), *adj.* Explanatory.
ex·plan′a·to′ry (ĕks·plăn′ȧ·tō′rĭ; ĭks-; *or, esp. Brit.*, -tẽr·ĭ), *adj.* Serving to explain; as, *explanatory* notes. — **ex·plan′a·to′ri·ly**, *adv.*
ex·plant′ (ĕks·plȧnt′), *v. t.* To remove to a place or medium outside the natural habitat, esp. in the culture of tissue in a medium outside of the body for purposes of study
ex′ple·tive (ĕks′plē·tĭv; *Brit. usu.* ĕks·plē′-, ĭks-), *adj.* [LL. *expletivus*, fr. *expletus*, past part. of *explere* to fill up, fr. *ex* out + *plere* to fill.] Filling up; hence, added merely to fill up. — *n.* Something added merely as a filling, as an extra word, phrase, or syllable; also, an oath or exclamation.
ex′ple·to′ry (ĕks′plē·tō′rĭ *or, esp. Brit.*, -tẽr·ĭ), *adj.* Expletive.
ex′pli·ca·ble (ĕks′plĭ·kȧ·b'l; ĕks·plĭk′ȧ-), *adj.* That may be explained.
ex′pli·cate (ĕks′plĭ·kāt), *v. t.* [L. *explicatus*, past part. of *explicare*. See EXPLOIT.] To unfold the meaning of; to explain. — **Syn.** See EXPLAIN. — **ex′pli·ca′tive** (-kā′tĭv; ĕks·plĭk′ȧ·tĭv), *adj.*
ex′pli·ca′tion (ĕks′plĭ·kā′shŭn), *n.* **1.** Explanation; exposition. **2.** A detailed description; a full account.
ex′pli·ca·to′ry (ĕks′plĭ·kȧ·tō′rĭ *or, esp. Brit.*, ĕks′plĭ·kā′tō·rĭ; ĕks·plĭk′ȧ·tẽr·ĭ), *adj.* Explanatory.
ex·plic′it (ĕks·plĭs′ĭt; ĭks-), *adj.* [L. *explicitus*, past part. of *explicare* to unfold. See EXPLOIT.] **1.** Distinctly stated; plain in language; clear; as, an *explicit* declaration. **2.** Having no disguised meaning; outspoken; — applied to persons; as, he was *explicit* in his statement. **3.** Clearly developed; with all its elements apparent. — **ex·plic′it·ly**, *adv.* — **ex·plic′it·ness**, *n.*
Syn. **Explicit, express, specific, definite** mean perfectly clear in meaning or reference, as an utterance. **Explicit** implies such plainness and distinctness that there is no reason for difficulty; **express** implies explicitness and utterance with directness, pointedness, or force; **specific** implies precision in reference or particularization in statement of the details covered or comprehended; **definite** stresses precise and determinate limitations, especially where they are necessary, as in orders, in recommendations, etc.
ex·plode′ (ĕks·plōd′; ĭks-), *v. t.* [L. *explodere, -plosum*, to drive out, as a player by clapping, fr. *ex* out + *plaudere, plodere*, to clap, applaud.] **1.** *Obs.* To drive (a play or actor) from the stage by noisy disapprobation; to hoot off. **2.** To bring into disrepute and reject; as, to *explode* a theory. **3.** To cause to burst noisily; to detonate. — *v. i.* **1.** To burst or expand violently and noisily as an effect of a sudden production or release of pressure. **2.** To burst forth with sudden violence and noise. — **ex·plod′er** (-plōd′ẽr), *n.*
ex·plod′ent (-plōd′ĕnt), *n.* An explosive consonant.
ex′ploit (ĕks′ploit; ĕks·ploit′), *n.* [OF. *esploit, espleit*, fr. L. *explicitum*, prop. past part. neut. of *explicare* to unfold, display, fr. *ex* + *plicare* to fold.] A deed or act; esp., a heroic act. — **Syn.** See FEAT.
ex·ploit′ (ĕks·ploit′; ĭks-), *v. t.* **1.** To utilize; to get the value out of. **2.** Hence, to make use of basely for one's own advantage or profit; as, to *exploit* one's friends. — **ex·ploit′a·ble**, *adj.* — **ex·ploit′er**, *n.*
ex′ploi·ta′tion (ĕks′ploi·tā′shŭn), *n.* Act of exploiting; utilization; now, esp., selfish or unfair utilization.
ex·ploit′a·tive (ĕks·ploit′ȧ·tĭv; ĭks-), *adj.* Pertaining to exploitation; exploiting.
ex·ploi′ter (ĕks·ploi′tẽr), *v. t.* To exploit, esp. so as to profit illegitimately.
ex′plo·ra′tion (ĕks′plō·rā′shŭn), *n.* **1.** Act of exploring, as for geographical discovery. **2.** *Med.* Physical examination, as of the chest.
ex·plor′a·tive (ĕks·plōr′ȧ·tĭv; 70), *adj.* Exploratory.
ex·plor′a·to′ry (ĕks·plōr′ȧ·tō′rĭ; ĕks·plōr′-; -tẽr·ĭ), *adj.* Of, relating to, used in, or connected with exploration.
ex·plore′ (ĕks·plōr′; ĭks-; 70), *v. t.* [F. *explorer*, fr. L. *explorare* to spy out, fr. *ex* out + *plorare* to cry, weep.] **1.** *Obs.* To seek for or after. **2.** To search through or into; to penetrate or range over for discovery. **3.** *Med.* To examine minutely, as by means of a probe; as, to *explore* a wound. — *v. i.* To make or conduct a systematic search.
ex·plor′er (-plōr′ẽr), *n.* **1.** One who or that which explores; esp., a traveler seeking geographical or scientific discovery. **2.** An instrument for exploring cavities, as in teeth.
ex·plo′sion (ĕks·plō′zhŭn; ĭks-), *n.* [See EXPLODE.] **1.** Act of exploding; a violent bursting, with noise, as in the case of explosives. **2.** A violent outburst of feeling. **3.** *Phonet.* Explosive release of breath at the end of a stop consonant.
ex·plo′sive (-sĭv), *adj.* **1.** Pertaining to, characterized or operated by, or suited to cause, explosion. **2.** Tending to explosion; as, an *explosive* temper. **3.** *Phonet.* Pronounced with an explosion, or puff of breath, after a complete closure of the breath passage. — *n.* **1.** An explosive substance, as gunpowder. **2.** *Phonet.* An explosive consonant. The stops *p, b, t, d, k, g* are called *explosives*. — **ex·plo′sive·ly**, *adv.* — **ex·plo′sive·ness**, *n.*
ex·po′nent (ĕks·pō′nĕnt), *n.* [L. *exponens, -entis*, pres. part. of *exponere* to set forth. See EXPOUND.] **1.** *Alg.* A symbol written above another symbol and on the right, denoting how many times the latter is repeated as a factor; thus, a^2 means $a \times a$. **2.** An expounder; interpreter, as of music. **3.** One who or that which exemplifies or represents; as, he is the *exponent* of his party's principles. — **ex′po·nen′tial** (ĕks′pō·nĕn′shăl), *adj.* — **ex′po·nen′tial·ly**, *adv.*
ex·po′ni·ble (ĕks·pō′nĭ·b'l), *adj.* Requiring explanation; — in logic said esp. of propositions needing restatement. — *n.* An exponible proposition.
ex·port′ (ĕks·pōrt′; *often* ĕks′pōrt, *esp. in contrast with import*; 70), *v. t.* [L. *exportare, -tatum*, fr. *ex* out + *portare* to carry.] To carry or send abroad, esp. to foreign countries, as merchandise or commodities in the way of commerce; — opposed to *import*. — **ex·port′a·ble**, *adj.*
ex′port (ĕks′pōrt; 70), *n.* **1.** Act of exporting; exportation. **2.** That which is exported; — opposed to *import*. — *adj.* Of or concerned with exportation or exports; suitable for exportation.
ex′por·ta′tion (ĕks′pōr·tā′shŭn), *n.* Act of exporting; also, commodity exported; an export.
ex·port′er (ĕks·pōr′tẽr *or, esp. in contrast*, ĕks′pōr·tẽr; 70), *n.* One who exports, as goods in the way of commerce.
ex·pos′al (ĕks·pōz′ăl; -'l), *n.* Exposure.

ex·pose′ (ĕks·pōz′; ĭks-), *v. t.* [OF. *exposer*, fr. *ex-* (fr. L. *ex* out) + *poser* to place. See POSE, *v.*] **1.** To lay open, as to attack, danger, test; to deprive of shelter or care; as, to *expose* troops needlessly; hence, to submit or subject to any action or influence; as, to *expose* iron to a magnet. **2.** To turn or cast out; to abandon; as, to *expose* an infant. **3.** To lay open to, or set out for, inspection; to exhibit, as goods for sale; to disclose; as, to *expose* a card in dealing, etc.; to lay or leave bare; as, winter clothing that leaves only one's face *exposed*. **4.** To disclose or unmask (something criminal, shameful, etc.); to disclose the faults or crimes of (a person). **5.** *Photog.* To subject (a sensitive film, plate, etc.) to the action of actinic rays. — **Syn.** See SHOW. — **ex·pos′er** (-pōz′ẽr), *n.*

ex′po·sé′ (ĕks′pō·zā′ *or, esp. Brit.,* ĕks·pō′zā), *n.* [F., prop. past part. of *exposer.*] An exposure of something discreditable.

ex·posed′ (ĕks·pōzd′; ĭks-), *adj.* **1.** Open to view. **2.** Unprotected, as from the weather, danger, etc. — **Syn.** See LIABLE.

ex·pos′er (-pōz′ẽr), *n.* One who or that which exposes.

ex′po·si′tion (ĕks′pō·zĭsh′ŭn), *n.* **1.** A setting forth of the meaning or purpose of a writing, discourse, law, etc. **2.** Discourse, or an example of it, designed to expound, explain, or appraise analytically. **3.** Act or practice of exposing; exposure; abandonment, as of infants. **4.** Condition of being exposed; exposure. **5.** A public exhibition or show. **6.** *Music.* **a** The first part of a sonata form. See SONATA FORM. **b** The opening section of a fugue.

ex·pos′i·tive (ĕks·pŏz′ĭ·tĭv), *adj.* Descriptive; expository.

ex·pos′i·tor (-tẽr), *n.* [L. See EXPOUND.] One who expounds or explains; an expounder; commentator.

ex·pos′i·to′ry (-tō′rĭ *or, esp. Brit.,* -tẽr·ĭ), *adj.* Of or relating to exposition; serving to explain or elucidate; as, *expository* writing.

ex post fac′to (ĕks pōst făk′tō). [L. *ex postfacto* from what is done afterwards.] Done or made after a thing but retroacting upon it; retrospective; as, an *ex post facto* law is any law enacted with a retrospective effect.

ex·pos′tu·late (ĕks·pŏs′tū·lāt; ĭks-), *v. i.* [L. *expostulatus*, past part. of *expostulare* to demand vehemently, fr. *ex* out + *postulare* to ask, require.] To reason earnestly with a person on some impropriety of his conduct; to remonstrate; — usually followed by *with*. — **Syn.** See OBJECT. — **ex·pos′tu·la′tor** (-lā′tẽr), *n.*

ex·pos′tu·la′tion (-lā′shŭn), *n.* Act of expostulating; earnest and kindly protest; remonstrance. — **ex·pos′tu·la′tive** (-pŏs′tū·lā′tĭv; -là·tĭv), *adj.* — **ex·pos′tu·la·to′ry** (-là·tō′rĭ *or, esp. Brit.,* -lā′tẽr·ĭ, -là·tẽr·ĭ), *adj.*

ex·po′sure (ĕks·pō′zhẽr; ĭks-), *n.* [From EXPOSE.] **1.** Act of exposing or state of being exposed. **2.** Position as to points of compass, or to influences of climate, etc.; as, a southern *exposure*. **3.** *Photog.* The act of exposing a sensitive surface.

exposure meter. *Photog.* An instrument for indicating correct exposure under varying conditions of illumination.

ex·pound′ (ĕks·pound′; ĭks-), *v. t.* [OF. *espondre*, fr. L. *exponere* to set out, expose, expound, fr. *ex* out + *ponere* to put.] **1.** To set forth; state; as, to *expound* a theory. **2.** To lay open the meaning of; interpret; as, to *expound* a text. — **Syn.** See EXPLAIN. — **ex·pound′er**, *n.*

ex·press′ (ĕks·prĕs′; ĭks-), *adj.* [OF. *expres*, fr. L. *expressus*, past part. of *exprimere* to express, fr. *ex* out + *premere* to press.] **1.** Directly and distinctly stated; definite; clear; explicit. **2.** Exact; precise. **3.** Of a special sort; as, he came for this *express* purpose. **4.** Adapted to or intended for a particular purpose. **5. a** Dispatched with or traveling at special speed, or with a limited number of stops; — often opp. to *local*; as, an *express* train. **b** Adapted for travel at special speed; as, an *express* highway. **6.** In the British postal service since 1891, designating immediate delivery by special messenger (of a letter or parcel) for which a fee is charged. Cf. SPECIAL DELIVERY. **7.** Of, pertaining to, or controlling an express (see EXPRESS, *n.*, 2, below); as, an *express* company. — **Syn.** See EXPLICIT.

— *adv.* Expressly; by express; as, to go *express*.

— *n.* **1.** A messenger sent on a special errand; also, a dispatch conveyed by a special messenger. **2.** A system for the prompt and safe transportation of parcels, money, or goods; also, a company operating such a system; also, the goods transported by such a system. **3.** An express train or other conveyance. **4.** An express rifle.

— *v. t.* [OF. *espresser*, fr. L. *ex* out + *pressare* to press.] **1.** To press or squeeze out, as the juice of a fruit; hence, to extort, as a confession; to exude, as a secretion. **2.** To represent in words; to state; to make known; exhibit. **3.** To delineate; depict. **4.** To make known the opinions or feelings of; — used reflexively; as, he *expressed* himself uncompromisingly. **5.** To represent by a sign or symbol; as, the sign = *expresses* equality. **6.** *Chiefly U. S.* To send by express. — **ex·press′er**, *n.* — **ex·press′i·ble**, *adj.*

Syn. **Express, vent, utter, voice, broach, air** mean to let out what one feels or thinks. **Express**, the general term, suggests an impulse to reveal in any way, as in words, in gestures, in what one makes or produces, etc.; **vent** stresses an inner compulsion to expression, especially in words; **utter** stresses use of voice though it may not imply speech; **voice** does not necessarily suggest vocal utterance but it invariably implies expression in words; **broach** adds the implication of disclosing; **air**, that of exposing one's opinions, one's ideas, etc.

ex·press′age (-ĭj), *n.* The carrying of parcels by express; also, the charge for such carrying.

ex·pres′sion (ĕks·prĕsh′ŭn; ĭks-), *n.* **1.** Act or product of pressing out. **2.** Act or process of representing, esp. by language. **3.** A form, pose, phrase, token, or the like, which manifests a thought, feeling, or quality; esp., a significant word or phrase; as, a common *expression*. **4.** Mode, means, or use of significant representation; as, to read or act with *expression*. **5.** Quality or fact of being indicative of character, feeling, etc.; also, facial aspect or intonation as indicative of feeling; as, a smiling *expression*. **6.** *Math.* A group of characters or signs, esp. algebraic symbols, representing a quantity or operation.

ex·pres′sion·ism (-ĭz′m), *n.* **1.** The theory or practice of freely expressing one's inner, or subjective, emotions and sensations; — a sense orig. developed in painting. Cf. IMPRESSIONISM. **2.** Belief in, or advocacy and practice of, the free expression of one's individuality, esp. as a means towards the acquiring of individual culture. — **ex·pres′sion·ist** (-ĭst), *n. & adj.* — **ex·pres′sion·is′tic** (-ĭs′tĭk), *adj.*

ex·pres′sive (ĕks·prĕs′ĭv; ĭks-), *adj.* **1.** Of, pertaining to, or marked by expression. **2.** Serving to express or represent; indicative. **3.** Full of expression; significant; as, *expressive* looks. — **-ly**, *adv.* — **-ness**, *n.*

ex·press′ly, *adv.* **1.** In an express manner; explicitly. **2.** For the express purpose; particularly.

ex·press′man (ĕks·prĕs′măn; ĭks-), *n.* *U. S.* A person employed in the express business.

express rifle. A sporting rifle for use at short ranges, employing a large charge of powder and a light (short) bullet, giving a high initial velocity and a flat trajectory.

ex·press′way′ (ĕks·prĕs′wā′; ĭks-), *n.* A superhighway.

ex·pro′pri·ate (ĕks·prō′prĭ·āt), *v. t.* [ML. *expropriatus*, past part. of *expropriare.*] **1.** To deprive of possession or proprietary rights. **2.** To take or transfer the ownership of from one owner to another. — **ex·pro′pri·a′tor** (-ā′tẽr), *n.*

ex·pro′pri·a′tion (-ā′shŭn), *n.* Act of expropriating, or state of being expropriated; specif., the action of the state in taking or modifying the property rights of individuals in the exercise of its sovereignty, as where property is sold under eminent domain.

ex·pul′sion (ĕks·pŭl′shŭn; ĭks-), *n.* [See EXPEL.] Act of expelling or state of being expelled; a driving or forcing out. — **ex·pul′sive** (ĕks-pŭl′sĭv), *adj.*

ex·punc′tion (ĕks·pŭngk′shŭn), *n.* Act of expunging.

ex·punge′ (-pŭnj′), *v. t.*; EX·PUNGED′ (-pŭnjd′); EX·PUNG′ING (-pŭn′jĭng). [L. *expungere, expunctum*, to prick out, mark for erasure by dots, fr. *ex* out + *pungere* to prick.] To blot out, as with a pen; to rub out. — **Syn.** See ERASE. — **ex·pung′er** (-pŭn′jẽr), *n.*

ex′pur·gate (ĕks′pẽr·gāt; *also* ĕks·pûr′-), *v. t.* [L. *expurgatus*, past part. of *expurgare* to purge, purify, fr. *ex* out, from + *purgare* to cleanse.] To clear from anything noxious, offensive, or erroneous; now, esp., to divest (a publication) of objectionable parts; as, to *expurgate* a book. — **ex′pur·ga′tion** (-gā′shŭn), *n.* — **ex′pur·ga′tor** (ĕks′pẽr·gā′tẽr; ĕks·pûr′gȧ-), *n.*

ex·pur′ga·to′ri·al (ĕks·pûr′gȧ·tō′rĭ·ăl; 70), *adj.* Expurgatory; pertaining to expurgation or expurgators.

ex·pur′ga·to′ry (ĕks·pûr′gȧ·tō′rĭ *or, esp. Brit.,* -tẽr·ĭ), *adj.* Serving to purify from anything noxious or erroneous.

ex′qui·site (ĕks′kwĭ·zĭt; *occas., esp. by way of emphasis,* ĕks·kwĭz′ĭt; ĭks-), *adj.* [L. *exquisitus*, past part. of *exquirere* to search out, fr. *ex* out + *quaerere* to search.] **1.** *Obs.* Carefully selected; choice. **2.** *Archaic.* Exact in operation; accurate. **3.** Carefully wrought; hence, of surpassing quality. **4. a** Highly accomplished; perfected; as, an *exquisite* gentleman. **b** Keenly appreciative; discriminating; fastidious; as, *exquisite* taste. **5.** Pleasing by reason of beauty, delicacy, or excellence. **6.** Keen; intense; as, *exquisite* pain. — **Syn.** See CHOICE. — *n.* A person who is overnice in dress; a fop; dandy. — **ex′qui·site·ly**, *adv.* — **ex′qui·site·ness**, *n.*

ex·san′guine (ĕks·săng′gwĭn), *adj.* Bloodless; anemic.

ex·scind′ (ĕk·sĭnd′), *v. t.* [L. *exscindere*, fr. *ex* out, from + *scindere* to cut.] To cut off or out; to excise.

ex·sect′ (ĕk·sĕkt′), *v. t.* [L. *exsectus*, past part. of *exsecare* to cut out.] To cut out. — **ex·sec′tion** (-sĕk′shŭn), *n.*

ex·sert′ (ĕks·sûrt′), *v. t.* [L. *exsertus*, past part. of *exserere* to stretch forth. See EXERT.] To thrust out; to protrude. — *adj.* Exserted. — **ex·ser′tion** (-sûr′shŭn), *n.*

ex·sert′ed (-sûr′tĕd; -tĭd), *adj.* *Bot. & Zool.* Protruding beyond some enclosing organ or part.

ex·ser′tile (-sûr′tĭl), *adj.* *Biol.* Capable of being protruded.

ex′sic·cate (ĕk′sĭ·kāt), *v. t. & i.* [L. *exsiccatus*, past part. of *exsiccare* to dry up, fr. *ex* out + *siccare* to make dry, fr. *siccus* dry.] To exhaust or evaporate moisture from; to dry up. — **ex′sic·ca′tion** (-kā′shŭn), *n.* — **ex·sic′ca·tive** (ĕks·sĭk′ȧ·tĭv), *adj. & n.* — **ex′sic·ca′tor** (ĕk′sĭ·kā′tẽr), *n.*

ex·stip′u·late (ĕks·stĭp′ū·lāt), *adj.* *Bot.* Without stipules, as a leaf.

ex·suf′fli·cate (ĕks·sŭf′lĭ·kāt), *adj.* [Cf. LL. *exsufflare* to blow upon.] Prob., inflated; empty; — a nonce use. *Shak.*

ex′tant (ĕks′tănt; ĕk·stănt′; ĭk-), *adj.* [L. *extans, -antis*, or *exstans, -antis*, pres. part. of *extare, exstare*, to stand out, fr. *ex* out + *stare* to stand.] **1.** *Now Rare.* Standing out; hence, conspicuous. **2.** In existence; not destroyed.

ex·tem′po·ral (ĕks·tĕm′pō·răl), *adj.* [L. *extemporalis*, fr. *ex tempore.*] Extemporaneous. — **ex·tem′po·ral·ly**, *adv.*

ex·tem′po·ra′ne·ous (-rā′nē·ŭs), *adj.* **1.** Unpremeditated; extemporary, as a speech. **2.** Given to, or clever at, extempore speaking. **3.** Made for the occasion; as, an *extemporaneous* shelter. — **ex·tem′po·ra·ne′i·ty** (-rȧ·nē′ĭ·tĭ), *n.* — **ex·tem′po·ra′ne·ous·ly**, *adv.* — **ex·tem′po·ra′ne·ous·ness**, *n.*

ex·tem′po·rar′y (ĕks·tĕm′pō·rĕr′ĭ *or, esp. Brit.,* -rẽr·ĭ; ĭks-), *adj.* **1.** Composed, performed, or uttered on the spur of the moment; not prepared beforehand; impromptu; as, an *extemporary* speech. **2.** Originated for or at the occasion; hence, sudden or unexpected. — **ex·tem′po·rar′i·ly**, *adv.* — **ex·tem′po·rar′i·ness**, *n.*

ex·tem′po·re (-rē), *adv.* [L., fr. *ex* out + *tempore*, abl. of *tempus* time.] Without previous study or meditation; extemporaneously. — *adj.* Extemporary.

ex·tem′po·rize (ĕks·tĕm′pō·rīz), *v. t. & i.* To do, make, or utter extempore, or offhand; to improvise. — **ex·tem′po·ri·za′tion** (-rĭ·zā′shŭn; -rī·zā′-), *n.* — **ex·tem′po·riz′er** (-rīz′ẽr), *n.*

ex·tend′ (ĕks·tĕnd′; ĭks-), *v. t.* [L. *extendere, extentum, extensum*, fr. *ex* out + *tendere* to stretch.] **1.** *Obs.* To take by force; to seize. **2.** To stretch or draw out; hence, to lengthen or prolong either in space or time. **3.** To straighten out, as a limb; to stretch. Cf. FLEX. **4.** To enlarge, as a surface or volume; to expand; spread. **5.** Hence: To broaden the application or action of, as, to *extend* power, influence, etc. **6.** To exaggerate. **7.** To hold out or reach forth, as the hand. **8.** To proffer or to bestow; as, to *extend* sympathy. **9.** *Finance.* To prolong the time of payment of, as a debt, beyond that originally stipulated. **10.** *Law.* **a** In Great Britain, to assess or value. **b** To take, assign, or levy upon by, or in execution of, a writ of extent. — *v. i.* To stretch out; to spread. — **ex·tend′i·ble** (-tĕn′dĭ·b'l), *adj.*

Syn. **Extend, lengthen, elongate, prolong, protract** mean to draw out or add to so as to increase in length. Both **extend** and **lengthen** may be used in reference to increase in time or space, but only *extend* to increase in range, as of influence, applicability, etc.; **elongate**, in technical rather than in general use, implies increase in dimension only; **prolong** suggests increase in duration chiefly, especially beyond usual or normal limits; **protract** adds to *prolong* the implications of indefiniteness, of needlessness, or the like.

ex·tend′ed (ĕks·tĕn′dĕd; -dĭd; ĭks-), *adj.* **1.** Stretched or drawn out; also, outstretched. **2.** *Print.* Of type, considerably wider than the standard for the same height. See TYPE. — **ex·tend′ed·ly**, *adv.*

ex·ten′si·ble (-tĕn′sĭ·b'l), *adj.* Capable of being extended. — **ex·ten′si·bil′i·ty** (-bĭl′ĭ·tĭ), **ex·ten′si·ble·ness**, *n.*

ex·ten′sile (ĕks·tĕn′sĭl; 56), *adj.* Extensible.

ex′ten·sim′e·ter (ĕks′tĕn·sĭm′ē·tẽr), *n.* An extensometer.

ex·ten′sion (ĕks·tĕn′shŭn; ĭks-), *n.* **1.** Act of extending, or state of being extended. **2.** A part constituting an addition; as, an *extension* to a house. **3.** *Com.* A written engagement on the part of a creditor, allowing a debtor further time to pay a debt. **4.** *Logic.* The number or aggregate of things named by a term or comprised in a concept; thus, the *extension* of "plant" is greater than that of "geranium"; denotation. Cf. INTENSION. **5.** *Physics.* That property of a body by which it occupies a portion of space. **6.** *Physiol.* The straightening of a limb. **7.** *Surg.* Stretching of a fractured or luxated limb so as to restore it to its natural position.

ex·ten′si·ty (ĕks·tĕn′sĭ·tĭ), *n.* **1.** The quality of extension. **2.** *Psychol.* Spatial quality as an attribute of sensation.

ex·ten′sive (ĕks·tĕn′sĭv; ĭks-), *adj.* **1.** Of, pertaining to, or characterized by, extension. **2.** Having wide extent; broad; wide. **3.** *Agric.* Designating, or pertaining to, any system of farming in which large areas of land are used with a minimum of labor and outlay; — opposed to *intensive.* — **ex·ten′sive·ly,** *adv.* — **ex·ten′sive·ness,** *n.*

ex′ten·som′e·ter (ĕks′tĕn·sŏm′ē·tẽr), *n.* [L. *extensus,* past part. + *-meter.*] An instrument for measuring any more or less minute deformation of a test specimen as caused by tension, compression, bending, twisting, etc.

ex·ten′sor (ĕks·tĕn′sẽr; -sôr), *n.* [LL., one who stretches.] *Anat.* A muscle serving to extend or straighten a limb or part. Cf. FLEXOR.

ex·tent′ (ĕks·tĕnt′; ĭks-), *n.* [OF. *estente,* fr. past part. of *estendre* to extend, fr. L. *extendere.* See EXTEND.] **1.** *Hist.* In Great Britain: Valuation or assessment, esp. of land. **2.** Space or amount to which a thing is extended; hence: **a** Compass; size; length. **b** Degree; measure; proportion. **3.** *Law.* **a** In Great Britain, a ***writ of extent,*** that is, a writ to recover judgments, under which the lands, goods, and person of the debtor may all be seized to secure payment. **b** A levy or seizure made under a writ of extent. **c** *Local, U. S.* A writ giving to a creditor temporary possession of his debtor's lands. **4.** *Logic.* Extension considered as a characteristic or function. **5.** *Math.* Continuous magnitude, esp. geometrical, of any number of dimensions, as a line, surface, space.

ex·ten′u·ate (ĕks·tĕn′ū·āt), *v. t.* [L. *extenuatus,* past part. of *extenuare* to make thin, loosen, weaken, fr. *ex* out + *tenuare* to make thin, fr. *tenuis* thin.] **1.** To make thin; to attenuate. **2.** To diminish; weaken. **3.** To underestimate; hence, *Obs.,* to disparage. **4.** To treat or represent (a crime, ill, or the like) as less than it appears to be; to excuse. — **ex·ten′u·a′tor** (-ā′tẽr), *n.*

ex·ten′u·at′ing (-āt′ĭng), *adj.* That extenuates.

ex·ten′u·a′tion (-ā′shŭn), *n.* Act of extenuating, or state of being extenuated; esp., palliation, as of a crime; also, something urged or done in palliation, as of a fault. — **ex·ten′u·a′tive** (-tĕn′ū·ā′tĭv; -ȧ·tĭv), *adj.* — **ex·ten′u·a·to′ry** (-ȧ·tō′rĭ *or, esp. Brit.,* -ā′tō·rĭ, -ȧ·tẽr·ĭ), *adj.*

ex·te′ri·or (ĕks·tēr′ĭ·ẽr; 2), *adj.* [L., compar. of *exterus* on the outside, foreign, compar. fr. *ex* out.] **1.** External, or outward. **2.** Being or occurring without; extrinsic. **3.** Relating to foreign nations; foreign. — *n.* **1.** The outward surface or part of a thing; outside. **2.** Outward or external deportment, form, or ceremony. — **ex·te′ri·or·ly,** *adv.*

ex·ter′mi·nate (ĕks·tûr′mĭ·nāt; ĭks-), *v. t.* [L. *exterminatus,* past part. of *exterminare* to abolish, fr. *ex* out + *terminus* limit.] To destroy utterly; to annihilate; to get rid of completely; as, to *exterminate* the termites infesting a building. — **ex·ter′mi·na′tor** (-nā′tẽr), *n.*

Syn. **Exterminate, extirpate, eradicate, uproot** mean to effect the destruction or abolition of something. **Exterminate** implies utter extinction, as by killing off; **extirpate** implies extinction of a race, a family, a species, etc., by destruction of the means by which it is propagated; **eradicate** implies the driving out or elimination of something that has established itself; **uproot** differs from *eradicate* in suggesting force or violence like that of a tempest tearing up trees by the roots.

ex·ter′mi·na′tion (-nā′shŭn), *n.* Act of exterminating; total destruction; eradication.

ex·ter′mi·na′tive (-tûr′mĭ·nā′tĭv; -nȧ·tĭv), *adj.* Exterminatory.

ex·ter′mi·na·to′ry (-nȧ·tō′rĭ *or, esp. Brit.,* -nā′tō·rĭ, -nȧ·tẽr·ĭ), *adj.* Of or relating to extermination; tending, as war, to exterminate.

ex·ter′mine (-mĭn), *v. t.* *Obs.* To exterminate.

ex′tern (ĕks′tûrn; ĕks·tûrn′), *adj.* *Obs.* External; extrinsic; not inherent.

ex′tern (ĕks′tûrn), *n.* [F. *externe,* n.] A person connected with an institution but not living in it. Cf. INTERN.

ex·ter′nal (ĕks·tûr′năl; -n'l; 2), *adj.* [L. *externus,* fr. *exter, exterus,* on the outside, outward. See EXTERIOR.] **1.** Outward; exterior; specif., applied or applicable to the outside of the body; as, *external* remedies. **2.** Outwardly perceptible; visible; physical, as disting. from mental or moral. **3.** Outside of a thing's extent, surface, constitution, etc. **4.** Not intrinsic; superficial. **5.** Foreign; as, *external* trade. **6.** *Anat.* Near the outside of the body; away from the median plane. **7.** *Philos.* Existing independently of mind. — *n.* Something external; outward part; visible form; — usually in *pl.* — **ex·ter′nal·ly,** *adv.*

ex·ter′nal–com·bus′tion en′gine. *Mach.* A heat engine which derives its heat from fuel consumed outside the engine cylinder. Cf. INTERNAL-COMBUSTION ENGINE.

ex·ter′nal·ism (ĕks·tûr′năl·ĭz'm), *n.* Quality or state of being manifest to the senses; also, regard for externals.

ex′ter·nal′i·ty (ĕk′stẽr·năl′ĭ·tĭ), *n.; pl.* -TIES (-tĭz). Quality or state of being external.

ex·ter′nal·ize (ĕks·tûr′năl·īz), *v. t.* To make external or externally manifest. — **ex·ter′nal·i·za′tion** (-ĭ·zā′shŭn; -ī·zā′-), *n.*

ex′ter·o·cep′tive (ĕk′stẽr·ō·sĕp′tĭv), *adj.* [L. *exter* outside + *-o* + *-ceptive* as in *receptive.*] *Physiol.* Activated by, pertaining to, or designating, stimuli impinging on the organism from without, as in touch, smell, sight, etc. Cf. INTEROCEPTIVE, PROPRIOCEPTIVE.

ex′ter·o·cep′tor (ĕk′stẽr·ō·sĕp′tẽr), *n.* [NL.] A sense organ excited by stimuli arising outside the body.

ex·ter′ri·to′ri·al (ĕks′tĕr·ĭ·tō′rĭ·ăl; 70), *adj.* [See EX-.] Beyond the territorial limits; extraterritorial. — **ex·ter′ri·to′ri·al′i·ty** (ĕks·tĕr′ĭ·tō′rĭ·ăl′ĭ·tĭ), *n.* — **ex′ter·ri·to′ri·al·ly,** *adv.*

ex·tinct′ (ĕks·tĭngkt′; ĭks-), *adj.* [L. *extinctus, exstinctus,* past part. See EXTINGUISH.] **1.** Extinguished; quenched. **2.** No longer living or active; passed away; that has died out; as, an *extinct* animal or plant; without a qualified heritor; as, an *extinct* title.

ex·tinc′tion (-tĭngk′shŭn), *n.* **1.** Act of extinguishing; state of being extinguished. **2.** Destruction; annihilation.

ex·tinc′tive (-tĭngk′tĭv), *adj.* Serving to extinguish.

ex·tin′guish (ĕks·tĭng′gwĭsh; ĭks-), *v. t.* [L. *extinguere, exstinguere,* to quench, prob. fr. *ex* out + *tinguere, tingere,* to wet, moisten.] **1.** To put out, as a light or fire; hence, to cause to die out; destroy. **2.** To obscure; eclipse, as by superior splendor. **3.** *Law.* To nullify. — **Syn.** See ABOLISH. — **ex·tin′guish·a·ble,** *adj.* — **ex·tin′guish·er,** *n.* — **ex·tin′guish·ment,** *n.*

ex′tir·pate (ĕk′stẽr·pāt; ĕks·tûr′pāt), *v. t.* [L. *extirpatus, exstirpatus,* past part. of *extirpare, exstirpare,* fr. *ex* out + *stirps* stock, stem.] To pluck up by the stem or root; to eradicate. — **Syn.** See EXTERMINATE. — **ex′tir·pa′tion** (ĕk′stẽr·pā′shŭn), *n.* — **ex′tir·pa′tive** (ĕk′stẽr·pā′tĭv), *adj.* — **ex′tir·pa′tor** (-pā′tẽr), *n.*

ex·tol′, ex·toll′ (ĕks·tōl′; -tŏl′; ĭks-), *v. t.* [L. *extollere,* fr. *ex* out + *tollere* to raise.] To elevate by praise; praise. — **ex·tol′ler** (-tōl′ẽr; -tŏl′ẽr), *n.* — **ex·tol′ment, ex·toll′ment,** *n.* *Rare.*

ex·tort′ (ĕks·tôrt′; ĭks-), *v. t.* [L. *extortus,* past part. of *extorquere* to twist out, extort, fr. *ex* out + *torquere* to twist.] To wrest from a person by force or any undue or illegal power or ingenuity; to wring (*from*); to exact. — **Syn.** See EDUCE. — **ex·tort′er,** *n.* — **ex·tor′tive,** *adj.*

ex·tor′tion (ĕks·tôr′shŭn; ĭks-), *n.* **1.** Act of extorting; act or practice of taking anything from a person by illegal use of fear; technically, *Law,* the offense committed by an officer who unlawfully, by color of his office, claims and takes money or other thing of value that is not due. **2.** That which is extorted.

ex·tor′tion·ar′y (-ĕr′ĭ; -ẽr·ĭ), *adj.* Extortionate.

ex·tor′tion·ate (-ĭt), *adj.* Characterized by extortion; oppressive; also, exorbitant. — **ex·tor′tion·ate·ly,** *adv.*

ex·tor′tion·er (-ẽr), *n.* One who practices extortion.

ex·tor′tion·ist (-ĭst), *n.* An extortioner.

ex′tra (ĕks′trȧ), *adj.* [From *extraordinary.* See EXTRA-.] Beyond, or greater than, what is due, usual, or necessary; additional; better or larger than ordinary. — *n.* **1.** Something in addition to what is due, expected, or customary; esp., an added charge or fee. **2.** An edition of a newspaper other than the regular one. **3.** *Cricket.* A run not made from a hit. **4.** Something of an extra quality or grade. **5.** *Colloq.* An extra workman; *Motion Pictures,* an actor employed by the day to enact a subordinate part, as one of a crowd. — *adv.* Beyond the usual size, extent, or degree. COMBINATIONS are:

extra-dry	**extra-hazardous**	**extra-strong**

ex′tra- (ĕks′trȧ-). [L., fr. *exter.* See EXTERIOR.] A combining form used to form adjectives, denoting *beyond, outside of, outside the scope of,* as in: **ex′tra·car′pal,** outside the carpal region; and in the following words:

extra-alimentary	**extragovernmental**	**extraorbital**
extracapsular	**extrahistoric**	**extraparental**
extracellular	**extralegal**	**extraparliamentary**
extracerebral	**extramarital**	**extraparochial**
extracorporeal	**extramolecular**	**extrasyllogistic**
extracutaneous	**extranuclear**	**extravaginal**
extraembryonic	**extraofficial**	**extravisceral**

ex′tra·bold′ (-bōld′; 2), *n.* *Print.* A style of type. See TYPE.

ex′tra·ca·non′i·cal (-kȧ·nŏn′ĭ·kăl), *adj.* *Eccl.* Not included in the canon, or list of authorized books.

ex′tra–con·densed′, *adj.* *Print.* Of type, having a narrower face than condensed type. See TYPE.

ex·tract′ (ĕks·trăkt′; ĭks-), *v. t.* [L. *extractus,* past part. of *extrahere* to extract, fr. *ex* out + *trahere* to draw.] **1.** To draw out or forth; hence, to derive as if by drawing out; to deduce. **2.** To withdraw by expression, distillation, treatment with a solvent, or other mechanical or chemical process. **3.** To choose out; to cite or quote. — *v. i.* To yield to the action of drawing out. — **Syn.** See EDUCE. — **ex·tract′a·ble, ex·tract′i·ble,** *adj.*

ex′tract (ĕks′trăkt), *n.* **1.** Something extracted; esp., something prepared from a substance by expression, solution, or the like; specif., a preparation supposed to possess the virtue of the original substance in concentrated form; as, *extract* of beef. **2.** A selection from a writing or discourse; quotation. **3.** *Chem.* The total solids obtained by evaporating wine, spirits, honey, etc. **4.** *Pharm.* A solid preparation obtained by evaporating a solution of a drug, the juice of a plant, or the like.

ex·trac′tion (ĕks·trăk′shŭn; ĭks-), *n.* **1.** Act of extracting, or drawing out. **2.** Derivation from a stock or family; lineage. **3.** That which is extracted; extract; essence.

ex·trac′tive (-tĭv), *adj.* **1.** Capable of being extracted. **2.** Tending or serving to extract; as, agriculture is an *extractive* industry. — *n.* Anything extracted; an extract.

ex·trac′tor (-tẽr), *n.* One who or that which extracts, as a device for withdrawing a cartridge or shell from the chamber of a breech-loading firearm (see GUNLOCK, *Illust.*).

ex′tra·cur·ric′u·lar (ĕks′trȧ·kŭ·rĭk′ū·lẽr), **ex′tra·cur·ric′u·lum** (-lŭm), *adj.* Not falling within the curriculum; esp., of or relating to those activities, as debating, dramatics, and athletics, which form part of the life of students, but are not part of the courses of study.

ex′tra·dite (ĕks′trȧ·dīt), *v. t.* To deliver up to a foreign jurisdiction; also, to procure the extradition of. — **ex′tra·dit′a·ble** (-dīt′ȧ·b'l), *adj.*

ex′tra·di′tion (-dĭsh′ŭn), *n.* [F., fr. L. *ex* out + *traditio* a delivering up.] The surrender of an alleged criminal by one state to another; hence, in general, the surrender of a prisoner by one authority to another.

ex·tra′dos (ĕks·trā′dŏs), *n.* [F., fr. L. *extra* outside + F. *dos* (fr. L. *dorsum*) the back.] *Arch.* The exterior curve of an arch.

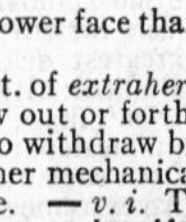

a Intrados, or Soffit; *b* Extrados.

ex′tra·ju·di′cial (ĕks′trȧ·jōō·dĭsh′ăl; 114), *adj.* Out of or beyond the proper authority of a court or judge. — **ex′tra·ju·di′cial·ly,** *adv.*

ex′tra·mun′dane (-mŭn′dān), *adj.* Beyond the material world.

ex′tra·mu′ral (-mū′răl), *adj.* **1.** Outside of the walls, as of a fortified city. **2.** Conducted or coming from outside of the precincts (of a given institution); — said of educational facilities, etc.

ex·tra′ne·ous (ĕks·trā′nē·ŭs), *adj.* [L. *extraneus.* See STRANGE.] Not essential or intrinsic; foreign; as, to separate gold from *extraneous* matter. — **Syn.** See EXTRINSIC. — **ex·tra′ne·ous·ly,** *adv.* — **ex·tra′ne·ous·ness,** *n.*

ex·traor′di·nar′i·ly (ĕks·trôr′dĭ·nĕr′ĭ·lĭ; ĭks-; *or, esp. Brit.,* -nẽr·ĭ·lĭ; -d'n·rĭ·lĭ; ĕks′trȧ·ôr′-), *adv.* In an extraordinary manner or degree.

ex·traor′di·nar′y (ĕks·trôr′dĭ·nĕr′ĭ; ĭks-; *or, esp. Brit.*, -dĭ·nĕr·ĭ; -d′n·rĭ; *or, esp. in sense* 3, ĕks′trȧ·ôr′-), *adj.* [L. *extraordinarius*, fr. *extra ordinem* outside the (usual) order. See EXTRA-; ORDINARY.] **1.** Beyond or out of the common order or method; not ordinary. **2.** Exceeding the common degree, measure, or condition; hence, remarkable. **3.** Employed for a special service; subordinate; as, an ambassador *extraordinary*.

ex′tra·phys′i·cal (ĕks′trȧ·fĭz′ĭ·kăl), *adj.* Not subject to physical laws or methods.

ex·trap′o·late (ĕks·trăp′ō·lāt), *v. t. & i.* [*extra-* + inter*polate*.] **1.** To project by inference into an unexplored situation (some sequent) from observations in an explored field, on the assumption of continuity or correspondence; as, meteorologists *extrapolate* local weather conditions from reports of distant stations; oil prospectors *extrapolate* from a knowledge of petrology. **2.** *Math.* To calculate (the value of the function lying beyond an interval) from values of the function within that interval. — **ex·trap′o·la′tion** (-lā′shŭn), *n.* — **ex·trap′o·la′tive** (-trăp′ō·lā′tĭv), *adj.* — **ex·trap′o·la′tor** (-tĕr), *n.*

ex′tra·pro·fes′sion·al (ĕks′trȧ·prō·fĕsh′ŭn·ăl; -′l), *adj.* Not within the ordinary limits of professional duty or business.

ex′tra·sen′so·ry (-sĕn′sō·rĭ), *adj.* Beyond, or outside the scope of, ordinary sense perception, as in **extrasensory perception** (abbr. *ESP*) — used by some psychologists of instances of perceptive powers not scientifically explained, as in clairvoyance and telepathy.

ex′tra·ter′ri·to′ri·al (ĕks′trȧ·tĕr′ĭ·tō′rĭ·ăl; 70), *adj.* Outside the territorial limits of a jurisdiction; exterritorial.

ex′tra·ter′ri·to′ri·al′i·ty (-ăl′ĭ·tĭ), *n.* Exemption from the jurisdiction of local tribunals, as in the case of diplomatic agents.

ex′tra·u′ter·ine (-ū′tĕr·ĭn; -īn), *adj.* Outside the uterus.

ex·trav′a·gance (ĕks·trăv′ȧ·găns; ĭks-), *n.* **1.** Quality of being extravagant; excess; esp., undue expenditure of money. **2.** An instance of excess; an action or thing which is extravagant.

ex·trav′a·gan·cy (-găn·sĭ), *n.*; *pl.* -CIES (-sĭz). Extravagance.

ex·trav′a·gant (-gănt), *adj.* [F. and ML.; F., fr. ML. *extravagans*, *-antis*, pres. part. of *extravagari*, fr. *extra* outside + *vagari* to wander.] **1.** *Obs.* Wandering. **2.** Exceeding due bounds; excessive; as, *extravagant* praise. **3.** Profuse in expenditure; wasteful. **4.** Excessively high; exorbitant. — **Syn.** See EXCESSIVE. — **Ant.** Restrained. — **ex·trav′a·gant·ly**, *adv.*

ex·trav′a·gan′za (-găn′zȧ), *n.* [It. *estravaganza*, *stravaganza*.] A wildly irregular musical or dramatic composition; esp., a spectacular drama like comic opera, with elaborate setting.

ex·trav′a·gate (ĕks·trăv′ȧ·gāt), *v. i.* To rove; to exceed normal limits.

ex·trav′a·sate (ĕks·trăv′ȧ·sāt), *v. t. & i.* [*extra-* + L. *vas* vessel.] **1.** To force or let out of the proper vessels, as blood; to force or pass by infiltration or effusion, as blood, lymph, etc., from its normal channel into surrounding tissue. **2.** *Geol.* To erupt in liquid form from a vent; as, *extravasated* lava. — **ex·trav′a·sa′tion** (-sā′shŭn), *n.*

ex′tra·vas′cu·lar (ĕks′trȧ·văs′kū·lĕr), *adj.* *Anat.* **a** Not contained in vessels. **b** Destitute of vessels; nonvascular.

ex′tra·ver′sion, ex′tra·vert. Vars. of EXTROVERSION, etc.

ex·treme′ (ĕks·trēm′; ĭks-; 2), *adj.* [OF., fr. L. *extremus*, superl. of *exter*, *exterus*. See EXTERIOR.] **1.** At the utmost point or border; utmost; most remote. **2.** Last; final; as, the *extreme* hour of life. **3.** Very far out; far toward the extreme. **4.** Existing in, or going to, the greatest degree; greatest. **5.** Very great; hence, immoderate. **6.** Radical; ultra; as, *extreme* opinions. — **Syn.** See EXCESSIVE. — (ĕks·trēm′; ĭks-), *n.* **1.** The utmost point; extremity. **2.** Furthest degree; undue departure from the mean; esp., *pl.*, things at an extreme distance from each other; as, *extremes* of heat and cold, of virtue and vice. **3.** An extreme state or condition; hence, danger, distress, etc. **4.** An excessive degree, measure, expedient, or the like. **5.** *Logic.* A term appearing in only one of the premises of a syllogism, as contrasted with the middle term. **6.** *Math.* The first or the last term of a proportion or series. — **ex·treme′ly**, *adv.* — **ex·treme′ness**, *n.*

extreme unction. *R.C.Ch.* The sacrament administered by a priest to one in danger of death, through application of holy oil to his organs of sense, and recital of prayers.

ex·trem′ism (ĕks·trēm′ĭz′m; ĭks-), *n.* Quality or state of being extreme; radicalism. — **ex·trem′ist** (-ĭst), *n.*

ex·trem′i·ty (-trĕm′ĭ·tĭ), *n.*; *pl.* -TIES (-tĭz). **1.** The utmost limit or part. **2.** A limb of the body; esp., the end part of it. **3.** The utmost point; highest degree. **4.** Greatest need or peril; necessity; esp., a state that makes immediate death probable. **5.** An extremely severe act or measure.

ex′tri·ca·ble (ĕks′trĭ·kȧ·b′l), *adj.* Capable of being extricated.

ex′tri·cate (ĕks′trĭ·kāt), *v. t.* [L. *extricatus*, past part. of *extricare*, fr. *ex* + *tricae* trifles, impediments, perplexities.] **1.** To free, as from difficulties; disentangle. **2.** To cause to be emitted or evolved; as, to *extricate* heat. — **ex′tri·ca′tion** (-kā′shŭn), *n.*

Syn. Extricate, disentangle, untangle, disencumber, disembarrass mean to free from that which binds or holds back. **Extricate** implies force or ingenuity in freeing from difficulties, perplexities, etc.; **disentangle** or, more rarely, **untangle** suggests a release of that which is actually entangled or complicated; **disencumber**, a release from that which weighs down, clogs, or the like; **disembarrass**, a release from that which impedes, hampers, or hinders.

ex·trin′sic (ĕks·trĭn′sĭk), *adj.* Also **ex·trin′si·cal** (-sĭ·kăl). [L. *extrinsecus*, adv., on the outside, fr. *exter* on the outside + *secus* otherwise, beside.] **1.** Not contained in or belonging to a body; unessential. **2.** Pertaining to, or derived from, things outside; extraneous. **3.** *Anat.* Originating outside a part and acting upon the part as a whole, as certain muscles. — **ex·trin′si·cal·ly**, *adv.*

Syn. Extrinsic, extraneous, foreign, alien mean external to a thing, its true nature, or its original character. **Extrinsic** applies to that which is distinctly outside the thing in question or is derived from something apart from it; **extraneous**, to that which is on or comes from the outside and may or may not be capable of becoming an integral part of it; **foreign**, to that which is so different from the thing considered that it is inadmissible because repellent or, if admitted, is incapable of becoming identified with or assimilated by it; **alien**, to a thing so foreign that it can never become an inherent or integral part of the thing.

ex·trorse′ (ĕks·trôrs′), *adj.* [F., fr. LL. *extrorsus* in an outward direction, fr. *extra* on the outside + *versus* towards.] Facing or turned outwards; *Bot.*, turned away from the axis of growth. Cf. INTRORSE.

ex′tro·ver′sion (ĕks′trō·vûr′shŭn), *n.* [See EXTROVERT.] **1.** *Med.* The condition of being turned inside out; as, *extroversion* of the bladder. **2.** Also **ex′tra·ver′sion** (ĕks′trȧ-). *Psychol.* Interest directed outward; a propensity for finding one's satisfactions in external things; — opposed to *introversion*.

ex′tro·vert (ĕks′trō·vûrt), *n.* [*extro-* (fr. *extra-*) + L. *vertere* to turn.] Also **ex′tra·vert** (ĕks′trȧ-). *Psychol.* One whose interest is centered in external objects and actions. Cf. INTROVERT.

ex·trude′ (ĕks·trōōd′), *v. t. & i.* [L. *extrudere*, *extrusum*, fr. *ex* out + *trudere* to thrust.] **1.** To force, press, or push out; to protrude. **2.** To shape by forcing (metal or plastic, softened usually by heat) through dies by pressure. — *v. i.* To be extruded; also, to protrude.

ex·tru′sion (-trōō′zhŭn), *n.* The act or process of extruding, as a metal or plastic; also, a form produced by the process; protrusion.

ex·tru′sive (-sĭv), *adj.* **1.** Expulsive; also, protrusive. **2.** *Geol.* Forced out at the surface; effusive, or volcanic. Cf. INTRUSIVE.

ex·u′ber·ance (ĕg·zū′bĕr·ăns; ĭg-), *n.* Also **ex·u′ber·an·cy** (-ăn·sĭ). **1.** State or quality of being exuberant; superabundance; profusion. **2.** An instance of exuberant action, growth, or the like.

ex·u′ber·ant (-ănt), *adj.* [L. *exuberans*, *-antis*, pres. part. of *exuberare* to be abundant, fr. *ex* + *uberare* to be fruitful, fr. *uber* fruitful.] **1.** Characterized by abundance or superabundance; plenteous; profuse. **2.** Maintained, experienced, or the like, to an extreme degree; effusive; lavish; — chiefly of persons, emotions, or their expression; as, *exuberant* praise, zeal. — **Syn.** See PROFUSE. — **ex·u′ber·ant·ly**, *adv.*

ex·u′ber·ate (-āt), *v. i.* To be in exuberance; to abound.

ex′u·date (ĕks′ū·dāt; 118), *n.* Exuded matter.

ex′u·da′tion (-dā′shŭn), *n.* Act of exuding; sweating; a discharge of moisture, juice, or gum, as through pores or incisions; also, the matter exuded. — **ex·u′da·tive** (ĕks·ū′dȧ·tĭv), *adj.*

ex·ude′ (ĕks·ūd′; ĕg·zūd′; ĭg-), *v. t. & i.* [L. *exudare*, *exsudare*, *-atum*, to sweat out, fr. *ex* out + *sudare* to sweat, fr. *sudor* sweat.] To discharge through pores or incisions, as moisture, juice, gum, etc.

ex·ult′ (ĕg·zŭlt′; ĭg-), *v. i.* [L. *exultare*, *exsultare*, *-atum*, to leap vigorously, exult, freq. fr. *exsilire* to spring out or up, fr. *ex* out + *salire* to leap.] **1.** *Obs.* To leap; spring. **2.** To be in high spirits; to rejoice in triumph; to glory, as in victory. — **ex·ult′ing·ly**, *adv.*

ex·ult′an·cy (ĕg·zŭl′tăn·sĭ; ĭg-), *n.* Exultation.

ex·ult′ant (-tănt), *adj.* Characterized by, or expressing, exultation; exulting. — **ex·ult′ant·ly**, *adv.*

ex′ul·ta′tion (ĕk′sŭl·tā′shŭn; ĕg′zŭl-), *n.* Act of exulting; lively joy at success or at any advantage gained.

ex·u′vi·ae (ĕg·zū′vĭ·ē; ĕks·ū′vĭ·ē), *n. pl.*; *sing.* EXUVIA. [L., fr. *exuere* to draw out or off.] Cast skins, shells, or coverings of animals, as the skins of snakes, etc. — **ex·u′vi·al** (-ăl), *adj.*

ex·u′vi·ate (-āt), *v. i. & t.* *Zool.* To shed an old covering; to molt. — **ex·u′vi·a′tion** (-ā′shŭn), *n.*

-ey (-ĭ). A form of *-y* (adj. suffix), used esp. after words ending in *y*, as in clay*ey*.

ey′as (ī′ăs), *n.* [F. *niais* fresh from the nest, fr. L. *nidus* nest. E. *an eyas* stands for *a nias*.] A nestling or unfledged bird.

eye (ī), *n.* [AS. *ēage*.] **1.** The organ of sight; esp., the nearly spherical mass, the **eye′ball′** (ī′bôl′), in a bony concavity of the skull, or the orbit; also, all the visible structures within and surrounding the orbit, including eyelids, eyelashes, eyebrows. **2. a** The faculty of seeing; vision; often, a developed visual perception; as, an *eye* for the beautiful. **b** The act of seeing; look. **c** Specif., attentive regard; inspection; hence, oversight. **3.** The faculty of intellectual discrimination or inner perception. **4.** In general, the most important part; essential place, spot, or location. **5.** Something suggestive of the organ of sight, as a spot on a peacock's tail, the center of a target, the hole through a needle, the center of a flower, the disk in composites, the undeveloped bud of a cutting, potato, etc. — ***in the eye of the wind.*** *Naut.* In a direction almost directly opposed to the wind; very close to the wind. — *v. t.*; EYED (īd); EY′ING (ī′ĭng) or EYE′ING. **1.** To view; to observe; esp., to watch with fixed attention. **2.** To make an eye in or on; as, to *eye* a needle. — *v. i.* *Obs.* To appear; to look.

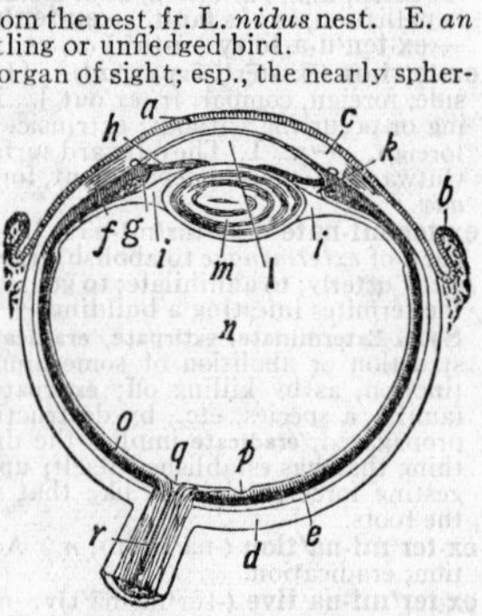

Horizontal section of Right Human Eyeball, seen from above, somewhat enlarged. *a b* Conjunctiva; *c* Cornea; *d* Sclerotic; *e* Chorioid; *f* Ciliary Muscle; *g* Ciliary Process; *h* Iris; *i* Suspensory Ligament; *k* Posterior Aqueous Chamber between *h* and *i*; *l* Anterior Aqueous Chamber; *m* Lens; *n* Vitreous Humor; *o* Retina; *p* Yellow Spot; *q* Center of Blind Spot; *r* Artery of Retina in the center of the Optic Nerve.

eye′beam′ (ī′bēm′), *n.* A glance of the eye.

eye′bolt′ (-bōlt′), *n.* A bolt with a looped head, or an opening in the head. See BOLT, *Illust.*

eye′bright′ (-brīt′), *n.* **a** A small European herb (*Euphrasia officinalis*) of the figwort family, formerly used as a remedy for diseases of the eye. **b** The scarlet pimpernel (see PIMPERNEL).

eye′brow′ (-brou′), *n.* The arch or ridge over the eye; also, the covering of soft hair growing on this ridge.

eye′cup′ (-kŭp′), *n.* A small oval cup having a rim curved to fit the orbit of the eye, and used in applying liquid remedies to the eyes.

eyed (īd), *adj.* Having eyes or eyelike spots.

eye′glass′ (ī′glȧs′), *n.* **1.** A lens of glass or rock crystal used to correct defects of vision; — when used singly, commonly called a *monocle*; when used in pairs, *eyeglasses* or *pince-nez*. Cf. SPECTACLE, 3. **2.** Eyepiece of a telescope, microscope, etc. **3.** A glass eyecup.

eye′hole′ (-hōl′), *n.* **1.** The orbit of the eye. **2.** A peephole. **3.** A circular opening to receive something, as a hook, cord, or rope; an eyelet.

eye′lash′ (-lăsh′), *n.* **a** The fringe of hair that edges the eyelid. **b** Now, usually, a single hair of this fringe.

eye′less (ī′lĕs; -lĭs), *adj.* Without eyes; blind.

eye′let (ī′lĕt; -lĭt), *n.* [OF. *oeillet*, dim. of *oeil* (F. *œil*) eye, fr. L. *oculus*.] **1.** A small hole, usually buttonholed, for decoration as in embroidery, or for receiving a cord. See GROMMET, *Illust.* **2.** A metal ring or grommet, used to line an eyelet hole. **3.** A small eye; an ocellus. **4.** A peephole or loophole. — *v. t.* To make eyelets in.

eye′lid′ (ī′lĭd′), *n.* That part of movable skin with which an animal covers or uncovers the eyeball.

ey′en (ī′ĕn). *Archaic & Dial. Eng. pl.* of EYE.

eye opener. That which makes the eyes open, as startling news, or, *U. S. Slang,* a drink of liquor.

eye′piece′ (ī′pēs′), *n.* *Optics.* The lens, or combination of lenses, at the eye end of an optical instrument. See MICROSCOPE, *Illust.*

eye rhyme. An imperfect rhyme appearing to have identical vowel sounds from similarity of spelling, as *move: love, bough: though;* — called also *sight rhyme.*

eye′serv′ant (ī′sûr′vănt), *n.* A servant who attends faithfully to his duty only when watched.

eye′serv′er (ī′sûr′vẽr), *n.* An eyeservant.

eye′serv′ice (-vĭs), *n.* **1.** Service performed only under inspection, as under the eye of an employer. **2.** Admiring looks or regard.

eye′shot′ (ī′shŏt′), *n.* Range, reach, or glance of the eye.

eye′sight′ (-sīt′), *n.* Sight; view; observation.

eye′some (-sŭm), *adj.* Charming to look upon.

eye′sore′ (-sōr′; 70), *n.* Something offensive to the sight.

eye′spot′ (-spŏt′), *n.* *Zool.* **a** A simple eye or visual organ in many invertebrates, consisting of pigment cells covering a sensory nerve termination. **b** An eyelike spot of color.

eye′stalk′ (-stôk′), *n.* *Zool.* One of the movable peduncles which, in the decapod Crustacea, bear the eyes at the tip, as in the lobster, crab, etc.

eye′stone′ (-stōn′), *n.* A small lenticular calcareous body, used to remove a foreign substance from the eye.

eye′strain′ (-strān′), *n.* Weariness or strained condition of the eye from overuse, uncorrected defects of vision, etc.

eye′string′ (-strĭng′), *n.* Any muscle, tendon, or nerve of the eye, formerly supposed to break at death or blindness.

eye′tooth′ (-tōōth′; 2), *n.; pl.* -TEETH (-tēth′). *Anat.* A canine tooth of the upper jaw. See TOOTH, *Illust.* — ***to cut one's eyeteeth.*** *Colloq.* To gain experience; become sophisticated.

eye′wash′ (ī′wŏsh′), *n.* **1.** Eyewater. **2.** *Slang.* Flattery intended to deceive.

eye′wa′ter (-wô′tẽr; -wŏt′ẽr), *n.* A lotion for the eyes.

eye′wink′ (-wĭngk′), *n.* A wink; also, a glance; look.

eye′wink′er (-ẽr), *n.* An eyelash.

eye′wit′ness (ī′wĭt′nĕs; -nĭs; 2), *n.* One who sees an object or act; esp., one who testifies what he has seen.

eyre (âr), *n.* [OF. *eire, erre,* journey, way, fr. L. *iter, itineris,* way, fr. root of *ire* to go.] **1.** A journey in circuit; — used in the phrase ***justices in eyre,*** itinerant judges who under temporary royal commissions rode circuit to hold courts in the different counties of England. **2.** The circuit or sessions held by the justices in eyre.

ey′rie, ey′ry (âr′ĭ; ẽr′ĭ; ī′rĭ), *n.* An aerie.

ey′rir (ā′rĭr), *n.; pl.* AURAR (oi′rär). [Icel.] A minor Icelandic coin, the hundredth part of a króna. See MONEY, *Tables.*

E·zek′iel (ē·zēk′yĕl; -zē′kĭ·ĕl; 58), *n.* *Douay Bib.* **E·zech′iel** (ē·zĕk′yĕl; -zē′kĭ·ĕl). [LL. *Ezechiel,* fr. Gr., fr. Heb. *Yeḥezqēl.*] **a** A Hebrew prophet of the 6th century B.C. **b** A book of the Old Testament. See BIBLE.

Ez′ra (ĕz′rȧ), *n.* [LL., fr. Heb. *'Ezrā.*] **a** A Hebrew priest of the 5th century B.C. **b** A book of the Old Testament. See BIBLE.

F

F, f (ĕf), *n.; pl.* F's, F's, Fs, FS (ĕfs). **1.** The sixth letter of the English alphabet. F comes from Latin F which, in form, came from obsolete Greek Ϝ. See DIGAMMA. **2.** The sound of this letter. See *Pron.,* § 43. **3.** *Music.* **a** The fourth tone of the model major scale (that of C), or the sixth tone of its relative minor scale (that of A minor). **b** Any symbol representing this tone. See PITCH, *Illust.* **c** A key or string producing this tone. **4.** As a *symbol,* the sixth in order or class. **5.** In Mendelian inheritance, a filial generation, the first and following generations being F_1, F_2, etc. Cf. P, 3 **b.**

F, F/, f, f:, f/, *f.*, etc. See F NUMBER.

fa (fä), *n.* [It.] *Music.* A syllable applied to the fourth tone of the diatonic scale in solmization.

fa·ba′ceous (fȧ·bā′shŭs), *adj.* [L. *fabaceus,* fr. *faba* bean.] Belonging to the pea family (Fabaceae). See PEA.

Fa′bi·an (fā′bĭ·ăn; 58), *adj.* **1.** In the manner of the Roman general Quintus Fabius Maximus, surnamed Cunctator (delayer), who avoided decisive contests in the defense of Rome against Hannibal; hence, cautious; dilatory; as, a *Fabian* policy. **2.** Designating or pertaining to a society of socialists, organized in England in 1884 to spread socialistic principles gradually. — *n.* A member of the Fabian Society. — **Fa′bi·an·ism** (-ĭz′m), *n.* — **Fa′bi·an·ist** (-ĭst), *n. & adj.*

fa′ble (fā′b'l), *n.* [OF., fr. L. *fabula,* fr. *fari* to speak, say.] **1.** A fictitious narrative or statement; specif.: **a** An untruth; falsehood. **b** A story of supernatural happenings, as in legend. **c** A narration enforcing some useful truth; esp., one in which animals speak and act like human beings. **2.** *Rare.* The plot of an epic or dramatic poem. — *v. i. & t.;* FA′BLED (-b'ld); FA′BLING (-blĭng). To compose fables; hence, to write or speak fiction; to talk idly; to feign or speak of as true or real. — **fa′bler** (-blẽr), *n.*

fa′bled (fā′b'ld), *adj.* **a** Told in fable; mythical; legendary. **b** Having no real existence; fictitious.

fab′li·au (făb′lĭ·ō; *F.* fȧ′blē·ō′), *n.; pl.* FABLIAUX (-ōz; *F.* -ō′). [F., fr. *fable* fable.] A short metrical tale, usually comic, frankly coarse, and often cynical, popular in the 12th and 13th centuries.

fab′ric (făb′rĭk), *n.* [F. *fabrique,* fr. L. *fabrica* fabric, workshop. See FORGE.] **1.** A structure. **2.** Act of constructing; erection; specif., construction and maintenance of a church building. **3.** Structural plan; workmanship; texture; as, cloth of a beautiful *fabric.* **4.** Anything manufactured; esp., cloth woven or knit from fibers. **5.** *Petrog.* The appearance or pattern produced by the shapes and arrangement of the crystal grains, or of these with glass, in a rock.

fab′ri·cant (făb′rĭ·kănt), *n.* A manufacturer.

fab′ri·cate (-kāt), *v. t.* [L. *fabricatus,* past part. of *fabricari, -care,* to build, forge, fr. *fabrica* fabric.] **1.** To construct; build. **2.** To construct by putting together standardized parts; as, a *fabricated* house. **3.** To form by art and labor; to manufacture. **4.** To invent (a legend, etc.); to devise falsely; as, to *fabricate* a story. — **Syn.** See MAKE. — **fab′ri·ca′tion** (-kā′shŭn), *n.* — **fab′ri·ca′tor** (-kā′tẽr), *n.*

Fab′ri·koid (făb′rĭ·koid), *n.* A trade-mark for a leatherlike fabric used in upholstery, bookbindings, etc.

fab′u·list (făb′ū·lĭst), *n.* One who invents or writes fables; also, an inventor of falsehoods; a liar.

fab′u·lous (-lŭs), *adj.* [L. *fabulosus.*] **1.** Feigned, as a fable; fictitious. **2.** Like a fable, esp. in exaggeration; astonishing. — **Syn.** See FICTITIOUS. — **fab′u·lous·ly,** *adv.* — **fab′u·lous·ness,** *n.*

fa·çade′ (fȧ·säd′; fȧ-), *n.* [F., fr. It., fr. VL. *facia.* See FACE.] **1.** *Arch.* The face of a building; esp., the principal face. **2.** Hence, the face or front of anything.

face (fās), *n.* [OF., fr. VL. *facia,* for L. *facies* form, shape, face, fr. *facere* to make.] **1.** The front part of the head; of man, the part of the head including the eyes, cheeks, nose, mouth, forehead, and chin. **2.** *Archaic.* Presence; view; sight. **3.** Expression of countenance. **4.** *Colloq.* A grimace; as, to make *faces* at one. **5.** *Colloq.* Confidence; also, boldness; as, to have the *face* to ask. **6.** Outward appearance; hence, disguise; pretense. **7.** Dignity; prestige; as, to save (one's) *face.* **8.** The exact amount expressed on a note, bond, etc. **9.** The physical features; — said of a country. **10.** The surface of anything; esp., the front, upper, or outer part or surface. **11.** The principal side or surface of anything; the front of a building, an arch, a cliff, etc. **12.** A side or surface dressed, finished, or specially prepared, as the finished side of cloth or leather, the inscribed or printed side of a document, the marked side of a playing card, watch, etc. **13.** The acting surface, esp. of a tool or implement. See FILE, *Illust.* **14.** *Fort.* **a** The portion of a work forming one side of a salient angle. **b** The front between two neighboring bastions or other salient works. See BASTION, *Illust.* **15.** *Math. & Cryst.* Any one of the plane surfaces that bound a polyhedron or other geometrical solid or a crystal. **16.** *Mil.* One of the sides of a formation, esp. of a square. **17.** *Mining.* The end or wall of the tunnel, drift, or excavation at which work is progressing; the breast. **18.** *Print.* **a** The upper or printing surface of a type, plate, etc. **b** The style or cut of type. See TYPE. — ***in (the) face of.*** In the immediate presence of; also, in opposition to; despite.

Syn. **Face, countenance, visage, physiognomy** denote the front part of the head from the forehead to the chin. **Face** is the simple, direct word, applicable either to one's own or another's; **countenance** applies to a face as seen and as revealing a mood, character, or the like; **visage** suggests attention to shape and proportions and, sometimes, expression; **physiognomy** suggests attention to the contours of the face and features, and to the characteristic expression as indicative of race, temperament, or the like.

— *v. t.;* FACED (fāst); FAC′ING (fās′ĭng). **1.** To confront impudently. **2.** To stand with the face toward. **3.** To meet face to face. **4.** To oppose firmly; resist. **5.** To contemplate the prospect of. **6.** To put a facing upon; as, a building *faced* with marble. **7.** To line near the edge, esp. with a different material; as, to *face* the front of a coat. **8.** To give a specious appearance, or "face," to; as, to *face* tea with coloring matter. **9.** *Card Playing.* To turn (a card) face upwards. **10.** *Mach.* To make flat or smooth the surface of, as a stone or a casting. **11.** *Mil.* To cause to turn or present a face or front. — *v. i.* To turn the face; as, to *face* to the right or left; to present a face or front. — **face′a·ble,** *adj.*

face card. *Card Playing.* The king, queen, or knave. Cf. COAT CARD.

face′-hard′en, *v. t.* To harden the face or surface of, as steel.

face lifting. An operation of plastic surgery for the removal of facial wrinkles or defects.

face′plate′ (fās′plāt′), *n.* *Mach.* A disk fixed with its face at right angles to the live spindle of a lathe for the attachment of the work.

fac′er (fās′ẽr), *n.* **1.** *Colloq.* A blow in the face, as in boxing; hence, any stunning defeat. **2.** One who or that which faces; specif., *Mach.,* a cutter for facing.

fac′et (făs′ĕt; -ĭt), *n.* [F. *facette.*] **1.** One of the small plane surfaces of a diamond or other cut gem or of a crystal. See BRILLIANT, *Illust.* **2.** A phase or aspect, as of a topic. **3.** *Anat.* A smooth, flat surface; as, the articular *facet* of a bone. **4.** *Arch.* The fillet between the flutes of a column. **5.** *Zool.* The surface of one of the visual units that make up a compound eye, as of an insect. — **Syn.** See PHASE. — *v. t.* To cut facets on. — **fac′et·ed** (făs′ĕt·ĕd; -ĭ·tĭd), *adj.*

fa·cete′ (fȧ·sēt′), *adj.* [L. *facetus* elegant, fine, facetious.] *Archaic.* Facetious; witty.

fa·ce′ti·ae (fȧ·sē′shĭ·ē), *n. pl.* [L., fr. *facetus.* See FACETE.] Witty or humorous writings or sayings.

fa·ce′tious (-shŭs), *adj.* Given to or characterized by pleasantry or levity; jocose; exciting laughter; — often applied to unseemly or inappropriate levity. — **Syn.** See WITTY. — **fa·ce′tious·ly,** *adv.* — **fa·ce′tious·ness,** *n.*

face value. **a** The value indicated on the face. **b** Nominal value, as of a bond. **c** Apparent value; as, words taken at their *face value.*

fa′cial (fā′shăl), *adj.* **1.** Of or pertaining to the face; as, the *facial* nerve. **2.** Concerned with or improving the freshness, etc., of the human face, esp. by massage, cosmetics, etc.; as, *facial* massages, etc. — *n.* *Colloq.* A facial treatment or massage.

facial angle. The angle made by the intersection of the axis of the face with the axis of the skull.

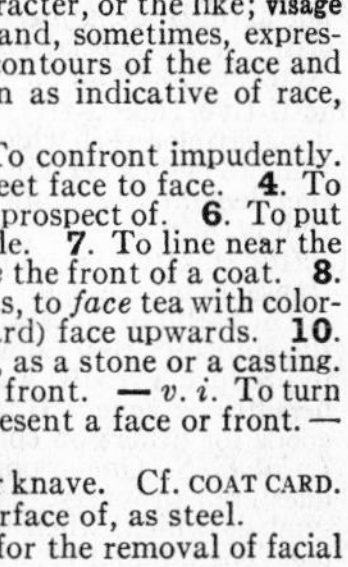

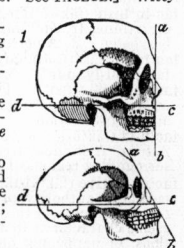

Facial Angles, 1, of an Orthognathous Skull and 2, of a Prognathous Skull. *a b* Axis of the Face; *c d* Axis of the Skull.

facial index. *Craniom.* Ratio of the breadth of the face to its length, usually expressed in hundredths of the latter. Cf. GNATHIC INDEX.

fa′ci·end (fā′shĭ·ĕnd), *n.* [From neut. of L. *faciendus,* gerundive of *facere* to do.] *Math.* A multiplicand.

-fa′cient (-fā′shĕnt). [L. *faciens, -entis,* pres. part. of *facere* to make, do.] A suffix signifying *making, causing,* as in cale*facient.*

fac′ile (făs′ĭl; 56), *adj.* [F., fr. L. *facilis,* fr. *facere* to make, do.] **1.** Easy to do; also, *Obs.,* easy to understand. **2.** Easy to surmount. **3.** Easy and mild in manner or disposition. **4.** Easily persuaded to good or bad; compliant. **5.** Expert; fluent; as, a *facile* speaker. — **Syn.** See EASY. — **fac′ile·ly,** *adv.* — **fac′ile·ness,** *n.*

‖**fa′ci·le prin′ceps** (făs′ĭ·lē prĭn′sĕps). [L.] Easily chief or first.

‖**fa′ci·lis de·scen′sus A·ver′no** *or* **A·ver′ni** (făs′ĭ·lĭs dē·sĕn′sŭs ȧ·vûr′nō, ȧ·vûr′nī). [L.] Descent to, or of, Avernus (the lower world, or hell) is easy; that is, the road to evil is easy.

fa·cil′i·tate (fȧ·sĭl′ĭ·tāt), *v. t.* To make easy or less difficult. — **fa·cil′i·ta′tion** (-tā′shŭn), *n.*

fa·cil′i·ty (-tĭ), *n.; pl.* -TIES (-tĭz). **1.** Quality of being easily performed; ease. **2.** Readiness from skill or use; dexterity. **3.** Easiness to be persuaded; — usually in a bad sense; pliancy. **4.** A thing that promotes the ease of any action, operation, or course of conduct; — usually in *pl.;* as, *facilities* for study.

fac′ing (făs′ĭng), *n.* **1.** A lining at the edge of a garment, as for ornament; *pl., Mil.,* the collar, cuffs, and trimmings of a uniform coat. **2.** A covering in front, for ornament or other purposes; as, the *facing* of an earthen slope, building, etc. **3.** Any material used for facing.

fa·cin′o·rous (fȧ·sĭn′ō·rŭs), *adj.* [L. *facinorosus,* fr. *facinus* deed, bad deed, fr. *facere* to do.] *Now Rare.* Atrociously wicked.

fac·sim′i·le (făk·sĭm′ĭ·lē; -lĭ), *n.; pl.* -LES (-lēz; -lĭz). [L. *fac simile* make like.] **1.** An exact copy. **2.** The process of transmitting and reproducing printed matter, still pictures, etc., by a system of telegraphic or radio communication. — **Syn.** See REPRODUCTION.

fact (făkt), *n.* [L. *factum* deed, act, fr. past part. of *facere* to do, make.] **1.** A thing done; deed; specif., an unlawful deed; crime. *Obs.,* except in "an accessory after the *fact,*" etc. **2.** That which has actual existence; an event. **3.** The quality of being actual; actuality; as, the realm of *fact* is distinct from that of fancy. **4.** The statement of a thing done or existing; as, his *facts* are false; loosely, the thing supposed (even though falsely) to be done or to exist. **5.** *Law.* Specif.: Usually in *pl.* Any of the circumstances or matters of a case as alleged; also, that which is of actual occurrence; reality as an event.

fac′tion (făk′shŭn), *n.* [F. and L.; F., fr. L. *factio* a making. See FASHION.] **1.** A party, combination, or clique within a state, party, or the like; — generally with the suggestion of contentiousness, self-seeking, or recklessness of the common good. **2.** Party spirit; also, dissension. **3.** *Obs.* A set or class of persons.

fac′tion·al (-ăl; -′l), *adj.* Of or pertaining to a faction; characterized by faction. — **fac′tion·al·ism** (-ĭz′m), *n.*

fac′tious (făk′shŭs), *adj.* [F. or L.; F. *factieux,* fr. L. *factiosus.*] **1.** Given to faction; raising dissensions; seditious. **2.** Proceeding from, or characterized by, faction. — **fac′tious·ly,** *adv.* — **fac′tious·ness,** *n.*

fac·ti′tious (făk·tĭsh′ŭs), *adj.* [L. *facticius,* fr. *facere* to make.] **1.** Artificial; sham. **2.** Formed by, or adapted to, an artificial standard; not natural; as, a *factitious* value; hence, induced or produced artificially or by special effort; as, the *factitious* vogue of an author. — **Syn.** See ARTIFICIAL. — **fac·ti′tious·ly,** *adv.* — **fac·ti′tious·ness,** *n.*

fac′ti·tive (făk′tĭ·tĭv), *adj.* [See FACT.] *Gram.* Pertaining to or designating a verb which expresses an idea of making or rendering anything to be of a certain character, and hence taking besides its object a complement (he *made* the water *wine;* ye *call* me *chief*). — **fac′ti·tive·ly,** *adv.*

fac′tor (făk′tẽr), *n.* [F. *facteur,* fr. L. *factor.*] **1.** One who acts, or transacts business, for another; an agent. **2.** *Obs. exc. Scot.* A steward or bailiff of an estate. **3.** The agent in charge of a trading post of the Hudson's Bay Company. **4.** One of the elements that contribute to produce a result; a constituent. **5.** *Biol.* The causative agent in heredity; a gene. **6. a** *Law.* A mercantile agent who sells or buys goods for others on commission; a commission merchant. **b** *Scot. & Local U. S.* One appointed by law to have charge of forfeited or sequestered property. **7.** *Math.* Any of the elements, quantities, or symbols which, when multiplied together, form a product. **8.** *Photog.* The number by which a given time is multiplied to give the complete time for developing or printing. **9.** *Physiol.* A substance involved in a physiological process, esp. nutrition, as a vitamin, a hormone, or a growth-promoting substance. — **Syn.** See AGENT; ELEMENT. — *v. t. Math.* To factorize. — **fac′tor·ship,** *n.*

fac′tor·age (-ĭj), *n.* **a** The business of a factor. **b** The commission or allowance of a factor.

fac·to′ri·al (făk·tō′rĭ·ăl; 70), *adj.* Of or relating to a factor or factors. — *n. Math.* A continued product of factors derived from any function $F(x)$ by successively increasing or decreasing the argument x by a constant, generally 1.

fac′tor·ize (făk′tẽr·īz), *v. t. Math.* To resolve into factors. — **fac′tor·i·za′tion** (-ĭ·zā′shŭn; -ī·zā′-), *n.*

fac′to·ry (făk′tō·rĭ), *n.; pl.* -RIES (-rĭz). **1.** A trading station where factors reside and transact business. **2.** A building, or collection of buildings, usually with equipment, for the manufacture of goods; a manufactory.

fac·to′tum (făk·tō′tŭm), *n.; pl.* FACTOTUMS (-tŭmz). [ML., lit., do everything, fr. *fac,* imper. of *facere* to do + *totus* all.] **1.** *Obs.* A busybody. **2.** A person employed to do all kinds of work.

fac′tu·al (făk′tū·ăl), *adj.* Relating to, or containing, facts; actual. — **fac′tu·al·ly,** *adv.*

fac′ture (făk′tūr), *n.* [F., fr. L. *factura* a making.] Act or manner of making or doing anything; — now used esp. of a literary, musical, or artistic production.

fac′u·la (făk′ū·lȧ), *n.; pl.* -LAE (-lē). [L., dim. of *fax, facis,* a torch.] *Astron.* A shining streak on the surface of the sun brighter than the surrounding regions of the photosphere. Cf. SUNSPOT.

fac′ul·ta′tive (făk′ŭl·tā′tĭv), *adj.* **1.** Having relation to the grant of a faculty, or authority, privilege, or the like; hence, optional; as, *facultative* enactments, or those which convey a faculty, or permission. **2.** Of such a character as to admit of existing under various forms or conditions, of happening or not happening, etc. **3.** *Biol.* Having the power to live under different conditions; as, a *facultative* parasite; — opp. to *obligate.* **4.** *Psychol.* Pertaining to a faculty or faculties.

fac′ul·ty (făk′ŭl·tĭ; -′l·tĭ), *n.; pl.* -TIES (-tĭz). [OF. *faculté,* fr. L. *facultas,* fr. *facilis* easy, fr. *facere* to make.] **1.** Ability to act or do. **2.** A physical power or function; as, the *faculty* of hearing. **3.** *Archaic.* That in which one is trained; trade. **4.** Natural aptitude. **5.** Power, authority, or prerogative given or conferred. **6.** A branch of learning or instruction in a university. **7.** The body of persons to whom are entrusted the government and instruction as of a university or college. **8.** The members of a profession or calling. **9.** *Psychol.* One of the powers into which psychologists formerly divided the mind (as will, reason, instinct), and through the interaction of which they endeavored to explain all mental phenomena. — **Syn.** See GIFT.

fad (făd), *n.* A custom, amusement, or the like, followed for a time with exaggerated zeal; a craze. — **Syn.** See FASHION. — **fad′dish** (făd′ĭsh), *adj.* — **fad′dist** (-ĭst), *n.* — **fad′dy** (-ĭ), *adj.*

fade (fād), *v. i.* [OF. *fader,* fr. *fade* pale, wan, dull.] **1.** To grow weak; to decay; wither, as a plant. **2.** To lose freshness or brilliance; to grow dim. **3.** To sink away; to vanish. **4.** *Motion Pictures & Radio.* To change gradually in distinctness or loudness, as a picture on a screen or a sound effect; — with *in* or *out.* — *v. t.* **1.** To cause to wither, dim, etc. **2.** *Motion Pictures & Radio.* To cause to fade; — with *in* or *out.* — *n.* Act or instance of fading; as, a *fade*-out of a motion-picture close-up.

‖**fade** (fȧd), *adj.* [F.] Insipid; flat; commonplace.

fade′less (fād′lĕs; -lĭs), *adj.* Unfading. — **fade′less·ly,** *adv.*

fadge (făj), *v. i. Rare.* To suit; hence, to succeed.

fae′cal, fae′ces, etc. Vars. of FECAL, etc.

fa′ẽr·ie, fa′ẽr·y (fā′ẽr·ĭ; fâr′ĭ), *n.* [See FAIRY.] **1.** *Archaic.* The world of fairies, esp. of such fairies as were first drawn by Spenser. **2.** *Obs.* A fairy.

faer′y (fâr′ĭ), *adj.* Also **faer′ie.** Fairy.

Faf′nir (fäv′nĭr), *n.* [ON. *Fāfnir.*] In the Eddas and the Volsunga Saga, a giant who, in the form of a dragon, guards the treasure of Andvari. He is slain by Sigurd.

fag (făg), *n. Colloq.* A cigarette.

fag (făg), *v. i.;* FAGGED (făgd); FAG′GING. [Perh. the same word as E. *flag* to droop.] **1.** To labor to weariness; to drudge. **2.** To act as a fag. — *v. t.* **1.** To tire by labor; to exhaust. **2.** To use or treat as a fag. — **Syn.** See TIRE. — *n.* **1.** *Colloq. Brit.* Toil; drudgery. **2.** In English schools, a boy who does service for another boy of a higher form; hence, a menial; a drudge.

fa·ga′ceous (fȧ·gā′shŭs), *adj.* [L. *fagus* beech.] *Bot.* Belonging to the beech family (Fagaceae). See BEECH.

fag end. The last part or coarser end of a web of cloth, the untwisted end of a rope, etc.; hence, a remnant; a worn, poor, or last part.

fag′ot, fag′got (făg′ŭt), *n.* [F. *fagot.*] **1.** A bundle of sticks or twigs, as for fuel or a fascine. **2.** *Ironworking.* A bundle of pieces of wrought iron to be worked over into bars or other shapes by rolling or hammering at a welding heat; a pile. — *v. t.* To make a fagot of; to bind in a fagot.

fag′ot·ing, fag′got·ing, *n. Embroidery.* A process of drawing out horizontal threads from a fabric, as linen, and tying the remaining cross threads into hourglass-shaped bunches; also, an openwork stitch joining hemmed edges.

Fahr′en·heit (făr′ĕn·hīt; fär′-), *adj.* Designating, or conforming to, the scale used by G. D. Fahrenheit (1686–1736) in the graduation of his thermometer. — *n.* The Fahrenheit thermometer or scale. On the Fahrenheit thermometer, under standard atmospheric pressure, the boiling point of water is at 212 degrees and the freezing point at 32 degrees above the zero of its scale. The zero point represents the temperature produced by mixing equal quantities, by weight, of snow and common salt. Abbr. *F.* or *Fahr.* Cf. CENTIGRADE THERMOMETER; see THERMOMETER, *Illust.*

fa′ïence′ (fȧ′yäNs′; fī′äNs′; fā′-), *n.* [F., fr. *Faenza,* Italy.] Decorative glazed earthenware or pottery, esp. ornamental tile.

fail (fāl), *v. i.* [OF. *faillir,* fr. L. *fallere, falsum,* to deceive, fail.] **1.** To be wanting; to fall short; to come to an end. **2.** To fall away; to decline; decay; also, to fade or die away. **3.** To become weaker; as, the old man is *failing* rapidly. **4.** To be found wanting in an action, a duty, an effect, etc.; to miss. **5.** *Rare.* To err; to be mistaken. **6.** To become bankrupt or insolvent. — *v. t.* **1.** To be wanting to; to disappoint; desert. **2.** *Rare.* To leave undone; to neglect. **3.** To reject as deficient, as in a test; as, to *fail* a student; also, to prove deficient in; as, to *fail* an examination. — *n.* Failure; — chiefly in *without fail.*

fail′ing, *adj.* That fails. — *n.* A failure; hence, a deficiency; weakness; as, a mental *failing.* — **Syn.** See FAULT. — *prep.* **a** Lacking; as, *failing* a purchaser, he rented the farm. **b** In case of failure of; as, *failing* his arrival, we shall stay here. — **fail′ing·ly,** *adv.*

faille (fīl), *n.* [F.] A ribbed silk fabric of plain weave, used for dresses, men's ties, etc.

fail′ure (fāl′ūr), *n.* [Earlier *failer,* fr. AF. *failer,* for F. *faillir,* the infin. used as n. See FAIL.] **1.** A falling short; a deficiency or lack. **2.** Omission to perform; as, *failure* to keep a promise. **3.** Want of success; as, *failure* in an examination. **4.** Deterioration; decay; as, *failure* of intellect. **5.** A becoming insolvent; bankruptcy. **6.** A person or thing that has failed.

fain (fān), *adj.* [AS. *fægen.*] **1.** Well-pleased; glad. **2.** Relatively satisfied or contented; also, constrained; obliged. **3.** *Archaic.* Inclined; desirous; as, *fain* to be wise. — *adv.* With joy; also, preferably; — now with *would.*

fai·naigue′ (fȧ·nāg′), *v. i. & t.;* FAI·NAIGUED′ (-nāgd′); FAI·NAI′GUING (-nā′gĭng). Also **fi·na′gle** (fĭ·nā′gl). To revoke at cards; hence, to shirk; to cheat; to use, or obtain by, devious methods. — **fai·nai′guer** (-nā′gẽr), *n.*

fai′ne·ance (fā′nē·ăns), **fai′ne·an·cy** (-ăn·sĭ), *n.* Literally, do-nothingness; inactivity; indolence.

fai′né·ant (fā′nē·ănt; *F.* fĕ′nā′äN′), *adj.* [F. (after *faire* to do and *neant* nothing), fr. OF. *feignant.*] Inactive; idle. — *n.* An idler; a sluggard.

faint (fānt), *adj.* [OF. *faint, feint,* past part. of *faindre, feindre,* to feign, shirk. See FEIGN.] **1.** Wanting in courage or spirit; timorous; cowardly. **2.** Lacking strength; weak; languid. **3.** Producing a sensation of faintness; oppressive. **4.** Performed weakly or feebly. **5.** Lacking distinctness; dim. — *n.* Act or state of fainting; a swoon. — *v. i.* **1.** *Archaic.* To sink into dejection; to lose courage or spirit. **2.** *Poetic.* To become weak. **3.** To swoon. **4.** *Rare.* To lose brightness. — **faint′er,** *n.* — **faint′ish,** *adj.* — **faint′ish·ness,** *n.* — **faint′ly,** *adv.* — **faint′ness,** *n.*

faint′heart′ed (-här′tĕd; -tĭd; 2), *adj.* Cowardly; timid. — **faint′heart′ed·ly,** *adv.* — **faint′heart′ed·ness,** *n.*

faints (fānts), *n. pl.* Also **feints** (fānts). [See FAINT weak.] The weak and impure spirit which comes over last in the distillation of whisky or other liquor.

fair (fâr), *adj.* [AS. *fæger.*] **1.** Pleasing to the eye; beautiful. **2. a** Plausible; inspiring hope; as, *fair* promises. **b** Gracious; courteous; as, *fair* speech. **3.** Ample in size; as, a *fair* estate. **4.** *Obs.* **a** Desirable. **b** Elegant. **5.** Light; blond, as opposed to brunet; as, *fair* hair. **6. a** Characterized by frankness, honesty, impartiality, or candor; just. **b** In conformity with the established rules of a game, task, etc.; as, a *fair* blow. **7.** Clean; pure; spotless; as, a *fair* name. **8.** Without sudden or angular deviation, as in line or surface; smooth; flowing; as, a ship's *fair* curves. **9.** Distinct; legible; as, *fair* handwriting. **10.** Open to legitimate pursuit; — in phrase ***fair game.*** **11.** Free from marked merit or defect; hence, average; pretty good; as, *fair* health. **12.** Free from obstacles; open; as, in *fair* view. **13. a** Not stormy; favorable; — said of the sky, weather, etc. **b** Specif., free or nearly free from rain, hail, or snow. **14.** Likely; promising; as, a *fair* chance of success.

Syn. (1) See BEAUTIFUL.

(2) **Fair, just, equitable, impartial, unbiased, dispassionate, objective** mean free from favor to either or any side. **Fair** implies an elimination of one's own feelings, prejudices, etc.; **just**, an exact following of a standard of what is right and proper without regard to other considerations; **equitable**, less rigid than *just*, generally implies fair and equal treatment of all concerned; **impartial** implies absence of favor for or prejudice against either or any person, party, or side; **unbiased**, even more strongly, the absence of all prejudice or prepossession and a disposition to be fair to all; **dispassionate**, freedom from the influence of strong feeling and great temperateness in judgment; **objective**, a tendency to view events, persons, etc., impartially and as apart from oneself.

— *adv.* **1.** In a fair manner. **2.** *Obs.* Quietly; moderately. **3.** Evenly; squarely; as, struck *fair* between the eyes.

— *n.* *Archaic.* **1.** Fairness; beauty. **2.** A fair woman; a sweetheart. **3.** That which is fair or fortunate.

— *v. i.* Of the weather, to clear.

fair (fâr), *n.* [OF. *feire* (F. *foire*), fr. L. *feria* holiday, pl. *feriae* days of rest, holidays, festivals.] **1.** A gathering of buyers and sellers at a stated time and place for trade. **2.** A festival, and sale of fancy articles, etc., usually for charity. **3.** A competitive exhibition of wares, farm products, etc.; as, a county *fair.*

fair and square. *Colloq.* Honest; firm; honestly; firmly.

fair ball. *Baseball.* A batted ball that first strikes the ground beyond first or third base and within the foul lines, or that comes to rest before passing first or third base and within the foul lines, or that after striking the ground passes first or third base within the foul lines.

fair catch. *Amer. Football.* A catch of a kicked ball made by a player on side who makes a prescribed signal that he will not attempt to advance the ball when caught. He may not then be interfered with.

fair copy. A neat and exact copy, esp. of a corrected draft.

Fair Deal. The national domestic program, including measures with far-reaching social implications, recommended for enactment to the Eighty-first Congress by President Harry S. Truman. — **Fair Dealer.**

fair green. *Golf.* A fairway.

fair′ing, *n.* **a** A present, orig. at or from a fair. **b** Due reward or punishment; deserts; as, to give one his *fairing.*

fair′ing, *n.* A member or structure whose primary function is to produce a smooth outline and to reduce drag, as in an aircraft.

fair′ish (fâr′ĭsh), *adj.* Tolerably good, well, or large.

fair′-lead′ (fâr′lēd′), *n.* *Naut.* **a** Also **fair′-lead′er** (-lēd′ẽr). A block, ring, or strip of plank with holes, serving as a guide for the running rigging or any rope, to keep it from chafing. **b** Sometimes **fair lead.** A course of running rope that avoids all chafing.

fair′ly, *adv.* **1.** *Obs.* **a** Handsomely; also, speciously. **b** Softly. **c** Courteously. **2.** Actually; positively; as, he is *fairly* exhausted. **3.** Favorably; as, a town *fairly* situated. **4.** In a fair manner; justly. **5.** Plainly; distinctly. **6.** Tolerably; as, she sings *fairly* well.

fair′-mind′ed (-mīn′dĕd; -dĭd; 2), *adj.* Unprejudiced; just; judicial; honest. — **fair′-mind′ed·ness,** *n.*

fair′ness (fâr′nĕs; -nĭs), *n.* State of being fair; honesty; impartiality.

fair′-spo′ken (-spō′kĕn; 2), *adj.* Using fair speech, or uttered with fairness; bland; civil; courteous; plausible.

fair′-trade′ a·gree′ment. An agreement, contract, or code executed between manufacturer and distributor prescribing a minimum price for resale of a commodity bearing the trade-mark of the manufacturer. This type of contract is legal, in the United States, under the Miller-Tydings Act (Aug. 17, 1937) for intrastate transactions in states in which a corresponding statute is in effect.

fair′way′ (fâr′wā′), *n.* **1.** The navigable part of a river, bay, etc. **2.** *Golf.* That part of a playing course exclusive of tees, putting greens, and hazards; — opposed to *rough.*

fair′y (fâr′ĭ), *n.*; *pl.* FAIRIES (-ĭz). [OF. *faierie, faerie,* enchantment, fairy folk, fr. LL. *fata* one of the Fates, hence, fairy, fr. L. *fatum* fate. See FATE.] A minor supernatural being, supposed to be able to assume human form (usually diminutive), and to meddle in human affairs. **— *adj.*** Of the nature of, or like, a fairy or fairies; belonging to or associated with fairies. — **fair′y·hood** (-hŏŏd), *n.* — **fair′y·ism** (-ĭz′m), *n.* — **fair′y·like′** (-līk′), *adj.*

fair′y·land′ (-lănd′), *n.* The land or abode of fairies.

fairy ring. A circle in a lawn or meadow consisting of luxuriant vegetation or of certain mushroom fungi.

fairy tale *or* **story.** A simple narrative concerning fairies, dwarfs, ogres, magicians, etc., told for the amusement of children; hence, *Colloq.*, a fib.

‖**fait′ ac′com′pli′** (fĕ′-tȧ′kôɴ′plē′). [F.] A thing accomplished and presumably irrevocable.

faith (fāth), *n.* [OF. *feid, feit,* later *fei,* F. *foi,* fr. L. *fides.*] **1.** Belief in God, revelation, or the like; as, soundness of *faith;* esp., orthodoxy in theology; in a practical religious sense, trust in God. **2.** Fidelity to one's promises, or allegiance to duty, or to a person; loyalty. **3.** That which is believed; esp., a system of religious beliefs. **4.** Complete confidence, esp. in someone or something open to question or suspicion. — **Syn.** See BELIEF. — ***interj.*** Also **in faith.** By my faith; verily.

faith cure. A method or practice of treating diseases by prayer and exercise of faith in God; also, a cure by this method.

faith′ful (fāth′fŏŏl; -f'l), *adj.* **1.** Full of faith; disposed to believe, esp. in God. **2.** Firm in adherence to promises, contracts, treaties, etc.; loyal. **3.** True in affection or allegiance. **4.** Worthy of confidence and belief; accurate. — **faith′ful·ly,** *adv.* — **faith′ful·ness,** *n.* — ***the faithful.*** **1.** Church members in good standing. **2.** The adherents of any system of religious belief, esp. of Mohammedanism. **3.** The devoted or loyal members of an organization.

Syn. Faithful, loyal, constant, stanch (*or* **staunch**), **steadfast** (*or* **stedfast**), **resolute** mean firmly adhering to a person or thing to which one is bound by love, allegiance, etc. **Faithful** implies unswerving adherence both to the person or thing and to the oath, pledge, or the like, by which the tie was contracted; **loyal** adds to *faithful* an implication of unwillingness to be tempted from that adherence; **constant** stresses firmness of devotion or attachment, but carries a weaker implication of strict adherence to one's vows, pledges, or the like; **stanch,** from its earlier sense of watertight, suggests an inherent imperviousness to all influences that would weaken one's loyalty; **steadfast** implies a steady and unwavering course not only in love, allegiance, etc., but more widely, as in quality or character; **resolute** implies steadfast determination, especially in adhering to a person, a cause, an end, or the like.

faith′less, *adj.* **1.** Not believing. **2.** Not believing in God or religion, esp. the Christian religion. **3.** Not observant of promises or covenants; false; disloyal. **4.** Delusive; unstable; unsatisfying. — **faith′less·ly,** *adv.* — **faith′less·ness,** *n.*

Syn. Faithless, false, disloyal, traitorous, treacherous, perfidious mean lacking in faithfulness. **Faithless** applies to any person, utterance, or act that implies in any degree a breach of a vow, a pledge, an allegiance, or the like; **false** stresses a failure to be faithful, loyal, or constant; **disloyal** implies lack of faithfulness in thought, in words, or in actions to a friend, superior, party, or the like; **traitorous** implies either actual treason or a serious betrayal of trust or confidence; **treacherous** implies, narrowly, readiness to betray trust or confidence but, loosely, especially in reference to things, a false and delusive appearance of safety; **perfidious** implies baseness or vileness as well as an incapacity for faithfulness in the person concerned.

fai′tour (fā′tẽr), *n.* [OF. *faitor* a doer, fr. L. *factor.*] **a** Formerly, an impostor. **b** *Dial.* A loafer.

fake (fāk), *n.* *Naut.* One loop of a coil of rope which is coiled free for running. — ***v. t.*** *Naut.* To coil (a rope, line, or hawser) in fakes.

fake, *v. t.* *Colloq.* To work upon in some special way, esp. so as to impart a false character or appearance to; to furbish or "doctor up" in order to deceive; also, to counterfeit; to simulate; feign. — ***v. i.*** To practice faking anything. — ***n.*** *Colloq.* **1.** A counterfeit or imitation presented as genuine with fraudulent intent; a fraud. **2.** A device or apparatus visible to the spectators, though they may not be aware of it, used by a magician in performing a trick. Cf. GIMMICK **b.** — **Syn.** See IMPOSTURE. — ***adj.*** *Colloq.* That is a fake; false; sham.

fake′ment (fāk′mĕnt), *n.* *Colloq.* A fake.

fak′er (fāk′ẽr), *n.* One who fakes; specif.: **a** *Colloq.* A peddler of petty things at fairs, etc. **b** *Colloq.* A fraud.

fa·kir′ (fȧ·kēr′; fā′kẽr), *n.* Also **fa·keer′.** [Ar. *faqīr* poor.] A member of any sect of Moslems taking a vow of poverty; a dervish; hence, a member of any of the religious orders of Islam; hence, loosely, and esp. in India, a mendicant or an itinerant wonder-worker of other religions; a yogi.

fa la, fal la, *or* **fa′-la′** (fä′lä′), *n.* *Music.* **a** A refrain in old songs. **b** Hence, a kind of part song with such a refrain.

Fa·lan′gist (fȧ·lăn′jĭst), *n.* [Sp. *Falangista,* fr. *falange* phalanx.] A member of a Spanish fascist organization, **Fa·lan′ge** (fä·läng′hā).

fal′ba·la (făl′bȧ·lȧ), **fal′be·lo** (-bĕ·lō), *n.* A furbelow.

fal′cate (făl′kāt), *adj.* [L. *falcatus,* fr. *falx, falcis,* sickle, scythe.] Hooked or curved like a sickle; as, a *falcate* leaf; a *falcate* claw.

fal′chion (fôl′chŭn; -shŭn), *n.* [OF. *fauchon,* fr. L. *falx, falcis,* sickle, scythe.] A broad-bladed sword, slightly curved, of the Middle Ages; hence, *Poetic,* a sword.

fal′ci·form (făl′sĭ·fôrm), *adj.* [L. *falx, falcis,* sickle + *-form.*] Having the shape of a scythe or sickle.

fal′con (fôl′kŭn; fô′kŭn), *n.* [OF. *faucon, faulcon,* fr. LL. *falco.*] **1. a** In old usage, any of various hawks trained for the sport of hawking, or falconry; esp., the ***peregrine falcon*** (*Falco peregrinus*). Cf. TERCEL. **b** Now, any of various hawks (see HAWK) constituting a subfamily (Falconinae, type genus *Falco*), having long wings and a notch and tooth (sometimes two teeth) on the edge of the upper mandible. See GYRFALCON; KESTREL; SPARROW HAWK, 2. **2.** A light piece of ordnance (15th–17th centuries).

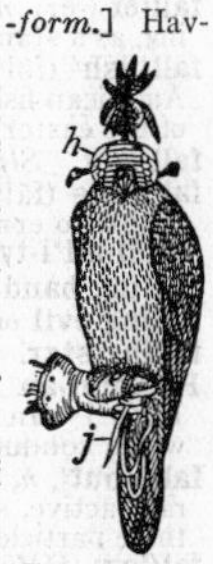

Falcon on fist of falconer. Head is enclosed in a Hood, *h,* with feathers; *j* Jesses. (1/12)

fal′con·er (-ẽr), *n.* A breeder or trainer of hawks for hunting; also, one who hunts with falcons.

fal′co·net (fôl′kŭn·ĕt; fô′-), *n.* [Dim. of *falcon.*] **1.** A smaller type falcon, or piece of ordnance. **2.** Any of several very small Asiatic falcons (genus *Microhierax*).

fal′con-gen′tle, *n.* [F. *faucon-gentil.* See FALCON; GENTEEL.] The female peregrine falcon.

fal′con·ry (fôl′kŭn·rĭ; fô′-), *n.* Art of training falcons; also, the sport of hunting with falcons.

fal′de·ral′ (făl′dĕ·răl′; -răl′), **fal′de·rol′** (-rŏl′; -rŏl′), **fol′de·rol′** (fŏl′-), *n.* **1.** A refrain in old songs. **2.** A trifle; a piece of finery; a bit of nonsense.

fald′stool′ (fôld′stōōl′), *n.* **1.** A folding stool or chair, esp. one used by a bishop. **2.** A similar stool or small desk at which one kneels during devotions; esp., one used by the king of England at his coronation. **3.** Specif., *Ch. of Eng.*, the desk from which the litany is read.

fall (fôl), *v. i.*; FELL (fĕl); FALL′EN (fôl′ĕn); FALL′ING. [AS. *feallan.*] **1.** To pass downwards freely; to drop; also, to hang or depend freely. **2.** Hence: **a** To become of lower degree; as, the temperature *fell.* **b** To come or come to pass as if by descending; as, the night *falls* swiftly. **c** To be uttered; as, words *fall* from the lips. **d** To be lowered, as the glance or the eyes. **e** To be dropped, or born; — said of the young of certain animals. **f** To take a lower tone; as, the voice *falls.* **3.** To cease to be erect; to take suddenly a recumbent posture; as, a child totters and *falls.* **4.** Hence: **a** To stumble; to be entrapped; as, to *fall* into error. **b** To become wounded or dead; esp., to die, as in battle. **c** To be overthrown or destroyed. **d** To break down; to collapse. **e** To lose station, dignity, etc. **5.** To move or extend downward; as, the land *falls* to a river. **6.** Hence: **a** To subside, abate, decline; to ebb, as the tide. **b** To lose strength, character, vigor, or activity; specif., to decline in value, price, etc.; as, stocks *fell* several points. **c** To assume a look of shame or dejection; — of the face. **7.** To occur; to arrive; as, Christmas *falls* on Friday. **8.** Specif.: **a** To happen; to come by chance. **b** To come or pass by lot, distribution, inheritance, or otherwise. **c** *Obs.* To result; to turn out. **9.** To pass somewhat suddenly, and passively, into a new state of body or mind; as, to *fall* asleep. **10.** To strike; to impinge; as, the shot *fell* near him. **11.** To find or have its place or station; as, the accent *falls* on the ultima. **12.** To be arranged or divisible (*into*). — *v. t. Dial.* To fell. **fall aboard.** *Naut.* To collide with. — **fall back.** To recede or retreat; to give way. — **fall behind** *or* **behindhand.** To drop to the rear; to lag behind; to be in arrears. — **fall flat.** To produce no response or result. — **fall foul of** *or* (*formerly*) **on** *or* **upon.** **a** *Naut.* To have a collision with; to become entangled with. **b** To attack. **c** To quarrel with; to have trouble with. — **fall from.** *Archaic.* **a** To depart from agreement with; to fail in duty to, as a king. **b** To give up, as a custom. — **fall from grace.** To sin; to backslide. — **fall home.** *Shipbuilding.* To curve inward; — said of the timbers or upper parts of a ship's side. — **fall in.** **a** To sink inwards; as, the roof *fell in.* **b** To agree or concur. **c** *Mil.* To take one's proper place in line. — **fall off.** **a** To drop, as ripe fruits. **b** To become estranged, as friends. **c** To diminish or deteriorate; to decline, as in health. **d** *Naut.* To deviate to leeward of the point to which the ship was headed. — **fall out.** **a** To quarrel. **b** To happen; to come to pass; hence, to prove to be; to turn out. **c** *Mil.* To leave one's place in the ranks. — **fall short.** **a** To become or be deficient. **b** To fail to attain, reach, or perform. — **fall through.** To come to nothing; to fail; miscarry. — **fall to.** **a** To begin; to set about actively. **b** To come to blows. — **fall upon.** **a** To attack. **b** To hit upon; to chance upon. **c** To devolve upon as a charge or responsibility.

— *n.* **1.** Act of falling; a dropping or descending. **2.** **a** Downfall; degradation; ruin. **b** The surrender or capture of a besieged place. **3.** A falling out, off, or away; a dropping or shedding; as, the *fall* of leaves. **4.** The season when leaves fall from trees; autumn. **5.** Act of dropping or tumbling from an erect posture; as, his *fall* on the ice. **6.** Lapse from innocence or goodness; specif., ***the Fall***, the act of Adam and Eve in eating the forbidden fruit, often called the **fall of man.** **7.** A sinking; subsidence; as, a *fall* in temperature. **8.** A downward direction; declivity. **9.** **a** The discharge of a stream into the ocean, lake, or pond. **b** A waterfall; — usually in *pl.* **10.** **a** A thing or quantity that falls; as, a two-inch *fall* of rain. **b** The distance which anything falls. **c** Decrease in price or value; as, the *fall* of prices. **11.** Dropping (birth), as of lambs; also, the number born. **12.** *Costume.* **a** Formerly, a wide turned-down ruff or collar. **b** A woman's veil hanging from a hat. **13.** *Mech.* **a** That part of the rope or chain of a tackle to which the power is applied in hoisting. **b** A hoisting-tackle rope. **14.** *Naut.* **a** A break in a deck line from one level to another. **b** *pl.* The tackle used in lowering and hoisting a ship's boat from or to the davits. **15.** *Wrestling.* Act or method of throwing an opponent; hence, a bout at the game.

— *adj.* Of or pert. to fall (the season); occurring or done in the fall; suitable for the fall; as, *fall* clothes.

fal·la′cious (fă·lā′shŭs), *adj.* **1.** Embodying a fallacy; misleading; as, *fallacious* reasoning. **2.** Disappointing; delusive; as, *fallacious* hopes. — **fal·la′cious·ly,** *adv.* — **fal·la′cious·ness,** *n.*

fal′la·cy (făl′à·sĭ), *n.; pl.* -CIES (-sĭz). [L. *fallacia*, fr. *fallax* deceitful, fr. *fallere* to deceive.] **1.** Deceptive appearance; deception. **2.** A false idea; also, the liability to err; fallaciousness. **3.** *Logic.* Any reasoning failing to satisfy the conditions of logical proof or violating the laws of valid argument.

fal′-lal′ (făl′lăl′), *n.* A bit of finery, esp. in dress. — *adj.* Fond of fal-lals; affected. — **fal′-lal′er·y** (-ẽr·ĭ), *n.*

fall dandelion. A European scapose herb (*Leontodon autumnalis*) of the chicory family, naturalized in the United States.

fall′en (fôl′ĕn), *adj.* Dropped; prostrate; degraded (of a woman, having lost chastity); ruined; decreased; dead.

fall′er (-ẽr), *n.* **1.** One who falls. **2.** *Mach.* A part that acts by falling, as a stamp in a fulling mill.

fall′fish′ (fôl′fĭsh′), *n.; pl.*, see FISH. Any of several common North American fishes of the carp family, esp. one (*Leucosomus corporalis*) of the eastern United States. Cf. CHUB, 2 **a**.

fall guy. *Slang, U. S.* One who is easily victimized.

fal′li·ble (făl′ĭ·b′l), *adj.* [ML. *fallibilis*, fr. L. *fallere* to deceive.] Liable to err; exposed to the danger of erring or of being deceived. — **fal′li·bil′i·ty** (-bĭl′ĭ·tĭ), *n.* — **fal′li·bly,** *adv.*

fall′ing band (fôl′ĭng). See BAND, 6 **b**.

falling evil *or* **sickness.** Epilepsy.

falling star. A meteor.

Fal·lo′pi·an tube (fă·lō′pĭ·ăn). [After *Fallopius* of Modena (d. 1562).] In female mammals, the oviduct; one of the pair of tubes which conduct the egg from the ovary to the uterus.

fall′-out′, *n.* The descent through the atmosphere of particles, often radioactive, stirred up by, or resulting from, a nuclear explosion; also, these particles, collectively.

fal′low (făl′ō), *n.* [ME. *falow;* akin to AS. *fealh* a harrow, *fælging* fallow land.] **1.** Land ordinarily used for crops, when allowed to lie idle during the growing season. **2.** The tilling of land, without sowing it, for a season. — *adj.* Left untilled or unsowed after plowing; uncultivated. — *v. t.* To plow, harrow, and break up, as land, without seeding, to destroy weeds and insects and render it mellow.

fal′low, *adj.* [AS. *fealu, fealo.*] Pale; pale-yellow; as, a *fallow* deer.

fallow deer. [From its *fallow* or pale-yellow color.] A European deer (*Dama dama*), much smaller than the red deer. In summer both sexes are spotted with white. Cf. DEER.

false (fôls), *adj.;* FALS′ER (fôl′sẽr); FALS′EST. [L. and OF.; OF. *fals, faus*, fr. L. *falsus*, past part. of *fallere* to deceive.] **1.** Not true; incorrect; as, a *false* statement. **2.** Uttering falsehood; dishonest. **3.** Not faithful or loyal; untrue; treacherous. **4.** Not genuine or real; hypocritical; sham; feigned. **5.** Not well founded; not trustworthy; wrong; as, a *false* claim. **6.** **a** Not properly so called; pseudo; as, *false* stratification. **b** In plant names, of a kind related to or like another species bearing the unqualified vernacular; as, *false* foxglove. **7** *Mach. & Building.* **a** Not essential or permanent; as, a *false* bottom, pillar. **b** Fitting over a main part to strengthen it, to protect it, or to disguise its appearance. **8.** Inaccurate in pitch; out of tune.

Syn. (1) **False, wrong** mean neither true nor right. **False,** however, nearly always carries an implication of deceiving or of being deceived, and **wrong** of deviation from that which is right, true, or correct. *Wrong* therefore is simple and direct, and *false* often complicated, in meaning; as, a *wrong* answer is merely not right or correct; a *false* answer is not only this but mendacious, misleading, or the like.

(2) See FAITHLESS.

false foxglove. Any herb of the genus *Aureolaria*, resembling the foxglove, but with yellow flowers.

false′heart′ed (fôls′här′tĕd; -tĭd; 2), *adj.* Treacherous; perfidious.

false′hood (fôls′hŏŏd), *n.* **1.** Want of truth or accuracy; falsity. **2.** A lie; also, the practice of lying. **3.** *Obs.* **a** Treachery; perfidy. **b** Imposture; a counterfeit.

false horizon. See HORIZON, 3 **c**.

false imprisonment. *Law.* The imprisonment of a person contrary to law.

false indigo. See BAPTISIA.

false keel. A thin keel below the main keel, to serve as a protection and to increase the ship's lateral resistance.

false′ly (fôls′lĭ), *adv.* In a false manner.

false′ness (-nĕs; -nĭs), *n.* State of being false; inaccuracy; deceitfulness; treachery.

false ribs. *Anat.* Those ribs the cartilages of which do not unite directly (or at all) with the sternum. Cf. FLOATING RIBS.

false topaz. See TOPAZ, 1 **c**.

fal·set′to (fôl·sĕt′ō), *n.; pl.* -TOS (-ōz). [It., dim. of *falso*, fr. L. *falsus.* See FALSE.] **1.** A false or artificial voice; specif., *Music & Phonet.*, that voice of a man which lies above his natural voice. **2.** A falsetto singer. — *adj.* Of the quality and compass of falsetto; also, singing in falsetto. — *adv.* In falsetto; as, to sing *falsetto.*

false wintergreen. See WINTERGREEN.

fal′si·fy (fôl′sĭ·fī), *v. t.;* -FIED (-fīd); -FY′ING. [F. *falsifier*, fr. ML. *falsificare.* See FALSE, *adj.;* -FY.] **1.** To make false; as: **a** To represent falsely. **b** To make false by mutilation or addition, as a record. **c** To alter from the normal form or correct standard. **2.** To prove to be false, or untrue. — *v. i.* To tell lies; to lie. — **fal′si·fi·ca′tion** (-fĭ·kā′shŭn), *n.* — **fal′si·fi′er** (fôl′sĭ·fī′ẽr), *n.*

fal′si·ty (-tĭ), *n.; pl.* -TIES (-tĭz). **1.** Character or quality of being false, or untrue. **2.** That which is false; a lie.

Fal·staff′i·an (fôl·stăf′ĭ·ăn; 58), *adj.* Like, or characteristic of, Shakespeare's Sir John Falstaff, a grossly fat, witty, convivial braggart; also, like the regiment of ragged rapscallions formed by him.

falt′boat′ (fält′bōt′; fôlt′-), *n.* [G. *faltboot* folding boat.] A collapsible boat made of rubberized sailcloth stretched over a knockdown framework, similar in size and shape to a kayak.

fal′ter (fôl′tẽr), *v. i.* [ME. *falteren, faltren*, of uncert. origin.] To move unsteadily or waveringly; as: **a** To stumble; totter. **b** To hesitate; to stammer. **c** To waver; flinch; give way. — *v. t.* To utter with hesitation, or in a broken manner; as, to *falter* an excuse. — **Syn.** See HESITATE. — *n.* A faltering or faltering sound; quaver; unsteadiness. — **fal′ter·er,** *n.*

fal′ter·ing, *adj.* That falters. — **fal′ter·ing·ly,** *adv.*

fame (fām), *n.* [OF., fr. L. *fama*, fr. root of *fari* to speak.] **1.** *Archaic.* Public report or rumor. **2.** **a** Public estimation; reputation. **b** Lofty reputation; renown. — *v. t.* **1.** *Archaic.* To report currently, widely, or honorably. **2.** To make famous or renowned. — **famed** (fāmd), *adj.*

Fa·meuse′ (fȧ·mūz′; *F.* fȧ′mûz′), *n.* [F., fem. of *fameux* famous.] A late autumn variety of apple; — called also *snow apple.*

fa·mil′ial (fȧ·mĭl′yăl), *adj.* [L. *familia* family.] Of, pertaining to, or characteristic of a family.

fa·mil′iar (fȧ·mĭl′yẽr), *adj.* [OF. *familier*, fr. L. *familiaris*, fr. *familia* family. See FAMILY.] **1.** *Archaic.* Of or pertaining to a family; domestic. **2.** **a** Closely acquainted or intimate. **b** Having an intimate knowledge of. **3.** **a** *Archaic.* Easy; affable; accessible. **b** Unduly or wrongly intimate; bold. **c** Unconstrained; free from formality or reserve; as, *familiar* conversation. **4.** Of animals, tamed; domesticated. **5.** Well known; frequent.

Syn. (1) **Familiar, intimate** mean close or indicative of closeness in relation or association. **Familiar** stresses characteristics associated with family life, such as informality, ease of address, readiness to take liberties, etc.; **intimate,** those associated with persons who are in very close contact through ties of blood, friendship, etc., and who have confidential relations with one another.

(2) See COMMON.

— *n.* **1.** An intimate; companion. **2.** *Obs.* A member of a family or household. **3.** A familiar spirit. **4.** *Court of Inquisition.* A confidential officer employed especially in apprehending the accused. **5.** *R.C.Ch.* A member of the household of a high church dignitary who renders domestic but not menial services.

fa·mil′i·ar′i·ty (fȧ·mĭl′ĭ·ăr′ĭ·tĭ; -yăr′ĭ·tĭ; 58), *n.; pl.* -TIES (-tĭz). **1.** State of being familiar; intimacy. **2.** Close acquaintance with, or knowledge of, anything. **3.** Anything said or done by one person to another informally; esp., *pl.*, such actions and words as propriety and courtesy do not warrant; liberties.

fa·mil′iar·ize (fȧ·mĭl′yẽr·īz), *v. t.* **1.** To make familiar; to accustom; to make to feel at ease. **2.** To make well known, accustomed, or familiar. — **fa·mil′iar·i·za′tion** (-ĭ·zā′shŭn; -ī·zā′-), *n.*

fa·mil′iar·ly (-lĭ), *adv.* In a familiar manner.

familiar spirit. A supernatural attendant that protects and prompts an individual man or woman. Cf. CONTROL, *n.*, 6; GENIUS, 2 **a**.

fam′i·ly (făm′ĭ·lĭ; făm′lĭ), *n.; pl.* -LIES (-lĭz). [L. *familia*, fr. *famulus* servant.] **1.** The body of persons who live in one house, and under one head; a household. **2.** **a** Those descended from a common progenitor; a tribe, clan, or race; kindred. **b** Lineage; esp., honorable lineage; as, a man of *family.* **c** One's children collectively. **3.** A group of closely related individuals or groups; as, a *family* of languages. **4.** A group comprising immediate kindred; esp., the group formed of parents and children. **5.** *Biol.* A group of related plants or animals forming a category ranking above a genus and below an order. Family names of animals end in *-idae*, of plants, in *-aceae.* See CLASSIFICATION, 2.

— *adj.* Of or pertaining to the (or a) family; as, *family* life; *family* prayers.

family circle. In a theater or opera house, a gallery or section usually above or behind one containing more expensive seats.

family man. **1.** A man who has a family. **2.** A man of domestic habits.

family name. That part of the name of individuals which is common to the family; surname.

fam′ine (făm′ĭn), *n.* [OF., fr. L. *fames* hunger.] **1.** General scarcity of food; destitution. **2.** Hunger; starvation. **3.** Extreme scarcity of something; as, a coal *famine.*

fam′ish (făm′ĭsh), *v. t.* [OF. *afamer*, fr. L. *fames* hunger.] **1.** To starve or destroy with hunger. **2.** To exhaust the strength of by hunger. — *v. i.* **1.** To die of hunger; to starve. **2.** To suffer extreme hunger, almost to the point of death. — **fam′ish·ment,** *n.*

fa′mous (fā′mŭs), *adj.* [L. *famosus*, fr. *fama* fame. See FAME.] **1.** Celebrated in fame; renowned. **2.** *Archaic.* Discreditably renowned; notorious. **3.** *Colloq.* Excellent; first-rate; as, a *famous* dinner. — **fa′mous·ly**, *adv.* — **fa′mous·ness**, *n.*

Syn. Famous, renowned, celebrated, noted, notorious, distinguished, eminent, illustrious mean known far and wide among men. **Famous** applies to men, events, and the like, widely and popularly known, especially for a time; **renowned** implies more glory and acclamation and **celebrated** more notice and attention, especially in print, than *famous;* **noted** implies more distinction, and **notorious**, especially in present use, more questionableness, in the person or thing than *celebrated;* **distinguished** implies an excellence or superiority that makes it or him marked in his class; **eminent** implies even greater conspicuousness for an outstanding quality or character; **illustrious** implies even more glory or luster that attaches itself to the person or thing so qualified.

fam′u·lus (făm′ū·lŭs), *n.; pl.* -LI (-lī). [L.] A servant or attendant, as upon a scholar or magician.

fan (făn), *n.* [AS. *fann*, fr. L. *vannus* fan, van for winnowing.] **1.** *Hist.* A basket or shovel used for tossing grain into the air to let the chaff be blown away. **2.** An instrument used for producing artificial currents of air, by the motion of a broad surface; as: **a** An instrument for cooling the person, made of feathers, paper, silk, etc., and often mounted on sticks all turning about the same pivot, so as when opened to radiate from the center and assume the figure of a sector of a circle. **b** *Mach.* Any revolving vane or vanes. **c** A wheel with revolving vanes for cooling a radiator. **3.** Something in the form of a spread fan. **4.** *Windmills.* One of the small vanes which receive the impulse of the wind and are so located as to keep the large sails in the direction of the wind.
— *v. t.;* FANNED (fănd); FAN′NING. **1.** To winnow. **2.** To move or impel (air) with or as with a fan. **3.** To blow or breathe upon; as, the breeze *fans* one. **4.** To direct a current of air upon with or as with a fan; as, to *fan* coals into a blaze; to stir up to activity as by fanning; stimulate. **5.** To spread like a fan; as, to *fan* out the cards. **6.** *Slang, Baseball.* To strike (the batter) out. — *v. i.* **1.** To spread like a fan; — often with *out.* **2.** *Slang, Baseball.* To strike out; — said of a batter.

fan, *n.* [Prob. fr. *fanatic.*] *Slang.* An enthusiastic devotee of a particular diversion, as baseball; hence, an ardent admirer or champion, as of some person or organization or movement.

fa·nat′ic (fȧ·năt′ĭk), *adj.* [L. *fanaticus* inspired by divinity, enthusiastic, frantic, fr. *fanum* fane.] Governed or produced by too great zeal; excessively enthusiastic, esp. on religious subjects. — *n.* A person affected by excessive enthusiasm, esp. on religious subjects.

fa·nat′i·cal (-ĭ·kăl), *adj.* Fanatic. — **fa·nat′i·cal·ly**, *adv.*

fa·nat′i·cism (-ĭ·sĭz′m), *n.* Excessive enthusiasm or unreasoning zeal on any subject, as religion.

fa·nat′i·cize (-sīz), *v. t.* To cause to become a fanatic. — *v. i.* To act or feel like a fanatic.

fan′ci·er (făn′sĭ·ẽr), *n.* **1.** One who is governed by fancy. **2.** One who has a special liking for, or interest in, something; esp., one who breeds or sells some kind of animal or plant for points of excellence; as, a pigeon *fancier.*

fan′ci·ful (făn′sĭ·fo͝ol; -f'l), *adj.* **1.** Full of or guided by fancy, rather than by reason and experience; whimsical. **2.** Conceived in the fancy; not based upon facts or reason; as, a *fanciful* scheme. **3.** Curiously shaped or constructed. — **Syn.** See IMAGINARY. — **fan′ci·ful·ly**, *adv.* — **fan′ci·ful·ness**, *n.*

fan′ci·less (-lĕs; -lĭs), *adj.* Having no fancy; without ideas or imagination.

fan′cy (făn′sĭ), *n.; pl.* -CIES (-sĭz). [Contr. fr. *fantasy*, fr. OF. *fantasie*, fr. L., fr. Gr. *phantasia* appearance, imagination, fr. *phantazein* to make visible, fr. *phainein* to show.] **1.** Inclination; liking formed by caprice rather than reason; as, to strike one's *fancy.* **2.** A caprice; whim; impression. **3.** Imagination, esp. of a capricious sort. **4.** Illusion; delusive imagination. **5.** Judgment or taste in matters of art, dress, etc. **6.** An image of anything formed in the mind; conception; idea. **7.** *Obs.* An apparition; phantom. **8.** Collectively (usually with *the*), all those intensely interested in some special art, practice, or amusement, as pugilism or the fancy breeding of animals; also, the object of their interest. **9.** That which pleases or entertains one's taste or caprice. **10.** *Aesthetics.* The power of conception and representation as found in poets, artists, etc.; imagination. — **Syn.** See IMAGINATION.
— *v. t.;* FAN′CIED (-sĭd); FAN′CY·ING. **1.** To have a fancy for; to like. **2.** To form a conception of; to imagine. **3.** To believe without being certain; to suppose. — **Syn.** See THINK.
— *adj.;* FAN′CI·ER (-sĭ·ẽr); FAN′CI·EST. **1.** Dependent upon fancy; whimsical; irregular. **2.** Adapted to please the fancy or taste; ornamental; — opposed to *plain;* as, *fancy* goods. **3.** Extravagant; above real value; as, *fancy* prices. **4.** Based on conceptions of the fancy; as, a *fancy* portrait. **5.** Bred for special points, as an animal. **6. a** Of particular excellence; — said of fruits, groceries, etc. **b** Executed with technical skill and superior grace; as, *fancy* skating.

fancy ball. A ball in which persons appear in fancy dress.

fancy diving. The art or practice of executing any of certain recognized or set dives into water. Cf. DIVE, *n.*, 4. — **fancy diver.**

fancy dress. Dress arranged according to fancy rather than to style, often representing the costume of some period, nation, or noted character. — **fan′cy–dress′**, *v. t. & adj.*

fan′cy–free′, *adj.* Free to imagine or fancy; not centering attentions or thoughts on one thing or person, especially one loved.

fancy man. 1. A woman's lover. **2.** A man who lives on the earnings of a prostitute.

fancy woman. A mistress; also, a prostitute.

fan′cy·work′ (făn′sĭ·wûrk′), *n.* Ornamental work done with a needle or hook, as embroidery, crocheting, etc.

fan·dan′go (făn·dăng′gō), *n.; pl.* -GOS (-gōz). [Sp.] A lively Spanish dance, or a tune in its rhythm.

fan delta. An alluvial fan.

fane (fān), *n.* [L. *fanum.*] *Archaic.* A temple; hence, a church.

fan′fare (făn′fâr; *Brit. also* făn′făr, făn′-, fōn′-), *n.* [F.] **1.** A flourish of trumpets. **2.** A showy outward display.

fan′fa·ron (făn′fȧ·rŏn), *n.* [F., fr. Sp. *fanfarrón.*] A braggart.

fan′fa·ron·ade′ (-rŏn·ād′), *n.* [F. *fanfaronnade*, fr. Sp. See FANFARON.] Swaggering; vain boasting; bluster.

fang (făng), *v. t.* [AS. *fōn.*] *Now Dial.* To seize; to lay hold of.

fang, *n.* **1.** A long sharp tooth by which the prey of an animal is seized and held or torn; any long pointed tooth; esp., one of the long, hollow or grooved, and often erectile, teeth of venomous snakes. **2.** The root of a tooth, or one of the prongs into which the root divides (see TOOTH, *Illust.*); hence, figuratively, any sharp prolongation or projection of an object. — **fanged** (făngd), *adj.*

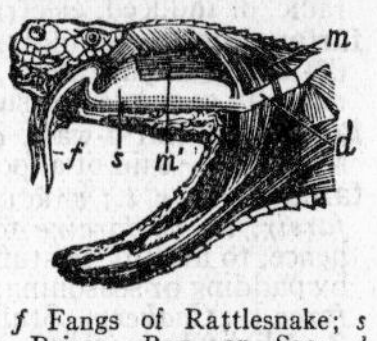

f Fangs of Rattlesnake; *s* Poison Bag or Sac; *d* Duct; *m, m′* Muscles.

fan′gle (făng′g'l), *n.* With *new:* A fashion, esp. a foppish or silly mode.

fan′gled (-g'ld), *adj.* Showily decorated; foppish; foolish; — usually with *new.* See NEWFANGLED.

fan′light′ (făn′līt′), *n.* *Arch.* A semicircular window with radiating sash bars, like the ribs of a fan, placed over a door or window.

fan′ner (făn′ẽr), *n.* One who or that which fans.

fan′on (făn′ŭn), *n.* Also **fan′o** (-ō), **fan′um** (-ŭm), **phan′o** (făn′ō). [OF. *fanon*, of Teut. origin.] *Eccl.* **a** A maniple. **b** A short cape or deep collar worn by the pope at solemn pontifical Mass.

fan palm. Any palm having simple, fan-shaped leaves (see 2d PALM, *n.*, 1), as the cabbage palmetto (see PALMETTO), talipot, and Washington palm.

fan′tail′ (făn′tāl′), *n.* **1.** A tail or end in the shape of a fan. **2. a** Among birds: (1) A variety of the domestic pigeon having a broad rounded tail. (2) Any Australian flycatcher (genus *Rhipidura*, family Muscicapidae) having a fanlike tail. **b** A goldfish of a fancy breed having anal and tail fins double. **3.** *Arch.* A structural part likened to a fan; specif., a centering, as of an arch, of radiating struts. **4.** *Naut.* A form of counter or after overhang of a vessel, which is shaped like a duck's bill.

fan′–tan′ (făn′tăn′), *n.* [Chin. (Pek.) *fan*[1]*-t'an*[1].] **1.** A Chinese gambling game. **2.** = NEWMARKET, the card game.

fan·ta′sia (făn·tā′zhȧ; făn′tȧ·zē′ȧ; făn·tä′zĭ·ȧ), *n.* [It. See FANCY.] **1.** A composition in which the author's fancy roves unrestricted by set form. **2.** *Music.* **a** An instrumental composition characterized by freedom of fancy unrestricted by set form. **b** A potpourri of familiar airs.

fan′tasm (făn′tăz'm). Var. of PHANTASM.

fan′tast (făn′tăst), *n.* A visionary; a dreamer.

fan·tas′tic (făn·tăs′tĭk; făn-), *adj.* [OF. *fantastique*, or ML. *fantasticus*, fr. LL., fr. Gr. *phantastikos* able to represent, fr. *phantazein* to make visible. See FANCY.] **1.** Imaginary; unreal; as, *fantastic* fears. **2.** Conceived or having the appearance of being conceived by wild and unrestrained fancy; grotesque; quaint. **3.** Characterized by extravagant fantasy or imagination; fanciful; hence, odd; eccentric. **4.** Due to fancies; capricious.

Syn. (1) See IMAGINARY.
(2) **Fantastic, bizarre, grotesque** mean conceived or made without reference to reality, truth, or common sense. **Fantastic** may connote absurd extravagance in conception or merely ingenuity in devising; **bizarre** applies to that which is unduly, often sensationally, queer and connotes violent contrasts, as in color or sound, or incongruous combinations, as of the tender and horrible; **grotesque** implies the distortion of the natural to the point of comic absurdity or aesthetically effective ugliness or, in popular use, exaggeration that is ridiculous and suggests caricature.
— *n. Archaic.* **a** One who has fantastic ideas. **b** A person given to fantastic dress, manners, etc.

fan·tas′ti·cal (-tĭ·kăl), *adj.* **1.** Indulging fantasy; whimsical. **2.** Marked by extravagance of imagination or by oddity or grotesqueness. — **fan·tas′ti·cal′i·ty** (-kăl′ĭ·tĭ), *n.* — **fan·tas′ti·cal·ly**, *adv.* — **fan·tas′ti·cal·ness**, *n.*

fan′ta·sy (făn′tȧ·sĭ; -zĭ), *n.; pl.* -SIES (-sĭz; -zĭz). Also **phan′ta·sy** (făn′-). [See FANCY.] **1. a** *Obs.* = PHANTASY, 1. **b** = FANCY, 3 & 4. **2.** A product of imagination; specif., an image; esp., an illusory image, phantasm. **3.** Mood, esp. a whimsical or capricious mood. **4.** *Music.* = FANTASIA, 2. — **Syn.** See IMAGINATION. — *v. t.;* -SIED (-sĭd; -zĭd); -SY·ING (-sĭ·ĭng; -zĭ·ĭng). To fancy; to imagine.

fan·tigue′ (făn·tēg′), **fan·teague′**, **fan·teeg′**, *n.* *Chiefly Dial. Eng.* A state of anxiety or unpleasant excitement.

fan′toc·ci′ni (făn′tŏ·chē′nē), *n. pl.* [It., dim. fr. *fantoccio* puppet, fr. *fante* child.] Puppets moved by machinery; also, the puppet shows in which they are used.

fan′tom. Var. of PHANTOM.

fan tracery. *Arch.* Decorative tracery on **fan vaulting**, vaulting in which the ribs diverge like the rays of a fan.

fan window. A window, as a fanlight, with radiating sash bars like the ribs of a fan.

fan′wort′ (făn′wûrt′), *n.* The water shield *Cabomba caroliniana*, commonly used in aquariums.

far (fär), *adv.* [AS. *feor.*] **1.** At or to a great distance of space; widely; afar. **2.** To a great distance in time from any point; remotely. **3.** In or to a great degree. **4.** In a great proportion; by a great interval; greatly. **5.** To, or at, a definite distance, point, or degree; as, so *far* I will go. — ***by far.*** By much; greatly. — ***far and away.*** By much; decidedly. — ***far and wide.*** Distantly and broadly.
— *adj.;* FAR′THER (fär′thẽr) and FAR′THEST (-thĕst; -thĭst) are used as the *compar.* and *superl.* of *far*, although they are corruptions arising from confusion with *further* and *furthest.* **1.** Distant; hence, widely different in time, quality, or nature. **2.** Extending to a distance; long. **3.** Being the more distant of two; as, the *far* side. **4.** Advanced; progressed; as, *far* in years. — **Syn.** See DISTANT.

far′ad (făr′ăd; -ȧd), *n.* [After Michael *Faraday*, Eng. physicist.] *Elec.* The unit of electrical capacity; the capacity of a condenser which, charged with one coulomb, gives a difference of potential of one volt. Abbr. *f.* or *F.*

far′a·day (făr′ȧ·dā; -dĭ), *n.* [See FARAD.] *Physics & Chem.* A unit of quantity of electricity, being 96,500 coulombs. It is the quantity carried in electrolysis by the ions of any substance whose mass equals the chemical equivalent of the substance.

fa·rad′ic (fȧ·răd′ĭk), *adj.* [See FARAD.] Of or pertaining to induced currents of electricity.

far′a·dism (făr′ȧ·dĭz'm), **far′a·di·za′tion** (-dĭ·zā′shŭn; -dī·zā′shŭn), *n.* *Med.* The application of faradic, or induced, currents of electricity for remedial purposes.

far'a·dize (făr'ȧ·dīz), *v. t. Med.* To stimulate with, or subject to, faradic, or induced, electric currents. — **far'a·diz'er** (-dīz'ẽr), *n.*

far'an·dole (făr'ăn·dōl; *F.* fȧ'räɴ'dôl'), *n.* Also **fa·ran'do·la** (fȧ·răn'-dō·lȧ). [F. *farandole*, fr. Pr. *farandoulo.*] **a** A lively Provençal dance in sextuple measure. **b** The music for such a dance.

far'a·way' (fär'ȧ·wā'), *adj.* **1.** Distant; remote. **2.** Dreamy; abstracted; — said of a look or eyes. — **Syn.** See DISTANT.

farce (färs), *v. t.;* FARCED (färst); FARC'ING (fär'sĭng). [OF. *farcir, farsir*, fr. L. *farcire* to stuff.] **1.** *Obs.* To stuff with forcemeat; hence, to fill full; to stuff. **2.** To make more pretentious or agreeable by padding or seasoning; as, to *farce* a book with wit. — *n.* **1.** [OF. *farce.*] *Cookery.* Stuffing as used in dressing a fowl; forcemeat. **2.** A light dramatic composition of satirical or humorous cast. **3.** The element of broad humor of farce (sense 2); comic trait or feature. **4.** Ridiculous or empty show; a mockery. — **far'cial** (fär'shăl), *adj.*

‖**far'ceur'** (fȧr'sûr'), *n.* [F.] A joker; wag; one skilled in farce; one who writes, or acts in, a farce.

far'ci·cal (fär'sĭ·kăl), *adj.* Pertaining to farce; ludicrous. — **Syn.** See LAUGHABLE. — **far'ci·cal'i·ty** (-kăl'ĭ·tĭ), *n.* — **far'ci·cal·ly**, *adv.*

far cry. A long distance; hence, a great contrast.

far'cy (fär'sĭ), *n.* [F. *farcin*, deriv. of L. *farciminum* a disease of horses.] *Veter.* A contagious, often fatal, disease of horses, characterized by painful ulcerating enlargements (**farcy buds** *or* **buttons**) of the lymphatics, esp. on the legs, and caused by the same organism as glanders.

fard (färd), *n.* [F.] *Archaic.* Cosmetic paint. — *v. t. Obs.* To paint, as with cosmetics; hence, to gloss over.

far'del (fär'dĕl; -d'l), *n.* [OF.] *Archaic & Dial.* **1.** A bundle; burden. **2.** A miscellaneous collection or lot. **3.** Clothing; as, women's *fardels.*

fare (fâr), *v. i.* [AS. *faran* to travel, fare.] **1.** To go; to pass; esp., to journey. **2.** To be in any state, or pass through any experience; as, to *fare* well. **3.** To happen or turn out; — used impersonally; as, we shall see how it will *fare* with him. **4.** To partake of fare, or food; to be entertained. — *n.* [AS. *faru* journey.] **1.** The price of transportation or passage. **2.** The passenger or passengers hiring a public vehicle. **3.** *Archaic & Dial.* State of things; fortune; hap; cheer. **4.** Range or stock of food; hence, anything that sustains or nourishes.

Far East. The countries of eastern Asia. See EAST, *n.*, 2 **a**; cf. MIDDLE EAST; NEAR EAST.

far'er (fâr'ẽr), *n.* A traveler.

fare'well' (fâr'wĕl'; *the accent shifts under influence of the sentence stress;* 2), *interj.* [*fare* (thou, you) + *well.*] An exclamation expressing at parting a wish for one's welfare; good-by; adieu.

fare'well' (fâr'wĕl'), *n.* **1.** A wish of welfare at parting; a good-by. **2.** A leave-taking; as, his *farewell* to life.

fare'well' (fâr'wĕl'; fâr'wĕl'; 2), *adj.* Parting; final.

far'fetched' (fär'fĕcht'; 2), *adj.* **1.** Brought from a remote place or time. **2.** Not easily or naturally deduced or introduced; forced.

far'–flung' (-flŭng'; 2), *adj.* Flung out to a distance; hence, having wide range; as, a *far-flung* empire.

far'–forth', *adv., or* **far forth**. *Archaic.* Far; to a great or definite distance, degree, or extent.

fa·ri'na (fȧ·rē'nȧ *or, esp. Brit.,* fȧ·rī'nȧ), *n.* [L., meal, flour, fr. *far* spelt.] **1.** A fine meal made from cereal grains, nuts, or sea moss, and used for puddings and breakfast cereal. **2.** Starch; esp., potato starch.

far'i·na'ceous (făr'ĭ·nā'shŭs), *adj.* **1.** Consisting or made of meal or flour; yielding farina or flour. **2.** Like meal; mealy.

far'i·nose (făr'ĭ·nōs), *adj.* **1.** Yielding farina; also, like farina. **2.** *Bot. & Zool.* Covered with a whitish mealy powder.

far'kle·ber'ry (fär'k'l·bĕr'ĭ), *n.* A shrub or small tree (*Vaccinium arboreum*) of the huckleberry family, of the southeastern United States.

farl, farle (färl), *n. Scot. & Ir.* A small scone.

farm (färm), *n.* [OF. *ferme* a lease, leased farm, fr. *fermer*, fr. L. *firmare*, fr. *firmus* firm.] **1.** *Obs.* A fixed sum or due payable at fixed intervals by way of rent, tax, or the like. **2.** Hence, a letting out of revenues or taxes for a fixed sum to one authorized to collect and retain them. **3.** The condition of being let, or farmed, out at a fixed rent. **4.** A district or division of a country leased (or farmed) out for the collection of the revenues of government. **5.** Any tract devoted to agricultural purposes. **6.** Hence, a plot or tract of land devoted to the raising of domestic or other animals; as, a chicken *farm.* By extension, a tract of water reserved for the artificial cultivation of some aquatic food; as, an oyster *farm.* **7.** *Sports.* A club, as of a minor league, associated with another club, as of a major league, as a subsidiary to which recruits are assigned until needed or for further training.

— *v. t.* **1.** To collect and take the fees or profits of (any occupation or business) on payment of a fixed sum. **2.** To give up to another, as an estate, a business, the revenue, etc., on condition of receiving in return a fixed sum. **3.** To contract for the care of (a person or thing) at a fixed price; as, the town *farms* its paupers. **4.** To devote (land) to agriculture; to cultivate (land). **5.** *Sports.* To assign to a farm (def. 7). — *v. i.* To till the soil; to manage a farm.

farm'er (fär'mẽr), *n.* One who farms; as: **a** One who takes taxes to collect, paying a fixed sum for the privilege. **b** One who conducts or manages a farm.

farm'er·ette' (-ĕt'), *n. Colloq.* A woman or girl who farms or works on a farm.

farm'er–gen'er·al, *n.; pl.* FARMERS-GENERAL. [F. *fermier général.*] *Fr. Hist.* One of the men who farmed certain taxes from 1697 to about 1789. — **farm'er–gen'er·al·ship'**, *n.*

farm hand. A farm laborer, esp. a hired laborer.

farm'house' (färm'hous' *or, esp. Brit.,* färm'hous'), *n.* The dwelling house of a farm.

farm'ing, *adj.* Pertaining to agriculture; devoted to, or engaged in, farming. — *n.* **1.** Act or custom of letting out to farm. **2.** Act or business of cultivating land.

farm'stead (färm'stĕd), *n.* Also **farm'stead'ing.** A farm.

farm'yard' (färm'yärd' *or, esp. Brit.,* färm'yärd'), *n.* The yard attached to a barn, or the space enclosed by farm buildings.

far'o (fâr'ō), *n.* A gambling game at cards.

far'–off' (fär'ôf'; 2), *adj.* Remote; distant. — **Syn.** See DISTANT.

‖**fa'rouche'** (fȧ'rōōsh'), *adj.* [F.] Wild; shy.

far·rag'i·nous (fă·răj'ĭ·nŭs), *adj.* [See FARRAGO.] *Rare.* Formed of various materials; mixed.

far·ra'go (fă·rā'gō; -rä'gō), *n.; pl.* -GOES (-gōz). [L. *farrago, -aginis*, mixed fodder, medley, fr. *far* a sort of grain.] A medley; mixture.

far'–reach'ing (fär'rēch'ĭng; 2), *adj.* Having a wide range or scope; having an influence reaching far in space, time, etc.

far'ri·er (făr'ĭ·ẽr), *n.* [OF. *ferrier*, fr. L. *ferrarius* blacksmith, fr. *ferrum* iron.] **1.** One, esp. a smith, who shoes horses. **2.** *Obs.* A veterinarian.

far'ri·er·y (făr'ĭ·ẽr·ĭ), *n.* **1.** The art or science of shoeing horses. **2.** *Obs.* The veterinary art.

far'row (făr'ō), *n.* [AS. *fearh* a little pig.] **a** *Obs.* A young pig. **b** A litter of pigs. — *v. t. & i.* To bring forth (young); — now said only of swine.

far'row, *adj.* [Cf. Scot. *ferry cow* a cow that is not with calf, Flem. *varvekoe, vervekoe.*] Not producing young in a given season or year; — said only of cows.

far'see'ing (fär'sē'ĭng; 2), *adj.* **a** Able to see to a great distance; farsighted. **b** Having foresight.

far'sight'ed (-sīt'ĕd; -ĭd; 2), *adj.* **1.** Seeing to a great distance; hence, of good judgment; sagacious. **2.** *Med.* Hyperopic. — **far'sight'ed·ly**, *adv.* — **far'sight'ed·ness**, *n.*

far'ther (fär'thẽr), *adj., compar.* of FAR. [For *farrer*, ME. *ferrer*, compar. of *far;* confused with *further.*] **1.** Beyond the present point; further. **2.** More remote. — *adv.* **1.** At or to a greater distance, as in space, time, or a progression. **2.** More completely.

Syn. Farther, further are not always differentiated in use. **Farther** strictly implies greater distance from a point in space or, less often, in time, and **further**, onwardness or advance not only in space or time, but also in quantity, degree, or the like; as, the *farther* tree; which is the *farther* country?; no *further* steps are necessary; let us go *further.* But sometimes, when both ideas are implied, either adjective or adverb may be used.

far'ther·most (-mōst; -mŭst), *adj.* Most remote; farthest.

far'thest (fär'thĕst; -thĭst), *adj., superl.* of FAR. [See FARTHER.] **1.** Most distant or remote. **2.** Longest; most extended. — *adv.* At or to the greatest distance.

far'thing (fär'thĭng), *n.* [AS. *fēorthung*, fr. *fēortha* fourth, fr. *fēor, fēower*, four.] **1.** The fourth of a penny, a small British bronze coin. See MONEY, *Tables.* **2.** *Obs.* A very small quantity or value.

far'thin·gale (fär'thĭng·gāl), *n.* [MF. *verdugale*, fr. Sp. *verdugado*, being named from its hoops, fr. *verdugo* young shoot of a tree, fr. *verde* green, fr. L. *viridis.* See VERDANT.] A hoop skirt or hoop petticoat, or a frame of hoops to extend the petticoat.

fas'ces (făs'ēz), *n. pl.* [L., pl. of *fascis* bundle.] *Rom. Antiq.* A bundle of rods having among them an ax with the blade projecting, borne before Roman magistrates as a badge of authority. — **fas'ci·al** (făsh'ĭ·ăl), *adj.*

fas'ci·a (făsh'ĭ·ȧ), *n.; pl.* -CIAE (-ē). [L., a band.] **1.** A band or fillet; esp., in surgery, a bandage. **2.** *Arch.* A flat member of an order or building, like a flat band, commonly under eaves and cornices; esp., in the Ionic order, one of the three bands which make up the architrave. See MOLDING, ORDER, *Illusts.* **3.** *Anat.* A layer of connective tissue covering, insheathing, supporting, or binding together internal parts of the body; hence, tissue of this character. **4.** *Zool.* A broad and well-defined band of color. — **fas'ci·al** (-ăl), *adj.*

fas'ci·ate (-āt), **fas'ci·at'ed** (-āt'ĕd; -ĭd), *adj.* [L. *fasciatus*, past part. of *fasciare* to envelop with bands, fr. *fascia* band.] **1.** Bound with a fillet, sash, or bandage. **2.** *Bot.* **a** Fascicled. **b** Exhibiting fasciation. **3.** *Zool.* Broadly banded with color.

fas'ci·a'tion (-ā'shŭn), *n.* **1.** Act or manner of binding up; bandage; also, condition of being fasciated. **2.** *Bot.* A common malformation in plant stems resulting in enlargement and flattening, as if several were fused.

fas'ci·cle (făs'ĭ·k'l), *n.* [L. *fasciculus*, dim. of *fascis* bundle.] **1.** A small bundle; cluster; as, a *fascicle* of fibers; specif., *Bot.*, a glomerule. **2.** One of the divisions of a book published in parts; a fasciculus. — **fas·cic'u·lar** (fă·sĭk'ū·lẽr), *adj.*

fas'ci·cled (-k'ld), *adj.* Arranged in fascicles; as, *fascicled* leaves.

fas·cic'u·late (fă·sĭk'ū·lāt), **fas·cic'u·lat'ed** (-lāt'ĕd; -ĭd), *adj.* Fascicled. — **fas·cic'u·late·ly**, *adv.* — **fas·cic'u·la'tion** (-lā'shŭn), *n.*

fas'ci·cule (făs'ĭ·kūl), *n.* [F.] A fasciculus.

fas·cic'u·lus (fă·sĭk'ū·lŭs), *n.; pl.* -LI (-lī). [L.] = FASCICLE. Specif., *Anat.*, a slender bundle of fibers, as of nerve fibers.

fas'ci·nate (făs'ĭ·nāt; 67), *v. t. & i.* [L. *fascinatus*, past part. of *fascinare*, fr. *fascinum* a spell.] **1.** *Obs.* To bewitch. **2.** To hold spellbound, as by some irresistible charm. **3.** To allure and hold intent, esp. by qualities that charm; to captivate. — **Syn.** See ATTRACT. — **fas'ci·nat'ed·ly** (-nāt'ĕd·lĭ; 30), *adv.*

fas'ci·nat'ing (-nāt'ĭng), *adj.* Exercising charm; attractive. — **fas'ci·nat'ing·ly**, *adv.*

fas'ci·na'tion (-nā'shŭn), *n.* **1.** Act or instance of fascinating; state of being fascinated. **2.** Quality or capability of fascinating; charming influence.

fas'ci·na'tor (făs'ĭ·nā'tẽr), *n.* **1.** One who fascinates. **2.** A crocheted head covering for women.

fas·cine' (fă·sēn'), *n.* [F., fr. L. *fascina* a bundle of sticks.] *Fort. & Engin.* A long bundle of sticks of wood, bound together, used in raising batteries, filling ditches, strengthening ramparts, making revetments for riverbanks, etc.

fas'cism (făsh'ĭz'm; făs'-), *n.* [It. *fascismo*, fr. *fascio* a (political) group, a club, lit. a bundle, fr. L. *fascis* a bundle.] **1.** [*often cap.*] The principles of the Fascisti; also, the movement or governmental regime embodying their principles. **2.** Any program for setting up a centralized autocratic national regime with severely nationalistic policies, exercising regimentation of industry, commerce, and finance, rigid censorship, and forcible suppression of opposition.

fas'cist (făsh'ĭst; făs'-), *n.* An adherent or advocate of fascism.

fas'cist, fa·scis'tic (fă·shĭs'tĭk), *adj.* Of, pertaining to, sponsored by, or embodying fascism; according with, or favoring, fascism; of or pertaining to fascists.

Fa·scis'ti (fă·shĭs'tē; *It.* fä·shē'stē), *n. pl.* [It., fr. *fascio* (see FASCISM), with ref. also to It. pl. *fasci* fasces and L. *fasces*, as if meaning "bearer of the fasces" because the Fascisti were supposed to typify obedience to the law as did the lictors in ancient Rome.] The members of an Italian organization, originated 1919, which under Benito Mussolini became identical with the government of the Italian state.

fash (făsh), *n. Scot.* Vexation. — *v. t. Scot.* To vex.

fash'ion (făsh'ŭn), *n.* [OF. *façon, fazon*, orig., a making, fr. L. *factio* a making, fr. *facere* to make.] **1.** The make or form of anything. **2.**

Obs. Act or process of making; hence, craftsmanship. **3.** Kind; sort. **4.** Mode of action or operation; also, method of conduct; behavior. **5.** Manner; custom; way. **6.** The prevailing conventional usage in dress, social forms, etc. **7.** The social group which conforms to the conventional ways of society; fashionable persons collectively.

Syn. (1) See METHOD.

(2) **Fashion, style, mode, vogue, fad, rage, craze** mean the accepted usage at a given time by those who wish to be regarded as up-to-date. **Fashion**, the most general term, implies any way of dressing, behaving, writing, etc., which is favored at the time; **style** usually implies a distinctive fashion, as in dress, furnishings, etc., adopted by those who have wealth or taste; **mode** suggests the fashion of the moment among those who cultivate elegance in dress, behavior, and the like; **vogue** stresses the prevalence or wide acceptance of the fashion; **fad** stresses caprice in its acceptance and in dropping; **rage** and **craze** stress short-lived and, often, senseless enthusiasm in the fashion.

— *v. t.* **1.** To give shape or figure to; to form. **2.** To bring about by devising; to contrive. **3.** To fit; adapt; accommodate; — with *to*. — **Syn.** See MAKE.

fash'ion·a·ble (făsh'ŭn·ȧ·b'l; făsh'nȧ·b'l), *adj.* **1.** *Obs.* Well-appearing. **2.** Conforming to the custom, fashion, or established mode. **3.** Of or pertaining to the world of fashion. — **Syn.** Modish, stylish, smart. — *n.* A fashionable person. — **fash'ion·a·ble·ness**, *n.* — **fash'ion·a·bly**, *adv.*

fash'ion·er (făsh'ŭn·ẽr), *n.* One who fashions, forms, or gives shape to anything; specif., a tailor; costumer.

fash'ion·mon'ger (făsh'ŭn·mŭng'gẽr), *n.* A person who studies, follows, and transmits fashions.

fash'ion·mon'ging (-gĭng), *n.* *Rare.* Behaving like a fashionmonger.

fashion plate. **a** A pictorial design showing the prevailing style or a new style of dress. **b** One whose clothes resemble such a design; one dressed in the height of fashion.

fast (fȧst; 9), *v. i.* [AS. *fæstan.*] **1.** To abstain from food. **2.** To practice abstinence as a religious exercise or as a token of grief. **3.** To eat sparingly or abstain from certain foods. — *n.* **1.** Abstinence from food, or from certain kinds of food. **2.** A time of fasting.

fast, *adj.* [ME., firm, strong, not loose, fr. AS. *fæst.*] **1.** Firmly fixed; specif.: **a** Stable; hence, unyielding. **b** Sound, as sleep. **c** Permanently dyed; unfadable. **d** Securely attached. **e** Firm in adherence; steadfast; also, narrowly confined. **f** Stuck, as on a reef. **g** Made firm; secure; hence, tenacious; as, a *fast* grip. **2.** Moving or able to move rapidly; hence: **a** Imparting quickness of motion; as, a *fast* pitcher. **b** Making for rapidity of action; as, a *fast* track. **c** Taking a comparatively short time; as, a *fast* race. **d** Registering in advance of that which is correct; — of a timepiece or a device for weighing. **3.** Impelled or characterized by zest for excitement or pleasure; hence, dissipated. **4.** Resistant to a (usually specified) agency or poisonous substance; as, arsenic-*fast* protozoa. **5.** *Photog.* = RAPID, *adj.*, 4.

Syn. **Fast, rapid, swift, fleet, quick, speedy, hasty, expeditious** mean moving or acting with celerity. **Fast** and **rapid** are often used without distinction, but *fast* is particularly applied to the thing which moves, and *rapid* to the movement itself (as, a *fast* horse, train; a *rapid* gait, current); **swift** suggests great rapidity coupled with ease of movement; **fleet** adds the implication of lightness or nimbleness; **quick** suggests promptness or taking of little time; **speedy** may imply extreme quickness or great velocity; **hasty** suggests hurry and precipitation, often also connoting carelessness; **expeditious** adds to *quick* or *speedy* the implications of efficiency and absence of bungling. — **Ant.** Slow.

— *adv.* [AS. *fæste* firmly, strongly.] **1.** In a fast or fixed manner. **2.** Close. *Obs.*, exc. in *fast by, fast beside.* **3.** Rapidly; swiftly; also, recklessly; dissipatedly.

fast (fȧst), *n.* [ME. *fest*, fr. ON. *festr*, a rope.] *Naut.* A mooring rope, hawser, or chain.

fast and loose. Now cohering, now disjoined; esp., in the phrase *to play fast and loose*, to act with reckless inconstancy or in a tricky manner; to say one thing and do another.

fas'ten (fȧs''n; 9), *v. t.* [AS. *fæstnian.*] **1.** To attach or join, as by pinning, tying, nailing, etc. **2.** To make fast, as that which is loose or free; also, to secure against opening, as by locking, clasping, etc. **3.** To fix or set steadily; as, to *fasten* the eyes, hopes, on something. **4.** To attach or affix, as something disagreeable or not obviously connected; hence, to impute; as, to *fasten* blame upon someone. — *v. i.* **1.** To get a firm hold, as with the hand, eye, attention, etc.; — with *on* or *upon*. **2.** To become firm, or set, as plaster. **3.** To be or become fastened. — **fas'ten·er** (fȧs''n·ẽr; fȧs'nẽr), *n.*

Syn. **Fasten, fix, attach, affix** mean to make something stay firmly in place. **Fasten** implies an action such as tying, binding, nailing, locking, or otherwise securing; **fix**, literally or figuratively, a driving in or implanting deeply; **attach**, a connecting or uniting by or as by a bond, link, or tie, in order to keep things together or to prevent their separation; **affix**, an imposing of one thing upon another, as by nailing, pasting, or otherwise impressing.

fas'ten·ing (fȧs''n·ĭng; fȧs'nĭng), *n.* A thing that fastens.

fas·tid'i·ous (făs·tĭd'ĭ·ŭs; 58), *adj.* [F. or L.; F. *fastidieux*, fr. L. *fastidiosus* disdainful, fr. *fastidium* loathing, aversion.] Difficult to please; delicate to a fault. — **Syn.** See NICE. — **fas·tid'i·ous·ly**, *adv.* — **fas·tid'i·ous·ness**, *n.*

fas·tig'i·ate (făs·tĭj'ĭ·āt), **fas·tig'i·at'ed** (-āt'ĕd; -ĭd), *adj.* [L. *fastigium* gable end, top, height, summit.] Narrowing toward the top; hence: **a** *Bot.* Erect and columnar. **b** *Zool.* United into a conical bundle.

fast'ness (fȧst'nĕs; -nĭs), *n.* **1.** State of being fast; as: **a** Fixedness; — chiefly of dyes. **b** Swiftness; speed. **c** Dissoluteness. **2.** A stronghold.

fat (făt), *adj.*; FAT'TER; FAT'TEST. [AS. *fætt.*] **1.** Abounding with fat; as: **a** Fleshy; plump. **b** Oily; unctuous; — of food. **2.** Thick; well filled out; as, a *fat* purse. **3.** Richly rewarding, as in income or success; as, a *fat* office. **4.** Fertile; as, a *fat* soil. **5.** Characterized by some element of richness; as, *fat* or resinous wood; *fat* coal (coal rich in volatile matter). **6.** Wealthy; affluent. **7.** Well stocked or supplied; as, a *fat* larder. **8.** Dull; stupid. — **Syn.** Obese, stout, corpulent, portly. — **Ant.** Lean.

— *n.* **1.** Any animal tissues consisting chiefly of cells distended with greasy or oily matter; adipose tissue; also, this oily or greasy substance or a like substance in plants, esp. in certain seeds; also, any such substance used in cookery. Cf. LEAN. **2.** The best or richest productions or part. **3.** Obesity. **4.** *Chem.* Any of a class of compounds of carbon, hydrogen, and oxygen (of which the natural fats are mixtures), chiefly glyceryl esters of certain acids, as stearic, palmitic, oleic, butyric, etc., soluble in ether but not in water. Fats constitute a major class of food for animals (see FOOD, *n.*, 1). **5.** *Theater.* Effective lines or business in an actor's part.

— *v. t. & i.*; FAT'TED; FAT'TING. To make or grow fat.

fa'tal (fā'tăl; -t'l), *adj.* [OF., fr. L. *fatalis*, fr. *fatum.* See FATE.] **1.** *Archaic.* Fated; inevitable; also, doomed. **2.** Fateful; fraught with fate; as, a *fatal* hour. **3.** Of, relating to, or like fate or the Fates; as, the *Fatal* sisters, and the *fatal* thread they spun; also, foreboding; ominous; as, *fatal* prophecy. **4.** Deadly; mortal; as, a *fatal* wound; calamitous; as, a *fatal* attack. — **Syn.** See DEADLY.

fa'tal·ism (-ĭz'm), *n.* **1.** The doctrine that all events are determined by necessity, or fate. **2.** The mental attitude of a believer in fatalism. — **fa'tal·ist** (-ĭst), *n.* — **fa'tal·is'tic** (-ĭs'tĭk), *adj.* — **fa'tal·is'ti·cal·ly** (-tĭ·kăl·ĭ), *adv.*

fa·tal'i·ty (fȧ·tăl'ĭ·tĭ; fā-), *n.*; *pl.* -TIES (-tĭz). **1.** The agent or agency of fate; as, an overruling *fatality.* **2.** A doctrine of a determining power superior to, and independent of, rational control; determinism. **3.** The quality or condition of being fated, esp. destined to disaster. **4.** The quality of being fatal; deadliness. **5.** A fatal outcome; specif., a disaster ending in death.

fa'tal·ly, *adv.* **1.** In a manner proceeding from, or determined by, fate. **2.** In a manner issuing in disaster.

fa'ta mor·ga'na (fä'tä môr·gä'nä). [It., i. e., Morgan the fay.] A mirage, esp. one seen at the Strait of Messina.

fate (fāt), *n.* [OF., fr. L. *fatum* oracle, what is ordained by the gods, fate, fr. *fari* to speak.] **1.** That principle, or determining cause or will, by which things in general are supposed to come to be as they are or events to happen as they do; destiny. **2.** That which is destined or decreed; appointed lot. **3.** Ultimate lot; final outcome; specif., ruin; disaster; death. **4.** [*cap.*] *Gr. & Roman Relig.* The goddess, or one of the goddesses, of fate or destiny; esp., *pl.* [L. *Fata*, pl. of *fatum*], the three goddesses supposed to determine the course of human life. They are ***Clotho*** (Spinner), who spins the thread of life, ***Lachesis*** (Disposer of Lots), who determines its length, and ***Atropos*** (Inflexible), who cuts it off. — *v. t. Obs. exc. in passive.* To foreordain; destine.

Syn. **Fate, destiny, lot, portion, doom** mean the state or end predetermined for one. **Fate** suggests inevitability and immutability in strict use, but usually carries no clear implication of whether it is good or evil; **destiny** implies something foreordained and inescapable, but the term rarely suggests, apart from the context, something to be feared; **lot** and **portion** carry a stronger implication of distribution in the decreeing of one's fate, but *lot* suggests the operation of blind chance, and *portion* the apportioning of good and evil; **doom** distinctly implies an unhappy or calamitous fate.

fat'ed (fāt'ĕd; -ĭd), *adj.* Decreed or controlled by fate.

fate'ful (fāt'fōōl; -f'l), *adj.* **1.** Fraught with fate; involving momentous consequences. **2.** Significant of fate; ominous. **3.** Controlled by irresistible and foreordained forces; as, *fateful* as a Greek tragedy. — **Syn.** See OMINOUS. — **fate'ful·ly**, *adv.* — **fate'ful·ness**, *n.*

fat'head' (făt'hĕd'), *n.* *Colloq.* A stupid person.

fa'ther (fä'thẽr), *n.* [AS. *fæder.*] **1.** One who has begotten a child; a male parent. **2.** [*usually cap.*] The Supreme Being and Creator; God. **3.** A forefather; *pl.*, ancestors. **4.** One who cares for as a father might; one to whom filial affection and respect are due. **5.** *Eccl.* As a title: **a** A dignitary of the church, as a bishop. **b** A confessor; — called also **father confessor.** **c** A priest. **6.** [*often cap.*] *Eccl.* Any early Christian writer accepted as a trustworthy witness to, or expositor of, the early history or teachings of the church. **7.** An originator; source or prototype. **8.** **a** A senator of ancient Rome. **b** *pl.* The leading men of a country, city, or council.

— *v. t.* **1.** To beget; also, to be the founder or author of. **2.** To accept or claim responsibility for. **3.** To treat as a father; to care for. **4.** To impose; to attach; fasten; as, to *father* a base meaning upon the Song of Songs.

fa'ther·hood (fä'thẽr·hōōd), *n.* State of being a father.

fa'ther-in-law', *n.*; *pl.* FATHERS-IN-LAW. The father of one's husband or wife; also, *Now Rare*, stepfather.

fa'ther·land' (fä'thẽr·lănd'), *n.* One's native land.

fa'ther·less (-lĕs; -lĭs), *adj.* Orphaned.

fa'ther·like' (-līk'), *adj. & adv.* Fatherly.

father longlegs. A crane fly.

fa'ther·ly (fä'thẽr·lĭ), *adj.* Like a father in affection, care, or demeanor; paternal. — *adv.* *Archaic.* In the manner of a father. — **fa'ther·li·ness** (-lĭ·nĕs; -nĭs), *n.*

Fa'ther's Day (fä'thẽrz). A day for honoring fathers, usually the third Sunday in June.

fath'om (făth'ŭm), *n.* [AS. *fæthm.*] A measure of length, containing six feet (orig., the space to which a man can extend his arms), used chiefly in measuring cables, cordage, and depth of water by soundings. See MEASURE, *Table* 9; cf. SOUNDING LINE, *Illust.* Abbr. *f.* or *fm.* — *v. t.* To measure by sounding; hence, to penetrate and comprehend; as, to *fathom* a mystery. — **fath'om·a·ble**, *adj.*

Fa·thom'e·ter (fȧ·thŏm'ē·tẽr), *n.* *Naut.* A trade-mark for a sonic depth finder.

fath'om·less (făth'ŭm·lĕs; -lĭs), *adj.* Incapable of being fathomed.

fa·tid'ic (fȧ·tĭd'ĭk; fā-), *adj.* [L. *fatidicus*, fr. *fatum* fate + *dicere* to say, tell.] Of or pertaining to foretelling; prophetic. — **fa·tid'i·cal** (-ĭ·kăl), *adj.*

fat'i·ga·ble (făt'ĭ·gȧ·b'l), *adj.* Easily tired.

fat'i·gate (-gāt), *adj.* [L. *fatigatus*, past part.] *Obs.* Fatigued. — *v. t. Obs.* To fatigue.

fa·tigue' (fȧ·tēg'), *n.* [F., fr. *fatiguer* to fatigue, fr. L. *fatigare.*] **1.** Weariness from labor or exertion; also, labor; toil. **2.** *Mech.* The action which takes place in material, esp. metals, causing deterioration and failure after a repetition of stress. **3.** *Mil.* **a** Fatigue duty. **b** *pl.* Fatigue clothes. **4.** *Physiol.* Condition of cells or organs which have undergone excessive activity with resulting loss of power or capacity to respond to stimulation. **5.** *Psychol.* A neurotic condition affecting combat personnel and characterized by anxiety, hysteria, and exhaustion. — *v. t.*; FA·TIGUED' (fȧ·tēgd'); FA·TI'GUING (-tē'gĭng). **1.** To weary; to tire. **2.** To induce a condition of fatigue in. — *v. i.* To become weary. — **Syn.** See TIRE.

fatigue clothes. *Mil.* Coarse, durable uniforms used for fatigue duties, field work, and fighting.

fatigue duty. *Mil.* Occasional work performed by selected details of soldiers in addition to drill duties, especially policing, painting, and camp maintenance.

Fat'i·ma (făt'ĭ·mȧ; *in the United States, usually* fȧ·tē'mȧ), *n.* **1.**

The favorite daughter of Mohammed. **2.** The last wife of Bluebeard. See BLUEBEARD.

Fat′i·mid (făt′ĭ·mĭd), **Fat′i·mite** (-mīt), *adj.* **a** Descended from Fatima, daughter of Mohammed. **b** Of, pertaining to, or characteristic of the period of the Fatimid dynasty. **—** *n.* A descendant of Fatima and Ali. The Fatimid dynasty ruled in portions of northern Africa (909–1171).

fat′ling (făt′lĭng), *n.* [*fat* + 1st *-ling.*] A calf, lamb, kid, or other young animal, fattened for slaughter.

fat′ly (-lĭ), *adv.* In a fat fashion; like a fat person.

fat′ness (-nĕs; -nĭs), *n.* Quality, state, or result of being fat; as: **a** Corpulence. **b** Oiliness. **c** Richness.

fat′–sol′u·ble, *adj.* Soluble in fats or fat solvents.

fat′ten (făt′'n), *v. t.* **1.** To make fat or plump. **2.** To make fertile and fruitful; as, to *fatten* land. **3.** *Poker.* To add chips to (an unopened jack pot). **—** *v. i.* To grow fat or corpulent. **— fat′ten·er** (-ẽr), *n.*

fat′ti ma′schii, pa·ro′le fe′mi·ne (făt′tē măs′kē, pä·rô′lā fā′mē·nā). [Abbr. and altered from Italian.] Literally, deeds masculine, words feminine; i. e., men act, women talk; — motto of Maryland.

fat′tish (făt′ĭsh), *adj.* Somewhat fat. **— fat′tish·ness,** *n.*

fat′ty (făt′ĭ), *adj.*; FAT′TI·ER (-ĭ·ẽr); FAT′TI·EST. Containing fat, or having the qualities of fat; adipose; greasy. **— fat′ti·ly,** *adv.* **— fat′ti·ness,** *n.*

fatty acid. *Chem.* Any one of the series of saturated acids ($C_nH_{2n}O_2$), some of which, as stearic and palmitic acids, occur in the natural fats, and are fatlike substances.

fatty degeneration. **1.** *Med.* Cell degeneration associated with the deposition of fat. **2.** Hence, figuratively, degeneration of character, esp. as caused by luxury.

fatty tumor. Lipoma.

fa·tu′i·tous (fȧ·tū′ĭ·tŭs), *adj.* Characterized by fatuity.

fa·tu′i·ty (-tĭ), *n.*; *pl.* -TIES (-tĭz). [F. *fatuité,* fr. L. *fatuitas,* fr. *fatuus* foolish.] **1.** Stupidity; unconscious dullness; also, anything fatuous. **2.** *Now Rare.* Idiocy; dementia.

fat′u·ous (făt′ū·ŭs), *adj.* [L. *fatuus.*] **1.** Foolish; blandly inane. **2.** Without reality; illusory, like the ignis fatuus. **— Syn.** See SIMPLE. **— fat′u·ous·ly,** *adv.* **— fat′u·ous·ness,** *n.*

fat′–wit′ted (făt′wĭt′ĕd; -ĭd; 2), *adj.* Dull; stupid.

‖**fau′bourg′** (fō′bōōr′; *E.* fō′bōōr, fō′bōōrg), *n.* [F.] A suburb of a French city; also, any quarter of a city.

fau′cal (fô′kăl), *adj.* Also **fau′cial** (-shăl). [L. *fauces* throat.] Pertaining to the fauces.

fau′ces (fô′sēz), *n. pl.* [L.] *Anat.* The narrow passage from the mouth to the pharynx.

fau′cet (fô′sĕt; -sĭt), *n.* [F. *fausset,* fr. Pr., fr. L. *falsare.*] *U. S. & Dial.* A fixture for drawing a liquid from a pipe, cask, etc.; — called also *tap* and *cock.* See BIBCOCK, *Illust.*

faugh (fô; *so pronounced as a word; the expression itself is* pf′ *or* f′), *interj.* An exclamation of contempt, disgust, etc.

fault (fôlt), *n.* [OF. *faute,* deriv. of L. *fallere* to deceive.] **1. a** *Obs.* Lack. **b** Neglect; default. **2.** A failing; flaw; blemish. **3.** A failure to do what is right; esp., a trifling misdemeanor; also, a mistake; error. **4.** Responsibility for wrongdoing or failure. **5.** *Geol. & Mining.* A fracture in the earth's crust, with displacement of one side of the fracture with respect to the other and in a direction parallel to the fracture. The surface along which the dislocated masses have moved is called, when not notably curved, the **fault plane.** **6.** *Hunting.* A lost scent; act of losing the scent. **7.** *Tennis, Rackets, etc.* Failure to serve the ball legitimately into the proper service court; also, a served ball that fails to land in the proper service court.

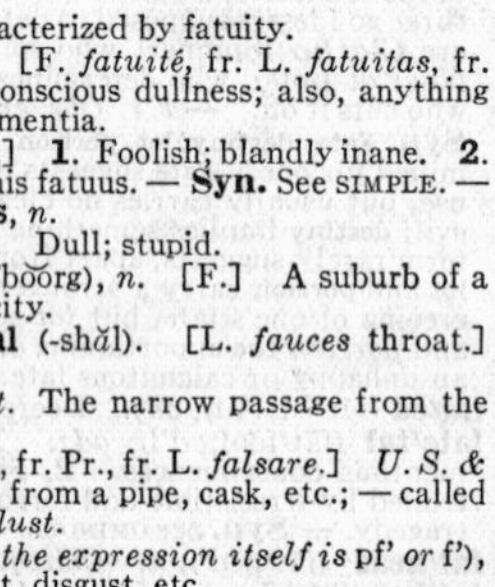

Faults. *F* Normal; *F′* Reverse. *Ff, F′f′* Fault Planes; inclination in the direction *af,* measured by angle *fac,* is the Hade; *ac* Throw; *bc* Heave; *ab* Displacement. 1–7 Strata.

Syn. **Fault, failing, frailty, foible, vice** mean an imperfection or weakness of character. **Fault** implies failure, but not necessarily serious or culpable failure, to reach perfection in disposition, deed, or habit; **failing** is less censorious than *fault,* for it usually implies a weakness of which one may not be aware; **frailty** implies a weakness which makes one prone to fall when tempted; **foible,** a temperamental failing that is harmless and, often, amiable; **vice,** as here compared, is a general term for any imperfection or weakness of character.

— ***at fault.*** **a** Unable to find the scent and continue chase; hence, in trouble and unable to proceed; puzzled. **b** *Colloq.* In fault. **—** ***in fault.*** Culpable; to blame. **—** ***to a fault.*** Excessively; very; as, gentle *to a fault.*

— *v. t.* **1.** *Now Dial.* **a** To blame. **b** To charge with a fault. **2.** *Geol.* To produce a fault in. **—** *v. i.* **1.** *Archaic.* To err; blunder. **2.** *Geol.* To fracture so as to produce a fault.

fault′find′ing (fôlt′fīn′dĭng), *n.* Act or practice of finding fault; esp., petty censure. **—** *adj.* Finding, or disposed to find, fault; captious; caviling. **— Syn.** See CRITICAL. **— fault′find′er,** *n.*

fault′less (-lĕs; -lĭs), *adj.* Without fault; free from defect, imperfection, failing, blemish, or error. **— fault′less·ly,** *adv.* **— fault′less·ness,** *n.*

fault′y (fôl′tĭ), *adj.*; FAULT′I·ER (-tĭ·ẽr); FAULT′I·EST. **1.** Of the nature of, or marked by, fault or faults; imperfect. **2.** *Obs.* Guilty of a fault; hence, blamable. **— fault′i·ly,** *adv.* **— fault′i·ness,** *n.*

faun (fôn), *n.* [L. *Faunus,* fr. *favere* to favor.] *Rom. Relig.* One of a class of rural deities, half goat and half man, or of human shape, with pointed ears, horns, and a goat's tail.

fau′na (fô′nȧ), *n.* [LL.] **1.** Animals or animal life, esp. as disting. from *flora,* of a region, period, environment, etc.; as, marine *fauna.* **2.** A systematic treatise upon the animals of a given area or period. **— fau′nal** (-năl; -n'l), *adj.* **— fau′nal·ly,** *adv.*

Fau′nus (fô′nŭs), *n.* [L. See FAUN.] *Rom. Relig.* A rural deity, god of animals and crops and of prophecy, — identified with Pan.

Faust (foust), *n.* The title and hero of a drama by Goethe. Faust deserts his studies and in association with Mephistopheles engages in a drinking bout, seduces Margaret, gains power in politics, weds Helen of Troy, wins a battle. His soul is snatched away from Mephistopheles to a new career. An opera by Gounod is based on the first part.

‖**fau′teuil′** (fō′tû′y′; *Angl.* fō′tĭl), *n.* [F., of Teut. origin.] An armchair.

Fau′vist (fō′vĭst), *n.* One of a group of French artists (Matisse, Derain, and others) who, about 1906, revolted from current tendencies in academic art, as well as from the scientific severity of the neoimpressionists.

‖**faux pas** (fō′ pä′); *pl.* FAUX PAS (fō′ pä′; *E.* fō′ päz′). [F.] A false step; esp., an offense against social convention.

fa·ve′o·late (fȧ·vē′ō·lāt), *adj.* [From dim. of L. *favus* honeycomb.] Honeycombed; alveolate.

fa·vo′ni·an (fȧ·vō′nĭ·ăn; 58), *adj.* [L. *Favonianus.*] Pertaining to the west wind; mild; favoring.

fa′vor, fa′vour (fā′vẽr), *n.* [OF. favor, fr. L. *favor,* fr. *favere* to be favorable.] **1.** Regard or esteem, as shown to another; hence, approbation. **2.** Act or instance of kindness; as: **a** A concession; privilege; as, a great *favor* was granted us. **b** Help; assistance. **c** A mark or token of favor; orig., a token of love; now, a token of an occasion, feast, etc. **d** A letter; as, your *favor* received; — now chiefly in acknowledging receipt. **3.** Indulgence; permission; also, indulgent treatment; hence, unfair indulgence; partiality. **4.** Favorable regard; hence, support; as, to win the *favor* of the voters. **5.** That which pleases; charm. **6.** *Archaic.* Appearance; look; also, countenance; face. **—** ***in favor of.*** **a** Approving; endorsing; in accord or sympathy with. **b** To (one) or to the order of (one); so as to be converted or utilized by (one); — of a check, etc.

Syn. **Favor, good will, countenance** mean a disposition to be friendly or helpful. **Favor** suggests an active interest and a willingness to give approval or support, sometimes implying partiality; **good will** usually implies positive friendliness and a willingness to contribute to the success or welfare of a person or group; **countenance** stresses approval or sanction but may or may not go so far as *favor* or *good will* in implying helpfulness or friendliness. **— Ant.** Animus.

— *v. t.* **1.** To regard with favor; specif.: **a** To show partiality towards. **b** To treat carefully; to spare. **2.** To oblige; to show kindness to. **3.** To afford advantages for success to; as, the darkness *favored* his attempt. **4.** To give support to; to sustain. **5.** To resemble in features; as, the child *favors* his father. **— fa′vor·er, fa′vour·er,** *n.*

fa′vor·a·ble, fa′vour·a·ble (fā′vẽr·ȧ·b'l), *adj.* **1.** Favoring; propitious; approving. **2.** Tending to favor; advantageous; as, a *favorable* breeze. **3.** That is in one's favor; as, a *favorable* answer. **— fa′vor·a·ble·ness,** *n.* **— fa′vor·a·bly,** *adv.*

Syn. **Favorable, auspicious, propitious** mean presaging a happy outcome. **Favorable** implies that the persons or circumstances involved are encouraging, as by being kindly disposed, advantageous, or the like; **auspicious** is applicable to anything that is taken as a favorable sign or omen; **propitious,** in earlier use applied to fate, omen, etc., in the sense of *favorable,* is now also applied to any time, condition, etc., that seems favorable for starting, proceeding, and the like.

fa′vored, fa′voured (fā′vẽrd), *adj.* **1.** Regarded with favor; aided; also, endowed with advantages; gifted. **2.** Having a certain favor or appearance; featured.

fa′vor·ite, fa′vour·ite (fā′vẽr·ĭt), *n.* [MF. *favorit* favored, fr. past part. of It. *favorire* to favor.] **1.** A person or thing regarded with peculiar favor; specif., one unduly loved, trusted, or enriched with favors. **2.** *Sports.* The competitor (as a horse in a race) judged most likely to win. **—** *adj.* Regarded with particular affection or esteem.

fa′vor·it·ism, fa′vour·it·ism (-ĭt·ĭz'm), *n.* **1.** Manifestation of partiality. **2.** State of being a favorite.

fa′vus (fā′vŭs), *n.* [L., honeycomb.] *Med.* A contagious skin disease caused by a fungus (*Trichophyton schoenleinii* and allied species).

fawn (fôn), *n.* [OF. *faon, feon,* deriv. of L. *fetus.* See FETUS.] **1.** *Zool.* A young deer; a buck or doe of the first year. **2.** A brown, redyellow in hue, of low saturation and medium brilliance. See COLOR. **—** *adj.* Of the color fawn.

fawn, *v. i.* [AS. *fagnian, fahnian,* to rejoice, var. of *fægnian.* See FAIN, *adj.*] **1.** To show delight or affection as a dog does, by crouching, wagging the tail, etc. **2.** To court favor by a cringing demeanor; — often with *on.*

— *n. Obs.* A cringing or fawning. **— fawn′er,** *n.* **— fawn′ing·ly,** *adv.*

Syn. **Fawn, toady, truckle, cringe, cower** mean to behave abjectly in a superior's presence. **Fawn** implies the courting of favor by servile flattery or exaggerated deference; **toady,** an attempt to ingratiate oneself as by a menial attitude; **truckle,** subordination of self and submission of one's desires, judgments, etc., to those of a superior; **cringe,** an obsequious bowing or crouching as if in fear; **cower,** abject fear, especially in the presence of those who domineer.

fay (fā), *v. t. & i.*; FAYED (fād); FAY′ING. [AS. *fēgan* to join.] *Shipbuilding.* To fit; to join; to unite closely.

fay, *n.* [OF. *fei.* See FAITH.] *Archaic.* = FAITH.

fay, *n.* [OF. *fae, faie* (F. *fée*).] A fairy; elf.

fay′al·ite (fā′ăl·īt; fī·äl′īt), *n.* [From the Azores island *Fayal.*] *Mineral.* An iron silicate, Fe_2SiO_4, of the chrysolite group.

faze (fāz), *v. t.* [See FEEZE to disturb.] *Colloq., U. S.* To disconcert; worry; daunt. Cf. FEEZE.

feal (fēl), *adj.* [OF., var. of *feeil, feoil,* fr. L. *fidelis* faithful, fr. *fides* faith.] *Obs.* Faithful; loyal.

fe′al·ty (fē′ăl·tĭ), *n.* [OF. *feauté, feeuté, feelté,* fr. L. *fidelitas,* fr. *fidelis* faithful.] **1.** Fidelity of a feudal tenant or vassal to his lord. **2.** Observance of allegiance; faithfulness as a duty; constancy; also, state of being faithful or loyal. **— Syn.** See FIDELITY.

fear (fēr), *n.* [AS. *fǣr* danger.] **1.** Painful emotion marked by alarm; dread; disquiet; also, an instance of this feeling. **2.** State or habit of fearing; anxious concern; solicitude. **3.** Awe; profound reverence, esp. for the Supreme Being. **4.** Ground for or occasion of alarm; danger. *Now Rare,* except in *no fear;* as, he will not fail, no *fear.*

Syn. **Fear, dread, fright, alarm, dismay, consternation, panic, terror, horror, trepidation** mean painful agitation in the presence or anticipation of danger. **Fear** and **dread** both imply apprehension and anxiety and, often, a complete loss of courage; **fright,** the shock of sudden, startling fear; **alarm,** the fright that comes from awareness of danger; **dismay** implies deprivation of courage or spirit by an alarming or disconcerting prospect; **consternation,** the prostration or confusion of one's faculties; **panic** stresses overmastering and, often, groundless fear or fright; **terror,** extreme consternation; **horror,** a shuddering fear mixed with abhorrence at something seen; **trepidation** adds to *dread* the implications of timidity and, often, trembling and hesitation.

— *v. t.* **1.** *Archaic & Dial.* To affright; terrify. **2.** *Archaic.* To be afraid; — used reflexively. **3.** To consider with alarm; to be afraid of.

4. To have a reverential awe of; as, to *fear* God. **— v. i. 1.** To be afraid. **2.** To feel painful uncertainty; to doubt. — **fear'er** (fēr'ẽr), *n.*

fear'ful (fēr'fo͝ol; -f'l), *adj.* **1.** Inspiring fear; exciting terror. **2.** Full of fear, alarm, awe, or apprehension; afraid; timorous. **3.** Indicating, or caused by, fear. **4.** Extremely bad, large, numerous, etc. — **fear'ful·ly**, *adv.* — **fear'ful·ness**, *n.*

Syn. (1) **Fearful, awful, dreadful, frightful, terrible, terrific, horrible, horrific, shocking, appalling** mean arousing a feeling akin to that suggested in the first part of the word. In very strict use they imply the suggested emotion, in very loose use they are merely intensives, but in loose but still correct usage each has a distinct value. **Fearful** suggests a disquieting; **awful**, an undue weighting with significance; **dreadful**, a power to make one shrink; **frightful**, a startling, outrageous quality; **terrible**, a painfulness too great to be borne; **terrific**, a capacity for stunning; **horrible** and **horrific**, outstanding hideousness or odiousness; **shocking**, a startling contrast to one's expectations, one's moral sense, etc.; **appalling**, a capacity to strike one forcibly as with dismay, amazement, etc.

(2) **Fearful, apprehensive, afraid** mean disturbed by fear or fears of something. **Fearful** connotes a timorous, worrying, or imaginative temperament more often than a real cause for fear; **apprehensive** implies good grounds for fear and, therefore, a state of mind; **afraid** may or may not imply good grounds for fear, but it usually suggests weakness or cowardice.

fear'less (-lĕs; -lĭs), *adj.* Free from fear; betraying no fear. — **fear'less·ly**, *adv.* — **fear'less·ness**, *n.*

fear'nought', fear'naught' (fēr'nôt'), *n.* **1.** A fearless person. **2.** A thick, stout woolen cloth.

fear'some (-sŭm), *adj.* **1.** Frightful; causing fear. **2.** Timid; timorous. — **fear'some·ly**, *adv.* — **fear'some·ness**, *n.*

fea'sance (fē'zăns), *n.* [F. *faisance.*] *Law.* The doing or performance of a condition, duty, etc.

fea'si·bil'i·ty (fē'zĭ·bĭl'ĭ·tĭ), *n.; pl.* -TIES (-tĭz). Quality of being feasible; practicability.

fea'si·ble (fē'zĭ·b'l), *adj.* [OF. *faisible, faisable,* fr. *faire* to make or do, fr. L. *facere.* See FACT.] **1.** Capable of being done or effected; practicable. **2.** Capable of being dealt with successfully. — **Syn.** See POSSIBLE. — **fea'si·ble·ness**, *n.* — **fea'si·bly**, *adv.*

feast (fēst), *n.* [OF. *feste* festival (F. *fête*), fr. L. *festum,* pl. *festa,* fr. *festus* joyful, festal.] **1.** A festival; esp., a religious festival of rejoicing as opposed to a fast. **2.** An elaborate meal; banquet. **3.** That which affords unusual pleasure to one's mind or senses. **— v. i.** To eat of a feast; hence, to enjoy some unusual pleasure or delight. **— v. t. 1.** To entertain lavishly, esp. at table. **2.** To delight; gratify. — **feast'er** (fēs'tẽr), *n.*

feast'ful (fēst'fo͝ol; -f'l), *adj.* Festive; festal.

Feast of Lanterns. a A Chinese festival on the 15th day of the first month, final part of the new-year celebration. **b** See BON.

feat (fēt), *n.* [OF. *fet, fait,* fr. L. *factum,* prop., past part. of *facere* to do.] **1.** An act; deed. **2.** A deed notable esp. for courage; exploit; as, *feats* in arms. **3.** An act or product of skill, dexterity, or ingenuity.

Syn. Feat, exploit, achievement mean a remarkable deed. **Feat** suggests an act of strength or dexterity, **exploit** an adventurous, heroic, or brilliant *feat,* **achievement** a distinguished endeavor, commonly in the face of difficulty or opposition.

feat, *adj.* [OF. *fait* made, shaped, fit, past part. of *faire* to make or do. See FEAT, *n.*] *Archaic & Dial.* Dexterous; skillful; apt; becoming; neat. — **Syn.** See DEXTEROUS.

feath'er (fĕth'ẽr), *n.* [AS. *fether.*] **1.** One of the light, horny, epidermal outgrowths which together make up the external covering of birds, and form the greater part of the surface of their wings. A typical feather consists of a shaft, the proximal part of which is hollow and is termed the *quill.* The distal part, called the *rachis,* bears processes on each side, called *barbs.* The barbs bear in like manner the *barbules,* which bear the *barbicels.* The barbicels often end in hooks, called *hamuli,* which hook on to the barbules of the next barb, uniting the processes in a vane or web. **2.** Usually *pl.* Plumage; hence, attire. **3.** Condition; hence, mood; spirits. **4.** Kind; nature; species; — from the phrase, "Birds of a *feather.*" **5.** A feathery tuft or fringe of hair. See DOG, *Illust.* **6.** A featherlike flaw, as in the eye or in a precious stone. **7.** [From FEATHER, *v.*] Act of feathering an oar, etc. **8.** *Archery.* A vane (see ARROW, *Illust.*); also, in yew, a layer of the grain. **9.** *Mach.* A projecting strip, rib, fin, or flange. — ***a feather in one's cap.*** *Colloq.* An honor, trophy, or mark of distinction.

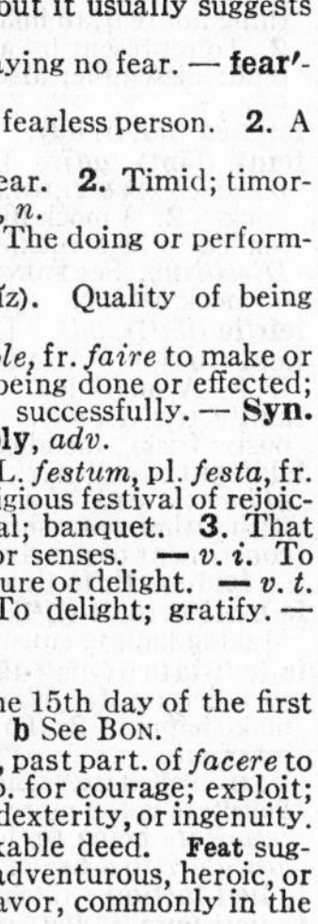

Feather, 1. *a* Shaft, with some of the barbs cut away on the left; *b* Aftershaft, with barbs cut away on the right; *c* Barbs; *d* Quill.

— v. t. 1. To furnish with a feather, as an arrow. **2.** To clothe; deck; adorn, as with feathers. **3.** To cover, or line, with feathers; as, to tar and *feather.* **4.** To join by a groove and tongue. **5.** *Aeronautics.* To rotate (propeller blades) about their span axes into such positions that, with the power off, there is no tendency for the propeller to rotate, or "windmill." When fully feathered, the propeller remains stationary and produces a minimum of aerodynamic drag. **6.** *Rowing.* To turn (an oar blade) almost horizontal as it is lifted from the water at the end of a stroke and to carry it thus until it is squared up for the next catch. **— v. i. 1.** To grow or form feathers; to become feathered. **2.** To move, spread, or grow like feathers. **3.** *Rowing.* To feather an oar. — ***feather one's nest.*** To provide for oneself, esp. from another's property confided to one's care.

feath'er·bed' (fĕth'ẽr·bĕd'), *v. i.;* FEATH'ER·BED'DED; FEATH'ER·BED'DING. To require unneeded workmen or the slowing up of work under a featherbed rule. — **feath'er·bed'ding**, *n.*

featherbed rule. A union rule requiring an employer to pay unneeded workmen, or to pay for unnecessary or duplicating jobs, or limiting the amount of work to be done in a day, as a means of stretching work.

feath'er·bone' (fĕth'ẽr·bōn'), *n.* A substitute for whalebone, made from the quills of geese and turkeys.

feath'er·brain' (-brān'), *n.* A weakbrained, foolish person.

feath'er·brained' (-brānd'), *adj.* Foolish; frivolous.

feath'er·cut' (-kŭt'), *n.* A style of cutting the hair to uneven lengths for shaping small upspringing curls with feathery effect at the tips, to suit head contour, often to form a halolike frame round the face.

feath'ered (fĕth'ẽrd), *adj.* **1.** Clothed, covered, or fitted with (or as with) feathers or wings. **2.** Winged; swift.

feath'er·edge' (fĕth'ẽr·ĕj'), *n.* A very thin edge that is easily broken or bent. — **feath'er·edged'** (-ĕjd'), *adj.*

feather grass. Any of several American grasses (genus *Stipa*) with a one-flowered spikelet, the lemma ending in a twisted awn.

feath'er·head' (fĕth'ẽr·hĕd'), *n.* **a** A frivolous person. **b** A weak head. — **feath'er·head'ed** (-hĕd'ĕd; -ĭd), *adj.*

feath'er·less, *adj.* Having no feathers.

feather palm. Any palm with pinnate leaves.

feather star. A comatulid.

feath'er·stitch' (fĕth'ẽr·stĭch'), *n.* A decorative stitch composed of stitches sewed to produce a branching zigzag line. See STITCH, *Illust.* **— v. t. & i.** To ornament with featherstitch. — **feath'er·stitch'ing**, *n.*

feath'er-veined' (-vānd'), *adj.* Having veins diverging from the midrib to the margin; — chiefly of leaves.

feath'er·weight' (-wāt'), *n.* **1.** A very light weight; specif.: **a** *Horse Racing.* The lightest weight carried by a horse in a handicap. **b** The weight of a boxer between 118 and 126 lbs. **2.** A person or thing of very light weight. — **feath'er·weight'**, *adj.*

feath'er·wood' (-wo͝od'), *n.* An Australian timber tree (*Polyosma cunninghamii*), with wood resembling hickory.

feath'er·y (fĕth'ẽr·ĭ), *adj.* **a** Like feathers; light; trivial. **b** Covered with or as with feathers. — **feath'er·i·ness**, *n.*

feat'ly (fēt'lĭ), *adv.* [From FEAT, *adj.*] **1.** Properly; neatly. **2.** *Archaic.* Nimbly; cleverly. — *adj.* Neat; graceful. — **feat'li·ness**, *n.*

fea'ture (fē'tūr), *n.* [OF. *faiture* fashion, make, fr. L. *factura* a making, fr. *facere, factum,* to make.] **1. a** The make, form, or appearance, esp. of a person. **b** Formerly, physical beauty. **2. a** The make or cast of a human face or of its parts; facial aspect. **b** A single part of the face; lineament. **3.** Any marked peculiarity; anything especially prominent; trait; characteristic. **4.** *U. S.* A special inducement or attraction; specif.: **a** The principal motion picture shown on a bill with other pictures. **b** A distinctive article, story, or picture, or a special department, in a newspaper or magazine. **— v. t. 1.** *Colloq.* To resemble as to features; to favor. **2.** To distinguish the face of; to be a feature of. **3.** To delineate the features of; to impress the shape of. **4.** *Colloq.* To make a feature of; to give special prominence to.

fea'tured (fē'tūrd), *adj.* **1.** Shaped; fashioned. **2.** Having features; formed into or expressed by features. **3.** *U. S.* Displayed or advertised as a special attraction.

fea'ture·less, *adj.* Having no distinctive features.

feaze (fēz), *v. t. & i.* *Now Dial.* To unravel; fray.

feaze (fēz; fāz). Var. of FEEZE, *n. & v.*

feb'ri- (fĕb'rĭ-). [L. *febris.*] Combining form meaning *fever,* as in **feb'ri·cide, feb'ri·fa'cient, fe·brif'er·ous.**

fe·bric'i·ty (fē·brĭs'ĭ·tĭ), *n.* *Med.* Feverishness.

fe·brif'ic (fē·brĭf'ĭk), *adj.* [*febri-* + *-fic.*] Producing fever; feverish.

fe·brif'u·gal (fē·brĭf'ū·găl; fĕb'rĭ·fū'găl), *adj.* Mitigating or removing fever.

feb'ri·fuge (fĕb'rĭ·fūj), *n.* [F. *fébrifuge,* fr. L. *febris* fever + *fugare* to put to flight, fr. *fugere* to flee.] *Med.* A remedy to mitigate or remove fever. — *adj.* Efficacious against fever.

fe'brile (fē'brĭl; fĕb'rĭl; 56), *adj.* [F. *fébrile.*] Feverish.

Feb'ru·ar'y (fĕb'ro͞o·ĕr'ĭ; fĕb'ū-; fĕb'o͞o-; -ẽr·ĭ), *n.; pl.* -ARIES (-ĭz). [L. *Februarius,* fr. *februa,* pl., feast of purification held on Feb. 15.] The second month in the year. In ordinary years it now has 28 days; in leap years, 29. Abbr. *Feb.*

fe'ces, fae'ces (fē'sēz), *n. pl.* [L. *faex,* pl. *faeces,* dregs.] **1.** Sediment; dregs. **2.** Excrement; ordure. — **fe'cal, fae'cal** (fē'kăl), *adj.*

‖**fe'cit** (fē'sĭt). [L.] He (or she) made (or executed) (it).

feck (fĕk), *n.* [Abbr. fr. *effect.*] *Scot.* Efficacy; value; also, amount; quantity.

feck'et (fĕk'ĭt), *n.* *Scot.* An under waistcoat.

feck'less (fĕk'lĕs; -lĭs), *adj.* *Orig. Dial.* Spiritless; weak; worthless. — **feck'less·ly**, *adv.* — **feck'less·ness**, *n.*

feck'ly (-lĭ), *adv.* *Chiefly Scot.* Mostly; almost.

fec'u·lence (fĕk'ū·lĕns), *n.* State or quality of being feculent; muddiness; also, sediment; dregs; feces.

fec'u·lent (-lĕnt), *adj.* [F. *féculent,* fr. L. *faeculentus,* fr. *faecula.* See FECULA.] Foul with impurities; fecal.

fe'cund (fē'kŭnd; fĕk'ŭnd), *adj.* [F. *fécond,* fr. L. *fecundus;* akin to FETUS, FEMININE.] Fruitful in offspring or vegetation; prolific; also, figuratively, rich in invention. — **Syn.** See FERTILE. — **Ant.** Barren.

fe'cun·date (fē'kŭn·dāt; fĕk'ŭn-), *v. t.* [L. *fecundare,* fr. *fecundus.*] **1.** To make fruitful or prolific. **2.** *Biol.* To impregnate; fertilize; pollinate. — **fe'cun·da'tion** (-dā'shŭn), *n.*

fe·cun'di·ty (fē·kŭn'dĭ·tĭ), *n.* Quality or power of producing offspring or fruit, esp. rapidly and in abundance; fertility; hence, productiveness.

fed (fĕd), *past & past part.* of FEED.

fed'er·a·cy (fĕd'ẽr·ȧ·sĭ), *n.; pl.* -CIES (-sĭz). An alliance; confederacy.

fed'er·al (fĕd'ẽr·ăl), *adj.* [L. *foedus* league, treaty, compact.] **1.** Pertaining to a compact between states that yield by its terms certain abatements of their sovereignty for uniting into a new state; as, a *federal* union. **2. a** Pertaining to a state consolidated from several states which retain limited powers; as, a *federal* government. **b** Of or pertaining to, or involving the principle of, the government of such a state (often specif. [*usually cap.*], the United States); as, the *Federal* legislation of the United States. **3.** [*cap.*] *U. S. Hist.* **a** Friendly to the principle of a federal government with strong centralized powers. **b** Of or relating to, or loyal to, the government or armies of the United States in the Civil War of 1861–65; as, *Federal* troops. — **fed'er·al·ly**, *adv.*

Fed'er·al, *n.* **1.** A Federalist. **2.** *U. S. Hist.* A supporter of the government of the United States in the Civil War; specif., a soldier in the Federal armies.

Federal Bureau of Investigation. *U. S.* A bureau of the Department of Justice established to conduct investigations in Federal crimes, such as espionage, bank robbery, bribery, kidnaping. Abbr. *FBI*

Federal Communications Commission. *U. S.* A board of seven commissioners, appointed by the president under the Communications Act of 1934, with power to regulate all electrical communications systems (radio, telegraph, cable, telephone) in the United States. Abbr. *FCC*

Federal Deposit Insurance Corporation. *U. S.* A corporation created under the Banking Act of 1933 to provide insurance of banks' deposits and to give aid in the liquidation of closed banks. Abbr. *FDIC*

fed′er·al·ism (fĕd′ẽr·ăl·ĭz′m), *n.* **1.** The federal principle of national organization; also, advocacy or support of this principle. **2.** [*cap.*] *U. S. Hist.* The principles of the Federalists.
fed′er·al·ist (-ĭst), *n.* **1.** An advocate of the federal system of national organization. **2.** [*cap.*] *U. S. Hist.* **a** An advocate of a federal union between the colonies after the War of Independence and of the formation and adoption of the Constitution. **b** A member or adherent of the Federal party (which see).
fed′er·al·ist, fed′er·al·is′tic (-ĭs′tĭk), *adj.* Of, pertaining to, or in favor of federalism or the Federalists.
fed′er·al·ize (fĕd′ẽr·ăl·īz), *v. t.* To unite by compact, as under a federal government; also, to bring under the sole jurisdiction of a federal government. — **fed′er·al·i·za′tion** (-ĭ·zā′shŭn; -ī·zā′-), *n.*
Federal party. A name given to the group of men most prominent in urging the formation and adoption of the Constitution of the United States, and later adopted by the political party favoring a strong centralized federal power.
Federal Reserve System. *U. S.* A banking system, including twelve **Federal reserve banks** throughout the country under the control of a central **Federal Reserve Board** of eight members, established in 1913 to concentrate the banking resources and to provide an elastic currency.
Federal Trade Commission. *U. S.* A commission of five members (created by an act of 1914) appointed by the president, to prevent unfair methods of commerce, to aid in enforcing antitrust laws, and to investigate business practice and management. Abbr. *FTC*
fed′er·ate (fĕd′ẽr·āt), *adj.* [L. *foederatus*, past part. of *foederare* to establish by treaty or league, fr. *foedus*. See FEDERAL.] United by compact; confederate.
fed′er·ate (-āt), *v. t. & i.* To unite in a league or federation.
fed′er·a′tion (fĕd′ẽr·ā′shŭn), *n.* **1.** A uniting by league or covenant, esp. in forming a sovereign power so that each of the uniting powers retains local powers. **2.** A federal or confederated government; now, esp., a sovereign state formed by federal union.
fed′er·a′tive (fĕd′ẽr·ā′tĭv; -*ȧ*·tĭv), *adj.* Of or relating to a federation; based on, or inclined to, federation. — **fed′er·a′tive·ly**, *adv.*
fe·do′ra (fē·dō′r*ȧ*; 70), *n.* [From the drama *Fédora* by Sardou.] *U. S.* Any low soft felt hat having the crown creased lengthwise.
fee (fē), *n.* [AF. *fee*, OF. *fiu, fieu, fief*, of G. origin.] **1.** In feudal law, any feudal benefice, or estate in land held of a feudal lord. **2.** *Law.* At the common law, an estate of inheritance in land, being either a ***fee simple***, a fee without limitation to any class of heirs or restrictions upon alienation, or a ***fee tail***, an estate of inheritance limited to a class of heirs. **3.** The territory held in fee. **4.** A charge fixed by law for certain services or privileges. **5.** Compensation for professional service. **6.** A fixed charge for admission, as to a museum, or for stated privileges; as, club *fees*. **7.** A gratuity; tip. — **Syn.** See WAGE. — *v. t.*; FEED (fēd); FEE′ING. **1.** To give a gratuity to; to tip. **2.** *Chiefly Scot.* To hire; employ.
fee′ble (fē′b'l), *adj.*; FEE′BLER (-blẽr); FEE′BLEST (-blĕst; -blĭst). [OF. *feble, foible*, fr. L. *flebilis* lamentable, fr. *flere* to weep.] **1.** Lacking in strength; weak; also, indicating weakness; as, a *feeble* moan. **2.** Deficient in qualities or resources that indicate vigor, authority, efficiency, etc.; ineffective; also, inadequate; inferior. — **Syn.** See WEAK. — **fee′ble·ness**, *n.* — **fee′bly**, *adv.*
fee′ble–mind′ed (-mīn′dĕd; -dĭd; 2), *adj.* **a** Weak in will or understanding. **b** *Psychol.* Abnormally lacking in intelligence. — **fee′ble–mind′ed·ly**, *adv.* — **fee′ble–mind′ed·ness**, *n.*
fee′blish (fē′blĭsh), *adj.* Somewhat feeble.
feed (fēd), *v. t.*; FED (fĕd); FEED′ING. [AS. *fēdan*.] **1.** To give food to. **2.** To furnish something essential as to the growth, sustenance, or maintenance of. **3.** To produce, or serve as, food for; as, enough wheat to *feed* all. **4.** To satisfy, as a desire for revenge or flattery; to gratify; also, to give support or cheer to. **5.** To supply or furnish for use or consumption; as, to *feed* coal to a furnace. **6.** *Mach.* To supply (the material to be operated upon) to a machine. **7.** *Theater.* To supply (a fellow actor) with the cue lines, etc., necessary to bring out his part. — *v. i.* **1.** To take food; to eat. **2.** To feed oneself; to prey; — with *on* or *upon*. **3.** To be nourished or satisfied, as if by food.
— *n.* **1.** *Now Colloq.* Act of eating; hence, a meal. **2.** **a** Food, esp. for livestock; fodder. **b** The amount given at each feeding; as, a *feed* of oats. **3.** *Mach.* **a** The motion, or act, of carrying forward the stuff to be operated upon, as in a machine. **b** Material supplied, as coal to a furnace. **c** The mechanism by which the action of feeding is produced.
feed′back′ (fēd′băk′), *n.* **1.** *Elec.* The returning of a fraction of the output of an electric oscillation to the input to which the fraction is added at the proper phase. **2.** Any partial reversion of the effects of a given process to its source; — esp. of biological, psychological, and social systems.
feed′er (fēd′ẽr), *n.* One who or that which feeds; specif.: **a** A device, apparatus, or organ for giving nourishment. **b** A worker who feeds material into a machine, furnace, etc. **c** A source of supply, as a tributary stream. **d** *Elec.* A heavy wire conductor supplying electricity at some point of a system of electric distribution. **e** *Theater.* An actor or part that feeds or serves as a foil for another.
feel (fēl), *v. t.*; FELT (fĕlt); FEEL′ING. [AS. *fēlan*.] **1.** To touch; handle; hence, to examine as by touching; to test. **2.** To perceive by sensation. **3.** To be aware of (an emotional reaction, etc.). **4.** To be aware of instinctively or intellectually. **5.** To be wounded in one's sensibilities by. — *v. i.* **1.** To receive or be able to receive a tactile sensation. **2.** To search for something with the fingers; to grope. **3.** To appear, esp. to the sense of touch; to seem; as, it *feels* cold to me. **4.** To be conscious of an inward impression, state of mind, etc.; as, to *feel* friendly. **5.** To have sympathy. — *n.* **1.** Feeling; perception by sensations. **2.** The sense of touch; as, it is soft to the *feel*. **3.** A quality of a thing as imparted through touch.
feel′er (fēl′ẽr), *n.* **1.** One who or that which feels. **2.** A tactile organ of an animal, as a tentacle. **3.** Anything, as a proposal, put forth to ascertain the views of others.
feel′ing, *n.* **1.** Act or condition of one that feels. **2.** That one of the five senses of which the skin is the chief end organ, and of which sensations of touch, pressure, etc., are characteristic; specif., touch. **3.** A sensation or a perception; bodily consciousness. **4.** Appreciative recognition; sense; as, a *feeling* of injury. **5.** Any emotional state; emotion; as, a kindly *feeling;* also, emotional responsiveness. **6.** Formerly, opinion; now, unreasoned opinion; sentiment. **7.** Character ascribed to a thing as a result of one's impression or emotional state; atmosphere; as, this has the *feeling* of a haunted house. **8.** **a** That quality of a work of art which embodies, and is calculated to convey, the emotion of the artist. **b** Sympathetic aesthetic response. **9.** *Psychol.* A state of consciousness, or consciousness in general considered in itself and apart from any reference to an object of perception or of thought. — *adj.* That feels; sensitive. — **feel′ing·ly**, *adv.*
Syn. **Feeling, affection, emotion, sentiment, passion** mean a partly mental and partly physical response that is painful or pleasurable or both in some degree. **Feeling**, apart from the context, gives no hint of the nature, the quality, or the intensity of the response; **affection**, once equal to *feeling*, now applies to such feelings as are also inclinations or likings; **emotion** carries a stronger implication of agitation or excitement; **sentiment** often implies a larger intellectual element in the feeling than the other terms but, occasionally, it connotes artificiality; **passion** suggests a powerful or controlling emotion.
fee simple, fee tail. See FEE.
feet (fēt), *n., pl.* of FOOT. Abbr. *ft.*
feeze, feaze (fēz; fāz), *v. t.* [AS. *fēsian, fȳsian*.] *Obs. exc. Dial.* To disturb; worry; also, to beat. Cf. FAZE.
feeze (fēz; fāz), *n.* **1.** *Obs. exc. Dial.* A rush. **2.** *Colloq., U. S.* Fretful alarm.
feice (fīs). Var. of FEIST.
feign (fān), *v. t.* [OF. *feindre* (pres. part. *feignant*), fr. L. *fingere* to form, shape, invent.] **1.** To give a mental existence to, as to something not real; to imagine; invent; hence, to form and relate as if true. **2.** To represent by a false appearance of; to sham. — *v. i.* To pretend; dissemble; also, to romance. — **Syn.** See ASSUME. — **feign′er** (-ẽr), *n.*
feigned (fānd), *adj.* **a** Fictitious. **b** Not real or genuine.
feint (fānt), *adj.* [OF.] *Obs.* Feigned. — *n.* [F. *feinte*, fr. *feindre*. See FEIGN.] **1.** That which is feigned; false appearance; trick. **2.** A mock blow or attack on one part when another part is intended to be struck, as in fencing, boxing, war, etc. **3.** Usually *pl. Distilling.* See FAINTS. — **Syn.** See TRICK. — *v. i.* To make a feint, or mock attack.
feir′ie (fẽr′ĭ), *adj.* [AS. *fēre* strong.] *Scot.* Nimble; active.
feist (fīst), *n.* Also **feice** (fīs), **fice** (fīs), **fist** (fīst), **fyce** (fīs). *Local, U. S.* A small dog.
feist′y (fīs′tĭ), *adj.* Also **fice′ty, fist′y** (fīs′tĭ). *Local, U. S.* Variously: frisky, meddlesome, pesky, cocky, touchy, or spunky.
feld′spar′ (fĕld′spär′; fĕl′-), *n.* [G. *feldspat*, fr. *feld* field + *spat* spar.] *Mineral.* Any of a group of crystalline minerals, aluminum silicates with either potassium, sodium, calcium, or barium, and an essential constituent of nearly all crystalline rocks. H., 6–6.5; sp. gr., 2.5–2.9. — **feld·spath′ic** (fĕld·spăth′ĭk; fĕl-), **feld′spath·ose** (-ōs), *adj.*
fe′li·cif′ic (fē′lĭ·sĭf′ĭk), *adj.* [L. *felix, -icis*, happy + *facere* to make.] Making happy; causing happiness.
fe·lic′i·tate (fē·lĭs′ĭ·tāt), *adj.* [LL. *felicitatus*, past part. of *felicitare* to felicitate, fr. *felix, -icis*, happy.] Made happy. — *v. t.* **1.** To make happy. **2.** To call happy or fortunate; to congratulate, as on a marriage.
Syn. **Felicitate, congratulate** mean to wish one joy or happiness. **Felicitate** is the more formal and **congratulate** the more intimate term, *felicitate* being preferred in wishing happiness to a bride, and *congratulate* to a bridegroom.
fe·lic′i·ta′tion (-tā′shŭn), *n.* Congratulation.
fe·lic′i·tous (fē·lĭs′ĭ·tŭs), *adj.* Happily applied or expressed; apt; as, a *felicitous* remark; also, happy in expression. — **Syn.** See FIT. — **fe·lic′i·tous·ly**, *adv.* — **fe·lic′i·tous·ness**, *n.*
fe·lic′i·ty (-tĭ), *n.*; *pl.* -TIES (-tĭz). [OF. *felicité*, fr. L. *felicitas*, fr. *felix, -icis*, happy, fruitful.] **1.** State of being happy; bliss; also, an instance of it. **2.** That which promotes happiness; success. **3.** A pleasing faculty, esp. in art or language; aptness or grace. **4.** An apt or peculiarly fitting expression; as, a style marked by many *felicities*.
fe′lid (fē′lĭd), *n.* Any animal of the cat family.
fe′line (fē′līn), *adj.* [L. *felinus*, fr. *feles, felis*, cat.] **1.** Of or pertaining to the cats (genus *Felis*) or the family (Felidae) which includes the cats, lions, tigers, leopards, pumas, lynxes, etc. **2.** Catlike; sly; stealthy. — *n.* An animal of the cat family. — **fe′line·ly**, *adv.* — **fe·lin′i·ty** (fē·lĭn′ĭ·tĭ), *n.*
feline enteritis. *Veter.* An acute, usually fatal, viral epizootic of cats characterized by fever, diarrhea and dehydration, and destruction of white blood cells; — called also *cat distemper, cat typhoid*.
fell (fĕl), *n.* [AS.] A skin or hide; pelt.
fell, *n.* [ON. *fjall*.] *Brit.* A moor; down.
fell, *v. t.*; FELLED (fĕld); FELL′ING (fĕl′ĭng). [AS. *fellan*.] **1.** To cut, beat, or knock down; as, to *fell* a tree. **2.** *Sewing.* To sew or hem down as shown in the illustration. — *n.* **1.** Timber cut down during one season. **2.** *Sewing.* A seam formed by felling.

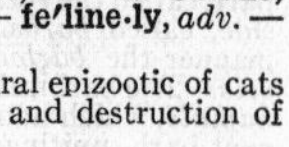

Fell, 2. *a* Original Seam joining pieces *A* and *B*; *b* Hemmed-down Fell.

fell, *adj.* [OF. *fel* cruel, fierce, orig. nom. of *felon*, n. See FELON.] **1.** Cruel; fierce. **2.** *Poetic.* Deadly. **3.** *Scot. & Dial.* **a** Sharp; pungent. **b** Spirited; doughty. **c** Great; mighty. — *adv. Obs. exc. Dial.* **a** Fiercely. **b** Vigorously. **c** Very; greatly.
fell, *past* of FALL.
fell′a·ble (fĕl′*ȧ*·b'l), *adj.* Fit to be felled.
fel′lah (fĕl′*ȧ*), *n.*; *pl.* Arabic FELLAHIN or -HEEN (fĕl′*ȧ*·hēn′), English FELLAHS (fĕl′*ȧ*z). [Ar. *fallāh*, pl. *fallahīn*.] A peasant in Egypt, Syria, and other Arabic-speaking countries.
fell′er (fĕl′ẽr), *n.* One who or that which fells.
fell′mon′ger (fĕl′mŭng′gẽr), *n.* A dealer in fells, esp. sheepskins. — **fell′mon′ger·ing, fell′mon′ger·y**, *n.*
fell′ness, *n.* Fierce barbarity; destructiveness.
fel′loe (fĕl′ō), *n.* A felly.
fel′low (fĕl′ō), *n.* [ME. *felawe, felaghe*, fr. late AS. *fēolaga*, fr. ON. *fēlagi* comrade, fr. *fēlag* partnership.] **1.** *Obs.* A sharer; partner. **2.** A comrade; associate. **3.** One of a pair; a mate. **4.** An equal, as in power, rank, character; peer. **5.** **a** *Obs.* A person of one of the lower social orders. **b** A man without good breeding or worth. **6.** *Colloq.* **a** A person; chap. **b** A beau; sweetheart. **7.** In certain universities, an incorporated member of a college; also, a graduate student appointed to a fellowship (def. 7 **c**). **8.** A member of an incorporated literary or scientific society; as, a *fellow* of the Royal Society. — *v. t.* **1.** To represent as equal to. **2.** To produce a fellow to; to match. — *adj.* Being a companion, mate, or associate.
fellow feeling. Sympathy; also, a feeling of mutual understanding.
fellow servant. **1.** One of two or more servants employed together. **2.** *pl. Law.* Persons employed by the same master and engaged in

promoting a common object under such relations to each other that the safety of any one in the ordinary course of events depends upon the exercise of due care and skill by the others.

fel'low·ship (fĕl'ō-shĭp), *n.* **1.** State or relation of being a fellow or associate. **2.** Community of interest, activity, feeling, etc. **3.** Friendliness; comradeship. **4.** Any union or association; esp., a company of equals or friends. **5.** *Obs.* Partnership; membership (in a society); intercourse. **6.** *Eccl.* Communion; mutual relation between members or branches of the same church. **7.** *Universities.* **a** The fellows of a college collectively. **b** The position of a fellow. **c** A foundation for maintenance of a graduate student called a *fellow,* who is pursuing some special line of study and usually resides at the university. — *v. t. & i.;* -SHIPED (-shĭpt) or -SHIPPED; -SHIP'ING (-shĭp'-ĭng) or -SHIP'PING. To admit to a fellowship or to join in fellowship.

fellow traveler. [Trans. of Russ. *popuchiki.*] One who sympathizes with and, often, furthers the ideals and program of, an organized group (originally, and chiefly, the Communist party) without membership in the group or participation in its activities.

fel'ly (fĕl'lĭ), *adv.* In a fell manner; cruelly.

fel'ly (fĕl'ĭ), *n.; pl.* -LIES (-ĭz). Also **fel'loe** (-ō). [AS. *felg.*] The exterior rim, or a segment of the rim, of a wheel, supported by the spokes. See WHEEL, *Illust.*

‖**fe'lo-de-se'** (fē'lō-dē-sē'; fĕl'ō-), *n.; pl.* FELONES-DE-SE (fĕl'ō-nēz-), FELOS-DE-SE (fē'lōz-; fĕl'ōz-). [Anglo-Lat., fr. *felo* felon + *de* of + *se* self.] *Law.* One who deliberately kills himself; a suicide.

fel'on (fĕl'ŭn), *adj.* [ME., adj., cruel, n., a villain, fr. OF. *felon,* adj. & n., perh. fr. L. *fel, fellis,* gall.] Cruel; wicked. — *n.* **1.** *Rare.* A villain. **2.** *Law.* A person who has committed a felony.

fel'on, *n. Med.* A whitlow.

fe·lo'ni·ous (fē-lō'nĭ-ŭs), *adj.* **1.** Of or relating to, or having the quality of, felony; malicious; villainous; traitorous. **2.** *Law.* Of the nature of a legal felony. — **fe·lo'ni·ous·ly,** *adv.* — **fe·lo'ni·ous·ness,** *n.*

fel'on·ry (fĕl'ŭn-rĭ), *n.* The class of felons; specif., the convict population of a penal colony.

fel'o·ny (fĕl'ō-nĭ), *n.; pl.* -NIES (-nĭz). **1.** *Common Law.* **a** In the early common law (with possibly some small anomalies), any crime that could be prosecuted by an appeal. **b** An offense which occasions a total forfeiture of either lands or goods, or both, at the common law, and to which capital or other punishment may be superadded, according to the degree of guilt. **2.** *Common & Statute Law.* Any of various crimes in general graver or more serious in their natures and penal consequences than those called *misdemeanors.*

fel'site (fĕl'sīt), *n.* [*fels*par (after G. *fels* rock, for *feldspar*) + *-ite.*] A dense, igneous rock chiefly of feldspar and quartz in minute crystals. — **fel·sit'ic** (fĕl-sĭt'ĭk), *adj.*

fel'spar' (fĕl'spär'). Var. of FELDSPAR.

felt (fĕlt), *n.* [AS.] **1.** A cloth made of matted fibers of wool, or wool and fur or hair, worked into a compact material by rolling and pressure. **2.** An article made of felt. **3.** A material resembling felt, as a fabric of fibrous asbestos. **4.** *Paper Mfg.* The web, usually a textile fabric, which carries the newly formed sheet of paper over the paper machine. — *v. t.* To make into felt; to cause to adhere and mat together; also, to cover with or as with felt. — *adj.* Pertaining to, or made of, felt.

felt (fĕlt), *past & past part.* of FEEL.

felt'ing, *n.* The material of which felt is made; also, felted cloth; also, the process by which it is made.

fe·luc'ca (fē-lŭk'ȧ), *n.* [It. *feluca.*] *Naut.* A narrow, fast, lateen-rigged vessel, common in the Mediterranean. See LATEEN SAIL, *Illust.*

fe'male (fē'māl), *n.* [OF. *femelle,* fr. L. *femella,* dim. of *femina* woman.] **1.** A woman or girl; a female human being; also, a female animal. **2.** *Bot.* A pistillate plant.

Syn. **Female, woman, lady** mean one of the sex that is the counterpart of the male. **Female,** the regular term where mere classification by sex is intended, whether of persons, animals, or plants, was once used by good writers in place of *woman* or *lady,* but is now avoided in reference to persons; **woman,** the now generally accepted term in reference to persons, applies to all members of that sex, regardless of any differentiating qualities, such as rank or breeding; **lady,** though often used to designate a woman of rank, now ordinarily connotes the possession of qualities befitting a woman of good class or breeding.

— *adj.* **1.** Of or pertaining to a human being of that sex which conceives and brings forth young; hence, by extension, of or pertaining to animals of the corresponding sex; — opposed to *male.* In *Nat. Hist.* the female sex or female animals or characters are denoted by the symbol of Venus (♀). **2.** Peculiar to, or carried on by, woman; feminine. **3.** *Obs.* Effeminate; weakly. **4.** *Bot.* **a** Pertaining to or designating any reproductive organ or portion in which large, nonmotile gametes requiring fertilization by smaller, motile gametes are organized, or any organ or reproductive body concerned in producing fruit after fecundation. **b** Of seed plants, loosely, pistillate. **5.** *Mach.* Designating a hollow part, tool, etc., into which is inserted a corresponding, or male, part.

Syn. **Female, feminine, womanly, womanlike, womanish, effeminate, ladylike** mean characteristic of a female. Since **female** suggests sex only, it applies to animals and plants as well as to human beings; **feminine** applies to features, qualities, etc., characteristic of women; **womanly** suggests qualities befitting a roundly developed woman, especially as a wife or mother; **womanlike,** usually, the typical faults and foibles of women; **womanish** implies behavior typical of a woman and, often, is used in reference to a man; **effeminate** emphasizes the weaker, more delicate aspects of woman's appearance, habits, etc., and is used most often in reference to a man; **ladylike** implies similarity to a lady in conduct, manner, etc., and applies especially to women and girls who evidence good breeding.

female suffrage. See WOMAN SUFFRAGE.

fe·mal'i·ty (fē-măl'ĭ-tĭ), *n.; pl.* -TIES (-tĭz). Femininity.

feme (fĕm), *n.* [OF. (F. *femme*), fr. L. *femina.*] Wife; also, *Obs.,* a woman.

feme cov'ert (kŭv'ērt). [OF. *coverte,* fem. of *covert* covered.] *Law.* A married woman; — disting. from **feme sole** (sōl) [OF. *sole* alone], a woman not married.

feme'-sole' trad'er *or* **mer'chant** (fĕm'sōl'). A married woman who engages in business on her own account, and, with respect to her trading, is treated at law as a feme sole. See SOLE, *adj.*

fem'i·na·cy (fĕm'ĭ-nȧ-sĭ), *n.; pl.* -CIES (-sĭz). Female nature.

fem'i·nal'i·ty (-năl'ĭ-tĭ), *n.; pl.* -TIES (-tĭz). Femininity.

fem'i·ne'i·ty (-nē'ĭ-tĭ), *n.; pl.* -TIES (-tĭz). [L. *femineus* feminine.] Womanliness; femininity.

fem'i·nin (fĕm'ĭ-nĭn), *n. Biochem.* Estrone.

fem'i·nine (-nĭn), *adj.* [OF. *feminin,* fr. L. *femininus,* fr. *femina* woman.] **1.** Female; of the female sex. **2.** Characteristic of women. **3.** *Gram.* Conforming or denoting conformity to the class of words viewed as distinguished for females. Abbr. *fem.* — **Syn.** See FEMALE, *adj.* — **Ant.** Masculine. — *n. Gram.* A noun, pronoun, adjective, or inflectional form or class of the feminine gender; also, the gender thus distinguished. — **fem'i·nine·ly,** *adv.* — **fem'i·nine·ness,** *n.*

feminine ending. *Prosody.* An ending of a verse with an unstressed and, usually, hypermetric syllable.

feminine rhyme. *Prosody.* Double rhyme in verse with feminine endings, as *motion, ocean.*

fem'i·nin'i·ty (fĕm'ĭ-nĭn'ĭ-tĭ), *n.; pl.* -TIES (-tĭz). **1.** The quality or nature of the female sex; womanliness. **2.** Women collectively; womankind.

fem'i·nism (fĕm'ĭ-nĭz'm), *n.* **1.** Feminine character or characteristics; also, a feminine expression. **2.** The theory, cult, or practice of those who advocate such legal and social changes as will establish political, economic, and social equality of the sexes. — **fem'i·nist** (-nĭst), *n. & adj.* — **fem'i·nis'tic** (-nĭs'tĭk), *adj.*

fe·min'i·ty (fē-mĭn'ĭ-tĭ), *n.; pl.* -TIES (-tĭz). Femininity.

fem'i·nize (fĕm'ĭ-nīz), *v. t.* To make effeminate. — **fem'i·ni·za'tion** (-nĭ-zā'shŭn; -nī-zā'-), *n.*

‖**femme** (fȧm), *n.* [F.] A woman; also, a feme.

‖**femme de cham'bre** (fȧm' dē shäɴ'br'). [F.] A lady's maid; a chambermaid.

fem'o·ral (fĕm'ō-răl), *adj.* [L. *femur, femoris,* thigh.] Pertaining to the femur or thigh; as, the *femoral* artery.

fe'mur (fē'mēr), *n.; pl.* FEMURS (-mērz), FEMORA (fĕm'ō-rȧ). [L., thigh.] *Anat.* The proximal bone of the hind limb; the thighbone.

fen (fĕn), *n.* [AS. *fen, fenn,* marsh, mud, dirt.] Low swampy land; moor; marsh; specif., ***the Fens,*** low-lying districts in Lincolnshire and some other English counties.

fence (fĕns), *n.* [From DEFENCE.] **1.** *Archaic.* A defense; bulwark. **2.** Self-defense by the sword; the art and practice of fencing; hence, skill in debate and repartee. **3.** An enclosure; esp., an enclosing barrier, as one to prevent straying from within or intrusion. **4.** A receiver of stolen goods, or a place where such goods are received. — ***on the fence.*** *Colloq.* Undecided or uncommitted in respect to two opposing parties, policies, theories, etc.

— *v. t.;* FENCED (fĕnst); FENC'ING (fĕn'sĭng). **1. a** To enclose with a fence. **b** To fend off danger from; protect. **c** *Archaic.* To repel; ward off. **2.** *Brit.* To prohibit hunting or fishing in. — *v. i.* **1.** *Obs.* To make a defense. **2.** To practice fencing. **3.** To fight or dispute in the manner of fencers; to parry arguments by shifting ground. — **fence'less,** *adj.* — **fence'less·ness,** *n.*

fenc'er (fĕn'sēr), *n.* One who fences; specif.: **a** One who teaches or practices the art of fencing with sword or foil. **b** One who builds or repairs fences.

fen'ci·ble (fĕn'sĭ-b'l), *adj. Chiefly Scot.* Capable of defending or being defended. — *n. Archaic. Mil.* A soldier enlisted for home service only; — usually in the *pl.*

fenc'ing (fĕn'sĭng), *n.* **1.** The art or practice of attack and defense with the sword or foil; hence, the art or practice of fencelike argument or debate. **2. a** *U.S.* Materials used for building fences. **b** Fences collectively.

fend (fĕnd), *v. t.* [From DEFEND.] **1.** *Archaic.* To defend. **2.** To keep off; to ward off; — often with *off;* as, to *fend* off blows. — *v. i.* **1.** To act on the defensive; to resist; parry. **2.** To strive; to make shift. — *n. Scot. & Dial.* An effort for oneself; a shift.

fend'er (fĕn'dēr), *n.* A device that defends or protects; as: **a** A cushion to lessen shock. **b** A splashboard. **c** A railing. **d** The device in front of locomotives and electric cars to lessen injury to pedestrians or animals in case of collision. **e** The guard over the wheel of a motor vehicle. **f** A low metal frame or a screen before an open fireplace.

fen'es·tel'la (fĕn'ĕs-tĕl'ȧ; fĕn'ĭs-), *n.* [L., dim. of *fenestra* window.] *Arch.* A small windowlike opening; specif., an opening in an altar front, allowing the relics within to be seen.

fe·nes'tra (fē-nĕs'trȧ), *n.; pl.* -TRAE (-trē). [L., window.] **1.** *Anat.* A small opening; esp., either of two apertures in the bone between the tympanum and internal ear. **2.** *Zool.* A transparent spot, as in the wings of certain moths. — **fe·nes'tral** (-trăl), *adj.*

fe·nes'trate (-trāt), *adj.* [L. *fenestratus,* past part. of *fenestrare* to furnish with openings and windows.] Having fenestrae or numerous openings; irregularly netted.

fe·nes'trat·ed (-trāt-ĕd; -ĭd), *adj.* Having windows; characterized by windows; also, fenestrate.

fen'es·tra'tion (fĕn'ĕs-trā'shŭn; fĕn'ĭs-), *n.* **1.** State of being or process of becoming fenestrated. **2.** *Arch.* The arrangement and proportioning of windows; hence, the decorating of an architectural composition by the window (and door) openings, their ornaments, and proportions. **3.** *Surgery.* The cutting of an opening in the bone between the tympanum and the internal ear to replace the obstructed natural opening (fenestra), as in ***fenestration operation.***

Fe'ni·an (fē'nĭ-ăn; fēn'yăn; 58), *n.* [Ir. *fiann,* confused with OIr. *Fēne,* a name of the old inhabitants of Ireland.] **1.** One of the ***Fi'an·na*** (fē'ȧ-nȧ), a body of soldiers who flourished in Ireland in the 2d and 3d centuries A.D. The mass of legends of their exploits constitutes the **Fenian cycle** of Irish romance. **2.** A member of the **Fenian Brotherhood,** a secret organization founded in New York in 1856, having for its aim the overthrow of British rule in Ireland. — **Fe'ni·an,** *adj.* — **Fe'ni·an·ism** (-ĭz'm), *n.*

fen'nec (fĕn'ĕk), *n.* [Ar. *fanak.*] *Zool.* A small pale-fawn African fox (*Vulpes zerda*) having large ears.

fen'nel (fĕn'ĕl; -'l), *n.* [AS. *fenol, finol,* deriv. of L. *feniculum, faeniculum,* dim. of *fenum, faenum,* hay.] **a** A perennial European herb (*Foeniculum vulgare*) of the carrot family, cultivated for the aromatic flavor of its seeds. **b** A staminate plant of the hemp (*Cannabis sativa*).

fen'nel·flow'er (fĕn'ĕl-flou'ēr; fĕn''l-), *n.* Any of a genus (*Nigella*) of erect annual herbs of the crowfoot family, esp. one species (*N. sativa*) which yields **fennel seed,** used as a condiment in India; also, its flower.

fen'ny (fĕn'ĭ), *adj.* [AS. *fennig.*] Pertaining to, inhabiting, or grown in, a fen; abounding in fens; boggy.

fen'u·greek (fĕn'ū-grēk), *n.* [F. *fenugrec,* fr. L. *faenugraecum,* fr. *faenum Graecum,* lit., Greek hay.] An annual Asiatic herb (*Trigonella foenumgraecum*) of the pea family, with aromatic seeds used in making curry.

feod (fūd), *n.* Var. of FEUD; specif., feudal estate; fee. — **feo'dal** (fū'dăl; -d'l), *adj.* — **feo·dal'i·ty** (fū·dăl'ĭ·tĭ), *n.* — **feo'da·to'ry** (fū'dȧ·tō'rĭ; -tẽr·ĭ), *n.*

feo'da·ry (fū'dȧ·rĭ), *n.; pl.* -RIES (-rĭz). [ML. *feodarius*, fr. *feodum*.] *Obs. exc. Hist.* **a** A vassal. **b** An accomplice.

feoff (fĕf; fēf), *v. t.* [AF. *feoffer*.] *Law.* To enfeoff.

feoff. Var. of FIEF.

feoff'ee' (fĕf'ē'; fēf'ē'), *n.* *Law.* The person to whom a feoffment is made.

feoff'ment (fĕf'mĕnt; fēf'-), *n.* *Eng. Law.* The grant of a feud or fee.

feof'for, feof'fer (fĕf'ẽr; fēf'ẽr), *n.* *Law.* One who makes a feoffment to another.

-fer (-fẽr). [See -FEROUS.] A suffix forming nouns denoting agents and materials corresponding to adjectives in *-ferous*, as in coni*fer*; Luci*fer*.

fe·ra'cious (fē·rā'shŭs), *adj.* [L. *ferax, -acis*, fr. *ferre* to bear.] Fruitful; fertile. — **fe·rac'i·ty** (fē·răs'ĭ·tĭ), *n.*

‖**fe'rae na·tu'rae** (fē'rē nȧ·tū'rē). [L.] Of a wild nature.

fe'ral (fēr'ăl), *adj.* [L. *fera* a wild animal, fr. *ferus* wild.] Untamed; undomesticated; hence, wild; savage.

fer'-de-lance' (fâr'dē·läns'), *n.* [F., the iron of a lance.] A large venomous snake (*Bothrops atrox*) of South and Central America, allied to the rattlesnake, but with no rattle.

fere (fēr), *n.* [AS. *gefēra*, fr. the root of *faran* to travel.] *Archaic & Dial.* A mate or companion.

fer'e·to'ry (fĕr'ē·tō'rĭ *or, esp. Brit.,* -tẽr·ĭ), *n.; pl.* -RIES (-rĭz). [ME. *fertre*, fr. OF. *fiertre*, fr. L. *feretrum*.] **a** An ornate, often portable, bier or shrine for the relics of a saint. **b** The chapel in which it was kept.

fe'ri·a (fē'rĭ·ȧ), *n.; pl.* FERIAE (-ē). [L.] **1.** *pl.* Festival days; holidays; as, **fe'ri·ae Jo'vi** (jō'vī), festivals of Jupiter. **2.** *Eccl.* A weekday, esp. one neither a festival nor a fast. — **fe'ri·al** (fēr'ĭ·ăl), *adj.*

fe'rine (fēr'īn; -ĭn), *adj.* [L. *ferinus*.] Feral.

Fe·rin'gi (fē·rĭng'gĭ), *n.* Also **Fe·rin'ghee.** [Per. *Firingi*, fr. Ar. *Faranji*, corrupt. of OF. *Franc* a Frank.] In India, a European; also, a Eurasian, esp. of Portuguese-Indian blood.

fer'i·ty (fĕr'ĭ·tĭ), *n.* [L. *feritas*, fr. *ferus* wild.] Wild or untamed state; hence, ferocity; rudeness; barbarity.

fer'ment (fûr'mĕnt), *n.* [F., fr. L. *fermentum*.] **1.** An agent capable of producing fermentation, esp. a living organism, as yeast. See ENZYME. **2.** Fermentation. **3.** State of unrest; agitation; tumult.

fer·ment' (fẽr·mĕnt'), *v. i.* **1.** To undergo fermentation; work. **2.** To be agitated; to seethe. — *v. t.* To cause fermentation in. — **fer·ment'a·ble,** *adj.*

fer'men·ta'tion (fûr'mĕn·tā'shŭn), *n.* **1.** A chemical change with effervescence, as that produced by yeast; any transformation, esp. of organic substances, by the action of ferments, as in the souring of milk or the formation of sugar from starch. **2.** Agitation; unrest.

fer·ment'a·tive (fẽr·mĕn'tȧ·tĭv), *adj.* Causing, having power to cause, or produced by, fermentation; fermenting.

fern (fûrn), *n.* [AS. *fearn*.] Any of a large order (Filicales) of flowerless seedless plants, like seed plants in being differentiated into root, stem, and leaves (fronds) and having vascular tissue, but reproducing by means of asexual spores. — **fern'like'** (-līk'), *adj.*

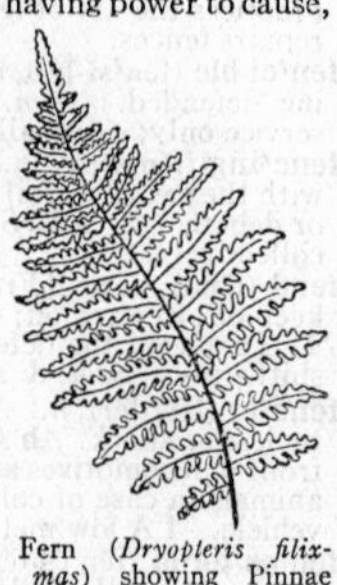

Fern (*Dryopteris filix-mas*) showing Pinnae and Pinnules. (¼)

fern'er·y (fûr'nẽr·ĭ), *n.; pl.* -ERIES (-ĭz). A collection of growing ferns; a place or stand where ferns grow.

fern seed. The dustlike asexual spores of ferns, formerly taken for seeds, and reputed to render one invisible.

fe·ro'cious (fē·rō'shŭs), *adj.* [L. *ferox, -ocis*, fierce.] **1.** Fierce; savage. **2.** *Colloq.* Unbearably intense. — **Syn.** See FIERCE. — **fe·ro'cious·ly,** *adv.* — **fe·ro'cious·ness,** *n.*

fe·roc'i·ty (fē·rŏs'ĭ·tĭ), *n.; pl.* -TIES (-tĭz). Quality of being ferocious; savage wildness; fierceness.

-fer·ous (-fẽr·ŭs). [L. *-fer*, fr. *ferre* to bear.] A suffix signifying *bringing, producing, yielding*, as in auri*ferous*, yielding gold. Hence: **-fer·ous·ly, -fer·ous·ness.**

fer'rate (fĕr'āt), *n.* [L. *ferrum* iron.] A salt of ferric acid.

fer'ret (fĕr'ĕt; -ĭt), *n.* [It. *fioretto*, dim. of *fiore* flower.] A type of narrow tape; — called also **fer'ret·ing.**

fer'ret, *n.* [OF. *fuiret, furet*, fr. *fuiron, furon*, fr. LL. *furo*, fr. L. *fur* thief.] An animal (*Mustela furo*) of the weasel family, kept for hunting rabbits and rats; also, *Western U. S.*, a related species (*M. nigripes*), that feeds on prairie dogs. — *v. t.;* FER'RET·ED (-ĕd; -ĭd); FER'RET·ING. To drive or hunt out of a lurking place, as a ferret does the rabbit; hence, to search (*out*), as by shrewd questioning. — *v. i.* To hunt with ferrets; hence, to search about. — **fer'ret·er,** *n.* — **fer'ret·y,** *adj.*

fer'ri- (fĕr'ĭ-; fĕr'ĭ-). [L. *ferrum* iron.] *Chem.* A combining form indicating *ferric iron* as an ingredient.

fer'ri·age (fĕr'ĭ·ĭj), *n.* The fare to be paid for passage at a ferry; also, conveyance over a ferry.

fer'ric (fĕr'ĭk), *adj.* [L. *ferrum* iron.] Pertaining to, derived from, or containing, iron; *Chem.*, denoting compounds in which iron has a higher valence than in the *ferrous* compounds, or iron with such a valence, as **ferric oxide**, Fe_2O_3, a compound found in nature as the mineral hematite and prepared in various ways as a red powder used as a pigment and for polishing.

fer'ri·cy·an'ic (fĕr'ĭ·sī·ăn'ĭk; fĕr'ĭ-), *adj.* [*ferri-* + *cyanic*.] *Chem.* Pertaining to or designating a brown, unstable, crystalline acid (**ferricyanic acid**, $H_3Fe(CN)_6$).

fer'ri·cy'a·nide (-sī'ȧ·nīd; -nĭd), *n.* *Chem.* A salt of ferricyanic acid.

fer·rif'er·ous (fĕ·rĭf'ẽr·ŭs), *adj.* [L. *ferrum* iron + *-ferous*.] Containing iron; iron-bearing.

Fer'ris wheel (fĕr'ĭs). An amusement device consisting of a giant power-driven steel wheel, carrying cars around its rim; — from its inventor, G. W. G. Ferris.

fer'rite (fĕr'īt), *n.* [L. *ferrum* iron + *-ite*.] **1.** *Petrog. & Metal.* **a** In rocks, any yellowish, reddish, or brownish amorphous substance apparently of iron compounds, but not certainly a particular mineral. **b** In iron and steel, pure metallic iron. **2.** *Chem.* Any of several compounds which may be regarded as metallic derivatives of the ferric hydroxide $Fe_2O_2(OH)_2$; as, franklinite is zinc *ferrite*.

fer'ro- (fĕr'ō-). [L. *ferrum* iron.] A combining form for *ferrous*, as in **fer'ro·al·loy'**, a crude alloy of iron with some other metal. *Ferro-* is used to indicate: **a** *Presence of*, or *connection with, iron*, as in *ferro*magnesian, *ferro*type. **b** In ironmaking and steelmaking, an *alloy of iron with a* (specified) *metal*, as in:

ferroaluminum	**ferromanganese**	**ferrosilicon**
ferrochrome	**ferromolybdenum**	**ferrotungsten**
ferrochromium	**ferronickel**	**ferrovanadium**

c In chemistry, *ferrous iron* as an ingredient, as in *ferro*cyanide.

fer'ro·cal'cite (-kăl'sīt), *n.* *Mineral.* Calcite containing ferrous carbonate, $FeCO_3$. It turns brown on exposure.

fer'ro·con'crete (-kŏn'krēt; -kŏn·krēt'), *n.* Reinforced concrete.

fer'ro·cy·an'ic (-sī·ăn'ĭk), *adj.* [*ferro-* + *cyanic*.] *Chem.* Pert. to or designating a colorless crystalline acid (**ferrocyanic acid**, $H_4Fe(CN)_6$), obtained by treating ferrocyanides with acids.

fer'ro·cy'a·nide (-sī'ȧ·nīd; -nĭd), *n.* A salt of ferrocyanic acid.

fer'ro·mag·ne'sian (-măg·nē'shăn), *adj.* *Mineral.* Containing iron and magnesium.

fer'ro·mag·net'ic (-măg·nĕt'ĭk), *adj.* *Magnetism.* **a** Formerly, paramagnetic, as disting. from diamagnetic and also from magnetic as relating to animal magnetism. **b** Now, usually, magnetic in a high degree, like iron, nickel, and cobalt; — disting. from *paramagnetic*. Cf. DIAMAGNETIC. — **fer'ro·mag'net·ism** (-măg'nē·tĭz'm; -nĭ·tĭz'm), *n.*

fer'ro·type (fĕr'ō·tīp), *n.* A photograph made on a thin iron plate by a process in which collodion is used as a vehicle for the sensitive salts; a tintype; also, the process. — *v. t.* *Photog.* To burnish (as a print) by squeegeeing while wet upon a japanned iron plate.

fer'rous (fĕr'ŭs), *adj.* [L. *ferrum* iron.] Pertaining to, or derived from, iron; specif., *Chem.*, denoting those compounds in which iron is bivalent, or iron with such a valence, as **ferrous sulfate**, $FeSO_4$, an astringent salt obtained as a by-product in certain processes and used as a mordant, in making ink and pigments, as a tonic medicine, etc.

fer'ru·gin'e·ous (fĕr'ōō·jĭn'ē·ŭs), *adj.* Ferruginous; rust-colored.

fer·ru'gi·nous (fĕ·rōō'jĭ·nŭs), *adj.* [L. *ferruginus, -neus*, fr. *ferrugo, -ginis*, iron rust, fr. *ferrum* iron.] **1.** Of, pert. to, or containing iron. **2.** Resembling iron rust in color.

fer'rule (fĕr'ĭl; -ōōl), *n.* [(After L. *ferrum* iron) fr. earlier *verrel*, fr. F. *virole*, fr. L. *viriola* little bracelet, dim. of *viriae* bracelets.] **1.** A ring or cap, usually of metal, put round a cane, tool handle, etc., to strengthen it or prevent splitting. **2.** *Mach.* A short tube or bushing. — *v. t.* To supply with a ferrule.

fer'ry (fĕr'ĭ), *v. t.;* FER'RIED (-ĭd); FER'RY·ING. [AS. *ferian* to convey.] **1.** To transport over a river, strait, etc., in a boat; to cross (a river, etc.) by ferry. **2.** To bring, deliver, or send as if by ferry; specif.: **a** To deliver (an air or naval craft) by operating under its own power. **b** To transport (troops, munitions, etc.) by regular scheduled air service. — *v. i.* To pass over water in a boat or by a ferry. — *n.; pl.* -RIES (-ĭz). **1.** A place or passage where persons or things are carried across a river, arm of the sea, etc., in a boat. **2.** A ferryboat. **3.** A franchise or right to ferry passengers or goods. **4.** An organized service and route for flying airplanes, esp. across a sea or continent, for delivery to the user. — **fer'ry·man,** *n.*

fer'ry·boat' (-bōt'), *n.* A vessel for conveying passengers, merchandise, etc., across a river or other narrow water.

fer'tile (fûr'tĭl; -t'l; *or, esp. Brit.,* -tīl; 56), *adj.* [F., fr. L. *fertilis*, fr. *ferre* to bear, produce.] **1.** Producing in abundance; productive. **2.** Causing fertility; promoting production. **3.** Plentiful. "*Fertile* tears." *Shak.* **4.** **a** As applied to seeds or eggs, capable of growing or developing. **b** Capable of breeding or reproducing. **5.** *Bot.* **a** Capable of producing fruit. **b** Containing pollen; — said of anthers. **c** Developing spores or spore-bearing organs. — **fer'tile·ly,** *adv.* — **fer'tile·ness,** *n.*

Syn. **Fertile, fecund, fruitful, prolific** mean showing power to produce fruit or offspring. **Fertile** applies to the soil, the egg or seed, a person or animal or pair that manifests this power, or to anything, such as a brain or an idea, that bears a figurative resemblance to them; **fecund** applies to that which produces in abundance fruit or offspring or, by extension, projects, inventions, works of art, etc.; **fruitful** may be preferred to *fecund* in reference to trees and plants, or to *fertile* in reference to soil or land, but it is very common in extended application to anything that bears fruit, or has useful or profitable results; **prolific**, which comes close to *fecund* in meaning, usually suggests greater rapidity in reproduction and is often used derogatorily of races, species, etc.

fer·til'i·ty (fẽr·tĭl'ĭ·tĭ), *n.; pl.* -TIES (-tĭz). **1.** State or quality of being fertile. **2.** *Biol.* The power or quality of producing offspring; reproductive capacity.

fer'ti·li·za'tion (fûr'tĭ·lĭ·zā'shŭn; -lī·zā'shŭn), *n.* **1.** Act or process of rendering fertile. **2.** *Biol.* Impregnation; specif. the union of a female and male germ cell, termed the *egg* and *sperm*, to form a new individual (*zygote*). The nuclei (usually *haploid*) fuse to form the (typically *diploid*) zygotic nucleus. Cf. CONJUGATION. **3.** *Bot.* Loosely, pollination in seed plants.

fer'ti·lize (fûr'tĭ·līz), *v. t.* **1.** To make fertile or enrich; to make productive; as, to *fertilize* land. **2.** *Biol.* To cause fertilization of; impregnate. — **fer'ti·liz'a·ble** (-līz'ȧ·b'l), *adj.*

fer'ti·liz'er (-līz'ẽr), *n.* A fertilizing agent or substance, esp. a manure for land, as guano, superphosphate, etc.

fer'u·la (fĕr'ū·lȧ; fĕr'ōō-), *n.; pl.* (sense 2) -LAE (-lē). [L., giant fennel (its stalks were used in punishing schoolboys), rod, whip.] **1.** *Bot.* Any of a very large genus (*Ferula*) of Old World plants of the carrot family, yielding various medicinal gum resins, as galbanum and asafetida. **2.** A ferule; a rod; hence, school discipline.

fer'ule (fĕr'ŭl; -ōōl), *n.* [L. *ferula*. See FERULA.] A rod or ruler, used in disciplining children; also, punishment. — *v. t.* To punish with a ferule.

fer'ule. Incorrect spelling of FERRULE.

fer'ven·cy (fûr'vĕn·sĭ), *n.* State of being fervent; hence, ardor; warmth of feeling or devotion.

fer'vent (-vĕnt), *adj.* [OF., fr. L. *fervens, -entis*, pres. part. of *fervere* to boil, glow.] **1.** Hot; glowing. **2.** Warm in feeling; ardent. — **Syn.** See IMPASSIONED. — **fer'vent·ly,** *adv.*

fer'vid (fûr'vĭd), *adj.* [L. *fervidus*, fr. *fervere*. See FERVENT.] **1.** Very hot; burning; boiling. **2.** Ardent; zealous. — **Syn.** See IMPASSIONED. — **fer'vid·ly,** *adv.* — **fer'vid·ness,** *n.*

‖**Fer'vi'dor'** (fĕr'vē'dôr'), *n.* [F.] See REVOLUTIONARY CALENDAR.

fer'vor, fer'vour (fûr'vẽr), *n.* [OF. *fervor, fervour*, fr. L. *fervor*, fr. *fervere*. See FERVENT.] **1.** Intense heat. **2.** Intensity of feeling or expression; glowing ardor. — **Syn.** See PASSION.

Fes′cen·nine (fĕs′ĕ·nīn; -nĭn), *adj.* [L. *Fescenninus*, fr. *Fescennia*, a city of Etruria, Italy.] Scurrilous; obscene.

fes′cue (fĕs′kū), *n.* [OF. *festu*, deriv. of L. *festuca* stalk, straw.] **1.** A straw, wire, stick, etc., used as a teacher's pointer. **2.** *Bot.* A tufted perennial grass (genus *Festuca*) with panicled spikelets; — called also **fescue grass**. Cf. SPIKELET, *Illust.*

fess (fĕs), *n.* Also **fesse** (fĕs). [OF. *fesse*, *faisse*, fr. L. *fascia* band.] *Her.* A band drawn horizontally across the center of an escutcheon. See ESCUTCHEON, *Illust.* — **fess′wise′**, **fesse′wise′** (-wīz′), *adv.*

fes′tal (fĕs′tăl; -t'l), *adj.* [OF., fr. L. *festum*. See FEAST.] Of, pertaining to, or characteristic of a holiday or a feast; festive. — **fes′tal·ly**, *adv.*

fes′ter (fĕs′tẽr), *v. i.* [ME. *festren*, fr. *fester*, n.] **1.** To generate pus. **2.** To cause progressive poisoning or inflammation; to rankle. **3.** To putrefy; rot. — *v. t.* To cause to fester or rankle. — *n.* [OF. *festre*, fr. L. *fistula* a sort of ulcer.] A small suppurating sore; a pustule.

‖**fe·sti′na len′te** (fĕs·tī′nȧ lĕn′tē). [L.] Make haste slowly.

fes′ti·nate (fĕs′tĭ·nāt), *v. i. & t.* [L. *festinatus*, past part. of *festinare* to hasten.] *Rare.* To hasten. — **fes′ti·nate** (-nāt), *adj.* — **fes′ti·nate·ly**, *adv.*

fes′ti·na′tion (-nā′shŭn), *n.* Haste.

fes′ti·val (fĕs′tĭ·văl), *adj.* [OF., fr. L. *festivus* festive, gay. See FESTIVE.] **1.** Of, pertaining to, appropriate to, or set apart as a festival. **2.** *Obs.* Festive. — *n.* **1.** A time of feasting or celebration; a feast. **2.** A periodical season of entertainment of a specific sort; as, a music *festival*. **3.** Revelry; festivity; — esp. in the phrase *hold*, *keep*, or *make festival*.

fes′tive (fĕs′tĭv), *adj.* [L. *festivus*, fr. *festum* holiday, feast. See FEAST.] Pertaining to or befitting a feast or festival; joyous; gay. — **fes′tive·ly**, *adv.* — **fes′tive·ness**, *n.*

fes·tiv′i·ty (fĕs·tĭv′ĭ·tĭ), *n.; pl.* -TIES (-tĭz). **1. a** *Obs.* Condition or quality of being festive. **b** Joyfulness; gaiety. **2.** A festival; now, often *pl.*, festive activities.

fes′ti·vous (fĕs′tĭ·vŭs), *adj.* *Rare.* Festive.

fes·toon′ (fĕs·to͞on′), *n.* [F. *feston*, fr. It. *festone*, fr. *festa* feast.] **1.** A garland or wreath hanging in a curve, used in decoration for festivals, etc. **2.** *Arch. & Sculp.* A carved or molded ornament representing a festoon. — *v. t. & i.* To form in, adorn with, or connect by, festoons.

fes·toon′er·y (-ẽr·ĭ), *n.* Festoonlike arrangement.

fet (fĕt), *v. t.;* FET; FET′TING. [AS. *fetian.*] *Obs.* To fetch.

fe′tal, **foe′tal** (fē′tăl; -t'l), *adj.* *Anat. & Zool.* Of, relating to, characteristic of, or in the condition of a fetus.

fe·ta′tion, **foe·ta′tion** (fē·tā′shŭn), *n.* The formation of a fetus, normally in the womb; pregnancy.

fetch (fĕch), *v. t.* [AS. *feccan*, *fetian.*] **1.** To go and get; to go and bring toward the person speaking. **2.** To cause to come; to bring to a particular state; as, to *fetch* the butter in the churn. **3.** *Now Dial.* To bring to accomplishment; to achieve. Also, to draw (a breath); heave (a sigh). **4.** *Dial.* To reach; to arrive at. **5.** To derive; deduce; as, to *fetch* analogies from nature. **6.** *Colloq.* To interest; attract. **7.** To bring, as a price; to sell for. **8.** *Colloq.* To strike; as, he *fetched* him a clip on the chin; to deal (a blow). — *v. i.* **1.** To get and bring things. Specif., *Hunting*, to retrieve killed game. **2.** *Naut.* To hold a course; also, to veer. **3.** To arrive at a point; — usually with *up* or *through*. — *n.* **1.** Act of fetching or reaching after; also, the distance so spanned or the effort involved. **2.** A stratagem; trick.

fetch, *n.* The apparition of a living person; a double.

fetch′er (fĕch′ẽr), *n.* One who or that which fetches.

fetch′ing, *adj.* *Colloq.* Pleasing; attractive. — **fetch′ing·ly**, *adv.*

fete, **fête** (fāt; *F.* fât), *n.* [F. *fête*. See FEAST.] A festival; esp., an outdoor entertainment on a lavish scale. — (fāt), *v. t.* To feast; to honor or commemorate by a fete.

‖**fête cham′pê′tre** (fât′ shäɴ′pâ′tr′). [F., a rural festival.] An entertainment in the open air.

fet′e·ri′ta (fĕt′ĕ·rē′tȧ), *n.* [Sudanese Ar.] A grain sorghum related to durra, grown in the southwestern U. S.

fe′ti·a′les (fē′shĭ·ā′lēz), *n. pl.* [L.] *Rom. Antiq.* A priestly board which conducted diplomatic negotiations and, if those failed, declared war. — **fe′tial** (fē′shăl), *adj. & n.*

fe′ti·cide, **foe′ti·cide** (fē′tĭ·sīd), *n.* Act of killing a fetus, causing an abortion. — **fe′ti·cid′al**, **foe′ti·cid′al** (-sīd′ăl; -'l; 2), *adj.*

fet′id (fĕt′ĭd; fē′tĭd), *adj.* [L. *fetidus*, *foetidus*, fr. *fetere*, *foetere*, to stink.] Having an offensive smell; stinking. — **Syn.** See MALODOROUS. — **fet′id·ly**, *adv.* — **fet′id·ness**, *n.*

fe′tish, **fe′tich** (fē′tĭsh; fĕt′ĭsh), *n.* [F. *fétiche*, fr. Pg. *feitiço*, adj., artificial, n., sorcery, charm, fr. L. *facticius* artificial.] **1.** An object supposed to possess magical powers, as in saving its owner from harm, in curing disease, etc. **2.** Any object of special devotion.

Syn. Fetish, talisman, charm, amulet mean an object believed useful in averting evil or in bringing good. **Fetish** applies literally to such an object held sacred by savage or barbarous peoples or, figuratively, to anything regarded unreasonably as sacrosanct; **talisman** applies literally to something such as a gem or a coin believed to have magical powers or, in figurative use, to anything that exerts a magical influence; **charm** applies to that (sometimes an object but often a form of words), superstitiously believed to repel evil spirits or influences or to attract their opposites; **amulet** applies to any charm worn on the person.

fe′tish·ism, **fe′tich·ism** (-ĭz′m), *n.* **1.** Devotion to or belief in fetishes. **2.** *Psychopathol.* Fixation of erotic interest on a part of the body, as the foot, or on an article of clothing. — **fe′tish·is′tic**, **fe′tich·is′tic** (-ĭs′tĭk), *adj.*

fe′tish·ist, **fe′tich·ist** (-ĭst), *n.* A believer in fetishes.

fet′lock (fĕt′lŏk), *n.* [ME. *fetlak*, *fitlok.*] The tufted cushionlike projection on the back side of the leg above the hoof of the horse and similar animals; also, the tuft of hair or the joint at this point. See HORSE, *Illust.*

fe′tor, **foe′tor** (fē′tẽr; -tôr), *n.* [L.] A stench.

fet′ter (fĕt′ẽr), *n.* [AS. *fetor*, *feter.*] Chiefly in *pl.* **1.** A shackle for the feet; a bond. **2.** Anything that restrains; a restraint. — *v. t.* **1.** To put fetters upon; shackle. **2.** To restrain from motion; to confine. — **Syn.** See HAMPER.

fetter bone. The great pastern bone (see PASTERN).

fet′ter·bush′ (-bo͝osh′), *n.* Either of two shrubs of the heath family, native to the southern U. S.: **a** A handsome shrub (*Neopieris nitida*) having small cylindric flowers followed by capsules. **b** An ornamental evergreen shrub (*Pieris floribunda*) having white bell-shaped flowers.

fet′ter·lock (-lŏk), *n.* Fetlock.

fet′tle (fĕt′'l), *v. t.;* FET′TLED (-'ld); FET′TLING (-lĭng). [ME. *fet(t)len* to fettle (in sense 1), orig., to gird up, fr. AS. *fetel* girdle, belt.] **1.** *Dial.* To put or set in order. **2.** *Dial.* To beat; thrash. **3.** *Metal.* To cover or line with loose material, as the hearth of a reverberatory furnace. — *n.* **1.** State of being fettled, or made ready; condition; as, in fine *fettle*. **2.** The fettling for a furnace.

fet′tling (-lĭng), *n.* *Metal.* Loose material, as ore, sand, etc., thrown on the hearth of a furnace, to protect it.

fe′tus, **foe′tus** (fē′tŭs), *n.; pl.* FETUSES, FOETUSES (-ĕz; -ĭz). [L., a bringing forth, offspring.] The young or embryo of an animal in the womb, or in the egg, esp. in the later stages of development (in man from the end of the third month until birth, *embryo* being applied to earlier stages).

feu (fū), *n.* [OF. *feu*, *fieu*, fief.] *Scots Law.* **a** A fee, or feudal benefice. **b** A tenure where the vassal, in place of military services, makes a return in grain or in money; also, a grant of land to be so held; hence, inaccurately, a perpetual lease for a fixed rent. **c** Land held under one of these tenures. — *v. t.* *Scots Law.* To grant (land) upon feu.

feu′ar (fū′ẽr), *n.* *Scots Law.* One who holds a feu.

feud (fūd), *n.* [ME. *feide*, fr. OF. *faide*, *feide*, fr. OHG. *fēhida.*] A contention or quarrel; esp., an inveterate strife between families, clans, etc.

feud, **feod** (fūd), *n.* [ML. *feudum*, *feodum*, of G. origin.] *Law.* A fee, or feudal benefice; a fief.

feu′dal (fū′dăl; -d'l), *adj.* Of or pertaining to a feud or state of hostility.

feu′dal, *adj.* **1.** Of, relating to, or of the nature of, feuds, fiefs, or fees. **2.** Of or pertaining to the feudal system; as, *feudal* law. — **feu′dal·ly**, *adv.*

feu′dal·ism (-ĭz′m), *n.* The feudal system, or its principles, relations, and usages. — **feu′dal·ist** (-ĭst), *n.* — **feu′dal·is′tic** (-ĭs′tĭk), *adj.*

feu·dal′i·ty (fū·dăl′ĭ·tĭ), *n.* **1.** Quality or state of being feudal; feudal practice. **2.** A feudal holding; a fief.

feu′dal·ize (fū′dăl·īz; fū′d'l-), *v. t.* To reduce to a feudal tenure; to conform to feudalism. — **feu′dal·i·za′tion** (-ĭ·zā′shŭn; -ī·zā′-), *n.*

feudal system. The system of polity which prevailed in Europe in the Middle Ages, based upon the relation of lord to vassal, with the holding of land in feud. The principal incidents of the feudal system were homage, service of the tenants, wardship, marriage, reliefs, aids, escheat, and forfeiture.

feu′da·ry (fū′dȧ·rĭ). Var. of FEODARY.

feu′da·to′ry (fū′dȧ·tō′rĭ *or, esp. Brit.,* -tẽr·ĭ), *n.; pl.* -RIES (-rĭz). **1.** One holding lands by feudal tenure. **2.** A feud or fief; a feudatory state. — *adj.* Standing in, or belonging to, the relation of a feudal vassal to his lord; hence, of a kingdom or state, under the overlordship of another state.

feud′ist (fūd′ĭst), *n.* *Law.* A person versed in feudal law.

feud′ist, *n.* *U. S.* One who is party to a (hostile) feud.

Feuil′lants′ (fû′y'·yäɴ′), *n. pl.* [F.] *Fr. Hist.* A political club of supporters of constitutional monarchy, formed in 1791. The Jacobins suppressed it in 1792.

‖**feuil′le·ton′** (fû′yĕ·tôɴ′; fû′ĕ-), *n.* [F., fr. *feuille* leaf.] A part of a French newspaper (usually the bottom of the page) devoted to light literature, criticism, etc.; also, the article thus printed. — **feuil′le·ton·ism** (-tŏn·ĭz′m), *n.* — **feuil′le·ton′ist** (-tŏn′ĭst), *n.* — **feuil′le·ton·is′tic** (-tŏn·ĭs′tĭk), *adj.*

‖**feux d'ar′ti′fice′** (fû′ dȧr′tē′fēs′). [F.] Fireworks; hence, a display of wit.

fe′ver (fē′vẽr), *n.* [AS. *fēfer*, fr. L. *febris.*] **1.** *Med.* **a** Elevation of the bodily temperature. **b** A diseased state marked by increased heat, accelerated pulse, and general functional derangement, usually with thirst and loss of appetite. **2.** Excessive excitement due to strong emotion. — *v. t.* To affect with fever. — **fe′vered** (-vẽrd), *adj.*

fe′ver·few (-fū), *n.* [AF. *fewerfue*, fr. LL. *febrifug(i)a*, fr. *febris* fever + *fugare* to put to flight.] A perennial European herb (*Chrysanthemum parthenium*) of the aster family.

fever heat. Heat of the body over the normal 98.6° Fahrenheit; hence, an abnormal condition of interest or excitement.

fe′ver·ish (fē′vẽr·ĭsh), *adj.* **1.** Having a fever; showing increased heat and thirst. **2.** Indicating, or pertaining to, fever. **3.** Causing fever; infected with fever. **4.** Disordered as by fever; excited. — **fe′ver·ish·ly**, *adv.* — **fe′ver·ish·ness**, *n.*

fe′ver·ous (-ŭs), *adj.* Feverish. — **fe′ver·ous·ly**, *adv.*

fe′ver·root′ (-ro͞ot′), *n.* A coarse American herb (*Triosteum perfoliatum*) of the honeysuckle family.

fever sore. **a** A carious ulcer or necrosis. **b** = COLD SORE.

fever therapy. *Med.* The treatment of disease by fever induced by various artificial means.

fever tree. Any of several trees which are thought to indicate regions free from fever or which yield febrifuges; esp.: **a** The blue gum *Eucalyptus globulus*. **b** An ornamental tree (*Pinckneya pubens*) of the madder family, of the southeastern U. S.

fe′ver·weed′ (fē′vẽr·wēd′), *n.* Any of several plants of a genus (*Eryngium*, esp. *E. aquaticum*) of coarse bristly herbs of the carrot family; — from their use in medicine.

fe′ver·wort′ (-wûrt′), *n.* **a** = FEVERROOT. **b** The boneset *Eupatorium perfoliatum*.

few (fū), *adj.* [AS. *fēawe*, pl.] Not many; of small number.

few′ness (-nĕs; -nĭs), *n.* State of being few; paucity.

few′trils (fū′trĭlz), *n. pl.* *Dial.* Little things; trifles.

fey (fā), *adj.* [AS. *fǣge.*] **1.** *Archaic & Scot.* Fated to die. **2.** Having the air of one under a doom or spell; also, visionary.

fez (fĕz), *n.; pl.* FEZZES (fĕz′ĕz; -ĭz). [F., fr. *Fez*, Morocco.] A form of felt or cloth cap, usually red and having a tassel, formerly worn as the national headdress of the Turks. — **fezzed** (fĕzd), *adj.*

fi·a′cre (fē·ä′kẽr; *F.* fyȧ′kr′), *n.* [F., fr. the Hotel St. *Fiacre*, Paris.] A small French hackney coach.

fi′an·cé′ (fē′än·sā′; fē·än′sā; *F.* fyäɴ′sā′), *n. masc.*, **fi′an·cée′** (*pron. as for preceding*), *n. fem.* [F.] A betrothed person.

Fi′an·na (fē′ă·nȧ), *n.*, *or* **Fi′an·na Eir′eann** (âr′ĭn). [Ir. *fianna* Fenians + *Eireann* of Ireland.] The Fenians.

Fi′an·na Fail (fôl′). [Ir. *Fianna Fáil*, lit., Fenians of Ireland.] *Irish Politics.* The party founded in 1926 by Eamon de Valera on his withdrawal from Sinn Fein.

fi′ar (fē′ẽr), *n.* *Scots Law.* One in whom the fee simple of an estate is vested.

fi·as'co (fē·ăs'kō), *n.; pl.* -COES or -COS (-kōz). [It., orig. bottle.] A crash; a complete or ridiculous failure.
fi'at (fī'ăt; -ăt), *n.* [L., let it be done.] A formula of sanction, consisting of the word *fiat*, by which authority is given; hence, a sanction; decree.
‖**fi'at jus·ti'ti·a, ru'at cae'lum** (*or* **mun'dus**) (fī'ăt jŭs·tĭsh'ĭ·ȧ, rōō'ăt sē'lŭm, mŭn'dŭs). [L.] Let justice be done, though the heavens fall (or, though the earth be shattered).
‖**fi'at lux** (lŭks'). [L.] Let there be light.
fiat money. *U. S.* Paper currency of government issue which is made legal tender by fiat or law, does not represent, or is not based upon, specie, and contains no promise of redemption.
fib (fĭb), *n.* [Perh. fr. *fable.*] A falsehood concerning a trivial matter. — *v. i.;* FIBBED (fĭbd); FIB'BING. To tell a fib. — **Syn.** See LIE. — **fib'ber** (-ẽr), *n.*
fib, *v. t. & i. Slang.* To beat; to pummel.
fi'ber, fi'bre (fī'bẽr), *n.* [F. *fibre*, fr. L. *fibra.*] **1.** A thread or threadlike structure or object. **2.** *Bot.* **a** A slender, threadlike root, as that of a grass. **b** A long slender thick-walled cell, as in sclerenchyma. **3.** Collectively, any tough substance composed of threadlike tissue, esp. when capable of being spun and woven. **4.** That which gives texture or substance; hence, essential character. **5.** *Chem.* Short for VULCANIZED FIBER.
fi'ber·board', fi'bre·board' (fī'bẽr·bōrd'; 70), *n.* A material made by compressing fibers, as of wood, into thin stiff sheets; also, one of the boards so made.
Fi'ber·glas' (fī'bẽr·glȧs'; 9), *n.* A trade-mark applied to fine, flexible glass fibers made by attenuating molten glass streams flowing from small holes, used esp. for making textile fabrics and, in cottonlike felted masses, for heat or sound insulation.
fi'bri·form (fī'brĭ·fôrm), *adj.* Like a fiber.
fi'bril (fī'brĭl), *n.* [NL. *fibrilla*, dim. of L. *fibra* fiber.] **1.** A small thread or fiber. **2.** *Bot.* A root hair. — **fi'bril·lar** (fī'brĭ·lẽr), **fi'bril·lar'y** (-lẽr'ĭ *or, esp. Brit.,* -lẽr·ĭ; fī·brĭl'ȧ·rĭ), *adj.* — **fi·bril'li·form** (fī·brĭl'ĭ·fôrm), *adj.* — **fi'bril·lose** (fī'brĭ·lōs), *adj.* — **fi'bril·lous** (-lŭs), *adj.*
fi·bril'la (fī·brĭl'ȧ), *n.; pl.* FIBRILLAE (-ē). [NL.] A fibril.
fi'bril·la'tion (fī'brĭ·lā'shŭn), *n.* **1.** Act or process of forming fibrils. **2.** A quivering or tremor of muscle fibers; specif., *Med.,* a condition occurring in organic disease of the heart, in which various groups of its muscle fibers beat independently and without rhythm.
fi'brin (fī'brĭn), *n. Biochem.* **a** A white insoluble fibrous protein, formed esp. in the coagulation of the blood. **b** Gluten; — called ***plant, or vegetable, fibrin.***
fi'bri·no- (fī'brĭ·nō-). Combining form for *fibrin*, as in *fibrino*lysin.
fi·brin'o·gen (fī·brĭn'ō·jĕn), *n.* [*fibrino-* + *-gen.*] *Biochem.* A soluble protein existing in the blood, and in other animal fluids, which by the action of fibrin ferment, or thrombin, yields the insoluble substance fibrin, thus producing coagulation. — **fi'bri·nog'e·nous** (fī'brĭ·nŏj'ē·nŭs), **fi'brin·o·gen'ic** (fī'brĭ·nō·jĕn'ĭk), *adj.*
fi'bri·no·ly'sin (fī'brĭ·nō·lī'sĭn; -nŏl'ĭ·sĭn), *n. Biochem.* An enzyme that causes the dissolution of fibrin, the process being called **fi'brin·ol'y·sis** (fī'brĭ·nŏl'ĭ·sĭs). — **fi'bri·no·lyt'ic** (-nō·lĭt'ĭk), *adj.*
fi'brin·ous (fī'brĭ·nŭs), *adj.* Having, or partaking of the properties of, fibrin; as, *fibrinous* exudation.
fi'bro- (fī'brō-), **fibr-.** A combining form for *fiber*, used in anatomy, physiology, etc., to indicate *connection with*, or *relation to, fibrous structure, fibrous tissue*, or *connective tissue;* also, *fibrous and.*
fi'broid (fī'broid), *adj.* Like, forming, or composed of, fibrous tissue or tissues; as, a *fibroid* tumor.
fi'bro·in (-brō·ĭn), *n.* [L. *fibra* a fiber.] *Biochem.* An albuminoid, the chief ingredient of raw silk.
fi·bro'ma (fī·brō'mȧ), *n.; pl.* -MATA (-mȧ·tȧ), -MAS (-mȧz). [NL., fr. *fibr-* + *-oma.*] *Med.* A benign tumor, mainly of fibrous tissue. — **fi·brom'a·tous** (-brŏm'ȧ·tŭs; -brō'mȧ·tŭs), *adj.*
fi·bro'sis (-brō'sĭs), *n.* [NL., fr. *fibr-* + *-osis.*] *Med.* A condition marked by increase of interstitial fibrous tissue.
fi'brous (fī'brŭs), *adj.* [NL. *fibrosus.*] Containing, or like, fibers; as, the *fibrous* husk of the coconut.
fi'bro·vas'cu·lar (fī'brō·văs'kū·lẽr), *adj. Bot.* Having or consisting of fibers and conducting cells, as vessels; as, a *fibrovascular* bundle.
fib'ster (fĭb'stẽr), *n. Colloq.* One who tells fibs.
fib'u·la (fĭb'ū·lȧ), *n.; pl.* -LAE (-lē), -LAS (-lȧz). [L., buckle.] **1.** *Gr. & Rom. Antiq.* A brooch or clasp. **2.** *Anat. & Zool.* The outer, and usually the smaller, of the two bones of the hind limb (or leg), below the knee. — **fib'u·lar** (-lẽr), *adj.*
-fic (-fĭk). [F. and L.; F., *-fique*, fr. L. *-ficus* (as in *somnificus* somnific), fr. *facere* to make.] A suffix signifying *making, causing,* as in sopori*fic.*
-fi·ca'tion (-fĭ·kā'shŭn). [F. and L.; F., fr. L. *-ficatio, -onis,* fr. *-ficare* (in comp.) to make.] A suffix denoting *a making, causing,* as in paci*fication.*
fice (fīs), **fice'ty** (fīs'tĭ). Vars. of FEIST, FEISTY.
Fich'te·an (fĭk'tē·ăn), *adj.* Pertaining to Johann Gottlieb Fichte (1762–1814) or his philosophy, an attempt to perfect the Kantian system. Cf. KANTIANISM. — *n.* An idealist of the Fichtean school. — **Fich'te·an·ism** (-ĭz'm), *n.*
fich'u (fĭsh'ōō; *F.* fē'shü'), *n.* [F., neckerchief.] An ornamental three-cornered cape, worn by women on the head, shoulders, or neck.
fick'le (fĭk''l), *adj.* [AS. *ficol.*] Liable to change; unstable; capricious. — **Syn.** See INCONSTANT. — **Ant.** Constant. — **fick'le·ness,** *n.*
fi'co (fē'kō), *n.; pl.* -COES (-kōz). [It., a fig, fr. L. *ficus.*] **1.** *Obs.* A fig, a sign of contempt made by the fingers. **2.** An insignificant trifle.
fic'tile (fĭk'tĭl *or, esp. Brit.,* -tīl), *adj.* [L. *fictilis.* See FICTION.] Molded, or capable of being molded, into form by art; made of molded clay; relating esp. to pottery.
fic'tion (fĭk'shŭn), *n.* [F., fr. L. *fictio,* fr. *fingere, fictum,* to form, invent, feign.] **1.** A feigning or imagining; as, by a *fiction* of the mind. **2.** That which is feigned or imagined; esp., a feigned or invented story. **3.** Fictitious literature; specif., novels. **4.** *Law.* An assumption of a possible thing as a fact irrespective of the question of its truth.
fic'tion·al (-ăl; -'l), *adj.* Pertaining to, or characterized by, fiction. — **fic'tion·al·ly,** *adv.*
fic'tion·ist (-ĭst), *n.* A writer of fiction; a storyteller.
fic·ti'tious (fĭk·tĭsh'ŭs), *adj.* [L. *ficticius.* See FICTION.] **1.** Feigned; imaginary; not genuine. **2.** Of, pertaining to, or like fiction. — **fic·ti'tious·ly,** *adv.* — **fic·ti'tious·ness,** *n.*

Syn. Fictitious, fabulous, legendary, mythical, apocryphal mean invented or imagined rather than true or genuine. **Fictitious** implies fabrication and, so, more often suggests artificiality or contrivance than intent to deceive or deliberate falsification; **fabulous** stresses the marvelousness or incredibility of that so described and only occasionally suggests impossibility or nonexistence; **legendary** suggests popular susceptibility to elaboration of details or distortion of historical facts as a basis for a thing's fictitious or fabulous character; **mythical** implies a purely fanciful explanation of facts or the creation of beings or events out of the imagination; **apocryphal** implies a mysterious or extremely dubious source or origin, as of an anecdote or a memoir.
fic'tive (fĭk'tĭv), *adj.* **1.** Capable of, or pertaining to, imaginative creation. **2.** Imaginary; feigned. — **fic'tive·ly,** *adv.*
fid (fĭd), *n.* [Dial. E. *fid* a small, thick lump.] **1.** *Naut.* A square bar of wood or iron, used to support the topmast. **2.** A wooden or metal bar or pin, used as a support. **3.** A tapering pin of wood or, loosely, iron, used to open the strands of a rope in splicing, to stretch eyes, etc. Cf. MARLINESPIKE, *Illust.*
-fid (-fĭd). [L. *-fidus* cleft, fr. root of *findere* to split.] A combining form denoting *divided into* (so many) *parts;* specif., *Bot., lobed* or *cleft,* as in pinnati*fid.*
fid'dle (fĭd''l), *n.* [AS. *fithele,* fr. L. *vitula.*] **1.** *Colloq. Music.* A violin. **2.** Something shaped like a violin. **3.** *Naut.* A rack or light railing of cords, or the like, to keep dishes from sliding off a cabin table in rough weather. — *v. i. & t.;* FID'DLED (-'ld); FID'DLING (-lĭng). **1.** *Colloq.* To play on a fiddle. **2.** To move the hands and fingers restlessly; hence, to trifle; to potter.
fid'dle·back' (-băk'), *n.* Anything thought of as shaped like a fiddle; specif., *Eccl.,* a type of chasuble. — **fid'dle·back',** *adj.*
fid'dle-fad'dle (fĭd''l·făd''l), *n. Colloq.* A trifle; trifling talk. — *v. i. Colloq.* To fuss; to fiddle with trifles.
fid'dle·head' (-hĕd'), *n. Naut.* An ornament on a ship's bow, curved like the scroll at the head of a violin.
fid'dler (fĭd'lẽr), *n.* **1.** One who fiddles. **2.** The fiddler crab (see CRAB, 1 **a**).
fid'dler·fish' (-fĭsh'), *n.; pl.,* see FISH. See 1st RAY.
fid'dle·stick' (fĭd''l·stĭk'), *n.* **1.** A violin bow. **2.** A mere nothing; — used, esp. in *pl.,* as an interjection.
fid'dle·wood' (-wŏŏd'), *n.* Any of a genus (*Citharexylum*) of tropical American trees of the verbena family, or their hard wood.
fid'dling (fĭd'lĭng), *adj. Colloq.* Trifling; petty.
‖**Fi'de·i De·fen'sor** (fī'dē·ī dē·fĕn'sôr). [L.] Defender of the Faith; — a title of the sovereigns of England.
fi·del'i·ty (fĭ·dĕl'ĭ·tĭ; fī-), *n.; pl.* -TIES (-tĭz). [F. *fidélité,* fr. L. *fidelitas.* See FEALTY.] **1.** Careful observance of duty, or discharge of obligations; esp.: **a** Loyalty. **b** Adherence to the marriage contract. **c** Exactness, as in a copy. **2.** *Elec.* The degree to which an electrical device, as a radio receiving set, accurately reproduces its effect.

Syn. Fidelity, allegiance, fealty, loyalty, devotion, piety mean faithfulness to that to which one is bound by pledge or duty. **Fidelity** implies strict adherence to that which is a matter of faith or of keeping faith, such as one's word, one's friends, one's mate, or the like; **allegiance,** adherence to something objective which one serves as a vassal his lord; **fealty,** adherence to a person or thing because of an obligation as compelling as one's sworn word; **loyalty** implies a close personal relationship that is steadfast even in temptation to renounce or ignore it; **devotion** stresses zeal and service amounting to self-dedication; **piety** emphasizes fidelity to obligations regarded as natural or fundamental, such as reverence for one's parents, one's race, one's God, etc., and observance of all the duties which such fidelity requires.
fidge (fĭj), *v. t. & i. Dial.* To fidget. — *n. Chiefly Scot.* A fidget.
fidg'et (fĭj'ĕt; -ĭt), *v. i.* To move restlessly. — *v. t.* To cause to fidget. — *n.* **1.** Uneasiness. **2.** *pl.* Restlessness, as shown by nervous movements. **3.** One who fidgets.
fidg'et·y (fĭj'ĕ·tĭ; -ĭ·tĭ), *adj.* Restless. — **fidg'et·i·ness,** *n.*
FI'DO (fī'dō), *n.* [*F*og *I*nvestigation *D*ispersal *O*perations.] A system in which fog above runways is evaporated by the heat from liquid-fuel burners at their sides to permit aircraft to operate.
fi·du'cial (fĭ·dū'shăl), *adj.* [L. *fiducia* trust, confidence.] **1.** Founded on faith or trust, esp. religious beliefs. **2.** Having the nature of a trust; fiduciary. **3.** *Physics, etc.* Taken as a standard of reference; as, a *fiducial* line, point, etc. — **fi·du'cial·ly,** *adv.*
fi·du'ci·ar'y (-shĭ·ĕr'ĭ *or, esp. Brit.,* -ẽr·ĭ; -shȧ·rĭ), *adj.* **1.** Holding, held, or founded, in trust. **2.** Of the nature of a trust; confidential; as, in a *fiduciary* capacity. **3.** Resting upon public confidence for value or currency; — esp. of fiat money. — *n.; pl.* -IES (-ĭz). One who holds a fiduciary relation or acts in a fiduciary capacity.
‖**fi'dus A·cha'tes** (fī'dŭs ȧ·kā'tēz). [L.] Faithful Achates (companion of Aeneas); hence, a trusty friend.
fie (fī), *interj.* Exclamation expressing disgust, dislike, or, now commonly, a humorous affectation of being shocked.
fief (fēf), *n.* [F.] *Law.* A feudal estate; a fee.
field (fēld), *n.* [AS. *feld.*] **1.** Chiefly *pl.* Open country. **2.** Cleared land; a tract, often enclosed, used for tillage or pasture. **3.** A natural area yielding some particular, esp. mineral, resource; as, a coal *field.* **4.** A piece of land put to a particular activity; as, a flying *field.* **5. a** A place where a battle is fought; also, the battle itself. **b** By extension, the country covered by military operations. **6.** An open extent or expanse. **7.** A space or ground on which something is drawn or projected; specif.: **a** In heraldry, the whole surface of an escutcheon (see ESCUTCHEON, *Illust.*). **b** In a flag, the ground of each division. **8.** A sphere of activity or opportunity; specif., the area visible through the lens of an optical instrument, as a telescope. **9.** *Elec.* Short for FIELD MAGNET, FIELD WINDING. See DYNAMO, *Illust.* **10.** *Physics.* A region or space traversed by lines of force, as of a magnet or electric current (magnetic force). **11.** *Sports.* **a** An athletic or playing area. **b** Specif., the central portion, usually enclosed by a racing track, of an athletic area, on which are contested such events as the high jump, pole vault, throwing of weights, etc. **c** All the players in action on a field; as, in football, to run through a broken *field.* **d** In cricket, etc., the side in the field, as opposed to the side at bat. **e** All the competitors in a sporting contest where more than two are entered; sometimes, specif., all except one or more specified, usually the favorite. — *adj.* **1.** Pertaining or belonging to the fields; made or conducted in, or used in the field; as, *field* operations or equipment. **2.** Growing in or inhabiting the fields or open country. **3.** *Sports.* Of or performed or contested on the field (def. 11 **b**) as disting. from the track. — *v. t. Sports.* **a** To catch, stop, throw, etc. (the ball), as a fielder.

b To put (a team or designated players) into the field for actual play; as, to *field* a weak team. — *v. i. Sports.* To play as a fielder.
field army. See ARMY, 1 **b**.
field artillery. *Mil.* **a** Artillery used with armies in the field. **b** [*caps.*] *U. S. Army.* An arm of the regular army under a major general known as the Chief of Field Artillery. See INSIGNIA, *Illust.*
field battery. *Mil.* A battery of field artillery.
field day. **1.** A day or occasion in the field, or out of doors, as by a group of naturalists seeking specimens, or by troops on maneuvers. **2.** A day of unusual exertion or display; a gala day; hence, an occasion of unusual success.
field'er (fēl'dẽr), *n.* One who fields; specif., a player stationed in the field, as in baseball or cricket.
field'er's choice (-dẽrz). *Baseball.* An attempt by a fielder, when handling a batted ball, to retire a base runner other than the batter, when a play to first base would have retired the batter.
field'fare' (fēld'fâr'), *n.* [AS. *feldeware,* for *feldefare.*] A medium-sized European thrush (*Turdus pilaris*) with ash-colored head and chestnut wings.
field glass. A small compact binocular telescope. See BINOCULAR, *Illust.*
field goal. **a** *American Football.* A score made from ordinary play by placement or drop kick not immediately after a touchdown. **b** *Basketball.* A basket thrown while the ball is in play.
field gun. = FIELDPIECE.
field hospital. A military organization of surgeons, nurses, etc., with equipment for establishing a temporary hospital in the field.
field magnet. A magnet used for producing and maintaining a magnetic field; — used esp. of the exciting magnets of dynamos and electric motors. See DYNAMO, *Illust.*
field marshal; *pl.* FIELD MARSHALS. *Mil.* In some armies, an officer next in rank below the commander in chief.
field mouse. See VOLE.
field mushroom. See MUSHROOM.
field music. *Mil. & Nav.* **a** The musicians, drummers, fifers, buglers, and pipers attached to military companies. **b** The music produced by drummers, fifers, pipers, or buglers.
field officer. *Mil.* A military officer of the rank of colonel, lieutenant colonel, or major.
field of force. *Physics.* = FIELD, *n.*, 10.
field of honor. **a** Formerly, a place where a duel was fought. **b** A battlefield.
field'piece' (fēld'pēs'), *n.* A gun mounted on wheels, for use in field campaigns.
field scabious. See SCABIOUS.
fields'man (fēldz'măn), *n. Cricket.* A fielder.
field spaniel. See SPANIEL.
field sparrow. See SPARROW, 2.
field trial. A trial of sporting dogs in actual performance. Cf. BENCH SHOW.
field winding. *Elec.* The winding of the field magnet of a dynamo or motor.
field'work' (fēld'wûrk'), *n. Mil.* Any temporary fortification thrown up by an army in the field.
field work. Work of gathering scientific data from the field. — **field'-work'er** (-wûr'kẽr), *n.*
fiend (fēnd), *n.* [AS. *fēond.*] **1.** Satan; the Devil; hence, any demon. **2.** A person of diabolical wickedness or, esp., cruelty. **3.** *Colloq.* A person who uses something, such as a drug, to excess; as, a dope *fiend;* also, one who is excessively devoted to some pursuit or object of interest; as, a golf *fiend.*
fiend'ish, *adj.* Like a fiend; diabolically wicked or cruel. — **fiend'ish·ly,** *adv.* — **fiend'ish·ness,** *n.*
fiend'like' (fēnd'līk'), *adj.* Fiendish.
fiend'ly (-lĭ), *adj. Rare.* Fiendlike; devilish.
fierce (fērs), *adj.;* FIERC'ER (fēr'sẽr); FIERC'EST. [OF. *fers, fiers,* nom. of *fer, fier,* fr. L. *ferus* wild, savage, cruel.] **1.** Vehement in anger or cruelty; of a nature to inspire terror. **2.** Furious; raging; also, extreme in intensity; overpowering. — **fierce'ly,** *adv.* — **fierce'ness,** *n.*
Syn. **Fierce, truculent, ferocious, barbarous, savage, inhuman, cruel** mean showing fury or malignity in looks or actions. **Fierce** applies largely to men and beasts that inspire terror because of their menacing aspect or fury in attack; **truculent** implies the adoption of a bullying or threatening attitude or aspect, often with the intent to inspire terror; **ferocious** not only implies extreme fierceness, but unrestrained violence and wanton brutality; **barbarous,** as here compared, implies a ferocity unworthy of civilized men; **savage** implies the absence of inhibitions characteristic of civilized men when filled with rage, lust, or other violent passion; **inhuman** implies absence of all feeling that normally characterizes a human being, such as pity, kindness, etc.; **cruel** implies indifference to suffering and even positive pleasure in inflicting it.
fiere. Var. of FERE.
‖**fi'e·ri fa'ci·as** (fī'ĕ·rī fā'shĭ·ăs). [L., cause it to be done.] *Law.* A common-law writ lying for one who has recovered judgment in debt or damages.
fi'er·y (fī'rĭ; fī'ẽr·ĭ), *adj.;* FI'ER·I·ER (fī'rĭ·ẽr); FI'ER·I·EST. **1.** Consisting of, containing, attended by, or bearing fire. **2.** Heated by fire, or as if by fire; hot; burning. **3.** Resembling fire; glowing. **4.** **a** Vehement; ardent. **b** Passionate; irritable. **5.** Inflammable; as, a *fiery* coal seam. — **fi'er·i·ly,** *adv.* — **fi'er·i·ness,** *n.*
‖**fies'ta** (fyās'tä; *Angl.* fĭ·ĕs'tȧ), *n.* [Sp. See FEAST.] A religious festival; a saint's day; also, any holiday or festivity.
fife (fīf), *n.* [MHG. *pfīfe* (whence F. *fifre*), G. *pfeife.*] *Music.* A small simple form of flute with shrill tone, used chiefly to accompany the drum. — *v. i. & t.* To play (on) a fife. — **fif'er** (fīf'ẽr), *n.*
fife rail. *Naut.* A rail about the mast, near the deck, to which running gear is belayed.
fif'teen' (fĭf'tēn'; 2), *n. & adj.* [AS. *fīftȳne, fīftēne.*] See NUMBER, *Table.* — **fif'teenth'** (-tēnth'; 2), *n. & adj.*
fifth (fĭfth), *n.* [AS. *fīfta.*] **1.** See NUMBER, *Table.* **2.** *Music.* **a** The interval embracing five diatonic degrees. **b** The tone at this interval. **c** The harmonic combination of two tones a fifth apart. **d** The fifth tone of a scale, reckoning up from the tonic; the dominant. **3.** One fifth of a U. S. gallon used as a measure of spirituous liquor. — **fifth,** *adj.* — **fifth'ly,** *adv.*
fifth column. **a** Originally, the Franco sympathizers within Madrid during the Spanish Civil War; — so described in a radio address by Gen. Mola when he was leading four columns of troops against the city. **b** Hence, secret sympathizers and supporters of the enemy, engaged in espionage, sabotage, and other subversive activities within defense lines. — **fifth col'umn·ist** (kŏl'ŭm·ĭst; -nĭst).
fifth monarchy. A universal monarchy, supposed to be prophesied in Daniel ii. See FIFTH MONARCHY MEN.
Fifth Monarchy Men. *Hist.* A fanatical sect in England, of the time of the Commonwealth (1649–1660), who maintained that the fifth monarchy, during which Christ would reign on earth a thousand years, was near at hand and that they must assist to establish it by force.
fifth wheel. **a** A horizontal segment made up of two parts rotating on each other above the fore axle of a carriage, forming a support to prevent careening. **b** An extra wheel carried for use as substitute for a disabled wheel. **c** Hence, a supernumerary or superfluous person or thing.
fif'ty (fĭf'tĭ), *n. & adj.* [AS. *fīftig.*] See NUMBER, *Table.* — **fif'ti·eth** (-tĭ·ĕth; -ĭth), *n. & adj.*
fif'ty·fold' (-fōld'; 2), *adj. & adv.* See -FOLD.
fig (fĭg), *n.* [OF. *figue,* fr. Pr. *figa,* fr. L. *ficus* fig tree, fig.] **1.** The oblong or pear-shaped fruit of the fig tree, pulpy when ripe, and eaten raw or preserved or dried with sugar. **2.** Any of a genus (*Ficus*) of trees of the mulberry family, distinguished by the peculiar fruit (syconium), esp. the cultivated fig tree (*F. carica*) native to southwestern Asia. See CAPRIFIG, CAPRIFICATION. **3.** *Australia.* Any of several trees resembling the true fig. **4.** **a** The value of a fig, practically nothing; a fico; — used in contempt. **b** A gesture of contempt.
fig, *v. t. Obs.* To insult with a fico. *Shak.*
fig (fĭg), *v. t.;* FIGGED (fĭgd); FIG'GING. To dress; to rig; — chiefly with *out* or *up.* — *n. Colloq.* **1.** Dress; array. **2.** Condition; form.

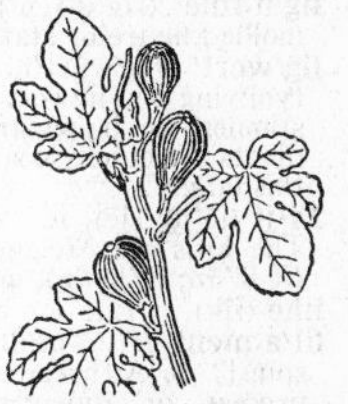
Fig. Leaves and Fruit. (⅙)

fig'eat'er (-ēt'ẽr), *n.* A large flower beetle (*Cotinus nitida*) of the southern United States.
fight (fīt), *n.* [AS. *feoht.*] **1.** A violent physical struggle for victory. **2.** Struggle; contest; as, fight the good *fight.* **3.** Strength or disposition for fighting; pugnacity. **4.** *Obs.* A screen for the combatants in ships. — *v. i.;* FOUGHT (fôt); FIGHT'ING. **1.** To attempt to defeat, subdue, or destroy an enemy; to engage in contest. **2.** To act in opposition to anything; to contend. — *v. t.* **1.** To carry on, or wage, as a battle; to win or gain by struggle, as one's way; to sustain by fighting, as one's case in the courts. **2.** To war against. **3.** To cause to engage in a fight; as, to *fight* cocks. — **fight'a·ble,** *adj.*
— ***fight shy of.*** To avoid meeting fairly or at close quarters. — ***fight (with) windmills.*** To combat imaginary evils, as Don Quixote tilted against windmills thinking them giants.
fight'er (fīt'ẽr), *n.* **1.** One who fights, as a soldier, a pugnacious person, or one not easily intimidated. **2.** In full, **fighter plane.** A military or naval airplane of high speed, high rate of climb, great maneuverability, and heavy firepower, primarily for overtaking and attacking enemy aircraft in the air.
fighting cock. **1.** A gamecock. **2.** A pugnacious person.
Fight'ing French. Prior to July 14, 1942, called **Free French.** Members of an organized group, **Free France,** headed by General Charles de Gaulle, as president of the French National Committee (set up Sept. 24, 1941) that rejected the 1940 armistice with Germany, repudiated the Vichy regime, and continued the war against Germany.
fighting top. The top on a war vessel. See TOP, *n.*, 14.
fig marigold. Any of several carpetweeds (genus *Mesembryanthemum*) with showy white or pink flowers.
fig'ment (fĭg'mĕnt), *n.* [L. *figmentum,* fr. *fingere* to form, invent.] An invention; a fiction; something feigned or imagined.
fig'u·rant (fĭg'ū·rănt; *F.* fē'gü'räN'), *n. masc.* [F., prop. pres. part. of *figurer* to figure, represent, make a figure.] One who dances at the opera as one of a group; an accessory character on the stage, with no speaking part.
fig'u·rante' (fĭg'ū·rănt'; *F.* fē'gü'räNt'), *n. fem.* [F.] A female figurant; esp., a ballet girl.
fig'ur·ate (fĭg'ūr·āt), *adj.* [L. *figuratus,* past part. of *figurare.* See FIGURE.] **1.** *Now Rare.* Of a definite form or figure. **2.** *Music.* Florid; involving passing discords by the freer melodic movement of one or more voice parts; as, *figurate* counterpoint. — **fig'ur·ate·ly,** *adv.*
fig'u·ra'tion (fĭg'ū·rā'shŭn), *n.* **1.** Act of giving figure, or determinate form. **2.** Form; shape; outline. **3.** Act of representation in figures and shapes; emblematical or typical representation. **4.** *Music.* **a** The ornamental treatment of a passage by the use of passing notes and other devices. **b** The figuring of a thorough bass.
fig'ur·a·tive (fĭg'ūr·ȧ·tĭv), *adj.* **1.** Representing by a figure, or by resemblance; typical; emblematical. **2.** Expressing one thing in terms normally denoting another with which it may be regarded as analogous; as, *figurative* language, sense. **3.** Abounding in figures of speech; flowery; as, a *figurative* description. **4.** Relating to the representation of form or figure by drawing, carving, etc. — **fig'ur·a·tive·ly,** *adv.* — **fig'ur·a·tive·ness,** *n.*
fig'ure (fĭg'ūr; *Brit.* fĭg'ẽr), *n.* [OF., fr. L. *figura.*] **1.** **a** A written or printed character representing a number, as 1, 2, 3, etc. **b** *pl.* Such characters used in reckoning; also, use of them in figuring; as, good at *figures.* **2.** A body; an object having shape or form. **3.** The form of anything; shape; outline. **4.** The representation of any form, as by drawing; a likeness; image. **5.** A person, thing, or action representative of another. **6.** An imagined form; phantasm. **7.** A diagram or drawing illustrating the text of a book; a cut. Abbr., *fig.* **8.** An outline traced by a series of evolutions, as with skates on ice or with an airplane in the air. **9.** A pattern; design. **10.** Appearance or impression made, esp. by a person; as, to present a sorry *figure.* **11.** A personage; character; as, the great *figures* of history. **12.** *Colloq.* Value, as expressed in numbers; price. **13.** *Dancing.* A set or group of evolutions in a dance. **14.** *Geom.* A drawing made to represent a magnitude or the relation of two or more magnitudes; a surface or space enclosed on all sides, — called ***plane or superficial*** when enclosed by lines, and ***solid*** when enclosed by surfaces. **15.** *Logic.* The form of a syllogism with respect to the relative position of the middle term. **16.** *Music.* A short, coherent group of tones or chords, which may grow into a phrase, a theme, or an entire composition. **17.** *Rhet.* A figure of speech (which see). — **Syn.** See FORM.

— *v. t.* **1.** To represent by a figure; as: **a** To trace the outline of. **b** To portray, as by description. **c** To fashion; shape. **2.** To represent by a metaphor. **3.** To adorn with figures. **4.** To indicate by numerals; also, to calculate. **5.** *Music.* To write figures over or under (the bass) to indicate the accompanying chords. — *v. i.* **1.** To make a figure; to be distinguished; to appear. **2.** *Colloq.* To reckon in figures; hence, to calculate; plan.

fig′ured (fĭg′ūrd; *Brit.* fĭg′ẽrd), *adj.* **1.** Represented by a figure, esp. a pictorial figure. **2.** Adorned with, formed into, or marked with, figures; as, *figured* muslin. **3.** Not literal; figurative. **4.** *Music.* **a** Figurate. **b** Indicated by figures, as a **figured bass**, a bass in which figures are put under the notes to represent the harmony.

fig′ure·head′ (fĭg′ūr·hĕd′; *Brit.* fĭg′ẽr-), *n.* **1.** *Naut.* The figure on the bow of a vessel. **2.** A nominal, but not real, head; esp., one who allows his name to be used to give standing to enterprises in which he has no responsible interest or duties.

fig′ure–of–eight′ knot. See KNOT, *Illust.* (2).

figure of speech. *Rhet.* A form of expression such as an allegory, metaphor, or simile, other than plain and normal, producing a stylistic effect.

fig′u·rine′ (fĭg′ū·rēn′), *n.* [F., fr. It. *figurina.*] A small carved or molded figure or statuette.

fig′wort′ (fĭg′wûrt′), *n.* Any of a genus (*Scrophularia*) of plants, typifying the figwort family (Scrophulariaceae), with leaves having no stipules, an irregular bilabiate corolla, and a 2-celled ovary. The plants are chiefly coarse herbs with small flowers. Also, any plant of this family.

Fi′ji (fē′jē; -jē), *n.* A member of the native race of the Fiji Islands. The Fijis are Melanesians with Polynesian intermixture. — **Fi·ji′an** (fē·jē′ăn; fē′jē·ăn), *adj.* & *n.*

fike (fīk), *v. i.* & *n.* *Scot.* & *Ir.* Fidget; fuss.

fil′a·ment (fĭl′ȧ·mĕnt), *n.* [F., fr. ML. *filamentum*, fr. *filare* to spin.] **1.** A thread, or a slender, threadlike object, process, or appendage. **2.** *Bot.* **a** The anther-bearing stalk of a stamen. **b** A threadlike series of cells or a very long cylindrical single cell, as of certain algae, fungi, and bacteria. **3** *Elec.* A threadlike conductor, as of carbon or metal, that is rendered incandescent by the passage of an electric current; in an electron tube, the heated wire forming the cathode. See INCANDESCENT LAMP, *Illust.* — **fil′a·men′ta·ry** (-mĕn′tȧ·rĭ), *adj.* — **fil′a·men′tous** (-tŭs), *adj.*

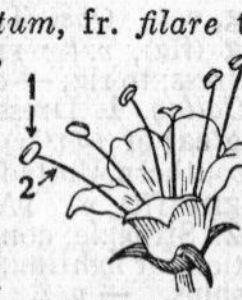
1 Anther; 2 Filament.

fi′lar (fī′lẽr), *adj.* [L. *filum* a thread.] Of or relating to a thread or line; characterized by threads stretched across the field of a view; as, a *filar* microscope.

fi·lar′i·a (fĭ·lâr′ĭ·ȧ), *n.; pl.* -IAE (-ē). [NL., fr. L. *filum* a thread.] *Zool.* Any of an important group of threadlike nematodes (Filariidae and allied families). These worms are parasites of the blood or tissues of vertebrates to which they are usually transmitted by certain flies or mosquitoes in which the larvae develop. — **fi·lar′i·al** (-ăl), **fi·lar′i·an** (-ăn), *adj.* — **fi·lar′i·id** (-ĭd), *adj.* & *n.*

fil′a·ri′a·sis (fĭl′ȧ·rī′ȧ·sĭs), *n.* [NL.] Infestation with filariae; also, the resulting diseased condition.

fil′a·ture (fĭl′ȧ·tūr), *n.* **a** A drawing out into threads; hence, the reeling of silk from cocoons. **b** A reel for drawing off silk from cocoons; also, an establishment for reeling silk.

fil′bert (fĭl′bẽrt), *n.* [F. dial.] Either of the two European hazels (*Corylus avellana pontica* and *C. maxima*); also, their thick-shelled and sweet-flavored nut.

filch (fĭlch), *v. t.* To steal; to pilfer. — **Syn.** See STEAL. — **filch′er** (fĭl′chẽr), *n.*

file (fīl), *n.* [F., row, fr. *filer* to spin, or, in some senses, F. *fil* thread, course; both fr. L. *filum* thread.] **1.** A line, wire, or other device by which papers are put and kept in order; now, any device, as a folder or cabinet, in which papers are preserved. **2.** An orderly collection of papers. **3.** *Obs.* A roll; list. **4.** A row of persons, animals, or things, arranged one behind the other. **5.** *Chess.* A row of squares from one player to his opponent across the chessboard. **6.** *Mil.* **a** A row of soldiers ranged one behind another; — opp. to *rank.* **b** A small number of soldiers detailed as a detachment. **c** *Colloq.* A number or numerical position on the lineal list for promotion.

file (fīl), *v. t.* To set in order; to lay away (papers, etc.), arranged in a methodical manner. — *v. i.* To march in a file or line, as soldiers.

file, *n.* [AS. *fīl, fēol.*] **1.** *Mach.* A hardened steel instrument having cutting ridges, or teeth, upon its surface, used for abrading or smoothing metal and other substances. Cf. RASP, *n.*, 1. **2.** *Slang.* A shrewd person; also, a fellow; cove. — *v. t.* **1.** To rub, smooth, or cut away, with or as if with a file. **2.** To remove with a file; — used with *off* and *away.*

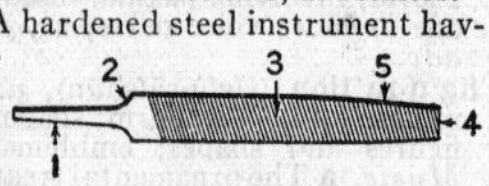
File. 1 Tang; 2 Heel; 3 Face; 4 Tip; 5 Edge.

file, *v. t.* [AS. *fȳlan*, fr. *fūl* foul.] *Archaic* & *Dial.* To defile.

file′fish′ (fīl′fĭsh′), *n.; pl.*, see FISH. Any of certain fishes with rough, leathery skins; specif.: **a** A triggerfish. **b** Any of many related oddly shaped plectognath fishes.

fil′er (fīl′ẽr), *n.* One who or that which files.

‖**fi′let′** (fē′lĕ′; *E.* fĭ·lā′, fĭl′ĭ, fē′lā; 2), *n.* [F.] **a** *Cookery.* Fillet. **b** Filet lace (see FILET, *adj.*).

fi′let′, *adj.* Designating a lace or net with square mesh.

‖**fi′let′ de sole** (d′ sôl′; *E.* dē sōl′). [F.] Fillet of sole.

‖**fi′let′ mi′gnon′** (mē′nyôN′; *E.* mēn·yŏn′). [F.] A round, relatively thick piece of beef garnished with pork or bacon before cooking.

fil′i·al (fĭl′ĭ·ăl; -yăl; 58), *adj.* [LL. *filialis*, fr. *filius* son, *filia* daughter.] **1.** Of or relating to a son or daughter; as, *filial* obedience. **2.** *Biol.* In Mendelian inheritance, designating any generation successive to the *parental.* They are distinguished as *first filial*, or F_1; *second filial*, or F_2; and so on. — **fil′i·al·ly**, *adv.*

fil′i·ate (fĭl′ĭ·āt), *v. t.* [ML. *filiatus*, past part.] To affiliate.

fil′i·a′tion (-ā′shŭn), *n.* [F., fr. ML. *filiatio.*] **1.** Relationship of a child to a parent, esp. to a father. **2.** Descent from, or as if from, a parent; as, to determine the *filiation* of a language. **3.** An offshoot. **4.** The formation of branches or offshoots. **5.** *Law.* Act of fixing the paternity of an illegitimate child upon some person.

fil′i·beg (fĭl′ĭ·bĕg), *n.* [Gael. *fèileadh* kilt + *beag* little.] A kilt.

fil′i·bus′ter (fĭl′ĭ·bŭs′tẽr), *n.* [Sp. *filibuster, flibustero*, ult. fr. D. *vrijbuiter.* See FREEBOOTER.] **1.** An irregular military adventurer; a freebooter. **2.** *U. S.* **a** A member of a deliberative body who obstructs action by use of dilatory tactics, such as speaking merely to consume time. **b** An instance of filibustering. — *v. i.* **1.** To act as a filibuster, or military freebooter. **2.** *U. S.* To delay action in an assembly by dilatory motions or other artifices. — **fil′i·bus′ter·er** (-bŭs′tẽr·ẽr), *n.*

fil′i·cide (fĭl′ĭ·sīd), *n.* [L. *filius* son, *filia* daughter + *-cide.*] Act of murdering a son or a daughter; also, the parent who does this. — **fil′i·cid′al** (-sīd′ăl; 2), *adj.*

fil′i·form (fĭl′ĭ·fôrm; fī′lĭ-), *adj.* [L. *filum* thread + *-form.*] Having the shape of a thread or filament.

fil′i·grain, fil′i·grane (fĭl′ĭ·grān), *n.* [F. *filigrane*, fr. It., fr. L. *filum* a thread + *granum* grain.] *Archaic.* Filigree.

fil′i·gree (fĭl′ĭ·grē), *n.* [Corrupted fr. *filigrane.*] **1.** Ornamental work, formerly with grains or beads, but now of fine wire, used chiefly in decorating gold and silver. **2.** Ornamental openwork of delicate or intricate design. — *v. t.* To adorn with, or work in, filigree.

fil′ing (fīl′ĭng), *n.* A fragment rubbed off in filing; — usually *pl.*; as, iron *filings.*

Fil′i·pi′no (fĭl′ĭ·pē′nō), *n.; pl.* -NOS (-nōz). [Sp.] **1.** A member of a native tribe, esp. of a Christianized tribe, of the Philippine Islands. **2.** A citizen of the Republic of the Philippines. — **Fil′i·pi′no**, *adj.*

fill (fĭl), *v. t.* [AS. *fyllan.*] **1.** To put or pour into, till no more can be received. **2.** To furnish a supply to. **3.** To feed; satiate. **4.** To occupy the whole of; as, he *filled* the chair. **5.** **a** To officiate in, as an incumbent; to occupy; as, a king *fills* a throne. **b** To supply with an incumbent; as, to *fill* an office. **6.** To stop up; to plug. **7.** To pour, or put, into a receptacle as if to fill it; as, to *fill* coal into vessels. **8.** *Civ. Engin.* To make an embankment in, or raise the level of (a low place), with earth, gravel, or rock. **9.** *Com.* To execute (a business order). **10.** *Naut.* **a** To dilate; to distend, as a sail. **b** To trim (a yard) so that the wind will blow on the after side of the sails. **11.** *Pharm., U. S.* To compound (a prescription). — *v. i.* **1.** To become full. **2.** To fill a cup or glass for drinking.

— ***fill away.*** *Naut.* To trim the sails so that the wind will catch them full; to proceed on the course after having been brought up in the wind. — ***fill in.*** To insert; also, to complete by insertions; as, to *fill in* an application. — ***fill out.*** **a** To enlarge to the desired limit; also, to fill in. **b** To distend. **c** To be distended to proper dimensions.

— *n.* **1.** A full supply; as much as supplies want. **2.** That which fills; esp., material filling a receptacle, cavity, or the like.

fil′la·gree (fĭl′ȧ·grē). Var. of FILIGREE.

‖**fille de cham′bre** (fē′y′ dē shäN′br′). [F.] A lady's maid.

filled gold (fĭld). *Jewelry.* A substitute for solid gold, consisting of a base metal, usually brass, mechanically covered with a layer of hard gold of appreciable thickness.

‖**fille d'hon′neur′** (fē′y′ dô′nûr′). [F.] A maid of honor.

filled milk. Skim milk enriched in fat content by the addition of vegetable oils.

fill′er (fĭl′ẽr), *n.* One who or that which fills; as: **a** Filling or a filling. **b** A substance added to another, as to increase bulk, weight, or viscosity. **c** *Arch.* & *Engin.* A plate or other piece to fill in a space between two parts of a structure. **d** *Painting.* A composition, as of powdered silica and oil, used to fill the pores and grain of wood before applying paint, varnish, etc. **e** *Tobacco.* The tobacco used for the interior portion of cigars.

fil′lér (fēl′lār), *n. sing.* & *pl.* [Hung.] A minor bronze coin of Hungary, the 100th part of a forint.

fil′let (fĭl′ĕt; -ĭt; *in sense* 7, *now often* fĭl′ā *or* fĭl′ĭ), *n.* [OF. *filet*, dim. of *fil* a thread. See FILE a row.] **1.** A little band, esp. one to encircle the hair. Cf. SNOOD, *Illust.* **2.** A narrow ribbon of any material, or a part or ornament resembling a ribbon. **3.** A concave junction formed where two surfaces meet; also, a curved strip, as of leather, to form such a junction. **4.** *Anat.* A band of fibers, esp. of white matter in the brain. **5.** *Arch.* A narrow flat member; esp., a flat molding separating other moldings; also, the space between two flutings in a shaft. See BASE, MOLDING, *Illusts.* **6.** *Bookbinding.* An ornamental line stamped or rolled on a book cover. **7.** *Cooking.* **a** A piece of lean meat without bone; sometimes, a long strip rolled up and tied. **b** A flat slice of fish without bone. — *v. t.* **1.** To bind, adorn, or make, with or as with a fillet. **2.** To cut into fillets, or slices.

fill′ing (fĭl′ĭng), *n.* **1.** Act of one who or that which fills; also, a making or becoming full. **2.** That which fills or is used to fill a container, cavity, or the like, or to supply a deficiency; filler. **3.** *Textiles.* The woof or weft in woven fabrics; also, yarn for the shuttle.

filling station. A retail station for gasoline and oil.

fil′lip (fĭl′ĭp), *v. t.* **1.** To snap with the finger. **2.** To snap; to project by or as by a fillip. **3.** To stimulate; urge. — *v. i.* To make a fillip. — *n.* **1.** A jerk of a finger forced suddenly from the thumb; a smart blow. **2.** Something serving to rouse or excite; a stimulus; as, to give a *fillip* to the fund raising, or to the dessert.

fil′lis·ter (fĭl′ĭs·tẽr), *n.* An adjustable rabbet plane; also, a rabbet, as on the outer edge of a window-sash bar.

fil′ly (fĭl′ĭ), *n.; pl.* -LIES (-ĭz). [ON. *fylja.*] A female foal or colt.

film (fĭlm), *n.* [AS. *filmen.*] **1.** A thin skin or membranous covering. **2.** Any thin, slight covering, veil, or layer; a haze; also, a pathological growth on or in the eye. **3.** A slender thread, as that of a cobweb. **4.** A thin, flexible, transparent sheet of cellulose nitrate or acetate or similar material coated with a light-sensitive emulsion, used for taking photographs. **5.** Hence, a motion picture; also, *pl.*, motion pictures collectively. — *v. t.* **1.** To cover with or as with a film. **2.** *Motion Pictures.* To photograph on a film; to make a motion picture from a scenario based upon; as, to *film* a novel. — *v. i.* **1.** To become covered with a film. **2.** **a** To be, or to be adapted to being, photographed for motion pictures. **b** To make a motion picture.

film′strip′ (fĭlm′strĭp′), *n.* A strip of film bearing a sequence of frames of still pictures with explanatory text and captions to be projected upon a screen as a teaching aid or to accompany a lecture.

film′y (fĭl′mĭ), *adj.*; FILM′I·ER (-mĭ·ẽr); FILM′I·EST. Composed of or resembling film; covered with or as if with a film; misty; clouded. — **film′i·ly**, *adv.* — **film′i·ness**, *n.*

fi′lose (fī′lōs), *adj.* [L. *filum* a thread.] **a** Threadlike. **b** Terminating in a threadlike process.

fils (fĭls), *n. sing.* & *pl.* A minor coin of Iraq, established 1932 as the thousandth part of a dinar.

‖**fils** (fēs), *n.* [F., fr. L. *filius.*] Son; — sometimes used after a proper name to distinguish a son; as, Dumas, *fils.*

fil′ter (fĭl′tẽr), *n.* [F. *filtre*, fr. ML. *filtrum, feltrum*, felt, fulled wool, used for filters.] **1.** A porous article or mass, as of cloth, charcoal, or diatomaceous earth, through which fluid is passed to separate from it matter held in suspension. **2.** *Physics.* A device for eliminating or minimizing waves of certain frequencies without greatly altering the intensity of others; specif.: **a** *Elec.* An electric circuit so designed that a certain selected range of frequencies is transmitted while other frequencies are almost entirely suppressed. In radiobroadcasting, a filter is used to change the character of sounds. **b** *Light.* A material or device which partly absorbs light rays. **c** *Photog.* A special colored screen for the lens, used in taking color plates. — *v. t.* **a** To subject to the action of a filter; to strain; also, to act as a filter toward. **b** To remove from a fluid by a filter. — *v. i.* **1.** To pass through, or as through, a filter; to percolate. **2.** *Brit.* To head one's vehicle into and join a line of traffic moving transversely. — **fil′ter·er,** *n.*

fil′ter·a·ble (fĭl′tẽr·ȧ·b'l), *adj.* Capable of being filtered; filtrable; as, a *filterable* virus. — **fil′ter·a·bil′i·ty** (-bĭl′ĭ·tĭ), *n.*

filter bed. A bed of sand, gravel, or the like, used for filtering large quantities of water or sewage.

filter paper. Porous unsized paper for filtering liquids, drying crystals, etc.

filth (fĭlth), *n.* [AS. *fȳlth.*] **1.** Foul matter; anything that soils or defiles disgustingly. **2.** Moral transgression or corruption; obscenity.

filth disease. A disease due to pollution of the soil or water or to insanitary and filthy surroundings and habits.

filth′y (fĭl′thĭ), *adj.;* FILTH′I·ER (-thĭ·ẽr); FILTH′I·EST. Defiled with filth; disgustingly dirty; foul; obscene. — **Syn.** See DIRTY. — **filth′i·ly,** *adv.* — **filth′i·ness,** *n.*

fil′tra·ble (fĭl′trȧ·b'l), *adj.* Capable of being filtered, or of passing through a filter; as, a *filtrable* virus (see VIRUS, 2 **b**). — **fil′tra·bil′i·ty** (-bĭl′ĭ·tĭ), *n.*

fil′trate (fĭl′trāt), *v. t. & i.* To filter. — *n.* The fluid which has passed through a filter.

fil·tra′tion (fĭl·trā′shŭn), *n.* Act or process of filtering.

‖**fi′lum** (fī′lŭm), *n.; pl.* FILA (-lȧ). [L., a thread.] *Anat.* A filament or threadlike structure.

fim′bri·ate (fĭm′brĭ·āt), *adj.* [L. *fimbriatus* fringed, fr. *fimbria* border, fringe.] *Bot. & Zool.* Fringed. — (-āt), *v. t.* To hem; fringe. — **fim′bri·at′ed** (-āt′ĕd; -ĭd), *adj.* — **fim′bri·a′tion** (-ā′shŭn), *n.*

fim·bril′late (fĭm·brĭl′āt), *adj.* *Bot.* Bordered with a fine fringe.

fin (fĭn), *n.* [AS. *finn.*] **1.** A membranous winglike or paddlelike process of an aquatic animal, used in propelling, balancing, or guiding the body. **2.** A finlike organ, part, or attachment; as: **a** *Slang.* The hand or arm. **b** Any of various small stationary surfaces attached to different parts of aircraft to secure stability; as, a tail *fin,* skid *fin,* etc. See AIRPLANE, *Illust.* **3.** *Mach.* Any of the projecting ribs on a radiator or internal-combustion engine cylinder. **4.** *Naut.* A finlike appendage, as of boats, esp. submarine boats; also, a fin keel (which see). — *v. t.;* FINNED (fĭnd); FIN′NING. **1.** To carve or cut up, as a chub; cut off the fins of. **2.** *Rare.* To progress, or make way, over by use of the fins. — *v. i.* To move the fins; to lash the water with the fins, as a dying whale.

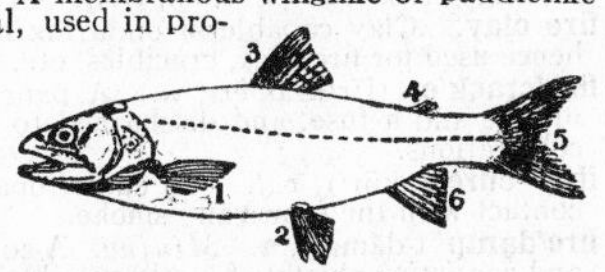

Fins. 1 Pectoral; 2 Pelvic or Ventral; 3 First Dorsal; 4 Second Dorsal; 5 Caudal; 6 Anal.

fi·na′gle (fĭ·nā′g'l), **fi·na′gler** (-glẽr). Vars. of FAINAIGUE, FAINAIGUER.

fi′nal (fī′năl; -n'l), *adj.* [OF., fr. LL. *finalis,* fr. L. *finis* limit, end.] **1.** Pertaining to, or occurring at, the end; last. **2.** Conclusive; decisive; as, a *final* judgment. **3.** Respecting an object to be gained; related to the purpose in view. — **Syn.** See LAST. — *n.* That which is final, as: (*pl.*) a final match, game, or the like; an examination at the end of a course, etc. — **fi′nal·ly,** *adv.*

fi·na′le (fē·nä′lā; -lē), *n.* [It.] Close; termination, as the last section of a musical composition.

fi′nal·ist (fī′năl·ĭst), *n.* *Sports.* Any of the contestants who meet in the finals of an elimination contest.

fi·nal′i·ty (fī·năl′ĭ·tĭ), *n.; pl.* -TIES (-tĭz). **1.** State of being final, settled, or complete. **2.** The doctrine or belief that change or advance is impossible. **3.** That which is final. **4.** *Philos.* Relation of end to means; teleology.

fi·nance′ (fĭ·năns′; fī·năns′; fī′năns; 2), *n.* [OF., fr. *finer* to pay, settle, end, fr. *fin* end.] **1.** Pecuniary resources, esp. of a government. **2.** The science and practice of raising and expending public revenue; the management of monetary affairs. — (fĭ·năns′; fī-), *v. t.;* -NANCED′ (-nănst′); -NANC′ING (-năn′sĭng). To conduct the finances of; to provide capital for.

finance bill. *Govt.* A revenue bill; a legislative act to provide the necessary funds for the public treasury.

fi·nan′cial (fĭ·năn′shăl; fī-), *adj.* Pertaining to finance, or financiers. — **fi·nan′cial·ly,** *adv.*

Syn. **Financial, monetary, pecuniary, fiscal** mean of or relating to money. **Financial** implies relation to money matters especially as conducted on a large scale; **monetary,** to money as coined, distributed, circulating, or the like; **pecuniary,** to money matters, especially as they affect the individual or a small business; **fiscal,** to money as providing revenue for the state.

financial year. *Brit.* The fiscal year.

fin′an·cier′ (fĭn′ăn·sēr′; fĭ′năn·sēr′; fĭ·năn′sĭ·ẽr), *n.* [F.] **1.** One engaged in financial operations; now, an investor on a large scale. **2.** One skilled in financial operations. — *v. t.* To finance.

fin′back′ (fĭn′băk′), *n.* Also **finback whale.** A rorqual; a whalebone whale (genus *Balaenoptera*). The common species of the Atlantic coast of the United States (*B. physalus*) attains a length of over sixty feet.

finch (fĭnch), *n.* [AS. *finc.*] *Zool.* Any of the numerous singing birds (family Fringillidae), including the sparrows, grosbeaks, crossbills, goldfinches, linnets, buntings, greenfinches, chaffinch, towhees, etc. The finches are small, stout birds, generally with a short conical bill adapted for crushing seeds. See BILL, *Illust.*

find (fīnd), *v. t.;* FOUND (found); FIND′ING. [AS. *findan.*] **1.** To meet with, or light upon, accidentally; hence, to fall in with, as a person. **2.** To come upon by seeking or by effort; as: **a** To discover by sounding; as, to *find* bottom. **b** To discover by study or experiment. **c** To gain, as the object of desire or effort. **d** To attain to; to arrive at; as, the bullet *found* its mark. **3.** To learn by experience or trial; to perceive; feel. **4.** To arrive at, as a conclusion; as, to *find* a verdict. **5.** To gain, or regain, the use of; as, to *find* one's tongue. **6.** To provide; supply; as, to *find* food for workmen. — *v. i.* *Law.* To determine and declare an issue by its verdict or decision, as a jury or court. — ***find fault.*** To criticize unfavorably. — ***find out.*** To detect (a thief); discover (a secret); solve; understand. — *n.* A finding, or something found.

find′er (fīn′dẽr), *n.* **1.** One who or that which finds (in various senses). **2.** *Astron.* A small telescope of low power and large field of view, attached to a larger telescope, for finding an object. **3.** *Photog.* A camera attachment which shows in miniature the view thrown by the camera lens upon the photographic plate. See KODAK, *Illust.*

‖**fin de siè′cle** (făN dĕ syâ′kl'). [F.] Literally, end of the century; hence, belonging to, or characteristic of, the close of the 19th century.

find′ing (fīn′dĭng), *n.* **1.** The act of one who finds something; also, that which is found. **2.** *pl.* That which an artisan finds or provides for himself, as tools, trimmings, etc.; as, shoemakers' *findings.* **3.** *Law.* The result of a judicial examination or inquiry, esp. into some matter of fact, as embodied in a jury's verdict, a court's decision, or a referee's report.

fine (fīn), *adj.;* FIN′ER (fīn′ẽr); FIN′EST. [OF. *fin,* deriv. of L. *finis* end or L. *finitus* finished.] **1.** Finished; brought to perfection; refined; hence, free from impurity; superior. **2.** Not large, thick, heavy, coarse, or the like; as, *fine* print; *fine* threads; *fine* sand; a *fine* point in an argument. **3.** Of an athlete or animal, trained to a point of weight and muscular activity close to the limit of efficiency. **4.** Of senses, emotions, reasoning, etc.: subtle; sensitive. **5.** *Obs.* Clever; ingenious; cunning. **6.** Superior in character, nature, or ability; as, a *fine* man, ship. — *adv.* **1.** *Now Dial. & Colloq.* Finely; well. **2.** *Billiards & Pool.* In a manner so that the driven ball strikes the object ball so far to one side as to be deflected but little. — *v. t. & i.* To make fine or grow fine or finer.

fine, *n.* [OF. *fin* end, settlement, arrangement, payment, fr. L. *finis* end.] **1.** *Obs.* End; conclusion. **2.** **a** Formerly, a sum paid by way of compensation or for exemption from punishment; now, a certain payment of money imposed as punishment for an offense; a mulct. **b** Any penalty or forfeiture. **3.** *Law.* **a** A compromise of a fictitious suit used as a form of conveyance of lands. **b** *Eng. Law.* A sum of money or charge for any benefit, favor, or privilege, as for obtaining or renewing a lease. — ***in fine.*** In conclusion; by way of termination. — *v. t.* To set a fine on by judgment of a court.

‖**fi′ne** (fē′nā), *n.* [It.] *Music.* The end; — used to mark the closing point after a repeat.

fine art. Art which is concerned with the creation of objects of imagination and taste for their own sake and without relation to the utility of the object produced.

fine arts. Painting, drawing, architecture, and sculpture; and sometimes, poetry, music, dancing, and dramatic art.

fine′-draw′ (fīn′drô′), *v. t.;* see DRAW. **1.** To draw together two edges of (a fabric, as when torn) by very fine stitches. **2.** To draw out to extreme fineness or subtlety; as, to *fine-draw* a wire; to *fine-draw* an argument.

fine′ly (fīn′lĭ), *adv.* In a fine manner; excellently; closely.

fine′ness (fīn′nĕs; -nĭs), *n.* **1.** Quality or condition of being fine. **2.** The proportion of pure silver or gold in jewelry, bullion, or coins, often expressed in parts per thousand. The fineness of United States coin is 9/10, or 0.900 fine; that of English gold coin is 11/12, or 0.9166 fine.

fin′er·y (fīn′ẽr·ĭ), *n.; pl.* -ERIES (-ĭz). Ornament; decoration; esp., showy clothes.

fin′er·y, *n.; pl.* -ERIES. *Ironworks.* A refinery.

fines (fīnz), *n. pl.* *Mining.* The material that has passed through a sieve.

fine′spun′ (fīn′spŭn′; 2), *adj.* Spun so as to be fine; attenuated; hence, unsubstantial; visionary.

fi·nesse′ (fĭ·nĕs′), *n.* [F., fr. *fin* fine.] **1.** Delicate skill; subtle discrimination; refinement. **2.** Subtlety of contrivance; cunning; stratagem. **3.** *Card Playing.* Act of finessing. — *v. i.;* FI·NESSED′ (-nĕst′); FI·NESS′ING. **1.** To use finesse, artifice, or stratagem. **2.** *Card Playing.* To attempt, when second or third player, to take a trick with a lower card, when a higher, not in sequence with it, is in the hand, in the hope that an intermediate card may be with the right-hand adversary. — *v. t.* *Card Playing.* To play (a card) as a finesse.

fine′-tooth′ (fīn′tōōth′), *or* **fine′-toothed′** (-tōōtht′; -tōōthd′), **comb.** A comb with teeth set close together; — used esp. in the phrase ***to go over with a fine-tooth comb,*** to search through or scrutinize minutely.

fin′ger (fĭng′gẽr), *n.* [AS.] **1.** One of the five terminating members of the hand, esp. one other than the thumb. **2.** Anything that resembles or does the work of a finger, as the pointer of a clock, watch, etc. **3.** The breadth of a finger, a measure varying from ¾ inch to one inch; also, the length of a finger, a measure of about four and a half inches. **4.** A part of a glove into which a finger is inserted. **5.** *Mach.* A projecting piece, which is brought into contact with an object to effect, direct, or restrain a motion, as a pawl for a ratchet. — *v. t.* **1.** To touch with the fingers; to handle. **2.** To pilfer; to purloin. **3.** *Music.* **a** To perform on (an instrument) with the fingers. **b** To perform with a certain fingering. **c** To mark the notes of (a piece) so as to guide the fingers in playing. — *v. i.* *Music.* **a** To use the fingers in playing. **b** To be fingered, as a musical instrument; as, it *fingers* like a cornet.

finger board. *Music.* **a** The part of a stringed instrument against which the fingers press the strings to vary the tone. See VIOLIN, *Illust.* **b** The keyboard of a piano, organ, etc.; manual.

finger bowl *or* **glass.** A bowl or basin to hold water for rinsing the fingers at table.

fin′ger·er (fĭng′gẽr·ẽr), *n.* One who fingers.

fin′ger·ing, *n.* **1.** Act or process of handling or touching with the fingers. **2.** *Music.* **a** Act or method of using the fingers in playing upon an instrument, as on a piano. **b** The marking of the method by figures on a piece of music.

fin′ger·ling (fĭng′gẽr·lĭng), *n.* [*finger* + 1st *-ling.*] Anything very small; specif., a small fish; esp., in Great Britain, the parr.

fin′ger·nail′ (-nāl′; 2), *n.* The horny scale on the upper surface of the end of a finger.

finger painting. A technique of spreading splotches of colored pigments (**finger paints**) on wet paper with the fingers, hand, or arm to form an original picture or design; also, a picture so produced. — **fin′ger-paint′,** *v. t. & i.*

finger post. A guidepost bearing an index finger.

fin′ger·print′ (-prĭnt′), *n.* The impression of a finger tip on any surface; esp., such an impression taken for identification; — often used in identifying criminals. — *v. i.* To make a fingerprint of.

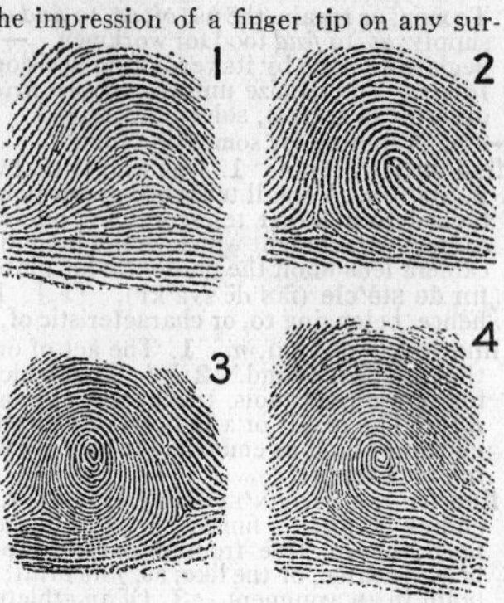

Fingerprints. 1 Arch; 2 Loop; 3 Whorl; 4 Composite.

finger wave. *Hairdressing.* A water wave in which the waves are made by the operator's fingers and set without heat.

fin′i·al (fĭn′ĭ·ăl; fī′nĭ·ăl), *n.* [L. *finis* end.] **a** The ornament that forms the upper extremity of a pinnacle, gable, or the like, esp. in Gothic architecture. **b** Hence, any crowning ornamental architectural detail.

fin′i·cal (fĭn′ĭ·kăl), *adj.* [From FINE, *adj.*] Affectedly fine; unduly dainty. — **Syn.** See NICE. — **fin′i·cal′i·ty** (-kăl′ĭ·tĭ), *n.* — **fin′i·cal·ly,** *adv.* — **fin′i·cal·ness,** *n.*

fin′ick·ing (fĭn′ĭ·kĭng), *adj.* Also **fin′ick·y** (-kĭ), **fin′i·kin** (-ĭ·kĭn). Finical; unduly particular; overprecise.

fi′nis (fī′nĭs), *n.; pl.* FINISES (-ĕz; -ĭz). [L.] An end; conclusion.

‖**fi′nis co·ro′nat o′pus** (fī′nĭs kō·rō′năt ō′pŭs). [L.] The end crowns the work.

fin′ish (fĭn′ĭsh), *v. t.* [OF. *fenir* (F. *finir*), fr. L. *finire* to limit, finish, end, fr. *finis* limit, end.] **1.** To arrive at the end of; to bring to an end. **2.** To complete; accomplish; also, to perfect. **3.** *Colloq.* To dispose of completely; to overthrow or exhaust utterly. — *v. i.* **1.** To come to an end; terminate. **2.** *Rare.* To die. — **Syn.** See CLOSE. — *n.* **1.** The conclusion; end. **2.** That which finishes, completes, or perfects. **3.** The result of completed labor, as on the surface of an object; manner or style of finishing; as, a rough, dead, or glossy *finish.* **4.** Cultivation in manners and speech; social polish. **5.** *Arch.* **a** The joiner work and other fine work required for the completion of a building, esp. of the interior. **b** The higher grades of lumber used for this work. **6.** *Painting.* A material used in finishing; as, oil *finish.*

fin′ished (fĭn′ĭsht), *adj.* **1.** Concluded; perfected. **2.** Polished to the highest degree of excellence; complete; consummate; as, a *finished* poem; a *finished* education.

fin′ish·er (fĭn′ĭsh·ẽr), *n.* One who or that which finishes.

fin′ish·ing school. A private school for girls which emphasizes cultural studies and prepares students for social life.

fi′nite (fī′nīt), *adj.* [L. *finitus,* past part. of *finire.* See FINISH.] **1.** Having definable limits. **2.** Having a character or being completely determinable (in theory or in fact), either as an object of thought, or as susceptible of complete enumeration or measurement. **3. a** Of numbers, attainable or surpassable by counting; less than an integer that may be assigned. **b** Of a magnitude, neither infinite nor infinitesimal. — *n.* A finite thing or being. — **fi′nite·ly,** *adv.* — **fi′nite·ness,** *n.*

finite verb. *Gram.* The predicative forms of a verb, taken collectively, as opposed to the verbals; a verb form limited as to tense, person, number, and mood.

fin′i·tude (fĭn′ĭ·tūd; fī′nĭ-), *n.* Finite state.

fink (fĭngk), *n.* **a** *Underworld Slang.* An informer, or squealer. **b** *Labor Union Slang.* A strikebreaker, esp. one supplied to employers by a strikebreaking agency.

fin keel. *Naut.* A plate of metal fixed to the keel of a shoal vessel to provide lateral resistance, usually with a cigar-shaped bulb of lead to provide stability.

Finn (fĭn), *n.* A native of Finland; also, a member of any of various allied races or of races speaking tongues allied to the Finnish. — **Finn′ic** (-ĭk), *adj.*

fin′nan had′die *or* **had′dock** (fĭn′ăn). A smoked haddock; — from Findon or Findhorn, towns in Scotland.

finned (fĭnd), *adj.* Having a fin or fins.

fin′nick·ing, fin′nick·y. Vars. of FINICKING, FINICKY.

Finn′ish (fĭn′ĭsh), *adj.* Of or pert. to Finland, the Finns, or their language. — *n.* The language of the Finns of Finland and adjacent parts of Russia. See LANGUAGE, *Table.*

Fin′no– (fĭn′ō-). A combining form for *Finn* or *Finnish,* as in **Fin′no–Hun·gar′i·an, Fin′no–Slav′,** etc.

Fin′no–U′gric (-ōō′grĭk), *adj.* **1.** Of or pertaining to the Finns and the Ugrians. **2.** Designating, or pertaining to, a subfamily of the Ural-Altaic languages containing the Finnish, Magyar, and Estonian languages. See LANGUAGE, *Table.* — **Fin′no–U′gric,** *n.*

fin′ny (fĭn′ĭ), *adj.* Having, abounding in, or resembling, fins; hence, pertaining to, or abounding in, fish.

fiord (fyôrd), *n.* Also **fjord.** [Nor. *fiord,* fr. ON. *fjörthr.*] A narrow inlet of the sea, between high banks or rocks, as on the coasts of Norway and Alaska.

fip′pen·ny bit (fĭp′ĕn·ĭ; fĭp′nĭ). The Spanish half real, a silver coin taken at 1/16 dollar; — formerly so called in Pennsylvania and the adjacent states.

fip′ple (fĭp′′l), *n.* In certain wind instruments, a block containing a "lip."

fir (fûr), *n.* [Dan. *fyr.*] **1.** Any of a genus (*Abies*) of trees of the pine family, often of large size, distinguished from the spruces by erect cones and persistent leaves. Some species (as the red fir; which see) are valued for timber, others (as *A. balsamea,* called specif. ***balsam fir***) for their fragrant resin (see CANADA BALSAM). Cf. CONE, *Illust.* **2.** Any of various related coniferous trees, as the Douglas fir (which see). **3.** The wood of any of these trees.

fire (fīr), *n.* [AS. *fȳr.*] **1.** The principle of combustion as manifested in light and heat, esp. flame. It was formerly classed with air, earth, and water as one of the four elements. **2.** Fuel in combustion, as on a hearth. **3.** A destructive burning as of a house or forest. **4.** *Poetic.* Lightning; a thunderbolt. **5.** The means of lighting a fire; also, an inflammable composition of a device for producing a fiery display; as, red *fire.* **6. a** Ardor of passion, spirit, or temperament. **b** Liveliness of imagination. **7.** Fever; inflammation. **8.** Brilliancy; luminosity; hence, a star. **9.** Torture by or as if by burning; hence, severe trial; affliction. **10.** The discharge of firearms; firing; as, exposed to a heavy *fire;* also, a running series, as of shots; as, a *fire* of reproaches. — ***on fire.*** Burning; hence, ardent; eager. — ***under fire.*** Exposed to an enemy's fire; hence, being attacked.
— *v. t.* **1.** To set on fire; to kindle; ignite. **2. a** To animate. **b** To inflame; irritate, as the passions. **3.** To light up as if by fire. **4. a** *Now Rare.* To drive out by or as if by fire. **b** *Colloq.* To eject forcibly; specif., to discharge from a position. **5.** To cause to explode; to discharge; to propel from or as if from a gun. **6.** To apply fire to; as: **a** To cauterize. **b** To subject to intense heat; to bake; to burn in a kiln. **c** To feed or serve the fire of; as, to *fire* a boiler. **d** To heat gently in order to dry; as, to *fire* tea. — *v. i.* **1.** To take fire; hence, to glow or redden. **2.** To be irritated or inflamed with passion. **3.** To discharge artillery or firearms. **4.** Of corn or grain, to turn yellow prematurely, as from drought. **5.** To undergo change by the action of fire, as pottery. — ***fire up.*** **a** To light a fire, as in a furnace. **b** To grow irritated or angry.

fire′arm′ (fīr′ärm′), *n.* Any weapon from which a shot is discharged by an explosive; — usually applied to small arms.

fire′ball′ (-bôl′), *n.* **1.** A ball of fire. **2.** A luminous meteor, resembling a ball of fire. **3.** Formerly, a ball filled with powder or other combustibles, to be thrown among the enemy.

fire beetle. Any of various beetles having light-producing organs; popularly, any of a genus (*Pyrophorus*) of elaterid beetles of tropical America. Cf. FIREFLY.

fire′bird′ (fīr′bûrd′), *n.* Any of several small bright-colored birds, as the Baltimore oriole and the scarlet tanager.

fire′boat′ (-bōt′), *n.* A vessel equipped with pumps and other apparatus for fighting fire on or from the water.

fire′box′ (-bŏks′), *n.* **1.** The chamber of a furnace, steam boiler, etc., for the fire. **2.** *Obs.* A tinderbox.

fire′brand′ (-brănd′), *n.* **1.** A piece of burning wood. **2.** One who inflames factions, or causes contention.

fire′break′ (-brāk′), *n.* A barrier, as of cleared or plowed land, intended to check or stop fires.

fire′brick′ (-brĭk′), *n.* A refractory brick, capable of sustaining high heat without fusion, used for lining furnaces, etc.

fire′bug′ (-bŭg′), *n.* *Colloq., U. S.* An incendiary or pyromaniac.

fire clay. Clay capable of enduring high heat without fusing, and hence used for firebrick, crucibles, etc.

fire′crack′er (fīr′krăk′ẽr), *n.* A paper cylinder, containing an explosive and a fuse, and discharged to make a noise, esp. for joyous celebrations.

fire′–cure′ (-kūr′), *v. t.* To cure (tobacco) over open fires in direct contact with the fumes and smoke.

fire′damp′ (-dămp′), *n.* *Mining.* A combustible gas formed in mines and consisting chiefly of methane; also, the explosive mixture formed by this gas with air. See DAMP, *n.,* 1.

fire′dog′ (-dŏg′; 74), *n.* One of a pair of supports for wood in a fireplace; an andiron.

fire′drake′ (-drāk′), **fire′drag′on** (-drăg′ŭn), *n.* [AS. *fȳrdraca,* fr. *fȳr* fire + *draca* dragon.] A drake, or dragon, breathing fire, a monster frequent in Teutonic mythology.

fire′–eat′er, *n.* **1.** A juggler who pretends to eat fire. **2.** *Colloq.* A quarrelsome person who seeks a fight.

fire engine. An engine for throwing an extinguishing agent, esp. a jet of liquid, usually water, upon fires.

fire escape. Any device for escape from a burning building.

fire extinguisher. A portable hand-operated contrivance for ejecting fire-extinguishing chemicals.

fire′fang′ (fīr′făng′), *v. i.* To deteriorate, often acquiring a smoky flavor or odor, through slow oxidation of its organic matter, as grain, cheese, or manure.

fire′flaught′ (-flôt′; *Scot.* -fläкt′), *n.* [*fire* + *flaught* a flake, flash.] *Scot.* Lightning; a gleam, as of fire; flash.

fire′fly′ (-flī′), *n.* Any nocturnal, winged, light-producing insect, esp. of either of two genera (*Photinus* and *Photuris*) of small, elongate, soft-bodied beetles (family Lampyridae), some having wingless females and some luminescent larvae (popularly called *glowworms*).

fire′guard′ (-gärd′), *n.* **1.** A wire screen or grating placed before or fitting over the front of an open fireplace. **2.** Land cleared of inflammable material as protection against forest or prairie fires.

fire irons. Utensils for a fireplace or grate, as tongs, poker, etc.

fire′lock′ (fīr′lŏk′), *n.* An old form of gunlock, as the wheel lock or flintlock; hence, a gun having such a lock.

fire′man (-măn), *n.* **1.** A member of a ***fire company,*** a company of men organized to extinguish fires. **2.** A man who tends or feeds fires; a stoker.

fire′–new′ (-nū′; 2), *adj.* Fresh from the forge; brand-new.

fire opal. = GIRASOL, 2.

fire pink. A scarlet-flowered sticky catchfly (*Silene virginica*) of the eastern United States.

fire′place′ (fīr′plās′), *n.* The part of a chimney used for the fire, usually an open recess in a wall; a hearth.

fire′plug′ (-plŭg′), *n.* A plug or hydrant for drawing water from the mains in a street, building, etc., for extinguishing fires.

fire′pow′er (-pou′ẽr), *n.* *Mil.* The aggregate of effective shells and missiles that can be placed upon a target; hence, the ability to deliver such fire.

fire′proof′ (-prōōf′), *v. t.* To render fireproof.

fire′proof′ (-prōōf′; 2), *adj.* Proof against fire; relatively incombustible. Degrees of fire resistance, in decreasing order, are designated by ***fire-resistive, fire-retardant,*** and ***flameproof.***

fir′er (fīr′ẽr), *n.* One who or that which fires.

fire ship. A vessel carrying combustibles or explosives, sent among the enemy's ships or works to set them on fire.

fire′side′ (fīr′sīd′), *n.* A place near the fire or hearth; hence, home; domestic life or retirement.

fire′stone′ (-stōn′), *n.* [AS. *fyrstān* flint, fr. *fȳr* fire + *stān* stone.] **1.** Iron pyrites, formerly used for striking fire; also, a flint. **2.** A stone which will endure high heat; — applied esp. to a sandstone found in the south of England.

fire′trap′ (-trăp′), *n.* A place, esp. a building, so constructed as to make egress hazardous in case of fire.

fire wall. A wall to prevent the spread of fire, as around an oil tank.
fire′ward′en (fīr′wôr′d'n), **fire′ward′** (-wôrd′), *n.* *U. S.* An officer with authority to take measures to prevent fires.
fire′wa′ter (-wô′tẽr; -wŏt′ẽr), *n.* Ardent spirits; — now jocular.
fire′weed′ (-wēd′), *n.* Any of several weeds troublesome in clearings or burned districts, esp. an American weed (*Erechtites hieracifolia*) of the aster family, and the Jimson weed.
fire′wood′ (-wŏŏd′), *n.* **1.** Wood for fuel. **2.** The ironwood *Cyrilla racemiflora* of the southeastern U. S.
fire′work′ (-wûrk′), *n.* Usually *pl.* A device for producing a striking display, as of light, noise, or smoke, by the combustion of explosive or inflammable compositions.
fire′worm′ (-wûrm′), *n.* The larva of a small tortricid moth (*Rhopobota naevana*), which eats cranberry leaves.
fir′ing (fīr′ĭng), *n.* **1. a** Act of discharging a firearm, a mine, etc. **b** Act or mode of introducing fuel into the furnace and working it. **c** Application of fire, or of a cautery. **d** *Ceramics.* Exposure to intense heat in a kiln in order to harden or glaze. **2.** Fuel; firewood or coal.
firing line. **1.** *Mil.* Any line delivering fire, or in a position to deliver fire, against the enemy; the front line. **2.** The forefront of any activity.
firing pin. In the breech mechanism of a firearm, the pin which strikes the head of the cartridge. See GUNLOCK, *Illust.*
fir′kin (fûr′kĭn), *n.* [Prob. fr. D. *vierde* fourth + *-kin.*] **1.** A small wooden vessel or cask for butter, lard, etc. **2.** A measure of capacity, usually one fourth part of a barrel.
firm (fûrm), *adj.* [OF. *ferm(e)*, fr. L. *firmus.*] **1.** Fixed; hence, closely compressed; solid. **2.** Not easily moved, shaken, or disturbed; steady; constant. **3.** Solid; — opposed to *fluid;* as, *firm* land. **4.** Indicating firmness; as, a *firm* voice or countenance. **5.** *Com.* Steady; not fluctuating markedly; — said of prices, a market, etc. — **firm′ly**, *adv.* — **firm′ness**, *n.*
Syn. **Firm, hard, solid** mean having a texture or consistency that completely or markedly resists deformation. **Firm** implies such compactness and coherence of substance or material that it is difficult to pull, distort, cut, or the like; **hard** implies impenetrability or virtually complete resistance to pressure, tension, or the like; **solid** implies a texture or construction of so uniform a density throughout that it is not only firm or hard but, usually, heavy. Figuratively, **firm** implies stability or resolution, **hard** obduracy or lack of feeling, and **solid** substantiality (that is, reliability, meatiness, or the like).
— *v. t. & i.* **1.** To make or become fast, secure, solid, or compact. **2.** *Archaic.* To confirm; establish.
firm, *n.* [Sp. & It. *firma*, fr. L. *firmare* to confirm, fr. *firmus* firm.] The name, title, or style under which a company transacts business; the firm name; hence, a partnership of two or more persons; as, the *firm* of Hope & Co. Under English and American law, a *firm* is not recognized as a legal person distinct from the members composing it.
fir′ma·ment (fûr′mȧ·mĕnt), *n.* [L. *firmamentum*, fr. *firmare* to make firm.] The vault or arch of the sky; the heavens. — **fir′ma·men′tal** (-mĕn′tăl; -t'l), *adj.*
fir′man (fûr′măn; fẽr·män′), *n.; pl.* -MANS (-mănz; -mänz′). [Turk. *fermān*, fr. Per. *fermān.*] Formerly in Turkey and still in some Oriental countries, a royal decree.
firm′er (fûr′mẽr), *adj.* [F. *fermoir.*] *Mech.* Designating a chisel, gouge, or the like, designed to withstand driving with a mallet or hammer. See CHISEL, *Illust.* — *n.* A firmer chisel.
firn (fĭrn), *n.* [G., last year's snow.] **1.** = NÉVÉ. **2.** *Skiing.* Granular snow.
fir′ry (fûr′ĭ), *adj.* Made of fir; abounding in firs.
first (fûrst), *adj.* [AS. *fyrst.*] **1.** Preceding all others; foremost; — used as an ordinal of *one* (see NUMBER, *Table*); as: **a** Earliest in time or succession. **b** Foremost in position. **c** Foremost in rank. **2.** *Automobiles.* Designating the lowest forward gear or speed. — *adv.* **1.** Before any or some other person or thing in time, space, rank, etc. **2.** For the first time. **3.** In preference to anything else; sooner. — *n.* **1.** Anything that is first; the beginning. See NUMBER, *Table.* **2.** The first, usually highest, class; also, a place, or a person, in such a class. **3.** The first year of a reign or the first day of a month. **4.** *Automobiles.* The first gear or speed. **5.** *pl. Com.* The finest grade of many articles of commerce, as lumber, butter, etc. **6.** *Music.* **a** The upper voice part of a duet, trio, etc. **b** The highest or chief voice or instrument of its class. **c** The prime, or unison. **7.** *Sports.* The winning place in a race or other contest.
first aid. More or less skilled emergency treatment given to sufferers from accident, battle, etc., before regular medical or surgical care can be given. — **first′–aid′** (*see Pron.*, § 2), *adj.*
first base. *Baseball.* **a** The base that must be touched first by a base runner. **b** A fielder stationed at this base.
first′–born′ (*see Pron.*, § 2), *adj.* First brought forth; eldest. — *n.* One that is first born; hence, an heir.
first cause. Prime mover; *Theol.*, God as a self-active being, source of all causality.
first′–class′ (fûrst′klȧs′; 2), *adj.* Of the highest class, quality, etc. — *adv.* By a first-class conveyance, etc.
first class. The highest class of accommodations in a passenger vessel, esp. one having three classes. First class was formerly sometimes called *cabin class* (which see).
first′hand′ (-hănd′; 2), *adv.* Directly from the original source. — *adj.* Obtained or coming directly from the first, or original, source.
first lieutenant. **1.** *Mil.* A commissioned officer of the army or marine corps next in rank below a captain and above a second lieutenant. **2.** *Nav.* An officer detailed as head of the construction and repair department of a man-of-war and responsible for her cleanliness and upkeep.
first′ling (fûrst′lĭng), *n.* The first of a class or kind; the first produce, offspring, or result of anything.
first′ly (fûrst′lĭ), *adv.* In the first place; first.
first mortgage. A mortgage which has priority as a lien over all other mortgages. — **first′–mort′gage**, *adj.*
first offender. One legally convicted of an offense for the first time.
first papers. *Colloq., U. S.* The papers declaring intention, filed by an applicant for citizenship as the first step towards naturalization.
first′–rate′ (fûrst′rāt′; 2), *adj.* **1.** Of the first rate or order. **2.** Of the highest efficiency; also, *Colloq.*, extremely good. — (fûrst′rāt′), *adv.* *Colloq.* Very or quite well.
first water. The highest quality or purest luster; — said of gems, esp. diamonds and pearls; hence, the highest grade.
firth (fûrth), *n.* [See FRITH.] A narrow arm of the sea; also, the opening of a river into the sea.
fisc (fĭsk), *n.* [F., fr. L. *fiscus* basket, money basket, treasury.] Any state or royal treasury; an exchequer.
fis′cal (fĭs′kăl), *adj.* [F., fr. LL. *fiscalis*, fr. *fiscus.* See FISC.] Of or pertaining to the public treasury or revenue; hence, of or pertaining to financial matters; as, *fiscal* control; a *fiscal* agent or period; the *fiscal* year, that is, the uniform period between one annual balancing of financial accounts and the next (the government fiscal year in the United States ends June 30, in Great Britain and Canada, March 31). — **Syn.** See FINANCIAL. — *n.* **1.** In some European countries, one of various officials having the character of public prosecutors, as, formerly, in Spain the king's solicitor. **2.** *Philately.* = REVENUE STAMP.
fiscal agent. A financial representative, as a trust company serving a corporation.
fish (fĭsh), *n.* [AS. *fisc.*] NOTE. — The word *fish* and its compounds, as black*fish*, normally use a plural form identical with the singular; they use a plural form in *-es* chiefly to signify diversity in kind or species; as, to distinguish the North Atlantic and Alaskan black*fishes;* except that to represent an emphatically distributive sense, *fishes* (*pron.* fĭsh′ĕz; -ĭz) is frequent. **1.** Broadly, almost any exclusively aquatic animal. **2.** Specif., any of numerous cold-blooded, strictly aquatic, water-breathing, craniate vertebrates having the limbs (when present) developed as fins, and typically a long, scaly, somewhat tapering body ending in a broad vertical caudal fin. See FIN, *Illust.* **3.** The flesh of fish, used as food. **4.** A piece of wood, iron, or other rigid material, fastened alongside another in order to strengthen it; a fishplate (see FISH JOINT). **5.** *Colloq.* A person resembling a fish, as in slipperiness, desirability, stupidity, etc. **6.** [*cap.*] Either of the two groups of stars which together form the constellation Pisces. **7.** *Naut.* **a** A purchase used to fish the anchor. **b** A fish-shaped piece of timber to strengthen a mast or yard.
— *adj.* Of or pertaining to fish, or to the catching or selling of fish.
— *v. i.* **1.** To attempt to catch fish, as by angling or drawing a net. **2.** To search for anything under water, hidden, buried, etc., with hook, dredge, etc. **3.** To seek to obtain by artifice, or indirectly to seek to draw forth; — often with *for;* as, to *fish* for compliments. — *v. t.* **1.** To catch, or try to catch; to draw (*out* or *up*). **2.** To try with a fishing rod; to fish in; as, to *fish* a stream. **3.** To strengthen (a beam, mast, etc.) by a fish. — **fish′a·ble** (fĭsh′ȧ·b'l), *adj.*
fish ball, fish cake. A cake made of fish (often codfish) shredded, mixed with mashed potato, and fried or sautéed.
fish′bolt′ (fĭsh′bōlt′), *n.* A bolt for securing a fishplate.
fish′er (fĭsh′ẽr), *n.* **1.** One who or that which fishes. **2.** A carnivorous arboreal mammal (*Martes pennanti*) of the weasel family, of eastern North America.
fish′er·man (-măn), *n.* **1.** One whose occupation is to catch fish; also, a ship or vessel used in fishing. **2.** One who fishes for sport.
fish′er·man's bend (-mănz). See KNOT, *Illust.* (14).
fish′er·y (-ĭ), *n.; pl.* -ERIES (-ĭz). **1.** Act, occupation, or season of taking fish or other sea products; fishing. **2.** A place for catching fish or taking other sea products. **3.** *Law.* The right to take fish at a certain place, or in particular waters, esp. by drawing a seine or net.
fish hawk. The osprey.
fish′hook′ (fĭsh′hŏŏk′), *n.* A hook for catching fish. Cf. LURE, *Illust.*
fish′ing (fĭsh′ĭng), *n.* Act of one that fishes: **a** Occupation or pastime of fishery. **b** A place for fishing; fishery.
fish joint. A butt joint in which the abutting members are held in alignment by one or more plates, called **fish′plates′**.

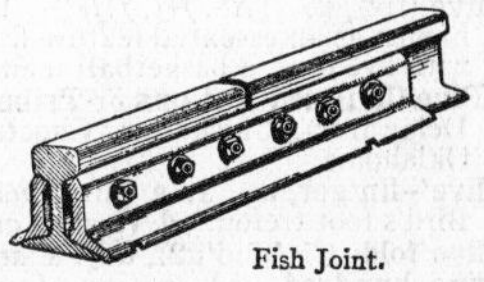

Fish Joint.

fish meal. Ground dried fish and fish waste, used as fertilizer and animal food.
fish′mon′ger (fĭsh′mŭng′gẽr), *n.* A person who buys and sells fish.
fish′pound′ (fĭsh′pound′), *n.* *Local, U. S.* A net attached to stakes, for entrapping and catching fish; a weir.
fish story. *Colloq.* An extravagant or incredible story.
fish tackle. *Naut.* A tackle or purchase used to raise the flukes of the anchor up to the gunwale.
fish′tail′ (fĭsh′tāl′), *v. i.* *Colloq., Aviation.* To skid or swing an aircraft or its tail from side to side to reduce speed.
fish′wife′ (-wīf′), *n.; pl.* -WIVES (-wīvz′). A woman who sells fish at retail; hence, a scurrilously abusive woman.
fish′y (fĭsh′ĭ), *adj.;* FISH′I·ER (-ĭ·ẽr); FISH′I·EST. **1.** Consisting of fish; having the qualities, taste, or odor of fish; abounding in fish. **2.** *Colloq.* Unreliable; improbable. **3.** Dull; lusterless; — said of the eyes or of a jewel. — **fish′i·ly**, *adv.* — **fish′i·ness**, *n.*
fis′sile (fĭs′ĭl; -īl), *adj.* [L. *fissilis*, fr. *fissus*, past part. of *findere* to split.] Capable of being split; cleavable. — **fis·sil′i·ty** (fĭ·sĭl′ĭ·tĭ), *n.*
fis′sion (fĭsh′ŭn), *n.* [L. *fissio.* See FISSURE.] **1.** A cleaving, or breaking up into parts. **2.** *Biol.* Reproduction by spontaneous division of the body into two or more parts, each of which grows into a complete organism, as in bacteria. **3.** *Physics & Chem.* The splitting of an atomic nucleus, as by bombardment with neutrons, resulting in the release of enormous quantities of energy when certain heavy elements, as uranium and plutonium, are split. — *v. t. & i.* To separate by fission.
fis′sion·a·ble (-ȧ·b'l), *adj.* Capable of undergoing fission.
fission bomb. An atomic bomb. Cf. FUSION BOMB.
fis·sip′a·rous (fĭ·sĭp′ȧ·rŭs), *adj.* [L. *fissus* cleft + *-parous.*] Producing new units or individuals by fission.
fis′si·ros′tral (fĭs′ĭ·rŏs′trăl), *adj.* [L. *fissus* cleft + *rostrum* beak.] Having the bill broad and deeply cleft, so that the mouth when opened is very large, as in swifts.
fis′sure (fĭsh′ẽr), *n.* [F., fr. L. *fissura*, fr. *findere, fissum*, to cleave, split.] **1.** A narrow opening made by the parting of any substance; a cleft. **2.** A cleaving, or state of being cleft; cleavage. **3.** *Anat.* One of the clefts or grooves separating certain lobes, bones, or tracts. — *v. t. & i.* To break into fissures; to cleave.
fist (fĭst). Var. of FEIST.
fist (fĭst), *n.* [AS. *fўst.*] **1.** The hand with fingers doubled into the palm; the clenched hand. **2.** *Now Colloq.* **a** The clutch; grasp. **b** The hand, whether closed or not; as, give me your *fist.* **c** Handwriting. **3.** *Print.* The index mark [☞]. — *v. t.* To strike with the fist; also, to clench.

fist'ic (fĭs'tĭk), *adj.* *Colloq.* Pertaining to boxing; pugilistic.
fist'i·cuff' (fĭs'tĭ·kŭf'), *n.* A blow with the fist; *pl.*, a fight with the fists. — *v. t. & i.* To cuff or strike with the fist; to resort to fisticuffs. — **fist'i·cuff'er** (-ẽr), *n.*
fis'tu·la (fĭs'tū·lȧ), *n.; pl.* -LAS (-lȧz), -LAE (-lē). [L.] *Med. & Veter.* An abnormal passage in an abscess or hollow organ; specif., a suppurative inflammation of the withers of the horse.
fis'tu·lar (-lẽr), *adj.* Fistulous.
fis'tu·lous (-lŭs), *adj.* **1.** *Med. & Veter.* Having the form or nature of a fistula. **2.** Hollow, like a pipe or reed.
fist'y (fĭs'tĭ). Var. of FEISTY.
fit (fĭt), *n.* [AS. *fitt.*] *Archaic.* A division of a poem or song; canto.
fit, *adj.;* FIT'TER (-ẽr); FIT'TEST. [ME. *fyt*, of uncertain origin.] **1.** Adapted to an end, object, or design; qualified. **2.** Proper, right, or becoming. **3.** Prepared; ready; as, *fit* for service. **4.** In fine physical condition; — said of an athlete, race horse, etc.; hence, in good health.
Syn. Fit, suitable, meet, proper, appropriate, fitting, apt, happy, felicitous mean right with respect to the nature, circumstances, use, etc., of the thing considered or qualified. **Fit** stresses adaptability or the possession of qualifications; **suitable,** an answering to requirements or demands; **meet,** a just proportioning; **proper,** a fitness or suitability by nature, custom, or the like; **appropriate,** eminent fitness or suitability; **fitting,** harmony of mood, spirit, or tone; **apt,** fitness by nature or construction; **happy,** singular appropriateness and aptness; **felicitous,** a happiness that is opportune, telling, or graceful.
— *v. t.;* FIT'TED (-ĕd; -ĭd); FIT'TING. **1.** To be suitable to; befit. **2.** To be correct in shape, size, adjustment, etc., for; as, the coat *fits* you; also, to make or adjust so as to fit a person or thing; as, to *fit* a coat. **3.** To make fit, ready, or qualified. **4.** To conform or cause to conform to. **5.** To supply with that, as a garment, which fits; outfit.
— *v. i.* **1.** To be befitting. **2.** To be (so) adjusted in shape, size, etc.; as, this cork *fits* tightly.
— *n.* **1.** Quality, condition, or manner of fitting or being fitted. **2.** *Colloq.* A making fit or ready. **3.** Something, as a garment or part, that fits. **4.** *Mach.* Coincidence of parts in contact; tightness of adjustment of adjacent parts.
— **fit'ly,** *adv.* — **fit'ness,** *n.* — **fit'ter,** *n.*
fit, *n.* [AS., strife, fight.] **1.** A sudden and violent attack of a disorder, esp. epilepsy or apoplexy; a convulsion; a paroxysm. **2.** A sudden outburst, as of anger; also, a passing mood, humor, etc. **3.** A sudden or transient manifestation; a spell. — ***by fits, by fits and starts.*** By intervals of action and repose; impulsively and irregularly.
fit. Scot. var. of FOOT.
fitch'ew (fĭch'ōō), *n.* Also **fitch** (fĭch), **fitch'et** (-ĕt; -ĭt). [OF. *fichau, fissel.*] The polecat of Europe, or its fur.
fit'ful (fĭt'fōōl; -f'l), *adj.* [From FIT a paroxysm.] Spasmodic; restless; impulsive and unstable. — **fit'ful·ly,** *adv.* — **fit'ful·ness,** *n.*
Syn. Fitful, spasmodic, convulsive mean lacking steadiness or regularity in movement. **Fitful** implies succession by fits and starts; **spasmodic** adds to *fitful* the implication of alternation of violent activity and of inactivity; **convulsive** suggests an abnormal period when something that is normally still or rhythmical in its movement acquires a jerky, heaving movement.
fit'ting (fĭt'ĭng), *n.* **1.** Act of one that fits. **2.** Anything used in fitting up; esp., *pl.*, fixtures, auxiliary parts, etc.; as, the *fittings* of a room, of a machine. Cf. FURNITURE, 2 **b.** — *adj.* Appropriate. — **Syn.** See FIT. — **fit'ting·ly,** *adv.* — **fit'ting·ness,** *n.*
five (fīv), *n.* [AS. *fīf, fīfe.*] **1.** See NUMBER, *Table.* **2.** Something having as an essential feature five units or members, as a playing card with five pips, a basketball team of five players, etc. — **five,** *adj.*
Five Civilized Nations *or* **Tribes.** The Cherokee (with the affiliated Delawares), Chickasaw, Choctaw, Creek, and Seminole nations of Oklahoma.
five'-fin'ger, *n.* **1. a** Cinquefoil. **b** The oxlip *Primula elatior.* **c** Bird's-foot trefoil. **d** Virginia creeper. **2.** A five-rayed starfish.
five'fold' (fīv'fōld'; 2), *adj. & adv.* See -FOLD.
five hundred. A variety of euchre, played with the joker and a widow, 500 points constituting a game.
Five Nations. See IROQUOIS.
five percenter. One who for a fee of five per cent aids businessmen to obtain government contracts or do other business with the government.
fiv'er (fīv'ẽr), *n.* *Slang.* **a** A five-dollar bill. **b** A five-pound note. **c** Something that counts or scores five.
fives (fīvz), *n.* A game similar to handball.
fix (fĭks), *v. t.;* FIXED (fĭkst) or FIXT; FIX'ING. [From *fix*, adj., fr. OF. *fixe*, or fr. ML. *fixare*, both fr. L. *fixus*, past part. of *figere* to fix.] **1.** To make firm, stable, or fast. **2.** To hold or direct steadily. **3.** To set or place definitely; establish; settle. **4.** To place or settle (authorship, blame, etc.) *on* or *upon.* **5.** To set or place in order; adjust. **6.** To render permanent; to give an unvarying form to. **7.** *Colloq.* **a** To put to rights; arrange. **b** To repair. **c** To get into a desired position, condition, or the like, by bribing or injuring, etc. (a person), by tampering with (a race horse), or the like. **8.** *Chem.* To render nonvolatile or solid; to cause to form a nonvolatile or solid compound; as, to *fix* ammonia. **9.** *Micros.* To kill, harden, and preserve, as organisms or fresh tissues, as for microscopic study. **10.** *Photog.* To render permanent by removing the unaffected light-sensitive material from a negative or positive. — *v. i.* To become fixed or stable. — **Syn.** See FASTEN.
— *n.* *Colloq.* **1.** A predicament; plight. **2.** The position, as of a ship or aircraft, obtained by bearings of objects on shore, by observations of heavenly bodies, or by radio means; also, a determination of the position. — **Syn.** See PREDICAMENT.
— **fix'a·ble,** *adj.* — **fix'er,** *n.*
fix'ate (fĭk'sāt), *v. t. & i.* [L. *fixus.* See FIX, *v.*] To render, or become, fixed; specif., *Psychol.:* **a** To direct upon an object; as, to *fixate* the eyes. **b** To look at. **c** To arrest in an immature stage of the development of sexual desire.
fix·a'tion (fĭks·ā'shŭn), *n.* Act or result of fixating; specif.: **a** *Psychol.* (1) The formation of a habit or association. (2) An arrest in the development of sexual desire by a strong attachment in childhood. **b** *Chem.* Process of making fixed, as an oil or a gas.
fix'a·tive (fĭk'sȧ·tĭv), *adj.* Having the power or quality of fixing, or making permanent. — *n.* That which fixes, or sets, anything.
fixed (fĭkst), *adj.* **1.** Securely placed or fastened. **2.** *Chem.* **a** Nonvolatile; as, a *fixed* acid. **b** Formed into a chemical compound; as, *fixed* nitrogen. — **fix'ed·ly** (fĭk'sĕd·lĭ; 30), *adv.* — **fix'ed·ness,** *n.*
fixed charge. *Finance.* In general, a charge that cannot be escaped or shifted, or altered; specif., such a charge becoming due at stated intervals, as rentals, taxes, etc.
fixed oil. *Chem.* A nonvolatile oil; — applied esp. to the liquid fats found in many animals and plants (usually in the seeds); — disting. from *volatile*, or *essential, oil.*
fixed star. *Astron.* A star whose apparent position relative to surrounding stars seems unvarying for long periods of time. Symbol, ✱ or ✻.
fix'ing, *n.* **a** Act of making fixed. **b** *pl.* *Colloq.* Arrangements; trimmings; accompaniments.
fix'i·ty (fĭk'sĭ·tĭ), *n.* Stability; also, that which is fixed; a fixture.
fixt (fĭkst). *Chiefly Poetic.* Past tense of FIX.
fix'ture (fĭks'tūr), *n.* [From *fixure*, after *mixture.*] **1.** Act of fixing, or state of being fixed. **2.** A person or, esp., a thing firmly fastened in place. **3.** Something firmly attached, as a part or an appendage; as, gas *fixtures;* specif., *Law*, anything of an accessory character annexed to houses and lands so as to legally constitute a part thereof; — often called an ***immovable fixture.***
fix'ure (fĭk'shẽr), *n.* [LL. *fixura* a fastening, fr. *figere* to fix.] *Archaic.* Fixed position; firmness.
fiz'gig' (fĭz'gĭg'), *n.* **1.** A gadding, flirting girl or woman. **2.** A firework which fizzes or hisses when it explodes; also, a whirligig; a kind of noisy toy.
fizz, fiz (fĭz), *v. i.;* FIZZED (fĭzd); FIZZ'ING. [Partly imitative.] To make a hissing or sputtering sound, as a burning fuse. — *n.* **1.** A hissing sound. **2.** An effervescing drink. — **fizz'er** (fĭz'ẽr), *n.*
fiz'zle (fĭz''l), *v. i.;* FIZ'ZLED (-'ld); FIZ'ZLING (-lĭng). **1.** To fizz. **2.** *Colloq.* To fail after a good start. — *n.* A fizzling; esp., *Colloq.*, a failure or an abortive effort.
fjeld (fyĕld), *n.* [Nor., fr. ON. *fjall.*] *Geog.* A barren plateau of the Scandinavian upland.
fjord (fyôrd). Var. of FIORD.
flab'ber·gast (flăb'ẽr·găst), *v. t.* [See FLABBY; AGHAST.] *Colloq.* To astonish, esp. by extraordinary statements. — **Syn.** See SURPRISE.
flab'by (flăb'ĭ), *adj.;* -BI·ER (-ĭ·ẽr); -BI·EST. [See FLAP.] Lacking firmness; soft and slack, as muscles; flaccid; also, having soft slack flesh or muscles; as, a *flabby* person; figuratively, feeble; weak. — **Syn.** See LIMP. — **flab'bi·ly,** *adv.* — **flab'bi·ness,** *n.*
fla·bel'late (flȧ·bĕl'āt), *adj.* Fan-shaped.
fla·bel'li- (flȧ·bĕl'ĭ-). [L. *flabellum* fan.] ‖ *Bot.* A combining form meaning *fanlike, fan-shaped*, as in **fla·bel'li·fo'li·ate, fla·bel'li·form** (see FOLIATE, -FORM).
fla·bel'lum (flȧ·bĕl'ŭm), *n.; pl.* -LA (-ȧ). [L., a fan, dim. of *flabrum* a breeze, fr. *flare* to blow.] **1.** A fan or fan-shaped organ or part. **2.** *Eccl.* A fan carried before the pope on state occasions.
flac'cid (flăk'sĭd), *adj.* [F. *flaccide*, fr. L. *flaccidus*, fr. *flaccus* flabby.] Yielding to pressure readily or without resistance; flabby. — **Syn.** See LIMP. — **flac·cid'i·ty** (flăk·sĭd'ĭ·tĭ), *n.* — **flac'cid·ly,** *adv.*
‖**fla'con'** (flȧ'kôN'), *n.* [F. See FLAGON.] Flask.
flag (flăg), *n.* [ME. *flagge.*] **1.** Any of various monocotyledonous plants having long, ensiform leaves; esp.: **a** The common yellow-flowered iris of Europe (*Iris pseudacorus*). **b** Either of two blue-flowered irises (*I. versicolor*, called ***blue flag,*** and *I. prismatica*) of the United States. **c** The cattail *Typha latifolia.* See CATTAIL, *Illust.* **2.** The leaf or blade of such a plant.
flag, *n.* [ON. *flaga.*] Any hard stone that splits into pieces suitable for paving; also, a piece of such stone; a flagstone. — *v. t.;* FLAGGED (flăgd); FLAG'GING. To lay with flags. — **flag'ger,** *n.*
flag, *n.* **1.** A light cloth bearing a device or devices to indicate nationality, party, etc., or to give or ask information; a standard; banner; ensign. **2. a** *pl.* The long feathers on the lower part of the legs of certain hawks, owls, etc. **b** *pl.* The secondaries of a bird's wing. **c** The tail of certain dogs, as setters and hounds; also, the tail of a deer. — *v. t.* **1.** To put a flag or flags on. **2.** To signal to with or as with a flag; also, to bring to a stop by signaling. **3.** To convey, as a message, by means of flag signals. **4.** To decoy (game) by waving a flag, handkerchief, or the like.
flag, *v. i.* **1.** To hang limply; droop. **2.** To lose vigor; show signs of exhaustion; languish; as, when energy *flags.* — *v. t.* To let droop; to cause to flag.
Flag Day. a *U. S.* June 14th, anniversary of the day in 1777 on which Congress formally adopted the Stars and Stripes as the national flag. **b** [*not caps.*] *Brit.* A day on which contributions are solicited for some fund, small flags being given to the contributors. Cf. TAG DAY.
flag'el·lant (flăj'ĕ·lănt; flȧ·jĕl'ănt), *n.* [L. *flagellans*, pres. part. See FLAGELLATE.] One who whips or scourges himself, esp. for a religious motive. — **flag'el·lant,** *adj.*
flag'el·late (flăj'ĕ·lāt), *v. t.* [L. *flagellatus*, past part. of *flagellare* to scourge, fr. *flagellum* whip.] To scourge; flog. — *adj.* Also **flag'el·lat'ed** (-lāt'ĕd; -ĭd). Having or bearing flagella; shaped like a flagellum. — **flag'el·la'tion** (-lā'shŭn), *n.* — **flag'el·la'tor** (-lā'tẽr), *n.*
fla·gel'li·form (flȧ·jĕl'ĭ·fôrm), *adj.* [*flagellum* + *-form.*] Shaped like a flagellum.
fla·gel'lum (-ŭm), *n.; pl.* -LUMS (-ŭmz), -LA (-ȧ). [L., whip.] *Biol.* A whiplike process or appendage, as of a cell, serving as the swimming organ of many zoospores and bacteria.
flag'eo·let' (flăj'ō·lĕt'), *n.* [F., dim. fr. OF. *flageol, flajol*, fr. L. *flabellum* fan.] A small wood-wind instrument of the flute class.
flag'ging (flăg'ĭng), *n.* A pavement of flagstones.
flag'ging, *adj.* Waning in force; drooping. — **flag'ging·ly,** *adv.*
fla·gi'tious (flȧ·jĭsh'ŭs), *adj.* [OF. *flagicieux*, fr. L. *flagitiosus*, fr. *flagitium* shame.] Shamefully criminal; grossly wicked; scandalous; also, guilty of enormities; villainous. — **Syn.** See VICIOUS. — **fla·gi'tious·ly,** *adv.* — **fla·gi'tious·ness,** *n.*
flag'man (flăg'măn), *n.* One who bears, or signals with, a flag.
flag officer. A naval officer in military command of combatant forces who is entitled to display a flag indicating his command rank, in the U. S. Navy having a rank of commodore (one-starred flag) or above, in the British Navy having a rank of rear admiral or above.
flag of truce. A white flag carried, or displayed to an enemy, as an invitation to conference or parley.
flag'on (flăg'ŭn), *n.* [OF. *flacon*, fr. VL. *flasco*, fr. *flasca.* See FLASK.] A vessel for liquors, esp. one with a handle and a spout, and usually a lid, but sometimes merely a large bulging bottle; also, its contents (as a measure, two quarts).

flag′pole′ (flăg′pōl′), *n.* A pole on which to raise a flag.
fla′gran·cy (flā′grăn·sĭ), *n.; pl.* -CIES (-sĭz). Also **fla′grance** (-grăns). Condition or quality of being flagrant.
fla′grant (-grănt), *adj.* [L. *flagrans, -antis,* pres. part. of *flagrare* to burn.] **1.** *Now Rare.* Burning. **2.** Flaming into notice; conspicuously bad; glaring. — **fla′grant·ly,** *adv.*
Syn. **Flagrant, glaring, gross, rank** mean conspicuously bad, unpleasant, disagreeable, or the like. **Flagrant** applies to that which cannot escape notice or be condoned (as, a *flagrant* abuse); **glaring** implies even more obtrusiveness than *flagrant* (as, a *glaring* fault in a design); **gross,** an exceeding the bounds so as to be wholly inexcusable (as, *gross* carelessness); **rank** applies chiefly to terms of reproach and means that the thing (sometimes person) described is utterly that which it is said to be (as, that is *rank* nonsense).
‖**fla·gran′te de·lic′to** (flȧ·grăn′tē dē·lĭk′tō). [L.] Literally, while the crime is blazing; in the very act.
flag′ship′ (flăg′shĭp′), *n.* *Naval.* The ship that carries the commander of a fleet or squadron and flies his flag.
flag′staff′ (-stȧf′; 9), *n.; pl.* -STAFFS (-stȧfs′) or -STAVES (-stāvz′). A staff on which a flag is hoisted.
flag′stone′ (-stōn′), *n.* Rock that splits into flags; flag.
flag stop *or* **station.** **a** A railroad station at which trains stop only if signaled, as by a flag. **b** A point along an air transportation line where a stop is made on the usual scheduled flight only by prearrangement.
flail (flāl), *n.* [OF. *flaiel,* fr. L. *flagellum* scourge, flail.] An instrument for threshing grain by hand, consisting of a wooden handle at the end of which a stouter and shorter stick, called a *swiple* or *swingle,* is so hung as to swing freely. — *v. t. & i.* To beat with or as if with a flail.

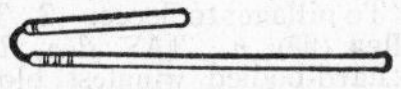
Flail.

flair (flâr), *n.* [OF. *flair* odor, fr. L. *fragrare.* See FRAGRANT.] **a** Instinctive power of discriminating or discerning. **b** Taste combined with aptitude; as, reporters with a *flair* for news; also, bent; aptitude. — **Syn.** See LEANING.
flak (flăk; *G.* fläk), *n.* [From G. *fl*ieger*a*bwehr*k*anone.] *Mil.* Antiaircraft artillery, or the bursting shells fired by such artillery. Hence, **flak ship, flak train.**
flake (flāk), *n.* [ON. *flaki, fleki.*] A rack, as for drying fish.
flake, *n.* A flat layer, or fake, of a coiled cable.
flake, *n.* [ME., of Scand. origin.] A loose filmy mass or a thin scalelike layer of anything; as, a *flake* of snow; fish *flakes;* also, a chiplike piece; as, cereal *flakes.* — *v. t. & i.* To form or separate into flakes; to cover with flakes; to make or become flaky. — **flak′er** (flāk′ẽr), *n.*
flak′y (flāk′ĭ), *adj.;* -I·ER (-ĭ·ẽr); -I·EST. Consisting of, lying, or cleaving off, in flakes or layers. — **flak′i·ly,** *adv.* — **flak′i·ness,** *n.*
flam (flăm), *n.* **1.** A falsehood; trick or deception. **2.** Humbug; flimflam. — *v. t. & i.;* FLAMMED (flămd); FLAM′MING. To deceive, as by lying; to trick; cheat.
flam, *n.* [Prob. imitative.] A drumbeat executed after the manner of a grace note, by allowing the sticks to strike the head so as just to be heard apart.
flam′beau (flăm′bō), *n.; pl.* -BEAUX (-bōz) or -BEAUS (-bōz). [F., fr. OF. *flambe* flame, fr. L. *flammula* a little flame, dim. of *flamma* flame.] A flaming torch.
flam·boy′ant (flăm·boi′ănt), *adj.* [F.] **1.** *Arch.* Characterized by waving or flamelike curves, as the tracery of windows, etc., in French Gothic style about 1450–1530; hence, designating this style of Gothic architecture. Cf. TRACERY, *Illust.* **2.** Florid; ornate; also, resplendent. **3.** Marked by ostentation and daring display; showy. — **flam·boy′ance** (-ăns), **flam·boy′an·cy** (-ăn·sĭ), *n.* — **flam·boy′ant·ly,** *adv.*
flame (flām), *n.* [OF. *flame,* fr. L. *flamma.*] **1.** A body of burning gas or vapor. **2. a** State of blazing combustion. **b** Any flamelike condition or appearance. **c** Brilliance. **3.** Burning zeal or passion; ardor. **4.** A sweetheart. **5.** In full **flame scarlet.** A color, reddish red-yellow in hue, of very high saturation and medium brilliance. See COLOR. — **Syn.** See BLAZE. — *v. i.* **1.** To burn with a flame; to burst into flame; blaze. **2.** To break out in violence of passion. **3.** To have a flamelike appearance; glow. — *v. t.* **1.** *Poetic.* To kindle; inflame; excite. **2.** To treat with flame; to pass (something) over or through a flame. — **flam′er** (flām′ẽr), *n.*
fla′men (flā′mĕn), *n.; pl.* FLAMENS (-mĕnz), FLAMINES (flăm′ĭ·nēz). [L.] *Rom. Relig.* A priest.
flame′proof′ (flām′pro͞of′; 2), *adj.* See FIREPROOF.
flame thrower. A device that expels from a nozzle a burning stream of fuel oil under pressure, used in war to penetrate portholes of tanks or pillboxes and in agriculture to kill weeds or insects; also, a person who operates such a device.
flam′ing (flām′ĭng), *adj.* **1.** Blazing; afire; also, flamelike. **2.** Ardent; passionate. — **flam′ing·ly,** *adv.*
fla·min′go (flȧ·mĭng′gō), *n.; pl.* -GOS or -GOES (-gōz). [Pg. *flamingo,* Sp. *flamenco.*] Any of a family (Phoenicopteridae) of aquatic birds with very long legs and neck and a broad bill bent abruptly downward. See BILL, *Illust.* Most species have rosy-white plumage with scarlet wing coverts, but one American species (now rare) is bright red.
flam′ma·ble (flăm′ȧ·b'l), *adj.* Capable of being easily ignited; inflammable; — preferred by many technical writers and publications to the older equivalent *inflammable* because of possible misinterpretation of the prefix *in-* as a negative. — **flam′ma·bil′i·ty** (-bĭl′ĭ·tĭ), *n.*
‖**flâ′ne·rie′** (flän′rē′), *n.* [F.] Aimlessness; idleness.
‖**flâ′neur′** (flä′nûr′), *n.* [F., fr. *flâner* to stroll.] One who strolls aimlessly; hence, an intellectual trifler.
flange (flănj), *n.* [OF. *flangir* to bend, turn.] **1.** A rib or rim, for strength, for guiding, or for attachment to another object; as, the *flange* of an iron beam, of a car wheel. **2.** A tool for forming flanges. — *v. t.;* FLANGED (flănjd); FLANG′ING (flăn′jĭng). To make a flange on; to furnish with a flange. — **flang′er** (flăn′jẽr), *n.*
flank (flăngk), *n.* [OF. *flanc.*] **1.** The side of an animal between the ribs and the hip; also, a cut of beef or lamb from this part. See BEEF, LAMB, *Illusts.* **2.** Loosely, the thigh. **3.** The side of anything. **4.** *Mil. & Nav.* **a** The right or left of an army, fleet, or any command. **b** That part of a bastion which reaches from the curtain to the face. See BASTION, *Illust.* **c** Either side of a fortification. — *v. t.* **1.** *Mil.* **a** To command or guard the flank of. **b** To attack the flank of. **c** To pass around, or turn, the flank of. **2.** To be situated at the flank or side of; border. — **flank′er** (flăng′kẽr), *n.*
flan′nel (flăn′ĕl; -'l), *n.* [W. *gwlanen* flannel, fr. *gwlân* wool.] **1.** A soft woolen cloth, of loose texture. **2.** Also **flan′nel·ette′, flan′nel·et′** (flăn′ĕl·ĕt′). A coarse soft cotton fabric napped on one or both sides; as, ***Canton,*** *or* ***cotton, flannel*** (used for underwear, infants' wear, etc.) and ***outing flannel*** (sometimes mixed with wool). See SWAN'S-DOWN, 2 **b**; SWANSKIN, 2. **3.** *pl.* Flannel clothing. — *v. t.;* FLAN′NELED (-ĕld; -'ld) or -NELLED; -NEL·ING or -NEL·LING. To clothe in, or rub with, flannel. — **flan′nel·ly** (flăn′ĕl·ĭ; -'l·ĭ), *adj.*
flap (flăp), *n.* [ME. *flappe,* fr. *flappen.*] **1.** Anything broad and limber or flat and thin that hangs loose, as a hinged leaf of a table, the lapel of a coat, brim of a hat, etc. **2.** The motion of anything broad and loose, or a stroke or sound made with it. **3.** *Aeronautics.* A movable auxiliary airfoil attached to the trailing edge of a wing, permitting a steeper angle in landing, etc. **4.** *Surg.* A piece of flesh partly severed from the adjoining tissues. — *v. t. & i.;* FLAPPED (flăpt); FLAP′PING. **1.** To strike or rouse with a flap. **2.** To turn, fold, or throw suddenly or violently. **3.** To move with a beating motion; as, to *flap* wings.
flap′doo′dle (flăp′do͞o′d'l), *n.* *Colloq.* Talk for fools; nonsense.
flap′drag′on (-drăg′ŭn), *n.* A game in which raisins or other tidbits are snatched from burning brandy and eaten.
flap′jack′ (-jăk′), *n.* A griddlecake.
flap′per (flăp′ẽr), *n.* **1.** One who or that which flaps. **2. a** *Colloq.* A young girl about 15 to 18 years of age, not yet introduced into society. **b** *Slang.* A girl or young woman whose conduct and dress are characterized by somewhat daring freedom and boldness. — **flap′per·dom** (-dŭm), *n.* — **flap′per·ish,** *adj.* — **flap′per·ism** (-ĭz'm), *n.*
flare (flâr), *v. i.* **1.** To burn or flame up with a sudden unsteady light. **2.** To become suddenly excited or angry; — usually with *up.* **3.** To open or spread outward as the bows of a ship. — *v. t.* To cause to flare; to display flaringly; also, to signal by fires or flares. — *n.* **1.** An unsteady glaring light. **2.** A blaze of fire or light used to signal, illuminate, or attract attention; also, the device or composition that produces the blaze. **3.** A sudden outburst, as of sound or anger. **4.** A spreading outward, or a part that spreads. **5.** *Optics & Photog.* Light resulting from interreflection between lens surfaces. — **Syn.** See BLAZE.
flare′back′ (-băk′), *n.* **1.** A burst, as of flame, back or out in a direction other than normal. **2.** An outburst of angry rebuke.
flare′–up′, *n.* A flaring up, as of flame, anger, etc.
flar′ing (flâr′ĭng), *adj.* **1.** That flares; dazzling; hence, gaudy. **2.** Opening or spreading outward.
flash (flăsh), *v. i.* [ME. *flaschen,* prob. of imitative origin.] **1.** *Archaic.* To dash or splash, as waves. **2.** To break forth in or like a sudden flame; to flare for a moment. **3.** To come or pass like a flash. **4.** To act, speak, perform, etc., with the suddenness, unexpectedness, or conspicuousness of a flash. **5.** To emit gleams; as, his eyes *flashed.* — *v. t.* **1.** *Archaic.* To dash or splash (water). **2.** To send out in, as in, or by, flashes; as, to *flash* the news abroad. **3.** *Colloq.* To display, esp. in a showy manner. **4.** *Building.* To protect against rain, as the valley, hip, or edge of a roof, by sheet metal or a substitute, laid under or over the roofing. **5.** *Glass Mfg.* **a** To coat (glass) with a film of different-colored glass. **b** To apply (this colored glass) to glass or glassware; — often with *on.*
Syn. **Flash, gleam, glance, glint, sparkle, glitter, glisten, scintillate, coruscate, glimmer, shimmer** mean to shoot forth light. **Flash** implies a sudden and transient outburst of light; **gleam,** a light that shines through a window, etc., or against a dark background; **glance,** a darting or obliquely reflected light; **glint,** quickly glancing or gleaming light; **sparkle** suggests quick, brief, innumerable small flashes; **glitter** connotes even greater brilliancy or showiness; **glisten** implies a somewhat subdued sparkling or gleaming and a lustrous quality; **scintillate,** the emission of sparks in a constant stream; **coruscate,** the emission of a brilliant flash or flashes; **glimmer** implies a faint or wavering sparkling or flashing, **shimmer** a soft lustrous sparkling or flashing.
— *n.* **1.** A sudden evanescent burst of light. **2.** A sudden and brilliant manifestation, as of wit or genius. **3.** The duration of a flash; an instant. **4.** Flashiness. **5.** Thieves' language. **6.** A stream or rush of water, as at a shoal or weir, for letting a boat descend. **7.** A device used to procure a flash of water, as a sluiceway. **8.** A preparation for coloring liquors. **9.** Something flashed, flashed on, etc. **10.** A movement of a light, a flag, etc., in signaling. **11.** *Colloq.* Short for FLASHLIGHT, 2. **12.** *Photog.* = FLASHLIGHT, 3.
— *adj.* **1.** Flashy; also, sporty; fast. **2.** Of or pertaining to thieves, tramps, and the like; as, *flash* language.
— **flash′er,** *n.* — **flash′ing·ly,** *adv.*
flash–. A combining form meaning *for,* or *in, a very short time,* as in *flash*-heated, *flash*-pasteurize.
flash back. A short interruption in the sequence of the plot, as of a motion picture, to introduce events prior to those last presented.
flash′board′ (flăsh′bōrd′; 70), *n.* A board placed on, or at the side of, a dam to increase the water's depth.
flash′ing (flăsh′ĭng), *n.* **1.** Act of one that flashes; specif., *Engineering,* the creation of an artificial flood by the sudden letting in of a body of water. **2.** Metal used in waterproofing roof valleys, hips, etc.
flashing point. = FLASH POINT.
flash lamp. *Photog.* A lamp for taking flashlights.
flash′light′ (flăsh′līt′), *n.* **1.** A flash of light, or a light that flashes; esp., a revolving light in lighthouses. **2.** A portable electric light. **3.** *Photog.* A sudden bright artificial light used in taking pictures, as at night; also, a picture taken by such a light. — **flash′light′,** *adj.*
flash point. The temperature at which an inflammable material will flash in air.
flash′y (flăsh′ĭ), *adj.;* FLASH′I·ER (-ĭ·ẽr); FLASH′I·EST. **1.** Flashing; dazzling for a moment. **2.** Showy; gay; sporty. — **Syn.** See GAUDY. — **flash′i·ly,** *adv.* — **flash′i·ness,** *n.*
flask (flȧsk; 9), *n.* [F. *flasque* powder flask, fr. It. *fiasca* a large flat bottle, fr. VL. *flasca* wine bottle.] **1.** A bottle-shaped vessel of metal, glass, etc., esp. one with a broad flat body, used to carry gunpowder, liquor, etc. **2.** The frame which holds the sand, etc., forming the mold used in a foundry.
flask′et (flȧs′kĕt; -kĭt), *n.* [OF. *flasquet,* dim.] **1.** *Eng.* A long shallow basket. **2.** A small flask.
flat (flăt), *adj.;* FLAT′TER (-ẽr); FLAT′TEST. [ON. *flatr.*] **1.** Having an even horizontal surface, or nearly so. **2.** Lying spread out; prostrate; hence, laid low; ruined. **3.** Having a surface, whether horizontal or not, that is smooth and even, or relatively so. **4.** Spread out, unrolled, arranged, etc. (upon or against a flat surface). **5.** Having broad and smooth lateral surfaces and little thickness. **6.** Unmistakable; positive; downright; as, a *flat* refusal. **7.** Unvarying; as, a

flat rate; also, exact; even; as, a *flat* ten seconds. **8.** Unanimated; dull; monotonous. **9.** Commercially inactive; depressed; as, a *flat* market. **10.** Tasteless; insipid; — of food and drink. **11.** Deflated; — of tires. **12.** Not clear, sharp, or sonorous; — of sounds. **13.** *Gram.* Not having an inflectional ending or sign, as a noun used as an adjective, an infinitive without *to*, and an adverb with no adverbial ending (speak *loud*). Many flat adverbs, as in run *fast*, buy *cheap*, are from AS. adverbs in *-ĕ*, the loss of this ending having made them like the adjectives. Some, as *exceeding*, *wonderful*, are now archaic. **14.** *Music.* Below the true pitch; hence, minor, or lower by a half step; as, A-*flat;* of keys or tonalities, having flats in the signature. **15.** *Naut.* Taut; — of a sail. **16.** *Painting.* **a** Uniform in hue or shade. **b** Monotonous in light and shade or in color. **c** Free from gloss. **17.** *Phonet.* **a** Of the vowel *a*, sounded as in *man* as contrasted with the broad *a* in *father*. **b** Of consonant sounds, soft or voiced. — **Syn.** See LEVEL: INSIPID.

— *adv.* **1.** Flatly. **2.** Exactly; precisely. **3.** *Finance.* Without interest charge. **4.** *Music.* Below the proper pitch.

— *n.* **1.** A level surface; a plain; esp., *U. S.*, a level tract along the bank of a river. **2.** A shoal; a shallow. **3.** The flat side or part; as, the *flat* of the hand. **4.** Something flat; as: **a** A punctured tire. **b** A flatcar. **c** A shallow box used for growing seedlings. **d** A flat-bottomed boat, with no keel. **5.** *Music.* A tone or note one half step lower than a tone or note named; also, the character (♭) indicating this change in pitch. A ***double flat*** (♭♭) indicates that a note is to be a whole step lower in pitch than it would be without any flat.

— *v. t. & i.;* FLAT′TED; FLAT′TING. To make or become flat. — **flat′ly**, *adv.* — **flat′ness**, *n.* — **flat′tish**, *adj.*

flat (flăt), *n.* [Scot. *flet*, fr. AS. *flet* ground, floor.] A floor, or story in a building; esp., a floor, or a suite of rooms on one floor, used as a residence. In the United States, residence flats of the better class are often called *apartments*.

flat′boat′ (flăt′bōt′), *n.* A boat with a flat bottom and square ends, used for transportation of bulky freight, esp. in shallow waters.

flat′car′ (-kär′), *n.* *Railroads.* A platform car for freight.

flat′fish′ (-fĭsh′), *n.; pl.*, see FISH. Any of a large group of teleost fishes including the halibuts, flounders, turbots, and soles, which have the body flattened dextrosinistrally, swim on one side, and have both eyes on the upper side.

flat foot. A foot in which the arch of the instep is flattened so that the entire sole rests upon the ground.

flat′foot′ (flăt′fo͝ot′), *n.* The deformity, usually congenital, exhibited by a flat foot.

flat′-foot′ed (-ĕd; -ĭd; 2), *adj.* **1.** Having a flat foot; hence, shambling. **2.** *Slang.* Standing square on the feet; hence, determined; forthright. — **flat′-foot′ed·ly**, *adv.* — **flat′-foot′ed·ness**, *n.*

Flat′head′ (flăt′hĕd′), *n.* **1.** A Chinook Indian. **2.** An American Indian of Salishan stock, specifically so called.

flat′i′ron (flăt′ī′ẽrn), *n.* An iron for pressing clothes; a sadiron.

flat knot. A reef knot. See KNOT, *Illust.* (28).

flat′ling (flăt′lĭng), *adv.* [*flat*, adj. + 2d *-ling*.] *Archaic.* Flat; with the flat side; — also **flat′lings** and, *Obs.*, **flat′long.** — *adj.* Dealt flatling, as a blow; hence, heavily pressing.

flat silver. Silver knives, forks, spoons, and the like.

flat spring. See SPRING, *Illust.*

flat′ten (flăt′'n), *v. t. & i.* To make or become flat, as in surface, position, or quality. — ***flatten out.*** *Aeronautics.* To manipulate an airplane so as to bring its longitudinal axis parallel with the ground, as after a climb or a dive; of an airplane, to assume such a position. — **flat′ten·er**, *n.*

flat′ter (flăt′ẽr), *n.* One who or that which makes flat; specif.: **a** *Metalworking.* A drawplate for drawing flat strips. **b** *Smithing.* A flat-faced swage.

flat′ter, *v. t.* [OF. *flater* to smooth, caress, flatter.] **1.** To shower praise or attentions upon, to gratify the recipient's vanity or to ingratiate oneself; blandish. **2.** To raise the hope or belief, esp. an unfounded one, in; as, he *flatters* himself that he will win. **3.** To beguile; charm. **4.** To portray too favorably. — *v. i.* To use flattery. — **flat′ter·a·ble**, *adj.* — **flat′ter·er**, *n.* — **flat′ter·ing·ly**, *adv.*

flat′ter·y (-ĭ), *n.; pl.* -TERIES (-ĭz). [OF. *flaterie* (F. *flatterie*), fr. *flater* to flatter.] Act of flattering; also, flattering speech or attentions; false, insincere, or excessive praise.

flat′top′ (flăt′tŏp′), *n.* *Slang.* An aircraft carrier.

flat′u·lent (flăt′ū·lĕnt), *adj.* [F., fr. L. *flatus* a blowing, *flatus ventris* windiness.] **1.** Marked by or affected with gases generated in the alimentary canal or in the stomach. **2.** Pretentious without substance; inflated; turgid. — **Syn.** See INFLATED. — **flat′u·lence** (-lĕns), **flat′u·len·cy** (-lĕn·sĭ), *n.* — **flat′u·lent·ly**, *adv.*

fla′tus (flā′tŭs), *n.* [L., fr. *flare* to blow.] **1.** A puff of wind. **2.** Gas generated in the stomach or bowels.

flat′ware′ (flăt′wâr′), *n.* Articles for the table that are flat, as platters, plates, etc.; esp., flat silver.

flat′wise′ (-wīz′), *adv.* Also **flat′ways′** (-wāz′). With the flat side downward, or next to another object; not edgewise.

flat′work′ (-wûrk′), *n.* *Laundry.* Articles such as sheets, towels, and tablecloths, which can be mangled, as distinguished from those requiring hand ironing.

flat′worm′ (-wûrm′), *n.* *Zool.* **a** Any platyhelminth. **b** In a narrower sense, any planarian.

flaunt (flônt; flänt), *v. i. & t.* [Of Scand. origin.] **1.** To wave or flutter showily. **2.** To move or display ostentatiously; to display boastfully, brazenly, or the like; to parade. — **Syn.** See SHOW. — *n.* Act of flaunting; display; something flaunted. — **flaunt′er**, *n.* — **flaunt′ing·ly**, *adv.* — **flaunt′y**, *adj.*

flau′tist (flô′tĭst), *n.* [It. *flautista.* See FLUTE.] A flutist.

fla·ves′cent (flȧ·vĕs′ĕnt; -'nt), *adj.* [L. *flavescens* turning yellow, fr. *flavus* yellow.] Turning yellow; yellowish.

fla′vin (flā′vĭn), *n.* [L. *flavus* yellow.] *Biochem.* **a** Any of a class of yellow, water-soluble nitrogenous pigments found in certain plant and animal products or prepared synthetically. **b** Specif., riboflavin, or vitamin B_2 (see VITAMIN).

fla′vone (flā′vōn; flȧ·vōn′; flăv′ōn), *n.* [L. *flavus* yellow + *-one.*] **a** A colorless crystalline compound, $C_{15}H_{10}O_2$, found on the leaves, seed capsules, etc., of many primroses, and also prepared synthetically. **b** Any derivative of this.

fla′vo·pur′pu·rin (flā′vō·pûr′pū·rĭn; flăv′ō-), *n.* [L. *flavus* yellow + E. *purpurin.*] A golden-yellow compound, $C_{14}H_8O_6$, found in commercial alizarin.

fla′vor, fla′vour (flā′vẽr), *n.* [OF. *fleur, flaur* (two syllables), odor.] **1.** Odor; fragrance. **2.** That quality of anything which affects the taste or gratifies the palate; relish; savor. **3.** A substance which flavors. **4.** Predominant or characterizing quality of anything, esp. of a literary or art work. — **Syn.** See TASTE. — *v. t.* To give flavor to. — **fla′vor·er, fla′vour·er** (-ẽr), *n.* — **fla′vor·less, fla′vour·less**, *adj.* — **fla′vor·ous, fla′vour·ous** (-ŭs), *adj.*

fla′vor·ing, fla′vour·ing, *n.* Anything, as an essence or extract, used to give a particular flavor.

flaw (flô), *n.* **1.** A crack; a gap; a faulty part. **2.** A defect; a fault; esp., in a legal paper, a fault that may nullify it. — **Syn.** See BLEMISH. — *v. t.* To make a flaw in. — *v. i.* To become defective; crack. — **flaw′less**, *adj.* — **flaw′y**, *adj.*

flaw, *n.* [Of Scand. origin.] **1.** A sudden brief burst of wind; a squall. **2.** *Obs.* An outburst, as of anger; uproar. — **flaw′y**, *adj.*

flax (flăks), *n.* [AS. *fleax.*] **1.** Any of a genus (*Linum*, family Linaceae, the flax family) of plants; esp., a slender erect annual (*L. usitatissimum*) with blue flowers, commonly cultivated for its fiber and seed. Linen is made from flax fiber. **2.** The fiber of the flax plant, prepared for spinning. **3.** Any of several plants resembling flax. Cf. TOADFLAX, WILD FLAX.

flax′en (flăk′s'n), *adj.* Pertaining to, made of, or resembling flax or its fibers; esp., of a light straw color; blond.

flax′seed′ (flăks′sēd′; flăk′sēd′), *n.* The seed of flax, used as a demulcent and emollient in medicine, and yielding an oil (*linseed oil*).

flay (flā), *v. t.* [AS. *flēan.*] **1.** To strip off the skin or surface of. **2.** To pillage; to fleece. **3.** To censure harshly. — **flay′er** (flā′ẽr), *n.*

flea (flē), *n.* [AS. *flēa, flēah.*] Any of an order (Siphonaptera) of hard-bodied, wingless, bloodsucking insects with extraordinary powers of leaping. They mostly infest warm-blooded animals, as the ***cat flea*** (*Ctenocephalis felis*) and the ***dog flea*** (*C. canis*). — ***a flea in the ear.*** An irritating hint, or rebuff.

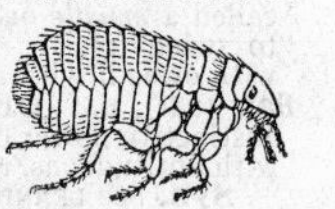

Flea (*C. canis*). (× 8)

flea′bane′ (-bān′), *n.* Any of various plants of the aster family supposed to drive away fleas.

flea′bite′ (-bīt′), *n.* **1.** The bite of a flea, or the red spot caused by the bite. **2.** A trifling pain or annoyance.

flea′-bit′ten (-bĭt′'n), *adj.* **1.** Bitten by a flea or fleas. **2.** White, flecked with dots of bay or sorrel; — said of a horse.

fleam (flēm), *n.* [OF. *flieme*, fr. VL. form of LL. *phlebotomus.* See PHLEBOTOMY.] *Surg.* A lancet for letting blood, lancing gums, etc.

flea′wort′ (flē′wûrt′), *n.* **1.** A European aromatic herb (*Inula squarrosa*) of the aster family, with rough leaves and yellow flower heads. **2.** A southern European plantain (*Plantago psyllium*), whose seeds are used as a laxative.

flèche (flāsh; *F.* flĕsh), *n.* [F., prop., an arrow.] **1.** *Fort.* A salient outwork of two faces with an open gorge. **2.** A spire, esp. a slender one above the intersection of the nave and transepts of a church.

flé·chette′ (flā·shĕt′), *n.* [F., dim. of *flèche* arrow.] A small steel dart with a vane or fluted shaft, to be dropped from an airplane as a missile.

fleck (flĕk), *n.* [ON. *flekkr.*] **1.** A spot; speck. **2.** A flake; particle. — *v. t.* To spot; streak; dapple. — **fleck′y**, *adj.*

flec′tion, flex′ion (flĕk′shŭn), *n.* [L. *flexio.*] **1.** A flexing. **2.** A part bent; a fold. **3.** *Gram.* Inflection. — **flec′tion·al, flex′ion·al**, *adj.*

fled (flĕd), *past & past part. of* FLEE.

fledge (flĕj), *v. i.;* FLEDGED (flĕjd); FLEDG′ING (flĕj′ĭng). [AS. *flycge.*] To acquire the feathers necessary for flight. — *v. t.* **1.** To care for (a bird) until its plumage is developed. **2.** To furnish with or as with feathers; as, to *fledge* an arrow. **3.** To make ready to fly, or strike out for oneself; — chiefly in past participle in combinations; as, full-*fledged*.

fledg′ling, fledge′ling (flĕj′lĭng), *n.* A young bird just fledged; hence, an immature person.

fledg′y (flĕj′ĭ), *adj.* Feathered; downy.

flee (flē), *v. i.;* FLED (flĕd); FLEE′ING. [AS. *flēon.*] **1.** To run away, as from danger or evil. **2.** To pass away swiftly; vanish. **3.** *Archaic.* To fly, as a bird or an arrow; speed. — *v. t.* To run away or escape from. — **fle′er** (flē′ẽr), *n.*

fleece (flēs), *n.* [AS. *flēos.*] **1.** The coat of wool that covers a sheep or similar animal; also, the quantity of wool shorn at one time. **2.** A fleecelike covering or mass. **3.** A fabric having a silky pile, used for warm linings; also, the pile. — *v. t.;* FLEECED (flēst); FLEEC′ING (flēs′ĭng). **1.** To shear (sheep). **2.** To strip of money or property by fraud; despoil. **3.** To spread over, or fleck, as with wool. — **fleece′a·ble**, *adj.* — **fleec′er** (flēs′ẽr), *n.*

fleec′y (flēs′ĭ), *adj.;* FLEEC′I·ER (-ĭ·ẽr); FLEEC′I·EST. Covered with, made of, or resembling fleece. — **fleec′i·ly**, *adv.* — **fleec′i·ness**, *n.*

fleer (flēr), *v. i. & t.* [ME. *flerien*, of Scand. origin.] To laugh or grimace coarsely or scornfully (at); sneer. — **Syn.** See SCOFF. — *n.* A word or look of derision or mockery. — **fleer′ing·ly**, *adv.*

fleet (flēt), *v. i.* [AS. *flēotan* to swim, float.] **1.** *Chiefly Dial.* To float; drift; hence, to sail; swim. **2.** *Archaic.* To glide along or away; hence, to dissolve; vanish. **3.** To fly swiftly; hasten; flit. **4.** *Naut.* To move, shift, or change in position; as, the crew *fleeted* aft. — *v. t.* **1.** To while away. **2.** *Naut.* To cause to fleet (see *v. i.*, 4). — **Syn.** See WHILE. — *adj.* **1.** Swift in motion; fast. **2.** Hence, evanescent; not lasting. **3.** *Chiefly Dial.* Shallow. — **Syn.** See FAST. — **fleet′ly**, *adv.* — **fleet′ness**, *n.*

fleet, *n.* [AS. *flēot* a place where vessels float, bay, river.] *Now Dial.* A creek or inlet; also, a sewer; — found in place names; as: **a** **Fleet Street**, a London street, center of the newspaper district. **b** **the Fleet**, a former debtors' prison in London named for its location near a creek or stream called *the Fleet*, now a covered sewer.

fleet, *n.* [AS. *flēot* ship, fr. *flēotan* to float, swim.] **1.** A number of war vessels under a single chief command; a naval force; also, the navy of a country. **2.** Any group, as of vessels, aircraft, vehicles, etc., which move together or operate under one control.

fleet admiral. A high-ranking admiral one grade higher than admiral; in the U. S. Navy, an admiral of the highest grade (insignia 5 stars), which is, according to statute, held by no more than four officers on the active list at one time.

fleet′ing, *adj.* Passing swiftly. — **Syn.** See TRANSIENT.

Flem′ing (flĕm′ĭng), *n.* A Flemish-speaking Belgian.

Flem′ish (flĕm′ĭsh), *adj.* Pertaining to Flanders, the Flemings, or Flemish. — *n.* The Low-German language of northern Belgium. See INDO-EUROPEAN LANGUAGES, *Table.*

flense (flĕns), *v. t.* Also **flench** (flĕnch). [Dan.] To strip the blubber or skin from, as from a whale. — **flens'er** (flĕn'sẽr), *n.*

flesh (flĕsh), *n.* [AS. *flǣsc.*] **1.** The soft parts of the body of an animal, esp. a vertebrate animal; more narrowly, only the parts composed chiefly of muscle. **2.** Animal food; meat; — often disting. from *fish* and, sometimes, *fowl.* **3.** The human body, as distinguished from the soul. **4. a** Mankind. **b** Living beings generally; animal life. **5.** Human nature: **a** In a good sense, tenderness of feeling. **b** In a bad sense, carnality; sensuality. **6.** Kindred. **7.** The pulp of fruit; also, the edible part of a root, fruit, etc. **8.** The external appearance of the body, esp. as to color. **9.** The average color of a white person's skin, red-yellow in hue, of very low saturation and high brilliance. See COLOR. **10.** *Christian Science.* An error of physical belief; a supposition that life, substance, and intelligence are in matter; an illusion; a belief that matter has sensation. *Mary Baker Eddy.*
— *v. t.* **1.** To feed (as dogs) with flesh, as an incitement to exertion. **2.** To initiate by giving a foretaste or first experience or by first use; as, to *flesh* raw troops in forays; to *flesh* a sword; hence, to incite to a desire for bloodshed, to rage, etc., by such fleshing. **3.** To glut; also, to harden; accustom. **4.** To cover with or as with flesh; hence, to fatten. **5.** To remove flesh, membrane, etc., from (hides). — *v. i.* To become fleshy. — **flesh'er,** *n.*

flesh fly. Any dipterous insect of a superfamily (Muscoidea), the larvae or maggots of which feed on flesh; esp., any of a genus (*Sarcophaga*) which deposit living larvae on fresh meat.

flesh'ings (flĕsh'ĭngz), *n. pl.* **1.** Flesh-colored tights. **2.** Scrapings from fleshed hides, used in making glue.

flesh'ly (-lĭ), *adj.* **1.** Corporeal; bodily. **2.** Sensual; lascivious. **3.** Worldly; mundane. **4.** Fleshy; plump. **5.** Sensuous; — applied to some 19th-century poets or their school (the **fleshly school**). — **Syn.** See CARNAL. — **flesh'li·ness,** *n.*

flesh'pot' (-pŏt'), *n.* A pot in which flesh is cooked; hence, *pl.*, plenty; luxury.

flesh'y (-ĭ), *adj.*; FLESH'I·ER (-ĭ·ẽr); FLESH'I·EST. **1.** Of, pertaining to, or resembling flesh; fleshly. **2.** Marked by abundant flesh; plump; corpulent. **3.** *Bot.* Succulent or pulpy, as certain fruits. — **flesh'i·ness,** *n.*

fletch (flĕch), *v. t.* To feather, as an arrow; fledge.

fletch'er (-ẽr), *n.* [OF. *flechier,* fr. *fleche* arrow.] One who fletches or makes arrows.

Fletch'er·ism (flĕch'ẽr·ĭz'm), *n.* [After Horace *Fletcher* (1849–1919), Am. author.] The practice of eating only when hungry, and of thoroughly masticating one's food. — **Fletch'er·ize** (-īz), *v. i.*

fleur'-de-lis' (flûr'dē·lē'; -lēs'), *n.*; *pl.* FLEURS-DE-LIS (flûr'dē·lēz'). [F., flower of the lily.] **1.** The iris. **2.** *Her.* A conventionalized flower (see *Illust.*), perhaps suggested by the iris.

Fleur-de-lis, 2.

flew (flōō; 114), *past* of FLY.

flews (flōōz; 114), *n. pl.* The chaps, or pendulous lateral parts of the upper lip, of dogs, esp. hounds. See DOG, *Illust.*

flex (flĕks), *v. t. & i.* [L. *flexus,* past part. of *flectere* to bend.] To bend; as, to *flex* the arm.

flex, *n.* **1.** Act or instance of bending or bowing. **2.** *Chiefly Brit.* An electric cord.

flex'i·ble (flĕk'sĭ·b'l), *adj.* [F., fr. L. *flexibilis.* See FLEX.] **1.** Capable of being flexed; pliable; not rigid. **2.** Ready to yield to influence; tractable. **3.** Capable of being adapted, modified, or molded; plastic; pliant; as, Latin is not a *flexible* language. **4.** Responsive to, or readily adjustable to, changing conditions; as, to hold *flexible* opinions. **5.** Not rigid. See AIRSHIP. — **Syn.** See ELASTIC. — **flex'i·bil'i·ty** (-bĭl'ĭ·tĭ), *n.* — **flex'i·bly,** *adv.*

flex'ile (flĕk'sĭl), *adj.* Flexible; mobile; plastic.

flex'ion, flex'ion·al. Vars. of FLECTION, FLECTIONAL.

flex'or (flĕk'sẽr; -sôr), *n.* [NL.] *Anat.* A muscle which serves to bend a limb or part. Cf. EXTENSOR.

flex'u·ous (flĕk'shōō·ŭs; flĕks'ū-; 118), *adj.* Also **flex'u·ose** (-ōs). [L. *flexuosus,* fr. *flexus* a bending.] **1.** Having turns or windings; sinuous; undulating. **2.** Not rigid in action; adaptable. — **flex'u·os'i·ty** (-ŏs'ĭ·tĭ), *n.* — **flex'u·ous·ly,** *adv.* — **flex'u·ous·ness,** *n.*

flex'ure (flĕk'shẽr), *n.* [L. *flexura.*] **1.** A flexing, or state of being flexed. **2.** A turn; bend; fold.

fley (flā), *v. t.* *Dial.* To frighten. — *n.* *Dial.* Fright.

flib'ber·ti·gib'bet (flĭb'ẽr·tĭ·jĭb'ĕt; -ĭt), *n.* A gossiper or chatterer; one who is giddy or frivolous, esp. a woman.

flicht'er (flĭk'tẽr), *v. i.* *Scot.* To flutter.

flick (flĭk), *n.* [Imitative.] **1** A light stroke, as with a whip; also, a quick jerk. **2.** A daub; a streak. — *v. t.* To whip, toss, etc., with a flick. — *v. i.* To flutter; flit. — **flick'er** (-ẽr), *n.*

flick'er (flĭk'ẽr), *v. i.* [AS. *flicorian.*] **1.** To flutter; to flap the wings without flying. **2.** To waver unsteadily; to burn fitfully, as a dying fire. — *v. t.* To cause to flicker. — *n.* **1.** A flickering; a brief interval of brightness. **2.** A rapidly scintillating light. **3.** A momentary quickening or stirring, as of an emotion. **4.** *Slang.* A motion picture; — esp. in *pl.* — **flick'er·y,** *adj.* — **flick'er·ing·ly,** *adv.*

flick'er, *n.* [Perh. imitative.] A woodpecker (*Colaptes auratus*), of eastern North America, with a black crescent on the breast, a red nape, white rump, and yellow shafts to the tail and wing feathers.

flick'er·tail' (flĭk'ẽr·tāl'), *n.* *Central U. S.* A spermophile (*Citellus richardsoni*).

flied (flīd). See FLY, *v. i.*, 7.

fli'er, fly'er (flī'ẽr), *n.* **1.** One who or that which flies; specif.: **a** An aircraft. **b** An airman. **2.** An uncommonly speedy coach, train, etc. **3.** *Slang.* A reckless venture, as in the stock market. **4.** Anything scattered or distributed in large numbers, as an advertising leaflet. **5.** *Arch.* Any of a flight of steps ascending without a turn.

flight (flīt), *n.* [AS. *fliht, flyht,* a flying; akin to E. FLY.] **1.** Act or mode of flying. **2.** Power of flying, or distance covered at a flight. **3.** A number of beings or things passing through the air together; as, a *flight* of arrows or birds. **4.** A passing above or beyond ordinary bounds; a soaring. **5.** The stairs from one landing to the next. **6.** *Angling.* Any arrangement for causing the bait to spin rapidly. **7.** *Archery.* **a** In full, **flight arrow.** A light low-feathered arrow for long-distance shooting. **b** A contest with such arrows. **8.** *Aviation.* A military formation of two or more elements flying together as a unit. — *v. i.* To take flight; to move in flights; migrate.

flight, *n.* [ME. *fliht, fluht;* akin to E. FLEE.] Act of fleeing; a running from danger.

flight'er (flĭk'tẽr). Var. of FLICHTER.

flight'less (flīt'lĕs; -lĭs), *adj.* Incapable of flight; — said of certain birds, as the ostrich, cassowary, and emu.

flight strip. See STRIP, *n.*, 4.

flight'y (flīt'ĭ), *adj.*; -I·ER (-ĭ·ẽr); -I·EST. **1.** *Rare.* Fleeting; transient. **2.** Indulging in flights of imagination, humor, caprice, etc.; volatile. **3.** Mildly insane. — **flight'i·ly,** *adv.* — **flight'i·ness,** *n.* — **Syn.** See LIGHTNESS.

flim'flam' (flĭm'flăm'), *n.* **1.** A trifle or conceit; also, a swindler's trick. **2.** Nonsense; humbug. — *adj.* Tricky; nonsensical. — *v. t.*; FLIM'FLAMMED' (-flămd'); FLIM'FLAM'MING. *Colloq.* To trick; swindle. — **flim'flam'mer,** *n.*

flim'sy (flĭm'zĭ), *adj.*; FLIM'SI·ER (-zĭ·ẽr); FLIM'SI·EST. Without strength or solidity; unsubstantial. — **Syn.** See LIMP. — *n.*; *pl.* -SIES (-sĭz). **1.** Something flimsy, frail, or unsubstantial; specif., *pl.*, *Colloq.*, women's delicate undergarments. **2.** *Newspapers.* Thin or transfer paper or manuscript on such paper. — **flim'si·ly,** *adv.* — **flim'si·ness,** *n.*

flinch (flĭnch), *v. i.* [OF. *flenchir,* of Teut. origin.] To draw back, as from pain or danger; wince. — **Syn.** See RECOIL. — *v. t.* To draw back from; hence, ***flinch the flagon,*** to refrain from drinking. — *n.* **1.** A flinching. **2.** *Cards.* A round game in which cards are built up on the table in a certain numerical order. — **flinch'er,** *n.* — **flinch'ing·ly,** *adv.*

flin'der (flĭn'dẽr), *n.* [ME. *flender.*] Piece, splinter, or fragment; — usually *pl.*; as, broken to *flinders.*

fling (flĭng), *v. t.*; FLUNG (flŭng); FLING'ING. [ME. *flingen, flengen,* to rush, hurl, of Scand. origin.] **1.** To cast from or as from the hand; throw; hurl. **2.** To put or send violently or suddenly; as, to *fling* one into prison. **3.** To throw aside; to cast off; as, to *fling* conventions to the winds. **4.** To project or extend suddenly or impetuously; toss; as, to *fling* back the head. **5.** To send forth; emit. **6.** To throw off or down; to prostrate; overthrow. — **Syn.** See THROW. — *v. i.* **1.** To rush, spring, plunge, etc., with violence or haste. **2.** To use abusive language; to curse. — *n.* **1.** Act or instance of flinging. **2.** *Colloq.* A try or attempt; a "shot." **3.** Scornful remark; a gibe. **4.** A lively gesticulatory dance; as, the Highland *fling.* **5.** Unconstrained action; dash; hence, a time of indulgence. — **fling'er** (flĭng'ẽr), *n.*

flint (flĭnt), *n.* [AS.] **1.** *Mineral.* A massive, very hard kind of quartz which strikes fire with steel. **2.** A piece of flint for striking fire. **3.** Anything hard and unyielding, like flint; as, a heart of *flint.* — *v. t.* To supply with flint.

flint corn. A type of Indian corn (*Zea mays indurata*) with hard, horny-coated kernels, which do not shrivel.

flint glass. A heavy brilliant glass containing lead and having a high dispersion relative to refractive index; crystal. Cf. CROWN GLASS, 2.

flint'lock' (flĭnt'lŏk'), *n.* An old-fashioned gun or pistol lock having a flint in the cock, or hammer, for striking a spark to ignite the charge; also, such a firearm.

flint'y (flĭn'tĭ), *adj.*; FLINT'I·ER (-tĭ·ẽr); FLINT'I·EST. Consisting of, abounding in, or resembling flint. — **flint'i·ly,** *adv.* — **flint'i·ness,** *n.*

flip (flĭp), *v. t.*; FLIPPED (flĭpt); FLIP'PING. To toss; fillip; flick. — *v. i.* **1.** To snap, as with a finger. **2.** To move with a jerk or flirt; flap. — *n.* **1.** Act of flipping. **2.** *Colloq.* A somersault, as in fancy diving.

flip, *n.* A spiced, sweetened drink of ale, beer, or the like, to which beaten egg is sometimes added.

flip (flĭp), *adj.* *Colloq.* Flippant; pert. — *n.* A flip person.

flip'pan·cy (flĭp'ăn·sĭ), *n.* State or quality of being flippant. — **Syn.** See LIGHTNESS. — **Ant.** Seriousness.

flip'pant (-ănt), *adj.* [Cf. dial. E. *flip* nimble, pliant.] **1.** *Now Rare.* Nimble, esp. in tongue; voluble. **2.** Treating with levity that which is serious or worthy of respect; pert. — **flip'pant·ly,** *adv.* — **flip'pant·ness,** *n.*

flip'per (flĭp'ẽr), *n.* **1.** A broad flat limb adapted for swimming, as of seals, whales, etc. **2.** *Slang.* The hand.

flirt (flûrt), *v. t.* **1.** To throw with a jerk; fling suddenly; fillip. **2.** To toss about jerkily; to open out or close briskly; as, to *flirt* a fan. — *v. i.* **1.** To move jerkily; dart; hence, to trifle. **2.** To play at courtship; coquet; trifle amorously. **3.** Hence, to dally, play, or toy; as, to *flirt* with an idea. — **Syn.** See TRIFLE. — *n.* **1.** Act or instance of flirting. **2.** One who flirts. — **flir·ta'tion** (flûr·tā'shŭn), *n.* — **flirt'er,** *n.* — **flirt'y,** *adj.*

flir·ta'tious (flûr·tā'shŭs), *adj.* Inclined to flirt; coquettish.

flit (flĭt), *v. i.*; FLIT'TED; FLIT'TING. [ON. *flytja* to carry away.] **1.** To pass or move suddenly or quickly; dart; fleet. **2.** *Now Dial.* To depart. **3.** To flutter; rove on the wing. **4.** *Obs.* To be shifting, evanescent, or the like. — *v. t.* *Archaic.* To transfer; remove. — *n.* Act or motion of flitting. — **flit'ter,** *n.*

flitch (flĭch), *n.* [AS. *flicce.*] **1.** The side of a hog salted and cured; a side of bacon. **2.** One of the parts secured together to make a large girder or built beam. — *v. t.* To cut into, or off in, flitches or strips.

flite, flyte (flīt), *v. i.* [AS. *flītan* to strive, contend, quarrel.] *Dial.* To quarrel; scold. — *n.* Strife; dispute.

flit'ter (flĭt'ẽr), *v. i. & t.* [Freq. of *flit.*] *Archaic & Dial.* To flutter.

flit'ter·mouse' (-mous'), *n.*; *pl.* -MICE (-mīs'). [*flitter,* v. i. + *mouse.*] A bat.

fliv'ver (flĭv'ẽr), *n.* *Slang.* A small inexpensive automobile; hence, anything small and cheap.

float (flōt), *n.* [AS. *flota* ship.] **1.** *Now Rare.* Act or state of floating. **2.** Anything that floats on a fluid; specif.: **a** A life preserver. **b** A hollow metallic ball at the end of a lever, in a cistern, tank, or boiler, for regulating the level of the water; also, a similar device in a carburetor. **c** The cork or quill used to support the bait line and to indicate the bite of a fish. **3.** A watertight structure attached to an aircraft to give it buoyancy on water. **4.** A trowel or other tool for smoothing. **5.** The footlights on a stage; — often in *pl.* **6.** A flat-topped vehicle for mounting a display in procession. — *v. i.* [AS. *flotian* to float, swim.] **1.** To rest on the surface of a fluid. **2.** To move quietly or gently on or as on water; drift along; also, to be suspended or to move within a fluid; as, to *float* in the air. **3.** To become detached, loose, or the like; hence, to be unstable, as in one's political affiliations. — *v. t.* **1.** To cause to float. **2.** To flood. **3.** To market, as an issue of bonds. **4.** To grind and pass through running water, as pigments, as a refining or levigating process. — **float'a·ble,** *adj.*

float'age, float·a'tion. Vars. of FLOTAGE, FLOTATION.

float'er (flōt'ẽr), *n.* **1.** One that floats. **2.** *Colloq.* A person, as a workman, who shifts often from one place of employment to another. **3.** A voter who votes illegally in various places.

float′–feed′ (flōt′fēd′), *adj.* *Mach.* Having a feed regulated by a float; as, a **float–feed carburetor.**

float′ing, *adj.* **1.** That floats. **2.** Not fixed or permanent in residence, occupation, form, use, etc.; as, the *floating* population. **3.** *Mach.* Connected or constructed so as to operate smoothly, as if floating; as, a *floating* axle. **4.** *Med.* Out of the normal position; abnormally movable; esp., subject to downward displacement; as, a *floating* kidney. — **float′ing·ly,** *adv.*

floating debt. *Finance.* A debt which is of a temporary and shifting nature; that is, one not funded.

floating dock. A dock which floats on the water and can be partly submerged to permit a ship to enter it and afterwards floated to raise the ship high and dry as in a dry dock; — called also **floating dry dock.** Cf. DRY DOCK.

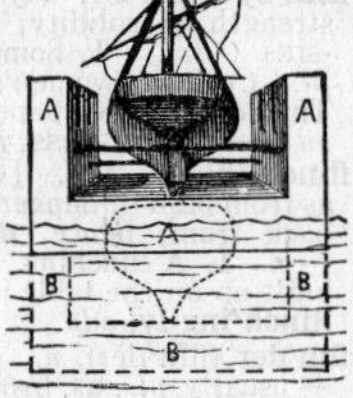

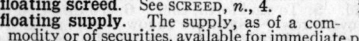

Floating Dock, supporting a ship. *A, A, A* Tanks filled with air; *B, B, B* Tanks filled with water when the Dock is submerged to allow the ship to float in or out.

floating heart. A small white-flowered aquatic plant (*Nymphoides lacunosum,* family Menyanthaceae) of the eastern United States, having heart-shaped leaves; also, any other species of this genus.

floating island. A dessert consisting of custard with floating masses of whipped cream or white of egg.

floating ribs. *Anat.* Ribs not connected with the sternum or cartilages of other ribs ventrally. In man they are the last two (eleventh and twelfth) pairs. Cf. FALSE RIBS. See THORAX, *Illust.*

floating screed. See SCREED, *n.*, 4.

floating supply. The supply, as of a commodity or of securities, available for immediate purchase, delivery, etc.

float′plane′ (flōt′plān′), *n.* A seaplane having one or twin watertight floats suspended from the underside of the fuselage for buoyancy and stability on the surface of the water; — distinguished from *flying boat.*

floc (flŏk), *n.* Also **flock.** [Abbr. fr. *floccule.*] *Physical Chem.* A small, light, loose mass, as of smoke or of a fine precipitate.

floc′cose (flŏk′ōs; flŏk·ōs′), *adj.* [LL. *floccosus.*] **1.** Woolly; flocculent. **2.** *Bot.* Having tufts of woolly hairs.

floc′cu·late (flŏk′ū·lāt), *v. t. & i.* To aggregate into small flocculent masses, as soils or sediments. — **floc′cu·la′tion** (-lā′shŭn), *n.*

floc′cule (flŏk′ūl), *n.* [See FLOCCULUS.] A detached mass of fibrous structure like a shredded tuft of wool; a floc.

floc′cu·lent (flŏk′ū·lĕnt), *adj.* **1.** Woolly; flocky. **2.** Containing, or consisting of, flocs or flocks; as, a *flocculent* precipitate. **3.** *Zool.* Covered with a soft, waxy substance, often resembling wool, as certain aphids, scale insects, etc. — **floc′cu·lence** (-lĕns), *n.*

floc′cu·lus (-lŭs), *n.; pl.* -LI (-lī). [NL., dim. of L. *floccus* flock of wool.] **1.** A small tuft of wool, hairs, etc.; esp., a floccule. **2.** *Anat.* A small lobe on the under surface of each hemisphere of the cerebellum. **3.** *Astron.* One of the tufty masses or cloudlike shapes in the solar atmosphere.

floc′cus (flŏk′ŭs), *n.; pl.* FLOCCI (-sī). [L.] A flock, as of wool; a floccule.

flock (flŏk), *n.* [OF. *floc,* fr. L. *floccus.*] **1.** A lock of wool or hair. **2.** Woolen or cotton refuse cut up and used for stuffing furniture, beds, etc. **3.** Very short wool fibers, or dust of vegetable fiber, used in weighting fabrics or as a coating for wallpaper. **4.** Floc. — *v. t.* To stuff, coat, etc., with flock.

flock, *n.* [AS. *flocc* flock, company.] **1.** A company of people; hence, *pl.*, multitudes; also, an aggregate, collection, or group; as, a *flock* of autumn novels. **2.** A number of birds or of animals of one kind living or herded together. **3.** All Christians in relation to Christ, the "Good Shepherd"; also, a congregation in relation to the pastor. — *v. i.* To gather or move in a flock or flocks.

flock′y (flŏk′ĭ), *adj.* Floccose; flocculent.

floe (flō), *n.* The floating ice formed in a large sheet on a body of water; also, a low, flat mass of floating ice.

flog (flŏg), *v. t.;* FLOGGED (flŏgd); FLOG′GING (flŏg′ĭng). To beat or strike with a rod or whip; lash. — *n.* Act of flogging; also, the sound as of a blow. — **flog′ger,** *n.*

flood (flŭd), *n.* [AS. *flōd.*] **1.** A great flow of water; esp., a body of water rising, swelling, and overflowing land; a deluge; inundation. **2.** In full, **flood tide.** The flowing in of the tide; — opposed to *ebb.* See TIDE. **3.** The watery element; specif., the sea. **4.** A great stream, flow, issue, etc.; hence, a superabundance. **5.** *Colloq.* Short for FLOODLIGHT. — *v. t.* To inundate or cause to be inundated; fill or cover with, or as with, a flood. — *v. i.* To pour or issue like a flood. — ***the Flood.*** The Deluge of the days of Noah (*Gen.* vii). — **flood′er,** *n.*

flood′gate′ (-gāt′), *n.* **1.** A gate for shutting out, admitting, or releasing, a body of water; a sluice. **2.** Something like a floodgate, as in restraining an outburst.

flood′light′ (-līt′), *n.* Artificial illumination in a broad bright beam; also, a lighting unit with a reflector for projecting a broad beam.

floor (flōr; 70), *n.* [AS. *flōr.*] **1.** The bottom or lower part of a room, on which one stands. **2.** Hence: **a** Any ground surface, as the bottom of the sea. **b** The platform of a bridge or similar structure. **3.** The structure dividing a building horizontally into stories; hence, a story. In the United States, the ground floor is called first floor, the floor above it being the second floor; in England and the Continent, first floor designates the one above the ground floor and so on. **4.** The main level space in an exchange, legislative chamber, etc., as distinguished from any platform or gallery; hence, with *the,* the right to speak from one's place on the floor; as, the senator from Maine has the *floor.* **5.** A minimum level, as of prices. Cf. CEILING, 2. **6.** *Shipbuilding.* **a** The flat part of the hull next to the keel. **b** A timber lying across the keel, or in a steel ship a vertical plate of the transverse framing, between the inner and outer bottoms. — *v. t.* **1.** To cover with a floor or flooring. **2.** To knock down to or as to the floor; hence, to silence, or defeat. — **floor′er,** *n.*

floor′age (flōr′ĭj; 70), *n.* The area, esp. the usable part, of a floor.

floor′ing (flōr′ĭng; 70), *n.* **a** A floor. **b** Material for a floor.

floor leader. *U.S.* In either house of Congress, a member chosen by his party to have charge of its organization and strategy on the floor.

floor show. An informal entertainment program presented in the midst of the patrons, as at a night club.

floor′walk′er (flōr′wôk′ẽr; 70), *n.* *U.S.* One who walks about in a large retail store as an overseer and director.

flop (flŏp), *v. i.;* FLOPPED (flŏpt); FLOP′PING. [Var. of FLAP.] *Colloq.* **1.** To strike about with something broad and flat, as a fish with its tail; to rise and fall; as, the brim of a hat *flops.* **2.** To throw oneself heavily, clumsily, or flabbily; as, to *flop* into a chair. **3.** To turn, move, or change suddenly. **4.** To fail, esp. completely. — *v. t.* *Colloq.* **1.** To flap, clap, or strike heavily or clumsily. **2.** To cause to flop, or drop. — *n.* **1.** *Colloq.* Act, sound, or instance of flopping. **2.** *Slang.* A failure; fizzle. — **flop′per,** *n.* — **flop′py,** *adj.*

flop′house′ (flŏp′hous′), *n.* *Slang, U.S.* A doss house.

flop′o′ver (-ō′vẽr), *n.* A defect in television reception in which a succession of frames appears to traverse the screen vertically.

Flo′ra (flō′rȧ; 70), *n.* [L., fr. *flos, floris,* flower.] **1.** *Rom. Relig.* Goddess of flowers. **2.** **a** [*not cap.; pl.* FLORAS (-rȧz), less often FLORAE (-rē).] Plants or plant life, esp. as distinguished from *fauna,* of a region, period, special environment, etc.; as, *flora* of the Devonian. **b** A systematic treatise on the plants of a given area.

flo′ral (flō′răl; 70), *adj.* [L. *Floralis* belonging to *Flora.*] Of, pertaining to, or like flowers. — **flo′ral·ly,** *adv.*

floral emblem. A plant or flower recognized as symbolic of a nation, state, territory, or the like. See STATE FLOWER.

‖**Flo′ré′al′** (flô′rā′ȧl′), *n.* [F.] See REVOLUTIONARY CALENDAR.

flo·res′cence (flō·rĕs′ĕns; -′ns), *n.* [L. *florescens,* pres. part. of *florescere* to begin to blossom, fr. *florere* to blossom, fr. *flos, floris,* flower.] State or period of being in bloom, or, figuratively, of flourishing. — **flo·res′cent** (-ĕnt; -′nt), *adj.*

flo′ret (flō′rĕt; -rĭt; 70), *n.* [OF. *florete,* dim. of OF. *flor* flower.] A small flower; specif., one of the small flowers which compose the head in composite plants, as the daisy. See COMPOSITE, *Illust.*

flo′ri·at′ed (flō′rĭ·āt′ĕd; -ĭd; 70), *adj.* Having floral ornaments or a floral form; as, *floriated* lace.

flo′ri·cul′ture (flō′rĭ·kŭl′tụ̈r; flŏr′ĭ-), *n.* [L. *flos, floris,* flower + *cultura* culture.] Cultivation of ornamental flowering plants. — **flo′ri·cul′tur·al,** *adj.* — **flo′ri·cul′tur·al·ly,** *adv.* — **-cul′tur·ist,** *n.*

flor′id (flŏr′ĭd), *adj.* [L. *floridus,* fr. *flos, floris,* flower.] **1.** Flowery; now, esp., flowery in style; embellished with figures of speech, as writing, or with rapid melodic figures, divisions, or passages, as musical composition; excessively ornate. **2.** Flushed with red; ruddy. — **flo·rid′i·ty** (flō·rĭd′ĭ·tĭ), *n.* — **flor′id·ly,** *adv.* — **flor′id·ness,** *n.*

Flor′i·da moss (flŏr′ĭ·dȧ; 74). = LONG MOSS.

flo·rif′er·ous (flō·rĭf′ẽr·ŭs), *adj.* [L. *florifer,* fr. *flos, floris,* flower + *ferre* to bear.] Bearing flowers.

flor′in (flŏr′ĭn), *n.* [F., fr. It. *fiorino,* fr. *fiore* a flower, fr. L. *flos* flower.] Orig., a gold coin with a lily on it, first struck in 1252 at Florence. Later: **a** An English gold six-shilling coin of Edward III. **b** A British silver coin worth 2 shillings. See MONEY, *Tables.* **c** An Austrian silver coin worth 48.2 cents, last coined in 1892. **d** The Dutch gulden.

flo′rist (flō′rĭst; flŏr′ĭst; 70), *n.* A cultivator of, or dealer in, flowers.

-florous. [L. *-florus,* fr. *flos, floris,* flower.] A combining form used after *i* to signify *flowered* or *flowering* (as specified); *-anthous;* as in multi*florous,* uni*florous.*

floss (flŏs; 74), *n.* Also **floss silk.** [F. *floche* soft, downy, fr. OF. *flochier* to form flocks.] **1.** Waste or unreelable silk fibers, or the untwisted thread spun from such fibers. **2.** **a** A soft lustrous silk thread used in embroidery; — called specif. ***embroidery floss.*** **b** Such thread, esp. when waxed, used for cleaning between the teeth; — called specif. ***dental floss.*** **3.** A fluffy substance, as silk cotton (see SILK COTTON). **4.** *Bot.* The styles of the pistillate flowers of maize; silk.

flo′tage (flō′tĭj), *n.* [Cf. OF. *flotage* (F. *flottage*). See FLOAT, *v.*] **1.** Act or state of floating; power to float. **2.** That which floats.

flo·ta′tion (flō·tā′shŭn), *n.* [For *floatation,* after F. *flottation* a floating.] **1.** Act, process, or state of floating. **2.** *Com. & Finance.* Act of financing a commercial venture or floating an issue of bonds, stock, or the like. **3.** *Ore Dressing.* The separation of the particles of a mass of pulverized ore according to their relative capacity for floating on a given liquid.

flo·til′la (flō·tĭl′ȧ), *n.; pl.* FLOTILLAS (-ȧz). [Sp., dim. of *flota* fleet.] A small fleet or a fleet of small vessels.

flot′sam (flŏt′săm), *n.* Also, formerly, **flot′san** (-săn), **flot′sen** (-sĕn), **flot′son** (-sŭn; -s′n), etc. [OF. *flotaison,* prop. a floating.] **1.** Wreckage of a ship or its cargo found floating on the sea. Cf. JETSAM, LAGAN. **2.** Drifting persons or things; driftage.

flounce (flouns), *v. i.;* FLOUNCED (flounst); FLOUNC′ING (floun′sĭng). To throw the limbs and body one way and the other; to spring or turn suddenly, as in anger; also, to flounder. — *n.* A flouncing.

flounce, *n.* [From earlier FROUNCE.] A strip gathered and sewed on by its upper edge only, as on a skirt. — *v. t.* To adorn with a flounce or flounces.

flounc′ing (floun′sĭng), *n.* Material suitable for flounces; also, a flounce or flounces.

floun′der (floun′dẽr), *n.;* see PLURAL, *Note,* 3. [OF. *flondre,* of Scand. origin.] Broadly, any flatfish; commonly, any of a certain genus (*Pleuronectes*) or allied genera of flatfishes; esp., in America, the ***summer flounder*** (*Paralichthys dentatus*), and the ***winter flounder*** (*Pseudopleuronectes americanus*), which are important food fishes.

floun′der, *v. i.* To struggle, as a horse in the mire; hence, to proceed clumsily; to muddle. — *n.* A floundering. — **floun′der·ing·ly,** *adv.*

flour (flour), *n.* [ME. *flour, flure,* flour, after F. *fleur de farine* the flower (i. e., the best) of meal. See FLOWER.] **1.** Finely ground and bolted meal of wheat. Cf. BRAN; SHORT, *n.*, 10. **2.** The finely ground meal of other cereals, as rye, barley, etc. **3.** The fine soft powder of any substance; as, *flour* of emery. — *v. t.* **1.** To grind and bolt; convert into flour. **2.** To sprinkle with flour. — **flour′y** (-ĭ), *adj.*

flour′ish (flûr′ĭsh; 117), *v. i.* [OF. *flurir, florir,* fr. L. *florere* to bloom, fr. *flos, floris,* flower.] **1.** *Obs.* To blossom. **2.** To grow luxuriantly; thrive. **3.** To increase in wealth, honor, etc.; also, to reach the climax of development or influence. **4.** To execute a flourish or flourishes. — *v. t.* **1.** To adorn with flowers or figures; ornament. **2.** To swing about flauntingly; brandish. — **Syn.** See SWING. — *n.* **1.** *Obs.* A blooming. **2.** Condition of flourishing, prospering, or of being in one's prime. **3.** Something executed or to be executed in a bold, dashing, or flaunting manner; as: **a** A fantastic or showy musical passage or its performance; esp., a fanfare, as of trumpets. **b** A brandishing, as of a sword. **c** A decorative stroke, as with a pen. — **flour′ish·er,** *n.*

flour′ish·ing, *adj.* That flourishes. — **flour′ish·ing·ly**, *adv.*

flout (flout), *v. t.* [Prob. fr. ME. *flouten* to play the flute.] To mock or insult; treat with contempt. — *v. i.* To practice mocking; sneer. — **Syn.** See SCOFF. — *n.* An insult; a jeer; hence, mockery. — **flout′er**, *n.* — **flout′ing·ly**, *adv.*

flow (flō), *v. i.* [AS. *flōwan*.] **1.** To move or circulate, as a liquid; run. **2.** To come (*in*), go (*away*), empty (*into*), issue (*from*), etc., in or as in a stream. **3.** To rise, as the tide; — opposed to *ebb*. **4.** To abound; be full, so as to run over. **5.** To manifest smoothness, continuity, and ease; as, *flowing* verse. **6.** To hang loose and waving. — **Syn.** See SPRING. — *v. t.* To cause to flow; flood. — *n.* **1.** Act or manner of flowing. **2.** The tidal flood. **3.** Something which flows or has flowed; a stream; an outpouring. **4.** The quantity that flows in a certain time. **5.** The form or artistic arrangement of something flowing; as, the *flow* of lines in a statue. **6.** *Physics.* The type of motion characteristic of fluids. — **flow′ing·ly**, *adv.* — **flow′ing·ness**, *n.*

flow′age (flō′ĭj), *n.* **1.** Act of flowing or flooding, or state of being flooded; also, the liquid that flows or overflows. **2.** *Mech.* Deformation by intermolecular shear, as distinguished from fracture.

flow′er (flou′ẽr), *n.* [OF. *flour, flor* (F. *fleur*), fr. L. *flos, floris*.] **1.** A bloom or blossom (see BLOSSOM, 1); also, bloom. **2.** The fairest or choicest part or specimen. **3.** *pl.* A powdery substance, esp. one condensed by sublimation; as, *flowers* of sulfur. **4.** Any plant grown or esteemed for its blossoms. **5.** An ornament; specif., a figure of speech. **6.** *Bot.* In higher plants, a short stem carrying leaves, some or all of which are sporophylls; narrowly, in seed-bearing plants, a similar structure protected by a floral envelope. — *v. i.* **1.** To blossom; produce flowers. **2.** To come into the finest or fairest condition. — *v. t.* To embellish with flowers or a floral design. — *adj.* Of or pertaining to a flower; of or for flowers; dealing in flowers.

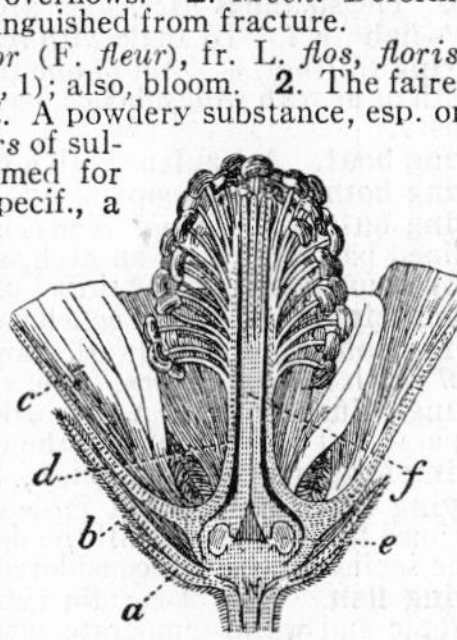

flow′er·age (-ĭj), *n.* A state of flowering; flowers in general; also, floral ornament.

flow′er·et (flou′ẽr·ĕt; -ĭt), *n.* A floret.

flower head. *Bot.* A capitulum.

flow′er·ing (flou′ẽr·ĭng), *adj.* **1.** In bloom. **2.** Having conspicuous flowers; as, the white-bracted **flowering dogwood** (*Cornus florida*), the flower of which is the State flower of Virginia and North Carolina.

flowering quince. = JAPANESE QUINCE.

flowering tobacco. See TOBACCO, 1.

flow′er·less (flou′ẽr·lĕs; -lĭs), *adj.* Having no flowers.

flow′er·pot′ (-pŏt′), *n.* A pot in which to grow plants.

flow′er·y (-ĭ), *adj.*; -ER (-ĭ·ẽr); -I·EST. **1.** Full of, or covered with, flowers. **2.** Highly embellished with figurative language; florid. — **flow′er·i·ly**, *adv.* — **flow′er·i·ness**, *n.*

flown (flōn), *past part.* of FLY. **1.** That have flown; transported by or as if by flying; as, far-*flown* seeds.

flown, *adj.* [Obs. past part. of *flow*.] Flushed; inflated.

flow sheet, *or* **flow′sheet′** (flō′shēt′), *n.* A diagram, chart, or expository outline showing the successive operations and apparatus through which material progresses in a metallurgical or manufacturing plant.

flu (flōō; 114), *n.* *Colloq.* Influenza.

fluc′tu·ant (flŭk′tụ·ănt), *adj.* [L. *fluctuans* fluctuating.] Undulating; wavering; fluctuating.

fluc′tu·ate (-āt), *v. i.* [L. *fluctuare* to wave, fr. *fluctus* wave, fr. *fluere, fluctum*, to flow.] **1.** To move as a wave; to roll back and forth. **2.** To be constantly changing, as between two points, states, etc.; waver; vary. — **Syn.** See SWING. — *v. t.* To cause to fluctuate. — **fluc′tu·a′tion** (-ā′shŭn), *n.*

flue (flōō; 114), *n.* [Flem. *vluwe*.] Light down, or fluff.

flue, *n.* A barb; esp., a fluke, as of an anchor; also, a barb of a feather.

flue, *n.* **1.** An enclosed passage for a current of air, gases, etc., as in a chimney, for conveying flame and smoke to the outer air. **2.** In a steam boiler, a pipe for conveying flame and hot gases around or through water. **3.** *Music.* **a** = FLUE PIPE. **b** In an organ flue pipe, the opening between the lower lip and the languet.

flu′ent (flōō′ĕnt; 114), *adj.* [L. *fluens, -entis*, pres. part. of *fluere* to flow.] **1.** Flowing, or capable of flowing; liquid; fluid. **2.** Ready in the use of words; voluble; ready; hence, flowing; smooth; facile; as, a *fluent* speaker. — **flu′en·cy** (-ĕn·sĭ), *n.* — **flu′ent·ly**, *adv.*

flue pipe. *Music.* A pipe, esp. an organ pipe, whose tone is produced by the impinging of a current of air upon an edge, or lip, causing a wave motion in the air within.

flue stop. An organ stop made up of flue pipes.

fluff (flŭf), *n.* **1.** Nap; down; also, a light mass as of dust and down. **2.** *Theater & Radio.* Act or instance of fluffing. — *v. t. & i.* **1.** To make or become fluffy. **2.** *Theater & Radio.* To forget or bungle, as a line or passage. — **fluff′er**, *n.*

fluff′y (flŭf′ĭ), *adj.*; -ER (-ĭ·ẽr); -I·EST. Covered with or consisting of fluff; like fluff. — **fluff′i·ly**, *adv.* — **fluff′i·ness**, *n.*

flu′gel·man (flōō′gĕl·măn). Var. of FUGLEMAN.

flu′id (flōō′ĭd; 114), *adj.* [F. or L.; F. *fluide*, fr. L. *fluidus*, fr. *fluere* to flow.] **1.** Having particles which easily move and change their relative position without a separation of the mass, and which easily yield to pressure; capable of flowing. **2.** Flowing, as style; fluent, as speech; tending or free to change in form; as, *fluid* consciousness. — **Syn.** See LIQUID. — *n.* A fluid substance; a liquid or gas. — **flu·id′ic** (flōō·ĭd′ĭk), *adj.* — **flu·id′i·ty** (-ĭ·tĭ), *n.* — **flu′id·ly**, *adv.*

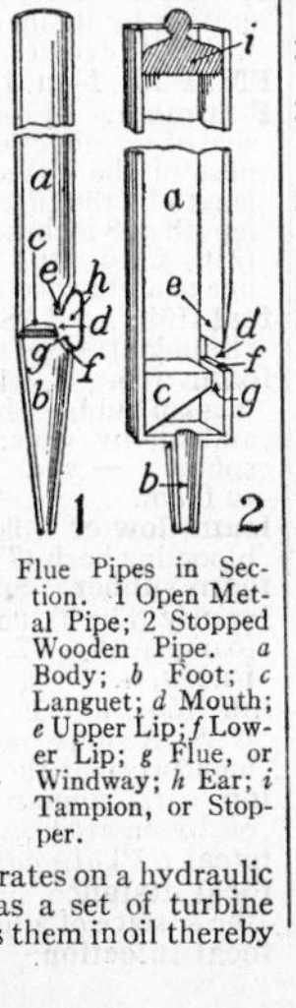

fluid dram *or* **drachm.** See MEASURE, *Table* 12.

fluid drive. An automotive power coupling that operates on a hydraulic turbine principle. The flywheel of the engine has a set of turbine blades (impellers) connected directly to it and drives them in oil thereby

Flower of Marsh Mallow in Section.
a Epicalyx; *b* Calyx; *c* Petal; *d* Androecium; *e* Ovule; *f* Gynoecium.

Flue Pipes in Section. 1 Open Metal Pipe; 2 Stopped Wooden Pipe. *a* Body; *b* Foot; *c* Languet; *d* Mouth; *e* Upper Lip; *f* Lower Lip; *g* Flue, or Windway; *h* Ear; *i* Tampion, or Stopper.

turning another set of turbine blades (runners) attached to the transmission gears of the automobile.

flu′id·ex′tract (flōō′ĭd·ĕks′trăkt), *n.* *Pharm.* A concentrated alcoholic preparation of a vegetable drug, one cubic centimeter of which closely represents the active ingredients of one gram of the dry drug.

fluid ounce. Also **flu′id·ounce′** (flōō′ĭd·ouns′), *n.* A measure for liquid medicines, etc. In the United States it equals ⅟₁₆ pint, or 29.6 cc.; in Great Britain, ⅟₂₀ imperial pint, or 28.4 cc. See MEASURE, *Table* 12.

fluke (flōōk; 114), *n.* [AS. *flōc*.] **1.** A flatfish or flounder. **2.** Any of various flattened, parasitic, trematode worms (order Digenetica). The best-known are the *liver flukes*, which infest the livers of cattle, sheep, swine, etc., and man.

fluke, *n.* **1.** That part of an anchor which fastens in the ground. See ANCHOR, *Illust.* **2.** The barbed head or one of the barbs of a harpoon, lance, arrow, etc. See ARROW, *Illust.* **3.** A lobe of a whale's tail.

fluke, *n.* *Slang.* An accidentally successful stroke at billiards or pool; hence, any accidental stroke of luck.

fluk′y (flōōk′ĭ), *adj.* Also **fluk′ey.** [From FLUKE successful stroke.] *Slang.* **a** Happening or obtained by chance. **b** Uncertain; unsteady.

flume (flōōm; 114), *n.* [OF. *flum* river, fr. L. *flumen*, fr. *fluere* to flow.] *U. S.* **a** A ravine or gorge with a stream running through it. **b** An inclined channel for conveying water from a distance for power, irrigation, etc. — *v. t.* *U. S.* To transport in a flume, as logs.

flum′mer·y (flŭm′ẽr·ĭ), *n.*; *pl.* -MERIES (-ĭz). [W. *llymru*, or *llymruwd*, a food made of steeped oatmeal.] **1.** A soft food like pap. **2.** A kind of custard. **3.** Something insipid; humbug; trash.

flum′mox (flŭm′ŭks), *v. t.* *Slang.* To perplex; confound.

flump (flŭmp), *v. t. & i.* [Imitative.] To set, move or fall suddenly and heavily. — **flump**, *n.*

flung (flŭng), *past & past part.* of FLING.

flunk (flŭngk), *v. i. & t.* *Colloq., U. S.* To fail, as in a recitation or examination; to back out, as through fear; to dismiss or be dismissed for deficiency, esp. from college. — *n.* *Colloq., U. S.* A failure.

flunk′y, flunk′ey (flŭngk′ĭ), *n.*; *pl.* FLUNKIES, -EYS (-ĭz). **1.** A somewhat contemptuous name for a liveried servant; esp., a footman. **2.** A snobbish or obsequious or cringing; toady. — -ism (-ĭz′m), *n.*

flu′o- (flōō′ō-; 114). [From FLUOR.] *Chem.* A combining form indicating *fluorine* as an ingredient, as in **flu′o·bro′mide, flu′o·car′bon·ate, flu′o·chlo′ride, flu′o·phos′phate, flu′o·sil′i·cate**; — used also for *fluorescent.* — **flu′o** (flōō′ō), *adj.*

flu′or (flōō′ôr; 114), *n.* [L., flux, fr. *fluere* to flow.] Fluorite.

fluor-. *Chem.* = FLUORO-.

flu′o·resce′ (flōō′ô·rĕs′), *v. i.* -RESCED′ (-rĕst′); -RESC′ING (-rĕs′ĭng). To produce, undergo, or exhibit fluorescence.

flu′o·res′ce·in (-rĕs′ĕ·ĭn), *n.* Also **flu′o·res′ce·ine.** *Chem.* A yellowish-red crystalline compound, $C_{20}H_{12}O_5$; — from the brilliant yellowish-green fluorescence of its alkaline solutions.

flu′o·res′cence (-ĕns; -′ns), *n.* [From FLUOR.] *Physics.* Property of emitting radiation as the result of, and only during, the absorption of radiation from some other source; also, the emitted radiation. Cf. PHOSPHORESCENCE.

flu′o·res′cent (-ĕnt; -′nt), *adj.* Having or showing fluorescence.

fluorescent lamp. A tubular electric lamp coated on its inner surface with a fluorescent material (phosphor) and containing mercury vapor whose bombardment by electrons from the cathode provides ultraviolet light which causes the phosphor to emit visible light, **fluorescent light**, either a close approximation of daylight or of a selected color.

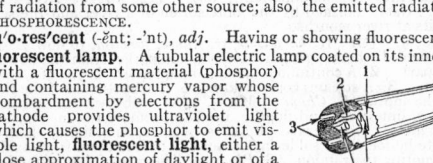

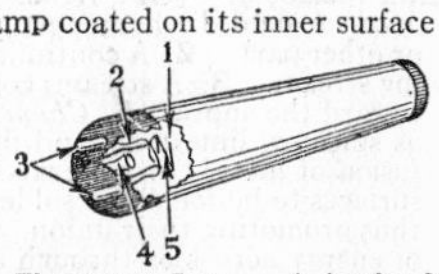

Fluorescent Lamp. 1 Anode; 2 Stem Press; 3 Base Pins; 4 Exhaust Tube; 5 Cathode.

flu·or′ic (flōō·ŏr′ĭk; 114), *adj.* [F. *fluorique*.] *Chem.* Pertaining to, obtained from, or containing fluorine.

flu′o·ri·date (flōō′ô·rĭ·dāt; flôôr′ĭ-), *v. t.* *Chem.* To treat with a fluoride; as, to *fluoridate* drinking water. — **flu′o·ri·da′tion** (-dā′shŭn), *n.*

flu′o·ride (flōō′ô·rīd; -rĭd; 114), *n.* Also **flu′o·rid.** *Chem.* A compound of fluorine with another element or radical.

flu′o·ri·nate (flōō′ô·rĭ·nāt; flôôr′ĭ-), *v. t.* *Chem.* To combine or treat with fluorine. — **flu′o·ri·na′tion** (-nā′shŭn), *n.*

flu′o·rine (-rēn; -rĭn), *n.* Also **flu′o·rin.** [Because found in the mineral *fluorite*.] *Chem.* An element of the chlorine family, a pungent, corrosive, greenish-yellow gas. Symbol, F; at. no., 9; at. wt., 19.00.

flu′o·rite (-rīt), *n.* [From FLUOR.] Calcium fluoride, CaF_2, a transparent or translucent mineral of different colors, used as a flux.

flu′o·ro- (flōō′ô·rō-), **fluor-.** *Chem.* A combining form for *fluorine, fluorescence*, etc.

flu′o·ro·scope (flōō′ô·rō·skōp; flôôr′ō-), *n.* [*fluorescence* + *-scope*.] An instrument for observing or exhibiting fluorescence.

flu′or·os′co·py (flōō′ôr·ŏs′kô·pĭ), *n.* Observation by means of fluorescence, esp. by observing the fluorescence of a screen, caused by X rays transmitted through the object.

flu′o·ro′sis (flōō′ô·rō′sĭs), *n.* [*fluor-* + *-osis*.] *Med.* An abnormal or poisoned condition caused by fluorine, as the spotting of the enamel of teeth caused by too much fluorine in the drinking water.

flu′or·spar′ (flōō′ôr·spär′), *n.* The mineral fluorite.

flur′ry (flûr′ĭ), *n.*; *pl.* -RIES (-ĭz). **1.** A sudden and brief commotion of the air. **2.** Nervous commotion; spasmodic agitation. **3.** A sudden shower or snowfall with a gust of wind. **4.** *Stock Exchange.* A sudden, temporary commotion in prices. — **Syn.** See STIR. — *v. t.*; FLUR′RIED (-ĭd); FLUR′RY·ING. To agitate; fluster. — **Syn.** See DISCOMPOSE.

flush (flŭsh), *v. i.* [ME. *fluschen* to fly up, influenced by *flash* and *blush*.] **1.** To flow and spread suddenly and freely; as, blood *flushes* into the face. **2.** To blush. **3.** To show red; to glow. — *v. t.* **1.** To animate; encourage. **2.** To draw water from, or pour it over or through (a pond, sewer, etc.); to wash out by a rush of water or other liquid. **3.** To make suddenly or temporarily red, rosy, or glowing. — *n.* **1.** A sudden flowing; a rush which fills or overflows, as of water for cleansing purposes. **2.** A sudden increase or expansion; now, esp., a sudden or abundant growth; as, the *flush* of grass. **3.** A sudden rush of feeling; a thrill. **4.** Any tinge of red or ruddy light or color. **b** Glow; vigor. **5.** A fit of extreme heat, as in a fever. — **flush′er**, *n.*

flush, *adj.* **1.** Fully supplied; well filled. **2.** Full of life and vigor; lusty; hence, of a ruddy color; flushed. **3.** Abundant; hence, lavish. **4.** Unbroken or even in surface; on a level with the adjacent surface; as, a *flush* panel, deck. **5.** Direct; full; as, a *flush* blow. **6.** *Naut.* Of a vessel, having a flush deck. **7.** *Printing.* Set even with the left edge of the type page; having no indention. — *adv.* Straight; squarely. — *v. t.* To make flush or level, as joints in masonry by pointing.

flush (flŭsh), *v. i.* [ME. *fluschen*, perh. of imitative origin.] To start up suddenly; to fly like a startled bird. — *v. t.* To cause to start up and fly, as a startled bird.

flush, *n.* [F. *flux*, fr. L. *fluxus* flow.] *Card Playing.* A hand of cards all of the same suit. In a ***straight flush*** the cards are in sequence. A ***royal flush***, the highest poker hand, is a straight flush from ace to ten. See POKER, *Illust.*

flus'ter (flŭs'tẽr), *v. t.* To make hot and rosy, as with drinking; to fuddle; confuse. — **Syn.** See DISCOMPOSE. — *v. i.* To be agitated and confused. — *n.* Formerly, heat or glow, as from drinking; now, agitation mingled with confusion.

flus'ter·ate (flŭs'tẽr·āt), **flus'trate** (-trāt), *v. t.* *Colloq.* To fluster. — **flus'ter·a'tion** (-ā'shŭn), **flus·tra'tion** (flŭs·trā'shŭn), *n.*

flute (flo͞ot; 114), *n.* [OF. *flaüte, fleüte*, fr. Pr. *flaut.*] **1.** A wind instrument consisting of a hollow cylinder or pipe, with holes along its length, stopped by the fingers or by keys. **2.** A channel or groove, as in plaited cloth. **3.** *Arch.* A groove of curved section, as one of the grooves used to decorate columns in classical architecture. **4.** Any of several flue organ stops of flutelike quality and of 8-foot or 4-foot pitch. See STOP, *n.*

flute, *v. i.* To play on or as on a flute. — *v. t.* **1.** To play, whistle, or sing with a note like that of a flute. **2.** To form flutes or channels in, as in a column.

flut'ed (flo͞ot'ĕd; -ĭd; 114), *adj.* **1.** Clear and mellow; flutelike; as, *fluted* notes. **2.** Decorated with flutes; grooved.

flut'er (-ẽr), *n.* **1.** A flutist. **2.** One who makes grooves or flutings; also, a tool for making flutings.

flut'ing (-ĭng), *n.* Decoration with flutes; flutes collectively; as, the *fluting* of a column, of a ruffle.

flut'ist (-ĭst), *n.* A performer on the flute.

flut'ter (flŭt'ẽr), *v. i.* [AS. *floterian* to float about.] **1.** To flap the wings rapidly, without flying. **2.** To move with quick vibrations; as, a sail *flutters* in the wind; his pulse *flutters.* **3.** To move about with great bustle and show but without much result. **4.** To be in agitation; to quiver. — *v. t.* **1.** To vibrate or move quickly. **2.** To throw into confusion. — *n.* **1.** A quick and irregular motion; vibration; as, the *flutter* of a fan. **2.** Agitation; confusion. **3.** *Swimming.* A movement, or kick, of the feet employed in the crawl and the backstroke; — called also **flutter kick.** — **flut'ter·er**, *n.* — **flut'ter·ing·ly**, *adv.* — **flut'ter·y**, *adj.*

flu'vi·al (flo͞o'vĭ·ăl), *adj.* [OF., fr. L. *fluvialis*, fr. *fluvius* river, fr. *fluere* to flow.] Of or relating to rivers; growing in streams or ponds; produced by river action.

flu'vi·a·tile (flo͞o'vĭ·ȧ·tĭl; 56), *adj.* [F., fr. L. *fluviatilis*, fr. *fluvius* river.] Fluvial.

flu'vi·o·ma·rine' (flo͞o'vĭ·ō·mȧ·rēn'), *adj.* [L. *fluvius* river + E. *marine.*] *Geol.* Formed by the joint action of a river and the sea, as deposits at river mouths.

flux (flŭks), *n.* [OF., fr. L. *fluxus*, fr. *fluere, fluxum*, to flow.] **1.** *Med.* A fluid discharge, esp. an excessive discharge, from the bowels or other part. **2.** A continuous moving on or passing by, as of a flowing stream. **3.** A stream; copious flow. **4.** The setting in of the tide toward the shore. **5.** *Chem. & Metal.* **a** Any substance or mixture, as silicates, limestone, and fluorite, used to promote fusion, esp. the fusion of metals or minerals. **b** Any substance, as rosin, applied to surfaces to be joined by soldering or welding to free them from oxide, thus promoting their union. **6.** *Physics.* The rate of flow of fluid or of energy across or through a surface. — *v. t.* **1.** To fuse; to treat with a flux. **2.** *Med.* To purge. — *v. i.* *Archaic.* To flow freely.

flux'ion (flŭk'shŭn), *n.* **1.** Act of flowing; hence, continuing motion or change. **2.** *Math.* In infinitesimal calculus, a differential. — **flux'ion·al**, *adj.* — **flux'ion·al·ly**, *adv.* — **flux'ion·ar'y** (-ĕr'ĭ *or, esp. Brit.*, -ẽr·ĭ), *adj.*

fly (flī), *v. i.*; FLEW (flo͞o); FLOWN (flōn); FLY'ING. [AS. *flēogan.*] **1.** **a** To move in or pass through the air with wings, as a bird. **b** To flee; as: (1) To run from danger. (2) To vanish; disappear. **2.** To move through the air or before the wind. **3.** To move or pass swiftly. **4.** To float, wave, or soar in the air, as a kite or flag. **5.** To be rapidly spent, as money; to seem to pass rapidly, as time. **6.** To traverse the air in an aircraft; to fly aircraft. **7.** *past & past part.* FLIED (flīd). *Baseball.* To hit a fly. **8.** *Hawking.* To hunt with a hawk; also, to attack in flight, as a hawk; as, to *fly* at higher game. — *v. t.* **1.** **a** To cause to fly or to float in the air, as a bird, a kite, a flag. **b** To fly or flee from; to shun. **2.** To pass or journey over by flying; as, to *fly* the Atlantic. **3.** *Aviation.* To manage or carry in flight; as, to *fly* an airplane. **4.** *Hawking.* To hunt with or as a hawk.
— *n.*; *pl.* FLIES (flīz). **1.** The course of anything projected through the air; esp., the flight of a batted ball before it strikes the ground. **2.** **a** *Obs. exc. Hist.* A passenger coach or parcels cart. **b** A covered pleasure carriage. **3.** A fold of material on a garment, as to conceal buttons. **4.** The outer canvas of a tent with double top. **5.** The length of an extended flag from its staff or support; also, the outer end of a flag. **6.** *Baseball.* A ball batted in the air. **7.** *Bookbinding.* A flyleaf. **8.** *Mach.* **a** A contrivance of rotating radial vanes, acting as a fan, or as a governor for clockwork or very light machinery. **b** A flywheel. **9.** *pl. Theaters.* The space over the whole stage, above the proscenium. — ***on the fly.*** Flying; hence, moving; without coming to a rest; of a batted ball, before it strikes the ground.

fly (flī), *n.*; *pl.* FLIES (flīz). [AS. *flȳge, flēoge.*] **1.** Orig., any winged insect; now, a dipterous insect of a family (Muscidae) of which the housefly (*Musca domestica*) is the most familiar form; loosely, almost any insect having transparent wings or otherwise resembling the housefly. With qualifying words *fly* forms the common names of many such insects of various orders, as in dragon*fly*, ichneumon *fly*, etc. **2.** *Angling.* A hook dressed with feathers, tinsel, etc., in imitation of a fly. **3.** *Print.* **a** Formerly, the person who took the printed sheets from the press. **b** A vibrating frame with fingers, attached to a power printing press for doing the same work.

Fly, 2. 1 Gut; 2 Head; 3 Wing; 4 Body; 5 Butt; 6 Tail; 7 Tag; 8 Hackle.

fly, *adj.* *Slang.* **a** Knowing; keen. **b** Nimble.

fly agaric *or* **amanita.** A common poisonous mushroom (*Amanita muscaria*) having a warty white or yellow pileus and a bulb at the base of the stipe.

fly'a·way' (flī'ȧ·wā'), *adj.* Flighty; light and free.

fly'belt' (flī'bĕlt'), *n.* Any area infested with tsetse. See TSETSE.

fly'blow' (flī'blō'), *n.* One of the eggs or young larvae deposited by a blowfly. — *v. t. & i.*; see BLOW. To deposit flyblows (in); hence, to taint or contaminate.

fly'boat' (-bōt'), *n.* [Prob. fr. *fly* + *boat.*] A fast vessel of any of various kinds.

fly'-by-night', *adj.* Insecurely financed; irresponsible.

fly'catch'er (flī'kăch'ẽr), *n.* Any of numerous passerine birds (esp. of the families Muscicapidae, the Old World or true flycatchers, and Tyrannidae, the American or ***tyrant flycatcher***) that feed upon insects, which they take on the wing. The ***crested flycatcher*** has a prominent crest, esp. a bird (*Myiarchus crinitus*) of eastern North America often called ***great crested flycatcher.*** The ***least flycatcher*** is a small plainly colored flycatcher (*Empidonax minimus*) common in eastern North America. See KINGBIRD, PEWEE.

fly'er (flī'ẽr), *n.* A flier.

☞ The spellings *flier, flyer* are both in good use.

fly'-fish', *v. i.* To angle with real or artificial flies.

fly'ing (flī'ĭng), *n.* Act of one that flies. — *adj.* Moving in the air with or as with wings; hence, passing about freely; fleeing; temporary; hasty.

flying boat. A seaplane with a hull adapted for floating.

flying bomb. See ROBOT BOMB.

flying buttress. *Arch.* A masonry structure, typically a straight inclined bar carried on an arch, and a solid buttress against which it abuts, for taking up the thrust of a roof or vault. See GOTHIC, *Illust.*

flying circus. A rotary echelon formation of airplanes in action.

flying colors. Flags unfurled and waving in the air; hence, ***to come off with flying colors***, to be victorious; to succeed thoroughly.

flying column. *Mil.* A strong detachment, usually of all arms, which operates at a distance from the main force.

flying dragon. See DRAGON, *n.*, 8.

Flying Dutchman. **a** A fabled Dutch mariner condemned for his crimes to sail the seas till the day of judgment. **b** His spectral ship, the seeing of which is considered a bad omen by sailors.

flying fish. Any of certain fishes (*Exocoetus* and allied genera) of tropic and warm-temperate seas, which have long winglike pectoral fins, and are capable of moving some distance through the air.

flying fox. Any of various large fruit-eating bats (esp. of the genera *Pteropus* and *Epomophorus*) with foxlike faces.

flying gurnard. Any of several gurnardlike spiny-finned fishes constituting a genus (*Dactylopterus*, family Dactylopteridae), with large pectoral fins. They can fly short distances. Cf. BATFISH, GURNARD.

flying jib. *Naut.* A sail set outside of the jib on an extension of the jib boom, called **flying jib boom.** See SAIL, *Illusts.*

flying lemur. An East Indian mammal (genus *Cynocephalus*) about the size of a cat, having a broad fold of skin which extends from the neck to the tail on each side, forming a parachute used in making long sailing leaps; — called also *colugo.* Flying lemurs are now classed as a separate order (Dermoptera) from the lemurs.

flying machine. *Aeronautics.* An apparatus for navigating the air; — sometimes restricted to an airplane.

flying mare. *Wrestling.* An attack in which the aggressor seizes his opponent's wrist, and, turning, jerks his opponent over his back.

flying mouse. See PHALANGER.

flying phalanger. See PHALANGER.

flying saucer. Also **flying disk.** Any of various unidentified moving objects repeatedly reported as seen in the air esp. over the United States, usually alleged to be saucer- or disk-shaped.

flying squirrel. See SQUIRREL, 3 **a.**

Flying Wing. A trade-mark applied to a tailless airplane accommodating substantially all of its parts within the outline of its single airfoil.

fly'leaf' (flī'lēf'), *n.*; *pl.* -LEAVES (-lēvz'). A blank leaf at the beginning or end of a book, circular, program, etc.

fly'pa'per (-pā'pẽr), *n.* Poisoned paper, or paper coated with a sticky substance, for killing flies.

fly'speck' (-spĕk'), *n.* A speck made by the excrement of a fly; hence, any small dot. — *v. t.* To soil with flyspecks.

flyte (flīt). Var. of FLITE.

fly'trap' (flī'trăp'), *n.* **1.** A trap for catching flies. **2.** **a** The pitcher plant. **b** Venus's-flytrap.

fly'way' (-wā'), *n.* An established air route of migratory birds.

fly'weight' (-wāt'), *n.* A boxer who weighs 112 pounds or less.

fly'wheel' (-hwēl'), *n.* *Mach.* A heavy wheel for opposing and moderating by its inertia any fluctuation of speed in the machinery with which it revolves.

FM, F.M., f-m, f.m. (ĕf'ĕm'). *Radio.* Frequency modulation.

F number. [From the initial of *focal.*] *Photog.* A number expressive of the effectiveness of the aperture of a lens in relation to brightness of the image. The number is obtained by dividing the focal length by the effective diameter of the lens. Thus, a lens having a focal length of 8 inches and a diameter of ½ inch is an F 16 (F/16, f 16, f:16, f/16, *f.* 16, etc.) lens. The lower the F number, the brighter the image and hence the shorter the exposure required.

foal (fōl), *n.* [AS. *fola.*] The young of an animal of the horse family (Equidae). See COLT, FILLY. — *v. t. & i.* To bring forth (a foal).

foam (fōm), *n.* [AS. *fām.*] The whitish substance, consisting of a mass of bubbles, formed on liquids, or in the mouth or on the skin of an animal, by violent agitation, fermentation, or perspiration; froth; spume. — *v. i.* To gather or form foam; to froth. — *v. t.* To cause to foam.

foam'flow'er (-flou'ẽr), *n.* An American white-flowered spring-blooming herb (*Tiarella cordifolia*) of the saxifrage family.

foam rubber. Spongy rubber produced for use as cushions, etc.

foam'y (fōm'ĭ), *adj.*; FOAM'I·ER (-ĭ·ẽr); FOAM'I·EST. **1.** Covered with foam; frothy. **2.** Full of, or like, foam. — **foam'i·ly**, *adv.* — **foam'i·ness**, *n.*

fob (fŏb), *n.* **1.** A little pocket in men's trousers for a watch. **2.** *U. S.* A short watch chain, ribbon, etc. **3.** A small weight or ornament worn at the end of a watch chain.

fob, *v. t.*; FOBBED (fŏbd); FOB'BING. To trick. — ***fob off.*** To shift off by an artifice; to put aside.

fo'cal (fō'kăl), *adj.* Of or pertaining to a focus.

focal distance *or* **length.** *Optics.* The distance of the focus from the surface of a lens or mirror.

focal infection. *Med. & Dent.* A persistent bacterial infection of some organ or region, as a tonsil or root of a tooth, esp. one causing infections elsewhere in the body.

fo'cal·ize (fō'kăl·īz), *v. t. & i.* **1.** To bring or come to a focus; to focus. **2.** *Med.* To confine, or become confined, to a limited area. — **fo'cal·i·za'tion** (-ĭ·zā'shŭn; -ī·zā'-), *n.*

fo'cus (fō'kŭs), *n.; pl.* FOCUSES (-ĕz; -ĭz), FOCI (fō'sī). [L., hearth, fireplace.] **1. a** Focal distance or length. **b** Adjustment, as of eye or eyepiece, for distinct vision. **2.** A central point; a center of activity, attraction, or attention. **3.** *Math.* **a** Either of the two fixed points on the principal axis of an ellipse. **b** Any analogous point in other conic sections. **4.** *Med.* A localized region of disease, or the chief site of a generalized disease. **5.** *Physics.* A point at which rays, as of light, heat, or sound, converge or from which they diverge or appear to diverge. Specif., *Optics*, the point where the geometrical lines (or their prolongations) conforming to the rays diverging from (or converging toward) another point, intersect and give rise to an image after reflection by a mirror or refraction by a lens or optical system. If the lines must be prolonged backward through the lens or mirror in order to intersect, the focus is called a ***virtual focus;*** otherwise it is called a ***real focus.*** **6.** *Seismol.* The place of origin of an earthquake.

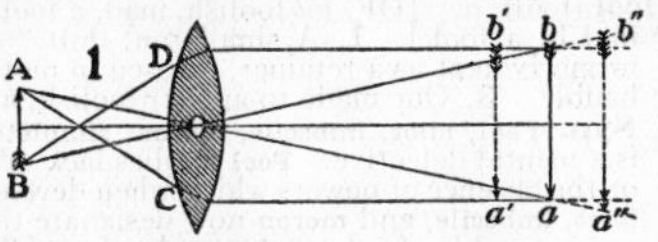

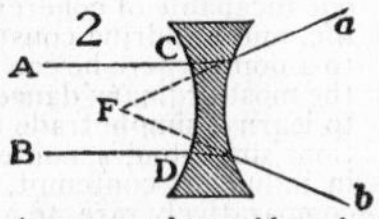

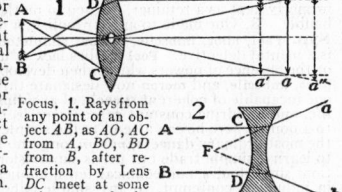

Focus. 1. Rays from any point of an object *AB*, as *AO, AC* from *A*, *BO, BD* from *B*, after refraction by Lens *DC* meet at some point, as *a, b*, the *Real Foci* for *A, B*. A screen at *ba* would receive the rays of all points in *AB*, and show a clear inverted image of *AB*. At *b'a'* or at *b''a''*, the screen would receive the rays from each point of *AB* at more than one point, and the image would be blurred (out of focus). 2. Parallel rays *AC, BD* refracted by Lens *CD* to *ab* appear to issue from *F*, the *Virtual Focus.*

— *v. t.;* FO'CUSED (fō'kŭst) or FO'CUSSED; FO'CUS·ING or FO'CUS·SING. **1.** To bring to a focus. **2.** To adjust the focus of (the eye, a lens, etc.). — *v. i.* To come to a focus.

fod'der (fŏd'ẽr), *n.* [AS. *fōdor.*] That which is fed out to domestic animals; esp., coarse food for cattle, horses, and sheep. — *v. t.* To feed with or as with fodder.

fodg'el (fŏj'ĕl), *adj. Scot.* Squat; plump.

foe (fō), *n.* [AS. *fāh* hostile, *gefā* foe.] **1.** One who entertains enmity, hatred, grudge, or malice against another; an enemy. **2.** An enemy in war; a hostile army; an adversary. **3.** One who opposes on principle; an ill-wisher. **4.** Anything prejudicial or injurious. — **Syn.** See ENEMY.

foehn (fûn), *n.* [G. dial. (Swiss), fr. L. *Favonius* west wind.] A warm dry wind blowing down a mountain side. Cf. CHINOOK, 3 **b.**

foe'man (fō'măn), *n.* A foe.

foe'tal, foe'tus, etc. Vars. of FETAL, etc.

fog (fŏg; 74), *n.* [ME. *fogge.*] **1.** A second growth of grass. **2.** *Scot.* Any moss.

fog, *n.* [Prob. fr. Dan. *fog* spray, shower, driving snow.] **1.** Vapor condensed to fine particles of water and obscuring vision near the ground. International symbol, ≡. It differs from cloud only in being near the ground. **2.** Any murky condition of the atmosphere, or any substance causing it. **3.** A state of mental confusion. **4.** *Photog.* Cloudiness of those parts of a developed film or a photograph which should be clear. — **Syn.** See HAZE. — *v. t.;* FOGGED (fŏgd); FOG'GING. **1.** To envelop as with fog; to obscure; hence, to perplex; confuse. **2.** *Photog.* To render semiopaque or cloudy, as a plate, as by exposure to stray light. — *v. i.* **1.** To become covered, or thick, with fog. **2.** To become blurred, as with fog. **3.** *Photog.* To show indistinctly, as the image on a negative.

fog'bow' (fŏg'bō'), *n.* A nebulous arch of white or yellowish light, sometimes seen in fog, etc.

fog'dog' (fŏg'dŏg'; 74), *n.* A luminous spot sometimes seen in fog near the horizon; — called also *seadog.*

fog'gage (fŏg'ĭj), *n. Scot.* Moss; fog.

fog'gy (fŏg'ĭ), *adj.;* FOG'GI·ER (-ĭ·ẽr); FOG'GI·EST. **1.** Filled or abounding with fog; misty. **2.** Beclouded; muddled. **3.** *Photog.* Fogged. — **fog'gi·ly,** *adv.* — **fog'gi·ness,** *n.*

fog'horn' (-hôrn'), *n.* A horn sounded as a fog signal; hence, figuratively, a loud hoarse voice.

fo'gram (fō'grăm), **fo'grum** (-grŭm), *adj.* Old-fashioned.

fo'gy (fō'gĭ), *n.; pl.* FOGIES (-gĭz). Also **fo'gey.** A person who is behind the times, overconservative, or slow; — usually with *old.* — **fo'gy·ish,** *adj.* — **fo'gy·ism** (-ĭz'm), *n.*

foi'ble (foi'b'l), *n.* [OF., feeble. See FEEBLE.] **1.** A failing; a weak point; frailty. **2.** The weaker part of a sword blade, between the middle and point; — opposed to *forte.* — **Syn.** See FAULT.

‖**foie gras** (fwȧ' grä'). [F.] Fat liver, esp. of a goose. It is usually imported in the form of a pâté. See PÂTÉ, 2.

foil (foil), *v. t.* [ME. *foilen,* irreg. fr. OF. *fouler* to trample.] **1.** *Obs. exc. Hunting.* To trample. **2.** To defeat; to render (an effort) vain; balk. — **Syn.** See FRUSTRATE. — *n.* **1.** Failure; defeat; frustration. **2.** A light, blunt sword, having a button at the point, for fencing; hence, *pl.*, the art or practice of fencing with a foil. **3.** The track or trail of an animal.

foil, *n.* [OF. *foil, fueil,* fr. L. *folium.*] **1.** A leaf or very thin sheet of metal; as, tin *foil.* **2.** Anything that serves by contrast of color or quality to adorn or set off another thing to advantage. **3.** *Arch.* The space between the cusps in Gothic architecture; a rounded or leaflike ornament, in windows, niches, etc. Cf. FOLIATION, 3; BALL-FLOWER, *Illust.* **4.** *Jewelry.* A thin leaf of metal silvered, burnished, and colored, used to give color or brilliancy to pastes and inferior stones. — *v. t.* **1.** To back, or cover, with foil. **2.** To enhance, or set off, by contrast. **3.** *Arch.* To adorn with foils.

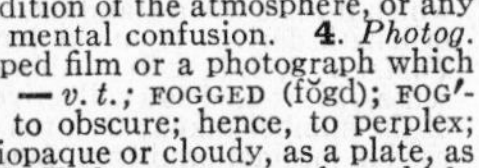

Foils, 3.

foils'man (foilz'măn), *n.* One who wields a foil, as in fencing.

foin (foin), *v. i. Archaic.* To thrust with a sword; lunge. — *n. Archaic.* A pass in fencing; a lunge.

foi'son (foi'z'n), *n.* [OF., fr. L. *fusio.* See FUSION.] **1.** *Archaic.* Rich harvest; abundance. **2.** *Obs. exc. Dial.* Vigor; strength; *pl.*, resources.

foist (foist), *v. t.* To insert surreptitiously; to pass off (something spurious) as genuine or worthy.

Fok'ker (fŏk'ẽr), *n.* A trade-mark for any of various airplanes.

fold (fōld), *v. t.* [AS. *fealdan.*] **1.** To lap or lay in plaits or folds. **2.** To lay or clasp together; to lay close to the body; as, the bird *folds* its wings; to *fold* one's arms. **3.** To enclose within, or as if within, folds; to envelop; embrace; surround. — *v. i.* **1.** To become folded, plaited, or doubled. **2.** To fail completely; collapse; — often with *up.* — *n.* **1.** A doubling or folding; also, a part laid over on another part; a plait. **2.** That which is folded together, or which infolds. **3.** *Geol.* A bend or flexure produced in rock by forces operative after the depositing or consolidation of the rock.

fold, *n.* [AS. *fald, falod.*] **1.** A pen, or enclosure, for sheep. **2.** A flock of sheep; figuratively, the church or a church. — *v. t.* To pen up, or confine in a fold, as sheep.

-fold. [AS. *-feald.*] A suffix used with numerals to form adjectives and adverbs, denoting multiplication or increase in a geometrical ratio, the doubling, tripling, etc., of anything; as, four*fold,* four times, increased in a quadruple ratio.

fold'boat' (fōld'bōt'), *n.* = FALTBOAT.

fold'er (fōl'dẽr), *n.* **1.** One who or that which folds. **2.** A small folded but unstitched booklet; as, a railroad timetable *folder.* **3.** A binder, as for loose papers.

fol'de·rol' (fŏl'dē·rŏl'; -rōl'). Var. of FALDERAL.

fo'li·a (fō'lĭ·ȧ), *n., pl.* of FOLIUM.

fo'li·a'ceous (-ā'shŭs), *adj.* [L. *foliaceus,* fr. *folium* leaf.] **1.** *Bot.* Belonging to, or like, a foliage leaf. **2.** *Mineral.* Consisting of leaves or thin laminae. **3.** *Zool.* Leaflike in form or mode of growth.

fo'li·age (fō'lĭ·ĭj; fōl'yĭj), *n.* [F. and L.; F. *feuillage,* fr. *feuille* leaf, fr. L. *folia.*] **1.** Collectively, the mass of leafage of a plant as produced in nature. **2.** A representation of leaves, flowers, and branches, in architecture, as an ornament. — **fo'li·aged** (fō'lĭ·ĭjd; fōl'yĭjd), *adj.*

fo'li·ar (fō'lĭ·ẽr), *adj.* Consisting of, or pertaining to, leaves.

fo'li·ate (-āt), *adj.* [L. *foliatus* leaved, leafy, fr. *folium* leaf.] **1.** *Bot.* Furnished with leaves; leafy; — often used in combination, as in flabelli*foliate.* **2.** Resembling a leaf or leaves; specif., having leaves, laminae, or leaflike projections. — (-āt), *v. t. & i.* **1.** To spread over with foil, esp. tin foil. **2.** To divide into leaves, or laminae. **3.** *Arch.* To form into, or ornament with, foils or foliage. — **fo'li·at'ed** (-āt'ĕd; -ĭd), *adj.*

fo'li·a'tion (-ā'shŭn), *n.* **1.** Act or process of forming into a leaf or leaves; also, state of being in leaf; — said of a plant. **2.** Act of coating with amalgam, as in making looking glasses. **3.** *Arch.* The enrichment of an opening by foils, etc. See FOIL, TRACERY, *Illusts.* **4.** *Art.* **a** Ornamentation with foliage. **b** A leaflike ornament or decoration. **5.** *Bot.* = VERNATION. **6.** *Goldbeating, etc.* Act of beating a metal into a thin plate, or foil. **7.** *Petrog.* Foliated texture.

fo'li·a·ture (fō'lĭ·ȧ·tūr), *n.* Foliage; leafage.

fo'lic (fō'lĭk; fŏl'ĭk), *adj.* [L. *folium* leaf.] Pert. to or designating a nitrogenous acid (**folic acid**), a growth-promoting vitamin belonging to the B complex, abundant in leaves and animal tissues.

fo'li·o (fō'lĭ·ō; fōl'yō; 58), *n.; pl.* FOLIOS (-ōz; -yōz). [Ablative of L. *folium* leaf.] **1.** A leaf of a book or manuscript. **2.** A sheet of paper once folded. **3.** A book made of sheets each folded once (four pages to the sheet); hence, a book of the largest kind; according to the American Library Association scale, a book more than 30 cm. in height. **4.** The size or form of a folio book. Abbr. *fol.* **5.** *Bookkeeping.* A page in an account book; sometimes, two opposite pages bearing the same serial number. **6.** *Law.* A certain number of words (England, 72 or 90; U. S., 100) taken as a unit in a document for measurement or reference. **7.** *Print.* The page number. Even folios are on the left-hand pages and odd folios on the right-hand. — *adj.* Formed of sheets each folded once, making two leaves, or four pages; as, a *folio* edition. — *v. t.;* -LI·OED (-ōd; -yōd); -LI·O·ING. To put a serial number on each folio or page of (a book or manuscript); to page.

fo'li·o·late (fō'lĭ·ō·lāt; fō·lī'ō·lāt), *adj.* [From *foliole,* fr. NL. *foliolum,* dim. fr. L. *folium* leaf.] *Bot.* Pertaining to, or consisting of, leaflets; — often used in combination.

fo'li·ose (fō'lĭ·ōs), *adj.* Also, *Rare,* **fo'li·ous** (-ŭs). [L. *foliosus,* fr. *folium* leaf.] *Bot.* Leafy; foliaceous.

-fo'li·ous (-fō'lĭ·ŭs). [L. *folium.*] An adjective suffix meaning *leaf.*

fo'li·um (fō'lĭ·ŭm), *n.; pl.* -UMS (-ŭmz), FOLIA (-ȧ). [L., a leaf.] **1.** *Geol.* A thin layer, esp. in metamorphic rocks. **2.** *Geom.* A loop; a leaf-shaped arc (of a curve) closed at both ends by the same node.

folk (fōk), *n.; pl.* FOLK and FOLKS (fōks). [AS. *folc.*] **1.** A group of kindred people, forming a tribe or nation. **2.** In a people bound together by ties of race, language, religion, etc., that great proportion of its number which determines the group character and tends to preserve its civilization, customs, etc., unchanged. **3.** People; persons; as, rural *folk; folks* say. **4.** *pl. Colloq.* The persons of one's own family; relatives.

— *adj.* Of or pertaining to the folk; designating songs, dances, etc., originated or used among the common people; as, **folk air, folk dance, folk laws, folk music, folk right, folk song, folk story, folk tale, folk tune.**

‖**Fol'ke·ting', -thing'** (fōl'kĕ·tĭng'), *n.* [Dan. See FOLK; THING assembly.] Lower house of the Danish legislature.

folk'lore' (fōk'lōr'; 70), *n.* Traditional customs, beliefs, tales, or sayings, preserved unreflectively among a people; hence, the science which investigates the life and spirit of a people as revealed in such lore.

folk'moot' (-mōōt'), **folk'mote'** (-mōt'), *n.* Also **folk'mot'** (-mōt'). [AS. *folcmōt* folk meeting.] *Hist.* An assembly of the people; esp., *A.-S. Law,* a general assembly of the people. Cf. GEMOT, MOOT, WITENAGEMOT.

folk'way' (-wā'), *n.* Any way of thinking, feeling, or acting, common to members of a social group.

fol'li·cle (fŏl'ĭ·k'l), *n.* [L. *folliculus* small bag, husk, pod, dim. of *follis* bellows, inflated ball.] **1.** *Bot.* A dry one-celled monocarpellary fruit, dehiscent only by one suture, as the fruits of the peony, larkspur, and milkweed. **2.** *Anat.* A small cavity; as, a hair *follicle,* the depression from which a hair grows; also, a crypt. — **fol·lic'u·lar** (fŏ·lĭk'ū·lẽr), *adj.* — **fol·lic'u·late** (-lāt), *adj.* — **fol·lic'u·lat'ed** (-lāt'ĕd; -ĭd), *adj.*

fol'low (fŏl'ō), *v. t.* [AS. *folgian, fylgan.*] **1.** To go or come after; to attend. **2.** To go in pursuit of; to seek to gain or attain. **3.** To accept as authority; to obey. **4.** To copy after; take after. **5.** To walk in, or proceed along, as a road or course; also, to attend upon closely, as a profession or calling. **6.** To pursue with hostility. **7.**

To succeed in order, as of time, rank, or natural sequence. **8.** To result from, as an effect from a cause. **9.** To keep the eyes or mind fixed upon; as, he *followed* the argument.

Syn. **Follow, pursue, chase, trail** mean to go immediately or shortly after. **Follow** usually implies a lead or, sometimes, a guidance; **pursue** suggests an attempt to overtake, reach, attain, or the like; **chase** suggests fast pursuit of something fleeing, running, or the like; **trail** suggests a following in one's tracks. — **Ant.** Precede.

— *v. i.* **1.** To go or come after a person or thing in place, time, or sequence; hence, to attend. **2.** To result or occur as a consequence. **3.** To pursue; to strive for attainment.

Syn. **Follow, succeed, ensue, supervene** mean to come after something or, less often, someone. **Follow** may imply a coming after in time, sequence, logic, and the like; **succeed** implies a coming after in a sequence, usually determined by inheritance, election, the laws of rank, or the like; **ensue** implies logical sequence or the operation of some principle such as necessity; **supervene** suggests the following of something added and, often, unforeseen or unpredictable.

— *n.* Act or process of following; specif., in billiards, a shot (**follow shot**) made by hitting the cue ball above the center and thus causing it to continue to roll after impact with the object ball.

fol'low·er (fŏl'ō·ẽr), *n.* **1.** One who follows; variously, a pursuer, attendant, disciple, dependent associate, retainer. **2.** *Colloq.* A sweetheart; beau. **3.** *Mach.* A part of a machine that receives motion from another part. See STUFFING BOX, *Illust.*

Syn. **Follower, adherent, disciple, partisan, satellite** mean one who attaches himself to the person or opinions of another. **Follower** implies nothing more than this; **adherent** suggests a close and persistent attachment; **disciple** suggests a devoted allegiance to the teaching of one regarded as a master; **partisan** suggests a zealous, often prejudiced, attachment; **satellite** suggests an attachment marked by constant and obsequious attendance.

fol'low·ing, *n.* One's followers, adherents, or dependents, collectively. — *adj.* **1.** Next after; succeeding. Abbr. (with reference to pages, chapters, etc.) *f.*, pl. *ff.* **2.** That is now immediately to follow or be treated of.

fol'low-through' (fŏl'ō·thro͞o'), *n.* Act of following through, as in the swing of a bat or club; also, that part of the stroke following the striking of the ball.

fol'low-up' (-ŭp'; 2), *adj.* **a** Of or pertaining to renewed or repeated action; as, a *follow-up* visit. **b** *Colloq. Com.* Pertaining to a second or later offer, as to a possible customer; as, a *follow-up* letter. — (fŏl'ō·ŭp'), *n.* *Colloq. Com.* A system of pursuing an initial effort, as in advertising, by supplementary action.

fol'ly (fŏl'ĭ), *n.; pl.* -LIES (-ĭz). [OF. *folie*, fr. *fol* foolish, mad. See FOOL.] **1.** State of being foolish; levity or weakness of mind. **2.** A foolish act or idea. **3.** Scandalous crime; sin. **4.** An unprofitable undertaking, esp. a building left unfinished because the cost proved too great for the builder's resources.

Fol'som man (fŏl'sŭm). *Anthropol.* One of a Stone Age people supposed to have lived in North America at the end of the last glacial period; — from artifacts found in 1925, near Folsom, New Mexico.

fo·ment' (fō·mĕnt'), *v. t.* [F. *fomenter*, fr. L. *fomentare*, fr. *fomentum* a warm application or lotion, fr. *fovere* to warm.] **1.** To bathe with warm water or medicated liquid. **2.** To nurse to life or activity; to excite, rouse, or instigate; as, to *foment* revolt. — **Syn.** See INCITE. — **fo·ment'er,** *n.*

fo'men·ta'tion (fō'mĕn·tā'shŭn), *n.* **1.** Excitation; instigation. **2.** *Med.* **a** Application of warm moist substances, as wet cloths, to the body to ease pain. **b** Lotion thus applied.

‖**fond** (fôN; *E.* fŏnd), *n.* [F. See FUND.] **1.** Background; basis; fundamental character. **2.** Fund, stock, or store.

fond (fŏnd), *adj.* [ME. *fonned*, past part. of *fonnen* to be foolish, fr. *fon* fool, foolish.] **1.** *Archaic & Dial.* Foolish; silly; simple. **2.** Greatly pleased; desirous. **3. a** Foolishly loving; weakly indulgent. **b** Affectionate; loving; as, a *fond* mother. **4.** Doted on; regarded with unreasoning affection.

Syn. **Fond, infatuated, insensate** mean made blindly or stupidly foolish. **Fond** implies judgment misled by excessive affection, undue optimism, or the like; **infatuated**, a weakening of judgment under the influence of passion or unreasoning emotion; **insensate**, the loss of feeling and judgment under the influence of greed, hatred, desire for revenge, and the like.

fon'dant (fŏn'dănt; *F.* fôN'däN'), *n.* [F., lit., melting, pres. part. of *fondre* to melt. See FOUND to cast.] A creamy preparation of sugar, used as the basis of much candy.

fon'dle (fŏn'd'l), *v. t.;* FON'DLED (-d'ld); FON'DLING (-dlĭng). [Freq. of obs. *fond* to dote.] **1.** *Obs.* To coddle. **2.** To handle tenderly or lovingly; to caress. — *v. i.* To manifest fondness, esp. by caresses. — **Syn.** See CARESS.

fon'dler (fŏn'dlẽr), *n.* One who fondles.

fond'ly (fŏnd'lĭ), *adv.* **1.** *Archaic.* Foolishly. **2.** In a fond manner; affectionately. **3.** In a willingly credulous manner.

fond'ness, *n.* **1.** *Obs.* Foolishness; folly; weakness. **2.** Doting affection; also, appetite or relish.

fon·due' (fŏn·do͞o'; fŏn'do͞o; *F.* fôN'dü'), *n.* Also **fon·du'.** [F. *fondue*, fr. fem. of *fondu*, past part. of *fondre*, to melt.] A dish made of melted cheese, butter, eggs, and, often, milk and bread crumbs.

F1 layer (ĕf'wŭn'). *Radio.* A layer in the ionosphere which reflects radio waves, occurring at varying heights, 90 to 150 miles above the earth's surface. It exists only in the daytime and at certain seasons.

‖**fons et o·ri'go** (fŏnz ĕt ō·rī'gō). [L.] Source and origin.

font (fŏnt), *n.* Also **fount** (fount; fŏnt). [F. *fonte*, fr. *fondre*. See FOUND to cast.] *Print.* An assortment of type of one size and style.

font, *n.* [AS., fr. L. *fons, fontis*, spring, fountain.] **1.** A basin in which water is contained for baptizing. **2.** A fountain; spring; a source; origin. **3.** A receptacle for holy water. Cf. STOUP, 2. — **font'al** (fŏn'tăl; -t'l), *adj.* *Rare.*

fon'ta·nel', fon'ta·nelle' (fŏn'tȧ·nĕl'), *n.* [F. *fontanelle*, prop. a little fountain, fr. *fontaine* fountain. See FOUNTAIN.] **1.** An opening for the discharge of secretions. **2.** *Anat.* One of the intervals, closed by membranous structures, between the incompleted angles of the parietal bones and the neighboring bones of a fetal or young skull.

food (fo͞od), *n.* [AS. *fōda.*] **1.** Nutritive material taken into an organism for growth, work, or repair and for maintaining the vital processes. The complex organic substances that form a large part of the food of animals fall into three main classes: proteins, carbohydrates, and fats. Cf. CALORIE **b**, VITAMIN. **2.** Nutriment in solid form, as opposed to *drink.* **3.** Anything that nourishes or sustains.

Syn. **Food, aliment, pabulum, nutriment, nourishment, sustenance** mean material feeding and supporting the body. **Food** applies to anything that enters the system, is assimilated by it, and contributes to its life, growth, and power for work; **aliment** and **pabulum**, now more common figuratively, are equivalents of *food*, but *aliment* applies usually to that which nourishes and *pabulum* to an article of diet; **nutriment** and **nourishment** imply that which is necessary for health and growth, and **sustenance** that which is necessary for the maintenance of life.

food'stuff' (-stŭf'), *n.* **1.** Anything used as food. **2.** Any substance of food value, as protein, fat, etc., entering into the composition of a food.

fool (fo͞ol), *n.* [OF. *fol* foolish, mad, a fool, fr. L. *follis* bellows, bag, in LL. a fool.] **1.** A simpleton; dolt. **2.** A professional buffoon formerly kept as a retainer, dressed in motley with cap and bells and bauble. **3.** One made to appear foolish; a dupe.

Syn. **Fool, idiot, imbecile, moron, simpleton, natural** mean one who is a mental defective. **Fool** implies lack of understanding and reason or the absence of powers which when developed make for intelligence; **idiot, imbecile,** and **moron** now designate three grades of fools; *idiot*, one incapable of coherent speech, of avoiding the common dangers of life, and requiring constant care; *imbecile*, one who can be educated to a point where he can attend to the simplest of his wants and avoid the most ordinary dangers; *moron*, one who has sufficient intelligence to learn a simple trade but needs supervision in his work and recreation; **simpleton**, a nontechnical term, applies to any fool or, as used in indulgent contempt, to any simple-minded person; **natural**, now comparatively rare, to anyone congenitally feeble-minded.

— *v. i.* **1.** To play the fool; to trifle. **2.** *Colloq.* To tamper; to waste time. **3.** *Archaic.* To act as a jester. — *v. t.* To deceive; dupe. — ***fool away.*** *Colloq.* To get rid of foolishly.

fool, *n.* [A special use of *fool*, n.] *Cookery.* A sweet made of stewed fruit and whipped cream.

fool'er·y (fo͞ol'ẽr·ĭ), *n.; pl.* FOOLERIES (-ĭz). **1.** The habit of fooling; behavior of a fool. **2.** A foolish act or deed.

fool'har'dy (fo͞ol'här'dĭ), *adj.;* FOOL'HAR'DI·ER (-dĭ·ẽr); FOOL'HAR'DI·EST. Daring without judgment; foolishly bold. — **Syn.** See ADVENTUROUS. — **fool'har'di·ly,** *adv.* — **fool'har'di·ness,** *n.*

fool'ing, *n.* Act of fooling or jesting; humor for fooling.

fool'ish (fo͞ol'ĭsh), *adj.* **1.** Exhibiting folly; unwise. **2.** Proceeding from folly. **3.** Absurd; preposterous; silly. **4.** *Archaic.* Paltry; humble. — **Syn.** See SIMPLE. — **fool'ish·ly,** *adv.* — **fool'ish·ness,** *n.*

fool'proof' (-pro͞of'; 2), *adj.* So simple, strong, etc., as not to be misused, damaged, etc., even by a fool.

fools'cap' (fo͞olz'kăp'), *n.* In senses 1 & 2 often **fool's cap.** **1.** A cap or hood, usually with bells, worn by jesters. **2.** A conical dunce's cap, sometimes worn by school children as a punishment. **3.** Paper in sheets measuring approximately 13 × 16 or 17 inches; — from the watermark used by old papermakers.

fool's errand. A silly, profitless adventure or undertaking.

fool's gold. Iron or copper pyrites, resembling gold in color.

fool's paradise. A state of illusive happiness.

fool's'-pars'ley, *n.* A European weed (*Aethusa cynapium*) resembling parsley but nauseous and poisonous.

foot (fo͝ot), *n.; pl.* FEET (fēt), sometimes FOOTS (fo͝ots). [AS. *fōt*, pl. *fēt.*] **1.** The terminal part of the leg; that part of an animal upon which it rests when standing, or upon which it moves. **2.** A measure of length derived from the length of the human foot (see MEASURE, *Tables* 1, 2, 3, 5, & 9). Abbr. *ft.* (sing. & pl.). Symbol '. In this sense, *foot* is used as a collective plural when preceded by a designation of the number taken; as, a ten-*foot* pole. **3.** The foot as the member used in locomotion; hence, figuratively, motion or power of walking or running; step; also, speed. **4.** Something resembling a foot in position or use; lowest part or base; bottom; also, the last of a series; the end. **5.** That part of anything that is in proximity to or covers the feet; as, the *foot* of a stocking. **6. a** That which is placed at the bottom or foot, as the sum of an account or the refrain of a song. **b** (*pl.* FOOTS) In refining processes, the bottom portion; sediment; dregs. **7.** *Mech.* In a sewing machine, the piece that holds the cloth steady; — called also *presser foot.* **8.** *Mil.* Soldiers who march and fight on foot; infantry. **9.** *Naut.* The lower edge (of a sail). **10** *Print.* Of a type, the lowest part of the body on either side of the groove. See TYPE, *Illust.* **11.** *Pros.* A group of syllables marked off as constituting a metrical unit in verse, analogous to a measure in music.

— *v. i.* **1.** To tread to measure or music; to dance. **2.** To walk; — opposed to *ride* or *fly.* **3.** To move, esp. as a ship; as, the yacht *foots* fast. — *v. t.* **1.** To tread; to walk, run, or dance, on, over, or through. **2. a** *Obs. exc. Dial.* To kick; to spurn. **b** To seize or strike with the talons, as a falcon. **3. a** To sum up, as the numbers in a column. **b** *Colloq.* To pay (a bill, expenses, etc.). **4.** To make or renew the foot of, as of a stocking.

foot'age (fo͝ot'ĭj), *n.* Length or quantity expressed in feet; specif.: **a** *Lumber.* Board feet. See BOARD FOOT. **b** *Motion Pictures.* The total number of running feet of film used in photographing any subject.

foot'-and-mouth' dis·ease'. *Veter.* An acute, contagious disease of cattle, sheep, swine, etc., caused by a filtrable virus, and characterized by vesicles and ulcers in the mouth and about the hoofs.

foot'ball' (fo͝ot'bôl'), *n.* **1.** An inflated ball to be kicked in sport. **2.** A field game played with a football, in which each of two contesting teams tries to kick or carry the ball to or through its opponent's goal or goal line. There are three principal varieties: ***Rugby***, in which the ball may be carried, kicked, or thrown, provided it is not thrown forward, and a player in possession of the ball may be tackled bodily; ***association*** (*or* ***soccer***), in which all use of the arms or hands is prohibited except to the goalkeeper, and the ball is propelled by kicking, or striking it with the head, shoulder, or other parts of the body except the arms; ***American***, a development of Rugby, in which one side is allowed undisputed possession of the ball at the moment when it is put in play, players may run ahead of the man with the ball to prevent his being tackled, the forward pass is permitted, and, in general, the play is more systematized and formal. The ball used in the Rugby and American games is ellipsoidal in shape, while the association football is spherical. **3.** Hence, a mere toy or plaything; as, the issue became a *football* of party politics.

foot'board' (-bōrd'; 70), *n.; pl.* FOOTBOARDS (-bōrdz'). **1.** A board or narrow platform on which to brace the feet or on which one may stand. **2.** A board forming the foot of a bedstead.

foot'boy' (-boi'), *n.* A page; an attendant.

foot brake. A brake operated by foot pressure.

foot′bridge′ (fo͝ot′brĭj′), *n.* A bridge for foot passengers only.
foot′–can′dle, *n. Photom.* A unit of illumination, being the direct illumination on a surface everywhere one foot from a uniform point source of one international candle. See CANDLE, *n.*, 3; LUMEN.
foot′cloth′ (fo͝ot′klôth′; 74), *n.; pl.* FOOTCLOTHS (-klôthz′; -klôths′). **1.** *Obs.* A caparison for a horse. **2.** A carpet.
foot′ed (fo͝ot′ĕd; -ĭd), *adj.* Having a foot or feet, or such or so many feet; — often used in combinations, as in bare*footed*, four-*footed*, splay*footed*, wing-*footed*.
foot′er (fo͝ot′ẽr), *n.* **1.** A walker. **2.** A person or thing a (specified) number of feet in measure; as, a six-*footer*.
foot′fall′ (-fôl′), *n.* A footstep; also, sound of a footstep.
foot′gear′ (-gēr′), *n.* Covering for the feet, as shoes.
foot′hill′ (-hĭl′), *n.* A hill at the foot of higher hills.
foot′hold′ (-hōld′), *n.* A hold for the feet; footing.
foot′ing, *n.* **1.** Standing; stable placing of the feet. **2.** Place for the foot to rest on; foothold; hence, basis for operation. **3.** A moving on foot; specif., walk; tread; dance; also, progress; coming. **4. a** Material for making the feet, as of stockings. **b** Act of putting a foot to anything. **5.** Relative position; status; condition. **6.** Act of adding up a column of figures; the sum total of such a column. **7.** *Arch.* An enlargement at the lower end of a wall, pier, or column, to distribute the load.
foo′tle (fo͞o′t'l; fo͝ot″l), *n. Slang.* Twaddle; drivel. — *adj. Slang.* Trivial; silly.
foot′less (fo͝ot′lĕs; -lĭs), *adj.* **1.** Having no feet; hence, without foundation; unsubstantial. **2.** *Colloq.* Clumsy; stupid.
foot′lights′ (-līts′), *n. pl.* **a** A row of lights in the front of the stage, and on a level therewith, in a theater, etc. **b** Figuratively, the stage or theater.
foo′tling (fo͞o′tlĭng; fo͝ot′lĭng), *adj.* [Prop., trifling, fr. FOOTLE.] *Slang.* Trivial; foolish and useless.
foot′–loose′ (fo͝ot′lo͞os′), *adj.* Free; untrammeled.
foot′man (-măn), *n.* **1.** *Archaic.* A walker. **2. a** *Obs.* A footpad. **b** *Rare.* A foot soldier. **3.** A male servant whose duties are to attend the door, table, etc.
foot′mark′ (-märk′), *n.* A footprint.
foot′note′ (-nōt′), *n.* A note at the foot of a page.
foot′pace′ (-pās′), *n.* A walking pace or step.
foot′pad′ (-păd′), *n.* [See 1st PAD.] A highwayman on foot.
foot′path′ (-pàth′), *n.* A narrow path for pedestrians only.
foot′–pound′, *n. Mech.* A unit of energy, or work, being equal to the work done in raising one pound avoirdupois against the force of gravity the height of one foot. Abbr. *fp.*, *F.P.*, or *f.p.*
foot′–pound′al, *n.* A unit of work, the work done when a force of one poundal acts through a distance of one foot. It is equal to a foot-pound divided by the acceleration of gravity (32.16) expressed in feet per second per second.
foot′print′ (fo͝ot′prĭnt′), *n.* An impression of the foot.
foot′rest′ (-rĕst′), *n.* A support for the feet.
foot′rope′ (-rōp′), *n. Naut.* **a** The rope rigged below a yard, on which men stand when reefing or furling. **b** That part of the boltrope sewed to the lower edge of a sail.
foot soldier. A soldier who serves on foot; infantryman.
foot′sore′ (-sōr′; 70), *adj.* Having sore or tender feet.
foot′stalk′ (-stôk′), *n.* A petiole, pedicel, or peduncle.
foot′stall′ (-stôl′), *n.* **1.** The stirrup of a woman's saddle. **2.** *Arch.* The plinth, base, or pedestal of a pillar.
foot′step′ (-stĕp′), *n.* **1.** A footfall; tread; also, distance covered by a step. **2.** The mark of the foot; track. **3.** A step on which to ascend or descend.
foot′stock′ (-stŏk′), *n. Mach.* A tailstock or loose headstock, as of a lathe.
foot′stool′ (-sto͞ol′), *n.* A low stool to support the feet.
foot′–ton′, *n. Mech.* A unit of energy or work, being equal to the work done in raising one ton against the force of gravity through the height of one foot.
foot′way′ (fo͝ot′wā′), *n.* A narrow way or path.
foot′wear′ (-wâr′), *n.* Wearing apparel for the feet, esp. boots or shoes.
foot′work′ (-wûrk′), *n.* The management of the feet, and work done with them, as in boxing, football, tennis, etc.
foot′worn′ (-wōrn′; 70), *adj.* Worn by, or wearied in, the feet; as, a *footworn* path; a *footworn* traveler.
foo′ty (fo͞o′tĭ), *adj.;* FOO′TI·ER (-tĭ·ẽr); FOO′TI·EST. [F. *foutu.*] *Slang & Dial. Eng.* Poor; paltry.
foo′zle (fo͞o′z'l), *v. t. & i.;* FOO′ZLED (-z'ld); FOO′ZLING (-zlĭng). To bungle; to manage or play unskillfully. — *n.* **1.** *Colloq.* A stupid fellow. **2.** A bungling act or stroke, as in golf.
fop (fŏp), *n.* **1.** *Obs.* A silly person; a conceited pretender to wit. **2.** A coxcomb; dandy. — *v. t. Obs.* To fool; dupe.
fop′per·y (fŏp′ẽr·ĭ), *n.; pl.* -IES (-ĭz). **1.** *Rare.* Foolishness; folly. **2.** The behavior, dress, or other mark of a fop.
fop′pish (-ĭsh), *adj.* **1.** *Obs.* Foolish. **2.** Foplike; dandyish. — **fop′pish·ly,** *adv.* — **fop′pish·ness,** *n.*
for (fôr; 4), *prep.* [AS. *for, fore.*] In the most general sense, indicating that in consideration of which, in view of which, or with reference to which, anything is, is done, or takes place; as: **1.** *Obs.* Before. **2.** Indicating the end with reference to which anything acts, serves, or is done; as, money *for* studying. **3.** Instead of; in place of; as, an eye *for* an eye. **4.** In behalf of; in support of; as, to campaign *for* a cause. **5.** Used with a noun or personal pronoun in the objective case followed by an infinitive to form an idiomatic equivalent for the noun clause; as, *for* him to submit (that he should submit) would be shameful; also, incumbent upon; as, debts *for* me to pay. **6.** Indicating that in the character of which anything is regarded or treated; as, to know *for* a fact. **7.** Indicating the cause, motive, or occasion of an act or condition; hence, because of; as, cursed himself *for* showing leniency. **8.** Notwithstanding; in spite of; — usually with *all;* as, you don't convince me *for* all your clever arguments. **9.** Indicating equality or proportion between numbers or quantities when compared; as, *for* one poet there are a dozen poetasters. **10.** As regards; concerning; as, so much *for* that. **11.** Expressing duration of time or extension of space; as, *for* miles about.
— ***for as much as,*** or ***forasmuch as.*** In consideration that; seeing that; since. — ***for ever.*** Eternally. — ***for ever and a day.*** Emphatically forever.
— *conj.* Because.

for-. [AS.] A prefix, no longer active in English, denoting *off, away.* It sometimes indicates neglect or refusal to do, but often has merely intensive force.
for′age (fŏr′ĭj), *n.* [OF. *fourage, forrage,* fr. *forre, fuerre,* fodder, straw, of Teut. origin.] **1.** Food for animals, esp. domestic animals. **2.** Act of foraging; search for provisions, etc. — *v. t.;* FOR′AGED (-ĭjd); FOR′AG·ING (-ĭj·ĭng). [F. *fourrager,* fr. *fourrage.* See FORAGE, *n.*] **1.** To strip of provisions; to collect forage from; now, rarely, to ravage. **2.** To supply with forage. **3.** To secure by foraging. — *v. i.* To wander in search of forage; to secure forage; hence, to ravage. — **for′ag·er** (-ĭj·ẽr), *n.*
for′ag·ing ant (-ĭj·ĭng). Any species of ant that goes out in search of food in companies, esp. the driver ant.
fo·ra′men (fō·rā′mĕn), *n.; pl.* FORAMINA (-răm′ĭ·nȧ), FORAMENS (-rā′mĕnz). [L., fr. *forare* to pierce.] A small opening, perforation, or orifice. See VERTEBRA, *Illust.*
‖**fo·ra′men mag′num** (măg′nŭm). [L., great opening.] The opening in the skull through which the spinal cord passes to become the medulla oblongata.
for′a·min′i·fer (fŏr′ȧ·mĭn′ĭ·fẽr), *n.* [L. *foramen, -aminis,* foramen + *ferre* to bear.] *Zool.* Any of an order (Foraminifera) of rhizopods, generally having a calcareous shell which in many forms is perforated with minute holes for protrusion of slender pseudopodia. The foraminifers are mostly marine and very small. Chalk and nummulitic limestone are composed chiefly of their shells. — **fo·ram′i·nif′er·al** (fō·răm′ĭ·nĭf′ẽr·ăl), *adj.* — **fo·ram′i·nif′er·ous** (-ŭs), *adj.*
fo·ram′i·nous (fō·răm′ĭ·nŭs), *adj.* Having foramina.
fo·rane′ (fō·rān′), *adj.* [See FOREIGN.] Pertaining to a remote place or thing; foreign; — chiefly in *vicar forane.*
for′ay (fŏr′ā), *v. t. & i.;* FOR′AYED (-ād); FOR′AY·ING. [OF. *forrer* to pillage, fr. *forre, fuerre.* See FORAGE.] To ravage in search of spoils; to pillage. — *n.* A sudden or irregular incursion for war or spoils; a raid. — **for′ay·er** (-ẽr), *n.*
for·bade′, for·bad′ (fŏr·băd′), *pasts of* FORBID.
for·bear′ (fôr·bâr′; 2), *v. t.;* FOR·BORE′ (-bōr′; 70); FOR·BORNE′ (-bōrn′; 70); FOR·BEAR′ING. *Archaic past* FOR·BARE′ (-bâr′). [AS. *forberan.* See FOR-; BEAR to support.] **1.** *Now Dial.* To endure. **2.** *Obs.* To avoid; shun; also, lose. **3.** To refrain from doing, using, expressing, injuring, etc. — *v. i.* **1.** To refrain; abstain; hold back. **2.** To control oneself; to be patient. — **Syn.** See REFRAIN. — **for·bear′er** (fôr·bâr′ẽr), *n.*
for′bear (fôr′bâr; fôr·bâr′). Var. of FOREBEAR, ancestor.
for·bear′ance (fôr·bâr′ăns), *n.* **1.** Act of forbearing; patience. **2.** A refraining from the enforcement of what is due. **3.** Quality of being forbearing; long-suffering.
for·bid′ (fŏr·bĭd′), *v. t.;* FOR·BADE′, FOR·BAD′ (-băd′); FOR·BID′DEN; FOR·BID′DING. *Archaic past* FOR·BID′. [AS. *forbēodan.* See FOR-; BID, *v.*] **1.** To prohibit; interdict. **2. a** To exclude from, or warn off, by command. **b** To bar from appearance or use, as in a sport. **3.** To oppose or prevent, as if by a command. **4.** To accurse; — now only in past part. — **for·bid′der** (-bĭd′ẽr), *n.*
Syn. **Forbid, prohibit, interdict, inhibit** mean to restrain from using, doing, entering, or the like. **Forbid** and **prohibit** are much alike, but *forbid* suggests the restraint of a parent, master, physician, or the like, and *prohibit* that of the law or of the state; **interdict** implies prohibition by civil or ecclesiastical authority, usually for a given time or for a salutary purpose; **inhibit** implies the imposition of restraints or restrictions not only by authority but by the exigencies of time or situation or, now commonly, by one's own conscience.
for·bid′dance (fŏr·bĭd′ăns; -'ns), *n.* Also **for·bid′dal** (-ăl; -'l). Act of forbidding; prohibition.
for·bid′den (-'n), *adj.* Prohibited; interdicted.
for·bid′ding, *adj.* That forbids; prohibiting; esp., repelling approach; repellent. — **for·bid′ding·ly,** *adv.* — **for·bid′ding·ness,** *n.*
for·bore′ (fôr·bōr′; 70), *past of* FORBEAR.
for·borne′ (-bōrn′; 70), *past part.* of FORBEAR.
for·by′, for·bye′ (fôr·bī′), *prep.* [*for* + *by.*] *Obs. exc. Dial.* **a** Hard by; close by. **b** Beside. — *adv. Now Dial.* **1.** Of time, gone by; of motion, to one side. **2.** Besides.
force (fōrs; 70), *n.* [OF., deriv. of L. *fortis* strong.] **1.** Strength or energy; vigor; as: **a** Physical strength or vigor. **b** Power to affect strongly in physical conditions; as, the *force* of a blow. **c** Power of effective action; as, *force* of character. **d** Power to persuade or convince. **2.** Strength for war; hence, any military body organized for offense or defense; *pl.* combined strength; as, the armed *forces.* Hence, a group prepared for action; as, the police *force.* **3.** Power, violence, or constraint exerted upon a person or thing. **4.** *Physics.* The cause of the acceleration of the movement of material bodies, as the cause of a body falling freely, of the movements of two billiard balls in collision, or of the movement of two related magnets. — **Syn.** See POWER. — *v. t.;* FORCED (fōrst); FORC′ING (fōr′sĭng). **1.** To do violence to; esp., to ravish; violate. **2.** To constrain or compel; to coerce. **3.** To impose or cause by necessity. **4.** To impel, wrest, extort, etc., by violence. **5.** To obtain or win by strength or struggle; specif.: **a** To capture by assault. **b** To break open, as a gate or lock. **c** To pass, or effect a passage, through by force, as a hostile country. **6.** To press or urge for acceptance; as, to *force* attentions upon one. **7.** To exert to the utmost; to urge; hence, to strain; to urge to, or produce, by unnatural effort; as, to *force* a laugh. **8.** To hasten, as in growth or productivity, by artificial means; as, to *force* bulbs. **9.** *Obs.* **a** To allow the force of; to value; to care for. **b** To provide with forces; to reinforce. **c** To put in force; to enforce. **10.** *Baseball.* **a** To cause (a base runner) to be put out by compelling him to leave his base and try to get to the next base. **b** To cause (a run) to be scored, or (a runner) to score, by compelling the runner to leave third base and cross home plate; — said of a pitcher who gives a base on balls when the bases are full. **11.** *Cards.* To cause (a player) to trump by leading a suit of which he has no cards, or to show the strength of his hand, or to play (a certain card). — **force′a·ble,** *adj.*
Syn. **Force, compel, coerce, constrain, oblige** mean to make a person or thing yield. **Force,** the general term, implies the exertion of strength, often physical strength, but sometimes something analogous, such as natural or logical necessity; **compel** typically requires a personal object (though sometimes it takes a personal reaction or response) and always suggests the working of irresistible force; **coerce** suggests the exertion of violence or duress; **constrain** suggests the power of that which presses and binds, such as restrictions imposed by nature, necessity, etc.; **oblige** usually implies the constraint of necessity, of law, or the like.

forced (fōrst; 70), *adj.* 1. Compelled by force or necessity; involuntary; compulsory; as, *forced* service; a *forced* landing (of an airplane). 2. Done or produced with force or labor, or by exertion; as, a *forced* laugh.

force feed. In internal-combustion engines, a lubricating system in which the lubricant is supplied under pressure.

force′ful (fōrs′fo͝ol; -f'l), *adj.* Full of, or possessing, force; effective. — **force′ful·ly**, *adv.* — **force′ful·ness**, *n.*

‖**force ma′jeure′** (fôrs′ma′zhûr′). [F.] Superior or irresistible force.

force′meat′ (fōrs′mēt′; 70), *n.* [F. *farce* stuffing + E. *meat.*] *Cookery.* Meat or fish chopped fine and highly seasoned, either served alone or used as a stuffing; farce.

for′ceps (fôr′sĕps), *n.; pl.* FORCEPS or, rarely, FORCEPSES (-ĕz; -ĭz), FORCIPES (-sĭ·pēz). [L. *forceps, -cipis.*] A pair of pincers or tongs, esp. for delicate operations, as those of watchmakers, surgeons, accoucheurs, dentists, etc.

force pump. *Mach.* A pump having a solid piston, or plunger, for drawing and forcing a liquid, as water, through valves. It is adapted for delivering liquid at a height above the pump, or under considerable pressure.

forc′er (fōr′sẽr; 70), *n.* One who or that which forces.

for′ci·ble (fōr′sĭ·b'l), *adj.* 1. Effected by force; as, *forcible* entry. 2. Characterized by force, efficiency, or energy; powerful. — **for′ci·ble·ness**, *n.* — **for′ci·bly**, *adv.*

ford (fōrd; 70), *n.* [AS.] A place where a river, or other water, may be passed by wading. — *v. t.* To cross by a ford. — **ford′a·ble**, *adj.*

for·do′ (fŏr·do͞o′), **fore·do′** (fōr-; 70), *v. t.;* see DO. [AS. *fordōn*, fr. *for-* + *dōn* to do.] 1. *Archaic.* To kill, abolish, or destroy. 2. To exhaust; — in past part.

fore (fōr; 70), *adv.* [AS., adv. & prep.; akin to E. FOR.] 1. In the part that precedes or goes first; — now only as opposed to *aft;* specif., *Naut.*, in or towards the bows of a ship. 2. *Obs.* Formerly; previously. — *prep.* Also **′fore.** *Obs.* **a** Before. **b** In the presence of; — used in oaths. — *conj. Dial.* = BEFORE. — *adj.* Advanced; being or coming first; forward. — *n.* The front; hence, that which is in front; specif., *Naut.*, the foremast, or, sometimes, the bows.

fore, *interj.* [Short for BEFORE.] *Golf.* A word cried by a player about to strike the ball to warn persons in the probable line of its flight.

fore- (fōr-; 70). [See FORE, *adv.*] A prefix denoting *before*, either in position or time; used: 1. (*Accent usually on verbal element*) In verbs, verbal adjectives and nouns, and nouns of agency or action, with the sense of: **a** *In front;* as, *fore*runner. **b** *Beforehand;* as, *fore*ordain. 2. (*Accent usually on prefix*) In other nouns, with the sense of: **a** *Front;* as, *fore*lock; *fore*arm. **b** *Preceding in time;* as, *fore*father.

☞ COMBINATIONS are:

forecited	forekeel	forerank
foreflank	forelimb	forerib
foreflipper	forepaw	foreshoulder
forehatch	forepayment	forespecified
forehatchway	forequoted	forewing

fore and aft. *Naut.* **a** From stem to stern; lengthwise of the vessel; — distinguished from *athwart.* **b** In, at, or towards both the bow and stern.

fore′–and–aft′, *adj. Naut.* 1. Lying, running, or acting in the general line of the length of a vessel; as, *fore-and-aft* sails. 2. Of a vessel or rig (**fore–and–aft rig**), having, mainly, sails bent to gaffs or set on the masts or on stays in the midship line of the vessel. Cf. SQUARE-RIGGED; see BARK, SAIL, YAWL, *Illusts.* — **fore′–and–aft′–rigged′**, *adj.*

fore′–and–aft′er, *n. Colloq. Naut.* A vessel, esp. a schooner, with a fore-and-aft rig.

fore–and–aft sail. Any sail not supported by a yard or yards, usually carried on a gaff, or stay.

fore′arm′ (fōr′ärm′; 70), *n.* In primates, that part of the arm or forelimb between the elbow and the wrist.

fore·arm′ (fōr·ärm′), *v. t.* To arm beforehand.

fore′bear (fōr′bâr; 70), **for′bear** (fôr′bâr), *n.* [*fore-* + *be* + *-er.*] An ancestor; a forefather; — usually in the *pl.*

fore·bode′ (fōr·bōd′; 70), *v. t. & i.* 1. To foretell; portend. 2. To have an inward conviction of, esp. of coming ill; to augur despondingly. **Syn.** See FORETELL. — **fore·bod′er** (-bōd′ẽr), *n.*

fore·bod′ing (-bōd′ĭng), *n.* A presage or presentiment esp. of coming evil.

fore′brain′ (fōr′brān′; 70), *n. Anat.* The anterior of the three primary divisions of the brain of vertebrates; — called also ***prosencephalon.*** It is subdivided into an anterior part (***telencephalon or endbrain***, composed chiefly of the cerebral hemispheres [see CEREBRUM]) and a posterior part (***diencephalon or betweenbrain*** comprising the thalamus and related structures). Cf. HINDBRAIN, MIDBRAIN.

fore·cast′ (fōr·kȧst′; fōr′kȧst′; 9), *v. t. & i.;* -CAST′, also -CAST′ED; -CAST′ING. 1. To plan ahead. 2. To foresee; to calculate beforehand. 3. To draw a forecast from the study of; to foretell; predict; as, to *forecast* the weather. 4. To serve as a forecast of. — **Syn.** See FORETELL.

fore′cast′ (fōr′kȧst′), *n.* 1. *Obs.* Previous determination; hence, a plan; design. 2. Foresight; forethought. 3. A prophecy or estimate of a future happening or condition.

fore·cast′er (fōr·kȧs′tẽr), *n.* One who forecasts; esp., one who officially forecasts the weather.

fore′cas·tle (fōk′s'l *or, esp. as a literary word,* fōr′kȧs·'l), *n. Naut.* **a** That part of the upper deck of a vessel forward of the foremast, or of the fore channels. **b** In merchant vessels, the forward part of the vessel, where the sailors live.

fore·close′ (fōr·klōz′), *v. t.* [OF. *forclos*, past part. of *forclore* to exclude, fr. *fors* except, outside (fr. L. *foris*) + *clore* to close. See CLOSE, *v.*] 1. To shut out; debar. 2. *Mortgages.* To subject to foreclosure proceedings. — *v. i.* To foreclose a mortgage.

fore·clo′sure (-klō′zhẽr), *n.* Act of foreclosing; specif., a proceeding which bars or extinguishes a mortgagor's right of redeeming a mortgaged estate.

fore′course′ (fōr′kōrs′; 70), *n. Naut.* The lowermost sail on the foremast of a square-rigged vessel; the foresail.

fore′date′ (fōr′dāt′), *v. t.* To antedate.

fore′deck′ (fōr′dĕk′), *n. Naut.* The fore part of a deck, esp. of the main deck.

fore·do′ (fōr·do͞o′). Var. of FORDO.

fore·doom′ (fōr·do͞om′), *v. t.* To doom beforehand.

fore′doom′ (fōr′do͞om′), *n.* Doom in advance; destiny.

fore′fa′ther (fōr′fä′thẽr), *n.* An ancestor.

Fore′fa′thers′ Day (-fä′thẽrz). *U. S.* The anniversary of the day (December 21, 1620) on which the Pilgrim Fathers landed at Plymouth, Massachusetts. On account of a mistake in reckoning the change from Old Style to New Style, it has generally been celebrated on the 22d.

fore·feel′ (fōr·fēl′), *v. t.;* see FEEL. To feel beforehand; to have a presentiment of. — **fore·feel′ing**, *n. & adj.*

fore·fend′ (fōr·fĕnd′). Var. of FORFEND.

fore′fin′ger (fōr′fĭng′gẽr), *n.* Finger next to the thumb.

fore′foot′ (-fo͝ot′), *n.; pl.* -FEET (-fēt′). 1. One of the front feet of a quadruped or multiped. 2. *Shipbuilding.* That point at the forward part of a ship where stem and keel meet.

fore′front′ (-frŭnt′), *n.* Foremost part or place.

fore·gath′er (fōr·găth′ẽr). Var. of FORGATHER.

fore′glimpse′ (fōr′glĭmps′), *n.* A glimpse of the future.

fore·go′ (fōr·gō′), *v. t. & i.;* see GO. [AS. *foregān*, fr. *fore* + *gān* to go.] To go before; precede. — **fore·go′er** (-gō′ẽr), *n.*

fore·go′, *v. t. & i.;* see GO. To forgo, or relinquish. See FORGO, *Note.* — **fore·go′er**, *n.*

fore·go′ing (2), *adj.* Going before. — **Syn.** See PRECEDING.

fore·gone′ (fōr·gŏn′; fōr′gŏn; 2), *adj.* That has gone before; previous; past. — **fore·gone′ness**, *n.*

foregone conclusion. **a** A conclusion that has preceded argument or examination. **b** An inevitable result.

fore′ground′ (fōr′ground′), *n.* In nature or in art, the part of the scene nearest to, and in front of, the spectator; — opposed to *background.*

fore′–gut′ (-gŭt′), *n. Embryol. & Zool.* The anterior part of the primitive alimentary canal of vertebrate embryos.

fore′hand′ (-hănd′), *n.* 1. Superior position. 2. All that part of a horse which is before the rider. 3. *Tennis, Rackets, etc.* A forehand stroke; also, manner of playing, or position when playing, such strokes. — *adj.* 1. Done beforehand; anticipative. 2. Heading; front. 3. *Tennis, Rackets, etc.* Of a stroke, made with the palm approximately to the front; hence, made without extending the arm across the body; — opp. to *backhand.*

fore′hand′ed (-hăn′dĕd; -dĭd; 2), *adj.* 1. Shaped as to the forehand or fore parts. 2. Early; timely. 3. *U. S.* Mindful of the future; thrifty; prudent. 4. *Tennis, Rackets, etc.* Forehand. — **fore′hand′ed·ness**, *n.*

fore′head (fŏr′ĕd; -ĭd; fōr′hĕd′; 74), *n.* [AS. *forhēafod.*] 1. The part of the face above the eyes. 2. The front or fore part of anything.

for′eign (fŏr′ĭn; 74), *adj.* [OF. *forain*, fr. LL. *foranus*, fr. L. *foras, foris*, out of doors, abroad, without.] 1. Situated outside a place or country, esp. outside one's own country or locality. 2. Not native or domestic; as, our *foreign* population. 3. Of, pertaining to, or proceeding from, some other person or material thing than the one under consideration. 4. Alien in character; not pertinent; not congruous; as, *foreign* to the purpose. 5. Related to, or dealing with, other countries, esp. nations; as, *foreign* trade. 6. Not organically connected or naturally related; as, a *foreign* body, a substance occurring in any part of the body or organism where it is not normally found. 7. *Obs.* Not of, or not pertaining to, one's home or household. 8. *Law.* Not within the sphere of operation of the laws of the country under consideration; — opposed to *domestic.* — **Syn.** See EXTRINSIC.

foreign bill, bill of exchange, draft, etc. *Law & Com.* Any bill, etc., with respect to any particular jurisdiction, not both drawn and payable within that jurisdiction.

for′eign·er (fŏr′ĭn·ẽr), *n.* A person belonging to or owing allegiance to a foreign country; an alien.

foreign exchange. **a** The process of settling accounts or debts between persons residing in different countries. **b** Bills or drafts against persons in a foreign country.

for′eign·ism (fŏr′ĭn·ĭz′m), *n.* Anything peculiar to a foreign language or people; a foreign idiom or custom.

for′eign·ness, *n.* Quality or condition of being foreign.

fore·judge′ (fōr·jŭj′; 70), *v. t.;* see JUDGE. 1. To judge beforehand, or before hearing the facts and proof. 2. To estimate beforehand.

fore·judge′. Var. of FORJUDGE.

fore·know′ (-nō′), *v. t.;* see KNOW. To have previous knowledge of; to know beforehand. — **Syn.** See FORESEE. — **fore·know′a·ble**, *adj.*

fore·knowl′edge (fōr·nŏl′ĕj; fōr′nŏl′ĕj; -ĭj; *cf.* KNOWLEDGE), *n.* Knowledge of a thing before it happens; prescience.

fore′la′dy (fōr′lā′dĭ), *n.; pl.* -LADIES (-dĭz). A forewoman.

fore′land (-lănd; -lănd′), *n.* A promontory; headland.

fore′leg′ (-lĕg′), *n.* A fore or forward leg.

fore′lock′ (-lŏk′), *n. Mach.* A cotter or split pin; a linchpin.

fore′lock′, *n.* [*fore-* + *lock* (of hair).] The lock of hair that grows from the fore part of the head.

fore′man (-măn), *n.* The first or chief man; specif.: **a** The chief man of a jury, who acts as speaker and chairman. **b** The chief workman in a gang or crew; one in charge of a room, department, etc. — **fore′man·ship**, *n.*

fore′mast′ (-mȧst′; *naut.* -mȧst), *n. Naut.* The mast nearest the bow.

fore′most (fōr′mōst; -mŭst), *adj.* [AS. *formest, fyrmest*, superl. to *forma* first, itself a superl. fr. the root of *fore* fore.] First in time, place, or series; most advanced. — *adv.* First; in the first place.

fore′name′ (-nām′), *n.* A Christian name.

fore′named′ (-nāmd′), *adj.* Named before; aforesaid.

fore′noon′ (fōr′no͞on′), *n.* The early part of the day, from morning to meridian, or noon. — **fore′noon′**, *adj.*

fo·ren′sic (fō·rĕn′sĭk), *adj.* Also, formerly, **fo·ren′si·cal** (-sĭ·kăl). [L. *forensis*, fr. *forum* public place.] Belonging to courts of judicature or to public discussion and debate; argumentative; rhetorical. — **fo·ren′si·cal·ly**, *adv.*

fore′or·dain′ (fōr′ôr·dān′; 70), *v. t.* To ordain beforehand; to predestinate. — **fore′or·dain′ment**, *n.*

fore·or′di·nate (fōr·ôr′dĭ·nāt), *v. t.* To foreordain.

fore′or·di·na′tion (fōr′ôr·dĭ·nā′shŭn), *n.* Previous ordination or appointment; esp., predestination.

fore part, *or* **fore′part′** (fōr′pärt′), *n.* The part most advanced, or first in time or in place.

fore·passed′, fore·past′ (fōr·pȧst′), *adj. Rare.* Bygone.

fore′peak′ (fōr′pēk′), *n.* *Naut.* The part of the hold which is farthest forward, in the angle of the ship's bows.

fore′quar′ter (fōr′kwôr′tẽr; 2), *n.* A front quarter or part; specif., the front part of the half of a carcass (as of beef, veal, or mutton).

fore·reach′ (fōr·rēch′; 70), *v. t. & i.* **1.** *Naut.* To overhaul and go ahead of when close-hauled. **2.** To gain an advantage over.

fore′roy′al (fōr′roi′ăl), *adj.* Designating the mast, sail, yard, etc., next above the fore-topgallant mast, sail, etc. See SAIL, *Illust.*

fore·run′ (fōr·rŭn′), *v. t.;* see RUN. **1.** To run before; to outrun; precede. **2.** To come before as an earnest of something to follow; to announce. **3.** To forestall; anticipate.

fore·run′ner (-rŭn′ẽr), *n.* **1.** A messenger sent before to give notice of the approach of others; precursor; harbinger. **2.** Specif. [*cap.*], with *the*, John the Baptist, as herald of the Christ. **3.** A predecessor; ancestor. *Shak.*

Syn. **Forerunner, precursor, harbinger, herald** mean one who goes before or announces another. **Forerunner**, literally a messenger who announces the approach of his master, is applicable to anything that serves as a sign or presage; **precursor**, literally *forerunner*, now applies to a person or thing paving the way for the success or accomplishments of another; **harbinger**, literally one who goes before his lord or master to provide lodgings for him, now implies someone or something that prepares for what is to come; **herald**, literally one who proclaims or announces a great event, similarly applies to that which proclaims an arrival.

fore′said′ (fōr′sĕd′; 70), *adj.* Aforesaid.

fore′sail′ (fōr′sāl′; *naut.* fōr′s'l *or* fō′s'l), *n.* *Naut.* **a** The sail carried on the foreyard of a square-rigged vessel, being the lowest sail on the foremast. See SAIL, *Illust.* **b** The lower sail set abaft the foremast of a schooner. **c** = FORESTAYSAIL.

fore·see′ (fōr·sē′), *v. t.;* see SEE. [AS. *foresēon*, fr. *fore* + *sēon* to see.] To see beforehand; foreknow. — **fore·see′a·ble**, *adj.* — **fore·se′er** (-sē′ẽr), *n.*

Syn. **Foresee, foreknow, divine, apprehend, anticipate** mean to know beforehand. **Foresee**, apart from its context, gives no hint of whether one knows by presentiment, inference, or inspiration; **foreknow** usually implies supernatural assistance, as through revelation; **divine** comes close to *foresee*, but usually suggests exceptional sagacity or discernment; **apprehend** implies an element of foresight mixed with great uncertainty and fear; **anticipate**, the most complex term, stresses action beforehand which usually connotes divining or foreseeing, but sometimes does not.

fore·shad′ow (-shăd′ō), *v. t.* To shadow or typify beforehand; to prefigure. — **fore·shad′ow·er** (-ẽr), *n.*

fore′shank′ (fōr′shăngk′), *n.* See BEEF, *Illust.*

fore′sheet′ (-shēt′), *n.* *Naut.* **a** One of the sheets of a foresail. **b** *pl.* The forward portion of an open boat.

fore′shore′ (-shōr′), *n.* The part of the shore between high-water and low-water marks.

fore·short′en (fōr·shôr′t'n), *v. t.* *Fine Arts.* To represent (objects) as diminished in such a way as to comply with the laws of perspective and thus seem relatively of the proper size.

fore·show′ (fōr·shō′), *v. t.;* see SHOW. [AS. *foresceawian* to foresee, fr. *fore* + *sceawian* to see.] To show or exhibit beforehand; to betoken.

fore′side′ (fōr′sīd′), *n.* **1.** The front side or part; the front. **2.** A stretch of country fronting the sea.

fore′sight′ (-sīt′), *n.* **1.** Act or power of foreseeing. **2.** Act of looking forward; a view forward. **3.** Action in reference to the future; provident care. — **fore′sight′ed** (-sīt′ĕd; -ĭd; 2), *adj.* — **fore′sight′ed·ness**, *n.*

fore′skin′ (-skĭn′), *n.* The prepuce.

fore·speak′ (fōr·spēk′), *v. t.;* see SPEAK. **1.** To foretell; predict. **2.** To bespeak in advance.

for′est (fŏr′ĕst; -ĭst), *n.* [OF., fr. ML. *(silva) forestis* (wood) lying outside (that for common use), hunting preserve, fr. L. *foris* outside.] **1.** A dense growth of trees and underbrush covering a large tract. **2.** *Eng. Law.* A tract of woodland, usually belonging to the sovereign, set apart for game, etc. — *adj.* Of or relating to a forest; sylvan. — *v. t.* To cover with trees or forests.

fore·stall′ (fōr·stôl′), *v. t.* [ME. *forstallen*, fr. *forstal* interception, fr. AS. *forsteal, foresteall*, prop., a placing oneself before another. See FORE; STALL.] **1.** To exclude, hinder, or prevent, by prior occupation, or by measures taken in advance. **2.** To get ahead of; anticipate. **3.** *Obs.* **a** To lie in wait for; to intercept. **b** To obstruct or beset. **4.** *Law.* To prevent normal trading in (a fair, market, etc.) by buying or diverting goods, persuading persons to raise prices, etc. — **Syn.** See PREVENT. — **fore·stall′er** (-ẽr), *n.*

for′est·a′tion (fŏr′ĕs·tā′shŭn; fŏr′ĭs-), *n.* Establishment of a forest.

fore′stay′ (fōr′stā′), *n.* *Naut.* A stay from the foremast head to the deck to support the foremast.

fore′stay′sail′ (fōr′stā′sāl′; *naut.* -s'l), *n.* *Naut.* The aftermost headsail of a schooner, ketch, yawl, or cutter, triangular in shape and set on hanks on the forestay. See SAIL, *Illust.*

for′est·ed (fŏr′ĕs·tĕd; fŏr′ĭs-; -tĭd), *adj.* Wooded.

for′est·er (fŏr′ĕs·tẽr; fŏr′ĭs-), *n.* **1.** A person trained in forestry, esp. one in charge of forests or trees. **2.** An inhabitant or denizen of a forest. **3.** Any of various moths (*Alypia* and allied genera, family Agaristidae). **4.** *Australia.* The giant kangaroo (*Macropus giganteus*).

for′est·ry (fŏr′ĕst·rĭ; fŏr′ĭst-), *n.* **1.** Forest land. **2.** The science and art of forming, caring for, or cultivating forests.

fore′taste′ (fōr′tāst′), *n.* A taste beforehand; anticipation. — **Syn.** See PROSPECT.

fore·taste′ (fōr·tāst′), *v. t.* To taste beforehand; anticipate.

fore·tell′ (fōr·tĕl′), *v. t. & i.;* see TELL. To tell beforehand; predict. — **fore·tell′er** (-ẽr), *n.*

Syn. **Foretell, predict, forecast, prophesy, prognosticate, augur, presage, portend, forebode** mean to tell beforehand by special knowledge or occult power. **Foretell** stresses the telling but does not, apart from the context, indicate how the information was gained; **predict** now commonly implies inference from facts or accepted laws of nature; **forecast**, in current use, adds the implication of anticipating eventualities; **prophesy** connotes inspired or mystic knowledge of what will occur; **prognosticate** implies prediction based upon signs or symptoms; **augur**, literally to interpret omens, now implies a similar reason for foretelling; **presage** and **portend** imply foreknowing as well as foretelling, but *presage* may be used of neutral or favorable prognostications whereas *portend* is used only of disastrous ones. **Forebode** implies prognostication from premonitions, presentiments, dreams, or the like.

fore′thought′ (fōr′thôt′), *n.* A thinking beforehand; anticipation; provident care. — *adj.* Thought of, or planned, beforehand; hence, deliberate.

fore′thought′ful (fōr′thôt′fo͝ol; fōr′thôt′-; -f'l), *adj.* Full of, or having, forethought. — **fore′thought′ful·ly**, *adv.* — **fore′thought′ful·ness**, *n.*

fore′time′ (fōr′tīm′), *n.* Former or past time.

fore′to′ken (fōr′tō′kĕn), *n.* [AS. *foretācen.*] Prognostic; premonitory sign.

fore·to′ken (fōr·tō′kĕn), *v. t.* To prognosticate.

fore′–tooth′, *n.; pl.* -TEETH. One of the teeth in the fore part of the mouth; an incisor.

fore′top′ (fōr′tŏp′), *n.* **1.** Forelock, formerly of a person, now of a horse. **2.** *Obs.* The front of a headdress; the top of a periwig. **3.** (*pron.* -tŏp′; *naut.* -tŭp) *Naut.* The platform at the head of the foremast.

fore′–top·gal′lant (-tŏp·găl′ănt; *naut.* -tō·găl′ănt), *adj.* Designating the mast, sail, yard, etc., next above the fore-topmast.

fore′–top′mast (fōr′tŏp′măst), *n.* A mast next above the foremast.

fore′–top′sail′ (-sāl′; *naut.* -s'l), *n.* The sail above the foresail, set on the fore-topmast. See SAIL, *Illust.*

for·ev′er (fŏr·ĕv′ẽr), *adv.* **1.** For a limitless time; eternally. **2.** At all times; incessantly.

☞ In England this is now usually written *for ever*.

for·ev′er·more′ (-mōr′), *adv.* Forever; — emphatic.

fore·warn′ (fōr·wôrn′), *v. t.* To warn beforehand. — **Syn.** See WARN.

fore′wom′an (fōr′wo͝om′ăn), *n.* A woman acting as a foreman.

fore′word′ (-wûrd′), *n.* A word said beforehand; a preface.

fore·worn′ (fōr·wōrn′). Var. of FORWORN.

fore′yard′ (fōr′yärd′), *n.* *Naut.* The lowest yard on a foremast.

for′feit (fôr′fĭt), *n.* [OF. *forfait* crime, prop. past part. of *forfaire* to forfeit, transgress, fr. ML. *forisfacere*, prop., to act beyond, fr. L. *foris* abroad, beyond + *facere* to do.] **1.** A thing forfeited; that which is lost by a crime, offense, neglect of duty, or breach of contract; hence, a fine; a penalty. **2.** Something deposited for making some mistake and redeemable by a sportive fine; — hence the game of **forfeits**. **3.** Forfeiture; as, the *forfeit* of civil rights. — *adj.* Lost or alienated for an error, fault, or crime. — *v. t.* To lose, or lose the right to, by some error, fault, offense, or crime; as, to *forfeit* an estate by treason. — **for′feit·a·ble**, *adj.* — **for′feit·er**, *n.*

for′fei·ture (fôr′fĭ·tūr), *n.* **1.** Act of forfeiting. **2.** That which is forfeited; a penalty; a fine or mulct.

for·fend′ (fôr·fĕnd′), **fore·fend′** (fōr-), *v. t.* [*for-* + *fend.*] **1.** *Archaic.* To prohibit; forbid; also, to avert; prevent. **2.** *Chiefly U. S.* To protect; preserve; secure.

for′fi·cate (fôr′fĭ·kāt), *adj.* [L. *forfex, forficis*, shears.] *Zool.* Deeply forked, as the tail of certain birds.

for·gath′er (fôr·găth′ẽr), **fore·gath′er** (fōr-; 70), *v. i.* **1.** To convene; assemble. **2.** To meet, esp. accidentally; to encounter. **3.** To fraternize; consort socially.

for·gave′ (fŏr·gāv′), *past* of FORGIVE.

forge (fôrj; fōrj; 70), *n.* [OF., fr. L. *fabrica* artisan's workshop, fr. *faber* artisan, smith, as adj., skillful.] **1.** A furnace, or a shop with its furnace, etc., where metal is heated and wrought; a smithy. **2.** A workshop where wrought iron is produced directly from the ore, or where iron is rendered malleable by puddling and shingling; a bloomery. — *v. t.;* FORGED (fôrjd; fōrjd); FORG′ING (fôr′jĭng; fōr′-). [OF. *forgier*, fr. L. *fabricare, fabricari*, to form, fashion, fr. *fabrica*. See FORGE, *n.*] **1.** To form by heating and hammering, as a metal. **2.** To form or shape out in any way; produce; fashion. **3.** To make or imitate falsely; to produce or devise (that which is untrue or not genuine); to fabricate; to counterfeit. — **Syn.** See MAKE. — *v. i.* **1.** To do forging; to work at a forge. **2.** To fabricate falsely; to commit forgery.

forge, *v. i. & t.* [Corrupt. of FORCE.] To move forward or ahead steadily but slowly or gradually.

forg′er (fôr′jẽr; fōr′-), *n.* One who forges; as: **a** Formerly, an author or maker; now, a fabricator; falsifier. **b** One who forges metals. **c** One guilty of forgery.

for′ger·y (fôr′jẽr·ĭ; fōr′-), *n.; pl.* -GERIES (-ĭz). **1.** *Poetic.* Act of forging or inventing; esp., feigning; fiction. **2.** Act of forging, fabricating, or producing falsely; esp., the crime of falsely and fraudulently making or altering a writing or instrument which if genuine would, or on its face might, be of some legal effect upon the rights of others. **3.** That which is forged, fabricated, or counterfeited.

for·get′ (fŏr·gĕt′), *v. t.; past* FOR·GOT′ (-gŏt′); *past part.* FOR·GOT′TEN (-gŏt′'n), FOR·GOT′; *pres. part.* FOR·GET′TING. *Archaic past* FOR·GAT′ (-găt′). [AS. *forgietan, forgitan.* See FOR-; GET.] **1.** To lose the remembrance of; to be unable to recall; also, formerly, to cease from doing. **2.** To omit or disregard unintentionally; to neglect. — **Syn.** See NEGLECT. — *v. i.* To cease remembering or noticing. — ***forget oneself.*** **a** To be entirely unselfish. **b** To become lost in thought. **c** To lose one's dignity, temper, or self-control. **d** To become unconscious, as in sleep.

for·get′ful (-fo͝ol; -f'l), *adj.* **1.** Apt to forget; having a poor memory. **2.** Heedless; inattentive. **3.** *Poetic.* Causing to forget; inducing oblivion. — **for·get′ful·ly**, *adv.* — **for·get′ful·ness**, *n.*

Syn. **Forgetful, oblivious, unmindful** mean letting go from one's mind something once known or learned. **Forgetful** usually implies a propensity not to remember or a defective memory; **oblivious**, in strict use, suggests forgetfulness because of a failure to remember; **unmindful** also stresses forgetfulness, usually because of a deliberate not keeping in mind.

for′ge·tive (fôr′jē·tĭv; fōr′-; 70), *adj.* [From FORGE.] Inventive; imaginative; — coined by Shakespeare.

for·get′–me–not′ (fŏr·gĕt′mē·nŏt′), *n.* Any of a genus (*Myosotis*) of small herbs of the borage family, having bright-blue or white flowers usually in a curving spike. The flowers (esp. of *M. palustris*) are widely treated as the emblem of friendship and fidelity. One species (*M. alpestris*) is the floral emblem of Alaska.

for·get′ta·ble (fŏr·gĕt′ȧ·b'l), *adj.* Liable to be forgotten.

for·get′ter (-ẽr), *n.* One who forgets.

for·give′ (fŏr·gĭv′), *v. t.;* -GAVE′ (-gāv′); -GIV′EN (-gĭv′ĕn); -GIV′ING. [AS. *forgiefan, forgifan.*] **1.** To give up claim to requital from (an offender); to pardon; as, to *forgive* one's enemies. **2.** To give up resentment or claim to requital on account of (an offense); to remit the penalty of; as, to *forgive* a wrong. — *v. i.* To grant forgiveness. — **Syn.** See EXCUSE. — **for·giv'a·ble** (fŏr·gĭv'ȧ·b'l), *adj.* — **for·giv'er** (-ẽr), *n.*

for·give'ness (fŏr·gĭv'nĕs; -nĭs), *n.* Act of forgiving; pardon.

for·giv'ing (fŏr·gĭv'ĭng), *adj.* That forgives; disposed to forgive. — **for·giv'ing·ly**, *adv.* — **for·giv'ing·ness**, *n.*

for·go' (fŏr·gō'), **fore·go'** (fōr-; 70), *v. t.*; see GO. [AS. *forgān*, prop., to go past, fr. *for-* + *gān* to go.] **1.** *Archaic.* **a** To pass by; hence, to neglect. **b** To depart from. **2.** To abstain from; renounce. — *v. i.* To refrain; forbear. — **for·go'er, fore·go'er** (-gō'ẽr), *n.*

☞ The prefix *for-*, which gives *forgo* its early meaning of passing over or neglecting and hence relinquishing, is distinct from *fore-* of *forego*, which means before; yet the spelling *forego* has been frequently used for *forgo* from the 16th century and in the United States is accepted usage.

for·got' (fŏr·gŏt'), *past & past part.* of FORGET.

for·got'ten (-gŏt''n), *past part.* of FORGET.

fo'rint (fō'rĭnt), *n.* [Hung., fr. It. *fiorino*. See FLORIN.] The monetary unit of Hungary authorized July 26, 1946, replacing the pengö, subdivided into 100 fillér. See MONEY, *Tables*.

for·judge' (fŏr·jŭj'), *v. t.*; see JUDGE. Also **fore·judge'** (fōr-; 70). [OF. *for(s)jugier*, fr. *fors* outside + *jugier* to judge.] *Obs. exc. Law.* To expel or put out by judgment of a court.

fork (fôrk), *n.* [AS. *forca*, *force* (fr. L.) and fr. ONF. *forque* (OF. *fourche*), fr. L. *furca*.] **1.** An implement with two or more prongs or tines, used for piercing, holding, taking up, or pitching anything. **2.** Anything like a fork in shape; as, a tuning *fork*. **3.** A barbed point, as of an arrow. **4.** A forking; bifurcation. **5.** One of the parts into which anything is divided; a branch of a stream, a road, etc. **6.** The place where a division or a union occurs; as, the *fork* of a tree; a road *fork*. **7.** A choice of alternatives; a dilemma.
— *v. i.* To divide into two or more branches; as, a road *forks*. — *v. t.* **1.** To give the form of a fork to. **2.** To raise or pitch with a fork.

forked (fôrkt; *poet. or rhetorical often* fôr'kĕd), *adj.* Formed into a forklike shape; dividing into prongs; as, *forked* lightning.

for·lorn' (fŏr·lôrn'), *adj.* [ME., past part. of *forlesen* to lose utterly, fr. AS. *forlēosan* (past part. *forloren*).] **1.** Deserted; forsaken; bereft. **2.** In pitiful plight; wretched. — **Syn.** See ALONE. — **for·lorn'ly**, *adv.* — **for·lorn'ness**, *n.*

forlorn hope. [D. *verloren hoop*, prop., a lost band or troop.] A body of men selected, usually from volunteers, for perilous service; hence, an almost hopeless undertaking.

form (fôrm), *n.* [OF. *forme*, *fourme*, fr. L. *forma*.] **1.** The shape and structure of anything; figure. **2. a** A body, esp. of a human being. **b** *Archaic.* Pleasing external appearance; beauty. **3.** The ideal or intrinsic character of anything, or that which imposes this character; hence, a pattern or schema. **4.** A manner or method, esp. as regulative or prescriptive; method of expression; formal way of proceeding. **5.** A prescribed or set order of words; a formula; as, a matter of *form*. **6. a** Conduct regulated by custom, etiquette, etc.; hence, empty ceremony. **b** A prescribed manner of behaving in society; a formality or conventionality. **c** Manner of performing something; as, his *form* in swimming is bad. **d** Manner or conduct as tested by a prescribed standard. **7.** Orderly arrangement; also, a particular species of such arrangement; as, the sonnet is a poetical *form*. **8.** A kind; species; variety; as, the *forms* of carbon. **9.** Physical and mental condition; esp., good or proper condition for competing, as in a sport or game. **10.** The seat, bed, or lair of a hare or other animal. **11.** (*pron. formerly generally, and still occas.*, fōrm) A long seat; bench; as, a school *form*. **12.** That by which shape is given or determined; a mold. **13.** A printed or typed document with blank spaces for insertion of information; as, a *form* for an income-tax report. **14.** *Educ.* A rank of students in a school; a class; grade. **15.** *Gram.* One of the different aspects a word may take as a result of inflection, or change of spelling or pronunciation; as, verbal *forms*. **16.** *Ling.* = LINGUISTIC FORM. **17.** *Philos.* The essential nature of a thing as distinguished from the matter in which it is embodied; specif.: **a** *Platonism.* = IDEA, 1 **b**. **b** *Aristotelianism.* That in a thing which determines it in its kind or species. **18.** *Print.* The type or other matter from which an impression is to be taken, arranged and secured in a chase.

Syn. **Form, figure, shape, conformation, configuration** mean the disposition or arrangement of content that gives a peculiar aspect or appearance to a thing. **Form** usually suggests reference to internal as well as external structure and, often, suggests the principle that gives unity to the whole; **figure** applies usually to the form as determined by the lines which bound or enclose a thing; **shape**, like *figure*, suggests an outline but it carries a stronger implication also of the mass or body; **conformation** implies a structure composed of related parts; **configuration** implies the disposition and arrangement of different parts, as in a relief map, or the like.

— *v. t.* **1.** To give form or shape to; to fashion. **2.** To give a particular form to; also, to model by instruction and discipline. **3.** To develop; to contract, as a habit. **4.** To go to make up; to act as constituent of; to take the shape of; — said of that out of which anything is formed. **5.** *Gram.* To construct or assume (an inflectional form, as the past tense of a verb); to construct (a compound word); to make up or constitute (a clause, sentence, etc.). **6.** *Mil. & Nav.* To arrange in order; as, the lines were *formed*. — **Syn.** See MAKE. — *v. i.* **1.** To become formed or shaped. **2.** To take form; arise. **3.** To take a definite shape or arrangement.

-form (-fôrm). [F. and L.; F. *-forme*, fr. L. *-formis*, fr. *forma* form.] A suffix denoting *in the form or shape of, resembling*, etc.; — used after *i*, as in oviform.

for'mal (fôr'măl), *adj.* **1.** Of or pertaining to form, esp. established form or custom; conventional. **2.** Characterized by due form; regular. **3.** Done in due form; ceremonial. **4.** Devoted to, or done in accordance with, forms or rules; methodical; also, ceremonious. **5.** Of the nature of form; as: **a** Of the nature of the inner form or reality; essential. **b** Of the nature of the external form; apparent. **6.** Having the form or appearance without the substance; external; as, *formal* worship. **7.** *Metaph.* Belonging to the essential constitution of a thing, as distinguished from the matter composing it. — **Syn.** See CEREMONIAL.

form·al'de·hyde (fôr·măl'dē·hīd), *n.* Also **form·al'de·hyd.** [*formic* + *aldehyde*.] *Chem.* A colorless gas, HCHO, with a sharp odor, formed by the partial combustion of methanol and in other ways. It is a preservative and disinfectant, and preparations of it, mostly aqueous solutions, are sold under various trade-marks, as **For'ma·lin** (fôr'mȧ·lĭn).

for'mal·ism (fôr'măl·ĭz'm), *n.* **1.** The practice or doctrine, or an instance, of strict adherence to prescribed forms, as in religion, art, etc. **2.** *Psychol.* Gestalt psychology. — **for'mal·ist** (-ĭst), *n.* — **for'mal·is'tic** (-ĭs'tĭk), *adj.*

for·mal'i·ty (fôr·măl'ĭ·tĭ), *n.*; *pl.* -TIES (-tĭz). **1.** Condition or quality of being formal, or ceremonious, precise, stiff, etc. **2.** Compliance with formal rules; ceremony. **3.** A legal, social, customary, or religious requirement; a form. **4.** A conventional, usual, or legal rule or method of procedure. **5.** *Obs.* Form without substance.

for'mal·ize (fôr'măl·īz), *v. t.* **1.** To give a certain or definite form to; to shape. **2.** To render formal. **3.** *Obs.* To cavil; scruple. — **for'mal·i·za'tion** (-ĭ·zā'shŭn; -ī·zā'-), *n.* — **for'mal·iz'er** (-īz'ẽr), *n.*

for'mal·ly, *adv.* In a formal manner.

for'mat (fôr'mä; -măt; *F.* fôr'mȧ'), *n.* [F., fr. L. *formatus*, past part.] Shape, size, and general make-up of a publication.

for'mate (fôr'māt), *n.* A salt of formic acid.

for·ma'tion (fôr·mā'shŭn), *n.* **1.** Act of giving form or shape to anything. **2.** That which is formed; as, new word *formations*. **3.** The manner in which a thing is formed; structure. **4.** *Geol.* Any sedimentary bed or series of beds sufficiently homogeneous or distinctive to be regarded as a unit. **5.** An arrangement of a body of troops.

form'a·tive (fôr'mȧ·tĭv), *adj.* **1.** Giving or having the power of giving form; plastic. **2.** *Gram.* Serving to form; derivative; not radical. — *n.* *Gram.* **a** That element which serves to give a word appropriate form, and is no part of the radical, as a prefix. **b** A word formed in accordance with some rule or usage, as from a root.

form class. *Ling.* A class of linguistic forms that have one or more morphological or syntactical features in common (*book-s, pipe-s; open-ed, walk-ed*). The parts of speech of traditional grammar are known as *major form classes*.

for'mée, for'mé (fôr'mā), *adj.* *Her.* Having the ends cut off square; — said of a cross. See CROSS, *Illust.* (16).

for'mer (fôr'mẽr), *adj.* [A compar. after ME. *formest*. See FOREMOST.] **1.** Preceding in time, place, or order; previous; hence, ancient. **2.** Of two things, being the one mentioned first; — opposed to *latter*. — **Syn.** See PRECEDING.

for'mer·ly (-lĭ), *adv.* **1.** In time past; of old; heretofore; once. **2.** *Obs.* In time just preceding.

for'mic (fôr'mĭk), *adj.* [L. *formica* ant.] *Chem.* Pertaining to or designating an acid (**formic acid**, HCO_2H), a colorless, mobile, vesicatory liquid, of pungent odor. It occurs naturally in some ants and various other insects and in plants.

for'mi·car'y (fôr'mĭ·kẽr'ĭ *or, esp. Brit.*, -kẽr·ĭ), *n.*; *pl.* -IES (-ĭz). [ML. *formicarium*, fr. L. *formica* ant.] An ants' nest.

for'mi·cate (-mĭ·kāt), *v. t.* [L. *formicare* to creep, fr. *formica* ant.] To swarm with or as if with ants.

for'mi·da·ble (fôr'mĭ·dȧ·b'l), *adj.* [F., fr. L. *formidabilis*, fr. *formidare* to fear.] Exciting fear or dread; adapted to excite fear or deter from approach or undertaking; redoubtable. — **for'mi·da·bil'i·ty** (-bĭl'ĭ·tĭ), *n.* — **for'mi·da·ble·ness**, *n.* — **for'mi·da·bly**, *adv.*

form'less, *adj.* Without determinate form; lacking regularity of shape. — **form'less·ly**, *adv.* — **form'less·ness**, *n.*

for'mu·la (fôr'mū·lȧ), *n.*; *pl.* -LAS (-lȧz), -LAE (-lē). [L., dim. of *forma* form.] **1.** A set form of words for use in any ceremony; as, a *formula* of faith. **2.** A prescription; a recipe. **3.** A prescribed or set form; a fixed or conventional method. **4.** *Chem.* A symbolic expression of the composition or constitution of a substance; as, the *formula* for water is H_2O. An ***empirical formula*** expresses the results of a quantitative analysis and indicates the number and kind of atoms (as, C_2H_2); a ***structural formula*** gives in addition information as to the relations of the atoms to each other (as, CH:CH). **5.** *Eccl.* A formal statement of doctrines. **6.** *Math.* Any general fact, rule, or principle expressed in algebraic symbols.

for'mu·lar·ize (fôr'mū·lẽr·īz), *v. t.* To state in a formula; to formulate. — **for'mu·lar·i·za'tion** (-ĭ·zā'shŭn; -ī·zā'-), *n.*

for'mu·lar'y (-lẽr'ĭ *or, esp. Brit.*, -lẽr·ĭ), *n.*; *pl.* -IES (-ĭz). **1.** A book of prescribed forms, as of oaths, prayers, etc.; a collection of formulas. **2.** A prescribed form or model; formula. **3.** *Pharm.* A book containing a list of medicinal substances and formulas. — *adj.* Of or relating to formulas; of the nature of a formula; prescribed.

for'mu·late (-lāt), *v. t.* To reduce to, or express in or as in, a formula; to put in a systematized statement. — **for'mu·la'tor** (-lā'tẽr), *n.*

for'mu·la'tion (-lā'shŭn), *n.* Act or result of formulating.

for'mu·lism (fôr'mū·lĭz'm), *n.* Attachment to, or reliance on, formulas; a system of formulas. — **for'mu·lis'tic** (-lĭs'tĭk), *adj.*

for'mu·lize (-līz), *v. t.* To formulate. — **for'mu·li·za'tion** (-lĭ·zā'shŭn; -lī·zā'-), *n.* — **for'mu·liz'er** (-līz'ẽr), *n.*

for'myl (fôr'mĭl), *n.* [*formic* + *-yl*.] *Chem.* The radical (H.C:O) of formic acid. See BENZOYL.

for·nent' (fŏr·nĕnt'), *prep.* Also **for·nenst'** (-nĕnst'). [*fore*, adv. + *anent*.] *Now Chiefly Dial.* **a** Opposite to; facing. **b** For; in exchange for. **c** Opposed to. **d** In connection with.

for'ni·cate (fôr'nĭ·kāt), *v. i.* [LL. *fornicatus*, past part. of *fornicari* to fornicate, fr. *fornix, -icis*, brothel, vault.] To commit fornication. — **for'ni·ca'tor** (-kā'tẽr), *n.*

for'ni·ca'tion (-kā'shŭn), *n.* **1.** Illicit sexual intercourse on the part of an unmarried person. Cf. ADULTERY. **2.** Figuratively, esp. in Scripture, idolatry.

for'nix (fôr'nĭks), *n.*; *pl.* FORNICES (-nĭ·sēz). [L., an arch or vault.] *Anat.* **a** An arch or fold. **b** A lamella composed of longitudinal white fibers, beneath the corpus callosum.

for'rit (fŏr'ĭt), *adj. & adv.* *Scot.* Forward.

for·sake' (fŏr·sāk'), *v. t.*; FOR·SOOK' (-sŏŏk'); FOR·SAK'EN (-sāk'ĕn); FOR·SAK'ING. [AS. *forsacan* to oppose, refuse, fr. *for-* + *sacan* to contend. See FOR-; SAKE end.] **1.** To renounce (something dear to one). **2.** To quit or leave entirely; to desert. — **Syn.** See ABANDON.

For'se·ti (fôr'sĕ·tē), *n.* *Teut. Relig.* A deity worshiped perhaps as a god of justice.

for·sooth' (fŏr·sōōth'), *adv.* [AS. *forsōth*, fr. *for*, prep. + *sōth* sooth, truth.] In truth; indeed; — now used ironically.

for·spend' (-spĕnd'), *v. t.* Usually in past part. FORSPENT. [AS. *forspendan* to consume.] *Archaic.* To waste in strength; to tire out.

for·swear' (fŏr·swâr'), *v. t.*; see SWEAR. [AS. *forswerian*, fr. *for-* + *swerian* to swear.] **1.** To reject or renounce upon oath; hence, to renounce earnestly. **2.** To deny upon oath. — **Syn.** See ABJURE. — *v. i.* To swear falsely; to commit perjury. — **for·swear'er** (-ẽr), *n.* — ***forswear oneself.*** To swear falsely; to perjure oneself.

for·sworn′ (fôr·swōrn′; 70), *adj.* Perjured.
for·syth′i·a (fôr·sĭth′ĭ·ȧ; -sī′thĭ·ȧ), *n.* [NL., after Wm. *Forsyth* (1737–1804), British botanist.] *Bot.* A plant of a genus (*Forsythia*) of ornamental shrubs of the olive family (Oleaceae), with opposite leaves and yellow bell-shaped flowers appearing before the leaves in early spring.
fort (fōrt; 70), *n.* [F., fr. *fort* strong, fr. L. *fortis.*] A strong or fortified place; usually, one occupied by troops and surrounded with defenses; a fortification. Abbr. *Ft.*
for′ta·lice (fôr′tȧ·lĭs), *n.* [ML. *fortalitia*, or OF. *fortelesce.*] *Mil.* Formerly, a fortress; now, a small fort.
forte (fōrt; 70), *n.* [F. *fort.*] **1.** One's strong point; that in which one excels. **2.** The stronger part of the blade of a sword, nearer the hilt; — opposed to *foible.*
for′te (fôr′tā), *adj.* [It., fr. L. *fortis* strong.] *Music.* Loud; powerful; — a direction, opposed to *piano.* — *adv. Music.* Loudly; powerfully. Abbr. *f* or *F* — *n. Music.* A tone or passage played forte.
‖**for′tes for·tu′na ju′vat** (fôr′tēz fôr·tū′nȧ jōō′văt). [L.] Fortune favors the brave.
forth (fōrth; 70), *adv.* [AS.] **1.** Forward; onward. **2.** Out, as from concealment. **3.** *Obs.* Away; abroad; out.
forth, *prep.* *Archaic.* Forth from; out of.
forth′com′ing (fōrth′kŭm′ĭng; 2), *adj.* About to appear; approaching. — (-kŭm′ĭng), *n.* A coming forth; approach.
forth′right′ (fōrth′rīt′; fōrth′rīt′; 2), **forth′rights′** (-rīts′; -rīts′), *adv.* **1.** Directly forth or ahead; also, frankly. **2.** Immediately; straightway.
forth′right′ (fōrth′rīt′; fōrth′rīt′; 2), *adj.* Proceeding straight on; direct; straightforward. — (fōrth′rīt′), *n.* *Archaic.* A straight path.
forth′with′ (fōrth′wĭth′; -wĭth′), *adv.* Immediately; promptly.
for′ti·eth (fôr′tĭ·ĕth; -ĭth), *n.* & *adj.* See NUMBER, *Table.*
for′ti·fi·ca′tion (fôr′tĭ·fĭ·kā′shŭn), *n.* **1.** Act of fortifying. **2.** That which fortifies or defends; esp., a defensive work or works. **3.** A fortified place or position.
for′ti·fy (fôr′tĭ·fī), *v. t.;* -FIED (-fīd); -FY′ING. [F. *fortifier*, fr. LL. *fortificare*, fr. *fortis* strong + *-ficare* (in comp.) to make.] To strengthen; specif.: **a** To give physical strength to; to invigorate. **b** To strengthen with alcohol, as wines. **c** To add mental or moral strength to; to confirm. **d** To strengthen and secure by forts or batteries. **e** To add nutritive value to; to enrich. — **for′ti·fi′er** (-fī′ẽr), *n.*
for·tis′si·mo (fôr·tĭs′ĭ·mō), *adj.* & *adv.* [It.] *Music & Speaking.* Very loud; — a direction. Abbr. *ff*
for′ti·tude (fôr′tĭ·tūd), *n.* [F., fr. L. *fortitudo*, fr. *fortis* strong.] **1.** *Obs.* Strength; impregnability. **2.** Firmness of mind in meeting danger or adversity; resolute endurance, — one of the cardinal virtues.
Syn. **Fortitude, grit, backbone, pluck, guts, sand** mean courage and staying power. **Fortitude** stresses endurance of physical or mental hardships or suffering without giving way under the strain; **grit**, an incapacity for being downed by difficulties and hardships; **backbone**, an ability to stand up in the face of opposition for one's principles or chosen objectives; **pluck**, stoutness of heart and gameness in fighting, especially against odds; **guts**, possession of stamina essential to facing that which repels or frightens one or to put up with the hardships a job imposes; **sand** comes close to *grit* but does not imply triumph over obstacles.
for′ti·tu′di·nous (-tū′dĭ·nŭs), *adj.* Courageous.
fort′night (fôrt′nīt; -nĭt), *n.* [For *fourteen nights.*] The space of fourteen days; two weeks.
fort′night·ly (-nīt·lĭ), *adj.* Occurring or appearing once in a fortnight. — *adv.* Once in a fortnight.
for′tress (fôr′trĕs; -trĭs), *n.* [OF. *forteresse*, fr. L. *fortis* strong.] A fortified place; esp., a large and permanent fortification; a stronghold. — *v. t.* To fortify.
for·tu′i·tism (fôr·tū′ĭ·tĭz′m), *n.* The doctrine or belief that evolutionary adaptations and progress are chance results rather than determined consequences of natural law or the outcome of teleology. — **for·tu′i·tist** (-tĭst), *n.* & *adj.*
for·tu′i·tous (-tŭs), *adj.* [L. *fortuitus*, fr. *forte*, adv., by chance, prop. abl. of *fors, fortis*, chance.] Happening by chance or accident; chance. — **Syn.** See ACCIDENTAL. — **for·tu′i·tous·ly**, *adv.* — **for·tu′i·tous·ness**, *n.*
for·tu′i·ty (-tĭ), *n.; pl.* -TIES (-tĭz). Fortuitousness; chance; also, a chance occurrence.
for′tu·nate (fôr′tū·nĭt), *adj.* [L. *fortunatus*, past part. of *fortunare* to make fortunate, fr. *fortuna* fortune.] **1.** Coming by good luck; bringing some good not foreseen as certain; auspicious. **2.** Receiving some unexpected good; lucky. — **Syn.** See LUCKY. — **for′tu·nate·ly**, *adv.* — **for′tu·nate·ness**, *n.*
for′tune (fôr′tŭn), *n.* [OF. *fortune*, fr. L. *fortuna.*] **1.** The supposed cause of that which befalls in a sudden or unexpected manner; chance; luck; also, [*sometimes cap.*] the personified power of chance. **2.** That which falls to one; good or ill success or luck; esp., favorable issue. **3.** Fate; destiny; as, to tell one's *fortune.* **4.** **a** Condition in life, esp. as determined by wealth; riches. **b** A store of wealth. — *v. t.* To provide with a fortune or dower. — *v. i.* To fall out; to happen; chance.
fortune hunter. One who seeks to acquire wealth, esp. by marriage. — **for′tune-hunt′ing**, *adj.*
for′tune·tell′er (-tĕl′ẽr), *n.* One who professes to tell future events. — **for′tune·tell′ing**, *n.* & *adj.*
for′ty (fôr′tĭ), *n.* & *adj.* [AS. *fēowertig.*] See NUMBER, *Table.*
for′ty·fold′ (-fōld′; 2), *adj.* & *adv.* See -FOLD.
for′ty-nin′er (-nīn′ẽr), *n.* *Collog., U. S.* One who went to California in the rush for gold in 1849; an "Argonaut"
Forty Thieves, the. See ALI BABA.
fo′rum (fō′rŭm; 70), *n.; pl.* FORUMS (-rŭmz), FORA (-rȧ). [L.] **1.** *Rom. Antiq.* The market place or public place of a city, center of judicial and public business. **2.** Tribunal; court. **3.** Hence, a public meeting place for open discussion.
for′ward (fôr′wẽrd), *adj.* [AS. *foreweard, forweard*, adj. & adv., fr. *for, fore* + *-weard, -ward.*] **1.** Near, at, or belonging to, the fore part. **2.** Advanced, esp. beyond the usual degree; specif., precocious. **3.** Extreme; radical. **4.** Moving, tending, or leading toward a position in front; onward. **5.** Ready; prompt; also, overready. **6.** Ardent; eager; in an ill sense, immodest; bold. **7.** *Com.* Of, pertaining to, or for, the future; as, *forward* buying or produce. — *adv.* Toward what is before or in front. — *n.* *Sports.* In certain games, as soccer, basketball, polo, etc., one of the players at or near the front of his side or team, whose chief duty is to carry on the offensive play; in American football, any player in the rush line. — *v. t.* **1.** To help onward; to advance; promote. **2.** To send forward; transmit. **3.** Specif., to send onward from an intermediate station in transit; of a letter, to send from one post office of address to another. **4.** *Bookbinding.* To put (a book) into its cover and otherwise prepare for the finisher by trimming, lining, etc. — **Syn.** See ADVANCE.
for′ward·er (fôr′wẽr·dẽr), *n.* **1.** One who or that which forwards. **2.** *Com.* One who receives goods for transportation, delivers them to the carrier by whom they are to be transported, but does not assume, and is not paid for, the transportation; a forwarding merchant or agent.
for′ward·ly, *adv.* **1.** With readiness, eagerness, or self-assurance. **2.** At or toward the front.
for′ward·ness, *n.* Quality or state of being forward; specif.: **a** Zeal. **b** An advanced stage of progress; precocity. **c** Boldness; esp., overboldness; presumption.
forward pass. *Football.* A pass made in the direction of the opponents' goal.
for′wards (fôr′wẽrdz), *adv.* [See -WARD.] Forward.
for·why′ (fôr·hwī′), *adv.* [AS. *for hwī* (*hwȳ*). See WHY.] *Archaic.* Why; wherefore. — *conj. Archaic.* Because.
for·worn′ (fŏr·wōrn′), **fore·worn′** (fōr-; 70), *adj.* *Archaic.* Worn out; wasted; used up; hackneyed.
‖**for·zan′do** (fôr·tsän′dō), *adj.* [It.] *Music.* Sforzando.
fos′sa (fŏs′ȧ), *n.; pl.* -SAE (-ē). [L., a ditch.] *Anat.* A pit or depression; as, the temporal *fossa* of the skull. See EAR, *Illust.*
fosse, foss (fŏs), *n.; pl.* FOSSES (fŏs′ĕz; -ĭz). [F. *fosse*, fr. L. *fossa*, fr. *fodere, fossum*, to dig.] A canal; a ditch; specif., *Fort.*, a ditch or moat.
fos·sette′ (fŏ·sĕt′), *n.* [F., dim. of *fosse* a fosse.] A small fossa; a little hollow; hence, a dimple.
fos′sick (fŏs′ĭk), *v. i.* & *t.* [Dial. E. *fussick* to potter over one's work, *fussock* to bustle about.] **1.** *Mining, Australia.* To search for gold by picking isolated spots, over abandoned workings, etc.; hence, to steal gold from another's claim. **2.** To rummage. — **fos′sick·er** (-ẽr), *n.*
fos′sil (fŏs′ĭl; -′l), *adj.* [F. *fossile*, fr. L. *fossilis*, fr. *fodere* to dig.] **1.** Of the nature of a fossil; as, *fossil* plants, resins, shells. **2.** Antiquated; dead to change or progress. — *n.* **1.** Orig., any rock, mineral, or other object dug out of the earth. **2.** Now, any impression, or trace, of an animal or plant of past geological ages, which has been preserved in the earth's crust. The term includes footprints or tracks. **3.** *Colloq.* A person whose opinions are extremely antiquated.
fos′sil·if′er·ous (fŏs′ĭ·lĭf′ẽr·ŭs), *adj.* Containing fossils.
fos′sil·ize (fŏs′ĭ·līz), *v. t.* & *i.* **1.** To convert into or become a fossil; to petrify. **2.** To become or cause to become antiquated, rigid, or fixed. **3.** To seek fossils for study; to collect fossils. — **fos′sil·i·za′tion** (-lĭ·zā′shŭn; -lī·zā′-), *n.*
fos·so′ri·al (fŏ·sō′rĭ·ăl; 70), *adj.* [L. *fossor* a digger.] Fitted for digging; as, a *fossorial* foot, animal.
fos′ter (fŏs′tẽr; 74), *adj.* [See FOSTER, *n.*] Affording, receiving, or sharing nourishment, nurture, or sustenance, though not related by blood, or, figuratively, by ties of nature, citizenship, or the like. Hence: **foster mother** *or* **father, foster parent**, a woman or man who has performed the duties of a parent to the child of another; **foster child, daughter,** *or* **son**, one who has been cared for by a foster parent; **foster brothers** *or* **sisters**, those reared as children in the same family. — *n.* [AS. *fōstre*, fr. *fōster, fōstor*, nourishment; akin to E. *food.*] *Obs.* A foster parent. — *v. t.* **1.** To feed; rear. **2.** To cherish; to sustain and promote. — **fos′ter·er**, *n.*
fos′ter·age (-ĭj), *n.* **1.** Care of a foster child. **2.** The entrusting of a child to foster parents. **3.** Act of encouraging development.
fos′ter·ling (-lĭng), *n.* [AS. *fōstorling.*] A foster child.
fos′tress (-trĕs; -trĭs), *n.* A woman who fosters; a nurse.
fou·droy′ant (fōō·droi′ănt; *F.* fōō′drwȧ′yäN′), *adj.* [F.] **1.** Thundering; stunning; dazzling. **2.** *Med.* Fulminant.
fought (fôt), *past & past part.* of FIGHT.
fought′en (fôt′′n; fŏk′tĕn). Archaic past part. of FIGHT.
foul (foul), *adj.* [AS. *fūl.*] **1.** Very offensive to the senses; loathsome; hence, charged or clogged with filth; as, a *foul* sewer. **2.** Covered with, or clogged by, dirt or foreign matter; soiled. **3.** Hence: **a** *Obs.* Disfigured. **b** Defaced, as by changes; as, a *foul* manuscript. **4.** Hateful; odious. **5.** Scurrilous; obscene or profane. **6.** Not favorable; as, a *foul* wind. **7.** *Now Dial.* Not attractive; ugly. **8.** Entangled; — opposed to *clear;* as, a cable may get *foul* while being paid out. **9.** Not conformed to the rules of a game, test, etc.; also, unfair; dishonest. **10.** *Baseball.* That is not fair (see FAIR BALL); pertaining to, or having to do with, fouls; as, the *foul* lines. — **Syn.** See DIRTY. — **Ant.** Fair.
— *adv. Now Rare.* In a foul manner; foully.
— *n.* **1.** That which is foul. **2.** In various sports, an act committed contrary to the rules; a foul stroke, hit, play, etc.; specif., in *Baseball*, a foul ball.
— *v. t.* **1.** To make foul; to soil. **2.** To disgrace; dishonor. **3.** To incrust (the bore of a gun) with residue from burnt powder from firing. **4.** **a** To cover (a ship's bottom) with anything that impedes its sailing; as, a bottom *fouled* with barnacles. **b** To entangle; as, to *foul* a cable. **c** To come into collision with; as, one boat *fouled* another. **5.** *Sports.* To make a foul against; as, in *Boxing*, to strike (an antagonist) a foul blow; in *Baseball*, to hit (a pitched ball) so as to make it a foul ball. — *v. i.* **1.** To become foul; as, a gun *fouls.* **2.** To become entangled, as ropes; to come into collision; as, the two boats *fouled.* **3.** *Sports.* To commit a foul; in *Baseball*, to hit a foul ball.
fou·lard′ (fōō·lärd′), *n.* [F.] A thin, soft material of silk, or silk and cotton, having a satin finish.
foul ball. *Baseball.* A batted ball that is not a fair ball.
foul line. *Baseball.* Either of two straight lines extending from the rear corner of the home plate through the outer corner of first and third base respectively and prolonged to the boundary of the field.
foul′ly (foul′lĭ), *adv.* In a foul manner.
foul′mouthed′ (foul′mouthd′; -moutht′; 2), *adj.* Using language scurrilous, opprobrious, obscene, or profane.
foul′ness (foul′nĕs; -nĭs), *n.* [AS. *fūlnes.*] Quality or state of being foul; also, that which is foul.
foul play. Unfair play; figuratively, unfair, perfidious, or dishonest conduct or dealing; specif., violence; murder.

foul tip. *Baseball.* A batted ball that goes sharp and direct, or but slightly deflected, to the catcher's hands and is legally caught. The batter is out on a foul tip only if he already has two strikes, the tip then counting as a third.

fou'mart (fōō'märt), *n.* [AS. *fūl* foul + *mearth* marten; influenced by OF. *marte, martre.*] The polecat (*Mustela putorius*) of Europe.

found (found), *past & past part.* of FIND; specif.: *adj.* Usually with qualifying adverb: Supplied, equipped, provided, or supported, esp. with food and lodging; as, his pay was $10 a week and *found.*

found, *v. t.* [OF. *fonder,* fr. L. *fundare,* fr. *fundus* bottom] **1.** To set, or place, as on something solid, for support; to ground; establish. **2.** To take the first steps in erecting or building up; to furnish the materials for beginning; originate. — *v. i.* To be founded or based.

found, *v. t.* [OF. *fondre,* fr. L. *fundere* to found, pour.] To melt and pour into a mold; to form by melting a metal and pouring it into a mold; to cast.

foun·da'tion (foun·dā'shŭn), *n.* **1.** Act of founding; state of being founded. **2.** Establishment of an institution with provision for maintenance. **3.** A donation to support a charitable institution, constituting a permanent fund. **4.** An endowed institution, corporation, or charity. **5.** That upon which anything is founded; base. **6.** A body, stock, or ground material, upon which anything is built up, as a fabric to stiffen a dress. **7.** = FOUNDATION GARMENT. **8.** *Arch.* The supporting member of a wall or structure. — **Syn.** See BASE. — **foun·da'tion·al** (-ăl; -'l), *adj.*

Foundation Day. In Australia, a holiday, Jan. 26, anniversary of the landing of the British under Arthur Philip at Sydney Cove, Australia, in 1788.

foundation garment. A woman's supporting undergarment; — applied variously to a corset, corselet, or girdle.

found'er (foun'dẽr), *n.* One who founds, or establishes.

found'er, *n.* One who founds or casts metals.

foun'der (foun'dẽr), *v. i.* [OF. *fondrer* to fall in, fr. *fond* bottom. See FOUND to establish.] **1.** To fall helplessly; to stumble; esp., to stumble and go lame, as a horse; also, of a horse, to be affected with founder (laminitis). **2.** To fail; miscarry. **3.** *Naut.* To become filled with water and sink, as a ship. — *v. t.* **1.** To cause to become lame; esp., to cause (a horse) to become affected with founder (laminitis). **2.** To dismay; dumfound. **3.** *Naut.* To cause (a ship) to founder; to sink.

foun'der, *n.* *Veter.* = LAMINITIS.

foun'der·ous (foun'dẽr·ŭs), **foun'drous** (-drŭs), *adj.* Causing foundering.

found'ers' shares (foun'dẽrz). *Finance.* Shares issued to the organizers of a public company, for some supposed right or property. Such shares are often given special privileges over other stock as to voting, and as to the division of profits in excess of a minimum dividend on the common stock.

found'ling (found'lĭng), *n.* [ME. See FIND, *v.;* 1st -LING.] An infant found after its unknown parents have deserted it.

found'ry (foun'drĭ), *n.; pl.* FOUNDRIES (-drĭz). [F. *fonderie.*] **1.** Act, process, or art of casting metals; also, castings. **2.** A building or works where metal or glass founding is carried on.

foundry proof. *Print.* A proof for a final reading before making electrotype or stereotype plates.

fount (fount), *n.* [F. *font,* fr. L. *fons, fontis,* fountain.] A fountain; a source.

fount (fount; fŏnt), *n.* *Print.* A font; — a British form.

foun'tain (foun'tĭn; -tĕn), *n.* [OF. *fontaine,* fr. LL. *fontana,* fr. L. *fontanus* of a spring, fr. *fons, fontis,* fountain.] **1.** A spring of water. **2.** An artificial jet of water; also, the structure in which such a jet rises or flows. **3.** A reservoir to contain a liquid which can be drawn off as needed. **4.** The source of anything; spring.

foun'tain·head' (-hĕd'; -hĕd'), *n.* **1.** A fountain which is the source of a stream. **2.** Primary source.

fountain pen. A pen with a reservoir in the holder which furnishes a supply of ink.

four (fōr; 70), *n.* [AS. *fēower.*] **1.** See NUMBER, *Table.* **2.** Something having as an essential feature four units or members, as a playing card with four pips, an internal-combustion engine having four cylinders, or an automobile having such an engine, etc. — **four,** *adj.*

four·chée', four·ché' (fōōr·shā'), *adj.* *Her.* Forked at the end; — said of a cross. See CROSS, *Illust.* (17).

four·chette' (fōōr·shĕt'), *n.* [F., dim. of *fourche.* See FORK.] *Anat.* **a** A small fold of membrane connecting the labia minora in the posterior part of the vulva. **b** The wishbone, or furculum, of birds. **c** The frog of a hoof.

four'-cy'cle, *n.* *Thermodyn.* A four-stroke cycle, as for an internal-combustion engine. Cf. TWO-CYCLE.

four'-di·men'sion·al, *adj.* Having, or relating to, four dimensions; esp., *Math.,* of an extent or space or assemblage each of whose elements requires four co-ordinates or determinations to distinguish it completely from all others.

Four·drin'i·er (fōōr·drĭn'ĭ·ẽr), *adj.* Designating or pertaining to a machine for making paper in an endless web, developed in England in the early 19th century chiefly by H. and S. Fourdrinier. — *n.* A Fourdrinier machine.

four'-flush', *v. i.* In poker, to bluff with a hand (**four flush**) with four cards of one suit but lacking the fifth of the same suit; hence, *Slang,* to bluff. — **four'flush'er,** *n.*

four'fold' (fōr'fōld'; 2), *adj. & adv.* See -FOLD.

four'-foot'ed (-fŏŏt'ĕd; -ĭd; 2), *adj.* Quadruped.

four freedoms. The four essential human freedoms set forth by President Franklin D. Roosevelt, January 6, 1941: freedom of speech and expression, freedom of worship, freedom from want, freedom from fear.

‖**four'gon'** (fōōr'gôN'), *n.* [F.] A van or wagon for carrying baggage, ammunition, etc.; also, a railroad baggage car.

four'-hand'ed (fōr'hăn'dĕd; -dĭd; 2), *adj.* Having, or requiring or participated in by, four hands.

four hundred, the. *U. S.* The exclusive social set of any place; — from a comment by Ward McAllister, a New York society leader, who stated, about 1889, that only this number of people were actually "in society" in that city.

Fou'ri·er·ism (fōō'rĭ·ẽr·ĭz'm), *n.* The co-operative socialistic system of F. M. C. Fourier (1772–1837), a Frenchman, who recommended the reorganization of society into small communities (phalansteries), living in common. — **Fou'ri·er·ist** (-ĭst), *n.* — **fou'ri·er·is'tic** (-ĭs'tĭk), *adj.*

Fou'ri·er·ite (fōō'rĭ·ẽr·īt), *n.* A Fourierist.

four'-in-hand' (fōr'ĭn·hănd'), *adj.* **1.** Consisting of, or drawn by, four horses arranged in two teams driven tandem by one person; as, a *four-in-hand* coach. **2.** Designating a kind of necktie tied with a slipknot. — *n.* **1.** A four-in-hand team or vehicle. **2.** A four-in-hand tie.

four'-mast'ed (-màs'tĕd; -tĭd; 2), *adj.* *Naut.* Having four masts.

four'-o'clock', *n.* Any plant of a genus (*Mirabilis*) typifying a family (Nyctaginaceae, the four-o'clock family) of chiefly American plants having apetalous flowers with an involucre simulating a calyx and the fruit enclosed by the persistent base of the perianth; esp.: **a** The common garden species (*Mirabilis jalapa*), with fragrant yellow, red, or white flowers opening late in the afternoon. **b** In California, a related species (*M. laevis*), with red flowers.

four of a kind. *Card Playing.* Four cards of the same denomination. See POKER, *Illust.*

four'pence (fōr'pĕns), *n.* The sum of four pence, or a British silver coin, not now current, of this value. — **four'pen·ny** (-pĕn·ĭ), *n. & adj.*

four'-post'er (-pōs'tẽr), *n.* A large bedstead with tall posts, often carved, at the corners to support curtains.

‖**four'ra'gère'** (fōō'rà'zhâr'), *n.* [F.] A French military decoration, presented to a unit of troops for distinguished service, consisting of a braided cord worn about the left shoulder seam by all the men of the unit honored.

four'score' (fōr'skōr'; 2), *adj.* Four times twenty.

four'some (-sŭm), *adj.* [*four* + 1st *-some.*] *Scot.* Consisting of four; requiring four participants. — *n.* **1.** *Golf.* A match between two sides, each of two players, each side playing but one ball, the partners striking alternately; also, the players in such a match. A four-ball match, in which each player plays his own ball and the best ball counts at each hole, is often in the United States called a ***Scotch foursome, or best-ball foursome.*** **2.** *Colloq.* A party of four.

four'square' (-skwâr'; 2), *adj. & adv.* **1.** Square; in a square form. **2.** With unshakable firmness; also, forthright; without equivocation. — **four'square'ly,** *adv.* — **four'square'ness,** *n.*

four'square', *n.* A foursquare figure; square.

four'teen' (fōr'tēn'; 2), *n. & adj.* [AS. *fēowertȳne, fēowertēne.*] See NUMBER, *Table.* — **four'teenth'** (-tēnth'; 2), *n. & adj.*

Fourteen Points *or* **Fourteen Peace Points.** Fourteen conditions or terms set forth by President Wilson in an address to Congress, January 8, 1918, as the basis of a world peace to follow World War I.

fourth (fōrth), *n.* [ME. *fourthe,* fr. *four.*] **1.** See NUMBER, *Table.* **2.** *Music.* **a** The interval embracing four diatonic degrees. See INTERVAL. **b** The tone at this interval. **c** The harmonic combination of two tones a fourth apart. **d** The fourth tone of a scale, reckoning up from the tonic; the subdominant. — **fourth,** *adj.*

fourth dimension. *Math.* The dimension added to a three-dimensional extent or aggregate to convert the former into a four-dimensional extent. Physical space is sometimes regarded, as in the theory of relativity, as consisting of the ordinary three spatial dimensions plus a fourth dimension, time, and is then known as a *space-time continuum.* — **fourth'-di·men'sion·al,** *adj.*

fourth estate. The public press; the newspapers.

fourth'ly (fōrth'lĭ), *adv.* In the fourth place.

Fourth of July. Independence Day in the United States.

four'-way', *adj.* Allowing passage in any of four directions; as, a *four-way* cock, or valve.

four'-wheel' (fōr'hwēl'), *adj.* **a** Four-wheeled. **b** *Automotive Vehicles.* Operative on four wheels; as, *four-wheel* brakes. See HYDRAULIC, *Illust.*

four'-wheel'er (-hwēl'ẽr), *n.* A vehicle with four wheels; specif., *Colloq., Eng.,* a public cab with four wheels.

fou'ter, fou'tre (fōō'tẽr), *n.* [OF. *foutre* to copulate with, fr. L. *futuere.*] A fig; — a word of contempt.

fo've·a (fō'vē·à), *n.; pl.* FOVEAE (-ē). [L., a small pit.] A small depression or pit; a fossa. — **fo've·al** (-ăl), *adj.*

‖**fo've·a cen·tra'lis** (sĕn·trā'lĭs). [L., central pit.] *Anat.* The small rodless area of the retina, affording acute vision.

fo've·ate (fō'vē·āt), *adj.* Pitted; having foveae.

fo·ve'o·la (fō·vē'ō·là), *n.; pl.* FOVEOLAE (-lē). [NL., dim. of L. *fovea.*] A very small pit; a small fovea.

fo've·o·late (fō'vē·ō·lāt), *adj.* Also **fo've·o·lat'ed** (-lāt'ĕd; -ĭd). *Bot. & Zool.* Having small pits; foveate.

fo've·ole (-ōl), **fo've·o·let** (-ō·lĕt), *n.* A foveola.

fowl (foul), *n.;* see PLURAL, *Note,* 3. [AS. *fugol.*] **1.** Orig., a bird of any kind; later, a large or edible bird; — now chiefly in combination, as in wild *fowl,* water*fowl.* **2.** When used alone, commonly, the domestic cock or hen (*Gallus gallus*), esp. when considered as an article of food. See POULTRY, *Illust.* Well-known breeds include *Andalusian, Brahma, Cochin, Dorking, Hamburg, Houdan, Leghorn, Minorca, Orpington, Plymouth Rock, Rhode Island Red, Wyandotte.* Cf. BANTAM. In combination, any of certain other gallinaceous birds, as the ***jungle fowl*** and ***guinea fowl*** (see these terms). **3.** The meat of fowls, esp. of the domestic fowl, used as food; also, a mature hen, as disting. from a *broiler, capon,* etc. — *v. i.* [AS. *fugelian.*] To seek for, catch, or kill wild fowl, for game or food. — **fowl'er** (-ẽr), *n.*

fowl'ing, *n.* The sport of hunting wild fowl.

fowling piece. A light gun, esp. for shooting birds.

fox (fŏks), *n.;* see PLURAL, *Note,* 3. [AS.] **1. a** Any of certain carnivorous mammals (family Canidae, esp. genus *Vulpes*), smaller than the wolves, and noted for craftiness. The common fox (*Vulpes vulpes*) of Europe and the ***red fox*** (*V. fulva*) of North America are very similar, and each exhibits color phases in which it is known as ***silver fox, black fox,*** etc. The ***gray fox*** (*Urocyon cinereoargenteus*) of North America usually frequents woods and lives in hollow logs or burrows. The ***arctic, or white, fox*** (*Alopex lagopus*) and its blue phase, the ***blue fox,*** generally inhabits the arctic lands and sea ice. Cf. FENNEC, FLYING FOX. **b** The fur or pelt of any of these animals. **2.** A sly, cunning fellow. **3.** [*cap.*] An Indian of an Algonquian tribe formerly dwelling in Wisconsin. In 1760 they united with the Sacs. **4.** *Obs.* A kind of sword. **5.** *Naut.* Rope yarn twisted and tarred, used for seizings, mats, etc.

— *v. t.* **1.** To intoxicate. **2.** *Slang.* To beguile; trick. **3.** To discolor with stains, as prints, book leaves, etc. **4.** To repair (a boot or shoe) with new front upper leather. — *v. i.* **1.** *Obs.* To become intoxicated. **2.** Of book leaves, to become foxed.

fox'glove' (fŏks'glŭv'), *n.* [AS. *foxesglōfa.*] Any plant of a genus (*Digitalis*) of the figwort family. The common foxglove (*D. purpurea*) is an ornamental European perennial or biennial, having racemes of dotted white or purple tubular flowers. Its leaves yield digitalis.

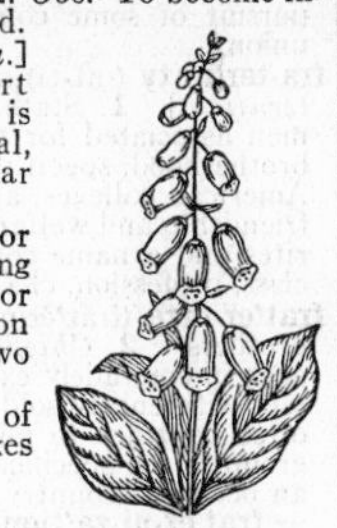

Common Foxglove. (1/16)

fox'hole' (-hōl'), *n.* *Mil.* An individual pit or trench, usually hastily dug with an entrenching tool, for shelter from enemy fire from ground or air, sometimes dug deep enough for a person standing or built with roof and sandbags for two persons.

fox'hound' (-hound'), *n.* A large, swift hound of a breed of great endurance, used in hunting foxes and other quarry.

fox squirrel. See SQUIRREL, 1 **a**.

fox'tail' (-tāl'), *n.* **1.** The tail, or brush, of a fox. **2.** *Bot.* Any of several grasses with brushlike spikes.

fox terrier. A small lively terrier of a breed formerly used to dig out foxes. There are two varieties, smooth-haired and wire-haired.

fox trot. **1.** An easy gait, with short steps, as that adopted by a horse in passing from a walk to a trot. **2.** A ballroom dance, in two-two or two-four time, including slow walking steps, quick trotting steps, etc.

fox'-trot', *v. i.;* FOX'TROT'TED; FOX'TROT'TING. To dance the fox trot.

fox'y (fŏk'sĭ), *adj.;* FOX'I·ER (-sĭ·ẽr); FOX'I·EST. **1.** Foxlike in disposition or looks; wily. **2.** Having the color of the common red fox. **3.** Defective in some way as to color or quality, as from age, decay, etc. **4.** Sour; unpleasant in taste; — said of wine, beer, etc. **5.** *Colloq.* Wide-awake or knowing. — **Syn.** See SLY. — **fox'i·ly,** *adv.* — **fox'i·ness,** *n.*

foy (foi), *n.* [MD. *foy, voye.*] *Dial.* A feast, gift, etc., given at a departure or at the end of harvest season.

foy, *n.* [F. *foi.* See FAITH.] *Obs.* Faith.

foy'er (foi'ā; foi'ẽr; fwä'yā), *n.* [F., fr. L. *focarium* fireplace.] A lobby, esp. in a theater.

fo'zy (fō'zĭ; fŏz'ĭ), *adj.* *Scot. & Dial.* Spongy; flabby; fat-witted; also, muggy.

fra (frä), *n.* [It., for *frate,* fr. L. *frater.*] Brother; — [*cap.*] a title of a monk or friar; as, *Fra* Angelo.

fra'cas (frā'kȧs; *Brit. usually* frăk'ä), *n.; pl.* FRACASES (frā'kȧs·ĕz; -ĭz), *Brit.* FRACAS (frăk'äz). [F., fr. It. *fracasso,* fr. *fracassare* to break in pieces.] Uproar; brawl.

frac'tion (frăk'shŭn), *n.* [OF., fr. L. *fractio* a breaking, fr. *frangere, fractum,* to break.] **1.** *Now Rare.* A breaking. **2.** A piece broken off; a fragment; scrap. **3.** *Colloq.* A little; bit. **4.** *Chem.* One of several separately collected portions, as of a distillate or precipitate. **5.** *Math.* One or more aliquot parts of a unit or integer; the indicated quotient of one integer divided by another. Fractions are known as: ***common, or vulgar, fraction,*** a fraction in which both numerator and denominator are expressed; ***complex, or compound, fraction,*** in which a fraction or mixed number is found in the numerator or denominator, or in each; ***continued fraction,*** in which the numerator is an integer and the denominator an integer plus a fraction whose numerator is an integer and whose denominator is an integer plus a fraction, and so on; ***decimal fraction*** (see NUMBER, *Table*); ***improper fraction,*** in which the numerator is greater than the denominator; ***partial fractions,*** the fractions into the sum of which a fraction may be decomposed; ***proper fraction,*** in which the numerator is less, or of lower degree, than the denominator; ***simple fraction,*** which is the ratio of two integers. See NUMBER, *Table.* — *v. t.* To separate into fractions.

frac'tion·al (-ăl; -'l), *adj.* **1.** Of or pertaining to fractions or a fraction; of the nature of, or constituting, a fraction. **2.** Relatively small; insignificant. **3.** *Chem.* Pertaining to or designating any process used to separate the constituents of a mixture through differences in boiling point, solubility, combustibility, or the like; — applied to various processes, as **fractional distillation, fractional crystallization, fractional combustion, fractional oxidation.** **4.** *Exchanges.* Being, or relating to, a number or amount less than the unit of dealing, which for shares is normally one hundred, and for grain 5,000 bushels. — **frac'tion·al·ly,** *adv.*

fractional currency. Small coin, or paper notes, in circulation, of less value than the monetary unit; specif., certain paper issues of the United States (1862 to 1876), and of Canada, ranging from three to fifty cents; — often called *shinplasters.*

frac'tion·ar'y (frăk'shŭn·ĕr'ĭ *or, esp. Brit.,* -ẽr·ĭ), *adj.* Fractional.

frac'tion·ate (-āt), *v. t.* *Chem.* To subject to fractional distillation, or the like. — **frac'tion·a'tion** (-ā'shŭn), *n.*

frac'tion·ize (-īz), *v. t. & i.* To separate into fractions. — **frac'tion·i·za'tion** (-ĭ·zā'shŭn; -ī·zā'-), *n.*

frac'tious (frăk'shŭs), *adj.* Apt to break out into a passion; cross; unruly. — **Syn.** Peevish, waspish, irritable. — **frac'tious·ly,** *adv.* — **frac'tious·ness,** *n.*

frac'tur·al (frăk'tūr·ăl), *adj.* Pertaining or due to, or of the nature of, a fracture.

frac'ture (frăk'tūr), *n.* [F., fr. L. *fractura,* fr. *frangere, fractum,* to break.] **1.** Act of breaking, or state of being broken; rupture; breach. **2.** That which is produced by breaking; crack. **3.** *Mineral.* The texture, etc., of a freshly broken surface; as, a conchoidal *fracture.* **4.** *Surg.* The breaking of a bone or (less often) of a cartilage. In a ***simple, or closed, fracture*** the skin remains unbroken; in a ***compound fracture*** an open wound is produced through which the bone often protrudes.

Syn. **Fracture, rupture** mean a break in tissue. **Fracture** commonly applies to hard substances such as bones, **rupture** to soft ones such as blood vessels.

— *v. t. & i.* To cause a fracture or fractures in; to break.

frae (frā). *Scot.* Fro; from.

frae'num. Var. of FRENUM.

frag'ile (frăj'ĭl; 56), *adj.* [F., fr. L. *fragilis,* fr. *frangere* to break.] Easily broken or destroyed; frail; delicate. — **frag'ile·ly,** *adv.* — **frag'ile·ness, fra·gil'i·ty** (frȧ·jĭl'ĭ·tĭ), *n.*

Syn. (1) **Fragile, frangible, brittle, crisp, friable** mean breaking easily. **Fragile** implies extreme delicacy of material or construction; **frangible,** a susceptibility to being broken; **brittle,** a hardness that makes for snapping or fracturing when subjected to any pressure or strain; **crisp,** a firmness and brittleness desirable especially in some foods; **friable,** a quality of some substances that are easily crumbled or pulverized. (2) See WEAK.

frag'ment (frăg'mĕnt), *n.* [F., fr. L. *fragmentum,* fr. *frangere* to break.] A part broken off; a small detached portion; an imperfect or incomplete part. — **Syn.** See PART.

frag·men'tal (frăg·mĕn'tăl; -t'l), *adj.* Fragmentary.

frag'men·tar'y (frăg'mĕn·tĕr'ĭ *or, esp. Brit.,* -tẽr·ĭ), *adj.* Composed of fragments; disconnected; not complete. — **frag'men·tar'i·ly,** *adv.* — **frag'men·tar'i·ness,** *n.*

frag'men·ta'tion (-tā'shŭn), *n.* Separation into segments or parts; specif., *Mil.,* the shattering into numerous and widely scattered fragments, as of a specially designed bomb, grenade, or shell.

frag'ment·ed (frăg'mĕn·tĕd; -tĭd), *adj.* Broken into fragments.

frag'ment·ize (frăg'mĕn·tīz), *v. t.* To break apart.

fra'grance (frā'grăns), *n.* Quality or state of being fragrant; sweetness of smell; also, a sweet smell; perfume.

Syn. **Fragrance, perfume, scent, incense, redolence, bouquet** mean a sweet or pleasant odor. **Fragrance** usually suggests the odors diffused by flowers or other growing things; **perfume,** in current use, the artificial odor (also called **scent**) which contains the essence of a fragrant flower or flowers (sometimes synthetically concocted) or a particularly heavy fragrance, such as of lilies; **incense,** the odorous smoke of burning spices, gums, etc., or any odor particularly grateful to the sense; **redolence,** a mixture of fragrant, often pungent, odors, as from a forest; **bouquet,** the distinctive and delicate odor especially of a good wine.

fra'gran·cy (-grăn·sĭ), *n.; pl.* -CIES (-sĭz). Fragrance.

fra'grant (-grănt), *adj.* [MF., fr. L. *fragrans, -antis,* pres. part. of *fragrare* to emit a fragrance.] Sweet or agreeable in smell. — **fra'grant·ly,** *adv.*

frail (frāl), *n.* [OF. *fraiel, freel.*] **1.** A basket made of rushes, as for figs or raisins. **2.** The quantity of raisins contained in such a basket, in Spain, 50 lb. avoirdupois.

frail, *adj.* [OF. *fraile, frele* (F. *frêle*), fr. L. *fragilis.* See FRAGILE.] **1.** Easily broken; fragile; not firm or durable; also, weak. **2.** Liable to fall from virtue or be led into sin. — **Syn.** See WEAK. — **frail'ly,** *adv.* — **frail'ness,** *n.*

frail'ty (frāl'tĭ), *n.; pl.* -TIES (-tĭz). **1.** Quality or state of being frail; frailness. **2.** A fault due to weakness; foible. — **Syn.** See FAULT.

fraise (frāz), *n.* [F., fr. *fraiser* to plait, ruffle.] **1.** A ruff for the neck. **2.** *Fort.* A defense of pointed stakes driven into ramparts in a horizontal or inclined position.

fram·be'si·a, fram·boe'si·a (frăm·bē'zhĭ·ȧ; -zĭ·ȧ), *n.* [NL., fr. F. *framboise* raspberry.] *Med.* A contagious disease of the skin, having many analogies with syphilis; — called also *yaws.*

frame (frām), *v. i.* [ME. *framen, framien,* to profit, to be of use, to fashion (in building), fr. AS. *framian* to profit, fr. *fram, from,* forth, from.] *Obs. exc. Dial.* **1.** To make progress; hence, to prosper. **2.** To proceed; go. **3.** To show promise; to be capable. **4.** To contrive; manage. — *v. t.* **1.** To shape or fashion; to form; also, to fit or adjust; to regulate. **2.** *Obs.* To determine or regulate the course of; to direct. **3.** To construct or make. **4.** To plan, devise, contrive, or compose; to invent or fabricate; to express or utter; to conceive or imagine. **5.** To enclose in or as in a frame; also, to be or serve as a frame to. **6.** *Slang.* To devise falsely, as a charge; to make (one) the victim of a false charge. **7.** To construct, as a building, by fitting and uniting the parts of the skeleton. — **fram'er** (frām'ẽr), *n.*

frame up. *Slang.* To prearrange by conspiracy, as a contest, or the fixing of guilt on (an innocent person).

— *n.* **1.** Anything composed of parts fitted and united together; a structure; esp., the constructional system that gives to a building, vessel, etc., its model and strength. **2.** The bodily structure; physical constitution. **3.** A kind of open case or structure made for admitting, enclosing, or supporting things, as a window, door, picture, etc. **4.** An enclosing border, esp. an ornamental one. **5.** *Obs.* Act of framing, or devising. **6.** The form in which anything is framed; structure. **7.** Particular disposition, as of the mind; humor; temper; as, a happy *frame* of mind. **8.** *Games.* **a** *Baseball Slang.* An inning. **b** *Bowling.* One of the several innings forming a game, as in tenpins. **c** *Pool.* The triangular form used in setting up the balls. **9.** *Mach.* Formerly, a loom; now, any of certain machines built upon or within framework; as, a spinning *frame.* **10.** *Motion Pictures.* One of the series of pictures on a film. **11.** *Shipbuilding.* Any of the skeleton structures forming the ribs or framework of a vessel; — called ***square frames*** when at right angles to the longitudinal vertical middle plane, and ***cant frames*** when at an oblique angle to it. **12.** *Television.* A picture of the image transmitted.

— *adj.* Framed; esp., of wood, as opposed to masonry.

frame house. A house of which the form and support is of wooden timbers, filled in with brick or plaster, or sheathed with clapboards or shingles, as commonly in the U. S.

frame'-up', *n.* *Slang.* A plot to incriminate a person or to further some fraudulent scheme.

frame'work' (frām'wûrk'), *n.* **1.** The work of framing, or the completed construction; as, the *framework* of a ship; the *framework* of society. **2.** *Hort.* The main branches of a tree.

frame'-work', (frām'wûrk'), *v. t.* *Hort.* To graft cions on the main branches (of fruit trees) after removal of fruit-bearing laterals, usually to obtain a preferred variety of fruit.

fram'ing (frām'ĭng), *n.* **a** Act, process, or style of putting together a frame; also, a frame; that which frames. **b** *Arch. & Engin.* A framework, or a system of frames.

franc (frăngk), *n.* [F., fr. *Franc* a Frank. See FRANK.] **1.** An old French gold coin; also, an old French silver coin. **b** An aluminum-bronze coin of modern France. **c** A silver coin of Switzerland. **2.** The monetary unit of France, Belgium, and Switzerland. See MONEY, *Tables.*

fran'chise (frăn'chīz), *n.* [OF., fr. *franchir* to free, fr. *franc,* fem. *franche,* free. See FRANK, *adj.*] **1.** Freedom or immunity from some burden, restriction, or the like; hence, a particular privilege conferred by grant from a sovereign or a government, and vested in an individual or individuals; a positive right to do something otherwise legally incompetent, such as: (1) the right to operate a ferry or a railroad; (2) to be, and exercise the powers of, a corporation; (3) to exercise the duties and perform the functions of a public office; (4) to have a patent right in an invention; etc. A franchise is a species of incorporeal hereditament, and is usually granted by a charter. **2.** Jurisdiction over which a franchise extends; hence, an asylum or sanctuary. **3.** A constitutional or statutory right, particularly the right of suffrage.

fran'chise (frăn'chīz), *v. t.* *Obs.* = ENFRANCHISE. — **fran'chise·ment** (-chĭz·mĕnt), *n.* *Obs.*

Fran·cis'can (frăn·sĭs'kăn), *adj.* *R.C.Ch.* Of or pertaining to St. Francis of Assisi, or to the Order of St. Francis, or to the Franciscans. — *n.* *R.C.Ch.* A member of one of the various religious foundations established by St. Francis of Assisi (see *Biog.*).

fran'ci·um (frăn'sĭ·ŭm), *n.* [NL., fr. *France* + *-ium.*] *Chem.* An element of the alkali-metal family, discovered in 1939 as a disintegration product of actinium. Symbol, *Fr;* at. no., 87.

Fran'co– (frăng'kō-). [ML., fr. *Francus* a Frank.] A combining form signifying *Frankish* or *French; pertaining to the French* or *France and* (the people specified); as in:

Franco-American **Franco-Prussian** **Franco-Soviet**

fran'co·lin (frăng'kō·lĭn), *n.* [F., fr. It. *francolino.*] Any of numerous partridges (*Francolinus* and allied genera) of southern Asia and Africa.

Fran'co·phile (frăng'kō·fīl; -fĭl), **Fran'co·phil** (-fĭl), *adj.* [*Franco-* + *-phile, -phil.*] Friendly to France. — *n.* A person, not French, friendly to France.

Fran'co·phobe (-fōb), *adj.* [*Franco-* + *-phobe.*] Fearing France. — *n.* One who dreads France or French influence. — **Fran'co·pho'bi·a** (-fō'bĭ·ȧ), *n.*

franc'–ti'reur' (fräN'tē'rûr'), *n.; pl.* FRANCS-TIREURS (fräN'tē'rûr'). [F., lit., free shooter.] *Mil.* A French partisan soldier, or one of a corps of detached light troops engaged in forays, etc.

fran'gi·ble (frăn'jĭ·b'l), *adj.* [OF.] Breakable; brittle; fragile. — **Syn.** See FRAGILE. — **fran'gi·bil'i·ty** (-bĭl'ĭ·tĭ), **fran'gi·ble·ness**, *n.*

fran'gi·pane (frăn'jĭ·pān), *n.* [F., appar. fr. It. family name *Frangipani.*] Frangipani.

fran'gi·pan'i (-păn'ĭ; -pä'nĭ), *n.* [See FRANGIPANE.] **1.** Any of certain tropical American shrubs or small trees (genus *Plumiera*) of the dogbane family, esp. one (*P. rubra*), often called *red jasmine*, and white-flowered species (*P. alba* and *P. acuminata*). **2.** A perfume derived from, or imitating the odor of, the flower of the red jasmine.

frank (frăngk), *adj.* [OF. *franc* free, frank, Frankish, fr. ML. *francus*, fr. *Francus* a Frank, fr. OHG. *Franko* the name of a Germanic people on the Rhine.] **1.** *Obs.* Free. **2.** *Now Rare.* Liberal; generous. **3.** Candid; outspoken.

Syn. **Frank, candid, open, plain** mean manifesting willingness to tell what one feels or thinks. **Frank** stresses lack of reserve or of reticence, and freedom from fear, shyness, secretiveness, etc.; **candid** suggests a refusal to dodge an issue or to be governed by bias or fear; **open** implies both frankness and candor but it suggests more witlessness than *frank* and less conscientiousness than *candid;* **plain** suggests outspokenness, downrightness, and freedom from affectation.

— *v. t.* **1.** To send by public conveyance free of expense, as a letter, package, telegram, etc. **2.** To enable to pass freely or easily. **3.** To exempt; to free; to render immune.

— *n.* [From FRANK, *v.*] **1.** The mark or sign denoting that a letter, telegram, etc., is to go free of postage. **2.** The privilege of franking letters, etc.

Frank (frăngk), *n.* [See FRANK, *adj.*] **1.** A member of the confederated German tribes who founded the Frankish Empire, which in the 9th century gave place to the medieval kingdoms that became France, Germany, and Italy. **2.** A native or inhabitant of western Europe; a European; — a term used in the Levant.

Frank'en·stein (frăngk'ĕn·stīn), *n.* **1.** A student of physiology in Mrs. Shelley's romance of the same name, who constructed a monster and gave it a sort of life. The monster inflicted the most dreadful retribution upon his creator. The name has become a synonym for one destroyed by his own works. **2.** Hence, a work or agency that ultimately ruins its originator.

frank'furt·er (frăngk'fĕr·tĕr), *n.* Also **frank'fort·er** (-fĕr·tĕr). [G. *Frankfurter* pert. to *Frankfurt*, Germany.] A beef or beef-and-pork sausage stuffed in casings, linked, and smoked; — called also **frankfurt,** *or* **frankfort, sausage.**

frank'in·cense (frăngk'ĭn·sĕns), *n.* [OF. *franc* free, pure + *encens* incense.] A fragrant gum resin obtained from various trees (genus *Boswellia;* family Burseraceae), chiefly of East Africa. It is an important incense resin.

Frank'ish (frăngk'ĭsh), *adj.* Like, or relating to, the Franks. — *n.* The Teutonic language of the Franks. See INDO-EUROPEAN LANGUAGES, *Table.*

frank'lin (frăngk'lĭn), *n.* [ME. *frankelein.*] An English freeholder, or substantial householder; in the 14th and 15th centuries, a middle-class landowner.

frank'lin·ite (-īt), *n.* [From *Franklin*, N. J., its locality.] *Mineral.* An iron-black, slightly magnetic oxide of iron, zinc, and manganese. It is a valuable ore.

Frank'lin stove (frăngk'lĭn). A kind of iron fireplace devised by Benjamin Franklin. It is connected to the chimney by a funnel. The term is now applied to any of various open stoves.

frank'ly (frăngk'lĭ), *adv.* In a frank manner; freely.

frank'ness, *n.* Candor; openness.

frank'pledge' (frăngk'plĕj'), *n.* [*frank* free + *pledge.*] *O. Eng. Law.* The system under which, with certain exceptions, each male member of a tithing of 12 years of age or upwards was responsible for the good conduct of other members of the tithing; also, the member himself, or the tithing.

fran'tic (frăn'tĭk), *adj.* [OF. *frenetique*, fr. L., fr. Gr. *phrenitikos.* See FRENZY.] **1.** *Rare.* Mentally deranged; insane. **2.** Wildly moved; frenzied. — **fran'ti·cal·ly** (-tĭ·kăl·ĭ), *adv.* — **fran'tic·ly**, *adv.* — **fran'tic·ness**, *n.*

frap (frăp), *v. t.;* FRAPPED (frăpt); FRAP'PING. [OF. *fraper* (F. *frapper*) to strike.] *Naut.* To tighten, as a tackle.

frap'pé' (frȧ'pā'), *adj.* [F., past part. of *frapper* to strike, chill.] Iced; frozen. — *n.* A frappé mixture or drink. — *v. t.;* FRAP'PÉED' (-pād'); FRAP'PÉ'ING. To freeze to a soft mush; hence, to chill; to cool.

fratch (frăch), *v. i. & n.* *Dial. Eng.* Dispute; quarrel.

fra'ter (frā'tĕr), *n.* [L.] Literally, a brother; hence: **a** *Obs.* A friar. **b** A comrade.

fra'ter, *n.* [OF. *freitor, refraitor, refeitor.* See REFECTORY.] *Hist.* A refectory of a monastery.

fra·ter'nal (frȧ·tûr'năl; -n'l), *adj.* [ML. *fraternalis*, fr. L. *fraternus*, fr. *frater* brother.] **1.** Of, pertaining to, or involving brethren. **2.** Like, or relating to, a fraternal society. **3.** *Biol.* Designating twins derived from two ova. Cf. IDENTICAL. — **fra·ter'nal·ism** (-ĭz'm), *n.* — **fra·ter'nal·ly**, *adv.*

fraternal society, association, *or* **order.** A society organized for the pursuit of some common object by working together in brotherly union.

fra·ter'ni·ty (-nĭ·tĭ), *n.; pl.* -TIES (-tĭz). [OF. *fraternité*, fr. L. *fraternitas.*] **1.** State of being brothers; brotherliness. **2.** A body of men associated for their common interest, business, or pleasure; a brotherhood; specif.: **a** A religious or ecclesiastical brotherhood. **b** In American colleges, a student organization formed chiefly to promote friendship and welfare among the members, and usually having secret rites and a name consisting of Greek letters. **3.** Men of the same class, profession, character, or tastes; as, the legal *fraternity.*

frat'er·nize (frăt'ĕr·nīz), *v. i.* **1.** To associate or hold fellowship as brothers. **2.** *Chiefly Brit.* To be friendly or amiable. **3.** To engage in comradely exchange of tokens or associate on intimate terms, esp. with enemy soldiers or with civilians of an occupied country and often contrary to military orders, also with members of any hostile group; often specifically, to engage in illicit relations with women of an occupied country. — *v. t.* To bring into fellowship, as nations. — **frat'er·ni·za'tion** (frăt'ĕr·nĭ·zā'shŭn; -nī·zā'-), *n.* — **frat'er·niz'er** (-nīz'ĕr), *n.*

frat'ri·cide (frăt'rĭ·sīd; frā'trĭ·sīd), *n.* [F., fr. L. *fratricidium* a brother's murder, fr. *fratricida* a brother's murderer, fr. *frater, fratris,* brother + *caedere* to kill.] **1.** Act of one who murders or kills one's own brother. Cf. SORORICIDE. **2.** [F., fr. L. *fratricida.*] One who murders or kills his own brother. — **frat'ri·cid'al** (-sīd'ăl; -'l; 2), *adj.*

‖**Frau** (frou), *n.; pl.* FRAUEN (frou'ĕn). [G.] In Germany, a married woman; a wife; — as a title, equiv. to *Mrs.*

fraud (frôd), *n.* [OF. *fraude*, fr. L. *fraus, fraudis.*] **1.** Deception; deceit; trickery. **2.** Artifice; trick. **3.** *Colloq.* A cheat; impostor. **4.** *Law.* An intentional perversion of truth to induce another to part with some valuable thing belonging to him, or to surrender a legal right. — **Syn.** See DECEPTION: IMPOSTURE.

fraud'u·lence (frôd'ū·lĕns), *n.* Quality or state of being fraudulent; deliberate deceit. — **fraud'u·len·cy** (-lĕn·sĭ), *n.*

fraud'u·lent (-lĕnt), *adj.* [OF., fr. L. *fraudulentus.*] **1.** Using fraud; deceitful. **2.** Characterized by or founded on fraud; of the nature of fraud. **3.** Obtained or performed by artifice. — **fraud'u·lent·ly**, *adv.*

fraught (frôt), *n.* [MD. *vracht, vrecht.*] *Obs.* A load; as, a *fraught* of water, i. e., two bucketfuls. — *v. t.* *Obs.* To freight; load. — *adj.* Freighted; laden; big or teeming (with); as, words *fraught* with meaning.

‖**Fräu'lein** (froi'līn), *n. sing. & pl.* [G., dim. of *frau* woman.] In Germany, a young lady; an unmarried woman; — as a title, equivalent to *Miss.*

Fraun'ho'fer lines (froun'hō'fĕr). [After J. von *Fraunhofer*, Bavarian physicist.] *Physics.* The dark lines in the solar spectrum, as observed on the earth.

frax'i·nel'la (frăk'sĭ·nĕl'ȧ), *n.* [NL. dim. of L. *fraxinus* the ash tree; — alluding to its leaves.] A Eurasian perennial herb (*Dictamnus albus*) of the rue family, with flowers which exhale an inflammable vapor in hot weather.

fray (frā), *n.* [Abbr. fr. AFFRAY.] A commotion; affray; combat; fight. — *v. t.* *Archaic.* To frighten; alarm. — *v. i.* *Obs.* To brawl; attack.

fray, *v. t. & i.* [OF. *freier, froier*, to rub, fr. L. *fricare.*] To wear, wear off, or wear into shreds, by rubbing; to ravel. — *n.* A fraying or a place injured by wear or rubbing.

fraz'zle (frăz''l), *v. t. & i.;* FRAZ'ZLED (-'ld); FRAZ'ZLING (-lĭng). *Chiefly U. S.* To fray; to wear or pull into tatters; also, to tire or fag. — *n.* *Chiefly U. S.* State of being frazzled; a frayed or tag end.

freak (frēk), *v. t.* *Poetic.* To variegate; checker; streak. — *n.* A streak; a fleck.

freak, *n.* **1.** A whim or fancy; a caprice. **2.** Freakish quality or disposition; whimsicality. **3.** An irregular or abnormal product of some process; also, a natural object, as an animal, plant, or flower, that exhibits markedly irregular or abnormal features; a lusus naturae; monstrosity. — **Syn.** See CAPRICE.

freak'ish (frēk'ĭsh), *adj.* Odd; whimsical; capricious. — **freak'ish·ly**, *adv.* — **freak'ish·ness**, *n.*

freak'y (-ĭ), *adj.;* FREAK'I·ER (-ĭ·ĕr); FREAK'I·EST. Freakish. — **freak'i·ly**, *adv.* — **freak'i·ness**, *n.*

freck'le (frĕk''l), *n.* [ME. *freken*, fr. ON. *freknur*, pl.] A small brownish spot in the skin, esp. on the face, neck, or hands; lentigo. — *v. t.;* FRECK'LED (-'ld); FRECK'LING (-lĭng). To mark with freckles. — *v. i.* To become marked with freckles. — **freck'ly** (-lĭ), *adj.*

free (frē), *adj.;* FRE'ER (frē'ĕr); FRE'EST. [AS. *frēo, frēoh, frī.*] **1.** Not subject to an arbitrary external power; independent; specif.: **a** Not in the condition of a slave or serf. **b** Enjoying political independence; as, a *free* city or nation. **2.** Of the nature of, pertaining to, or characteristic of, that which is free, or independent; as, *free* labor; a *free* state. **3.** Not subject to some particular authority or obligation; released, as from a tax, duty, etc.; hence, released from any onerous condition; as, *free* from pain. **4.** **a** Having no trade restrictions; open for commercial purposes to all; as, a *free* port, ship, road. **b** Given without cost or payment; gratuitous; as, *free* admission; a *free* pass. **5.** Not determined by anything beyond its own nature or being; choosing or capable of choosing for itself; as, a *free* agent; *free* will. **6.** Denoting unconstrained or uncontrolled action; as: **a** Made voluntarily or spontaneously; as, a *free* offer. **b** Liberal; lavish; as, *free* with his money. **c** Profuse; copious. **d** Frank; often, overfree; forward. **e** Loose; licentious. **7.** Not confined, restrained, or restricted. **8.** Hence, not held to strict form or narrow limitations; specif.: **a** Not observant of conventional or established forms, esp. in composition; as, *free* verse. **b** Not literal or exact; as, a *free* translation. **c** Allowable; as, it is *free* for him to think so; of a competition, without restrictions as to contestants; open. **9.** Devoid; also, outside; beyond. **10.** Not united with anything else; as, a *free* caryatid; *free* ore. **11.** *Naut.* Favorable; — of a wind blowing from a direction more than six points from straight ahead.

Syn. **Free, independent, sovereign, autonomous** mean not subject to the rule or control of another. **Free** stresses the absence of external compulsion or determination rather than the absence of all restraint; **independent** implies a standing alone but especially, when applied to a state or government, it implies lack of connection with any other that has power to interfere with its citizens, its laws, etc.; **sovereign** stresses the absence of a superior power and implies supremacy within a thing's own domain or sphere; **autonomous** implies strict independence in the-

ory, but in practice often implies self-government, as in matters pertaining to the country itself.
— *adv.* **1.** Freely. **2.** Without charge; as, admitted *free.* **3.** *Naut.* With the wind more than six points from dead ahead; as, sailing, steering, etc., *free.*
— *v. t.;* FREED (frēd); FREE'ING. To make free; to set at liberty; to exempt; relieve; disengage; clear; — often with *from* or *of.*
Syn. Free, release, liberate, emancipate, manumit, discharge mean to set loose from anything that restrains or constrains. Free refers not only to persons, but to things, whether held under restraint as a prisoner or a captive or by being entangled, encumbered, or the like; release chiefly implies a setting loose of a person from that which restrains him by keeping him confined, under obligation, or the like; liberate implies a setting at liberty, not only of a person under restraint, but a person or thing attached in some way to another; emancipate implies the liberation of a person from subjection; manumit implies emancipation from servitude or slavery; discharge, a more general term, implies a liberation of a person or thing from that which confines, whether it also restrains or not.
free alongside ship *or* **vessel**. Delivered at the side of the ship free of charges, the buyer's liability then beginning. Abbr. *f.a.s.* Cf. FREE ON BOARD.
free'board' (frē'bōrd'; 70), *n.* **a** *Naut.* A vessel's side, or the distance, between water line and deck. See DECK, *Illust.* **b** In automobiles, the space between the ground and the undercarriage.
free'boot' (-bōōt'), *v. i.* To act as a freebooter.
free'boot'er (-bōōt'ẽr), *n.* [D. *vrijbuiter,* fr. *vrij* free + *buit* booty.] One who goes about plundering; pirate.
free'boot'y (-ĭ), *n.* *Obs.* Plunder or plundering.
free'born' (-bôrn'; 2), *adj.* Born free; not born in vassalage; also, pertaining or suitable to one born free.
free companion. In the Middle Ages, one of a band (**free company**) of mercenaries who could be hired by any prince or country. Cf. CONDOTTIERE, FREE LANCE.
freed'man (frēd'măn), *n.* A man freed from slavery.
free'dom (frē'dŭm), *n.* [AS. *frēodōm.*] **1.** Quality or state of being free; as: **a** Liberation from slavery, imprisonment, or restraint. **b** Exemption from necessity, in choice and action; as, the *freedom* of the will. **c** Frankness; outspokenness. **d** Improper familiarity. **e** Ease; facility. **f** Boldness of conception or performance. **g** Exemption; immunity; as, *freedom* from care. **h** Possession of the rights or privileges of a citizen, as of a city. **i** Unrestricted use; as, the *freedom* of my house is his. **2.** A privilege; franchise. **3.** *Philos.* The status of the will as an uncaused cause of human actions; also, sometimes, as with Hegelians, self-determination; spiritual self-fulfillment.
Syn. Freedom, liberty, license mean, as here compared, the power or condition of acting without compulsion. Freedom, a very general term, may imply at one extreme total absence of restraint and at the other, an unawareness of being hampered in any way; liberty often differs from *freedom* in implying a power to say, do, etc., what one wishes, as distinguished from being uninhibited in doing, thinking, etc., or a release from restraint or compulsion (as, to have the *liberty* to come and go; to set at *liberty*); license implies liberty that consists in breaking laws or rules, and is sometimes regarded as an abuse and other times as a privilege.
freedom of the seas. The doctrine that merchant ships of all nonbelligerent nations shall be free to traverse all the seas, outside of territorial waters, alike in peace and war.
freed'wom'an (frēd'wŏŏm'ăn), *n.* A woman freed from slavery.
free enterprise. Freedom of private business to organize and operate for profit in a competitive system without interference by government beyond regulation necessary for keeping the national economy in balance.
free'-for-all', *n.* A competition or fight open to or entered by all.
free form. *Ling.* A linguistic form which can be used alone with meaning (*child, children, redemption*). Cf. BOUND FORM, MORPHEME.
Free French, Free France. See FIGHTING FRENCH.
free gold. **a** Gold in the United States treasury not required to redeem gold certificates. It includes the legal reserve. **b** *Mining.* Gold not combined with another element.
free'hand' (frē'hănd'; 2), *adj.* Done by the hand, without support, the guidance of instruments, measurements, etc.; — said of a style of drawing or of a drawing thus executed.
free hand. The right to act or decide on one's own responsibility; as, to give a subordinate a *free hand.*
free'hand'ed (-hăn'dĕd; -dĭd; 2), *adj.* Done with a free hand; also, openhanded; liberal.
free'heart'ed (-här'tĕd; -tĭd; 2), *adj.* Having a free heart; frank; liberal; generous; spontaneous.
free'hold' (-hōld'), *n.* *Law.* A tenure of real property by which an estate of inheritance or for life is held, or the estate itself; also, a similar tenure of an office or dignity. — **free'hold'**, *adj.* — **free'hold'er** (-hōl'dẽr), *n.*
free lance. **a** Formerly, a knight whose services were purchasable by any state or commander; hence, a person who acts on his own responsibility without regard to authority. Cf. CONDOTTIERE, FREE COMPANION. **b** One who writes, esp. for newspapers or magazines, without being regularly employed; hence, an artist or actor who moves from one engagement to another. — **free'-lance'** (frē'láns'; 2), *adj.* & *v. i.*
free liver. One who gratifies his appetites without stint. — **free'-liv'ing** (frē'lĭv'ĭng; 2), *adj.*
free love. The doctrine or practice of living openly with one of the opposite sex at pleasure, without marriage.
free'ly (frē'lĭ), *adv.* In a free manner.
free'man (-măn), *n.* **1.** One who enjoys liberty, esp. civil or political liberty. **2.** A citizen of a borough, town, or state.
free'mar'tin (-mär'tĭn), *n.* A sexually imperfect, usually sterile, female calf, twinborn with a male.
Free'ma'son (frē'mā's'n; frē'mā's'n), *n.* A member of a celebrated secret society (more fully *Free and Accepted Masons*), consisting of persons who are united for fraternal purposes. — **free'ma·son'ic** (frē'mȧ·sŏn'ĭk), *adj.*
Free'ma'son·ry (-rĭ; 2), *n.* **1.** Principles, institutions, or practices of Freemasons. Cf. SCOTTISH RITE; YORK RITE; SHRINE, 4; KNIGHT TEMPLAR. **2.** [*not cap.*] Natural or instinctive fellowship.
free'ness (frē'nĕs; -nĭs), *n.* Condition of being free.
free on board. Delivered free of charge on the means of conveyance, as a train or vessel; — said of goods or freight; — usually abbreviated *f.o.b.*; as, *f.o.b.* Detroit. Cf. FREE ALONGSIDE SHIP.
free port. *Com.* An enclosed, guarded port, or section of a port, where goods may be received and shipped free of customs duty and of most customs regulations. Cf. FREE ZONE.
free'si·a (frē'zhĭ·ȧ; -zĭ·ȧ), *n.* [NL., after E. M. *Fries,* Sw. botanist.] Any of a genus (*Freesia*) of sweet-scented South African herbs of the iris family.
free silver. *Econ.* The free coinage of silver, often specif. at a fixed ratio with gold, as at the ratio of 16 to 1. — **free'-sil'ver**, *adj.*
free soil. *Hist.* Territory in which no slaves can be held.
free'-soil' (frē'soil'; 2), *adj.* *U. S. Hist.* Pertaining to or advocating the nonextension of slavery; — applied [*caps.*] esp. to a party (**Free-Soil party**) active in opposing the extension of slavery to the Territories during the period 1848–56; also, of or pertaining to this party or its principles. — **free'-soil'er, Free'-soil'er**, *n.*
free'-spo'ken (-spō'kĕn; 2), *adj.* Outspoken. — **free'-spo'ken·ly**, *adv.* — **free'-spo'ken·ness**, *n.*
free'stone' (-stōn'), *n.* **1.** Any stone, but esp. sandstone or limestone, that may be cut freely without splitting. **2.** *Hort.* A stone which, in certain varieties of peach, plum, cherry, etc., does not adhere to the flesh; hence, any fruit having such a stone. Cf. CLINGSTONE.
Freestone State. Connecticut; — from its freestone quarries.
free'-swim'ming (*see Pron.,* § 2), *adj.* *Zool.* Able to swim about; — opposed to *attached.* — **free'-swim'mer**, *n.*
free'think'er (frē'thĭngk'ẽr; 2), *n.* One who forms opinions independently, esp. independently of the authority of revelation or the church; hence, an agnostic. See FREE THOUGHT. — **Syn.** See ATHEIST. — **free'think'ing**, *n.* & *adj.*
free thought. Thought which is free of traditional authority in matters of opinion, esp. in respect to religion.
free trade. **a** Commerce not subjected to burdens or restrictions, as by tariff regulations. **b** Specif.: Trade free from any restrictions, burdens, or differences in treatment intended to change its natural course; also, the system, policy, or maintenance of such trade; — opp. to *protection.* **c** *Archaic Dial.* Smuggling. — **free'-trade'** (2), *adj.*
free verse. = VERS LIBRE. — **free'-ver'si·fi'er** (-vûr'sĭ·fī'ẽr), *n.*
free'way' (frē'wā'), *n.* **1.** A multilane highway with access only at established points and with usually complete grade separation at intersections. **2.** A toll-free expressway.
free'wheel' (frē'hwēl'), *n.* **1.** A transmission system in an automotive vehicle with a device permitting the propeller shaft to run freely when its speed becomes greater than that of the engine shaft. **2.** *Mach.* A clutch fitted in the rear hub of a bicycle, which permits the rear wheel to run on free from the rear sprocket when the pedals are stopped. — **free'wheel'ing**, *n.* & *adj.*
free will. Unhampered or uncoerced choice; specif., the doctrine that human beings are not controlled in their choices by physical or divinely imposed necessity.
free'will' (-wĭl'; 2), *adj.* Voluntary; spontaneous.
freeze (frēz), *v. i.;* FROZE (frōz); FRO'ZEN (frō'z'n); FREEZ'ING. [AS. *frēosan.*] **1.** To be hardened by cold into ice or a like solid. **2.** To become coldly formal in manner. **3.** To adhere by or as if by freezing; as, the tool *froze* to the walls of the well. **4.** To become clogged with ice; as, the water pipes *froze.* **5.** To be at a temperature cold enough to freeze water. **6.** *Colloq.* To stand motionless. — *v. t.* **1.** To congeal; to harden into ice. **2.** To chill; sometimes, to discourage by coldness of demeanor; also, to anesthetize (a part) by cold. **3.** To harden, damage, kill, or the like, by frost. **4.** To clog with ice; as, the intense cold *froze* the pipes. **5.** *Financial Cant, U. S.* To fix or stabilize a price, as of a security or a commodity. **6.** To fix inflexibly, as by executive order, at the point or level or in the status governing on a given day; as, to *freeze* a price, wage, machine design, etc.; also, to forbid further manufacture, use, or sale of (a raw material). **7.** *Finance.* To immobilize completely (foreign-owned bank balances) by legislation or governmental edict prohibiting exchange, withdrawal, or even expenditure within the country. Cf. BLOCK, *v. t.,* 5 **a**.
— *n.* **a** Act of freezing, or state of being frozen. **b** A state of the weather characterized by low temperature.
freez'er (frēz'ẽr), *n.* One who or that which cools or freezes; esp., a compartment or apparatus for keeping food, etc., at a temperature below freezing, or for freezing perishable food rapidly at a temperature of −10° to −30° F. for storage in a locker, or for both freezing and storage.
freez'ing point (frēz'ĭng). *Physical Chem.* The temperature at which a liquid solidifies; — applied esp. to water, whose freezing point is 32° F. or 0° C. Abbr. *f.p.*
free zone. An area within which goods may be received and stored without payment of duty. Cf. FREE PORT.
freight (frāt), *n.* [ME. *freyte,* fr. MD. *vrecht.*] **1.** Compensation paid for the transport of goods. **2.** That with which anything is laden for transportation; lading; cargo. **3.** **a** Transportation of goods, or a line (railroad, motor, airplane, or steamship) used esp. for this business; specif., the ordinary transportation of goods afforded by a common carrier (esp. a railroad company). **b** A train carrying freight (def. 2); a freight train; — in England called *goods train.* — *v. t.* **1.** To load with goods for transportation; in general, to load or burden. **2.** To transport or ship by freight.
freight'age (-ĭj), *n.* **1.** Charge for transportation. **2.** Freight; cargo. **3.** The transportation of freight.
freight'er (-ẽr), *n.* **1.** One who loads a ship. **2.** One employed in receiving and forwarding freight. **3.** One for whom freight is transported. **4.** A vessel used mainly to carry freight.
fremd (frĕmd; frāmd), *adj.* [AS. *fremede, fremde.*] *Obs. exc. Dial.* Strange; foreign; hostile.
frem'i·tus (frĕm'ĭ·tŭs), *n. sing.* & *pl.* [L., a murmuring, roaring.] *Med.* Palpable vibration or thrill.
French (frĕnch), *adj.* [AS. *frencisc.*] Of or pertaining to France or its inhabitants or their language. — *n.* **1.** Collectively, the people of France. **2.** The chief language of the French people, descended from Latin. It is commonly divided by periods into ***Old French*** (9th–16th cent. or, sometimes, 9th–13th cent., the term ***Middle French*** being then applied to the language of the 14th–16th. cent.) and ***Modern French.*** See INDO-EUROPEAN LANGUAGE, *Table.* — *v. t.* To prepare in a French manner or style, as rib chops by trimming the meat from the ends of the ribs. — **French'man, French'wom'an**, *n.*
French Academy. See IMMORTAL, *n.,* 2 **b**.
French Canadian. **1.** A Canadian descended from early French colonists. Cf. HABITANT, 2. **2.** French as spoken in Canada. **3.** An

animal of a small hardy breed of black or brown dairy cattle originating in Quebec and resembling Jerseys.
French chalk. A soft white granular variety of steatite used for drawing lines on cloth, in dry cleaning, etc.
French chop. A rib chop with the meat trimmed from the outer end of the rib. See LAMB, *Illust.*
French dressing. A salad dressing of oil and vinegar seasoned with salt, and pepper, mustard, or other spice.
French endive. See ENDIVE.
French fried potatoes. Potatoes cut into strips and cooked by frying in deep fat.
French heel. A high curved heel, pitched well forward, used on some kinds of women's shoes.
French horn. A brass-wind instrument derived from the hunting horn.
French'i·fy (frĕn'chĭ·fī), *v. t. & i.*; -FIED (-fīd); -FY'ING. Also **french'i·fy.** To make or become French.
French leave. An informal, hasty, or secret departure.
French pastry. Fancy pastry baked in individual portions varying in shape, and filled variously, as with custards or preserved fruits.
French Revolution. See REVOLUTION, 5.
French telephone. A handset.
French toast. Bread dipped in egg and milk and sautéed.
French window. *Arch.* A casement window, usually reaching to the floor, opening like folding doors.
fre·net'ic (frē·nĕt'ĭk), **fre·net'i·cal** (-ĭ·kăl), *adj.* [See PHRENETIC.] Frantic. Cf. PHRENETIC. — *n.* A frantic person. — **fre·net'i·cal·ly,** *adv.*
fre'num, frae'num (frē'nŭm), *n.*; *pl.* -NUMS (-nŭmz), -NA (-nȧ). [L., a bridle.] *Anat. & Zool.* A connecting fold of membrane serving to support or restrain any part, as that which binds down the under side of the tongue.
fren'zied (frĕn'zĭd), *adj.* Affected with frenzy; frantic.
fren'zy (-zĭ), *n.*; *pl.* -ZIES (-zĭz). [OF. *frenesie,* fr. ML., fr. Gr. *phrenēsis, phrenitis,* disease of the mind, fr. *phrēn* mind.] Any violent mental agitation approaching to distraction; wild emotional excitement; as, a *frenzy* of grief, despair, or joy. — **Syn.** See INSPIRATION. — *v. t.*; FREN'ZIED (-zĭd); FREN'ZY·ING. To affect with frenzy; to drive to madness.
Fre'on (frē'ŏn), *n.* A trade-mark applied to a group of halogenated hydrocarbons having one or more fluorine atoms in the molecule, used as refrigerants.
fre'quence (frē'kwĕns), *n.* Frequency.
fre'quen·cy (-kwĕn·sĭ), *n.*; *pl.* -CIES (-sĭz). **1.** Quality or state of being frequent; as: **a** *Archaic.* A crowded state; hence, a crowd. **b** Fact or condition of returning frequently; occurrence often repeated. **2.** *Math.* The ratio of the number of actual occurrences of an event to the number of possible occurrences (in the same time). In statistics, frequency is the ratio of the number of individuals falling within a single class to the total number of individuals classified or classifiable. The distribution of the individuals among the various classes is called the **frequency distribution.** **3.** *Physics.* In periodic motion, the number of vibrations or cycles in a unit of time; specif.: *Elec.* The number of complete cycles of current per second produced by an alternating-current generator.
frequency modulation. *Radio.* Modulation of the frequency of the transmitting wave in accordance with speech or a signal; specif., the practically static-free system of broadcasting using this method of modulation. Abbr. *FM* or *F.M.* Contrasted with ***amplitude modulation*** (abbr. *AM* or *A.M.*), modulation of the amplitude of the transmitting wave, or the system using such modulation.
fre'quent (frē'kwĕnt), *adj.* [F. or L.; F. *fréquent,* fr. L. *frequens, -entis,* crowded, frequent.] **1.** *Obs.* Filled; thronged. **2.** Happening at short intervals; often repeated. **3.** Habitual; persistent.
fre·quent' (frē·kwĕnt'), *v. t. & i.* To visit often; to associate with, to be in, or to resort to, habitually.
Syn. **Frequent, haunt, habituate** mean to resort to frequently or habitually. **Frequent** implies little more than this and is used often in reference to places but sometimes to the sacraments, persons, etc.; **haunt** implies a continual or pertinacious frequenting or, by extension, a frequent obsessing as thoughts, fears, etc.; **habituate** adds to *frequent* the implication of a fixed habit.
fre'quen·ta'tion (frē'kwĕn·tā'shŭn), *n.* Act or habit of frequenting, or visiting often.
fre·quen'ta·tive (frē·kwĕn'tȧ·tĭv), *adj.* *Gram.* Serving to express frequent repetition; as, the *frequentative* verbs *babble, chatter, stutter.* — *n.* A frequentative verb.
fre·quent'er (frē·kwĕn'tẽr), *n.* One who frequents.
fre'quent·ly, *adv.* At frequent or short intervals.
‖**frère** (frâr), *n.* [F.] **a** Brother. **b** Friar.
fres'co (frĕs'kō), *n.*; *pl.* -COES or -COS (-kōz). [It., fr. *fresco* fresh.] **1.** *Obs.* Cool air; shade. Cf. ALFRESCO. **2. a** The art or method of painting on freshly spread plaster before it dries. **b** A fresco painting. — *v. t.*; FRES'COED (-kōd); FRES'CO·ING. To paint in fresco, as walls. — **fres'co·er** (-kō·ẽr), *n.*
fresh (frĕsh), *adj.* [ME. fr. OF. and AS.; ME. *fresch,* fr. OF. *fres, freis,* fem. *fresche;* ME. *fersch,* fr. AS. *fersc.*] **1.** Newly produced, gathered, or made; hence, not stored or preserved. **2.** Not salt; as, *fresh* water. **3.** Pure; refreshing; cool; brisk. **4.** Of the wind, strong; specif., according to the latest wind scale of the U. S. Weather Bureau, designating a velocity of 19 to 24 miles per hour. Cf. BEAUFORT'S SCALE. **5.** *Slang.* Intoxicated; tipsy. **6.** Coming or experienced anew; recent; as, *fresh* news; hence, additional; further; as, a *fresh* start. **7.** Having its original qualities unimpaired: **a** Not stale, sour, or decayed. **b** Not faded, tarnished, or the like. **8.** Full of, or renewed in, vigor, alacrity, etc. In dairy farming said specif. of a cow that has recently calved. **9.** Having little or no experience; raw; green. **10.** *Slang.* Presumptuous, obtrusive, or meddlesome. — **Syn.** See NEW. — **Ant.** Stale. — *n.* **1.** A freshet of water. **2.** A stream, spring, or pool of fresh water. — *v. t. & i. Now Dial.* To refresh. — *adv. Colloq.* Freshly.
fresh'en (frĕsh'ĕn; -'n), *v. t.* **1.** To make fresh; esp., to refresh; revive. **2.** *Naut.* To relieve, as a rope, by change of place where friction wears it. — *v. i.* To grow or become fresh; specif.: **a** To grow more brisk or strong; as, the wind *freshens.* **b** To become fresh in appearance; to brighten. **c** To lose saltness. **d** Of a cow, to calve.
fresh'et (-ĕt; -ĭt), *n.* [*fresh,* n. + *-et.*] **1.** *Obs.* A stream of fresh water. **2.** An overflowing of a stream.
fresh'ly, *adv.* In a fresh manner.
fresh'man (frĕsh'măn), *n.*; *pl.* -MEN (-mĕn). A novice; esp., a student during his or her first year, as in a college.
fresh'ness, *n.* Fresh state, quality, or character.
fresh'-wa'ter, *adj.* **1.** Of, pertaining to, or living in fresh water. **2.** Accustomed to navigate fresh waters only; unskilled as a seaman. **3.** Hence, untrained; unskilled.
fret (frĕt), *v. t.*; FRET'TED; FRET'TING. [ME. *freten* to eat, fr. AS. *fretan.* See FOR-; EAT.] **1.** To eat away; gnaw; also, to wear away; rub; chafe. **2.** To make by gnawing or wearing away a substance; as, to *fret* a hole in cloth. **3.** To roughen, agitate, or disturb; to ripple. **4.** To tease; irritate; vex; worry. — *v. i.* **1.** To gnaw; — with *into, on, upon.* **2.** To make way by corrosion; hence, to rankle. **3.** To chafe; fray. **4.** To be vexed or irritated. **5.** To be agitated, as a stream of water. — *n.* **1.** Act or state of erosion; a wasting away. **2.** A worn or eroded spot. **3.** Agitation of mind.
fret, *n.* [OF. *frette* latticework, fr. *fretté,* past part., adorned with interlaced work.] **1.** Ornamental network, esp. a woman's headdress of former times. **2.** An ornament of small straight lines or bars, arranged in symmetrical patterns. **3.** *Arch.* Ornamental work in relief; fretwork. — *v. t.* **1.** To adorn with lines or figures that interlace; to embroider with gold or silver; hence, to variegate; checker. **2.** *Arch.* To enrich with embossed, or pierced, carved patterns.
fret, *n.* *Music.* A ridge of metal, ivory, etc., fixed across the finger board of a guitar or similar instrument. — *v. t.* To furnish with frets.
fret'ful (frĕt'fo͝ol; -f'l), *adj.* Disposed to fret; peevish; irritable; querulous. — **fret'ful·ly,** *adv.* — **fret'ful·ness,** *n.*
fret saw. A saw for cutting frets, scrolls, etc. — **fret'-saw',** *v. t.*
fret'ty (frĕt'ĭ), *adj.*; FRET'TI·ER (-ĭ·ẽr); FRET'TI·EST. **a** Fretful. **b** *Colloq.* Festering; inflamed, as a sore.
fret'ty, *adj.* [See FRET network.] Marked as by fretwork.

Frets, 2. 1, 2, 3, 4 Greek Frets; 5 Japanese Fret.

fret'work' (frĕt'wûrk'), *n.* Work adorned with frets; ornamental openwork or work in relief, esp. when elaborate; hence, any play of light and shade, or the like.
Freud'i·an (froid'ĭ·ăn), *adj.* Relating to, or according with, the theories or practices of Sigmund Freud, in regard esp. to the causes and treatment of hysteria and other psychopathic phenomena, and the interpretation of dreams and other mental products, as based upon a psychology of the unconscious. See PSYCHOANALYSIS. — **Freud'i·an,** *n.* — **Freud'i·an·ism** (-ĭz'm), *n.*
Frey (frā), **Freyr** (frâr), *n.* [ON. *Freyr.*] *Norse Relig.* God of fertility and the crops, of peace and prosperity. See VANIR.
Frey'a (frā'ä), **Frey'ja** (frā'yä), *n.* [ON. *Freyja.*] *Norse Relig.* The goddess of love and beauty. Her famous possession is the jewel, or necklace, ***Brisingamen,*** obtained from the dwarfs, which Loki tried to steal and Heimdall defended. See VANIR.
fri'a·ble (frī'ȧ·b'l), *adj.* [F., fr. L. *friabilis,* fr. *friare* to rub or crumble into small pieces.] Easily crumbled or pulverized; as, *friable* soil. — **Syn.** See FRAGILE. — **fri'a·bil'i·ty** (-bĭl'ĭ·tĭ), **fri'a·ble·ness,** *n.*
fri'ar (frī'ẽr), *n.* [OF. *frere, fredre,* brother, friar, fr. L. *frater* brother.] *R.C.Ch.* A member of a religious order, esp. of one of the four mendicant orders: Dominicans, Franciscans, Carmelites, and Augustinians. Cf. BLACK FRIAR, GRAY FRIAR, WHITE FRIAR. — **Syn.** See RELIGIOUS.
fri'ar·bird' (-bûrd'), *n.* An Australian honey eater (*Philemon corniculatus*) with bare head; also, a bird of any allied species.
fri'ar's lan'tern (frī'ẽrz). Ignis fatuus, or will-o'-the-wisp.
fri'ar·y (frī'ẽr·ĭ), *n.*; *pl.* FRIARIES (-ĭz). A monastery; a brotherhood of friars.
frib'ble (frĭb''l), *adj.* Frivolous; trifling. — *n.* A frivolous person or thing; also, frivolity. — *v. i.*; FRIB'BLED (-'ld); FRIB'BLING (-lĭng). **1.** To act in a trifling manner; to act frivolously. **2.** *Obs.* To totter; falter. — *v. t.* To trifle or fool (away); as, to *fribble* away a fortune. — **frib'bler** (-lẽr), *n.*
fric'an·deau' (frĭk'ăn·dō'; frĭk'ăn·dō), *n.* [F. *fricandeau.*] Larded veal, roasted and glazed in its own juices.
fric'as·see' (frĭk'ȧ·sē'; 2), *n.* [F. *fricassée,* fr. *fricasser* to fry, fricassee.] A dish made of fowls, veal, or other meat cut into pieces, and stewed in a gravy. — (-sē'), *v. t.*; FRIC'AS·SEED' (-sēd'); FRIC'AS·SEE'ING. To cook as a fricassee.
fric'a·tive (frĭk'ȧ·tĭv), *adj.* [See FRICTION.] *Phonet.* Characterized by frictional rustling of the breath as it is emitted; — said of certain consonants (*f, v, s, z,* etc.). — *n.* A fricative consonant.
fric'tion (frĭk'shŭn), *n.* [F., fr. L. *frictio,* fr. *fricare, frictum,* to rub.] **1.** Act of rubbing one body against another; attrition. **2.** Clashing between two persons or parties in opinions or work; disagreement tending to prevent or retard progress. **3.** *Mech.* The resistance to relative motion between two bodies in contact.
fric'tion·al (-ăl; -'l), *adj.* Relating to, or moved or produced by, friction; as, *frictional* electricity. — **fric'tion·al·ly,** *adv.*
friction clutch *or* **coupling.** *Mach.* Any clutch or coupling operating by friction, for engaging or disengaging revolving parts or for use as a safety appliance.
friction drive. *Automobiles.* A power-transmission system having a **friction gear** (gearing for transmitting motion by surface friction instead of teeth), the driver and follower of which are arranged so that by varying their position relative to one another a full range of variation in desired speed ratios may be obtained.
friction match. A match that is ignited by friction.
friction tape. *Elec.* A tape impregnated with some insulating material and an adhesive, used to protect, insulate, and support electrical conductors.
Fri'day (frī'dĭ), *n.* [AS. *frīgedæg,* fr. *Frīg,* name of a goddess + *dæg* day.] The sixth day of the week. Abbr. *Fri.*
fried (frīd), *past & past part.* of FRY.
fried'cake' (-kāk'), *n.* A cake in the form of a ring, twist, ball, or strip, fried in deep fat; a doughnut; cruller.
friend (frĕnd), *n.* [AS. *frēond,* orig. pres. part. of a verb meaning to love, AS. *frēon, frēogan.*] **1.** One attached to another by esteem, respect, and affection; an intimate. **2.** One not hostile; one not a foe; also, one of the same nation, party, kin, etc. **3.** A favorer; a promoter; as, a *friend* to commerce. **4.** *Scot.* A kinsman. **5.** [*cap.*]

One of a religious sect who lay especial stress upon the guidance of the Holy Spirit, reject outward rites and an ordained ministry, practice simplicity of dress and speech, and oppose war. They are popularly called *Quakers*.

friend'ed (frĕn'dĕd; -dĭd), *adj.* Having, or accompanied by, friends.

friend'less, *adj.* Destitute of friends. — **friend'less·ness**, *n.*

friend'ly (frĕnd'lĭ), *adj.*; FRIEND'LI·ER (-lĭ·ẽr); FRIEND'LI·EST. [AS. *frēondlīc.*] **1.** Kindly disposed; hence, amicable; not hostile. **2.** Favorable; propitious. — **Syn.** See AMICABLE. — *n.*; *pl.* -LIES (-lĭz). A friendly person or act. — *adv.* Amicably. — **friend'li·ly**, *adv.* — **friend'li·ness**, *n.*

friend'ship, *n.* State of being friends; friendly attachment; friendliness; amity.

fri'er (frī'ẽr), *n.* A fryer.

Frie'sian (frē'zhăn), *adj.* & *n.* Frisian.

Fries'ic (frēz'ĭk), *adj.* & *n.* Frisian.

frieze (frēz), *n.* [F. *frise.*] A shaggy-piled woolen fabric.

frieze, *n.* [F. *frise*, fr. ML. *frisium* fringe, lappet.] *Arch.* **a** That part of an entablature between the architrave and the cornice, sometimes enriched with sculpture. See ORDER, *Illust.* **b** Any ornamented band in a building, as on a wall; also, a similar band on furniture.

frig'ate (frĭg'ĭt), *n.* [F. *frégate*, fr. It. *fregata.*] **a** Orig., a light vessel propelled by sails and by oars; later, a ship-rigged war vessel intermediate between a corvette and a ship of the line. **b** *Brit. & Canadian Navies.* An antisubmarine escort vessel, smaller than a destroyer.

frigate bird. A long-winged web-footed sea bird (genus *Fregata*), noted for its powers of flight and rapacious habits.

Frigg (frĭg), *n.* Also **Frig'ga** (frĭg'ä). [ON. *Frigg.*] *Norse Myth.* Wife of Odin and goddess of the sky. She presides over marriage and the home, and, with Odin, shares dominion in heaven and knowledge of the world's fate. Cf. FREYA.

fright (frīt), *n.* [AS. *fryhto, fyrhto.*] **1.** Fear excited by sudden danger; alarm. **2.** A thing that frightens; hence, *Colloq.*, anything ugly or shocking. — **Syn.** See FEAR. — *v. t.* To frighten.

fright'en (frīt''n), *v. t.* **1.** To throw into a state of fright; to alarm; scare. **2.** To drive (away or into), force (out), etc., by frightening. — **fright'en·er**, *n.* — **fright'en·ing·ly**, *adv.*

fright'ened (-'nd), *adj.* Affected with fright; made afraid; also, *Colloq.*, afraid.

fright'ful (frīt'fŏŏl; -f'l), *adj.* **1.** Exciting alarm; frightening; also, shocking. **2.** *Colloq.* Excessive; extreme. — **Syn.** See FEARFUL. — **fright'ful·ly**, *adv.*

fright'ful·ness, *n.* **1.** State or quality of being frightful. **2.** Action or policy, esp. in warfare, intended to terrorize; — a translation of German *Schrecklichkeit.*

frig'id (frĭj'ĭd), *adj.* [L. *frigidus*, fr. *frigere* to be cold.] **1.** Intensely cold. **2.** Lacking warmth, ardor, vivacity, etc.; forbidding; stiff and formal. **3.** Abnormally averse to sexual intercourse. — **fri·gid'i·ty** (frĭ·jĭd'ĭ·tĭ), *n.* — **frig'id·ly**, *adv.* — **frig'id·ness**, *n.*

Frigid Zone. See ZONE, *n.*

frig'o·rif'ic (frĭg'ō·rĭf'ĭk), **frig'o·rif'i·cal** (-ĭ·kăl), *adj.* [L. *frigorificus*, fr. *frigus, frigoris*, cold + *facere* to make.] Cooling; chilling.

fri'jol, fri'jole (frē'hōl), *n.*; *pl.* FRIJOLES (frē'hōlz; *Sp.* frē·hō'lās). [Sp. *frijol, fréjol.*] Any cultivated bean of the genus *Phaseolus*, esp. the black seed of a variety of *P. vulgaris.*

frill (frĭl), *n.* **1.** A gathered, fluted, or crimped edging of lace, lawn, etc. **2.** *Colloq.* A showy superfluity in dress, manners, etc. **3.** Something frill-like; as: **a** A wrinkling of the edge of the gelatin film, as of a photographic plate. **b** A fold of hair or feathers about the neck of some animals. — *v. t.* & *i.* To furnish or become furnished with a frill or frills. — **frill'er**, *n.* — **frill'y**, *adj.*

frill'ing, *n.* Frills; also, edging suitable for frills.

‖**Fri'maire'** (frē'mâr'), *n.* [F., fr. *frimas* hoarfrost.] See REVOLUTIONARY CALENDAR.

fringe (frĭnj), *n.* [OF. *frenge, fringe*, fr. L. *fimbria* fringe.] **1.** An edging or trimming made of projecting ends of a fabric, or of loose threads, or strips, twisted or plaited together at the top. **2.** Something resembling such an edging or trimming; a border; margin; also, a fringelike growth or edge, as of hair. **3.** *Optics.* One of a number of light or dark bands, produced by the interference or diffraction of light. **4.** That which lies at the borderline of an activity or a process or is additional to what is basic in importance; — also used attributively, as in *fringe* area, *fringe* benefits. — *v. t.*; FRINGED (frĭnjd); FRING'ING (frĭn'jĭng). To furnish with or as with a fringe; to serve as a fringe for.

fringed gen'tian (frĭnjd). See GENTIAN.

fringed orchis. See ORCHIS.

fringe tree. A small tree (*Chionanthus virginica*) of the olive family, of the southern U. S., having clusters of white flowers.

frin·gil'line (frĭn·jĭl'ĭn; -īn), *adj.* [L. *fringilla* a chaffinch.] Belonging to a family (Fringillidae) of birds, including the finches, sparrows, and usually the buntings.

frip'per·y (frĭp'ẽr·ĭ), *n.*; *pl.* -PERIES (-ĭz). [F. *friperie*, fr. OF. *freperie.*] **1.** *Obs.* Castoff clothes or a place where they are sold; old clothes. **2.** Cheap, tawdry finery; hence, affected elegance.

fri·sette', fri·zette' (frĭ·zĕt'), *n.* [F. *frisette* curl.] A fringe of hair or curls worn about the forehead by women.

‖**fri'seur'** (frē'zûr'), *n.* [F.] A hairdresser.

Fri'sian (frĭzh'ăn; frĭz'ĭ·ăn; 58), *adj.* Of or pertaining to Friesland, the Frisians, or Frisian. — *n.* **1.** One of an ancient Teutonic tribe of Holland; also, an inhabitant of Friesland. **2.** The language of the Frisians, a Low German tongue, closely related to Anglo-Saxon. See INDO-EUROPEAN LANGUAGES, *Table.*

frisk (frĭsk), *adj.* [F. *frisque.*] Frisky. — *n.* **1.** *Obs.* A caracole; caper. **2.** A frolic; a gambol. **3.** A frisking. — *v. i.* To frolic; gambol. — *v. t.* **1.** To move in a frisking manner. **2.** To search (a person) by running the hand over the clothing, through pockets, etc.; hence, to steal from in such a manner. — **frisk'er**, *n.*

frisk'y (frĭs'kĭ), *adj.*; FRISK'I·ER (-kĭ·ẽr); -I·EST. Inclined to frisk; frolicsome. — **frisk'i·ly**, *adv.* — **frisk'i·ness**, *n.*

frit (frĭt), *n.* Also **fritt.** [F. *fritte*, fr. *frit* fried.] **1.** The calcined or partly fused, but yet unvitrified, materials of which glass is made. **2.** *Ceramics.* **a** A partly or wholly fused compound used as a basis for certain glazes. **b** A semifused substance used to impart density to soft porcelain. — *v. t.* & *i.*; FRIT'TED; FRIT'TING. To prepare by heat (materials for glass); to fuse partly.

frith (frĭth), *n.* [ON. *fjörthr.*] An estuary; a firth.

frit'il·lar'y (frĭt'ĭ·lĕr'ĭ *or, esp. Brit.*, frĭ·tĭl'ẽr·ĭ), *n.*; *pl.* -IES (-ĭz). [L. *fritillus* dicebox, from the checkered markings of the petals.] **1.** Any of a genus (*Fritillaria*) of herbs of the lily family having nodding mottled or checkered flowers. **2.** Any of numerous butterflies (*Argynnis* and allied genera) distinguished for their spotted coloration.

frit'ter (frĭt'ẽr), *n.* [F. *friture*, fr. L. *frigere* to fry. See FRY, *v.*] A small quantity of fried batter or batter-covered fruit, corn, etc.

frit'ter, *n.* [OF. *freture, fraiture*, a breaking, thing broken, fr. L. *fractura.*] A fragment; a shred. — *v. t.* To cut or break into fritters; hence, to scatter; waste. — ***fritter away.*** To reduce or waste piecemeal; as, to *fritter away* time. — **frit'ter·er** (-ẽr), *n.*

friv'ol (frĭv'ŭl), *v. i.*; -OLED (-ŭld) or -OLLED; -OL·ING or -OL·LING. To act frivolously; to trifle. — **friv'ol·er** (-ẽr), **friv'ol·ler**, *n.*

fri·vol'i·ty (frĭ·vŏl'ĭ·tĭ), *n.*; *pl.* -TIES (-tĭz). Frivolousness; also, a frivolous act or thing. — **Syn.** See LIGHTNESS.

friv'o·lous (frĭv'ō·lŭs), *adj.* [L. *frivolus.*] **1.** Of little weight or importance; slight. **2.** Given to trifling; marked with unbecoming levity. — **friv'o·lous·ly**, *adv.* — **friv'o·lous·ness**, *n.*

friz, frizz (frĭz), *v. t.*; FRIZZED (frĭzd); FRIZ'ZING, FRIZZ'ING. [F. *friser* to curl, crimp, roll up.] To form into small curls, as hair, or into burrs or tufts, as the nap of cloth. — *v. i.* To be or become frizzed. — *n.* That which is frizzed, as a wig or hair.

frizz (frĭz), *v. t.* & *i.* [From FRY, with imitative ending.] To fry or sear with a sizzling noise.

friz'zle (frĭz''l), *v. t.* & *i.*; -ZLED (-'ld); -ZLING (-lĭng). To sizzle or make sizzle, as in cooking.

friz'zle (frĭz''l), *v.* & *n.* Friz; crimp. — **friz'zly** (-lĭ), *adj.*

friz'zy (-ĭ), *adj.* Frizzly. — **friz'zi·ly**, *adv.* — **friz'zi·ness**, *n.*

fro (frō), *adv.* [ON. *frā.*] From; away; back; — now only in *to and fro.* — *prep. Chiefly Scot.* From.

frock (frŏk), *n.* [OF. *froc*, fr. OHG. *hroc.*] **1.** A coarse gown or habit worn by monks or friars; hence, clerical office. **2.** Any of several garments; as: **a** A tunic or mantle. **b** A smock. **c** A sailor's woolen jersey. **d** A frock coat. **e** A dress; gown. — *v. t.* **1.** To clothe in a frock. **2.** Hence, to make a cleric of.

frock coat. A coat for men, usually double-breasted, having skirts reaching about to the knees. Cf. PRINCE ALBERT.

froe (frō), *n.* Also **frow.** A cleaving tool with handle at right angles to the blade, used for splitting cask staves and shingles from the block.

frog (frŏg), *n.* [AS. *frogga.*] **1.** Any of numerous tailless leaping amphibians (genus *Rana* and allied genera of the family Ranidae), of aquatic habits. The young hatch out as tadpoles. See TADPOLE, *Illust.* Among the best-known American species are the ***bullfrog*** (a large frog, esp. *R. catesbeiana*, *R. grylio*, and *R. aurora*, uttering loud, guttural notes), ***leopard frog*** (*Rana pipiens*), and ***pickerel frog*** (*Rana palustris*). A typical frog differs from a typical toad in its more aquatic habits, smooth skin, webbed feet, and greater agility. Cf. TOAD, TREE TOAD. **2.** In full, **frog in the throat.** A soreness or swelling in the throat; hence, hoarseness. **3.** The triangular elastic horny pad in the middle of the sole of a horse's foot. See HOOF, *Illust.* **4. a** A loop, as on a belt, for receiving a sword, or the like. **b** [Perh. fr. Pg. *froco* tuft of wool or silk, fr. L. *floccus.*] An ornamental braiding sewed on a coat or dress, often in loops and with a fastening for a button. **5.** A device permitting wheels on one rail of a track to cross an intersecting rail. — *v. i.*; FROGGED (frŏgd); FROG'GING. To catch, or look for, frogs.

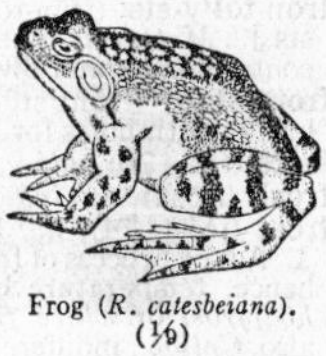

Frog (*R. catesbeiana*). (⅙)

frog'eye' (frŏg'ī'), *n.* Any leaf disease characterized by concentric rings about spots; esp., a tobacco disease caused by a parasitic fungus.

frog'fish' (-fĭsh'), *n.*; *pl.*, see FISH. Any of certain pediculate fishes, as the angler; — from the broad mouth and limblike fins.

frog'hop'per (-hŏp'ẽr), *n.* A spittle insect; also, any small, leaping insect of the same family (Cercopidae), feeding on plant juices.

frog'man (-măn; -măn'), *n.*; *pl.* -MEN (-mĕn; -mĕn'). A person equipped for extended periods of underwater swimming, usually for military reconnaissance and demolition of underwater obstacles.

frog spit *or* **spittle.** See CUCKOO SPIT **a.**

frol'ic (frŏl'ĭk), *adj.* [D. *vroolijk*, fr. MD. *vrō.*] Full of fun or mirth; frisk; merry. — *n.* **1.** A prank; flight of gaiety, or mirth. **2.** Merrymaking. — *v. i.*; FROL'ICKED (-ĭkt); FROL'ICK·ING. To play pranks; make merry; to caper about; to play. — **frol'ick·er** (-ĭk·ẽr), *n.* — **frol'ick·y** (-ĭ), *adj.*

frol'ic·some (-sŭm), *adj.* Full of gaiety; sportive. — **-ly**, *adv.* — **-ness**, *n.*

from (frŏm; 4), *prep.* [AS. *fram, from.*] Forth out of; away out of contact with or proximity to; out of, as a starting point, place, etc., or as an origin, source, or cause; as, to go *from* home; measure *from* here.

fro'men·ty (frō'mĕn·tĭ). Var. of FRUMENTY.

frond (frŏnd), *n.* [L. *frons, frondis*, a leafy branch.] **1.** *Now Poetic.* A leaf, esp. that of a palm. **2.** *Bot.* **a** Any leaflike thallus or thalloid shoot; as, the *frond* of a lichen. **b** The leaf of a fern, including foliage leaves and sporophylls. See FERN, *Illust.* — **frond'ed**, *adj.*

‖**Fronde** (frôɴd), *n.* [F.] A political party in France, during the minority of Louis XIV, which opposed the government and the court party.

front (frŭnt), *n.* [OF., forehead, fr. L. *frons, frontis.*] **1.** The forehead or brow; sometimes, the whole face. **2.** The countenance or bearing, as expressive of character or temper; as, a bold *front.* **3.** *Colloq.* The appearance, often feigned, of wealth, standing, etc. **4.** The fore or forward part or surface of a thing. **5.** A position before a person or thing. **6.** The beginning; as, summer's *front.* **7. a** Land which faces or abuts on a body of water, a road, etc.; frontage. **b** A promenade along the beach at a seaside resort. **8.** A thing attached in front; as: **a** A shirt front, or dickey. **b** A cravat. **9.** In hotels, the first bellboy in line. **10.** [*often cap.*] The zone of conflict. **11.** A widespread movement arraying diverse forces in the battle for certain common political or ideological objectives; as, labor's united *front.* **12. a** A person appointed as official, often nominal, head of an enterprise to lend it prestige; a figurehead. **b** A person or group acting for another, as to establish liaison or gain favorable publicity. **c** A person or group serving, often under guise of patriotic or other fair-seeming activity, as public representative of a pressure group or an illegal or subversive organization, for the end of public delusion. **13.** *Arch.* Any face of a building; esp., the one having the main entrance. **14.** *Meteorol.* The forward boundary of a discrete current of air; as, a warm *front*, a polar *front.* **15.** *Mil.* **a** The van. **b** The most advanced portion of the field of operations.

— *adj.* **1.** Being of, on, at, or in, the front. **2.** *Phonet.* Pronounced

with closure or narrowing of the oral passage at the front of the mouth, or between the tongue and the hard palate (*p, s, ē* in *ēve, ā* in *āle*).
— *v. t.* **1.** To confront. **2.** To appear before. **3.** To be in front of. **4.** To face toward. **5.** To supply a front to.
— *v. i.* **1.** To face; as, the house *fronts* toward the east. **2.** To serve as a front (*for*).

front′age (frŭn′tĭj), *n.* **1.** The front face of a building; also, the direction it faces; exposure. **2.** The part of a lot between a building and the street. **3.** The front boundary line of a lot that abuts on a street; also, its length.

fron′tal (frŭn′tăl; frŏn′-; -t'l), *n.* [OF. *frontel, frontal,* fr. L. *frontale* an ornament for the forehead, frontlet.] **1.** A band, piece, guard, etc., worn over the forehead or face. **2.** A façade. **3.** A hanging for the front of an altar. **4.** *Anat.* A frontal bone, scale, or shield. — *adj.* Of or pertaining to the front, or esp., to the forehead; as, the *frontal* bone. — **fron′tal·ly,** *adv.*

fron·tier′ (frŭn·tēr′; frŏn′tēr), *n.* [OF. (F. *frontière*). See FRONT.] **1.** That part of a country facing another country or an unsettled region; hence: **a** The border or advance region of settlement and civilization. **b** An advance or not fully explored region, as of thought, sentiment, etc. **2.** *Obs.* A stronghold upon a frontier. — *adj.* Of, relating to, or lying on the frontier.

fron·tiers′man (frŭn·tērz′măn), *n.* A man living on the frontier.

fron′tis·piece (frŭn′tĭs·pēs; frŏn′-), *n.* [F. *frontispice,* fr. ML. *frontispicium* beginning, front of a church, fr. L. *frons* front + *spicere, specere,* to view.] **1.** The part which first meets the eye; specif.: *Arch.* **a** A façade. **b** A pediment over a portico, window, etc. **2.** An illustration fronting the first page or title page of a book; formerly, the title page.

front′less (frŭnt′lĕs; -lĭs), *adj.* *Now Rare.* Shameless.

front′let (-lĕt; -lĭt), *n.* [OF. *frontelet.*] **1.** A frontal or brow band. **2.** The forehead, esp. of an animal. **3.** In birds, the forehead, when marked by a different color or texture of plumage. **4.** A frontstall.

fron′to- (frŏn′tō-). [L. *frons, frontis,* the forehead.] *Anat.* A combining form denoting *connection with the frontal bone* or *region,* as in **fron′to·au·ric′u·lar, fron′to·ma′lar, fron′to·na′sal.**

fron′to·gen′e·sis (frŏn′tō·jĕn′ē·sĭs), *n.* [NL. See FRONT, 14; -GENESIS.] *Meteorol.* The bringing together of two masses or currents of air which differ and commonly so react upon each other as to induce cloud and precipitation.

fron·tol′y·sis (frŭn·tŏl′ĭ·sĭs; frŏn-), *n.* [NL. See FRONT, 14; -LYSIS.] *Meteorol.* The process tending to destroy a front, as by horizontal mixing and divergence of the air.

front′stall′ (frŭnt′stôl′), *n.* *Armor.* A plate attached to a horse's bridle, with holes for the eyes and nostrils.

frore (frōr; 70), *adj.* [AS. *froren.*] *Archaic.* Frozen; frosty.

frosh (frŏsh), *n. sing. & pl.* *U. S.* A freshman in school or college.

frost (frŏst; 74), *n.* [AS. *frost, forst;* akin to AS. *frēosan* to freeze.] **1.** Act or process of freezing. **2.** Temperature which causes freezing; hence, temperature below freezing. **3.** Frozen dew; — called also *hoarfrost* or *white frost.* **4.** Coldness of temperament; austerity; also, *Colloq.,* indifference; a coolness. **5.** *Slang.* A play, book, or the like, that meets with a cool reception; a failure. — *v. t.* **1.** To injure by frost; freeze. **2.** To quick-freeze. **3.** To cover with frost; to make frostlike in surface, as a cake by icing or glass by matting.

frost′bite′ (-bīt′), *v. t.;* see BITE. To blight or nip with frost, as a part of the body. — *n.* An instance or effect of frostbiting. — **frost′bit′ten** (-bĭt′'n), *adj.*

frost′fish′ (-fĭsh′), *n.; pl.,* see FISH. The common tomcod, abundant on the New England coast in early winter.

frost′flow′er (-flou′ẽr), *n.* A small bulbous herb (*Milla biflora*) of the lily family, of southwestern U. S. and Mexico; also, its star-shaped flower.

frost′ing, *n.* **1.** Icing for cake. **2.** Lusterless finish of metal or glass; mat. **3.** Pulverized glass mixed with varnish and glue, used in frosting lamp shades.

frost′work′ (frŏst′wûrk′), *n.* Delicate tracery formed by frost, as on glass; also, decorative designs like such tracery.

frost′y (frŏs′tĭ), *adj.;* FROST′I·ER (-tĭ·ẽr); FROST′I·EST. **1.** Attended with, or producing, frost; freezing. **2.** Covered with frost; frosted. **3.** Hoary; white-haired; hence, aged. **4.** Without ardor, warmth, or cordiality. — **frost′i·ly,** *adj.* — **frost′i·ness,** *n.*

froth (frŏth; 74), *n.* [ON. *frotha, frauth.*] **1.** The bubbles caused in fluids or liquors by fermentation or agitation; spume; foam. **2.** A spume of saliva caused by disease or nervous excitement. **3.** Anything light, unsubstantial, or frivolous. — *v. t.* **1.** To cause to foam. **2.** To eject as froth. **3.** To cover with froth. — *v. i.* To throw up or cast out froth; foam. — **froth′er** (-ẽr), *n.*

froth′y (frŏth′ĭ), *adj.;* -I·ER (-ĭ·ẽr); -I·EST. **1.** Full of or consisting of froth. **2.** Light as froth; lacking in substance or weight. — **froth′i·ly,** *adv.* — **froth′i·ness,** *n.*

‖**frot′tage′** (frô′tȧzh′), *n.* *Painting.* A composition, based upon outlines derived by rubbing a surface with charcoal or lead-coated paper and recording the texture of materials.

frou′frou′ (frōō′frōō′), *n.* [F.] **1.** A rustling, esp. of a skirt. **2.** Frilly trimming on women's garments, esp. trimming that rustles. **3.** Fussy details or showy accessories.

frounce (frouns), *v. t. & i.;* FROUNCED (frounst); FROUNC′ING (froun′sĭng). [OF. *froncir, froncier.*] *Archaic.* To adorn with plaits, curls, etc. — *n.* A frouncing; hence, affectation.

frous′y, frouz′y (frouz′ĭ). Vars. of FROWZY.

frow (frō), *n.* *U. S.* A froe (the cleaving tool).

fro′ward (frō′wẽrd; -ẽrd), *adj.* [*fro* + *-ward.*] **1.** Obstinately willful; refractory. **2.** *Obs.* Adverse. — **Syn.** See CONTRARY. — **Ant.** Compliant. — **fro′ward·ly,** *adv.* — **fro′ward·ness,** *n.*

frown (froun), *v. i.* [OF. *froignier.*] **1.** To contract the brow, as in displeasure or sternness; scowl. **2.** To indicate disapproval or displeasure. — *v. t.* To affect, express, silence, etc., with a frown. — *n.* **1.** A wrinkling of the brow, as in displeasure; a scowl. **2.** Any expression of displeasure. — **frown′er,** *n.* — **frown′ing·ly,** *adv.*

Syn. **Frown, scowl, glower, lower** mean to put on a dark or gloomy aspect. **Frown** implies a stern face and contracted brows that express disapprobation or anger; **scowl,** wrinkled drawn-down brows expressing ill humor or sullenness; **glower,** a more direct stare than *frown* or *scowl,* expressive of contempt or defiance; **lower,** a menacing blackness and sullenness.

frowst′y (frous′tĭ), *adj.* *Colloq.* Fusty; musty.

frowz′y, frows′y (frouz′ĭ), *adj.;* -I·ER (-ĭ·ẽr); -I·EST. Disordered and offensive; musty; slovenly; unkempt. — **frowz′i·ly,** *adv.* — **frowz′i·ness,** *n.*

froze (frōz), *past* of FREEZE.

fro′zen (frō′z'n), *adj.* **1.** Congealed with cold; made into, covered with, or affected by, ice **2.** Having a frigid climate. **3.** Coldhearted; unsympathetic. **4.** Fixed in form or character; as, *frozen* truth. **5.** Refrigerated; — of foods prepared for the table. **6.** Fixed at a particular point or level, as by executive order; as, *frozen* prices or wages. **7.** *Com.* Not liquid; not immediately marketable; as, **frozen credit,** credit on collateral that cannot at a given time be marketed to advantage, **frozen asset,** an asset that cannot quickly be turned into cash.

‖**Fruc′ti′dor′** (frük′tē′dôr′), *n.* [F., fr. L. *fructus* fruit + Gr. *dōron* gift.] See REVOLUTIONARY CALENDAR.

fruc·tif′er·ous (frŭk·tĭf′ẽr·ŭs), *adj.* [L. *fructifer,* fr. *fructus* fruit + *ferre* to bear.] Bearing fruit.

fruc′ti·fy (frŭk′tĭ·fī), *v. i.;* -FIED (-fīd); -FY′ING. [OF. *fructifier,* fr. L. *fructificare,* fr. *fructus* fruit. See FRUIT; -FY.] To bear fruit. — *v. t.* To make fruitful; fertilize. — **fruc′ti·fi·ca′tion** (-fĭ·kā′shŭn), *n.*

fruc′tose (frŭk′tōs; frōōk′-), *n.* [L. *fructus* fruit.] *Chem.* A sugar, $C_6H_{12}O_6$, occurring in three optically different forms, the best-known being levulose, or fruit sugar.

fruc′tu·ous (frŭk′tū·ŭs), *adj.* [OF., fr. L. *fructuosus.*] Fruitful.

fru′gal (frōō′găl), *adj.* [F., fr. L. *frugalis,* fr. *frugi,* lit., for fruit, hence, fit for food, useful, temperate, dative of *frux, frugis,* fruit.] **1.** Economical in the use of resources; saving; provident. **2.** Obtained by, or appropriate to, economy. — **Syn.** See SPARING. — **fru·gal′i·ty** (frōō·găl′ĭ·tĭ), *n.* — **fru′gal·ly,** *adv.* — **fru′gal·ness,** *n.*

fru·giv′o·rous (frōō·jĭv′ō·rŭs), *adj.* [L. *frux, frugis,* fruit + *-vorous.*] Feeding on fruit.

fruit (frōōt; 114), *n.* [OF., fr. L. *fructus* enjoyment, product, fruit, fr. *frui,* past part. *fructus,* to enjoy.] **1.** Any product of plant growth useful to man or animals, as grain, vegetables, cotton, etc.; — commonly in *pl.;* as, the *fruits* of the earth. **2.** The edible, more or less succulent, product of a perennial or woody plant, consisting of the ripened seeds and adjacent tissues, or of the latter alone. In popular usage there is no exact distinction between a *fruit* and a *vegetable,* except where the latter consists of the stem, leaves, or root of the plant. **3.** *Archaic.* Offspring. **4.** Product or result, as of work, training, idleness, etc.; reward; outcome; consequence. **5.** *Bot.* **a** In general, any product of fertilization with its modified envelopes or appendages. **b** Specif., the ripened ovary of a seed plant, and its contents, as the pod of a pea, a nut, grain, berry, etc. — *v. t. & i.* To bear or cause to bear fruit; develop fruit on.

fruit′age (-ĭj), *n.* [F.] **1.** Fruit. **2.** State or process of bearing fruit. **3.** Effect (good or ill) of any action.

fruit′cake′ (-kāk′) *n.* A rich cake usually containing raisins, citron, and currants, and often highly spiced.

fruit′er (frōōt′ẽr), *n.* **1.** A ship for carrying fruit. **2.** A fruit tree.

fruit′er·er (-ẽr), *n.; fem.* **fruit′er·ess** (-ĕs; -ĭs). A fruit dealer; also, a fruiter, a ship for carrying fruit.

fruit fly. Any of various small flies whose larvae feed on fruit, as drosophila (which see) and the ***Mediterranean fruit fly*** (*Ceratitis capitata*).

fruit′ful (frōōt′fōōl; -f'l), *adj.* **1.** Full of fruit; producing fruit abundantly; bearing results; prolific. **2.** Beneficial; productive; as, his studies proved *fruitful.* — **Syn.** See FERTILE. — **fruit′ful·ly,** *adv.* — **fruit′ful·ness,** *n.*

fru·i′tion (frōō·ĭsh′ŭn), *n.* [OF., fr. LL. *fruitio* enjoyment, fr. *frui,* past part. *fruitus,* to use or enjoy.] **1.** Use or possession of anything; enjoyment. **2.** State of bearing fruit; hence, realization; — through confusion with *fruit.* — **Syn.** See PLEASURE.

fruit′less, *adj.* **1.** Lacking, or not bearing, fruit; barren. **2.** Ineffectual; vain; unprofitable. — **Syn.** See FUTILE. — **fruit′less·ly,** *adv.* — **fruit′less·ness,** *n.*

fruit sugar. = LEVULOSE.

fruit′y (frōōt′ĭ), *adj.;* FRUIT′I·ER (-ĭ·ẽr); FRUIT′I·EST. **1.** Like fruit, esp. in taste or odor; of wines, rich in flavor, esp. of the grape. **2.** *Slang.* Easy and enjoyable. — **fruit′i·ness,** *n.*

fru′men·ta′ceous (frōō′mĕn·tā′shŭs), *adj.* [LL. *frumentaceus,* fr. *frumentum* corn or grain.] Made of, or resembling, wheat or other grain.

fru′men·ty (frōō′mĕn·tĭ), *n.* [OF. *frumentée,* fr. L. *frumentum* grain.] A pudding made with hulled wheat.

frump (frŭmp), *n.* **1.** *pl.* *Now Dial.* Sulks. **2.** A cross, old-fashioned person; esp., a dowdy woman. — **frump′ish,** *adj.* — **frump′y,** *adj.*

frus′trate (frŭs′trāt), *adj.* [L. *frustratus,* past part. of *frustrare* to deceive, frustrate, fr. *frustra* in vain.] *Archaic.* **1.** Frustrated. **2.** Vain; useless. — (-trāt), *v. t.* **1.** To prevent from attaining a purpose; to thwart. **2.** To bring to nothing; defeat; also, to nullify. — **frus′trat·er** (-trāt·ẽr), *n.* — **frus·tra′tion** (frŭs·trā′shŭn), *n.* — **frus′tra·tive** (frŭs′trā·tĭv; -trȧ·tĭv), *adj.*

Syn. **Frustrate, thwart, foil, baffle, balk, circumvent, outwit** mean to defeat a hope, attempt, or desire. **Frustrate** implies a rendering vain or ineffectual all efforts, however feeble or vigorous; **thwart,** frustration by running counter to one making headway; **foil,** a repulse that destroys one's inclination to go further; **baffle,** a frustration by confusing or puzzling; **balk** implies frustration by interposing obstacles or hindrances; **circumvent,** by stratagem; **outwit,** by craft or cunning.

frus′tum (frŭs′tŭm), *n.; pl.* -TUMS (-tŭmz), -TA (-tȧ). [L., piece, bit.] *Geom.* The part of a conical-shaped solid, formed by cutting off the top by a plane parallel to the base; also, the part of any solid, as of a cone or pyramid, intersected between two (usually parallel) planes.

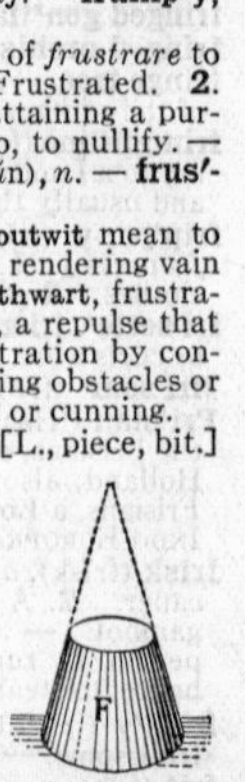

F Frustum of Cone.

fru·tes′cent (frōō·tĕs′ĕnt; -'nt), *adj.* [Irreg. fr. L. *frutex, fruticis,* shrub, bush.] Shrubby. — **fru·tes′cence** (-ĕns; -'ns), *n.*

fru′ti·cose (frōō′tĭ·kōs), *adj.* [L. *fruticosus,* fr. *frutex, fruticis,* shrub.] Pertaining to, or resembling, a shrub.

fry (frī), *n. sing. & pl.* [ME. *fri, fry,* seed, descendants, fr. OF. *froi* spawning, or ON. *fræ, frjō* seed.] **1.** The young of fishes. **2.** Very small adult fishes, esp. in schools. **3.** Young; offspring; esp., a swarm or brood of young; also, a crowd of insignificant persons or things.

fry (frī), *v. t. & i.;* FRIED (frīd); FRY′ING. [OF. *frire,* fr. L. *frigere* to roast, parch, fry.] **1.** To cook or be cooked over a flame in a pan, esp. with fat; to brown or sear in hot fat. **2.** To cause strong agitation in, or to be strongly agitated; to vex; also, *Obs.*, to seethe; boil. — *n.; pl.* FRIES (frīz). **1.** A dish of anything fried. **2.** *Local.* An internal part or organ of an animal, usually eaten fried, as pigs' liver, calves' pluck, or lambs' testicles; — usually in *pl.*

fry'er, fri'er (frī'ẽr), *n.* One who or that which fries; also, something intended for frying; specif., a young chicken.

F2 layer (ĕf'tōō'). *Radio.* A layer in the ionosphere which reflects radio waves, occurring at varying heights from about 125 miles up.

fub (fŭb), *v. t.* Var. of FOB, to trick.

fub'sy (fŭb'zĭ), *adj.; FUB'SI·ER* (-zĭ·ẽr); *FUB'SI·EST.* *Colloq.* Plump; chubby; soft and well-stuffed.

fuch'sia (fū'shȧ; -shĭ·ȧ; *as a generic name,* fŏŏk'sĭ·ȧ), *n.* [NL., after Leonhard *Fuchs,* Ger. botanist.] **1.** Any of a genus (*Fuchsia*) of decorative shrubs of the evening-primrose family, having handsome nodding flowers, usually in deep pinks, reds, and purples. **2.** Usually **California fuchsia.** An herb (genus *Zauschneria,* esp. *Z. californica*) with brilliant scarlet flowers.

fuch'sin (fŏŏk'sĭn), **fuch'sine** (-sĭn; -sēn), *n.* [*fuchsia* + *-ine;* — named from its color.] A dye produced by oxidation of a mixture of aniline and toluidines. It is metallic-green superficially, but when dissolved yields a brilliant bluish red.

fu'coid (fū'koid), *adj.* [*fucus* + *-oid.*] *Bot.* Pertaining to, or resembling, algae of a family (Fucaceae) which includes the rockweeds and gulfweed. — *n.* A fucoid seaweed.

fu'cus (fū'kŭs), *n.; pl.* FUCI (-sī) or (in sense 2) -CUSES (-kŭs·ĕz; -ĭz). [L., orchil, used as a red dye.] **1.** *Obs.* A paint; dye. **2.** Any of a genus (*Fucus,* family Fucaceae) of olive-green or brown algae; a rockweed.

fud'dle (fŭd''l), *v. t.;* -DLED (-'ld); -DLING (-lĭng). *Colloq.* To make confused, as with drink; muddle. — *v. i.* *Colloq.* To tipple.

fudge (fŭj), *n.* **1.** A made-up story; nonsense; humbug; — often used as an exclamation of contempt. **2.** A patch of print, as of colored print, or an insertion of late matter, in a newspaper page; also, a machine or cylinder for printing such patches. **3.** A soft sugary candy, often containing chocolate and nuts. — *v. t.;* FUDGED (fŭjd); FUDG'ING. To patch together; fake; devise.

Fu·e'gi·an (fū·ē'jĭ·ăn; fwā'jĭ·ăn), *adj.* [Sp. Tierra del *Fuego,* lit., Land of Fire.] Of or pertaining to Tierra del Fuego, or its native Indians. — *n.* A Fuegian Indian.

Fueh'rer (fü'rẽr), *n.* See FÜHRER.

fu'el (fū'ĕl; -ĭl), *n.* [OF. *fouaille, fuaille,* fr. LL. *focalia,* fr. L. *focus* fireplace, in LL., fire.] **1.** Any matter used to produce heat or power by combustion. **2.** Anything that increases passion, excitement, etc. — *v. t. & i.;* FU'ELED (fū'ĕld; -ĭld) or -ELLED; -EL·ING or -EL·LING. To feed with, or procure, fuel. — **fu'el·er, fu'el·ler,** *n.*

fu·ga'cious (fū·gā'shŭs), *adj.* [L. *fugax, fugacis,* fr. *fugere* to flee.] **1.** Flying, or disposed to fly; hence, evanescent; volatile. **2.** *Bot.* Falling soon after blossoming, as a flower. Cf. CADUCOUS, DECIDUOUS. — **fu·ga'cious·ly,** *adv.* — **fu·ga'cious·ness, fu·gac'i·ty** (fū·găs'ĭ·tĭ), *n.*

-fuge (-fūj). A combining form denoting in adjectives and derivative nouns *that* (*which*) *causes to flee* or *drives away,* as in febri*fuge,* vermi*fuge.* Derivative adjectives are formed in **-fugal.**

fu'gi·tive (fū'jĭ·tĭv), *adj.* [OF. *fugitif,* fr. L. *fugitivus,* fr. *fugere* to flee.] **1.** Resorting to flight; fleeing, as from danger. **2.** Itinerant; vagabond. **3.** Not fixed, established, or firmly held; evanescent; liable to fade; as, *fugitive* colors or impressions. **4.** Dealing with topics of temporary interest; occasional; as, *fugitive* verse. — **Syn.** See TRANSIENT. — *n.* **1.** One who flees from pursuit, danger, service, etc. **2. a** *Obs.* A deserter. **b** A refugee or exile. **3.** Something fugitive, evanescent, or intangible. — **fu'gi·tive·ly,** *adv.* — **fu'gi·tive·ness,** *n.*

fu'gle (fū'g'l), *v. i.;* FU'GLED (-g'ld); FU'GLING (-glĭng). *Colloq.* To act as guide, or model; also, to motion as if signaling.

fu'gle·man (-măn), *n.; pl.* FUGLEMEN (-mĕn). Also **flu'gel·man** (flōō'g'l-); *pl.* FLUGELMEN. [G. *flügelmann* file leader, fr. *flügel* wing + *mann* man.] **1.** *Hist.* A trained soldier placed in front of a company, as a guide for the others in their exercises. **2.** Hence, a model; example.

fugue (fūg), *n.* [F., fr. It. *fuga,* fr. L. *fuga* a fleeing, flight.] *Music.* A polyphonic composition, developed from a given theme, according to strict contrapuntal rules.

‖**Füh'rer** (fü'rẽr), *n.* Also **Fueh'rer.** [G.] In Germany, a leader or guide; specif., **der Füh'rer** (dĕr), the chancellor of the Third Reich; also, a leader of a local Nazi party. See REICH.

-ful (-fŏŏl). [See FULL, *adj.*] **1.** (*pron.* -fŏŏl; -f'l) An adjective suffix, denoting *full of, abounding in, characterized by;* also, *able to* or *tending to;* as in grace*ful.* **2.** (*pron.* -fŏŏl) A noun suffix, denoting *quantity that would fill,* as in cup*ful.*

Fu'lah, Fu'la (fōō'lä), *n. sing. & pl.* A native of Sudan of a race of Hamitic stock with Negro admixture.

ful'crum (fŭl'krŭm), *n.; pl.* FULCRUMS (-krŭmz), FULCRA (-krȧ). [L., bedpost, fr. *fulcire* to prop.] **1.** A prop; support. **2.** The support, as a wedge, about which a lever turns. See LEVER, *Illust.*

ful·fill', ful·fil' (fŏŏl·fĭl'), *v. t.;* -FILLED' (-fĭld'); -FILL'ING. [AS. *fulfyllan.*] To carry into effect, as an intention; to bring to pass, as a design; also, reflexively, to realize or manifest completely. — **Syn.** See PERFORM. — **ful·fill'er,** *n.* — **ful·fill'ment, ful·fil'ment,** *n.*

ful'gent (fŭl'jĕnt), *adj.* [L. *fulgens, -entis,* pres. part. of *fulgere* to flash, glitter.] Dazzlingly bright; shining. — **ful'gent·ly,** *adv.*

ful'gid (-jĭd), *adj.* [L. *fulgidus.*] Shining; glittering.

ful'gor, ful'gour (fŭl'gẽr), *n.* [L. *fulgor,* fr. *fulgere* to shine.] *Archaic.* Dazzling brightness; splendor.

ful'gu·rant (fŭl'gū·rănt), *adj.* [L. *fulgurans,* pres. part. of *fulgurare.*] Resembling lightning; flashing. — **ful'gu·rant·ly,** *adv.*

ful'gu·rate (-rāt), *v. i.* [L. *fulgurare* to flash, fr. *fulgur* lightning.] To flash as lightning. — **ful'gu·ra'tion** (-rā'shŭn), *n.*

ful'gu·rat'ing (-rāt'ĭng), *adj.* *Med.* Resembling lightning; — used to describe sudden intense stabbing pains.

ful'gu·rite (-rīt), *n.* [L. *fulgur* lightning.] *Geol.* A vitrified crust, often tubular, produced by the fusion of rock, sand, etc., by lightning.

ful'gu·rous (-rŭs), *adj.* [L. *fulgur* lightning.] Flashing with light or lightning; fulgurant.

ful'ham (fŏŏl'ăm), *n.* Also **ful'lam, ful'lom** (-ŭm). *Slang.* A loaded die.

fu·lig'i·nous (fū·lĭj'ĭ·nŭs), *adj.* [LL. *fuliginosus,* fr. *fuligo* soot.] Smoky; sooty; dusky. — **fu·lig'i·nous·ly,** *adv.*

full (fŏŏl), *v. t. & i.* [OF. *fuler, fouler,* fr. L. *fullo* a fuller.] To thicken by moistening, heating, and pressing, as cloth; to scour, cleanse, and thicken cloth in a mill.

full, *adj.* [AS.] **1.** Filled; holding all it can contain. **2.** Having an incumbent; not vacant. **3.** Satisfied or serving to satisfy; also, sated. **4.** Complete as in quota, quantity, duration, etc.; as, a *full* jury, quart, or hour; being at the maximum in size, development, etc.; as, a *full* moon; of sounds, having volume or depth; as, *full* tones. **5.** That fills; as, a *full* cargo. **6.** Abundantly supplied; as, a *full* purse. **7.** Filled out; distended; as, *full* sails. **8.** Being engrossed with a thought, plan, etc. **9.** Hanging in folds or gathers; as, a *full* skirt.

Syn. **Full, complete, plenary, replete. Full,** the general term, implies either the inclusion of all that is required or the presence of all that may be held, contained, etc. (as, a *full* meal; a *full* basket); **complete** means full in the sense of having everything needed; **plenary** adds to complete the implication of fullness without qualification (as, *complete* control; *plenary* powers); **replete** (with) means full in the sense of being filled to the brim or, sometimes, to satiety.

— *n.* Full measure, length, size, etc.; maximum.

— *adv.* Entirely; completely; to the utmost extent; as, *full*-blown.

— *v. t. & i.* To make or become full; to give or attain fullness; esp., to gather, as cloth. — **full'ness, ful'ness,** *n.* — **ful'ly** (fŏŏl'ĭ; -lĭ), *adv.*

full and by. *Naut.* Sailing close-hauled, with all sails full, and lying as near the wind as possible.

full'back' (fŏŏl'băk'), *n.* *Football.* One of the backs; orig., the back stationed farthest from the opponent's goal.

full blood. **a** Unmixed descent; as, a Negro of *full* blood. **b** Relationship through both parents. — **full'blood'** (fŏŏl'blŭd'), *adj.*

full'-blood'ed (fŏŏl'blŭd'ĕd; -ĭd; 2), *adj.* **1.** Having a full supply of blood; hence, rubicund; florid. **2.** Of pure blood; thoroughbred.

full'-blown' (-blōn'; 2), *adj.* **1.** Fully expanded or open; as, a *full-blown* rose. **2.** Fully distended, as a sail.

full'-bod'ied (-bŏd'ĭd; 2), *adj.* Substantial in quality; rich in flavor.

full dress. The style of dress prescribed for occasions of ceremony; esp., customary formal dress for evening.

full'er (fŏŏl'ẽr), *n.* [From FULL to make full.] *Blacksmithing.* A hammer for grooving and spreading iron; also, a groove; fluting. — **full'er,** *v. t.*

full'er, *n.* [AS. *fullere,* fr. L. *fullo.* See FULL to thicken.] One who fulls cloth.

full'er's earth (fŏŏl'ẽrz). A claylike earthy substance used in fulling cloth, as a filter medium, and as a catalyst.

fuller's teasel. See TEASEL.

full'er·y (fŏŏl'ẽr·ĭ), *n.; pl.* -ERIES (-ĭz). A mill for fulling cloth.

full'-fash'ioned (fŏŏl'făsh'ŭnd; 2), *adj.* Knitted so as to conform to the shape of the leg and foot by dropping stitches as the contour narrows; — used of hosiery, underwear, etc.

full'-fledged' (fŏŏl'flĕjd'; 2), *adj.* Fully developed; mature; of birds, having full plumage; hence, figuratively, having reached the developed stage; as, a *full-fledged* lawyer.

full house. Also **full hand.** *Poker.* A hand containing three of a kind and a pair, as three kings and two tens. See POKER, *Illust.*

full'-rigged' (-rĭgd'; 2), *adj.* *Naut.* Having three or more masts, each with its full complement of square sails. See SAIL, *Illust.*

full sentence. *Gram.* See SENTENCE.

full stop. *Punctuation.* A period.

ful'mar (fŏŏl'mẽr), *n.* [ON. *full* foul + *mār* sea mew.] An Arctic sea bird (*Fulmarus glacialis*) of the petrel family. The related ***giant fulmar*** (*Macronectes giganteus*) of southern seas is nearly as large as an albatross.

ful'mi·nant (fŭl'mĭ·nănt), *adj.* [F. or L.; F., fr. L. *fulminans,* pres. part. of *fulminare* to lighten.] **1.** Fulminating. **2.** *Med.* Coming on suddenly with great severity, as a disease.

ful'mi·nate (-nāt), *v. i. & t.* [L. *fulminatus,* past part. of *fulminare* to lighten, strike with lightning, fr. *fulmen* thunderbolt.] **1.** *Rare.* To thunder and lighten. **2.** To explode suddenly and violently; detonate. **3.** To thunder forth, as censures or decrees; to utter or issue with threats or denunciation. **4.** To attack with suddenness and violence; — of a disease. — *n.* [From FULMINIC.] *Chem.* **1.** A salt of fulminic acid. **2.** A fulminating powder. — **ful'mi·na'tion** (-nā'shŭn), *n.* — **ful'mi·na'tor** (-nā'tẽr), *n.* — **ful'mi·na·to'ry** (-nȧ·tō'rĭ *or, esp. Brit.,* -tẽr·ĭ), *adj.*

ful'mi·nat'ing pow'der (-nāt'ĭng). *Chem.* Any violently explosive powder, esp. one of the salts of fulminic acid.

ful'mine (fŭl'mĭn), *v. i. & t.* [F. *fulminer.*] To fulminate.

ful·min'ic (fŭl·mĭn'ĭk), *adj.* [L. *fulmen* lightning.] *Chem.* Designating a strong, poisonous, unstable acid, C:N.OH, which forms highly explosive salts.

ful'mi·nous (fŭl'mĭ·nŭs), *adj.* [L. *fulmen* thunderbolt.] Of, pertaining to, or resembling, thunder and lightning.

ful'some (fŏŏl'sŭm; fŭl'-), *adj.* [*full,* adj. + 1st *-some.*] **1.** Offensive; disgusting; esp., offensive because of insincerity or baseness of motive; as, *fulsome* praise. **2.** *Rare.* Lustful; wanton. — **ful'some·ly,** *adv.* — **ful'some·ness,** *n.*

ful'vous (fŭl'vŭs), *adj.* [L. *fulvus.*] Tawny; dull yellow.

fu·mar'ic (fū·măr'ĭk), *adj.* [L. *fumus* smoke, fume.] Designating a white, crystalline acid, $C_2H_2(CO_2H)_2$, occurring in fumitory and other plants, and made artificially.

fu'ma·role (fū'mȧ·rōl), *n.* [From F., fr. LL. *fumariolum,* fr. *fumarium,* fr. *fumus* smoke.] A hole or orifice in a volcanic region, from which issue hot gases and vapors.

fu'ma·to'ri·um (-tō'rĭ·ŭm), *n.; pl.* -RIA (-ȧ). [NL., fr. L. *fumare, fumatum,* to smoke.] An airtight compartment in which vapor may be generated to destroy fungous or insect pests on growing plants.

fu'ma·to'ry (fū'mȧ·tō'rĭ *or, esp. Brit.,* -tẽr·ĭ), *adj.* [See FUMATORIUM.] Pertaining to, or concerned with, smoking. — *n.; pl.* -RIES (-rĭz). A place for subjecting things to the action of smoke or vapor; a fumatorium.

fum'ble (fŭm'b'l), *v. i. & t.;* -BLED (-b'ld); -BLING (-blĭng). **1.** To feel or grope about clumsily; to seek awkwardly. **2.** To handle or manage awkwardly; specif., in certain games, as baseball and football, to fail to hold, catch, or handle (the ball) properly. — *n.* Act of fumbling. — **fum'bler** (-blẽr), *n.*

fume (fūm), *n.* [OF. *fum,* fr. L. *fumus.*] **1.** Smoke. **2.** Aromatic smoke, as of incense. **3.** A vaporous or odorous exhalation, esp. if noxious or stifling. **4.** Something fumelike; a vaporing. **5.** An emotional outburst; esp., a fit of anger or vexation. — *v. i.* **1.** To smoke; to throw off fumes; rise up, as vapor. **2.** To give vent to rage or annoyance. — *v. t.* **1.** To fill with, or expose to, fumes; to treat with vapors, smoke, etc. **2.** To throw off in fumes. — **fum'er** (fūm'ĕr), *n.* — **fum'ing·ly**, *adv.*

fu'met (fū'mĕt), *n.* Also **fu·mette'** (fū·mĕt'). [F. *fumet* odor, fume of wine or meat, fr. *fumer* to fume.] The odor of long-kept game or other meat or of meat in cooking.

fu'mi·gant (fū'mĭ·gănt), *n.* Any substance used for fumigation.

fu'mi·gate (fū'mĭ·gāt), *v. t.* [L. *fumigatus*, past part. of *fumigare* to fumigate, fr. *fumus* smoke.] **1.** To apply smoke, vapor, or gas to, esp. as a means of disinfecting or disinfesting. **2.** To perfume. — **fu'mi·ga'tion** (-gā'shŭn), *n.* — **fu'mi·ga'tor** (-gā'tĕr), *n.*

fu'mi·to'ry (fū'mĭ·tō'rĭ *or, esp. Brit.*, -tĕr·ĭ), *n.; pl.* -RIES (-rĭz). [OF. *fumeterre*, prop., smoke of the ground, fr. L. *fumus* smoke + *terra* earth.] Any of a genus (*Fumaria*) typifying a family (Fumariaceae, the fumitory family) of erect or climbing herbs; esp., the common fumitory or ***hedge fumitory*** (*F. officinalis*), used in medicine as a tonic, alterative, and diaphoretic.

fun (fŭn), *n.* [From *fun* to trick, cajole, prob. fr. *fon* to befool. See FOND, *adj.*] Sport; merriment; playful action or speech. — *v. i. Colloq.* To act in fun; to make fun; joke.

Syn. **Fun, jest, sport, game, play** mean activity, utterance, etc., intended to amuse or regard as amusing. **Fun** usually implies the provocation or eliciting of laughter but it may imply merely a lack of serious purpose (as, he is full of *fun;* she writes for the *fun* of it); **jest** always implies a lack of earnestness in what is said or done and may suggest raillery, hoaxing, or the like; **sport**, especially in the phrases *in sport* and *to make sport*, implies the arousing of laughter against one who is the butt of a joke; **game**, often close to *sport*, emphasizes mischievous or malicious fun (as, to find *sport* in his embarrassment; to make *game* of his scruples); **play** implies nothing more than opposition to the noun *earnest* and is sometimes substituted for *fun* or *sport*.

fu·nam'bu·list (fū·năm'bū·lĭst), *n.* [L. *funambulus*, fr. *funis* rope + *ambulare* to walk.] A ropewalker or ropedancer. — **fu·nam'bu·lism** (-lĭz'm), *n.*

func'tion (fŭngk'shŭn), *n.* [F. and L.; F. *fonction*, fr. L. *functio*, fr. *fungi* to perform.] **1.** The natural, proper, or characteristic action of anything; esp., the normal and special action of any organ or part of a living animal or plant; as, the *functions* of digestion and assimilation. **2.** Special purpose, office, duty, or the like; as, the *function* of education. **3.** Profession; occupation; as, the clerical *function*. **4.** A formal, elaborate, or impressive ceremony or social affair. **5.** Any quality, trait, or fact so related to another that it is dependent upon and varies with that other. **6.** *Math.* A magnitude so related to another magnitude that to values of the latter there correspond values of the former. See ARGUMENT, 7.

Syn. **Function, office, duty, province** mean the acts or operations expected of a person or thing. **Function** is the most widely applicable of these terms, being used in reference to all living things, their organs, members, etc., and to all created or manufactured things; **office** applies usually, but not exclusively, to the work to be performed by a person as a result of his trade, profession, position, or the like; **duty** applies not only to a task required by one's occupation but to one which is imposed by one's rank, status, or calling; **province** applies to any function, office, or duty which comes within one's range of jurisdiction, one's powers, or one's competence.

— *v. i.* To perform or fulfill its function; act; operate; work.

func'tion·al (-ăl; -'l), *adj.* **1.** Of, pertaining to, or connected with a function or functions. **2.** Serving a function, as a useful purpose or special activity; designed, developed, considered, etc., with reference to functioning; as, a *functional* plan, style. **3.** *Med.* Affecting functions but not structure; as, a *functional* disease. Cf. ORGANIC. — **func'tion·al·ly**, *adv.*

func'tion·al·ism (-ăl·ĭz'm), *n.* Any doctrine or practice that lays stress upon function, use, and adaptation, as, in architecture, conscious adaptation of form to use, structure, and material. — **func'tion·al·ist** (-ĭst), *n.*

func'tion·ar'y (-ĕr'ĭ *or, esp. Brit.*, -ĕr·ĭ), *n.; pl.* -IES (-ĭz). One charged with the performance of a function; an official.

fund (fŭnd), *n.* [F. *fond* bottom, foundation, *fonds* fund, deriv. of L. *fundus* bottom.] **1.** An accumulation or deposit of resources; a store; supply. **2.** A sum of money, esp. one the principal or interest of which is appropriated or devoted to a specific object, as the carrying on of some commercial undertaking; stock or capital; in *pl.*, available pecuniary resources. **3.** *Eng. pl.* The stock of a national debt; public securities; — with *the.* — *v. t.* **1.** To provide a fund to pay the interest of. **2.** To convert into a more or less permanent debt bearing regular interest; as, to *fund* a floating debt. **3.** To place in a fund; accumulate. **4.** *Obs.* To finance.

fun'da·ment (fŭn'dȧ·mĕnt), *n.* [OF. *fondement*, fr. L. *fundamentum* foundation, fr. *fundare* to lay the bottom.] **1.** Foundation; basis. **2.** The buttocks; specif., the anus.

fun'da·men'tal (-mĕn'tăl; -t'l), *adj.* **1.** Of or pertaining to the foundation or basis; essential; basal. **2.** *Music.* Having the root in the bass; — of a chord or its position. **3.** *Physics.* Pertaining to or designating a fundamental. — **Syn.** See ESSENTIAL. — *n.* **1.** A principle, law, or article, which serves as the groundwork of a system; essential part. **2.** *Music.* A fundamental bass or tone. **3.** *Physics.* The principal component of a wave, the component of lowest frequency or greatest wave length. — **fun'da·men'tal·ly**, *adv.*

fun'da·men'tal·ism (fŭn'dȧ·mĕn'tăl·ĭz'm), *n.* [*often cap.*] **a** A recent movement in American Protestantism re-emphasizing as fundamental to Christianity belief in the inerrancy of the Scriptures, Biblical miracles, especially the virgin birth and physical resurrection of Christ, etc. **b** The beliefs so emphasized. **c** The state or fact of being an adherent of this belief. — **fun'da·men'tal·ist** (-ĭst), *n. & adj.*

fun'dus (fŭn'dŭs), *n.; pl.* FUNDI (-dī). [L., bottom.] The bottom or base of (or part opposite the aperture of) the internal surface of a hollow organ; as, the *fundus* of the bladder is the lower back part, of the eye is the part opposite the pupil.

fu'ner·al (fū'nĕr·ăl), *adj.* [OF., fr. ML. *funeralis* of a funeral, fr. L. *funus, funeris*, funeral.] Pertaining to or befitting a funeral; used at the burial of the dead. — *n.* [F. *funérailles*, pl.] **1.** The rites used in the disposition of a dead human body, esp. by interment; obsequies. **2.** The procession attending the burial of the dead.

fu·ne're·al (fū·nēr'ē·ăl), *adj.* [L. *funereus.*] Appropriate to a funeral; sad and solemn. — **fu·ne're·al·ly**, *adv.*

fu·nest' (fū·nĕst'), *adj.* [F. *funeste*, fr. L. *funestus*, fr. *funus* a funeral, destruction.] Fatal; dire; doleful.

fun'gal (fŭng'găl), *adj. Bot.* Fungus. — *n.* A fungus.

fun'gi (fŭn'jī), *n., pl.* of FUNGUS.

fungi-. A combining form for *fungus*, as in **fun·gif'er·ous, fun'gi·form, fun·giv'o·rous** (see -FEROUS, etc.).

fun'gi·ble (fŭn'jĭ·b'l), *adj. Law.* Of such kind or nature that one specimen or part may be used in place of another in the satisfaction of an obligation, as money, food, etc. — *n.* [ML. (*res*) *fungibiles*, fr. L. *fungi* to discharge.] A thing that is fungible. — **fun'gi·bil'i·ty** (-bĭl'ĭ·tĭ), *n.*

fun'gi·cide (fŭn'jĭ·sīd), *n.* [*fungi-* + *-cide.*] Any substance that destroys fungi or inhibits the growth of the spores or hyphae. — **fun'gi·cid'al** (-sīd'ăl; -'l), *adj.*

fun'goid (fŭng'goid), *adj.* [*fungus* + *-oid.*] Resembling, or characteristic of, a fungus; fungal. — *n.* A fungus.

fun·gos'i·ty (fŭng·gŏs'ĭ·tĭ), *n.; pl.* -TIES (-tĭz). Fungus quality; a fungus excrescence.

fun'gous (fŭng'gŭs), *adj.* [L. *fungosus.*] Fungus.

fun'gus (fŭng'gŭs), *n.; pl.* FUNGI (fŭn'jī), FUNGUSES (fŭng'gŭs·ĕz; -ĭz). [L., a mushroom.] **1.** Any of a group (Fungi) of thallophytic plants comprising the molds, mildews, rusts, smuts, mushrooms, etc. They are destitute of chlorophyll and reproduce mainly by means of asexual spores. **2.** *Med.* A morbid spongy growth, esp. of granulations. — *adj.* Of the nature of, pertaining to, or like, a fungus; caused by a fungus; as, a *fungus* disease.

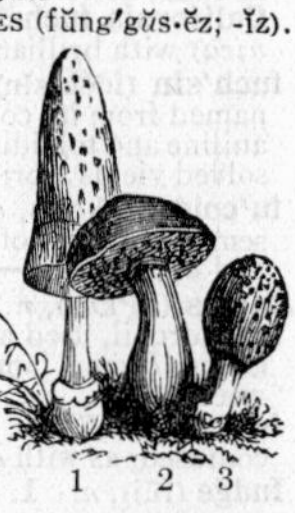

1 2 3

Fungi. 1 Shaggy-mane or Horsetail Mushroom (*Coprinus comatus*); 2 Mushroom *Boletus edulis*; 3 Morel or Cup Fungus (*Morchella esculenta*).

fu'ni·cle (fū'nĭ·k'l), *n.* [L. *funiculus*, dim. of *funis* cord.] A small cord; a funiculus.

fu·nic'u·lar (fū·nĭk'ū·lĕr), *adj.* **1.** Pertaining to, like, or consisting of, a funicle, a funiculus, or funiculi. **2.** Pertaining to, or dependent on, the tension of a cord. — *n.* In full **funicular railway.** A cable railway; esp. any form of mountain railway in which the ascending car and the descending car counterbalance each other in weight.

fu·nic'u·lus (-lŭs), *n.; pl.* -LI (-lī). [L., a little cord. See FUNICLE.] **1.** *Anat.* **a** The umbilical cord. **b** A cord, band, or bundle of fibers. **c** The spermatic cord. **2.** *Bot.* The stalk of an ovule.

funk (fŭngk), *n. Colloq.* **1.** A shrinking back through fear; panic. **2.** One who shirks through fear. — *v. i. Colloq.* To shrink back through fear; flinch. — *v. t. Colloq.* **1.** To shrink from or shirk because of fright. **2.** To cause to flinch.

fun'nel (fŭn'ĕl; -'l), *n.* [Pr. *founil*, *enfounilh*, fr. L. *fundibulum*, *infundibulum*, funnel, deriv. of *in* in + *fundere* to pour.] **1.** A vessel (usually an inverted cone) with a tube at the point, through which liquids, powders, etc., may be run into another vessel. **2.** A flue for air, light, smoke, or vapor; a smokestack, esp. of a steamship. — *v. i. & t.;* -NELED; -NELLED (-ĕld; -'ld); -NEL·ING, -NEL·LING. To pass through a funnel; as, to *funnel* wheat from an elevator into a freighter; to move or guide in the direction of a focal point.

fun'nel·form' (fŭn'ĕl·fôrm'; fŭn''l-), *adj. Bot.* Shaped like a funnel; as, the *funnelform* corolla of the morning-glory.

fun'ny (fŭn'ĭ), *adj.;* FUN'NI·ER (-ĭ·ĕr); FUN'NI·EST. [From FUN.] **1.** Laughable, esp. from oddness or absurdity; humorous. **2.** *Colloq.* Strange; queer; odd. — **Syn.** See LAUGHABLE. — **fun'ni·ly**, *adv.* — **fun'ni·ness**, *n.*

fun'ny, *n.; pl.* FUNNIES (-ĭz). Something funny; esp., *pl., Colloq., U. S.*, comic strips, books, etc. See COMIC, *n.*, 2.

funny bone. [Perh. a joke on *humerus, humorous;* — from the tingling felt when it receives a blow.] The place at the back of the elbow where the ulnar nerve rests against a prominence of the elbow joint in the bone of the upper arm; crazy bone.

fur (fûr; 117), *n.* [ME. *furre.* See FUR, *v.*] **1.** A strip or piece of the dressed pelt of any of certain animals (as the sable, ermine, or fur seal), worn as a trimming or lining to a garment; hence, such a dressed pelt or pelts as a material. **2.** An article of clothing made of, or trimmed or lined with, fur; esp., a fur tippet. **3.** The hairy coat of a mammal, esp. when fine, soft, and thick. **4.** *pl.* The skins of such animals with the fur; peltry. **5.** Any coating suggestive of fur, as morbid matter on the tongue. — *adj.* Pertaining to, or made of, fur.

fur, *v. t.;* FURRED (fûrd); FUR'RING. [OF. *forrer*, fr. *fuerre, forre*, sheath, case, covering.] **1.** To line, face, cover, or clothe with fur. **2.** *Arch.* To apply furring to.

fu'ran (fū'răn; fū·răn'), **fu'rane** (-rān), *n.* [L. *furfur* bran.] *Chem.* A colorless mobile liquid, C_4H_4O, of peculiar odor, obtained from wood tar by distillation, and in other ways.

fur'be·low (fûr'bē·lō), *n.* [F. dial. *farbala*, equiv. to F. *falbala.*] A flounce, ruffle, or frill; hence, any showy or fussy trimming. — *v. t.* To deck with furbelows.

fur'bish (fûr'bĭsh), *v. t.* [OF. *forbir, furbir*, fr. OHG. *furban* to clean.] To rub or scour to brightness; burnish; freshen; renovate. — **fur'bish·er**, *n.*

fur'cate (fûr'kāt), *adj.* [ML. *furcatus*, fr. L. *furca* fork.] Forked; branching like a fork. — (-kāt), *v. i.* To branch like a fork. — **fur'cate·ly**, *adv.* — **fur·ca'tion** (fûr·kā'shŭn), *n.*

fur'cu·la (fûr'kū·lȧ), *n.; pl.* -LAE (-lē). *Anat. & Zool.* A forked process or structure, esp. the wishbone or furculum.

fur'cu·lum (-lŭm), *n.; pl.* -LA (-lȧ). [NL., dim. of L. *furca* a fork.] *Anat.* A forked part; esp., the wishbone.

fur'fur (fûr'fĕr), *n.; pl.* FURFURES (-fū·rēz). [L.] Scurf; dandruff; *pl.*, scurfy particles.

fur'fu·ra'ceous (-fū·rā'shŭs), *adj.* Of or like bran; scurfy; covered with furfures. — **fur'fu·ra'ceous·ly**, *adv.*

fur'fur·al (fûr'fĕr·ăl; fûr'fĕr·ăl'), *n.* [L. *furfur* bran.] *Chem.* An oily liquid, $C_4H_3O.CHO$, of pleasant odor, obtained by distillation of bran, wood, etc. It is used for making lacquers and dyes; — called also **fur'fur·al'de·hyde** (-ăl'dē·hīd).

fur'fur·an (-ăn; -ăn'), **fur'fur·ane** (-ān), *n.* Furan.

fu'ri·bund (fū'rĭ·bŭnd), *adj.* [L. *furibundus*, fr. *furere* to rage.] Full of fury; raging; frenzied.

fu'ri·ous (fū'rĭ·ŭs), *adj.* [OF. *furieus*, fr. L. *furiosus*, fr. *furia* rage, fury.] **1.** Full of, or transported with, passion or fury; frenzied; frantic. **2.** Moving with violence; rushing; vehement. — **fu'ri·ous·ly**, *adv.* — **fu'ri·ous·ness**, *n.*

furl (fûrl), *v. t.* [F. *ferler*, fr. OF. *fermlier*, fr. *ferm, ferme*, fast + *lier* to tie, bind.] To wrap or roll tightly, as a sail or a flag. — *v. i.* To curl or fold as in being furled. — *n.* A furling; also, a furled coil.

fur′long (fûr′lŏng; 74), *n.* [AS. *furlang, furlung,* fr. *furh* furrow + *lang* long.] A measure of length. See MEASURE, *Tables* 1 & 2.

fur′lough (fûr′lō), *n.* [D. *verlof.*] Leave of absence, esp. to a soldier; also, the official paper authorizing such a leave. — *v. t.* To grant a furlough to.

fur′men·ty (fûr′mĕn·tĭ), **fur′me·ty.** Vars. of FRUMENTY.

fur′nace (fûr′nĭs; -nĭs), *n.* [OF. *fornais, fornaise,* fr. L. *fornax.*] An enclosed place in which heat is produced, as for reducing ores, melting metals, warming a house, etc.

fur′nish (fûr′nĭsh), *v. t.* [OF. *furnir, fornir,* to furnish, finish, fr. OHG. *frumjan* to further, execute, do.] **1.** To provide what is necessary for; equip; fit out or fit up. **2.** To provide; supply; give. — **fur′nish·er,** *n.*

Syn. Furnish, equip, outfit, appoint, accouter (*or* **accoutre**), **arm** mean to supply with necessary or appropriate adjuncts. **Furnish** implies the provision of all essentials that make a person or thing ready to perform its functions; **equip,** the provision of a thing or things making for efficiency in action or use; **outfit,** provision for a journey, an expedition, an occupation, or the like; **appoint,** provision of complete, often elegant, equipment; **accouter,** provision of dress, array, or other personal equipment; **arm,** provision for effective action or operation, especially in war.

fur′nish·ing, *n.* **1.** Act of supplying furniture or fittings. **2.** Ornament; adornment. **3.** *pl.* Furniture, fixtures, etc.

fur′ni·ture (fûr′nĭ·tụ̄r), *n.* [F. *fourniture.*] **1.** *Archaic.* A furnishing or state of being furnished. **2.** Necessary equipment; furnishings; specif.: **a** A set or supply of articles constituting the fittings of a bed, ship, automobile, etc. **b** Movable articles, as chairs, tables, beds, etc., used in furnishing a room or rooms; — usually disting. from *fittings,* or permanent adjuncts, as gas fixtures, sanitary appliances, etc. **3.** *Print.* Pieces, as of wood or metal, of less height than type, placed around and between matter to give blank spaces and, with quoins, to fasten the matter in the chase.

fu′ror (fū′rôr), *n.* [F. and L.; F. *fureur,* fr. L. *furor.*] **1.** Fury; frenzy. **2.** Poetic or religious enthusiasm. **3.** A public excitement or enthusiasm; esp., a prevalent and excited admiration; a "rage"; a craze. — **Syn.** See INSPIRATION.

fu′rore (fū′rōr; fū·rō′rē), *n.* [It.] Furor; a "rage."

furred (fûrd), *adj.* **1.** Bearing, wearing, or trimmed with fur. **2.** *Arch.* Provided with furring. **3.** *Med.* Having a morbid coating; — of the tongue.

fur′ri·er (fûr′ĭ·ẽr; 117), *n.* A dresser of or dealer in furs.

fur′ri·er·y (-ĭ), *n.; pl.* -ERIES (-ĭz). **1.** Furs, in general. **2.** The business of a furrier; trade in furs.

fur′ring (fûr′ĭng), *n.* **1.** Fur trimmings or lining. **2.** A supply or accumulation of fur. **3.** *Arch.* **a** The application of thin wood, brick, or metal to a surface to level it, as for lathing, plastering, etc., or to make an air space. **b** The material so applied.

fur′row (fûr′ō), *n.* [AS. *furh.*] **1.** A trench in the earth made by or as by a plow. **2.** Any narrow channel, or groove; a wrinkle. **3.** *Poetic.* Plowed land; field. — *v. t. & i.* To make furrows (in); plow. — **fur′row·er,** *n.*

fur′ry (fûr′ĭ), *adj.* **1.** Covered with or dressed in fur; furred. **2.** Consisting of or like fur. — **fur′ri·ness,** *n.*

fur seal. See SEAL.

fur′ther (fûr′thẽr), *adj. compar.; positive wanting; superl.* FUR′-THEST. [A compar. fr. the stem of *forth;* ME. *further, forther,* fr. AS. *furthra.*] **1.** More remote; farther. **2.** Going or lying beyond; additional. — *adv.* **1.** To or at a greater distance; to a greater extent or degree. **2.** In addition; furthermore. — **Syn.** See FARTHER. — *v. t.* To help forward; promote. — **Syn.** See ADVANCE. — **Ant.** Hinder. — **fur′ther·er,** *n.*

fur′ther·ance (-ăns), *n.* Act of furthering; advancement.

fur′ther·more′ (-mōr′; 2), *adv.* Moreover; besides.

fur′ther·most (-mōst; -mŭst), *adj.* Most remote; furthest.

fur′thest (fûr′thĕst; -thĭst), *adj. & adv. superl.* [Formed as a superl. under influence of *further.*] Most remote; at the greatest distance; farthest.

fur′tive (fûr′tĭv), *adj.* [F. *furtif,* fr. L. *furtivus,* fr. *furtum* theft, fr. *fur* thief.] Done by stealth; hence, sly; stealthy. — **Syn.** See SECRET. — **fur′tive·ly,** *adv.* — **fur′tive·ness,** *n.*

fu′run·cle (fū′rŭng·k'l), *n.* [L. *furunculus* a petty thief, a boil, dim. of *fur* thief.] *Med.* A boil. — **fu·run′cu·lar** (fū·rŭng′kū·lẽr), *adj.* — **fu·run′cu·lous** (-lŭs), *adj.*

fu′ry (fū′rĭ), *n.; pl.* FURIES (-rĭz). [OF. *furie,* fr. L. *furia;* akin to L. *furor, furere* to rage.] **1.** Violent anger; rage. **2.** [*cap.*] *Gr. & Rom. Myth.* One of the Erinyes; hence, any avenging spirit. **3.** A person given to rages; esp., a virago. **4.** Fierceness; vehemence. **5.** Frenzy; enthusiasm of one possessed as by a god. — **Syn.** See ANGER: INSPIRATION.

furze (fûrz), *n.* [AS. *fyrs.*] A spiny evergreen shrub (*Ulex europaeus*) of the pea family, with yellow flowers, common in Europe; gorse; whin.

fu′sain′ (fü′zăN′), *n.* [F., the spindle tree, charcoal made from it.] *Fine Arts.* Fine charcoal used in drawing, or a drawing made with it.

fus′cous (fŭs′kŭs), *adj.* [L. *fuscus.*] Dusky or somber in hue.

fuse, fuze (fūz), *n.* [It. *fuso* spindle, fr. L. *fusus.*] **1.** (usually **fuse**) A tube or cord filled or impregnated with combustible matter for igniting an explosive charge after a predetermined interval, as in firing a cannon or in blasting. **2.** (**fuze** in U. S. mil. use) A mechanical detonating device for an explosive charge, as in a shell, bomb, grenade, or other projectile. **3.** (usually **fuse**) An electrical safety device consisting of a wire or a strip of fusible metal inserted in a circuit and melting when the current becomes too strong. — *v. t.* To attach a fuse or fuze to.

fuse (fūz), *v. t. & i.* [L. *fusus,* past part. of *fundere* to pour.] **1.** To liquefy by heat; melt. **2.** To unite or blend, as if melted together. **3.** *Elec.* To fail, or cause to fail, because of the blowing of a fuse. — **Syn.** See MIX.

fu·see′, fu·zee′ (fū·zē′), *n.* [F. *fusée* a spindleful, fusee, fr. ML., fr. L. *fusus* spindle.] **1.** A friction match with a bulbous head, not easily blown out. **2.** *Horol.* A conoidal spirally grooved pulley from which a chain or cord is unwound onto the barrel which contains the spring. The lessening of the power of the spring is compensated for by the increasing diameter of the fusee. **3.** *Railroads.* A warning signal, esp. a kind of flare.

fu′se·lage (fū′zĕ·lĭj; fū′zĕ·läzh′), *n.* [F.] The elongated structure to which are attached the wings and tail unit of an airplane and which holds passengers, power plant, cargo, etc. See AIRPLANE, *Illust.*

fu′sel oil, *or* **fu′sel** (fū′zĕl, -z'l; -sĕl, -s'l), *n.* [G. *fusel* bad liquor.] An acrid, oily liquid, occurring in insufficiently distilled alcoholic liquors and consisting chiefly of amyl alcohol; also, amyl alcohol.

fu′si·bil′i·ty (fū′zĭ·bĭl′ĭ·tĭ), *n.* Quality of being fusible; also, relative reaction to heat in the process of fusion, esp. as expressed in terms of a recognized scale.

fu′si·ble (fū′zĭ·b'l), *adj.* Capable of being fused, esp. of being melted or liquefied; as, **fusible metal,** an easily melted metal such as lead. — **fu′si·ble·ness,** *n.* — **fu′si·bly,** *adv.*

fu′si·form (fū′zĭ·fôrm; fū′sĭ-), *adj.* [L. *fusus* spindle + *-form.*] Spindle-shaped; tapering at each end.

fu′sil (fū′zĭl), *n.* [F., fr. OF. *foisil, fuisil,* steel for striking fire, deriv. of L. *focus* hearth, in VL. fire.] A light flintlock musket.

fu′sil (fū′zĭl; fū′sĭl), **fu′sile** (fū′zĭl; -sĭl; -sīl), *adj.* [L. *fusilis* molten, fluid, fr. *fundere, fusum,* to pour.] **1.** *Rare.* Fusible; also, fusing. **2.** Fused; hence, cast; founded.

fu′sil·ier′, fu′sil·eer′ (fū′zĭ·lēr′), *n.* [F. *fusilier.*] **1.** *Obs.* A soldier armed with a fusil. **2.** *pl.* A title now borne by some British regiments.

fu′sil·lade′ (fū′zĭ·lād′), *n.* [F. See FUSIL musket.] A simultaneous or rapidly repeated discharge of, or as of, firearms. — *v. t.* To shoot down or attack by a fusillade.

fu′sion (fū′zhŭn), *n.* [L. *fusio,* fr. *fundere, fusum,* to pour, melt.] **1.** Act or operation of melting or of melting together. **2.** State of being fused; hence, a blending; coalescence; coalition. **3.** Something formed by fusing.

fusion bomb. A bomb in which nuclei of a light chemical element unite with a release of energy, as in the hydrogen bomb. Cf. ATOMIC BOMB.

fu′sion·ism (-ĭz'm), *n.* Policy or practice of bringing political parties into a coalition. — **fu′sion·ist** (-ĭst), *n. & adj.*

fuss (fŭs), *n.* **1.** Unnecessary or annoying ado about trifles; pother. **2.** A fussy person. — **Syn.** See STIR. — *v. i.* To fidget or be unduly anxious, esp. about trifles. — *v. t. Colloq.* To annoy with trifles; bother. — **fuss′er** (-ẽr), *n.*

fuss′y (-ĭ), *adj.;* FUSS′I·ER (-ĭ·ẽr); FUSS′I·EST. **1.** Disposed to fuss; finical. **2.** Showing or requiring unusual care. — **fuss′i·ly,** *adv.* — **fuss′i·ness,** *n.*

fus′tian (fŭs′chăn; fŭst′yăn), *n.* [OF. *fustaigne,* fr. ML. *fustaneum,* fr. L. *fustis* stick of wood.] **1.** Formerly, cotton and linen cloth; now, corduroy or velveteen. **2.** Bombast; claptrap. — **Syn.** See BOMBAST. — **fus′tian,** *adj.*

fus′tic (fŭs′tĭk), *n.* [F. *fustoc,* fr. Sp., fr. Ar. *fustuq,* fr. Gr. *pistakē* pistachio.] **1.** The wood of a tropical American tree (*Chlorophora tinctoria*) of the mulberry family, which yields a light-yellow dye much used in the arts; also, the tree itself. **2.** Any of several other dyewoods.

fus′ti·gate (fŭs′tĭ·gāt), *v. t.* [L. *fustigare,* fr. *fustis* stick.] To cudgel. — **fus′ti·ga′tion** (-gā′shŭn), *n.*

fust′y (fŭs′tĭ), *adj.;* FUST′I·ER (-tĭ·ẽr); FUST′I·EST. [OF. *fust* cask, fr. L. *fustis* stick.] **1.** Moldy; musty. **2.** Old-fashioned; old-fogyish; esp., obstinately or pedantically fogyish. — **Syn.** See MALODOROUS. — **fust′i·ly,** *adv.* — **fust′i·ness,** *n.*

fu′thorc, fu′thork (fōō′thôrk), *n.* Also **fu′tharc, fu′thark** (-thärk). The runic alphabet; — so called from the first six letters, *f, u, þ* (*th*), *o* (or *a*), *r, c* (= *k*).

fu′tile (fū′tĭl, -t'l; 56), *adj.* [F. or L.; F., fr. L. *futilis* that easily pours out, vain, worthless.] **1.** Useless; vain; ineffectual; as, a *futile* struggle. **2.** Trifling; frivolous; as, *futile* talk. — **fu′tile·ly,** *adv.* — **fu′tile·ness,** *n.* — **fu·til′i·ty** (fū·tĭl′ĭ·tĭ), *n.*

Syn. Futile, vain, fruitless mean barren of result. **Futile** and **vain** are synonyms only when they imply failure to realize a result, but *futile* also connotes completeness of failure or unwisdom of undertaking. **Fruitless** comes close to *vain* but is especially applicable when long and arduous effort or severe disappointment is implied.

fu·til′i·tar′i·an (fū·tĭl′ĭ·târ′ĭ·ăn), *adj.* [From *futility,* after *utilitarian.*] Holding the doctrine that all human endeavor and aspiration are futile. — **fu·til′i·tar′i·an,** *n.* — **fu·til′i·tar′i·an·ism,** *n.*

fut′tock (fŭt′ŭk), *n.* [Prob. for *foothook.*] *Naut.* One of the crooked timbers scarfed together to form the lower part of the compound rib of a vessel.

futtock shroud. One of the short, usually iron, shrouds, connecting the topmast rigging with the lower mast.

fu′tur·al (fū′tụ̄r·ăl), *adj.* Pert. to the future or futures.

fu′ture (fū′tụ̄r), *adj.* [OF. *futur,* fr. L. *futurus,* used as fut. part. of *esse* to be.] **1.** That is to be or come hereafter. **2.** *Gram.* Expressive of time yet to come; as, *future* tense. — *n.* **1.** Time that is to come; time subsequent to the present. **2.** The life after death; the future state. **3.** *pl.* Things bought and sold for delivery at a future time, esp. in speculation, as grain, provisions, and stocks. **4.** *Gram.* The future tense, or a verb in it. Abbr. *fut.*

fu′ture·less, *adj.* Without prospect of future success.

future perfect. *Gram.* Expressing a future act or event as past in relation to a given future time (By noon I *shall have gone*); also, the future perfect tense, or a verb in it.

fu′tur·ism (fū′tụ̄r·ĭz'm), *n.* A movement in the arts originating about 1910 and characterized by rejection of tradition and convention, and by efforts to express the dynamic energy and movement of contemporary life. — **fu′tur·ist** (-ĭst), *n. & adj.*

fu·tu′ri·ty (fū·tū′rĭ·tĭ), *n.; pl.* -TIES (-tĭz). **1.** Future state or time. **2.** A future event; specif., a futurity race.

futurity race. *Racing.* A race for futurity stakes.

futurity stakes. *Racing.* Stakes to be raced for long after the nominations or entries are made, the competitors (in animal races) being often nominated before birth; loosely, a futurity race.

fuze (fūz), **fu·zee′** (fū·zē′). See FUSE, FUSEE.

fuzz (fŭz), *n.* Fine, light particles or fibers; down; fluff. — *v. i. & t.* To fly off in, or cover with, fuzz; to become, or cause to be, fuzzy.

fuzz′y (-ĭ), *adj.;* FUZZ′I·ER (-ĭ·ẽr); FUZZ′I·EST. **1.** Covered with fuzz; also, like fuzz. **2.** Indistinct; not clear; as, *fuzzy* outlines, sounds.

-fy (-fī). [Through F. verbs in *-fier,* fr. L. *-ficare,* fr. *-ficus.* See -FIC.] A suffix signifying *to make, to form into,* etc.; — usually following *i,* as in ampli*fy,* Frenchi*fy.*

fyce (fīs), *n.* Var. of FEIST.

fyke (fīk), *n.* [D. *fuik* a bow net.] A long bag fish net.

fyl′fot (fĭl′fŏt), *n.* The swastika.

G

G, g (jē), *n.; pl.* G's, g's, Gs, gs (jēz). **1.** The seventh letter of the English alphabet, as of the Latin, whence it came. **2.** The sound of this letter. See *Pron.*, § 44. **3.** *Music.* **a** The fifth tone in the model major scale (that of C), or the seventh tone of its relative minor scale (that of A minor). **b** Any symbol representing, or a key or string producing, this tone. See PITCH, *Illust.* **4.** As a *symbol*, seventh in order or class.

G′-1′, G′-2′, G′-3′, G′-4′, G′-5′ (jē′wŭn′, etc.). [*G* for *G*eneral Staff.] *U. S. Army.* The designations, in a division or larger unit, of the sections of the executive officer's staff or the heads of these sections: G-1 personnel and administration, G-2 military intelligence, G-3 operations and training, G-4 supply and evacuation, G-5 civil affairs in occupied territory. Cf. S-1, S-2, etc.

gab (găb; *Scot.* gȧb), *n. Scot.* The mouth.

gab (găb), *v. i. & n. Colloq.* Chatter; gabble.

gab′ar·dine′ (găb′ẽr·dēn′; găb′ẽr·dēn), *n.* **1.** = GABERDINE. **2.** A woolen fabric closely resembling serge, but twilled on one side only; also, a similar fabric of cotton or rayon.

gab′bard (găb′ẽrd), **gab′bart** (-ẽrt), *n.* [F. *gabare, gabarot.*] *Obs. exc. Scot.* A lighter, barge, or similar vessel.

gab′ble (găb′'l), *v. i. & t.;* GAB′BLED (-'ld); GAB′BLING (-lĭng). **1.** To jabber; chatter. **2.** To utter inarticulate sounds rapidly, as fowls. — **gab′ble,** *n.* — **gab′bler** (-lẽr), *n.*

gab′bro (găb′rō), *n.* [It., fr. L. *glaber* bare, smooth.] *Petrog.* Any of a family of granular, igneous rocks essentially of plagioclase with a ferromagnesian mineral and accessory iron ore, etc.

gab′broid (-roid), *adj. Petrog.* Resembling gabbro.

gab′by (găb′ĭ), *adj. Colloq.* Loquacious; talkative.

ga·belle′ (gȧ·bĕl′), *n.* [F., through Pr. & It., fr. Ar. *qabālah.*] A tax; specif., an impost on salt, levied in France for several centuries prior to 1790, and in use down to the present day in China.

gab′er·dine′ (găb′ẽr·dēn′; găb′ẽr·dēn), *n.* [Sp. *gabardina.*] **1.** A coarse loose frock or coat; — chiefly of medieval costume. **2.** The medieval Jewish gown or mantle. **3.** Var. of GABARDINE.

gab′er·lun′zie (găb′ẽr·lŭn′zĭ; *Scot.* gȧb′ẽr·lün′yĭ, -lo͞on′yĭ, -lo͞on′ĭ), *n. Scot.* A wandering beggar.

ga′bi·on (gā′bĭ·ŭn; 58), *n.* [F., fr. It. *gabbione* a large cage, fr. *gabbia* cage, fr. L. *cavea.*] A hollow cylinder of wickerwork, iron, or the like. Gabions are filled with earth and used in building fieldworks, mining, etc.

ga′bi·on·ade′ (gā′bĭ·ŭn·ād′), *n.* [F. *gavionnade.*] A work made with gabions.

ga′ble (gā′b'l), *n.* [OF., fr. ON. *gafl.*] *Arch.* **a** The vertical triangular portion of the end of a building, from the level of the cornice or eaves to the ridge of the roof. Also, a similar end when not triangular in shape, as of a gambrel roof. Hence: **b** The end wall of a building, as distinguished from the front or rear side. **c** A decorative member having the shape of a triangular gable, such as that above a Gothic arch in a doorway. — *v. t. & i.;* GA′BLED (-b'ld); GA′BLING (-blĭng). To furnish with gables; to terminate in a gable; as, a *gabled* roof.

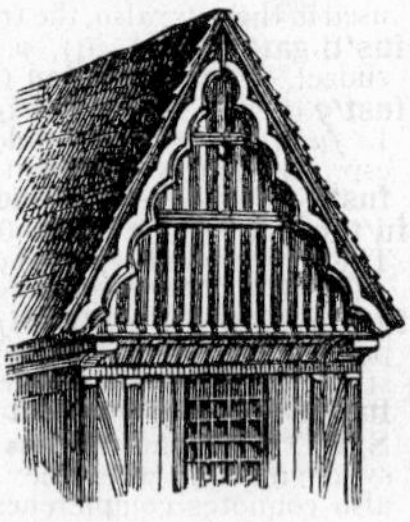

Gable **a**.

gable roof. A roof which forms a gable at each end.

gable window. A window in a gable, or one with a gable.

Ga′bri·el (gā′brĭ·ĕl), *n.* [Heb. *Gabhrī'ēl.*] An angel of comfort to man (*Dan.* viii and ix), a herald declaring the coming of the Messiah. In Jewish and Christian tradition, he is one of the seven archangels. He is believed by Mohammedans to have dictated the Koran to their prophet.

ga′by (gā′bĭ; *dial. also* gô′bĭ), *n. Colloq.* A simpleton.

gad (găd), *n.* [ON. *gaddr* a sting, spike.] **1.** A goad; as, upon the *gad,* that is, suddenly, as if goaded. **2.** *Mining, etc.* A pointed iron or steel bar for loosening ore, etc.

gad (găd), *v. i.;* GAD′DED (-ĕd; -ĭd); GAD′DING. To wander about idly. — *n. Colloq.* A gadding, or rambling; — only in *on,* or *upon, the gad.*

Gad (găd), *n.* A softened form of *God,* used as a mild oath, as in **Gads′bod′i·kins** (gădz′bŏd′ĭ·kĭnz), **Gads′woons′** (-wo͞onz′), **Gad′-zooks′** (găd′zo͞oks′), etc.

Gad (găd), *n. Bib.* See JACOB.

gad′a·bout′ (găd′ȧ·bout′), *adj.* Gadding; roving. — *n. Colloq.* One who gads about.

gad′bee′ (găd′bē′), *n.* A gadfly.

gad′der (găd′ẽr), *n.* One who roves about idly; a gadabout.

gad′fly′ (găd′flī′), *n.; pl.* -FLIES (-flīz′). [1st *gad* + *fly.*] A fly that bites cattle; a horsefly.

gadg′et (găj′ĕt; -ĭt), *n.* A small contrivance, object, or device for doing something; esp., a part of machinery.

Ga·dhel′ic (gȧ·dĕl′ĭk; -dē′lĭk; găd′ĕ·lĭk). Var. of GOIDELIC.

ga′did (gā′dĭd), *n* [See GADOID.] A fish of the cod family (Gadidae). — **ga′did,** *adj.*

ga′doid (-doid), *adj.* [NL. *gadus* cod + *-oid.*] Like or pertaining to the cod family (Gadidae), a large family of soft-finned, chiefly marine food fishes, including the cod and haddock, having a rather elongated body and a large mouth. — *n.* A fish of the cod family or of a group (Anacanthini) of teleost fishes that comprises the codfishes, hakes, and their allies.

gad′o·lin·ite (găd′ō·lĭn·īt), *n.* [After J. *Gadolin* (1760–1852), Finnish chemist.] A black or brown vitreous silicate of iron, beryllium, yttrium, cerium, erbium, etc. H., 6.5–7. Sp. gr., 4–4.5. It is a source of rare earths.

gad′o·lin′i·um (-lĭn′ĭ·ŭm; 58), *n.* [NL.] *Chem.* A metallic element, one of the rare-earth metals, found in combination in gadolinite and certain other minerals. Symbol, *Gd;* at. no., 64; at. wt., 156.9.

ga·droon′ (gȧ·dro͞on′), *n.* [F. *godron* a round plait, gadroon.] **a** *Arch.* An ornament made by notching or carving a rounded molding. **b** A fluting or reeding, often nearly oval, used in silverware, etc.

gad′wall (găd′wôl), *n.;* see PLURAL, *Note,* 3. A wild duck (*Chaulelasmus streperus*), of about the size of the mallard.

Gae′a (jē′ȧ), *n.* [Gr. *Gaia.*] *Gr. Myth.* Earth as a goddess.

Gaek′war (gīk′wär), *n.* Also **Gaik′war, Gaek′wad** (-wäd). [Marathi *Gāekvād,* family name, lit., cowherd.] The title of the ruling prince of Baroda, India.

Gael (gāl), *n.* [Gael. *Gāidheal.*] One of the Celtic inhabitants of Ireland, Scotland, and the Isle of Man; esp., a Scottish Highlander of Gaelic speech.

Gael′ic (gāl′ĭk), *adj.* Of or pertaining to the Gaels or their language. — *n.* The Goidelic speech of the Celts of Ireland (called also *Irish*), the Isle of Man (*Manx*), and, specif. (sometimes called *Erse*), of the Highlands of Scotland, the Hebrides, and other Scottish islands. See INDO-EUROPEAN LANGUAGES, *Table.*

gaff (găf), *n.* [F. *gaffe,* fr. Pr. *gaf.*] **1.** A barbed spear or iron hook for securing heavy fish, as in lifting them into a boat. **2.** A metal spur for a gamecock. **3.** *Slang.* Something difficult to bear; — esp. in the phrase *to stand the gaff.* **4.** *Slang, Eng.* [Where "fish" or "suckers" are gaffed.] A cheap place of amusement. **5.** *Naut.* The spar upon which the head, or upper edge, of a fore-and-aft sail is extended.
— *v. t.* **1.** To strike or secure with a gaff; as, to *gaff* turtles, salmon. **2.** *Slang.* To trick; fleece.

‖**gaffe** (găf), *n.* [F.] *Colloq.* A clumsy mistake; faux pas.

gaf′fer (găf′ẽr), *n.* [Contr. fr. *godfather.*] **1.** *Originally Respectful; now Contemptuous.* An old man; an aged rustic. Cf. GAMMER. **2.** *Eng.* A foreman, or overseer, of labor.

gaff′-top′sail′ (găf′tŏp′sāl′; *naut.* -s'l), *n.* A topsail, usually triangular, with its foot extended upon the gaff and its luff upon the topmast. See SAIL, *Illust.*

gag (găg), *v. t.;* GAGGED (găgd); GAG′GING. [Of imitative origin.] **1.** To cause to heave as with nausea; to retch. **2.** To stop the mouth of, by something thrust in, and hinder speaking; hence, to silence by authority or by violence; to prevent from free speech. **3.** *Slang.* To perpetrate a gag or gags upon; to hoax. — *v. i.* **1.** To heave; to retch. **2.** *Slang.* To introduce gags in acting.
— *n.* **1.** A mouthful that makes one retch; a choking bit. **2.** Something thrust into the mouth or throat to hinder speaking; hence, any forcible restraint of speech. **3. a** A made-up story told plausibly to hoax or impose on someone or to provide oneself an evasive pretext; also, an often-used fabrication of this kind that has become a cliché. **b** Hence, any trick of imposture or deception for making someone a butt of ridicule, as in vaudeville. **4.** An interpolation, originally of an amusing local or topical allusion or bit of byplay, by an actor in his lines; hence, use of any pat or clever comment, joke, pantomime, or episode in stage or motion-picture presentation, often one with a contrived climax of a laughter-provoking situation.

gage (gāj), **gag′er** (gāj′ẽr). Vars. of GAUGE, etc.

gage (gāj), *n.* [OF. *gage, guage, wage,* of Teut. origin.] **1.** Something deposited as a security for the performance of some act by the person depositing it; security. **2.** A pledge, as a glove or cap cast on the ground, of one's appearance to support one's claims; hence, a challenge; defiance; as, to throw down the *gage.* — *v. t.;* GAGED (gājd); GAG′ING (gāj′ĭng). **1.** *Obs. exc. Hist.* To give or deposit as a gage or pledge. **2.** *Archaic.* To wager. **3.** *Archaic.* To bind as by a pledge.

gage, *n.* The greengage (which see).

gag′ger (găg′ẽr), *n.* One who or that which gags.

gag law *or* **rule.** *Colloq.* A ruling prohibiting free debate, as in a legislative body; also, legislation restricting freedom of the press.

gag′man′ (găg′măn′), *n.* One who contrives gags for comedians or other entertainers.

gahn′ite (gän′īt), *n.* [After J. G. *Gahn* (1745–1818), Sw. chemist.] *Mineral.* A member of the spinel group, being pure zinc aluminate, $ZnAl_2O_4$, or the same with partial replacement by manganese and iron.

gai′e·ty, gay′e·ty (gā′ĕ·tĭ), *n.; pl.* -TIES (-tĭz). [F. *gaieté.*] **1.** State of being gay; merriment; jollity; also, a gay or merry affair, entertainment, or the like; as, the season's *gaieties.* **2.** Finery; as, *gaiety* of dress.

gail·lar′di·a (gȧ·lär′dĭ·ȧ), *n.* [NL., after *Gaillard* de Marentonneau, French botanist.] *Bot.* Any of a genus (*Gaillardia*) of chiefly western American herbs of the aster family.

gai′ly, gay′ly (gā′lĭ), *adv.* In a gay manner.

gain (gān), *n.* [F., fr. OF. *gaain,* fr. *gaaignier.* See GAIN to acquire.] **1.** Increase in profit, resources, or advantage acquired; profit; — opposed to *loss.* **2.** Act of gaining something; acquisition; accumulation.
— *v. t.* [F. *gagner,* fr. OF. *gaaignier,* fr. OHG. *weidenen* to pasture, hunt, fr. *weida* pasturage.] **1.** To get; acquire; earn; as, to *gain* a living. **2.** Ironically, to get or incur, as loss, or damage. **3.** To get in competition; to win. **4.** To win to one's side; to persuade; — often with *over.* **5.** To reach; to arrive at; as, to *gain* the top. **6.** To get as by a natural development, advance, or increment, or by a normal exercise of function; as, to *gain* strength slowly. — *v. i.* To secure advantage; to acquire gain. — **Syn.** See GET (**Ant.** forfeit, lose): REACH.

gain (gān), *n. Carpentry, etc.* A notch or mortise, as in a timber, wall, etc., for a girder, joist, etc. — *v. t.* To make a gain or gains in; to join or secure by a gain.

gain′er (gān′ẽr), *n.* **1.** One who or that which gains. **2.** *Fancy Diving.* A dive executed as a back somersault but from a front-dive take-off position. Cf. HALF GAINER.

gain′ful (-fo͝ol; -f'l), *adj.* Productive of gain; profitable; lucrative. — **gain′ful·ly,** *adv.* — **gain′ful·ness,** *n.*

gain′giv′ing (-gĭv′ĭng), *n. Archaic.* A misgiving.

gain′less, *adj.* Unprofitable. — **gain′less·ness,** *n.*

gain′ly (gān′lĭ), *adj.* [ME. *gayn* near, active, kindly + *-ly,* 1.] Having good form or appearance; shapely; graceful. — **gain′li·ness,** *n.*

gain′say′ (gān′sā′; gān′sā′; 2), *v. t.;* -SAID′ (-sĕd′; -sĕd′); -SAY′ING. To speak against; contradict; controvert; dispute; forbid. — **Syn.** See DENY. — **gain′say′er** (gān′sā′ẽr), *n.*

gain′say′ (gān′sā′), *n.* A gainsaying; contradiction.

'gainst, gainst (gĕnst *or, esp. Brit.,* gānst), *prep. & conj.* Aphetic form of AGAINST.

gait (gāt), *n.* [Special use of GATE a way.] **1.** Manner of walking, running, or moving on foot. **2.** Specif., of horses, foot movement in going. The principal gaits are the amble, canter, pace, rack, run, single-foot, trot, and walk. — *v. t.* **1.** To train to a regular gait; as, to *gait* a horse. **2.** To prepare for work; as, to *gait* a loom.

gait'ed (-ĕd; -ĭd), *adj.* Having a (certain) gait; as, slow-*gaited.*

gai'ter (gā'tẽr), *n.* [F. *guêtre.*] **1.** A covering for the ankle and instep, or for the leg from the knee to the instep. **2.** A button shoe, covering the ankle, orig. with a cloth upper, later either with or without cloth. **3.** A kind of overshoe, with a cloth upper.

ga'la (gā'lȧ; gä'lȧ), *n.* [F. and It.; F., fr. It. *gala* finery, fr. OF. *gale* merrymaking.] **1. a** Festive dress; — now only in *in gala.* **b** *Obs.* Festivity. **2.** A festival; celebration. — *adj.* Pertaining to or attended by festivities; suitable for festivity; as, a *gala* day; a *gala* dress.

ga·lac'tic (gȧ·lăk'tĭk), *adj.* [Gr. *galaktikos* milky, fr. *gala, -aktos,* milk.] **1.** = LACTIC. **2.** *Astron.* Of or pertaining to the Milky Way, or Galaxy, to the great circle (**galactic circle** *or* **equator**) passing through its central line, to the plane of this circle (**galactic plane**), or to the poles of this circle (**galactic poles**).

ga·lac'to- (gȧ·lăk'tō-), **galact-.** [Gr. *gala, galaktos.*] A combining form meaning *milk, milky fluid,* as in **ga·lac'ta·gogue** (-tȧ·gŏg), promoting secretion of milk; specif., *Chem.,* denoting *galactose.*

ga·lac'tose (gȧ·lăk'tōs), *n.* [*galact-* + *-ose.*] *Chem.* A white, crystalline sugar, $C_6H_{12}O_6$. The D variety is obtained by the hydrolysis of lactose and from certain gums.

Gal'a·had, Sir (găl'ȧ·hăd). In late Arthurian legend, a knight of the Round Table, surnamed "the chaste," who achieved the quest of the Holy Grail.

gal'an·gal (găl'ăn·găl), **gal'an·gale** (găl'ăn·gāl). Vars. of GALINGALE.

gal'an·tine (găl'ăn·tēn; găl'ăn·tēn'), *n.* [F.] A dish of poultry, fish, game, or other meat, freed of bones, stuffed, cooked, pressed, covered with aspic, and served cold.

ga·lan'ty show (gȧ·lăn'tĭ). A pantomime made by throwing shadows on a wall or screen.

gal'a·te'a (găl'ȧ·tē'ȧ), *n.* [After the *Galatea,* a British man-of-war, the material being used for children's sailor suits (*Oxf. E. D.*).] A striped cotton fabric used for women's dresses and children's play suits.

Gal'a·te'a, *n.* [L., fr. Gr. *Galateia.*] An ivory statue of a maiden, by Pygmalion, a king of Cyprus. He fell in love with the statue, and at his prayer Aphrodite gave it life.

Ga·la'tians (gȧ·lā'shănz), *n. pl., construed as sing.* The Epistle to the Galatians in the New Testament. See BIBLE.

gal'a·vant' (găl'ȧ·vănt'). Var. of GALLIVANT.

ga'lax (gā'lăks), *n.* [NL.] A plant of a genus (*Galax*) of evergreen herbs (family Diapensiaceae). Its leaves are widely used for funeral decorations.

gal'ax·y (găl'ăk·sĭ), *n.; pl.* GALAXIES (-sĭz). [F. and L.; F. *galaxie,* fr. L. *galaxias,* fr. Gr. *galaxias* (sc. *kyklos* circle), fr. *gala, -aktos,* milk.] **1.** *Astron.* **a** [*usually cap.*] The Milky Way. **b** A milky way or island universe. See ISLAND UNIVERSE. **2.** An assemblage of brilliant or noted persons or things.

gal'ba·num (găl'bȧ·nŭm), *n.* [L., fr. Gr. *chalbanē,* fr. Heb. *helbenāh.*] A brownish gum resin of aromatic odor and unpleasant taste, derived from certain Asiatic plants, mostly species of one genus (*Ferula*). It resembles asafetida, and is used for similar medicinal purposes, and in the arts.

gale (gāl), *n.* [AS. *gagel.*] A bog shrub (*Myrica gale,* family Myricaceae) of the North Temperate Zone, with bitter fragrant leaves; — commonly called ***sweet gale.***

gale, *n.* [Origin uncert.] **1.** A strong wind of a velocity between 39 and 54 miles per hour (U. S. Weather Bureau wind scale). A ***whole gale*** is a wind with a velocity between 55 and 75 miles per hour. International symbol, ⫫. Cf. BEAUFORT'S SCALE, BREEZE, HURRICANE. **2.** *Poetic.* A breeze. **3. a** Gust; outburst; as, *gales* of laughter. **b** *Colloq.* A state of excitement, passion, etc.

gale, *n.* [From GAVEL tribute.] *Rare.* A periodical payment, as for rent.

ga'le·a (gā'lē·ȧ), *n.; pl.* GALEAE (-ē). [L., helmet.] *Bot.* Any helmet-shaped part of a calyx or corolla, esp. the upper lip of a ringent or labiate corolla.

ga'le·ate (-āt), **ga'le·at'ed** (-āt'ĕd; -ĭd), *adj.* Helmet-shaped; as, a *galeate* corolla.

ga·le'i·form (gȧ·lē'ĭ·fôrm), *adj.* [*galea* + *-form.*] Helmet-shaped.

Ga'len (gā'lĕn), *n.* A physician; — from Galen (A.D. 130 or 131–c. 200), a physician of Pergamum in Asia Minor.

ga·le'na (gȧ·lē'nȧ), *n.* [L., lead ore.] *Mineral.* Native lead sulfide, PbS, the chief ore of lead. It is bluish gray with metallic luster, and shows highly perfect cubic cleavage.

Ga·len'ic (gȧ·lĕn'ĭk; -lē'nĭk), **Ga·len'i·cal** (-ĭ·kăl), *adj.* Of or relating to Galen, or his medical principles.

Galenic pharmacy. The preparation of a medicine (**ga·len'i·cal**) or medicines from crude drugs or chemical substances by physical means (solution, decoction, etc.).

Ga'len·ism (gā'lĕn·ĭz'm), *n.* The Galenic system or practice of medicine. — **Ga'len·ist** (-ĭst), *n.*

ga·le'nite (gȧ·lē'nīt), *n.* Galena.

Ga·li'cian (gȧ·lĭsh'ăn), *adj.* from GALICIA (Spain), *Gaz.* — *n.* A native of Galicia; also, the language of the Galicians, a dialect of Portuguese. See INDO-EUROPEAN LANGUAGES, *Table.*

Gal'i·le'an (găl'ĭ·lē'ăn), *adj.* from GALILEE, *Gaz.* — *n.* A native or inhabitant of Galilee. Hence, a Christian; — after the epithet ***the Galilean*** applied to Jesus.

Gal'i·le'an, *adj.* Of or relating to the Italian Galileo Galilei (1564–1642), founder of experimental physics and astronomy; as, the *Galilean* telescope.

gal'i·lee (găl'ĭ·lē), *n.* [OF., fr. ML. *galilaea.*] In certain English churches, a chapel or porch at the entrance, used as an accessory room.

gal'i·ma'ti·as (găl'ĭ·mā'shĭ·ăs; -măt'ĭ·ăs), *n.* [F.] Nonsense; gibberish; confused and unmeaning talk; jargon.

gal'in·gale (găl'ĭn·gāl), *n.* [OF. *galingal,* fr. Ar., fr. Per. *khalanjān.*] **1.** The pungent aromatic rhizome of various plants related to the true ginger. **2.** An English sedge (*Cyperus longus*) with a pungent root.

gal'i·ot, gal'li·ot (găl'ĭ·ŭt), *n.* [F. *galiote,* dim. fr. OF. *galie.* See GALLEY.] *Naut.* **a** A small swift galley, formerly used in the Mediterranean. **b** A long, narrow, light-draft Dutch merchant vessel. **c** *Obs.* A Roman galley.

gal'i·pot, gal'li·pot (găl'ĭ·pŏt), *n.* [F. *galipot.*] The crude turpentine oleoresin exuded from a pine (*Pinus pinaster*) in southern Europe, esp. France.

gall (gôl), *n.* [AS. *gealla.*] **1.** Bile, as from the ox, used in arts and in medicine. **2.** The gall bladder. **3.** Anything bitter to endure. **4.** Bitterness of spirit; rancor. **5.** *Slang, U. S.* Impudence; brazen assurance. — **Syn.** See TEMERITY.

gall, *n.* [ME. *galle* a sore spot. See GALL to chafe.] **1.** A sore in the skin from rubbing, esp. one on the back of a horse. **2.** A cause, or a state, of irritation; exasperation. **3.** A bare or weak spot; flaw. — *v. t.* [ME. *gallen,* fr. *galle,* fr. AS. *gealle* blister, windgall, but influenced by OF. *galle,* a galling.] **1.** To fret and wear away by friction; to chafe. **2.** To vex; irritate. **3.** To injure; harass. — *v. i.* To become sore or worn by rubbing.

gall, *n.* [OF. *galle,* fr. L. *galla.*] A swelling on the tissues of plants, caused by the attacks of certain parasites, as the *gallfly* (Cynipoidea), the *gall midge* (Itonididae), and certain aphids. Many galls contain much tannic acid and are important in commerce, esp. those produced on certain oaks (esp. *Quercus lusitanica*).

gal'lant (găl'ănt; *see sense* 4), *adj.* [F. *galant,* prop. pres. part. of OF. *galer* to rejoice, fr. *gale.* See GALA.] **1.** Showy; esp., gay or smart in dress. **2.** Stately in appearance or action; as, a *gallant* ship. **3.** Noble in bearing or spirit; brave. **4.** (*pron.* gă·lănt'; găl'ănt) **a** Courteously attentive to women. **b** Amorous; amatory. — **Syn.** See CIVIL. — (găl'ănt; gă·lănt'), *n.* **1.** A gay, fashionable person, usually a man. **2.** One gallant to ladies; hence, a lover; in a bad sense, a paramour. — **gal'lant·ly,** *adv.*

gal·lant' (gȧ·lănt'), *v. t.* **1.** To bestow gallant attentions on (a lady). **2.** To act as escort to (a lady); hence, to escort; conduct. — *v. i.* To act the gallant; to make love.

gal'lant·ry (găl'ăn·trĭ), *n.; pl.* -RIES (-trĭz). **1.** *Obs.* Gallants collectively. **2.** *Archaic.* Gallant appearance; display; hence, a bit of finery. **3.** Bravery; as, the *gallantry* of soldiers. **4.** The life or conduct of a gallant. **5.** A gallant action or speech. **6.** Civility or polite attention to ladies. — **Syn.** See HEROISM.

gall bladder. *Anat.* The bladder which receives the bile.

gal'le·ass (găl'ē·ăs), *n.* [F. *galéasse, galéace,* fr. It. See GALLEY.] *Naut.* A large galley mounting heavy guns; esp., such a vessel used by nations of southern Europe in the 16th and 17th centuries.

gal'le·on (găl'ē·ŭn), *n.* [F. *galion* (fr. OF. *galie*) and Sp. *galeón,* fr. *galea.* See GALLEY.] A sailing vessel of the 15th and following centuries, often having three or four decks, and used for war or commerce.

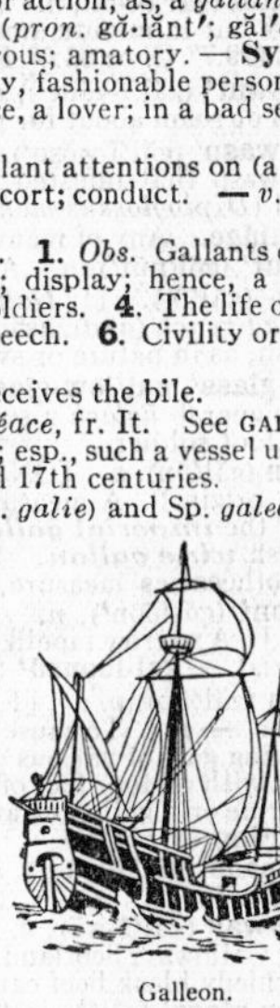
Galleon.

gal'ler·y (găl'ẽr·ĭ), *n.; pl.* -LER·IES (-ĭz). [F. *galerie,* fr. It. *galleria,* fr. ML. *galilaea.*] **1.** A long narrow room, hall, or other passage; esp., in the southern U. S., a veranda. **2.** A room for the exhibition of works of art; as, a picture *gallery;* hence, a collection of paintings. **3.** A structure attached to one or more sides of an auditorium above the main floor, to accommodate part of the audience; specif., in a theater, the highest of such structures, usually having the cheapest seats. **4.** The occupants of a gallery; hence, the general public; also, any body of spectators at a game, as of golf or tennis. **5.** By extension: **a** A place of business shaped like or analogous to a gallery; as, a photograph *gallery;* a shooting *gallery.* **b** An underground passage made by an animal, as by moles or ants. **6.** *Fort.* Any sunk or cut passageway covered overhead as well as at the sides. **7.** *Mining.* A working drift or level. **8.** *Naut.* A platform at the quarters or around the stern, common in old-time vessels (the ***quarter gallery*** and ***stern gallery***). — *v. t. & i.;* GAL'LER·IED (-ĭd); GAL'LER·Y·ING. To provide with, or to make, a gallery or galleries.

gal'ley (găl'ĭ), *n.; pl.* -LEYS (-ĭz). [OF. *galie, galee,* fr. ML., fr. MGr. *galea, galaia.*] **1.** A large, low, usually one-decked, vessel propelled by both oars and sails, used throughout the Middle Ages, esp. in the Mediterranean. **2.** *Class. Antiq.* A seagoing vessel propelled chiefly by oars. **3.** A large open rowing boat. **4.** The kitchen and cooking apparatus of a vessel. **5.** [F. *galée.*] *Print.* **a** An oblong tray, with upright sides, to hold type which has been set. **b** A galley proof.

galley proof. *Print.* A proof from type on a galley before it is made up in pages; also, such proofs collectively.

galley slave. A slave acting as a rower on a galley; also, a criminal condemned to such work; figuratively, a drudge.

gall'fly' (gôl'flī'), *n.; pl.* -FLIES (-flīz'). An insect that deposits its eggs in plants, and occasions galls. See GALL.

gal'liard (găl'yẽrd), *adj.* [OF. *gaillard.*] *Archaic.* **1.** Gay; lively; gallant. **2.** Hardy; valiant. — *n.* A gay, lively, 16th century dance with five steps to a phrase.

gal'liard·ise (găl'yẽr·dēz), *n.* [F. *gaillardise.* See GALLIARD, *adj.*] *Archaic.* Excessive gaiety; merriment.

gal'li·ass (găl'ĭ·ăs). Var. of GALLEASS.

gal'lic (găl'ĭk), *adj.* [From *gallium.*] Of, relating to, or containing, gallium.

gal'lic, *adj.* [From GALL excrescence.] *Chem.* Pertaining to or designating a white crystalline acid, $C_6H_2(OH)_3CO_2H$, widely distributed among plants, esp. in galls, tea, etc.

Gal'lic (găl'ĭk), *adj.* [L. *Gallicus,* fr. *Galli* Gauls, *Gallia* Gaul.] Of or relating to Gaul or France; Gallican; French.

Gal'li·can (găl'ĭ·kăn), *adj.* Gallic.

Gal'li·can·ism (-ĭz'm), *n.* A theory or policy regarding the relations between the papacy and the French church, tantamount to a demand for an autonomous national church.

Gallican Liberties. The ancient liberties of the Gallican church as maintained by Gallicanism.

‖**Gal'li·ce** (găl'ĭ·sē), *adv.* In French; after the French manner.

Gal'li·cism, gal'li·cism (găl'ĭ·sĭz'm), *n.* A word or idiom peculiar to French, and borrowed for use in another language, as English.

Gal'li·cize, gal'li·cize (-sīz), *v. t. & i.* To conform to the French mode or idiom.

gal'li·gas'kin (găl'ĭ·găs'kĭn), *n.* **1.** *pl.* Loose, wide hose or breeches, esp. of the 17th century; now, jocosely, loose breeches. **2.** *Dial. Eng.* A gaiter or legging.

gal'li·mau'fry (găl'ĭ·mô'frĭ), *n.; pl.* -FRIES (-frĭz). [F. *galimafree.*] **1.** A meat ragout. **2.** A hodgepodge.

gal'li·na'ceous (găl'ĭ·nā'shŭs), *adj.* [L. *gallinaceus*, fr. *gallina* hen, fr. *gallus* cock.] *Zool.* Resembling domestic fowls; of or belonging to a group (Gallinae, order Galliformes) of birds including the pheasants, turkeys, grouse, etc.

gall'ing (gôl'ĭng), *adj.* Such as to gall or chafe; irritating. — **gall'ing·ly,** *adv.*

gal'li·nip'per (găl'ĭ·nĭp'ẽr), *n.* *Colloq.* A large mosquito or other stinging insect; also, a crane fly.

gal'li·nule (găl'ĭ·nūl), *n.* [L. *gallinula* chicken, dim. of *gallina* hen.] Any of certain birds of the rail family (Rallidae), related to the coots, as the European gallinule (*Gallinula chloropus*), called also *water hen* or *moor hen.* The related American subspecies is known as the ***Florida gallinule*** (*G. c. cachinnans*).

gal'li·ot (găl'ĭ·ŭt). Var. of GALIOT.

gal'li·pot (-pŏt), *n.* [Prob. *galley* + *pot*, as being brought in galleys.] A small vessel, esp. one used by apothecaries to hold medicines, etc.; hence, *Colloq.*, a druggist.

gal'li·pot, *n.* A resin; — var. of GALIPOT.

gal'li·um (găl'ĭ·ŭm), *n.* [NL.] *Chem.* A metallic element occurring widely but in minute amounts. It is remarkable for its low melting point (29.7° C. or 85.5° F.). Symbol, *Ga*; at. no., 31; at. wt., 69.72.

gal'li·vant' (găl'ĭ·vănt'), *v. i.* **1.** To play the gallant. **2.** Hence, to travel or roam about for pleasure.

gal'li·wasp' (găl'ĭ·wŏsp'), *n.* [*galley* + *wasp*; — appar. applied first to a wasp that infested ships in West Indian ports.] A harmless lizard (*Diploglossus monotropis*) of eastern Central America.

gall midge. Any of many gall-making gnats. See GALL.

gall'nut' (gôl'nŭt'), *n.* A nutlike gall. See 3d GALL.

Gal'lo- (găl'ō-). [L. *Gallus* a Gaul, Gallic.] A combining form denoting *French (and)*, as in **Gal'lo–Brit'on,** a person both French and British, as in nature or sympathies.

gal'lo·glass', gal'low·glass' (găl'ō·glȧs'), *n.* [Ir. *gallōglach*, fr. *gall* a foreigner + *ōglach* a servant, soldier.] *Obs. exc. Hist.* An armed Irish foot soldier.

gal'lon (găl'ŭn), *n.* [ONF. *galon*, OF. *jalon, jallon*, of obscure, perh. Celt., origin.] A measure of capacity: the British standard gallon being the ***imperial gallon,*** the U. S. standard gallon being the old English ***wine gallon.*** See MEASURE, *Tables* 11 & 12. Abbr. *gal.* In apothecaries' measure, it is denoted by the symbol *C.* (L. *congius*).

gal·loon' (gȧ·lōōn'), *n.* [F. *galon*, fr. *galonner* to adorn with galloons.] A narrow tapelike binding or trimming; esp., a binding of rich material. — **gal·looned'** (-lōōnd'), *adj.*

gal'lop (găl'ŭp), *v. i.* [F. *galoper.*] To move or go at, or as if at, a gallop. — *v. t.* To cause to gallop; as, to *gallop* a horse. — *n.* **1.** A springing gait of various quadrupeds, esp. a fast springing gait of the horse, with all four feet off the ground once in each stride, as in a leap. **2.** A ride on a galloping animal. **3.** Rapid progression, as if by leaps. — **gal'lop·er** (-ẽr), *n.*

gal'lo·pade' (găl'ō·pād'), *n.* [F. *galopade.*] A kind of lively dance, or music for it.

Gal'lo·way (găl'ō·wā), *n.* **1.** A breed of small hardy horses originating in Galloway, Scotland. **2.** A hardy breed of medium-sized, hornless, chiefly black beef cattle, native to southwestern Scotland.

gal'low·glass' (găl'ō·glȧs'), *n.* See GALLOGLASS.

gal'lows (găl'ōz; -ŭs), *n. sing.; pl.* GALLOWSES (-ĕz; -ĭz) or, *Archaic,* GALLOWS. [ME. *galwes*, pl., fr. AS. *galga, gealga*, gallows, cross.] **1.** A frame, usually of two upright posts and a crossbeam, from which criminals are hanged. **2.** A gallows bird. **3.** Any upright frame with crosspiece. **4.** *pl.* (*pron.* găl'ŭs·ĭz). *Chiefly Dial.* A pair of suspenders, or braces. — *adj. Dial.* Deserving the gallows; villainous. — *adv. Slang & Dial.* Extremely; very.

gallows bird. *Colloq.* A person who deserves hanging.

gallows tree, gal'low tree (găl'ō). The gallows.

gall'stone' (gôl'stōn'), *n.* A concretion, or calculus, formed in the gall bladder or biliary passages. See CALCULUS, *n.*, 1.

gal'lus·es (găl'ŭs·ĭz), *n. pl. Dial.* Suspenders; braces. See GALLOWS, *n.*, 4.

ga·loot' (gȧ·lōōt'), *n.* *Slang.* An uncouth, awkward fellow.

gal'op (găl'ŭp), *n.* [F.] A lively dance in duple measure; also, its music.

ga·lore' (gȧ·lōr'; 70), *adj.* [Ir. *go leōr* enough.] *Colloq.* Abundant; plentiful; copious; as, bandits *galore*; evidence *galore.* — *adv. Colloq.* In abundance; plentifully. — *n. Colloq.* Abundance.

ga·losh', ga·loshe' (gȧ·lŏsh'), *n.* [OF. *galoche.*] **1.** *Obs.* A clog; a shoe with a heavy sole; hence, a boot or shoe of any sort. **2.** An overshoe worn in wet weather.

gal·van'ic (găl·văn'ĭk), *adj.* Also **gal·van'i·cal** (-ĭ·kăl). [After Luigi *Galvani*, of Bologna, Italy, on account of his connection (about 1780) with the discovery of dynamical electricity.] **1.** Of or relating to a direct current of electricity, esp. from a battery (**galvanic battery**); voltaic; — disting. from *faradic.* **2.** Figuratively, affected, or affecting, by or as by an electric shock. — **gal·van'i·cal·ly,** *adv.*

galvanic pile. See PILE, *n.*, 3 **a**.

gal'va·nism (găl'vȧ·nĭz'm), *n.* *Physics.* **a** Dynamical, or current, electricity. **b** The branch of physical science treating of the properties and effects of electrical currents.

gal'va·nize (-nīz), *v. t.* **1.** To affect with galvanism; to subject to the action of electrical currents; hence, to stimulate or excite as if by an electric shock. **2.** To coat (iron or steel) with zinc; as, *galvanized* iron. — **gal'va·ni·za'tion** (-nĭ·zā'shŭn; -nī·zā'-), *n.* — **gal'va·niz'er** (-nīz'ẽr), *n.*

gal'va·no- (găl'vȧ·nō-; găl·văn'ō-). [From *Galvani.* See GALVANIC.] A combining form used for *galvanic, galvanism*; also, *employing or produced by the galvanic current*, as in **gal'va·no·cau'ter·y, gal'va·no·sur'ger·y, gal'va·no·tax'is, gal'va·not'ro·pism.** See CAUTERY, etc.

gal'va·nom'e·ter (găl'vȧ·nŏm'ē·tẽr), *n.* [*galvano-* + *-meter.*] *Elec.* An instrument for measuring a small electric current by movements of a magnetic needle or of a coil in a magnetic field. — **gal'va·no·met'ric** (-nō·mĕt'rĭk; găl·văn'ō-), **gal'va·no·met'ri·cal** (-rĭ·kăl), *adj.*

gal'va·nom'e·try (-trĭ), *n.* Art or process of measuring the force of electric currents.

gal'va·no·scope' (găl'vȧ·nō·skōp'; găl·văn'ō·skōp), *n.* [*galvano-* + *-scope.*] *Elec.* An instrument or apparatus, as a magnetic needle, for detecting the presence and direction of electric currents, esp. those of feeble intensity. — **gal'va·no·scop'ic** (-skŏp'ĭk), *adj.* — **gal'va·nos'co·py** (găl'vȧ·nŏs'kō·pĭ), *n.*

gal'va·no·ther'my (-thûr'mĭ), *n.* [*galvano-* + Gr. *thermē* heat.] Production of heat by electricity.

Gal'ves·ton plan *or* **sys'tem** (găl'vĕs·tŭn). [From *Galveston*, Texas.] *Govt.* = COMMISSION PLAN.

Gal'ways (gôl'wāz), *n. pl.* [Prob. fr. *Galway*, Eire.] *Slang, U. S.* Whiskers following the line of the chin.

gal'yak (găl'yăk), *n.* Also **gal'yac.** [Russ. *golyak* naked one, poor fellow.] A flat fur from the pelt of a lamb or kid.

gam (găm), *n.* *Naut.* **a** A herd, or school, of whales. **b** A visit between whalers at sea; hence, *Local, U. S.*, social intercourse between persons ashore. — *v. i.;* GAMMED (gămd); GAM'MING. *Naut.* **a** To gather in a gam; — said of whales. **b** To engage in a gam, or, *Local, U. S.*, in social intercourse. — *v. t. Naut.* To have a gam or visit with.

ga·mash'es (gȧ·măsh'ĕz; găm'ȧsh-), *n. pl.* [F. *gamaches.*] *Archaic exc. Scot.* A type of leggings or gaiters worn, as by horseback riders, to protect the legs.

gamb, gambe (gămb), *n.* [ONF. *gambe*, OF. *jambe.* See JAMB.] A leg or shank; specif., *Her.*, the leg of a beast.

gam·ba'do (găm·bā'dō), *n.; pl.* -BADOS or -BADOES (-dōz). [Sp. *gambada.* See GAMBOL.] **1.** A spring of a horse. **2.** A fantastic movement as in dancing; hence, an antic.

gam·ba'do, *n.;* usually in *pl.* -DOS or -DOES (-dōz). [It. *gamba* leg.] A long legging attached to a saddle instead of stirrups; any long gaiter.

gam'be·son (găm'bē·sŭn; -s'n), *n.* [OF., of Teut. origin.] A medieval padded cloak, worn as a defensive garment.

gam'bier, gam'bir (găm'bḗr), *n.* [Malay *gambir.*] See CATECHU.

gam'bit (găm'bĭt), *n.* [F., fr. Pr. *cambi* an exchange.] **1.** A chess opening in which the first player offers to sacrifice a pawn or a piece for advantage in position. **2.** Hence, an opening move or series of moves, esp. one inviting discussion.

gam'ble (găm'b'l), *v. i.;* GAM'BLED (-b'ld); GAM'BLING (-blĭng). **1.** To play or game for money or other stake. **2.** To hazard; wager. — *v. t.* **1.** To lose by gaming; — with *away.* **2.** To stake or wager in gaming. — *n. Colloq.* A transaction involving gambling; hence, anything involving a like risk or uncertainty.

gam'bler (găm'blẽr), *n.* One who gambles.

gam'bling (-blĭng), *n.* The action of one who gambles.

gam·boge' (găm·bōj'; -bōōj'; -bōōzh'), *n.* [NL. *gambogium*, ult. fr. *Cambodia.*] **1.** An orange-red gum resin, derived from certain trees (genus *Garcinia*, family Clusiaceae) and used by artists as a yellow pigment, also in medicine as a cathartic. **2.** A color, reddish-yellow in hue, of high saturation and high brilliance. See COLOR.

gam'bol (găm'bŭl; -b'l), *n.* [F. *gambade* gambol, fr. It. *gambata* kick, fr. *gamba* leg.] A skipping or leaping about in frolic. — *v. i.;* -BOLED (-bŭld; -b'ld), -BOLLED; -BOL·ING, -BOL·LING. To bound or spring as in dancing or play; frisk.

gam'brel (găm'brĕl), *n.* [OF. *gamberel* a crooked stick or iron used by butchers, dim. fr. OF. *gambe, jambe*, leg.] **1.** The hock of an animal, esp. a horse. **2.** A gambrel roof.

gambrel roof. *Arch.* A curb roof of the same section in all parts, with a lower steeper slope and an upper flatter one, so that each gable is pentagonal.

Gam·bri'nus (găm·brī'nŭs), *n.* A mythical king, possibly Flemish, said to have been the inventor of beer.

game (gām), *n.* [AS. *gamen, gomen*, play, sport.] **1.** Sport of any kind; fun. **2.** An amusement or diversion. **3.** A scheme; plan; project. **4.** A contest, physical or mental, according to set rules, undertaken for amusement or for a stake. **5.** *Slang.* The contest for success in a vocation or business; as, the advertising *game.* **6.** An animal or animals pursued or taken in hunting; also, the flesh of game animals considered as food. **7.** Pluck or intrepidity, like that of a game animal. **8.** That which is made a subject of sport or ridicule. **9.** An objective which one holds in view or pursues. **10. a** A single contest lasting until a (certain) limit is reached. **b** That which is gained as the result of a game; the number of points necessary to be scored in order to win. **c** *pl.* Organized athletics. **11.** *Sports.* A manner or style of playing in a contest; as, a kicking *game.* — **Syn.** See FUN.

☞ COMBINATIONS and PHRASES (in sense 6) are:

gamebag	**game fish**	**game preserve**
game bird	**gamekeeper**	**game sanctuary**
game dog	**game laws**	**game warden**

— *v. i.* To play, as with cards, dice, billiards, etc., for a wager. — *v. t.* To squander, lose, or dispose of by gaming.

— *adj.* **1.** Having a resolute, unyielding spirit, like the gamecock. **2.** Of or pertaining to game (sense 6).

game (gām), *adj. Colloq.* Lame; as, a *game* leg.

game'cock' (gām'kŏk'), *n.* A male game fowl.

game'ly (gām'lĭ), *adv.* In a plucky manner.

game'ness, *n.* Endurance; pluck.

game'some (gām'sŭm), *adj.* Gay; sportive; playful; frolicsome; merry. — **game'some·ly,** *adv.* — **game'some·ness,** *n.*

game'ster (-stẽr), *n.* [*game* + *-ster.*] **1.** A person who plays at games; esp., a gambler. **2.** *Obs.* A merry frolicsome person. **3.** *Obs.* A lewd person.

gam'e·tan'gi·um (găm'ē·tăn'jĭ·ŭm), *n.; pl.* -GIA (-ȧ). [NL. See GAMETE; ANGIO-.] *Bot.* The cell or organ in which gametes are developed. Cf. SPORANGIUM.

gam'ete (găm'ēt; gȧ·mēt'; *the latter usually in compounds*), *n.* [NL. *gameta*, fr. Gr. *gametē* wife, or *gametēs* husband, fr. *gamein* to marry.] *Biol.* A matured sex cell or germ cell, usually haploid in chromosome number, capable of uniting with another of like origin to form a new plant or animal. Cf. ZYGOTE. — **ga·met'ic** (gȧ·mĕt'ĭk), *adj.* — **ga·met'i·cal·ly** (-ĭ·kăl·ĭ), *adv.*

gameto-. *Biol.* A combining form for *gamete*, as in **ga·me'to·cyte, gam'e·to·gen'e·sis.**

ga·me'to·phore (gȧ·mē'tō·fōr; 70), *n.* [*gameto-* + *-phore.*] *Bot.* A modified branch bearing sex organs, or gametangia, as in the thalloid liverworts.

ga·me'to·phyte (-fīt), *n.* [*gameto-* + *-phyte.*] *Bot.* In the alternation of generations in plants, the generation which bears sex organs; — disting. from *sporophyte.*

gam'ic (găm'ĭk), *adj.* [Gr. *gamos* marriage.] *Biol.* **a** Sexual. **b** Developing after fertilization.

gam'i·ly (găm'ĭ·lĭ), *adv.* In a gamy, or plucky, manner.
gam'in (găm'ĭn; *F.* gȧ'măN'), *n.* [F.] A street Arab.
gam'i·ness (găm'ĭ·nĕs; -nĭs), *n.* Quality of being gamy.
gam'ing (găm'ĭng), *n.* Act or practice of gambling.
gam'ma (găm'ȧ), *n.; pl.* GAMMAS (-ȧz). [Gr.] **1.** The third letter (Γ, γ) of the Greek alphabet, equivalent to English *g* (as in *go*). It is often used to designate something third in position, order, importance, etc. **2.** *pl.* GAMMA. A microgram. **3.** *Photog.* The degree of contrast of a printed-out or developed exposure.
gam·ma'di·on (gă·mā'dĭ·ŏn), *n.; pl.* -DIA (-ȧ). [MGr., dim. of *gamma.*] A cross formed of four capital gammas (Γ), esp. in the figure of a swastika. Gamma among early Christians symbolized Christ as cornerstone of the church.
gamma globulin. A fraction of blood plasma rich in antibodies and used against measles, hepatitis, etc.
gamma rays. *Physics.* Radiation, similar to X rays but of shorter wave length, emitted during some nuclear transformations. Gamma rays are used in treating cancer by means of radioactive substances such as radium.
gam'mer (găm'ẽr), *n.* [Contr. fr. *godmother.*] An old wife; an old woman; — correlative of *gaffer.*
Gam·mex'ane (găm·ĕk'sān), *n.* A trade-mark applied to a powerful insecticide (chemically, the gamma isomer of benzene hexachloride or hexachlorocyclohexane, $C_6H_6Cl_6$, "666").
gam'mon (găm'ŭn), *n.* [ONF. *gambon,* fr. *gambe* leg.] A ham or flitch of bacon salted and smoked or dried; also, the lower end of a side of bacon.
gam'mon, *n.* [See GAME sport.] **1.** *Obs.* Backgammon. **2.** *Backgammon.* A double game, won by the player who bears off all his men before his adversary removes any. — *v. t.* To beat at backgammon by getting a gammon.
gam'mon, *v. t.* *Naut.* To fasten (a bowsprit) to the stem of a vessel by lashings of rope or chain, or by an iron band.
gam'mon, *n.* *Colloq.* Talk intended to deceive; humbug. — *v. i.* *Colloq.* To talk gammon; hence, to feign. — *v. t.* *Colloq.* To influence with gammon. — **gam'mon·er,** *n.*
gam'o- (găm'ō-). [Gr. *gamos* marriage.] A combining form denoting: **a** *Biol. Sexual union,* as in *gamo*genesis. **b** *Bot. Union or fusion of parts,* as in *gamo*petalous. For the meanings of the following, see the definitions of their elements: **gam'o·ma'ni·a, gam'o·trop'ic, ga·mot'ro·pism, gam'o·phyl'lous.**
gam'o·gen'e·sis (-jĕn'ĕ·sĭs), *n.* [*gamo-* + *-genesis.*] *Biol.* Reproduction by means of gametes; sexual reproduction. — **gam'o·ge·net'ic** (-jĕ·nĕt'ĭk), *adj.* — **gam'o·ge·net'i·cal·ly** (-ĭ·kăl·ĭ), *adv.*
gam'o·pet'al·ous (-pĕt'ăl·ŭs), *adj.* [*gamo-* + *petalous.*] *Bot.* Having the petals united; — opp. to *choripetalous,* or *polypetalous.*
gam'o·sep'al·ous (-sĕp'ăl·ŭs), *adj.* [*gamo-* + *sepalous.*] *Bot.* Having the sepals united.
-gamous. [Gr. *gamos* marriage.] A combining form meaning *marrying, uniting for propagation,* as in mono*gamous,* phanero*gamous;* — used chiefly in *Biol.* and *Bot.*
gamp (gămp), *n.* A large umbrella; — alluding to Mrs. Gamp's umbrella, in Dickens's *Martin Chuzzlewit.*
gam'ut (găm'ŭt), *n.* [*gamma,* a name used formerly for the first note of the early scale + *ut.*] **1.** The series of recognized musical notes; sometimes, any recognized scale; specif., the major scale. **2.** An entire range or series.
gam'y (gām'ĭ), *adj.;* GAM'I·ER (-ĭ·ẽr); GAM'I·EST. **1.** Abounding in game. **2.** *Sporting.* Plucky; game. **3.** Having the flavor of game, esp. of game kept until it is high (see HIGH, *adj.,* 15).
-gamy. [See -GAMOUS.] A combining form denoting *marriage, union for propagation* or *reproduction,* as in poly*gamy,* oö*gamy;* — used chiefly in *Biol.* and *Bot.*
gan (găn), *past of* GIN, begin. It was formerly used with the infinitive to form compound preterits, as *did* is now sometimes used. "This man *gan* fall (i. e., fell) in great suspicion." *Chaucer.*
gan'der (găn'dẽr), *n.* [AS. *gandra, ganra.*] **1.** The adult male goose. **2.** A simpleton.
ga'nef (gä'nĕf), **ga'nof** (-nŭf), *n.* Also **gon'oph, gon'of.** [Yiddish *ganef, gannef,* fr. Heb. *gannabh.*] *Yiddish.* A thief.
gang (găng), *n.* [AS.] **1.** *Scot.* A walk for cattle; pasturage. **2.** A set of articles; an outfit. **3.** A number going in or forming a company; as, a *gang* of sailors. Specif.: **a** A group of persons associated under the same direction; as, a *gang* of slaves. **b** A company of persons acting together for some purpose, usually criminal; as, a *gang* of thieves. **4.** A combination of similar implements or devices arranged for convenience to act together; as, a *gang* of saws; — also attributively; as, a **gang condenser, gang cultivator, gang plow, gang punch, gang switch,** etc. — *v. i. & t.* To form or act with a gang or gangs.
gang, *v. i.* [AS. *gangan.*] *Obs. exc. Scot.* To go; walk.
gang. Var. of GANGUE.
gang'er (găng'ẽr), *n.* Foreman over a gang of workmen.
gang hook. *Angling.* Two or three fishhooks with their shanks joined.
gan'gli- (găng'glĭ-). = GANGLIO- (which see), as in **gan'gli·as·the'ni·a, gan'gli·ec'to·my, gan'gli·i'tis.**
gan'gli·a (găng'glĭ·ȧ), *n., pl.* of GANGLION.
gan'gli·at'ed (-āt'ĕd; -ĭd), **gan'gli·ate** (-āt), *adj.* *Anat. & Zool.* Furnished with ganglia; as, *gangliated* nerves.
gan'gling (găng'glĭng), *adj.* *Colloq.* Of a spindling or awkwardly long growth; loosely built; lanky.
gan'gli·o- (găng'glĭ·ō-). A combining form meaning *ganglion,* as in **gan'gli·o·plex'us,** a spreading ganglion in a mesh of fibers.
gan'gli·on (-ŭn), *n.; pl.* -GLIA (-ȧ), -GLIONS (-ŭnz). [LL., sort of swelling or excrescence, fr. Gr. *ganglion.*] **1.** *Anat. & Zool.* A mass of nervous tissue containing nerve cells, esp. when external to the brain or spinal cord. Cf. NUCLEUS, 3. **2.** Figuratively, a center or focus of energy, strength, etc. **3.** *Med.* A small hard tumor, connected either with a joint or tendon sheath. It is caused by inflammation. — **gan'gli·on'ic** (-ŏn'ĭk), *adj.*
gan'gli·on·ec'to·my (-ĕk'tō·mĭ), *n.* [*ganglion* + *-ectomy.*] Surgical removal of a ganglion.
gang'plank' (găng'plăngk'), *n.* A long, narrow, movable platform or bridge, used in entering or leaving a vessel.
gan'grel (găng'grĕl; găng'rĕl), *n.* *Scot.* A vagrant.
gan'grene (găng'grēn), *n.* [L. *gangraena,* fr. Gr. *gangraina.*] *Med.* Mortification of a part of the body caused by interference with the local nutrition. — *v. t. & i.* To produce gangrene in; to be affected with gangrene. — **gan'gre·nous** (-grē·nŭs), *adj.*
gang'ster (găng'stẽr), *n.* [*gang* + *-ster.*] *Colloq., U. S.* A member of a gang of roughs, thieves, or the like.
gangue (găng), *n.* [F., fr. G. *gang* a metallic vein.] *Mining.* The worthless rock or vein matter in which valuable metals or minerals occur; veinstone; matrix.
gang'way' (găng'wā'), *n.* [AS. *gangweg.*] **1.** A passage or way into, through, or out of, any enclosed place, esp. a temporary way of planks. **2.** Specif.: **a** In the British House of Commons, a narrow aisle across the house. **b** *Naut.* (1) Either of the sides of the upper deck between the deckhouse and the rail and the quarter-deck and forecastle. (2) The passageway through the bulwarks of a vessel. (3) A gangplank. **c** *Mining.* A main level, as in a coal mine. **d** *Logging.* The incline up which logs are moved from the water into a sawmill. — *interj.* *Orig. Naut.* Stand aside! Make way!
gan'is·ter (găn'ĭs·tẽr), *n.* [G. dial. *ganster,* MHG. *ganeister,* a spark.] **a** *Petrog.* A siliceous sandstone of England, used to make a material for lining furnace hearths, for macadamizing roads, etc. **b** A mixture of ground quartz and fire clay for lining certain metallurgical furnaces.
gan'net (găn'ĕt; -ĭt), *n.* See PLURAL, *Note,* 3. [AS. *ganot* a sea fowl.] Any of several large web-footed sea birds (genera *Sula* and *Moris*). The common gannet of the North Atlantic (*M. bassana*) is, when adult, mostly white and measures about six feet in extent of wings.
ga'nof (gä'nŭf). Var. of GANEF.
gan'oid (găn'oid), *adj.* [Gr. *ganos* brightness + *-oid.*] Of or pertaining to a superorder (Ganoidei) of fishes containing the sturgeons, paddlefishes, gars, the bowfins, and many extinct forms, and having hard scales (**ganoid scales**) often composed of an inner layer of bone and an outer enamellike layer known as **gan'o·in** (găn'ō·ĭn). Cf. PLACOID. — *n.* A ganoid fish.
gan'te·lope, gant'lope, *n.* *Obs.* The gantlet.
gant'let (gänt'lĕt; gănt'-; -lĭt), *n.* A gauntlet, or glove.
gant'let (gônt'lĕt; gănt'-; -lĭt; 9), *n.* [Earlier *gantlope,* fr. Sw. *gatlopp,* orig., a running down a lane, fr. *gata* street, lane + *lopp* career.] **1.** A former military punishment wherein the offender ran between two files of men, who struck him with switches, clubs, etc., as he passed. **2.** A stretch of railroad track, as over a bridge, where (to obviate switching) two lines of track overlap so that one rail of each track is within the rails of the other. — *v. t.* To run together (railroad tracks) so as to make a gantlet.
gant'line' (gănt'līn'), *n.* *Naut.* A line rove through a block, as at a bowsprit end for hoisting rigging, etc.
gan'try (găn'trĭ), **gaun'try** (gôn'trĭ), *n.* [OF. *gantier, chantier,* fr. L. *cantherius,* fr. Gr. *kanthēlios* pack ass.] **1.** A frame for supporting barrels, as in a cellar. **2.** *Engin.* A frame structure raised on side supports so as to span over something; as: **a** A bridge or platform carrying a traveling crane. **b** A structure supporting a number of railroad signals for several tracks.
Gan'y·mede (găn'ĭ·mēd), *n.* [L. *Ganymedes,* fr. Gr. *Ganymēdēs.*] **1.** *Class. Myth.* A beautiful boy who was carried up to Olympus by the eagle of Zeus, to be the cupbearer of the gods. Cf. HEBE. **2.** A youth who serves liquors; a cupbearer. **3.** *Astron.* The so-called third (really the fourth) satellite of Jupiter, discovered by Galileo in 1610. This and Callisto are the largest known satellites in the solar system.
gaol (jāl), *n.* [See JAIL.] A place of confinement. = JAIL. — **gaol'-bird', gaol'er,** etc.
☞ In the United States the forms *gaol, gaoler,* etc., are obsolete, except for occasional legal use. In Great Britain they are still current, esp. in official use.
gap (găp), *n.* [ON. *gap.*] **1.** An opening in anything made by breaking or parting; breach. **2.** A mountain pass, cleft, or ravine. **3.** Any break in continuity; interval; hiatus. **4.** *Aeronautics.* The shortest distance between the planes of the chords of the upper and lower wings of a biplane. — *v. t.;* GAPPED (găpt); GAP'PING. To make an opening in.
gape (gāp; găp; gäp), *v. i.* [ON. *gapa.*] **1.** To open the mouth wide, as indicating: **a** A desire for food. **b** Sleepiness. **c** Self-forgetfulness in surprise. **d** A desire to injure, devour, or overcome. **2.** To open or part widely; to exhibit a gap. — **Syn.** See GAZE. — *n.* **1.** Act of gaping; specif.: **a** A yawn. **b** An openmouthed stare; hence, a state of wonder. **2.** A gap; rent. **3.** *Zool.* **a** The median margin-to-margin length of the open mouth. **b** The line along which the mandibles of a bird close. — **gap'er** (gāp'ẽr; găp'-; gäp'-), *n.* — **gap'ing·ly,** *adv.* — **gap'y,** *adj.*
— ***the gapes.*** **a** A fit of yawning. **b** A disease of young poultry, etc., attended with gaping. See GAPEWORM.
gape'seed' (gāp'sēd'; găp'-; gäp'-), *n.* Anything that causes gaping looks.
gape'worm' (-wûrm'), *n.* A parasitic nematode worm (*Syngamus trachealis*) infesting the trachea and bronchi of birds and causing the gapes.
gar (gär), *n.* [AS. *gār* spear.] *Zool.* Any of certain fishes having an elongate pikelike body and long narrow jaws; — called also *garfish* and *gar pikes.* The marine gars are teleost fishes, called also *billfishes* and *needlefishes.* The common European species (*Belone vulgaris*) is a good food fish. The fresh-water gars of North America are ganoids constituting a family (Lepisosteidae), whose members are destructive of other fish.
gar, *v. t.* [ON. *gera, gōra,* to make, do.] *Dial.* To cause; make; compel.
ga·rage' (gȧ·räzh'; gȧ·räj'; *esp. Brit.,* găr'äzh), *n.* [F.] **1.** A building for housing automobiles; also, a repair shop for such vehicles. **2.** *Aeronautics.* A hangar. — *v. t.;* -RAGED' (-räzhd'; -räjd'; găr'äzhd); -RAG'ING. *Colloq.* To keep or put in a garage.
Gar'a·mond (găr'ȧ·mŏnd), *n.* A style of type, orig. produced in 1540 and based upon the design of Claude Garamond, French type founder. See TYPE, *n.,* 9.
Gar'and ri'fle (găr'ănd). [After John C. *Garand* (b. 1888), its inventor.] A semiautomatic rifle having a rapid fire and a light recoil. See RIFLE, *Illust.*
garb (gärb), *n.* [F. *garbe,* now *galbe,* graceful outline, contour, fr. It. *garbo* grace.] **1.** *Obs.* Personal bearing. **2.** *Obs.* Custom; method. **3.** Fashion or style of dress, esp. as distinctive of rank or standing; clothing; hence, outward appearance. — *v. t.* To clothe; array.
gar'bage (gär'bĭj), *n.* [Origin uncert.] Offal; refuse animal or vegetable matter, as from a kitchen or a store; hence, anything worthless or filthy; trash.

‖**gar·ban′zo** (gär·vän′thō; -sō; 17), *n.*; *pl.* -ZOS (-thōs; -sōs). [Sp.] The chick-pea.

gar′ble (gär′b'l), *v. t.*; GAR′BLED (-b'ld); GAR′BLING (-blĭng). [It. *garbellare*, through Ar., fr. LL. *cribellum*, dim. of *cribrum* sieve.] **1.** *Now Rare.* To select the best parts of. **2.** *Obs. exc. Trade.* To sift or bolt; as, to *garble* spices. **3.** To pick out such parts of as may serve a purpose, usually unfair; to mutilate (a text, story, record, or the like) in such a way as to mislead; as, to *garble* an account. — *n.* Act or instance of garbling; a garbled work or passage. — **gar′bler** (-blẽr), *n.*

gar′board (gär′bōrd; 70), *n.* *Shipbuilding.* The planks or plates next to the keel; — called also **garboard strake.**

gar′boil (-boil), *n.* [MF. *garbouil.*] *Archaic & Dial.* Broil; confusion.

‖**gar′çon′** (gȧr′sôɴ′), *n.*; *pl.* -ÇONS (*F.* -sôɴ′). [F.] A boy; a waiter.

‖**gar′çon′ d'hon′neur′** (dô′nûr′). [F.] A groomsman; a best man.

‖**garde à che·val′** (gȧr′-dȧsh·vȧl′). [F.] A mounted guard.

‖**garde du corps** (gȧrd′ dü kôr′). [F.] A bodyguard.

‖**garde–feu** (gȧr′dē·fû′), *n.* [F.] A fire screen or fender.

gar′den (gär′d'n), *n.* [ONF. *gardin* (F. *jardin*), of Teut. origin.] **1.** A piece of ground for the cultivation of herbs, fruits, flowers, or vegetables; commonly, such a piece adjoining a dwelling. **2.** Hence, a rich, well-cultivated tract of country. **3.** An enclosure for displaying to the public selected plant or animal life; as, zoological *gardens.* **4.** *Baseball Slang.* Outfield. — *v. i.* To lay out, cultivate, or labor in, a garden. — *v. t.* To cultivate as a garden. — *adj.* Grown, or such as grows, in gardens; hence, hardy; also, figuratively, commonplace.

garden balm. See BALM, *n.*, 4.

garden buttercup. See CROWFOOT, 1.

gar′den·er (gär′d'n·ẽr; gärd′nẽr), *n.* One who gardens or is versed in gardening.

gar·de′ni·a (gär·dē′nĭ·ȧ; -dēn′yȧ), *n.* [NL., after Alexander *Garden* (1730–91), Am. botanist.] Any plant of a genus (*Gardenia*) of Old World tropical trees and shrubs, of the madder family, with showy, fragrant, white or yellow flowers. The ***Cape jasmine*** (see JASMINE, 3) is the gardenia commonly cultivated by florists.

Garden of Eden. = EDEN.

garden sauce. See SAUCE, 4.

Garden State. New Jersey; — a nickname.

garde′robe (gärd′rōb), *n.* [F. See WARDROBE.] *Hist.* **a** A wardrobe or its contents. **b** A private room.

‖**gar′dez′ la foi** (gȧr′dā′ lȧ fwä′). [F.] Keep the faith.

gar′dy·loo′ (gär′dĭ·lōō′), *n.* [F. *gare l'eau* beware of the water.] A warning cry uttered on throwing water, etc., into the streets from the windows in old Edinburgh.

Gar′eth (găr′ĕth), *n.* In Arthurian romance, a knight of the Round Table, a nephew of King Arthur.

gar′fish′ (gär′fĭsh′), *n.*; *pl.*, see FISH. A gar.

gar′ga·ney (gär′gȧ·nĭ), *n.* [It. dial. *garganello.*] A European teal (*Querquedula circia*) related to the American blue-winged teal.

Gar·gan′tu·a (gär·găn′tụ̈·ȧ; *F.* gȧr′gäɴ′twȧ′), *n.* [F.] Hero of a satirical romance (1535) by Rabelais. He is a gigantic king, educated according to the noblest ideas of the humanist Renaissance. Cf. PANTAGRUEL. — **Gar·gan′tu·an** (gär·găn′tụ̈·ăn), *adj.*

gar′get (gär′gĕt; -gĭt), *n.* [OF. *gargate*, fr. L. *gurges* whirlpool.] **1.** A disease in swine and cattle marked by inflammation of the head or throat; also, a distemper in hogs. **2.** A diseased condition of the udders of cows, etc.

gar′gle (gär′g'l), *v. t.*; GAR′GLED (-g'ld); GAR′GLING (-glĭng). [F. *gargouiller* to dabble, gargle.] **1.** To rinse, as the throat, agitating the liquid by expelling air from the lungs. **2.** To utter as if gargling. — *v. i.* **1.** To use a gargle. **2.** To make a sound as if gargling. — *n.* A liquid used in gargling.

gar′goyle (gär′goil), *n.* [OF. *gargouille*, fr. L. *gurgulio* gullet, windpipe.] **1.** *Arch.* A waterspout, often carved grotesquely, projecting at the upper part of a building, usually from the roof gutter. **2.** Hence, a grotesque figure resembling a gargoyle. — **gar′goyled** (-goild), *adj.*

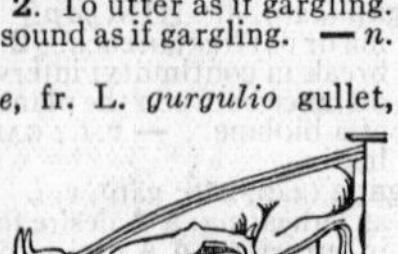
Gargoyle.

gar′i·bal′di (găr′ĭ·bôl′dĭ; -băl′dĭ), *n.* A kind of shirtwaist worn by women; — from its resemblance in shape to the red shirt of the Italian patriot Garibaldi.

gar′ish (gâr′ĭsh), *adj.* **1.** Showy; harsh and glaring. **2.** Gay to extravagance; flighty. — **Syn.** See GAUDY. — **Ant.** Somber. — **gar′ish·ly**, *adv.* — **gar′ish·ness**, *n.*

gar′land (gär′lănd), *n.* [OF. *garlande.*] **1.** A wreath made of branches, flowers, leaves, etc.; chaplet. **2.** A book of extracts; an anthology; esp., a chapbook or broadside containing one or more ballads or songs. **3.** *Naut.* **a** A grommet or ring of rope lashed to a spar for hoisting, to prevent chafing, etc. **b** A band of rope, iron, or wood for retaining shot in place. **c** A sort of netted bag used by sailors to keep provisions in. — *v. t.* To form into, or deck with, a garland.

gar′lic (gär′lĭk), *n.* [AS. *gārlēac*, fr. *gār* spear, lance + *lēac* leek.] A European bulbous herb (*Allium sativum*) of the lily family; also, its pungent, strong-scented bulb, composed of smaller bulbs called *cloves.* Garlic is much used in cooking, esp. in Europe. — **gar′lick·y** (-lĭk·ĭ), *adj.*

gar′ment (gär′mĕnt), *n.* [OF. *garnement, garniment*, fr. *garnir* to garnish.] Any article of clothing; in women's wear, often specif. = FOUNDATION GARMENT. — *v. t.* To clothe with or as if with a garment.

gar′ner (gär′nẽr), *n.* [OF. *gernier, grenier*, fr. L. *granarium*, fr. *granum* grain.] A granary; hence, a store. — *v. t.* To gather for preservation; to store.

gar′net (gär′nĕt; -nĭt), *n.* [OF. *grenat*, fr. L. *granatus*, fr. *granum* grain.] **1.** A hard, brittle, glasslike mineral, occurring massive and in grains, and common in gneiss and mica schist. H., 6.5–7.5. Sp. gr., 3.15–4.3. The ***precious garnet*** is a deep red. The ***common garnet*** includes the coarser kinds of almandite and andradite, and is used as an abrasive. Garnets are often found as crystals. **2.** A color, red in hue, of medium saturation and low brilliance. See COLOR.

gar′net, *n.* *Naut.* A hoisting tackle, usually rigged on the mainstay.

gar′ni·er·ite (gär′nĭ·ẽr·īt), *n.* [After Jules *Garnier*, French geologist.] *Mineral.* A soft, amorphous, hydrous nickel magnesium silicate, of apple-green or pale-green color. Sp. gr., 2.3–2.8. It is an important ore of nickel.

gar′nish (gär′nĭsh), *v. t.* [OF. *garnir, guarnir*, to provide, prepare, garnish, warn, of Teut. origin.] **1.** To adorn; deck. **2.** *Cookery.* To ornament, as a dish, with something bright and savory; as, fish *garnished* with parsley. **3.** *Law.* To warn, or bring into court, by garnishment; to garnishee. — **Syn.** See ADORN. — *n.* **1.** Decoration; ornament; also, *Rare*, dress; garments. **2. a** *Obs. exc. Hist.* A fee; in English jails, an unauthorized fee demanded by old prisoners of a newcomer. **b** *Slang.* A fee or treat from a new workman. **3.** *Cookery.* That which garnishes a dish. — **gar′nish·er** (gär′nĭsh·ẽr), *n.*

gar′nish·ee′ (-ē′), *n.* *Law.* One who is garnished. — *v. t.* GAR′NISH-EED′ (-ēd′); GAR′NISH·EE′ING. *Law.* **a** To make (a person) a garnishee; to garnish. **b** To attach (the fund or property sought to be secured by garnishment); to trustee.

gar′nish·ment (gär′nĭsh·mĕnt), *n.* **1.** Ornament. **2.** *Law.* Legal notice to one to appear in court, specif.: **a** A notice summoning a third party to appear in a suit. **b** Warning to a person holding another's attached property not to deliver it to him but to account for it in court.

gar′ni·ture (gär′nĭ·tụ̈r), *n.* [F.] That which garnishes; embellishment; trimming.

ga·rotte′. Var. of GARROTE.

gar pike. A gar (esp. of the family Lepisosteidae).

gar′ret (găr′ĕt; -ĭt), *n.* [OF. *garite* watchtower, place of refuge, fr. *garir, guarir*, to preserve, defend.] That part of a house just under or within the roof. Cf. ATTIC **b**.

gar′ri·son (găr′ĭ·sŭn; -s'n), *n.* [OF. *garison*, fr. *garir.* See GARRET.] *Mil.* **a** A fortified place in which troops are quartered. **b** A body of troops stationed in a fort. — *v. t.* *Mil.* **a** To place troops in, as a fortification, for its defense; to furnish with soldiers. **b** To secure by fortresses manned with troops. **c** To place on duty in a garrison. **d** To guard or occupy as a garrison; as, the regiment *garrisoned* the town.

gar·rote′ (gă·rōt′; -rŏt′), **gar·rotte′** (-rŏt′), *n.* [Sp. *garrote.*] **1.** A Spanish mode of execution by strangulation with an iron collar tightened by a screw; also, the collarlike device. **2.** Throttling as if with the garrote, esp. for robbery. — *v. t.*; -ROT′ED, -ROT′TED; -ROT′ING, -ROT′TING. To strangle with the garrote; hence, to throttle and rob. — **gar·rot′er** (-rōt′ẽr; -rŏt′ẽr), **gar·rot′ter** (-rŏt′ẽr), *n.*

gar·ru′li·ty (gă·rōō′lĭ·tĭ; 114), *n.* Talkativeness.

gar′ru·lous (găr′ŭ·lŭs; -ōō·lŭs), *adj.* [L. *garrulus*, fr. *garrire* to chatter, talk.] Talking much; also, long-winded; diffuse. — **Syn.** See TALKATIVE. — **gar′ru·lous·ly**, *adv.* — **gar′ru·lous·ness**, *n.*

gar′ter (gär′tẽr), *n.* [ONF. *gartier*, fr. *garet* bend of the knee.] **1.** A band or supporting strap worn to hold up a stocking. **2.** [*usually cap.*] The distinguishing blue badge of the ***Order of the Garter***, the highest order of British knighthood; also, this order or membership in it. — *v. t.* To bind or support with or as with a garter.

garter snake. Any of numerous harmless viviparous American snakes (genus *Thamnophis*) with yellow stripes on the back.

garth (gärth), *n.* [ON. *garthr* yard.] *Archaic.* A close; yard; croft.

gas (găs), *n.*; *pl.* GASES (găs′ĕz; -ĭz). [Invented by the chemist Van Helmont of Brussels (d. 1644); — suggested by L. *chaos*, Gr. *chaos*, chaos.] **1.** An aeriform fluid, having neither independent shape nor volume, but tending to expand indefinitely. **2.** In popular usage, any gaseous mixture except atmospheric air; specif.: **a** Any gas used to produce anesthesia. **b** Any combustible gaseous mixture for illuminating or fuel. **3.** Any substance, as chlorine, used to produce a poisonous or irritant atmosphere, as in warfare. **4.** *Slang.* Empty, boasting, or humbugging talk. **5.** *Colloq.* Gasoline. **6.** *Mining.* Firedamp mixed with air, so as to become liable to explosion.
— *v. t.*; GASSED (găst); GAS′SING. **1.** To affect or treat with gas; as: **a** *Textiles.* To singe, as in a gas flame, to remove loose fibers. **b** To subject to the action of gas; as, to *gas* lime with chlorine in making bleaching powder. **c** To poison with gas, esp. in warfare. **2.** To replenish or supply with gas. **3.** *Slang.* To talk "gas" or empty talk to. — *v. i.* **1.** To give off gas, as a storage battery during charging. **2.** *Slang.* To indulge in idle talk.

gas black. A fine, bulky carbon obtained as soot by the direct impingement of a burning flame on a metal surface; — often called simply *carbon black.*

Gas′con (găs′kŏn), *adj.* [F.] Of or relating to Gascony, in France, or its people, who were noted for boasting; also [*not cap.*], braggart; swaggering. — *n.* One of the natives of Gascony; hence [*not cap.*], a boaster; swashbuckler.

gas′con·ade′ (găs′kŏn·ād′), *n.* [F. *gasconnade.*] A boast or boasting; bravado. — *v. i.* To boast. — **gas′con·ad′er** (-ād′ẽr), *n.*

gas′e·lier′ (găs′ĕ·lēr′), *n.* A chandelier arranged to burn gas.

gas′e·ous (găs′ē·ŭs; *Brit. usually* gā′zē·ŭs *or* gā′sē·ŭs), *adj.* **1.** In the form, or of the nature, of gas; pertaining to gases; as, *gaseous* matter; *gaseous* laws. **2.** Lacking substance or solidity; tenuous.

gas fitter. A workman who installs or repairs gas pipes.

gash (găsh), *v. t.* [For older *garsh* or *garse*, fr. OF. *garser, jarser*, to scarify.] To make a long, deep incision in. — *n.* A deep and long cut.

gash (gȧsh), *adj.* *Scot.* **1.** Knowing; witty. **2.** Well-dressed.

gas helmet. *Mil.* A gas mask. See MASK.

gas′hold′er (găs′hōl′dẽr), *n.* A receptacle for gas; specif., a gasworks, a huge metal cylinder or reservoir, commonly in two parts, one of which telescopes into the other according to the volume of gas or the pressure required; — called also *gasometer.*

gas′house′ (-hous′), *n.* A gasworks.

gas′i·form (găs′ĭ·fôrm), *adj.* In the form of gas; gaseous.

gas′i·fy (-fī), *v. t.*; -FIED (-fīd); -FY′ING. To convert into gas, as by heat or a chemical process. — *v. i.* To become gas. — **gas′i·fi′a·ble** (-fī′ȧ·b'l), *adj.* — **gas′i·fi·ca′tion** (-fĭ·kā′shŭn), *n.* — **gas′i·fi′er** (găs′ĭ·fī′ẽr), *n.*

gas′ket (găs′kĕt; -kĭt), *n.* **1.** *Naut.* A line or band used to lash a furled sail securely. **2.** *Mach.* Plaited hemp or tallowed rope for packing pistons, making pipe joints, etc.; hence, packing of any other suitable material.

gas′kin (-kĭn), *n.* **1.** *Obs. pl.* Gaiters; galligaskins. **2.** That part of the hind leg of a horse or other quadruped between the stifle and the hock. See HORSE, *Illust.* (39).

gas′kin, *n.* Also **gas′king** (-kĭng). *Rare.* A gasket.

gas′light′ (găs′līt′), *n.* **1.** The light yielded by illuminating gas. **2.** A burner using gas; also, a lamp lighted by gas.

gas log. A hollow perforated device imitating a log, used as a gas burner in a fireplace.

gas mask. A face covering that constitutes, or forms part of, a respirator to protect a person from poison gases.

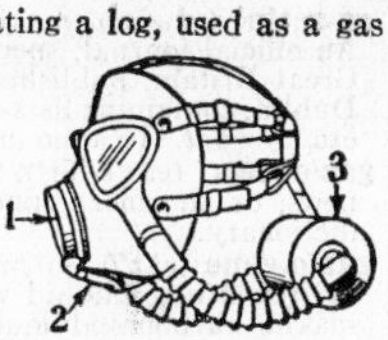

Gas Mask. 1 Diaphragm; 2 Outlet Valve; 3 Canister.

gas'o·gene (găs'ō·jēn). Var. of GAZOGENE.

gas'o·lier' (găs'ō·lēr'), *n.* Var. of GASELIER.

gas'o·line (găs'ō·lēn; găs'ō·lēn'; 2), **gas'o·lene,** *n.* [*gas* + *-ol*, 2 + *-ine*.] A volatile, inflammable, liquid hydrocarbon mixture used as a fuel, esp. for internal-combustion engines, as a solvent for oils, fats, etc., and as a carburetant; — called also *petrol.* It is made by the refining or the cracking of petroleum, by recovery from natural gas, by hydrogenation of coal or water gas, distillation of oil shale, etc.

gas·om'e·ter (găs·ŏm'ē·tēr), *n.* [See GAS; -METER.] **1.** An instrument for holding and measuring gas. **2.** Less properly, a gasholder.

gasp (gȧsp; 9), *v. i.* [ON. *geispa* to yawn.] To catch the breath sharply, with wide open mouth; to pant. Hence, to pant with eagerness; to show vehement desire. — *v. t.* To emit or utter with gasps; — with *forth, out, away,* etc. — *n.* Act of gasping; a gasping utterance.

gas plant. The fraxinella.

gas'sing (găs'ĭng), *n.* **1.** Act or process of subjecting to gas, as the subjection of lime to chlorine gas in making bleaching powder. **2.** A poisoning by exposure to noxious gases.

gas station. A station for the sale of gasoline and oil.

gas'sy (găs'ĭ), *adj.;* GAS'SI·ER (-ĭ·ēr); GAS'SI·EST. Full of or containing gas; like gas; *Colloq.*, full of boastful talk.

gas'ter·o·pod' (găs'tēr·ō·pŏd'). Var. of GASTROPOD.

gast'ful (gȧst'fo͝ol; -f'l). Var. of GHASTFUL.

gas'tight' (găs'tīt'; 2), *adj.* **a** Impervious to gas. **b** So constructed that a specified gas will not enter the enclosing case under specified pressure conditions.

gastr-. = GASTRO-, as in **gas·trec'to·my** (see -ECTOMY).

gas·tral'gi·a (găs·trăl'jĭ·ȧ), *n.* [NL., fr. *gastr-* + *-algia.*] Pain, esp. neuralgic pain, in the stomach or epigastrium.

gas'tric (găs'trĭk), *adj.* [Gr. *gastēr, gastros,* stomach.] Of, pertaining to, or situated near the stomach.

gastric juice. *Physiol.* The digestive fluid secreted by the glands in the mucous membrane of the stomach. It is a thin watery fluid having an acid reaction, and contains several enzymes, esp. pepsin and rennin.

gastric ulcer. *Med.* An ulcer of the inner wall of the stomach.

gas'trin (găs'trĭn), *n.* [*gastric* + *-in.*] *Biochem.* A hormone causing secretion of the gastric juice.

gas·tri'tis (găs·trī'tĭs), *n.* [NL., fr. *gastr-* + *-itis.*] *Med.* Inflammation of the stomach, esp. its mucous membrane.

gas'tro- (găs'trō-), **gastr-.** [Gr. *gastēr, gastros.*] A combining form meaning: **a** *Stomach* or *belly*, as in **gas·trol'o·gy.** **b** *Gastric* (*and*), as in **gas'tro·en·ter'ic, gas'tro·he·pat'ic, gas'tro·in·tes'ti·nal, gas·tros'to·my, gas·trot'o·my** (see -STOMY, -TOMY).

gas'tro·col'ic (-kŏl'ĭk), *adj.* Pertaining to the stomach and colon; as, the **gastrocolic omentum.** See OMENTUM.

gas'tro·en'ter·i'tis (-ĕn'tēr·ī'tĭs), *n.* [NL.] *Med.* Inflammation of the lining membrane of the stomach and the intestines. — **gas'tro·en'ter·it'ic** (-ĭt'ĭk), *adj.*

gas'tro·en'ter·o- (găs'trō·ĕn'tēr·ō-). [*gastro-* + *entero-.*] A combining form denoting *pertaining to the stomach and intestine*, as in **gas'tro·en'ter·ol'o·gy,** the anatomy and pathology of the stomach and intestine, **gas'tro·en'ter·os'to·my, gas'tro·en'ter·ot'o·my** (see -STOMY, -TOMY).

gas'tro·nome (găs'trō·nōm), *n.* [F.] An epicure.

gas·tron'o·my (găs·trŏn'ō·mĭ), *n.* [F. *gastronomie*, fr. Gr. *gastronomia*, fr. *gastēr, gastros,* stomach + *nomos* law.] The art or science of good eating; epicurism. — **gas'tro·nom'ic** (găs'trō·nŏm'ĭk), *adj.* — **gas'tro·nom'i·cal** (-ĭ·kăl), *adj.* — **gas'tro·nom'i·cal·ly,** *adv.* — **gas·tron'o·mist** (găs·trŏn'ō·mĭst), *n.*

gas'tro·pod (găs'trō·pŏd), *n.* Also **gas'ter·o·pod'** (găs'tēr·ō·pŏd'). [*gastro-* + *-pod.*] *Zool.* Any of a large class (Gastropoda) of mollusks including most forms having a univalve shell and many having no shell; a snail, slug, or allied mollusk. — **gas'tro·pod, gas·trop'o·dous** (găs·trŏp'ō·dŭs), *adj.*

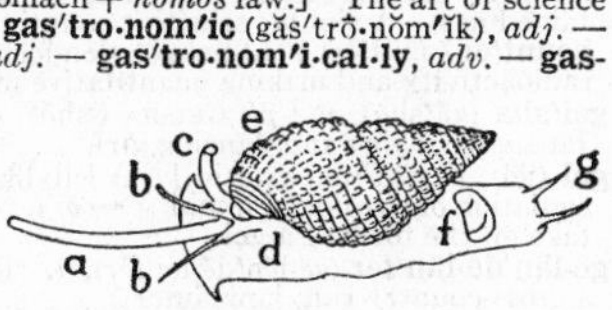

Dog Whelk (*Alectrion trivittata*), a Gastropod. *a* Proboscis exserted; *b, b* Tentacles; *c* Siphon; *d* Foot; *e* Shell; *f* Operculum; *g* Caudal Cirri. Nat. size.

gas'tro·scope (găs'trō·skōp), *n.* [*gastro-* + *-scope.*] *Med.* An instrument for viewing the interior of the stomach. — **gas'tro·scop'ic** (-skŏp'ĭk), *adj.* — **gas·tros'co·py** (găs·trŏs'kō·pĭ), *n.*

gas·trot'ri·chan (găs·trŏt'rĭ·kăn), *n.* *Zool.* Any of a small group of minute fresh-water many-celled animals superficially like infusorians, having cilia on the ventral side. — **gas·trot'ri·chan,** *adj.*

gas'tro·vas'cu·lar (găs'trō·văs'kū·lēr), *adj.* [*gastro-* + *vascular.*] *Zool.* Functioning both as digestive and circulatory organs; as, the *gastrovascular* canals of coelenterates.

gas'tru·la (găs'tro͝o·lȧ), *n.; pl.* -LAE (-lē). [NL., dim. fr. Gr. *gastēr* stomach.] *Embryol.* An embryo consisting typically of a cup or openmouthed sac with walls composed of two layers of cells, an outer (epiblast) and an inner (hypoblast). The mouth is called the *blastopore* and the interior cavity the *archenteron.* A recognizable gastrula stage occurs in the early development of most metazoans. Cf. BLASTULA. — **gas'tru·lar** (-lēr), *adj.*

gas'tru·late (-lāt), *v. i.* *Embryol.* To become or form a gastrula. — **gas'tru·la'tion** (-lā'shŭn), *n.*

gas'works' (găs'wûrks'), *n. pl., usually construed as a singular.* A place where gas, esp. illuminating gas, is manufactured.

gat (găt). Archaic & dial. past of GET.

gat, *n.* [Scand. or LG. *gat* hole, opening.] A natural or artificial channel or passage, as between sandbanks or cliffs.

gat, *n.* [Short for *Gatling gun.*] *Slang.* Revolver; gun.

ga'ta (gä'tȧ), *n.* See 1st SHARK.

gate (gāt), *n.* [AS. *gæt, gat, geat,* gate, door.] **1.** An opening for passage in an enclosing wall, fence, or barrier; esp., such an opening with a movable frame or door for closing it. **2.** A structure or part of a structure comprising a passageway together with towers, approaches, etc. **3.** The frame or door which closes a gate. **4. a** Any means of entrance or egress. **b** Specif., a pass or defile in mountains. **5.** Something shaped or functioning like a gate; as: **a** A valve for controlling the passage of fluid. **b** A stretching frame for a saw or saws. **6.** Aggregate money paid for admission; also, the number admitted.

☞ COMBINATIONS (in various senses) are:

gatehouse	**gateman**	**gateway**
gatekeeper	**gatetender**	**gatewoman**

— *v. t. Eng. Schools & Univ.* To punish by confinement to the school or college grounds, entirely or for certain hours.

gate, *n.* [ON. *gata.*] **1.** *Archaic.* A way; path. **2.** *Now Dial.* Manner of acting or doing; habitual mode.

gate, *n.* *Founding.* **a** The channel in a mold through which the molten metal flows into the cavity made by the pattern. **b** The waste piece of metal cast in the opening.

gate'-leg', or gate'-legged', ta'ble (gāt'lĕg', -lĕgd'). A style of table with drop leaves supported by gatelike legs that fold against the frame when the leaves are dropped.

gate money. *Sports.* Money paid for admission.

gate'post' (gāt'pōst'), *n.* A post to which a gate is hung; also, a post against which a gate closes.

gath'er (găth'ēr), *v. t.* [AS. *gaderian, gadrian;* akin to AS. *gæd* fellowship, *gador, geador,* together.] **1.** To bring together; to collect. **2.** To pick out and collect, as a harvest; to cull; pick. **3.** To accumulate by collecting and saving little by little. **4.** To summon up a reserve of (strength, voice, etc.), preparatory to exertion; also, to draw (one's limbs or oneself) together; as, to *gather* one's wits. **5.** To gain or win as by gradual increase. **6.** To bring closely together the parts of; to draw together, as a piece of cloth by a thread. **7.** To derive, or deduce, as an inference; to infer; conclude. — *v. i.* **1.** To come together; to assemble. **2.** To come to a head, as a sore, and generate pus. **3.** To grow larger by accretion; to increase. **4.** To bring things together by way of increase; acquire.

Syn. (1) **Gather, collect, assemble, congregate** mean to come or bring together in a group. **Gather** may be used not only of persons and objects but of intangible things; **collect,** often but not always, implies careful selection, orderly arrangement, or the like; **assemble** stresses a close union of persons or things and a definite end in their coming or being brought together; **congregate** implies a flocking together to form a crowd, a huddle, or the like.
(2) See INFER.

— ***gathered to one's people*** or ***fathers.*** Dead.

— *n.* A drawing together; fold; specif., a plait in cloth.

gath'er·er (-ēr), *n.* One who or that which gathers.

gath'er·ing (-ĭng), *n.* **1.** A crowd; assembly. **2.** A charitable contribution; collection. **3.** A gather (of cloth). **4.** *Med.* A boil; abscess.

Gat'ling gun (găt'lĭng). [After the Amer. inventor R. J. *Gatling.*] A machine gun consisting of a cluster of barrels revolved by a crank, and loaded and fired once each during a revolution of the group. The service rate of fire was about 600 shots a minute.

gauche (gōsh), *adj.* [F.] Left-handed; hence, awkward; esp., lacking the social graces. — **Syn.** See AWKWARD. — **gauche'ly,** *adv.* — **gauche'ness,** *n.*

gau'che·rie' (gō'shē·rē'; gō'shē·rē; *F.* gōsh'rē'), *n.* [F.] Awkwardness; tactlessness; a tactless or awkward action.

Gau'cho (gou'chō), *n.; pl.* GAUCHOS (-chōz). [Sp.] A cowboy of the pampas, famous for horsemanship and for skill in guerrilla fighting.

gaud (gôd), *n.* [ME. *gaude*, appar. fr. OF. *gaudir*, fr. L. *gaudere* to rejoice.] An ornament; a trinket.

‖**gau'de·a'mus i'gi·tur** (gô'dē·ā'mŭs ĭj'ĭ·tēr; gou'dā·ä'mo͝os ĭg'ĭ·to͝or). [L.] Let us then be merry; — first words of a favorite Latin song of students. Its present form, dating from about 1781, is probably based on a 13th-century Latin song.

gaud'er·y (gôd'ēr·ĭ), *n.* Finery; ostentatious display.

gaud'y (gôd'ĭ), *adj.;* GAUD'I·ER (-ĭ·ēr); GAUD'I·EST. Ostentatiously fine; showy; now esp., tastelessly fine. — *n.* **1.** *Obs.* A gaud. **2.** *Eng.* A festival or entertainment, as an annual college dinner. — **gaud'i·ly,** *adv.* — **gaud'i·ness,** *n.*

Syn. **Gaudy, tawdry, garish, flashy, meretricious** mean vulgarly or cheaply showy. **Gaudy** implies use of gay colors and lavish and tasteless ornamentation; **tawdry** implies both gaudiness and cheapness; **garish,** a dazzling or offensive brightness; **flashy,** a dazzling yet shallow and vulgar display; **meretricious,** an alluring but deceitful show of worth, value, brilliancy, etc. — **Ant.** Quiet.

gaud'y (gôd'ĭ), *n.* [Prob. fr. L. *gaudium* joy.] *Eng.* A feast, as an annual college dinner in an English university.

gauf'fer (gôf'ēr). Var. of GOFFER.

gauge, gage (gāj), *v. t.;* GAUGED, GAGED (gājd); GAUG'ING, GAG'ING (gāj'ĭng). [ONF. *gauger.*] **1.** To find the exact measurement of. **2.** To measure the contents or capacity of, as of a keg. **3.** To measure the capacity, character, or ability of; to estimate. **4.** To limit by or as by a gauge, esp. so as to conform to a standard; as, to *gauge* a line, work; hence, to set bounds to. **5.** To render (bricks or stones) of a uniform size or shape by cutting or rubbing. **6.** *Plastering.* To mix (plaster) in certain definite proportions, as for quick drying.

— *n.* **1.** A measure; a standard measure. **2.** Dimensions; extent. **3.** An instrument for or means of measuring or testing; as, a rain *gauge;* a wind *gauge.* **4.** *Building.* That part of a shingle, slate, or tile, exposed to the weather when laid; also, one course as laid. **5.** *Firearms.* The interior diameter of the barrel of a shotgun expressed by the number of spherical lead bullets fitting it required to make a pound; — chiefly in combination; as, a ten-*gauge* shotgun. Cf. 1st BORE, *n.* **6.** *Mach.* A device for determining whether a specified dimension is within specified limits. **7.** *Naut.* Relative position of a vessel with reference to another vessel and the wind. **8.** *Plastering.* The quantity of plaster of Paris used with common plaster to accelerate its setting. **9. a** *Railroads.* The distance between the rails of a railroad. ***standard gauge*** in most countries is now 4 feet 8½ inches; ***broad,*** or ***wide, gauge*** is any larger gauge than this, and ***narrow gauge*** is any smaller gauge. **b** Distance between the wheels of a vehicle. — **Syn.** See STANDARD.

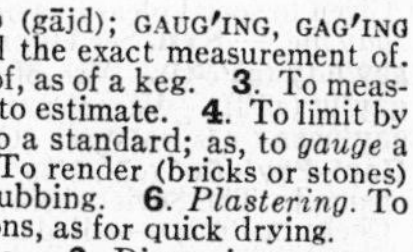

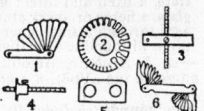

Gauges, 6. 1 Feeler, or Thickness; 2 Wire, or Sheet Metal; 3 Depth; 4 Scratch, or Marking; 5 Go-Not Go; 6 Thread, or Screw Pitch.

gaug'er, gag'er (gāj'ẽr), *n.* One that gauges; esp., an officer who gauges casks; hence, an exciseman.

gauge wheel. A wheel on the underside of a plow beam which limits the depth of plowing.

Gaul (gôl), *n.* [F. *Gaule;* cf. L. *Gallia,* fr. *Gallus* a Gaul.] **1.** One of the natives or inhabitants of ancient Gaul, or a member of the race to which they belonged. **2.** A Frenchman.

gau'lei'ter (gou'lī'tẽr), *n.* [G., fr. *gau* district + *leiter* leader.] A district leader of the German National Socialist party, acting in his territory as provincial political governor.

Gaul'ish (gôl'ĭsh), *adj.* Of or pertaining to Gaul or the Gauls. — *n.* The Celtic language of ancient Gaul, once spoken over a considerable area in western and central Europe, and even in Asia Minor (Galatia), but extinct since the 5th or 6th century A.D.; — called also *Continental Celtic.* See INDO-EUROPEAN LANGUAGES, *Table.*

Gaull'ist (gōl'ĭst), *n.* = DE GAULLIST.

gaul·the'ri·a (gôl·thē'rĭ·ȧ), *n.* [NL., after M. *Gaulthier,* Can. botanist and physician.] A plant of a large genus (*Gaultheria*) of shrubs of the heath family, including the American wintergreen. Oil of wintergreen is also called **gaultheria oil.**

gaum (gôm), *v. t. Dial.* To smear, as with grease.

gaunt (gônt; gänt), *adj.* **1.** Attenuated, as with fasting or suffering; haggard. **2.** Forbidding; grim. — **Syn.** See LEAN. — **gaunt'ly,** *adv.* — **gaunt'ness,** *n.*

gaunt'let (gônt'lĕt; gänt'lĕt; -lĭt), *n.* [F. *gantelet,* dim. of *gant* glove, of Teut. origin.] **1.** A glove to defend the hand from wounds. **2.** Hence: **a** With *the,* a challenge; — from former use of a glove as a symbol of defiance; as, to fling down the *gauntlet;* to take up the *gauntlet.* **b** A long stout glove, covering part of the arm. **c** The part of a glove covering the wrist. — **gaunt'let·ed,** *adj.*

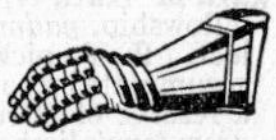

Gauntlet, 1.

gaunt'let. Var. of GANTLET.

gaun'try (gôn'trĭ). Var. of GANTRY.

gauss (gous; gôs), *n.* [After Karl F. *Gauss,* Ger. mathematician.] *Elec.* The C.G.S. unit of magnetic flux density. It is equal to one maxwell per square centimeter.

gauze (gôz), *n.* [F. *gaze,* appar. fr. *Gaza* (Ar. *Ghazze*), a city in Palestine.] **1.** A very thin transparent material of silk, cotton, or linen; also, a fabric resembling this, as one of wire. **2.** A haze or mist. — *adj.* Made of or like gauze.

gauz'y (gôz'ĭ), *adj.;* GAUZ'I·ER (-ĭ·ẽr); GAUZ'I·EST. Thin and slight as gauze. — **gauz'i·ly,** *adv.* — **gauz'i·ness,** *n.*

‖**ga'vage'** (gȧ'vȧzh'), *n.* [F., fr. *gaver* to gorge.] **a** Feeding by means of a stomach tube. **b** Cramming poultry.

gave (gāv), *past of* GIVE.

gav'el (găv'ĕl; -'l), *n. U. S.* The mallet of the presiding officer in a legislative body, court, etc.

gav'el, *n.* [AS. *gafol.*] *Obs. exc. Hist.* Tribute or rent, as in **gavel bread, gavel corn, gavel swine,** etc.

gav'el·kind' (-kīnd'), *n.* [ME. *gavelkynde, gavelkende.* See GAVEL tribute; KIND, *n.*] *Law.* **1.** A common-law tenure of land (now abolished) providing that: (1) Upon the death of the tenant in fee intestate the land is divided equally among all the sons, or among brothers or other collateral heirs on failure of direct or nearer heirs. (2) A tenant in fee can make disposal of his land by feoffment at the age of 15. **2.** The custom of dividing an intestate's estate equally among the sons, or other heirs.

gav'e·lock (găv'ĕ·lŏk), *n.* [AS. *gafeluc.*] *Dial.* An iron lever.

ga'vi·al (gā'vĭ·ăl), *n.* [F., fr. Hind. *ghariyāl.*] A large harmless crocodilian (*Gavialis gangeticus*) of India.

ga·votte' (gȧ·vŏt'), **ga·vot'** (gȧ·vŏt'; găv'ŏt), *n.* [F. *gavotte,* fr. Pr. *gavoto,* fr. *Gavots,* the Alpine mountaineers.] **1.** A lively dance of French peasant origin in which the feet were raised in the step instead of sliding. **2.** Music for this dance, in moderately quick duple measure, having two parts, the first of four measures and the second of eight.

Ga'wain (gä'wān; -wĭn), *n.* A nephew of King Arthur and a knight of the Round Table.

gawk (gôk), *n.* [E. dial *gawk* left, left-handed.] A clumsy, stupid person; lout. — *v. i. Colloq.* To act like a gawk; stare.

gawk'y (gôk'ĭ), *adj.;* GAWK'I·ER (-ĭ·ẽr); GAWK'I·EST. Foolish and awkward; clumsy. — *n.* A gawk. — **gawk'i·ly,** *adv.* — **gawk'i·ness,** *n.*

gaw'sie (gô'sĭ), *adj.* Also **gaw'sy.** *Scot.* Large and jolly or good-looking; lusty; big.

gay (gā), *adj.;* GAY'ER (-ẽr); GAY'EST. [OF. *gai.*] **1.** Excited with merriment; merry. **2.** Bright in appearance; brilliant in color. **3.** Given to social pleasures or indulgence; hence, loose; licentious; as, a *gay* life. — **Syn.** See LIVELY. — **Ant.** Sober.

gay'e·ty (gā'ĕ·tĭ). Var. of GAIETY.

gay'ly (gā'lĭ). Var. of GAILY.

gay'ness (-nĕs; -nĭs), *n.* Gaiety.

Gay'–Pay'–Oo' (gā'pā'ōō'), *n.* [Russ., fr. the initials (*G.P.U.*) of its name.] The Soviet secret service organization which succeeded the Cheka in 1922; — called also *Ogpu.* See NKVD.

gay'wings' (gā'wĭngz'), *n.* A small American herb (*Polygala paucifolia*), with leaves somewhat like wintergreen.

gaze (gāz), *v. i.* [ME. *gasen.*] To fix the eyes in a steady and intent look; to look with eagerness, as in wonder or with studious attention. **Syn. Gaze, gape, stare, glare, peer, gloat** mean to look at long and attentively. **Gaze** implies fixed and prolonged attention as in admiration or wonder; **gape,** a stupid or openmouthed wonder or indecision; **stare,** a fixed and direct gazing, connoting curiosity, insolence, etc.; **glare,** a fierce or angry staring; **peer,** a gazing narrowly and curiously, as if through a small aperture; **gloat,** a prolonged or frequent gazing, often with undue or malignant satisfaction.
— *n.* **1.** *Archaic.* An object gazed on. **2.** An intent look.

ga·ze'bo (gȧ·zē'bō), *n.; pl.* -BOS, -BOES (-bōz). A balcony with windows.

gaze'hound' (gāz'hound'), *n.* A hound that pursues by sight rather than by scent.

ga·zelle' (gȧ·zĕl'), *n.;* see PLURAL, *Note,* 3. [F., fr. Ar. *ghazāl.*] Any of numerous small graceful and swift antelopes (*Gazella* and allied genera), with lustrous eyes, found esp. in South Africa, northern Africa, Persia, and India.

gaz'er (gāz'ẽr), *n.* One who gazes.

ga·zette' (gȧ·zĕt'), *n.* [F., fr. It. *gazzetta.*] **1.** A newspaper. **2.** An official journal; specif. [*cap.*], one of the three official papers of Great Britain, published twice a week in London, Edinburgh, and Dublin, containing lists of honors, names of bankrupts, public notices, etc. — *v. t.* To announce or publish in a gazette.

gaz'et·teer' (găz'ĕ·tēr'), *n.* [F. *gazettier, gazetier.*] **1.** A writer of news, or an officer appointed to publish news. **2.** A geographical dictionary.

gaz'o·gene (găz'ō·jēn), *n.* An apparatus for generating gases or for impregnating a liquid with a gas; specif., a portable apparatus for making carbonated liquids.

gean (gēn), *n.* A cultivated sweet cherry, having tender heart-shaped fruit. See CHERRY, 1.

ge'an'ti·cline (jē'ăn'tĭ·klīn), **ge'an·ti·cli'nal** (jē'ăn·tĭ·klī'năl; -n'l), *n.* (See GEO-; ANTICLINAL.] *Geol.* A great upward flexure of the earth's crust. Cf. GEOSYNCLINE; ANTICLINE, *Illust.* — **ge'an·ti·cli'nal,** *adj.*

gear (gēr), *n.* [ME. *gere.*] **1.** Clothing; garments. **2.** Hence: **a** *Archaic.* Warlike accouterments. **b** The harness, esp. of horses. **c** Tools; implements. **3.** Goods; movable property. **4.** *Archaic & Dial.* **a** Property in general; wealth. **b** Matter; stuff; also, rubbish. **c** Business; affair. **5.** *Mach.* **a** An accessory mechanism that performs a specific function in a complete machine; as, a steering *gear.* **b** A toothed wheel, or cogwheel; as, a train of *gears.* See BEVEL GEAR, *Illust.* **c** Working relation or adjustment; as, in *gear.* **d** The diameter in inches of a hypothetical wheel, whose circumference equals the distance a bicycle moves in one complete revolution of the pedal cranks. **6.** *Naut.* The rigging in general. — *v. t.* **1.** To equip; also, *Mach.,* to provide with or connect by gearing; to put into gear. **2.** To adjust so as to match or blend with something; as, production *geared* to war needs. — *v. i.* **1.** *Mach.* To be in, or come into, gear. **2.** To blend.

gear'ing (gēr'ĭng), *n.* **1.** Act or manner of fitting a machine with a gear or gears. **2.** *Mach.* The parts, collectively, by which motion is transmitted from one portion of machinery to another; gear or a train of gear wheels.

gear'less (-lĕs; -lĭs), *adj.* Without gear.

gear'shift' (-shĭft'), *n.* A mechanism by which the transmission gears in a power transmission system are engaged and disengaged.

gear wheel, *or* **gear'wheel'** (gēr'hwēl'), *n. Mach.* A wheel that gears with another piece; specif., a cogwheel. See IDLE WHEEL, *Illust.*

geck (gĕk), *n.* [MD. *gec,* MLG. *geck.*] *Obs. exc. Dial.* An object of scorn; a dupe; a gull.

geck, *v. t. & i. Scot. & Ir.* To deride; toss the head, as in derision.

geck'o (gĕk'ō), *n.; pl.* GECKOS, GECKOES (-ōz). [Malay *geko';* — from its cry.] Any of a family (Gekkonidae) of small harmless lizards.

ged, gedd (gĕd), *n.* [ON. *gedda.*] *Scot.* The pike.

gee (jē), *n.; pl.* GEES (jēz). The letter G, g.

gee (jē), *interj. & n.* A command used in guiding teams without reins, to turn to the off side, or to the right; also, used (esp. with *up*) to urge on an animal. — *v. t. & i.* To turn to the off side; to evade.

gee (jē), *v. i. Slang & Dial.* To agree; harmonize; fit.

geese (gēs), *n., pl.* of GOOSE.

geest (gēst), *n.* [LG. *geest, geest*land, sandy, dry land.] *Geol.* **a** Alluvial matter on the surface of land, not of recent origin. **b** *Rare.* Loose material, earth or soil, formed by decay of rocks in a place.

gee'zer (gē'zẽr), *n.* [Dial. corrupt. of *guiser* a mummer.] *Slang.* A queer old fellow; an old chap; an old woman.

Ge·hen'na (gē·hĕn'ȧ; gĕ-), *n.* [LL., fr. Gr. *Geenna,* fr. Heb. *Gē Hinnōm.*] The Valley of Hinnom, near Jerusalem, used as a receptacle for refuse, fires being kept up to prevent pestilence. Hence, in the New Testament, hell.

Gei'ger count'er (gī'gẽr). [After Hans *Geiger* (b. 1882), German physicist.] *Physics.* A thin-walled metallic cylindrical tube with a needlelike electrode projecting within, which detects the passage through its walls of every ionizing particle, such as a cosmic-ray particle, by the momentary current set up on ionization of the contained gas. A similar sensitive counting tube, the **Gei'ger–Mül'ler count'er** (-mül'ẽr), containing a slender axial wire, is used for detecting radioactivity and making quantitative measurements.

gei'sha (gā'shȧ), *n.; pl.* GEISHA (-shȧ), GEISHAS (-shȧz). [Jap.] A Japanese singing and dancing girl.

gel (jĕl), *n.* [From *gel*atin.] A jellylike material formed by the coagulation of a colloidal liquid. — *v. i.;* GELLED (jĕld); GEL'LING. To take on the form of a gel.

ge·län'de·läu'fer (gĕ·lĕn'dĕ·loi'fẽr), *n.* [G.] *Skiing.* A skier making a cross-country run; langläufer.

ge·län'de·sprung' (gĕ·lĕn'dĕ·shprōōng'), *n.* [G., fr. *gelände* level or open field + *sprung* jump.] *Skiing.* A jump made from a low crouching position with the aid of both ski poles, usually over an obstacle, with a return to the crouch in the moment of landing; — called also **ge·län'de jump.**

gel'a·tin (jĕl'ȧ·tĭn), **gel'a·tine** (-tĭn; -tēn), *n.* [F. *gélatine,* fr. L. *gelata,* fr. *gelare* to freeze.] **1.** Animal jelly; glutinous material (as in glue or isinglass) obtained from animal tissues by boiling; specif., the protein so extracted. **2.** Any of various substances likened to this; as, vegetable *gelatins* (agar-agar, etc.). **3.** A jelly formed with gelatin.

ge·lat'i·nate (jē·lăt'ĭ·nāt), *v. t. & i.* To turn to gelatin or a jellylike substance. — **gel'a·tin·a'tion** (jĕl'ȧ·tĭn·ā'shŭn), *n.*

ge·lat'i·nize (-nīz), *v. t.* To convert into gelatin or jelly; also, *Photog.,* to coat or treat with gelatin. — *v. i.* To be converted into gelatin or a jelly. — **ge·lat'i·ni·za'tion** (-nĭ·zā'shŭn; -nī·zā'shŭn), *n.*

ge·lat'i·noid (jē·lăt'ĭ·noid; jĕl'ȧ·tĭn·oid'), *adj.* [*gelatin* + *-oid.*] Resembling gelatin. — *n.* A gelatinoid substance.

ge·lat'i·nous (jē·lăt'ĭ·nŭs), *adj.* **1.** Jellylike; viscous. **2.** Of, pertaining to, or containing gelatin.

ge·la'tion (jē·lā'shŭn), *n.* [L. *gelatio* a freezing, fr. *gelare* to freeze.] A cooling and solidifying.

geld (gĕld), *v. t.;* GELD'ED or GELT (gĕlt); GELD'ING. [ON. *gelda,* fr. *geldr* barren.] **1.** To castrate; hence, to spay. **2.** To deprive of anything essential; to lessen the force of.

geld (gĕld), *n.* Also, incorrectly, **gelt** (gĕlt), **gheld** (gĕld). [AS. *gild, gield, geld,* tribute, payment, fr. the root of *gieldan* to pay, render.] The crown tax paid under the Anglo-Saxon and Norman kings.

geld'ing (gĕl'dĭng), *n.* [ON. *geldingr.*] A castrated animal; specif., a castrated horse; formerly, also, a eunuch.

gel'id (jĕl'ĭd), *adj.* [L. *gelidus,* fr. *gelu* frost, cold.] Cold; frozen. — **ge·lid'i·ty** (jē·lĭd'ĭ·tĭ), *n.* — **gel'id·ly,** *adv.*

gel·se′mi·um (jĕl·sē′mĭ·ŭm), *n.* [NL., fr. It. *gelsomino* jessamine.] **1.** Any of a genus (*Gelsemium*, family Loganiaceae) of woody vines containing two Asiatic species and one species of the southern United States (*G. sempervirens*, the yellow jasmine or Carolina jessamine: see JASMINE, 2). **2.** *Pharm.* The root of *G. sempervirens*, used in the treatment of spasms and neuralgia.

gelt (gĕlt), *n.* [G. *geld* money, fr. MHG. *gelt*.] *Now Humorous.* Money; gold.

gelt (gĕlt), *past & past part.* of GELD.

gem (jĕm), *n.* [OF. *jamme, gemme*, fr. L. *gemma* a precious stone, bud.] **1.** Any jewel; a precious or, sometimes, a semiprecious stone cut and polished for ornament. See BRILLIANT, *Illust.* **2.** Something prized for great beauty or perfection, esp. when small or brief, as a poem. **3.** A muffin made of coarse flour and sometimes unleavened. **4.** *Print.* An old size of type between brilliant and diamond. — *v. t.*; GEMMED (jĕmd); GEM′MING. To adorn with or as with gems.

Ge·ma′ra (gĕ·mä′rä; -mô′rä), *n.* [Aram. *gemārā* completion.] *Jewish Lit.* The commentary of the Talmud.

gem′i·nate (jĕm′ĭ·nāt), *adj.* [L. *geminatus*, past part. of *geminare* to double, fr. *geminus* a twin.] In pairs; coupled. — *v. t. & i.* To double; to become double or paired. — **gem′i·na′tion** (-nā′shŭn), *n.*

Gem′i·ni (jĕm′ĭ·nī), *n. pl.*; *gen.* GEMINORUM (-nō′rŭm; 70). [L., twins.] *Astron.* **a** The third zodiacal constellation, pictorially represented as the twins, Castor and Pollux, sitting together. It is on the opposite side of the Milky Way from Taurus and Orion. **b** The third sign [II, □, or)(] of the zodiac, which the sun enters about May 21. See ZODIAC.

gem′ma (jĕm′ȧ), *n.*; *pl.* -MAE (-ē). [L., a bud.] *Biol.* In reproduction, a bud or budlike body.

gem′mate (-āt), *adj.* [L. *gemmatus*, past part.] *Biol.* Having or reproducing by buds or gemmae.

gem·ma′tion (jĕm·ā′shŭn), *n.* *Biol.* Reproduction by gemmae.

gem·mip′a·rous (jĕ·mĭp′ȧ·rŭs), *adj.* *Biol.* Producing buds; reproducing by buds. — **gem·mip′a·rous·ly**, *adv.*

gem·mol′o·gy (jĕm·ŏl′ō·jĭ), *n.* Also **gem·ol′o·gy**. [L. *gemma* gem + *-logy*.] The science of gems. — **gem′mo·log′i·cal** (jĕm′ō·lŏj′ĭ·kăl), *adj.* — **gem·mol′o·gist** (jĕm·ŏl′ō·jĭst), *n.*

gem′mu·la′tion (jĕm′ū·lā′shŭn), *n.* [See GEMMULE.] *Biol.* The formation of, or reproduction by, gemmules.

gem′mule (jĕm′ūl), *n.* [F., fr. L. *gemmula*, dim. of *gemma* bud.] *Biol.* **a** One of the hypothetical supramolecular units assumed in Darwin's theory of pangenesis. **b** A gemma.

gem′my (jĕm′ĭ), *adj.* Full of gems; glittering.

ge·mot′ (gĕ·mōt′), **ge·mote′**, *n.* [AS. *gemōt*. See MOOT.] *Anglo-Saxon Hist.* A meeting or assembly; a court. Cf. FOLKMOOT, MOOT, WITENAGEMOT.

gems′bok′ (gĕmz′bŏk′), *n.*; see PLURAL, *Note*, 3. [D.] The largest and handsomest species of oryx (*Oryx gazella*).

-gen (-jĕn; -jĕn). [F. *-gène*, fr. Gr. *-genēs* born, fr. root of *gignesthai* to be born, become.] A combining form used in forming nouns denoting: **a** *A substance that produces* or *generates*, used chiefly in *Chem.*, as in oxy*gen*, halo*gen*. **b** *Biol.* *A thing produced* or *generated*, as in anti*gen*, exo*gen*, phello*gen*.

gen·darme′ (zhän·därm′; zhän′därm; *F.* zhäɴ′dȧrm′), *n.*; *pl.* GENDARMES (zhän·därmz′; *F.* zhäɴ′dȧrm′). [F.] One of a body of policemen organized, armed, and drilled as soldiers, in France and some other European countries.

gen·darm′er·y (zhän·där′mẽr·ĭ), ‖**gen′dar′me·rie′** (zhäɴ′dȧr′mĕ·rē′), *n.* [F. *gendarmerie*.] A body of gendarmes.

gen′der (jĕn′dẽr), *n.* [OF. *genre, gendre* (with excrescent *d*), fr. L. *genus, generis*, birth, race, kind, gender.] **1.** *Archaic.* Kind; sort. **2.** *Colloq.* Sex, male or female. **3.** *Gram.* Form of a noun or form or selection of other words (as adjectives, participles, pronouns) used with the noun as a mark of the noun's membership in a distinct class; also, one of the classes, or such classes, so distinguished. In most Indo-European languages (as Latin, English, and German) there are three genders, *masculine*, *feminine*, and *neuter*; in some (as French and Italian) there are only two, *masculine* and *feminine*. Some non-Indo-European languages have many genders.

gen′der, *v. t. & i.* *Archaic.* To engender.

gene (jēn), *n.* [See -GEN, GENUS.] *Biol.* An entity concerned with the transmission and development or determination of hereditary characters; an element of the germ plasm, regarded as a small part of a chromosome; a factor.

gen′e·al′o·gist (jĕn′ē·ăl′ō·jĭst; jē′nē-), *n.* One who traces genealogies or studies the descent of persons or families.

gen′e·al′o·gy (-jĭ), *n.*; *pl.* -GIES (-jĭz). [OF. *genealogie*, fr. LL., fr. Gr. *genealogia*, fr. *genealogos* genealogist, fr. *genea* descent + *logos* discourse.] **1.** A history of the descent of a person or family from an ancestor. **2.** Regular descent of a person or family from a progenitor; pedigree; lineage. **3.** The study of family pedigrees. — **gen′e·a·log′i·cal** (-ȧ·lŏj′ĭ·kăl), *adj.* — **gen′e·a·log′i·cal·ly**, *adv.*

gen′er·a (jĕn′ẽr·ȧ), *n.*, *pl.* of GENUS.

gen′er·a·ble (-ȧ·b'l), *adj.* Capable of being generated.

gen′er·al (jĕn′ẽr·ăl), *adj.* [OF., fr. L. *generalis*, fr. *genus, -eris*, class, kind.] **1.** Of or pertaining to the whole; not local; as, a *general* election; *general* anesthesia; also, taken as a whole; (the) whole. **2.** Pertaining to, affecting, or applicable to, each and all of a class, kind, or order; as, a *general* law. **3.** Not limited to a precise import or application; not specific. **4.** Of or pertaining to the typical or generic; generic and abstract; not concrete. **5.** Pertaining to many persons, cases, or occasions; prevalent. **6.** Not special or specialized; as, a *general* store. **7.** Not precise or definite; as, *general* comments. **8.** As a second term in some nonmilitary titles, indicating superiority in rank; as, governor *general*. — **Syn.** See UNIVERSAL.
— *n.* **1.** *Archaic.* The whole; total; a general proposition, fact, principle, etc.; — opposed to *particular*. **2.** The general public; the people. **3.** *Eccl.* The chief of a religious order. **4.** *Mil.* **a** *U. S. Army.* (1) A general officer (four stars) who ranks next above a lieutenant general and next below a general of the army. (2) Inclusively: an officer of one of the first six grades of general officer, namely, general of the armies (a rank created for John J. Pershing), general of the army (five stars), general (four stars), lieutenant general (three stars), major general (two stars), brigadier general (one star). **b** *Brit. Army.* A commander of an independent army, ranking next above a lieutenant general and next below a field marshal. **c** A title used in addressing a general officer.
— ***in general***. Generally; for the most part.

General Assembly. See ASSEMBLY, 2.

General Court. *U. S.* The legislature of a state. In the colonial days it had judicial power. *Obs.*, except where (Massachusetts and New Hampshire) it is the legal title.

gen′er·al·cy (jĕn′ẽr·ăl·sĭ), *n.* Office or term of a general.

General Election Day. See HOLIDAY, 3.

gen′er·al·is′si·mo (jĕn′ẽr·ăl·ĭs′ĭ·mō), *n.*; *pl.* -MOS (-mōz). [It.] The chief commander, as of a combined military and naval force.

gen′er·al′i·ty (jĕn′ẽr·ăl′ĭ·tĭ), *n.*; *pl.* -TIES (-tĭz). **1.** State or quality of being general. **2.** That which is general; a general or vague statement or phrase. **3.** The main body; the bulk; the greatest part.

gen′er·al·i·za′tion (-ăl·ĭ·zā′shŭn; -ī·zā′shŭn), *n.* **1.** Act or process of generalizing. **2.** A general inference.

gen′er·al·ize (jĕn′ẽr·ăl·īz), *v. t.* **1.** To make general; to reduce to general laws. **2. a** To derive (a general conception or principle) from particulars. **b** To derive or induce a general conception, principle, or inference from; to use with a more extensive application. **3.** To give general applicability to; as, to *generalize* a law. — *v. i.* To form generalizations. — **gen′er·al·iz′er** (-īz′ẽr), *n.*

gen′er·al·ly (jĕn′ẽr·ăl·ĭ), *adv.* In a general manner.

general officer. *U. S. Army.* Any officer above the rank of colonel.

general of the army. *U. S. Army.* A general officer of the highest rank, established by act of Congress (Dec. 14, 1944) to be held by no more than four officers on the active list at one time.

general paralysis *or* **paresis.** *Med.* Insanity caused by syphilitic degeneration of the brain, terminating in dementia and paralysis.

gen′er·al–pur′pose, *adj.* Of general utility; — applied specif. to animals, breeds, implements.

gen′er·al·ship′ (jĕn′ẽr·ăl·shĭp′), *n.* **1.** Office or tenure of office of a general; exercise of the functions of a general. **2.** Military skill in a general officer. **3.** Leadership; management.

general staff. *Mil.* A group of officers in the headquarters of a division or larger unit who assist the commander in administrative and executive duties. See G-1, G-2, etc.

gen′er·ate (jĕn′ẽr·āt), *v. t.* [L. *generatus*, past part. of *generare* to generate, fr. *genus*. See GENUS.] **1.** To beget; procreate. **2.** To originate, esp. by a vital or chemical process; to produce. **3.** *Math.* To trace out (a line, figure, or solid) by the motion of a point or a magnitude of inferior order.

gen′er·a′tion (-ā′shŭn), *n.* **1.** Act or process of producing offspring; procreation. **2. a** A single stage in the succession of natural descent; hence, the body of men, animals, or plants of the same genealogical rank or remove from an ancestor. **b** The ordinary period of time at which one rank follows another, or father is succeeded by child, — usually taken to be about 33 years. **3.** Origination by some mathematical, chemical, or other process; production. **4.** *Obs.* **a** Progeny; offspring. **b** Race; kind; breed; stock. **5.** *Geom.* The formation of any geometrical figure by the motion, in accordance with a mathematical law, of some other figure; as, the *generation* of a line by a point.

gen′er·a′tive (jĕn′ẽr·ā′tĭv; -ȧ·tĭv), *adj.* Having the power, or function, of generating or reproducing.

gen′er·a′tor (-ā′tẽr), *n.* [L.] **1.** One who or that which generates. **2.** An apparatus in which vapor or gas is formed. **3.** *Elec.* Any machine by which mechanical energy is changed into electrical energy; a dynamo. See DYNAMO, *Illust.*

gen′er·a′trix (-ā′trĭks), *n.*; *pl.* -ATRICES (-ȧ·trī′sēz). [L.] **1.** A female that generates. **2.** *Math.* That which generates.

ge·ner′ic (jĕ·nĕr′ĭk), *adj.* Also **ge·ner′i·cal** (-ĭ·kăl). [L. *genus, generis*, race, kind.] **1.** *Biol.* Pertaining to, or having the rank of, a genus; as, a *generic* name. **2.** General (sense 4); typical; not concrete; — opp. to *specific*. — **Syn.** See UNIVERSAL. — **ge·ner′i·cal·ly**, *adv.*

gen′er·os′i·ty (jĕn′ẽr·ŏs′ĭ·tĭ), *n.*; *pl.* -TIES (-tĭz). **1.** Liberality in spirit or act. **2.** A generous act.

gen′er·ous (jĕn′ẽr·ŭs), *adj.* [F. *généreux*, fr. L. *generosus* of noble birth, magnanimous, fr. *genus* birth, race.] **1.** *Archaic.* Of honorable birth or origin. **2.** Exhibiting qualities regarded as belonging to high birth; honorable; magnanimous. **3.** Liberal; openhanded. **4.** Characterized by munificence; abundant; ample. **5.** Full of spirit or strength; rich; as, *generous* wine. — **Syn.** See LIBERAL. — **gen′er·ous·ly**, *adv.* — **gen′er·ous·ness**, *n.*

gen′e·sis (jĕn′ē·sĭs), *n.*; *pl.* GENESES (-sēz). [L., fr. Gr. *genesis*, fr. root of *gignesthai* to be born.] **1.** [*cap.*] The first book of the Pentateuch, containing an account of creation. See BIBLE. **2.** The coming into being of anything.

-gen′e·sis (-jĕn′ē·sĭs). A combining form of *genesis* signifying *origination, generation, development, evolution of.*

gen′et (jĕn′ĕt; jĕ·nĕt′), **ge·nette′** (jĕ·nĕt′), *n.* [F. *genette*, fr. Sp. *gineta*, fr Ar. *jarnayt*.] Any of a genus (*Genetta*) of small Old World flesh-eating mammals, allied to the civets but without a pouch and with perfectly retractile claws.

gen′et (jĕn′ĕt; -ĭt). Var. of JENNET, a horse.

ge·neth′li·ac (jĕ·nĕth′lĭ·ăk), *adj.* Also **gen′eth·li′a·cal** (jĕn′ĕth·lī′ȧ·kăl). [From F., fr. L. *genethliacus*, fr. Gr. *genethliakos*, fr. *genethlios* of one's birth.] Pertaining to birthdays; showing position and influence of stars at one's birth. — **gen′eth·li′a·cal·ly**, *adv.*

ge·net′ic (jĕ·nĕt′ĭk), *adj.* Also **ge·net′i·cal** (-ĭ·kăl). [From *genesis*, after *antithetic*, etc. See GENESIS.] **1.** Pertaining to the genesis of anything, or its mode of development. **2.** Of or pertaining to genetics. **3.** Of, pert. to, or produced by a gene; genic. — **ge·net′i·cal·ly**, *adv.*

ge·net′i·cist (-ĭ·sĭst), *n.* A specialist in genetics.

ge·net′ics (-ĭks), *n.*; see -ICS. **1. a** The branch of biology dealing with heredity and variation among related organisms, largely in their evolutionary aspects. As an applied science it deals with the fundamentals of plant and animal breeding, esp. in the production and development of improved strains, varieties, breeds, etc. Cf. EUGENICS. **b** A treatise on this subject. **2.** The genetic make-up and phenomena of an organism, type, or group.

ge·ne′va (jĕ·nē′vȧ), *n.* [D. *genever, jenever*, fr. OF. *genevre*, fr. L. *juniperus* juniper.] Holland gin.

Geneva bands. See BAND, *n.*, 6 c.

Geneva cross. *Mil.* A red Greek cross on a white ground; — more commonly called *red cross*.

Geneva gown. The loose, large-sleeved, black academic gown adopted as a vestment for preaching by the Calvinistic clergy of Geneva, and widely used by Protestants.

Ge·ne′van (jĕ·nē′văn), *adj.* **1.** Of or pertaining to Geneva, in Switzerland; Genevese. **2.** Of or relating to ecclesiastical authorities in control in Geneva about the time of Calvin; Calvinistic. — *n.* **1.** A native or inhabitant of Geneva. **2.** A supporter of Genevan doctrines.

gen'ial (jēn'yăl; jē'nĭ·ăl), *adj.* [L. *genialis*, fr. *genius.*] **1.** (*pron.* jē'nĭ·ăl) Of or pertaining to marriage or generation; nuptial. **2.** Favorable to growth or comfort; hence, contributing to enjoyment of life; cheerful and cheering; enlivening; kindly. **3.** *Obs.* Native; inborn. **4.** Denoting or marked with genius. — **Syn.** See GRACIOUS. — **gen'ial·ly**, *adv.* — **gen'ial·ness**, *n.*

ge·ni'al (jē·nī'ăl), *adj.* [Gr. *geneion* chin.] *Anat. & Zool.* Of or pertaining to the chin; mental.

ge'ni·al'i·ty (jē'nĭ·ăl'ĭ·tĭ; jēn·yăl'-), *n.* The quality of being genial; esp., sympathetic cheerfulness.

gen'ic (jĕn'ĭk), *adj.* *Biol.* Of, pert to, produced by, or of the nature of a gene; genetic; as, *genic* balance.

-gen'ic (-jĕn'ĭk). **1.** A combining form for adjectives (see -IC) corresponding to nouns ending in *-gen* and *-geny*. **2.** [From photo*genic*, 2.] A combining form meaning *eminently suitable for production or reproduction by a* (given) *medium*, as in radio*genic*, tele*genic*.

ge·nic'u·late (jē·nĭk'ū·lāt), *adj.* [L. *geniculatus*, fr. *geniculum* little knee, knot or joint, dim. of *genu* knee.] Bent abruptly at an angle, like the bent knee.

ge·nic'u·la'tion (-lā'shŭn), *n.* [LL. *geniculatio* a kneeling.] **1.** State of being bent abruptly at an angle. **2.** A geniculate part, process, or formation.

ge'nie (jē'nĭ), *n.* [F. *génie.*] A genius (def. 2 **b**), or jinni.

ge'ni·i (jē'nĭ·ī), *n., pl. of* GENIUS.

gen'i·pap (jĕn'ĭ·păp), *n.* [Sp. *genipe*, Pg. *genipapo*, of Tupian origin.] The edible orange-sized fruit of a tree (*Genipa americana*) of the madder family, of the West Indies and South America; also, the tree itself.

ge·nis'ta (jē·nĭs'tȧ), *n.* [L. broom.] Any plant of a genus (*Genista*) of often spiny shrubs of the pea family, including the woodwaxen. Cf. BROOM, 1 **b**.

gen'i·tal (jĕn'ĭ·tăl; -t'l), *adj.* [OF., fr. L. *genitalis*, fr. *genere*, *gignere*, to beget.] Relating to generation or the sexual organs.

gen'i·tals (-tălz; -t'lz) *n. pl.* The organs of reproduction; esp. the external sexual organs.

gen'i·ti'val (-tī'văl), *adj.* Possessing genitive form; relating to, or derived from, the genitive case; as, "needs" is a *genitival* adverb.

gen'i·tive (jĕn'ĭ·tĭv), *adj.* [L. *genitivus.*] *Gram.* Designating, or pertaining to, that case of inflected nouns which expresses primarily the relation of source or possession, and also analogous relations. In English these various relations are often expressed by means of prepositional phrases with *of* (Latin *amor dei, God's* love, the love of God). The genitive in English now prevailingly denotes the relation of possession, and is therefore commonly called the *possessive*. — *n. Gram.* The genitive case, or a word in it. Abbr. *gen.*

gen'i·to- (jĕn'ĭ·tō-). *Anat.* A combining form, French *genito-*, denoting *genital* (*and*).

gen'i·tor (jĕn'ĭ·tẽr; -tôr), *n.* *Rare.* One who begets.

gen'i·to·u'ri·nar'y (jĕn'ĭ·tō·ū'rĭ·nĕr'ĭ; -nẽr·ĭ), *adj.* Pertaining to the genital and urinary organs or functions.

gen'i·ture (jĕn'ĭ·tūr), *n.* [L. *genitura.*] *Obs.* **a** Generation; birth. **b** *Astrol.* Nativity.

gen'ius (jēn'yŭs *or, esp. in senses* 1 & 2, jē'nĭ·ŭs), *n.; pl.* GENIUSES (-ĕz; -ĭz), GENII (jē'nĭ·ī) (see note, below). [L., tutelar deity, taste, talent, genius, fr. *genere, gignere*, to beget.] **1.** [*often cap.*] *Rom. Relig.* An attendant spirit; tutelar deity. **2.** Hence: **a** [*often cap.*] A spirit presiding over the destiny of a person or place. **b** A nature spirit, esp. a spirit of fire or air; specif., in Arabian and Mohammedan lore, a jinni. **3.** By extension, a person who influences another in character, behavior, or the like; as, his evil *genius*. **4.** Inborn mental gift or endowment; talent. **5.** Peculiar nature; esp., animating spirit, as of a nation; as, the *genius* of the 18th century. **6.** Extraordinary power of invention or origination of any kind; as, a man of *genius*; also, a person endowed with transcendent ability. Cf. TALENT, 4. **7.** The associations and influences (of a place); as, the *genius* of Edinburgh. — **Syn.** See GIFT.

☞ In the senses of defs. 1 and 2 the Latin plural, *genii* is now the only correct plural form. For the other senses *geniuses* is the correct plural.

‖**ge'ni·us lo'ci** (jē'nĭ·ŭs lō'sī). [L.] The tutelary of a place; hence, the pervading spirit of a place or institution, as of a college, etc.

gen'o·cide (jĕn'ō·sīd), *n.* [Gr. *genos* race + *-cide.*] The use or a user of deliberate, systematic measures toward the extermination of a racial, political, or cultural group. — **gen'o·cid'al** (-sīd'ăl; -'l; 2), *adj.*

gen'ome (jē'nōm), **gen'om** (-ŏm), *n.* [*gene* + chromo*some.*] *Biol.* One haploid set of chromosomes with the genes they contain; thus, a diploid cell has two *genomes*, a tetraploid, four *genomes*, etc. — **ge·no'mic** (jē·nō'mĭk; -nŏm'ĭk), *adj.*

gen'o·type (jĕn'ō·tīp), *n.* [Gr. *genos* race, kind + *-type.*] *Biol.* **1.** The type species of a genus. **2.** The genetic make-up of an individual or group; also, a group of individuals sharing a (specified) genetic make-up. Cf. PHENOTYPE. — **gen'o·typ'ic** (-tĭp'ĭk), **gen'o·typ'i·cal** (-ĭ·kăl), *adj.* — **gen'o·typ'i·cal·ly**, *adv.*

-genous. [*-gen* + *-ous.*] A suffix in adjectives corresponding to nouns ending in *-gen, -geny* signifying: **a** *Producing, yielding.* **b** *Produced by* or *arising in.*

gen're (zhäN'r'), *n.* [F.] **1.** A kind, sort, or species; category; — applied esp. to works of literature or art as falling into distinctive groups with respect to style, form, purpose, etc. **2.** *Fine Arts.* A class of art, esp. painting, in which subjects of everyday life are treated realistically; — also used attributively; as, a *genre* painter.

gen'ro' (gĕn'rō'), *n.* [Jap. *genrō*, lit., first (of the) elders.] See ELDER STATESMEN.

gens (jĕnz), *n.; pl.* GENTES (jĕn'tēz). [L. See GENTLE, *adj.*] *Rom. Hist.* A clan embracing the families of the same stock in the male line.

gent (jĕnt), *adj.* [OF.] *Obs.* **1.** Of gentle birth. **2.** Graceful; pretty; elegant.

gent (jĕnt), *n.; pl.* GENTS (jĕnts). *Vulgar.* Shortened form of GENTLEMAN.

gen·teel' (jĕn·tēl'), *adj.* [F. *gentil.* See GENTLE.] **1.** Having qualities regarded as belonging to high birth and breeding; polite; well-bred. **2.** Graceful in mien or form; elegant. **3.** Suited to a lady or a gentleman; stylish. — **gen·teel'ly**, *adv.* — **gen·teel'ness**, *n.*

☞ *Genteel* is now regarded as at least inelegant, except when used humorously or somewhat sarcastically.

gen'tian (jĕn'shăn), *n.* [OF. *gentiane*, fr. L. *gentiana*, fr. *Gentius*, an Illyrian king.] **1.** Any plant (genera *Gentiana* or *Dasystephana*) typifying a family (Gentianaceae, the gentian family) of smooth, opposite-leaved bitter herbs, prized for their handsome flowers, usually blue, as the ***five-flowered gentian*** (*G. quinquefolia*) of eastern North America. The North American ***closed gentian*** (*Dasystephana andrewsii*) blooms in the early fall and has clusters of blue tubular flowers which never open. The eastern North American ***fringed gentian*** (*Gentiana crinita*) has blue tubular, deeply fringed flowers. **2.** The roots of the yellow gentian (*G. lutea*), used as a tonic and stomachic. — **gen'ti·a·na'ceous** (jĕn'shĭ·ȧ·nā'shŭs), *adj.*

gen'tian·el'la (jĕn'shăn·ĕl'ȧ; jĕn'shĭ·ȧ·nĕl'ȧ), *n.* [NL., dim. of L. *gentiana* gentian.] Any of several gentians, esp. the blue-flowered alpine species (*Gentiana acaulis*).

gentian violet. A purple dye, a mixture of methyl derivatives, used as a microscopic stain and bactericide.

‖**gen'til'** (zhäN'tē'), *adj.* [F.] Gentle; well-bred.

gen'tile (jĕn'tīl), *n.* [L. and F.; F. *gentil*, fr. L. *gentilis* of the same clan or race.] **1.** As used by the Jews, one of non-Jewish faith or race; as used by the Christians, one not a Jew; esp., a Christian as distinguished from a Jew; formerly, as used by Christians, a heathen. **2.** Among the Mormons, a non-Mormon. — *adj.* **1.** [*often cap.*] Belonging to the nations at large, as distinguished from the Jews; also, belonging or pertaining to Christians, as distinguished from Jews; by extension, belonging or pertaining to non-Mormons. **2.** Heathen; pagan. **3.** (*pron.* -tĭl; -tīl) Pertaining to a nation, tribe, or clan.

gen'ti·lesse' (jĕn'tĭ·lĕs'), *n.* [OF. *gentilesce, gentelise.* See GENTLE.] *Archaic.* Quality of being gentle.

gen'til·ism (jĕn'tīl·ĭz'm; -tĭ·lĭz'm), *n.* **1.** Heathenism; paganism. **2.** Tribal feeling; devotion to one's gens.

gen·til'i·ty (jĕn·tĭl'ĭ·tĭ), *n.* **1.** Gentle birth. **2.** Qualities appropriate to those who are wellborn, as self-respect, dignity, courage, courtesy. **3.** *Rare.* The gentry.

gen'tle (jĕn't'l), *adj.;* GEN'TLER (-tlẽr); GEN'TLEST (-tlĕst; -tlĭst). [OF. *gentil* noble, of high birth, fr. L. *gentilis* of the same clan, fr. *gens, gentis*, tribe, race.] **1.** Wellborn. **2.** Honorable; as, of *gentle* extraction; of, or appropriate to, good birth or high position. **3.** *Archaic.* Chivalrous. **4.** Hence, used as an epithet of respect or conciliation; as, *gentle* reader. **5.** Tamed; docile; as, a *gentle* horse. **6.** Refined in manners; not harsh; as, a *gentle* nature. **7.** Soft; soothing; as, a *gentle* touch. **8.** Moderate; as, a *gentle* warmth. **9.** Of the wind, designating a velocity of, usually, 8 to 12 miles per hour. Cf. BEAUFORT'S SCALE. — **Syn.** See SOFT.

— *n. Archaic.* One wellborn; a gentleman.

— *v. t.;* GEN'TLED (-t'ld); GEN'TLING (-tlĭng). **1.** *Obs.* To raise from the vulgar; to ennoble. **2.** To render gentle, smooth, or easy. **3.** *Colloq.* To make docile, as a horse.

gentle craft. **a** *Obs.* The art or trade of shoemaking. **b** Angling, for sport; — so called by Izaak Walton.

gen'tle·folk' (jĕn't'l·fōk'), **gen'tle·folks'** (-fōks'), *n. pl.* Persons of gentle or good family and breeding.

gen'tle·man (-măn), *n.; pl.* -MEN (-mĕn). **1.** *Chiefly Hist.* A man wellborn; sometimes, anyone above the social condition of a yeoman. **2.** A well-bred man of fine feelings, good education, and social position. **3.** A servant, esp. a valet, of a person of high rank. **4.** A man, irrespective of condition; — esp. in *pl.*, as in addressing a group of men.

gen'tle·man-at-arms', *n.; pl.* GENTLEMEN-AT-ARMS. One of a band of forty gentlemen who attend the sovereign on state occasions, formerly called **gen'tle·men-pen'sion·ers.**

gen'tle·man-com'mon·er, *n.; pl.* GENTLEMEN-COMMONERS. One of a privileged class of commoners at Oxford and Cambridge, paying higher fees than ordinary commoners.

gen'tle·man·like' (jĕn't'l·măn·līk'), *adj.* Resembling or appropriate to a gentleman. — **gen'tle·man·like'ness**, *n.*

gen'tle·man·ly (-lĭ), *adj.* Having the character of, or characteristic of, a gentleman, in nature, behavior, etc.

gentleman of fortune. A gentleman seeking fortune by hazard; hence, a sharper; also, an adventurer.

gentleman of the road. A highwayman.

gentleman's, *or* **gentlemen's, agreement.** An informal substitute for an agreement, secured only by the honor of the participants.

gentleman's gentleman; *pl.* GENTLEMEN'S GENTLEMEN. A valet.

gen'tle·ness (jĕn't'l·nĕs; -nĭs), *n.* Quality or state of being gentle; esp., softness of manners, disposition, etc.

gentle sex, the. The female sex; women in general.

gen'tle·wom'an (jĕn't'l·wŏŏm'ăn), *n.; pl.* -WOMEN (-wĭm'ĕn; -ĭn). A woman of good family or breeding; also, *Now Hist.*, a woman attending a lady of rank.

gen'tly (jĕn'tlĭ), *adv.* In a gentle, soothing manner.

Gen·too' (jĕn·tōō'), *n.; pl.* -TOOS (-tōōz'). [Pg. *gentio* gentile, heathen. See GENTILE.] A Hindu; specif., a Telugu.

gen'trice (jĕn'trĭs), *n.* [OF. *genterise.*] *Archaic.* **1.** Gentility of birth; rank. **2.** Gentle feeling; good breeding.

gen'try (jĕn'trĭ), *n.* [OF. *genterise, gentelise.*] **1.** *Obs.* Birth; rank by birth; esp., gentle birth. **2.** People of education and good breeding; specif., *Eng.*, those between the nobility and the yeomanry. **3.** *Archaic.* The qualities appropriate to those of gentle birth, as courtesy, generosity, good breeding. **4.** People; persons of a class; — usually with contemptuous or humorous significance; as, the light-fingered *gentry*.

gen'ty (jĕn'tĭ), *adj.* [F. *gentil.*] *Dial.* Neat; trim.

gen'u·flect (jĕn'ū·flĕkt; jĕn'ū·flĕkt'), *v. i.* [See GENUFLECTION.] To bend the knee, as in worship.

gen'u·flec'tion, gen'u·flex'ion (jĕn'ū·flĕk'shŭn), *n.* [ML. *genuflexio*, fr. L. *genu* knee + *flexio* a bending. See FLEX.] Act of bending the knee, esp. in worship.

gen'u·ine (jĕn'ū·ĭn), *adj.* [L. *genuinus*, fr. the root of *genere, gignere*, to beget.] **1.** Actually belonging to, or proceeding from, the reputed source, origin, or author; authentic. **2.** Of or pert. to the original stock or source; as, the *genuine* Aztecs. **3.** Sincere; free from hypocrisy. — **Syn.** See AUTHENTIC. — **gen'u·ine·ly**, *adv.* — **gen'u·ine·ness**, *n.*

ge'nus (jē'nŭs), *n.; pl.* GENERA (jĕn'ẽr·ȧ), rarely GENUSES (jē'nŭs·ĕz; -ĭz). [L., birth, race, kind, sort.] **1.** *Logic.* A class of objects divided into several subordinate species. See SPECIES, 6. **2.** *Biol.* A category of classification between family and species; a group of structurally or phylogenetically related species, or an isolated species exhibiting unusual differentiation. The first word of the scientific name of a species is the genus name, and is capitalized. **3.** A class; order; kind; sort.

-geny. [Gr. suffix *-geneia.* See -GEN.] A suffix denoting *generation, production, origin* and *development of,* as in biogeny, ontogeny.

ge'o- (jē'ō-). [Gr. prefix *geō-,* fr. *gaia, gē,* the earth.] A combining form signifying *earth, ground,* as in *geo*centric.

ge'o·cen'tric (-sĕn'trĭk), **ge'o·cen'tri·cal** (-trĭ·kăl), *adj.* [*geo-* + Gr. *kentron* center.] Relating to or measured from the earth's center; having, or relating to, the earth as a center.

ge'o·chem'is·try (-kĕm'ĭs·trĭ), *n.* The study of the chemical composition of, and chemical changes in, the crust of the earth. — **ge'o·chem'i·cal** (-ĭ·kăl), *adj.*

ge'ode (jē'ōd), *n.* [L. *geodes,* fr. Gr. *geōdēs* earthlike, fr. *gaia, gē,* earth + *eidos* form.] *Geol.* A nodule of stone having a cavity lined with crystals or mineral matter.

ge'o·des'ic (jē'ō·dĕs'ĭk; -dē'sĭk), *adj.* Also **ge'o·des'i·cal** (-ĭ·kăl). *Math.* Of or pertaining to geodesy; geodetic.

ge·od'e·sist (jē·ŏd'ē·sĭst), *n.* One versed in geodesy.

ge·od'e·sy (-sĭ), *n.* [Gr. *geōdaisia,* fr. *gaia, gē,* the earth + *daiein* to divide.] *Math.* That branch of applied mathematics which determines the exact positions of points and the figures and areas of large portions of the earth's surface, or the shape and size of the earth, and the variations of terrestrial gravity.

ge'o·det'ic (jē'ō·dĕt'ĭk), *adj.* Also **ge'o·det'i·cal** (-ĭ·kăl). Of or pertaining to, or determined by, geodesy; geodesic; as, *geodetic* surveying. — **ge'o·det'i·cal·ly,** *adv.*

ge'o·dy·nam'ic (jē'ō·dī·năm'ĭk; -dĭ-), **ge'o·dy·nam'i·cal** (-ĭ·kăl), *adj.* Of, pert. to, or noting the forces or processes within the earth. — **ge'o·dy·nam'ics** (-ĭks), *n.;* see -ICS.

ge·og'no·sy (jē·ŏg'nō·sĭ), *n.* [F. *géognosie,* fr. Gr. *gaia, gē,* the earth + *gnōsis* knowing, knowledge, fr. *gignōskein* to know.] That part of geology treating of the materials of the earth and its constitution.

ge·og'ra·pher (jē·ŏg'rȧ·fēr), *n.* One versed in geography.

ge'o·graph'i·cal (jē'ō·grăf'ĭ·kăl), *adj.* Also **ge'o·graph'ic** (-ĭk). Of or pertaining to geography; also, belonging to or characteristic of a particular region. — **ge'o·graph'i·cal·ly,** *adv.*

ge·og'ra·phy (jē·ŏg'rȧ·fĭ), *n.; pl.* -PHIES (-fĭz). [F. *géographie,* fr L. *geographia,* fr. Gr. *geōgraphia,* fr. *gaia, gē,* the earth + *graphē* description.] **1.** The science of the earth and its life; esp., the description of land, sea, air, and the distribution of plant and animal life, including man and his industries. **2.** A treatise on this science; also, a geographic description. **3.** The natural features, collectively, of an area; as, the *geography* of Cuba.

ge'oid (jē'oid), *n.* The figure of the earth; the mean sea level conceived as extended continuously through all the continents. The figure of the geoid is a spheroid.

ge'o·log'ic (jē'ō·lŏj'ĭk), **ge'o·log'i·cal** (-ĭ·kăl), *adj.* Of or relating to geology. — **ge'o·log'i·cal·ly,** *adv.*

ge·ol'o·gist (jē·ŏl'ō·jĭst), *n.* One versed in geology.

ge·ol'o·gize (-jīz), *v. i.* To study geology or make geological investigations; to discourse as a geologist.

ge·ol'o·gy (-jĭ), *n.; pl.* -GIES (-jĭz). [*geo-* + *-logy.*] **1.** The science which treats of the history of the earth and its life, esp. as recorded in the rocks. **2.** A treatise on this science. **3.** The materials of this science; rocks, collectively; as, the *geology* of Utah.

ge'o·man'cer (jē'ō·măn'sēr), *n.* One who practices geomancy.

ge'o·man'cy (-sĭ), *n.* [OF. *geomance, geomancie,* fr. ML. *geomantia,* fr. Gr. *gaia, gē,* the earth + *manteia* divination.] Divination by means of figures or lines. — **ge'o·man'tic** (-măn'tĭk), *adj.*

ge·om'e·ter (jē·ŏm'ē·tēr), *n.* [L. *geometres, geometra,* fr. Gr. *geōmetrēs,* fr. *gaia, gē,* the earth + *metron* measure.] A geometrician.

ge'o·met'ric (jē'ō·mĕt'rĭk), **ge'o·met'ri·cal** (-rĭ·kăl), *adj.* **1.** Pertaining or according to the methods or principles of geometry; determined by geometry; as, ***geometric mean*** (see MEAN, *n.,* 5); ***geometric progression*** *or* ***series*** (see PROGRESSION, 4); ***geometric proportion*** (see PROPORTION, 4 **a**). **2.** [*cap.*] *Gr. Antiq.* Designating, or pertaining to, a style of Greek pottery marked by simple geometric designs, usually rectilinear, such as bands, zigzags, triangles, etc. **3.** *Design.* Utilizing geometric motives, outlines, etc.; as, a *geometric* pattern in a rug. Cf. FRET, PARQUETRY, *Illusts.* — **ge'o·met'ri·cal·ly,** *adv.*

ge·om'e·tri'cian (jē·ŏm'ē·trĭsh'ăn; jē'ō·mē-), *n.* One skilled in geometry; a geometer; a mathematician.

ge·om'e·trid (jē·ŏm'ē·trĭd), *n.* [L. *geometra* geometer.] Any of a family (Geometridae) of medium-sized moths with large wings, whose larvae usually have two pairs of prolegs and progress by a looping movement, whence they are called *measuring worms, loopers,* etc. — **ge·om'e·trid,** *adj.*

ge·om'e·trize (-trīz), *v. i.* To make geometrical constructions; to work by geometrical principles.

ge·om'e·try (-trĭ), *n.; pl.* -TRIES (-trĭz). [OF. *geometrie,* fr. L. *geometria,* fr. Gr. *geōmetria,* fr. *geōmetrein* to measure land, fr. *gaia, gē,* the earth + *metrein* to measure.] **1.** That branch of mathematics which investigates the relations, properties, and measurement of solids, surfaces, lines, and angles; the theory of space and of figures in space. Cf. ANALYTIC GEOMETRY. **2.** A treatise on this science.

ge'o·mor'phic (jē'ō·môr'fĭk), *adj.* Of or pert. to the figure of the earth or the form of its surface; like the earth.

ge'o·mor·phol'o·gy (-môr·fŏl'ō·jĭ), *n.* That department of physical geography which deals with the form of the earth, the general configuration of its surface, the distribution of land and water, and the changes that take place in the evolution of land forms. — **ge'o·mor'pho·log'i·cal** (-môr'fō·lŏj'ĭ·kăl), *adj.*

ge·oph'a·gy (jē·ŏf'ȧ·jĭ), *n.* [*geo-* + Gr. *phagein* to eat.] The practice of eating earthy substances, esp. clay. — **ge·oph'a·gism** (-jĭz'm), *n.* — **ge·oph'a·gist** (-jĭst), *n.*

ge'o·phys'ics (jē'ō·fĭz'ĭks), *n.;* see -ICS. *Geol.* The physics of the earth, or the science treating of the agencies which modify the earth. — **ge'o·phys'i·cal** (-ĭ·kăl), *adj.* — **ge'o·phys'i·cist** (-ĭ·sĭst), *n.*

ge'o·phyte (jē'ō·fīt), *n.* *Phytogeog.* A plant growing in earth; — contrasted with *hydrophyte* and *epiphyte.*

ge'o·po·lit'i·cal (-pō·lĭt'ĭ·kăl), **ge'o·pol'i·tic** (-pŏl'ĭ·tĭk), *adj.* Of or according or relating to geopolitics. — **ge'o·po·lit'i·cal·ly,** *adv.*

ge'o·pol'i·ti'cian (-pŏl'ĭ·tĭsh'ăn), *n.* Also **ge'o·pol'i·tist** (-pŏl'ĭ·tĭst). An expert or specialist in geopolitics.

ge'o·pol'i·tics (-pŏl'ĭ·tĭks), *n.;* see -ICS. [From G. *Geopolitik,* coined c. 1916 by Rudolf Kjellen (1864–1922), Swedish political scientist and Pan-German geographer.] **1.** Systematic study of internal and continental geographical features, physical, economic, and anthropographic, as essential factors in shaping governmental policies, esp. foreign policy, for achieving national security, — distinguished, by its dynamic quality viewing the state as an organism with requirements for growth, from political geography, which treats static conditions. **2.** A German Nazi expansionist doctrine based upon politico-geographical studies but, as popularized by retired Major General Karl Haushofer, emphasizing strategic frontiers, demand for living space (Lebensraum), and racial, economic, and social pressures as factors demanding reallocation of the earth's surface and resources to effect Nazi dominance of the world island.

ge'o·pon'ic (-pŏn'ĭk), *adj.* [Gr. *geōponikos,* fr. *gaia, gē,* earth + *ponikos* toilsome, fr. *ponos* labor.] Pert. to tillage or agriculture; agricultural; also, rustic.

ge'o·pon'ics (-ĭks), *n.;* see -ICS. The art or science of cultivating the earth; agriculture; also, a treatise on it.

George (jôrj), *n.* **1.** A jewel showing a figure of St. George, forming part of the insignia of the Order of the Garter. **2.** *Obs. Slang.* An English coin bearing St. George's image.

Geor·gette' crepe, *or* **Geor·gette'** (jôr·jĕt'), *n.* A trade-mark applied to a thin silk crepe of very fine texture.

Geor'gi·an (jôr'jĭ·ăn; -jăn; -jyăn), *adj.* **1.** Of or relating to the reigns of the four Georges (1740–1830), or the reign of George V (1910–1936), Kings of Great Britain. **2.** Of or pertaining to Georgia, one of the United States. — *n.* **1.** A native or inhabitant of Georgia, U. S. **2. a** One belonging to the Georgian period. **b** Georgian taste or style.

Geor'gi·an, *adj.* Of or pertaining to Georgia, in Transcaucasia, or the Georgians. — *n.* A member of a race of mountaineers of the Caucasus; also, their agglutinative language.

Geor'gia pine (jôr'jȧ; -jyȧ; -jĭ·ȧ). See PINE.

geor'gic (jôr'jĭk), *adj.* [L. *georgicus,* fr. Gr. *geōrgikos,* fr. *geōrgia* tillage.] Relating to agriculture and rural affairs. — *n.* A poetical composition on husbandry; as, the *Georgics* of Vergil.

ge'o·stat'ic (jē'ō·stăt'ĭk), *adj.* [*geo-* + *static.*] *Civ. Engin.* Relating to pressure exerted by earth or a similar substance.

ge'o·stat'ics (-ĭks), *n.;* see -ICS. *Physics.* That part of the mechanics of rigid bodies which deals with balanced forces; statics as applied to rigid bodies.

ge'o·stroph'ic (jē'ō·strŏf'ĭk), *adj.* [*geo-* + Gr. *strophikos,* fr. *strephein* to turn, twist.] *Meteorol.* Of or pertaining to deflective force due to the rotation of the earth.

ge'o·syn'cline (-sĭn'klīn), **ge'o·syn·cli'nal** (-sĭn·klī'năl; -n'l), *n* *Geol.* A great downward flexure of the earth's crust. Cf. GEANTICLINE. — **ge'o·syn·cli'nal,** *adj.*

ge'o·tax'is (-tăk'sĭs), *n.* [NL., fr. *geo-* + *-taxis.*] *Biol.* A taxis in which the force of gravity is the directive factor. — **ge'o·tac'tic** (-tăk'tĭk), *adj.* — **ge'o·tac'ti·cal·ly** (-tĭ·kăl·ĭ), *adv.*

ge'o·tec·ton'ic (-tĕk·tŏn'ĭk), *adj.* *Geol.* Structural; relating to form, arrangement, and structure of rock masses of the earth's crust; as, *geotectonic* geology.

ge'o·trop'ic (-trŏp'ĭk), *adj.* *Biol.* Characterized by, showing, or pert. to, geotropism. — **ge'o·trop'i·cal·ly** (-ĭ·kăl·ĭ), *adv.*

ge·ot'ro·pism (jē·ŏt'rō·pĭz'm), *n.* [*geo-* + *-tropism.*] *Biol.* Tropism in which gravitational attraction is the orienting factor, as in roots growing down, shoots growing upward, the right-side-up orientation of certain animals; — sometimes, when not otherwise qualified, applied restrictedly to turning or movement toward, rather than away from, the earth. Cf. APOGEOTROPISM.

ge'rah (gē'rȧ), *n.* [Heb. *gērāh,* lit., a bean.] A small Hebrew weight; 1/20th of a shekel.

ge·ra'ni·um (jē·rā'nĭ·ŭm; 58), *n.* [L., fr. Gr. *geranion,* fr. *geranos* crane.] **1.** *Bot.* **a** Any of a large genus (*Geranium*) of plants typifying a family (Geraniaceae, the geranium family) and having, usually, pink or purple flowers and leaves with a pungent odor, including the ***wild geranium*** (*G. maculatum*) of eastern North America, with rose-purple flowers, and the ***herb Robert*** (*G. robertianum*) with small red-purple flowers. The species are also known, from the long slender beak of the carpels, as ***crane's-bill*** (*or* ***cranesbill***). **b** The flower of this plant. **2.** A flower or plant of related genera of this family, esp. of: (1) *Pelargonium,* a genus of South African plants, species of which with showy, chiefly red or white flowers, are widely cultivated as garden plants under the name *geranium,* as the ***fish geranium*** (*P. hortorum*); and (2) *Erodium,* including the forage plant *alfilaria* (which see). The species of both genera are often called *stork's-bill,* and those of *Erodium* called also *heron's-bill.* — **ge·ra'ni·a'ceous** (jē·rā'nĭ·ā'shŭs), *adj.*

ger'bil, ger'bille (jûr'bĭl), *n.* [F. *gerbille.*] Any of various Old World burrowing leaping desert rodents forming a subfamily of the vole family (Cricetidae).

ge'rent (jēr'ĕnt), *n.* [L. *gerens* bearing, managing.] One who rules or manages.

ger'fal'con (jûr'fôl'kŭn; -fô'kŭn), *n.* Gyrfalcon.

ger'i·at'rics (jĕr'ĭ·ăt'rĭks), *n.;* see -ICS. [Gr. *gēras* old age + *-iatrics.*] *Med.* The subdivision of medicine which is concerned with old age and its diseases. — **ger'i·a·tri'cian** (-ȧ·trĭsh'ăn), *n.*

germ (jûrm), *n.* [F. *germe,* fr. L. *germen, germinis,* sprout, germ.] **1.** An embryo in its early stages; a bud; seed. **2.** *Biol.* The germ cells collectively; — disting. from *soma.* **3.** Any microorganism, esp. any of the pathogenic bacteria; a microbe. **4.** That from which anything springs; a rudiment. — *adj.* **a** Germinal. **b** Of, pertaining to, or produced by disease germs.

ger'man (jûr'măn), *adj.* [OF. *germain,* fr. L. *germanus* full, own, having the same parents.] Literally, near of kin; specif.: **a** Of the same parentage; own (brother or sister); — in brother-*german* and sister-*german.* **b** Being the child of one's parent's own brother or sister; own, or first (cousin); — in *cousin-german.* Cf. CONSANGUINITY, *Illust.*

Ger'man, *n.* [L. *Germanus,* prob. of Celtic origin.] **1.** A native or one of the people of Germany. **2. a** The Teutonic language of the Germans, including ***High German*** and ***Low German.*** See INDO-EUROPEAN LANGUAGES, *Table.* **b** The literary and official language of Germany; High German. The older forms are called ***Old High German*** (800–1100) and ***Middle High German*** (1100–1500). **3.** [*not cap.*] **a** A dance consisting of capriciously involved figures intermingled with waltzes, etc.; a cotillion. **b** A social party at which the german is danced. — *adj.* **1.** Of or relating to Germany or the Germans. **2.** Of, belonging to, or in German (the language).

ger·man′der (jûr·măn′dẽr), *n.* [Through corrupted OF. and ML. forms fr. Gr. *chamaidrys*, fr. *chamai* on the ground + *drys* tree.] **a** Any plant of a genus (*Teucrium*) of the mint family. **b** Any plant of a genus (*Veronica*) of the figwort family. See SPEEDWELL.

ger·mane′ (jûr·mān′), *adj.* **1.** = 1st GERMAN. **2.** Closely allied; appropriate. — **Syn.** See RELEVANT. — **ger·mane′ly**, *adv.*

Ger·man′ic (jûr·măn′ĭk), *adj.* **1.** German. **2.** Of or pertaining to the Teutons, or designating or belonging to the Teutonic languages; Teutonic. — *n.* The Teutonic, or Germanic, languages.

Ger′man·ism (jûr′măn·ĭz′m), *n.* **1.** A German idiom. **2.** A characteristic German mode of thought, doctrine, etc. **3.** Adoption or imitation of German habits or traits.

ger·ma′ni·um (jûr·mā′nĭ·ŭm), *n.* [NL., fr. L. *Germania* Germany.] *Chem.* A grayish-white, brittle, metallic element. Symbol, *Ge;* at. no., 32; at. wt., 72.60. It resembles carbon and silicon in some respects and tin in others.

Ger′man·ize (jûr′măn·īz), *v. t.* **1.** To translate into German. **2.** To make German, or like what is distinctively German. — **Ger′man·i·za′tion** (-ĭ·zā′shŭn; -ī·zā′-), *n.* — **Ger′man·iz′er** (-īz′ẽr), *n.*

German measles. Rubella.

Ger′ma·no- (jûr′mȧ·nō-). A combining form for *German*, as in **Ger·man′o·phile** (jûr·măn′ō·fīl; -fĭl), **Ger′ma·no·pho′bi·a** (jûr′mȧ·nō·fō′bĭ·ȧ).

German shepherd dog. A shepherd dog of a breed originating in northern Europe at an uncertain date. It is intelligent and trains well and is often used in police work; — hence often called **German police dog.**

German silver. A silver-white alloy of copper, zinc, and nickel; — now usually called *nickel silver.*

German text. *Print.* The modern German type, used in English printing for ornamental headings, etc., as in the words 𝔊𝔢𝔯𝔪𝔞𝔫 𝔗𝔢𝔵𝔱.

German tinder. Punk; amadou.

germ cell. An egg or sperm cell; — opp. to *somatic cell.*

ger′men (jûr′mĕn), *n.; pl.* -MENS (-mĕnz), -MINA (-mĭ·nȧ). [L.] *Obs. exc. Figurative.* A germ.

ger′mi·cide (jûr′mĭ·sīd), *n.* [*germ* + *-cide.*] Any agent which destroys germs or microorganisms, esp. disease germs. — **ger′mi·cid′al** (-sīd′ăl; -′l; 2), *adj.*

ger′mi·nal (jûr′mĭ·năl; -n′l), *adj.* Pertaining to a germ or germ cell; embryonic; as, *germinal* band, groove, etc.

‖**Ger′mi′nal′** (zhĕr′mē′nȧl′; jûr′mĭ·năl), *n.* [F.] **a** See REVOLUTIONARY CALENDAR. **b** [*not cap.*] Springtime.

germinal disk. *Embryol.* **a** A disklike area of the blastoderm of eggs of certain vertebrates, in which the embryo proper first appears. **b** In meroblastic eggs with much yolk, the disklike protoplasmic part, which undergoes segmentation.

germinal vesicle. **a** *Embryol.* The nucleus of the egg before the formation of the polar bodies. **b** *Bot.* = OÖSPHERE.

ger′mi·nant (jûr′mĭ·nănt), *adj.* Germinating; sprouting.

ger′mi·nate (-nāt), *v. i.* [L. *germinatus*, past part. of *germinare* to sprout, fr. *germen* germ.] To begin to grow or develop; — said esp. of a spore or seed, and, by extension, of a bud or plant; to sprout. — *v. t.* To cause to sprout or develop.

ger′mi·na′tion (-nā′shŭn), *n.* Process of germinating; beginning of vegetation or growth.

ger′mi·na′tive (jûr′mĭ·nā′tĭv; -nȧ·tĭv), *adj.* Pert. to germination; having power to grow or develop.

germ layer. *Embryol.* Any of the layers of cells differentiated in the early stages of embryonic development.

germ plasm *or* **plasma.** *Biol.* The substance contained in the germ cells, by which hereditary characters are transmitted; idioplasm.

germ theory. **a** *Biol.* The theory that living organisms can be produced only by the development of living germs. Cf. BIOGENESIS, ABIOGENESIS. **b** *Med.* The theory which attributes contagious and infectious diseases, suppurative lesions, etc., to germs or microparasites.

ge·ron′to- (jĕ·rŏn′tō-), **geront-.** A combining form (from Greek *gerōn, gerontos*, an old man) meaning *old people* or *old age*, as in **ger′on·toc′ra·cy** (jĕr′ŏn·tŏk′rȧ·sĭ), government by the old; **ger′on·tol′o·gy** (-tŏl′ō·jĭ), the scientific study of the phenomena of old age.

-gerous. [L. *-ger*, fr. *gerere* to bear, carry.] A suffix signifying *bearing, producing*, as in crystalli*gerous*, producing crystals.

ger′ry·man′der (gĕr′ĭ·măn′dẽr; jĕr′ĭ·măn′dẽr), *v. t.* [*Gerry* + sala*mander;* after Gov. Elbridge *Gerry*, whose party, in 1812, divided Essex Co., Mass., so as to form a dragon-shaped district.] *Political Cant, U. S.* To divide (a state, county, etc.) into election districts or other civil divisions in an unnatural and unfair way, esp. to give a political party an advantage over its opponent. — (gĕr′ĭ·măn′dẽr; jĕr′ĭ·măn′dẽr), *n.* The act or method of gerrymandering, or its result.

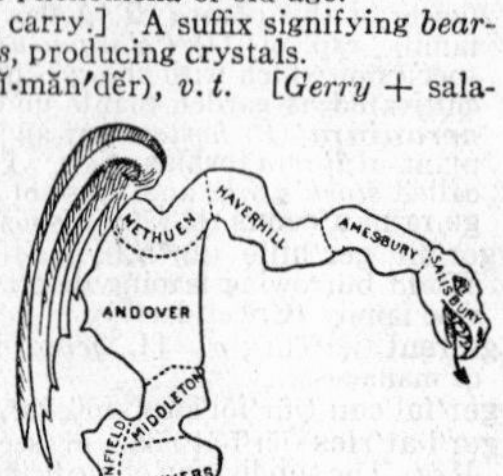

Gerrymander.

ger′und (jĕr′ŭnd), *n.* [LL. *gerundium*, fr. *gerere* to bear, carry.] *Gram.* **a** In Latin, the verbal noun expressing the action of the verb as generalized or in continuance (ars *vivendi*, the art of living). **b** In modern English, the verbal noun in *-ing* in certain uses in which it performs the function of a substantive, often taking the case phrase construction (we did not dream *of its being* she), and at the same time shows the verbal features of tense and voice (*choosing, having chosen, being chosen*), taking adverbial qualifiers, and governing objects. — **ge·run′di·al** (jĕ·rŭn′dĭ·ăl), *adj.*

ge·run′dive (jĕ·rŭn′dĭv), *adj.* [LL. *gerundivus.*] *Gram.* (*Chiefly Lat.*) Pertaining to, or partaking of the nature of, the gerund; gerundial. — *n. Gram.* **a** The Latin adjective having the same suffix as the gerund, expressing necessity, fitness, etc., and serving as the future passive participle. **b** An analogous verbal adjective in another language.

Ge′ry·on (jē′rĭ·ŏn; gĕr′ĭ·ŭn), *n.* [L., fr. Gr. *Gēryōn.*] *Gr. Myth.* A three-bodied winged monster, slain by Hercules.

ges′so (jĕs′ō), *n.* [It., chalk, plaster.] Plaster of Paris, or gypsum, esp. as prepared for use in painting, etc.

gest, geste (jĕst), *n.* [OF. *geste.* See JEST.] **1.** A deed; adventure; exploit. **2.** A tale of adventures; a romance, esp. in meter. Cf. CHANSON DE GESTE.

gest, geste, *n.* [F. *geste*, fr. L. *gestus*, fr. *gerere* to conduct (oneself).] *Archaic.* Gesture; deportment.

gest (jĕst), *n.* [OF. *giste* abode.] *Obs.* A stage or route in traveling, esp. in a royal progress.

Ge·stalt′ psy·chol′o·gy (gĕ·shtält′). [G. *gestalt* form.] Psychology based on the theory that physical, psychological, and biological events do not occur through the summation of separate elements, as sensations or reflexes, but through formed patterns of these, integrated units which function singly or in interrelation; configurationism. Each of these patterns is called a **Gestalt** (*pl.* GESTALTEN).

Ge·sta′po (gĕ·stä′pō; gĕ·shtä′pō), *n.* [G., fr. *Ge*heime *Sta*ats *po*lizei, lit., secret state police.] The German secret state police organized under the Nazi regime for operation especially against political and treasonable offenses.

ges′tate (jĕs′tāt), *v. t.* [See GESTATION.] To carry in the uterus during pregnancy.

ges·ta′tion (jĕs·tā′shŭn), *n.* [L. *gestatio* a bearing, fr. *gestare* to bear, carry, intens. fr. *gerere, gestum*, to bear.] Act or period of carrying young in the uterus; pregnancy. — **ges·ta′tion·al** (-ăl; -′l), *adj.*

ges′tic (jĕs′tĭk), **ges′ti·cal** (-tĭ·kăl), *adj.* [See GEST gesture.] Relating to bodily motion, esp. dancing.

ges·tic′u·late (jĕs·tĭk′ū·lāt), *v. i.* [L. *gesticulatus*, past part. of *gesticulari* to gesticulate, fr. *gesticulus* a mimic gesture, dim. of *gestus* gesture.] To make gestures, esp. when speaking. — **ges·tic′u·la′tive** (-lā′tĭv; -lȧ·tĭv), *adj.* — **ges·tic′u·la′tor** (-lā′tẽr), *n.*

ges·tic′u·la′tion (-lā′shŭn), *n.* **1.** Act of gesticulating, or making gestures. **2.** A gesture, as in representing passion, or enforcing arguments.

ges·tic′u·la·to′ry (jĕs·tĭk′ū·lȧ·tō′rĭ *or, esp. Brit.*, -tẽr·ĭ), *adj.* Representing by, belonging to, or resembling, gesticulation.

ges′tion (jĕs′chŭn), *n.* [L. *gestio* a managing, fr. *gerere* to bear, manage.] *Archaic.* Management; conduct.

ges′ture (-tūr), *n.* [ML. *gestura* mode of action, fr. L. *gerere, gestum*, to bear, behave, act.] **1.** *Obs.* Carriage; posture. **2.** A motion of the body or limbs intended to express an idea or a passion, or to enforce or emphasize an argument, assertion, or opinion. **3.** The use of motions of the limbs or body as a mode of expression. **4.** [Influenced by F. *geste.*] Something done or said merely by way of formality, courtesy, or diplomacy.
— *v. i.* To make gestures or a gesture; gesticulate. — **ges′tur·er** (-tūr·ẽr), *n.*

‖**Ge·sund′heit** (gĕ·zŏŏnt′hīt), *n.* [G.] (To your) health; — a salutation, as when drinking, or after a sneeze.

get (gĕt), *v. t.; past* GOT (gŏt), *Archaic & Dial.* GAT (găt); *past part.* GOT, *or* (*esp. in U. S.*) GOT′TEN (gŏt′′n); *pres. part.* GET′TING. [ON. *geta.*] **1.** To come into possession of; to obtain; acquire; receive. **2.** Hence, in idiomatic uses: **a** To reach by some process, as hunting, sounding, etc.; as, to *get* a fine stag; to *get* bottom. **b** *Colloq.* To receive a sentence of; as, to *get* three months. **c** *Slang.* To hit; strike; as, the blow *got* him in the mouth. **d** Procure as by fetching; as, let me *get* my hat. **e** To establish communication with, as by telephone. **3.** Specif.: *Chiefly Colloq.* To obtain the mastery over; as: **a** To overmaster; as, a bad habit *gets* one at last. **b** To capture; as, the police *got* the thief. **c** To baffle; puzzle; as, this problem *gets* me; also, to annoy; irritate. **d** To pen; trap; hence, to bring to retribution; also, to kill; as, to *get* the murderer. **e** In certain sports, to retire, or put out (a player), esp. by making a catch. **4.** With *have* and *had*: Pleonastically, *Colloq.*, to be obliged to; as, he has *got* to do it. **5.** **a** To cause to be in any position or condition; as, to *get* one's feet wet. **b** To cause to move or be removed; as, to *get* him away. **c** To get ready; prepare; as, to *get* dinner. **6.** To induce; as, to *get* him to go. **7.** To betake; — reflexively; as, let us *get* us away. **8.** To beget; — now of animals.
— *v. i.* **1.** To arrive at, or bring oneself or itself into, a state, condition, or position; as, to *get* to be friends; to *get* free. **2.** To make acquisition; to profit.

Syn. **Get, obtain, procure, secure, acquire, gain, win, earn** mean to come into possession of. **Get**, a very general term, may or may not imply effort or initiative; **obtain** suggests the attainment of an end sought for or hoped for; **procure**, effort in obtaining something for oneself or another; **secure**, difficulty in obtaining and fixing that obtained in one's possession or under one's control; **acquire** stresses addition, as by inevitable result, to something already possessed; **gain** adds to *obtain* the implications of struggle and, usually, of material value in the thing obtained; **win** adds to *gain* the implication of qualities or circumstances that favor; **earn** implies a correspondence between the effort and what one gets by effort.

— ***get ahead of.*** *Colloq.* To surpass.
— *n.* **1.** An offspring (of an animal); breed. **2.** Begetting; as, colts of Man o' War's *get.* **3.** In certain games, as lawn tennis and handball, a return of a shot that ordinarily would score for the opponent.

get′-at′-a·ble (gĕt′ăt′ȧ·b′l), *adj.* Possible to be reached, attained, got, or known; approachable; accessible.

get′a·way′ (gĕt′ȧ·wā′), *n.* The act or fact of getting away, starting, going, etc.

Geth·sem′a·ne (gĕth·sĕm′ȧ·nē), *n.* [Gr. *Gethsēmanē, Gethsēmanei*, fr. Aram. *gath shemānī(m)* oil press.] **1.** *Bib.* The enclosure outside of Jerusalem, scene of the agony and arrest of Jesus. **2.** [*sometimes not cap.*] Any place or occasion of great, esp. mental or spiritual, suffering. Cf. CALVARY, 3.

get′ter (gĕt′ẽr), *n.* **1.** One who gets. **2.** *Elec.* A substance placed in a vacuum tube to remove traces of free gas.

get′up′ (gĕt′ŭp′), *n. Colloq.* General composition or structure; make-up.

ge′um (jē′ŭm), *n.* [L., herb bennet.] = AVENS.

gew′gaw (gū′gô), *n.* A showy trifle; bauble. — *adj.* Showy.

gey (gā), *adj. Scot.* Considerable; tolerable. — *adv. Scot.* Considerably; very; pretty.

gey′lies, gay′lies (gā′lĭs), *adv. Scot.* Fairly well; very much.

gey′ser (gī′zẽr; gī′sẽr; *Brit. also* gā′zẽr, gē′-, *usually* gē′- *in sense* 2), *n.* [Icel. *geysir*, the name of a certain hot spring, fr. *geysa* to rush furiously.] **1.** A spring which throws forth intermittent jets of heated water and steam. **2.** *Brit.* An apparatus for heating water rapidly, esp. by injected steam.

gey′ser·ite (gī′zẽr·īt; gī′sẽr-), *n.* [From GEYSER.] Hydrous silica, a variety of opal, deposited in white or grayish concretionary masses around some hot springs and geysers.

ghar'ry, ghar'ri (gär'ĭ), *n.* [Hind. *gāṛī.*] *India.* Any wheeled cart or carriage, usually one plying for hire.

ghast (gȧst), *adj. Archaic.* Ghastly.

ghast'ful, gast'ful (gȧst'fo͝ol; -f'l), *adj.* [See GHASTLY, *adj.*] *Archaic.* Fit to make one aghast; dreadful.

ghast'ly (gȧst'lĭ; 9), *adj.*; -LI·ER (-lĭ·ẽr); -LI·EST. [ME. *gastlich, gastli,* fearful, causing fear, fr. *gasten* to terrify, fr. AS. *gæstan.*] **1.** Horrible; shocking. **2.** Like a ghost in appearance; deathlike; pallid. **3.** *Obs.* Terrified. — *adv.* In a ghastly manner. — **ghast'li·ness,** *n.*

Syn. **Ghastly, grisly, gruesome** (*or* **grewsome**), **macabre, grim, lurid** mean horrifyingly repellent in appearance. **Ghastly** suggests the terrifying aspects of death or bloodshed; **grisly** and **gruesome**, an inspiring of shuddering horror; **macabre**, preoccupation with the horrors of death; **grim**, a fierce and forbidding aspect; **lurid**, ghastliness and sinisterness.

ghat, ghaut (gôt), *n.* [Hind. *ghāṭ.*] **1.** *India.* A mountain pass. **2.** A mountain range; esp., in *pl.*, the two coastal ranges of the peninsula of India, the Eastern and Western Ghats. **3.** In India, a landing place, with stairs descending to a river for purposes of bathing, etc. The ***burning ghat*** is the level space at the head of a ghat, the space where Hindus cremate their dead.

gha'zi (gä'zē), *n.* [Ar. *ghāzi.*] **1.** Among Moslems, a warrior champion, esp. in the destruction of infidels. **2.** [*cap.*] In the Turkish republic, a title indicating the highest rank, esp. as applied to the president. — **gha'zism** (-zĭz'm), *n.*

Ghe'ber, Ghe'bre (gā'bẽr; gē'bẽr), *n.* [F. *guèbre,* fr. Per. *gabr.*] One of the Zoroastrian fire worshipers remaining in Persia after the Moslem conquest. Cf. PARSI.

ghee (gē), *n.* [Hind. *ghī* clarified butter, fr. Skr. *ghṛta.*] A semifluid butter made chiefly in India, usually by melting buffalo butter, cooling, and pouring off the more liquid portion, which is the *ghee.*

gheld (gĕld). Incorrect var. of GELD.

gher'kin (gûr'kĭn), *n.* [D. *agurkje.*] *Bot.* **a** The small prickly fruit of a species of cucumber (*Cucumis anguria*), used for pickling; also, the plant producing it. **b** The immature common garden cucumber, used for the same purpose.

ghet'to (gĕt'ō), *n.*; *pl.* GHETTOS (-ōz), GHETTI (-tē). [It.] **1.** *Hist.* The quarter of a city to which Jews were restricted for residence. **2.** A quarter of a city in which members of a racial group are segregated.

Ghib'el·line (gĭb'ĕ·lĭn; -lēn; -līn), *n.* [It.*Ghibellino.*] *Hist.* A member of a great political faction in medieval Italy which upheld the authority of the German emperors in Italy. See GUELPH. — *adj.* Of or pertaining to this faction. — **Ghib'el·lin·ism** (-ĭz'm), *n.*

ghost (gōst), *n.* [AS. *gāst* breath, spirit, soul.] **1.** *Archaic.* The soul as the seat of life or intelligence; hence, the spirit of man as distinguished from the body. **2.** A spirit or daemon. **3.** A disembodied soul; the soul or spirit of a deceased person conceived either as a denizen of the unseen world or as appearing to the living in bodily likeness; hence, specter; spook. **4.** *Obs.* The Holy Ghost. **5.** Any faint shadowy semblance; a glimmering; as, he didn't have a *ghost* of a chance to escape. **6.** One who does work, esp. literary or artistic work, for another who takes the credit. — *v. i. & t.* **1.** To float about, or to haunt, as a ghost. **2.** To act as a literary or artistic ghost (for); esp., to ghostwrite. — **ghost'like'** (gōst'līk'), *adj. & adv.*

ghost dance. A religious dance of the North American Indians, looked upon as a rite of invocation to bring the dancer into communion with the spirits of departed friends.

ghost'ly (gōst'lĭ), *adj.*; GHOST'LI·ER (-lĭ·ẽr); GHOST'LI·EST. **1.** Relating to the soul; spiritual; as, a *ghostly* confessor. **2.** Of or pertaining to an apparition. — **ghost'li·ness,** *n.*

ghost writer. A literary ghost (see GHOST, 6). — **ghost'write'** (gōst'rīt'), *v. i. & t.*; GHOST'WROTE' (-rōt'); GHOST'WRIT'TEN (-rĭt''n); GHOST'WRIT'ING (-rīt'ĭng).

ghoul (go͞ol), *n.* [Ar. *ghūl,* fr. *ghāla* to seize.] **1.** Among Eastern nations, an imaginary evil being who robs graves and feeds upon corpses. **2.** A person whose pursuits suggest those of a ghoul, as a blackmailer, grave robber, etc. — **ghoul'ish,** *adj.* — **ghoul'ish·ly,** *adv.* — **ghoul'ish·ness,** *n.*

ghyll (gĭl). Var. of 2d GILL.

GI, G.I. (jē'ī'), *adj.* **1.** *U.S. Armed Services.* **a** *Orig., abbr., U.S. Army.* General issue or government issue; — applied to anything provided by an official supply department; as, *GI* field boots. **b** Prescribed for enlisted personnel or according strictly to regulations or custom; as, a *GI* haircut. **2.** Of or characteristic of enlisted, or former enlisted, personnel; as, *GI* morale. **3.** Designed for the benefit of service or ex-service personnel; as, *GI* housing. — *n.*; *pl.* GIs, GI's, G.I.'s, G.I.s (jē'īz'). An enlisted, or former enlisted, person in the U. S. armed forces; in civilian use, any ex-serviceman or ex-service woman. — **GI Joe** (jē'ī' jō'), **GI Jane** (jān'), **ex-GI.**

gi'ant (jī'ănt), *n.* [ONF. *gaiant* (OF. *jaiant,* F. *géant*), fr. L. *gigas,* fr. Gr. *gigas, gigantos.*] **1.** A huge mythical manlike or monstrous being of more than mortal, but less than godlike, power and endowment. **2.** A person, animal, plant, or thing of extraordinary size or power. **3.** *Astron.* In full, **giant star.** One of a class of stars of relatively great mass whose average luminosity is about one hundred times that of the sun. — *adj.* **1.** Like a giant in size, strength, or power. **2.** In plant and animal names, designating a species which is huge, as contrasted with related or similar species. — **gi'ant·ess,** *n.*

giant cane. See CANE, 3 **b**.

giant fulmar. See FULMAR.

gi'ant·ism (-ĭz'm), *n.* **1.** The condition or quality of being a giant; peculiarity, or practices, of a giant. **2.** *Med.* = GIGANTISM, 3.

giant panda. See PANDA, 2.

giant sequoia. See SEQUOIA.

giant star. One of a class of stars of great mass whose luminosity is about one hundred times that of the sun.

‖**giaour** (jour), *n.* [Turk. *giaur* infidel, fr. Per. *gaur, gabr.* See GHEBER.] An infidel; — applied by Turks to non-Moslems, esp. Christians.

gib (gĭb), *n.* [Abbr. fr. *Gilbert,* name of a cat.] A familiar name for a cat; hence, a cat, esp. a tomcat.

gib (gĭb), *n. Mach.* A plate of metal or wood, machined to hold other parts in place, to afford a bearing surface, or to provide means for taking up wear. — *v. t.*; GIBBED (gĭbd); GIB'BING. To fasten with a gib or gibs.

gibbed (gĭbd), *adj.* Castrated; — said of a cat.

gib'ber (jĭb'ẽr; gĭb'ẽr), *v. i. & t.* [Prob. imitative.] To talk volubly and foolishly. — *n.* Gibberish.

gib'ber·ish (-ĭsh), *n.* Voluble and foolish talk; a gibbering.

gib'bet (jĭb'ĕt; -ĭt), *n.* [OF. *gibet.*] A kind of gallows on which, formerly, malefactors were hanged in chains and allowed to remain as a warning. — *v. t.* **1.** To execute by hanging. **2. a** To hang on a gibbet. **b** Figuratively, to expose to infamy.

gib'bon (gĭb'ŭn), *n.* [F.] Any of two genera (*Hylobates* and *Symphalangus*) of apes of Asia and the East Indies, the lowest, smallest, and most perfectly arboreal of the anthropoid apes.

gib·bos'i·ty (gĭ·bŏs'ĭ·tĭ), *n.*; *pl.* -TIES (-tĭz). **1.** State or quality of being gibbous. **2.** A protuberance; swelling.

gib'bous (gĭb'ŭs), **gib'bose** (gĭb'ōs; gĭ·bōs'), *adj.* [L. *gibbus* a hunch, hump.] **1.** Swelling by a regular curve; protuberant; convex; — said specif., *Astron.* of the moon between half-moon and full moon, when both limbs are convex. **2.** Hunched; humpbacked. — **gib'bous·ness,** *n.*

gibe, jibe (jīb), *v. i.* [Origin obscure.] To utter taunting, sarcastic words; to flout; scoff. — *v. t.* To deride; scoff at. — **Syn.** See SCOFF. — *n.* An expression of sarcastic scorn; a scoff.

Gib'e·on·ites (gĭb'ē·ŭn·īts), *n. pl. Bib.* Inhabitants of Gibeon, who asked for alliance with Joshua, pretending to have come from afar, and who were condemned to be hewers of wood and drawers of water because of their deceptions.

gib'er, jib'er (jīb'ẽr), *n.* One who gibes.

gib'let (jĭb'lĕt; -lĭt), *n.* [OF. *gibelet* game.] Usually *pl.* The edible viscera of a fowl or the like.

Gi·bral'tar (jĭ·brôl'tẽr), *n.* [Ar. *jabal* mount (of) + *Ṭāriq,* name of the Moslem general who landed there in 711 and invaded Spain.] An impregnable stronghold; — from GIBRALTAR (see *Gaz.*).

gi'bus (jī'bŭs; *F.* zhē'büs'), *n.*, *or* **gibus hat.** An opera hat; — so named from the original maker in Paris.

gid (gĭd), *n.* [See GIDDY, *adj.*] *Veter.* A disease chiefly of sheep, produced by a larval tapeworm (*Multiceps multiceps*) in the brain. See COENURUS.

gid'dy (gĭd'ĭ), *adj.*; GID'DI·ER (-ĭ·ẽr); GID'DI·EST. [ME. *gidi* mad, silly, fr. AS. *gydig* insane.] **1.** Having a sensation of whirling or reeling about; dizzy. **2. a** Promoting or inducing giddiness; as, a *giddy* height. **b** Turning round with bewildering speed. **3.** Characterized by inconstancy; fickle; also, flighty; heedless. — *v. t. & i.*; -DIED (-ĭd); -DY·ING. To make or become giddy. — **gid'di·ly,** *adv.* — **gid'di·ness,** *n.*

Gid'e·on (gĭd'ē·ŭn), *n.* [Heb. *Gid'ōn.*] In the Bible, an Israelitish hero who defeated the Midianites and ruled Israel for 40 years.

gie (gē; gĭ). Scot. & dial. Eng. var. of GIVE.

gier'-ea'gle (jēr'ē'g'l), *n.* [D. *gier* vulture.] A bird referred to in the Bible (*Lev.* xi. 18 and *Deut.* xiv. 17) as unclean, probably the Egyptian vulture.

gift (gĭft), *n.* [ME. *gift,* fr. ON. *gift, gipt.*] **1.** The act, right, or power of giving; as, the office is not in his *gift.* **2.** Anything given; a present. **3.** A special talent or aptitude; as, the *gift* of wit; (*Colloq.*) the *gift* of gab (a talent for talking fluently). **4.** *Obs.* A bribe.

Syn. **Gift, faculty, aptitude, genius, talent, knack, bent** mean a special ability or a capacity for a definite work. **Gift** often implies favor by God, nature, or fortune; **faculty** applies to an innate or acquired ability or capacity that is distinctive and requires skill in its exercise; **aptitude** implies a natural liking for some activity and the likelihood of success in it; **genius** suggests an inborn gift, usually of an exalted character; **talent,** often contrasted with *genius,* usually, but not invariably, suggests an inborn gift which depends upon its possessor's industry for development; **knack** implies a slight gift which makes for ease or dexterity in performance; **bent** is almost equal to *aptitude,* but is less formal.

— *v. t.* **1.** To endow with a gift, esp. of some power or faculty. **2.** *Scot.* To make a gift of; to present.

gift'ed (gĭf'tĕd; -tĭd), *adj.* Endowed by nature with gifts or a gift; talented.

gig (gĭg), *n.* **1.** Anything that whirls or is whirled; specif., *Obs.*, a top. **2.** Something odd or grotesque.

gig, *n.* **a** A fish spear. **b** An arrangement of hooks to be drawn through a school of fish when they will not bite, in order to hook them in the bodies. — *v. t. & i.*; GIGGED (gĭgd); GIG'GING. To fish with a gig; to spear with a gig.

gig, *n.* **1.** A light two-wheeled, one-horse carriage. **2. a** *Naut.* A long, light ship's boat for oars or sail; as, the captain's *gig.* **b** A rowboat made for speed rather than for work or carrying. — *v. i.* To travel in a gig; — often with *it.*

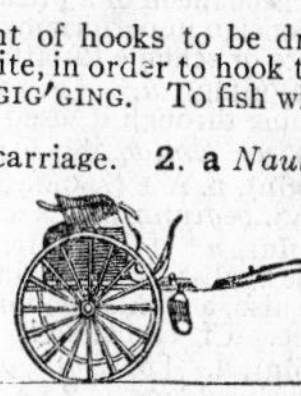
Gig, 1.

gi'gan·te'an (jī'găn·tē'ăn), *adj.* [L. *giganteus.*] Gigantic.

gi'gan·tesque' (-tĕsk'), *adj.* [F., fr. It. *gigantesco.*] Like a giant; befitting a giant.

gi·gan'tic (jī·găn'tĭk), *adj.* Also, formerly, **gi·gan'ti·cal** (-tĭ·kăl). [L. *gigas, -antis,* giant.] **1.** Of, pertaining to, or like a giant. **2.** Such as a giant might use, make, or cause; huge. — **Syn.** See ENORMOUS.

gi·gan'tism (-tĭz'm), *n.* **1.** Giantism (sense 1). **2.** *Biol.* Excessive vegetative growth, often accompanied by the inhibiting of reproduction. **3.** *Med.* Development to abnormally large size.

gi'gan·tom'a·chy (jī'găn·tŏm'ȧ·kĭ), *n.* Also **gi·gan'to·ma'chi·a** (jī·găn'tō·mā'kĭ·ȧ). [LL. *gigantomachia,* fr. Gr. *gigantomachia,* fr. *gigas, -antos,* giant + *machē* battle.] A war of giants; esp. [*cap.*], *Gr. Myth.,* the war between the Olympians and the giants.

gig'gle (gĭg''l), *v. i.*; GIG'GLED (-'ld); GIG'GLING (-lĭng). [Of imitative origin.] To laugh with short, convulsive catches of the breath; to titter nervously. — *n.* Act of giggling; a light, silly laugh. — **gig'gler** (-lẽr), *n.* — **gig'gling·ly,** *adv.* — **gig'gly** (-lĭ), *adj.*

gig'let (gĭg'lĕt; -lĭt), *n.* Also **gig'lot** (-lŏt). **1.** *Archaic.* A lascivious woman. **2.** A giddy, frivolous, frolicsome girl.

gig'o·lo (jĭg'ō·lō; *F.* zhē'gô'lō'), *n.*; *pl.* GIGOLOS (-lōz). [F.] **1.** A man who lives upon the earnings of a professional prostitute. **2.** A paid dancing partner or male escort, as at a cabaret.

gig'ot (jĭg'ŏt), *n.* [F.] **1.** Leg, as of lamb, when cooked. **2.** A leg-of-mutton sleeve; — called also **gigot sleeve.**

Gi'la mon'ster (hē'lȧ). Also **Gi'la,** *n.* [From the *Gila* River, Arizona.] A large orange-and-black venomous lizard (*Heloderma suspectum*) of Arizona, New Mexico, etc.; also, an allied form (*H. horridum*) of Mexico.

gil'bert (gĭl'bẽrt), *n.* [After William *Gilbert,* Eng. physicist.] *Elec.*

The C.G.S. unit of magnetomotive force, equivalent to $10 \div 4\pi$, or 0.7958, ampere turns.

gild (gĭld), *v. t.;* GILD'ED or GILT (gĭlt); GILD'ING. [AS. *gyldan*, fr. *gold* gold.] **1.** To overlay with a thin covering of gold; to adorn with a golden color. **2.** *Now Rare.* To make ruddy or smear (with blood). **3.** To give a fair but deceptive outward appearance to; as, to *gild* a lie. **4.** To make attractive; to brighten. — **gild'a·ble** (gĭl'dȧ·b'l), *adj.*

gild (gĭld), **gilds'man**, etc. Vars. of GUILD, etc.

gild'er (gĭl'dẽr), *n.* One who gilds.

gil'der (gĭl'dẽr). Var. of GUILDER.

gild'ing (gĭl'dĭng), *n.* **1. a** Art or practice of overlaying or covering with gold. **b** The material used in gilding. **2.** A superficial coating or appearance.

gill (jĭl), *n.* [OF. *gille, gelle*, a wine measure.] A small liquid measure. See MEASURE, *Table* 11.

gill, ghyll (gĭl), *n.* [ON. *gil.*] *Chiefly Scot.* **a** A ravine. **b** A brook.

gill (gĭl), *n.* [ME. *gile*, of Scand. origin.] **1.** An organ for respiration under water, as in fish; a branchia. In fish, gills are commonly leaflike processes situated at each side of the pharynx; water, taken in at the mouth, passes out through the branchial clefts, bathing the gills. **2. a** A fowl's wattle. **b** The flesh about the chin or jaws. **3.** *Bot. pl.* Gill-shaped plates on the under surface of the top in mushroom fungi. — *v. t.* **1.** To gut (fish). **2.** To catch (fish) by the gills in a gill net.

gill (jĭl), *n.* **1.** A girl; wench. **2.** *Dial.* = GROUND IVY.

gill fungus (gĭl). An agaric.

gil'lie, gil'ly (gĭl'ĭ), *n.; pl.* GILLIES (-ĭz). [Gael. *gille*, Ir. *giolla*, boy, servant.] **1.** In the Scottish Highlands, a male attendant; now, an attendant on a hunter. **2.** A follower; a servant.

gill net (gĭl). A flat net suspended vertically in the water, having meshes that allow the heads of fishes to pass, but catch them in the gills as they seek to withdraw.

gil'ly (gĭl'ĭ), *n.; pl.* -LIES (-ĭz). [Cf. GILL a two-wheeled frame, in the *Dict.*] A lumber wagon or any local wagon or truck, hired for hauling circus or carnival paraphernalia. — *v. t. & i.;* GIL'LIED (-ĭd); GIL'LY·ING. To transport or be transportable by such means. *Both Cant.*

gil'ly·flow'er (jĭl'ĭ·flou'ẽr), *n.* Also **gil'li·flow'er.** [OF. *girofle*, fr. Gr. *karyophyllon* clove tree, fr. *karyon* nut + *phyllon* leaf.] **1. a** The clove pink (*Dianthus caryophyllus*). See PINK. **b** The common wallflower of Europe (*Cheiranthus cheiri*). **c** Any plant of related species of the genus *Matthiola*, esp. the common stock (*M. incana*). **2.** [*cap.*] *Hort.* An old-time favorite apple of mild flavor.

gil'son·ite (gĭl'sŭn·īt), *n.* *Mineral.* Uintaite.

gilt (gĭlt), *n.* Gold, or that which resembles gold, laid on the surface of a thing; gilding. — *adj.* Gilded.

gilt, *n.* [ON. *gyltr.*] A young sow.

gilt, *past & past part.* of GILD.

gilt'-edge' (gĭlt'ĕj'; 2), *adj.* Gilt-edged.

gilt'-edged' (-ĕjd'; 2), *adj.* **1.** Having a gilt edge. **2.** *Colloq.* Of the best quality; as, *gilt-edged* securities.

gilt'head' (-hĕd'), *n.* Any or several marine fishes so named from their colors; esp.: **a** A valuable sparoid food fish (*Sparus auratus*) of the Mediterranean. **b** The English cunner. See CUNNER.

gim'bals (jĭm'bălz; gĭm'-), *n. pl.* [See GIMMAL.] A contrivance for permitting a body to incline freely in any direction, or for suspending anything, as a barometer, ship's compass, etc., so that it will remain plumb, or level, when its support is tipped.

gim'crack' (jĭm'krăk'), *n.* A fanciful trifle or ornament; a bauble; gewgaw. — *adj.* Showy, but of little worth. — **-crack'er·y** (-ẽr·ĭ), *n.*

gim'let (gĭm'lĕt; -lĭt), *n.* [OF. *guimbelet, guibelet.*] A small tool with a screw point, grooved shank, and cross handle, for boring holes.

gim'mal (gĭm'ăl; jĭm'ăl), *n.* [OF. *gemel* twin, fr. L. *gemellus.*] In machinery, connecting parts which move within each other; a pair or series of interlocked rings.

gim'mick (gĭm'ĭk), *n.* **1.** A secret device by which a grifter controls the mechanism of a prize wheel. **2.** Any small device used secretly by a magician in performing a trick. Cf. 2d FAKE, *n.*, 2. **3.** An ingenious device or scheme for attaining an end, often one artfully concealed.

gimp (gĭmp), *n.* [F. *guimpe.*] A narrow fabric, often with a wire running through it, used as trimming for dresses, furniture, etc.

gimp, *n.* *Colloq.* Spirit; vim.

gin (gĭn), *v. i. & t.;* GAN (găn); GIN'NING. [ME. *ginnen*, fr. *beginnen*, fr. AS. *beginnan.*] *Archaic.* Short for BEGIN.

gin (jĭn), *n.* [Contr. fr. GENEVA liquor.] A strong alcoholic liquor made by distilling a grain (esp. rye) mash in pot stills with juniper berries; also, a similar liquor made from plain spirit flavored with an aromatic. Cf. HOLLANDS.

gin (jĭn), *n.* [ME. *gin, gynne*, fr. OF. *engin.*] **1.** *Obs.* Contrivance; artifice; scheme. **2.** Any of various tools or mechanical devices; as: **a** A trap for game. **b** A machine for raising or moving heavy weights. **c** A cotton gin. — *v. t.;* GINNED (jĭnd); GIN'NING. **1.** To catch in a gin; to snare. **2.** To clear of seeds by a gin, as cotton.

gin (gĭn), *conj.* *Scot.* If; whether.

gin'gal, gin'gall (jĭn'gôl). Vars. of JINGAL.

gin'ger (jĭn'jẽr), *n.* [ME. *ginger, gingivere*, fr. AS. *gingiber* and fr. OF. *gengibre, gingimbre*, both fr. L. *gingiber, zingiber*, fr. Gr. *zingiberis.*] **1.** Any plant of a genus (*Zingiber*, esp. *Z. officinale*) of tropical Asiatic and Polynesian herbs, typifying a family (Zingiberaceae, the ginger family), and having pungent, aromatic rootstalks, used as a condiment and in medicine as a stimulant and a carminative; also, the rootstalk of this plant. **2.** *Colloq.* Mettle; spirit. — *v. t.* **1.** To treat with ginger. **2.** To make lively or animated.

ginger ale *or* **beer.** A nonalcoholic beer or beverage impregnated with ginger.

gin'ger·bread' (jĭn'jẽr·brĕd'), *n.* [OF. *gingebras, gingembras, gingimbrat*, fr. ML. *gingiber.* See GINGER.] **1.** A kind of plain cake flavored with ginger and usually sweetened with molasses. **2.** Something showy but tawdry.

gin'ger·ly (-lĭ), *adv.* **1.** *Obs.* Daintily; mincingly. **2.** Very cautiously. — *adj.* Very cautious; careful.

gin'ger·snap' (-snăp'), *n.* A thin brittle cooky flavored with ginger and usually sweetened with molasses.

gin'ger·y (-ĭ), *adj.* Having the characteristics of ginger; flavored with ginger; sharp; spicy.

ging'ham (gĭng'ăm), *n.* [F. *guingan*, fr. Malay *ginggang* gingham, striped.] A cotton cloth, usually in stripes or checks, of two or more colors, woven of dyed yarn and used for dresses, aprons, etc.

gin·gi'val (jĭn·jī'văl; jĭn'jĭ·văl), *adj.* [L. *gingiva* the gum.] Of or pertaining to the gums; specif., *Phonet.*, alveolar.

gin'gi·vi'tis (jĭn'jĭ·vī'tĭs), *n.* *Med.* Inflammation of the gums.

gink (gĭngk), *n.* *Slang, U. S.* An absurd, eccentric person.

gink'go (gĭng'kō; jĭng'kō), *n.; pl.* -GOES (-kōz). Also **ging'ko** (gĭng'kō); *pl.* -KOES (-kōz). [NL., fr. Jap. *gingko.*] A handsome gymnospermous tree (*Ginkgo biloba*), with fan-shaped leaves and yellow fruit, native to eastern China.

gin'ner (jĭn'ẽr), *n.* One who gins cotton.

gin rum'my (jĭn' rŭm'ĭ). A variety of rummy, in which a player whose unmatched cards count to ten or less may "knock," winning the number of points by which his opponent's unmatched cards exceed his or losing the points by which his exceed his opponent's plus a penalty of ten points. A score of 100 points wins the game.

gin'seng (jĭn'sĕng), *n.* [Chin. (Pek.) *jen*[2]*-shen*[1].] **a** A perennial herb (*Panax schinseng*) of China, typifying a widely distributed family (Araliaceae, the ginseng family) having compound and often aromatic leaves, umbellate flowers, and drupaceous fruits. The Chinese ginseng has 5-foliolate leaves, scarlet berries, and an aromatic root valued in China as a medicine. **b** The root of the Chinese ginseng. **c** Any of various related plants, esp. one (*P. quinquefolium*) of North America.

Gio·con'da, La (lä jō·kōn'dä). = MONA LISA.

gip (jĭp), **gip'sy**, etc. Vars. of GYP, GYPSY, etc.

gi·pon' (jĭ·pŏn'; jĭp'ŏn), *n.* [See JUPON.] A quilted doublet, often worn over (originally under) armor.

gi·raffe' (jĭ·răf'; 9), *n.* See PLURAL, *Note*, 3. [F. *girafe*, fr. It. *giraffa*, fr. Ar. *zirāfah, zarāfah.*] **1.** A large ruminant mammal (*Giraffa camelopardalis*) of Africa; the camelopard. It has a very long neck and is the tallest of quadrupeds. **2.** [*cap.*] The constellation Camelopard.

gir'an·dole (jĭr'ăn·dōl), *n.* Also **gi·ran'do·la** (jĭ·răn'dō·lȧ). [F. *girandole*, fr. It. *girandola*, dim. of *giranda*, fr. *girare* to revolve, fr. L. *gyrare* to gyrate.] **1.** A radiating and showy composition, as a cluster of skyrockets fired together. **2.** An ornamental, branched candleholder.

gir'a·sol, gir'a·sole (jĭr'ȧ·sŏl; -sōl), *n.* [It. *girasole*, fr. *girare* to turn + *sole* sun. See GIRANDOLE; SOLAR.] **1.** A sunflower (*Helianthus*), esp., the Jerusalem artichoke (*H. tuberosus*). **2.** *Mineral.* An opal giving out firelike reflections in a bright light; — called also *fire opal.*

gird (gûrd), *v. t.;* GIRT (gûrt) or GIRD'ED; GIRD'ING. [AS. *gyrdan.*] **1.** To encircle or bind with any flexible band, as a belt; hence, to make fast, as a sword by a belt or clothing with a cord. **2. a** To equip, esp. with the sword of knighthood. **b** To clothe or invest, as with a robe confined by a girdle, or with powers or attributes. **c** To prepare; brace; as, to *gird* oneself for a contest. **3.** To surround; encircle.

gird (gûrd; *Scot.* gĭrd), *v. t. & i.* To sneer at; mock; jeer. — **Syn.** See SCOFF. — *n.* *Archaic.* A sarcastic remark; a gibe; sneer.

gird'er (gûr'dẽr), *n.* [From GIRD to encircle.] **1.** Any heavy, strong, or principal member, usually horizontal, on which the weight of a floor or partition is carried. **2.** *Arch. & Engin.* An iron or steel beam, either made in a single piece or built up in plates, bars, latticework, etc., often of very large size (as in bridge construction), used for the same or a similar purpose.

gir'dle (gûr'd'l), *n.* [AS. *gyrdel.*] **1.** That which girds or encircles; esp., a belt or sash. **2.** A ring made by removing the bark around the trunk of a tree. **3.** A woman's close-fitting undergarment, either lightly boned or boneless and partly or wholly of elastic fabric, extending from just above the waist to below the hips, of step-in style or opening with hooks or slide fastener, and usually having garters attached. **4.** *Jewelry.* That edge of a gem grasped by the setting. See BRILLIANT, *Illust.* **5.** *Zool.* A bony arch for support of a limb.

gir'dle (gûr'd'l), *v. t.;* GIR'DLED (-d'ld); -DLING (-dlĭng). **1.** To bind or encircle with or as with a belt or sash. **2.** To make a circular cut around (a tree, etc.) through the outer bark and cortex, thus killing it.

gir'dler (-dlẽr), *n.* **1.** A maker of girdles. **2.** One who girdles. **3.** Any insect that girdles stems, twigs, etc.; specif., an American beetle (*Oncideres cingulata*), laying its eggs on twigs of the hickory, pear, etc.

girl (gûrl; 117), *n.* [ME. *girle, gerle, gurle*, young person.] **1.** A female child; a maiden; also, a young unmarried woman; — in familiar, affectionate, or jocular use applied to any woman, and often to a mare or filly. **2.** A female servant. **3.** *Colloq.* A sweetheart.

girl'hood (-hŏŏd), *n.* State or time of being a girl.

girl'ish, *adj.* Like, or characteristic of, a girl or girlhood. — **girl'ish·ly**, *adv.* — **girl'ish·ness**, *n.*

girl scout. A member of the **Girl Scouts**, an American organization of girls, formed by Juliette Low in Savannah, Ga., in 1912, under the name of **Girl Guides** (which is still the name of the British organization). Cf. BROWNIE, 2; BOY SCOUT.

girn (gûrn; gĭrn), *v. i. & t.* [Var. of GRIN to snarl.] *Dial.* To snarl or utter with a snarl. — *n.* A snarl.

gi'ro (jī'rō), *n.* A type of aircraft bearing the trade-mark *Autogiro.*

Gi·ron'dist (jĭ·rŏn'dĭst), *n.* [F. *Girondiste.*] A member of the moderate republican party in the French legislative assembly in 1791, called ***the Gi'ronde'*** (zhē'rôɴd'; *E.* jĭ·rŏnd') because the leaders were deputies from the Department of Gironde. — **Gi·ron'dism** (-dĭz'm), *n.*

gir'o·sol. Var. of GIRASOL.

girsh (gĭrsh), *n. sing. & pl.* [Ar.] A coin of Ethiopia, equal to 1/16 talari.

girt (gûrt), *past & past part.* of GIRD.

girt (gûrt), *n.* = GIRTH, *n.*

girt, *v. t.* To gird. — *v. i.* To measure in girth.

girth (gûrth), *n.* [ON. *gjörth* girdle.] **1.** A band or strap which encircles the body of a horse or other animal, to fasten a saddle, pack, blanket, etc. See HARNESS, *Illust.* **2.** The measure round the body, as at the waist; the circumference of anything. **3.** A girdle; belt.

girth, *v. t.* **1.** To gird; encircle. **2.** To bind with a girth.

girth. *Hist.* Var. of GRITH.

gi·sarme' (gĭ·zärm'), *n.* [OF.] A medieval weapon mounted on a long staff and carried by foot soldiers.

gist (jĭst), *n.* [OF. *gist* (F. *gît*), 3d pers. sing. ind. of *gesir* to lie, fr. L. *jacēre.*] The ground of a legal action; hence, the main point of a question, debate, or the like; the pith of a matter.

git'tern (gĭt'ẽrn), *n.* [OF. *guiterne.*] A medieval wire-strung instrument like a guitar.

give (gĭv), *v. t.;* GAVE (gāv); GIV'EN (gĭv'ĕn); GIV'ING. [ME. *given*, prob. of Scand. origin.] **1.** To bestow without a return; to grant or confer, as authority, a favor, etc.; to accord, as trust. **2.** To deliver, as property, in exchange for something or in discharge of a debt. **3.** Variously: **a** To furnish or serve; as, to *give* a drink. **b** To administer; as, to *give* the sacrament. **c** To commit; as, to *give* a letter to the postman. **d** To transfer from one's authority or care; as, to *give* a daughter in marriage. **e** To execute and deliver; as, to *give* one's bond as security. **4.** To bestow freely; as, to *give* one's energies to a cause. **5.** To deliver or deal by bodily action; as, to *give* a blow. **6.** To deliver in words; to utter, as an oath; to proffer, as a reply; to announce, as tidings, etc.; to issue, as a command; to pronounce, as an opinion, sentence, etc.; to award, as a prize. **7.** To furnish or supply by way of entertainment; as, to *give* a dinner. **8.** To yield as a product or effect; produce; as, flint and steel *give* sparks. **9.** To offer to the action of another; to proffer; as, to *give* a person one's hand. **10.** To present for consideration; as, to *give* a reason. **11.** To cause to have; to impart; as, to *give* a disease to another. **12.** To grant; permit. — *v. i.* **1.** To make gifts or presents. **2.** To yield to force or pressure; as, the earth *gives* under the feet. **3.** To accommodate oneself or itself; as, he *gave* to the motion of the horse. **4.** To open; to afford a view or passage. *A Gallicism.*

Syn. **Give, present, donate, bestow, confer, afford** mean to pass over to another something which becomes his own. **Give**, the general term, implies a passing over for use, enjoyment, or the like; **present** is more formal and ceremonious; **donate**, an Americanism, implies publicity (in some degree) in giving; **bestow**, the settling of something on one as a gift; **confer**, a giving graciously or as a favor or honor; **afford**, a giving as a natural or legitimate consequence of that which gives.

give a good account of. To meet with success in, against, or for; to bear (oneself) with credit. — ***give birth to.*** To bear or bring forth, as a child. — ***give tongue.*** *Hunting.* To begin barking; — of hounds. — ***give up.*** **a** To abandon. **b** To devote or addict; — used esp. reflexively. **c** To cease from; relinquish. **d** To pronounce incurable or insoluble. **e** To cease from effort; to yield. — ***give way.*** **a** To give ground. **b** To yield to force or pressure. **c** To give oneself up. **d** To lose control of oneself. **e** *Stock Exchange.* To decline in value, esp. under attack.

— *n.* Act of giving; esp., act or process of yielding to force or strain; a giving way; also, springiness; elasticity.

give′-and-take′ (gĭv′ănd·tāk′), *n.* A giving and taking by way of compromise, equalization, or the like; also, exchange, as of repartee, ideas, etc., esp. upon fair terms.

give′a·way′ (gĭv′ȧ·wā′), *n.* *Slang.* A betrayal, esp. one made unintentionally.

giv′en (gĭv′ĕn), *adj.* **1.** Bestowed; presented; as, one's *given* name. **2.** Disposed; addicted; as, *given* to drink. **3.** Stated; fixed; as, in a *given* time. **4.** Executed; dated; — used in official documents; as, *given* under my hand and seal this 10th day of June. **5.** *Math. & Logic.* Granted; assumed.

given name. The Christian name, or name *given* by one's parents or guardians. Cf. SURNAME.

giv′er (gĭv′ẽr), *n.* One who gives; a donor.

giz′zard (gĭz′ẽrd), *n.* [OF. *giser, gisier,* F. *gésier,* fr. L. *gigeria,* pl., cooked entrails of poultry.] **1.** The second (posterior) stomach of birds, having thick walls and horny lining for grinding food. Cf. CROP, *n.,* 1; PROVENTRICULUS. **2.** *Humorous & Colloq.* Stomach; interior (of a person).

gla·bel′la (glȧ·bĕl′ȧ), *n.; pl.* -LAE (-ē). [NL., fr. L. *glabellus* hairless, fr. *glaber* bald.] *Anat.* The smooth prominence between the eyebrows.

gla′brate (glā′brāt), *adj.* *Bot. & Zool.* Glabrous; tending to be glabrous.

gla′brous (-brŭs), *adj.* [L. *glaber.*] Smooth; having a surface without hairs or projections.

‖**gla·cé′** (glȧ′sā′), *adj.* [F., past part. of *glacer* to freeze, to ice.] **1.** Made with a smooth glossy surface; — said of cloth, leather, etc.; hence, smooth and glossy; as, a *glacé* finish. **2.** Coated with icing; as, marrons *glacés;* also, frozen.

gla·cé′, *v. t.;* GLA·CÉED′ (-săd′); GLA·CÉ′ING. To make glacé; to ice.

gla′cial (glā′shăl), *adj.* [F., fr. L. *glacialis,* fr. *glacies* ice.] **1.** Pertaining to ice or to its action; frozen; icy; esp., pertaining to, or produced by the action of, glaciers; as, *glacial* soil. **2.** *Geol.* **a** [*cap.*] = PLEISTOCENE. **b** Of, pertaining to, or designating any of those parts (**glacial epochs**) of geological time when a much larger portion of the earth was covered by glaciers than at present. **3.** *Chem.* Resembling ice in appearance; — of certain compounds. **4.** As cold and hard as ice; calm; also, slow-moving. — **gla′cial·ly,** *adv.*

gla′cial·ist (glā′shăl·ĭst), *n.* A supporter of the glacier theory; also, a student of glaciers.

gla′ci·ate (glā′shĭ·āt), *v. t.* **1.** To freeze. **2.** *Geol.* To subject to glacial action, as in the scoring or erosion of rocks. — **gla′ci·a′tion** (glā′sĭ·ā′shŭn; glā′shĭ-), *n.*

gla′cier (glā′shẽr; glăs′ĭ·ẽr), *n.* [F., fr. VL. *glacia* ice, for L. *glacies.*] A field or body of ice, formed in a region where snowfall exceeds melting, and moving slowly down a mountain slope or valley, as in the Alps, or over a wide area, as in Greenland. Cf. ICEBERG. — **gla′ciered** (glā′shẽrd; glăs′ĭ·ẽrd), *adj.*

glacier theory. *Geol.* The theory that the drift was deposited by the agency of glaciers during the Glacial epoch.

gla′cis (glā′sĭs; glăs′ĭs), *n.* [F., fr. OF. *glacier* to slip, slide, fr. *glace* ice. See GLACIER.] A gentle slope; esp., *Fort.,* the slope from the top of the counterscarp toward the open country.

glad (glăd), *adj.; comp.* GLAD′DER (-ẽr); GLAD′DEST. [AS. *glæd* bright, glad.] **1.** Characterized by joy or pleasure; happy; pleased. **2.** Expressive of, or caused by, gladness; bringing or exciting gladness; as, *glad* tidings. **3.** Characterized by brightness and beauty; gay; beautiful.

Syn. **Glad, happy, cheerful, lighthearted, joyful, joyous** mean showing or expressing pleasure or delight. **Glad** and **happy** may express gratification, but the usual implication of *glad* is elation, and of *happy* a sense of well-being and of complete satisfaction; **cheerful** suggests a strong and, often, a spontaneous flow of good spirits; **lighthearted** suggests freedom from care, worry, and discontent; **joyful** and **joyous** suggest exultant rejoicing.

— *v. i. & t.;* GLAD′DED; GLAD′DING. *Archaic.* To gladden.

glad′den (glăd′'n), *v. t. & i.* To make or become glad.

glad′den·er (-ẽr), *n.* One who or that which gladdens.

glade (glād), *n.* A grassy open space in a forest.

glad′i·ate (glăd′ĭ·āt; glā′dĭ-), *adj.* [L. *gladius* sword.] *Bot.* Sword-shaped; ensiform.

glad′i·a′tor (glăd′ĭ·ā′tẽr), *n.* [L., fr. *gladius* sword.] **1.** *Rom. Hist.* One who fought with a weapon in public for the amusement of the people, as at a festival. **2.** One who engages in any fierce combat or controversy.

glad′i·a·to′ri·al (-ȧ·tō′rĭ·ăl; 70), *adj.* Of or pertaining to gladiators, combatants, or combats or controversies.

glad′i·o′la (glăd′ĭ·ō′lȧ; glȧ·dī′ō·lȧ), *n.* [NL.] A gladiolus.

glad′i·o′lus (glăd′ĭ·ō′lŭs; glȧ·dī′ō·lŭs; *see note below*), *n.; pl.* GLADIOLI (-lī), GLADIOLUSES (-lŭs·ĕz; -ĭz). [L., a small sword.] **1.** A plant (genus *Gladiolus*) of the iris family (Iridaceae), natives chiefly of Africa, with erect sword-shaped leaves and spikes of brilliantly colored irregular flowers, springing from flat corms; also, a corm or flower of this plant. **2.** *Anat.* The bladelike compound middle part of the sternum, esp. in man and many mammals.

☞ The proper pronunciation for the genus name is glȧ·dī′ō·lŭs, although glăd′ĭ·ō′lŭs is now more usual for the plant name.

glad′ly (glăd′lĭ), *adv.* With gladness; cheerfully.

glad′ness, *n.* State or quality of being glad; joy.

glad′some (glăd′sŭm), *adj.* **1.** Causing joy; expressive of, or indicating, gladness; gay. **2.** Pleased; cheerful. — **glad′some·ly,** *adv.* — **glad′some·ness,** *n.*

Glad′stone (glăd′stōn; -stŭn), *n.* [After W. E. *Gladstone.*] **1.** A four-wheeled pleasure carriage with two inside seats. **2.** Short for GLADSTONE BAG, GLADSTONE WINE.

Gladstone bag. A traveling bag with flexible sides and hinged so as to open flat into two equal compartments.

Gladstone wine *or* **claret.** *Humorous, Eng.* Any of the cheap French wines, tariffs on which were reduced by Gladstone in 1860.

glaik′et, glaik′it (glāk′ĭt), *adj.* *Scot.* Foolish; thoughtless; giddy.

glair (glâr), *n.* [OF. *glaire.*] **1.** White of egg; also, a size or glaze made from it, as used in bookbinding, pastry, etc. **2.** A viscous substance, like white of egg.

glair′y (glâr′ĭ), *adj.* Like glair, or partaking of its qualities; covered with glair. — **glair′i·ness** (-ĭ·nĕs; -nĭs), *n.*

glaive (glāv), *n.* [OF.] *Archaic.* A sword; esp., a broadsword.

glam′or·ize (glăm′ẽr·īz), *v. t.* To make glamorous or glorify; to extol the accomplishments or attractiveness of, through lavish publicity.

glam′or·ous (glăm′ẽr·ŭs), *adj.* Also **glam′our·ous.** Full of glamour. — **glam′or·ous·ly,** *adv.*

glam′our (glăm′ẽr), *n.* Also **glam′or.** [Scot. *glamour, glamer,* modification of E. *gramarye* magic.] **1.** Magic; a spell or charm. **2.** Any association with an object or person, through which the object or person appears delusively glorified; a deceptive or enticing charm.

glance (glȧns; 9), *v. i.;* GLANCED (glȧnst); GLANC′ING (glȧn′sĭng). [OF. *glacier* to slip, slide.] **1.** To strike obliquely and fly off or turn aside. **2.** To make an indirect, incidental, or passing reference; to allude. **3.** To shoot or emit a flash of light; to flash. **4.** To gaze with a sudden, rapid look; — said of the eye. — *v. t.* **1.** To shoot or dart suddenly or obliquely; to glance at; to catch a glimpse of. **2.** *Obs.* To hint at. — **Syn.** See FLASH.

— *n.* **1.** A rapid oblique movement or indirect hit. **2.** A movement causing a flash of light; a flash thus produced. **3.** A quick cast of the eyes; a quick look. **4.** *Cricket.* A stroke to leg off a slanting bat.

glance, *n.* [G. *glanz,* prop. brightness, or D. *glans.*] Any of several mineral sulfides with a metallic luster.

gland (glănd), *n.* *Mach.* The movable part of a stuffing box by which the packing is compressed. See STUFFING BOX, *Illust.*

gland, *n.* [F. *glande,* fr. OF. *glandre,* fr. L. *glandula,* dim. of *glans, glandis,* acorn.] *Anat.* An organ for secreting a substance or substances to be used in, or eliminated from, the body; as, the salivary *glands* of the mouth. The essential elements of a gland are the epithelial cells, which select out from the blood and in many cases build up into new chemical compounds the constituents of the secretion. In some glands (see DUCTLESS GLAND) the blood itself carries away the secretion, and there is no cavity or duct. Certain structures, not true glands, are still often called *glands* in conformity with old usage, esp. the lymphatic glands.

gland, *n.* [F., fr. L. *glans, glandis.* See 2d GLAND.] *Bot.* **a** Any special secreting organ, as the hairs on the leaves of a sundew. **b** Any small protuberance, as on the petiole of a peach leaf.

glan′dered (glăn′dẽrd), *adj.* Affected with glanders.

glan′ders (glăn′dẽrz), *n.* [OF. *glandres,* pl., glands.] *Veter.* A contagious and very destructive disease of horses, mules, etc., caused by a bacterium (*Pfeifferella mallei*). It may be transmitted to dogs, goats, sheep, and man, but bovines are immune. While the same in cause it is more generalized than farcy. — **glan′der·ous** (-dẽr·ŭs), *adj.*

glan′du·lar (glăn′dū·lẽr), *adj.* Containing or bearing glands or gland cells; of, pertaining to, or like, a gland.

glan′du·lous (-lŭs), *adj.* [L. *glandulosus.*] Of or pertaining to a gland; glandular.

glans (glănz), *n.; pl.* GLANDES (glăn′dēz). [L. See GLAND organ.] *Anat.* The conical vascular body which forms the extremity of the penis (**glans pe′nis** [pē′nĭs]) or of the clitoris (**glans cli·tor′i·dis** [klĭ·tŏr′ĭ·dĭs]).

glare (glâr), *v. i.* [ME. *glaren.*] **1.** To shine with a dazzling light. **2.** To be bright and intense, as certain colors; also, to be ostentatiously splendid. **3.** To stare with fierce, piercing eyes. — *v. t.* To shoot out, emit, or express with a glare. — **Syn.** See GAZE. — *n.* **1.** A bright, dazzling light; hence, glitter. **2.** Ostentatious fineness of appearance; showiness. **3.** A fierce or piercing look or stare. — **Syn.** See BLAZE.

glare, *n.* *U. S.* A smooth, glassy surface; as, a *glare* of ice. — *adj.* *U. S.* Smooth and bright; as, *glare* ice.

glar′ing (glâr′ĭng), *adj.* **1.** Staring fiercely; — said of eyes. **2.** Emitting a dazzling light; vivid. **3.** Vividly conspicuous; as, a *glaring* error. — **Syn.** See FLAGRANT. — **glar′ing·ly,** *adv.*

glar′y (-ĭ), *adj.;* GLAR′I·ER (-ĭ·ẽr); GLAR′I·EST. Of a dazzling luster; glaring; shining. — **glar′i·ness,** *n.*

glar′y, *adj.* [From 2d GLARE.] *U. S.* Very smooth; slippery.

glass (glȧs; 9), *n.* [AS. *glæs.*] **1.** An amorphous substance, usually transparent, consisting ordinarily of a mixture of silicates, but in some cases of borates, phosphates, etc. Most glass is made by fusing silica, as sand, an alkali, as potash or soda, and some other base, as lime or lead oxide. See CROWN GLASS, CUT GLASS, FLINT GLASS, VENETIAN GLASS. **2.** Collectively, articles made of glass; as, dinner *glass.* **3.** Anything made of glass, as a goblet, an hourglass, a windowpane, a mirror, a thermometer, a pair of binoculars, etc.; *pl.* eyeglasses; spectacles. **4.** The contents of a goblet or drinking glass. — *v. t.* **1.** **a** *Rare.* To cover or protect with glass; to case in glass. **b** To pack and seal in glass containers, for shipment. **2.** To reflect; to mirror. **3.** *Rare.* To make glassy. — *adj.* Of, pertaining to, or made of, glass.

glass blowing. Art of shaping a mass of glass, when heated to a viscid state, by inflating it through a tube. — **glass blower.**

glass'ful (glȧs'fo͝ol), *n.; pl.* GLASSFULS (-fo͝olz). The contents of a glass; as much as a glass will hold.

glass'house' (-hous'), *n.* A building constructed chiefly of glass and used for growing plants. Cf. GREENHOUSE.

glass'mak'er (-māk'ẽr), *n.* A maker of glass.

glass'man (-măn), *n.; pl.* GLASSMEN (-mĕn). **1.** One who sells glassware. **2. a** A glassmaker. **b** A glazier.

glass snake. A limbless lizard (*Ophisaurus ventralis*) of the southern U. S., superficially like a snake; — from its fragility, the long tail easily breaking into pieces.

glass'ware' (glȧs'wâr'), *n.* Ware made of glass.

glass wool. Spun glass resembling wool, used in the filtration of acids, heat insulation, etc.

glass'work' (glȧs'wûrk'), *n.* **1.** *pl.* A glass factory. **2.** Manufacture of glass or glassware; also, glaziery. **3.** Articles or ornamentation made of glass.

glass'work'er (-wûr'kẽr), *n.* One who works with glass.

glass'wort' (-wûrt'), *n.* **a** Any plant of the genus *Salicornia*, esp. *S. europaea*, of the goosefoot family. **b** The related saltwort (*Salsola kali*).

glass'y (glȧs'ĭ), *adj.;* GLASS'I·ER (-ĭ·ẽr); GLASS'I·EST. **1.** Resembling glass, as in smoothness. **2.** Dull; wanting life or fire. — **glass'i·ly,** *adv.* — **glass'i·ness,** *n.*

Glas·we'gian (glȧs·wē'jăn; -jĭ·ăn), *adj.* Of or pertaining to Glasgow. — *n.* A native or inhabitant of Glasgow.

Glau'ber's salt (glou'bẽrz), **Glau'ber salt** (glou'bẽr). [After J. R. *Glauber*, Ger. chemist.] Often also *pl.* A colorless crystalline sodium salt, $Na_2SO_4.10H_2O$, used as a cathartic, aperient, and diuretic.

glau·co'ma (glô·kō'mȧ), *n.* [L., fr. Gr. *glaukōma*, fr. *glaukos* light gray, blue gray.] A condition of the eye marked by hardness of the eyeball, causing impairment of vision or blindness. — **glau·co'ma·tous** (-kō'mȧ·tŭs; -kŏm'ȧ·tŭs), *adj.*

glau'co·nite (glô'kō·nīt), *n.* [Gr. *glaukos* bluish-green or gray.] *Mineral.* A dull-green amorphous iron potassium silicate, occurring abundantly in greensand.

glau'cous (glô'kŭs), *adj.* [L. *glaucus*, fr. Gr. *glaukos*.] **1.** Yellowish-green in hue and of low saturation and very high brilliance. See COLOR. **2.** *Bot.* Having the surface covered with a waxy bloom, a whitish or grayish powdery coating that gives a frosted appearance, as a plum, a cabbage leaf, or a leaf of blue spruce.

glaze (glāz), *v. t.* [ME. *glasen*, fr. *glas* glass.] **1.** To furnish or fit (a window, a sash, etc.) with glass. **2.** To overlay with a thin surface consisting of, or resembling, glass; as, to *glaze* earthenware. **3.** To coat with glaze, as meat or fish. **4.** *Paint.* To apply a semitransparent color to (a painted surface or another color), to modify the effect. — *v. i.* To become glazed or glassy. — *n.* **1. a** A substance used for glazing. **b** The vitreous coating of pottery or porcelain, esp. one that is transparent, as distinguished from *enamel*. **c** Figuratively, a film or coating; as, the *glaze* of death over his eyes. **2.** A smooth glassy surface or bright polish. **3.** *Cookery.* Broth boiled to a gelatinous paste, and spread thinly over braised dishes. **4.** *Meteorol.* Sleet. **5.** *Painting.* A coat of semitransparent color applied to modify the effect of another color. — **glaz'er** (glāz'ẽr), *n.* — **glaz'i·ness** (-ĭ·nĕs; -nĭs), *n.* — **glaz'y** (-ĭ), *adj.*

gla'zier (glā'zhẽr *or, esp. Brit.,* -zĭ·ẽr), *n.* [ME. *glasier*, fr. *glas*, after F. nouns in *-ier*.] One whose business is to set glass in window frames, etc. — **gla'zier·y** (-ĭ), *n.*

glaz'ing (glāz'ĭng), *n.* **1.** Act, art, or trade of setting glass. **2.** The glass set, or to be set, in a sash, frame, etc. **3.** The glass or glasslike substance with which anything, as pottery, paper, etc., is overlaid. **4.** Act of laying on glaze; also, the glaze applied.

gleam (glēm), *n.* [AS. *glǣm*.] Formerly, a bright light, as of the sun; now, a moderate brightness or a transient illumination. — *v. i.* To shoot or dart, as rays of light; to send out gleams. — *v. t.* To shoot or emit (flashes of light, etc.). — **Syn.** See FLASH. — **gleam'y** (-ĭ), *adj.*

glean (glēn), *v. t.* [OF. *glener*, fr. LL. *glenare*, of Celt. origin.] **1.** To gather after a reaper, as grain. **2.** To gather from (a field or vineyard) what has been left by the reapers. **3.** To collect with patient labor; to pick out. — *v. i.* **1.** To gather what is left by reapers. **2.** To pick up or gather anything by degrees. — **glean'er,** *n.*

glean'ing, *n.* Act of one who gleans; also, usually *pl.*, that which is collected by gleaning.

glebe (glēb), *n.* [L. and F.; F. *glèbe*, fr. L. *gleba*, *glaeba*, land, soil.] **1.** *Now Poetic.* Soil; sod. **2.** *Archaic.* A plot of cultivated ground; a field. **3.** *Eccl. Law.* The land belonging, or yielding revenue, to a parish church or ecclesiastical benefice.

glede (glēd), *n.* Also **gled.** [AS. *glida*.] The common European kite (*Milvus milvus*).

glee (glē), *n.* [AS. *glēo* music, minstrelsy, mirth.] **1.** *Music.* An unaccompanied song for three or more solo voices. Cf. MADRIGAL, PART SONG. **2.** Exultant, sometimes malicious, joy. — **Syn.** See MIRTH.

glee club. A club or company organized for singing glees, and (by extension) part songs, ballads, etc.

gleed (glēd), *n.* [AS. *glēd*.] *Dial.* A glowing coal.

glee'ful (glē'fo͝ol; -f'l), *adj.* Full of glee; merry; gay; joyous. — **glee'ful·ly,** *adv.* — **glee'ful·ness,** *n.*

gleek (glēk), *n. Obs. exc. Dial.* A jest or scoff; a trick. — *v. i. & t. Obs.* To gibe; sneer; cheat; trick.

gleek, *n.* [OF. *glic*.] *Obs.* A three-handed card game.

glee'man (glē'măn), *n. Archaic.* A minstrel.

glee'some (-sŭm), *adj.* Merry; joyous; gleeful.

gleet (glēt), *n.* [OF. *glete*, *glette* (F. *glette* litharge).] **1.** *Obs. exc. Scot.* Slime; ooze. **2.** *Med.* A persistent transparent mucous discharge from the urethra; formerly, any morbid discharge. **3.** *Veter.* A chronic inflammation of the nasal cavities.

gleg (glĕg), *adj.* [ON. *glöggr*.] *Scot.* Quick; alert.

glen (glĕn), *n.* [Of Celt. origin.] A secluded narrow valley.

Glen·gar'ry (glĕn·găr'ĭ), *n.,* or **Glengarry bonnet** *or* **cap.** [Name of a valley in Scotland.] A type of cap worn by Scottish Highlanders.

gle'noid (glē'noid), *adj.* [Gr. *glēnoeidēs*, fr. *glēnē* socket of a joint + *eidos* form.] *Anat.* Having the form of a smooth shallow depression, as the cavity of the scapula.

gley (glē; glī), *n. & v. Scot. & Dial. Eng.* Squint.

gli'a·din (glī'ȧ·dĭn), *n.* [F. *gliadine*, fr. Gr. *glia* glue.] *Biochem.* **a** An alcohol-soluble plant protein found in wheat and rye. **b** = PROLAMIN.

glib (glĭb), *adj.;* GLIB'BER (-ẽr); GLIB'BEST. **1.** *Dial.* Smooth; slippery. **2.** Characterized by ease, as action or manner. **3.** Speaking or spoken smoothly and flippantly; fluent. — **glib'ly,** *adv.* — **glib'ness,** *n.*

glid'der (glĭd'ẽr), *v. t.* [AS. *glidder* slippery.] *Obs. exc. Dial.* To glaze. — *v. i. Dial. Eng.* To slip.

glide (glīd), *v. i.* [AS. *glīdan*.] **1.** To move gently and smoothly; to pass with a smooth, silent motion. **2.** To pass gradually or without break; to shade. **3.** *Aviation.* To descend at a normal angle of attack without engine power sufficient for level flight; to volplane. **4.** *Phonet.* To pass (from one definite sound to another) with a glide, as of the voice. See GLIDE, *n.*, 5. — *v. t.* To cause to glide. — *n.* **1.** Act of gliding or moving smoothly. **2.** *Aviation.* The act or action of gliding. **3.** *Dancing.* In ballroom dances, a smooth sliding step used with other steps. **4.** *Music.* A slur. **5.** *Phonet.* A transitional sound produced while the vocal organs are assuming, or passing from, the position for a definite speech sound, such as the indefinite sound produced in passing from the back position of *g* to the front one of *ā* in *gay*.

glide'-bomb' (glīd'bŏm'), *v. t. & i.* To descend upon (a target) at an angle between 45° and 60°; — distinguished from *dive-bomb*.

glid'er (glīd'ẽr), *n.* **1.** One who or that which glides. **2.** A form of aircraft similar to an airplane but with no engine. **3.** A porch swing with cushioned seat or couch suspended by links from an upright framework.

glid'ing (-ĭng), *adj.* That glides. — **glid'ing·ly,** *adv.*

gliff (glĭf), *n. Scot.* A moment; instant.

glim (glĭm), *n.* **1.** *Scot.* A small bit. **2.** *Slang.* **a** A light, as a lamp. **b** Eye.

glime (glīm), *n. Dial.* A sly or sidelong look or glance. — *v. i. Dial.* To look askance, or slyly.

glim'mer (glĭm'ẽr), *v. i.* [Akin to G. *glimmer* a faint, trembling light, mica, *glimmern* to glimmer.] To give feeble rays of light; to shine faintly and unsteadily. — **Syn.** See FLASH. — *n.* **1.** A faint unsteady light; gleam. **2.** A slight perception; a bit; as, a *glimmer* of hope.

glim'mer·ing, *n.* A faint, unsteady light; a glimmer; hence, a faint view or idea; a glimpse; an inkling.

glimpse (glĭmps; 89), *n.* **1.** A sudden flash; transient luster. **2.** A faint passing appearance; hence, a trace; tinge. **3.** A short hurried view. **4.** A faint idea; inkling. — *v. i.* **1.** To shine faintly or unsteadily; to glimmer. **2.** To take a glimpse; to glance. — *v. t.* To catch a glimpse of.

glint (glĭnt), *n.* **1.** A gleam; also, brightness; luster. **2.** *Scot.* A glimpse; a glance. — *v. i. & t.* [ME. *glenten* to turn aside, glance, of Scand. origin.] **1.** To make a quick or sudden movement; dart. **2.** To flash; gleam. — **Syn.** See FLASH.

gli·o'ma (glī·ō'mȧ), *n.; pl.* -MATA (-mȧ·tȧ), -MAS (-mȧz). [NL., fr. Gr. *glia* glue + *-oma*.] *Med.* A tumor springing from the neuroglia of the brain, spinal cord, or the like. — **gli·o'ma·tous** (-ō'mȧ·tŭs; -ŏm'ȧ·tŭs), *adj.*

glisk (glĭsk), *n. Scot.* A glance; glimpse.

glis·sade' (glĭ·säd'; -sād'), *n.* [F., fr. *glisser* to slip.] **1.** A sliding descent down a snow slope. **2.** In ballet dancing, a gliding step to one side. — *v. i.* To slide; to glide, as in mountaineering.

glis·san'do (glē·sän'dō), *n.; pl.* GLISSANDI (-dē). [As if It. = F. *glissant* sliding.] *Music.* A gliding effect, as produced by sounding in quick succession adjacent tones.

glis'ten (glĭs''n), *v. i.* [AS. *glisnian*.] To sparkle or shine; esp., to shine with a mild fitful luster. — **Syn.** See FLASH. — *n.* A glistening; a shining brightness.

glis'ter (glĭs'tẽr), *v. i.* [ME. *glistren*.] To be bright or brilliant; to sparkle. — *n.* Glitter; luster.

glit'ter (glĭt'ẽr), *v. i.* [ON. *glitra*.] **1.** To sparkle with light; to gleam. **2.** To be showy or striking, and hence attractive. — **Syn.** See FLASH. — *n.* A bright, sparkling light; brilliant and showy luster; brilliancy.

glit'ter·y (-ĭ), *adj.* Full of glitter.

gloam (glōm), *n. Poetic.* The twilight; gloaming.

gloam'ing (-ĭng), *n.* [AS. *glōmung*, fr. *glōm* twilight.] Twilight; dusk.

gloat (glōt), *v. i.* [ON. *glotta* to smile scornfully.] To look steadfastly; esp., to gaze with malignant satisfaction, ardent desire, lust, or avarice. — **Syn.** See GAZE. — **gloat'er** (-ẽr), *n.*

glob'al (glōb'ăl), *adj.* Spherical; also, relating to the globe, esp. as an entirety; world-wide; as, *global* war. — **glob'al·ly,** *adv.*

glo'bate (glō'bāt), **glo'bat·ed** (-bāt·ĕd; -ĭd), *adj.* [L. *globatus*, past part., fr. *globus* ball.] Spherical.

globe (glōb), *n.* [F., fr. L. *globus*.] **1.** A round or spherical body; a ball; sphere. **2. a** The earth; — usually with *the*. **b** Hence, any planet. **3.** A round model of the earth or heavens. **4.** A golden ball carried as an emblem of authority. **5.** Anything which is nearly spherical in shape. **6.** An appliance for protecting a lamp or for diffusing its light. — *v. t. & i.* To gather or form into a globe.

globe'fish' (-fĭsh'), *n.; pl.*, see FISH. = PUFFER, 2.

globe'flow'er (-flou'ẽr), *n.* Any of a genus (*Trollius*) of plants of the crowfoot family, with globose yellow flowers.

globe'-trot'ter, *n. Colloq.* One who travels widely, or in all parts of the world. — **globe'-trot'ting,** *n. & adj.*

glo'bin (glō'bĭn), *n.* [L. *globus* globe + *-in*.] *Biochem.* A histone formed as a cleavage product of hemoglobin.

glo'boid (-boid), *adj.* Approximately globular; globate. — *n.* A globoid figure or body.

glo'bose (glō'bōs; glō·bōs'), *adj.* [L. *globosus*.] Globular; spherical. — **glo·bos'i·ty** (glō·bŏs'ĭ·tĭ), *n.*

glo'bous (glō'bŭs), *adj.* [L. *globosus*.] Globose.

glob'u·lar (glŏb'ū·lẽr), *adj.* **1.** Globe-shaped; round. **2.** Consisting of globules.

glob'ule (glŏb'ūl), *n.* [F., fr. L. *globulus*, dim. of *globus* globe.] A small spherical particle.

glob'u·lif'er·ous (glŏb'ū·lĭf'ẽr·ŭs), *adj.* [*globule* + *-ferous*.] Bearing or containing globules.

glob′u·lin (glŏb′ū·lĭn), *n.* [From GLOBULE.] *Biochem.* Any of a group of proteins insoluble in pure water, but soluble in dilute solutions of neutral salts.

glo·chid′i·ate (glō·kĭd′ĭ·āt), *adj.* [Gr. *glōchis* point of an arrow.] *Bot.* Bearing barbs; barbed.

glock′en·spiel′ (glŏk′ĕn·spēl′), *n.* [G., fr. *glocke* bell + *spiel* play.] *Music.* A percussion instrument consisting typically of a series of metal bars tuned to the chromatic scale and played with two hammers. Cf. XYLOPHONE.

glom′er·ate (glŏm′ẽr·āt), *adj.* [L. *glomeratus*, past part., fr. *glomus* a ball.] Clustered together.

glom′er·a′tion (-ā′shŭn), *n.* **1.** Act of forming or gathering into a round mass; conglomeration. **2.** That which is formed into a ball; a ball.

glom′er·ule (glŏm′ẽr·ōōl), *n.* [NL. *glomerulus*, dim. fr. L. *glomus* ball.] *Bot.* An inflorescence consisting of a compacted, or sessile, cyme, as that of the box tree.

glo·mer′u·lus (glō·mĕr′ū·lŭs; -ōō·lŭs), *n.; pl.* GLOMERULI (-lī). [NL.] *Anat.* A tuft of capillaries at the origin of each uriniferous tubule.

gloom (glōōm), *n.* [From GLOOM, *v.*] **1.** *Scot.* A frown or sullen look. **2.** Partial or total darkness; thick shade. **3.** A shady, gloomy, or dark place. **4.** Cloudiness or heaviness of mind; low spirits. — **Syn.** See SADNESS. — *v. i.* [ME. *gloum(b)en.*] **1.** To look sullen; to frown; also, to look dismal or gloomy. **2.** To become dark or threatening, as the sky. **3.** To be or appear dark, somber, or gloomy. — *v. t.* To render gloomy; to obscure.

gloom′ing (glōōm′ĭng), *n.* **1.** A scowl; a sullen fit. **2.** *Poetic.* Twilight; gloaming.

gloom′y (glōōm′ĭ), *adj.;* GLOOM′I·ER (-ĭ·ẽr); GLOOM′I·EST. **1.** Dark; murky. **2.** Affected with gloom; melancholy. **3.** Producing, or characterized by, gloom or melancholy. — **Syn.** See DARK: SULLEN. — **gloom′i·ly**, *adv.* — **gloom′i·ness**, *n.*

Glo′ri·a (glō′rĭ·ȧ; 70), *n.* [L., glory.] **1.** *Eccl.* One of certain Latin doxologies beginning with this word; also, its English version; esp.: **a** The **Glo′ri·a in Ex·cel′sis De′o** (ĭn ĕk·sĕl′sĭs dē′ō), "Glory be to God on high" based on the angelic hymn of Luke ii. 14. **b** The **Glo′ri·a Pa′tri** (pā′trī; pä′trĭ), "Glory be to the Father." **2.** [*not cap.*] A nimbus; aureole; also, an imitation of one. **3.** [*not cap.*] A glossy fabric of silk and wool or silk and cotton.

glo′ri·fi·ca′tion (glō′rĭ·fĭ·kā′shŭn), *n.* **1.** A glorifying, or state of being glorified. **2.** A festivity; jollification.

glo′ri·fi′er (glō′rĭ·fī′ẽr), *n.* One who glorifies.

glo′ri·fy (glō′rĭ·fī; 70), *v. t.;* -FIED (-fīd); -FY′ING. [OF. *glorifier*, fr. LL. *glorificare*, deriv. of *gloria* glory + *-ficare* (in comp.) to make.] **1.** To make glorious by bestowing glory upon; esp., to elevate to celestial glory. **2.** To shed radiance or splendor on. **3.** To make glorious by presentation in a favorable aspect; as, to *glorify* everyday life. **4.** To magnify in worship; to adore; exalt.

glo′ri·ole (glō′rĭ·ōl), *n.* [F., fr. L. *gloriola* a small glory, dim. of *gloria* glory.] An aureole; halo; nimbus; glory.

glo′ri·ous (-ŭs; 70), *adj.* [OF. *glorios, glorious*, fr. L. *gloriosus.*] **1.** *Obs.* Boastful; vainglorious. **2.** Exhibiting attributes, qualities, or acts that deserve or receive glory; praiseworthy. **3.** Splendid in appearance; resplendent. **4.** *Colloq.* Delightful; magnificent. — **Syn.** See SPLENDID. — **Ant.** Inglorious. — **glo′ri·ous·ly**, *adv.* — **glo′ri·ous·ness**, *n.*

glo′ry (glō′rĭ; 70), *n.; pl.* -RIES (-rĭz). [OF. *glorie* (F. *gloire*), fr. L. *gloria.*] **1.** Praise, honor, or distinction, accorded by common consent; renown. **2.** That which secures praise or renown; an occasion for praise. **3.** Honor and praise accorded in worship. **4.** Brilliancy; splendor. **5.** Celestial bliss; heaven. **6.** Height of prosperity or splendor; as, Spain in its *glory.* **7.** An emanation of light supposed to proceed from beings of peculiar sanctity; also, in art, a representation of such light by rays of gold, a golden disk, etc., around the head or body; an aureole, nimbus, or halo. — *v. i.;* -RIED (-rĭd); -RY·ING. **1.** To exult with joy or triumph; to be proud or boastful. **2.** To form a glory; to spread like a glory.

gloss (glŏs; 74), *n.* **1.** Brightness or luster; polish; as, the *gloss* of silk. **2.** A specious appearance; superficial quality or show. — *v. t.* **1.** To give luster or gloss to. **2.** To give a gloss, or specious appearance, to; to color.

gloss, *n.* [OF. *glose*, fr. L. *glossa* a word needing explanation, fr. Gr. *glōssa*, lit., tongue.] **1.** An interpretation, as of marginal or interlinear words; a note of explanation; loosely, a running commentary. **2.** Hence: **a** A glossary. **b** An interlinear translation. **3.** A false interpretation; a deceiving explanation. — *v. t.* **1.** To furnish with glosses; to explain by notes. **2.** To interpret speciously, or to pervert in this way. — *v. i.* To make glosses; to comment. — **Syn.** See ANNOTATE.

glos′sa (glŏs′ȧ), *n.; pl.* GLOSSAE (-ē). [NL., fr. Gr. *glōssa* the tongue.] *Zool.* The median anterior part of the labium of many insects.

glos′sal (glŏs′ăl), *adj.* Of or relating to the tongue.

glos·sar′i·al (glŏ·sâr′ĭ·ăl; 6), *adj.* Of, pertaining to, or of the nature of a glossary. — **glos·sar′i·al·ly**, *adv.*

glos′sa·rist (glŏs′ȧ·rĭst), *n.* A writer of glosses or compiler of a glossary; a commentator; scholiast.

glos′sa·ry (-rĭ), *n.; pl.* -RIES (-rĭz). [L. *glossarium.*] A collection of glosses; a partial dictionary of a work, an author, a science, explaining terms or words.

glos·sa′tor (glŏ·sā′tẽr), *n.* [ML.] A writer of glosses.

gloss′er (glŏs′ẽr), *n.* [See 1st GLOSS.] A polisher.

gloss′er, *n.* [See 2d GLOSS.] A writer of glosses.

glos′so- (glŏs′ō-), **gloss-**. [Gr. *glōssa* tongue.] A combining form denoting: **a** *Chiefly Med.* The *tongue*, as in **glos·sec′to·my, glos·sot′o·my** (see -ECTOMY, -TOMY). **b** A *gloss* or *glossary.* **c** *Anat. & Zool. Glossal* (and). **d** *Bot. & Zool. A tonguelike formation.*

glos·sog′ra·pher (glŏ·sŏg′rȧ·fẽr), *n.* [Gr. *glōssographos*, fr. *glōssa* tongue + *graphein* to write.] A writer of glosses.

glos·sol′o·gy (glŏ·sŏl′ō·jĭ), *n.; pl.* -GIES (-jĭz). [*glosso-* + *-logy.*] The science of language; linguistics. — **glos′so·log′i·cal** (glŏs′ō·lŏj′ĭ·kăl), *adj.* — **glos·sol′o·gist** (glŏ·sŏl′ō·jĭst), *n.*

gloss′y (glŏs′ĭ; 74), *adj.;* GLOSS′I·ER (-ĭ·ẽr); GLOSS′I·EST. [From GLOSS luster.] **1.** Smooth and shining; polished. **2.** Smooth; specious; plausible; as, *glossy* deceit. — **gloss′i·ly**, *adv.* — **gloss′i·ness**, *n.*

glost (glŏst), *n.* Glazed ware.

-glot (-glŏt). [Gr. *glōtta* tongue.] A combining form denoting *mastery of* or *expression in* (a specified number of) *languages*, as in *polyglot.*

glot′tal (glŏt′ăl; -'l), *adj.* Of, relating to, or produced in the glottis.

glot′tic (glŏt′ĭk), *adj.* **a** Glottal. **b** Of, relating to, or based upon, language; linguistic.

glot′tis (glŏt′ĭs), *n.* [NL., fr. Gr. *glōttis, glōssis*, fr. *glōtta, glōssa*, the tongue.] *Anat. & Zool.* The space between the vocal fold and arytenoid cartilage of one side of the larynx, and those of the other side.

glotto-. [See GLOTTIS.] A combining form denoting *language.*

glot·tol′o·gy (glŏ·tŏl′ō·jĭ), *n.* [*glotto-* + *-logy.*] Glossology; linguistics. — **glot′to·log′ic** (glŏt′ō·lŏj′ĭk), **glot′to·log′i·cal** (-ĭ·kăl), *adj.* — **glot·tol′o·gist** (glŏ·tŏl′ō·jĭst), *n.*

glove (glŭv), *n.* [AS. *glōf.*] **1.** A cover for the hand, now always with a separate sheath for each finger. Cf. MITTEN. **2.** A boxing glove. — *v. t.* To cover with or as with a glove.

glov′er (glŭv′ẽr), *n.* One who makes or sells gloves.

glow (glō), *v. i.* [AS. *glōwan.*] **1.** To shine with an intense or white heat. **2.** To exhibit a strong, bright color; to be brilliant or red, as with heat, animation, blushes, etc. **3.** To feel hot; to burn. **4.** To feel the heat of passion; to be animated. — *v. t.* **1.** To cause to glow. **2.** *Rare.* To express by glowing. — *n.* **1.** Light such as is emitted by a solid body heated to luminosity; incandescence. **2.** Brightness or warmth of color; redness. **3.** Intense excitement; vehemence or heat of emotion. **4.** Heat of body; a sensation of warmth, as from exercise, etc. — **Syn.** See BLAZE.

glow′er (glou′ẽr), *v. i.* **1.** *Scot.* To look intently. **2.** To stare or look angrily or with a scowl. — **Syn.** See FROWN. — *n.* Act of glowering; an angry stare.

glow′er·ing (glou′ẽr·ĭng), *adj.* That glowers. — **glow′er·ing·ly**, *adv.*

glow′fly′ (glō′flī′), *n.; pl.* -FLIES (-flīz′). A firefly.

glow′ing (glō′ĭng), *adj.* That glows. — **glow′ing·ly**, *adv.*

glow′worm′ (glō′wûrm′), *n.* Any of various luminous insects; as: **a** The wingless females and larvae of certain European beetles (genus *Lampyris*), which emit light from some of the abdominal segments. **b** In America, the larvae of certain fireflies and fire beetles, and the wingless adult females of the genus *Phengodes* (family Cantharidae).

glox·in′i·a (glŏk·sĭn′ĭ·ȧ; 58), *n.* [NL., after B. P. *Gloxin*, Ger. botanist.] *Hort.* A popular greenhouse herb (genus *Sinningia*, esp. the Brazilian *S. speciosa*), with large bell-shaped flowers, often handsomely spotted.

gloze (glōz), *n.* [ME. *glose* explanation, flattery, fr. OF. *glose.*] **1.** *Archaic.* A note or gloss. **2.** *Rare.* Flattery. **3.** *Rare.* Specious show; gloss. — *v. t.* **1.** *Obs.* To make glosses on; to explain. **2.** To smooth over; to palliate; gloss. — *v. i.* To make a gloss; to comment.

gloze, *v. t. & i.* To shine; glow; gleam.

glu·ci′num (glōō·sī′nŭm), *n.* Also **glu·cin′i·um** (-sĭn′ĭ·ŭm). [NL., deriv. of Gr. *glykys* sweet.] *Chem.* Beryllium. Symbol, *Gl*

glu′co·pro′te·in (glōō′kō·prō′tē·ĭn). Var. of GLYCOPROTEIN.

glu′cose (glōō′kōs; 114), *n.* [F., irreg. fr. Gr. *gleukos* must, sweet wine.] **1.** *Chem.* A sugar, $C_6H_{12}O_6$, occurring in three optically different forms, of which only one (dextrose, D-glucose, dextroglucose, or ordinary glucose) occurs in nature. See DEXTROSE. **2.** *Com.* A light-colored, uncrystallizable sirup obtained by the incomplete hydrolysis of starch and containing chiefly maltose, dextrin, and dextrose. In U. S., it is made chiefly from cornstarch and is called also *corn sirup* or *starch sirup.* Cf. SIRUP, 2.

glu′co·side (glōō′kō·sīd; -sĭd), *n.* Also **glu′co·sid.** [See GLUCOSE.] *Chem.* **a** Properly, any of certain compounds yielding glucose on hydrolysis. **b** Often, a glycoside.

glue (glōō; 114), *n.* [OF. *glu*, fr. LL. *glus, glutis.*] **1.** A hard gelatin, obtained esp. by boiling to a jelly the skins, hoofs, bones, etc., of animals. When heated with water, it is used for sticking things together. **2.** By extension, any of various adhesive or viscous substances. — *v. t.;* GLUED (glōōd); GLU′ING (glōō′ĭng). To cause to stick or hold fast, with or as with glue. — **glue′y** (glōō′ĭ), *adj.*

glum (glŭm), *adj.;* GLUM′MER (-ẽr); GLUM′MEST. [ME. *glomen* to look sullen, var. of *gloumen.*] Moody; gloomy. — **Syn.** See SULLEN. — **glum′ly**, *adv.* — **glum′ness**, *n.*

glu·ma′ceous (glōō·mā′shŭs; 114), *adj. Bot.* Consisting of, or of the nature of, glumes.

glume (glōōm), *n.* [L. *gluma* hull, husk, fr. root of *glubere* to peel.] *Bot.* A chaffy bract; specif., one of the two empty bracts at the base of the spikelet in grasses. See SPIKELET, *Illust.*

glump′y (glŭmp′ĭ), *adj.;* GLUMP′I·ER (-ĭ·ẽr); GLUMP′I·EST. *Colloq.* Glum; sullen; sulky. — **glump′i·ly**, *adv.*

glunch (glōōnsh; glŭnsh), *adj. Scot.* Frowning. — *n.* A sullen look. — *v. i.* To frown.

glut (glŭt), *v. t.;* GLUT′TED; GLUT′TING. [OF. *glotir, gloutir*, fr. L. *glutire, gluttire.*] To swallow, esp. greedily.

glut, *v. t.* [ME. *glotten.*] **1.** To fill to satiety; to satiate. **2.** To oversupply any article so that there is no sale for it at the price at which it is offered; — chiefly in *to glut the market.* — *v. i.* To eat gluttonously. — **Syn.** See SATIATE. — *n.* **1.** Act of glutting, or state of being glutted; a full supply; hence, often, a surfeit. **2.** A supply of mercantile goods in excess of the demand at the seller's price; an oversupply.

glu′ta·mine (glōō′tȧ·mēn; -mĭn), *n.* [*gluten* + *amine.*] *Chem.* A crystalline compound, $C_5H_{10}N_2O_3$, widely distributed in plants.

glu·te′al (glōō·tē′ăl; glōō′tē·ăl), *adj.* [From GLUTEUS.] Pert. to, or in the region of, the gluteus muscles.

glu′ten (glōō′tĕn; -t'n), *n.* [F. or L.; F., fr. L. *gluten* glue.] The viscid substance which gives adhesiveness to dough, esp. that made from wheat flour.

gluten bread. Bread made of **gluten flour**, which is a flour containing a high gluten and a low starch content.

glu′te·nous (glōō′tē·nŭs), *adj.* Resembling gluten; rich in, or possessing a high content of, gluten.

glu·te′us (glōō·tē′ŭs), *n.; pl.* -TEI (-ī). [NL., fr. Gr. *gloutos* rump, pl. the buttocks.] *Anat.* Any of the three muscles of the buttocks.

glu′ti·nous (glōō′tĭ·nŭs), *adj.* [L. *glutinosus*, fr. *gluten* glue.] Of the nature of glue; gluey. — **glu′ti·nous·ly**, *adv.* — **glu′ti·nous·ness**, *n.*

glut′ton (glŭt′'n), *n.* [OF. *glutun, glouton*, fr. L. *gluto, glutto.*] **1.** One who eats voraciously, or to excess; a gormandizer. **2.** [Trans. of G. *vielfrass* gormandizer, wolverine.] A shaggy, thickset, carnivorous mammal (*Gulo gulo*, family Mustelidae) of northern Europe and Asia, related to the martens and sables; also, the closely related wolverine (*Gulo luscus*) of North America. — **Syn.** See EPICURE.

glut′ton·ize (-īz), *v. i. & t.* To gormandize.

glut′ton·ous (glŭt′'n·ŭs), *adj.* Given to gluttony; voracious. — **glut′ton·ous·ly**, *adv.* — **glut′ton·ous·ness**, *n.*

glut′ton·y (-ĭ), *n.; pl.* GLUTTONIES (-ĭz). Excess in eating.

glyc′er·al′de·hyde (glĭs′ẽr·ăl′dē·hīd), *n.* [*glycer-*, a combining form for *glycerol* + *aldehyde*.] *Chem.* A sweet crystalline compound, $CH_2OHCHOHCHO$, formed by oxidation of glycerol.

gly·cer′ic (glĭ·sĕr′ĭk; glĭs′ẽr·ĭk), *adj.* *Chem.* Designating an acid (**glyceric acid**, $CH_2OHCHOHCO_2H$), obtained by partly oxidizing glycerol, and in other ways.

glyc′er·ide (glĭs′ẽr·īd; -ĭd), *n.* Also **-id.** [See GLYCERIN.] *Chem.* An ester of glycerol, either natural, as various fats, or artificial. See ESTER.

glyc′er·in (-ĭn), **glyc′er·ine** (-ĭn; -ēn), *n.* [F. *glycérine*, fr. Gr. *glykeros, glykys*, sweet.] Glycerol, esp. for industrial use. *Glycerin* was the original name and is still widely used.

glyc′er·ol (-ōl; -ŏl), *n.* *Chem.* A sweet, sirupy, trihydroxy alcohol, $C_3H_5(OH)_3$, colorless, odorless, and hygroscopic, obtained by saponifying natural fats and fixed oils. It is an excellent solvent.

glyc′er·yl (-ĭl), *n.* [*glycerin* + *-yl.*] *Chem.* A trivalent radical, CH_2CHCH_2, of which glycerol is the hydroxide.

gly·cine′ (glī·sēn′; glī′sēn; -sĭn), *n.* [Gr. *glykys* sweet.] *Chem.* A sweet-tasting crystalline acid, $NH_2CH_2CO_2H$, obtained from certain proteins, etc.

gly′co·gen (glī′kō·jĕn), *n.* [Gr. *glykys* sweet + *-gen.*] *Biochem.* A white, amorphous, tasteless carbohydrate, $(C_6H_{10}O_5)x$, related to starch and dextrin, found abundantly in the liver of most animals.

gly′co·gen′ic (-jĕn′ĭk), *adj.* Pertaining to, or caused by, glycogen; as, the *glycogenic* function of the liver.

gly′col (glī′kōl; -kŏl), *n.* [*glycerin* + *-ol.* See GLYCERIN.] *Chem.* **a** A thick, sweet, colorless liquid, $C_2H_4(OH)_2$, produced from certain ethylene compounds. **b** Any of the class of dihydroxy alcohols, of which glycol proper is the type.

gly·col′ic (glī·kŏl′ĭk), *adj.* *Chem.* Designating an acid (**glycolic acid**, CH_2OHCO_2H), in unripe grapes and in the leaves of the Virginia creeper, and made artificially.

gly′co·pro′te·in (glī′kō·prō′tē·ĭn; -tēn), **gly′co·pro′te·id** (-tē·ĭd), *n.* [Gr. *glykys* sweet + *protein.*] *Biochem.* Any of a class of compounds of a protein with a substance or substances (other than nucleic acid) containing a carbohydrate group.

gly′co·side (glī′kō·sīd; -sĭd), **gly′co·sid** (-sĭd), *n.* [From *glycose* glucose.] *Chem.* Any of a class of compounds, as amygdalin and salicin, which on hydrolysis yield a sugar (most commonly glucose).

gly′co·su′ri·a (-sū′rĭ·ȧ), *n.* [NL., fr. *glycose* glucose + *-uria.*] *Med.* A condition in which sugar, esp. glucose, is excreted in the urine, as in diabetes mellitus. — **gly′co·su′ric** (-rĭk), *adj.*

glyph (glĭf), *n.* [Gr. *glyphē* carving, fr. *glyphein* to carve.] **1.** *Arch.* A channel or groove, usually vertical. **2.** *Archaeol.* A carved figure; hence, a pictograph representing a form for sculpture. — **glyph′ic** (-ĭk), *adj.*

glyp′tic (glĭp′tĭk), *adj.* [Gr. *glyptos* fit for carving, carved. See GLYPH.] Pert. to carving or engraving, esp. on gems.

glyp′to·dont (glĭp′tō·dŏnt), *n.* [Gr. *glyptos* carved + *-odont.*] *Paleontol.* Any of a genus (*Glyptodon*) of large extinct mammals related to the armadillos.

glyp·tog′ra·phy (glĭp·tŏg′rȧ·fĭ), *n.* [Gr. *glyptos* carved + *-graphy.*] Art or process of engraving gems; also, the description or study of engraved gems. — **glyp·tog′ra·pher** (-fẽr), *n.* — **glyp′to·graph′ic** (glĭp′tō·grăf′ĭk), *adj.*

G man. [For *G*overnment *man.*] *U.S.* A special agent of the Federal Bureau of Investigation.

gnar, gnarr (När), *v. i.*; GNARRED (närd); GNAR′RING. To snarl; growl; — chiefly of dogs.

gnarl (närl), *v. i.* To growl; snarl.

gnarl, *v. t.* To twist or contort. — **Syn.** See DEFORM. — *n.* A knot in wood; a large or hard knot on a tree. — **gnarl′y**, *adj.*

gnarled (närld), *adj.* [Var. of KNURLED.] Knotty; full of knots or gnarls; twisted; cross-grained; rugged.

gnash (năsh), *v. i. & t.* [ME. *gnasten, gnaisten.*] To grind or strike together, as the teeth in anger. — **gnash**, *n.*

gnat (năt), *n.* [AS. *gnæt.*] Any of various small dipterous insects or flies, esp. such as bite; — applied in England chiefly to mosquitoes, in America to smaller forms.

gnath′ic (năth′ĭk), *adj.* [Gr. *gnathos* jaw.] Of or pertaining to the jaw.

gnathic index. *Craniom.* The ratio of the distance from nasion to basion (taken as 100) to that from the basion to the point on the alveolar process midway between the median upper incisor teeth. Cf. FACIAL INDEX.

gna′thi·on (nā′thĭ·ŏn; năth′ĭ·ŏn), *n.* [NL.] *Craniol.* The lower end of the symphysis of the jaw.

gna·thon′ic (nă·thŏn′ĭk), *adj.* [From *Gnatho*, a parasite in a play of Terence.] Flattering; deceitful.

-gnathous. A combining form meaning *-jawed.*

gnaw (nô), *v. t.*; GNAWED (nôd); GNAWED OR GNAWN (nôn); GNAW′ING. [AS. *gnagan.*] **1.** To bite so as to wear away or remove a part from; to eat away by scraping or biting with the teeth; loosely, to chew upon. **2.** To corrode; to fret away. **3.** To produce a pain in (the stomach or bowels) likened to that caused by gnawing. — *v. i.* **1.** To bite with repeated effort; as, *gnawing* on a crust of bread. **2.** To have an effect like gnawing with the teeth. — **gnaw′er** (-ẽr), *n.*

gnaw′ing, *n.* A pain (in the stomach) likened to that caused by gnawing; in *pl.*, pangs; as, *gnawings* of hunger.

gneiss (nīs), *n.* [G.] *Petrog.* A laminated or foliated metamorphic rock, corresponding in composition to granite or some other feldspathic plutonic rock. — **gneiss′ic** (-ĭk), *adj.* — **gneiss′oid** (-oid), *adj.*

gnome (nōm; nō′mē), *n.* [Gr. *gnōmē*, fr. root of *gignōskein* to know.] A brief reflection or maxim; aphorism; saw.

gnome (nōm), *n.* [F.] One of a fabled race of diminutive subterranean beings, guardians of mines, quarries, etc.

gno′mic (nō′mĭk; nŏm′ĭk), *adj.* Also **gno′mi·cal** (nō′mĭ·kăl; nŏm′ĭ-). [Gr. *gnōmikos*, fr. *gnōmē*. See GNOME maxim.] Uttering or containing maxims; aphoristic; also, pertaining to the **gnomic poets**, certain Greek poets whose writings are of a gnomic character.

gno·mol′o·gy (nō·mŏl′ō·jĭ), *n.* [Gr. *gnōmologia*, fr. *gnōmē* judgment, maxim + *logos* discourse.] Gnomic discourse, or a collection of gnomes.

gno′mon (nō′mŏn), *n.* [L., fr. Gr. *gnōmōn* one that knows, the index of a sundial.] **1.** Any object which by the position or length of its shadow serves as an indicator, esp. of the time, as the style of a sundial, a column erected perpendicularly to the horizon, etc. **2.** *Geom.* The remainder of a parallelogram after removal of a similar parallelogram containing one of its corners; as, the *gnomon bcdefg* in the *Illust.*

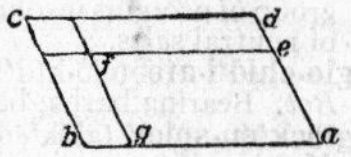

Gnomon, 2.

gno·mon′ic (nō·mŏn′ĭk), *adj.* Also **gno·mon′i·cal** (-ĭ·kăl). Of or pertaining to the gnomon or the art of indicating time by means of a gnomon.

gno′sis (nō′sĭs), *n.* [NL., fr. Gr. *gnōsis.*] *Metaph.* Positive knowledge, esp. of spiritual truth, such as was claimed by the Gnostics.

-gnosis. [See GNOSIS.] *Med. & Psychol.* A combining form denoting *cognition*, or *recognition*, as in psycho*gnosis*. Corresponding adjectives are formed in **-gnostic.**

gnos′tic (nŏs′tĭk), *adj.* Also **gnos′ti·cal** (-tĭ·kăl). **1.** Of, pertaining to, or characterized by knowledge or gnosis. **2.** [*cap.*] Of or pertaining to Gnosticism or the Gnostics. — **gnos′ti·cal·ly**, *adv.*

Gnos′tic, *n.* [LL. *gnosticus*, fr. Gr. *gnōstikos* sagacious, fr. *gignōskein* to know.] An adherent of Gnosticism.

Gnos′ti·cism (-tĭ·sĭz'm), *n.* A philosophicoreligious movement of pre-Christian times and later, having several forms, Pagan and Christian, all of which were characterized by the central doctrine that emancipation came through knowledge, gnosis, the possession of which saved the initiates from the clutch of matter.

gno′thi se·au·ton′ (g′nō′thĭ sĕ·ou·tŏn′). [Gr.] Know thyself; — maxim inscribed on the ancient temple of Apollo at Delphi.

gnu (nōō; nū), *n.*; see PLURAL, *Note*, 3. [Cape Bushman *nqu.*] Any of a genus (*Connochaetes*) of African antelopes, with an oxlike head, short mane, downward-curved horns, and long tail.

go (gō; 4), *v. i.*; WENT (wĕnt); GONE (gŏn; 74); GO′ING. *Went* comes from the AS. *wendan*. See WEND, *v.* [AS. *gān.*] **1.** To move on a course; to proceed. **2.** To depart; — opposed to *come.* **3.** To pass about or abroad (in a certain state); as, to *go* armed. **4.** To be rejected, relinquished, displaced, or abolished; to cease to operate or be efficient; hence, of a person, to faint; fail; die. **5.** To be kept in motion or action; to operate; — said of a machine. **6.** Of time, to pass; to elapse. **7.** To pass current or have currency. **8.** To follow a given course or procedure. **9.** To proceed or happen in a given manner. **10.** To be expressed or phrased; as, the second clause *goes* thus. **11.** To give way; to break; as, the sails *went* in the gale. **12.** To extend along a denoted space; to reach; as, this road *goes* to London. **13.** To have recourse or resort; as, to *go* to the country with a political issue. **14.** To put oneself, as to trouble or expense. **15.** To participate equally in; as, to *go* shares, etc., with someone. **16.** To enter a given relation; as, to *go* bail. **17.** To have its usual or proper place; to belong; as, that book *goes* on the second shelf. **18.** To harmonize; also, to suit; fit; as, congenial men who *go* with any group. — *v. t.* **1.** *Colloq.* To endure; tolerate. **2.** To bet or wager.

☞ *Go* is used, with many prepositions and adverbs, to denote motion of the kind indicated by the preposition or adverb, in which, and not in the verb, lies the main force of the expression; as, to *go against, go out, go astray*, etc.

Syn. **Go, leave, depart, quit, withdraw, retire** mean to move out of or away from the place where one is. **Go**, the most general term, is often used as the opposite of *come;* **leave** usually implies in addition a separation from somebody expressed or understood; **depart**, a more formal or less colloquial term, usually has as its opposite *arrive;* **quit** adds to *leave* an implication of getting free from that which holds, burdens, or the like; **withdraw** implies a deliberate removal for some just reason and rarely connotes, as *quit* often does, instability, cowardice, or the like; **retire**, close to *withdraw*, is preferred when a relinquishing, a retreat, a recoil, etc., is also implied. — **Ant.** Come.

go about. *Naut.* To tack. — ***go behind.*** **a** To investigate the elements which have produced (some result); as, to *go behind* the returns of an election. **b** To lose money. — ***go better.*** In poker, etc., to raise the previous bet; hence, *Colloq.*, to outbid or surpass; to exceed. — ***go under.*** To sink, as under water; to go to ruin; succumb.

— (gō), *n.*; *pl.* GOES (gōz). **1.** *Colloq.* Power of going or doing; energy; spirit. **2.** *Colloq.* With *the*, the fashion; the rage. **3.** *Colloq.* A circumstance; incident; as, a pretty *go.* **4.** Something that goes or is successful; a success; also, a bargain. **5.** *Colloq.* An attempt, or try; as, a brief *go* at farming. **6.** *Colloq.* Quantity used or furnished at one time, as of liquor. — ***no go.*** *Colloq.* Useless; hopeless; as, that plan is *no go.* — ***on, or upon, the go.*** In a state of activity, esp. restless activity.

go′a (gō′ȧ), *n.* [Tibetan *dgoba* (pronounced *gowa*).] A common gazelle (*Gazella picticaudata*) of Tibet.

goad (gōd), *n.* [AS. *gād* spear, point, arrow.] **1.** A pointed rod used to urge on a beast. **2.** Something that produces the effect of a goad; a spur. — **Syn.** See MOTIVE. — *v. t.* To prick; to drive with or as with a goad.

go′-a·head′, *adj.* Advancing; hence, *Colloq.*, enterprising.

goal (gōl; *dial.* gōōl), *n.* [ME. *gol*, of uncert. origin.] **1.** The mark set to bound a race; the end of a race or a journey. **2.** The end to which a design tends; objective; aim. **3.** In various games, one of the stations or bounds towards which the players strive to advance the ball, puck, etc., to score points; also, act of causing the ball, etc., to go through or into a goal, or the point or score thus made. — **Syn.** See INTENTION. — ***goal from the field.*** In American football, a goal made by a drop kick or from placement.

goal′ee, goal′ie (gōl′ē), *n.* *Colloq.* A goalkeeper.

goal′keep′er (gōl′kēp′ẽr), *n.*, *or* **goal tender.** In certain games, a player whose duty it is to defend the goal.

Go′a pow′der (gō′ȧ). [From *Goa*, India.] *Pharm.* A bitter powder found in the interspaces of the wood of a Brazilian tree (*Vataireopsis araroba*) of the pea family. See CHRYSAROBIN.

goat (gōt), *n.*; see PLURAL, *Note*, 3. [AS. *gāt.*] **1.** Any of certain hollow-horned ruminant mammals allied to the sheep, but of lighter build, with backwardly arching horns, a short tail, and (usually) straight hair. The true goats constitute a genus (*Capra*, family Bovidae). See ANGORA GOAT, IBEX. **2.** In medieval bestiary lore, the animal type of lechery; hence, a libidinous man. **3.** *Slang.* A scapegoat; as, they made him the *goat.* **4.** [*cap.*] *Astron.* = CAPRICORN. — **goat′like′** (-līk′), *adj.* — **goat′skin′** (-skĭn′), *n.*

goat antelope. Any of certain ruminants intermediate between the goats and antelopes, as the chamois and goral.

goat′ee′ (gō′tē′; 2), *n.* A man's beard on the chin, trimmed to a point.
goat′fish′ (gōt′fĭsh′), *n.; pl.*, see FISH. Any of certain mullets (family Mullidae), esp. the ***red goatfish*** (*Upeneus maculatus*) and the ***yellow goatfish*** (*U. martinicus*), of the West Indies, Florida, etc.
goat′–god′, *n.* Pan.
goat′herd′ (gōt′hûrd′), *n.* A herder of goats.
goat′ish, *adj.* Characteristic of a goat; goatlike; hence, coarse; lecherous. — **goat′ish·ly**, *adv.* — **goat′ish·ness**, *n.*
goat, *or* **goat's, pepper**. The chili. See PEPPER, 3.
goats′beard′ (gōts′bẽrd′), *n.* **a** Any of a genus (*Tragopogon*) of plants of the chicory family; salsify. **b** An herb (*Aruncus sylvester*) of the rose family, grown for its small white flowers.
goat's′–rue′ (-rōō′), *n.* In Europe, a plant (*Galega officinalis*) of the pea family.
goat′suck′er (gōt′sŭk′ẽr), *n.* Any of numerous fissirostral birds which constitute two families (Caprimulgidae and Podargidae, order Caprimulgiformes), including the nightjar (*Caprimulgus europaeus*), called *goatsucker* under the mistaken notion that it sucks the milk of goats. Among American species are the whippoorwill, chuck-will's-widow, and nighthawks.
gob (gŏb), *n.* [OF. *gobe.*] *Dial. & Slang.* A mass; lump.
gob, *n.* *Slang.* A sailor of the U. S. Navy.
gob′bet (gŏb′ĕt; -ĭt), *n.* [OF. *gobet.*] **1.** A portion or fragment; — now chiefly of flesh. **2.** A lump; mass.
gob′ble (gŏb′'l), *v. t. & i.;* GOB′BLED (-'ld); GOB′BLING (-lĭng). [F. *gober* to swallow, fr. *gobet* mouthful, lump.] To swallow or eat greedily; *Slang*, to take eagerly.
gob′ble, *v. i.* [Imitative.] To make its characteristic guttural noise; — said of a turkey cock, or **gob′bler** (gŏb′lẽr). — **gob′ble**, *n.*
gob′ble·dy·gook′ (gŏb′'l·dĭ·gōōk′), *n.* [Coined by U. S. Representative Maury Maverick (b. 1895), of Texas, after the gobbling of turkeys.] *Slang, U. S.* Inflated, involved, and obscure verbiage characteristic of the pronouncements of officialdom.
Gob′e·lin (gŏb′ĕ·lĭn; gô′blăN′), *adj.* Designating tapestry produced in the famous Gobelin works in Paris.
go′–be·tween′, *n.* An intermediate agent; a broker.
go′bi·oid (gō′bĭ·oid), *adj.* [See GOBY, -OID.] Of or pertaining to the gobies. — *n.* A gobioid fish.
gob′let (gŏb′lĕt; -lĭt), *n.* [OF. *gobelet.*] **1.** *Archaic.* A type of cup without a handle; loosely, any wine cup. **2.** A drinking glass with a foot and stem. Cf. TUMBLER, 3.
gob′lin (gŏb′lĭn), *n.* [F. *gobelin*, fr. ML. *gobelinus.*] A sprite usually conceived as ugly or grotesque and either as evil and malicious or as merely mischievous. — **gob′lin**, *adj.*
go′bo (gō′bō), *n.; pl.* GOBOS (-bōz). *Motion Pictures, Television, etc.* **a** A dark strip, as of wallboard, to shield a camera lens from lights. **b** A device to shield a microphone from sounds.
go′by (gō′bĭ), *n.; see* PLURAL, *Note*, 3. [L. *gobius, gobio*, a kind of fish, fr. Gr. *kōbios.*] Any of a large, widely distributed family (Gobiidae) of spiny-finned, mostly marine fishes, with thoracic pelvic fins often united to form a sucking disk.
go′cart′ (gō′kärt′), *n.* **1.** A framework on casters, to support children while learning to walk. **2.** A baby carriage, esp. one with front wheels smaller than the rear wheels. **3.** A type of light carriage.
god (gŏd; *often* gôd *or even* gôd, *especially in speaking with reverence of the Divine Being*), *n.* [AS.] **1.** A being of more than human attributes and powers; a deity, esp. a male deity; anything worshiped by man as a deity, as **earth′–god′**, **moon′–god′**, **rain′–god′**, **sun′–god′**, **wind′–god′**. **2.** An idol. **3.** **God.** The Supreme Being; the eternal and infinite Spirit, Creator and Sovereign of the universe. **4.** The ruler or sovereign embodiment of some aspect, attribute, or department of reality; as, the *god* of love; also, a supreme being conceived as a world soul; as, the pantheistic *god.* **5.** A person or thing deified. **6.** **God.** *Christian Science.* Incorporeal, divine, supreme, infinite Mind, Spirit, Soul, Principle, Life, Truth, Love. *Mary Baker Eddy.* — *v. t.;* GOD′DED (-ĕd; -ĭd); GOD′DING. To treat as a god; to deify.
god′child′ (gŏd′chīld′), *n.* One for whom a person becomes sponsor at baptism; a godson or goddaughter.
god′daugh′ter (-dô′tẽr), *n.* A female godchild.
god·den′. Dial. var. of "good even."
god′dess (gŏd′ĕs; -ĭs), *n.* **1.** A female god. **2.** A woman of great charms, or one whom one adores.
go′–dev′il (gō′dĕv′'l), *n.* Any of various machines; as: **a** A weight which is dropped into a bored hole, as of an oil well, to explode a cartridge. **b** A scraper for cleaning oil pipe lines. **c** *Local, U. S.* A rough sled used for dragging logs, stone, etc. **d** *Railroads.* A handcar for transporting laborers and supplies.
god′fa′ther (gŏd′fä′thẽr), *n.* **1.** A man who becomes sponsor for a child at baptism or confirmation. **2.** One having a relation to someone else analogous to that of a male sponsor to his godchild. — *v. t.* To act as godfather to.
god′head (-hĕd), *n.* **1.** Divine nature or essence. **2.** [*cap.*] The Deity; God. **3.** *Rare.* A divinity.
god′hood (-hŏŏd), *n.* Godhead; godship.
Go·di′va (gō·dī′vȧ; -dē′vȧ), *n.* According to a legend, a Saxon lady who rode naked through the streets of Coventry to fill a condition upon which her husband had promised to relieve the town of a tax.
god′less (gŏd′lĕs; -lĭs), *adj.* Having, or acknowledging, no God; ungodly; impious. — **god′less·ness**, *n.*
god′like′ (-līk′), *adj.* Like, or befitting, a god or God; divine; hence, pre-eminently good. — **god′like′ness**, *n.*
god′ling (-lĭng), *n.* An inferior or purely local deity.
god′ly (-lĭ), *adj.;* GOD′LI·ER (-lĭ·ẽr); GOD′LI·EST (-ĕst; -ĭst). **1.** Divine. **2.** Pious; devout; righteous. — **god′li·ly**, *adv.* *Rare.* — **god′li·ness**, *n.*
god′moth′er (-mŭth′ẽr), *n.* A woman sponsor for a child in baptism. — *v. t.* To act as a godmother to.
go·down′ (gō·doun′), *n.* [Corrupt. of Malay *godon* warehouse.] In eastern Asia, the Philippines, etc., a warehouse.
god′par′ent (gŏd′pâr′ĕnt), *n.* A sponsor at baptism.
go·droon′ (gō·drōōn′). Var. of GADROON.
God's acre (gŏdz). A churchyard; a burying ground.
god′send′ (gŏd′sĕnd′), *n.* [For *God's send*, fr. ME. *sande, sonde*, a sending, message.] Some desirable or needed thing which comes unexpectedly as if sent by God.
god′ship (-shĭp), *n.* The character of a god; deity; divinity.
god′son′ (gŏd′sŭn′), *n.* A male godchild.
God′speed′ (-spēd′), *n.* Success; prosperous journeying; — a contraction of "God speed you."
God′ward (-wẽrd), **God′wards** (-wẽrdz), *adv.* Toward God; also, in relation or with reference to God.
god′wit (-wĭt), *n.* Any of a genus (*Limosa*) of long-billed wading birds of the snipe family, much like the curlews.
go′er (gō′ẽr), *n.* One who or that which goes.
goe′thite (gō′thīt; gû′tīt). Var. of GÖTHITE.
gof′fer (gŏf′ẽr), **gauf′fer** (gôf′-), *v. t.* [F. *gaufrer* to figure cloth, velvet, etc., fr. *gaufre* honeycomb, waffle.] To plait, crimp, or flute, as lace, paper, etc. — *n.* **1.** A goffering iron or press. **2.** A crimping or fluting.
go′–get′ter (gō′gĕt′ẽr; 2), *n.* *Slang.* An aggressive person who goes after and gets what he wants; a hustler.
gog′gle (gŏg′'l), *v. i.;* GOG′GLED (-'ld); GOG′GLING (-lĭng). **1.** To squint; to roll the eyes; stare. **2.** To turn to one side; to squint; roll; — said of the eyes. — *v. t.* To turn (the eyes) to one side or from side to side. — *n.* **1.** An affected rolling of the eye. **2.** *pl.* A kind of protective spectacles. — *adj.* Protruding; staring; — said of the eyes.
gog′gle–eyed′, *adj.* Having bulging or rolling eyes.
gog′let (gŏg′lĕt; -lĭt), *n.* [Pg. *gorgoleta.*] *Anglo-Ind.* A long-necked vessel, of porous earthenware, for cooling water by evaporation.
Goid′el·ic (goi·dĕl′ĭk; gȧ·thĕl′ĭk; gâl′ĭk), *adj.* [See GAEL.] Of, belonging to, or designating, the Gaels or their language. Cf. BRYTHONIC. — *n.* That branch of Celtic which comprises Irish, Gaelic, and Manx. See INDO-EUROPEAN LANGUAGES, *Table.*
go′ing (gō′ĭng), *n.* **a** Departure. **b** Course of life; behavior; — usually *pl.* **c** *Obs.* Gait. **d** Condition of the ground for traveling, crossing, or racing. — *adj.* **a** That goes; in existence; obtainable; also, working; in operation. **b** Carrying on its ordinary business; — in the phrases *a going business, a going concern*, etc. **c** Of or pertaining to a going business; as, the *going* value of a company.
goi′ter, goi′tre (goi′tẽr), *n.* [F. *goitre*, fr. OF. *goitron* throat, deriv. of L. *guttur.*] *Med.* An enlargement of the thyroid gland, seen as a swelling on the anterior part of the neck; also, the diseased condition. In ***exophthalmic goiter*** there are diffuse increase of glandular tissue, prominence of the eyeballs, nervous excitability, accelerated heart beat, muscular tremor, and loss of weight. — **goi′trous** (-trŭs), *adj.*
Gol·con′da (gŏl·kŏn′dȧ), *n.* A rich mine; hence, any source of great wealth; — from the city of Golconda, in India.
gold (gōld), *n.* [AS.] **1.** A yellow metallic element, the most precious metal used as a common commercial medium of exchange. Symbol, *Au* (for Lat. *aurum*); at. no., 79; at. wt., 197.2. It is the most malleable and ductile of all the metals, and very heavy (sp. gr., 19.3). **2.** Gold coin; hence, riches. **3.** The yellow color of the metal. — *adj.* Made or consisting of gold; having the color of gold; golden; also, pertaining to or payable in gold.
gold′beat′er (gōld′bēt′ẽr), *n.* One who beats gold into gold leaf.
gold′beat′er's skin (-bēt′ẽrz). The membrane of the large intestine of the ox, used to separate the leaves of metal in goldbeating.
gold′beat′ing (-bēt′ĭng), *n.* Also **gold beating**. Act, art, or process of hammering pieces of gold into extremely thin leaves.
gold beetle. Also, *U. S.*, **gold′bug′** (gōld′bŭg′), *n.* Any of various beetles (subfamily Cassidinae) having a golden luster.
gold brick. *Colloq., U. S.* A pretended or real brick of gold, sold by a swindler to his victim, to whom is delivered the spurious brick or some substitute for the genuine one.
gold′brick′ (gōld′brĭk′), **gold′brick′er** (-brĭk′ẽr), *n.* *U. S. Army Slang.* **a** Orig., a soldier who, because of assignment to special duty, is free from army routine such as drill or K.P. **b** Usually, a soldier who uses excuses or devious means to evade assigned work; a shirker. — **gold′brick′**, *v. i.*
gold certificate. *U. S.* A certificate, issued by the secretary of the Treasury, that gold coin or bullion of a stated value in dollars has been deposited in the Treasury and is payable on demand to the bearer.
gold′cup′ (-kŭp′), *n.* See CROWFOOT, 1.
gold digger. **1.** One who digs gold. **2.** *Slang, U. S.* A woman whose relations with men are primarily for selfish mercenary advantages.
gold′en (gōl′dĕn; -d'n), *adj.* **1.** Made of gold; pertaining to gold. **2.** Containing, or abounding in, gold. **3.** Having the color of gold; as, the *golden* grain. **4.** Very precious; as, *golden* hours. **5.** Prosperous and happy; flourishing. — **gold′en·ly**, *adv.*
golden age. A period of great prosperity and progress or of the flowering of civilization or art.
golden aster. See ASTER.
golden buck. Welsh rabbit with a poached egg on it.
golden eagle. See EAGLE, 1.
gold′en·eye′ (gōl′dĕn·ī′; -d'n·ī′), *n.;* see PLURAL, *Note*, 3. A duck (*Glaucionetta clangula*) found in Europe and Asia, and represented in North America by a related variety, the ***American goldeneye*** (*G. c. americana*). The goldeneyes are expert divers and are noted for their swift whistling flight. Cf. BUFFLEHEAD.
Golden Fleece. *Gr. Myth.* The fleece of gold placed by the king of Colchis in a sacred grove, where it was guarded by a dragon. See JASON.
golden glow. A tall branching herb (*Rudbeckia laciniata hortensia*) with showy, yellow, much-doubled flower heads. See RUDBECKIA.
golden goose. The goose which, according to an ancient Greek fable, laid golden eggs, but was killed by its owner, who hoped to get all the gold at once.
golden mean. [Trans. of L. *aurea mediocritas.*] The way of wisdom and safety between extremes; moderation.
golden nematode. A small yellowish Old World nematode worm (*Heterodera rostochiensis*), a serious potato pest on Long Island.
gold′en·ness, *n.* Quality of being golden.
golden oriole. See ORIOLE, 1.
golden pheasant. See PHEASANT.
golden robin. The Baltimore oriole (see ORIOLE, 2).
gold′en·rod′ (gōl′dĕn·rŏd′; gōl′d'n-), *n.* Any of a genus (*Solidago*) or of several related genera (*Brachychaeta*, etc.) of summer-blooming and fall-blooming perennials or biennials of the aster family, with wandlike stems, variously shaped leaves, and heads of small yellow, or rarely white, flowers, often clustered in panicles. Species have been adopted as State flowers by Alabama, Kentucky, and Nebraska.
golden rule. The rule of doing to others as we would have them do to us. *Matt.* vii. 12; *Luke* vi. 31.
gold′en·seal′ (gōl′dĕn·sēl′; gōl′d'n-), *n.* A perennial American herb

(*Hydrastis canadensis*) of the crowfoot family, with a thick, knotted, yellow rootstock and large rounded leaves. See HYDRASTINE.

Golden State. California; — a nickname, from its gold mines.

golden warbler. The yellow warbler (*Dendroica aestiva*) or other closely allied species, chiefly yellow in color.

golden wattle. *Australasia.* Any of various yellow-flowered species of a genus (*Acacia*, esp. *A. pycnantha* and *A. longifolia*) of the mimosa family. It is the unofficial floral emblem of Australia.

gold′-ex·change′ stand′ard. *Finance.* A currency system in which the domestic currency is kept at a parity with the standard money of a foreign gold-standard country.

gold′-filled′ (gōld′fĭld′; 2), *adj.* *Jewelry.* Covered with a layer of gold so as to constitute filled gold. See FILLED GOLD.

gold′finch′ (-fĭnch′), *n.* [AS. *goldfinc.*] **a** A small brightly colored European finch (*Carduelis carduelis*), often kept as a cage bird; — so called from the yellow on the wings. **b** In America, any of various small finches (genus *Spinus*, esp. *S. tristis*). In summer the male becomes bright yellow, with black wings, tail, and crown. See BILL, *Illust.*

gold′fin′ny (gōld′fĭn′ĭ), *n.; pl.* -NIES (-ĭz). A small brightly colored European wrasse (*Ctenolabrus rupestris*); also, any of several related European wrasses, as the cunner.

gold′fish′ (-fĭsh′), *n.; pl.*, see FISH. **1.** A small fish (*Carassius auratus*) of the carp family, chiefly golden-yellow or orange, kept in aquariums and ponds. **2.** *Army Slang.* Salmon.

gold foil. Gold beaten or rolled out very thin; specif., gold in sheets thicker than gold leaf. — **gold′-foil′**, *adj.*

gold′i·locks′ (gōl′dĭ·lŏks′), *n.* **1.** A person with golden hair. **2. a** A European herb (*Linosyris vulgaris*) of the aster family, with heads of flowers resembling those of goldenrod. **b** A European buttercup (*Ranunculus auricomus*).

gold leaf. A leaf of gold, of extreme thinness, used for gilding, etc. It varies ordinarily from 0.000005 to 0.000004 of an inch in thickness. Cf. GOLD FOIL. — **gold′-leaf′**, *adj.*

gold note. *Banking.* A note payable in gold.

gold′-of-pleas′ure, *n.* A European herb (*Camelina*, esp. *C. sativa*) of the mustard family, with yellow flowers, widely naturalized in North America.

gold point. *Finance.* In foreign exchange, the rate of exchange at which it is as cheap to settle accounts by the shipment of gold as it is to do so by buying exchange.

gold reserve. A fund of gold; specif.: **a** The gold held by the United States Treasury for the redemption of United States notes and treasury notes. **b** *Banking.* The amount of gold held by the central bank of a country.

gold′smith′ (gōld′smĭth′), *n.* An artisan who manufactures vessels and ornaments, etc., of gold. Goldsmiths commonly acted as bankers as late as the 18th century.

goldsmith beetle. A large, bright-yellow American beetle (*Cotalpa lanigera*, family Scarabaeidae), which eats the foliage of various trees.

gold standard. *Econ.* A standard, consisting solely of gold, used for measuring values; usually, a certain weight of gold declared to constitute a standard coin. The United States in 1933 substituted for the gold standard a managed gold reserve standard by which gold is held as bullion, not coined, often called a "gold-bullion standard."

gold′stone′ (gōld′stōn′), *n.* Aventurine of jewellike appearance in which the gold spangles are very close and fine.

gold′thread′ (-thrĕd′), *n.* **a** A North American herb (*Coptis groenandica*) with fibrous yellow roots. **b** Dodder.

golf (gŏlf), *n.* [Late ME., prob. fr. MD. *colf*, *colve* (D. *kolf*), club, *colven* to play a game with sticks or clubs.] A game which consists in striking a small, resilient ball (**golf ball**) with clubs (**golf clubs**) having heads (wooden or metal), into a series of holes (usually nine or eighteen) situated at varying distances on a course (**golf links**) with natural or artificial obstacles, or hazards, irregularly interposed. The object is to put the ball into each hole in as few strokes as possible. — *v. i.* To play golf. — **golf′er** (gŏl′fẽr), *n.*

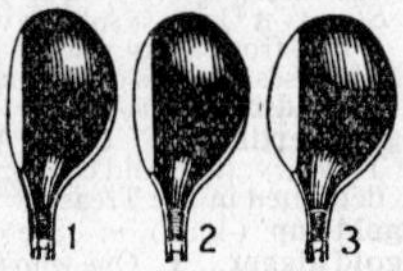

Golf, fig. 1. Wooden Clubs. 1 Driver; 2 Brassie; 3 Spoon.

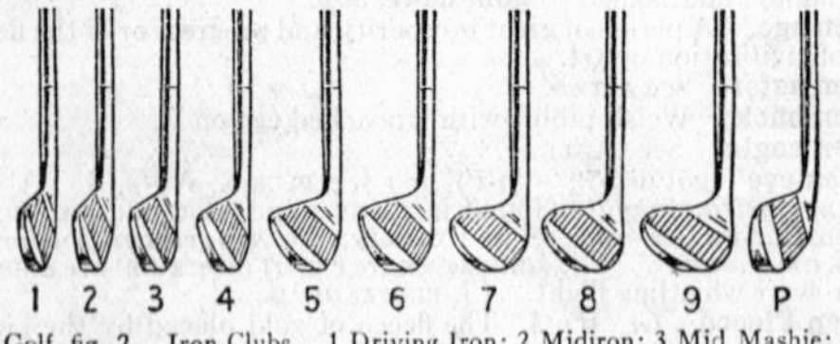

Golf, fig. 2. Iron Clubs. 1 Driving Iron; 2 Midiron; 3 Mid Mashie; 4 Mashie Iron; 5 Mashie; 6 Mashie Niblick; 7 Pitcher; 8 Pitching Niblick; 9 Niblick; *P* Putter.

Gol′go·tha (gŏl′gō·thȧ), *n.* [LL. & Gr., fr. Aram. *gūlgūlthā*, fr. Heb. *gulgōleth* skull.] **1.** Calvary. **2.** [*not cap.*] **a** A burial place. **b** A place of torment or martyrdom.

gol′iard (gōl′yẽrd), *n.* [OF., jester, glutton, fr. *gole* gullet.] One of a class of wandering students, chiefly of the 12th and 13th centuries, who composed loose and satirical Latin verse, and served as jesters or minstrels. — **gol·iar′der·y** (gōl·yär′dẽr·ĭ), *n.* — **gol·iar′dic** (-dĭk), *adj.*

Go·li′ath (gō·lī′ăth), *n.* [LL., fr. Heb. *Golyōth.*] *Bib.* The Philistine giant killed by David with a sling.

gol′li·wogg (gŏl′ĭ·wŏg), *n.* Orig., a kind of grotesque black doll, as in Florence K. Upton's illustrations (1895) of the Golliwogg books; hence, a grotesque person.

go·losh′ (gō·lŏsh′). Var. of GALOSH.

gom′bo. Var. of GUMBO.

gom′er·al (gŏm′ẽr·ăl), **gom′er·el** (-ĕl), **gom′er·il** (-ĭl), *n.* *Scot.* A simpleton; fool.

Go·mor′rah, Go·mor′rha (gō·mŏr′ȧ). See SODOM.

gom·pho′sis (gŏm·fō′sĭs), *n.* [NL., fr. Gr. *gomphōsis*, prop., a bolting together, deriv. of *gomphos* bolt, nail.] *Anat.* A form of immovable articulation where a hard part is received into a bone cavity, as the teeth into the jaws.

go·mu′ti (gō·mōō′tē), *n.* [Malay *gumuti.*] **1.** Also **gomuti palm.** A Malayan feather palm (*Arenga saccharifera*) having large leaves with the bases densely clothed with fibers. **2.** The black, wiry fiber from this palm.

-gon (-gŏn; -gŭn). [Gr. *gōnia* angle.] *Geom.* A combining form denoting *a figure having a* (specified) *number of angles*, as in deca*gon*, penta*gon*, etc.

gon′ad (gŏn′ăd), *n.* [Gr. *gonē* that which generates.] *Anat. & Zool.* An essential sexual gland; an ovary, testis, or hermaphrodite gland. — **gon′ad·al** (-ăl), **go·na′di·al** (gō·nā′dĭ·ăl), **go·nad′ic** (-năd′ĭk), *adj.*

gon′a·do·trop′ic (gŏn′ȧ·dō·trŏp′ĭk; gō·năd′ō-), *adj.* [See GONAD; -TROPIC.] *Biochem.* Influencing, usually as a stimulant, the growth, activity, or the like, of the gonads; as, a *gonadotropic* substance.

Gond (gŏnd), *n.* A member of an important Dravidian people of low culture, dwelling chiefly in Central India.

gon′do·la (gŏn′dō·lȧ), *n.* [It., of Venetian, and prob. ult. of imitative, origin.] **1.** A long, narrow, flat-bottomed boat with a high prow and stern, used in the canals of Venice. **2.** *U.S.* A heavy flat-bottomed barge, used esp. in parts of New England. **3.** *U.S.* = GONDOLA CAR. **4.** A long car attached to the under part of an airship.

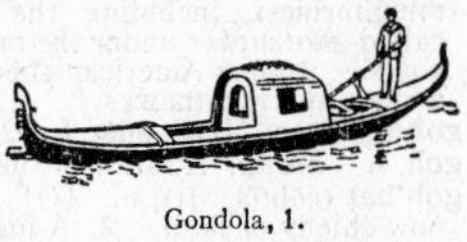
Gondola, 1.

gondola car. *U.S.* A railroad car with sides and ends but without a top, for freight in bulk.

gon′do·lier′ (gŏn′dō·lēr′), *n.* [F.] A man who rows a gondola.

gone (gŏn; 74), *past part.* of GO, used in many special senses; as: **a** *Colloq.* Infatuated; with *on* or *upon*, in love with. **b** With *far*, much advanced; deeply involved; also, much wearied. **c** Lost; ruined. **d** With an expression denoting time, ago; since; as, these ten years *gone.*

gone′ness, *n.* A state of exhaustion; faintness.

Gon′er·il (gŏn′ẽr·ĭl), *n.* See KING LEAR.

gon′fa·lon (gŏn′fȧ·lŏn; -lŭn), *n.* [From F. *gonfalon* or It. *gonfalone.* See GONFANON.] **1.** The ensign of certain princes or states, as the medieval republics of Italy. **2.** Loosely, any flag which hangs from a crosspiece or frame.

gon′fa·lon·ier′ (-ēr′), *n.* He who bears the gonfalon; esp., an official of certain republics in medieval Italy.

gon′fa·non (gŏn′fȧ·nŏn), *n.* [OF. *gonfanon*, fr. OHG. *gundfano* war flag.] *Obs. exc. Hist.* A gonfalon.

gong (gŏng), *n.* [Jav. *goṅ*, Malay *guṅ*, of imitative origin.] **1.** A disk-shaped instrument of percussion, that produces a resounding tone. **2.** A flat saucerlike bell.

go·nid′i·um (gō·nĭd′ĭ·ŭm), *n.; pl.* GONIDIA (-ȧ). [NL., fr. *gon-* + dim. suffix *-idium.*] *Bot.* **a** An asexual reproductive cell or spore arising on the gametophyte. **b** One of the green chlorophyll-bearing cells found within the thallus of a lichen. — **go·nid′i·al** (-ăl), *adj.*

go′ni·o- (gō′nĭ·ō-). [Gr. *gōnia.*] A combining form meaning *corner, angle*, as in *gonio*meter; specif., *Craniol.*, equivalent to GONION.

go′ni·om′e·ter (gō′nĭ·ŏm′ē·tẽr), *n.* [F. *goniomètre*, fr. Gr. *gōnia* angle + *metron* measure.] **1.** An instrument for measuring angles, as in surveying, craniometry, mineralogy. **2.** *Radio.* A direction finder. — **go′ni·o·met′ric** (-ō·mĕt′rĭk), **go′ni·o·met′ri·cal** (-rĭ·kăl), *adj.* — **go′ni·om′e·try** (-ŏm′ē·trĭ), *n.*

go′ni·on (gō′nĭ·ŏn), *n.; pl.* GONIA (-ȧ). [NL., fr. Gr. *gōnia* angle.] *Craniol.* The point at the angle of the lower jaw on either side.

go′ni·um (gō′nĭ·ŭm), *n.; pl.* GONIA (-ȧ). [NL.] *Biol.* An undifferentiated primitive germ cell; an oögonium or spermatogonium.

-go′ni·um (-gō′nĭ·ŭm). [See GONO-.] *Biol.* A combining form denoting *a cell from which*, or *a structure in which, germ cells are formed*, as in spermato*gonium*, arche*gonium*.

gon′o- (gŏn′ō-), **gon-**. [Gr. *gonos*, *gonē*, procreation, offspring, semen, fr. the root of *gignesthai* to be born.] A combining form used to signify *sexual, generative.*

gon′o·coc′cus (-kŏk′ŭs), *n.; pl.* GONOCOCCI (-sī). [NL., fr. *gono-* + *-coccus.*] *Bacteriol.* The pus-producing bacterium (*Neisseria gonorrheae*), which causes gonorrhea. — **gon′o·coc′cal** (-ăl), *adj.* — **gon′o·coc′cic** (-sĭk), *adj.*

gon′of, gon′oph (gŏn′ŭf). Vars. of GANEF.

gon′o·phore (gŏn′ō·fōr), *n.* [*gono-* + *-phore.*] **1.** *Bot.* Any sporophyll-bearing prolongation of the axis. **2.** *Zool.* A reproductive zooid of a hydroid colony.

gon′or·rhe′a, gon′or·rhoe′a (gŏn′ŏ·rē′ȧ), *n.* [LL. *gonorrhoea*, fr. Gr. *gonorrhoia*, fr. *gonē* that which begets, semen + *rhein* to flow.] *Med.* A contagious inflammatory disease of the genitourinary tract affecting esp. the urethra and vagina. — **gon′or·rhe′al, gon′or·rhoe′al** (-ăl), *adj.*

-gony. [L. *-gonia*, fr. Gr. *-gonia*, fr. root of *gignesthai* to be born.] A combining form used to signify *generation, reproduction, manner of coming into being*, as in cosmo*gony.*

goo′ber (gōō′bẽr), *n.* Also **goober pea.** [From a Bantu language, *nguba.*] *Southern U.S.* The peanut.

good (gŏŏd), *adj.; BET′TER; BEST.* [AS. *gōd.*] **1.** Sufficient or satisfactory for its purpose. **2.** In excess; ample; full. **3.** Considerable; not insignificant; — esp. in the phrases *a good deal, a good share, a good while*, etc. **4.** Possessing attractive qualities; specif.: **a** Stouthearted; as, *good* men and true. **b** Kind; friendly. **c** Well-behaved. **5.** Agreeable; pleasant. **6.** Adapted to a useful end; beneficial; as, *good* advice. **7. a** Proper; becoming. **b** Virtuous; also, pious or devout. **8.** Of a reliable character; hence: valid; adequate; also, actual; honest; sincere. **9.** Of comparative excellence in its kind; admirable. **10. a** Honorable; untainted. **b** In unquestioned standing; orthodox; as, *good* Republicans. **11.** Commercially sound or reliable; as, a *good* risk. **12.** *Law.* Valid or effectual for the transfer of title or the creation or vesting of rights; as, a *good* deed.

— *n.* **1.** That which is serviceable, fit, etc.; — opposed to *ill, evil.* **2.** *Ethics.* That which is conceived as fitting in the moral order of the universe. **3.** Prosperity; benefit; — opposed to *harm*, etc. **4.** An object of desire or endeavor; as, an economic *good.* **5.** *pl.* Wares; commodities. In law, a comprehensive name for almost all personal property, as disting. from land or real property. **6.** Collectively, good persons.

— *interj.* An exclamation of satisfaction.

— *adv.* Well; — in *as good*, with a following *as* expressed or implied, equally well. — ***as good as.*** In effect; virtually; the same as.

good book. [*often caps.*] The Bible; — often with *the.*

good′–by′, good′–bye′ (gŏŏd′bī′; 2), *n. & interj.* [Contr. of *God be with ye.*] Farewell.

Good Conduct Medal. *Mil., U. S.* A medal awarded to enlisted personnel for honorable completion of a specified term of service, under various standards of military efficiency, obedience, etc.

good fellow. A person of companionable qualities. — **good′–fel′low·hood, good′–fel′low·ship,** *n.*

Good Friday. The Friday of Holy Week, observed as the anniversary of the Crucifixion of Christ.

good′heart′ed (gŏŏd′här′tĕd; -tĭd; 2), *adj.* Of a kind disposition. — **good′heart′ed·ly,** *adv.* — **good′heart′ed·ness,** *n.*

good humor. A cheerful or pleasant temper or state of mind.

good′–hu′mored, good′–hu′moured (-hū′mērd; -ū′mērd; 2), *adj.* Characterized by or indicating good humor. — **good′–hu′mored·ly, good′–hu′moured·ly,** *adv.*

good′ish (gŏŏd′ĭsh), *adj.* Rather good.

good′ly (gŏŏd′lĭ), *adj.;* GOOD′LI·ER (-lĭ·ēr); GOOD′LI·EST. **1.** Of pleasing appearance, character, or quality. **2.** Large; considerable. — **good′li·ness,** *n.*

good′man (gŏŏd′măn), *n. Archaic.* **1.** The master (of the house); householder; husband. **2.** An appellation of civility, equivalent to "Mister," prefixed to the names of persons under the rank of gentlemen.

good nature. Pleasant or kindly nature; a sunny nature.

good′–na′tured (gŏŏd′nā′tūrd; 2), *adj.* Characterized by good nature. — **Syn.** See AMIABLE. — **good′–na′tured·ly,** *adv.* — **good′–na′tured·ness,** *n.*

good′ness (gŏŏd′nĕs; -nĭs), *n.* Excellence; virtue.

goods (gŏŏdz), *n. pl.* Wares; merchandise; — often used attributively; as, **goods engine, goods train, goods wagon** (car), **goods yard.** This attributive use is chiefly British, the common word in the United States being *freight.*

Good Shepherd. Christ. See *John* x. 11, 14.

good speed. Good luck; good success; Godspeed.

good′–tem′pered (gŏŏd′tĕm′pērd; 2), *adj.* Having a good temper. — **good′–tem′pered·ly,** *adv.*

good′wife′ (gŏŏd′wīf′), *n. Archaic & Dial.* The mistress of a house or other establishment. Formerly used as an appellation of civility, equivalent to "Mrs."

good will. Also **good′will′** (gŏŏd′wĭl′; 2), *n.* **1.** Good intention or inclination. **2.** Kindly feeling; benevolence. **3.** Cheerful consent; heartiness; readiness. **4.** *Law.* The favor or advantage in the way of custom which a business has acquired beyond the mere value of what it sells. — **Syn.** See FAVOR. — **Ant.** Ill will.

good′will′y (gŏŏd′wĭl′ĭ), *adj. Scot.* Liberal; cordial.

good′y (gŏŏd′ĭ), *n.; pl.* -IES (-ĭz). *Colloq.* Anything regarded as especially good to eat, as a bonbon; — usually *pl.* — *adj. Colloq.* Weakly or affectedly good; — often in the reduplicated form **good′y–good′y.**

good′y, *n.* [From *goodwife.*] An appellation of civility formerly applied to a woman, esp. a married one, of lowly station; hence, such a woman.

goof (gōōf), *n. Slang, U. S.* A ridiculous, stupid person.

goof′y (-ĭ), *adj. Slang.* Foolish; silly; also, gullible. — **goof′i·ly,** *adv.* — **goof′i·ness,** *n.*

goo′gly (gōō′glĭ), *n. Cricket.* A ball so bowled that it swerves one way and breaks the other.

goo′gol (gōō′gŏl), *n.* The figure 1 followed by 100 zeros (= 10^{100}), whence **goo′gol·plex′** (-plĕks′), the figure 1 followed by a googol of zeros (= $10^{10^{100}}$); — coined by Dr. Edward Kasner (1878–), American mathematician.

goon (gōōn), *n.* [Prob. fr. gorilla + baboon.] *Slang, orig. Western U. S.* One hired as a slugger, bomber, incendiary, or the like, by racketeers or outlaw unionists for terrorizing industry or workers; — from the subhuman creatures of a comic strip by E. C. Segar (d. 1938).

Goop (gōōp), *n.* A nonsense creature invented by Gelett Burgess (see *Biog.*). The Goops are often presented as "horrible examples" of naughtiness or boorish manners.

goos·an′der (gōōs·ăn′dēr), *n.* The merganser.

goose (gōōs), *n.; pl.* GEESE (gēs), rarely GOOSE. [AS. *gōs,* pl. *gēs.*] **1.** Any of a subfamily (Anserinae) of lamellirostral birds, intermediate between the swans and ducks, with long necks, feathered lores, and reticulate tarsi. See BARNACLE GOOSE, BRANT, CANADA GOOSE, GRAYLAG. **2.** A female goose as distinguished from a gander. **3.** The flesh of a goose, used as food. **4.** A silly creature; a simpleton. **5.** *Obs.* A game played with counters on a board. **6.** *pl.* GOOSES. A tailor's smoothing iron; — from its curved handle.

goose′ber′ry (gōōz′bĕr′ĭ; gōōs′-; -bēr·ĭ), *n.* **1.** Any shrub of the genus *Ribes* (family Saxifragaceae). **2.** The acid, usually hairy, berry of a shrub of the genus *Ribes,* used chiefly in making jam or preserves, tarts, pies, etc.

goose flesh. Also **goose pimples, goose skin.** A roughness of the skin produced by erection of its papillae, caused by cold or fear.

goose′foot′ (gōōs′fŏŏt′), *n.; pl.* -FOOTS (-fŏŏts′). Any of a genus (*Chenopodium*) of glabrous herbs typifying a family (Chenopodiaceae, the goosefoot family), distinguished by the utricular fruit; also, any plant of this family.

goose′herd′ (-hûrd′), *n.* One who tends geese.

goose′neck′ (-nĕk′), *n.* Anything curved like the neck of a goose, as a kind of clamp, a flexible iron pipe joint, etc.

goose step. *Mil.* **a** A drill in which the soldier stands alternately on each foot and sharply raises the other, as in marking time. **b** The straight-legged parade step of German infantry; — so called by English and Americans.

goose′–step′, *v. i. Colloq.* To move in a goose step.

go′pher (gō′fēr), *n.* [F. *gaufre* waffle, honeycomb; — from their burrows.] **1.** Any of certain genera (*Geomys, Thomomys* and allies, family Geomyidae) of burrowing rodents the size of a large rat, having small eyes and short ears, strong claws on the forelimbs, and very large cheek pouches, whence they are also called ***pocket gophers.*** **2.** See SPERMOPHILE. **3.** A burrowing land tortoise (*Gopherus polyphemus*) of the coast region of the southern U. S. **4.** [*cap.*] *U. S.* A native or inhabitant of Minnesota (nicknamed the **Gopher State**).

gopher snake. A large harmless burrowing snake (*Drymarchon corais couperi*) of the southern United States.

go′pher·wood′ (gō′fēr·wŏŏd′), *n.* [Heb. *gōpher.*] The unidentified wood used in building Noah's ark. *Gen.* vi. 14.

go′ral (gō′răl), *n.;* see PLURAL, *Note,* 3. Any of several species of goat antelopes (genus *Naemorhedus*), found from the southern Himalayas to parts of China.

gor′bel′ly (gôr′bĕl′ĭ), *n.* [See GORE blood.] *Obs.* A prominent belly; also, a big-bellied person. — **gor′bel′lied** (-ĭd), *adj.*

gor′cock′ (-kŏk′), *n.* The moor cock, or male red grouse.

Gor′di·an (gôr′dĭ·ăn; 58), *adj.* Intricate; complicated, like the **Gordian knot** tied by Gordius, King of Phrygia. An oracle having declared that he who should untie the knot should be master of Asia, Alexander the Great cut it with his sword.

Gor′don set′ter (gôr′d′n). See SETTER.

gore (gōr; 70), *n.* [AS. *gor* dirt, dung.] Blood; esp., clotted blood.

gore, *n.* [AS. *gāra* triangular piece of land.] **1.** *Now Dial.* A small triangular piece of land. **2.** Any tapering or triangular piece of cloth, canvas, etc., used to give a varying width, as in a skirt, or in a sail. — *v. t.* To cut into a tapering or triangular form.

gore, *v. t.* **1.** *Obs.* To pierce or stab, as with a spear. **2.** To pierce with horns or tusks; — of bulls, boars, etc.

gorge (gôrj), *n.* [OF., fr. LL. *gurga* whirlpool, for L. *gurges.*] **1.** The throat. **2.** *Archaic & Dial.* **a** A hawk's crop; hence, stomach; appetite. **b** A hawk's meal; hence, a meal, esp. a full meal. **3.** That which is gorged, or swallowed. **4.** A kind of earthenware pitcher; as, white *gorges. Obs.* **5.** A narrow passage, as a defile, ravine, etc. **6.** A mass of matter that chokes up a passage; as, an ice *gorge* in a river. **7.** Act of gorging, or eating voraciously. **8.** *Fort.* Rear entrance into a bastion or other outwork. See BASTION, *Illust.*

gorge, *v. i.;* GORGED (gôrjd); GORG′ING (gôr′jĭng). [OF. *gorger.*] To fill the gorge or crop; to eat greedily and to satiety; as, to *gorge* on books. — *v. t.* **1.** To fill the gorge or crop of; to glut. **2.** To swallow with greediness. — **Syn.** See SATIATE.

gor′geous (gôr′jŭs), *adj.* [OF. *gorgias* beautiful, glorious.] Resplendently beautiful; magnificent. — **Syn.** See SPLENDID. — **gor′geous·ly,** *adv.* — **gor′geous·ness,** *n.*

gorg′er (gôr′jēr), *n.* One who or that which gorges.

gor′get (gôr′jĕt; -jĭt), *n.* [OF. *gorgete,* dim. of *gorge* throat.] **1.** A piece of armor protecting the throat. See ARMOR, *Illust.* **2.** Hence: **a** A collar. **b** A kind of covering for the neck and breast, worn by women; a wimple. **3.** *Zool.* A specially colored patch on the throat.

Gor′gon (gôr′gŭn), *n.* [L. *Gorgo, -onis,* fr. Gr. *Gorgō,* fr. *gorgos* terrible.] **1.** *Gr. Myth.* One of three snaky-haired sisters, whose terrific aspect turned the beholder to stone; esp., Medusa (which see). **2.** [*not cap.*] Any ugly or repulsive woman.

Gor·go′ni·an (gôr·gō′nĭ·ăn; 58), *adj.* Pertaining to, or resembling, a Gorgon; petrifying.

gor′gon·ize (gôr′gŭn·īz), *v. t.* To have the effect of the Gorgon's look upon; to petrify; also, to stare at with a Gorgon's look.

Gor′gon·zo′la (gôr′gŭn·zō′lȧ), *n., or* **Gorgonzola cheese.** [It.] A kind of Italian pressed milk cheese resembling Roquefort; — from a village near Milan.

gor′hen′ (gôr′hĕn′), *n.* [*gor-* as in *gorcock* + *hen.*] The female red grouse; a moor hen.

go·ril′la (gō·rĭl′ȧ), *n.* [An African word.] **1.** The largest anthropoid ape (*Gorilla gorilla*), of equatorial West Africa. It is closely related to the chimpanzee, but much larger, the males being more powerful than a man. **2.** *Slang.* An ugly brute of a man. **3.** *Slang.* A thief who resorts to violence; also, a ruffian; a tough.

gor′mand (gôr′mănd), **gor′mand·ism,** etc. Vars. of GOURMAND, etc.

gor′mand·ize (gôr′măn·dīz), *v. i. & t.* [From F. *gourmandise* gluttony.] To eat greedily or ravenously. — *n.* Experience, taste, or indulgence in the pleasures of the table. — **gor′mand·iz′er** (-dīz′ēr), *n.*

gorse (gôrs), *n.* [ME. & AS. *gorst.*] *Eng.* Furze. — **gors′y,** *adj.*

gor′y (gōr′ĭ; 70), *adj.;* GOR′I·ER (-ĭ·ēr); GOR′I·EST. **1.** Covered with gore; bloodstained. **2.** Bloody. — **gor′i·ness,** *n.*

gos′hawk′ (gŏs′hôk′), *n.* See HAWK.

Go′shen (gō′shĕn), *n. Bib.* The land of plenty allotted to the Israelites in Egypt; hence, a land or place of plenty.

gos′ling (gŏz′lĭng), *n.* [ME. *gōs* goose + 1st *-ling.*] **a** A young goose. **b** A foolish or callow person.

gos′pel (gŏs′pĕl), *n.* [AS. *godspell,* as if fr. *god* God, but prop. *gōdspell* good tidings. See SPELL a tale.] **1.** Glad tidings; esp., the good news concerning Christ, the Kingdom of God, and salvation; hence, the teachings of Christ and the apostles; the Christian faith, revelation, or dispensation. **2. a** The story or record of Christ's life and doctrines, contained in the first four books of the New Testament (**Matthew, Mark, Luke,** and **John**). **b** [*cap.*] Esp., one of the four New Testament books containing narratives of the life and death of Jesus Christ, ascribed respectively to Matthew, Mark, Luke, and John. **3.** [*usually cap.*] *Eccl.* A selection from one of the four Gospels, read in a religious service at the left side (**gospel side**) of the altar. **4.** Anything propounded or accepted as infallibly true. **5.** Any guiding principle for action; often, any doctrine of political or social philosophy; as, this political *gospel.*

gos′pel·er, gos′pel·ler (gŏs′pĕl·ēr), *n.* **1.** One who reads or sings the Gospel. **2.** *Hist.* A Protestant, esp. one holding views now called fundamentalist; a Puritan or other evangelical sectary.

gos′port (gŏs′pōrt), *n.* [From GOSPORT, Eng.] A flexible speaking tube for one-way communication from flight instructor to student pilot during training.

gos′sa·mer (gŏs′ȧ·mēr), *n.* [ME. *gossomer, gossummer,* appar. for *goose summer,* referring to a period of mild weather in November, when geese were eaten.] **1.** A film of cobwebs floating in the air in calm clear weather. **2.** Any gauzelike fabric. **3.** *U. S.* A thin waterproof fabric, or a garment of it. — **gos′sa·mer, gos′sa·mer·y** (-ĭ), *adj.*

gos′san (gŏs′ăn; gŏz′-), *n.* [Cornish.] Decomposed rock of rusty color (owing to oxidized pyrites).

gos′sip (gŏs′ĭp), *n.* [AS. *godsibb,* fr. *god* God + *sibb* related, a relation.] **1.** *Archaic.* **a** A godparent. **b** A friend; crony. **2.** An idle tattler; a newsmonger. **3.** A gossip's tattle; groundless rumor; also, chatter. — *v. i.;* -SIPED (-ĭpt); -SIP·ING. To act as gossip; to spread gossip. — **gos′sip·er,** *n.* — **gos′sip·ing·ly,** *adv.*

gos′sip·ing (gŏs′ĭ·pĭng), *n.* **1.** Act of one who gossips. **2.** *Now Dial.* **a** A christening or christening feast. **b** A meeting of friends, as at a lying-in; also, a merrymaking.

gos′sip·red (gŏs′ĭp·rĕd), *n.* **1.** *Hist.* Spiritual relationship between sponsor and sponsored. **2.** *Rare.* Gossip; chatter.

gos′sip·ry (-rĭ), *n.* Gossip; also, a body of gossips.

gos′sip·y (gŏs′ĭ·pĭ), *adj.* Full of, or given to, gossip.

gos·soon′ (gŏ·so͞on′), *n.* [F. *garçon*.] A boy; lad.

got (gŏt; 73), *past & past part.* of GET.

Goth (gŏth), *n.* [LL. *Gothi*, pl.] **1.** One of an ancient Teutonic race (divided into two groups, ***Ostrogoths*** and ***Visigoths***, or ***East Goths*** and ***West Goths***) which early in the Christian Era overran the Roman Empire. **2.** One who is rude or uncivilized; a barbarian.

Go′tham, *n.* **1.** (gō′tăm; gŏt′ăm) A village in England whose inhabitants were proverbial for their follies. **2.** (gŏth′ăm; gō′thăm) New York City. — **Go′tham·ite** (-īt), *n.*

Goth′ic (gŏth′ĭk), *adj.* [F. and LL.; F. *gothique*, fr. LL. *Gothicus*.] **1.** Of or pertaining to the Goths or their language. **2.** *Obs.* Teutonic; Germanic. **3.** [*often not cap.*] Of, pertaining to, or characteristic of, the Middle Ages; medieval; romantic as opposed to classical; derogatorily, rude; barbarous. See GOTHICISM. **4.** Pertaining to, or designating, a style of building, **Gothic architecture**, which originated in France and spread through western Europe (approximately 1160–1530) and which is typically characterized by the converging of weights and strains at isolated points upon slender vertical piers and counterbalancing buttresses and by pointed arches and vaulting. **5.** *Print.* Designating or pertaining to a style of type. See GOTHIC, *n.*, 3, below; TYPE. — *n.* **1.** The language of the Goths, known only from a few scattered remains. See INDO-EUROPEAN LANGUAGES, *Table*. **2.** Gothic architecture, ornament, etc. **3.** Gothic type: **a** *Eng.* Black letter. **b** *U. S.* [*usually not cap.*] A square-cut type with no serifs; — in England called *grotesque*. See TYPE. — **Goth′i·cal·ly** (-ĭ·kăl·ĭ), *adv.*

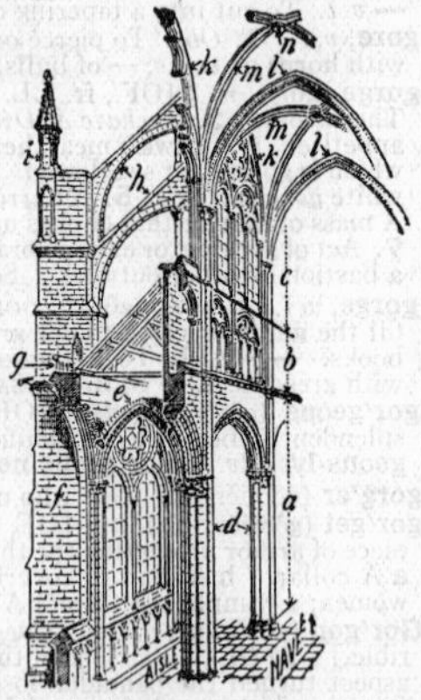

Gothic Church. *a* Nave Arcade; *b* Triforium; *c* Clerestory; *d* Piers; *e* Aisle Vaulting; *f* Buttress; *g* Parapet; *h* Flying Buttress; *i* Pinnacle; *k* Wall Ribs; *l* Transverse Ribs; *m* Diagonal Ribs; *n* Boss.

Gothic arch. The pointed arch, esp. one with a joint instead of a keystone at its apex.

Goth′i·cism (gŏth′ĭ·sĭz′m), *n.* The principles, style, or characteristics of Gothic art, literature, etc.; specif.: **a** Rudeness; inelegance or an instance of it. **b** Lack of classical simplicity or unity; combination of sublime and grotesque.

Goth′i·cize (-sīz), *v. t.* To make Gothic.

gö′thite, goe′thite (gō′thīt; gû′tīt), *n.* [After the poet *Goethe*.] *Mineral.* A hydrous iron oxide, $Fe_2O_3.H_2O$.

got′ten (gŏt′'n), *past part.* of GET.

Göt′ter·däm′mer·ung (gût′ĕr·dĕm′ĕr·o͝ong), *n.* [G., twilight of the gods.] The fourth and last opera of Wagner's tetralogy of *The Ring of the Nibelung*.

‖**gouache** (gwäsh), *n.* [F., fr. It. *guazzo*, fr. L. *aquatio* watering, pool.] A method of painting with opaque colors which have been ground in water and mingled with a preparation of gum; also, the pigment.

gouge (gouj), *n.* [F., fr. LL. *gubia*, *gulbia*.] **1.** A kind of chisel with a concavo-convex cross section. **2.** *U. S.* **a** *Colloq.* Act of scooping out with or as with such a chisel; a groove or cavity so made. **b** *Slang.* An imposition; also, an impostor. — *v. t.*; GOUGED (goujd); GOUG′ING (gouj′ĭng). **1.** To scoop out with or as with a gouge. **2.** To scoop out (an eye) or the eye of, as with the thumbnail. **3.** *Colloq., U. S.* To defraud. — **goug′er** (gouj′ĕr), *n.*

gou′lash (go͞o′läsh; -lăsh), *n.*, *or* **Hungarian goulash.** [Hung. *gulyás*, lit., (meat of a) herdsman.] A ragout of beef or veal flavored with paprika and vegetables.

gourd (gōrd *or, esp. Brit.*, go͝ord), *n.* [OF. *gourde*, fr. L. *cucurbita*.] **1.** Any plant of a genus (*Cucurbita*) typifying a family (Cucurbitaceae, the gourd family) of chiefly herbaceous, tendril-bearing vines, including the cucumber, melon, squash, and pumpkin; also, any plant of this family. **2.** The fruit of any of certain plants of the gourd family (Cucurbitaceae), including esp. the pumpkin and squash, and also, the hard-shelled ***bottle gourd*** (*Lagenaria vulgaris* and its varieties). Cf. CALABASH. **3.** The cleaned dried shell of the fruit, used as a dipper, bottle, etc. **4. a** Drinking vessel; bottle. **b** *Chem.* A cucurbit.

gourde (go͞ord), *n.* [F. *gourde*, fem., numb, dull, heavy, fr. L. *gurdus*.] **a** The monetary unit of Haiti, established in 1920 at 20 cents, U. S. money. It is subdivided into 100 centimes. **b** The former unit and coin, equal to five francs ($0.965).

gour′mand (go͞or′mănd; *F.* go͞or′mäN′), *n.* [F., fr. OF. *gromet*, *gormet*, servant.] A hearty or, sometimes, greedy eater; also, one who delights in luxurious food. — **Syn.** See EPICURE. — **gour′mand·ism,** *n.*

gour′met (go͞or′mā; *F.* go͞or′mĕ′), *n.* [F.] A connoisseur in eating and drinking. — **Syn.** See EPICURE.

gout (gout), *n.* [OF. *goute*, *goutte*, fr. L. *gutta* drop.] **1.** A drop; a clot. **2.** A metabolic disease marked by painful inflammation of the joints, deposits of urate of sodium in and around the joints, and an excess of uric acid in the blood.

‖**goût** (go͞o), *n.* [F., fr. L. *gustus* taste.] Taste.

gout′y (gout′ĭ), *adj.*; GOUT′I·ER (-ĭ·ĕr); GOUT′I·EST. Having or manifesting gout; of, like, or causing, gout. — **gout′i·ly,** *adv.* — **gout′i·ness,** *n.*

‖**gou′ver′nante′** (go͞o′vĕr′näNt′), *n.* [F.] Housekeeper; chaperon; governess.

gov′ern (gŭv′ĕrn), *v. t.* [OF. *governer*, fr. L. *gubernare* to steer, govern, fr. Gr. *kybernan*.] **1.** To direct and control; rule. **2.** To regulate; restrain. **3.** To be a rule or law for; to determine. **4.** *Gram.* To require to be (in a certain case or mood); as, a transitive verb *governs* a noun in the objective case; or to require (a certain case or mood); as, a transitive verb *governs* the objective case. — *v. i.* To exercise authority; to rule. — **gov′ern·a·ble,** *adj.*

Syn. **Govern, rule** mean to exercise power or authority in controlling others. **Govern** connotes as its end a keeping in a straight course or smooth operation for the good of the individual and the whole; **rule** more often suggests the exercise of despotic or arbitrary power.

gov′ern·ance (gŭv′ĕr·năns), *n.* Government.

gov′ern·ess (-ĕr·nĕs; -nĭs), *n.* **1.** A female governor; *Jocular*, a governor's wife. **2.** A woman who teaches and trains a child or children, esp. in a private home. — *v. t. & i.* To act or serve as governess.

gov′ern·ment (gŭv′ĕrn·mĕnt), *n.* **1.** A governing; exercise of administrative powers. **2.** The mode or system of governing; specif., the established form of political administration. Abbr. *govt.*, *Govt.* **3.** *Obs.* Demeanor; conduct. **4.** Function, office, right, or power of governing. **5.** Territory or country governed; also, sometimes, an administrative subdivision of a country, as formerly in Russia and France. **6.** The governing body; the administration. **7.** *Gram.* The influence of a word that governs the case and mood of another; also, syntactical relationship. — **gov′ern·men′tal** (-mĕn′tăl; -t'l), *adj.* — **gov′ern·men′tal·ly,** *adv.*

gov′er·nor (gŭv′ĕr·nĕr; -ĕ·nĕr; 93), *n.* [OF. *governeor* (F. *gouverneur*).] **1.** One who governs; a chief ruler or magistrate; specif.: **a** A person appointed to govern a province, town, fortress, prison, etc.; esp., the official representing the crown in a British dependency. Abbr. *Gov.* **b** The person elected as chief executive of a state in the United States. Abbr. *Gov.* **2.** A tutor. **3.** One who directs, or administers the affairs of a society, club, or the like. **4.** *Slang.* **a** One's employer; chief. **b** One's father or guardian. **5.** An automatic attachment to an engine, turbine, and the like, for controlling its speed.

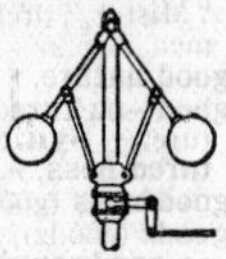

Governor, 5 (Conical-Pendulum type).

governor general *or, esp. Brit.*, **gov′er·nor–gen′er·al,** *n.*; *pl.* GOVERNORS GENERAL, GOVERNORS-GENERAL. A governor who has lieutenant or deputy governors under him, as of Canada and the Australian Commonwealth. — **gov′er·nor–gen′er·al·ship′,** *n.*

gov′er·nor·ship′, *n.* Office, function, term, etc., of a governor.

gow′an (gou′ăn), *n.* *Scot. & N. of Eng.* The common British daisy (*Bellis perennis*). — **gow′an·y** (-ĭ), *adj.*

gowd (goud), *n.* *Scot. & Dial. Eng.* Gold.

gowk (gouk; gōk), *n.* [ON. *gaukr*.] **1.** *Scot.* A cuckoo. **2.** A simpleton.

gown (goun), *n.* [OF. *gone*, *gonne*, fr. LL. *gunna*.] **1.** An outer garment; esp.: **a** The ordinary outer dress of a woman. **b** A garment falling in soft folds, worn by the ancients, as the toga; hence, *Poetic*, the dress of peace. **c** A loose robe, as a dressing gown or a nightgown. **d** Official or distinctive robe of certain officers, professional men, or scholars. Cf. GENEVA GOWN. **2.** College students, collectively; — disting. from *town* (townspeople); as, town and *gown*. — *v. t.* To clothe in, or invest with, a gown.

gowns′man (gounz′măn), *n.* **1.** *Rare.* A civilian. **2.** One whose professional, official, or scholastic habit is a gown.

Graaf′i·an fol′li·cle *or* **ves′i·cle** (gräf′ĭ·ăn). [After Regnier de *Graaf*, Dutch physician of the 17th century.] *Anat.* One of the small sacs or follicles in which the eggs are enclosed in the ovary.

Graal. Var. of GRAIL (Holy Grail).

grab (grăb), *v. t.*; GRABBED (grăbd); GRAB′BING. [MD. *grabben*.] **1.** To snatch; seize. **2.** To take unscrupulously. — **Syn.** See TAKE. — *n.* **1.** A grabbing; also, that which is grabbed or one who grabs. **2.** An instrument or device for clutching objects, as for hauling or hoisting them. Cf. GRAPNEL, GRAPPLING IRON. — **grab′ber** (-ĕr), *n.*

grab, *n.* [Ar. *ghurāb*, colloq. *ghrāb*, raven, a kind of ship.] A sharp-bowed, light-draft coasting vessel with lateen sails and, usually, two masts, used in the East.

grab′ble (grăb′'l), *v. i.*; GRAB′BLED (-'ld); GRAB′BLING (-lĭng). [D. *grabbelen*, freq.] **1.** To move the hand in a groping fashion; to grope. **2.** To sprawl; grovel. **3.** To grab.

grab rope. *U. S. Navy.* = GUEST ROPE **b**.

grace (grās), *n.* [OF., fr. L. *gratia*, fr. *gratus* beloved, dear.] **1.** Favor, kindness, mercy, etc.; also, an act or an exhibition of such favor, etc.; as, to sue for *grace*. **2.** *pl.* State of being favored or in favor; as, to be in one's bad *graces*. **3.** A short prayer in which a blessing is asked, or thanks rendered, at a meal. **4.** *Obs.* Lot; fate. **5.** Virtue; esp., sense of right; graciousness; as, he had the *grace* to refuse. **6.** [*usually cap.*] Title given to a duke, duchess, or archbishop, and formerly to the English sovereign. **7.** Temporary exemption, as from a penalty, or relief, as by postponement of a settlement; reprieve; as, a day or year of *grace*. **8.** Attractiveness; charm; easy, natural elegance or harmony; beauty of line, movement, etc. **9.** A pleasing or charming characteristic, feature, manner, etc. **10.** *Eccl.* **a** Divine mercy or forgiveness. **b** Divine assistance given man for his regeneration or sanctification. **c** In full ***state of grace***. State of being pleasing to God because of responsiveness to grace; also, state of the elect. **d** A Christian virtue. **11.** *pl.* [*cap.*] *Gr. Myth.* Graceful and beautiful maidens, sister goddesses, intimate with the Muses and attendants oftenest of Eros, Aphrodite, and Dionysus. Three were commonly mentioned: Aglaia (Brilliance), Euphrosyne (Joy), and Thalia (Bloom). **12.** *Music.* An embellishment consisting of notes not essential to the melody or harmony, as the trill, turn, etc., indicated by special symbols or written small. — **Syn.** See MERCY.

— *v. t.*; GRACED (grāst); GRAC′ING (grās′ĭng). **1.** To honor. **2.** To endow with grace or graces; adorn; embellish. **3.** *Music.* To add grace notes, cadenzas, etc., to.

grace cup. A cup used in drinking a final health after the grace at the end of a meal, or a health drunk from it.

grace′ful (grās′fo͝ol; -f'l), *adj.* Displaying grace or beauty in form or action; elegant; also, happily timed or done; tactful. — **grace′ful·ly,** *adv.* — **grace′ful·ness,** *n.*

grace′less, *adj.* Lacking in grace; depraved; also, ungraceful. — **grace′less·ly,** *adv.* — **grace′less·ness,** *n.*

grace note. *Music.* A grace, esp. an appoggiatura. See APPOGGIATURA, *Illust.*; cf. MORDENT.

grac′ile (grăs′ĭl; 56), *adj.* [L. *gracilis*.] Slender; esp., gracefully slender; slight. — **gra·cil′i·ty** (grȧ·sĭl′ĭ·tĭ), *n.*

gra′ci·o′so (grā′shĭ·ō′sō; *Sp.* grä·thyō′sō), *n.* [Sp.] **1.** A favorite. **2.** A buffoon; a comic character.

gra′cious (grā′shŭs), *adj.* [OF. (F. *gracieux*), fr. L. *gratiosus*.] **1.** *Obs.* Pleasing; acceptable. **2.** Attractive; full of grace or charm. **3.** Granting or bestowing grace; merciful; benignant; now, esp., kindly and courteous. — **gra′cious·ly,** *adv.* — **gra′cious·ness,** *n.*

Syn. **Gracious, cordial, affable, genial, sociable** mean markedly pleasant and at ease in social intercourse. **Gracious** implies kindliness and courtesy, especially to inferiors, strangers, etc.; **cordial**, warmth and heartiness; **affable**, approachability and readiness to talk in the person conversed with or addressed; **genial**, the qualities that make for good cheer, such as warm human sympathy, a fine sense of humor; **sociable**, a genuine liking for the companionship of others and readiness to engage in social intercourse.

grack'le (grăk''l), *n.* [L. *graculus* jackdaw.] **a** Any of certain Old World birds (family Sturnidae), as the mynas. **b** Any of certain American blackbirds (genera *Quiscalus, Cassidix* and *Euphagus*, family Icteridae) with glossy iridescent black plumage; esp., the ***purple grackle*** (*Q. quiscula*) and the ***bronzed grackle*** (*Q. q. aeneus*).

gra'date (grā'dāt), *v. i. & t.* To grade or arrange so as to blend, harmonize, show differences in rank, order, etc.; esp., to shade into another or each other, as colors.

gra·da'tion (grȧ·dā'shŭn), *n.* **1.** A gradating. **2.** A series or succession resulting from, or as if from, a gradating; also, successive or hierarchical arrangement. **3.** *pl.* The steps, stages, degrees, etc., in a gradated series; esp., the transitional steps or stages, etc. — **gra·da'tion·al**, *adj.* — **gra·da'tion·al·ly**, *adv.*

grade (grād), *n.* [F., fr. L. *gradus* step, grade.] **1.** A stage; step; degree; as, *grades* of military rank. **2.** Relative position or standing or a class of things having the same relative position, standing, or value; as, crimes of every *grade.* **3.** The rate of ascent or descent of a road, track, etc.; also, a graded ascending, descending, or level portion of a road; a gradient. **4.** Of animals, a hybrid, specif., *Stock Breeding*, an animal having one purebred parent. **5.** *U. S.* **a** One of the divisions of the school course, each representing a year's work; — formerly restricted to the elementary school but now used also of the high schools; also, the body of pupils in any one of these divisions. **b** *pl.* The (or an) elementary school. **c** A school mark or rating. — ***at grade.*** *U. S.* On the same level; — of a railroad crossing. See GRADE CROSSING.

— *v. t.* **1.** To arrange in grades; class; sort. **2.** To gradate. **3.** To reduce to a level, or to an evenly progressive ascent, as the line of a canal or road. **4.** To assign to a grade or assign a grade to; as, to *grade* pupils; also, to divide into grades; as, a *graded* school. **5.** *Stock Breeding.* To improve the blood of; — often with *up.* — *v. i.* To be graded; to be of a grade. — **grad'er** (grād'ẽr), *n.*

-grade (-grād). [L. *gradi* to step, walk.] A combining form used chiefly in zoology, to signify *walking, going* (in a certain manner), as in digiti*grade*, planti*grade.*

grade crossing *or, Brit.,* **level crossing.** A crossing, or intersection, of a railroad and a highway or another railroad on the same level or grade. Cf. OVERPASS, UNDERPASS.

gra'di·ent (grā'dĭ·ĕnt; 58), *adj.* [L. *gradiens*, pres. part. of *gradi* to step, go.] **1.** Moving by steps; walking; as, *gradient* automata. **2.** Adapted for walking, as the feet of certain birds. — *n.* **1.** Of roads, ways, etc.: **a** *Chiefly Brit.* The grade, or rate of ascent or descent. **b** An ascending or descending part; a slope. **2.** A ramp. **3.** Rate of increase or decrease of a variable magnitude, or the curve that represents it. **4.** A series of transitional forms, states, or qualities connecting related extremes.

gra'din (grā'dĭn; *F.* grȧ'dăN'), **gra·dine'** (grȧ·dēn'), *n.* [F. *gradin*, fr. It. *gradino*, dim. of *grado*, fr. L. *gradus* step.] One of a series of tiered steps, seats, or shelves.

grad'u·al (grăd'ū·ăl), *adj.* [ML. *gradualis.*] Proceeding or changing by steps or degrees; made or effected by slow, easy, or not clearly marked stages. — *n.* *Eccl.* **a** [*cap.*] An antiphon between the Epistle and the Gospel of the Mass. **b** A service book containing the portion of the Mass sung by the choir. — **grad'u·al·ly**, *adv.* — **grad'u·al·ness**, *n.*

grad'u·al·ism (grăd'ū·ăl·ĭz'm), *n.* The doctrine of proceeding by gradual degrees toward a desired end. — **grad'u·al·ist** (-ĭst), *n.* — **grad'u·al·is'tic** (-ĭs'tĭk), *adj.*

grad'u·ate (-āt), *adj.* [ML. *graduatus*, past part. of *graduare* to admit to a degree, fr. L. *gradus* grade.] **1.** That has been graduated, esp. from college; holding a bachelor's degree; as, a *graduate* student. **2.** Of, pert. to, or designed for, graduate students.

— *n.* **1.** One who has received an academic or professional degree; *U. S.*, one who has completed the prescribed course of study in a college or school. **2.** A graduated, or measuring, cup, tube, or flask.

— (-āt), *v. t.* **1.** To admit to a certain grade or degree; esp., in schools, colleges, etc., to admit, at the close of a course, to a standing defined by a diploma. **2.** To mark with degrees of measurement, weight, etc.; as, to *graduate* a cup. **3.** To divide into grades according to a scale; as, to *graduate* a tax. — *v. i.* **1.** To become a graduate. **2.** To pass by degrees; change gradually. — **grad'u·a'tor** (-ā'tẽr), *n.*

grad'u·a'tion (grăd'ū·ā'shŭn), *n.* **1.** Act of graduating or state of being graduated. **2.** Any of the marks on an instrument or vessel to indicate degrees or quantity; also, these marks collectively. **3.** *Educ.* Commencement.

gra'dus (grā'dŭs), *n.* [L., step, grade.] A dictionary of prosody to aid in writing Greek or other poetry.

Grae'ae (grē'ē), **Gra'iae** (grā'yē; grī'ē), *n. pl.* *Gr. Myth.* Three daughters of a sea deity, sentinels for the Gorgons. They had but one eye and one tooth among them.

Grae'cism, Grae'cize, etc. Vars. of GRECISM, etc.

‖**Graf** (gräf), *n.; pl.* GRAFEN (grä'fĕn). A German, Austrian, and Swedish title of nobility, equivalent to *earl* in English.

graf·fi'to (grȧ·fē'tō), *n.; pl.* -TI (-tē). [It., fr. *graffio* a scratching.] A rude inscription, drawing, or the like, found on rocks, walls, etc.

graft (grȧft; 9), *n.* [OF. *greffe* graft, cion, *grafe, greffe*, stylus, fr. LL. *graphium* grafting knife, L. *graphium* stylus, fr. Gr. *graphion, grapheion*, fr. *graphein* to write.] **1.** *Hort.* **a** A cion. **b** A grafted plant or tree. **c** The point of insertion of a cion upon a stock. **2.** A grafting; that which is grafted. **3.** *Surg.* A piece of living tissue used in grafting. **4.** [Prob. orig. because such profit was a sort of excrescence, or *graft*, on a legitimate business undertaking.] Acquisition of money, position, etc., by dishonest or questionable means, as by taking advantage of one's official position; also, anything thus gained.

— *v. t.* **1.** *Hort.* **a** To insert (a cion) into a stem, root, or branch of another plant, so that a permanent union is effected. **b** To propagate (a flower, fruit, etc.) by grafting a cion. **2.** To join (one thing) to another by or as if by grafting. **3.** *Colloq.* To get by graft. **4.** *Surg.* To implant (living tissue), as in a lesion, so as to form an organic union. — *v. i.* **1.** To be or become grafted. **2.** To perform the operation of grafting cions or living tissues. **3.** *Colloq.* To practice graft. — **graft'er**, *n.*

graft'age (grȧf'tĭj), *n.* The principles and practice of grafting.

graft hybrid. *Hort.* A graft exhibiting characters of both cion and stock.

gra'ham flour (grā'ăm). [After Sylvester *Graham* (1794–1851), Am. physician.] Flour made from entire kernels of wheat. — **gra'ham**, *adj.*

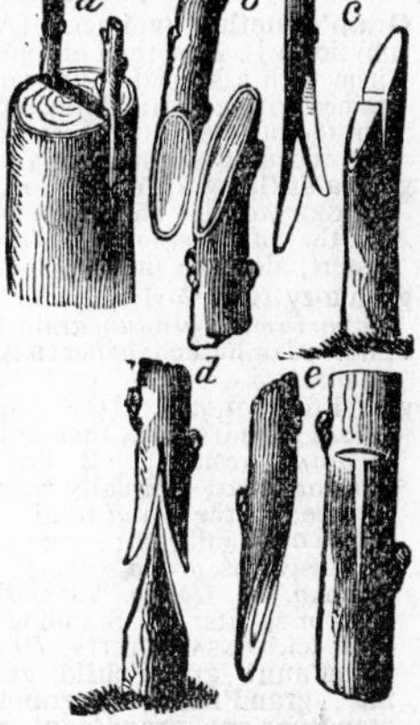

Graftage. *a* Cleft; *b* Splice; *c* Whip or Tongue; *d* Saddle; *e* Side.

grail (grāl), *n.* [OF. *graal.*] A platter; cup; — used only [*cap.*] of the ***Holy Grail***, which in some medieval legends was the platter, in others, the cup, used by Christ at the Last Supper. The Grail was brought to Britain but disappeared in time when its keepers became impure. Knight after knight engaged in the search for it, but only Percivale, Galahad, and Bors proved worthy of achieving the quest.

grain (grān), *n.* [OF., fr. L. *granum* grain, seed; in sense 5 fr. OF. *graine* crimson dye, kermes, prop. seed, fr. L. *grana*, pl. of *granum.*] **1.** The seed or seedlike fruit of any cereal grass, as wheat, maize, or oats. **2.** Collectively, the seeds or fruits of various food plants, now usually the cereal grasses; also, the plants themselves. In British usage all kinds of grain are popularly known as *corn.* **3.** Any small, hard particle, as of sand or sugar; hence, a particle; the smallest amount. **4.** The unit of the English system of weights, derived from the weight of a grain of wheat. Abbr. *gr.*, or *g.* (*sing. & pl.*) See WEIGHT, *Tables* 1, 2, 3, & 4. **5. a** *Hist.* Kermes or, sometimes, cochineal; also, a red dye made from either of them; hence, crimson, scarlet, or the like; also, any dye, esp. a fast one. **b** Color; hue. **6.** A granulated surface or appearance. **7.** The hair side of a piece of leather, or the marking on that side. **8. a** The fiber which forms the substance of wood or other fibrous material. **b** Direction, arrangement, or appearance of the fibers in wood, of strata in stone, etc. **9.** Texture and compactness of constituent particles, as in sugar or stone; as, marble of fine *grain.* **10.** Temper; natural disposition. **11.** State of being crystallized; as, syrup boiled to the *grain.* **12.** *pl.* Remains of grain after the mashing process, as in brewing. **13.** The fiber or yarn, as disting. from the woven fabric; as, carpets dyed in the *grain.* — ***in grain.*** Dyed in grain (sense 5 **a**), or scarlet or crimson; of a fast color; deeply seated.

— *v. i. & t.* **1.** To form grains or into grains; granulate; crystallize. **2.** To paint in imitation of the grain of wood, marble, etc.; also, to give a granular surface (to). **3.** To dye in grain. **4.** To take the hair off (skins); to soften and raise the grain of (leather, etc.). — **grain'er**, *n.*

grain alcohol. Ethyl alcohol, C_2H_5OH; — properly so called when made from grain.

grain'y (grān'ĭ), *adj.;* GRAIN'I·ER (-ĭ·ẽr); GRAIN'I·EST. **1.** Granular in texture. **2.** Full of grain. **3.** Resembling the grain of wood.

gral'la·to'ri·al (grăl'ȧ·tō'rĭ·ăl; 70), *adj.* [L. *grallator* one who runs on stilts, fr. *grallae* stilts.] Belonging or pert. to a former order (Grallatores), the wading birds, including shore birds, as snipe, and inland water birds, as herons.

gram (grăm), *n.* [Pg. *grão*, fr. L. *granum* grain.] In India esp., one of certain leguminous plants grown for their seed; as: **a** The chick-pea. **b** The bean *Phaseolus aureus.*

gram, gramme (grăm), *n.* [F. *gramme*, fr. LL., fr. Gr. *gramma* that which is written, a letter, a small weight, fr. *graphein* to write.] A unit of mass and weight in the metric system. See METRIC SYSTEM, *Table* 5. Abbr. *g., gm., gr.*

-gram (-grăm). [See GRAMMAR.] A combining form denoting *something drawn* or *written, a drawing, writing*, etc.

gra'ma (grä'mȧ), *n., or* **grama grass.** [Sp. *grama* grass, fr. L. *gramen.*] A pasture grass (genus *Bouteloua*) of the western United States.

gram'a·rye, gram'a·ry (grăm'ȧ·rĭ), *n.* [OF. *gramaire.* See GRAMMAR.] *Archaic.* Occult science; magic.

gram atom, gram'-a·tom'ic weight. *Chem.* The quantity of an element which has a weight in grams equal numerically to the number expressing the atomic weight of the element; as, a *gram atom* of oxygen is sixteen grams.

gra·mer'cy (grȧ·mûr'sĭ), *interj.* [F. *grand-merci.*] *Archaic.* An exclamation, as of thanks or surprise.

gram'i·ci'din (grăm'ĭ·sī'dĭn; grȧ·mĭs'ĭ·dĭn), *n.* [*gram* (fr. *Gram*-positive) + *-cide* + *-in.*] An antibacterial substance obtained from certain soil bacteria, that is active against certain (Gram-positive) harmful bacteria.

gra·min'e·ous (grȧ·mĭn'ē·ŭs), *adj.* [L. *gramineus*, fr. *gramen*, *-minis*, grass.] **a** Of or like grass. **b** Of the grass family; poaceous.

gram'mar (grăm'ẽr), *n.* [OF. *gramaire*, fr. L. *grammatica*, fr. Gr. *grammatikē*, fem. of *grammatikos* skilled in grammar, fr. *gramma* letter, fr. the root of *graphein* to write.] **1.** The science treating of the classes of words, their inflections, and their syntactical relations and functions; also, the phenomena with which this science deals. Abbr. *gram.* **2.** A treatise on grammar. **3.** Manner of speaking or writing, with reference to grammatical rules. **4.** The elements or principles of any science or art; — chiefly in book titles.

gram·mar'i·an (grȧ·mâr'ĭ·ăn; 6), *n.* One versed in grammar.

grammar school. **a** Orig., a school for the teaching of Latin; now, esp. in England, a college preparatory school in which Latin, Greek, etc., are taught. **b** *U. S.* The school grades between those called primary and high school.

gram·mat'i·cal (grȧ·măt'ĭ·kăl), *adj.* **1.** Of or pertaining to grammar. **2.** According to the rules of grammar. — **gram·mat'i·cal·ly**, *adv.*

grammatical meaning. *Ling.* The part of meaning that varies from one form of a paradigm to another (*plays, played, playing*). Cf. LEXICAL MEANING.

gramme (grăm). Var. of GRAM, weight.

gram molecule. Also **gram'-mo·lec'u·lar weight.** *Chem.* The quantity of a compound or element which has a weight in grams equal numerically to its molecular weight.

Gram'o·phone (grăm'ō·fōn), *n.* A trade-mark for talking machines and records.

gram'pus (grăm'pŭs), *n.; pl.* GRAMPUSES (-ĕz; -ĭz). **a** A cetacean (*Grampus griseus*) allied to the blackfish; also, one of other cetaceans of like size, as the blackfish. **b** The common killer whale.

Gram's method (grămz). [After H. C. J. *Gram* (1853–1938), Dan. physician.] A method of differential staining of bacteria by treating them with a special iodine solution (**Gram's solution**) after being stained with gentian violet. Certain species (**Gram'–pos'i·tive**) retain the purple dye and others (**Gram'–neg'a·tive**) are decolorized, thus affording a basis for classification.

gran'a·dil'la (grăn'ȧ·dĭl'ȧ), *n.* [Sp., dim. of *granada* pomegranate. See GRENADE.] The edible fruit of certain species of passionflower, esp. that of *Passiflora quadrangularis* of tropical America, used as a dessert; also, the vine.

gran'a·ry (grăn'ȧ·rĭ; *popularly* grān'ȧ·rĭ), *n.; pl.* -RIES (-rĭz). [L. *granarium*, fr. *granum* grain.] A storehouse for grain, esp. after it is threshed or husked; hence: **a** A region fertile in grain. **b** An abundant supply.

grand (grănd), *adj.* [OF. *grant, grand*, fr. L. *grandis*.] **1.** Higher in rank, dignity, etc., than others having the same title or designation; as, *grand* president. **2.** Pre-eminent; foremost; chief. **3.** Notably large or great; — usually with an added significance; as: **a** Comprehensive; as, the *grand* total. **b** Main; principal; as, the *grand* staircase. **c** Magnificent; sumptuous; as, *grand* banquets. **d** Imposing; impressive; as, *grand* scenery. **e** Illustrious; also, stately; as, a *grand* old man. **4.** *Colloq.* Variously: admirable, excellent, fine, in best of looks or spirits. **5.** Standing in the second degree of ancestry or descent (cf. CONSANGUINITY, *Illust.*); — generally in composition, as in **grand'aunt', grand'child', grand'daugh'ter, grand'fa'ther, grand'-ma', grand'moth'er, grand'neph'ew, grand'niece', grand'pa', grand'par'ent, grand'son', grand'un'cle. 6.** *Music.* Of full dimensions or for full orchestra; as, a *grand* chorus. — **grand'ly**, *adv.* — **grand'ness**, *n.*

Syn. **Grand, magnificent, imposing, stately, majestic, august, noble, grandiose** mean large and impressive. **Grand** is distinguished from other words meaning huge or colossal by its implications of handsomeness and dignity; **magnificent** implies an impressive largeness proportionate to the thing's scale and in accordance with the canons of good taste; **imposing** stresses impressiveness because of size and dignity; **stately** implies dignity, handsomeness, and impressiveness; **majestic** combines the implications of *imposing* and *stately* but adds a connotation of solemn grandeur; **august** implies an impressiveness that awes; **noble** implies the power to impress the imagination, emotions, or the intellect as incomparably great or excellent; **grandiose**, often but not always used derogatorily, implies a grandeur or majesty exceeding that of life or experience.

gran'dam (grăn'dăm; -dăm), *n.* Also **gran'dame** (-dām; -dăm). [F. *grande*, fem. of *grand* + *dame*.] An old woman; esp., a grandmother.

grand duchess. **a** The wife or widow of a grand duke. **b** A lady who is sovereign of a grand duchy in her own right. **c** Formerly, in Russia, a daughter of a tsar, or one of his female descendants through the male line.

grand duchy. A territory of which a grand duke or grand duchess is sovereign; as, the *grand duchy* of Luxembourg.

grand duke. **a** A sovereign duke of certain countries, one degree below a king. **b** Formerly, in Russia, a son of a tsar or one of his male descendants through the male line.

gran·dee' (grăn·dē'), *n.* [Sp. *grande*.] A man of elevated rank or station, or of eminence. In Spain and Portugal, a nobleman of the first rank.

||**grande pas'sion'** (gräɴd' pä'syôɴ'). [F.] Great passion; love.

gran'deur (grăn'dūr; 118), *n.* [F., fr. *grand* grand.] Grandness; eminence; magnificence; sublimity; also, an instance of such greatness or magnificence.

gran·dil'o·quence (grăn·dĭl'ō·kwĕns), *n.* [L. *grandis* grand + *loqui* to speak.] Use of lofty, swelling language or the quality resulting from such use; pompous eloquence. — **gran·dil'o·quent** (-kwĕnt), *adj.* — **gran·dil'o·quent·ly**, *adv.*

gran'di·ose (grăn'dĭ·ōs), *adj.* [F., fr. It. *grandioso*.] **1.** Impressive or imposing; displaying grandeur. **2.** Characterized by affectation of grandeur or splendor; flaunting. — **Syn.** See GRAND. — **gran'di·ose·ly**, *adv.* — **gran'di·os'i·ty** (-ŏs'ĭ·tĭ), *n.*

||**gran·dio'so** (grän·dyō'sō), *adj.* [It.] *Music.* Broad and noble in style; — a direction.

grand jury. *Law.* A jury that examines accusations against persons charged with crime, and finds bills of indictment, if the evidence warrants.

Grand Lama. See LAMAISM.

grand larceny. See LARCENY.

||**grand mal** (gräɴ' mȧl'). [F., lit., great sickness.] *Med.* A strongly marked form of epilepsy. Cf. PETIT MAL.

Grand Mo'narque', le (lẽ gräɴ' mô'nȧrk'). [F.] Literally, the Great Monarch; — applied to Louis XIV of France.

||**grand monde'** (gräɴ' môɴd'). [F.] The great world; specif., high society.

grand opera. Opera in which the plot is elaborated as in serious drama, and the entire text set to music.

grand'sire' (grănd'sīr'), *n.* Also **grand'sir'** (-sûr'). *Archaic.* **a** A grandfather. **b** An ancestor; a forefather. **c** An aged man.

grand'stand' (-stănd'), *n.* The principal stand at a racecourse, athletic field, etc.

grandstand play. *Colloq.* A play executed more showily than necessary to draw applause from the grandstand; hence, an act done to draw applause or make an impression.

grand tour. An extended tour on the Continent formerly commonly taken by youth of the British aristocracy as a part of their education; hence, any similar extended tour.

grand vizier. The chief officer of state of a Moslem country, esp., formerly, of the Turkish Empire.

grange (grānj), *n.* [OF., fr. VL. *granica*, fr. L. *granum* grain.] **1.** *Archaic.* A granary. **2.** A farm; esp., a farmhouse with outbuildings. **3.** *Hist.* An outlying farmhouse, with its barns and other buildings, belonging to a monastery or to a feudal lord. **4.** *U.S.* **a** One of the lodges of the "Patrons of Husbandry," a secret association of farmers to further their interests. **b** [*cap.*] Also, popularly, the association itself.

grang'er (grān'jẽr), *n.* *U.S.* **a** A member of a grange or the Grange (def. 4). **b** A farmer. — **grang'er·ism** (-ĭz'm), *n.*

grang'er·ize (-īz), *v. t. & i.* [After Rev. James *Granger*, whose *Biographical History of England* (1769) was prepared for illustration in this manner.] *Chiefly Brit.* To illustrate by inserting engravings, etc., collected from other sources; also, to mutilate (books, etc.) to obtain material for such illustration. — **grang'er·ism** (-ĭz'm), *n.* — **grang'er·i·za'tion** (-ĭ·zā'shŭn; -ī·zā'-), *n.* — **grang'er·iz'er** (-īz'ẽr), *n.*

grani-. [L. *granum*.] A combining form meaning *grain*, as in **gran'i·form.** See -FORM.

gran'ite (grăn'ĭt), *n.* [It. *granito* granite, adj., grainy, deriv. of L. *granum* grain.] **1.** Any very hard natural igneous rock formation of visibly crystalline texture, consisting essentially of quartz and orthoclase or microcline. **2.** Figuratively, unyielding firmness or endurance. — **gra·nit'ic** (grȧ·nĭt'ĭk), *adj.* — **gran'it·oid** (grăn'ĭt·oid), *adj. & n.*

granite paper. A thin, wove paper containing tiny pieces of colored silk thread, giving it a mottled appearance.

Granite State. New Hampshire; — a nickname, from the granite in its mountains.

gran'ite·ware' (grăn'ĭt·wâr'), *n.* Enameled ironware.

gran'it·ite (grăn'ĭt·īt), *n.* *Petrog.* Granite that contains biotite.

gra·niv'o·rous (grȧ·nĭv'ō·rŭs), *adj.* [*grani-* + *-vorous*.] Feeding on seeds or grain. — **gran'i·vore** (grăn'ĭ·vōr), *n.*

gran'ny, gran'nie (grăn'ĭ), *n.; pl.* -NIES (-ĭz). **1.** Grandmother. **2.** An old woman. **3.** *Colloq.* **a** *Southern U.S.* A nurse. **b** A fussy person. **4.** A granny knot.

gran'ny knot, gran'ny's bend, gran'ny's knot (grăn'ĭz). A kind of readily jammed and insecure knot often made by the inexperienced instead of a reef knot. See KNOT, *Illust.* (29).

gran'o- (grăn'ō-). [L. *granum* grain.] A combining form meaning *granite, granitic, granular*, as in **gran'o·di'o·rite, gran'o·gab'bro, gran'o·lite.**

gran'o·phyre (-fīr), *n.* [*grano-* + *-phyre*.] *Petrog.* A porphyritic igneous rock, chiefly of feldspar and quartz, having a granular groundmass. — **gran'o·phy'ric** (-fī'rĭk), *adj.*

grant (grȧnt; 9), *v. t.* [OF. *graanter, craanter, creanter*, to promise, yield, fr. L. *credens*. See CREDENCE.] **1.** To agree to; allow to be fulfilled; accord. **2.** To give, esp. in answer to a prayer, request, or petition; esp., *Law*, to bestow formally, as a privilege; make conveyance of; give the possession or title of, esp. by a deed or formal writing; convey. **3.** To admit as true (what is not yet satisfactorily proved); concede.

Syn. **Grant, concede, vouchsafe, accord, award** mean to give as a favor or a right. **Grant** implies an act of justice or indulgence in answering a request or demand; **concede**, a yielding with reluctance because of some compelling force in the claim or claimant; **vouchsafe**, a granting as a courtesy that which is prayed for or begged for or expected; **accord**, a granting of that which is due one or in keeping with his character or status; **award**, the granting of that which has been merited or earned.

— *n.* **1.** Act of granting; concession; allowance; bestowal. **2.** Thing or property granted; gift; esp., a tract of land, a monopoly, or the like, granted by the government. **3.** In Maine, New Hampshire, and Vermont, a kind of minor territorial division, usually unincorporated, and originally granted to some individual or individuals. **4.** A transfer of property, by deed or writing.

— **grant'a·ble**, *adj.* — **grant'er**, *n.*

gran'tee' (grȧn'tē'), *n.* *Law.* One to whom a grant is made.

grant'–in–aid', *n.; pl.* GRANTS-IN-AID. **1.** A grant or subsidy from public funds paid by a central to a local government in aid of some public undertaking. **2.** Any similar financial aid by a private organization.

grant'or (grȧn'tẽr; grȧn'tôr', *esp. in contrast with* grantee), *n.* A granter; esp., *Law*, the person by whom a grant or conveyance is made.

gran'u·lar (grăn'ū·lẽr), *adj.* **1.** Consisting of or appearing to consist of grains or granules; of the nature of granules; as, a *granular* rock. **2.** *Med.* Granulated; showing granulation. — **gran'u·lar'i·ty** (-lăr'ĭ·tĭ), *n.*

gran'u·late (-lāt), *v. t. & i.* **1.** To form, crystallize, or collect, into grains or granules, as sugar. **2.** To make or become rough, esp. on the surface, by the formation of small elevations or granules. — **gran'u·lat'ed** (-lāt'ĕd; -ĭd), *adj.* — **gran'u·lat'er** (-lāt'ẽr), **gran'u·la'tor** (-lā'tẽr), *n.* — **gran'u·la'tive** (-lā'tĭv), *adj.*

gran'u·la'tion (-lā'shŭn), *n.* **1.** A granulating; state of being granulated. **2.** One of the elevations or granules in a granulated surface or condition, as of the eyelids in trachoma; also, one of the minute red prominences, made up of new tissue, which form on a raw surface, as of a wound or ulcer, and are the active agents in the process of healing.

gran'ule (grăn'ūl), *n.* [LL. *granulum*, dim. of *granum* grain.] A small grain or grainlike particle.

gran'u·lite (grăn'ū·līt), *n.* *Petrog.* **a** A whitish, granular rock, consisting of feldspar, quartz, and small red garnets. **b** Aplite. **c** Any rock which, by recrystallization after crushing, has become granular. — **gran'u·lit'ic** (-lĭt'ĭk), *adj.*

gran'u·lose (-lōs), *adj.* Granular.

gran'u·lose, *n.* A polysaccharide forming the inner part of starch granules and convertible to maltose by diastase.

grape (grāp), *n.* [OF., bunch of grapes, fr. *graper, craper*, to gather grapes.] **1.** Any vine of a family (Vitaceae, the grape family) of woody or herbaceous vines, with leaves that have, usually, tendril-bearing stems, and with small, greenish, clustered flowers succeeded by several-seeded berries. **2.** A smooth-skinned juicy berry, the edible fruit of two genera (*Vitis* and *Muscadinia*) of vines of the grape family (Vitaceae). **3.** A color, bluish blue-red in hue, of low saturation and very low brilliance. See COLOR. **4.** *Mil.* Grapeshot; — formerly also used in *pl.*

grape'fruit' (-frōōt'), *n.* A large citrus fruit that has a bitter yellow rind and somewhat acid juicy pulp and grows in clusters; also, the tree bearing this fruit.

grape hyacinth. Any of a genus (*Muscari*, esp. *M. botryoides*, called also *bluebell*, and *M. racemosum*) of plants of the lily family, bearing racemes of blue flowers.

grap'er·y (grāp'ẽr·ĭ), *n.; pl.* -ERIES (-ĭz). A building used for the cultivation of grapes.

grape′shot′ (grāp′shŏt′), *n.* A cluster of small iron balls used as a cannon charge.
grape′stone′ (-stōn′), *n.* A seed of the grape.
grape sugar. Dextrose, found naturally in ripe grapes. See DEXTROSE.
grape′vine′ (grāp′vīn′), *n.* **1.** Any grape-bearing vine; esp., any plant (genus *Vitis*) typifying the grape family (Vitaceae). **2.** A rumor, esp. a false rumor, conveyed by signals, underground channels, etc. (**grapevine telegraph**); also, an underground channel of information.

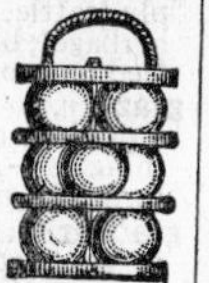
Grapeshot.

-graph (-grăf; 9). [Gr. *graphein* to write.] A combining form meaning *a writing;* also, *a writer, an instrument for making records* or *for transmitting.*
graph (grăf; 9), *n.* [See -GRAPH.] **1.** A diagram symbolizing a system of interrelations by spots, all distinguishable and some connected by lines of the same kind. **2.** *Math.* A curve or surface, the locus of a point whose co-ordinates are the variables in the equation of the locus. — *v. t.* To plot or trace, as a curve from its equation.
graph′al·loy′ (grăf′ă·loi′), *n.* [*graph*ite + *alloy.*] Graphite impregnated with molten metal under hydraulic pressure. It is made into bushings, electrical contacts, etc.
-grapher. A combining form denoting *one who writes;* — in nouns corresponding to those in *-graph* and *-graphy.*
graph′ic (grăf′ĭk), *adj.* Also **graph′i·cal** (-ĭ·kăl). [L. *graphicus,* fr. Gr. *graphikos,* fr. *graphein* to write.] **1.** Well delineated; vividly described; also, describing clearly and vividly. **2.** Of or pertaining to the arts (**graphic arts**) of painting, drawing, engraving, and any other arts which pertain to the expression of ideas by means of lines, marks, or characters impressed on a surface. **3.** Of or pertaining to writing or to representation by graphs or diagrams. **4.** *Mineral.* Exhibiting on the surface or in transverse section the appearance of written or printed characters; as, *graphic* granite. — **graph′i·cal·ly,** *adv.*
Syn. **Graphic, vivid, picturesque, pictorial,** as applied to writings, mean giving a clear visual impression. **Graphic** stresses the evoking of a clear-cut lifelike picture; **vivid,** impressing upon the mind the vigorous aliveness of something; **picturesque,** the presentation of a striking or effective picture, sometimes without regard to reality; **pictorial,** representation in the manner of painting, with emphasis upon colors, shapes, etc.
-graph′ic (-grăf′ĭk). Also **-graph′i·cal** (-ĭ·kăl). A combining form in adjectives corresponding to nouns ending in *-graphy* or *-graph* (see -IC).
graph′ics (grăf′ĭks), *n.;* see -ICS. Art or science of drawing, esp. according to mathematical rules, as in perspective, projection, etc.; specif., calculation, as of stresses in engineering, by the use of geometrical constructions.
graph′ite (-īt), *n.* [G. *graphit,* fr. Gr. *graphein* to write.] *Mineral.* Soft, black native carbon of metallic luster; — often called *plumbago* or *black lead.* It is used for lead pencils, crucibles, lubricants, etc. H., 1–2. Sp. gr., 2.09–2.23. — **gra·phit′ic** (gră·fĭt′ĭk), *adj.*
grapho-. [Gr. *graphē* writing, *graphein* to write.] A combining form meaning *writing* or *to write,* as in **graph′o·ma′ni·a** (grăf′ō·mā′nĭ·ȧ), **graph′o·spasm** (grăf′ō·spăz′m).
graph·ol′o·gy (grăf·ŏl′ō·jĭ), *n.* The study of handwriting, as for detecting forgeries, determining character or aptitudes, or diagnosing nervous diseases. — **graph·ol′o·gist** (-jĭst), *n.*
graph′o·mo′tor (grăf′ō·mō′tẽr), *adj.* [*grapho-* + *motor.*] *Med.* Relating to, or affecting, movements made in writing.
Graph′o·phone (grăf′ō·fōn), *n.* A trade-mark applied to sound-recording and reproducing machines and records.
graph paper. Paper ruled into small squares for drawing graphs, plotting curves, making diagrams, etc.; plotting paper.
-graphy. [Gr. *-graphia,* fr. *graphein* to write.] A combining form denoting: **a** *A writing* or *describing.* **b** *A branch of learning descriptively treated.* **c** *A treatise.*
grap′lin, grap′line (grăp′lĭn). Corrupt. of GRAPPLING, a grapnel.
grap′nel (grăp′nĕl; -n'l), *n.* [ME. *grapenel,* dim. fr. OF. *grapin, grapil,* fr. Pr. *grapin, grapil,* fr. *grapa* hook, fork.] A small anchor with four or five flukes or claws; hence, a grappling iron; a grab.
grap′ple (grăp′'l), *n.* [OF. *grappil, grapil.* See GRAPNEL.] **1.** A grapnel. **2.** A grappling; a seizing or seizure, as in wrestling. — *v. t.;* GRAP′PLED (-'ld); GRAP′PLING (-lĭng). To seize, hold, as with a grapnel; to grip. — *v. i.* **1.** To use a grapple; hence, to contend in close fight; seize one another. **2.** To make grasping motions; grope. — **grap′pler** (-lẽr), *n.*
grap′pling (grăp′lĭng), *n.* A grapnel.
grappling iron *or* **hook.** A hooked iron for grappling a vessel or other object, under water, etc.; a grapnel.
grap′y (grāp′ĭ), *adj.* Of, pertaining to, or like, grapes or the vine.
grasp (gràsp; 9), *v. i.* [ME. *graspen* to grope, grasp at.] To make the motion of seizing or trying to seize; clutch; — now with *at.* — *v. t.* **1.** To take or seize eagerly. **2.** To seize and hold by or as by clasping or clutching; grip. **3.** To lay hold of with the mind; comprehend. — **Syn.** See TAKE. — *n.* **1.** A grasping; handgrip; also, an embrace. **2.** Forcible holding; possession; control. **3.** Reach of the arms; hence, the power of seizing, holding, or comprehending. **4.** Proficiency in comprehending. — **grasp′er,** *n.*
grasp′ing, *adj.* That grasps; esp., avaricious; covetous. — **Syn.** See COVETOUS. — **grasp′ing·ly,** *adv.* — **grasp′ing·ness,** *n.*
grass (gràs; 9), *n.* [AS. *græs, gærs.*] **1.** Green herbage affording food for cattle or other grazing animals; esp., herbage provided by the true grasses (see def. 2), the sedges, and the rushes, in which the leaves have narrow and spear-shaped blades. **2.** Any plant of a family (Poaceae, the grass family), distinguished by their jointed stems, sheathing leaves, flowers borne in spikelets of bracts, and fruit of a seedlike grain. **3.** Land on which grass is grown for hay or pasture. **4.** A blade or leaf of grass; — now only in *pl.* **5.** Grass-covered ground. **6.** A grass sponge. — *v. t.* **1.** To graze, as cattle. **2.** To cover with grass. **3.** To expose on the grass for bleaching. **4.** *Sports.* To bring to the ground; fell. — **grass′land′** (-lănd′), *n.* — **grass′plot′** (-plŏt′), *n.*
grass′hop′per (-hŏp′ẽr), *n.* **1.** Any of numerous leaping orthopterous insects of the families Acridiidae and Locustidae, feeding on plants and often very destructive. Those of the Acridiidae, also called *locusts,* have short antennae and ovipositor and three-jointed tarsi; those of the Locustidae have long antennae and ovipositor and four-jointed tarsi. Among American forms of the Acridiidae are the widely distributed ***red-legged grasshopper*** (*Melanoplus femur-rubrum*) and the ***Rocky Mountain grasshopper*** (*M. spretus*) which often migrates in vast swarms over the plains west of the Mississippi River destroying all vegetation in that area. American forms of the Locustidae include the ***meadow, or green, grasshopper*** and the *katydids.* See LOCUST; KATYDID; INSECT, *Illust.;* cf. CICADA. **2.** A light unarmed scouting and liaison airplane used esp. in directing field-artillery fire.
grass′-of-Par·nas′sus, *n.* Any of a genus (*Parnassia,* family Parnassiaceae) of smooth bog herbs with basal entire leaves and white flowers, natives of arctic and temperate regions.
grass roots. **1.** Roots of grass; also, fig., the very source. **2.** The farming district or the people of a farming district thought of as a politico-economic group holding firm independent views.
grass snipe. The pectoral sandpiper.
grass sponge. A harsh, usually dark-brown, often very large sponge (*Hippospongia equima cerebriformis* and allied species), of inferior commercial quality, found in the Gulf of Mexico, off Florida, and in the West Indies.
grass tree. **a** Any of a genus (*Xanthorrhoea*) of Australian plants of the lily family, with a thick woody trunk bearing a cluster of stiff linear leaves and a terminal spike of small flowers; — called also *blackboy.* Some species yield a red and yellow resin (*acaroid resin* or *gum*) used in paper size, varnish, etc. **b** Any of several Australasian trees of grass-like foliage, as the ti of New Zealand.
grass widow. A woman separated from her husband, esp. by divorce or by his absence. Hence, **grass widower.**
grass′y (gràs′ĭ), *adj.;* GRASS′I·ER (-ĭ·ẽr); GRASS′I·EST. **1.** Covered with grass; consisting of grass. **2.** Also **grass′y-green′.** Resembling grass in color. — **grass′i·ness,** *n.*
grate (grāt), *v. t.* [OF. *grater* to scrape, scratch, of Teut. origin.] **1.** *Archaic.* To scrape; abrade. **2.** To pulverize by rubbing against a rough or indented surface; as, to *grate* a nutmeg. **3.** To grind (the teeth) or rub against (something) so as to make a rasping noise; also, *Rare,* to produce (a noise) by grinding or friction. **4.** To fret; irritate; offend. — *v. i.* **1.** To rub or grind with a rasping sound. **2.** To have a rasping or exasperating effect. — **grat′er** (grāt′ẽr), *n.* — **grat′ing·ly,** *adv.*
grate, *n.* [ML. *grata,* fr. L. *cratis* hurdle.] **1.** A frame of parallel or crossed bars, as in a prison window or in a coal-burning furnace. **2.** Hence: **a** *Obs.* A grated cage; also, a prison. **b** A fireplace. **3.** A screen or sieve for use in stamp mills for grading ore. — *v. t.* To furnish with a grate or grates.
grate′ful (grāt′fo͝ol; -f'l), *adj.* [Obs. *grate,* adj., agreeable (fr. L. *gratus*) + *full.*] **1.** Appreciative of benefits received; thankful. **2.** Affording pleasure; gratifying; welcome; as, *grateful* coolness after heat. **3.** Expressing gratitude. — **grate′ful·ly,** *adv.* — **grate′ful·ness,** *n.*
Syn. (1) **Grateful, thankful** mean feeling or expressing gratitude. **Grateful** more commonly expresses a proper sense of favors received from one's fellow men; **thankful,** acknowledgment of divine favor, or of what is vaguely felt to be providential. (2) See PLEASANT.
grat′i·fi·ca′tion (grăt′ĭ·fĭ·kā′shŭn), *n.* **1.** A gratifying, or state of being gratified. **2.** A reward; a recompense; a gratuity. **3.** A source of satisfaction or pleasure.
grat′i·fy (grăt′ĭ·fī), *v. t.;* -FIED (-fīd); -FY′ING. [F. or L.; F. *gratifier,* fr. L. *gratificari,* fr. *gratus* pleasing + *-ficare* (in comp.) to make.] **1.** **a** *Obs.* To requite in gratitude. **b** *Archaic.* To remunerate. **2.** To give or be a source of pleasure or satisfaction to; as, beauty *gratifies* the eye; hence, to oblige; favor; indulge; humor. — **grat′i·fi′er** (-fī′ẽr), *n.* — **grat′i·fy′ing,** *adj.* — **Syn.** See PLEASANT. — **-ing·ly,** *adv.*
‖**gra′tin′** (grȧ′tăN′; *Angl.* grăt′'n), *n.* [F.] *Cookery.* The brown crust formed upon a gratinated dish; also, the dish. Cf. AU GRATIN.
grat′i·nate (grăt′ĭ·nāt), *v. t.* [F. *gratiner,* v. i., to form a crust.] To cook with a covering of buttered crumbs or grated cheese, until a crust forms.
grat′ing (grāt′ĭng), *n.* **1.** A partition, covering, or frame of parallel bars or crossbars; a grate. **2.** *Optics.* A system of close equidistant and parallel lines or bars, esp. lines ruled on a polished surface, used for producing spectra by diffraction.
grat′ing, *adj.* Harsh in sound.
gra′tis (grā′tĭs; grăt′ĭs), *adv.* [L., contr. fr. *gratiis* out of favor, fr. *gratia* favor.] Without recompense. — *adj.* Gratuitous.
grat′i·tude (grăt′ĭ·tūd), *n.* [F. or L.; F., fr. LL. *gratitudo,* fr. *gratus* agreeable, grateful.] State of being grateful; thankfulness.
gra·tu′i·tant (grȧ·tū′ĭ·tănt), *n.* The receiver of a gratuity.
gra·tu′i·tous (-tŭs), *adj.* [L. *gratuitus,* fr. *gratus* pleasing.] **1.** Given freely, without recompense, or regardless of merit. **2.** Not called for by the circumstances; unwarranted. **3.** *Econ.* Designating goods, or utilities, which are the free gifts of nature and not the products of effort. **4.** *Law.* Not involving a return, compensation, or consideration, as in **gratuitous contract,** one solely for the benefit of one of the parties. — **Syn.** See SUPEREROGATORY. — **gra·tu′i·tous·ly,** *adv.* — **gra·tu′i·tous·ness,** *n.*
gra·tu′i·ty (-tĭ), *n.; pl.* -TIES (-tĭz). **1.** Something given gratuitously. **2.** A voluntary return for a favor or for service, as a tip.
grat′u·lant (grăt′ū·lănt), *adj.* [L. *gratulans,* pres. part.] Showing gratification; congratulatory.
grat′u·late (-lāt), *v. t.* [L. *gratulatus,* past part. of *gratulari* to congratulate, fr. *gratus* pleasing, agreeable.] *Now Rare.* To salute joyfully; congratulate. — *adj. Obs.* Gratifying. — **grat′u·la′tion** (-lā′shŭn), *n.* — **grat′u·la·to′ry** (-lȧ·tō′rĭ *or, esp. Brit.,* -lā′tẽr·ĭ), *adj.*
grau′pel (grou′pĕl), *n.* [G. *graupeln* to sleet, hail.] Granular snow pellets; soft hail. International symbol, △.
gra·va′men (grȧ·vā′mĕn), *n.; pl.* -VAMINA (-văm′ĭ·nȧ), -MENS (-vā′mĕnz). [LL., fr. *gravare* to load, fr. *gravis* heavy.] The material part of a grievance, charge, etc.
grave (grāv), *v. t.* [F. *grave, grève,* beach.] *Naut.* To clean and pay with pitch, as a barnacled vessel.
grave (grāv), *adj.* [F., fr. L. *gravis* heavy.] **1.** Deserving serious consideration; important; momentous. **2.** Sedate and dignified; solemn. **3.** Sober; somber; as, *grave* colors. **4.** *Music.* Low in pitch; not acute; — said of sound. **5.** *Phonet.* **a** Characterized by the tone or quality indicated by the grave accent; marked with this accent; as, *grave* e (è). **b** Entirely unaccented, as a syllable. — **Syn.** See SERIOUS. — **Ant.** Gay. — *n.* In full **grave accent.** A mark (`) indicating: **a** The open quality of a French *e.* **b** A falling inflection. **c** Pronunciation of a final *ed* (*armèd*). — **grave′ly,** *adv.* — **grave′ness,** *n.*
‖**gra′ve** (grä′vā), *adj.* [It.] *Music.* Slow; serious; — designating the slowest tempo used in music. — ‖**gra′ve,** *adv.*
grave (grāv), *v. t.;* GRAVED (grāvd); GRAV′EN (grāv′ĕn) or GRAVED;

GRAV′ING. [AS. *grafan* to dig, engrave.] **1.** *Archaic.* **a** To dig. **b** To bury. **2. a** To carve out with a chisel; sculpture. **b** To carve or cut, as letters or figures, on some hard substance; engrave. **3.** To impress deeply; fix indelibly.

grave (grāv), *n.* [AS. *græf.*] An excavation in the earth as a place of burial; a tomb; sepulcher; hence, death.

grave′clothes′ (grāv′klōthz′; *see* CLOTHES), *n. pl.* The clothes or dress in which the dead are interred.

grav′el (grăv′ĕl; -'l), *n.* [OF. *gravele, gravelle,* dim. of *grave, greve* (F. *grève* sandy shore, strand), of Celt. origin.] **1.** *Obs.* Sand. **2.** Loose rounded fragments of rock, such as pebbles. **3.** *Med.* A deposit of small calculous concretions in the kidneys and urinary bladder; also, the disease causing it. — *v. t.;* -ELED (-ĕld; -'ld) or -ELLED; -ELING or -EL·LING. **1.** To cover with gravel. **2.** *Colloq.* To baffle; embarrass. **3.** To ground (a ship) on gravel. — **grav′el·ly** (grăv′ĕl·ĭ; -'l·ĭ), *adj.*

grav′el–blind′ (-blīnd′), *adj.* Having very dim sight.

grav′en (grāv′ĕn), *adj.* Sculptured; engraved; hence, **graven image,** an idol.

Grav′en·stein (grăv′ĕn·stīn; *popularly* -stēn), *n.* [From *Gravenstein,* a place in Slesvig.] A large fall apple with streaks of deep red and orange.

grav′er (grāv′ẽr), *n.* One that graves; specif.: **a** An engraver. **b** Any of various cutting or graving tools, as an engraver's burin.

Graves′ disease (grāvz). [After R. J. *Graves* (1796–1853), Irish physician.] Exophthalmic goiter.

grave′stone′ (grāv′stōn′), *n.* A stone marking a grave.

grave′yard′ (-yärd′), *n.* A burial yard; cemetery.

grav′id (grăv′ĭd), *adj.* [L. *gravidus,* fr. *gravis* heavy, loaded.] Pregnant. — **gra·vid′i·ty** (grȧ·vĭd′ĭ·tĭ), *n.* — **grav′id·ly,** *adv.* — **grav′id·ness,** *n.*

gra·vim′e·ter (grȧ·vĭm′ē·tẽr), *n.* [F. *gravimètre,* fr. L. *gravis* heavy. See -METER.] A kind of hydrometer.

grav′i·met′ric (grăv′ĭ·mĕt′rĭk), *adj.* Also **grav′i·met′ri·cal** (-rĭ·kăl). *Chem.* Of or pertaining to measurement by weight; measured by weight. — **grav′i·met′ri·cal·ly,** *adv.*

gra·vim′e·try (grȧ·vĭm′ē·trĭ), *n.* [L. *gravis* heavy + *-metry.*] The measurement of weight or density.

grav′ing dock (grāv′ĭng). A dock for holding a ship for cleaning the bottom, etc.; a dry dock.

grav′i·tate (grăv′ĭ·tāt), *v. i.* To obey the law of gravitation; to tend to move as if influenced by gravitation. — **grav′i·tat′er** (-tāt′ẽr), *n.*

grav′i·ta′tion (-tā′shŭn), *n.* **1.** A gravitating. **2.** *Physics.* The phenomenon that any two material particles or bodies, if free to move, will be accelerated toward each other. — **grav′i·ta′tion·al,** *adj.* — **grav′i·ta′tion·al·ly,** *adv.* — **grav′i·ta′tive** (grăv′ĭ·tā′tĭv; -tȧ·tĭv), *adj.*

grav′i·ty (grăv′ĭ·tĭ), *n.; pl.* -TIES (-tĭz). [F. or L.; F. *gravité,* fr. L. *gravitas,* fr. *gravis* heavy.] **1.** State or quality of being grave; seriousness; solemnity; importance; enormity. **2.** *Archaic.* A grave matter. **3.** Ponderability; also, weight; — now chiefly in *center of gravity.* **4.** *Physics.* **a** Terrestrial gravitation; specif., the gravitational acceleration of terrestrial bodies toward the center of the earth. **b** Loosely, gravitation in general. **c** Specific gravity. — *adj.* Using gravity; working or operated by gravity; as, a *gravity* railroad.

gravity cell. *Elec.* A type of cell in which the two fluids remain separate because of the greater specific gravity of the copper sulfate solution.

gra·vure′ (grȧ·vūr′; grā′vūr), *n.* [F.] An engraved copper plate or block of wood; also, a print made from such a plate or block. Cf. PHOTOGRAVURE, ROTOGRAVURE.

gra′vy (grā′vĭ), *n.; pl.* -VIES (-vĭz). **1.** A sauce for meat, fish, vegetables, etc. **2.** The juice that drips from meat in cooking; — usually called *dish gravy.* **3.** *Slang.* Something got without effort; also, graft; illegal profits.

gray, grey (grā), *adj.* [AS. *grǣg, grēg.*] **1.** Of the color gray; hence, dull; not bright; also, cheerless; dismal. **2.** Gray-haired; hence, elderly or mature. **3.** Clothed or habited in gray; as, **Gray Friars,** or Franciscans. **4.** Manipulated in restraint of trade by undercover methods not actually or explicitly illegal; as, a *gray* market in metals. — *n.* **1. a** Any color formed by blending black and white. **b** Technically, a color which has no hue and hence no saturation. **2.** A gray animal or thing; also, a person wearing a gray uniform. **3.** State of being unbleached and undyed; — of fabrics, hosiery, etc.; — esp. in phrase ***in the gray.*** — *v. t. & i.* To make or become gray or grayish. — **gray′ly, grey′ly,** *adv.* — **gray′ness, grey′ness,** *n.*

gray′back′, grey′back′ (grā′băk′), *n.* Any of various animals distinguished by their gray or grayish upper parts, as a whalebone whale (*Rhachianectes glaucus*), the hooded crow (*Corvus cornix*), etc.

gray′beard′, grey′beard′ (-bẽrd′), *n.* One whose beard is gray; an old and experienced man.

gray birch. See BIRCH.

gray′fish′, grey′fish′ (grā′fĭsh′), *n.; pl.,* see FISH. The dogfish (either *Cynias canis* or *Squalus acanthias*).

gray fox. See FOX.

Gray Friar. A friar of the Franciscan order.

gray goods *or* **cloth.** Fabric just as it leaves the loom or knitting machine, unbleached, undyed, unprinted, and unfinished, but not necessarily gray in color; greige.

gray gum. See GUM, 5 a.

gray′ish, grey′ish (grā′ĭsh), *adj.* Somewhat gray. — **gray′ish, grey′ish,** *n.*

gray′lag′, grey′lag′ (-lăg′), *n.* The common gray wild goose (*Anser anser*) of Europe.

gray′ling (grā′lĭng), *n.* **1.** *pl.,* see PLURAL, *Note,* 6. Any of several fresh-water game fishes constituting a genus (*Thymallus*), allied to the trouts. **2.** Any of various gray and brown butterflies (subfamily Satyrinae).

gray manganese ore. = MANGANITE, 1.

gray matter. a Nerve tissue (esp. of the brain and spinal cord) which contains nerve cells as well as fibers, and has a brownish-gray color. **b** *Colloq.* Brains; intellect.

Gray's Inn (grāz). See INN OF COURT.

gray squirrel. See SQUIRREL, 1 a.

gray′wacke′, grey′wacke′ (grā′wăk′; -wăk′ĕ), *n.* [G. *grauwacke,* fr. *grau* gray + *wacke* wacke.] *Petrog.* A coarse sandstone or fine-grained conglomerate, usually dark gray, composed of firmly cemented, somewhat rounded, fragments of quartz, feldspars, etc.

graze (grāz), *v. t.* [AS. *grasian,* fr. *græs* grass.] **1.** To feed or supply (cattle, sheep, etc.) with grass or pasture. **2.** To feed on (growing herbage); browse. **3.** To tend (cattle, etc.) while grazing. — *v. i.* To feed on growing herbage. — *n. Colloq.* A grazing or cropping.

graze, *v. t.* **1.** To touch lightly in passing; to glance off from. **2.** To scratch or abrade. — *v. i.* To graze, brush, or scrape against something. — *n.* A grazing; an abrasion made by scraping. — **graz′er** (grāz′ẽr), *n.* — **graz′ing·ly,** *adv.*

gra′zier (grā′zhẽr *or, esp. Brit.,* -zĭ·ẽr), *n.* **1.** One who grazes cattle. **2.** In Australia, a person occupying crown or other land for sheep raising. Cf. SQUATTER.

graz′ing (grāz′ĭng), *n.* A pasture; growing grass.

grease (grēs), *n.* [OF. *gresse, graisse, craisse,* fr. L. *crassus* fat, gross.] **1.** Fat, or fatness, in an animal's body; — now only a hunting term. **2.** Rendered animal fat; hence, oily matter; esp., a thick lubricant; as, axle *grease.* **3. a** Also **grease wool.** Wool as shorn, before cleansing. **b** Of wools, furs, etc., state of being uncleansed; as, furs in the *grease.* **4.** Also **grease′–heels′.** An inflammation of the skin of the fetlocks and pasterns of horses marked by an oily secretion, ulcerations, and in severe cases, by grapes and swelling of the legs.

grease (grēs *or, esp. Brit. & southern U. S.,* grēz), *v. t.* **1.** To smear, daub, soil, etc., with grease; lubricate. **2.** In full **grease the hand** *or* **palm.** To bribe; to influence by presents.

greas′er (grēs′ẽr; grēz′ẽr), *n.* **1.** One that greases. **2.** A Mexican or Spanish American; — usually derogatory.

grease′wood′ (grēs′wŏŏd′), *n.* Also **grease′bush′** (-bŏŏsh′). A low stiff shrub (*Sarcobatus vermiculatus*) of the goosefoot family, common in alkaline soils in the western U. S.; also, any of various related or similar shrubs.

greas′y (grēs′ĭ; grēz′ĭ), *adj.;* GREAS′I·ER (-ĭ·ẽr); GREAS′I·EST. **1.** Greased; soiled with grease. **2.** Oily; unctuous; hence, slippery. **3.** Affected with grease-heels. See GREASE, *n.,* 4. — **greas′i·ly,** *adv.* — **greas′i·ness,** *n.*

great (grāt), *adj.* [AS. *grēat.*] **1.** Large in size; big; — opposed to *small* and *little.* **2.** Specif.: **a** *Archaic.* Pregnant. **b** Grown large; as, *great* girls. **c** Elaborately full; as, in *great* detail. **d** Designating a species distinguished by the size of its members; as, *great* auk, lobelia, etc. **3.** Numerous; as, a *great* company. **4.** Long continued; as, a *great* while. **5.** Being much above the average in magnitude, intensity, importance, etc.; as, *great* winds, bloodshed, or pain; of persons, their work, etc., eminent; distinguished. **6.** *Colloq.* **a** Remarkably adept or proficient; as, he is *great* at chess. **b** Particularly favored; much used or repeated; as, that's a *great* trick of his. **c** Capital; excellent. **7.** In genealogy, older, younger, or more remote, by a single generation; — often used before *grand* or another *great* to indicate one degree more remote in the direct line of descent. See CONSANGUINITY, *Illust.* — **Syn.** See LARGE.

☞ COMBINATIONS are:

great-grandchild	**great-grandmother**	**great-grandparent**
great-granddaughter	**great-grandnephew**	**great-grandson**
great-grandfather	**great-grandniece**	**great-granduncle**

— *adv. Colloq.* Successfully; well. — *n.* **1.** The whole; the gross; as, a contract to build a ship by the *great.* **2.** *pl. Slang, Oxf. Univ.* In full **great go.** The final examination for the bachelor's degree in classics and mathematics. — **great′ly,** *adv.* — **great′ness,** *n.*

great albacore. See ALBACORE **b.**

great auk. See AUK.

great′–aunt′ (grāt′ănt′; -änt′; 2), *n.* A grandaunt.

Great Bear. *Astron.* The constellation Ursa Major. See URSA MAJOR, *Illust.*

great circle. See CIRCLE, *n.,* 9. — **great′–cir′cle,** *adj.*

great′–cir′cle sail′ing. See SAILING.

great′coat′ (grāt′kōt′; grāt′kōt′; 2), *n.* An overcoat.

Great Dane. A large smooth-coated dog of a breed of massive size and great strength. Cf. BOARHOUND.

Great Divide. 1. A chief mountain watershed, esp. that of the Rocky Mountains. **2.** Death; also, a significant crisis.

great′en (grāt′'n), *v. t. & i.* To make or become greater; enlarge; magnify; increase.

great gross. Twelve gross.

great′heart′ed (grāt′här′tĕd; -tĭd), *adj.* **a** High-spirited; fearless. **b** Generous; magnanimous.

great laurel. See RHODODENDRON.

Great Mogul. a The sovereign of the empire founded in Hindustan by the Mongols in the 16th century. **b** [*not caps.*] A very important personage; a lord.

great morel. The belladonna *Atropa belladonna.*

great′–neph′ew, *n.* A grandnephew.

great′–niece′, *n.* A grandniece.

Great Rebellion. See CIVIL WAR.

great rhododendron. See RHODODENDRON.

Great Russian. See RUSSIAN.

great seal. The principal seal of a kingdom or state; also [*caps.*], the British lord chancellor (custodian of this seal) or his office.

great′–un′cle, *n.* A granduncle.

Great Week. *Eastern Ch.* Holy Week.

great white trillium. A showy perennial herb (*Trillium grandiflorum,* family Trilliaceae) of eastern North America.

Great White Way. That part of Broadway, in New York City, centering about Times Square; — from its brilliant electric illumination, esp. of the theaters, at night.

great willow herb. See WILLOW HERB.

great year. = PLATONIC YEAR. See PRECESSION OF THE EQUINOXES.

greave (grēv), *n.* [OF. *greves* greaves, shins.] Armor for the leg below the knee; — usually *pl.*

greaves (grēvz), *n. pl.* [LG. *greven.*] Refuse of tallow melting, used as food for dogs.

grebe (grēb), *n.;* see PLURAL, *Note,* 3. [F. *grèbe.*] Any of a family (Colymbidae) of swimming birds closely related to the loons, but having lobate toes. They are expert divers. The family includes the ***little grebe*** (*Podiceps ruficollis*) of Europe and the ***pied-billed grebe*** (*Podilymbus podiceps*) of America. See DABCHICK.

Gre′cian (grē′shăn), *adj.* Greek. — *n.* **1.** A Greek. **2.** One versed in Greek language and literature; a Hellenist.

Gre′cism, Grae′cism (grē′sĭz'm), *n.* **1.** A Greek idiom. **2.** The spirit of Greek art or culture.

Gre'cize, Grae'cize (grē'sīz), **gre'cize, grae'cize,** *v. t.* [F. *gréciser*, fr. L. *Graecizare.*] To render Greek; to give a Greek form or character to; Hellenize. — *v. i.* To conform to Greek usage.

Gre'co-, Grae'co- (grē'kō-). [L. *Graecus.*] A combining form denoting *Greek*, as in **Gre'co·ma'ni·a**; *the Greeks*, as in **Gre'co·phil** (see -PHIL); *Greek and*, as in **Gre'co–Ro'man.**

gree (grē), *n.* [OF. *gré.*] *Archaic.* Good will; favor; as, to take or accept in *gree*, to take favorably.

gree, *v. i. & t. Obs. exc. Dial.* To agree.

gree, *n.* [OF. *gre*, fr. L. *gradus.*] **1.** *Obs.* Degree. **2.** *Chiefly Scot.* Superiority; mastery; hence, a prize.

greed (grēd), *n.* [From GREEDY.] Acquisitive desire beyond reason; greediness.

greed'y (-ĭ), *adj.*; GREED'I·ER (-ĭ·ẽr); -I·EST. [AS. *grǣdig.*] **1.** Having a keen appetite for food or drink; ravenous. **2.** Eagerly desirous, esp. of wealth; hence, avaricious or grasping. — **Syn.** See COVETOUS. — **greed'i·ly,** *adv.* — **greed'i·ness,** *n.*

gree'gree (grē'grē). Var. of GRIGRI.

Greek (grēk), *n.* [AS. *Grēcas, Crēcas*, pl., fr. L. *Graecus*, sing., fr. Gr. *Graikos.*] **1.** A native or citizen of Greece, or often, specif., of ancient Greece. **2.** A person using the Greek language as his native tongue. **3.** [*not cap.*] A swindler or sharper; esp., a card cheat; also, a roisterer; a boon companion; — usually derogatory. **4.** The language of the Greeks, primarily of the classical Greeks; with its various dialects, constitutes the Hellenic subfamily of Indo-European languages. Four dialects are of special importance: (1) ***Ionic***, spoken on the coast of Asia Minor and on many of the islands of the Aegean; divided into ***Old Ionic, or Epic***, the language of Homer, and ***New Ionic***, used by Herodotus and spoken in the Ionian cities of Asia; (2) ***Attic***, orig. the dialect of Attica, the standard form of classical Greek; the language of the great dramatists, philosophers, and historians of ancient Greece, and as later modified, of Plutarch and the New Testament; (3) ***Aeolic***, the dialects of Aeolis, Thessaly, and Boeotia; (4) ***Doric***, used by Pindar and Theocritus, and spoken especially in the Peloponnesus, Crete, and Greek colonies. It is sometimes divided chronologically into ***Greek*** proper (to end of 2d century A.D.), ***Late Greek*** (to end of 6th century), ***Middle Greek*** (to end of 15th century), and ***Modern, or New, Greek.*** *Modern Greek* closely resembles classical Greek but has lost some inflectional forms and certain features of accent and vowel change; ***Romaic*** is its common speech form. See INDO-EUROPEAN LANGUAGES, *Table.* **5.** Something unintelligible. — *adj.* Of or pertaining to Greece, the Greeks, or their language.

Greek calends. A time that will never come, since the Greeks had no calends.

Greek Catholic. **a** A member of any Orthodox Church. **b** A Uniat Greek or Byzantine.

Greek Church, *or* **Greek Orthodox Church.** **a** The Orthodox Church; — disting. from the Latin, or Roman Catholic, Church. **b** The established church of Greece, a part of the Orthodox Church.

Greek cross. See CROSS, *Illust.* (6).

Greek fire. An incendiary composition said to take fire on wetting; also, wildfire.

green (grēn), *adj.* [AS. *grēne.*] **1.** Of the color green. **2.** Characterized by green growth; verdant; of climate or weather, snowless; hence, mild; as, a *green* winter. **3.** Full of life and vigor; as, *green* memories. **4.** Having a sickly color, as from fear, jealousy, etc. **5.** Grown above the ground; more narrowly, leafy; — of a type of vegetable. **6.** Not ripened; immature. **7.** Inexperienced or untrained; hence, simple; gullible. **8.** Not seasoned, mellowed, cured, etc.; not fully processed; raw. — **Syn.** See RUDE.
— *n.* **1.** A color the hue of which is somewhat less yellow than that of growing fresh grass or of the emerald, or is that of the portion of the color spectrum lying between yellow and blue; one of the four psychologically primary hues. See COLOR. **2.** Any pigment or dye which colors green. **3.** Something green or of which green is a symbol or emblem; specif.: **a** *pl.* Decorations of fresh leaves or branches; also, wreaths. **b** *pl.* A dish of a cooked green, or leafy, vegetable, as spinach. **c** A grassy plain or plat, as a village common, a golf course, or a putting green.
— *v. t. & i.* To make, grow, or become green.

green algae. See ALGA.

green'back' (grēn'băk'), *n.* Any United States legal-tender notes having the devices on the back printed in green.

Greenback party. *U. S. Polit. Hist.* A party, known as the Independent party, opposed to the retirement, or reduction in amount, of the greenbacks, and to all currency except government paper "based on the faith and resources of the nation." Its first convention was in 1874. — **Green'back'er** (-băk'ẽr), *n.*

green'belt' (grēn'bĕlt'), *n.* [From *Green Belt*, a strip encircling outer London, Eng.] A belt of parkways or farm lands around a planned town or community, that prevents undesirable encroachments.

green'bri'er (grēn'brī'ẽr), *n.* Any of a genus (*Smilax*) of plants of the smilax family; esp., a thorny vine (*S. rotundifolia*) of the eastern U. S., bearing umbels of small greenish flowers.

green corn. The immature ears of sweet corn. See SWEET CORN.

green dragon. See DRAGON, 4.

green'er·y (grēn'ẽr·ĭ), *n.*; *pl.* -ERIES (-ĭz). **1.** Verdure; a greenness. **2.** A place for raising or keeping plants, as a greenhouse.

green'–eyed' (-īd'; 2), *adj.* **1.** Having green eyes. **2.** Seeing with jealous eyes; biased by jealousy. Cf. GREEN, *adj.*, 4.

green'finch' (-fĭnch'), *n.* **a** A common European finch (*Chloris chloris*) with olive-green and yellow plumage. **b** The Texas sparrow.

green'gage' (grēn'gāj'; 2), *n.* [After Sir Wm. *Gage*, of Suffolk, who imported it from France about 1725.] Any of a group of greenish-yellow plums of high quality.

green'gro'cer (grēn'grō'sẽr), *n.* A retailer of fresh vegetables and fruit. — **green'gro'cer·y** (-ĭ), *n.*

green gum. See GUM, 5 **a.**

green'heart' (-härt'), *n.* Any of several tropical American trees furnishing somewhat greenish, usually hard, valuable wood; also, the wood; specif., the evergreen tree ***bebeeru*** (*Nectandra rodioei*) whose wood is esp. valued for shipbuilding and turnery, and whose bark yields a medicinal alkaloid.

green'horn' (-hôrn'), *n.* A raw, inexperienced person.

green'house' (-hous'), *n.* A glasshouse devoted to the protection or cultivation of tender plants.

green'ing (-ĭng), *n.* [MD. *groeninc.*] Any of several green-skinned apples, as the well-known greenish-yellow winter apple, ***Rhode Island greening.***

green'ish, *adj.* Somewhat green; tinged with green.

green lead ore (lĕd). Pyromorphite.

green'let (grēn'lĕt; -lĭt), *n.* Any vireo.

green light. *Chiefly Colloq.* Authoritative permission to go ahead with a specified project.

green'ling (grēn'lĭng), *n.* Any of several rather large carnivorous food fishes of a group (*Scleroparei*) of the rocky North Pacific coasts, constituting a genus (*Hexagrammos*).

green manure. *Agric.* **a** A herbaceous crop, as clover, vetch, etc., plowed under while green for the purpose of enriching the soil. **b** Fresh or undecayed stable manure.

green monkey. A West African long-tailed monkey (*Cercopithecus callitrichus*) with slightly greenish hair.

Green Mountain State. Vermont; — a nickname.

green'ness (grēn'nĕs; -nĭs), *n.* Quality or state of being green.

green'ock·ite (grēn'ŭk·īt; grĭn'-; grĕn'-), *n.* [After C. M. Cathcart, Lord *Greenock* (1783–1859).] *Mineral.* Native cadmium sulfide, CdS, occurring in yellow, translucent, hexagonal crystals, and as an earthy incrustation.

green pepper. See PEPPER, 3.

green'room' (grēn'rōōm'), *n.* In old theaters, a waiting room for the players between cues or scenes.

green'sand' (-sănd'), *n.* A sedimentary deposit consisting of dark, greenish grains of glauconite, often mingled with clay or sand.

green'shank' (-shăngk'), *n.* An Old World sandpiper (*Glottis nebularia*) related to the American yellowlegs.

green'sick'ness (-sĭk'nĕs; -nĭs), *n. Med.* Chlorosis. — **green'sick',** *adj.*

green soap. A soft soap, orig. green, used in skin diseases.

green'stone' (grēn'stōn'), *n.* **1.** *Petrog.* Any of various dark-green compact rocks, usually altered, as diorite, etc. **2.** Nephrite.

green'sward' (-swôrd'), *n.* Turf green with grass.

green tea. See TEA, 1 **b.**

greenth (grēnth), *n.* Green growth; verdure.

green thumb. An unusual ability to make plants grow; also, a person with such an ability.

Green'wich time (grĭn'ĭj; grĕn'-, -ĭch). See STANDARD TIME.

green'wood' (grēn'wood'), *n.* A forest in foliage.

greet (grēt), *v. t.* [AS. *grētan* to address, approach.] **1.** To address, esp. with expressions of kind wishes; hail; welcome. **2.** To meet or receive demonstratively; as, the team was *greeted* with cheers. **3.** To appear or present itself to; to come to, as if in greeting; as, jeers *greeted* the candidate. — *v. i.* To meet and give salutations. — **greet'er,** *n.*

greet'ing (grēt'ĭng), *n.* Salutation at meeting; also, a compliment from one who is absent.

greg'a·rine (grĕg'ȧ·rīn; -rĭn), *adj.* Belonging to an order or subclass (Gregarinida) of minute wormlike sporozoans parasitic on earthworms, crustaceans, insects, etc.

gre·gar'i·ous (grē·gâr'ĭ·ŭs), *adj.* [L. *gregarius*, fr. *grex, gregis*, herd, flock.] **1.** Habitually living or moving in flocks or herds; tending to flock or herd together. **2.** Pertaining to, or affecting, a flock, crowd, or community. **3.** *Bot.* Growing in clusters or colonies. — **gre·gar'i·ous·ly,** *adv.* — **gre·gar'i·ous·ness,** *n.*

gre'go (grē'gō; grā'gō), *n.* [From It. *Greco* Greek, or Sp. *Griego*, or Pg. *Grego.*] A short jacket or cloak, of thick, coarse cloth, with a hood attached, worn in the Levant; hence, *Obs.*, a rough greatcoat.

Gre·go'ri·an (grē·gō'rĭ·ăn; 70), *adj. & n.* from GREGORY (see in *Biog.*), esp. one of the popes of that name.

Gregorian calendar. The calendar, now in general use, introduced by Pope Gregory XIII in 1582 to correct a slight error in the Julian calendar. The date Oct. 5, 1582 was called Oct. 15, 1582, thus dropping 10 days, and to prevent future errors it was provided that of the centesimal years (1600, 1700, etc.), only those exactly divisible by 400 should be leap years. It was adopted in Great Britain and the English colonies in America in 1752, at which time the difference between the two calendars was 11 days (12 days from 1800 to 1900, 13 days since 1900). The two modes of reckoning are also called *Old Style* (abbr. *O.S.*) and *New Style* (abbr. *N.S.*); thus Nov. 13, Old Style, is the same as Nov. 26, New Style (since 1900). Cf. JULIAN CALENDAR.

Gregorian chant. The ritual plain song, or cantus firmus, in use in the Roman Catholic Church; — after Gregory I.

greige (grā; grāzh), *adj.* [From F. *grège* raw (of silk), fr. It. *greggio*, of unknown origin; probably influenced by *beige.*] In untreated condition just as it comes from the loom, uncoverted by bleaching, dyeing, or finishing; — of fabrics. — *n.* = GRAY GOODS.

grei'sen (grī'zĕn; -z'n), *n.* [G.] *Petrog.* A crystalline rock of quartz and mica, found in Cornwall and Saxony.

gre'mi·al (grē'mĭ·ăl; 58), *n.* [L. *gremium* lap, bosom.] A silk or linen apron used by a bishop when seated at Mass or when anointing.

grem'lin (grĕm'lĭn), *n.* [Perhaps fr. Ir. *gruaimin* ill-humored little fellow, by confusion with *goblin.*] One of the impish foot-high gnomes whimsically blamed by airmen for interfering with motors, instruments, machine guns, etc.; hence, any like disruptive elf.

gre·nade' (grē·nād'), *n.* [F., grenade, pomegranate, fr. OF. *grenate*, fr. L. (*malum*) *granatum*, lit., (apple) having many grains or seeds. See GARNET.] **1.** *Mil.* A bomb or small shell filled with high explosive, gas, etc. Cf. HAND GRENADE. **2.** A glass bottle or globe, containing volatile chemicals, to be thrown and burst, as for extinguishing a fire.

gren'a·dier' (grĕn'ȧ·dēr'), *n.* [F.] **1.** Orig., a soldier who carries and throws grenades; later, one of a company wearing a distinctive uniform; now, specif., a member of a special regiment or corps; as, a *grenadier* of Napoleon's guard. **2.** Any of a family (Macrouridae) of soft-finned, mostly deep-sea, fishes having a tapering body. — **gren'a·dier'i·al** (-ĭ·ăl), *adj.* — **gren'a·dier'ly** (-lĭ), *adv.*

gren'a·dine' (grĕn'ȧ·dēn'; grĕn'ȧ·dēn), *n.* [F.] A sirup of pomegranates or red currants used in various mixed drinks.

gren'a·dine' (*see Pron.*, § 2), *n.* [F. *grenadin*, fr. *grenade* pomegranate.] A gauzelike, plain or figured fabric of silk, wool, or cotton.

Gresh'am's law, *or, sometimes,* **Gresh'am's the'o·rem** (grĕsh'ămz). [After Sir Thomas *Gresham*, Eng. financier.] The tendency, when two or more coins are equal in debt-paying power but unequal in intrinsic value, for the one having the least intrinsic value to remain in circulation and for the other to be hoarded.

gres·so′ri·al (grĕ·sō′rĭ·ăl; 70), **gres·so′ri·ous** (-ŭs), *adj.* [L. *gressus*, past part. of *gradi* to step, go.] Adapted for walking, as the feet of certain birds and insects; gradient.

Gret′na Green marriage (grĕt′nȧ). A runaway marriage; — so called from Gretna Green, a Scottish village just across the English border, once much resorted to by runaway couples from England.

grew (grōō; 114), *past* of GROW.

grew′some (-sŭm), etc. Vars. of GRUESOME, etc.

grey (grā), *adj.*, *n.*, & *v.* Gray; — common in British use.

☞ For some words and phrases beginning *grey-*, *grey*, see forms in GRAY-, GRAY.

grey′hound′ (-hound′), *n.* Rarely **gray′hound′**. [AS. *grīghund.*] **1.** A tall, slender, smooth-coated dog of a very swift, keen-sighted breed. **2.** A swift steamer, esp. an ocean steamer.

grib′ble (grĭb′'l), *n. Zool.* A small marine isopod crustacean (*Limnoria lignorum* or *L. terebrans*), which burrows into submerged timber.

grice (grīs), *n.* [ON. *grīss.*] *Scot. & Dial.* A young pig.

grid (grĭd), *n.* [From GRIDIRON.] **1.** A grating or gridiron, or something likened to one. **2.** *Elec.* **a** A perforated or ridged plate of lead for use in a storage battery. **b** The control electrode of an electron tube. It consists usually of an assemblage of parallel wires.

grid circuit. *Elec.* The electric circuit including the grid and cathode of an electron tube.

grid condenser. *Elec.* A condenser connected in series in the grid circuit of an electron tube.

grid current. *Elec.* Current flowing between the grid and cathode of an electron tube.

grid′dle (grĭd′'l), *n.* [ME. *gridel*, *gredil.*] An iron, aluminum, or soapstone plate or pan for cooking cakes. — *v. t.*; GRID′DLED (-'ld); GRID′DLING (-lĭng). To cook on a griddle.

grid′dle·cake′ (-kāk′), *n.* A thin-batter cake, as of buckwheat or wheat flour, griddled on both sides.

gride (grīd), *v. t. & i.* [From GIRD to sneer.] To cut or pierce; specif., to cut or scrape raspingly or with a grating sound. — *n.* A griding or a grating sound.

grid′i′ron (grĭd′ī′ẽrn), *n.* [ME. *gredirne*, *gredire*, var. of *gredil*; — confused with *iron*. See GRIDDLE.] **1.** A grated iron utensil for broiling food. **2.** Something likened to a gridiron; as: **a** A network of pipes, tracks, or the like. **b** *Colloq.* A football field.

grid leak. *Elec.* A resistor used with an electron tube.

grief (grēf), *n.* [OF. *grief*, *gref*, fr. *grever* to distress, burden. See GRIEVE, *v.*] **1.** *Obs.* Suffering; pain; also, a cause of these, as a wound, disease, or grievance. **2.** Mental suffering from bereavement, remorse, or the like, or a cause of it. **3.** A mishap; disaster; failure; — esp. in *to come*, or *bring*, *to grief*. — **Syn.** See SORROW.

☞ COMBINATIONS are: **grief′-bowed′**, **grief′-strick′en**, **grief′-worn′**.

grie′shoch (grē′shŭκ), *n. Scot. & Ir.* Hot embers.

griev′ance (grēv′ăns), *n.* **1.** *Obs.* **a** Suffering, or its infliction; affliction. **b** Aggrieved state; anger. **2.** A cause of uneasiness and complaint; a wrong. — **Syn.** See INJUSTICE.

grieve (grēv), *v. t.* [OF. *grever*, fr. L. *gravare* to burden, fr. *gravis* heavy.] **1.** *Archaic.* To injure; harm. **2.** To occasion grief to; to try; afflict. — *v. i.* To feel grief; sorrow; lament. — **griev′er** (grēv′ẽr), *n.* — **griev′ing·ly**, *adv.*

griev′ous (grēv′ŭs), *adj.* [OF. *grevous*, *grevos.*] **1.** *Archaic.* Heavy; oppressive. **2.** Causing, or characterized by, physical pain or suffering; hence, severe; intense. **3.** Causing or expressing grief. **4.** Heinous; serious; grave; as, a *grievous* sin. — **griev′ous·ly**, *adv.* — **griev′ous·ness**, *n.*

griff (grĭf), *n.* [F. *griffe* a claw.] A claw.

griff, *n. India.* A griffin, or Occidental newcomer in India.

griffe (grĭf), *n.* [F., fr. Sp. *grifo.*] *Local, U. S.* The offspring of a mulatto woman and a Negro; also, a mulatto.

griffe, *n.* [F.] *Arch.* A clawlike ornament projecting from the round base of a column.

grif′fin (grĭf′ĭn), *n.* Also **grif′fon** (-ŏn). [OF. *grifoun*, fr. OHG. *grīfo*, fr. L. *gryphus*, *gryps*, fr. Gr. *gryps.*] *Gr. Myth.* A monster half lion and half eagle.

grif′fin, *n.* A white person new to the East; one recently come from the Occident. — **grif′fin·age** (-ĭj), *n.*

grif′fin, *n. Local, U. S.* A griffe, or mulatto.

grif′fon (grĭf′ŏn), *n.* [F.] **1.** *Gr. Myth.* A griffin. **2.** A wiry-haired dog of a European breed; — so called because of resemblances to the griffin.

grift′er (grĭf′tẽr), *n. Slang, U. S.* A trickster, esp. one who operates a wheel of chance or other device upon circus grounds.

grig (grĭg), *n.* **1.** *Dial.* **a** Cricket; grasshopper. **b** A small eel. **2.** A lively person; — usually with *merry*.

gri′gri, **gree′gree** (grē′grē), *n.* [From a Sudanese language.] *Southern U. S.* A Negro charm, or fetish. — *v. t.* To bewitch.

gri′gri (grē′grē). Var. of GRUGRU (palm).

grill (grĭl), *n.* [F. *gril*, fr. OF. *graïl*, fr. L. *craticulum*, dim. of L. *crates* hurdle.] **1.** A gridiron. **2.** [From the verb.] **a** A broiling. **b** Something broiled; a dish of broiled meat, etc.; as, a mixed *grill*. **c** In full **grill′room′**. In a hotel or clubhouse, a room specially fitted for serving broiled foods. — *v. t.* **1.** To broil on a grill. **2. a** To torment by or as by broiling. **b** To question or cross-examine with distressing persistency. — **Syn.** See AFFLICT. — *v. i.* To undergo broiling, severe questioning, etc. — **grill′er** (grĭl′ẽr), *n.*

grill, *n.* Var. of GRILLE; specif., a rectangular figure of crossed rows made by a metal roll with points, as on some postage stamps. — *v. t.* To emboss with a grill.

gril′lage (grĭl′ĭj), *n.* [F.] *Arch. & Engin.* A framework of sleepers and crossbeams of timber or steel forming a foundation in marshy or treacherous soil.

grille (grĭl), *n.* Also **grill**. [F., fr. OF. *graïlle* grille, grill, fr. L. *craticula.*] **1.** A grating of wrought iron, bronze, etc., forming an openwork barrier or screen. **2.** A window with such a grille, as in a ticket office, bank, etc. **3.** *Court Tennis.* A square opening in the corner at the farther end of the court, on the hazard side.

grilled (grĭld), *adj.* Provided with a grille.

grill′room′ (grĭl′rōōm′), *n.* See GRILL, *n.*, 2 c.

grilse (grĭls), *n.*; *pl.* GRILSE, rarely GRILSES (grĭl′sĕz; -sĭz). The young of the salmon (*Salmo salar*) after its first return from the sea; also, a similar stage in other species. Cf. SMOLT.

grim (grĭm), *adj.*; GRIM′MER (-ẽr); GRIM′MEST. [AS.] **1.** Savage and merciless; fierce. **2.** Harsh and forbidding; hence, ghastly; repellent; as, a *grim* task. **3.** Unyielding; relentless; stern. — **grim′ly**, *adv.* — **grim′ness**, *n.* — **Syn.** See GHASTLY.

gri·mace′ (grĭ·mās′), *n.* [F., fr. Sp. *grimazo.*] A distortion of the countenance expressing contempt, disapproval, self-satisfaction, etc.; a wry face. — *v. i.*; -MACED′ (-māst′); -MAC′ING (-mās′ĭng). To make grimaces. — **gri·mac′er** (-mās′ẽr), *n.*

gri·mal′kin (grĭ·măl′kĭn; -môl′kĭn), *n.* [For *graymalkin*, fr. *gray* + *malkin.*] A cat, esp. a she-cat; also, *Contemptuous*, an old woman.

grime (grīm), *n.* [Of LG. origin.] Soot, smut, or dirt, rubbed in. — *v. t.* To soil deeply; begrime.

Grimes Golden, *or* **Grimes** (grīmz), *n.* [After Thomas P. *Grimes*, of W. Va.] A late, golden-yellow dessert apple.

Grimm's law (grĭmz). [After Jacob *Grimm*, Ger. philologist.] *Philol.* A statement of the regular changes which the stops, or mute consonants, of the primitive Indo-European consonant system have undergone in the Teutonic languages. The principal changes, which took place independently and at different times, may be set forth as follows: **a** The Indo-European voiceless stops, *k*, *t*, *p*, become in early Teutonic voiceless spirants, *h*, *th*, *f* (Gr. *pous*, *pŏs*, L. *pes*, Goth. *fotus*, E. *foot*). **b** The voiced stops, *g*, *d*, *b*, become voiceless stops, *k*, *t*, *p* (L. *duo*, Goth. *twai*, E. *two*). **c** The voiced aspirates, *gh*, *dh*, *bh* (Gr. *ch*, *th*, *ph*) become voiced stops, *g*, *d*, *b* (Skr. *bharāmi* [I bear], Gr. *pherō*, L. *fero*, Goth. *baira*, E. *bear*).

grim′y (grīm′ĭ), *adj.*; GRIM′I·ER (-ĭ·ẽr); GRIM′I·EST. Full of grime; dirty. — **grim′i·ly** (grīm′ĭ·lĭ), *adv.* — **grim′i·ness** (-ĭ·nĕs; -nĭs), *n.*

grin (grĭn), *v. i.*; GRINNED (grĭnd); GRIN′NING. [AS. *grennian.*] To draw back the lips so as to show the teeth as a dog in snarling, or a person in laughter or pain; esp., to do this in merriment or good humor, as in a broad smile. — *v. t.* To make or express by grinning. — *n.* A facial expression due to grinning. — **grin′ner**, *n.* — **grin′ning·ly**, *adv.*

grin, *n.* [AS.] *Dial.* A snare; a gin; a noose.

grind (grīnd), *v. t.*; GROUND (ground), also, *Rare*, GRIND′ED; GRIND′ING. [AS. *grindan.*] **1.** To reduce to powder by friction; to crush into small fragments. **2.** To wear down, polish, or sharpen by friction; whet. **3.** To grate or grit, as the teeth. **4.** To oppress; harass. **5.** To operate or produce by or as by turning a crank. **6.** *Colloq.* To study hard and constantly. — *v. i.* **1.** To perform the operation of grinding. **2.** To become ground. **3.** To grate. **4.** *Colloq.* To drudge, esp. in study. — *n.* **1.** Act of grinding. **2.** *Colloq.* **a** Hard unremitting labor; drudgery; esp., a study requiring drudgery. **b** *U. S.* A student who grinds. — **Syn.** See WORK. — **grind′ing·ly**, *adv.*

grind′er (grīn′dẽr), *n.* **1.** One who grinds. **2.** A machine for grinding. **3.** A molar; hence, *pl.*, teeth. **4.** Two slabs of bread cut lengthwise and containing ham or spiced meat, cheese, pickle, tomato, and lettuce.

grind′er·y (grīn′dẽr·ĭ), *n.*; *pl.* -ERIES (-ĭz). **1.** *Brit.* Leatherworkers' materials. **2.** A place where tools, etc., are ground.

grind′stone′ (grīnd′stōn′), *n.* **1.** A millstone. **2.** A flat, circular stone, revolving on an axle, for grinding, shaping, or smoothing objects.

grin′go (grĭng′gō), *n.*; *pl.* -GOS (-gōz). [Amer. Sp., fr. Sp. *gringo* gibberish.] Among Spanish Americans, a foreigner, esp. an Englishman or American; — contemptuous.

grip (grĭp), *n.* [AS. *gripe.*] **1.** A strong or tenacious grasp. **2.** Power or force of hold or domination; as, the *grip* of disease; also, mental grasp. **3.** A spasm of pain. **4.** A peculiar mode of clasping the hand by which members of a secret association recognize or greet one another. **5.** A device for gripping, clutching, etc. **6.** A handle or part of a handle adapted to grasping. **7.** *U. S. Colloq.* A gripsack or valise. **8.** [See GRIPPE.] Influenza; grippe. — *v. t.*; GRIPPED (grĭpt) or GRIPT; GRIP′PING. **1.** To grasp grimly; hold tenaciously. **2.** To give a grip, or handclasp, to. **3.** To fasten or attach by a grip or clutch. **4.** To hold riveted in attention. — *v. i.* To take firm hold. — **grip′per**, *n.* — **grip′ping·ly**, *adv.*

gripe (grīp), *v. t.* [AS. *grīpan.*] **1.** To grasp; esp., to seize and hold; clasp closely. **2.** To distress; afflict. **3.** To cause spasmodic pain in the bowels of. **4.** *Colloq.*, *U. S.* To pain mentally; to vex. — *v. i.* **1.** *Archaic.* To grasp. **2.** To experience griping pains. **3.** *Slang*, *U. S.* To grumble; complain. — *n.* **1.** A griping; hence, control. **2.** Pinching distress; as, the *gripe* of poverty. **3.** Spasmodic intestinal pain; — chiefly in *pl.* **4.** A handle, or grip; also, a device for griping, as a brake. **5.** *Colloq.*, *U. S.* Vexation; complaint. — **grip′er** (grīp′ẽr), *n.*

grippe (grĭp), *n.* [F., fr. Russ. *khrip* hoarseness.] An acute catarrhal disease identical with, or like, influenza. — **grip′pal** (grĭp′ăl), *adj.*

grip′ple (grĭp′'l), *adj.* [AS. *gripul.*] *Dial.* Avaricious.

grip′sack′ (grĭp′săk′), *n. Colloq.*, *U. S.* A traveler's handbag.

gri·saille′ (grĭ·zāl′; *F.* grē′zä′y′), *n.* [F., fr. *gris* gray.] Decorative painting in gray monochrome; — in English applied esp. to glass so painted.

Gri·sel′da (grĭ·zĕl′dȧ; -sĕl′dȧ), *n.* [It., of G. origin.] A lady in old romance proverbial for virtue and patience.

gris′e·ous (grĭs′ē·ŭs; grĭz′-), *adj.* [ML. *griseus.*] Of a light color, mottled with black or brown; grizzled.

gri·sette′ (grĭ·zĕt′; *F.* grē′zĕt′), *n.* [F., fr. *grisette* a gray woolen cloth, fr. *gris* gray; — orig. from their gowns of this stuff.] A French girl of the working class, of lively and free manners.

gris′kin (grĭs′kĭn), *n. Eng.* Pork loin.

gris′ly (grĭz′lĭ), *adj.*; GRIS′LI·ER (-lĭ·ẽr); GRIS′LI·EST. [AS. *grislic*, fr. *grīsan* (in comp.) to shudder.] Horrifying; ghastly. — **Syn.** See GHASTLY. — **gris′li·ness**, *n.*

gris′ly (grĭz′lĭ). Var. of GRISTLY, GRIZZLY.

grist (grĭst), *n.* [AS. *grīst*, fr. *grindan.*] **1.** Grain to be, or that has been, ground; esp., as much grain as is carried to the mill at one time, or the meal it produces. **2.** *Colloq.*, *U. S.* A lot; quantity; as, a *grist* of bees.

gris′tle (grĭs′'l), *n.* [AS.] Cartilage; also, a cartilaginous part. — **gris′tly** (-lĭ), *adj.* — **gris′tli·ness** (-lĭ·nĕs; -nĭs), *n.*

grist′mill′ (grĭst′mĭl′), *n.* A mill for grinding grain.

grit (grĭt), *n.* [AS. *grēot* grit, sand, dust.] **1.** Sand; also, sandlike particles. **2.** Structure of stone, as adapted to grinding; as, a hone of good *grit*. **3.** *Petrog.* One of certain sandstones, distinguished by a coarse sharp grain. **4.** Firmness; unyielding courage; stamina. — **Syn.** See FORTITUDE. — *v. t. & i.*; GRIT′TED; GRIT′TING. **1.** To cover or fill with grit. **2.** To grate; also, to make a grating sound.

grith (grĭth), *n.* [AS., fr. ON. *grith.*] *Hist.* Peace; security; sanctuary; also, a refuge or asylum.

grits (grĭts), *n. pl.* Hulled and coarsely ground grain; esp., *U. S.*, coarse hominy.

grit′ty (grĭt′ĭ), *adj.;* GRIT′TI·ER (-ĭ·ẽr); GRIT′TI·EST. **1.** Containing or resembling grit. **2.** Courageously persistent; plucky. — **grit′ti·ly,** *adv.* — **grit′ti·ness,** *n.*

griv′et (grĭv′ĕt; -ĭt), *n.* A monkey (*Cercopithecus griseoviridis*) of the upper Nile and Ethiopia.

griz′zle (grĭz″l), *adj.* [OF. *grisel,* fr. *gris* gray.] Gray. — *n.* **1.** Gray hair; also, a gray wig. **2.** The color gray. — *v. t. & i.;* GRIZ′ZLED (-′ld); GRIZ′ZLING (-lĭng). To make or become grizzly, or grayish.

griz′zle, *v. i. Brit.* To grin; also, to fret; complain.

griz′zled (grĭz″ld), *adj.* Sprinkled or streaked with gray.

griz′zly (-lĭ), *adj.;* GRIZ′ZLI·ER (-lĭ·ẽr); GRIZ′ZLI·EST. Somewhat gray; grizzled. — *n.; pl.* -ZLIES (-lĭz). In full **grizzly bear.** See 2d BEAR, 1.

groan (grōn), *v. i.* [AS. *grānian.*] **1.** To utter a moaning sound, expressive of pain, grief, or disapproval. **2.** To express longing by groans. **3.** To be burdened or oppressed beyond endurance; hence, to creak from weight or pressure. — *v. t.* To utter or give forth with groans. — *n.* A sound uttered in groaning. — **groan′er,** *n.* — **groan′ing·ly,** *adv.*

groat (grōt *or, esp. formerly in Brit. use,* grôt), *n.* [MD. *groot,* prop., great, thick.] An old English silver coin worth fourpence.

groats (grōts), *n. pl.* [AS. *gratan.*] Grits; esp., coarse cracked wheat; also, the edible parts of oat kernels.

gro′cer (grō′sẽr), *n.* [ME. *grosser,* fr. OF. *grossier,* fr. ML. *grossarius,* fr. *grossus* thick.] A dealer in tea, sugar, spices, coffee, fruits, and other commodities, chiefly foodstuffs.

gro′cer·y (-ĭ), *n.; pl.* -CERIES (-ĭz). **1.** The commodities sold by grocers; — usually *pl.* in *U. S.* **2.** The trade, business, or store of a grocer. **3.** *Southern U. S.* A barroom.

grog (grŏg), *n.* [From "Old *Grog,*" a nickname of the English admiral Edward Vernon, in allusion to his wearing a *grogram* cloak. He issued an order to dilute the sailors' rum.] An unsweetened mixture of spirit and water; hence, any intoxicating liquor.

grog′ger·y (-ẽr·ĭ), *n.; pl.* -GERIES (-ĭz). A grogshop.

grog′gy (grŏg′ĭ), *adj.;* GROG′GI·ER (-ĭ·ẽr); GROG′GI·EST. *Colloq.* Tipsy; unsteady on the legs; in pugilistic cant, so weakened in a fight as to stagger. — **grog′gi·ness,** *n.*

grog′ram (grŏg′răm), *n.* [F. *gros grain* large grain, of a coarse texture.] A coarse, often stiffened, fabric of silk and mohair, or of silk.

grog′shop′ (-shŏp′), *n.* A dramshop; a barroom.

groin (groin), *n.* [ME. *grynde.*] **1.** The fold or depression between the lower part of the abdomen and the thigh, or the region about it. **2.** *Arch.* The projecting solid angle formed by the meeting of two vaults, growing more obtuse at the top. See VAULT, *Illust.* — *v. t.* To build or furnish with groins.

Gro′li·er (grō′lĭ·ẽr; *F.* grô′lyā′), *adj.* Designating an early 16th-century style of bookbinding designed by Jean Grolier de Servières (1479–1565), or its characteristic delicate design of interlacing bars, bands, and scrollwork in slender gold lines.

grom′met (grŏm′ĕt; -ĭt), *n.* [Prob. fr. F. *grommette,* now *gourmette* curb of a bridle.] **1.** *Naut.* A ring of rope. **2.** A metal eyelet such as those along the edges of sails, on mailbags, etc.

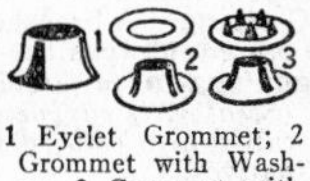

1 Eyelet Grommet; 2 Grommet with Washer; 3 Grommet with Teeth.

grom′well (grŏm′wĕl), *n.* [OF. *gromil, gremil,* fr. LL. *gruinum milium.*] Any of a genus (*Lithospermum,* esp. *L. officinale*) of plants of the borage family, having polished white, stony nutlets.

groom (grōōm), *n.* [OF. *gromet* servant, assistant.] **1.** *Archaic.* A man, esp. a man of inferior station. **2.** A manservant; now, esp., one in charge of horses. **3.** One of several officers of the English royal household. **4.** A bridegroom. — *v. t.* **1.** To attend to the needs of (a horse), as by currying. **2.** To make neat, smart, or tidy. **3.** To prepare; as, to *groom* a candidate for office. — **groom′er,** *n.*

grooms′man (grōōmz′măn), *n.; pl.* -MEN (-mĕn). A male friend who attends a bridegroom at his wedding.

groove (grōōv), *n.* [MD. *groeve.*] **1.** A furrow, channel, or rut; also, a rectangular rabbet. **2.** Habitual course; a fixed routine. **3.** The channel on the bottom of a type. See TYPE, *Illust.* — ***in the groove.*** *Swing Music Cant.* Playing swing music in exalted mood and in top form. — *v. t.* To form a groove or grooves in. — **groov′er** (grōōv′ẽr), *n.*

grope (grōp), *v. i. & t.* [AS. *grāpian* to touch, grope.] To search (out) by feeling, as in the dark; to feel one's way. — *n.* A groping. — **grop′er** (grōp′ẽr), *n.* — **grop′ing·ly,** *adv.*

gros′beak′ (grōs′bēk′), *n.* [F. *grosbec.*] Any of various species of finch having a large stout conical bill. The common European grosbeak is the ***hawfinch*** (*Coccothraustes coccothraustes*). Well-known North American species include the eastern ***rose-breasted grosbeak*** (*Hedymeles ludovicianus*), the western ***black-headed grosbeak*** (*Hedymeles melanocephala*), the western ***evening grosbeak*** (*Hesperiphona vespertina*), the ***cardinal grosbeak*** (see CARDINAL BIRD), and the gray-and-red ***gray grosbeak*** (genus *Pyrrhuloxia*) of Mexico and Texas. Cf. BULLFINCH.

gro′schen (grō′shĕn; *Ger.* grô′shĕn), *n. sing. & pl.* [G.] **a** A former silver coin of Germany varying in value; now, *Colloq.*, the 10-pfennig piece. **b** In Austria, a minor bronze coin worth $\frac{1}{100}$ schilling.

gros′grain′ (grō′grān′), *adj.* [F. See GROGRAM.] Designating silk fabrics having heavy transverse cords. — *n.* Grosgrain silk or ribbon.

gross (grōs), *adj.* [OF. *gros,* fr. L. *grossus* thick.] **1.** Big; bulky; massive. **2.** *Archaic.* Plain; manifest; obvious. **3.** Burly; fat. **4.** Rank; heavy; dense. **5.** Coarse; not fine or delicate. **6.** Whole; entire; total; of earnings, etc., without deductions; — opposed to *net.* **7.** *Obs.* Compact; close. **8.** Unrefined; insensitive; undiscriminating; dull. **9.** Vulgar; sensual; obscene. **10.** Flagrant; shameful. **11.** Large enough to be seen with the naked eye; macroscopic. — **Syn.** See WHOLE; COARSE; FLAGRANT. — *n.* [F. *gros, grosse* (in sense 2).] **1.** The main body; also, the undivided whole; bulk; mass. **2.** *sing. & pl.* The number of twelve dozen. Abbr. *gr., gro.* — **gross′ly,** *adv.* — **gross′ness,** *n.*

gros′su·lar·ite (grŏs′ū·lẽr·īt), *n.* [*grossular* pert. to or resembling a gooseberry (genus *Ribes,* syn. *Grossularia*) + *-ite.*] A colorless, green, yellow, red, or brown variety of garnet, chemically $Ca_3Al_2(SiO_4)_3$.

gross weight. Total weight of merchandise or goods, without deduction for tare, tret, or waste. Abbr. *gr. wt.*

grosz (grôsh), *n.; pl.* GROSZY (grôsh′ĭ). [Pol., fr. Ger. *gross.*] The hundredth part of a zloty; also, the bronze coin of this value.

grot (grŏt), *n.* [F. *grotte,* fr. It. *grotta.*] A grotto.

gro·tesque′ (grō·tĕsk′), *n.* [See GROTESQUE, *adj.*] **1.** A fanciful painting, sculpture, or the like representing human and animal forms amid foliage, flowers, fruit, wreaths, etc. **2.** Grotesque quality or character. **3.** See GOTHIC, *n.*, 3 **b.** — *adj.* [F., fr. It. *grottesca,* fr. *grotta* grotto. See GROTTO.] **1.** Of or characteristic of grotesques; hence, combining heterogeneous and incongruous details or employing distortion for artistic effect. **2.** Absurdly incongruous; bizarre. — **Syn.** See FANTASTIC. — **gro·tesque′ly,** *adv.* — **gro·tesque′ness,** *n.*

gro·tes′quer·ie (-tĕs′kẽr·ĭ), *n.; pl.* -QUERIES (-ĭz). Also **gro·tes′quer·y.** Grotesque quality, action, speech, or manners; also, a grotesque object or work.

grot′to (grŏt′ō), *n.; pl.* -TOES or -TOS (-ōz). [It. *grotta,* fr. VL. *grupta, crupta,* for L. *crypta* a vault, cavern. See CRYPT.] A cave; also, an artificial recess or place of retreat like or suggestive of a cave.

grouch (grouch), *v. i. Colloq.* To sulk or grumble. — *n.* A fit of sulkiness; also, a sulky person. — **grouch′i·ly,** *adv.* — **grouch′i·ness,** *n.* — **grouch′y,** *adj.*

ground (ground), *past & past part.* of GRIND. Specif.: *adj.* Reduced to small particles by grinding.

ground, *n.* [AS. *grund* bottom, earth.] **1.** The surface of the earth, or the earth as a basis or abode. **2.** A region, territory, or field resorted to for a particular purpose; as, a hunting *ground.* **3.** Land; estate; specif., *pl.*, gardens, lawns, etc., of a homestead. **4.** An extent to be covered; an area or distance; as, to gain or lose *ground.* **5.** The soil; soil; earth. **6.** A position to be maintained; basic belief, assumption, etc.; as, to shift one's *ground* in argument; also, topic; subject. **7.** Bottom, as of the sea. **8.** *pl.* Sediment; dregs; lees. **9.** Foundation; substratum; specif.: **a** The data, premises, or evidence, on which a conclusion, a theory, a belief, etc., rests for support; — sometimes in *pl.* **b** Hence, sufficient or good reason; as, to have *ground* for complaint. **c** Foundation on which anything is wrought or displayed; background. **10.** *Elec.* The connection made in grounding a circuit. **11.** *Radio.* Place to which the ground wire is connected. **12.** *Theater.* The pit. — **Syn.** See BASE.
— *v. t.* **1.** To bring down to, place on, or cause to touch, the ground. **2.** To found; establish; to fix or set, as on a foundation, reason, or principle; to fix firmly. **3.** To instruct in elements or first principles. **4.** *Elec.* To connect with the ground so as to make the earth part of a circuit. **5.** To provide with a ground or background. — *v. i.* **1.** To have a ground, or basis; rely; found; — usually with *in* or *upon.* **2.** To run aground; strike bottom. **3.** To fall or light on the ground. **4.** *Baseball.* To hit a grounder.
— *adj.* Associated with the ground by situation or use.

ground bait. *Angling.* Bait that sinks or is held down by a sinker.

ground bass (bās). *Music.* A short bass passage continually repeated to a constantly changing melody and harmony.

ground cherry. See STRAWBERRY TOMATO.

ground crew. A crew of mechanics and technicians charged with the maintenance and servicing of aircraft.

ground′er (groun′dẽr), *n.* **1.** One that grounds. **2.** *Baseball, etc.* A moving ball, esp. a struck ball, that rolls along the ground.

ground fir. See GROUND PINE **b.**

ground floor. The floor of a house most nearly on a level with the ground; — called also, in America, *first floor.*

ground glass. Glass with a light-diffusing surface.

ground hog. The woodchuck.

ground′-hog′ day. Candlemas Day; — from the tradition that the ground hog then emerges to see if winter is over.

ground ivy. A trailing herb (*Glecoma hederacea*) of the mint family, with round leaves and blue-purple flowers.

ground′less, *adj.* Without ground; unwarranted; unfounded. — **ground′less·ly,** *adv.* — **ground′less·ness,** *n.*

ground′ling (ground′lĭng), *n.* **1.** One that keeps close to the ground or bottom; — applied esp. to certain fishes. **2.** A spectator in the pit of a theater; hence, one of inferior taste.

ground loop. *Aviation.* A sharp uncontrollable turn on the ground in landing or taking off.

ground′mass′ (-măs′), *n. Petrog.* The fine-grained base of a porphyry in which the larger distinct crystals are embedded.

ground′nut′ (-nŭt′), *n.* Any of several plants having edible tuberous roots; also, the root of any of these plants; as: **a** A North American vine (*Apios tuberosa*) of the pea family. **b** The peanut.

ground pine. **a** A European herb (*Ajuga chamaepitys*) of the mint family, of resinous odor. **b** Any of several club mosses often used in Christmas decoration, esp. *Lycopodium clavatum,* with long creeping stems and erect branches, and *L. complanatum,* with fan-shaped branches, also species having a stiff erect habit and known more commonly as *ground fir,* as *L. selago* and *L. obscurum.*

ground pink. The moss pink.

ground plan. A plan of the ground floor of any building; hence, any first, or basic, plan.

ground plate. **a** *Arch.* A timber laid horizontally on or near the ground to support uprights. **b** *Elec.* A metallic plate buried in the ground to connect a circuit to earth. **c** *Railroads.* A bedplate for sleepers or ties.

ground plum. **a** A milk vetch (*Geoprumnon crassicarpum*) of the western United States; also, its plumlike pod. **b** Any of several related species (as *G. mexicanum*).

ground rent. A price per year or term of years paid for the right to occupy and improve a piece of land; also, money or compensation so paid.

ground′sel (ground′sĕl; *colloq.* groun′s'l), *n.* Also **ground′sill** (ground′sĭl). [*ground* + *sill.*] A foundation timber; a ground plate.

ground′sel, *n.* [AS. *grundeswylige, grundeswelge.*] Any herb of an immense genus (*Senecio,* esp. the English *S. vulgaris* or the American *S. aureus*) of plants of the aster family, having mostly yellow flowerheads.

ground squirrel. See SQUIRREL, 1.

ground swell. A broad, deep undulation of the ocean, caused by, and felt at a distance from, a gale or earthquake.

ground water. Water within the earth, such as supplies wells and springs.

ground wave. *Radio.* That portion of electric waves which is propagated along the surface of the earth. Cf. SKY WAVE.

ground wire. A conductive connection from a radio set to the ground.

ground′work′ (ground′wûrk′), *n.* Foundation; basis. — **Syn.** See BASE.

group (gro͞op), *n.* [F. *groupe*, fr. It. *gruppo, groppo*, cluster, packet, group, prob. of Teut. origin.] **1.** Two or more figures forming a design or a unit in a design. **2.** An assemblage of persons or things forming a separate unit; a cluster; an aggregation. **3.** An assemblage of objects having some relationship, resemblance, or common characteristic; specif.: **a** *Biol.* Any assemblage of animals or plants classed as having natural relationship to each other, as plants of the fungus family (Fungi). **b** *Chem.* An assemblage of atoms forming part of a molecule; a radical; as, a methyl *group* (CH_3). **c** *Ethnol.* A classificatory division less inclusive than a branch. **d** *Geol.* A division of rocks comprising those formed during an era. Cf. ERA, 5; SYSTEM, 7. — *v. t.* To arrange or combine in a group or in groups. — *v. i.* To form a group; be a member of a group.

group′er (gro͞op′ẽr), *n.*; see PLURAL, *Note*, 3. [Pg. *garoupa*.] Any of numerous fishes of warm seas, constituting certain genera (*Epinephelus, Mycteroperca*, and allied genera, family Epinephelidae) closely resembling the sea basses. Many are important food fishes of Florida, the West Indies, etc. The tripletail and some of the Californian rockfishes are also called *groupers*. See CABRILLA; BONACI; 2d HIND, 2; 2d HAMLET.

grouse (grous), *n. sing. & pl.* [Origin uncert.] Any of a number of birds (order Galliformes), having a plump body, strong, feathered legs, and plumage usually mottled with red-brown, or other color adapted to concealment. Included among the grouse are the ***red grouse*** (*Lagopus scoticus*) and the ***ruffed grouse*** (*Bonasa umbellus*), both game birds. Cf. CAPERCAILLIE, BLACK GROUSE, PRAIRIE CHICKEN, SAGE GROUSE, PTARMIGAN, RUFFED GROUSE.

grouse (grous; gro͞os), *v. i.* *Slang, Brit.* To grumble; complain. — **grouse**, *n.*

grout (grout; *dial. also* gro͞ot), *n.* [AS. *grūt*.] **1.** Coarse meal; *pl.*, groats. **2.** *Eng.* Lees; dregs; grounds; — usually *pl.* **3. a** Thin mortar. **b** A kind of plaster or cement. — *v. t.* [See GROUT, *n.*, 3.] To fill or finish as with grout. — **grout′er**, *n.*

grout′y (grout′ĭ), *adj.*; GROUT′I·ER (-ĭ·ẽr); GROUT′I·EST. *Colloq., U. S.* Cross; sulky; sullen.

grove (grōv), *n.* [AS. *grāf*.] A small wood; a group of trees without underwood, planted or growing naturally.

grov′el (grŏv′'l; grŭv′'l), *v. i.*; GROV′ELED (-'ld) or GROV′ELLED; -EL·ING or -EL·LING. [From ME. *grovelinge, grufelinge*, adv., on the face, prone.] **1.** To creep or lie with the face to the ground; to lie prone or crawl, in abjectness. **2.** To tend to, or delight in, what is sensual or base; to be low, abject, or mean. — **grov′el·er, grov′el·ler**, *n.* — **grov′el·ing·ly, grov′el·ling·ly**, *adv.*

grow (grō), *v. i.*; GREW (gro͞o), GROWN (grōn); GROW′ING. [AS. *grōwan*.] **1.** To spring up and mature; to be developed or produced naturally. **2.** To thrive; flourish. **3.** To increase in size by assimilation of new matter into the living organism; — chiefly of animals, plants, and their organs. **4.** To increase in any way; to become larger, stronger, etc.: wax. **5.** To come to be by degrees; become; as, to *grow* pale. **6.** To become united by or as by growth. — *v. t.* **1.** To cause to grow; cultivate; produce. **2.** In the passive, to be covered with a growth; as, land well *grown* with trees. **3.** To develop, as a taste. — **grow′er**, *n.*

grow′ing pains. Neuralgic pains or cramp in the limbs occurring during growth; — rarely in *sing.*

growl (groul), *v. i. & t.* To utter or express with a growl or growls. — *n.* The deep threatening sound made by a surly dog; hence, a grumbling or rumbling sound; esp., a low muttered complaint.

growl′er (-ẽr), *n.* **1.** One who or that which growls. **2.** *Slang.* **a** *Eng.* A four-wheeled cab. **b** *U. S.* A can, pitcher, etc., for beer bought by measure. **c** *Elec.* An electromagnetic device with two adjustable pole pieces, used for finding short-circuited coils and for magnetizing and demagnetizing; — so called from a growling noise caused by a short-circuited coil.

grown (grōn), *adj.* Full-grown; mature.

grown′-up′ (grōn′ŭp′; 2), *adj.* Adult; *Colloq.*, characteristic of adults.

grown′up′ (grōn′ŭp′), *n.* *Colloq.* An adult.

growth (grōth), *n.* **1.** A growing; increase; esp., progressive development of an organism, or the like. **2.** Origin and development; as, a custom of English *growth*. **3.** That which has grown or is growing; produce or product. **4.** A morbid formation, as a tumor.

GR–S (jē′är′ĕs′). [From *G*overnment *R*ubber + *s*tyrene.] A synthetic rubber made by copolymerization of butadiene and styrene; — called also *buna S*.

grub (grŭb), *v. i.*; GRUBBED (grŭbd); GRUB′BING. [ME. *grubben, gruben*.] **1.** To dig laboriously, as for a root. **2.** To plod; drudge. **3.** *Slang.* To eat. — *v. t.* **1.** To clear or break up (land) by digging. **2.** To root out by digging; — with *up*. **3.** *Slang.* To supply with food. — *n.* **1.** Any thick wormlike larva, as of a beetle. **2.** One who grubs; drudge. **3.** *Slang.* Food. — **grub′ber** (-ẽr), *n.*

grub′by (grŭb′ĭ), *adj.*; GRUB′BI·ER (-ĭ·ẽr); GRUB′BI·EST. [From GRUB.] **1.** Infested with grubs; specif., *Western U. S.*, of cattle or sheep, affected by the larvae of botflies or warble flies. **2.** Dirty; slovenly; grimy. — **grub′bi·ly**, *adv.* — **grub′bi·ness**, *n.*

grub hoe. A heavy hoe for grubbing. See HOE, *Illust.*

grub′stake′ (grŭb′stāk′), *n.* *Western U. S.* Supplies or funds furnished a prospector on promise of a share in his finds. — **grub′stake′**, *v. t.* — **grub′stak′er** (-stāk′ẽr), *n.*

Grub Street. Also **Grub′street′** (-strēt′), *n.*, or, as an adjective, **grub′street′**. A London street (now *Milton Street*), described by Dr. Johnson as "much inhabited by writers of small histories, dictionaries, and temporary poems, whence any mean production is called *grubstreet*"; hence, petty and needy writers, or literary hacks.

grudge (grŭj), *v. t.*; GRUDGED (grŭjd); GRUDG′ING. [ME. *grutchen, gruchen*, to grumble, fr. OF. *groucher, groucier*.] To be loath to give, or let have (something); give reluctantly; begrudge; envy. — *v. i.* *Obs.* To grumble. — *n.* Sullen malice; cherished ill will. — **Syn.** See MALICE. — **grudg′er**, *n.* — **grudg′ing·ly**, *adv.*

gru′el (gro͞o′ĕl; -ĭl), *n.* [OF.] **1.** A thin porridge. **2.** *Colloq.* Punishment; — in *take one's gruel*, etc. — *v. t.*; -ELED (-ĕld), -ELLED; -EL·ING, -EL·LING. To punish, work, question, etc., to the point of exhaustion; to try beyond one's endurance. — **gru′el·er, gru′el·ler**, *n.* — **gru′el·ing, gru′el·ling**, *adj. & n.*

grue′some, grew′some (gro͞o′sŭm; 114), *adj.* [Cf. Dan. *gru* horror, *grusom*. See 1st -SOME.] Horrifying and repulsive; grisly. — **Syn.** See GHASTLY. — **grue′some·ly, grew′some·ly**, *adv.* — **grue′some·ness, grew′some·ness** *n.*

gruff (grŭf), *adj.* [D. *grof*.] **1.** Rough and surly in manner, speech, or countenance. **2.** Hoarse; deep and harsh; — of the voice. — **Syn.** See BLUFF. — **gruff′ly**, *adv.* — **gruff′ness**, *n.*

gruff′y (-ĭ), *adj.*; GRUFF′I·ER (-ĭ·ẽr); GRUFF′I·EST. Gruff. — **gruff′i·ly**, *adv.* — **gruff′i·ness**, *n.*

gru′gru (gro͞o′gro͞o), *n.* [Sp. *grugrú*, of Cariban origin.] **1.** Also **grugru palm.** Any of several tropical American spiny palms, esp. a West Indian species *Acrocomia aculeata*) and a Brazilian species (*A. sclerocarpa*). **2.** Also **grugru worm.** The edible wormlike larva of a large weevil (*Rhyncophorus ferrugineus* or allied species), the **grugru beetle**, which lives in the pith of palm trees in tropical America.

grum (grŭm), *adj.*; GRUM′MER (-ẽr); -MEST. Morose; glum.

grum′ble (grŭm′b'l), *v. i. & t.*; -BLED (-b'ld); -BLING (-blĭng). [F. *grommeler*, of Teut. origin.] **1.** To murmur or mutter in complaint. **2.** To growl; snarl in deep tones. **3.** To rumble. — *n.* A grumbling; a growl; a rumble. — **grum′bler** (-blẽr), *n.* — **grum′bling·ly**, *adv.* — **grum′bly**, *adj.*

Grum′ble·to′ni·an (-b'l·tō′nĭ·ăn), *n.* [From GRUMBLE, *v.*] *Hist.* A member of a certain English political party in the 17th century; — so called by their opponents.

grume (gro͞om), *n.* [F. *grume*, fr. L. *grumus* a little heap.] A thick, viscid fluid; a clot, as of blood.

grum′met (grŭm′ĕt; -ĭt), *n.* A grommet.

gru′mose (gro͞o′mōs), *adj.* *Bot.* Formed of clustered grains or granules.

gru′mous (-mŭs), *adj.* [See GRUME.] **1.** Resembling, or containing, grume; clotted. **2.** Grumose.

grumph′y (grŭm′fĭ; gro͞om′pĭ), *n.* *Scot.* A pig; a sow.

grump′y (grŭmp′ĭ), *adj.*; GRUMP′I·ER (-ĭ·ẽr); GRUMP′I·EST. Also **grump′ish** (-ĭsh). Surly; moodily cross. — *n.* A grumpy person. — **grump′i·ly**, *adv.* — **grump′i·ness**, *n.*

Grun′dy, Mrs. (grŭn′dĭ). A person referred to in Thomas Morton's comedy (1798) *Speed the Plough* by characters asking, "What will Mrs. Grundy say?"; hence, narrowly conventional society; prudish persons. — **Grun′dy·ism** (-ĭz'm), *n.* — **Grun′dy·ist** (-ĭst), **Grun′dy·ite** (-īt), *n.*

grun′ion (grŭn′yŭn), *n.* [Prob. fr. Sp. *gruñón* grunter.] A silversides (*Leuresthes tenuis*) of the California coast.

grunt (grŭnt), *v. i. & t.* [AS. *grunnettan*, fr. *grunian* to grunt.] **1.** To make or to utter with a deep guttural sound. **2.** *Obs.* To groan. — *n.* **1.** A short deep guttural sound, as that made by a hog. **2.** Any of numerous marine fishes (genus *Haemulon* and allied genera) allied to the snappers. They make a grunting noise when taken from the water. Many are valuable food fishes. — **grunt′er**, *n.* — **grunt′ing·ly**, *adv.*

grush′ie (grŭsh′ĭ; gro͞osh′ĭ), *adj.* *Scot.* Of thriving growth.

grutch (grŭch; gro͞och), *v. t. & i. & n.* *Dial.* Grudge; grumble.

Gru′yère′ cheese (grü′yâr′). Also **Gru′yère′**, *n.* [From *Gruyère*, Switz.] A pressed, pale-yellow, whole-milk cheese of nutty flavor, made chiefly in Switzerland.

gryph′on (grĭf′ŏn; grī′fŏn). Var. of GRIFFIN.

G string. A breechcloth worn by savages consisting of a strip of cloth passed between the legs and supported by a waist cord.

gua′cha·ro (gwä′chä·rō), *n.* [Sp. *guácharo*.] A nocturnal bird (*Steatornis caripensis*) of northern South America and Trinidad; — called also *oilbird* because an oil is extracted from the young by the natives.

gua′co (gwä′kō), *n.* [Sp.] **a** A tropical American vine (*Mikania guaco*) of the aster family; also, its aromatic dried leaves, reputed to be an antidote to snake bites. **b** A tropical American vine (*Aristolochia maxima*) of the birthwort family, also used as a remedy for snake bites.

guai′ac (gwī′ăk), *n.* [See GUAIACUM.] = GUAIACUM, 2, 3.

guai′a·col (gwī′ȧ·kōl; -kŏl), *n.* [*guaiacum* + *-ol*.] A colorless liquid or white crystalline solid, *o*-$CH_3OC_6H_4OH$, obtained by distilling guaiacum, from wood-tar creosote, and in other ways. It has been used in treating tuberculosis.

guai′a·cum (-kŭm), **guai′o·cum** (-ō·kŭm), *n.* [NL., fr. Sp. *guayacán, guayaco*, fr. Taino *guayacan*.] **1.** Any of a genus (*Guaiacum*) of tropical American trees and shrubs of the bean-caper family, having pinnate leaves, mostly blue flowers, and capsular fruit. **2.** The hard greenish-brown wood yielded by trees of this genus (esp. by *G. officinale*). **3.** A resin with a faint balsamic odor, obtained from the trunk of *G. officinale* or *G. sanctum*, and used esp. as a remedy for gout, rheumatism, and skin diseases.

guan (gwän), *n.* [Sp. *guan, cuan*, of Cariban origin.] Any of a subfamily (Penelopinae) of large gallinaceous birds, of Central and South America.

gua·na′co (gwä·nä′kō), *n.*; see PLURAL, *Note*, 3. [Sp., fr. Quechua *huanacu*.] A South American mammal (*Lama guanicoe*) related to the llama but larger and more graceful.

gua′nase (gwä′nās), *n.* *Biochem.* An enzyme that transforms guanine into xanthine.

guan′i·dine (gwăn′ĭ·dēn; gwä′nĭ·dēn; -dĭn), *n.* Also **guan′i·din.** *Chem.* A strong, deliquescent crystalline base, $NH{:}C(NH_2)_2$, formed by the oxidation of guanine, and in other ways.

gua′nine (gwä′nēn; go͞o′ȧ·nēn; go͞o·än′ĭn), *n.* Also **gua′nin.** [From GUANO.] *Chem.* A base, $C_5H_5N_5O$, occurring in guano, in liver, pancreas, muscle, etc., and in many plants, and obtained as a white amorphous powder.

gua′no (gwä′nō), *n.*; *pl.* -NOS (-nōz). [Sp., fr. Quechua *huanu* dung.] **1.** A substance composed chiefly of the excrement of seafowl, and used extensively as a fertilizer. **2.** Any similar manure.

Gua′ra·ni′ (gwä′rä·nē′), *n.*; *pl.* GUARANI (-nē′), -NIS (-nēz′). **1.** An Indian of a group of Tupian tribes formerly dwelling in central South America. **2.** The language of the Guarani, developed from the southern Tupian dialects. See LANGUAGE, *Table*. **3.** [*not cap.*] The monetary unit of Paraguay. See MONEY, *Tables*.

guar′an·tee′ (găr′ăn·tē′), *n.*; *pl.* -TEES (-tēz′). **1.** A guarantor. **2.** A guaranteeing; guaranty (sense 1). **3.** An agreement by which one person guarantees something held, enjoyed, etc., by another; guaranty (def. 2). **4.** That given or held as security; guaranty (def. 3). — *v. t.* **1.** To undertake to answer for the debt, default, miscarriage, or nonfulfillment of; as, to *guarantee* a contractor or the execution of a contract. **2.** To engage for the existence, permanence, nature, or the like, of (something); warrant. **3.** To give security to; to secure.

guar′an·tor (găr′ăn·tôr *or, esp. Brit.,* găr′ăn·tôr′), *n. Law.* One who makes or gives a guaranty or surety; one who enters in a guaranty.

guar′an·ty (găr′ăn·tĭ), *n.; pl.* -TIES (-tĭz). [OF. *guarantie, garantie,* fr. OF. *guarantir.* See WARRANT.] **1.** An undertaking to answer for the payment of another's debt, the performance of another's duty, or the like, in case of that other's default or miscarriage. **2.** An agreement by which one person promises to make another secure in the possession, continued enjoyment, or the like, of something. **3.** Something given or held as security; a security or pledge. **4.** A guarantor. — *v. t.;* GUAR′AN·TIED (-tĭd); GUAR′AN·TY·ING. To guarantee.

guard (gärd), *v. t.* [OF. *guarder, garder* (ONF. *warder*), of Teut. origin.] **1.** To protect the edge of, esp. with an ornamental border. **2.** To protect from danger; defend; shield. **3.** *Archaic.* To escort. **4.** To watch over so as to restrain, check, or keep under control; as, to *guard* a prisoner or one's tongue. — *v. i.* To watch; stand guard; take precautions. — **Syn.** See DEFEND.

— *n.* **1.** *Obs.* Guardianship. **2.** A posture of defense, as in fencing. **3.** Act or duty of guarding; state of being guarded; protection; defense; watch; as, to stand or keep *guard;* responsible for the *guard* of a child. **4.** *Archaic.* Caution; also, a safeguard; precaution. **5.** A person that guards; specif.: **a** One or more persons on sentinel duty; a watch. **b** A railway brakeman or gateman or, *Brit.,* conductor. **c** *Amer. Football.* One of two players, called ***right guard*** and ***left guard,*** next to the center in the line-up. **d** *Basketball.* Either of two players, ***right guard*** and ***left guard,*** stationed at the rear of the court, whose play is primarily defensive. **6.** A protective or safety device; a shield; esp., a part or attachment to protect against injury, soiling, loss, or the like. **7.** *pl.* In the British Army, certain troops attached to the person of the sovereign. — **guard′er,** *n.*

guard′ed, *adj.* Protected; also, cautious; circumspect; wary; framed or uttered with caution. — **guard′ed·ly,** *adv.* — **guard′ed·ness,** *n.*

guard′house′ (gärd′hous′), *n.* A building occupied by the guard, usually one for prisoners; hence, a military lockup.

guard′i·an (gär′dĭ·ăn), *n.* [OF. *gardien.*] **1.** One who guards, keeps safe, or secures; a custodian. **2.** *Law.* One who has, or is entitled to, the care and management of the person or property, or both, of another, as of a minor or of a person incapable of managing his own affairs. — *adj.* Performing, or appropriate to, the office of a protector. — **guard′i·an·ship′,** *n.*

guard′room′ (gärd′rōōm′), *n. Mil.* **a** The room occupied by the guard during its term of duty. **b** Room where prisoners are confined.

guards′man (gärdz′măn), *n.; pl.* GUARDSMEN (-mĕn). **1.** A guard. **2.** A member, officer or private, of any military body called Guards.

Guar·ne′ri·us (gwär·nā′rĭ·ŭs), *n. Music.* A violin made by one of the famous Italian Guarnieri family in the 17th and 18th centuries.

gua′va (gwä′vȧ), *n.* [Sp. *guayaba,* the fruit, *guayabo,* the tree, of Arawakan origin.] **1.** Any of several tropical American shrubs or small trees (genus *Psidium,* esp. *P. guajava* and *P. cattleyanum*) of the myrtle family. **2.** The small fruit of these trees, used in making jelly, jam, etc.

gua·yu′le (gwä·yōō′lā; wĭ·ōō′lā), *n.* [Sp., fr. Nahuatl *quauholli,* fr. *quauitl* plant + *olli, ulli,* gum, lit., ball; — used by the Aztecs for making footballs.] A shrubby herb (*Parthenium argentatum*) of the aster family, of northern Mexico and adjacent Texas; also, the rubber, **guayule rubber,** which it yields.

gu′ber·na·to′ri·al (gū′bĕr·nȧ·tō′rĭ·ăl; 70), *adj.* [L. *gubernator* governor.] Pert. to a governor, or to government.

gudg′eon (gŭj′ŭn), *n.* [OF. *goujon,* fr. L. *gobio.*] **1.** A small European fresh-water fish (*Gobio gobio*), allied to the carps; also, any of certain gobies, or, in America, killifishes. **2. a** A person easily duped. **b** A bait. **c** A worthless catch. — *v. t.* To cheat; dupe.

gudg′eon, *n.* [OF. *goujon.*] *Mach.* A pivot or journal.

gudgeon pin. A wrist pin.

Gud′run, Guth′run (gŏŏd′rōōn; gŏŏth′rōōn), *n.* [ON. *Guthrūn.*] See BRYNHILD, ATLI.

guel′der-rose′ (gĕl′dĕr·rōz′), *n.* [From *Gelderland* (see *Gaz.*).] A cultivated variety of the cranberry tree with sterile flowers in globose heads. See CRANBERRY, 2 **a**; SNOWBALL, 2.

Guelph, Guelf (gwĕlf), *n.* [It. *Guelfo,* ML. *Guelphus,* fr. MHG. *Welf.*] *Hist.* **a** A member of a German princely family, so called from *Welf,* its founder. **b** A member of a medieval faction in Italy that opposed the authority of the German emperors in Italy, which was upheld by the other faction, the Ghibellines. — **Guelph′ic, Guelf′ic** (gwĕl′fĭk), *adj.*

gue·non′ (gĕ·nôN′), *n.* [F.] Any of numerous long-tailed African monkeys constituting a genus (*Cercopithecus*), as the green monkey and grivet.

guerche (gĕrsh). Var. of GIRSH.

guer′don (gûr′dŭn), *n. & v. t.* [OF. *guerdon, guerredon,* fr. ML. *widerdonum,* fr. OHG. *widarlōn,* fr. *widar* again, against + *lōn* reward.] Reward; recompense. — **guer′don·er** (-ĕr), *n.*

Guern′sey (gûrn′zĭ), *n.; pl.* GUERNSEYS (-zĭz). [From the island of *Guernsey.*] **1.** [*not cap.*] A close-fitting knitted woolen shirt or vest. **2.** One of a breed of dairy cattle originating in Guernsey, usually fawn and white, and larger than Jerseys.

‖**guerre à ou′trance′** (gâr′ ȧ ōō′träNs′). [F.] War to the uttermost, or death.

guer·ril′la (gĕ·rĭl′ȧ), *n.* Also **gue·ril′la.** [Sp. *guerrilla,* dim. of *guerra* war, fr. OHG. *werra* strife.] **1.** *Rare.* An irregular war by independent bands. **2.** One who engages in irregular warfare in connection with a regular war, esp. as a member of a predatory band.

guess (gĕs), *v. t. & i.* [ME. *gessen,* of Scand. or LG. origin.] **1.** To form an opinion (of) from good but not sufficient evidence. **2.** To form an opinion (of) without evidence; conjecture. **3.** To conjecture rightly. **4.** To think; suppose; believe; — with an objective clause, and properly implying some uncertainty. — **Syn.** See CONJECTURE. — *n.* A guessing; a conjecture; a surmise. — **guess′er** (-ĕr), *n.*

guess′work′ (-wûrk′), *n.* Work performed, or results obtained, by guess; conjecture.

guest (gĕst), *n.* [AS. *gæst, gest.*] **1.** *Obs.* A stranger. **2.** A person entertained in one's house or at one's table; a visitor entertained without pay; hence, a person to whom the hospitality of a home, club, etc., is extended. **3.** Any person who lodges, boards, or receives refreshment, for pay, at a hotel, or the like; patron. **4.** *Biol.* An inquiline; — used esp. of insects inhabiting or breeding in the nests or galls of other insects, and more fully termed **guest ants, guest bees, guest moths,** etc. — *v. t.* To receive or entertain as a guest; to give refreshment to. — *v. i.* To be a guest; to lodge.

guest rope. Also **guess′-rope′,** *n. Naut.* **a** An additional line from a ship to a boat being towed astern, to keep the latter steady. **b** A line run along a vessel's side or out to the end of a boom for small boats to hold to.

guff (gŭf), *n.* [Prob. imitative.] *Slang.* Idle talk; humbug.

guf·faw′ (gŭ·fô′), *n.* A loud burst of laughter; a horselaugh. — *v. i.;* GUF·FAWED′ (-fôd′); GUF·FAW′ING. To laugh noisily or coarsely.

gug′gle (gŭg′'l), *v. i. & n.* Gurgle.

guib (gwĭb; gēb), *n.* See HARNESSED ANTELOPE.

guid′ance (gīd′ăns), *n.* A guiding; direction; also, a guide.

guide (gīd), *v. t.* [F. *guider,* fr. OF. *guier,* of Teut. origin.] **1.** To act as a guide to; to direct in a way; conduct. **2.** To regulate and manage; direct; order; govern; hence, to superintend the training of; instruct. — *v. i.* To act or work as guide.

Syn. **Guide, lead, steer, pilot, engineer** mean to direct the course of or to show the way to those following. **Guide** implies intimate knowledge of the course or way and of all its difficulties or dangers; **lead,** a going in advance to show the way and, often, to keep those that follow in order or under control; **steer,** an ability to control a mechanism which determines the course or direction and so, figuratively, an ability to maneuver correctly; **pilot,** guidance over a course where one might easily lose one's way and run afoul of difficulties or dangers; **engineer,** guidance in the manner of an expert engineer, by one who finds a way to avoid or overcome difficulties in achieving an end, or the like.

— *n.* **1.** One who guides, as tourists in a strange land or hunters in a forest. **2.** In full **guide′book′.** A handbook of information for travelers. **3.** A post (**guide′post′**), as at the fork of a road, with an attached board (**guide′board′**) giving directions or information about routes. **4.** Any contrivance serving to steady or to direct the motion of something, to guide a tool or instrument, to mark a position, etc. **5.** *Mil.* A member of a unit upon whom the movements or alignments of the unit are regulated. The commands ***guide center, guide right, guide left,*** indicate upon which element of a line a movement is to be regulated.

— **guid′a·ble** (gīd′ȧ·b'l), *adj.* — **guid′er,** *n.*

guid′ed mis′sile (gīd′ĕd; -ĭd). **a** Any missile whose course toward a target may be altered during passage by means of its own mechanism controlled by radio signals, a built-in target-seeking radar device, or similar means. **b** Less strictly, a missile guided by a preset control, as the V-1 or the torpedo.

guide rope. 1. A rope leading laterally from a rope by which any object is lifted or hauled, for directing its motion. **2.** *Aeronautics.* A rope hung from a balloon or dirigible so as to trail along the ground for about half its length, used esp. to preserve altitude automatically (by variation of the length dragging) without loss of ballast or gas.

gui′don (gī′dŭn), *n.* [F., fr. It. *guidone.*] **1.** A small flag or streamer carried by troops, formerly to show the position of the guide or the line on which a formation was to be made, or, now, *U. S. Army,* to distinguish a company. **2.** One who carries such a flag.

guid′will′ie (güd′wĭl′ĭ; gwēd′-). Var. of GOODWILLY.

guild, gild (gĭld), *n.* [ON. *gildi* guild, tribute.] **1.** An association of men with kindred pursuits or common interests or aims for mutual aid and protection. **2.** Specif., any of various medieval associations, as of merchants (***merchant guild***) or tradesmen (***trade guild***), formed to protect the interests of their members and in some cases developing into the governing bodies of their respective boroughs. **3.** Any fellowship or society. **4.** An ecological group of plants distinguished from the ordinary herbs, shrubs, and trees by a special mode of life. The four recognized guilds are the *saprophytes, parasites, epiphytes,* and *lianas.* — **guild′ship,** *n.* — **guilds′man** (gĭldz′măn), *n.*

guil′der (gĭl′dĕr), *n.* [D. *gulden,* orig., golden.] A gulden.

guild′hall′ (gĭld′hôl′; 2), *n.* The hall where a guild or corporation usually assembles; a town hall.

guild socialism. An English socialistic theory (developed 1907–15) advocating state ownership of industries and control and management by guilds of workers. — **guild socialist.** — **guild′-so′cial·is′tic,** *adj.*

guile (gīl), *n.* [OF. *guile, guille,* fr. AS. *wigle* divination, sorcery. See WILE.] **1.** Deceitful cunning; craft and treachery. **2.** *Obs.* A stratagem; a trick. — *v. t. Archaic.* To beguile. — **guile′ful** (-fōōl; -f'l), *adj.* — **guile′ful·ly,** *adv.* — **guile′ful·ness,** *n.*

guile′less (-lĕs; -lĭs), *adj.* Lacking guile; hence, innocent. — **guile′less·ness,** *n.*

guil′le·mot (gĭl′ĕ·mŏt), *n.* [F., fr. *Guillaume* William.] Any of certain narrow-billed auks (family Alcidae) of northern seas, constituting two genera (*Uria* and *Cepphus*), including the ***black guillemot*** (*C. grylle* and allied species) and ***foolish guillemot*** (*U. aalge*). Cf. MURRE, DOVEKIE **a.**

guil·loche′ (gĭ·lōsh′), *n.* [F. *guillochis.*] An ornamental design formed of loosely interlaced bands, the openings being filled with round ornaments.

guil′lo·tine (gĭl′ō·tēn), *n.* [F., after J. I. *Guillotin* (1738–1814), French physician, who in 1789 proposed its use.] A machine for beheading persons by means of a heavy ax or blade sliding in vertical guides. — (gĭl′ō·tēn′), *v. t.* To behead with a guillotine.

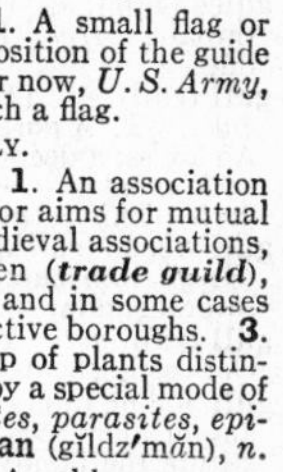
Guillotine.

guilt (gĭlt), *n.* [AS. *gylt* crime.] **1.** The fact of having committed a breach of conduct, esp. such as violates law and involves a penalty; as, to establish one's *guilt.* **2.** Guilty conduct; sin; as, a life free from *guilt.* **3.** Guiltiness; culpability; as to confess one's *guilt.*

guilt′less, *adj.* **1.** Free from guilt; innocent. **2.** Devoid of experience, mark, or sign; — with *of.* — **guilt′less·ly,** *adv.* — **guilt′less·ness,** *n.*

guilt′y (gĭl′tĭ), *adj.;* GUILT′I·ER (-tĭ·ĕr); GUILT′I·EST. [AS. *gyltig.*] **1.** Having one's guilt established; justly chargeable with, or responsible for, delinquency, crime, or sin. **2.** Conscious of, or suffering from, guilt; also, evincing, indicating, or involving guilt. **3.** *Obs.* Justly liable (to) or deserving (of). — **Syn.** See BLAMEWORTHY. — **guilt′i·ly,** *adv.* — **guilt′i·ness,** *n.*

guimpe (gămp), *n.* [F.] A chemisette, with sleeves.

guin′ea (gĭn′ĭ), *n.* **1.** An English gold coin issued from 1663 to 1813, supposedly first struck out of gold from Guinea. In 1717 its value was fixed at 21 shillings; hence, a money of account, the sum of 21 shillings. See MONEY, *Tables.* **2.** Short for GUINEA FOWL.

Guinea corn. Durra.

guinea fowl, guinea hen. A gallinaceous bird (*Numida meleagris*) with dark slaty plumage speckled with white; also, any of the subfamily (Numidinae) of which this species is the type; — called also ***helmeted guinea fowl.*** Certain domesticated strains are raised for food.

Guinea pepper. **a** The pungent aromatic fruits of a tropical African tree (*Xylopia aethiopica*, family Annonaceae); also, this tree. **b** See PEPPER, *n.*, 3.

guinea pig. [Prob. from being carried from S. America to England by slave ships from *Guinea.*] **1.** A stout, short-eared, nearly tailless domesticated cavy, usually black, white, or tawny, and about seven inches long. It may be a form of the restless cavy. See CAVY. **2.** Any subject of experimentation or testing designed to yield data for scientific conclusions or large-scale calculations.

Guinea worm. A slender nematode worm (*Dracunculus medinensis*) of warm countries. It infests the horse and dog and also man.

Guin'e·vere (gwĭn'ē·vēr), *n.* Also **Guin'e·ver** (-vēr). Queen to King Arthur, beloved by Lancelot du Lac.

gui·pure' (gē·pūr'; *F.* gē'pür'), *n.* [F., fr. *guiper* to cover with silk.] A heavy, large-patterned decorative lace.

guise (gīz), *n.* [OF., way, manner, of Teut. origin.] **1.** Customary way of speaking or acting; fashion; behavior. **2.** External appearance, esp. as to dress; hence, semblance; aspect. **3.** Cover; cloak; mask. — *v. t.* **1.** To dress, attire, or arrange, as in a certain manner. **2.** *Dial.* To disguise. — *v. i.* *Dial.* To appear in disguise, esp. as a mummer.

gui·tar' (gĭ·tär'), *n.* [F. *guitare*, fr. Sp. *guitarra*, fr. Gr. *kithara.*] An instrument of the lute class, having a long fretted neck and six strings plucked with the fingers.

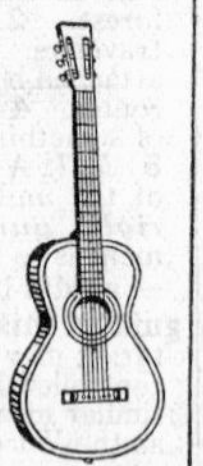
Guitar.

gui·tar'fish' (-fĭsh'), *n.; pl.*, see FISH. See 1st RAY.

Gu'ja·ra'ti (goo͝'jȧ·rä'tĭ), *n.* The Sanskritic language of Gujarat and neighboring Indian states. See INDO-EUROPEAN LANGUAGES, *Table.*

gu'lar (gū'lēr), *adj.* [L. *gula* throat.] On, or pertaining to, the throat.

gulch (gŭlch), *n.* *Orig. Western U. S.* A deep or precipitous cleft, esp. the sharply hollowed bed of a torrent; a ravine.

gul'den (goo͝l'dĕn), *n.* [D. & G.] A coin and money of account; — called also *guilder* and *florin*; as: **a** Any of various obsolete German and Dutch coins. **b** The Dutch gold monetary unit; also, a current silver coin of this value. See MONEY, *Tables.* **c** The former Austrian florin. **d** Formerly, the monetary unit of the Free City of Danzig; originally, a silver, later a nickel coin used in the Free City of Danzig.

gules (gūlz), *n.* [OF. *gueules*, fr. *gole* fur neckpiece dyed red, fr. *gole* throat.] *Her.* Red, represented in engravings by parallel vertical lines.

gulf (gŭlf), *n.* [F. *golfe*, fr. It. *golfo*, fr. LGr., fr. Gr. *kolpos* bosom, gulf.] **1.** A portion of an ocean or sea extending into the land. **2.** An abyss; a deep chasm; hence, a wide separation. **3.** A whirlpool; sucking eddy. — *v. t.* To plunge into, or swallow up in or as in, a gulf; engulf. — **gulf'y**, *adj.*

gulf'weed' (gŭlf'wēd'), *n.* A tropical Atlantic olive-brown seaweed (*Sargassum bacciferum*) having berrylike air vesicles; also, any of several similar species of this genus.

gull (gŭl), *v. t.* To delude; trick; dupe. — **Syn.** See DUPE. — *n.* **1.** One easily cheated; a dupe. **2.** *Archaic.* A trick; fraud.

gull, *n.; pl.* GULLS (gŭlz), rarely GULL. [Of Celt. origin.] **a** Broadly, any of numerous long-winged, web-footed, aquatic birds which constitute the family Laridae, including the *terns* and, sometimes, the *jaegers* or *skuas.* **b** Narrowly, any bird of the genus *Larus* and closely allied genera, usually larger and stouter than the terns and with thicker bill, hooked at the tip, less pointed wings, and short, unforked tail, including: the ***black-backed gull*** (esp. *L. marinus*), ***black-headed gull*** (*L. ridibundus* of Europe and *L. atricilla* of America), ***herring gull*** (*L. argentatus* of Europe and *L. a. smithsonianus* of Atlantic coast and interior of North America), and the *kittiwake* and *mew* (which see).

gull'a·ble, gull'a·bil'i·ty. Vars. of GULLIBLE, etc.

Gul'lah (gŭl'ȧ), *n.* One of a group of Negroes inhabiting the sea islands and coast districts of South Carolina and Georgia; also, their dialect, now essentially a corrupt form of English.

gul'let (gŭl'ĕt; -ĭt), *n.* [OF. *goulet*, dim. of *gole*, *goule*, throat, fr. L. *gula.*] **1.** The esophagus; hence, the throat. **2.** Hence: **a** A channel for water. **b** *Now Rare.* A gully.

gul'li·ble (gŭl'ĭ·b'l), *adj.* Easily gulled, duped, or imposed upon. — **gul'li·bil'i·ty** (-bĭl'ĭ·tĭ), *n.* — **gul'li·bly**, *adv.*

Gul'li·ver, Lem'u·el (gŭl'ĭ·vēr). In **Gul'li·ver's Trav'els** (-vērz), a satirical romance (1726) by Jonathan Swift, an Englishman who makes four voyages to fabulous lands. See BROBDINGNAG; LAPUTA; LILLIPUTIAN; YAHOO.

gul'ly (gŭl'ĭ), *n.; pl.* -LIES (-ĭz). [For GULLET.] A miniature valley or gorge excavated by running water, esp. after rains. — *v. t. & i.;* GUL'LIED (-ĭd); GUL'LY·ING. To wear a gully or gullies in.

gul'ly (gŭl'ĭ; goo͝l'ĭ), *n.* *Scot. & Ir.* A large knife.

gu·los'i·ty (gū·lŏs'ĭ·tĭ), *n.* Greediness.

gulp (gŭlp), *v. t.* [D. *gulpen.*] To swallow eagerly, or in large drafts; also, to suppress as if swallowing; — often with *down;* as, to *gulp* down a drink or a sob. — *v. i.* To catch the breath as if in taking a long drink. — *n.* Act of gulping; a swallow, or as much as is swallowed at once. — **gulp'er**, *n.* — **gulp'ing·ly**, *adv.*

gum (gŭm), *n.* [AS. *gōma* palate, pl. jaws.] The tissue which surrounds the necks of teeth, and covers the alveolar parts of the jaws; the portion of it in either jaw or attached to a single tooth.

gum, *n.* [OF. *gomme*, fr. L. *gummi*, *cummi*, fr. Gr. *kommi*, fr. Egypt. *qemai.*] **1.** **a** Any of a class of colloidal substances, glutinous when moist but hardening on drying, exuded by or extracted from plants, and usually soluble in water. The essential constituents of gums are complex organic acids (**gum acids**) or their salts. **b** Loosely, any of various plant exudations, such as the resins. **2.** A natural gum prepared for industrial or other use. **3.** A gumlike substance, as an adhesive. **4.** Short for: **a** *U. S.* GUMSHOE (def. 1 **a**). **b** CHEWING GUM. **c** GUM ELASTIC. **5.** **a** Short for **gum tree.** Any of several gum-yielding trees, as: (1) *U. S.* Any tree of the genus *Nyssa*, of the dogwood family, the ***tupelo gums or tupelos***, esp.: *N. sylvatica*, the ***black gum***, called also ***tupelo (gum)***, ***sour gum***, and ***yellow gum or pepperidge***, of the eastern, central, and southern U. S., having blue-black drupaceous fruit; *N. aquatica* of the southeastern U. S., called variously ***tupelo (gum), cotton gum, or sour gum.*** (2) *U. S.* A North American tree (*Liquidambar styraciflua*), called specif. ***sweet gum, white gum, red gum, or copalm,*** with corky branches and hard wood used sometimes as an imitation of mahogany. It yields a yellowish fragrant balsam called *copalm* or *liquidambar.* (3) *Australia.* Any eucalyptus; — variously called according to characteristic features, ***blue, cider, gray, green, red, white, or yellow gum.*** (4) Any of several other trees, as the sapodilla (which yield chicle). **b** Short for **gumwood.** The wood of any of these trees, esp. of a eucalyptus or of the sweet gum. **6.** *Southern U. S.* A hive, trough, etc., made of a hollowed log from a gum tree. Cf. BEE GUM. **7.** *Philately.* The adhesive substance on the back of postage stamps. A stamp having this gum intact is said to be with ***original gum*** (abbr. *O.G.*).
— *v. t.;* GUMMED (gŭmd); GUM'MING. To smear with gum; unite or stiffen by gum or a gumlike substance; also, *Slang*, to impede or clog as if with gum. — *v. i.* To exude or form gum; to become gummy or clogged as if with gum. — **gum'mer**, *n.*

gum am·mo'ni·ac (ă·mō'nĭ·ăk). Ammoniac.

gum ar'a·bic (ăr'ȧ·bĭk). A gum, obtained from several species of plants (genus *Acacia*, esp. *A. senegal* and *A. arabica*) of the mimosa family, composed chiefly of the calcium, magnesium, and potassium salts of arabic acid.

gum'bo (gŭm'bō), *n.* Also **gom'bo.** [From dialects of Cen. Africa.] **1.** A soup thickened with the mucilaginous pods of the okra. **2.** The okra plant or its pods. **3.** In full **gumbo soil.** Any of a class of fine-grained silty soils, esp. in the western U. S., which become soapy, sticky, or waxy when wet. — **gum'bo**, *adj.*

gum'boil' (gŭm'boil'), *n.* A small abscess on the gums.

gum'drop' (-drŏp'), *n.* A gumlike candy drop made with gum arabic, gelatin, or the like.

gum elastic. Rubber; caoutchouc.

gum el'e·mi (ĕl'ē·mĭ). **a** Elemi. **b** A small tropical American tree (*Bursera simaruba*) yielding an aromatic resin.

gum'ly (gŭm'lĭ), *adj.* *Scot.* Turbid; gloomy.

gum'ma (gŭm'ȧ), *n.; pl.* -MATA (-ȧ·tȧ). [NL. So called from its gummy contents. See 2d GUM.] *Med.* A growth of syphilitic origin, and of gummy or rubbery consistency. — **gum'ma·tous** (-tŭs), *adj.*

gum·mo'sis (gŭ·mō'sĭs), *n.* [NL. See 2d GUM; -OSIS.] A symptom of disease in plants, characterized by the formation of gummy exudates, the products of cell degeneration.

gum'mous (gŭm'ŭs), *adj.* Also **gum'mose** (-ōs). [L. *gummosus.*] Gumlike; composed of gum; gummy.

gum'my (gŭm'ĭ), *adj.;* GUM'MI·ER (-ĭ·ēr); GUM'MI·EST. Consisting of, producing, or containing or covered with gum; viscous. — **gum'mi·ness**, *n.*

gump (gŭmp), *n.* *Dial. & Slang.* A silly, stupid fellow.

gum plant. Any of several plants (genus *Grindelia*, esp. *G. robusta*) of the aster family, with gummy-coated foliage.

gump'tion (gŭmp'shŭn), *n.* *Colloq.* **a** Common sense; shrewdness. **b** Enterprise; initiative. — **Syn.** See SENSE.

gum resin. A product consisting essentially of a mixture of gum and resin, usually obtained by making an incision in a plant and allowing the juice which exudes to solidify.

gum'shoe' (gŭm'shoo͞'), *n.* **1.** **a** A rubber overshoe. **b** *pl.* Sneakers. **2.** *Slang.* A detective. — *v. i.* *Slang, U. S.* To go stealthily.

gum tree, gum'wood' (gŭm'wo͝od'). See GUM, *n.*, 5.

gun (gŭn), *n.* [ME. *gunne*, *gonne.*] **1.** A piece of ordnance; a cannon. **2.** Any portable firearm except a pistol or revolver; a rifle, shotgun, carbine, etc. **3.** Any similar tubular device for throwing a projectile; as, air *gun.* **4.** A discharge of a cannon as in a salute. **5.** *Colloq.* A revolver or pistol. **6.** Something suggestive of a gun, esp. in shape or function. **7.** *Aviation.* The throttle or the throttle lever.

☞ COMBINATIONS are:

gunbearer	**gunmaking**	**gunshop**
gunbuilder	**gunplay**	**gunsmith**
gunmaker	**gunrack**	**gunstock**

— *v. i.;* GUNNED (gŭnd); GUN'NING. To hunt with a gun; to go hunting. — *v. t.* **a** *Colloq.* To shoot. **b** To fire on. **c** *Chiefly Aviation.* To open up the throttle of (an engine) so as to increase the speed.

gun'boat' (-bōt'), *n.* *Nav.* An armed vessel of light draft.

gun'cot'ton (-kŏt''n), *n.* An explosive usually made by nitrating purified cotton waste with a mixture of nitric and sulfuric acids.

gun dog. A trained dog, as a pointer, setter, or the like, that accompanies sportsmen when they hunt with guns.

gun'fire' (gŭn'fīr'), *n.* *Mil. & Nav.* **a** The firing, or the time of firing, of a gun. **b** *Chiefly Mil.* Use of artillery, rifles, etc., as weapons of war, as disting. from the use of the bayonet, sword, torpedoes, etc., and esp. as disting. from *shock tactics* or the *charge.*

gun'flint' (-flĭnt'), *n.* A small, sharp flint for use in a flintlock, to produce a spark of fire to ignite the priming.

gun'lock' (-lŏk'), *n.* The mechanism attached to some firearms, by which the charge is ignited.

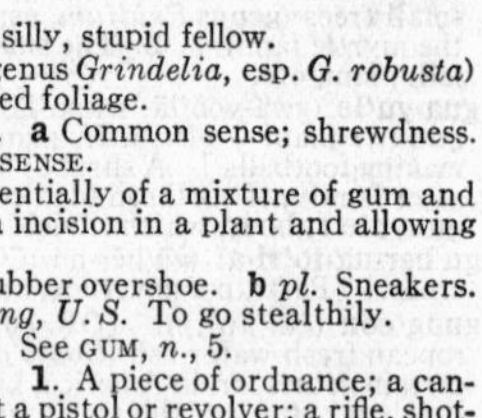

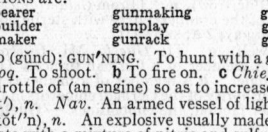

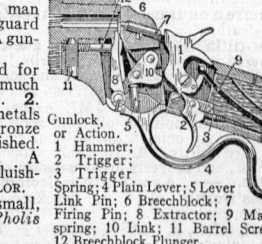

Gunlock, or Action. 1 Hammer; 2 Trigger; 3 Trigger Spring; 4 Plain Lever; 5 Lever Link Pin; 6 Breechblock; 7 Firing Pin; 8 Extractor; 9 Mainspring; 10 Link; 11 Barrel Screw; 12 Breechblock Plunger.

gun'man (-măn), *n.* **1.** A man armed with a gun; an armed guard or, *U. S.*, an armed thug. **2.** A gunmaker.

gun metal. **1.** A metal used for guns; specif., a bronze once much used as a material for cannon. **2.** Any of various alloys or metals treated so as to imitate this bronze when nearly black and tarnished. **3.** Also **gun'-met'al gray.** A nearly neutral gray, slightly bluish-red, of low brilliance. See COLOR.

gun'nel (gŭn'ĕl; -'l), *n.* A small, slimy North Atlantic blenny (*Pholis gunnellus*).

gun'nel. Var. of GUNWALE.

gun'ner (gŭn'ēr), *n.* **1.** A cannoneer. **2.** A warrant officer in the navy having charge of the ordnance on a vessel. **3.** *Brit.* An artilleryman. **4.** One who hunts with a gun.

gun'ner·y (-ĭ), *n.* **1.** Guns collectively. **2.** Science of the flight of projectiles and use of guns. **3.** The practical use of cannon.

gun'ning (gŭn'ĭng), *n.* Hunting game with a gun.

gun′ny (gŭn′ĭ), *n.; pl.* -NIES (-ĭz). [Hind. *gonī*, fr. Skr. *goṇī*.] Coarse jute sacking or a bag made of it. Hence, **gunny bag** *or* **sack**, etc.
gun′pow′der (gŭn′pou′dẽr), *n.* **1.** An explosive mixture of saltpeter, charcoal, and sulfur, used in gunnery and blasting. **2.** Any of various powders used in guns as propelling charges. **3.** A Chinese green tea (see TEA, 1 **b**) with leaves rolled in small pellets.
gun room. In the British Navy, the quarters used by midshipmen and junior officers, orig. assigned to the gunner and his mates.
gun′run′ning (gŭn′rŭn′ĭng), *n.* Contraband traffic in arms and ammunition. — **gun′run′ner,** *n.*
gun′shot′ (gŭn′shŏt′), *n.* **1.** Shot fired from a gun. **2.** A wound made by shot. **3.** Effective reach or range of a gun.
Gun′ter's chain (gŭn′tẽrz). See CHAIN, *n.*, 4.
Gun′ther (gōōn′tẽr), *n.* See BRUNHILD, SIEGFRIED.
gun′wale (gŭn′ĕl; -′l), *n.* Also **gun′nel.** [*gun* + *wale;* because the upper guns were pointed from it.] That part of a vessel where topsides and deck meet.
gup′py (gŭp′ĭ), *n.* A small minnow (*Lebistes reticulatus*) of Barbados, Trinidad, and Venezuela, frequently kept as an aquarium fish.
gurge (gûrj), *n. & v. i.* [L. *gurges* whirlpool.] Swirl.
gur′gi·ta′tion (gûr′jĭ·tā′shŭn), *n.* [LL. *gurgitare* to flood, fr. *gurges, -itis,* whirlpool.] Boiling of a liquid; violent ebullition.
gur′gle (gûr′g′l), *v. i.;* -GLED (-g′ld); -GLING (-glĭng). To flow in a broken, noisy current; also, to sound like a liquid flowing in this way. — *v. t.* To utter with a gurgling sound. — *n.* Act or sound of gurgling.
gur′glet (gûr′glĕt; -glĭt). Var. of GOGLET.
gur′nard (gûr′nẽrd), *n.;* see PLURAL, *Note,* 3. [OF. *gornart.*] Any of a family (Triglidae) of marine spiny-finned fishes having an armored head and three pairs of feelers. Cf. FLYING GURNARD.
gu′ru (gōō′rōō; gōō·rōō′), *n.* [Skr., venerable one.] *India.* A teacher, esp. a religious teacher.
gush (gŭsh), *v. i.* [ME. *guschen.*] **1.** To issue copiously or violently; to spout. **2.** To emit a flood of tears, blood, etc.; to break (into tears, etc.). **3.** To exhibit or express affection, enthusiasm, etc., effusively. — *v. t.* To emit freely. — *n.* **1.** A gushing; also, that which gushes forth. **2.** A free outpouring. **3.** *Colloq.* Effusive display of sentiment. — **gush′i·ness,** *n.* — **gush′ing·ly,** *adv.* — **gush′y,** *adj.*
gush′er (gŭsh′ẽr), *n.* One that gushes; specif., an oil well with a copious natural flow.
gus′set (gŭs′ĕt; -ĭt), *n.* [F. *gousset* armpit, fob, gusset, dim. of *gousse* pod, husk.] A triangular piece, inserted in a garment, glove, etc., to give width or strength. — *v. t.;* GUS′SET·ED (-ĕd; -ĭd); GUS′SET·ING. To provide with a gusset.
gust (gŭst), *n.* [ON. *gustr.*] **1.** A sudden brief blast of wind. **2.** A sudden outburst, as of temper.
gust, *n.* [L. *gustus.*] *Archaic.* **a** Taste; relish; gusto. **b** Flavor, or savor. **c** Gratification; enjoyment. — *v. t. Scot.* To taste; relish. — **gust′a·ble,** *adj. & n.*
gus·ta′tion (gŭs·tā′shŭn), *n.* Act or faculty of tasting. — **gus′ta·tive** (gŭs′tȧ·tĭv), *adj.* — **gus′ta·tive·ness,** *n.* — **gus′ta·to′ry** (-tō′rĭ *or, esp. Brit.,* -tẽr·ĭ), *adj.*
gus′to (gŭs′tō), *n.* [It., fr. L. *gustus.*] **1.** Taste; liking. **2.** Keen or zestful appreciation; great relish. **3.** Artistic style or taste. — **Syn.** See TASTE.
gust′y (gŭs′tĭ), *adj.;* GUST′I·ER (-tĭ·ẽr); GUST′I·EST. Marked by gusts; windy. — **gust′i·ly,** *adv.* — **gust′i·ness,** *n.*
gust′y (gŭs′tĭ; gōōs′tĭ), *adj.* *Chiefly Scot.* Savory.
gut (gŭt), *n.* [AS. pl. *guttas.*] **1. a** *pl. Now Coarse.* Bowels; entrails. **b** An intestine; the alimentary canal or part of it. Cf. CAECUM. **2.** A narrow passage, as a strait or defile. **3.** A prepared gut (sense 1 **b**) esp. of a sheep, used in making sausage cases, catgut, etc. **4.** The sac of silk taken from a silkworm ready to spin its cocoon and drawn out into a thread for use as a snell. **5.** *pl. Slang.* Stamina; grit. — **Syn.** See FORTITUDE. — *v. t.;* GUT′TED (-ĕd; -ĭd); GUT′TING. **1.** To eviscerate. **2.** To destroy or remove the interior or contents of. — **gut′ter,** *n.*
Gu·tru′ne (gōō·trōō′nĕ), *n.* See SIEGFRIED.
gut′ta (gŭt′ȧ), *n.; pl.* -TAE (-ē). [L.] A drop; a droplike marking; esp., *Arch.,* one of a series of droplike ornaments, as on the lower face of a mutule in a Doric entablature.
gut′ta–per′cha (-pûr′chȧ), *n.* [Malay *gĕtah* gum + *pĕrca* the tree producing it.] A whitish-to-brown substance resembling rubber but containing more resin and changing less on vulcanization, from the latex of several Malaysian trees of the sapodilla family, of the genera *Payena* and *Palaquium.*
gut′tate (gŭt′āt), *adj.* Also **gut′tat·ed** (-āt·ĕd; -ĭd). [L. *guttatus.*] Droplike; having guttae.
gut′ter (gŭt′ẽr), *n.* [OF. *goutiere,* fr. L. *gutta* drop.] **1.** A channel worn by running water. **2.** A channel at the eaves for conveying away the rain. **3.** A narrow ditch, esp. at the roadside, to lead off surface water; hence, low life; as, slang of the *gutter.* **4.** Any similar narrow channel or groove, as one on each side of a bowling alley to catch balls rolled wide. **5.** *Philately.* The spaces between the stamps of a printed sheet to allow for separation or perforation. **6.** *Print.* The blank space between pages of a book, along their inside margins. — *v. t.* To form gutters in. — *v. i.* **1.** To flow in streams. **2.** To become channeled, as a flaring candle. — **gut′ter·y,** *adj.*
gut′ter·snipe′ (gŭt′ẽr·snīp′), *n.* **1.** A street Arab; a ragamuffin. **2.** A disreputable or despicable person.
gut′tle (gŭt′′l), *v. t. & i.;* -TLED (-′ld); -TLING (-lĭng). [From GUT, *n.*] To gormandize. — **gut′tler** (-lẽr), *n.*
gut′tur·al (gŭt′ẽr·ăl), *adj.* [F., fr. L. *guttur* throat.] **1.** Of or pertaining to the throat. **2. a** Sounded in the throat; popularly, harsh or rasping, as resembling a throat sound. **b** *Phonet.* Velar. — *n.* A guttural sound or its symbol; guttural utterance. — **gut′tur·al′i·ty** (-ăl′ĭ·tĭ), *n.* — **gut′tur·al·ly,** *adv.* — **gut′tur·al·ness,** *n.*
gut′tur·al·ize (-īz), *v. t.* To speak gutturally; *Phonet.,* velarize. — **gut′tur·al·i·za′tion** (-ĭ·zā′shŭn; -ī·zā′-), *n.*
gut′tur·o- (gŭt′ẽr·ō-). [L. *guttur* throat.] A combining form denoting *guttural (and),* as in **gut′tur·o·na′sal,** *Phonet.,* having both a guttural and a nasal character; **gut′tur·o·pal′a·tal.**
guy (gī), *n.* [OF. *gui, guie,* a guide.] A rope, chain, or rod attached to anything to steady it. — *v. t.;* GUYED (gīd); GUY′ING. To steady with a guy.
guy, *n.* **1.** In English popular custom, a grotesque effigy of Guy Fawkes paraded and burned on the anniversary of his plot to blow up the king and parliament, Nov. 5, 1605. **2.** A person of grotesque appearance or dress. **3.** *Colloq.* A person; fellow. — *v. t. Colloq.* To make fun of; chaff. — **guy′er** (gī′ẽr), *n.*
guz′zle (gŭz′′l), *v. i. & t.;* GUZ′ZLED (-′ld); GUZ′ZLING (-lĭng). To drink greedily, excessively, or continually. — **guz′zler** (-lẽr), *n.*
gybe (jīb). Var. of JIBE.
gym (jĭm), *n.* *Colloq.* Short for GYMNASIUM.
gym·kha′na (jĭm·kä′nȧ), *n.* [(After *gym*nastics), fr. Hind. *gẽdkhānā* racket court, fr. Per. *khāna* house.] *Orig. Anglo-Indian.* A meeting for athletic contests, mainly racing.
gym·na′si·arch (-nā′zĭ·ärk), *n.* [L. *gymnasiarchus,* fr. Gr. *gymnasiarchos,* fr. *gymnasion* + *archein* to govern.] *Gr. Antiq.* One who trained athletes or assumed financial responsibility for their training. — **gym·na′si·arch·y** (-är·kĭ), *n.*
gym·na′si·ast (-ăst), *n.* **1.** A gymnast. **2.** A student or graduate of a Gymnasium.
gym·na′si·um (jĭm·nā′zĭ·ŭm; 58), *n.; pl.* -SIUMS (-ŭmz), -SIA (-ȧ). [L., fr. Gr. *gymnasion,* fr. *gymnazein* to exercise (naked), fr. *gymnos* naked.] **1.** A place or building for athletic exercises; a school for gymnastics. **2.** [*cap.*] (*Ger. pron.* gĭm·nä′zĭ·ōōm; gŭm-) In Europe, esp. Germany, a secondary school preparing for the university.
gym′nast (jĭm′năst), *n.* [Gr. *gymnastēs* a trainer of athletes.] A teacher of, or an expert in, gymnastics.
gym·nas′tic (jĭm·năs′tĭk), *adj.* Also **gym·nas′ti·cal** (-tĭ·kăl). Pertaining to exercise, esp. of the body; athletic. — **gym·nas′ti·cal·ly,** *adv.*
gym·nas′tics (-tĭks), *n. sing. & pl.;* see -ICS. Physical exercises performed in, or adapted to performance in, a gymnasium.
gym′no- (jĭm′nō-), **gymn-.** [Gr. *gymnos.*] A combining form, meaning *naked, bare, uncovered,* as in **gym′no·car′pous, gym·nog′e·nous, gym·nog′y·nous, gym′no·plast, gym′no·spore** (see -CARPOUS, -GENOUS, -GYNOUS, etc.). Cf. ANGIO-.
gym·nos′o·phist (jĭm·nŏs′ō·fĭst), *n.* [L. *gymnosophistae,* pl., fr. Gr. *gymnosophistai,* fr. *gymnos* naked + *sophistēs* philosopher.] **1.** One of a sect of ascetic philosophers, found in India by Alexander the Great. **2.** A nudist. — **gym·nos′o·phist,** *adj.* — **gym·nos′o·phy** (-fĭ), *n.*
gym′no·sperm (jĭm′nō·spûrm), *n.* [Gr. *gymnospermos,* fr. *gymnos* naked + *sperma* seed.] Any plant of a class (Gymnospermae) having seeds naked, or not enclosed in an ovary. Cf. ANGIOSPERM. — **gym′no·sper′mous** (-spûr′mŭs), *adj.*
gyn-. = GYNO-.
gyn′ae·ce′um (jĭn′ē·sē′ŭm; jī′nē-), *n.; pl.* -CEA (-ȧ). Also **gyn′ae·ci′um** (-sĭ′ŭm; jĭ·nē′sĭ·ŭm). [L., fr. Gr. *gynaikeion,* fr. *gynē* woman.] **1.** *Gr. & Rom. Antiq.* The women's apartments in a house. **2.** *Bot.* The gynoecium.
gy·nan′drous (jĭ·năn′drŭs; jī-), *adj.* [Gr. *gynandros* of doubtful sex, fr. *gynē* woman + *anēr, andros,* man.] **1.** *Bot.* Having the androecium and gynoecium united in a column, as orchids. **2.** Characterized by gynandry.
gy·nan′dry (-drĭ), *n.* Hermaphroditism.
gyn′arch·y (jĭn′är·kĭ; jī′nȧr·kĭ), *n.* [*gyn-* + *-archy.*] Government by a woman or women. — **gyn·arch′ic** (jĭ·när′kĭk; jī-), *adj.*
gyn′e·co- (jĭn′ē·kō-; jī′nē-; *in learned words, esp. medical terms, often* gī·nē′kō-), **gynec-.** [Gr. *gynē, gynaikos.*] A combining form meaning *woman, womanish, female.*
gyn′e·coc′ra·cy, gyn′ae·coc′ra·cy (jĭn′ē·kŏk′rȧ·sĭ; jī′nē-), *n.* [Gr. *gynaikokratia,* fr. *gynē, gynaikos,* woman + *kratein* to rule.] Government by women; in a depreciative sense, petticoat rule. See MATRIARCHY. — **gy·ne′co·crat, gy·nae′co·crat** (jĭ·nē′kō·krăt; jī-), *n.* — **gyn′e·co·crat′ic** (jĭn′ē·kō·krăt′ĭk; jī·nē′-), **gyn′e·co·crat′i·cal** (-ĭ·kăl), *adj.*
gyn′e·col′o·gy, gyn′ae·col′o·gy (jĭn′ē·kŏl′ō·jĭ; gī′nē-; jī′nē-), *n.* [*gyneco-* + *-logy.*] The branch of medicine which treats of women, their diseases, their hygiene, etc. — **gyn′e·co·log′ic, gyn′ae·co·log′ic** (-kō·lŏj′ĭk), *adj.* — **gyn′e·col′o·gist, gyn′ae·col′o·gist** (-kŏl′ō·jĭst), *n.*
gyn′e·co·mor′phous, gyn′ae·co·mor′phous (jĭn′ē·kō·môr′fŭs; jī·nē′kō-), *adj.* [Gr. *gynaikomorphos* in woman's shape. See GYNECO-; -MORPHOUS.] Having the form or morphological characters of a woman or female.
gyneo-, gynaeo-. [Gr. *gynaios* of or for woman.] A combining form equivalent to *gyneco-,* as in **gyn′e·oc′ra·cy, gyn′ae·oc′ra·cy, gyn′e·ol′a·try, gyn′ae·ol′a·try** (see -CRACY, -LATRY).
gyn′i·at′rics (jĭn′ĭ·ăt′rĭks; jī′nĭ-), *n.;* see -ICS. [*gyn-* + *-iatrics.*] *Med.* Treatment of diseases of women.
gyn′o- (jĭn′ō-; jī′nō-), **gyn-.** [Gr. *gynē* woman.] A combining form meaning woman; specif., *Bot. & Med., a female reproductive organ, a pistil* or *ovary.*
gy·noe′ci·um (jĭ·nē′sĭ·ŭm; jī-), *n.; pl.* -CIA (-ȧ). Also **gy·ne′ci·um.** [NL., fr. *gyn-* + Gr. *oikos* house.] *Bot.* The aggregate of carpels or megasporophylls in the flower of a seed plant; the part of a flower consisting of the pistils. See FLOWER, *Illust.*
gyn′o·phore (jĭn′ō·fōr; jī′nō-; 70), *n.* [*gyno-* + *-phore.*] *Bot.* A stipe bearing the gynoecium. — **gyn′o·phor′ic** (-fŏr′ĭk), *adj.*
-gynous. [Gr. *gynē* woman.] A combining form meaning *woman, female;* specif., *Bot., having* or *pertaining to* (such or so many) *female organs* or *pistils,* as in andro*gynous.* Corresponding nouns denoting *condition* are formed in **-gyny.**
gyp (jĭp), *n.* *Eng.* A college servant.
gyp (jĭp), *n. & v. t. & i.;* GYPPED (jĭpt); GYP′PING. *Slang.* Cheat; swindle.
gyp′se·ous (jĭp′sē·ŭs), *adj.* [LL. *gypseus.* See GYPSUM.] Resembling, containing, or consisting of gypsum.
gyp·sif′er·ous (jĭp·sĭf′ẽr·ŭs), *adj.* [*gypsum* + *-ferous.*] Bearing gypsum.
gyp·soph′i·la (jĭp·sŏf′ĭ·lȧ), *n.* [NL. See GYPSUM; -PHIL.] Any of a large genus (*Gypsophila*) of Old World herbs of the pink family, having small delicate paniculate flowers. *G. paniculata* is called also *babies'-breath.*
gyp′sum (jĭp′sŭm), *n.* [L. *gypsum,* fr. Gr. *gypsos* chalk, gypsum.] *Mineral.* Hydrous calcium sulfate, $CaSO_4.2H_2O$. H., 2. Sp. gr., 2.31–2.32. Gypsum is used as a dressing for soils, for making plaster of Paris, etc. — *v. t.;* GYP′SUMED (-sŭmd); GYP′SUM·ING. To treat with gypsum, as soil or water.
gyp′sy, gip′sy (jĭp′sĭ), *n.; pl.* -SIES (-sĭz). [Earlier *Gipcyan,* fr. *Egypcyan* Egyptian, gypsy.] **1.** [*often cap.*] **1.** One of a wandering Caucasian race coming from India into Europe in the 14th or 15th

century, some settling down, some maintaining their itinerant life and tribal organization, and everywhere noted for skill in metalworking and music. **2.** *U. S.* A member of any itinerant dark-skinned family, who live a nomadic life. **3.** [*cap.*] The language of the gypsies (sense 1), divided into many dialects. Cf. ROMANY. — *v. i.;* -SIED (-sĭd); -SY·ING. To live or roam like a gypsy. — **gyp′sy, gip′sy,** *adj.* — **gyp′sy·dom, gip′sy·dom,** *n.* — **gyp′sy·hood, gip′sy·hood,** *n.*

gypsy moth. An Old World tussock moth (*Porthetria,* syn. *Ocneria, dispar*) introduced into Massachusetts about 1869, now found beyond New England. The caterpillars eat the leaves of fruit and forest trees.

gy′rate (jī′rāt), *adj.* [L. *gyratus* made in a circular form, past part. of *gyrare* to gyrate.] Winding or coiled round; curved. — (jī′rāt; jī-rāt′), *v. i.* To revolve round a central point; move spirally about an axis. — **gy·ra′tion** (jī·rā′shŭn), *n.* — **gy′ra′tor** (jī′rā′tẽr; jī·rā′-), *n.*

gy′ra·to′ry (jī′rȧ·tō′rĭ *or, esp. Brit.,* -tẽr·ĭ), *adj.* Gyrating; whirling.

gyre (jīr), *n.* [L. *gyrus,* fr. Gr. *gyros.*] **1.** A circle described by a moving body; revolution. **2.** A circular or spiral form; also, a vortex.

gy·rene′ (jī·rēn′; jī′rēn), *n.* [*GI* + *marine.*] *Slang.* A marine.

gyr′fal′con, ger′fal′con (jûr′fôl′kŭn; -fô′kŭn), *n.* [OF. *gerfaucon, gerfauc,* of Teut. origin.] Any of the large falcons of the arctic regions which constitute a subgenus (*Hierofalco*), as the European falcon *Falco rusticolus rusticolus.*

gy′ro (jī′rō), *n.; pl.* -ROS -rōz). *Colloq.* Short for GYROSCOPE, GYROCOMPASS, etc.

gy′ro- (jī′rō-), **gyr-.** [Gr. *gyros* ring.] A combining form denoting: **a** *A ring or circle.* **b** *Spiral,* as in **gy·roi′dal.**

gy′ro·com′pass (-kŭm′pȧs), *n.* A compass consisting of a continuously driven gyroscope whose spinning axis is confined to a horizontal plane, so that the earth's rotation causes it to assume a position parallel to the earth's axis, and thus point to the true north; — called also **gyrostatic compass.**

gyro horizon. = ARTIFICIAL HORIZON, 2.

gy′ro·mag·net′ic (jī′rō·măg·nĕt′ĭk), *adj.* [See GYRATE; MAGNETIC.] *Physics.* Of or pertaining to the magnetic properties of a rotating electrical particle, esp. the spinning electron in the atom.

gy′ro·pi′lot (jī′rō·pī′lŭt), *n.* *Aeronautics.* A control mechanism consisting of two vacuum-driven gyroscopes, one in vertical, one in horizontal position, for automatically controlling elevators, rudder, and ailerons, thus maintaining the plane in straight level flight and on a set course.

gy′ro·plane′ (-plān′), *n.* [*gyro*scope + air*plane.*] A flying machine balanced and supported by rapidly rotating horizontal or slightly inclined planes.

gy′ro·scope (-skōp), *n.* [F. See GYRE; -SCOPE.] A wheel or disk mounted to spin rapidly about an axis, and also free to rotate about one or both of two axes perpendicular to each other and to the axis of spin. The spinning gyroscope offers considerable resistance, depending on the angular momentum, to any torque which would change the direction of the axis of spin; it can therefore be used as a stabilizer to resist the rolling of a ship or airplane, or to maintain the equilibrium of a monorail car, or as a steering apparatus, etc. — **gy′ro·scop′ic** (-skŏp′ĭk), *adj.* — **gy′ro·scop′i·cal·ly** (-ĭ·kăl·ĭ), *adv.*

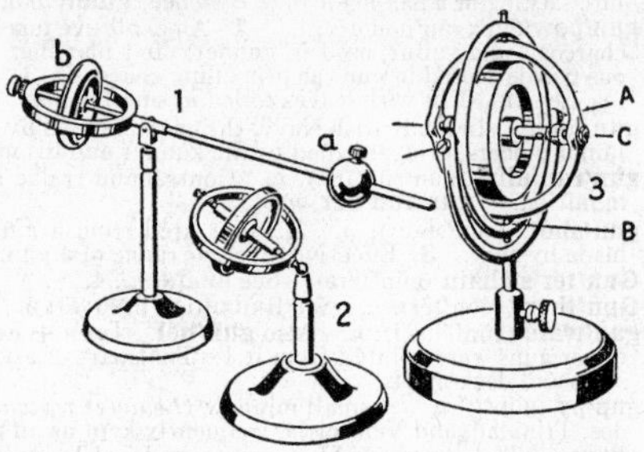

Gyroscopes. 1 Balanced (*a* Counterweight; *b* Gyroscope); 2 Unbalanced; 3 Supported (*A* Horizontal Axis, *B* Vertical Axis, *C* Spinning Axis).

gy′rose (jī′rōs), *adj.* [See GYRE.] Marked with wavy lines.

gy′ro·sta′bi·liz′er (jī′rō·stā′bĭ·līz′ẽr; -stăb′ĭ-), *n.* A stabilizing device, as for a ship or airplane, consisting of a continuously driven gyroscope whose spinning axis is confined to a fore-and-aft movement in a vertical plane.

gy′ro·stat (jī′rō·stăt), *n.* A device consisting of a gyroscope in a case.

gy′ro·stat′ic (-stăt′ĭk), *adj.* *Physics.* Of or pert. to the gyrostat or gyrostatics. — **gy′ro·stat′i·cal·ly** (-ĭ·kăl·ĭ), *adv.*

gy′ro·stat′ics (-ĭks), *n.;* see -ICS. That branch of physical science which deals with the phenomena of rotating bodies.

gy′rus (jī′rŭs), *n.; pl.* GYRI (-rī). [L. See GYRE, *n.*] *Anat.* A convoluted ridge between grooves.

gyve (jīv), *n.* [ME. *give.*] A shackle; — usually in *pl.* — *v. t.* To shackle.

H

H, h (āch), *n.; pl.* H's, H's, Hs, HS (āch′ĕz; -ĭz). **1.** The eighth letter of the English alphabet. It came through the Latin from the Greek H (eta) which was derived from a Phoenician letter, corresponding to Hebrew *cheth,* that stood for a strong guttural aspirate. **2.** The sound of this letter. In English, its sound is usually that of an aspiration or breathing. See *Pron.,* § 49, and for the various combinations of *h* see under the initial letter. **3.** Anything having the shape of the letter H. **4.** As a *symbol,* the eighth in order or class.

haaf (häf), *n.* [ON. *haf* the high sea.] Deep-sea fishing grounds off the Shetland and Orkney Islands.

haar (här), *n.* *Scot.* A fog; esp., a chill fog.

Hab′ak·kuk (hăb′ȧ·kŭk; hȧ·băk′ŭk), *n.* *Douay Bible.* **Hab′a·cuc** (hăb′ȧ·kŭk; hȧ·băk′ŭk). **a** A Hebrew prophet of unknown date. **b** A book of the Old Testament. See BIBLE.

ha′ba·ne′ra (ä′vä·nā′rä; 17), *n.* [Sp., of Habana (Havana).] *Music.* **a** A dance of voluptuous character in slow duple measure, imported into Cuba from Africa. **b** The music for this dance.

ha′be·as cor′pus (hā′bē·ăs kôr′pŭs). [L., (that) you have the body.] *Law.* Any of several common-law writs having for their object to bring a party before a court or judge; esp., the prerogative writ, more fully ‖**ha′be·as cor′pus ad sub·ji′ci·en′dum** (ăd sŭb·jĭs′ĭ·ĕn′dŭm), for inquiring into the lawfulness of the restraint of a person who is imprisoned or detained in another's custody.

hab′er·dash′er (hăb′ẽr·dăsh′ẽr), *n.* **1.** A dealer in small wares, as tapes, pins, needles, and thread, and formerly also hats; now, esp., a dealer in linens, trimmings, etc. **2.** *U. S.* One who keeps a men's furnishing store.

hab′er·dash′er·y (-ĭ), *n.; pl.* -ERIES (-ĭz). The goods and wares sold by a haberdasher; also, a haberdasher's shop.

hab′er·geon (hăb′ẽr·jŭn), *n.* [OF. *haubergeon* a small hauberk, dim. of *hauberc.*] A jacket of mail, shorter than a hauberk; loosely, a hauberk.

hab′ile (hăb′ĭl), *adj.* [F., fr. L. *habilis.*] Able; expert; adroit; skillful; clever.

ha·bil′i·ment (hȧ·bĭl′ĭ·mĕnt), *n.* [OF. *habillement,* fr. *habiller* to dress.] Dress; attire; also, *Obs.,* accouterment; equipment; — chiefly in *pl.*

ha·bil′i·tate (-tāt), *v. t.* [ML. *habilitatus,* past part. of *habilitare,* fr. *habilitas.* See ABILITY.] **1.** *Local, U. S.* To fit out, or equip for working, as a mine. **2.** To clothe; dress. — **ha·bil′i·ta′tion** (-tā′shŭn), *n.*

hab′it (hăb′ĭt), *n.* [OF. *habit, abit,* fr. L. *habitus* state, appearance, dress, fr. *habere* to have.] **1.** Dress; garb; attire. **2.** A particular costume indicative of rank, calling, or occupation; specif.: **a** The gown or dress of a religious. **b** The riding costume of a lady. **3.** Bodily appearance; hence, bodily constitution. **4.** Mental or moral constitution or bearing; disposition; mental make-up. **5.** A custom or practice; esp., an aptitude or inclination for some action, acquired by repetition and showing itself in facility of performance or in decreased power of resistance; as, the opium *habit.* **6.** Characteristic form or mode of occurrence or growth; as, elms have a spreading *habit.* **7.** *Rare.* Familiarity or terms of familiarity.

Syn. **Habit, habitude, practice, usage, custom, use, wont** mean a way of behaving, proceeding, etc., that has become fixed through constant repetition. **Habit** specifically implies a doing unconsciously or without premeditation; **habitude,** a fixed attitude or habitual response to a given stimulus; **practice,** an act or method at first chosen, but followed so regularly that it has become a habit; **usage,** a long-continued and generally adopted practice as in a country or among a class; **custom,** any practice or usage so associated with an individual or a group as to have the force of an unwritten law. **Use** and **wont** are slightly archaic synonyms of *custom.*

hab′it, *v. t.* [OF. *habiter,* fr. L. *habitare,* intens. fr. *habere* to have.] **1.** To dress; array. **2.** *Archaic.* To inhabit. **3.** *Obs.* To accustom.

hab′it·a·ble (hăb′ĭ·tȧ·b′l), *adj.* Capable of being inhabited. — **hab′it·a·bil′i·ty** (-bĭl′ĭ·tĭ), **hab′it·a·ble·ness,** *n.* — **hab′it·a·bly,** *adv.*

hab′it·ant (hăb′ĭ·tănt), *n.* [F.] **1.** An inhabitant. **2.** Also **ha′bi·tan′** (ȧ′bē′täN′) One of the settlers, or their descendants, of French descent in Canada or Louisiana, of the farming class.

hab′i·tat (hăb′ĭ·tăt), *n.* [L., it dwells.] **1.** *Biol.* The natural abode of a plant or animal, esp. the particular location where it normally grows or lives, as the seacoast, desert, etc. **2.** Place where a thing is commonly found.

hab′i·ta′tion (-tā′shŭn), *n.* **1.** Act of inhabiting; occupancy. **2.** Place of abode; settled dwelling; residence.

hab′it·ed (hăb′ĭt·ĕd; -ĭd), *adj.* Clothed; arrayed.

ha·bit′u·al (hȧ·bĭt′ū·ăl), *adj.* **1.** Of the nature of a habit; according to habit; customary; as, *habitual* practice. **2.** Doing, practicing, or acting in some manner by force of habit; as, a *habitual* drunkard. **3.** Usual; customary; as, a *habitual* topic. — **Syn.** See USUAL. — **ha·bit′u·al·ly,** *adv.* — **ha·bit′u·al·ness,** *n.*

ha·bit′u·ate (-āt), *v. t.* [LL. *habituatus,* past part. of *habituare* to bring into a habit of body.] **1.** To accustom; familiarize. **2.** *Colloq.* To frequent. — **Syn.** See FREQUENT. — **ha·bit′u·a′tion** (-ā′shŭn), *n.*

hab′i·tude (hăb′ĭ·tūd), *n.* [F., fr. L. *habitudo* condition.] **1.** Native character; hence, habitual attitude. **2.** *Archaic.* Habitual association. **3.** Habitual disposition or mode of procedure. — **Syn.** See HABIT.

ha·bit′u·é′ (hȧ·bĭt′ū·ā′; hȧ·bĭt′ū·ā; *F.* ȧ′bē′tü′ā′), *n.* [F., past part.] One who frequents a place or class of places.

Habs′burg (hăps′bûrg; *G.* häps′bo͝ork). Var. of HAPSBURG.

ha·chure′ (hă·shūr′; hăsh′ūr), *n.* [F., fr. *hacher* to hack.] *Fine Arts.* A short line used in drawing and engraving, esp. in shading and denoting different surfaces. — (hă·shūr′), *v. t.* To shade with, or show by, hachures.

ha·cien′da (ä·syān′dä; *Angl.* hăs′ĭ·ĕn′dȧ), *n.* [Sp., fr. OSp. *facienda* employment, estate, fr. L. *facienda,* pl., things to be done, fr. *facere* to do.] *Sp. Amer.* A large estate, or a works or establishment.

hack (hăk), *v. t.* [AS. *hæccan, haccian* (in comp.).] **1.** To cut irregularly, as if by repeated strokes of a cutting instrument; as, to *hack* a post. **2.** To break up (land) or cultivate with a hack. **3.** *Rugby Football.* To kick the shins of (an opposing player). — *v. i.* **1.** To make hacks, or rough cuts. **2.** To cough in a short, broken manner. **3.** *Rugby Football.* To kick or kick at an opponent's shins deliberately. — *n.* **1.** A tool or implement for hacking, as a pick, mattock, hoe, or the like. **2.** A notch; cut; nick. **3.** A breaking or stumbling in speech. **4.** A hacking; a short, broken cough. **5.** *Rugby Football.* A kick on the shins, or a cut from a kick. — **hack′er** (-ẽr), *n.*

hack, *n.* [From HACKNEY.] **1.** **a** A horse let out for hire; also, a horse used in all kinds of work, or a horse trained for saddle use. **b** Hence, a horse worn out in service; a jade. **2.** A coach or carriage let for hire; a hackney. **3.** One who hires himself out for any sort of literary work;

a drudge. — *v. t.* **1.** To use often, so as to render trite and commonplace. **2.** To use as a hack; to let out for hire. — *v. i.* To ride at an ordinary pace, or over the roads, as disting. from riding across country. — *adj.* **a** That is used as a hack; as, a *hack* horse. **b** Performed by a hack; as, *hack* work. **c** Hackneyed.

hack'a·more (hăk'ȧ·mōr; 70), *n.* [Prob. fr. Sp. *jáquima* headstall of a halter.] *Western U.S.* A variety of halter, used chiefly for breaking horses; hence, a loop of rope passed around a horse's neck and through his mouth, serving a similar purpose.

hack'ber'ry (hăk'bĕr'ĭ; -bĕr·ĭ), *n.* [Var. of HAGBERRY.] Any of a genus (*Celtis*) of trees of the elm family, with small fruit; also, its wood.

hack'but (hăk'bŭt), **hag'but** (hăg'-), *n.* [F. *haquebute*, fr. D. *haakbus*, fr. *haak* hook + *bus* gun barrel.] A harquebus of which the butt was bent down or hooked for convenience in taking aim. — **hack'but·eer'** (-ēr'), **hack'but·ter** (hăk'bŭt·ẽr), *n.*

hack hammer. A hammer resembling an adz, used in dressing stone.

hack'le (hăk''l), *n.* [Akin to *heckle.*] **1.** A hatchel. **2. a** A long, narrow feather, as a neck feather of certain birds, esp. the domestic fowl. **b** The neck plumage collectively of the domestic fowl. See POULTRY, *Illust.* (5). **3.** *pl.* Erectile bristles along a dog's neck and back. **4.** *Angling.* **a** The legs of an artificial fly represented by filaments of feathers from the neck of a rooster. See FLY, *Illust.* **b** A hackle fly. — *v. t.*; HACK'LED (-'ld); HACK'LING (-lĭng). **1.** To comb out (flax or hemp) with a hackle; to hatchel. **2.** To furnish with a hackle for fishing. — **hack'ler** (-lẽr), *n.*

hack'le, *v. t. & i.* [Freq. of HACK.] To cut roughly; hack.

hackle fly. An artificial fly tied without feather wings.

hack'man (hăk'măn), *n.*; *pl.* HACKMEN (-mĕn). The driver of a hack.

hack'ma·tack' (hăk'mȧ·tăk'), *n.* [Of Algonquian origin.] **a** The American larch, or tamarack (*Larix laricina*); also, its wood. **b** The common juniper.

hack'ney (hăk'nĭ), *n.* [ME. *hakeney, hakenai*, fr. *Hackney*, in Middlesex, Eng.] **1.** A horse for ordinary riding or driving. **2.** [*cap.*] A horse of an English breed with compact build and high knee action. **3.** A carriage kept for hire; a hack. **4.** A hired drudge. — *adj.* Let out for hire; hence, trite; mean. — *v. t.* To devote to common use, as a horse; to wear out in common service; hence, to make trite, vulgar, or commonplace.

hackney coach. A coach standing or plying for hire; a four-wheeled carriage drawn by two horses and seated for six persons.

hack'neyed (hăk'nĭd), *adj.* **1.** Commonplace; trite. **2.** Worn, or habituated, by long use or practice; practiced. — **Syn.** See TRITE.

hack saw, *or* **hack'saw'** (hăk'sô'), *n.* A fine-toothed, narrow-bladed saw stretched in a frame, for cutting metal.

had (hăd; 4), *past & past part.* of HAVE. [AS. *hæfde*, in past part. *hæfed, gehæfed.*] See HAVE. Specif.: **a** *Archaic.* Equivalent to *would have* or *should have.* **b** With adjectives, adverbs, or phrases of comparison, as *as well, as lief, rather, better, liefer, best*, and the like, followed by an infinitive or by a clause introduced by *that*, used to indicate preference or advisability; as, I *had* rather go than stay.

had'dock (hăd'ŭk), *n.*; see PLURAL, *Note*, 6. [ME. *haddok, hadok.*] An important food fish (*Melanogrammus aeglefinus*), allied to, but smaller than, the cod, found on both sides of the Atlantic.

hade (hād), *n.* *Geol.* The angle made by a fault plane or a vein with the vertical. See FAULT, *Illust.* — *v. i.* *Geol.* To deviate from the vertical, as a vein, fault, or lode.

Ha'des (hā'dēz), *n.* [Gr. *Haidēs, haidēs.*] **1.** *Gr. Myth.* **a** See PLUTO. **b** The abode of the dead, a gloomy subterranean realm or a remote island beyond the Western Ocean. **2.** The abode or state of the dead; the place of departed spirits; — esp. in Revised Version of New Testament. **3.** [*sometimes not cap.*] *Colloq.* Hell.

hadj (hăj), *n.* [Ar. *ḥajj.*] A pilgrimage, esp. of a Moslem to Mecca.

hadj'i (hăj'ē), *n.* [Turk. *ḥājjī*, colloq. *ḥādjī*, fr. Ar. *ḥājj* pilgrim.] **a** A Moslem who has made his hadj; — sometimes prefixed as a title. **b** A Greek or Armenian who has visited the holy sepulcher at Jerusalem.

hae (*Scot.* hā, hă). *Obs. exc. Dial.* Var. of HAVE.

haem-, hae'ma-, haemat-, haem'a·to-, hae'mo-. Vars. of HEM-, HEMA-, HEMAT-, HEMATO-, HEMO-.

☞ The spelling *haem-* (from Greek *haima*, blood) is preferred in scientific names of botanical and zoological groups and derivatives. Otherwise, *hem-* is preferred.

haem'a·to·cry'al, hem'a·to·cry'al (hĕm'ȧ·tō·krī'ăl; hē'mȧ·tō-), *adj.* *Zool.* Cold-blooded, as reptiles and fishes.

haem'a·to·ther'mal, hem'a·to·ther'mal (-thûr'măl), *adj.* [*haemato-* + Gr. *thermos* warm.] *Zool.* Warm-blooded, as birds and mammals.

hae'ma·tox'y·lin, he'ma·tox'y·lin (hē'mȧ·tŏk'sĭ·lĭn; hĕm'ȧ-), *n.* [*haemato-* + Gr. *xylon* wood.] **1.** *Bot.* **a** Any of a genus (*Haematoxylon*) of tropical American trees of the senna family, containing the logwood. **b** The wood or a dye derived from the logwood. **2.** *Chem.* A colorless crystalline compound, $C_{16}H_{14}O_6$, occurring in logwood and easily oxidizable to the dye hematein. It is used as a stain in microscopy and as an indicator.

-hae'mi·a (-hē'mĭ·ȧ). Var. of -EMIA.

haet, hate (hāt), *n.* *Scot.* A whit; atom; bit.

haf'fet, haf'fit (hăf'ĕt; -ĭt), *n.* [AS. *healfhēafod* the fore part of the head, lit., halfhead.] *Scot. & Ir.* Cheek; temple.

ha'fiz (hä'fĭz), *n.* [Ar. *ḥāfiẓ*, lit., one who remembers.] A Moslem who knows the Koran by heart; — a title of respect.

haf'ni·um (hăf'nĭ·ŭm; hăf'-), *n.* [NL., fr. *Hafnia*, L. name of Copenhagen.] *Chem.* A quadrivalent metallic element discovered in 1922 in a Norwegian zircon. Symbol, *Hf*; at. no., 72; at. wt., 178.6.

haft (hȧft; 9), *n.* [AS. *hæft.*] A handle; usually, the hilt of a knife, sword, or dagger. — *v. t.* To set in, or furnish with, a haft.

haft (hȧft), *n.* [Origin obscure.] *Scot.* A place devoted to a settled use, as for pasture; also, a dwelling.

hag (hăg), *n.* [ME. *hagge, hegge*, witch, hag, fr. AS. *hægtesse.*] **1.** *Archaic.* A female demon, ghost, or goblin. **2.** A witch. **3.** An ugly old woman, esp. one of evil nature. **4.** = HAGFISH.

hag (hăg; hȧg; ȧg), *v. t.* *Obs.* To harass or terrify.

hag, *n.* [Scot. *hag* to cut. See HAGGLE.] *Scot. & Dial. Eng.* A part of a wood felled or marked off for felling.

hag, *n.* [ON. *högg* a ravine.] *Scot.* **a** A quagmire; marsh; bog. **b** A firm spot in a bog.

Ha'gar (hā'gär; hā'gẽr), *n.* [Heb. *Hāghār.*] *Bib.* An Egyptian concubine of Abraham and slave of Sarah, who was driven into the desert with her son Ishmael, because of Sarah's jealousy.

hag'ber'ry (hăg'bĕr'ĭ; -bĕr·ĭ), *n.* [Of Scand. origin.] The hackberry.

hag'born' (-bôrn'), *adj.* Born of a hag or witch.

hag'bush' (-bo͝osh'), *n.* The China tree.

hag'but (hăg'bŭt). Var. of HACKBUT.

hag'don (-dŭn), *n.* A shearwater; — applied to the several species of the North Atlantic by sailors.

Ha'gen (hä'gĕn), *n.* [G.] **a** In the *Nibelungenlied*, Gunther's uncle, who murders Siegfried. **b** In Wagner's *Ring of the Nibelung*, the half brother of Gunther, who tried to get Siegfried's ring.

hag'fish' (hăg'fĭsh'), *n.*; *pl.*, see FISH. Any of several slimy, eellike marine cyclostomes, the lowest existing craniate vertebrates, allied to the lampreys and constituting an order (Hyperotreta). Hagfishes devour other fishes.

hag·ga'da, hag·ga'dah (hȧ·gä'dȧ), *n.*; *pl.* -DOTH (-dōth). [Rabbinic Heb. *haggādāh*, fr. *higgīd* to relate.] **a** In Jewish rabbinical literature, a story, legend, or explanatory narration; hence [*cap.*], collectively, the nonlegal portion of Rabbinical literature. **b** [*cap.*] In a restricted sense, that exegesis or exposition of the Scriptures consisting chiefly in imaginative developments of thoughts suggested by the text, or a didactic or homiletic exposition. Cf. HALAKAH, MIDRASH. — **hag·gad'ic** (hȧ·găd'ĭk; -gä'dĭk), **hag·gad'i·cal** (-găd'ĭ·kăl; -gä'dĭ·kăl), *adj.*

hag·ga'dist (hȧ·gä'dĭst), *n.* A haggadic writer, or a student of the Haggada. — **hag'ga·dis'tic** (hăg'ȧ·dĭs'tĭk), *adj.*

Hag'ga·i (hăg'ā·ī), *n.* *Bib.* **a** A Hebrew prophet who flourished about 520 B.C. **b** A book of the Old Testament. See BIBLE.

hag'gard (hăg'ẽrd), *adj.* [MF. *hagard.*] **1.** Wild or intractable; untamed; — said esp., *Falconry*, of a hawk caught after acquiring adult plumage. **2.** Wild-eyed; later, esp., having the expression of one wasted by want, suffering, anxiety, or age; gaunt. — *n.* **1.** *Falconry.* A haggard hawk. **2.** *Obs.* An intractable person; a coy woman. — **hag'gard·ly,** *adv.* — **hag'gard·ness,** *n.*

hagged (hăgd; hăg'ĕd; -ĭd), *adj.* *Obs. exc. Dial.* **a** Bewitched; haglike. **b** Haggard; gaunt.

hag'gis (hăg'ĭs), *n.* *Scot.* A pudding made of the heart, liver, lights, etc., of a sheep or a calf, minced with suet, onions, oatmeal, etc., seasoned, and boiled in the stomach of the animal.

hag'gish (-ĭsh), *adj.* Like, or characteristic of, a hag.

hag'gle (hăg''l), *v. t.*; HAG'GLED (-'ld); HAG'GLING (-lĭng). [Freq. of Scot. *hag*, fr. ON. *höggva.*] **1.** To cut roughly; to hack. **2.** To subject to caviling or chaffering. — *v. i.* To wrangle; esp., to make difficulties in bargaining; to stickle. — *n.* Act of haggling. — **hag'gler** (-lẽr), *n.*

hag'i·arch'y (hăg'ĭ·är'kĭ; hā'jĭ-), *n.* Government by men in holy orders.

hag'i·o- (hăg'ĭ·ō-; hā'jĭ·ō-), **hagi-.** [Gr. *hagios.*] A combining form meaning *sacred, holy*, as in *hagio*logy.

Hag'i·og'ra·pha (-ŏg'rȧ·fȧ), *n. pl.* [LL., fr. Gr. *hagiographa*, fr. *hagios* holy + *graphein* to write.] The last of the three Jewish divisions of the Old Testament, or that portion not in the Law and the Prophets.

hag'i·og'ra·pher (-fẽr), *n.* One of the writers of the Hagiographa; also, a writer of lives of the saints.

hag'i·og'ra·phist (-fĭst), *n.* A hagiographer.

hag'i·og'ra·phy (hăg'ĭ·ŏg'rȧ·fĭ; hā'jĭ-), *n.* Biography of saints; saints' lives; hagiology. — **hag'i·o·graph'ic** (-ō·grăf'ĭk), **hag'i·o·graph'i·cal** (-ĭ·kăl), *adj.*

hag'i·ol'a·try (-ŏl'ȧ·trĭ), *n.* [*hagio-* + *-latry.*] The invocation or worship of saints. — **hag'i·ol'a·ter** (-tẽr), *n.* — **hag'i·ol'a·trous** (-trŭs), *adj.*

hag'i·ol'o·gy (hăg'ĭ·ŏl'ō·jĭ; hā'jĭ-), *n.*; *pl.* -GIES (-jĭz). [*hagio-* + *-logy.*] The history of the sacred writings or of sacred persons; a narrative of the lives of the saints; a catalogue of saints. — **hag'i·o·log'ic** (-ō·lŏj'ĭk), **hag'i·o·log'i·cal** (-ĭ·kăl), *adj.* — **hag'i·ol'o·gist** (-ŏl'ō·jĭst), *n.*

hag'i·o·scope' (hăg'ĭ·ō·skōp'; hā'jĭ·ō-), *n.* [*hagio-* + *-scope.*] An opening in the interior walls of a cruciform church to afford a view of the altar to those in the transepts. — **hag'i·o·scop'ic** (-skŏp'ĭk), *adj.*

hag'ride' (hăg'rīd'), *v. t.*; see RIDE. To ride or harass (a person) in the manner of a hag, or witch.

hag'seed' (-sēd'), *n.* Offspring of a hag.

ha'-ha' (hä'hä'), *n.* [F. *haha.*] A sunk fence, wall, or ditch.

Hai'duk (hī'do͝ok), *n.* Also **Hey'duck, -duke, -duc,** etc. [G. *haiduck, heiduck*, fr. Hung. *hajduk*, pl.] **1.** One of the bandit mountaineers among the Balkan Slavs; also, in Hungary, one of a class of mercenary foot soldiers who received privileges of nobility and local independence in 1605. **2. a** In Hungary and Poland, a domestic in the household of a noble. **b** Formerly, in France, an outrider in Hungarian costume.

haik (hīk; hāk), *n.* [Ar. *ḥayk*, fr. *ḥāka* to weave.] A piece of cloth worn in North Africa as an outer garment.

hai'kwan' (hī'kwän'), *n.* [Chin. (Pek.) *hai³-kuan¹*, lit., sea gate.] Chinese maritime customs.

haikwan tael. **a** A Chinese weight (1⁄16 catty) equivalent to 1⅓ oz. or 37.80 g. **b** The former Chinese customs unit upon which the other local taels were based. It was superseded 1935 by establishment of the yuan, or Chinese dollar, as legal tender. See TAEL, YUAN.

hail (hāl), *n.* [AS. *hægel, hagol.*] **1.** Small, roundish lumps of ice precipitated during thunderstorms. International symbol, ▲. **2.** *Now Rare.* A hailstorm. **3.** Hence, a shower of anything likened to hail; as, a *hail* of bullets. — *v. i.* To precipitate hail. — *v. t.* To shower forcibly down, as hail.

hail, *v. t.* [From ME. *heil, hail*, n. & adj., used in greeting, fr. ON. *heill* hale, sound.] **1.** To salute, as by saying "hail"; to greet; also, with a complementary object, to name in greeting; as, they *hailed* him king. **2.** To call loudly to, or after. — *v. i.* *Chiefly Naut.* To call out in order to attract attention, extend greetings, etc. — ***hail from.*** To come, or claim to come, from as one's home or home port; as, to *hail from* Nantucket. — *interj.* An exclamation expressing respectful or reverent salutation or, occasionally, familiar greeting. — *n.* **1.** Act of hailing; a salutation. **2.** Hailing distance; as, within *hail.* — **hail'er,** *n.*

hail. *Chiefly Scot.* Var. of HALE, *adj.*

hail fellow, *or* **hail'-fel'low.** A phrase used as an adjective, noun, or adverb, signifying familiarity or comradeship. The phrase **hail fellow well met,** *or* **hail'-fel'low-well'-met',** is similarly used; as, to be *hail fellow well met* with everyone.

Hail Mary. = AVE MARIA, 1 & 3.

hail′stone′ (hāl′stōn′), *n.* [AS. *hagolstān.*] A pellet of hail.

hail′storm′ (-stôrm′), *n.* A storm accompanied with hail.

hair (hâr), *n.* [AS. *hǣr.*] **1.** A slender threadlike outgrowth of an animal; esp., one of the filaments which form the characteristic coat of mammals; also, the coat or some part of it, esp. that of the human head. **2.** Any very small distance, degree, or quantity. **3.** Fabric made of hair; haircloth; a mat of such fabric. **4.** *Bot.* A slender outgrowth of the epidermis.

hair′breadth′ (-brĕdth′), *n.* Also **hairs′breadth′** (hârz′-). The diameter or breadth of a hair; a very small distance.

hair′breadth′, *adj.* Very narrow; as, a *hairbreadth* escape.

hair′brush′ (-brŭsh′), *n.* A brush for the hair.

hair′cloth′ (-klŏth′; 74), *n.* A fabric of camel's hair or horsehair, used for furniture covering, stiffening, etc.

hair′cut′ (-kŭt′), *n.* The act, process, or style of cutting the hair. — **hair′cut′ter**, *n.* — **hair′cut′ting**, *n. & adj.*

hair′do′ (-dōō′), *n.; pl.* HAIRDOS (-dōōz′). A way of dressing the hair; coiffure.

hair′dress′er (-drĕs′ẽr), *n.* One who dresses or cuts hair. — **hair′dress′ing**, *n. & adj.*

hair′less (-lĕs; -lĭs), *adj.* Having no hair.

hair′line′ (-līn′), *n.* **1.** A very slender line, as in a type. **2.** In textiles, a narrow color striping, or striped cloth. **3.** Outline of the scalp, or of the growth of hair on a head.

hair′pin′ (-pĭn′), *n.* A pin, usually forked, used for fastening the hair, or a headdress, in place. — *adj.* Designating a sharp complete turn, as in a road.

hair shirt. A shirt of horsehair, worn as a penance.

hair space. *Print.* The thinnest metal space made by type founders, commonly 6 to the em.

hair′split′ter (hâr′splĭt′ẽr), *n.* One who makes excessively nice or needless distinctions in reasoning; a quibbler. — **hair′split′ting**, *adj. & n.*

hair′spring′ (-sprĭng′), *n.* *Horol.* The slender recoil spring which regulates the motion of the balance.

hair′streak′ (-strēk′), *n.* Any of certain small butterflies (*Thecla* and allied genera, family Lycaenidae) with striped markings under the wings. The ***purple hairstreak*** (*T. halesus*) has wings bluish-green above.

hair stroke. A delicate stroke in writing or printing.

hair trigger. *Firearms.* A trigger so adjusted as to permit the piece to be fired by a very slight pressure.

hair′-trig′ger (hâr′trĭg′ẽr), *adj.* *Colloq.* Acting, or operative, under a slight provocation; easily moved.

hair′y (hâr′ĭ), *adj.;* HAIR′I·ER (-ĭ·ẽr); HAIR′I·EST. Bearing, or covered with, hair; made of, or like, hair; hirsute. — **hair′i·ness**, *n.*

haj′i, haj′ji. Vars. of HADJI.

hake (hāk), *n.;* see PLURAL, *Note,* 3. **1.** Any of several fishes (genus *Merluccius*), allied to the cods. The New England ***silver hake*** (*M. bilinearis*) is an important food fish. **2.** Any of certain marine codlike fishes (*Phycis* and allied genera) having filamentous pelvic fins under the throat; — called also *codling.* The ***white hake*** (*P. tenuis*) and the common ***squirrel hake*** (*P. chuss*) are valued as food, for their oil, etc.

ha·keem′, ha·kim′ (hȧ·kēm′), *n.* [Ar. *ḥakīm,* lit., wise one.] In Moslem countries, a physician.

ha′ken·kreuz′ (hä′kĕn·kroits′), *n.* [G., lit., hook-cross.] Swastika; — used in Germany, Austria, etc., from 1918 as a symbol of anti-Semitism or as the emblem of organizations (**Ha′ken·kreuz′ler** [-lẽr]) of extreme nationalist tendencies. See SWASTIKA.

ha′kim (hä′kēm), *n.* [Ar. *ḥākim.*] In Moslem countries, a ruler or a judge.

ha′la·kah′, ha′la·cha′ (hä′lä·kä′; hä·lä′kä), *n.; pl.* -KOTH, -CHOTH (-kōth′; -kōth). [Rabbinic Heb. *hălākhāh* practice, rule.] *Rabbinical Lit.* Literally, usage or custom; hence [*cap.*], the Jewish oral laws supplementing or explaining the law of the Scriptures, or these laws as later reduced to writings; also [*not cap.*], a single tradition or law. Cf. HAGGADA, MIDRASH. — **ha′la·kist, ha′la·chist** (hä′lȧ·kĭst; hȧ·lä′kĭst), *n.*

ha·la′tion (hă·lā′shŭn; hă-), *n.* [See HALO.] *Photog.* A spreading of light beyond its proper boundaries, such as may appear, in an interior view, around a window facing the sky.

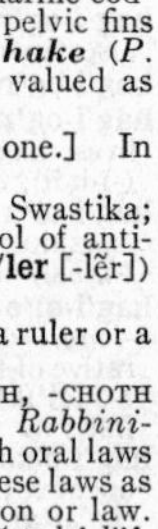

Head of a Halberd.

hal′berd (hăl′bẽrd; *formerly* hôl′bẽrd, hô′-), **hal′bert** (-bẽrt), *n.* [F. *hallebarde, alabarde,* fr. It., fr. MHG. *helmbarte* (G. *hellebarde*).] *Mil.* A kind of long-handled weapon, esp. in use in the 15th and 16th centuries. — **hal′berd·ier′** (hăl′bẽr·dēr′), *n.*

hal′cy·on (hăl′sĭ·ŭn), *n.* [L. *halcyon, alcyon,* fr. Gr. *halkyōn, alkyōn,* kingfisher.] A bird, identified with the kingfisher, fabled to nest at sea about the winter solstice and calm the waves; hence, *Poetic,* the kingfisher. — *adj.* Relating to, or like, the halcyon; hence, calm; peaceful.

hale (hāl), *v. t.* [ME. *halen.*] To haul; draw; hence, to compel to go along; as, to *hale* one to prison.

hale (hāl), *adj.* Also **hail** (hāl). [AS. *hāl.*] Free from defect, disease, or infirmity; sound; healthy. — **Syn.** See HEALTHY.

ha′ler (hä′lẽr), *n.; pl.* HALERU (-ōō). [Czech, fr. MHG. *haller, heller.*] = HELLER **b.**

half (hăf; hȧf; 9), *n.; pl.* HALVES (hävz; hȧvz). [AS. *healf* half.] **1.** One of two equal parts of anything. **2.** Hence, a part of anything approximately equal to the remainder; as, the larger *half* of one's fortune. **3.** *Golf.* The same score as the opponent on a hole or round. **4.** *Football, etc.* Either of the equal divisions of a game, between which the players rest. — *adj.* **1.** Consisting of a moiety, or one of two equal parts. **2.** Consisting of a portion that may or may not be an exact half; hence, partial; imperfect. **3.** *Bookbinding.* Half-bound in a (specified) material; as, *half* calf. — *adv.* **1.** In an equal part or degree; also, partly; imperfectly. **2.** With a negative: Not by a great deal; very little or not at all. **3.** In various idiomatic uses, as in expressing the time of day, in which the English idiom is *half past* or *half after,* that is, half an hour past or after the hour named.

half′-and-half′, *n.* That which is half one thing and half another; specif., a mixture of two malt liquors, esp. porter and ale, in about equal parts. — *adj.* Half one thing and half another. — *adv.* In equal measure or in equal parts.

half′back′ (hăf′băk′; hȧf′-), *n.* *Football.* One of the backs.

half′-baked′ (-bākt′; 2), *adj.* **1.** Baked imperfectly. **2.** *Colloq.* **a** Not thought out completely. **b** Lacking in intelligence and experience.

half binding. A book binding in which the material of the back and sometimes the corners is different from that of the sides. — **half′-bound′** (-bound′; 2), *adj.*

half blood, *or* **half′-blood′**, *n.* **1.** (In this sense always *half blood.*) The relation between persons having one parent, but not both, in common; as, a brother or sister of the *half blood.* **2.** A person so related to another. **3.** A half-breed.

half′-blood′ed (hăf′blŭd′ĕd; -ĭd; hȧf′-), *adj.* Having half blood; also, having one parent of good and one of inferior stock; as, a *half-blooded* sheep.

half boot. A boot with a top somewhat above the ankle.

half′-bred′, *adj.* Half-blooded. — *n.* A half-bred animal.

half′-breed′, *n.* The offspring of parents of different races, esp., *U. S.,* of the American Indian and the white race. — *adj.* Half-blooded.

half brother. A boy or man related to a brother or sister through one parent only.

half′-caste′, *n.* **1.** One born of a European parent on the one side, and of a Hindu or Mohammedan on the other. **2.** One born of two distinct races; a half-breed. — *adj.* Of the rank of, or pertaining to, a half-caste or half-castes.

half cock. The position of the hammer of a gun when about half retracted and held by the sear so that it cannot be operated by a pull on the trigger. Cf. 1st COCK, *n.,* 6; COCK, *v. i. & t.*

half′cocked′ (-kŏkt′; 2), *adj.* **a** At half cock. **b** *Colloq., U. S.* Figuratively, not fully prepared.

half crown. An English coin, originally of gold, but now of silver, worth 2s. 6d. See MONEY, *Tables.*

half dollar. *U. S. & Canada.* Fifty cents, a half of a dollar; also, a silver coin of this value.

half eagle. *U. S.* A five-dollar gold piece.

half gainer. *Fancy Diving.* A dive executed as a back dive, with or without an accompanying jackknife, but from a front-dive take-off position. Cf. GAINER, 2.

half′heart′ed (hăf′här′tĕd; -tĭd; hȧf′-; 2), *adj.* Wanting in heart or interest. — **half′heart′ed·ly**, *adv.* — **half′heart′ed·ness**, *n.*

half hitch. *Naut.* A simple knot or noose, so made as to be easily unfastened. See KNOT, *Illust.* (19, 20).

half hose. Short stockings; socks.

half′-hour′, *n.* The mid point of an hour. — **half′-hour′**, *adj.* — **half′-hour′ly**, *adj. & adv.*

half′-length′ (*see Pron.,* § 2), *adj.* Of half the full length; specif., designating a portrait showing only the upper half of the person. — **half′-length′**, *n.*

half life, half′-life′ pe′ri·od. *Physical Chem.* The time required for half of the atoms of a radioactive element present to become disintegrated. Since there will still be one quarter of the element left at the end of two half-life periods and one eighth at the end of three, etc., the time for complete disintegration of the element is indefinitely large.

half′-light′, *n.* The grayish light of dim interiors, evening, mist, etc. — **half′-light′**, *adj.*

half′-long′ (hăf′lŏng′; hȧf′-; 2), *adj.* *Phonet.* Having to a recognizable degree the quality of the so-called long vowel (ā, ē, ō, ū) but shortened in duration by occurrence in an unaccented syllable (in Merriam-Webster dictionaries indicated by the symbols ȧ, ė, ȯ, ů). Cf. §§ 12, 35, 79, 118 in the *Guide to Pronunciation.*

half′-mast′ (*see Pron.,* § 2), *n.* A point some distance, not necessarily halfway down, below the top of a mast or staff or peak of a gaff; as, a flag at *half-mast* (a token of mourning, or, sometimes, of distress). — *v. t.* To hang at half-mast, as a flag. In lowering a half-masted flag it is first hoisted to the truck.

half′-moon′, *n.* **1.** The moon at the quarters, when half its disk appears illuminated. **2.** Something shaped like a half-moon or like a crescent. — **half′-moon′**, *adj.*

half mourning. **a** The period of mourning succeeding that of deep mourning. **b** Mourning dress lightened by the use of white, gray, or lavender.

half nelson. *Wrestling.* A hold in which one arm is thrust under the corresponding arm of the opponent, generally from behind, and the hand placed upon the back of his neck.

half note. *Music.* See NOTE, *n.*

half pay. Half, or approximately half, of the usual wages or salary; reduced pay; specif., the reduced pay of an army or navy officer when not on active service. — **half′-pay′** (-pā′; 2), *adj.*

half′pen·ny (hā′pĕn·ĭ; hăp′nĭ; hăf′pĕn′ĭ *is a mere spelling pron.*), *n.; pl.* -PENCE (hā′pĕns) or -PENNIES (hā′pĕn·ĭz; hăp′nĭz) (see PENNY). *Eng.* Half a penny, or a coin of this value. — **half′pen·ny**, *adj.*

half relief (hăf; hȧf). See RELIEF, *n.,* 6.

half sister. A girl or woman related to a brother or sister through one parent only.

half sole. A shoe sole extending from the shank forward; a tap. — **half′-sole′**, *v. t.*

half sovereign. A British gold coin worth ten shillings.

half′-staff′, *n.* Half-mast.

half step. **a** *Mil.* In the United States infantry, a step of fifteen inches, or, in double time, of eighteen inches. **b** *Music.* The smallest pitch interval used in modern music, produced by sounding any two adjacent keys on a keyboard instrument; semitone.

half tide. Time or state halfway between flood and ebb.

half′-tim′bered, *adj.* *Arch.* Constructed of a timber frame having the spaces filled in with masonry or with plaster on laths; — said of buildings.

half title. *Print.* The name of a book placed at the head of the first page of text; or a title, as of a subdivision, standing alone on a page introducing the subdivision.

half tone, *or, esp. Photoengraving,* **half′tone′** (hăf′tōn′; hȧf′-), *n.* **1.** *Fine Arts.* **a** An intermediate tone in a painting, engraving, photograph, etc.; a middle tint, neither very dark nor very light. **b** A halftone photoengraving. **2.** *Music.* A half step.

half′tone′ (hăf′tōn′; hȧf′-), *adj.* Having, consisting of, or pertaining to or designating plates, processes, or pictures in which the gradation of tone in the photograph is reproduced by spots caused by interposing a screen between the sensitive surface and the object.

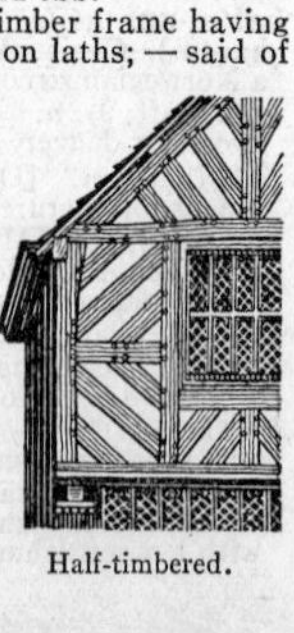

Half-timbered.

half′-track′, *n.* Also **half′track′** (hăf′trăk′; hȧf′-). **a** A chain-track drive system consisting of an endless metal belt driven by one of two inside sprockets, running on bogie wheels mounted on the frame, and laying down on the ground as it revolves a flexible track of cleated steel or hard rubber plates and serving, one on each side, to propel a vehicle supported in front by a pair of wheels. **b** *U. S. Army.* An armored personnel carrier equipped with half-tracks in the rear and wheels forward, and armed. — **half′-track′, half′-tracked′** (-trăkt′), *adj.*

half′-truth′, *n.* A statement of part of the facts, the remaining facts being purposely suppressed; an incomplete recital, — usually intended to evade blame, or to deceive. "Putting her off with *half-truths.*" *Stephen McKenna.* — **half′-truth′**, *adj.*

half volley. In cricket, tennis, football, etc., a "ball" or return played by striking the ball at the instant of its bouncing from the ground. — **half′-vol′ley**, *v. t. & i.*

half′way′ (hăf′wā′; hȧf′-; 2), *adj.* Midway between points, conditions, etc.; partial. — *adv.* In the middle; partially.

half′-wit′, *n.* A foolish person; a dolt.

half′-wit′ted (*see Pron.*, § 2), *adj.* Mentally deficient; imbecile. — **half′-wit′ted·ly**, *adv.* — **half′-wit′ted·ness**, *n.*

hal′i·but (hăl′ĭ·bŭt; hŏl′-), *n.*; see PLURAL, *Note*, 6. Also **hol′i·but.** [ME. *hali* holy + *but, butte,* flounder; as being eaten on holy days.] **a** The largest species of flatfish (*Hippoglossus hippoglossus*), one of the finest of food fishes, found in northern seas. The halibut is among the largest of teleost fishes, the female sometimes weighing several hundred pounds. **b** The flesh of this fish cooked and served as food.

hal′ide (hăl′īd; -ĭd; hā′līd; -lĭd), *n.* Also **hal′id.** [*halogen* + *-ide, -id.*] *Chem.* A binary compound (a chloride, bromide, iodide, or fluoride) of a halogen with an element or radical. — *adj.* Haloid.

hal′i·dom (hăl′ĭ·dŭm), **hal′i·dome** (-dōm), *n.* [AS. *hāligdōm,* fr. *hālig* holy + *-dōm.* See -DOM.] *Archaic.* Holiness; sanctity; also a sanctuary or holy relics.

hal′ite (hăl′īt; hā′līt), *n.* [Gr. *hals* salt.] *Mineral.* Native salt.

hal′i·to′sis (hăl′ĭ·tō′sĭs), *n.* [NL., fr. L. *halitus* breath + *-osis.*] *Med.* Condition of having foul or offensive breath.

hal′i·tus (hăl′ĭ·tŭs), *n.* [L., fr. *halare* to breathe.] Exhalation; breath; vapor.

Hal′iv′er (hăl′ĭv′ẽr; -ĭ·vẽr), *n.* A trade-mark applied to an oil obtained from the liver of the halibut. Its use is similar to that of cod-liver oil.

hall (hôl), *n.* [AS. *heal, heall.*] **1.** The public dwelling of a Teutonic chieftain. **2.** *Chiefly Brit.* The manor house of a landed proprietor. **3.** [*sometimes cap.*] A large building used for public or semipublic purposes; often, specif., a town hall. **4.** [*sometimes cap.*] *Colleges & Universities.* **a** At Oxford and Cambridge: Orig., any university building for the residence or instruction of students; now, a building for the use of students in university branches who may or may not have university privileges; in both these senses, the institution formed by the officers and members or residents of such a hall. **b** In the United States, a college building devoted to any special purpose; as, Science *Hall.* **5.** An assembly room. **6.** [*sometimes cap.*] The common dining apartment at an English university; hence, the dinner. **7.** The entrance room of a building; also, a corridor or passage.

hal′lan (hăl′ăn; häl′ăn), *n.* *Scot. & Ir.* A partition in a cottage, esp. between the door and the fireplace.

hal·lel′ (hȧ·lāl′; hăl′ĕl), *n.* [Heb. *hallēl* praise.] *Jewish Ritual.* A selection of certain psalms of praise.

hal′le·lu′jah, hal′le·lu′iah (hăl′ē·lōō′yȧ), *n. & interj.* [Heb. *hallĕlū-yāh.* See ALLELUIA.] Praise ye Yah (*Jehovah*); praise ye the Lord; — an exclamation used chiefly in songs of praise.

hal′liard (hăl′yẽrd). Var. of HALYARD.

hall′mark′ (hôl′märk′), *n.* Also **hall mark.** The official mark stamped on gold and silver articles at Goldsmiths' Hall in London to attest their purity; hence, any mark similarly used.

hall′mark′, *v. t.* Also **hall′-mark′.** To stamp with a hallmark. — **hall′mark′er** (-mär′kẽr), *n.*

hal·lo′, hal·loa′ (hă·lō′). Vars. of HOLLO.

hal·loo′ (hă·lōō′), *interj.* A shout or call to incite an animal or attract attention. — **hal·loo′** (hă·lōō′; hăl′ōō), *n.*

hal·loo′ (hă·lōō′), *v. i.* [Prob. fr. earlier *hallow,* fr. OF. *halloer* to pursue with shouts.] To cry out, as by shouting *Halloo!* — *v. t.*; HAL·LOOED′ (-lōōd′); HAL·LOO′ING. **1.** To encourage, or incite, with shouts. **2.** To call or shout to; to hail. **3.** To shout loudly.

hal′low (hăl′ō), *v. t.* [AS. *hālgian,* fr. *hālig* holy.] To make holy; to consecrate. — **Syn.** See DEVOTE.

hal′low (hăl′ō), *n.* Halloo. — **hal′low**, *v.*

hal·low′ (hă·lō′), *interj.* Halloo!

hal′lowed (hăl′ōd; *in the solemn or liturgical style often* hăl′ō·ĕd), *adj.* Blessed; consecrated.

Hal′low·een′ (hăl′ō·ēn′; *sometimes* hŏl′-), *n.* The evening preceding Allhallows, or All Saints' Day; the evening of October 31.

Hal′low·mas (hăl′ō·mȧs), *n.* The feast of Allhallows.

Hall′statt civ′i·li·za′tion (hôl′stăt; *G.* häl′shtät). A prehistoric civilization of central Europe, dated from about 1000 B.C. (or 1500 B.C.) to about 500 B.C. (**Hallstatt epoch**), usually associated with the Celtic or Alpine race. It was characterized by expert use of bronze, knowledge of iron, possession of domestic animals, agriculture, and skill in making pottery, etc.

hal·lu′ci·nate (hă·lū′sĭ·nāt), *v. t. & i.* [L. *hallucinatus, alucinatus,* past part. of *hallucinari, alucinari,* to wander in mind, dream, fr. Gr. *alyein* to wander in mind.] To affect or be affected with visions or imaginary perceptions.

hal·lu′ci·na′tion (hă·lū′sĭ·nā′shŭn), *n.* **1.** Perception of objects with no reality, or experience of sensations with no external cause, usually arising from disorder of the nervous system, as in delirium tremens. **2.** The object of a hallucinatory perception. — **Syn.** See DELUSION.

hal·lu′ci·na·to′ry (hă·lū′sĭ·nȧ·tō′rĭ *or, esp. Brit.,* -tẽr·ĭ), *adj.* Partaking of, or tending to produce, hallucination.

hal·lu′ci·no′sis (-nō′sĭs), *n.* *Psychiatry.* Mental disorder characterized by hallucinations.

hal′lux (hăl′ŭks), *n.*; *pl.* -LUCES (-ū·sēz). [NL., fr. L. *hallex, allex.*] *Anat. & Zool.* The first, or preaxial, digit of the hind limb; in man, the great toe; in birds, the hind toe.

hall′way′ (hôl′wā′), *n.* *U. S.* An entrance hall; a corridor.

halm (hôm). Var. of HAULM.

ha′lo (hā′lō), *n.*; *pl.* HALOS, HALOES (-lōz). [L. *halos,* acc. *halo,* fr. Gr. *halōs* a threshing floor, also, disk of the sun or moon, and later a halo round it.] **1.** A circle of light, appearing to surround a luminous body. International symbols: solar halo, ⨁; lunar halo, ▽. **2.** The glory investing an object idealized by sentiment; as, the *halo* surrounding medieval chivalry. **3.** *Art.* A glory; nimbus. — *v. t. & i.* To form, or surround with, a halo.

hal′o·gen (hăl′ō·jĕn; *sometimes* hā′lō-), *n.* [Gr. *hals, halos,* the sea, salt + *-gen.*] *Chem.* An element or nonoxygenated radical (chlorine, bromine, iodine, fluorine, and cyanogen) which forms salts by direct union with metals. — **ha·log′e·nous** (hȧ·lŏj′ē·nŭs), *adj.*

hal′o·gen·ate (hăl′ō·jĕn·āt), *v. t.* *Chem.* To combine with halogen; to subject to the action of a halogen. — **hal′o·gen·a′tion** (-jĕ·nā′shŭn), *n.*

hal′oid (hăl′oid; hā′loid), *adj.* [Gr. *hals, halos,* salt + *-oid.*] *Chem.* Resembling salt. — *n.* A halide.

hal′o·phyte (hăl′ō·fīt), *n.* [Gr. *hals, halos,* salt + *-phyte.*] *Bot.* A plant which grows naturally in soil impregnated with salts, as that of the seacoast or alkaline deserts. Cf. MESOPHYTE, XEROPHYTE. — **hal′o·phyt′ic** (-fĭt′ĭk), *adj.*

halt (hôlt), *n.* [Sp. *alto* and F. *halte,* both fr. G. *halt,* fr. *halten* to hold.] A stop in marching or walking, or in any action; arrest of progress. — *v. i.* To cease progress; to stop. — *v. t.* To cause to cease marching; to stop.

halt, *adj.* [AS. *healt.*] Having a halting walk; lame. — *n.* Act of limping; lameness. — *v. i.* **1.** To limp. **2.** To stand in doubt whether to proceed, or what to do. **3.** To be imperfect in the relating of the successive steps; as, a *halting* argument.

hal′ter (hôl′tẽr), *n.* [AS. *hælfter.*] **1.** A rope or strap, with or without a headstall, for leading or tying an animal. **2.** A noose; hence, death by hanging. **3.** A woman's waist, esp. for sports wear, held in place by straps about the neck and across the back, leaving the arms and back exposed. — *v. t.* **1.** To catch with or as if with a halter; to put a halter on, as a horse. **2.** To put a hangman's halter on; to hang.

hal′ter (hăl′tẽr), *n.*; *pl.* HALTERES (hăl·tē′rēz). [NL., fr. Gr. *haltēr,* pl. *haltēres,* leaping weight.] In dipterous insects, one of a pair of club-shaped organs believed to be sense organs and to assist in balancing.

halt′ing (hôl′tĭng), *adj.* Lame; limping. — **halt′ing·ly**, *adv.*

halve (häv; hȧv; 9), *v. t.* **1.** To divide into two equal parts; to share equally with; also, to reduce to one half. **2.** *Golf.* Of a hole, match, etc., to reach or play in the same number of strokes as an opponent.

halves (hävz; hȧvz), *n.*, *pl.* of HALF.

hal′yard (hăl′yẽrd), *n.* [For earlier *hallier,* prop., a puller or hauler, fr. *hale,* v.] *Naut.* A rope or tackle for hoisting and lowering yards, sails, flags, etc.

ham (hăm), *n.* [AS.] **1.** *Anat.* **a** The region behind the knee joint. **b** In quadrupeds, the hock. **2.** The thigh and buttock; — usually *pl.* **3.** The thigh of any animal, esp. a hog, prepared for food. See PORK, *Illust.* **4.** *Slang.* **a** An amateur, inexperienced, or bungling actor or performer of any sort; hence, **ham actor**, esp. a self-assertive, affected strutter. **b** A government-licensed operator of an amateur radio station. — *v. i. & t.*; HAMMED (hămd); HAM′MING. *Slang.* To play (as a part or scene) in an artificial, affected, or inflated style.

Ham (hăm), *n.* *Bib.* The youngest son of Noah.

ham′a·dry′ad (hăm′ȧ·drī′ăd; -ăd), *n.*; *pl.* -DRYADS (-ădz; -ădz), -DRYADES (-drī′ȧ·dēz). [L. *Hamadryas, -adis,* fr. Gr. *Hamadryas,* fr. *hama* together with + *drys* oak, tree.] **1.** *Gr. Myth.* A dryad. **2. a** The king cobra. See COBRA. **b** The sacred baboon.

ha·mal′ (hȧ·mäl′; -môl′), *n.* Also **ham·mal′, ha·maul′**, etc. [From Ar. *ḥammāl* carrier, porter, partly through Turk. *ḥamāl.*] In the Orient, a porter or burden bearer.

ham′a·me′li·da′ceous (hăm′ȧ·mē′lĭ·dā′shŭs; -mĕl′ĭ·dā′-), *adj.* [Gr. *hamamēlis* a kind of medlar or service tree.] *Bot.* Belonging to the witch-hazel family (Hamamelidaceae). See WITCH HAZEL.

Ha′man (hā′măn), *n.* *Bib.* An enemy of the Jews, hanged on the gallows prepared for Mordecai.

Ham′ble·to′ni·an (hăm′b'l·tō′nĭ·ăn), *n.* A superior race or strain of American trotting horses descended from a stallion called Hambletonian (1849–76).

Ham′burg (hăm′bûrg), *n.* [From *Hamburg,* Ger.] A European breed of rather small domestic fowls with rose combs and lead-blue legs.

ham′burg·er (hăm′bûr·gẽr) *or* **ham′burg**, *n.* **1.** = HAMBURG STEAK. **2.** A patty of Hamburg steak. **3.** A sandwich consisting of a patty of Hamburg steak typically between the halves of a round flat roll.

Ham′burg steak (hăm′bûrg). [*sometimes not cap.*] **a** Finely ground or chopped beef. **b** This meat when cooked.

hame (hām), *n.* [AS. *hama* a cover, skin.] One of the two curved pieces in heavy-draft harness, to which the traces are fastened.

Ham′ite (hăm′īt), *n.* **1.** A descendant of Ham, Noah's youngest son. *Gen.* x. 6–20. **2.** *Ethnol.* A member of the chief native race of North Africa. The Hamites are Caucasians, characterized by tall stature, dark, or even black skin, wavy hair, and oval face.

Ham·it′ic (hăm·ĭt′ĭk; hă·mĭt′-), *adj.* Of or pertaining to the Hamites, or the family of languages (**Hamitic languages**) which includes ancient Egyptian, Coptic, and various modern languages. See LANGUAGE, *Table.* — *n.* Any of the Hamitic languages.

ham′let (hăm′lĕt; -lĭt), *n.* [OF. *hamelet,* dim. of *hamel* (F. *hameau*), fr. *ham,* of Teut. origin.] A little cluster of houses in the country, esp. belonging to a parish or village.

ham′let, *n.* A large grouper (*Epinephelus striatus*) common from Key West to Brazil and at Bermuda.

Ham′let (hăm′lĕt; -lĭt), *n.* The title and hero of a tragedy (1602?) by Shakespeare.

ham′mer (hăm′ẽr), *n.* [AS. *hamer, hamor.*] **1.** An instrument for driving nails, beating metals, and the like, consisting of a head, usually of steel, fixed crosswise to a handle. **2.** Something in form or action resembling or likened to a hammer; as: **a** A lever for ringing a bell or striking a gong. **b** Any of the padded mallets in a piano action for striking the wires. **3.** A gavel with which an auctioneer indicates that an

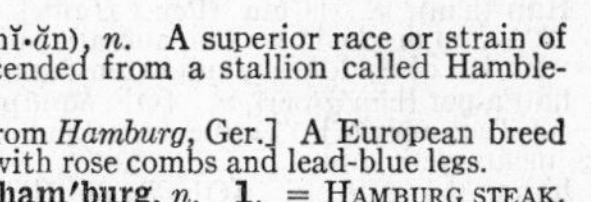

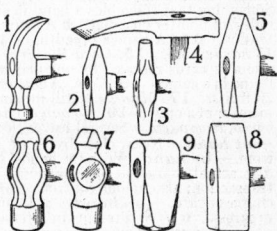

Hammers, 1. 1 Claw; 2 Riveting; 3 Boilermaker's; 4 Bricklayer's; 5 Blacksmith's; 6 Machinist's with Ball Peen; 7 Machinist's with Cross Peen; 8 Stone or Spalling; 9 Prospecting.

article is sold to the last bidder; hence, an auction sale. **4.** *Anat.* The malleus. **5.** *Athletics.* A spherical weight attached to a flexible handle and hurled from a circle. **6.** *Firearms.* That part of a gunlock which strikes the percussion cap, or firing pin; the cock. See GUNLOCK, *Illust.* **7.** *Mach.* A machine, esp. a power-driven machine, in which a block of metal or other hard substance is used to strike something, as the work in forging or striking up metal. — *v. t.* **1.** To beat, strike, or shape with a hammer; to beat with heavy blows. **2.** To fasten or build with a hammer, as by nailing. **3.** To produce by repeated blows; as, to *hammer* out a tune on the piano; also, to formulate or create as if by hammer strokes. **4.** To force or drive as if by repeated blows from a hammer. — *v. i.* To strike repeated blows as with a hammer; to make reiterated efforts. — **ham′mer·er,** *n.*

hammer and sickle. An emblem consisting of a crossed sickle and hammer, used as a symbol of peasant and worker and adopted (1923) by the U.S.S.R. on its national flag.

hammer and tongs. *Colloq.* With great force and violence.

ham′mered work (hăm′ẽrd). *Art.* Work in thin metal, as repoussé work, where plate is beaten up by hand.

ham′mer·head′ (hăm′ẽr·hĕd′), *n.* Any of certain active voracious sharks found in warm seas, and having the sides of the head produced into long flat processes, which bear the eyes. With the shovelhead, they constitute a family (Sphyrnidae).

ham′mer·less, *adj.* *Firearms.* Without a visible hammer; — of a gun having a firing pin or striker inside the lock.

hammer lock. *Wrestling.* A hold in which a wrestler's arm is held twisted and bent behind his back by his opponent.

ham′mer·toe′ (hăm′ẽr·tō′), *n.* *Med.* **a** A toe deformed by permanent angular flexion. **b** The deformity of a foot with one or more such toes.

ham′mock (hăm′ŭk), *n.* [Sp. *hamaca,* of Arawakan origin.] A swinging couch, usually of netting or canvas, suspended by cords at each end.

ham′mock, *n.* [Var. of HUMMOCK.] In the southern U. S., esp. in Florida, an area with deep, rich soil and hardwood vegetation.

ham′per (hăm′pẽr), *n.* [From HANAPER.] A large basket, usually with a cover; as, a *hamper* of wine.

ham′per, *v. t.* [ME. *hampren.*] To put a hamper or fetter on; to shackle; hence, to impede; encumber.

Syn. **Hamper, trammel, clog, fetter, shackle, manacle** mean to impede one so that he cannot move or act freely. **Hamper** implies embarrassment by an impediment or restraining influence; **trammel,** an entangling and restraining, as if enmeshed in a net; **clog,** a hampering of movement, often of efforts to ascend, by something that weights one down; **fetter,** a confining or restraining so that one's freedom or power to progress is almost lost; **shackle** and **manacle,** such interference with one's freedom that if one is to make headway the bonds must be broken.

— *n.* *Naut.* Articles ordinarily indispensable, but in the way at certain times.

Hamp′shire Down (hămp′shĭr; -shẽr). Also **Hamp′shire,** *n.* A breed of Down sheep which are large, thick-fleshed and hornless.

ham′ster (hăm′stẽr), *n.* [G.] Any of several thick-bodied, short-tailed Old World rodents (of *Cricetus* and allied genera) having very large cheek pouches. The ***golden hamster*** (*C. auratus*) is much used in medical research.

ham′string′ (hăm′strĭng′), *n.* [*ham* + *string.*] **a** In man, either of two groups of tendons at the back of the knee. **b** In quadrupeds, the large tendon above and behind the hock. — *v. t.;* see STRING. To lame or disable by cutting the hamstring; hence, to cripple; disable.

ham′u·lus (hăm′ū·lŭs), *n.; pl.* -LI (-lī). [L., a little hook.] *Anat. & Zool.* A hook or hooklike process, as the process terminating some barbicels of feathers.

Han (hän), *n.* [Chin. (Pek.) *Han⁴.*] A Chinese dynasty (206 B.C.–220 A.D.) marked by a bureaucratic monarchy, revival of letters, introduction of Buddhism, and extension of Chinese rule.

han′a·per (hăn′ȧ·pẽr), *n.* [OF. *hanapier,* fr. *hanap* a drinking vessel, of Teut. origin.] Formerly, a kind of small hamper in which documents were kept.

hance (hȧns; 9), *n.* [OF. *hauce* (F. *hausse*) a rise.] **1.** *Naut.* A sudden fall, as of the fife rail to the gangway. **2.** *Arch.* The arc of minimum radius at the springing of an elliptical or similar arch; hence, the haunch of an arch.

hand (hănd), *n.* [AS. *hand, hond.*] **1.** The terminal part of the arm when, as in man and the apes, it is specially modified as a grasping organ. The hand, or *manus,* includes the *phalanges,* or fingers and thumb; the *metacarpus,* or hand proper; and the *carpus,* or wrist. **2.** A part serving the function of or like a hand; as: **a** The foot of an ape. **b** The chela of a crustacean. **3.** Personal possession; hence, control; direction. **4.** Agency; part in any action. **5.** Side; part; direction; hence, tendency or trend of events; also, figuratively, side or aspect of a subject, argument, or the like. **6.** A pledge, esp. of betrothal or bestowal in marriage; as, he asked for her *hand.* **7.** Ability; skill. **8.** Handwriting or style of handwriting; also, a signature. **9.** **a** The hand as a means of assistance; as, to bear, or lend, a *hand;* a helping *hand.* **b** A round of applause; as, to give one a *hand.* **10.** **a** A performer of some work; as, two portraits by the same *hand.* **b** One employed at manual labor; as, a farm *hand.* **11.** *Archaic.* Handiwork; workmanship. **12.** Source; as, knowledge at first *hand.* **13.** Something that resembles a hand in shape, function, or use; as: **a** An index, or pointer on a dial. **b** A figure [☞] to point a way or call attention. **14.** A hand's breadth, or 4 inches (10.16 cm.); as, a horse 15 *hands* high. **15.** *Card Playing.* **a** One of the players. **b** The quota of cards received by one player during one round. **c** A single round in a game. **16.** *Com.* A cluster of bananas containing from 8 to 20 fruits. **17.** *Manège.* Skill in handling the reins. **18.** *Naut.* A member of a crew. **19.** *Roman & Civil Law.* = MANUS, 2. **20.** *Tobacco, Hemp, etc.* Several leaves tied together.

— ***at hand.*** Near; close by. — ***at the hand of.*** By the act of; from. — ***by hand.*** With the hands, or by manual labor. — ***in hand.*** **a** In actual charge; at one's disposal. **b** In preparation; in course of transaction; also, under control. — ***off one's hands.*** Out of one's charge or care. — ***on hand.*** **a** In present possession. **b** Pending; in progress. **c** *U. S.* Present; in attendance. — ***on one's hands.*** In one's care; resting on one as a responsibility or burden. — ***out of hand.*** **a** Forthwith; without delay. **b** Done with; also, beyond control. — ***to hand.*** Into possession; within reach; under control; as, his letter is *to hand.*

— *adj.* Of or pertaining to the hand; worn on or carried in the hand; operated by hand.

— *v. t.* **1.** *Obs.* To manage, or manipulate, with the hands. **2.** To lead, guide, or assist with the hand; as, to *hand* a lady into a carriage. **3.** To give, pass, or transmit with, or as with, the hand. **4.** *Naut.* To furl, as a sail.

hand down. **a** To transmit in succession, as from father to son. **b** To deliver to the proper officer of an inferior court (the decision of an appellate court); less properly, to announce (the opinion of any court). — ***hand on.*** To transmit. — ***hand over.*** To yield control of.

hand′bag′ (hănd′băg′), *n.* A satchel; a grip; a small bag for carrying parcels or one for money, cosmetics, etc.

hand′ball′ (-bôl′), *n.* A game played in a walled court by players who use the hands in striking a ball.

hand′bar′row (-băr′ō), *n.* A frame or flat barrow, without a wheel, carried by handles. Cf. WHEELBARROW.

hand′bill′ (-bĭl′), *n.* A loose printed sheet to be distributed by hand.

hand′book′ (-bŏŏk′), *n.* **1.** A book, esp. a reference book, that can be easily handled or consulted; a manual. **2.** A betting book of a bookmaker carried in the hand or on the person to evade the laws against making books of bets.

hand′breadth′ (-brĕdth′), *n.* A linear measure varying from about 2½ to 4 inches; a palm.

hand′car′ (-kär′), *n.* *Railroads, U. S.* A small car propelled by hand.

hand′cart′ (-kärt′), *n.* A cart drawn or pushed by hand.

hand′cuff′ (-kŭf′), *n.* A metal ringlike fastening which can be locked around the wrist; a manacle; — usually *pl.* — *v. t.* To manacle.

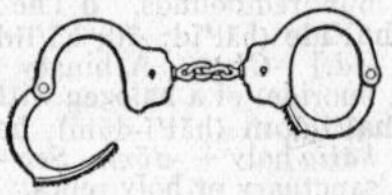

Handcuffs, open and closed.

hand′ed (hăn′dĕd; -dĭd), *adj.* Having a hand or hands, esp. a peculiar or characteristic hand.

hand′fast′ (hănd′făst′), *n.* *Archaic.* **1.** Firm hold. **2.** A clasping of hands to bind an agreement; hence, a contract or covenant, esp. of betrothal or marriage.

hand′fast′ing, *n.* **1.** *Archaic.* A betrothal. **2.** *Hist.* A form of irregular or probationary marriage contracted by the parties joining hands and agreeing to live together.

hand′ful (hănd′fŏŏl), *n.; pl.* -FULS (-fŏŏlz). **1.** As much or many as the hand will grasp. **2.** A small quantity or number.

hand glass. **1.** A small mirror with a handle. **2.** A magnifying reading glass held in the hand.

hand grenade. *Mil.* A grenade to be thrown by hand.

hand′grip′ (hănd′grĭp′), *n.* [AS. *handgripe.*] **1.** A grasping with the hand; a grip. **2.** *pl.* Hand-to-hand combat.

hand′i·cap (hăn′dĭ·kăp), *n.* [From *hand in cap,* in allusion to a certain old sport.] **1.** A race or contest in which, in order to equalize chances of winning, an artificial disadvantage is imposed on a supposedly superior contestant or an artificial advantage is given to one supposedly inferior; also, the advantage given or the disadvantage imposed. **2.** Figuratively, any disadvantage that renders success more difficult. — *v. t.;* -CAPPED (-kăpt); -CAP′PING. **1.** To encumber with a handicap; hence, to place at a disadvantage. **2.** To assign handicaps to, as to horses in a race. — **hand′i·cap′per,** *n.*

hand′i·craft (hăn′dĭ·krȧft; 9), *n.* [(After *handiwork*) fr. *handcraft,* fr. AS. *handcræft.*] **1.** A trade requiring skill of hand; manual skill. **2.** *Obs.* A handicraftsman.

hand′i·crafts′man (-krȧfts′măn), *n.* A man skilled in handicraft. — **hand′i·crafts′man·ship,** *n.*

Hand′ie–Talk′ie (hăn′dĭ·tôk′ĭ), *n.* A trade-mark applied to a small portable radio transmitter-receiver.

hand′i·ly (hăn′dĭ·lĭ), *adv.* In a handy manner.

hand′i·ness (-dĭ·nĕs; -nĭs), *n.* Quality of being handy.

hand′i·work′ (hăn′dĭ·wûrk′), *n.* [AS. *handgeweorc,* fr. *hand* hand + *geweorc* work.] Work done by the hands; hence, any work done personally.

hand′ker·chief (hăng′kẽr·chĭf), *n.* **1.** A small piece of cloth, usually square and often embroidered or trimmed with lace, carried for wiping the face, nose, or eyes. **2.** A neckerchief; neckcloth.

hand′–knit′, hand′–knit′ted (*see Pron.,* § 2), *adj.* Knitted by hand.

han′dle (hăn′d'l), *v. t.;* HAN′DLED (-d'ld); HAN′DLING (-dlĭng). [AS. *handlian.*] **1.** To touch, hold, take up, move, or otherwise affect, with the hand. **2.** To deal with or manage in writing or speaking or in the arts; to treat, as a theme or subject. **3.** To treat; to use, well or ill. **4.** To manage in using with the hands, as a spade, an oar, or a weapon; manipulate. **5.** To manage; control; direct. **6.** To deal with; as, much mail matter was *handled.* **7.** *Chiefly U. S.* To deal or trade in; as, they *handle* only fruit. — *v. i.* **1.** To use the hands. **2.** To act, behave, or feel, in a certain way when handled; as, this boat *handles* easily.

Syn. **Handle, manipulate, wield** mean to manage dexterously as or as if a tool. **Handle** implies acquired skill directed to the accomplishment of ends and is used especially in reference to men and situations; **manipulate** implies adroitness in handling, often suggesting the use of craft or of fraud; **wield** implies mastery and vigor in handling, especially of authority, influence, power, and the like.

— *n.* **1.** That part of vessels, instruments, etc., which is held in the hand. **2.** Something that resembles a handle in appearance, use, or function. **3.** *Dyeing.* A mordant.

handle bar. Often in *pl.,* **handle bars.** A straight or bent bar with a handle, specif. one used to steer a bicycle. See BICYCLE, MOTORCYCLE, *Illusts.*

han′dler (hăn′dlẽr), *n.* **1.** One who or that which handles. **2.** *Sporting.* A man who holds and incites a dog, gamecock, or the like, in a match; esp., one who helps train a pugilist, or acts as his second during a match.

hand′less, *adj.* Inefficient with the hands; clumsy.

han′dling (hăn′dlĭng), *n.* **1.** A touching, controlling, dealing with, etc., with or as with the hands. **2.** The mode of treatment, as in writing or the arts.

hand′made′ (hănd′mād′; 2), *adj.* Made by hand as distinguished from natural, or from manufactured, objects.

hand′maid′ (-mād′), *n.* *Archaic,* **hand′maid′en** (-mād′'n). A female servant or attendant.

hand′–me–down′, *adj.* *Slang.* Ready-made; hence, cheap; lacking style; also, secondhand; — applied esp. to garments. — *n.* *Slang.* Such a garment.

hand of writ *or* **write.** *Scot.* Handwriting.

hand organ. *Music.* A barrel organ cranked by hand.

hand′out′ (hănd′out′), *n.* **1.** *Slang, U.S.* Food or clothing given to a beggar at a house door. See HOBO, *Illust.* **2.** A folder or circular of information for free distribution. **3.** A press release by a news service. **4.** A prepared official statement released to the press.

hand′rail′ (-rāl′), *n.* A rail to be grasped by the hand as a support; a railing serving as a guard.

hand′saw′ (-sô′), *n.* A saw used with one hand.

hand′sel (hănd′sĕl; hăn′-), **han′sel** (hăn′sĕl), *n.* [ON. *handsal* the closing of a bargain by shaking hands, fr. *hand* hand + *sal* sale, bargain.] A gift as a token of good luck, esp. in an enterprise or experience; as: **a** A first gift on any occasion. **b** A gift at the new year. — *v. t.*; -SELED (-sĕld) or -SELLED; -SEL·ING or SEL·LING. **1.** To give a handsel to. **2.** To inaugurate with some token of pleasure. **3.** To use or do for the first time.

hand′set′ (hănd′sĕt′), *n.* A combined telephone transmitter and receiver mounted on a handle. See TELEPHONE, *Illust.*

hand′some (hăn′sŭm), *adj.* [*hand* + *-some.*] **1.** *Dial. & Colloq.* Dexterous. **2.** *Dial. & Colloq.* Suitable; becoming; appropriate. **3.** Moderately large; considerable; ample. **4.** Gracious; liberal; generous. **5.** Having a pleasing appearance; comely. — **Syn.** See BEAUTIFUL. — **hand′some·ly**, *adv.* — **hand′some·ness**, *n.*

hand′spike′ (hănd′spīk′), *n.* [(After *spike*) fr. D. *handspaak*, lit., hand pole or beam.] A bar used as a lever.

hand′spring′ (-sprĭng′), *n.* A feat of tumbling, consisting in turning in the air as in a somersault, with the aid of a push from both hands, or one hand, on the ground.

hand to hand. Attributively, **hand′-to-hand′.** In close proximity; at close quarters.

hand′-to-mouth′, *adj.* Consuming at once what is obtained; improvident; as, a *hand-to-mouth* existence.

hand′wheel′ (hănd′hwēl′), *n.* Any wheel worked by hand, esp. one whose rim serves as a handle for operating a valve, brake, or other part.

hand′work′ (hănd′wûrk′), *n.* Work done with the hands, as distinguished from work done by a machine.

hand′write′ (-rīt′), *v. t. & i.*; HAND′WROTE′ (-rōt′); HAND′WRIT′TEN (-rĭt′'n); HAND′WRIT′ING (-rīt′ĭng). To write by hand.

hand′writ′ing (-rīt′ĭng), *n.* **1.** Writing done with the hand; esp., the cast or form of writing peculiar to each hand or person; chirography. **2.** *Archaic.* That which is written by hand; manuscript.

hand′y (hăn′dĭ), *adj.*; HAND′I·ER (-dĭ·ẽr); HAND′I·EST. **1.** *Obs.* Performed by the hand. **2.** Ready to the hand; conveniently near; also, convenient or suited for use; as, a *handy* tool. **3.** Skillful in using the hand; dexterous. **4.** *Naut.* Easily managed or handled; esp., obedient to the helm; — said of a vessel.

handy man. A man serviceable for odd jobs.

hang (hăng), *v. t.*; HUNG (hŭng) or HANGED (hăngd); HANG′ING. With reference to the death penalty *hanged* is preferred to *hung*. [AS. *hangian*, v. i., *hōn*, v. t. (pret. *heng*, past part. *hongen*).] **1.** To fasten to some elevated point without support from below; suspend. **2.** To put to death by suspending from a cross, gibbet, or gallows; specif., to suspend by the neck until life is extinct; — also used in mild oaths; as, *hang* it. **3.** To fasten so as to allow free motion upon the point of suspension; as, to *hang* a pendulum, a swing, a door, etc. **4.** To cover, decorate, or furnish by hanging pictures, trophies, drapery, etc.; also, to fasten or adjust (drapery, a skirt, etc.) so as to fall gracefully or evenly. **5.** To hold or bear in a suspended or inclined manner or position; to droop. **6.** To fit or fix in position, as at a proper angle (a part of an implement that is swung in using), as a scythe to its snath, or an ax to its helve. **7.** To prevent, as a jury, from reaching a decision, as by one member's refusal to join in a verdict which must be unanimous. — *v. i.* **1.** To be suspended; to dangle. **2.** To die or be put to death by hanging. **3.** To lean or incline over or downward; to slope down. **4.** To be fastened so as to allow free motion on the point of suspension; as, the door *hangs* on its hinges. **5.** To be suspended as if without support; hover; impend. **6.** To depend; as, his election *hangs* on one vote. **7.** To hold for support; to cling; as, she *hung* on his arm. **8.** To be in a state of rapt attention; as, he *hung* on her words. **9.** To be uncertain; to be in suspense; also, to linger; loiter.
hang fire. *Ordn.* To be slow in explosion; as, the gun *hangs fire;* hence, figuratively, to hesitate; to be dilatory. — ***hang together.*** **a** To remain united. **b** *Colloq.* To be self-consistent. — ***hang out.*** *Slang.* To live; lodge; also, to loiter idly. — ***hang up.*** To keep or remain suspended or in abeyance; as, the plans were *hung up*.
— *n.* **1.** Manner in which a thing hangs; as, the *hang* of a scythe; the *hang* of a gown. **2.** Meaning; plan; as, to get the *hang* of an argument; also, method of use; knack; as, to get the *hang* of handling a boat. **3.** A hesitancy, pause, or slackening, in motion. **4.** The least bit; — used in mild oaths; as, to care not a *hang*.
— **hang′a·ble**, *adj.*

hang′ar (hăng′ẽr; hăng′gär) *n.* [F.] **1.** A shelter or shed, as for a coach. **2.** A shelter for housing aircraft.

hang′bird′ (hăng′bûrd′), *n.* The Baltimore oriole (see ORIOLE, 2).

hang′dog′ (-dŏg′; 74), *n.* A person fit only to hang a dog or to be hanged like a dog. — *adj.* Sneaking; ashamed; base.

hang′er (hăng′ẽr), *n.* **1.** One who hangs, or causes to be hung or hanged, as a hangman, a paper hanger, etc. **2.** That which hangs; specif., a short, usually slightly curved, sword, formerly much used, esp. by seamen. **3.** Any of various hanging devices, esp. for supporting something; as: **a** A strap by which a dagger or sword was suspended. **b** A loop on a collar, by which a garment is hung up. **c** A form on which a garment is hung to retain its pressed shape. **4.** *Automobiles.* A bracket connecting the spring shackle to the chassis frame.

hang′er-on′, *n.*; *pl.* HANGERS-ON. One who hangs on, or sticks to, a person, place, or service; a dependent.

hang′ing (hăng′ĭng), *n.* **1.** A suspending or state of being suspended. **2.** Execution by hanging. See HANG, *v. t.*, 2. **3.** That which is hung, as drapery, wallpaper, etc.; — chiefly in *pl.* — *adj.* **1.** Suspended; leaning over or downward. **2.** Situated on steeply sloping grounds. **3.** Downcast in appearance. **4.** Adapted for sustaining a hanging object; as, the *hanging* post of a gate. **5.** Deserving, likely to cause, or prone to inflict, death by hanging; as, a *hanging* crime.

hanging indention. *Print.* Indention of all the lines of a paragraph except the first.

hang′man (hăng′măn), *n.* One who hangs another; esp., a public executioner.

hang′nail′ (-nāl′), *n.* [Corrupt. of AGNAIL.] A strip of epidermis hanging loose at the root of a fingernail.

hang′out′ (-out′), *n.* A place where one "hangs out"; a rendezvous.

hang′-o′ver (-ō′vẽr), *n.* **1.** Something that remains from what is past, as a surviving custom. **2.** *Slang.* The aftereffect of dissipation, esp. of overindulgence in intoxicating liquor.

hank (hăngk), *n.* [Of Scand. origin.] **1.** A coil or loop; specif., a coil or skein of yarn. A hank of cotton yarn contains 840 yd.; of worsted, 560 yd. **2.** *Naut.* A ring of wood, iron, or, rarely, rope attached to the edge of a jib or staysail and running on a stay.

han′ker (hăng′kẽr), *v. i.* To long (*for*); — usually with *for* or *after*. — **Syn.** See LONG. — **han′ker·er**, *n.* — **han′ker·ing**, *n.*

han′ky-pan′ky (hăng′kĭ-păng′kĭ), *n.* *Colloq.* Hocus-pocus; hence, jugglery; trickery.

Han′o·ve′ri·an (hăn′ō·vẽr′ĭ·ăn), *adj.* Of, pert. to, or supporting, the former ducal house of Hanover, founded about 1125, to which belonged the four Georges and William IV, of England, and, by birth, Queen Victoria and her descendants. — **Han′o·ve′ri·an**, *n.*

Han′sard (hăn′sẽrd), *n.* An official report of proceedings in the British Parliament; — from the name of the compilers during a long period.

hanse (hăns), *n.* [ML. *hansa* and OF. *hanse*, fr. MHG. *hanse, hans*, merchant guild, association.] **1.** *Hist.* A merchant guild, as of a town. **2.** A fee or tribute paid to a merchant guild. **3.** [*cap.*] Also **Han′se·at′ic League.** *Hist.* A medieval league of merchants of various free Germanic towns dealing abroad, and later of the towns themselves, formed to protect their trade.

Han′se·at′ic (hăn′sē·ăt′ĭk), *adj.* Pertaining to the Hanse towns, or to their confederacy.

han′sel (hăn′sĕl). Var. of HANDSEL.

Han′sen's dis·ease′ (hăn′sĕnz). [After the Norwegian physician G.H.A. *Hansen* (1841–1912), who first described (1869) *Mycobacterium leprae.*] *Med.* Leprosy.

han′som (hăn′sŭm), *n.*, *or* **hansom cab.** [After J. A. *Hansom* (1803–82), Eng. inventor.] A light two-wheeled covered carriage with the driver's seat elevated behind.

Hansom.

han′tle (hăn′t'l), *n.* *Scot. & Dial. Eng.* A good many.

Ha′nuk·kah, Ha′nuk·ka (hä′nŏŏ·kä; *Heb.* KÄ′-), *n.* [Heb. *ḥănūkkāh* dedication.] See JEWISH HOLIDAYS.

hap (hăp), *n.* [ON. *happ* good luck.] Chance; happening; luck. — *v. i.*; HAPPED (hăpt); HAP′PING. [ME. *happen.* See HAP chance.] To happen; befall.

hap (hȧp; ȧp), *v. t.* *Dial.* To cover up; wrap. — *n.* *Dial.* Any covering, as a cloak.

‖**ha′pax le·go′me·non** (hā′păks lĕ·gŏm′ē·nŏn). [Gr.] Said or used but once, as a rare word or phrase, evidenced by a single citation.

hap′haz′ard (hăp′hăz′ẽrd), *n.* [*hap* + *hazard.*] Chance; accident; random. — (hăp′hăz′ẽrd; 2), *adj.* Random; determined by chance. — (hăp′hăz′ẽrd; 2), *adv.* In a haphazard manner. — **Syn.** See RANDOM. — **hap′haz′ard·ly**, *adv.*

haph′ta·rah′ (häf′tä·rä′; häf·tô′rȧ), *n.*; *pl.* -TAROTH (-rōth′). [Heb. *haphtārāh* conclusion.] One of the lessons from the Nebiim (or Prophets) read in the Jewish synagogue after the parashoth. See PARASHAH.

hap′less (hăp′lĕs; -lĭs), *adj.* Without hap; unlucky. — **hap′less·ly**, *adv.* — **hap′less·ness**, *n.*

hap′lo- (hăp′lō-), **hapl-.** [Gr. *haploos.*] A combining form meaning *single, simple,* as in **hap′lo·scope**, a simple form of stereoscope.

hap′loid (hăp′loid), *adj.* Single; specif., *Biol.*, having the basic chromosome number or half the diploid number characteristic of a species or other group, as most germ cells. Cf. DIPLOID. — **hap′loid**, *n.* — **hap′loid·y** (hăp′loid·ĭ), *n.* — **hap·loi′dic** (hăp·loi′dĭk), *adj.*

hap·lo′sis (hăp·lō′sĭs), *n.* [NL., fr. *hapl-* + *-osis.*] *Biol.* The reducing of the chromosome number by the division into two haploid sets in meiosis. Cf. DIPLOSIS.

hap′ly (hăp′lĭ), *adv.* By hap, chance, luck, or accident.

hap′pen (hăp′ĕn), *v. i.* [ME. *happenen, hapnen.* See HAP to happen.] **1.** To occur by chance. **2.** To come to pass; to befall. **3.** To chance; as, I *happened* to hear it. **4.** *Obs. exc. Dial.* To be (*in, at,* etc.) by chance. **5.** To come (*on, upon,* rarely *of*) by chance.

Syn. Happen, chance, occur, transpire mean to come about. **Happen** may imply obvious causation or seeming accident in both personal and impersonal uses; **chance** differs from *happen* in uniformly implying lack of design; **occur** always implies a presentation to sight, to mind, etc. (as, the accident *happened* [or *occurred*] Friday; the word rarely *occurs* [never *happens*] in print); **transpire**, often used in this sense, is acceptable only when its primary implication is a leaking out or becoming known (as, what the chief said has never *transpired*).

hap′pen·ing, *n.* Occurrence.

hap′pi·ly (hăp′ĭ·lĭ), *adv.* **1.** *Archaic.* = HAPLY. **2.** By good fortune. **3.** In a happy manner or state. **4.** With dexterity; felicitously.

hap′pi·ness (hăp′ĭ·nĕs; -nĭs), *n.* **1.** Good luck; good fortune; prosperity. **2.** A state of well-being and pleasurable satisfaction; bliss. **3.** Graceful aptitude; felicity; — used esp. of language.

hap′py (hăp′ĭ), *adj.*; HAP′PI·ER (-ĭ·ẽr); HAP′PI·EST. [From HAP chance.] **1.** Favored by hap, luck, or fortune; fortunate; prosperous. **2.** Dexterous; apt; felicitous. **3.** Enjoying well-being, peace, and comfort; joyous. **4.** Expressing happiness; as, *happy* laughter. **5.** (In slang combinations) in a dazed, irresponsible state of unpredictableness, as in blitz-*happy*, trigger-*happy;* also, obsessed, as in ski-*happy*, pun-*happy*. — **Syn.** See LUCKY: FIT: GLAD.

hap′py-go-luck′y, *adj.* Trusting to luck; easygoing.

Haps′burg (hăps′bûrg), *n.* [From *Habsburg*, Aargau, Switzerland.] A member of a German family, founded about 1100, to which belonged the rulers of Austria from 1276 (Rudolph I) to 1918, of Spain from 1516 (Charles I) to 1700, and many of the Holy Roman Emperors.

hap′ten (hăp′tĕn), **hap′tene** (-tēn), *n.* [Gr. *haptein* to fasten + *-ene.*] *Immunol.* A substance that, when injected, unites with a protein to form a compound having specific antigenic properties.

har′a-kir′i (hăr′ȧ·kĭr′ĭ; hä′rȧ-), *n.* Also, incorrectly, **har′a-kar′i** (-kăr′ĭ; -kä′rĭ), **har′i-kar′i** (hăr′ĭ-; hä′rĭ-), etc. [Jap., belly cutting.] Suicide by disembowelment, formerly practiced by the samurai in cases of disgrace or by government order; — a term rarely used by the Japanese, the proper word being *seppuku*.

ha·rangue′ (hȧ·răng′), *n.* [F., fr. ML. *harenga*, fr. OHG. *hari* host, army + *hringa* assembly, ring.] A speech addressed to a multitude; often, a noisy, ranting speech. — *v. i. & t.*; HA·RANGUED′ (-răngd′);

HA·RANGU′ING (hȧ·răng′ĭng). To make, or address in, a harangue. — **ha·rangu′er** (hȧ·răng′ẽr), *n.*

har′ass (hăr′ȧs; hȧ·răs′), *v. t.* [F. *harasser*, fr. MF. *harer* to set (a dog) on.] **1.** To tire with repeated and exhausting efforts; to weary by importunity; to fatigue. **2.** To harry; to lay waste; to raid. **3.** *Mil.* To worry by repeated attacks. — **Syn.** See WORRY. — **har′ass·er,** *n.* — **har′ass·ment,** *n.*

har′bin·ger (här′bĭn·jẽr), *n.* [OF. *herbergeor* a provider of lodging, deriv. of *herberge* lodging, inn.] **1.** One sent before to arrange for lodgings. **2.** A forerunner; a precursor. — **Syn.** See FORERUNNER. — *v. t.* To be a harbinger of; to presage.

har′bor, har′bour (här′bẽr), *n.* [ME. *herbore, herberwe.*] **1.** A place of security and comfort; a refuge. **2.** A portion of a body of water so protected as to be a place of safety for vessels; a port or haven. — *v. t.* To entertain as a guest; to shelter; to give a refuge to; to indulge or cherish (a thought or feeling). — *v. i.* To lodge, or abide for a time; to take shelter, as in a harbor. — **har′bor·er, har′bour·er,** *n.* — **har′bor·less, har′bour·less,** *adj.*

har′bor·age, har′bour·age (-ĭj), *n.* Shelter; harbor.

harbor master. An officer charged with the duty of executing the regulations respecting the use of a harbor.

harbor seal. = SEA DOG, 1 **b**.

hard (härd), *adj.* [AS. *heard.*] **1.** Not easily penetrated; firm; solid; — opposed to *soft.* **2.** Physically fit for exertion or endurance. **3. a** Carried on energetically or persistently; as, *hard* study. **b** Earnest; persevering; as, a *hard* student. **4.** Characterized by or displaying severity; harsh; as, *hard* words. **5. a** Obdurate; unfeeling; as, a *hard* heart. **b** *Chiefly Dial.* Close in money matters. **6.** Rigid; ungraceful; repelling; as, a *hard* style. **7.** Inclement; — of weather. **8. a** Rough; sour, as liquors. **b** *U. S.* Strong; spirituous, as distilled liquors. **9.** Characterized by the presence of substances which prevent lathering with soap; — of water. **10.** *Colloq.* Disreputable; as, a *hard* character. **11.** Difficult to bear or endure; hence, oppressive; distressing; as, a *hard* lot. **12.** Having difficulty in doing something or in exercising some faculty. *Now Rare,* exc. in *hard of hearing.* **13.** Difficult; laborious; fatiguing. **14.** Difficult to manage or deal with. **15.** *Agric.* Having flinty kernels high in gluten which yield a strong flour; — of wheats. **16.** *Phonet.* **a** Of *c* and *g*, pronounced as stop sounds, as in *picnic, geese,* in contrast to the "*soft*" fricatives or affricates in *city, ocean, gem.* **b** Voiceless; — of the stops *p, t, k,* and sometimes also of the fricatives and affricates *s, f, th, sh, ch,* in contrast to the "*soft,*" or voiced, *z, v, th, zh, j.* **17.** *Physics.* Designating or pertaining to rays, esp. X rays, of high penetrating power.

Syn. (1) See FIRM. — **Ant.** Soft.

(2) **Hard, difficult, arduous** mean demanding great toil or effort. **Hard,** the simple and blunt term, implies the opposite of all that is easy; **difficult** commonly implies the presence of obstacles to be surmounted and suggests the need of skill, ingenuity, or courage; **arduous** stresses the need of laborious and persistent or persevering exertion.

— *adv.* **1.** With pressure, tension, or strain; with energy; vigorously. **2.** Tightly; firmly; as, to hold *hard.* **3.** So as to involve pain or trouble; severely. **4.** With difficulty. **5.** Close or near; as, they waited *hard* by. **6.** *Naut.* With the utmost energy, or to the extreme limit; — esp. in directions to the helmsman; as, *Hard* aport!

hard and fast. Rigidly binding; strict.

hard′-bit′ten (härd′bĭt′'n), *adj.* Hard in biting; — of dogs; hence, tough; dogged; as, a *hard-bitten* corporal.

hard′-boiled′ (-boild′; 2), *adj.* **1.** Boiled until both white and yolk have solidified; — said of an egg. **2.** *Colloq.* Fixed and unyielding in opinion or character; callous.

hard coal. Anthracite coal.

hard′en (här′d'n), *v. t.* **1.** To make hard or harder; to make firm, tight, or compact; to indurate. **2.** To make unimpressionable or callous. **3.** To confirm in disposition, feeling, or actions. **4.** To make hardy or robust; as, to *harden* troops. — *v. i.* **1.** To become hard or harder; to acquire solidity. **2.** To become confirmed or strengthened, in either a good or a bad sense; esp., to become hard in disposition. **3.** *Colloq. Com.* Of prices, the market, etc., to become higher or less subject to fluctuations downward.

hard′en·er (-d'n·ẽr), *n.* One who or that which hardens; specif.: **a** One whose work is to harden a (specified) thing. **b** A substance added to a paint, varnish, or the like, to impart greater hardness to the film.

hard′en·ing, *n.* That which hardens, as a material used for converting the surface of iron into steel.

hard′-fa′vored, hard′-fa′voured (härd′fā′vẽrd; 2), *adj.* Hard-featured; ill-looking. — **hard′-fa′vored·ness, hard′-fa′voured·ness,** *n.*

hard′-fea′tured (-fē′tūrd; 2), *adj.* Having coarse, unattractive, or stern features. — **hard′-fea′tured·ness,** *n.*

hard′fist′ed (härd′fĭs′tĕd; -tĭd; 2), *adj.* Hardhanded; also, closefisted; niggardly. — **hard′fist′ed·ness,** *n.*

hard′hack′ (härd′hăk′), *n.* An American spiraea (*Spiraea tomentosa*) with rusty hairy leaves and dense terminal panicles of pink or, rarely, white flowers.

hard′hand′ed (-hăn′dĕd; -dĭd), *adj.* **1.** Having hard hands, as a manual laborer. **2.** Oppressive; as, a *hardhanded* despot.

hard′head′ (-hĕd′), *n.* **1.** A shrewd, unfeeling person; also, a blockhead. **2.** Any of various fishes, as the menhaden or any of certain gurnards or sculpins. **3.** A **hardhead sponge,** any of certain commercial sponges having a harsh but elastic and durable fiber.

hard′head′ed (-hĕd′ĕd; -ĭd; 2), *adj.* **1.** Stubborn; willful. **2.** Of sound judgment; shrewd. — **hard′head′ed·ness,** *n.*

hard′heart′ed (-här′tĕd; -tĭd; 2), *adj.* Unsympathetic; unfeeling; callous; cruel; pitiless. — **hard′heart′ed·ly,** *adv.* — **hard′heart′ed·ness,** *n.*

har′di·hood (här′dĭ·hŏŏd), *n.* Boldness, united with firmness of mind; also, impudence. — **Syn.** See TEMERITY.

har′di·ly, *adv.* In a hardy manner; boldly; stoutly.

har′di·ment (här′dĭ·mĕnt), *n.* [OF. See HARDY.] *Archaic.* Hardihood; boldness; courage.

har′di·ness, *n.* Hardy quality or state; physical vigor; robustness; endurance.

hard labor. *Law.* Compulsory labor such as that which is imposed upon imprisoned criminals as a part of the prison discipline.

hard′ly (härd′lĭ), *adv.* **1.** Severely; harshly. **2.** In a difficult manner; with difficulty. **3.** Scarcely; barely; only just; not probably; as, it will *hardly* be possible.

hard′ness (-nĕs; -nĭs), *n.* **1.** Quality or state of being hard. **2.** The peculiar quality exhibited by water containing certain dissolved salts. See HARD, *adj.*, 9. **3.** *Mineral.* The cohesion of the particles on the surface of a body, as determined by its capacity to scratch another, or be itself scratched. The *hardness* of a mineral is expressed in terms of the following scale, introduced by Mohs: 1, talc; 2, gypsum; 3, calcite; 4, fluorite; 5, apatite; 6, orthoclase (feldspar); 7, quartz; 8, topaz; 9, sapphire (corundum); 10, diamond. "H., 3.5" means that a mineral is harder than calcite, but softer than fluorite.

hard′pan′ (härd′păn′), *n.* *Chiefly U. S.* **1.** A cementlike or compacted layer in soils through which it is difficult to dig. **2.** Hard unbroken ground. **3.** The firm, solid, substantial part of anything.

hard rubber. Firm and relatively inelastic vulcanized rubber, obtained by heating crude rubber with a large amount of sulfur (usually 30–50 per cent).

hards (härdz), *n. pl.* Hurds.

hard sauce. A creamed mixture of butter and powdered sugar, to which, often, cream and flavoring are added.

hard′-set′ (*see Pron.,* § 2), *adj.* **1.** Hard pressed; in a hard position. **2.** Hard; firm; fixed in rigidity; hence, stubborn.

hard′-shell′, hard′-shelled′, *adj.* **1.** Having a hard shell; as a *hard-shelled* clam (see CLAM); *hard-shelled,* or *hard-shell,* crab (see CRAB). **2.** *Colloq., U. S.* Unyielding; uncompromising.

hard′ship (härd′shĭp), *n.* **1.** Hardness. **2.** That which is hard to bear, as privation, injury, etc. — **Syn.** See DIFFICULTY.

hard′-spun′, *adj.* Firmly twisted in spinning.

hard′tack′ (-tăk′), *n.* A type of hard biscuit or sea bread.

hard up. *Colloq.* Without money or resources.

hard′ware′ (härd′wâr′), *n.* Ware made of metal, as fittings, trimmings, cutlery, tools, parts of machines, etc.

hard′wood′ (-wŏŏd′), *n.* **a** Any heavy, close-grained, and resistant wood. **b** In forestry, the wood of any broad-leaved deciduous tree as disting. from that of a coniferous tree. **c** Any tree having hardwood (sense **a** or **b**). — **hard′wood′** (*see Pron.,* § 2), *adj.*

har′dy (här′dĭ), *adj.;* HAR′DI·ER (-dĭ·ẽr); HAR′DI·EST. [OF. *hardi,* past part. fr. *hardir* to make bold, of Teut. origin.] **1.** Bold; brave; resolute. **2.** Confident; full of assurance. **3.** Strong; firm. **4.** Inured to fatigue or hardships; robust. **5.** *Hort.* Capable of living over winter without artificial protection.

hare (hâr), *n.;* see PLURAL, *Note,* 3. [AS. *hara.*] **1.** Any of certain swift, timid, long-eared mammals (mostly of the genus *Lepus,* family Leporidae), technically lagomorphs, having a divided upper lip, long hind legs, and a short, cocked tail. The American forms are generally called *rabbits.* See LEPORID. **2.** One of those chased in the game of hare and hounds.

hare and hounds. A sport in which two or more players, the *hares,* having a few minutes' start, and scattering bits of paper, called "scent," are chased by others, the *hounds.*

hare′bell′ (hâr′bĕl′), *n.* **a** See BLUEBELL, 1. **b** = WOOD HYACINTH.

hare′brained′ (-brānd′), *adj.* Giddy; volatile; heedless.

hare′lip′ (hâr′lĭp′; hâr′lĭp′; 2), *n.* A congenitally divided lip, like that of a hare, or this deformity.

ha′rem (hā′rĕm; hâr′ĕm), *n.* [Ar. *ḥarīm,* orig., anything forbidden or sacred.] **1.** The apartments in a Mohammedan house allotted to females; a seraglio. **2.** The wives, concubines, and other females occupying a harem. **3.** A Mohammedan sacred place, forbidden to infidels. **4.** A group of females associated with a single male; — applied specif. to certain animals.

har′i·cot (hăr′ĭ·kō), *n.* [F., fr. OF. *harigoter* to cut in pieces.] A ragout of meat, esp. mutton or lamb.

har′i·cot, *n.* [F., fr. Nahuatl *ayecotli.*] The seeds, or the unripe pod, of the string bean.

har′i-kar′i (hăr′ĭ·kăr′ĭ; hä′rĭ·kä′rĭ). Var. of HARA-KIRI.

hark (härk), *v. i.* [ME. *herken.* See HEARKEN.] To listen; hearken; — used chiefly in the imperative, formerly often with *ye,* whence the contraction **hark′ee.** — *v. t.* To listen to. — ***hark back.*** To go back a little for a fresh start, as a hound that has lost the scent; hence, to revert.

— *n.* A shout of encouragement or guidance to hounds.

hark′en (här′kĕn). Var. of HEARKEN.

harl (härl), *v. t.* [ME. *harlen* to drag.] *Scot.* **1.** To drag or scrape along; to scrape. **2.** To plaster with roughcast. — *v. i. Scot.* To drag oneself along; also, to peel off, as skin after sunburn. — *n. Scot.* A dragging; something harled; a small quantity; also, a road scraper.

harl, *n.* [ME. *herle.*] **1.** A filamentous substance; esp., the filaments of flax or hemp. **2.** A herl.

Har′le·ian (här′lē·ăn; här·lē′ăn), *adj.* Of Robert Harley (1661–1724), and his son Edward or belonging to their collection of books and manuscripts, now in the British Museum.

Har′le·quin (här′lē·kwĭn; -kĭn), *n.* [F. *harlequin, arlequin,* fr. It. *arlecchino,* fr. OF. *Herlekin* a demon, goblin.] **1.** A character in comedy and pantomime having shaven head, masked face, parti-colored tights, and a sword of lath. See COLUMBINE. **2.** [*not cap.*] A buffoon. — *adj.* [*not cap.*] Parti-colored.

har′le·quin·ade′ (här′lē·kwĭn·ād′), *n.* [F. *arlequinade.*] That part of a play in which the Harlequin is conspicuous; hence, buffoonery.

har′lot (här′lŏt), *n.* [OF. *harlot, herlot, arlot,* a rogue.] **1.** *Obs.* **a** A rogue; rascal. **b** A male servant. **c** A juggler; entertainer. **2.** A loose woman; specif., a prostitute. — *adj.* Wanton; lewd.

har′lot·ry (-rĭ), *n.* Prostitution; also, a harlot.

harm (härm), *n.* [AS. *hearm.*] **1.** Injury; hurt; damage. **2.** Evil; wrong. — *v. t.* To hurt; injure; damage. — **Syn.** See INJURE.

har′mat·tan′ (här′mă·tăn′), *n.* [Sp. *harmatán,* fr. Ar. *harām* forbidden or evil thing.] A dust-laden land wind on the Atlantic coast of Africa in certain seasons.

harm′ful (härm′fŏŏl; -f'l), *adj.* Injurious; hurtful; mischievous. — **harm′ful·ly,** *adv.* — **harm′ful·ness,** *n.*

harm′less (-lĕs; -lĭs), *adj.* **1.** Free from harm, liability, or loss. **2.** Free from power to harm; inoffensive; innocuous. — **harm′less·ly,** *adv.* — **harm′less·ness,** *n.*

har·mon′ic (här·mŏn′ĭk), *adj.* [L. *harmonicus,* fr. Gr. *harmonikos,* fr. *harmonia.* See HARMONY.] **1.** Of or pertaining to harmonics. **2.** Concordant; consonant. **3.** *Math.* Having relations bearing some resemblance to those of musical consonances; as, ***harmonic progression*** (see PROGRESSION, 4). **4.** *Music.* Relating to harmony as distinguished from melody or rhythm. — *n.* **1.** *Music & Acoustics.* **a** An overtone, esp. one produced by a vibration frequency which is an integral multiple of the vibration rate producing the fundamental. **b** A flutelike tone produced on a stringed instrument, by touching a vibrating string at a nodal point. **2.** *Elec.* One of the component frequencies of a wave or alternating current which is an integral multiple of the fundamental frequency. — **har·mon'i·cal·ly** (-ĭ·kăl·ĭ), *adv.*

har·mon'i·ca (här·mŏn'ĭ·kȧ), *n.* [Fem. fr. L. *harmonicus* harmonic.] *Music.* **a** An instrument consisting of a series of hemispherical glasses played by touching the edges with the dampened finger. **b** An instrument of the glockenspiel type having strips of glass or metal. **c** A small wind instrument, played by the mouth, in which the tones are produced by free metallic reeds, one set being sounded by exhaling, another by inhaling; a mouth organ.

harmonic motion. *Physics.* A vibratory motion, as that of a sounding violin string or of a swinging pendulum, in which the force causing the motion is always directly proportional but oppositely directed to the displacement of the body from an equilibrium position.

har·mon'i·con (här·mŏn'ĭ·kŏn), *n.; pl.* -ICA (-kȧ). [Gr. *harmonikon*, neut. of *harmonikos* harmonic]. *Music.* **a** A harmonica. **b** An orchestrion.

har·mon'ics (här·mŏn'ĭks), *n.;* see -ICS. The science of musical sounds.

har·mo'ni·ous (här·mō'nĭ·ŭs), *adj.* **1.** Having parts adapted and proportioned to each other; symmetrical; congruous. **2.** Marked by harmony of feeling or of sound; free from discord. — **har·mo'ni·ous·ly,** *adv.* — **har·mo'ni·ous·ness,** *n.*

har'mo·nist (här'mō·nĭst), *n.* **1.** *Music.* **a** A musical composer or performer. **b** One skilled in harmony. **2.** One who shows the agreement of corresponding passages of different authors, as of the Evangelists. **3.** A harmonizer. — **har'mo·nis'tic** (-nĭs'tĭk), *adj.*

har·mo'ni·um (här·mō'nĭ·ŭm; 58), *n.* [NL.] A small reed organ, in which a bellows forces air outward through free metallic reeds.

har'mo·nize (här'mō·nīz), *v. i.* To be harmonious; to unite in an effect of consonance. — **Syn.** See AGREE. — **Ant.** Clash. — *v. t.* To bring into harmony; *Music*, to accompany with harmony, as melody. — **har'mo·ni·za'tion** (-nĭ·zā'shŭn; -nī·zā'-), *n.* — **har'mo·niz'er** (-nīz'ẽr), *n.*

har'mo·ny (här'mō·nĭ), *n.; pl.* -NIES (-nĭz). [OF. *armonie*, fr. L. *harmonia*, fr. Gr. *harmonia* joint, proportion, concord, fr. *harmos* a fitting.] **1.** Musical consonance; tuneful sound; a concord. **2.** Just adaptation of parts to each other; agreement between the parts of a design or composition giving unity of effect or an aesthetically pleasing whole. **3.** Concord in facts, opinions, interests, etc. **4.** A systematic arrangement of parallel passages, as of the Gospels, to show their agreement. **5.** *Music.* **a** The combination of tones into a chord; a triad. **b** The structure of a piece of music according to the composition, progression, and modulation of its chords; — disting. from *melody* and *rhythm.* **c** The science of the structure, relation, and progression of chords.

har'mo·tome (här'mō·tōm), *n.* [F., fr. Gr. *harmos* joint + *temnein* to cut.] *Mineral.* A hydrous silicate of aluminum, barium, and potassium.

har'ness (här'nĕs; -nĭs), *n.* [OF. *harneis, herneis*, fr. ON. *herr* army + *nest* provisions.] **1.** *Archaic.* The complete trappings, esp. in a military sense, of a man or a horse. **2.** The gear or tackle (other than a yoke) of a draft animal, esp. of a horse, dog, or goat. **3.** Tackle, gear, or equipment of any kind. **4.** The part of a loom comprising the heddles, by which the warp threads are raised and depressed. — *v. t.* **1.** *Archaic.* To accouter. **2.** To put harness on, as a horse. **3.** To provide with apparatus so as to secure mechanical power.

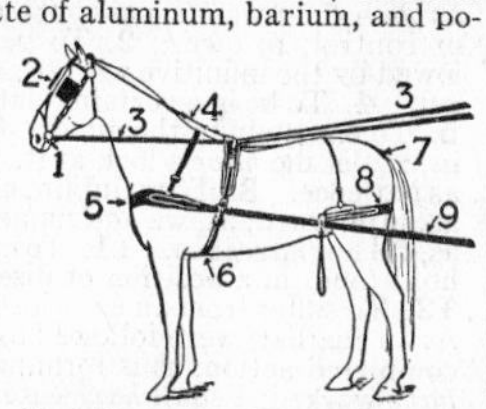

Single Harness. 1 Bit; 2 Blinder; 3, 3 Reins; 4 Checkrein; 5 Breast Collar; 6 Bellyband or Girth; 7 Crupper; 8 Breeching; 9 Trace. See also BIT, *Illust.*

har'nessed an'te·lope (här'nĕst; -nĭst). Any antelope of the genus *Tragelaphus*, having striped markings, as the ***bushbuck or boschbok*** (*T. sylvaticus*) of South Africa and the ***guib*** (*T. scriptus*) of West Africa.

harness hitch. See KNOT, *Illust.* (9).

harns (härnz; *dial. also* änz), *n. pl.* *Scot.* The brains.

harp (härp), *n.* [AS. *hearpe.*] **1.** A musical instrument of strings generally set in an open frame and plucked with the fingers. **2.** Any of various contrivances suggestive of a harp. **3.** [*cap.*] *Astron.* The constellation Lyra. — *v. t.* **1.** To give expression to; to voice. **2.** To bring by harping. — *v. i.* **1.** To play a harp; to sound like a harp. **2.** To dwell on or recur to a subject tediously or monotonously. — **harp'er,** *n.*

harp'ist (här'pĭst), *n.* A harp player.

har·poon' (här·po͞on'), *n.* [F. *harpon*, fr. *harpe* claw, clamp.] A barbed spear or javelin used to strike large fish, whales, etc. — *v. t.* To strike or catch with a harpoon. — **har·poon'er,** *n.*

harp'si·chord (härp'sĭ·kôrd), *n.* [MF. *harpechorde*, fr. It. *arpicordo*, fr. LL. *harpa* harp (of Teut. origin) + *chorda*, It. *corda* string.] A harp-shaped wire-stringed keyboard instrument, immediate precursor of the piano, and resembling a grand piano, but producing its tones by the plucking of its strings with quill or leather points, in use from the 16th to the 18th century.

Har'py (här'pĭ), *n.; pl.* -PIES (-pĭz). [F. *harpie*, fr. L. *harpyia*, fr. Gr. *harpyia*, prob. akin to Gr. *harpazein* to snatch.] **1.** *Class. Myth.* One of a group of foul, malign creatures, part woman, part bird, that snatched away the souls of the dead or seized or defiled the food of their victims. **2.** [*not cap.*] A rapacious person. **3.** [*not cap.*] Short for HARPY EAGLE.

harpy eagle. See EAGLE, 1.

har'que·bus (här'kwē·bŭs; -bŭs), **ar'que·bus** (är'-), *n.; pl.* -BUSES (-bŭs·ĕz; -ĭz). Also **har'que·buse, har'que·buss.** [F. *arquebuse*, fr. It. *archibuso*, fr. D. *haakbus*, prop., a gun with a hook.] An obsolete portable firearm originally having a matchlock operated by a trigger and supported for firing by a hook.

har'que·bus·ier' (här'kwē·bŭs·ēr'; är'-), **ar'que·bus·ier'** (är'kwē-), *n.* A soldier armed with a harquebus.

har'ri·dan (hăr'ĭ·dăn), *n.* [F. *haridelle* a worn-out horse, jade.] A worn-out strumpet; a vixenish woman; a hag.

har'ri·er (hăr'ĭ·ẽr), *n.* [From HARE, *n.*] **a** A dog of an English breed used to hunt hares. **b** A cross-country runner.

har'ri·er, *n.* [From HARRY.] **1.** One who harries. **2.** Any of certain hawks of the genus *Circus*, which feed chiefly on small mammals, reptiles, and insects, as the ***marsh hawk*** (*C. hudsonius*) of America.

Har·ro'vi·an (hă·rō'vĭ·ăn; hă-), *n.* A student or former student of Harrow, the boys' school in England. — **Har·ro'vi·an,** *adj.*

har'row (hăr'ō), *v. t.* [See HARRY.] *Archaic.* To harry.

har'row (hăr'ō), *n.* [ME. *harwe.*] A cultivating implement set with spikelike or spring teeth or disks, used primarily for pulverizing and smoothing the soil. — *v. t.* **1.** To draw a harrow over (land). **2.** To lacerate; torment; vex; — often with *up.* — *v. i.* To be affected by harrowing. — **har'row·er,** *n.*

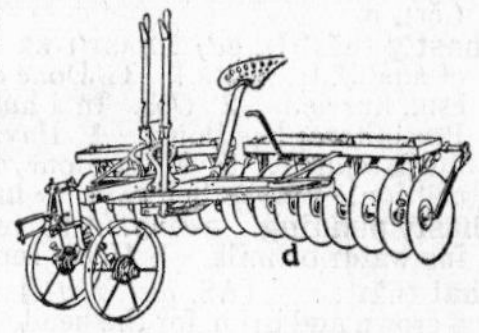

Disk Harrow. *d* Disks.

har'row·ing, *adj.* Grievously distressing; acutely painful; as, a *harrowing* experience.

har'ry (hăr'ĭ), *v. t.;* HAR'RIED (-ĭd); HAR'RY·ING. [AS. *hergian* to afflict with an army, to ravage.] **1.** To make a raid upon, with destruction or seizure of property; to ravage; despoil; pillage. **2.** To persecute as by constant ill-treatment or annoyance; to harass. **3.** *Obs. exc. Scot.* To take in a raid or foray. — **Syn.** See WORRY.

harsh (härsh), *adj.* [ME. *harsk*, of Scand. origin.] **1.** Offensive to sense as being coarse, rough, grating, discordant, astringent, etc.; lacking harmony or smoothness; rasping; repellent. **2.** Offensive to one's feeling of aesthetic or intellectual propriety. **3.** Offensive to a sense of justice; severe; unduly rigorous; as, a *harsh* parent or punishment. — **Syn.** See ROUGH. — **harsh'ly,** *adv.* — **harsh'ness,** *n.*

harsh'en (här'shĕn), *v. t.* To make harsh.

hars'let (härs'lĕt; -lĭt). Var. of HASLET.

harst (härst; hârst). Scot. var. of HARVEST.

hart (härt), *n.; pl.* HARTS (härts), HART; see PLURAL, *Note*, 3. [AS. *heort, heorot.*] = STAG, 1 **a.**

har·tal' (här·täl'), *n.* [Hind. *hartāl*, fr. *hāṭ* shop + *tālā* a lock.] In India, concerted cessation of work and business, esp. as a protest against a political situation.

har'te·beest' (här'tē·bēst'; härt'bēst'), *n.; pl.* -BEESTS (-bēsts'), -BEEST; see PLURAL, *Note*, 3. [S. Afr. D., fr. D. *hert*, earlier also *hart* + *beest.*] A large swift-footed African antelope (*Alcelaphus caama*), having ringed lyrate horns.

harts'horn' (härts'hôrn'), *n.* **1.** A hart's horn. **2.** *Old Chem.* **a** Aqua ammoniae. **b** Sal volatile.

har'um-scar'um (hâr'ŭm-skâr'ŭm; 2), *adj.* *Colloq.* Reckless; wild; irresponsible. — *n.* *Colloq.* Harum-scarum person or conduct.

ha·rus'pex (hȧ·rŭs'pĕks; hăr'ŭs·pĕks), *n.; pl.* -PICES (hȧ·rŭs'pĭ·sēz). [L.] *Rom. Relig.* A diviner who interpreted lightning and natural prodigies, and read the entrails of sacrificial victims. Cf. AUGUR, 1. — **ha·rus'pi·cal** (-pĭ·kăl), *adj.* — **ha·rus'pi·cy** (-pĭ·sĭ), *n.*

har'vest (här'vĕst; -vĭst), *n.* [AS. *haerfest.*] **1.** The season of gathering grain and fruits; also, the gathering of a crop. **2.** A crop, as of grain or fruit; also, the yield, as of honey. **3.** The product or reward of any exertion. — *v. t. & i.* To reap or gather (a crop).

harvest bug *or* **tick.** = CHIGGER **b.**

har'vest·er (här'vĕs·tẽr; -vĭs-), *n.* One who or that which harvests; a machine for harvesting field crops; a reaper.

harvest fly. See CICADA.

harvest home. The gathering or the time of harvest; also, a feast at the close of harvest; hence, the song sung by the reapers.

har'vest·man (här'vĕst·măn; här'vĭst-), *n.* **1.** A man engaged in harvesting. **2.** Any of an order (*Phalangida*) of arachnids resembling the true spiders, most of which have very long slender legs and are called *daddy longlegs.*

harvest moon. The full moon nearest the autumnal equinox.

Har'vey·ize (här'vĭ·īz), *v. t.* [After H. A. *Harvey* (1824–93), Am. inventor.] To face-harden (steel, esp. armor plate) by carburizing the surface at high heat and then suddenly chilling.

has (hăz; 4), *3d pers. sing. pres.* of HAVE.

has'-been' (hăz'bĭn'; -bēn'), *n.* *Colloq.* A person or thing that has had his or its day; that which belongs to the past.

ha'sen·pfef'fer (hä'zĕn·(p)fĕf'ẽr), *n.* [G., fr. *hase* hare + *pfeffer* pepper.] A highly seasoned stew made of pickled rabbit's flesh.

hash (hăsh), *v. t.* [F. *hacher* to hash, fr. *hache* hatchet.] To chop into small pieces and mix; to make a mess of. — *n.* **1.** Meat and vegetables, esp. such as have been already cooked, chopped into small pieces, mixed, and, usually, browned by baking or sautéing. **2.** A new mixture of old matter. **3.** A mixture; a jumble; a mess. **4.** *Chiefly Scot.* A slovenly person; a stupid fellow.

Hash'im·ite (hăsh'ĭm·īt), *n.* A member of the Arabic dynasty founded by Husein ibn-Ali, King of the Hejaz 1916–24. — **Hash'im·ite,** *adj.*

hash'ish (hăsh'ēsh; -ĭsh), *n.* [Ar. *ḥashīsh* hemp.] Also **hash'eesh.** Cannabis, chewed or smoked in the East for its intoxicating effect.

hash mark. *Mil. Slang.* A service stripe.

has'let (hăs'lĕt; hās'-; hăz'-; -lĭt), *n.* [F. *hâtelettes* broil, fr. OF. *haste*, fr. OHG. *harst* gridiron.] The edible viscera (heart, liver, etc.) of a beast, esp. of a hog.

hasp (hȧsp; 9), *n.* [AS. *hæpse.*] A clasp or fastening as for a lid or book covers; esp., a hinged metal strap designed to be passed over a staple and to be secured by a pin, padlock, or the like. — *v. t.* To shut or fasten with a hasp.

has'sle, has'sel (hăs''l), *n.* [Perh. blend of *haggle* and *tussle.*] *Slang.* A confused struggle; a mix-up; also, an argument or quarrel.

has'sock (hăs'ŭk), *n.* [AS. *hassuc* a tuft of bog grass.] **1.** A tuft of bog grass or sedge; tussock. **2.** A stuffed cushion used as a footstool, or a cushion used under the knees when praying.

hast (hăst; 4), *2d pers. sing. pres.* of HAVE.

has'tate (hăs'tāt), *adj.* [L. *hastatus*, fr. *hasta* spear.] Spear-shaped; of leaves, triangular, with the basal angles or lobes spreading. See LEAF, *Illust.* (20).

haste (hāst), *n.* [OF. *haste*, of Teut. origin.] **1.** Celerity of motion; swiftness; dispatch. **2.** Undue celerity; unthinking or rash quickness of action. **3.** Urgency.

Syn. **Haste, hurry, speed, expedition, dispatch** (*or* **despatch**) mean quick or swift in movement or action. **Haste** implies urgency or precipitancy, usually in persons; **hurry** carries a stronger implication of confusion, agitation, or bustle; **speed,** used of things as well as persons, suggests swiftness of movement, or performance, etc., without bustle or confusion and, often, with success; **expedition** and **dispatch** both

imply speed and efficiency, *expedition* often suggesting ease, and *dispatch*, promptness.
— *v. t. & i. Now Literary & Dial.* To hasten; hurry.
has'ten (hās''n), *v. t.* To drive or urge forward; to accelerate; expedite; hurry. **—** *v. i.* To make haste; to hurry. — **has'ten·er** (-ẽr), *n.*
hast'y (hās'tĭ), *adj.;* HAST'I·ER (-tĭ·ẽr); HAST'I·EST. [OF. *hasti*, var. of *hastif*, fr. *haste*.] **1.** Done or made quickly; speedy; expeditious; esp., hurried. **2.** *Obs.* In a hurry; impatient; — with infinitive. **3.** Precipitate; headlong. **4.** Having, proceeding from, or indicating, a quick temper. **5.** Made, done, or reached, without deliberation or due caution. — **Syn.** See FAST. — **hast'i·ly**, *adv.* — **hast'i·ness**, *n.*
hasty pudding. **a** *Eng.* A batter of flour or oatmeal stirred into boiling water or milk. **b** *U. S.* Indian-meal mush.
hat (hăt), *n.* [AS. *hæt, hætt*.] **1.** A shaped covering, esp. one with a crown and brim, for the head. **2.** The red hat, hence, the office, of a cardinal. — ***throw, toss,*** etc., ***one's hat in the ring.*** *Colloq.* To announce one's entry, or readiness to enter, into a contest. — ***pass the hat.*** To take up a collection. — ***under one's hat.*** In one's head; also, to oneself; secret.
— *v. t.;* HAT'TED (hăt'ĕd; -ĭd); HAT'TING. To furnish or cover with a hat.
hat'a·ble (hāt'*à*·b'l), *adj.* Hateable; odious.
hat'band' (hăt'bănd'), *n.* A band round the crown of a hat; sometimes, a black band worn as a badge of mourning.
hat'box' (-bŏks'), *n.* A box for holding a hat or hats.
hatch (hăch), *n.* [AS. *hæc*.] **1.** A lower half of a divided door, gate, etc. **2.** *Naut.* **a** The covering of an opening in the deck, orig. a grating of wood or metal, but now usually solid. **b** A hatchway. **3. a** An opening in a floor, covered with a grating or trap door. **b** A floodgate.
hatch, *v. t.* [ME. *hacchen*.] **1.** To produce (young) from an egg or eggs by incubation, natural or artificial; to produce young from (eggs). **2.** To originate; concoct; contrive. **—** *v. i.* To produce young. **—** *n.* Act of hatching; also, that which is hatched; hence, outcome. — **hatch'er,** *n.*
hatch, *v. t.* [F. *hacher* to chop, hack. See HASH.] **1.** To mark with hatching. **2.** To inlay in fine lines. **—** *n. Fine Arts.* A stroke or line, esp. for shading.
hatch'el (hăch'ĕl), *n.* [For *hetchel*, ME. *hechele*.] A toothed instrument for cleansing flax or hemp from the tow, hurds, or coarse part. **—** *v. t.;* -ELED (-ĕld) or -ELLED; -EL·ING or -EL·LING. To dress with a hatchel.
hatch'er·y (hăch'ẽr·ĭ), *n.; pl.* -ERIES (-ĭz). A place for hatching eggs, esp. those of poultry or fish.
hatch'et (hăch'ĕt; -ĭt), *n.* [F. *hachette*, dim. of *hache* ax, of Teut. origin.] A short-handled ax with a hammer head, to be used with one hand; sometimes, a tomahawk, esp. in ***to dig up or to bury the hatchet***, to go to war or make peace.

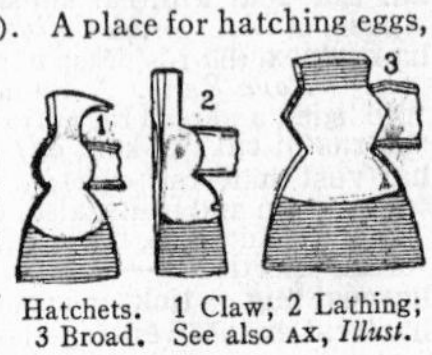
Hatchets. 1 Claw; 2 Lathing; 3 Broad. See also AX, *Illust.*

hatchet face. Thin, sharp face. — **hatch'et–faced',** *adj.*
hatch'ing, *n.* [See HATCH to mark.] In engraving, drawing, etc., the process or result of making fine lines in close proximity as shading.
hatch'ment (hăch'mĕnt), *n.* [Corrupt. fr. *achievement*.] *Her.* A panel on which the arms of a deceased person are temporarily displayed.
hatch'way' (-wā'), *n.* An opening, usually square or oblong, in a deck or floor, from one deck or story to another; also, any similar opening, as to a cellar.
hate (hāt), *v. t.* [AS. *hatian*.] **1.** To feel an intense aversion to; detest; abhor. **2.** To dislike exceedingly; — with an infinitive. **—** *v. i.* To feel hate or hatred.
Syn. **Hate, detest, abhor, abominate, loathe** mean to dislike extremely. **Hate** implies aversion often coupled with enmity or malice; **detest,** violent antipathy; **abhor,** profound, often shuddering, repugnance; **abominate,** strong detestation, as of something ill-omened or shameful; **loathe,** utter disgust and intolerance. — **Ant.** Love.
— *n.* [AS. *hete*.] **1.** Intense aversion; hatred. **2.** An object of hatred.
— **hate'a·ble** (hāt'*à*·b'l), *adj.* — **hat'er** (hāt'ẽr), *n.*
hate (hāt). Var. of HAET.
hate'ful (hāt'fŏŏl; -f'l), *adj.* **1.** *Archaic.* Full of hate; malevolent. **2.** Exciting or deserving hate; odious. — **hate'ful·ly,** *adv.* — **hate'ful·ness,** *n.*
Syn. **Hateful, odious, abhorrent, detestable, abominable** mean intensely disagreeable. **Hateful** applies to that which excites actual hatred; **odious,** to that which arouses offense or repugnance; **abhorrent,** to that which outrages one's sense of what is just, right, honorable, or decent; **detestable,** to that which deserves scorn or contempt; **abominable,** to that which is so abhorrent as to deserve execration.
hath (hăth; 4). *Archaic 3d pers. sing. pres.* of HAVE.
Hath'or (hăth'ôr), *n.* [Gr. *Hathōr*, fr. Egypt. *Het-Hert* the house above, var. *Het-Heru* the house of Horus.] *Egypt. Relig.* The goddess of love, mirth, and social joy, often represented with a cow's head or ears.
Ha·thor'ic (hă·thŏr'ĭk), *adj.* Of the goddess Hathor; *Arch.*, pertaining to a type of Egyptian column (**Hathor column**) having the capital sculptured with heads or masks representing Hathor.
ha'tred (hā'trĕd; -trĭd), *n.* [ME. *hatred, hatreden*, in which *-reden* is fr. AS. *rǣden* condition.] Strong aversion or detestation coupled with ill will.
hat'ter (hăt'ẽr), *n.* One who makes or sells hats.
hat tree. A stand with spreading arms for hats.
hau'berk (hô'bûrk), *n.* [OF. *hauberc*, fr. OHG. *halsberg*.] In medieval armor, a coat of mail developed into a long tunic of chain mail (see 2d MAIL, 1, and *Illust.*).
haugh (häk; häf), *n. Chiefly Scot.* A low-lying meadow by a river.
haugh'ty (hô'tĭ), *adj.;* HAUGH'TI·ER (-tĭ·ẽr); HAUGH'TI·EST. [F. *haut* high, fr. L. *altus*.] **1.** Disdainfully or contemptuously proud. **2.** *Archaic.* Noble; exalted. — **Syn.** See PROUD. — **haugh'ti·ly,** *adv.* — **haugh'ti·ness,** *n.*
haul (hôl), *v. t.* [Earlier *hall*, fr. ME. *halen*, fr. OF. *haler*, fr. ON. *hala*.] **1.** To pull or draw with force; to transport by drawing, esp. by conveyance. **2.** To call to account; — usually with *up*. **3.** *Naut.* To shift the course of (a ship), esp. so as to sail closer to the wind. **—** *v. i.* **1.** To pull; tug; drag. **2.** To change direction, as the wind, more often counterclockwise; to shift; — often with *around*. **3.** *Naut.* To shift the course of a ship, esp. closer to the wind. — **Syn.** See PULL. — ***haul off.*** To draw back one's arm so as to gain impetus for a blow. **—** *n.* **1.** A violent pull; a tug. **2.** A single draft of a net. **3.** That which is caught, taken, or gained at once, as by hauling a net; hence, loot. **4.** Transportation by hauling, or the distance or route covered.
haul'age (-ĭj), *n.* **1.** Act of hauling, or the force expended in hauling. **2.** Charge for hauling; specif., a charge made by a railroad for handling foreign cars.
haul'er (-ẽr), *n.* One who hauls; — in Eng. called also **haul'ier** (hôl'yẽr; *dial.* ôl'-).
haulm (hôm), *n.* [AS. *healm*.] **1.** *Eng.* Collectively, the stems or stalks of peas, beans, cereals, etc., without pods, etc. **2.** The culm or stem of a plant.
haunch (hônch; hänch), *n.* [OF. *hanche*, of Teut. origin.] **1.** The hip; hence, *pl.*, the hindquarters. **2.** Of meats: The leg and loin taken together; as, a *haunch* of venison. See LAMB, *Illust.* **3.** [Cf. HANCE, 2.] *Arch.* Either of the sides of an arch between the crown and the springings. See ARCH, *Illust.*
haunt (hônt; hänt), *v. t.* [OF. *hanter* to frequent, dwell, fr. AS. *hāmettan* to house, fr. *hām* abode.] **1.** To frequent; to visit intrusively. **2.** To inhabit or frequent as a specter; to pervade with spectral activities; as, a room reputed to be *haunted*. **3.** To recur to (the mind, etc.) frequently and spontaneously; as, *haunted* by vague dreams. **—** *v. i.* To persist in staying or visiting. — **Syn.** See FREQUENT. **—** *n.* **1.** A place to which one often resorts; a den or lair. **2.** (*pron.* hånt; hănt) *Dial.* A ghost. — **haunt'ing·ly,** *adv.*
Hau'sa (hou'sä), *n. sing. & pl.* One of a numerous and important Negroid people of Northern Nigeria and the Sudan; also, their language.
hau'sen (hô'z'n; *G.* hou'z'n), *n.* [G.] = BELUGA, 1.
haus·tel'lum (hôs·tĕl'ŭm), *n.; pl.* -LA (-*à*). [NL., fr. L. *haurire, haustum*, to drink.] *Zool.* A proboscis adapted to suck blood or juices of plants, as in many insects.
haus·to'ri·um (hôs·tō'rĭ·ŭm), *n.; pl.* -RIA (-*à*). [NL., fr. L. *haurire, haustum*, to draw, drink.] In parasitic plants, a specialized outgrowth of stem or root or a hyphal outgrowth (in fungi), serving for the absorption of food.
haut'boy (hō'boi; ō'boi), *n.* [F. *hautbois*, fr. *haut* high (in tone) + *bois* wood.] *Music.* An oboe. See OBOE, *Illust.*
hau·teur' (hō·tûr'; ō-), *n.* [F., fr. *haut* high.] Haughtiness; pride; arrogance.
Ha·van'a (h*à*·văn'*à*), *n.* [From *Havana*, Cuba.] A cigar made in Cuba or from Cuban tobacco.
have (hăv; 4), *v. t.;* HAD (hăd; 4); HAV'ING (hăv'ĭng). Indic. present, I *have*, thou *hast*, he *has*, or (archaic) *hath;* we, ye, they *have*. [AS. *habban* (imp. *hæfde*, past part. of *gehæfd*).] **1.** To hold in possession or control; to own. **2.** To be under necessity or obligation; — followed by the infinitive with *to;* as, he *had* to leave. **3.** To bear or beget. **4.** To be in a certain relation to; as, we *had* the sea on our right. **5.** To entertain in the mind. **6.** To perform; experience; participate in; as, let me *have* a look at it. **7.** To give expression to; to exercise, as patience. **8.** To maintain; assert; as, rumor *had* it. **9.** To obtain; acquire; learn; as, we *had* no news. **10.** To approve; tolerate; allow; as, I'll not *have* it so. **11.** To cause to be, go, or do; to effect. **12.** To hold (one) in a position of disadvantage; to hold an advantage over. **13.** To suffer from an exterior source; as, he *had* his leg broken. **14.** As an auxiliary verb followed by a past participle, expressing a sense of completed action, thus forming the perfect tenses of any verb; as, I *have* worked; I shall *have* eaten.
Syn. **Have, hold, own, possess** mean to control as one's own. **Have,** the general term, may imply any one of numerous reasons for regarding as one's own; **hold** usually suggests a grasp upon, an occupancy of, or a bond between; **own** implies a natural or legal right to regard as under one's full control; **possess** is preferred in law as implying a full title as well as a right, but may refer to other things such as power, a quality, etc.
have'lock (hăv'lŏk), *n.* [After Sir Henry *Havelock*, Eng. general.] A cloth covering for the cap, with flap shielding the neck as a protection from the sun.
ha'ven (hā'vĕn), *n.* [AS. *hæfen, hæfene*.] **1.** A harbor; port. **2.** A place of safety; an asylum. **—** *v. t.* To shelter.
hav'er (hȧv'ẽr; ȧv'-), *n.* [ME., of Scand. origin.] *Dial.* The oat.
ha'ver (hā'vẽr), *v. i. Chiefly Scot.* To maunder; babble.
ha'ver·el (hā'v'rĕl; ā'-), *n. Chiefly Scot.* A babbler; fool.
ha'vers (hā'vẽrz), *interj. Brit.* Nonsense.
hav'er·sack (hăv'ẽr·săk), *n.* [F. *havresac*, fr. G. *habersack* sack for oats.] A bag or case for carrying provisions on a march; — distinguished from *knapsack*.
hav'ior, hav'iour (hāv'yẽr), *n. Archaic.* Behavior.
hav'oc (hăv'ŭk), *n.* [OF. *havot* plunder, *crier havot* to cry havoc.] **1.** In medieval war the order to fall to pillage. **2.** Wide and general destruction; devastation. **—** *v. t. & i.;* HAV'OCKED (-ŭkt); HAV'OCKING. To devastate.
haw (hô), *n.* [AS. *haga*.] A hawthorn berry; hence, the hawthorn.
haw, *interj. & n.* A command used in guiding teams without reins, to turn to the near side, or to the left. **—** *v. t. & i.* To turn to the near side.
haw, *n.* The nictitating membrane, esp. when inflamed.
Ha·wai'ian (h*à*·wī'[y]*ă*n; -wô'y*ă*n), *adj.* from HAWAII, *Gaz.* **—** *n.* **1.** A native or citizen of Hawaii. **2.** The Hawaiian language, an Austronesian tongue. See LANGUAGE, *Table.*
haw'finch' (hô'fĭnch'), *n.* See GROSBEAK.
hawk (hôk), *n.* [AS. *hafoc, heafoc*.] Any of a family (Falconidae) of diurnal birds of prey, excepting the eagles and vultures and including besides the falcons, typified in America by the small ***pigeon hawk*** (*Falco columbarius*), the buzzards, harriers, kites, caracaras, and osprey (or fish hawk). Typically, any of a genus (*Accipiter*) including the sparrow hawk (which see) of Europe and the ***sharp-shinned hawk*** (*A. velox*) and ***Cooper's hawk*** (*A. cooperi*) of America (these two being also called ***chicken hawk***), or of a genus (*Astur*) consisting of the ***goshawks***, all of which are large short-winged hawks noted for powerful flight, activity, and courage. See BILL, *Illust.;* RAPTORIAL, *Illust.* **—** *v. i.* **1.** To pursue birds by means of hawks trained for the purpose; to practice falconry. **2.** To soar and strike like a hawk.
hawk (hôk), *v. i.* [Imitative.] To utter a harsh palatal sound, as

in clearing the throat. — *v. t.* To raise by hawking, as phlegm. — *n.* An audible effort to raise phlegm from the throat.
hawk, *v. t.* [From HAWKER one who sells.] To offer for sale by outcry in the street; to peddle. — *v. i.* To cry, or peddle, goods about.
hawk, *n.* A small board or metal sheet, with a handle on its under side, for holding mortar.
hawk′er (hôk′ẽr), *n.* A falconer.
hawk′er, *n.* [LG. *höker.* The E. form was influenced by *hawker* falconer, peddler of hawks.] One who sells wares from place to place or by crying them in the street; hence, a peddler.
Hawk′eye′ (hôk′ī′), *n.* A native or inhabitant of Iowa, the **Hawkeye State**; — a nickname.
hawk′-eyed′ (-īd′), *adj.* Having a keen eye; sharp-sighted.
hawk′ie (hôk′ĭ), *n. Scot.* A cow with a white face.
hawk′ing, *n.* Falconry. See FALCON, *Illust.*
hawk moth. Any of a numerous family (Sphingidae) of large graceful moths which have a stout body and a long proboscis, usually kept coiled up, and which suck the nectar of flowers; — called also *sphinx.*
hawk′s′-beard′ (hôks′bẽrd′), *n.* Any of a genus (*Crepis*) of plants of the chicory family having a copious bristly pappus.
hawks′bill′ tur′tle *or* **hawks′bill′** (-bĭl′), *n.* See TURTLE, 1.
hawk′s′-eye′ (-ī′), *n.* See TIGEREYE.
hawk′weed′ (hôk′wēd′), *n.* Any of a genus (*Hieracium*) of weedy herbs of the chicory family, having flowers with orange or red rays.
hawse (hôz; hôs), *n.* [Earlier *halse*, fr. ON. *hals* neck, part of the bows of a ship.] *Naut.* **1.** A hawsehole; also, that part of the bow in which are the hawseholes. **2.** The distance forward from bow to anchor. **3.** The situation of a vessel's cables when port and starboard anchors are used.
hawse′hole′ (-hōl′), *n. Naut.* One of the holes in the bow of a ship, through which a cable passes.
haw′ser (hô′zẽr; hô′sẽr), *n.* [OF. *haucier* to hoist.] A large rope for towing, warping, or mooring a ship.
hawser bend. See KNOT, *Illust.* (34).
haw′ser-laid′ (-lād′), *adj.* Cable-laid.
haw′thorn (hô′thôrn), *n.* [AS. *hagathorn, hægthorn.*] Any of a genus (*Crataegus*, esp. the European *C. oxyacantha* and the American *C. coccinea*) of spring-flowering spiny shrubs of the apple family, with glossy, and often lobed, leaves, white or pink fragrant flowers, and small red fruits called *haws.* The blossom of the ***downy hawthorn*** (*C. mollis*) is the State flower of Missouri. See COCKSPUR, 2.
hay (hā), *n.* [AS. *hēg, hīg, hīeg.*] Grass or other plant, as clover, mowed and cured for fodder. — *v. i.* To cut and cure grass for hay. — **hay′field′** (-fēld′), *n.*
hay, *n.* [AS. *hege* and OF. *haie.*] *Obs.* A hedge; a fence.
hay, *n.* [MF. *haye.*] A rustic dance with interweaving of couples.
hay′cock′ (hā′kŏk′), *n.* A conical pile or heap of hay.
hay fever. A catarrhal affection of the mucous membranes of eyes, nose, and respiratory tract, often with fever and asthma, caused chiefly by inhaled pollen of various plants.
hay′fork′ (-fôrk′), *n.* A hand fork or esp. a mechanically operated fork for loading or unloading hay.
hay′lift′ (-lĭft′), *n.* An airlift engaged in dropping emergency food to cattle isolated by deep snow.
hay′loft′ (-lôft′; 74), *n.* A loft for hay.
hay′mak′er (hā′māk′ẽr), *n.* **1.** A person engaged in making hay. **2.** *Boxing Slang.* A wild swing.
Hay′mar′ket (hā′mär′kĕt; -kĭt), *n.* A street in London, between Pall Mall and Piccadilly Circus, famous as a theater center.
hay′mow′ (hā′mou′), *n.* A mow of hay; a hayloft.
hay′rack′ (-răk′), *n.* **1.** A frame mounted on the running gear of a wagon, for hauling hay, straw, etc. **2.** A feeding rack to hold hay for cattle or horses.
hay′seed′ (-sēd′), *n.* Grass seed, esp. that gathered from a haymow; also, the bits of straw, chaff, etc., from hay.
hay′stack′ (hā′stăk′), *n.* Also **hay′rick′** (-rĭk′). A heap or pile of hay in the open air, often covered for preservation.
hay′ward′ (hā′wôrd′), *n.* [*hay* a hedge + *ward.*] An officer charged with care of fences for keeping out cattle.
hay′wire′ (hā′wīr′), *n.* **a** Wire used to bind bales of hay, straw, etc.; esp., such wire in a tangled mass after removal from the bales. **b** Hence, *Slang,* anything tangled, amiss, or out of order; — used esp. in the predicate with adverbial or adjectival force.
ha·zan′. Variant of HAZZAN.
haz′ard (hăz′ẽrd), *n.* [OF. *hasard*, fr. Ar. *al-zahr* the die.] **1.** An old dice game of which craps is a simplified form. **2.** Chance; a chance. **3. a** Risk; danger; peril; also, a source of risk. **b** *Shak.* Anything risked; a stake. **4.** *Court Tennis.* One of the winning openings in a court. **5.** *Eng. Billiards.* A stroke which pockets an object ball, called ***winning hazard,*** or a cue ball after contact, called ***losing hazard.*** **6.** *Golf.* Any obstruction in playing a stroke, including bunkers, traps, ponds, roadways, etc. — *v. t.* **1.** To venture; to risk. **2.** To run, or take, the risk of; to venture upon.
haz′ard·ous (-ẽr·dŭs), *adj.* **1.** Depending on chance or luck; aleatory. **2.** Dangerous; risky. — **Syn.** See DANGEROUS. — **haz′ard·ous·ly,** *adv.* — **haz′ard·ous·ness,** *n.*
haze (hāz), *n.* [Origin uncert.] **1.** Light vapor or smoke in the air impeding vision; a lack of transparency in the air, caused by dust or heat. **2.** A slightly clouded mental condition.
Syn. Haze, mist, fog mean a clouding of the atmosphere. **Haze** suggests a diffusion of dust, smoke, and the like; **mist**, a suspension of fine particles of water; **fog**, a denser condition than mist, with power to cut off the vision. Figuratively, **haze** suggests a vagueness, **mist** a dimness or indistinctness, **fog** a blinding of mental or spiritual vision.
haze, *v. t.* [OF. *haser* to irritate, vex.] **1.** *Chiefly Naut.* To harass by exacting unnecessary or difficult work. **2.** *U. S.* In schools, etc., to harass with abusive or ridiculous tricks. — **haz′er** (hāz′ẽr), *n.*
ha′zel (hā′z'l), *n.* [AS. *hæsel.*] **1.** Any of a genus (*Corylus*) of shrubs or small trees of the birch family (in U. S. esp. *C. americana* and *C. cornuta*) bearing nuts enclosed in a leafy involucre and called **ha′zel·nuts′** or *filberts.* See COBNUT. **2.** A stick from the wood of the hazel. **3.** The brown of the hazelnut, red-yellow in hue, of medium saturation and medium brilliance. See COLOR. — *adj.* **1.** Of hazels or hazel wood. **2.** Of the color hazel. — **ha′zel·ly** (-ĭ), *adj.*
haz′ing (hāz′ĭng), *n.* **1.** Infliction of excessive work. **2.** *Chiefly U. S.* A harassment by abusive or ridiculous treatment.
ha′zy (hā′zĭ), *adj.;* HA′ZI·ER (-zĭ·ẽr); HA′ZI·EST. **1.** Characterized by haze, usually by obscuring vapor less dense than fog or mist. **2.** Vague in thought or sense. — **ha′zi·ly,** *adv.* — **ha′zi·ness,** *n.*
haz·zan′, ha·zan′ (kä·zän′; käz′ăn), *n.* [Heb. *ḥazzān* superintendent, officer.] *Jewish Hist.* **1.** In the Talmudic period, a synagogue official. **2.** In modern times, a cantor.
H′-bomb′ (āch′bŏm′), *n.* See HYDROGEN BOMB.
he (hē; 4), *pron.; nom.* HE; *poss.* HIS (hĭz); *obj.* HIM (hĭm); *pl. nom.* THEY (thā); *poss.* THEIR (thâr) or THEIRS (thârz); *obj.* THEM (thĕm). [AS. *hē*, masc., *hēo*, fem., *hit*, neut.; pl. *hī*, or *hīe.*] **1.** The man or male being previously designated. **2.** That or any man or person; anyone; as, *he* who will may believe. — *n.* A man; a male.
he-. A combining form of *he*, denoting *a male of a* (specified) *class*, as in **he′-goat′.**
head (hĕd), *n.* [AS. *hēafod.*] **1.** The anterior division of the human or animal body, containing the brain, enclosed in the skull, the chief sense organs, and the mouth. **2.** The seat of the intellect; hence, a person; as, crowned *heads;* also, natural aptitude; as, a good *head* for figures; poise; mental balance; as, he kept his *head.* **3.** A representation of a head as on a coin. **4.** An individual; — often used as a plural; as, six *head* of cattle. **5.** The end of anything regarded as the upper end, through being higher, being associated with the head of a person, being opposite to the foot, or the like; as, the *head* of a bed or a valley; hence, either end. **6.** A director; chief; specif., a headmaster. **7.** The place of leadership or command. **8.** Culminating point or crisis; hence, strength; force. **9.** The source, as of a stream. **10.** A body of water kept in reserve at a height, as for a mill or in a reservoir; hence, pressure exerted by a body or column of fluid; as, a *head* of steam. **11.** A heading; hence, a separate part, or topic; as, the *heads* of a sermon. **12.** The top part of a plant, esp. when compact; *Bot.,* the capitulum. **13.** A headland or a projecting sand bar. **14.** The foremost, or front, part, as of a pier. **15.** The uppermost extremity or projecting part of an inanimate object, whether fixed or removable; as, the *head* of a cane, a nail, the femur, a sail, a page, a staircase; hence, either end, as of a cask. **16.** Hence, specif.: **a** The foam or scum on a fermenting or effervescing liquid. **b** The part of a boil, pimple, abscess, or the like, at which it is likely to break. **17.** *Linguistics.* The modified word or words in an endocentric construction. Thus, in "a very polite old man" *very polite old man, polite, old man,* and *man* are heads. The ultimate head, *man*, is called also *center.* **18.** *Mach.* A part or attachment of a machine or machine tool containing the cutter or cutters; as, the turret*head* of a lathe. **19.** *Mil.* The leading element of a column. **20.** *Mining.* A heading. **21.** *Music.* **a** The membrane of a drum or tambourine. See DRUM, *Illust.* **b** In a violin, lute, etc., the part above the neck. See LUTE, VIOLIN, *Illusts.* **c** The oval part of a note. **22.** *Naut.* The bow and adjacent parts. **23.** *Newspapers.* The headlines of an article taken as a whole.
— ***by,*** *or* ***down by, the head.*** *Naut.* Having the bows lower in the water than the stern. — ***out of one's head.*** *Colloq.* Delirious. — ***over one's head.*** **a** Beyond one's comprehension. **b** Passing over one with a higher position; — of promotions. — ***to go to one's head.*** To make one dizzy or conceited. — ***to lay heads together.*** To scheme together.
— *adj.* **1.** Principal; chief. **2.** Situated at the head; as, *head* sails. **3.** Coming from in front; as, a *head* sea.
— *v. t.* **1.** To behead. **2.** To lop off the top branches of; to poll. **3.** To fit or furnish with a head; to form the head of. **4.** To be or put oneself at the head of; to lead. **5.** To go round the head or source of. **6.** To get in the front of, so as to stop or turn back; hence, to restrain; as, to *head* a drove of cattle. **7.** To put something at the head of; to be placed, or stand, at the head of; as, his name *heads* the list; also, to excel. **8.** To shape the course of. — *v. i.* **1.** To form a head, as cabbage. **2.** To go or point in a certain direction; to tend. **3.** To have its source, as a river.
-head (-hĕd). *Now Rare.* = -HOOD, as in God*head.*
head′ache′ (hĕd′āk′), *n.* **1.** Pain in the head. **2.** A vexatious situation or baffling problem confronting one; also, a vexing worriment.
head′band′ (-bănd′), *n.* **1.** *Costume.* A band for the head; a fillet. **2.** *Books.* **a** *Chiefly U. S.* A decorative printed or engraved band at the head of a page or chapter. **b** A narrow strip of cloth glued to a book at the head and tail of the inner back.
head′board′ (-bōrd′; 70), *n.* A board forming the head, as of a bed.
head′cheese′ (hĕd′chēz′), *n. U. S.* Portions of the meat of the head or head and feet, esp. of swine, cut up fine, boiled, and pressed.
head′dress′ (-drĕs′), *n.* A covering or ornament for the head; also, a manner of dressing or adorning the hair.
head′ed (hĕd′ĕd; -ĭd), *adj.* **1.** Furnished with a head or a heading. **2.** Formed into a head.
-head′ed (*see Pron.,* § 2). A combining form of *headed*, denoting *having* (so many or such) *heads* or *a head*, as in wrong*headed.*
head′er (hĕd′ẽr), *n.* **1.** One who or that which heads nails, rivets, etc. **2.** A tube, chamber, or the like, to which a series of tubes or connections are joined so as to permit fluid to pass freely from one to another. **3.** *Colloq.* A fall or plunge headforemost; a dive. **4.** In framing, a piece of timber fitted between two trimmers; and carrying the ends of the tailpieces. **5.** *Agric. Mach.* A grain-harvesting machine which cuts off the grain heads and raises them to a wagon. **6.** *Masonry.* A brick or stone laid with its end toward the face of the wall.

Header, 4. *a, a* Trimmers; *b* Header; *c, c, c* Tailpieces or Tail Beams.

head′first′ (hĕd′fûrst′; 2), **head′-fore′most** (-fōr′mōst; -mŭst), *adv.* With the head foremost; headlong.
head gate. a An upper canal-lock gate. **b** A gate by which water is admitted to a race, sluice, or the like.
head′gear′ (hĕd′gēr′), *n.* **1.** Headdress, as a hat or cap; also, a guard or helmet to protect the head. **2.** Harness for a horse's head.
head′-hunt′ing, *n.* The custom, esp. of Malayan and Melanesian peoples, of decapitating enemies and preserving their heads. — **head′-hunt′er,** *n.* — **head′-hunt′ing,** *adj.*
head′i·ly (hĕd′ĭ·lĭ), *adv.* In a heady manner; headlong.
head′i·ness (-nĕs; -nĭs), *n.* Quality or state of being heady.
head′ing (hĕd′ĭng), *n.* **1.** That which serves to form a head or stands at the head; title. **2.** Material for the heads of casks, barrels, etc. **3.** *Aeronautics.* The compass direction in which the longitudinal axis of an aircraft points in flight. **4.** *Mining.* A horizontal passage or drift of a tunnel; also, the end of a drift.

head'land' (hĕd'lănd'; *sense 2 usually* -lănd), *n.* **1.** Unplowed land at the ends of furrows, or near a fence. **2.** A cape or promontory.

head'less, *adj.* [AS. *hēafodlēas.*] **1.** Having no head; acephalous; also, beheaded. **2.** Destitute of a chief or leader. **3.** Destitute of brains or prudence; foolish.

head'light' (hĕd'līt'), *n.* A light with reflector and lens, as at the front of a locomotive; also, a masthead light.

head'line' (-līn'), *n. Print.* A line at the top of a page, giving the running title, the page number, etc.; also, a title line over an article in a newspaper, or over an item.

head'lin'er (-līn'ẽr), *n.* **1.** A writer of headlines. **2.** A performer whose name is given prominent billing.

head'lock' (-lŏk'), *n. Wrestling.* A hold in which the head of one contestant is locked between the body and encircling arm of the opponent.

head'long (-lŏng; 74), *adv.* [ME. *hedling, hevedlynge,* confused with E. *long,* adj. & adv.] **1.** Headforemost. *Acts* i. 18. **2.** Precipitately. — *adj.* **1.** Rash; precipitate. **2.** Plunging headfirst. **3.** *Poetic.* Precipitous. — **Syn.** See PRECIPITATE.

head'man (-măn), *n.* [AS. *hēafodman.*] **1.** A leading man; a chief. **2.** An executioner.

head'mas'ter (-más'tẽr; 2), *n., or* **head master.** In some schools, the principal master, or principal. — **head'mas'ter-ship,** *n.*

head'mis'tress (-mĭs'trĕs; -trĭs), *n., or* **head mistress.** In some schools, the principal mistress or principal. — **head'mis'tress-ship,** *n.*

head money. **1.** A capitation tax. **2.** Prize money for a person captured or for the head of an outlaw or enemy.

head'-on', *adj.* Having the front facing, esp. in colliding.

head'most (hĕd'mōst; -mŭst), *adj.* Most advanced; foremost.

head'phone' (hĕd'fōn'), *n.* **a** A telephone receiver or a pair of them held over the ear or ears by a band. **b** A receiver like a telephone headphone for radio reception.

head'piece' (hĕd'pēs'), *n.* **1.** A covering for the head, as a helmet, an attachment with headphones for listening to a telephone, etc. **2.** The head; intellect. **3.** An engraved ornament at the head of a chapter.

head pin. *Tenpins.* The pin which stands at the head of the pins when set up.

head'quar'ters (hĕd'kwôr'tẽrz; 2), *n. pl., sometimes construed as sing.* The quarters of any chief officer, or head of a police force; the center of operations and of authority.

head'race' (-rās'), *n.* In a millrace, the current of water flowing down to the mill wheel.

head'rest' (hĕd'rĕst'), *n.* A support for the head.

head'sail' (-sāl'; *naut.* hĕd's'l), *n. Naut.* Any sail set forward of the foremast, as a jib or foretaysail. See SAIL, *Illust.*

head'set' (hĕd'sĕt'), *n. Elec.* A pair of headphones.

head'ship (-shĭp), *n.* The chief authority; chief place.

heads'man (hĕdz'măn), *n.; pl.* HEADSMEN (-mĕn). One who beheads.

head spin. *Wrestling.* A maneuver for escaping a half nelson, consisting in throwing the feet in the air and spinning round on the head.

head'spring' (hĕd'sprĭng'), *n.* Fountain; source.

head'stall' (hĕd'stôl'), *n.* That part of a bridle or halter which encircles the head.

head'stock' (-stŏk'), *n. Mach.* A bearing for a revolving part; specif., the part of a lathe that holds the spindle. Cf. TAILSTOCK.

head'stone' (-stōn'), *n.* **1.** The principal stone in a foundation; the cornerstone. **2.** The stone at the head of a grave.

head'stream' (-strēm'), *n.* A stream which is the source, or one of the sources, of a river.

head'strong (-strŏng; 74), *adj.* **1.** Not easily restrained; willful. **2.** Directed by ungovernable will. — **Syn.** See UNRULY.

head'wait'er (hĕd'wāt'ẽr; 2), *n.* The attendant in charge of the waiters in a dining room, as of a hotel.

head'wa'ter (-wô'tẽr; -wŏt'ẽr), *n.* Source of a stream; — used chiefly in *pl.*

head'way' (-wā'), *n.* **1.** Motion forward, as of a ship. **2.** Clear space under an arch, or the like. **3.** The time interval between two trains traveling the same route.

head wind. *Naut.* A wind directly ahead, or opposed to a ship's course.

head'work' (hĕd'wûrk'), *n.* Mental labor.

head'y (hĕd'ĭ), *adj.;* HEAD'I·ER (-ĭ-ẽr); HEAD'I·EST. [From HEAD.] **1.** Willful; rash; hence, violent; impetuous. **2.** Apt to affect the head; intoxicating. **3.** *Colloq.* Showing good judgment; as, a *heady* player.

heal (hēl), *v. t.* [AS. *hǣlan.*] **1.** To make hale, sound, or whole; to restore to health. **2.** To cure or restore to a sound or healthy condition (a disease or wound); to remedy or amend (any evil, as grief). **3.** To restore to original purity or integrity. — **Syn.** See CURE. — *v. i.* To return to a sound state. — **heal'er,** *n.* — **heal'ing·ly,** *adv.*

health (hĕlth), *n.* [AS. *hǣlth,* fr. *hāl* hale, sound, whole.] **1.** State of being hale or sound in body, mind, or soul; esp., freedom from physical disease or pain. **2.** A wish of health and happiness, as in pledging in a toast.

health'ful (-fŏŏl; -f'l), *adj.* **1.** Serving to promote health of body or mind; wholesome; salutary. **2.** Enjoying health; sound. — **health'ful·ly,** *adv.* — **health'ful·ness,** *n.*

health'y (hĕl'thĭ), *adj.;* HEALTH'I·ER (-thĭ-ẽr); HEALTH'I·EST. **1.** Being in a state of health; well. **2.** Evincing health; as, a *healthy* complexion. **3.** Conducive to health; as, *healthy* exercise. — **health'i·ly,** *adv.* — **health'i·ness,** *n.*

Syn. Healthy, sound, wholesome, robust, hale, well mean having or showing health of mind or body. Healthy implies full strength and vigor as well as freedom from signs of disease; sound suggests the proved possession of perfect health and absence of all signs of disease; wholesome implies a healthiness indicative of a person's physical, mental, and moral soundness; robust implies the attributes of all that is delicate; hale applies chiefly to the elderly who show no signs of infirmity or senility; well, a less explicit term, means merely freedom from disease or illness.

heap (hēp), *n.* [AS. *hēap* heap, multitude.] **1.** A pile or mass. **2.** *Now Colloq.* A great number or large quantity. — *v. t.;* HEAPED (hĕpt) *or* HEAP'ING. **1.** To throw or lay in a heap; to amass; lay up; accumulate. **2.** To bestow in large quantities. **3.** To fill (a measure) more than even full.

hear (hẽr), *v. t.;* HEARD (hûrd; *formerly* hẽrd); HEAR'ING. [AS.

hēran, hȳran, hēran.] **1.** To perceive by the ear. **2.** Hence, to gain knowledge or appreciation of by hearing, as the news. **3.** To listen to; to heed. **4.** To accede to the demand or wishes of. **5.** To examine or judge in hearing, as a recitation; specif., *Law,* to give a hearing to. **6.** To attend, or be present at, as a hearer or worshiper. — *v. i.* **1.** To have the sense or faculty of perceiving sound. **2.** To be informed. — **hear'er,** *n.*

hear'ing (hẽr'ĭng), *n.* **1.** The process, function, or power of perceiving sound; the special sense by which noises and tones are received as stimuli through a characteristic end organ, the ear; the auditory sense. **2.** Opportunity to be heard; audience. **3.** Extent within which sound may be heard; earshot. **4.** A listening to arguments or proofs by an officer, court, or the like; *Law,* in equity practice, a trial.

hark'en, hark'en (här'kĕn), *v. i.* [AS. *hercnian, heorcnian,* fr. the source of E. *hark.*] To listen; to give ear; to give heed. — *v. t. Archaic.* To hear; to give heed to.

hear'say' (hẽr'sā'), *n.* Something heard from another; report; rumor; common talk. — **hear'say',** *adj.*

hearsay evidence. *Law.* Such evidence as does not derive its value solely from the credit given to the witness himself as such, but rests in part on the veracity and competency of some other person; it is, with a few exceptions, inadmissible as testimony.

hearse (hûrs), *n.* [OF. *herce* harrow, hearse (in sense 1), fr. L. *hirpex, irpex,* harrow.] **1.** A framework with prickets used as a candelabrum in Tenebrae or over a coffin in church. **2.** *Hist.* An elaborate framework erected over a coffin or royal tomb to which verses or epitaphs were attached. **3.** *Archaic.* A bier. **4.** A vehicle for conveying the dead to the grave. — *v. t.;* HEARSED (hûrst); HEARS'ING. **1.** To place on or in a hearse; to bury. **2.** To shroud.

heart (härt), *n.* [AS. *heorte.*] **1.** *Anat. & Zool.* A hollow muscular organ, which, by contracting rhythmically, keeps up the circulation of

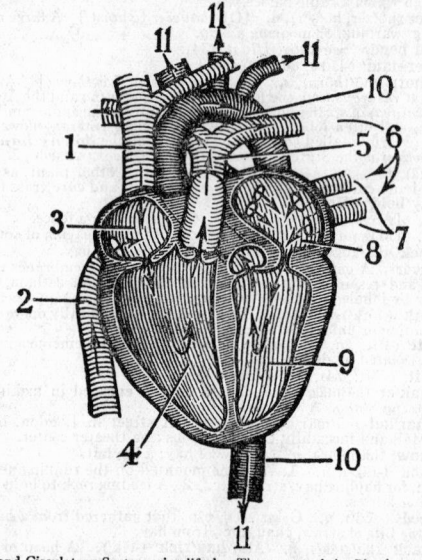

Heart and Circulatory System, simplified. The course of the Blood may be followed, coming from the extremities and entering from the Superior Vena Cava (1) and from the Inferior Vena Cava (2) into the Right Auricle (3), to the Right Ventricle (4), and to the Pulmonary Artery (5); thence to the Lungs (6, not shown), returning by the Pulmonary Vein (7), into the Left Auricle (8), the Left Ventricle (9), and the Aorta (10), from which it goes out (by 11) to the extremities, to return again by 1 and 2.

the blood. **2.** The part nearest the center; specif., the core of a tree, the pith of wood, or the like. **3.** The inmost or most essential part of any body or system. **4.** The bosom. **5.** Something resembling a heart in shape; specif., a conventionalized representation of a heart, as a decorative figure (see *Illust.*) or a trinket. **6.** The heart regarded as the seat of spiritual or conscious life; soul; spirit; specif.: **a** The emotional as distinguished from the intellectual nature; as, *heart* and head often disagree; hence, emotion, esp. a benevolent emotion as sympathy or love. **b** Courage; spirit. **c** Memory; — in the phrase *to learn by heart.* **d** *Obs.,* exc. in *after one's own heart,* intent, desire. **e** Conscience; moral sensibility. **f** Temperament; mood; as, a heavy *heart.* **7.** Vital part; secret meaning. **8.** Power of fertile production. **9.** One of a suit of playing cards with the figure of the heart in red; *pl.* this suit, also, a game, somewhat like whist, in which the object is to avoid taking tricks containing hearts. **10.** A man; a person; as, stout *hearts* that followed me. Heart, 5.

— **at heart.** In the inmost character; at bottom. — **from one's heart.** From one's inmost soul; sincerely. — **to have at heart.** To desire (anything) earnestly. — **to have the heart.** To be sufficiently hardhearted. — **with all one's heart.** Very earnestly.

— *v. t. Now Rare.* **a** To hearten. **b** To fix in the heart.

heart'ache' (härt'āk'), *n.* Sorrow; anguish of mind.

heart and soul. With the utmost earnestness.

heart block. *Med.* A pathological condition in which the ventricular beat of the heart does not follow the auricular beat with normal regularity.

heart'break' (härt'brāk'), *n.* Crushing sorrow or grief.

heart'break'ing (-brāk'ĭng; 2), *adj.* Causing overpowering sorrow.

heart'bro'ken (-brō'kĕn; 2), *adj.* Overcome by sorrow.

heart'burn' (-bûrn'), *n.* **1.** = CARDIALGIA. **2.** Heartburning; envy.

heart'burn'ing, *n.* Discontent; secret enmity.

heart cam. See CAM, *Illust.*

heart cherry. A race of cherries with heart-shaped fruit, derived from the sweet cherry (*Prunus avium*).
heart disease. Any abnormal or morbid condition of the heart.
-heart'ed (-här'tĕd; -tĭd). A combining form denoting *having* (such) *a heart;* as, faint*hearted;* stout*hearted.*
heart'en (här't'n), *v. t.* To give heart to; to encourage.
heart'felt' (härt'fĕlt'), *adj.* Deeply felt; sincere. — **Syn.** See SINCERE.
heart'-free' (-frē'; 2), *adj.* Having the affections disengaged; not in love.
hearth (härth; *now poet. or dial.* hûrth), *n.* [AS. *heorth.*] **1.** The pavement on which a fire is made, usually in a chimney; the floor of a fireplace; also, a corresponding part of a stove. **2.** The fireside; the home itself. **3.** *Metal.* **a** The crucible of a blast furnace. **b** The bottom of a reverberatory or open-hearth furnace on which the ore or metal is exposed to the flame. **c** A bloomery. **d** The inside bottom of a cupola.
hearth'stone' (härth'stōn'), *n.* **1.** Stone forming the hearth; hence, fireside; home. **2.** A composition of powdered stone and pipe clay, used to scour hearths, doorsteps, etc.
heart'i·ly (här'tĭ·lĭ), *adv.* **1.** With sincerity. **2.** With zest or zeal. **3.** Abundantly.
heart'i·ness (-tĭ·nĕs; -nĭs), *n.* Quality of being hearty.
heart'land' (härt'lănd'), *n.* In geopolitics, a central land area conceived to be capable of self-sufficiency as an economic and military unit, invulnerable to seapower and holding mastery of the world island and thereby of the world; specif., northern Eurasia from the Elbe to the Amur.
heart'less, *adj.* **1.** Destitute of courage or zeal; spiritless. **2.** Destitute of feeling; unsympathetic; merciless. — **heart'less·ly,** *adv.* — **heart'less·ness,** *n.*
heart point. See ESCUTCHEON, *Illust.*
heart'-rend'ing (härt'rĕn'dĭng; 2), *adj.* Causing anguish.
heart'scald' (härt'- *or* hĕrt'skôld'; -skäld'; -skôd'; -skäd'), *n. Dial.* Heartburn; hence, remorse.
hearts'ease' (härts'ēz'), *n.* Also **heart's'-ease'.** **1.** [Prop. two words, *heart's ease.*] Ease of heart; peace. **2.** The wild pansy. See PANSY. **3.** *U. S.* The common persicary.
heart'sick' (härt'sĭk'), *adj.* Sick at heart; very despondent.
heart'some (härt'sŭm; hĕrt'-), *adj. Chiefly Scot.* Animating; also, merry; lively. — **heart'some·ly,** *adv.*
heart'sore' (härt'sōr'), *adj.* Grieved; indicative of grief.
heart'-strick'en (-strĭk'ĕn), **heart'-struck'** (-strŭk'), *adj.* Struck to the heart with grief, dismay, or the like.
heart'string' (-strĭng'), *n.* A nerve once supposed to sustain the heart; hence, the deepest emotions or affections.
heart'-to-heart', *adj.* Sincere; frank.
heart'-whole' (härt'hōl'; 2), *adj.* **1.** Having the heart or affections free. **2.** Of a single and sincere heart.
heart'wood' (-wŏŏd'), *n.* The hard central part of the trunk of a dicotyledonous tree. See DURAMEN.
heart'y (här'tĭ), *adj.;* HEART'I·ER (-tĭ·ĕr); HEART'I·EST. **1.** Pertaining to, or proceeding from, the heart; warm; cordial; also, energetic. **2.** Exhibiting strength; sound; healthy. **3.** Promoting strength; nourishing; abundant; as, *hearty* food; also, enjoying abundant food. **4.** Fertile; — of land. — **Syn.** See SINCERE. — *n.; pl.* HEARTIES (-tĭz). Comrade; — in addressing sailors; hence, a sailor.
heat (hēt), *n.* [AS. *hǣtu, hǣto;* akin to E. HOT.] **1.** That which causes a body to rise in temperature, fuse, evaporate, or undergo related phenomena as a result of interaction with another body of higher temperature; the energy involved in such phenomena; in terms of the kinetic theory, the energy associated with the minute parts of a body because of their random motions and mutual forces. **2.** High temperature; also, a period of heat; a hot place. **3.** Intensity of feeling; also, an instance of it. Specif.: **a** Rage; vehemence. **b** Agitation of mind; exasperation. **c** Animation, as in discourse; ardor. **4.** A single effort. **5.** A single complete operation of heating, as at a forge or in a furnace; also, the quantity so heated. **6.** Appearance, condition, or color of a body, as indicating its temperature; degree of temperature to which something is heated. **7.** The height or stress of an action or condition. **8.** Sexual excitement; specif., the period during which the female of mammals will accept service by the male; oestrus; as, to be in *heat.* **9.** *Slang.* **a** Extreme pressure, as in police investigation of crime, a racer's spurt or the like; — esp. in *to turn on the heat.* **b** *Underworld Slang.* The relentless trailing of a lawbreaker. **c** *Underworld Slang.* Coercive application of torture, as for extorting a confession. **d** Coercion, whether by legal proceedings or by underhand compulsion or intimidation. **10.** *Psychol.* A sensation resulting from the simultaneous stimulation of warm and cold spots on the skin. **11.** *Sports.* **a** A single course in a race or other contest. **b** When contestants are too many to compete at once, a division of a contest in which the losers are eliminated. — *v. t. & i.* To make or grow hot; hence, to excite; inflame. — **heat'ed·ly** (hēt'ĕd·lĭ; -ĭd·lĭ), *adv.*
heat engine. An engine for converting the energy of heat into mechanical energy, as in steam and gas engines.
heat'er (hēt'ĕr), *n.* **1.** A contrivance to impart heat or hold a thing to be heated; as: **a** A stove, furnace, steam radiator, etc. **b** In an electron tube, an element for supplying heat indirectly to a cathode. **2.** One whose work is to heat something; as, an ingot *heater;* a rivet *heater.*
heath (hēth), *n.* [ME. *heth* waste land, the plant heath, fr. AS. *hǣth.*] **1.** A tract of waste land; esp., in Great Britain, an open, level area with a characteristic vegetation of low shrubs. Cf. MOOR. **2.** Any of a large genus (*Erica*) of low evergreen undershrubs having whorls of needlelike leaves and clusters of small white, pink, or yellow flowers; often, any plant of the family (Ericaceae, the heath family), typified by this genus and including the rhododendrons, azaleas, and sometimes the huckleberries and wintergreens. **3.** The common heather (*Calluna vulgaris*).
heath aster. A common aster (*Aster ericoides*) of the eastern United States, with small white flower heads.
heath'ber'ry (hēth'bĕr'ĭ; -bĕr·ĭ), *n.* Any berry growing on a heath, esp. the crowberry and bilberry.
heath'bird' (-bûrd'), *n.* The black grouse.
heath cock. The blackcock.
hea'then (hē'thĕn), *n.; pl.* HEATHENS (-thĕnz) or, collectively, HEATHEN. [AS. *hǣthen,* prob. connected with *hǣth* heath, meaning orig. one who lives in the country or on the heaths.] **1.** An unconverted member of a people that does not acknowledge the God of the Bible; a pagan; specif., *Bib.,* an idolater. **2.** An unenlightened or irreligious person. — *adj.* **1.** Gentile; pagan; hence, unenlightened; irreligious. **2.** Of or pertaining to the heathen. — **hea'then·dom** (-dŭm), *n.* — **hea'then·ry** (-rĭ), *n.*
hea'then·esse' (-ĕs'), *n. Archaic.* Heathenism; heathendom.
hea'then·ish (-ĭsh), *adj.* Of the heathen; heathenlike, pagan, or barbarous. — **hea'then·ish·ly,** *adv.* — **hea'then·ish·ness,** *n.*
hea'then·ism (-ĭz'm), *n.* The rites of heathens; idolatry; also, heathenish manners or morals.
hea'then·ize (-īz), *v. t. & i.* To render or become heathen or heathenish.
heath'er (hĕth'ĕr), *n.* [ME. *hadder, hathir,* perh. fr. ON. *heithr.*] A species of heath (*Calluna vulgaris*) having a rose-colored calyx with a whorl of green bracts at the base; ling; also, any of several other British heaths (genus *Erica*).
heath'er·y (-ĭ), *adj.* Abounding in or like heather.
heath, *or* **heather, grass.** A European perennial grass (*Sieglingia decumbens*) growing on heaths and moors.
heath hen. **a** The female of the black grouse. **b** A grouse (*Tympanuchus cupido*) closely related to the prairie chicken.
heath'y (hēth'ĭ), *adj.* Of or like heath; heathery.
heat lightning. Vivid electric flashes, without thunder, ascribed to far-off lightning, reflected by high clouds. It is seen near the horizon, especially at the close of a hot day.
heat'stroke' (hēt'strōk'), *n. Med.* Exhaustion or illness caused by exposure to excessive heat.
heaume (hōm), *n.* [F.] A great helmet, worn over a hood of mail or close-fitting steel cap. See HELMET, *Illust.* (9).
heave (hēv), *v. t.;* HEAVED (hēvd) or HOVE (hōv); HEAV'ING. [AS. *hebban* (pret. *hōf,* past part. *hafen*).] **1.** To lift or raise, now usually with exertion. **2.** *Chiefly Naut.* To throw; to cast. **3.** To force from the breast; to utter with effort; as, to *heave* a sigh. **4.** To cause to swell or rise, as the breast. **5.** *Geol.* To displace (a stratum), as by a fault. **6.** *Naut.* To draw or pull; to haul on. — **Syn.** See LIFT. — *v. i.* **1.** To be thrown up or raised, as ground. **2.** To rise and fall with alternate motions. **3.** To strain to do something difficult; specif.: **a** To pant. **b** To retch. **4.** *Naut.* To haul or push; to move a vessel in a (specified) direction or manner; also, of the vessel, to move.
heave in sight. To seem to rise above the horizon and come in sight. — ***heave to.*** *Naut.* To bring (a vessel) to a standstill by heading into the wind with headsails aback.
— *n.* **1.** An effort to heave or to raise something. **2.** An upward motion; a rising; esp., a rhythmical rising. **3.** *Geol.* The horizontal displacement by a faulting. See FAULT, *Illust.* **4.** *pl.* (HEAVES) *construed as sing.* A disease, chiefly of horses, marked by permanent distention of the air vesicles, heaving of the flanks, and a persistent cough; broken wind.
heav'en (hĕv'ĕn), *n.* [AS. *heofon.*] **1.** *Chiefly pl.* The expanse of space surrounding the earth, esp., that arching over the earth; the firmament; empyrean; the sky. **2.** The abode of the Deity and of the blessed dead. **3.** [*cap.*] God; Providence. **4.** Any place of supreme happiness or great comfort; also, perfect felicity. **5.** The sky or climate of a particular region. **6.** *Christian Science.* Harmony; the reign of Spirit; government by divine Principle; spirituality; bliss; the atmosphere of Soul. *Mary Baker Eddy.*
heav'en·ly, *adj.* **1.** Of or dwelling in heaven; celestial. **2.** Of the heavens. **3.** Divine; also, of more than earthly purity or beauty. — **heav'en·li·ness,** *n.*
Heavenly City. See NEW JERUSALEM.
heav'en·ward (-wĕrd), **heav'en·wards** (-wĕrdz), *adv.* Toward heaven.
heav'en·ward, *adj.* Directed or tending toward heaven.
heav'er (hēv'ĕr), *n.* One who heaves; *Naut.,* a bar used as a lever in twisting rope, etc.
heav'i·ly (hĕv'ĭ·lĭ), *adv.* **1.** In a heavy manner; with great weight. **2.** Slowly and laboriously; dully.
heav'i·ness (-ĭ·nĕs; -nĭs), *n.* Heavy state or quality.
Heav'i·side, *or* **Ken'nel·ly-Heav'i·side** (kĕn''l·ĭ·hĕv'ĭ·sīd), **lay'er.** [After O. *Heaviside,* Brit. physicist, and A. E. *Kennelly,* Am. elec. engineer.] = IONOSPHERE.
heav'y (hĕv'ĭ), *adj.;* -I·ER (-ĭ·ĕr); -I·EST. [AS. *hefig;* akin to AS. *hefe* weight, *hebban* to lift, heave. See HEAVE.] **1.** Heaved or lifted with labor; weighty; hence, of high specific gravity. **2.** Not easy to bear; burdensome; oppressive; hence, afflictive. **3.** Of weighty import; grave; consequential. **4.** Deep; intense; as, a *heavy* silence. **5.** Burdened; bowed down with care, grief, etc. **6.** Great with young. **7.** Slow or dull; sluggish; stupid; as, a *heavy* gait or style; also, lacking mirth or gaiety; doleful. **8.** Overcome with weariness or dull with sleep. **9.** Of more than the usual amount or quantity; as, a *heavy* rain; specif.: **a** Violent; as, a *heavy* storm. **b** Gloomy; overcast; lowering; as, a *heavy* sky. **c** Cloggy; clayey. **d** Loud; deep; as, a *heavy* sound. **e** Thick; massive; as, *heavy* features. **f** Oppressive; as, a *heavy* odor. **g** Steep; as, a *heavy* grade. **10.** Of foods, etc.: **a** Not easily digested. **b** Not properly leavened. **11.** Above a certain usual weight; as, *heavy* woolens. **12.** *Mil.* Heavy-armed. **13.** *Theater.* Of a grave or somber nature; as, the *heavy* villain.
Syn. **Heavy, weighty, ponderous, cumbrous, cumbersome** mean not easy to bear. **Heavy** implies greater density and compactness in substance than the average of its kind and class; **weighty,** actual and not relative heaviness; **ponderous,** extreme heaviness because of size and massiveness; **cumbrous** and **cumbersome,** heaviness and bulkiness that make for difficulty in moving or carrying. Figuratively, **heavy** applies to a person or thing that weighs on the senses, the spirit, the mind, etc.; **weighty,** to things momentous or deeply impressive; **ponderous,** to things unduly labored, complicated, or the like; **cumbrous** and **cumbersome,** to things both ponderous and unwieldy.
— *n.; pl.* HEAVIES (-ĭz). *Theater.* **a** A role or actor representing a grave or imposing person. **b** The villain.
heav'y-armed' (hĕv'ĭ·ärmd'; 2), *adj.* Wearing heavy armor; having or carrying heavy arms.
heav'y-du'ty (-dū'tĭ; 2), *adj.* Able to withstand unusual strain, exposure, wear, etc.; also, subject to a high tariff rate.
heavy earth. Baryta, or barium monoxide.
heav'y-heart'ed (-här'tĕd; -tĭd; 2), *adj.* Despondent.
heavy hydrogen. *Chem.* Deuterium; also, tritium.
heavy spar. See BARIUM SULFATE.
heavy water. *Chem.* **a** Any species of water heavier than ordinary water; specif., deuterium oxide, D_2O. **b** Any water mixture heavier

than ordinary water, esp. that containing a higher than usual proportion of deuterium oxide, D_2O.

heav'y·weight' (hĕv'ĭ·wāt'), *n.* In wrestling, boxing, etc., one in the heaviest of the classes of contestants; esp., any contestant weighing not less than 175 pounds.

heb'do·mad (hĕb'dō·măd), *n.* [L. *hebdomas, -adis,* fr. Gr. *hebdomas* the number seven, seven days, fr. *hebdomos* seventh.] **1.** The number seven. **2.** A week.

heb·dom'a·dal (hĕb·dŏm'ȧ·dăl; -d'l), *adj.* [LL. *hebdomadalis.*] Of, or occurring at intervals of, seven days.

He'be (hē'bē), *n.* [L., fr. Gr. *hēbē* youth, *Hēbē* Hebe.] *Gr. Relig.* The goddess of youth, daughter of Zeus and Hera, and cupbearer of the gods before Ganymede.

he'be·phre'ni·a (hē'bē·frē'nĭ·ȧ), *n.* [NL., fr. Gr. *hēbē* youth, puberty + *phrēn* mind.] A form of dementia praecox occurring usually at puberty. — **he'be·phren'ic** (-frĕn'ĭk), *adj.*

heb'e·tate (hĕb'ē·tāt), *v. t. & i.* [L. *hebetatus,* past part. of *hebetare* to dull.] To make or become dull; to blunt. — **heb'e·ta'tion** (-tā'shŭn), *n.*

he·bet'ic (hē·bĕt'ĭk), *adj.* [Gr. *hēbētikos,* fr. *hēbē* puberty.] Of, pertaining to, or occurring at puberty.

heb'e·tude (hĕb'ē·tūd), *n.* [LL. *hebetudo.*] Obtuseness.

He·bra'ic (hē·brā'ĭk), *adj.* [LL. *Hebraicus,* fr. Gr. *Hebraïkos.*] Of or pertaining to the Hebrews, or to Hebrew.

He'bra·ism (hē'brā·ĭz'm), *n.* **1.** A Hebrew idiom or attribute. **2.** Hebrew institutions; Judaism. **3.** Hebrew character, spirit, or mode of thought. Cf. HELLENISM.

He'bra·ist (-ĭst), *n.* **1.** One versed in the Hebrew language and learning. **2.** One having the qualities of Hebraism; also, an adherent of Judaism.

He'bra·is'tic (-ĭs'tĭk), **He'bra·is'ti·cal** (-tĭ·kăl), *adj.* Hebraic; marked by Hebraism or characteristic of Hebraists.

He'bra·ize (hē'brā·īz), *v. t. & i.* [Gr. *hebraizein* to speak Hebrew.] To make or become Hebrew or Hebraic; to speak Hebrew or use a Hebraism.

He'brew (hē'broo), *n.* [OF. *Ebreu,* fr. L. *Hebraeus,* fr. Gr. *Hebraios,* fr. Heb. *'Ibhri.*] **1.** A member of one of a group of northern Semitic tribes, including the Israelites; usually, specif., an Israelite. **2.** The Semitic language of the ancient Hebrews. See LANGUAGE, *Table.* — *adj.* Of or pertaining to the Hebrews or Hebrew.

Hebrew calendar. = JEWISH CALENDAR.

He'brews (hē'brooz), *n. pl., construed as sing.* The Epistle to the Hebrews, in the New Testament. See BIBLE.

Hec'a·te, Hek'a·te (hĕk'ȧ·tē; -tē; *formerly often* hĕk'ăt), *n.* [L., fr. Gr. *Hekatē.*] *Gr. Relig.* A goddess of the moon, earth, and underworld; later, dark goddess of magic.

hec'a·tomb (hĕk'ȧ·tōm; -tōom), *n.* [L. *hecatombe,* fr. Gr. *hekatombē,* fr. *hekaton* hundred + *bous* ox.] *Gr. Antiq.* A sacrifice of a hundred oxen or cattle at one time; hence, a great slaughter.

hecht (hĕkt). Scot. var. of HIGHT.

heck'le (hĕk''l), *v. t.;* HECK'LED (-'ld); HECK'LING (-lĭng). [ME. *hekelen,* var. of *hechelen.* See HATCHEL.] **1.** To hackle. **2.** To badger with questions, comments, or gibes. — **Syn.** See BAIT. — *n.* Hackle. — **heck'ler** (-lẽr), *n.*

hec'tare (hĕk'târ), *n.* [F., fr. Gr. *hekaton* hundred + F. *are* an are.] See METRIC SYSTEM, *Table* 3.

hec'tic (hĕk'tĭk), *adj.* [F. *hectique,* fr. LL., fr. Gr. *hektikos* habitual, consumptive.] **1.** Pertaining to slow waste of animal tissue, as in consumption. **2.** In a hectic condition; having hectic fever. **3.** *Colloq.* Filled with excitement; restless. — *n. Med.* **a** A hectic fever; also, a consumptive. **b** A hectic flush. — **hec'ti·cal·ly** (-tĭ·kăl·ĭ), *adv.*

hectic fever. A type of fever occurring usually at an advanced stage of exhausting disease, as in pulmonary tuberculosis, and marked by a daily recurring rise of temperature, profuse perspiration, and flushed face (**hectic flush**).

hec'to- (hĕk'tō-), **hect-.** [Gr. *hekaton.*] A combining form meaning *hundred,* as in **hec'to·gram** *or* **hec'to·gramme, hec'to·li'ter** *or* **hec'to·li'tre, hec'to·me'ter** *or* **hec'to·me'tre, hec'to·stere.** See METRIC SYSTEM, *Tables.*

hec'to·cot'y·lus (-kŏt'ĭ·lŭs), *n.; pl.* -LI (-lī). [NL., fr. *hecto-* + Gr. *kotylē* hollow vessel.] *Zool.* One of the arms of the male of most cephalopods, which is modified in various ways to effect the fertilization of the eggs.

hec'to·graph (hĕk'tō·grăf; 9), *n.* [*hecto-* + *-graph.*] A contrivance for manifolding a writing by transferring it to a slab of gelatin treated with glycerin, and then taking transcripts from the gelatin. — *v. t.* To copy with a hectograph. — **hec'to·graph'ic** (-grăf'ĭk), *adj.*

Hec'tor (hĕk'tẽr), *n.* [L., fr. Gr. *Hektōr,* prop., holding fast.] **1.** In Homer's *Iliad,* a son of Priam, husband of Andromache, and bravest of the Trojans. He slew Patroclus, and was slain by Achilles. **2.** [*not cap.*] One who hectors; a bully; roisterer. — *v. t.* [*not cap.*] To bully; hence, to torment by words; to irritate by bullying. — **Syn.** See BAIT.

Hec'u·ba (hĕk'ū·bȧ), *n.* [L., fr. Gr. *Hekabē.*] In the *Iliad,* the wife of Priam and mother of Hector.

hed'dle (hĕd''l), *n.* One of the sets of cords or wires which compose the harness to guide the warp threads in a loom.

hedge (hĕj), *n.* [AS. *hecg, hegg.*] **1.** A thicket, esp. when planted as a fence or boundary. **2.** A barrier; limit.

— *adj.* Of or for a hedge; as, *hedge* plants; born, living, or done near hedges; roadside; clandestine; as, a *hedge* marriage; hence, low in class or quality.

— *v. t.;* HEDGED (hĕjd); HEDG'ING. **1.** To enclose or separate with a hedge. **2.** To obstruct as with a barrier; to hinder. **3.** To surround as for defense; guard. **4.** To surround so as to prevent escape. **5.** To safeguard oneself from loss on (a risk) by making compensatory arrangements on the other side. — *v. i.* **1.** To shelter oneself from danger, duty, etc., as if by hiding behind a hedge. **2.** To arrange a way of escape from any position taken; specif., to use qualifications in one's speech to avoid committing oneself definitely. **3.** *Betting.* To reduce the risk of a wager by making a bet against the side one has bet on. **4.** *Stock Exchange.* To counterbalance a sale or purchase of one security by making a purchase or sale of another.

hedge garlic. A wild mustard (*Alliaria officinalis*) with a strong odor of garlic.

hedge'hog' (hĕj'hŏg'), *n.* **1. a** Any of a genus (*Erinaceus*) of Old World, nocturnal, insectivorous mammals having both hair and spines which they present outwardly by rolling themselves up. **b** In America, the porcupine. **2.** *Mil.* **a** A defensive stronghold fortified with mine fields and pillboxes and concentrations of artillery and supplies, for sustained resistance to frontal attack, encirclement, and siege. **b** A wire entanglement made of barbed wire.

hedge'hop' (hĕj'hŏp'), *v. i. & t.;* -HOPPED' (-hŏpt'); -HOP'PING. *Aviation Slang.* To fly (an airplane) so close to the ground (often at 25-foot elevation) that it is necessary to "hop" over trees, hedges, etc. — **hedge'hop'per** (-hŏp'ẽr), *n.*

hedge hyssop. **a** Any of a genus (*Gratiola*) of herbs of the figwort family (esp. *G. aurea*). **b** In Great Britain, any of several similar plants (as *Scutellaria minor,* etc.).

hedg'er (hĕj'ẽr), *n.* One who makes, trims, or mends hedges; also, one who hedges, as in betting, evading, etc.

hedge'row' (hĕj'rō'), *n.* A row of shrubs or trees, planted for enclosure or separation of fields.

hedge sparrow. See SPARROW, 3 **a.**

he·don'ic (hē·dŏn'ĭk), *adj.* [Gr. *hēdonikos,* fr. *hēdonē* pleasure; akin to Gr. *hēdys* sweet, pleasant.] **1.** Pertaining to, or consisting in, pleasure. **2.** Of or pertaining to hedonism, hedonists, or hedonics.

he·don'ics (-ĭks), *n.;* see -ICS. **a** Ethics which treats of the relation of duty to pleasure. **b** Psychology which treats of pleasurable and unpleasant states of consciousness.

he'don·ism (hē'dŏn·ĭz'm), *n.* **1.** *Ethics.* The doctrine that pleasure is the sole or chief good in life and that moral duty is fulfilled in the gratification of pleasure-seeking instincts and dispositions. Cf. EUDAEMONISM. **2.** The manner of life of a hedonist; a living for pleasure. — **he'don·ist** (-ĭst), *n. & adj.* — **he'do·nis'tic** (hē'dō·nĭs'tĭk), *adj.* — **he'do·nis'ti·cal·ly** (-tĭ·kăl·ĭ), *adv.*

-he'dron (-hē'drŭn). [Gr. *hedra* seat, base.] A combining form denoting *a geometrical figure,* or *a crystal, having a* (specified) *form* or *number of surfaces,* as in tetra*hedron.* Corresponding adjectives usually end in **-he'dral** (-drăl).

hee'bie jee'bies (hē'bĭ jē'bĭz). [Origin uncert.] *Slang.* Jitters; also, delirium tremens.

heed (hēd), *v. t.* [AS. *hēdan.*] To regard with care; to take notice of. — *v. i.* To pay attention; to have a care. — *n.* Attention; notice; regard. — **heed'er,** *n.*

heed'ful (-fōol; -f'l), *adj.* That takes heed; mindful. — **heed'ful·ly,** *adv.* — **heed'ful·ness,** *n.*

heed'less, *adj.* Without heed; inattentive; careless. — **heed'less·ly,** *adv.* — **heed'less·ness,** *n.*

hee'haw' (hē'hô'), *n.* [Imitative.] The bray of an ass; a guffaw. — *v. i.* To bray, or utter heehaws.

heel (hēl), *n.* [AS. *hēla.*] **1. a** The hind part of the human foot. **b** In other vertebrates, the part of the hind limb homologous with the human heel. **2.** Anything regarded as like a human heel in shape, position, etc., as the crust at the bottom end of a loaf of bread, a cake of cheese, etc., the part of any tool next to the tang or handle, the small projection at the back of the bowl of a spoon, etc., the crook of the head of a golf club where it joins the shaft. **3.** The hinder part of any covering for the foot, as of a shoe, sock, etc.; specif., a solid part projecting downward from the hinder part of the sole of a boot or shoe. See SHOE, *Illust.* **4.** *Hort.* The base of a tuber, cutting, or other part of a plant separated for propagation, esp. when including a portion of the wood or stem of the parent branch. **5.** *Naut.* The lower end of a mast, a boom, the sternpost, etc. **6.** *Orig. Underworld Slang, U. S.* A contemptibly mean-spirited scoundrel likely to double-cross a pal. — ***down at the heel*** *or* ***at heel.*** In a poor plight; in an embarrassed condition; seedy. — ***to heel.*** Close at the heels, as a hunting dog following the hunter; close behind; hence, obediently following. — *v. t.* **1.** To add a heel to; as, to *heel* a shoe. **2. a** To arm with a gaff, as a cock for fighting. **b** *Slang, U. S.* To supply or equip, as with money. — ***heel in.*** To cover (the roots of a plant) temporarily with soil.

heel (hēl), *v. t. & i.* [AS. *heldan, hyldan.*] To tilt or incline; — esp. of ships. — *n.* Act or amount of heeling.

heel'-and-toe', *adj.* Designating a form of speed walking in which each step begins on the heel and ends on the toe.

heeled (hēld), *adj.* Having a heel; hence, *Colloq., U. S.,* provided with money; also, armed, as with a revolver.

heel'er (hēl'ẽr), *n.* **1.** One who heels, or puts on heels. **2.** *Colloq., U. S.* One who follows at the heels; specif., a subservient hanger-on of a political patron; one who canvasses for votes, gives bribes, and does other dishonest work for a boss; — called also *ward heeler.*

heel'less (-lĕs; -lĭs), *adj.* Having no heel.

heel'piece' (-pēs'), *n.* A piece at or for the heel of something; as: **a** The heel of a shoe. **b** *Teleg.* An iron bar connecting the soft-iron cores of an electromagnet.

heel'post' (-pōst'), *n.* A post supporting the heel or outer end of a thing, as one to which a door is hinged.

heel'tap' (-tăp'), *n.* **1.** A lift for the heel of a shoe. **2.** A small portion of liquor left in a glass after drinking.

heeze (hēz), *v. t.* [See HOISE.] *Scot.* To raise; hoist.

heft (hĕft), *n.* [From HEAVE.] **1.** *Obs.* Violent strain or exertion. **2.** *Colloq.* Weight; figuratively, influence. **3.** *Colloq., U. S.* The greater part or bulk of anything. — *v. t.* **1.** To heave up; to raise aloft. **2.** *Colloq.* To prove or try the weight of by raising.

heft'y (hĕf'tĭ), *adj.;* HEFT'I·ER (-tĭ·ẽr); HEFT'I·EST. *Colloq.* **a** Moderately heavy; weighty. **b** Vehement or vigorous.

he·gar'i (hē·gâr'ĭ; hĕg'ȧ·rĭ), *n.* [Ar. (Sudan) *hegiri,* fr. Ar. *ḥajari, ḥijāri,* stony, stonelike.] A grain sorghum native to the Sudan region of Africa, an early-maturing variety of which is grown in the southwestern U. S.

He·ge'li·an (hā·gā'lĭ·ăn; hē·jē'-), *adj.* Of or pertaining to Hegel or his philosophy. — *n.* A follower of Hegel.

He·ge'li·an·ism (-ĭz'm), *n.* The philosophy of Georg Wilhelm Friedrich Hegel (1770–1831), an attempt to unite and harmonize the Greek ontology with the Kantian psychology.

he·gem'o·ny (hē·jĕm'ō·nĭ; hĕj'ē·mō'nĭ; hē'jē-; *some prefer "hard" g* [*as in go*]), *n.; pl.* -NIES (-nĭz). [Gr. *hēgemonia,* deriv. of *hēgeisthai* to lead.] Leadership; preponderant influence or authority, esp. of a government or state. — **heg'e·mon'ic** (hĕj'ē·mŏn'ĭk; hē'jē-), *adj.*

he·gi'ra (hē·jī'rȧ; hĕj'ĭ·rȧ), *n.* Also **he·ji'ra.** [ML., fr. Ar. *hijrah* flight.] [*often cap.*] The flight of Mohammed from Mecca, A.D. 622 (later taken as the first year of the Moslem era); hence, any similar flight or exodus. See MOHAMMEDAN CALENDAR.

he·gu'men (hē·gū'mĕn), *n.* [ML. *hegumenus*, fr. Gr. *hēgoumenos*, pres. part. of *hēgeisthai* to lead.] *Eastern Ch.* The head of a religious community, specif., of a smaller monastery. Cf. ARCHIMANDRITE.

Hei'del·berg jaw (hī'd'l·bûrg; *G.* hī'dĕl·bĕrk). *Anthropol.* A human lower jaw of great geological age, found near Heidelberg, Germany, 1907, and regarded as belonging to an extinct species of man (called **Heidelberg man**). See MAN, *n.*, 9. — **Heidelberg race.**

Hei'duc, Hei'duk. Vars. of HAIDUK.

heif'er (hĕf'ẽr), *n.* [AS. *hēahfore.*] A young cow; a cow that has not had a calf.

heigh (hā; hī), *interj.* An exclamation used to attract attention, to encourage, to express exultation, etc.; hey.

heigh (hēk). Scot. var. of HIGH.

heigh'-ho' (hā'hō'; hī'hō'; 2), *interj.* An exclamation expressing dejection, uneasiness, weariness, etc.

height (hīt; *dial.* hītth, hīth), *n.* Also **highth** (hītth; hīth). [AS. *hīehthu, hēahthu, hēhthu;* akin to AS. *hēah* high.] **1.** The condition of being high. **2.** An eminence; a hill or mountain; elevated point or position. **3.** Highest part; summit; hence, utmost degree; extreme limit; as, the *height* of a fever; climax, as of action. **4.** Altitude; stature. **5.** *Obs.* **a** An advanced social rank. **b** Hauteur.

Syn. **Height, stature, elevation, altitude** mean the distance a thing rises from its base or the level on which it stands. **Height** may be used of anything so measured, whether high or low; **stature**, except in a figurative sense, is confined to animal bodies, especially to the human body, and may be used without a figure, as in full *stature*, average *stature*, etc.; **elevation** is applicable to things which are raised or thought of as raised and it, often, and **altitude**, chiefly, are applicable to things which are exceedingly, and not relatively, high.

height'en (hīt''n), *v. t.* **1.** To make high; elevate. **2.** To carry forward; advance; augment; hence, to render more conspicuous; specif., to render more luminous or intense. **3.** *Obs.* To exalt or elate. — *v. i.* To rise in height; to increase; augment. — **Syn.** See INTENSIFY. — **height'en·er**, *n.*

height'-to-pa'per, *n.* *Print.* The standard height of type, 0.9186 of an inch. See TYPE.

‖**heil** (hīl), *interj.* [G.] Hail! Greeting! — **heil**, *v. t.*

Heim'dall (hām'däl), *n.* [ON. *Heimdallr.*] *Norse Myth.* The warder of Asgard, who can see a hundred leagues by day or by night, can hear the grass grow, and needs less sleep than a bird. At the end of the world Loki and he kill each other.

hei'nous (hā'nŭs), *adj.* [OF. *haïnos* hateful, fr. *haïne* hate, fr. *haïr* to hate, of Teut. origin.] Hateful; hatefully bad; odious; atrocious; giving great offense. — **Syn.** See OUTRAGEOUS. — **hei'nous·ly**, *adv.* — **hei'nous·ness**, *n.*

heir (âr), *n.* [OF. *heir, eir*, fr. L. *heres, -edis.*] **1.** One who inherits, or is entitled to inherit; specif.: **a** *Eng. Common Law.* The one in whom the fee of the real property of an intestate is vested by law at his death, called ***legal heir*** *or* ***heir-at-law***. **b** *Civil Law.* The successor of a deceased person, succeeding orig. to both rights and liabilities. **c** In modern civil codes based upon the civil law, as in Europe, the person who succeeds to the (entire) estate of a person. **d** Loosely, any person inheriting property of a deceased person. **2.** One who receives or is entitled to receive any endowment or quality from a parent, or predecessor; the rightful future recipient or possessor; as, the *heir* of one's virtues. **3.** *Obs.* Offspring; product. — *v. t.* To inherit.

heir apparent (âr); *pl.* HEIRS APPARENT. *Law.* An heir whose right is indefeasible if he survives the ancestor; — disting. from *heir presumptive.* — **heir apparency.**

heir'dom (âr'dŭm), *n.* State or inheritance of an heir.

heir'ess (-ĕs; -ĭs), *n.* A female heir, esp. to wealth.

heir'loom' (âr'lōōm'; 2), *n.* [*heir* + *loom* implement, tool.] Any personal chattel, which descends to the heir with the inheritance; hence, any piece of personal property owned by a family for several generations.

heir presumptive. One who, if the ancestor should die immediately, would be his heir, but whose right to the inheritance may be defeated by the birth of a nearer relative, or by some other contingency.

heir'ship (âr'shĭp), *n.* Right of inheriting; inheritance.

he·ji'ra (hē·jī'rȧ; hĕj'ĭ·rȧ). Var. of HEGIRA.

hek'tare, hek'to·gram, hek'to·graph, hek'to·li'ter, hek'to·me'ter. Vars. of HECTARE, etc.

Hel (hĕl), *n.* [ON.] *Norse Myth.* Orig., the underworld (cf. Gr. HADES). In Old Norse, the goddess of the dead and queen of the underworld, the daughter of Loki.

held (hĕld), *past & past part.* of HOLD.

Hel'en of Troy (hĕl'ĕn; -ĭn). See APPLE OF DISCORD.

he·li'a·cal (hē·lī'ȧ·kăl), *adj.* Also **he'li·ac** (hē'lĭ·ăk). [Gr. *hēliakos* of the sun, fr. *hēlios* sun.] *Astron.* Pertaining to, or near, the sun; — said esp. of the last setting of a star before, and its first rising after, invisibility due to conjunction with the sun. — **he·li'a·cal·ly**, *adv.*

he'li·an'thus (hē'lĭ·ăn'thŭs), *n.* [NL., fr. Gr. *hēlios* sun + *anthos* flower.] A sunflower (genus *Helianthus*).

hel'i·cal (hĕl'ĭ·kăl), *adj.* [From HELIX.] Of or pertaining to, or in the form of, a helix; spiral. — **hel'i·cal·ly**, *adv.*

hel'i·ces (hĕl'ĭ·sēz), *n., pl.* of HELIX.

hel'i·cline (hĕl'ĭ·klīn), *n.* [Gr. *helix, helikos*, a spiral + stem of *klinein* to slope.] A gradually ascending and curving ramp.

hel'i·co- (hĕl'ĭ·kō-), **helic-.** [Gr. *helix, helikos.*] A combining form meaning *helix, spiral.*

hel'i·coid (hĕl'ĭ·koid), *adj.* [Gr. *helikoeidēs*, fr. *helix, -ikos*, spiral + *eidos* shape.] Spiral; curved, as the spire of a univalve shell. Cf. SYMPODIUM, *Illust.* — *n.* *Geom.* Any of several screw-shaped surfaces. — **hel'i·coi'dal** (-koi'dăl; -d'l), *adj.* — **hel'i·coi'dal·ly**, *adv.*

Hel'i·con (-kŏn; -kŭn), *n.* [L., fr. Gr. *Helikōn.*] **1.** A mountain in Boeotia, supposed by the Greeks to be the residence of Apollo and the Muses. The name is often used allusively of poetry and poets. **2.** [*not cap.*] *Music.* A very large bass tuba used in military bands. — **Hel'i·co'ni·an** (-kō'nĭ·ăn), *adj.*

hel'i·cop'ter (hĕl'ĭ·kŏp'tẽr; hē'lĭ-), *n.* [F. *hélicoptère*, fr. Gr. *helix, -ikos*, spiral + *pteron* wing.] *Aeronautics.* A form of aircraft whose support in the air is derived solely from the reaction of a stream of air driven downward by propellers revolving around a vertical axis.

he'li·o- (hē'lĭ·ō-), **heli-.** [Gr. *hēlios.*] A combining form meaning *the sun*, as in *helio*taxis, *helio*tropism.

he'li·o (hē'lĭ·ō), *n.* *Colloq.* Short for HELIOGRAM, HELIOGRAPH.

he'li·o·cen'tric (hē'lĭ·ō·sĕn'trĭk), *adj.* Also **he'li·o·cen'tri·cal** (-trĭ·kăl). [*helio-* + *centric, centrical.*] *Astron.* Pertaining to, or measured from, the sun's center, or appearing to be seen from it; having, or relating to, the sun as a center.

he'li·o·chrome' (hē'lĭ·ō·krōm'), *n.* [*helio-* + *-chrome.*] A photograph in natural colors, orig. one made by use of a form of silver chloride. — **he'li·o·chro'mic** (-krō'mĭk), *adj.*

he'li·o·gram' (-grăm'), *n.* [*helio-* + *-gram.*] A message transmitted by a heliograph.

he'li·o·graph' (-grȧf'; 9), *n.* [*helio-* + *-graph.*] **1.** A photoengraving. **2.** An instrument for taking photographs of the sun. **3.** An apparatus for telegraphing by means of the sun's rays thrown from a mirror. — *v. t. & i.* To signal by means of a heliograph. — **he'li·og'ra·pher** (-ŏg'rȧ·fẽr), *n.* — **he'li·o·graph'ic** (-ō·grăf'ĭk), *adj.* — **he'li·og'ra·phy** (-ŏg'rȧ·fĭ), *n.*

he'li·o·gra·vure' (hē'lĭ·ō·grȧ·vūr'; -grā'vūr), *n.* [F. *héliogravure.*] Any of various photoengraving processes.

he'li·ol'a·try (hē'lĭ·ŏl'ȧ·trĭ), *n.* = SUN WORSHIP. — **he'li·ol'a·ter** (-tẽr), *n.* — **he'li·ol'a·trous** (-trŭs), *adj.*

he'li·om'e·ter (-ŏm'ē·tẽr), *n.* [F. *héliomètre.* See HELIO-; -METER.] *Astron.* A double-image micrometer, devised orig. for measuring the diameter of the sun, but now used for accurate measurement of any short arc of the celestial sphere. — **he'li·o·met'ric** (-ō·mĕt'rĭk), **he'li·o·met'ri·cal** (-rĭ·kăl), *adj.* — **he'li·o·met'ri·cal·ly**, *adv.*

He'li·os (hē'lĭ·ŏs), *n.* [Gr. *hēlios* sun, *Hēlios.*] *Gr. Relig.* The sun-god, represented as driving a four-horse chariot through the heavens. See APOLLO, PHAËTHON.

he'li·o·scope' (hē'lĭ·ō·skōp'), *n.* [F. *hélioscope.* See HELIO-; -SCOPE.] *Astron.* A telescope or instrument for viewing the sun without injury to the eyes.

he'li·o·stat' (-stăt'), *n.* [*helio-* + *-stat.*] A mirror mounted on an axis moved by clockwork, by which a sunbeam is steadily reflected to one spot.

he'li·o·tax'is (-tăk'sĭs), *n.* [NL., fr. *helio-* + *-taxis.*] Phototaxis in which sunlight is the stimulus.

he'li·o·ther'a·py (-thĕr'ȧ·pĭ), *n.* [*helio-* + *therapy.*] *Med.* Treatment of disease by sun baths.

he'li·o·trope (hē'lĭ·ō·trōp; *Brit. commonly* hĕl'ĭ·ō·trōp; -yō·trōp), *n.* [F. *héliotrope*, fr. L. *heliotropium*, fr. Gr. *hēliotropion*, fr. *hēlios* the sun + *trepein* to turn.] **1. a** Any plant which turns toward the sun, as the sunflower, the marigold. **b** Any of a genus (*Heliotropium*, esp. *H. peruvianum*) of herbs of the borage family, having fragrant white or purple flowers; turnsole. **c** The common valerian (*Valeriana officinalis*). **2.** *Mineral.* = BLOODSTONE. **3.** A color, reddish bluered in hue, of medium saturation and low brilliance. See COLOR.

he'li·ot'ro·pism (hē'lĭ·ŏt'rō·pĭz'm), *n.* Tropism in which sunlight is the orienting stimulus. The movement may be toward the sunlight or (*apheliotropism*) away from it. Cf. PHOTOTROPISM. — **he'li·o·trop'ic** (-ō·trŏp'ĭk; -trō'pĭk), *adj.*

he'li·um (hē'lĭ·ŭm; 58), *n.* [NL., fr. Gr. *hēlios* the sun.] An inert, colorless, gaseous element, first observed spectroscopically in the sun's atmosphere. Next to hydrogen, it is the lightest of gases and because of its noninflammability is separated from natural gas for use in dirigibles, etc. Symbol, *He;* at. no., 2; at. wt., 4.003. It is a product of radioactive transformations.

he'lix (hē'lĭks), *n.; pl.* HELICES (hĕl'ĭ·sēz), HELIXES (hē'lĭk·sĕz; -sĭz). [L., anything of spiral shape, fr. Gr. *helix, -ikos.*] **1.** Anything having a spiral form. **2.** The incurved rim of the external ear. See EAR, *Illust.* **3.** *Arch.* A spiral ornament, esp. a volute in an Ionic or a Corinthian capital. **4.** *Math.* The curve formed on any cylinder by a straight line in a plane that is wrapped round the cylinder, as an ordinary screw thread.

hell (hĕl), *n.* [AS.] **1.** [*sometimes cap.*] The place of the dead, or of souls after death; the grave; — corresponding to *Sheol* and *Hades.* **2.** The place or state of punishment for the wicked after death; the abode of evil spirits, corresponding to *Gehenna, Tartarus;* hence: **a** Any place or state of misery or wickedness. **b** That which causes torment. **3.** The evil spirits who dwell in torment; the powers of darkness. **4.** A place where outcast persons or things are gathered; as: **a** A dungeon. **b** A gambling house. **c** A receptacle into which a tailor throws his shreds, or a printer his broken type. **5.** *Christian Science.* Mortal belief; error; lust; remorse; hatred; revenge; sin. *Mary Baker Eddy.*

hell'bend'er (-bĕn'dẽr), *n.* A large aquatic salamander (*Cryptobranchus alleganiensis*) of the Ohio Valley.

hell'box' (hĕl'bŏks'), *n.* *Print.* A hell (def. 4 **c**).

hell'broth' (-brŏth'; 74), *n.* A composition for working black magic.

hell'cat' (-kăt'), *n.* A witch; also, a malicious person.

hell'-div'er (-dīv'ẽr), *n.* A dabchick or other small grebe.

hel'le·bore (hĕl'ē·bōr; 70), *n.* [L. *helleborus*, fr. Gr. *helleboros.*] **1. a** Any of a genus (*Helleborus*) of herbs of the crowfoot family, as the medicinal herb *H. foetidus* (called also *bear's-foot*), with digitate leaves and offensive smell. **b** Any herb of a genus (*Veratrum*, esp. *V. album* and *V. viride*) having short poisonous root stocks. Both of the above species are called ***white hellebore***, and one (*V. viride*) is called also ***American hellebore*** *or* ***false hellebore***. **2. a** The dried rhizome and roots of a medicinal herb (*Helleborus niger*), containing helleborin and helleborein. **b** The dried rhizome and roots of white hellebore used as a parasiticide and insecticide.

hel'le·bo're·in (-bō'rē·ĭn), *n.* *Chem.* A poisonous glucoside accompanying helleborin in several species of hellebore and acting strongly on the heart.

hel·leb'o·rin (hĕ·lĕb'ō·rĭn; hĕl'ē·bō·rĭn), *n.* *Chem.* A poisonous crystalline glucoside occurring in hellebore.

Hel'len (hĕl'ĕn; -ĭn), *n.* [Gr. *Hellēn.*] The eponymous ancestor of the Hellenic race.

Hel'lene (hĕl'ēn), *n.; pl.* HELLENES (-ēnz). [Gr. *Hellēn.*] A Greek.

Hel·len'ic (hĕ·lĕn'ĭk; -lē'nĭk), *adj.* Pert. to the Hellenes. — *n.* Classical Greek, esp. of the later period.

Hel'len·ism (hĕl'ĕn·ĭz'm; hĕl'ĭn-; hĕl'ēn-), *n.* **1.** A Greek phrase or idiom. **2.** Greek character or civilization; esp., the culture represented by the ideals of the classical Greeks. **3.** Adoption of the Greek language, thought, and ideals.

Hel'len·ist (-ĭst), *n.* [Gr. *Hellēnistēs.*] **1.** One who affiliates with Greeks, or imitates Greek manners; esp., a Jew who used the Greek language as his mother tongue. **2.** One skilled in the Greek language and literature. **3.** One of the Greek scholars who disseminated Byzantine culture in the Renaissance.

Hel·len·is'tic (hĕl'ĕ·nĭs'tĭk; hĕl'ĭ-), *adj.* Also **Hel·len·is'ti·cal** (-tĭ·kăl). **1.** Of or pertaining to Greek history, culture, or art after Alexander the Great. **2.** Of or pertaining to the Hellenists.

Hel'len·ize (hĕl'ĕn·īz; hĕl'ĭn-), *v. i.* [Gr. *Hellenizein.*] To use the Greek language; to play the Greek. — *v. t.* To give a Greek form or character to. — **Hel'len·i·za'tion** (-ĭ·zā'shŭn; -ĭ·zā'-), *n.* — **Hel'len·iz'er** (hĕl'ĕn·īz'ẽr; hĕl'ĭn-), *n.*

hel'ler (hĕl'ẽr), *n.; pl.* HELLER (-ẽr). [G.] **a** In Austria, up to 1925, a small copper coin equivalent to $\frac{1}{100}$ krone. **b** In Czechoslovakia, $\frac{1}{100}$ koruna.

hell'-fire' (hĕl'fīr'; 2), *n.* **1.** The fire of hell. **2.** Burning spite resentment, or the like.

hell'gram·mite (hĕl'gră·mīt), *n.* The carnivorous, aquatic larva of a large North American insect (*Corydalis cornuta*), much used as a fish bait; the dobson.

hell'hound' (hĕl'hound'), *n.* [AS. *helle hund.*] A dog of hell (cf. CERBERUS); hence, a fiend; a demon.

hel'lion (hĕl'yŭn), *n. Colloq.* One given to deviltry.

hell'ish, *adj.* Of or pertaining to hell; like hell; infernal. — **hell'ish·ly,** *adv.* — **hell'ish·ness,** *n.*

hell'kite' (hĕl'kīt'), *n.* A person who shows hellish cruelty.

hel·lo' (hĕ·lō'; *various shifts in accent & intonation occur when the word expresses surprise*), *interj.* [See HOLLO.] **1.** An exclamation used to call attention or to greet persons, esp. in connection with the telephone, as the common form of call; — apparently a form of HOLLO, first appearing about 1880. **2.** An exclamation expressing surprise, etc. — **hel·lo'** (hĕ·lō'; hĕl'ō), *n.*

helm (hĕlm), *n.* [AS. *helma* rudder.] **1.** *Naut.* The apparatus by which a ship is steered, comprising rudder, tiller, wheel, etc.; commonly, the tiller or wheel alone; also, a turn of the helm. **2.** In figurative use, guidance or steering of anything. — *v. t.* To steer; direct.

helm, *n.* [AS.] *Archaic.* A helmet. — *v. t.* To cover or furnish with a helmet.

hel'met (hĕl'mĕt; -mĭt), *n.* [OF., dim. of *helme,* of Teut. origin.] **1.** A defensive covering for the head. Specif.: **a** The headpiece in armor (see ARMOR, *Illust.*). **b** The military hat, often made of or

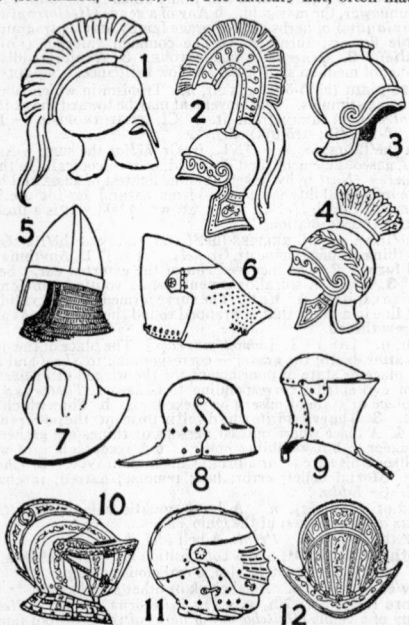

Hellgrammite. (½)

Helmets. 1, 2 Greek; 3, 4 Roman; 5 Norman Casque with fixed Nosepiece, 11th cent.; 6 Basinet, 14th cent.; 7, 8 Sallets, 15th cent.; 9 Tilting Heaume, 15th and 16th cents.; 10, 11 Armets, 16th cent.; 12 Morion, late 16th cent.

strengthened with metal, worn as a guard against head wounds. **c** A domed hat with a visor and a neckguard, such as worn by policemen, firemen, or by Europeans in hot countries. **d** The headpiece of a diver's armor, provided with air pipes and glass windows. **e** A leather covering for the head worn by players in certain sports, as American football. **2.** That which resembles a helmet in form or position, as the hood-shaped upper sepal or petal of some flowers. **3.** *Fencing, Singlestick, etc.* A head covering with a mesh, usually of wire, to protect the face. — **hel'met·ed,** *adj.*

hel'minth (hĕl'mĭnth), *n.* [Gr. *helmins, -inthos,* worm.] A worm; esp., an intestinal worm.

hel·min·thi'a·sis (hĕl'mĭn·thī'ȧ·sĭs), *n.* [NL., fr. Gr. *helminthian* to suffer from worms, fr. *helmins, -inthos,* worm.] *Med.* A disease in which worms are present in the body.

hel·min'thic (hĕl·mĭn'thĭk), *adj.* Of, relating to, or expelling worms, or helminths.

hel·min·thol'o·gy (hĕl'mĭn·thŏl'ō·jĭ), *n.* The natural history, or study, of worms, esp. parasitic worms.

helms'man (hĕlmz'măn), *n.* A steersman.

Hel'ot (hĕl'ŏt), *n.* [L. *Helotes, Hilotae,* pl., fr. Gr. *Heilōtes, Heilōtai,* bondsmen or serfs.] **1.** One of the lowest class (serfs) of the people of ancient Sparta. **2.** [*often not cap.*] Hence, a slave or serf.

hel'ot·ism (-ĭz'm), *n.* Serfdom.

hel'ot·ry (-rĭ), *n.* Helots, collectively; slaves; also, slavery; serfdom.

help (hĕlp), *v. t.; past* HELPED (hĕlpt), *Archaic* HOLP (hō(l)p); *past part.* HELPED, *Archaic* HOL'PEN (hō(l)'pĕn), *Obs.* HOLP; *pres. part.* HELP'ING. [AS. *helpan.*] **1.** To aid; assist. **2.** To furnish with relief, as from pain, disease, or distress; to succor; to be of avail against (an ill). **3.** To aid in bringing about, causing, etc.; as, caste feeling *helps* prejudice. **4. a** To change for the better; to improve. **b** To prevent; as, we cannot *help* his fall. **5.** To forbear; avoid; as, we cannot *help* liking him. **6.** To wait upon, as a guest at table; to serve (food), as at table. — *v. i.* **1.** To lend aid; to avail or be of use; to assist. **2.** To serve food, as at table. **3.** To avoid or prevent; as, no more than I can *help.*

Syn. (1) Help, aid, assist mean to furnish what is needed to accomplish work or to attain an end. **Help** contains a strong implication of advance toward an objective; **aid** strongly suggests the need of help or relief and therefore imputes weakness to the one aided and strength to the one aiding; **assist** (etymologically, to stand by) suggests a secondary role in the assistant or a subordinate character in the assistance. (2) See IMPROVE.

— *n.* **1.** Aid; assistance; also, one furnishing aid. **2.** Remedy; relief. **3. a** A helper; assistant, esp. a hired one. **b** The whole force of hired helpers. **c** *Rural, U. S.* A domestic servant or farm hand. **4.** A portion of food.

help'er (hĕl'pẽr), *n.* One who or that which helps.

help'ful (hĕlp'fŏŏl; -f'l), *adj.* Furnishing help; assistant; useful; salutary. — **help'ful·ly,** *adv.* — **help'ful·ness,** *n.*

help'ing, *n.* The act of one who helps; also, a portion, as of food, to which one is helped.

help'less, *adj.* **1.** Destitute of help or strength; weak; also, incompetent. **2.** *Now Rare.* Bringing no help; unaiding. — **help'less·ly,** *adv.* — **help'less·ness,** *n.*

help'mate' (hĕlp'māt'), *n.* [Corrupt. of the "*help meet* for him" of Genesis ii. 18.] A helper; companion; specif., a wife.

help'meet' (-mēt'), *n.* A helpmate; esp., a wife.

hel'ter-skel'ter (hĕl'tẽr-skĕl'tẽr), *adv. Colloq.* In hurry and confusion; in disorder. — *adj.* Characterized by confused hurry. — *n.* Anything that is helter-skelter.

helve (hĕlv), *n.* [AS. *hielf, helf, hylf.*] The handle of a tool or weapon, as an ax, hatchet, or adz. Cf. HAFT. — *v. t.;* HELVED (hĕlvd); HELV'ING. To furnish or fit with a helve. — **helv'er** (hĕl'vẽr), *n.*

Hel·ve'tian (hĕl·vē'shăn), *adj.* [L. *Helvetius.*] Of or pertaining to the Helvetii or Helvetia; Swiss. — *n.* One of the Helvetii; a Swiss.

Hel·vet'ic (-vĕt'ĭk), *adj.* Helvetian; Swiss. — *n.* A Swiss Protestant; a follower of Zwingli.

Hel·ve'ti·i (hĕl·vē'shĭ·ī), *n. pl.* [L.] In the time of Julius Caesar, the inhabitants of the Alpine regions.

hem (hĕm), *n.* [AS. *hem, hemm,* border, margin.] **1.** The edge or border of a garment or cloth; now, a border formed by doubling back the edge and sewing it. **2.** Border; margin. — *v. t.;* HEMMED (hĕmd); HEM'MING. **1.** To fold and sew down the edge of; hence, to border; edge. **2.** To enclose and confine; to surround.

hem, *interj.* An exclamation to call attention, to express hesitation, etc., or to represent a clearing of the throat. — *n.* An uttering or the sound of "hem." — *v. i.;* HEMMED (hĕmd); HEM'MING. To utter the sound represented by *hem;* hence, to hesitate in speaking.

hem-, haem-. = HEMO-; see HAEM-.

he'ma-, hae'ma- (hē'mȧ-; hĕm'ȧ-). [Gr. *haima.*] Irregular combining form signifying *blood.* See HEMO-, HAEM-.

he'ma·cy·tom'e·ter (-sī·tŏm'ē·tẽr). Var. of HEMOCYTOMETER.

he'mal, hae'mal (hē'măl), *adj.* [Gr. *haima* blood.] **1.** Pertaining to the blood or blood vessels. **2.** *Zool.* In vertebrates, pertaining to the side of the spinal cord where the heart and chief blood vessels are.

he'ma·tal, hae'ma·tal (hē'mȧ·tăl; hĕm'ȧ-; -t'l), *adj. Anat.* Relating to the blood or blood vessels.

he'ma·te'in, hae'ma·te'in (hē'mȧ·tē'ĭn; hĕm'ȧ-), *n.* [See HEMATO-.] *Chem.* A reddish-brown crystalline compound, $C_{16}H_{12}O_6$, the essential dye in logwood extracts.

he'ma·ther'mal, hem'a·to·ther'mal. Vars. of HAEMATHERMAL, HAEMATOTHERMAL.

he·mat'ic, hae·mat'ic (hē·măt'ĭk), *adj.* [Gr. *haimatikos.*] **1.** Of, pertaining to, containing, full of, or having the color of blood. **2.** *Med.* Acting on the blood. — *n.* A medicine acting on the blood.

hem'a·tin, haem'a·tin (hĕm'ȧ·tĭn; hē'mȧ-), *n.* Also -tine. [Gr. *haima, haimatos,* blood.] **1.** *Chem.* Hematein. **2.** *Biochem.* A bluish-black substance containing iron, formed by the decomposition of hemoglobin.

hem'a·tin'ic, haem'a·tin'ic (-tĭn'ĭk), *n. Med.* Any substance, such as an iron salt, tending to increase the hemoglobin content of the blood; a hematic.

hem'a·tin'ic, haem'a·tin'ic, *adj.* **a** Pertaining to, or derived from, hematin. **b** = HEMATIC, 1.

hem'a·tite, haem'a·tite (hĕm'ȧ·tīt; hē'mȧ-), *n.* [L., *haematites,* fr. Gr. *haimatitēs* bloodlike, fr. *haima, haimatos,* blood.] *Mineral.* An important ore of iron, Fe_2O_3, red when powdered. The term **brown** hematite is a synonym for *limonite.* — **hem'a·tit'ic, haem'a·tit'ic** (-tĭt'ĭk), *adj.*

hem'a·to-, haem'a·to- (hĕm'ȧ·tō-; hē'mȧ·tō-), hemat-, haemat-. [Gr. *haima, haimatos,* blood.] = HEMO-, as in **hem'a·to·cele', hem'a·tol'y·sis.**

hem'a·to·crit', haem'a·to·crit' (-krĭt'), *n.* [*hemato-* + Gr. *kritēs* judge.] *Physiol.* An instrument for determining the relative amounts of plasma and corpuscles in blood, generally some form of centrifugal apparatus.

hem'a·tog'e·nous, haem'a·tog'e·nous (hĕm'ȧ·tŏj'ē·nŭs; hē'mȧ-), *adj. Physiol.* **a** Producing blood. **b** Produced by or arising in the blood.

he'ma·toid, haem'a·toid (hē'mȧ·toid; hĕm'ȧ-), *adj.* [*hemat-* + *-oid.*] *Physiol.* Resembling blood.

hem'a·tol'o·gy, haem'a·tol'o·gy (hĕm'ȧ·tŏl'ō·jĭ; hē'mȧ-), *n.* The science dealing with the blood. — **hem'a·to·log'i·cal, haem'a·to·log'i·cal** (-tō·lŏj'ĭ·kăl), *adj.* — **hem'a·tol'o·gist, haem'a·tol'o·gist** (-tŏl'ō·jĭst), *n.*

he'ma·to'ma, hae'ma·to'ma (hē'mȧ·tō'mȧ; hĕm'ȧ-), *n.; pl.* -TOMATA (-tō'mȧ·tȧ), -TOMAS (-mȧz). [NL., fr. *hemat-* + *-oma.*] A tumor or swelling containing blood.

hem'a·to·poi·e'sis, haem'a·to·poi·e'sis (hĕm'ȧ·tō·poi·ē'sĭs; hē'mȧ-), *n.* [NL., fr. *hemato-* + Gr. *poiēsis* a making.] The formation of blood. — **hem'a·to·poi·et'ic, haem'a·to·poi·et'ic** (-ĕt'ĭk), *adj.*

hem′a·tose, haem′a·tose (hĕm′ȧ·tōs; hē′mȧ-), *adj. Med.* Full of blood; bloody.
he′ma·to′sis, hae′ma·to′sis (hē′mȧ·tō′sĭs; hĕm′ȧ-), *n.* [NL., fr. Gr. *haimatōsis*, fr. *haimatoein* to change into blood.] *Physiol.* **a** Formation of blood. **b** Arterialization of the blood in the lungs.
he′ma·tox′y·lin. Var. of HAEMATOXYLIN.
hem′a·to·zo′on, haem′a·to·zo′on (hĕm′ȧ·tō·zō′ŏn; hē′mȧ-), *n.; pl.* -ZOA (-ȧ). [NL., fr. *hemato-* + Gr. *zōion* animal.] *Zool.* Any animal parasite inhabiting the blood, as filariae. — **-zo′al** (-ăl), **-zo′ic** (-ĭk), *adj.*
hem·el′y·tron (hĕm·ĕl′ĭ·trŏn), **hem·el′y·trum** (-trŭm), *n.; pl.* -TRA (-trȧ). [NL. See HEMI-; ELYTRON.] *Zool.* One of the partly thickened anterior wings of certain insects, as of hemipterous insects. — **hem·el′y·tral** (-trăl), *adj.*
hem′er·o·cal′lis (hĕm′ẽr·ō·kăl′ĭs), *n.* [NL., fr. Gr. *hēmerokallis*, fr. *hēmera* day + *kallos* beauty.] = DAY LILY, 1.
hem′i- (hĕm′ĭ-). [Gr. *hēmi-*. Cf. SEMI-.] A prefix signifying *half.*
-he′mi·a, -hae′mi·a (-hē′mĭ·ȧ). Vars. of -EMIA, -AEMIA.
hem′i·al′gi·a (hĕm′ĭ·ăl′jĭ·ȧ), *n.* [NL., fr. *hemi-* + *-algia.*] *Med.* Pain upon only one side of the body, esp. on one side of the head.
he′mic, hae′mic (hē′mĭk; hĕm′ĭk), *adj.* Of or pertaining to the blood.
hem′i·cel′lu·lose (hĕm′ĭ·sĕl′ū·lōs), *n. Chem.* Any of a group of polysaccharides less complex than cellulose and easily hydrolyzable to simple sugars.
hem′i·cra′ni·a (-krā′nĭ·ȧ), *n.* [LL.] *Med.* Hemialgia of the head.
hem′i·cy′cle (hĕm′ĭ·sī′k'l), *n.* [F. *hémicycle*, fr. L. *hemicyclus*, fr. Gr. *hēmikyklon*, fr. *hēmi-* + *kyklos.*] **1.** A half circle; a semicircle. **2.** A curved or approximately semicircular structure.
hem′i·dem′i·sem′i·qua′ver (hĕm′ĭ·dĕm′ĭ·sĕm′ĭ·kwā′vẽr), *n.* [*hemi-* + *demisemiquaver.*] *Music.* See NOTE, *n.*
hem′i·el′y·tron, hem′i·el′y·trum. Vars. of HEMELYTRON, etc.
hem′i·he′dral (hĕm′ĭ·hē′drăl), *adj.* [*hemi-* + Gr. *hedra* seat, base.] *Cryst.* Having half of the similar parts of a crystal form, instead of all; consisting of half the faces which full symmetry would require; — opposed to *holohedral.* Cf. HOLOHEDRAL, TETARTOHEDRAL. — **hem′i·he′dral·ly**, *adv.*
hem′i·hy′drate (-hī′drāt), *n. Chem.* A hydrate containing half a molecule of water to one of the compound forming the hydrate.
hem′i·mor′phic (-môr′fĭk), *adj. Cryst.* Unsymmetrical in form as regards the two ends of an axis. — **hem′i·mor′phism** (-fĭz'm), *n.*
hem′i·mor′phite (-môr′fīt), *n. Mineral.* Calamine (sense **a**).
he′min, hae′min (hē′mĭn), *n.* [Gr. *haima* blood.] *Biochem.* A reddish-brown substance obtained in the form of microscopic, prismatic crystals by the action on blood of hydrochloric acid or of glacial acetic acid and salt. The obtaining of these crystals, as from suspected stains, is evidence of the presence of blood.
hem′i·ple′gi·a (hĕm′ĭ·plē′jĭ·ȧ), *n.* Also **hem′i·ple′gy** (hĕm′ĭ·plē′jĭ). [NL., fr. *hemi-* + *-plegia.*] *Med.* Paralysis of one lateral half of the body. — **hem′i·pleg′ic** (-plĕj′ĭk; -plē′jĭk), *adj.*
he·mip′ter·ous (hē·mĭp′tẽr·ŭs), **he·mip′ter·al** (-ăl), *adj.* [*hemi-* + Gr. *pteron* wing.] Belonging to a large order (Hemiptera) of insects, which have a more or less flattened form, a proboscis adapted for piercing and sucking, and two pairs of wings — an anterior with the basal part thickened and the distal membranous, a posterior wholly membranous. This order comprises those insects to which the term *bug* is most properly applied, as the bedbug, squash bug, etc.
hem′i·sphere (hĕm′ĭ·sfẽr), *n.* [F. and L.; F. *hémisphère*, fr. L., fr. Gr. *hēmisphairion*, fr. *hēmi-* half + *sphaira* sphere.] **1.** A half sphere. **2.** Half of the celestial or terrestrial globe, or a projection of it as in a map. The terrestrial hemispheres are customarily divided (1) by the equator, into ***Northern Hemisphere*** and ***Southern Hemisphere***, or (2) by a meridian, so that North and South America are contained in the ***Western Hemisphere***, and the other continents chiefly in the ***Eastern Hemisphere***. The celestial hemispheres are customarily divided by the horizon, the celestial equator, or the ecliptic. **3.** Figuratively: **a** A realm; a sphere. **b** The inhabitants of a hemisphere. **4.** *Anat.* Either of the two parts (***cerebral hemispheres***) chiefly composing the cerebrum. See CEREBRUM, FOREBRAIN.
hem′i·spher′i·cal (-sfĕr′ĭ·kăl), *adj.* Also **hem′i·spher′ic** (-ĭk). Of, pertaining or belonging to, or like a hemisphere.
hem′i·sphe′roid (-sfē′roid), *n.* A half spheroid.
hem′i·stich (hĕm′ĭ·stĭk), *n.* [From L., fr. Gr. *hēmistichion*, fr. *hēmi-* half + *stichos* row, line, verse.] Half a poetic verse or line, esp. as divided by a caesura, etc. — **he·mis′ti·chal** (hē·mĭs′tĭ·kăl; hĕm′ĭ·stĭk·ăl), *adj.*
hem′i·ter′pene (-tûr′pēn), *n. Chem.* One of a series of isomeric hydrocarbons, C_5H_8. Cf. TERPENE.
hem′i·trope (hĕm′ĭ·trōp), *adj.* [F. *hémitrope.* See HEMI-; -TROPE.] Half turned round; half inverted; *Cryst.*, having a twinned structure. See TWIN.
hem′i·trop′ic (-trŏp′ĭk), *adj. Cryst.* Hemitrope.
hem′lock (hĕm′lŏk), *n.* [AS. *hemlic, hymlic.*] **1.** Any of several poisonous herbs of the carrot family, having finely cut leaves and small white flowers, esp. the ***poison hemlock***, *Comium maculatum* and species of *Cicuta*, the latter known also as ***water hemlock*** or *cowbane* (which see). **2.** Any of a genus (*Tsuga*) of trees of the pine family, esp. the ***Canadian***, *or* ***eastern***, ***hemlock*** (*T. canadensis*), and any of several species (esp. *T. mertensiana*) of western United States.
hem′mer (hĕm′ẽr), *n.* One who or that which hems.
he′mo-, hae′mo- (hē′mō-; hĕm′ō-). [Gr. *haima* blood.] A combining form denoting *blood.*
he′mo·cy·tom′e·ter, hae′mo·cy·tom′e·ter (-sī·tŏm′ē·tẽr), *n.* An apparatus for determining the number of corpuscles in a given quantity of blood.
he′mo·flag′el·late, hae′mo·flag′el·late (-flăj′ĕ·lāt), *n. Zool.* Any flagellate protozoan, as a trypanosome, which is a blood parasite.
he′mo·glo′bin, hae′mo·glo′bin (-glō′bĭn), *n. Biochem.* The respiratory pigment in the red corpuscles of vertebrates, a compound of hematin and globin. Hemoglobins from different animals crystallize in different forms. In the lungs or gills it combines loosely with oxygen, becoming ***oxyhemoglobin*** (*or* ***oxyhaemoglobin***), which is brighter in color.
he′moid, hae′moid (hē′moid), *adj. Physiol.* Resembling blood; hematoid.
he′mo·leu′co·cyte, hae′mo·leu′co·cyte, -leu′ko·cyte (hē′mō·lū′kō·sīt; hĕm′ō-), *n. Anat.* Any circulating leucocyte. — **he′mo·leu′co·cyt′ic, hae′mo·leu′co·cyt′ic, -leu′ko·cyt′ic** (-sĭt′ĭk), *adj.*
he′mo·ly′sin, hae′mo·ly′sin (-lī′sĭn), *n. Biochem.* A substance developed in the blood serum, capable of liberating hemoglobin from red corpuscles, esp. those from another animal.
he·mol′y·sis, hae·mol′y·sis (hē·mŏl′ĭ·sĭs), *n.* [*hemo-* + *-lysis.*] *Immunol.* The dissolution of red blood corpuscles with liberation of their hemoglobin. — **he′mo·lyt′ic, hae′mo·lyt′ic** (hē′mō·lĭt′ĭk; hĕm′ō-), *adj.*
he′mo·phile, hae′mo·phile (hē′mō·fīl; -fĭl; hĕm′ō-), *n.* **a** A hemophiliac. **b** A hemophilic organism. — **he′mo·phile, hae′mo·phile,** *adj.*
he′mo·phil′i·a, hae′mo·phil′i·a (hē′mō·fĭl′ĭ·ȧ; hĕm′ō-), *n.* [NL., fr. *hemo-* + *-phil* + *-ia.*] *Med.* A tendency, usually hereditary, to profuse bleeding even from slight wounds.
he′mo·phil′i·ac, hae′mo·phil′i·ac (-fĭl′ĭ·ăk), *n.* One afflicted with hemophilia.
he′mo·phil′ic, hae′mo·phil′ic (-ĭk), *adj.* **1.** *Med.* Pert. to, of the nature of, or affected with, hemophilia. **2.** *Biol.* Growing well in blood, as certain bacteria.
he·mop′ty·sis, hae·mop′ty·sis (hē·mŏp′tĭ·sĭs; hĕm·ŏp′-), *n.* [NL., fr. *hemo-* + Gr. *ptyein* to spit.] *Med.* Expectoration of blood, due usually to hemorrhage of the lungs.
hem′or·rhage, haem′or·rhage (hĕm′ŏ·rĭj), *n.* [F. *hémorragie*, fr. L., fr. Gr. *haimorrhagia*, fr. *haima* blood + *rhēgnynai* to break, burst.] *Med.* Any discharge of blood from the blood vessels, caused by injury. — **hem′or·rhag′ic, haem′or·rhag′ic** (-răj′ĭk), *adj.*
hem′or·rhoid, haem′or·rhoid (hĕm′ŏ·roid), *n.* [F. *hémorroïdes*, fr. L., pl., fr. Gr. deriv. of *haima* blood + *rhein* to flow.] *Med.* A livid and painful swelling formed by dilatation of a vein at the anus; — often in *pl.* and called *piles.* — **hem′or·rhoi′dal, haem′or·rhoi′dal** (-roi′dăl; -d'l), *adj.*
he′mo·stat, hae′mo·stat (hē′mō·stăt; hĕm′ō-), *n.* [From HEMOSTATIC.] An agent which checks hemorrhage; specif., an instrument for compressing a bleeding vessel.
he′mo·stat′ic, hae′mo·stat′ic (-stăt′ĭk), *adj.* [*hemo-* + Gr. *statikos* causing to stand.] *Med.* Serving to arrest hemorrhage; styptic. — *n.* A hemostat.
hemp (hĕmp), *n.* [AS. *henep, hænep.*] **1. a** A tall, widely cultivated Asiatic herb (*Cannabis sativa*, family Cannabinaceae, the hemp family); — called also *cannabis, Indian hemp, marijuana,* and (in India) *bhang.* **b** Its tough bast fiber, used for making cloth, floor covering, and cordage. **c** A narcotic drug from this plant. See BHANG, CANNABIS, HASHISH, MARIJUANA. **2.** A similar fiber from various other plants, or any of the plants, as jute, Manila hemp or abacá, ramie, sisal. **3.** *Slang.* A gallows rope. — **hemp′en**, *adj.*
hemp agrimony. A coarse European herb (*Eupatorium cannabinum*) of the aster family, with reddish flower heads and sessile leaves.
hemp nettle. Any of a genus (*Galeopsis*) of coarse Old World herbs of the mint family, esp. a bristly Eurasian herb (*G. tetrahit*), common as a weed in the United States.
hemp′seed′ (hĕmp′sēd′), *n.* The seed of hemp; figuratively, *Slang*, a rogue; a gallows bird.
hemp′y (-ĭ), *adj.* Hempen; *Dial.*, fit for hanging.
hem′stitch′ (hĕm′stĭch′), *v. t.* [*hem* + *stitch.*] To ornament at the head of a hem by drawing out a few parallel threads and fastening the cross threads in successive small clusters. — *n. Sewing.* Ornamental needlework done by hemstitching, or the stitch used in it. — **hem′stitch′er**, *n.*

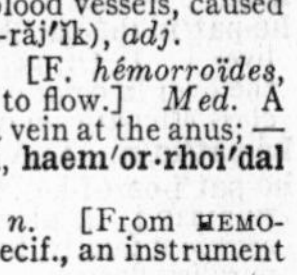
Hemstitch.

hen (hĕn), *n.* [AS. *henn, hen, hæn.*] **1.** The female of the domestic fowl, or of any of various other birds. Cf. POULTRY, *Illust.* **2.** *Colloq.* The female of any of certain other animals, as the lobster. **3.** *Humorous.* A woman.
hen and chickens, *or* **hen′–and–chick′ens,** *n.* Any of several plants marked by offsets, runners, proliferous flowers, etc.; esp.: **a** A European houseleek (*Sempervivum globiferum*). **b** Ground ivy.
hen′bane′ (hĕn′bān′), *n.* [*hen* + *bane.*] A fetid Old World herb (*Hyoscyamus niger*) of the nightshade family, with sticky, hairy, dentate leaves and yellowish-brown flowers. It is a deadly poison, esp. to fowls. See HYOSCYAMINE.
hen′bit′ (-bĭt′), *n.* A mint (*Lamium amplexicaule*) having leaves like those of the nettle but without stinging hairs.
hence (hĕns), *adv.* [ME. *hennes, hens* (the *s* is adv. gen. ending), fr. AS. *heonan, heonon.*] **1.** From this place; away; specif., from this world or life. **2.** From this time; as, a week *hence.* **3.** Consequently; therefore; — used conjunctively. **4.** From this source or origin.
hence′forth′ (hĕns′fōrth′; hĕns′fōrth′; 70), **hence′for′ward** (hĕns′fôr′wẽrd), *adv.* From this time forward.
hench′man (hĕnch′măn), *n.; pl.* -MEN (-mĕn). [ME. *hencheman, henxman*, appar. fr. AS. *hengest* horse + E. *man*, i. e., a groom.] **1.** *Obs.* An attendant, squire, or page. **2.** A trusted follower and supporter. **3.** A political follower; esp., one serving for personal advantage.
hen·dec′a·gon (hĕn·dĕk′ȧ·gŏn), *n.* [Gr. *hendeka* eleven + *gōnia* angle.] *Geom.* A (plane) polygon of 11 angles and therefore 11 sides. — **hen′de·cag′o·nal** (hĕn′dē·kăg′ō·năl), *adj.*
hen′dec·a·syl′la·ble (hĕn′dĕk·ȧ·sĭl′ȧ·b'l), *n.* [From L., fr. Gr. deriv. of *hendeka* eleven + *syllabē* syllable.] A metrical line of eleven syllables. — **hen′dec·a·syl·lab′ic** (-sĭ·lăb′ĭk), *adj. & n.*
hen·di′a·dys (hĕn·dī′ȧ·dĭs), *n.* [LL., fr. Gr. *hen dia dyoin* one by two.] *Gram.* Expression of an idea by two nouns connected by *and*, instead of by a noun and an adjunct (we drink from *cups and gold*, for *golden cups*).
hen′e·quen (hĕn′ē·kĕn; hĕn′ē·kĕn′), *n.* Also **hen′e·quin** (-kĭn). [Sp. *henequén, jeniquén*, fr. Taino *henequén.*] **a** A strong, yellowish leaf fiber, derived from the leaves of a Yucatán plant (*Agave fourcroydes*) of the amaryllis family. **b** The plant yielding this fiber. Cf. SISAL.
hen hawk. See BUZZARD, 1.
Hen′ley (hĕn′lĭ), *n.* The Henley Regatta, held annually since 1839 at Henley-on-Thames, in Oxfordshire, England.
hen′na (hĕn′ȧ), *n.* [Ar. *ḥinnā'.*] **1.** An Old World tropical shrub (*Lawsonia inermis*, family Lythraceae) with small opposite leaves and axillary panicles of fragrant white flowers; camphire. Its leaves yield a reddish-orange dye and a cosmetic for tinting the hair red. **2.** The dye and cosmetic yielded by this shrub. **3.** A brown, reddish red-yellow in hue, of medium saturation and low brilliance. See COLOR. — *v. t.*; HEN′NAED (-ȧd); HEN′NA·ING. To dye or paste with henna.

hen'ner·y (hĕn'ẽr·ĭ), *n.; pl.* -NERIES (-ĭz). A poultry farm; also, an enclosure for keeping hens.
hen'o·the·ism (hĕn'ō·thē·ĭz'm), *n.* [Gr. *heis, henos,* one + *theism.*] Belief in one god, though not to the exclusion of belief in others. — **hen'o·the·ist** (-ĭst), *n.* — **hen'o·the·is'tic** (-ĭs'tĭk), *adj.*
hen'peck' (hĕn'pĕk'), *v. t.* To subject to petty attempts to rule; — said of a wife who thus treats her husband.
hen'ry (hĕn'rĭ), *n.; pl.* -RYS, -RIES (-rĭz). [After Joseph *Henry,* Am. physicist.] *Elec.* The unit of inductance; inductance of a circuit in which an electromotive force of one volt is induced by a current varying at the rate of one ampere per second. Abbr. *H.*
hent (hĕnt), *v. t.;* HENT; HENT'ING. [AS. *hentan.*] *Archaic.* To seize.
hep (hĕp), *adj.* [Appar., with the sense of in step, in line, fr. the drill sergeant's *hep, hep,* for *step, step.*] *Slang.* Having intimate knowledge; informed; "wise"; as, to be, or to put one, *hep* to anything.
he'par (hē'pär), *n.* [ML., fr. Gr. *hēpar* liver.] *Old Chem.* **a** Any of several sulfur compounds, liver-colored, made by fusing sulfur or a sulfide with an alkali metal compound or metallic oxide. **b** In homeopathy, calcium sulfide.
hep'a·rin (hĕp'ȧ·rĭn), *n.* [Gr. *hēpar* liver + *-in.*] *Biochem.* A substance found in liver and other body tissues, used, either by injection or by addition to drawn blood, to render blood nonclotting.
hepat-. = HEPATO-, as in **hep'a·tat'ro·phy, hep'a·tec'to·my.**
he·pat'ic (hē·păt'ĭk), *adj.* [L. *hepaticus,* fr. Gr. *hēpatikos,* fr. *hēpar* liver.] **1.** Of, pertaining to, or affecting the liver; also, resembling the liver in color or form; as, *hepatic* aloes. **2.** *Bot.* Pertaining to a class (Hepaticae) of plants, the liverworts.
he·pat'ic, *n.* **1.** A hepatic medicine, or the like. **2.** *Bot.* A liverwort.
he·pat'i·ca (-ĭ·kȧ), *n.* [NL.; from the shape of the lobed leaves. See HEPATIC.] A plant or flower of a genus (*Hepatica*) of herbs of the crowfoot family, having lobed leaves and delicate white, pink, blue, or purplish flowers.
he·pat'i·co- (hē·păt'ĭ·kō-). Comb. form for *hepatic,* as in **he·pat'i·co-gas·tros'to·my, he·pat'i·co·pul'mo·nar'y, he·pat'i·cot'o·my.**
hep'a·ti'tis (hĕp'ȧ·tī'tĭs), *n.* [NL., fr. *hepat-* + *-itis.*] *Med.* Inflammation of the liver.
hep'a·ti·za'tion (-tĭ·zā'shŭn; -tī·zā'-), *n.* *Med.* Conversion of tissue into a substance resembling the liver, as of the lungs in pneumonia, in which the affected tissue becomes solidified and airless.
hep'a·to- (hĕp'ȧ·tō-), **hepat-.** [Gr. *hēpar, hēpatos.*] A combining form, meaning *the liver,* as in **hep'a·tec'to·my, hep'a·tot'o·my** (see -ECTOMY, -TOMY).
hep'cat' (hĕp'kăt'), *n., or* **hep cat.** [*hep* + *cat.*] *Swing Music.* A musician in a swing band; — called also *cat.*
He·phaes'tus (hē·fĕs'tŭs *or, esp. Brit.,* -fēs'tŭs), **He·phais'tos** (-fīs'tŏs), *n.* [Gr. *Hēphaistos.*] *Gr. Relig.* The god of fire and of metalworking, son of Zeus and Hera and husband of Aphrodite.
Hep'ple·white (hĕp''l·hwīt), *adj.* Designating a style of furniture developed in England under George III, chiefly by A. Hepplewhite & Co. This style is often distinguishable from Sheraton by its greater use of curves, as in the favored shield and heart backs of its chairs.
hep'ta- (hĕp'tȧ-), **hept-.** [Gr. *hepta.*] A combining form meaning *seven,* as in *heptagon;* specif., *Chem.,* denoting *the presence of seven atoms* or *equivalents of a* (specified) *substance,* as in: **hep'tane,** any of nine isomeric hydrocarbons, C_7H_{16}, of the paraffin series; **hep'ta·he'dral; hep'ta·he'dron; hep·tan'gu·lar.**
hep'ta·chord (-kôrd), *n.* [Gr. *heptachordos* seven-stringed, fr. *hepta* seven + *chordē* chord.] *Greek Music.* **a** The lyre of seven strings. **b** A diatonic system of seven tones. **c** The interval of a major seventh.
hep'tad (hĕp'tăd), *n.* [L. *heptas* the number seven, fr. Gr. *heptas, -ados,* fr. *hepta* seven.] The sum or number, or a group, of seven.
hep'ta·gon (hĕp'tȧ·gŏn), *n.* [Gr. *heptagōnos* seven-cornered, fr. *hepta* seven + *gōnia* angle.] *Geom.* A (plane) polygon of seven angles and therefore seven sides. — **hep·tag'o·nal** (hĕp·tăg'ō·năl; -n'l), *adj.*
hep·tam'er·ous (hĕp·tăm'ẽr·ŭs), *adj.* [*hepta-* + *-merous.*] *Bot.* Consisting of seven parts, or having the parts of the flower in sevens; — often written 7-*merous.*
hep·tam'e·ter (hĕp·tăm'ē·tẽr), *n.* [*hepta-* + *-meter.*] *Pros.* A verse of seven metrical feet or measures.
hep'tane (hĕp'tān), *n.* [Gr. *hepta* seven.] *Chem.* Any of nine isomeric hydrocarbons, C_7H_{16}, of the methane series.
hep'tarch·y (hĕp'tär·kĭ), *n.; pl.* -TARCHIES (-kĭz). [*hept-* + *-archy.*] A government by seven persons; also, a group of seven friendly or allied districts or kingdoms, each under its own ruler; as, the Anglo-Saxon *heptarchy* in England.
hep'ta·stich (hĕp'tȧ·stĭk), *n.* [*hepta-* + Gr. *stichos* line, verse.] *Pros.* A poem or strophe of seven lines or verses.
Hep'ta·teuch (-tūk), *n.* [L. *heptateuchos,* fr. Gr. *hepta* seven + *teuchos* tool, book.] The first seven books of the Old Testament. See BIBLE.
her (hûr; 4), *pron.* [AS. *hire,* gen. and dat. sing. of *hēo* she.] **1.** The objective case of *she.* **2.** The possessive case of *she.* — *adj.* Of, belonging to, or relating to that female (person or thing personified).
He'ra (hē'rȧ), **He're** (hē'rē), *n.* [L., fr. Gr. *Hēra, Hērē.*] *Gr. Relig.* An Olympian goddess, queen of heaven, sister and wife of Zeus. She is goddess of women and marriage.
Her'a·cli'dae (hĕr'ȧ·klī'dē), *n. pl.; sing.* **Her'a·clid** (hĕr'ȧ·klĭd). [Gr. *Hērakleidai.*] *Gr. Myth.* The descendants of Hercules, fabled to have conquered the Peloponnesus. — **Her'a·cli'dan** (-klī'dăn), *adj.*
Her'a·kles, Her'a·cles (hĕr'ȧ·klēz), *n.* Hercules.
her'ald (hĕr'ăld), *n.* [OF. *heralt, heraut,* deriv. of OHG. *hari, heri,* army + *waltan* to manage, govern.] **1. a** An officer who proclaimed war or peace, bore messages to or from rulers or commanders, made solemn announcements, etc. **b** In tourneys, an official who issued and announced challenges, marshaled combatants, etc. **2.** In Great Britain and Ireland, a similar officer charged also with the care of genealogies, and esp. of armorial bearings. **3.** Hence, one who proclaims, publishes, or announces; a messenger; precursor; harbinger. — **Syn.** See FORERUNNER. — *v. t.* To introduce, or give tidings of, as by a herald; to proclaim; to announce; to foretell; to usher in.
he·ral'dic (hē·răl'dĭk), *adj.* Of or pertaining to heralds or heraldry; as, *heraldic* blazoning.
her'ald·ry (hĕr'ăld·rĭ), *n.; pl.* -RIES (-rĭz). **1.** The art or science of a herald; the science of recording genealogies and blazoning arms or ensigns armorial. **2.** An emblazonment; heraldic symbol; armorial bearing. See ESCUTCHEON. **3.** Heraldic pomp or ceremony.
Her'alds' Col'lege (hĕr'ăldz). In England, a corporation which retains from the Middle Ages the charge of the armorial bearings of persons privileged to bear them, as well as of genealogies and kindred subjects.
herb (ûrb; hûrb), *n.* [OF. *herbe, erbe,* fr. L. *herba.*] **1.** A seed plant which does not develop woody persistent tissue, as that of a shrub or tree, but is more or less soft or succulent; specif., one used for medicinal purposes, or for its sweet scent or flavor. **2.** Grass; herbage.
her·ba'ceous (hûr·bā'shŭs), *adj.* [L. *herbaceus* grassy.] **1.** Pertaining to, or having the characteristics of, an herb. **2.** Of the texture, color, or appearance of an ordinary foliage leaf; as, *herbaceous* sepals.
herb'age (ûr'bĭj; hûr'bĭj), *n.* [F.] **1.** Herbaceous vegetation; green plants collectively, esp. those used for pasturage. **2.** The succulent parts of herbaceous plants, esp. the foliage and young stems.
herb'al (hûr'băl; ûr'-), *adj.* Pertaining to, or made of, herbs. — *n.* *Hist.* A book describing plants.
herb'al·ist (-ĭst), *n.* Orig., a botanist; in later usage, a collector of, or dealer in, herbs, esp. medicinal herbs.
her·bar'i·um (hûr·bâr'ĭ·ŭm), *n.; pl.* -IUMS (-ŭmz), -IA (-ȧ). [LL., fr. L. *herba* herb.] A collection of dried plants, usually mounted and classified; also, the room or building where the collection is kept.
herb bennet. The common avens (*Geum urbanum*). See AVENS.
herb doctor. One who cures, or professes to cure, by means of herbs.
her'bi·vore (hûr'bĭ·vōr), *n.* An animal feeding chiefly on herbage; esp., *Zool.,* any of a group (**Her·biv'o·ra** [hûr·bĭv'ō·rȧ]) of mammals, mostly feeding on herbage.
her·biv'o·rous (hûr·bĭv'ō·rŭs), *adj.* [L. *herba* herb + *-vorous.*] *Zool.* Eating, or living on, plants; — opposed to *carnivorous.*
herb Paris. A European herb (*Paris quadrifolia,* family Trilliaceae) resembling members of a related genus (*Trillium*), and commonly reputed to be poisonous.
herb Robert. See GERANIUM, 1.
Her·cu'le·an (hûr·kū'lē·ăn; hûr'kū·lē'ăn), *adj.* **1.** Of or pertaining to Hercules. **2.** [*often not cap.*] Requiring the strength of Hercules; hence, very difficult or dangerous. **3.** [*often not cap.*] Having extraordinary strength or size.
Her'cu·les (hûr'kū·lēz), *n.* [L., fr. Gr. *Hēraklēēs,* fr. *Hēra* Hera + *kleos* glory.] **1.** *Class. Myth.* A hero, the son of Zeus (Jupiter) and Alcmene, celebrated for strength and esp. for achieving twelve great tasks, or "labors," imposed on him as a result of the hatred of Hera (Juno). See NESSUS. **2.** [*gen.* HERCULIS.] A northern constellation between Corona Borealis and Lyra.
Her'cu·les'-club' (hûr'kū·lēz-), *n.* A small prickly tree (*Aralia spinosa*) of the ginseng family, of the eastern United States, with compound leaves; — called also *angelica tree.*
herd (hûrd), *n.* [AS. *heord.*] **1.** A number of beasts, esp. of large animals, assembled together. **2.** The common people in the aggregate; rabble; crowd. — *v. i.* **1.** To unite or associate in a herd. **2.** To associate; to ally oneself with a group or company. — *v. t.* To form or put into a herd.
herd, *n.* [AS. *hierde, hirde, hyrde, heorde.*] A herdsman; — chiefly in composition, as shep*herd,* goat*herd.* — *v. t.* To tend, lead, or drive as a herdsman.
herd'er (hûr'dẽr), *n.* One who herds; a herdsman.
her'dic (hûr'dĭk), *n.* [After Peter *Herdic,* the inventor.] A type of low-hung cab, usually with two wheels, but sometimes four, with side seats, and entrance at the back.
herd'man (hûrd'măn), *n.* *Obs.* A herdsman.
herd's'-grass' (hûrdz'grȧs'), *n.* **a** Timothy. **b** Redtop (*Agrostis stolonifera major*).
herds'man (hûrdz'măn), *n.* **1.** One who owns, keeps, or tends a herd. **2.** [*cap.*] *Astron.* = BOÖTES.
here (hēr; 27), *adv.* [AS. *hēr.*] **1.** In this place; — opposed to *there.* **2.** In the present life or state. **3.** To or into this place; hither. **4.** At this point; now. — ***here and there.*** In one place and another; irregularly. — ***neither here nor there.*** To no purpose; irrelevant.
He're (hē'rē). Var. of HERA.
here'a·bout' (hēr'ȧ·bout'; 2), **here'a·bouts'** (-bouts'), *adv.* About this place; in this vicinity.
here·aft'er (hēr·ȧf'tẽr; 9), *adv.* [AS. *hēræfter.*] After this time or order; in some future time or state. — *n.* The future; a future existence or state, esp. after death.
here·at' (hēr·ăt'), *adv.* At, or by reason of, this.
here·by' (-bī'), *adv.* **1.** *Obs.* Close by. **2.** By means of this.
he·red'i·ta·ble (hē·rĕd'ĭ·tȧ·b'l), *adj.* [MF., fr. ML. *hereditabilis,* fr. *hereditare* to inherit, fr. L. *heres* heir.] Heritable. — **he·red'i·ta·bil'i·ty** (-bĭl'ĭ·tĭ), *n.* — **he·red'i·ta·bly,** *adv.*
her'e·dit'a·ment (hĕr'ē·dĭt'ȧ·mĕnt), *n.* [ML. *hereditamentum.*] *Law.* Any property that may be inherited.
he·red'i·tar'y (hē·rĕd'ĭ·tĕr'ĭ *or, esp. Brit.,* -tẽr·ĭ), *adj.* [L. *hereditarius,* fr. *hereditas* heirship, inheritance, fr. *heres* heir.] **1.** Descended, or capable of descending, from an ancestor to an heir at law. **2.** Having title or possession through inheritance. **3.** Transmitted, or transmissible, as a constitutional quality or condition from parent to offspring. Cf. CONGENITAL, 2. **4.** Of or pertaining to inheritance or heredity. — **Syn.** See INNATE. — **he·red'i·tar'i·ly,** *adv.* — **he·red'i·tar'i·ness,** *n.*
he·red'i·ty (hē·rĕd'ĭ·tĭ), *n.; pl.* -ITIES (-tĭz). [F. *hérédité,* fr. L. *hereditas* heirship.] **1.** *Biol.* Hereditary transmission of the physical and psychical characters of parents to their offspring. **2.** That which is derived by such hereditary transmission.
Her'e·ford (hĕr'ē·fẽrd; *U. S. chiefly* hûr'fẽrd), *n.* One of a breed of hardy beef cattle originating in Herefordshire, England. Herefords are red with white faces and markings.
here·in' (hēr·ĭn'), *adv.* [AS. *hērinne.*] In or into this.
here'in·aft'er (hēr'ĭn·ȧf'tẽr), *adv.* In the following part of this (writing, document, book, etc.).
here·in'be·fore' (hēr·ĭn'bē·fōr'), *adv.* In the preceding part of this (writing, document, book, etc.).
here·in'to (hēr·ĭn'tōō), *adv.* Into this (place, matter, etc.).
here·of' (hēr·ŏv'), *adv.* Of this; concerning this.
here·on' (-ŏn'), *adv.* On or upon this; hereupon.
he·re'si·arch (hē·rē'sĭ·ärk; hĕr'ē·sĭ·ärk), *n.; pl.* -ARCHS (-ärks). [F. or L.; F. *hérésiarque,* fr. L. *haeresiarcha,* fr. Gr. *hairesiarchēs,* fr. *hairesis* heresy + *archos* leader, *archein* to lead.] A leader in heresy; the chief of a sect of heretics.

her'e·sy (hĕr'ĕ·sĭ), *n.; pl.* -SIES (-sĭz). [OF. *heresie, eresie,* fr. L., fr. Gr. *hairesis* a taking, choice, sect, heresy, fr. *hairein* to take, choose.] **1.** Religious opinion opposed to the authorized doctrinal standards of any particular church, and tending to promote schism. **2.** An opinion held in opposition to the commonly received doctrine, and tending to promote division or dissension.

her'e·tic (hĕr'ĕ·tĭk), *n.* [OF. *heretique,* fr. L., fr. Gr. *hairetikos* able to choose, heretical.] One who holds to a heresy; esp., one who, having made a profession of Christian belief, deliberately upholds a doctrine varying from that of his church, or rejects one prescribed by his church.

he·ret'i·cal (hē·rĕt'ĭ·kăl), *adj.* Also **her'e·tic** (hĕr'ĕ·tĭk). Of the nature of, or characterized by, heresy. — **Syn.** See HETERODOX. — **he·ret'i·cal·ly,** *adv.*

here·to' (hēr·to͞o'), *adv.* To this; hereunto.

here'to·fore' (hēr'to͞o·fōr'; 70), *adv.* Up to this time.

here'un·to' (-ŭn·to͞o'), *adv.* Unto this; up to this time.

here'up·on' (hēr'ŭ·pŏn'), *adv.* On this; hereon.

here·with' (hēr·wĭth'; -wĭth'), *adv.* With this.

her'i·ot (hĕr'ĭ·ŏt), *n.* [AS. *heregeatu* military equipment, fr. *here* army + *geatwe,* pl., arms.] *Eng. Law.* A feudal duty or tribute due to a lord upon the death of a tenant.

her'it·a·ble (hĕr'ĭt·ȧ·b'l), *adj.* [OF.] **1.** Capable of being inherited; inheritable. **2.** Capable of inheriting. — **her'it·a·bil'i·ty** (-bĭl'ĭ·tĭ), *n.*

her'it·age (hĕr'ĭ·tĭj), *n.* [OF., fr. *heriter* to inherit, fr. LL. *hereditare,* fr. L. *heres* heir.] **1.** That which is inherited; inheritance; hence, the lot, condition, or status into which one is born; birthright. **2.** *Bib.* God's chosen people; Israel; also, the Christian church.

Syn. **Heritage, inheritance, patrimony, birthright** mean something which one receives or will receive from a parent or predecessor. **Heritage,** the most comprehensive term, may imply anything passed on to one's heirs or to generations that succeed, such as an estate, a tradition, a right, etc.; **inheritance** applies to that which passes from parents to children, whether it be money, property, traits of character, or the like; **patrimony** applies strictly to an inherited estate, but is also used of anything inherited from one's ancestors; **birthright,** as here compared, applies to the property that has come or will come to one by right of birth, usually by primogeniture.

her'it·ance (-tăns), *n.* [OF.] Heritage; inheritance.

her'i·tor (hĕr'ĭ·tẽr), *n.* [OF. *heritier.*] An inheritor; specif., *Scots Law,* the owner in fee of heritable property in a parish.

herl (hûrl), *n.* A barb, or barbs, of a feather, used in dressing artificial flies; also, a fly so dressed.

her'ma (hûr'mȧ), *n.; pl.* HERMAE (-mē), HERMAI (-mī). [L. *Herma,* fr. Gr. *Hermēs,* pl. *Hermai.*] *Gr. Antiq.* An image in the form of a stone pillar, usually square, surmounted by a head of Hermes, generally bearded, set up in many gymnasia and streets.

her·maph'ro·dite (hûr·măf'rō·dīt), *n.* [From L., fr. Gr. *hermaphroditos,* so called from the myth of *Hermaphroditus.*] **1.** *Biol.* An individual having both male and female reproductive organs. **2.** *Naut.* A hermaphrodite brig. — *adj.* Of or pertaining to hermaphrodites; characterized by hermaphroditism.

hermaphrodite brig. *Naut.* A two-masted vessel, square-rigged forward and schooner-rigged aft.

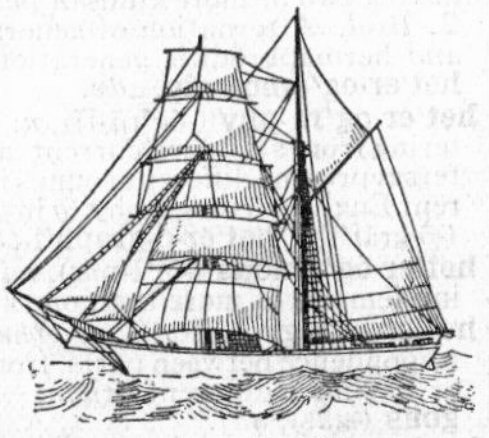

Hermaphrodite Brig.

her·maph'ro·dit'ic (-dĭt'ĭk), *adj.* Also **her·maph'ro·dit'i·cal** (-ĭ·kăl). Relating to a hermaphrodite or to hermaphroditism; hence, uniting contrary natures; joining discordant elements. — **her·maph'ro·dit'i·cal·ly,** *adv.*

her·maph'ro·dit·ism (hûr·măf'rō·dīt·ĭz'm), *n.* *Biol.* The union of the two sexes in the same individual, rare and abnormal in higher vertebrates, but normal in some fishes and many invertebrates.

Her·maph'ro·di'tus (-dī'tŭs), *n.* [Gr. *Hermaphroditos.*] *Gr. Myth.* A son of Hermes and Aphrodite, who while bathing became joined in one body with a nymph.

her'me·neu'tic (hûr'mē·nū'tĭk), **her'me·neu'ti·cal** (-tĭ·kăl), *adj.* [Gr. *hermēneutikos,* fr. *hermēneuein* to interpret.] Unfolding the signification; interpretative.

her'me·neu'tics (-tĭks), *n.; see* -ICS. The science of interpretation and explanation; esp., that branch of theology which defines the laws applied by exegesis.

Her'mes (hûr'mēz), *n.* [L., fr. Gr. *Hermēs.*] *Gr. Relig.* An Olympian god, son of Zeus and Maia. He was herald and messenger of the gods, giver of increase to herds, guardian of boundaries and of roads and their commerce. He was further god of science and invention, of eloquence, of cunning, trickery, and theft, of luck and treasure-trove, and conductor of the dead to Hades. His attributes are the winged sandals (talaria), caduceus, and winged hat (petasos).

Her'mes Tris'me·gis'tus (trĭs'mē·jĭs'tŭs). [Gr. *Hermēs trismegistos,* lit., Hermes thrice greatest.] A late name of Hermes, as identified with the Egyptian god Thoth. He was the fabled author of works embodying magical, astrological, and alchemical doctrines.

her·met'ic (hûr·mĕt'ĭk), **her·met'i·cal** (-ĭ·kăl), *adj.* [ML. *hermeticus,* fr. *Hermes.*] **1.** [*usually cap.*] Of, pertaining to, taught by, or derived from Hermes Trismegistus or his teachings; hence, alchemical; magical. **2.** Made perfectly close or airtight by, or as by, fusion, so that no gas or spirit can enter or escape; as, a *hermetic* seal. — **her·met'i·cal·ly,** *adv.*

Her·mi'o·ne (hûr·mī'ō·nē), *n.* *Gr. Myth.* Daughter of Menelaus and Helen.

her'mit (hûr'mĭt), *n.* [OF. *hermite, ermite,* fr. L. *eremita,* fr. Gr. *erēmitēs,* fr. *erēmos* solitary.] **1.** A person who retires from society and lives in solitude, esp. from religious motives; recluse; anchorite. Cf. CENOBITE. **2.** *Obs.* A beadsman. **3.** *Cookery.* A spiced molasses cooky, with chopped raisins and nuts.

her'mit·age (hûr'mĭ·tĭj), *n.* **1.** The habitation of a hermit; a secluded residence. **2.** [*cap.*] [F. *Vin de l'Hermitage.*] Wine made in a certain locality in the Department of the Drôme, France.

hermit crab. Any of numerous, mostly marine, decapod crustaceans (families Paguridae and Parapaguridae) which occupy the empty shells of snails and other gastropods. See CRAB, 1 **b**; PURSE CRAB.

her·mit'ic (hûr·mĭt'ĭk), **her·mit'i·cal** (-ĭ·kăl), *adj.* Pertaining to, or suited for, a hermit. — **her·mit'i·cal·ly,** *adv.*

hern (hûrn). Scot. var. of HERON.

her'ni·a (hûr'nĭ·ȧ), *n.; pl.* -NIAS (-ȧz), -NIAE (-ē). [L.] *Med.* Protrusion of an organ or part through some opening in the walls of its natural cavity; rupture. — **her'ni·al** (-ăl), *adj.*

hernio-. A combining form for *hernia,* as in **her'ni·ot'o·my** (see -TOMY).

he'ro (hē'rō; 27), *n.; pl.* -ROES (-ōz). [L. *heros,* fr. Gr. *hērōs.*] **1.** *Myth. & Relig.* **a** A man, esp. a warrior, of the Greek epic or heroic age. **b** A man honored after death by public worship, because of exceptional service to mankind, and usually held to be in part at least of divine descent. **2.** The principal male personage, usually of noble character, in a poem, story, drama, or the like. **3.** A person of distinguished valor or fortitude. **4.** A central personage taking an admirable part in any remarkable action or event; hence, a person regarded as a model.

He'ro and Le·an'der (lē·ăn'dẽr). [L. *Hero,* fr. Gr. *Hērō;* L. *Leander,* fr. Gr. *Leiandros.*] In Greek legend, a pair of lovers. Hero was a priestess of Aphrodite at Sestos on the Hellespont, and Leander, who lived at Abydos, swam the strait nightly to visit her. One night he was drowned, and Hero, in grief, cast herself into the sea.

he·ro'ic (hē·rō'ĭk), *adj.* Also **he·ro'i·cal** (-ĭ·kăl). **1.** Of, pertaining to, or like, a hero or heroes; of the nature of heroes; distinguished by the existence of heroes; as, the *heroic* age; a *heroic* people. **2.** Worthy of a hero; brave; valiant; illustrious. **3.** Treating of, or suitable to or used in the treatment of, heroes and their deeds; as, *heroic* poetry, verse. **4.** In the fine arts, larger than life size, but smaller than colossal; hence, often humorously, huge; enormous. **5.** Large; powerful; as, a *heroic* dose of medicine; hence, utmost; extreme; as, *heroic* measures, treatment. — **he·ro'i·cal·ly,** *adv.*

he·ro'ic (hē·rō'ĭk), *n.* **1.** A heroic verse or poem. **2.** *pl.* Extravagant expression in words or actions.

heroic couplet. A rhyming couplet used in heroic verse, specif. one in iambic pentameter, usually forming a distinct rhetorical as well as metrical unit.

heroic verse. **1.** The verse form in which the heroic poetry of a particular language is or should be composed, as the Alexandrine in French. **2.** Specif., in English poetry, the iambic pentameter.

her'o·in (hĕr'ō·ĭn; hēr'ō·ĭn; hē·rō'ĭn), *n.* A white crystalline narcotic, $C_{21}H_{23}NO_5$; diacetyl-morphine.

her'o·ine (hĕr'ō·ĭn), *n.* [L. *heroina,* fr. Gr. *hērōinē,* fem. of *hērōs.*] **1.** *Myth.* A woman of qualities like those of a hero. **2.** A woman of heroic spirit. **3.** The principal female person figuring in a remarkable action, or as the main subject of a poem, story, or the like.

her'o·ism (-ĭz'm), *n.* The qualities characteristic of a hero; also, display of such qualities.

Syn. **Heroism, valor, prowess, gallantry** mean conspicuous bravery or courage, especially in conflict. **Heroism** implies superlative, often transcendent, courage especially in fulfilling a superhumanly high purpose where the odds are against one; **valor** implies illustrious bravery, especially in fighting, and fearlessness and audacity; **prowess** stresses brilliant achievements or exploits in arms; **gallantry,** mettle and spirit as well as high courage, and an almost gay indifference to danger or hardship.

her'on (hĕr'ŭn), *n.;* see PLURAL, *Note,* 3. [OF. *hairon* (F. *héron*), of Teut. origin.] Any of a family (Ardeidae) of wading birds with long neck and legs, long tapering bill, large wings, and soft plumage, including the common European species (*Ardea cinerea*), the ***great blue heron*** (*A. herodias;* a slaty-blue American species about 50 inches long), the ***great white heron*** (*A. occidentalis*) of Florida and Mexico, and the egrets. See EGRET; CRANE, *n.,* 2; NIGHT HERON; BITTERN. Cf. STORK, IBIS.

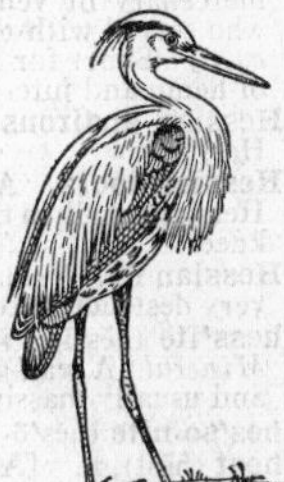

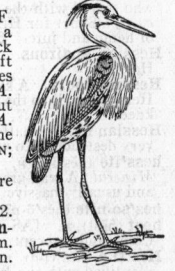

Great Blue Heron. (1/30)

her'on·ry (-rĭ), *n.; pl.* -RIES (-rĭz). A place where herons breed.

her'on's-bill' (hĕr'ŭnz·bĭl'), *n.* See GERANIUM, 2.

her'on·sew (hĕr'ŭn·sō; -sū), **her'on·sewe, her'on·shaw** (-shô), *n.* [OF. *heroncel,* later *-ceau,* dim. of *héron.* See HERON.] *Obs. exc. Dial.* A heron.

her'pes (hûr'pēz), *n.* [L., fr. Gr. *herpēs,* fr. *herpein* to creep.] *Med.* Any of various acute inflammations of the skin and mucous membrane, in which clusters of small vesicles spread from one part to another; now, esp. shingles (‖**her'pes zos'ter** [zŏs'tẽr]) or cold sores (‖**her'pes la'bi·a'lis** [lā'bĭ·ā'lĭs]). — **her·pet'ic** (hûr·pĕt'ĭk), *adj.*

her'pe·tol'o·gy (hûr'pē·tŏl'ō·jĭ), *n.* [Gr. *herpeton* reptile, fr. *herpein* to creep + *-logy.*] That branch of zoology which relates to reptiles and amphibians, their structure, classification, and habits. — **her'pe·to·log'i·cal** (-tō·lŏj'ĭ·kăl), *adj.* — **her'pe·tol'o·gist** (-tŏl'ō·jĭst), *n.*

‖**Herr** (hĕr), *n.; pl.* HERREN (hĕr'ĕn). Lord; master; also, now, commonly, a title of respect equivalent to English *mister.*

Her'ren·volk' (hĕr'ĕn·fōlk'), *n.* [G. *herren* lords, masters + *volk* people.] A supposed pre-eminently superior race fitted to impose itself by force as ruler and model of the world; — in the Nazi-fostered myth, the Germans.

her'ring (hĕr'ĭng), *n.;* see PLURAL, *Note,* 6. [AS. *hǣring, hēring.*] A very valuable clupeid physostomous food fish (*Clupea harengus*), the type of a family (Clupeidae), extremely abundant in the North Atlantic. The adults are smoked or salted and the young are canned as sardines. A closely allied species, the ***California herring*** (*C. pallasii*) replaces the true herring in the North Pacific. The name *herring* is extended to many members of the herring family and also to some fishes of more or less similar families. Cf. SPRAT.

her'ring·bone' (-bōn'), *adj.* Resembling the spine of a herring; esp., arranged in rows of parallel lines, which in any two successive rows slope in reverse directions. — *n.* A herringbone arrangement or pattern. — *v. t.* To produce a herringbone pattern on (a surface); also, to arrange in a herringbone pattern. — *v. i.* To make a herringbone pattern; hence, *Skiing,* to proceed, as in a steep ascent, by placing the skis, alternately, at an angle to each other and to the line of progress.

herringbone stitch. *Needlework.* A kind of cross-stitch used to fasten down material too thick to be hemmed; also, an embroidery stitch.

her'ry (hĕr'ĭ). Scot. var. of HARRY, *v.* — **her'ry·ment,** *n.*

hers (hûrz), *pron.* The form of the possessive *her* when it is used absolutely, that is, without a following noun. Like *yours* and *theirs*, *hers* is the form used after *of*; as, a gift of *hers*.

herse (hûrs), *n.* [F., harrow, portcullis.] A harrowlike battle formation, as of pikemen or archers.

her·self′ (hûr·sĕlf′; hĕr-), *pron.* An emphasized form of the pronoun for the third person sing. feminine. Its uses are: **1.** For emphasis; as, she *herself* said it. **2.** Specif., esp. after *be, become*, etc.: Her normal, proper, or true self; as, she was demented, but is now *herself* again. **3.** As a reflexive; as, she blames *herself*.

hertz′i·an (hĕrt′sĭ·ăn), *adj.* Of or pertaining to the type of experiments, apparatus, etc., used by the German physicist Heinrich Hertz about 1886; as, *hertzian* oscillator, telegraphy; esp., **hertzian wave**, an electric wave.

Hesh′van (hĕsh′văn), *n.* Also **Hesh′wan.** See JEWISH CALENDAR.

hes′i·tance (hĕz′ĭ·tăns), *n.* Hesitation.

hes′i·tan·cy (-tăn·sĭ), *n.; pl.* -CIES (-sĭz). Hesitation.

hes′i·tant (hĕz′ĭ·tănt), *adj.* Hesitating. — **Syn.** See DISINCLINED. — **hes′i·tant·ly**, *adv.*

hes′i·tate (-tāt), *v. i.* [L. *haesitare*, intens. fr. *haerere, haesum*, to hesitate, stick fast.] **1.** To be in uncertainty as to what to do, say, or the like; to pause undecidedly. **2.** To stammer. — **hes′i·tat′ing** (-tāt′ĭng), *adj.* — **hes′i·tat′ing·ly**, *adv.*

Syn. **Hesitate, waver, vacillate, falter** mean to show irresolution or uncertainty. **Hesitate** implies a pause or other sign of indecision before making up one's mind what to do, say, choose, or the like; **waver**, hesitation after a decision and so, usually, connotes weakness or a retreat; **vacillate**, prolonged hesitation resulting from one's inability to make a fixed and final decision; **falter**, a wavering in purpose or action, usually made evident in trembling, the breaking of the voice, or the like.

hes′i·ta′tion (-tā′shŭn), *n.* **1.** Act or fact of hesitating; vacillation. **2.** A faltering in speech; stammering.

hes′i·ta′tive (hĕz′ĭ·tā′tĭv; -tȧ·tĭv), *adj.* Showing, or characterized by, hesitation. — **hes′i·ta′tive·ly**, *adv.*

Hes′per (hĕs′pẽr), *n.* Hesperus.

Hes·pe′ri·a (hĕs·pē′rĭ·ȧ), *n.* [L., fr. Gr.] The Western Land; — a name given by the Greek poets to Italy and by the Roman poets to Spain and sometimes to Italy.

Hes·pe′ri·an (hĕs·pē′rĭ·ăn), *adj.* [L. *hesperius*, fr. *hesperus* the evening star, fr. Gr. *hesperos* evening, *hesperos astēr* the evening star.] **1.** Western; occidental; specif., of or pertaining to Hesperia. **2.** *Poetic.* Of or pertaining to the Hesperides.

Hes·per′i·des (hĕs·pĕr′ĭ·dēz), *n. pl.* [L., fr. Gr. *Hesperides.*] *Class. Myth.* **1.** *sing.* HES′PER·ID (hĕs′pẽr·ĭd). The nymphs who guarded with the aid of a dragon the garden in which grew the golden apples which Gaea gave as a wedding present to Hera. **2.** The garden producing the golden apples, located in the extreme west.

hes·per′i·din (hĕs·pĕr′ĭ·dĭn), *n.* [From *hesperidium*, the fruit of the orange. See HESPERIDES.] A white crystalline glucoside, $C_{50}H_{60}O_{27}$, found in citrus fruit.

Hes′per·us (hĕs′pẽr·ŭs), *n.* [L.] The evening star; Venus.

Hes′sian (hĕsh′ăn), *adj.* Of or pertaining to Hesse, in Germany, or the Hessians. — *n.* **1.** A native or inhabitant of Hesse. **2.** *U. S.* A mercenary or venal person; — alluding to the Hessian mercenaries who served with the British in the Revolutionary War. **3.** *pl.* [*not cap.*] Short for HESSIAN BOOTS. **4.** [*not cap.*] A coarse sacking of hemp and jute. **5.** *pl.* Short for HESSIAN ANDIRONS.

Hessian andirons. Andirons having uprights shaped to represent Hessians.

Hessian boots. A kind of high boots introduced into England by the Hessians early in the 19th century. The top extended to just below the knee.

Hessian fly. A small two-winged fly, or midge (*Mayetiola destructor*), very destructive to wheat in America.

hess′ite (hĕs′īt), *n.* [After G. Y. *Hess* (1802–50), Swiss chemist.] *Mineral.* A lead-gray sectile silver telluride, Ag_2Te, often auriferous, and usually massive.

hes′so·nite (hĕs′ō·nīt), *n.* *Mineral.* Essonite.

hest (hĕst), *n.* [AS. *hǣs*, fr. root of *hātan* to call, bid.] **1.** *Archaic.* Command; precept. **2.** *Obs.* A pledge.

Hes′ti·a (hĕs′tĭ·ȧ), *n.* [Gr.] *Gr. Relig.* Goddess of the hearth; — identified with the Roman *Vesta.*

Hes′y·chast (hĕs′ĭ·kăst), *n.* [Gr. *hēsychastēs* hermit, fr. *hēsychazein* to be still or quiet, fr. *hēsychos* still, calm.] One of a sect of mystics or quietists in the Eastern Church, which originated among the monks of Mt. Athos, in the 14th century. — **Hes′y·chas′tic** (-kăs′tĭk), *adj.*

he·tae′ra (hē·tē′rȧ), **he·tai′ra** (-tī′rȧ), *n.; pl.* HETAERAE (-rē), HETAIRAI (-rī). [NL. *hetaera*, Gr. *hetaira.*] *Gr. Antiq.* A female paramour of the better class. The hetaerae were usually slaves.

he·tae′rism ((hē·tēr′ĭz′m), **he·tai′rism** (-tī′rĭz′m), *n.* [Gr. *hetaira* companion, concubine, fem. of *hetaros, hetairos*, comrade.] **1.** Concubinage. **2.** A supposed primitive state of society, in which women were held in common.

het′er·o- (hĕt′ẽr·ō-), **heter-.** [Gr. *heteros* other.] A combining form signifying: **a** *Other, other than usual, different.* **b** *Immunol. For, from,* or *to, a different species.* **c** *Chem.* (1) (Used adjectively in the form **het′er·o.**) Designating an atom other than carbon, esp. when part of a ring. (2) Denoting an isomer or close relative of the compound to whose name it is prefixed.

het′er·o·cer′cal (-sûr′kăl), *adj.* [*hetero-* + Gr. *kerkos* tail.] *Zool.* Having the upper lobe larger than the lower with the end of the vertebral column prolonged and somewhat upturned, in the upper lobe; — said of the tail fin of certain fishes; also, having, or pertaining to, such a tail fin.

het′er·o·chro·mat′ic (-krō·măt′ĭk), *adj.* [*hetero-* + *chromatic.*] Of, having, or pertaining to different colors, specif. a more or less complex pattern of colors; — opposed to *homochromatic.*

het′er·o·chro′ma·tin (-krō′mȧ·tĭn), *n.* [*hetero-* + *chromatin.*] *Biol.* A densely staining nuclear material appearing as nodules in or along chromosomes and thought to influence the physiology of the cell.

het′er·o·chrome′ (hĕt′ẽr·ō·krōm′), *adj.* Heterochromatic.

het′er·o·chro′mo·some (-krō′mō·sōm), *n.* *Biol.* A sex chromosome, as an X or Y chromosome.

het′er·o·chro′mous (-krō′mŭs), *adj.* [*hetero-* + Gr. *chrōma* color.] Of different colors; — opposed to *homochromous.*

het′er·och′tho·nous (-ŏk′thō·nŭs), *adj.* [See HETERO-; AUTOCHTHON.] Not indigenous; foreign; naturalized.

het′er·o·clite′ (hĕt′ẽr·ō·klīt′), *adj.* [F. *hétéroclite*, fr. LL., fr. Gr. *heteroklitos*, fr. *heteros* other + *klinein* to lean, incline, inflect.] Deviating from ordinary forms or rules; irregular; anomalous; abnormal. — *n.* **1.** *Gram.* A word deviating from the ordinary inflection of like words. **2.** Any thing or person deviating from the common rule, or from common forms.

het′er·o·cy′clic (-sī′klĭk; -sĭk′lĭk), *adj.* [*hetero-* + *cyclic.*] *Chem.* Pertaining to, containing, or designating a ring composed of atoms of different kinds.

het′er·o·dox (hĕt′ẽr·ō·dŏks), *adj.* [Gr. *heterodoxos*, fr. *heteros* other + *doxa* opinion.] **1.** Contrary to, or different from, some acknowledged standard, as the Bible, a creed, etc.; not orthodox; heretical. **2.** Holding unorthodox opinions or doctrines.

Syn. **Heterodox, heretical** mean not in conformity with orthodox teachings. **Heterodox** implies merely this; **heretical**, in addition, suggests a point of view that regards such teachings as destructive of truth.

het′er·o·dox′y (-dŏk′sĭ), *n.; pl.* -DOXIES (-sĭz). **1.** Quality of being heterodox. **2.** A heterodox opinion or doctrine.

het′er·o·dyne′ (-dīn′), *adj.* [*hetero-* + *dyne.*] *Radio.* Pertaining to the production of a difference frequency (beats) between two radio frequencies, one of them usually being that of a received signal-carrying current and the other that of an uninterrupted current introduced for the purpose into the apparatus. The beat frequency, being lower than the original frequency, is more readily subjected to the processes of amplification and the like. Cf. SUPERHETERODYNE. — **het′er·o·dyne′**, *v.*

het′er·oe′cious (hĕt′ẽr·ē′shŭs), *adj.* [*heter-* + Gr. *oikia* house.] *Biol.* Parasitic on an alternation of hosts, as rusts, some insects, etc. Cf. AUTOECIOUS. — **het′er·oe′cism** (-sĭz′m), *n.*

het′er·o·ga·mete′ (hĕt′ẽr·ō·gȧ·mēt′), *n.* [*hetero-* + *gamete.*] *Biol.* A gamete of a type exhibiting sexual or other differentiation; — opposed to *isogamete.*

het′er·og′a·mous (-ŏg′ȧ·mŭs), *adj.* [*hetero-* + *-gamous.*] **1.** **a** *Biol.* Having conjugation of unlike gametes. Cf. ISOGAMOUS. **b** Having alternation of generations in which two kinds of sexual generation alternate. **2.** *Bot.* **a** Bearing flowers of two different kinds; — opposed to *homogamous.* **b** Characterized by indirect methods of pollination; — opposed to *orthogamous.* — **het′er·og′a·my** (-mĭ), *n.*

het′er·o·ge·ne′i·ty (hĕt′ẽr·ō·jē·nē′ĭ·tĭ), *n.; pl.* -TIES (-tĭz). Heterogeneous state or quality.

het′er·o·gen′e·sis (-jĕn′ē·sĭs), *n.* [NL., fr. *hetero-* + *-genesis.*] *Biol.* Alternation of generations; esp., alternation of a dioecious and one or more parthenogenetic generations.

het′er·o·ge′ne·ous (-jē′nē·ŭs), *adj.* [From ML., fr. Gr. *heterogenēs*, fr. *heteros* other + *genos* race, kind.] Differing in kind; having unlike qualities; dissimilar; — opposed to *homogeneous.* — **het′er·o·ge′ne·ous·ly**, *adv.* — **het′er·o·ge′ne·ous·ness**, *n.*

het′er·og′e·nous (-ŏj′ē·nŭs), *adj.* [*hetero-* + *-genous.*] *Biol. & Med.* Of other origin; not originating within the body; — opposed to *autogenous.*

het′er·og′e·ny (-ŏj′ē·nĭ), *n.* *Biol.* Heterogenesis.

het′er·og′o·ny (-ŏg′ō·nĭ), *n.* [*hetero-* + *-gony.*] **1.** *Bot.* State of having two or more kinds of perfect flowers; — opposed to *homogony.* **2.** *Biol.* Alternation of generations; esp., alternation of a dioecious and hermaphroditic generation. — **het′er·og′o·nous** (-nŭs), *adj.* — **het′er·og′o·nous·ly**, *adv.*

het′er·og′ra·phy (-ŏg′rȧ·fĭ), *n.* [*hetero-* + *-graphy.*] **a** Spelling differing from standard current usage. **b** Spelling in which the same letters represent different sounds in different words or syllables, as in current English orthography (*g* in *get* and in *ginger*). — **het′er·o·graph′ic** (-ō·grăf′ĭk), **het′er·o·graph′i·cal** (-ĭ·kăl), *adj.*

het′er·og′y·nous (-ŏj′ĭ·nŭs), *adj.* [*hetero-* + *-gynous.*] *Zool.* Having females of more than one kind, as bees.

het′er·ol′o·gy (-ŏl′ō·jĭ), *n.* [*hetero-* + *-logy.*] *Biol.* The lack of correspondence between parts, from being composed of different elements, or having a different origin; — opposed to *homology.* — **het′er·ol′o·gous** (-gŭs), *adj.*

het′er·ol′y·sis (-ŏl′ĭ·sĭs), *n.* [NL., fr. *hetero-* + *-lysis.*] *Biochem.* Destruction by an outside agent, as of a cell by lysins or enzymes from another source; — opp. to *autolysis.* — **het′er·o·lyt′ic** (-ō·lĭt′ĭk), *adj.*

het′er·om′er·ous (-ŏm′ẽr·ŭs), *adj.* [*hetero-* + *-merous.*] *Bot.* Having one or more whorls the number of whose members differs from that of the remaining whorls; — said of a flower, and opposed to *isomerous.*

het′er·o·mor′phic (-ō·môr′fĭk), **het′er·o·mor′phous** (-fŭs), *adj.* [*hetero-* + *-morphic, -morphous.*] Deviating from the normal or usual form; exhibiting diversity of form; specif.: **a** *Zool.* Having different forms at different stages, as insects which undergo a complete metamorphosis. **b** *Biol.* Unlike in form or size. — **het′er·o·mor′phism** (-fĭz′m), *n.*

het′er·on′o·mous (hĕt′ẽr·ŏn′ō·mŭs), *adj.* [*hetero-* + Gr. *nomos* law.] **1.** Subject to the law of another. **2.** *Biol.* Subject to, or involving, different laws of growth; specialized along different lines.

het′er·on′o·my (-mĭ), *n.* Condition or state of being heteronomous, or not self-governing, not self-determining, etc.; — opp. to *autonomy.*

het′er·o·nym′ (hĕt′ẽr·ō·nĭm′), *n.* A word spelled like another, but differing in sound and sense; — opp. to *homonym.*

het′er·on′y·mous (-ŏn′ĭ·mŭs), *adj.* [*hetero-* + Gr. *onyma*, for *onoma* a name.] **1.** Standing in opposite relations; *Optics*, pertaining to or designating crossed images of an object seen double. **2.** Pertaining to or designating a heteronym. — **het′er·on′y·mous·ly**, *adv.*

Het′er·o·ou′si·an (hĕt′ẽr·ō·ōō′sĭ·ăn; -ou′sĭ·ăn), *n. & adj.* [Gr. *heteroousios*, fr. *heteros* other + *ousia* being, essence.] *Eccl. Hist.* (One) holding that the Son of God was not of the same substance as the Father; Arian. Cf. HOMOOUSIAN.

het′er·o·phyl′lous (-fĭl′ŭs), *adj.* *Bot.* Bearing foliage leaves of more than one form on the same plant or stem, as many eucalypts. — **het′er·o·phyl′ly** (hĕt′ẽr·ō·fĭl′ĭ), *n.*

het′er·o·plas′ty (hĕt′ẽr·ō·plăs′tĭ), *n.* Surgical grafting of tissues taken from another individual. Cf. AUTOPLASTY.

het′er·o·po′lar (-pō′lẽr), *adj.* [*hetero-* + *polar.*] *Chem.* Polar. — **het′er·o·po·lar′i·ty** (-pō·lăr′ĭ·tĭ), *n.*

het′er·o·sex′u·al (-sĕk′shōō·ăl; *cf.* SEXUAL), *adj.* **1.** Characterized by or pert. to sexual passion for one of the opposite sex; — opp. to *homosexual.* **2.** *Biol.* Of or pert. to different sexes. — *n.* A heterosexual individual. — **het′er·o·sex′u·al′i·ty** (-sĕk′shōō·ăl′ĭ·tĭ; -shŭ-), *n.*

het′er·o′sis (-ō′sĭs), *n.* [NL., fr. Gr. *heterōsis* alteration, fr. *heteros* other.] *Biol.* Increased vigor or capacity for growth often displayed by crossbred animals or plants.

het′er·os′po·rous (hĕt′ĕr·ŏs′pō·rŭs; -ō·spō′rŭs), *adj.* *Bot.* **a** Bearing asexual spores of more than one kind. **b** Producing microspores and megaspores, as seed plants; — opposed to *homosporous.*

het′er·o·tax′is (hĕt′ĕr·ō·tăk′sĭs), *n.* Also **het′er·o·tax′i·a** (-tăk′sĭ·ȧ), **het′er·o·tax′y** (hĕt′ĕr·ō·tăk′sĭ). [NL., fr. *hetero-* + *-taxis.*] Abnormal arrangement, as of organs or parts of the body, geological strata, etc. — **het′er·o·tac′tic** (-tăk′tĭk), **het′er·o·tax′ic** (-tăk′sĭk), *adj.*

het′er·o·thal′lic (-thăl′ĭk), *adj.* [*hetero-* + Gr. *thallos* young shoot.] *Bot.* Having two physiologically distinct types of mycelium, which function as opposite sexes in reproduction; — opposed to *homothallic.*

het′er·o·to′pi·a (-tō′pĭ·ȧ), *n.* Also **het′er·ot′o·py** (-ŏt′ō·pĭ). [NL. *heterotopia,* fr. *hetero-* + Gr. *topos* place.] *Biol.* Displacement, as of an organ or growth. — **het′er·o·top′ic** (-ō·tŏp′ĭk), **het′er·ot′o·pous** (-ŏt′ō·pŭs), *adj.*

het′er·o·troph′ic (-trŏf′ĭk), *adj.* [See HETERO-; TROPHIC.] *Physiol.* Obtaining nourishment from organic matter, as most animals and the saprophytic plants. Cf. AUTOTROPHIC.

het′er·o·typ′ic (-tĭp′ĭk), **het′er·o·typ′i·cal** (-ĭ·kăl), *adj.* *Biol.* Designating meiosis, as contrasted with typical, or somatic, cell division.

het′er·o·zy′gote (-zī′gōt; -zĭg′ōt), *n.* [*hetero-* + *-zygote.*] *Biol.* An animal or plant containing genes for both members of at least one pair of allelomorphic Mendelian characters. Cf. HOMOZYGOTE. — **het′er·o·zy′gous** (-zī′gŭs), *adj.*

het′man (hĕt′măn), *n.; pl.* -MANS (-mănz). [Pol.] A Cossack headman.

heugh, heuch (hūk), *n.* *Chiefly Scot.* **a** Crag. **b** Pit.

heu′land·ite (hū′lăn·dīt), *n.* [After H. *Heuland,* Eng. mineralogist.] *Mineral.* A hydrous calcium aluminum silicate, $H_4CaAl_2(SiO_3)_6.3H_2O$, of the zeolite family.

heu·ris′tic (hū·rĭs′tĭk), *adj.* [Gr. *heuriskein* to discover.] Serving to discover or to stimulate investigation; — of methods of demonstration which tend to lead a person to investigate further by himself.

hew (hū), *v. t.;* HEWED (hūd); HEWED or HEWN (hūn); HEW′ING. [AS. *hēawan.*] **1.** To cut by blows with an ax or other sharp instrument; chop. **2.** To fell, as trees, by cutting. **3.** To form or shape by, or as by, blows with a sharp instrument. — *v. i.* To make cutting blows, as with an ax. — **hew′er** (hū′ĕr), *n.*

hex (hĕks), *n.* [G. *hexe* witch.] *Local, U. S.* Witch; also, a spell; enchantment. — *v. t. Local, U. S.* To bewitch; to practice witchcraft upon.

hex′a- (hĕk′sȧ-), **hex-.** [Gr. *hex* six, *hexa-* (in comp.).] A combining form, meaning *six,* as in **hex′a·syl·lab′ic**; specif., *Chem.,* denoting *the presence of six atoms* or *equivalents of* (specified) *substance,* as in **hex′a·car′bon.**

hex′a·bas′ic (-bās′ĭk), *adj.* [*hexa-* + *basic.*] *Chem.* **a** Having six hydrogen atoms capable of replacement by basic atoms or radicals; — said of acids. **b** Containing six atoms of a univalent metal, or their equivalent.

hex′a·chord (hĕk′sȧ·kôrd), *n.* [*hexa-* + Gr. *chordē* string, chord.] *Medieval Music.* A diatonic series of six tones with their intervals of steps (—) and half steps (◡) as follows: 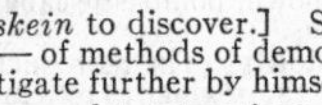

hex′ad (hĕk′săd), *n.* [L. *hexas, hexadis,* the number six, fr. Gr. *hexas, hexados,* fr. *hex* six.] A group or series of six. — **hex·ad′ic** (hĕks·ăd′ĭk), *adj.*

hex′a·em′er·on (hĕk′sȧ·ĕm′ĕr·ŏn), **hex′a·hem′er·on** (-hĕm′ĕr·ŏn), *n.* [L. *hexaëmeron,* fr. Gr. *hex* six + *hēmera* day.] The six days of the Creation, or a history of them as contained in Genesis; also, a treatise on it. — **hex′a·em′er·ic, hex′a·hem′er·ic** (-ĭk), *adj.*

hex′a·gon (hĕk′sȧ·gŏn), *n.* [L. *hexagonum,* fr. Gr. *hexagōnos,* six-cornered, fr. *hex* six + *gōnia* angle.] A polygon of six angles and therefore six sides.

hex·ag′o·nal (hĕks·ăg′ō·năl; -n′l), *adj.* **a** Having six angles and six sides; six-sided; divided into hexagons. **b** Having a hexagon as section or base. **c** Designating, or belonging to, a crystal system (**hexagonal system**) in which six-sided forms occur. — **hex·ag′o·nal·ly,** *adv.*

hex′a·gram (hĕk′sȧ·grăm), *n.* [*hexa-* + *-gram.*] **1.** A figure formed by completing externally an equilateral triangle on each side of a regular hexagon. **2.** *Geom.* The figure formed by any six intersecting lines.

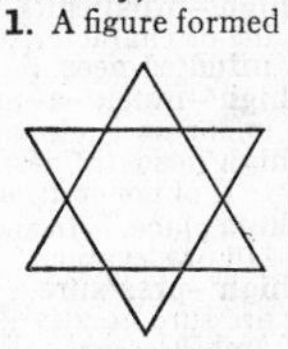

Hexagram.

hex′a·he′dron (-hē′drŭn), *n.; pl.* -DRONS (-drŭnz), -DRA (-drȧ). [NL., fr. *hexa-* + Gr. *hedra* seat, base.] A polyhedron of six faces. — **hex′a·he′dral** (-drăl), *adj.*

hex′a·hy′drate (-hī′drāt), *n.* [*hexa-* + *hydrate.*] *Chem.* A compound containing six molecules of water.

hex′a·hy′dric (-drĭk), *adj.* *Chem.* Containing six hydroxyl groups.

hex·am′er·ous (hĕks·ăm′ĕr·ŭs), *adj.* [*hexa-* + *-merous.*] **1.** *Bot.* Having floral whorls composed of six members; — frequently written *6-merous.* **2.** *Zool.* Having six parts, or parts in multiples of six, arranged radially. — **hex·am′er·ism** (-ĭz′m), *n.*

hex·am′e·ter (-ăm′ē·tĕr), *n.* [L., fr. Gr. *hexametros* of six meters, fr. *hex* six + *metron* measure.] *Pros.* A verse of six metrical feet or dipodies; esp., the six-foot dactylic verse of Greek and Latin epic poetry, of which the first four feet may be either dactyls or spondees, the fifth is regularly a dactyl, and the sixth a spondee; thus, —

Arma vi|rumque ca|no ‖ Tro|jae qui | primus ab | oris.
(‒ ◡ ◡ | ‒ ◡ ◡ | ‒ ‖ ‒ | ‒ ‒ | ‒ ◡ ◡ | ‒ ‒)

— **hex·am′e·ter, hex·am′e·tral** (-trăl), **hex′a·met′ric** (hĕk′sȧ·mĕt′rĭk), *adj.*

hex′a·meth′yl·ene·tet′ra·mine′ (hĕk′sȧ·mĕth′ĭ·lēn·tĕt′rȧ·mēn′), *n.* Also -in. [*hexa-* + *methylene* + *tetra-* + *amine.*] *Chem.* A crystalline compound, $C_6H_{12}N_4$, used as an accelerator in vulcanizing rubber, as an absorbent for phosgene, etc., and as a diuretic.

hex′ane (hĕk′sān; hĕks·ān′), *n.* [Gr. *hex* six.] *Chem.* Any of five volatile liquid hydrocarbons, C_6H_{14}, of the paraffin series.

hex·an′gu·lar (hĕks·ăng′gū·lĕr), *adj.* Having six angles.

hex′a·pla (hĕk′sȧ·plȧ), *n. pl., construed as sing.* [NL., fr. Gr. *hexapla,* fr. *hexaploos,* contr. *hexaplous,* sixfold.] An edition or work in six texts or versions in parallel columns; specif. [*cap.*], the edition of the Old Testament compiled by Origen. — **hex′a·plar** (-plĕr), *adj.*

hex′a·pod (hĕk′sȧ·pŏd), *adj.* [Gr. *hexapous, hexapodos,* six-footed, fr. *hex* six + *pous, podos,* foot.] Having six feet. — *n.* A hexapod animal; specif., one of the true insects (Hexapoda or Insecta in its narrower sense). — **hex·ap′o·dous** (hĕks·ăp′ō·dŭs), *adj.*

hex·ap′o·dy (hĕks·ăp′ō·dĭ), *n.; pl.* -DIES (-dĭz). *Pros.* A verse or group of six feet.

hex′arch·y (hĕk′sär·kĭ), *n.; pl.* HEXARCHIES (-kĭz). [*hex-* + *-archy.*] A group of six states. Cf. HEPTARCHY.

hex′a·stich (hĕk′sȧ·stĭk), *n.; pl.* -STICHS (-stĭks). Also **hex·as′ti·chon** (hĕks·ăs′tĭ·kŏn); *pl.* -CHA (-kȧ). [From L., fr. Gr. *hexastichos,* fr. *hex* six + *stichos* row, line, verse.] *Pros.* A poem or stanza of six verses or lines. — **hex′a·stich′ic** (-stĭk′ĭk), *adj.*

Hex′a·teuch (hĕk′sȧ·tūk), *n.* [*hexa-* + Gr. *teuchos* tool, book.] The first six books of the Old Testament. See BIBLE.

hex′en·be′sen (hĕk′sĕn·bā′zĕn), *n.* [G., lit., witches'-broom.] *Plant Pathol.* Witches'-broom.

hex′o·san (hĕk′sō·săn), *n.* [*hexose* + *-an.*] *Chem.* Any of a class of polysaccharides yielding hexoses on hydrolysis.

hex′ose (hĕk′sōs), *n.* *Chem.* Any of a group of simple sugars containing six oxygen atoms in the molecule.

hex′yl (hĕk′sĭl), *n.* [*hex-* + *-yl.*] *Chem.* A univalent hydrocarbon radical, C_6H_{13}, the radical of hexane.

hex′yl·res·or′cin·ol (-rĕz·ôr′sĭ·nōl; -nŏl), *n.* *Chem.* A white crystalline solid, $C_6H_{13}C_6H_3(OH)_2$, used in medicine as a germicide.

hey (hā), *interj.* An exclamation as of surprise, joy, etc.

hey′day′ (hā′dā′), *interj.* An exclamation of joy or wonder. — *n.* Time of highest strength, vigor, or bloom; hence, joy; high spirits.

Hey′duck, -duke, -duc, etc. Vars. of HAIDUK.

Hez′e·ki′ah (hĕz′ē·kī′ȧ), *n.* [Heb. *Ḥizqīyāh.*] The name of several Old Testament characters; esp., a king of Judah.

hi·a′tus (hī·ā′tŭs), *n.; pl.* HIATUSES (-ĕz; -ĭz), HIATUS. [L., fr. *hiare, hiatum,* to gape.] **1.** An opening; a gap; esp., a break with a part missing. **2.** A slight pause between two vowels each of which is to be distinctly pronounced, as in *co-operate.*

Hi′a·wa′tha (hī′ȧ·wô′thȧ; -wŏth′ȧ; hē′ȧ-), *n.* **1.** A Mohawk Indian chief who effected the confederation known as the Five Nations or League of the Iroquois. **2.** The Indian hero of the poem *The Song of Hiawatha* (1855), by Longfellow.

hi′ber·nac′u·lum (hī′bĕr·năk′ū·lŭm), *n.; pl.* -LA (-lȧ). [L., a winter residence.] *Zool.* **a** A case or covering for protection during the winter. **b** In certain fresh-water bryozoans, an encysted bud which survives the winter and develops into a colony in the spring.

hi·ber′nal (hī·bûr′năl; -n′l), *adj.* [L. *hibernalis.*] Wintry.

hi′ber·nate (hī′bĕr·nāt), *v. i.* [L. *hibernare, -natum,* fr. *hiberna* winter quarters, *hibernus* wintry.] To winter; to pass the winter in close quarters, in a torpid or lethargic state, as do many animals. — **hi′ber·na′tion** (-nā′shŭn), *n.*

Hi·ber′ni·a (hī·bûr′nĭ·ȧ; 58), *n.* [L.] Ireland.

Hi·ber′ni·an (-ăn), *adj.* [L. *Hibernia* Ireland.] Irish. — *n.* An Irishman. — **Hi·ber′ni·an·ism** (-ĭz′m), *n.*

Hi·ber′ni·cism (hī·bûr′nĭ·sĭz′m), *n.* Irish quality, character, trait, custom, etc.; esp., an Irish idiom.

hi·bis′cus (hī·bĭs′kŭs; hĭ-), *n.* [L., marsh mallow, fr. Gr. *hibiskos.*] *Bot.* Any of a large genus (*Hibiscus*) of herbs, shrubs, or small trees of the mallow family, the rose mallows, having large showy flowers. *H. rosa-sinensis,* the China rose, is the floral emblem of the Territory of Hawaii.

hic′cup, hic′cough (hĭk′ŭp), *n.* [Earlier *hickup, hicket, hickock,* prob. of imitative origin.] *Physiol.* A spasmodic inspiration with closure of the glottis, producing a peculiar sound. — *v. i.* To make a hiccup or hiccups.

‖**hic et u·bi′que** (hĭk′ ĕt ū·bī′kwē). [L.] Here and everywhere.

‖**hic ja′cet** (jā′sĕt). [L.] Here lies; — used in epitaphs.

hick (hĭk), *n.* [Familiar form of *Richard.*] An awkward uncouth rustic; a rube; bumpkin. — *adj.* Of or like hicks; countrified; rustic.

hick′ey (hĭk′ĭ), *n.* A device or gadget; specif., *Elec.:* **a** A threaded coupling for attaching a fixture to an outlet box. **b** A device for bending pipe and conduit.

hick′o·ry (hĭk′ō·rĭ), *n.; pl.* -RIES (-rĭz). [Virginian *pawcohiccora* a preparation of pounded kernels.] **1. a** Any of a genus (*Carya*) of North American hardwood trees of the walnut family, esp. the shagbark, or shellbark (*C. ovata*) or one of its allies. Some species yield a sweet edible nut (**hickory nut**). See PECAN; PIGNUT, 2; cf. WALNUT, 2. **b** The valuable hard wood of certain of these trees. **2.** A switch, cane, etc., of hickory wood. — *adj.* Of, pertaining to, or made of hickory.

hid (hĭd), *past & past part.* of HIDE, to conceal.

hi·dal′go (hĭ·dăl′gō), *n.; pl.* -GOS (-gōz). [Sp., contr. fr. *hijo de algo,* i. e., son of something.] A Spanish nobleman of the lower class.

hid′den (hĭd′'n), *past part.* of HIDE, to conceal. Specif.: *adj.* Concealed; secret; not known; mysterious.

hid′den·ite (hĭd′'n·īt), *n.* [After W. E. *Hidden* (b. 1853), of N. Y.] *Mineral.* A yellow to green variety of spodumene found in North Carolina, used as a gem.

hide (hīd), *n.* [AS. *hīd.*] *Eng. Hist.* A measure of land, varying from 80 to 120 acres; — common in old English charters.

hide, *n.* [AS. *hȳd.*] **1.** The skin of an animal, either raw or dressed. See SKIN, *n.,* 1. **2.** *Chiefly Humorous.* The human skin. — *v. t.* **1.** To take the hide from. **2.** *Colloq.* To flog severely.

hide (hīd), *v. t.;* HID (hĭd); HID′DEN (hĭd′'n) or HID; HID′ING (hīd′ĭng). [AS. *hȳdan.*] **1.** To conceal; withdraw from sight; put out of view; secrete. **2.** To withhold from knowledge; keep secret. **3.** To obstruct or bar the view of. **4.** To shelter. **5.** To turn away, as the eyes or face, in displeasure, shame, etc. — *v. i.* To lie concealed; keep oneself out of view. — **hid′er** (hīd′ĕr), *n.*

Syn. **Hide, conceal, screen, secrete, bury** mean to withhold or withdraw from sight. **Hide** may or may not suggest intent but **conceal** usually does, often specifically implying a refusal to divulge; **screen** implies an interposition of something that prevents discovery; **secrete** implies a depositing in a place of concealment unknown to others; **bury** implies a covering with something that effectively hides.

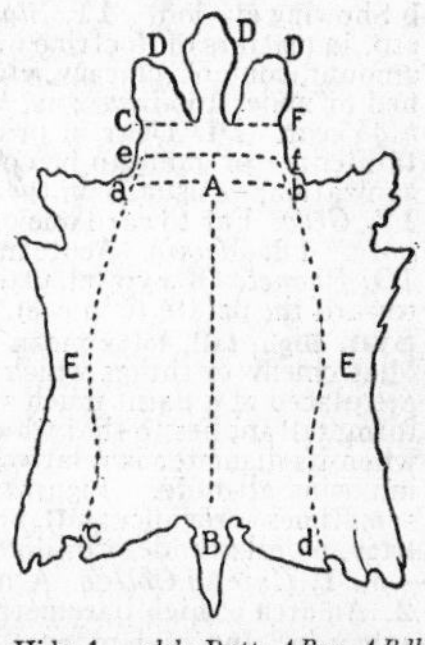

Hide, 1. *abdc* Butt; *ABca, ABdb* Bends; *abFC* Shoulder; *abfe* Range; *E, E* Belly offal; *D, D, D* Cheeks and Faces.

hide′bound′ (hīd′bound′), *adj.* **1.** Having the skin adhering closely to the ribs and back; — of an animal. **2.** Obstinately narrow; stupidly conservative. **3.** Kept from growing by having bark too firm or close; — of trees.

hid′e·ous (hĭd′ē·ŭs), *adj.* [OF. *hidous, hisdos,* fr. *hide, hisde,* fright.] **1.** *Now Colloq.* Dreadful; awful. **2.** Revolting; horribly ugly or discordant; shocking; morally detestable. — **hid′e·ous·ly,** *adv.* — **hid′e·ous·ness,** *n.*

hid′ing (hīd′ĭng), *n.* *Colloq.* A flogging.

hid′ing, *n.* Concealment; also, place or means of concealment.

hi·dro′sis (hĭ·drō′sĭs), *n.* [NL., fr. Gr. *hidroun* to sweat, *hidrōs* sweat.] **1.** *Physiol.* Perspiration. **2.** *Med.* Excessive perspiration or any skin disease characterized by it.

hie (hī), *v. i.;* HIED (hīd); HY′ING, HIE′ING. [AS. *hīgian.*] To hasten; go in haste; — often reflexively.

hi′er·a′co·sphinx (hī′ẽr·ā′kō·sfĭngks), *n.* [Gr. *hierax, -akos,* hawk + *sphinx.*] A hawk-headed sphinx. See SPHINX, 3.

hi′er·arch (hī′ẽr·ärk), *n.* [ML. *hierarcha,* fr. Gr. *hierarchēs,* fr. *hieros* sacred + *archos* leader, ruler, fr. *archein* to rule.] One having authority in sacred things; the chief of a sacred order. — **hi′er·ar′chal** (-är′kăl), *adj.*

hi′er·ar′chism (-är′kĭz′m), *n.* The principles or authority of a hierarchy. — **hi′er·arch′ist** (-är′kĭst), *n.*

hi′er·arch′y (hī′ẽr·är′kĭ), *n.; pl.* -ARCHIES (-kĭz). **1.** A rank or order of holy beings, esp. of angels; also, usually ***celestial hierarchy,*** the angelic orders collectively. **2.** A body of rulers, esp. of ecclesiastics, disposed organically in ranks and orders each subordinate to the one above it; also, such a system of church government or its authority. **3.** A series of objects, or items divided or classified in ranks or orders, as in natural science or logic; a hierarchical arrangement. — **hi′er·ar′chic** (-är′kĭk), **hi′er·ar′chi·cal** (-kĭ·kăl), *adj.* — **-ar′chi·cal·ly,** *adv.*

hi′er·at′ic (hī′ẽr·ăt′ĭk), *adj.* Also **hi′er·at′i·cal** (-ĭ·kăl). [L. *hieraticus,* fr. Gr. *hieratikos.*] **1.** Consecrated to sacred uses; sacerdotal; pertaining to, or originated by, priests. **2.** *Egypt. Archaeol.* Designating an abridged and somewhat cursive form of hieroglyphic writing which in late use was reserved for religious writings. — **hi′er·at′i·cal·ly,** *adv.*

hi′er·o- (hī′ẽr·ō-), **hier-.** [Gr. *hieros.*] A combining form meaning *sacred,* as in **hi′er·o·gram′** (see -GRAM).

hi′er·oc′ra·cy (hī′ẽr·ŏk′rȧ·sĭ), *n.; pl.* -CIES (-sĭz). [*hiero-* + *-cracy.*] Government by ecclesiastics; a hierarchy. — **hi′er·o·crat′ic** (-ō·krăt′ĭk), **hi′er·o·crat′i·cal** (-ĭ·kăl), *adj.*

hi′er·o·dule (hī′ẽr·ō·dūl), *n.* [LL., *hierodulus,* fr. Gr. *hierodoulos,* fr. *hieron* temple or *hieros* sacred + *doulos* slave.] *Gr. Relig.* A slave attached to the service of a temple. — **hi′er·o·du′lic** (-dū′lĭk), *adj.*

hi′er·o·glyph′ (hī′ẽr·ō·glĭf′), *n.* A hieroglyphic.

hi′er·o·glyph′ic (-glĭf′ĭk), *adj.* Also **hi′er·o·glyph′i·cal** (-ĭ·kăl). [F. or L.; F. *hiéroglyphique,* fr. L., fr. Gr. *hieroglyphikos,* fr. *hieros* sacred + *glyphein* to carve.] Of the nature of a hieroglyph or hieroglyphics; inscribed with hieroglyphics. — *n.* **1.** A sacred character; a character in the picture writing of the ancient Egyptians, Mexicans, etc., or the mode of writing in such characters. **2.** Any obscure or unintelligible symbol, sign, etc.; also, *pl.,* illegible writing. — **hi′er·o·glyph′i·cal·ly,** *adv.* — **hi′er·og′ly·phist** (-ŏg′lĭ·fĭst), *n.*

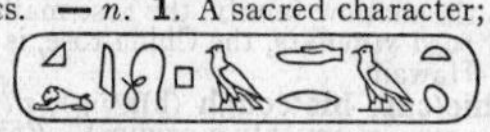
Hieroglyphics (Egyptian).

hi′er·ol′o·gy (hī′ẽr·ŏl′ō·jĭ), *n.; pl.* -GIES (-jĭz). [*hiero-* + *-logy.*] A body of knowledge of sacred things; literary or traditional embodiment of the religious beliefs of a people.

Hi′er·o·nym′ic (-ō·nĭm′ĭk), **Hi′er·o·nym′i·an** (-ĭ·ăn), *adj.* Made by St. Jerome (L. *Hieronymus*).

Hi′er·on′y·mite (-ŏn′ĭ·mīt), *n.* A member of any of various hermit orders named after St. Jerome.

hi′er·o·phant (hī′ẽr·ō·fănt; hī·ẽr′-), *n.* [From LL., fr. Gr. *hierophantēs,* fr. *hieros* sacred + *phainein* to show.] **1.** *Gr. Antiq.* A priest; specif., the chief priest of the Eleusinian mysteries. **2.** Hence, an expositor of sacred mysteries. — **hi′er·o·phan′tic** (-făn′tĭk), *adj.*

hi′-fi′ (hī′fī′), *n.* [By shortening.] = HIGH FIDELITY. — **hi′-fi′,** *adj.*

hig′gle (hĭg′′l), *v. i.;* -GLED (-′ld); -GLING (-lĭng). To stickle for small advantage; chaffer. — **hig′gler** (-lẽr), *n.*

hig′gle·dy-pig′gle·dy (hĭg′′l·dĭ·pĭg′′l·dĭ), *adv.* In confusion. — *adj.* Jumbled. — *n.* Confusion; jumble.

high (hī), *adj.* [AS. *hēah, hēh.*] **1.** Lifted up; lofty; tall; elevated. **2.** Having (the specified) altitude or elevation; as, ten stories *high.* **3.** Advanced to or toward its mid, acme, or fullness of character; as, *high* summer. **4.** Long past; ancient; remote; as, *high* antiquity. **5.** Sharp; shrill; — of sound. **6.** Elevated or exalted in character or quality; noble; sublime. **7.** Intellectually deep; profound. **8.** Of great importance; first; chief; as: **a** Exalted in standing, rank, dignity, etc. **b** Grave; serious; as, a *high* crime. **9.** Forcible; powerful; strong; mighty; as, *high* winds; *high* speed. **10. a** Arrogant; boastful. **b** Showing elation. **11.** *Slang.* Intoxicated. **12.** Extreme or rigid, esp. in matters of doctrine or ceremony. **13.** Of greater degree, size, amount, content, efficacy, etc., than ordinary; superior in some specified or understood way; as, *high* stakes; iron *high* in phosphorus; in *high* gear. **14.** Dear in price; costly. **15.** Strong-scented; slightly tainted; — of game to be cooked. **16.** *Biol.* Having a complex organization; — usually in the comparative degree; as, the *higher* apes. **17.** *Geog.* Far toward one of the poles; — chiefly in phrase *high latitude.* **18.** *Music.* Acute in pitch; sharp; — opposed to *grave* or *low.* **19.** *Phonet.* Of a vowel, uttered with some part of the tongue high up toward the palate (ē in *eve*).

Syn. **High, tall, lofty** mean above the average in height. **High** applies chiefly to things which rise from a base or foundation or which are placed at a point much above a lower level such as a floor or platform; **tall** applies to that which grows or seems to grow high, especially when its diameter is relatively narrow; **lofty** implies, usually, great or imposing altitude. Figuratively, **high** implies elevation, distinction, sometimes arrogance; **tall,** now chiefly in humorous use, exaggeration; **lofty,** moral grandeur or dignity. — **Ant.** Low.

— *n.* **1.** *Chiefly Colloq.* A high place, condition, level, etc.; a height. **2.** An area of high barometric pressure.

high, *adv.* In a high manner, degree, station, etc.; at or to a high place, altitude, pitch, etc. — **high′ly,** *adv.*

high′ball′ (hī′bôl′), *n., or* **high ball.** A drink of diluted spirits, usually whisky, served with ice in a tall glass.

high′ball′, *n.* **1.** A railroad signal for a train to proceed at full speed. **2.** A fast train. — *v. i. & t.* To go, or to operate or drive, at high speed.

high′bind′er (hī′bīn′dẽr), *n.* *U. S.* One of a band of Chinese criminals in a Chinese quarter, hirable as assassins.

high blower. See BLOWING, *n.,* 2.

high′born′ (hī′bôrn′; 2), *adj.* Of noble birth.

high′boy′ (-boi′), *n.* A chest of drawers mounted on a tablelike base or lowboy. Cf. LOWBOY, *Illust.*

high′bred′ (hī′brĕd′; 2), *adj.* Of superior blood or breeding; aristocratic.

high′brow′ (hī′brou′), *n.* A person of superior learning or culture; an intellectual; — often used derisively. — **high′brow′,** *adj.* — **high′-browed′** (-broud′), *adj.* — **high′brow′ism** (-brou′ĭz′m), *n.*

High Church. In churches of the Anglican Communion, a party that stresses the ecclesiastical, liturgical, and sacerdotal aspects of Anglicanism. — **High′-Church′** (-chûrch′; 2), *adj.*

high comedy. Comedy which depends more on fine characterization and witty dialogue than on ludicrous situations.

high command. *Mil.* The supreme headquarters of a nation's organized forces in the field.

high day. *Bib.* A holy or feast day.

high′er crit′i·cism (hī′ẽr). The use of scientific and historical methods in the study of literature, esp. of the Bible. Cf. LOWER CRITICISM.

higher education. Education of collegiate or more advanced grade.

high explosive. An explosive, as trinitrotoluene, that generates gas with extreme rapidity and has a shattering effect. — **high′-ex·plo′sive,** *adj.*

high′fa·lu′tin (hī′fȧ·lū′tĭn; -t′n), **high′fa·lu′ting** (-tĭng), *n.* *Colloq.* High-flown, bombastic language. — *adj.* *Colloq.* High-flown; pretentious.

high fidelity. The reproduction of sound with a high degree of faithfulness to the original, as by a radio or phonograph. — **high′-fi·del′i·ty,** *adj.*

high′fli′er, high′fly′er (hī′flī′ẽr; hī′flī′ẽr), *n.* One that flies high. Hence: **a** One notably pretentious, extravagant, etc. **b** In the 18th century, an extreme partisan, as of the High-Church or Tory party. — **high′fly′ing** (hī′flī′ĭng; 2), *adj.*

high′-flown′ (hī′flōn′; 2), *adj.* **1.** Elevated; proud. **2.** Turgid; bombastic; inflated; as, *high-flown* language.

high′-fre′quen·cy (-frē′kwĕn·sĭ), *adj.* *Elec.* Of a frequency between 3 and 30 megacycles per second. Abbr. *H.F., HF, h.f., hf,* etc.

High German. The language of the (southern) highlands of Germany. See GERMAN, 2.

high hand. Highhanded use of power.

high′hand′ed (hī′hăn′dĕd; -dĭd; 2), *adj.* Overbearing; arbitrary. — **high′hand′ed·ly,** *adv.* — **high′hand′ed·ness,** *n.*

high hat. A top hat.

high′-hat′ (hī′hăt′; 2), *n.* One who wears a high hat; hence, a snob. — *adj.* Characteristic of a high-hat; aristocratic; snobbish. — *v. t.;* HIGH′-HAT′TED; HIGH′-HAT′TING. To act as a snob toward (another person).

high′-hold′er (-hōl′dẽr), **high′hole′** (-hōl′) *n.* *Local, U.S.* The flicker.

high′jack′ (-jăk′), **high′jack′er.** Vars. of HIJACK, HIJACKER.

high jinks. Noisy revelry; wild behavior.

high jump. *Athletics.* The jump for height. Cf. BROAD JUMP.

high′land (hī′lănd), *n.* Hilly or mountainous land; specif., **the High′lands** (hī′lăndz; *Scot.* hē′lȧnts), the elevated region of Scotland. — **high′land·er, High′land·er** (hī′lăn·dẽr; *Scot.* hē′lȧn-), *n.*

Highland fling. A lively folk dance of the Highlands.

high light. The brightest spot in a painting, drawing, etc.; hence, an event, scene, etc., of paramount interest.

high′light′ (hī′līt′), *v. t.;* -LIGHT′ED; -LIGHT′ING. To throw a strong light upon; to emphasize or make prominent in any of various ways.

High Mass. *R.C.Ch.* Mass with incense, music, the assistance of a deacon, subdeacon, etc.

high′-mind′ed (*see Pron.,* § 2), *adj.* **1.** Proud; arrogant. **2.** Having or characterized by high or noble principles or feelings. — **high′-mind′ed·ness,** *n.*

high′-muck′-a-muck′ (-mŭk′ȧ·mŭk′), *n.* *Slang, U. S.* A person of importance, esp. as marked by arrogance or conceit. Cf. BIGWIG.

high′ness (hī′nĕs; -nĭs), *n.* **1.** Elevation; loftiness. **2.** [*cap.*] A title of honor given to kings, princes, etc.

high place. In ancient Semitic religions, a temple or altar, usually on a hill or elevation.

high′-pres′sure (*see Pron.,* § 2), *adj.* **1.** Having or involving a pressure greatly exceeding that of the atmosphere. **2.** Urgent; as, *high-pressure* salesmanship. **3.** Having a high barometric pressure.

high priest. A chief priest; esp., the head of the Jewish priesthood.

high proof. Also **high′-proof′** (*see Pron.,* § 2), *adj.* Highly rectified; strongly alcoholic; as, *high-proof* spirits.

high relief. See RELIEF, *n.,* 6.

high′road′ (hī′rōd′), *n.* A highway; hence, an easy way.

high school. *U. S.* A school composed of the grades above those of the elementary school, and preparing for college, business, a trade, etc.

high sea. The open, unenclosed portion of the sea or ocean; specif., *pl., Brit.,* that part of the sea which does not lie within the body of a country. — **high′-sea′** (-sē′; 2), *adj.*

high′-sound′ing (*see Pron.,* § 2), *adj.* Pompous or imposing in sound.

high′-spir′it·ed (*see Pron.,* § 2), *adj.* Characterized by a bold or lofty spirit; having mettle. — **high′-spir′it·ed·ness,** *n.*

high′-strung′ (*see Pron.,* § 2), *adj.* In a state of tense or quick sensibility; highly sensitive or nervous.

hight (hīt), *v. t. & i.; past & past part.* HIGHT. [AS. *hātan* to call, name.] **1.** *Archaic.* To name; to call oneself; — chiefly in *past part.* **2.** *Scot.* To promise; to assure.

hight. *Chiefly Dial.* Var. of HEIGHT.

high tea. Tea (a meal) with meats and extra relishes.

high′-ten′sion (*see Pron.,* § 2), *adj.* *Elec.* Having a high potential, or pertaining to apparatus to be used at high potentials.

high′-test′ (*see Pron.,* § 2), *adj.* That passes a difficult test; specif., having a low boiling-point range, as certain gasolines.

highth (see HEIGHT). Var. of HEIGHT.

high tide. The tide at **high water,** that is, when the water is at the greatest elevation; hence, culminating point.

high time. **a** Quite time; none too soon. **b** *Slang.* A time of great excitement or enjoyment; a carousal.
high′-toned′ (hī′tōnd′; 2), *adj.* **1.** High in tone or sound. **2.** Elevated; dignified. **3.** *Colloq., U. S.* Stylish.
high treason. Treason against the sovereign or the state.
high′ty-tigh′ty (hī′tĭ-tī′tĭ), *interj. & adj.* Hoity-toity.
high′way′ (hī′wā′), *n.* A main road or thoroughfare; hence, a road or way open to the use of the public.
high′way′man (hī′wā′măn; hī·wā′-), *n.* One who robs on the public road; a highway robber.
high′-wrought′ (hī′rôt′; 2), *adj.* **1.** Elaborated. **2.** Turbulent; worked-up.
hi′jack′, high′jack′ (hī′jăk′), *v. t.* [Origin obscure.] To hold up or rob, esp. of goods being transported in quantity, often illicitly; to steal (such goods); as, to *hijack* a truck or a liquor shipment; also, to force, coerce, or steal. — **hi′jack′er, high′jack′er** (-ẽr), *n.*
hike (hīk), *v. i.* **1.** To proceed with exertion or effort. **2.** To walk or tramp, esp. for some distance in rural areas. **3. a** To travel; journey. **b** To hitchhike. **c** To decamp. **4.** To increase or rise, as prices. **5.** To gather or bunch together; — of clothing. — *v. t.* To cause to hike. — *n.* Act of hiking; esp., a walk or tramp. — **hik′er** (hīk′ẽr), *n.*
hi·lar′i·ous (hĭ·lâr′ĭ·ŭs; hī-), *adj.* Noisily merry; boisterous. — **hi·lar′i·ous·ly,** *adv.* — **hi·lar′i·ous·ness,** *n.*
hi·lar′i·ty (hĭ·lăr′ĭ·tĭ; hī-), *n.* [F. *hilarité,* fr. L. *hilaritas,* fr. *hilaris, hilarus,* cheerful, fr. Gr. *hilaros.*] Boisterous mirth; hilariousness. — **Syn.** See MIRTH.
hilch (hĭlsh), *n. & v.* *Scot. & Ir.* Limp; halt.
hil′ding (hĭl′dĭng), *n.* *Archaic.* A base wretch or jade. — *adj.* *Archaic.* Base; spiritless.
hill (hĭl), *n.* [AS. *hyll.*] **1.** A natural elevation of land lower than a mountain and usually rounded. **2.** An artificial heap or mound, as of earth; as, a *hill* made by ants. **3.** Specif., a heap of earth raised about the roots of a plant or cluster of plants; also, the plant or cluster of plants so cultivated; as, a *hill* of corn.
☞ COMBINATIONS are: **hill′man, hill′side′, hill′top′.**
— *v. t.* **1.** To form into a hill, heap, or mound. **2.** To surround with earth; as, to *hill* corn. — **hill′er,** *n.*
hill′bil′ly (hĭl′bĭl′ĭ), *n.* [*hill* + 2d *billy.*] *Colloq., U. S.* A backwoodsman or mountaineer of the South.
hill myna. An Asiatic bird (*Eulabes religiosa*) allied to the starlings. It is often tamed and taught to speak.
hil′lo, hil′loa (hĭl′ō; hĭ·lō′), *n. & interj.* *Archaic.* = HOLLO.
hill′ock (hĭl′ŭk), *n.* A small hill. — **hill′ock·y** (-ĭ), *adj.*
hill station. In India, a village or government post in the hills or low mountain ranges, usually a health resort for Europeans in the hot season.
hill′y (hĭl′ĭ), *adj.*; HILL′I·ER (-ĭ·ẽr); HILL′I·EST. **1.** Abounding with hills. **2.** Steep. — **hill′i·ness,** *n.*
hilt (hĭlt), *n.* [AS. *hilt, hilte.*] A handle, as of a sword or dagger. — *v. t.* To furnish with a hilt.
hi′lum (hī′lŭm), *n.*; *pl.* HILA (-lȧ). [L., a little thing, trifle.] **1.** *Bot.* **a** The mark at the point of attachment of an ovule forming the "eye," as of a bean. See SEED, *Illust.* **b** The nucleus of a starch grain. **2.** *Anat. & Zool.* A mark, notch, or opening.
him (hĭm; 4), *pron.* [AS., dat. of *hē.*] Objective case of HE.
hi·mat′i·on (hĭ·măt′ĭ·ŏn), *n.*; *pl.* HIMATIA (-ȧ). [Gr.] *Gr. Antiq.* A garment consisting of a rectangular cloth draped over the left shoulder and about the body.
Him′a·vat (hĭm′ȧ·văt), *n.* See DEVI.
him·self′ (hĭm·sĕlf′; 4), *pron.* An emphasized form of the pron. for the third person sing. masculine. Its uses are: **1.** For emphasis: **a** As a simple objective; as, it is for *himself.* **b** In apposition; as, John *himself* told us. **c** As a predicate nominative; as, he went *himself.* **d** *Dial.* As a subject nominative, esp. when referring to the master or head of a household. **2.** Specif., esp. after *be, become,* etc.: His proper or normal self or state of mind. **3.** As a reflexive; as, he hurt *himself.*
Him′yar·ite (hĭm′yȧr·īt), *n.* [From Ar. *Ḥimyar,* a legendary king in Yemen.] **1.** One of an important Arab tribe of antiquity dwelling in southern Arabia. **2.** An Arab of a group of related ancient tribes of southern Arabia, or of their descendants. — **Him′yar·ite, Him′yar·it′ic** (-ĭt′ĭk), *adj.*
hin (hĭn), *n.* A Hebrew liquid measure, between one and two gallons.
‖**hinc il′lae la′cri·mae** (hĭngk ĭl′ē lăk′rĭ·mē). [L.] Hence these tears.
hind (hīnd), *n.* [AS. *hīne, hīna,* orig. gen. pl. of *hīwan* domestics.] **1.** A farm assistant. **2.** *Eng.* A peasant.
hind (hīnd), *n.*; see PLURAL, *Note,* 3. [AS.] **1.** The adult female of the red deer. See RED DEER. **2.** Any of various groupers, as the niggerfish; — applied esp. to certain spotted or speckled species, as the ***red hind*** (*Epinephelus guttatus*) important as a food fish in Cuba (where it is called *cabrilla*), and the ***rock hind*** (*E. adscensionis*), a brown-spotted fish of the West Indies and southern U. S.
hind (hīnd), *adj.*; HIND′ER (hīn′dẽr); HIND′MOST or HIND′ER·MOST. Of or pertaining to the part or end which follows or is behind; rear.
hind′brain′ (-brān′), *n.* *Anat.* The posterior of the three primary divisions of the brain of vertebrates; — called also ***rhombencephalon.*** It is subdivided into the ***metencephalon*** (including the *cerebellum* and *pons Varolii*) and the ***myelencephalon*** or ***afterbrain*** (comprising the *medulla oblongata*). Cf. FOREBRAIN, MIDBRAIN.
hind′er (hīn′dẽr), *adj.* Of or pertaining to a part that follows or is in the rear.
hin′der (hĭn′dẽr), *v. t.* [AS. *hindrian.*] **1.** To keep back or behind; check; obstruct. **2.** To prevent; embarrass; debar. — *v. i.* To interpose obstacles or impediments; to be a hindrance. — **hin′der·er,** *n.*
Syn. Hinder, impede, obstruct, block mean to put obstacles in the way of one in action. **Hinder** stresses harmful or annoying interference with progress; **impede** implies a slowing up, as by clogging, hampering, or fettering; **obstruct** implies interference with something in motion or in progress or the placing of obstacles in a path or channel; **block** implies more effective, but not necessarily insurmountable, obstruction. — **Ant.** Further.
hind′er·most (hīn′dẽr·mōst; -mŭst), *adj.* See HIND, *adj.*
hind′-gut′ (hīnd′gŭt′), *n.* The posterior part of the alimentary canal.
Hin′di (hĭn′dē), *n.* [Hind. *hindī,* fr. *Hind* India, fr. Per.] An Indo-Aryan language, the chief vernacular of northern India. It is divided into ***Eastern Hindi,*** and ***Western Hindi*** (of which the chief dialect is Hindustani). See INDO-EUROPEAN LANGUAGES, *Table.*
hind′most (hīnd′mōst; -mŭst), *adj.* See HIND, *adj.*
hind′quar′ter (hīnd′kwôr′tẽr; 2), *n.* The back part of the half of a carcass (beef, veal, lamb, mutton), divided usually between the twelfth and thirteenth ribs. Cf. BEEF, *Illust.*
hin′drance (hĭn′drăns), *n.* A hindering or a state of being hindered; also, that which hinders; impediment; obstruction.
hind′sight′ (hīnd′sīt′), *n.* **1.** The rear sight of a firearm. **2.** *Humorous.* Perception of the nature and demands of an event after it has happened; — opposed to *foresight.*
Hin′du, Hin′doo (hĭn′dōō; hĭn′dōō′), *n.* [Per. *Hindū,* fr. *Hind* India.] **1.** An adherent of Hinduism. **2.** In Continental and American usage, a member of one of the native races of India. — **Hin′du, Hin′doo,** *adj.* — **Hin′du·ize, Hin′doo·ize** (hĭn′dōō·īz), *v. t.*
Hin′du·ism, Hin′doo·ism (hĭn′dōō·ĭz′m), *n.* The native religious and social system of India. It is a devotional theism of various forms with a philosophical background, and a social system based on the idea of function (*dharma*) and caste observances. The number of sects is very large.
Hin′du·sta′ni, Hin′doo·sta′ni (hĭn′dōō·stä′nē; -stăn′ĭ), *adj.* [Hind. *Hindūstānī* an Indian, fr. Per. *Hindūstān* India.] Of or pertaining to Hindustan or its people or Hindustani. — *n.* Also **Hin′do·sta′ni** (hĭn′dō-). The most important dialect of Hindi, written in both the Arabic and the Devanagari character. Its subdialect, Urdu, is spoken by Mohammedans. It is current as a lingua franca over nearly all India. See INDO-EUROPEAN LANGUAGES, *Table.*
hinge (hĭnj), *n.* [ME. *heng, heeng.*] **1.** The joint, or flexible piece, on which a door, gate, lid, etc., turns or swings. **2.** An articulated joint, as of a bivalve shell. **3.** That on which anything turns or depends. **4.** *Obs.* The earth's axis, or a cardinal point of the compass. **5.** *Philately.* A small piece of thin gummed paper used in fastening a postage stamp in an album or on a sheet. — *v. t.*; HINGED (hĭnjd); HING′ING (hĭn′jĭng). To attach by, or furnish with, hinges. — *v. i.* To stand, hang, or turn, as on a hinge; to depend (*on*), as for a decision or for validity. — **hing′er** (hĭn′jẽr), *n.*

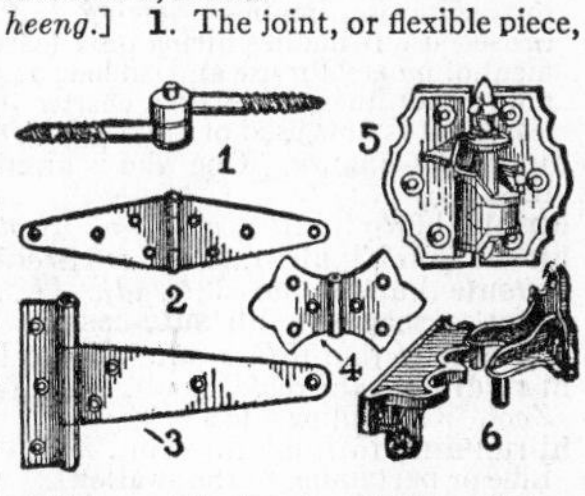

Hinges. 1 Hook-and-eye; 2 Strap; 3 T; 4 Flap; 5 Blind; 6 Gate.

hin′ny (hĭn′ĭ), *n.*; *pl.* HINNIES (-ĭz). [L. *hinnus.*] A hybrid between a stallion and a she ass. Cf. MULE.
hin′ny, *v. i.* [L. *hinnire.*] To neigh; whinny. *Rare.*
hint (hĭnt), *n.* [ME. *henten* to seize, catch, fr. AS. *hentan.*] **1.** *Obs.* An occasion; moment; time; turn. **2.** A remote allusion; intimation; insinuation; a covert suggestion. — *v. t.* To bring to mind by a hint; suggest indirectly. — *v. i.* To make a hint or hints. — **Syn.** See SUGGEST. — **hint′er,** *n.* — **hint′ing·ly,** *adv.*
hin′ter·land′ (hĭn′tẽr·lănd′; *G.* -länt′), *n.* [G.] The region lying behind the coast district; hence, a region remote from cities and towns.
hip (hĭp), *interj.* A call to attention, as in beginning a cheer.
hip (hĭp), *n.* [AS. *hype.*] **1.** The projecting region of each side of the body below the waist, formed by the lateral parts of the pelvis and upper part of the thigh; haunch. The **hip joint** is the ball-and-socket joint between the femur and the innominate bone, or **hip′bone′** (hĭp′-bōn′). **2.** *Arch.* The external angle formed by the meeting of two sloping sides of a roof, which have their wall plates running in different directions. — ***on, or upon, the hip.*** At a disadvantage; as, to take or have one *on the hip;* — a phrase derived from wrestling. — *v. t.*; HIPPED (hĭpt); HIP′PING. To make with a hip or hips, as a roof.
hip, *n.* [AS. *hēope.*] The ripened fruit of a rosebush.
hip and thigh. Overwhelmingly; unsparingly.
hip′parch (hĭp′ärk), *n.* [Gr. *hipparchos, hipparchēs,* fr. *hippos* horse + *archein* to lead, rule.] *Gr. Antiq.* A commander of cavalry.
hipped (hĭpt), *adj.* **1.** Having hips of a specified kind; as, large-*hipped;* narrow-*hipped.* **2.** Hipshot. **3.** Designating a roof having hips.
hipped, *adj.* *Colloq.* **a** Depressed. **b** Obsessed.
hip′pish (hĭp′ĭsh), *adj.* *Colloq.* Morbidly depressed.
hip′po- (hĭp′ō-), **hipp-.** [Gr. *hippos.*] A combining form meaning *horse,* as in **hip·pol′o·gy, hip′po·phile.**
hip′po·cam′pus (-kăm′pŭs), *n.*; *pl.* -PI (-pī). [L., the sea horse, fr. Gr. *hippokampos,* fr. *hippos* horse + *kampos* a sea monster.] **1.** *Gr. & Rom. Myth.* A sea monster with head and forequarters like a horse and tail like a dolphin or fish. **2.** *Anat.* A ridge extending throughout the length of the descending horn of each lateral ventricle of the brain. — **hip′po·cam′pal** (-păl; -p′l), *adj.*
hip′po·cras (hĭp′ō·krăs), *n.* [OF. *ypocras,* prop., Hippocrates.] *Hist.* A highly spiced wine.
Hip′po·crat′ic (hĭp′ō·krăt′ĭk), *adj.* from HIPPOCRATES, *Biog.*
Hippocratic oath. An oath, embodying a code of medical ethics, generally taken by recipients of the M.D. degree.
Hip′po·crene (hĭp′ō·krēn; hĭp′ō·krē′nē), *n.* [L., fr. Gr. *hippokrēnē,* fr. *hippos* horse + *krēnē* fountain.] A fountain on Mount Helicon in Boeotia, fabled to have burst forth when the ground was struck by the hoof of Pegasus. Also, its waters, supposed to impart poetic inspiration.
hip′po·drome (hĭp′ō·drōm), *n.* [F., fr. L. *hippodromos,* fr. Gr. *hippodromos,* fr. *hippos* horse + *dromos* course.] **1.** *Gr. Antiq.* An oval track for horse and chariot races, with tiers of seats for spectators. **2.** An arena for equestrian performances; a circus.
hip′po·griff, hip′po·gryph (hĭp′ō·grĭf), *n.* [F. *hippogriffe.*] A fabulous winged animal, half horse and half griffin.
Hip·pol′y·tus (hĭ·pŏl′ĭ·tŭs), *n.* [L., fr. Gr. *Hippolytos.*] *Gr. Myth.* A son of Theseus. His stepmother, Phaedra, fell in love with him, but he repulsed her advances. Phaedra hanged herself accusing Hippolytus of ravishment. Poseidon, answering the imprecation of Theseus, sent a sea monster which so terrified the horses of Hippolytus that they dragged him to death.
Hip·pom′e·nes (hĭ·pŏm′ē·nēz), *n.* See ATALANTA.
hip·poph′a·gous (hĭ·pŏf′ȧ·gŭs), *adj.* [*hippo-* + *-phagous.*] Eating horseflesh. — **hip·poph′a·gy** (-jĭ), *n.*

hip′po·pot′a·mus (hĭp′ō·pŏt′ȧ·mŭs), *n.; pl.* HIPPOPOTAMUSES (-ĕz; -ĭz), HIPPOPOTAMI (-mī), sometimes HIPPOPOTAMUS. [L., fr. Gr. *hippopotamos,* fr. *hippos* horse + *potamos* river.] Any of a family (Hippopotamidae) or of its typical genus (*Hippopotamus*) of herbivorous mammals allied to the hogs, and largely aquatic in habits; esp., one (*Hippopotamus amphibius*) found in African rivers, and, next to the elephant, the largest existing quadruped.

-hip′pus (-hĭp′ŭs). [Gr. *hippos.*] *Zool.* A combining form meaning *horse,* used in generic names, esp. in paleontology, as eo*hippus.*

hip roof. A roof with sloping ends and sides; hipped roof.

hip′shot′ (hĭp′shŏt′), *adj.* [*hip* + *shot.*] Having the hip dislocated; hence, having one hip lower than the other.

hir′cine (hûr′sĭn; -sīn), *adj.* [L. *hircinus,* fr. *hircus* he-goat.] Goatlike, esp. in smell; also, goatish; lecherous.

hire (hīr), *n.* [AS. *hȳr.*] **1.** The price paid for the use of a thing or a place, for personal service, or for labor; pay. **2.** Act of hiring something. — **Syn.** See WAGE. — *v. t.* **1.** To engage the labor or services of, for hire. **2.** To procure for temporary use, for a compensation. **3.** To grant temporary use of, for compensation; let; lease. — *v. i. Colloq.* To give one's services for hire. — **hir′a·ble** (hīr′ȧ·b'l), **hire′a·ble,** *adj.* — **hir′er** (hīr′ẽr), *n.*

Syn. (1) See EMPLOY.

(2) **Hire, let, lease, rent, charter** mean to engage or grant for use at a price or rate. **Hire** and **let** are usually complementary terms, *hire* implying the act of engaging and *let,* the act of granting for use; **lease,** in precise use, implies a letting, but in current and not always approved use it implies hiring on a lease; **rent** strictly implies the payment of money for use and, so long as this idea is stressed, it may connote either hiring or letting; **charter** strictly implies hiring a ship on a lease, but is now used of any vehicle, especially a public one.

hire′ling (-lĭng), *n.* One who is hired; hence, a mercenary. — **hire′-ling,** *adj.*

hir′ple (hûr′p'l; hĭr′-), *v. i. & n. Scot.* Hobble; limp.

hir′sle (hûr′s'l; hĭr′-), *v. i. & t. Scot.* To hitch along.

hir′sute (hûr′sūt; hûr·sūt′), *adj.* [L. *hirsutus.*] Rough with hair or bristles; shaggy. — **hir′sute·ness,** *n.*

hir·tel′lous (hûr·tĕl′ŭs), *adj.* [From L. *hirtus* hairy.] Finely hirsute.

hi·ru′di·noid (hĭ·rōō′dĭ·noid), *adj.* [L. *hirudo, -inis,* leech + *-oid.*] *Zool.* Resembling a leech.

hi·run′dine (hĭ·rŭn′dĭn; -dīn), *adj.* [L. *hirundo* swallow.] *Zool.* Like or pertaining to the swallows.

his (hĭz; 4), *pron.* [AS. *his* of him, his, gen. masc. & neut. of *hē,* neut. *hit.* See HE.] Of him; — the possessive case of *he* used as an objective genitive (as, *his* memory will live long) or absolutely (as, the book is *his*). — *adj.* Belonging or pert. to him; made, done, etc., by him.

His·pa′ni·a (hĭs·pā′nĭ·ȧ; -pän′yȧ), *n.* [L.] An ancient country comprising modern Spain and Portugal; now, *Poetic,* Spain.

His·pan′ic (hĭs·păn′ĭk), *adj.* Pert. to or deriving from the people, speech, or culture of Spain, of Spain and Portugal, or of the regions colonized by the Spanish and Portuguese. — **His·pan′i·cism** (-ĭ·sĭz′m), *n.*

his′pa·ni·dad′ (ēs′pä·nē·thäth′), *n.* [Sp. See HISPANIA.] A movement based on assertion of the spiritual unity of Latin culture in Europe and America and the doctrine that Spain is destined to control Latin America.

his′pid (hĭs′pĭd), *adj.* [L. *hispidus.*] Rough with bristles, stiff hairs, or minute spines. — **his·pid′i·ty** (hĭs·pĭd′ĭ·tĭ), *n.*

his·pid′u·lous (hĭs·pĭd′ū·lŭs), *adj.* [Dim. of *hispid.*] *Bot. & Zool.* Minutely hispid.

hiss (hĭs), *v. i.* [ME. *hissen,* of imitative origin.] To make a sharp sibilant sound like the prolonged sound of the letter *s* or the sound emitted by an angered goose or snake; esp., to make such a sound as an expression of hatred or disapproval. — *v. t.* **1.** To condemn by hissing. **2.** To utter with a hiss. — *n.* The sound made in hissing or one like it, esp. as an expression of hatred or disapproval. — **hiss′er,** *n.*

hiss′ing, *n.* **1.** Act of emitting a hiss or hisses. **2.** *Archaic.* An object of scorn or contempt.

hist (hĭst), *interj.* Hush! Be silent! Listen!

his′ta·mine (hĭs′tȧ·mēn; -mĭn), *n.* [*hist*idine + *amine.*] *Biochem.* A compound, $C_5H_9N_3$, occurring in ergot and many animal tissues, also made synthetically. It is thought to be responsible for the dilatation and increased permeability of blood vessels which play a major role in allergic reactions, as in hives and asthma, and in certain respiratory affections. — **his′ta·min′ic** (-mĭn′ĭk), *adj.*

his′ti·dine (hĭs′tĭ·dēn; -dĭn), *n.* Also **his′ti·din.** [Gr. *histion* tissue.] *Biochem.* A crystalline basic amino acid, $C_6H_9N_3O_2$, formed in the splitting of proteins.

his′tie (hĭs′tĭ), *adj. Scot.* Bare; barren.

his′to- (hĭs′tō-), **hist-.** [Gr. *histos* loom, warp, web.] *Chiefly Biol.* A combining form, meaning *tissue;* as in:

histoblast	**histography**	**histopathology**
histochemistry	**histolysis**	**histophysiology**
histogenesis	**histomorphology**	**histotome**

his′to·gram (hĭs′tō·grăm), *n.* [*histo-* + *-gram.*] *Statistics.* A graphical representation of a frequency distribution by a series of rectangles which have for one dimension a distance proportional to a definite range of frequencies and for the other dimension a distance proportional to the number of frequencies appearing within the range.

his′toid (hĭs′toid), *adj.* [*hist-* + *-oid.*] *Med.* Resembling the normal tissues; as, *histoid* tumors.

his·tol′o·gy (hĭs·tŏl′ō·jĭ), *n.* [*histo-* + *-logy.*] **1.** That branch of science which treats of the minute structure of animal and vegetable tissues. **2.** The tissue structure or organization, as of an organism. — **his′to·log′i·cal** (hĭs′tō·lŏj′ĭ·kăl), *adj.* — **his·tol′o·gist** (hĭs·tŏl′ō·jĭst), *n.*

his′tone (hĭs′tōn), *n.* Also **his′ton** (-tŏn). [Gr. *histos* tissue.] *Biochem.* Any of a class of basic proteins, soluble in water and dilute acids, yielding amino acids on hydrolysis. Injected into an animal, they show a toxic action and prevent coagulation of the blood.

his·to′ri·an (hĭs·tō′rĭ·ăn; 70), *n.* **1.** A writer of history; chronicler; annalist. **2.** One versed in history.

his·tor′ic (-tŏr′ĭk), *adj.* Historical; esp., famous in history.

his·tor′i·cal (-ĭ·kăl), *adj.* [L. *historicus,* fr. Gr. *historikos.* See HISTORY.] **1.** Of, pertaining to, or of the nature of history; narrating, dealing with, or based upon history; true to history; as, *historical* evidence, fidelity, or novels; few details were *historical.* **2.** Not now used except in historical accounts; — of words. **3.** Famous in history; associated with history. — **his·tor′i·cal·ly,** *adv.* — **-cal·ness,** *n.*

historical, *or* **historic, present.** See PRESENT, *adj.,* 5.

historical school. A number of economists who have been variously classed together as pursuing the **historical method,** that is, basing their teaching upon the facts revealed by historical research and the inductions to be drawn from them.

his′to·ric′i·ty (hĭs′tō·rĭs′ĭ·tĭ), *n.* Actual occurrence or existence; historical genuineness.

his′to·ried (hĭs′tō·rĭd), *adj.* Having a history; storied.

his·to′ri·og′ra·pher (hĭs·tō′rĭ·ŏg′rȧ·fẽr), *n.* [F. *historiographe,* fr. L., fr. Gr. *historiographos,* fr. *historia* history + *graphein* to write.] A historian; esp., one designated to write a history. — **his·to′ri·og′ra·phy** (-fĭ), *n.*

his′to·ry (hĭs′tō·rĭ; -trĭ), *n.; pl.* -RIES (-rĭz; -trĭz). [L. *historia,* fr. Gr. *historia* history, information, fr. *histōr* knowing.] **1. a** A narrative of events; a tale; story. **b** A record of facts about a person, as a ***case history,*** which lists details relating to ancestry, environment, experiences, and the like, for use in analyzing a case as for treatment or discipline. **2.** A systematic written account of events, particularly of those affecting a nation, institution, science, or art, usually connected with a philosophical explanation of their causes. **3.** The branch of knowledge that records and explains past events. **4.** Events which form the subject matter of a history; as, to survey the *history* of a movement. **5.** Something that belongs to the past; as, that is all *history.*

his′tri·on′ic (hĭs′trĭ·ŏn′ĭk), *adj.* [LL. *histrionicus,* fr. L. *histrio* an actor.] Of or pertaining to the stage or actors; theatrical. — **Syn.** See DRAMATIC. — *n.* An actor; also, *pl.,* dramatic representation; theatricals. — **his′tri·on′i·cal** (-ĭ·kăl), *adj.* — **his′tri·on′i·cal·ly,** *adv.* — **his′tri·on′i·cism** (-ĭ·sĭz′m) *or* **his′tri·o·nism** (hĭs′trĭ·ō·nĭz′m), *n.*

hit (hĭt), *v. t.;* HIT; HIT′TING. [ON. *hitta.*] **1.** To reach with or as if with a stroke; to strike or touch, usually with force and often as a result of an aim. **2.** Hence: **a** To bring into violent contact; knock; as, to *hit* one's head in falling. **b** To deliver; as, to *hit* a blow. **3.** To affect to one's detriment, discomfort, or discomfiture, as, the taunt *hit* him hard. **4.** To come upon or meet with as after search or by chance; arrive at; as, to *hit* the answer to a riddle. **5.** To accord precisely with; suit. **6.** To represent, mimic, or reproduce; as, to *hit* the right note. **7.** To set in operation as by striking or touching. — *v. i.* **1.** To deliver a blow; make thrusts; strike; — often with *out.* **2.** To come in contact forcibly; collide. **3.** To come, happen, or light (*upon*); as, to *hit* upon a solution. **4.** To accord; suit; agree. **5.** Of an internal-combustion engine, to fire the charge in its cylinders. — **Syn.** See STRIKE. — ***hit off.*** To improvise, imitate, etc., neatly and easily.

hit, *n.* **1.** A blow striking the object aimed at. **2.** A collision. **3. a** A stroke of success. **b** A conspicuously successful play, book, etc. **4.** An effectively turned or directed phrase; esp., a stinging remark. **5.** *Backgammon.* A game won after the adversary has removed some of his men, counting less than a gammon; sometimes, any game won. **6.** *Ball Games.* A stroke by which the ball is hit so as to result in a score, or some other advantage; specif., *Baseball,* a base hit. — **hit′-ter,** *n.*

hit′-and-miss′, *adj.* Sometimes hitting, or corresponding in position, and sometimes not.

hit′-and-run′, *adj.* **1.** *Baseball.* Designating or pert. to a play in which a base runner starts for the next base as the pitcher starts to pitch, and the batsman attempts to hit the ball. **2.** That hits and runs away; — orig. and esp. used of motor-vehicle drivers who flee after being involved in an accident.

hitch (hĭch), *v. t.* **1.** To move with jerks. **2.** To catch or fasten as by a hook or knot; to make fast, unite, or yoke. — *v. i.* **1.** To move haltingly, jerkily, or discontinuously; hobble; hop. **2.** To become entangled, caught, or yoked; to catch or cling to something. **3.** *Colloq.* To agree; harmonize. — *n.* **1.** A sudden movement or pull; a jerk. **2.** A hobble; a hop. **3.** A stop or sudden halt; impediment; obstacle. **4.** Act of catching hold of or on something. **5.** A connection between a portable implement, as a plow, and the source of draft, as a tractor. **6.** *Naut.* A knot or noose that can be easily untied; — used for temporary fastening. See KNOT, *n., Illust.* — **hitch′er,** *n.*

hitch′hike′ (hĭch′hīk′), *v. i.* To make one's way, esp. when hiking, by getting rides in automobiles.

hith′er (hĭth′ẽr), *adv.* [AS. *hider.*] To this place. — *adj.* Being on the side next or toward the person speaking; nearer; also, of time, earlier.

hith′er·most (hĭth′ẽr·mōst), *adj.* Nearest on this side.

hith′er·to′ (hĭth′ẽr·tōō′; 2), *adv.* **1.** To this place. **2.** Up to this time; as yet; until now.

hith′er·ward (hĭth′ẽr·wẽrd), *adv.* Also **hith′er·wards** (-wẽrdz). Toward this place; hither.

Hit′ler·ism (hĭt′lẽr·ĭz′m), *n. Ger. Hist.* The extreme nationalistic doctrines of the National Socialist party under the leadership of Adolf Hitler, from about 1930; German fascism. — **Hit′ler·ite** (-īt), *n. & adj.*

hit or miss. Haphazardly. — **hit′-or-miss′,** *adj.*

Hit′tite (hĭt′īt), *n.* [Heb. *Ḥittīm* Hittites.] **1.** One of an ancient people (or group of peoples), of undetermined origin, who invaded and conquered Asia Minor and Syria in the 2d millennium B.C. **2.** The official language of the Hittite empire. — **Hit′tite,** *adj.*

hive (hīv), *n.* [AS. *hȳf.*] **1.** A beehive. **2.** The bees of one hive; a swarm of bees. **3.** Something suggestive of a beehive as in a place swarming with busy occupants. — *v. t.* **1.** To collect into, or cause to enter, a hive. **2.** To store up in a hive, as honey; hence, to lay up a store of. — *v. i.* To enter a hive together, as bees; to reside in a body. — **hiv′er** (hīv′ẽr), *n.*

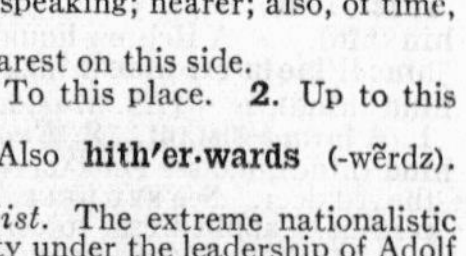

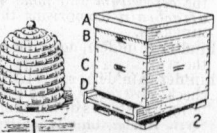

Hives, 1. 1 Old-fashioned; 2 Modern; *A* Cover; *B* Super; *C* Brood Chamber; *D* Bottom.

hives (hīvz), *n.* [Scot.] Urticaria; any eruptive skin disease.

ho (hō), *interj.* [OF.] Stop! Stand still! Whoa!

ho (hō), *interj.* Also **hoa.** **1.** A cry of surprise, delight, etc., or when repeated, of derisive laughter. **2.** Halloo! Attend! **3.** Expressing a (specified) direction or destination; as, westward *ho.*

ho·ac′tzin (hō·äk′tsĭn). Var. of HOATZIN.

hoar (hōr; 70), *adj.* [AS. *hār* gray, old.] **1.** White or light gray. **2.** Gray or white with age; hoary; venerable. **3.** *Now Dial.* Moldy; musty; stale. — *n.* **1.** Hoariness. **2.** Hoarfrost.

hoard (hōrd; 70), *n.* [AS. *hord.*] A store laid up; a hidden supply. — *v. t.* To collect and lay up; amass and conceal. — *v. i.* To hoard money or the like. — **hoard′er,** *n.*

hoard′ing (hōr′dĭng), *n.* Act of one who hoards; also, something hoarded.

hoard′ing, *n.* [From OF. *hourd* barrier, palisade, of Teut. origin.] A temporary screen of boards enclosing a construction; hence, a billboard.

hoar′frost′ (hōr′frŏst′; 74), *n.* A silvery-white deposit of ice needles formed during still, clear nights.

hoar′hound′ (-hound′). Var. of HOREHOUND.

hoarse (hōrs; 70), *adj.* [ME. *hors,* also *hos, has,* fr. AS. *hās.*] **1.** Harsh; grating; discordant; — of sounds. **2.** Having a rough grating voice, as when affected with a cold; making a hoarse cry or sound. — **hoarse′ly,** *adv.* — **hoarse′ness,** *n.*

hoars′en (hōr′s′n), *v. t. & i.* To make or become hoarse.

hoar′y (hōr′ĭ), *adj.;* -I·ER (-ĭ·ẽr); -I·EST. **1.** White or whitish; white or gray with age. **2.** Remote in time past. — **hoar′i·ness,** *n.*

ho·at′zin (hō·ăt′sĭn), **ho·ac′tzin** (hō·ăk′tsĭn), *n.* [Sp., fr. Nahuatl *uatzin.*] A peculiar crested South American bird (*Opisthocomos cristatus*) smaller than a pheasant, with olive-colored plumage marked with white above.

hoax (hōks), *n.; pl.* HOAXES (-ĕz; -ĭz). [Prob. contr. fr. *hocus,* in *hocus-pocus.*] A deception for mockery or mischief; a practical joke. — *v. t.* To deceive by a hoax. — **Syn.** See DUPE. — **hoax′er** (hōk′sẽr), *n.*

hob (hŏb), *n.* [Orig. a familiar alteration of *Robin, Robert.*] **1.** *Dial. Eng.* **a** A rustic; clown. **b** A fairy; sprite; elf. Orig. [*cap.*] = ROBIN GOODFELLOW. **2.** *Colloq.* Mischief; as, to raise *hob.*

hob, *n.* [Origin uncert.] **1.** A projection at the back or side of a fireplace on which something may be kept warm. **2.** A peg, pin, or mark used as a target in some games, as in quoits; also, the game.

hob′–and–nob′, *adj., or* **hob and nob.** On familiar terms; in close companionship; intimate.

Hob′bism (hŏb′ĭz′m), *n.* The philosophical system of Thomas Hobbes (1588–1679); esp., his theory that absolutism in government is necessary to prevent the anarchy to which natural selfishness and warring interests of men inevitably lead. — **Hob′bist** (-ĭst), *n.*

hob′ble (hŏb″l), *v. i.;* -BLED (-′ld); -BLING (-lĭng). [ME. *hobelen, hoblen.*] **1.** To go unevenly; wobble. **2.** To walk lame; limp. — *v. t.* **1.** To cause to limp; make lame. **2.** To fetter; hopple; clog. — *n.* **1.** A hobbling gait; limp. **2.** *Colloq.* A difficulty. **3.** A fetter; hopple; clog. — **hob′bler** (-lẽr), *n.* — **hob′bling·ly,** *adv.*

hob′ble·bush′ (hŏb″l·bo͝osh′), *n.* A North American shrub (*Viburnum alnifolium*) of the honeysuckle family.

hob′ble·de·hoy′ (-dē·hoi′), *n.* A youth between boy and man; an awkward, gawky fellow.

hobble skirt. A woman's skirt so scant at the bottom as to restrain freedom of movement as a hobble does.

hob′by (hŏb′ĭ), *n.; pl.* -BIES (-ĭz). [OF. *hobé, hobet,* dim. of *hobe* hobby, falcon.] A small Old World falcon (*Falco subbuteo*), formerly trained and flown at small birds.

hob′by, *n.* [ME. *hoby, hobyn,* prop. orig. an ambling or pacing horse.] **1.** *Dial.* A strong medium-sized horse. **2.** An engrossing topic, plan, etc., to which one constantly reverts; also, an occupation or interest to which one gives his spare time.

hob′by·horse′ (hŏb′ĭ·hôrs′), *n.* **1.** A figure of a horse fastened to the waist of a performer in the morris dance, pantomimes, etc.; also, the performer. **2.** *Obs.* **a** A buffoon. **b** A prostitute. **3.** A stick, often with a horse's head or figure, on which children pretend to ride; hence, an imitation horse of wood, as one on rockers used as a child's plaything. **4.** = 2d HOBBY.

hob′gob′lin (hŏb′gŏb′lĭn), *n.* **1.** A mischievous sprite; esp. [*cap.*], Robin Goodfellow, or Puck. **2.** A bogy.

hob′nail′ (-nāl′), *n.* [*hob* peg + *nail.*] **1.** A short, large-headed nail for studding shoe soles. **2.** A rustic; a clownish person. — **hob′nailed′** (-nāld′), *adj.*

hob′nob′ (-nŏb′), *adv.* [AS. *hæbbe* have + *næbbe* have not, fr. *ne* not + *habban* to have.] Hit or miss.

hob′nob′, *v. i.;* -NOBBED′ (-nŏbd′); -NOB′BING. To drink familiarly; hence, to be on intimate terms; — with *with.* — *n.* A drinking together; a familiar chat.

ho′bo (hō′bō), *n.; pl.* HOBOES, HOBOS (-bōz). [Origin unknown.] **a** A migratory worker. **b** A professional tramp. — **ho′bo·ism** (-ĭz′m), *n.*

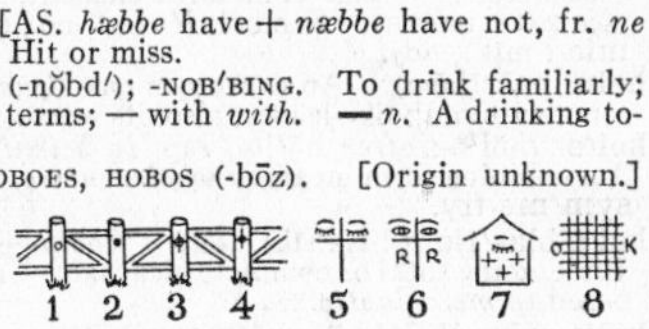

Hobo, or Tramp, Signs. 1 Good for a handout; 2 Cranky woman or bad dog; 3 Not generous; 4 Stay away; 5 Police not hostile; 6 Police hostile (*R R* used for Railroad Police, if applicable); 7 Jail good for a night's lodging; 8 Clean jail; 9 Jail food no good; 10 "Cooties" in jail; 11 Jail has rock pile; 12 Jail is a workhouse; 13 Saloons in town; 14 Town is hostile; 15 Streets good for begging; 16 Plain-clothes detectives here.

Hob′son's choice (hŏb′s′nz). A choice without an alternative; the thing offered or nothing; — so-called in allusion to the practice of Thomas Hobson (d. 1631), at Cambridge, England, who let horses, and required every customer to take the horse which stood nearest the door.

hock (hŏk), *n.* [AS. *hōh* heel.] The tarsal joint in the hind limb of digitigrade quadrupeds, as the horse, corresponding to the ankle of man, but elevated and bending backward; also, the corresponding joint of a fowl's leg. See DOG, HORSE, POULTRY, *Illusts.* — *v. t.* To hamstring.

hock, *n.* A certain white Rhine wine (**Hoch′hei′mer** [hŏk′hī′mẽr; *G.* hōk′-, hōκ′-]); hence, any white Rhine wine.

hock, *n. & v. Slang, U. S.* Pawn; pledge.

hock′ey (hŏk′ĭ), *n.* [Perh. fr. OF. *hoquet* shepherd's crook, fr. *hoc* hook, fr. MD. *hoek.*] **1.** A field or ice-rink game (***field hockey*** or ***ice hockey***) in which the players on the two sides try to score goals by driving the ball or the puck (a vulcanized-rubber disk) into the opponents' goal. **2.** *pl.* -EYS (-ĭz). In full **hockey stick.** The stick, curved or hooked at the end, used in driving in this game.

ho′cus (hō′kŭs), *v. t.* **1.** To cheat. **2.** To adulterate; drug.

ho′cus–po′cus (-pō′kŭs), *n.* [Prob. invented by jugglers in imitation of Latin.] **1.** A juggler's formula. **2.** A juggler. **3.** A juggler's trick; sleight of hand; hence, nonsense intended to cloak deception. — *v. t. & i. Colloq.* To cheat; trick.

hod (hŏd), *n.* [MD. *hodde.*] **1.** A wooden tray or trough with a handle, borne on the shoulder, for carrying mortar, brick, etc. **2.** A coal scuttle.

hod carrier. Also **hod′man** (hŏd′măn). A laborer whose business is to carry mortar, brick, etc., in a hod.

hod′den (hŏd″n), *n. Chiefly Scot.* Coarse cloth of undyed wool.

hodge′podge′ (hŏj′pŏj′), *n.* [From HOTCHPOTCH.] A stew of various ingredients; hence, a mixture; medley.

hoe (hō), *n.* [OF. *houe,* fr. OHG. *houwa,* fr. *houwan* to hew.] A long-handled implement with a thin, flat blade set transversely, used for weeding, cultivating, etc. — *v. t. & i.;* HOED (hōd), HOE′ING. To dig, scrape, clean, etc., with a hoe. — **ho′er** (hō′ẽr), *n.*

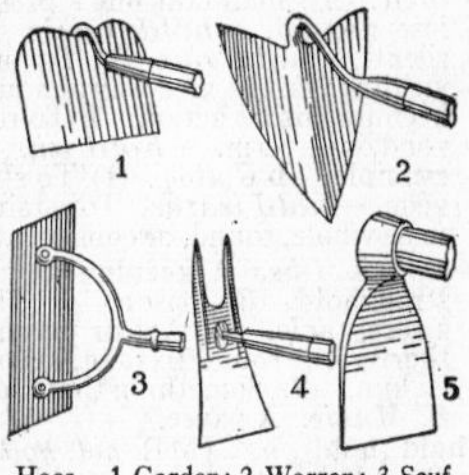

Hoes. 1 Garden; 2 Warren; 3 Scuffle; 4 Weeding; 5 Grub.

hoe′cake′ (hō′kāk′), *n. Southern U. S.* A cake of Indian meal, baked before the fire or in the ashes, originally on a hoe.

hog (hŏg; 74), *n.* [AS. *hogg,* prob. of Celt. origin.] **1.** A swine; a pig, sow, or boar; esp., an adult animal suitable for market. See SWINE, 1. **2.** *Dial.* A young unshorn sheep. **3.** *Colloq.* A selfish, gluttonous, or filthy person. — *v. t.;* HOGGED (hŏgd); HOG′GING. **1.** To cause to arch like a hog's back. **2.** To cut short (a horse's mane) so as to make it bristly. **3.** *Slang.* To take selfishly or in excess of one's due. — *v. i.* To become curved upward like a hog's back; — of a ship's bottom or keel.

ho′gan (hō′gôn), *n.* [Navaho *qoghan* house, hut.] An earth-covered lodge of the Navaho Indians.

hog′back′ (hŏg′băk′), *n. Geol.* A ridge formed by the outcropping edges of tilted strata; any ridge with a sharp summit and steeply sloping sides.

hog cholera. A highly infectious, often fatal disease of swine, caused by a filtrable virus and characterized by fever, diarrhea, hemorrhages (esp. in the kidneys and lymph glands), etc.

hog′fish′ (-fĭsh′), *n.; pl.,* see FISH. **1.** Any of various fishes usually so called from some fancied resemblance to a hog; esp.: **a** A large West Indian and Florida wrasse (*Lachnolaimus maximus*) used for food. **b** The pigfish *Orthopristis chrysopterus.* **2.** *Obs.* **a** A porpoise. **b** A manatee.

hog′gish (hŏg′ĭsh), *adj.* Grossly selfish, gluttonous, or filthy. — **hog′gish·ly,** *adv.* — **hog′gish·ness,** *n.*

hog′ma·nay′ (hŏg′mȧ·nā′), *n. Scot.* New Year's Eve, when children go about singing, and soliciting gifts.

hog′nose′, *or* **hog′–nosed′, snake** (hŏg′nōz′, -nōzd′). Any of several rather small, harmless, stout-bodied North American snakes constituting a genus (*Heterodon*). Cf. ADDER **b.**

hog′nut′ (hŏg′nŭt′), *n.* **a** The earthnut *Conopodium denudatum.* **b** In the United States, the pignut.

hog peanut. The earthpea.

hogs′head (hŏgz′hĕd), *n.* [That is, *hog's head;* why so called is unknown.] **1.** A large cask, esp. one containing from 63 to 140 gallons. **2.** A large measure for liquids, of varying content, esp. one of 63 U. S. gallons, or 238.5 liters. Cf. 1st BUTT; PIPE, 7. Abbr. *hhd.*

hog′–tie′ (hŏg′tī′), *v. t.;* -TIED′ (-tīd′); -TY′ING. **1.** To tie together the four feet of (a hog or other animal). **2.** *Colloq.* To tie down; bind fast.

hog′wash′ (hŏg′wŏsh′), *n. Colloq.* Swill for hogs; refuse.

hog′weed′ (-wēd′), *n.* Any of various weeds or coarse plants, as ragweed, knotweed, sow thistle, dog fennel.

Ho′hen·stau′fen (hō′ĕn·shtou′fĕn), *n.* A member of a German princely family, of Swabian origin, which furnished sovereigns of Germany, 1138–1254, and of Sicily, 1194–1266.

Ho′hen·zol′lern (hō′ĕn·tsôl′ẽrn), *n.* A member of a German princely family, founded about the 11th century, from which came the kings of Prussia from 1701 to 1918 and the German emperors from 1871 to 1918.

hoicks (hoiks), **hoick** (hoik), *interj. Hunting.* A call used to incite the hounds. — *v. t. & i.* To urge by or as by the cry "hoicks."

hoi′den (hoi′d′n). Var. of HOYDEN.

‖**hoi pol·loi′** (hoi′ pŏ·loi′). [Gr.] The many; the masses; the populace.

hoise (hoiz), *v. t.;* HOISED (hoizd) or HOIST (hoist); HOIS′ING (hoiz′-). [See HOIST.] To hoist; — now chiefly in ***hoist with his own petard,*** blown up by his own bomb.

hoist (hoist; *dial.* hīst), *v. t.;* HOIST′ED; HOIST′ING. [Earlier *hoise, hyse,* fr. D. *hijschen,* LG. *hissen.*] To raise; elevate; esp., to lift with tackle. — *v. i.* To rise, or be hoisted. — **Syn.** See LIFT. — *n.* **1.** *Colloq.* Act of hoisting; a lift; a boost. **2.** A lifting apparatus; esp., an elevator, or lift, for heavy loads. **3. a** The perpendicular edge or height of a flag, as when flying from a staff. **b** The height or depth of any sail except a course. Cf. DROP, *n.,* 9. — **hoist′er,** *n.*

hoi′ty–toi′ty (hoi′tĭ·toi′tĭ; 2), *adj.* Giddy; flighty; also, haughty; patronizing. — *n.* A hoity-toity person or action. — *interj.* A mildly contemptuous exclamation of surprise or disapproval.

ho′key·po′key (hō′kĭ·pō′kĭ), *n.* Hocus-pocus.

ho′kum (hō′kŭm), *n.* [Cf. HOCUS-POCUS.] *Slang.* In a play, speech, etc., deliberate stimulation of emotion by artificial means; also, the means so used; bunk.

hold (hōld), *v. t.;* HELD (hĕld); HOLD′ING. HOLD′EN (hōl′dĕn), *past part.,* is now rare, archaic, or legal. [AS. *healdan, haldan.*] **1.** To maintain possession of, or authority over; to retain by force. **2.** To retain in love or affection. **3.** To receive and retain; contain. **4.** To have or keep, as in the grasp; to cause to remain in a given position, relation, or the like; sustain; support. **5.** To impose restraint upon; specif.: **a** To keep from relaxing or letting go, as interest, attention, etc. **b** To keep from advance or attack or from gaining an advantage. **c** To keep bound; oblige; as, to *hold* one to his word. **6.** To entertain; harbor; as, to *hold* no prejudice; to accept; as, to *hold* a theory. **7.** To consider; regard; judge; as, to *hold* one guiltless. **8.** To carry on or join in, as something which is the result of united action; as, to *hold* a meeting, a session, or conversation; also, to invoke, conduct, or preside at; as, a judge *holds* a court. **9.** To maintain in being, action, a specified state, etc.; as, to *hold* oneself in readiness. **10.** To bear, carry, or manage; as, he *holds* himself erect. **11.** To own or possess; occupy;

derive title to. **12.** *Obs.* To undergo; bear; endure. **— *v. i.* 1.** To remain steadfast or faithful; cleave; adhere. **2.** To endure a test; not to fail; continue; persist. **3.** To maintain a grasp on, or a connection with, something; to remain fast. **4.** To remain unbroken or unsubdued; not to give way. **5.** To derive right or title; — generally with *of* or *from*. **6.** To be valid; as, the rule *holds* in all cases. **7.** To continue, obtain, or occur, as a state or event; as, winter still *holds*. **8.** To restrain oneself; forbear. — **Syn.** See HAVE: CONTAIN.
hold forth. To harangue or preach at length. — ***hold in.*** To restrain, esp. oneself. — ***hold off.*** To keep aloof. — ***hold one's own.*** To maintain one's present condition, advantage, etc.; not to lose ground. — ***hold one's peace or one's tongue.*** To keep silent. — ***hold out.*** **a** To offer, as a reward. **b** To keep from yielding; fail to give way; endure. — ***hold over.*** **a** To postpone; to keep for future action. **b** To remain in possession or enjoyment of beyond one's term. — ***hold up.*** **a** To exhibit; display; as, *held up* as an example. **b** *Colloq.* (1) To stop in order to rob. (2) To stop or impede. — ***hold water.*** To retain water without leaking; hence, *Colloq.*, to be whole, sound, or consistent; as, his contention will not *hold water*.
— *n.* 1. *Obs.* A keeping in charge; possession; protection. **2.** A stronghold. **3.** Prison. **4.** That which holds something, as a lock or a receptacle. **5.** Act or manner of holding; seizure; grasp. **6.** Authority or ground to take, keep, restrain, etc.; as, the law has no *hold* on him. **7.** Something that may be grasped or held; means of support. **8.** *Music.* A pause.

hold (hōld), *n.* [ME. *hol, holl,* hole, and D. *hol* hold, hole.] *Naut.* The whole interior of a vessel below decks, or, strictly, below the lower deck, where cargo is stowed.

hold'all' (-ôl'), *n.* A container for all sorts of things; esp., a kind of portable case used by tourists, soldiers, etc.

hold'back' (-băk'), *n.* **1.** A check or hindrance. **2.** A device to enable a horse to back or hold back a vehicle. **3.** A device for holding a door open.

hold'er (hōl'dẽr), *n.* **1.** One who or that which holds. **2.** A tenant. **3.** The person in possession of, and legally entitled to receive payment of, a bill, note, or check.

hold'fast' (hōld'fȧst'), *n.* **1.** A tight hold or grasp. **2.** Something, as a long, flat-headed nail, a catch, or a clamp, used to secure and hold in place something else.

hold'ing (hōl'dĭng), *n.* **1.** Land held, esp. of a superior. **2.** Property owned, of any description, as bonds or stocks.

holding company. *Finance.* **a** A company the principal business of which is to own the stocks or securities of other companies. **b** An operating company which acquires all or part of the stock of subsidiaries.

hold'o'ver (hōld'ō'vẽr), *n.* **1.** Something that remains or lasts beyond the normal period of termination. **2.** A person who remains in an office or station after the departure of his associates. **3.** *Educ.* A repeater. **4.** *Logging.* A tree left in cutting, reserved for a future crop.

hold'up' (hōld'ŭp'), *n.* A holding up; specif., *Slang,* an assault for the purpose of robbery.

hole (hōl), *n.* [AS. *hol* hole, cavern, fr. *hol,* adj., hollow.] **1.** An opening into or through anything. **2.** A hollow place; a cavity; a pit. **3.** A deep place in a stream; as, a swimming *hole*. **4.** A den or burrow. **5.** A defect; flaw; as, to pick *holes*. **6.** *Colloq.* An embarrassing position. **7.** *Games.* A small cavity into which a marble or ball is to be played; hence, a score made by so playing. **— *v. t.* 1.** To cut, dig, or bore a hole or holes in. **2.** To drive into a hole, as an animal, or a golf ball. **— *v. i.*** To go or get into a hole. — ***hole out.*** *Golf.* To hole a ball.

hole'y (hōl'ĭ), *adj.* Having a hole or holes.

hol'i·but (hŏl'ĭ·bŭt). Var. of HALIBUT.

hol'i·day (hŏl'ĭ·dā *or, esp. Brit.,* -dĭ), *n.* [*holy* + *day*.] **1.** *Now* **ho'ly·day'** (hō'lĭ·dā'). A religious feast day. **2.** Any day of exemption from labor or work; hence, often *pl.,* a period of recreation or rest; vacation. **3.** A day fixed by law for the suspension of business in whole or in part; a legal holiday (which see). In the United States the ***legal holidays*** are determined by law, commonly by the statutes of the several states. There is no national legal holiday, and the only common-law holiday is Sunday (not generally called a holiday). The holidays most widely observed in the UNITED STATES are: ***New Year's Day,*** January 1; ***Lincoln's Birthday,*** February 12; ***Washington's Birthday,*** February 22; ***Memorial, or Decoration, Day,*** May 30; ***Independence Day,*** July 4; ***Labor Day,*** the first Monday in September; ***Columbus Day,*** October 12; ***Veterans Day,*** November 11; ***Christmas Day,*** December 25. The fourth Thursday in November is now regularly appointed by proclamation, by the national and state executives, as ***Thanksgiving Day,*** a day of thanksgiving and praise. In various states a day in the spring, as ***Good Friday,*** or the first Thursday in April, is regularly appointed by executive proclamation as a day of fasting and prayer, and observed as a holiday. In nearly all states ***General Election Day,*** the first Tuesday after the first Monday in November, is a legal holiday.
The HAWAIIAN ISLANDS, besides observing most of the holidays usual in the United States, have one special holiday: ***Kamehameha Day*** (June 11).
PUERTO RICO observes, besides the usual American holidays, ***Occupation Day*** (July 25), anniversary of the landing (1898) of U. S. troops.
In the PHILIPPINES the legal holidays (established by act of the Philippine Government) are ***New Year's Day*** (Jan. 1), ***Thursday*** and ***Friday of Holy Week, Labor Day*** (May 1), ***Independence Day*** (July 4), ***National Heroes' Day*** (Nov. 30), ***Christmas Day*** (Dec. 25), and ***Rizal Day*** (Dec. 30). ***General Election Day,*** as appointed by law, is also a legal holiday.
In the BRITISH COMMONWEALTH, the ***Queen's Birthday*** (either actual or arbitrary) and ***Victoria, or Empire, Day*** (the birthday of Queen Victoria, May 24) are observed as imperial holidays.
In ENGLAND, WALES, NORTHERN IRELAND, and the REPUBLIC OF IRELAND, the days of the greater church feasts are observed as church holidays. The bank holidays include Good Friday, Christmas Day, and these statute holidays: ***Easter Monday, Whitmonday, first Monday in August,*** and ***Boxing Day,*** December 26 (in some years 27), for Northern Ireland, ***Orangemen's Day,*** July 12, and for both parts of Ireland, ***St. Patrick's Day,*** March 17.
In SCOTLAND the bank holidays are ***New Year's Day, Good Friday, first Monday in May, first Monday in August,*** and ***Christmas Day.***
In the DOMINION OF CANADA, the public statutory holidays are ***Sundays, New Year's Day, Good Friday, Easter Monday,*** the two imperial holidays (the ***Queen's Birthday*** and ***Victoria Day***), ***Dominion Day*** (July 1), ***Labour Day*** (first Monday in September), ***Thanksgiving Day*** (when proclaimed — usually early in October), ***Remembrance Day*** (November 11), ***Christmas Day,*** and any day appointed by proclamation for a general fast or thanksgiving. Several of the provinces in their local use omit some of the dominion holidays, and Quebec observes several in addition.
See JEWISH HOLIDAYS.
— *adj.* 1. Joyous; gay; as, *holiday* attire. **2.** Occasional.

ho'li·ly (hō'lĭ·lĭ), *adv.* [From HOLY.] Piously; also, sacredly.

ho'li·ness (-nĕs; -nĭs), *n.* [AS. *hālignes.*] **1.** State or character of being holy. **2.** [*cap.*] A title of the pope; — used with *his* or *your*.

hol'la (hŏl'ȧ *or, esp. as an exclamation,* hŏ·lä'), *interj.* [F. *holà,* fr. *ho* ho + *là* there.] An exclamation meaning: Stop! Ho there! Hey!

hol'land (hŏl'ănd), *n.* [*rarely cap.*] A cotton or linen, glazed or unglazed, fabric used for window shades, furniture coverings, etc.; — also used in *pl.* with singular construction.

hol'lan·daise' sauce, *or* **hol'lan·daise'** (hŏl'ăn·dāz'), *n.* [F. *hollandaise,* fem. of *hollandais* Dutch.] *Cookery.* A sauce consisting essentially of a seasoned emulsion of butter and yolk of eggs with a little lemon juice or vinegar.

Hol'land·er (hŏl'ăn·dẽr), *n.* A native of Holland; a Dutchman.

Hol'lands (hŏl'ăndz), *n., or* **Holland gin.** Gin made in Holland.

hol'ler (hŏl'ẽr), *v. i. & t.* [Var. of *hollo.*] To cry out, as in pain or complaint; also, to shout. — **hol'ler,** *n.*

hol'lo (hŏl'ō *or, esp. as an exclamation,* hŏ·lō'), *interj.* Also **hol'loa** (hŏl'ō; hŏ·lō'). An exclamation used as a call to stop or pay attention, or to incite dogs in the chase. **— *n.*** A call of "hollo." — (hŏl'ō), *v. i.;* HOL'LOED (-ōd); HOL'LO·ING. To call out or exclaim; halloo. **— *v. t.*** To shout aloud; chase or incite with shouts; shout to.

hol'low (hŏl'ō), *adj.* [AS. *holh* a hollow, hole.] **1.** Having a cavity within a solid substance; not solid. **2.** Depressed; concave; sunken. **3.** Empty; hence, hungry. **4.** Reverberated, or sounding as if reverberated, from a cavity; deep; muffled; as, a *hollow* roar. **5.** False; deceitful; faithless; as, *hollow* praise; also, worthless; vain; as, a *hollow* victory. — **Syn.** See VAIN. **— *adv.* 1.** Hollowly. **2.** *Colloq.* Wholly; completely; utterly; — usually in phrase ***to beat all hollow.*** **— *n.* 1.** A cavity; a hole. **2.** A surface depression; a channel, basin, or valley. **— *v. t. & i.*** To make, or to become, hollow. — **hol'low·ly,** *adv.* — **hol'low·ness,** *n.*

hol'low·heart'ed (hŏl'ō·här'tĕd; -tĭd; 2), *adj.* Insincere; deceitful. — **hol'low·heart'ed·ness,** *n.*

hol'lus·chick' (hŏl'ŭs·chĭk'), *n.; pl.* HOLLUSCHICKIE (-chĭk'ĭ). [Prob. fr. Russ. *golyshka* bare of possessions, offspring, etc., fr. *golyĭ* naked.] A young male fur seal; a bachelor.

hol'ly (hŏl'ĭ), *n.; pl.* -LIES (-ĭz). [AS. *holen, holegn.*] **1.** Any of a genus (*Ilex,* family Ilicaceae) of trees and shrubs having thick, glossy, spiny-margined leaves and bright-red berries. Cf. INKBERRY **a**. **2.** The foliage or branches of the holly.

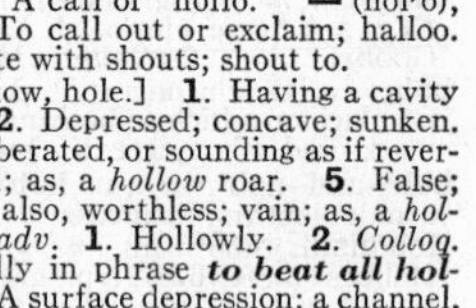
European Holly (*I. aquifolium*). (⅛)

hol'ly·hock (hŏl'ĭ·hŏk), *n.* [ME. *holihoc,* fr. *holi* holy + *hoc* mallow.] A tall perennial Chinese herb (*Althaea rosea*) of the mallow family, cultivated in gardens as a biennial; also, its flower. It has large, coarse, rounded leaves.

Hol'ly·wood' (hŏl'ĭ·wŏŏd'), *n.* **a** A suburb of Los Angeles, Calif., famous for the motion-picture industry established there. **b** Hence, the American motion-picture industry. **— *adj.*** Of, pert. to, or characteristic of Hollywood.

holm (hōm), *n.* [AS. *holen* holly.] **a** The holm oak. **b** *Now Dial.* The holly.

holm, *n.* [AS., hill, island, (high) sea.] **1.** An islet in a river or lake or near the mainland; — common in English place names. **2.** *Eng.* Low, flat land near a river; bottoms.

hol'mi·um (hōl'mĭ·ŭm), *n.* [NL., fr. *Holmia,* Latinized form of *Stockholm.*] *Chem.* A metallic element, one of the rare-earth metals (see RARE EARTH). Symbol, *Ho;* at. no., 67; at. wt., 164.94. — **hol'mic** (-mĭk), *adj.*

holm oak (hōm). An evergreen oak (*Quercus ilex*) of southern Europe, with hollylike leaves; also, its wood.

hol'o- (hŏl'ō-; *often* hō'lō-, *esp. in scientific words*). [Gr. *holos.*] A combining form meaning *whole, entire,* as in **hol'o·cryp'tic, hol'o·sym'me·try.**

hol'o·blas'tic (-blăs'tĭk), *adj.* [*holo-* + *-blast* + *-ic.*] *Embryol.* Undergoing total or complete cleavage; — said of certain eggs, and opposed to *meroblastic.*

hol'o·caine (hŏl'ō·kān; hō'lō-), *n.* *Pharm.* = PHENACAINE.

hol'o·caust (hŏl'ō·kôst), *n.* [F. *holocauste,* fr. L., fr. Gr. *holokauston,* neut. of *holokaustos,* fr. *holos* whole + *kaustos* burnt.] **1.** A sacrificial offering the whole of which is consumed by fire. **2.** Hence, a complete or thorough sacrifice or destruction, esp. by fire, as of large numbers of human beings. — **hol'o·caus'tal** (-kôs'tăl; -t'l), *adj.* — **hol'o·caus'tic** (-tĭk), *adj.*

Hol'o·cene (hŏl'ō·sēn), *adj.* [*holo-* + Gr. *kainos* recent.] *Geol.* Pertaining to or designating the Recent epoch and the development of man from the neolithic stage onward.

Hol'o·fer'nes (hŏl'ō·fûr'nēz), *n.* See JUDITH.

hol'o·graph (hŏl'ō·gráf; 9), *n.* [F. or L.; F. *holographe,* fr. L., fr. Gr. *holographos,* fr. *holos* whole + *graphein* to write.] A document, as a will, wholly in the handwriting of the purported author. Cf. ONOMASTIC. — **hol'o·graph, hol'o·graph'ic** (-grăf'ĭk), **hol'o·graph'i·cal** (-ĭ·kăl), *adj.*

hol'o·he'dral (hŏl'ō·hē'drăl; hō'lō-), *adj.* [*holo-* + Gr. *hedra* seat, base.] *Cryst.* Having all the faces required by complete symmetry. Cf. HEMIHEDRAL, TETARTOHEDRAL.

hol'o·mor'phic (-môr'fĭk), *adj.* *Cryst.* Symmetrical in form as regards the two ends.

hol'o·phote (hŏl'ō·fōt), *n.* [*holo-* + Gr. *phōs, phōtos,* light.] An apparatus used in lighthouses, etc., in which, by means of lenses or reflectors, or both, a large amount of the light from the lamp is collected and thrown in the desired direction. — **hol'o·pho'tal** (-fō'tăl; -t'l), *adj.*

hol'o·phras'tic (-frăs'tĭk), *adj.* [*holo-* + Gr. *phrastikos* suited for expressing, fr. *phrazein* to speak.] Expressing a complex of ideas in a single word.

hol'o·thu'ri·an (hŏl'ō·thū'rĭ·ăn; hō'lō-), *n.* [L. *holothuria,* pl., a sort of water polyp, fr. Gr. *holothourion.*] *Zool.* Any of a class (Holo-

thurioidea) of echinoderms having an elongate, flexible, tough, muscular body; a sea cucumber. See TREPANG. — **hol'o·thu'ri·an**, *adj.*
hol'o·type (hŏl'ō·tīp), *n.* [*holo-* + *-type.*] *Biol.* That single specimen designated as the type of a species or lower group by the original author. Cf. TYPE SPECIMEN, TYPE SPECIES.
holp (hō(l)p), **hol'pen** (hō(l)'pĕn). See HELP.
Hol'stein–Frie'sian (hōl'stīn·frē'zhăn), *n.* Also **Hol'stein** (hōl'stīn; *popularly* -stēn). [From *Holstein* and *Friesland.* (See *Gaz.*)] One of a breed of black-and-white dairy cattle of very large size, orig. from North Holland and Friesland.
hol'ster (hōl'stẽr), *n.* [D.] A leather case for a pistol.
holt (hōlt), *n.* [AS.] *Archaic.* A wood; copse; wooded hill.
ho'lus–bo'lus (hō'lŭs·bō'lŭs), *adv.* All at once; altogether.
ho'ly (hō'lĭ), *adj.*; HO'LI·ER (-lĭ·ẽr); HO'LI·EST. [AS. *hālig;* akin to AS. *hāl* whole, well.] **1.** Set apart to the worship of God; hallowed; sacred. **2.** Worthy of adoration or veneration. **3.** Associated with Christ or events of his life; as, *holy* places, the *holy* cross. **4.** Spiritually whole; of unimpaired innocence or proved virtue; godly. — *n.*; *pl.* HOLIES (-lĭz). A holy thing or place, as a sanctuary.
holy city. A city which is the center of religious worship and traditions, as Jerusalem, Mecca, Rome, etc.; — *Holy City* [*caps.*] when used specifically.
Holy Communion. = EUCHARIST, 1 **a**.
ho'ly·day' (hō'lĭ·dā'), *n.* Also **holy day.** A religious feast day; holiday (sense 1).
Holy Father. A title of the pope.
Holy Ghost. The third person of the Trinity.
Holy Grail. See GRAIL.
Holy Innocents' Day. *Eccl.* A day (Dec. 28) commemorating the children slain by Herod (*Matt.* ii); — called also *Childermas.*
Holy Land. Palestine; — so called first in Zechariah ii. 12.
Holy Office. The tribunal of the Curia once called *Inquisition.*
holy of holies. The innermost apartment of the Jewish tabernacle and temple, where the ark was kept.
holy orders. The ranks, or orders, of the Christian ministry; specif.: **a** *R.C.Ch.* The orders of priest, deacon, and subdeacon. **b** *Anglican Communion.* The orders of bishop, priest, and deacon.
Holy Roman Empire. The medieval and modern empire of the German-speaking peoples of central Europe, from the crowning of Charlemagne as Emperor of the West at Rome in 800 (or from Otto I, 962–973) to Francis II (Francis I of Austria) in 1806.
Holy Saturday. The Saturday before Easter Sunday.
Holy See. *R.C.Ch.* The Apostolic See. See SEE, *n.*, 2.
Holy Spirit. The Holy Ghost.
ho'ly·stone' (hō'lĭ·stōn'), *n.* *Naut.* A soft sandstone used to scrub decks. — *v. t. & i.* To scrub with a holystone.
Holy Synod. The governing body in any of the Orthodox Churches.
Holy Thursday. **1.** *R.C.Ch.* The Thursday in Holy Week. **2.** *Anglican Communion.* The Thursday on which the Ascension is commemorated.
ho'ly·tide' (hō'lĭ·tīd'), *n.* A time devoted to religion.
holy water. Water blessed by a priest.
Holy Week. *Eccl.* The week before Easter, in which the passion of Christ is commemorated.
Holy Writ. The sacred Scriptures.
hom-. = HOMO-.
hom'age (hŏm'ĭj; ŏm'-), *n.* [OF., fr. ML. *hominaticum,* fr. L. *homo* a man, ML. also, a client, vassal.] *Feudal Law.* **1.** A ceremony by which a man acknowledged himself the vassal of a lord; also, the relation between the lord and his vassal. Cf. FEALTY. **2.** An act done or thing rendered as an acknowledgment of, or as part of the services required by, vassalage. **3.** Respect or reverential regard; deference; esp., respect paid by external action· obeisance. — **Syn.** See HONOR.
hom'ag·er (hŏm'ĭj·ẽr), *n.* A vassal.
hom'a·lo·graph'ic (hŏm'ȧ·lō·grăf'ĭk), *adj.* [Gr. *homalos* even + *-graphic.*] Preserving the mutual relations of parts; esp., **homalographic projection,** in map making, an equal-area projection in the form of an ellipse. See MOLLWEIDE PROJECTION.
hom'bre (ŏm'bẽr). Var. of OMBER.
‖**hom'bre** (ôm'brā), *n.*; *pl.* HOMBRES (-brās). [Sp.] Man; fellow.
Hom'burg hat (hŏm'bûrg; *Ger.* hôm'bŏŏrk). A man's soft felt hat with dented crown, first worn in Homburg, Germany.
home (hōm), *n.* [AS. *hām.*] **1.** One's dwelling place; abode of one's family. **2.** One's abode after death; the grave. **3.** The abiding place of the affections, esp. domestic affections. **4.** One's native land or place. **5.** Habitat; seat. **6.** An asylum. **7.** The social unit or center formed by a family living together. **8.** In various games, the goal; esp., *Baseball,* the plate, called also **home base** *or* **home plate.** — *adj.* **1.** Of or pertaining to home; domestic. **2.** That strikes home; poignant; intimate; effective; as, a *home* thrust. — *adv.* **1.** To one's home or country. **2.** To the vital center or seat; to the heart or core. **3.** To the place where it belongs; to the point aimed at; as, to drive a nail *home.* **4.** *Naut.* **a** To or towards the ship or its interior; as, the anchor came *home* slowly. **b** To or towards the land. — *v. t. & i.* To send to or place in a home; to go to or be in a home.
home-. = HOMEO-.
home'bred' (hōm'brĕd'; 2), *adj.* **1.** Bred at home; domestic; not foreign. **2.** Not polished; rude; uncultivated.
home'–brew', *n.* Drink, esp. malt liquor, brewed at home.
home economics. The science and art dealing with homemaking, esp. the selection and preparation of food and clothing, conditions of living, the use of income, the care and training of children, etc. Cf. HOUSEHOLD ARTS.
home'less, *adj.* Having no home. — **home'less·ness,** *n.*
home'like' (hōm'līk'), *adj.* Like a home; comfortable; cheerful; cozy; friendly. — **home'like·ness,** *n.*
home'ly (hōm'lĭ), *adj.*; HOME'LI·ER (-lĭ·ẽr); HOME'LI·EST. **1.** *Chiefly Archaic & Dial.* **a** Familiar; friendly; intimate. **b** Fond of one's home and home life. **2.** Characteristic of home life; simple; plain; unpretending; as, *homely* phrases; also (depreciatively) wanting polish or refinement; rude. **3.** Of plain or coarse features; plain; not comely. — **home'li·ness** (-lĭ·nĕs; -nĭs), *n.*
home'made' (hōm'mād'; 2), *adj.* Made at home; of domestic manufacture; hence, simple; plain.
home'mak'er (-māk'ẽr), *n.* One whose occupation is household management. — **home'mak'ing,** *n. & adj.*

ho'me·o-, ho'moe·o- (hō'mē·ō-; hŏm'ē·ō-), **ho·moi'o-** (hō·moi'ō-). [Gr. *homoios.*] A combining form meaning *like, similar,* as in *homeopathy.*
ho'me·o·mor'phism, ho'moe·o·mor'phism (-môr'fĭz'm), *n.* [Gr. *homoiomorphos* of like form, fr. *homoios* like + *morphē* form.] *Cryst.* A near similarity of crystalline forms between unlike chemical compounds. Cf. ISOMORPHISM. — **ho'me·o·mor'phous** (-fŭs), *adj.*
ho'me·o·path, ho'moe·o·path (hō'mē·ō·păth; hŏm'ē·ō-), *n.* A practitioner of homeopathy.
ho'me·o·path'ic, ho'moe·o·path'ic (-păth'ĭk), *adj.* Of or pert. to, or according to the principles of, homeopathy.
ho'me·op'a·thist, ho'moe·op'a·thist (-ŏp'ȧ·thĭst), *n.* A believer in, or practitioner of, homeopathy.
ho'me·op'a·thy, ho'moe·op'a·thy (-ŏp'ȧ·thĭ), *n.* [*homeo-, homoeo-* + *-pathy.*] *Med.* The theory or system of medical practice holding that disease is cured by remedies which produce on a healthy person effects similar to the symptoms of the complaint of the patient, the remedies being usually administered in minute doses. Cf. ALLOPATHY.
ho'me·o·sta'sis (hō'mē·ō·stā'sĭs; hŏm'ē·ō-), *n.* [NL., fr. *homeo-* + Gr. *stasis* condition.] A relatively stable state of equilibrium, or a tendency toward such a state, between the different but interdependent elements and subsystems of an organism of any kind. — **ho'me·o·stat'ic** -(stăt'ĭk), *adj.*
ho'me·o·ther'mal (-thûr'măl), **ho'me·o·ther'mic, ho'me·o·ther'mous.** Vars. of HOMOIOTHERMAL, etc.
ho'me·o·typ'ic, ho'moe·o·typ'ic (-tĭp'ĭk), **ho'me·o·typ'i·cal, ho'moe·o·typ'i·cal** (-ĭ·kăl), *adj.* *Biol.* Designating the second nuclear division in meiosis, in which the chromosomes divide equally.
ho'mer (hō'mẽr), *n.* [Heb. *hōmer.*] A Hebrew measure of capacity equal to ten ephahs; a kor.
hom'er (hōm'ẽr), *n.* **1.** *Colloq. Baseball.* A home run. **2.** = HOMING PIGEON.
Ho·mer'ic (hō·mĕr'ĭk), *adj.* Also **Ho·mer'i·cal** (-ĭ·kăl). Relating to, or characteristic or suggestive of, the Greek epic poet Homer, his age, style, or poems, or their contents. — **Ho·mer'i·cal·ly,** *adv.*
Homeric laughter. Inextinguishable or irrepressible laughter.
home rule. Government of a country, colony, district, etc., as to local and internal legislation, by power vested in the people within the country, district, etc. — **home ruler.**
home run. *Baseball.* A hit enabling the batter to make the complete circuit of the bases without the aid of an error by the opponents.
home'sick' (hōm'sĭk'), *adj.* Pining for home; in a nostalgic condition. — **home'sick'ness,** *n.*
home'spun' (-spŭn'), *adj.* **1.** Spun or wrought at home; coarse; plain. **2.** Made of homespun. — *n.* **1.** Cloth made at home, or of yarn spun at home, or like that of home make. **2.** *Obs.* A rustic.
home'stead (-stĕd), *n.* **1.** The home place; a home and the ground immediately connected with it. **2.** *Law.* The land and buildings thereon occupied by the owner as a home for himself and his family, and protected by law from the claims of creditors. — *v. t.*; HOME'STEAD·ED; HOME'STEAD·ING. *U. S.* To acquire or occupy as a homestead under homestead laws.
home'stead·er (-stĕd·ẽr), *n.* One who holds a homestead; specif., *U. S.*, one who has entered upon or acquired a homestead under provisions of homestead laws.
homestead law. **a** A law conferring special privileges or exemptions upon owners of homesteads; esp., a law exempting a homestead from attachment or sale under execution for general debts. **b** *U. S.* Any of several acts of Congress, esp. the first (**Homestead Act**), passed in 1862, authorizing the sale of public lands, in parcels of 160 acres each (*homesteads*), to settlers.
home'stretch' (hōm'strĕch'), *n.* That part of a racecourse between the last curve and the winning post; hence, the last part of any course, operation, etc.
home'ward (-wẽrd), **home'wards** (-wẽrdz), *adv.* Toward home.
home'ward (-wẽrd), *adj.* Being in the direction of home.
home'work' (-wûrk'), *n.* Work done or to be done at home; specif.: **a** Work let out by manufacturers or middlemen to be done in the home of the worker. **b** *Educ.* Any assignment for study or preparation outside the classroom.
home'y (hōm'ĭ), *adj.* Pertaining to home; homelike; intimate.
hom'i·cide (hŏm'ĭ·sīd), *n.* [OF., fr. L. *homicidium,* fr. *homicida* a manslayer, fr. *homo* man + *caedere* to cut, kill.] **1.** The killing of one human being by another. **2.** [OF., fr. L. *homicida.*] A manslayer. — **hom'i·cid'al** (-sīd'ăl; -'l; 2), *adj.*
hom'i·let'ic (-lĕt'ĭk), *adj.* Also **hom'i·let'i·cal** (-ĭ·kăl). [Gr. *homilētikos,* fr. *homilein* to be in company with.] Having the nature of a homily; of or pertaining to homiletics.
hom'i·let'ics (-ĭks), *n.*; see -ICS. The art of preaching; that branch of theology which treats of homilies or sermons.
hom'i·list (hŏm'ĭ·lĭst), *n.* One who delivers homilies.
hom'i·ly (-lĭ), *n.*; *pl.* -LIES (-lĭz). [OF. *omelie,* fr. LL., fr. Gr. *homilia* communion, converse, fr. *homilos* an assembly, fr. *homos* same + *ilē* a crowd.] **1.** A discourse or sermon. **2.** A tedious exhortation on some moral point.
hom'ing (hōm'ĭng), *adj.* Home-returning; also, dwelling.
homing pigeon. A pigeon trained to return home from a distance, often up to 500 miles. See CARRIER PIGEON.
hom'i·noid (hŏm'ĭ·noid), *adj.* [L. *homo, hominis,* man + *-oid.*] Resembling man; — applied esp. to certain fossils of uncertain relationship. — *n.* A manlike being.
hom'i·ny (hŏm'ĭ·nĭ), *n.* [From *rockahominy,* of Algonquian origin.] A food product prepared by removing the hulls from kernels of maize (hulled corn) and, in **hominy grits,** by grinding them into fragments coarser than in corn meal; also, a cooked dish of this product.
‖**homme d'es·prit'** (ôm' dĕs'prē'). [F.] A wit.
ho'mo (hō'mō), *n.*; *pl.* HOMINES (hŏm'ĭ·nēz). [L., man.] **1.** Man; a man. **2.** [*cap.*] *Zool.* The genus of mammals consisting of mankind, usually considered as belonging to the order (Primates) which contains also the monkeys, apes, and lemurs.
ho'mo- (hō'mō-; hŏm'ō-; *the accent & pron. vary with the number of syllables*), **hom-.** [Gr. *homos.*] **1.** A combining form denoting *one and the same, common, joint, like;* — often opp. to *hetero-,* as in *homogeneous, homonym.* **2.** *Chem.* Designating a *homologue* (usually the next higher) *of a* (specified) *compound,* as in **ho'mo·cre'o·sol,** $C_9H_{12}O_2$. **3.** *Immunol.* *For,* or *from,* or *to the same species,* as in **ho·mol'y·sin,** a form of hemolysin.

ho′mo·cen′tric (hō′mō·sĕn′trĭk; hŏm′ō-), *adj.* Having the same center.

ho′mo·cer′cal (-sûr′kăl), *adj.* [*homo-* + Gr. *kerkos* tail.] Having the upper and lower lobes nearly or quite symmetrical, with the vertebral column ending at or near the middle of the base; — said of the tail fin of certain fishes; also, having or pertaining to a tail fin of this structure.

ho′mo·chro·mat′ic (-krō·măt′ĭk), *adj.* [*homo-* + *chromatic.*] Consisting of, having, or pertaining to one color or hue; homochromous; — opposed to *heterochromatic.* — **ho′mo·chro′ma·tism** (-krō′mȧ·tĭz′m), *n.* — **ho′mo·chrome** (hō′mō·krōm; hŏm′ō-), *adj.*

ho′mo·chro′mous (-krō′mŭs), *adj.* [*homo-* + Gr. *chrōma* color.] Of the same or uniform color; — opposed to *heterochromous.*

ho′moe·o- (hō′mē·ō-; hŏm′ē·ō-). Var. of HOMEO-, as in:
homoeomorphism homoeopathic homoeopathy
homoeopath homoeopathist homoeotypic

ho′mo·er′o·tism (hō′mō·ĕr′ō·tĭz′m; hŏm′ō-), *n.* [*homo-* + *erotism.*] *Psychoanalysis.* Homosexuality. — **ho′mo·e·rot′ic** (-ē·rŏt′ĭk; -ĕ-), *adj.*

ho·mog′a·my (hō·mŏg′ȧ·mĭ), *n.* [Gr. *homogamos* married together, fr. *homos* the same + *gamos* marriage.] **1.** *Bot.* **a** State of having flowers alike throughout, as in the heads of plants of the chicory family; — opposed to *heterogamy.* **b** Maturing of the stamens and pistils at the same period; — opposed to *dichogamy.* **2.** The mating of like with like. — **ho·mog′a·mous** (-mŭs), *adj.*

ho′mo·ge·ne′i·ty (hō′mō·jē·nē′ĭ·tĭ; hŏm′ō-), *n.; pl.* -TIES (-tĭz). Homogeneous character.

ho′mo·ge′ne·ous (-jē′nē·ŭs; 58), *adj.* [ML. *homogeneus,* fr. Gr. *homogenēs,* fr. *homos* the same + *genos* race, kind.] **1.** Of the same kind or nature; consisting of similar parts or elements; — opposed to *heterogeneous.* **2.** *Math.* **a** Alike in nature and therefore comparable in size. **b** Of the same degree or dimensions; as, a *homogeneous* equation. — **Syn.** See SIMILAR. — **ho′mo·ge′ne·ous·ly,** *adv.* — **ho′mo·ge′ne·ous·ness,** *n.*

ho′mo·gen′e·sis (hō′mō·jĕn′ē·sĭs; hŏm′ō-), *n.* [*homo-* + *-genesis.*] *Biol.* That method of reproduction in which the successive generations are alike, no alternation of generations taking place.

ho·mog′e·nize (hō·mŏj′ē·nīz), *v. t.* To make homogeneous; specif., to pass (milk, cream, etc.) through an apparatus to break up the fat globules, casein shreds, etc., increasing digestibility. — **ho·mog′e·ni·za′tion** (-nĭ·zā′shŭn; -nī-), *n.* — **ho·mog′e·niz′er** (-nīz′ẽr), *n.*

ho·mog′e·nous (hō·mŏj′ē·nŭs), *adj.* *Biol.* Having a resemblance in structure due to descent from a common progenitor.

ho·mog′e·ny (-nĭ), *n.* [Gr. *homogeneia,* fr. *homos* the same + *genos* race, kind.] *Biol.* = HOMOLOGY, 2.

ho·mog′o·ny (hō·mŏg′ō·nĭ), *n.* [Gr. *homogonos,* fr. *homos* the same + *gonos* offspring.] *Bot.* The condition of having one kind of flowers with the androecium and gynoecium of uniform relative length; — opposed to *heterogony.* — **ho·mog′o·nous** (-nŭs), *adj.* — **ho·mog′o·nous·ly,** *adv.*

hom′o·graph (hŏm′ō·grăf; hō′mō-; 9), *n.* [Gr. *homographos* with the same letters, fr. *homos* + *graphein* to write.] One of two or more words identical in orthography, but different in derivation and meaning, as *fair,* market, and *fair,* beautiful; *lead,* to conduct, and *lead,* metal. — **hom′o·graph′ic** (-grăf′ĭk), *adj.*

ho·moi′o- (hō·moi′ō-). Var. of HOMEO-.

ho·moi′o·ther′mic (-thûr′mĭk), *adj.* Also **ho·moi′o·ther′mal** (-măl), **ho·moi′o·ther′mous** (-mŭs). *Physiol. & Zool.* Having a relatively uniform body temperature; warm-blooded.

Ho′moi·ou′si·an (hō′moi·ōō′sĭ·ăn; -ou′sĭ·ăn), *n. & adj.* [Gr. *homoiousios, homoioousios,* of like substance, fr. *homoios* like + *ousia* the substance, being, essence.] *Eccl. Hist.* (One) holding a doctrine midway between that of the Homoousians and Heteroousians, and affirming the essential likeness of the Son to the Father. — **Ho′moi·ou′si·an·ism** (-ĭz′m), *n.*

ho·mol′o·gate (hō·mŏl′ō·gāt), *v. t.* [ML. *homologatus,* past part. of *homologare* to homologate, fr. Gr. *homologein* to assent, agree.] *Civil Law.* To approve; allow; confirm. — *v. i.* To be or act in accord or agreement.

ho′mo·log′i·cal (hō′mō·lŏj′ĭ·kăl; hŏm′ō-), *adj.* Also **ho′mo·log′ic** (-ĭk). Homologous. — **ho′mo·log′i·cal·ly,** *adv.*

ho·mol′o·gize (hō·mŏl′ō·jīz), *v. t.* To make homologous; specif., *Biol.,* to determine the existence of homology between, as parts.

ho·mol′o·gous (-gŭs), *adj.* [ML. or Gr.; ML. *homologus,* fr. Gr. *homologos* assenting, agreeing, fr. *homos* the same + *logos* speech, proportion.] **1.** Having the same relative position, proportion, value, or structure. **2.** *Biol.* Exhibiting homology. **3.** *Chem.* Having the relation of compounds of a series whose successive members possess similarity in structure but regular difference in formula. **4.** *Immunol., Med., etc.* Having the relation of an immune serum and the particular species of bacterium by means of which it is prepared.

hom′o·lo·graph′ic (hŏm′ō·lō·grăf′ĭk), *adj.* = HOMALOGRAPHIC.

hom′o·logue (hŏm′ō·lŏg; 74), *n.* Also **hom′o·log.** That which is homologous to something else; as, the members or terms of a homologous series in chemistry are the *homologues* of each other; specif., *Biol.,* a part or organ exhibiting homology.

ho·mol′o·gy (hō·mŏl′ō·jĭ), *n.* [Gr. *homologia* agreement. See HOMOLOGOUS.] **1.** Quality of being homologous. **2.** *Biol.* Fundamental similarity of structure, regardless of function, due to descent from a common ancestral form; as, the wing of a bird and the forelimb of a horse exhibit *homology;* — opposed to *heterology* and distinguished from *analogy.* **3.** *Chem.* The relation existing between the compounds of a series whose successive members possess, in addition to similarity of structure, a regular difference in formula.

ho·mol′o·sine (hō·mŏl′ō·sĭn; -sīn), *adj.* [*homolo-* for *homalo-,* fr. Gr. *homalos* even + L. *sinus* curve.] Preserving proportional areas by sinusoids; specif., **homolosine projection,** a map first developed in 1923 by the American geographer J. Paul Goode, showing the land areas of the globe on a sinusoidal projection from the equator to latitude 40° and on a homalographic (Mollweide) projection for the outer areas. The map is interrupted and presents a minimum of distortion.

ho′mo·mor′phism (hō′mō·môr′fĭz′m; hŏm′ō-), *n.* Likeness in form; as: **a** *Biol.* = HOMOMORPHY. **b** *Bot.* State of having perfect flowers of only one type or kind. **c** *Zool.* Similarity of the larva and the adult. — **ho′mo·mor′phic** (-fĭk), *adj.* — **ho′mo·mor′phous** (-fŭs), *adj.*

ho′mo·mor′phy (hō′mō·môr′fĭ; hŏm′ō-), *n.* [*homo-* + Gr. *morphē* form.] *Biol.* Similarity of form with different fundamental structure; superficial resemblance between organisms of different groups.

hom′o·nym (hŏm′ō·nĭm; hō′mō-), *n.* [See HOMONYMOUS.] **1.** A word having the same pronunciation as another, but differing from it in origin, meaning, and often, in spelling, as *bare* and *bear;* a homophone. **2.** One of two or more having the same name; a namesake. **3.** *Biol.* A preoccupied generic or specific name, rejected on the basis of the law of priority, which requires the use of the oldest published available name. — **ho′mo·nym′ic** (hō′mō·nĭm′ĭk; hŏm′ō-), *adj.*

ho·mon′y·mous (hō·mŏn′ĭ·mŭs), *adj.* [L. *homonymus,* fr. Gr. *homōnymos,* fr. *homos* the same + *onyma,* for *onoma* name.] **a** Having the same name. **b** Having the qualities of a homonym or homonyms.

ho·mon′y·my (-mĭ), *n.* Homonymous state or character.

Ho′mo·ou′si·an (hō′mō·ōō′sĭ·ăn; -ou′sĭ·ăn; hŏm′ō-), *n. & adj.* [Gr. *homoousios,* fr. *homos* the same + *ousia* being, essence, substance.] *Eccl. Hist.* (One) holding that the Son of God is of the same essence or substance with the Father. Cf. HOMOIOUSIAN, HETEROOUSIAN. — **Ho′mo·ou′si·an·ism** (-ĭz′m), *n.*

hom′o·phone (hŏm′ō·fōn; hō′mō-), *n.* **1.** A letter or character expressing a like sound with another. **2.** A homonym (sense 1).

hom′o·phon′ic (-fŏn′ĭk), *adj.* [Gr. *homophōnos,* fr. *homos* the same + *phōnē* sound, tone.] *Music.* **a** Orig., sounding alike; of the same pitch; unisonous. Cf. ANTIPHONAL. **b** Of or pertaining to homophony; monodic; monophonic.

ho·moph′o·nous (hō·mŏf′ō·nŭs), *adj.* **1.** = HOMOPHONIC **a.** **2.** Having or representing the same sound (Greek ϕ and English *ph*). Cf. HOMOPHONE.

ho·moph′o·ny (hō·mŏf′ō·nĭ; hŏm′ō·fō′nĭ), *n.* Sameness of sound; specif.: *Music.* **a** Unison. **b** = MONODY, 3 **a.**

ho·mop′la·sy (hō·mŏp′lȧ·sĭ; hō′mō·plăs′ĭ; hŏm′ō-), *n.* [*homo-* + *-plasy.*] *Biol.* Correspondence between parts or organs not due to their modification from a common ancestral type, but acquired independently; analogy. — **ho′mo·plas′tic** (hō′mō·plăs′tĭk; hŏm′ō-), *adj.*

ho′mo·po′lar (hō′mō·pō′lẽr; hŏm′ō-), *adj.* [*homo-* + *polar.*] *Chem.* Designating, pert. to, or characterized by a union of atoms of like state as regards polarity, as in the ordinary covalent bond; — dist. from *heteropolar, polar,* or *ionic.* — **ho′mo·po·lar′i·ty** (-pō·lăr′ĭ·tĭ), *n.*

ho·mop′ter·ous (hō·mŏp′tẽr·ŭs), *adj.* [*homo-* + Gr. *pteron* wing.] *Zool.* Belonging to a large order (Homoptera) of insects having sucking mouth parts, comprising the cicadas, aphids, scale insects, etc. — **ho·mop′ter·an** (-ăn), *adj. & n.*

Ho′mo sa′pi·ens (hō′mō sā′pĭ·ĕnz). [L. See HOMO; SAPIENT.] Man, regarded as a biological species.

ho′mo·sex′u·al′i·ty (hō′mō·sĕk′shōō·ăl′ĭ·tĭ; hŏm′ō-), *n.* Eroticism for one of the same sex. — **ho′mo·sex′u·al** (-sĕk′shōō·ăl; *cf.* SEXUAL), *adj. & n.*

ho·mos′po·rous (hō·mŏs′pō·rŭs; hō′mō·spō′rŭs; 70), *adj.* [*homo-* + *-sporous.*] *Bot.* Having asexual spores of one kind only; — opposed to *heterosporous.* — **ho·mos′po·ry** (hō·mŏs′pō·rĭ), *n.*

ho′mo·tax′is (hō′mō·tăk′sĭs; hŏm′ō-), *n.* [NL., fr. *homo-* + *-taxis.*] Similarity in arrangement; esp., *Geol.,* similarity in fossils and in order of arrangement of stratified deposits which are not necessarily contemporaneous. — **ho′mo·tax′ic** (-sĭk), *adj.*

ho′mo·thal′lic (-thăl′ĭk), *adj.* [*homo-* + Gr. *thallos* young shoot.] *Bot.* Having a single type of mycelium with two kinds of branches (hyphae), which function as opposite sexes in reproduction; — opp. to *heterothallic.*

ho′mo·zy·go′sis (-zī·gō′sĭs; -zĭ-), *n.* [NL., fr. *homo-* + Gr. *zygōsis* a balancing, fr. *zygon* yoke.] *Biol.* The union of gametes to form a homozygote; the state of being a homozygote.

ho′mo·zy′gote (-zī′gōt; -zĭg′ōt), *n.* [*homo-* + *zygote.*] *Biol.* An animal or plant containing either member (not both) of at least one pair of allelomorphic Mendelian characters. Cf. HETEROZYGOTE. — **ho′mo·zy′gous** (-zī′gŭs), *adj.*

ho·mun′cu·lus (hō·mŭng′kū·lŭs), *n.; pl.* -CULI (-lī). [L., dim. of *homo* man.] A little man; a dwarf; manikin; also, the human fetus.

hom′y (hōm′ĭ), *adj.;* HOM′I·ER (hōm′ĭ·ẽr); HOM′I·EST. Homey.

hone (hōn), *n.* [AS. *hān* a stone.] **1.** A fine whetstone, esp. for razors. **2.** A tool for enlarging holes to precise tolerances and controlled finishes by means of a mechanically rotated and expanded abrasive. — *v. t.* To sharpen, dress, or enlarge with a hone.

hone, *v. i.* [F. *hogner.*] *Dial.* To grumble; lament; also, to yearn.

hon′est (ŏn′ĕst; -ĭst), *adj.* [OF. *honeste, oneste,* fr. L. *honestus,* fr. *honos, honor,* honor.] **1.** *Archaic.* Honorable; hence, creditable. **2.** Characterized by integrity and straightforwardness in conduct, thought, speech, etc.; free from fraud. **3.** Genuine, full, or unadulterated; as, *honest* goods. **4.** Open; frank; as, an *honest* countenance. **5.** *Archaic.* Chaste. — **Syn.** See UPRIGHT. — **hon′est·ly,** *adv.*

hon′es·ty (ŏn′ĕs·tĭ; -ĭs·tĭ), *n.* **1.** Quality or state of being honest; specif.: **a** *Obs.* Honor. **b** Integrity; truthfulness; freedom from fraud. **c** *Archaic.* Chastity. **2.** Any of a genus (*Lunaria*) of European plants of the mustard family.

Syn. Honesty, honor, integrity, probity mean uprightness as shown in one's character or action. **Honesty** implies a refusal to lie, steal, or deceive in any way; **honor,** a fastidious allegiance to the standards of one's profession, calling, or position; **integrity,** such rectitude that one is incapable of being false to a trust, a responsibility, a pledge, etc.; **probity,** tried and proved honesty or integrity.

hone′wort′ (hōn′wûrt′), *n.* Any of several plants of the carrot family, as the stone parsley.

hon′ey (hŭn′ĭ), *n.; pl.* HONEYS (-ĭz). [AS. *hunit.*] **1.** A sweet viscid material produced in the honey sac of bees out of the nectar of flowers. **2.** Honeylike quality or character. **3.** Sweet one; — a term of endearment. — *adj.* Resembling honey; sweet; hence, dear; precious. — *v. t.;* HON′EYED or HON′IED (-ĭd); HON′EY·ING. **1.** To make sweet, as with honey. **2.** To make (speech, language, etc.) affectedly endearing or intimate; hence, to flatter or conciliate. — *v. i.* To be gentle, agreeable, or coaxing; also, to become obsequious; to fawn.

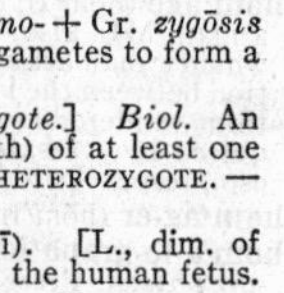

Honeybee (Worker). (⅔)

hon′ey·bee′ (-bē′), *n.* Any of certain social honey-producing bees (genus *Apis* and allied genera), esp. those of the species *Apis mellifera,* native to Europe, kept for their honey and wax in most parts of the world.

hon′ey·comb′ (hŭn′ĭ·kōm′), *n.* [AS. *hunigcamb.*] **1.** The mass of hexagonal cells of wax built by honeybees. **2.** Any substance, as cast iron, tripe, etc., having cells suggesting a honeycomb. — *v. t. & i.* To make or become full of holes or cavities like a honeycomb. — *adj.* **1.** Of, like, or pertaining to honeycomb; esp., having a pattern resembling that of honeycomb; as, a *honeycomb* radiator. **2.** *Radio.* Pertaining to a type of basket-weave coil winding in which spaces are left which suggest cells of a honeycomb.

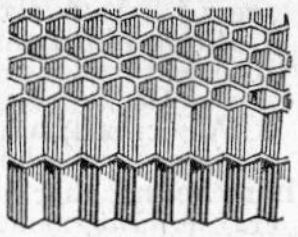
Honeycomb, 1.

hon′ey·dew′ (hŭn′ĭ·dū′), *n.* **a** The sweet material exuding from the leaves of many plants in hot weather. **b** A honeylike secretion produced by many homopterous insects.

honeydew melon. A sweet, smooth-skinned, white variety of muskmelon.

honey eater. Also **hon′ey·suck′er** (hŭn′ĭ·sŭk′ẽr), *n.* Any of a numerous family (Meliphagidae) of oscine birds of Australasia which extract nectar and insects from flowers. Well-known species are the wattlebirds and the friarbirds.

hon′eyed (hŭn′ĭd), *past & past part.* of HONEY. Specif., *adj.* Abounding with, or like, honey; sweet.

honey guide. Any of two genera (*Indicator* and *Prodotiscus*) of small, plainly colored nonpasserine birds of Africa, the Himalayas, and the East Indies. They lead men and animals to the nests of bees.

honey locust. An ornamental North American tree (*Gleditsia triacanthos*) of the senna family, bearing spines on the trunk and having bipinnate leaves.

hon′ey·moon′ (hŭn′ĭ·mōōn′), *n.* The first month or so after marriage; the holiday spent by a couple after marriage. — **hon′ey·moon′**, *v. i.*

honey sac. In bees, the distention of the esophagus, in which the honey is produced.

hon′ey·suck′er (hŭn′ĭ·sŭk′ẽr), *n.* The honey eater.

hon′ey·suck′le (-sŭk″l), *n.* [AS. *hunigsūce* privet. See HONEY; SUCK.] **1.** *Obs.* Clover. **2.** Any of a genus (*Lonicera*) of shrubs typifying a family (Caprifoliaceae, the honeysuckle family) of woody vines, shrubs, or perennial herbs having opposite leaves and, often, showy flowers. See TRUMPET FLOWER, 2 **b**. **3.** Any of several other fragrant-flowered plants; — usually with qualifying adjective; as, the ***bush honeysuckle*** (*Diervilla*), esp. the yellow-flowered species (*D. lonicera*) of northeastern U. S., blooming in early summer, and the ***swamp honeysuckle, or swamp azalea*** (*Azalea viscosa*) of the eastern United States. See AZALEA.

hong (hŏng), *n.* [Chin. (Pek.) *hang*², Cant. *hong* a mercantile house, factory.] An establishment, warehouse, or trading station for foreign trade in China, as formerly at Canton.

Hong Kong dollar (hŏng′ kŏng′; 2). See DOLLAR, 1 **a**.

hon′ied (hŭn′ĭd). Var. of HONEYED.

‖**ho′ni′ soit qui mal y pense** (ô′nē′ swȧ′ kē mȧl′ ē päɴs′). [F.] Shamed be he who thinks evil of it; — motto of the Order of the Garter, being a reputed remark of Edward III when (c. 1344) he tied upon his own leg the Countess of Salisbury's garter, which had fallen off while he danced with her.

honk (hŏngk; 74), *n.* [Imitative.] The cry of a wild goose or a sound likened to it, as the noise of a horn. — **honk**, *v. i.*

honk′y–tonk′ (hŏngk′ĭ·tŏngk′), *n.* [Cf. E. dial. *honk* to idle about.] *U. S.* A low drinking resort.

hon′or, hon′our (ŏn′ẽr), *n.* [OF. *honor, onur*, fr. L. *honor, honos.*] **1.** Esteem due or paid to worth; manifestation of respect; hence, fame; credit; good name. **2.** That to which esteem is paid; distinguished position. **3.** A token of esteem paid to worth; as: **a** A mark of respect, as a title. **b** *Obs.* A bow; a curtsy. **c** A ceremonial sign of consideration; as, civil *honors*. **d** *pl.* Social courtesies; as, to do the *honors* of the table. **4.** A title applied to the holders of certain civil offices; as, His *Honor* the Mayor. **5. a** That which rightfully attracts esteem, as dignity and courage; esp., excellence of character; in men, integrity; uprightness; in women, purity; chastity. **b** A nice sense of what is right, just, and true; as, a man of *honor*. **6.** One whose worth brings respect and fame; as, he is an *honor* to his nation. **7.** *pl. Educ.* A grade of academic distinction awarded for high proficiency **8.** *Games.* **a** *Cards. pl.* (1) *Whist.* The ace, king, queen and jack of trumps. (2) *Bridge.* The five highest cards of the trump suit, or the four aces at no-trump; also, all scores above the line, counting nothing toward game, but affecting the value of the rubber. **b** *Golf.* The privilege of playing first from the tee.

Syn. (1) **Honor, homage, reverence, deference, obeisance** mean respect and honor shown to another. **Honor** implies both the recognition of one's title to respect and esteem or any manifestation of such recognition; **homage** specifically implies accompanying praise and tributes; **reverence**, profound respect mingled with love or devotion; **deference**, such respect for the person or the position, such reverence for his personality, or the like, that one courteously yields one's judgment or preference to his; **obeisance**, a show of honor or reverence by some act or gesture that indicates humility, submission, or the like
(2) See HONESTY.

— *v. t.* **1.** To regard or treat with honor, as by due obedience and courtesy; also, as used of the Supreme Being, to adore; worship. **2.** To bestow honor upon; to elevate in rank or station; to ennoble; exalt. **3.** *Com.* To accept and pay when due; as, to *honor* a draft.

hon′or·a·ble, hon′our·a·ble (ŏn′ẽr·ȧ·b′l), *adj.* **1.** Worthy of honor: **a** Noble; illustrious. **b** Commendable; estimable. **c** Of reputable association or use; respectable. **2.** Performed or accompanied with marks of honor; as, an *honorable* burial. **3.** Conferring honor, or procured by noble deeds. **4.** Entitled to honor; — a title of distinction given to certain officials, usually simply as a courtesy title. Abbr. *Hon.* **5.** Characterized or actuated by honor; as, an *honorable* man. — **Syn.** See UPRIGHT. — **hon′or·a·ble·ness**, *n.* — **hon′or·a·bly**, *adv.*

hon′o·rar′i·um (ŏn′ō·râr′ĭ·ŭm; hŏn′ō-), *n.; pl.* -IA (-ȧ), -IUMS (-ŭmz). [L. (sc. *donum*), fr. *honorarius.*] An honorary payment or reward, usually in recognition of gratuitous or professional services on which custom or propriety forbids any price to be set.

hon′or·ar′y (ŏn′ẽr·ẽr′ĭ *or, esp. Brit.*, -ẽr·ĭ), *adj.* [L. *honorarius*, fr. *honor* honor.] **1.** Done or conferred as a sign of honor. **2.** Designating a title or place which is held without rendering service or receiving the emoluments or privileges usual to it; also, holding such a title or place. **3.** Depending on one's honor, as for fulfillment; as, an *honorary* debt.

hon′or·er, hon′our·er (ŏn′ẽr·ẽr), *n.* One who honors.

hon′or·if′ic (-ĭf′ĭk), *adj.* Also **hon′or·if′i·cal** (-ĭ·kăl). [L. *honorificus.* See HONOR; -FIC.] Conferring or importing honor or respect; esp., designating a class of epithets in Chinese, Japanese, etc., used in respectful address. — *n.* An honorific word or phrase. — **hon′or·if′i·cal·ly**, *adv.*

honor point. See ESCUTCHEON, *Illust.*

hon′ors of war (ŏn′ẽrz). *Mil.* Distinctions or privileges granted to a vanquished enemy, as of marching out from a camp or town armed and with colors flying.

hon′our, hon′our·a·ble, etc. Brit. spelling of HONOR, HONORABLE, etc.

hooch (hōōch), *n.* Short for HOOCHINOO; hence, *Slang, U. S.*, crude ardent spirits, esp. liquor surreptitiously made or obtained.

hoo′chi·noo′ (hōō′chĭ·nōō′), *n.* [Var. of *Hutsnuwu*, name of a Tlingit tribe, applied to an alcoholic drink made by the Indians.] A distilled liquor made by Alaska Indians.

hood (hŏŏd), *n.* [AS. *hōd.*] **1.** A flexible covering for the head and neck, as on a robe or mantle. **2.** Hence: **a** A monk's cowl. **b** An ornamental fold at the back of an academic gown or ecclesiastical vestment. **c** A covering for a horse's head. **3.** Something resembling a hood in form or use, as the top of a carriage or automobile, a chimney top, a hood-shaped flower petal, etc. **4.** *Falconry.* A covering for a hawk's head and eyes. See FALCON, *Illust.* **5.** *Mach.* A cover for parts of mechanisms; specif., the removable metal covering over the engine of an automobile; bonnet. Cf. COWL, 3. **6.** *Zool.* A crest. — *v. t.* To cover with or as with a hood; to furnish with a hood or hood-shaped appendage.

hood, *n.* [By shortening.] *Slang.* A hoodlum.

-hood (-hŏŏd). [ME. *-hod, -had*, fr. *hod, had*, rank, condition, fr. AS. *hād.*] A noun-forming suffix, denoting in general *state, condition, quality, character*, as in man*hood*, state or character of being a man. These nouns often develop various secondary senses, esp.: (1) A concrete instance or example of the quality or state, as a false*hood*. (2) A collective total of those having the given character or state, as a brother*hood*.

hood′ed (hŏŏd′ĕd; -ĭd), *adj.* **1.** Covered or furnished with a hood. **2.** Hood-shaped; esp., *Bot.*, cucullate, as the spathe of the jack-in-the-pulpit. See SPADIX, *Illust.* **3.** *Zool.* **a** Having the head conspicuously different in color from the rest of the plumage; — said of birds. **b** Having a hoodlike crest on the head. **c** Having the skin at each side of the neck capable of expansion by movements of the ribs, as the cobra.

hooded seal. A large North Atlantic seal (*Cystophora cristata*). The male has a large, inflatable, hoodlike sac upon the fore part of the head.

hood′ie, hood′y (hŏŏd′ĭ; *Scot.* hŏŏd′ĭ), *n.; pl.* HOODIES (-ĭz). The European hooded crow (*Corvus cornix*).

hood′lum (hōōd′lŭm), *n.* *Colloq.* A young rowdy; also, a gangster.

hood′man (hŏŏd′măn), *n.* *Archaic.* The person blindfolded in **hood′man–blind′** (-blīnd′), or blindman's buff.

hoo′doo (hōō′dōō), *n.* **1.** = VOODOO. **2.** *Colloq.* One who or that which brings bad luck. **3.** *Western U. S.* A natural rock pile of fantastic shape. — *v. t.;* HOO′DOOED (-dōōd); HOO′DOO·ING. *Colloq.* To be a hoodoo to; to bring bad luck to.

hood′wink (hŏŏd′wĭngk), *v. t.* [*hood* + *wink.*] **1.** To blind by covering the eyes. **2.** To cover; to hide, as by dissembling. **3.** To deceive; to impose upon. — **hood′wink·er**, *n.*

hoo′ey (hōō′ĭ), *interj. & n.* *Slang, U. S.* Nonsense.

hoof (hōōf; 85), *n.; pl.* HOOFS (hōōfs), HOOVES (hōōvz). [AS. *hōf.*] **1.** The covering of horn which protects the ends of the digits of ungulates, as the horse, swine, etc.; also, the foot as a whole, esp. of a horse. **2.** A hoofed animal; a beast. — *v. t. & i.* **a** To walk. **b** To trample with the hoofs.

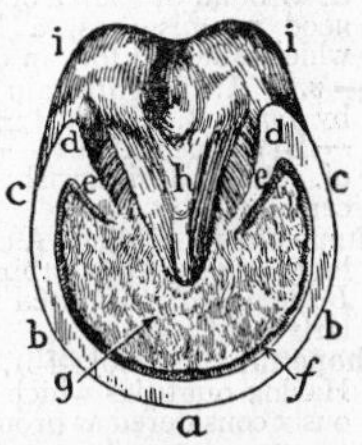

Hoof of a Horse, unshod. *a, b, c, d* Parts of Wall (*a* Toe, *b, b* Side Walls, *c, c* Quarters, *d, d* Buttresses); *e, e* Bars; *f* White Line; *g* Sole; *h* Frog; *i, i* Bulbs.

hoof′bound′ (-bound′), *adj.* Having a dry and contracted hoof.

hoofed (hōōft), *adj.* Furnished with hoofs; ungulate.

hoof′er (hōōf′ẽr), *n.* *Slang.* A clog dancer or a tap dancer.

hoof′print′ (hōōf′prĭnt′), *n.* An impression made by a hoof.

hook (hŏŏk), *n.* [AS. *hōc.*] **1.** A curved or bent implement for catching, holding, sustaining, or pulling anything. **2.** An implement for cutting or lopping, as a sickle. **3.** A snare; trap. **4.** Something resembling a hook in form, as a spit or narrow cape turned landward at the outer end, an angular or recurved mark in a written character, a recurved part of a plant or animal, etc. **5.** *Baseball.* A curve. **6.** *Boxing.* A short swinging blow with the elbow bent and rigid. **7.** *Golf.* A stroke in which the ball curves to the left of the intended line of play (with a right-handed player). Cf. SLICE, *v. t.*, 5. **8.** *Music.* One of the cross strokes on notes of small denomination; — called also *pennant.* The eighth note 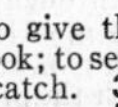 has one hook, the 16th note 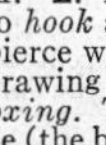 has two, etc. — ***by hook or by crook.*** One way or other; by any means. — *v. t.* **1.** To give the form of a hook to; crook. **2.** To catch or fasten with a hook; to seize or hold with a hook; as, to *hook* a trout; hence, to secure; catch. **3.** To steal; pilfer. **4.** To pierce with the horns, as cattle; to gore. **5.** To work, as canvas, by drawing loops of yarn, etc., through it with a hook. **6.** *Sports.* **a** *Boxing.* To strike with a hook. **b** *Cricket.* To pull. **c** *Golf.* To strike (the ball) so that a hook results. — *v. i.* **1.** To bend; to curve as a hook. **2.** *Slang.* To make off; clear out; — often with *it.* **3.** To be caught or fastened by or as if by a hook; as, a dress that *hooks.*

hook′ah, hook′a (hŏŏk′ȧ), *n.* [Ar. *huqqah* a round box, a bottle through which tobacco fumes pass.] A pipe with a long flexible stem, so arranged that the smoke is cooled by passing through water. Cf. HUBBLE-BUBBLE, NARGHILE.

hooked (hŏŏkt *or* hŏŏk′ĕd; -ĭd), *adj.* **1.** Having the form of a hook. **2.** Provided with a hook or hooks; made with hooks; as, a *hooked* rug. — **hook′ed·ness** (hŏŏk′ĕd·nĕs; -ĭd-; -nĭs), *n.*

hook′er (hŏŏk′ẽr), *n.* [D. *hoeker* fishing vessel, fr. *hoek* hook.] **a** A fishing boat with one mast, used on the coasts of England and Ireland. **b** A sailor's contemptuous term for any old or clumsy seagoing craft.

hook′up′ (-ŭp′), *n.* **1.** An assemblage of apparatus, circuits, etc., used for a specific purpose, as for radio transmission or reception; also, the plan of such an assemblage. **2.** *Colloq.* Establishment of relations or connections; alliance; as, a *hookup* between two governments.

hook′worm′ (hŏŏk′wûrm′), *n.* Any of certain parasitic nematode worms (genera *Ancylostoma, Necator,* etc.) having strong buccal hooks or plates.

hookworm disease. *Med.* Disease caused by hookworms; ancylostomiasis; uncinariasis.

hook′y (hŏŏk′ĭ), *n.* A word used in the phrase ***to play hooky,*** to run away, to play truant.

hoo′li·gan (hōō′lĭ·găn), *n.* [After an Irish family in London.] *Orig. Slang, Eng.* A loafer or ruffian, like the hoodlum. — **hoo′li·gan,** *adj.* — **hoo′li·gan·ism** (-ĭz′m), *n.*

hoo′ly (hōō′lĭ; *dial. also* **hŭ′lĭ, hü′lĭ**), *adj. & adv. Scot.* Wary; soft; slow.

hoop (hōōp; 85), *n.* [AS. *hōp.*] **1.** A circular strip for holding together the staves of casks, tubs, etc., or any of various purposes. **2.** Something resembling a hoop; a ring; circlet; specif., a finger ring. **3.** A circle, or combination of circles, of elastic material, used for expanding the skirts (***hoop skirts***) of ladies' dresses; — chiefly in *pl.* **4.** *Croquet.* An arch or wicket. — *v. t.* To bind or fasten with hoops; hence, to clasp; surround.

hoop′er (hōōp′ẽr), *n.* One who puts hoops on casks or tubs; a cooper.

hoo′poe (hōō′pōō), *n.* [F. *huppe,* fr. L. *upupa.*] Any of a family (Upupidae) of Old World nonpasserine birds having a slender curved bill.

hoo·ray′ (hŏŏ·rā′). Var. of HURRAH.

hoose′gow, hoos′gow (hōōs′gou; -gô), *n.* Also **hoose′-gaw.** [Perh. fr. Sp. *juzgado* a court.] *Slang, U. S.* A jail; lockup; guardhouse.

Hoo′sier (hōō′zhẽr), *n. U. S.* An inhabitant of the State of Indiana, the **Hoosier State;** — a nickname.

hoot (hōōt), *v. i.* **1.** To utter a loud shout; now usually, to cry out in contempt. **2.** To make a sound resembling that of *hoot;* specif., to utter the cry of an owl. — *v. t.* **1.** To assail with contemptuous cries. **2.** To express in hoots. — *n.* **1.** A loud inarticulate shout or noise; esp., a derisive shout. **2.** The cry of an owl. — **hoot′er,** *n.*

hoot (hōōt; ōōt), **hoots** (hōōts; ōōts), *interj. Scot.* Hush; tut; — an exclamation of impatience, dissatisfaction, etc.

hooves (hōōvz), *n., pl.* of HOOF.

hop (hŏp), *v. i.;* HOPPED (hŏpt); HOP′PING. [AS. *hoppian* to leap, dance.] **1.** To move by a quick springy leap or successive leaps, as do birds, toads, grasshoppers, etc.; also, to spring or jump on one foot. **2.** *Colloq.* To dance. **3.** *Slang.* Loosely, to go; as, *hop* to it. — *v. t.* **1.** To hop, or leap, about or over. **2.** *Colloq.* To get upon by or as by hopping; as, to *hop* a freight. — *n.* **1.** A short brisk leap, esp. on one leg. **2.** *Colloq.* A dance; esp., an informal dance or ball. **3.** A flight in an aircraft.

hop, *n.* [MD. *hoppe* (D. *hop*).] **1.** A twining vine (*Humulus lupulus*) with 3-lobed or 5-lobed leaves and inconspicuous flowers, the pistillate ones in glandular, conelike catkins. **2.** *pl.* The ripe dried pistillate catkins of these plants used in medicine, and to impart a bitter flavor to malt liquors.

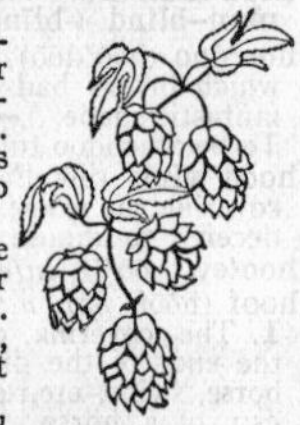

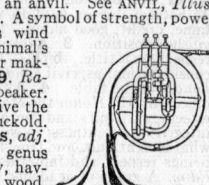

Hop, leaves and strobiles. (⅓)

hope (hōp), *n.* [AS. *hopa, tōhopa.*] **1.** Desire with expectation of obtaining what is desired, or belief that it is obtainable. **2.** Trust; reliance. **3.** Ground or source of happy expectation; hence, good promise; as, a land of *hope.* **4.** That which is hoped for; an object of hope. — *v. i.* **1.** To entertain hope; — usually followed by *for.* **2.** To trust; — usually followed by *in.* — **Syn.** See EXPECT. — *v. t.* **1.** To cherish hope of. **2.** To desire; wish; trust; — often used colloquially regarding uncertainties.

hope chest. *Colloq.* A chest or box in which a young woman accumulates an outfit of clothing, linen, etc., in anticipation of her marriage. *Bottom drawer* is used in England of a drawer, as in a dresser, similarly used.

hope′ful (hōp′fŏŏl; -f'l), *adj.* **1.** Full of hope; inclined to hope. **2.** Having qualities which excite hope. — *n.* A young person humorously considered as promising. — **-ful·ly,** *adv.* — **-ful·ness,** *n.*

hope′less (-lĕs; -lĭs), *adj.* **1.** Destitute of hope; despairing. **2.** Giving no ground of hope; desperate; as, a *hopeless* cause. — **Syn.** See DESPONDENT. — **hope′less·ly,** *adv.* — **hope′less·ness,** *n.*

Ho′pi (hō′pē), *n.* One of a Shoshonean tribe of Pueblo Indians, noted for their weaving and dyeing and their religious ceremonies.

hop′lite (hŏp′līt), *n.* [Gr. *hoplitēs,* fr. *hoplon* tool, weapon.] *Gr. Antiq.* A heavy-armed infantry soldier.

hop′-o′-my-thumb′ (hŏp′ō·mĭ·thŭm′; *Brit.* -mĭ·thŭm′), *n.* A very diminutive person; a pygmy.

hop′per (hŏp′ẽr), *n.* **1.** One that hops. **2.** The larva of a fly (*Piophila casei*) infesting cheese; also, any of various other leaping insects; as, the leaf*hopper,* grass*hopper.* **3.** A chute, box, or receptacle, usually funnel-shaped, for delivering any material, as to animals or to a machine; as, the *hopper* in a grain elevator; the *hopper* which feeds coal to a furnace. **4.** A tank holding liquid and having a device for releasing its contents through a pipe; as, the *hopper* of a toilet.

hop′ple (hŏp′'l), *v. t. & n.* Hobble; fetter.

hop′scotch′ (hŏp′skŏch′), *n.* [*hop* to leap + *scotch* a line, scratch.] A child's game in which the player tosses a pebble, block, or the like, from one compartment to another of a figure traced, or scotched, on the ground, and after each toss hops on one foot through the spaces of the figure to get the object, and back again.

hop′vine′ (hŏp′vīn′), *n.* **a** The stem of the hop. **b** = 2d HOP, 1.

Ho′rae (hō′rē; 70), *n. pl.* [L., fr. Gr. *Hōrai.*] *Gr. Relig.* Goddesses of the seasons, hence of orderliness.

ho′ral (hō′răl), *adj.* [L. *horalis,* fr. *hora* hour.] Of or relating to an hour or hours; hourly.

ho′ra·ry (hō′rȧ·rĭ), *adj.* [ML. *horarius,* fr. L. *hora* hour.] **1.** Of or pertaining to an hour; noting the hours. **2.** Occurring once an hour; hourly. **3.** *Astrol.* Of or pertaining to specific or fitting times, or their determination.

Ho·ra′tian (hō·rā′shăn; -shĭ·ăn), *adj.* Of the Latin poet Horace (Quintus Horatius Flaccus, 65–8 B.C.), or resembling his poetic style.

Ho·ra′tius Co′cles (hō·rā′shŭs kō′klēz; hō·rā′shĭ·ŭs; kŏk′lēz). In Roman legend, a famous hero who defended a bridge at Rome against the Etruscan army under Lars Porsena.

horde (hōrd; 70), *n.* [F., through G. & Pol., fr. Turk. *ordu* camp, army.] **1.** A clan or tribal group of Mongolian nomads; as, the ***Golden Horde*** of Mongol Tatars that overran eastern Europe in the 13th century (so called from the magnificent tent of Batu Khan, grandson of Genghis Khan). **2.** Any loosely organized group of nomads. **3.** Any crowd; swarm; pack. — **Syn.** See CROWD. — *v. i.* To associate in or form a horde.

hore′hound′ (hōr′hound′), *n.* [AS. *hārhūne, hārehūne,* fr. *hār* hoar, gray + *hūne,* name of a plant.] **1.** A bitter mint (*Marrubium vulgare*) with hoary downy leaves. **2.** An extract or confection made from this plant. **3.** Any of several other mints.

ho·ri′zon (hō·rī′z'n), *n.* [OF. *orizonte,* fr. L., fr. Gr. *horizōn* (sc. *kyklos*) the bounding line, horizon, fr. *horizein* to bound, fr. *horos* boundary.] **1.** The apparent junction of earth and sky, called the ***apparent, local, or visible horizon.*** **2.** Figuratively, range of perception or experience. **3.** *Astron.* **a** A plane passing through the eye of the spectator and at right angles to the vertical at a given place; — called the ***sensible horizon.*** **b** A plane parallel to the sensible horizon, and passing through the earth's center, or the great circle formed by the intersection of this plane with the celestial sphere; — called the ***celestial, rational, geometrical, or true horizon.*** **c** A level mirror, as the surface of mercury in a shallow vessel, or a plane reflector adjusted to the true level artificially, used in observing altitudes; — called ***artificial, or false, horizon.*** **4.** *Geol.* The deposit of a particular time, usually identified by distinctive fossils. **5.** *Painting.* In a picture, the imaginary line on which is projected the point of sight of the spectator, esp. in landscapes, where this horizon replaces the natural horizon. **6.** *Soils.* A layer of soil or its underlying material as seen in a vertical section of land. Distinct layers are gradually developed as a result of soil-forming processes.

hor′i·zon′tal (hŏr′ĭ·zŏn′tăl; -t'l), *adj.* **1. a** Of, pertaining to, or near the horizon. **b** Parallel to the horizon; on a level. **c** Measured or contained in a plane of the horizon. **2.** Designating any of various machines placed or operating chiefly along a plane parallel to the horizon; as, a *horizontal* engine. — *n.* A thing that is horizontal. — **hor′i·zon′tal·ly,** *adv.*

horizontal union. = CRAFT UNION.

hor′mic (hôr′mĭk), *adj.* Striving; purposive; as, the *hormic* activities of an organism.

hor′mone (hôr′mōn), *n.* [Gr. *hormōn,* pres. part. of *hormaein* to excite.] *Physiol.* A substance, esp. a specific organic product of the cells of one part, as of the adrenal glands, transported in the body fluid or the sap of an organism and producing a specific effect on the activity of cells remote from its source; an internal secretion; an autacoid; strictly, one which is excitatory, as distinguished from *chalone.* Cf. ANDROGEN, ESTROGEN, ESTRONE. — **hor·mo′nal** (hôr·mō′năl; -n'l), **hor·mon′ic** (hôr·mŏn′ĭk), *adj.*

horn (hôrn), *n.* [AS.] **1.** One of the hard processes borne on the head of many hoofed mammals, and used chiefly as weapons of offense or defense. Those of cattle, sheep, goats, and true antelopes are unbranched and permanent. Those of deer, called *antlers,* are solid, bony, and branched, and are shed and renewed annually. **2.** Any natural projection from an animal, suggestive of a horn, as a tuft of feathers on the head of a bird. **3.** An emblem of a cuckold, cuckolds being reputed to wear horns. **4.** The tough, fibrous material, keratin, of which true horns are composed; also, any similar substance. **5. a** A drinking cup, or beaker; hence, a drink. **b** The cornucopia, or horn of plenty. **c** A vessel made of a horn, esp. one for containing powder. **6.** Something resembling a horn; as: **a** One of the curved ends of a crescent. **b** The beak-shaped point of an anvil. See ANVIL, *Illust.* **c** The high pommel of a saddle. **7.** *Bib.* A symbol of strength, power, glory, or pride. **8. a** Any of various wind instruments somewhat resembling an animal's horn; as, a French *horn.* **b** A device for making sound signals; as, an electric *horn.* **9.** *Radio.* A tube used in some types of loud-speaker. — *v. t.* **1.** To furnish with horns; to give the shape of a horn to. **2.** *Archaic.* To cuckold. **3.** To gore with the horns. — **horn′less,** *adj.*

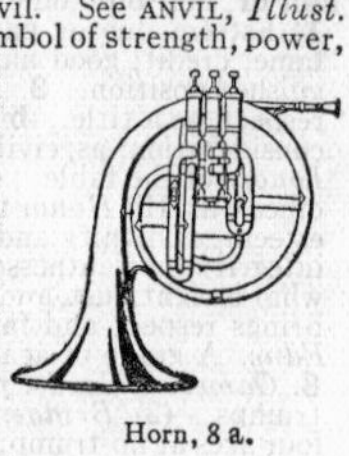

Horn, 8 a.

horn′beam′ (-bēm′), *n.* Any of a genus (*Carpinus*) of trees of the birch family, having smooth gray bark and hard white wood.

horn′bill′ (-bĭl′), *n.* Any of a family (Bucerotidae) of large nonpasserine Old World birds having enormous bills.

horn′blende′ (-blĕnd′), *n.* [G., fr. *horn* horn + *blende* blende.] *Mineral.* Amphibole, properly the common dark aluminous variety. — **horn·blen′dic** (hôrn·blĕn′dĭk), *adj.*

hornblende schist. *Petrog.* See AMPHIBOLITE.

horn′book′ (hôrn′bŏŏk′), *n.* A kind of child's primer formerly in use, consisting typically of a sheet of parchment protected by a sheet of transparent horn. Hence, a rudimentary treatise.

horned (hôrnd *or, poet. or rhetorical,* hôr′nĕd, -nĭd), *adj.* Furnished with a horn or horns; having a hornlike process; — often used in combinations in the sense of *having* (such or so many) *horns,* as in broad-*horned,* four-*horned.*

horned pout. A bullhead, esp. one species (*Ameiurus nebulosus*) which is common in the eastern United States and has been introduced into streams of the Pacific coast.

horned toad. Any of certain small, harmless, scaly, insectivorous lizards (genus *Phrynosoma*) having hornlike spines, of Mexico and western United States.

hor′net (hôr′nĕt; -nĭt), *n.* [AS. *hyrnet.*] A large strong wasp whose sting is very severe; esp., a European species (*Vespa crabro*) and the American ***white-faced hornet*** (*V. maculata*).

Horn′ie (hôr′nĭ), *n. Scot.* The Devil.

hor·ni′to (hôr·nē′tō; *Sp.* ôr·nē′tō), *n.* [Sp., dim. fr. *horno* oven, fr. L. *furnus.*] *Geol.* A low, dome-shaped mound, in volcanic regions, emitting smoke and vapors.

horn′-mad′ (hôrn′măd′; 2), *adj.* Enraged enough to gore; hence, furious; raving crazy. — **horn′-mad′ness,** *n.*

horn of plenty. A cornucopia. See AMALTHAEA.

horn′pipe′ (hôrn′pīp′), *n.* **a** A musical instrument formerly popular in Wales, consisting of a wooden pipe and a reed mouthpiece. **b** A lively dance, orig. accompanied by hornpipe playing, popular among sailors. **c** A lively tune for such a dance.

horn pout. The horned pout.

horn′stone′ (hôrn′stōn′), *n. Mineral.* A variety of quartz much like flint, but more brittle.

horn'swog'gle (hôrn'swŏg''l), *v. t.* *Slang.* To bamboozle; to hoax.
horn'tail' (hôrn'tāl'), *n.* Any of certain hymenopterous insects (superfamily Siricoidea) related to the sawflies, the female commonly having a stout ovipositor. Their larvae burrow in plants, often in trees.
horn'worm' (-wûrm'), *n.* The larva of various hawk moths, having a hornlike process, as the tobacco worm.
horn'wort' (-wûrt'), *n.* Any of a genus (*Ceratophyllum*, family Ceratophyllaceae) of aquatic herbs found in quiet fresh waters.
horn'y (hôr'nĭ), *adj.;* HORN'I·ER (-nĭ·ẽr); HORN'I·EST. **1.** Of horn, or a hornlike substance. **2.** Having horns or hornlike projections. **3.** Hard, callous, or semiopaque, like horn; — often in combination, as in **horn'y-hand'ed.**
hor'o·loge (hŏr'ō·lōj; -lŏj), *n.* [OF. *horloge, orloge*, fr. L., fr. Gr. *hōrologion*, fr. *hōra* hour + *legein* to say, tell.] A timepiece; a watch, clock, or dial.
ho·rol'o·ger (hō·rŏl'ō·jẽr), *n.* A maker or vender of clocks and watches; one skilled in horology.
hor'o·log'ic (hŏr'ō·lŏj'ĭk), *adj.* Also **hor'o·log'i·cal** (-ĭ·kăl). Of or pertaining to a horologe or horology.
ho·rol'o·gist (hō·rŏl'ō·jĭst), *n.* A horologer.
ho·rol'o·gy (-jĭ), *n.* The science of measuring time, or the art of constructing clocks, dials, etc., for indicating time.
hor'o·scope (hŏr'ō·skōp), *n.* [F., fr. L., fr. Gr. *hōroskopos*, fr. *hōra* hour + *skopos* watcher.] *Astrol.* **a** Aspect of the stars at a particular time, as at the moment of a person's birth; horoscopy (def. 2). **b** A diagram or scheme of the twelve houses of heaven, showing the relative positions of planets and signs of the zodiac, by which astrologers profess to foretell the events of a person's life or to answer horary questions.
ho·ros'co·py (hō·rŏs'kō·pĭ), *n.* **1.** The art or practice of casting horoscopes, or observing the disposition of the stars, with a view to predicting events. **2.** Aspect of the stars at a specific time, as at one's birth.
hor·ren'dous (hŏ·rĕn'dŭs), *adj.* [L. *horrendus.*] Fearful; frightful; horrible. — **hor·ren'dous·ly,** *adv.*
hor'rent (hŏr'ĕnt), *adj.* [L. *horrens*, pres. part. of *horrere* to bristle.] **1.** Standing erect, as bristles; bristling. **2.** *Rare.* Horrified; horrible; expressing horror.
hor'ri·ble (hŏr'ĭ·b'l; 74), *adj.* [OF. *horrible*, fr. L. *horribilis*, fr. *horrere.*] Exciting, or tending to excite, horror; dreadful; shocking. — **Syn.** See FEARFUL. — **hor'ri·ble·ness,** *n.* — **hor'ri·bly,** *adv.*
hor'rid (hŏr'ĭd), *adj.* [L. *horridus.*] **1.** *Archaic.* Rough; bristling. **2.** Hideous; shocking; hence, very offensive; now often, *Colloq.*, rather objectionable; offensive. — **hor'rid·ly,** *adv.* — **hor'rid·ness,** *n.*
hor·rif'ic (hŏ·rĭf'ĭk), *adj.* [F. or L.; F. *horrifique*, fr. L. *horrificus*, fr. *horrere* to be horrible.] Causing horror; horrifying; frightful. — **Syn.** See FEARFUL.
hor'ri·fy (hŏr'ĭ·fī), *v. t.;* -FIED (-fīd); -FY'ING. [L. *horrificare.*] To strike with horror. — **Syn.** See DISMAY. — **hor'ri·fi·ca'tion** (-fĭ·kā'shŭn), *n.*
hor·rip'i·la'tion (hŏ·rĭp'ĭ·lā'shŭn), *n.* [L. *horripilatio*, fr. *horripilare* to bristle, fr. *horrere* to bristle + *pilus* the hair.] *Med.* A bristling of the hair of the head or body, resulting from disease, terror, chilliness, etc.; goose flesh.
hor'ror (hŏr'ẽr), *n.* [OF., fr. L. *horror*, fr. *horrere* to bristle, shiver, be dreadful.] **1.** *Archaic.* A bristling up; a roughness. **2.** A shivering, as in the cold fit which precedes a fever. **3.** A painful emotion of fear, dread, and abhorrence; great aversion and repugnance. **4.** The quality of exciting horror; that which excites horror or dread, or is horrible. — **Syn.** See FEAR. — ***the horrors.*** **a** The blues. **b** *Colloq.* A spasm, or spasms, of horror.
‖**hors de com'bat'** (ôr' dē kôɴ'bȧ'; *formerly, and still by many*, hôr'). [F.] Out of the combat; disabled from fighting.
hors d'oeu'vre (dû'vr'); *pl.* D'OEUVRES (dû'vr'). [F. *hors d'œuvre*, lit., outside of work.] A relish or appetizer, served usually at the beginning of a meal; — chiefly in *pl.*
horse (hôrs), *n.; pl.* HORSES (hôr'sĕz; -sĭz). [AS. *hors.*] **1.** [*pl.* also rarely HORSE. See PLURAL, *Note*, 2.] **a** A large, solid-hoofed,

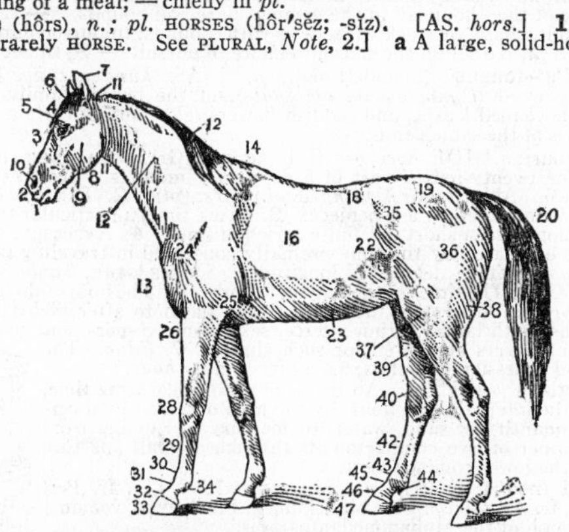

Horse. 1 Lips; 2 Nose; 3 Face; 4 Forehead; 5 Eyebrows; 6 Forelock; 7 Ears; 8 Lower Jaw; 9 Cheek; 10 Nostril; 11 Poll; 12 Mane; 13 Chest; 14 Withers; 16 Ribs; 18 Loin; 19 Croup; 20 Tail; 22 Flank; 23 Belly; 24 Shoulder; 25 Elbow; 26 Forearm; 28 Knee; 29 Cannon or Shank; 30 Fetlock Joint; 31 Pastern; 32 Coronet; 33 Hoof; 34 Fetlock; 35 Haunch; 36 Thigh; 37 Stifle; 38 Buttock; 39 Gaskin; 40 Hock; 42 Cannon or Shank; 43 Fetlock Joint; 44 Fetlock; 45 Pastern; 46 Coronet; 47 Hoof. See also HARNESS, HOOF, *Illusts.*

herbivorous mammal (*Equus caballus*) domesticated by man since a prehistoric period, used as a beast of burden, a draft animal, or for riding or driving. Well-known breeds include *Arab, Belgian, Clydesdale, Galloway, Hambletonian, Morgan, Percheron, Shetland pony, Shire, Suffolk, Thoroughbred.* **b** Any of certain closely allied extinct species. **2.** The male of the horse; usually, a gelding, but sometimes a stallion. **3.** Anything on which one rides, sits, exercises, or is carried as on a horse. **4.** A frame, usually with legs, to support something, as planks, a staging, or clothing; specif., a sawhorse. **5.** A jocular, friendly, or, sometimes, opprobrious, name for a man; as, old *horse.* **6.** *Student Slang.* **a** A translation or other illegitimate aid in study or examination; — called also *trot, pony.* **b** Horseplay; tomfoolery. **7.** *Colloq. Chess.* A knight. **8.** *Gymnastics.* An apparatus shaped somewhat like the body of a small horse, used for vaulting exercises, etc. **9.** *Mil.* [*pl.* HORSE.] Mounted soldiery; cavalry; as, a regiment of *horse.* **10.** *Mining Geol.* A mass of the same character as the wall rock, occurring in a vein. **11.** *Zool.* In a broad sense, any member of the horse family (Equidae), including the ass, zebra, etc.
— *v. t.* **1.** To provide with a horse, or with horses; to place on a horse. **2.** To place on the back of another, or on a wooden horse, etc., to be flogged; hence, to flog. **3.** *Slang.* To make (one) the object of horseplay; also, to ridicule.
— *v. i.* To get, or go, on horseback.
— *adj.* **1.** Pertaining to a horse or horses. **2.** Large or coarse of its kind or genus; as, a *horse* mackerel. **3.** Mounted on horses; for mounted troops; as, *horse* archers.
horse'back' (hôrs'băk'), *n.* **1.** The back of a horse. **2.** A natural ridge; a hogback. — *adv.* On horseback.
horse block. A block or platform for mounting or dismounting from a horse.
horse'car' (hôrs'kär'), *n.* *U. S.* **a** A railroad car or streetcar drawn by horses. **b** A car fitted for transporting horses.
horse chestnut. The large nutlike seed of a tree (*Aesculus hippocastanum*) brought from Constantinople in the 16th century, now common in the temperate zones; also, the tree. See BUCKEYE, 1.
horse'cloth' (hôrs'klŏth'), *n.* A cloth for a covering or trapping of a horse.
horse'flesh' (-flĕsh'), *n.* **1.** The flesh of the horse, esp. when slaughtered for food. **2.** *Colloq.* Horses collectively.
horse'fly' (-flī'), *n.* **1.** Any of a family (Tabanidae) of swift two-winged flies, sometimes large; — called also *gadfly.* The females suck the blood of animals. **2.** Any of various other flies annoying to horses.
horse gentian. Any of a genus (*Triosteum*, esp. *T. perfoliatum*, the feverroot) of plants of the honeysuckle family.
Horse Guards. *Mil.* **1.** A picked body of cavalry so called; esp., the cavalry brigade of the English household troops, which furnishes guards of state for the sovereign. **2.** *Colloq.* The building opposite Whitehall, London, serving as headquarters for several regiments of the guards, and as offices for some departments of the War Office.
horse'hair' (hôrs'hâr'), *n.* **a** A hair of a horse, esp. one from the mane or tail. **b** Haircloth. — **horse'hair',** *adj.*
horse'hide' (-hīd'), *n.* A horse's hide or leather made from it.
horse'jock'ey (-jŏk'ĭ), *n.* A professional rider or driver of race horses; — usually merely *jockey.*
horse latitudes. *Naut.* Either of two belts or regions in the neighborhood of 30° N. and 30° S. latitude, characterized by high pressure, calms, and light baffling winds.
horse'laugh' (hôrs'läf'; -láf'), *n.* A loud, boisterous laugh.
horse'leech' (-lēch'), *n.* Also formerly **horse leach.** **1.** *Archaic.* A veterinary surgeon. **2.** A common European leech (*Haemopis gulo*), said (perhaps incorrectly) to attack the nose and mouth of horses when drinking.
horse'less (-lĕs; -lĭs), *adj.* Without a horse; specif., not requiring a horse; — said of self-propelled vehicles.
horse mackerel. **a** The common tunny. **b** Locally, any of several other large fishes, as the bluefish, saurel, etc.
horse'man (hôrs'măn), *n.; pl.* HORSEMEN (-mĕn). A rider on horseback; one skilled in the management or care of horses; specif., *Obs.*, a cavalryman. — **horse'man·ship,** *n.*
horse marine. One of a mythical body of marine cavalry; also, a marine or sailor on mounted duty ashore or a cavalryman on shipboard; hence, a man out of his element.
horse'mint' (hôrs'mĭnt'), *n.* **a** Any of several European mints, esp. *Mentha longifolia* and *M. aquatica.* **b** *U. S.* Any of several coarse herbs of the genus *Monarda*, with yellow or white flowers.
horse nettle. A prickly weed (*Solanum carolinense*) of the nightshade family, with yellow berrylike fruit.
horse opera. *Motion Picture Slang.* A western, esp. a thriller.
horse pistol. A large pistol, formerly carried by horsemen.
horse'play' (hôrs'plā'), *n.* Rude, boisterous play.
horse'pow'er (-pou'ẽr; 2), *n.* **1.** The power which a horse exerts in pulling. **2.** *Mech.* A unit of power, numerically equal to a rate of 33,000 foot-pounds of work per minute (= 550 foot-pounds per second). Abbr. *h.p.* or *hp.*
horse'pow'er-hour', *n.* *Mech.* The work performed or energy consumed by working at the rate of one horsepower for one hour. It is equal to 1,980,000 foot-pounds.
horse'-rad'ish (-răd'ĭsh; 2), *n.* A tall coarse white-flowered herb (*Armoracia lapathifolia*) of the mustard family, the pungent root of which is used as a condiment.
horse rake. A horse-drawn rake.
horse sense. *Colloq., U. S.* Practical common sense.
horse'shoe' (hôrs'shōō'; hôrsh'-), *n.* **1.** A shoe for horses, usually a narrow plate of iron conformed to the rim of a horse's hoof. **2.** Anything shaped like a horseshoe. **3.** *pl.* A game like quoits played with horseshoes or horseshoe-shaped pieces of metal. **4.** Short for HORSESHOE CRAB. — *v. t.;* -SHOED' (-shōōd'); -SHOE'ING. To furnish with horseshoes; to shoe (a horse). — **horse'sho'er** (-shōō'ẽr), *n.*
horseshoe arch. See ARCH, *Illust.*
horseshoe crab. = KING CRAB.
horse'tail' (hôrs'tāl'), *n.* **1.** The tail of a horse. **2.** **a** Any of a genus (*Equisetum*) of perennial flowerless plants related to the ferns; an equisetum. Cf. SCOURING RUSH. **b** = MARE'S-TAIL, 2 **a.** **3.** A Turkish standard, denoting a pasha's rank. Commanders were distinguished by the number of horsetails carried before them.
horsetail agaric, fungus, *or* **mushroom.** The shaggy-mane.
horse'weed' (hôrs'wēd'), *n.* A North American weed (*Leptilon canadense*) of the aster family, with yellowish flowers.
horse'whip' (-hwĭp'), *n.* A whip for horses. — *v. t.;* see WHIP. To flog with a horsewhip.
horse'wom'an (-wŏŏm'ăn), *n.* A woman who rides on horseback.
Horst Wes'sel song (hôrst' vĕs'ĕl). A song by Horst Wessel, young storm trooper (died 1930), sung from 1933, after the national anthem, as the official Nazi rallying song.
hors'y (hôr'sĭ), *adj.;* HORS'I·ER (-sĭ·ẽr); HORS'I·EST. **1.** Pertaining

to, of the nature of, or suggestive of, a horse. **2.** Addicted to, or having to do with, horses or horse racing; as, a *horsy* man; *horsy* talk. — **hors'i·ness** (hôr'sĭ·nĕs; -nĭs), *n.*

hor'ta·tive (hôr'tȧ·tĭv), *adj.* [L. *hortativus*, fr. *hortari* to incite.] Giving exhortation; advisory; exhortative. — **hor'ta·tive·ly**, *adv.*

hor'ta·to'ry (-tō'rĭ *or, esp. Brit.*, -tẽr·ĭ), *adj.* [L. *hortatorius.*] Giving, or characterized by, exhortation; exhortatory.

hor'ti·cul'ture (hôr'tĭ·kŭl'tūr), *n.* [L. *horti* (gen. of *hortus*) *cultura* cultivation of a garden.] Cultivation of a garden or orchard; art of growing fruits, vegetables, ornamental plants. — **hor'ti·cul'tur·al** (-kŭl'tūr·ăl), *adj.* — **hor'ti·cul'tur·ist** (-kŭl'tūr·ĭst), *n.*

hor'tus sic'cus (hôr'tŭs sĭk'ŭs). [L., a dry garden.] A collection of dried botanical specimens; a herbarium.

Ho'rus (hō'rŭs), *n.* [L., fr. Gr. *Hōros*, fr. Egypt. *Ḥeru.*] *Egypt. Relig.* The hawk-headed god of day.

ho·san'na (hō·zăn'ȧ), *interj.* [LL., fr. Gr. *hōsanna*, fr. Heb. *hōshīʽāh nnā* save now, we pray.] An exclamation of praise to the Lord or the Saviour. — *n.; pl.* HOSANNAS (-ȧz). A cry of "hosanna."

hose (hōz), *n.; pl.* HOSE, formerly HOSEN (hō'z'n). [AS.] **1.** A leg covering, in modern use covering also the foot; a stocking, or stockings. **2.** Close-fitting coverings for the legs and waist as formerly worn, often fastened to the doublet by ribbons or strings called *points;* later, breeches reaching only to the knee. **3.** *pl.* sometimes HOSES. A flexible pipe, as of rubber, for conveying fluids from a faucet, hydrant, etc. — *v. t.* To drench by means of a hose; as, to *hose* the garden.

Ho·se'a (hō·zē'ȧ; -zā'ȧ), *n.* [Heb. *Hōshēaʽ.*] **a** A Hebrew prophet of the 8th century B.C. **b** A book of the Old Testament. See BIBLE.

ho'sier (hō'zhẽr), *n.* One who deals in hose, or in clothing knit or woven like hose.

ho'sier·y (-ĭ), *n.* **1.** The business of a hosier. **2.** Hose in general; goods knit or woven like hose.

hos'pice (hŏs'pĭs), *n.* [F., fr. L. *hospitium* hospitality, an inn, fr. *hospes* stranger, guest.] An inn for travelers, esp. one kept by a religious order.

hos'pi·ta·ble (hŏs'pĭ·tȧ·b'l; *Brit. also* hŏs·pĭt'ȧ·b'l), *adj.* [MF., fr. L. *hospitare* to receive as a guest.] **1.** Receiving and entertaining guests generously and kindly. **2.** Proceeding from or suggestive of kindness and generosity to guests or strangers. **3.** Liberally receptive; as, a mind *hospitable* to ideas. — **hos'pi·ta·bly** (-blĭ), *adv.*

hos'pi·tal (hŏs'pĭt·ăl; -'l), *n.* [OF. (F. *hôpital*), fr. ML., fr. L. *hospitalis* relating to a guest, fr. *hospes* guest.] **1.** *Hist.* A place for shelter or entertainment of travelers, strangers, etc. **2.** *Obs. exc. Hist.* A charitable institution for the refuge, maintenance, or education of needy, aged, infirm, or young persons. **3.** An institution in which patients or injured persons are given medical or surgical care.

hos'pi·tal·er, hos'pi·tal·ler (hŏs'pĭt·'l·ẽr), *n.* [OF. *hospitalier.* See HOSPITAL.] **1.** One residing in a hospital; in some London hospitals, once religious establishments, the title of a chief religious officer. **2.** *Obs. exc. Hist.* A member of any of many religious orders whose chief purpose was to care for the sick or needy. **3.** [*cap.*] One of a religious military order called the ***Knights of St. John of Jerusalem***, growing out of a hospital founded at Jerusalem about 1048.

hos'pi·tal'i·ty (hŏs'pĭ·tăl'ĭ·tĭ), *n.; pl.* -TIES (-tĭz). Hospitable treatment, reception, or disposition.

hos'pi·tal·ize (hŏs'pĭt·'l·īz), *v. t.* *Med.* To place in a hospital for treatment. — **hos'pi·tal·i·za'tion** (-ĭ·zā'shŭn; -ī·zā'-), *n.*

hos·pi'ti·um (hŏs·pĭsh'ĭ·ŭm), *n.; pl.* HOSPITIA (-ȧ). [L.] *Hist.* A hospice.

hos'po·dar (hŏs'pō·där), *n.* [Romanian.] A title formerly borne by the princes or governor of Moldavia and Walachia as vassals of the Sultan.

host (hōst), *n.* [OF., fr. L. *hostis* enemy, ML., army.] **1.** An army. **2.** Any great multitude; a throng.

host, *n.* [OF. *hoste*, fr. L. *hospes* stranger, guest, host.] **1.** One who receives or entertains another; specif., a landlord. **2.** *Biol.* Any living animal or plant affording subsistence or lodgment to a parasite. Some parasites pass successive stages in ***alternate hosts***, or different species. The one of these in which the parasite attains maturity or passes its sexual stage is the ***primary host;*** in the ***secondary host*** the parasite is larval or asexual.

host, *n.* [OF. *oiste*, fr. L. *hostia* sacrifice, victim.] [*now often cap.*] *Eccl.* The Eucharistic wafer, or bread, before or after consecration.

hos'tage (hŏs'tĭj), *n.* [OF., fr. ML. *hostaticus*, prob. for *hospitaticum*, fr. L. *hospes* guest.] State of a person given or kept as a pledge, as for the fulfillment of a treaty; hence, a person in such a state or position; as, held as *hostage.*

hos'tel (hŏs'tĕl; -t'l), *n.* [OF., fr. ML. *hospitale.* See HOSPITAL.] **1.** A place of lodging; inn. **2.** One of a system of supervised lodgings or shelters for use by youth, as on hiking trips.

hos'tel·er (-ẽr), *n.* *Archaic.* The keeper of a hostel or inn.

hos'tel·ry (hŏs'tĕl·rĭ), *n.; pl.* -RIES (-rĭz). [OF. *hostelerie.* See HOSTEL.] *Archaic.* An inn; a lodginghouse.

host'ess (hōs'tĕs; -tĭs), *n.* A female host.

hos'tile (hŏs'tĭl *or, esp. Brit.*, -tīl; 56), *adj.* [F. or L.; F., fr. L. *hostilis*, fr. *hostis* enemy.] Belonging or appropriate to an enemy; having or showing ill will; inimical; unfriendly. — **hos'tile·ly**, *adv.*

hos·til'i·ty (hŏs·tĭl'ĭ·tĭ), *n.; pl.* -TIES (-tĭz). **1.** State of being hostile; enmity. **2.** An act of open enmity; a hostile deed; esp., *pl.*, acts of warfare. — **Syn.** See ENMITY.

hos'tler (hŏs'lẽr; ŏs'lẽr), *n.* Also **os'tler** (ŏs'lẽr). [OF. *hostelier* innkeeper.] One who takes care of horses at an inn or stable; hence, anyone who takes care of horses; a groom.

hot (hŏt), *adj.;* HOT'TER (-ẽr); HOT'TEST. [AS. *hāt.*] **1.** Having, or characterized by, a (relatively) high temperature; — opposed to *cold* and exceeding *warm* in degree. **2.** Characterized by violent activity, emotion, or passion; as: **a** Ardent; fiery. **b** Violent; raging. **c** Excited; urgent. **d** Lustful. **e** Kindled with eager desire; as, *hot* for reform. **3.** Inducing or suggesting heat; as: **a** Pressing hard or close; as, a *hot* chase. **b** Fresh; recent; as, *hot* from the press. **c** Producing a sensation as of heat; pungent; as, *hot* as mustard. **d** *Slang.* Highly exciting, novel, or otherwise fashionably taking. **4.** *Slang.* **a** Impassioned and exciting in rhythm and mood, often also vehement in execution; as, *hot* jazz; a *hot* dancer. **b** *Swing Music.* Inspired by the music to such a degree as to break free from the score, interpolating variations without losing the original melody and rhythm; of music, played in this style. **c** Exciting, or of an excellence to excite, warm admiration. **5.** *Orig. Underworld Slang.* Recently stolen or otherwise illegally obtained; as, *hot* goods or bonds; also, contraband; specif., of oil (petroleum), illegally pumped and shipped in excess of regulations for proration. **6.** *Games.* Very near to the object or solution sought. **7.** *Hunting.* Strong; intense; clear; — said of the scent.

hot'bed' (-bĕd'), *n.* **1.** *Hort.* A bed of soil enclosed in glass heated by fermenting manure, etc., for raising seedlings. **2.** A place or environment which favors rapid growth or development.

hot'–blood'ed (*see Pron.*, § 2), *adj.* **1.** Excitable; high-spirited; ardent; — opp. to *cold-blooded.* **2.** Having Thoroughbred blood; — said esp. of horses.

hot'box' (hŏt'bŏks'), *n.* A journal box, as on a railroad car, overheated by friction.

hotch (hŏch), *v. t. & i.* [F. *hocher* to shake, fr. D. *hotsen* to shake, jolt.] *Scot.* To jog; joggle; fidget.

hotch'pot' (-pŏt'), *n.* [See HOTCHPOTCH.] **1.** *Law.* A throwing into a common lot or stock, of property for equality of division. **2.** A hotchpotch.

hotch'potch' (hŏch'pŏch'), *n.* [From earlier *hotchpot*, fr. F. *hochepot*, fr. D. *hutspot* hotchpotch.] **1.** A mingled mass; a stew of various ingredients; a hodgepodge. **2.** *Law.* A hotchpot.

hot cockles. A rustic, or childish, play, in which one covers his eyes, and guesses who strikes him.

hot dog. *Slang.* A heated wienerwurst or frankfurter, esp. one placed in a split roll.

ho·tel' (hō·tĕl'; *Brit. also* ō·tĕl'), *n.* [F. *hôtel*, fr. OF. *hostel.* See HOSTEL.] **1.** A house providing lodging and usually meals for the public, esp. for transients; an inn. **2.** (*F. pron.* ō'tĕl') In French usage: **a** The mansion of a person of rank or wealth. **b** A public building.

‖**hô'tel' de ville** (ō'tĕl' dẽ vēl'). [F.] A town hall.

hot'foot' (hŏt'fo͝ot'; 2), *adv.* *Colloq.* In impulsive haste. — (hŏt'fo͝ot'), *v. i.* *Colloq.* To hurry; to go hotfoot.

hot'head' (-hĕd'), *n.* A hotheaded person.

hot'head'ed (-hĕd'ĕd; -ĭd; 2), *adj.* Fiery; hasty; impetuous. — **hot'head'ed·ly**, *adv.* — **hot'head'ed·ness**, *n.*

hot'house' (-hous'), *n.* **1.** *Obs.* **a** A bathhouse. **b** A bagnio; a brothel. **2.** A glasshouse artificially heated for growing or keeping tender or tropical plants.

hot'ly (hŏt'lĭ), *adv.* In a hot or fiery manner; ardently.

hot'ness (-nĕs; -nĭs), *n.* Quality or state of being hot.

hot plate. **a** A heated iron plate or stove lid for use in cooking. **b** A covered plate or electrical appliance for keeping food warm. **c** A simple portable gas or electric heater with one or more flat burners or heating elements mounted on a low frame.

hot pot. Mutton or beef cooked with potatoes in a tight-covered pot.

hot rod. An automobile rebuilt or modified for high speed and fast acceleration.

hot seat. *Underworld Slang, U. S.* The electric chair.

hot spring. See THERMAL SPRING.

hot'spur' (hŏt'spûr'), *n.* A rash, hotheaded man.

Hot'ten·tot (hŏt''n·tŏt), *n.* [S. Afr. D., lit., *hot* and *tot.*] **1.** One of a South African race apparently allied to both the Bushmen and Bantus. **2.** The Hottentot language. — **Hot'ten·tot**, *adj.*

hot'ter (hŏt'ẽr), *v. i. & t.* *Scot.* To shake, as with rage or laughter.

Hou'dan (ho͞o'dăn), *n.* [F., fr. *Houdan*, town in northern France.] One of a French breed of crested domestic fowls with black-and-white or white plumage, and five toes.

hough (hŏk; *Scot.* hŏκ), *n.* *Chiefly Scot.* The hock.

hound (hound), *n.* [ME. *hune*, fr. or akin to ON. *hūnn* knob.] **1.** *pl. Shipbuilding.* The framing at the masthead of a vessel to support the heel of the topmast and the upper parts of the lower rigging. **2.** *pl. Vehicles.* Certain side bars that add rigidity to the parts they connect.

hound, *n.* [AS. *hund.*] **1.** Orig., a dog; now, specif., a dog of any of certain breeds used in the chase. The typical hounds have large drooping ears and hunt by scent. **2.** A despicable person. **3.** A player who is one of the "hounds" in the game of hare and hounds. — *v. t.* **1.** To hunt, chase, or track with, or as with, hounds; to pursue unrelentingly. **2.** To set on the chase; to incite to pursuit. — **Syn.** See BAIT.

hound's'–tongue' (houndz'tŭng'), *n.* [AS. *hundes tunge.*] A coarse weed (*Cynoglossum officinale*), of the borage family, with tongue-shaped leaves, and reddish flowers; also, any of certain other species of the same genus.

hour (our), *n.* [OF. *hore, ore*, fr. L. *hora*, fr. Gr. *hōra* a season, hour.] **1.** The twenty-fourth part of a day; sixty minutes. See MEASURE, *Table* 6. Abbr. *hr.* or *h.* (*sing. & pl.*); *hrs.* (*pl*). **2.** The time of the day, as indicated by a timepiece. **3.** Fixed time; a particular time or occasion; also, a short indefinite period of time. **4.** A measure of distance estimated by the time normally consumed in traveling it. **5.** *Astron.* Fifteen degrees of longitude. See MEASURE, *Table* 8. **6.** *pl. Eccl.* **a** The times of the day set for prayer. The hours (also called ***canonical hours***) in their order from dawn to after nightfall are matins (with lauds), prime, tierce, sext, none, vespers, and complin. **b** The prayers appointed for such times. **7.** *Educ.* The period of session of a class; as, a fifty-minute *hour.*

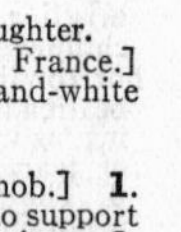

Hour-glass.

hour'glass' (-glȧs'), *n.* An instrument for measuring time, esp. the interval of an hour, by the time occupied by a certain quantity of sand, water, or mercury in running from the upper of two compartments through a small aperture into the lower compartment.

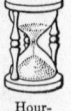

hou'ri (ho͞o'rĭ; hou'rĭ), *n.; pl.* -RIS (-rĭz). [F., fr. Per. *ḥūri*, fr. Ar. *ḥūrīyah* a white-skinned, black-eyed woman.] A nymph of the Mohammedan paradise.

hour'ly (our'lĭ), *adv.* Every hour; frequently; continually. — *adj.* Happening or done every hour; frequent.

house (hous), *n.; pl.* HOUSES (houz'ĕz; -ĭz). [AS. *hūs.*] **1.** A structure for human habitation; esp., a human habitation which is fixed in place and is intended for the private occupation of a family or families. **2.** **a** Anything serving an animal other than man for habitation, as the shell of a snail, the nest of bird, etc. **b** A building in which something is housed; as, a coach *house.* **3.** Any place of abode or deposit, as the body as the habitation of the soul, the grave as the final abode of man, etc. **4.** Those who dwell in the same house; a household. **5.** A family of kindred; esp., a noble family or an illustrious race; as, the *House* of Windsor. **6.** A religious fraternity or its place of abode. **7.** A college in a university; a boardinghouse or dormitory in a college or school; also, the students in either collectively. **8.** One of the estates of a kingdom or other government assembled in parliament or legislature; as, the *House* of Representatives; also, the building, or chamber, where it meets. **9.** A body of men forming a deliberative or consultative assembly, esp. of an ecclesiastical or a collegiate character; as, the *house* of bishops. **10.** A theater; hence, an audience, as at a theater. **11.** *Astrol.* **a** A twelfth part of the heavens as divided by six circles intersecting at the north and south points of the horizon, used by astrologers in noting the positions of the heavenly bodies, and casting horoscopes or nativities. **b** A zodiacal sign regarded as the seat of a planet's greatest influence. **12.** *Com.* A place of business; hence, a firm or commercial establishment; as, the *house* of Morgan.

house (houz), *v. t.* **1.** To lodge in a house; also, to store in a house. **2.** To cover, enclose, or shelter as if by putting in a house. **3.** *Obs.* To drive to shelter in a house. **4.** *Naut.* To stow or secure in a safe place; as, to *house* a yacht for the winter. — *v. i.* To take shelter or lodgings.

house'boat' (hous'bōt'), *n.* A covered boat used as a dwelling, esp. a large, flat-bottomed boat with a superstructure much like a house, used for leisurely cruising.

house'break'ing (-brāk'ĭng), *n.* **1.** The act of breaking open and entering, with a felonious purpose, the dwelling house of another, by day or night. Cf. BURGLARY. **2.** The act of pulling down old buildings. — **house'break'er,** *n.*

house'bro'ken (-brō'kĕn), **house'broke'** (-brōk'), *adj.* Trained to live in a house, as a dog.

house'carl' (-kärl'), *n.* [AS. *hūscarl,* fr. ON. *hūskarl.* See HOUSE; CARL.] A member of the household or bodyguard of a Danish or early English king or noble.

house'coat' (-kōt'), *n.* A woman's long-skirted garment worn in place of a dress in the home.

house'fly' (-flī'), *n.* A two-winged fly (*Musca domestica*) found in all habitable parts of the world. It is occasionally an agent in transmitting diseases, esp. typhoid fever.

house'ful (-fo͝ol), *n.* As much or as many as a house will accommodate; as, a *houseful* of guests.

house'hold (-hōld; -ōld), *n.* Those who dwell as a family under one roof. — *adj.* Of or pertaining to a household; hence, domestic; familiar; common; as, *household* tasks.

household arts. The occupations connected with a household or similar group; hence, *Educ.*, a group of courses covering instruction and practice in such occupations. Cf. HOME ECONOMICS.

house'hold'er (hous'hōl'dẽr), *n.* The master or head of a family; one who occupies a house with his family or alone; specif., in Great Britain, one who occupies such a dwelling as to qualify him to exercise the franchise.

household troops. Troops appointed to attend and guard a sovereign or his residence.

house'keep'er (-kēp'ẽr), *n.* One who does or oversees the work of keeping house. — **house'keep'ing,** *n.*

hou'sel (hou'z'l), *n.* [AS. *hūsel.*] *Archaic.* The Eucharist. — *v. t.* To administer the Eucharist to.

house'leek' (hous'lēk'), *n.* [*house* + *leek.*] A pink-flowered plant (*Sempervivum tectorum*) of the orpine family, of Europe, found on old walls and roofs.

house'less (hous'lĕs; -lĭs), *adj.* **1.** Homeless. **2.** Destitute of houses; as, a *houseless* plain.

house'line' (-līn'), *n.* *Naut.* A small line of three strands laid left-handed, for seizing.

house'maid' (-mād'), *n.* A female house servant.

house'maid's' knee (hous'mādz'). A swelling due to an enlargement of the sac in the front of the kneepan.

House of Assembly. In South Africa, the lower house of the legislature.

House of Bur'gess·es (bûr'jĕs·ĕz; -jĭs-; -ĭz). The colonial representative assembly of Virginia.

House of Commons. **a** The lower house of the Parliament of Great Britain and Northern Ireland. **b** The lower house of the Parliament of the Dominion of Canada.

house of correction. An institution where persons are confined who have committed a minor offense and who are considered capable of reformation.

House of Delegates. *U. S.* The name of the lower house in some states, as Virginia and Maryland.

House of Keys. See KEYS.

House of Lords. The upper house of the Parliament of Great Britain and Northern Ireland.

House of Peers. The upper legislative house in Japan.

House of Representatives. The lower, or popular, branch of the United States Congress and many state and other legislatures, as of Mexico, Japan, and Australia.

house organ. A publication of a business concern, containing articles of interest to employees and customers.

house party. A gathering and entertainment, lasting over one or more nights, of a party of guests in a house, usually in the country; also, the guests collectively.

house physician *or* **surgeon.** A senior resident physician or surgeon of a hospital or other public institution.

house'-rais'ing (hous'rāz'ĭng), *n.* In rural districts, the joint erection of a house or its framework by a gathering of neighbors.

house'room' (-ro͞om'), *n.* Space for accommodation in a house; lodging; as, to give anyone *houseroom.*

house sparrow. See SPARROW, 1.

house'top' (hous'tŏp'), *n.* A roof.

house'warm'ing (-wôr'mĭng), *n.* A merrymaking made by or for those taking possession of a new house.

house'wife' (hous'wīf'; *still occas.* hŭz'ĭf; *in sense* 3 *usually* hŭz'ĭf), *n.; pl.* -WIVES (hous'wīvz'; hŭz'ĭvz). **1.** The female head of a household. **2.** *Obs.* A hussy; — usually written *huswife.* **3.** A little case or bag for needles, thread, pins, etc.; — called also *hussy.* Sometimes spelled *huswife.* — (hous'wīf'; hŭz'ĭf), *v. t. & i.;* -WIFED' (-wīfd'; -ĭft); -WIF'ING (-wīf'ĭng; -ĭf·ĭng). To manage with skill and economy, as a housewife.

house'wife'ly (hous'wīf'lĭ), *adj.* Pertaining or appropriate to, or of the character of, a housewife; domestic; thrifty. — *adv.* In a housewifely manner. — **house'wife'li·ness,** *n.*

house'wif'er·y (hous'wīf'ẽr·ĭ; -rĭ; hŭz'ĭf·rĭ), *n.* The business of a housewife; female management of a house.

house'wive' (hous'wīv'), *v. t. & i.;* -WIVED' (-wīvd'); -WIV'ING (-wīv'ĭng). To housewife.

house'work' (hous'wûrk'), *n.* The work of housekeeping.

hous'ing (houz'ĭng), *n.* [See HOUSE to shelter. In some senses confused with the following word.] **1.** Act of putting or receiving under shelter; also, dwelling in a habitation. **2.** That which shelters or covers; shelter. **3.** Provision of dwelling quarters, esp. of houses. **4.** *Arch.* **a** The space taken out of one solid to admit the insertion of part of another, as the end of one timber in the side of another. **b** A niche, as for a statue. **5.** *Mach.* An upright, frame, or other support to hold a thing in place, as journal-box supports. **6.** *Naut.* That portion of a mast which is beneath the deck, or of a bowsprit which is inboard.

hous'ing, *n.* [OF. *houce* (F. *housse*).] A cover, esp. one of cloth for a horse's saddle, as an ornamental or military appendage; a saddlecloth; a horsecloth; *pl.*, trappings.

hous'ing, *n.* *Naut.* A houseline.

hous·to'ni·a (ho͞os·tō'nĭ·ȧ), *n.* [NL., after Wm. *Houston* (1695?–1733), Eng. botanist.] *Bot.* Any of a genus (*Houstonia*) of herbs of the madder family, including the common bluet.

Hou·yhn'hnm (ho͞o·ĭn'ŭm; hwĭn'ŭm), *n.* In Swift's *Gulliver's Travels,* one of a race of horses endowed with reason and noble qualities and ruling the Yahoos.

hove (hōv), *past & past part.* of HEAVE.

hov'el (hŏv'ĕl; hŭv'-; -'l), *n.* [ME. *hovel, hovyl.*] **1.** An open shed for sheltering cattle, protecting produce, etc. **2.** A shed or shelter for human beings; also, a small, mean house; a hut. — *v. t.;* -ELED (-ĕld) or -ELLED; -EL·ING or -EL·LING. To put in a hovel; shelter.

hov'er (hŭv'ẽr; hŏv'ẽr), *v. i.* [ME. *hoveren,* fr. ME. *hoven* to hover, linger.] **1.** To hang fluttering in the air, or on the wing; to remain suspended about or over a place or object. **2.** To move to and fro near a place, watchfully or irresolutely; hence, figuratively, to be in a state of irresolution or suspense. — *n.* Act or state of hovering. — **hov'er·er,** *n.* — **hov'er·ing·ly,** *adv.*

how (hou), *adv.* [AS. *hū.*] **1.** In what manner or way. **2.** To what degree or extent, number or amount. **3.** In what state or condition. **4.** For what reason; why. **5.** By what name or title; with what meaning; to what effect. **6.** At what price; how dear; as, *how* are stocks today? **7.** What; as, *how* about a game of tennis? — *n.* A way, method, or manner, or a question in regard to this.

how·be'it (hou·bē'ĭt), *conj.* [*how* + *be* + *it.*] **1.** *Archaic.* Be it as it may; nevertheless. **2.** *Obs.* Although; albeit.

how'dah (hou'dȧ), *n.* [Hind. *hawdah,* fr. Ar. *hawdaj.*] A seat or pavilion, generally covered, on the back of an elephant.

how'die, how'dy (hou'dĭ; ou'dĭ; hō'dĭ; ō'-), *n.* *Chiefly Scot.* A midwife.

howe (hou), *n.* *Chiefly Scot.* A hollow; a dell.

how·ev'er (hou·ĕv'ẽr), *adv.* Contr. **how·e'er'** (-âr'; -ār'). **1.** In whatever manner, way, or degree; by whatever means or to whatever extent. **2.** Nevertheless; yet. — *conj. Obs.* Although.

howff, howf (houf; ouf; hōf; ōf), *v. i., v. t., & n.* *Scot.* Haunt; resort.

how'itz·er (hou'ĭt·sẽr), *n.* [G. *haubitze,* fr. Czech *houfnice,* orig., a catapult.] *Ordn.* A short, light cannon, used to deliver shells with a curved trajectory, with shells of lower muzzle velocities than those from guns, at angles between 20 and 45 degrees.

howk (houk; ouk; hōk; ōk), *v. t. & i.* [ME. *holken.*] *Now Dial.* To hollow out by digging; to dig.

howl (houl), *v. i.* [ME. *houlen,* fr. or akin to MD. *hulen, huylen.*] **1.** To utter a loud, long, mournful cry, as dogs. **2.** To lament; wail. **3.** To make a noise resembling the cry of a wild beast. — *v. t.* **1.** To utter with howling. **2.** To affect, effect, or bring by howling. — *n.* **1.** The loud, long, mournful cry of a dog or a wolf, or other like sound. **2.** A wail, or cry of disappointment, rage, or the like.

howl'er (-ẽr), *n.* **1.** One who or that which howls. **2.** = HOWLING MONKEY. **3.** *Slang.* Anything exaggerated, esp. a stupid and ridiculous blunder.

howl'et (hou'lĕt; -lĭt), *n.* *Archaic.* Owl.

howl'ing mon'key. Any of a genus (*Alouatta*) of South American and Central American monkeys having a long prehensile tail, and making remarkable howling noises, as the ***ursine howler*** (*A. ursina*) of Brazil.

how'so·ev'er (hou'sō·ĕv'ẽr), *adv.* In what manner soever; to whatever degree or extent.

hoy (hoi), *n.* [MD. *hoey, hoei* (D. *hui, heu*).] *Naut.* A former type of sloop-rigged coasting vessel; now, a heavy barge.

hoy, *interj.* An exclamation used in calling attention. Cf. AHOY. — *n.* A call of "hoy."

hoy'den, hoi'den (hoi'd'n), *n.* A rude, bold girl. — *adj.* Rude; roistering. — *v. i.* To act like a hoyden.

Hoyle (hoil), *n.* [After Edmond *Hoyle* (1672–1769), English authority on whist, who first systematized its rules.] An encyclopedia of indoor games, esp. card games. — ***according to Hoyle.*** In conformity with Edmond Hoyle's rules of whist or, by extension, with standard rules or usage.

hub (hŭb), *n.* **1.** The central part of a wheel; the nave. See WHEEL, *Illust.* **2.** A center of activity; specif., ***the Hub*** (***of the Universe***), Boston, U. S.; — a nickname.

hub'ba-hub'ba (hŭb'ȧ·hŭb'ȧ), *interj.* [Perh. fr. Ar. *habba* love.] *Slang, U. S.* An exclamation of delighted approval.

hub'ble-bub'ble (hŭb''l·bŭb''l), *n.* **1.** A tobacco pipe so arranged that the smoke passes through water, making a bubbling noise. Cf. HOOKAH, NARGHILE. **2.** A bubbling sound; confused chatter.

hub'bub (hŭb'ŭb), *n.* **1.** A loud noise of many voices shouting at once; uproar. **2.** Tumult; confusion; rumpus.

huck'a·back (hŭk'ȧ·băk), *n.* A strong fabric of linen, or linen and cotton, much used for towels.

huck'le (hŭk''l), *n.* [ME. *hoke, huke.*] The hip; the haunch; also, a bunch or part projecting like the hip.

huck'le·ber'ry (-bĕr'ĭ), *n.* [See WHORTLEBERRY.] Any of a genus (*Gaylussacia*) of American shrubs (of the family Vacciniaceae, the huckleberry family); also, the berry, esp. the fruit of *G. baccata,* a common market berry. In parts of U. S., *huckleberry* is also applied, commonly but incorrectly, to various species of blueberry (*Vaccinium,* the type genus of Vacciniaceae), from which it differs in containing the nutlets instead of numerous minute seeds and in being more acid and shiny black in color.

huck'le·bone' (-bōn'), *n.* **a** The hipbone. **b** The anklebone. See ASTRAGALUS.

huck′ster (hŭk′stẽr), *n.* [MD. *hokester, hoekster*, fem. of *hoeker*. See HAWKER.] **1.** A peddler; hawker. **2.** A mean, mercenary person. **3.** One whose business is advertising for commercial clients, esp. preparation of advertising programs for radiobroadcasting; — usually implying showmanship. — **huck′ster·ess, huck′stress,** *n.*

hud′dle (hŭd′'l), *v. i.;* HUD′DLED (-'ld); HUD′DLING (-lĭng). **1.** To crowd together, from confusion, fear, or the like. **2.** *Amer. Football.* To gather in a huddle. — *v. t.* **1.** To crowd together. **2.** To do, make, or put, in haste or roughly; hence, to do imperfectly. **3.** To drive, push, or thrust, hurriedly or in disorder. **4.** To draw (oneself) into a contracted heap; — usually with *up;* as, he was *huddled* up close to the fire. — *n.* **1.** A number of persons or things crowded together confusedly; a jumble. **2. a** *Amer. Football.* A close grouping together of the members of a team behind their line of scrimmage, as to receive signals. **b** Hence, *Slang*, a secret conference.

Hud′son seal (hŭd′s'n). The fur of the muskrat plucked and dyed to resemble seal.

hue (hū), *n.* [AS. *hīew, hīw, hēow.*] **1.** *Obs.* Form; appearance. **2.** Color. **3.** That one of the three attributes of some colors by virtue of which they differ characteristically from the gray of the same brilliance, and in respect to which they fall into classes which may be designated as red, yellow, green, blue, or intermediates of these. See COLOR. — **Syn.** See COLOR.

hue, *n.* [OF. *hu*, fr. *huer* to shout.] A shouting; an outcry, esp. in the chase. *Obs.*, exc. in **hue and cry,** *Law*, a loud outcry with which felons were anciently pursued; also, the pursuit; hence, any clamor of alarm, pursuit, or assault.

hued (hūd), *adj.* Having color; — usually in combination; as, bright-*hued.*

huff (hŭf), *v. t.* [Imitative.] **1.** To swell; to puff up. **2.** To treat with arrogance; to offend; to make angry or sulky. — *v. i.* **1.** To puff; to blow. **2.** *Obs.* To bluster or swell with anger or arrogance. — *n.* A surge of sudden anger or arrogance; a fit of petulance. — **Syn.** See OFFENSE.

huff′–duff′ (hŭf′dŭf′), *n.* [From pronunciation popularly given to abbreviations *HF* and *DF* (*high-frequency* and *direction finder*).] A radio receiving device that indicates on the screen of a cathode-ray tube the direction from which high-frequency signals are received. By means of the bearings indicated by two or more of these devices at separated points, the position of the sender may be determined.

huff′ish (hŭf′ĭsh), *adj.* **a** *Obs.* Disposed to be blustering or arrogant. **b** Petulant. — **huff′ish·ly,** *adv.* — **huff′ish·ness,** *n.*

huff′y (-ĭ), *adj.;* HUFF′I·ER (-ĭ·ẽr); HUFF′I·EST. **1.** *Obs.* Arrogant. **2.** Easily offended; pettish. — **huff′i·ly,** *adv.* — **huff′i·ness,** *n.*

hug (hŭg), *v. t.;* HUGGED (hŭgd); HUG′GING. **1.** To clasp to the bosom; to embrace. **2.** To hold fast; to cherish. **3.** To keep very close to; as, the ship *hugged* the coast. — *n.* A close embrace.

huge (hūj), *adj.* [ME. *huge, hoge*, fr. OF. *ahuge, ahoge.*] Very large; enormous. — **Syn.** See ENORMOUS. — **huge′ly,** *adv.* — **huge′-ness,** *n.*

huge′ous (hūj′ŭs), *adj.* *Colloq. or Humorous.* Huge.

hug′ger-mug′ger (hŭg′ẽr-mŭg′ẽr), *n.* **1.** *Archaic.* Privacy; secrecy; — chiefly in *in huggermugger*, with haste and secrecy. **2.** Confusion; a muddle. — *adj.* **1.** Secret; sly. **2.** Confused; disorderly. — *v. t.* To keep secret; hush up. — *v. i.* To act or confer stealthily.

hug′–me–tight′ (hŭg′mē·tīt′), *n.* A close-fitting knitted jacket, with or without sleeves.

Hu′gue·not (hū′gē·nŏt), *n.* [F., fr. *eiguenot*, fr. G. *eidgenoss* confederate.] *Eccl. Hist.* A French Protestant in the 16th and 17th centuries; one of the members of the Reformed or Calvinistic communion. — **Hu′gue·not·ism** (-ĭz'm), *n.*

hu′la (hōō′lä), **hu′la–hu′la,** *n.* [Hawaiian.] A native Hawaiian mimetic dance performed by men and women, singly or together, and accompanied by chants and rhythmic drumming.

hulk (hŭlk), *n.* [AS. *hulc* a light, swift ship.] **1.** A ship; now, only a heavy ship of clumsy build. **2. a** The body of an old vessel laid by as unfit for sea. **b** A vessel built for other purposes than seagoing; specif., usually *pl.*, one used as a prison. **3.** Anything or anyone bulky or unwieldy. — *v. i.* To grow or rise in bulky form; — usually with *up.*

hulk′ing (hŭl′kĭng), **hulk′y** (-kĭ), *adj.* Bulky; loutish.

hull (hŭl), *n.* [AS. *hulu.*] **1.** The outer covering, or husk, of any fruit or seed, as of a pea pod; also, the calyx or involucre of certain fruits, as the strawberry. **2.** Hence, any covering or casing. **3.** *Naut.* The frame or body of a vessel, exclusive of masts, yards, sails, and rigging. **4.** *Aeronautics.* **a** The portion of a flying boat which furnishes buoyancy when in contact with the water, and to which the main supporting surfaces and other parts are attached. **b** The main structure of a rigid airship. — *v. t.* **1.** To strip or take off the hull of, as corn. **2.** To pierce or strike the hull of (a ship) with a shot, torpedo, or the like. — **hull′er,** *n.*

hul′la·ba·loo′ (hŭl′ȧ·bȧ·lōō′; hŭl′ȧ·bȧ·lōō′), **hul′la·bal·loo′,** *n.* A confused noise; uproar.

hull down. Of a ship, so distant that her hull is concealed by the convexity of the sea.

hul·lo′ (hŭ·lō′), *interj.* An exclamation of greeting; hollo.

hum (hŭm), *v. i.;* HUMMED (hŭmd); HUM′MING. [Imitative.] **1.** To utter a sound like, or suggestive of, that of the letter *m* prolonged, without opening the mouth. **2.** To drone; buzz; as, a *humming* top. **3.** To sing with closed lips and without articulating. **4.** To give forth a low, murmuring sound, as from the blending of many voices; as, the street *hums.* **5.** *Colloq.* To be very active or spirited; as, to make things *hum.* — *v. t.* **1.** To sing with the lips closed and without articulation; as, to *hum* a tune. **2.** To affect or effect by humming; as, he *hummed* me to sleep. — *n.* Act of humming, or sound made by humming.

hu′man (hū′măn), *adj.* [OF. *humain*, fr. L. *humanus.*] **1.** Belonging or relating to man; characteristic of man. **2.** Designating, or being, a man; consisting of men; having human form or attributes. — *n.* A human being.

hu·mane′ (hū·mān′), *adj.* [L. *humanus.* See HUMAN.] **1.** Having feelings and inclinations creditable to man; kind; benevolent. **2.** Humanizing; refining; as, *humane* studies. — **hu·mane′ly,** *adv.* — **hu·mane′ness,** *n.*

hu′man·ism (hū′măn·ĭz'm), *n.* **1.** Human nature; humanity. **2.** The study of the humanities; polite learning; esp. [*often cap.*], the learning, or cultural impulse, imparted by those who brought the Greek and Roman classics into new vogue during the Renaissance. **3.** A mode or attitude of thought or action centering upon distinctively human interests or ideals. — **hu′man·ist** (-ĭst), *n. & adj.* — **hu′man·is′tic** (-ĭs′tĭk), *adj.*

hu·man′i·tar′i·an (hū·măn′ĭ·târ′ĭ·ăn), *n.* **1.** An adherent of humanitarianism (senses 1 & 2). **2.** A philanthropist. — *adj.* Of or pertaining to, or characteristic of, humanitarianism.

hu·man′i·tar′i·an·ism (-ĭz'm), *n.* **1.** *Theol.* The tenet denying the divinity of Christ. **2.** *Ethics.* **a** The doctrine that man's obligations are limited to, and dependent alone on, man and human relations. **b** The doctrine that man's nature is perfectible through his own efforts without divine grace. **3.** Regard for the interests of mankind; benevolence.

hu·man′i·ty (hū·măn′ĭ·tĭ), *n.; pl.* -TIES (-tĭz). [OF. *humanité*, fr. L. *humanitas.*] **1. a** Quality of being human; the peculiar nature of man, by which he is distinguished from other beings. **b** *pl.* Human characteristics and attributes. **2.** Quality of being humane; the kind feelings, dispositions, and sympathies of man. **3. a** *Archaic.* Mental cultivation; liberal education, as through the study of classical and polite literature. **b** Usually in *pl.*, with *the.* The branches of polite learning, esp. the ancient classics and belles-lettres. **4.** Mankind; human beings collectively.

hu′man·ize (hū′măn·īz), *v. t.* **1.** To make human; to adapt to human nature or use. **2.** To render humane; to refine or civilize. — **hu′man·i·za′tion** (-ĭ·zā′shŭn; -ī·zā′-), *n.* — **hu′man·iz′er** (-īz′ẽr), *n.*

hu′man·kind′ (-kīnd′), *n.* Mankind; the human race.

hu′man·ly, *adv.* In a human manner; after the manner of men; according to the knowledge and wisdom of men.

‖**hu·ma′num est er·ra′re** (hū·mā′nŭm ĕst ĕ·rā′rē). [L.] To err is human.

hum′ble (hŭm′b'l; *formerly, and still occas.*, ŭm′b'l), *adj.* [OF. *humble, umble*, fr. L. *humilis* on the ground, low, fr. *humus* ground.] **1.** Not proud or assertive; lowly. **2.** Near the ground; not high; hence, not pretentious; unassuming.

Syn. Humble, meek, modest, lowly mean lacking in pride or self-sufficiency. Humble and meek strictly suggest virtues, one consisting in absence of pride in oneself or in one's achievements, the other, in absence of passion or wrath and in a consistent mildness of temper but, in current loose use, *humble* implies undue self-depreciation, and *meek*, spiritlessness and timid submissiveness; modest implies a lack of boastfulness or show of conceit; lowly comes very close to *humble* in its older underogatory sense. All but *meek* are applied to things, *humble* and *lowly* suggesting insignificance as in station, and *modest* unobtrusiveness, as in way of living.

— *v. t.;* HUM′BLED (-b'ld); HUM′BLING (-blĭng). **1.** To bring low; to reduce the power or exaltation of; to lower. **2.** To make humble or lowly in mind. — **Syn.** See ABASE.

— **hum′ble·ness,** *n.* — **hum′bler,** *n.* — **hum′bly,** *adv.*

hum′ble·bee′ (hŭm′b'l·bē′), *n.* The bumblebee.

humble pie. a Umble pie, or pie made of the inferior parts of a deer and served to the huntsman and other servants. **b** In the phrase *to eat humble pie*, humiliation.

hum′bug′ (hŭm′bŭg′), *n.* [Origin unknown.] **1.** Something contrived to deceive and mislead; fraud; sham. **2.** A spirit of deception; imposture. **3.** One who deceives or misleads. — **Syn.** See IMPOSTURE. — *v. t.;* -BUGGED′ (-bŭgd′); -BUG′GING. To deceive; to impose on; hoax. — **hum′bug′ger,** *n.* — **hum′bug′ger·y,** *n.*

hum′ding′er (hŭm′dĭng′ẽr), *n.* *Slang, U. S.* A person or thing of striking excellence.

hum′drum′ (hŭm′drŭm′), *adj.* Monotonous; dull. — *n.* **1.** A dull fellow; bore. **2.** Monotonous and tedious commonplaceness.

hu′mer·al (hū′mẽr·ăl), *adj.* [L. *humerus* the shoulder.] **1.** *Anat. & Zool.* Of or pertaining to, or in the region of, the humerus; brachial. **2.** Of or pertaining to the shoulder.

hu′mer·us (-ŭs), *n.; pl.* -MERI (-ī). [L., better *umerus*, shoulder.] *Anat. & Zool.* **a** The bone of the upper part of the arm or forelimb from the shoulder to the elbow. **b** The part of the limb containing this bone; the brachium.

hu′mic (hū′mĭk), *adj.* [L. *humus* the earth, ground.] *Chem.* Pertaining to or derived from humus; as, *humic* acid.

hu′mid (hū′mĭd), *adj.* [F. *humide*, fr. L. *humidus, umidus*, fr. *humere, umere*, to be moist.] Damp; moist. — **Syn.** See WET. — **hu′mid·ly,** *adv.* — **hu′mid·ness,** *n.*

hu·mid′i·fy (hū·mĭd′ĭ·fī), *v. t.;* -FIED (-fīd); -FY′ING. [*humid* + *-fy.*] To render humid, as the atmosphere; to moisten; damp. — **hu·mid′i·fi·ca′tion** (-fĭ·kā′shŭn), *n.* — **hu·mid′i·fi′er** (hū·mĭd′ĭ·fī′ẽr), *n.*

hu·mid′i·stat (hū·mĭd′ĭ·stăt), *n.* An instrument for regulating or maintaining the degree of humidity.

hu·mid′i·ty (hū·mĭd′ĭ·tĭ), *n.* Moisture; dampness; a moderate degree of wetness, esp. of the atmosphere. In meteorology, ***relative humidity*** is the ratio of the quantity of vapor actually present to the greatest amount possible at the given temperature. In reports of the U. S. Weather Bureau, complete saturation of the air is designated by "*humidity* 100," and partial saturation by smaller numbers.

hu′mi·dor (hū′mĭ·dôr), *n.* A case, as for storing cigars, in which the air is kept properly humidified; also, a contrivance, as a tube containing moistened sponges, placed in a case to keep the air moist.

hu·mil′i·ate (hū·mĭl′ĭ·āt), *v. t.* [L. *humiliatus*, past part. of *humiliare*, fr. *humilis.* See HUMBLE.] To reduce to a lower position in one's own eyes, or in the eyes of others; humble; mortify. — **Syn.** See ABASE.

hu·mil′i·at′ing (-āt′ĭng), *adj.* Humbling; mortifying. — **hu·mil′i·at′ing·ly,** *adv.*

hu·mil′i·a′tion (-ā′shŭn), *n.* Act of humiliating, or state of being humiliated; mortification.

hu·mil′i·a·to′ry (hū·mĭl′ĭ·ȧ·tō′rĭ *or, esp. Brit.*, -tẽr·ĭ), *adj.* Tending to humiliate.

hu·mil′i·ty (hū·mĭl′ĭ·tĭ), *n.; pl.* -TIES (-tĭz). [OF. *humilité*, fr. L. *humilitas.*] **1.** State or quality of being humble in spirit; freedom from pride and arrogance. **2.** An act of submission or humble courtesy. **3.** *Obs.* Humble condition or estate; humbleness.

hum′mer (hŭm′ẽr), *n.* One who or that which hums.

hum′ming (hŭm′ĭng), *adj.* **a** Droning; buzzing. **b** *Colloq.* Active or spirited; big; as, business is *humming.* **c** *Colloq.* Frothing; strong; — of ale, beer, etc. — **hum′ming·ly,** *adv.*

hum′ming·bird′ (-bûrd′), *n.* Any of a family (Trochilidae) of chiefly small, brilliantly colored, nonpasserine birds. In flying, the wings beat so rapidly that a humming sound is produced, and only a blur is visible. The ***ruby-throated hummingbird*** (*Archilochus*, syn. *Trochilus, colubris*) is found in eastern United States and Canada.

hum′mock (hŭm′ŭk), *n.* **1.** A rounded knoll or hillock. **2.** A ridge of ice, as in an ice field. **3.** *Southern U. S.* = 2d HAMMOCK. — **hum′mock·y** (-ĭ), *adj.*

hu′mor, hu′mour (hū′mẽr; ū′-), *n.* [OF. *humor, umor*, fr. L. *humor, umor*, moisture, fluid.] **1.** *Archaic.* Moisture; vapor. **2.** **a** In old physiology, a fluid or juice, esp. one of the four fluids — blood, phlegm, choler (yellow bile), and melancholy (black bile) — conceived as determining a person's health and temperament. **b** Hence, one's disposition or state of mind; mood. **3.** A changing and uncertain state of mind; a caprice; whim; fancy. **4.** *pl.* Whimsical or freakish actions or happenings. **5.** **a** That quality which appeals to a sense of the ludicrous or absurdly incongruous; comicality. **b** The mental faculty of discovering, expressing, or appreciating ludicrous or absurdly incongruous elements. **6.** *Biol.* A normal, functioning fluid or semifluid of the body, as the blood, lymph, or bile. **7.** *Med.* Any chronic cutaneous affection supposedly arising from a morbid state of the blood. — **Syn.** See MOOD: WIT. — ***out of humor.*** Displeased; dissatisfied. — *v. t.* **1.** To comply with the humor of; to indulge. **2.** To adapt oneself to. — **Syn.** See INDULGE. — **hu′mor·al, hu′mour·al** (hū′mẽr·ăl), *adj.*

hu′mor·esque′ (hū′mẽr·ĕsk′), *n.* [G. *humoreske.*] *Music.* A composition of a humorous or fanciful character; a caprice.

hu′mor·ist, hu′mour·ist (hū′mẽr·ĭst; ū′-), *n.* **1.** One subject to humors or eccentricities, which he indulges in whimsical ways. **2.** One who displays humor in speaking or writing; a wag; droll.

hu′mor·is′tic (-ĭs′tĭk), *adj.* Also **hu′mour·is′tic.** Of or pertaining to humor or a humorist.

hu′mor·ous (hū′mẽr·ŭs; ū′-), *adj.* Also **hu′mour·ous. 1.** *Obs.* Moist; watery. **2.** Capricious; whimsical. **3.** Full of, or characterized by, humor; jocular; funny. **4.** *Obs. Med.* Humoral. — **Syn.** See WITTY. — **hu′mor·ous·ly,** *adv.* — **hu′mor·ous·ness,** *n.*

hump (hŭmp), *n.* **1.** A rounded protuberance, esp. one formed by a crooked back in human beings, or by a fleshy mass on the back of some animals, as the camel, bison, and whale. **2.** A mound or hummock. **3.** *Slang, Brit.* A fit of the blues; sulks. **4.** A difficult, trying, or critical phase or period, as of an undertaking or of an illness; — esp. in *over the hump.* **5.** *Slang, Australia.* A long tramp with a bundle on one's back. — ***the Hump.*** The Himalaya Mountains; — used esp. by Allied aviators in World War II.
— *v. t.* **1.** To make hump-shaped; to hunch. **2.** *Slang, Australia.* To put or carry on the back; hence, to carry. Cf. *hump bluey*, under BLUEY, *n.* **3.** *Slang, U. S.* To exert; as, *hump* yourself.

hump′back′ (hŭmp′băk′), *n.* **1.** A crooked back; a humped back. **2.** A humpbacked person; a hunchback. **3.** Any whalebone whale (genus *Megaptera*) related to the rorquals, but having very long flippers.

hump′backed′ (-băkt′), *adj.* Having a humped back.

humped (hŭmpt), *adj.* Having a hump; humpbacked.

humph (hŭmf: *the conventional pronunciation of the word; the actual sound made varies, as* hŭmf, hmf, hŭ, etc.), *interj.* An exclamation expressing doubt, contempt, etc.

hump′y (hŭmp′ĭ), *adj.*; HUMP′I·ER (-ĭ·ẽr); -I·EST. Full of humps or bunches; covered with protuberances; humped.

hu′mus (hū′mŭs), *n.* [L., the earth, soil.] A brown or black material formed by the partial decomposition of vegetable or animal matter in or on the soil; the organic portion of soil.

Hun (hŭn), *n.* [L. *Hunni*, *pl.*] **1.** One of a barbarous Asiatic people that invaded Europe about A.D. 450, controlling for a time a large portion of central and eastern Europe. **2.** One wantonly destructive; a vandal. **3.** *Opprobrious.* A German.

hunch (hŭnch), *v. t.* **1.** *Obs.* To jostle, esp. with the elbow; to shove. **2.** To thrust out in a hump; to bend into an arch or hump. — *v. i.* To thrust, shove, or move oneself forward jerkily. — *n.* **1.** A lump; a hunk **2.** A hump; protuberance. **3.** *Colloq.* A strong, intuitive impression that something will happen; — from the gambler's superstition that it brings luck to touch the hump of a hunchback.

hunch′back′ (-băk′), *n.* A back with a hunch or hump; also, a hunchbacked person.

hunch′backed′ (-băkt′), *adj.* Having a humped back.

hun′dred (hŭn′drĕd), *n.* [AS., fr. the stems of AS. *hund* hundred + *-red* (akin to Goth. *rathjo* number).] **1.** See NUMBER, *Table.* **2.** *Brit. Hist.* A division of a county. **3.** *U. S. Hist.* A small political division, still surviving in Delaware. — **hun′dred,** *adj.*

hun′dred·fold′ (hŭn′drĕd·fōld′), *adj., adv., & n.* See -FOLD.

hun′dred–per·cent′er, *n.* A person, esp. an American, of thoroughgoing, unqualified, and often blatant patriotism.

hun′dredth (hŭn′drĕdth), *adj. & n.* See NUMBER, *Table.*

hun′dred·weight′ (hŭn′drĕd·wāt′), *n.* An avoirdupois weight. Abbr. *cwt.* See WEIGHT, *Table* 1. Cf. CENTAL, CENTNER.

hung (hŭng), *past & past part.* of HANG. See HANG.

Hun·gar′i·an (hŭng·gâr′ĭ·ăn; 6), *adj.* **1.** Of or pertaining to Hungary or its people. **2.** *Obs. Slang.* Thievish; beggarly. — *n.* **1.** A native or citizen of Hungary; esp., a Magyar. **2.** The language of the Magyars. See MAGYAR.

hun′ger (hŭng′gẽr), *n.* [AS. *hungor.*] **1.** **a** A craving or need for food. **b** An uneasy sensation occasioned normally by the want of food. **c** The weakened condition brought about by lack of food; as, to die of *hunger.* **2.** Any strong or eager desire; craving. — *v. i.* **1.** To feel, or be oppressed by, hunger. **2.** To have an eager desire; to long. — **Syn.** See LONG. — *v. t.* To famish; starve.

hun′ger·ing·ly (-ĭng·lĭ), *adv.* Hungrily.

hun′ger·ly (-lĭ), *adj. Archaic.* Hungry-looking.

hunger strike. Refusal, as of a prisoner, to eat enough to sustain life, so as to obtain his demands.

hun′gry (hŭng′grĭ), *adj.*; HUN′GRI·ER (-grĭ·ẽr); HUN′GRI·EST. [AS. *hungrig.*] **1.** Feeling hunger; hence, having an eager desire or craving. **2.** *Obs.* Marked by lack of food; famine-stricken. **3.** Showing, or characterized by, hunger or a craving desire. **4.** Not rich or fertile; barren; as, a *hungry* soil. — **hun′gri·ly,** *adv.* — **hun′gri·ness,** *n.*

hunk (hŭngk), *n. Colloq.* A large lump or piece; a hunch; as, a *hunk* of bread.

hun′kers (hŭng′kẽrz), *n. pl. Scot. & Dial.* Haunches.

hunks (hŭngks), *n. sing. & pl.* A surly, ill-natured person; a covetous, sordid man; a miser.

hunk′y (hŭngk′ĭ), *adj. Slang, U. S.* All right; in a good condition; also, even; square.

hunk′y, *n.*; *pl.* HUNKIES (-ĭz). *Slang, U. S.* Also **hunks** (hŭngks). A foreign-born laborer, usually unskilled, esp. a Hungarian or Yugoslav.

hunk′y–do′ry (-dō′rĭ; 70), *adj. Colloq.* Quite to one's content; comfortably nice.

Hun′nish (hŭn′ĭsh), *adj.* Of, like, or pertaining to the Huns; barbarous. — **Hun′nish·ness,** *n.*

hunt (hŭnt), *v. t.* [AS. *huntian.*] **1.** To follow or search for (game) for the purpose of capturing or killing; to pursue (game or prey) for food or in sport. **2.** To search diligently after; to seek. **3.** To drive; chase; hence, to follow up with, or as with, persecutions or annoyances; as, he was *hunted* from the parish. **4.** To traverse in pursuit of game; as, he *hunts* the woods; hence, to search carefully; as, he *hunted* the house for the papers. **5.** To use or manage in the chase, as hounds or a horse. **6.** *Change Ringing.* To shift the order of (a bell) in a hunt. — *v. i.* **1.** To follow the chase; to pursue game. **2.** To seek; pursue; search. **3.** *Change Ringing.* To shift the order of bells in a hunt. — *n.* **1.** Act or practice of hunting; chase. **2.** An association of huntsmen. **3.** A district hunted over. **4.** A regular course of changes on a series of from five to twelve bells. See CHANGE RINGING.

hunt′er, *n.* **1.** One who hunts wild animals; a huntsman. **2.** One who hunts or seeks after anything, as if for game. **3.** **a** A dog that scents game, or is trained to the chase. **b** One of a class of horses adapted for use in hunting, esp. in fox hunting. **4.** A watch having a hunting case.

hunt′ing, *n.* **1.** Act of one that hunts; specif., the pursuit of game. **2.** *Elec.* A periodic variation in speed of a synchronous machine from that of the true synchronous speed. — *adj.* Of, pertaining to, or adapted for use in hunting; as, a *hunting* dog; a *hunting* horn.

hunting case. A watchcase with a hinged cover to protect the crystal from accidents, as on the hunting field.

hunting knife. A large, stout, very sharp knife used to skin and cut up, and sometimes to dispatch, game. See KNIFE, *Illust.* (18).

hunting lodge. Also **hunting box.** A lodge used during a season of hunting.

hunting watch. = HUNTER, 4.

hunt′ress (hŭn′trĕs; -trĭs), *n.* A woman who hunts.

hunts′man (hŭnts′măn), *n.*; *pl.* -MEN (-mĕn). **1.** One who hunts. **2.** The person whose office it is to manage the hunt.

hunts′man's–cup′ (hŭnts′mănz-), *n.* The common pitcher plant (*Sarracenia purpurea*) of the northeastern United States; — so called from the shape of its pitchers, or leaves.

hunt′s–up′, *n.* A tune played on the hunting horn to call out the hunters; hence, any rousing tune.

Hu′on pine (hū′ŏn). [From the river *Huon* in Tasmania, named after a French officer.] A large Tasmanian timber tree (*Dacrydium franklinii*) of the yew family.

hur′cheon (hûr′chŭn), *n. Dial.* A hedgehog; also, an urchin.

hur′dies (hûr′dĭz), *n. pl. Scot.* The buttocks; rump.

hur′dle (hûr′d'l), *n.* [AS. *hyrdel.*] **1.** A movable frame, as of wattled twigs, for enclosing land, for folding sheep, etc. **2.** In England, a sled or crate on which criminals were formerly drawn to the place of execution. **3.** An artificial barrier over which men or horses leap, as in a race; hence, figuratively, a barrier to be surmounted. **4.** *pl.*, with *the.* A race (**hurdle race** *or* **the hurdles**) in which these barriers are used. — *v. t.*; HUR′DLED (-d'ld); HUR′DLING (-dlĭng). **1.** To hedge, cover, make, or enclose with hurdles. **2.** To leap over while running, as one leaps a hurdle; figuratively, to surmount (an obstacle). — *v. i.* **1.** To hurdle an obstacle. **2.** To compete in a hurdle race or specialize in hurdle racing. — **hur′dler** (-dlẽr), *n.*

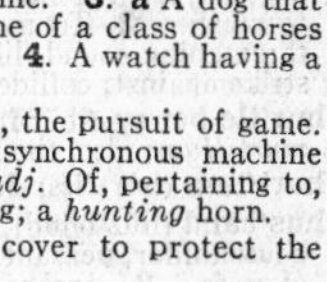
Hurdle, 3.

hurds (hûrdz), *n. pl.* [AS. *heordan.*] The refuse or coarse part of flax, hemp, or other textile plants; tow.

hur′dy–gur′dy (hûr′dĭ·gûr′dĭ), *n.*; *pl.* -DIES (-dĭz). *Music.* **a** A lutelike stringed instrument, in which the sound is produced by the friction of a resined wheel turned by a crank at the end. **b** Any instrument, esp. of street music, played by turning a handle; specif., a hand organ.

hurl (hûrl), *v. t.* [ME. *hurlen, hourlen*, prob. of imitative origin.] **1.** To throw or cast with violence. **2.** To overthrow; to cast down. **3.** To utter with vehemence; as, to *hurl* invective. — *v. i.* **1.** *Archaic.* To hurl oneself; to rush. **2.** To throw something (at another). **3.** *Baseball Slang.* To pitch. — **Syn.** See THROW. — *n.* A violent throw; cast. — **hurl′er,** *n.*

hurl′ey, hurl′y (hûr′lĭ), *n.*; *pl.* HURLEYS, HURLIES (-lĭz). **1.** The Irish game of hurling. **2.** The stick, club, or ball used in this game.

hurl′ing (hûr′lĭng), *n. Ireland.* A game resembling hockey.

hurl′y (hûr′lĭ), *n.*; *pl.* HURLIES (-lĭz). Turmoil; uproar.

hurl′y–burl′y (-bûr′lĭ), *n.*; *pl.* -IES (-lĭz). Tumult; uproar; also, a storm. — *adj.* Tumultuous; confused.

Hu′ron (hū′rŭn), *n.* [F., lit., unkempt person, ruffian.] One of a tribe of Iroquoian Indians, formerly occupying the country between Lake Huron and Lake Ontario.

hur·rah′ (hŏŏ·rô′; hŭ-; -rä′), *interj.* A shout expressing joy, triumph, applause, etc. — *n.* A cheer; a shout of joy. — *v. i. & t.* To utter hurrahs; to cheer.

hur·ray′ (hŏŏ·rā′; hŭ-). *Colloq.* var. of HURRAH.

hur′ri·cane (hûr′ĭ·kān; -kĭn), *n.* [Sp. *huracán*, fr. Taino *huracan, hurricán*, hurricane, evil spirit.] A cyclone of large extent, usually with rain, thunder, and lightning. It is the highest term in scales of wind force, but does not imply so great a velocity as tornadic winds, rarely exceeding 100 miles an hour. Cf. CYCLONE, GALE, TORNADO.

hurricane deck. The upper deck, usually a light structure, on a river steamer or like boat.

hur′ried (hûr′ĭd), *adj.* **1.** Going or working at speed. **2.** Done in a hurry; hasty. — **hur′ried·ly,** *adv.* — **hur′ried·ness,** *n.*

hur′ry (hûr′ĭ; 117), *v. t.*; HUR′RIED (-ĭd); HUR′RY·ING. **1.** To move, carry, or make to move, with great or flurried haste. **2.** To impel to hasty action. **3.** To urge on; to hasten the preparation or progress of. — *v. i.* To move or act with haste. — *n.*; *pl.* HURRIES (-ĭz). **1.**

Quick, hurried motion; rush; scurry. **2.** Act of hurrying, or state of being obliged to hurry; flurried haste or eagerness. — **Syn.** See HASTE.

hur′ry-scur′ry, hur′ry-skur′ry (hûr′ĭ-skûr′ĭ; 117), *n.* [*hurry* + *scurry*.] Flustered haste; disorderly confusion. — *v. t. & i.*; -SCUR′RIED (-skûr′ĭd) or -SKUR′RIED; -SCUR′RY·ING or -SKUR′RY·ING. To move or act hurry-scurry. — *adj.* Marked by, or full of, haste and confusion. — *adv.* Confusedly.

hurt (hûrt), *v. t.*; HURT; HURT′ING. [OF. *hurter* to knock, thrust, of Teut. origin.] **1.** To cause physical pain to. **2.** To impair the value, usefulness, beauty, or pleasure of; to damage. **3.** To wound the feelings of; to distress. — **Syn.** See INJURE. — *v. i.* **1.** To cause pain, injury, or damage of any kind. **2.** *Colloq.* To give the sensation of pain; as, my back *hurts*. — *n.* **1.** A wounding blow; also, the wound or injury caused by a blow; any bodily injury causing severe pain, or the pain itself. **2.** An injury causing pain of mind or conscience. **3.** Injury; damage. — **hurt′er**, *n.*

hurt′er (hûr′tẽr), *n.* [OF. *hurtoir.*] A strengthening piece; esp., *Ordn.*, a buffer or the like to check the motion of a gun carriage as the piece is run into position for firing.

hurt′ful (hûrt′fo͝ol; -f′l), *adj.* Tending to impair, damage, or pain; harmful; injurious. — **hurt′ful·ly**, *adv.* — **hurt′ful·ness**, *n.*

hur′tle (hûr′t′l), *v. i.*; HUR′TLED (-t′ld); HUR′TLING (-tlĭng). [ME. *hurtlen*, freq. of *hurten* to hurt.] **1.** To meet with violence or shock; to clash. **2.** To move rapidly; to rush suddenly. **3.** To make a threatening sound, like the clash of arms. — *v. t.* **1.** *Archaic.* To strike against; collide with. **2.** To drive or throw violently.

hur′tle·ber′ry (-bĕr′ĭ), *n.* The European whortleberry (*Vaccinium myrtillus*); also, the American huckleberry (genus *Gaylussacia*).

hurt′less (hûrt′lĕs; -lĭs), *adj.* Harmless; also, unhurt.

hus′band (hŭz′bănd), *n.* [AS. *hūsbonda*, fr. ON. *hūsbōndi* husband, householder, peasant.] **1.** A man who has a wife; — the correlative of *wife*. **2.** *Archaic.* A steward; manager. — *v. t.* **1.** To direct and manage with frugality; to spend, apply, or use with economy; as, to *husband* one's resources or one's strength. **2.** *Archaic.* To furnish with a husband; to mate. **3.** To become, or act as, the husband of; to marry.

hus′band·man (-măn), *n.* A farmer; a tiller of the ground.

hus′band·ry (-rĭ), *n.* **1.** Care of domestic affairs; hence, thrift; wise management. **2.** The business of a husbandman; farming. **3.** Management of one's affairs.

hush (hŭsh), *v. t.*; HUSHED (hŭsht) or, chiefly *Obs.*, HUSHT; HUSH′ING. [ME. *hussht* silent, taken as a past part., of interjectional origin.] **1.** To make quiet, still, or calm. **2.** To allay; soothe. **3.** To procure silence concerning; — usually with *up*. — *v. i.* To become or to keep still or quiet. — *adj. Archaic.* Still; hushed. — *n.* Stillness or silence, esp. following noise; quiet. — *interj.* An exclamation enjoining silence.

hush′-hush′, *adj.* Made or carried on with secrecy.

hush′ion (hŭsh′ŭn), *n. Scot.* A stocking without a foot.

hush money. Money paid to secure silence, or secrecy.

husk (hŭsk), *n.* [MD. *huuskijn*, dim. fr. *huus* (D. *huis*) house.] **1.** The outer covering, or envelope, of various seeds or fruits; *U. S.*, the bracts investing an ear of Indian corn. The *husks* referred to in the story of the prodigal son (*Luke* xv. 16) were carob pods. **2.** The outside covering of anything, esp. when rough or worthless. — *v. t.* To strip the husk from. — **husk′er**, *n.*

husk′ing, *n. U. S.* A meeting of neighbors or friends for husking Indian corn; — called also **husking bee**.

husk′y (hŭs′kĭ), *adj.*; HUSK′I·ER (-kĭ·ẽr); HUSK′I·EST. [From HUSK, *n.*] **1.** Abounding with, consisting of, or like, husks. **2.** Dry in the throat; rough in tone; harsh; as, a *husky* voice. — **husk′i·ly**, *adv.* — **husk′i·ness**, *n.*

hus′ky (hŭs′kĭ), *adj. Colloq.* Powerful; strong; burly. — *n. Colloq.* A husky person. — **hus′ki·ly**, *adv.* — **hus′ki·ness**, *n.*

Hus′ky (hŭs′kĭ), *n.*; *pl.* -KIES (-kĭz). [Origin uncert.] **a** An Eskimo. **b** An Eskimo dog of an unstandardized breed. **c** The Eskimo language.

hus·sar′ (ho͝o·zär′), *n.* [Hung. *huszár*, orig., a freebooter, fr. Serb. *husar*, *gusar*, fr. ML. *cursarius*.] *Mil.* Orig., one of the light cavalry of Hungary and Croatia; now, one of a class of cavalry of European armies, usually brilliantly uniformed. Cf. BUSBY, *Illust.*

Huss′ite (hŭs′īt), *n. Eccl. Hist.* A follower of John Huss, Bohemian reformer, who was adjudged a heretic by the Council of Constance (1414–18) and burned alive in 1415. He taught largely the doctrines of Wycliffe except upon the Eucharist, whereon he was orthodox. — **Huss′ite**, *adj.* — **Huss′it·ism** (-īt·ĭz′m), *n.*

hus′sy (hŭz′ĭ; hŭs′ĭ), *n.*; *pl.* -SIES (-ĭz). [Contr. fr. *huswife*.] **1.** *Contemptuous.* A worthless woman or girl; a jade. **2.** *Jocose.* A pert girl. **3.** *Now Dial.* A small case for needles, thread, etc.; a housewife.

hus′tings (hŭs′tĭngz), *n. pl.*, *usually construed as sing.* [AS. *hūsting*, fr. ON. *hūsthing*, fr. *hūs* house + *thing* thing, assembly.] **1.** *Hist.* A court formerly held in various English boroughs or cities. It still survives in London. **2.** The platform from which candidates for Parliament were formerly nominated; also, the proceedings at an election; now, any place where political campaign speeches are made. **3.** Any of various local courts of Virginia; — called usually **hustings court**.

hus′tle (hŭs′′l), *v. t. & i.*; HUS′TLED (-′ld); HUS′TLING (-lĭng). [D. *hutselen* to shake.] **1.** To shake together in confusion; to push, jostle, or crowd rudely. **2.** *Colloq.* To force onward rapidly; as, he *hustled* the work. **3.** *Colloq.* To move or act with resolute energy. — *n.* The act of one who hustles; specif.: **a** A pushing or shoving. **b** *Colloq.* Energetic activity; push.

hus′tler (hŭs′lẽr), *n.* One who hustles; specif., *Colloq.*, one who works with indefatigable rapidity and energy.

hus′wife (hŭz′ĭf). Var. of HOUSEWIFE. *Obs.* exc. in sense 3.

hut (hŭt), *n.* [F. *hutte*, fr. MLG. *hütte*, fr. OHG. *hutta*, *huttea*.] **1.** A rude small house, hovel, or cabin. **2.** *Mil.* A structure of varying size for housing troops. Cf. NISSEN HUT. **3.** *Australasia.* A house, sometimes a large permanent structure, for shearers or other workers on a station. — *v. t. & i.*; HUT′TED; HUT′TING. To place in a hut or huts; to live in a hut or huts; to furnish with huts.

hutch (hŭch), *n.* [OF. *huche*, *huge*, fr. LL. *hutica*.] **1.** A chest, box, coffer, bin, coop, or the like; as, a grain *hutch*; a rabbit *hutch*. **2.** A hut; hovel. — *v. t.* To put away; hoard.

huz·za′ (hŭ·zä′; ho͞o·zä′), *interj.* Hurrah! — *n.* A shout of *huzza*. — *v. i. & t.*; HUZ·ZAED′ (-zäd′); HUZ·ZA′ING. To applaud with huzzas; to cheer.

hy′a·cinth (hī′ȧ·sĭnth), *n.* [L. *hyacinthus* a kind of flower, also a proper name. See HYACINTHUS.] **1.** A precious stone of the ancients, perhaps the sapphire. **2. a** A plant fabled in classic myth to have sprung from the blood of Hyacinthus, variously identified as the Turk's-cap lily (*Lilium martagon*), the iris, larkspur, or gladiolus. **b** Commonly, a well-known plant (genus *Hyacinthus*) of the lily family, having spikes of bell-shaped flowers; also, the bulb or flower of the plant. **3.** A color, bluish blue-red in hue, of medium saturation and medium brilliance. See COLOR. **4.** *Mineral.* A transparent red or brownish variety of zircon, sometimes used as a gem. See JACINTH.

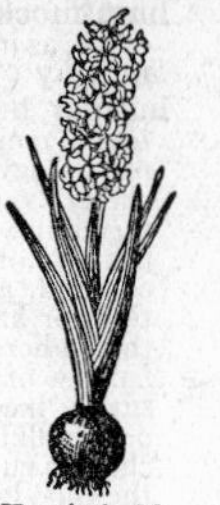

Hyacinth, 2 b. (⅛)

hy′a·cin′thine (-sĭn′thĭn; -thīn), *adj.* Of, or decked with, the hyacinth; resembling the hyacinth, as in color.

Hy′a·cin′thus (-sĭn′thŭs), *n. Gr. Myth.* A youth beloved by Apollo and accidentally killed by him. From his blood Apollo caused the hyacinth to spring.

Hy′a·des (hī′ȧ·dēz), **Hy′ads** (hī′ădz), *n. pl.* [L. *Hyades*, fr. Gr. *Hyades*.] **1.** *Gr. Myth.* Nymphs, daughters of Atlas and nurses of Dionysus, placed by Zeus in the heavens. **2.** *Astron.* A V-shaped cluster of stars in the head of the constellation Taurus, supposed by the ancients to indicate rainy weather when they rose with the sun.

hy·ae′na (hī·ē′nȧ). [L.] Var. of HYENA.

hy′a·line (hī′ȧ·lĭn; -līn), *adj.* [L. *hyalinus*, fr. Gr. *hyalinos*, fr. *hyalos* glass.] Glassy; specif., *Bot.*, transparent or translucent. — *n.* **1.** *Poetic.* The sea or the atmosphere when smooth or clear; anything transparent. **2.** (*pron.* -lēn; -lĭn) [In this use also **hy′a·lin**.] *Biochem.* **a** A nitrogenous substance closely related to chitin, forming the main constituent of the walls of hydatid cysts. **b** Any of several similar substances yielding a carbohydrate as a cleavage product.

hyaline cartilage. *Anat.* Typical cartilage consisting of a homogeneous intercellular matrix in which are small cavities, each containing one or more protoplasmic cells, the ***cartilage cells***.

hy′a·lite (hī′ȧ·līt), *n.* [*hyal-* + *-ite*.] *Mineral.* A colorless variety of opal, sometimes clear as glass, sometimes translucent or whitish.

hy′a·lo- (hī′ȧ·lō-), **hyal-**. [Gr. *hyalos* glass.] **a** A combining form meaning *glass*, *glassy character*. **b** Hence, a combining form for *hyaline* and *hyaloid*.

hy·al′o·gen (hī·ăl′ō·jĕn), *n.* [*hyalo-* + *-gen*.] *Biochem.* Any of several insoluble substances related to mucoids, found in many animal structures, as hydatids, sponges, etc., and yielding hyalines on hydrolysis.

hy′a·loid (hī′ȧ·loid), *adj.* [Gr. *hyaloeidēs* glassy. See -OID.] *Anat.* Glassy; transparent.

hyaloid membrane. *Anat.* A very delicate membrane enclosing the vitreous humor of the eye.

hy′a·lo·plasm (hī′ȧ·lō·plăz′m), *n.* [*hyalo-* + *-plasm*.] *Biol.* The clear, more fluid ground substance of protoplasm as distinguished from the reticulum, or from the granules or microsomes. — **hy′a·lo·plas′mic** (-plăz′mĭk), *adj.*

hy′brid (hī′brĭd), *n.* [L. *hybrida*, *hibrida*, the offspring of a tame sow and wild boar.] **1.** The offspring of the union of a male of one race, variety, species, genus, etc., with the female of another; a crossbred animal or plant. Artificial hybrids are obtained among plants by cross-pollinating the flowers of distinct species. By many plant and animal breeders the term *hybrid* is limited to a cross between different species, *crossbreed* being used for a cross between races or varieties of the same species. **2.** *Philol.* A word composed of elements from different languages (Eng. *bureaucracy*, *speedometer*). **3.** Anything of heterogeneous origin or composition. — *adj.* **1.** Of, pertaining to, or of the nature of a hybrid. **2.** Derived from unlike sources.

hy′brid·ism (-ĭz′m), *n.* **1.** Hybridity. **2.** Production of hybrids; crossbreeding; interbreeding.

hy·brid′i·ty (hī·brĭd′ĭ·tĭ), *n.* Hybrid state or quality.

hy′brid·ize (hī′brĭd·īz), *v. t. & i.* To produce, or to cause to produce, hybrid words or, esp., hybrid offspring, as, in *Bot.*, by cross-pollination; to interbreed; to cross. — **hy′brid·i·za′tion** (-ĭ·zā′shŭn; -ī·zā′-), *n.* — **hy′brid·iz′er** (-īz′ẽr), *n.*

hy′da·tid (hī′dȧ·tĭd), *n.* [Gr. *hydatis*, *-idos*, a watery vesicle, fr. *hydōr*, *hydatos*, water.] *Zool. & Med.* A cyst, filled with a pellucid fluid, sometimes found in various parts of the body of man and animals, enclosing larval tapeworms. — **hy′da·tid**, *adj.*

hyd′no·car′pate (hĭd′nō·kär′pāt), *n.* [Gr. *hydnon* an edible fungus + *-carp* + 1st *-ate*, 3.] *Chem.* A salt or ester of **hyd′no·car′pic ac′id** (-pĭk), $C_{15}H_{27}COOH$. Sodium hydnocarpate and ethyl hydnocarpate are used in the treatment of leprosy.

hydr-. = HYDRO-.

Hy′dra (hī′drȧ), *n.*; *gen.* HYDRAE (-drē); *pl.* HYDRAS (-drȧz), HYDRAE (-drē). [OF. *ydre*, fr. L. *hydra*, fr. Gr. *hydra*.] **1.** *Gr. Myth.* A serpent or monster slain by Hercules. It had nine heads, any of which, when cut off, was succeeded by two others, unless the wound was cauterized. **2.** [*not cap.*] Hence: A multifarious evil, or an evil having many sources, not to be overcome by a single effort. **3.** *Astron.* A southern constellation of great length lying south of Cancer, Sextans, Corvus, and Virgo. It is represented on old maps by a serpent. **4.** [*not cap.*] *Zool.* Any of a genus (*Hydra*) of small fresh-water hydrozoan polyps.

hy·drac′id (hī·drăs′ĭd), *n.* [*hydr-* + *acid*.] *Chem.* An acid which contains no oxygen.

hy·dran′ge·a (hī·drān′jē·ȧ; -drăn′-), *n.* [NL., fr. *hydr-* + Gr. *angeion* vessel, capsule.] Any of a genus (*Hydrangea*) of shrubs and one woody vine, typifying a family (Hydrangeaceae, the hydrangea family). Hydrangeas have opposite leaves and corymbose clusters of usually showy white or tinted flowers.

hy′drant (hī′drănt), *n.* [Gr. *hydōr* water.] A discharge pipe with a valve and spout at which water may be drawn from the mains of waterworks.

hy′dranth (-drănth), *n.* [*hydra* + Gr. *anthos* a flower.] *Zool.* One of the nutritive zooids of a hydroid colony.

hy·drar′gy·rism (hī·drär′jĭ·rĭz′m), *n.* [*hydrargyrum* + *-ism*.] *Med.* Mercurialism.

hy·drar′gy·rum (hī·drär′jĭ·rŭm), *n.* [NL., fr. L. *hydrargyrus*, fr. Gr. *hydrargyros*, fr. *hydōr* water + *argyros* silver.] Mercury. Chem. symbol, *Hg* (no period). — **hy′drar·gyr′ic** (hī′drär·jĭr′ĭk), *adj.*

hy·dras′tine (hī·drăs′tēn; -tĭn), *n.* Also **hy·dras′tin.** [NL. *Hydrastis*, genus name, fr. Gr. *hydōr* water.] *Chem.* A bitter crystalline nonpoisonous alkaloid, $C_{21}H_{21}O_6N$, found in the rootstock of the goldenseal and used as a tonic.

hy′drate (hī′drāt), *n.* [Gr. *hydōr* water.] *Chem.* A compound formed by the union of water with some other substance. — *v. t. & i.* *Chem.* To cause to become, or to become, a hydrate; in general, to combine with water or the elements of water. — **hy·dra′tion** (hī·drā′shŭn), *n.*

hy′drat·ed (-drāt·ĕd; -ĭd), *adj.* *Chem. & Mineral.* Containing water chemically combined, as in hydrates.

hy·drau′lic (hī·drô′lĭk), *adj.* Also, formerly, **hy·drau′li·cal** (-lĭ·kăl). [L. *hydraulicus*, fr. Gr. *hydraulikos*, fr. *hydraulis*, *-los*, a water organ, fr. *hydōr* water + *aulos* flute.] **1.** Of or relating to hydraulics; as, *hydraulic* engineering; conveying, or acting by, water; operated or effected by water; as, a *hydraulic* crane, press, or ram; *hydraulic* mining. **2.** Specif.: Designating a machine or device operating by the resistance offered when a quantity of water or other liquid is forced through a small orifice; as, a *hydraulic* brake; *hydraulic* elevator. **3.** Hardening or setting under water; as, *hydraulic* cement. — **hy·drau′li·cal·ly**, *adv.*

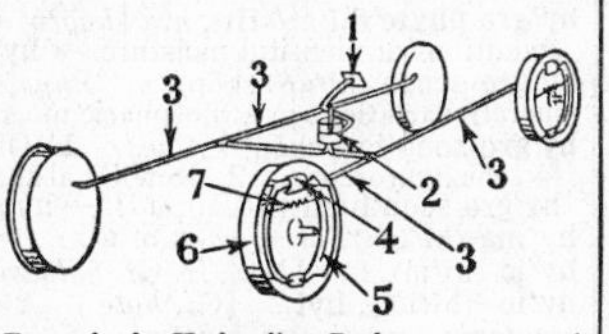

Four-wheel Hydraulic Brake system. 1 Pedal; 2 Master Cylinder (containing Piston); 3, 3, 3, 3 Lines to each Wheel; 4 Wheel Cylinder (containing opposed Pistons); 5 Shoe; 6 Drum; 7 Return Spring.

hy·drau′lics (-lĭks), *n.;* see -ICS. That branch of science, or of engineering, which treats of water or other liquid in motion, its action, the machinery for conducting or raising it, its use in driving machinery, etc. Cf. HYDRODYNAMICS, HYDROSTATICS.

hy′dra·zine (hī′drȧ·zēn; -zĭn), *n.* Also **hy′dra·zin.** [*hydr-* + *az-* + *-ine.*] *Chem.* **a** A colorless, fuming, corrosive liquid base, NH_2NH_2, made by reducing hyponitrous acid and in other ways. It forms a monohydrate, $NH_2NH_2.H_2O$, resembling it in properties, and a series of salts (as the sulfate). **b** Any of various organic bases derived from it.

hy·draz′o- (hī·drăz′ō-; hī′drȧ·zō-). [*hydr-* + *azo-.*] *Chem.* A combining form denoting the *presence of the group* -HNNH- *united to two hydrocarbon radicals.* — **hy·draz′o** (-ō), *adj.*

hy′dra·zo′ic (hī′drȧ·zō′ĭk), *adj.* [*hydr-* + *azo-* + *-ic.*] *Chem.* Pertaining to or designating an acid, HN_3, obtained by the action of nitrous acid on hydrazine, by heating sodium amide with nitrous oxide, and by other methods. In anhydrous form it is a colorless, mobile, volatile, poisonous liquid of unbearable odor. It and its salts (called **hy′dra·zo′ates** [-āts]), esp. those of silver and mercury, are explosive.

hy′dric (hī′drĭk), *adj.* Pert. to or containing hydrogen.

hy′dride (-drīd; -drĭd), *n.* Also **hy′drid.** [*hydr-* + *-ide.*] *Chem.* **a** Formerly, a hydroxide. **b** A compound of hydrogen with some element or radical.

hy′dri·od′ic (hī′drĭ·ŏd′ĭk), *adj.* [*hydr-* + *iodic.*] *Chem.* Pertaining to or designating an acid (**hydriodic acid**, HI), formed by the direct union of its elements, hydrogen and iodine, and in other ways.

hy′dro (hī′drō), *n.; pl.* -DROS (-drōz). Colloquial contraction of HYDROPLANE.

hy′dro- (hī′drō-), **hydr-.** [Gr. *hydōr.*] A combining form meaning: **a** *Water*, as in *hydrogen.* **b** *Chem. Presence of hydrogen*, as in *hydrochloric.* — **hy′dro** (-drō), *adj.*

hy′dro·air′plane′ (-âr′plān′), *n.* = HYDROPLANE, 2.

hy′dro·bi′plane′ (-bī′plān′), *n.* A hydroplane having two main supporting planes, one above the other.

hy′dro·bomb′ (hī′drō·bŏm′), *n.* A torpedo dropped from an aircraft into water, where it is propelled by a rocket engine.

hy′dro·bro′mic (-brō′mĭk), *adj.* [*hydro-* + *bromic.*] *Chem.* Pertaining to or designating an acid (**hydrobromic acid**, HBr) formed by the direct union of its elements, hydrogen and bromine, and in other ways.

hy′dro·car′bon (-kär′bŏn; *cf.* CARBON), *n.* [*hydro-* + *carbon.*] *Chem.* A compound containing only hydrogen and carbon, as acetylene, benzene, etc.

hy′dro·cele (hī′drō·sēl), *n.* [L., fr. Gr. *hydrokēlē*, fr. *hydōr* water + *kēlē* tumor.] *Med.* An accumulation of serous fluid in a sacculated cavity, specif. in the scrotum.

hy′dro·ceph′a·lus (hī′drō·sĕf′ȧ·lŭs), *n.* [NL., fr. Gr. *hydrokephalon*, fr. *hydōr* water + *kephalē* head.] *Med.* A condition marked by an excessive amount or pressure of the cerebrospinal fluid in the cranial cavity. — **hy′dro·ceph′a·loid** (-loid), *adj.* — **hy′dro·ceph′a·lous** (-lŭs), *adj.*

hy′dro·ceph′a·ly (-lĭ), *n.* Hydrocephalus.

hy′dro·chlo′ric (hī′drō·klō′rĭk; -klŏr′ĭk), *adj.* [*hydro-* + *chloric.*] *Chem.* Pertaining to or designating an acid (**hydrochloric acid**, HCl) formed by the explosive union of its elements, hydrogen and chlorine, by the action of acids on chlorides, and in other ways. The acid is a colorless, incombustible, pungent gas that fumes strongly in moist air, and is commonly known in the form of its solution in water. It is useful in commercial and general chemical work.

hy′dro·chlo′ride (-klō′rīd; -rĭd), *n.* Also **hy′dro·chlo′rid.** *Chem.* A compound of hydrochloric acid.

hy′dro·cy·an′ic (-sī·ăn′ĭk), *adj.* [*hydro-* + *cyanic.*] *Chem.* Pertaining to or designating a very weak acid (**hydrocyanic acid**, HCN), formed by combination of hydrogen and cyanogen, and in other ways. The acid is a colorless, mobile, volatile liquid of peach-blossom odor, and is a deadly poison; — called also *prussic acid.*

hy′dro·dy·nam′ic (-dī·năm′ĭk; -dĭ·năm′ĭk), **hy′dro·dy·nam′i·cal** (-ĭ·kăl), *adj.* Relating to, or derived from, the dynamical action of water or a liquid; of or pertaining to water power.

hy′dro·dy·nam′ics (-ĭks), *n.;* see -ICS. That branch of the science of mechanics which relates to fluids, or, as usually limited, which treats of the laws of motion and action of liquids; the principles of dynamics as applied to water and other fluids. Cf. HYDRAULICS, HYDROSTATICS.

hy′dro·e·lec′tric (-ē·lĕk′trĭk), *adj.* Pertaining to, or employed in, production of electricity by water power or the friction of water, steam, etc. — **hy′dro·e·lec′tric′i·ty** (-ē·lĕk′trĭs′ĭ·tĭ), *n.*

hy′dro·flu·or′ic (-flōō·ŏr′ĭk), *adj.* [*hydro-* + *fluoric.*] *Chem.* Pertaining to or designating an acid (**hydrofluoric acid**, HF or H_2F_2), a compound of hydrogen and fluorine. The acid is a colorless, mobile, volatile, fuming liquid, very corrosive in its action, and having a pungent, suffocating odor. It attacks all silicates, as glass or porcelain, and is chiefly used in etching glass.

hy′dro·gen (hī′drō·jĕn), *n.* [F. *hydrogène;* — because water is generated by its combustion. See HYDRO-; -GEN.] An element commonly isolated as a colorless, tasteless, odorless gas, inflammable, and lighter than any other known substance (sp. gr., compared with air, 0.0695). Symbol, *H*; at. no., 1; at. wt., 1.0080. The hydrogen atom is the simplest of all atoms, the ordinary isotope (H^1) consisting of a single proton in the nucleus and a single electron outside of the nucleus. It is accompanied by a minute amount of a heavier isotope called *deuterium* (H^2 or D), the nucleus of which is called *deuteron* or *deuton.*

hy′dro·gen·ate (-āt), *v. t.* *Chem.* To combine with hydrogen; also, to treat with, or expose to, hydrogen; as, to *hydrogenate* an oil. — **hy′dro·gen·a′tion** (-ā′shŭn), *n.*

hydrogen bomb. Also **H′–bomb′** (āch′bŏm′), *n.* A bomb designed to release an enormous quantity of atomic energy as a result of the union of (heavy) hydrogen nuclei at very high temperature and pressure to form helium nuclei; — called also *fusion bomb.* Cf. ATOMIC BOMB, ATOMIC ENERGY.

hydrogen ion. *Chem.* The positive (H^+) ion of all acids.

hy·drog′e·nous (hī·drŏj′ē·nŭs), *adj.* Of or pertaining to hydrogen; containing hydrogen.

hydrogen peroxide. An unstable compound, H_2O_2, used as an oxidizing and bleaching agent, and as antiseptic.

hydrogen sulfide. An inflammable poisonous gas, H_2S, of disagreeable odor, found in many mineral waters.

hy·drog′ra·phy (hī·drŏg′rȧ·fĭ), *n.* [F. *hydrographie.* See HYDRO-; -GRAPHY.] **1.** The description and study of seas, lakes, rivers, and other waters; specif.: **a** The measurement of flow of streams, esp. with reference to utilization of their waters. **b** The charting of water bodies. — **hy·drog′ra·pher** (-fẽr), *n.* — **hy′dro·graph′ic** (hī′drō·grăf′ĭk), **hy′dro·graph′i·cal** (-ĭ·kăl), *adj.*

hy′droid (hī′droid), *adj.* [*hydra* + *-oid.*] *Zool.* Of or pertaining to a hydrozoan (order Hydroidea); resembling the hydra; polyplike. — *n.* **a** A hydrozoan. **b** The polyp form of a hydrozoan, as distinguished from the *medusa* or *jellyfish* form.

hy′dro·ki·net′ic (hī′drō·kĭ·nĕt′ĭk; -kī·nĕt′-), **hy′dro·ki·net′i·cal** (-ĭ·kăl), *adj.* *Physics.* Of or relating to the motions of fluids, or the forces which produce or affect such motions.

hy′dro·ki·net′ics (-ĭks), *n.;* see -ICS. That branch of kinetics which relates to liquids. Cf. HYDRAULICS.

hy·drol′o·gy (hī·drŏl′ō·jĭ), *n.* [*hydro-* + *-logy.*] The science treating of water, its properties, phenomena, and distribution, esp. with reference to water on the surface of the land, in the soil and underlying rocks, and in the atmosphere. — **hy′dro·log′ic** (hī′drō·lŏj′ĭk), **hy′dro·log′i·cal** (-ĭ·kăl), *adj.* — **hy·drol′o·gist** (hī·drŏl′ō·jĭst), *n.*

hy·drol′y·sis (-ĭ·sĭs), *n.; pl.* HYDROLYSES (-sēz). [*hydro-* + *-lysis.*] *Chem.* A chemical process of decomposition involving addition of the elements of water.

hy′dro·lyte (hī′drō·līt), *n.* Any substance subjected to hydrolysis.

hy′dro·lyt′ic (-lĭt′ĭk), *adj.* Of, pert. to, or causing hydrolysis.

hy′dro·lyze (hī′drō·līz), *v. t. & i.* *Chem.* To subject to, or undergo, hydrolysis. — **hy′dro·lyz′a·ble** (-līz′ȧ·b′l), *adj.* — **hy′dro·ly·za′tion** (-lī·zā′shŭn), *n.*

hy′dro·man′cy (-măn′sĭ), *n.* [F. *hydromancie*, fr. L. *hydromantia.* See HYDRO-; -MANCY.] Divination by water or other liquid, as in observing ebb and flow of tides. — **hy′dro·manc′er** (-măn′sẽr), *n.*

hy′dro·me·chan′ics (-mē·kăn′ĭks), *n.;* see -ICS. That branch of physics which treats of the mechanics, or laws of equilibrium and motion, of liquids. See HYDRAULICS. — **hy′dro·me·chan′i·cal** (-ĭ·kăl), *adj.*

hy′dro·me·du′sa (-mē·dū′sȧ), *n.; pl.* -SAE (-sē). [NL. See HYDRA; MEDUSA.] *Zool.* Any medusa, or jellyfish, produced by budding from a hydroid.

hy′dro·mel (hī′drō·mĕl), *n.* [F. and L.; F., fr. L., fr. Gr. *hydromeli*, fr. *hydōr* water + *meli* honey.] A liquor consisting of honey diluted in water, and after fermentation called *mead.*

hy′dro·met′al·lur′gy (-mĕt′'l·ûr′jĭ), *n.* Treatment of ores by wet processes. — **hy′dro·met′al·lur′gi·cal** (-ûr′jĭ·kăl), *adj.*

hy′dro·me′te·or (hī′drō·mē′tē·ẽr), *n.* A meteor, or atmospheric phenomenon, dependent upon the vapor of water, as rain, hail, etc. — **hy′dro·me′te·or·ol′o·gy** (-ŏl′ō·jĭ), *n.*

hy·drom′e·ter (hī·drŏm′ē·tẽr), *n.* [*hydro-* + *-meter.*] *Physics.* A floating instrument for determining specific gravities, esp. of liquids, and thence the strength of spirituous liquors, saline solutions, etc. — **hy′dro·met′ric** (hī′drō·mĕt′rĭk), **hy′dro·met′ri·cal** (-rĭ·kăl), *adj.*

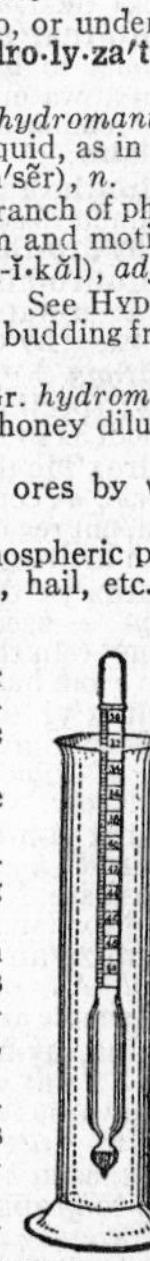
Hydrometer.

hy·drom′e·try (-trĭ), *n.* The art or operation of using the hydrometer; hence, formerly, hydrodynamics.

hy′dro·mon′o·plane′ (hī′drō·mŏn′ō·plān′), *n.* *Aeronautics.* A hydroplane having but one main supporting plane.

hy·drop′a·thy (hī·drŏp′ȧ·thĭ), *n.* [*hydro-* + *-pathy* as in homeo*pathy.*] A mode of treating diseases by copious use of water, internally and externally; water cure. — **hy′dro·path′ic** (hī′drō·păth′ĭk), **hy′dro·path′i·cal** (-ĭ·kăl), *adj.* — **hy·drop′a·thist** (hī·drŏp′ȧ·thĭst), *n.*

hy′dro·phane (hī′drō·fān), *n.* [*hydro-* + *-phane.*] *Mineral.* A semitranslucent variety of opal that becomes translucent or transparent on immersion in water. — **hy·droph′a·nous** (hī·drŏf′ȧ·nŭs), *adj.*

hy′dro·pho′bi·a (hī′drō·fō′bĭ·ȧ; 58), *n.* [L., fr. Gr. *hydrophobia*, fr. *hydōr* water + *phobos* fear.] *Med.* **a** A morbid dread of water. **b** Rabies, or canine madness. The disease is marked in human beings by mental depression, and by convulsions stimulated by any attempt to swallow water. — **hy′dro·pho′bic** (-fō′bĭk; -fŏb′ĭk), *adj.*

hy′dro·phone (hī′drō·fōn), *n.* [*hydro-* + *-phone.*] **a** An instrument for listening to sound transmitted through water, as in detecting submarines from the noise of their propellers. **b** An instrument, embodying a microphone, for detecting by sound a flow of water in a pipe.

hy′dro·phyte (-fīt), *n.* A plant which grows in water or in saturated soil; — contrasted with *epiphyte* and *geophyte.* — **hy′dro·phyt′ic** (-fĭt′ĭk), *adj.*

hy·drop′ic (hī·drŏp′ĭk), **hy·drop′i·cal** (-ĭ·kăl), *adj.* [OF. *idropique*, fr. L. *hydropicus*, fr. Gr. *hydrōpikos.* See DROPSY.] Dropsical.

hy′dro·plane (hī′drō·plān), *n.* **1.** A form of motorboat that glides on the water and receives its support, when in motion, from the dynamic reaction of the water upon a number of planes projecting from the hull. **2.** An airplane which is built to rise from or alight upon water; a seaplane. **3.** *Naut.* A rudder hung on a horizontal axis on a submarine for steering it upward or downward. — *v. i.* To glide like a hydroplane; also, to drive or ride in a hydroplane.

hy′dro·pon′ics (hī′drō·pŏn′ĭks), *n.;* see -ICS. [*hydro-* + Gr. *ponos* labor. Cf. GEOPONIC.] The growing of plants, esp. vegetables, with their roots immersed in an aqueous solution containing the essential mineral nutrient salts, instead of in soil; — called also *tray agriculture, tank farming, water culture.* — **hy′dro·pon′ic** (-ĭk), *adj.* — **hy·drop′o·nist** (hī·drŏp′ō·nĭst), *n.*

hy′dro·qui·none′ (hī′drō·kwĭ·nōn′; -kwĭn′ōn), *n.* Also **hy′dro·quin′ol** (-kwĭn′ōl; -ŏl). [*hydro-* + *quinone.*] *Chem.* A white crystalline compound, $C_6H_4(OH)_2(p)$, obtained by reduction of quinone and otherwise, used as a photographic developer and as an antiseptic and antipyretic agent.

hy′dro·scope (hī′drō·skōp), *n.* A device for enabling a person to see at considerable depths below the surface of water. — **hy′dro·scop′ic** (-skŏp′ĭk), *adj.*

hy′dro·sol (-sŏl; -sōl), **hy′dro·sole** (-sōl), *n.* [*hydro-* + *sol*ution.] *Chem.* An aqueous colloidal solution.

hy′dro·some (-sōm), **hy′dro·so′ma** (-sō′mȧ), *n.* [NL. *hydrosoma.* See HYDRA; 2d -SOME.] *Zool.* The entire colony of a compound hydrozoan; a hydroid.

hy′dro·sphere (-sfēr), *n.* **a** The aqueous vapor of the atmosphere. **b** The aqueous envelope of the earth.

hy′dro·stat (-stăt), *n.* **1.** A contrivance to prevent the explosion of steam boilers. **2.** A device, usually electrical, for indicating or regulating the height of water in a reservoir or receptacle.

hy′dro·stat′ic (-stăt′ĭk), **hy′dro·stat′i·cal** (-ĭ·kăl), *adj.* [*hydro-* + Gr. *statikos* causing to stand.] Of or relating to hydrostatics; as, a *hydrostatic*, or hydraulic, press.

hy′dro·stat′ics (-ĭks), *n.;* see -ICS. That branch of physics which relates to the pressure and equilibrium of liquids; the principles of statics applied to liquids. Cf. HYDRAULICS, HYDRODYNAMICS.

hy′dro·sul′fide, hy′dro·sul′phide (hī′drō·sŭl′fīd; -fĭd), *n.* Also **hy′dro·sul′fid, hy′dro·sul′phid.** *Chem.* A compound derived from hydrogen sulfide by the replacement of half its hydrogen by an element or radical.

hy′dro·sul′fite, hy′dro·sul′phite (-fīt), *n.* *Chem.* A salt of hydrosulfurous acid; specif., sodium hyposulfite, used as a reducing and bleaching agent.

hy′dro·sul·fu′rous, hy′dro·sul·phu′rous (-sŭl·fū′rŭs; -sŭl′fŭ·rŭs), *adj.* *Chem.* Hyposulfurous.

hy′dro·tax′is (-tăk′sĭs), *n.* [NL., fr. *hydro-* + *-taxis.*] *Biol.* A taxis in which the proximity of water is the directive factor. — **hy′dro·tac′tic** (-tăk′tĭk), *adj.*

hy′dro·ther′a·py (-thĕr′ȧ·pĭ), *n.; pl.* -PIES (-pĭz). [*hydro-* + *therapy.*] *Med.* A system of treating disease by baths and mineral waters. — **hy′dro·ther′a·peu′tic** (-thĕr′ȧ·pū′tĭk), *adj.* — **hy′dro·ther′a·peu′tics** (-tĭks), *n.;* see -ICS. — **hy′dro·ther′a·pist** (-thĕr′ȧ·pĭst), *n.*

hy′dro·ther′mal (-thûr′măl), *adj.* [*hydro-* + *thermal.*] Of or pertaining to hot water; — used esp. with reference to the action of heated waters in dissolving, redepositing, and otherwise causing mineral changes within the earth's crust (**hydrothermal metamorphism**).

hy′dro·tho′rax (-thō′răks), *n.* [NL.] *Med.* An abnormal condition characterized by an accumulation of serous fluid in the pleural cavity. — **hy′dro·tho·rac′ic** (-thō·răs′ĭk), *adj.*

hy·drot′ro·pism (hī·drŏt′rō·pĭz′m), *n.* *Biol.* A tropism in which water or water vapor constitutes the orienting factor, as in many plant roots. — **hy′dro·trop′ic** (hī′drō·trŏp′ĭk), *adj.*

hy′drous (hī′drŭs), *adj.* [Gr. *hydōr* water.] Containing water; watery; specif., *Chem. & Mineral.*, containing water chemically combined, as in hydrates.

hy·drox′ide (hī·drŏk′sīd; -sĭd), *n.* Also **hy·drox′id.** [*hydr-* + *oxide.*] *Chem.* A compound of an element or radical with hydrogen and oxygen, not regarded as present in the form of water; usually, a compound with hydroxyl (OH).

hy·drox′y- (hī·drŏk′sĭ-). *Chem.* A combining form for *hydroxyl; oxy-;* — used in organic compounds, as in **hy·drox′y·an′thra·qui·none′** (-ăn′thrȧ·kwĭ·nōn′; -kwĭn′ōn), anthraquinone in which a hydrogen atom has been replaced by hydroxyl. — **hy·drox′y** (-sĭ), *adj.*

hy·drox′yl (hī·drŏk′sĭl), *n.* [*hydr-* + *oxy*gen + *-yl.*] *Chem.* The univalent group or radical OH, consisting of one atom of hydrogen and one of oxygen. It is a characteristic part of bases, alcohols, oxygen acids, etc. See HYDROXIDE.

hy·drox′yl·a·mine′ (-sĭl·ȧ·mēn′; hī′drŏk·sĭl′ȧ·mēn; -mĭn), *n.* Also **-min.** [*hydroxyl* + *amine.*] *Chem.* A colorless, odorless, nitrogenous base, NH_2OH, resembling ammonia in its reactions but less basic. Hydroxylamine is a strong reducer.

hy′dro·zo′an (hī′drō·zō′ăn), *n.* [*hydra* + Gr. *zōion* an animal.] *Zool.* Any of a class (Hydrozoa) of coelenterates which includes various simple and compound polyps and jellyfishes. — **hy′dro·zo′an,** *adj.*

hy·e′na, hy·ae′na (hī·ē′nȧ), *n.* [L. *hyaena*, fr. Gr. *hyaina*, fr. *hys* hog.] Any of a family (Hyaenidae) of large and strong, but cowardly, carnivorous mammals of Asia and Africa.

hy′e·to- (hī′ē·tō-), **hyet-.** [Gr. *hyetos.*] A combining form meaning *rain*, as in *hyeto*graphy.

hy′e·to·graph′ (-grăf′; 9), *n.* [*hyeto-* + *-graph.*] A chart showing the average annual rainfall.

hy′e·tog′ra·phy (hī′ē·tŏg′rȧ·fĭ), *n.* Scientific description of the geographical distribution of rain. — **hy′e·to·graph′ic** (-tō·grăf′ĭk), **hy′e·to·graph′i·cal** (-ĭ·kăl), *adj.* — **hy′e·to·graph′i·cal·ly,** *adv.*

hy′e·tol′o·gy (-tŏl′ō·jĭ), *n.* [*hyeto-* + *-logy.*] The science which treats of the precipitation of rain, snow, etc. — **hy′e·to·log′i·cal** (-tō·lŏj′ĭ·kăl), *adj.*

Hy·ge′ia (hī·jē′ȧ; -jē′yȧ), *n.* [From L., fr. Gr. *hygieia, hygeia* health.] *Gr. Myth.* Goddess of health.

hy′ge·ist, hy′gie·ist (hī′jē·ĭst), *n.* A hygienist.

hy′giene (hī′jēn; hī′jĭ·ēn), *n.* [F. *hygiène*, fr. Gr. *hygieinos* healthful.] The science of the preservation of health; sanitary science; a system of principles or rules designed for the promotion of health.

hy′gi·en′ic (hī′jĭ·ĕn′ĭk; hī·jē′nĭk), **hy′gi·en′i·cal** (-ĭ·kăl), *adj.* Of or pertaining to health or hygiene; sanitary. — **hy′gi·en′i·cal·ly,** *adv.*

hy′gi·en′ics (-ĭks), *n.;* see -ICS. The science of health.

hy′gi·en·ist (hī′jĭ·ĕn·ĭst), *n.* One versed in hygiene; specif., in full ***dental hygienist***, a trained worker, usually a woman, who cleanses teeth and, esp. in schools, instructs in the hygienic care of the teeth and mouth.

hy′gro- (hī′grō-), **hygr-.** [Gr. *hygros.*] A combining form meaning *wet, moist*, usually denoting *moisture, humidity*, as in *hygro*meter.

hy′gro·graph (hī′grō·grăf; 9), *n.* An instrument for recording automatically the variations of atmospheric humidity.

hy·grom′e·ter (hī·grŏm′ē·tēr), *n.* [*hygro-* + *-meter.*] *Physics.* An apparatus for measuring the degree of moisture of the atmosphere. — **hy′gro·met′ric** (hī′grō·mĕt′rĭk), *adj.* — **hy·grom′e·try** (hī·grŏm′ē·trĭ), *n.*

hy′gro·phyte (hī′grō·fīt), *n.* [*hygro-* + *-phyte.*] A plant living under conditions of plentiful moisture. — **hy′gro·phyt′ic** (-fĭt′ĭk), *adj.*

hy′gro·scope (hī′grō·skōp), *n.* *Physics.* An instrument which shows merely variations in atmospheric moisture.

hy′gro·scop′ic (-skŏp′ĭk), *adj.* **1.** Of or pertaining to, or indicated by, the hygroscope. **2.** Readily absorbing and retaining moisture. — **hy′gro·scop′i·cal** (-ĭ·kăl), *adj.* — **hy′gro·scop′i·cal·ly,** *adv.*

hy′ing (hī′ĭng), *pres. part.* of HIE.

hy′la (hī′lȧ), *n.* [NL., fr. Gr. *hylē* wood.] A tree toad.

hy′lo- (hī′lō-), **hyl-.** [Gr. *hylē.*] A combining form meaning *wood, material, substance, matter.*

hy′lo·zo′ism (-zō′ĭz′m), *n.* [*hylo-* + Gr. *zōē* life.] The doctrine that matter is animated, or that matter and life are inseparable; — often applied specif. to the crude theories of the early Ionian philosophers. — **hy′lo·zo′ic** (-ĭk), *adj.* — **hy′lo·zo′ist** (-ĭst), *n.* — **hy′lo·zo·is′tic** (-zō·ĭs′tĭk), *adj.* — **hy′lo·zo·is′ti·cal·ly** (-tĭ·kăl·ĭ), *adv.*

hy′men (hī′mĕn), *n.* [Gr. *hymēn* skin, membrane.] *Anat.* A fold of mucous membrane partly closing the orifice of the vagina.

Hy′men, *n.* [L., fr. Gr. *Hymēn.*] **1.** *Gr. Myth.* God of marriage. **2.** [*not cap.*] Marriage; also, a wedding song.

hy′me·ne′al (hī′mĕ·nē′ăl), *adj.* Of or pertaining to marriage. — *n.* A marriage song. — **hy′me·ne′al·ly,** *adv.*

hy·me·ne′an (-ăn), *adj.* Hymeneal.

hy′me·no- (hī′mĕ·nō-), **hymen-.** [Gr. *hymēn.*] A combining form meaning *membrane*, as in *hymeno*pterous.

hy′me·nop′ter·on (hī′mĕ·nŏp′tēr·ŏn), *n.; pl.* -TERA (-ȧ). Also **hy′me·nop′ter** (hī′mĕ·nŏp′tēr). A hymenopterous insect.

hy′me·nop′ter·ous (-ŭs), *adj.* [Gr. *hymenopteros* membrane-winged, fr. *hymēn* membrane + *pteron* wing.] *Zool.* Belonging to an extensive and highly specialized order (Hymenoptera) of insects, including the bees, wasps, ants, ichneumons, sawflies, true gallflies, etc. When winged they have four membranous wings. Taking into account both their structure and their instincts (apparently not unmixed with true intelligence), exhibited in the provision for their young and in the remarkable social organization of the communities of many of the social forms, they are the most specialized group not only of insects, but of invertebrates. — **hy′me·nop′ter·an** (-ăn), *adj. & n.*

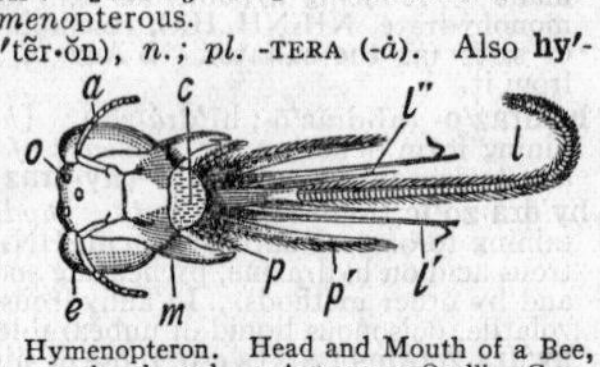

Hymenopteron. Head and Mouth of a Bee, much enlarged. *a* Antenna; *o* Ocelli; *c* Compound Eye; *c* Labrum; *m* Mandible; *p* Maxillary Palpus; *p′* Maxilla; *l* Ligula or Tongue; *l′* Labial Palpus; *l″* Paraglossa.

hymn (hĭm), *n.* [From AS. *ymen, hymen* (fr. LL.), and fr. OF. *ymne* (F. *hymne*), fr. LL. *ymnus, hymnus*, fr. Gr. *hymnos.*] An ode or song of praise or adoration; esp., a religious ode or song; as, the Homeric *hymns.* — *v. t. & i.* To praise, worship, or extol by singing hymns.

hym′nal (hĭm′năl; -n'l), *adj.* Pertaining to, or using, hymns. — *n.* A collection of hymns.

hymn′book′ (hĭm′bŏŏk′), *n.* A book containing a collection of hymns, as for use in churches; a hymnal.

hym′nist (hĭm′nĭst), *n.* A writer of hymns.

hym′no·dy (hĭm′nō·dĭ), *n.* [Gr. *hymnōidia*, fr. *hymnos* hymn + *ōidē* a song, a singing.] **1.** Act or art of singing hymns. **2.** Hymns collectively. — **hym′no·dist** (-dĭst), *n.*

hym·nol′o·gy (hĭm·nŏl′ō·jĭ), *n.* [Gr. *hymnos* hymn + *-logy.*] **a** The composition of hymns. **b** The study or science of hymns. **c** Hymns collectively. — **hym·nol′o·gist** (-jĭst), *n.*

hy′oid (hī′oid), *adj.* [F. *hyoïde*, fr. Gr. *hyoeidēs*, fr. the letter Υ (upsilon) + *eidos* form.] *Anat. & Zool.* Designating, or pertaining to, a bone (U-shaped in man) or bones at the base of the tongue. — *n.* The hyoid bone.

Hy′os·cine (hī′ō·sēn; -sĭn), *n.* Also **Hy′os·cin.** *Chem.* A trade-mark for levo scopolamine; also, any variety of scopolamine.

hy′os·cy′a·mine (hī′ō·sī′ȧ·mēn; -mĭn), *n.* Also **hy′os·cy′a·min.** [L. *hyoscyamus* henbane, fr. Gr. *hyoskyamos*, fr. *hys* sow, hog + *kyamos* bean.] *Chem.* **a** A colorless crystalline alkaloid, $C_{17}H_{23}NO_3$, found in henbane (*Hyoscyamus niger*) and other plants of the nightshade family. **b** Specif., the levo variety, used as a hypnotic and sedative and locally as a mydriatic.

hyp (hĭp), *n.* *Colloq.* Short for HYPOCHONDRIA.

hyp-. = HYPO-.

hyp′a·byss′al (hĭp′ȧ·bĭs′ăl; -'l), *adj.* *Petrog.* Partly crystalline in texture, as formed at a moderate depth below the surface. Cf. PLUTONIC.

hyp′aes·the′si·a, hyp′aes·the′sic. Vars. of HYPESTHESIA, etc.

hy·pae′thral, hy·pe′thral (hĭ·pē′thrăl; hī·pē′-), *adj.* [L. *hypaethrus* in the open air, uncovered, fr. Gr. *hypaithros*, fr. *hypo* under + *aithēr* ether, the clear sky.] Open to the sky; not roofed over; — applied, *Class. Arch.*, to a building, court, etc.

hy·pan′thi·um (hĭ·păn′thĭ·ŭm; hī·păn′-), *n.; pl.* HYPANTHIA (-ȧ). [NL., fr. *hyp-* + Gr. *anthos* flower.] *Bot.* Any enlargement or special development of the torus below the calyx, as in the rose hip, or fruit. — **hy·pan′thi·al** (-ăl), *adj.*

hy′per- (hī′pēr-). [Gr. *hyper* over, above.] **1.** A prefix meaning *over, above, beyond, beyond the ordinary* or *norm;* used: **a** Prepositionally; *super-;* — chiefly in adjectives, as in *hyper*barbarous. **b** Adverbially; *extra-;* — chiefly in adjectives and nouns, as in *hyper*critical, *hyper*acidity. **c** *Anat. & Zool.* Denoting *position above.* **2.** *Chem.* = PER-, 2, as in **hy′per·ox′ide,** peroxide. **3.** *Med.* Denoting:

Abnormal excess in extent or *degree;* — opposite of *hypo-*, as in *hyperesthesia.*

☞ COMBINATIONS are:

hyperacid	hyperdelicate	hyperphenomena
hyperacidity	hyperdiabolical	hyperpigmentation
hyperactive	hyperexcitable	hyperrational
hyperactivity	hyperexcitement	hyperridiculous
hyperacute	hyperextension	hypersceptical
hyperbarbarous	hyperfunction	hypersensual
hypercathartic	hyperfunctional	hypersensuous
hypercivilized	hyperhypocrisy	hypersentimental
hyperclassical	hyperimmunity	hypersophisticated
hyperconfident	hyperingenuity	hyperspeculative
hyperconscientious	hyperintellectual	hypertechnical
hyperconscious	hypermoral	hypertoxicity
hyperconservatism	hypermystical	hypertragical
hypercriticism	hyperneurotic	hypervigilant

hy′per·ae′mi·a, hy′per·ae′mic. Vars. of HYPEREMIA, etc.

hy′per·aes·the′si·a, hy′per·aes·thet′ic. Vars. of HYPERESTHESIA, etc.

hy′per·al·ge′si·a (hī′pẽr·ăl·jē′zĭ·ȧ; -sĭ·ȧ), **hy′per·al·ge′sis** (-sĭs), *n.* [NL., fr. *hyper-* + Gr. *algēsis* sense of pain.] Excessive sensitiveness to pain. — **hy′per·al·ge′sic** (-sĭk), *adj.*

hy·per′bo·la (hī·pûr′bō·lȧ), *n.; pl.* -BOLAS (-lȧz). [NL., fr. Gr. *hyperbolē*, prop., an overshooting, excess. See HYPERBOLE.] *Geom.* A curve formed by a section of a right circular cone when the cutting plane makes a greater angle with the base than the cone's side makes.

hy·per′bo·le (-lē; -lē), *n.* [L., fr. Gr. *hyperbolē*, prop., an overshooting, excess, deriv. of *hyper* over + *ballein* to throw.] *Rhet.* Extravagant exaggeration of statement; a statement exaggerated fancifully, as for effect.

hy′per·bol′ic (hī′pẽr·bŏl′ĭk), **hy′per·bol′i·cal** (-ĭ·kăl), *adj.* **1.** *Math.* Of or pertaining to the hyperbola. **2.** *Rhet.* Of the nature of, or given to, hyperbole. — **hy′per·bol′i·cal·ly** (-ĭ·kăl·ĭ), *adv.*

hy·per′bo·lism (hī·pûr′bō·lĭz′m), *n.* Use of hyperbole.

hy·per′bo·lize (-līz), *v. t. & i.* To state, speak, or write with hyperbole.

Hy′per·bo′re·an (hī′pẽr·bō′rē·ăn; 70), *n.* [L. *hyperboreus*, fr. Gr. *hyperboreos*, perh. prop., beyond the mountains. See HYPER-; BOREAS.] *Gr. Myth.* One of a people beyond the north wind in a region of perpetual sunshine. — *adj.* Of or in the far north; hence, cold.

hy′per·cat′a·lec′tic (hī′pẽr·kăt′ȧ·lĕk′tĭk), *adj.* [From L., fr. Gr. *hyperkatalēktos.* See HYPER-; CATALECTIC.] *Pros.* Having a syllable or two beyond the last regular measure, esp. when such a measure ends in a long or accented syllable.

hy′per·crit′ic (-krĭt′ĭk), *n.* [*hyper-* + *critic.*] One who is critical beyond measure or reason; a carping critic.

hy′per·crit′i·cal (-ĭ·kăl), *adj.* Overcritical; also, excessively nice or exact. — **Syn.** See CRITICAL. — **hy′per·crit′i·cal·ly**, *adv.*

hy′per·du·li′a (-dū·lī′ȧ), *n.* [*hyper-* + *dulia.*] *R.C.Ch.* The veneration given to the Virgin Mary as the most exalted of mere creatures; higher veneration than dulia.

hy′per·e′mi·a, hy′per·ae′mi·a (-ē′mĭ·ȧ), *n.* [NL.] *Med. & Physiol.* A superabundance or congestion of blood in any part. — **hy′per·e′mic, hy′per·ae′mic** (-ē′mĭk; -ĕm′ĭk), *adj.*

hy′per·es·the′si·a, hy′per·aes·the′si·a (-ĕs·thē′zhĭ·ȧ; -zhȧ; -zĭ·ȧ; -sĭ·ȧ), *n.* [NL.] A state of exalted or morbidly increased sensibility. — **hy′per·es·thet′ic, hy′per·aes·thet′ic** (-thĕt′ĭk), *adj.*

hy′per·eu·tec′tic (-ū·tĕk′tĭk), *adj.* *Physics, Metal., & Chem.* Containing the minor constituent in an amount in excess of that contained in the eutectic mixture; — opposed to *hypoeutectic.*

hy′per·fo′cal (-fō′kăl), *adj.* *Photog.* Designating the nearest distance upon which a lens may be focused to produce satisfactory definition at infinity.

Hy·pe′ri·on (hī·pē̃r′ĭ·ŏn; *L.* hī′pẽr·ĭ′ŏn), *n.* [L., fr. Gr. *Hyperiōn.*] *Gr. Myth.* **a** A Titan, father of Helios; also (as a patronymic), Helios. **b** In later myth, Apollo.

hy′per·ir′ri·ta·bil′i·ty (hī′pẽr·ĭr′ĭ·tȧ·bĭl′ĭ·tĭ), *n.* *Med.* Excessive irritability. — **hy′per·ir′ri·ta·ble** (-ĭr′ĭ·tȧ·b'l), *adj.*

hy′per·ki·ne′si·a (-kĭ·nē′sĭ·ȧ; -zĭ·ȧ; -kī-), *n.* Also **hy′per·ki·ne′sis** (-nē′sĭs). [NL., fr. *hyper-* + Gr. *kinēsis* motion.] *Med.* Abnormally increased muscular movement. — **hy′per·ki·net′ic** (-nĕt′ĭk), *adj.*

hy′per·met′ric (-mĕt′rĭk), **hy′per·met′ri·cal** (-rĭ·kăl), *adj.* *Pros.* Having a redundant syllable; exceeding the common measure.

hy′per·me·tro′pi·a (hī′pẽr·mē·trō′pĭ·ȧ), *n.* [NL., fr. Gr. *hypermetros* excessive + *ōps, ōpos*, the eye.] = HYPEROPIA. — **hy′per·me·trop′ic** (-trŏp′ĭk), **hy′per·me·trop′i·cal** (-ĭ·kăl), *adj.* — **hy′per·met′ro·py** (-mĕt′rō·pĭ), *n.*

Hy′perm·nes′tra (hī′pẽrm·nĕs′trȧ), *n.* [L., fr. Gr. *Hypermnēstra.*] *Gr. Myth.* See DANAÏDES.

hy′per·o′pi·a (hī′pẽr·ō′pĭ·ȧ), *n.* [NL., fr. *hyper-* + *-opia.*] *Med.* A condition of the eye in which vision for distant objects is better than for near objects so that the individual is said to be farsighted. — **hy′per·op′ic** (-ŏp′ĭk), *adj.*

hy′per·os·to′sis (-ŏs·tō′sĭs), *n.; pl.* HYPEROSTOSES (-sēz). [NL., fr. *hyper-* + Gr. *osteon* bone + *-osis.*] *Anat. & Med.* Outgrowth or marked local thickening of bony tissue, normal or abnormal. — **hy′per·os·tot′ic** (-tŏt′ĭk), *adj.*

hy′per·phys′i·cal (-fĭz′ĭ·kăl), *adj.* **1.** Beyond, or more than, the physical. **2.** Independent of the physical.

hy′per·pi·e′si·a (-pī·ē′zhĭ·ȧ; -sĭ·ȧ), **hy′per·pi·e′sis** (-sĭs), *n.* [NL., fr. *hyper-* + Gr. *piesis* pressure, fr. *piezein* to press.] *Med.* Abnormally high blood pressure.

hy′per·pi·tu′i·ta·rism (-pĭ·tū′ĭ·tȧ·rĭz′m), *n.* [*hyper-* + *pituitary* + *-ism.*] *Med. & Psychol.* Excessive activity of the pituitary body; also, the resultant abnormal state. Cf. HYPOPITUITARISM.

hy′per·pla′si·a (-plā′zhĭ·ȧ; -zĭ·ȧ), *n.* [NL., fr. *hyper-* + *-plasia.*] *Med. & Biol.* An abnormal increase in the elements composing a part, as of the cells of a tissue. Cf. HYPOPLASIA. — **hy′per·plas′tic** (-plăs′tĭk), **hy′per·plas′tic** (-tĭk), *adj.*

hy′per·ploid (hī′pẽr·ploid), *adj.* [*hyper-* + Gr. *-ploos* -fold.] *Biol.* Having or designating a chromosome number greater than the basic chromosome number but usually not a simple multiple of it. Cf. HYPOPLOID — **hy′per·ploid, hy′per·ploid′y**, *n.*

hy′perp·ne′a, hy′per·pnoe′a (hī′pẽrp·nē′ȧ; hī′pẽr·nē′ȧ), *n.* [NL., fr. *hyper-* + Gr. *pnoē, pnoiē*, breath.] *Physiol.* Abnormally rapid breathing, as from deficient arterialization of the blood. Cf. EUPNEA, DYSPNEA.

hy′per·py·rex′i·a (hī′pẽr·pī·rĕk′sĭ·ȧ), *n.* [NL.] *Med.* Abnormally high fever (for a given disease). — **hy′per·py·ret′ic** (-rĕt′ĭk), **hy′per·py·rex′i·al** (-rĕk′sĭ·ăl), *adj.*

hy′per·sen′si·tive (-sĕn′sĭ·tĭv), *adj.* Excessively sensitive. — **hy′per·sen′si·tive·ness, hy′per·sen′si·tiv′i·ty** (-tĭv′ĭ·tĭ), *n.*

hy′per·son′ic (hī′pẽr·sŏn′ĭk), *adj.* [*hyper-* + *sonic.*] Designating any speed approximately five times that of sound in air or greater; also, moving, capable of moving, or utilizing air currents moving at such a speed. Cf. SUPERSONIC.

hy′per·sthene (hī′pẽr·sthēn), *n.* [*hyper-* + Gr. *sthenos* strength.] *Mineral.* An orthorhombic grayish or greenish-black or dark-brown mineral of the pyroxene group. — **hy′per·sthen′ic** (-sthĕn′ĭk), *adj.*

hy′per·ten′sion (hī′pẽr·tĕn′shŭn), *n.* [*hyper-* + *tension.*] *Med.* **a** Abnormally high arterial blood pressure, either: (1) without apparent or determinable organic changes in the tissues, resulting partly from factors such as a hereditary tendency, fear and other emotions, and hormonal action, or (2) with demonstrable organic changes, such as in nephritis, diabetes, hyperthyroidism, etc., and old age. **b** The resulting condition, which may be symptomless or accompanied by nervousness, headache, dizziness, etc.

hy′per·ten′sive (-sĭv), *adj.* *Med.* Characterized by a rise in blood pressure; suffering hypertension. — *n.* A hypertensive person.

hy′per·therm (hī′pẽr·thûrm), *n.* [*hyper-* + Gr. *thermē* heat.] *Med.* An apparatus using hot humid air to produce artificial fever for remedial purposes.

hy′per·thy′roid·ism (-thī′roid·ĭz′m), *n.* *Med.* Excessive functional activity of the thyroid gland; also, the resultant abnormal state. Cf. HYPOTHYROIDISM. — **hy′per·thy′roid**, *n.*

hy′per·ton′ic (-tŏn′ĭk), *adj.* *Physiol.* **a** Having excessive tone. Cf. HYPOTONIC **a.** **b** Having a greater osmotic pressure than an isotonic fluid. See ISOTONIC. — **hy′per·to·nic′i·ty** (-tō·nĭs′ĭ·tĭ), *n.*

hy·per′tro·phied (hī·pûr′trō·fĭd), *adj.* *Med. & Biol.* Excessively developed; characterized by hypertrophy.

hy·per′tro·phy (hī·pûr′trō·fĭ), *n.* [*hyper-* + *-trophy.*] *Med. & Biol.* A condition of excessive development of an organ or part, as from excessive use. Cf. ATROPHY. — **hy′per·troph′ic** (hī′pẽr·trŏf′ĭk), *adj.* — **hy·per′tro·phy** (hī·pûr′trō·fĭ), *v. i.*

hy′per·ven′ti·la′tion (hī′pẽr·vĕn′tĭ·lā′shŭn), *n.* *Med.* Excessive respiration, leading to abnormal loss of carbon dioxide from the blood.

hy′per·vi′ta·mi·no′sis (-vī′tȧ·mĭ·nō′sĭs), *n.* *Med.* The condition produced by excessive administration of any vitamin.

hyp′es·the′si·a, hyp′aes·the′si·a (hĭp′ĕs·thē′zhĭ·ȧ; -zhȧ; -zĭ·ȧ; -sĭ·ȧ), *n.* [NL., fr. *hyp-* + *esthesia.*] *Med.* Imperfect power of sensation. — **hyp′es·the′sic, hyp′aes·the′sic** (-sĭk), *adj.*

hy·pe′thral (hĭ·pē′thrăl; hī·pē′-), *adj.* Hypaethral.

hy′pha (hī′fȧ), *n.; pl.* -PHAE (-fē). [NL., fr. Gr. *hyphē* a web.] *Bot.* One of the threadlike elements of the mycelium of a fungus. — **hy′phal** (-făl), *adj.*

hy′phen (hī′fĕn), *n.* [LL., fr. Gr. *hyphen*, fr. *hyph' hen* under one, into one, together, fr. *hypo* + *hen*, neut. of *heis* one.] A punctuation point [-] used between the syllables of a divided word or between the parts of a compound word. — *v. t.* To connect or mark with a hyphen.

hy′phen·ate (-āt), *v. t.* To hyphen. — *n.* A hyphenated American. — **hy′phen·a′tion** (-ā′shŭn), *n.*

hy′phen·at′ed (-āt′ĕd; -ĭd), *adj.* Pertaining to citizens of the United States of foreign birth whose origin is designated by hyphened words, as in German-American, Anglo-American, etc.; — chiefly used opprobriously.

hy′phen·ize (-īz), *v. t.* To hyphen. — **hy′phen·i·za′tion** (-ĭ·zā′shŭn; -ī·zā′-), *n.*

hyp′no- (hĭp′nō-), **hypn-.** [Gr. *hypnos.*] A combining form meaning *sleep* or *hypnotism.*

hyp′no·a·nal′y·sis (-ȧ·năl′ĭ·sĭs), *n.* [*hypnosis* + psycho*analysis.*] *Med.* The treatment of mental disease using hypnosis and certain psychoanalytical methods.

hyp′no·gen′e·sis (-jĕn′ē·sĭs), *n.* [NL.] The production of the hypnotic state. — **hyp′no·ge·net′ic** (-jē·nĕt′ĭk), *adj.*

hyp′noid (hĭp′noid), **hyp·noi′dal** (hĭp·noi′dăl; -d'l), *adj.* *Psychol.* Akin to sleep or to hypnosis.

hyp·nol′o·gy (hĭp·nŏl′ō·jĭ), *n.* [*hypno-* + *-logy.*] That branch of science which treats of sleep, esp. of hypnotic sleep. — **hyp′no·log′ic** (hĭp′nō·lŏj′ĭk), **hyp′no·log′i·cal** (-ĭ·kăl), *adj.* — **hyp·nol′o·gist** (hĭp·nŏl′ō·jĭst), *n.*

hyp·no′sis (hĭp·nō′sĭs), *n.; pl.* -SES (-sēz). [NL. See HYPNOTIC.] **1.** A state resembling normal sleep, differing in being induced by the suggestions and operations of the hypnotizer, with whom the hypnotized subject remains in rapport, responsive to his suggestions. **2.** Hence, a similar sleeplike condition.

hyp′no·ther′a·py (hĭp′nō·thĕr′ȧ·pĭ), *n.* [*hypno-* + *therapy.*] Treatment of disease, esp. mental disease, that uses hypnosis.

hyp·not′ic (hĭp·nŏt′ĭk), *adj.* [F. or L.; F. *hypnotique*, fr. L., fr. Gr. *hypnōtikos* inclined to sleep, fr. *hypnos* sleep.] **1.** Tending to produce sleep; soporific. **2.** Of or pertaining to hypnotism; in a state of hypnotism; liable to hypnotism. — *n.* **1.** Any agent that produces, or tends to produce, sleep; an opiate; a soporific; a narcotic. **2.** A person who is subject to, or under the influence of, hypnotism. — **hyp·not′i·cal·ly** (-ĭ·kăl·ĭ), *adv.*

hyp′no·tism (hĭp′nō·tĭz′m), *n.* The study of hypnosis, or the act or practice of inducing it.

hyp′no·tist (-tĭst), *n.* One who practices hypnotism.

hyp′no·tize (hĭp′nō·tīz), *v. t.* **1.** To induce hypnosis in. **2.** To entrance or overcome by suggestion. — **hyp′no·tiz′a·ble** (-tīz′ȧ·b'l), *adj.* — **hyp′no·ti·za′tion** (-tĭ·zā′shŭn; -tī·zā′-), *n.* — **hyp′no·tiz′er**, *n.*

hy′po (hī′pō), *n.* [Abbr. from *hyposulfite.*] *Photog.* Sodium hyposulfite, used as a fixing agent.

hy′po (hī′pō), *n.; pl.* HYPOS (-pōz). *Colloq.* Short for HYPODERMIC INJECTION and HYPODERMIC SYRINGE.

hy′po, *n.* *Colloq.* Hypochondria.

hy′po- (hī′pō-; hĭp′ō-), **hyp-.** [Gr. *hypo.*] **1.** A prefix meaning *under, beneath, down, less than the ordinary* or *norm;* — used: **a** Prepositionally; *sub-;* — chiefly in adjectives, as in *hypo*dermic. **b** Adverbially or adjectively; — chiefly in adjectives and nouns, as in *hypo*thermal. **2.** *Anat., Bot., & Zool.* Denoting *position below*, as in *hypo*branchial. **3.** *Chem.* Indicating a lower state of oxidation, or a low (usually, the lowest) position in a series of compounds. **4.** *Med.* Denoting: *Abnormal decrease, deficiency,* or *weakness.*

☞ Combinations include:

hypoacid	hypoalkaline	hypokinetic
hypoacidity	hypoalkalinity	hypomotility
hypoactive	hypofunction	hyposecretion
hypoactivity	hypokinesis	hypotoxic

hy′po·blast (hī′pō·blăst; hĭp′ō-), *n.* *Embryol. & Zool.* The inner or lower layer of the blastoderm; the inner of the germ layers of the embryo; the endoderm (which see); endoblast. — **hy′po·blas′tic** (-blăs′tĭk), *adj.*

hy′po·bran′chi·al (-brăng′kĭ·ăl), *adj.* *Zool.* Below the gills.

hyp′o·caust (hĭp′ō·kôst; hī′pō-), *n.* [L. *hypocaustum*, fr. Gr. *hypokauston*, fr. *hypo* under + *kaiein* to burn.] *Anc. Arch.* A series of small chambers and flues through which the heat of a fire was distributed to rooms.

hy′po·chlo′rous (hī′pō·klō′rŭs; hĭp′ō-), *adj.* [*hypo-* + *chlorous.*] *Chem.* Pertaining to or designating an acid (**hypochlorous acid,** $HClO$), obtained in aqueous solution by the distillation of a bleaching-powder solution with dilute nitric acid, and otherwise. Hypochlorous acid is very unstable and acts as an oxidizing and bleaching agent. Its salts, the **hy′po·chlo′rites** (-rīts), are also easily decomposed.

hy′po·chon′dri·a (-kŏn′drĭ·ȧ), *n.* [L., pl., the abdomen, supposed formerly to be the seat of hypochondria, fr. Gr. *hypochondria*, pl. fr. *hypochondrios*, adj., under the cartilage of the breastbone, fr. *hypo* under + *chondros* cartilage.] Morbid depression of mind or spirits; specif., *Med.*, morbid anxiety as to one's own health, with conjuring up of imaginary ailments.

hy′po·chon′dri·ac (-ăk), *adj.* **1.** *Anat. & Zool.* Below the costal cartilages; designating the two regions of the abdomen lying on either side of the epigastric region and above the lumbar regions. **2.** *Med.* Affected, or produced, by hypochondria. — *n.* A person affected with hypochondria.

hy′po·chon·dri′a·cal (-kŏn·drī′ȧ·kăl), *adj.* Hypochondriac. — **hy′po·chon·dri′a·cal·ly**, *adv.*

hy′po·chon·dri′a·sis (-kŏn·drī′ȧ·sĭs), *n.* [NL., see HYPOCHONDRIA.] *Med.* Hypochondria in its pathological aspects.

hy′po·chon′dri·um (-kŏn′drĭ·ŭm), *n.; pl.* -DRIA (-ȧ). [NL.] *Anat.* Either hypochondriac region.

hy·poc′o·rism (hĭ·pŏk′ō·rĭz′m; hī-), *n.* [From Gr. *hypokorisma.*] A hypocoristic name; also, formation or use of hypocoristic terms.

hyp′o·co·ris′tic (hĭp′ō·kō·rĭs′tĭk; hī′pō-), **hyp′o·co·ris′ti·cal** (-tĭ·kăl), *adj.* [Gr. *hypokoristikos*, fr. *hypo* under, secretly + *korizesthai* caress, fr. *koros* child.] Adopted or modified, as by the affixing of a diminutive ending or by abbreviation, for use as a pet name, nickname, or euphemism (as *babykins* for baby, *Billy* for William, *tell a story* for lie). — **hyp′o·co·ris′ti·cal·ly**, *adv.*

hy′po·cot′yl (hī′pō·kŏt′ĭl; hĭp′ō-), *n.* [*hypo-* + *cotyl*edon.] *Bot.* That portion of the stem or axis below the cotyledons in the embryo of a seed plant. See RADICLE, 2; EMBRYO, PLUMULE, SEED, *Illusts.* Cf. EPICOTYL. — **hy′po·cot′y·lous** (-ĭ·lŭs), *adj.*

hy·poc′ri·sy (hĭ·pŏk′rĭ·sĭ), *n.; pl.* -SIES (-sĭz). [OF. *ypocrisie* (F. *hypocrisie*), fr. L. *hypocrisis*, fr. Gr. *hypokrisis* the playing a part on the stage, simulation, deriv. of *hypo* + *krinein* to decide, (in middle voice) to dispute.] Act or practice of feigning to be what one is not, or to feel what one does not feel; esp., the false assumption of an appearance of virtue or religion; canting simulation of goodness.

hyp′o·crite (hĭp′ō·krĭt), *n.* [OF. *ipocrite*, *ypocrite*, fr. L., fr. Gr. *hypokritēs* one who plays a part on the stage, a dissembler. See HYPOCRISY.] One who feigns to be other and better than he is; a false pretender to virtue or piety. — **hyp′o·crit′i·cal** (-krĭt′ĭ·kăl), *adj.* — **hyp′o·crit′i·cal·ly**, *adv.*

hy′po·cy′cloid (hī′pō·sī′kloid; hĭp′ō-), *n.* *Geom.* A curve traced by a point on the circumference of a circle rolling internally on another circle. Cf. EPICYCLOID. — **hy′po·cy·cloi′dal** (-sī·kloi′dăl; -d'l), *adv.*

hy′po·der′ma (hī′pō·dûr′mȧ; hĭp′ō-), *n.* [NL., fr. *hypo-* + *derma.*] **1.** *Bot.* Any layer of tissues beneath the epidermis, serving to strengthen the latter. In seed plants it is usually developed as *collenchyma*. **2.** *Zool.* = HYPODERMIS, 1.

hy′po·der′mal (-măl), *adj.* **1.** *Bot.* **a** Pertaining to the hypoderma. **b** Situated beneath the epidermis; as, a *hypodermal* gland. **2.** *Zool.* Hypodermic.

hy′po·der′mic (-mĭk), *adj.* **1.** Of or pert. to the parts under the skin. **2.** *Zool.* Pert. to the hypodermis. — *n.* Short for HYPODERMIC INJECTION, HYPODERMIC SYRINGE, etc.—**hy′po·der′mi·cal·ly** (-mĭ·kăl·ĭ), *adv.*

hypodermic injection. *Med.* An injection made into the subcutaneous tissues.

hypodermic medication. Application of remedies by injection under the epidermis.

hypodermic needle. **a** The needle of a hypodermic syringe. **b** Popularly, a hypodermic syringe.

hypodermic syringe. A small syringe equipped with a hollow needle-like point, used in hypodermic medication.

hy′po·der′mis (hī′pō·dûr′mĭs; hĭp′ō-), *n.* [NL.] **1.** *Zool.* The cellular layer which lies beneath, and which secretes, the chitinous cuticle of arthropods, annelids, and some other invertebrates. **2.** *Bot.* = HYPODERMA, 1.

hy′po·eu·tec′tic (-ū·tĕk′tĭk), *adj.* *Physics, Metal., & Chem.* Containing the minor constituent in an amount less than that in the eutectic mixture; — opposed to *hypereutectic*.

hy′po·gas′tric (-găs′trĭk), *adj.* *Anat.* Designating, or pertaining to, the lower median region of the abdomen.

hy′po·gas′tri·um (-găs′trĭ·ŭm), *n.; pl.* -TRIA (-ȧ). [NL., fr. Gr. *hypogastrion*, fr. *hypo* under + *gastēr* belly.] The hypogastric region.

hy′po·ge′al (-jē′ăl), *adj.* [*hypo-* + Gr. *gē* the earth.] **1.** Of, pertaining to, or occurring below the surface of the earth, or within the earth. **2.** *Bot.* Hypogeous.

hyp′o·gene (hĭp′ō·jēn; hī′pō-), *adj.* [*hypo-* + *-gene* (= *-gen*).] Formed or crystallized at depths beneath the earth's surface; also, plutonic; — said of granite, gneiss, and other rocks; as, *hypogene* action. Opposed to *epigene*.

hy·pog′e·nous (hĭ·pŏj′ē·nŭs; hī-), *adj.* *Bot.* Growing on the lower side of anything, as fungi on the under surface of leaves. Cf. EPIGENOUS.

hy′po·ge′ous (hī′pō·jē′ŭs; hĭp′ō-), *adj.* Also **hy′po·gae′ous.** [*hypo-* + Gr. *gē* the earth.] *Bot. & Zool.* Growing or ripening underground, as the peanut. Cf. EPIGEOUS.

hyp′o·ge′um (hĭp′ō·jē′ŭm; hī′pō-), *n.; pl.* -GEA (-ȧ). [L., fr. Gr. *hypogaios*, *hypogeios*, subterranean, fr. *hypo* under + *gaia*, *gē*, the earth.] *Anc. Arch.* The subterranean portion of a building; a cellar.

hy′po·glos′sal (hī′pō·glŏs′ăl; hĭp′ō-; -'l), *adj.* [*hypo-* + Gr. *glōssa* tongue.] *Anat.* Designating the last pair of cranial nerves in reptiles, birds, and mammals, distributed to the region of the base of the tongue, of which they are the motor nerves. — *n.* A hypoglossal nerve.

hy·pog′y·nous (hĭ·pŏj′ĭ·nŭs; hī-), *adj.* [*hypo-* + *-gynous.*] *Bot.* **a** Inserted upon the torus or axis below the gynoecium and free from it; — said of sepals, petals, and stamens. **b** Having these parts so inserted; — said of a flower. — **hy·pog′y·ny** (-nĭ), *n.*

hy′po·ma′ni·a (hī′pō·mā′nĭ·ȧ; hĭp′ō-), *n.* [*hypo-* + *-mania.*] *Psychiatry.* A mild degree of manic excitement. — **hy′po·ma′nic** (-mā′nĭk; -măn′ĭk), *adj. & n.*

hy′po·nas′ty (hī′pō·năs′tĭ; hĭp′ō-), *n.* [*hypo-* + Gr. *nastos* close-pressed.] *Plant Physiol.* That state in which the more vigorous growth of the lower surface of an organ, as a young fern frond, causes an upward curvature. Cf. EPINASTY. — **hy′po·nas′tic** (-năs′tĭk), *adj.* — **hy′po·nas′ti·cal·ly** (-tĭ·kăl·ĭ), *adv.*

hy′po·ni′trous (hī′pō·nī′trŭs), *adj.* *Chem.* Pertaining to or designating a white crystalline nitrogenous diacid, $H_2N_2O_2$ (probably HON.NOH), formed by condensation of hydroxylamine and nitrous acid, and otherwise. As a solid, hyponitrous acid is explosive; in solution, it is more stable.

hy′po·phar′ynx (hī′pō·făr′ĭngks; hĭp′ō-), *n.; pl.*, see PHARYNX. [NL. See HYPO-; PHARYNX.] *Zool.* An appendage or membranous fold on the floor of the mouth of many insects.

hy′po·phos′phite (hī′pō·fŏs′fīt), *n.* *Chem.* A salt of hypophosphorous acid.

hy′po·phos′pho·rous (-fŏs′fō·rŭs; -fŏs·fō′rŭs), *adj.* *Chem.* Pertaining to or designating a monoacid of phosphorus, H_3PO_2. It is a white crystalline solid, and has a powerful reducing action.

hy·poph′y·sis (hī·pŏf′ĭ·sĭs; hĭ-), *n.* [NL., fr. Gr. *hypophysis* an undergrowth, fr. *hypo* under + *physis* nature, origin.] *Anat.* The pituitary body. — **hy′po·phys′e·al** (hī′pō·fĭz′ē·ăl; hĭp′ō-; hī·pŏf′ĭ-sē′ăl; hĭ-), **hy′po·phys′i·al** (hī′pō·fĭz′ĭ·ăl; hĭp′ō-), *adj.*

hy′po·pi·tu′i·ta·rism (hī′pō·pĭ·tū′ĭ·tȧ·rĭz′m; hĭp′ō-), *n.* [*hypo-* + *pituitary* + *-ism.*] *Med.* Deficient activity of the pituitary body; also, the resultant abnormal state. Cf. HYPERPITUITARISM.

hy′po·pla′si·a (-plā′zhĭ·ȧ), *n.* [NL., fr. *hypo-* + *-plasia.*] *Med.* A condition of arrested development in which an organ or part remains below the normal size or in an immature state. Cf. HYPERPLASIA. — **hy′po·plas′tic** (-plăs′tĭk), *adj.*

hy′po·ploid (hī′pō·ploid; hĭp′ō-), *adj.* [*hypo-* + Gr. *-ploos* -fold.] *Biol.* Having or designating a chromosome number which is less than the basic chromosome number. Cf. HYPERPLOID. — **hy′po·ploid, hy′po·ploid′y**, *n.*

hy′po·po′di·um (-pō′dĭ·ŭm), *n.; pl.* -DIA (-ȧ). [NL., fr. *hypo-* + *-podium.*] *Bot.* The base of a foliage or floral leaf, including the stalk or petiole if present.

hy·po′py·on (hī·pō′pĭ·ŏn; hĭ-), *n.* [NL., fr. Gr. *hypopyon* a sort of ulcer, deriv. of *hypo* under + *pyon* pus.] *Med.* A collection of pus in the anterior chamber of the eye.

hy·pos′ta·sis (hī·pŏs′tȧ·sĭs; hĭ-), *n.; pl.* -SES (-sēz). [L., fr. Gr. *hypostasis* subsistence, substance, deriv. of *hypo* under + *histasthai* to stand, middle voice of *histanai* to cause to stand.] **1.** *Eccl. Hist.* **a** In the original Nicene use, equivalent to *ousia*; specif., the unique essence of the Godhead, and as such, of the three persons of the Trinity, Father, Son, and Holy Spirit. **b** In later use, one of the persons of the Godhead. Also, the whole personality of Christ as distinguished from his two natures, human and divine. **2.** *Med.* **a** That which is deposited at the bottom of a fluid; sediment. **b** Hyperemia caused by settling of blood in the dependent parts of an organ. **3.** *Philos.* Substance, subsistent principle, or essential nature of anything.

hy′po·stat′ic (hī′pō·stăt′ĭk; hĭp′ō-), *adj.* [Gr. *hypostatikos.*] **1.** Of or relating to hypostasis; hence, constitutive, or elementary. **2.** Personal, or distinctly personal; relating to the divine hypostases, or subsistences. **3.** *Med.* Depending on, or due to, deposition; as, *hypostatic* congestion, due to settling of blood by gravitation; *hypostatic* pneumonia.

hy′po·stat′i·cal (-ĭ·kăl), *adj.* Hypostatic (senses 1 & 2).

hy·pos′ta·tize (hī·pŏs′tȧ·tīz; hĭ-), *v. t.* To make into, or regard as, a separate and distinct substance; also, to assume as a reality. — **hy·pos′ta·ti·za′tion** (-tĭ·zā′shŭn; -tī·zā′-), *n.*

hyp′o·style (hĭp′ō·stīl; hī′pō-), *adj.* [Gr. *hypostylos* resting on pillars, fr. *hypo* under + *stylos* a pillar.] *Arch.* Having the roof resting upon rows of columns; constructed by means of columns, as the hall at Karnak in Egypt.

hy′po·sul′fite, hy′po·sul′phite (hī′pō·sŭl′fīt), *n.* *Chem.* **a** A thiosulfate; as, *hyposulfite* of soda (sodium thiosulfate, $Na_2S_2O_3$), a crystalline salt used in photography as a fixing agent. **b** A salt of hyposulfurous acid proper. Sodium hyposulfite, $Na_2S_2O_4$, is used in dyeing, etc., as a reducing agent.

hy′po·sul·fu′rous, hy′po·sul·phu′rous (-sŭl·fū′rŭs; -sŭl′fū·rŭs), *adj.* *Chem.* Pertaining to or designating an unstable diacid, $H_2S_2O_4$, obtained by reducing sulfurous acid. The acid and its salts are strong reducing and bleaching agents.

hy′po·tax′is (hī′pō·tăk′sĭs; hĭp′ō-), *n.* [NL., fr. *hypo-* + *-taxis.*] *Gram.* Subordinative expression of the syntactic relation between main and qualifying elements; — opposed to *parataxis*. — **hy′po·tac′tic** (-tăk′tĭk), *adj.*

hy′po·ten′sion (-tĕn′shŭn), *n.* *Med.* **a** Low blood pressure. **b** The condition of one having low blood pressure. — **hy′po·ten′sive** (-sĭv), *adj. & n.*

hy·pot′e·nuse (hī·pŏt′ē·nūs; hĭ-; -nūz), **hy·poth′e·nuse** (-pŏth′-), *n.* [L. *hypotenusa*, fr. Gr. *hypoteinousa*, prop., subtending (sc. *grammē*), deriv. of *hypo* under + *teinein* to stretch.] *Geom.* The side of a right-angled triangle that is opposite the right angle.

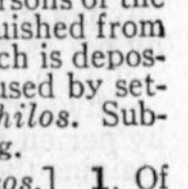

h Hypotenuse.

hy′po·thal′a·mus (hī′pō·thăl′ȧ·mŭs; hĭp′ō-), *n.; pl.* HYPOTHALAMI (-mī). [NL., fr. *hypo-* + *thalamus.*] *Anat.* The basal part of the diencephalon, believed to contain vital autonomic nervous centers and fiber tracts. — **hy′po·tha·lam′ic** (-thȧ·lăm′ĭk), *adj.*

hy·poth′ec (hĭ·pŏth′ĕk; hī-), *n.* [F. and L.; F. *hypothèque*, fr. L. *hypotheca*, fr. Gr. *hypothēkē* a thing subject to some obligation, fr. *hypotithenai*. See HYPOTHESIS.] **1.** *Roman Law & Civil Law System.* An obligation, right, or security given to a creditor over property of the debtor without transfer of possession or title to the creditor; — distinguished from a *pignus* or *pledge*. **2.** *Scot.* Affair; — usually in the phrase ***the whole or hale hypothec.***

hy·poth′e·car′y (hĭ·pŏth′ē·kĕr′ĭ *or, esp. Brit.,* -kēr·ĭ; hī-), *adj.* *Law.* Of or pertaining to, or created or secured by, a hypothec.

hy·poth′e·cate (hĭ·pŏth′ē·kāt; hī-), *v. t.* [ML. *hypothecatus*, past part. of *hypothecare* to pledge, fr. L. *hypotheca* pledge.] **1.** *Law.* To subject to a hypothec; to pledge without delivery of title or possession. **2.** *Commerce.* To deposit as security for a loan.

hy·poth'e·ca'tion (-kā'shŭn), *n.* *Law.* Act or contract by which property is hypothecated. — **hy·poth'e·ca'tor** (-pŏth'ē·kā'tẽr), *n.*

hy'po·ther'mal (hī'pō·thûr'măl; hĭp'ō-), *adj.* [*hypo-* + *thermal.*] Moderately warm; tepid.

hy·poth'e·sis (hī·pŏth'ē·sĭs; hĭ-), *n.; pl.* -SES (-sēz). [NL., fr. Gr. *hypothesis* foundation, supposition, fr. *hypotithenai* to place under, fr. *hypo* under + *tithenai* to put. See HYPO-; THESIS.] **1.** A tentative theory or supposition provisionally adopted to explain certain facts and to guide in the investigation of others; — frequently called a *working hypothesis;* as, the nebular *hypothesis.* **2.** Something assumed or conceded merely for the purposes of argument or action; as, start with this *hypothesis.*

Syn. **Hypothesis, theory, law** mean a formula derived by inference from scientific data explaining a principle operating in nature. **Hypothesis** implies insufficiency of presently attainable evidence and, therefore, a tentative explanation; **theory** implies a much greater range of evidence and greater likelihood of truth; **law** implies a statement of order and relation in nature that has been found to be invariable under the same conditions. The terms are not rigidly applied, however, as the discovery of new evidence often changes the status of the formula.

hy·poth'e·size (-sīz), *v. i. & t.* To make a hypothesis; to make a hypothesis of; to assume.

hy'po·thet'i·cal (hī'pō·thĕt'ĭ·kăl; hĭp'ō-), *adj.* Also **hy'po·thet'ic** (-ĭk). [L. *hypotheticus,* fr. Gr. *hypothetikos.*] **1.** Involving a formal hypothesis or condition; as, a *hypothetical* proposition or judgment; — in logic, as applied to propositions, contrasted with *categorical.* **2.** Characterized by, or of the nature of, a hypothesis; assumed without proof, for the purpose of reasoning and deducing proof, or of accounting for some fact. **3.** Concerned with hypotheses; given to making hypotheses; as, a *hypothetical* thinker. — **hy'po·thet'i·cal·ly,** *adv.*

hy'po·thy'roid·ism (-thī'roid·ĭz'm), *n.* *Med.* Deficient activity of the thyroid gland; also, the resultant abnormal state. Cf. HYPERTHYROIDISM. — **hy'po·thy'roid,** *n.*

hy'po·ton'ic (-tŏn'ĭk), *adj.* *Physiol.* **a** Having less than the normal tone. Cf. HYPERTONIC **a.** **b** Having a lower osmotic pressure than an isotonic fluid. See ISOTONIC. — **hy'po·to·nic'i·ty** (-tō·nĭs'ĭ·tĭ), *n.*

hy'po·xan'thine (hī'pō·zăn'thēn; -thĭn), *n.* Also **hy'po·xan'thin.** *Biochem.* A crystalline nitrogenous compound, $C_5H_4N_4O$, closely related to xanthine and occurring with it, esp. in muscle tissue. — **hy'po·xan'thic** (-thĭk), *adj.*

hyps (hĭps), *n., pl.* of HYP. *Colloq.* Hypochondria.

hyp'so- (hĭp'sō-). [Gr. *hypsos.*] A combining form meaning *height,* as in *hyps*ometry.

hyp·sog'ra·phy (hĭp·sŏg'rȧ·fĭ), *n.* [*hypso-* + *-graphy.*] *Geog.* **a** Topographic relief. **b** The observation or description of topographic relief. **c** The parts of a map, collectively, which represent topographic relief. **d** Hypsometry, or the measurement of heights. — **hyp'so·graph'ic** (hĭp'sō·grăf'ĭk), **hyp'so·graph'i·cal** (-ĭ·kăl), *adj.*

hyp·som'e·ter (hĭp·sŏm'ē·tẽr), *n.* [*hypso-* + *-meter.*] An apparatus for determining heights, as of mountains, by finding the boiling point of a liquid.

hyp·som'e·try (-trĭ), *n.* In geodesy, the measurement of heights, as with reference to the sea level. — **hyp'so·met'ric** (hĭp'sō·mĕt'rĭk), **hyp'so·met'ri·cal** (-rĭ·kăl), *adj.* — **hyp'so·met'ri·cal·ly,** *adv.* — **hyp·som'e·trist** (hĭp·sŏm'ē·trĭst), *n.*

hy'rax (hī'răks), *n.; pl.* -RAXES (-răk·sēz; -sĭz), -RACES (hī'rȧ·sēz). [NL., fr. Gr. *hyrax* shrew mouse.] *Zool.* The daman.

hy'son (hī's'n), *n.* [Chin. (Pek.) *hsi*[1]*-ch'un*[1], lit., blooming spring.] A green tea (see TEA, 1 **b**) from China having a special twist. The early crop [called *yü*[3]*-ch'ien*[2], lit., "before the rains"] is ***young hyson.*** The light and inferior leaves winnowed from the hyson are called ***hyson skin.***

hys'sop (hĭs'ŭp), *n.* [OF. *ysope,* fr. L. *hysopum, hyssopum, -pus,* fr. Gr. *hyssōpos, -pon,* an aromatic plant, fr. Heb. *ēzōb.*] **1.** A European mint (*Hyssopus officinalis*) with highly aromatic and pungent leaves. The hyssop of Scripture is supposed to be a species of caper (*Capparis spinosa*). **2.** *Local, U.S.* Any of several species of a genus (*Artemisia*) of the thistle family. **3.** *Eccl.* The holy water sprinkled in the Asperges; also, the aspergillum.

hyster-. Var. of HYSTERO-.

hys'ter·ec'to·my (hĭs'tẽr·ĕk'tō·mĭ), *n.* [*hyster-* + *-ectomy.*] The surgical removal of the uterus.

hys'ter·e'sis (-ē'sĭs), *n.* [NL., fr. Gr. *hysterein* to be behind, to lag.] *Physics.* **a** A retardation of the effect, when the forces acting upon a body are changed, as if from viscosity or internal friction. **b** In a magnetic material, as iron, a lagging in the values of resulting magnetization due to a changing magnetizing force.

hys'ter·et'ic (hĭs'tẽr·ĕt'ĭk), *adj.* Of or relating to hysteresis; as, **hysteretic loss,** a loss of energy due to molecular change manifest in heat; **hysteretic constant,** the hysteretic loss in ergs per cubic centimeter per cycle.

hys·te'ri·a (hĭs·tē'rĭ·ȧ), *n.* [NL. See HYSTERICAL.] **1.** *Med.* A psychoneurosis characterized by emotional excitability and various vasomotor derangements, probably due to mental causes, as autosuggestion, dissociation, or repressed emotion. **2.** Any outbreak of wild emotionalism; as, war *hysteria.*

hys·ter'ic (-tĕr'ĭk), *adj.* Hysterical.

hys·ter'i·cal (-ĭ·kăl), *adj.* [L. *hystericus,* fr. Gr. *hysterikos,* fr. *hystera* womb.] **1.** Pertaining to, or affected by hysteria. **2.** Wildly emotional. — **hys·ter'i·cal·ly,** *adv.*

hys·ter'ics (-ĭks), *n. pl.; see* -ICS. A hysterical fit; hysteria.

hys'ter·o- (hĭs'tẽr·ō-), **hyster-.** [Gr. *hystera* the womb.] A combining form denoting *connection with,* or *relation to, the uterus* or *hysteria.*

hys'ter·o·cat'a·lep'sy (-kăt'ȧ·lĕp'sĭ), *n.* *Med.* Hysteria attended with catalepsy.

hys'ter·o·gen'ic (-jĕn'ĭk), *adj.* *Med.* Producing hysteria; as, the **hysterogenic pressure points** on the surface of the body, pressure upon which may produce or arrest an attack of hysteria.

hys'ter·oid (hĭs'tẽr·oid), *adj.* Also **hys'ter·oi'dal** (-oi'dăl; -d'l). [*hyster-* + *-oid.*] *Med.* Resembling hysteria.

hys'ter·o·neu'ras·the'ni·a (-ō·nū'răs·thē'nĭ·ȧ; -thē·nī'ȧ), *n.* [NL.] *Med.* Neurasthenia associated with hysteria.

hys'ter·on prot'er·on (hĭs'tẽr·ŏn prŏt'ẽr·ŏn). [LL., fr. Gr. *hysteros* the latter + *proteros* before others, sooner.] **1.** An arrangement reversing the natural or rational order, specif.: *Rhet.* A figure in which the natural order of the sense is reversed (*valet atque vivit,* "he is well and lives"). **2.** *Logic.* The fallacy of explaining a thing by that which presupposes it and so inverting the natural order of reason.

hys'ter·ot'o·my (hĭs'tẽr·ŏt'ō·mĭ), *n.* [*hystero-* + *-tomy.*] *Med.* **a** The Caesarean section. **b** Incision or section of the uterus, esp. of the neck of the uterus.

hys'tri·co·mor'phic (hĭs'trĭ·kō·môr'fĭk), *adj.* [Gr. *hystrix* porcupine + *-morphic.*] Of, belonging to, or designating a suborder (Hystricomorpha) of rodents, comprising the porcupines, cavies, agoutis, chinchillas, and allies.

hyte (hīt), *adj.* *Scot.* Mad.

I

I, i (ī), *n.; pl.* I's, i's, Is, is (īz). **1.** The ninth letter of the English alphabet. It came through Greek (the *iota*) and Latin from Phoenician (the Semitic *yodh*), and probably ultimately from Egyptian. **2.** The sound of this letter. In Anglo-Saxon the value of the vowel when short was that of modern short *i* as in *pin,* but when long its value was practically the same as that of Italian long *i* or English "long *e*" as in *mete* (see E). It was only in the early modern period that it developed the present diphthongal sound of English "long *i*" as in *pine.* *I* also represents other sounds in English: that of *u* in *urn,* as in *thirst;* that of *e* in *mete* (in words of foreign origin), as in *pique, machine;* and that of consonant *y* (in many words in which it precedes another vowel), as in *onion, million.* See *Pron.,* § 50; J. **3.** [*cap.*] In Roman numerals, 1. **4.** Anything having the shape of the letter I. **5.** As a *symbol,* the ninth in order or class.

I (ī), *pron.; poss.* MY (mī; *cf.* MY) or MINE (mīn); *object.* ME (mē; *cf.* ME); *pl. nom.* WE (wē; *cf.* WE); *poss.* OUR (our) or OURS (ourz); *object.* US (ŭs; *cf.* US). [AS. *ic.*] The nominative case of the pronoun of the first person, by which a person denotes himself. — *n.* The pronoun *I* regarded as a word or represented as a person; specif., *Metaph.,* the ego.

i-. Archaic var. of Y-.

i-. *Chem.* Inactive; — in optic polarization.

-ia. [L. *-ia* or Gr. *-ia,* an ending of fem. nouns, usually abstract, and of neut. plurals.] A noun suffix occurring in: **a** Names of diseases, as in neural*gia.* **b** Names of countries, as in Tasman*ia.* **c** Names of alkaloids, as in morph*ia.* **d** Generic names of plants, as in Dahl*ia.* **e** Names of classical festivals, mostly plural, as in Saturnal*ia.* **f** Names of classes, orders, and other divisions of plants and animals, all plural, as in Mammal*ia.* **g** Various other words from Latin or Greek, as in *sep*ia, and the plurals memorabil*ia,* bacter*ia,* etc.

I·a'go (ē·ä'gō), *n.* The ancient, or ensign, of Othello, in Shakespeare's *Othello,* a subtle and malignant villain.

-ial. An adjective suffix composed of the connective *i* and *-al,* as in connub*ial,* fluv*ial.*

i'amb (ī'ămb), *n.* [F. *iambe,* fr. L. *iambus,* fr. Gr. *iambos.*] *Pros.* A foot consisting of a short syllable followed by a long one, as in *ămāns,* or of an unaccented syllable followed by an accented one, as in *invent.*

i·am'bic (ī·ăm'bĭk), *adj.* **1.** *Pros.* Consisting of an iamb or of iambics. **2.** *Gr. Lit.* Designating a type of poetry, chiefly satirical, characterized by iambic meter. — *n.* **1.** *Pros.* **a** An iambic foot. **b** A verse composed of iambic feet. **2.** A satirical poem.

i·am'bus (-bŭs), *n.; pl.* -BI (-bī). [L.] An iamb.

-ian. [F. or L.; F. *-ien,* fr. L. *-ianus.* See -AN.] An adjective suffix, composed of thematic or (rarely) connective *i* and *-an,* as in Christ*ian,* barbar*ian,* Jefferson*ian.*

-iana. = -ANA; — from use of *-ana* after stems ending in *i.*

iar'o·vize (yär'ō·vīz), *v. t.* Var. of JAROVIZE. — **iar'o·vi·za'tion** (-vĭ·zā'shŭn; -vī·zā'-), *n.*

-i'a·sis (-ī'ȧ·sĭs). [NL.] A combining form signifying *a process* or *course of action,* as in odont*iasis;* specif., *Med.,* denoting *a morbid condition,* as in mydr*iasis.*

i·at'ric (ī·ăt'rĭk), **i·at'ri·cal** (-rĭ·kăl), *adj.* [Gr. *iatrikos* healing, fr. *iatros* physician, fr. *iasthai* to heal.] Of or relating to medicine or a medical practitioner; medical.

-i·at'rics (-ĭ·ăt'rĭks). *Med.* A combining form, denoting *treatment of disease,* as in ped*iatrics.*

i·at'ro- (ī·ăt'rō-; ī·ā'trō-). [Gr. *iatro-,* fr. *iatros* physician.] A combining form meaning *physician* or *medicine* (*and*), as in **i·at'ro·chem'is·try,** chemistry united with medicine.

-i'a·try (-ī'ȧ·trĭ). [Gr. *iatreia.*] A combining form meaning *medical treatment, healing,* as in psych*iatry.*

I·be'ri·an (ī·bē'rĭ·ăn), *adj.* **1.** Of or pertaining to Iberia (the Spanish peninsula; see *Gaz.*), its inhabitants, or the Iberian race. **2.** Of or pertaining to the ancient Iberians of the Caucasus (of modern Georgia). — *n.* **1.** One of the ancient inhabitants of Iberia, early known to the Greeks and conquered by the Romans. **2.** Hence, a member of the **Iberian race** (of which the Spanish Iberians are typical), a short, dark, dolichocephalic race, probably the neolithic inhabitants of western Europe. **3.** One of an ancient people of the Caucasus, probably ancestors of the modern Georgians. **4.** A native or inhabitant of Spain or Portugal.

i'bex (ī'bĕks), *n.; pl.* IBEXES (-bĕk·sēz; -sĭz), IBICES (ĭb'ĭ·sēz; ī'bĭ-), sometimes IBEX. [L., the chamois.] Any of certain wild goats, esp. the ***Alpine ibex*** (*Capra ibex*), of the Old World, having large recurved horns.

||**i·bi′dem** (ĭ·bī′dĕm), *adv.* [L.] In the same place; — commonly abbreviated *ibid.*

i′bis (ī′bĭs), *n.; see* PLURAL, *Note,* 3. [L., fr. Gr. *ibis,* fr. Egypt. *hab.*] Any of certain wading birds (family Threskiornithidae) related to the herons. The best-known species, the ***sacred ibis*** (*Threskiornis aethiopica*), common in the Nile basin, was venerated by the ancient Egyptians.

-i·ble (-ĭ·b'l). [L. *-ibilis.*] An adjective suffix. See -ABLE. — **-i·bil′i·ty** (-ĭ·bĭl′ĭ·tĭ).

-ic (-ĭk). [F. or L. or Gr.; F. *-ique,* fr. L. *-icus,* native suff. or fr. Gr. *-ikos.*] A suffix signifying, in general, *of* or *pertaining to,* and forming: **1.** Adjectives, denoting: **a** *Of the nature of, consisting of, characterized by,* as in angel*ic,* iamb*ic.* **b** *Of* or *belonging to,* as in apostol*ic,* volcan*ic.* **c** *After the manner of, characteristic of, resembling,* as in Byron*ic,* quixot*ic.* **d** *Connected* or *dealing with,* as in aquat*ic,* dramat*ic.* **e** *Chem.* Specif., denoting that the element indicated enters into certain compounds with its *highest valence,* or with a *valence relatively higher* than in compounds named with an adjective ending in *-ous;* as, ferr*ic,* sulfur*ic.* **2.** Nouns from: **a** The substantive use of adjectives in any of the senses preceding, as in mag*ic,* class*ic,* mechan*ic,* Icelandi*c.* **b** Greek or Latin nouns that were originally adjectives used substantively and adopted into English, as in mus*ic,* publ*ic.* See -ICS.

☞ Adjectives in *-ic* often have a parallel form in *-ical,* sometimes with a distinction in meaning, the form in *-ic* denoting the senses having closer relation to the subject denoted by the root and the form in *-ical* denoting the remoter senses. Thus, a histor*ic* event, one that is a part of history, but a histor*ical* treatise, one that deals with history; a com*ic* opera, a com*ical* grimace. In terms of chemistry and adjectives from proper names, *-ical* is seldom used.

☞ Adverbs are formed from adjectives in *-ic* by adding *-ly* or (usually) *-ally.*

-i·cal (-ĭ·kăl). [LL. *-icalis,* fr. *-icus* + *-alis.*] A compound suffix forming adjectives: **a** From nouns in *-ic, -ics,* as in mus*ical,* eth*ical.* **b** Parallel to adjectives in *-ic,* as in fantast*ical,* com*ical.* See -IC.

I·car′i·an (ī·kâr′ĭ·ăn), *adj.* Of, pertaining to, or characteristic of Icarus; hence, soaring too high for safety.

Ic′a·rus (ĭk′ȧ·rŭs; ī′kȧ-), *n.* See DAEDALUS.

ice (īs), *n.* [AS. *īs.*] **1.** Water frozen. **2.** Any frozen dessert, esp. one not containing cream, as a water ice, sherbet, or frappé. **3.** Any substance looking like ice; as, camphor *ice.* **4.** Icing; frosting. **5.** A coldness, as of formality or reserve. **6.** *Slang.* A diamond. — *v. t.;* ICED (īst); IC′ING (īs′ĭng). **a** To cover or supply with ice; to convert into ice. **b** To cover with icing. **c** To chill or cool, as with ice. — *adj.* Of ice; connected with ice.

-ice (-ĭs). [OF. *-ice, -ise,* fr. L. *-itius, -itia, -itium.*] A suffix denoting *act, quality, condition,* as in serv*ice.*

ice age. *Geol.* = GLACIAL EPOCH (see GLACIAL, 2 **b**).

ice apron. See ICEBREAKER, 1.

ice bag. *Med.* A rubber bag to hold crushed ice.

ice′berg′ (īs′bûrg′), *n.* [Of Scand. origin, perh. through D.] A huge, floating mass of ice, detached from a glacier.

ice′blink′ (-blĭngk′), *n.* = BLINK, *n.,* 4.

ice′boat′ (-bōt′), *n.* **1.** A skeleton boat or frame on runners propelled on ice by sails. **2.** A strong steam vessel for breaking through ice.

ice′bound′ (-bound′), *adj.* Surrounded or obstructed with ice; as, an *icebound* vessel; an *icebound* harbor.

ice′box′ (-bŏks′), *n.* A refrigerator.

ice′break′er (-brāk′ẽr), *n.* **1.** A device for breaking ice, as a wedge-shaped structure (called specif. ***ice apron***) to protect a bridge pier from floating ice. **2.** A vessel equipped with a reinforced bow for making and maintaining a channel through ice, as in a river or harbor.

ice′cap′ (-kăp′), *n.* **1.** A perennial mantle of ice and snow covering a tract and moving in all directions from the center. A very large icecap is an ***ice sheet,*** or continental glacier. **2.** *Med.* An ice bag shaped to be fitted to the head.

ice cream (īs′ krēm′). A frozen food containing cream, or butterfat, flavoring, sweetening, and, usually, eggs.

iced (īst), *adj.* **a** Covered with ice; also, chilled with ice. **b** Covered with icing; frosted.

ice field. An extensive sheet of sea ice.

ice foot. A wall or belt of ice that forms along the shore in arctic regions between high and low watermarks.

ice′house′ (īs′hous′), *n.* A building for storing ice.

Ice·lan′dic (īs·lăn′dĭk), *adj.* Of, or pertaining or relating to, Iceland, the Icelanders, or Icelandic. — *n.* The language of the Icelanders, a Scandinavian tongue divided into ***Old*** and ***Modern Icelandic.*** Old Icelandic possesses a literature of sagas, or prose tales, valuable as a chief source of knowledge of the life of the ancient Scandinavian north; Modern Icelandic dates from about 1540. See INDO-EUROPEAN LANGUAGES, *Table.*

Ice′land moss (īs′lănd). A lichen (*Cetraria islandica*), of arctic regions, sometimes used medicinally or as food.

Iceland spar. *Mineral.* A doubly refracting, transparent variety of calcite, the best of which is obtained in Iceland.

ice′man′ (īs′măn′), *n.* A man who deals in or delivers ice.

ice needle. A slender ice particle that floats in the air in clear, cold weather. International symbol, ⟵.

I·ce′ni (ī·sē′nī), *n. pl.* [L.] An ancient tribe of Britons which under its queen Boadicea (Boudicca) revolted against the Romans, A.D. 61. — **I·ce′nic** (-nĭk), *adj.*

ice pack. **1.** A large area of floating pieces of ice driven more or less closely together. **2.** A container in which cracked ice is packed for use in making cold applications.

ice plant. An Old World plant (***Mesembryanthemum crystallinum***) of the carpetweed family, with foliage covered with glistening papillose dots or vesicles.

ice sheet. See ICECAP, 1.

||**ich dien** (ĭĸ dēn′). [G.] I serve; — motto of the Prince of Wales.

ich·neu′mon (ĭk·nū′mŏn), *n.* [L., fr. Gr. *ichneumōn,* lit., the tracker, so called because it hunts out the eggs of the crocodile.] **1.** A mongoose, supposed by the ancient Egyptians to devour crocodiles' eggs. **2.** An ichneumon fly.

ichneumon fly. Any of a large group of insects (order Hymenoptera, chiefly of the family Ichneumonidae) whose larvae are for the most part internal parasites on the larvae of other insects, esp. on caterpillars.

ich·nog′ra·phy (ĭk·nŏg′rȧ·fĭ), *n.* [Through F. & L., fr. Gr. *ichnographia,* fr. *ichnos* track, footstep + *graphein* to describe.] A horizontal section, as of a building, drawn to scale; ground plan.

ich·nol′o·gy (ĭk·nŏl′ō·jĭ), *n.* *Geol.* The study of fossil footprints.

i′chor (ī′kôr; ī′kẽr), *n.* [NL., fr. Gr. *ichōr.*] **1.** *Class. Myth.* An ethereal fluid that supplied the place of blood in the veins of the gods. **2.** A thin, acrid discharge, as from an ulcer. — **i′chor·ous** (ī′kŏr·ŭs), *adj.*

ich′thy·ic (ĭk′thĭ·ĭk), *adj.* [Gr. *ichthys, -yos,* a fish.] *Zool.* Pertaining to fishes; having the characteristics of a fish.

ich′thy·o- (ĭk′thĭ·ō-), **ich′thy-.** [Gr. *ichthys, -yos.*] A combining form meaning *fish,* as in *ichthyo*logy.

ich′thy·og′ra·phy (ĭk′thĭ·ŏg′rȧ·fĭ), *n.* A treatise on fishes.

ich′thy·oid (ĭk′thĭ·oid), *adj.* [Gr. *ichthyoeidēs.*] Resembling a fish. — *n. Old Zool.* A fishlike animal. — **ich′thy·oi′dal** (-oi′dăl; -d'l), *adj.*

ich′thy·ol′o·gy (-ŏl′ō·jĭ), *n.* [*ichthyo-* + *-logy.*] **a** The department of zoology which treats of fishes. **b** A treatise on fishes. — **ich′thy·o·log′ic** (-ō·lŏj′ĭk), **ich′thy·o·log′i·cal** (-ĭ·kăl), *adj.* — **ich′thy·ol′o·gist** (-ŏl′ō·jĭst), *n.*

ich′thy·oph′a·gy (-ŏf′ȧ·jĭ), *n.* [F. *ichthyophagie,* fr. Gr. *ichthyophagia.*] The practice of eating, or living on, fish. — **ich′thy·oph′a·gous** (-gŭs), *adj.*

ich′thy·or′nis (-ôr′nĭs), *n.* [NL., fr. *ichthy-* + Gr. *ornis* bird.] *Paleontol.* Any of a genus (*Ichthyornis*) of extinct toothed birds. The best-known species (*I. victor*) was about the size of a gull.

ich′thy·o·saur′ (ĭk′thĭ·ō·sôr′), **ich′thy·o·sau′rus** (-sô′rŭs), *n.* [*ichthyo-* + Gr. *sauros* lizard.] Any of an order (Ichthyosauria) of extinct marine reptiles, with fish-shaped body and porpoiselike snout.

ich′thy·o′sis (ĭk′thĭ·ō′sĭs), *n.* [NL., fr. *ichthy-* + *-osis.*] *Med.* A disease, usually congenital, in which the skin is thick, rough, and scaly. — **ich′thy·ot′ic** (-ŏt′ĭk), *adj.*

-i′cian (-ĭsh′ăn). [F. *-icien,* fr. *-ien* added to nouns.] A suffix denoting *a specialist* or *practitioner in a* (specified) *field,* as in mus*ician,* techn*ician,*

i′ci·cle (ī′sĭk·'l), *n.* [ME. *isikel,* fr. AS. *īs* ice + *gicel* icicle.] A pendent mass of ice, formed by the freezing of dripping water. — **i′ci·cled** (-'ld), *adj.*

i′ci·ly (ī′sĭ·lĭ), *adv.* In an icy manner.

i′ci·ness (ī′sĭ·nĕs; -nĭs), *n.* Quality or state of being icy.

ic′ing (īs′ĭng), *n.* A coating for cakes, made from sugar combined with water, milk, or egg white; frosting.

||**i′ci′ on parle fran′çais′** (ē′sē′ ôɴ′ pȧr′lẽ fräɴ′sĕ′). [F.] French is spoken here.

ick′er (ĭk′ẽr), *n.* [AS. *eher.*] *Scot.* An ear of corn.

i′con (ī′kŏn), *n.; pl.* ICONS (ī′kŏnz), ICONES (ī′kō·nēz). [L., fr. Gr. *eikōn, eikonos.*] **1.** An image or representation; a portrait; picture; illustration; now usually, a monumental portrait statue. **2.** *Eastern Ch.* An image of Christ, the Virgin Mary, or a saint, in painting, bas-relief, or mosaic (but never in sculpture).

i·con′ic (ī·kŏn′ĭk), *adj.* Also **i·con′i·cal** (-ĭ·kăl). [L. *iconicus,* fr. Gr. *eikonikos,* fr. *eikōn* image.] Of or pertaining to an icon, image, or other representation; — applied specif. in art to statues and busts sculptured according to fixed or conventional representation or symbolism.

i·con′o- (ī·kŏn′ō-), **icon-.** [See ICON.] A combining form meaning *image,* as in **i·con′o·clasm,** image breaking.

i·con′o·clast (-klăst), *n.* [ML. *iconoclastes,* fr. MGr. *eikonoklastēs,* fr. *eikōn* image + *klastēs* a breaker, fr. *klan* to break.] **1.** A breaker of icons, or images; an opponent of religious use of images. **2.** One who attacks cherished beliefs as shams. — **i·con′o·clas′tic** (-klăs′tĭk), *adj.*

i·con′o·graph′ic (-grăf′ĭk), **i·con′o·graph′i·cal** (-ĭ·kăl), *adj.* Of or pert. to iconography; representing by pictures or diagrams.

i′co·nog′ra·phy (ī′kō·nŏg′rȧ·fĭ), *n.* [ML. *iconographia,* fr. Gr. *eikonographia* a sketch or description, fr. *eikōn* image + *graphein* to describe.] **1.** Art of representation by pictures or images; the description or study of portraiture or representation. **2.** A record or representation by means of pictures or diagrams.

i′co·nol′a·try (-nŏl′ȧ·trĭ), *n.* [*icono-* + *-latry.*] Image worship. — **i′co·nol′a·ter** (-tẽr), *n.*

i′co·nol′o·gy (-ō·jĭ), *n.* [*icono-* + *-logy.*] Science or lore of icons; study of the use of icons; also, icons collectively. — **i·con′o·log′i·cal** (ī·kŏn′ō·lŏj′ĭ·kăl), *adj.*

i·con′o·scope (ī·kŏn′ō·skōp), *n.* *Television.* An electron-gun pickup or camera tube employing the storage principle in its operation and utilizing an electron scanning beam to convert photoemission effects into video signals.

i′co·nos′ta·sis (ī′kō·nŏs′tȧ·sĭs), *n.; pl.* -SES (-sēz). Also **i·con′o·stas** (ī·kŏn′ō·stăs), **i·con′o·sta′si·on** (-stā′sĭ·ŏn). [NL., fr. NGr. *eikonostasis,* fr. Gr. *eikōn* image + *stasis* a standing.] *Eastern Ch.* The partition with doors, adorned with icons, which separates the bema of a church from the choir or from the nave.

i′co·sa·he′dron (ī′kō·sȧ·hē′drŭn), *n.; pl.* -DRA (-drȧ). [Gr. *eikosaedron,* fr. *eikosi* twenty + *hedra* seat, base.] *Geom.* A polyhedron of twenty faces. — **i′co·sa·he′dral** (-drăl), *adj.*

i′co·si- (ī′kō·sĭ-), **icos-.** [Gr. *eikosi.*] A combining form meaning *twenty,* as in **i′co·si·tet′ra·he′dron,** a twenty-four-sided solid.

-ics (-ĭks). [See -IC.] A suffix used in the names of many sciences, arts, and systematic studies. Form: Such nouns as acoust*ics,* athlet*ics,* dynam*ics,* polit*ics,* statist*ics* originally had in English the singular form, as still in arithmet*ic,* log*ic,* mus*ic,* rhetor*ic;* but since 1600 their plurals have been the regular forms, probably in imitation of the Greek *ta physika, ta ethica,* etc., although the singular of certain words also occurs, after French and German usage, as diagnost*ic,* eth*ic,* and metaphys*ic.* Scientific and technical nouns have regularly adopted the plural form, as bionom*ics,* ceram*ics,* demot*ics,* electron*ics,* homilet*ics,* kinet*ics,* logist*ics,* mnemon*ics,* nucleon*ics,* opt*ics,* pediatr*ics,* pedagog*ics,* prosthet*ics,* systemat*ics,* therapeut*ics,* pyrotechn*ics.* Construction: As denoting a science or art or its subject matter nouns in *-ics* are now construed as singular (all linguist*ics* is descriptive; genet*ics* is an example of extreme specialization; strategy wins wars, tact*ics* wins battles). As denoting concrete activities, practices, or phenomena such nouns are usually construed as plural (it has been questioned if gymnast*ics* give real endurance; the mechan*ics* of the gyroscope explain the gyrocompass; the phonet*ics* of the language are minutely observed). A few nouns in *-ics* have acceptable uses in both singular and plural in the same sense (polit*ics* is, or are, completely barred; his polit*ics* was reactionary; his polit*ics* are the subject of debate; Russian tact*ics* is to plunge forward; Japanese tact*ics* were easily diagnosed).

ic·ter′ic (ĭk·tĕr′ĭk), *adj.* Also **ic·ter′i·cal** (-ĭ·kăl). [L. *ictericus*, fr. Gr. *ikterikos*, fr. *ikteros* jaundice.] Pertaining to, affected with, or serving as a cure for jaundice. — *n.* A remedy for jaundice.

ic′ter·us (ĭk′tĕr·ŭs), *n.* [NL., fr. Gr. *ikteros* jaundice.] **1.** *Med.* Jaundice. **2.** *Plant Pathol.* A diseased condition, as of grain, in which the foliage turns yellow.

ic′tus (ĭk′tŭs), *n.; pl.* ICTUSES (-ĕz; -ĭz), ICTUS. [L., fr. *icere, ictum*, to strike.] **1.** *Pros.* Metrical or rhythmical stress or beat in utterance. **2.** *Med.* **a** A stroke or blow, as in a sunstroke. **b** A sudden attack; a fit.

i′cy (ī′sĭ), *adj.;* I′CI·ER (-sĭ·ĕr); I′CI·EST. [AS. *īsig.*] **1.** Having ice within, about, or over; cold; frosty; as, *icy* seas. **2.** Resembling ice; chilling; frigid; cold.

id (ĭd), *n.* [G., short for *idioplasma.* See IDIOPLASM.] *Psychoanalysis.* The fundamental mass of life tendencies, out of which the ego and libido tendencies develop.

I′d (īd). A contraction of *I would* or *I had;* — often used for *I should.*

-id (-ĭd). [L. *-is*, pl. *-ides*, patronymic suffix, daughter(s) of, fr. Gr. *-is*, pl. *-ides.*] **a** *Astron.* A suffix used with the name of a constellation in naming meteors which appear to radiate from it, as in Perse*id.* **b** A suffix used in names of epic poems, as in Aene*id.*

-id (-ĭd). [Cf. F. *-ide.* See -IDAE.] *Zool.* A suffix, derived from *-idae*, used to form English nouns and adjectives designating members of zoological families, as in clupe*id.*

-id. [F. *-ide*, fr. L. *-idus.*] *Chem.* = -IDE.

-i·dae (-ĭ·dē). [Pl. of L. *-ides*, patronymic suffix, son of, fr. Gr. *-idēs.*] *Zool.* The suffix with which, in modern classifications, all names of families of animals are formed, as in Fel*idae* (the cat family).

-ide (-īd; -ĭd; 56). [From ox*ide.*] *Chem.* A suffix used in names of compounds, as in chlor*ide.* In binary compounds it denotes the nonmetallic or negative element or radical, as in hydrogen sulf*ide.*

i·de′a (ī·dē′ȧ; ī·dē̦′ȧ: *see note below*), *n.; pl.* IDEAS (-ȧz). [L., fr. Gr., fr. *idein* to see.] **1.** *Philos.* **a** A concept; also, a percept. **b** *Platonism.* One of the archetypes, or patterns, of which existing things are imperfect copies. **2.** A design; a preliminary plan; often, a plan or purpose of action; project. **3.** *Archaic.* A visible representation of a conception; a realized ideal. **4. a** *Obs.* An image, or picture recalled by memory. **b** An indefinite or fanciful notion; a fancy. **5.** Broadly, any object of the mind existing in thought; a concept, a notion, or mental impression. **6.** A formulated thought or opinion.

☞ The pronunciation ī′dē·ȧ is a common provincialism esp. throughout the southern United States.

Syn. Idea, concept, conception, thought, notion, impression mean something existing in the mind as the result of apprehension, comprehension, or the formulation of an opinion, a plan, or the like. **Idea** may apply to a mental image of something seen or heard of or fancied, a pure abstraction, a mere supposition, or the like; **concept,** logically, applies to the idea of a species or genus formed by the mind but, popularly, to any idea of what a thing should be; **conception,** often used in place of *concept* in the latter sense, primarily implies something expressed as a result of an individual's or group's conceiving; **thought** applies to an idea expressed or unexpressed that has come to the mind as a result of reflection; **notion** implies more vagueness or caprice than *thought;* **impression,** an idea stimulated by something seen, heard, read, etc.

i·de′al (ī·dē′ăl; ī·dē̦′ăl), *adj.* [F. *idéal*, fr. L. *idealis.*] **1.** Existing as a pattern, or archetypal idea. **2. a** Existing as a mere mental image; existing in fancy or imagination only. Cf. PRACTICAL, 1. **b** Pertaining to, or of the nature of, mental images; conceptual. **3.** Of or pertaining to an ideal or to perfection of kind; existing as a perfect exemplar. **4.** *Philos.* Of or pertaining to idealism; idealistic. — *n.* A standard of perfection, beauty, or excellence. — **Syn.** See MODEL.

i·de′al·ism (ī·dē′ăl·ĭz′m), *n.* **1.** *Philos.* Any theory which affirms the central importance of mind, or the spiritual and ideal, in reality; specif.: **a** Theory which regards reality as essentially spiritual or the embodiment of mind or reason. **b** Theory which identifies reality with perceptibility or denies the possibility of knowing anything except the mental life. **2.** The practice of forming ideals; the tendency to idealize; also, that which is idealized. **3.** In literature and art, the theory or practice which values ideal or subjective types or aspects of beauty more than formal or sensible qualities, or that which affirms the pre-eminent value of imagination as compared with faithful copying of nature; — opposed to *realism.*

i·de′al·ist (-ĭst), *n.* **1. a** An adherent of a theory of idealism in philosophy. **b** An artist or author who advocates or practices idealism in art, writing, etc. **2.** One who idealizes; hence, a visionary; a dreamer. Cf. REALIST, 2.

i·de′al·is′tic (-ĭs′tĭk), *adj.* Also **i·de′al·is′ti·cal** (-tĭ·kăl). Of or pertaining to idealists or idealism. — **i·de′al·is′ti·cal·ly,** *adv.*

i′de·al′i·ty (ī′dē·ăl′ĭ·tĭ), *n.; pl.* -TIES (-tĭz). **1.** Quality or state of being ideal; also, existence only in idea. **2.** The capacity to form or entertain ideals.

i·de′al·ize (ī·dē′ăl·īz), *v. t.* To give an ideal form or value to; to attribute ideal characteristics to. — *v. i.* To form ideals; to work idealistically. — **i·de′al·i·za′tion** (-ĭ·zā′shŭn; -ī·zā′-), *n.* — **i·de′al·iz′er** (-īz′ĕr), *n.*

i·de′al·ly (-ĭ), *adv.* **a** In idea or imagination; mentally. **b** Conformably to an ideal; perfectly; as, an actor *ideally* suited to the part.

i·de′ate (ī·dē′āt), *v. t.* **1.** To form in idea; to conceive. **2.** To have ideas, thoughts, or impressions of.

i·de′ate (-āt), *n.* *Philos.* An actual existence supposed to correspond with an idea.

i′de·a′tion (ī′dē·ā′shŭn), *n.* Function or capacity of the mind whereby it entertains ideas. — **i′de·a′tion·al,** *adj.* — **i′de·a′tion·al·ly,** *adv.*

‖**i′dée′ fixe** (ē′dā′ fēks′). [F.] A fixed idea.

‖**i′dem** (ī′dĕm), *pron. & adj.* [L.] The same; the same as that mentioned above; — often abbreviated *id.*

i·den′tic (ī·dĕn′tĭk), *adj.* Identical; specif., in diplomacy, designating an action or expression in which two or more governments follow precisely the same course or employ the same form; — distinguished from a *joint* action.

i·den′ti·cal (-tĭ·kăl), *adj.* [ML. *identicus.* See IDENTITY.] **1.** The same; not different or other. **2.** Exactly alike or equal. **3.** *Biol.* Designating the similar twins derived from a single ovum. Cf. FRATERNAL. — **Syn.** See SAME. — **i·den′ti·cal·ly,** *adv.* — **i·den′ti·cal·ness,** *n.*

i·den′ti·fi·ca′tion (ī·dĕn′tĭ·fĭ·kā′shŭn), *n.* **1.** Act of identifying, or state of being identified. **2.** Something that identifies, or establishes the identity of, a person or thing.

i·den′ti·fy (ī·dĕn′tĭ·fī), *v. t.;* -FIED (-fīd); -FY′ING. **1.** To make to be the same; to consider as the same in any relation; as, to *identify* the interests of subjects and their sovereigns. **2.** To establish the identity of; to prove the same (with something described, claimed, or asserted). **3.** *Biol.* To determine the species of. **4.** *Colloq.* To associate (oneself), as with a business or a social or political group. — **i·den′ti·fi′er** (-fī′ĕr), *n.*

i·den′ti·ty (-tĭ), *n.; pl.* -TIES (-tĭz). [F. *identité*, fr. LL. *identitas*, irreg. fr. L. *idem* the same.] **1. a** Sameness of essential character. **b** Sameness in all that constitutes the objective reality of a thing; self-sameness; oneness. **2.** Unity and persistence of personality; individuality; as, to forget one's *identity.* **3.** The condition of being the same with something described or asserted; as, to establish the *identity* of stolen goods.

id′e·o- (ĭd′ē·ō-; ī′dē·ō-). [F. *idéo-*, fr. Gr. *idea.*] A combining form meaning *idea*, as in *ideology.*

id′e·o·gram′ (-grăm′), *n.* [*ideo-* + *-gram.*] **1.** A picture or pictorial symbol as an original (not phonetic) element of writing; an early form of hieroglyph. Cf. PICTOGRAPH. **2.** A graphic symbol used for convenience and representing an idea rather than a word; as, 3 (read as *three* in English, *drei* in German, *trois* in French).

id′e·o·graph′ (-grăf′), *n.* [*ideo-* + *-graph.*] An ideogram. — **id′e·o·graph′ic** (-grăf′ĭk), **id′e·o·graph′i·cal** (-ĭ·kăl), *adj.* — **id′e·o·graph′i·cal·ly,** *adv.*

id′e·og′ra·phy (ĭd′ē·ŏg′rȧ·fĭ; ī′dē-), *n.* Employment of ideograms; representation of ideas by graphic symbols.

id′e·ol′o·gy (-ŏl′ō·jĭ), *n.; pl.* -GIES (-jĭz). [F. *idéologie.* See IDEO-; -LOGY.] **1.** *Philos.* The science of ideas; specif., a theory of the origin of ideas which derives them exclusively from sensation. **2.** Visionary theorizing. **3.** Manner or content of thinking characteristic of an individual or class; as, bourgeois *ideology.* **4.** The intellectual pattern of any widespread culture or movement; as, exposure to Anglo-Saxon *ideology;* specif., the integrated assertions, theories, and aims constituting a politico-social program, often with an implication of factitious propagandizing; as, Fascism was altered in Germany to fit the Nazi *ideology.* — **id′e·o·log′ic** (-ō·lŏj′ĭk), **id′e·o·log′i·cal** (-ĭ·kăl), *adj.* — **id′e·ol′o·gist** (-ŏl′ō·jĭst), *n.*

id′e·o·mo′tion (ĭd′ē·ō·mō′shŭn; ī′dē·ō-), *n.* [*ideo-* + *motion.*] Nonvoluntary movement produced as the direct expression of an idea. — **id′e·o·mo′tor** (-mō′tĕr), *adj.*

ides (īdz), *n. pl.* [F., fr. L. *idus.*] See ROMAN CALENDAR.

‖**id est** (ĭd ĕst). [L.] That is. Abbr. *i. e.*

id′i·o- (ĭd′ĭ·ō-). [Gr. *idios.*] A combining form meaning: **a** *One's own, personal, separate, distinct*, as in *idio*syncrasy. **b** *Biochem. & Med. Self-produced.*

id′i·o·blast′ (-blăst′), *n.* [*idio-* + *-blast.*] **a** *Biol.* A hypothetical structural unit of the cell. **b** *Bot.* An isolated cell differing from neighboring cells. — **id′i·o·blas′tic** (-blăs′tĭk), *adj.*

id′i·oc′ra·sy (ĭd′ĭ·ŏk′rȧ·sĭ), *n.; pl.* -SIES (-sĭz). [Gr. *idiokrasia.* See IDIO-; CRASIS.] Peculiarity of constitution; idiosyncrasy.

id′i·o·cy (ĭd′ĭ·ō·sĭ), *n.* [From IDIOT.] **1.** Extreme deficiency in intelligence, commonly due to incomplete or abnormal development of the brain. See IDIOT, MENTAL DEFICIENCY. **2.** Anything idiotic.

id′i·o·e·lec′tric (ĭd′ĭ·ō·ē·lĕk′trĭk), *adj.* Also **id′i·o·e·lec′tri·cal** (-trĭ·kăl), *adj.* [*idio-* + *electric.*] *Physics.* Capable of becoming electrified by friction.

id′i·om (ĭd′ĭ·ŭm), *n.* [F. and L.; F. *idiome*, fr. L. *idioma*, fr. Gr. *idiōma*, fr. *idioun* to make a person's own, fr. *idios* one's own, proper.] **1.** The language peculiar to a people (a tongue), or to a district, community, or class (a dialect). **2.** The structural form peculiar to any language. **3.** An expression in the usage of a language, that is peculiar to itself either in grammatical construction or in having a meaning which cannot be derived as a whole from the conjoined meanings of its elements (as, *the more the merrier, a picture of the king's, to make friends with him*). **4.** A form of expression characteristic of an author.

id′i·o·mat′ic (ĭd′ĭ·ō·măt′ĭk), *adj.* Also **id′i·o·mat′i·cal** (-ĭ·kăl). Of or pertaining to, or conforming to, idiom. — **id′i·o·mat′i·cal·ly,** *adv.* — **id′i·o·mat′i·cal·ness,** *n.*

id′i·o·mor′phic (-môr′fĭk), *adj.* [*idio-* + *-morphic.*] **1.** Having a form of its own. **2.** *Cryst.* Having its proper crystallographic form or shape; as, an *idiomorphic* mineral; — opposed to *xenomorphic.* — **id′i·o·mor′phi·cal·ly** (-fĭ·kăl·ĭ), *adv.*

id′i·op′a·thy (ĭd′ĭ·ŏp′ȧ·thĭ), *n.; pl.* -THIES (-thĭz). [Gr. *idiopatheia*, fr. *idios* proper, peculiar + *pathein, paschein*, to suffer.] *Med.* A morbid state not preceded or caused by any other disease; a primary disease. — **id′i·o·path′ic** (-ō·păth′ĭk), *adj.*

id′i·o·plasm (ĭd′ĭ·ō·plăz′m), *n.* [*idio-* + *-plasm.*] *Biol.* That portion of the cell protoplasm supposed to determine the character of the species and to be the physical basis of hereditary transmission; germ plasm. Cf. TROPHOPLASM. — **id′i·o·plas·mat′ic** (-plăz·măt′ĭk), *adj.*

id′i·o·syn′cra·sy (ĭd′ĭ·ō·sĭng′krȧ·sĭ), *n.; pl.* -SIES (-sĭz). [Gr. *idiosynkrasia*, fr. *idios* proper, peculiar + *synkrasis* a mixing together.] **1.** A peculiarity of constitution or temperament; a characteristic distinguishing an individual; specif., an eccentricity. **2.** *Med.* Individual hypersensitiveness to a drug, food, or other agent, as in a person in whom a sulfa drug causes anemia. — **Syn.** See ECCENTRICITY. — **id′i·o·syn·crat′ic** (-sĭn·krăt′ĭk), *adj.* — **id′i·o·syn·crat′i·cal·ly** (-ĭ·kăl·ĭ), *adv.*

id′i·ot (ĭd′ĭ·ŭt), *n.* [OF. *idiot*, fr. L. *idiota, idiotes*, ignorant person, fr. Gr. *idiōtēs*, also and orig., a private person, fr. *idios* proper, peculiar.] **1.** A person afflicted with idiocy. Idiots are incapable of connected speech or of avoiding the common dangers of life. **2.** A fool; simpleton; — a term of reproach. — **Syn.** See FOOL.

id′i·ot′ic (ĭd′ĭ·ŏt′ĭk), **id′i·ot′i·cal** (-ĭ·kăl), *adj.* [L. *idioticus* ignorant, fr. Gr. *idiōtikos.* See IDIOT.] Foolish; senseless. — **id′i·ot′i·cal·ly,** *adv.*

id′i·ot·ism (ĭd′ĭ·ŭt·ĭz′m), *n.* [In sense 1, fr. F. *idiotisme*, fr. L. *idiotismus* the way of a private person, the common or vulgar manner of speaking, fr. Gr. *idiōtismos*, deriv. of *idiōtēs.* See IDIOT.] **1.** *Obs.* Idiom. **2.** [F. *idiotisme*, fr. *idiot.*] Character or quality of being idiotic; specif.: **a** *Rare.* Idiocy. **b** *Obs.* Ignorance. **3.** A foolish act.

i′dle (ī′d'l), *adj.;* I′DLER (ī′dlĕr); I′DLEST (ī′dlĕst; -dlĭst). [AS. *īdel* vain, useless.] **1.** Without worth or basis; useless; vain; as, *idle* theorizing. **2.** Not occupied or employed; as: **a** Not turned to appropriate use; as, *idle* funds; *idle* hours. **b** Unemployed; inactive; as, *idle* workmen. **3.** Lazy; slothful; as, an *idle* fellow. — **Syn.** See VAIN: INACTIVE. — *v. i.; I′DLED* (-d'ld); *I′DLING* (-dlĭng). **1.** To lose time in idleness; esp., to saunter idly. **2.** *Mach.* To run disconnected, as from the transmission, so that power is not used for work; — said of machines, etc. — *v. t.* To spend in idleness; waste. — **i′dle·ness**, *n.* — **i′dly** (ī′dlĭ), *adv.*

idle, *or* **idler, pulley.** *Mach.* A guide or tightening pulley for a belt.

i′dler (ī′dlẽr), *n.* **1.** One who idles. **2.** *Mach.* An idle wheel or idle pulley. See TANK, *Illust.*

i′dlesse (ī′dlĕs), *n.* *Archaic.* Idleness.

idle wheel. *Mach.* **a** A gear wheel placed between two others, to transfer motion from one to the other without changing the direction of revolution or the velocity ratio. **b** A guide or tightening pulley for a belt.

C Idle Wheel.

i′do·crase (ī′dō·krās; ĭd′ō-), *n.* [F., fr. Gr. *eidos* form + *krasis* mixture.] Vesuvianite.

i′dol (ī′dŭl; -d'l), *n.* [OF. *idole*, *idele*, fr. L. *idolum*, fr. Gr. *eidōlon* image, phantom, idol, fr. *eidos* that which is seen, form, shape; akin to Gr. *idein* to see.] **1.** An image or representation of a deity, made or used as an object of worship; in Scriptural language, a false god; a heathen deity. **2.** *Obs.* Any image or representation; also, an impostor. **3.** A form or appearance visible but without substance, as an image in a mirror. **4.** An object of passionate devotion.

i·dol′a·ter (ī·dŏl′ȧ·tẽr), *n.* [F. *idolâtre*, fr. L., fr. Gr. *eidōlolatrēs* See IDOLATRY.] **1.** A worshiper of idols. **2.** An adorer; admirer. — **i·dol′a·tress** (-trĕs; -trĭs), *n.*

i·dol′a·trize (-trīz), *v. i.* To worship idols; to pay idolatrous worship. — *v. t.* To make an idol of; to idolize.

i·dol′a·trous (-trŭs), *adj.* Of or pertaining to idolatry; of the nature of idolatry; given to idolatry. — **i·dol′a·trous·ly**, *adv.* — **i·dol′a·trous·ness**, *n.*

i·dol′a·try (-trĭ), *n.; pl.* -TRIES (-trĭz). [OF. *idolatrie*, fr. L. *idololatria*, fr. Gr. *eidōlolatreia*, fr. *eidōlon* idol + *latreia* service.] **1.** Worship of a made image as a god. **2.** Excessive love or veneration for anything. **3.** An idol.

i′dol·ism (ī′dŭl·ĭz'm; ī′d'l-), *n.* Worship of idols; idolization; also, false thinking; a fallacy.

i′dol·ist (-ĭst), *n.* An idolater.

i′dol·ize (-īz), *v. t.* To make an idol of; esp., to love to excess; adore. — *v. i.* To practice idolatry. — **i′dol·i·za′tion** (-ĭ·zā′shŭn; -ī·zā′-), *n.* — **i′dol·iz′er** (-īz′ẽr), *n.*

i·do′ne·ous (ī·dō′nē·ŭs), *adj.* [L. *idoneus*.] Suitable.

i′dyl, i′dyll (ī′dĭl *or*, *Brit.*, ĭd′ĭl), *n.* [L. *idyllium*, fr. Gr. *eidyllion*, fr. *eidos* form.] **1.** Any simple description, either in poetry or prose, of rustic life, pastoral scenes, or the like; bucolic; eclogue. **2.** A fit subject for an idyl.

i′dyl·ist, i′dyll·ist (-ĭst), *n.* A composer of idyls; an idyllic poet.

i·dyl′lic (ī·dĭl′ĭk; ĭ-), *adj.* Of, pertaining to, or of the nature of an idyl; pleasing or picturesque in its natural simplicity. — **i·dyl′li·cal·ly** (-ĭ·kăl·ĭ), *adv.* — **i·dyl′li·cism** (-ĭ·sĭz'm), *n.*

-ie (-ĭ). A former spelling of *-y;* — now used as a diminutive suffix, as in bird*ie*.

-ier (-ẽr). [F., fr. L. *-arius*.] A noun suffix equivalent to *-eer*, as in gondol*ier*, cash*ier*, caval*ier*, grenad*ier*.

if (ĭf), *conj.* [AS. *gif*.] **1.** In case that; granting, allowing, or supposing that; — introducing a condition or supposition. **2.** Whether; — introducing indirect questions. — *n.* The conjunction *if;* hence, a condition; supposition.

if′fy (ĭf′ĭ), *adj.* *Colloq.* Abounding in ifs; contingent; provisory.

Ig′dra·sil, Ig′dra·syl, Igg′dra·sil. Vars. of YGGDRASILL.

ig′loo, ig′lu (ĭg′lōō), *n.* [Eastern Eskimo *igdlu* snow house.] **1.** An Eskimo house or hut, often made of snow blocks and in the shape of a dome. **2.** A building or structure of similar shape.

ig′ne·ous (ĭg′nē·ŭs), *adj.* [L. *igneus*, fr. *ignis* fire.] **1.** Pertaining to, having the nature of, or like fire; containing fire. **2.** *Petrol.* Resulting from the action of heat within the earth, usually accompanied by fusion; of rocks, formed by solidification of a molten magma.

ig·nes′cent (ĭg·nĕs′ĕnt; -'nt), *adj.* [L. *ignescens*, pres. part. of *ignescere* to become inflamed, fr. *ignis* fire.] Emitting sparks when struck with steel; hence, becoming inflamed; inflammatory; as, *ignescent* hate. — *n.* An ignescent substance.

‖**ig′nis fat′u·us** (ĭg′nĭs făt′ū·ŭs); *pl.* IGNES FATUI (ĭg′nēz făt′ū·ī). [ML., fr. L. *ignis* fire + *fatuus* foolish; — from its tendency to mislead travelers.] **1.** A light that appears in the night over marshy grounds, supposed to be caused by the combustion of marsh gas (methane); — popularly called also *will-o'-the-wisp*. **2.** A misleading influence or thing.

ig·nite′ (ĭg·nīt′), *v. t.* [L. *ignitus*, past part. of *ignire* to ignite, fr. *ignis* fire.] To subject to fire; to heat strongly; to render luminous by heat; also, to kindle. — *v. i.* To take fire; to begin to burn. — **ig·nit′er** (-nīt′ẽr), **ig·ni′tor** (-nī′tẽr), *n.* — **ig·nit′i·ble** (-nīt′ĭ·b'l), **ig·nit′a·ble** (-ȧ·b'l), *adj.*

ig·ni′tion (ĭg·nĭsh′ŭn), *n.* **1.** Act of igniting; a setting on fire; loosely, burning. **2.** Means of igniting. **3.** In internal-combustion engines, the process or the means of igniting the mixture, as an electric spark from a magneto.

ig·ni′tron (ĭg·nī′trŏn), *n.* [*ignite* + elec*tron* tube.] *Elec.* A mercury-containing half-wave rectifier tube in which the arc is restruck at the beginning of each cycle by a special electrode separately energized by an auxiliary circuit.

ig·no′ble (ĭg·nō′b'l), *adj.* [F., fr. L. *ignobilis*, fr. *in-* not + *gnobilis*, *nobilis*, noble.] **1.** Of low birth or family; not noble; humble. **2.** Not honorable; base; mean. **3.** *Falconry.* Designating the short-winged hawks (as the goshawk) which rake for their prey instead of pouncing. — **Syn.** See MEAN. — **Ant.** Noble. — **ig·no′ble·ness**, *n.* — **ig·no′bly**, *adv.*

ig′no·min′i·ous (ĭg′nō·mĭn′ĭ·ŭs), *adj.* [F. *ignominieux*, fr. L. *ignominiosus*.] **1.** Marked with, or full of, ignominy; dishonorable. **2.** Deserving ignominy; despicable. **3.** Humiliating; degrading. — **ig′no·min′i·ous·ly**, *adv.*

ig′no·min·y (ĭg′nō·mĭn·ĭ), *n.; pl.* -IES (-ĭz). [F. *ignominie*, fr. L. *ignominia* ignominy (i. e., a deprivation of one's good name), fr. *in-* not + *nomen* name.] **1.** Disgrace or dishonor. **2.** Quality or conduct deserving disgrace. — **Syn.** See DISGRACE.

ig′no·ra′mus (-rā′mŭs), *n.* [L., we do not know. See IGNORE.] An ignorant person; a dunce.

ig′no·rance (ĭg′nō·răns), *n.* State of being ignorant; want of knowledge.

ig′no·rant (-rănt), *adj.* [OF., fr. L. *ignorans*, *-antis*, pres. part. See IGNORE.] **1.** Destitute of knowledge; uninstructed or uninformed. **2.** Uninformed (in); unaware (of). **3.** Resulting from, or showing, ignorance. — **ig′no·rant·ly**, *adv.*

Syn. **Ignorant, illiterate, unlettered, untutored, unlearned, nescient** mean not having knowledge. **Ignorant** may imply a general condition but more often implies lack of knowledge of a particular thing such as a fact or a body of facts; **illiterate** usually implies a failure to attain a standard set (as, *illiterate* draftees; *illiterate* candidates for the Ph.D.); **unlettered** implies ignorance of knowledge gained by reading; **untutored, unlearned** imply lack of training in the schools or under teachers or an ignorance suggesting such a lack; **nescient** implies ignorance that is invincible or merely the result of unawareness, or the like.

‖**ig·no·ran′ti·a ju′ris,** *or* **le′gis, ne′mi·nem ex·cu′sat** (ĭg′nō·răn′shĭ·ȧ jōō′rĭs, lē′jĭs, nĕm′ĭ·nĕm ĕks·kū′săt). [L.] *Law.* Ignorance of the law, or a law, excuses no one; — expressing a general rule of criminal law.

‖**ig′no·ra′ti·o e·len′chi** (ĭg′nō·rā′shĭ·ō ē·lĕng′kī). [L.] *Logic.* Fallacy of supposing a point proved or disproved by an argument proving or disproving something not at issue.

ig·nore′ (ĭg·nōr′; 70), *v. t.* [F. *ignorer*, fr. L. *ignorare*, fr. *in-* not + the root of *gnarus* knowing, *noscere* to become acquainted with.] To refuse to take notice of; to disregard willfully. — **Syn.** See NEGLECT. — **Ant.** Heed. — **ig·nor′er** (-nōr′ẽr), *n.*

I′go·rot′ (ē′gō·rōt′), *n.; pl.* -ROT (-rōt′), -ROTS (-rōts′). Also **I′gor·ro′te** (ē′gôr·rō′tā). [Sp. *Igorrote*.] **1.** A member of any one of the three Indonesian groups of northern Luzon, Philippine Islands. **2.** The language, or group of dialects, spoken by the Igorot.

I·graine′ (ē·grān′), *n.* In Arthurian legend, the wife of Uther, and mother of Arthur.

i·gua′na (ĭ·gwä′nȧ), *n.* [Sp., of Arawakan and Cariban origin.] Any of several large tropical American lizards of several genera (esp. *Iguana* and *Metopoceros*, family Iguanidae). The best-known (*I. iguana*) attains a length of five or six feet.

i·guan′o·don (ĭ·gwăn′ō·dŏn), *n.* [NL., fr. *iguana* + Gr. *odōn*, *odontos*, tooth.] *Paleontol.* Any of a genus (*Iguanodon*) of gigantic herbivorous dinosaurs (group Ornithopoda), known from the early Cretaceous of Belgium and England.

ih·ram′ (ē·räm′), *n.* [Ar. *iḥrām* interdiction.] The peculiar dress worn by pilgrims to Mecca. It consists of a white cotton cloth thrown over the back, leaving the right arm and shoulder exposed, and another wrapped round the loins.

IHS. A symbol or monogram representing the Greek IHΣ, contraction of IH(ΣΟΥ)Σ, Jesus.

i′kon. Var. of ICON.

il- (ĭl-). An assimilated form of *in-*, not, as in *il*logical; and of *in-*, in, as in *il*lumine.

i′lang-i′lang (ē′läng·ē′läng), *n.* [Tag.] **a** A tree (*Canangium odoratum*) of the custard-apple family (Annonaceae) of Malaysia, the Philippines, etc., with greenish-yellow, very fragrant flowers. **b** An essence or perfume distilled from its flowers.

-ile (-ĭl; *Brit. usually* -īl; 56), **-il** (-ĭl). [F. or L.; F. *-il*, *-ile*, fr. L. *-ilis*.] A suffix in adjectives (and their derivative nouns) signifying *of*, or *pertaining to*, *appropriate to*, *suited for*, *capable of*, etc., as in doc*ile*, vir*ile*; civ*il*, utens*il*.

il′e·o- (ĭl′ē·ō-), **il′e-.** A combining form for *ileum*, as in **il′e·os′to·my**, **il′e·ot′o·my** (see -STOMY, -TOMY); denoting also, *ileac and*, as in **il′e·o·cae′cal**, **il′e·o·ce′cal**, pert. to the ileum and caecum; **il′e·o·col′ic**, **il′e·o·co·li′tis**.

il′e·um (ĭl′ē·ŭm), *n.* [L. *ile*, *ileum*, *ilium*, pl. *ilia*, groin, flank.] *Anat.* The last division of the small intestine; the part between the jejunum and large intestine. — **il′e·ac** (-ăk), *adj.*

il′e·us (-ŭs), *n.* [NL., fr. L. *ileus*, *ileos*, fr. Gr. *eileos*, *ileos*.] *Med.* A morbid condition due to intestinal obstruction, marked by complete constipation. — **il′e·ac** (-ăk), *adj.*

i′lex (ī′lĕks), *n.; pl.* ILEXES (ī′lĕk·sĕz; -sĭz). [L., holm oak.] **1.** The holm oak. **2.** A shrub or tree of a genus (*Ilex*) having small flowers and berrylike fruits; a holly.

il′i·a (ĭl′ĭ·ȧ), *n.*, *pl.* of ILIUM.

il′i·ac (ĭl′ĭ·ăk), *adj.* [F. or L.; F. *iliaque* relating to the colic, fr. L. *iliacus*, fr. *ileus* colic, confused with *ilium* ileum.] **1.** *Obs.* Ileac. **2.** *Anat.* Pertaining to the ilium; of or in the region of the ilium.

Il′i·ad (ĭl′ĭ·ăd), *n.* [L. *Ilias*, *-adis*, fr. Gr. *Ilias*, *-ados* (sc. *poiēsis*), fr. *Ilios*, *Ilion*, Ilium, the city of Ilus, a son of Tros, founder of Ilium (Troy).] **1.** A Greek epic poem ascribed to Homer. It narrates events of the last year of the Trojan War. **2.** An epic resembling Homer's *Iliad*; also, a long series, as of woes; a long account.

il′i·o- (ĭl′ĭ·ō-). A combining form for *ilium*, denoting in adjectives *iliac and*, as in **il′i·o·sa′cral**, iliac and sacral.

-il′i·ty (-ĭl′ĭ·tĭ). [F. *-ilité*, fr. L. *-ilitas*.] A suffix forming nouns denoting *quality* or *condition*, correspondent to adjectives ending in *-able*, *-ible*, *-il*, and *-ile*, as in affab*ility*.

il′i·um (ĭl′ĭ·ŭm), *n.; pl.* ILIA (-ȧ). [See ILEUM.] *Anat.* The dorsal and upper one of the three bones composing either lateral half of the pelvis.

ilk (ĭlk), *pron.* [AS. *ilca*.] *Obs.* With *the* or *that*, the same person or persons; the same thing. — ***of that ilk.*** *Scot.* Of the same (name, surname, place, or territorial designation); as, *Grant of that ilk*, i. e., *Grant of Grant*.

ilk, *n.* Family; kind; breed; class; — a use arising from a misunderstanding of *of that ilk* and still regarded as improper by many authorities.

ilk, *adj. & pron.* [Northern form of *each*.] *Scot. & Dial.* Each; every.

il′ka (ĭl′kȧ), *adj.* [*ilk* each + *a*, indef. article.] *Scot.* Each; every.

ill (ĭl), *adj.; compar.* WORSE (wûrs); *superl.* WORST (wûrst). [ON. *illr*, of uncert. origin.] **1.** *Archaic.* Evil; wrong. **2.** Contrary to advantage, happiness, etc.; bad; unwholesome; unfortunate; unlucky; painful; disagreeable. **3.** Defective; of persons, unskillful; not accordant with rule, fitness, or propriety; incorrect; unpolished. **4.** Characterized by bad intention; malevolent; unkind. **5.** Not healthy; hence, sick; indisposed. — **Syn.** See BAD: SICK. — *adv.* In an ill manner; badly; — often used in combination, as in:

ill-assorted	**ill-defined**	**ill-mated**
ill-conceived	**ill-informed**	**ill-pleased**
ill-contrived	**ill-kept**	**ill-timed**

— *n.* Whatever annoys or impairs happiness, or prevents success; evil; misfortune; disease; pain.

I'll (īl). Colloq. contr. of *I will;* — often used for *I shall.*

ill′–ad·vised′ (ĭl′ăd·vīzd′; 2), *adj.* Exhibiting, or due to, lack of due or wise consideration or counsel; injudicious.

il·la′tion (ĭ·lā′shŭn), *n.* [L. *illatio,* fr. *illatus,* used as past part. of *inferre* to carry or bring in.] Inference from premises or reasons; hence, that which is inferred or deduced.

il′la·tive (ĭl′ȧ·tĭv; ĭ·lā′tĭv), *adj.* [L. *illativus.*] Inferential; as, an *illative* consequence; an *illative* word, as *then, therefore,* etc.

il·laud′a·ble (ĭl·lôd′ȧ·b'l), *adj.* Not laudable.

ill′–be′ing (ĭl′bē′ĭng), *n.* Ill state or condition.

ill′–bod′ing (-bōd′ĭng; 2), *adj.* Inauspicious; ill-omened.

ill′–bred′ (-brĕd′; 2), *adj.* Badly brought up; impolite.

il·le′gal (ĭl·lē′găl), *adj.* [F. *illégal,* or ML. *illegalis.*] Not according to, or authorized by, law; unlawful; illicit; also, not sanctioned by official rules. — **il·le′gal·ly,** *adv.*

il′le·gal′i·ty (ĭl′lē·găl′ĭ·tĭ), *n.; pl.* -TIES (-tĭz). Quality or condition of being illegal; unlawfulness; also, an illegal act.

il·leg′i·ble (ĭl·lĕj′ĭ·b'l), *adj.* [*il-* not + *legible.*] Not legible; undecipherable. — **il·leg′i·bil′i·ty** (-bĭl′ĭ·tĭ), *n.* — **il·leg′i·ble·ness,** *n.* — **il·leg′i·bly,** *adv.*

il′le·git′i·ma·cy (ĭl′lē·jĭt′ĭ·mȧ·sĭ), *n.; pl.* -CIES (-sĭz). State or quality of being illegitimate; specif., bastardy.

il′le·git′i·mate (-mĭt), *adj.* **1.** Unlawfully begotten; bastard. **2.** Not legitimately deduced or inferred; illogical. **3.** Not according to law; unlawful. **4.** Not authorized by good usage. — **il′le·git′i·mate·ly,** *adv.* — **il′le·git′i·mate·ness,** *n.*

ill′–fat′ed (ĭl′făt′ĕd; -ĭd; 2), *adj.* Having an evil fate; doomed to, or fraught with, misfortune or disaster.

ill′–fa′vored *or* **–fa′voured** (-fā′vẽrd; 2), *adj.* **1.** Ugly; esp., evil-looking. **2.** Offensive; unpleasant. — **ill′–fa′vored·ly, -voured·ly,** *adv.* — **ill′–fa′vored·ness, -voured·ness,** *n.*

ill′–got′ten (-gŏt′'n; 2), *adj.* Acquired by evil means.

ill′–hu′mor, ill′–hu′mour (-hū′mẽr), *n.* Moody crossness; a mood of bad temper. — **ill′–hu′mored,** *or* **ill′–hu′moured** (-mẽrd; 2), *adj.* — **ill′–hu′mored·ly, ill′–hu′moured·ly,** *adv.* — **ill′–hu′mored·ness, ill′–hu′moured·ness,** *n.*

il·lib′er·al (ĭl·lĭb′ẽr·ăl), *adj.* [F. *illibéral,* fr. L. *illiberalis.*] **1.** Not liberal; esp., without a liberal education; lacking culture; ungentlemanly. **2.** Indicating a lack of culture or breadth of view; bigoted. **3.** Not generous; stingy. — **il·lib′er·al′i·ty** (-ăl′ĭ·tĭ), *n.* — **il·lib′er·al·ly,** *adv.* — **il·lib′er·al·ness,** *n.*

il·lic′it (ĭl·lĭs′ĭt; ĭ·lĭs′ĭt), *adj.* [F. *illicite,* fr. L. *illicitus,* fr. *il-* not + *licitus,* past part. of *licere* to be permitted.] Not permitted; improper; unlawful. — **il·lic′it·ly,** *adv.* — **il·lic′it·ness,** *n.*

il·lim′it·a·ble (ĭl·lĭm′ĭt·ȧ·b'l), *adj.* Incapable of being limited; immeasurable. — **il·lim′it·a·bil′i·ty** (-bĭl′ĭ·tĭ), **il·lim′it·a·ble·ness,** *n.* — **il·lim′it·a·bly,** *adv.*

il·lin′i·um (ĭ·lĭn′ĭ·ŭm), *n.* [NL., fr. *Illinois* + *-ium.*] *Chem.* The element of atomic number 61; — a former name. See PROMETHIUM.

Il′li·nois′ (ĭl′ĭ·noi′; -noiz′), *n.* [F., of Am. Indian origin.] An Indian of a confederacy of Algonquian tribes, formerly occupying Illinois and parts of Iowa and Wisconsin.

il·liq′uid (ĭl·lĭk′wĭd), *adj.* **1.** Not liquid; — said of assets, as of a bank. **2.** *Law.* That has not been made clear and certain; — said esp. of a right or claim not fixed by a written instrument or by a decree of the court.

il·lit′er·a·cy (ĭl·lĭt′ẽr·ȧ·sĭ), *n.; pl.* -CIES (-sĭz). **1.** Quality or state of being illiterate; want of learning; specif., inability to read and write. **2.** An instance of such ignorance; a literary blunder.

il·lit′er·ate (-ĭt), *adj.* [L. *illiteratus,* fr. *il-* not + *literatus* learned.] **1.** Ignorant of letters or books; uneducated; specif., unable to read. **2.** Unlearned; unrefined; as, *illiterate* style. — **Syn.** See IGNORANT. — *n.* An illiterate person. — **-ate·ly,** *adv.* — **-ate·ness,** *n.*

ill′–look′ing (ĭl′lo͝ok′ĭng; 2), *adj.* Ill-favored; homely; also, evil-looking; sinister.

ill′–man′nered (-măn′ẽrd; 2), *adj.* Impolite; rude. — **ill′–man′nered·ly,** *adv.* — **ill′–man′nered·ness,** *n.*

ill nature. Bad disposition or temperament; churlishness.

ill′–na′tured (-nā′tụrd; 2), *adj.* Cross; crabbed; surly. — **ill′–na′tured·ly,** *adv.* — **ill′–na′tured·ness,** *n.*

ill′ness (ĭl′nĕs; -nĭs), *n.* **1.** *Obs.* Wickedness; also, unfavorableness. **2.** Disease; malady; sickness.

il·log′i·cal (ĭl·lŏj′ĭ·kăl), *adj.* Not observing the rules of logic or correct reasoning. — **il·log′i·cal·ly,** *adv.* — **il·log′i·cal·ness,** *n.*

ill′–o′mened (ĭl′ō′mĕnd; 2), *adj.* Having bad omens; inauspicious.

ill′–sort′ed, *adj.* Poorly arranged; also, badly suited or matched.

ill′–starred′, *adj.* Born under, or having one's affairs controlled by, an evil star; ill-fated; unlucky; — from astrological beliefs.

ill temper. Bad temper; crossness. — **ill′–tem′pered** (-tĕm′pẽrd; 2), *adj.* — **ill′–tem′pered·ly,** *adv.*

ill′–treat′ (ĭl′trēt′), *v. t.* To treat cruelly or improperly; to maltreat; abuse. — **ill′–treat′ment,** *n.*

il·lume′ (ĭ·lūm′), *v. t.* To illuminate.

il·lu′mi·nant (ĭ·lū′mĭ·nănt), *n.* That which illuminates.

il·lu′mi·nate (-nāt), *v. t.* [L. *illuminatus,* past part. of *illuminare,* fr. *il-* in + *luminare* to enlighten, fr. *lumen* light.] **1.** To make light; to light up; to enlighten. **2.** To throw light on; to elucidate. **3.** To render illustrious; to cause to be resplendent. **4.** To adorn, as an initial letter, with designs in gold, brilliant colors, or the like, or a book or page, with borders, initial letters, or pictures in colors and gold, as in medieval manuscripts. **5.** To decorate with artificial lights, as a building on a gala occasion. — *v. i.* To light up in token of rejoicing. — (-nāt), *adj.* Illuminated; specif., *Obs.,* enlightened. — (-nāt), *n.* One who is enlightened; one of the illuminati.

il·lu′mi·na′ti (-nā′tī; -nä′tē), *n. pl.; sing.* ILLUMINATO (-tō). [L. *illuminatus,* sing., It. *illuminato.* See ILLUMINATE, *v.*] Those who claim special illumination, spiritual or intellectual; — usually capitalized when applied to the members of various special sects or groups.

il·lu′mi·na′tion (ĭ·lū′mĭ·nā′shŭn), *n.* **1.** An illuminating, or state of being illuminated; a lighting up; specif.: the lighting up or decoration of buildings, towns, etc.; also, *pl.,* the lights, lighting equipment, etc., with which this is done. **2.** Enlightenment, spiritual or mental. **3.** Adornment of a letter, manuscript, book, etc., with brilliant colors, gold, silver, elaborate flourishes, miniature designs, or the like; also, the colors, designs, etc., thus used. **4.** *Photom.* The surface light density, or luminous flux or power per unit area, on an intercepting surface at a point.

il·lu′mi·na′tive (ĭ·lū′mĭ·nā′tĭv; -nȧ·tĭv), *adj.* Tending to illuminate; illuminating; enlightening.

il·lu′mi·na′tor (-nā′tẽr), *n.* One who or that which illuminates; as: **a** One who illuminates manuscripts, etc. **b** Any of various devices or instruments for lighting.

il·lu′mine (ĭ·lū′mĭn), *v. t. & i.* [F. *illuminer,* fr. L. *illuminare.*] To illuminate or be illuminated; to light up; enlighten. — **il·lu′mi·na·ble** (-mĭ·nȧ·b'l), *adj.*

Il·lu′mi·nism (-mĭ·nĭz′m), *n.* The principles of the Illuminati, esp. the claim to a special enlightenment not accessible to mankind in general. — **Il·lu′mi·nist** (-nĭst), *n.*

ill′–us′age (ĭl′ūs′ĭj; -ūz′ĭj), *n.* Abusive treatment.

ill′–use′ (-ūz′), *v. t.* To subject to bad or cruel treatment; to abuse. — (-ūs′), *n.* Ill-usage; abuse.

il·lu′sion (ĭ·lū′zhŭn), *n.* [OF., fr. L. *illusio,* fr. *illudere, illusum,* to deride.] **1.** An unreal or misleading image presented to the vision; a deceptive appearance. **2.** State or fact of being deceived; false impression; misconception. **3.** A perception which fails to give the true character of an object perceived. Psychologists recognize *normal* illusions, and *abnormal* or *pathological* illusions, which are often not distinguishable from hallucinations. **4.** A delicate net lace, for veils, scarfs, etc.; tulle. — **Syn.** See DELUSION.

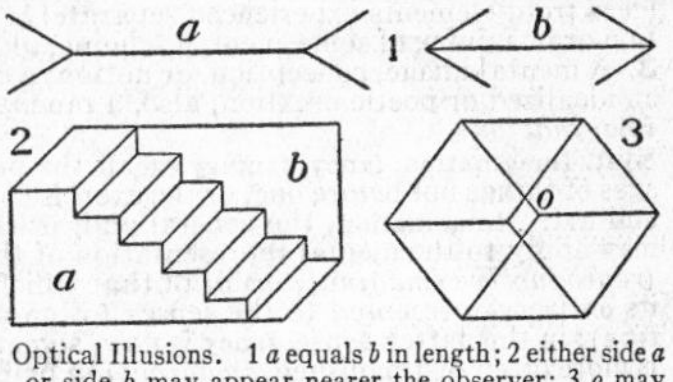

Optical Illusions. 1 *a* equals *b* in length; 2 either side *a* or side *b* may appear nearer the observer; 3 *o* may appear to be either the near or the far corner of the cube.

il·lu′sion·al (-ăl; -'l), *adj.* Of the nature of illusion.

il·lu′sion·ism (-ĭz′m), *n.* Any doctrine which affirms that the material world is wholly illusory.

il·lu′sion·ist (-ĭst), *n.* **1.** One given to illusion; a visionary. **2.** An adherent of illusionism. **3.** A conjurer.

il·lu′sive (ĭ·lū′sĭv), *adj.* Deceiving by false show; illusory; unreal. — **il·lu′sive·ly,** *adv.* — **il·lu′sive·ness,** *n.*

il·lu′so·ry (-sō·rĭ), *adj.* Deceiving; illusive. — **Syn.** See APPARENT.

il′lus·trate (ĭl′ŭs·trāt; ĭ·lŭs′trāt), *v. t.* [L. *illustratus,* past part. of *illustrare* to illuminate.] **1.** *Archaic.* To enlighten; illuminate. **2.** *Obs.* To make illustrious. **3.** *Obs.* To make luminous; to light up. **4.** To make clear; to explain, as by figures and examples. **5.** To provide with pictures or designs for elucidation or adornment; of pictures, etc., to elucidate or adorn.

il′lus·tra′tion (ĭl′ŭs·trā′shŭn), *n.* **1.** Act of illustrating, or state of being illustrated; specif.: **a** A making illustrious; distinction, or an instance or cause of it. **b** A making clear, evident, or distinct; elucidation. **c** Pictorial elucidation; adornment with pictures. **2.** That which illustrates; a comparison or example intended to make clear. **3.** A picture designed to elucidate or decorate a book, article, etc. Abbr. *illust.* — **Syn.** See INSTANCE.

il·lus′tra·tive (ĭ·lŭs′trȧ·tĭv; ĭl′ŭs·trā′tĭv), *adj.* Tending or designed to illustrate. — **il·lus′tra·tive·ly,** *adv.*

il′lus·tra′tor (ĭl′ŭs·trā′tẽr; ĭ·lŭs′trā·tẽr), *n.* One who or that which illustrates; esp., a person who designs illustrations for books, etc.

il·lus′tri·ous (ĭ·lŭs′trĭ·ŭs), *adj.* [L. *illustris;* akin to L. *illustrare* to illuminate.] **1.** *Archaic.* Brilliant; lustrous. **2.** Characterized by greatness, nobleness, or the like; famous. — **Syn.** See FAMOUS. — **il·lus′tri·ous·ly,** *adv.* — **il·lus′tri·ous·ness,** *n.*

il·lu′vi·al (ĭ·lū′vĭ·ăl), *adj.* [*il-* + *alluvial.*] Of or pertaining to illuviation or illuviated materials or areas, as soils or soil horizons.

il·lu′vi·a′tion (-ā′shŭn), *n.* The process of accumulation of dissolved or suspended material in a soil area or horizon due to eluviation (which see). — **il·lu′vi·ate** (ĭ·lū′vĭ·āt), *v. i.*

ill will. Inimical, esp. malevolent, feeling. — **Syn.** See MALICE. — **ill′–willed′** (ĭl′wĭld′; 2), *adj.*

ill′–wish′er, *n.* One who wishes ill to another.

il′ly (ĭl′lĭ), *adv.* Badly; ill.

Il·lyr′i·an (ĭ·lĭr′ĭ·ăn), *adj.* Of or pertaining to ancient Illyria. — *n.* **1.** One of the race of people inhabiting ancient Illyria. They were nearly related to the Thracians and are probably represented by the Albanians of today. **2.** The language of the Illyrians. See INDO-EUROPEAN LANGUAGES, *Table.*

il′men·ite (ĭl′mĕn·īt), *n.* [From *Ilmen,* a chain of the Ural Mountains.] *Mineral.* An iron-black mineral composed of iron, titanium, and oxygen, usually massive.

I′lo·ka′no (ē′lō·kä′nō; *Sp.* -nō), *n.; pl.* -NOS (-nōz; *Sp.* -nōs). [Sp. *Ilocano,* fr. *Iloko,* native name.] **1.** A member of one of the chief native peoples of the Philippines. They are Christian Malays. **2.** Their language, a Malayan tongue.

im- (ĭm-). An assimilated form: **a** Of *in-,* not, as in *im*mature. **b** Of Latin or English *in-,* in, sometimes for earlier *em-,* as in *im*bue.

I'm (īm). Colloq. contraction of *I am.*

im′age (ĭm′ĭj), *n.* [OF., fr. L. *imago, imaginis,* fr. the root of *imitari* to imitate.] **1. a** An imitation or likeness of any person or thing, sculptured, drawn, painted, or the like; esp., an imitation in solid form, as a sculptured figure; statue. **b** Hence, form; aspect; likeness; semblance. **2.** A copy or counterpart. **3.** A mental representation of anything not actually present to the senses; a picture drawn by the fancy; broadly, a conception; idea. **4.** *Archaic.* An illusory appearance; an apparition. **5.** A type; as, she is the *image* of devotion. **6.** A symbol; a representation. **7.** The optical counterpart of an object, produced by a lens, mirror, or other optical system. A ***real image*** is one formed of real foci, as on a photographic plate; a ***virtual image*** is one formed of virtual foci, as one seen in a plane mirror.

— *v. t.;* IM′AGED (-ĭjd); IM′AG·ING (-ĭj·ĭng). **1.** To exhibit or represent in language; to describe or portray. **2.** To represent to the fancy or recollection; to conceive; imagine. **3.** To form an image of; to portray; also, to reflect; mirror. **4.** To represent symbolically; to typify.

im′age·ry (ĭm′ĭj·rĭ; -ẽr·ĭ), *n.* **1.** Images in general. **2.** Mental images taken collectively; broadly, the work of memory, imagination, or fancy. **3.** Figurative language, esp. when used as ornament.

im·ag′i·na·ble (ĭ·măj′ĭ·nȧ·b′l), *adj.* Capable of being imagined; conceivable. — **im·ag′i·na·bly,** *adv.*

im·ag′i·nal (-năl; -n′l), *adj.* *Zool.* Of or pertaining to an imago.

im·ag′i·nar′y (-nĕr′ĭ *or, esp. Brit.,* -nẽr·ĭ), *adj.* **1.** Existing only in imagination or fancy; not real; fancied. **2.** *Alg.* Designating or pertaining to the square root of a negative number or to a quantity containing such a square root.

Syn. Imaginary, fanciful, visionary, fantastic, chimerical, quixotic mean out of keeping with things as they are, or conceiving such things. Imaginary implies fictitiousness or the product of an excited imagination; fanciful, a giving rein to the fancy or power of producing things which have no counterpart in nature or in fact; visionary, impracticality or incapability of realization; fantastic, incredibility or strangeness past belief; chimerical combines the implications of *visionary* and *fantastic;* quixotic implies an extravagantly chivalrous devotion to visionary ideals.

im·ag′i·na′tion (-nā′shŭn), *n.* **1.** The act or power of imagining; formation of mental images of objects not present to the senses, esp. of those never perceived in their entirety; hence, mental synthesis of new ideas from elements experienced separately. **2.** *Archaic.* A conception or imagining of some event; a scheme, plot, or project, esp. of evil. **3.** A mental image, conception, or notion; a creation of the mind, esp. an idealized or poetic creation; also, a fanciful or vain notion; as, idle *imaginations.*

Syn. Imagination, fancy, fantasy mean the power to form mental images of things not before one, or the exercise of that power in literature and art. Imagination, the general and, usually, underogatory term, may apply to the mental representation of that which is remembered (*reproductive imagination*) or of that which has never been (esp. in its entirety) presented to the senses (often called *creative imagination*): in this latter sense, fancy is now, sometimes, its equivalent, but is more often distinguished, *imagination* being the power to represent the real more fully and truly than it appears to the senses and in its ideal or universal character, and *fancy* to the power of inventing the novel and unreal by recombining the elements of reality; fantasy applies to the power of unrestrained (often extravagant or delusive) fancy, esp. as exhibited in art.

im·ag′i·na′tion·al (-ăl; -′l), *adj.* Pertaining to, involving, or caused by the imagination.

im·ag′i·na′tive (ĭ·măj′ĭ·nā′tĭv; -nȧ·tĭv), *adj.* **1.** Of or pertaining to the imagination; proceeding from, or characterized by, imagination; as, *imaginative* literature. **2.** Given to imagining; full of fancies. — **im·ag′i·na′tive·ly,** *adv.* — **im·ag′i·na′tive·ness,** *n.*

im·ag′ine (ĭ·măj′ĭn), *v. t.* [OF. *imaginer,* fr. L. *imaginari,* past part. *imaginatus,* fr. *imago* image. See IMAGE.] **1.** To form a mental image of; to represent or picture to oneself; to produce by the imagination. **2.** *Archaic.* To contrive in purpose; to scheme. **3.** *Colloq.* To suppose or think to be; guess. — *v. i.* **1.** To form images; to exercise the imagination. **2.** *Colloq.* To fancy; think; suppose. — **Syn.** See THINK.

im′ag·ist (ĭm′ĭj·ĭst), *n.* Any of a group of modern poets who compose chiefly in vers libre and express their ideas and emotions through a series of clear, precise images. — **im′ag·ism** (-ĭz′m), *n.* — **im′ag·ist, im′ag·is′tic** (ĭm′ĭ·jĭs′tĭk), *adj.*

i·ma′go (ĭ·mā′gō), *n.; pl.* IMAGOES (-gōz), IMAGINES (ĭ·măj′ĭ·nēz). [L.] **1.** An image. **2.** *Zool.* An insect in its final adult, sexually mature, and usually winged, state. See BOLL WEEVIL, *Illust.* **3.** *Psychoanalysis.* The more or less infantile conception of the parent retained in the unconscious.

i·mam′ (ĭ·mäm′), **i·maum′** (ĭ·mäm′; -môm′), *n.* [Ar. *imām.*] **1.** A Mohammedan priest. **2.** Among the Moslems, any of various persons called by this name (which is capitalized when used as or in a title) as: **a** The spiritual and temporal head of Islam. **b** The caliph, or any of various other sovereign princes. **c** Any of the twelve heads of Islam recognized by the Shiites. **d** Any person who is followed as an authority in theology and law.

i·mam′ate (ĭ·mäm′āt), *n.* The region or country ruled over by an imam; as, the *Imamate* of Yemen.

i·ma′ret (ĭ·mä′rĕt), *n.* [Turk. *ʻimāret,* fr. Ar. *ʻimārah* building.] In Turkey, an inn; hospice.

im·bal′ance (ĭm·băl′ăns), *n.* [*im-* not + *balance.*] Lack of balance; state of being out of equilibrium or out of proportion; as, a dietary or an economic *imbalance;* specif., lack of the muscular balance of the eyes, or of the functioning of the endocrine glands.

im·balm′ (ĭm·bäm′), **im·bark′** (ĭm·bärk′), etc. Vars. of EMBALM, EMBARK, etc.

im′be·cile (ĭm′bē·sĭl, -s′l, *or, esp. Brit.,* ĭm′bē·sēl, -sīl), *adj.* [F. *imbécile,* fr. L. *imbecillus* weak, feeble.] **1.** Weak; feeble; esp., mentally weak; feeble-minded. Imbecile persons are commonly incapable of earning a living. **2.** Stupid; fatuous; idiotic. — *n.* An imbecile person. — **Syn.** See FOOL.

im′be·cil′i·ty (-sĭl′ĭ·tĭ), *n.; pl.* -TIES (-tĭz). **1.** Quality of being imbecile; weakness, esp. of mind. See MENTAL DEFICIENCY. **2.** Incapacity; inability. **3.** Foolishness; fatuity, or an instance of it.

im·bed′ (ĭm·bĕd′), *v. t.;* see BED. To embed.

im·bibe′ (ĭm·bīb′), *v. t.* [F. and L.; F. *imbiber,* fr. L. *imbibere* to drink in, fr. *im-* in + *bibere* to drink.] **1.** *Obs.* To saturate; soak; steep. **2.** To receive or absorb into the mind and retain; as, to *imbibe* principles. **3.** To drink or drink in; hence, to inhale; absorb. — *v. i.* To drink; take in liquid; absorb; assimilate. — **Syn.** See ABSORB. — **im·bib′er** (-bīb′ẽr), *n.* — **im′bi·bi′tion** (ĭm′bĭ·bĭsh′ŭn), *n.*

im·bit′ter (ĭm·bĭt′ẽr), *v. t.* To embitter.

im·bod′y (ĭm·bŏd′ĭ), *v. t.* To embody.

im·bold′en (ĭm·bōl′dĕn; -d′n), *v. t.* To embolden.

im·bos′om (ĭm·bo͝oz′ŭm; -bo͞o′zŭm), *v. t.* To embosom.

im·bow′er (ĭm·bou′ẽr), *v. t. & i.* To embower.

im′bri·cate (ĭm′brĭ·kāt), **im′bri·cat′ed** (-kāt′ĕd; -ĭd), *adj.* [L. *imbricatus,* past part. of *imbricare* to cover with tiles, fr. *imbrex, -icis,* a hollow tile, fr. *imber* rain.] **1.** Lying lapped over each other in regular order, like tiles or shingles on a roof; — said of bud scales, involucral bracts, the scales of fishes, etc. **2.** *Decorative Art.* Having regularly overlapping scales, or a representation of such scales. — **im′bri·cate·ly,** *adv.*

im′bri·cate (-kāt), *v. t. & i.* To lay or lie in order, one lapping over another, so as to form an imbricate surface; to overlap like tiles.

im′bri·ca′tion (ĭm′brĭ·kā′shŭn), *n.* An overlapping of the edges, like that of tiles or shingles; also, a decoration suggesting such a structure.

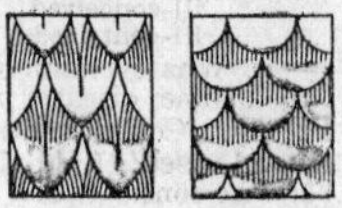

Imbrication.

im·bro′glio (ĭm·brōl′yō), *n.; pl.* -GLIOS (-yōz). [It.] **1.** *Rare.* A confused mass. **2.** An intricate or complicated situation; also, a complicated and embarrassing state of things; a serious misunderstanding.

im·brown′ (ĭm·broun′). Var. of EMBROWN.

im·brue′ (ĭm·bro͞o′), *v. t.;* IM·BRUED′ (-bro͞od′); IM·BRU′ING (-bro͞o′ĭng). [OF. *embreuver, embrevrer,* to give to drink, soak.] To stain; drench; — now only of blood, gore, etc.

im·brute′ (ĭm·bro͞ot′), *v. t. & i.* [*im-* in + *brute.*] To degrade or sink to the state of a brute.

im·bue′ (ĭm·bū′), *v. t.;* IM·BUED′ (-būd′); IM·BU′ING (-bū′ĭng). [L. *imbuere.*] **1.** To saturate; to tinge deeply; imbrue. **2.** To cause to become impressed or penetrated; as, *imbued* with wisdom or with grace. — **Syn.** See INFUSE.

im′id·az′ole (ĭm′ĭd·ăz′ōl; -ȧ·zōl′), *n.* Also **im′id·az′ol.** [*imide* + *azole.*] *Chem.* A white crystalline base, $C_3H_4N_2$.

im′ide (ĭm′ĭd; -īd), *n.* Also **im′id.** [From AMIDE.] *Chem.* A compound of the bivalent group NH; specif., a compound of this group with a bivalent acid radical.

i·mi′do- (ĭ·mē′dō-; ĭm′ĭ·dō-). *Chem.* A combining form for *imide,* meaning: Pertaining to, containing, or designating, the bivalent group NH, united to or in a radical of acid character; — distinguished from *imino-.* — **i·mi′do** (-dō), *adj.*

i·mid′o·gen (ĭ·mĭd′ō·jĕn; ĭ·mē′dō-), *n.* [*imido-* + hydro*gen.*] *Chem.* The bivalent radical NH; the imido or imino group.

i·mine′ (ĭ·mēn′; ĭm′ĭn), *n.* [Arbitrary variation of *amine.*] *Chem.* A compound of the group NH with a bivalent hydrocarbon radical.

i·mi′no- (ĭ·mē′nō-; ĭm′ĭ·nō-). *Chem.* A combining form for *imine,* meaning: Pertaining to, containing, or designating, the bivalent group NH when united to or in nonacid radicals (as imines); — distinguished from *imido-.* — **i·mi′no** (-nō), *adj.*

im′i·ta·ble (ĭm′ĭ·tȧ·b′l), *adj.* Capable of being imitated.

im′i·tate (ĭm′ĭ·tāt), *v. t.* [L. *imitatus,* past part. of *imitari* to imitate.] **1.** To follow as a pattern, model, or example; to copy, or strive to copy. **2.** To be or appear like; to resemble. **3.** To mimic. — **Syn.** See COPY.

im′i·ta′tion (-tā′shŭn), *n.* **1.** An imitating; a copying. **2.** That which is made or produced as a copy; an artificial likeness. **3.** Properly, a literary work designed to reproduce the style or manner of another author. **4.** *Biol.* Mimicry. **5.** *Music.* The repetition in a voice part of the melodic theme, phrase, or motive previously found in another part. Imitation is *strict* when the original theme or phrase and its repeated form are identical in intervals and note values, *free* when the repetition has some modification. — *adj.* Simulating something superior; as, *imitation* lace.

im′i·ta′tive (ĭm′ĭ·tā′tĭv; -tȧ·tĭv), *adj.* **1.** Marked by imitation. **2.** Inclined to imitate, or copy. **3.** Imitating something superior; imitation; counterfeit. **4.** *Zool.* Mimicking. — **im′i·ta′tive·ly,** *adv.* — **im′i·ta′tive·ness,** *n.*

im′i·ta′tor (-tā′tẽr), *n.* One who imitates.

im·mac′u·late (ĭ·măk′ū·lĭt), *adj.* [L. *immaculatus,* fr. *im-* not + *maculatus,* past part., spotted.] **1.** Without stain or blemish; pure. **2.** Without flaw, fault, or error. **3.** Without spot; spotlessly clean. — **im·mac′u·late·ly,** *adv.* — **im·mac′u·late·ness,** *n.*

Immaculate Conception. *R.C.Ch.* The miraculous conception by which the Virgin Mary "in the first instant of her conception by a singular privilege and grace granted by God, was preserved free from all stain of original sin." Immaculate Conception is not the same as virgin birth.

im·mane′ (ĭ·mān′), *adj.* [L. *immanis.*] *Archaic.* Very great; huge; also, monstrous in character; inhuman.

im′ma·nence (ĭm′ȧ·nĕns), **im′ma·nen·cy** (-nĕn·sĭ), *n.* **1.** Immanent state; an indwelling. **2.** *Theol.* The indwelling presence of God in the world (including man).

im′ma·nent (-nĕnt), *adj.* [L. *immanens,* pres. part. of *immanere* to remain in or near, fr. *im-* in + *manere* to remain.] Remaining or operating within the subject considered; indwelling; inherent; as, the belief that God is *immanent* in nature; often, as applied to a mental event, confined to consciousness or to the mind; subjective; as, an *immanent* act. — **im′ma·nent·ly,** *adv.*

Im·man′u·el (ĭ·măn′ū·ĕl), *n.* [Heb. *ʻImmānūēl,* fr. *ʻim* with + *ānū* us + *ēl* God.] God with us; — an appellation of the Christ. *Is.* vii. 14. *Matt.* i. 23.

im′ma·te′ri·al (ĭm′mȧ·tẹ̄r′ĭ·ăl), *adj.* [ML. *immaterialis.*] **1.** Not consisting of matter; incorporeal; spiritual. **2.** Of no substantial consequence; unimportant. — **im′ma·te′ri·al·ly,** *adv.* — **im′ma·te′ri·al·ness,** *n.*

im′ma·te′ri·al·ism (-ĭz′m), *n.* The doctrine that external bodies are of the essence of mind; Berkeleianism. — **im′ma·te′ri·al·ist** (-ĭst), *n.*

im′ma·te′ri·al′i·ty (ĭm′mȧ·tẹ̄r′ĭ·ăl′ĭ·tĭ), *n.; pl.* -TIES (-tĭz). State or quality of being immaterial; also, something immaterial.

im′ma·te′ri·al·ize (ĭm′mȧ·tẹ̄r′ĭ·ăl·īz), *v. t.* To render immaterial.

im′ma·ture′ (ĭm′ȧ·tūr′), *adj.* [L. *immaturus,* fr. *im-* not + *maturus* mature, ripe.] **1.** *Archaic.* Premature. **2.** Not mature; not arrived at full development; unripe; unfinished. **3.** *Phys. Geog.* Youthful; not yet mature; — said of topographic features, esp. valleys, drainage, etc., so long as most of the area is well above base level. — **im′ma·ture′ly,** *adv.* — **im′ma·ture′ness,** *n.* — **im′ma·tu′ri·ty** (-tū′rĭ·tĭ), *n.*

im·meas′ur·a·ble (ĭ·mĕzh′ẽr·ȧ·b′l; ĭm·mĕzh′-), *adj.* Incapable of being measured; illimitable. — **im·meas′ur·a·bly,** *adv.*

im·me′di·a·cy (ĭ·mē′dĭ·ȧ·sĭ), *n.* **1.** Quality or state of being immediate; specif., freedom from intervention of a medium; directness; direct presence. **2.** *Philos.* The direct content of consciousness, or consciousness itself, as distinguished from what consciousness represents or mediates a knowledge of.

im·me′di·ate (-dĭ·ĭt; *Brit. also* -jĭt), *adj.* [ML. *immediatus.*] **1.** Having no intermediary or intermediation. Specif.: **a** Next in line or relation; not secondary or remote. **b** Acting without the intervention of another object, cause, or agency. **c** Direct; intuitive. **d** Directly or intimately touching or affecting. **2.** Not distant or separated in

time or space; adjoining; nearest; next; hence, made or done at once. — **Syn.** See DIRECT. — **im·me′di·ate·ness**, *n.*
immediate constituent. *Ling.* See CONSTITUENT.
im·me′di·ate·ly, *adv.* In an immediate manner; specif.: **a** Without intermediary; closely. **b** Without delay. — *conj.* As soon as.
im·med′i·ca·ble (ĭm·mĕd′ĭ·kȧ·b'l), *adj.* Incurable.
Im′mel·mann turn (ĭm′ĕl·män; -măn). [After Max *Immelmann* (1890–1916), Ger. aviator.] *Aviation.* A maneuver in which an airplane is first made to complete half of a loop and is then rolled half of a complete turn.
im′me·mo′ri·al (ĭm′mē·mō′rĭ·ăl; 70), *adj.* [ML. *immemorialis.*] Extending beyond the reach of memory, record, or tradition; indefinitely ancient. — **im′me·mo′ri·al·ly**, *adv.*
im·mense′ (ĭ·mĕns′), *adj.* [F., fr. L. *immensus*, fr. *im-* not + *mensus*, past part. of *metiri* to measure.] **1.** Unmeasured; infinite. Commonly: Very great; huge; vast. **2.** *Slang.* Hyperbolically, of surpassing excellence. — **Syn.** See ENORMOUS. — **im·mense′ly**, *adv.* — **im·mense′ness**, *n.*
im·men′si·ty (ĭ·mĕn′sĭ·tĭ), *n.; pl.* -TIES (-tĭz). State or quality of being immense; hugeness; also, infinite being, existence, or space.
im·men′su·ra·ble (ĭm·mĕn′shōō·rȧ·b'l), *adj.* [F., or LL. *immensurabilis.*] Not mensurable; immeasurable.
im·merge′ (ĭ·mûrj′), *v. t. & i.;* see MERGE. [L. *immergere*, fr. *im-* in + *mergere* to dip.] To immerse.
im·merse′ (ĭ·mûrs′), *v. t.* [See IMMERGE.] **1.** To plunge into anything that surrounds or covers, esp. into a fluid. **2.** To baptize by immersion. **3.** To engage deeply; to engross; to absorb. — **im·mersed′** (ĭ·mûrst′), *adj.*
im·mer′sion (ĭ·mûr′shŭn), *n.* **1.** Act of immersing, or state of being immersed; specif., baptism by submersion of the person in water. **2.** *Astron.* Disappearance of a celestial body behind, or into the shadow of, another.
im·mer′sion·ism (-ĭz'm), *n.* The doctrine that immersion is essential to Christian baptism; the practice of baptism by immersion. — **im·mer′sion·ist** (-ĭst), *n.*
im·mesh′ (ĭm·mĕsh′). Var. of ENMESH.
im′me·thod′i·cal (ĭm′mē·thŏd′ĭ·kăl), *adj.* Not methodical.
im′mi·grant (ĭm′ĭ·grănt; -grănt), *n.* One who immigrates. — **Syn.** See EMIGRANT. — *adj.* Immigrating.
im′mi·grate (-grāt), *v. i.* [L. *immigrare, -gratum*, to immigrate, fr. *im-* in + *migrare* to migrate.] To come into a country of which one is not a native, for permanent residence. — *v. t.* To bring in or send as immigrants.
im′mi·gra′tion (-grā′shŭn), *n.* **1.** An immigrating. **2.** The number of immigrants during a given period.
im′mi·nence (ĭm′ĭ·nĕns), **im′mi·nen·cy** (-nĕn·sĭ), *n.* **1.** Condition or quality of being imminent. **2.** That which is imminent; impending evil or danger.
im′mi·nent (-nĕnt), *adj.* [L. *imminens*, pres. part. of *imminere* to project, fr. *im-* in + *minere* (in comp.) to project.] **1.** Threatening to occur immediately; impending; — said esp. of misfortune or peril. **2.** Projecting over; overhanging. — **Syn.** See IMPENDING. — **im′mi·nent·ly**, *adv.*
im·min′gle (ĭm·mĭng′g'l), *v. t. & i.;* see MINGLE. To mix intimately; to blend; intermingle.
im·mis′ci·ble (ĭ·mĭs′ĭ·b'l), *adj.* Not capable of being mixed or mingled. — **im·mis′ci·bil′i·ty** (-bĭl′ĭ·tĭ), *n.* — **im·mis′ci·bly** (ĭ·mĭs′ĭ·blĭ), *adv.*
im·mit′i·ga·ble (ĭ·mĭt′ĭ·gȧ·b'l), *adj.* [L. *immitigabilis*, fr. *im-* not + *mitigare* to mitigate.] Not capable of being mitigated. — **im·mit′i·ga·bly**, *adv.*
im·mix′ (ĭm·mĭks′), *v. t. & i.;* see MIX. [L. *immixtus*, past part.] To mix intimately; commingle.
im·mix′ture (ĭm·mĭks′tūr), *n.* Act of immixing, or quality or state of being immixed; involvement.
im·mo′bile (ĭm·mō′bĭl; -bēl; 56), *adj.* [F., fr. L. *immobilis.*] Incapable of motion or of being moved; immovable; fixed; also, motionless.
im′mo·bil′i·ty (ĭm′ō·bĭl′ĭ·tĭ), *n.* Fixedness; also, motionlessness.
im·mo′bi·lize (ĭm·mō′bĭ·līz), *v. t.* [F. *immobiliser.*] To make immobile, as troops or a fleet; in surgery, to make immovable, as a joint by use of splints or stiffened bandages; in finance, to withhold (specie) from circulation for the purpose of having it as security for other money; to convert (circulating capital) into fixed capital. — **im·mo′bi·li·za′tion** (-lĭ·zā′shŭn; -lī·zā′-), *n.*
im·mod′er·a·cy (ĭm·mŏd′ẽr·ȧ·sĭ), *n.* Lack of moderation; excess.
im·mod′er·ate (-ĭt), *adj.* [L. *immoderatus*, fr. *im-* not + *moderatus* moderate.] **1.** Not moderate; unreasonable; extreme. **2.** *Obs.* **a** Characterized by excess; intemperate. **b** Without limits; boundless. — **Syn.** See EXCESSIVE. — **Ant.** Moderate. — **im·mod′er·ate·ly**, *adv.* — **im·mod′er·ate·ness**, *n.*
im·mod′er·a′tion (-ā′shŭn), *n.* Lack of moderation; excess.
im·mod′est (ĭm·mŏd′ĕst; -ĭst; ĭ-), *adj.* Not modest; forward; bold; often, specif., indecent. — **im·mod′est·ly**, *adv.* — **im·mod′es·ty**, *n.*
im′mo·late (ĭm′ō·lāt), *v. t.* [L. *immolatus*, past part. of *immolare* to sacrifice, orig., to sprinkle with sacrificial meal, fr. *im-* in + *mola* grits mixed with salt.] To sacrifice; esp., to kill as a sacrificial victim. — **im′mo·la′tor** (-lā′tẽr), *n.*
im′mo·la′tion (-lā′shŭn), *n.* Act of immolating; also, a sacrifice.
im·mor′al (ĭm·mŏr′ăl; ĭ-), *adj.* Not moral; contrary to conscience or moral law; licentious. — **im·mor′al·ly**, *adv.*
im′mo·ral′i·ty (ĭm′mō·răl′ĭ·tĭ), *n.; pl.* -TIES (-tĭz). State or quality of being immoral; vice; wickedness; specif., unchastity; also, an immoral act or practice; a vice.
im·mor′tal (ĭ·môr′tăl; -t'l), *adj.* [L. *immortalis*, fr. *im-* not + *mortalis* mortal.] **1.** Not mortal; imperishable. **2.** Connected with, or pertaining to, immortality. **3.** Destined to live in all ages of this world; abiding. — *n.* **1.** An immortal being; esp., *pl., Gr. & Rom. Myth.*, the gods. **2. a** A person, esp. an author, whose fame is lasting. **b** [*cap.*] A member of the French Academy, a society of 40 eminent Frenchmen, chiefly men of letters, whose chief function is registration of correct usage of the French language. — **im·mor′tal·ly**, *adv.*
im′mor·tal′i·ty (ĭm′ôr·tăl′ĭ·tĭ), *n.* Quality or state of being immortal; esp.: **a** Unending existence. **b** Enduring fame.
im·mor′tal·ize (ĭ·môr′tăl·īz), *v. t.* To render immortal.
im′mor·telle′ (ĭm′ôr·tĕl′), *n.* [F.] = EVERLASTING, *n.*, **3.**
im·mo′tile (ĭm·mō′tĭl; 56), *adj.* Not motile.
im·mov′a·ble (ĭm·mōōv′ȧ·b'l), *adj.* **1.** That cannot be moved; firmly fixed; hence: **a** Stationary. **b** Steadfast; unyielding. **c** Unimpressible; impassive. **2.** *Law.* Not liable to be removed; permanent in place or tenure. — *n. pl. Law.* Lands and things adherent thereto, as trees, buildings, etc.; — opposed to *movable.* — **im·mov′a·bil′i·ty** (-bĭl′ĭ·tĭ), **im·mov′a·ble·ness**, *n.* — **im·mov′a·bly**, *adv.*
im·mune′ (ĭ·mūn′), *adj.* [F., fr. L. *immunis.* See IMMUNITY.] Exempt, as from a tax; protected against a disease, as by inoculation; enjoying immunity. — *n.* One that is immune.
im·mu′ni·ty (ĭ·mū′nĭ·tĭ), *n.; pl.* -TIES (-tĭz). [F. *immunité*, fr. L. *immunitas*, fr. *immunis* free from a public service, fr. *im-* not + *munia* services, obligations.] **1.** Freedom or exemption from any charge, duty, tax, etc. **2.** State or power of resisting the development of a (given) disease, esp. of resisting infecting microorganisms or their products. ***active immunity*** is acquired through production of antibodies within the immune organism; ***passive immunity***, by injection of serum from another individual.
im′mu·nize (ĭm′ū·nīz; ĭ·mūn′īz), *v. t.* To render immune. — **im′mu·ni·za′tion** (ĭm′ū·nĭ·zā′shŭn; ĭ·mūn′ĭ-), *n.*
im·mu′no- (ĭ·mū′nō-). A combining form for *immune.*
im·mu′no·gen (ĭ·mū′nō·jĕn), *n.* [*immuno-* + *-gen.*] *Immunol.* An antigen, esp. one inducing a highly specific immunity to disease. — **im·mu′no·gen′ic** (-jĕn′ĭk), *adj.* — **im·mu′no·gen·ic′i·ty** (-jĕn·ĭs′ĭ·tĭ), *n.*
im·mu′no·ge·net′ics (-jē·nĕt′ĭks), *n.;* see -ICS. [*immuno-* + *genetics.*] **1.** *Immunol.* The branch of immunology which deals with the interrelation of the immunity to disease and the genetic make-up of the individual. **2.** *Biol.* The study of biological interrelationships by serological means. — **im·mu′no·ge·net′ic** (-ĭk), *adj.*
im′mu·nol′o·gy (ĭm′ū·nŏl′ō·jĭ), *n.* [*immuno-* + *-logy.*] The bacteriological and chemical science treating of immunity to disease. — **im·mu′no·log′i·cal** (ĭ·mū′nō·lŏj′ĭ·kăl), *adj.* — **im′mu·nol′o·gist** (ĭm′ū·nŏl′ō·jĭst), *adj. & n.*
im·mu′no·re·ac′tion (ĭ·mū′nō·rē·ăk′shŭn), *n.* *Immunol.* A reaction between antigen and antibody, as in the blood.
im·mure′ (ĭ·mūr′), *v. t.* [F. *emmurer*, or ML. *immurare.* See IM-in; MURE.] To enclose within or as within walls; hence, to imprison; also, to entomb. — **im·mure′ment**, *n.*
im·mu′si·cal (ĭm·mū′zĭ·kăl; ĭ·mū′-), *adj.* Unmusical.
im·mu′ta·ble (ĭ·mū′tȧ·b'l), *adj.* Not mutable; unchangeable; invariable. — **im·mu′ta·bil′i·ty** (-bĭl′ĭ·tĭ), **im·mu′ta·ble·ness**, *n.* — **im·mu′ta·bly**, *adv.*
imp (ĭmp), *n.* [ME., a graft, fr. AS. *impa.*] **1.** *Obs.* A shoot (of a plant); cion; graft; also, offspring; child; scion. **2.** A young, petty, or little devil; — from the phrase **imp of Satan**, often applied to human beings. **3.** A mischievous child.
imp, *v. t. & i. Archaic.* **a** To engraft; also, implant. **b** *Falconry.* To graft or repair (a wing, tail, or feather) with a feather or feathers. **c** Hence, to fasten (wings) on or to equip with (wings) so as to develop in power of flight; — often used figuratively.
im·pact′ (ĭm·păkt′), *v. t.* [L. *impactus*, past part. of *impingere.* See IMPINGE.] To drive close; fix firmly; pack; wedge. — (ĭm′păkt), *n.* **1.** A striking together; a collision communicating force. **2.** *Mech.* Act of impinging, as of a stream against a vane; also, the single instantaneous stroke of a body in motion against another either in motion or at rest. **3.** An impacting; forcible contact.
im·pact′ed (ĭm·păk′tĕd; -tĭd), *adj.* Driven together or close; esp., *Dent.*, wedged between the jawbone and another tooth.
im·pac′tion (ĭm·păk′shŭn), *n.* [L. *impactio* a striking.] **1.** Act of becoming, or state of being, impacted. **2.** *Dent.* The lodgment of a tooth in the jawbone.
im·pair′ (ĭm·pâr′), *v. t.* [OF. *empeirier*, deriv. of L. *im-* in + *pejorare* to make worse, fr. *pejor* worse.] To make worse; to diminish in quantity, value, or strength. — **Syn.** See INJURE. — *n. Archaic.* Impairment; deterioration. — **im·pair′er**, *n.* — **im·pair′ment**, *n.*
im·pale′ (ĭm·pāl′), *v. t.* [OF. & F. *empaler*, fr. *em-* (fr. L. *in*) + *pal* a pale, stake.] **1.** *Rare.* To enclose with or as with pales; hem in. **2.** To pierce with or as with a pale; to torture or punish by fixing on a sharp stake. — **im·pale′ment**, *n.* — **im·pal′er** (ĭm·pāl′ẽr), *n.*
im·pal′pa·ble (ĭm·păl′pȧ·b'l), *adj.* **1.** Not palpable; that cannot be felt; intangible. **2.** So fine, delicate, etc., as not to be easily perceived, discerned, or apprehended. — *n.* Anything impalpable. — **im·pal′pa·bil′i·ty** (-bĭl′ĭ·tĭ), *n.* — **im·pal′pa·bly**, *adv.*
im′pa·na′tion (ĭm′pȧ·nā′shŭn), *n.* [ML. *impanatio*, fr. *impanatus*, past part., deriv. of L. *im-* in + *panis* bread.] A doctrine that the body of Christ is present in the Eucharistic bread and wine without any change in their substance; — distinguished from *consubstantiation* and *transubstantiation.*
im·pan′el (ĭm·păn′ĕl; -'l), *v. t.;* see PANEL. To enter in or on a panel, or list; enroll; as, to *impanel* a jury.
im·par′a·dise (-păr′ȧ·dīs; -dīz), *v. t.* To put in, or as in, paradise.
im·par′i- (ĭm·păr′ĭ-). A combining form, from Latin *impar*, unequal, equivalent to *odd-*, as in **im·par′i·pin′nate.** See PINNATE, *adj.*
im·par′i·ty (ĭm·păr′ĭ·tĭ), *n.* Inequality; disparity.
im·park′ (ĭm·pärk′), *v. t.* [OF. *emparquer*, fr. *parc* park.] To enclose in or for a park; shut up or off.
im·part′ (ĭm·pärt′), *v. t.* [OF. *impartir, empartir*, fr. L. *impartire*, fr. *im-* in + *partire* to part, divide, fr. *pars, partis*, part, share.] **1.** To bestow a share of; give from one's store or abundance. **2.** To communicate by words or signs; make known; disclose. — **Syn.** See COMMUNICATE. — **im·part′a·ble**, *adj.* — **im′par·ta′tion** (ĭm′pär·tā′shŭn), *n.* — **im·part′er**, *n.* — **im·part′ment**, *n.*
im·par′tial (ĭm·pär′shăl), *adj.* Not partial; not favoring one more than another; unbiased; equitable; just. — **Syn.** See FAIR. — **im·par′tial·ly**, *adv.* — **im·par′tial·ness**, *n.*
im′par·ti·al′i·ty (ĭm′pär·shĭ·ăl′ĭ·tĭ; -shăl′ĭ·tĭ), *n.* Freedom from favoritism or bias; fairness; disinterestedness.
im·part′i·ble (ĭm·pär′tĭ·b'l), *adj.* [LL. *impartibilis.*] Not subject to partition; indivisible, as an estate. — **im·part′i·bil′i·ty** (-bĭl′ĭ·tĭ), *n.* — **im·part′i·bly**, *adv.*
im·part′i·ble, *adj.* [From IMPART.] Capable of being imparted. — **im·part′i·bil′i·ty**, *n.* — **im·part′i·bly**, *adv.*
im·pass′a·ble (ĭm·pȧs′ȧ·b'l), *adj.* Incapable of being passed, traversed, or circulated; as, an *impassable* road or coin. — **im·pass′a·bil′i·ty** (-bĭl′ĭ·tĭ), **im·pass′a·ble·ness**, *n.* — **im·pass′a·bly**, *adv.*
im·passe′ (ĭm·pȧs′; ĭm′pȧs; 9; *F.* ăN′pȧs′), *n.; pl.* IMPASSES (ĭm·pȧs′ĕz; -ĭz; *F.* ăN′pȧs′). [F.] An impassable road or way; a blind alley; hence, a predicament affording no escape.

im·pas'si·ble (ĭm·păs'ĭ·b'l), *adj.* [F., fr. LL. *impassibilis*, fr. *im-* not + *passibilis* passible.] **1.** *Archaic.* Incapable of suffering; inaccessible to harm. **2.** Not to be emotionally moved or touched; unfeeling. Cf. IMPASSIVE. — **im·pas'si·bil'i·ty** (-bĭl'ĭ·tĭ), **im·pas'si·ble·ness**, *n.* — **im·pas'si·bly**, *adv.*

im·pas'sion (ĭm·păsh'ŭn), *v. t.* To fill with passion; to arouse the passions of.

im·pas'sion·ate (-ĭt), *adj.* *Rare.* Dispassionate; calm.

im·pas'sion·ate, *adj.* [It. *impassionato*, past part.] Impassioned. — **im·pas'sion·ate·ly**, *adv.*

im·pas'sioned (ĭm·păsh'ŭnd), *adj.* Full of passion or warm feeling; ardent.

Syn. **Impassioned, passionate, ardent, fervent, fervid, perfervid** mean actuated by or showing intense feeling. **Impassioned** implies intensity without violence that passes naturally from the person into his expression; **passionate** implies vehemence and, often, violence and wasteful diffusion of emotion; **ardent**, vehemence showing itself in eagerness, enthusiasm, acts of devotion, etc.; **fervent**, intensity of feeling that glows rather than bursts into flame; **fervid**, intensity of feeling manifesting itself in warm, spontaneous, and, sometimes, feverish expression or acts; **perfervid** carries an implication of exaggerated and overwrought feelings or of their expression.

im·pas'sive (ĭm·păs'ĭv), *adj.* **1.** *Now Rare.* Impassible; also, insensible; inanimate. **2.** Devoid of emotion or of signs of emotion; showing indifference, stoicism, apathy, etc.; also, calm; serene. — **im·pas'sive·ly**, *adv.* — **im·pas'sive·ness, im'pas·siv'i·ty** (ĭm'pă·sĭv'ĭ·tĭ), *n.*

Syn. **Impassive, stoic, phlegmatic, apathetic, stolid** mean unresponsive to something that might normally excite interest or emotion. **Impassive** implies showing or feeling no emotion or sensation, without necessarily implying insusceptibility; **stoic** implies indifference to pain or pleasure and, usually, connotes unflinching fortitude; **phlegmatic** implies a temperament or constitution hard to arouse; **apathetic** now usually implies a state of mind from which it is difficult to arouse one; **stolid**, applied usually to the countenance or its expression, suggests an inattentiveness due to a plodding, mechanical adherence to routine.

im·paste' (ĭm·pāst'), *v. t.* [It. *impastare*. See IM- in; PASTE.] **1.** To enclose in or as in a paste. **2.** To solidify. **3.** To decorate by impasto. — **im'pas·ta'tion** (ĭm'păs·tā'shŭn), *n.*

im·pas'to (ĭm·päs'tō; 9), *n.* [It.] *Painting.* The thick application of a pigment to a canvas or panel; also, the body of pigment so applied.

im·pa'tience (ĭm·pā'shĕns), *n.* State, quality, or instance of being impatient; specif.: **a** Lack of endurance, as of pain, suffering, opposition, or delay. **b** Restless or eager desire or longing; as, *impatience* to set out.

im·pa'ti·ens (ĭm·pā'shĭ·ĕnz; *often* ĭm·pā'shĕns), *n.* [L., impatient.] Any of a widely distributed genus (*Impatiens*) of annual plants, type genus of the family Balsaminaceae (order geraniales), distinguished from the geraniaceae by the irregular flowers. The impatiens has irregular spurred or saccate flowers and dehiscent capsules.

im·pa'tient (ĭm·pā'shĕnt), *adj.* [OF. *impacient*, fr. L. *impatiens*, fr. *im-* not + *patiens* patient.] **1.** Not patient; restless because of pain, delay, or opposition; uneasy. **2.** Prompted by, affected by, or indicating impatience. — **Syn.** Nervous, fidgety, jittery. — **im·pa'tient·ly**, *adv.* — **im·pa'tient·ness**, *n.*

im·pav'id (ĭm·păv'ĭd), *adj.* [L. *impavidus*, fr. *im-* not + *pavidus* timid.] Fearless. — **im'pa·vid'i·ty** (ĭm'pȧ·vĭd'ĭ·tĭ), *n.* — **im·pav'id·ly**, *adv.*

im·pawn' (ĭm·pôn'), *v. t.* To put in pawn; to pledge.

im·peach' (ĭm·pēch'), *v. t.* [OF. *empeechier* to prevent, hinder, fr. LL. *impedicare* to entangle, fr. *im-* in + *pedica* fetter, fr. *pes, pedis*, foot.] **1.** To bring an accusation against; specif., to charge with a crime or misdemeanor; to accuse; esp., to charge (a public officer), before a competent tribunal, with misbehavior in office. See IMPEACHMENT, 2 **b**. **2.** To impute some fault or defect to; to call in question; as, to *impeach* one's motives; specif., to challenge the credibility or validity of, as a witness or a promissory note. — *n.* Impeachment. — **im·peach'a·bil'i·ty** (-bĭl'ĭ·tĭ), *n.* — **im·peach'a·ble**, *adj.* — **im·peach'er**, *n.*

im·peach'ment (-mĕnt), *n.* **1.** Act of impeaching. **2.** *Law.* **a** Accusation or liability thereto. **b** Arraignment, esp. of a public officer for misconduct while in office. In the U. S. it is the right of the House of Representatives to impeach and of the Senate to try and determine impeachments; similarly, in most of the states the lower house impeaches and the upper house tries the impeachment. In England, the House of Commons impeaches, the House of Lords tries the impeachment.

im·pearl' (ĭm·pûrl'), *v. t.* *Poetic.* To form into, or as into, pearls; to adorn with or as with pearls.

im·pec'ca·ble (ĭm·pĕk'ȧ·b'l), *adj.* [LL. *impeccabilis*, fr. *im-* not + *peccare* to err, sin.] **1.** Not liable to sin. **2.** Free from fault, blemish, or error; faultless. — *n.* One who is impeccable. — **im·pec'ca·bil'i·ty** (-bĭl'ĭ·tĭ), *n.* — **im·pec'ca·bly**, *adv.*

im·pec'cant (-pĕk'ănt), *adj.* Sinless; inerrant. — **im·pec'cance** (-ăns), **im·pec'can·cy** (-ăn·sĭ), *n.*

im'pe·cu'ni·ous (ĭm'pē·kū'nĭ·ŭs), *adj.* [F. or L.; F. *impécunieux*, fr. L. *im-* not + *pecuniosus* rich, fr. *pecunia* money.] Not having money; habitually without money; poor. — **im'pe·cu'ni·os'i·ty** (-ŏs'ĭ·tĭ), *n.* — **im'pe·cu'ni·ous·ly**, *adv.* — **im'pe·cu'ni·ous·ness**, *n.*

im·ped'ance (ĭm·pēd'ăns), *n.* [*impede* + *-ance*.] **1.** *Elec.* The apparent resistance in a circuit to the flow of an alternating current, analogous to the actual resistance to a direct current. **2.** *Acoustics.* The ratio of the pressure to the volume displacement at a given surface in a sound-transmitting medium.

im·pede' (ĭm·pēd'), *v. t.* [L. *impedire*, lit., to entangle the feet, fr. *im-* in + *pes, pedis*, foot.] To stop in progress; obstruct; hinder. — **Syn.** See HINDER. — **im·ped'er** (-pēd'ēr), *n.*

im·pe'di·ent (ĭm·pē'dĭ·ĕnt), *adj.* & *n.* [L. *impediens*, *-entis*, pres. part.] (One) that impedes.

im·ped'i·ment (ĭm·pĕd'ĭ·mĕnt), *n.* [L. *impedimentum*.] **1.** Obstruction; also, a hindrance; obstacle. **2.** A bodily defect obstructing functions; — *Obs.*, exc. of organic obstructions to speech. **3.** *Law & Canon Law.* A cause or fact, as lack of legal age, compulsion, or impotence, which prevents the formation of a valid marriage; — usually called ***diriment impediment*** and called specif.: ***absolute impediment*** when it prevents a person from marrying at all; ***relative impediment*** when it only forbids marriage with reference to certain persons or facts. — **im·ped'i·men'tal** (-mĕn'tăl; -t'l), **im·ped'i·men'ta·ry** (-tȧ·rĭ), *adj.*

im·ped'i·men'ta (-mĕn'tȧ), *n. pl.* [L.] **1.** Encumbrances; baggage. **2.** *Law.* Impediments. **3.** *Mil.* Supply trains.

im·ped'i·tive (-pĕd'ĭ·tĭv), *adj.* Hindering; obstructive.

im·pel' (ĭm·pĕl'), *v. t.* & *i.*; -PELLED' (-pĕld'); -PEL'LING. [L. *impellere*, fr. *im-* in + *pellere, pulsum*, to drive.] To drive or urge forward or on; give an impulse to; propel; force; constrain. — **Syn.** See MOVE.

im·pel'lent (-ĕnt), *adj.* Impelling. — *n.* An impelling agent, force, etc.

im·pel'ler (ĭm·pĕl'ēr), *n.* One who or that which impels, as the rotor of a centrifugal pump or air compressor.

im·pend' (ĭm·pĕnd'), *v. i.* [L. *impendēre*, fr. *im-* in + *pendēre* to hang.] To hang (*over*) threateningly; hence, to be imminent.

im·pend'ent (-pĕn'dĕnt), *adj.* Impending; threatening; imminent. — **im·pend'ence** (-dĕns), **im·pend'en·cy** (-dĕn·sĭ), *n.*

im·pend'ing, *adj.* Threatening to occur soon; approaching.

Syn. **Impending, imminent** mean threatening to occur very soon. But **impending** implies signs that keep one in suspense; **imminent** more strongly suggests the shortness of time before happening.

im·pen'e·tra·bil'i·ty (ĭm·pĕn'ē·trȧ·bĭl'ĭ·tĭ), *n.* **1.** Quality or state of being impenetrable. **2.** That property in virtue of which two portions of matter cannot at the same time occupy the same space.

im·pen'e·tra·ble (-pĕn'ē·trȧ·b'l), *adj.* **1.** Incapable of being penetrated or pierced; impervious. **2.** Incapable of being comprehended; unfathomable. **3.** Inaccessible, as to knowledge, reason, sympathy, etc.; as, an *impenetrable* heart or mind. **4.** Having the property of impenetrability. — **im·pen'e·tra·ble·ness**, *n.* — **im·pen'e·tra·bly**, *adv.*

im·pen'i·tence (ĭm·pĕn'ĭ·tĕns), **im·pen'i·ten·cy** (-tĕn·sĭ), *n.* Fact, quality, or condition of being impenitent; failure or refusal to repent.

im·pen'i·tent (ĭm·pĕn'ĭ·tĕnt), *adj.* Not penitent; unrepentant. — **im·pen'i·tent·ly**, *adv.* — **im·pen'i·tent·ness**, *n.*

im·pen'nate (ĭm·pĕn'āt), *adj.* [L. *im-* not + *penna* feather.] *Zool.* Belonging to an order (Sphenisciformes, or Impennes) of flightless aquatic birds, comprising the penguins.

im·per'a·tive (ĭm·pĕr'ȧ·tĭv), *adj.* [L. *imperativus*, fr. *imperare* to command.] **1.** *Gram.* Expressive of command, entreaty, or exhortation. **2.** Expressive of, or of the nature of, command; directive; commanding; authoritative. **3.** Not to be avoided or evaded; obligatory; binding; compulsory; as, an *imperative* task. — **Syn.** See MASTERFUL. — *n.* **1.** *Gram.* The imperative mood; also, a verb or verbal form denoting it. Abbr. *imp.*, *imper.*, or *impr.* **2.** Something which is imperative; a command. See CATEGORICAL IMPERATIVE. — **im·per'a·tive·ly**, *adv.* — **im·per'a·tive·ness**, *n.*

im'pe·ra'tor (ĭm'pē·rā'tôr; -tēr), *n.* [L.] Commander; emperor. — **im·per'a·to'ri·al** (ĭm·pĕr'ȧ·tō'rĭ·ăl), *adj.* — **im·per'a·to'ri·al·ly**, *adv.*

im'per·cep'ti·ble (ĭm'pēr·sĕp'tĭ·b'l), *adj.* Not perceptible by the senses or mind; hence, very slight, gradual, or subtle. — **im'per·cep'ti·bil'i·ty** (-bĭl'ĭ·tĭ), **im'per·cep'ti·ble·ness**, *n.* — **im'per·cep'ti·bly**, *adv.*

im'per·cep'tive (-tĭv), *adj.* Without, or lacking in, perception; not perceiving or discerning. — **im'per·cep·tiv'i·ty** (-sĕp·tĭv'ĭ·tĭ), **im'per·cep'tive·ness**, *n.*

im·per'fect (ĭm·pûr'fĕkt; -fĭkt), *adj.* [L. *imperfectus*, fr. *im-* not + *perfectus* perfect.] **1.** Not perfect; defective; incomplete. **2.** *Gram.* Expressive of action or state as incomplete or in continuance; commonly, expressive of incomplete past action (*I was choosing*); as, an *imperfect* tense. **3.** *Law.* Not enforceable; having no sanction. **4.** *Music.* Diminished. — *n.* *Gram.* The imperfect tense, or a verb or verbal form denoting it. Abbr. *imp.*, *imperf.*, or *impf.* — **im·per'fect·ly**, *adv.* — **im·per'fect·ness**, *n.*

imperfect flower. *Bot.* A diclinous flower.

im'per·fec'tion (ĭm'pēr·fĕk'shŭn), *n.* Quality or state of being imperfect; also, deficiency, fault, blemish, or flaw.

im·per'fo·rate (ĭm·pûr'fō·rāt), *adj.* Also **im·per'fo·rat'ed** (-rāt'ĕd; -ĭd). **1.** Not perforated; having no opening or aperture. **2.** *Philately.* Without perforations or roulettes separating the individual stamps. Abbr. *imperf.* — *n.* An imperforate stamp. — **im·per'fo·ra'tion** (-rā'shŭn), *n.*

im·pe'ri·al (ĭm·pēr'ĭ·ăl), *adj.* [OF. *emperial*, *imperial*, fr. L. *imperialis*, fr. *imperium*. See EMPIRE.] **1.** Of or pertaining to an empire or an emperor. **2.** Supreme; sovereign. **3.** Of or pertaining to a state as sovereign and supreme over colonies, and the like. **4.** Of superior or unusual size or excellence. **5.** Designating the weights and measures established by law in the United Kingdom. See GALLON. — *n.* [Cf. F. *impériale*, for senses 3 & 5.] **1.** [*cap.*] An adherent of the Holy Roman emperor, or a soldier of his troops. **2.** An article of unusual size or excellence. **3.** The top or roof of a coach, esp. of a diligence. **4.** A Russian gold coin of 15 rubles, not coined since 1917. **5.** [After Napoleon III, emperor of the French.] A pointed tuft of hair on a man's chin. **6.** A size of paper (*U. S.* 23 in. × 31 in.; Eng. 22 in. × 30 in.). — **im·pe'ri·al·ly**, *adv.*

imperial eagle. See EAGLE, 1.

im·pe'ri·al·ism (ĭm·pēr'ĭ·ăl·ĭz'm), *n.* **1.** Imperial government, authority, or system. **2.** The policy, practice, or advocacy of seeking to extend the control, dominion, or empire of a nation. — **im·pe'ri·al·ist** (-ĭst), *n.* & *adj.* — **im·pe'ri·al·is'tic** (-ĭs'tĭk), *adj.* — **im·pe'ri·al·is'ti·cal·ly** (-tĭ·kăl·ĭ), *adv.*

imperial moth. A large handsome American moth (*Basilona imperialis*), yellow with brown bands.

im·per'il (ĭm·pĕr'ĭl), *v. t.*; see PERIL. To endanger.

im·pe'ri·ous (-pēr'ĭ·ŭs), *adj.* [L. *imperiosus*.] **1.** Befitting an emperor; lordly. **2.** Arrogant; overbearing; domineering. **3.** Imperative; urgent; compelling. — **Syn.** See MASTERFUL. — **im·pe'ri·ous·ly**, *adv.* — **im·pe'ri·ous·ness**, *n.*

im·per'ish·a·ble (-pĕr'ĭsh·ȧ·b'l), *adj.* Not perishable; indestructible. — **im·per'ish·a·bil'i·ty** (-bĭl'ĭ·tĭ), **im·per'ish·a·ble·ness**, *n.* — **im·per'ish·a·bly**, *adv.*

im·pe'ri·um (ĭm·pēr'ĭ·ŭm), *n.*; *pl.* -RIA (-ȧ). [L. See EMPIRE.] **1.** Supreme power; absolute dominion; empire. **2.** *Law.* Right to command; right to employ the force of the state to enforce the laws.

‖**im·pe'ri·um in im·pe'ri·o** (ĭm·pēr'ĭ·ŭm ĭn ĭm·pēr'ĭ·ō). [L.] A sovereignty within a sovereignty.

im·per'ma·nent (ĭm·pûr'mȧ·nĕnt), *adj.* Not permanent. — **im·per'ma·nence** (-nĕns), *n.* — **im·per'ma·nent·ly**, *adv.*

im·per'me·a·ble (-pûr'mē·ȧ·b'l), *adj.* Not permeable; impervious. — **im·per'me·a·bil'i·ty** (-bĭl'ĭ·tĭ), **im·per'me·a·ble·ness**, *n.* — **im·per'me·a·bly**, *adv.*

im·per'son·al (ĭm·pûr'sŭn·ăl), *adj.* [L. *impersonalis.*] **1.** Not personal; specif.: **a** Without personal reference or connection; as, *impersonal* criticism. **b** Not having personality; as, an *impersonal* God. **2.** *Gram.* **a** Of certain verbs, denoting the action of an unspecified agent, and hence used either with no subject or a merely formal one (it *rains*). **b** Indefinite. — *n.* **1.** That which is impersonal. **2.** *Gram.* An impersonal verb. Abbr. *imp.*, or *impers.* — **im·per'son·al'i·ty** (-ăl'ĭ·tĭ), *n.* — **im·per'son·al·ize** (ĭm·pûr'sŭn·ăl·īz), *v. t.* — **im·per'son·al·ly,** *adv.*

im·per'son·ate (ĭm·pûr'sŭn·āt), *v. t.* **1.** To invest with personality; personify. **2.** To assume or act the person or character of; personate. — *adj.* Invested with personality. — **im·per'son·a'tion** (-ā'shŭn), *n.* — **im·per'son·a'tor** (-ā'tẽr), *n.*

im·per'ti·nence (ĭm·pûr'tĭ·nĕns), *n.; pl.* -NENCES (-nĕn·sĕz; -sĭz). Also **im·per'ti·nen·cy** (-nĕn·sĭ); *pl.* -NENCIES (-sĭz). **1.** The fact or action of being impertinent; specif.: **a** Irrelevance; unfitness; impropriety. **b** Incivility; insolence. **2.** An impertinent, irrelevant, or uncivil remark, action, etc.

im·per'ti·nent (-nĕnt), *adj.* [F., fr. L. *impertinens, -entis,* fr. *im-* not + *pertinens.*] **1.** Not pertinent; irrelevant; inapplicable. **2.** Not congruous; inappropriate. **3.** Not restrained within due or proper bounds; rudely officious; pert; saucy; insolent. — **im·per'ti·nent·ly,** *adv.*

Syn. **Impertinent, officious, meddlesome, intrusive, obtrusive** mean unduly concerned in affairs other than one's own. **Impertinent** implies one's exceeding the bounds of propriety in interest, in curiosity, or the like; **officious,** the offering of services, attentions, or assistance that are unwelcome or offensive; **meddlesome** carries a strong implication of annoying interference in others' affairs, often connoting a prying or inquisitive nature; **intrusive** and **obtrusive** both imply a thrusting oneself, often boldly, into others' affairs, but *intrusive* generally suggests an objectionable disposition, and *obtrusive,* objectionable actions.

im'per·turb'a·ble (ĭm'pẽr·tûr'bȧ·b'l), *adj.* Incapable of being disturbed or disconcerted; calm; serene. — **Syn.** See COOL. — **Ant.** Choleric. — **im'per·turb'a·bil'i·ty** (-bĭl'ĭ·tĭ), **im'per·turb'a·ble·ness,** *n.* — **im'per·turb'a·bly,** *adv.*

im'per·tur·ba'tion (-tẽr·bā'shŭn), *n.* Calmness; quietude.

im·per'vi·a·ble (ĭm·pûr'vĭ·ȧ·b'l), *adj.* Impervious.

im·per'vi·ous (-vĭ·ŭs; 58), *adj.* Not pervious; impenetrable, as by light rays, moisture, etc.; — often figurative. — **im·per'vi·ous·ly,** *adv.* — **im·per'vi·ous·ness,** *n.*

im'pe·ti'go (ĭm'pē·tī'gō; -tē'gō), *n.* [L., fr. *impetere* to attack.] *Med.* A pustulous skin disease. — **im'pe·tig'i·nous** (-tĭj'ĭ·nŭs), *adj.*

im'pe·trate (ĭm'pē·trāt), *v. t.* [L. *impetratus,* past part. of *impetrare* to obtain, fr. *im-* in + *patrare* to bring to pass.] **1.** To obtain by entreaty. **2.** To entreat; beseech. — **im'pe·tra'tion** (-trā'shŭn), *n.* — **im'pe·tra'tive** (-trā'tĭv), *adj.* — **im'pe·tra'tor** (-trā'tẽr), *n.*

im·pet'u·os'i·ty (ĭm·pĕt'ū·ŏs'ĭ·tĭ), *n.* Impetuousness.

im·pet'u·ous (ĭm·pĕt'ū·ŭs), *adj.* [F. *impétueux,* fr. L. *impetuosus.* See IMPETUS.] **1.** Rushing with force and violence; furious. **2.** Hastily or rashly energetic; impulsive and vehement in action or feeling. — **Syn.** See PRECIPITATE. — **im·pet'u·ous·ly,** *adv.* — **im·pet'u·ous·ness,** *n.*

im'pe·tus (ĭm'pē·tŭs), *n.; pl.* -TUSES (-ĕz; -ĭz). [L., fr. *impetere* to rush upon, fr. *im-* in + *petere* to seek.] **1.** The property possessed by a moving body in virtue of its mass and its motion; — applied commonly to bodies moving suddenly or violently, and indicating the origin and intensity of the motion. Cf. MOMENTUM, 1. **2.** Impulse; incentive; stimulus.

im'pi (ĭm'pĭ), *n.* [Zulu.] *S. Africa.* A body of Kaffir warriors.

im·pi'e·ty (ĭm·pī'ĕ·tĭ), *n.; pl.* -TIES (-tĭz). **1.** Want of piety; irreverence; ungodliness; undutifulness. **2.** An impious act.

im·pig'no·rate (-pĭg'nō·rāt), *v. t.* [ML. *impignoratus,* past part. of *impignorare.*] To pledge; pawn; mortgage. — **im·pig'no·ra'tion** (-rā'shŭn), *n.*

im·pinge' (ĭm·pĭnj'), *v. i.;* IM·PINGED' (-pĭnjd'); IM·PING'ING (-pĭn'jĭng). [L. *impingere,* fr. *im-* in + *pangere* to strike, fix.] **1.** To strike or dash (*on, upon, against*), esp. with a clash or with sharp collision; of radiant or aerial waves, to come sharply (*on* or *upon* a body). **2.** To encroach or infringe (*on* or *upon*). **3.** To come into close contact. — **im·pinge'ment,** *n.* — **im·ping'er** (-pĭn'jẽr), *n.*

im'pi·ous (ĭm'pĭ·ŭs; 58), *adj.* Not pious; lacking piety; specif.: **a** Irreverent; profane. **b** Lacking in respect, as for parents; unfilial; undutiful. — **im'pi·ous·ly,** *adv.* — **im'pi·ous·ness,** *n.*

imp'ish (ĭmp'ĭsh), *adj.* Having the characteristics of an imp; mischievous. — **imp'ish·ly,** *adv.* — **imp'ish·ness,** *n.*

im·pla'ca·ble (ĭm·plā'kȧ·b'l; -plăk'ȧ·b'l), *adj.* Not of a nature to be placated, appeased, or pacified; inexorable. — **im·pla'ca·bil'i·ty** (-bĭl'ĭ·tĭ), **im·pla'ca·ble·ness,** *n.* — **im·pla'ca·bly,** *adv.*

im'pla·cen'tal (ĭm'plȧ·sĕn'tăl; -t'l), *adj.* [See IM- not; PLACENTAL.] *Zool.* Belonging to a primary division (Implacentalia) of the Mammalia, including the monotremes and marsupials, most of which have no placenta. — **im'pla·cen'tal,** *n.* — **im'pla·cen'tate** (-tāt; ĭm-plăs'ĕn-), *adj.*

im·plant' (ĭm·plȧnt'; 9), *v. t.* **1.** To plant or set securely or deeply; hence, to instill or inculcate thoroughly. **2.** To move or insert living tissue in a living site, as in skin grafting.

Syn. **Implant, inculcate, instill, inseminate, infix** mean, in their extended senses, to introduce into the mind. **Implant** (literally, to plant in the soil so that it will take root and grow) implies teaching that makes for permanence of that learned; **inculcate** (etymologically, to tread on with the heels), persistent or repeated endeavor to impress on the mind; **instill** (literally, to pour in drop by drop), gradual, gentle imparting of knowledge, esp. from infancy to adolescence; **inseminate** (literally, to sow, as seed where it will germinate and sprout), a sowing, as of ideas, in many minds, so that they spread throughout a class, community, nation, or the like; **infix** (literally, to set one thing fixedly in another) stresses a deeply implanted or firmly inculcated habit.

— (ĭm'plȧnt; ĭm·plȧnt'; 9), *n.* Something implanted; specif., *Med.,* a small tube containing radium or radon inserted in tissue, as for cancer treatment.

— **im·plant'er,** *n.*

im'plan·ta'tion (ĭm'plăn·tā'shŭn), *n.* **1.** An implanting. **2.** *Med.* **a** Introduction of a drug beneath the skin. **b** The artificial moving of living tissue into a new site, as in skin grafting. **c** Spontaneous passage of cells, esp. tumor cells, to a new site.

im·plau'si·ble (ĭm·plô'zĭ·b'l), *adj.* Not plausible; not such as to be believed. — **im·plau'si·bly,** *adv.*

im·plead' (ĭm·plēd'), *v. t. & i.* [OF. *emplaidier.*] **1.** To sue or prosecute at law; hence, to accuse. **2.** To plead, as a cause. — **im·plead'a·ble,** *adj.* — **im·plead'er,** *n.*

im'ple·ment (ĭm'plē·mĕnt), *n.* [LL. *implementum* a filling up, fr. L. *implere, impletum,* to fill up, finish, fr. *im-* in + *plere* to fill.] An article of equipment; esp., a tool, utensil, instrument, etc., essential to the performance or execution of something.

Syn. **Implement, tool, instrument, appliance, utensil** mean, specifically, any relatively simple device used in performing work. **Implement,** which implies an effecting of the end in view, ordinarily applies to any device used by farmers, masons, or the like; **tool,** which implies a facilitation of work, applies usually, but not exclusively, to contrivances used by carpenters, mechanics, etc.; **instrument,** which implies a means of accomplishing an end, is most often applied to precise and delicate tools requiring expert manipulation used by surgeons, dentists, draftsmen, etc.; **appliance** refers to a tool or instrument moved by electric or other power but guided, usually, by the hand; **utensil** applies commonly to any device used in domestic or similar work including not only tools or instruments, but pots, pans, pails, etc.

— (-mĕnt), *v. t.* **1.** To accomplish; fulfill; complete; carry out; as, to *implement* one's revenge. **2.** To give practical effect to and insure of actual fulfillment by concrete measures; as, to *implement* a treaty. **3.** To provide with an implement or implements. — **Syn.** See ENFORCE. — **im'ple·men'tal** (-mĕn'tăl; -t'l), *adj.* — **im'ple·men·ta'tion** (-mĕn-tā'shŭn), *n.*

im·ple'tion (ĭm·plē'shŭn), *n.* [LL. *impletio.* See IMPLEMENT.] Act of filling or state of being full; also, that which fills.

im'pli·cate (ĭm'plĭ·kāt), *v. t.* [L. *implicatus,* past part. of *implicare* to involve.] **1.** To fold or twist together; entwine. **2.** To imply. **3.** To bring into intimate or incriminating connection; involve.

im'pli·ca'tion (-kā'shŭn), *n.* **1.** Act of implicating or state of being implicated; involvement; close connection. **2.** Act of implying or state of being implied; also, that which is implied; inference. — **im'pli·ca'tion·al, im'pli·ca'tive** (ĭm'plĭ·kā'tĭv; ĭm·plĭk'ȧ·tĭv), *adj.* — **im'pli·ca'tive·ly,** *adv.* — **im'pli·ca·to'ry** (ĭm'plĭ·kȧ·tō'rĭ *or, esp. Brit.,* -kā'tō·rĭ), *adj.*

im·plic'it (ĭm·plĭs'ĭt), *adj.* [F. or L.; F. *implicite,* fr. L. *implicitus,* past part. of *implicare* to entwine.] **1.** *Obs.* Implicated; entangled. **2.** Tacitly comprised; fairly to be understood, though not expressed; implied; as, an *implicit* condition of an agreement. **3.** Involved in the nature or being of something, though not shown, expressed, or realized; virtual or potential; as, the oak is *implicit* in the acorn. **4.** Unreserved; unquestioning; complete; as, *implicit* obedience. — **im·plic'it·ly,** *adv.* — **im·plic'it·ness,** *n.*

im·plied' (ĭm·plīd'), *adj.* Virtually involved or included; inferential; not expressly stated. See IMPLY.

im·plore' (ĭm·plōr'), *v. t.* [L. *implorare,* fr. *im-* in + *plorare* to cry aloud.] To call upon, or for, in supplication; pray to, or for, earnestly; beseech; entreat. — **Syn.** See BEG. — **im·plor'er** (-plōr'ẽr), *n.* — **im·plor'ing·ly,** *adv.* — **im·plor'ing·ness,** *n.*

im·plo'sion (ĭm·plō'zhŭn), *n.* [*im-* + *explosion.*] **1.** A bursting inwards; — contrasted with *explosion.* **2.** *Phonet.* **a** Compression of air between the closed glottis and the closed oral and nasal passages, as in forming the voiceless stops *p, t, k.* **b** The inrush of air in forming a suction stop. — **im·plo'sive** (-sĭv), *adj. & n.*

im·ply' (ĭm·plī'), *v. t.;* IM·PLIED' (-plīd'); IM·PLY'ING. [OF. *emplier,* fr. L. *implicare.*] **1.** *Obs.* To infold. **2.** To involve in substance, or by fair inference, or by construction of law, when not expressly stated; to contain by implication; as, war *implies* fighting. **3.** To express indirectly; to hint or hint at. **4.** Of words or phrases, to involve as a meaning or meanings. — **Syn.** See INCLUDE: SUGGEST.

im·pol'i·cy (-pŏl'ĭ·sĭ), *n.* Unwise policy; inexpediency.

im'po·lite' (ĭm'pō·līt'), *adj.* Not polite; uncivil; rude. — **im'po·lite'ly,** *adv.* — **im'po·lite'ness,** *n.*

im·pol'i·tic (ĭm·pŏl'ĭ·tĭk), *adj.* Not politic; unwise; inexpedient. — **im·pol'i·tic·ly,** *adv.* — **im·pol'i·tic·ness,** *n.*

im·pon'der·a·ble (-pŏn'dẽr·ȧ·b'l), *adj.* Not ponderable; incapable of being weighed. — *n.* An imponderable thing, substance, etc.; — chiefly *pl.;* as, spiritual *imponderables.* — **im·pon'der·a·bil'i·ty** (-bĭl'ĭ·tĭ), *n.* — **im·pon'der·a·ble·ness,** *n.* — **im·pon'der·a·bly,** *adv.*

im·pone' (-pōn'), *v. t.* [L. *imponere, impositum,* to place upon.] *Obs.* To stake; pledge. *Shak.*

im·port' (ĭm·pōrt'; *often* ĭm'pōrt, *esp. in contrast with export*), *v. t.* [L. *importare* to bring in, to occasion, to cause, fr. *im-* in + *portare* to bear. Sense 3 & v. i. come through F.] **1.** To bear or carry with it; specif.: **a** To purport; mean; signify. **b** To express or state. **c** To imply. **2.** To introduce from without; esp., to bring (wares) into one country from another country in commerce; — opposed to *export.* **3.** To be of importance to; concern. — *v. i.* To be of importance; matter; — with *little, much,* etc. — **im·port'a·bil'i·ty** (-pōr'tȧ·bĭl'ĭ·tĭ), *n.* — **im·port'a·ble** (ĭm·pōr'tȧ·b'l), *adj.* — **im·port'er,** *n.*

im'port (ĭm'pōrt; *formerly also* ĭm·pōrt'), *n.* **1.** Meaning or signification, as of a word, phrase, or document. **2.** Importance. **3.** Merchandise imported; — generally in *pl.,* and opposed to *export.* — **Syn.** See MEANING.

im·por'tance (ĭm·pôr'tăns), *n.* Also, *Obs.,* **im·por'tan·cy** (-tăn·sĭ). **1.** Quality or state of being important; consequence; moment; weight; significance. **2.** *Obs.* **a** A weighty matter. **b** Importunity. **c** Import; meaning.

Syn. **Importance, consequence, moment, weight, significance** mean the quality or character of that which impresses one as of great worth, influence, or the like. **Importance** implies a judgment of the mind which ascribes superiority of this sort to a person or thing; **consequence** may imply importance in rank or station but it usually implies importance because of possible or probable effects or results; **moment** implies conspicuous or self-evident consequence; **weight** implies a judgment of the relative importance of a thing; **significance** implies a quality or character in a person or thing which ought to mark it as of importance or consequence.

im·por'tant (ĭm·pôr'tănt), *adj.* [F.] **1.** Having consequence; momentous; weighty; significant. **2.** Consequential; pompous. **3.** *Obs.* Importunate; urgent. — **im·por'tant·ly,** *adv.*

im'por·ta'tion (ĭm'pōr·tā'shŭn), *n.* Act or practice of importing; also, that which is imported.

im·por'tu·na·cy (ĭm·pôr'tū·nȧ·sĭ), *n.* Importunateness.

im·por'tu·nate (-nĭt), *adj.* **1.** *Obs.* Troublesome. **2.** Troublesomely urgent; too solicitous in request or demand; urgent. — **im·por′tu·nate·ly**, *adv.* — **im·por′tu·nate·ness**, *n.*

im′por·tune′ (ĭm′pôr·tūn′; ĭm·pôr′tŭn), *adj.* [F. *importun*, fr. L. *importunus*, fr. *im-* not + *portus* port, harbor, prop., entrance, access.] Importunate; urgent. — *v. t.* **1.** *Obs.* **a** To annoy. **b** To press on; impel. **2.** To ply or press with requests; to urge persistently. **3.** *Now Rare.* To request or solicit with urgency. — *v. i.* To be importunate. — **Syn.** See BEG. — **im′por·tune′ly**, *adv.* — **im′por·tun′er** (ĭm′pôr·tūn′ẽr), *n.*

im′por·tu′ni·ty (ĭm′pôr·tū′nĭ·tĭ), *n.; pl.* -TIES (-tĭz). Quality of being importunate; troublesome pertinacity in requesting or demanding.

im·pose′ (ĭm·pōz′), *v. t.* [F. *imposer*, fr. *im-* in + *poser* to place.] **1.** To subject (one) *to* a charge, penalty, or the like. **2.** To lay as a charge, duty, command, etc.; hence, to levy; inflict; as, to *impose* burdens or a penalty. **3.** *Eccl.* To lay on (the hands), as in confirmation. **4.** *Archaic.* To place; deposit. **5.** To pass or palm off; as, to *impose* inferior goods on a buyer. **6.** To obtrude; as, to *impose* oneself upon others. **7.** *Print.* To arrange in order on a table of stone or metal (**imposing stone** *or* **table**) and lock up in a chase. — *v. i.* **1.** To impress oneself or itself, esp. obnoxiously; presume; as, to *impose* upon good nature. **2.** To practice tricks or deception; — with *on* or *upon.* — **im·pos′er** (-pōz′ẽr), *n.*

im·pos′ing (ĭm·pōz′ĭng), *adj.* Impressive because of size, power, etc. — **Syn.** See GRAND. — **im·pos′ing·ly**, *adv.*

im′po·si′tion (ĭm′pō·zĭsh′ŭn), *n.* **1.** Act of imposing. **2.** That which is imposed; specif.: **a** A levy or tax. **b** An excessive, unwarranted, or uncalled-for requirement or burden. **c** A trick or deception; imposture. **3.** Act of laying on the hands as a religious ceremony, as in ordination. **4.** *Print.* Act or process of imposing pages of type.

im·pos′si·bil′i·ty (ĭm·pŏs′ĭ·bĭl′ĭ·tĭ), *n.; pl.* -TIES (-tĭz). **1.** Quality of being impossible. **2.** An impossible thing.

im·pos′si·ble (ĭm·pŏs′ĭ·b′l), *adj.* [OF., fr. L. *impossibilis.*] **1.** Not possible; incapable of being or of occurring. **2.** Utterly impracticable or hopeless. **3.** *Colloq.* Without chance of favor or acceptance; highly unsuitable. — **im·pos′si·ble·ness**, *n.* — **im·pos′si·bly**, *adv.*

im′post (ĭm′pōst), *n.* [OF., fr. L. *impositus*, past part. of *imponere* to impose.] **1.** A tax; esp., a customs duty. **2.** *Slang.* The weight carried by a horse in a handicap. — *v. t. U. S. Customs.* To classify (imports) in order to fix the duties. — **im′post·er**, *n.*

im′post, *n.* [F. *imposte*, fr. It. *imposta*, fr. L.] *Arch.* The top member of a pillar, pier, wall, etc., upon which the weight of an arch rests. See ARCH, *Illust.*

im·pos′tor (ĭm·pŏs′tẽr), *n.* [LL.] One who imposes upon others for the purpose of deception; a pretender.

im·pos′ture (-tŭr), *n.* [F., fr. LL. *impostura.*] Act or conduct of an impostor; fraud; deception.

Syn. **Imposture, cheat, fraud, sham, fake, humbug, deceit, deception, counterfeit** mean a thing which is imposed upon one by false pretenses. **Imposture** applies to anything foisted upon one as genuine, authentic, or the like; **cheat**, to anything which one believes genuine through being deliberately misled or the victim of delusion or illusion; **fraud**, to any imposture or impostor that positively reveals perversion of the truth in the claims made for it or him; **sham**, to any fraudulent imitation of a thing; **fake**, to a sham that is not necessarily dishonest; **humbug**, to someone or something making pretenses to be what he or it is not; **deceit** and **deception**, to anything that deceives one as to its true character, *deceit* also often connoting that which leads one astray; **counterfeit**, to a very close imitation of a genuine thing that is valuable.

im′po·tence (ĭm′pō·tĕns), *n.* Also **im′po·ten·cy** (-tĕn·sĭ). **1.** Quality or state of being impotent; weakness. **2.** *Poetic.* Want of self-control. **3.** Incapacity for sexual intercourse.

im′po·tent (-tĕnt), *adj.* **1.** Not potent; lacking power, strength, or vigor, whether physical, intellectual, or moral; deficient in capacity. **2.** *Obs.* Ungovernable. **3.** Unable to copulate; sometimes, sterile. — **Syn.** See STERILE. — **im′po·tent·ly**, *adv.* — **im′po·tent·ness**, *n.*

im·pound′ (ĭm·pound′), *v. t.* **1.** To shut up or place in or as in a pound; hence, to seize and hold in legal custody; as, to *impound* stray cattle; to *impound* goods or documents. **2.** To collect (water) for irrigation purposes, or the like, as a reservoir. — **im·pound′age**, *n.* — **im·pound′er**, *n.*

im·pov′er·ish (ĭm·pŏv′ẽr·ĭsh), *v. t.* [OF. *empovrir*, fr. *em-* (fr. L. *in*) + *povre* poor.] **1.** To make poor; reduce to poverty. **2.** To exhaust the strength, richness, or fertility of (land). — **Syn.** See DEPLETE. — **im·pov′er·ish·er**, *n.* — **im·pov′er·ish·ment**, *n.*

im·pow′er (ĭm·pou′ẽr). Var. of EMPOWER.

im·prac′ti·ca·ble (ĭm·prăk′tĭ·kȧ·b′l), *adj.* **1.** Not practicable; infeasible; also, not usable. **2.** Unmanageable; intractable. — **im·prac′ti·ca·bil′i·ty** (-bĭl′ĭ·tĭ), *n.* — **im·prac′ti·ca·ble·ness**, *n.* — **im·prac′ti·ca·bly**, *adv.*

im·prac′ti·cal (ĭm·prăk′tĭ·kăl), *adj.* Not practical; theoretical; also, not useful. — **im·prac′ti·cal′i·ty** (-kăl′ĭ·tĭ), **im·prac′ti·cal·ness**, *n.*

im′pre·cate (ĭm′prē·kāt), *v. t. & i.* [L. *imprecatus*, past part. of *imprecari* to imprecate, fr. *im-* in, on + *precari* to pray.] To invoke, as evil, by prayer; hence, to curse. — **im′pre·ca′tor** (-kā′tẽr), *n.* — **im′pre·ca·to′ry** (-kȧ·tō′rĭ *or, esp. Brit.,* -kā′tō·rĭ), *adj.*

im′pre·ca′tion (-kā′shŭn), *n.* An imprecating; esp., a curse.

im·preg′na·ble (ĭm·prĕg′nȧ·b′l), *adj.* [F. *imprenable*, fr. *im-* not + *prenable* pregnable.] Not to be taken by assault; able to resist attack; unconquerable. — **im·preg′na·bil′i·ty** (-bĭl′ĭ·tĭ), **im·preg′na·ble·ness**, *n.* — **im·preg′na·bly**, *adv.*

im·preg′na·ble, *adj.* Capable of being impregnated, as an egg.

im·preg′nate (-nāt), *adj.* [LL. *impraegnatus*, past part. of *impraegnare* to impregnate, fr. L. *im-* in + *praegnans* pregnant.] Impregnated. — (-nāt), *v. t.* **1.** To make pregnant; get with child or young. **2.** To infuse particles of another substance into; cause to be permeated or saturated. **3.** To infuse an active principle into; render fruitful or fertile. **4.** *Biol.* To introduce sperm cells into; fecundate. — **Syn.** See SOAK. — **im′preg·na′tion** (ĭm′prĕg·nā′shŭn), *n.* — **im·preg′na·tor** (ĭm·prĕg′nā·tẽr), *n.*

im·pre′sa (ĕm·prā′zä), **im·prese′** (ĭm·prēz′), *n.* [It. *impresa* undertaking.] *Hist.* A device or motto on a shield.

im′pre·sa′ri·o (ĭm′prā·sä′rĭ·ō), *n.; pl.* -RIOS (-ōz); -SARI (-sä′rē). [It., fr. *impresa* enterprise.] **1.** The projector, manager, or conductor of an opera or concert company. **2.** One who puts on or sponsors a show, concert, radio program, art exhibition, sports contest, or the like.

im′pre·scrip′ti·ble (ĭm′prē·skrĭp′tĭ·b′l), *adj.* Not subject to prescription; inalienable; as, the *imprescriptible* rights of man; also, absolute. — **im′pre·scrip′ti·bil′i·ty** (-bĭl′ĭ·tĭ), *n.* — **im′pre·scrip′ti·bly**, *adv.*

im·press′ (ĭm·prĕs′), *v. t.* [L. *impressus*, past part. of *imprimere* to impress, fr. *im-* in, on + *premere* to press.] **1.** **a** To apply with pressure so as to imprint. **b** To produce, as a mark or stamp, by such pressure. **2.** **a** To produce a vivid impression of; as, to *impress* ideas on the mind. **b** To affect, esp. forcibly or deeply; as, to *impress* one favorably. **3.** To press, stamp, or print something in or upon. **4.** *Elec.* To create or establish (an electromotive force or difference of potential) in a conductor. — **Syn.** See AFFECT. — **im·press′er**, *n.*

im′press (ĭm′prĕs; *formerly also* ĭm·prĕs′), *n.* **1.** Act of impressing. **2.** A mark made by pressure; imprint; the image, figure or other result of impressing; an impression. **3.** Characteristic; mark of distinction; stamp; as, the work bore the *impress* of a great artist.

im·press′ (ĭm·prĕs′), *v. t.* [*im-* in + *press* to force into service.] To levy for public service; specif., to take by force for public service; esp., to force into the naval service. — (ĭm′prĕs; *formerly* ĭm·prĕs′), *n.* Impressment.

im·press′i·ble (-prĕs′ĭ·b′l), *adj.* Capable of being impressed; susceptible. — **im·press′i·bil′i·ty** (-bĭl′ĭ·tĭ), *n.*

im·pres′sion (ĭm·prĕsh′ŭn), *n.* **1.** An impressing. **2.** Effect produced by impressing; specif.: **a** An impress; indentation; stamp; imprint. **b** A characteristic, trait, or feature, resulting from immaterial or indirect influence. **c** Influence or effect on feeling, sense, or the intellect; esp., a lively or profound effect. **d** A vague or indefinite remembrance, belief, or opinion. **3.** *Dent.* An imprint of the teeth and adjacent parts. **4.** *Print.* **a** Pressure of type, plates, etc., on paper, or its result as to appearance; as, a heavy or a clear *impression.* **b** A printed copy from type, an engraved block, etc. **5.** *Psychol.* The immediate conscious effect produced by stimulation of the senses; also, the stimulation apart from the sensation aroused. **6.** *Publishing.* The whole number of copies printed for one issue; esp., those reprinted without alteration. — **Syn.** See IDEA. — **im·pres′sion·al**, *adj.*

im·pres′sion·a·ble (-ȧ·b′l), *adj.* Liable or subject to impression; capable of being molded; plastic; also, impressible; susceptible. — **im·pres′sion·a·bil′i·ty** (-bĭl′ĭ·tĭ), **im·pres′sion·a·ble·ness**, *n.*

im·pres′sion·ism (-ĭz′m), *n.* **1.** *Art.* A type of realism (see REALISM, 3) the aim of which is to render the immediate sense impression of the artist apart from any element of inference or study of detail; specif., the theory and practice of a school of French painters originating with Édouard Manet (1832–83) and including Monet, Degas, Pissarro, and Renoir. Since with all of this group, study and depiction of light became the chief aim and divisionism (which see) their usual method, these impressionists are called also *luminists* and *plein-airists.* Cf. NEOIMPRESSIONISM, POSTIMPRESSIONISM. **2.** In literature, depiction of scene, emotion, or character with broad simplicity and little elaboration of detail. **3.** *Music.* A style of composition designed to create descriptive impressions by evoking moods. — **im·pres′sion·ist** (-ĭst), *n. & adj.* — **im·pres′sion·is′tic** (-ĭs′tĭk), *adj.*

im·pres′sive (ĭm·prĕs′ĭv), *adj.* [From 1st IMPRESS.] Making, or tending to make, an impression; having power to impress; adapted to touch the sensibilities, or affect the conscience. — **Syn.** See MOVING. — **im·pres′sive·ly**, *adv.* — **im·pres′sive·ness**, *n.*

im·press′ment (ĭm·prĕs′mĕnt), *n.* Act of seizing for public use, or of impressing into public service; as, the *impressment* of sailors.

im·pres′sure (ĭm·prĕsh′ẽr), *n.* Impression.

im·prest′ (ĭm·prĕst′). Archaic past & past part. of IMPRESS.

im′prest (ĭm′prĕst), *adj.* Advanced; lent. — *n.* [*im-* + *prest*, after It. *imprestare.* See PREST, *n.*] A loan or advance of money; esp., an advance from government funds to enable a person to discharge his duties.

im′pri·ma′tur (ĭm′prĭ·mā′tẽr; -prī-), *n.* [NL., let it be printed.] **1.** *Law.* A license to print or publish a book, paper, etc.; also, where censorship of the press exists, approval of that which is published. **2.** Hence, sanction; approval.

‖**im·pri′mis** (ĭm·prī′mĭs), *adv.* [L., for *in primis* among the first, chiefly.] In the first place.

im·print′ (ĭm·prĭnt′), *v. t.* [OF. *empreinter*, fr. *empreinte*, deriv. of L. *im-* in + *premere* to press.] **1.** To impress; mark by pressure; stamp. **2.** To stamp or mark, as letters on paper, by means of type, plates, stamps, etc. **3.** To fix indelibly, as in the memory. — **im·print′er**, *n.*

im′print (ĭm′prĭnt), *n.* **1.** Whatever is imprinted; an impress. **2.** The place of publication, publisher's name, and date, etc., now usually printed at the foot of a title page; the name of the printer, etc., on any printed sheet.

im·pris′on (ĭm·prĭz′'n), *v. t.* To put in prison; to confine. — **im·pris′on·ment**, *n.*

im′prob·a·bil′i·ty (ĭm′prŏb·ȧ·bĭl′ĭ·tĭ), *n.; pl.* -TIES (-tĭz). Quality or state of being improbable; unlikelihood; also, that which is improbable; an improbable event or result.

im·prob′a·ble (ĭm·prŏb′ȧ·b′l), *adj.* Not probable; unlikely to be true or to occur; not to be readily believed; not to be expected. — **im·prob′a·ble·ness**, *n.* — **im·prob′a·bly**, *adv.*

im·pro′bi·ty (ĭm·prō′bĭ·tĭ; -prŏb′ĭ·tĭ), *n.* [L. *improbitas*, fr. *im-* not + *probitas* probity.] Lack of probity; want of integrity.

im·promp′tu (ĭm·prŏmp′tū), *adv. & adj.* [F., fr. L. *in promptu* in readiness, at hand, fr. *in* + *promptus* visibility, readiness.] Made or done without previous study or preparation; offhand; extemporaneous; extempore; as, an *impromptu* verse. — *n.* An impromptu address, composition, etc.

im·prop′er (ĭm·prŏp′ẽr), *adj.* Not proper; specif.: **a** Not appropriate, fit, or congruous; as, *improper* dress. **b** Not accordant with fact, truth, or right procedure; incorrect; inaccurate; as, an *improper* conclusion. **c** Not regularly or normally formed, or not properly so called; as, an *improper* fraction (see FRACTION). **d** Not accordant with propriety or good taste; indecorous. — **Syn.** See INDECOROUS. — **im·prop′er·ly**, *adv.*

im·pro′pri·ate (ĭm·prō′prĭ·āt), *adj.* [*im-* in + L. *propriatus*, past part. of *propriare.* See APPROPRIATE.] *Eng. Eccl. Law.* Impropriated. — (-āt), *v. t.* **1.** *Obs.* To appropriate. **2** *Eng. Eccl. Law.* To transfer to lay control or ownership (monastic properties). — **im·pro′pri·a′tion** (-ā′shŭn), *n.* — **im·pro′pri·a′tor** (-ā′tẽr), *n.*

im′pro·pri′e·ty (ĭm′prō·prī′ĕ·tĭ), *n.; pl.* -TIES (-tĭz). **1.** Quality or fact of being improper. **2.** An improper or indecorous act. **3.** An incorrect use of a word; a violation of linguistic good usage. Cf. BARBARISM, 1; SOLECISM, 1.

im·prove′ (ĭm·pro͞ov′), *v. t.* [Earlier *improue, enprowe*, fr. OF. *en* in (fr. L. *in*) + *prou* profit, excellent, fr. L. *pro, prod* in *prodesse* to be useful.] **1.** To turn to profit or good account; to use to advantage; as, to *improve* one's time. **2.** *Now Dial.* To make use of; employ.

3. To augment or enhance in value or good quality; make better; as, to *improve* one's health by exercise. 4. Specif., *U. S.*, to enhance in value, as land by cultivation or reclamation, or property by erection of buildings, or the laying out of streets and installing of utilities. — *v. i.* 1. To increase; rise in value. 2. To grow better. 3. To make improvements; — usually with *on* or *upon*. — **im·prov'a·bil'i·ty** (-proov'ȧ·bĭl'ĭ·tĭ), *n.* — **im·prov'a·ble**, *adj.* — **im·prov'a·ble·ness**, *n.* — **im·prov'a·bly**, *adv.* — **im·prov'er**, *n.* — **im·prov'ing·ly**, *adv.*

Syn. Improve, better, help, ameliorate mean to mend or correct in some degree. Improve (the general term) and better (more vigorous and homely) apply both to objects and to states and conditions, not of necessity bad, but capable of being made better; help implies improvement while leaving something to be desired; ameliorate implies conditions hard to bear and their betterment by being made tolerable.

im·prove'ment (ĭm·proov'mĕnt), *n.* 1. An improving; esp., betterment. 2. State of being improved; esp., enhanced value or excellence. 3. A result of improving, or that which constitutes it; as, macadam roads were an *improvement* on the old dirt roads. 4. An addition or modification that improves land, a machine, a manufacture, etc.

im·prov'i·dent (ĭm·prŏv'ĭ·dĕnt), *adj.* Not provident; lacking foresight or forethought; not providing for the future; thriftless. — **im·prov'i·dence** (-dĕns), *n.* — **im·prov'i·dent·ly**, *adv.*

im'pro·vi·sa'tion (ĭm'prō·vĭ·zā'shŭn; ĭm'prŏv·ĭ-), *n.* Act, art, or result, of composing and rendering music, poetry, etc., extemporaneously. — **im'pro·vi·sa'tion·al** (-ăl; -'l), *adj.*

im·prov'i·sa'tor (ĭm·prŏv'ĭ·zā'tẽr; ĭm'prō·vĭ-), *n.* An improviser. — **im·prov'i·sa·to'ri·al** (ĭm·prŏv'ĭ·zȧ·tō'rĭ·ăl), *adj.* — **im·prov'i·sa·to'ri·al·ly**, *adv.* — **im'pro·vi'sa·to'ry** (ĭm'prō·vī'zȧ·tō'rĭ, -vĭz'ȧ·tō'rĭ *or, esp. Brit.*, -tẽr·ĭ), *adj.*

im'pro·vise (ĭm'prō·vīz; ĭm'prō·vīz'), *v. t. & i.* [F. *improviser*, fr. It. *improvvisare*, fr. *improvviso* unprovided, sudden, extempore, fr. L. *improvisus*, fr. *im-* not + *provisus* foreseen, provided.] 1. To compose, recite, sing, act, etc., extemporaneously; extemporize. 2. To make, do, or provide, offhand; as, to *improvise* a hammer out of a stone. — **im'pro·vis'er** (-vīz'ẽr), *n.*

||**im'prov·vi'sa·to're** (ēm'prŏv·vē'zä·tō'rā), *n.; pl.* -TORI (-rē). [It.] One who composes and sings or recites short poems extemporaneously; an improviser.

im·pru'dent (ĭm·proo'dĕnt), *adj.* [L. *imprudens, -entis*, fr. *im* not + *prudens* prudent.] Not prudent; lacking in discretion or caution; indiscreet; injudicious; as, *imprudent* behavior. — **im·pru'dence**, *n.* — **im·pru'dent·ly**, *adv.* — **im·pru'dent·ness**, *n.*

im'pu·dence (ĭm'pū·dĕns), *n.* Also **im'pu·den·cy** (-dĕn·sĭ). Quality of being impudent; shameless effrontery; brazenness; insolence.

im'pu·dent (-dĕnt), *adj.* [L. *impudens, -entis*, fr. *im-* not + *pudens* ashamed, modest, pres. part. of *pudere* to feel shame.] 1. *Obs.* Lacking modesty; shameless. 2. Bold or pert, with contempt or disregard of others; unblushingly forward; insolent. — **im'pu·dent·ly**, *adv.* — **im'pu·dent·ness**, *n.*

im'pu·dic'i·ty (ĭm'pū·dĭs'ĭ·tĭ), *n.* Immodesty.

im·pugn' (ĭm·pūn'), *v. t.* [OF. *impugner*, fr. L. *impugnare*, fr. *in* on, against + *pugnare* to fight.] To assail by words or arguments; to call in question; oppose as false; as, to *impugn* one's veracity. — **Syn.** See DENY. — **im·pugn'a·ble**, *adj.* — **im'pug·na'tion** (ĭm'pŭg·nā'shŭn), *n.* — **im·pugn'er** (ĭm·pūn'ẽr), *n.*

im·pu'is·sant (ĭm·pū'ĭ·sănt; ĭm'pū·ĭs'ănt; ĭm·pwĭs'ănt), *adj.* [F., fr. *im-* not + *puissant*.] Powerless; impotent; feeble. — **im·pu'is·sance** (-săns; -ăns), *n.*

im'pulse (ĭm'pŭls), *n.* [L. *impulsus*, fr. *impellere*. See IMPEL.] 1. Act of impelling, or driving onward with sudden force; impulsion; also, the motion produced by such an impulsion. 2. A sudden incitement to action, insight, etc.; a spontaneous inclination; as, to act on *impulse*. 3. A motive, propensity, or tendency, that is not instinctive and not governed by reason; as, a man of good *impulses*. 4. *Elec.* A unidirectional surge of current or voltage. 5. *Mech.* The product of the average value of a force and the time during which it acts, a quantity equal to the change in momentum produced by the force. 6. *Physiol.* A change transmitted through certain tissues, esp. nerve fibers and muscles, and resulting in physiological activity or inhibition. — **Syn.** See MOTIVE.

im·pul'sion (ĭm·pŭl'shŭn), *n.* [F., fr. L. *impulsio*. See IMPEL.] 1. Act of impelling, or state of being impelled; also, the impelling force. 2. An impulse, or sudden inclination to do or not to do something. 3. Onward tendency derived from an impulsion; impetus.

im·pul'sive (-sĭv), *adj.* 1. Having the power of driving or impelling; giving an impulse; moving; impellent. 2. Actuated or characterized by impulse or impulses; impetuous. 3. *Mech.* Acting momentarily, or by impulse. — **Syn.** See SPONTANEOUS. — **im·pul'sive·ly**, *adv.* — **im·pul'sive·ness**, *n.*

im·pu'ni·ty (ĭm·pū'nĭ·tĭ), *n.* [F. *impunité*, fr. L. *impunitas*, fr. *impunis* without punishment, fr. *im-* not + *poena* punishment.] Exemption or freedom from punishment, harm, or loss.

im·pure' (ĭm·pūr'), *adj.* [L. *impurus*, fr. *im-* not + *purus* pure.] Not pure; specif.: **a** Containing something unclean; dirty; unwholesome. **b** Adulterated. **c** Of art, etc., mixed; not of one style, tone, period, etc. **d** Unclean ceremonially; not purified; defiled. **e** Unchaste; lewd; obscene. **f** Characterized by an intermixture of foreign elements (as, an *impure* dialect) or by incorrect, incongruous, or objectionable locutions (as, an *impure* style). — **im·pure'ly**, *adv.* — **im·pure'ness**, *n.*

im·pu'ri·ty (ĭm·pū'rĭ·tĭ), *n.; pl.* -TIES (-tĭz). 1. Condition or quality of being impure. 2. That which is, or which renders, impure.

im·put'a·ble (ĭm·pūt'ȧ·b'l), *adj.* That may be imputed; ascribable; referable; attributable. — **im·put'a·bil'i·ty** (-bĭl'ĭ·tĭ), **im·put'a·ble·ness**, *n.* — **im·put'a·bly**, *adv.*

im'pu·ta'tion (ĭm'pū·tā'shŭn), *n.* Act of imputing; ascription; attribution; also, thing imputed; specif., attribution of evil; insinuation. — **im·put'a·tive** (ĭm·pūt'ȧ·tĭv), *adj.* — **im·put'a·tive·ly**, *adv.* — **im·put'a·tive·ness**, *n.*

im·pute' (ĭm·pūt'), *v. t.* [F. *imputer*, fr. L. *imputare* to bring into the reckoning, charge, impute, fr. *im-* in + *putare* to reckon, think.] 1. To ascribe (to one) as author, responsible originator, or possessor; to charge (a fault or the like); to credit (a virtue or good); as, to *impute* the theft to a tramp. 2. *Law.* To impose as a charge; arraign. 3. *Theol.* To ascribe vicariously. — **Syn.** See ASCRIBE. — **im·put'er** (-pūt'ẽr), *n.*

in (ĭn; 4), *prep.* [AS.] Primarily, *in* denotes situation or position with respect to a surrounding, encompassment, or enclosure. It may indicate either simple location or direction, the latter sense in modern English being generally distinguished by the use of *into*. See AT, *Note*. *In* is specifically used as: 1. Indicating being within, as a bounded place, a limited time, an encompassing material, a class or group, etc.; as, to travel *in* Italy; *in* one's childhood; dressed *in* silk. 2. Indicating inclusion in a whole; as, the tallest boy *in* the class. 3. Indicating inclusion with respect to scope, influence, occupation, condition, nature, participation, etc.; as, to be *in* difficulties, *in* business, or *in* ruins. 4. Indicating being limited with respect to manner, quality, means, substance, etc.; as, to argue *in* a circle; to be, *in* truth, a sorry lot; a statue *in* marble. — ***in as much as***. See INASMUCH AS. — ***in so far as***. To the extent that; as fully or widely as.

— *adv.* [AS.] 1. To or towards the inside, as of a house, harbor, etc.; as, come *in*; a ship on the way *in*. 2. So as to be mingled, form a part of, or the like; as, mix *in* the flour; paint *in* another figure. 3. So as to be in place, in line, in agreement, etc.; as, their plans fell *in* with ours; to fit *in* a piece. — *adj.* 1. Being inside or within an understood place, condition, connection, etc.; as, he is not *in*; the *in* party. 2. Coming, bound, etc., in; as, the *in* train.

in (ĭn), *n.* 1. One who is in, esp. in office; — usually *pl.* 2. A reentrant angle; a nook or corner. — **ins and outs.** Nooks and corners; twists and turns; peculiarities; details. — *v. t. Dial.* To enclose; also, to take in; specif., to harvest.

in- (ĭn-). A prefix from Eng. prep. and adv. *in*, also from Lat. prep. *in*, meaning *in, within, into, toward, on*, as in income, *in*side, *in*deed, *in*cline. In words from the Latin, *in-* regularly appears as *il-* before *l*, *ir-* before *r*, and *im-* before a labial, as in *il*lusion, *ir*ruption, *im*bue, *im*part. It is often merely intensive, and sometimes its force is entirely lost. In native words *in-* is generally unchanged by the following consonant, as in *in*land, *in*road, *in*mate.

in- (ĭn-). [L.; akin to E. *un-*.] An inseparable prefix, or particle, meaning *not, non-, un-*, as in *in*active, *in*capable. *In-* becomes *il-* before *l*, *ir-* before *r*, etc. See 1st IN-.

-in. *Chem.* A suffix. See 2d -INE.

in'a·bil'i·ty (ĭn'ȧ·bĭl'ĭ·tĭ), *n.* Quality or state of being unable; insufficiency, as of power, strength, or resources.

||**in ab·sen'ti·a** (ĭn ăb·sĕn'shĭ·ȧ). [L.] In absence, as of the accused or of a person receiving a degree.

in'ac·ces'si·ble (ĭn'ăk·sĕs'ĭ·b'l), *adj.* Not accessible. — **in'ac·ces'si·bil'i·ty** (-bĭl'ĭ·tĭ), *n.* — **in'ac·ces'si·ble·ness**, *n.* — **in'ac·ces'si·bly**, *adv.*

in·ac'cu·ra·cy (ĭn·ăk'ū·rȧ·sĭ), *n.; pl.* -CIES (-sĭz). Quality or fact of being inaccurate; also, a mistake; an error.

in·ac'cu·rate (-rĭt), *adj.* Not accurate; hence, incorrect; erroneous. — **in·ac'cu·rate·ly**, *adv.* — **in·ac'cu·rate·ness**, *n.*

in·ac'tion (ĭn·ăk'shŭn), *n.* Lack of action; idleness; inertness.

in·ac'ti·vate (-tĭ·vāt), *v. t.* To render inactive; specif., *Immunol.*, to destroy certain biological activities of, as to destroy the complement action of normal serum by heat. — **in·ac'ti·va'tion** (-vā'shŭn), *n.*

in·ac'tive (-tĭv), *adj.* Not active; as: **a** Inert; having inertia; not having active properties. **b** Sluggish; indolent. **c** *Physics & Chem.* Optically neutral in polarized light; — said of certain isomeric forms; as, *inactive* fructose. — **in·ac'tive·ly**, *adv.* — **in·ac'tive·ness**, *n.* — **in'ac·tiv'i·ty** (ĭn'ăk·tĭv'ĭ·tĭ), *n.*

Syn. Inactive, idle, inert, passive, supine mean not engaged in work or activity. Inactive is applicable to anyone or anything that for any reason is not in action, operation, use, work, or the like; idle applies chiefly to persons that are not busy or occupied but is also applicable to their powers, organs, implements, etc.; inert, as applied to things, implies inherent powerlessness to move or produce effects, but as applied to persons suggests an inherent or habitual indisposition to be aroused to activity; passive usually suggests immobility or lack of response to influences that act upon one (whether a person or thing); supine, applicable only to persons, implies cowardly inertia or passivity, esp. when danger threatens.

in·ad'e·quate (ĭn·ăd'ē·kwĭt), *adj.* Not adequate; deficient; insufficient. — **in·ad'e·qua·cy** (-kwȧ·sĭ), *n.* — **in·ad'e·quate·ly**, *adv.* — **in·ad'e·quate·ness**, *n.*

in'ad·mis'si·ble (ĭn'ăd·mĭs'ĭ·b'l), *adj.* Not admissible. — **in'ad·mis'si·bil'i·ty** (-bĭl'ĭ·tĭ), *n.* — **in'ad·mis'si·bly**, *adv.*

in'ad·vert'ence (-vûr'tĕns), *n.; pl.* -CES (-tĕn·sĕz; -sĭz). [ML. *inadvertentia*.] Fact, action, or result of being inadvertent; inattention or an error resulting from it; an oversight.

in'ad·vert'en·cy (-tĕn·sĭ), *n.* Heedlessness; inadvertence.

in'ad·vert'ent (-tĕnt), *adj.* 1. Not turning the mind to a matter; heedless; inattentive. 2. Unintentional. — **in'ad·vert'ent·ly**, *adv.*

in'ad·vis'a·ble (-vīz'ȧ·b'l), *adj.* Not advisable; inexpedient. — **in'ad·vis'a·bil'i·ty** (-bĭl'ĭ·tĭ), **in'ad·vis'a·ble·ness**, *n.*

-i'nae (-ī'nē). [L. fem. pl. ending of adjectives in *-inus*.] *Zool.* A termination (in recent classifications) for all names of subfamilies. Cf. -IDAE.

||**in ae·ter'num** (ĭn ē·tûr'nŭm). [L.] Forever; everlastingly; always.

in·al'ien·a·ble (ĭn·āl'yĕn·ȧ·b'l; -ā'lĭ·ĕn-), *adj.* Incapable of being alienated, surrendered, or transferred. — **in·al'ien·a·bil'i·ty** (-bĭl'ĭ·tĭ), *n.* — **in·al'ien·a·bly**, *adv.*

in·al'ter·a·ble (-ôl'tẽr·ȧ·b'l), *adj.* Not alterable. — **in·al'ter·a·bil'i·ty** (-bĭl'ĭ·tĭ), *n.* — **in·al'ter·a·bly**, *adv.*

in·am'o·ra'ta (ĭn·ăm'ō·rä'tȧ), *n.; pl.* INAMORATAS (-tȧz). [It. *innamorata*, fem., *innamorato*, masc., past part. of *innamorare* to inspire with love.] A woman in love or beloved. — **in·am'o·ra'to** (-tō), *n. masc.; pl.* -TOS (-tōz).

in'–and–in', *adv. & adj.* Repeated(ly) in generations of the same or closely related stocks; — of mating, breeding, etc.

in·ane' (ĭn·ān'), *adj.* [L. *inanis*.] Without contents; empty; esp., void of sense or significance; pointless. — **Syn.** See INSIPID. — *n.* That which is inane; esp., the void of space. — **in·ane'ly**, *adv.*

in·an'i·mate (ĭn·ăn'ĭ·māt), *adj.* 1. Not animate; not endowed with life and spirit. 2. Bereft of life or consciousness; as, an *inanimate* body. 3. Not animated; dull; spiritless. — **Syn.** See DEAD. — **in·an'i·mate·ly**, *adv.* — **in·an'i·mate·ness**, *n.*

in'a·ni'tion (ĭn'ȧ·nĭsh'ŭn; ĭn'ă-), *n.* [F. or L.; F., fr. LL. *inanitio* emptiness, fr. *inanire* to empty, fr. *inanis* empty.] 1. Inanity; emptiness. 2. Exhaustion from lack or nonassimilation of food.

in·an'i·ty (ĭn·ăn'ĭ·tĭ), *n.; pl.* -TIES (-tĭz). 1. State or quality of being inane. 2. An inane thing; esp., a senseless remark.

in'ap·peas'a·ble (ĭn'ă·pēz'ȧ·b'l), *adj.* Not appeasable.

in·ap'pe·tence (ĭn·ăp'ē·tĕns), **in·ap'pe·ten·cy** (-tĕn·sĭ), *n.* Lack of appetite or desire. — **in·ap'pe·tent** (-tĕnt), *adj.*

in·ap′pli·ca·ble (ĭn·ăp′lĭ·kȧ·b'l), *adj.* Not applicable; unsuitable; irrelevant. — **in·ap′pli·ca·bil′i·ty** (-bĭl′ĭ·tĭ), **in·ap′pli·ca·ble·ness**, *n.* — **in·ap′pli·ca·bly**, *adv.*

in·ap′po·site (-ăp′ō·zĭt), *adj.* Not apposite or pertinent.

in′ap·pre′ci·a·ble (ĭn′ȧ·prē′shĭ·ȧ·b'l), *adj.* **a** *Rare.* Invaluable. **b** Too small to be perceived. — **in′ap·pre′ci·a·bly**, *adv.*

in′ap·pre′ci·a′tive (-ā′tĭv; -ȧ·tĭv), *adj.* Not appreciative.

in′ap·pre·hen′si·ble (ĭn′ăp·rē·hĕn′sĭ·b'l), *adj.* Not apprehensible; unthinkable.

in′ap·pre·hen′sion (-shŭn), *n.* Lack of apprehension.

in′ap·pre·hen′sive (-sĭv), *adj.* **1.** Deficient in power of apprehension. **2.** Without apprehension of danger.

in′ap·proach′a·ble (ĭn′ȧ·prōch′ȧ·b'l), *adj.* Not approachable; also, unrivaled. — **in′ap·proach′a·bil′i·ty** (-bĭl′ĭ·tĭ), *n.* — **in′ap·proach′a·bly**, *adv.*

in′ap·pro′pri·ate (-prō′prĭ·ĭt), *adj.* Not appropriate. — **in′ap·pro′pri·ate·ly**, *adv.* — **in′ap·pro′pri·ate·ness**, *n.*

in·apt′ (ĭn·ăpt′), *adj.* Not apt; not suitable; also, not ready; inept. — **in·apt′ly**, *adv.* — **in·apt′ness**, *n.*

in·apt′i·tude (-ăp′tĭ·tūd), *n.* Lack of aptitude.

in·arch′ (ĭn·ärch′), *v. t.* [*in-* in + *arch*, v.] To graft by bringing cion and stock into contact while both are growing on their own roots.

in·arm′ (-ärm′), *v. t.* To surround by or as if by the arms.

in′ar·tic′u·late (ĭn′är·tĭk′ū·lāt), *adj.* [L. *inarticulatus*, fr. *in-* not + *articulatus* articulate.] **1.** Of sounds, uttered without the definite articulations of intelligible speech. **2.** Incapable of articulating; dumb; hence, unable to speak intelligibly or expressively. **3.** *Zool.* **a** Not jointed or articulated; having no distinct body segments; as, an *inarticulate* worm. **b** Without a hinge; pertaining to a primary division (Inarticulata, or Lyopomata) of brachiopods. — **in′ar·tic′u·late·ly**, *adv.* — **in′ar·tic′u·late·ness**, *n.*

‖**in ar·tic′u·lo mor′tis** (ĭn är·tĭk′ū·lō môr′tĭs). [L.] At the point of death.

in·ar′ti·fi′cial (ĭn·är′tĭ·fĭsh′ăl), *adj.* **1.** Not artificial; natural; artless; simple; direct. **2.** Inartistic; clumsy. — **in·ar′ti·fi′ci·al′i·ty** (-fĭsh′ĭ·ăl′ĭ·tĭ), *n.* — **in·ar′ti·fi′cial·ly**, *adv.*

in′ar·tis′tic (ĭn′är·tĭs′tĭk), *adj.* Also **in′ar·tis′ti·cal** (-tĭ·kăl). Not artistic; lacking in artistic taste. — **in′ar·tis′ti·cal·ly**, *adv.*

in′as·much′ as (ĭn′ăz·mŭch′). Seeing that; since.

in′at·ten′tion (ĭn′ȧ·tĕn′shŭn), *n.* Lack of attention.

in′at·ten′tive (-tĭv), *adj.* Not attentive; heedless; negligent. — **in′at·ten′tive·ly**, *adv.* — **in′at·ten′tive·ness**, *n.*

in·au′di·ble (ĭn·ô′dĭ·b'l), *adj.* Not audible. — **in·au′di·bil′i·ty** (-bĭl′ĭ·tĭ), **in·au′di·ble·ness**, *n.* — **in·au′di·bly**, *adv.*

in·au′gu·ral (ĭn·ô′gū·răl), *adj.* [F.] Pertaining to an inauguration. — *n.* *U. S.* An inaugural address.

in·au′gu·rate (-rāt), *v. t.* [L. *inauguratus*, past part. of *inaugurare* to take omens; hence, to consecrate, inaugurate, fr. *in-* in + *augurare* to augur.] **1.** To introduce or induct into an office formally; install. **2.** To begin or initiate under favorable or auspicious circumstances or with ceremony. **3.** To commence or enter upon (esp. something beneficial); to set in motion. — **Syn.** See BEGIN. — **in·au′gu·ra′tion** (-rā′shŭn), **in·au′gu·ra′tor** (-rā′tēr), *n.*

In·au′gu·ra′tion Day. The day on which the president of the United States is inaugurated, now the 20th of January in every year next after a year divisible by four, but previous to 1934, the 4th of March in such years.

in′aus·pi′cious (ĭn′ôs·pĭsh′ŭs), *adj.* Not auspicious; ill-omened; unlucky. — **in′aus·pi′cious·ly**, *adv.* — **in′aus·pi′cious·ness**, *n.*

in′be′ing (ĭn′bē′ĭng), *n.* **1.** Inherence; immanence. **2.** Inner or inmost being; essence.

in′board′ (ĭn′bōrd′; 70), *adj. & adv.* **1.** *Naut.* Inside the line of a vessel's bulwarks or hull. Cf. OUTBOARD. **2.** *Mach.* From without inward; toward the inside.

in′born′ (-bôrn′; 2), *adj.* Born in or with one; natural; such by nature. — **Syn.** See INNATE.

in′bound′ (-bound′), *adj.* Inward bound.

in·breathe′ (ĭn·brēth′), *v. t.* **1.** To breathe (something) in; to inhale. **2.** To infuse by breathing; to inspire.

in′bred′ (ĭn′brĕd′; 2), *adj.* **1.** Bred within; innate. **2.** (*pron.* ĭn′brĕd′; 2) Subjected to or produced by inbreeding. — **Syn.** See INNATE.

in·breed′ (ĭn·brēd′), *v. t.*; IN·BRED′ (-brĕd′; *cf. the adj.*); IN·BREED′ING. **1.** To produce or generate within. **2.** To subject to inbreeding.

in′breed′ing (ĭn′brēd′ĭng), *n.* Breeding or mating of closely related individuals or stocks, to preserve or fix favorable or eliminate unfavorable characters. Cf. OUTBREEDING.

in′burst′ (-bûrst′), *n.* A bursting in or into; an irruption.

in′by′, in′bye′ (ĭn′bī′), *adv.* [*in-* in + *by.*] *Scot.* In an inward direction; within; near. — *adj.* *Scot.* Situated close by. — *prep.* *Scot.* Close to.

In′ca (ĭng′kȧ), *n.* [Sp., fr. Quechua *ynca* prince of the ruling family.] **1.** An Indian of a Quechuan tribe or group of tribes of the highlands of Peru, predominant in South America at the advent of the Spaniards. **2.** Specif., one of the ruling family; esp., the ruling chief. — **In′can** (-kăn), *n. & adj.*

in·cage′ (ĭn·kāj′). Var. of ENCAGE.

in·cal′cu·la·ble (ĭn·kăl′kū·lȧ·b'l), *adj.* Not capable of being calculated; very great; also, undeterminable; uncertain. — **in·cal′cu·la·bil′i·ty** (-bĭl′ĭ·tĭ), **in·cal′cu·la·ble·ness**, *n.* — **in·cal′cu·la·bly**, *adv.*

in′ca·les′cent (ĭn′kȧ·lĕs′ĕnt; -'nt), *adj.* [L. *incalescens*, *-entis*, pres. part. of *incalescere* to grow hot.] *Rare.* Growing warm. — **in′ca·les′cence** (-ĕns; -'ns), *n.*

‖**in ca′me·ra** (ĭn kăm′ē·rȧ). [L.] In a chamber; in private; specif., *Law*, in the chambers, or private office, of a judge.

in′can·desce′ (ĭn′kăn·dĕs′), *v. i. & t.*; -DESCED′ (-dĕst′); -DESC′ING (-dĕs′ĭng). [L. *incandescere.*] To be or become, or cause to become, incandescent.

in′can·des′cence (-ĕns; -'ns), *n.* Glowing due to heat; emission by a hot body of radiation that renders it visible.

in′can·des′cent (-ĕnt; -'nt), *adj.* [L. *incandescens*, *-entis*, pres. part. of *incandescere* to become hot, fr. *in-* in + *candescere* to become red-hot, incho. fr. *candere* to be of a glittering whiteness.] **1.** White, glowing, or luminous, with intense heat; hence, clear; shining; brilliant. **2.** Pertaining to or designating a lamp (**incandescent lamp**) whose light is produced by incandescence of some specially prepared material, as the filament of an electric bulb. — **in′can·des′cent·ly**, *adv.*

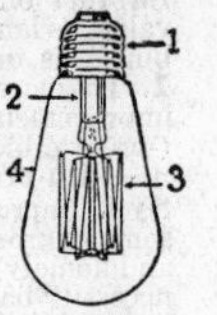

Incandescent Lamp. 1 Base; 2 Stem; 3 Filament; 4 Bulb.

in′can·ta′tion (ĭn′kăn·tā′shŭn), *n.* [F., fr. LL. *incantatio*, fr. *incantare* to chant a magic formula over one. See ENCHANT.] **1.** The use of spells or verbal charms, spoken or sung, as a part of the ritual of magic; also, the verbal formula chanted or recited. **2.** Loosely, magic; sorcery; enchantment.

in·ca′pa·ble (ĭn·kā′pȧ·b'l), *adj.* [F., fr. LL. *incapabilis.*] **1.** Not capable; lacking in capacity, ability, or qualification; incompetent; unqualified. **2.** *Archaic.* Not in a state to receive so as to be affected or moved by, or so as to be sensible; not receptive; not susceptible; — with *of*; as, *incapable* of pain. **3.** Not in a state or of a kind to admit; insusceptible; — now only with *of*; as, *incapable* of measurement. **4.** Not able or fit for the doing or performance (of some specified action). **5.** *Law.* Lacking legal qualification or power; disqualified; ineligible. — *n.* One who is incapable. — **in′ca·pa·bil′i·ty** (ĭn′kā·pȧ·bĭl′ĭ·tĭ), *n.* — **in·ca′pa·ble·ness**, *n.* — **in·ca′pa·bly**, *adv.*

in′ca·pa′cious (ĭn′kȧ·pā′shŭs), *adj.* [LL. *incapax.*] Not capacious; of insufficient capacity; specif., deficient mentally. — **in′ca·pa′cious·ness**, *n.*

in′ca·pac′i·tate (-păs′ĭ·tāt), *v. t.* To deprive of capacity or capability; disable; disqualify. — **in′ca·pac′i·ta′tion** (-tā′shŭn), *n.*

in′ca·pac′i·ty (-tĭ), *n.*; *pl.* -TIES (-tĭz). [F. *incapacité.*] Quality or state of being incapable; lack of physical or intellectual power, or of natural or legal qualification.

in·car′cer·ate (ĭn·kär′sēr·āt), *v. t.* [ML. *incarceratus*, past part. of *incarcerare* to imprison, fr. *in-* in + *carcer* prison.] To imprison; hence, to confine; hem in. — (-āt), *adj.* *Now Rare.* Imprisoned. — **in·car′cer·a′tion** (-ā′shŭn), *n.* — **in·car′cer·a′tor** (-ā′tēr), *n.*

in·car′di·nate (-kär′dĭ·nāt), *v. t.* [ML. *incardinare.*] **a** *R.C.Ch.* To accept canonically (a candidate for the priesthood) or to receive formally (a priest from another diocese) as a diocesan subject. **b** To make (one) a cardinal. — **in·car′di·na′tion** (-nā′shŭn), *n.*

in·car′na·dine (-kär′nȧ·dīn; -dĭn), *adj.* [F. *incarnadin*, fr. It. *incarnatino*, fr. *incarnato*. See INCARNATE.] **a** Of the color flesh. **b** By extension, red, esp. blood-red. — *n.* Incarnadine color. — *v. t.* To make incarnadine; to color pink, red, or crimson.

in·car′nate (-nāt), *adj.* [LL. *incarnatus*, past part. of *incarnare* to incarnate, fr. *in-* in + *caro*, *carnis*, flesh.] **1.** Invested with flesh or bodily nature and form; esp., embodied in human form; hence, personified. **2. a** Of the color flesh or flesh pink. **b** Red; rosy. — (-nāt), *v. t.* **1.** To make incarnate; to invest with flesh; embody. **2.** Hence: **a** To give a concrete or actual form to; realize; actualize. **b** To show itself as the embodiment of.

in′car·na′tion (ĭn′kär·nā′shŭn), *n.* **1.** An incarnating; a clothing, or state of being clothed, with flesh. **2.** [*usually cap.*] *Theol.* The union of Divinity with humanity in Christ. **3.** A person, animal, or other being, embodying a spirit or deity. **4.** Any concrete or actual form incorporating or exemplifying a principle, ideal, or the like; esp., a person showing a trait or typical character to a marked degree.

in·case′ (ĭn·kās′), *v. t.* [*in-* in + *case* a box.] To enclose in or as in a case. — **in·case′ment**, *n.*

in·cau′tion (ĭn·kô′shŭn), *n.* Lack of caution; heedlessness.

in·cau′tious (-shŭs), *adj.* Not cautious; heedless; rash. — **in·cau′tious·ly**, *adv.* — **in·cau′tious·ness**, *n.*

in·cen′di·a·rism (ĭn·sĕn′dĭ·ȧ·rĭz'm; 58), *n.* Incendiary action or practice. Cf. ARSON.

in·cen′di·ar′y (ĭn·sĕn′dĭ·ĕr′ĭ *or, esp. Brit.*, -ēr·ĭ), *adj.* [L. *incendiarius*, fr. *incendium* a fire. See INCENSE, *v.*] **1.** Of or pertaining to the malicious burning of property; as, *incendiary* material; an *incendiary* crime. **2.** Tending to excite or inflame factions, sedition, or quarrel; inflammatory; seditious. **3.** Pertaining to or designating missiles containing chemicals which ignite at a bursting of the shell. — *n.*; *pl.* -IES (-ĭz). **1.** One who maliciously or willfully sets fire to a building or other property. **2.** One who excites faction, quarrels, or sedition; an agitator. **3.** *Obs.* Anything that excites passion, strife, or evil-doing. **4.** An incendiary bomb or the like.

in·cense′ (ĭn·sĕns′), *v. t.* [OF. *incenser*, fr. L. *incensus*, past part. of *incendere* to burn, fr. *in-* + root of *candēre* to be of a glowing white.] To enkindle or excite, as a passion; now, specif., to inflame with anger; madden. — **in·cense′ment**, *n.*

in′cense (ĭn′sĕns), *n.* [OF. *encens*, fr. LL. *incensum*, fr. *incensus*, past part. of *incendere* to burn.] **1.** Material used to produce a perfume when burned. **2.** The perfume or the smoke exhaled from spices and gums when burned in celebrating religious rites; hence, any pleasing scent or fragrance. **3.** Pleasing attention; homage; flattery. — **Syn.** See FRAGRANCE. — *v. t.* **1.** To burn incense before. **2.** To perfume as if with incense. — *v. i.* To burn or offer incense.

in·cen′tive (ĭn·sĕn′tĭv), *adj.* [L. *incentivus*, fr. *incinere* to strike up or set the tune, fr. *in-* + *canere* to sing.] **1.** Inciting; stimulative. **2.** *Obs.* Kindling. — *n.* [L. *incentivum.*] That which incites, or tends to incite, to determination or action; motive; spur. — **Syn.** See MOTIVE.

in·cept′ (ĭn·sĕpt′), *v. t.* [L. *inceptare* to undertake, begin, v. freq. of *incipere* to begin.] **1.** To begin; commence; undertake. **2.** To take in; to intussuscept. — *v. i.* **1.** To complete the taking of the degree of master or doctor; — now used only at Cambridge University, England. **2.** Hence, to enter upon a career of any sort. — **in·cep′tion** (-sĕp′shŭn), *n.* — **Syn.** See ORIGIN. — **in·cep′tor** (-tēr), *n.*

in·cep′tive (-sĕp′tĭv), *adj.* **1.** Beginning, or relating to a beginning. **2.** *Gram.* Denoting the beginning of an action, state, or occurrence; — said of a verb or verb form. — *n.* An inceptive word, phrase, etc.

in·cer′ti·tude (-sûr′tĭ·tūd), *n.* [F., fr. ML. *incertitudo*, fr. L. *incertus* uncertain.] Uncertainty of mind; doubtfulness; indecision; hence, insecurity.

in·ces′sant (-sĕs′ănt; -'nt), *adj.* [F., fr. LL. *incessans*, *-antis*, fr. *in-* not + *cessare* to cease.] Continuing or following without interruption; unceasing. — **Syn.** See CONTINUAL. — **in·ces′san·cy** (-ăn·sĭ), *n.* — **in·ces′sant·ly**, *adv.*

in′cest (ĭn′sĕst), *n.* [L. *incestus*, *incestum*, unchastity, incest, fr. *incestus* unchaste, fr. *in-* not + *castus* chaste.] **1.** The crime of cohabitation between persons related within the degrees wherein marriage is prohibited by law. **2.** *Eccl.* = SPIRITUAL INCEST.

in·ces'tu·ous (ĭn·sĕs'tū·ŭs), *adj.* Guilty of incest; also, involving, or pertaining to, incest. — **in·ces'tu·ous·ly**, *adv.*
inch (ĭnch), *n.* [AS. *ynce*, fr. L. *uncia* the twelfth part, inch, ounce.] **1.** A measure of length. See MEASURE, *Tables* 1 & 2. Abbr. *in.*, pl. *in.* or *ins.* Symbol ″. **2.** Hence: **a** Of rain, snow, etc.: A fall sufficient to cover the surface or to fill a gauge to the depth of one inch; as, two *inches* of rain. **b** A degree of pressure sufficient to balance the weight of a liquid column one inch high in a barometer or manometer (when the liquid is not named mercury is understood); as, an atmospheric pressure of 30 *inches*. **c** Short for WATER-INCH. **3.** A small distance or degree; hence, a critical moment. — *v. t.* To drive or move by inches or small degrees. — *v. i.* To advance or retire by small degrees.
inch, *n.* [Gael. *innis*.] *Scot. & Ir.* An island.
inch'meal' (-mēl'), *adv.* Also **by inchmeal.** Little by little; gradually.
in·cho'ate (ĭn·kō'ĭt; ĭn'kō·āt), *adj.* [L. *inchoatus*, better *incohatus*, past part. of *incohare* to begin.] Recently or just begun; being in the first stages; rudimentary. — **in·cho'ate·ly**, *adv.* — **in·cho'ate·ness**, *n.* — **in'cho·a'tion** (ĭn'kō·ā'shŭn), *n.*
in·cho'a·tive (ĭn·kō'ȧ·tĭv; ĭn'kō·ā'tĭv), *adj.* **1.** *Rare.* Inchoate. **2.** Inceptive; — esp. of a verb. — *n.* An inceptive verb.
inch'worm' (ĭnch'wûrm'), *n.* A measuring worm. Cf. GEOMETRID.
in'ci·dence (ĭn'sĭ·dĕns), *n.* **1.** Act, fact, or manner of falling upon or affecting; also, range of occurrence or influence. **2.** *Physics.* The falling of a projectile, ray of light, etc., on a surface; specif., usually ***angle of incidence***, the angle formed by the line of a falling projectile, ray, etc., and a perpendicular arising from the point of incidence. See REFRACTION, *Illust.* **3.** *Geom.* Partial coincidence or community of elements between two figures, as of a point and a line containing it.
in'ci·dent (-dĕnt), *adj.* [F. and L.; F., fr. L. *incidens*, *-entis*, pres. part. of *incidere* to fall into or upon, fr. *in-* in, on + *cadere* to fall.] **1.** Liable to happen; apt to occur; hence, naturally happening or appertaining, esp. as a subordinate or subsidiary feature. **2.** *Now Rare.* Incidental; fortuitous. **3.** Falling or striking, as a ray of light on a surface. **4.** *Law.* Dependent on, or appertaining to, another thing (the *principal*); directly and immediately pertaining to, or involved in, something else, though not an essential part of it. — **Syn.** See LIABLE. — *n.* **1.** That which happens or takes place; an event; occurrence. **2.** A subordinate action or event; an accidental occurrence; hence, a slight matter. **3.** *Law.* Something that is incident to another. — **Syn.** See OCCURRENCE.
in'ci·den'tal (ĭn'sĭ·dĕn'tăl; -t'l), *adj.* **1.** Happening as a chance or undesigned feature of something; casual; hence, minor; of secondary importance; as, an *incidental* expense. **2.** Liable to happen or to follow as a chance feature or incident; as, trials *incidental* to married life. — **Syn.** See ACCIDENTAL. — *n.* **1.** That which is incidental; esp., *pl.*, subordinate items not particularized. **2.** *Music.* A tone, as a grace note, foreign to a chord. — **in'ci·den'tal·ly**, *adv.*
in·cin'er·ate (ĭn·sĭn'ẽr·āt), *v. t. & i.* [ML. *incineratus*, past part. of *incinerare* to incinerate, fr. *in-* in + *cinis*, *cineris*, ashes.] To burn to ashes; to consume, or be consumed, by fire; cremate. — **in·cin'er·a'tion** (-ā'shŭn), *n.*
in·cin'er·a'tor (-ā'tẽr), *n.* One who or that which incinerates; esp., a furnace for incinerating substances.
in·cip'i·ence (ĭn·sĭp'ĭ·ĕns), *n.* Also **in·cip'i·en·cy** (-ĕn·sĭ). The fact of being incipient; beginning; commencement.
in·cip'i·ent (ĭn·sĭp'ĭ·ĕnt), *adj.* [L. *incipiens*, pres. part. of *incipere* to begin.] Beginning to be, or to show itself; commencing; initial. — **in·cip'i·ent·ly**, *adv.*
‖**in'ci·pit** (ĭn'sĭ·pĭt). [L.] Literally, here begins; — used by medieval scribes at the beginning of a manuscript.
in·cise' (ĭn·sīz'), *v. t.* [F. *inciser*, fr. OF. *enciser*, fr. L. *incisus*, past part. of *incidere* to incise, fr. *in-* in + *caedere* to cut.] To cut into with a sharp instrument; to depict or inscribe by carving or engraving.
in·cised' (-sīzd'), *adj.* **1.** Cut in; engraved. **2.** Having the margin deeply and sharply notched. See LEAF, *Illust.*
in·ci'sion (-sĭzh'ŭn), *n.* **1.** An incising. **2.** A cut; gash; also, a marginal notch. **3.** Acuteness of understanding or expression; incisiveness.
in·ci'sive (-sī'sĭv), *adj.* Cutting; penetrating; hence, acute; clear-cut; trenchant; also, biting. — **in·ci'sive·ly**, *adv.* — **in·ci'sive·ness**, *n.*
Syn. **Incisive, trenchant, clear-cut, cutting, biting, crisp** mean having or showing sharpness, keenness, or acuteness, esp. of mind. **Incisive** specifically implies a power to penetrate the senses, the mind, etc.; **trenchant**, literally applied to a weapon with an extremely sharp edge or point, implies a power of cutting so sharply and clearly as to reveal distinctions, classes, and the like, or of probing deeply into the nature of the thing considered; **clear-cut** suggests the absence of all soft edges, blurring, or the like, in the things presented, described, or defined, so that each stands out in sharp clearness; **cutting** is often used in place of *incisive* when sarcasm or penetrating truthfulness is to be implied; **biting** suggests a power to grip and deeply impress itself on the mind or memory, as acid bites into an etcher's plate; **crisp** suggests not only incisiveness but a vigorous terseness.
in·ci'sor (-sī'zẽr), *n.* [NL.] *Zool.* A tooth adapted for cutting; specif., in mammals, any of the cutting teeth in front of the canines in either jaw. See TOOTH, RODENT, *Illusts.*
in·ci'so·ry (-sī'sō·rĭ), *adj.* Adapted for cutting.
in'ci·ta'tion (ĭn'sī·tā'shŭn; ĭn'sĭ-), *n.* An inciting; stimulation; also, an incitement; incentive.
in·cite' (ĭn·sīt'), *v. t.* [F. *inciter*, fr. L. *incitare*, fr. *in-* in + *citare* to rouse, stir up.] To arouse to action; spur or urge on. — **in·cite'ment**, *n.* — **in·cit'er** (-sīt'ẽr), *n.*
Syn. **Incite, instigate, abet, foment** mean to excite to action. **Incite** stresses stirring up and urging on: though *incite* often also suggests prompting, **instigate** invariably does and further connotes underhandedness or an evil intention; **abet** now implies a seconding or supporting but it definitely also suggests an encouraging; **foment** implies persistence in goading and does not necessarily carry any implication of instigation.
in'ci·vil'i·ty (ĭn'sĭ·vĭl'ĭ·tĭ), *n.*; *pl.* -TIES (-tĭz). **1.** Quality or state of being uncivil; rudeness; discourtesy. **2.** A rude or discourteous act.
in'ci·vism (ĭn'sĭ·vĭz'm), *n.* Lack of civism or of patriotism.
in·clasp' (ĭn·klȧsp'). Var. of ENCLASP.
in·clem'ent (ĭn·klĕm'ĕnt), *adj.* [L. *inclemens*, fr. *in-* not + *clemens* mild.] Not clement; harsh; severe; of weather, stormy; of temper, acts, etc., unmerciful. — **in·clem'en·cy** (-ĕn·sĭ), *n.* — **in·clem'ent·ly**, *adv.*
in·clin'a·ble (ĭn·klīn'ȧ·b'l), *adj.* Having a propensity or inclination; hence, favorably disposed.
in'cli·na'tion (ĭn'klĭ·nā'shŭn), *n.* [F., fr. L. *inclinatio*.] **1.** A particular disposition; propensity; bent; bias. **2.** A tendency; trend. **3.** An act or practice to which one is inclined. **4.** An inclining, bending, or bowing; esp., a bow; nod. **5.** A deviation from the true vertical or horizontal; a slant; also, the amount or degree of such deviation. **6.** An inclined surface; a slope. **7.** *Geom.* The angle determined by two lines or planes; as, the *inclination* of two rays of light.
in·cli'na·to'ry (ĭn·klī'nȧ·tō'rĭ *or, esp. Brit.*, -tẽr·ĭ), *adj.* Leaning or inclining.
in·cline' (ĭn·klīn'), *v. i.* [OF. *encliner*, *incliner*, fr. L. *inclinare*, fr. *in-* in + *clinare* to bend, incline.] **1.** To bow; to incline the head or body forward. **2.** To lean or tend, as to an opinion or a person; be favorably disposed. **3.** To deviate from a line, direction, or course; to slope; slant. — *v. t.* **1.** To cause to incline, bend, slant, etc. **2.** To turn; dispose; influence. — **in·clin'er** (-klīn'ẽr), *n.* — ***incline one's ear.*** To listen favorably.
Syn. **Incline, bias, dispose, predispose** mean to influence one to take or to have an attitude toward a thing. **Incline** implies a tendency to favor one of two or more conclusions, projects, or the like; **bias**, a stronger and more settled leaning, usually connoting a prejudice for or against; **dispose**, an affecting of one's disposition, mood, or temper so that one inclines to a certain thing; **predispose**, a disposing in advance of the opportunity to reveal itself in action.
in'cline (ĭn'klīn; ĭn·klīn'), *n.* An inclined plane; an ascent or descent; a slope.
in·clined' (ĭn·klīnd'), *adj.* **1.** Having inclination; disposed, esp. favorably. **2.** Sloping; leaning. **3.** *Math.* Making an angle with some line or plane.
inclined plane. *Mech.* A plane surface that makes an oblique angle with the plane of the horizon; a sloping plane. When used as one element of a machine, the machine is classed as a *simple machine* (which see).
in·clin'ing (ĭn·klīn'ĭng), *n.* **a** Inclination; disposition. **b** *Archaic.* Party or following.
in'cli·nom'e·ter (ĭn'klĭ·nŏm'ē·tẽr), *n.* [*incline* + *meter*.] **1.** *Magnetism.* An apparatus to determine the direction of the earth's magnetic force with relation to the plane of the horizon; a dip needle with its accessories. **2.** A machinist's clinometer. See CLINOMETER. **3.** An instrument or device for indicating the inclination to the horizontal of an axis of an aircraft.
in·close' (ĭn·klōz'), *v. t.* [See ENCLOSE.] To enclose. In legal use in the United States, *inclose* is preferred in speaking of land. — **in·clos'er** (ĭn·klōz'ẽr), *n.*
in·clo'sure (ĭn·klō'zhẽr), *n.* Enclosure.
in·clude' (ĭn·klōōd'; 114), *v. t.* [L. *includere*, *inclusum*, fr. *in-* in + *claudere* to shut.] **1.** To confine; shut up; enclose. **2.** To comprehend or comprise, as the whole comprises a part; contain; embrace. — **in·clud'a·ble** (-klōōd'ȧ·b'l), **in·clud'i·ble** (-ĭ·b'l), *adj.*
Syn. **Include, comprehend, embrace, involve, imply** mean to contain something within itself as part of the whole. **Include** suggests that it forms a constituent, component, or subordinate part (as, the exhibit *includes* every work of this artist); **comprehend**, that it comes within the range or scope of a statement, a definition, or the like, whether clearly mentioned or not (as, the term "dog" *comprehends* every known variety); **embrace**, that it is gathered within a whole, such as a view, a course, an interpretation as of a law, etc. (as, from that high point, the scene *embraced* hills, valleys, and distant mountains); **involve**, that it is rolled up in a whole, as by being its consequence or an element of its definition (as, surrender *involves* submission); **imply**, that it is involved because it can be inferred through a hint or as a necessary cause or effect (as, gaudy *implies* gay colors and lavish display; a watch *implies* a watchmaker). — **Ant.** Exclude.
in·clud'ed (-klōōd'ĕd; -ĭd), *adj.* **1.** Enclosed; embraced. **2.** *Bot.* Not projecting beyond the mouth of the corolla; said of stamens and pistils; — opposed to *exserted*.
in·clu'sion (-klōō'zhŭn), *n.* **1.** Act of including, or state of being included. **2.** That which, or anything that, is included; specif.: **a** A foreign body, gaseous, liquid, or solid, enclosed in the mass of a mineral. **b** *Biol.* A passive product, as of cell activity, as a starch grain.
inclusion body. A characteristic stainable particle in the nucleus or cytoplasm in tissues infected with a filtrable virus, as in smallpox and rabies.
in·clu'sive (ĭn·klōō'sĭv), *adj.* **1.** Including or tending to include. **2.** Comprehending the stated limit or extremes; as, from Monday to Friday *inclusive*. Abbr. *incl.* — **in·clu'sive·ly**, *adv.* — **in·clu'sive·ness**, *n.*
in'co·er'ci·ble (ĭn'kō·ûr'sĭ·b'l), *adj.* **1.** Not coercible. **2.** *Physics.* Not capable of reduction to a liquid by pressure.
in·cog' (ĭn·kŏg'), *adj.*, *adv.*, & *n.* *Colloq.* Incognito.
in·cog'i·ta·ble (ĭn·kŏj'ĭ·tȧ·b'l), *adj.* [L. *incogitabilis*, fr. *in-* not + *cogitabilis* cogitable.] Not cogitable; inconceivable.
in·cog'i·tant (-tănt), *adj.* Thoughtless; inconsiderate.
in·cog'ni·ta (ĭn·kŏg'nĭ·tȧ; ĭn'kŏg·nē'tȧ), *adj.* & *n.* Fem. of INCOGNITO.
in·cog'ni·to (-tō), *adj.* & *adv.* [It. *incognito*, masc., *incognita*, fem., fr. L. *incognitus* unknown, fr. *in-* not + *cognitus* known, past part. of *cognoscere*.] With (one's) identity concealed; esp., in a capacity other than one's official capacity, or under a name or title not calling for special recognition. — *n.*; *pl.* -TOS (-tōz). One appearing incognito; also, the state or disguise or name of such a one.
in·cog'ni·zant (ĭn·kŏg'nĭ·zănt; ĭn·kŏn'ĭ-), *adj.* Not cognizant; unaware; — with *of*.
in'co·her'ence (ĭn'kō·hēr'ĕns), *n.*; *pl.* -ENCES (-ĕn·sĕz; -sĭz). **1.** The state or fact of being incoherent. **2.** That which is incoherent.
in'co·her'en·cy (-ĕn·sĭ), *n.*; *pl.* -ENCIES (-sĭz). Incoherence.
in'co·her'ent (-ĕnt), *adj.* Not coherent; as: **a** Lacking cohesion; loose; disconnected. **b** Lacking agreement or co-ordination; incongruous; inconsistent. — **in'co·her'ent·ly**, *adv.*
in'com·bus'ti·ble (ĭn'kŏm·bŭs'tĭ·b'l), *adj.* Not combustible; not inflammable. — *n.* An incombustible substance. — **in'com·bus'ti·bil'i·ty** (-bĭl'ĭ·tĭ), **in'com·bus'ti·ble·ness**, *n.* — **in'com·bus'ti·bly**, *adv.*
in'come (ĭn'kŭm), *n.* **1.** A coming in; specif., beginning; advent. **2.** Something that comes in as addition. **3.** That gain or recurrent

benefit (usually measured in money) which proceeds from labor, business, or property; revenue; receipts.

income account. In corporation finance, the account that records the amounts, sources, and expenditure of income. Cf. CAPITAL ACCOUNT.

in'com'er (ĭn'kŭm'ēr), *n.* One that comes in.

income tax. A tax on a person's incomes, emoluments, profits, etc., or on the excess over a certain amount.

in'com'ing (ĭn'kŭm'ĭng), *adj.* Coming in; accruing, as profit; taking possession, as a tenant; beginning, as a year. — *n.* **1.** A coming in. **2.** That which comes in; an income.

in'com·men'su·ra·ble (ĭn'kŏ·mĕn'shŏŏ·rȧ·b'l), *adj.* **1.** Not commensurable; having no common measure, as quantities when no third quantity can be found that is an aliquot part of each. **2.** Having no common basis of comparison as to value, size, etc. — *n.* **a** That which is incommensurable. **b** One of two or more quantities having no common measure. — **in'com·men'su·ra·bil'i·ty** (-bĭl'ĭ·tĭ), **in'com·men'su·ra·ble·ness**, *n.* — **in'com·men'su·ra·bly**, *adv.*

in'com·men'su·rate (-rĭt), *adj.* Not commensurate; specif.: **a** Incommensurable. **b** Inadequate; disproportionate. — **in'com·men'su·rate·ly**, *adv.* — **in'com·men'su·rate·ness**, *n.*

in'com·mode' (ĭn'kŏ·mōd'), *v. t.* [F. *incommoder*, fr. L. *incommodare*, fr. *incommodus* inconvenient, fr. *in-* not + *commodus* convenient.] To give inconvenience or trouble to; put out; discommode; inconvenience.

in'com·mo'di·ous (-mō'dĭ·ŭs), *adj.* Not commodious; not affording ease or advantage; inconvenient. — **in'com·mo'di·ous·ly**, *adv.* — **in'com·mo'di·ous·ness**, *n.*

in'com·mod'i·ty (-mŏd'ĭ·tĭ), *n.* Inconvenience; trouble; annoyance; disadvantage.

in'com·mu'ni·ca·ble (-mū'nĭ·kȧ·b'l), *adj.* Not communicable; incapable of being communicated, told, or imparted. — **in'com·mu'ni·ca·bil'i·ty** (-bĭl'ĭ·tĭ), **in'com·mu'ni·ca·ble·ness**, *n.* — **in'com·mu'ni·ca·bly**, *adv.*

in'com·mu'ni·ca'do (ĭn'kŏ·mū'nĭ·kä'dō), *adj.* [Sp. *incomunicado.*] Without means of communication; also, in solitary confinement.

in'com·mu'ni·ca'tive (-mū'nĭ·kā'tĭv; -kȧ·tĭv), *adj.* Not communicative; reserved; exclusive. — **in·com·mu'ni·ca'tive·ness**, *n.*

in'com·mut'a·ble (-mūt'ȧ·b'l), *adj.* Not commutable; as: **a** Unchangeable. **b** Unexchangeable. — **in'com·mut'a·bil'i·ty** (-bĭl'ĭ·tĭ), **in'com·mut'a·ble·ness**, *n.* — **in'com·mut'a·bly**, *adv.*

in'com·pact' (ĭn'kŏm·păkt'), *adj.* Not compact; not solid; loose; discrete. — **in'com·pact'ly**, *adv.* — **in'com·pact'ness**, *n.*

in·com'pa·ra·ble (ĭn·kŏm'pȧ·rȧ·b'l), *adj.* **1.** Beyond comparison. without a peer or equal; matchless. **2.** Incommensurable; not suitable for comparison; — followed by *with* or *to.* — **in·com'pa·ra·bil'i·ty** (-bĭl'ĭ·tĭ), **in·com'pa·ra·ble·ness**, *n.* — **in·com'pa·ra·bly**, *adv.*

in'com·pat'i·ble (ĭn'kŏm·păt'ĭ·b'l), *adj.* **1.** Of offices, dignities, etc., incapable of being held at the same time by the same person. **2.** Not compatible; incapable of association because contradictory, incongruous, discordant, or the like; irreconcilable. **3.** *Pharm. & Med.* Incapable of being put or used together because of undesirable chemical or physiological effects; — said of drugs or the like, and of different blood types. — *n.* One that is incompatible; esp., *pl.:* **a** Incompatible drugs. **b** *Logic.* Incompatible propositions. — **in'com·pat'i·bil'i·ty** (-bĭl'ĭ·tĭ), **in'com·pat'i·ble·ness**, *n.* — **in'com·pat'i·bly**, *adv.*

in·com'pe·tence (ĭn·kŏm'pē·tĕns), *n.* Also **in·com'pe·ten·cy** (-tĕn·sĭ). Quality, state or fact of being incompetent; inadequacy; specif., lack of legal qualification or fitness.

in·com'pe·tent (-tĕnt), *adj.* [F. *incompétent*, fr. LL. *incompetens.*] Not competent; wanting in adequate strength, capacity, qualifications, or the like; specif., not having the necessary legal qualifications. — *n.* One who is incompetent, as one incapable of managing his affairs because mentally deficient or undeveloped. — **in·com'pe·tent·ly**, *adv.*

in'com·plete' (ĭn'kŏm·plēt'), *adj.* [LL. *incompletus.*] **1.** Not complete; not finished; not having all its parts; imperfect; defective. **2.** *Bot.* Of a flower, lacking one or more floral whorls; — opposed to *complete.* — **in'com·plete'ly**, *adv.* — **in'com·plete'ness**, *n.* — **in'com·ple'tion** (-plē'shŭn), *n.*

in'com·pli'ant (-plī'ănt), *adj.* Not compliant; unyielding; of substances, not pliant. — **in'com·pli'ance** (-ăns), **in'com·pli'an·cy** (-ăn·sĭ), *n.* — **in'com·pli'ant·ly**, *adv.*

in'com·pre·hen'si·ble (ĭn'kŏm·prē·hĕn'sĭ·b'l), *adj.* **1.** *Archaic.* That no limits can contain; illimitable. **2.** Not capable of being comprehended; unintelligible. — **in'com·pre·hen'si·bil'i·ty** (-bĭl'ĭ·tĭ), **in'com·pre·hen'si·ble·ness**, *n.* — **in'com·pre·hen'si·bly**, *adv.*

in'com·pre·hen'sive (-sĭv), *adj.* Not comprehensive.

in'com·press'i·ble (ĭn'kŏm·prĕs'ĭ·b'l), *adj.* Not compressible; resisting, or incapable of, compression. — **in'com·press'i·bil'i·ty** (-bĭl'ĭ·tĭ), *n.*

in'com·put'a·ble (-pūt'ȧ·b'l), *adj.* Not computable.

in'con·ceiv'a·ble (ĭn'kŏn·sēv'ȧ·b'l), *adj.* Not conceivable; incapable of being conceived, imagined, or believed; unthinkable, unimaginable, or incredible. — **in'con·ceiv'a·bil'i·ty** (-bĭl'ĭ·tĭ), **in'con·ceiv'a·ble·ness**, *n.* — **in'con·ceiv'a·bly**, *adv.*

in'con·clu'sive (-klōō'sĭv), *adj.* Not conclusive; leading to no conclusion; not leading to a definite result. — **in'con·clu'sive·ly**, *adv.* — **in'con·clu'sive·ness**, *n.*

in'con·den'sa·ble (-dĕn'sȧ·b'l), *adj.* Also **in'con·den'si·ble** (-sĭ·b'l). Not condensable; incapable of being condensed. — **in'con·den'sa·bil'i·ty, in'con·den'si·bil'i·ty** (-bĭl'ĭ·tĭ), *n.*

in·con'dite (ĭn·kŏn'dĭt), *adj.* [L. *inconditus*, fr. *in-* not + *conditus*, past part. of *condere* to put or join together.] Badly put together; unformed; crude.

in'con·form'i·ty (ĭn'kŏn·fôr'mĭ·tĭ), *n.* Lack of conformity.

in·con'gru·ent (ĭn·kŏng'grōō·ĕnt), *adj.* Incongruous; not congruent; unsuitable. — **in·con'gru·ence** (-ĕns), *n.* — **in·con'gru·ent·ly**, *adv.*

in'con·gru'i·ty (ĭn'kŏng·grōō'ĭ·tĭ), *n.; pl.* -TIES (-tĭz). **1.** Quality or state of being incongruous; unsuitableness; inconsistency; disagreement. **2.** That which is incongruous.

in·con'gru·ous (ĭn·kŏng'grōō·ŭs), *adj.* [L. *incongruus.*] Not congruous or congruent; specif.: **a** Incompatible; as, *incongruous* beliefs. **b** Not conforming (*to*); being at variance (*with*); as, conduct *incongruous* with one's ethics. **c** Lacking propriety or suitability. **d** Having inconsistent or inharmonious parts, qualities, etc.; as, an *incongruous* story. — **in·con'gru·ous·ly**, *adv.* — **in·con'gru·ous·ness**, *n.*

in'con·sec'u·tive (ĭn'kŏn·sĕk'ū·tĭv), *adj.* Not consecutive.

in·con'se·quent (ĭn·kŏn'sē·kwĕnt *or, esp. Brit.*, -kwĕnt), *adj.* [L. *inconsequens.* See IN- not; CONSEQUENT.] **1.** Not following from the premises; illogical; inconsistent. **2.** Not in sequence; inconsecutive. **3.** Characterized by want of logic or relevancy; irrelevant. — **in·con'se·quence** (-kwĕns; -kwĕns), *n.* — **in·con'se·quent·ly**, *adv.*

in·con'se·quen'tial (-kwĕn'shăl), *adj.* **1.** Inconsequent; irrelevant. **2.** Unimportant; of no consequence. — **in·con'se·quen'ti·al'i·ty** (-kwĕn'shĭ·ăl'ĭ·tĭ), *n.* — **in·con'se·quen'tial·ly**, *adv.*

in'con·sid'er·a·ble (ĭn'kŏn·sĭd'ēr·ȧ·b'l), *adj.* Not considerable; slight; trivial. — **in'con·sid'er·a·bly**, *adv.*

in'con·sid'er·ate (-ĭt), *adj.* **1.** Not adequately considered; ill-advised. **2.** Not considerate; not regarding the rights or feelings of others; thoughtless. — **in'con·sid'er·ate·ly**, *adv.* — **in'con·sid'er·ate·ness**, *n.* — **in'con·sid'er·a'tion** (-ā'shŭn), *n.*

in'con·sist'ence (ĭn'kŏn·sĭs'tĕns), *n.* Inconsistency.

in'con·sist'en·cy (-tĕn·sĭ), *n.; pl.* -CIES (-sĭz). Quality, state, or an instance of being inconsistent.

in'con·sist'ent (-tĕnt), *adj.* Not consistent; incompatible; incongruous; inharmonious; specif.: **a** Of propositions, ideas, beliefs, etc., so related that both (or all) cannot be true. **b** Of persons, incoherent or illogical in thought or actions; hence, inconstant; fickle. **c** In respect to character, sentiment, etc., incongruous; incompatible; irreconcilable. — **in'con·sist'ent·ly**, *adv.*

in'con·sol'a·ble (ĭn'kŏn·sōl'ȧ·b'l), *adj.* Not consolable; disconsolate. — **in'con·sol'a·bil'i·ty** (-bĭl'ĭ·tĭ), **in'con·sol'a·ble·ness**, *n.* — **in'con·sol'a·bly**, *adv.*

in·con'so·nant (ĭn·kŏn'sō·nănt), *adj.* Not consonant; discordant. — **in·con'so·nance** (-năns), *n.* — **in·con'so·nant·ly**, *adv.*

in'con·spic'u·ous (ĭn'kŏn·spĭk'ū·ŭs), *adj.* Not conspicuous; hardly discernible; not prominent or striking. — **in'con·spic'u·ous·ly**, *adv.* — **in'con·spic'u·ous·ness**, *n.*

in·con'stant (ĭn·kŏn'stănt), *adj.* Not constant; not stable or uniform; changeable; fickle. — **in·con'stan·cy** (-stăn·sĭ), *n.* — **in·con'stant·ly**, *adv.*

Syn. Inconstant, fickle, capricious, mercurial, unstable mean lacking in steadiness, esp. in purpose or attachment. Inconstant implies an incapacity for fixity or steadiness and an inherent tendency to change; fickle, an unreliability that shows itself in an incapacity for being true or steadfast or certain, esp. in affections; capricious, variableness that suggests guidance by whim, mood, or freak; mercurial, a pleasing but baffling variability and volatility; unstable, a constitutional incapacity for remaining in a fixed position or state mentally or emotionally as well as physically.

in'con·sum'a·ble (ĭn'kŏn·sūm'ȧ·b'l), *adj.* Not consumable; incapable of being consumed, wasted, or spent.

in'con·test'a·ble (-tĕs'tȧ·b'l), *adj.* Not contestable; not to be disputed or controverted; indisputable; incontrovertible; unquestionable. — **in'con·test'a·bil'i·ty** (-bĭl'ĭ·tĭ), *n.* — **in'con·test'a·bly**, *adv.*

in·con'ti·nent (ĭn·kŏn'tĭ·nĕnt), *adj.* [OF., or fr. L. *incontinens.* See IN- not; CONTINENT.] **1.** Not continent; esp., not restraining the passions or appetites, particularly the sexual appetite; also, unable to contain, keep, or restrain; as, *incontinent* of secrets. **2.** *Med.* Unable to restrain natural evacuations. — **in·con'ti·nence** (-nĕns), *n.* — **in·con'ti·nent·ly**, *adv.*

in·con'ti·nent, *adv.* Also **in·con'ti·nent·ly**. [F. *incontinent*, fr. L. *in continenti* (sc. *tempore*), lit., in continuous time.] *Archaic.* At once; immediately.

in'con·tin'u·ous (ĭn'kŏn·tĭn'ū·ŭs), *adj.* Not continuous.

in'con·trol'la·ble (ĭn'kŏn·trōl'ȧ·b'l), *adj.* Uncontrollable.

in'con·tro·vert'i·ble (ĭn'kŏn·trŏ·vûr'tĭ·b'l), *adj.* Not controvertible; indisputable. — **in'con·tro·vert'i·bil'i·ty** (-bĭl'ĭ·tĭ), **in'con·tro·vert'i·ble·ness**, *n.* — **in'con·tro·vert'i·bly**, *adv.*

in'con·ven'ience (ĭn'kŏn·vēn'yĕns), *n.* **1.** Quality or condition of being inconvenient; discomfort; incommodiousness. **2.** That which is inconvenient; esp., that which gives trouble, embarrassment, or uneasiness. — *v. t.;* -IENCED (-yĕnst); -IENC·ING (-yĕn·sĭng). To put to inconvenience; to incommode.

in'con·ven'ien·cy (-yĕn·sĭ), *n.* Inconvenience.

in'con·ven'ient (-yĕnt), *adj.* [OF., fr. L. *inconveniens.*] **1.** *Obs.* Not suitable; inexpedient. **2.** Not convenient; giving trouble, annoyance, or delay; inopportune; incommodious. — **in'con·ven'ient·ly**, *adv.*

in'con·vert'i·ble (ĭn'kŏn·vûr'tĭ·b'l), *adj.* Not convertible; of paper money, not exchangeable on demand for specie. — **in'con·vert'i·bil'i·ty** (-bĭl'ĭ·tĭ), **in'con·vert'i·ble·ness**, *n.*

in'con·vin'ci·ble (-vĭn'sĭ·b'l), *adj. & n.* (One) incapable of being convinced. — **in'con·vin'ci·bil'i·ty** (-bĭl'ĭ·tĭ), *n.* — **in'con·vin'ci·bly**, *adv.*

in'—co—or'di·nate (ĭn'kō·ôr'dĭ·nāt), *adj.* Not co-ordinate.

in'—co—or'di·na'tion (-nā'shŭn), *n.* Lack of co-ordination.

in·cor'po·ra·ble (ĭn·kôr'pō·rȧ·b'l), *adj.* Capable of being incorporated.

in·cor'po·rate (-rāt), *adj.* [L. *incorporatus.* See IN- not; CORPORATE.] Incorporeal; spiritual.

in·cor'po·rate, *adj.* [L. *incorporatus*, past part. of *incorporare* to incorporate, fr. *in-* in + *corporare* to make into a body. See CORPORATE.] **1.** Made one in body; intimately united or blended. **2.** Formed into or associated as part of a corporation; incorporated. — (-rāt), *v. t.* **1.** To unite or introduce (*with, in, into* a body or mass already formed); as, to *incorporate* new laws in a constitution. **2.** To unite intimately; to blend or combine so as to form one body, organization, etc.; as, the thirteen colonies were *incorporated.* **3.** To admit as member of a corporation. **4.** To form into a legal corporation. See CORPORATION, 2. **5.** To give a material form to; to embody. — (-rāt), *v. i.* **1.** To unite in or as one body. **2.** To constitute or to become a corporation. — **in·cor'po·ra'tion** (-rā'shŭn), *n.* — **in·cor'po·ra'tive** (-rā'tĭv; -rȧ·tĭv), *adj.* — **in·cor'po·ra'tor** (-rā'tēr), *n.*

in·cor'po·rat'ed (-rāt'ĕd; -ĭd), *adj.* United in one body; esp., forming a legal corporation. Abbr. *inc.*

in'cor·po're·al (ĭn'kôr·pō'rē·ăl), *adj.* **1.** Not corporeal; immaterial; sometimes, of spirits, angelic. **2.** *Law.* Existing only in contemplation of law; not having physical existence, but existing as an immaterial right. — **in'cor·po're·al·ly**, *adv.*

in·cor'po·re'i·ty (ĭn·kôr'pō·rē'ĭ·tĭ), *n.; pl.* -TIES (-tĭz). Quality or state of being incorporeal; immateriality; also, an incorporeal attribute or entity.

in'cor·rect' (ĭn'kŏ·rĕkt'), *adj.* **1.** Not correct; faulty. **2.** Unbecoming; improper. **3.** Untrue; inaccurate. — **in'cor·rect'ly**, *adv.* — **in'cor·rect'ness**, *n.*

in·cor′ri·gi·ble (ĭn·kŏr′ĭ·jĭ·b'l), *adj.* **1.** Not corrigible; incapable of being corrected or amended; not reformable. **2.** Unmanageable; unruly; delinquent. — *n.* One who is incorrigible. — **in·cor′ri·gi·bil′i·ty** (-bĭl′ĭ·tĭ), **in·cor′ri·gi·ble·ness**, *n.* — **in·cor′ri·gi·bly**, *adv.*

in′cor·rupt′ (ĭn′kŏ·rŭpt′), *adj.* Not corrupt; sound; pure; untainted; also, incorruptible. — **in′cor·rupt′ly**, *adv.* — **in′cor·rupt′ness**, *n.*

in′cor·rupt′i·ble (ĭn′kŏ·rŭp′tĭ·b'l), *adj.* Not corruptible; incapable of being bribed or morally corrupted; inflexibly just and upright. — **in′cor·rupt′i·bil′i·ty** (-bĭl′ĭ·tĭ), **in′cor·rupt′i·ble·ness**, *n.* — **in′cor·rupt′i·bly**, *adv.*

in′cor·rup′tion (ĭn′kŏ·rŭp′shŭn; *in contrast with* corruption, ĭn′kŏ·rŭp′shŭn), *n. Archaic.* Condition or quality of being incorrupt or incorruptible.

in·cras′sate (ĭn·krăs′āt), *adj.* Also **in·cras′sat·ed** (-āt·ĕd; -ĭd). [L. *incrassatus*, past part. of *incrassare*, fr. *in* in + *crassus* thick.] *Bot. & Zool.* Thickened or swollen.

in·cras′sate (-āt), *v. t. & i.* To thicken; inspissate. — **in′cras·sa′tion** (ĭn′kră·sā′shŭn), *n.*

in·crease′ (ĭn·krēs′), *v. i.* [OF. *encreistre*, fr. L. *increscere*, fr. *in-* in + *crescere* to grow.] **1.** To become greater; to grow; augment; wax. **2.** To multiply by the production of young. — *v. t.* To augment; add to; enhance. — **in·creas′a·ble**, *adj.* — **in·creas′ing·ly**, *adv.*

Syn. **Increase, enlarge, augment, multiply** mean to become or cause to become greater in size, number, etc. **Increase**, esp. as an intransitive verb, implies progressive growth, as in size, amount, intensity, and the like, but as a transitive it sometimes loses its implication of progressiveness; **enlarge** implies expansion or extension so that what is affected is greater in size, in capacity, or in what it comprehends; **augment**, like *increase*, implies growth but seldom suggests growth by degrees for it is commonly used in reference to things already well grown, well developed, or the like; **multiply** commonly implies increase in number, as by generation or mechanically. — **Ant.** Decrease.

in′crease (ĭn′krēs), *n.* **1.** An increasing; enlargement; augmentation; multiplication, esp. of young. **2.** That which results from increasing; as: **a** Addition; increment. **b** Progeny; issue; offspring. **c** Produce; profit; interest.

in·creas′er (ĭn·krēs′ẽr), *n.* One who or that which increases; as: **a** A breeder. **b** *Archaic.* A promoter. **c** *Mech.* Any device to increase size, strength, etc.; as, a traction *increaser.*

in′cre·ate′ (ĭn′krē·āt′; ĭn′krē·āt; 2), *adj.* Uncreated; self-existent.

in·cred′i·ble (ĭn·krĕd′ĭ·b'l), *adj.* Not credible; too extraordinary and improbable to admit of belief. — **in·cred′i·bil′i·ty** (-bĭl′ĭ·tĭ), **in·cred′i·ble·ness**, *n.* — **in·cred′i·bly**, *adv.*

in′cre·du′li·ty (ĭn′krē·dū′lĭ·tĭ), *n.* State, quality, or instance of being incredulous; a withholding or refusal of belief. — **Syn.** See UNBELIEF.

in·cred′u·lous (ĭn·krĕd′ū·lŭs), *adj.* **1.** Not credulous; skeptical. **2.** Indicating, or caused by, disbelief. — **in·cred′u·lous·ly**, *adv.* — **in·cred′u·lous·ness**, *n.*

in′cre·ment (ĭn′krē·mĕnt; ĭng′-), *n.* [L. *incrementum*, fr. *increscere.* See INCREASE.] **1.** An increasing; enlargement; increase. **2.** That which is gained or added; esp., one of a series of additions, or, sometimes, of minute additions; — opposed to *decrement.* **3.** *Math.* A change, generally arbitrary, either positive or negative, in the value of an independent variable; also, the corresponding change in the value of the dependent function. — **in′cre·men′tal** (-mĕn′tăl; -t'l), *adj.*

in·cres′cent (ĭn·krĕs′ĕnt; -'nt), *adj.* [L. *increscens, -entis*, pres. part. of *increscere.*] Increasing; waxing; as, the *increscent* moon.

in·cre′tion (ĭn·krē′shŭn), *n.* [*in-* + secretion.] Internal secretion or a product of it; an autacoid. — **in·cre′tion·ar′y** (-ẽr′ĭ *or, esp. Brit.*, -ẽr·ĭ), **in′cre·to′ry** (ĭn′krē·tō′rĭ; -tẽr·ĭ), *adj.*

in·crim′i·nate (ĭn·krĭm′ĭ·nāt), *v. t.* [ML. *incriminatus*, past part. of *incriminare*, fr. *in-* in + *criminare, criminari*, to accuse one of a crime. See CRIMINATE.] To charge with, or involve in, a crime or fault; accuse. — **in·crim′i·na′tion** (-nā′shŭn), *n.* — **in·crim′i·na′tor** (-nā′tẽr), *n.* — **in·crim′i·na·to′ry** (-nȧ·tō′rĭ *or, esp. Brit.*, -tẽr·ĭ, -nā′tẽr·ĭ), *adj.*

in·crust′ (ĭn·krŭst′), *v. t.* [F. *incruster*, fr. L. *incrustare*, fr. *in-* in + *crustare* to cover with a crust.] To cover or line with or as with a crust, or hard coat.

in′crus·ta′tion (ĭn′krŭs·tā′shŭn), *n.* **1.** Act of incrusting, or state of being incrusted. **2.** A crust or hard coating.

in′cu·bate (ĭn′kū·bāt; ĭng′-), *v. t.* [L. *incubatus*, past part. of *incubare* to lie on, fr. *in-* in, on + *cubare* to lie down.] To sit upon (eggs) to hatch them; brood; hence, to maintain (eggs, embryos, or the like) under conditions favorable for hatching or development. — *v. i.* To sit on eggs; brood; also, to undergo incubation. — **in′cu·ba′tive** (-bā′tĭv), *adj.*

in′cu·ba′tion (-bā′shŭn), *n.* **1.** Act or process of incubating, as eggs, bacteria, etc. **2.** Brooding or brooding upon. **3.** *Med.* The development of an infectious disease from inception to visible manifestation. — **in′cu·ba′tion·al**, *adj.*

in′cu·ba′tor (ĭn′kū·bā′tẽr; ĭng′-), *n.* [L.] One who or that which incubates; specif., any apparatus for incubating eggs, microorganisms, prematurely born babies, etc.

in′cu·bus (ĭn′kū·bŭs; ĭng′-), *n.; pl.* INCUBI (-bī), -BUSES (-bŭs·ĕz; -ĭz). [LL., the nightmare, ML., a demon, fr. L. *incubare.* See INCUBATE.] **1.** An evil spirit, supposed to lie upon persons in their sleep, and esp. to have sexual intercourse with women by night. Cf. SUCCUBUS. **2.** Any person or thing that oppresses or burdens. **3.** *Med.* Nightmare.

in·cu′des (ĭn·kū′dēz), *n., pl.* of INCUS.

in·cul′cate (ĭn·kŭl′kāt; ĭn′kŭl·kāt), *v. t.* [L. *inculcatus*, past part. of *inculcare* to tread on, fr. *in-* in, on + *calcare* to tread, fr. *calx* the heel.] To teach and impress by frequent repetitions or admonitions; to urge on the mind; — with *on* or *upon.* — **Syn.** See IMPLANT. — **in′cul·ca′tion** (ĭn′kŭl·kā′shŭn), *n.* — **in·cul′ca·tor** (ĭn·kŭl′kā·tẽr; ĭn′kŭl·kā′tẽr), *n.*

in·cul′pa·ble (ĭn·kŭl′pȧ·b'l), *adj.* Not culpable; blameless; innocent.

in·cul′pate (ĭn·kŭl′pāt; ĭn′kŭl·pāt), *v. t. & i.* [ML. *inculpatus*, past part. of *inculpare* to blame, fr. L. *in-* in + *culpa* fault.] To impute guilt (to); to involve or implicate in guilt; incriminate. — **in′cul·pa′tion** (ĭn′kŭl·pā′shŭn; ĭng′-), *n.* — **in·cul′pa·to′ry** (ĭn·kŭl′pȧ·tō′rĭ *or, esp. Brit.*, -tẽr·ĭ), *adj.*

in·cult′ (ĭn·kŭlt′), *adj.* [L. *incultus*, fr. *in-* not + *cultus*, past part. of *colere* to cultivate.] Uncultivated; uncivilized; crude; rude; rough.

in·cum′ben·cy (ĭn·kŭm′bĕn·sĭ), *n.; pl.* -CIES (-sĭz). State or quality of being incumbent, or that which is incumbent; specif.: **a** That which is imposed as a duty, obligation, or responsibility. **b** State of holding a benefice; possession and exercise of any office. **c** An incumbent, or overlying, weight or mass.

in·cum′bent (-bĕnt), *adj.* [L. *incumbens, -entis*, pres. part. of *incumbere* to lie down upon, press upon.] **1.** Lying or reclining, esp. with downward pressure; hence, impending. **2.** Imposed as a duty or obligation; obligatory; — with *on* or *upon.* **3.** Lying upon or opposed to; as, an *incumbent* anther. **4.** *Geol.* Overlying. — *n.* One holding a benefice or office. — **in·cum′bent·ly**, *adv.*

in·cum′ber (-bẽr), *v. t.* To encumber. — **in·cum′brance** (-brăns), *n.*

in′cu·nab′u·la (ĭn′kū·năb′ū·lȧ), *n. pl.; sing.* -LUM (-lŭm). [L., pl., cradle, birthplace, origin.] **1.** Cradle period or state; beginnings; infancy. **2.** *Bibliog.* Works of an early epoch; specif., books printed before A.D. 1501. — **in′cu·nab′u·lar** (-lẽr), *adj.*

in·cur′ (ĭn·kûr′), *v. t.;* -CURRED′ (-kûrd′); -CUR′RING. [L. *incurrere* to run into or toward, fr. *in-* in + *currere* to run.] To meet with, as a thing inconvenient or harmful; become liable to; bring down on oneself.

Syn. **Incur, contract, catch** mean to bring something upon oneself. **Incur** may or may not imply foreknowledge, but it usually implies responsibility for the act or acts which bring something upon one; **contract** implies more strongly effective acquirement, but is equally inexplicit as to the part played by accident; **catch**, a more popular term, implies infection or something comparable in tracing the means of communication.

in·cur′a·ble (ĭn·kūr′ȧ·b'l), *adj.* Not curable; irremediable. — *n.* A person diseased beyond cure. — **in·cur′a·bil′i·ty** (-bĭl′ĭ·tĭ), *n.* — **in·cur′a·ble·ness**, *n.* — **in·cur′a·bly**, *adv.*

in·cu′ri·ous (ĭn·kū′rĭ·ŭs), *adj.* Not curious, or inquisitive; indifferent; uninterested. — **Syn.** See INDIFFERENT. — **in′cu·ri·os′i·ty** (ĭn′kū·rĭ·ŏs′ĭ·tĭ), *n.* — **in·cu′ri·ous·ly**, *adv.* — **in·cu′ri·ous·ness**, *n.*

in·cur′rence (ĭn·kûr′ĕns), *n.* Act or process of incurring; as, *incurrence* of debt.

in·cur′rent (-ĕnt), *adj.* [L. *incurrens, -entis*, pres. part. See INCUR.] *Zool.* Characterized by an inward-flowing current. Cf. CLAM, *Illust.*

in·cur′sion (-zhŭn; -shŭn), *n.* [L. *incursio.* See INCUR.] A running in, into, or against; hence, a hostile entrance into a territory; a sudden invasion; raid; inroad.

in·cur′sive (-sĭv), *adj.* Making incursions; invasive.

in·cur′vate (ĭn·kûr′vāt; ĭn′kûr-), *adj.* [L. *incurvatus*, past part. of *incurvare* to crook, fr. *in-* in + *curvus* bent.] Incurved; incurvated. — (-vāt), *v. t. & i.* To bend; crook; specif., to curve inwards. — **in′cur·va′tion** (ĭn′kûr·vā′shŭn), *n.* — **in·cur′va·ture** (ĭn·kûr′vȧ·tūr), *n.*

in′curve′ (ĭn′kûrv′), *n.* Also **in′–curve′**, **in curve.** A curving in; *Baseball*, a ball that curves in. See CURVE, 4.

in·curve′ (ĭn·kûrv′), *v. t. & i.* [See INCURVATE.] To curve, esp. inward.

in′cus (ĭng′kŭs), *n.; pl.* INCUDES (ĭn·kū′dēz). [L., anvil.] *Anat.* The middle one of the chain of three small bones in the ear of mammals; the anvil. See EAR, *Illust.*

in·cuse′ (ĭn·kūz′), *adj.* [L. *incusus*, past part. of *incudere* to forge with the hammer.] Struck or stamped in; — esp. of ancient coins. — *n.* An impression, usually square or oblong, produced on the obverse of a coin by the punch with which it was struck; an incuse figure or design.

Ind (ĭnd), *n. Chiefly Poetic.* **a** India. **b** Indies.

Ind-. = INDO-.

in·da′ba (ĭn·dä′bä), *n.* [Zulu *in-daba*, prop., matter, affair.] Among South African natives, a conference.

in′da·gate (ĭn′dȧ·gāt), *v. t.* [L. *indagatus*, past part. of *indagare* to seek.] To investigate. — **in′da·ga′tion** (-gā′shŭn), *n.* — **in′da·ga′tor** (-gā′tẽr), *n.*

in′da·mine (ĭn′dȧ·mēn; -mĭn), *n.* Also **in′da·min.** [Prob. fr. *indigo* + *amine.*] *Chem.* Any of a series of organic bases, the simplest of which has the formula $NH:C_6H_4:NC_6H_4NH_2$. Their salts are unstable blue and green dyes.

in·debt′ (ĭn·dĕt′), *v. t.* [OF. *endetter*, fr. *en-* (fr. L. *in*) + *dette* debt.] To bring into debt; place under obligation. — **in·debt′ed** (-ĕd; -ĭd), *adj.*

in·debt′ed·ness, *n.* **1.** State of being indebted. **2.** The sum owed; debts, collectively.

in·de′cent (ĭn·dē′sĕnt; -s'nt), *adj.* Not decent; specif.: **a** Unbecoming or unseemly; indecorous. **b** Morally offensive; unfit to be seen or heard. — **Syn.** See INDECOROUS. — **in·de′cen·cy** (-sĕn·sĭ; -s'n·sĭ), *n.* — **in·de′cent·ly**, *adv.*

in′de·cid′u·ate (ĭn′dē·sĭd′ū·āt), *adj.* Having no decidua.

in′de·cid′u·ous (-ŭs), *adj.* Not deciduous, as leaves; evergreen, as trees.

in′de·ci′pher·a·ble (ĭn′dē·sī′fẽr·ȧ·b'l), *adj.* Not decipherable. — **in′de·ci′pher·a·bil′i·ty** (-bĭl′ĭ·tĭ), *n.*

in′de·ci′sion (-sĭzh′ŭn), *n.* Want of decision, settled purpose, or firmness; hesitation; vacillation; irresolution.

in′de·ci′sive (-sī′sĭv), *adj.* **1.** Not decisive; inconclusive. **2.** Prone to indecision; irresolute. **3.** Not certain; dubious; indefinite. — **in′de·ci′sive·ly**, *adv.* — **in′de·ci′sive·ness**, *n.*

in′de·clin′a·ble (ĭn′dē·klīn′ȧ·b'l), *adj.* Not declinable; as: **a** *Obs.* Incapable of being avoided; unavoidable. **b** *Gram.* Not varied by inflectional terminations.

in′de·com·pos′a·ble (ĭn′dē·kŏm·pōz′ȧ·b'l), *adj.* Not decomposable; not resolvable into constituent parts. — **in′de·com·pos′a·ble·ness**, *n.*

in·dec′o·rous (ĭn·dĕk′ō·rŭs; ĭn′dē·kō′rŭs), *adj.* Not decorous; violating good manners; unbecoming. — **in·dec′o·rous·ly**, *adv.* — **in·dec′o·rous·ness**, *n.*

Syn. **Indecorous, improper, unseemly, indecent, unbecoming, indelicate** mean not conforming to the accepted standard of what is right or fitting. **Indecorous** suggests a transgression of what polite society regards as good manners; **improper**, of what the authorities in etiquette, language, aesthetics, etc., regard as right or correct; **unseemly** adds to these a suggestion of offensiveness to persons of good taste; **indecent**, once meaning great unseemliness, now more often implies gross offensiveness to persons of sound morals; **unbecoming** suggests behavior, expressions, etc., that do not befit one's character or standing; **indelicate** suggests a lack of modesty or the like which betrays lack of tact or of refined perceptions.

in′de·co′rum (ĭn′dē·kō′rŭm), *n.* [L., fr. *indecorus* unbecoming.] **1.** Want of decorum; impropriety, now esp. of behavior. **2.** An indecorous action.

in·deed′ (ĭn·dēd′), *adv.* [*in*, prep. + *deed.*] In reality; in truth; in fact; to be sure. — *interj.* An exclamation of surprise, irony, incredulity, etc.

in′de·fat′i·ga·ble (ĭn′dē·făt′ĭ·gȧ·b'l), *adj.* [L. *indefatigabilis.*] Incapable of being fatigued, or not yielding to fatigue; untiring; tireless. — **in′de·fat′i·ga·bil′i·ty** (-bĭl′ĭ·tĭ), **in′de·fat′i·ga·ble·ness**, *n.* — **in′de·fat′i·ga·bly**, *adv.*

in′de·fea′si·ble (ĭn′dē·fē′zĭ·b'l), *adj.* Not defeasible; incapable of being annulled or made void. — **in′de·fea′si·bil′i·ty** (-bĭl′ĭ·tĭ), *n.* — **in′de·fea′si·bly**, *adv.*

in′de·fect′i·ble (-fĕk′tĭ·b'l), *adj.* Not liable to defect, failure, or decay; also, faultless. — **in′de·fect′i·bil′i·ty** (-bĭl′ĭ·tĭ), *n.* — **in′de·fect′i·bly**, *adv.*

in′de·fen′si·ble (-fĕn′sĭ·b'l), *adj.* Not defensible; unjustifiable; untenable. — **in′de·fen′si·bil′i·ty** (-bĭl′ĭ·tĭ), **in′de·fen′si·ble·ness**, *n.* — **in′de·fen′si·bly**, *adv.*

in′de·fin′a·ble (-fīn′ȧ·b'l), *adj.* Incapable of being defined or exactly described. — *n.* Anything indefinable. — **in′de·fin′a·ble·ness**, *n.* — **in′de·fin′a·bly**, *adv.*

in·def′i·nite (ĭn·dĕf′ĭ·nĭt), *adj.* [L. *indefinitus.*] **1.** Not definite; undetermined or indeterminate; specif.: **a** Vague or general; not precise or certain; as, an *indefinite* plan. **b** Having no prescribed limit or known limits; as, an *indefinite* supply, or area. **2.** Unmeasured or unmeasurable, though not infinite; as, an *indefinite* number. **3.** *Bot.* Very numerous or not easily counted; — of members of a floral whorl. **4.** *Gram.* Not defining or determining; as, "any" is an *indefinite* pronoun. Abbr. *indef.* — **in·def′i·nite·ly**, *adv.* — **in·def′i·nite·ness**, *n.*

indefinite article. *Gram.* The article *a* or *an.*

in′de·his′cent (ĭn′dē·hĭs′ĕnt; -'nt), *adj.* *Bot.* Remaining closed at maturity; not dehiscent; — said specif. of many fruits. — **in′de·his′cence** (-ĕns; -'ns), *n.*

in′de·lib′er·ate (-lĭb′ẽr·ĭt), *adj.* Without deliberation; unpremeditated. — **in′de·lib′er·ate·ly**, *adv.* — **in′de·lib′er·ate·ness**, *n.*

in·del′i·ble (ĭn·dĕl′ĭ·b'l), *adj.* [L. *indelebilis*, fr. *in-* not + *delebilis* capable of being destroyed.] That cannot be removed, washed away, blotted out, or effaced; also, making marks not readily erased. — **in·del′i·bil′i·ty** (-bĭl′ĭ·tĭ), **in·del′i·ble·ness**, *n.* — **in·del′i·bly**, *adv.*

in·del′i·ca·cy (-kȧ·sĭ), *n.; pl.* -CIES (-sĭz). **1.** Quality of being indelicate. **2.** Anything indelicate.

in·del′i·cate (-kĭt), *adj.* Not delicate; offensive to good manners, or to purity of mind; coarse; gross; immodest. — **Syn.** See INDECOROUS. — **in·del′i·cate·ly**, *adv.* — **in·del′i·cate·ness**, *n.*

in·dem′ni·fi·ca′tion (ĭn·dĕm′nĭ·fĭ·kā′shŭn), *n.* **1.** An indemnifying or being indemnified; reimbursement of loss, damage, or penalty. **2.** A payment or recompense which indemnifies. — **in·dem′ni·fi·ca′to·ry** (-dĕm′nĭ·fĭ·kā′tō·rĭ), *adj.*

in·dem′ni·fy (ĭn·dĕm′nĭ·fī), *v. t.;* -FIED (-fīd); -FY′ING. [L. *indemnis* unhurt (fr. *in-* not + *damnum* hurt, damage) + *-fy.*] **1.** To secure against loss or damage. **2.** To make restitution or compensation to; reimburse; also, to make good (a loss). — **Syn.** See PAY. — **in·dem′ni·fi′er** (-fī′ẽr), *n.*

in·dem′ni·tor (-tẽr), *n.* One who gives indemnity.

in·dem′ni·ty (-tĭ), *n.; pl.* -TIES (-tĭz). [F. *indemnité*, fr. LL. *indemnitas*, fr. *indemnis* uninjured.] **1.** Protection or exemption from loss or damage, past or to come; security; insurance; specif., immunity from penalty for past offenses; amnesty. **2.** Indemnification, compensation, or remuneration for loss or injury sustained.

in′de·mon′stra·ble (ĭn′dē·mŏn′strȧ·b'l; ĭn·dĕm′ŭn-), *adj.* Not demonstrable; not subject to proof. — **in′de·mon′stra·bil′i·ty** (-bĭl′ĭ·tĭ), *n.* — **in′de·mon′stra·bly**, *adv.*

in′dene (ĭn′dēn), *n.* [*indole* + *-ene.*] *Chem.* An oily hydrocarbon, C_9H_8, obtained especially in the fractional distillation of coal tar.

in·dent′ (ĭn·dĕnt′), *v. t.* [OF. *endenter*, fr. ML. *indentare*, fr. L. *in* in + *dens, dentis*, tooth.] **1.** To make a notch or a series of notches in the border of; to make jagged or serrate. **2.** To cut into (a board, etc.) for mortising or dovetailing; to join together by so doing. **3.** To sever the parts of (a document) by way of indenture; to draw up (an agreement or the like) in duplicate. **4.** To indenture. **5.** To make an order upon; to draw upon, as for stores; also, *Com.*, to make an indent, or order, for (goods). **6.** To set (a line or lines) in from the margin; to form an indention in (a paragraph, etc.). — *v. i.* **1.** To form a recess or indentation. **2.** To agree by indenture; contract. **3.** To make out a written order with a duplicate or counterfoil; hence, to make a requisition; to draw (*on*).
— (ĭn·dĕnt′; ĭn′dĕnt), *n.* **1.** A notch in a margin, or a recess like a notch; *Print.*, an indention. **2.** An indented writing; an indenture. **3.** An indented certificate issued by the government of the United States at the close of the Revolution, for the principal or interest of the public debt. **4.** *Eng.* An official requisition or order for supplies. **5.** *Com.* A foreign order for goods; esp., one with detailed specifications. — **in·dent′er**, *n.*

in·dent′ (ĭn·dĕnt′), *v. t.* [*in-* in + *dent.*] To dent; impress; stamp or press in; as, to *indent* a pattern in metal; also, to form a dent or dents in. — (ĭn·dĕnt′; ĭn′dĕnt), *n.* A dent.

in′den·ta′tion (ĭn′dĕn·tā′shŭn), *n.* **1.** An indenting or state of being indented; also, the result of indenting; as: **a** A notch or recess in a border. **b** *Print.* Indention. **2.** A denting; a dent.

in·den′tion (ĭn·dĕn′shŭn), *n.* **1.** The result of indenting; a cut, notch, recess, or the like, in a margin; an indentation or dent. **2.** *Print.* **a** Act of setting a line or lines in from the margin or a little within the flush line of the text. **b** The blank space so left. Cf. HANGING INDENTION.

in·den′ture (-tūr), *n.* [OF. *endenture, endenteure.*] **1.** An agreement in writing (usually in duplicate, the parts originally being notched or cut so as to correspond to each other). **2.** Specif., usually *pl.*, a contract by which an apprentice is bound to a master, or a servant to service in a colony, etc. **3.** A formal or official document, as a certificate or an inventory (originally one prepared in duplicate). **4.** An indenting; state of being indented; an indentation. — *v. t.* **1.** To bind by indenture. **2.** To indent; furrow.

in′de·pend′ence (ĭn′dē·pĕn′dĕns), *n.* **1.** State or quality of being independent; freedom from control by others; self-government. **2.** A sufficiency of means for a livelihood; a competency.

Independence Day. *U. S. & Phil. I.* A holiday, the 4th of July, anniversary, in the U. S., of the adoption of the Declaration of Independence in 1776 and, in the Philippines, of the transfer of sovereignty from the U. S. in 1946.

in′de·pend′en·cy (ĭn′dē·pĕn′dĕn·sĭ), *n.; pl.* -CIES (-sĭz). **1.** Independence. **2.** An independent state, province, etc. **3.** [*cap.*] *Eccl.* Doctrine and polity of the Independents.

in′de·pend′ent (-dĕnt), *adj.* **1.** Not dependent; not subject to control by others; self-governing. **2.** **a** Irrespective of others, each other, or another; as, an *independent* inquiry. **b** Irrespective; exclusive; — with *of.* **3.** [*cap.*] Of or pertaining to the Independents. **4.** Not being a dependent (of), as for support; hence: **a** Earning or earned. **b** Having or forming a competency. **5.** Not subject to bias or influence; hence, self-reliant, self-confident, self-respecting, or the like; not subservient. **6.** *Gram.* Not subordinate; main; — of a clause. **7.** *Math.* Not dependent on another quantity in respect of value or rate of variation; — said of quantities and functions. **8.** *Politics.* Not bound by party; exercising a free choice in voting. — **Syn.** See FREE.
— *n.* **1.** [*cap.*] *Eccl.* **a** One who believes that the local Christian church is complete in itself and independent of all external ecclesiastical authority. **b** *Eng.* A Congregationalist. **2.** An independent person or thing; esp., *Politics*, one who does not acknowledge an obligation to support a party's candidate under all circumstances.
— **in′de·pend′ent·ly**, *adv.*

in′de·scrib′a·ble (ĭn′dē·skrīb′ȧ·b'l), *adj.* That cannot be described; surpassing description. — **in′de·scrib′a·bly**, *adv.*

in′de·struct′i·ble (-strŭk′tĭ·b'l), *adj.* Not destructible; incapable of being destroyed. — **in′de·struct′i·bil′i·ty** (-bĭl′ĭ·tĭ), *n.* — **in′de·struct′i·bly**, *adv.*

in′de·ter′mi·na·ble (-tûr′mĭ·nȧ·b'l), *adj.* Not determinable; impossible to be definitely known, defined, or limited. — *n.* An indeterminable thing or question.

in′de·ter′mi·nate (-nāt), *adj.* **1.** Not determinate; indefinite; not distinct or precise; vague. **2.** Not fixed; not predetermined; also, not leading to a definite end or result. **3.** *Bot.* **a** Racemose. **b** Having the parts of the perianth separate and not overlapping in the bud. — **in′de·ter′mi·nate·ly**, *adv.* — **in′de·ter′mi·nate·ness**, *n.*

in′de·ter′mi·na′tion (-nā′shŭn), *n.* **1.** Lack of determination. **2.** State of being indeterminate or undefined.

in′de·ter′min·ism (ĭn′dē·tûr′mĭn·ĭz'm), *n.* *Philos.* The doctrine that the will is free, or esp., that one's deliberate choices or acts are not completely determined by, or predictable from, antecedent causes. — **in′de·ter′min·ist** (-ĭst), *n. & adj.* — **in′de·ter′min·is′tic** (-ĭs′tĭk), *adj.*

in′de·vout′ (ĭn′dē·vout′), *adj.* Not devout; irreverent.

in′dex (ĭn′dĕks), *n.; pl.* INDEXES (-dĕk·sĕz; -sĭz), INDICES (ĭn′dĭ·sēz). [L., fr. *indicare* to point out. See INDICATE.] **1.** In full **index finger.** The forefinger. **2.** A pointer or indicator. **3.** That which indicates or discloses; a token or indication. **4.** *Obs.* Table of contents, argument, preface, or prologue. **5.** [*pl.* commonly *indexes.*] A table, list, or file, usually arranged alphabetically, for facilitating reference to topics, names, objects, etc., esp. in a book or a collection. **6.** The ratio, or formula expressing the ratio, of one dimension of a thing to another dimension. Cf. CEPHALIC INDEX. **7.** A ratio or other number derived from a series of observations and used as an indicator or measure of a certain condition; as, an *index* of intelligence. **8.** [*pl.* always *indices.*] *Math.* The figure, letter, or expression showing the power or root of a quantity; exponent. **9.** *Print.* A sign [☞] used to direct particular attention to a note or paragraph; a "fist." See FIST, 3; HAND, 13 **b**. **10.** [*cap.*] *R.C.Ch.* A list of books the reading of which is prohibited or restricted by the church authorities. The ***In′dex Li·bro′rum Pro·hib′i·to′rum*** (lī·brō′rŭm prō·hĭb′ĭ·tō′rŭm) [L.], *or* ***Prohibitory Index*** is a list of books forbidden as dangerous to faith and morals. The ***In′dex Ex·pur′ga·to′ri·us*** (ĕks·pûr′gȧ·tō′rĭ·ŭs), is a list of books interdicted until amended. — *v. t.* **1.** To provide with, or put into, an index. **2.** To put on the Index. See INDEX, *n.*, 10. **3.** To be an index of. — **in′dex·er**, *n.*

index of refraction. *Optics.* A measure of refracting power, being either (***absolute index of refraction***) the ratio of the velocity of light in a vacuum (or, commonly, in air) to that in a given medium, or (***relative index of refraction***) the ratio of the velocity of light in two different media.

In′di·a ink (ĭn′dĭ·ȧ; *esp. Brit.*, -dyȧ; 58). A black pigment used for writing, painting, etc., brought chiefly from China and Japan, now consisting of specially prepared lampblack or ivory black.

In′di·a·man (-măn), *n.; pl.* -MEN (-mĕn). *Naut.* A vessel in the India trade; specif., a large vessel belonging to the East India Company.

In′di·an (ĭn′dĭ·ăn; 58), *adj.* [From *India*, fr. L. *India*, fr. Gr. *India*, fr. *Indos* the Indus river, fr. OPer. & Av. *Hindu* India.] **1.** Of or pertaining to India or the East Indies; designating the Indians or their civilization. **2.** Of, pertaining to, or designating the aborigines, or Indians, of America. **3.** Made of Indian corn; as, *Indian* pudding. — *n.* **1.** A member of one of the native races of India or of Indochina, whether Hindu, Moslem, or animist. **2.** A member of the aboriginal American race; an American, or Red, Indian. **3.** An American Indian language; any one of the many, diverse languages spoken by members of the aboriginal races of North and South America. See LANGUAGE, *Table.*

Indian club. A form of wooden club which is swung for gymnastic exercise.

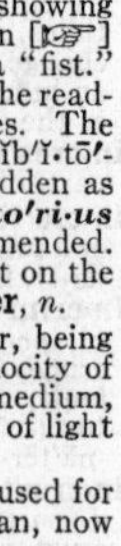
Indian Club.

Indian corn. **1.** A native American cereal grass (*Zea mays*); maize; — called *corn* in the United States, Canada, and Australia. **2.** **a** The ripened ears of this plant; also, the seeds, widely used as food for human beings and livestock. **b** A crop of this cereal.

Indian file. Single file, the Indian way of traversing woods.

Indian gift. *Colloq., U. S.* A gift for which an equivalent or more is expected in return, or which is expected to be returned. — **Indian giver.**

Indian hemp. **a** An American herb (*Apocynum cannabinum*) of the dogbane family, having milky juice, and tough, fibrous bark. The root is emetic and cathartic. **b** The common hemp (*Cannabis sativa*), esp. the variety cultivated in India. Cf. HEMP, CANNABIS, HASHISH, BHANG.

Indian licorice. An East Indian herb (*Abrus precatorius*) of the pea family, whose root is a substitute for licorice.

Indian mallow. An East Indian yellow-flowered mallow (*Abutilon theophrasti*), widely naturalized as a weed.

Indian meal. Ground Indian corn, or maize.

Indian millet. **a** Durra. **b** Pearl millet.

Indian paintbrush. = PAINTED CUP.

Indian pipe. A waxy-white leafless saprophytic herb (*Monotropa uniflora*, family Monotropaceae), native to Asia and the U. S.

Indian pudding. A pudding whose chief ingredients are Indian meal, milk, and molasses.
Indian red. A yellowish-red earth, orig. from the Persian Gulf, used as a pigment; also, a pigment of similar color made by calcining iron salts.
Indian summer. A period of warm or mild weather late in autumn or in early winter.
Indian tobacco. An American wild lobelia (*Lobelia inflata*) with small blue flowers.
Indian turnip. The jack-in-the-pulpit; also, its root.
India paper. **a** A thin, delicate paper made in China, and used for prints of engravings, etc. **b** A very thin opaque printing paper.
India rubber *or, often,* **in′di·a·rub′ber** (ĭn′dĭ·ȧ·rŭb′ẽr), *n.* **1.** Rubber; caoutchouc. **2.** A piece of this substance or an article made from it; a rubber.
India silk. A soft, thin silk fabric in plain weave.
In′dic (ĭn′dĭk), *adj.* [L. *Indicus*, fr. Gr. *Indikos* Indian.] **1.** Of or pertaining to India; Indian. **2.** Designating, or belonging to, the Indian branch of the Indo-Iranian languages. See INDO-EUROPEAN LANGUAGES, *Table*.
in′di·can (ĭn′dĭ·kăn), *n.* [See INDIGO.] **1.** *Chem.* A glucoside, $C_{14}H_{17}NO_6$, occurring in the indigo plant, woad, etc. It is the source of natural indigo. **2.** *Biochem.* An indigo-forming substance, $C_8H_6NOSO_2OH$, found (as a salt) in urine and other animal fluids; — called also *uroxanthin*.
in′di·cant (-kănt), *adj.* Serving to point out; indicating. — *n.* That which indicates or points out.
in′di·cate (ĭn′dĭ·kāt), *v. t.* [L. *indicatus*, past part. of *indicare* to indicate, fr. *in-* in + *dicare* to proclaim. See DICTION.] **1.** To point out or to; to be an index, sign, or token of; betoken. **2.** To state or sketch briefly; to intimate or show indirectly. **3.** *Med.* To manifest by symptoms; to point to as the proper remedy or treatment.
in′di·ca′tion (-kā′shŭn), *n.* **1.** An indicating; suggestion. **2.** That which serves to indicate or point out; sign. **3.** The degree indicated by a thermometer, gauge, etc.; a reading.
in·dic′a·tive (ĭn·dĭk′ȧ·tĭv *or, in sense* 2, *esp. Brit.*, ĭn′dĭ·kā′tĭv), *adj.* **1.** Designating, or pertaining to, that mood, **indicative mood**, of the verb which represents the denoted act or state as an objective fact, as distinguished from a mood representing an act or state merely entertained in thought. **2.** Pointing out; giving intimation or knowledge (of something not visible or obvious); suggestive. — (ĭn·dĭk′ȧ·tĭv), *n.* *Gram.* The indicative mood or a verbal form denoting it. Abbr. *ind.* or *indic.* — **in·dic′a·tive·ly**, *adv.*
in′di·ca′tor (ĭn′dĭ·kā′tẽr), *n.* **1.** One that shows or points out; an indication or sign. **2.** Specif., any device or apparatus for indicating something; as: **a** An index hand or pointer. **b** A gauge, as to show pressure. **c** A dial which registers, as the positions of trains, the movement of an elevator, etc. **d** *Mach.* An instrument for automatically making a diagram which shows the pressure of the working fluid in an engine at every point of the stroke. **3.** *Chem.* A substance used to indicate to the eye the condition of a solution as to the presence of free acid, alkali, or other substance. Thus, litmus is blue in alkalies, violet in neutral solutions, and red in acids. — **in′di·ca·to′ry** (-kȧ·tō′rĭ *or, esp. Brit.*, -kā′tẽr·ĭ, -kȧ·tẽr·ĭ), *adj.*
in′di·ces (ĭn′dĭ·sēz), *n., pl.* of INDEX.
in·di′ci·a (ĭn·dĭsh′ĭ·ȧ), *n. pl.; sing.* INDICIUM (-ŭm). [L., pl. of *indicium* sign, token.] Signs; indications; appearances; specif., *U. S. Post Office*, the markings printed in place of stamp, cancellation, postmark, etc., on envelopes in bulk mail.
in·dict′ (ĭn·dīt′), *v. t.* [See INDITE.] To charge with an offense; esp., *Law*, to find an indictment against. — **in·dict′a·ble**, *adj.* — **in·dict′er** *or, esp. in Law,* **in·dict′or** (-dīt′ẽr), *n.*
in·dic′tion (ĭn·dĭk′shŭn), *n.* [OF. or L.; OF., fr. L. *indictio*, fr. *indicere* to announce, appoint. See DICTION.] **1.** *Rare.* Proclamation. **2.** The edict of a Roman emperor establishing the valuation for assessment of property tax every fifteen years; hence, a tax so levied. **3.** *Chron.* A recurring cycle of fifteen years, called in full the ***cycle of indiction***, formerly used as a method of reckoning periods of time.
in·dict′ment (ĭn·dīt′mĕnt), *n.* **1.** Act or process, esp. the legal process, of indicting; state of being indicted. **2.** *Law.* The formal written statement charging one or more persons with an offense, as framed by the prosecuting authority of the state, and found by the grand jury.
in·dif′fer·ence (ĭn·dĭf′ẽr·ĕns), *n.* Quality, state, or fact of being indifferent; specif.: **a** Lack of feeling for or against anything; apathy. **b** Lack of distinction or difference. **c** Lack of sufficient importance to constitute a difference or consideration; insignificance.
in·dif′fer·en·cy (-ĕn·sĭ), *n.* Indifference.
in·dif′fer·ent (-ĕnt), *adj.* [F. or L.; F. *indifférent*, fr. L. *indifferens, -entis*.] **1.** Having a neutral or unbiased disposition; specif.: **a** *Chiefly Legal.* Impartial; unprejudiced. **b** Not interested in or concerned about something; esp., without predilection or choice; as, *indifferent* to discomfort; *indifferent* to heat or cold. **c** Hence, apathetic; not easily interested or moved. **2.** Neutral; neither good nor bad, large nor small, desirable nor undesirable, etc.; as, in *indifferent* health; a room in *indifferent* order. **3.** Having no preponderating influence or value; hence, unimportant; as, *indifferent* matters; also, of a rite or custom, observable at one's option. **4.** Characterized by lack of active quality; as, the *indifferent* part of a magnet. **5.** *Biol.* Undifferentiated; as, *indifferent* tissue. — **in·dif′fer·ent·ly**, *adv.*
Syn. **Indifferent, unconcerned, incurious, aloof, detached, disinterested** mean not feeling or showing interest. **Indifferent**, in strict use, implies neutrality of attitude when two or more persons or things are considered; **unconcerned** implies indifference arising from unconsciousness, insensitiveness, selfishness, or the like, which prevents one from being moved, worried, solicitous, or the like; **incurious**, indifference caused by lack of interest or normal curiosity; **aloof**, indifference resulting from a sense of superiority, an aversion to the inferior, or the like; **detached**, a commendable aloofness resulting from freedom from all bias; **disinterested**, freedom from all concern for personal or party advantage that permits one to see or tell the truth.
in·dif′fer·ent·ism (-ĭz′m), *n.* State of being indifferent, esp. to what is true or false; systematic want of interest or earnestness. — **in·dif′fer·ent·ist** (-ĭst), *n.*
in′di·gence (ĭn′dĭ·jĕns), *n.* Condition of being indigent; penury; poverty. — **Syn.** See POVERTY.
in′di·gene (-jēn), **in′di·gen** (-jĕn), *n.* [F. *indigène*, fr. L. *indigena*.] An indigenous animal or plant; a native.
in·dig′e·nous (ĭn·dĭj′ē·nŭs), *adj.* [LL. *indigenus* native, fr. L. *indigena* a native, fr. *indu, endo*, in, within + the root of L. *gignere* to beget, bear.] **1.** Produced, growing, or living naturally in a country or climate; native. **2.** Inborn; inherent; innate. — **Syn.** See NATIVE. — **in·dig′e·nous·ly**, *adv.* — **in·dig′e·nous·ness**, *n.*
in′di·gent (ĭn′dĭ·jĕnt), *adj.* [F., fr. L. *indigens*, pres. part. of *indigere* to stand in need of, fr. *indu* in, within + *egere* to need.] **1.** *Archaic.* Wanting; also, destitute. **2.** Needy; poor.
in′di·gest′ed (ĭn′dĭ·jĕs′tĕd; -tĭd; ĭn′dī-), *adj.* Not digested; hence not properly ordered or considered; as, an *indigested* array of facts.
in′di·gest′i·ble (-jĕs′tĭ·b'l), *adj.* Not digestible; not readily digested. — **in′di·gest′i·bil′i·ty** (-bĭl′ĭ·tĭ), **in′di·gest′i·ble·ness**, *n.*
in′di·ges′tion (ĭn′dĭ·jĕs′chŭn), *n.* Lack of digestion; dyspepsia; incomplete or difficult digestion. — **in′di·ges′tive** (-tĭv), *adj.*
in·dign′ (ĭn·dīn′), *adj.* [F. *indigne*, fr. L. *indignus*.] *Obs. exc. Poetic.* Undeserving; disgraceful; undeserved.
in·dig′nant (ĭn·dĭg′nănt), *adj.* [L. *indignans, -antis*, pres. part. of *indignari* to be indignant, disdain, fr. *indignus* unworthy, fr. *in-* not + *dignus* worthy. See DIGNITY.] Affected with indignation; wrathful because of unworthy or unjust treatment, mean action, etc. — **Syn.** See ANGRY. — **in·dig′nant·ly**, *adv.*
in′dig·na′tion (ĭn′dĭg·nā′shŭn), *n.* Anger excited by that which is unworthy, base, or disgraceful; righteous wrath. — **Syn.** See ANGER.
in·dig′ni·ty (ĭn·dĭg′nĭ·tĭ), *n.; pl.* -TIES (-tĭz). [L. *indignitas*.] **1.** Unworthy or disgraceful quality, state, or act. **2.** Any action toward another which shows contempt for him; an offense against personal dignity; contumely. — **Syn.** See AFFRONT.
in′di·go (ĭn′dĭ·gō), *n.; pl.* -GOS or -GOES (-gōz). [Sp. *índigo, indico*, fr. L. *indicum* indigo, fr. Gr. *indikon*, fr. *Indikos* Indian.] **1.** A blue dye obtained from several plants, esp. species of *Indigofera* and woad, but now chiefly made synthetically from aromatic amino compounds. **2.** Any plant (**indigo plant**) which yields indigo; specif. any of a genus (*Indigofera*) of herbs of the pea family, esp. the indigo-producing *I. tinctoria, I. anil*, and *I. articulata*. Cf. WILD INDIGO. **3.** A color, reddish-blue in hue, of low saturation and low brilliance, one of Newton's seven prismatic colors. See COLOR. — **in′di·go**, *adj.*
indigo blue. **a** Indigotin. **b** The color indigo. — **in′di·go–blue′**, *adj.*
indigo bunting *or* **bird.** A small finch (*Passerina cyanea*) of the eastern U. S. The male is indigo-blue.
in′di·goid (ĭn′dĭ·goid), *adj.* [*indigo* + *-oid*.] Designating, or belonging to, an important class of vat dyes, characterized by the same color-producing atoms as indigo. — *n.* An indigoid dye.
in·dig′o·tin (ĭn·dĭg′ō·tĭn; ĭn′dĭ·gō′tĭn), *n.* Also **in·dig′o·tine** (-tĭn; -tēn). The essential coloring principle, $C_{16}H_{10}N_2O_2$, of indigo. It is a dark-blue earthy powder with a coppery luster.
in′di·rect′ (ĭn′dĭ·rĕkt′; ĭn′dī-), *adj.* Not direct; specif.: **a** Not straight or rectilinear; circuitous. **b** Not straightforward; dishonest; misleading; as, *indirect* dealing. **c** Not directed straight to the point, the person involved, etc.; roundabout; as, an *indirect* accusation. **d** Remotely, not directly, connected; not immediate or primary; as, *indirect* causes or results. **e** Quoted after a verb of saying, thinking, asking, etc., with changes in person and tense; as, ***indirect discourse*** (He said that he could come when I call him), ***indirect question*** (He asked me what was my view). — **in′di·rect′ly**, *adv.* — **in′di·rect′ness**, *n.*
in′di·rec′tion (ĭn′dĭ·rĕk′shŭn), *n.* **1.** Indirect procedure; an indirect act or means. **2.** An act or practice not fair or open; deceit.
indirect lighting. See LIGHTING, *n.*, 3.
indirect object. See OBJECT, *n.*, 4.
indirect tax. A tax exacted from a person other than the one who is to bear the ultimate burden.
in′dis·cern′i·ble (ĭn′dĭ·zûr′nĭ·b'l; -dĭ·sûr′-), *adj.* Not discernible; imperceptible; undistinguishable.
in′dis·cov′er·a·ble (ĭn′dĭs·kŭv′ẽr·ȧ·b'l), *adj.* Undiscoverable.
in′dis·creet′ (ĭn′dĭs·krēt′), *adj.* Not discreet; wanting in discretion; injudicious; unwise. — **in′dis·creet′ly**, *adv.* — **in′dis·creet′ness**, *n.*
in′dis·crete′ (ĭn′dĭs·krēt′; ĭn·dĭs′krēt), *adj.* [L. *indiscretus* unseparated.] Not discrete or separated; compact.
in′dis·cre′tion (ĭn′dĭs·krĕsh′ŭn), *n.* Lack of discretion; imprudence; also, an imprudent or unwise act. — **in′dis·cre′tion·ar′y** (-ĕr′ĭ *or, esp. Brit.*, -ẽr·ĭ), *adj.*
in′dis·crim′i·nate (-krĭm′ĭ·nĭt), *adj.* Not discriminate; showing lack of discrimination or distinction. — **in′dis·crim′i·nate·ly**, *adv.* — **in′dis·crim′i·nate·ness**, *n.* — **in′dis·crim′i·na′tion** (-nā′shŭn), *n.*
Syn. **Indiscriminate, wholesale, sweeping** mean including all within the range of choice or operation. **Indiscriminate** implies lack of consideration of individual deserts or merits (as, *indiscriminate* charity); **wholesale**, the failure to escape of any person or thing within the set limits (as, *wholesale* slaughter of a people); **sweeping**, a reaching out so as to bring all or everything within its range (as, *sweeping* accusations).
in′dis·crim′i·nat′ing (ĭn′dĭs·krĭm′ĭ·nāt′ĭng), *adj.* Not discriminating, or distinguishing. — **in′dis·crim′i·nat′ing·ly**, *adv.*
in′dis·pen′sa·ble (ĭn′dĭs·pĕn′sȧ·b'l), *adj.* Not dispensable; essential. — *n.* An indispensable person or thing. — **in′dis·pen′sa·bil′i·ty** (-bĭl′ĭ·tĭ), **in′dis·pen′sa·ble·ness**, *n.* — **in′dis·pen′sa·bly**, *adv.*
in′dis·pose′ (ĭn′dĭs·pōz′), *v. t.* **1.** To render unfit; disqualify. **2.** To disorder as regards health; — chiefly as *part. adj.* **in′dis·posed′** (-pōzd′), slightly ill. **3.** To render averse or unfavorable; disincline.
in′dis·po·si′tion (-pō·zĭsh′ŭn), *n.* State of being indisposed; as: **a** A slight or temporary illness. **b** State of not being favorably disposed; disinclination.
in·dis′pu·ta·ble (ĭn·dĭs′pū·tȧ·b'l; ĭn′dĭs·pūt′ȧ·b'l), *adj.* Not disputable; incontestable. — **in·dis′pu·ta·bil′i·ty** (-bĭl′ĭ·tĭ), **in·dis′pu·ta·ble·ness**, *n.* — **in·dis′pu·ta·bly**, *adv.*
in′dis·sol′u·ble (ĭn′dĭ·sŏl′ū·b'l; ĭn·dĭs′ō·lū·b'l), *adj.* Not dissoluble; not capable of being dissolved, annulled, disintegrated, or the like. — **in′dis·sol′u·bil′i·ty** (-bĭl′ĭ·tĭ), **in′dis·sol′u·ble·ness**, *n.* — **in′dis·sol′u·bly**, *adv.*
in′dis·tinct′ (ĭn′dĭs·tĭngkt′), *adj.* [L. *indistinctus*.] **1.** Not clear; difficult to distinguish, as from faintness, blurring, etc.; obscure. **2.** Not separate or separable; hence, not distinguished or not readily distinguishable; confused. — **in′dis·tinct′ly**, *adv.* — **in′dis·tinct′ness**, *n.*
in′dis·tinc′tive (-tĭngk′tĭv), *adj.* Not distinctive; without distinction.
in′dis·tin′guish·a·ble (-tĭng′gwĭsh·ȧ·b'l), *adj.* Not distinguishable; as: **a** Not capable of being discriminated. **b** Not discernible; indiscernible; imperceptible. — **in′dis·tin′guish·a·ble·ness**, *n.* — **in′dis·tin′guish·a·bly**, *adv.*

in·dite' (ĭn·dīt'), v. t. [OF. enditer to indicate, dictate, write, inform, fr. L. in- in, upon, against + dictare to declare, proclaim.] **1.** To compose, or to compose and write; hence, to describe or phrase; also, to put in writing. **2.** Obs. To dictate; prompt. — **in·dite'ment**, n. Now Rare. — **in·dit'er** (-dīt'ẽr), n.

in'di·um (ĭn'dĭ·ŭm), n. [NL., fr. indicum + -ium. See INDIGO.] Chem. A white, malleable, easily fusible metallic element combined in many ores, esp. zinc blende. It has two indigo-blue lines in its spectrum. Symbol, In; at. no., 49; at. wt., 114.76.

in'di·vert'i·ble (ĭn'dĭ·vûr'tĭ·b'l), adj. Not to be diverted or turned.

in'di·vid'u·al (-vĭd'ů·ăl), adj. [ML. individualis, fr. L. individuus indivisible, fr. in- not + dividuus divisible.] **1.** Obs. **a** Not divisible; of one essence. **b** Inseparable. **c** Identical. **2.** Arising from, pertaining to, or possessed or used by an individual. **3.** Existing as a distinct entity; particular; — opposed to general and universal. **4.** Of the character of an individual, or indivisible entity. **5.** Having individuality of a peculiar, striking, or idiosyncratic character; as, an individual style. — **Syn.** See SPECIAL: CHARACTERISTIC. — n. A single or particular being or group of beings; esp.: **a** A person. **b** An instance, case, or unit. **c** An indivisible entity or a totality. **d** Biol. A single organism as distinguished from a group. — **in'di·vid'u·al·ly**, adv.

in'di·vid'u·al·ism (-ĭz'm), n. **1. a** Individuality; personality. **b** An individual peculiarity; idiosyncrasy. **2.** Egoism. **3.** Any doctrine or practice based on the assumption that the individual and not society is the paramount consideration or end; specif.: **a** Econ. A theory maintaining that individual initiative, action, and interests should be independent of governmental or social control. **b** Ethics. The conception that all values, rights, and duties originate in individuals, and not in the social whole. — **in'di·vid'u·al·ist** (-ĭst), n. & adj. — **in'di·vid'u·al·is'tic** (-ĭs'tĭk), adj.

in'di·vid'u·al'i·ty (-ăl'ĭ·tĭ), n.; pl. -TIES (-tĭz). **1.** The quality which distinguishes one person or thing from another; distinctive character. **2.** Separate or distinct existence. **3.** Obs. Indivisibility or inseparability. **4.** An individual; esp., a person. — **Syn.** See DISPOSITION.

in'di·vid'u·al·ize (-vĭd'ů·ăl·īz), v. t. **1.** To make individual; mark as an individual. **2.** To treat or notice individually; particularize. — **in'di·vid'u·al·i·za'tion** (-ĭ·zā'shŭn; -ĭ·zā'-), n.

in'di·vid'u·ate (ĭn'dĭ·vĭd'ů·āt), v. t. [ML. individuatus, past part. of individuare. See INDIVIDUAL.] **1.** To distinguish from others of the species; form into an individual. **2.** To endow with individuality.

in'di·vid'u·a'tion (-ā'shŭn), n. **1.** Process by which an individual develops his or its peculiar character. **2.** Personal or individual existence. **3.** Philos. The development of the individual from the universal, or the determination of the individual in the general.

in'di·vis'i·ble (ĭn'dĭ·vĭz'ĭ·b'l), adj. Not divisible or separable into parts. — n. An indivisible thing. — **in'di·vis'i·bil'i·ty** (-bĭl'ĭ·tĭ), **in'di·vis'i·ble·ness**, n. — **in'di·vis'i·bly**, adv.

In'do- (ĭn'dŏ), **Ind-**. [Gr., fr. Indos (L. Indus) East Indian. See INDIAN.] A combining form meaning Indian (East Indian), denoting: **a** Pertaining to, belonging to, or derived from, India; of Indian (or Hindu) stock. **b** Indian and, as in **In'do-Brit'ish**, **In'do-Ma·lay'an**.

In'do-Ar'y·an, adj. Pertaining to the Indo-Aryans, or designating, or of, the Aryan languages of India (see INDO-EUROPEAN). — n. A member of one of the native races of India of Aryan speech and blood, characterized by tall stature, dolichocephaly, fair complexion with dark hair and eyes, plentiful beard, and narrow and prominent nose.

In'do-Chi·nese', adj. **1.** Usually **In'do-chi·nese'**. Of or pertaining to Indochina. **2.** Of or pertaining to the Mongoloid races of Indochina; pertaining to or designating a family of languages spoken by them. See LANGUAGE, Table.

In'do-chi·nese', n. sing. & pl. An inhabitant of Indochina.

in·doc'ile (ĭn·dŏs'ĭl; Brit. -dŏ'sīl, -dŏs'ĭl), adj. Not docile; unteachable; intractable. — **in'do·cil'i·ty** (ĭn'dŏ·sĭl'ĭ·tĭ), n.

in·doc'tri·nate (ĭn·dŏk'trĭ·nāt), v. t. [ML. in- in + doctrinare to teach, fr. doctrina teaching.] To instruct in the rudiments or principles of learning, or of a branch of learning; to instruct (in), or imbue (with), as principles or doctrines; sometimes, in a derogatory sense, to imbue with a partisan or sectarian point of view. — **in·doc'tri·na'tion** (-nā'shŭn), n. — **in·doc'tri·na'tor** (-nā'tẽr), n.

In'do-Eu'ro·pe'an, adj. Designating, or belonging to, certain languages constituting a linguistic family comprising the Indo-European languages. See also LANGUAGE, Table. — **In'do-Eu'ro·pe'an**, n.

Indo-European languages. The most important linguistic family of the globe, comprising the chief languages of Europe together with the Indo-Iranian and other Asiatic tongues. In the 19th century, comparative and historical study of these languages, called also Indo-Germanic or Aryan, established their descent from a common ancestor, spoken in the late Stone Age, probably in eastern Europe, by a people or group of peoples of unknown, perhaps mixed, race. This unrecorded language and, in some degree, the civilization and religion of those who spoke it, have been largely hypothetically reconstructed by scientific philological method. The prehistoric dialects of the primitive Indo-Europeans accompanied their migrations into India, Persia, Greece, Rome, and the western borders of Europe, where they are found at the beginning of history. The parent speech was highly inflected, but historically the general tendency of the Indo-European languages has been toward the analytic type, as in French or English. The broadest classification of these languages is that into two great divisions, the centum and the satem, depending, among other criteria, upon the development of prehistoric palatal gutturals into stops, or mutes, in the western division, and into spirants, or sibilants, in the eastern, as illustrated by the word for hundred (for example, Latin centum, pronounced kentum, but Avestan satem). They are further classified into eight main subfamilies, as shown in the Table herewith. Cf. ARYAN, SOGDIAN, TOCHARIAN.

TABLE OF INDO–EUROPEAN LANGUAGES

DIVISION	SUBFAMILY	BRANCH	LANGUAGES AND DIALECTS *	CHIEF LOCALITY †
EASTERN OR SATEM	INDO-IRANIAN or ARYAN	Indic	Sanskrit (Vedic, Classical); Pali; Prakrit; Kashmiri, Sindhi; Marathi; Oriya; Bengali; Eastern Hindi; Western Hindi (Hindustani, incl. Urdu), Rajasthani, Gujarati, Panjabi, Singhalese, Romany or Gypsy	India
EASTERN OR SATEM	INDO-IRANIAN or ARYAN	Iranian	EAST: Afghan or Pashto; Baluchi	Afghanistan, Baluchistan, etc.
EASTERN OR SATEM	INDO-IRANIAN or ARYAN	Iranian	WEST: Avestan, Old Persian, Middle Persian (Pahlavi, Parsi), Modern Persian; Kurdish; Scythian, Ossetic	Iran (Persia), Kurdistan, Caucasia
EASTERN OR SATEM	THRACO-PHRYGIAN	Phrygian	Phrygian	Ancient Phrygia
EASTERN OR SATEM	THRACO-PHRYGIAN	Armenian	Armenian (Old or Classical, Modern)	Armenia
EASTERN OR SATEM	THRACO-ILLYRIAN		Thracian, Illyrian, Albanian	Balkan Peninsula
EASTERN OR SATEM	BALTO-SLAVIC	Slavic or Slavonic	SOUTH: Church Slavic or Old Bulgarian; Bulgarian, Serbo-Croatian (Serbian, Croatian), Slovenian	Bulgaria, Yugoslavia
EASTERN OR SATEM	BALTO-SLAVIC	Slavic or Slavonic	EAST: Great Russian or Russian, White Russian, Little Russian or Ukrainian	Russia
EASTERN OR SATEM	BALTO-SLAVIC	Slavic or Slavonic	WEST: Czechoslovak (Czech, Moravian, Slovak); Sorbian or Wendish; Polish	Czechoslovakia, Poland, Germany
EASTERN OR SATEM	BALTO-SLAVIC	Baltic or Lettic	Old Prussian, Lithuanian, Lettish	East Prussia, Lithuania, Latvia
WESTERN OR CENTUM	HELLENIC	Greek	(Old Ionic or Epic, New Ionic, Attic; Doric; Aeolic), Modern Greek (Romaic)	Greece and Asia Minor
WESTERN OR CENTUM	ITALIC	Osco-Umbrian	Oscan; Umbrian	Italy
WESTERN OR CENTUM	ITALIC	Sabellian	(Sabine, Volscian)	Italy
WESTERN OR CENTUM	ITALIC	Latinian	Latin; Romance languages: langue d'oïl, langue d'oc, French, Provençal, Franco-Provençal, Catalan; Spanish (Castilian), Portuguese (Galician); Italian (Tuscan or standard Italian); Rhaeto-Romanic (Romansh, Ladin); Romanian	Italy, France, Spain, Portugal, Switzerland, Romania
WESTERN OR CENTUM	CELTIC	Continental	Gaulish	Ancient Gaul
WESTERN OR CENTUM	CELTIC	Insular	CYMRIC: Cornish, Welsh, Breton	Cornwall, Wales, Brittany
WESTERN OR CENTUM	CELTIC	Insular	GOIDELIC: Irish, Gaelic, Manx	Ireland, Scotland, Isle of Man
WESTERN OR CENTUM	TEUTONIC or GERMANIC	East	Gothic	Ancient Germany, etc.
WESTERN OR CENTUM	TEUTONIC or GERMANIC	North or Scandinavian	Old Norse, Icelandic, Swedish, Danish, Norwegian	Scandinavia
WESTERN OR CENTUM	TEUTONIC or GERMANIC	West	HIGH: Old High German (Frankish in part, Bavarian), Middle High German, German	Germany, Austria
WESTERN OR CENTUM	TEUTONIC or GERMANIC	West	LOW: Old Saxon, Low German or Plattdeutsch, Dutch, Flemish, Frisian; Anglo-Saxon, Middle English, English (Scottish)	Germany, Netherlands, Belgium, England, etc.

* Semicolons [;] divide subgroups; parentheses [( )] indicate dialects. Small capitals indicate groups; italics show dead languages.
† Localities where Indo-European languages have been carried in recent times by immigration, as North America for English, Spanish America for Spanish, are not here indicated.

In'do–Ger·man'ic, *adj.* Indo-European.

In'do–I·ra'ni·an, *adj.* [*Indo-* + *Iranian*.] Belonging to or designating the subfamily of Indo-European languages spoken chiefly in India and Iran (Persia). See INDO-EUROPEAN LANGUAGES, *Table*.

in'dole (ĭn'dōl), *n.* Also **in'dol** (-dōl; -dŏl). [*indigo* + *-ol* of phen*ol*.] *Chem.* A white, crystalline, feebly basic compound, C_8H_7N, obtained by reduction from indigo blue and in other ways, and formed from proteins by putrefaction; also, a derivative of this substance.

in'do·lence (ĭn'dō·lĕns), *n.* [F. or L.; F., fr. L. *indolentia* freedom from pain.] Quality, condition, or instance of being indolent; indisposition to labor; sloth.

in'do·lent (-lĕnt), *adj.* [F. or L.; F., fr. LL. *indolens, -entis*, fr. *in-* not + *dolens*, pres. part. of *dolere* to feel pain.] **1.** *Med.* Causing little or no pain; as, an *indolent* tumor. **2.** Indulging in ease; avoiding exertion; lazy. — **Syn.** See LAZY. — **Ant.** Industrious. — **in'do·lent·ly**, *adv.*

in·dom'i·ta·ble (ĭn·dŏm'ĭ·tȧ·b'l), *adj.* [LL. *indomitabilis*, fr. *in-* not + *domitare*, intens. fr. *domare* to tame.] Not to be subdued; unconquerable; invincible. — **in·dom'i·ta·bly**, *adv.*

In'do·ne'sian (ĭn'dō·nē'zhăn; -shăn), *adj.* [*Indo-* + Gr. *nēsos* island.] **1.** Of or pertaining to Indonesia or the Indonesians. **2.** Designating the subfamily of Austronesian languages spoken chiefly in the Malay Peninsula and Archipelago. See LANGUAGE, *Table*. — *n.* A member of a race forming the chief part of the population of the Malay Archipelago preceding the Malays, and probably sprung from a mixture of Polynesian and Mongoloid immigrants.

in'door' (ĭn'dōr'; 70), *adj.* **1.** Of or pert. to the interior of a building. **2.** Done, living, or belonging within doors.

in'doors' (ĭn'dōrz'; ĭn'dōrz'), *adv.* In or into a building.

in'do·phe'nol (ĭn'dō·fē'nōl; -nŏl), *n.* [*indigo* + *phenol*.] Any of a series of synthetic blue dyes, derivatives of quinonimines.

in·dors'a·ble, in·dorse'ment, in·dors'er. Vars. of ENDORSABLE, etc.

in·dorse' (ĭn·dôrs'), *v. t.* [After ML. *indorsare*. See ENDORSE.] To endorse.

in·dox'yl (ĭn·dŏk'sĭl; ĭn'dŏk·sēl'), *n.* [*indigo* + hydr*oxyl*.] *Chem.* A crystalline compound, C_8H_7NO, occurring in plants and animals, and made artificially as a step in indigo manufacture.

In'dra (ĭn'drȧ), *n.* [Skr.] *Hindu Relig.* In Vedic mythology, the great national god of the Indo-Aryans. Later he sinks to secondary rank.

in'draft', in'draught' (ĭn'drȧft'), *n.* **1.** Drawing or pulling in; inward attraction. **2.** An inward flow or current, as of air, water, etc.

in'drawn' (ĭn'drôn'; 2), *adj.* Drawn in.

in'dri (ĭn'drĭ), *n.* [F. *indri*, a mistaken application of the Malagasy *indry* lo! or *indry izy* there he is. *Oxf. E. D.*] The largest of the lemurs of Madagascar (*Indris brevicaudatus*), about two feet long.

in·du'bi·ta·ble (ĭn·dū'bĭ·tȧ·b'l), *adj.* Not dubitable; too evident for doubt; unquestionable. — **in·du'bi·ta·ble·ness**, *n.* — **in·du'bi·ta·bly**, *adv.*

in·duce' (ĭn·dūs'), *v. t.*; -DUCED' (-dūst'); -DUC'ING (-dūs'ĭng). [L. *inducere, inductum*, fr. *in-* in + *ducere* to lead.] **1.** To lead on; prevail on; to move by persuasion or influence. **2.** *Obs.* **a** To introduce. **b** To imply. **c** To overspread. **3.** To bring on or about; effect; cause; as, a fever *induced* by exposure. **4.** *Logic.* To conclude or infer from particulars or by induction. Cf. DEDUCE. **5.** *Physics.* **a** To produce by induction, as an electric current. **b** To produce (radioactivity) in an element by artificial means, as by bombardment. — **in·duc'er** (-dūs'ẽr), *n.* — **in·duc'i·ble**, *adj.*

Syn. **Induce, persuade, prevail on** *or* **upon** mean to move another to act in a certain way. **Induce** implies influence over the reason or judgment; **persuade** implies an appeal to a person's emotions; **prevail on** *or* **upon** may be used in place of *induce* or *persuade* but it usually carries a stronger implication of opposition to be faced or of arguments to be overcome.

in·duce'ment (-mĕnt), *n.* **1.** Act of inducing or state of being induced. **2.** That which induces; motive; consideration. **3.** *Law.* Matter stated by way of explanatory preamble or introduction to the main allegations of a pleading. — **Syn.** See MOTIVE.

in·duct' (ĭn·dŭkt'), *v. t.* [L. *inductus*, past part. of *inducere*. See INDUCE.] **1.** To introduce, as into an office; install; specif., to introduce ceremonially into a benefice; — in the Church of England, disting. from *institute*. **2.** To bring in; introduce; hence, initiate. **3.** *Mil.* To enroll for training and service under a selective-service act or bring into federal service as part of the National Guard of the U. S.

in·duct'ance (-dŭk'tăns), *n.* *Elec.* **a** That property of an electric circuit by virtue of which a varying current induces an electromotive force in that circuit or in a neighboring circuit. **b** The property of an electric circuit by which it lags in receiving in full measure the force of a current or, when the current is cut off, in decreasing to zero. **c** A circuit or a device possessing inductance, as a reactor.

in'duc·tee' (ĭn'dŭk·tē'), *n.* A person inducted into the armed forces.

in·duc'tile (ĭn·dŭk'tĭl; 56), *adj.* Not ductile; inflexible; unyielding. — **in'duc·til'i·ty** (ĭn'dŭk·tĭl'ĭ·tĭ), *n.*

in·duc'tion (ĭn·dŭk'shŭn), *n.* **1.** An inducting; installation, as in an official position; initiation. **2.** An inducing; specif.: **a** A bringing forward of facts to prove something. **b** A causing or bringing about something, as a fever or disease. **3.** *Archaic.* An introduction or introductory scene; preface; prelude. **4.** *Elec. & Magnetism.* Act or process by which: (1) an electrical conductor becomes electrified when near a charged body (***electrostatic induction***); (2) a magnetizable body becomes magnetized when in a magnetic field or in the magnetic flux set up by a magnetomotive force (***magnetic induction***); (3) an electromotive force is produced in a circuit by varying the magnetic field linked with the circuit (***electromagnetic induction***). **5.** *Engin.* In internal-combustion engines, the inspiration of the fuel-air charge from the carburetor into the cylinders. **6.** *Logic.* Act or process of reasoning from a part to a whole, from particulars to generals, or from the individual to the universal; the inference so reached. Cf. DEDUCTION. **7.** *Mil.* The formality by which a civilian is inducted into military service under the provisions of a draft law.

induction coil. *Elec.* An apparatus for transforming a direct current, such as an ordinary battery current, by induction into an alternating current of high potential.

in·duc'tive (ĭn·dŭk'tĭv), *adj.* **1.** Inducing; persuasive; tempting. **2.** Of or pertaining to logical induction; as, *inductive* reasoning; also, employing the methods of induction; as, *inductive* science. **3.** *Elec.* Pertaining to inductance or electric induction. **4.** *Physiol.* Producing internal change, and response. — **in·duc'tive·ly**, *adv.* — **in·duc'tive·ness**, *n.*

in'duc·tiv'i·ty (ĭn'dŭk·tĭv'ĭ·tĭ), *n.* *Elec.* **a** Capacity for induction; specif., inductance. **b** Specific inductive capacity.

in·duc'tor (ĭn·dŭk'tẽr), *n.* **1.** One who inducts. **2.** *Biol.* A substance capable, under certain circumstances, of inducing a specific type of development in embryonic or other undifferentiated tissue; as, the dorsal margin of the blastopore is an *inductor* of embryonic differentiation. **3.** *Elec.* **a** A part of an electrical apparatus which acts upon another, or is itself acted upon, by induction. **b** A reactor.

in·due' (ĭn·dū'), *v. t.* [L. *induere* to put on, clothe.] **1.** To assume; put on, as clothes; draw on. **2.** To clothe; invest; hence, endow; furnish; supply, esp. with moral, mental, or spiritual qualities.

in·dulge' (ĭn·dŭlj'), *v. t.*; -DULGED' (-dŭljd'); -DULG'ING (-dŭl'jĭng). [L. *indulgere* to be kind to, to yield to.] **1.** To be complacent or tolerant toward; to give way to; specif.: **a** Of a habit, desire, etc., to give oneself up to. **b** Of a person, to yield to the desire of; humor; as, to *indulge* children. **2.** To grant as by favor. — *v. i.* To indulge oneself; gratify one's tastes or desires. — **in·dulg'er** (-dŭl'jẽr), *n.* — **in·dulg'ing·ly**, *adv.*

Syn. **Indulge, pamper, humor, spoil, baby, mollycoddle** mean to show undue favor or attention to a person or his desires. **Indulge** implies complaisance or even weakness in gratifying another's desires; **pamper** implies inordinate gratification of taste for that which is luxurious or dainty (and, therefore, enervating in its effects); **humor** stresses a yielding to a person's moods, whims, or caprices; **spoil** stresses indulging or pampering with injurious effects on character or disposition; **baby** stresses the giving of the excessive care and attention proper only when its recipient is a baby; **mollycoddle** stresses inordinate attention to another's health or welfare, or undue efforts to relieve him of strain or hardships.

in·dul'gence (ĭn·dŭl'jĕns), *n.* **1.** Act, fact, or practice of indulging; gratification; humoring. **2.** An indulgent act; favor granted. **3.** Self-gratification; self-indulging; also, an act or habit indulged in. **4.** *Com. & Law.* An extension of the time for payment or performance, granted as a favor. Cf. MORATORIUM. **5.** *Eng. & Scot. Hist.* **a** [*sometimes cap.*] The grant or offer of certain religious liberties as special favors, made by Charles II and James II to Protestant dissenters and Roman Catholics. **b** The permission given during the same reigns to Scotch Presbyterian ministers to hold services. **6.** *R.C.Ch.* Remission of the temporal (usually purgatorial) punishment due for sins whose eternal punishment has been remitted and whose guilt has been pardoned by the reception of the sacrament of penance. — *v. t.*; -GENCED (-jĕnst); -GENC·ING (-jĕn·sĭng). *R.C.Ch.* To attach an indulgence to.

in·dul'gent (-jĕnt), *adj.* [L. *indulgens, -entis*, pres. part.] Indulging or prone to indulge; showing indulgence; compliant; lenient. — **in·dul'gent·ly**, *adv.*

in'du·line (ĭn'dū·lēn; -lĭn), *n.* Also **in'du·lin.** [From *indigo*.] *Chem. & Dyes.* Any of a large series of blue or violet dyes prepared by heating certain nitrogen compounds with amines in presence of a mineral acid, and in other ways.

in·dult' (ĭn·dŭlt'), *n.* [F. or L.; F., fr. LL. *indultum* indulgence, favor. See INDULGE.] *Canon Law.* A special privilege granted by ecclesiastical authority for a definite or indefinite period of time.

in'du·men'tum (ĭn'dū·mĕn'tŭm), *n.* [L., a covering.] **1.** *Zool.* The feathery covering of a bird. **2.** *Bot.* A dense woolly pubescence.

in·du'pli·cate (ĭn·dū'plĭ·kāt), *adj.* [*in-* in + *duplicate*.] *Bot.* **a** Having the edges bent abruptly toward the axis; — said of the parts of the calyx or corolla in estivation. **b** Having the edges rolled inward and then arranged about the axis without overlapping; — said of leaves in vernation. — **in·du'pli·ca'tion** (-kā'shŭn), *n.* — **in·du'pli·ca'tive** (-kā'tĭv), *adj.*

in'du·rate (ĭn'dū·rāt), *adj.* [L. *induratus*, past part. of *indurare*. See ENDURE.] Hardened, physically or morally. — (-rāt), *v. t. & i.* **1.** To make grow hard; to harden; as, great heat *indurates* clay. **2.** To make unfeeling; render stubborn or obdurate. **3.** To make or become hardy or enduring; inure. — **in'du·ra'tion** (-rā'shŭn), *n.* — **in'du·ra'tive** (-rā'tĭv), *adj.*

in·du'si·um (ĭn·dū'zĭ·ŭm; -zhĭ·ŭm), *n.*; *pl.* -SIA (-ȧ). [L., an undergarment, fr. *induere* to put on.] **1.** *Bot.* In ferns, an outgrowth of the leaf which covers or invests the sori in many species. **2.** *Anat. & Zool.* Any membrane serving as a covering, as the amnion. — **in·du'si·al** (-ăl), *adj.* — **in·du'si·ate** (-āt), *adj.*

in·dus'tri·al (ĭn·dŭs'trĭ·ăl), *adj.* [From F. *industriel* and ML. *industrialis*. See INDUSTRY.] Having to do with industry; as: **a** Of the nature of, or constituting, an industry or industries. **b** Characterized by highly developed industries; as, an *industrial* nation; the *industrial* revolution (see REVOLUTION, 4). **c** Engaged in industries, esp. in the manual labor of industries; as, the *industrial* classes. **d** Derived from industry, or human toil; as, *industrial* wealth. **e** Pertaining to or aiding those engaged in industries; as *industrial* medicine or training. **f** Produced by an organized industry; — applied to products. — *n.* **1.** A person employed in an industrial pursuit; esp., one engaged in manufacturing industry. **2.** A stock, bond, or other security based upon the assets of an industrial corporation or enterprise. — **in·dus'tri·al·ly**, *adv.*

in·dus'tri·al·ism (-ĭz'm), *n.* Social organization in which industries, esp. large-scale industries, are dominant.

in·dus'tri·al·ist (-ĭst), *n.* A person engaged in, or connected with, some industry; a manufacturer or operative.

in·dus'tri·al·ize (-īz), *v. t.* To make industrial; affect with, or give over to, industrialism. — **in·dus'tri·al·i·za'tion** (-ĭ·zā'shŭn; -ī·zā'-), *n.*

industrial school. A school giving education for participation in industry; specif., a public institution of this type for young persons committed to it by legal proceedings.

industrial union. A labor union, local or national, which admits to membership workmen in an industry irrespective of their occupation or craft; — called also *vertical union*. Cf. CRAFT UNION.

in·dus'tri·ous (ĭn·dŭs'trĭ·ŭs), *adj.* [From L. *industriosus*, perh. through F. *industrieux*.] **1.** *Obs.* Exhibiting or marked by intelligent work; skillful. **2.** Steadily and perseveringly active; painstaking; busy; diligent; — commonly implying devotion to lawful and useful labor. — **Syn.** See BUSY. — **-ous·ly**, *adv.* — **-ous·ness**, *n.*

in'dus·try (ĭn'dŭs·trĭ), *n.*; *pl.* -TRIES (-trĭz). [F. *industrie*, fr. L. *industria*.] **1.** *Obs.* Skill; ingenuity. **2.** Habitual diligence in any employment or pursuit; steady attention to business; assiduity. **3.** Any department or branch of art, occupation, or business; esp., one which employs much labor and capital and is a distinct branch of trade; as, the sugar *industry*. **4.** *Econ.* Systematic labor or habitual employment. — **Syn.** See BUSINESS.

in′dwell′ (ĭn′dwĕl′), *v. t. & i.*; IN′DWELT′ (-dwĕlt′); IN′DWELL′ING (-dwĕl′ĭng; 2). To dwell in; abide within; inhabit. — **in′dwell′er** (ĭn′dwĕl′ẽr), *n.*

-ine (*see Pron.*, § 56). [F. or L.; F. *-in, -ine*, fr. L. *-inus, -ina, -inum*, an adj. ending.] **1.** A suffix in adjectives, denoting *of* or *pertaining to, like, characterized by*, as in femin*ine*, can*ine*, Levant*ine*. **2.** [F. *-ine*, L. *-ina*, an abstract fem. ending.] A suffix in abstract nouns, as in discipl*ine*, rap*ine*, medic*ine*. **3.** A feminine suffix, commonly from French *-ine*, of varying origin, as in hero*ine*, Joseph*ine*.

-ine (-ēn; -ĭn; 56). Also **-in**. [Cf. F. *-ine*, L. *-inus*, fem. *-ina*, adj. suffix.] *Chem.* A suffix used in forming the names of certain elements, as chlor*ine*, and compounds, as ars*ine*. Names of organic bases, as alkaloids, are systematically written with the ending *-ine*; those of neutral substances, as fats, most proteins, glucosides, etc., with *-in*; as, stear*in* gelat*in*, amygdal*in*, etc. This rule does not apply to the many commercial or popular names in *-ine*, as gasol*ine*. Some chemists prefer *-in* for basic substances also.

-ine (*see Pron.*, § 56). [L. *-inus*, fr. Gr. *-inos*.] A suffix in adjectives, denoting *of the nature of, like*, esp. *a* (specified) *material*, as in crystall*ine*, opal*ine*, adamant*ine*.

in·earth′ (ĭn·ûrth′), *v. t.* To inter; bury.

in·e′bri·ant (ĭn·ē′brĭ·ănt), *adj.* Intoxicating. — *n.* An intoxicant.

in·e′bri·ate (ĭn·ē′brĭ·āt), *adj.* [L. *inebriatus*, past part. of *inebriare* to inebriate, fr. *in-* in + *ebriare* to make drunk, fr. *ebrius* drunk.] Intoxicated; habitually given to drink. — (-āt), *v. t.* **1.** To make drunk; intoxicate. **2.** Hence, to exhilarate or stupefy as if by liquor. — (-āt), *n.* A drunkard; esp., a habitual drunkard. — **in·e′bri·at′ed** (-āt′ĕd; -ĭd), *adj.* — **Syn.** See DRUNK. — **in·e′bri·a′tion** (-ā′shŭn), *n.*

in′e·bri′e·ty (ĭn′ē·brī′ĕ·tĭ), *n.* Inebriation; drunkenness.

in·ed′i·ble (ĭn·ĕd′ĭ·b′l), *adj.* Not edible; not fit for food. — **in·ed′i·bil′i·ty** (-bĭl′ĭ·tĭ), *n.*

in·ed′it·ed (-ĭ·tĕd; -tĭd), *adj.* Not edited; unpublished.

in·ef′fa·ble (-ĕf′ȧ·b′l), *adj.* [F., fr. L. *ineffabilis*. See IN- not; FAME.] **1.** Incapable of being expressed in words; unutterable; indescribable; as, *ineffable* anguish or joys. **2.** Not to be uttered; as, the *ineffable* name of Jehovah. — **in·ef′fa·bil′i·ty** (-bĭl′ĭ·tĭ), **in·ef′fa·ble·ness**, *n.* — **in·ef′fa·bly**, *adv.*

in′ef·face′a·ble (ĭn′ĕ·fās′ȧ·b′l; ĭn′ĭ-), *adj.* Not effaceable; indelible; ineradicable. — **in′ef·face′a·bil′i·ty** (-bĭl′ĭ·tĭ), *n.* — **-face′a·bly**, *adv.*

in′ef·fec′tive (-fĕk′tĭv), *adj.* **1.** Not effective; productive of no effect; ineffectual. **2.** Not efficient; incapable; incompetent. — **in′ef·fec′tive·ly**, *adv.* — **in′ef·fec′tive·ness**, *n.*

in′ef·fec′tu·al (-tụ̈·ăl), *adj.* Not effectual; not producing the proper or usual effect; useless; futile; unavailing. — **in′ef·fec′tu·al′i·ty** (-ăl′ĭ·tĭ), *n.* — **in′ef·fec′tu·al·ly**, *adv.* — **in′ef·fec′tu·al·ness**, *n.*

in′ef·fi·ca′cious (ĭn′ĕf·ĭ·kā′shŭs), *adj.* Not efficacious; not having power to produce the effect desired; inadequate; inefficient. — **in′ef·fi·ca′cious·ly**, *adv.* — **in′ef·fi·ca′cious·ness**, *n.*

in·ef′fi·ca·cy (ĭn·ĕf′ĭ·kȧ·sĭ), *n.* Lack of efficacy; character of being inefficacious; inefficiency; futility.

in′ef·fi′cien·cy (ĭn′ĕ·fĭsh′ĕn·sĭ; -′n·sĭ; ĭn′ĭ-), *n.* Quality, state, or fact of being inefficient; lack of efficiency.

in′ef·fi′cient (-ĕnt; -′nt), *adj.* Not efficient; as: **a** Not producing the effect intended or desired; inefficacious. **b** Not competent, capable, or proficient. — *n.* An inefficient person. — **in′ef·fi′cient·ly**, *adv.*

in′e·las′tic (ĭn′ē·lăs′tĭk), *adj.* Not elastic; hence, inflexible; unyielding. — **in′e·las·tic′i·ty** (-lăs·tĭs′ĭ·tĭ), *n.*

in·el′e·gance (ĭn·ĕl′ē·găns), *n.*; *pl.* INELEGANCES (-găn·sĕz; -sĭz). Also **in·el′e·gan·cy** (-găn·sĭ); *pl.* INELEGANCIES (-sĭz). **1.** Lack of elegance; lack of grace, taste, or beauty, in language, manners, etc. **2.** Anything inelegant.

in·el′e·gant (-gănt), *adj.* Not elegant; deficient in beauty, polish, grace, or ornament; lacking in anything required by good taste. — **in·el′e·gant·ly**, *adv.*

in·el′i·gi·ble (ĭn·ĕl′ĭ·jĭ·b′l), *adj.* Not eligible; not qualified, as for an office. — *n.* A person ineligible, esp. as a suitor. — **in·el′i·gi·bil′i·ty** (-bĭl′ĭ·tĭ), **in·el′i·gi·bly**, *adv.*

in·el′o·quent (-ō·kwĕnt), *adj.* Not eloquent; lacking eloquence. — **in·el′o·quence** (-kwĕns), *n.* — **in·el′o·quent·ly**, *adv.*

in′e·luc′ta·ble (ĭn′ē·lŭk′tȧ·b′l), *adj.* [L. *ineluctabilis*, fr. *in-* not + *eluctabilis* to be surmounted, fr. *eluctari* to struggle out of, to surmount.] Not to be overcome; irresistible; inevitable. — **in′e·luc′ta·bil′i·ty** (-bĭl′ĭ·tĭ), *n.* — **in′e·luc′ta·bly**, *adv.*

in′e·lud′i·ble (-lūd′ĭ·b′l), *adj.* That cannot be eluded.

in′e·nar′ra·ble (ĭn′ē·năr′ȧ·b′l), *adj.* [F. *inénarrable*, fr. L. *inenarrabilis*, fr. *in-* not + *enarrabilis* that may be related.] Incapable of being narrated; indescribable; ineffable.

in·ept′ (ĭn·ĕpt′), *adj.* [F. or L.; F. *inepte*, fr. L. *ineptus*, fr. *in-* not + *aptus* apt, fit.] **1.** Not apt; devoid of fitness or aptitude. **2.** Inappropriate; out of place. **3.** Absurd; foolish. — **Syn.** See AWKWARD. — **in·ept′i·tude**, *n.* — **in·ept′ly**, *adv.* — **in·ept′ness**, *n.*

in′e·qual′i·ty (ĭn′ē·kwŏl′ĭ·tĭ), *n.*; *pl.* -TIES (-tĭz). [MF. *inequalité*, fr. L. *inaequalitas*.] **1.** Quality of being unequal; want of equality; also, an instance of such inequality. **2.** Specif.: **a** Social disparity. **b** Lack of proper proportion or distribution. **c** Unevenness; want of levelness. **d** Variableness; inconstancy. **e** Inadequacy for any office or purpose. **3.** A variation, as in height of tide, motion of a planet, etc.; also, the amount of such variation. **4.** *Math.* Also **in′e·qua′tion** (-kwā′zhŭn; -shŭn). An expression consisting of two unequal quantities, with the sign of inequality (>, <, or ≠) between them; as, the *inequality* 2<3, or 4>1.

in′e·qui- (ĭn′ē·kwĭ-). [*in-* not + L. *aequus* equal.] A combining form meaning *unequal, unequally*, as in:

inequiaxial	**inequilateral**	**inequipotential**
inequicostate	**inequilobate**	**inequivalve**

in·eq′ui·ta·ble (ĭn·ĕk′wĭ·tȧ·b′l), *adj.* Not equitable; unjust.

in·eq′ui·ty (ĭn·ĕk′wĭ·tĭ), *n.*; *pl.* -TIES (-tĭz). Want of equity or an instance of it; injustice; unfairness.

in′e·rad′i·ca·ble (ĭn′ē·răd′ĭ·kȧ·b′l), *adj.* That cannot be eradicated; ineffaceable. — **in′e·rad′i·ca·bly**, *adv.*

in′e·ras′a·ble (-rās′ȧ·b′l; -rāz′-), *adj.* Incapable of being erased.

in·er′ra·ble (ĭn·ĕr′ȧ·b′l; -ûr′-), *adj.* [L. *inerrabilis*.] Incapable of erring; infallible. — **in·er′ra·bil′i·ty** (-bĭl′ĭ·tĭ), **in·er′ra·ble·ness**, *n.* — **in·er′ra·bly**, *adv.*

in·er′rant (-ănt), *adj.* [L. *inerrans, -antis*, not wandering. See IN- not; ERR.] Exempt from error; free from mistake; infallible. — **in·er′ran·cy** (-ăn·sĭ), *n.*

in′er·rat′ic (ĭn′ē·răt′ĭk), *adj.* Not erratic; settled; established.

in·ert′ (ĭn·ûrt′), *adj.* [L. *iners, inertis*, unskilled, idle, fr. *in-* not + *ars* art.] **1.** Destitute of power to move itself or actively to resist motion impressed; having inertia; as, matter is *inert*. **2.** Not having active properties; powerless for a desired effect, as a drug. **3.** Sluggish; indolent. — **Syn.** See INACTIVE. — **in·ert′ly**, *adv.* — **in·ert′ness**, *n.*

in·er′tia (ĭn·ûr′shȧ; -shĭ·ȧ), *n.* [L., idleness, fr. *iners* idle.] **1.** *Physics.* **a** The property of matter by which it will remain at rest, or in uniform motion in the same straight line or direction unless acted upon by some external force. **b** An analogous property of other physical quantities, as electricity. **2.** Indisposition to exertion or action; inertness. — **in·er′tial** (-shăl; -shĭ·ăl), *adj.*

in′es·cap′a·ble (ĭn′ĕs·kāp′ȧ·b′l; ĭn′ĭs-), *adj.* That cannot be escaped; inevitable. — **in′es·cap′a·bly**, *adv.*

‖**in es′se** (ĭn ĕs′ē). [L.] In actual existence. Cf. IN POSSE.

in′es·sen′tial (ĭn′ĕ·sĕn′shăl; ĭn′ĭ-), *adj.* Having no essence or being; also, not essential; unessential. — *n.* Anything inessential. — **in′es·sen′ti·al′i·ty** (-sĕn′shĭ·ăl′ĭ·tĭ), *n.*

in·es′ti·ma·ble (ĭn·ĕs′tĭ·mȧ·b′l), *adj.* [OF., fr. L. *inaestimabilis*.] Incapable of being estimated; esp., too valuable or excellent to be measured or fully appreciated. — **in·es′ti·ma·bly**, *adv.*

in·ev′i·ta·ble (-ĕv′ĭ·tȧ·b′l), *adj.* [L. *inevitabilis*. See IN- not; EVITABLE.] Incapable of being avoided, evaded, or shunned; bound to come, happen, etc. — **in·ev′i·ta·bil′i·ty** (-bĭl′ĭ·tĭ), **in·ev′i·ta·ble·ness**, *n.* — **in·ev′i·ta·bly**, *adv.*

in′ex·act′ (ĭn′ĕg·zăkt′; ĭn′ĭg-), *adj.* Not exact; not precisely correct or true; inaccurate. — **in′ex·act′ly**, *adv.* — **in′ex·act′ness**, *n.*

in′ex·act′i·tude (-zăk′tĭ·tūd), *n.* [F.] Inexactness.

in′ex·cus′a·ble (ĭn′ĕks·kūz′ȧ·b′l; ĭn′ĭks-), *adj.* Not excusable; not admitting excuse or justification. — **in′ex·cus′a·bil′i·ty** (-bĭl′ĭ·tĭ), **in′ex·cus′a·ble·ness**, *n.* — **in′ex·cus′a·bly**, *adv.*

in′ex·haust′i·ble (ĭn′ĕg·zôs′tĭ·b′l; ĭn′ĭg-), *adj.* Incapable of being exhausted; as: **a** Exhaustless. **b** Indefatigable. — **in′ex·haust′i·bil′i·ty** (-bĭl′ĭ·tĭ), *n.* — **in′ex·haust′i·bly**, *adv.*

in′ex·ist′ent (-zĭs′tĕnt), *adj.* Not having being; not existing. — **in′ex·ist′ence** (-tĕns), **in′ex·ist′en·cy** (-tĕn·sĭ), *n.*

in·ex′o·ra·ble (ĭn·ĕk′sō·rȧ·b′l), *adj.* [L. *inexorabilis*. See IN- not; EXORABLE.] Not to be persuaded or moved by entreaty; inflexible; relentless. — **Syn.** See INFLEXIBLE. — **in·ex′o·ra·bil′i·ty** (-bĭl′ĭ·tĭ), *n.* — **in·ex′o·ra·ble·ness**, *n.* — **in·ex′o·ra·bly**, *adv.*

in′ex·pe′di·ent (ĭn′ĕks·pē′dĭ·ĕnt; ĭn′ĭks-), *adj.* Not expedient; not practicable, advisable, or politic. — **in′ex·pe′di·ence** (-ĕns), **in′ex·pe′di·en·cy** (-ĕn·sĭ), *n.* — **in′ex·pe′di·ent·ly**, *adv.*

in′ex·pen′sive (-pĕn′sĭv), *adj.* Not expensive. — **in′ex·pen′sive·ly**, *adv.* — **in′ex·pen′sive·ness**, *n.*

in′ex·pe′ri·ence (-pẽr′ĭ·ĕns), *n.* Lack of experience; lack of personal and experimental knowledge. — **in′ex·pe′ri·enced** (-ĕnst), *adj.*

in′ex·pert′ (-pûrt′; 2), *adj.* Not expert; unskilled. — *n.* An inexpert person. — **in′ex·pert′ly**, *adv.* — **in′ex·pert′ness**, *n.*

in·ex′pi·a·ble (ĭn·ĕks′pĭ·ȧ·b′l), *adj.* [L. *inexpiabilis*.] **1.** Admitting of no expiation or atonement. **2.** *Archaic.* Unappeasable; implacable. — **in·ex′pi·a·ble·ness**, *n.* — **in·ex′pi·a·bly**, *adv.*

in′ex·plain′a·ble (ĭn′ĕks·plān′ȧ·b′l; ĭn′ĭks-), *adj.* Not explainable; inexplicable.

in·ex′pli·ca·ble (ĭn·ĕks′plĭ·kȧ·b′l), *adj.* [F., fr. L. *inexplicabilis*.] Not explicable; incapable of being explained, interpreted, or accounted for. — **in·ex′pli·ca·bil′i·ty** (-bĭl′ĭ·tĭ), **in·ex′pli·ca·ble·ness**, *n.* — **in·ex′pli·ca·bly**, *adv.*

in′ex·plic′it (ĭn′ĕks·plĭs′ĭt; ĭn′ĭks-), *adj.* [L. *inexplicitus*. See IN- not; EXPLICIT.] Not explicit; not definite and unequivocal.

in′ex·press′i·ble (-prĕs′ĭ·b′l), *adj.* Not capable of being expressed; ineffable; unutterable. — **in′ex·press′i·bil′i·ty** (-bĭl′ĭ·tĭ), **in′ex·press′i·ble·ness**, *n.* — **in′ex·press′i·bly**, *adv.*

in′ex·press′i·bles (-b′lz), *n. pl. Humorous.* Breeches.

in′ex·pres′sive (-prĕs′ĭv), *adj.* **1.** *Rare.* Inexpressible. **2.** Not expressive; dull. — **in′ex·pres′sive·ly**, *adv.* — **in′ex·pres′sive·ness**, *n.*

in′ex·pug′na·ble (-pŭg′nȧ·b′l), *adj.* [F., fr. L. *inexpugnabilis*.] Impregnable; unconquerable; stable. — **in′ex·pug′na·bil′i·ty** (-bĭl′ĭ·tĭ), **in′ex·pug′na·bly**, *adv.*

in′ex·ten′si·ble (-tĕn′sĭ·b′l), *adj.* Not extensible.

‖**in ex·ten′so** (ĭn ĕks·tĕn′sō). [ML.] At full length.

in′ex·tin′guish·a·ble (ĭn′ĕks·tĭng′gwĭsh·ȧ·b′l; ĭn′ĭks-), *adj.* Not extinguishable; unquenchable. — **in′ex·tin′guish·a·bly**, *adv.*

in′ex·tir′pa·ble (ĭn′ĕks·tûr′pȧ·b′l; ĭn′ĭks-), *adj.* Not capable of being extirpated; ineradicable. — **in′ex·tir′pa·ble·ness**, *n.*

‖**in ex·tre′mis** (ĭn ĕks·trē′mĭs). [L.] In extremity; dying.

in·ex′tri·ca·ble (ĭn·ĕks′trĭ·kȧ·b′l), *adj.* [F. or L.; F. *inextricable*, fr. L. *inextricabilis*.] **1.** Not permitting extrication; forming a maze from which it is impossible to get free. **2.** Incapable of being disentangled or untied; hence, unsolvable; indissoluble. — **in·ex′tri·ca·bil′i·ty** (-bĭl′ĭ·tĭ), **in·ex′tri·ca·ble·ness**, *n.* — **in·ex′tri·ca·bly**, *adv.*

in·fal′li·ble (ĭn·făl′ĭ·b′l), *adj.* [ML. *infallibilis*.] **1.** Not fallible; not liable to err. **2.** Indubitable; certain; as, an *infallible* symptom. **3.** *R.C.Ch.* Incapable of error in defining doctrines touching faith or morals. — *n.* An infallible person, remedy, etc. — **in·fal′li·bil′i·ty** (-bĭl′ĭ·tĭ), *n.* — **in·fal′li·bly**, *adv.*

in′fa·mous (ĭn′fȧ·mŭs), *adj.* [ML. *infamosus*, L. *infamis*, fr. *in-* not + *fama* fame.] **1.** Of very bad report; held in abhorrence; notoriously base. **2.** Causing or producing infamy; scandalous to the last degree. **3.** *Law.* Branded with infamy by conviction. — **Syn.** See VICIOUS. — **in′fa·mous·ly**, *adv.* — **in′fa·mous·ness**, *n.*

in′fa·my (-mĭ), *n.*; *pl.* -MIES (-mĭz). [F. *infamie*, fr. L. *infamia*, fr. *infamis* infamous.] **1.** Evil fame or reputation; public disgrace, dishonor, or reproach. **2.** Quality of being infamous; also, an infamous act. **3.** *Law.* That public disgrace or loss of character incurred by a person convicted of any of certain crimes. — **Syn.** See DISGRACE.

in′fan·cy (ĭn′făn·sĭ), *n.*; *pl.* -CIES (-sĭz). [L. *infantia*. See INFANT.] **1.** Babyhood. **2.** Beginning or early period of existence. **3.** *Law.* The state of an infant; minority.

in′fant (ĭn′fănt), *n.* [OF. *enfant*, fr. L. *infans*, fr. *in-* not + *fari* to speak.] **1.** A child in the first period of life; a babe. **2.** *Law.* A person not of full age; a minor. At the common law any person under 21 is an infant; but this rule is varied from in some states of the United States. — *adj.* **1.** Of, pert. to, or being in infancy. **2.** Intended for young children; as, an *infant* school.

in·fan′ta (ĭn·făn′tȧ), *n.* [Sp. & Pg., fem.] Any daughter of a king of Spain or Portugal; also, the wife of an infante.

in·fan′te (-tā), *n.* [Sp. & Pg.] Any son of a king of Spain or Portugal except the eldest (*principe*); — also used as a title.

in·fan′ti·cide (ĭn·făn′tĭ·sīd), *n.* **1.** [F., fr. LL. *infanticidium* child murder, fr. *infans, -antis*, child + *caedere* to kill.] The killing of an infant. **2.** [F., fr. LL. *infanticida*.] One who commits infanticide.

in′fan·tile (ĭn′făn·tīl; -tĭl; -tēl; *occas.* ĭn·făn′tĭl), *adj.* **1.** Of or pertaining to infancy or an infant; childish. **2.** *Phys. Geog.* In an early stage of development, following an uplift or equivalent change with respect to base level; — said of topographic features.

infantile paralysis. *Med.* An acute virus disease, chiefly in infants and children, characterized by febrile symptoms, motor paralysis, and muscular atrophy, often producing permanent deformities. The paralysis is due to degeneration of the nerve cells in the anterior horns of the gray substance of the spinal cord. Called also *acute anterior poliomyelitis.*

in·fan′ti·lism (ĭn·făn′tĭ·lĭz′m), *n.* *Med.* Condition of being abnormally infantile or childlike; retardation of physical, intellectual, or emotional development.

in′fan·tine (ĭn′făn·tīn; -tĭn; -tēn), *adj.* Infantile.

in′fan·try (ĭn′făn·trĭ), *n.; pl.* -TRIES (-trĭz). [F. *infanterie*, fr. It. *infanteria*, fr. *infante* infant, boy, servant, foot soldier, fr. L. *infans, -antis*, child.] Soldiers, or a body of soldiers, equipped for service on foot. — **in′fan·try·man** (-măn), *n.*

in·farct′ (ĭn·färkt′), *n.* [ML. *infarctus*, for L. *infartus*, past part. of *infarcire*, fr. *in-* in + *farcire* to stuff.] A sharply limited region of necrosis and hemorrhage in an organ, resulting from obstruction of the local circulation by a thrombus or embolus. — **in·farc′tion** (-färk′shŭn), *n.*

in′fare′ (ĭn′fâr′), *n.* [AS. *infær* a going in.] *Chiefly Dial.* A housewarming, esp. one for a bride.

in·fat′u·ate (ĭn·făt′ū·āt), *adj.* [L. *infatuatus*, past part. of *infatuare*, fr. *in-* in + *fatuus* foolish.] Infatuated; marked by infatuation. — (-āt), *v. t.* **1.** To make foolish; affect with folly; deprive of sound judgment. **2.** To inspire with a foolish and extravagant passion. — (-āt), *n.* An infatuated person. — **in·fat′u·at′ed** (-āt′ĕd; -ĭd), *adj.* — **Syn.** See FOND: ENAMORED. — **in·fat′u·a′tion** (-ā′shŭn), *n.*

in·fea′si·ble (ĭn·fē′zĭ·b'l), *adj.* Not feasible; impracticable.

in·fect′ (ĭn·fĕkt′), *v. t.* [L. *infectus*, past part. of *inficere* to put or dip into, to stain, infect, fr. *in-* in + *facere* to make.] **1.** To taint with morbid matter; contaminate with a disease-producing substance, germs, or bacteria; as, to *infect* a lancet. **2.** To affect with infectious disease; to communicate infection to. **3. a** Contaminate; corrupt. **b** To work upon or affect (another) so as to communicate one's mood, feeling, etc.; as, to *infect* one with enthusiasm. **4.** *Law.* To contaminate with illegality or to expose to penalty. — **in·fec′tor** (-fĕk′tẽr), *n.*

in·fec′tion (ĭn·fĕk′shŭn), *n.* **1.** An infecting, as with disease; communication of a disease from one organism to another. **2.** State of being infected; the state produced by the entrance into, and multiplication within the body, of pathogenic microorganisms. **3.** A prevailing disease; epidemic. **4.** That which infects, or causes the communicated disease. **5.** Communication of qualities or emotions by influence of sympathy, example, etc. **6.** *Humorous Misuse.* Affection.

in·fec′tious (-shŭs), *adj.* **1.** Having qualities that may infect; germbearing or germ-laden; as, *infectious* breath. **2.** Communicable or caused by infection. See INFECTIOUS DISEASE. **3.** Tending to infect or corrupt; vitiating. **4.** Capable of being easily diffused or spread; as, *infectious* mirth. **5.** *Obs.* Infected. **6.** *Law.* Contaminating with illegality; exposing to seizure and forfeiture or other penalty. — **in·fec′tious·ly**, *adv.* — **in·fec′tious·ness**, *n.*

infectious disease. Any disease caused by the entrance, growth, and multiplication of bacteria, protozoans, or analogous organisms (filtrable viruses) in the body; a germ disease. It may or may not be contagious (see CONTAGIOUS DISEASE).

in·fec′tive (ĭn·fĕk′tĭv), *adj.* Producing infection; infectious.

in·fe′cund (ĭn·fē′kŭnd; -fĕk′ŭnd), *adj.* Not fecund or fruitful; barren. — **in′fe·cun′di·ty** (ĭn′fē·kŭn′dĭ·tĭ), *n.*

in′fe·lic′i·tous (ĭn′fē·lĭs′ĭ·tŭs), *adj.* Not felicitous; not appropriate in application or expression. — **in′fe·lic′i·tous·ly**, *adv.*

in′fe·lic′i·ty (-tĭ), *n.; pl.* -TIES (-tĭz). **1.** State or quality of being infelicitous. **2.** An infelicitous act, remark, etc.

in′felt′ (ĭn′fĕlt′), *adj.* Felt inwardly; heartfelt.

in·fer′ (ĭn·fûr′), *v. t.;* -FERRED′ (-fûrd′); -FER′RING. [L. *inferre* to bring into, occasion, infer, fr. *in-* in + *ferre* to bring.] **1.** *Obs.* To bring on; induce; inflict. **2.** To derive by reasoning or implication; conclude from facts or premises; to derive as a consequence, conclusion, or probability. **3.** *Colloq.* To surmise; guess. **4.** To indicate; point out. **5.** *Erroneous.* To imply, or hint. **6.** *Obs.* To bring forward; adduce; allege. — *v. i.* To draw inferences. — **in·fer′a·ble** (ĭn·fûr′ȧ·b'l; ĭn′fẽr·ȧ·b'l), *adj.* — **in·fer′rer** (-ẽr), *n.*

Syn. Infer, deduce, conclude, judge, gather mean to arrive at through reasoning from evidence or from premises. In logical use **infer** means just this, but in popular use it often comes close to *surmise;* **deduce**, in nontechnical use, equals *infer* as used in logic, but in strict logical use it means to derive a particular inference from a generalization; **conclude** is often used as an equivalent of *deduce* in its nontechnical sense, but strictly it means to draw the inference that is the necessary consequence of a chain of reasoning; **judge** is near to *conclude* in this latter sense, but sometimes implies more critical testing of the relation of the conclusion to the evidence or premises. **Gather**, a colloquial term, may be used in place of any of these words.

in′fer·ence (ĭn′fẽr·ĕns), *n.* **1.** An inferring; esp., the act of passing from one judgment to another, or from a belief or cognition to a judgment. **2.** That which is inferred; a logical conclusion from given data or premises.

in′fer·en′tial (-ĕn′shăl), *adj.* Deduced or deducible by inference. — **in′fer·en′tial·ly**, *adv.*

in·fe′ri·or (ĭn·fēr′ĭ·ẽr), *adj.* [L., compar. of *inferus* that is below, underneath.] **1.** Situated lower down; lower; nether. **2.** Of low or lower degree or rank, in any scale. **3.** Of little or less importance, value, or merit; of poor or poorer quality; mediocre; second-rate. **4.** *Astron.* **a** Nearer the sun than is the earth; — said of the planets Mercury and Venus. **b** Nearer the earth than is the sun; as, an *inferior* conjunction of Venus. **c** Below the celestial pole (see 2d POLE, 1); as, the *inferior* part of the meridian. **5.** *Bot.* **a** Situated below some other organ, as a calyx when free from the ovary. **b** On the side of a flower which is next the bract; opposite or farthest from the axis. **6.** *Print.* Standing at the bottom of the line, as small figures or letters; as, in A_2, B_n, *2* and *n* are *inferior.* — *n.* An inferior person or thing. — **in·fe′ri·or′i·ty** (-ŏr′ĭ·tĭ), *n.* — **in·fe′ri·or·ly**, *adv.*

in·fe′ri·or′i·ty com′plex. See COMPLEX, *n.*, 2.

in·fer′nal (ĭn·fûr′năl; -n'l), *adj.* [OF., fr. LL. *infernalis*, fr. *infernus* that which lies beneath, the lower. See INFERIOR.] **1.** Of or pertaining to the nether world, the realm of the dead. **2.** Of or pertaining to, or inhabiting, hell; hence, hellish; diabolic; fiendish. **3.** *Colloq.* Detestable; plaguy; as, an *infernal* nuisance. — **in·fer′nal·ly**, *adv.*

infernal machine. A machine or apparatus maliciously designed to explode, and destroy life or property.

in·fer′no (ĭn·fûr′nō), *n.; pl.* -NOS (-nōz). [It.] **1.** The infernal regions; hell; hence, a place likened to it. **2.** [*cap.*] The first part of Dante's *Divina Commedia*, representing hell as a huge pit, formed of gradually concentric circles, in which the damned souls suffer.

in′fe·ro- (ĭn′fē·rō-). [L. *inferus* lower.] *Anat. & Zool.* A combining form meaning: **a** *On the under side.* **b** *Below and;* — in adjectives, as in **in′fe·ro·an·te′ri·or.**

in·fer′ri·ble (ĭn·fûr′ĭ·b'l), *adj.* Inferable; — a spelling chiefly used in logic.

in·fer′tile (ĭn·fûr′tĭl; -t'l; *or, esp. Brit.*, -tīl; 56), *adj.* Not fertile; sterile. — **Syn.** See STERILE. — **in′fer·til′i·ty** (ĭn′fûr·tĭl′ĭ·tĭ), *n.*

in·fest′ (ĭn·fĕst′), *v. t.* [F. *infester*, fr. L. *infestare*, fr. *infestus* disturbed, hostile.] To trouble greatly by numbers or by frequency of presence; as, a sea *infested* with pirates; to assail persistently and in numbers; as, fleas *infest* dogs. — **in·fest′er**, *n.*

in′fes·ta′tion (ĭn′fĕs·tā′shŭn), *n.* Act of infesting, or state of being infested; molestation; also, anything infesting.

in′feu·da′tion (-fū·dā′shŭn), *n.* [ML. *infeudatio*, fr. *infeudare* to enfeoff. See FEUD a fief.] *Eng. Law.* **a** Enfeoffment. **b** The granting of tithes to laymen.

in′fi·del (ĭn′fĭ·dĕl), *adj.* [F. *infidèle*, fr. L. *infidelis*, fr. *in-* not + *fidelis* faithful, fr. *fides* faith.] **1.** Not holding the faith; esp., non-Christian; also, opposing or unfaithful to Christianity. **2.** Of or pertaining to infidels. — *n.* An unbeliever; a disbeliever; specif.: **a** A non-Christian; one who does not accept Christianity. **b** A non-Mohammedan. — **Syn.** See ATHEIST.

in′fi·del′i·ty (ĭn′fĭ·dĕl′ĭ·tĭ; ĭn′fī-), *n.; pl.* -TIES (-tĭz). **1.** Lack of belief in (a certain) religion. **2.** Breach of trust; unfaithfulness to a charge or a moral obligation; also, an unfaithful act. **3.** Marital unfaithfulness; adultery.

in′field′ (ĭn′fēld′), *n.* **1.** A field near a farmhouse. **2.** *Baseball.* **a** The square, the corners of which form the four bases, marked off on a baseball playing field; the diamond. **b** The players on this square, comprising the first, second, and third basemen and the shortstop.

in′field′er (-fēl′dẽr), *n.* *Baseball.* One of the infield (sense 2 **b**).

in·fil′trate (ĭn·fĭl′trāt), *v. t. & i.* [*in-* in + *filtrate.*] **1.** To enter or cause to enter by or as by penetrating the pores or interstices of a substance. **2.** To pass through or into as in filtering; as, to *infiltrate* troops into or nearer to hostile territory by sending single men or small groups through gaps in the enemy's line or in his position. — *n.* That which infiltrates; a substance passing into the tissues and forming an abnormal accumulation. — **in′fil·tra′tion** (ĭn′fĭl·trā′shŭn), *n.* — **in·fil′tra·tive** (ĭn·fĭl′trȧ·tĭv), *adj.*

in′fi·nite (ĭn′fĭ·nĭt), *adj.* [OF. or L.; OF. *infinit*, fr. L. *infinitus*. See IN- not; FINITE.] **1.** Without limits of any kind; undetermined or indeterminate; — said esp. of God and the Absolute. **2.** Without end; boundless; immeasurable. **3.** Indefinitely large, extensive, or numerous; hence, vast; immense; also, inexhaustible. **4.** *Math.* **a** Greater than any assignable quantity of the same kind; — said esp. of a variable. **b** Equivalent to, or having the same power as, some proper part of itself; — said of an assemblage. — **Syn.** Illimitable, boundless, uncircumscribed. — **Ant.** Finite. — (-nĭt; *in church singing often* -nīt), *n.* That which is infinite; specif.: **a** Boundless space or duration; infinity. **b** [*cap.*, with *the.*] The Infinite Being; God. **c** *Math.* An infinite quantity or magnitude. — **in′fi·nite·ly**, *adv.* — **in′fi·nite·ness**, *n.*

in′fin·i·tes′i·mal (ĭn′fĭn·ĭ·tĕs′ĭ·măl), *adj.* **1.** That approaches zero as a limit. **2.** Immeasurably or incalculably small; very minute. — *n.* An infinitesimal quantity. — **in′fin·i·tes′i·mal·ly**, *adv.*

infinitesimal calculus. The differential calculus and the integral calculus. See CALCULUS, 2 **b**.

in·fin′i·tive (ĭn·fĭn′ĭ·tĭv), *adj.* [LL. *infinitivus*. See INFINITE.] *Gram.* Of, belonging to, or formed with the infinitive; as, an ***infinitive clause,*** a construction following verbs of making, telling, thinking, or wishing, in which the infinitive has predicative force with subject in the objective case (we believe him *to be honest*). — *n.* *Gram.* A form of verbal noun which performs functions of a noun and at the same time shows the verbal features of taking objects and adverbial qualifiers and of having tense forms (in English only for present and perfect, *to see, to have seen*). In Modern English the infinitive is usually preceded by *to* except after auxiliary verbs showing mood (*can, may*, etc.) and some other verbs, as *let, dare, make*, etc. The verbal noun in *-ing*, once classed as an infinitive, is now usually called a *gerund.* Abbr. *inf.* or *infin.* — **in·fin′i·ti′val** (ĭn·fĭn′ĭ·tī′văl; ĭn·fĭn′ĭ·tĭv·ăl), *adj.*

in·fin′i·tude (-tūd), *n.* **1.** Quality of being infinite; infiniteness; also, that which is infinite; infinity; eternity; boundlessness. **2.** Innumerable quantity.

in·fin′i·ty (-tĭ), *n.; pl.* -TIES (-tĭz). [OF. *infinité*, fr. L. *infinitas*.] **1.** The quality of being infinite; also, that which is infinite; unlimited extent of time, space, or quantity; eternity; boundlessness. **2.** An indefinitely great number or amount. **3.** *Math.* **a** An infinite; — denoted by ∞. **b** *Geom.* That region of a line, plane, or space, which is infinitely distant from the finite region regarded.

in·firm′ (ĭn·fûrm′), *adj.* **1.** Not firm or sound physically; weak, esp. from age; feeble. **2.** Weak of mind or will; irresolute; vacillating. **3.** Not solid or stable; insecure. — **Syn.** See WEAK. — *v. t.* *Rare.* To weaken; impair; also, to invalidate, or challenge the validity of.

in·fir′ma·ry (ĭn·fûr′mȧ·rĭ), *n.; pl.* -RIES (-rĭz). [ML. *infirmaria*, fr. *infirmus* infirm.] A hospital, or place where the infirm or sick are lodged and nursed.

in·fir′mi·ty (-mĭ·tĭ), *n.; pl.* -TIES (-tĭz). [L. *infirmitas*.] **1.** Character or state of being infirm; feebleness; frailty. **2.** An instance of such infirmity; as: **a** A disease; a malady. **b** A personal failing; foible; defect.

in·fix′ (ĭn·fĭks′), *v. t.* [OF. *infixer,* fr. L. *infixus,* past part. of *infigere* to infix, fr. *in-* in + *figere* to fix.] **1.** To fasten or fix by piercing or thrusting in. **2.** To implant; instill; inculcate. **3.** *Gram.* To insert as an infix. — **Syn.** See IMPLANT.

in′fix (ĭn′fĭks), *n. Gram.* A derivative or formative element sometimes analogous to a suffix, inserted in the body of a word, as *n* in L. *vinco* from the stem *vic.*

in·flame′ (ĭn·flām′), *v. t.* [OF. *enflamer,* fr. L. *inflammare, -matum,* fr. *in-* in + *flammare* to flame, fr. *flamma* flame.] **1.** To set on fire. **2.** To kindle or intensify, as passion or appetite. **3.** To incense; enrage; also, to cause to redden as from anger. **4.** *Med.* To cause inflammation in. — *v. i.* To burst into flame; become inflamed; esp.: **a** To become excited or angered. **b** To become morbidly congested or affected with inflammation. — **in·flam′er** (-flām′ẽr), *n.* — **in·flam′ing·ly,** *adv.*

in·flam′ma·ble (ĭn·flăm′ȧ·b'l), *adj.* **1.** Capable of being easily set on fire; combustible. See FLAMMABLE. **2.** Easily inflamed, excited, or angered; irascible. — *n.* An inflammable thing or substance. — **in·flam′ma·bil′i·ty** (-bĭl′ĭ·tĭ), *n.* — **in·flam′ma·ble·ness,** *n.* — **in·flam′ma·bly,** *adv.*

in′flam·ma′tion (ĭn′flă·mā′shŭn), *n.* **1.** Act of inflaming; state of being inflamed. **2.** *Med.* A local response to cellular injury marked by capillary dilatation, leucocytic infiltration, redness, and heat. It serves as a mechanism initiating the elimination of noxious agents and the repair of damaged tissue.

in·flam′ma·to′ry (ĭn·flăm′ȧ·tō′rĭ *or, esp. Brit.,* -tẽr·ĭ), *adj.* **1.** Tending to inflame, kindle, or irritate. **2.** Tending to excite anger, animosity, tumult, or sedition; seditious; as, *inflammatory* writings. **3.** *Med.* Accompanied by, or tending to cause, inflammation.

in·flate′ (ĭn·flāt′), *v. t.* [L. *inflatus,* past part. of *inflare* to inflate, fr. *in-* in + *flare* to blow.] **1.** To swell with air or gas; expand; distend. **2.** To puff up; elate. **3.** To expand or increase abnormally or improperly; to extend imprudently; as, to *inflate* currency or credit. — **Syn.** See EXPAND. — **Ant.** Deflate. — **in·flat′a·ble** (-flāt′ȧ·b'l), *adj.* — **in·flat′er** (-flāt′ẽr), **in·fla′tor** (-flā′tẽr), *n.*

in·flat′ed (-flāt′ĕd; -ĭd), *adj.* **1.** Distended, as with air. **2.** Turgid; bombastic; as, an *inflated* style. **3.** Expanded abnormally or unjustifiably, as prices. **4.** *Bot.* Hollow and distended, as a stem or capsule; open and swelled out, as a perianth.

Syn. **Inflated, flatulent, tumid, turgid** mean filled with or as if with air or gas. **Inflated** implies stretching to the point of tautness or tension or, in figurative use, to a point not justified by value, use, etc.; **flatulence** implies a distention, literally of stomach and bowels by gases generating from within, and figuratively, therefore, empty of substance but seemingly full; **tumid** implies an abnormal or conspicuous increase in volume without a proportionate increase in mass or weight; **turgid** implies distention due to the presence of some vital fluid such as blood or sap or, in figurative use, of something such as vital but undisciplined emotion which makes the thing so described unrestrained or unmeasured (as, *inflated* currency or style; *flatulent* stomach or bombast; *tumid* limbs or language; *turgid* woody tissue or prose).

in·fla′tion (-flā′shŭn), *n.* **1.** An inflating; state of being inflated. **2.** Disproportionate and relatively sharp and sudden increase in the quantity of money or credit, or both, relative to goods available for purchase. Inflation always produces a rise in the price level.

in·fla′tion·ar′y (-ẽr′ĭ *or, esp. Brit.,* -ẽr·ĭ), *adj.* Of or pertaining to inflation, esp. as an economic process; producing or tending to produce inflation; as, an *inflationary* policy.

inflationary spiral. See SPIRAL, *n.,* 5.

in·fla′tion·ist (-ĭst), *n.* One who favors inflation, esp. inflation of the currency by the issue of paper money. — **in·fla′tion·ism** (-ĭz'm), *n.* — **in·fla′tion·ist,** *adj.*

in·flect′ (ĭn·flĕkt′), *v. t.* [L. *inflectere, inflexum,* fr. *in-* in + *flectere* to bend.] **1.** To turn from a direct line; bend; deflect. **2.** To modulate, as the voice; to vary in pitch. **3.** *Biol.* To bend inward, or toward the main axis. **4.** *Gram.* To vary (a word) by inflection; to decline, as a noun, or conjugate, as a verb. — **in·flec′tive** (-flĕk′tĭv), *adj.* — **in·flec′tor** (-flĕk′tẽr), *n.*

in·flec′tion (-flĕk′shŭn), **in·flex′ion** (-flĕk′shŭn), *n.* **1.** An inflecting; state of being inflected. **2.** A bend; curve; angle. **3.** A change in pitch or tone of voice. **4.** *Gram.* **a** The change of form which words undergo to mark distinctions of case, gender, number, tense, person, mood, voice, etc. **b** A form, suffix, or element involved in such variation. **5.** *Math.* Change of curvature from concave to convex or conversely; also, the point where it takes place.

in·flec′tion·al, in·flex′ion·al (-ăl; -'l), *adj. Gram.* Designating or pertaining to an affix used in inflection (John′*s*; sing*s*; play*ed*; long*er*); — distinguished from *derivational* (*un*happy; child*hood*). — **in·flec′tion·al·ly, in·flex′ion·al·ly,** *adv.*

in·flexed′ (ĭn·flĕkst′), *adj.* **1.** Turned; bent. **2.** *Bot. & Zool.* Bent or turned abruptly inward or downward, or toward the axis, as the petals of a flower.

in·flex′i·ble (-flĕk′sĭ·b'l), *adj.* [L. *inflexibilis.* See IN- not; FLEXIBLE.] **1.** Not capable of being bent; rigid. **2.** Firm in will or purpose; unyielding; inexorable. **3.** Incapable of change; unalterable. — **in·flex′i·bil′i·ty** (-bĭl′ĭ·tĭ), **in·flex′i·ble·ness,** *n.* — **in·flex′i·bly,** *adv.*

Syn. (1) See STIFF.

(2) **Inflexible, inexorable, obdurate, adamant** mean incapable of being moved from one's course or purpose. **Inflexible** implies rigid adherence to principle, but sometimes also connotes slavish conformity; **inexorable,** deafness to entreaty but, in extended use, relentlessness or, as applied to things, inevitableness; **obdurate,** hardness of heart or insensitiveness to external influences such as divine grace or appeals for mercy; **adamant,** impenetrability to temptation or entreaty.

in·flict′ (ĭn·flĭkt′), *v. t.* [L. *inflictus,* past part. of *infligere* to strike on, inflict, fr. *in-* in, on + *fligere* to strike.] To give or cause by, or as if by, striking (a blow, pain, etc.); cause to suffer; impose, as a penalty. — **in·flict′er, in·flic′tor** (-flĭk′tẽr), *n.* — **in·flic′tive** (-flĭk′tĭv), *adj.*

in·flic′tion (-flĭk′shŭn), *n.* Act of inflicting; also, that which is inflicted, as punishment or disgrace.

in′flo·res′cence (ĭn′flō·rĕs′ĕns; -'ns), *n.* [NL. *inflorescentia,* fr. LL. *inflorescens,* pres. part. of *inflorescere* to begin to blossom, fr. *in-* in + *florescere* to begin to blossom.] **1.** A flowering. **2.** *Bot.* **a** General arrangement and disposition of the flowers on an axis; mode of development of the flowers. **b** A floral axis with its appendages; flowers collectively; as now commonly restricted, a flower cluster; also, a solitary flower. Excluding the solitary flower, the principal types of

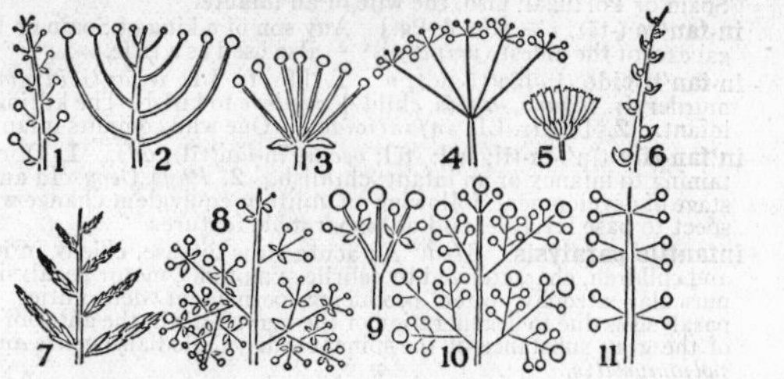

Types of Inflorescence. *Racemose:* 1 Raceme; 2 Corymb; 3 Umbel; 4 Compound Umbel; 5 Capitulum, or Head; 6 Spike; 7 Compound Spike; 8 Panicle. *Cymose:* 9 Cyme. *Mixed:* 10 Thyrsus; 11 Verticillaster.

inflorescence are shown in the *Illust.* — **-res′cent** (-ĕnt; -'nt), *adj.*

in′flow′ (ĭn′flō′), *n.* A flowing in; influx.

in′flu·ence (ĭn′flōō·ĕns; 118), *n.* [OF., fr. LL. *influentia,* fr. L. *influens, -entis,* pres. part. See INFLUENT.] **1.** *Astrol.* Orig., an ethereal fluid thought to flow from the stars and to affect the actions of men; later, a supposed emanation of occult power from stars. **2.** *Poetic.* Emanation or effusion, esp. of a spiritual or moral force. **3.** The act or the power of producing an effect without apparent force or direct authority; as, *influence* by suggestion. **4.** Hence, power arising from station, character, wealth, etc. **5.** A person or thing that exerts influence, esp. considerable influence. **6.** *Elec.* Induction.

Syn. **Influence, authority, prestige, weight, credit** mean power exerted over the minds or acts of others. **Influence** originally implied and still often implies an affecting insensibly but, in current use, it often suggests conscious and, sometimes, underhanded power used in affecting a person or in effecting a result; **authority** implies the power resident in a person or thing to win devotion or allegiance and to gain (rather than exact) obedience and belief; **prestige** implies power to gain ascendancy over the minds of men for conspicuous excellence in its kind; **weight** implies measurable influence, esp. in determining the acts of others; **credit,** influence that arises from one's reputation for inspiring confidence.

— *v. t.;* -ENCED (-ĕnst); -ENC·ING (-ĕn·sĭng). **1.** To exert influence upon; as, to *influence* a person for good. **2.** To modify or determine; as, prices *influence* the demand. — **Syn.** See AFFECT. — **in′flu·enc·er** (-ĕn·sẽr), *n.*

in′flu·ent (-ĕnt), *adj.* [L. *influens, -entis,* pres. part. of *influere, influxum,* to flow in, fr. *in-* in + *fluere* to flow.] Flowing in. — *n.* That which flows in; inflow.

in′flu·en′tial (-ĕn′shăl), *adj.* [See INFLUENCE.] Exerting or possessing influence; hence, potent; effective. — **in′flu·en′tial·ly,** *adv.*

in′flu·en′za (-ĕn′zȧ), *n.* [It., influence, an epidemic formerly attributed by astrologers to the influence of the heavenly bodies, influenza.] **1.** *Med.* An epidemic disease characterized by acute inflammation of the throat and bronchi, and accompanied by great muscular prostration and often severe neuralgic pains. **2.** *Veter.* A contagious disease of horses, affecting the mucous membrane of the air passages and the eyelids, and often complicated with diseases of the liver and intestines.

in′flux (ĭn′flŭks), *n.* [F. or L.; F., fr. LL. *influxus,* fr. *influere.* See INFLUENT.] **1.** A flowing in; inflow; an inpouring. **2.** The mouth or debouchment of a river.

in·fold′ (ĭn·fōld′), *v. t.* **1.** To wrap up or cover with folds; envelop. **2.** To embrace. **3.** To fold or fold over.

in·form′ (ĭn·fôrm′), *adj.* [F. *informe,* fr. L. *informis,* fr. *in-* not + *forma* form.] **1.** Shapeless; deformed; as, an *inform* monster. **2.** Without form or an informing principle; unformed.

in·form′, *v. t.* [OF. *enformer,* fr. L. *informare,* fr. *in-* in + *formare* to form, fr. *forma* form.] **1.** To give form to; to be the formative principle of; hence, to animate. **2.** *Now Rare.* To train; instruct. **3.** *Obs.* To communicate knowledge of; to make known. **4.** To communicate knowledge to; to acquaint; tell; enlighten. **5.** To tell by way of accusation. **6.** To permeate or impregnate as an animating and characterizing quality; — usually followed by *with.* — *v. i.* To give intelligence or information, esp. in accusation. — **in·form′ing·ly,** *adv.*

Syn. **Inform, acquaint, apprise, notify** mean to make one aware of something. **Inform** implies impartation of knowledge, esp. of occurrences or facts; **acquaint** puts more stress upon introduction, as into knowledge, experience, or the like; **apprise** implies a message or sign communicating something of interest or importance; **notify** implies sending a notice or the like concerning a thing requiring attention.

in·for′mal (ĭn·fôr′măl), *adj.* Not in conventional or customary form; as, *informal* evening dress; hence, without ceremony or formality; as, an *informal* meeting. — **in′for·mal′i·ty** (ĭn′fôr·măl′ĭ·tĭ), *n.* — **in·for′mal·ly,** *adv.*

in·form′ant (ĭn·fôr′mănt), *n.* One who gives information; specif., a native speaker engaged to repeat words, phrases, and sentences in his own language or dialect as a model for imitation and a source of information for one learning, transcribing, or teaching it; hence, anyone supplying linguistic data for scientific study.

‖**in for′ma pau′pe·ris** (ĭn fôr′mȧ pô′pĕ·rĭs). [L.] *Law.* In the form of a pauper; as a poor man.

in′for·ma′tion (ĭn′fŏr·mā′shŭn), *n.* **1.** Act or process of informing; specif., communication of knowledge or intelligence; also, accusation. **2.** Knowledge derived from reading, observation or instruction; esp., unorganized or unrelated facts or data. **3.** News; advices; intelligence. **4.** An employee whose work is to answer queries. **5.** *Law.* **a** A kind of prosecution for an offense that differs from an indictment chiefly in not being based on the finding of a grand jury. **b** A formal accusation by the public prosecutor, substituted for indictment by a grand jury in many states. — **in′for·ma′tion·al,** *adj.*

in·form′a·tive (ĭn·fôr′mȧ·tĭv), *adj.* Informing; instructive.

in·form′er (ĭn·fôr′mẽr), *n.* **1.** One who imparts knowledge or news; an informant. **2.** One who informs against another; specif., one (often called a ***common informer***) who, esp. for a financial reward, makes a practice of informing against others for violation of penal laws.

in·for′tune (ĭn·fôr′tŭn), *n.* [OF., fr. L. *infortunium.*] **1.** *Obs.* Misfortune. **2.** *Astrol.* One of the malevolent planets, Saturn, Mars, or sometimes Mercury.

in′fra- (ĭn′frȧ-). [L. *infra*, adv. & prep.] A prefix meaning *below, beneath, lower, inferior*, as in:

infra-anal	**inframarginal**	**infranatural**
infracostal	**inframaxillary**	**infrarenal**
infrahuman	**inframundane**	**infrasternal**

in·fract′ (ĭn·frăkt′), *v. t.* [L. *infractus*, past part. of *infringere.* See INFRINGE.] To break; infringe; violate, as a law or right. — **in·frac′tor** (-frăk′tẽr), *n.*

in·frac′tion (-frăk′shŭn), *n.* Act of infracting, or breaking; breach; violation; as, *infraction* of a treaty, law, regulation.

in′fra dig′ (ĭn′frȧ dĭg′). Colloq. for **in′fra dig′ni·ta′tem** (dĭg′nĭ·tā′-tĕm) [L.], beneath one's dignity; undignified.

in′fra·lap·sar′i·an (ĭn′frȧ·lăp·sâr′ĭ·ăn), *n. & adj.* [*infra-* + L. *lapsus* a falling, fall. See LAPSE.] Sublapsarian. — **in′fra·lap·sar′i·an·ism,** (-ĭz′m), *n.*

in′fra·me′di·an (-mē′dĭ·ăn), *adj.* *Zoogeog.* Designating a zone of the sea bottom lying at the depth of between fifty and one hundred fathoms. — **in′fra·me′di·an,** *n.*

in·fran′gi·ble (ĭn·frăn′jĭ·b'l), *adj.* **1.** Not capable of being broken or separated into parts. **2.** Not to be infringed or violated. — **in·fran′gi·bil′i·ty** (-bĭl′ĭ·tĭ), **in·fran′gi·ble·ness,** *n.* — **in·fran′gi·bly,** *adv.*

in′fra·red′ (ĭn′frȧ·rĕd′), *adj.* Pertaining to or designating those rays lying just beyond the red end of the visible spectrum, such as are emitted by a hot nonincandescent body. Their wave lengths are longer than those of visible light and shorter than those of radio waves. Cf. ULTRAVIOLET.

in·fre′quen·cy (ĭn·frē′kwĕn·sĭ), *n.* State of rarely occurring; uncommonness; rarity.

in·fre′quent (-kwĕnt), *adj.* **1.** Happening or occurring seldom; rare. **2.** Placed or occurring at considerable distances or intervals; occasional; sparse. — **in·fre′quent·ly,** *adv.*

Syn. **Infrequent, uncommon, scarce, rare, sporadic** mean not common or abundant. **Infrequent** implies occurrence at wide intervals in time or in space; **uncommon,** singularity or exceptionality; **scarce,** a not existing or being produced in sufficient quantities; **rare,** uncommonness because of extreme fewness of specimens, instances, etc.; **sporadic,** occurrence only in rare and, usually, isolated instances.

in·fringe′ (ĭn·frĭnj′), *v. t.;* -FRINGED′ (-frĭnjd′); -FRING′ING (-frĭn′-jĭng). [L. *infringere*, fr. *in-* in + *frangere* to break.] **1.** *Obs.* To break or break down; specif.: **a** To destroy. **b** To frustrate. **c** To impair. **2.** To commit a breach of; violate. **3.** To commit an infringement of; as, to *infringe* a patent. — *v. i.* To encroach; to trespass; — with *on* or *upon.* — **Syn.** See TRESPASS. — **in·fring′er** (-frĭn′jẽr), *n.*

in·fringe′ment (-mĕnt), *n.* **1.** Act of infringing; breach; violation. **2.** An encroachment or trespass on a right or privilege, as of a patent, copyright, or trade-mark.

in′fun·dib′u·lar (ĭn′fŭn·dĭb′ū·lẽr), *adj.* Also **in′fun·dib′u·late** (-lāt). **1.** Funnel-shaped. **2.** Pertaining to or having an infundibulum.

in′fun·dib′u·li·form′ (-lĭ·fôrm′), *adj.* Funnel-shaped.

in′fun·dib′u·lum (-lŭm), *n.; pl.* -ULA (-lȧ). [L., a funnel, fr. *infundere* to pour in or into.] Any of various funnel-shaped or dilated organs or parts; as: *Anat.* **a** The hollow, conical process of gray matter to which the pituitary body is attached. **b** Any of the small spaces in which the bronchial tubes terminate in the lungs.

in·fu′ri·ate (ĭn·fū′rĭ·āt), *adj.* [ML. *infuriatus*, past part. of *infuriare*, fr. *in-* in + L. *furia* fury.] Furiously angry. — (-āt), *v. t.* To render furious; enrage; madden. — **in·fu′ri·ate·ly,** *adv.* — **in·fu′ri·a′tion** (-ā′shŭn), *n.*

in·fuse′ (ĭn·fūz′), *v. t.* [F. or L.; F. *infuser*, fr. L. *infusus*, past part. of *infundere* to pour in or into, fr. *in-* in + *fundere* to pour.] **1.** To pour in, as a liquid; to pour (*into* or *upon*). **2.** To instill, as principles or qualities; introduce; insinuate. **3.** To imbue (*with*); animate; fill. **4.** To steep in water or other fluid without boiling, for extracting useful qualities. — **in·fus′er** (-fūz′ẽr), *n.*

Syn. **Infuse, suffuse, imbue, engrain** (*or* **ingrain**), **inoculate, leaven** mean to introduce one thing into another so as to affect it. **Infuse** implies a pouring in of something that gives new life, new vigor, new significance, etc.; **suffuse,** a spreading, through a surface or extent, of something that gives color, texture, quality, etc.; **imbue,** an infusion into someone or something (the object of the verb) that gives him (or it) new life, vigor, etc. (as, to *infuse* courage into his soldiers; to *imbue* his soldiers with courage); **engrain,** an incorporation with the substance or nature of that which is affected (as, love so deeply *ingrained* in a mother); **inoculate,** an imbuing (a person) with something that acts in the manner of a disease germ; **leaven,** a transforming or tempering of a mass so as to produce effects like yeast in dough.

in·fu′si·ble (-fū′zĭ·b'l), *adj.* [*in-* not + *fusible.*] Not fusible; not easily fused. — **in·fu′si·bil′i·ty** (-bĭl′ĭ·tĭ), *n.*

in·fu′sion (ĭn·fū′zhŭn), *n.* **1.** Act, process, or result of infusing; a tincture; admixture. **2.** *Surg.* The introduction of a solution, esp. a saline solution, into a vein.

in·fu′sive (ĭn·fū′sĭv), *adj.* Inspiring; influencing.

in′fu·so′ri·an (ĭn′fū·sō′rĭ·ăn), *n.* Any member of a heterogeneous group of minute organisms (formerly classed as Infusoria), found in decomposing infusions of organic matter, in stagnant water, etc. Today the term is usually limited to the ciliated protozoans (Ciliophora), esp. to the free-living members of this group, which are present in almost any exposed body of water although only the largest are visible to the naked eye. — **in′fu·so′ri·an,** *adj.*

in′fu·so′ri·al (-ăl), *adj.* **1.** Pertaining to, or having the characters of, the infusorians. **2.** Composed of, or containing infusorians, as **infusorial earth,** or kieselguhr.

-ing (-ĭng). [AS. *-ing.*] A suffix denoting *belonging to, of the kind of, descended from,* used to form nouns, esp. patronymics and diminutives, as in athel*ing*, shill*ing*.

-ing (-ĭng). [For ME. *-end, -and, -ind*, fr. AS. *-ende.*] The suffix of the present participle; as, sing*ing* birds.

-ing. [ME. *-ing*, fr. AS. *-ing, -ung.*] A suffix used to form nouns from verbs, and also, by analogy, from nouns, adverbs, and other words. It means: **a** *Act, fact, art,* etc., *of doing* (what the verbal root denotes); as, public speak*ing;* fond of boat*ing.* **b** *That which does* or *that which results from, accompanies,* etc., *the act of* (what the verbal root denotes); as, a cover*ing;* sweep*ings;* a moor*ing.* **c** *Material for;* as, bedd*ing;* roof*ing.*

in·gem′i·nate (ĭn·jĕm′ĭ·nāt), *v. t.* [L. *ingeminatus*, past part. of *ingeminare* to double, fr. *in-* in + *geminare.* See GEMINATE.] To redouble or repeat; reiterate. — **in·gem′i·na′tion** (-nā′shŭn), *n.*

in·gen′er·ate (-jĕn′ẽr·āt), *adj.* [L. *ingeneratus*, past part. of *ingenerare.* See ENGENDER.] Inborn; innate. — (-āt), *v. t.* To generate within; beget; cause.

in·gen′ious (ĭn·jēn′yŭs; 58), *adj.* [F. *ingénieux*, fr. L. *ingeniosus*, fr. *ingenium* natural quality or capacity, genius.] **1.** *Obs.* Possessed of genius or unusual mental powers. **2.** Possessed of ingenuity; inventive. **3.** Proceeding from or characterized by cleverness or ingenuity; curiously or cleverly fashioned; as, an *ingenious* machine; also, of ideas, adroit; shrewd; as, an *ingenious* solution. — **Syn.** See CLEVER. — **in·gen′ious·ly,** *adv.* — **in·gen′ious·ness,** *n.*

in′gé·nue′ (ăN′zhā′nü′; *Angl.* ĭn′jĕ·nōō), *n.; pl.* -NUES (-nüz′; -nōōz). [F., fem. of *ingénu* ingenuous.] An ingenuous or naïve girl or young woman, or an actress representing such a person.

in′ge·nu′i·ty (ĭn′jĕ·nū′ĭ·tĭ), *n.* [L. *ingenuitas* ingenuousness.] **1.** Ingenuousness; candor. **2.** Ingeniousness; inventiveness; skill in devising or combining; also, cleverness of design or contrivance.

in·gen′u·ous (ĭn·jĕn′ū·ŭs), *adj.* [L. *ingenuus* inborn, freeborn, noble, frank.] **1.** Of a superior character; noble; honorable **2.** Free from reserve, disguise, or dissimulation; open; frank; candid; also, naïve; artlessly frank. **3.** Erron. for INGENIOUS. — **Syn.** See NATURAL. — **Ant.** Disingenuous. — **in·gen′u·ous·ly,** *adv.* — **in·gen′u·ous·ness,** *n.*

in·gest′ (ĭn·jĕst′), *v. t.* [L. *ingestus*, past part. of *ingerere* to put in, fr. *in-* in + *gerere* to bear.] To take in for digestion, as into the stomach. — **in·ges′tion** (-jĕs′chŭn), *n.* — **in·ges′tive** (-tĭv), *adj.*

in·ges′ta (ĭn·jĕs′tȧ), *n. pl.* [NL.] That which is ingested; — opposed to *egesta.*

in·gine′ (ĭn·jīn′), *n.* *Scot.* Genius; ingenuity.

in′gle (ĭng′g'l), *n.* [Scot., prob. fr. Gael. *aingeal* fire.] Flame; blaze; also, a fireplace.

in′gle·nook′ (-nŏŏk′), *n., or* **ingle nook.** Chimney corner.

in′gle·side′ (-sīd′), *n.* A fireside.

in·glo′ri·ous (ĭn·glō′rĭ·ŭs; 70), *adj.* **1.** Not glorious; not famous or honored. **2.** Shameful; ignominious; as, *inglorious* defeat. — **in·glo′ri·ous·ly,** *adv.* — **in·glo′ri·ous·ness,** *n.*

in′go′ing (ĭn′gō′ĭng), *adj.* Going in; entering.

in′got (ĭng′gŏt), *n.* [ME., fr. AS. *in* in + *goten*, past part. of *geotan* to pour.] **1.** A mold in which metal is cast. **2.** A mass of metal cast into some convenient shape for storage or transportation, to be later remelted for casting or finished by rolling, forging, etc. — *v. t.* To turn into ingots.

ingot iron. A commercial form of iron cast from the molten state into malleable masses which do not harden when quenched. It usually contains less than 0.1 per cent carbon. See WROUGHT IRON.

in·graft′ (ĭn·grȧft′; 9), *v. t.* To graft or engraft.

in·grain′ (ĭn·grān′), *v. t.* To engrain. In the past participle and participial adjective, *ingrained* is the usual spelling. — **Syn.** See INFUSE. — (ĭn′grān′; 2), *adj.* Ingrained; specif.: **a** Dyed in the fiber or yarn before being woven or knitted, as carpets; hence, fast-dyed. **b** Thoroughly inwrought; inherent. — (ĭn′grān′), *n.* Something ingrain or ingrained; esp., an ingrain carpet or ingrain yarn.

in′grained′ (ĭn′grānd′; 2), *adj.* Wrought into the grain or fiber; hence, deep-seated.

in′grate (ĭn′grāt; ĭn·grāt′; 2), *adj.* [OF. *ingrat*, fr. L. *ingratus.* See IN- not; GRATEFUL.] *Archaic.* Ungrateful. — (ĭn′grāt *or, esp. Brit.,* ĭn·grāt′), *n.* An ingrate, or ungrateful, person.

in·gra′ti·ate (ĭn·grā′shĭ·āt), *v. t.* [*in-* in + L. *gratia* favor.] To bring or work (esp. oneself) into another's favor. — **in·gra′ti·at′ing** (-āt′ĭng), *adj.* — **Syn.** See DISARMING. — **in·gra′ti·at′ing·ly,** *adv.* — **in·gra′ti·a′tion** (-ā′shŭn), *n.* — **in·gra′ti·a·to′ry** (-ȧ·tō′rĭ *or, esp. Brit.,* -tẽr·ĭ), *adj.*

in·grat′i·tude (ĭn·grăt′ĭ·tūd), *n.* Lack of gratitude; insensibility to, or ill return for, kindness.

in′gra·ves′cent (ĭn′grȧ·vĕs′ĕnt; -'nt), *adj.* [L. *ingravescens, -entis*, pres. part.] *Med.* Gradually increasing in severity.

in·gre′di·ent (ĭn·grē′dĭ·ĕnt), *n.* [F. and L.; F. *ingrédient*, fr. L. *ingrediens, -entis*, entering into, pres. part. of *ingredi* to enter, fr. *in-* in + *gradi* to walk, go.] That which enters into a compound or is a component part of any combination or mixture; a constituent. — *adj.* Present as, or forming, an ingredient; component. — **Syn.** See ELEMENT.

in′gress (ĭn′grĕs), *n.* [L. *ingressus*, fr. *ingredi.*] **1.** Act of entering; entrance. **2.** Power or liberty of entrance; access. **3.** A place for entering; an entrance.

in·gres′sion (ĭn·grĕsh′ŭn), *n.* Entrance.

in·gres′sive (-grĕs′ĭv), *adj.* Of or pertaining to ingress; entering; specif., *Gram.*, inceptive. — **in·gres′sive·ness,** *n.*

in′grow′ (ĭn′grō′), *v. i.;* see GROW. To grow within or inward, as the edges of a nail (**in′grow′ing nail**) into the adjacent flesh. — **in′grown′** (-grōn′; 2), *adj.* — **in′growth′** (-grōth′), *n.*

in′gui·nal (ĭng′gwĭ·năl; -n'l), *adj.* [L. *inguinalis*, fr. *inguen, inguinis*, the groin.] *Anat. & Med.* Of, pertaining to, or in the region of the groin; as, an *inguinal* hernia.

in′gui·no- (ĭng′gwĭ·nō-), **inguin-.** A combining form meaning *groin, inguinal and.*

in·gulf′ (ĭn·gŭlf′), *v. t.* To engulf.

in·gur′gi·tate (ĭn·gûr′jĭ·tāt), *v. t. & i.* [L. *ingurgitatus* poured in, fr. *in-* in + *gurges* whirlpool.] To swallow greedily or in large quantity; guzzle. — **in·gur′gi·ta′tion** (-tā′shŭn), *n.*

in·hab′it (ĭn·hăb′ĭt), *v. t.* [OF. *enhabiter*, fr. L. *inhabitare*, fr. *in-* in + *habitare* to dwell.] **1.** To live in; to occupy as a place of residence or habitat. **2.** *Obs.* **a** To settle; people. **b** To establish as resident. — *v. i.* *Archaic.* To dwell; abide. — **in·hab′it·a·bil′i·ty** (-ĭ·tȧ·bĭl′ĭ·tĭ), *n.* — **in·hab′it·a·ble,** *adj.* — **in·hab′it·er,** *n.*

in·hab′it·an·cy (ĭn·hăb′ĭ·tăn·sĭ), *n.; pl.* -CIES (-sĭz). **1.** An inhabiting; state of being inhabited; occupancy. **2.** Place of residence; abode.

in·hab′it·ant (-tănt), *n.* [OF., fr. L. *inhabitans, -antis*, pres. part. of *inhabitare.*] A permanent resident in a place, as distinguished from a transient lodger or visitor.

in·hab′i·ta′tion (ĭn·hăb′ĭ·tā′shŭn), *n.* An inhabiting.

in·hab′it·ed (ĭn·hăb′ĭ·tĕd; -tĭd), *adj.* Having inhabitants.

in·hal′ant (ĭn·hāl′ănt), *adj.* Inhaling; used for inhaling. — *n.* **1.** An inhaler. **2.** That which is to be inhaled.

in′ha·la′tion (ĭn′hȧ·lā′shŭn), *n.* An inhaling; also, an inhalant.

in′ha·la′tor (ĭn′hȧ·lā′tẽr; ĭn′hȧ·lā′tẽr), *n.* = INHALER, 2.

in·hale′ (ĭn·hāl′), *v. t.* [L. *inhalare*, fr. *in-* in, on, against + *halare* to breathe.] To breathe or draw in, esp. into the lungs. — *v. i.* To inhale air, smoke, etc.

in·hal′er (-hāl′ẽr), *n.* **1.** One who inhales. **2.** An apparatus facilitating inhalation of a gas, spray, etc.; also, one for filtering air, etc.

in′har·mon′ic (ĭn′här·mŏn′ĭk), *adj.* Also **in′har·mon′i·cal** (-ĭ·kăl). Not harmonic; discordant.

in′har·mo′ni·ous (-mō′nĭ·ŭs), *adj.* [*in-* not + *harmonious.*] Not harmonious or in harmony; discordant. — **in′har·mo′ni·ous·ly,** *adv.* — **in′har·mo′ni·ous·ness,** *n.*

in′haul′ (ĭn′hôl′), **in′haul′er** (-ẽr), *n.* *Naut.* A rope used to draw in a sail, as a spanker on its gaff.

in·here′ (ĭn·hēr′), *v. i.* [L. *inhaerere*, fr. *in-* in + *haerere* to stick, hang.] To be inherent; to be a fixed element or attribute; to belong, as attributes, rights, etc.; as, in a democracy sovereignty *inheres* in the people.

in·her′ence (-hēr′ĕns), *n.* State, quality, or fact of inhering or of being inherent; specif., *Philos.*, the relation of a quality to a substance or subject.

in·her′en·cy (-ĕn·sĭ), *n.; pl.* -CIES (-sĭz). Inherence; also, an inherent character, attribute, or the like.

in·her′ent (-ĕnt), *adj.* [L. *inhaerens*, *-entis*, pres. part. See INHERE.] Firmly infixed; esp., involved in the constitution or essential character of anything; belonging by nature or settled habit; intrinsic. — **in·her′ent·ly,** *adv.*

in·her′it (ĭn·hĕr′ĭt), *v. t.* [OF. *enheriter* to appoint as heir, fr. LL. *inhereditare*, fr. *in-* in + *hereditare* to inherit, fr. *heres* heir.] **1.** *Obs.* To make heir; put in possession. **2.** To come into possession of. **3.** To receive by law from an ancestor or from another at his death; as, to *inherit* property from a relative. **4.** To derive or acquire from an ancestor; as, to *inherit* a strong constitution. **5.** To have in turn or to receive from a predecessor; as, they *inherited* that problem from the previous administration. — *v. i.* **1.** To take or hold a possession or rights by inheritance. **2.** To derive its nature or character (*from*).

in·her′it·a·ble (-ȧ·b'l), *adj.* **1.** Capable of being inherited; transmissible; descendible, as a title or an estate. **2.** Capable of inheriting; hence, entitled (*to*), as a birthright. — **in·her′it·a·bil′i·ty** (-bĭl′ĭ·tĭ), — **in·her′it·a·ble·ness,** *n.*

in·her′it·ance (-ĭ·tăns), *n.* **1.** An inheriting. **2.** That which is or may be inherited; that which is derived from an ancestor or as a legacy or which is transmissible to an heir or to offspring. **3.** A possession or blessing, esp. one received by gift or without purchase; a benefaction. **4.** Possession; ownership. — **Syn.** See HERITAGE.

inheritance tax. *Law. U. S.* A death duty.

in·her′i·tor (ĭn·hĕr′ĭ·tẽr), *n.* One who inherits; an heir. — **in·her′i·tress** (-três; -trĭs), **in·her′i·trix** (-trĭks), *n. fem.*

in·hib′it (ĭn·hĭb′ĭt), *v. t.* [L. *inhibitus*, past part. of *inhibere*, fr. *in-* in + *habere* to have, hold.] **1.** To forbid; interdict. **2.** To hold in check; restrain. — **Syn.** See FORBID. — **in·hib′it·a·ble,** *adj.* — **in·hib′i·tive** (-ĭ·tĭv), **in·hib′i·to′ry** (-ĭ·tō′rĭ *or, esp. Brit.*, -tẽr·ĭ), *adj.*

in′hi·bi′tion (ĭn′hĭ·bĭsh′ŭn), *n.* **1.** Act of inhibiting, or state of being inhibited; restraint; prohibition. **2.** Any inner impediment to free activity, expression, or functioning; esp., any psychical activity imposing restraint upon another activity. **3.** *Physiol.* A restraining of the function of an organ or an agent.

in·hib′i·tor (ĭn·hĭb′ĭ·tẽr), *n.* One who or that which inhibits, as a nerve. Specif., *Physical Chem.*, any substance which interferes with or retards a chemical reaction.

‖**in hoc sig′no vin′ces** (ĭn hŏk sĭg′nō vĭn′sēz). [L.] In, or by, this sign thou shalt conquer; — motto said to have been adopted by the emperor Constantine after seeing a vision of the cross.

in·hos′pi·ta·ble (ĭn·hŏs′pĭ·tȧ·b'l), *adj.* **1.** Not hospitable. **2.** Affording no shelter or sustenance; barren; desert. — **in·hos′pi·ta·ble·ness,** *n.* — **in·hos′pi·ta·bly,** *adv.*

in·hos′pi·tal′i·ty (-tăl′ĭ·tĭ), *n.* Inhospitableness.

in·hu′man (ĭn·hū′măn), *adj.* [F. *inhumain*, fr. L. *inhumanus.*] **1.** Destitute of human or humane feeling; cruel; brutish. **2.** Unlike what is normally human; nonhuman. — **Syn.** See FIERCE. — **in·hu′man·ly,** *adv.* — **in·hu′man·ness,** *n.*

in′hu·mane′ (ĭn′hū·mān′), *adj.* [*in-* not + *humane;* formerly a form of *inhuman.*] Not humane; lacking humanity; inhuman. — **in′hu·mane′ly,** *adv.*

in′hu·man′i·ty (-măn′ĭ·tĭ), *n.; pl.* -TIES (-tĭz). Quality, state, or instance of being inhuman or inhumane; cruelty.

in′hu·ma′tion (-mā′shŭn), *n.* Burial; interment.

in·hume′ (ĭn·hūm′), *v. t.* [L. *inhumare*, fr. *in-* in + *humare* to cover with earth.] To deposit, as a dead body, in the earth; bury; inter. — **in·hum′er** (-hūm′ẽr), *n.*

in·im′i·cal (ĭn·ĭm′ĭ·kăl), *adj.* [LL. *inimicalis*, fr. L. *inimicus* unfriendly, hostile, fr. *in-* not + *amicus* friendly.] **1.** Having the disposition of an enemy; unfriendly. **2.** Opposed, adverse; antagonistic. — **in·im′i·cal·ly,** *adv.*

in·im′i·ta·ble (-ĭ·tȧ·b'l), *adj.* Not capable of being imitated; matchless. — **in·im′i·ta·bil′i·ty** (-bĭl′ĭ·tĭ), **in·im′i·ta·ble·ness,** *n.* — **in·im′i·ta·bly,** *adv.*

in′i·on (ĭn′ĭ·ŏn), *n.* [NL., fr. Gr. *inion* the back of the head.] The external occipital protuberance of the skull.

in·iq′ui·tous (ĭ·nĭk′wĭ·tŭs), *adj.* Characterized by iniquity; unjust; wicked. — **Syn.** See VICIOUS. — **in·iq′ui·tous·ly,** *adv.* — **in·iq′ui·tous·ness,** *n.*

in·iq′ui·ty (ĭ·nĭk′wĭ·tĭ), *n.; pl.* -TIES (-tĭz). [OF. *iniquité*, fr. L. *iniquitas* inequality, injustice, fr. *iniquus* uneven, unjust, fr. *in-* not + *aequus* even, equal.] **1.** Absence of, or deviation from, just dealing; gross injustice; wickedness. **2.** An iniquitous act or thing; an offense; a heinous sin.

in·i′tial (ĭ·nĭsh′ăl), *adj.* [F. and L.; F., fr. L. *initialis*, fr. *initium* entrance, beginning, fr. *inire* to go into, fr. *in-* in + *ire* to go.] **1.** Of or pertaining to the beginning; marking the commencement; incipient. **2.** Placed at the beginning; first. — *n.* The first letter of a name; also, a large letter beginning a text or a division or paragraph. — *v. t.;* -TIALED (-ăld) or -TIALLED; -TIAL·ING or -TIAL·LING. To mark with initials. — **in·i′tial·ly,** *adv.*

in·i′ti·ate (ĭ·nĭsh′ĭ·āt), *v. t.* [L. *initiatus*, past part. of *initiare* to begin, fr. *initium* beginning. See INITIAL.] **1.** To introduce by a first act; begin. **2.** To instruct in the rudiments or principles. **3.** To admit to a club, sect, or the like, as by special rites. **4.** *Polit. Sci.* To cause or bring to pass by the initiative (see INITIATIVE, 3 **b**). — **Syn.** See BEGIN. — (-ăt), *adj.* **1.** Initiated; also, pertaining to an initiate. **2.** In the initial stage; begun; commenced. — (-ăt), *n.* One who is, or is to be, initiated. — **in·i′ti·a′tor** (-ā′tẽr), *n.*

in·i′ti·a′tion (-ā′shŭn), *n.* **1.** An initiating; process of being initiated. **2.** The rites, ceremonies, ordeals, or instructions with which one is made a member of a sect, society, etc.

in·i′ti·a′tive (ĭ·nĭsh′ĭ·ā′tĭv; -ȧ·tĭv; -nĭsh′ȧ·tĭv), *adj.* Of or pertaining to initiation; serving to initiate; introductory; preliminary. — *n.* **1.** An introductory step. **2.** Energy or aptitude displayed in the initiation of action; self-reliant enterprise; self-initiated activity. **3.** *Polit. Sci.* **a** The right or power to introduce a new measure or course of action, as in legislation; as, the *initiative* in respect to revenue bills is in the House of Representatives. **b** The procedure or device by which legislation may be introduced or enacted directly by the people, as in the Swiss Confederation and in many of the states of the United States; — chiefly used with *the.* — **in·i′ti·a′tive·ly,** *adv.*

in·i′ti·a·to′ry (-ȧ·tō′rĭ *or, esp. Brit.*, -tẽr·ĭ), *adj.* **1.** Introductory; prefatory. **2.** Tending or serving to initiate; used in initiation; as, *initiatory* rites. — **in·i′ti·a·to′ri·ly,** *adv.*

in·ject′ (ĭn·jĕkt′), *v. t.* [L. *injectus*, past part. of *inicere*, *injicere*, to throw in, fr. *in-* in + *jacere* to throw.] **1.** To throw, drive, or force in. **2.** Hence, to throw in by way of suggestion, interruption, etc.; interject. **3.** To force a fluid into (a vessel, cavity, or organic tissue), as for preserving or hardening, for relieving pain, or for preventing disease.

in·jec′tion (-jĕk′shŭn), *n.* **1.** An injecting, esp. by means of a syringe, pump, etc. **2.** That which is injected; esp., a liquid medicine injected into the subcutaneous tissue or a cavity of the body; an enema.

in·jec′tor (-tẽr), *n.* One who or that which injects; specif., a device for injecting feed water into a steam boiler by the direct action of live steam.

in′ju·di′cious (ĭn′jōō·dĭsh′ŭs; 114), *adj.* Not judicious; indiscreet; unwise. — **in′ju·di′cious·ly,** *adv.* — **in′ju·di′cious·ness,** *n.*

in·junc′tion (ĭn·jŭngk′shŭn), *n.* [LL. *injunctio*, fr. *injungere*, *injunctum*, to join into, to enjoin. See ENJOIN.] **1.** An enjoining; act of directing, commanding, or prohibiting. **2.** That enjoined; an order; precept. **3.** *Law.* A writ or process, granted by a court of equity, requiring a party to do or to forbear certain acts.

in′jure (ĭn′jẽr), *v. t.* [F. *injurier*, fr. L. *injuriari*, fr. *injuria* injury. See INJURY.] To do harm to; hurt; impair, as health; to wound, as the person; to damage or lessen the value of, as goods or estate; to tarnish, as reputation; to give pain to, as the feelings. — **in′jur·er** (-jẽr·ẽr), *n.*

Syn. Injure, harm, hurt, damage, impair, mar mean to rob of soundness or perfection. Injure, in current use, implies the infliction of anything detrimental to one's appearance, health, success, comfort, or the like; harm often carries a stronger implication of pain, suffering, or annoyance inflicted; hurt, of a wound not only to the body but to the feelings; damage, of an injury that lowers value or involves loss of efficiency or the like; impair, of deterioration or diminution, as in value, strength, validity, etc.; mar, of an injury that disfigures or maims.

in·ju′ri·ous (ĭn·jōōr′ĭ·ŭs; 84), *adj.* [F. *injurieux*, fr. L. *injuriosus.* See INJURY.] **1.** Inflicting or tending to inflict injury; hurtful; harmful; detrimental. **2.** Slanderous; abusive; defamatory. — **in·ju′ri·ous·ly,** *adv.* — **in·ju′ri·ous·ness,** *n.*

in′ju·ry (ĭn′jẽr·ĭ), *n.; pl.* -RIES (-ĭz). [AF. *injurie*, fr. L. *injuria*, fr. *injurius* injurious, unjust, fr. *in-* not + *jus, juris*, right, law, justice.] **1.** Damage or hurt done or suffered; detriment to, or violation of, person, character, feelings, rights, property, or interests, or the value of a thing. **2.** An act which injures. **3.** *Obs.* Abusive speech; an insult. **4.** *Law.* An actionable wrong. — **Syn.** See INJUSTICE.

in·jus′tice (ĭn·jŭs′tĭs), *n.* [F., fr. L. *injustitia.*] **1.** Want of justice; violation of another's rights; wrong. **2.** An unjust act; a wrong.

Syn. Injustice, injury, wrong, grievance mean an act that inflicts loss, hardship, or the like. Injustice, the general term, applies to any (or all) acts that involve unfairness to another or a violation of his rights; injury (in this sense a legal term) applies to any injustice for which a person may sue to recover compensation or specific property or both; wrong, in law, applies not only to an injury as defined but to any misdemeanor or crime punishable according to the criminal code, but in general use it applies to a flagrant injustice; grievance applies to any circumstance or condition that to the sufferer constitutes a wrong and gives him just ground for complaint.

ink (ĭngk), *n.* [OF. *enque*, fr. LL. *encaustum* the purple-red ink with which the Roman emperors signed their edicts, fr. Gr. *enkauston*, fr. *enkaustos* burnt in, encaustic. See ENCAUSTIC.] **1.** A fluid or viscous material, of various colors, but commonly black, used for writing and printing. **2.** *Zool.* The black protective secretion of a cephalopod. — *v. t.* To put ink upon; to blacken or color with or as with ink. — **ink′er** (-ẽr), *n.*

ink′ber′ry (-bĕr′ĭ; -bẽr·ĭ), *n.; pl.* -RIES (-ĭz). **a** The holly (*Ilex glabra*) of eastern North America, with evergreen oblong leathery leaves, and small black berries. **b** The pokeweed. **c** The fruit of either of these plants.

ink′horn′ (-hôrn′), *n.* A small bottle of horn or other material for holding ink. — *adj.* Pedantic; affectedly learned.

in′kle (ĭng′k'l), *n.* A type of linen tape or braid; also, the thread or yarn from which it is made.

ink′ling (ĭngk′lĭng), *n.* [ME. *inclen* to hint, of uncert. origin.] **1.** A hint; an intimation. **2.** A slight knowledge or vague notion; — usually with *of.*

ink′stand′ (ĭngk′stănd′), *n.* An inkwell; also, a device for holding ink, pens, etc.

ink′well′ (-wĕl′), *n.* A container for writing ink.

ink′wood′ (-wŏŏd′), *n.* A tree (*Exothea paniculata*) of the soapberry family, of Florida and the West Indies, having dark wood.

ink′y (ĭngk′ĭ), *adj.;* INK′I·ER (-ĭ·ẽr); INK′I·EST. Consisting of, using, or resembling ink; soiled with ink; black.

inky cap. Any mushroom of the genus *Coprinus.* Its pileus melts into an inky fluid after maturation of the spores.

in·laid′ (ĭn·lād′; ĭn′lād′), *adj.* Set into a surface so as to form a design; also, decorated with a design so formed.

in′land (ĭn′lănd; ĭn′lănd′), *n.* The interior part of a country, or the part or parts near the centers of population. — (ĭn′lănd), *adj.* **1.**

Of, pertaining to, or limited to the inland; not coastal or frontier. 2. Within the land; not bordering on the sea; as, *inland* transportation. 3. Confined to a country or state; domestic; as, *inland* commerce. — (ĭn′lănd′; -lănd; 2), *adv.* Into, or toward, the inland; away from the frontier or coast.

in′land·er (ĭn′lăn·dẽr), *n.* One who lives inland.

in·law′ (ĭn·lô′), *v. t.* [AS. *inlagian.* See IN; LAW.] *O. Eng. Law.* To clear of outlawry or attainder; to place under the protection of the law. — **in′law·ry** (ĭn′lô·rĭ), *n.*

in′-law′ (ĭn′lô′), *n.* *Colloq.* A relative by marriage.

in·lay′ (ĭn·lā′), *v. t.*; see LAY. 1. To set into the body of a surface; also, to adorn (a surface or ground) by the insertion of other material. 2. To insert (a print, a printed page, etc.) in a heavier or stouter sheet serving as a mat or frame for it; to provide (a book) with inlaid illustrations. — **in′lay′er** (ĭn′lā′ẽr), *n.*

in′lay′ (ĭn′lā′), *n.* 1. Material inlaid; inlaid work. 2. *Dent.* A filling made and then cemented into a tooth.

in′let (ĭn′lĕt; *Brit. also* -lĭt), *n.* 1. *Now Rare.* Act of letting in. 2. A place of ingress; entrance. 3. A recess in a shore; a narrow strip of water running into the land or between islands; a creek. 4. That which is let in or inlaid.

in′li′er (ĭn′lī′ẽr), *n.* *Geol.* A mass of stratified rock whose outcrop is wholly surrounded by rock of later deposition.

‖**in li′mi·ne** (ĭn lĭm′ĭ·nē). [L.] On the threshold; at the beginning.

‖**in lo′co** (lō′kō). [L.] In (the proper or natural) place.

‖**in lo′co pa·ren′tis** (pȧ·rĕn′tĭs). [L.] In the place of a parent.

in′ly (ĭn′lĭ), *adv.* [AS. *inlīce.*] **a** Internally; in the heart. **b** Hence, heartily; intimately. — *adj.* Internal; felt inly.

in′mate (ĭn′māt), *n.* [*in* + *mate* an associate.] 1. One who lives in the same house or apartment with another. 2. One of a family or community occupying a single dwelling or home; now esp., one kept in an institution, as an asylum or poorhouse. 3. An inhabitant.

‖**in me′di·as res** (ĭn mē′dĭ·ăs rēz). [L.] Into the midst of things; — used specif. of the method of beginning a narrative with an important event rather than with the first in time, as in some old epics.

in me·mo′ri·am (ĭn mē·mō′rĭ·ăm). [L.] In memory (of); to the memory (of); — used in epitaphs, etc.

in·mesh′ (ĭn·mĕsh′). Var. of ENMESH.

in′most (ĭn′mōst; -mŭst), *adj.* [AS. *innemest,* a double superlative of *inne* within.] Deepest within; innermost.

inn (ĭn), *n.* [AS., house, chamber, lodging.] 1. *Obs.* A place of shelter; hence, dwelling; abode. 2. A public house for the lodging and entertainment of travelers or wayfarers for a compensation; hotel; also, tavern. 3. A residence or hostel for students; — *Obs.* except in names of buildings. See INN OF COURT. — *v. t. & i. Now Rare.* To lodge, stop, or put up (at, or as at, an inn).

in′nards (ĭn′ẽrdz), *n. pl.* *Colloq.* = INWARD, *n.*, **a**.

in′nate (ĭn′nāt; ĭ·nāt′; 2), *adj.* [L. *innatus,* fr. *in-* in + *natus* born, past part. of *nasci* to be born.] 1. Inborn; native; natural; not acquired; as, *innate* vigor; of nonliving things, existing within; belonging to the essential nature of; as, an *innate* defect in a plan. 2. *Philos.* Originating in, or derived from, the constitution of the intellect; not acquired from experience; as, *innate* ideas. — **in′nate·ly,** *adv.* — **in′nate·ness,** *n.*

Syn. **Innate, inborn, inbred, congenital, hereditary** mean not acquired after birth. **Innate** and **inborn** often apply to qualities, characters, etc., but *innate* suggests them as part of one's constitution and *inborn* as so natural or deep-seated as to seem to have been born in one; **inbred** implies reference to the processes of generation and nourishment of offspring and suggests something deeply rooted and ingrained; **congenital** and **hereditary** refer to something coming before birth, *congenital* implying acquirement during the development of the fetus in the womb, and *hereditary* implying transmission from an ancestor through the germ plasm.

in′ner (ĭn′ẽr), *adj.* [AS. *innerra,* compar. of *inne* within.] 1. Farther in; interior; internal; — opp. to *outer.* 2. Of or pertaining to the mind or spirit or its phenomena. 3. Near to a center, esp. of influence; as, *inner* circles. 4. Not obvious or easily discovered. — *n.* The inside part. — **in′ner·ly,** *adv.*

Inner Light. In Quaker doctrine, a Divine presence in the soul, enlightening and guiding it.

in′ner·most (ĭn′ẽr·mōst; -mŭst), *adj.* [From *inmost,* after *inner.*] Farthest inward; inmost. — *n.* Inmost part or being.

Inner Temple. See INN OF COURT.

in·ner′vate (ĭ·nûr′vāt; ĭn·nûr′-), *v. t.* [See INNERVE.] 1. To supply with nerves. 2. To stimulate (a nerve or an organ) to activity.

in′ner·va′tion (ĭn′ẽr·vā′shŭn), *n.* 1. *Anat.* The distribution of nerves to or in a part. 2. *Physiol.* The nervous excitation necessary for the maintenance of the life and functions of the various organs. — **in′ner·va′tion·al,** *adj.*

in·nerve′ (ĭ·nûrv′; ĭn·nûrv′), *v. t.* [*in-* in + *nerve.*] To give nervous energy or power to; invigorate; stimulate.

inn′hold′er (ĭn′hōl′dẽr), *n.* An innkeeper.

in′ning (ĭn′ĭng), *n.* [AS. *innung.*] 1. Act of taking in, gathering, enclosing, reclaiming, etc. 2. *pl.* Reclaimed lands. 3. **a** *Baseball.* A division of the game in which each side, or, occasionally, only one side, has a full turn at bat. **b** *Cricket.* [*In this sense,* **in′nings** (ĭn′ĭngz), *n. sing. & pl.*] A turn at bat of a side or of an individual player. **c** The turn of a person, or party, in power.

inn′keep′er (ĭn′kēp′ẽr), *n.* The landlord of an inn.

in′no·cence (ĭn′ō·sĕns; -s′ns), *n.* 1. State or quality of being innocent; as: **a** Freedom from sin; purity of heart. **b** Guilelessness; simplicity. **c** Guiltlessness. **d** Harmlessness; innocuousness. 2. An innocent person. 3. **a** The bluet. **b** A small herb (*Collinsia verna*) of the figwort family, of the central United States; also, a related species (*C. bicolor*) of California.

in′no·cen·cy (-sĕn·sĭ; -s′n·sĭ), *n.* Innocence or an instance of it.

in′no·cent (-sĕnt; -s′nt), *adj.* [OF., fr. L. *innocens, -entis,* fr. *in-* not + *nocens,* pres. part. of *nocere* to harm.] 1. Free from guilt or sin, or from evil action or effect; specif.: **a** Doing or thinking no evil; unacquainted with evil; pure. **b** Free from blame, censure, or guilt; not guilty. **c** Without evil influence or effect, or not arising from evil intention; as, an *innocent* deception. 2. Spotless; unsullied; as, the *innocent* snow. 3. Guileless, ignorant, or simple; naïve; hence, simple-minded. 4. Innocuous; harmless. 5. Free or devoid (*of*); destitute; as, *innocent* of clothes. 6. Lawful; permitted; specif., *Internat. Law,* not contraband. — *n.* 1. One who is innocent; esp.: **a** A young child. **b** A simpleton; also, an idiot. 2. *pl. U. S.* Bluets. See INNOCENCE, 3 **a**. — **in′no·cent·ly,** *adv.*

in·noc′u·ous (ĭ·nŏk′ū·ŭs), *adj.* [L. *innocuus,* fr. *in-* not + *nocuus* hurtful, fr. *nocere* to hurt.] Harmless; producing no ill effect or no injury. — **in·noc′u·ous·ly,** *adv.* — **in·noc′u·ous·ness,** *n.*

Inn of Court. *Eng.* One of the four sets of buildings in London (*Inner Temple, Middle Temple, Lincoln's Inn,* and *Gray's Inn*) belonging to the four societies of "students and practisers of the law of England" which alone admit to practice at the bar; *pl.*, the four societies.

in·nom′i·nate (ĭ·nŏm′ĭ·nāt; ĭn·nŏm′-), *adj.* [LL. *innominatus,* fr. *in-* not + *nominare* to name.] Having no name.

innominate bone. *Anat.* The great bone which makes a lateral half of the pelvis in mammals; hipbone. It is composed of three bones, ilium, ischium, and pubis, consolidated into one in the adult.

in′no·vate (ĭn′ō·vāt), *v. t. & i.* [L. *innovatus,* past part. of *innovare* to renew, fr. *in-* in + *novare* to make new, fr. *novus* new.] To make changes or innovations (in). — **in′no·va′tive** (-vā′tĭv), *adj.* — **in′no·va′tor** (-vā′tẽr), *n.*

in′no·va′tion (-vā′shŭn), *n.* Act of introducing something new or novel as in customs, rites, etc.; also, a change effected by innovating; a novelty added or substituted. — **in′no·va′tion·al,** *adj.* — **in′no·va′tion·ist,** *n.*

in′nu·en′do (ĭn′ū·ĕn′dō), *n.; pl.* -DOES (-dōz). [L., by intimation, by hinting, gerund of *innuere, innutum,* to give a nod, to intimate, fr. *in-* in, to + *-nuere* (in comp.) to nod.] 1. **a** Meaning; namely; to wit; — a term formerly employed in legal documents to introduce matter explanatory of the text. **b** Hence, the parenthesis or explanation so introduced, esp. an interpretation of expressions alleged to be injurious or libelous. 2. Remote and derogatory reference, esp. to a person; a depreciatory allusion; insinuation.

in·nu′mer·a·ble (ĭ·nū′mẽr·ȧ·b′l; ĭn·nū′-), *adj.* 1. Too many to be counted; indefinitely numerous; numberless. 2. Characterized by vast or countless number. — **in·nu′mer·a·ble·ness,** *n.* — **in·nu′mer·a·bly,** *adv.*

in·nu′mer·ous (-ŭs), *adj.* Numberless; innumerable.

in′nu·tri′tion (ĭn′ū·trĭsh′ŭn; ĭn′nū-), *n.* Lack of nutrition; failure of nourishment. — **in′nu·tri′tious** (-ŭs), *adj.*

in′ob·serv′ance (ĭn′ŏb·zûr′văns), *n.* 1. Lack of attention; heedlessness. 2. Nonobservance, as of a treaty, law, regulation, etc. — **in′ob·serv′ant** (-vănt), *adj.*

in·oc′u·la·ble (ĭn·ŏk′ū·lȧ·b′l), *adj.* Susceptible to, or transmissible by, inoculation.

in·oc′u·lant (-lănt), *n.* Inoculum.

in·oc′u·late (-lāt), *v. t.* [L. *inoculatus,* past part. of *inoculare* to engraft, fr. *in-* in, on + *oculare* to furnish with eyes, fr. *oculus* an eye, a bud.] 1. *Obs.* To graft by budding. 2. **a** To communicate a disease to, by inserting its virus into the tissues. **b** To introduce an immunizing serum into. **c** To introduce (a microorganism, virus, etc.) by inoculation. 3. To introduce into the mind of, usually with harmful effects. — **Syn.** See INFUSE. — **in·oc′u·la′tive** (-lā′tĭv), *adj.* — **in·oc′u·la′tor** (-lā′tẽr), *n.*

in·oc′u·la′tion (-lā′shŭn), *n.* 1. Act, process or art of inoculating. 2. The introduction of minute organisms or of serum or the like into living tissues, milk, culture media, soil, etc.; in medicine, such communication of a disease virus to a healthy individual in order to induce a mild form of the disease and produce immunity.

in·oc′u·lum (ĭn·ŏk′ū·lŭm), *n.* [NL.] Material, as spores, bacteria, etc., used in making an inoculation.

in′of·fen′sive (ĭn′ŏ·fĕn′sĭv), *adj.* Not offensive; not offending or annoying; unobjectionable; also, harmless. — **in′of·fen′sive·ly,** *adv.* — **in′of·fen′sive·ness,** *n.*

‖**in om′ni·a pa·ra′tus** (ĭn ŏm′nĭ·ȧ pȧ·rā′tŭs). [L.] Ready for all things.

in·op′er·a·ble (ĭn·ŏp′ẽr·ȧ·b′l), *adj.* 1. Not operable. 2. *Surg.* Not suitable for operation; as, *inoperable* cases.

in·op′er·a′tive (ĭn·ŏp′ẽr·ā′tĭv; -ȧ·tĭv), *adj.* Not operative; not in operation; producing no effect, as laws that are not enforced. — **in·op′er·a′tive·ness,** *n.*

in·op′por·tune′ (ĭn·ŏp′ŏr·tūn′), *adj.* Not opportune; unseasonable. — **in·op′por·tune′ly,** *adv.* — **in·op′por·tune′ness,** *n.*

in·op′por·tun′ist (-tūn′ĭst), *n.* One who holds an action, policy, etc., inopportune; esp. [*cap.*], any member of the Vatican Council (1870) who opposed promulgation of the dogma of papal infallibility, as inopportune.

in·or′di·nate (ĭn·ôr′dĭ·nĭt), *adj.* [L. *inordinatus* disordered.] Not ordered or kept within bounds; unregulated; unrestrained; hence, excessive; immoderate. — **Syn.** See EXCESSIVE. — **in·or′di·nate·ly,** *adv.* — **in·or′di·nate·ness,** *n.*

in′or·gan′ic (ĭn′ôr·găn′ĭk), *adj.* Not organic; specif.: **a** Designating, or composed of, matter other than animal or vegetable; hence, inanimate. **b** Not forming, or not characteristic of, an organism. **c** Designating, or pertaining to, the branch of chemistry treating all substances but those called organic. See CHEMISTRY, 1.

in·os′cu·late (ĭn·ŏs′kū·lāt), *v. i. & t.* [*in-* in + *osculate.*] To unite by apposition or contact, as two tubular vessels at their extremities; to anastomose; hence, to unite or join so as to become or make as one; to blend. — **in·os′cu·la′tion** (-lā′shŭn), *n.*

in·o′si·tol (ĭn·ō′sĭ·tōl; -tŏl), *n.* Also **in′o·site** (ĭn′ō·sīt). [Gr. *is, inos,* muscle, fiber + *-ite* + *-ol.*] *Chem.* A white, crystalline alcohol, $C_6H_6(OH)_6$, existing in several isomeric modifications. The inactive variety is found in certain animal tissues and fluids and in some plants. It is a growth-promoting vitamin of the B complex.

in·o′wer (ĭn·ō′ẽr), *adv. & prep.* *Scot.* In toward; inby.

in·ox′i·dize (-ŏk′sĭ·dīz), *v. t.* To keep from oxidation.

in′pa′tient (ĭn′pā′shĕnt), *n.* A patient who receives lodging and food, as well as treatment, in a hospital or infirmary.

‖**in per·pe′tu·um** (ĭn pẽr·pĕt′ū·ŭm). [L.] Forever.

in per·so′nam (pẽr·sō′năm). [L.] *Law.* 1. Against a particular person. 2. Against the person, as distinguished from things.

‖**in pet′to** (ĭn pĕt′tō). [It.] In the breast; secretly; — applied specif. to cardinals appointed by the pope but not named in consistory.

in′phase′ (ĭn′fāz′), *adj.* *Elec.* Being of the same phase.

‖**in pos′se** (ĭn pŏs′ē). [ML.] Potentially; in possibility or capacity. Cf. IN ESSE.

in′pour′ (ĭn′pōr′; 70), *v. i. & t.* To pour in.

‖**in prae·sen′ti** (ĭn prē·zĕn′tī). [L.] At the present (time).

‖**in pro'pri·a per·so'na** (ĭn prō'prĭ·ȧ pẽr·sō'nȧ). [L.] In one's own person or character.

in'put' (ĭn'po͝ot'), *n.* That which is put in; specif., *Mech.*, power or energy put into a machine, storage battery, etc.

in'quest (ĭn'kwĕst), *n.* [OF. *enqueste*, deriv. of past part. of L. *inquaerere*. See INQUIRE.] **1.** *Law.* **a** Judicial or official inquiry, esp. before a jury; as, a coroner's *inquest* (see CORONER). **b** A jury or body assembled to hold such an inquiry. **c** The finding of such a jury. **2.** Inquiry; investigation.

in·qui'et (ĭn·kwī'ĕt), *adj.* Disturbed; uneasy. — **in·qui'et·ly**, *adv.* — **in·qui'et·ness**, *n.* — **in·qui'e·tude** (-ĕ·tūd), *n.*

in'qui·line (ĭn'kwĭ·līn; -lĭn), *n.* [L. *inquilinus* tenant, lodger.] An animal, esp. a hymenopteran, that lives habitually in the nest or abode of some other species; a guest; a commensal. — **in'qui·line**, *adj.*

in·quire' (ĭn·kwīr'), *v. t.* [OF. *enquerre*, deriv. of L. *inquirere*, *inquisitum*, fr. *in-* in + *quaerere* to seek.] **1.** *Obs.* **a** To interrogate; question. **b** To seek; — often with *out*. **2.** To seek to know by asking; make examination or inquiry respecting. — *v. i.* **1.** To ask a question; to put queries. **2.** To make an investigation, examination, or the like. — **Syn.** See ASK. — **in·quir'er**, *n.* — **in·quir'ing·ly**, *adv.*

in·quir'y (ĭn·kwīr'ĭ; ĭn'kwĭ·rĭ), *n.; pl.* -QUIRIES (-ĭz; -rĭz). An inquiring; specif.: **a** Search for truth, information, or knowledge; research; investigation. **b** A seeking for information by asking questions; interrogation; a question or questioning.

in'qui·si'tion (ĭn'kwĭ·zĭsh'ŭn), *n.* [OF., fr. L. *inquisitio*. See INQUIRE.] **1.** Act or instance of inquiring; inquiry. **2.** A judicial or official inquiry before a jury; also, the finding of the jury. **3.** [*cap.*] *R.C.Ch.* The systematic pursuit of heresy and the punishment of heretics; a tribunal (the ***Holy Office***) established for that purpose. The ***Spanish Inquisition***, as reorganized and put under state control in 1480, conducted its proceedings from the beginning through the 16th century with extreme severity. — **in'qui·si'tion·al** (-ăl; -'l), *adj.*

in'qui·si'tion·ist (-ĭst), *n.* An inquisitor.

in·quis'i·tive (ĭn·kwĭz'ĭ·tĭv), *adj.* **1.** Given to examination, investigation, or research. **2.** Disposed to ask questions; improperly curious. — *n.* An inquisitive person. — **Syn.** See CURIOUS. — **in·quis'i·tive·ly**, *adv.* — **in·quis'i·tive·ness**, *n.*

in·quis'i·tor (-tẽr), *n.* One who inquires or makes inquisition, esp. officially, as a coroner, sheriff, or member of the Inquisition.

in·quis'i·to'ri·al (-tō'rĭ·ăl; 70), *adj.* **1.** Pertaining to, or of the nature of, an inquisitor or inquisitors; making rigorous or obnoxious inquiry. **2.** *Law.* Designating, or pertaining to, that system of criminal procedure in which the judge also acts as prosecutor, or in which the proceedings are secretly conducted. — **in·quis'i·to'ri·al·ly**, *adv.* — **in·quis'i·to'ri·al·ness**, *n.*

‖**in re** (ĭn rē'). [L.] In the matter of; concerning.

‖**in rem** (rĕm'). [L.] *Law.* In or against a (or the) thing; — used esp. of any right available over its subject without reference to one person more than another.

in'road' (ĭn'rōd'), *n.* **1.** A sudden or desultory hostile incursion; raid; foray; hence, forcible entrance; encroachment. **2.** A serious encroachment, often by wasteful consumption or destruction; as, *inroads* on one's time or one's health.

in'rush' (-rŭsh'), *n.* A rushing in; inpour; influx.

‖**in sae'cu·la sae'cu·lo'rum** (ĭn sĕk'ū·lȧ sĕk'ū·lō'rŭm). [L.] For ages and ages; forever and ever.

in·sal'i·vate (ĭn·săl'ĭ·vāt), *v. t.* *Physiol.* To mix with the saliva. — **in·sal'i·va'tion** (-vā'shŭn), *n.*

in'sa·lu'bri·ous (ĭn'sȧ·lū'brĭ·ŭs), *adj.* Not salubrious; unwholesome. — **in'sa·lu'bri·ty** (-brĭ·tĭ), *n.*

in·sane' (ĭn·sān'; 2), *adj.* [L. *insanus*. See IN- not; SANE.] **1.** Unsound; — said of the mind; exhibiting unsoundness or disorder of mind; not sane; mad. See INSANITY. **2.** Used by, or for, persons not of sound mind. **3.** Characterized by the utmost folly; chimerical; unpractical; as, an *insane* plan. — **in·sane'ly**, *adv.* — **in·sane'ness**, *n.*

in·san'i·tar'y (ĭn·săn'ĭ·tĕr'ĭ *or, esp. Brit.*, -tẽr·ĭ), *adj.* Not sanitary; unhealthy; liable to promote disease.

in·san'i·ta'tion (-tā'shŭn), *n.* Lack of sanitation; unsanitary condition.

in·san'i·ty (ĭn·săn'ĭ·tĭ), *n.* **1.** State of being insane; unsoundness or derangement of mind, esp. without recognition of one's own illness. *Insanity* is rather a social and legal than a medical term, and implies mental disorder resulting in inability to manage one's affairs and perform one's social duties. The term covers a variety of disorders, such as manic-depressive insanity, dementia praecox, paranoia, general paralysis, and the alcoholic insanities. Mental deficiency is not usually included. **2.** *Law.* Such unsoundness of mental condition as, with regard to any matter under action, modifies or does away with individual legal responsibility or capacity. **3.** Extravagant folly, or an example of it.

Syn. **Insanity, lunacy, psychosis, mania, dementia** denote a serious mental disorder. **Insanity**, chiefly a legal term, implies unfitness to manage one's own affairs or perform one's social duties, and is usually distinguished from inborn mental deficiency and from temporary neurosis or delirious conditions; **lunacy**, in Great Britain, is still to an extent used in place of *insanity*, but ordinarily it suggests occasional spells of fury intermingled with lucid periods; **psychosis** is the medical term for any mental disease; **mania** definitely implies insanity but is often used specifically for one of the spells of extreme mental derangement that characterize some mental diseases; **dementia**, a technical psychiatric term, applies to any mental disease or any condition of one that involves marked mental deterioration.

in·sa'ti·a·ble (ĭn·sā'shĭ·ȧ·b'l; -shȧ·b'l), *adj.* Not satiable; incapable of being satisfied or appeased. — **in·sa'ti·a·bil'i·ty** (-bĭl'ĭ·tĭ), *n.* — **in·sa'ti·a·ble·ness**, *n.* — **in·sa'ti·a·bly**, *adv.*

in·sa'ti·ate (ĭn·sā'shĭ·āt), *adj.* Not satiated; insatiable.

in·scribe' (ĭn·skrīb'), *v. t.* [L. *inscribere*. See IN- in; SCRIBE.] **1.** To write or engrave (words or characters); also, to mark or engrave (a tablet or the like). **2.** To enter the name of, as upon a list; enroll. **3.** To address; dedicate informally. **4.** To stamp deeply; impress. **5.** *Brit.* To register the names of the holders of (securities, as stocks, etc.). **6.** *Geom.* To draw (one figure within another) so as to have as many incidences as possible. — **in·scrib'er** (-skrīb'ẽr), *n.*

in·scrip'tion (-skrĭp'shŭn), *n.* **1.** Act or process of inscribing. **2.** That which is inscribed; esp., an engraved text or record. **3.** An address, or informal dedication, as of a book. **4.** *Brit.* Registration, or inscribing, of securities; also, *pl.*, securities so inscribed. — **in·scrip'tion·al** (-ăl; -'l), *adj.*

in·scrip'tive (ĭn·skrĭp'tĭv), *adj.* Pertaining to, or of the nature of, an inscription.

in·scroll' (ĭn·skrōl'), *v. t.* To write on a scroll; record.

in·scru'ta·ble (-skro͞o'tȧ·b'l), *adj.* [LL. *inscrutabilis*. See IN- not; SCRUTINY.] Incapable of being searched into and understood; incomprehensible; unfathomable. — **Syn.** See MYSTERIOUS. — **in·scru'ta·bil'i·ty** (-bĭl'ĭ·tĭ), *n.* — **in·scru'ta·ble·ness**, *n.* — **in·scru'ta·bly**, *adv.*

in·sculp' (ĭn·skŭlp'), *v. t.* [L. *insculpere*.] *Now Rare.* To engrave; sculpture.

in'sect (ĭn'sĕkt), *n.* [L. *insectum*, fr. *insectus*, past part. of *insecare* to cut in; — because their bodies appear *cut in*, or almost divided.] **1.** Strictly (*Zool.*), any of a class (Insecta) of small invertebrate animals, with three clearly defined body regions, *head*, *thorax*, and *abdomen*, with only three pairs of legs, and usually with wings, as beetles, bugs, bees, flies, etc. **2.** Popularly, also, any of certain allied classes of arthropods whose members are wingless and usually have more than six legs, as spiders, mites, ticks, etc. **3.** A small, contemptible person. — *adj.* Pertaining to or like insects; as, *insect* eggs; for insects; as, an *insect* cabinet.

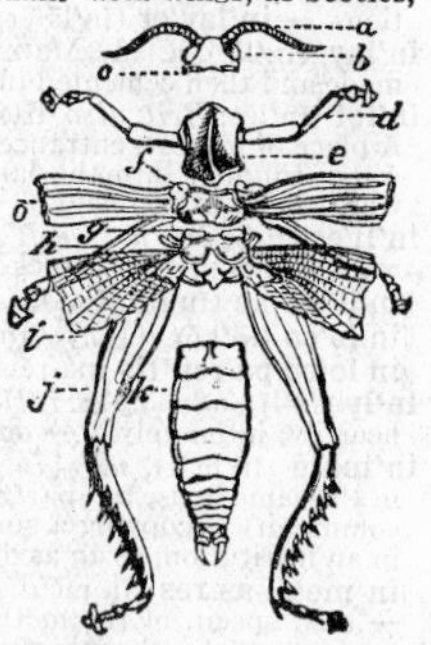

Parts of an Insect (Grasshopper). *a* Antennae; *b* Eyes; *c* Head; *d* Anterior Legs; *e* Prothorax; *f* Mesothorax; *g* Metathorax; *h* Middle Legs; *i* Base of Posterior Wing; *j* Posterior Legs; *k* Abdomen; *o* Base of Anterior Wing.

in'sec·tar'i·um (ĭn'sĕk·târ'ĭ·ŭm; 6), *n.; pl.* -IA (-ȧ). Also **in'sec·tar'y** (ĭn'sĕk·tẽr'ĭ *or, esp. Brit.*, -tẽr·ĭ). [NL. *insectarium*.] A place in which living insects are kept and propagated; also, the collection in such a place.

in·sec'ti·cide (ĭn·sĕk'tĭ·sīd), *n.* [L. *insectum* insect + *-cide*, 1.] An agent or preparation for destroying insects.

in·sec'ti·fuge (-fūj), *n.* An agent or preparation for repelling or destroying insects.

in·sec'tile (ĭn·sĕk'tĭl; 56), *adj.* Like, or of the nature of, an insect; consisting of insects.

in'sec·ti'val (ĭn'sĕk·tī'văl; ĭn·sĕk'tĭ·văl), *adj.* Of, pertaining to, or like an insect.

in'sec·tiv'o·rous (ĭn'sĕk·tĭv'ō·rŭs), *adj.* [L. *insectum* an insect + *vorare* to devour.] **a** Feeding on insects. **b** Belonging to an order (Insectivora) of mammals including the moles, shrews, hedgehogs, and their allies, which are mostly small, terrestrial, nocturnal, and feed on insects. — **in·sec'ti·vore** (ĭn·sĕk'tĭ·vōr; 70), *n.*

in'se·cure' (ĭn'sē·kūr'), *adj.* Not secure; specif.: **a** Not effectually protected or sustained; unsafe. **b** Not tightly fastened or firmly fixed; loose or shaky.

in'se·cu'ri·ty (-kū'rĭ·tĭ), *n.; pl.* -TIES (-tĭz). Condition or quality of being insecure; want of safety or assurance; also, an insecure condition or circumstance.

in·sem'i·nate (ĭn·sĕm'ĭ·nāt), *v. t.* [L. *inseminatus*, past part. of *inseminare* to sow. See IN- in; SEMINAL.] **1.** To sow or sow in; implant. **2.** To introduce spermatozoa into the vagina of; to impregnate. — **Syn.** See IMPLANT. — **in·sem'i·na'tion** (-nā'shŭn), *n.*

in·sen'sate (ĭn·sĕn'sāt), *adj.* **1.** Without sensation; inanimate. **2.** Without sense; foolish; fatuous. **3.** Without sensibility; unfeeling; brutal. — **Syn.** See FOND. — **in·sen'sate·ly**, *adv.* — **in·sen'sate·ness**, *n.*

in·sen'si·bil'i·ty (ĭn·sĕn'sĭ·bĭl'ĭ·tĭ), *n.* State or quality of being insensible; lack of feeling.

in·sen'si·ble (ĭn·sĕn'sĭ·b'l), *adj.* **1.** Incapable or bereft of feeling or sensation; specif.: **a** Not endowed with consciousness; inanimate; insentient. **b** Deprived of consciousness; unconscious; as, to fall *insensible*. **c** Not endowed with acute sense perception; as, *insensible* to cold, pain, etc. **2.** Not apparent or clearly apparent to the senses; hence, imperceptible. **3.** Devoid of sensibility or sensitiveness; apathetic; indifferent; also, unaware; as, *insensible* of their danger. **4.** *Now Rare.* Devoid of sense, reason, meaning, etc. — **in·sen'si·bly**, *adv.*

in·sen'si·tive (-tĭv), *adj.* Not sensitive; esp., not quick to react; unimpressionable or unresponsive. — **in·sen'si·tiv'i·ty** (-tĭv'ĭ·tĭ), **in·sen'si·tive·ness**, *n.*

in·sen'ti·ent (ĭn·sĕn'shĭ·ĕnt; -shĕnt), *adj.* Not sentient; nonconscious or inanimate. — **in·sen'ti·ence** (-shĭ·ĕns), *n.* — **in·sen'ti·en·cy** (-shĭ·ĕn·sĭ), *n.*

in·sep'a·ra·ble (ĭn·sĕp'ȧ·rȧ·b'l), *adj.* Not separable; incapable of being separated or disjoined. — *n.* One of inseparable things or persons; — usually in *pl.* — **in·sep'a·ra·bil'i·ty** (-bĭl'ĭ·tĭ), *n.* — **in·sep'a·ra·bly**, *adv.*

in·sert' (ĭn·sûrt'), *v. t.* [L. *insertus*, past part. of *inserere* to insert, fr. *in-* + *serere* to place, connect.] **1.** To set so as to be within; to put or thrust in; to introduce; as, to *insert* a cion in a stock or a letter in a word. **2.** *Zool., Bot., etc.* To attach by natural growth, as the parts of a flower, or a muscle or tendon; — only in *past part.* — **Syn.** See INTRODUCE. — **in·sert'er**, *n.*

in'sert (ĭn'sûrt), *n.* A thing inserted or to be inserted; esp., *U. S.*, an extra leaf or leaves, a circular, or the like, placed within the leaves of a pamphlet, the folds of a newspaper, etc.

in·ser'tion (ĭn·sûr'shŭn), *n.* **1.** Act or process of inserting. **2.** That which is set in, or inserted; esp.: **a** Embroidery or needlework made to be inserted into plain material to ornament it; also, a piece of such work. **b** Each appearance of an advertisement, as in a newspaper. **3.** *Zool., Bot., etc.* **a** The mode or place of attachment of an organ or part. **b** *Anat.* The end or part of a muscle by which it is attached to the part to be moved.

in'ses·so'ri·al (ĭn'sĕ·sō'rĭ·ăl), *adj.* [L. *insessor* a sitter in, fr. *insidere*, *insessum*, to sit in or down. See INSIDIOUS.] *Zool.* Perching, or adapted for perching.

in·set' (ĭn·sĕt'), *v. t.;* IN·SET' *or, occasionally Brit.*, IN·SET'TED; IN·SET'TING. To set in; insert as an inset.

in'set' (ĭn'sĕt'), *n.* **1.** Act of setting in; inflow; as, the *inset* of the tide. **2.** That which is inserted, or set in. **3.** One or more separate leaves inserted in a book, usually before binding. **4.** A piece of cloth set or let into a garment. **5.** A small map, illustration, etc., set within a larger one.

in·sheathe' (ĭn·shēth'), *v. t.;* -SHEATHED' (-shēthd'); -SHEATH'ING (-shēth'ĭng). To insert as in a sheath.

in′shoot′ (ĭn′shōōt′), *n.* *Baseball.* A pitched ball (or its course) that curves toward a right-handed batter; incurve.

in′shore′ (ĭn′shōr′; ĭn′shōr′; 2), *adj.* Near, or directed in toward, the shore. — (ĭn′shōr′), *adv.* In toward the shore; as, he was headed *inshore.*

in′side′ (ĭn′sīd′; 2), *n.* **1.** The inner side, surface, or part; interior. **2.** Inward nature or being. **3.** *Colloq.* **a** *pl.* Entrails. **b** An inside passenger, as in a coach. **4.** *Print.* The side of a sheet containing the second page. — *adj.* **1.** Internal; interior. **2.** Employed or working indoors; as, an *inside* man. **3.** Pertaining or known to insiders; as, *inside* information. **4.** Placed on or toward the inner side of any curve or turn; as, edge the *inside* ski. **5.** Engaged to work within a plant or organization as a spy upon workers or members. *Slang.* — *adv.* Within. — (ĭn′sīd′; 2), *prep.* Inside of; within.

in′sid′er (ĭn′sīd′ẽr), *n.* A person inside; hence, one in a position to have firsthand information.

inside track. The inner side of a curved racecourse; hence, *Colloq.*, advantage of place, facilities, etc., in competition.

in·sid′i·ous (ĭn·sĭd′ĭ·ŭs; 58), *adj.* [F. *insidieux*, fr. L. *insidiosus*, fr. *insidiae* an ambush, fr. *insidere* to sit in, fr. *in-* in + *sedere* to sit.] **1.** Full of plots; watching for an opportunity to ensnare; devised so as to entrap; wily; sly; treacherous. **2.** Having a more serious effect than is apparent; as, an *insidious* disease or poison. — **in·sid′i·ous·ly,** *adv.* — **in·sid′i·ous·ness,** *n.*

in′sight′ (ĭn′sīt′), *n.* Keen discernment or understanding; penetration; also, intuition; immediate apprehension or cognition. — **Syn.** See DISCERNMENT.

‖**in·sig′ne cum lau′de.** See CUM LAUDE.

in·sig′ni·a (ĭn·sĭg′nĭ·ȧ; 58), *n. pl.; sing.* INSIGNE (-nē). [L. *insigne*, pl. *insignia*, fr. *insignis* distinguished by a mark, fr. *in-* + *signum* a

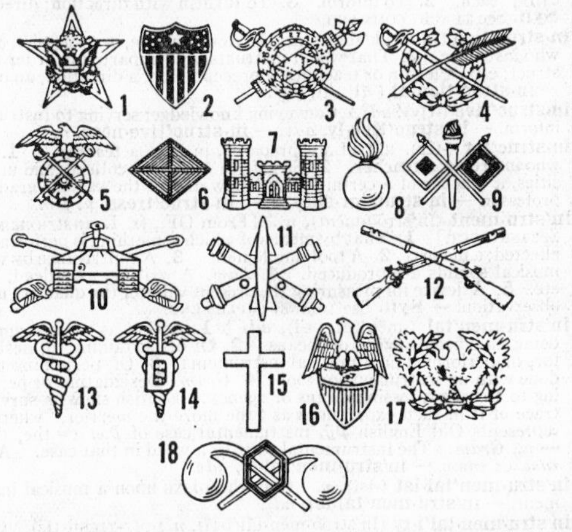

Insignia of the United States Army. 1 General Staff; 2 Adjutant General's Corps; 3 Inspector General; 4 Judge Advocate General's Corps; 5 Quartermaster Corps; 6 Finance Corps; 7 Corps of Engineers; 8 Ordnance Corps; 9 Signal Corps; 10 Armor; 11 Artillery; 12 Infantry; 13 Medical Corps; 14 Dental Corps; 15 Chaplain (Christian faith); 16 Aide (to a Brigadier General); 17 Warrant Officer; 18 Chemical Corps. Cf. WINGS, *Illust.*

mark, sign.] **1.** Distinguishing marks of authority, office, or honor; badges; emblems; as, the *insignia* of royalty or of an order. **2.** Typical and characteristic marks or signs by which anything is distinguished; as, the *insignia* of a trade.

in′sig·nif′i·cance (ĭn′sĭg·nĭf′ĭ·kăns), *n.* Condition or quality of being insignificant; lack of significance.

in′sig·nif′i·can·cy (-kăn·sĭ), *n.; pl.* -CIES (-sĭz). Insignificance; also, an insignificant thing or person.

in′sig·nif′i·cant (-kănt), *adj.* Not significant; as: **a** Meaningless; void of sense. **b** Unimportant; trifling; without weight. **c** Not conspicuous for size, influence, etc.; small; little; mean. — **in′sig·nif′i·cant·ly,** *adv.*

in′sin·cere′ (ĭn′sĭn·sēr′), *adj.* Not sincere; hypocritical; dissembling. — **in′sin·cere′ly,** *adv.* — **in′sin·cer′i·ty** (-sĕr′ĭ·tĭ), *n.*

in·sin′u·ate (ĭn·sĭn′ū·āt), *v. t.* [L. *insinuatus*, past part. of *insinuare* to insinuate, fr. *in-* + *sinus* the bosom.] **1.** To introduce gently or gradually; hence, to introduce or work (in) artfully, indirectly, etc.; infuse; instill. **2.** To hint indirectly; suggest; imply. — *v. i. Obs.* **a** To creep, wind, or flow in. **b** To ingratiate oneself. — **Syn.** See INTRODUCE; SUGGEST. — **in·sin′u·at′ing** (-āt′ĭng), *adj.* — **Syn.** See DISARMING. — **in·sin′u·at′ing·ly,** *adv.* — **in·sin′u·a′tive** (-ā′tĭv; -ȧ·tĭv), *adj.* — **in·sin′u·a′tor** (-ā′tẽr), *n.*

in·sin′u·a′tion (-ā′shŭn), *n.* **1.** An insinuating; esp., covert suggestion. **2.** That which is insinuated; specif.: **a** An ingratiating act or speech. **b** An intimation by indirect or remote allusion.

in·sip′id (ĭn·sĭp′ĭd), *adj.* [F. and L.; F. *insipide*, fr. LL. & ML. *insipidus*, fr. *in-* not + *sapidus* savory, fr. *sapere* to taste.] **1.** Without taste or savor; vapid. **2.** Lacking in spirit or animation; uninteresting; flat; dull. — **in′si·pid′i·ty** (ĭn′sĭ·pĭd′ĭ·tĭ), **in·sip′id·ness,** *n.* — **in·sip′id·ly,** *adv.*

Syn. **Insipid, vapid, flat, jejune, banal, inane** mean lacking in qualities that give spirit, character, or substance. **Insipid**, literally without taste or savor, applies not only to food or drink but to persons, works of art, and the like, which are thin, weak, and characterless; **vapid** applies to that which has lost its freshness, sparkle, or tang and is stale, pointless, or the like; **flat** implies extreme vapidness; **jejune** implies an absence of substance or nutritive quality; **banal** implies a commonplaceness that makes for flatness or jejuneness; **inane** implies an absence of sense, significance, or point.

in·sip′i·ence (ĭn·sĭp′ĭ·ĕns; 58), *n.* [OF., fr. L. *insipientia*.] Lack of intelligence; stupidity. — **in·sip′i·ent** (-ĕnt), *adj.*

in·sist′ (ĭn·sĭst′), *v. i.* [F. or L.; F. *insister*, fr. L. *insistere* to set foot on, follow, persist, fr. *in-* in + *sistere* to stand, cause to stand, fr. *stare* to stand.] To take a stand and refuse to give way; to hold to something firmly; to be persistent, urgent, or pressing.

in·sist′ence (-sĭs′tĕns), *n.* Also **in·sist′en·cy** (-tĕn·sĭ). Act or instance of insisting; state or quality of being insistent; persistence; urgency.

in·sist′ent (-tĕnt), *adj.* Insisting or disposed to insist; persistent; hence, compelling attention. — **in·sist′ent·ly,** *adv.*

‖**in si′tu** (ĭn sī′tū). [L.] In its natural or original position.

in·snare′ (ĭn·snâr′). Var. of ENSNARE.

in·so′cia·ble (ĭn·sō′shȧ·b'l), *adj.* Unsociable. — **in·so′cia·bil′i·ty** (-bĭl′ĭ·tĭ), *n.* — **in·so′cia·bly,** *adv.*

in so far. In such measure; to such extent or degree; — properly written as one word, **in′so·far′** (ĭn′sō·fär′), and usually followed by *as.*

in′so·late (ĭn′sō·lāt), *v. t.* [L. *insolatus*, past part. of *insolare* to expose to the sun, fr. *in-* in + *sol* the sun.] To expose to the sun's rays, as for drying, ripening, etc.

in′so·la′tion (-lā′shŭn), *n.* **1.** An insolating. **2.** *Med.* **a** Sunstroke. **b** Treatment of disease by sun baths. **3.** *Meteorol.* **a** Received solar radiation, as by the earth. **b** Rate of delivery of all direct solar energy per unit of horizontal surface.

in′sole′ (ĭn′sōl′), *n.* The inside sole of a shoe; also, a loose, thin inner sole added for warmth or ease. See SHOE, *Illust.*

in′so·lence (ĭn′sō·lĕns), *n.* **1.** Quality of being insolent; contemptuous and overbearing demeanor. **2.** An insult.

in′so·lent (-lĕnt), *adj.* [L. *insolens*, *-entis;* akin to L. *insolescere* to be insolent.] **1.** Haughty and contemptuous or brutal in behavior or language; overbearing; grossly disrespectful. **2.** Proceeding from, or characterized by, insolence. — **Syn.** See PROUD. — **Ant.** Deferential. — *n.* An insolent person. — **in′so·lent·ly,** *adv.*

in·sol′u·ble (ĭn·sŏl′ū·b'l), *adj.* Not soluble; specif.: **a** *Rare.* Indissoluble. **b** Not to be solved or explained; insolvable. **c** Incapable or very difficult of being dissolved (in a liquid). — **in·sol′u·bil′i·ty** (-bĭl′ĭ·tĭ), **in·sol′u·ble·ness,** *n.* — **in·sol′u·bly,** *adv.*

in·solv′a·ble (ĭn·sŏl′vȧ·b'l), *adj.* Admitting no solution; as, an *insolvable* problem.

in·sol′ven·cy (ĭn·sŏl′vĕn·sĭ), *n.* State of being insolvent.

in·sol′vent (-vĕnt), *adj.* *Law.* **a** Not solvent; unable to pay one's debts. **b** Not sufficient to pay all the debts enforceable against it; as, an *insolvent* estate. **c** Relating to insolvents; as, *insolvent* laws. — *n.* An insolvent debtor.

in·som′ni·a (ĭn·sŏm′nĭ·ȧ), *n.* [L., fr. *insomnia* sleepless, fr. *in-* not + *somnus* sleep.] Prolonged inability to obtain due sleep; sleeplessness. — **in·som′ni·ous** (-ŭs), *adj.*

in·som′ni·ac (-ăk), *n.* A person affected with insomnia.

in′so·much′ (ĭn′sō·mŭch′), *adv.* So much; to such a degree; in such wise; so; — usually followed by *that* or *as.*

in·sou′ci·ance (ĭn·sōō′sĭ·ăns; *F.* ăN′sōō′syäNs′), *n.* [F.] Want of concern; indifference, esp. as an attitude of mind. — **in·sou′ci·ant** (-ănt; *F.* -syäN′), *adj.* — **in·sou′ci·ant·ly** (ĭn·sōō′sĭ·ănt·lĭ), *adv.*

in·soul′ (ĭn·sōl′), *v. t.* To ensoul.

in·span′ (ĭn·spăn′), *v. t. & i.;* see SPAN. [D. *inspannen.*] *S. Africa.* To yoke or harness.

in·spect′ (ĭn·spĕkt′), *v. t.* [L. *inspectus*, past part. of *inspicere* to inspect, fr. *in-* in + *specere* to look at.] **1.** To look upon; to view closely and critically; scrutinize. **2.** To view and examine officially, as troops, arms, etc. — **Syn.** See SCRUTINIZE. — **in·spec′tive** (-spĕk′tĭv), *adj.*

in·spec′tion (ĭn·spĕk′shŭn), *n.* An inspecting; critical, esp. official, examination; scrutiny. — **in·spec′tion·al,** *adj.*

in·spec′tor (-tẽr), *n.* [L.] **1.** One who inspects. **2.** A police officer in charge of a number of precincts, ranking below a superintendent or deputy superintendent. — **in·spec′to·ral** (-tō·răl), *adj.* — **in·spec′tor·ate** (-tẽr·āt), *n.*

in·sphere′ (ĭn·sfēr′), *v. t.* To ensphere.

in·spir′a·ble (ĭn·spīr′ȧ·b'l), *adj.* Capable of being inspired.

in′spi·ra′tion (ĭn′spĭ·rā′shŭn; *Brit. also* ĭn′spī-), *n.* **1.** Act of breathing in; specif., the drawing of air into the lungs; — the opposite of *expiration.* **2.** Act or state of being intellectually or emotionally inspired. **3.** *Theol.* A supernatural influence which qualifies men to receive and communicate divine truth. **4.** Any inspiring influence, person, etc. **5.** That which results from inspiration.

Syn. **Inspiration, enthusiasm, afflatus, fury, furor** (*or* **furore**), **frenzy,** esp. when qualified by *divine* or *poetic*, mean a power compelling creation or expression. **Inspiration** implies an infusion of divine power or a preternatural enlightening of the mind; **enthusiasm**, its now rare equivalent, derived from Greek, stresses the first implication and came to be applied to some preachers; **afflatus**, a bookish term, implies merely an inspiring influence; **fury, furor,** and **frenzy** stress the emotional excitement which carries the artist out of himself.

in′spi·ra′tion·al (-ăl; -'l), *adj.* **1.** Produced by, or moved by, inspiration; inspired. **2.** Of, pertaining to, or communicating inspiration. — **in′spi·ra′tion·al·ly,** *adv.*

in·spir′a·to′ry (ĭn·spīr′ȧ·tō′rĭ *or, esp. Brit.*, -tẽr·ĭ), *adj.* Pertaining to, aiding, used for, or marked by inspiration.

in·spire′ (ĭn·spīr′), *v. t.* [OF. *enspirer, inspirer*, fr. L. *inspirare*, fr. *in-* in + *spirare* to breathe.] **1.** *Archaic.* **a** To blow or breathe into or upon. **b** To infuse by breathing. **2.** To inhale; — opp. to *expire.* **3.** To fill with or as with a supernatural power or energy; to affect so as to enliven, animate, or esp., impel or stimulate; as, the success of his first play *inspired* him to write even better. **4.** To infuse into the mind; to communicate by or as by supernatural influence; as, behavior that *inspires* confidence. — *v. i.* **1.** To inhale. **2.** To impart inspiration. — **in·spir′er** (-spīr′ẽr), *n.* — **in·spir′ing·ly,** *adv.*

in·spir′it (ĭn·spĭr′ĭt), *v. t.* To infuse life or spirit into; animate; encourage. — **in·spir′it·ing·ly,** *adv.*

in·spis′sate (ĭn·spĭs′āt), *v. t. & i.* [LL. *inspissatus*, past part. of *inspissare* to thicken, fr. *in-* + *spissare* to thicken, fr. *spissus* thick.] To thicken, as by evaporation. — **in′spis·sa′tion** (ĭn′spĭ·sā′shŭn), *n.* — **in′spis·sa′tor** (ĭn′spĭ·sā′tẽr), *n.*

in′sta·bil′i·ty (ĭn′stȧ·bĭl′ĭ·tĭ), *n.; pl.* -TIES (-tĭz). Quality or condition of being unstable, or an instance of it; specif.: **a** Want of firmness; in security. **b** Lack of determination; inconstancy.

in·sta′ble (ĭn·stā′b'l), *adj.* Not stable; unstable.

in·stall′, in·stal′ (ĭn·stôl′), *v. t.;* IN·STALLED′ (-stôld′); IN·STALL′ING.

[F. *installer*, fr. ML. *installare*, fr. *in-* in + *stallum*, fr. OHG. *stal* a place, stall.] **1.** To place in office or dignity by seating in a stall or official seat; hence, to place formally in an office, rank, or order; induct. **2.** To set in a seat; to establish in a place. **3.** To set up or fix, as a lighting system, for use or service. — **in·stall'er** (ĭn·stôl'ẽr), *n.*

in'stal·la'tion (ĭn'stă·lā'shŭn; ĭn'stô-), *n.* **1.** Act of installing or state of being installed. **2.** That which is installed, or set up; specif., *pl.*, appointments; furnishings.

in·stall'ment, in·stal'ment (ĭn·stôl'mĕnt), *n.* [*install* + *-ment.*] Installation.

in·stall'ment, in·stal'ment, *n.* [From earlier *estallment*, fr. *estall* to agree upon payment by installments, fr. OF. *estaler* to stop, fix.] **1.** Any portion of a debt or sum of money divided into portions that are made payable at different times; as, to pay for a new automobile by monthly *installments*. **2.** One of several parts, as of a novel presented at intervals.

in'stance (ĭn'stăns), *n.* [OF., fr. L. *instantia*, fr. *instans*. See INSTANT.] **1.** *Archaic.* Urgent or earnest solicitation; insistence. **2.** Instigation; suggestion; request; as, a book written at the *instance* of the publishers. **3.** An illustrative case; an example. **4.** Step in an action; occasion; as, in the first *instance*. **5.** *Obs.* **a** Impelling motive or cause. **b** A token; a sign. **c** A detail or circumstance. **6.** *Law.* The institution and prosecution of a suit; a proceeding or process; suit; as, a court of the first *instance*.

Syn. **Instance, case, illustration, example, sample, specimen** mean a concrete thing which represents a type, a homogeneous whole, or the like. **Instance** applies to any individual person, act, or the like, brought forth in support or disproof of a general statement; **case,** to an instance that shows the occurrence or existence of something being considered, studied, dealt with, etc.; **illustration,** to an instance or case cited as a means of throwing light upon what has been discussed in general terms; **example,** to a typical, representative, or illustrative instance or case; **sample,** to a part of a larger whole, offered as an indication of its qualities; **specimen,** to any example or sample.

in'stance, *v. t.*; IN'STANCED (-stănst); IN'STANC·ING (-stăn·sĭng). **1.** *Rare.* To demonstrate by an instance, or example. **2.** To mention as an example; to cite.

in'stan·cy (ĭn'stăn·sĭ), *n.* Quality or state of being instant; as: **a** Urgency; insistence. **b** Instantaneousness.

in'stant (-stănt), *adj.* [OF., fr. L. *instans, -antis*, pres. part. of *instare* to stand or press upon, fr. *in-* in, on + *stare* to stand.] **1.** Pressing; urgent; importunate; as, continuing *instant* in prayer. **2.** Present; current; — used with dates to indicate the current month (abbr. *inst.*); as, the 10th *inst.* **3.** Closely pressing in respect to time; immediate; as, this matter demands *instant* attention. **4.** Not mediate; direct. — *adv. Poetic.* Instantly. — *n.* **1.** A point in duration; a moment; esp., an infinitesimal portion of time; also, any particular moment. **2.** The present or current month. Abbr. *inst.*

in'stan·ta'ne·ous (ĭn'stăn·tā'nē·ŭs; 58), *adj.* **1.** Done or occurring in an instant; as, an *instantaneous* flash. **2.** Done instantly; prompt; as, an *instantaneous* reply. — **in'stan·ta'ne·ous·ly,** *adv.* — **in'stan·ta'ne·ous·ness,** *n.*

in·stan'ter (ĭn·stăn'tẽr), *adv.* [L., earnestly.] Immediately; instantly; at once.

in'stant·ly (ĭn'stănt·lĭ), *adv.* **a** With urgency or importunity; pressingly. **b** Without the least delay; at once. — *conj.* As soon as; directly.

in'star (ĭn'stär), *n.* [L., form.] An insect or other arthropod in any of the forms assumed between successive molts. Thus the pupa and imago of a butterfly are *instars*.

in·star' (ĭn·stär'), *v. t.*; see STAR. **1.** To place as a star; turn into a star. **2.** To stud with or as with stars.

in·state' (ĭn·stāt'), *v. t.* **1.** To set or establish, as in a rank or office; install. **2.** *Obs.* **a** To invest; endow. **b** To bestow; confer.

‖**in sta'tu quo** (ĭn stā'tū kwō'). [L.] In the state in which (it is or was); in the former (or same) state.

in'stau·ra'tion (ĭn'stô·rā'shŭn), *n.* [L. *instauratio*, fr. *instauratus*, past part. of *instaurare* to renew.] Restoration after decay, lapse, or dilapidation.

in·stead' (ĭn·stĕd'), *adv.* [*in-* + *stead* place.] **1.** In the place; in lieu. **2.** In its stead; rather.

in'step (ĭn'stĕp), *n.* [Appar., but obscurely, fr. *in-* in + *step.*] **1.** The arched part of the human foot in front of the ankle joint; also, the upper portion of this part. **2.** That part of the hind leg of the horse between the hock, or ham, and the pastern joint. **3.** That part of a shoe, stocking, etc., over the instep (sense 1).

in'sti·gate (ĭn'stĭ·gāt), *v. t.* [L. *instigatus*, past part. of *instigare* to instigate, fr. *in-* in + *stigare* (in comp.) to prick.] To goad or urge forward; to set on; provoke; incite. — **Syn.** See INCITE. — **in'sti·ga'tion** (-gā'shŭn), *n.* — **in'sti·ga'tive** (-gā'tĭv), *adj.* — **in'sti·ga'tor** (-gā'tẽr), *n.*

in·still', in·stil' (ĭn·stĭl'), *v. t.*; -STILLED' (-stĭld'); -STILL'ING. [F. or L.; F. *instiller*, fr. L. *instillare, -latum*, fr. *in-* in + *stillare* to drop, fr. *stilla* a drop.] To drop in; to pour in drop by drop; hence, to impart gradually; infuse slowly. — **Syn.** See IMPLANT. — **in'stil·la'tion** (ĭn'stĭ·lā'shŭn), *n.* — **in·still'er,** *n.* — **in·still'ment, in·stil'ment,** *n.*

in·stinct' (ĭn·stĭngkt'), *adj.* [L. *instinctus*, past part. of *instinguere* to instigate, incite.] Impelled by an inner or animating agency; hence, imbued; filled; charged; as, a poem *instinct* with passion.

in'stinct (ĭn'stĭngkt; 68), *n.* [F. or L.; F., fr. L. *instinctus*. See INSTINCT, *adj.*] **1.** A natural aptitude or knack; as, an *instinct* for order. **2. a** A tendency to actions which lead to the attainment of some goal natural to the species; natural and unreasoning prompting to action; as, the web-building *instinct* of spiders. **b** The native or hereditary factor in behavior; as, habit is based upon *instinct*.

in·stinc'tive (ĭn·stĭngk'tĭv), *adj.* Of, pertaining to, or of the nature of, instinct; derived from, or prompted by, instinct; determined by natural impulse. — **Syn.** See SPONTANEOUS. — **in·stinc'tive·ly,** *adv.*

in'sti·tute (ĭn'stĭ·tūt), *v. t.* [L. *institutus*, past part. of *instituere* to place in, institute, fr. *in-* in + *statuere* to set.] **1.** To set up; originate and establish; found; organize; hence, to set on foot; initiate; as, to *institute* an inquiry. **2. a** To appoint, specif., as heir; to install, as in a benefice. **b** *Ch. of Eng.* Specif., to invest with spiritual charge of a benefice; — disting. from *induct*. — *n.* **1.** *Obs.* Act of instituting; institution. **2.** That which is instituted; specif.: **a** An elementary principle; a precept or rule, recognized as authoritative; usually, *pl.*, a collection of such institutes; esp., a comprehensive summary of legal principles and decisions; as, the *Institutes* of Justinian. **b** An institution; an organization to promote art, science, or the like, as a society, college or technical school; also, a building devoted to its work. **c** Also ***teachers' institute***. A meeting of schoolteachers for instruction. — **in'sti·tut'er** (-tūt'ẽr), **in'sti·tu'tor** (-tū'tẽr), *n.*

in'sti·tu'tion (ĭn'stĭ·tū'shŭn), *n.* **1.** Act or process of instituting; establishment. **2.** *Obs. exc. in Law.* A textbook; a system of elements or rules. **3.** That which is instituted: as: **a** An established practice, law, custom, etc. **b** An established society or corporation; an establishment, esp. one of a public character; a foundation; as, a charitable *institution*; also, the building or buildings used by such organization. **4.** *Eccl.* **a** The designation, authorization, or ordination by Christ of certain signs or ceremonies as sacraments. **b** The instituting of a clergyman into a benefice.

in'sti·tu'tion·al (-ăl· -'l), *adj.* **1.** Of, pertaining to, or characteristic of institution or an institution; as, *institutional* ceremonies or management. **2.** Highly organized so as to include various charitable, educational, and other activities; — of religion, a church or the like. **3.** *Advertising Cant.* Designed to create good will and prestige for a company and its products, and not aimed at immediate sales. — **in'sti·tu'tion·al·ize** (-īz), *v. t.* — **in'sti·tu'tion·al·ly,** *adv.*

in'sti·tu'tion·al·ism (-ĭz'm), *n.* The upholding of institutions, of their usefulness, validity, or, in the case of established institutions, of their authority and sanctity.

in'sti·tu'tion·ar'y (-ĕr'ĭ *or, esp. Brit.,* -ẽr·ĭ), *adj.* Of or pert. to legal institutes, to clerical institution, or to an institution or institutions.

in'sti·tu'tive (ĭn'stĭ·tū'tĭv), *adj.* **1.** Tending or intended to institute; of or pertaining to institution. **2.** Established; conventional. — **in'sti·tu'tive·ly,** *adv.*

in·struct' (ĭn·strŭkt'), *v. t.*; IN·STRUCT'ED; IN·STRUCT'ING. [L. *instructus*, past part. of *instruere* to furnish, provide, instruct, fr. *in-* in, on + *struere* to build.] **1.** To impart knowledge to, esp. methodically; teach. **2.** To inform. **3.** To furnish with direction; direct. — **Syn.** See TEACH; COMMAND.

in·struc'tion (ĭn·strŭk'shŭn), *n.* **1.** Act, practice, or profession of one who instructs. **2.** That which instructs or is imparted in order to instruct; esp., a lesson or teaching; a precept; also, a direction; an order. — **in·struc'tion·al** (-ăl; -'l), *adj.*

in·struc'tive (-tĭv), *adj.* Conveying knowledge; serving to instruct or inform. — **in·struc'tive·ly,** *adv.* — **in·struc'tive·ness,** *n.*

in·struc'tor (-tẽr), *n.* [L., a preparer, in ML. a teacher.] **1.** One who instructs; a teacher. **2.** Specif., in American colleges and universities, a teacher of a certain rank below any of the various grades of professor. — **in·struc'tor·ship,** *n.* — **in·struc'tress,** *n. fem.*

in'stru·ment (ĭn'stro͝o·mĕnt), *n.* [From OF., fr. L. *instrumentum*. See INSTRUCT.] **1.** That by means of which something is performed or effected; a means. **2.** A tool; implement. **3.** A contrivance by which musical sounds are produced. **4.** *Law.* A writing, as a deed, writ, etc. **5.** A device for measuring the present value of the quantity under observation. — **Syn.** See MEANS; IMPLEMENT.

in'stru·men'tal (-mĕn'tăl; -t'l), *adj.* **1.** Acting as an instrument; being an efficient agent or means. **2.** Of or pertaining to, designed for, or performed on a musical instrument. **3.** Of, pertaining to, or done with an instrument or tool. **4.** *Gram.* Designating or pertaining to a case expressing means or agency. English shows a surviving trace of it in such expressions as "the more the merrier," where *the* represents Old English *þȳ*, instrumental case of *þæt* (= the, that). — *n. Gram.* The instrumental case, or a word in that case. Abbr. *inst.* or *instr.* — **in'stru·men'tal·ly,** *adv.*

in'stru·men'tal·ist (-ĭst), *n.* One who plays upon a musical instrument. — **in'stru·men'tal·ist,** *adj.*

in'stru·men·tal'i·ty (ĭn'stro͝o·mĕn·tăl'ĭ·tĭ), *n.*; *pl.* -TIES (-tĭz). Quality or fact of being instrumental or an instrument; agency.

in'stru·men·ta'tion (-tā'shŭn), *n.* **1.** A use of, or operation with, instruments. **2.** *Music.* The arrangement or composition of music for instruments, as for a band.

instrument board. = DASHBOARD, 2.

instrument flying. Navigation of an aircraft solely according to data given by instruments within it; — opp. to *contact flying*. — **instrument flight, instrument landing.**

in'sub·or'di·nate (ĭn'sŭ·bôr'dĭ·nĭt), *adj.* Not subordinate; specif., not submitting to authority; disobedient; mutinous. — *n.* An insubordinate person. — **in'sub·or'di·nate·ly,** *adv.* — **in'sub·or'di·na'tion** (-nā'shŭn), *n.*

in'sub·stan'tial (ĭn'sŭb·stăn'shăl), *adj.* Not substantial; as: **a** Immaterial; apparitional. **b** Unsubstantial; flimsy. — **in'sub·stan'ti·al'i·ty** (-shĭ·ăl'ĭ·tĭ), *n.*

in·suf'fer·a·ble (ĭn·sŭf'ẽr·ȧ·b'l), *adj.* Incapable of being endured; intolerable; as, *insufferable* wrongs. — **in·suf'fer·a·ble·ness,** *n.* — **in·suf'fer·a·bly,** *adv.*

in'suf·fi'cience (ĭn'sŭ·fĭsh'ĕns), *n.* *Rare.* Insufficiency.

in'suf·fi'cien·cy (-ĕn·sĭ), *n.* Lack of sufficiency; as: **a** Inability; incompetency. **b** Lack of sufficient force, quantity, etc.; inadequacy.

in'suf·fi'cient (-ĕnt), *adj.* Not sufficient; inadequate to need, use, purpose, etc.; also, incompetent. — **in'suf·fi'cient·ly,** *adv.*

in·suf'flate (ĭn·sŭf'lāt; ĭn'sŭ·flāt), *v. t.* [LL. *insufflatus*, past part. of *insufflare.*] **1.** To breathe upon, as a person being baptized in certain Christian rites, to symbolize the inspiration of a new spiritual life and the expulsion of evil spirits. **2.** To blow upon or into; as, to *insufflate* a room with an insecticide. **3.** To blow, as air into the lungs in cases of asphyxia. — **in'suf·fla'tion** (ĭn'sŭ·flā'shŭn), *n.*

in'suf·fla'tor (ĭn'sŭ·flā'tẽr), *n.* A device for insufflating; specif.: **a** A device for blowing air into a person's lungs. **b** A kind of injector for blowing the powder used in fingerprinting.

in'su·lar (ĭn'sū·lẽr), *adj.* [L. *insularis*, fr. *insula* island.] **1.** Of, pertaining to, or like an island; dwelling or situated on, or forming, an island. **2.** Insulated; isolated; detached, as a column. **3.** Of or pertaining to islanders; hence, narrow; circumscribed; illiberal. **4.** *Med.* **a** Arranged in or characterized by isolated patches or spots. **b** Of or pertaining to islands of tissue, specif. to the islands of Langerhans in the pancreas. — **in'su·lar'i·ty** (-lăr'ĭ·tĭ), *n.*

Insular Celtic. The Cymric (Welsh) and Goidelic (Irish, Gaelic, Manx) languages of the Celtic subfamily spoken in the British Isles. See INDO-EUROPEAN LANGUAGES, *Table.*

in'su·late (ĭn'sū·lāt; ĭn'sŭ-), *v. t.* [L. *insulatus* insulated, fr. *insula* island.] To place in a detached situation; isolate; specif., *Physics & Elec.*, to separate from conducting bodies by means of nonconductors, as to prevent transfer of electricity, heat, or sound.

in·su·la′tion (ĭn′sū·lā′shŭn; ĭn′sŭ-), *n.* An insulating, state of being insulated; also, *Physics,* material used in insulating.

in′su·la′tor (ĭn′sū·lā′tẽr; ĭn′sŭ-), *n.* One who or that which insulates; specif., *Elec.,* a nonconducting substance or body, as porcelain or glass, used in insulating wires, etc. Cf. CONDUCTOR, NONCONDUCTOR.

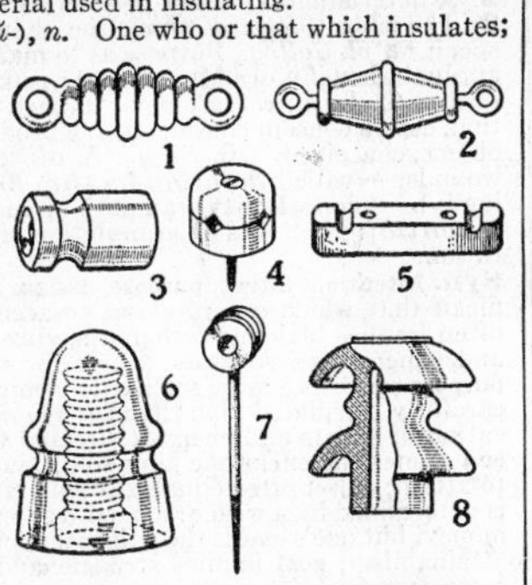

Insulators. 1, 2 Antennae; 3 Knob; 4 Splitknob; 5 Cleat; 6, 8 Petticoat; 7 Standoff.

in′su·lin (-lĭn), *n.* [L. *insula* island + *-in.*] **a** The crystalline active principle of the islands of Langerhans in the pancreas, which promotes the utilization of sugar in the organism. **b** [*cap.*] A trade-mark applied to a solution of this, made from the pancreas of sheep or oxen, and used hypodermically as a specific for diabetes.

in·sult′ (ĭn·sŭlt′), *v. t.* [F. or L.; F. *insulter,* fr. L. *insultare,* freq. fr. *insilire* to leap into or upon, fr. *in-* in, on + *salire* to leap.] **1.** To treat with insolence; affront wantonly. **2.** *Obs.* To assault; specif., *Mil.,* to attack suddenly. — **Syn.** See OFFEND. — *v. i. Archaic.* To display insolence; to exult insolently. — **in·sult′er,** *n.* — **in·sult′ing,** *adj.* — **in·sult′ing·ly,** *adv.*

in′sult (ĭn′sŭlt), *n.* **1.** *Archaic.* Act of attacking; onset; attack. **2.** Gross indignity offered to another; an insulting speech or act; an affront. **3.** *Med.* That which produces injury; also, the injury (frequently subclinical) so produced. — **Syn.** See AFFRONT.

in′sul·ta′tion (ĭn′sŭl·tā′shŭn), *n. Archaic.* Insult.

in·su′per·a·ble (ĭn·sū′pẽr·*á*·b'l), *adj.* Not superable; incapable of being surmounted, overcome, or passed over; as, an *insuperable* difficulty or barrier. — **in·su′per·a·bil′i·ty** (-bĭl′*ĭ*·tĭ), *n.* — **in·su′per·a·bly,** *adv.*

in′sup·port′a·ble (ĭn′s*ŭ*·pōr′t*á*·b'l; 70), *adj.* Not supportable; unendurable. — **in′sup·port′a·bly,** *adv.*

in′sup·press′i·ble (-prĕs′*ĭ*·b'l), *adj.* Not suppressible; irrepressible. — **in′sup·press′i·bly,** *adv.*

in·sur′a·ble (ĭn·shŏŏr′*á*·b'l), *adj.* Capable of being insured against loss, damage, death, etc.; affording a sufficient ground for insurance. — **in·sur′a·bil′i·ty** (-bĭl′*ĭ*·tĭ), *n.*

in·sur′ance (ĭn·shŏŏr′*ă*ns; 84), *n.* **1.** Act of insuring; a contract whereby one party undertakes to indemnify or guarantee another against loss by a contingent event; also, the business of making such contracts. In U. S. and popular British use, *insurance* is the term for all forms of insurance. By the majority of British insurance companies, *assurance* is used for life insurance, and *insurance* for marine, fire, or accident insurance. **2.** Premium paid for insuring. **3.** Sum for which anything is insured.

in·sur′ant (-*ă*nt), *n.* The person insured.

in·sure′ (ĭn·shŏŏr′; 84), *v. t.* [ME. *ensuren,* prob. for *assuren,* by a change of prefix.] **1.** To assure against loss by a contingent event; to give, take, or procure an insurance on or for; to enter into, or carry, a contract of insurance on. **2.** To ensure; make certain. — *v. i.* To give, take, or procure insurance; specif., to underwrite. — **Syn.** See ENSURE.

in·sured′ (ĭn·shŏŏrd′), *n.; pl.* INSUREDS (-shŏŏrdz′). A person whose life or property is insured.

in·sur′er (ĭn·shŏŏr′ẽr), *n.* One who or that which insures; specif., an insurance underwriter.

in·sur′gence (ĭn·sûr′j*ĕ*ns), *n.* An uprising; insurrection.

in·sur′gen·cy (-j*ĕ*n·sĭ), *n.* **1.** Quality, state, or fact of being insurgent; insurrection. **2.** *Int. Law.* A revolt against a government, not reaching the proportions of an organized revolution, and not recognized as belligerency.

in·sur′gent (-j*ĕ*nt), *adj.* [L. *insurgens,* pres. part. of *insurgere* to rise up, fr. *in-* in + *surgere* to rise.] Rising in opposition to authority; rebellious; manifesting insurgency. — *n.* **1.** An insurgent person; one participating in an insurgency; often, a rebel not recognized as a belligerent. **2.** *U. S.* One who acts contrary to the policies and decisions of his political party.

in′sur·mount′a·ble (ĭn′sûr·moun′t*á*·b'l), *adj.* Incapable of being surmounted; insuperable. — **in′sur·mount′a·bly,** *adv.*

in′sur·rec′tion (ĭn′s*ŭ*·rĕk′shŭn), *n.* [F., fr. LL. *insurrectio,* fr. *insurgere.* See INSURGENT.] A rising up against civil or political authority. — **Syn.** See REBELLION. — **in′sur·rec′tion·al** (-*ă*l; -'l), *adj.*

in′sur·rec′tion·ar′y (-ĕr′ĭ *or, esp. Brit.,* -ẽr·ĭ), *adj. & n.* Rebel; insurgent.

in′sur·rec′tion·ist (-ĭst), *n.* One who favors, or takes part in, insurrection; an insurgent. — **in′sur·rec′tion·ism** (-ĭz′m), *n.*

in′sus·cep′ti·ble (ĭn′s*ŭ*·sĕp′t*ĭ*·b'l), *adj.* Not susceptible; not impressible. — **in′sus·cep′ti·bil′i·ty** (-bĭl′*ĭ*·tĭ), *n.* — **in′sus·cep′ti·bly,** *adv.*

in·swathe′ (ĭn·swāth′). Var. of ENSWATHE.

in′swept′ (ĭn′swĕpt′), *adj.* Narrowed at the forward end; — said of an automobile frame.

in·tact′ (ĭn·tăkt′), *adj.* [L. *intactus,* fr. *in-* not + *tactus,* past part. of *tangere* to touch.] Untouched, esp. by anything that harms, defiles, etc.; uninjured; unimpaired; left complete or entire. — **Syn.** See PERFECT.

in·tagl′io (ĭn·tăl′yō; -täl′lĭ·ō; *It.* ēn·tä′lyō), *n.; pl.* INTAGLIOS (ĭn·tăl′yōz), INTAGLI (ēn·tä′lyē). [It., fr. *intagliare* to engrave, carve, fr. *in-* in + *tagliare* to cut, carve.] **1.** An engraving; esp., an incised figure or design in stone or the like, depressed below the surface of the material so that an impression from it yields an image in relief; — opposed to *cameo.* **2.** Art or process of executing intaglios. **3.** Anything, esp. a gem, carved in intaglio.

in′take′ (ĭn′tāk′), *n.* **1.** Place where a fluid is taken into a channel, conduit, etc. **2.** A taking in; as: **a** Suction. **b** A narrowing; contraction. **3.** A thing or the amount taken in; specif., *Mech.,* energy taken in.

in·tan′gi·ble (ĭn·tăn′j*ĭ*·b'l), *adj.* Not tangible; incorporeal. — *n.* Anything intangible; esp., an asset which is not corporeal, as good will, a patent right, etc. — **in·tan′gi·bil′i·ty** (-bĭl′*ĭ*·tĭ), **in·tan′gi·ble·ness,** *n.* — **in·tan′gi·bly,** *adv.*

in·tar′si·a (ĭn·tär′sĭ·*á*), *n.* [It. *intarsio.*] A decoration in woodwork, much used in Italy in the 15th century and later, in which designs were produced by inlaying wood in a background of wood; also, the art or process of making such work. — **in·tar′si·ate** (-āt), *adj.*

in·tar′sist (-sĭst), *n.* One who works in intarsia.

in′te·ger (ĭn′tē·jẽr), *n.* [L., untouched, whole.] A complete entity; esp., a whole (not fractional or mixed) number.

‖**in′te·ger vi′tae sce′le·ris′que pu′rus** (vī′tē skĕl′*ĕ*·rĭs′kwē pū′rŭs). [L.] Blameless of life and free from guilt.

in′te·gra·ble (ĭn′tē·gr*á*·b'l), *adj. Math.* That may be integrated, as a function or differential equation.

in′te·gral (ĭn′tē·gr*ă*l), *adj.* [ML. *integralist,* fr. *integer* entire.] **1.** Essential to completeness; integrant; as, an *integral* part. **2.** Composed of constituent parts making a whole; composite; as, an *integral* whole. **3.** Lacking nothing of completeness; entire; as, *integral* repentance. **4.** *Math.* **a** Of, being, or pertaining to an integer. **b** Relating to, or concerned with, integrals or integration. — *n.* **1.** A whole; an entire thing; a totality. **2.** *Math.* The result of an integration either of a function or of an equation; an expression whose derivative is the integrand. — **in′te·gral′i·ty** (ĭn′tē·grăl′*ĭ*·tĭ), *n.* — **in′te·gral·ly,** *adv.*

integral calculus. See CALCULUS, 2 **b.**

In′te·gral·ist (ĭn′tē·gr*ă*l·ĭst), *n.* Also ‖**In′te·gra·lis′ta** (ēnn′tĕ·grȧ·lēs′tȧ); *pl.* INTEGRALISTAS (-tȧs). [Pg. *Integralista.* See INTEGRAL; -IST.] A member or adherent of the Brazilian fascist party.

in′te·grand′ (ĭn′tē·grănd′), *n.* [L. *integrandus,* gerundive of *integrare* to make whole.] *Math.* The expression to be integrated.

in′te·grant (-gr*ă*nt), *adj. & n.* [L. *integrans, -antis,* pres. part.] Constituent; component; integral.

in′te·grate (-grāt), *v. t. & i.* [L. *integratus,* past part. of *integrare* to make whole, renew, fr. *integer* whole.] **1.** To form into a whole; to unite or become united so as to form a complete or perfect whole; unify; as, to *integrate* the plots of a play. **2.** To indicate the whole of; to give the sum or total of. **3.** *Math.* To subject to integration. — **in′te·gra′tive** (-grā′tĭv; -gr*á*·tĭv), *adj.*

in′te·gra′tion (-grā′shŭn), *n.* [L. *integratio* a renewing, restoring.] **1.** Act or process of integrating; specif., act or process of making whole or entire. **2.** *Math.* The operation of finding a function of which the integrand is the derivative, or of finding an equation among finite variables that is the equivalent of the differential equation integrated. The sign of integration is $\int$. **3.** *Psychol.* **a** Co-ordination and relation of the total processes of perception, interpretation, and reaction insuring a normal, effective life. **b** Harmonious co-ordination of behavior and personality with one's environment.

in′te·gra′tor (ĭn′tē·grā′tẽr), *n.* **a** One who or that which integrates. **b** An instrument for performing mechanically the calculations formerly made through calculus.

in·teg′ri·ty (ĭn·tĕg′r*ĭ*·tĭ), *n.* [F. and L.; F. *intégrité,* fr. L. *integritas.* See INTEGER.] **1.** State or quality of being complete, undivided, or unbroken; entirety. **2.** Unimpaired state; soundness; purity. **3.** Moral soundness; honesty; uprightness. — **Syn.** See UNITY: HONESTY.

in·teg′u·ment (-ū·m*ĕ*nt), *n.* [L. *integumentum,* fr. *integere* to cover, fr. *in-* in, on + *tegere* to cover.] A covering; investment; external coating or skin. — **in·teg′u·men′ta·ry** (-mĕn′t*á*·rĭ), *adj.*

in′tel·lect (ĭn′tĕ·lĕkt), *n.* [F. and L.; F., fr. L. *intellectus,* fr. *intellegere, -ligere, intellectum,* to understand. See INTELLIGENT.] **1.** The power or faculty of knowing as distinguished from the power to feel and to will; esp., the power of reasoning, judging, comprehending, etc.; understanding. **2.** A mind or intelligence; also, a person of intelligence.

in′tel·lec′tion (-lĕk′shŭn), *n.* Exercise of the intellect; cognition; comprehension; also, a specific act of the intellect; a notion.

in′tel·lec′tive (-tĭv), *adj.* Pertaining to, possessed of, or characterized by intellect; rational. — **in′tel·lec′tive·ly,** *adv.*

in′tel·lec′tu·al (ĭn′tĕ·lĕk′t*ū*·*ă*l), *adj.* **1.** Belonging or relating to, or performed by, the intellect or understanding; as, *intellectual* processes. **2.** Endowed with intellect; having unusual mental capacity; much above the average in intelligence. **3.** Suitable for the exercise of intellect; as, an *intellectual* occupation. — *n.* **1.** *pl.* **a** *Archaic.* Intellectual powers or faculties. **b** Things pertaining to the intellect. **2.** An intellectual person; *pl.,* such persons as a social class. — **in′tel·lec′tu·al′i·ty** (-ăl′*ĭ*·tĭ), *n.* — **in′tel·lec′tu·al·ly,** *adv.*

in′tel·lec′tu·al·ism (-ĭz′m), *n.* **1.** Quality of being intellectual. **2.** The doctrine that knowledge is derived from pure reason; also, the doctrine that the ultimate principle of reality is reason. — **in′tel·lec′tu·al·ist** (-ĭst), *n.* — **in′tel·lec′tu·al·is′tic** (-ĭs′tĭk), *adj.*

in′tel·lec′tu·al·ize (-īz), *v. t. & i.* To make or become intellectual; also, to think.

in·tel′li·gence (ĭn·tĕl′*ĭ*·j*ĕ*ns), *n.* **1.** The power or act of understanding; intellect or mind in operation; also, mental acuteness or sagacity. **2.** The power of meeting any situation, esp. a novel situation, successfully by proper behavior adjustments; also, the ability to apprehend the interrelationships of presented facts in such a way as to guide action towards a desired goal. **3.** Information; news; advice. **4.** The obtaining or dispensing of information, particularly secret information; also, the persons engaged in obtaining information; secret service. **5.** [*often cap.*] An intelligent being or spirit; specif., an angel. **6.** *Christian Science.* The primal and eternal quality of infinite Mind. *Mary Baker Eddy.*

intelligence bureau *or* **department.** A bureau for collecting information or statistics of a particular character; esp., one dealing with military or naval information.

intelligence office. *U. S.* An office established to bring together workers seeking employment and employers seeking workers.

intelligence quotient. A number denoting the intelligence of a person, determined by multiplying his mental age by 100 (to eliminate decimals) and dividing by his chronological age. Abbr. *IQ* or *I.Q.*

in·tel′li·genc·er (ĭn·tĕl′*ĭ*·j*ĕ*n·sẽr), *n.* One who or that which conveys intelligence or news; esp., a secret agent; spy.

intelligence test. Any psychological test designed to determine the relative mental capacity of the persons examined.

in·tel′li·gent (ĭn·tĕl′*ĭ*·j*ĕ*nt), *adj.* [L. *intelligens, intellegens, -entis,* pres. part. of *intelligere, -legere,* to perceive, fr. *inter* between + *legere* gather, choose.] **1.** Endowed with intelligence or intellect. **2.** Exhibiting a high or fitting degree of intelligence. **3.** Cognizant or aware; skilled or versed. — **in·tel′li·gent·ly,** *adv.*

Syn. **Intelligent, clever, alert, quick-witted, knowing** mean intellectually keen. **Intelligent** stresses success in meeting or solving problems, esp. new or abstruse problems; **clever** implies native ability or aptness more than *intelligent;* **alert** implies quickness in apprehending or comprehending a situation; **quick-witted** implies alertness and promptness in action, speech, or the like; **knowing** stresses the possession of knowledge necessary or useful under the circumstances but, sometimes, connotes sophistication, secretiveness, or the like.

in·tel′li·gen′tial (ĭn·tĕl′ĭ·jĕn′shăl), *adj.* **1.** Of, like, pertaining to, or having intelligence. **2.** Transmitting news.

in·tel′li·gent′si·a (-jĕnt′sĭ·ȧ; -gĕnt′-), *n. pl.* [Russ. *intelligentsiya,* fr. It. *intelligenzia.* See INTELLIGENT.] Informed intellectual people collectively; the educated class.

in·tel′li·gi·bil′i·ty (ĭn·tĕl′ĭ·jĭ·bĭl′ĭ·tĭ), *n.* **1.** Clearness; perspicuity; definiteness. **2.** That which is intelligible.

in·tel′li·gi·ble (ĭn·tĕl′ĭ·jĭ·b′l), *adj.* [L. *intelligibilis.*] **1.** Capable of being understood; comprehensible. **2.** *Philos.* Apprehensible by the intellect only; purely conceptual. — **in·tel′li·gi·bly,** *adv.*

in·tem′er·ate (ĭn·tĕm′ẽr·ăt), *adj.* [L. *intemeratus,* fr. *in-* not + *temeratus* defiled.] Inviolate; pure; undefiled.

in·tem′per·ance (ĭn·tĕm′pẽr·ăns), *n.* **1.** Quality or state of being intemperate; want of moderation or restraint. **2.** Any immoderate indulgence of appetites or passions; esp., habitual or excessive indulgence in intoxicants.

in·tem′per·ate (-ĭt), *adj.* **1.** Not temperate; immoderate; excessive; inclement, as weather; inordinate, as zeal; violent, as language. **2.** Characterized by intemperance, esp. in use of intoxicants. — **in·tem′per·ate·ly,** *adv.* — **in·tem′per·ate·ness,** *n.*

in·tend′ (ĭn·tĕnd′), *v. t.* [OF. *entendre,* fr. L. *intendere, -tentum, -tensum,* to intend, attend, extend, fr. *in-* in + *tendere* to stretch.] **1.** To understand; also, to signify. **2.** To have in mind as a design or purpose; plan; purpose. **3.** To direct oneself to; to be intent upon. **4.** *Archaic.* To direct or turn, as one's mind, course, etc.; bend. **5.** *Obs.* To stretch; extend; strain; expand. **6.** *Law.* To give effect or construction to as having a certain meaning; construe by intendment. — *v. i.* **1.** To have an intention. **2.** *Archaic.* To direct or bend one's course or way.

in·tend′ance (ĭn·tĕn′dăns), *n.* **1.** Management; superintendence. **2.** An administrative department. **3.** An intendant's office or headquarters; intendancy.

in·tend′an·cy (-dăn·sĭ), *n.; pl.* -CIES (-sĭz). **1.** The office, function, or employment of an intendant; also, a body of intendants. **2.** [Sp. *intendencia.*] A district under an intendant.

in·tend′ant (-dănt), *n.* [F., fr. L. *intendere* to direct (one's thoughts) to a thing. See INTEND.] One who has the direction or management of some public business; a superintendent; — used specif. of various foreign officials; as, an *intendant* of finance, of marine.

in·tend′ed (ĭn·tĕn′dĕd; -dĭd), *adj.* **1.** Purposed; intentional. **2.** *Colloq.* Betrothed; affianced. — *n. Colloq.* An affianced lover.

in·tend′ment (ĭn·tĕnd′mĕnt), *n.* **1.** *Archaic.* Intention; design; purpose. **2.** *Obs. exc. Law.* Meaning; intent.

in·ten′er·ate (ĭn·tĕn′ẽr·āt), *v. t.* [*in-* in + L. *tener* soft, tender.] To make tender; soften. — **in·ten′er·a′tion** (-ā′shŭn), *n.*

in·tense′ (ĭn·tĕns′), *adj.* [F., fr. L. *intensus* stretched, tight, past part. of *intendere* to stretch.] **1.** In a strained or extreme degree; having or showing its distinctive quality or character in a high degree; as, an *intense* light; the *intense* sun. **2.** Strained or straining to the utmost; profoundly earnest or intent; as, *intense* study or thought. **3.** Feeling deeply; characterized by or expressive of strong emotion, earnest purpose, or the like; as, an *intense* person or expression. **4.** *Photog.* Intensified; dense. — **in·tense′ly,** *adv.* — **in·tense′ness,** *n.*

in·ten′si·fy (ĭn·tĕn′sĭ·fī), *v. t. & i.;* -FIED (-fīd); -FY′ING. **1.** To render or become intense or more intense. **2.** *Photog.* To increase the intensity of (an image) by treating a film or plate with any of various solutions (*intensifiers*). — **in·ten′si·fi·ca′tion** (-fĭ·kā′shŭn), *n.* — **in·ten′si·fi′er** (-fī′ẽr), *n.*

Syn. **Intensify, aggravate, heighten, enhance** mean to increase markedly in degree or measure. **Intensify** implies a deepening or strengthening of a thing or its characteristic quality; **aggravate** implies a manifest increase in gravity or seriousness; **heighten** and **enhance** both imply a lifting or raising, *heighten* a lifting above the ordinary, the trite, the commonplace, and *enhance* a lifting above the norm or the average in desirability or attractiveness.

in·ten′sion (ĭn·tĕn′shŭn), *n.* **1.** *Now Rare.* Tension. **2.** Intensity. **3.** Intensification. **4.** Energetic use or exercise, as of the mind; determination. **5.** Intensiveness. **6.** *Logic.* All or any of the attributes, qualities, or characteristics comprised in a concept or implied by a term; thus, the *intension* of "triangle" implies that of "plane figure"; — opposed to *extension.*

in·ten′si·ty (-sĭ·tĭ), *n.; pl.* -TIES (-tĭz). **1.** State or quality of being intense; extreme or very high degree. **2.** Degree or amount of strength, force, energy, radiation, or the like; specif.: **a** *Elec.* (1) Current strength. (2) Current density. (3) Potential, or electromotive force. **b** *Photog.* Degree of opacity. **c** *Photom.* = CANDLE POWER. **d** *Physics.* Magnitude of force or energy per unit of surface, charge, mass, or the like; as, *intensity* of electric field; *intensity* of radiation.

in·ten′sive (-sĭv), *adj.* **1.** Of, pertaining to, or marked by intensity or intensification. **2.** Exhaustive or concentrated; as, *intensive* preparations, bombings. **3.** *Agric.* Designating, or pertaining to, a method of cultivating land designed to increase the productivity of a given area by the expenditure of more capital and labor upon it; — opp. to *extensive.* **4.** *Gram.* Intensifying; esp., serving to give force or emphasis; as, an *intensive* verb. **5.** *Med.* Marked by increased intensity or strength of treatment in successive operations. — *n.* That which intensifies; specif., *Gram.*, an intensive word, prefix, etc. — **in·ten′sive·ly,** *adv.* — **in·ten′sive·ness,** *n.*

in·tent′ (ĭn·tĕnt′), *adj.* [L. *intentus,* past part. See INTEND.] **1.** Directed with keen, eager, or fixed attention; as, mind *intent* on a problem. **2.** Having the mind or attention closely directed; engrossed. — **in·tent′ly,** *adv.* — **in·tent′ness,** *n.*

Syn. **Intent, engrossed, absorbed, rapt** mean having one's mind or attention deeply fixed on something. **Intent** suggests the direction or end to which the mind is bent; **engrossed,** monopolization of one's attention by an interest, an emotion, or the like; **absorbed,** a capturing of one's attention so firmly that it is not easily distracted; **rapt,** complete absorption as though one were taken out of oneself.

in·tent′, *n.* [OF. *entent, entente,* understanding, purpose, fr. L. *intendere, intentum.* See INTEND.] An intending; also, that which is intended; hence: **a** Design; purpose; intention. **b** Meaning; import; significance. — **Syn.** See INTENTION.

in·ten′tion (ĭn·tĕn′shŭn), *n.* **1.** *Archaic.* Close attention; intentness. **2.** A determination to act in a certain way or to do a certain thing. **3.** The object toward which the thoughts are directed; end; aim; specif.: **a** *pl. Colloq.* Purpose as to marriage. **b** *R.C.Ch.* The will to apply the benefits of a Mass, prayers, etc., to a particular person or purpose. **4.** *Archaic.* Intent, or import. **5.** *Logic.* A concept or notion; esp., a concept considered as a product of attention directed to the object conceived. **6.** *Surg.* A process or manner of healing of wounds; — called (***healing by the***) ***first intention*** when the healing is by union without granulation, and (***healing by the***) ***second intention*** when it is by granulation of the surfaces following suppuration.

Syn. **Intention, intent, purpose, design, aim, end, object, objective, goal** mean that which one proposes to accomplish or attain. **Intention** often implies little more than a having in mind; **intent,** both in legal and general use, suggests clearer formulation or more deliberation; **purpose** suggests a more settled determination; **design** suggests a more carefully calculated plan than *intention;* **aim** adds to these an implication of efforts and energies directed to accomplishing or attaining; **end** names the effect one aims to produce or the condition one hopes to attain; **object** often equals *end,* but is used more often when the end is determined by a wish or a need (as, one's *object* in writing is to earn money, but one's *end* is the edification of the reader); **objective** implies attainability; **goal** implies struggle and endurance of hardships but cessation of effort at attainment.

in·ten′tion·al (-ăl; -′l), *adj.* **1.** Done by design; intended. **2.** Of or pertaining to intention. — **Syn.** See VOLUNTARY. — **in·ten′tion·al·ly,** *adv.*

in·ter′ (ĭn·tûr′), *v. t.;* -TERRED′ (-tûrd′); -TER′RING. [OF. *enterrer,* deriv. of *interrare,* fr. *in-* in + *terra* the earth.] To deposit (a corpse) in the earth or in a tomb; bury.

in′ter- (ĭn′tẽr-). [L., fr. *inter,* prep., among, between, a compar. form of *in* in.] A prefix meaning: **1.** *Among; between; together;* as, *inter*lace, to lace together; **in′ter·ja′cent,** lying among or between; — chiefly with verbs and their derivatives; as in:

interbedded	**intergrowth**	**intermesh**
interblend	**interjoin**	**intermingle**
interflow	**interknit**	**intertwine**
interfluent	**interknot**	**intertwist**
interfold	**interlay**	**interwind**
interglow	**interlink**	**interwreathe**

2. *Mutual* or *mutually; reciprocal* or *reciprocally;* as, **in′ter·ac·cuse′,** to accuse each other in turn; *inter*play, mutual or reciprocal action or influence; — chiefly in verbs and their derivatives; as in:

interagree	**interconversion**	**interrelate**
intercommunicate	**intermigration**	**interrelation**
intercommunication	**interreaction**	**interrelationship**
intercommunion	**interreflection**	**interwork**

3. *Between the parts, individuals, units, etc., of;* as, *inter*continental, between or among continents; — chiefly in adjectives derived from nouns; as in:

inter-Allied	**intercollegiate**	**intermunicipal**
inter-American	**intercolonial**	**interoceanic**
inter-Andean	**intercolumnar**	**interplanetary**
interarmy	**intercontinental**	**interpolar**
interatomic	**interdenominational**	**interracial**
interborough	**interdepartmental**	**interscholastic**
intercellular	**interfibrillar**	**interterritorial**
interchurch	**interisland**	**intertribal**
intercollege	**intermolecular**	**interurban**

4. *Placed, occurring, etc., between; intervening; intermediate* or *intermediary;* as, *inter*paroxysmal, occurring between paroxysms; also, something between; as, *inter*node, the part between two nodes; — chiefly in nouns and their derivative adjectives, as in:

interepidemic	**intermural**	**interscapular**
interequinoctial	**internode**	**interseptal**
intermundane	**interparoxysmal**	**intertidal**

in′ter·act′ (ĭn′tẽr·ăkt′), *v. i.* To act upon each other.

in′ter·ac′tion (-ăk′shŭn), *n.* Mutual or reciprocal action or influence. — **in′ter·ac′tive** (-tĭv), *adj.*

‖**in′ter a′li·a** (ĭn′tẽr ā′lĭ·ȧ). [L.] Among other things.

‖**in′ter a′li·os** (ā′lĭ·ōs). [L.] Among other persons.

in′ter·brain′ (ĭn′tẽr·brān′), *n.* = DIENCEPHALON (see FOREBRAIN).

in′ter·breed′ (ĭn′tẽr·brēd′), *v. t. & i.;* see BREED. To breed by crossing different stocks, varieties, or species.

in·ter′ca·lar′y (ĭn·tûr′kȧ·lẽr′ĭ *or, esp. Brit.,* -lẽr·ĭ), *adj.* [L. *intercalaris, intercalarius.*] **1.** *Chron.* Inserted or introduced in the calendar; as, an *intercalary* month or day (as Feb. 29 in leap years); also, of a year, having such an inserted month, day, etc. **2.** Inserted or introduced between the original or usual elements; interpolated; as, *intercalary* matter in a document.

in·ter′ca·late (-lāt), *v. t.* [L. *intercalatus,* past part. of *intercalare* to intercalate, fr. *inter-* + *calare* to proclaim.] To insert, as a day in a calendar; also, to insert among others; interpolate. — **Syn.** See INTRODUCE. — **in·ter′ca·la′tion** (-lā′shŭn), *n.* — **in·ter′ca·la′tive** (-lā′tĭv; -lȧ·tĭv), *adj.*

in′ter·cede′ (ĭn′tẽr·sēd′), *v. i.* [L. *intercedere, intercessum,* fr. *inter-* + *cedere* to pass.] **1.** *Rom. Hist.* To interpose a veto; — said of a magistrate, esp. a tribune. **2.** To act between parties with a view to reconcile differences; mediate; — usually followed by *with* and *for.* — **Syn.** See INTERPOSE. — **in′ter·ced′er** (-sēd′ẽr), *n.*

in′ter·cept′ (-sĕpt′), *v. t.* [F. or L.; F. *intercepter,* fr. L. *interceptus,* past part. of *intercipere* to intercept, fr. *inter-* + *capere* to take, seize.] **1.** To take or seize by the way, or before arrival at destination; to interrupt the course of; as, to *intercept* a letter. **2.** To prevent; hinder. **3.** To cut off communication with, a view of, etc. **4.** *Math.* To include between; as, the part *intercepted* between two points. — **in′ter·cep′tion** (-sĕp′shŭn), *n.* — **in′ter·cep′tive** (-tĭv), *adj.*

in′ter·cept′ (ĭn′tẽr·sĕpt′), *n.* *Math.* A part intercepted.

in′ter·cep′tor (-sĕp′tẽr), *n., or* **interceptor plane.** A fighter; often specif., a defensive fighter of high rate of climb for intercepting enemy raiders.

in′ter·ces′sion (-sĕsh′ŭn), *n.* [F. or L.; F., fr. L. *intercessio* an intervention, a becoming surety. See INTERCEDE.] Act of interceding; mediation; prayer, petition, or entreaty in behalf of another or others. — **in′ter·ces′sion·al** (-ăl; -′l), *adj.*

in′ter·ces′sor (ĭn′tẽr·sĕs′ẽr; ĭn′tẽr·sĕs′ẽr), *n.* One who intercedes; a mediator.

in′ter·ces′so·ry (ĭn′tẽr·sĕs′ō·rĭ), *adj.* Pertaining to, or of the nature of, intercession.

in′ter·change′ (ĭn′tẽr·chānj′), *v. t.;* see CHANGE. [OF. *entrechangier.* See INTER-; CHANGE.] **1.** To put each in the place of the other; reciprocate in giving and taking. **2.** To alternate; vary. — *v. i.* To make an interchange. — (ĭn′tẽr·chānj′), *n.* **1.** An interchanging; mutual exchange; specif., barter; also, alternation. **2.** An intersection or junction of highways, involving a separation of levels and roadways to permit traffic to pass from one highway to another.

in′ter·change′a·ble (-chān′jȧ·b'l), *adj.* Capable of being interchanged; specif., admitting of mutual substitution; as, *interchangeable* parts in a machine. — **in′ter·change′a·bil′i·ty** (-bĭl′ĭ·tĭ), *n.* — **in′ter·change′a·ble·ness,** *n.* — **in′ter·change′a·bly,** *adv.*

in′ter·clav′i·cle (-klăv′ĭ·k'l), *n. Zool.* A ventral median bone in front of the sternum and between the clavicles in certain vertebrates.

in′ter·co·lum′ni·a′tion (-kō·lŭm′nĭ·ā′shŭn), *n.* [L. *intercolumnium.*] *Arch.* **a** The clear space between two columns. **b** The system of spacing between columns.

in′ter·com′ (ĭn′tẽr·kŏm′), *n., or* **in′ter·com·mu′ni·ca′tion sys′tem.** A two-way communication system with microphone and loud-speaker at each station for localized use, as in a ship, airplane, or building.

in′ter·com·mu′ni·ty (-kŏ·mū′nĭ·tĭ), *n.* Quality of being common to two or more; participation in common.

in′ter·con·nect′ (-kŏ·nĕkt′), *v. t.* To connect mutually or with one another. Specif., *Mach.*, to connect so that the movement of any part causes the movement of the rest. — **in′ter·con·nec′tion** (-nĕk′shŭn), *n.*

in′ter·cos′tal (-kŏs′tăl; -t'l), *adj.* [NL. *intercostalis,* fr. L. *inter* between + *costa* rib.] **1.** *Anat. & Physiol.* Between the ribs. **2.** *Bot.* Between the veins or nerves of a leaf. — **in′ter·cos′tal·ly,** *adv.*

in′ter·course (ĭn′tẽr·kōrs; 70), *n.* [OF. *entrecours* commerce, exchange, deriv. of L. *intercurrere* to run between. See INTER-; COURSE.] **1.** Dealings or connection between persons, organizations, or nations, as in common affairs, civilities, or business; communication. **2.** Sexual connection.

in′ter·crop′ (-krŏp′), *v. t. & i.;* see CROP. To grow (crops) simultaneously, as in alternate rows; as, to *intercrop* an orchard.

in′ter·cross′ (-krŏs′; 74), *v. t. & i.* **1.** To cross each other, as lines. **2.** To interbreed. — *n.* An interbreeding or its result.

in′ter·cur′rent (-kûr′ĕnt), *adj.* [L. *intercurrens,* pres. part. of *intercurrere.* See INTERCOURSE.] Running or coming between or among; specif.: **a** Intervening. **b** *Med.* Occurring in and modifying the course of another disease.

in′ter·den′tal (-dĕn′tăl; -t'l), *adj.* Situated between teeth; *Phonet.*, articulated with the tongue between the front teeth.

in′ter·de·pend′ent (-dē·pĕn′dĕnt), *adj.* Mutually or reciprocally dependent. — **in′ter·de·pend′ence** (-dĕns), **in′ter·de·pend′en·cy** (-dĕn-sĭ), *n.* — **in′ter·de·pend′ent·ly,** *adv.*

in′ter·dict (ĭn′tẽr·dĭkt), *n.* [OF. *entredit,* fr. L. *interdictum,* fr. *interdicere* to interpose, prohibit, fr. *inter-* + *dicere* to say.] **1.** A prohibitory decree; a prohibition. **2.** *Law.* **a** *Roman Civil Law.* An administrative order, usually a prohibition, of the praetor. **b** In the Scots law, Dutch law, etc., an order corresponding to the injunction. **3.** *R.C.Ch.* A punitive censure restraining certain persons or peoples from the sacraments, Christian burial, etc. — (ĭn′tẽr·dĭkt′), *v. t.* To prohibit; debar; esp., to lay under, or prohibit by, an interdict. — **Syn.** See FORBID. — **in′ter·dic′tion** (-dĭk′shŭn), *n.* — **in′ter·dic′tive** (-dĭk′tĭv), *adj.* — **in′ter·dic′tor** (-tẽr), *n.* — **in′ter·dic′to·ry** (-tō-rĭ), *adj.*

in′ter·est (ĭn′tẽr·ĕst; -ĭst; *or, esp. Brit.,* ĭn′trĭst), *n.* [ML. *interesse* usury, compensation, fr. L. *interesse* to be between, be different, be of importance, fr. *inter* between + *esse* to be; influenced by OF. *interest,* fr. L. *interest* it interests, is of interest, 3d sing. pres. of *interesse.*] **1.** A right, title, or share in a thing, participation in advantage, profit, and responsibility. **2.** The business or affairs in which one has such an interest; business. **3.** Advantage; good; benefit. **4.** The price or rate of premium per unit of time paid by a borrower for use of what he borrows; specif., a rate per cent of money paid for the use of money or on an overdue debt; also, the money so paid. Interest paid only on the principal lent is called ***simple interest;*** when paid on unpaid interest (usually periodically added to the principal) besides the original capital, it is called ***compound interest.*** **5.** Payment of more than is due or deserved. **6.** Influence; esp., personal, social, or political influence. **7.** Persons interested, as in a particular industry or measure; as, the iron *interest; pl.*, such groups of persons collectively; as, the *interests.* **8.** Excitement of feeling, accompanying special attention to some object; concern; also, that which causes or holds such interest; power to interest.
— *v. t.* **1.** To involve the interest or welfare of; affect; concern. **2.** To cause or induce to have a share or interest. **3.** To engage the attention of; to excite interest in.

in′ter·est·ed (ĭn′tẽr·ĕs·tĕd; -ĭs·tĭd; *or, esp. Brit.,* ĭn′trĭs·tĕd; -tĭd), *adj.* **1.** Having the attention aroused; as, an *interested* listener. **2.** Having a share or concern in some project; liable to be affected or prejudiced; as, an *interested* witness; also, having self-interest; not disinterested. — **in′ter·est·ed·ly,** *adv.* — **in′ter·est·ed·ness,** *n.*

in′ter·est·ing (ĭn′tẽr·ĕs·tĭng; -ĭs·tĭng; *or, esp. Brit.,* ĭn′trĭs-), *adj.* Engaging the attention; arousing interest. — **in′ter·est·ing·ly,** *adv.* — **in′ter·est·ing·ness,** *n.*

in′ter·face′ (ĭn′tẽr·fās′), *n.* A surface, esp. a plane surface, forming a common boundary of two bodies or spaces. — **in′ter·fa′cial** (-fā′shăl), *adj.*

in′ter·fere′ (ĭn′tẽr·fẽr′), *v. i.* [OF. *entreferir* to strike (each other), fr. *entre* between (fr. L. *inter*) + *ferir* to strike, fr. L. *ferire.*] **1.** To strike one foot against the opposite foot or ankle in the action of going; — said esp. of a horse. **2.** To collide; clash; as, *interfering* claims. **3.** To enter into, or take a part in, the concerns of others; meddle; intervene. **4.** *Patent Law.* To claim substantially the same invention so that the question of the priority of invention is involved between the claimants. Cf. INFRINGE. **5.** *Physics.* To act reciprocally, so as to affect one another; — said of waves. **6.** *Sports.* To hamper or obstruct an opposing player illegally. — **Syn.** See INTERPOSE. — **in′ter·fer′er** (-fẽr′ẽr), *n.* — **in′ter·fer′ing·ly,** *adv.*

in′ter·fer′ence (-fẽr′ĕns), *n.* **1.** An interfering. **2.** *Physics.* The mutual effect, on meeting, of two beams of light or of two series of pulsations of sound or, generally, of two waves or vibrations of any kind. In the case of light, interference produces lines, bands, or fringes either alternately light and dark or variously colored. In the case of sounds, interference produces silence, increased intensity, or beats. **3.** *Radio.* **a** Confusion of received signals due to strays, undesired signals, etc. **b** That which produces such confusion. **4.** *Sports.* **a** Action of illegally hampering an opponent. **b** *Amer. Football.* Action of protecting a ball carrier or passer by blocking would-be tacklers; also, players affording this protection. — **in′ter·fe·ren′tial** (-fē·rĕn′-shăl), *adj.*

in′ter·fer·om′e·ter (-fẽr·ŏm′ē·tẽr), *n.* [See INTERFERE; -METER.] *Physics.* An instrument that uses light interference phenomena for measurement of wave lengths, etc., and for the analysis of a narrow spectrum region.

in′ter·fuse′ (ĭn′tẽr·fūz′), *v. t.* [L. *interfusus,* past part. of *interfundere* to pour between, fr. *inter-* + *fundere* to pour.] **1.** To combine by scattering, mixing, or fusing; intermingle. **2.** To pass into or through others; infuse; diffuse. **3.** To permeate; pervade. — *v. i.* To blend; fuse. — **in′ter·fu′sion** (-fū′zhŭn), *n.*

in′ter·gla′cial (-glā′shăl), *adj. Geol.* Occurring between two glacial epochs; as, an *interglacial* climate.

in′ter·grade′ (ĭn′tẽr·grād′), *n.* An intermediate or transitional form.

in′ter·grade′ (-grād′), *v. i.* To merge gradually one with another through a continuous series of intermediate forms, kinds, or types. — **in′ter·gra·da′tion** (-grā·dā′shŭn), *n.* — **in′ter·gra′di·ent** (-grā′dĭ-ĕnt), *adj.*

in′ter·im (ĭn′tẽr·ĭm), *n.* [L., adv., meanwhile, fr. *inter* between.] The meantime; time intervening; interval. — *adj.* Done, made, occurring, etc., for or during an interim; as, an *interim* dividend.

in·te′ri·or (ĭn·tẽr′ĭ·ẽr), *adj.* [OF., fr. L. *interior,* compar. fr. *inter* between.] **1.** Being within; inside; inner; — opp. to *exterior,* or *superficial.* **2.** Remote from the limits, frontier, or shore; inland. **3.** Belonging to the inner constitution of a thing, or the inner life of a person; hidden, private, spiritual, etc. — *n.* **1.** That which is interior; as: **a** The inside. **b** The inland. **c** Inner nature or character. **2.** The internal affairs of a state or nation; as, the Department of the *Interior.* **3.** A scene or view of the interior of a building. — **in·te′ri·or′i·ty** (-ŏr′ĭ·tĭ), *n.* — **in·te′ri·or·ly,** *adv.*

in′ter·ject′ (ĭn′tẽr·jĕkt′), *v. t. & i.* [L. *interjectus,* past part. of *interjicere* to interject, fr. *inter* between + *jacere* to throw.] To throw in or come between; interpose; interpolate. — **Syn.** See INTRODUCE. — **in′ter·jec′tor** (-jĕk′tẽr), *n.* — **in′ter·jec′to·ri·ly** (-tō·rĭ·lĭ), *adv.* — **in′ter·jec′to·ry** (-tō·rĭ), *adj.*

in′ter·jec′tion (-jĕk′shŭn), *n.* **1.** An interjecting; also, that which is interjected. **2.** *Gram.* An ejaculatory word or form of speech, usually thrown in without grammatical connection (*O! Alas!*); also, a mere cry rather than a real word (*whew! hem! bah!*). Abbr. *int.* or *interj.* — **in′ter·jec′tion·al,** *adj.* — **in′ter·jec′tion·al·ly,** *adv.*

in′ter·lace′ (ĭn′tẽr·lās′), *v. t. & i.;* see LACE. To unite as by lacing together; to twine or weave together; also, to vary by alternation; intersperse; mix. — **in′ter·lace′ment,** *n.*

in′ter·lam′i·nate (ĭn′tẽr·lăm′ĭ·nāt), *v. t.* To insert between laminae; also, to arrange in alternate laminae. — **in′ter·lam′i·na′tion** (-nā′-shŭn), *n.*

in′ter·lard′ (-lärd′), *v. t.* [F. *entrelarder.* See INTER-; LARD.] **1.** *Now Rare.* To alternate with layers or strips of fat; to insert lard or bacon in; to lard. **2.** To introduce that which is foreign or irrelevant into; as, to *interlard* a conversation with oaths.

in′ter·leaf′ (ĭn′tẽr·lēf′), *n.; pl.* -LEAVES (-lēvz′). A leaf inserted between other leaves; also, the matter printed or written on it.

in′ter·leave′ (-lēv′), *v. t.* To insert a leaf or leaves in; to bind with blank leaves inserted between the others.

in′ter·line′ (-līn′), *v. t. & i.* To write or print something between the lines (of).

in′ter·line′, *v. t.* To insert a lining in (a garment) beneath the ordinary lining.

in′ter·lin′e·al (-lĭn′ē·ăl; 58), *adj.* Interlinear; also, disposed in alternate lines. — **in′ter·lin′e·al·ly,** *adv.*

in′ter·lin′e·ar (-ẽr), *adj.* **1.** Contained between lines; interlined. **2.** Written or printed in different languages or texts in alternate lines; as, an *interlinear* Bible. — *n.* An interlinear translation.

in′ter·lin′e·ate (ĭn′tẽr·lĭn′ē·āt), *v. t. & i.* To interline, as a document, page, book, etc. — **in′ter·lin′e·a′tion** (-ā′shŭn), *n.*

in′ter·lin′ing (ĭn′tẽr·līn′ĭng), *n.* Interlineation.

in′ter·lin′ing (ĭn′tẽr·līn′ĭng), *n.* A lining inserted beneath the ordinary lining of a garment; also, a cotton or wool fabric for such linings.

in′ter·lock′ (-lŏk′), *v. i. & t.* **1.** To unite, engage, or interrelate with one another; lock into one another. **2.** *Mach.* To connect in such a way that the motion of any part is constrained by another part or parts; esp., *Railroads,* to arrange the connections of (switches, signals, etc.) so that one lever cannot be worked independently. — **in′ter·lock′,** *n.*

in′ter·lo·cu′tion (-lō·kū′shŭn), *n.* [L. *interlocutio,* fr. *interloqui, -locutus,* to speak between, fr. *inter-* + *loqui* to speak.] Interchange of speech; conversation.

in′ter·loc′u·tor (-lŏk′ū·tẽr), *n.* One who takes part in dialogue or conversation; a talker, interpreter, or questioner; specif., in a minstrel show, the man in the middle of the line, who questions the end men.

in′ter·loc′u·to′ry (-tō′rĭ *or, esp. Brit.,* -tẽr·ĭ), *adj.* **1.** Consisting of, or having the nature of, dialogue; conversational. **2.** Interruptive; interjected. **3.** *Law.* Intermediate; not final or definitive; as, an *interlocutory* decree.

in′ter·loc′u·tress (-trĕs; -trĭs), **in′ter·loc′u·trice** (-trĭs), **in′ter·loc′u·trix** (-trĭks), *n.* A female interlocutor.

in′ter·lope′ (ĭn′tẽr·lōp′), *v. i.* [Prob. fr. D. *enterlooper,* fr. *entre* between (fr. L. *inter*) + D. *looper* a runner.] To run between parties and intercept without right the advantage that one should gain from the other; to intrude; intermeddle. — **Syn.** See INTRUDE. — **in′ter·lop′er** (ĭn′tẽr·lōp′ẽr), *n.*

in′ter·lude (ĭn′tẽr·lūd), *n.* [ML. *interludium,* fr. L. *inter* between + *ludus* play, fr. *ludere* to play.] **1.** *Hist.* A light or farcical entertainment introduced between acts of the old mystery or morality plays or presented in fetes; hence, a farce, comedy, or an early type of drama. **2.** A performance or entertainment between the acts of a play. **3.** A short piece of instrumental music played between the parts of a song, the acts of a drama, etc. **4.** An intervening or interruptive space, feature, event, or the like.

in′ter·lu′nar (-lū′nẽr), *adj.* Relating to the interval between old and new moon, when the moon is invisible.

in′ter·mar′ry (ĭn′tẽr·măr′ĭ), *v. i. & t.;* see MARRY. To become connected by marriage between their members; — said of families, ranks, castes, etc. — **in′ter·mar′riage** (-măr′ĭj; ĭn′tẽr·măr′ĭj), *n.*

in′ter·med′dle (-mĕd′'l), *v. t.;* see MEDDLE. To mix or mingle together. — *v. i.* To meddle with the affairs of others; meddle officiously. — **in′ter·med′dler** (-lẽr), *n.*

in'ter·me'di·a·cy (ĭn'tẽr·mē'dĭ·ȧ·sĭ), *n.* Intermediateness.
in'ter·me'di·ar'y (-ĕr'ĭ *or, esp. Brit.,* -ẽr·ĭ), *adj.* **1.** Intermediate. **2.** Acting as a mediating agent or agency. — *n.; pl.* -IES (-ĭz). **1. a** A mediator. **b** A mediating agency; means. **2.** An intermediate form, stage, or product.
in'ter·me'di·ate (-ĭt), *adj.* [ML. *intermediatus,* fr. L. *intermedius.*] Lying or being in the middle place or degree; between extremes or limits; coming or done between. — *n.* **1.** Something intermediate. **2.** A mediator or an intermediary. **3.** *Chem.* A compound formed as an intermediate step between the initial material and the final product. — **in'ter·me'di·ate·ly,** *adv.* — **in'ter·me'di·ate·ness,** *n.*
in'ter·me'di·ate (-āt), *v. i.* To come between; also, to mediate. — **in'ter·me'di·a'tion** (-ā'shŭn), *n.* — **in'ter·me'di·a'tor** (-ā'tẽr), *n.*
in·ter'ment (ĭn·tûr'mĕnt), *n.* Act or ceremony of interring; burial.
in'ter·mez'zo (ĭn'tẽr·mĕd'zō; -mĕt'sō), *n.; pl.* -MEZZI (-mĕd'zē; -mĕt'sē), -MEZZOS (-zōz; -sōz). [It.] **1.** A short, light entr'acte. **2.** *Music.* **a** A movement in a symphony or other extended work. **b** A short independent instrumental composition.
in·ter'mi·na·ble (ĭn·tûr'mĭ·nȧ·b'l), *adj.* [OF. or LL., fr. L. *interminabilis.*] Without termination; endless. — **in·ter'mi·na·bly,** *adv.*
in'ter·mis'sion (ĭn'tẽr·mĭsh'ŭn), *n.* [L. *intermissio.* See INTERMIT.] **1.** Act of intermitting, or state of being intermitted; interruption; discontinuance. **2.** Cessation for a time; a pause; respite; also, an intervening period of time; an interval. — **in'ter·mis'sive** (-mĭs'ĭv), *adj.*
in'ter·mit' (-mĭt'), *v. t. & i.;* -MIT'TED; -MIT'TING. [L. *intermittere,* fr. *inter* between + *mittere, missum,* to send.] To stop or cease for a time, or at intervals; discontinue; to make or be intermittent. — **Syn.** See DEFER. — **in'ter·mit'ter,** *n.*
in'ter·mit'tent (-mĭt'ĕnt), *adj.* Coming and going at intervals; alternating; recurrent; periodic. — **in'ter·mit'tence** (-ĕns), **in'ter·mit'ten·cy** (-ĕn·sĭ), *n.* — **in'ter·mit'tent·ly,** *adv.*
Syn. **Intermittent, recurrent, periodic, alternate** mean happening or appearing in interrupted sequence. **Intermittent** implies repeated omission or disappearance with invariably a return; **recurrent**, the repeated returning after a period of intermission; **periodic**, recurrence at fairly regular intervals; **alternate**, usually said of two things, implies both intermittence and recurrence, each one following the other.
intermittent current. *Elec.* A current that flows and ceases to flow at intervals, but is not reversed.
intermittent fever. *Med.* A form of fever in which there is a fall of temperature to normal at periodical intervals, as in malarial fevers.
in'ter·mix' (ĭn'tẽr·mĭks'), *v. t. & i.* To mix or mingle together.
in'ter·mix'ture (-mĭks'tûr), *n.* **1.** An intermixing, or state of being intermixed; also, a mass formed by mixture. **2.** Admixture; an additional ingredient.
in'tern, in'terne (ĭn'tûrn; ĭn·tûrn'), *adj.* [L. *internus.*] *Archaic.* Internal. — *n. Poetic.* Internal nature.
in·tern' (ĭn·tûrn'), *v. t.* To segregate and detain, as suspicious persons; also, to hold; detain in port, as ships carrying contraband.
in'tern (ĭn'tûrn), *n.* [F. *interne.*] **1.** Also **in'terne** (ĭn'tûrn; ĭn·tûrn'). *Med.* A resident physician, surgeon, or officer in a hospital; esp., one serving in preparation for independent practice. Cf. EXTERN. **2.** A person interned, as an alien during a war. — **in'tern·ship** (ĭn'tûrn·shĭp; ĭn·tûrn'-), *n.*
in'tern, *v. i. Med.* To act as a hospital intern.
in·ter'nal (ĭn·tûr'năl; -n'l), *adj.* [ML. *internalis,* fr. L. *internus,* fr. *in* in.] **1.** Enclosed; inward; interior; — opposed to *external.* **2.** Inner; spiritual. **3.** Inwardly taken or applied; as, *internal* remedies. **4.** Belonging to or inherent in the thing itself; not derived from or dependent on anything external; as, *internal* evidence. **5.** Domestic; not foreign; hence, *U. S.,* derived from taxes or duties on domestic commerce, trade, industries, etc.; as, *internal* revenue. **6.** *Anat.* Near or toward the inside of the body. **7.** *Psychol.* Occurring or arising within the organism; as, an *internal* stimulus. — **in'ter·nal'i·ty** (ĭn'tẽr·năl'ĭ·tĭ), *n.* — *n.* **1.** *pl.* The internal organs of the body. **2.** Inner or essential nature or quality. — **in·ter'nal·ly,** *adv.*
in·ter'nal–com·bus'tion en'gine. *Mach.* A heat engine in which the pressure necessary to produce motion of the mechanism results from the ignition or burning of a fuel-air mixture within the engine cylinder. Cf. EXTERNAL-COMBUSTION ENGINE.
internal medicine. *Med.* The branch of medicine dealing with the diagnosis and treatment of diseases of the interior of the body.
in'ter·na'tion·al (ĭn'tẽr·năsh'ŭn·ăl; -'l), *adj.* [*inter-* + *national.*] **1.** Common to or affecting two or more nations. **2.** [*cap.*] Of or concerning any of the associations called *International.* — *n.* **1.** A participant in any international contest. **2.** [*cap.*] Any of several working-class Socialist organizations of international scope; esp.: **a** ***First International*** (1864–1876), founded in London, with Karl Marx as moving spirit. **b** ***Second International,*** founded in Paris in 1889. **c** ***Third International,*** founded at Moscow in 1919 under the leadership of the Russian Communist party and composed of affiliated national Communist parties. It called upon the world proletariat to support the Bolshevik Revolution of November, 1917, and to overthrow everywhere the existing "capitalistic" governments. It was officially disbanded at Moscow May 23, 1943, but Communist activities were carried on by the various national Communist parties. Called also ***Communist, or Red, International;*** also ***Comintern.*** **d** ***Labor and Socialist International,*** formed at Hamburg, Germany, in 1923, by the merging of the Second International and the ***Vienna International*** (1921). **3.** [*cap.*] A rallying song of communism, composed in French by Eugène Pottier in 1871 and set to music by Adolphe Degeyter. — **in'ter·na'tion·al·ism** (-ĭz'm), *n.* — **in'ter·na'tion·al·ist** (-ĭst), *n.* — **in'ter·na'tion·al'i·ty** (-ăl'ĭ·tĭ), *n.* — **in'ter·na'tion·al·ize** (-ăl·īz; -'l·īz), *v. t.* — **in'ter·na'tion·al·ly,** *adv.*
international candle. See CANDLE, 3.
international code. *Teleg.* See MORSE CODE.
international date line. The date line.
‖**In'ter'na'tio'nale'** (ăN'tĕr'nȧ'syō'nȧl'), *n.* [F.] = INTERNATIONAL, *n.*, 2 & 3.
International Labor Organization. A body created by the Treaty of Versailles to promote uniform labor legislation among member nations. Abbr. ILO
international law. The body of rules which modern civilized nations regard as binding them in their mutual intercourse.
International Monetary Fund. A fund established, under terms of an agreement adopted at the Bretton Woods conference July, 1944, and made effective Dec. 27, 1945, to promote international monetary cooperation and exchange stability, and to aid the contributing nations in current monetary transactions.
International Phonetic Association. A society founded in 1886 "to promote the scientific study of phonetics." In its **International Phonetic Alphabet** the pronunciation of practically any language can be represented. Abbr. (for either association or alphabet), *IPA*
in'terne (ĭn'tûrn; ĭn·tûrn'). See 1st & 3d INTERN.
in'ter·ne'cine (ĭn'tẽr·nē'sĭn; -sīn), *adj.* [L. *internecinus* deadly, fr. *internecare* to kill, slaughter, fr. *inter-* + *necare* to kill.] Mutually slaughterous or destructive of life.
in'tern·ee' (ĭn'tûrn·ē'), *n.* One interned, as an enemy alien during a war.
in·tern'ment (ĭn·tûrn'mĕnt), *n.* An interning; state of being interned. See 2d INTERN.
‖**in'ter nos** (ĭn'tẽr nōs'). [L.] Between ourselves; entre nous.
in'ter·nun'ci·o (ĭn'tẽr·nŭn'shĭ·ō), *n.; pl.* -CIOS (-ōz). [It. *internunzio,* fr. L. *internuntius,* fr. *inter-* + *nuntius, nuncius,* messenger.] **1.** An envoy. **2.** A diplomatic representative of the pope, of lower rank than a nuncio.
in'ter·o·cep'tive (ĭn'tẽr·ō·sĕp'tĭv), *adj. Physiol.* Activated by, pertaining to, or designating stimuli arising in the viscera. Cf. EXTEROCEPTIVE, PROPRIOCEPTIVE.
in'ter·o·cep'tor (-tẽr; 2), *n.* [NL.] *Physiol.* A receptor for stimuli of visceral origin.
in'ter·os'cu·late (ĭn'tẽr·ŏs'kū·lāt), *v. i.* To osculate with each other; intermix; specif., *Biol.,* of species, etc., to have characters in common. — **in'ter·os'cu·la'tion** (-lā'shŭn), *n.*
in'ter·pel'lant (-pĕl'ănt), *adj.* [L. *interpellans,* pres. part. See INTERPELLATE.] Interrupting. — *n.* One who interpellates.
in'ter·pel'late (ĭn'tẽr·pĕl'āt; ĭn·tûr'pĕ·lāt), *v. t.* [L. *interpellatus,* past part. of *interpellare,* fr. *inter-* + *pellare* (in comp.), akin to *pellere* to drive.] To question formally, as a minister, or other executive officer, in order to obtain a statement or defense of his policy, conduct, etc. — **in'ter·pel·la'tion** (-pĕ·lā'shŭn), *n.* — **in'ter·pel·la'tor** (-lā'tẽr), *n.*
in'ter·pen'e·trate (ĭn'tẽr·pĕn'ē·trāt), *v. t. & i.* To penetrate between, within, or throughout; permeate; also, to penetrate mutually. — **in'ter·pen'e·tra'tion** (-trā'shŭn), *n.*
in'ter·phone' (ĭn'tẽr·fōn'), *n.* A telephone system for intercommunication between points within a small area, as in an airplane, tank, ship, or office building.
in'ter·play' (ĭn'tẽr·plā'), *n.* Mutual action or influence; interaction; reciprocal or contrasting action or effect.
in'ter·play' (-plā'), *v. i.* To exert interplay.
in'ter·plead' (ĭn'tẽr·plēd'), *v. i. Law.* To plead, or go to trial, with each other in order to determine a right on which the action of a third party depends.
in'ter·plead'er (-ẽr), *n.* One who interpleads.
in'ter·plead'er, *n. Law.* A proceeding to enable a person to compel parties making the same claim against him to litigate the matter between themselves.
in·ter'po·late (ĭn·tûr'pō·lāt), *v. t.* [L. *interpolatus,* past part. of *interpolare* to form anew, interpolate, fr. *interpolus, interpolis,* falsified, vamped up, fr. *inter-* + root of *polire* to polish.] **1.** To alter or corrupt, as a text, by inserting new or foreign matter. **2.** To insert between other things or parts; intercalate. **3.** *Math.* To insert intermediate terms in, as a series according to the law of the series. — *v. i.* To make interpolations. — **Syn.** See INTRODUCE. — **in·ter'po·lat'er** (-lāt'ẽr), **in·ter'po·la'tor** (-lā'tẽr), *n.* — **in·ter'po·la'tion** (-lā'shŭn), *n.* — **in·ter'po·la'tive** (-lā'tĭv), *adj.*
in'ter·pose' (ĭn'tẽr·pōz'), *v. t.* [F. *interposer.* See INTER-; POSE, v.] **1.** To place between; as, to *interpose* a screen. **2.** To thrust in; intrude. **3.** To introduce or inject between parts of a conversation or argument. — *v. i.* **1.** To be or come between. **2.** To mediate; intervene. **3.** To interrupt. — **in'ter·pos'al** (-pōz'ăl; -'l), *n.* — **in'ter·pos'er** *n.* — **in'ter·pos'ing·ly,** *adv.* — **in'ter·po·si'tion** (-pō·zĭsh'ŭn), *n.*
Syn. (1) See INTRODUCE.
(2) **Interpose, interfere, intervene, mediate, intercede** mean to come or go between two (persons or things, or persons and things). **Interpose**, in its general use, implies no more than this, gaining additional implications only from the context; **interfere** implies a getting in the way as by crossing a path or, more often, by creating a condition that hinders movement, activity, view, or free operation; **intervene**, the interposition of something, often, but not always, in space or time, or of someone, interested in conciliation or the like; **mediate**, intervention between those that are hostile, antagonistic, or otherwise opposed; **intercede**, intervention on a person's (usually an offender's) behalf.
in·ter'pret (ĭn·tûr'prĕt; -prĭt), *v. t.* [OF. *interpreter,* fr. L. *interpretari,* past part. -*tatus,* whence L. *interpres* interpreter, negotiator.] **1.** To explain or tell the meaning of; translate; elucidate. **2.** To construe in the light of individual belief, judgment, or interest; as, to *interpret* a contract. **3.** To apprehend and represent by means of art; show by illustrative representation; as, an actor who *interprets* Hamlet. — *v. i.* To act as an interpreter; translate. — **Syn.** See EXPLAIN. — **in·ter'pret·a·bil'i·ty** (-ȧ·bĭl'ĭ·tĭ), *n.* — **in·ter'pret·a·ble** (-ȧ·b'l), *adj.* — **in·ter'pret·er,** *n.* — **in·ter'pre·tive** (-prĕ·tĭv), *adj.* — **in·ter'pre·tive·ly,** *adv.*
in·ter'pre·ta'tion (ĭn·tûr'prĕ·tā'shŭn), *n.* **1.** An interpreting. **2.** Explanation, construction, or sense given by an interpreter. **3.** A person's conception of a work of art, subject, etc., as shown in performance, criticism, artistic representation, or the like. — **in·ter'pre·ta'tion·al** (-ăl; -'l), *adj.* — **in·ter'pre·ta'tive** (ĭn·tûr'prĕ·tā'tĭv; -tȧ·tĭv), *adj.* — **in·ter'pre·ta'tive·ly,** *adv.*
in'ter·reg'num (ĭn'tẽr·rĕg'nŭm), *n.; pl.* -NA (-nȧ). [L., fr. *inter-* + *regnum* dominion.] **1.** The time during which a throne is vacant between two successive reigns. **2.** Any period during which the functions of government or any kind of control are suspended. **3.** Hence, a break, lapse, or pause in a continuous series.
in·ter'ro·gate (ĭn·tĕr'ō·gāt), *v. t. & i.* [L. *interrogatus,* past part. of *interrogare* to ask, fr. *inter-* + *rogare* to ask.] To question; esp., to examine by asking questions; as, to *interrogate* a witness. — **Syn.** See ASK. — **in·ter'ro·gat'ing·ly** (-gāt'ĭng·lĭ), *adv.* — **in·ter'ro·ga'tion** (-gā'shŭn), *n.* — **in·ter'ro·ga'tion·al,** *adj.* — **in·ter'ro·ga'tor** (-gā'tẽr), *n.*
in·ter'ro·ga'tion point *or* **mark** (-gā'shŭn). The mark [?] indicating that the preceding sentence is a direct question.
in'ter·rog'a·tive (ĭn'tĕ·rŏg'ȧ·tĭv), *adj.* Interrogatory. — *n.* A word used in asking questions, as *who? what? which?* Abbr. *interrog.* — **in'ter·rog'a·tive·ly,** *adv.*

in′ter·rog′a·to′ry (ĭn′tĕ·rŏg′ȧ·tō′rĭ *or, esp. Brit.*, -tẽr·ĭ), *adj.* Containing, expressing, or implying a question. — *n.* A formal question or inquiry. — **in·ter·rog′a·to′ri·ly**, *adv.*

in′ter·rupt′ (ĭn′tĕ·rŭpt′), *v. t.* [L. *interruptus*, past part. of *interrumpere* to interrupt, fr. *inter-* + *rumpere* to break.] **1.** To break into, or between; to hinder by or as by breaking in. **2.** To make a break in the continuity, uniformity, monotony, etc. of. — *v. i.* To break in upon some action or discourse, esp. with questions or remarks. — **in′ter·rup′tive** (-rŭp′tĭv), *adj.*

in′ter·rupt′er (-rŭp′tẽr), *n.* One who or that which interrupts; specif., *Elec.*, any of various devices to interrupt or make and break an electric current, usually automatically.

in′ter·rup′tion (-rŭp′shŭn), *n.* **1.** An interrupting. **2.** A break caused by the abrupt intervention of something foreign; intervention; interposition. **3.** Obstruction of current, progress, or motion. **4.** Intermission; suspension.

‖**in′ter se** (ĭn′tẽr sē′). [L.] Among, or between, themselves.

in′ter·sect′ (ĭn′tẽr·sĕkt′), *v. t. & i.* [L. *intersectus*, past part. of *intersecare* to intersect, fr. *inter-* + *secare* to cut.] To pierce or divide by passing through or athwart; cut across; cross.

in′ter·sec′tion (-sĕk′shŭn), *n.* Act or place of intersecting; as, the *intersection* of two roads.

in′ter·sec′tion·al (-ăl; -′l), *adj.* **a** Between sections; as, an *intersectional* contest; drawn from various sections; as, an *intersectional* gathering. **b** Of or pertaining to an intersection.

in′ter·sex′u·al (-sĕk′shōō·ăl; -sĕks′ū-), *adj.* [*inter-* + *sexual*.] **1.** Between the sexes. **2.** *Biol.* Designating or pertaining to an individual (an **in′ter·sex′**) intermediate in sexual characters between a typical male and a typical female. — **in′ter·sex′u·al′i·ty** (-ăl′ĭ·tĭ), *n.*

in′ter·space′ (ĭn′tẽr·spās′), *n.* Intervening space; interval.

in′ter·sperse′ (ĭn′tẽr·spûrs′), *v. t.* [L. *interspersus* interspersed, fr. *inter-* + *spargere* to scatter.] **1.** To scatter or set here and there among other things. **2.** To diversify or adorn with things so set or scattered. — **in′ter·spers′ed·ly** (-spûr′sĕd·lĭ; -sĭd·lĭ), *adv.* — **in′ter·sper′sion** (-spûr′shŭn), *n.*

in′ter·state′ (ĭn′tẽr·stāt′; 2), *adj.* Pertaining to the mutual relations of states; existing between, or including, different states; as, *interstate* commerce.

in′ter·stel′lar (-stĕl′ẽr), *adj.* Located among the stars or passing from one to another; as, *interstellar* space.

in·ter′stice (ĭn·tûr′stĭs), *n.; pl.* -STICES (-stĭ·sēz; -sĭz). [F., fr. L. *interstitium*, fr. *inter-* + *sistere, statum*, to place, stand.] A space between one thing and another, esp. between things closely set, or between the parts of a body; chink; crevice. — **Syn.** See APERTURE.

in′ter·sti′tial (ĭn′tẽr·stĭsh′ăl), *adj.* Of or pertaining to interstices; of, pertaining to, or situated in, the interstices of a tissue. — **in′ter·sti′tial·ly**, *adv.*

in′ter·strat′i·fy (-străt′ĭ·fī), *v. t. & i.*; -FIED (-fīd); -FY′ING. To insert, or to lie, between other strata; to arrange, or to lie, in alternate strata. — **in′ter·strat′i·fi·ca′tion** (-fĭ·kā′shŭn), *n.*

in′ter·tex′ture (-tĕks′tūr), *n.* An interweaving; also, that which is interwoven.

in′ter·trop′i·cal (-trŏp′ĭ·kăl), *adj.* Situated between or within the tropics; relating to regions within the tropics.

in′ter·val (ĭn′tẽr·văl), *n.* [F. *intervalle*, fr. L. *intervallum* interval, orig., space between ramparts, fr. *inter-* + *vallum* a wall.] **1.** A space of time between any two points or events, esp. between recurrent conditions or states. **2.** A pause or break in the course of something, as sessions. **3.** A space, gap, or distance between objects, states, qualities, etc. **4.** *Music.* The relation of two tones with regard to pitch. An interval is ***harmonic*** if between simultaneous tones; ***melodic*** if between successive tones.

in′ter·vale (-vāl), *n.* [Same word as *interval* a space between, influenced by E. *vale*.] *Local, U. S. & Canada.* A tract of low, usually alluvial, ground between hills, or along the banks of a stream.

in′ter·vene′ (ĭn′tẽr·vēn′), *v. i.* [L. *intervenire, interventum*, to intervene, hinder, fr. *inter-* + *venire* to come.] **1.** To enter or appear as an irrelevant or extraneous feature or circumstance; to come (in between). **2.** To occur, fall, or come between points of time or events. **3.** To come in or between by way of hindrance or modification; to interpose; as, to *intervene* to settle a quarrel. **4.** To lie or have its place (*between*); as, the Mediterranean *intervenes* between Europe and Africa. **5.** *Law.* To become a party to an action or other legal proceeding, for the protection of an alleged interest therein; — said of a third person not originally a party thereto. — **Syn.** See INTERPOSE. — **in′ter·ven′er** (-vēn′ẽr), **in′ter·ve′nor** (-vē′nẽr), *n.* — **in′ter·ven′ient** (-vēn′yĕnt), *adj. & n.*

in′ter·ven′tion (-vĕn′shŭn), *n.* **1.** An intervening; interposition. **2.** Any interference that may affect the interests of others; specif., *Internat. Law*, the interference of a state in the affairs of another state for the purpose of compelling it to do or forbear certain acts or to maintain or alter an internal condition. — **in′ter·ven′tion·al** (-ăl; -′l), *adj.*

in′ter·ven′tion·ist (-ĭst), *n.* One who intervenes, or who favors intervention. — **in′ter·ven′tion·ist**, *adj.* — **in′ter·ven′tion·ism** (-ĭz′m), *n.*

in′ter·view (ĭn′tẽr·vū), *n.* [F. *entrevue*, fr. *entrevoir* to see imperfectly, have a glimpse of, *s'entrevoir* to visit each other. See INTER-; VIEW.] **1.** A mutual sight or view; a meeting face to face; usually, a formal consultation. **2.** A meeting between a representative of the press with a person from whom he seeks information for publication; also, the press article giving this information. — *v. t.* To have an interview with. — **in′ter·view′er**, *n.*

‖**in′ter vi′vos** (ĭn′tẽr vī′vōs). [L.] Between living persons; specif., *Law*, designating a gift which passes title from one living person to another.

in′ter·vo·cal′ic (ĭn′tẽr·vō·kăl′ĭk), *adj.* Situated between vowels; immediately preceded and followed by vowel sounds.

in′ter·weave′ (-wēv′), *v. t. & i.*; see WEAVE. **1.** To weave together; to intermix or unite in texture or construction. **2.** To mingle together; unite or connect closely. — **in′ter·wo′ven** (-wō′vĕn), *adj.*

in·tes′ta·cy (ĭn·tĕs′tȧ·sĭ), *n.* State of being or dying intestate.

in·tes′tate (-tāt), *adj.* [L. *intestatus*, fr. *in-* not + *testatus*, past part. of *testari* to make a will.] **1.** Without having made a valid will. **2.** Not disposed of by will. — *n. Law.* A person who dies intestate.

in·tes′ti·nal (ĭn·tĕs′tĭ·năl; -n′l; *rare & esp. Brit.*, ĭn′tĕs·tī′-), *adj.* Of or pertaining to the intestine.

in·tes′tine (ĭn·tĕs′tĭn), *adj.* [L. *intestinus*, fr. *intus* on the inside, within, fr. *in* in.] Internal, esp. with regard to a state or country; domestic; — applied usually to disorders, calamities, etc. — *n.* The tubular part of the alimentary canal, terminating at the anus; the bowels; — commonly *pl.* In the human adult the ***small intestine*** comprises the duodenum, jejunum, and ileum; the ***large intestine***, the caecum and vermiform appendix, the colon, and the rectum. See RUMINANT, *Illust.*

in·thrall′, in·thral′ (ĭn·thrôl′), *v. t.* To enthrall. — **in·thrall′ment, in·thral′ment**, *n.*

in·throne′ (ĭn·thrōn′). Var. of ENTHRONE.

in′ti·ma (ĭn′tĭ·mȧ), *n.; pl.* -MAE (-mē). [NL., fr. L. *intimus* innermost.] *Anat. & Zool.* The innermost coat of an organ, esp. of a blood vessel or lymphatic.

in′ti·ma·cy (ĭn′tĭ·mȧ·sĭ), *n.; pl.* -CIES (-sĭz). State or instance of being intimate; close association; familiarity.

in′ti·mate (-māt), *v. t.* [L. *intimatus*, past part. of *intimare* to put, drive, or press into, to announce, fr. *intimus* the inmost. See INTIMATE, *adj.*] **1.** To announce; notify. **2.** To suggest obscurely or indirectly; hint. — **Syn.** See SUGGEST. — **in′ti·mat′er** (-māt′ẽr), *n.* — **in′ti·ma′tion** (-mā′shŭn), *n.*

in′ti·mate (-mĭt), *adj.* [Formerly *intime*, fr. L. *intimus* a superl. corresponding to the compar. *interior*. The form *intimate* is due to confusion with L. *intimatus*, past part. See INTIMATE, *v. t.*] **1.** Intrinsic; innermost; inmost; hence, very personal; private. **2.** Characterized by or arising from close union, contact, association, acquaintance, investigation, or the like; as, *intimate* friends or knowledge. **3.** Having illicit sexual relations (*with*). **4.** Closely personal; — of garments. — **Syn.** See FAMILIAR. — *n.* An intimate friend or associate. — **in′ti·mate·ly**, *adv.* — **in′ti·mate·ness**, *n.*

in·tim′i·date (ĭn·tĭm′ĭ·dāt), *v. t.* [ML. *intimidatus*, past part. of *intimidare* to frighten, fr. *in-* in + *timidus* timid.] To make timid or fearful; to inspire or affect with fear; specif., to deter, as by threats; overawe; cow. — **in·tim′i·da′tion** (-dā′shŭn), *n.* — **in·tim′i·da′tor** (-dā′tẽr), *n.*

in·tinc′tion (ĭn·tĭngk′shŭn), *n.* [LL. *intinctio*.] *Eccl.* Administration of the sacrament by dipping the bread or wafer in the wine and administering both together.

in·ti′tle (ĭn·tī′t′l). Var. of ENTITLE.

in·tit′ule (ĭn·tĭt′ūl), *v. t.* [F. *intituler*, fr. LL. *intitulare*.] To give a title to, as a legislative act.

in′to (ĭn′tōō; -tŏŏ; 4), *prep.* [*in* + *to*.] **1.** From being outside of, as in place, state, form, etc., to within; to the place, state, form, etc., of; — usually after verbs of motion, change, or the like. **2.** *Math.* By or together with; — with *multiply* expressed or understood; as, $a \times b$ may be read *a* is multiplied *into b*.

in·tol′er·a·ble (ĭn·tŏl′ẽr·ȧ·b′l), *adj.* Not tolerable; insufferable. — *adv.* Intolerably. — **in·tol′er·a·bil′i·ty** (-bĭl′ĭ·tĭ), *n.* — **in·tol′er·a·ble·ness**, *n.* — **in·tol′er·a·bly**, *adv.*

in·tol′er·ance (-ăns), *n.* Quality or instance of being intolerant; incapacity to endure; esp., refusal to tolerate others' opinions, religious beliefs, etc.; illiberality; bigotry.

in·tol′er·ant (-ănt), *adj.* Manifesting intolerance. — *n.* An intolerant person. — **in·tol′er·ant·ly**, *adv.*

in·tomb′ (ĭn·tōōm′), **in·tomb′ment.** Vars. of ENTOMB, etc.

in′to·nate (ĭn′tō·nāt), *v. t.* [See INTONE.] **1.** To intone. **2.** *Phonet.* To utter with voice.

in′to·na′tion (-nā′shŭn), *n.* **1.** The act of intoning or chanting, as a part of a liturgy; esp., act of sounding musical tones, as of a scale. **2.** That which is intoned; specif., the opening tones of a Gregorian chant. **3.** Manner of singing, playing, or uttering tones, esp. with relation to pitch or harmony. **4.** *Phonet.* The rise and fall in pitch of the voice in speech.

in·tone′ (ĭn·tōn′), *v. t. & i.* [ML. *intonare, -natum*, fr. *in-* in + L. *tonus* tone.] To utter in musical or prolonged tones; chant; recite in singing tones or in monotone. — **in·ton′er** (-tōn′ẽr), *n.*

in·tort′ (ĭn·tôrt′), *v. t.* [L. *intortus*, past part. of *intorquere* to twist.] To twist inwards or in and out; twine. — **in·tor′sion** (-tôr′shŭn), *n.*

‖**in to′to** (ĭn tō′tō). [L.] In the whole; entirely.

in·tox′i·cant (ĭn·tŏk′sĭ·kănt), *adj.* Intoxicating. — *n.* That which intoxicates; an intoxicating agent, as alcohol.

in·tox′i·cate (-kāt), *adj.* [ML. *intoxicatus*, past part. of *intoxicare* to drug or poison, fr. *in-* in + L. *toxicum* poison. See TOXIC.] Intoxicated. — (-kāt), *v. t.* **1.** *Obs.* To poison. **2.** To make drunk; inebriate. **3.** To excite to a frenzy; elate excessively. — **in·tox′i·ca′tive** (-kā′tĭv), *adj.* — **in·tox′i·ca′tor** (-kā′tẽr), *n.*

in·tox′i·cat′ed (-kāt′ĕd; -ĭd), *adj.* Affected by an intoxicant; also, emotionally wrought up, as by sorrow or joy. — **Syn.** See DRUNK.

in·tox′i·ca′tion (-kā′shŭn), *n.* **1.** An intoxicating; specif., *Med.*, a poisoning, as by a spirituous substance, or by serum injections, by bacterial toxins, etc. **2.** State of being intoxicated, or drunk. **3.** Transport; frenzy.

in′tra- (ĭn′trȧ-). [L. *intra*, prep., within, on the inside.] A prefix meaning: **1.** *Within; inside;* as in:

intra-abdominal	intracranial	intranational
intra-atomic	intracutaneous	intranuclear
intracardiac	intradermal	intraspinal
intracellular	intramarginal	intrastate
intracollegiate	intramundane	intra-uterine

2. *Into; intro-;* as in **in′tra·sus·cep′tion**, intussusception.

in·trac′ta·ble (ĭn·trăk′tȧ·b′l), *adj.* Not tractable; specif.: **a** Not easily governed, managed, or directed; not disposed to be taught, disciplined, or tamed; stubborn; obstinate. **b** Not easily manipulated, wrought, cured, or the like; refractory. — **Syn.** See UNRULY. — **in·trac′ta·bil′i·ty** (-bĭl′ĭ·tĭ), **in·trac′ta·ble·ness**, *n.* — **in·trac′ta·bly**, *adv.*

in·trac′tile (-tĭl), *adj.* Not tractile; not ductile.

in·tra′dos (ĭn·trā′dŏs), *n.* [F., fr. L. *intra* within + F. *dos* the back.] *Arch.* The interior curve of an arch. See ARCH, EXTRADOS, *Illusts.*

in′tra·mo·lec′u·lar (ĭn′trȧ·mō·lĕk′ū·lẽr), *adj.* Existing or acting within the molecule; formed by reaction between different parts of the same molecule.

in′tra·mu′ral (-mū′răl), *adj.* **1.** Within the walls, as of a city; of collegiate activities, confined to members of the college; as, *intramural* games. **2.** *Anat. & Med.* Within the substance of the walls or boundaries of an organ.

‖**in′tra mu′ros** (ĭn′trȧ mū′rōs). [L.] Within the walls, esp. city walls or the precincts of a college.

in′tra·mus′cu·lar (ĭn′trȧ·mŭs′kū·lẽr), *adj.* *Med.* In or within a muscle; specif., into muscular tissue, esp. by injection.

‖**in′tran′si′geant′** (ăN′trăN′zē′zhäN′), *n. & adj.* [F.] (An) intransigent. — ‖**in′tran′si′geance′** (-zhäNs′), *n.*

in·tran′si·gent (ĭn·trăn′sĭ·jĕnt), *adj.* [F. *intransigeant*, fr. Sp. *intransigente*, fr. L. *in-* not + *transigere* to come to an agreement. See TRANSACT.] Refusing compromise; uncompromising; irreconcilable. — *n.* A radical or irreconcilable (in politics). — **in·tran′si·gence** (-jĕns), **in·tran′si·gen·cy** (-jĕn·sĭ), *n.* — **in·tran′si·gent·ly,** *adv.*

in·tran′si·tive (ĭn·trăn′sĭ·tĭv), *adj.* Not transitive; specif., *Gram.*, not passing over to an object; as, an *intransitive* action; expressing an action or state as limited to the agent or subject, or as ending in itself; as, an *intransitive* verb (e.g., *seem, die, exist*) or construction. Abbr. *int., intr., intrans.* — **in·tran′si·tive·ly,** *adv.* — **in·tran′si·tive·ness,** *n.*

in′trant (ĭn′trănt), *n.* [L. *intrans*, pres. part. of *intrare* to enter. See ENTER.] One who enters; esp., a person entering upon some office, station, order, or association.

in′tra·ve′nous (ĭn′trȧ·vē′nŭs), *adj.* In or within a vein or veins; specif., into a vein, esp. by injection. — **in′tra·ve′nous·ly,** *adv.*

in·treat′ (ĭn·trēt′), *v. t.* To entreat.

in·trench′ (ĭn·trĕnch′), *v. t. & i.* **1.** To cut in; furrow. **2.** To surround with a trench; to entrench. — **Syn.** See TRESPASS. — **in·trench′er,** *n.* — **in·trench′ment,** *n.*

in·trep′id (ĭn·trĕp′ĭd), *adj.* [L. *intrepidus.* See IN- not; TREPIDATION.] Not trembling or shaking with fear; fearless; bold; undaunted. — **Syn.** Dauntless, valiant, brave, courageous. — **in·trep′id·ly,** *adv.*

in′tre·pid′i·ty (ĭn′trē·pĭd′ĭ·tĭ), *n.* Quality of being intrepid; boldness; dauntlessness.

in′tri·ca·cy (ĭn′trĭ·kȧ·sĭ), *n.; pl.* -CIES (-sĭz). State, quality, or an instance of being intricate; complexity.

in′tri·cate (-kĭt), *adj.* [L. *intricatus*, past part. of *intricare* to entangle, perplex.] Entangled; involved; complicated; difficult to understand, follow, etc. — **Syn.** See COMPLEX. — **in′tri·cate·ly,** *adv.*

in′tri·gant (ĭn′trĭ·gănt; *F.* ăN′trē′gäN′), *n. masc.; pl.* -GANTS (-gănts; *F.* -gäN′); **in′tri·gante′** (ĭn′trĭ·gănt′; *F.* ăN′trē′gäNt′), *n. fem.; pl.* -GANTES (-gănts′; *F.* -gäNt′). [F., fr. It. *intrigante.*] An intriguer.

in·trigue′ (ĭn·trēg′), *v. t.;* IN·TRIGUED′ (-trēgd′); IN·TRI′GUING (-trē′gĭng). [F. *intriguer*, fr. It. *intrigare*, fr. L. *intricare.* See INTRICATE.] **1.** To cheat; trick; contrive by intrigue; also, to bring about or get by intrigue. **2.** To entangle; complicate. **3. a** To puzzle; perplex. **b** To arouse the interest, desire, or curiosity of, as by an engaging, beguiling, or baffling quality. — *v. i.* **1.** To carry on a secret and illicit amour. **2.** To plot or scheme; to contrive to accomplish a purpose by secret artifice. — (ĭn·trēg′; ĭn′trēg), *n.* **1.** A plot or plotting to gain a desired end; machination. **2.** A secret amour. — **Syn.** See PLOT. — **in·tri′guer** (ĭn·trē′gẽr), *n.* — **in·tri′guing·ly,** *adv.*

in·trin′sic (ĭn·trĭn′sĭk), *adj.* [F. *intrinsèque*, fr. ML. *intrinsecus*, fr. L. *intrinsecus*, adv., inward, on the inside.] **1.** Belonging to the constitution, nature, or essence of a thing; essential; inherent. **2.** *Anat.* Included wholly within an organ or limb, as certain groups of muscles. Cf. EXTRINSIC. — **in·trin′si·cal** (-sĭ·kăl), *adj.* — **in·trin′si·cal·ly,** *adv.*

in′tro- (ĭn′trō-). [L., fr. *intro*, adv., inwardly, within. See INTER-.] A prefix signifying *to; into; within; inward.*

in′tro·duce′ (ĭn′trō·dūs′), *v. t.;* -DUCED′ (-dūst′); -DUC′ING (-dūs′ĭng). [L. *introducere, -ductum*, fr. *intro* within + *ducere* to lead.] **1.** To bring into play; hence, to bring into practice or use; institute; as, to *introduce* a new fashion. **2.** To lead or bring in; contrive the entrance of; conduct or usher in; as, to *introduce* European birds into America. **3.** To lead to and make known formally; esp.: **a** To cause to be acquainted; as, to *introduce* strangers. **b** To present formally as at court or to society. **4. a** To begin or present; as, to *introduce* a subject. **b** To make known to; to call to the attention of; as, to *introduce* readers to a poem. **5.** To insert, as a probe. **6.** To bring forward formally or in an official manner; as, to *introduce* a bill into Congress. — **in′tro·duc′er** (-dūs′ẽr), *n.* — **in′tro·duc′tive** (-dŭk′tĭv), *adj.*

Syn. **Introduce, insert, insinuate, interpolate, intercalate, interpose, interject** mean to put something among or between other things. **Introduce** suggests a bringing in of a thing (or person) into a group, collection, or the like (as, to *introduce* an amendment into the bill); **insert,** introduction into a fixed space between or among; **insinuate,** introduction by pushing or worming its way through; **interpolate,** insertion of something extraneous or spurious; **intercalate,** intrusive insertion of something in a sequence or series; **interpose,** insertion of some obstacle, obstruction, or cause of delay; **interject,** introduction of something that breaks in.

in′tro·duc′tion (-dŭk′shŭn), *n.* **1.** An introducing or bringing to notice. **2.** That part of a book, discourse, etc., introducing the main subject or part; a preface. **3.** A formal preliminary treatise; a guide. **4.** Act of formally making persons known to each other.

in′tro·duc′to·ry (-dŭk′tō·rĭ), *adj.* Serving to introduce; preliminary. — **in′tro·duc′to·ri·ly** (-rĭ·lĭ), *adv.*

in·tro′it (ĭn·trō′ĭt), *n.* [F. *introït*, fr. L. *introitus*, fr. *introire* to go into, enter, fr. *intro* within + *ire* to go.] **1.** [*cap.*] *R.C.Ch.* The first part of the proper of the Mass. It now consists usually of an antiphon and verse from one of the psalms followed by the *Gloria Patri.* **2.** In Anglican churches, a psalm, anthem, or hymn, sung or played at the beginning of the Communion service.

in′tro·jec′tion (ĭn′trō·jĕk′shŭn), *n.* [*intro-* + L. *jacere* to throw.] *Psychol.* The adoption of externals (persons or objects) into the self, so as to have a sense of oneness with them and to feel personally affected by what happens to them; — opp. to *projection.*

in′tro·mit′ (-mĭt′), *v. t.;* -MIT′TED; -MIT′TING. [L. *intromittere, -missum*, fr. *intro-* + *mittere* to send.] To send or put in; insert; also, to let pass in; admit. — **in′tro·mis′sion** (-mĭsh′ŭn), *n.* — **in′tro·mit′tent** (-mĭt′ĕnt; -′nt), *adj.* — **in′tro·mit′ter** (-ẽr), *n.*

in·trorse′ (ĭn·trôrs′), *adj.* [L. *introrsus* inward, contr. fr. *introversus.* See INTROVERT.] *Bot.* Facing inward, or toward the axis of growth. Cf. EXTRORSE. — **in·trorse′ly,** *adv.*

in′tro·spect′ (ĭn′trō·spĕkt′), *v. t. & i.* [L. *introspectus*, past part. of *introspicere* to look into, fr. *intro* within + *specere* to look.] To look into or within, as one's own mind; to inspect, as one's own thoughts or feelings; to practice self-examination. — **in′tro·spec′tion** (-spĕk′shŭn), *n.* — **in′tro·spec′tive** (-tĭv), *adj.* — **in′tro·spec′tive·ly,** *adv.*

in′tro·ver′sion (-vûr′shŭn; -zhŭn), *n.* **1.** Act of introverting, or directing one's attention within oneself. **2.** *Psychol.* Interest directed inward; a propensity for finding one's satisfactions in the inner life of thought and fancy; — opp. to *extroversion.* — **in′tro·ver′sive** (-sĭv), *adj.*

in′tro·vert′ (-vûrt′), *v. t. & i.* [*intro-* + L. *vertere, versum*, to turn.] **1.** To direct (the mind, thought, or effort) within oneself; practice introversion. **2.** To turn or bend inward. **3.** *Zool.* To draw in or invaginate (one tubular part or organ within another).

in′tro·vert′ (ĭn′trō·vûrt′), *n.* **1.** That which is or can be introverted, as the eyestalks of certain snails. **2.** *Psychol.* A person strongly inclined to introversion. Cf. EXTROVERT. — *adj.* Characterized by or characteristic of introversion.

in·trude′ (ĭn·trōōd′; 114), *v. t.* [L. *intrudere, intrusum*, fr. *in-* in + *trudere* to thrust.] **1.** To thrust or force (something) in or upon; esp., to force (oneself) in without leave or welcome. **2.** *Geol.* To enter, or cause to enter, by force. — *v. i.* To thrust oneself in; to enter; encroach; trespass. — **in·trud′er** (-trōōd′ẽr), *n.* — **in·trud′ing·ly,** *adv.*

Syn. **Intrude, obtrude, interlope** mean to thrust oneself or something in without invitation or authorization. **Intrude** usually implies rudeness, officiousness, or invasion of another's property, time, etc.; **obtrude** suggests even more strongly the impropriety, the boldness, or the futility of the act and the disagreeableness of the offense; **interlope** (chiefly in present participle) implies an interposing oneself in a place or position with advantage to oneself and injury to one or both of the persons or things originally concerned.

in·tru′sion (ĭn·trōō′zhŭn), *n.* **1.** An intruding; esp., the forcing of oneself into a place without right or welcome; specif., *Law*, the act of wrongfully entering upon, seizing, or taking possession of, the property of another. **2.** *Geol.* The forcible entry of molten rock or magma into or between other rock formations; also, the intruded mass.

in·tru′sive (-sĭv), *adj.* **1.** Apt to intrude; characterized by intrusion; entering without right or welcome. **2.** Intruded, or thrust in, as a foreign element; also, thrusting inward; intruding. **3.** *Geol.* **a** Formed by solidification of a molten magma forced into fissures or between layers of older rock formations; as, an *intrusive* sheet or dike. Cf. EXTRUSIVE. **b** Plutonic. — **Syn.** See IMPERTINENT. — **in·tru′sive·ly,** *adv.* — **in·tru′sive·ness,** *n.*

in·trust′ (ĭn·trŭst′), *v. t.* To entrust.

in′tu·ba′tion (ĭn′tū·bā′shŭn), *n.* [*in-* in + *tube.*] The introduction of a tube into a hollow organ to keep the latter open, esp. into the larynx through the glottis. — **in′tu·bate** (ĭn′tū·bāt), *v. t.*

in′tu·it (ĭn′tū·ĭt), *v. t. & i.* To apprehend by intuition.

in′tu·i′tion (-ĭsh′ŭn), *n.* [ML. *intuitio*, fr. L. *intueri* to look on, fr. *in-* in, on + *tueri.* See TUITION.] The power of knowing, or the knowledge obtained, without recourse to inference or reasoning; innate or instinctive knowledge; familiarly, a quick or ready apprehension. — **in′tu·i′tion·al** (-ăl; -′l), *adj.*

in′tu·i′tion·ism (-ĭz′m), *n.* **1.** *Ethics.* The doctrine that moral values are intuitively apprehended. **2.** *Philos.* **a** The doctrine that there are self-evident truths, intuitively known, which form the basis of human knowledge. **b** The doctrine that objects of perception are intuitively known to be real. — **in′tu·i′tion·ist** (-ĭst), *n. & adj.*

in·tu′i·tive (ĭn·tū′ĭ·tĭv), *adj.* **1.** Knowing, or perceiving, by intuition; having, or characterized by, intuition. **2.** Received, known, reached, or perceived by intuition. — **in·tu′i·tive·ly,** *adv.* — **in·tu′i·tive·ness,** *n.*

in·tu′i·tiv·ism (-tĭv·ĭz′m), *n.* **1.** = INTUITIONISM, 1. **2.** Intuitive character, quality, faculty, or power. — **in·tu′i·tiv·ist** (-ĭst), *adj.*

in′tu·mesce′ (ĭn′tū·mĕs′), *v. i.;* -MESCED′ (-mĕst′); -MESC′ING (-mĕs′ĭng). [L. *intumescere*, fr. *in-* in + *tumescere* to swell up, incho. fr. *tumere* to swell.] To enlarge or expand with heat; to swell or bubble up.

in′tu·mes′cence (-mĕs′ĕns; -′ns), *n.* **1.** An intumescing; also, state of being swollen; inflation. **2.** Anything swollen or enlarged, as a tumor. — **in′tu·mes′cent** (-ĕnt; -′nt), *adj.*

in′turn′ (ĭn′tûrn′), *n.* An inward turn or bend, as of toes.

in′tus·sus·cept′ (ĭn′tŭs·sŭ·sĕpt′), *v. t.* To receive into some other thing or part; invaginate. — **in′tus·sus·cep′tive** (-sĕp′tĭv), *adj.*

in′tus·sus·cep′tion (-sĕp′shŭn), *n.* [L. *intus* within + *susceptio*, fr. *suscipere* to take up.] An intussuscepting; reception of one part within another; specif.: **a** *Med.* The slipping of one part of the intestine into an adjacent part, esp. of the small intestine into the large. **b** *Biol.* The deposition of new particles of formative material among those already embodied in a tissue or structure, as in the growth of living organisms. Cf. APPOSITION, 3.

in·twine′ (ĭn·twīn′). Var. of ENTWINE.

in·twist′ (ĭn·twĭst′), *v. t.* To entwist.

in′u·lase (ĭn′ū·lās), *n.* [*inulin* + *-ase.*] *Biochem.* An enzyme capable of converting inulin into levulose.

in′u·lin (-lĭn), *n.* [L. *inula* elecampane + *-in.*] A tasteless, white, semicrystalline polysaccharide, found dissolved in the sap of the roots and rhizomes of many plants.

in·unc′tion (ĭn·ŭngk′shŭn), *n.* [L. *inunctio*, fr. *inunguere, inunctum*, to anoint. See UNCTION.] **1.** An anointing, or state of being anointed; specif., *Med.*, the rubbing of ointments into the skin. **2.** An ointment.

in·un′dant (ĭn·ŭn′dănt), *adj.* Overflowing; inundating.

in′un·date (ĭn′ŭn·dāt), *v. t.* [L. *inundatus*, past part. of *inundare* to inundate, fr. *in-* in + *undare* to rise in waves, to overflow, fr. *unda* a wave.] To cover with or as with a flood; overflow; deluge. — **in′un·da′tion** (-dā′shŭn), *n.* — **in′un·da′tor** (-dā′tẽr), *n.* — **in·un′da·to′ry** (ĭn·ŭn′dȧ·tō′rĭ *or, esp. Brit.,* -tẽr·ĭ), *adj.*

in′ur·bane′ (ĭn′ûr·bān′), *adj.* Not urbane; uncivil; discourteous. — **in′ur·ban′i·ty** (-băn′ĭ·tĭ), *n.*

in·ure′ (ĭn·ūr′ *or, esp. Brit.,* ĭn·yŏor′), *v. t.* [*in-* in + *ure* use, work.] To accustom to something hard or painful; harden; habituate. — *v. i.* To pass into use; to be applied; as, a gift of lands *inures* to the heirs. — **in·ure′ment,** *n.*

in·urn′ (ĭn·ûrn′), *v. t.* To put in an urn; hence, entomb.

in·u′tile (ĭn·ū′tĭl; 56), *adj.* [F., fr. L. *inutilis.*] Useless; unprofitable. — **in·u′tile·ly,** *adv.* — **in′u·til′i·ty** (ĭn′ū·tĭl′ĭ·tĭ), *n.*

‖**in vac′u·o** (ĭn văk′ū·ō). [L.] In a vacuum.

in·vade′ (ĭn·vād′), *v. t.* [L. *invadere, invasum*, fr. *in-* in + *vadere* to go.] **1.** To enter for conquest or plunder. **2.** To infringe; or encroach on; as, to *invade* the rights of the people. **3.** To spread over injuriously and progressively; as, gangrene *invades* healthy tissue. **4.** To enter with a rush or make an irruption into, with or as if with intent to take possession; as, a crowd of tourists *invaded* the village. — *v. i.* To make an invasion. — **Syn.** See TRESPASS. — **in·vad′er** (-vād′ẽr), *n.*

in·vag′i·na·ble (ĭn·văj′ĭ·nȧ·b′l), *adj.* Capable of invagination.

in·vag′i·nate (-nāt), *v. t.* [L. *in-* in + *vagina* sheath.] To insert as in a sheath; cause to infold so that an outer becomes an inner surface. — *v. i.* To have one portion (of a hollow organ) drawn back within another; undergo invagination.

in·vag'i·nate (ĭn·văj'ĭ·nāt), *adj.* Showing invagination.

in·vag'i·na'tion (-nā'shŭn), *n.* **1.** An invaginating or state of being invaginated; also, an invaginated part. **2.** *Embryol.* Formation of a gastrula by ingrowth or infolding of part of the wall of the blastula; — more fully, ***embolic invagination.*** **3.** *Med.* Intussusception.

in·val'id (ĭn·văl'ĭd), *adj.* [L. *invalidus* not strong, infirm, inadequate. See IN- not; VALID.] Not valid; of no force, weight, or cogency; void; null.

in'va·lid (ĭn'vȧ·lĭd *or, esp. Brit.,* -lēd), *adj.* [L. & F.; F. *invalide*, adj. & n., fr. L. *invalidus*, adj.] **1.** Not well; sickly. **2.** Adapted for a sick person; as, *invalid* diet. — (ĭn'vȧ·lĭd *or, esp. Brit.,* ĭn'vȧ·lēd *or* ĭn'vȧ·lēd'), *n.* A person weak and infirm, esp. one in chronic ill health, or disabled for active service. — (ĭn'vȧ·lĭd *or, esp. Brit.,* ĭn'vȧ·lēd *or* ĭn'vȧ·lēd'), *v. t.* **1.** To make or render invalid or infirm. **2.** To classify, enroll, or dismiss from duty, as an invalid. — *v. i.* **1.** To lose health. **2.** Of a soldier or sailor, to retire because of ill health.

in·val'i·date (ĭn·văl'ĭ·dāt), *v. t.* To render invalid or null; to weaken or destroy the force of. — **Syn.** See NULLIFY. — **in·val'i·da'tion** (-dā'shŭn), *n.* — **in·val'i·da'tor** (-dā'tẽr), *n.*

in'va·lid·ism (ĭn'vȧ·lĭd·ĭz'm; *see* INVALID, *n.*), *n.* Chronic condition of being an invalid.

in'va·lid'i·ty (ĭn'vȧ·lĭd'ĭ·tĭ), *n.* Lack of validity or cogency.

in·val'u·a·ble (ĭn·văl'ū·ȧ·b'l), *adj.* Valuable beyond estimation; inestimable; priceless. — **Syn.** See COSTLY. — **in·val'u·a·bly**, *adv.*

In·var' (ĭn·vär'), *n.* A trade-mark for a nickel steel, containing about 36 per cent nickel, that expands practically not at all at ordinary temperatures.

in·var'i·a·ble (ĭn·vâr'ĭ·ȧ·b'l; 6), *adj.* Not given or subject to variation or change; unchangeable or unchanging; constant; uniform. — **in·var'i·a·bil'i·ty** (-bĭl'ĭ·tĭ), **in·var'i·a·ble·ness**, *n.* — **in·var'i·a·bly**, *adv.*

in·var'i·ant (-ănt), *adj.* Not variant; constant. — *n. Math.* An invariable quantity.

in·va'sion (ĭn·vā'zhŭn), *n.* [F., fr. LL. *invasio.* See INVADE.] **1.** Act of invading; incursion of an army for conquest or plunder. **2.** The incoming, or first attack, of anything hurtful.

in·va'sive (-sĭv), *adj.* Of, pertaining to, or characterized by invasion; tending to invade; aggressive; encroaching.

in·vec'tive (ĭn·vĕk'tĭv), *adj.* [F. *invectif*, fr. LL. *invectivus.* See INVEIGH.] Characterized by invective; using, or given to the use of, invective. — *n.* A violent or railing denunciation or accusation; hence, harsh, censorious, or denunciatory expression. — **Syn.** See ABUSE. — **in·vec'tive·ly**, *adv.* — **in·vec'tive·ness**, *n.*

in·veigh' (ĭn·vā'), *v. i.* [L. *invehere, invectum*, to carry or bring into or against, in passive, to attack with words, inveigh, fr. *in-* in + *vehere* to carry.] To declaim or rail bitterly; to utter severe denunciations; — with *against.* — **in·veigh'er**, *n.*

in·vei'gle (ĭn·vē'g'l; -vā'g'l), *v. t.;* IN·VEI'GLED (-g'ld); IN·VEI'GLING (-glĭng). [F. *aveugler* to blind, delude, fr. *aveugle* blind, fr. VL. *aboculus.* The pref. *in-* was substituted for *a-* taken as the pref. F. *à*, L. *ad.* See OCULAR.] To lead on or astray by blinding, or deceiving; to ensnare or win over by guile; to cajole. — **Syn.** See LURE. — **in·vei'gle·ment**, *n.* — **in·vei'gler** (-glẽr), *n.*

‖**in·ve'nit** (ĭn·vē'nĭt). [L.] (He or she) devised or invented it.

in·vent' (ĭn·vĕnt'), *v. t.* [L. *inventus*, past part. of *invenire* to come upon, find, invent, fr. *in-* in + *venire* to come.] **1.** *Archaic.* To come upon; find. **2.** To fabricate mentally; create or devise in the imagination; as, to *invent* a plot. **3.** To discover, as by study or experiment; produce for the first time; as, to *invent* printing. — **in·ven'tor, in·vent'er** (-vĕn'tẽr), *n.* — **in·vent'i·ble** (-vĕn'tĭ·b'l), *adj.*

Syn. Invent, create, discover mean to bring into being something new. Invent always implies fabrication, now especially as a result of study, experiment, etc.; create implies an evoking into being, originally out of nothing but, later, as if out of nothing; discover presupposes preexistence of something and lack of knowledge of it, and therefore implies its finding by exploration, investigation, etc. (as, one *invents* a device, *creates* a work of art, *discovers* the laws of motion).

in·ven'tion (ĭn·vĕn'shŭn), *n.* **1.** *Archaic.* Act of finding or finding out; discovery. **2.** The power of inventing, or conceiving, devising, originating, etc.; inventive skill or ingenuity. **3.** Act of inventing. **4.** Something invented; specif.: **a** A fabrication of the imagination; fiction; hence, falsehood. **b** A device, contrivance, or the like, originated after study and experiment. — **in·ven'tion·al** (-ăl; -'l), *adj.*

in·ven'tive (-tĭv), *adj.* Able and apt to invent; quick at contrivance. — **in·ven'tive·ly**, *adv.* — **in·ven'tive·ness**, *n.*

in'ven·to'ry (ĭn'vĕn·tō'rĭ *or, esp. Brit.,* -tẽr·ĭ, -trĭ), *n.; pl.* -RIES (-rĭz). [ML. *inventorium*, for L. *inventarium.* See INVENT.] **1.** A catalogue or schedule of the property of a person or an estate; hence, an itemized list of goods with their estimated worth; specif., an annual account of stock taken in any business. **2.** Goods or stock comprising an inventory. — *v. t.;* -RIED (-tō'rĭd; -tẽr·ĭd; -trĭd); -RY·ING. To make an inventory of. — **in'ven·to'ri·al** (-tō'rĭ·ăl), *adj.* — **in'ven·to'ri·al·ly**, *adv.*

in've·rac'i·ty (ĭn'vẽ·răs'ĭ·tĭ), *n.* Lack of veracity; also, a lie.

In'ver·ness' (ĭn'vẽr·nĕs'; 2), *n., or* **Inverness cape.** [From *Inverness*, Scotland.] A full sleeveless cape.

in·verse' (ĭn·vûrs'; ĭn'vûrs; 2), *adj.* [L. *inversus*, past part. of *invertere.* See INVERT.] Opposite in order, relation, or effect to that which is under consideration or is usual; reversed; inverted. — *n.* That which is inverse or the result of an inversion. — (ĭn·vûrs'), *v. t.* To invert or reverse. — **in·verse'ly** (ĭn·vûrs'lĭ; 2), *adv.*

in·ver'sion (ĭn·vûr'shŭn; -zhŭn), *n.* **1.** Act of inverting, or state or position of being inverted; a turning upside down or inside out; also, an inversing; reversal of position, order, or relation. **2.** *Chem.* **a** Conversion of a substance showing dextrorotation into one showing levorotation, or vice versa. Thus, cane sugar, which is dextrorotatory, yields by hydrolysis or *inversion* a levorotatory mixture of dextrose and levulose. **b** Improperly, the hydrolysis of any carbohydrate. **3.** *Meteorol.* Increase, instead of the usual decrease, of temperature of the air with increase of height. **4.** *Music.* Process or result of changing or reversing the relative positions of the elements of an interval, chord, phrase, or voice part, as by raising the lower or dropping the upper tone of an interval by an octave, or by repeating a phrase with its intervals in the contrary direction, etc. **5.** *Phonet.* The turning upward and backward of the tip of the tongue. **6.** *Psychopathol.* Homosexuality. **7.** *Rhet.* A change in the normal order of words and phrases.

in·ver'sive (ĭn·vûr'sĭv), *adj.* Manifesting inversion.

in·vert' (ĭn·vûrt'), *v. t.* [L. *invertere, inversum*, fr. *in-* in + *vertere* to turn.] **1.** To turn upside down, outside in, or inside out; as, to *invert* a cone. **2.** To reverse, as in order or relations; change to the reverse order, sense, condition, etc.; as, to *invert* a phrase. **3.** To subject to inversion (which see), as sugar or a chord. — **Syn.** See REVERSE. — **in·vert'i·ble** (-vûr'tĭ·b'l), *adj.*

in'vert (ĭn'vûrt), *adj. Chem.* Inverted. — *n.* **1.** One who or that which is inverted or is transformed by inversion. **2.** *Psychiatry.* = HOMOSEXUAL.

in·vert'ase (ĭn·vûr'tās), *n.* [*invert* + *-ase.*] *Biochem.* An enzyme, found in many plants and in animal intestines, capable of effecting the inversion of cane sugar.

in·ver'te·brate (ĭn·vûr'tē·brāt), *adj.* **1.** Without a backbone, or spinal column; of or pertaining to the invertebrates. **2.** Of persons, without moral backbone; weak-willed. — *n.* An invertebrate animal or person; specif., one of an obsolete division (Invertebrata) of the animal kingdom including all except the vertebrates.

in·vert'ed com'mas (ĭn·vûr'tĕd; -tĭd). Quotation marks.

in·vert'er (ĭn·vûr'tẽr), *n.* One who or that which inverts; specif., *Elec.*, a device for converting direct current into alternating current by either mechanical or electronic means.

invert sugar. A mixture of dextrose and levulose, found in fruits, and artificially formed by the inversion of sucrose; also, less properly, dextrose obtained from starch.

in·vest' (ĭn·vĕst'), *v. t.* [L. *investire, investitum*, fr. *in-* in + *vestire* to clothe, fr. *vestis* clothing.] **1.** *Now Rare.* To clothe, dress, or array. **2.** To envelop as, or as with, a garment; hence, to surround or endue as with something extrinsic; as, dignity *invests* every speech of his. **3.** To vest with the insignia of office; install ceremonially; as, to *invest* a king. **4.** *Now Rare.* **a** To confer or grant, as power; to vest, as a right (*in*). **b** To put on; to don. **5.** [It. *investire.*] To lay out (money or capital) in business with the view of obtaining an income or profit; to convert into some form of wealth other than money, as securities or real estate, with the expectation of deriving income. **6.** *Mil.* To surround with troops or ships so as to prevent escape or entry; to lay siege to; as, to *invest* a town. — *v. i.* To make an investment.

in·ves'ti·ga·ble (ĭn·vĕs'tĭ·gȧ·b'l), *adj.* That may be investigated.

in·ves'ti·gate (-gāt), *v. t. & i.* [L. *investigatus*, past part. of *investigare* to investigate, fr. *in-* in + *vestigare* to track, trace.] To follow up or make research by patient inquiry and observation and examination of facts. — **in·ves'ti·ga'tion** (-gā'shŭn), *n.* — **in·ves'ti·ga'tive** (-gā'tĭv), *adj.* — **in·ves'ti·ga'tor** (-gā'tẽr), *n.* — **in·ves'ti·ga·to'ry** (-gȧ·tō'rĭ *or, esp. Brit.,* -gā'tẽr·ĭ, -gȧ·tẽr·ĭ), *adj.*

in·ves'ti·tive (ĭn·vĕs'tĭ·tĭv), *adj. Law.* Operating to vest (a right); of or pertaining to such vesting.

in·ves'ti·ture (-tūr), *n.* **1.** Act or right of investing, as with an office; formal installation. **2.** That which invests, or clothes; vesture. **3.** *Feudal Law.* Livery of seizin.

in·vest'ment (ĭn·vĕst'mĕnt), *n.* **1.** Act of investing, or state of being invested; also, vestment; clothing; covering. **2.** The investing of money or capital for income or profit; also, the sum invested or the property purchased.

investment trust. An organization, frequently a corporation, for the purpose of investing moneys subscribed or loaned thereto and distributing the net return to stockholders or beneficiaries.

in·ves'tor (ĭn·vĕs'tẽr), *n.* One who invests.

in·vet'er·a·cy (ĭn·vĕt'ẽr·ȧ·sĭ), *n.* Inveterate character or condition.

in·vet'er·ate (-ĭt), *adj.* [L. *inveteratus*, past part. of *inveterare* to render old, fr. *in-* in + *vetus, veteris*, old.] **1.** Firmly established by age; deep-rooted; ineradicable; as, an *inveterate* dislike. **2.** Confirmed in a habit; habitual; as, an *inveterate* smoker. — **in·vet'er·ate·ly**, *adv.*

Syn. Inveterate, confirmed, chronic, deep-seated, deep-rooted mean firmly established, as a habit or disease. Inveterate implies such length of existence, as of a habit, a feeling, a tradition, etc., as to be practically ineradicable or unalterable; confirmed implies a growing stronger and firmer with time so that it (a habit, etc.) resists all attempts to uproot it; chronic applies to diseases, habits, conditions, etc., which persist in spite of all efforts to cure or alleviate them; deep-seated and deep-rooted stress the extent to which something has become imbedded in one's body, one's mind, etc.

in·vid'i·ous (ĭn·vĭd'ĭ·ŭs; 58), *adj.* [L. *invidiosus.* See ENVIOUS.] **1.** Tending to excite odium, ill will, or envy; likely to give offense; esp., unjustly discriminating. **2.** *Rare.* Envious. — **Syn.** See REPUGNANT. — **in·vid'i·ous·ly**, *adv.* — **in·vid'i·ous·ness**, *n.*

in·vig'i·late (ĭn·vĭj'ĭ·lāt), *v. i.* [L. *invigilare, -latum*, fr. *in-* in, on + *vigilare* watch.] To watch diligently; specif., *Brit.*, to proctor an examination. — **in·vig'i·la'tion** (-lā'shŭn), *n.* — **in·vig'i·la'tor** (-lā'tẽr), *n.*

in·vig'or·ant (ĭn·vĭg'ẽr·ănt), *n.* An invigorating agent.

in·vig'or·ate (-āt), *v. t.* [L. *in-* in + *vigor.*] To give vigor, life, or energy to; strengthen; animate. — **in·vig'or·at'ing·ly** (-āt'ĭng·lĭ), *adv.* — **in·vig'or·a'tion** (-ā'shŭn), *n.* — **in·vig'or·a'tive** (-ā'tĭv), *adj.* — **in·vig'or·a'tive·ly**, *adv.* — **in·vig'or·a'tor** (-ā'tẽr), *n.*

in·vin'ci·bil'i·ty (ĭn·vĭn'sĭ·bĭl'ĭ·tĭ), *n.* Quality or state of being invincible.

in·vin'ci·ble (ĭn·vĭn'sĭ·b'l), *adj.* [F., fr. L. *invincibilis.*] Incapable of being conquered, overcome, or subdued. — **in·vin'ci·ble·ness**, *n.* — **in·vin'ci·bly**, *adv.*

‖**in vi'no ve'ri·tas** (ĭn vī'nō vĕr'ĭ·tăs). [L.] (There is) truth in wine.

in·vi'o·la·ble (ĭn·vī'ō·lȧ·b'l), *adj.* **1.** Not violable or not to be violated; proof or secure against profanation, corruption, breach, etc. **2.** Incapable of being harmed, destroyed, etc., by violence. — **in·vi'o·la·bil'i·ty** (-bĭl'ĭ·tĭ), **in·vi'o·la·ble·ness**, *n.* — **in·vi'o·la·bly**, *adv.*

in·vi'o·late (-lāt), *adj.* Not violated; unimpaired; unprofaned. — **in·vi'o·late·ly**, *adv.* — **in·vi'o·late·ness**, *n.*

in·vis'i·ble (ĭn·vĭz'ĭ·b'l), *adj.* **1.** Incapable of being seen; not perceptible by vision; as, *invisible* beings. **2.** Not in sight; not presently apparent. **3.** Not manifest or obvious; indistinct; as, an *invisible* stripe; not acknowledged; as, *invisible* government. **4.** *Com. & Finance.* Not appearing in the regular statements; as, *invisible* assets. — *n.* One that is invisible; specif. [*cap.*], with *the*, God, or the unseen world. — **in·vis'i·bil'i·ty** (-bĭl'ĭ·tĭ), **in·vis'i·ble·ness**, *n.* — **in·vis'i·bly**, *adv.*

invisible ink. = SYMPATHETIC INK.

in'vi·ta'tion (ĭn'vĭ·tā'shŭn), *n.* **1.** Act of inviting; solicitation; also,

the written, printed, or spoken expression by which one is invited. **2.** A drawing one on; allurement; enticement. — **in′vi·ta′tion·al** (ĭn′vĭ·tā′shŭn·ăl; -′l), *adj.*
in·vi′ta·to′ry (ĭn·vī′tȧ·tō′rĭ *or, esp. Brit.,* -tĕr·ĭ), *adj.* Containing invitation.
in·vite′ (ĭn·vīt′), *v. t.* [F. *inviter*, fr. L. *invitare*.] **1.** To request graciously, politely, or formally, the presence or attendance of; to ask to come as a guest, a participant, etc. **2.** To urge courteously; also, to request a person or persons to give, pay, utter, etc.; as, to *invite* donations. **3.** To induce by encouraging; tempt; as, the quiet *invites* sleep. — **in·vit′er** (-vīt′ẽr), *n.*
Syn. **Invite, solicit, court** mean to encourage a falling in with one's plans or desires. **Invite** often implies a courteous or attractive method of requesting one's presence, one's participation, or the like, but sometimes implies merely an attracting or tempting; **solicit** suggests urgency rather than courtesy in encouraging; **court** suggests an endeavor to win something, such as the love of a lady or the favor of the public, by suitable words or acts.
in·vit′ing (ĭn·vīt′ĭng), *adj.* That invites; alluring; tempting. — **in·vit′ing·ly**, *adv.* — **in·vit′ing·ness**, *n.*
in vi′tro (ĭn vī′trō). [L.] In glass; hence, in a test tube, beaker, etc.; as, digestion *in vitro* Cf. IN VIVO.
in vi′vo (vī′vō). In a living organism, as a man, animal, or plant. Cf. IN VITRO.
in′vo·cate (ĭn′vō·kāt), *v. t. & i.* [L. *invocatus*, past part. of *invocare*. See INVOKE.] *Now Rare.* To make an invocation (to). — **in·voc′a·tive** (ĭn·vŏk′ȧ·tĭv; ĭn′vō·kā′tĭv), *adj.* — **in′vo·ca′tor** (ĭn′vō·kā′tẽr), *n.* — **in·voc′a·to′ry** (ĭn·vŏk′ȧ·tō′rĭ *or, esp. Brit.,* -tẽr·ĭ), *adj.*
in′vo·ca′tion (-kā′shŭn), *n.* **1.** Act of invoking; prayer or solemn entreaty, esp. for a blessing, aid, or intercession. **2.** An invocatory prayer or plea; specif.: **a** A prayer, esp. one offered at the beginning of a service. **b** In the classic epic or similar poems, a formal introductory appeal for the aid, as of a Muse. **3.** Act of, or formula for, conjuring, or summoning devils, spirits, etc.; incantation. **4.** *Law.* A judicial calling in of papers or evidence from another case into court.
in′voice (ĭn′vois), *n.* [F. *envois* things sent, goods forwarded, pl. of *envoi*, fr. *envoyer* to send. See ENVOY.] **1.** An itemized statement of merchandise shipped or sent to a purchaser, consignee, etc., with the quantity, value or prices, and charges annexed. **2.** The lot or set of goods as shipped or received. — *v. t.;* -VOICED (-voist); -VOIC·ING (-vois·ĭng). To make an invoice of; to enter in an invoice.
in·voke′ (ĭn·vōk′), *v. t.* [F. *invoquer*, fr. L. *invocare*, fr. *in-* in, on + *vocare* to call, fr. *vox* voice.] **1.** To call on for aid or protection; to address an invocation, or prayer, to. **2.** To call forth by incantation, etc.; conjure. **3.** To appeal to for support; to cite; as, to *invoke* Plato. — **in·vok′er** (ĭn·vōk′ẽr), *n.*
in·vol′u·cel (ĭn·vŏl′ū·sĕl), *n.* *Bot.* A secondary involucre, subtending the branches of a compound umbel. See INVOLUCRE, *Illust.*
in′vo·lu′cral (ĭn′vō·lū′krăl), *adj.* *Bot.* Pertaining to, or resembling, an involucre.
in′vo·lu′crate (-krāt), *adj.* *Bot.* Having an involucre.
in′vo·lu′cre (ĭn′vō·lū′kẽr), *n.* Also **in′vo·lu′crum** (ĭn′vō·lū′krŭm); *pl.* -CRA (-krȧ). [F., fr. L. *involucrum* a covering, fr. *involvere*. See INVOLVE.] *Bot.* In seed plants, a whorl or rosette of bracts, often resembling an ordinary calyx, subtending or supporting a flower cluster or fruit. Involucres are characteristic of all composites, as the daisy.

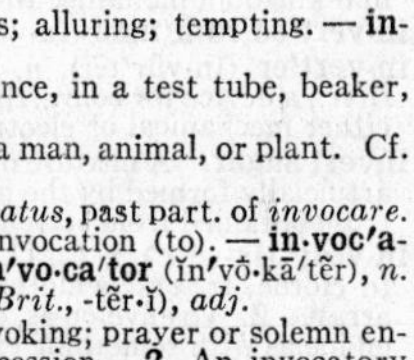

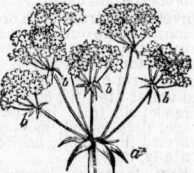

a Involucre, and *b, b, b, b* Involucels, of a Compound Umbel.

in·vol′un·tar′y (ĭn·vŏl′ŭn·tĕr′ĭ *or, esp. Brit.,* -tẽr·ĭ, -trĭ), *adj.* **1.** Not voluntary; not done, given, etc., willingly, by choice, or by an act of the will; as, *involuntary* submission or weeping. **2.** Not under the control of the will, as an organ or its action; as, an *involuntary* muscle. — **in·vol′un·tar′i·ly**, *adv.* — **in·vol′un·tar′i·ness**, *n.*
in′vo·lute (ĭn′vō·lūt; 114), *adj.* [L. *involutus*, past part. of *involvere*. See INVOLVE.] **1.** Involved; intricate; as, an *involute* plot. **2.** *Bot.* Rolled inward at the margin or edges, as foliage leaves in vernation, or floral leaves in estivation. **3.** *Zool.* Having the whorls closely coiled; convolute; as, an *involute* shell. — *n.* Something intricate or involved; specif., *Geom.*, a curve traced by any point of a perfectly flexible inextensible thread kept taut as it is wound upon or unwound from another curve. See EVOLUTE.
in′vo·lut′ed (-lūt′ĕd; -ĭd), *adj.* Involute. — **in′vo·lut′ed·ly**, *adv.*
in′vo·lu′tion (-lū′shŭn), *n.* [L. *involutio*. See INVOLVE.] **1.** An involving or infolding; also, that which is involved. **2.** State of being involved; complication; entanglement; hence, something entangled. **3.** *Biol.* Retrograde development; degeneration. **4.** *Gram.* An involved construction; esp., one caused by inserting clauses between the subject and predicate. **5.** *Math.* Act or process of raising a quantity or symbol to any assigned power; — the inverse of *evolution.* **6.** *Med.* The return of an enlarged part or organ to its normal size, as of the uterus after pregnancy. **7.** *Physiol.* Presenile decline, marked by the menopause in women and by the decrease of vital force in both sexes. — **in′vo·lu′tion·al** (-ăl; -′l), *n.* — **in′vo·lu′tion·ar′y** (-ĕr′ĭ *or, esp. Brit.,* -ẽr·ĭ), *adj.*
in·volve′ (ĭn·vŏlv′), *v. t.* [OF. or L.; OF. *involver*, fr. L. *involvere*, *involutum*, to roll about, wrap up, fr. *in-* in + *volvere* to roll.] **1.** To roll about, or infold, esp. so as to conceal, obscure, cause perplexity, etc.; envelop. **2.** To draw into a complication; implicate. **3.** To complicate or make intricate in thought or form. **4.** To wind or coil; roll up intricately. **5.** To roll up in itself so as to gather in, embrace, or comprehend; include; as, this problem *involves* the others. **6.** To contain by implication; to require, as implied conditions, effect, etc.; as, surrender *involves* submission. **7.** To occupy (oneself) absorbingly or engrossingly; — usually passive. — **Syn.** See INCLUDE. — **in·volve′ment**, *n.* — **in·volv′er**, *n.*
in·volved′ (ĭn·vŏlvd′), *adj.* **1.** That is involved; complex. **2.** *Zool.* = INVOLUTE, 3. — **Syn.** See COMPLEX.
in·vul′ner·a·ble (ĭn·vŭl′nẽr·ȧ·b′l), *adj.* Incapable of being wounded or injured; hence, proof against attack; unassailable. — **in·vul′ner·a·bil′i·ty** (-bĭl′ĭ·tĭ), **in·vul′ner·a·ble·ness**, *n.* — **in·vul′ner·a·bly**, *adv.*
in′wall′ (ĭn′wôl′), *n.* An inner wall, as of a blast furnace.
in·wall′ (ĭn·wôl′), *v. t.* To enclose with or as with a wall.
in′ward (ĭn′wẽrd) **in′wards** (-wẽrdz), *adv.* [AS. *inweard.*] **1.** Toward the inside, center, or interior. **2.** *Obs.* Internally. **3.** Into, or toward, the mind or thoughts.
in′ward, *adj.* **1.** Being or placed within; inner; — opposed to *outward.* **2.** Specif.: **a** Of or belonging to the inner life; spiritual. **b** Inland; interior; as, *inward* Africa. **3.** *Archaic.* Domestic; intestine. **4.** Going inward; ingoing. **5.** *Obs.* **a** Intimate; familiar. **b** Secret; private. — *n.* That which is inward; esp., *pl.:* **a** (*colloq.* ĭn′ẽrdz) The entrails. **b** *Eng.* Imports or dues on imports.
in′ward·ly (ĭn′wẽrd·lĭ), *adv.* **1.** Internally. **2.** In spirit; secretly. **3.** Toward the center. **4.** *Archaic.* Intimately.
in′ward·ness, *n.* **1.** Internal or true state; intrinsic nature. **2.** Quality or state of being inward, esp. spiritually. **3.** *Now Rare.* Intimacy. **4.** Sincerity.
in′wards (ĭn′wẽrdz), *adv.* Inward.
in·weave′ (ĭn·wēv′), *v. t.;* see WEAVE. To weave in or together; interweave; interlace.
in·wind′ (ĭn·wīnd′), **en·wind′** (ĕn-), *v. t.;* see WIND. To wind in or about; entwine.
in·wo′ven (ĭn·wō′vĕn), *adj.* Woven in; interwoven.
in·wrap′ (ĭn·răp′), *v. t.;* see WRAP. To enwrap.
in·wreathe′ (ĭn·rēth′), *v. t.* To enwreathe.
in·wrought′ (ĭn·rôt′; ĭn′rôt′; 2), *adj.* Wrought or worked in or among other things; inwoven into a fabric; of a fabric, wrought or adorned, as with figures.
I′o (ī′ō), *n.* [L., fr. Gr. *Iō.*] *Gr. Myth.* A maiden loved by Zeus. Hera, from jealousy, changed her into a heifer and set the hundred-eyed Argus to watch her.
i′o·date (ī′ō·dāt), *v. t.* To impregnate or treat with iodine. — *n.* *Chem.* A salt of iodic acid, HIO_3. — **i′o·da′tion** (-dā′shŭn), *n.*
i·od′ic (ī·ŏd′ĭk), *adj.* [See IODINE.] Pertaining to, caused by, or containing iodine; specif., *Chem.*, denoting those compounds in which iodine has a valence of five.
i′o·dide (ī′ō·dīd; -dĭd), *n.* Also **i′o·did.** *Chem.*, A compound of iodine with another element or radical; a salt or ester of hydriodic acid.
i′o·dine (ī′ō·dīn; -dĭn; *by chemists generally* -dēn *or, less often,* -dĭn), *n.* Also **i′o·din.** [F. *iode* iodine (fr. Gr. *iōdēs* violetlike, fr. *ion* a violet + *eidos* form) + E. chlor*ine;* — from its violet vapor.] *Chem.* A nonmetallic element of the halogen group, isolated as a shining, blackish-gray, crystalline solid of peculiar chlorinelike odor. Symbol, *I;* at. no., 53; at. wt., 126.91.
i′o·dism (ī′ō·dĭz′m), *n.* *Med.* A morbid state produced by the use of iodine and its compounds.
i′o·dize (-dīz), *v. t.* To treat with iodine or an iodide, as a photographic plate.
i·o′do- (ī·ō′dō-; ī′ō·dō-), **iod-**. [NL. *iodum* iodine.] *Chem.* A combining form meaning *iodine;* denoting also *an iodine compound.*
i·o′do·form (ī·ō′dō·fôrm; ī·ŏd′ō-), *n.* [*iodo-* + *formyl.*] *Chem.* A crystalline, volatile compound, CHI_3, used as a healing and antiseptic dressing for wounds and sores.
i′o·dol (ī′ō·dōl; -dŏl), *n.* [*iod-* + pyrr*ole.*] A crystalline compound, C_4HI_4N, used like iodoform.
i·o′dous (ī·ō′dŭs; ī·ŏd′ŭs), *adj.* Pert. to or containing iodine; as, **iodous acid** (a hypothetical acid, HIO_2).
i′o·lite (ī′ō·līt), *n.* [Gr. *ion* violet + *-lite.*] *Mineral.* An orthorhombic mineral of various shades of blue, with glassy luster and strong dichroism. It is a silicate of aluminum, iron, and magnesium, easily altered by exposure.
I′o moth (ī′ō). [See IO.] A large handsome American moth (*Automeris io*), with a spot on each hind wing, resembling the spots on the tail of a peacock.
i′on (ī′ŏn), *n.* [Gr. *ion*, neuter of *iōn*, pres. part. of *ienai* to go.] *Chem. & Physics.* An electrically charged atom or group of atoms. Some compounds (salts, bases, acids) are thought to consist wholly or partly of ions held together by electric attraction. In electrolysis the negative ions (*anions*, containing an excess of one or more electrons, denoted by minus signs, as Cl^-, SO_4^{--}) move toward the anode, while the positive ions (*cations*, deficient in electrons, as Na^+, Ba^{++}) move toward the cathode. In gases a molecule may lose an electron, as by the action of X rays, thus becoming a positive ion; the free electron may attach itself to another molecule, forming a negative ion.
-ion. [F. or L.; F. *-ion*, fr. L. *-io, -ionis.*] A suffix forming nouns meaning: **a** Act or process; also, its result; as in solut*ion*, rebell*ion*. **b** State or condition; also, a thing acted upon or so conditioned; as in subject*ion*, ambit*ion*.
i·on′ic (ī·ŏn′ĭk), *adj.* [*ion* + *-ic.*] Of, pertaining to, or existing in the form of ions or an ion; as, *ionic* hydrogen.
I·on′ic (ī·ŏn′ĭk), *adj.* [L. *Ionicus*, fr. Gr. *Iōnikos.*] **1.** Of or pertaining to Ionia (see *Gaz.*) or the Ionians. **2.** *Arch.* Of, pertaining to, or designating the Ionic order of architecture, distinguished esp. by the spiral volutes of its capital. See ORDER, *Illust.* **3.** *Pros.* Designating a kind of foot, verse, or meter. See IONIC, *n.*, 2. — *n.* **1.** The Ionic dialect. See GREEK, *n.*, 4. **2.** *Gr. & Lat. Pros.* **a** A foot consisting of four syllables: either two long and two short (––⏑⏑), called the ***greater Ionic***, or two short and two long (⏑⏑––), called the ***smaller Ionic.*** **b** A verse or meter of Ionic feet. **3.** *Print.* A kind of heavy-faced, legible type.

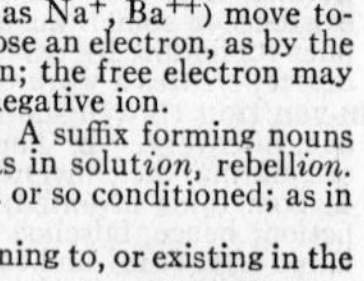

Greek Ionic Capital. **1** Volute; **2** Listel; **3** Bolster; **4** Necking; **5** Shaft; **6** Abacus; **7** Anthemion Band.

i·o′ni·um (ī·ō′nĭ·ŭm; 58), *n.* [*ion* + *-ium;* — from its ionizing action.] *Chem.* A radioactive isotope of thorium, of at. wt. 230.
i′on·ize (ī′ŏn·īz), *v. t. & i.* [*ion* + *-ize.*] *Physics & Chem.* **a** To convert or be converted (wholly or partly) into ions. **b** To render or become conducting, supposedly by formation of ions. — **i′on·i·za′tion** (-ĭ·zā′shŭn; -ī·zā′-), *n.* — **i′on·iz′er** (-īz′ẽr), *n.*
i′o·none (ī′ō·nōn), *n.* [Gr. *ion* violet + ket*one.*] *Chem.* Either of two isomeric compounds ($C_{13}H_{20}O$) with the scent of violets, found in orrisroot, also prepared from citral.
i·on′o·sphere (ī·ŏn′ō·sfēr; ī·ō′nō-), *n.* *Radio.* A region of electrically charged (ionized) air beginning about 25 miles above the surface of the earth, by means of which radio waves are transmitted to great distances. It includes several layers (D layer, E layer, F1 layer, F2 layer) that vary in height and ionization with season and time of day. The air particles in the ionosphere are ionized by the ultraviolet rays from the sun, and to a less extent by the charged particles from the sun. — **i·on′o·spher′ic** (-sfĕr′ĭk), *adj.*

i·o'ta (ī·ō'tȧ), *n.* [L., fr. Gr. *iōta.*] **1.** The ninth (and smallest) letter (I, ι) of the Greek alphabet, corresponding to the English *I, i.* **2.** A very small quantity; a jot.

i·o'ta·cism (ī·ō'tȧ·sĭz'm), *n.* [LL. *iotacismus,* fr. Gr. *iōtakismos.*] Excessive use of the letter iota or I or of its sound.

I O U (ī' ō' ū'). [I owe you.] A paper having on it the letters *I O U,* with a sum named, and signed as an acknowledgment of debt.

-ious. An adjective suffix, *-ous* following thematic *-i,* as in ambit*ious,* invid*ious;* — often in adjectives corresponding to nouns in *-ion.*

ip'e·cac (ĭp'ē·kăk), **ip'e·cac'u·an'ha** (-kăk'ū·ăn'ȧ), *n.* [Pg. *ipecacuanha,* fr. Tupi *ipe-caa-goéne,* lit., small roadside emetic plant.] **1.** A tropical South American creeping plant (*Cephaëlis ipecacuanha*) of the madder family, with drooping flowers. **2.** The dried rhizome and roots of this plant, or a tincture from them, used esp. as an expectorant and emetic, and as a specific in amoebic dysentery.

Iph'i·ge·ni'a (ĭf'ĭ·jē·nī'ȧ), *n.* [L., fr. Gr. *Iphigeneia.*] *Greek Mythology.* A daughter of Agamemnon and Clytemnestra, offered by her father as a sacrifice to Artemis, who saved and made her a priestess.

ip'o·moe'a (ĭp'ō·mē'ȧ; ī'pō-), *n.* [NL., fr. Gr. *ips, ipos,* a kind of worm + *homoios* like.] Any of a genus (*Ipomoea*) of herbaceous vines, the morning-glories.

ip'se dix'it (ĭp'sē dĭk'sĭt). [L.] Literally, he himself has said (it); hence, an assertion made but not proved. Cf. DIXIT.

‖**ip·sis'si·ma ver'ba** (ĭp·sĭs'ĭ·mȧ vûr'bȧ). [L.] The very words, or language.

‖**ip'so fac'to** (ĭp'sō făk'tō). [L.] By the fact or act itself; by the very nature of the case.

‖**ip'so ju're** (jōō'rē). [L.] By the law itself; by operation of law.

IQ, I. Q. (ī'kū'); *pl.* IQs or I.Q.'s (ī'kūz'). Intelligence quotient.

ir- (ĭr-). An assimilated form of *in-,* as in *ir*rational.

i'ra·cund (ī'rȧ·kŭnd), *adj.* [L. *iracundus,* fr. *ira* anger.] Irascible; choleric. — **i'ra·cun'di·ty** (-kŭn'dĭ·tĭ), *n.*

i·ra'de (ē·rä'dĕ), *n.* [Turk., fr. Ar. *irādah* will, desire.] A decree of a Mohammedan ruler, as formerly of the sultan.

I·ra'ni·an (ī·rā'nĭ·ăn; 58), *adj.* Of or pertaining to Iran (see *Gaz.*), the Iranians, or their speech. — *n.* **1.** A native of Iran; specif., a Caucasian of Iranian speech. **2.** A branch of the Indo-Iranian subfamily of languages; Modern Persian. See PERSIAN, *n.,* 2; INDO-EUROPEAN LANGUAGES, *Table.*

I·ra'qi (ē·rä'kē), *n.* **1.** One of the natives of Iraq (see *Gaz.*), chiefly of Arabic race. **2.** The modern Arabic dialect spoken in Iraq. — **I·ra'qi, I·ra'qi·an** (-kĭ·ăn), *adj.*

Iraqi dinar. See DINAR, 3.

i·ras'ci·ble (ī·răs'ĭ·b'l; ĭ·răs'-), *adj.* [F., fr. LL. *irascibilis,* fr. *irasci* to be angry, fr. *ira* anger.] Prone to anger; choleric. — **i·ras'ci·bil'i·ty** (-bĭl'ĭ·tĭ), **i·ras'ci·ble·ness,** *n.* — **i·ras'ci·bly,** *adv.*

Syn. **Irascible, choleric, splenetic, testy, techy, touchy, cranky, cross** mean easily angered. **Irascible** implies an inflammable temper or a disposition to be incensed on slight provocation; **choleric,** excitability, unreasonableness, and an impatient and irritable frame of mind; **splenetic** a temperament given to moroseness and fits of spleen; **testy,** irascibility occasioned by small annoyances; **techy** and **touchy,** undue irritability or oversensitiveness; **cranky** and **cross,** a difficulty in pleasing or satisfying, *cranky* because of fixed notions, standards, or the like, *cross* because one is out of sorts.

i'rate (ī'rāt; ī·rāt'), *adj.* [L. *iratus,* fr. *irasci* to be angry.] Angry; enraged. — **Syn.** See ANGRY. — **i'rate·ly,** *adv.*

ire (īr), *n.* [OF., fr. L. *ira.*] Anger; wrath. — **Syn.** See ANGER.

ire'ful (-fōōl; -f'l), *adj.* Full of ire; angry; irascible. — **ire'ful·ly,** *adv.*

i·ren'ic (ī·rĕn'ĭk; -rē'nĭk), *adj.* Also **i·ren'i·cal** (-ĭ·kăl). [Gr. *eirēnikos.*] Pacific; peaceful; conciliatory.

i·ren'ics (ī·rĕn'ĭks; -rē'nĭks), *n.;* see -ICS. *Eccl.* Irenical, as distinguished from polemical, theology; theology concerned with securing Christian unity.

irid-. = IRIDO-, as in **ir'i·dec'to·my** (see -ECTOMY).

i'ri·da'ceous (ī'rĭ·dā'shŭs; ĭr'ĭ-), *adj.* [See IRIS.] Belonging to the iris family (Iridaceae). See IRIS.

ir'i·des'cence (ĭr'ĭ·dĕs'ĕns; -'ns), *n.* A rainbowlike play of colors, as in the soap bubble, mother-of-pearl, etc.

ir'i·des'cent (-ĕnt; -'nt), *adj.* [L. *iris, iridis,* the rainbow.] Having or exhibiting iridescence. — **ir'i·des'cent·ly,** *adv.*

i·rid'ic (ī·rĭd'ĭk), *adj.* *Chem.* Of or pertaining to iridium.

i·rid'i·um (ī·rĭd'ĭ·ŭm; ĭ-), *n.* [NL., fr. L. *iris, iridis,* the rainbow; — from the iridescence of some of its solutions.] A rare silver-white metallic element resembling platinum, but harder and brittle. It is one of the heaviest substances known (sp. gr., 22.4). Symbol, *Ir;* at. no., 77; at. wt., 193.1.

ir'i·do- (ĭr'ĭ·dō-; ī'rĭ·dō), **irid-.** [Gr. *iris, iridos.*] A combining form denoting *the iris,* used chiefly in *Anat., Med., & Surg.,* as in **ir'i·dot'o·my** (see -TOMY).

ir'i·dos'mine (ĭr'ĭ·dŏz'mĭn; ī'rĭ-; -dŏs'mĭn), *n.* Also **ir'i·dos'mi·um** (-mĭ·ŭm). [See IRIDIUM; OSMIUM.] *Mineral.* A native alloy of iridium and osmium, containing some rhodium, platinum, etc., used for pen points, compass bearings, etc. H., 7.

i'ris (ī'rĭs), *n.; pl.* IRISES (-ĕz; -ĭz), IRIDES (ĭr'ĭ·dēz; ī'rĭ-). [L. *Iris, Iridis,* the goddess, the rainbow, a sweet-smelling plant, fr. Gr. *Iris, Iridos,* also (l.c.) iris of the eye.] **1.** [*cap.*] *Gr. Relig.* Goddess of the rainbow; in the *Iliad,* messenger of Zeus and Hera. **2.** The rainbow. **3.** A rainbowlike play of colors. **4.** *Anat.* The opaque contractile diaphragm perforated by the pupil and forming the colored portion of the eye. See EYE, *Illust.* **5.** Any of a large genus (*Iris*) typifying a family (Iridaceae, the iris family) of perennial plants. The irises have large, handsome flowers of many colors. See BLUE FLAG.

iris diaphragm. *Optics.* An adjustable diaphragm of thin opaque plates which can be turned by a ring so as to change the diameter of a central opening, usually employed to regulate the aperture of a lens in cameras, microscopes, and other optical instruments.

I'rish (ī'rĭsh), *adj.* [ME. also *Irisc,* fr. stem of AS. *Īras,* ON. *Īrar,* the Irish (fr. OIr. *Ériu,* Ir. *Éire,* Ireland) + *-isc* -ish.] **1.** Of, pertaining to, or characteristic of Ireland or its inhabitants. **2.** Designating or pertaining to the Celtic speech of Ireland. — *n.* **1.** *pl.* IRISH. Natives or inhabitants of Ireland or their immediate descendants, esp. those of Celtic race. **2.** The Irish language (see INDO-EUROPEAN LANGUAGES, *Table*); specif.: **a** The Irish branch of Goidelic; the Celtic speech of Ireland. **b** English as spoken by the Irish.

Irish bull. = 1st BULL (a blunder).

Irish daisy. The dandelion.

I'rish·ism (ī'rĭsh·ĭz'm), *n.* An action, expression, idiom, etc., peculiar to the Irish; a Hibernicism.

I'rish·man (-măn), *n.* A man born in Ireland or of Irish descent; a Hibernian. — **I'rish·wom'an** (-wŏŏm'ăn), *n.*

Irish moss. See CARRAGEEN.

Irish potato. The ordinary white potato.

Irish setter. See SETTER.

Irish stew. A stew having as chief ingredients meat, potatoes, and onions, cut small, and having a thick gravy.

Irish terrier. A small dog of an old Irish breed having a dense wiry coat, usually red, and famous for gameness.

i·ri'tis (ī·rī'tĭs), *n.* [NL. See IRIS; -ITIS.] Inflammation of the iris of the eye. — **i·rit'ic** (ī·rĭt'ĭk), *adj.*

irk (ûrk), *v. t.* [ME. *irken.*] To weary or trouble; to annoy; bore. — **Syn.** See ANNOY.

irk'some (-sŭm), *adj.* Wearisome; tedious; formerly, disgusting; painful. — **irk'some·ly,** *adv.* — **irk'some·ness,** *n.*

i'ron (ī'ērn; *by some,* ī'rŭn), *n.* [AS. *īren, īsen, īsern.*] **1.** A silver-white metallic element, malleable and ductile, strongly attracted by magnets, readily oxidized (rusted) in moist air. Symbol, *Fe* (Latin *ferrum*); at. no., 26; at. wt., 55.85. Found almost universally in combined forms, it constitutes about 5 per cent of the earth's crust. Pure iron melts at 1535° C. (2795° F.), has a sp. gr. of 7.86, and weighs 491 lbs. per cu. foot. The chief commercial forms of iron are *steel, cast iron, wrought iron,* and *ingot iron* (see these terms). Cf. PIG IRON. **2.** An iron weapon; specif.: **a** *Obs.* A sword. **b** *Slang.* A portable firearm; — more fully a *shooting iron.* **3.** *pl.* Iron fetters, chains, or shackles; manacles. **4.** An instrument, utensil, appliance, etc., made of iron; specif.: **a** A branding or cauterizing iron. **b** A harpoon. **c** A flatiron. **5.** Strength; power; firmness; as, rule with a rod of *iron.* **6.** *Golf.* A golf club with an iron head; also, specif., a midiron. See GOLF, *Illust.* — ***in,* or *into, irons.*** *Naut.* Of a sailing vessel, incapable of coming about or filling away.

— *adj.* **1.** Of, or made of, iron; consisting of iron; as, an *iron* bar; also, loosely, made of or consisting of steel. **2.** Like iron in appearance or in strength, inflexibility, insensibility, etc.; robust; unrelenting; cruel.

— *v. t.* **1.** To furnish, arm, or cover with iron. **2.** To shackle with irons. **3.** To smooth with an instrument of iron, esp. a heated flatiron. — *v. i.* To iron clothes.

Iron Age. **a** *Archaeol.* An epoch (c. 1000 B.C.–A.D. 100) marked by expert use of bronze, knowledge of iron, use of domestic animals, and skill in pottery. **b** [*not cap.*] *Class. Myth.* The last and worst age of the world, marked by toil, selfishness, and degeneracy.

i'ron·bark' (ī'ērn·bärk'; *see* IRON, *n.*), *n., or* **ironbark tree.** Any of several Australian eucalypti (as *Eucalyptus sideroxylon, E. paniculata*) having hard gray bark and useful timber.

i'ron·bound' (-bound'; 2), *adj.* Bound with iron or as if with iron; hence: **a** Harsh or rugged; as, an *ironbound* coast. **b** Rigid; unyielding; as, *ironbound* traditions.

i'ron·clad' (-klăd'; 2), *adj.* **1.** Clad in iron. **2.** *Colloq.* Rigorous; exacting.

i'ron·clad', *n.* An ironclad or armored naval vessel.

iron curtain. A barrier created by censorship, prohibition of free travel, etc., to isolate Russian-controlled territory from outside contact and communication; — a term made popular by Winston Churchill.

i'ron·er (ī'ērn·ēr; *see* IRON), *n.* One that irons.

iron gray. A nearly neutral gray, somewhat resembling the color of cast iron freshly broken. — **i'ron–gray', i'ron–grey'** (*see Pron.,* § 2), *adj.*

iron horse. *Colloq.* A locomotive engine; also, a bicycle or a tricycle.

i·ron'i·cal (ī·rŏn'ĭ·kăl), *adj.* Also **i·ron'ic** (-ĭk). [LL. *ironicus,* fr. Gr. *eirōnikos* dissembling. See IRONY, *n.*] **1.** Of, using, or of the nature of irony. **2.** Addicted to the use of irony. — **i·ron'i·cal·ly,** *adv.* — **i·ron'i·cal·ness,** *n.*

iron lung. A device for artificial respiration in which rhythmic alternations in the air pressure in a chamber surrounding a patient's chest force air into and out of the lungs. It is of special value when the nerves governing the chest muscles fail to function because of infantile paralysis.

i'ron·mas'ter (ī'ērn·măs'tēr), *n.* A manufacturer of iron.

i'ron·mon'ger (-mŭng'gēr), *n.* *Chiefly British.* A dealer in iron goods or hardware. — **i'ron·mon'ger·y** (-ĭ), *n.*

iron pyrites. See PYRITES.

iron ration. An emergency ration, esp. D ration.

i'ron·side' (ī'ērn·sīd'), *n.* **1.** A man of great strength or bravery; specif. [*cap.*], also **I'ron·sides'** (-sīdz'), Oliver Cromwell. **2.** [*cap.*] *pl.* Cromwell's cavalry in the English Civil War. **3.** *pl. Nav.* An ironclad.

i'ron·smith' (-smĭth'), *n.* An ironworker; a blacksmith.

i'ron·stone' (-stōn'), *n.* Any hard ore of iron; siderite.

i'ron·ware' (-wâr'), *n.* Articles made of iron; hardware.

i'ron·weed' (-wēd'), *n.* In America, any of a genus (*Vernonia*) of herbs or shrubs of the aster family, having terminal cymose heads of tubular flowers, mostly red or purple.

i'ron·wood' (-wŏŏd'), *n.* Any of many trees or shrubs with unusually hard, strong, or heavy wood; also, their wood.

i'ron·work' (-wûrk'), *n.* **1.** Work in iron. **2.** *pl., sometimes construed as a sing.* A mill or building where iron or steel is smelted, or heavy iron or steel products are made. — **i'ron·work'er** (-wûr'kēr), *n.*

i'ro·ny (ī'rō·nĭ), *n.; pl.* IRONIES (-nĭz). [L. *ironia,* fr. Gr. *eirōneia* dissimulation, fr. *eirōn* a dissembler in speech.] **1.** Simulation of ignorance, chiefly in Socratic irony (see SOCRATIC IRONY). **2. a** A sort of humor, ridicule, or light sarcasm, the intended implication of which is the opposite of the literal sense of the words; also, the figure of speech using this. **b** An ironical utterance or expression. **3.** A state of affairs or a result opposite to and as if in mockery of the appropriate result; as, the *irony* of fate. — **Syn.** See WIT.

Ir'o·quoi'an (ĭr'ō·kwoi'ăn), *adj.* Of, pertaining to, or designating one of the principal linguistic families of the North American Indians, including the Cherokee, Erie, Wyandot or Huron, and the six Iroquois tribes.

Ir'o·quois (ĭr'ō·kwoi; ĭr'ō·kwoiz), *n. sing. & pl.* [F., fr. the Algonquin name.] An Indian of a powerful and warlike confederacy (the Five Nations) formerly inhabiting central New York. The original tribes were the Mohawk, Oneida, Onondaga, Cayuga, and Seneca; in 1722 the Tuscarora were admitted.

ir·ra'di·ant (ĭ·rā'dĭ·ănt), *adj.* Irradiating or illuminating. — **ir·ra'di·ance** (-ăns), *n.* — **ir·ra'di·an·cy** (-ăn·sĭ), *n.*

ir·ra'di·ate (-āt), *v. t.* [L. *irradiatus,* past part. of *irradiare* to irradiate.] **1.** To throw rays of light upon; to illuminate; to brighten. **2.** To enlighten intellectually or spiritually. **3.** To radiate, shed, or diffuse. **4.** To treat by radiant heat or other radiant energy; specif., *Med., Chem., etc.,* to treat by exposure to radiation, as of ultraviolet light, radium, etc. — *v. i.* To emit rays; to be radiant. — (-āt), *adj.* Made brilliant; illuminated. — **ir·ra′di·a′tive** (-ā′tĭv; -ȧ·tĭv), *adj.*

ir·ra′di·a′tion (ĭ·rā′dĭ·ā′shŭn), *n.* **1.** An irradiating; state of being irradiated; illumination; irradiance. **2.** Mental light or illumination. **3.** A ray, as of light. **4. a** Exposure to any type of rays, as ultraviolet light. **b** Application of X rays, radium rays, or other radiation, as for therapeutic purposes. **5.** *Physics.* The radiant power per unit area on an intercepting surface at a point.

ir·ra′tion·al (ĭr·răsh′ŭn·ăl; -′l), *adj.* [L. *irrationalis.*] Not rational; specif.: **a** Not endowed with reason or understanding. **b** Not according to reason; unreasonable. **c** *Gr. & Lat. Pros.* Not preserving the normal ratio between arsis and thesis (see RATIONAL); — applied to (1) a long syllable used where the normal measure calls for a short; or (2) a foot containing such a syllable. **d** *Math.* Not expressible as an integer or as the quotient of two integers; surd. — **ir·ra′tion·al·ly,** *adv.* — **ir·ra′tion·al·ness,** *n.*

Syn. **Irrational, unreasonable** mean not governed or guided by reason. **Irrational** may imply mental derangement, but more often it suggests actions, words, etc., directly in conflict with reason; **unreasonable** suggests guidance by some force other than reason (such as self-will) that makes one deficient in good sense (as, *irrational* beliefs; *unreasonable* demands).

ir·ra′tion·al·ism (-ĭz′m), *n.* Irrational belief or action.

ir·ra′tion·al′i·ty (-ăl′ĭ·tĭ), *n.* Quality of being irrational.

ir′re·claim′a·ble (ĭr′rē·klām′ȧ·b′l), *adj.* Incapable of being reclaimed. — **ir′re·claim′a·bil′i·ty** (-bĭl′ĭ·tĭ), **ir′re·claim′a·ble·ness,** *n.* — **ir′re·claim′a·bly,** *adv.*

ir·rec′on·cil′a·ble (ĭr·rĕk′ŏn·sīl′ȧ·b′l; ĭr·rĕk′ŏn·sīl′ȧ·b′l), *adj.* Not reconcilable; implacable; incompatible; inconsistent; as, *irreconcilable* enemies, statements. — *n.* One who is irreconcilable; one who refuses to compromise. — **ir·rec′on·cil′a·bil′i·ty** (-bĭl′ĭ·tĭ), **ir·rec′on·cil′a·ble·ness,** *n.* — **ir·rec′on·cil′a·bly,** *adv.*

ir′re·cov′er·a·ble (ĭr′rē·kŭv′ẽr·ȧ·b′l), *adj.* Not capable of being recovered or rectified; irreparable; irremediable. — **ir′re·cov′er·a·bly,** *adv.*

ir′re·cu′sa·ble (-kū′zȧ·b′l), *adj.* [F. or LL.; F. *irrécusable,* fr. LL., fr. *ir-* not + *recusabilis* that should be rejected, fr. *recusare* to reject.] Not liable to exception or rejection. — **ir′re·cu′sa·bly,** *adv.*

ir′re·deem′a·ble (-dēm′ȧ·b′l), *adj.* **1.** Not redeemable; specif.: **a** Not convertible into specie at the pleasure of the holder; inconvertible; — said of paper money. **b** Not terminable by payment of the principal; as, an *irredeemable* bond. **2. a** Admitting of no change; as, *irredeemable* gloom. **b** Beyond redemption; irreclaimable. — **ir′re·deem′a·bly,** *adv.*

Ir′re·den′tist (ĭr′ē·dĕn′tĭst), *n.* [It. *irredentista,* fr. *irredento* unredeemed, fr. L. *in-* not + *redemptus* redeemed.] **1.** *Italian Politics.* One of a party formed about 1878, for incorporating with Italy neighboring regions (called ***Italia irredenta,*** unredeemed Italy), largely Italian in population but subject to other governments. **2.** Any advocate of policies for regaining for the country territory formerly belonging therein but later lost. — **Ir′re·den′tism** (ĭr′ē·dĕn′tĭz′m), *n.*

ir′re·duc′i·ble (ĭr′rē·dūs′ĭ·b′l), *adj.* Not reducible; incapable of being brought into a proper or normal state; as, an *irreducible* formula; an *irreducible* equation.

ir·ref′ra·ga·ble (ĭr·rĕf′rȧ·gȧ·b′l), *adj.* **1.** Not refragable; unanswerable; undeniable; as, an *irrefragable* argument. **2.** Unbreakable; indestructible. — **ir·ref′ra·ga·bil′i·ty** (-bĭl′ĭ·tĭ), *n.* — **ir·ref′ra·ga·bly,** *adv.*

ir′re·fran′gi·ble (ĭr′rē·frăn′jĭ·b′l), *adj.* **1.** Inviolable. **2.** Not refrangible; that cannot be refracted.

ir·ref′u·ta·ble (ĭr·rĕf′ū·tȧ·b′l; ĭr′rē·fūt′ȧ·b′l), *adj.* Incapable of refutation or disproof. — **ir·ref′u·ta·bil′i·ty** (-bĭl′ĭ·tĭ), *n.* — **ir·ref′u·ta·bly,** *adv.*

ir·reg′u·lar (ĭr·rĕg′ū·lẽr), *adj.* [OF. *irreguler,* fr. ML. *irregularis.*] **1.** Not regular; not according to established law, method, or usage; not conformable to nature or to the rules of moral rectitude; immethodical; not straight; not uniform. **2.** Not belonging to, or having conformed to, the requirements of some particular organized body; as, an *irregular* physician. **3.** *Bot.* Showing a lack of uniformity; as, an *irregular* corolla; zygomorphic; — said specif. of flowers. **4.** *Gram.* **a** Not conforming to the normal manner of inflection; as, sell and cast are *irregular* verbs. **b** Specif., strong; — of verbs. Abbr. *irreg.* **5.** *Mil.* Not belonging to the regular army organization, but raised for a special purpose. — **ir·reg′u·lar·ly,** *adv.*

Syn. **Irregular, anomalous, unnatural** mean outside the sphere of that which conforms to law, rule, or the like. **Irregular** especially implies a not conforming to a law or regulation imposed for the sake of uniformity in method, practice, or conduct; **anomalous,** a not conforming to what might be expected because of the class or type to which it belongs, the laws which govern its existence, or the like; **unnatural,** a contrariness to nature or to natural law (i. e., principles accepted by all civilized men as essential to the well-being of society); as, *irregular* conduct; an *anomalous* situation; an *unnatural* appetite; an *unnatural* deed.

— *n.* One who is not regular; esp., *Mil.* (usually in *pl.*), a soldier not in regular service.

ir·reg′u·lar′i·ty (-lăr′ĭ·tĭ), *n.; pl.* -TIES (-tĭz). Quality or state of being irregular; that which is irregular.

ir·rel′a·tive (ĭr·rĕl′ȧ·tĭv), *adj.* **1.** Not relative; unrelated; also, irrelevant. **2.** *Music.* Not having tones in common; as, *irrelative* chords, keys, etc. — **ir·rel′a·tive·ly,** *adv.* — **ir·rel′a·tive·ness,** *n.*

ir·rel′e·vance (ĭr·rĕl′ē·văns), *n.* Irrelevancy.

ir·rel′e·van·cy (-văn·sĭ), *n.; pl.* -CIES (-sĭz). Quality or state of being irrelevant; that which is irrelevant.

ir·rel′e·vant (-vănt), *adj.* Not relevant, not applicable or pertinent; extraneous. — **ir·rel′e·vant·ly,** *adv.*

ir′re·liev′a·ble (ĭr′rē·lēv′ȧ·b′l), *adj.* Not relievable.

ir′re·li′gion (ĭr′rē·lĭj′ŭn), *n.* State of being irreligious; lack of religion; impiety. — **ir′re·li′gion·ist** (-ĭst), *n.*

ir′re·li′gious (-ŭs), *adj* [L. *irreligiosus.*] **1.** Disregardful of religion; ungodly. **2.** Indicating irreligion; profane; as, *irreligious* speech. — **ir′re·li′gious·ly,** *adv.*

ir·rem′e·a·ble (ĭr·rĕm′ē·ȧ·b′l; ĭr·rē′mē-), *adj.* [L. *irremeabilis,* fr. *ir-* not + *remeabilis* returning, fr. *remeare.*] Admitting no return. — **ir·rem′e·a·bly,** *adv.*

ir′re·me′di·a·ble (ĭr′rē·mē′dĭ·ȧ·b′l), *adj.* Not remediable; not capable of being remedied; specif., incurable. — **ir′re·me′di·a·ble·ness,** *n.* — **ir′re·me′di·a·bly,** *adv.*

ir′re·mis′si·ble (ĭr′rē·mĭs′ĭ·b′l), *adj.* Not remissible; unpardonable; as, *irremissible* crimes; also, obligatory; as, *irremissible* duties. — **ir′re·mis′si·bly,** *adv.*

ir′re·mov′a·ble (-mōōv′ȧ·b′l), *adj.* Not removable. — **ir′re·mov′a·bil′i·ty** (-bĭl′ĭ·tĭ), *n.* — **ir′re·mov′a·bly,** *adv.*

ir·rep′a·ra·ble (ĭ·rĕp′ȧ·rȧ·b′l), *adj.* Not reparable; irretrievable; irremediable. — **ir·rep′a·ra·bil′i·ty** (-bĭl′ĭ·tĭ), **ir·rep′a·ra·ble·ness,** *n.* — **ir·rep′a·ra·bly,** *adv.*

ir′re·peal′a·ble (ĭr′rē·pēl′ȧ·b′l), *adj.* Not repealable.

ir′re·place′a·ble (-plās′ȧ·b′l), *adj.* Not replaceable.

ir′re·press′i·ble (-prĕs′ĭ·b′l), *adj.* Not repressible; unrestrainable; uncontrollable. — **ir′re·press′i·bil′i·ty** (-bĭl′ĭ·tĭ), *n.* — **ir′re·press′i·bly,** *adv.*

ir′re·proach′a·ble (-prōch′ȧ·b′l), *adj.* Not reproachable; blameless. — **ir′re·proach′a·ble·ness,** *n.* — **ir′re·proach′a·bly,** *adv.*

ir′re·sist′i·ble (-zĭs′tĭ·b′l), *adj.* That cannot be successfully resisted; resistless. — **ir′re·sist′i·bil′i·ty** (-bĭl′ĭ·tĭ), **ir′re·sist′i·ble·ness,** *n.* — **ir′re·sist′i·bly,** *adv.*

ir·res′o·lu·ble (ĭ·rĕz′ō·lū·b′l), *adj.* **1.** Incapable of being resolved; insoluble. **2.** Incapable of being relieved or loosened.

ir·res′o·lute (-lūt), *adj.* Not resolute; wavering; vacillating. — **ir·res′o·lute·ly,** *adv.* — **ir·res′o·lute·ness,** *n.*

ir·res′o·lu′tion (-lū′shŭn), *n.* Want of resolution; irresoluteness; indecision; vacillation.

ir′re·solv′a·ble (ĭr′rē·zŏl′vȧ·b′l), *adj.* Incapable of being resolved; not solvable; insoluble; not separable into component parts.

ir′re·spec′tive (-spĕk′tĭv), *adj.* *Rare.* Having no regard for persons, conditions, or consequences. — **ir′re·spec′tive·ly,** *adv.*

irrespective of. Without regard to; independent of.

ir′re·spir′a·ble (ĭr′rē·spīr′ȧ·b′l; ĭ·rĕs′pĭ·rȧ·b′l), *adj.* Not respirable (so as to sustain life).

ir′re·spon′si·bil′i·ty (ĭr′rē·spŏn′sĭ·bĭl′ĭ·tĭ), *n.; pl.* -TIES (-tĭz). Lack of, or freedom from, responsibility.

ir′re·spon′si·ble (-spŏn′sĭ·b′l), *adj.* **1.** Free from, or incapable of incurring, responsibility. **2.** Not able to answer for consequences; not able to render satisfaction; insolvent. — *n.* An irresponsible person. — **ir′re·spon′si·bly,** *adv.*

ir′re·spon′sive (ĭr′rē·spŏn′sĭv), *adj.* Not responsive; not able, ready, or inclined to respond. — **ir′re·spon′sive·ness,** *n.*

ir′re·ten′tive (ĭr′rē·tĕn′tĭv), *adj.* Not retentive.

ir′re·trace′a·ble (-trās′ȧ·b′l), *adj.* Not retraceable.

ir′re·triev′a·ble (-trēv′ȧ·b′l), *adj.* Not retrievable; irrecoverable; irreparable. — **ir′re·triev′a·bil′i·ty** (-bĭl′ĭ·tĭ), *n.* — **ir′re·triev′a·bly,** *adv.*

ir·rev′er·ence (ĭ·rĕv′ẽr·ĕns), *n.* **1.** Lack of reverence; disrespect to what is sacred; also, an irreverent act or utterance. **2.** State of not being reverenced.

ir·rev′er·ent (-ĕnt), *adj.* [OF., fr. L. *irreverens, -entis.*] Not reverent; showing lack of reverence. — **ir·rev′er·ent·ly,** *adv.*

ir′re·vers′i·ble (ĭr′rē·vûr′sĭ·b′l), *adj.* Incapable of being reversed. — **ir′re·vers′i·bil′i·ty** (-bĭl′ĭ·tĭ), *n.* — **ir′re·vers′i·bly,** *adv.*

ir·rev′o·ca·ble (ĭ·rĕv′ō·kȧ·b′l), *adj.* Incapable of being revoked; unalterable. — **ir·rev′o·ca·bil′i·ty** (-bĭl′ĭ·tĭ), **ir·rev′o·ca·ble·ness,** *n.* — **ir·rev′o·ca·bly,** *adv.*

ir′ri·ga·ble (ĭr′ĭ·gȧ·b′l), *adj.* That can be irrigated.

ir′ri·gate (ĭr′ĭ·gāt), *v. t.* [L. *irrigatus,* past part. of *irrigare* to irrigate, fr. *ir-* in + *rigare* to water.] **1.** To subject to irrigation; to supply (land) with water by causing a stream to flow upon, over, or through it, as in artificial channels. **2.** To refresh as if by watering. — **ir′ri·ga′tor** (-gā′tẽr), *n.*

ir′ri·ga′tion (-gā′shŭn), *n.* **1.** Act or process of irrigating, or state of being irrigated; specif., the artificial watering of farm land by canals, ditches, flooding, etc., to supply growing crops with moisture. **2.** *Med.* Application of a continuous stream of liquid to an affected part for cleansing, disinfecting, etc. — **ir′ri·ga′tion·al** (-ăl; -′l), *adj.*

ir′ri·ga′tive (ĭr′ĭ·gā′tĭv; -gȧ·tĭv), *adj.* Serving to irrigate.

ir·rig′u·ous (ĭ·rĭg′ū·ŭs), *adj.* [L. *irriguus.*] **1.** Well-watered. **2.** Irrigative.

ir′ri·ta·bil′i·ty (ĭr′ĭ·tȧ·bĭl′ĭ·tĭ), *n.; pl.* -TIES (-tĭz). [L. *irritabilitas.*] Quality or state of being irritable; specif.: **a** Quick excitability to annoyance, impatience, or anger; petulance; fretfulness. **b** *Med.* A condition of morbid excitability of an organ or part; undue susceptibility to stimuli. **c** *Physiol.* The characteristic property of living organisms, and, specif., their protoplasm, of responding to environmental changes (*stimuli*), as by change in shape or by production or cessation of motion.

ir′ri·ta·ble (ĭr′ĭ·tȧ·b′l), *adj.* [L. *irritabilis.*] Capable of being irritated; specif.: **a** Very susceptible of impatience, anger, or passion; easily exasperated. **b** Easily excitable. **c** *Med.* Susceptible of irritation; unduly sensitive to irritants or stimuli. **d** *Physiol.* Responsive to stimuli. — **Syn.** Peevish, fretful, querulous. — **ir′ri·ta·ble·ness,** *n.* — **ir′ri·ta·bly,** *adv.*

ir′ri·tan·cy (-tăn·sĭ), *n.* Irritating quality; irritation.

ir′ri·tant (-tănt), *adj.* [L. *irritans, -antis,* pres. part. of *irritare.*] Producing irritation or inflammation. — *n.* That which irritates or excites; specif., *Physiol. & Med.,* any agent by which irritation is produced.

ir′ri·tate (-tāt), *v. t.* [L. *irritatus,* past part. of *irritare.*] **1.** To excite impatience, anger, or displeasure in; to provoke; exasperate. **2.** To cause to be irritable, as a wound. **3.** *Physiol.* To produce irritation in; to stimulate, as a muscle to contraction by artificial stimulation.

Syn. **Irritate, exasperate, nettle, provoke, roil, peeve** mean to excite angry annoyance. **Irritate** suggests a provocation that greatly displeases and evokes momentary impatience or an outburst of rage; **exasperate,** bitter and keen irritation at something not to be endured; **nettle,** a stinging and piquing rather than enraging; **provoke,** an arousing of a feeling of strong annoyance or vexation; **roil,** angry agitation that disturbs one's peace of mind; **peeve,** a tendency to be easily irritated and to become fretful.

ir′ri·tat′ing (-tāt′ĭng), *adj.* Provoking; causing displeasure. — **ir′ri·tat′ing·ly,** *adv.*

ir′ri·ta′tion (-tā′shŭn), *n.* An irritating, or state of being irritated; annoyance; anger; specif., *Med.,* a condition of morbid excitability of an organ or part of the body.

ir′ri·ta′tive (ĭr′ĭ·tā′tĭv), *adj.* **1.** Serving to irritate; irritating. **2.** Accompanied with, or produced by, irritation.

ir·rup′tion (ĭ·rŭp′shŭn), *n.* [L. *irruptio*, fr. *irrumpere, irruptus*, fr. *ir-* in + *rumpere* to break.] **1.** A bursting in. **2.** A sudden and violent inroad or invasion.

ir·rup′tive (-tĭv), *adj.* **1.** Rushing in or upon; tending to irruption. **2.** *Petrology.* Intrusive; — of igneous rocks.

is (ĭz; 4). [AS.] A verb form supplying the third person singular present indicative of the verb *be;* as, he *is* a man.

is-. = ISO-.

I′saac (ī′zȧk; -zĭk), *n.* [LL., fr. Heb. *Yitsḥāq*, lit., laughter.] *Bib.* A Hebrew patriarch, son of Abraham and Sarah, husband of Rebekah, and father of Jacob and Esau.

is′a·cous′tic (ĭs′ȧ·kōōs′tĭk; -kous′tĭk), *adj.* [*is-* + *acoustic.*] Of or pertaining to equal intensity of sound.

i′sa·go′ge (ī′sȧ·gō′jē), *n.* [L., fr. Gr. *eisagōgē*, fr. *eisagein* to introduce, fr. *eis* into + *agein* to lead.] An introduction, as to a subject of research. — **i′sa·gog′ic** (-gŏj′ĭk), *adj.*

i′sa·gog′ics (-gŏj′ĭks), **i′sa·gog′ic** (-ĭk), *n.; see* -ICS. Introductory study; esp., *Theol.*, that part of theology directly preliminary to actual exegesis and concerned with the literary history of the Bible.

I·sa′iah (ī·zā′yȧ; ī·zī′ȧ), *n.* *Douay Bib.* **I·sa′ias** (ī·zā′yăs; ī·zī′ăs). [Heb. *Yĕsha′yāh*, lit., salvation.] **a** A major Hebrew prophet in Judah (about 740 to 701 B.C.). **b** A book of the Old Testament. See BIBLE.

i·sal′lo·bar (ī·săl′ō·bär), *n.* [*is-* + *allo-* + Gr. *baros* weight.] *Meteorol.* An imaginary line, or a line upon a chart, connecting the places of equal change of atmospheric pressure within a specified time.

i′sa·tin (ī′sȧ·tĭn; ĭz′ȧ-), *n.* Also, less properly, **i′sa·tine** (-tĭn; -tēn). [NL. *Isatis*, a genus of plants, fr. L. *isatis* a kind of plant, fr. Gr. *isatis* woad.] *Chem.* An orange-red crystalline compound, $C_8H_5NO_2$, obtained by oxidation of indigotin, and from certain other aromatic compounds.

is·ba′, iz·ba′ (ĭz·bä′; ĭz′bȧ), *n.* In Russia, a log hut.

Is·car′i·ot (ĭs·kăr′ĭ·ŏt), *n.* [L. *Iscariota*, fr. Gr. *Iskariōtēs*, fr. Heb. *īsh-qĕrīyōth* the man of Kerioth (a village in Palestine).] Surname of Judas, who betrayed Christ; hence, a traitor.

is·che′mi·a, is·chae′mi·a (ĭs·kē′mĭ·ȧ), *n.* [NL., fr. Gr. *ischein* to check + *-emia.*] *Med.* Deficiency of blood in a part; local anemia. — **is·che′mic** (-kē′mĭk; -kĕm′ĭk), *adj.*

is′chi·um (ĭs′kĭ·ŭm), *n.; pl.* -CHIA (-ȧ). [L., fr. Gr. *ischion.*] *Anat.* The dorsal and posterior of the three principal bones composing either half of the pelvis. — **is′chi·al** (-ăl), **is′chi·ad′ic** (-ăd′ĭk), **is′chi·at′ic** (-ăt′ĭk), *adj.*

-ise (-īz). A suffix, in verbs, equivalent to -IZE.

I·seult′ (ĭ·sōōlt′). Var. of ISOLDE.

-ish (-ĭsh). [AS. *-isc.*] A suffix used to form adjectives: **a** On names of peoples, as in Scott*ish*, Turk*ish*. **b** On nouns, with the meaning of *the nature of, belonging to*, as in boy*ish*, clown*ish*; — now often derogatory in force, with the sense *having* or *showing the undesirable traits of*, as in child*ish* petulancy. **c** On nouns, with the sense of *verging upon, suggestive of, resembling*, as in book*ish* phrases. **d** On adjectives, with the sense of *somewhat*, as in whit*ish*.

Ish′ma·el (ĭsh′mā·ĕl), *n.* [Heb. *Yishmā′ē′l*, i. e., God hears.] *Bib.* Son of Abraham and Hagar (see HAGAR); hence, a social outcast.

Ish′ma·el·ite (-īt), *n.* **1.** A descendant of Ishmael. **2.** An outcast. — **Ish′ma·el·it′ish** (-īt′ĭsh), *adj.*

Ish′tar (ĭsh′tär), *n.* [Assyr.-Bab.] *Babylon. Relig.* The chief goddess of the pantheon; the goddess of love and of the reproductive forces of nature; also, esp. with the Assyrians, goddess of war.

i′sin·glass′ (ī′zĭng·glȧs′; ī′zĭn-), *n.* [Obs. D. *huysenblas*, lit., bladder of the *huso*, or large sturgeon.] **1.** A semitransparent, whitish, and very pure form of gelatin, prepared from the air bladders of certain fish (originally sturgeons, now largely cod, ling, and carp), used in making jellies, glue, etc. **2.** *Colloq.* Mica, esp. in thin transparent sheets.

I′sis (ī′sĭs), *n.* [L., fr. Gr. *Isis*, fr. Egypt. *Ȧst.*] *Egypt. Relig.* An Egyptian goddess of motherhood and fertility, sometimes represented as cow-headed. She is sister and wife of Osiris.

Is′lam (ĭs′lȧm; ĭz′-; ĭs·läm′), *n.* [Ar. *Islām*, lit., submission (to the will of God).] **1.** The religion of the Moslems; Islamism. Their creed, or formula of faith, is: There is no god but Allah, and Mohammed is his prophet. **2.** The whole body of Moslems, or the countries they occupy. — **Is·lam′ic** (ĭs·lăm′ĭk; ĭz-; ĭs·läm′ĭk), *adj.* — **Is′lam·it′ic** (ĭs′lȧm·ĭt′ĭk; ĭz′-), *adj.*

Is′lam·ism (ĭs′lȧm·ĭz′m; ĭz′-), *n.* The faith, doctrines, or religious system, or sway, of the Moslems; Islam.

Is′lam·ite (-īt), *n.* A Moslem.

Is′lam·ize (-īz), *v. i. & t.* To conform, or convert, to Islam.

is′land (ī′lănd), *n.* [AS. *īgland, ēgland, ēglond*, fr. *īg, ēg, īeg*, island + *land, lond*, land.] **1.** A tract of land surrounded by water, and smaller than a continent. Abbr. *I., Is.* (*sing. & pl.*). **2.** Anything that is regarded as resembling an island in position, isolation, etc., as a safety zone on a street. **3.** *Anat.* Any group of cells differentiated from the surrounding tissue, as in structure or staining properties, as the **is′lands of Lang′er·hans** (läng′ĕr·häns), groups of granular cells among the gland tubules and alveoli of the pancreas, which produce an internal secretion controlling the oxidation of sugar. **4.** The superstructure on the starboard side of an aircraft carrier, flanking the flight deck, and containing usually the signal bridge, navigation office, cranes, and fire-fighting equipment. — *v. t.* **1.** To isolate. **2.** To furnish with or as with islands.

is′land·er (ī′lăn·dẽr), *n.* A native or inhabitant of an island.

Islands of the Blessed. *Class. Myth.* Islands of the Western Ocean, where favorites of the gods dwell, after death.

island universe. *Astron.* Any of the million or more galaxies of stars like our own Galaxy.

isle (īl), *n.* [OF. *ile, isle*, fr. L. *insula.*] *Chiefly Poetic.* An island; now, usually, a small island. — *v. t. & i.;* ISLED (īld); ISL′ING (īl′ĭng). To cause to become an island, or like an island; to put in, or as in, an island; also, stay in an isle.

is′let (ī′lĕt; -lĭt), *n.* [OF. *islette*, dim. of *isle.*] A little island.

-ism (-ĭz′m). [F. or L.; F. *-isme*, fr. L. *ismus*, fr. Gr. *-ismos.*] A suffix forming nouns, with the meaning of: **a** *Action:* (1) *Act* or *fact of doing* (what the corresponding verb denotes), often also the *result*, as in baptism, ostracism, plagiarism. (2) *Manner of action* or *conduct characteristic of* (the person or kind of person indicated), as in despot*ism*, heathen*ism*. **b** *State, condition,* or *fact of being;* — from passive or neutral verb senses, or from adjectives or nouns of state or condition, as in hypnot*ism*, barbar*ism*. **c** (1) *Doctrine* or *practice of* (a religious or philosophical system or a theory or principle), as in Quaker*ism*, Berkeleian*ism*. (2) *Adherence* or *attachment to* (a system or idea), as in Anglican*ism*. **d** *A characteristic* or *peculiarity of* (esp. language), as in an American*ism*, a colloquial*ism*. **e** *Med. An abnormal condition from excess of a* (specified) *thing*, as in alcohol*ism*.

ism (ĭz′m), *n.* [See -ISM.] A distinctive doctrine, ideal, system, or practice; — usually disparaging.

i′so- (ī′sō-), **is-.** [Gr. *isos* equal.] A combining form meaning *equal, alike, the same:* **a** Denoting *equality, similarity, uniformity,* or *identity*, as in *iso*chronal. **b** (*pron.* ī′sō-; *occas.* ē′sō-) [From *isomeric.*] *Chem.* Denoting *isomeric with*, as **i′so·cy·an′ic** acid, which is isomeric with cyanic acid; **i′so·bu′tane, i′so·bu′tyl.**

i′so·ag·glu′ti·na′tion (-ă·glōō′tĭ·nā′shŭn), *n.* *Med.* The agglutination of the blood corpuscles of an animal (or man) by the serum of another animal of the same species.

i′so·ag·glu′ti·nin (-ă·glōō′tĭ·nĭn), *n.* *Immunol.* An agglutinin specific for the cells of another individual of the same species.

i′so·bar (ī′sō·bär), *n.* [*iso-* + Gr. *baros* weight.] **1.** *Meteorol.* A line marking places upon the earth's surface where the height of the barometer reduced to sea level is the same either at a given time or for a certain period. **2.** *Chem.* One of two atoms or elements having the same atomic weights or mass numbers but different atomic numbers. — **i′so·bar′ic** (-băr′ĭk), *adj.*

i′so·cheim (ī′sō·kīm), *n.* [*iso-* + Gr. *cheima* winter.] *Phys. Geog.* An imaginary line connecting places having the same mean winter temperature. Cf. ISOTHERE. — **i′so·chei′mal** (-kī′măl), **i′so·chei′me·nal** (-kī′mē·năl), *adj.*

i′so·chor (ī′sō·kôr), *n.* Also **i′so·chore.** [*iso-* + Gr. *chōra* space.] *Thermodyn.* A line representing the variation of pressure with temperature when the volume of the substance operated on is constant.

i′so·chro·mat′ic (-krō·măt′ĭk), *adj.* **1.** *Optics.* Of the same color; — said of lines or curves of the same tint appearing in figures formed by interfering light waves passing through biaxial crystals. **2.** *Photog.* = ORTHOCHROMATIC.

i·soch′ro·nal (ī·sŏk′rō·năl; -n′l), *adj.* Uniform in time; of equal time; recurring at regular intervals. — **i·soch′ro·nal·ly**, *adv.* — **i·soch′ro·nism** (-nĭz′m), *n.*

i·soch′ro·nize (-nīz), *v. t.* To render isochronal.

i·soch′ro·nous (-nŭs), *adj.* [Gr. *isochronos*, fr. *isos* equal + *chronos* time.] Isochronal. — **i·soch′ro·nous·ly**, *adv.*

i·soch′ro·ous (-ŭs), *adj.* [*iso-* + *-chroous.*] Of the same tint or color throughout.

i′so·cli′nal (ī′sō·klī′năl; -n′l), *adj.* [*iso-* + Gr. *klinein* to incline.] Of, having, or indicating equality of inclination or dip, as of a dip needle; as, *isoclinal* lines joining points on the earth's surface. — *n.* An isoclinal line.

i′so·cline (ī′sō·klīn), *n.* [See ISOCLINAL.] An anticline or syncline so closely folded that the rock beds of the two sides have the same dip.

i′so·clin′ic (-klĭn′ĭk), *adj. & n.* Isoclinal.

i·soc′ra·cy (ī·sŏk′rȧ·sĭ), *n.* [Gr. *isokratia.* See ISO-; DEMOCRACY.] A system of government in which all have equal political power. — **i′so·crat′ic** (ī′sō·krăt′ĭk), *adj.*

i′so·cy′a·nine (ī′sō·sī′ȧ·nēn; -nĭn), *n.* Also **i′so·cy′a·nin.** [See ISO-; CYANO-.] Any of a certain series of dyes capable of sensitizing photographic material.

i′so·di′a·met′ric (-dī′ȧ·mĕt′rĭk), *adj.* Having equal diameters.

i′so·di·mor′phism (-dī·môr′fĭz′m), *n.* *Mineral.* Isomorphism between the two forms, severally, of two dimorphous substances. — **i′so·di·mor′phous** (-fŭs), *adj.*

i′so·dy·nam′ic (-dī·năm′ĭk; -dĭ-), *adj.* Also **i′so·dy·nam′i·cal** (-ĭ·kăl). Of, having, or denoting equality of force; marking points of the same magnetic intensity.

i′so·e·lec′tric (-ē·lĕk′trĭk), *adj.* *Physics.* Having the same electric potential; as, *isoelectric* points.

i′so·e·lec′tron′ic (-ē·lĕk′trŏn′ĭk; -ĕl′ĕk-), *adj.* *Physics.* Having the same number of extranuclear electrons.

i′so·ga·mete′ (-gȧ·mēt′), *n.* *Biol.* A gamete of a type not exhibiting sexual or other differentiations; — opposed to *heterogamete*.

i·sog′a·mous (ī·sŏg′ȧ·mŭs), *adj.* [*iso-* + *-gamous.*] *Biol.* Characterized by the conjugation of similar gametes. — **i·sog′a·my** (-mĭ), *n.*

i·sog′e·nous (ī·sŏj′ē·nŭs), *adj.* [*iso-* + *-genous.*] *Biol.* Having the same origin. — **i·sog′e·ny** (-nĭ), *n.*

i′so·ge′o·therm (ī′sō·jē′ō·thûrm), *n.* [*iso-* + *geo-* + Gr. *thermē* heat.] *Geol.* A line or curved surface beneath the earth's surface passing through points having the same mean temperature. — **i′so·ge′o·ther′mal** (-thûr′măl), **i′so·ge′o·ther′mic** (-mĭk), *adj.*

i′so·gloss (ī′sō·glŏs), *n.* *Ling.* **a** In a speech area, a line between places which delimits any feature of language, such as pronunciation, inflection, vocabulary, or syntax. **b** A line on a map representing an isogloss.

i·sog′o·nal (ī·sŏg′ō·năl; -n′l), *adj.* Having equal angles; isogonic.

i′so·gon′ic (ī′sō·gŏn′ĭk), *adj.* [Gr. *isogōnios* having equal angles.] Pertaining to, or noting, equal angles. An **isogonic line,** *or* **isogonic,** is an imaginary line joining places on the earth's surface at which the variation of the magnetic needle from the meridian or true north is the same. See VARIATION, *Illust.*

i′so·gram (ī′sō·grăm), *n.* A line on a chart connecting points having equal values of some phenomenon, as temperature, pressure, rainfall.

i′so·hel (ī′sō·hĕl), *n.* [*iso-* + Gr. *hēlios* sun.] *Meteorol.* A line on a chart connecting places having equal duration of sunshine.

i′so·hy′et (ī′sō·hī′ĕt), *n.* [*iso-* + Gr. *hyetos* rain.] *Meteorol.* A line on a chart connecting places having equal rainfall.

i′so·late (ī′sō·lāt; ĭs′ō-), *v. t.* [From *isolated*, fr. F. *isolé*, fr. It. *isolato*, past part. of *isolare* to isolate, fr. *isola* island, fr. L. *insula.*] **1.** To place apart by itself. **2.** *Chem.* To separate from all other substances. **3.** *Med.* To separate (a patient with an infectious disease) from persons not similarly infected. — **i′so·la·ble** (-lȧ·b′l), *adj.*

i′so·la′tion (ī′sō·lā′shŭn; ĭs′ō-), *n.* Act of isolating, or state of being isolated; loneliness. — **Syn.** See SOLITUDE.

i′so·la′tion·ist (-ĭst), *n.* **1.** One who favors or advocates isolation, esp. keeping aloof politically from other countries. **2.** An advocate or adherent of a strict national policy of nonparticipation in alliances, engagements, or conflicts with other nations.

I·solde′ (ĭ·sōld′), *n.* [OF. *Isolt, Iseut.*] See TRISTRAM.

i·sol′o·gous (ī·sŏl′ō·gŭs), *adj.* [*iso-* + Gr. *logos* proportion.] *Chem.* Pertaining to or designating any of two or more compounds of related structure and a characteristic difference of composition other than CH_2, or the series which they form. Cf. HOMOLOGOUS.

i′so·mag·net′ic (ī′sō·măg·nĕt′ĭk), *adj.* Of, pertaining to, or indicating equality of magnetic force. — *n.* An isomagnetic line.

i′so·mer (ī′sō·mẽr), *n.* *Physics & Chem.* A substance or nucleus isomeric with another or others.

i′so·mer′ic (-mĕr′ĭk), *adj.* [*iso-* + Gr. *meros* part.] **1.** *Chem.* Composed of the same elements united in the same proportion by weight, but differing in one or more properties because of difference in structure. **2.** *Physics & Chem.* Having the same atomic number and mass number but differing in one or more properties, as in the rate of radioactive decay; — said of atomic nuclei.

i·som′er·ism (ī·sŏm′ẽr·ĭz′m), *n.* *Chem.* State, quality, or relation of being isomeric. See ISOMERIC.

i·som′er·ous (-ŭs), *adj.* Having an equal number of parts, ridges, markings, etc.; specif., *Bot.*, having the members of each floral whorl equal in number; — opposed to *heteromerous*.

i′so·met′ric (ī′sō·mĕt′rĭk), *adj.* Also **i′so·met′ri·cal** (-rĭ·kăl). [*iso-* + Gr. *metron* measure.] **1.** Of, pertaining to, or indicating equality of measure. **2.** *Crystallog.* Pertaining to or designating a system characterized by three equal axes at right angles, as in the cube and regular octahedron. — *n.* Also **isometric line**. *Thermodyn.* A line representing changes of pressure or temperature under conditions of constant volume. — **i′so·met′ri·cal·ly**, *adv.*

i′so·me·tro′pi·a (-mē·trō′pĭ·ȧ), *n.* [NL., fr. *iso-* + Gr. *metron* measure + *-opia*.] Equality in refraction in the two eyes.

i·som′e·try (ī·sŏm′ē·trĭ), *n.* [*iso-* + *-metry*.] Equality of, or in respect of, measure; specif., *Geog.*, equality of elevation; as, the *isometry* of Alpine summits.

i′so·morph (ī′sō·môrf), *n.* One of two or more substances or organisms isomorphic with each other.

i′so·mor′phic (-môr′fĭk), *adj.* Of identical or like form; specif., *Biol. & Cryst.*, exhibiting isomorphism.

i′so·mor′phism (-fĭz′m), *n.* **1.** *Biol.* Similarity in organisms of different ancestry resulting from convergence. **2.** *Chem. & Cryst.* A similarity of crystalline form between substances of similar composition. Cf. HOMEOMORPHISM.

i′so·mor′phous (-fŭs), *adj.* [*iso-* + *-morphous*.] Isomorphic.

i·son′o·my (ī·sŏn′ō·mĭ), *n.* [Gr. *isonomia*, fr. *isos* equal + *nomos* law.] Equality of laws or rights.

i′so–oc′tane (ī′sō·ŏk′tān), *n.* *Chem.* An octane (2,2,4-trimethylpentane) which because of its branched structure has high antiknock value.

i′so·pi·es′tic (ī′sō·pī·ĕs′tĭk), *adj.* [*iso-* + Gr. *piezein* to press.] Denoting equal pressure; isobaric. — *n.* An isopiestic line; isobar.

i′so·pleth (ī′sō·plĕth), *n.* [Gr. *isoplēthēs* equal in quantity or number, fr. *isos* equal + *plēthos* quantity, number.] **1.** A graph showing the occurrence or frequency of any phenomenon as a function of two variables, generally used with reference to meteorological elements. **2.** *Math.* The straight line on which lie corresponding values of the dependent and independent variables.

i′so·pod (-pŏd), *n.* [*iso-* + *-pod*.] Any of a large order (Isopoda) of small sessile-eyed crustaceans in which the body is composed of seven free thoracic segments each bearing a pair of legs typically alike in size and direction. — **i′so·pod**, *adj.* — **i·sop′o·dan** (ī·sŏp′ō·dăn), *adj. & n.*

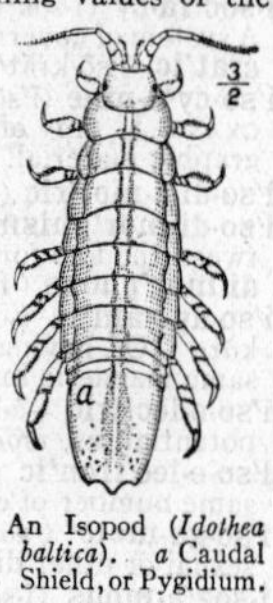

An Isopod (*Idothea baltica*). *a* Caudal Shield, or Pygidium.

i′so·prene (ī′sō·prēn), *n.* [Appar. an arbitrary formation. Cf. -ENE.] *Chem.* A volatile liquid unsaturated hydrocarbon, C_5H_8, obtained by heating rubber and otherwise.

i′so·pro′pyl (-prō′pĭl), *n.* *Chem.* A univalent radical, $(CH_3)_2CH$, isomeric with normal propyl.

i′so·pyre (ī′sō·pīr), *n.* [*iso-* + Gr. *pyr* fire.] *Mineral.* An impure opal containing iron, alumina, etc.

i·sos′ce·les (ī·sŏs′ĕ·lēz), *adj.* [L., fr. Gr. *isoskelēs*, fr. *isos* equal + *skelos* leg.] *Geom.* Having two equal sides; — of a triangle. See TRIANGLE, *Illust.*

i′so·seis′mal (ī′sō·sīz′măl; -sīs′măl), *adj.* Isoseismic. — *n.* An isoseismal line.

i′so·seis′mic (-mĭk), *adj.* [*iso-* + *seismic*.] Affected with, pertaining to, or indicating equal intensity in an earthquake shock.

i·sos′ta·sy (ī·sŏs′tȧ·sĭ), *n.* [*iso-* + Gr. *stasis* a standing still.] The state or quality of being isostatic; specif., *Geol.*, general equilibrium in the earth's crust, supposed to be maintained by the yielding or flow of rock material beneath the surface under gravitative stress.

i′so·stat′ic (ī′sō·stăt′ĭk), *adj.* *Physics & Geol.* Subjected to equal pressure from every side; being in hydrostatic equilibrium, as a body submerged in a liquid at rest.

i′so·there (ī′sō·thēr), **i·soth′er·al** (ī·sŏth′ẽr·ăl; ī′sō·thēr·ăl), *n.* [*iso-* + Gr. *theros* summer.] *Phys. Geog.* A line joining points on the earth's surface having the same mean summer temperature. Cf. ISOCHEIM. — **i·soth′er·al**, *adj.*

i′so·therm (-thûrm), *n.* [*iso-* + Gr. *thermē* heat.] **1.** *Phys. Geog.* A line joining points on the earth's surface having the same temperature at a given time, or the same mean temperature for a given period. **2.** *Physics & Chem.* An isothermal line.

i′so·ther′mal (ī′sō·thûr′măl), *adj.* Of, pert. to, or indicating equality of temperature; specif., *Phys. Geog.*, relating to the geographical distribution of temperature, as shown by isotherms. — *n.* An isothermal line.

isothermal line *or* **curve**. **a** *Physics & Chem.* A line representing changes of volume or pressure under conditions of constant temperature. **b** *Phys. Geog.* = ISOTHERM, 1.

i′so·ton′ic (-tŏn′ĭk), *adj.* [Gr. *isotonos*. See ISO-; TONIC.] **1.** Having, or indicating, equal tones, or tension. **2.** *Biochem., Physical Chem., & Physiol.* Having the same or equal osmotic pressure; — esp. of solutions containing the proper percentage of salts to keep the red blood corpuscles unaltered in form and to prevent the removal of the hemoglobin. — **i′so·to·nic′i·ty** (-tō·nĭs′ĭ·tĭ), *n.*

i′so·tope (ī′sō·tōp), *n.* [*iso-* + Gr. *topos* place.] *Chem. & Physics.* Any of two or more forms of the same element, occupying the same position in the periodic table (that is, having the same atomic number), closely similar in chemical behavior, but distinguishable by radioactive transformations, differences in atomic weight, etc. According to present theory the nuclei of the isotopes of an element contain the same number of protons but different numbers of neutrons. — **i′so·top′ic** (-tŏp′ĭk), *adj.* — **i·sot′o·py** (ī·sŏt′ō·pĭ), *n.*

i′so·trop′ic (-trŏp′ĭk; -trō′pĭk), *adj.* [*iso-* + *tropic*.] **1.** *Physics.* Having the same properties in all directions. **2.** *Biol.* Not having predetermined axes, as certain eggs. — **i·sot′ro·py** (ī·sŏt′rō·pĭ), *n.*

i·sot′ro·pous (ī·sŏt′rō·pŭs), *adj.* Isotropic.

Is′ra·el (ĭz′rĭ·ĕl; -rā·ĕl), *n.* [L., fr. Gr. *Israēl*, fr. Heb. *Yisrā'ēl*, lit., contender with God.] **1.** *Bib.* Jacob. *Gen.* xxxii. 28. **2.** The northern Hebrew kingdom. **3.** Jacob's descendants; the Jews. **4.** Figuratively, God's chosen people; the elect; Christians collectively. **5.** The Jewish state in Palestine proclaimed May 15, 1948.

Is·rae′li (ĭz·rā′lĭ), *adj.* Of or pert. to the state of Israel. — *n.; pl.* ISRAELIS (-lĭz). An inhabitant of the state of Israel.

Is′ra·el·ite (ĭz′rĭ·ĕl·īt), *n.* **1.** A descendant of Israel, or Jacob; a Jew. **2.** One of God's chosen people. — *adj.* Israelitish; Jewish.

Is′ra·el·it′ish (-īt′ĭsh), *adj.* Also **Is′ra·el·it′ic** (-ĭt′ĭk). Of or pertaining to Israel or the Israelites.

Is′sa·char (ĭs′ȧ·kär), *n.* *Bib.* See JACOB.

is′sei′ (ēs′sā′), *n.; pl.* ISSEI, ISSEIS (-sāz′). [Jap. *is* first + *sei* generation.] A Japanese immigrant in the U. S., ineligible for citizenship. Cf. NISEI, KIBEI.

is′su·a·ble (ĭsh′ū·ȧ·b'l), *adj.* [From ISSUE.] **1.** Leading to an issue; capable of being made an issue at law. **2.** Lawful or liable to be issued; as, a writ *issuable* on these grounds. **3.** That may issue, as rents.

is′su·ance (-ăns), *n.* Act of issuing, or giving out; issue.

is′su·ant (-ănt), *adj.* Issuing; — in *Her.* said of a beast with only the upper part visible.

is′sue (ĭsh′ū; -ōō), *n.* [OF. *issue, eissue*, fr. *issir, eissir*, to go out, fr. L. *exire*, fr. *ex* out of, from + *ire* to go.] **1.** A going, passing, or flowing out; egress; exit. **2.** A means or place of issue; an exit, outlet, or vent. **3.** The outcome or result; upshot; event. **4.** *Obs.* An action or deed. *Shak.* **5.** Progeny; offspring. **6.** Produce; profits from property. **7.** A point in debate on which the parties take affirmative and negative positions. **8.** Act of sending out; delivery; issuance. **9.** That which is issued; the whole quantity emitted at one time; as, an *issue* of stock or stamps. **10.** *Med.* **a** A discharge, or flux, as of blood. **b** An artificial ulcer made, as by incision, to secure discharge of pus. — **Syn.** See EFFECT. — ***at issue***. At variance; disputed.

— *v. i.* **1.** To pass or flow out, esp. through an opening, from an enclosed place. **2.** To sally forth; emerge. **3.** To proceed, as progeny; to be descended. **4.** To accrue, as rents. **5.** To be derived; to emanate; to be produced as an effect; result. **6.** To be given out officially, as a proclamation, or emitted, as money. **7.** To terminate; as, how will the cause *issue?* — **Syn.** See SPRING. — *v. t.* **1.** To cause to issue; to discharge. **2.** To deliver, or give out, as provisions. **3.** To send out officially; to publish; to emit. — **is′su·er** (ĭsh′ū·ẽr; -ōō·ẽr), *n.*

-ist (-ĭst). [F. or L. or Gr.; F. *-iste*, fr. L. *-ista*, fr. Gr. *-istēs*.] A suffix forming agent nouns denoting: **a** *One who does*, or *makes a practice of* (1) a given action, commonly expressed by a corresponding verb in *-ize*, as in monopol*ist*; or (2) a specified class of conduct, as in bigam*ist*. **b** *One who practices* a given art, as in rhapsod*ist*; *one professionally* or *particularly occupied with*, or *skilled in*, a given department of knowledge or a (specified) musical instrument, as in botan*ist*, organ*ist*; or a given subject or thing, as in humor*ist*, balloon*ist*. **c** *One who professes*, or *adheres to*, or *advocates to an extreme*, a given doctrine, system, or cult, commonly denoted by a corresponding noun in *-ism*, as in athe*ist*, hedon*ist*.

isth′mi·an (ĭs′mĭ·ăn; ĭsth′-), *adj.* Of or pertaining to an isthmus; as [*cap.*]: **a** The Isthmus of Panama. **b** The Isthmus of Corinth, Greece, or the games anciently celebrated there. — *n.* A native or inhabitant of an isthmus.

isth′mus (ĭs′mŭs; ĭsth′-), *n.; pl.* ISTHMUSES (-ĕz; -ĭz), ISTHMI (-mī). [L., fr. Gr. *isthmos* isthmus, neck, narrow passage.] **1.** *Geog.* A neck or narrow strip of land by which two larger portions of land are connected. **2.** *Anat. & Zool.* A contracted part or passage connecting two larger structures or cavities.

is′tle (ĭs′tlĕ), *n.* Also **ix′tle** (ĭks′tlĕ; -tlĭ; ĭs′-). [Sp. *ixtle*, fr. Nahuatl *ichtli*.] **a** The fiber from the leaves of a kind of wild pineapple (*Bromelia sylvestris*). **b** The fiber from various Mexican agaves, used for cordage, basketry, etc.

it (ĭt; 4), *pron.; poss.* ITS; *obj.* IT. [ME. *it, hit*, fr. AS. *hit*, neut. of *hē*.] The neuter pronoun of the third person, singular number, used: **1.** As a substitute for any neuter noun in the nominative or objective case. **2.** As a demonstrative; as, what is *it?* **3.** As an indefinite nominative for an impersonal verb; as, *it* snows. **4.** As a substitute for such general terms as the state of affairs or the circumstances; as, how fares *it?* **5.** As a grammatical (usually anticipatory) subject or object of a verb; as, *it* is hard to believe what one hears. **6.** *Colloq.* As an indefinite object after some verbs, or after a substantive used as a verb; as, to foot *it*. — *n.* In certain games, as tag, the player who must perform a given task, as catching another player.

it′a·col′u·mite (ĭt′ȧ·kŏl′ū·mīt), *n.* [From *Itacolumi*, a mountain of Brazil.] *Petrog.* A micalike quartzite which in thin layers is flexible (called *flexible sandstone*).

I·tal′ian (ĭ·tăl′yăn), *adj.* Of or pertaining to Italy or its people, or their language or literature. — *n.* **1.** A native or citizen of Italy, or a member of one of its native races. **2.** The language of the Italians, developed from the vulgar, or popular, Latin of ancient times, the standard dialect being the Tuscan. See INDO-EUROPEAN LANGUAGES, *Table*.

I·tal′ian·ate (-āt), *adj.* Having an Italian form, character, or appearance. — (-āt), *v. t.* To Italianize.

I·tal′ian·ism (-ĭz′m), *n.* A practice, phrase, or idiom peculiarly Italian; Italian quality, spirit, etc.

I·tal′ian·ize (-īz), *v. i.* To speak or become Italian. — *v. t.* To render Italian in any respect. — **I·tal′ian·i·za′tion** (-ĭ·zā′shŭn; -ī·zā′-), *n.*

I·tal′ic (ĭ·tăl′ĭk), *adj.* [L. *Italicus*.] **1.** Of or pertaining to ancient Italy or its peoples. **2.** [*not cap.*] Designating type in which the letters slope up toward the right, as in *these words*. See TYPE, *n.* — *n.* **1.** A subfamily of the western division of Indo-European languages comprising the Osco-Umbrian, Sabellian, and Latinian branches. See INDO-EUROPEAN LANGUAGES, *Table*. **2.** [*not cap.*] An italic letter or type, or such letters, print, etc., collectively, called also **italics** (-ĭks) and now used chiefly to distinguish words for emphasis, importance, antithesis, etc. See TYPE, *n.*

I·tal′i·cism (-ĭ·sĭz′m), *n.* An Italianism.

i·tal′i·cize (-sīz), *v. t. & i.* To print in italics; to underline (written letters or words) with a single line.

itch (ĭch), *n.* [AS. *gicce.* See ITCH, *v.*] **1.** An itching, contagious eruption of the skin; specif., one caused by a certain parasitic mite, the **itch mite** (*Sarcoptes scabiei*), that burrows and breeds in the skin of man and animals; scabies. **2.** A sensation in the skin occasioned, or like that occasioned, by the itch eruption. **3.** A constant irritating desire or longing. — *v. i.* [ME. *icchen, yicchen*, fr. AS. *giccan.*] **1.** To have an uneasy sensation in the skin, which inclines the person to scratch the part affected. **2.** To have a constant desire; to long. — **itch'y** (ĭch'ĭ), *adj.*

itch'ing palm. Avaricious desire, as for bribes.

-ite (-īt). [F. or L. or Gr.; F. *-ite*, fr. L. *-ita, -ites*, fr. Gr. *-itēs*, fem. *-itis.*] **1.** A noun suffix denoting: **a** *A native* or *citizen of*, as in Gotham*ite*. **b** *One of a party, a sympathizer with* or *adherent of*, as in Bentham*ite*. **2.** *An explosive* or any of various other manufactured substances, as in melin*ite*. **3.** *Chem.* = -ITOL, as in mann*ite*. **4.** *Mineral. A mineral* or *rock*, as in anthrac*ite*, syen*ite*. **5.** *Paleontology. A fossil*, as in trilob*ite*. **6.** *Zool. A division of the body* or *of a part*, as in som*ite*.

-ite. [L. *-itus*, an ending of past participles.] A suffix in adjectives and verbs formed from Latin past participle stems, as in favor*ite*, exquis*ite*, exped*ite*, un*ite*.

-ite. [Arbitrary var. of *-ate* (see 1st -ATE, 3).] *Chem.* A suffix denoting a *salt* or *ester* formed from an acid whose name ends in *-ous*, as nitr*ite*, from nitr*ous* acid.

i'tem (ī'tĕm; ī'tĕm), *adv.* [L.] Also; — used to introduce each article in an enumeration. — *n.* **1.** *Obs.* A warning; a hint. **2.** An article; a separate particular in an enumeration or account; a detail. **3.** A separate piece of news or information; a short article; paragraph. — *v. t.* To set or note down as an item, or by or in items.

Syn. Item, detail, particular mean one of the distinct parts of a whole. **Item** applies usually to each thing specified in a list, an account, or the like; **detail**, to each thing which enters into a construction, a performance, etc., such as a house, a painting, a job, a way of living, or the like; **particular**, often implying a relation to the general or universal, may be used in place of *item* or *detail* when it stresses the smallness, singleness, or concreteness of each thing.

i'tem·ize (ī'tĕm·īz), *v. t.* *Chiefly U.S.* To state in items, or by particulars; as, to *itemize* charges or an invoice.

it'er·ance (ĭt'ĕr·ăns), *n.* Iteration; repetition.

it'er·ant (-ănt), *adj.* [L. *iterans*, pres. part.] Iterating.

it'er·ate (-āt), *v. t.* [L. *iteratus*, past part. of *iterare* to repeat, fr. *iterum* again.] To utter or do a second time or many times; to repeat. — **Syn.** See REPEAT. — **it'er·a'tion** (-ā'shŭn), *n.*

it'er·a'tive (-ā'tĭv; -ȧ·tĭv), *adj.* Repeating; repeated.

ith'er (ĭth'ĕr). Scot., N. of Eng., and Ir. var. of OTHER, EITHER.

I'thunn, I'thun (ē'thōōn), *n.* *Norse Myth.* The wife of Bragi, having the golden apples of youth in her keeping.

I·thu'ri·el (ĭ·thū'rĭ·ĕl), *n.* [Heb. *yithūrī'ēl* the superiority of God.] In Milton's *Paradise Lost*, an angel who found Satan "squat like a toad, close at the ear of Eve," and transformed him by a touch of his spear to his proper shape.

ith'y·phal'lic (ĭth'ĭ·făl'ĭk), *adj.* [L. *ithyphallicus*, fr. Gr. *ithyphallikos*, fr. *ithyphallos* membrum virile erectum, or a figure thereof.] **1.** Of the phallus carried in the festivals of Bacchus; hence, lewd. **2.** Written in the meter of the Bacchic hymns; esp., consisting of a trochaic tripody.

i·tin'er·a·cy (ī·tĭn'ĕr·ȧ·sĭ; ĭ-), *n.* Also **i·tin'er·an·cy** (-ăn·sĭ). **1.** Act of itinerating, or state of being itinerant; a passing from place to place. **2.** A discharge of official duty involving frequent change of residence; also, a body of itinerants. **3.** Itinerant preaching, or system of rotation, of ministers.

i·tin'er·ant (-ănt), *adj.* [LL. *itinerans, -antis*, pres. part. of *itinerari* to make a journey, fr. L. *iter, itineris*, a walk, journey.] Passing about a country; as, *itinerant* laborers; going or preaching on a circuit; as, an *itinerant* preacher. — *n.* One who travels from place to place. — **i·tin'er·ant·ly**, *adv.*

i·tin'er·ar'y (ī·tĭn'ĕr·ĕr'ĭ; ĭ-; *or, esp. Brit.*, -ĕr·ĭ), *adj.* Pertaining to a route, or journeying, or roads. — *n.; pl.* -ARIES (-ĭz). **1.** A route. **2.** A record of a journey. **3.** A traveler's guidebook or outline of a route.

i·tin'er·ate (ī·tĭn'ĕr·āt; ĭ-), *v. i.* [LL. *itineratus*, past part.] To travel about or on a circuit, esp. to preach. — **i·tin'er·a'tion** (-ā'shŭn), *n.*

-i'tion (-ĭsh'ŭn). [F. or L.; F. *-ition*, fr. L. *-itionem.*] A noun suffix equivalent to -ATION, as in aud*ition*, trans*ition*.

-i'tious (-ĭsh'ŭs). [L. *-icius.*] An adjective suffix denoting *of the nature of* or *characterized by*, as in fict*itious*.

-i'tis (-ī'tĭs; *by some*, -ē'tĭs). [Gr. *-itis*, orig. fem. adj. suffix.] A noun suffix used to denote: *A disease*; specif., *an inflammatory disease of a* (specified) *part*, as in bronch*itis*.

-i·tol (-ĭ·tōl; -ĭ·tŏl). [1st *-ite* + *-ol*, 1.] *Chem.* A compound suffix used in naming certain alcohols having more than one hydroxyl group.

its (ĭts), *adj.* [*it*, pron. + *'s*, possessive case ending; formerly written *it's.*] **1.** Of or belonging to it, that object, or itself, as possessor. **2.** Of or relating to it as source, cause, agent, etc. **3.** Of or relating to it as object.

it's (ĭts). Contraction of *it is*.

it·self' (ĭt·sĕlf'), *pron.* Emphasized or reflexive form of *it*.

it's me. See *Note* under ME.

-i·ty (-ĭ·tĭ). [F. or L.; F. *-ité*, fr. L. *-itas.* See -TY.] A suffix denoting *state, condition, quality*, or *degree*, as in acid*ity*, calam*ity*.

-i·um (-ĭ·ŭm). *Chem.* A modern Latin suffix used in forming the names of elements, as in uran*ium*, sod*ium*, hel*ium*.

-ive (-ĭv). [F. or L.; F. *-if*, fem. *-ive*, fr. L. *-ivus.*] A suffix signifying: **a** *Having the nature* or *quality of* (a thing), as in affirmat*ive*. **b** *Given* or *tending to* (an action), as in conclus*ive*.

I've (īv). Colloq. contraction of *I have*.

i'vied (ī'vĭd), *adj.* Overgrown with ivy.

i'vo·ry (ī'vō·rĭ), *n.; pl.* -RIES (-rĭz). [AF. *ivorie*, ONF. *ivurie*, OF. (& F.) *ivoire*, fr. L. *eboreus* made of ivory, fr. *ebur, eboris*, ivory.] **1.** The hard, creamy-white, opaque, fine-grained dentine composing elephants' tusks; also, the dentine of the tusks of other large mammals, or of any tooth. **2. a** A color, reddish-yellow in hue, of low saturation and very high brilliance. See COLOR. **b** Whiteness, as of the skin. **3.** A tusk, esp. of the elephant. **4.** An ivorylike substance; as, vegetable *ivory*. **5.** *Slang.* Any article made of ivory, as, *pl.*, dice or piano keys. — *adj.* Of or like ivory; of the color ivory.

ivory black. A fine black pigment made by calcining ivory.

ivory nut. The nutlike seed of a South American palm, the ***ivory palm*** (*Phytelephas macrocarpa*), containing a very hard endosperm (called ***vegetable ivory***) used for turning and carving, as for buttons.

ivory tower. A retreat; a secluded place for meditation; — figuratively; as, an *ivory tower* of aloofness from life.

i'vy (ī'vĭ), *n.; pl.* IVIES (-vĭz). [AS. *īfig.*] **1.** A well-known climbing or prostrate woody vine (*Hedera helix*) of the ginseng family, with evergreen leaves, small yellowish flowers, and black berries; — called in the United States ***English ivy***. **2.** Any of various other plants resembling the true ivy; as, ***American ivy*** (see VIRGINIA CREEPER); ***poison ivy*** (see POISON IVY, *Illust.*). Cf. JAPANESE IVY.

i'vy·ber'ry (-bĕr'ĭ), *n.* *U.S.* The wintergreen *Gaultheria procumbens.*

i·wis', y·wis' (ĭ·wĭs'), *adv.* [AS. *gewis* certain.] *Archaic.* Certainly; — often mistakenly written *I wis*, as if from the verb *wit*, to know.

ix'i·a (ĭk'sĭ·ȧ), *n.* [NL., fr. Gr. *ixos* birdlime; — from the viscid nature of some species.] A bulb, plant, or flower of a genus (*Ixia*) of South African bulbous plants of the iris family.

Ix·i'on (ĭks·ī'ŏn), *n.* *Gr. Myth.* A king of the Lapithae, a Thessalian people, bound in Tartarus to an endlessly revolving wheel for aspiring to the love of Hera.

ix'tle. See ISTLE.

I'yar, Iy'yar (ē'yär), *n.* [Heb. *iyyār.*] See JEWISH CALENDAR.

-i·za'tion (-ĭ·zā'shŭn; -ī·zā'shŭn). A compound suffix forming nouns derived from verbs in *-ize*, as in steril*ization*.

iz·ba'. Var. of ISBA.

-ize (-īz). [F. or L. or Gr.; F. *-iser*, fr. LL. *-izare*, fr. Gr. *-izein.*]. A suffix forming verbs with the following senses: **1.** (Transitive verbs) **a** *To subject to* (action, treatment, or process), as in catech*ize*, cauter*ize*, satir*ize*. **b** *To render, make into, put into conformity with*, or *make like* (thing, character, or quality), as in Christian*ize*, steril*ize*. **c** *Chem. To impregnate, treat*, or *combine with*, as in oxid*ize*. **2.** (Intransitive verbs) *To act in the way of*, or *practice*, or *carry on*, as in apostat*ize*, botan*ize*.

☞ Certain words ending with the sound of īz are always spelled with *-ise* after the French *-iser* or *-ise*, as dev*ise*, surpr*ise*. But the great body of words so ending are spelled either *-ize* or *-ise*. There is a tendency to prefer the *-ize* spelling. In general, the forms in *-ise* are not entered in this dictionary. See *Orthography*, § 18.

iz'zard (ĭz'ĕrd), *n.* [Formerly *ezed.*] *Dial.* The letter Z, z.

J

J, j (jā), *n.; pl.* J's, j's, Js, JS (jāz). **1.** The tenth letter of the English alphabet. J is a late variant of the Latin I, which was used indifferently as a vowel or as a consonant (English *y* in *yet*). As the form prolonged above or below the line was often initial, and the initial was usually consonantal, the *j* gradually became differentiated from *i* in function as well as form until in the 17th century the distinction of *j* as consonant and *i* as vowel was fully established. **2.** The sound of this letter. In English, the regular sound of *j* is as in *jet* (= *dzh*), the same as *g* in *gem*. See *Pron.*, § 59. Etymologically, English *j* is of varied origin (cf. the etymologies of *conjure, jelly, jot, journey, joy*). **3.** As a *symbol*, tenth in order or class.

jab (jăb), *v. t. & i.*; JABBED (jăbd); JAB'BING. [Var. of JOB to stab.] To thrust abruptly with something sharp; to poke. — *n.* A jabbing; a quick or abrupt thrust or stab.

jab'ber (jăb'ĕr), *v. i. & t.* To talk or utter rapidly, indistinctly, or unintelligibly; to chatter. — *n.* Act of jabbering; incoherent utterance; gibberish. — **jab'ber·er**, *n.*

jab'i·ru (jăb'ĭ·rōō), *n.* [Sp. & Pg. *jabirú*, fr. Tupi *jabirú, jaburú.*] The wood ibis (*Mycteria americana*).

jab'o·ran'di (jăb'ō·răn'dĭ), *n.* [Pg. & Sp., fr. Tupi *jaborandi.*] *Pharm.* The dried leaflets of a shrub (*Pilocarpus jaborandi*) of the rue family, containing alkaloids, as pilocarpine.

ja'bot' (zhȧ'bō' *or, esp. Brit.*, zhă'bō), *n.; pl.* JABOTS (zhȧ'bōz'; zhă'bōz; *F.* zhȧ'bō'). [F.] **1.** Originally, a ruffle worn by men on the shirt bosom. **2.** A trimming of lace, tulle, chiffon, etc., worn by women down the dress front.

ja'ça·na' (zhä'sȧ·nä'), *n.* [Pg., fr. Tupi *jaçanam, jassanam.*] Any of a family (Jacanidae) of wading birds having extremely long toes, enabling them to run about on floating lily pads.

jac'a·ran'da (jăk'ȧ·răn'dȧ), *n.* [NL., fr. Pg. *jacarandá*, fr. Tupi *jacarandá.*] A tropical American tree (family Bignoniaceae) having pinnate leaves and showy blue flowers; also, its wood.

ja'cinth (jā'sĭnth; jăs'ĭnth), *n.* [OF. *iacinte, iacincte* (F. *jacinthe*), fr. L. *hyacinthus.*] Hyacinth, the gem, esp. when nearly pure orange in color.

jack (jăk), *n.; pl.* JACKS (jăks), *sometimes* JACK. [Pg. *jaca*, fr. Malayalam *cakka.*] The fruit of a large East Indian tree (*Artocarpus integra*) of the mulberry family, allied to the breadfruit; also, the tree, or its fine-grained yellow wood, used in cabinetwork.

jack (jăk), *n.* [OF. *jaque*, fr. Sp. *jaco* jacket, coat of mail.] **1.** A medieval coat of defense, esp. one of leather. **2.** [Perhaps from resemblance to a *jack boot.*] *Archaic.* A pitcher or can for liquor, orig. of waxed leather.

jack, *n.* [OF. *Jaques* James, fr. LL. *Jacobus*, fr. Gr. *Iakōbos*, fr. Heb. *Ya'ăqōbh* Jacob, prop., supplanter. Also, in E., a familiar form

of *John*.] **1.** [*cap.*] A familiar nickname of the masculine proper name *John*. **2. a** [*cap.*] A man of the common people. **b** [*often cap.*] A sailor. **c** [*sometimes cap.*] A doer of odd jobs. **3.** A figure, esp. on old clocks, which strikes the time on the bell. **4.** The male of certain animals. **5.** Short for JACKASS, JACK RABBIT, JACKDAW, JACKSNIPE, etc. **6.** Any of various contrivances, orig. one that took the place of a boy; as: **a** A contrivance for turning a spit. **b** A hood placed over a chimney or vent pipe. **c** A bootjack. **7.** *Bowls.* The small ball used as a mark. **8.** *Card Playing.* Any of the knaves in a pack. **9.** *Elec.* A receptacle with connections to electric circuits, arranged for convenient plugging in. **10.** *Hunting, U.S.* The pan for the fuel of the torch used in attracting game or fish at night. **11.** *Mech. & Mach.* A portable machine, for exerting great pressure, or lifting a heavy body through a small distance, as a jackscrew, a ratchet jack, a hydraulic jack. **12.** *Naut.* A bar of iron at a topgallant masthead, to support a royal mast and spread the royal shrouds. **13.** *Nav.* A small flag used as a signal, usually the same as the union (and then often called *union jack*).
— v. t. 1. To move or lift by means of a jack (sense 11); — with *up*; hence, *Colloq.*: **a** To increase, as prices. **b** To bring up to one's duty. **2.** *U.S.* To hunt or fish for at night with a jack.

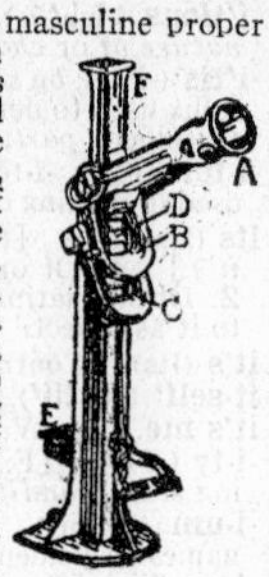

Jack, 11 (Ratchet Jack with Foot Lift). *A* Socket for Elevating Lever; *B* Lifting Pawl; *C* Detent; *D* Rack; *E* Lifting Foot; *F* Lifting Head.

jack'–a–dan'dy, *n.* A little dandy, or foppish fellow.
jack'al (jăk'ôl), *n.*; see PLURAL, *Note*, 3. [Turk. *chaqāl*, fr. Per. *shagāl, shaghāl*.] **1.** Any of several wild dogs (esp. *Canis aureus*) of the Old World, smaller, more yellowish, and much more cowardly than wolves. **2.** One who does mean work for another's advantage.
jack'a·napes' (jăk'ȧ·nāps'), *n.* [For *Jack o'* (= *of*) *Napes* (for *Naples*) a Jack (monkey or ape) from Naples in Italy.] **1.** *Archaic.* A monkey; an ape. **2.** A coxcomb; an impertinent or conceited fellow.
jack'a·roo' (jăk'ȧ·rōō'), *n.* [*Jack* + kang*aroo*.] *Colloq., Australia.* A young apprentice on a sheep station, or otherwise engaged in acquainting himself with colonial life.
jack'ass' (jăk'ăs'; 9), *n.* [*Jack* + *ass*.] **1.** A male ass. **2.** A dolt; a blockhead.
jack boot, *or* **jack'boot'** (jăk'bōōt'), *n.* A type of large boot reaching above the knee, formerly worn by cavalrymen.
jack'daw' (jăk'dô'), *n.* [*Jack* + *daw*, n.] A common glossy-black crowlike bird (*Corvus monedula*) of Europe, similar to the American grackles.
jack'et (jăk'ĕt; -ĭt), *n.* [F. *jaquette*, dim. of *jaque*. See 2d JACK.] **1.** A short coat without skirts, usually with sleeves. **2.** Any of various outer coverings or casings; as: **a** *U.S.* A wrapper for an official document. **b** A tough metal covering on a bullet or projectile. **c** A coating or lagging of some nonconducting material, used to prevent heat radiation. **d** An outer casing through which can be passed a fluid for maintaining a predetermined temperature. **e** A detachable outer paper wrapper, issued with a bound book. **— v. t.** To put a jacket on; to furnish with a jacket.
Jack Frost. Frost or frosty weather personified.
jack'–in–a–box', *n.* A tropical tree (*Hernandia sonora*) typifying a family (Hernandiaceae, the jack-in-a-box family), bearing a drupe that rattles in the calyx when dry.
jack'–in–the–box', *n.*; *pl.* JACK-IN-THE-BOXES. A child's toy, consisting of a box, out of which, when the lid is raised, a figure springs.
jack'–in–the–pul'pit, *n.*; *pl.* -PULPITS. An American spring-flowering woodland herb (*Arisaema atrorubens*) of the arum family, bearing an upright club-shaped spadix with an overarching green and purple spathe; — called also *Indian turnip*. See SPADIX, *Illust.*
Jack Ketch (kĕch). [After a notorious executioner.] *Eng.* A public hangman.
jack'knife' (jăk'nīf'), *n.*; *pl.* -KNIVES (-nīvz'). **1.** A large, strong pocketknife. See KNIFE, *Illust.* (2). **2.** A dive in which the diver bends from the waist and touches his ankles while holding his knees unflexed.
jack light. *U.S.* A torch used in hunting or fishing at night.
Jack'–of–all'–trades', *n.* A person who can do passable work at various trades; a handy man.
jack'–o'–lan'tern, *n.*; *pl.* -LANTERNS. **1.** An ignis fatuus; a will-o'-the-wisp. **2.** A lantern made of a pumpkin, so as to show features of a human face.
jack plane. See PLANE, *Illust.*
jack pot. *Poker.* A pot or pool which cannot be opened until some player has a pair of jacks or better. Cf. POKER, *Illust.*
jack rabbit. Any of several large hares (genus *Lepus*) of western North America, having very long ears and long hind legs.
jack'screw' (jăk'skrōō'), *n.* A jack in which a screw is used for lifting or for exerting pressure.
jack'snipe' (-snīp'), *n.*; see PLURAL, *Note*, 3. **a** A true snipe (*Limnocryptes gallinula*) of the Old World, smaller than the common snipe. **b** The pectoral sandpiper.
jack'–span'iard, *n.* Any of numerous tropical social wasps, esp. of the genus *Polistes*, which build paper nests.
jack'stay' (-stā'), *n.* *Naut.* **a** An iron rod, wooden bar, or wire rope, stretching along a yard of a vessel, to which the sails are fastened. **b** A support of wood, iron, or rope, running up and down a mast, on which a yard travels.
jack'stone' (-stōn'), *n.* **a** *pl.* A game played with five or six small stones or specially shaped pieces of metal. **b** One of such metal pieces.
jack'straw' (-strô'), *n.* **1.** An effigy stuffed with straw. **2.** One of a set of straws or of strips of ivory, bone, etc., thrown in a heap, to be plucked out without disturbing the rest; also, *pl.*, the game so played.
jack'–tar' (jăk'tär'), *n.* *Colloq.* A sailor.
jack towel. A coarse towel, hung on a roller.
Ja'cob (jā'kŭb), *n.* [LL. *Jacobus*. See 3d JACK.] *Bib.* Hebrew patriarch, son of Isaac and Rebekah, father (*Gen.* xxv–l) of the twelve patriarchs, ancestors of the twelve tribes of Israel: Reuben, Simeon, Levi, Judah, Dan, Naphtali, Gad, Asher, Issachar, Zebulun, Joseph (his tribe later dividing and being named for his two sons Manasseh and Ephraim), and Benjamin.
Jac'o·be'an (jăk'ō·bē'ăn), *adj.* [NL. & LL. *Jacobaeus*, fr. *Jacobus* Jacob, James.] Of or pertaining to James I, of England, or his reign or times; specif., designating, or pertaining to, a style of architecture and decoration prevailing in England in the early 17th century, a continuation of the Elizabethan, with freer use of the classical orders. **— n.** A Jacobean statesman or writer.
Jac'o·bin (jăk'ō·bĭn), *n.* [F.] **1.** *Eccl. Hist.* A Dominican friar. **2.** One of a society or club of radical democrats in France during the revolution of 1789; hence, a plotter against an existing government; a violent radical or turbulent demagogue. **3.** [*not cap.*] A breed of fancy pigeons having the neck feathers reversed, forming a fluffy hood.
Jac'o·bin'ic (-bĭn'ĭk), **Jac'o·bin'i·cal** (-ĭ·kăl), *adj.* Of or pertaining to the Jacobins of France; violently radical.
Jac'o·bin·ism (jăk'ō·bĭn·ĭz'm), *n.* **1.** The principles of the French Jacobins; violent radicalism, esp. in politics. **2.** A Jacobinic idea or trait. — **Jac'o·bin·ize** (-īz), *v. t.*
Jac'o·bite (-bīt), *n.* [LL. *Jacobus* James. See JACOBEAN.] *Eng. Hist.* A partisan or adherent of James II, after his abdication, or of his descendants. — **Jac'o·bit'i·cal** (-bĭt'ĭ·kăl), *adj.* — **Jac'o·bit·ism** (jăk'ō·bīt·ĭz'm), *n.*
Ja'cob's lad'der (jā'kŭbz). **1.** The ladder which Jacob saw in his dream. (*Gen.* xxviii. 12). **2.** *Naut.* A rope or wire ladder with wooden or iron rungs.
Ja'cob's–lad'der, *n.* A pinnate-leaved European perennial herb (*Polemonium caeruleum*) with bright-blue or white flowers; also, any of several related American species.
ja·co'bus (jȧ·kō'bŭs), *n.* [See JACOBITE.] The English gold coin unite.
Jac·quard' loom (jă·kärd'). [After J. M. *Jacquard* (1752–1834), a French mechanician.] A loom fitted with a mechanism controlled by a chain of perforated cards, for weaving figured fabrics.
Jacque'mi·not (jăk'mĭ·nō; *F.* zhȧk'mē'nō'), *n.* [After a French general.] A deep crimson perennial rose.
‖**Jac'que·rie'** (zhȧk'rē'), *n.* [F.] A revolt of French peasants against the nobles in 1358, named from the contemptuous title, **Jacques Bon'homme'** (zhȧk' bô'nôm'), given by the nobles to the peasantry; hence, any revolt of peasants.
jac·ta'tion (jăk·tā'shŭn), *n.* [L. *jactatio*, fr. *jactare* to throw, boast.] **1.** *Med.* Jactitation. **2.** Boasting.
jac'ti·ta'tion (jăk'tĭ·tā'shŭn), *n.* [ML. *jactitatio*.] **1.** Boasting; bragging; specif., *Law*, false boasting or assertions repeated to another's prejudice; false claim. **2.** *Med.* A tossing or jerking of the body; excessive restlessness.
jac'u·late (jăk'ū·lāt), *v. t. & i.* [L. *jaculatus*, past part. See EJACULATE.] To throw, as a dart. — **jac'u·la'tion** (-lā'shŭn), *n.*
jade (jād), *n.* [F., fr. Sp. piedra de *ijada* (stone of the side, fr. *ijada* flank, side, pain in the side (the stone being supposed to cure this pain), fr. L. *ilia* flanks.] **1.** A tough, compact gem stone, commonly green, capable of a high polish, cut from two minerals: **a** Jadeite, or ***true jade***. **b** Nephrite. **2.** The color jade green.
jade (jād), *n.* Also, *Scot.*, **jad** (jȧd; jăd). **1.** A horse; a mean, tired, vicious, or worn-out horse. **2.** A woman; a disreputable woman; a wench. **— v. t. & i.** To tire or wear out by or from severe or tedious tasks. — **Syn.** See TIRE. — **jad'ish** (jād'ĭsh), *adj.*
jad'ed (jād'ĕd; -ĭd), *adj.* Exhausted; worn out; also, dulled; surfeited.
jade green. A color varying from yellowish-green to greenish-yellow in hue. — **jade'–green'**, *adj.*
jade'ite (jād'īt), *n.* *Mineral.* A monoclinic mineral of the pyroxene group, constituting a valuable variety of jade.
‖**j'a'doube'** (zhȧ'dōōb'). [F.] Literally, I adjust; — used in playing chess and checkers when a player touches a piece without meaning to make a move.
jae'ger (yā'gẽr; *in sense* 2 *also* jā'gẽr), *n.* **1.** Var. of JÄGER. **2.** Any bird (esp. of genus *Stercorarius*) of the family Stercorariidae (sometimes ranked as a subfamily of Laridae: see 2d GULL **a**), noted for harassing weaker birds until they drop or disgorge their prey; — called also *skua*.
jag (jăg), *n.* Also **jagg**. A sharp projecting part; a tooth.
jag, *v. t.*; JAGGED (jăgd); JAG'GING. **1.** *Dial.* To prick, stab, or jab. **2.** To pink or slash, as a garment; to cut into teeth as those of a saw; to cut indentations in; to notch.
jag, *n.* Also **jagg**. [Origin unknown.] **1.** *Dial.* A small load, as of hay. **2.** *Slang, U.S.* Enough liquor to make one noticeably drunk; a spree; — esp. in the phrase *to have a jag on*, to be drunk.
Jag'an·nath (jŭg'ȧ·nät; -nôt), **Jag'an·na'tha** (-nät'hȧ), *n.* Also **Jug'ger·naut** (jŭg'ẽr·nôt). [Hind. *Jagannāth* lord of the world, fr. Skr. *jagannātha*.] *Hinduism.* A form of Vishnu, or of Krishna, whose chief idol during festival is drawn upon a car adorned with obscene paintings, under the wheels of which it was once supposed that devotees allowed themselves to be crushed.
jä'ger (yā'gẽr), *n.* [G. *jäger*, fr. root of *jagen* to hunt.] **1.** A hunter. **2.** [*often cap.*] A German or Austrian rifleman. **3.** (yā'gẽr; jā'-) A jaeger.
jag'ged (jăg'ĕd; -ĭd), *part. adj.* Having jags or sharp notches; sharply pointed. — **jag'ged·ly**, *adv.* — **jag'ged·ness**, *n.*
jag'ger·y (jăg'ẽr·ĭ), *n.* [Hind. *jāgrī*, fr. Skr. *śarkarā*.] A coarse brown East Indian sugar made from palm sap.
jag'uar (jăg'wär; -ū·är; -ū·ẽr), *n.*; see PLURAL, *Note*, 3. [Sp. & Pg., of Tupian origin.] A large powerful cat (*Felis onca*), brownish yellow or buff marked with black spots, ranging from Texas to Paraguay.
Jah've, Jah'veh (yä'vĕ), **Jah'vism**, etc. Vars. of YAHWEH, etc.
‖**jai a·lai'** (hī' ä·lī'), *n* [Sp., fr. Basque *jai* festival + *alai* merry.] A court game, resembling rackets, played with a ball and wicker rackets by two players on each side.
jail (jāl), *n.* Also **gaol** (jāl). [OF. *jaiole*, ONF. *gaiole*, fr. VL. *cabeola*, dim. fr. L. *cavea* cage.] A building for the confinement of persons held in lawful custody, esp. for minor offenses or pending judicial proceeding; a lockup. **— v. t.** To confine in or as in a jail.
jail'bird' (-bûrd'), *n.* Also **gaol'bird'**. *Colloq.* A prisoner in jail, esp. a habitual criminal.
jail delivery. **1.** *Eng. Law.* The clearing of a jail by bringing the prisoners to trial, esp. at the assizes. **2.** Deliverance from a jail, whether by force or otherwise.
jail'er (jāl'ẽr), *n.* Also **jail'or, gaol'er**. The keeper of a jail.
Jain (jīn), **Jai'na** (jī'nȧ). [Hind. *Jaina*, fr. Skr. *Jaina*, fr. *jina* saint, fr. *jina* victorious.] An adherent of Jainism.
Jain'ism (-ĭz'm), *n.* A heterodox Hindu religion founded about the 6th century B.C. in which the Vedas are rejected, as in Buddhism, and respect for the lives of animals is carried to great lengths.

jal′ap (jăl′ăp), *n.* [F., fr. Sp. *jalapa*, fr. *Jalapa*, town in Mexico.] **a** The purgative tuberous root of a Mexican plant (*Exogonium purga*) of the morning-glory family; also, a powdered drug prepared from it. **b** Any plant yielding jalap.

jal′a·pin (jăl′ȧ·pĭn), *n.* *Chem.* An ether-soluble glucoside constituent (about ten per cent) of true jalap resin.

ja·lop′y, ja·lop′py (jȧ·lŏp′ĭ), *n.; pl.* -IES (-ĭz). [Origin obscure.] *U. S.* A dilapidated automobile or airplane.

jal′ou·sie (zhăl′o͝o·sē; zhăl′o͝o·zē; *also* jăl′o͝o·sē′; zhăl′o͝o·zē′), *n.* [F., prop., jealousy.] A blind or a shutter having horizontal slats sloping like louver boards, to admit air and light and exclude sun and rain.

jam (jăm), *v. t.;* JAMMED (jămd); JAM′MING. Also **jamb** (jăm). **1.** To press into a close or tight position; to crowd; squeeze; wedge in; also, to thrust or apply with force and suddenness; as, to *jam* one's brakes on; to force as if by jamming; as, to *jam* a bill through a legislature. **2.** To crush or bruise. **3.** To cause to be wedged or fixed so as to be unworkable, as some movable part of a machine. **4.** *Radio.* To render (radio signals) unintelligible by sending interfering signals. — *v. i.* **1.** To become blocked, wedged, or fixed. **2.** To become unworkable through the wedging or fixing of some part or parts. **3.** *Swing Music.* To participate in a jam session. — *n.* **1.** Act of jamming; state of being jammed; a crush. **2.** *Colloq., U. S.* A state of involved affairs; a "tight place." — **Syn.** See PREDICAMENT.

jam, *n.* Fruit boiled with sugar to a thick consistency, without preserving the shape of the fruit.

jamb (jăm), *n.* Also **jambe**. [F. *jambe* leg, *jambe de force* a principal rafter, fr. L. *gamba, camba*.] **1.** An upright piece forming the side of an opening, as of a door or fireplace. **2.** *Armor.* A jambeau. See ARMOR, *Illust.*

jam′beau (jăm′bō), *n.; pl.* JAMBEAUX (-bōz). [F. *jambe* leg.] A piece of armor for the leg. See ARMOR, *Illust.*

jam′bo·ree′ (jăm′bō·rē′), *n.* [Origin uncert.] **1.** *Slang.* A noisy carousal or merrymaking. **2.** An international, national, or intersectional gathering of boy scouts. Cf CAMPOREE.

James (jāmz), *n.* [F., fr. LL. *Jacobus*.] *Bib.* **a** An apostle, son of Zebedee. **b** An apostle, son of Alphaeus. **c** James the Less, often identified with James, son of Alphaeus. **d** The James called the Lord's brother in Gal. i. 19. **e** The Epistle of James in the New Testament. See BIBLE.

jam session. [See 1st JAM, *n.*] *Swing Music.* A meeting of musicians for playing without scores in the impromptu swing-music style for their own entertainment.

Jam·shid′, Jam·shyd′ (jăm·shēd′), *n.* [Per. *Jamshīd*.] *Persian Myth.* The king of the peris, who, in punishment for his boast of immortality, was compelled to assume a human form and dwell on earth, where he became a mighty king of Persia.

jan′gle (jăng′g'l), *v. i.;* JAN′GLED (-g'ld); JAN′GLING (-glĭng). [OF. *jangler*.] **1.** To talk idly; to prate. **2.** To quarrel in words; to wrangle. **3.** To sound discordantly, as bells out of tune. — *v. t.* To cause (bells) to jangle. — *n.* Act or sound of jangling.

jan′i·tor (jăn′ĭ·tẽr), *n.* [L.; akin to L. *janua* door.] **1.** A doorkeeper; porter. **2.** *U. S.* One having the care of a building, offices, etc. — **jan′i·to′ri·al** (-tō′rĭ·ăl), *adj.* — **jan′i·tress** (-trĕs; -trĭs), *n. fem.*

Jan′i·zar′y (jăn′ĭ·zĕr′ĭ *or, esp. Brit.,* -zẽr·ĭ), *n.; pl.* -IES (-ĭz). Also **Jan′is·sar′y** (-sĕr′ĭ; -sẽr·ĭ). [F. and It.; F. *janissaire*, (prob. fr.) It. *giannizzero*, fr. Turk. *yeñicheri* new troops.] [*often not cap.*] A soldier of a body of Turkish infantry that existed from the 14th century, consisting at first of slaves, and later forming the main fighting force of the Turks until abolished 1826; also, any Turkish soldier.

Jan′sen·ism (jăn′sĕn·ĭz'm), *n.* *Eccl. Hist.* The doctrines of Cornelis Jansen (1585–1638), bishop of Ypres, including total depravity, irresistible grace, loss of free will, predestination, and limited atonement. — **Jan′sen·ist** (-ĭst), *n.* — **Jan′sen·is′tic** (-ĭs′tĭk), **Jan′sen·is′ti·cal** (-tĭ·kăl), *adj.*

Jan′u·ar′y (jăn′ū·ĕr′ĭ *or, esp. Brit.,* -ẽr·ĭ), *n.* [L. *Januarius*, fr. *Janus*, Latin deity to whom the month was sacred.] The first month of the year, having 31 days. Abbr. *Jan.*

Ja′nus (jā′nŭs), *n.* [L.] An ancient Roman deity, primarily god of gates and doors, and hence, of all beginnings. He was represented with two opposite faces, probably symbolizing the faces of a door. — **Ja′nus-faced′** (-fāst′), *adj.*

ja·pan′ (jȧ·păn′), *n.* [From *Japan*, the country.] **1.** Any varnish yielding a hard brilliant coating, as the natural Japanese lacquer (see LACQUER, 1 **b**). **2.** Work varnished and figured in the Japanese manner. — *adj.* Of, pertaining to, or coated or treated with japan. — *v. t.;* JA·PANNED′ (-pănd′); JA·PAN′NING. To cover with a coat of japan, or of some other hard, brilliant varnish; to lacquer.

Jap′a·nese′ (jăp′ȧ·nēz′; -nēs′; 2), *n.* **1.** *sing. & pl.* A member of the native race of Japan; also, a native or inhabitant of Japan **2.** The language of the Japanese, an agglutinative tongue, forming a family by itself. It is distantly related to Korean and perhaps to the Ural-Altaic family. See LANGUAGE, *Table.* — *adj.* Of or pertaining to Japan, its inhabitants, or their language.

Japanese beetle. *Zool.* A small green-and-brown leaf chafer (*Popillia japonica*) introduced into America from Japan. The adults eat foliage and fruits; the grubs feed on the roots of grasses. It is a serious pest.

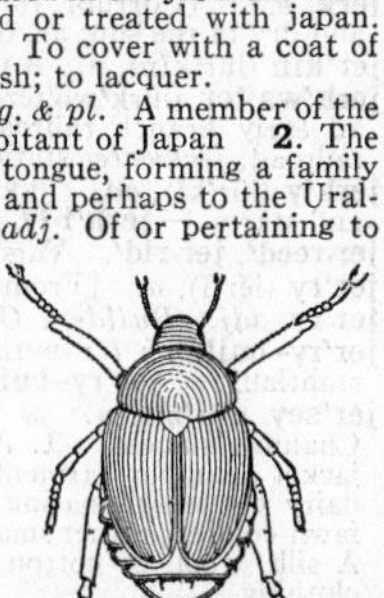

Japanese Beetle.

Japanese ivy. A woody Chinese and Japanese vine (*Parthenocissus tricuspidata*) having 3-lobed, or trifoliolate, leaves and clinging to walls by its disk-bearing tendrils.

Japanese lantern. = CHINESE LANTERN.

Japanese quince. A hardy Chinese shrub (*Chaenomeles lagenaria*) with handsome scarlet flowers, grown chiefly for ornament, often under the syn. *Cydonia japonica*. A similar smaller-flowered species (*Chaenomeles japonica*) is called ***dwarf Japanese quince.*** Both are known also as *flowering quince* and *japonica*.

Japanese yew. See YEW, *n.*, 1.

jape (jāp), *v. i.* To jest; to play tricks; to jeer. — *v. t.* To trick; fool; deride; mock. — *n.* A jest; fraud; now usually, a joke; a jibe. — **jap′er** (jāp′ẽr), *n.* — **jap′er·y** (-ĭ), *n.*

Ja′pheth (jā′fĕth), *n.* [L. *Japheth* or Gr. *Iapheth*, fr. Heb. *Yepheth*.] *Bib.* One of the sons of Noah.

Ja·phet′ic (jȧ·fĕt′ĭk), *adj.* Pertaining to, or derived from, Japheth, a son of Noah; — formerly used vaguely of the Caucasians of Europe and some adjacent parts of Asia.

ja·pon′i·ca (jȧ·pŏn′ĭ·kȧ), *n.* [NL., Japanese, fr. *Japonia* Japan.] *Hort.* **1.** = CAMELLIA. **2.** = JAPANESE QUINCE.

Ja′ques (jā′kwēz; -kwĭz), *n.* A lord attending the exiled duke in *As You Like It.* He affects a cynical philosophy.

jar (jär), *n.* [F. *jarre*, fr. Pr. *jarro*, fr. Ar. *jarrah* earthen water vessel.] **1.** A deep, broadmouthed vessel of earthenware or glass, for holding preserves, etc., or for ornament. **2.** Such a vessel and its contents; a jarful.

jar, *n.* [See AJAR.] A turn; — only in phrase ***on the jar,*** on the turn, ajar, as a door.

jar, *v. i.;* JARRED (järd); JAR′RING. **1.** To sound harshly, esp. with a grating noise; to give forth rude discords; of notes, tones, etc., to be discordant. **2.** To make a jarring sound; esp., to shake or vibrate so as to cause such a sound; hence, to shiver; quake. **3.** To have or exert a discordant or harshly disagreeable effect. **4.** To be or act at variance; to clash; conflict. — *v. t.* **1.** To cause to shake, esp. so as to produce a harsh sound; also, to produce discordant (music, notes, etc.). **2.** To affect (a person, one's nerves, etc.) painfully; to shock; — now usually regarded as slang or inelegant. — *n.* **1.** A harshly discordant sound; also, a rattling vibration. **2.** A state of discord or disharmony; clash, as of interests or opinions; hence, dispute; esp., a petty dispute. **3.** A painful effect, as that produced by discords or concussion; a shock, as to the nerves.

jar′di·niere′ (jär′dĭ·nēr′; zhär′-; *F.* zhȧr′dē′nyâr′), *n.* [F. *jardinière*, orig. adj. fr. *jardinier* gardener.] **1** An ornamental stand or receptacle for plants, flowers, etc. **2.** *Ceramics.* A large flowerpot.

jar′gon (jär′gŏn; -gŭn), *n.* [OF. *jargon, gargon*, a chattering, warbling.] Confused, unintelligible language; gibberish; hence: **a** A language, speech, or dialect regarded as barbarous or outlandish. **b** A hybrid speech or dialect arising from a mixture of languages, as a lingua franca. **c** The technical or secret vocabulary of a science, art, trade, sect, profession, or other special group; a lingo. — **Syn.** See DIALECT. — *v. i.* To utter jargon; talk unintelligibly.

jar′gon (jär′gŏn), **jar·goon′** (jär·go͞on′), *n.* [F. *jargon*, through Pg. & Ar., fr. Per. *zargūn* gold-colored.] *Mineral.* A variety of zircon. See ZIRCON.

jar′go·nelle′ (jär′gō·nĕl′), *n.* Also **jar′go·nel′**. [F. *jargonelle*.] An early variety of pear.

jar′gon·ize (jär′gŏn·īz), *v. i.* To utter jargon. — *v. t.* To utter in, or render into, jargon.

jarl (yärl), *n.* [ON., nobleman, chief.] A Danish or Norse chieftain or headman below the king.

jar′o·site (jăr′ō·sīt; jȧ·rō′sīt), *n.* [From Barranco *Jaroso*, in Spain.] *Mineral.* An ocher-yellow or brown mineral, $K_2O.3Fe_2O_3.4SO_3.6H_2O$, occurring in minute rhombohedral crystals or massive.

jar′o·vize (yär′ō·vīz), **iar′o·vize** (yär′ō·vīz), **yar′o·vize,** *v. t.* [Russ. *yar′* spring grain.] = VERNALIZE. — **jar′o·vi·za′tion** (-vĭ·zā′shŭn; -vī-), *n.*

jar′vey (jär′vĭ), *n.; pl.* JARVEYS (-vĭz). [From the name *Jarvis, Jervis*.] *Slang, Eng.* **1.** The driver of a hackney coach or of a jaunting car. **2.** *Obs.* A hackney coach.

ja′sey (jā′zĭ), *n.; pl.* JASEYS (-zĭz). *Colloq., Eng.* A wig, esp. a worsted one.

jas′mine (jăz′mĭn; jăs′-), **jes′sa·mine** (jĕs′ȧ·mĭn), *n.* Also **jas′min.** [F. *jasmin*, fr. Ar. *yāsamīn*, colloq. *yāsmīn*, fr. Per. *yāsaman*.] **1.** Any of a genus (*Jasminum*) of shrubs of the olive family, the species of which are noted for their fragrant flowers, esp. *J. officinale*, the *jessamine* of poetry. **2.** A plant (*Gelsemium sempervirens*) of southern U. S., usually called ***yellow jasmine*** or ***Carolina jessamine.*** It is the State flower of South Carolina. Its root is used medicinally (see GELSEMIUM). **3.** Any of numerous other plants having sweet-scented flowers, as ***Cape jasmine*** (*Gardenia jasminodes*) and ***red jasmine*** (*Plumiera rubra:* see FRANGIPANI, 1).

Ja′son (jā′sŭn; -s'n), *n.* [L. *Iason*, fr. Gr. *Iasōn*.] *Gr. Myth.* Nephew of Pelias, King of Iolcus, who, to keep him from the throne, sent him in quest of the Golden Fleece, kept by Aeëtes, King of Colchis. With the help of Medea, Jason fulfilled the conditions imposed upon him by Aeëtes and secured the fleece. See MEDEA, ARGONAUT.

jas′per (jăs′pẽr), *n.* [OF. *jaspre, jaspe*, fr. L. *iaspis*, fr. Gr. *iaspis*, of Semitic origin.] An opaque, compact, uncrystalline variety of quartz, stained red, brown, green, yellow, etc. The jasper of the Bible was probably a dark-green or opalescent stone.

Jat (jät; jôt), *n.* [Hind. *Jāṭ*.] A member of an important Indo-Aryan people or caste, dwelling chiefly in the Punjab, Rajputana, and the United Provinces.

ja′to u′nit (jā′tō). [*jet* + *assisted* + *take-off*.] *Aeronautics.* An auxiliary means of propulsion for assisting the take-off of an airplane, consisting of one or more rocket engines which are usually discarded after the fuel has been consumed.

jauk (jäk; jôk), *v. i.* *Scot.* To dally; trifle.

jaun′dice (jôn′dĭs; jän′-), *n.* [OF. *jaunisse*, fr. *jaune, jalne*, yellow, fr. L. *galbinus* yellowish, fr. *galbus* yellow.] *Med.* A morbid condition characterized by yellowness of the skin and eyes and deep-yellow color of the urine, due to the presence of bile pigments in the blood and tissues — *v. t.;* -DICED (-dĭst); -DIC·ING (-dĭs·ĭng). To affect with jaundice, or to make yellow as if with jaundice; hence, to color by prejudice or envy.

jaunt (jônt; jänt), *v. i.* **1.** *Obs.* To go to and fro wearily; to trudge about. **2.** To ramble here and there, esp. for pleasure; to stroll. — *n.* **1.** *Rare.* A wearisome journey. **2.** A short excursion for pleasure or recreation.

jaunt′ing car. *Ir.* A light two-wheeled open vehicle with seats placed lengthwise, face to face or back to back.

jaun′ty (jôn′tĭ; jän′-), *adj.;* -TI·ER (-tĭ·ẽr); -TI·EST. [Formerly spelled *janty*, fr. F. *gentil*. See GENTLE.] **1.** *Obs.* Genteel; gentlemanly. **2.** Stylish; showy. **3.** Having an air of easy unconcern or sprightliness. — **jaun′ti·ly,** *adv.* — **jaun′ti·ness,** *n.*

jaup (jäp; jôp), *v. i., v. t., & n.* *Scot.* Splash.

Ja′va (jä′vȧ; jăv′ȧ), *n.* [From *Java* (see *Gaz.*).] A variety of coffee.

Java man. See PITHECANTHROPUS. See MAN, *Illust.*

Jav′a·nese′ (jăv′ȧ·nēz′; -nēs′; 2), *n.* **1.** *sing. & pl.* A native of Java. **2.** The language of the natives of Java, closely akin to Malay. See LANGUAGE, *Table.* — *adj.* Of or pertaining to Java, its inhabitants, or their language.

Java sparrow. See SPARROW, 3 **b**.

jave'lin (jăv'lĭn; jăv'ĕ·lĭn), *n.* [F. *javeline.*] **1.** A light spear, to be thrown or cast either as a weapon of war or in hunting. **2.** *Athletics.* A slender spearlike shaft of wood, not less than 260 centimeters (approximately 8½ feet) long, thrown for distance as an athletic feat.

Ja·velle', *or* **Ja·vel', wa'ter** (zhȧ·vĕl'). An aqueous solution of (now usually) sodium hypochlorite, NaOCl, used as an antiseptic, bleaching agent, etc.

jaw (jô), *n.* [Perh. akin to *chaw, chew,* influenced by F. *joue* the cheek.] **1. a** In most vertebrates, either of two complex cartilaginous or bony structures bordering the mouth, a relatively fixed ***upper jaw*** (cf. MAXILLA) and a hinged movable ***lower jaw*** or *mandible.* **b** Usually *pl.* The bones, muscles, nerves, and other structures surrounding the mouth and serving to open and close it. **2.** *Zool.* Any comparable structure in an invertebrate animal. Cf. MANDIBLE **b. 3.** Anything resembling or suggesting the jaw of an animal in form or action; esp., *pl.,* the mouth or entrance; specif., either of two or more opposing parts movable so as to open and close, for grasping or crushing anything between them; as, the *jaws* of a vise. **4.** *Slang.* Talk, esp. when offensive; impudent talk. — *v. i. Slang.* To talk, esp. offensively; to scold.

jaw, *n. Chiefly Scot.* A wave, or dash, or considerable quantity, of water or other liquid. — *v. t. & i. Chiefly Scot.* To splash; pour.

jaw'bone' (jô'bōn'; 2), *n.* One of the bones of a vertebrate's jaw, esp. of the lower jaw.

jaw'break'er (-brāk'ĕr), *n.* Literally, something that breaks the jaws, as, *Slang,* a word difficult to pronounce, or a hard kind of candy.

jay (jā), *n.* [OF. (F. *geai*), fr. VL. *gaius,* perh. fr. L. *Gaius,* prop. name.] **1.** *Zool.* A European bird (*Garrulus glandarius*), type of a subfamily (Garrulinae) of the crow family (Corvidae); hence, any of numerous birds of this subfamily, as the *blue jay* and *Canada jay* (which see). The jays are smaller and more arboreal than the crows, more graceful, and more highly colored. **2. a** An impertinent chatterer. **b** *Slang.* A stupid, gullible, or gawky person.

jay'hawk'er (jā'hôk'ĕr), *n.* **1.** *Slang, U.S.* A member of a band of guerrillas, orig. antislavery men, esp. in Kansas and Missouri, before and during the Civil War; hence, an irregular soldier. **2.** [*cap.*] A native or resident of Kansas; — a nickname.

jay'walk' (jā'wôk'), *v. i.* To cross a street carelessly, so as to be endangered by the traffic. — **jay'walk'er,** *n.* — **jay'walk'ing,** *n. All Colloq.*

jazz (jăz), *n.* [Creole *jazz* to speed up, applied to syncopated music, of Am. Negro, and prob. African, origin.] **a** *Music.* A type of American music, characterized by melodious themes, subtly syncopated dance rhythms, and varied orchestral coloring. **b** A dance to jazz music. **c** A quality suggestive of jazz music, esp. in literary style. — *adj.* Of, pertaining to, or characterized by jazz. — *v. t. Slang.* To transform into, or infuse with, jazz. — **jazz'er** (-ĕr), *n.* — **jazz'y** (-ĭ), *adj.*

jeal'ous (jĕl'ŭs), *adj.* [OF. *jelous, gelos* (F. *jaloux*), fr. (assumed) VL. *zelosus.* See ZEALOUS.] **1.** Exacting exclusive devotion; intolerant of rivalry. **2. a** Disposed to suspect rivalry in matters of interest and affection. **b** Prompted by such apprehension; as, *jealous* fears. **3.** Suspiciously watchful. **4.** *Archaic & Dial.* Zealous; devoted. **5.** *Now Dial.* Distrustful; suspicious. **6.** Vigilant or exact in observation. — **Syn.** See ENVIOUS. — **jeal'ous·ly,** *adv.* — (*Now Rare*) **jeal'ous·ness,** *n.*

jeal'ous·y (jĕl'ŭs·ĭ), *n.; pl.* -IES (-ĭz). **1.** Unpleasant fear, suspicion, or resentment, arising from mistrust of another; specif.: **a** Unpleasant suspicion of the faithfulness of husband, wife, or lover. **b** Grudging; envy; as, *jealousy* of rank. **2.** State or quality of being jealous.

jean (jēn; jān), *n.* [Prob. fr. F. *Gênes* Genoa.] A twilled cotton cloth used for overalls, etc.; *pl.,* a garment of this.

jee (jē). Scot. var. of GEE, *v.*

jeep (jēp), *n.* [From *GP* (general purpose) through association with the sound "jeep" made by a rodentlike wonderworker (Eugene) in a comic strip ("Popeye") by E. C. Segar.] **1.** *U.S.Army.* **a** A diminutive multipurpose cross-country vehicle of 80-inch wheelbase and quarter-ton capacity, weighing 2200–2300 lbs., equipped with four-wheel drive, and capable of a speed of 60 miles per hour. Called also *bantam, blitzbuggy,* and (by armored forces) *peep.* **b** A raw recruit; rookie. **c** A tiny 2100 lb. airplane for reconnaissance and liaison. **d** A diminutive amphibious truck capable of carrying five men. **2.** *U.S. Navy Slang.* An escort carrier. **3.** [*cap.*] A trade-mark applied to a civilian automotive vehicle.

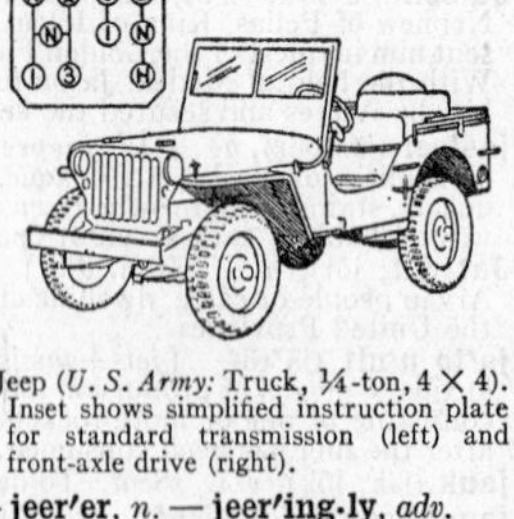

Jeep (*U. S. Army:* Truck, ¼-ton, 4 × 4). Inset shows simplified instruction plate for standard transmission (left) and front-axle drive (right).

jeer (jēr), *v. i. & t.* To utter sarcastic or scoffing reflections; to taunt; flout. — **Syn.** See SCOFF. — *n.* A railing remark; a taunt. — **jeer'er,** *n.* — **jeer'ing·ly,** *adv.*

jeer, *n. Naut.* Usually *pl.* An assemblage of tackles, for hoisting or lowering the lower yards.

‖**je'fe** (hā'fā), *n.* [Sp.] Chief; military commander.

Jef'fer·so'ni·an (jĕf'ĕr·sō'nĭ·ăn; 58), *adj.* Pertaining to, or characteristic of, Thomas Jefferson (third President of the United States) or his political doctrines, which were those of the Republicanism of his time, as opposed to those of the Federalists. — **Jef'fer·so'ni·an·ism** (-ĭz'm), *n.*

je·had' (jē·häd'). Var. of JIHAD.

Je·hosh'a·phat (jē·hŏsh'ȧ·făt), *n. Bib.* A king of Judah.

Je·ho'vah (jē·hō'vȧ), *n.* [Heb. usually *Yĕhōwāh;* prob. properly *Yahweh.*] God; — a Christian form given to the Tetragrammaton.

Je·ho'vah's Wit'ness·es (-vȧz). Members of a Christian sect founded by Charles T. Russell and under the leadership of "Judge" Rutherford from 1916 to 1942. The members, known originally as *Russellites,* constitute a society known as the International Bible Students' Association.

Je·ho'vist (-vĭst), *n. Hist.* One who maintains that the vowel points of the Hebrew word translated *Jehovah* are the proper vowels of that word.

Je'ho·vis'tic (jē'hō·vĭs'tĭk), *adj.* Marked by the use of *Jehovah* (properly *Yahweh*) as a name of God; Yahwistic.

Je'hu (jē'hū), *n.* **1.** *Bib.* King of Israel (841–815? B.C.). **2.** [*not cap.*] *Humorous.* A fast driver; a coachman.

je·june' (jē·jōōn'; 2), *adj.* [L. *jejunus* hungry, dry, barren.] **1.** Lacking nourishing quality. **2.** Void of interest or satisfaction; dry; insipid. — **Syn.** See INSIPID. — **je·june'ly,** *adv.* — **je·june'ness,** *n.*

je·ju'no- (jē·jōō'nō-), **jejun-**. *Med.* A combining form for *jejunum,* denoting *the jejunum;* — in nouns, as in **je'ju·nec'to·my, je'ju·nos'to·my, je'ju·not'o·my** (see -ECTOMY, -STOMY, etc.).

je·ju'num (jē·jōō'nŭm), *n.* [NL., fr. L. *jejunus* empty, dry.] *Anat.* The middle division of the small intestine, between the duodenum and ileum; — so called because formerly supposed to be empty after death.

jell (jĕl), *n. Colloq.* Jelly. — *v. i.* **1.** To jelly. **2.** Also *v. t. Colloq.* To solidify or crystallize; as, public opinion has *jelled* on the question.

jel'lied (jĕl'ĭd), *adj.* Brought to the state or consistency of jelly; furnished or covered with jelly.

jel'li·fy (jĕl'ĭ·fī), *v. t. & i.; -*FIED (-fīd); -FY'ING. To make, or to become, gelatinous; to jelly. — **jel'li·fi·ca'tion** (-fĭ·kā'shŭn), *n.*

jel'ly (jĕl'ĭ), *n.; pl.* -LIES (-ĭz). [OF. *gelée* jelly, frost, fr. L. *gelata* (that which is) congealed, fr. *gelare.*] **1.** A food preparation with a soft, somewhat elastic, homogeneous consistency, owing to the presence of gelatin, pectin, or a similar substance. **2.** Anything of the consistency of jelly (in sense 1). — *v. i. & t.;* JEL'LIED (-ĭd); JEL'LY·ING. To become jelly; to come, or to bring, to the consistency of jelly; to set in jelly; as, *jellied* tongue.

jel'ly·fish' (-fĭsh'), *n.;* see FISH. **1.** Any of various marine free-swimming coelenterates (classes Hydrozoa and Scyphozoa) having a body of jellylike consistency; a medusa. Many have long tentacles with stinging hairs. **2.** A person without stamina.

jem'a·dar (jĕm'ȧ·där), *n.* [Hind. *jamaʻdār,* fr. Per. *jamāʻat* body of men + *-dār* holder.] In the native army of India, a native officer second to the subahdar; also, one of several Indian government police or other officials.

‖**je main'tien'drai'** (zhĕ măɴ'tyăɴ'drā'). [F.] I will maintain; — motto of the Netherlands.

jem'my (jĕm'ĭ), *n.; pl.* JEMMIES (-ĭz). [i. e., *Jimmy,* a familiar form of *James.*] **1.** *Obs.* A type of riding boot. **2.** A short crowbar; a jimmy. **3.** *Slang, Eng.* A sheep's head used for food.

‖**je ne sais quoi** (zhĕn sā' kwȧ'). [F.] I know not what; an inexpressible something.

jen'net (jĕn'ĕt; -ĭt), *n.* [F. *genet,* fr. Sp. *jinete,* orig., a mounted soldier.] A small Spanish horse.

jen'ny (jĕn'ĭ), *n.; pl.* JENNIES (-ĭz). **1.** [*cap.*] A familiar or pet form of the feminine proper name *Jane.* **2.** With names of animals, often used to denote a female (as in **jenny ass, jenny wren,** etc.); hence, loosely, any of these animals. **3.** Short for SPINNING JENNY.

jeop'ard (jĕp'ĕrd), *v. t.* To put in jeopardy; to risk.

jeop'ard·ize (jĕp'ĕr·dīz), *v. t.* To expose to loss or injury; to risk.

jeop'ard·ous (-dŭs), *adj.* Exposing to death, loss, or injury; perilous. — **Syn.** See DANGEROUS.

jeop'ard·y (-dĭ), *n.* [OF. *jeu parti* an even game, fr. L. *jocus partitus.* See JOKE; PART, *v.*] **1.** Exposure to death, loss, or injury; peril; danger. **2.** *Law.* The danger that an accused person is subjected to when duly put upon trial for a criminal offense.

je·quir'i·ty (jē·kwĭr'ĭ·tĭ), *n., or* **jequirity bean.** [F. *jéquirity,* fr. Pg. *jequiriti.*] The seed of the Indian licorice (*Abrus precatorius*), used for beads in rosaries and necklaces, as a standard weight, etc.; also, the plant.

jer·bo'a (jĕr·bō'ȧ), *n.* [NL., fr. Ar. *yarbūʻ.*] Any of several social, nocturnal, jumping rodents (family Dipodidae) inhabiting arid parts of the Old World; esp., *Jaculus jaculus* of northern Africa.

je·reed', je·rid' (jĕ·rēd'), *n.* [Ar. *jarīd* shaft, rod.] A blunt javelin used in military games in Moslem countries.

jer'e·mi'ad (jĕr'ē·mī'ăd), *n.* [F. *jérémiade,* fr. *Jérémie* Jeremiah, alluding to the *Lamentations of Jeremiah.*] A lamenting and denunciatory complaint; a dolorous tirade.

Jer'e·mi'ah (jĕr'ē·mī'ȧ), *n. Douay Bib.* **Jer'e·mi'as** (-ăs). [LL. *Jeremias,* fr. Heb *Yirmĕyāh.*] A major Hebrew prophet whose preaching of denunciation and judgment is recorded in the Old Testament books of ***Jeremiah*** (*D.V.* ***Jeremias***) and ***Lamentations.*** See BIBLE.

jerk (jûrk), *v. t. & i.* **1.** To give a quick and suddenly arrested push, pull, or twist. **2.** To throw with a quick motion suddenly arrested. **3.** To utter in a snappy or sharply broken manner. **4.** To dispense (sodas) as a soda jerk. — *n.* **1.** A sharp, suddenly arrested pull, twitch, or the like. **2.** = SODA JERK. **3.** *Slang.* A despicable or worthless person. **4.** *Physiol.* An involuntary spasmodic muscular movement due to reflex action; in *pl.* with *the,* chorea or involuntary twitchings due to nervous excitement.

jerk, *v. t.* [Corrupt. fr. CHARQUI.] To cut into long slices or strips and dry in the sun; as, to *jerk* beef. See CHARQUI.

jer'kin (jûr'kĭn), *n.* A jacket or short coat.

jerk'wa'ter (jûrk'wô'tĕr; -wŏt'ĕr), *n.* [*jerk* + *water.*] A train on an early branch railroad; — also used attributively; as, *jerkwater* railroad; *jerkwater* station.

jerk'y (jûr'kĭ), *adj.;* JERK'I·ER (-kĭ·ĕr); JERK'I·EST. Moving by jerks and starts. — **jerk'i·ly,** *adv.* — **jerk'i·ness,** *n.*

jer·reed', jer·rid'. Vars. of JEREED.

jer'ry (jĕr'ĭ), *n.* [From *German.*] *Slang.* A German.

jer'ry, *adj. Builders' Cant.* Flimsy; jerry-built.

jer'ry–build', *v. t.;* -BUILT'; -BUILD'ING. To build cheaply and unsubstantially. — **jer'ry–build'er,** *n.*

jer'sey (jûr'zĭ), *n.; pl.* JERSEYS (-zĭz). [From *Jersey,* one of the Channel Islands.] **1.** A kind of knitted jacket; hence, a close-fitting jacket or upper garment of an elastic fabric. **2.** [*cap.*] A breed of dairy cattle originating on the island of Jersey. They are usually fawn-colored, rather small, and yield rich milk. **3.** Also **jersey cloth.** A silk, wool, or cotton knitted fabric, sometimes napped, used for clothing.

Je·ru'sa·lem ar'ti·choke (jē·rōō'sȧ·lĕm). [Corrupt. of It. *girasole.*] A perennial American sunflower (*Helianthus tuberosus*); also, the tuber of the plant, used as a vegetable.

jess (jĕs), *n.* [OF. *gies, giez,* prop. pl. of *giet, get, jet.* See JET a gush.] *Falconry.* A short strap secured round the leg of a hawk and usually provided with a ring. See FALCON, *Illust.* — **jessed** (jĕst), *adj.*

jes'sa·mine (jĕs'ȧ·mĭn), *n.* [MF. *jessemin.*] See JASMINE.

jes'sant (jĕs'ănt), *adj. Her.* Lying over; also, issuing.

Jes'se (jĕs'ē), *n. Bib.* The father of David.

jest (jĕst), *n.* [OF. *geste,* fr. L. *gesta* deeds, exploits, neut. pl. fr. *gestus,* past part. of *gerere* to bear, accomplish.] **1.** *Obs.* **a** An exploit. **b** A story of action; a tale; a gest. **2.** A jeering or satirical remark; also, something done or said in banter or raillery. **3.** A joke;

also, a thing not to be taken seriously. **4.** Sport or fun. **5.** A laughingstock; a butt.

Syn. (1) **Jest, joke, quip, witticism, wisecrack** mean something said (occasionally, done) for the purpose of evoking laughter. **Jest** now carries a stronger implication of banter than formerly but it often also suggests raillery; **joke**, applied as often to an act as an utterance, suggests no intent to hurt feelings; **quip** implies more lightness and neatness of expression than *jest;* **witticism**, the bookish term, and **wisecrack**, slang, denote a clever or witty retort, comment, or the like.
(2) See FUN.

— *v. i.* To make merriment by words or actions; to joke; to make a jest or jests. — *v. t.* To ridicule; banter.

jest'er (jĕs'tẽr), *n.* **1.** A buffoon; a merry-andrew; a court fool. **2.** A person addicted to jesting.

jest'ing, *n.* The making of jests; joking; pleasantry. — *adj.* Sportive; not serious. — **jest'ing·ly**, *adv.*

Je'su (jē'zū; -sū; yā'so͞o), *n.* [L.] *Poetical.* Jesus.

Jes'u·it (jĕz'ū·ĭt; jĕzh'-), *n.* [NL. *Jesuita*, fr. *Jesus*.] **1.** A member of the clerks regular of the ***Company*** (*or* ***Society***) ***of Jesus***, a religious order founded by Ignatius Loyola in 1534. Abbr. *S. J.* **2.** One likened to a Jesuit; specif., a casuist; hence, a crafty person; an intriguer; — a derogatory use. — **Jes'u·it'ic** (-ĭt'ĭk), **Jes'u·it'i·cal** (-ĭ·kăl), *adj.* — **Jes'u·it'i·cal·ly**, *adv.*

Jes'u·it·ism (-ĭz'm), *n.* **1.** The principles, doctrines, or organization and practice of Jesuits. **2. a** Jesuitry. **b** [*not cap.*] A quibble.

Jes'u·it·ry (-rĭ), *n.* Principles or practices ascribed in derogation to the Jesuits, such as the practice of mental reservation; hence, casuistry.

Je'sus (jē'zŭs), *n.* [L., fr. Gr. *Iēsous*, fr. Heb. *Yēshūa'*.] **1.** *Bib.* The son of Mary, the source of the Christian religion and Saviour in the Christian faith. Since *Jesus* is the personal name it is often combined with *Christ* (see CHRIST, *n.*, 1 & 2); as, *Jesus Christ* or *Christ Jesus.* **2.** *Bib.* Any of various persons, as the author (Jesus, son of Sirach) of the Apocryphal wisdom book commonly known as *Ecclesiasticus.* **3.** *Christian Science.* The highest human corporeal concept of the divine idea, rebuking and destroying error and bringing to light man's immortality. *Mary Baker Eddy.*

jet (jĕt), *n.* [OF. *jet, jayet*, fr. L. *gagates*, fr. Gr. *gagatēs;* — from *Gagas* or *Gangai*, a town and river in Lycia.] **1.** A very compact velvet-black mineral of the nature of coal, susceptible of a good polish. **2. a** *Obs.* Black marble. **b** Lustrous black. — **jet**, *adj.*

jet, *n.* [OF. *get, giet*, a throw, a cast (F. *jet*), fr. *jeter* to throw.] **1.** A sudden rush or gush of liquid or gas through a narrow opening or a nozzle; also, that which issues in a jet. **2.** A nozzle for a jet of gas, water, or other fluid. **3.** Short for *jet engine, jet airplane*, etc., which see, under JET PROPULSION.

jet (jĕt), *v. i. & t.;* JET'TED; JET'TING. [F. *jeter*, fr. VL. *jectare*, for L. *jactare*, freq. fr. *jacere* to throw.] To spout out in a stream; to shoot forth; to spurt.

jet'-black' (-blăk'; 2), *adj.* Black as jet; deep-black.

jet motor. A jet engine. See JET PROPULSION.

jet propeller. *Aeronautics.* A propeller driven directly by the reaction forces produced by jets that are discharged through nozzles or orifices in or adjacent to the rearmost edges of the propeller blades.

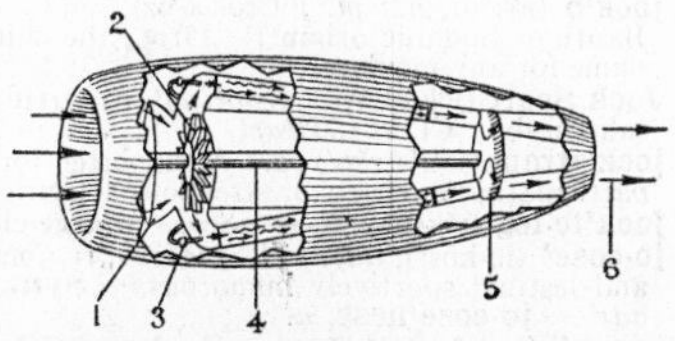

Jet Engine (simplified cutaway). 1 Air Intake; 2 Impeller, or Compressor; 3 Fuel Injection; 4 Drive Shaft; 5 Turbine; 6 Exhaust.

jet propulsion. *Aeronautics.* Propulsion of a body produced by the forwardly directed forces of the reaction resulting from the rearward discharge from the body of a jet (a high-speed stream of fluid) through a nozzle or orifice. The forces responsible for the propulsion are exerted usually against the inside of the forward part of the body and are opposed to those expended by the rearward discharge of the jet. A simple example of jet propulsion is the motion given to an inflated toy balloon when the compressed air is allowed to escape through the neck. Another example is the forward propulsion of a rocket by the rearward discharge of a high-speed stream of hot gases produced by the combustion of the rocket fuel. Rocket-type jet propulsion is independent of the surrounding air and may occur in a vacuum. A jet-propulsion engine, or **jet engine**, has essentially one or more combustion chambers and one or more exhaust nozzles for discharging rearwards a continuous or intermittent stream of fluid, usually heated air and exhaust gases. A **jet airplane**, *or* **jet plane**, may be powered by a jet engine that utilizes the surrounding air in the combustion of fuel or by a jet engine of the rocket type that carries its fuel and all the oxygen necessary for combustion, and therefore functions independently of atmospheric oxygen. — **jet'-pro·pul'sion**, *adj.* — **jet'-propelled'**, *adj.*

jet'sam (jĕt'săm), *n.* [See JETTISON.] *Mar. Law.* Goods cast overboard to lighten a vessel in distress; often specif., such goods when washed ashore. Cf. FLOTSAM.

jet'ti·son (jĕt'ĭ·sŭn; -s'n), *n.* [OF. *getaison* a throwing, fr. L. *jactatio*, fr. *jactare* to throw. See JET, *v.*] *Mar. Law.* **a** The throwing overboard of goods, esp. to lighten a vessel in danger. **b** = JETSAM. — *v. t.* **1.** *Mar. Law.* To make jettison of (goods). **2.** Hence, to cast off as an incumbrance; to discard. **3.** *Mil.* To get rid of (as bombs or auxiliary equipment) by casting loose or dumping, as for lightening an aircraft to increase its range or maneuverability or for freeing a tank for fighting; as, a rocket launcher carried under each wing to be *jettisoned* in an emergency. — **jet'ti·son·a·ble** (-ȧ·b'l), *adj.*

jet'ton (jĕt'ŭn; -'n), *n.* [F. *jeton*, fr. *jeter* to throw.] Any of various counters or tokens of metal, bone, etc.

jet'ty (jĕt'ĭ), *n.; pl.* -TIES (-ĭz). [F. *jetée*, fr. *jeter* to throw.] **a** A structure, as a pier or mole, extended into a sea, lake, or river, to influence the current or tide or to protect a harbor; also, a starling, or protecting frame of a pier. **b** A wharf or pier.

‖**jeu** (zhû), *n.; pl.* JEUX (zhû). [F.] Game; amusement.

‖**jeu de mots** (zhûd' mō'). [F.] A play on words; a pun.

‖**jeu d'es'prit'** (zhû' dĕs'prē'). [F., play of mind.] A sally giving play to cleverness or wit.

‖**jeune fille** (zhûn' fē'y'). [F.] Young girl; miss.

‖**jeu'nesse' do'rée'** (zhû'nĕs' dô'rā'). [F.] Young people of wealth and fashion.

Jew (jo͞o; jū; 114), *n.* [OF. *giu, jueu*, fr. L. *Judaeus*, fr. Gr. *Ioudaios*, fr. Heb. *Yĕhūdhi* one belonging to Judah.] Orig., one of the tribe of Judah; hence, any person of the Hebrew people or anyone whose religion is Judaism.

jew'el (jo͞o'ĕl; jū'ĕl; -ĭl; 114), *n.* [OF. *juel, joel*, fr. LL. *jocalis* pert. to play, fr. *jocus* play, jest.] **1.** A costly ornament of gold, silver, or the like, usually for personal wear and having enamel or precious stones as a part of its design. **2.** An object regarded with special affection. **3.** A precious stone; a gem. See BRILLIANT, *Illust.* **4.** A bearing for a pivot in a watch, formed of a crystal or precious stone, as a ruby. **5.** An ornamental boss of glass or glaze.
— *v. t.;* -ELED (-ĕld; -ĭld) or -ELLED; -EL·ING or -EL·LING. To dress, adorn, or supply with jewels, as a dress or watch.

jew'el·er, jew'el·ler (-ẽr), *n.* One who makes, or deals in, jewels, precious stones, etc.

jew'el·ry (jo͞o'ĕl·rĭ; jū'ĕl-; -ĭl·rĭ), *or, British,* **jew'el·ler·y** (jo͞o'ĕl·rĭ; jū'ĕl-; -ĭl·rĭ), *n.* Jewels collectively; personal ornaments set or studded with jewels.

jew'el·weed' (-wēd'), *n.* Either of two American plants (genus *Impatiens*) of the family Balsaminaceae, the jewelweed family; as, the ***spotted jewelweed*** (*I. biflora*) with orange-yellow brown-spotted flowers, and *I. pallida* with pale-yellow unmarked flowers.

Jew'ess (jo͞o'ĕs; jū'ĕs; -ĭs), *n.* A female Jew.

jew'fish' (jo͞o'fĭsh'; jū'-), *n.; pl.*, see FISH. **1.** Any of certain large sluggish groupers, usually dusky green and rough scaled. The largest species (*Promicrops lanceolata*) of the South Pacific reaches a length of twelve feet. **2.** Any of various large fishes of other families.

Jew'ish (jo͞o'ĭsh; jū'ĭsh; 114), *adj.* Of or pertaining to Jews or Hebrews; Israelitish.

Jewish calendar. A lunisolar calendar in use among Hebraic peoples, reckoning from the year 3761 B.C., the date traditionally given for the Creation. It received its present fixed form from Hillel II about A.D. 360. Nineteen years constitute a lunar cycle, of which the 3d, 6th, 8th, 11th, 14th, 17th, and 19th years are leap years. The year 5682 [A.D. 1921–22] was the first year of the 300th lunar cycle. The common year is said to be a ***defective, regular, or perfect*** (*or* ***abundant***) ***year*** according as it has 353, 354, or 355 days. The leap year has an intercalary month, and a total of 383 (defective), 384 (regular), or 385 (perfect, or abundant) days. The calendar is complicated by various rules providing for the harmonious arrangement of festivals, etc. (see JEWISH HOLIDAYS), so that no simple perpetual calendar can be constructed. The following table gives the months in order, with the number of days assigned to each. Only three months vary in length. The ecclesiastical year commences with Nisan and the civil year with Tishri. The date of the first of Tishri, or the Jewish New Year (Rosh Hashana), is also given for the Jewish years 5706–5723 (A.D. 1945–1962).

MONTHS OF THE JEWISH YEAR

	days		days		days
1 **Tishri**	30	5 **Shebat**	30	7 **Nisan**	30
2 **Heshvan**	29 or 30	6 **Adar**	29 or 30	8 **Iyar**	29
				9 **Sivan**	30
3 **Kislev**	29 or 30	— **Veadar** (*occurring only in leap years*)	29	10 **Tammuz**	29
				11 **Ab**	30
4 **Tebet**	29			12 **Elul**	29

JEWISH YEAR		A.D.	JEWISH YEAR		A.D.
5706 *d. l.*	begins	Sept. 8, 1945	5715 *r.*	begins	Sept. 28, 1954
5707 *r.*	"	" 26, 1946	5716 *p.*	"	" 17, 1955
5708 *p. l.*	"	" 15, 1947	5717 *p. l.*	"	" 6, 1956
5709 *p.*	"	Oct. 4, 1948	5718 *r.*	"	" 26, 1957
5710 *d.*	"	Sept. 24, 1949	5719 *d. l.*	"	" 15, 1958
5711 *r. l.*	"	" 12, 1950	5720 *p.*	"	Oct. 3, 1959
5712 *p.*	"	Oct. 1, 1951	5721 *r.*	"	Sept. 22, 1960
5713 *p.*	"	Sept. 20, 1952	5722 *d. l.*	"	" 11, 1961
5714 *d. l.*	"	" 10, 1953	5723 *p.*	"	" 29, 1962

d. = defective year; *d. l.* = defective leap year; *p.* = perfect year; *p. l.* = perfect leap year; *r.* = regular year; *r. l.* = regular leap year.

Jewish holidays. The holidays observed in Judaism; esp.: ***Rosh Hashana***, New Year, 1st and 2d of Tishri; ***Yom Kippur***, Day of Atonement, 10th of Tishri; ***Sukkoth***, Feast of Tabernacles, 15th to 22d (incl.) of Tishri; ***Simhath Torah***, Rejoicing over the Law, 23d of Tishri; ***Hanukkah***, Feast of the Dedication, 25th of Kislev to 2d (incl.) or, when Kislev has 29 days, to 3d (incl.) of Tebet; ***Purim***, Feast of Lots, 14th of Adar; ***Pesach***, the Passover, 15th to 22d (incl.) of Nisan; ***Lag b'Omer***, thirty-third day of counting the omer; ***Shabuoth***, Feast of Weeks, or Pentecost, seven weeks from the 16th of Nisan, usually 6th and 7th of Sivan; ***Tishah b'ab or bov***, fast day, 9th of Ab.

Jew'ry (jo͞o'rĭ; jū'rĭ), *n.; pl.* JEWRIES (-rĭz). [OF. *juerie*.] **1.** Judea; also, a district inhabited by Jews; a ghetto. **2.** The Jewish people.

jew's'-harp', jews''-harp' (jo͞oz'härp'; jūz'-), *n.* [*Jew* + *harp*.] A small lyre-shaped instrument which, when placed between the teeth, gives tones from a bent metal tongue struck by the finger.

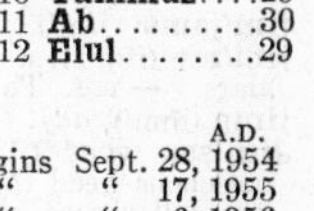
Jew's-harp.

Jew's, *or* **Jews', pitch.** Asphalt.

Jez'e·bel (jĕz'ĕ·bĕl; -b'l), *n.* **1.** *Bib.* Wife of Ahab, a king of Israel. She introduced Baal worship, persecuted Elijah, instigated the murder of Naboth, and made her name a term of reproach. **2.** A wicked or bold woman.

JHS. = IHS.

JHVH, JHWH. See TETRAGRAMMATON.

jib (jĭb), *v. t. & i.;* JIBBED (jĭbd); JIB'BING. Also **jibb.** [Var. of JIBE.] *Chiefly Naut.* To shift, or swing round, as a sail, boom, yard, etc., as in tacking.

jib, *n. Naut.* A triangular sail set upon a stay or its own luff, extending from the head of the foremast to the bowsprit or the jib boom. See SAIL, SLOOP, *Illusts.* — ***the cut of one's jib.*** *Colloq.* One's outward appearance.

jib, *n.* The projecting arm of a crane.

jib (jĭb), *v. i.* Of an animal in harness, to move restively backward or sidewise; to balk. — *n.* One that jibs, or balks; a jibber. — **jib′ber**, *n.*

jib boom, *or* **jib′boom′** (jĭb′bo͞om′; jĭ·bo͞om′), *n.* *Naut.* A spar or boom which serves as an extension of the bowsprit.

jibe (jīb), *v. i.* Also **gybe**. [D. *gijben, gijpen.* Cf. 1st JIB.] *Naut.* **1.** To shift suddenly from one side to the other; — said of a fore-and-aft sail or its boom when the vessel is steered off the wind until the sail fills on the opposite side. **2.** To change the course of a vessel so that the sail jibes. — *v. t.* To cause to jibe.

jibe, *v. i.* [Origin uncert.] *Colloq., U.S.* To agree; to harmonize; as, his words and actions do not *jibe.*

jibe (jīb), **jib′er** (jīb′ẽr). Vars. of GIBE, GIBER.

jif′fy (jĭf′ĭ), *n.; pl.* JIFFIES (-ĭz). Also **jiff**. *Colloq.* A moment; instant; as, I will go in a *jiffy.*

jig (jĭg), *v. t.;* JIGGED (jĭgd); JIG′GING. [OF. *giguer* to hop, dance, fr. *gigue* a fiddle, of Teut. origin.] **1.** To sing, play, or dance as a jig. **2.** To jerk or jolt up and down, or to and fro. **3.** *Mach.* To treat, cut, or form in or with a jig, as a piece of metal in a jigging machine. — *v. i.* **1.** To dance a jig. **2.** To move jerkily. **3. a** To fish with a jig. **b** To work with the aid of a jig. — *n.* [From JIG, *v.*] **1.** Any of several lively springy dances in triple rhythm; also, its music **2.** *Now Slang.* A piece of sport; a trick; — now chiefly in ***the*** (***his***, etc.) ***jig is up***, the game is ended; the time of reckoning has come. **3.** Any of several devices used in fishing, as a kind of spoon hook, jerked up and down through the water, esp. in fishing through the ice. **4.** *Mach.* A contrivance with hard steel surfaces to guide a tool, as a drill, or to form a shield or template to work to, as in filing. **5** A device in which crushed ore is concentrated, or coal is cleaned, by agitating it in water.

jig′ger (jĭg′ẽr), *n.* [Corrupt. of CHIGOE.] **a** = CHIGOE **a**; — called also **jigger flea**. **b** = CHIGGER **b**.

jig′ger, *n.* [See JIG, *n.* & *v.*] **1.** One who dances a jig. **2.** One who jigs something, as the strings of a puppet. **3.** A small measure of liquor; a dram; also, a small glass used in mixing drinks, holding one and one half ounces. **4.** Any of various mechanical devices or contrivances; a gadget. **5.** *Angling.* A jig used to catch fish. **6.** *Billiards & Pool.* A kind of bridge. **7.** *Golf.* An iron club with a narrow, fairly well-lofted face. **8.** *Mining & Ore Dressing.* A jig. **9.** *Naut.* **a** A light tackle. **b** A small vessel, rigged like a yawl. **c** Also **jigger mast**. A small mast stepped in the stern, as in a yawl or ketch; also, the aftermost mast of a four-masted vessel.

jig′gle (jĭg′'l), *v. i.* & *t.;* JIG′GLED (-'ld); JIG′GLING (-lĭng). [Freq. of JIG.] To move with quick little jerks. — *n.* Light, rapidly repeating, jerky motion.

jig saw. A sawing machine with a narrow, vertically reciprocating saw, used to cut curved and irregular lines, or ornamental patterns in openwork. — **jig′-saw′** (jĭg′sô′), *v. t.*

jig′saw′ (jĭg′sô′), *adj.* Made up of pieces cut by a jig saw; as, a **jigsaw puzzle**, a picture puzzle so made.

ji·had′, je·had′ (jē·häd′), *n.* [Ar. *jihād.*] *Moham.* A religious war against infidels; also, a crusade for a principle.

jill′et (jĭl′ĕt; -ĭt), *n.* [Dim. of *Jill, Gill,* a woman's name.] *Chiefly Scot.* A jilt or flirt.

jilt (jĭlt), *n.* A woman who capriciously casts off a man previously accepted as a lover. — *v. t.* To cast off capriciously or unfeelingly, as a lover. — **jilt′er**, *n.*

jim′jams′ (jĭm′jămz′), *n. pl.* *Slang, U. S.* Delirium tremens.

jim′my (jĭm′ĭ), *n.; pl.* JIMMIES (-ĭz). A short crowbar used by burglars. — *v. t.* To open with or as with a jimmy.

jimp (jĭmp), *adj.* *Scot. & Dial.* Slender; spruce; trim.

Jim′son weed (jĭm′s'n). [From *Jamestown,* Va.] An intensely poisonous weed (*Datura stramonium*) of the nightshade family. It is a tall coarse annual with rank-smelling foliage and large white trumpet-shaped flowers.

jin. Var. of JINN.

jin′gal (jĭn′gôl), *n.* [Hind. *janjāl.*] A long, heavy musket or rude cannon fired from a rest, used in central Asia.

jing′ko (jĭng′kō). Corruption of GINGKO.

jin′gle (jĭng′g'l), *v. i.* & *t.;* JIN′GLED (-g'ld); JIN′GLING (-glĭng). [ME. *gingelen, ginglen,* of imitative origin.] **1.** To sound with fine, sharp, continued clinking or tinkling sounds. **2.** To rhyme or sound with a jingling effect. — *n.* **1.** A jingling sound, or that which makes it, as one of the disks on a tambourine. **2.** A catchy repetition or correspondence of sounds in verse, or the verse itself. **3.** A two-wheeled covered car used in parts of Ireland and Australia. — **jin′gly** (jĭng′glĭ), *adj.;* JIN′GLI·ER (-glĭ·ẽr); JIN′GLI·EST.

jin′go (jĭng′gō), *n.; pl.* JINGOES (-gōz). **1.** *Colloq.* A word used as a jocular oath; — chiefly in *by jingo.* **2.** One who favors or supports a bellicose policy in foreign affairs. — **jin′go**, *adj.*

jin′go·ism (-ĭz'm), *n.* Belief, policy, or practice of or characteristic of jingoes. Cf. CHAUVINISM. — **jin′go·ist** (-ĭst), *n.* & *adj.* — **jin′go·is′tic** (-ĭs′tĭk), *adj.*

jink (jĭngk), *v. i.* & *t.* *Orig. Scot.* To move quickly, esp. with a sudden turn; to dodge; to escape by a quick turn. — *n.* **1.** *Chiefly Scot.* Evasion. **2.** *pl.* Pranks; frolics; — esp. in the phrase *high jinks.* — **jink′er**, *n.*

jinn (jĭn), *n.* **1.** *pl.* of JINNI. **2.** (*pl.* JINNS) Improperly, a jinni.

jin·ni′, jin·nee′ (jĭ·nē′), *n.; pl.* JINN (jĭn). [Ar. *jinnī,* pl. *jinn;* in English somewhat confused with *genie, genius.*] In Mohammedan belief, one of a class of supernatural beings, subject to magic control.

jin·rik′i·sha (jĭn·rĭk′shä; -shô), *n.* Also **jin·rick′sha**. [Jap. *jin* man + *riki* power + *sha* carriage.] A small two-wheeled hooded vehicle drawn by one or more men, orig. used in Japan.

jinx (jĭngks), *n.* & *v.* *Slang.* Hoodoo.

ji′pi·ja′pa (hē′pē·hä′pä), *n.* [Sp., fr. *Jipijapa,* town in Ecuador.] A Central and South American palmlike plant (*Carludovica palmata,* family Cyclanthaceae); also, a Panama hat made from its young leaves.

jit′ney (jĭt′nĭ), *n.* *Slang.* **a** Five cents; a nickel. **b** An automotive vehicle which carries passengers for a small, orig. a five-cent, fare.

jit′ter (jĭt′ẽr), *v. i.* *Slang, U. S.* To be or act nervous.

jit′ter·bug′ (jĭt′ẽr·bŭg′), *n.* [*jitter,* v. + *bug* enthusiast (*Slang*).] A devotee of swing music impelled by the rhythm to athletic dancing expressive of vigorous youth. — **jit′ter·bug′**, *v. i.;* -BUGGED′ (-bŭgd′); -BUG′GING.

jit′ters (jĭt′ẽrz), *n. pl.* *Slang, U. S.* Extreme nervousness; nerves. — **jit′ter·y** (-ẽr·ĭ), *adj.*

jiu·jit′su, jiu·jut′su. Vars. of JUJITSU.

jive (jīv), *n.* **1.** Swing music or selections in this style; also, the lingo of swing musicians. **2.** *Slang.* **a** Any unintelligible jargon. **b** Idle chatter; bunk. — *v. i.* To play swing music; also, to jitterbug.

jo (jō), *n.; pl.* JOES (jōz). *Scot.* Sweetheart; darling.

jo·an′nes (jō·ăn′ēz; -ĭz). Var. of JOHANNES.

job (jŏb), *v. t.* & *i.;* JOBBED (jŏbd); JOB′BING. [ME. *jobben* to peck.] *Rare in U. S.* To strike, stab, or dig with something pointed, esp. a knife or dagger; to jab. — *n.* A jab.

job, *n.* [Origin uncert.; cf. ME. *jobbe* a lump.] **1. a** A piece of work; specif., any definite work undertaken in gross, esp. for a fixed price; also, a piece of work of the small miscellaneous kind taken as it comes from the public. **b** The material thing on which work is being done. **2.** A piece of business done ostensibly as an official duty, but really for private gain. **3.** *Colloq.* Any affair, circumstance, or event. **4.** *Colloq.* A situation or employment. — **Syn.** See TASK; POSITION. — *v. i.;* JOBBED (jŏbd); JOB′BING. **1.** To do odd or occasional pieces of work for hire. **2.** To seek private gain under pretense of public service. — *v. t.* **1.** To buy and sell as a broker; to deal in as a middleman. **2.** To sublet (work); as, to *job* a contract. **3** To make a job of (a matter of public trust or duty). **4.** To hire or let by the job or for a period of service. — *adj.* For hire or sale by the job.

Job (jōb), *n.* [L., fr. Gr. *Iōb,* fr. Heb. *Iyyōbh.*] *Bib.* **a** The Old Testament patriarch who undergoes afflictions with fortitude and faith. **b** A book of the Old Testament. See BIBLE.

job′ber (jŏb′ẽr), *n.* **1.** One who buys goods from importers or producers and sells to other dealers; a middleman. **2.** One who works by the job; a pieceworker; hack. **3.** *Eng.* A dealer in stock-exchange securities; a stockjobber. **4.** One who jobs in official or public business; hence, one who does corrupt work in office, politics, etc.

job′ber·y (jŏb′ẽr·ĭ), *n.* Act or practice of jobbing; esp., the conduct of matters of public trust or duty for private graft; corruption in public office.

job′hold′er (jŏb′hōl′dẽr), *n.* One who has a regular job; specif., *U. S.,* a government employee.

job lot. Any miscellaneous, presumably inferior, collection

job printer. One who does miscellaneous printing, as circulars, cards, billheads, etc. — **job printing**.

Job's com′fort·er (jōbz). One who maliciously afflicts with words ostensibly meant to comfort.

Job′s′-tears′ (jōbz′tērz′), *n. pl.* The hard, pearly-white, capsulelike seeds of an Asiatic grass (*Coix lacryma-jobi*) often used as beads; also, the plant itself.

Jo·cas′ta (jō·kăs′tȧ), **Jo·cas′te** (-tē), *n.* [L., fr. Gr. *Iokastē.*] See OEDIPUS.

jock (jŏk), *n.* **1.** A jockey. **2.** A jockstrap.

jock′ey (jŏk′ĭ), *n.* [Dim. of *Jock,* Scot. form of JACK.] **1.** One who rides or drives a horse; now, a professional rider of horses in races. **2.** *Hist.* A wandering minstrel; a vagabond. — *v. t.* **1.** To cheat, outwit, or overreach. **2.** To manage with skill; esp., to treat trickily; to effect, put, or the like, by tricky dealing. — *v. i.* To cheat; to take unfair advantage; also, to maneuver for advantage.

jock′o (jŏk′ō), *n.; pl.* JOCKOS (-ōz). [F., fr. earlier (E.) *engeco,* of Bantu or Sudanic origin.] Orig., the chimpanzee; often, a familiar name for any monkey.

Jock Scott (jŏk skŏt). *Angling* An artificial varicolored trout and salmon fly. Cf. FLY, *Illust.*

jock′strap′ (jŏk′străp′), *n.* A supporter for the genitals worn by men participating in sports or strenuous activities.

jock′te·leg (jŏk′tĕ·lĕg), *n.* *Scot.* A large clasp knife.

jo·cose′ (jō·kōs′), *adj.* [L. *jocosus,* fr. *jocus* joke.] Given to jokes and jesting; sportively humorous. — **Syn.** See WITTY. — **jo·cose′ly**, *adv.* — **jo·cose′ness**, *n.*

jo·cos′i·ty (jō·kŏs′ĭ·tĭ), *n.; pl.* -TIES (-tĭz). A jocose act or saying; jocoseness.

joc′u·lar (jŏk′ū·lẽr), *adj.* [L. *jocularis,* fr. *joculus,* dim. of *jocus* joke.] **1.** Given or disposed to jesting; acting in jest; overtly jocose; as, a *jocular* person. **2.** Said or done in joke; sportive; merry. — **Syn.** See WITTY. — **joc′u·lar′i·ty** (-lăr′ĭ·tĭ), *n.* — **joc′u·lar·ly**, *adv.*

joc′und (jŏk′ŭnd; jō′kŭnd), *adj.* [OF. *jocond, jocund,* fr. LL. *jocundus* (after *jocus* joke), fr. L. *jucundus* pleasant, orig., helpful, fr. *juvare* to help.] Feeling, exhibiting, or characteristic of mirth or good cheer; merry; gay. — **Syn.** See MERRY. — **joc′und·ly**, *adv.*

jo·cun′di·ty (jō·kŭn′dĭ·tĭ), *n.; pl.* -TIES (-tĭz). State or quality of being jocund; also, a jocund action or speech.

jodh′purs (jŏd′pẽrz), *n. pl., or* **jodh′pur breech′es** (-pẽr). [From *Jodhpur,* Rajputana.] Riding breeches that fit closely from the knee to just above the ankle.

joe (jō). Var. of JO, a sweetheart.

Jo′el (jō′ĕl; -ĕl), *n.* [L., fr. Gr. *Iōel,* fr. Heb. *Yō′ēl.*] *Bib.* **a** A Hebrew prophet of uncertain date, assigned by some to about 830 B.C.; by others, to a postexilic period. **b** A book of the Old Testament. See BIBLE.

joe′-pye′ weed (jō′pī′). Either of two tall perennial American herbs (*Eupatorium maculatum* and *E. purpureum*), having whorled leaves and terminal flower clusters.

jo′ey (jō′ĭ), *n.* [Australian *joè. Oxf. E. D.*] *Australia.* The young of an animal; esp., a young kangaroo.

jog (jŏg), *v. t.;* JOGGED (jŏgd); JOG′GING. [Partly of imitative origin, and partly fr. earlier SHOG.] **1.** To push or shake, as with the elbow or hand; to jostle; nudge. **2.** To suggest to; to remind; to call the attention of; as, to *jog* the memory. — *v. i.* To move slowly, leisurely, or monotonously. — *n.* **1.** A slight shake; a push; jolt. **2.** A slow motion or pace with marked jogs or beats. **3.** *Chiefly U. S.* A projecting or retreating part, as in a wall.

jog′gle (jŏg′'l), *v. t.;* JOG′GLED (-'ld); JOG′GLING (-lĭng). [Freq. of JOG.] **1.** To shake slightly; to jostle; jog. **2.** To join by means of a joggle or joggles; sometimes, loosely, to dowel. — *v. i.* To shake slightly to and fro; to totter. — *n.* **1.** A jog; a jog trot. **2.** A notch in the joining surface of any piece of building material to prevent slipping.

jog trot. A slow, regular, jolting gait; a routine habit or method persistently adhered to; a slow, easygoing way.

jo·han′nes (jō·hăn′ēz; -ĭz), *n. sing.* & *pl.* Also **jo·an′nes** (jō·ăn′-). [NL. See JOHN.] A Portuguese gold coin (1722–1835) worth about $8.81 and named from John V. See DOBRA.

John (jŏn), *n.* [LL. & ML. *Joannes,* ML. *Johannes,* fr. Gr. *Iōannēs,* fr. Heb. *Yōḥānān.*] **a** Any of various Biblical characters; esp.: (1)

John the Baptist. (2) John the Apostle, whose name is attached to the Fourth Gospel, three Epistles, and the Book of Revelation. **b** (1) The Gospel of John. (2) One of the three Epistles of John. See BIBLE.

John Bull (bŏŏl). The English nation personified; the English people; also, the, or a, typical Englishman.

John Doe (dō). *Law.* The fictitious lessee acting as plaintiff in the common-law action of ejectment. Hence, a fictitious name for a party, real or fictitious, to any transaction, action, or proceeding.

John Do′ry (dō′rĭ; 70); *pl.* JOHN DORYS (-rĭz). Also **John Do′ree** (-rē). [*John* + *doree, dory,* the fish.] A marine fish of the family Zeidae; specif., a common yellow to olive European food fish (*Zeus faber*), or an allied Australian fish (*Zeus australis*).

John Han′cock (hăn′kŏk). An autograph signature; — from the legibility of the handwriting of John Hancock.

john′ny·cake′ (jŏn′ĭ·kāk′), *n.* [For *journey cake.*] *U.S.* A bread made of Indian meal, flour, eggs, milk, etc.

John′ny–jump′–up′, *n.* Also **Johnny jumper. a** Any of several American violets, as the bird's-foot violet. **b** *U.S.* The wild pansy.

John′son·ese′ (jŏn′sŭn·ēz′; -ēs′), *n.* The diction or literary style of Dr. Samuel Johnson, or one formed in imitation of it; — used derogatorily of stilted or pompous style.

John′son grass (jŏn′s′n). [After W. *Johnson* of Alabama, who planted it about 1840–45.] A tall perennial European grass (*Sorghum halepense*) valuable in southern and western U. S. for pasture and hay.

John·so′ni·an (jŏn·sō′nĭ·ăn; 58), *adj.* Pertaining to, or resembling, Dr. Samuel Johnson or his style; derogatorily, pompous; inflated. — *n.* A follower or copier of Dr. Johnson. — **John·so′ni·an·ism** (-ĭz′m), *n.*

‖**joie de vi′vre** (zhwȧ′ dẽ vē′vr′). [F.] Literally, joy in living; hence, zest; keen enjoyment of the pleasures of life.

join (join), *v. t.* [OF. *joindre,* fr. L. *jungere* to yoke, join.] **1.** To connect physically; to fasten or put together; to couple. **2.** To unite in association, specif., in marriage; to associate oneself with; as, to *join* the church. **3.** To unite in time, effort, action, consideration, or other immaterial manner; as, to *join* prayers. **4.** To assemble in a group; as, to *join* forces. **5.** To accept, or engage in, as a contest; as, to *join* battle. **6.** *Colloq.* To be adjacent to; adjoin. **7.** *Geom.* To connect by a line, esp. by a straight line. — *v. i.* **1.** To come together so as to be connected; to unite. **2.** To engage; to join battle.

Syn. Join, combine, unite, connect, link, associate, relate mean to attach or fasten two or more things to each other or to become so attached or fastened. **Join** presupposes prior detachment and the bringing of them into contact or conjunction; **combine** usually implies a mingling or merging, often suggesting the loss of identity of each unit; **unite** implies a oneness that results from a joining or combining; **connect** implies a loose or obvious attachment without loss of any unit's identity; **link** implies the strength of the connection; **associate,** referring more often to persons than to things, suggests a connection based upon companionship or the like; **relate,** if used of persons, suggests a connection by blood, or if used of things, a connection based on some logical principle, such as cause of an effect, effect of a cause, subordination, etc. (as, to *join* hands; to *combine* ingredients; to *unite* churches; to *connect* railway coaches; to *link* persons in marriage; to *associate* ideas; to *relate* one event to another).

— *n.* Act of joining; place or point of junction.

join′der (join′dẽr), *n.* [F. *joindre,* inf. as n.] **1.** Act of joining; a putting together; a conjunction. **2.** *Law.* **a** A joining of parties as plaintiffs or defendants in a suit. **b** Acceptance of an issue tendered. **c** A joining of causes of action or defense.

join′er (join′ẽr), *n.* **1.** One who or that which joins. **2.** One whose occupation is to construct articles by joining pieces of wood; a skilled woodworker who does the woodwork (as doors, stairs, etc.) necessary for the finishing of buildings.

join′er·y (-ĭ), *n.* Also **joiner work.** Art or trade of a joiner; the work of a joiner; also, things made by a joiner.

joint (joint), *n.* [OF. *joint, jointe,* fr. L. *junctus,* past part. of *jungere, junctum,* to join.] **1.** The part, or the arrangement of the part, where two bones of an animal's body, or parts of an invertebrate's body, are joined, esp. so as to admit of motion; hence, a part in a plant where branches give off. **2.** The part or space included between two articulations, knots, or nodes. **3.** Specif., any of the large pieces of meat as cut for roasting. **4.** The place or part where two things or parts are joined or united; junction; as, a *joint* in a pipe; a *joint* between two pieces of timber. **5.** *Slang.* A gathering place; loosely, any establishment, resort, etc. **6.** *Geol.* A fracture in rock, smaller than a fault and not accompanied by dislocation.

— *adj.* [OF., past part. of *joindre.*] **1.** Joined; combined; specif., *Law,* of the lives of two or more persons, united in time; concurrent. **2.** Common to two or more; as: **a** Involving the united activity of two or more. **b** Shared by, or affecting, two or more; as, a *joint* account; a *joint* fine; specif., in diplomacy, designating an action or expression in which two or more governments unite (dist. from *identic*). **3.** United, joined, or sharing with another or with others; acting together; as, *joint* creditor; *joint* debtor. **4.** *Parl. Practice.* Of or pertaining to the two branches of a legislative body; as, a *joint* committee.

— *v. t.* **1.** To unite by a joint or joints; to fit together. **2.** To separate the joints of; cut up into joints, as meat. **3.** To provide with a joint or joints; to articulate.

joint′ed (join′tĕd; -tĭd), *adj.* Having joints.

joint′er (join′tẽr), *n.* **1.** One that joints; esp., any various tools used in making joints. **2.** *Agric. Mach.* A triangular-shaped edged attachment to a plow beam for covering trash in plowing. See PLOW, *Illust.*

joint′ly, *adv.* In a joint manner; together; unitedly.

joint resolution. A resolution adopted jointly by the two branches of a legislative body.

joint′ress (join′trĕs; -trĭs), *n.* *Law.* A woman who has a jointure.

joint stock. Stock or capital held in company; capital held as a common stock or fund.

joint′–stock′ com′pa·ny. *Law.* A company or association, consisting of a number of individuals organized to conduct a business for gain, with a joint stock, the shares owned by any member being transferable without the consent of the rest.

join′ture (join′tūr), *n.* [OF., fr. L. *junctura,* fr. *jungere* to join.] **1.** *Obs.* A joining; union. **2.** *Law.* The joint tenancy of an estate, or the estate so held. *Obs.,* except specif., an estate settled on a wife to be taken by her in lieu of dower.

joint′weed′ (joint′wēd′), *n.* *U.S.* An American herb (*Polygonella articulata*) of the buckwheat family, with jointed, almost leafless stems, and spikelike racemes of small white flowers.

joint′worm′ (-wûrm′), *n.* The larva of any of several small chalcid flies (genus *Harmolita,* family Eurytomidae), which attack the stems of grain and cause gall-like swellings.

joist (joist), *n.* [OF. *giste,* fr. L. *jacēre* to lie.] **a** Any of the small timbers or beams ranged parallelwise from wall to wall in a building to support the floor, or to support the laths or furring strips of a ceiling. **b** *U.S.* A stud or scantling about 3 by 4 inches in section. — *v. t.* To furnish with joists.

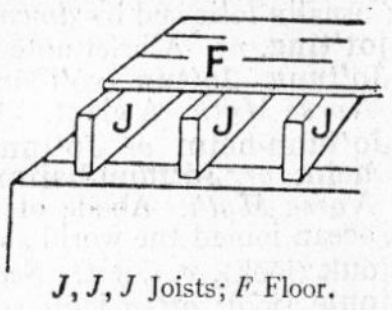

J, J, J Joists; *F* Floor.

joke (jōk), *n.* [L. *jocus* joke, jest, game.] **1.** Something said or done to excite a laugh; something witty or sportive; jest; witticism. **2.** Something said or done in sport and not seriously. **3.** A laughingstock; as, he is a *joke* — **Syn.** See JEST. — *v. i.* To do something as a joke; to be merry; to jest. — *v. t.* To make merry with; to rally; banter; as, to *joke* a comrade. — **jok′ing·ly** (jōk′ĭng·lĭ), *adv.*

jok′er (jōk′ẽr), *n.* **1.** One who jokes; a jester. **2. a** *Political Cant.* An apparently harmless clause inserted in a legislative bill to render it inoperative or uncertain in some respect without arousing opposition at the time of its passage. **b** Hence, an unsuspected clause in a document, or the like, which in effect nullifies or greatly alters its apparent terms. **3.** *Card Playing.* An extra card now usually made to accompany the regulation pack. When used, it has special privileges; thus, in euchre it is the best trump.

jole (jōl). Var. of JOWL.

jol′li·er (jŏl′ĭ·ẽr), *n.* *Colloq.* One who jollies, flatters, etc.

jol′li·fi·ca′tion (jŏl′ĭ·fĭ·kā′shŭn), *n.* [*jolly* + *-fication.*] *Colloq.* A merrymaking; jovial festivity.

jol′li·fy (jŏl′ĭ·fī), *v. t. & i.;* -FIED (-fīd); -FY′ING. *Colloq.* To make, or to be, jolly.

jol′li·ty (jŏl′ĭ·tĭ), *n.; pl.* -TIES (-tĭz). **1.** State or quality of being jolly; gaiety. **2.** *Brit.* A festive gathering. — **Syn.** See MIRTH.

jol′ly (jŏl′ĭ), *adj.;* JOL′LI·ER (-ĭ·ẽr); JOL′LI·EST. [OF. *joli, jolif,* joyful, merry.] **1.** Full of spirits; joyful. **2.** Full of life and mirth; jovial; merry. **3.** Expressing or inspiring mirth. **4.** *Colloq.* Splendid; pleasant; also, large; strong. — **Syn.** See MERRY. — *n.; pl.* JOLLIES (-ĭz). **1.** *Brit. Sailors' Slang.* A marine. **2.** *Colloq.* Something said or done to keep a person or people in good humor or quiet. **3.** *Slang, Eng.* A social meeting for mirth and good cheer. — *v. t.;* JOL′LIED (-ĭd); JOL′LY·ING. *Colloq.* To encourage to feel pleasant or cheerful; — often implying a bantering spirit; hence, to poke fun at; rally. — *v. i.* **1.** To be or act jolly. **2.** *Colloq.* To jolly a person or people. — **jol′li·ly,** *adv.* — **jol′li·ness,** *n.*

jolly boat. *Naut.* A boat of medium size belonging to a ship, used for general rough or small work.

Jolly Roger. See ROGER, 2.

jolt (jōlt), *v. i. & t.* **1.** To shake with short, abrupt risings and fallings, as a carriage moving on rough ground; to jar. **2.** *Boxing.* To jar with a hard blow. — *n.* A butt, knock, or blow; a sudden shock or jerk; in boxing, a jarring blow. — **jolt′er,** *n.*

Jo′nah (jō′nȧ), *n.* [Heb. *Yōnāh,* lit., dove.] **1.** *Bib.* A Hebrew prophet, who, during a tempest sent by God because of his disobedience, was cast overboard from his ship, swallowed by a great fish, and remained in its belly three days before being cast out. **2.** The book of the Old Testament that tells his story. See BIBLE. **3.** One who brings ill luck.

Jo′nas (-năs), *n.* *Douay Bib.* Jonah.

Jon′a·than (jŏn′ȧ·thăn), *n.* [Heb. *Yōnāthān.*] *Bib.* Son of Saul, and friend of David.

Jon′a·than, *n.* *Hort.* A late autumn variety of red apple.

jon′gleur′ (zhôN′glûr′; jŏng′glẽr), *n.* [F. See JUGGLER.] In medieval France and Norman England, an itinerant minstrel who recited or sang by way of entertainment, as at courts.

jon′quil (jŏng′kwĭl; jŏn′-; *still by some,* jŭng′kwĭl), *n.* [F. *jonquille,* fr. Sp. *junquillo* jonquil, reed, dim. of *junco* a rush, fr. L. *juncus.*] A bulbous plant (*Narcissus jonquilla*) of southern Europe and Algeria, with long, rushlike leaves, and yellow or white, single or double fragrant flowers resembling those of the daffodil; also, a bulb or flower of the plant. See CORONA, *Illust.*

jook joint (jŏŏk; jōōk). See JUKE JOINT.

jor′dan (jôr′d′n), **jor′den,** *n.* *Obs. exc. Dial.* A chamber pot.

Jor′dan al′monds (jôr′d′n). [ME. *jardyne almaunde* (*jardyne,* fr. OF. *jardin* garden); hence, prop., a cultivated almond.] Almonds imported from Málaga, used in confectionery.

‖**jor·na′da** (hôr·nä′thä), *n.* [Sp.] The toil, travel, or the like, of a day; hence, *Southwest U. S. & Mexico,* a long stretch of desert region.

jo′rum (jō′rŭm; 70), *n.* [Prob. from *Joram,* in 2 Sam. viii. 10, who brought vessels of silver, etc.] *Colloq.* A large drinking vessel, or its contents.

Jo′seph (jō′zĕf; -zĭf), *n.* [L. *Joseph, Josephus,* fr. Gr. *Iōsēph,* fr. Heb. *Yōsēph.*] **1.** *Bib.* **a** A Hebrew patriarch, son of Jacob, who gave him a "coat of many colors." See JACOB. **b** The husband of Mary, mother of Jesus. **c** The rich councilor of Arimathea, ***Joseph of Arimathea,*** who placed the body of Jesus in his tomb. **2.** [*not cap.*] An 18th-century cloak, esp. a woman's riding coat.

josh (jŏsh), *v. t. & i.* *Slang, U. S.* To make fun (of); to chaff; banter. — *n.* *Slang, U. S.* A bantering joke. — **josh′er** (-ẽr), *n.*

Josh′u·a (jŏsh′ū·ȧ), *n.* [Heb. *Yĕhōshūa′.*] *Bib.* **a** The successor of Moses, who led the Israelites into Canaan. **b** A book of the Old Testament. See BIBLE.

Joshua tree. A branched treelike yucca (*Yucca brevifolia*) of the southwestern U. S., often 25 feet high, with short leaves and clustered greenish-white flowers.

jos′kin (jŏs′kĭn), *n.* *Slang.* A bumpkin; a boor.

joss (jŏs), *n.* [Pidgin English, fr. Pg. *deos, deus,* a god, fr. L. *deus.*] *Pidgin English.* A Chinese household divinity; also, a cult image.

joss house. *Pidgin English.* A Chinese temple.

joss stick. A reed covered with, or a cylinder of, paste made of the dust of odoriferous woods. The Chinese burn joss sticks as incense.

jos′tle (jŏs′'l), *v. t. & i.;* JOS′TLED (-'ld); JOS′TLING (-lĭng). [Dim. of *joust, just,* v. See JOUST.] To run against and shake; to elbow; to hustle; to crowd. — *n.* A crowding or bumping together; interference. — **jos′tler** (-lẽr), *n.*

Jos′u·e (jŏs′ū·ē), *n.* *Douay Bib.* Joshua.

jot (jŏt), *n.* [L. *iota*, fr. Gr. *iōta*, the smallest letter of the alphabet.] An iota; a point; a tittle.

jot, *v. t.;* JOT′TED; JOT′TING. To set down; to make a brief note of; — usually followed by *down*.

jot′ting, *n.* A brief note or memorandum.

Jo′tunn, Jo′tun (yô′to͝on), **Jö′tunn** (yû′to͝on), *n.* [ON. *jötunn*.] *Norse Myth.* A giant.

Jo′tunn·heim *or* **Jo′tunn·heimr** (yô′to͝on·hām, -hām′r), **Jö′tunn·heim** *or* **Jö′tunn·heimr** (yû′to͝on-), *n.* [ON. *jötunheimar*, pl.] *Norse Myth.* Abode of the giants, in the far northwest where the ocean joined the world's edge.

jouk (jo͞ok), *v. i. & t.* *Scot.* To dodge or duck; skulk; bow.

joule (jo͞ol; *often* joul; *see note below*), *n.* [After James P. *Joule*, Eng. physicist.] *Physics.* A unit of work or energy equal to 10^7 ergs, and practically the energy expended in one second by an electric current of one ampere in a resistance of one ohm. One joule is approximately equal to 0.738 foot-pound, or 0.24 small calorie. Abbr. *J.*

☞ The physicist's own pronunciation was pretty certainly jo͞ol, and may originally have been jōl; joul is frequent for the unit, however, throughout the English-speaking world.

jounce (jouns), *v. t. & i.;* JOUNCED (jounst); JOUNC′ING (joun′sĭng). To shake, esp. by rough riding; to jolt. — *n.* A shaking bump; a jolt.

jour′nal (jûr′năl; -n′l), *n.* [F., fr. L. *diurnalis*. See DIURNAL.] **1.** A diary; an account of daily transactions and events. **2.** The record of transactions kept by a deliberative body. **3.** A newspaper published daily; by extension, any periodical publication; a magazine. **4.** *Bookkeeping.* **a** A daybook. **b** In double entry, a book of original entry. When specialized cash, sales, purchase, and other journals are used, the journal is the original entry book for transactions which cannot be recorded properly in the specialized journals. **5.** *Mach.* That portion of a rotating shaft, axle, spindle, etc., which turns in a bearing. See CRANK, *Illust.*

journal box. *Mach.* A box or bearing for a journal.

jour′nal·ese′ (jûr′năl·ēz′; -ēs′), *n.* *Colloq.* Language of a style considered characteristic of newspaper writing.

‖jour′nal′ in′time′ (zhōōr′nȧl′ ăN′tēm′). [F.] Private diary.

jour′nal·ism (jûr′năl·ĭz′m), *n.* The business of managing, editing, or writing for journals or newspapers; also, journals or newspapers collectively.

jour′nal·ist (-ĭst), *n.* **1.** An editor or other professional writer for a periodical; now, esp., one who conducts a public journal. **2.** One who keeps a journal, or diary.

jour′nal·is′tic (-ĭs′tĭk), *adj.* Characteristic of journalism or journalists. — **jour′nal·is′ti·cal·ly** (-tĭ·kăl·ĭ), *adv.*

jour′nal·ize (jûr′năl·īz), *v. t.* **1.** To enter or record in a journal, or book for accounts or records, as in bookkeeping. **2.** To enter, narrate, or describe in a diary, or journal.

jour′ney (jûr′nĭ), *n.* [OF. *journee* a day, a day's work or travel, fr. L. *diurnum* day, fr. *diurnus* daily.] **1.** Travel or passage from one place to another; hence, a trip. Cf. VOYAGE, *n.*, 1. **2.** *Now Dial.* A day's travel (in the Middle Ages estimated at 20 miles). — *v. i.* To travel from place to place; to go on a journey.

jour′ney·er (jûr′nĭ·ẽr), *n.* One who journeys.

jour′ney·man (-măn), *n.* A worker who has learned a handicraft or trade; — distinguished from *apprentice*, *foreman*, and *master*.

jour′ney·work′ (-wûrk′), *n.* Work done by a journeyman.

joust (jŭst; joust; jo͞ost), *v. i.* Also **just** (jŭst). [OF. *juster*, *jouster*, *joster*, fr. L. *juxta* near to, nigh, fr. root of *jungere* to join.] **1.** *Obs.* To join battle; to engage, esp. on horseback, as men-at-arms. **2.** To engage in a joust; to tilt. — *n.* A combat on horseback between two knights with lances; specif., a combat (often mock) of this kind as part of a tournament; often, *pl.*, a tournament. — **joust′er** (jŭs′tẽr; jous′-; jo͞os′-), **just′er** (jŭs′tẽr), *n.*

Jove (jōv), *n.* [L. *Jovis*, used as gen. of *Jupiter* and as a nom., god of the sky.] Jupiter (deity or planet).

jo′vi·al (jō′vĭ·ăl), *adj.* [F., fr. LL. *Jovialis* pertaining to Jove. The planet Jupiter was thought to make those born under it joyful or jovial.] **1.** [*cap.*] Of or pertaining to Jupiter, the god (Jove) or the planet. **2.** Characterized by mirth or jollity; merry; hilarious; jolly. — **Syn.** See MERRY. — **jo′vi·al·ly**, *adv.* — **jo′vi·al·ness**, *n.*

jo′vi·al′i·ty (-ăl′ĭ·tĭ), *n.* Quality or state of being jovial.

Jo′vi·an (jō′vĭ·ăn), *adj.* Of or pertaining to or like Jove.

jow (jou; jō), *v. t. & i.* *Scot.* To ring (a bell); clang; toll.

jowl (joul; jōl), *n.* [(After F. *joue* cheek), fr. ME. *chauel*, *chavel*, fr. AS. *ceafl* jaw.] **1.** A jaw, esp. the under jaw. **2.** The cheek; a cheek.

jowl, *n.* [ME. *cholle*, of uncert. origin.] The hanging part of a double chin; the dewlap (of cattle); the wattle (of a fowl).

jowl, *n.* The head, or head and adjacent parts, of a fish.

joy (joi), *n.* [OF. *joie*, fr. L. *gaudia*, pl. of *gaudium* joy, fr. *gaudere* to rejoice, be glad.] **1.** The emotion excited by the acquisition or expectation of good; gladness; delight. **2.** State of happiness; bliss. **3.** That which causes happiness. **4.** The exhibition of joy; gaiety. — **Syn.** See PLEASURE. — *v. i. & t.* To rejoice; delight; also, *Archaic*, to enjoy.

joy′ance (joi′ăns), *n.* Enjoyment; delight; gaiety.

joy′ful (-fo͝ol; -f'l), *adj.* Full of joy; having or causing joy; very glad. — **Syn.** See GLAD. — **joy′ful·ly**, *adv.* — **joy′ful·ness**, *n.*

joy′less, *adj.* Not having or causing joy; unenjoyable. — **joy′less·ly**, *adv.* — **joy′less·ness**, *n.*

joy′ous (joi′ŭs), *adj.* Glad; joyful; also, affording joy. — **Syn.** See GLAD. — **joy′ous·ly**, *adv.* — **joy′ous·ness**, *n.*

joy ride. *Colloq.* A pleasure ride, esp. in an automobile, often a surreptitious one with companions and characterized by reckless driving. — **joy rider.** — **joy riding.**

jub′bah (jo͝ob′bȧ), *n.* [Ar. *jubbah*.] A long garment worn in Mohammedan countries by both sexes.

ju′bi·lant (jo͞o′bĭ·lănt), *adj.* [L. *jubilans*, *-antis*, pres. part.] Shouting with joy; exulting. — **ju′bi·lance** (-lăns), **ju′bi·lan·cy** (-lăn·sĭ), *n.* — **ju′bi·lant·ly**, *adv.*

ju′bi·late (-lāt), *v. i. & t.* [L. *jubilatus*, past part. of *jubilare*, fr. *jubilum* a wild cry, shout.] To exult; rejoice.

Ju′bi·la′te (jo͞o′bĭ·lā′tē; -lä′tē), *n.* [L., imper. of *jubilare* to shout for joy.] **1.** The 100th Psalm (99th in the Vulgate and the Douay Version); — from its opening word in the Latin version. **2.** Third Sunday after Easter; — from first word of the Introit for that day.

ju′bi·la′tion (jo͞o′bĭ·lā′shŭn), *n.* A triumphant shouting; rejoicing; exultation.

ju′bi·lee (jo͞o′bĭ·lē; 114), *n.* [OF. *jubilé*, fr. LL. *jubilaeus*, fr. Gr. *iōbēlaios*, fr. Heb. *yōbēl* ram's horn, jubilee; confused with L. *jubilum* a shout.] **1.** *Jewish Hist.* An institution (Lev. xxv. 8–17) to be kept every fiftieth year by the liberation of all slaves who were Hebrews, the restoration of alienated lands, and omission of sowing and reaping of any kind. **2.** A plenary indulgence proclaimed by the pope every 25 years (***ordinary jubilee***) or during a time of stress, as a plague, or of rejoicing, as an anniversary (***extraordinary jubilee***). Paul II in 1470 fixed the interval between ordinary jubilees at 25 years. **3.** The anniversary completing fifty (sometimes twenty-five) years in continuance, service, etc., or a joyful commemoration on such an anniversary. **4.** A season or occasion of general joy. **5.** A state of exultation; jubilation.

Ju′dah (jo͞o′dȧ), *n.* *Douay Bib.* **Ju′da.** *Bib.* Son of Jacob, and founder of the tribe of Judah, which constituted one of the main elements of the Kingdom of Judah (933–586 B.C.) in southern Palestine.

Ju·da′ic (jo͞o·dā′ĭk), *adj.* Also **Ju·da′i·cal** (-ĭ·kăl). Of or pertaining to the Jews; Jewish.

Ju′da·ism (jo͞o′dā·ĭz′m), *n.* **1.** The religious doctrines and rites of the Jews. **2.** Conformity to the Jewish rites and ceremonies. — **Ju′da·ist** (-ĭst), *n.* — **Ju′da·ist, Ju′da·is′tic** (-ĭs′tĭk), *adj.*

Ju′da·ize (-īz), *v. i. & t.* To conform, or to convert, to the doctrines, observances, or methods of the Jews. — **Ju′da·iz′er** (-īz′ẽr), *n.*

Ju′das (jo͞o′dăs), *n.* [LL. See JUDE.] **1.** The disciple, called Iscariot, who betrayed Christ. **2.** A treacherous person; a traitor. **3.** *Bib.* **a** One of the twelve apostles, not Iscariot (*Luke* vi. 16, *Acts* i. 13, and *John* xiv. 22). **b** A brother of James (*Matt.* xiii. 55; *Mark* vi. 3).

Judas tree. Any of a genus (*Cercis*) of shrubs and trees of the senna family, including the tree (*C. siliquastrum*) on which Judas Iscariot is said to have hanged himself.

Jude (jo͞od), *or* **Ju′das** (jo͞o′dăs), *n.* [LL. *Judas*, fr. Gr. *Ioudas*; same name as *Judah*.] Author of the Epistle of Jude in the New Testament. See BIBLE.

Ju·de′an, Ju·dae′an (jo͞o·dē′ăn), *adj.* [L. *Judaeus*.] Of or pertaining to Judea or the Jews. — *n.* A Jew.

judge (jŭj), *n.* [OF. *juge*, fr. L. *judex*, *judicis*, fr. *jus* law + the root of *dicere* to say.] **1.** A public officer who is invested with authority to determine litigated questions; esp., the presiding magistrate in a court of justice. **2.** An umpire, as of a race. **3.** One who has knowledge sufficient to decide on the merits of a question; a connoisseur; a critic. **4.** *Jewish Hist.* One of the magistrates who governed Israel for more than four hundred years after Joshua's death. — *v. t. & i.;* JUDGED (jŭjd); JUDG′ING (jŭj′ĭng). **1.** To hear and determine the case of (a person or persons) in a court of justice; to hear and determine (a matter) judicially; to try. **2.** To conclude or decide by the exercise of the judgment; to estimate; suppose. **3.** To decree or adjudge to be or be done. **4.** *Archaic.* To govern. — **Syn.** See INFER. — **judge′ship**, *n.*

judge advocate; *pl.* JUDGE ADVOCATES. *Mil. & Nav., U. S.* An officer appointed to act as prosecutor at a court-martial.

judge′-made′, *adj.* Created by judges or judicial decision.

judg′er (jŭj′ẽr), *n.* One who judges.

Judg′es (jŭj′ĕz; -ĭz), *n. pl., construed as sing.* The seventh book of the Old Testament, recording the history of the judges. See BIBLE.

judg·mat′ic (jŭj·măt′ĭk), **judg·mat′i·cal** (-ĭ·kăl), *adj.* [*judge* + *-matic* as in *dogmatic*.] *Colloq.* Judicious. — **judg·mat′i·cal·ly**, *adv.*

judg′ment, judge′ment (jŭj′mĕnt), *n.* **1.** The pronouncing of a formal opinion or decision; also, the opinion or decision given. **2.** A calamity regarded as sent by God, by way of punishment. **3.** *Archaic.* Justice. **4.** The result of judging; opinion; decision. **5.** The mental act of judging; the operation of the mind, involving comparison and discrimination, by which knowledge of values and relations is mentally formulated. **6.** The power of arriving at a wise decision; discretion; discernment. **7.** *Law.* **a** The act of determining, as in courts, what is conformable to law and justice; also, the decree or sentence of a court. **b** The obligation, esp. a debt, created by the decision or decree of a court; also, the official certificate evidencing such a decision or decree. **8.** *Theol.* The mandate or sentence of God as the judge of all; esp., ***Last Judgment***, God's or Christ's final judgment of mankind; also, the time of it; as, the great Day of *Judgment*. — **Syn.** See SENSE.

judgment day. [*often caps.*] *Theol.* The day of the last judgment; the last day; doomsday.

ju′di·ca·ble (jo͞o′dĭ·kȧ·b'l), *adj.* Capable of being, or liable to be, judged.

ju′di·ca′tive (jo͞o′dĭ·kā′tĭv; -kȧ·tĭv), *adj.* Having power to judge; judicial; as, the *judicative* faculty.

ju′di·ca′tor (-kā′tẽr), *n.* [LL.] One who judges; a judge.

ju′di·ca·to′ry (-kȧ·tō′rĭ *or, esp. Brit.*, -tẽr·ĭ), *adj.* Of or pertaining to judgment; exercising judicial functions; judicial; as, *judicatory* tribunals. — *n.; pl.* -RIES (-rĭz). [LL. *judicatorium*.] **1.** A court of justice; a tribunal. **2.** Administration of justice; judicature.

ju′di·ca·ture (-tūr), *n.* [F., fr. ML. *judicatura*.] **1.** State, profession, or function of those employed in the administration of justice; also, the action of judging. **2.** Judges collectively; a court of justice; a judicatory. **3.** The right of judicial action; jurisdiction.

ju·di′ci·a·ble (jo͞o·dĭsh′ĭ·ȧ·b'l; 58), *adj.* Judicable.

ju·di′cial (jo͞o·dĭsh′ăl; 114), *adj.* [OF. or L.; OF., fr. L. *judicialis*, fr. L. *judicium* judgment, fr. *judex* judge.] **1.** Of or pertaining or appropriate to the administration of justice, or courts of justice, or a judge thereof, or the proceedings therein; as, *judicial* power; *judicial* proceedings; — distinguished in general from *legislative*, *executive*, *administrative*, *ministerial*. **2.** Sanctioned, ordered, or enforced by a court; as, *judicial* sale. **3.** Disposed to form or pass judgment; critical; exercising, involving, or relative to judgment; as, a *judicial* mind. **4.** Belonging or proper to a judge or the judiciary; as, the *judicial* ermine. **5.** *Theol.* Arising from a judgment of God; coming as a divine punishment; as, a *judicial* pestilence. — **ju·di′cial·ly**, *adv.*

ju·di′ci·ar′y (jo͞o·dĭsh′ĭ·ĕr′ĭ *or, esp. Brit.*, -ẽr·ĭ), *adj.* Of or pertaining to courts, or a judge thereof or the procedure therein; judicial. — *n.* That branch of government in which judicial power is vested; the system of courts of justice in a country; the judges, taken collectively; judicature.

ju·di′cious (jo͞o·dĭsh′ŭs), *adj.* [F. *judicieux*.] Directed or governed by sound judgment; wise. — **Syn.** See WISE. — **ju·di′cious·ly**, *adv.* — **ju·di′cious·ness**, *n.*

Ju′dith (jōō′dĭth), *n.* [L., fr. Gr. *Ioudith*, fr. Heb. *Yĕhūdhīth*.] A book of the Old Testament Apocrypha that tells the story of Judith, slayer of Holofernes, the general of Nebuchadnezzar; also, a book in the Douay Bible. See BIBLE.

ju′do (jōō′dō), *n.* = JUJITSU.

Ju′dy (jōō′dĭ), *n.* [Familiar form of JUDITH.] A character in the puppet show of *Punch and Judy*. See PUNCH.

jug (jŭg), *n.* [A corruption of, or nickname for, *Joan*, or *Joanna*.] **1.** A pitcher or ewer; specif., *U. S.*, a deep, large vessel of earthenware, with a narrow mouth and a handle; also, the contents of such a vessel. **2.** *Slang.* A prison; a jail; a lockup. — *v. t.;* JUGGED (jŭgd); JUG′GING. **1.** To seethe or stew, as a hare, in a jar. **2.** *Slang.* To commit to jail.

ju′gal (jōō′găl; 114), *adj.* [L. *jugalis*, fr. *jugum* yoke.] *Anat. & Zool.* Pertaining to or designating a bone of the lateral part of the face below the eye; zygomatic.

ju′gate (-gāt), *adj.* [L. *jugatus*, past part. of *jugare* to join.] **1.** *Biol.* Paired. **2.** *Bot.* Having leaflets in pairs, as a pinnate leaf.

Jug′ger·naut (jŭg′ẽr-nôt), *n.* [See JAGANNATH.] **1.** *Hinduism.* A form of Vishnu. See JAGANNATH. **2.** [*not cap.*] A belief calling for blind self-sacrifice. **3.** [*not cap.*] Any massive inexorable force that advances irresistibly, crushing whatever is in its path.

jug′gins (jŭg′ĭnz), *n.* *Slang.* A simpleton.

jug′gle (jŭg′'l), *v. i.;* JUG′GLED (-'ld); JUG′GLING (-lĭng). [OF. *jogler, jugler*. See JUGGLER.] **1.** To perform the tricks of a juggler. **2.** To practice artifice or imposture. — *v. t.* **1.** To beguile or deceive, as by jugglery. **2.** To perform juggling tricks with; as, to *juggle* knives. — *n.* An act or piece of juggling; an imposture; deception.

jug′gler (-lẽr), *n.* [OF. *jogleor, jugleor, jongleor*, fr. L. *joculator* a jester, joker, fr. *joculari* to jest, fr. *joculus* a little jest or joke, dim. of *jocus* jest, joke.] **1.** One who entertains people by tricks of illusion, esp. sleight of hand. **2.** A deceiver; a cheat.

jug′gler·y (-ĭ), *n.; pl.* -IES (-ĭz). **1.** Art or act of a juggler; sleight of hand. **2.** Trickery; imposture.

jug′gling (jŭg′lĭng), *n.* Jugglery. — *adj.* Cheating; tricky.

ju′glan·da′ceous (jōō′glăn-dā′shŭs), *adj.* [L. *juglans* walnut.] *Bot.* Belonging to the walnut family (Juglandaceae). See WALNUT.

Ju′go·slav′, Ju′go·slav′ic, etc. Vars. of YUGOSLAV, etc.

jug′u·lar (jŭg′ū-lẽr; jōō′gū-), *adj.* [NL. *jugularis*, fr. L. *jugulum* the collarbone.] *Anat.* **a** Of or pertaining to the throat or neck; as, the *jugular* vein. **b** Of or pertaining to the jugular vein (see JUGULAR, *n.*, below). — *n.* *Anat.* Short for **jugular vein**, any of several veins of each side of the neck; esp., one of the large veins returning the blood from the head.

juice (jōōs; 114), *n.* [OF. *jus* broth, juice, fr. L. *jus*.] **1.** The fluid contents of plant cells or structures. **2.** The fluid content of animal flesh; esp., *pl.*, all the fluids in the body. **3.** Any liquid extracted from a body; also, an essence. **4.** *Slang.* A medium that supplies power, as electricity, gasoline, or oil. — **juice′less**, *adj.*

juic′y (jōōs′ĭ), *adj.;* JUIC′I·ER (-ĭ-ẽr); -I·EST. **a** Abounding with juice; succulent. **b** Rich in interest or coloring; esp., *Colloq.*, racy or piquant. — **juic′i·ly**, *adv.* — **juic′i·ness**, *n.*

ju·jit′su (jōō-jĭt′sōō; *Jap.* jōō′jĭt′sōō), *n.* Also **ju·jut′su** (jōō-jōōt′sōō; *Jap.* jōō′jōōt′sōō), **jiu·jit′su, jiu·jut′su** (jōō-). [Jap. *jūjutsu*, fr. *jū* soft, pliant, yielding + *jutsu* art.] The Japanese art of self-defense without weapons, depending largely upon the principle of making use of an opponent's strength and weight to disable or injure him — **ju·jit′su, ju·jut′su**, etc., *adj. & v.*

ju′ju (jōō′jōō), *n.* A fetish, charm, or amulet of West African tribes, or the magic attributed to it; also, the beliefs connected with the use of jujus. — **ju′ju·ism** (-ĭz'm), *n.*

ju′jube (jōō′jōōb; 114), *n.* [F., fr. L. *zizyphum*, fr. Gr. *zizyphon*, fr. Per. *zīzafūn*.] **1. a** The edible drupaceous fruit of any of several trees (genus *Zizyphus*) of the buckthorn family. **b** Any tree producing this fruit. Cf. CHRIST'S-THORN. **2. a** A jelly made from this fruit. **b** A lozenge made of, or flavored with, this fruit.

juke, *or* **jook, joint** (jōōk; jŏŏk). [Appar. of West African origin.] *Orig. Southern U. S.* Orig., an out-of-the-way shack used by Negro turpentine workers as a drinking and dancing resort; hence, any roadhouse or dance hall or like resort for drinking and dancing, esp. to the music of an automatic player of phonograph records that plays one record on deposit of a coin in the slot, called a **juke′box′** (-bŏks′) *or* **juke**.

ju′lep (jōō′lĕp; -lĭp), *n.* [F., fr. Ar. *julāb*, fr. Per. *gulāb* rose water, julep, fr. *gul* rose + *āb* water.] **1.** A refreshing drink flavored with aromatic herbs. **2.** *U. S.* A beverage of brandy or whisky, with sugar, ice, and sprigs of mint; — called also ***mint julep***.

Jul′ian (jōōl′yăn; 58), *adj.* [L. *Julianus*, fr. *Julius*.] Relating to Julius Caesar.

Julian calendar. The calendar introduced by Julius Caesar in 46 B.C., in which the year consisted of 365 days, each fourth year (leap year) having 366 days, and the months having the same names, order, and length as now. Cf. GREGORIAN CALENDAR.

ju′li·enne′ (jōō′lĭ-ĕn′; *F.* zhü′lyĕn′), *n.* [F.] A clear soup containing thin strips of carrots, onions, etc. — *adj.* Designating vegetables cut in matchlike strips.

Ju′li·et (jōō′lĭ-ĕt; -ĕt; jōō′lĭ-ĕt′; jōōl′yĕt; 58), *n.* See ROMEO.

Ju·ly′ (jōō-lī′; 114), *n.; pl.* JULIES (-līz′). [AF. *Julie*, fr. L. *Julius*; — from Gaius *Julius* Caesar, born in this month.] The seventh month of the year, having 31 days. Abbr. *Jul.*

Ju·ma′da (jōō-mä′dä), *n.* [Ar. *Jumāda*.] See MOHAMMEDAN CALENDAR.

jum′ble (jŭm′b'l), *v. t. & i.;* JUM′BLED (-b'ld); JUM′BLING (-blĭng). To mix in a confused mass. — *n.* **1.** A confused mixture. **2.** A shaking or jolting about. **3.** A small, thin, sugared cake, usually ring-shaped.

jum′bo (jŭm′bō), *n.; pl.* JUMBOS (-bōz). A big, clumsy thing or person; esp. [*cap.*], a very large African elephant, weighing 6½ tons, formerly exhibited in Barnum's circus. — *adj.* Huge of its kind; as, a *jumbo* roll.

jump (jŭmp), *v. i.* [ML. *jumpare*, of obscure origin.] **1.** To spring or leap free from the ground; to project oneself through the air. **2.** To bounce; jolt. **3.** To change or pass abruptly as if by a leap; as, the price *jumped*. **4.** To coincide; agree; — followed by *with*. **5.** To undergo a displacement, as the images of a motion picture, owing to improper alignment of the film on the mechanism. **6.** *Checkers.* To move over a square occupied by an opponent's man, capturing the man. — *v. t.* **1.** To pass over or across by a spring or leap. **2.** *Obs.* To risk; hazard. **3.** To evade as if by a jump; as, to *jump* bail. **4.** To come down upon and seize, as a mining claim. **5.** To cause to jump; as, he *jumped* his horse across the ditch. **6. a** *U. S.* To leap aboard of; as, to *jump* a train. **b** To leave as if by a leap; as, to *jump* the track. **7.** *Bridge.* To increase (the partner's bid), usually to show four trumps; also, at contract, to make any unnecessarily high bid in (a partner's suit). **8.** *Checkers.* To capture (a man) by jumping. **9.** *Sporting.* To flush; to start, as game.
— *n.* **1.** Act of jumping; a leap; spring; hence, a transition as if by jumping over; as, a *jump* in the price. **2. a** The space traversed by a leap; as, a *jump* of twelve feet; also, something to be jumped over; as, a racecourse with *jumps*. **b** *Colloq.* Space gained as if by jumping at starting a race; advantage. **3.** A start; a twitch; *pl.*, convulsive twitchings, as in chorea; hence (usually ***the jumps***), *Slang:* **a** Chorea. **b** Delirium tremens. **4.** *Checkers.* A move made by jumping. **5.** *Sports.* In athletic games, any of various competitions featuring a leap, spring, or bound.
— *adv. Obs.* Exactly; pat.

jump bid. *Bridge.* Any declaration which is more than necessary to overcall the previous bid.

jump′er (jŭmp′ẽr), *n.* [From E. dial. *jump* a jacket.] **1.** A sort of blouse or loose jacket worn by workmen, sailors, etc.; also, a loose blouse or jacket, often a slip-on, for women and children. **2.** A sleeveless, low-necked, one-piece dress worn over a blouse or sweater. **3.** Usually *pl.* Rompers.

jump′er, *n.* One who or that which jumps; as: **a** Any of various devices operating with a jumping motion. **b** Any of various kinds of sleds, as one used by boys in coasting. **c** *Elec.* A short wire used to close a break or cut out part of a circuit. **d** *Mining, etc.* A drill consisting of a bar which is jumped up and down in the bore hole.

jump′ing bean. A seed of any of certain Mexican shrubs (genera *Sebastiania* and *Sapium*, family Euphorbiaceae), which tumbles about because of movements of the contained larva of a small moth (*Carpocapsa saltitans*).

jumping jack. A toy figure of a man, jointed and made to jump or dance by means of strings or a sliding stick.

jump spark. A spark produced by the jumping of electricity across a permanent gap.

jump′y (jŭmp′ĭ), *adj.;* JUMP′I·ER (-ĭ-ẽr); JUMP′I·EST. Jumping, or inducing to jump; characterized by jumps or sudden variations; hence, nervous; apprehensive; irritable.

jun·ca′ceous (jŭng-kā′shŭs), *adj.* [L. *juncus* rush + *-aceous*.] Belonging to the rush family (Juncaceae, order Liliales). See RUSH.

jun′co (jŭng′kō), *n.; pl.* JUNCOS, *sometimes* JUNCOES (-kōz). [NL., fr. Sp. *junco* a rush. See JONQUIL.] Any of a genus (*Junco*) of small American finches found from the Arctic Circle to Guatemala; as, the ***slate-colored junco*** (also known as the *snowbird*), common in northeastern North America.

junc′tion (jŭngk′shŭn), *n.* [L. *junctio*, fr. *jungere*, *junctum*, to join.] **1** Act of joining, or state of being joined. **2.** The place or point of union; specif., the place where lines of a railway meet or cross.

junc′ture (jŭngk′tūr), *n.* [L. *junctura*.] **1.** A joining; junction. **2.** A joint; articulation; connection; seam. **3.** A point of time, esp. one made critical by a concurrence of circumstances; a conjuncture; hence, a crisis; emergency.

Syn. **Juncture, pass, exigency, emergency, contingency, pinch, strait, straits, crisis** mean a critical or crucial time or state of affairs. **Juncture** stresses the concurrence or convergence of events that, in combination, threaten, warn, etc.; **pass**, a state of affairs, usually evil, brought about, usually, by a combination of causes; **exigency**, the pressure of restrictions or the urgency of demands created by a juncture or pass; **emergency**, a sudden and unforeseen juncture, often having the character of an exigency; **contingency**, an exigency or emergency seen as possible or as about to happen; **pinch**, a juncture that resembles an exigency; **strait**, or more commonly **straits**, a situation from which it is extremely difficult to escape; **crisis**, a juncture or pass the outcome of which serves as a turning point, as in a life, a history, etc.

jun′dy, jun′die (jŭn′dĭ), *v. t. & i. & n.* *Scot.* Jostle; jog.

June (jōōn; 114), *n.* [OF. *juin*, fr. L. *Junius*; from name of a Roman gens.] The sixth month of the year, containing 30 days. Abbr. *Je.*

June beetle *or* **bug.** **a** In the northern U. S., any of several species of large brown beetles (genus *Phyllophaga* and related genera) related to the rose beetles. **b** In the southern U. S., the figeater.

June′ber′ry (jōōn′bĕr′ĭ; -bẽr-ĭ), *n.* The pome of any of several shadbushes (*Amelanchier*); also, any of these trees.

June grass. See MEADOW GRASS **a**.

jun′gle (jŭng′g'l), *n.* [Hind. *jaṅgal* desert, forest, fr. Skr. *jaṅgala* waste ground, desert.] **1. a** Any impenetrable thicket or tangled mass of vegetation. **b** Any dense intermingled growth. **2.** *Slang, U. S.* A hobo camp.

jungle fever. *Med.* A severe form of malaria endemic to East India.

jungle fowl. Any of several Asiatic wild birds (genus *Gallus*); esp., one species (*G. gallus*) of India, from which domestic fowls are believed to have descended. — **jungle cock.** — **jungle hen.**

jun′ior (jōōn′yẽr; 114), *adj.* [L., compar. of *juvenis* young.] **1.** Younger; — opposed to *senior* or *elder*; as, John Smith, *Junior*. Abbr. *Jr.* or *jr.* **2.** Lower in standing or in rank; as, a *junior* partner. **3.** Composed of juniors; as, the *junior* class; of or pertaining to juniors or a junior class. **4.** Of more recent date, and hence, of a mortgage, lien, or the like, inferior or subordinate as to right of preference. — *n.* **1.** A younger person. **2.** Hence: One of a lower or later standing; specif., in American colleges and schools, one in the third year of a four-year course, or one in the second year of a three-year course.

jun′ior·ate (-āt), *n.* *R.C.Ch.* A two-year course of instruction for Jesuits preparatory to an extended course in logic, metaphysics, etc.; also, a seminary for this course.

junior college. A college providing courses of freshman, and often of sophomore, grade, either as an independent unit or as part of a standard college or of a secondary school.

junior high school. A school including either the 7th and 8th grades of the elementary school and the 1st year of the high school, or only the 7th and 8th or the 8th and 9th grades, permitting limited election of subjects, and having some subjects usually taught in the high school.

Junior League. One of the organizations, the first of which was established in New York in 1901, making up the Association of the Junior Leagues of America, Inc. (founded 1921), composed of young women of leisure and dedicated to the "education of the members for intelligent citizen participation," esp. through direct volunteer service in agencies for social betterment.

ju'ni·per (jo͞o'nĭ·pẽr; 114), *n.* [L. *juniperus.*] **1.** Any of a genus (*Juniperus*) of evergreen shrubs or trees, esp. of those having a prostrate or shrubby habit. Cf. CEDAR, 1 **b**. The blue, berrylike fruits of common juniper (*J. communis*) have a warm, pungent taste. The acrid oil is employed in medicine, in the manufacture of varnish, etc. Cf. 2d CADE. **2. a** *U. S.* Loosely, any of several coniferous trees resembling the juniper, as the larch. **b** In the English version of the Old Testament, the retem (*Retama raetam*).

junk (jŭngk), *n.* [Pg. *junco*, fr. Jav. *joṅ.*] *Naut.* Any of various vessels of Chinese waters having as common features bluff lines, very high poop and overhanging stem, little or no keel, and pole masts.

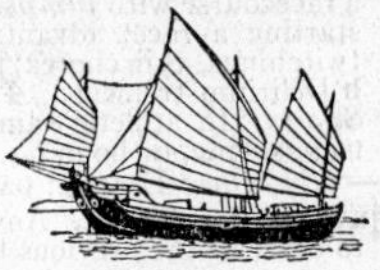

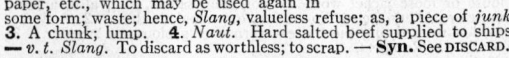

Chinese Junk.

junk, *n.* [Prob. fr. Pg. *junco* junk, cordage, rush, fr. L. *juncus* a bulrush.] **1.** Pieces of old cordage used for making gaskets, mats, oakum, etc. **2.** Old iron, glass, paper, etc., which may be used again in some form; waste; hence, *Slang*, valueless refuse; as, a piece of *junk*. **3.** A chunk; lump. **4.** *Naut.* Hard salted beef supplied to ships. — *v. t. Slang.* To discard as worthless; to scrap. — **Syn.** See DISCARD.

‖**Jun'ker** (yo͝ong'kẽr), *n.* [G.] A young German noble; esp., a member, of any age, of the Prussian aristocracy; — often implying conservatism, haughtiness, etc. — **Jun'ker, jun'ker**, *adj.* — **Jun'ker·dom, jun'ker·dom** (-dŭm), *n.* — **Jun'ker·ism, jun'ker·ism** (-ĭz'm), *n.*

jun'ket (jŭng'kĕt; -kĭt), *n.* [It. *giuncata* cream cheese, served in a wicker or rush basket, fr. *giunco* rush, fr. L. *juncus.*] **1. a** A cream cheese, or a dish of curds and cream. **b** A dish of sweetened, flavored milk set in a smooth jelly by rennet. **2.** *Obs.* A sweetmeat; any delicate food. **3.** A banquet; often, esp. in the U. S., opprobriously, an outing or excursion at the public cost. — *v. i. & t.* To feast; banquet; often, esp. in the U. S., opprobriously, to go on an outing at public cost. — **jun'ket·er**, *n.*

Ju'no (jo͞o'nō), *n.*; *pl.* JUNOS (-nōz). [L.] **1.** *Rom. Relig.* An ancient Italian goddess, identified with the Greek Hera. **2.** A stately, matronly woman.

jun'ta (jŭn'tȧ), *n.* [Sp., fr. L. *jungere, junctum*, to join.] **1.** A council, tribunal, or committee, esp. one for legislation or administration, as in Spain. **2.** A junto.

jun'to (jŭn'tō), *n.*; *pl.* -TOS (-tōz). [Corrupt. of JUNTA.] A number of men combined for some purpose, esp. a political one; a faction; cabal.

jupe (jo͞op; *F.* zhüp), *n.* [From OF. *jupe, gipe*, and fr. F. *jupe*. See JUPON.] *Scot.* **1.** A man's coat or tunic. **2.** A man's shirt; a woman's bodice; *pl.*, stays.

Ju'pi·ter (jo͞o'pĭ·tẽr; 114), *n.* [L. *Jupiter, Juppiter*, orig. a vocative.] **1.** *Rom. Relig.* An ancient Italian god identified with the Greek Zeus. **2.** *Astron.* The largest of the planets, having a mean diameter of 87,000 miles. It ranks second only to Venus in brightness. It revolves around the sun in 11.86 years, at a mean distance of 483,000,000 miles. Symbol, ♃. See PLANET, *Table*.

ju'pon (jo͞o'pŏn; jo͞o·pŏn'; *F.* zhü'pôɴ'), *n.* [OF., fr. *jupe*, fr. Sp. *aljuba* a Moorish garment, fr. Ar.] A gipon.

Ju'ra (jo͝or'ȧ), *n.* [F. & L.] *Geol.* The Jurassic period or the rocks belonging to it.

ju'ral (jo͝or'ăl; 114), *adj.* [L. *jus, juris*, right.] Of or pert. to law; juristic; also, of or pert. to rights or obligations.

ju'ra·men·ta'do (ho͞o'rä·mĕn·tä'thō), *n.*; *pl.* -DOS (-thōs). [Sp., bound by an oath.] A (Mohammedan) Moro who has taken an oath to die while engaged in killing Christians.

ju'rant (jo͝or'ănt), *adj.* [L. *jurans, -antis*, pres. part.] Making oath. — *n.* One who makes oath.

Ju·ras'sic (jo͝o·răs'ĭk), *adj.* [F. *jurassique*, fr. the *Jura* mountains between France and Switzerland.] *Geol.* Of, pertaining to, or designating the period of the Mesozoic era between the Triassic and the Cretaceous, or the system of rocks formed during this period. In this period ichthyosaurs, plesiosaurs, and other reptiles abounded in the sea, dinosaurs, pterosaurs, etc., on land, and birds first appeared. — **Ju·ras'sic**, *n.*

ju'rat (jo͝or'ăt), *n.* [F. & Pr. *jurat* and ML. *juratus*, fr. L. *juratus* sworn, past part. of *jurare* to swear.] **1.** *Hist.* A person under oath, as a juror. **2.** [L. *juratum*, neut. past part.] *Law.* A memorandum added to an affidavit, stating when, before whom, and (in British practice) where, it was made.

ju·rel' (ho͞o·rĕl'), *n.* [Sp.] Any of several carangoid food fishes of warm seas, as *Paratractus*, or *Caranx, crysos* of the Atlantic and *P. caballus* of the Pacific.

ju·rid'ic (jo͝o·rĭd'ĭk), *adj.* Juridical.

ju·rid'i·cal (jo͝o·rĭd'ĭ·kăl), *adj.* [L. *juridicus*, fr. *jus, juris*, right, law + root of *dicere* to say.] **1.** Of or pertaining to the administration of justice, or the office of a judge. **2.** Of or pertaining to law in general, or jurisprudence; legal. — **ju·rid'i·cal·ly**, *adv.*

juridical days. Days on which courts are open.

ju'ris·con·sult' (jo͝or'ĭs·kŏn·sŭlt'; -kŏn'sŭlt), *n.* [L. *jurisconsultus*, fr. *jus, juris*, right + *consultus* skillful. See CONSULT.] A man learned in law; a jurist.

ju'ris·dic'tion (jo͝or'ĭs·dĭk'shŭn; *esp. Brit.*, jôr'ĭs-; 114), *n.* [OF. *juridiction, juredicion*, fr. L. *jurisdictio*, fr. *jus, juris*, right, law + *dictio* a saying, speaking.] **1.** *Law.* The legal power, right, or authority to hear and determine a cause or causes. **2.** Authority of a sovereign power to govern or legislate; control. **3.** Sphere of authority. — **Syn.** See POWER. — **ju'ris·dic'tion·al**, *adj.* — **ju'ris·dic'tion·al·ly**, *adv.*

ju'ris·pru'dence (-pro͞o'dĕns), *n.* [F. or L.; F., fr. L. *jurisprudentia*, fr. *jus, juris*, right, law + *prudentia* a foreseeing, prudence.] **1.** The science of law. **2.** Law, or a system of laws; a department of law. — **ju'ris·pru·den'tial** (-pro͞o·dĕn'shăl), *adj.*

ju'ris·pru'dent (-dĕnt), *n.* One skilled in jurisprudence; a jurist. — **ju'ris·pru'dent**, *adj.*

ju'rist (jo͝or'ĭst *or, esp. Brit.*, jôr'ĭst), *n.* [F. *juriste*, fr. ML. *jurista*, fr. L. *jus, juris*, law.] One who professes or is versed in the law.

ju·ris'tic (jo͝o·rĭs'tĭk), *adj.* Of or pertaining to a jurist or jurisprudence; relating to, created by, or recognized in law. — **ju·ris'ti·cal** (-tĭ·kăl), *adj.* — **ju·ris'ti·cal·ly**, *adv.*

ju'ror (jo͝or'ẽr; *esp. Brit.*, jôr'-; 114), *n.* [OF. *jureor* one who takes oath, fr. L. *jurator* a swearer, fr. *jurare, jurari*, to swear.] **1.** *Law.* A member of a jury, or one summoned to serve on a jury. **2.** A member of any jury for awarding prizes, etc.

ju'ry (jo͝or'ĭ; *esp. Brit.*, jôr'ĭ), *n.*; *pl.* JURIES (-ĭz). [OF. *jurée* an oath, juridical inquiry, fr. *jurer* to swear, fr. L. *jurare, jurari.*] **1.** *Law.* A body of men sworn to give a true answer, or verdict, upon some matter submitted to them; esp., a body of men legally selected to inquire into any matter of fact, and to render their verdict according to the evidence. **2.** A committee for determining relative merit or awarding prizes at an exhibition or competition.

ju'ry, *adj.* [First in *jury mast*, prob. fr. OF. *ajurie* relief, help, fr. L. *adjutare* to help.] *Naut.* For temporary use, usually in an emergency; as, a *jury* mast.

ju'ry·man (-măn), *n.*; *pl.* -MEN (-mĕn). A juror.

ju'ry–rigged', *adj.* *Naut.* Rigged for temporary use.

‖**jus** (zhü), *n.* [F.] Juice; gravy.

‖**jus** (jŭs), *n.*; *pl.* JURA (jo͞o'rȧ). [L. See JURY.] *Law.* Law; laws, collectively; a rule or principle of law; a law; also, legal right; legal power.

‖**jus ca·no'ni·cum** (kȧ·nŏn'ĭ·kŭm). [L.] Canon law.

‖**jus ci·vi'le** (sĭ·vī'lē). [L.] Civil law.

‖**jus di·vi'num** (dĭ·vī'nŭm). [L.] Divine law or right.

‖**jus gen'ti·um** (jĕn'shĭ·ŭm). [L.] The law of nations; international law.

‖**jus post'li·mi'ni·i** (pōst'lĭ·mĭn'ĭ·ī). [L.] See POSTLIMINIUM.

jus'sive (jŭs'ĭv), *adj.* [L. *jubere, jussum*, to command.] *Gram.* Expressing, or having the effect of, a command. — *n. Gram.* A word, form, case, or mood, expressing command.

just (jŭst), *adj.* [OF. *juste*, fr. L. *justus*, fr. *jus* right, law, justice.] **1.** Conforming to spiritual law; righteous, esp. before God. **2.** Righteous or equitable in action or judgment; impartial; hence, as of punishments, merited. **3.** Legally right; as, a *just* title. **4.** Conformed to the truth of things; well-founded; as, a *just* statement. **5.** Exact; accurate. — **Syn.** See UPRIGHT: FAIR. — *adv.* **1.** Precisely; exactly; as, it was placed *just* so. **2.** Closely; nearly; almost. **3.** Precisely at the time referred to or implied; now, or but a moment ago; as, one *just* dead. **4.** Barely; by a very small space or time; as, *just* too late. **5.** *Colloq.* Simply; quite; — intensive; as, *just* tired out.

just (jŭst), **just'er** (jŭs'tẽr). Vars. of JOUST, JOUSTER.

‖**juste'–mi'lieu'** (zhüs'tĕ-mē'lyû'). [F.] The just or golden mean.

jus'tice (jŭs'tĭs), *n.* [OF. *justice, justise*, fr. L. *justitia*, fr. *justus* just.] **1.** The maintenance or administration of that which is just; also, merited reward or punishment. **2.** A person duly commissioned to hold courts, or to try and decide controversies and administer justice; a judge or magistrate. **3.** Administration of law, according to the rules of law or equity. **4.** The principle of rectitude and just dealing of men with each other; also, conformity to it; integrity; rectitude; — one of the cardinal virtues. **5.** Rightfulness; as, the *justice* of a cause. **6.** *Obs.* A court of justice or its jurisdiction. — **jus'tice·ship**, *n.*

justice of the peace. *Law.* A subordinate magistrate appointed (first in 1327) for the conservation of the peace in a specified district, with, esp. formerly in England, other incidental powers specified in his commission. In Great Britain and the United States his principal duties are to administer summary justice in minor cases and to commit for trial in a superior court on cause shown, and, in Great Britain, to grant licenses and, if a county justice, act as judge at the quarterly sessions.

jus'tic·er (jŭs'tĭs·ẽr), *n.* [OF. *justicier.*] *Archaic.* A judge.

jus·ti'ci·a·ble (jŭs·tĭsh'ĭ·ȧ·b'l), *adj.* Liable to trial in a court of justice; as, a *justiciable* dispute.

jus·ti'ci·ar (jŭs·tĭsh'ĭ·ẽr), *n.* Also **jus·ti'ci·ar'y** (-ẽr'ĭ; -ẽr·ĭ). [ML. *justitiarius.*] *Eng. Hist.* **a** The chief political and judicial officer of the Norman and later kings until the 13th century. **b** A high royal judicial officer.

jus'ti·fi'a·ble (jŭs'tĭ·fī'ȧ·b'l), *adj.* Capable of being justified, or shown to be just. — **jus'ti·fi'a·bil'i·ty** (-bĭl'ĭ·tĭ), *n.* — **jus'ti·fi'a·ble·ness**, *n.* — **jus'ti·fi'a·bly**, *adv.*

jus'ti·fi·ca'tion (-fĭ·kā'shŭn), *n.* **1.** Act of justifying, or state of being justified; also, that which justifies; vindication. **2.** *Print.* Adjustment, as of type, by spacing it so as to make it exactly fill a line, or of a cut so as to hold it in place. **3.** *Theol.* A being accepted by or made acceptable to God, as righteous or worthy of salvation; — chiefly in phrases giving grounds of such acceptance, as **justification by faith.** — **jus'ti·fi·ca'tive** (jŭs'tĭ·fĭ·kā'tĭv), *adj.*

jus'ti·fi·ca'to·ry (jŭs'tĭ·fĭ·kā'tō·rĭ; jŭs·tĭf'ĭ·kȧ-), *adj.* Tending or serving to justify; vindicatory.

jus'ti·fi'er (jŭs'tĭ·fī'ẽr), *n.* One who or that which justifies.

jus'ti·fy (jŭs'tĭ·fī), *v. t.*; -FIED (-fīd); -FY'ING. [OF. *justifier*, fr. LL. *justificare*, fr. *justus* just + *-ficare* (in comp.) to make.] **1.** To prove or show to be just; to vindicate. **2.** To pronounce free from guilt or blame; to absolve. **3.** To adjust or arrange exactly. **4.** *Law.* **a** To show to have had a sufficient legal reason for an act made the subject of a charge or accusation. **b** To qualify (oneself) as a surety by taking oath to the ownership of sufficient property. **5.** *Print., etc.* To space (a line of type) so that it is exactly the intended length. — **Syn.** See MAINTAIN. — *v. i.* **1.** *Law.* **a** To show a sufficient lawful reason for an act done. **b** To qualify as bail or surety. **2.** *Print.* To form an even surface or true line with something else; to fit exactly; — of type.

Jus·tin'i·a'ni·an (jŭs·tĭn'ĭ·ā'nĭ·ăn), *adj.* Of or pertaining to Justinian (483–565), the Byzantine emperor under whom the laws were codified in what is called the **Jus·tin'i·an** (jŭs·tĭn'ĭ·ăn), *or, rarely*, **Justinianian, Code.** See CORPUS JURIS CIVILIS.

‖**jus·ti'ti·a om'ni·bus** (jŭs·tĭsh'ĭ·ȧ ŏm'nĭ·bŭs). [L.] Justice to all; — motto of the District of Columbia.

jus'tle (jŭs''l). Var. of JOSTLE.

just'ly (jŭst'lĭ), *adv.* In a just manner.

just'ness, *n.* Quality or state of being just.

jut (jŭt), *v. i. & t.*; JUT'TED; JUT'TING. [Corrupt. of JET, *v.*] To shoot out or forward; to project; protrude. — *n.* That which projects or juts; a projection.

jute (jo͞ot; 114), *n.* [Bengali *jūt*, fr. Skr. *jūṭa* matted hair.] **a** The glossy fiber of either of two East Indian plants (*Corchorus olitorius* and *C. capsularis*) of the linden family. It is used chiefly for sacking, burlap, and twine. **b** The plant producing this fiber. — **jute**, *adj.*

Jute, *n.* A member of one of the Low German tribes of Jutland, some of whom settled in Kent, England, in the 5th century. — **Jut′ish** (jo͞ot′ĭsh), *adj.*

jut′ty (jŭt′ĭ), *n.; pl.* -TIES (-ĭz). [See JETTY, *n.*] A projection in a building; also, a pier or mole; a jetty. — *v. t. & i. Obs.* To project beyond; to jut.

ju′ve·nes′cent (jo͞o′vē·nĕs′ĕnt; -′nt), *adj.* [L. *juvenescens*, pres. part. of *juvenescere* to grow young again, fr. *juvenis* young.] Growing young. — **ju′ve·nes′cence** (-ĕns; -′ns), *n.*

ju′ve·nile (jo͞o′vē·nĭl; -nīl: -nīl *usual in British usage, and not uncommon in America, esp. for the noun*), *adj.* [L. *juvenilis*, fr. *juvenis* young.] **1.** Young; youthful; immature or undeveloped. **2.** Of, pertaining to, characteristic of, or suitable for youth. — *n.* **1.** A young person or youth. **2.** *Theat.* An actor of youthful parts. **3.** A book for children.

‖**ju′ve·nil′i·a** (jo͞o′vē·nĭl′ĭ·ȧ), *n. pl.* [L.] Youthful compositions; immature work, esp. literary or artistic.

ju′ve·nil′i·ty (-nĭl′ĭ·tĭ), *n.; pl.* -TIES (-tĭz). **1.** Youthfulness or youthful manner or character. **2.** Juveniles as a body; *pl.*, juvenile traits, acts, etc.

jux′ta- (jŭks′tȧ-). [L. *juxta* by the side of, near.] A combining form denoting *situated near*, as in **jux′ta–am·pul′lar, jux′ta–ar·tic′u·lar, jux′ta·ma·rine′, jux′ta·spi′nal, jux′ta·trop′i·cal.** See AMPULLAR, etc.

jux′ta·pose′ (jŭks′tȧ·pōz′), *v. t.* To place side by side.

jux′ta·po·si′tion (-pō·zĭsh′ŭn), *n.* [F., fr. L. *juxta* near + F. *position.*] A placing or being placed side by side.

‖**j′y suis, j′y reste** (zhē swē′, zhē rĕst′). [F.] I am here; here I remain; — attributed to MacMahon in 1855 when advised to abandon the Malakoff.

K

K, k (kā), *n.; pl.* K′S, K′S, KS, KS (kāz). **1.** The eleventh letter of the English alphabet. It came through the Latin from Greek Κ (*kappa*), which took it from the Phoenician (Hebrew *caph*, or *kaph*). Its value is that of a voiceless velar, or guttural, stop, or mute consonant. See *Pron.*, § 60. **2.** The sound or any sound of the letter K. **3.** As a *symbol*, the tenth or (when J is used for the tenth) the eleventh, in order or class.

Kaa′ba (kä′bȧ; kä′ȧ·bȧ), *n.* Also **Caa′ba, Kaa′beh** (-bĕ). [Ar. *ka‛bah*, lit., a square building, fr. *ka‛b* cube.] The small stone building in the court of the Great Mosque at Mecca which contains the famous Black Stone said to have been given by Gabriel to Abraham. The Kaaba represents the direction (*kiblah*) to which Moslems turn in praying. Since the time of Mohammed the Kaaba has been the chief object of pilgrimage of the Islamic world.

kab. Var. of CAB.

kab′a·la, kab′ba·la. Vars. of CABALA.

ka·bob′ (kȧ·bŏb′). Var. of CABOB.

Ka·byle′ (kȧ·bīl′), *n.* [Ar. *qabīlah* tribe, pl. *qabā′il.*] **a** A Berber of Algeria or Tunisia. **b** The Hamitic language of these Berbers.

ka′di. Var. of CADI.

Ka·diak′ (*Russian* kŭ·dyăk′), *or* **Ko′di·ak** (kō′dĭ·ăk), **bear.** A brown bear (*Ursus middendorffi*), larger than the grizzly bear, found on Kodiak island.

Kaf′fir, Kaf′ir (kăf′ẽr), *n.* [Ar. *kāfir* infidel, fr. *kafara* to be skeptical in religious matters.] A member of the most intelligent and powerful of the Bantu races of South Africa; also, their language.

kaf′ir (kăf′ẽr), *n.* Any of certain grain sorghums derived from one species (*Sorghum vulgare*), and cultivated for grain and forage in dry regions. Called erron. **kafir corn.**

Kaf′ir (kăf′ẽr; kä′fẽr), **Kaf′fir** (kăf′ẽr), *n.* One of a small group of tribes in the Hindu Kush, Kafiristan (see *Gaz.*).

kaf′tan. Var. of CAFTAN.

kai′ak. Var. of KAYAK.

kail (kāl). Var. of COLE, KALE.

kail′yard′ (kāl′yärd′). Var. of KALEYARD; — applied to a type of fiction which describes Scottish life with much use of the vernacular. The writers of it, as Ian Maclaren and Sir J. M. Barrie, are alluded to as the **kailyard school.**

ka′i·nite (kā′ĭ·nīt; kī′nīt), *n.* Also **ka′i·nit** (-nĭt) (following the Ger. form). [G. *kainit*, fr. Gr. *kainos* recent.] *Mineral.* A natural salt containing when pure 35.1% of potassium sulfate, 24.2% of magnesium sulfate, 18.9% of magnesium chloride, and 21.8% of water of hydration. It is used as a fertilizer and as a source of potash.

kai′ser (kī′zẽr), *n.* [G., fr. L. *Caesar.*] Emperor; — a title of: **a** *Obs. exc. Hist.* Heads of the Holy Roman Empire. **b** Emperors of Austria (1804–1918). **c** Esp., the German emperors (1871–1918).

Kai′ser·ism (-ĭz′m), *n.* = CAESARISM.

kaj′e·put. Var. of CAJUPUT.

ka′ka (kä′kȧ), *n.* [Maori *kaka* a parrot; — from its note.] A New Zealand parrot (*Nestor meridionalis*), olive brown with gray and red markings.

ka′ka·po′ (kä′kä·pō′), *n.* [Maori.] A parrot (*Strigops habroptilus*), peculiar to New Zealand, living in holes or burrows in the ground.

‖**ka′ke·mo′no** (kä′kĕ·mō′nō), *n.* [Jap.] *Japan.* A picture or writing on silk or paper, suitable for hanging, and usually having a roller at its lower edge.

ka′ki (kä′kē), *n.* [Jap.] The Japanese persimmon. See PERSIMMON.

kale (kāl), *n.* [Scot. *kale*, *kail*, *cale*, the northern form of COLE.] **1.** Cole or colewort; in Scotland, *Colloq.*, any plant of the cabbage tribe. **2.** Specif., a very hardy type of cabbage with curled leaves. See CABBAGE. **3.** *Dial.* A broth or soup of kale; any vegetable soup. **4.** *Slang, U. S.* Money; cash.

ka·lei′do·scope (kȧ·lī′dō·skōp), *n.* [Gr. *kalos* beautiful + *eidos* form + *-scope.*] **1.** An instrument containing loose fragments of colored glass, and two plane mirrors, so arranged that changes of position exhibit its contents in an endless variety of symmetrical varicolored forms. **2.** A variegated changing pattern, scene, or the like. — **ka·lei′do·scop′ic** (-skŏp′ĭk), **ka·lei′do·scop′i·cal** (-ĭ·kăl), *adj.* — **ka·lei′do·scop′i·cal·ly**, *adv.*

kal′en·dar. Var. of CALENDAR.

kal′ends (kăl′ĕndz; -ĭndz). Var. of CALENDS.

Ka′le·va′la (kä′lā·vä′lä), *n.* [Finn., from the country (Finland) of the giant hero *Kaleva.*] A collection of Finnish heroic poetry, systematized as a national epic by Elias Lönnrot. The original songs, dating from the Middle Ages, deal with mythic-heroic material but are dominantly lyric and characterized by a love of magic.

kale′yard′ (kāl′yärd′), *n. Scot.* A kitchen garden. See KAILYARD.

kal′i (kăl′ĭ; kā′lĭ), *n.* [Ar. *qili.* See ALKALI.] = GLASSWORT **b.**

kal·ian′ (kăl·yän′), *n.* [Per. *kaliān.*] A Persian form of the hookah.

ka′lif (kā′lĭf; kăl′ĭf). Var. of CALIPH.

kal′mi·a (kăl′mĭ·ȧ), *n.* [NL., after Peter *Kalm* (1715–1779), Sw. botanist.] *Bot.* A plant of a small genus (*Kalmia*) of North American evergreen shrubs of the heath family, with handsome corymbose flowers. See MOUNTAIN LAUREL.

Kal′muck, Kal′muk (kăl′mŭk), *n.* [Turki *kalmuk* the part of a nomad Tatar tribe remaining at home, prop., past part. of *kalmak* to remain.] **1.** A member of any of a confederacy of Buddhist Mongol tribes, mostly of western China. **2.** The language of the Kalmucks.

ka′long (kä′lŏng), *n.* [Jav. *kaloṅ.*] A large fruit-eating bat of warm parts of the Old World; a flying fox (which see).

kal′pak. Var. of CALPAC.

kal′so·mine (kăl′sō·mīn). Var. of CALCIMINE.

ka·ma′la (kȧ·mä′lȧ; kăm′ȧ·lȧ), *n.* [Skr.] **a** An East Indian tree (*Mallotus philippinensis*). **b** The orange-red powder from its capsules, used for dyeing silk and wool.

kame (kām), *n.* **1.** Scot. & Northern Eng. var. of COMB. **2.** A short ridge, hill, or hillock of stratified drift; esker.

Ka·me′ha·me′ha Day (kä·mā′hä·mā′hä). June 11, the birthday (1736) of Kamehameha, first king of Hawaii, celebrated as a holiday. See HOLIDAY, 3.

‖**Ka′me·rad′** (kä′mĕ·rät′), *n.* [G.] Comrade; — an appeal for quarter by German soldiers.

ka′mi·ka′ze (kä′mĭ·kä′zē), *n.* [Jap., *divine wind.*] The pilot of an explosives-laden Japanese plane whose sole mission was a suicidal crash dive upon a target, esp. a ship; also, such a plane.

kam·seen′, kam′sin. Vars. of KHAMSIN.

Kan′a·ka (kăn′ȧ·kȧ; kȧ·năk′ȧ), *n.* [Polynesian, prop., man.] A Hawaiian; a Polynesian or Melanesian.

Ka′na·rese′ (kä′nȧ·rēz′; -rēs′), *adj.* Of or pertaining to Kanara, India. — *n.* (*sing. & pl.*) One of a civilized Dravidian people of southern India; also, their language.

kane (kān), **kain** (kān), *n. Scot.* Produce paid as rent in kind.

kan′ga·roo′ (kăng′gȧ·ro͞o′), *n.;* see PLURAL, *Note*, 3. [Said to be a native name.] Any of a family (Macropodidae) of herbivorous leaping marsupial mammals of Australia, New Guinea, and adjacent islands; esp., the larger species of one genus (*Macropus*). Kangaroos have a small head, large ears, small forelegs, long and powerful hind legs, and a long thick tail, used as a support in standing or walking.

kangaroo court. *Slang, U. S.* An irresponsible, unauthorized, or irregular tribunal, or one in which the principles of law and justice are disregarded or perverted.

kangaroo rat. Any of numerous pouched, nocturnal, jerboalike burrowing rodents (genus (*Dipodomys*) of arid parts of western U. S.

Kant′i·an (kăn′tĭ·ăn), *adj.* Of or pert. to Immanuel Kant; conformed or relating to Kantianism. — *n.* A follower of Kant.

Kant′i·an·ism (-ĭz′m), *n.* The philosophy of Immanuel Kant (1724–1804). He held that the mind furnished the forms of experience and the sense organs furnish only impressions. Our knowledge is therefore only subjective. But Kant shows the necessity of a belief in God, freedom, and immortality, if we are to have the institutions of civilization. And he further shows that without the a priori idea of intelligent design in nature we could not recognize any phenomena of life in plants or animals or other organisms.

ka′o·li·ang′ (kä′ō·lē·ăng′), *n.* [Chin. (Pek.) *kao*[1] *liang*[2], lit., tall grain.] Any of a group of grain sorghums derived from *Sorghum vulgare*, having open erect panicles and slender, dry, pithy stalks.

ka′o·lin (kā′ō·lĭn), *n.* Also **ka′o·line.** [F. *kaolin*, fr. Chin. (Pek.) *kao*[1]*-ling*[3], lit., high hill, from the place where it was found.] A very pure white clay, used to form the paste of porcelain.

ka′o·lin·ite (-īt), *n. Mineral.* Pure kaolin.

‖**Ka·pell′meis′ter** (kä·pĕl′mīs′tẽr), *n. sing. & pl.* [G., fr. *kapelle* chapel, private band of a prince + *meister* a master.] *Music.* A choirmaster or orchestra conductor.

ka′pok (kā′pŏk; kăp′ŏk), *n.* [Jav. *kapuk.*] The mass of silky fibers investing the seeds of the silk-cotton tree, or **kapok tree** (*Ceiba pentandra*), used as a filling for mattresses, etc.; — called also *ceiba* and *silk cotton.* **kapok oil**, from the seeds, is used for soapmaking.

kap′pa (kăp′ȧ), *n.* [Gr.] The tenth letter (Κ, κ) of the Greek alphabet. It is equivalent to Eng. *k*, but is often transliterated by *c.*

ka·put′ (kä·po͝ot′), *adj. used predicatively.* [G.] Finished; done for; ruined.

kar′a·kul (kăr′ȧ·kŭl), *n.* Also **kar′a·kule.** [From *Kara Kul*, lake in the Pamirs, lit., black lake.] **1.** A broadtail sheep of a hardy breed (**Karakul**) from the province of Bokhara. **2.** The tightly curled, glossy, black coat of the newborn lambs of this breed, valued as fur. Cf. ASTRAKHAN, 1; BROADTAIL, 2; PERSIAN LAMB.

kar′at (kăr′ăt). Var. of CARAT.

Ka·ren′ (kȧ·rĕn′), *n.* **a** One of a people living in eastern and southern Burma. **b** Their language. — **Ka·ren′**, *adj.*

kar′ma (kär′mȧ; kŭr′mȧ), *n.* [Skr. *karman*, nom. *karma.*] **1.** In Hinduism and Buddhism, the whole ethical consequence of one's acts considered as fixing one's lot in the future existence. **2.** Hence, loosely, destiny; fate.

ka·ross′ (kȧ·rŏs′), *n.* [Prob. fr. D. *kuras*, but perh. of Hottentot origin.] *S. Africa.* A square garment or rug of skins worn by native blacks.

kar·roo′, ka·roo′ (kă·ro͞o′), *n.; pl.* -ROOS (-ro͞oz′). [Prob. fr. a Cape Hottentot word meaning red soil.] One of the dry table lands of South Africa.

Kar·roo′ (kă·ro͞o′), *adj.* *Geol.* Pertaining to or designating a major division of the Paleozoic and Mesozoic of South Africa, nearly 30,000 feet thick.

kar′y·o- (kăr′ĭ·ō-), **kar′y-** (kăr′ĭ-). Also **car′y·o-, car′y-.** [Gr. *karyon.*] A combining form meaning *nut, kernel,* used specif. in biology to denote *nucleus of a cell.*

kar′y·o·ki·ne′sis (-kĭ·nē′sĭs; -kī-), *n.* [NL., fr. *karyo-* + Gr. *kinein* to move.] *Biol.* **a** A Mitosis. **b** In a narrower sense, nuclear division only. See CYTOKINESIS. — **kar′y·o·ki·net′ic** (-nĕt′ĭk), *adj.*

kar′y·om′i·tome (-ŏm′ĭ·tōm), *n.* [*karyo-* + Gr. *mitos* thread.] *Biol.* The network of fibers of which the nucleus of a cell is in part composed.

kar′y·o·plasm (kăr′ĭ·ō·plăz′m), *n.* Also **kar′y·o·plas′ma** (-plăz′mȧ). [*karyo-* + *-plasm.*] *Biol.* The protoplasm of the nucleus. Cf. CYTOPLASM. — **kar′y·o·plas′mic** (-plăz′mĭk), **kar′y·o·plas·mat′ic** (-plăz·măt′ĭk), *adj.*

kar′y·o·some′ (-sōm′), *n.* [*karyo-* + 2d *-some.*] *Biol.* **a** A nucleolus-like body in the chromatin network of the cell nucleus, as opposed to the true nucleolus, or plasmosome. See CELL, 4, *Illust.* **b** A chromosome. **c** The nucleus of a cell.

kar′y·o′tin (kăr′ĭ·ō′tĭn), *n.* [*karyo-* + chroma*tin.*] *Biol.* The stainable, often reticular, material of the nucleus.

ka′sher (kä′shĕr). Var. of KOSHER, *adj. & n.*

ka′sher (kä′shĕr; *Heb.* kä·shăr′), *v. t.* Also **kosh′er** (kŏsh′ĕr). To make or pronounce *kasher,* or legally sanctioned.

Kash·mi′ri (kăsh·mēr′ĭ), *n.* The language of the Kashmirians (natives of Kashmir), a Sanskritic tongue with many Arabic and Persian words, and a considerable literature. See INDO-EUROPEAN LANGUAGES, *Table.*

kata-. Variant of CATA-, as in:

katabolic	**katalase**	**katalytic**
katabolically	**katalysis**	**katalyze**
katabolism	**katalyst**	**kataplasia**

ka·tab′a·sis (kȧ·tăb′ȧ·sĭs), *n.; pl.* -SES (-sēz). [Gr., fr. *katabainein* to go down.] Literally, a going down; specif., the return march to the sea of the Greek auxiliaries of the Anabasis; hence, any similar retreat.

ka·thar′sis (kȧ·thär′sĭs), *n.* [Gr., fr. *kathairein* to cleanse.] Catharsis. — **ka·thar′tic** (-tĭk), *adj.*

kath′ode, ka·thod′ic, etc. Vars. of CATHODE, etc.

kat′i′on. Var. of CATION.

ka′ty·did′ (kā′tĭ·dĭd′), *n.* Any of several large, green, arboreal American orthopterous insects of the grasshopper family Locustidae; — from the sound made by the males in summer and fall.

kau′ri, kau′ry (kou′rĭ), *n.* [Maori.] **a** A tall timber tree of New Zealand (*Agathis australis*) of the pine family. **b** The wood of this tree. **c** Kauri resin. **d** By extension, any other species of *Agathis,* as the ***red kauri*** (*A. lanceolata*).

kauri resin, gum, *or* **copal.** A resinous product of the kauri, found in the form of colorless, yellow, or brown lumps in the ground where the trees have grown. It is used for making varnish, and as a substitute for amber.

ka′va (kä′vä), *n.* Also **ka′va·ka′va** (kä′vä·kä′vä). [Maori, etc., *kawa,* lit., bitter.] Either of two Australasian peppers (*Piper methysticum* and *P. excelsum*), from which an intoxicating beverage is made; also, the beverage.

Kay, Sir (kā). A boastful malicious knight of the Round Table, foster brother and seneschal of King Arthur.

kay′ak (kī′ăk), *n.* [Of Eskimauan origin.] An Eskimo canoe, usually of sealskin and completely decked, the covering being laced about the paddler.

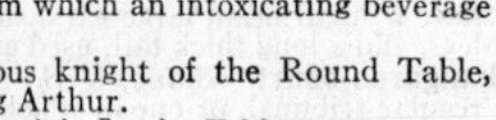

Kayak.

ka·zoo′ (kȧ·zo͞o′), *n.* [Origin uncert.] A toy or rough musical instrument consisting of a tube containing a strip of catgut made to vibrate by singing or humming into it.

ke′a (kā′ä; *colloq.* kē′ȧ), *n.* [Maori.] A large, chiefly dull-green New Zealand parrot (*Nestor notabilis*). Normally insectivorous, it has learned to attack live sheep, and inflicts lethal wounds by devouring their kidney fat.

keb′ar. Scot. var. of CABER, a beam.

keb′buck, keb′bock (kĕb′ŭk), *n.* [Gael. *ceapag, cepac,* a cheese, wheel.] *Dial.* A cheese.

keck (kĕk), *v. i.;* KECKED (kĕkt); KECK′ING. [Imitative.] To retch; to feel or show disgust.

keck′sy (kĕk′sĭ), *n.; pl.* -SIES (-sĭz). = KEX.

ked′dah (kĕd′ȧ), *n.* [Hind. *khedā.*] *India.* An enclosure constructed to entrap wild elephants.

kedge (kĕj), *v. t. & i.;* KEDGED (kĕjd); KEDG′ING. [Origin uncert.; cf. *cadge* to carry.] *Naut.* To move (a vessel, raft, etc.) by carrying out a kedge in a boat, dropping it overboard, and hauling the vessel up to it.

kedge, *n., or* **kedge anchor.** *Naut.* A small anchor, used in light work, as kedging.

ke·ef′ (kē·ēf′). Var. of KEF.

keek (kēk), *v.* [ME. *kiken* to peer, prob. fr. MD. *kiken* (D. *kijken*).] *Dial. Eng., Scot., & Ir.* To peep.

keel (kēl), *n.* [ON. *kjölr* keel (Sw. *köl,* Dan. *kjöl*).] **1.** A longitudinal timber, or series of timbers, or in a metal vessel a combination of plates, extending along the center of the bottom of a vessel. It often projects below the bottom. **2.** *Poetic.* A ship. **3.** Something resembling a ship's keel in form, position, or function. **4.** *Aeronautics.* The assembly of members at the bottom of the hull of a semirigid or rigid airship. **5.** *Bot. & Zool.* Any ridgelike process; a carina. — *v. t. & i.* To turn up the keel (of); to turn over.

keel over. *Colloq.* To upset; to capsize; to fall suddenly.

keel, *n.* [MD. *kiel* ship.] **a** A flat-bottomed ship, esp. a barge or lighter used on the Tyne to carry coal; also, a bargeload of coal. **b** A British weight for coal, equal to 21.2 long tons avoirdupois.

keel, *v. t. & i.* [AS. *cēlan* to cool.] *Dial.* To cool; to prevent boiling over, as by skimming, etc.

keel, *n.* [Origin uncert.; cf. Ir. & Gael. *cīl* ruddle.] A red ocher used for marking lumber, sheep, etc.; ruddle.

keel′boat′ (kēl′bōt′), *n.* *U. S.* A shallow, covered freight boat with a keel but no sails, used on western rivers.

keel′haul′ (kēl′hôl′), *v. t.* Also **keel′hale′** (-hāl′). [D. *kielhalen.*] *Naut.* To haul under the keel of a ship as a punishment or mode of torture.

keel′son (kĕl′s'n; kēl′-), **kel′son** (kĕl′-), *n.* *Shipbuilding.* A longitudinal structure incorporated with the framing of a ship to stiffen it; esp., such a structure above, and fastened to, the keel.

keen (kēn), *adj.* [AS. *cēne* bold, wise.] **1.** Sharp; having a fine edge or point; as, a *keen* razor. **2.** Sharply painful; bitter; piercing; as, *keen* sarcasm; a *keen* wind. **3. a** Pungent or stinging to touch or taste. **b** Vivid, shrill, or strong; as, a *keen* scent. **4. a** Eager; vehement. **b** Greatly interested, eager, or enthusiastic. **c** Intense; — of emotion, desire, etc. **5.** Acute; sensitive; — of sight, smell, etc. **6.** Acute of mind; expressing mental acuteness; sharp; as, *keen* questions. — **Syn.** See SHARP; EAGER. — **keen′ly,** *adv.* — **keen′ness,** *n.*

keen (kēn), *n.* [Ir. *caoine.*] *Ir.* A lamentation or dirge for the dead. — *v. t. & i.* To wail, or bewail, with the keen. — **keen′er** (-ẽr), *n.*

keep (kēp), *v. t.;* KEPT (kĕpt); KEEP′ING. [AS. *cēpan* to observe, notice.] **1.** To observe (anything prescribed or obligatory); to adhere to; to practice or perform, as duty. **2.** Specif.: **a** To observe duly (a rite, festival, or the like); to celebrate. **b** *Archaic.* To conform one's habits or conduct to (anything prescribed); to attend regularly, as church or chapel. **3.** To preserve or maintain; — in various senses, as: **a** To guard; defend. **b** To have the care of; tend. **c** To continue to hold; to maintain; as, to *keep* silence. **d** To cause to remain; to maintain unchanged. **e** *Obs.* To behave. **f** To supply with necessaries of life; to support. **g** To have in one's service; to have and maintain, as a servant, mistress, horse, etc.; also, to lodge or feed for pay; as, to *keep* boarders. **h** To maintain a record of transactions, accounts, or events in; as, to *keep* books. **i** To have habitually in stock for sale. **4.** To restrain from departure or removal; to hold; retain; detain. **5.** Hence: **a** To reserve; to withhold, as evil tidings. **b** To refrain from communicating, as a secret; to conceal. **c** To confine oneself to; to remain in; as, to *keep* one's house. **6.** To conduct or carry on; to maintain; to manage; continue. — *v. i.* **1.** *Now Colloq. Chiefly U. S.* To reside for a time; lodge. **2.** To remain in any position or state; to continue. **3.** To abstain or refrain; as, unable to *keep* from talking. **4.** To persevere or continue; as, to *keep* to the right. **5.** To last; to endure; not to sour or spoil; as, milk will not *keep* in such heat. **6.** *Colloq.* To be in session; as, school *keeps* today.

Syn. (1) **Keep, observe, celebrate, commemorate** mean to pay due attention to something prescribed, obligatory, or the like. **Keep** stresses the idea of not neglecting or violating (as, to *keep* a promise, the commandments); **observe,** of punctiliousness in performance of the required acts, rites, etc. (as, to *observe* the Sabbath); **celebrate,** of demonstrations such as demanded, esp. by a festive or joyous occasion (as, to *celebrate* Independence Day); **commemorate,** of observances that call to mind the event, the day, the season, etc., celebrated.
(2) **Keep, retain, detain, withhold, reserve** mean not to let go from one's possession or control. **Keep** implies nothing additional; **retain** suggests continued keeping, esp. against a threat to seize or of forced loss; **detain** suggests a delay in letting go; **withhold** suggests, usually, a refusal to let go, often for some good reason; **reserve** suggests either a keeping in store for future use or a withholding from others' use, enjoyment, or the like.

keep company. To go together in courtship. — ***keep tab*** *or* ***tabs.*** To keep count (*of*) or a check (*on*). — ***keep track.*** To keep oneself informed, as of some matter.

— *n.* **1.** *Archaic.* Custody; guard. **2.** A fortress; a castle; specif., the donjon of a medieval castle. **3.** *Rare.* State of being kept; hence, the resulting condition; as, to be in good *keep.* **4.** The means or provisions by which one is kept; support. **5.** *pl.* The right to retain after having won; also, a game played for keeps. — ***for keeps.*** *Colloq.* For the recipient or winner to retain; for good.

keep′er (kēp′ẽr), *n.* **1.** One who watches, guards, maintains, etc. **2.** Specif.: **a** One who has care of a prison. **b** In England, a gamekeeper. **c** One who maintains an establishment, as for eating, lodging, or sale of specified articles; as, an inn*keeper;* store*keeper.* **d** A custodian, as in a museum. **3.** Any of various devices to keep something in position, as a lock nut. **4.** One that may be kept; as: **a** A fruit that keeps well. **b** A fish not undersized.

keep′ing (kēp′ĭng), *n.* **1.** Act of one who keeps; observance; custody; maintenance; also, the state of being so kept; retention; preservation. **2.** Means of maintenance; keep; support. **3.** Conformity; harmony; as, a remark not in *keeping* with the tone of the meeting.

keep′sake′ (kēp′sāk′), *n.* Anything kept, or given to be kept, for the sake of the giver; a token of friendship; specif., an early 19th-century type of giftbook.

kef (kāf), *n.* [Ar. *kayf,* colloq. *kef,* enjoyment.] **1.** Languor; dreamy tranquillity, as from drugs. **2.** The smoking material used to produce this state, esp. Indian hemp; — in this sense often spelled *kief, keef.*

keg (kĕg), *n.* [Earlier *cag,* fr. *cagge,* of Scand. origin.] **a** A small cask, usually of ten gallons or less. **b** *U. S.* A weight for nails, equal to 100 lb.

keg′ler (kĕg′lẽr), *n.* [G.] *Tenpins. Colloq.* A bowler.

Ke′ku·le's for′mu·la (kā′ko͞o·lāz). See BENZENE RING, *Illust.*

kel′leg, kel′lick, kel′lock. Vars. of KILLICK.

ke′loid (kē′loid), *n.* [F. *kéloïde, chéloïde,* fr. Gr. *chēlē* crab's claw + *-oid.*] *Med.* A dense fibrous tumor of the skin, an overgrowth of scar tissue. — **ke′loid,** *adj.*

kelp (kĕlp), *n.* [Formerly *kilpe,* fr. ME. *culp* or *culpe.*] **1.** The ashes of seaweed; — now used chiefly as a source of iodine. **2.** Any of various large brown seaweeds (families Laminariaceae and Fucaceae), as the ***giant kelp*** of the Pacific coast (*Macrocystis pyrifera*).

kel′pie, kel′py (kĕl′pĭ), *n.; pl.* -PIES (-pĭz). *Gael. Myth.* A water sprite, usually equine in form, believed to warn those who are to be drowned or to assist in their drowning.

kel′son (kĕl′s'n). Var. of KEELSON.

Kelt, Kelt′ic, etc. Vars. of CELT, etc.

kel′ter (kĕl′tẽr). Var. of KILTER.

Kel′vin scale (kĕl′vĭn). [After Wm. Thompson, 1st Baron *Kelvin,* Brit. scientist.] *Physical Chem.* The scale of absolute temperature, in which the zero is approximately −273.1° C.; — called also *absolute scale.*

kemp (kĕmp), *n.* [AS. *cempa.*] *Scot.* A champion; warrior or athlete. — *v. i. Scot.* To contend, esp. in reaping.

ken (kĕn), *v. t.;* KENNED (kĕnd); KEN′NING. [ME. *kennen* to teach, make known, (after ON.) to know, fr. AS. *cennan* to make known.] **1.** *Archaic & Dial.* To recognize; discern. **2.** *Scot.* To know; understand. **3.** To recognize or admit. *Obs.,* except *Scots Law.* To recognize as heir. — *v. i. Archaic & Dial.* To know (*of* or *about*). — *n.* Cognizance; sight; esp., range of sight; understanding.

ke·naf′ (kĕ·năf′), *n.* [Per. *kanaf.*] = AMBARY.

kench (kĕnch), *n. U. S.* An enclosure in which fish or skins are salted.

Ken′dal green (kĕn′d'l), *or* **Ken′dal,** *n.* A cloth colored green by Flemish weavers at Kendal, England; also, the color of this cloth.

ken′nel (kĕn′ĕl; -'l), *n.* [From ONF. *canel* channel.] The watercourse of a street; a gutter.

ken′nel, *n.* [F. *chenil,* fr. LL. *canile,* fr. L. *canis* a dog.] **1.** A house for a dog or for dogs. Also (often in *pl.*), an establishment where dogs are bred. **2.** A pack of dogs. — *v. i.;* KEN′NELED (-ĕld; -'ld) or KEN′NELLED; KEN′NEL·ING or KEN′NEL·LING. To lie or lodge in a kennel. — *v. t.* To put or keep in a kennel.

Kennelly–Heaviside layer. See HEAVISIDE LAYER.

ken′ning (kĕn′ĭng), *n.* [See KEN, *v.*] **1.** *Scot.* **a** Recognition. **b** A perceptible portion; a small amount. **2.** In Norse and early Teutonic literature, a metaphorical name having a conventional meaning in poetic diction, as, "home of the whale" for "sea."

Ken′ny meth′od *or* **treat′ment** (kĕn′ĭ). A method of treating poliomyelitis developed by Elizabeth Kenny, Australian nurse.

ke′no (kē′nō), *n.* A form of lotto used in gambling.

ke′no·gen′e·sis (kē′nō·jĕn′ē·sĭs; kĕn′ō-), **ke′no·ge·net′ic.** Vars. of CENOGENESIS, CENOGENETIC.

ke·no′sis (kē·nō′sĭs), *n.* [NL., fr. Gr. *kenōsis* an emptying, fr. *kenos* empty.] *Theol.* Christ's action of "emptying himself" on becoming man (*Phil.* ii. 7, R. V.), humbling himself even to suffering death; also, any of various theories based upon this. — **ke·not′ic** (-nŏt′ĭk), *adj.*

ken′speck′le (kĕn′spĕk′'l), *adj. Scot.* Conspicuous.

kent′ledge (kĕnt′lĕj), *n. Naut.* Pig-iron ballast.

Ken·tuck′y blue′grass′ (kĕn·tŭk′ĭ). See BLUEGRASS.

Kentucky coffee tree. A tall North American tree (*Gymnocladus dioica*) of the senna family, with large woody brown pods, the seeds (**Kentucky coffee beans**) of which have been used as a substitute for coffee.

Kentucky Der′by (dûr′bĭ; *by some* där′bĭ, *after the British pron.*). The foremost American Derby (see DERBY, 2), run since 1875 at Churchill Downs, Louisville, Ky.

kep (kĕp), *v. t. & i.* [Differentiated form of *keep. Oxf. E. D.*] *Dial. Eng., Scot., & Ir.* To catch; also, to intercept.

kep′i (kĕp′ē), *n.; pl.* KEPIS (-ēz). [F. *képi,* fr. G. dial. *käppi.*] A military cap having a round flat top sloping toward the front, and a visor.

kept (kĕpt), *past & past part.* of KEEP.

ke·ram′ic (kē·răm′ĭk), **ke·ram′ics.** Vars. of CERAMIC, CERAMICS.

kerat-. = KERATO- (which see), as in **ker′a·tal′gi·a, ker′a·tec·ta′si·a, ker′a·tec′to·my, ker′a·ti′tis, ker′a·to′ma.**

ker′a·tin (kĕr′ȧ·tĭn), *n.* [Gr. *keras, -atos,* horn.] *Biochem.* An albuminoid forming the chemical basis of epidermal tissues, as horn, hair, nails, feathers, and the like. — **ke·rat′i·nous** (kē·răt′ĭ·nŭs), *adj.*

ker′a·to- (kĕr′ȧ·tō-), **kerat-.** [Gr. *keras, keratos,* horn.] A combining form meaning: **a** *Horn,* as in **ker′a·tog′e·nous. b** *Horny tissue.* **c** [From *keratoid.*] *Anat., Med., & Surg. The cornea,* as in **ker′a·tot′o·my** (see -TOMY).

ker′a·toid (kĕr′ȧ·toid), *adj.* [*kerat-* + *-oid.*] Horny.

ker′a·tose (-tōs), **ker′a·tode** (-tōd), *n.* [Gr. *keras, -atos,* horn.] A tough, horny animal substance, part of the skeleton of sponges and other invertebrates. — **ker′a·tose,** *adj.*

kerb (kûrb), **kerb′stone′.** Vars. of CURB, CURBSTONE.

ker′chief (kûr′chĭf), *n.* [OF. *cuevrechief, couvrechef,* fr. *couvrir* to cover + *chief* head. See COVER; CHIEF.] **1.** A cloth worn by women as a covering for the head; hence, a similar cloth worn or carried as for ornament. **2.** A handkerchief. — **ker′chiefed, ker′chieft** (-chĭft), *adj.*

kerf (kûrf), *n.* [AS. *cyrf* a cutting off, fr. *ceorfan* to cut, carve.] **1.** Act of cutting; a cut or stroke. **2.** The slit or notch made in cutting, as by a saw. **3.** Something cut off; a cutting, as of wool in shearing.

Ker·man′shah′ (kĕr·män′shä′), *n.* See KIRMAN.

ker′mes (kûr′mēz), *n.* [F. *kermès,* fr. Ar. *qirmiz.*] **1.** The dried bodies of the females of certain scale insects (genus *Kermes*) allied to the cochineal insect, which are found on an oak (*Quercus coccifera*) of the Mediterranean region. They contain a purplish-red coloring matter. **2.** Also **kermes oak.** The oak on which kermes insects feed.

ker′mis (kûr′mĭs), **ker′mess** (-mĕs), *n.* [D. *kermis,* fr. *kerk* church + *mis* Mass.] **a** In the Low Countries, a local outdoor festival. **b** *U. S.* An indoor entertainment and fair.

kern, kerne (kûrn), *n.* [Ir. *ceatharnach* a foot soldier, *ceatharn* a band of soldiers.] **a** A light-armed Celtic foot soldier of Ireland or Scotland; — used chiefly of medieval times; also, a body of kerns. **b** A rude peasant; a boor.

kern (kûrn), *n.* [F. *carne* a projecting angle, fr. L. *cardo, cardinis,* a hinge. *Oxf. E. D.*] *Type Founding.* A part of the face of a type which projects beyond the body, or shank. — *v. t. Type Founding.* To form with a kern; also, to smooth (type) about the kern.

ker′nel (kûr′nĕl; -n'l), *n.* [AS. *cyrnel,* dim. of *corn* grain.] **1.** A whole grain or seed of a cereal, as of wheat or corn. **2.** The inner portion of a seed within the integuments; hence, the endocarp in nuts, drupes, or other seedlike fruits. **3.** The essential part of anything; gist; core.

ker′o·sene′ (kĕr′ō·sēn′; kĕr′ō·sēn′; 2), *n.* Also **ker′o·sine′** (-sēn′; -sēn′). [Gr. *kēros* wax.] A thin mineral oil used for burning in lamps, and also in oil stoves, etc. It is produced by distillation, chiefly from petroleum but also from oil shale. Called also *coal oil.*

Ker′ry (kĕr′ĭ), *n.; pl.* -RIES (-ĭz). [From County *Kerry,* Eire.] An Irish breed of small black dairy cattle.

Kerry blue terrier. A terrier of a breed originating in Ireland before 1800, with a long head, a deep chest, and a silky blue coat.

ker·sen′neh (kĕr·sĕn′ĕ), *n.* [Ar. *kirsannah.*] Also **ker·san′né** (-săn′ā). [F.] A variety of vetch.

ker′sey (kûr′zĭ), *n.* [From *Kersey,* village in Suffolk, Eng.] **1.** A kind of woolen cloth, usually coarse and ribbed. **2.** *pl.* Varieties of kersey; trousers made of kersey. — **ker′sey,** *adj.*

ker′sey·mere (-mēr), *n.* [From *cassimere,* after *kersey.*] Cassimere, a kind of woolen cloth.

kes′trel (kĕs′trĕl), *n.* [ME. *castrel,* fr. OF. *cresserelle.*] A small European falcon (*Falco tinnunculus*) noted for its habit of hovering in the air against a wind. It is about a foot long, bluish gray above in the male and reddish brown in the female.

ketch (kĕch), *n.* [Prob. fr. *catch,* n. or v.] *Naut.* A fore-and-aft rigged vessel with mainmast and mizzenmast, similar to a yawl, but with mizzenmast stepped farther forward and a larger mizzen.

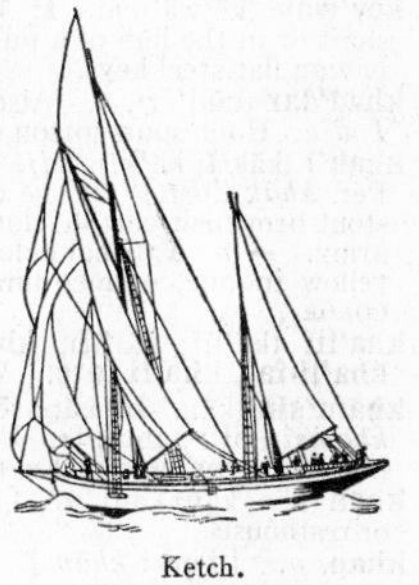
Ketch.

ketch′up (kĕch′ŭp), *n.* See CATCHUP.

ke′tene (kē′tēn), *n.* Also **ke′ten** (-tĕn). [*ketone* + *-ene.*] *Chem.* A colorless gas, $H_2C:CO$, of penetrating odor, prepared by decomposition of acetone, ethyl acetate, or acetic anhydride, by high heat.

ke′to- (kē′tō-), **ket-.** *Chem. & Med.* A combining form for *ketone,* meaning *relating to,* or *denoting, ketones or ketone bodies,* as in **ke′to·gen′e·sis, ke·tol′y·sis, ke′to·ne′mi·a, ke′to·nu′ri·a.** — **ke′to** (-tō), *adj.*

ke′tone (kē′tōn), *n.* [G. *keton,* fr. F. *acétone.*] *Chem.* A compound containing the carbonyl group (CO) doubly united with carbon, as with two hydrocarbon radicals, with a single bivalent radical, or with derivatives of these. — **ke·ton′ic** (kē·tŏn′ĭk), *adj.*

ke·to′sis (kē·tō′sĭs), *n.* [NL., fr. *ketone* + *-osis.*] *Med.* Excess of acetone or other ketones in the organism, occurring in diabetes, acidosis, etc.

ket′tle (kĕt′'l), *n.* [ON. *ketill,* like AS. *cetel,* D. *ketel,* etc., fr. L. *catillus,* dim. of *catinus* a deep vessel, bowl.] **1.** A metallic vessel for boiling liquids; a pot; now, esp., a teakettle. **2.** Short for KETTLEDRUM. **3.** *Geol.* Also **kettle hole.** A steep-sided hollow, without surface drainage, esp. in a deposit of glacial drift.

ket′tle·drum′ (-drŭm′), *n. Music.* A drum made of a hollow hemisphere of brass or copper with a parchment head.

kev′el (kĕv′ĕl; -'l), *n.* [ONF. *keville,* fr. L. *clavicula* fork, peg.] *Naut.* A strong timber, bollard, or cleat, for making fast the heavier lines of a vessel.

kex (kĕks), *n. Chiefly Dial. Eng.* The dry stalk of various hollow-stemmed plants, as cow parsnip, wild chervil, etc.

key (kē), *n.* [Sp. *cayo,* fr. Taino *cayo, caya,* small island.] A low island or reef, as off the southern coast of Florida.

key (kē), *n.* [AS. *cæg, cæge.*] **1.** An instrument by which the bolt of a lock is shot or drawn. **2.** That which affords or prevents entrance, possession, etc.; as, the *key* of a line of defense. **3.** A piece inserted between other pieces, as a bolt, cotter, pin, or wedge. **4.** A tool or other device like a key in form or function; as, a watch *key.* **5.** That which serves to reveal, discover, or solve something; as, the *key* to a riddle; hence, an outline map, a word-for-word translation, a book containing solutions to problems, etc. **6.** General pitch or tone of the speaking voice; also, a certain tone of voice; as, a plaintive *key.* **7.** Characteristic style or tone; as, writings all in the same *key.* **8.** *Advertising.* The matter used to key an advertisement. See KEY, *v. t.,* 2. **9. a** *Bot. & Zool.* A table in which the salient characters of a group of plants or animals (or of species, genera, etc.) are arranged so as to facilitate the determination of their names and taxonomic relationships. **b** *Bot.* = KEY FRUIT. **10.** *Building.* A keystone in an arch. **11.** *Carp.* A tapered piece of wood driven in a mortise between the parts of a scarfed joint to bring them together. **12.** *Elec.* A small switch for opening or closing a circuit. **13.** *Mach.* **a** A small, parallel-sided piece, flat or tapered on top, for securing pulleys, cranks, etc., to shafts. **b** In such instruments as the typewriter, linotype, etc., any of a set of levers analogous to the keys of a piano. See TYPEWRITER, *Illust.* **14.** *Music.* **a** In keyboard instruments, one of the levers, or esp. the exposed front end of it, by depressing which the player actuates the mechanism that produces the tones. **b** *Obs.* The keynote of a scale. **c** A system of tones based on their relation to a keynote, or tonic, from which it is named; the tonality of a certain scale; as, the *key* of C major.

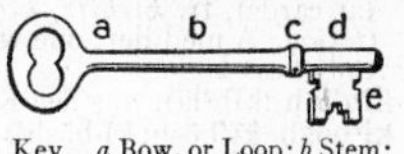

Key. *a* Bow, or Loop; *b* Stem; *c* Collar; *d* Pin; *e* Bit, or Web. See also LOCK, *Illust.*

— *v. t.* **1.** To lock with a key; to fix the key or keys of; esp., figuratively, to harmonize; to attune. **2.** *Advertising.* To insert in (an advertisement) some direction or other matter intended to identify answers to it. **3.** *Mach.* **a** To secure by a key, as a pulley on a shaft. **b** To finish off (an arch) by inserting the keystone. **4.** *Music.* To regulate the pitch of; as, to *key* the strings.

key up. To raise in key, as by tightening the strings; hence, to produce or cause a nervous tension in; to excite.

key′board′ (kē′bōrd′; 70), *n.* **1.** The bank or row of keys on an organ, piano, etc. **2.** The whole arrangement, or one range, of the keys of an organ, typewriter, linotype, etc. See TYPEWRITER, *Illust.* — *v. t. & i. Printing.* To set type by using a keyboard.

keyed (kēd), *adj.* **a** Furnished with keys. **b** Reinforced by a key or keystone. **c** Set to a key, as a tune.

key fruit. A samara. See SAMARA, *Illust.*

key′hole′ (kē′hōl′), *n.* A hole for receiving a key.

key industry. An industry whose output is essential to the successful operation of many other industries.

key man. Also **key′man′** (kē′măn′), *n.* A person doing such work in an organization that his services are indispensable.

key′note′ (kē′nōt′; 2), *n.* **1.** *Music.* The tonic of a key or scale as written or sounded. When sounded it is called also **key tone. 2.** The fundamental fact or idea; as, *keynote* of a policy. — (kē′nōt′), *v. t. & i.* To sound the keynote (of); also, to deliver a keynote address. — **key′not′er** (-nōt′ĕr), *n.*

keynote address *or* **speech.** An address, as at a political convention, that presents the essential issues of interest to the assembly.

Keys (kēz), *n. pl.* The twenty-four officials constituting the ***House of Keys,*** the representative branch of the legislature of the Isle of Man.

key signature. *Music.* The sign, composed of one or more sharps or flats, placed after the clef at the beginning of a staff to designate the key.

key'stone' (kē'stōn'), *n.* **1.** *Arch.* The voussoir at the crown of an arch, regarded as binding the whole. See ARCH, *Illust.* **2.** A part or force on which associated things depend.

Keystone State. Pennsylvania; — a nickname alluding to its central position among the original 13 colonies.

key'way' (kē'wā'), *n.* **1.** *Mach.* A groove or channel for a key, as in a shaft or in the hub of a pulley. **2.** The aperture for the key in locks having flat steel keys.

khad'dar (kŭd'ẽr), *n.* Also **kha'di** (kä'dē). [Hind. *khādar, khādī.*] *India.* Homespun cotton cloth.

khak'i (kăk'ĭ; kä'kĭ), *adj.* [Hind. *khākī*, lit., dusty, dust-colored, fr. Per. *khāk* dust.] Of the color khaki; — applied to cloth, orig. to a stout brownish cotton cloth used for uniforms in the Anglo-Indian army. — *n.* **1.** Khaki cloth or uniform. **2.** A brown, yellowish red-yellow in hue, of medium saturation and medium brilliance. See COLOR.

kha'lif (kā'lĭf; kăl'ĭf), **kha·li'fa** (kȧ·lē'fȧ), **kha'liff, kha'lee·fate, kha'li·fat, kha'li·fate.** Vars. of CALIPH, CALIPHATE.

kham'sin (kăm'sĭn; kăm·sēn'), *n.* Also **kham·seen', kam'sin.** [Ar. *khamsīn* fifty, abbr. fr. *rīḥ al-khamsīn* the wind of fifty (days).] A hot southerly wind in Egypt, coming from the Sahara.

khan (kän; kăn; Kän), *n.* [Ar. *khān.*] In the Near East, a caravansary, or resthouse.

khan, *n.* [Turki *khān.*] Literally, lord; prince; — a Tatar title of sovereignty of the successors of Genghis Khan now applied to dignitaries of various rank in Persia, Afghanistan, etc. — **khan'ate** (-āt), *n.*

khed'ah (kĕd'ȧ). Var. of KEDDAH.

khe·dive' (kĕ·dēv'), *n.* [F. *khédive*, fr. Turk. *khidīv*, fr. Per. *khidīw* a prince.] The title from 1867 to 1914 of Turkish viceroys in Egypt. — **khe·di'vi·al** (kĕ·dē'vĭ·ăl), *adj.* — **khe·di'vi·ate** (-āt), *n.*

khid'mat·gar, khid'mut·gar (kĭd'mȧt·gär), *n.* [Hind. & Per. *khidmatgār.*] *India.* A male waiter.

Khmer (k'mĕr), *n.* **1.** One of the native race of Cambodia, of undetermined origin. The Khmers developed a great Hindu and Buddhistic civilization during the Middle Ages. **2.** The language of the Khmers.

ki·ang' (kĭ·ăng'), *n.; pl.* KIANGS (-ăngz'), *sometimes* KIANG. A Tibetan wild ass (*Equus kiang*). See ONAGER.

kiaugh (kyäK), *n.* *Scot.* Trouble; anxiety.

kibe (kīb), *n.* A chapped or ulcerated chilblain.

ki'bei' (kē'bā'), *n.; pl.* KIBEI, KIBEIS (-bāz'). [Jap.] An American born of Japanese parents in the United States, who has acquired all or part of his education in Japan. Cf. NISEI, ISSEI.

kib'itz (kĭb'ĭts), *v. i.;* KIB'ITZED (-ĭtst); KIB'ITZ·ING. *Colloq.* To act as a kibitzer.

kib'itz·er (kĭb'ĭt·sẽr), *n.* [Yiddish, fr. colloq. G. *kiebitzen* to look on (at cards), fr. *kiebitz, kibitz*, a looker-on, a meddlesome spectator.] *Colloq.* A meddler; one who gives gratuitous advice; specif., a spectator at cards.

kib'lah (kĭb'lä), *n.* See KAABA.

ki'bosh (kī'bŏsh; kĭ·bŏsh'), *n.* *Slang.* Nonsense; stuff. — ***to put the kibosh on.*** *Slang.* To do for finally; squelch.

kick (kĭk), *v. i.* [ME. *kiken.*] **1.** To strike out with the foot or feet, as in defense or in bad temper, or at a ball in games, or in swimming. **2.** *Now Colloq.* To show opposition or ill temper; to object strenuously; as, to *kick* against a decision. **3.** *Slang.* To die; — often ***kick in, kick off, kick the bucket.*** **4.** Of a firearm, to recoil when fired. — **Syn.** See OBJECT. — *v. t.* **1.** To strike, thrust, or hit violently with the foot. **2.** To strike violently as if with the foot, or as a gun does in recoiling; to impel or drive as by kicking. **3.** *Football.* To score (a goal) by kicking. — **kick'er,** *n.*

kick back. **a** *Colloq.* To recoil upon one in an unexpected manner. **b** *Slang.* To return (part of a sum received as wages, fees, etc.).

— *n.* **1.** A blow with the foot or feet; power to kick. **2.** *Eng. Slang.* A pocket. **3.** Any movement resembling a kick; specif., the recoil of a firearm. **4. a** *Slang.* A distinct protest. **b** *Slang, U. S.* Grounds of objection or complaint. **5.** *Slang.* **a** Strongly stimulating effect, as of liquor. **b** Pleasurable excitement. **6.** The indentation at the bottom of a molded glass bottle to lessen its holding capacity. **7.** *Football.* Act or instance of kicking the ball.

kick'back' (-băk'), *n.* **1.** *Colloq.* A reaction, esp. when sharp or violent. **2. a** *Thieves' Slang.* A restoration by a thief of part or all of stolen property. **b** A return of a part of a sum received, as of wages, commissions, fees, etc., specif. because of confidential agreement or coercion.

kick'off' (-ôf'; 74), *n.* **a** *Football.* Act of starting play by a place kick at or near the center of the field. **b** *Colloq.* Figuratively, a commencement.

kick'shaw' (-shô'), **kick'shaws'** (-shôz'), *n.* [F. *quelque chose* something.] **1.** Something fantastical; a toy; bauble. **2.** A fancy dish; a tidbit; a delicacy.

kick turn. *Skiing.* A method of reversing direction by swinging first one ski high with a jerk and planting it in the desired direction, then lifting the other ski into a parallel position. — **kick'-turn',** *v. i.*

kick'up' (-ŭp'), *n.* *Slang.* A row; a disturbance.

kid (kĭd), *n.* A small wooden tub. esp. a sailors' mess tub.

kid, *n.* [ON. *kith.*] **1.** A young goat. **2.** The flesh, fur, or skin of a kid; also, a thing made of kid; specif.: **a** = KIDSKIN. **b** *pl.* Kid gloves. **3.** *Colloq.* A child; a youngster. — *v. i.;* KID'DED; KID'DING. To bring forth young; — said of a goat or an antelope.

kid, *v. t. & i.;* KID'DED; KID'DING. *Slang.* **a** To hoax; humbug. **b** To make fun (of), esp. by deceptive talk; rally; jolly. — *n. Slang.* Humbug; a hoax. — **kid'der,** *n.*

Kid'der·min'ster (kĭd'ẽr·mĭn'stẽr), *n.* Ingrain carpet; — from the English town where first made.

kid'nap (kĭd'năp; *formerly* kĭd·năp'), *v. t.;* -NAPED (-năpt) or -NAPPED; -NAP'ING or -NAP'PING. [*kid* a child + E. dial. *nap* to seize, to grasp.] To carry (anyone) away by unlawful force or by fraud, and against his will, or to seize and detain him for the purpose of so carrying him away. — **kid'nap'er** (-năp'ẽr), **kid'nap'per,** *n.*

kid'ney (kĭd'nĭ), *n.* [ME. *kydney, kidenei;* first element of unknown origin; second is ME. *ey* egg.] **1.** In vertebrates, one of a pair of glands, situated in the body cavity near the spinal column, and serving to excrete urea, uric acid, and other waste products of metabolism. In man, the kidneys are bean-shaped organs, about 4½ inches long. Each kidney is made up chiefly of epithelial tubules (*uriniferous tubules*) which secrete urine, collect it, and discharge it into a main cavity whence it is conveyed by the ureter to the bladder for periodical discharge. Each tubule begins as a thin-walled invagination or capsule surrounding the *glomerulus*, or *Malpighian tuft*, the capsule and glomerulus together constituting a **kidney corpuscle.** **2.** Temperament; disposition; sort; kind. **3.** The tissue of the kidney of an animal, as of the ox or sheep, used as an article of food; as, grilled *kidneys.*

kidney bean. a *Eng.* The common bean *Phaseolus vulgaris.* **b** The scarlet runner (*P. coccineus*).

kidney vetch. A perennial Eurasian herb (*Anthyllis vulneraria*) of the pea family, with cloverlike heads of red or yellow flowers, once used as a remedy for renal disorders.

kid'skin' (kĭd'skĭn'), *n.* The skin of a young goat, used for footwear, gloves, etc. — **kid'skin',** *adj.*

kief (kēf). Var. of KEF.

kier (kẽr), *n.* [ON. *ker* a tub.] A large vat in which textile goods, cotton, etc., are boiled, bleached, etc.

kie'sel·guhr', kie'sel·gur' (kē'zĕl·gŏŏr'), *n.* [G., fr. *kiesel* flint + *guhr* sediment.] Loose or porous diatomite. See DIATOM.

kie'ser·ite (kē'zẽr·īt), *n.* [After D. G. *Kieser*, of Jena.] *Mineral.* Hydrous magnesium sulfate, $MgSO_4.H_2O$.

kil'der·kin (kĭl'dẽr·kĭn), *n.* [MD. *kinderkijn, kinneken*, fr. ML. *quintale.* See QUINTAL.] A cask, or small barrel; hence, an old English measure usually equal to 18 gallons.

kil'erg' (kĭl'ûrg'), *n.* [*kilo-* + *erg.*] *Physics.* A unit of work equal to one thousand ergs.

Kil·ken'ny cats (kĭl·kĕn'ĭ). Two cats which fought till nothing was left but their tails; — probably a parable of a local contest between Kilkenny and Irishtown.

kill (kĭl), *v. t.* [ME. *killen, kellen, cullen*, to kill, strike.] **1.** To deprive of life; to slay. **2.** To slaughter (an animal for food); hence, to convert a food animal into (beef, pork, or the like); as, to *kill* beef. **3.** To deprive of vital quality; to destroy. **4.** Specif.: **a** To consume (time). **b** To defeat or veto. **c** To stop; as, to *kill* an engine. **5.** *Elec.* To cut off (a live circuit). **6.** *Lawn Tennis, etc.* To play (a ball) so hard that it cannot be returned. **7.** *Print.* To mark or designate (matter) as not to be used.

Syn. Kill, slay, murder, assassinate, dispatch (*or* despatch), execute mean to deprive of life. Kill, the general term, may or may not suggest human agency or a human victim or even, in figurative use, an animate victim; slay implies killing wantonly or deliberately; murder, a motive and, usually, premeditation; assassinate, murder by stealth or treachery, esp of an important person; dispatch, getting rid of a person or the like or killing him quickly; execute, the carrying out of a sentence to death.

— *n.* **a** The act of killing. **b** An animal, or, collectively, the animals, killed in a hunt or by hunting.

kill, *n.* [D. *kil*, MD. *kille.*] *Local, U. S.* A channel; creek; stream; as, the *Kills*, between Staten Island and Bergen Neck; — also used in combination; as, Cats*kill.*

kill'deer' (kĭl'dẽr'), *n.;* see PLURAL, *Note*, 3. Also **kill'dee'** (-dē'). [So named from its notes.] A plover (*Oxyechus vociferus*) found throughout temperate North America. It has a plaintive and penetrating cry.

kill'er (kĭl'ẽr), *n.* **1.** One who or that which kills, as an assassin. **2.** Also **killer whale.** Any of several rapacious gregarious cetaceans of the dolphin family, mostly of northern seas. The common Atlantic species (*Orcinus orca*) is 20 to 30 feet long.

kil'lick (kĭl'ĭk), *n.* Also **kil'lock** (-ŭk). A small anchor; also, a kind of anchor formed by a stone, usually enclosed by pieces of wood; loosely, any anchor.

kil'lick·in·nic', kil'li·ki·nick' (kĭl'ĭ·kĭ·nĭk'). Vars. of KINNIKINNICK.

kil'li·fish' (kĭl'ĭ·fĭsh'), *n.; pl.*, see FISH. Any of numerous small American cyprinodont fishes (genus *Fundulus* and allied genera), some of which live equally well in fresh, brackish, or sea water. They are much used as bait.

kill'ing (kĭl'ĭng), *n.* **1.** Act of one who kills; esp., homicide; murder. **2.** That which is killed, as the amount of game taken on one hunt. **3.** *Colloq.* A large gain or profit acquired; as, to make a *killing* on the stock market. — *adj.* That kills or pertains to killing; also, *Colloq.*, captivating; irresistibly amusing. — **kill'ing·ly,** *adv.*

kill'-joy', *n.* One who causes gloom; a dispiriting person.

kiln (kĭl; kĭln), *n.* [AS. *cyln, cylen*, fr. L. *culina* kitchen.] A large stove or oven, or furnace of brick or stone, or a heated chamber, for hardening, burning, or drying anything; as, a lime*kiln* or cement *kiln.* — *v. t.;* KILNED (kĭld; kĭlnd); KILN'ING. To burn, bake, or dry in a kiln.

kiln'-dry' (-drī'), *v. t.;* see DRY. To dry in a kiln.

ki'lo (kē'lō; kĭl'ō), *n.; pl.* KILOS (-lōz). [F.] A kilogram; a kilometer; — shortened form.

kil'o- (kĭl'ō-). [F. *kilo-*. See KILOGRAM.] A prefix meaning *thousand*, used chiefly in names of units in the metric system, as in **kil'o·am'pere**, one thousand amperes, **kil'o·dyne, kil'o·gauss', kil'o·joule', kil'o·lu'men, kil'o·volt'.**

kil'o·cal'o·rie (-kăl'ō·rĭ), *n.* *Physics.* A great calorie. See CALORIE.

kil'o·cy'cle (-sī'k'l), *n.* A thousand cycles; also, esp. *Radio*, one thousand cycles per second. Abbr. *kc.*

kil'o·gram, kil'o·gramme (-grăm), *n.* [F. *kilogramme*, fr. *kilo-* (fr. Gr. *chilioi* a thousand) + *gramme* gram.] See METRIC SYSTEM, *Table* 5. Abbr. *kg.*

kil'o·gram-me'ter, kil'o·gram-me'tre (-mē'tẽr), *n.* *Mech.* A unit of energy or work, being the amount expended in raising one kilogram through the height of one meter, in the latitude of Paris. It is nearly equal to 7¼ foot-pounds.

kil'o·li'ter, kil'o·li'tre (-lē'tẽr), *n.* [F. *kilolitre.*] See METRIC SYSTEM, *Table* 4. Abbr. *kl.*

kil'o·me'ter, kil'o·me'tre (kĭl'ō·mē'tẽr; *sometimes* kĭ·lŏm'ē·tẽr), *n.* [F. *kilomètre.*] See METRIC SYSTEM, *Tables* 1, 2, & 3. Abbr. *kil., kilom.*, or *km.* — **kil'o·met'ric** (-mĕt'rĭk), **-met'ri·cal** (-rĭ·kăl), *adj.*

kil'o·ton' (kĭl'ō·tŭn'), *n.* [*kilo-* + *ton.*] A thousand tons.

kil'o·watt' (kĭl'ō·wŏt'), *n.* [See KILOGRAM; WATT.] *Elec.* A unit of power, equal to one thousand watts. Abbr. *kw.*

kil'o·watt'-hour', *n.* *Elec.* A unit of work or energy equal to that done by one kilowatt acting for one hour, — approx. = 1.34 horsepower hour. Abbr. *kw-hr* (no period).

kilt (kĭlt), *n.* [From KILT, *v.*] A type of short plaited petticoat worn in the Highlands of Scotland by men; hence, any similar garment.

— *v. t.* [Of Scand. origin.] **1.** *Scot.* To tuck up. **2.** To lay in plaits like those of a Highland kilt.
kil'ter (kĭl'tẽr), **kel'ter** (kĕl'tẽr), *n.* *Colloq. & Dial.* Order; proper condition; — chiefly in phrases; as, *out of*, or *in, kilter*.
kilt'ie, kilt'y (kĭl'tĭ), *n.; pl.* KILTIES (-tĭz). One who wears a kilt, specif. a regimental kilt.
kilt'ing, *n.* *Dressmaking.* A series of perpendicular flat plaits, each folded so as to cover about half of the preceding.
kim'mer (kĭm'ẽr). Scot. & dial. var. of CUMMER, lass.
ki·mo'no (kĭ·mō'nŭ; kĭ·mō'nō), *n.; pl.* -NOS (-nŭz; -nōz). [Jap.] **1.** A type of loose robe or gown tied with a sash, worn as an outer garment by Japanese men and women. **2.** A similar gown worn as a dressing gown by women of Western nations.
kin (kĭn), *n.* [AS. *cynn* kin, race, people.] **1.** *Archaic.* A group of persons of the same stock, race, or family; a sept, clan, or tribe. **2.** One's relatives, collectively; kindred; also, formerly, a kinsman. **3.** *Rare.* Relationship; connection by birth or marriage. — *adj.* Kindred; related.
-kin (-kĭn). [ME. *-kin*, fr. MD. *-kin, -kijn*.] A diminutive suffix, as in mani*kin*.
kin'aes·the'si·a, kin'aes·the'sis, kin'aes·thet'ic. Vars. of KINESTHESIA, etc.
ki'nase (kī'nās; kĭn'ās), *n.* [*kinetic* + *-ase*.] *Biochem.* A substance that converts a zymogen into an enzyme.
kin'chin (kĭn'chĭn), *n.* *Slang.* A child.
kin'chin·mort' (-môrt'), *n.* *Slang.* A girl or infant.
kind (kīnd), *n.* [AS. *cynd, gecynd, gecynde*, fr. the root of E. KIN.] **1.** *Archaic.* Nature; character; style; mode of action. **2.** A natural group, class, or division; as, the bird *kind*. **3.** A class; sort; variety; description; as, several *kinds* of eloquence. **4.** The generic or specific quality or character of anything; as, differences in *kind*. — **Syn.** See TYPE. — ***in kind.*** **1.** In the same or like manner. **2.** In produce or commodities, instead of in money; as, payment *in kind*. — ***of a kind.*** Of the same class, sort, value, etc.
kind, *adj.* [AS. *cynde, gecynde*, natural, innate. See KIND, *n.*] **1.** *Obs.* Natural; native; hence, appropriate; rightful. **2.** Having feelings befitting our common nature; benevolent; well-disposed; also, showing kindness or tenderness; gracious. **3.** Proceeding from, or characterized by, goodness or benevolence; as, a *kind* act. **4.** *Now Chiefly Dial.* Loving; affectionate. **5.** Gentle; tractable; as, a horse sound and *kind* in harness.
Syn. **Kind, kindly, benign, benignant** mean showing a gentle, considerate nature. **Kind** and **kindly** both imply interest in another's welfare, and sympathy, humaneness, and the like, but *kind* stresses a disposition to be helpful, and *kindly* the expression of a benevolent nature, mood, or impulse (as, to have a *kind* heart; to take a *kindly* interest); **benign** and **benignant** stress mildness, graciousness, and mercifulness, and apply more often to superiors than to equals, but *benign*, usually, describes a person, and *benignant* his acts, words, etc. (as, a *benign* master; a *benignant* influence).
kin'der·gar'ten (kĭn'dẽr·gär't'n), *n.* [G., lit., children's garden.] A school for young children conducted on the theory that education should be begun by cultivating the normal aptitude for exercise, play, observation, imitation, and construction, and emphasizing the necessity of social training.
kin'der·gart'ner (-gärt'nẽr), *n.* Also **kin'der·gar'ten·er.** **1.** A kindergarten teacher. **2.** A kindergarten pupil.
kind'heart'ed (kīnd'här'tĕd; -tĭd; 2), *adj.* Having kindness of nature; sympathetic. — **kind'heart'ed·ly,** *adv.* — **kind'heart'ed·ness,** *n.*
kin'dle (kĭn'd'l), *v. t.;* KIN'DLED (-d'ld); KIN'DLING (-dlĭng). [ON. *kynda*.] **1.** To set on fire; to ignite; light. **2.** To inflame, as the passions; to rouse; excite. **3.** To light up or inflame as if with flame. — *v. i.* **1.** To take fire. **2.** To begin to be excited; to grow warm or animated.
kin'dle, *v. t. & i.* [ME. *kindlen, cundlen*.] To bring forth young.
kind'less (kīnd'lĕs; -lĭs), *adj.* Destitute of kindness; also, *Obs.*, unnatural. — **kind'less·ly,** *adv.*
kin'dling (kĭn'dlĭng), *n.* **1.** Act of causing to burn, or of exciting the passions. **2.** Material, easily lighted, for starting a fire.
kind'ly (kīnd'lĭ), *adj.;* KIND'LI·ER (-lĭ·ẽr); KIND'LI·EST. [AS. *cyndelīc, gecyndelīc*.] **1.** *Archaic.* Natural; native; hereditary. **2.** Humane; sympathetic; hence, benevolent; gracious; kind. **3.** Favorable; genial; agreeable. — **Syn.** See KIND. — *adv.* [AS. *gecyndelīce*.] **1.** Naturally; fitly. **2.** In a kind manner; agreeably; pleasantly. **3.** *Colloq.* As a considerate, courteous, or gracious act; as a favor or gesture of good will; as, I would take it *kindly* if you would come; will you *kindly* fill out this blank? — **kind'li·ness,** *n.*
kind'ness (-nĕs; -nĭs), *n.* **1.** State or quality of being kind; specif., beneficence; rarely, kind feeling; affection. **2.** A kind act; an act of good will.
kind of. *Colloq.* In a way; somewhat; rather; as, he is *kind of* queer.
kin'dred (kĭn'drĕd; -drĭd), *n.* [ME. *kinrede, kynrede, kunreden*, fr. AS. *cynn* kin, race + the termination *-rǣden* condition, rule.] **1.** Relationship; affinity; kinship. **2.** The family, or the like, to which one belongs; collectively, relations; persons related to each other. — *adj.* Belonging to the same family or race; related; of the like nature or properties; cognate.
kine (kīn), *n. pl.* [For older *kyen*, formed like *oxen*, fr. AS. *cȳ*, pl. of *cū* cow.] *Archaic & Dial.* Cows; cattle.
kin'e·mat'ics (kĭn'ē·măt'ĭks; kī'nē-), *n.;* see -ICS. [Gr. *kinēma, kinēmatos*, motion, fr. *kinein* to move.] *Physics.* The science which treats of motions considered in themselves, or apart from their causes; also, the application of this science to mechanical contrivances. — **kin'e·mat'ic** (-ĭk), **kin'e·mat'i·cal** (-ĭ·kăl), *adj.*
kin'e·mat'o·graph (kĭn'ē·măt'ō·grȧf; kī'nē-; 9), **kin'e·ma·tog'ra·phy,** etc. Vars. of CINEMATOGRAPH, etc.
kin'e·scope (kĭn'ē·skōp; kī'nē-), *n.* *Television.* A cathode-ray tube having at one end a screen of luminescent material on which are produced visible images, such as pictures or oscillograph curves. Cf. ICONOSCOPE.
kin'es·the'si·a (kĭn'ĕs·thē'zhĭ·ȧ, -zhȧ, -zĭ·ȧ; kī'nĕs-), **kin'es·the'sis** (-thē'sĭs). [NL., fr. Gr. *kinein* to move + *aisthēsis* perception.] The sense whose end organs lie in the muscles, tendons, and joints and are stimulated by bodily tensions; the muscle sense. — **kin'es·thet'ic** (-thĕt'ĭk), *adj.*
ki·net'ic (kĭ·nĕt'ĭk; kī-), *adj.* [Gr. *kinētikos*, fr. *kinein* to move.] *Physics.* Of, pertaining to, or due to motion; — often contr. with *potential;* as, *kinetic* energy.
ki·net'ics (-ĭks), *n.;* see -ICS. The branch of dynamics treating of the changes of motion produced by forces.
kinetic theory of matter. *Physics.* The theory that the minute particles of substances are in vigorous motion. The **kinetic theory of gases** assumes that the particles of a gas move in straight lines with high average velocity, continually encountering one another and, hence, changing their individual velocities and directions, and that the pressure of the gas is due to the impact of the particles against the walls of the containing vessel. The **kinetic theory of heat** assumes that the temperature of a substance depends on the average kinetic energy of the minute particles, and that when heat is added to a substance there is an increase in this average kinetic energy.
ki·ne'to·graph (kĭ·nē'tō·grȧf; kĭ·nĕt'ō-; kī-; 9), *n.* [Gr. *kinētos* moving + *-graph*.] An apparatus for taking a series of photographs of moving objects; a form of cinematograph. — **ki·ne'to·graph,** *v. t.* — **kin'e·tog'ra·pher** (kĭn'ē·tŏg'rȧ·fẽr; kī'nē-), *n.* — **ki·ne'to·graph'ic** (kĭ·nē'tō·grăf'ĭk; kĭ·nĕt'ō-; kī-), *adj.* — **kin'e·tog'ra·phy** (kĭn'ē·tŏg'rȧ·fĭ; kī'nē-), *n.*
kin'folk', kin'folks'. Dial. variants of KINSFOLK.
king (kĭng), *n.* [AS. *cyng, cyning*.] **1.** A male sovereign; the monarch of a state distinctively called a kingdom, and usually independent. **2.** One that holds a pre-eminent position or rank; as, a railroad *king*. **3.** *Cards.* A card conventionally picturing a king. **4.** *Checkers.* A crowned man. **5.** *Chess.* The principal piece, moving ordinarily one square in any direction, but obliged never to enter or remain in check. Abbr. *K* (no period). — *adj.* Chief; most important; — often in combination, as in *king*bolt.
King apple. A red-striped variety of winter apple.
King Arthur. See ARTHURIAN.
king'bird' (kĭng'bûrd'), *n.* Any of several American tyrant flycatchers (genus *Tyrannus*), some species of which are noted for their pugnacity, as the common kingbird (*T. tyrannus*) of the eastern U. S.
king'bolt' (-bōlt'), *n.* A vertical bolt by which the forward axle and wheels of a vehicle or the trucks of a railroad car are connected with the other parts.
King Charles spaniel. See SPANIEL.

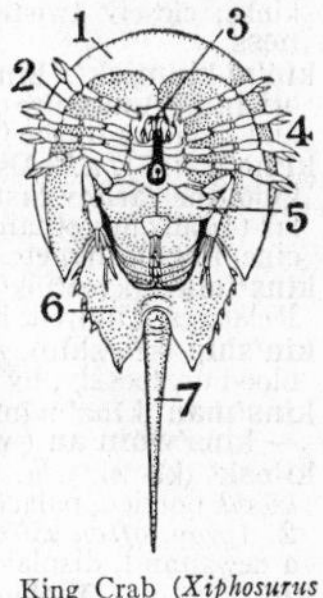

King Crab (*Xiphosurus sowerbyi*), ventral aspect. (⅐) 1 Carapace; 3 Anterior Appendages; 4 Ambulatory Appendages of Cephalothorax, 2; 5 Operculum; 6 Abdomen; 7 Caudal Spine, or Telson.

king crab. Any of several closely related species of large marine arthropods (order Xiphosura and class Merostomata); a horseshoe crab; a xiphosuran. Cf. CRAB.
king'craft' (kĭng'krȧft'), *n.* The art of governing as a sovereign.
king'cup' (-kŭp'), *n.* See CROWFOOT, 1.
king'dom (kĭng'dŭm), *n.* [AS. *cyningdōm*.] **1.** *Archaic.* The rank, state, or attributes of a king; royal authority. **2.** A state or monarchy the head of which is a king; dominion; realm. **3.** *Nat. Hist.* One of the three grand divisions into which all natural objects are commonly classified, the ***mineral kingdom*** comprising all unorganized and lifeless substance and objects, the ***vegetable kingdom*** containing all plants, the ***animal kingdom*** containing all animals. **4.** *Theol.* The spiritual realm having God as its head.
king'fish' (-fĭsh'), *n.; pl.,* see FISH. **1. a** An American marine sciaenoid food fish (genus *Menticirrhus*), esp. one (*M. saxatilis*) of the Atlantic coast. **b** The opah. **c** Either of two sierras, the cero (*Sierra cavalla*) or the pintado. **2.** *Colloq* The undisputed master in a community, faction, legislature, etc.
king'fish'er (-fĭsh'ẽr), *n.* Any of a family (Alcedinidae) of nonpasserine birds, mostly crested and bright-colored, with a short tail and long, stout, sharp bill, as the slate-blue ***belted kingfisher*** (*Megaceryle alcyon*) of the United States, with a chestnut band across a white breast.
King Horn. The title and hero of various old metrical romances in English, Scotch, and French.
King James Bible. The Authorized Version of the Bible. See BIBLE.
King Lear (lēr). The title and hero of a tragedy by Shakespeare. Lear is a legendary king of Britain, who divides his kingdom between his elder daughters, Goneril and Regan, and disinherits his youngest daughter, Cordelia. The elder daughters drive the old man to madness by neglect and abuse. Cordelia, with her husband, the king of France, enters Britain with an army to rescue her father, but is defeated, captured, and hanged in prison. Lear dies of grief.
king'let (kĭng'lĕt; -lĭt), *n.* **1.** A little or insignificant king. **2.** Any of several very small birds (genus *Regulus*), resembling the warblers, as the ***golden-crowned kinglet*** (*R. satrapa*) and ***ruby-crowned kinglet*** (*R. calendula*).
king'ly (-lĭ), *adj.;* -LI·ER (-lĭ·ẽr); -LI·EST. Belonging to, suitable to, or befitting a king; characteristic of, or resembling, a king; royal; august; noble; grand. — *adv.* In a kingly manner. — **king'li·ness,** *n.*
king'-of-arms', *n., or* **king of arms.** [*also caps.*] The chief heraldic officer of a country.
king'pin' (kĭng'pĭn'), *n.* **1.** *Bowling.* **a** A tall pin, or any pin, in the center of the frame. **b** The head pin. **2.** *Colloq.* The chief person in a group or undertaking. **3.** A kingbolt.
king post. *Carp.* A vertical member connecting the apex of a triangular truss with the base. Cf. QUEEN POST; see ROOF, *Illust.*
Kings (kĭngz), *n. pl., construed as sing.* One of two (or, in Douay Bible, four) books of the Old Testament recording the reigns of Jewish kings. See BIBLE.
King's, *or* **Queen's, Bench.** *Eng. Law.* A former court of record and the highest court of common law in England. The sovereign used to sit there in person.
King's, *or* **Queen's, Birthday.** *Brit.* The birthday of the sovereign, whether actual or arbitrary. See HOLIDAY, 3.
king's counsel. *Brit.* Barristers, or a barrister, designated as counsel for the king; — called ***queen's counsel*** when the sovereign is a queen. Abbr. *K.C.* or *Q.C.*
king's, *or* **queen's, English, the.** English speech or usage regarded as if sanctioned by royal, or official, authority.
king's, *or* **queen's, evidence.** *Eng. Law.* Evidence for the king or queen, that is, the crown or state; esp., the evidence voluntarily given by an accomplice who confesses the crime and testifies against his accomplices. It is called ***state's evidence*** in the United States.

king's evil. Scrofula; — so called because formerly supposed to be healed by the touch of a king.

king'ship (kĭng'shĭp), *n.* **a** State, office, or dignity of a king. **b** Royal government. **c** Personality of a king; majesty.

king snake. A large, harmless snake (*Lampropeltis getulus*, family Colubridae) of the southern United States. It kills other snakes, but lives chiefly on mice and rats.

king's, *or* queen's, proctor. In England, an officer of the court who may intervene in actions for divorce, chiefly to prevent collusive proceedings.

king's, *or* queen's, shilling. A shilling given by a recruiting officer to a recruit, the taking of which, until 1879, constituted a binding enlistment in the British Army.

king truss. A truss framed with a king post.

king'wood' (kĭng'wŏŏd'), *n.* A handsome violet-marked wood from a tree (*Dalbergia cearensis*) of the pea family, of Brazil; also, this tree.

kink (kĭngk), *n.* [From D. *kink* or Sw. *kink* a twist in a rope.] **1.** A short and often tight twist, loop, or curl as in a rope, thread, hair, etc., caused by a doubling or winding upon itself. **2.** A cramp in some part of the body; a crick. **3.** A peculiarity; a quirk; also, a mental twist; crotchet. — *v. i. & t.* To wind into or form a kink.

kin·kaid'er (kĭn·kād'ẽr), *n.* [After Moses P. *Kinkaid* (1854–1922), Am. Congressman.] *Local, U.S.* One of the settlers on free land in Nebraska under terms of the Kinkaid Act (1904), which allowed each bona fide settler 640 acres upon payment of a filing fee of fourteen dollars.

kin'ka·jou (kĭng'kȧ·jōō), *n.* [From F., Sp., or Pg., fr. Tupi *kinkajú, kinkajou.*] A nocturnal arboreal carnivorous mammal (*Potos caudivolvulus*, family Procyonidae), inhabiting Mexico and Central and South America. It is about three feet long, and has a slender body, long prehensile tail, large lustrous eyes, and soft woolly yellowish-brown fur. It may easily be tamed.

kin'kle (kĭng'k'l), *n.* A little kink. — **kin'kled** (-k'ld), *adj.*

kink'y (kĭngk'ĭ), *adj.*; KINK'I·ER (-ĭ·ẽr); KINK'I·EST. Full of, or having, kinks; closely twisted; as, *kinky* hair. — **kink'i·ly**, *adv.* — **kink'i·ness**, *n.*

kin'ni·kin·nick', kin'ni·ki·nic' (kĭn'ĭ·kĭ·nĭk'), *n.* [Of Algonquian origin.] A mixture of leaves and bark formerly smoked by the Indians and pioneers in the Ohio Valley.

ki'no (kē'nō), *n.* Also **kino gum**. [Mandingo *keno* or *kano* African kino (the variety first known).] A dark-red or blackish product similar to catechu, obtained from various tropical trees and used in medicine, in tanning, etc.

kins'folk' (kĭnz'fōk'), *n. pl.* Formerly also **kins'folks'** (-fōks'). Relatives; kindred; kin; persons closely related.

kin'ship (kĭn'shĭp), *n.* Quality or state of being kin; relationship by blood or, loosely, by marriage.

kins'man (kĭnz'măn), *n.* A man of the same race or family; relative. — **kins'wom'an** (-wŏŏm'ăn), *n.*

ki·osk' (kē·ŏsk'), *n.* [F. *kiosque*, fr. Turk. *kiūshk* pavilion, fr. Per. *kūshk* portico, palace.] **1.** A Turkish open summerhouse or pavilion. **2.** (*pron. often* kī'ŏsk) A similar light ornamental structure used as a newsstand, display stand, bandstand, etc.

kip (kĭp), *n.* **1.** The undressed hide of a young steer, cow, or horse. **2.** A set or bundle of such hides.

kip, *n.* [AS. *cip* brothel.] *Slang.* **a** *Obs.* A brothel. **b** A lodginghouse; a lodging or bed in one; hence, a bed.

kip'per (kĭp'ẽr), *n.* **a** A male salmon or sea trout during or after spawning. **b** A kippered salmon or herring. Cf. BLOATER. **c** *Slang, Eng.* A fellow; chap. — *v. t.* To cure by cleaning, salting, and, often, treating with pepper, spice, etc., and then drying or smoking.

Kir·ghiz' (kĭr·gēz'), *n.*; *pl.* KIRGHIZ or KIRGHIZES (-ēz; -ĭz). **1.** A member of a widespread people of Turkic speech and Mongolian race, chiefly of the Central Asian steppes. **2.** The language of the Kirghiz, a Turkic tongue. See LANGUAGE, *Table.*

kirk (kûrk; *Scot.* kĭrk), *n.* [Scot. See CHURCH.] **1.** *Scot. & N. of Eng.* A church. **2.** [usually *cap.*, and with *the.*] Esp., in English usage, the national church of Scotland as distinguished from the Church of England or from the Scottish Episcopal Church.

kirk'man (-măn), *n.* **1.** *Scot.* An ecclesiastic; a churchman. **2.** A member or adherent of the Church of Scotland.

Kir·man' (kĭr·män'), *n.* [From Per. *Kirmān* Kerman (see *Gaz*).] A carpet or rug woven in Kerman province, Persia, characterized by elaborate fluid designs and soft colors. The ***Kir·man'-La·vehr'*** (-lȧ·vâr') is the highest quality; the ***Ker·man'shah'*** (kẽr·män'shä'), *or* ***Kir·man'shah'***, is a cheaper grade.

kir'mess (kûr'mĕs). Var. of KERMIS.

kirn (kûrn; *Scot. also* kĭrn), *n. & v.* *Chiefly Scot.* Churn.

kirn, *n.* *Chiefly Scot.* **1.** A merrymaking at the end of the harvest. **2.** Last handful or sheaf reaped at harvest.

kirsch (kĭrsh), **kirsch'was'ser** (-väs'ẽr), *n.* [G., fr. *kirsche* cherry + *wasser* water.] An alcoholic liquor made by distilling the fermented juice of the morello cherry.

kir'sen, kir'sten (kûr'sĕn). Dial. vars. of CHRISTEN.

kir'tle (kûr't'l), *n.* [AS. *cyrtel.*] *Archaic.* **1.** A man's tunic or coat. **2.** A woman's gown. — **kir'tled** (-t'ld), *adj.*

Kis'lev (kĭs'lĕf), *n.* Also **Kis'leu, Kis'lew** (-lĕf). [Heb. *Kislēw.*] See JEWISH CALENDAR.

kis'met (kĭz'mĕt; kĭs'-), *n.* Also **kis'mat** (-mŭt). [Turk. *qismet*, fr. Ar. *qismah* portion, lot.] Destiny; fate.

kiss (kĭs), *v. t. & i.* [AS. *cyssan*; akin to AS. *coss* a kiss.] **1.** To touch or press with the lips, as in love, affection, greeting, etc. **2.** To touch gently, as if fondly or caressingly; to touch or hit lightly. — *n.* **1.** Act of kissing; a touch or caress with the lips; as, a *kiss* of pardon. **2.** A gentle touch or contact. **3.** A sweetmeat made of beaten egg whites and sugar, baked lightly. — **kiss'er**, *n.*

kiss'ing bug. Any of several species of bloodsucking, venomous insects (order Hemiptera), as the conenose, which sometimes bite the lips, causing painful sores.

kist (kĭst), *n.* [ON. *kista*, fr. L. *cista.*] *Scot. & Dial.* A chest; jocularly, the counter of a shop.

kist. Var. of CIST.

kit (kĭt), *n.* A kitten.

kit, *n.* *Music.* A small violin; — more fully, **kit violin**.

kit, *n.* [MD. *kitte* (D. *kit* jug).] **1.** *Chiefly Scot. & Dial.* A wooden tub of various sizes, kinds, and uses. **2.** A set of implements or of personal effects forming part of one's equipment; an outfit; also, the box, bag, etc., in which such a kit is carried. **3.** *Colloq.* A set or collection; as, the whole *kit* and boodle of them (see BOODLE).

kitch'en (kĭch'ĕn; -ĭn), *n.* [AS. *cycene*, fr. L. *coquina*, fr. *coquere* to cook.] **1.** A room or part of an establishment appropriated to cookery. **2.** The cooking department; cuisine. **3.** *Scot. & Dial.* Food eaten as a relish to other food. — *v. t.* *Scot. & Dial.* To impart relish to; to season.

kitch'en·er (kĭch'ĕ·nẽr), *n.* A kitchen servant; a cook.

kitch'en·ette' (kĭch'ĕ·nĕt'), *n.* Also **kitch'en·et'**. A very small room or an alcove combining kitchen and pantry, with the conveniences compactly arranged.

kitchen garden. A garden in which vegetables are cultivated; — called also **kitchen ground, garth,** *or* **plot**.

kitchen midden. See MIDDEN.

kitchen police. *Mil.* Enlisted men detailed to assist the cooks in an army mess; also, their work. Abbr. *K.P.*

kitch'en·ware' (kĭch'ĕn·wâr'), *n.* Hardware for kitchen use.

kite (kīt), *n.* [AS. *cȳta.*] **1.** Any of certain birds of the hawk family (Falconidae; *Milvus, Elanus*, and other genera), mostly of rather small or medium size, with long narrow wings. See GLEDE. **2.** One who is rapacious; a sharper, rogue, or rascal. **3.** A light framework covered with paper or cloth, intended to be flown in the air at the end of a string. See BOX KITE, *Illust.* **4.** *Com.* A piece of fictitious commercial paper used for raising money or to sustain credit, as a check which represents no deposit in bank. **5.** *Aeronautics.* A form of heavier-than-air aircraft pulled by a towline, having as its only support the force of the wind moving past its surfaces. **6.** *pl. Naut. & Nav.* The lightest and, usually, the loftiest sails, supposed to be carried only in light breezes, as skysails.
— *v. i.* **1.** *Colloq. & Dial.* To fly, soar, or glide like a kite. **2.** *Com.* To get money or credit by kites. — *v. t.* *Com.* To use (a kite) to get money or credit.

kith (kĭth), *n.* [AS. *cȳththe, cȳth*, native land, fr. *cūth* known.] Familiar friends, neighbors, or relatives, collectively. *Archaic*, except in **kith and kin**, friends and kindred; now, often, kindred; relations.

kithe, kythe (kīth), *v. t.* [AS. *cȳthan*, fr. *cūth* known.] To make known; to manifest. — *v. i.* To show oneself; to become known; appear. *Both Now Scot. & Dial.*

kit'ling (kĭt'lĭng), *n.* *Now Scot. & Dial.* A kitten.

kit'ten (kĭt''n), *n.* [ME. *kitoun*, fr. OF. *caton, chaton*, dim. of *chat* cat.] A young cat; also, sometimes, the young of other animals, as rabbits. — *v. t. & i.* To give birth to (a kitten or kittens).

kit'ten·ish, *adj.* Resembling, or like that of, a kitten; playful. — **kit'ten·ish·ly**, *adv.* — **kit'ten·ish·ness**, *n.*

kit'ti·wake (kĭt'ĭ·wāk), *n.*; see PLURAL, *Note*, 3. [In imitation of its cry.] Any of several gulls (genus *Rissa*), having the hind toe short or rudimentary. See 2d GULL **b**.

kit'tle (kĭt''l), *v. t.* [MD. *kitelen.*] *Scot.* **a** To tickle; enliven. **b** To perplex. — *adj.* Ticklish; hence, difficult to manage, understand, or pronounce.

kit'ty (kĭt'ĭ), *n.*; *pl.* -TIES (-ĭz). A kitten; — a pet name.

kit'ty, *n.* [Origin uncert.] **a** A pool, as in a poker game, formed by contributions from the players for some special purpose. **b** In some card games, an extra hand or part of a hand, as one dealt to the table.

kit'ty-cor'nered. *U. S.* Var. of CATER-CORNERED.

ki'va (kē'vȧ), *n.* [Native name.] In Pueblo Indian architecture, a ceremonial chamber or structure.

Ki·wa'ni·an (kē·wä'nĭ·ăn), *n.* A member of any of a large number of clubs (**Ki·wa'nis** [-nĭs] **Clubs**), in the United States and Canada, having the same constitution, the first organized in 1915 at Detroit. The Kiwanian principles are fair dealing and the observance of the golden rule.

ki'wi (kē'wĭ), *n.* [Maori.] An apteryx. See APTERYX, *Illust.*

Klam'ath weed (klăm'ăth). [From *Klamath* River, California.] The St.-John's-wort *Hypericum perforatum.*

Klan (klăn), *n.* The Ku Klux Klan, or one of its local units. — **Klans'man** (klănz'măn), *n.*

Klebs'-Löf'fler ba·cil'lus (klāps'lûf'lẽr). See DIPHTHERIA.

klepht (klĕft), *n.* [NGr. *klephtēs* robber, fr. Gr. *kleptēs.*] One of the Greeks who, after the Turkish conquest of Greece, formed communities of brigands.

klep'to·ma'ni·a (klĕp'tō·mā'nĭ·ȧ), *n.* [NL., fr. Gr. *kleptēs* thief + *mania.*] A persistent neurotic impulse to steal, esp. without economic motive.

klep'to·ma'ni·ac (-ăk), *n.* A person having kleptomania.

klieg eyes (klēg). Eyes inflamed from excessive exposure to light from klieg lights; also, the affliction itself.

klieg, *or* **kleig, light** (klēg). [After *Kliegl* brothers, the inventors.] A type of arc light, used in taking motion pictures, with carbons that emit a light rich in actinic rays.

Kling'sor (klĭng'zōr), *n.* [G.] In Wagner's *Parsifal*, a magician who, having been refused admission to the knighthood of the Grail, takes revenge by setting fair women to seduce the knights, from whose chief, Amfortas, he takes the sacred spear.

klip'spring'er (klĭp'sprĭng'ẽr), *n.*; see PLURAL, *Note*, 3. [D., lit., cliff springer.] A small African antelope (*Oreotragus oreotragus*) somewhat like the chamois in habits, found from Cape Colony to Somaliland.

klis'ter (klĭs'tẽr), *n.* [Nor.] *Skiing.* Soft wax used esp. for corn snow or crust.

‖**kloof** (*Cape D.* klōōf), *n.* [D.] *S. Africa.* A deep glen; ravine; gorge.

klys'tron (klĭs'trŏn), *n.* [From Gr. *klystēr* syringe + *-tron* as in *electron.*] *Physics.* An electron tube that converts direct current into ultra-high-frequency current through electromagnetic sorting of electronic velocities.

knack (năk), *n.* A sharp sound; a crack. — *v. t. & i.* *Now Dial.* To strike sharply; to crack.

knack, *n.* **1.** A trick; device; now esp., a clever way of doing something; an ingenious expedient. **2.** Aptness at doing something; facility; dexterity. **3.** A clever contrivance; a knickknack. — **Syn.** See GIFT.

knack'er (năk'ẽr), *n.* **1.** *Eng.* One who buys and slaughters worn-out or useless horses and sells their flesh for dog's meat, etc. **2.** A buyer of old ships, houses, etc., for their materials.

knap (năp), *n.* [AS. *cnæp, cnæpp*, top, knob, button.] A top or crest (of a hill); a summit.

knap (năp), *v. t. & i.*; KNAPPED (năpt); KNAP′PING. *Now Dial.* **1.** To rap; snap. **2.** To shape or dress by breaking off pieces, as flints; to chip. **3.** To bite smartly; to snap; nibble. — *n. Dial.* A sharp or abrupt blow; a rap.

knap′sack′ (năp′săk′), *n.* [D. *knapzak,* fr. *knappen* to eat + *zak* bag.] A case of canvas or leather for carrying on the back a soldier's necessaries or a traveler's clothing, etc.; — disting. from *haversack.*

knap′weed′ (năp′wēd′), *n.* [From KNAP top.] A plant of a genus (*Centaurea*) of the aster family; esp., a common European plant (*C. nigra*) having knoblike heads of purple flowers. See STAR THISTLE.

knar (när), *n.* A knot or burr in wood. — **knarred** (närd), *adj.* — **knar′ry** (när′ĭ), *adj.*

knave (nāv), *n.* [AS. *cnafa* a boy, youth.] **1.** *Archaic.* A boy servant; hence, a male servant; also, a man of humble birth or position. **2.** A tricky, deceitful fellow; a rogue. **3.** A playing card marked with the figure of a servant or soldier; a jack.

knav′er·y (nāv′ẽr·ĭ), *n.; pl.* -ERIES (-ĭz). **1.** Practices of a knave; petty villainy; fraud; rascality. **2.** *Obs.* Roguishness; mischievous sportiveness.

knav′ish (nāv′ĭsh), *adj.* Like or characteristic of a knave. — **knav′ish·ly,** *adv.* — **knav′ish·ness,** *n.*

knead (nēd), *v. t.* [AS. *cnedan.*] **1.** To work and press into a mass, as dough, usually with the hands. **2.** To treat or form as by kneading; to mix or operate on as if by kneading. — **knead′er** (-ẽr), *n.*

knee (nē), *n.* [AS. *cnēo, cnēow.*] **1.** In man, the joint, or the region of the joint, in the middle part of the leg. **2.** In animals: **a** The joint in the hind limbs of vertebrates homologous with the knee of man. See DOG, *Illust.* **b** In the forelimb of hoofed quadrupeds, the carpal joint (corresponding to the wrist in man). **c** In birds, the tarsal joint. **3.** Something suggestive of the human knee, esp. when bent, as a crook in a tree branch. **4.** That part of a garment which covers the knee. — *v. t.*; KNEED (nēd); KNEE′ING. To strike or touch with the knee.

knee action. *Automobiles.* A type of front-wheel suspension permitting independent vertical movement of each front wheel. — **knee′-ac′tion** (2), *adj.*

knee′cap′ (nē′kăp′), *n.* The patella; kneepan.

knee′-deep′ (-dēp′; 2), *adj.* **1.** Rising to the knees; knee-high. **2.** Sunk to the knees; as, men *knee-deep* in water.

knee′-high′, *adj.* Rising or reaching upward to the knees.

knee′hole′ (nē′hōl′), *n.* An open space for the knees, as under a desk.

knee jerk. A kick produced by a light blow on the tendon below the kneecap.

kneel (nēl), *v. i.*; KNELT (nĕlt) or KNEELED (nēld); KNEEL′ING. [AS. *cnēowlian.*] To bend the knee; to fall or rest on the knees. — *n.* Act of kneeling. — **kneel′er** (nēl′ẽr), *n.*

knee′pad′ (nē′păd′), *n.* A pad to protect stockings, etc., at the knee.

knee′pan′ (-păn′), *n.* The patella; kneecap.

knee′-sprung′, *adj. Veter.* Having the knees bent when they should normally be straight, as from straining, etc.

knell (nĕl), *v. t.* [AS. *cnyllan.*] **1.** *Obs.* To ring, esp. to toll (a bell). **2.** To summon by or as by a knell. **3.** To announce by or as by a knell. — *v. i.* To ring; esp., to toll; hence, to sound as a warning or evil omen. — *n.* The stroke or sound of a bell, esp. when tolled at a funeral; hence, a warning of, or a sound indicating, death.

knelt (nĕlt), *past & past part.* of KNEEL.

knew (nū; 114), *past* of KNOW.

Knick′er·bock′er (nĭk′ẽr·bŏk′ẽr), *n.* **1.** A descendant of the old Dutch settlers of New York; more widely, any New Yorker; — from Diedrich *Knickerbocker,* the pretended author of Irving's (1809) *History of New York.* **2.** [*not cap.*] *pl.* A style of short breeches, gathered at the knee; also, the costume of which these are a part.

knick′ers (nĭk′ẽrz), *n. pl.* Short for KNICKERBOCKERS; hence, a woman's undergarment similar to bloomers.

knick′knack′ (nĭk′năk′), *n.* [Redupl. of KNACK.] A small article, as of furniture, dress, etc., rather for ornament than for use; a gimcrack; a gewgaw.

knife (nīf), *n.; pl.* KNIVES (nīvz). [AS. *cnīf.*] **1.** An instrument consisting (in its modern form) of a thin blade, usually of steel and having a sharp edge for cutting, fastened to a handle. **2.** A weapon consisting of or like a knife. **3.** *Mach.* A cutting blade or tool in a machine. — *v. t.*; KNIFED (nīft); KNIF′ING (nīf′ĭng). **1.** To use a knife on; cut or stab with a knife. **2.** *Slang, U. S.* To try to defeat by underhand means, esp. in politics. — **knife′like′** (-līk′), *adj.*

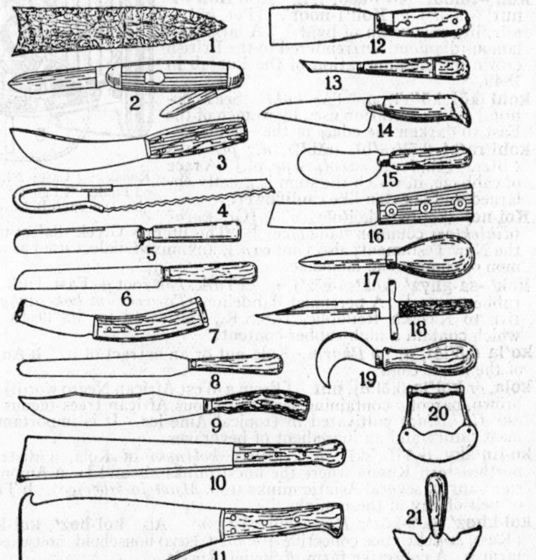

Knives. 1 Indian Jasper Blade; 2 Pocketknife; 3 Skinning Knife; 4 Bread Knife; 5 Table Knife; 6 Goldbeater's Knife; 7 Farrier's Knife; 8 Palette Knife; 9 Carving Knife; 10 Corn Knife; 11 Cane Knife; 12 Putty Knife; 13 Wood Carver's Knife; 14 Felt Knife; 15 Paper Hanger's Knife; 16 Hacking Knife; 17 Oyster Knife; 18 Hunting, or Bowie, Knife; 19 Oilcloth Knife; 20, 21 Chopping Knives. See also DRAWKNIFE, *Illust.*

knife′-edge′, *n.* **1.** Edge of a knife, or an edge likened to that of a knife in sharpness. **2.** *Mach.* A sharp hardened steel wedge used as a fulcrum for a lever beam in instruments of precision, as scales, testing machines, etc.

knight (nīt), *n.* [AS. *cniht, cneoht,* boy, youth, attendant, military follower.] **1.** A military attendant or follower; hence, one who devotes himself to a lady as her attendant or champion. **2. a** In feudal times, a mounted man-at-arms serving a superior; esp., one who, after serving as page and squire, was admitted to a special military rank and bound to chivalrous conduct. **b** In modern times, a man upon whom a corresponding dignity has been conferred by a sovereign. In Great Britain the knight ranks next below a baronet. He has the title *Sir* prefixed to his name. The dignity is not hereditary. **3.** A person of ancient history regarded as of a rank equivalent to that of knight. **4.** A member of an order or society, or the holder of a degree or rank in such an order or society, whose official title is "knight." **5.** *Chess.* A piece, usually bearing a horse's head, having a move of two squares such that it passes over any adjacent square whether occupied or not, and alights on a square of different color from that from which it started. Abbr. *Kt* (no period). — *v. t.* To dub or create (one) a knight.

knight bachelor; *pl.* KNIGHTS BACHELORS. A knight of the most ancient, but the lowest, order of English knights.

knight′-er′rant, *n.; pl.* KNIGHTS-ERRANT. A wandering knight; a knight traveling in search of adventures in which to exhibit military skill, prowess, and generosity.

knight′-er′rant·ry, *n.; pl.* KNIGHT-ERRANTRIES (-rĭz). The character or actions of knights-errant; practice of wandering in quest of adventures; quixotic conduct.

knight′hood (nīt′hŏŏd), *n.* **1.** The rank, dignity, profession, or vocation of a knight, or of knights as a class. **2.** Knightliness; chivalry. **3.** The whole body of knights.

knight′ly, *adj.* Of or pertaining to a knight; chivalrous; also, made up of knights. — *adv.* In a knightly manner. — **knight′li·ness,** *n.*

Knights of Columbus. A fraternal and benevolent society of Roman Catholic men, founded in 1882.

Knights of St. John of Jerusalem. See HOSPITALER, 3.

Knight Templar. 1. *pl.* KNIGHTS TEMPLARS. See TEMPLAR, **1. 2.** *pl.* KNIGHTS TEMPLAR. A member of a certain order of Freemasonry, claimed to be a lineal descendant of the ancient order of Templars.

knit (nĭt), *v. t.*; KNIT or KNIT′TED; KNIT′TING. [AS. *cnyttan;* akin to E. KNOT.] **1.** *Archaic & Dial.* To tie together, as cord; to fasten by or as by knots. **2.** To form, as a fabric, by interlacing a single yarn or thread in loops, by means of long thin bluntly pointed rods (***knitting needles***). Cf. CROCHET. **3.** To bring or bind together as by knitting; to interlock; as, to *knit* the hands; to conjoin, cement, consolidate; as, to *knit* the parts of a fractured bone. **4.** To draw together; to contract into wrinkles; as, he *knit* his brow in thought. **5.** To bind by a social, legal, or similar tie; as, to *knit* persons together by marriage. — *v. i.* **1.** To form a fabric by interlacing a single yarn or thread in a series of loops. **2.** To become drawn together or contracted into wrinkles; also, to become compact; to consolidate. **3.** To become united closely; to grow together, as bones. — **knit′ter** (nĭt′ẽr), *n.*

knit′ting (nĭt′ĭng), *n.* **a** The action of one who knits. **b** The work or product made by one who knits.

knit′wear′ (nĭt′wâr′), *n.* Knit goods for clothing.

knives (nīvz), *n., pl.* of KNIFE.

knob (nŏb), *n.* **1.** A rounded protuberance or mass; a bunch; lump. **2.** A knoblike ornament or handle; as, a door*knob.* **3.** A rounded hill or mountain, esp. an isolated one. — **knobbed** (nŏbd), *adj.* — **knob′by** (nŏb′ĭ), *adj.*

knob′ker′rie (-kĕr′ĭ), *n.* [S. Afr. D. *knopkirie,* fr. D. *knop*hout, knotty stick + Hottentot *kīrri* club.] A short club with a knobbed end used as a missile weapon, esp. by Kaffirs; — called also **knob′stick′** (-stĭk′).

knock (nŏk), *v. i. & t.* [AS. *cnocian, cnucian.*] **1.** To strike a sharp or resounding blow; to rap. **2.** To drive or be driven against something; to collide; bump. **3.** Of machinery, to rattle or make a pounding noise, as, in an internal-combustion engine, from a detonation of the charge. **4.** *Slang, U. S.* To find fault; to criticize captiously.

knock down. **a** To strike down; hence, to vanquish. **b** To assign to a bidder at an auction, as by the fall of the hammer. **c** To separate (a manufactured article) into parts for convenience of transportation or storage; — opposed to *set up.* — ***knock off.*** **a** To leave off (work, etc.). **b** To deduct; as, to *knock off* five dollars from a bill. **c** To cease as from work; to stop working. — ***knock out.*** To defeat; vanquish; specif.: **a** *Baseball,* more fully ***knock out of the box.*** To cause (a pitcher) to retire or be taken from the box by hitting the balls pitched by him hard or often. **b** *Pugilism.* To disable (an opponent) so that he is unable to rise before the referee has completed a count of ten seconds. — ***knock up.*** **a** To arouse by knocking. **b** *Colloq., Eng.* To tire out; to fatigue.

— *n.* **1.** An act of knocking; specif.: **a** A sharp or resounding blow. **b** In an internal-combustion engine, the sound produced by improper operation, due either to a mechanical defect, as a loose connecting rod, or improperly timed or uneven combustion; also, detonation. **2.** *Slang, U. S.* A piece of severe faultfinding.

knock′a·bout′ (nŏk′ȧ·bout′), *adj.* **1.** Marked by roughness; boisterous. **2.** Characterized by, or suitable for, knocking about, or traveling hither and thither. — *n. Naut.* A sloop-rigged yacht of 21-foot water line, without a bowsprit, designed for sailing on open waters.

knock′down′ (nŏk′doun′), *adj.* **1.** Of such force as to fell or overthrow; overwhelming. **2.** Made so as to be capable of being knocked down or taken apart, as for transportation. — *n.* **1.** That which knocks one down. **2.** A knocking down; a felling by a blow. **3.** Something that takes apart, for packing or removal, as a piece of furniture.

knock′er (-ẽr), *n.* One who or that which knocks; as: **a** One who raps at a door. **b** A kind of hammer hinged to a door, with which to knock for admittance.

knock′-knee′, *n.* A condition in which the knees bend in so as to touch each other in walking. — **knock′-kneed′,** *adj.*

knock′out′ (nŏk′out′), *adj.* That knocks out; as, a *knockout* blow. — *n.* **1.** Act of knocking out, or state of being knocked out. **2.** *Slang, U.S.* A striking or attractive person or thing. **3.** *Boxing.* Act of knocking out an opponent; also, a knockout blow.

knoll (nōl), *v. & n. Archaic & Dial. Eng.* Knell.

knoll, *n.* [AS. *cnoll.*] A little round hill; a mound.

knop (nŏp), *n.* A knob; a stud, boss, or bunch.

knosp (nŏsp), *n.* [G. *knospe* bud.] A knop; a boss.

knot (nŏt), *n.* [Origin unknown.] A sandpiper (*Calidris canutus*) which breeds in Arctic regions and migrates south.

knot, *n.* [AS. *cnotta.*] **1.** An interlacement of the parts of one or more flexible bodies, as cordage, forming a lump or knob; any tie or fastening formed with a cord, rope, or the like, including bends, hitches, splices, etc. **2.** Figuratively: **a** Something not easily solved; a difficulty; a problem. **b** A bond of union; a tie; specif., the tie or bond of marriage. **3.** A bow, cockade, or epaulet. **4.** A place where several or many lines, nerves, etc., meet or intersect and form a thickening. **5.** A figure the lines of which are interwoven, as in embroidery, etc. **6.** A knob or protuberance, as in a muscle. **7.** A cluster of persons or things; group. **8. a** Any swelling in the tissues of a plant, as the node of a grass; hence, the hard, irregular lump formed at the point of insertion of a branch in a tree trunk; also, a cross section of this in the surface of wood. **b** Any fungous disease of trees characterized by the development of abnormal excrescences. **9.** *Archaic.* A flower garden elaborate in design. **10.** *Naut.* **a** A division of the log line, serving to measure the rate of a vessel's motion. Hence: **b** A unit of speed, equivalent to one nautical mile, or 6,080.20 feet, an hour; as, when a ship goes eight nautical miles an hour, her speed is eight *knots.* **c** Loosely, a nautical mile.
— *v. t.;* KNOT′TED; KNOT′TING. **1.** To tie in or with, or form into, a knot or knots. **2.** To unite closely or intricately; to entangle. — *v. i.* **1.** To form knots, as in a cord; to become entangled. **2.** To knit knots for fringe or trimming.

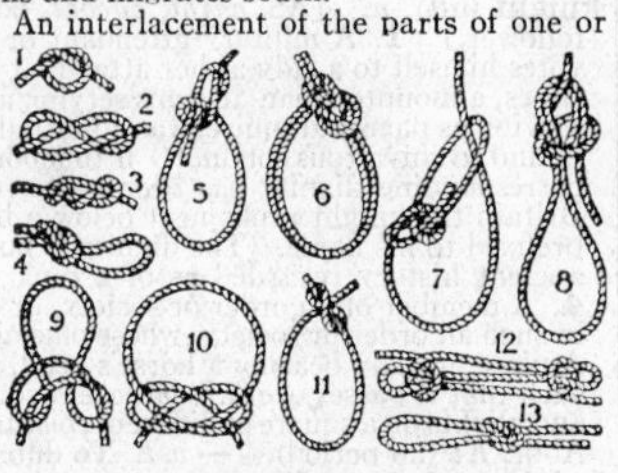
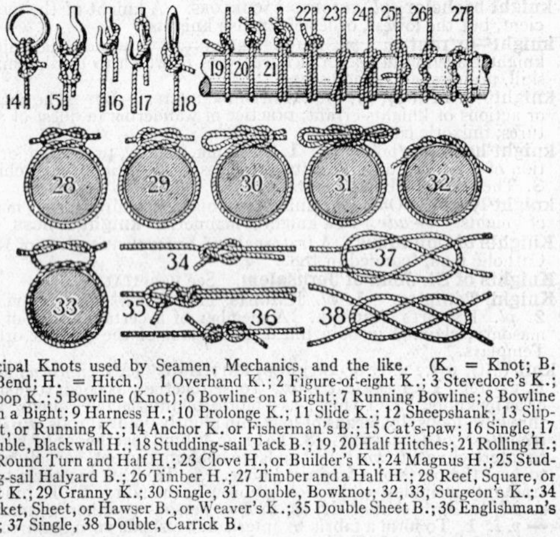

Principal Knots used by Seamen, Mechanics, and the like. (K. = Knot; B. = Bend; H. = Hitch.) 1 Overhand K.; 2 Figure-of-eight K.; 3 Stevedore's K.; 4 Loop K.; 5 Bowline (Knot); 6 Bowline on a Bight; 7 Running Bowline; 8 Bowline with a Bight; 9 Harness H.; 10 Prolonge K.; 11 Slide K.; 12 Sheepshank; 13 Slipknot, or Running K.; 14 Anchor K. or Fisherman's B.; 15 Cat's-paw; 16 Single, 17 Double, Blackwall H.; 18 Studding-sail Tack B.; 19, 20 Half Hitches; 21 Rolling H.; 22 Round Turn and Half H.; 23 Clove H., or Builder's K.; 24 Magnus H.; 25 Studding-sail Halyard B.; 26 Timber H.; 27 Timber and a Half H.; 28 Reef, Square, or Flat K.; 29 Granny K.; 30 Single, 31 Double, Bowknot; 32, 33, Surgeon's K.; 34 Becket, Sheet, or Hawser B., or Weaver's K.; 35 Double Sheet B.; 36 Englishman's Tie; 37 Single, 38 Double, Carrick B.

knot′grass′ (nŏt′grȧs′; 9), *n.* **a** A cosmopolitan weed (*Polygonum aviculare,* family Polygonaceae) having jointed stems, linear leaves, and minute greenish flowers. **b** Any of several grasses with geniculate stems, as oat grass, etc.

knot′hole′ (-hōl′), *n.* A hole in a board, tree trunk, etc., where a knot or branch has come out.

knot stitch. Any of a variety of stitches which are used in embroidery to form lines ornamented at intervals with knots, and in drawn work to tie threads. See STITCH, *Illust.*

knot′ted (nŏt′ĕd; -ĭd), *adj.* **1.** Tied in or with a knot or knots. **2.** Full of knots or knobs; gnarled. **3.** Having intersecting lines or figures; laid out in elaborate patterns; as, a *knotted* flower garden. **4.** Entangled; puzzling. **5.** Ornamented with knots, or bosses.

knot′ter (nŏt′ẽr), *n.* **1.** One that knots, as a machine for tying knots. **2.** One who removes knots, as from yarn.

knot′ty (nŏt′ĭ), *adj.;* KNOT′TI·ER (-ĭ·ẽr); KNOT′TI·EST. **1.** Full of knots; tied in knots; knotted. **2.** Difficult; perplexing; puzzling. — **Syn.** See COMPLEX. — **knot′ti·ness,** *n.*

knot′weed′ (nŏt′wēd′), *n.* Knapweed; also, knotgrass.

knout (nout; nōōt; *sometimes* k′nōōt), *n.* [Russ. *knut.*] A type of whip for flogging criminals. — *v. t.* To punish with the knout.

know (nō), *v. t.;* KNEW (nū; 114); KNOWN (nōn); KNOW′ING. [AS. *cnāwan.*] **1.** To perceive directly; to recognize; to discern the character of; hence, to recognize as distinct from something else; to distinguish. **2.** To recognize as valid or as fact on the basis of information possessed or of one's understanding. **3.** To be more or less familiar with the person, character, etc., of; as, to *know* an author. **4.** To have sexual intercourse with. **5.** To have practical knowledge of; to be skilled in; as, to *know* carpentry. — *v. i.* **1.** To have knowledge. **2.** To be or become cognizant. — *n.* Knowledge; — chiefly in colloq. phrase ***in the know,*** having special, often somewhat exclusive, knowledge or information. — **know′a·ble,** *adj. & n.* — **know′-er,** *n.*

knowe, know (nou; nō), *n. Scot.* A knoll or mound.

know′-how′ (nō′hou′), *n.* Technical expertness and accumulated practical skill in lining up a complicated operation for smooth and efficient execution.

know′ing (nō′ĭng), *n.* Acquaintance; cognizance; hence, *Obs.,* an experience. — *adj.* **1.** Informed; intelligent. **2.** Having or displaying discernment; shrewd; wide-awake. — **Syn.** See INTELLIGENT. — **know′ing·ly,** *adv.* — **know′ing·ness,** *n.*

knowl′edge (nŏl′ĕj; -ĭj; *by some, esp. in Brit. usage,* nō′lĕj; -lĭj), *n.; pl.* KNOWLEDGES (-ĕz; -ĭz). **1.** Familiarity gained by actual experience; practical skill. **2.** Acquaintance with fact; hence, scope of information; as, it has not come to my *knowledge.* **3.** The act or state of understanding; clear perception of truth; cognition. **4.** That which is gained and preserved by knowing; enlightenment; learning; also, broadly, the sum of information conserved by civilization; — often personified. **5.** A thing that is or may be known; — chiefly in the *pl.* **6.** Sexual intercourse; as, carnal *knowledge.*

knowl′edge·a·ble (nŏl′ĕj·ȧ·b′l; nŏl′ĭj-), *adj. Colloq.* Having or showing knowledge or shrewdness.

known (nōn), *past part.* of KNOW.

know′-noth′ing, *n.* **1.** An ignoramus; also, an agnostic. **2.** [*caps.*] *U.S. Hist.* A member of a secret political party (*American party*) which flourished 1853–56 and advocated rigid measures to restrict the political power of the foreign-born population.

knuck′le (nŭk′′l), *n.* [ME. *knokel, knokil.*] **1.** The rounded prominence formed by the ends of the two adjacent bones at a joint; also, the joint itself; — in man now commonly restricted to those at the joints of the fingers. **2.** The knee or hock joint of a quadruped, used chiefly for soups, stews, etc. See BEEF, *Illust.* **3.** *pl.* A knuckle-duster; as, brass *knuckles.* **4.** *Mech.* Any of the joining parts of a hinge through which the pin or rivet passes; also, a knuckle joint. **5.** *Shipbuilding.* The meeting of any two surfaces of a vessel at an angle instead of a continuous curve. — *v. i.;* KNUCK′LED (-′ld); KNUCK′LING (-lĭng). **1.** To place the knuckles on the ground in shooting a marble; — often with *down;* as, to *knuckle* at the taw. **2.** To yield; to submit; — usually with *down* or *under.* **3.** To apply oneself earnestly; as, to *knuckle* to work.

knuckle ball. *Baseball.* A slow ball delivered with the thumb and little finger grasping the sides of the ball and the first joints of the remaining fingers bent and pressing against the top of the ball.

knuck′le·bone′ (nŭk′′l·bōn′), *n.* The bone of a knuckle joint; — in man, now only of a finger; in an animal, a limb bone with a knob at the joint end, or the knob itself.

knuck′le–dust′er, *n.* A metal weapon fitting over the front of the doubled fist.

knuckle joint. **a** A joint forming a knuckle. **b** *Mach.* A hinge joint in which a projection with an eye on one piece enters a jaw between two corresponding projections with eyes on another piece, and is retained by a pin.

knur (nûr), *n.* [ME. *knorre.*] A knot, as in a tree trunk; a gnarl.

knurl (nûrl), *n.* **1.** A knot in wood; a knob; also, a ridge or one of a series of small beads on a metal surface, as on a circular nut, to aid in gripping it. **2.** *Scot.* A thickset person. — **knurled** (nûrld), *adj.*

K.O. (kā′ō′). A knockout. — *v. t.;* K.O.′D (-ōd′); K.O.′ING. To knock out.

ko′a (kō′ȧ), *n.* A Hawaiian timber tree (*Acacia koa*) with valuable fine-grained wood.

ko·a′la (kō·ä′lȧ; *native pron.* kōō′lȧ), *n.* [Native name.] An Australian arboreal marsupial (*Phascolarctos cinereus*), about two feet long, with large hairy ears, gray fur, and sharp claws. It feeds upon eucalyptus leaves.

ko′bold (kō′bŏld; -bōld), *n.* [G.] In German folklore: **a** A domestic spirit, often mischievous. **b** A gnome haunting underground places.

Ko′dak (kō′dăk), *n.* A trade-mark applied (originally) to a small hand camera.

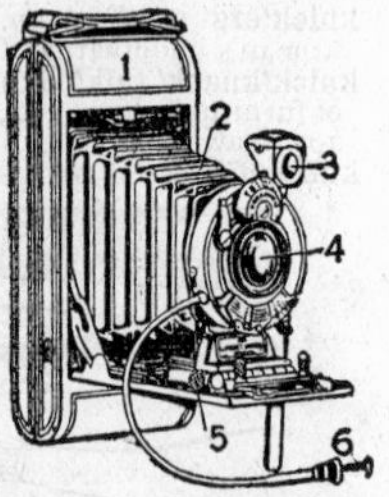

Kodak. 1 Case; 2 Bellows; 3 Finder; 4 Lens; 5 Focusing Device; 6 Release.

Ko′di·ak bear. See KADIAK BEAR.

ko′el (kō′ĕl), *n.* [Hind. *koel, koyal,* fr. Skr. *kokila.*] Any of several cuckoos (genus *Eudynamys*) of India, the East Indies, and Australia.

Koh′–i·noor′ (kō′ĭ·nŏŏr′), *n.* Also **Koh′–i·nur′** (-nŏŏr′), *or* **Koh′i·noor′.** [Per. *kōh-i-nūr,* lit., mountain of light.] A large and famous diamond, surrendered to the British crown on the annexation of the Punjab in 1849.

kohl (kōl; kō′h′l), *n.* [Ar. *kuḥl.* See ALCOHOL.] A preparation used by women of the East to darken the edges of the eyelids.

kohl′ra′bi (kōl′rä′bĭ; -răb′ĭ), *n.; pl.* -BIES (-bĭz). [G., fr. It. *cavoli rape,* pl.] A race of cabbage, in which the stem is greatly enlarged and is eaten like cauliflower.

Koi·ne′ (koi·nā′; koi′nē), *n.* [Gr. *koinē* (*dialektos*) common (language).] The literary Greek dialect used in the New Testament; also [*not cap.*], any mixed dialect used as a common or commercial language.

kok′–sa·ghyz′ (kōk′sȧ·gēz′), *n.* [Turk. *kök* root + East Turk. *sagïz* rubber, gum.] A perennial dandelion (*Taraxacum kok-saghyz*) native to Kazakh Republic, U.S.S.R., cultivated for its fleshy roots, which contain a high rubber content.

ko′la (kō′lȧ), *n.* **a** *Pharm.* Kola nut or an extract of it. **b** Any tree of the genus *Cola.*

kola, *or* **kol′la** (kŏl′ȧ), **nut.** [From a West African Negro word.] The brown, narcotic-containing seed of various African trees (genus *Cola,* esp. *C. nitida*) cultivated in tropical America. It is important as a masticatory and an ingredient of beverages.

ko·lin′sky (kō·lĭn′skĭ), *n.* [Russ. *kolinski* of Kola, a district in northeastern Russia where the finest minks abound.] **a** Among furriers, any of several Asiatic minks (esp. *Mustela siberica*). **b** The fur or pelt of any of these minks.

kol·khoz′ (kŏl·kŏz′; *Russ.* kŭl·κôs′), *n.* Also **kol·hoz′, kol·khos′.** [Russ. *kollektivnoe* collective + *khozyaĭstvo* household, housekeeping, farm.] A collective farm of Soviet Russia.

Kom′in·tern′. Var. of COMINTERN (see INTERNATIONAL, *n.,* **2 c**).

kon·ta′ki·on (kŏn·tä′kĭ·ŏn; *Gr.* kôn·tä′kyē·ôn), *n.* [MGr.] *Eastern Ch.* **a** A short hymn in praise of a saint. **b** A small book or folder containing the prayers of a priest or deacon at a given service.

koo′doo (kōō′dōō). Var. of KUDU.

kook′a·bur′ra (kŏŏk′ȧ·bŭr′ȧ; kŏŏk′ȧ·bŭr′ȧ), *n.* [Native name.] *Australia.* = LAUGHING JACKASS.

koo′ra·jong (koo͞o′rȧ·jŏng). Var. of KURRAJONG.

‖**kop** (kŏp), n. [S. Afr. D., fr. D. kop head.] S. Africa. Hill; mountain.

ko′peck (kō′pĕk), n. Also **ko′pek, co′peck**, etc. [Russ. kopeĭka.] A minor Russian bronze (orig. silver) coin and money of account, $\frac{1}{100}$ ruble. Abbr. kop.

‖**kop′je** (kŏp′ĭ), n. [S. Afr. D., dim. of kop.] S. Africa. A hillock; a small kop.

kor (kôr; kōr), n. [Heb. kōr.] An ancient Hebrew measure of capacity; a homer.

Ko·ran′ (kō·răn′; -rän′; Ar. kō͞or·än′), n. [Ar. Qur′ān, fr. qara′a to read.] The scriptures of the Mohammedans, containing the professed revelations to Mohammed.

Ko·re′an (kō·rē′ăn), n. 1. A member of the native race of Korea, a mixed race of Mongoloid type. 2. The language of the Koreans, an agglutinative tongue related to Japanese. — **Ko·re′an**, adj.

ko′ru·na (kô′ro͞o·nȧ), n.; pl. KORUNY (-nĭ), KORUN (kô′ro͞on). [Czech, fr. L. corona.] The monetary unit of Czechoslovakia, stabilized (1945) at two United States cents. Abbr. K or (pl.) Kč or Kčs

kos (kōs), n. sing. & pl. [Hind. kos, fr. Skr. krośa.] A measure of distance in India varying from 1½ to 3 miles.

ko′sher (kō′shēr), adj. Also **ka′sher** (kä′-). [Heb. kāshēr fit, proper.] 1. Jewish Relig. Sanctioned by Jewish law; especially, designating food that may be eaten as ritually clean. 2. Slang. Right; legitimate; proper; genuine. — n. Kosher food; also, a kosher shop.

kosh′er (kŏsh′ēr), v. t. To kasher.

ko′tow′ (kō′tou′). Var. of KOWTOW.

kou′mis, kou′miss, kou′myss. Vars. of KUMISS.

kour′bash. Var. of KURBASH.

kow′tow′ (kou′tou′; kou′tou′), v. i. [Chin. (Pek.) k′o¹-t′ou² knockhead.] 1. Chinese. To kneel and touch the forehead to the ground by way of homage, worship, or deep respect. 2. Hence, to treat (one) with obsequious deference. — n. Chinese. The prostration made by kneeling and touching the forehead to the ground.

kraal (kräl), n. [D., a village, enclosure, park, fr. Pg. curral a cattle pen.] 1. A village of South African natives; also, the social unit which the kraal represents. 2. S. Africa. An enclosure for cattle or sheep. — v. t. To confine in a kraal.

kraft (kráft), n. Also **kraft paper**. [G., strength.] A strong paper, usually dark brown, made from sulfate pulp.

Krag (kräg; krăg), n. Colloq. Mil. A Krag-Jörgensen rifle.

Krag′-Jör′gen·sen ri′fle (-yûr′gĕn·sĕn). [After Capt. O. Krag and E. Jörgensen of Norway, the inventors.] A type of breechloading rifle, used by Denmark and Norway. With modifications, it was the standard arm of the United States Army from 1892 to 1898.

krait (krīt), n. [Hind. karait.] A very venomous snake (Bungarus coeruleus) of India, allied to the cobra, which causes more deaths than any other snake.

kra′ken (krä′kĕn; krä′-), n. [Nor. dial. krake (the final n is the article).] A fabulous Scandinavian sea monster.

kra′ter, n. See CRATER, 1.

K ration (kā). U. S. Army. A heatproof and coldproof 32 oz. package containing three boxes of concentrated foods providing three meals (3726 calories) including bread, meat, beverage, and confection.

krem′lin (krĕm′lĭn), n. [F., fr. Russ. kreml′.] Russia. The citadel of a city, esp. [cap.] of Moscow.

kreut′zer (kroit′sēr), n. Also **kreu′zer** (kroit′sĕr). [G. kreuzer.] An old German or Austrian copper coin worth about half a cent.

krieg′spiel (krēg′spēl′), ‖**Kriegs′spiel** (krēks′shpēl′; krēgz′spēl′), n. [G. kriegsspiel, fr. krieg war + spiel game.] A game in which blocks, pins, flags, etc., representing contending forces, guns, etc., are moved about according to rules representing conditions of actual warfare.

Kriem′hild (krēm′hĭlt), n. [MHG. Chriemhilt, Kriemhilt.] In the Nibelungenlied, the wife of Siegfried. After his death she marries Etzel and instigates the slaughter of her kinsmen in revenge for Hagen′s murder of Siegfried. See BRUNHILD.

krim′mer (krĭm′ēr), **crim′mer**, n. [G. krimmer, fr. Krim Crimea.] A gray fur resembling astrakhan, made from the pelts of young lambs of the Crimean Peninsula region. Cf. ASTRAKHAN.

kris (krēs). Var. of CREESE.

Krish′na (krĭsh′nȧ), n. [Skr. Kṛṣṇa.] Hindu Relig. The eighth avatar of Vishnu and one of the most widely worshiped of the Hindu deities. — **Krish′na·ism** (-ĭz′m), n.

Kriss Krin′gle (krĭs krĭng′g′l). [G. Christkindl, -del, Christ child, Christmas gift, a dim. of Christkind.] St. Nicholas, or Santa Claus.

kró′na (krō′nȧ), n.; pl. KRÓNUR (-nĕr). [Icel.] The monetary unit of Iceland, containing 100 aurar. See MONEY, Tables.

kro′na (krō′nȧ; Sw. krō͞o′nȧ), n.; pl. KRONOR (-nôr). [Sw.] The monetary unit and a silver coin of Sweden, containing 100 öre. See MONEY, Tables.

kro′ne (krō′nĕ), n.; pl. KRONER (-nĕr). [Dan.] The gold monetary unit of Denmark and Norway, equal to 100 öre; — called also crown. See MONEY, Tables.

kro′ne (krō′nĕ), n.; pl. KRONEN (-nĕn). [G.] a The German gold 10-mark coin, discontinued in 1924. b The former monetary unit of Austria-Hungary (1892–1925); also, the corresponding coin, equivalent to 100 heller.

Kro′nos (krō′nŏs). Var. of CRONUS.

kroon (kro͞on), n.; pl. KROONS (kro͞onz) or KROONI (kro͞o′nĭ). [Estonian kron.] Formerly, the coin unit of Estonia, equal to the Swedish krona.

krul′ler. Var. of CRULLER.

kry′o-. Var. of CRYO-.

kryp′ton (krĭp′tŏn), n. [NL., fr. Gr. krypton, neut. of kryptos hidden.] Chem. An element, one of the inert gases, occurring in air (one volume in about a million). Symbol, Kr; at. no., 36; at. wt., 83.80.

Kshat′ri·ya (kshăt′rĭ·yȧ), n. [Skr. kṣatriya.] One belonging to the governing and military caste, second of the four great Hindu castes.

ku′chen (ko͞o′kĕn), n. [G. See CAKE.] A variety of German cake, typically one made from sweetened yeast dough, rolled thin, covered with a coating of sugar and spices, and baked.

ku′dos (kū′dŏs; ko͞o′dŏs), n. [Gr. kydos glory.] Colloq. Glory; fame; renown; praise.

ku′du (ko͞o′do͞o), n. [Hottentot.] A large grayish-brown African antelope (Strepsiceros strepsiceros).

Ku′fic (kū′fĭk), adj. Also **Cu′fic**. Of or pertaining to Al Kufa, or Cufa, a town on the Euphrates, south of Babylon; — applied esp. to an Arabic alphabet early employed there.

Ku′–Klux′, Ku′klux′ (kū′klŭks′; ko͞o′-), n. [Gr. kyklos circle.] U. S. Hist. a A secret political organization in the Southern States, active after the close of the Civil War, and having for its chief aim the establishment of white control; — called also **Ku–Klux Klan**. b Hence, a member of the Ku-Klux.

Ku Klux Klan. a = KU-KLUX **a. b** A fraternal secret order, ostensibly reviving the Ku-Klux, incorporated in Georgia in 1915 as the Invisible Empire, Knights of the Ku Klux Klan. Its membership is said to be confined to American-born Protestant whites. — **Ku Klux Klanner.**

ku′lak (k[y]o͞o′lăk; k[y]o͞o·lăk′), n. [Russ., lit., fist, fr. Estonian kulak.] Russia. A rich peasant; esp., a farmer or peasant who has made money out of the poorer class or who refuses to co-operate with the government. — **ku′lak·ism** (-ĭz′m), n.

‖**Kul·tur′** (ko͞ol·to͞or′), n. [G.] Culture regarded as an evolutionary force developing advanced stages of social organization; hence, a stage or type of such organization.

Kul·tur′kampf (ko͞ol·to͞or′kämpf), n. [G., fr. kultur civilization + kampf fight.] Ger. Hist. The struggle (1872–87) between the Roman Catholic Church and the German government, chiefly over the latter′s efforts to control educational and ecclesiastical appointments.

ku′miss, kou′miss (ko͞o′mĭs), n. [Russ. kumys, fr. Tatar kumiz.] An intoxicating fermented (or distilled) liquor originally made by the Tatars from mare′s or camel′s milk.

küm′mel (kĭm′ĕl; G. küm′ĕl), n. [G., cumin, caraway seed, fr. OHG. kumil, kumīn, fr. L. cuminum.] A liqueur flavored with caraway seed, anise, etc. It is made chiefly at Riga.

kum′mer·bund. Var. of CUMMERBUND.

kum′quat (kŭm′kwŏt), n. [From Cant. pron. of Chin. (Pek.) chin¹-chü², lit., golden orange.] a A Chinese citrus fruit cultivated for making preserves and confectionery. b The tree (genus Fortunella, of the rue family) which bears it.

kunz′ite (ko͞onts′īt), n. [After Geo. F. Kunz (1856–1932), Am. gem expert.] Mineral. A variety of spodumene occurring in beautiful lilac crystals.

Kuo′min′tang′ (gwô′mĭn′däng′), n. [Chin. (Pek.) kuo² nationalist + min³ people′s + tang³ party.] The revolutionary and nationalist party in the Chinese Republic organized chiefly by Sun Yat-sen. It gained control of China in 1926–27.

kur′bash (ko͞or′băsh), n. [Turk. qirbāch.] A lash or whip of hide used as an instrument of punishment in Turkey, Egypt, etc. — v. t. To lash with the kurbash.

Kurd (kûrd; properly ko͞ord), n. One of a numerous Moslem people dwelling chiefly in Kurdistan.

Kurd′ish (kûr′dĭsh; ko͞or′-), adj. Of or pertaining to the Kurds; also, designating a Kurdistan. — n. The Iranian language of the Kurds. See INDO-EUROPEAN LANGUAGES, Table.

Kur·di·stan′ (ko͞or·dĭ·stän′), n. [See KURDISTAN, in Gaz.] Any of the rugs of several varieties woven by Kurds in Turkey or, mainly, in Persia; — called also **Kurdish rug**.

kur′ra·jong (kŭr′ȧ·jŏng), n. Also **koo′ra·jong** (ko͞o′rȧ-), **cur′ra·jong**. [Native name.] Any of several trees or shrubs (families Malvaceae and Sterculiaceae) from the fiber of which Australian aborigines make cordage, nets, and matting.

‖**Kur′saal** (ko͞or′zäl′), n.; pl. KURSÄLE (-zä′lĕ). [G., fr. kur cure + saal hall.] A public hall for visitors at watering places.

ku·ruş′ (ko͞o·ro͞osh′), n. sing. & pl. [Turk.] The legal monetary unit of Turkey, equivalent to $\frac{1}{100}$ of a Turkish pound. See MONEY, Tables.

kvass (kväs), n. Also **kvas, quass**, etc. [Russ. kvas.] A thin sour beer, commonly made by pouring warm water on rye or barley and letting it ferment.

ky′ack (kī′ăk), n. Western U. S. A packsack to be swung on either side of a packsaddle.

ky′a·nite (kī′ȧ·nīt). Var. of CYANITE.

kyle (kīl), n. [Gael. caol.] Scot. A firth.

ky′mo·graph (kī′mô·gráf; 9), n. [Gr. kyma wave + -graph.] a An automatic apparatus on which curves of pressure, etc., may be traced. b An instrument for recording the rotary motions of an airplane in flight. — **ky′mo·graph′ic** (-gráf′ĭk), adj.

Kym′ri (kĭm′rĭ), **Kym′ry, Kym′ric.** Vars. of CYMRY, CYMRIC.

ky·pho′sis (kī·fō′sĭs), n. [NL., fr. Gr. kyphōsis, fr. kyphos humpbacked.] Angular curvature of the spine; condition of one who is humpbacked. — **ky·phot′ic** (-fŏt′ĭk), adj.

Kyr′i·e e·le′i·son (kĭr′ĭ·ē ĕ·lā′ĭ·sŏn; kē′rĭ·ē). [LL., fr. Gr. kyrie eleēson.] Eccl. The Greek words, or their English translation "Lord have mercy upon us," used in various offices, esp. of the Roman Catholic and Anglican churches, as one of a series of petitions or as a response; also, a musical setting for such a petition or response.

kyte (kīt), n. Scot. Stomach; belly.

kythe. Var. of KITHE.

L

L, l (ĕl), *n.; pl.* L's, l's, Ls, ls (ĕlz). **1.** The twelfth letter of the English alphabet. L comes through the Latin from the Greek (*lambda*), which took it from the Phoenician. **2.** The sound of this letter. In English L normally represents a voiced lateral continuant, loosely classed as a liquid consonant. See *Pron.*, § 61. **3.** [*cap.*] In Roman numerals, 50 or, in the form L̄, 50,000. **4. a** Anything having the shape of the capital letter L, as an extension on a building constructed at right angles to the length of the building. **b** As a *symbol*, the eleventh or (cf. K, 3) twelfth in order.

L (ĕl), *adj. Chem.* [*cap.* or *small cap.*] Similar in configuration to *l*-glyceraldehyde; as, L-glucose, the L family.

la (lä), *n. Music.* A syllable applied to the sixth tone of the diatonic scale in solmization.

laa'ger, la'ger (lä'gẽr), *n.* [D. (in South Africa), also *leger.*] *S. Africa.* A camp, esp. one with a defensive barrier of travelers' wagons. — *v. t. & i. S. Africa.* To form into, or camp in, a laager.

lab'a·rum (lăb'ȧ·rŭm), *n.; pl.* -RA (-rȧ). [LL.] The imperial standard of the later Roman emperors, esp. that adopted by Constantine after his conversion to Christianity. It bore a monogram of the first two letters (XP) of the name of Christ in its Greek form.

lab'da·num (lăb'dȧ·nŭm), *n.* Also **lad'a·num** (lăd'ȧ-). [ML. & L., fr. Gr. *ladanon, lēdanon,* fr. *lēdon* mastic, fr. Ar. *lādan,* fr. Per. *lādan.*] A soft dark oleoresin derived from various species of rockrose (genus *Cistus*), used in making perfumes.

lab'e·fac'tion (lăb'ē·făk'shŭn), *n.* [L. *labefacere* to cause to totter, weaken.] A weakening; impairment.

la'bel (lā'bĕl; -b'l), *n.* [OF. *label, lambel,* sort of ribbon or fringe.] **1.** A band, fillet, or the like. **2.** A slip of ribbon, parchment, etc., on a document, to hold the seal. **3.** A slip of paper, cloth, leather, metal, etc., affixed to anything, and indicating the contents, ownership, destination, rating, etc. **4.** A term or phrase attached by way of classification or characterization. **5.** *Arch.* A projecting molding by the sides, and over the top, of an opening; a dripstone. — *v. t.;* LA'BELED (-bĕld; -b'ld) or LA'BELLED; LA'BEL·ING or LA'BEL·LING. **1.** To affix a label to; to mark with a name, etc. **2.** To describe or designate as by a label; to tag. — **la'bel·er, la'bel·ler,** *n.*

‖**la belle dame sans mer'ci'** (lȧ bĕl dȧm säɴ mĕr'sē'). [F.] The beautiful lady without mercy.

la·bel'lum (lȧ·bĕl'ŭm), *n.; pl.* -LA (-ȧ). [L., dim. of *labrum* lip.] *Bot.* The lip, or median member of the inner perianth or corolla, of an orchid. Cf. LADY'S-SLIPPER, *Illust.*

la'bi·a (lā'bĭ·ȧ), *n., pl.* of LABIUM.

la'bi·al (lā'bĭ·ăl), *adj.* [ML. *labialis,* fr. L. *labium* lip.] **1.** Of or pertaining to the lips, or labia. **2.** *Music.* Giving its tones from impact of an air current on a liplike edge, as a flute. **3.** *Phonet.* **a** Articulated, as a consonant, mainly by the lips (*b, p, m*). **b** Modified, as a vowel, by circular contraction of the lip opening (o͞o in fo͞od; ō in ōld). — *n.* **1.** *Music.* A labial organ pipe. Cf. FLUE PIPE. **2.** *Phonet.* A labial consonant.

la'bi·al·ism (-ĭz'm), *n. Phonet.* Quality of being labial; tendency to labialize sounds.

la'bi·al·ize (-īz), *v. t. Phonet.* To make labial; to round (a vowel or a consonant, as *o* or *r*). — **la'bi·al·i·za'tion** (-ĭ·zā'shŭn; -ī·zā'-), *n.*

la'bi·ate (lā'bĭ·āt), *adj.* Having lips; lipped; specif., *Bot.,* having the limb of a tubular corolla or calyx divided into two parts, one projecting over the other, as in the snapdragon.

la'bile (lā'bĭl; -b'l; 56), *adj.* [L. *labilis* apt to slip, fr. *labi* to slip.] **1.** Characterized by adaptability to change or modification; plastic; unstable. **2.** *Chem. & Physics.* Readily undergoing change, as in cleavage or molecular rearrangement.

la'bi·o- (lā'bĭ·ō-). [See LABIUM.] A combining form denoting: **a** *The lips.* **b** *Labial and,* as in *labio*dental.

la'bi·o·den'tal (-dĕn'tăl; -t'l), *adj.* [*labio-* + *dental.*] *Phonet.* Formed with the lips, or one lip, and the teeth, as *f* and *v.* — *n.* A labiodental consonant.

la'bi·o·na'sal (-nā'zăl; -z'l), *adj.* [*labio-* + *nasal.*] *Phonet.* Uttered with the joint use of the lips and the nasal passage, as *m.* — *n.* A labionasal consonant.

la'bi·o·ve'lar (-vē'lẽr), *adj.* [*labio-* + *velar.*] *Phonet.* Formed with the lips rounded, narrowed, or closed, and with the back of the tongue touching or near the velum, as *w.* — *n.* A labiovelar vowel or consonant.

la'bi·um (lā'bĭ·ŭm), *n.; pl.* LABIA (-ȧ). [L.] **1.** A lip. **2.** *pl. Anat.* The folds of integument at the opening of the vulva; as, the **la'bi·a ma·jo'ra** (lā'bĭ·ȧ mȧ·jō'rȧ), the outer folds, and the **la'bi·a mi·no'ra** (mĭ·nō'rȧ), the inner folds of the vulva. **3.** *Bot.* The lower lip of a labiate corolla. **4.** *Zool.* The lower lip of an insect, formed by the second pair of maxillae. See HYMENOPTERON, *Illust.*

la'bor, la'bour (lā'bẽr), *n.* [OF. *labour, labor,* fr. L. *labor.*] **1.** Physical or mental work; toil. **2.** That which requires effort for its accomplishment; a task. **3.** The service rendered or part played by the laborer, operative, and artisan in the production of wealth, as distinguished from the service rendered by capitalists or by those whose exertion is primarily and almost entirely mental. **4.** Laborers, operatives, and artisans as a body or class, esp. as united in efforts to secure economic rights and better living and working conditions. **5.** *Med.* Travail; childbirth. — **Syn.** See WORK. — *v. i.* **1.** To perform labor; to work; hence, to strive; take pains. **2.** To be in travail. **3.** To be oppressed with difficulties or disease; to do one's work under conditions that make it hard, wearisome, or grievous. **4.** *Naut.* To pitch or roll heavily, as a ship. — *v. t.* **1.** *Now Chiefly Literary.* To expend labor on; specif., to till; cultivate. **2.** *Archaic.* To form, perform, or bring with labor. **3.** To treat or work out with effort and in detail; as, to *labor* a point.

‖**la'bo·ra're est o·ra're** (lăb'ō·rā'rē ĕst ō·rā'rē). [L.] To work is to pray.

lab'o·ra·to'ry (lăb'ō·rȧ·tō'rĭ; *Brit.* lȧ·bŏr'ȧ·tẽr·ĭ, lăb'ō·rȧ·tẽr·ĭ, -trĭ), *n.; pl.* -RIES (-rĭz). Orig., the workroom of a chemist; hence, a place devoted to experimental study in any science, or to the testing and analysis of drugs, chemicals, explosives, etc.; by extension, a place where something is prepared or some operation is performed. — *adj.* Of or pert. to, or used or done in, a laboratory.

Labor Day. In most states of the United States, the first Monday of September, set aside as a legal holiday in honor of, or in the interest of, workingmen as a class; also, a similar holiday (**Labour Day**) in Canada, Australia, etc. In many European countries and in the Philippine Islands the first day of May is observed as Labor Day.

la'bored, la'boured (lā'bẽrd), *adj.* Produced or performed with labor; elaborately wrought; not easy or natural; as, a *labored* style or speech.

la'bor·er, la'bour·er (lā'bẽr·ẽr), *n.* One who labors; specif.: **a** One who does physical labor; one who does work that requires strength rather than skill. **b** A person who performs labor of any kind.

la·bo'ri·ous (lȧ·bō'rĭ·ŭs; 70), *adj.* [OF. *laborios,* fr. L. *laboriosus,* fr. *labor* labor.] **1.** Requiring much work; toilsome. **2.** Devoted to labor; industrious. — **la·bo'ri·ous·ly,** *adv.* — **la·bo'ri·ous·ness,** *n.*

La'bor·ite, La'bour·ite (lā'bẽr·īt), *n.* [*sometimes not cap.*] A member of a labor party, esp. of the British Labor party.

‖**la'bor om'ni·a vin'cit** (lā'bôr ŏm'nĭ·ȧ vĭn'sĭt). [L.] Labor conquers all things; — motto of Oklahoma.

labor party. A political party claiming to represent especially the economic interests of wage earners.

la'bor·sav'ing, la'bour·sav'ing (lā'bẽr·sāv'ĭng), *adj.* Adapted to replace or decrease the labor, esp. manual labor, of men; as, *laborsaving* devices.

labor union. A trade-union. See TRADE-UNION.

la'bour, la'bour·er, etc. Brit. spelling of LABOR, LABORER, etc.

lab'ra·dor·ite (lăb'rȧ·dôr·īt; lăb'rȧ·dôr'īt), *n.* [*Labrador* + *-ite.*] A triclinic feldspar showing a beautiful play of colors.

la'bret (lā'brĕt), *n.* [L. *labrum* lip.] A piece, as of wood, shell, or stone, worn in a perforation of the lip, as among various peoples of low culture.

lab'roid (lăb'roid), *adj.* [L. *labrus, labros,* a kind of fish.] *Zool.* Belonging to the wrasse family (Labridae) or to a former superfamily (Labroidea) that included the wrasses, the parrot fishes, etc. — *n.* A labroid fish.

la'brum (lā'brŭm; lăb'rŭm), *n.; pl.* -BRA (-brȧ). [L.] **1.** A lip or edge, as of a basin. **2.** *Zool.* **a** The upper or anterior lip of arthropods. See HYMENOPTERON, *Illust.* **b** The external margin of a gastropod shell.

la·bur'num (lȧ·bûr'nŭm), *n.* [L.] *Bot.* One of a genus (*Laburnum*) of Eurasian poisonous shrubs and trees of the pea family, having bright-yellow flowers.

lab'y·rinth (lăb'ĭ·rĭnth), *n.* [L. *labyrinthus,* fr. Gr. *labyrinthos.*] **1.** A place full of intricate passageways; a maze; specif., in Greek myth, the maze in Crete in which the Minotaur was confined. **2.** Any intricate enclosure; esp., a maze of paths in a park or garden. **3.** Any inextricable or bewildering state of things, etc.; a perplexity. **4.** *Anat. & Zool.* The internal ear. See EAR, 1.

lab'y·rin'thi·an (-rĭn'thĭ·ăn), **lab'y·rin'thic** (-thĭk), **lab'y·rin'thi·cal** (-thĭ·kăl), *adj.* Labyrinthine.

lab'y·rin'thine (-thĭn *or, esp. Brit.,* -thīn), *adj.* Like, or of the nature of, a labyrinth; intricate; involved.

lac (lăk), *n.* [Per. *lak* or Hind. *lākh,* fr. Skr. *lākṣā.*] A resinous substance secreted by a scale insect (*Tachardia lacca*) widely cultivated, esp. in northern India. This resin is melted, purified, and then solidified in thin layers, which form the shellac of commerce.

lac, lakh (lăk), *n.* [Hind. *lākh,* fr. Skr. *lakṣa* mark, sign, lac.] *India.* One hundred thousand; also, a great number; specif., 100,000 rupees (written Rs. 1,00,000).

lac'co·lith (lăk'ō·lĭth), **lac'co·lite** (-līt), *n.* [Gr. *lakkos* a cistern + *-lith, -lite.*] *Geol.* A mass of igneous rock intruded between sedimentary beds and producing a domical bulging of the overlying strata.

lace (lās), *n.* [OF. *laz,* fr. L. *laqueus* noose, snare.] **1.** A cord, band, or line, esp. one used in drawing together parts of a garment, a shoe, etc. **2.** An ornamental braid for trimming men's hats, coats, uniforms, etc.; — now only in ***gold lace*** and ***silver lace.*** **3.** A delicate openwork fabric, usually figured, of fine threads, used in handkerchiefs, table covers, etc., or worn as an ornament of dress. **4.** A dash of spirits (or formerly sugar) added to coffee or some other beverage. — *v. t.;* LACED (lāst); LAC'ING (lās'ĭng). **1.** To fasten or unite with or as with a lace or laces. **2.** To compress the waist of (a person) by tightening the laces of a garment, as a corset. **3.** To beat; lash. **4.** To adorn with or as if with lace. **5.** To interlace; intertwine. **6.** To add a dash of spirits, or formerly sugar, to (a beverage). — *v. i.* **1.** To be fastened, or to admit of being fastened, with a lace or laces. **2.** To use lacing for compression of the waist, as by a corset.

lac'er·ate (lăs'ẽr·āt), *v. t.* [L. *laceratus,* past part. of *lacerare* to lacerate; akin to L. *lacer* mangled.] To rend; to mangle; hence, to afflict; harrow.

lac'er·ate (-āt), **lac'er·at'ed** (-āt'ĕd; -ĭd), *adj.* **1.** Torn; mangled; also, harrowed; distracted. **2.** *Bot. & Zool.* Having the edges deeply and irregularly cut.

lac'er·a'tion (-ā'shŭn), *n.* **a** Act of lacerating. **b** A breach or wound made by lacerating.

la·cer'ti·an (lȧ·sûr'shĭ·ăn; 58), *adj. & n. Zool.* Lacertilian.

lac'er·til'i·an (lăs'ẽr·tĭl'ĭ·ăn; 58), *adj.* [L. *lacertus, lacerta,* lizard.] *Zool.* Of or belonging to a division (Lacertilia) of reptiles, comprising lizards, chameleons, geckos, and allied limbless forms. — **lac'er·til'i·an,** *n.*

lace'wing' (lās'wĭng'), *n.* Any of certain insects (order Neuroptera) of *Chrysopa, Hemerobius,* and allied genera. They have delicate, lacelike wings and brilliant eyes.

lach'es (lăch'ĕz; -ĭz), *n.* [OF. *laschesse,* ult. fr. L. *laxus* loose, lax.] *Law.* Neglect to do a thing at the proper time; undue delay in asserting a right, or in claiming or asking for a privilege.

Lach'e·sis (lăk'ē·sĭs), *n.* [L., fr. Gr. *Lachesis,* lit., lot, fr. *lanchanein, lachein,* to obtain by lot.] See FATE, *n.,* 4.

lach'ry·mal (lăk'rĭ·măl), *adj.* Also **lac'ri·mal.** [ML. *lachrymalis, lacrimalis,* fr. L. *lacrima* a tear.] **1.** Of or pertaining to tears. **2.** *Anat.* Designating, pertaining to, or situated near, the organs (**lachrymal glands**) producing tears. — *n.* **1.** *pl.* Lachrymal organs. **2.** = LACHRYMATORY.

lach′ry·ma′tor (lăk′rĭ·mā′tẽr), *n.* A tear-producing substance.
lach′ry·ma·to′ry (-mȧ·tō′rĭ *or, esp. Brit.,* -tẽr·ĭ, -mā′tẽr·ĭ), *n.; pl.* -RIES (-rĭz). A vase for tears; esp., *Archaeol.*, one of a class of narrow-necked vessels found in ancient tombs, and so called from a former notion that the tears of the deceased person's friends were collected in them. — *adj.* Of or pert. to tears; tending to make tears flow.
lach′ry·mose (lăk′rĭ·mōs), *adj.* [L. *lacrimosus.*] Generating or shedding tears; tearful. — **lach′ry·mose·ly,** *adv.*
lac′ing (lās′ĭng), *n.* **1.** Action of one that laces. **2.** Any of various things that lace; a lace.
la·cin′i·ate (lȧ·sĭn′ĭ·āt), **la·cin′i·at′ed** (-āt′ĕd; -ĭd), *adj.* [L. *lacinia* lappet.] Fringed; *Bot.*, cut into deep irregular lobes; narrowly incised.
lack (lăk), *n.* [ME. *lac.*] **1.** Fact or state of being deficient or wanting; deficiency; want; need. **2.** That which is lacking; thing needed. — *v. i.* **1.** To be wanting, missing, or deficient. **2.** To have need; to be short; — with *of* or *in*. Specif., to be in want or need. — *v. t.* **1.** To be without, destitute of, or deficient in. **2.** To want; need; require.
Syn. **Lack, want, need, require** mean to be without something essential or greatly desired. **Lack** may imply either an absence or a shortage in supply (as, the house *lacks* a dining room; the army *lacks* airplanes); **want** frequently adds to *lack* the implication of a pressing desire but more often of necessity (as, the house *wants* painting); **need** clearly suggests urgent necessity (as, the man *needs* food and clothing); **require** heightens this implication by suggesting imperativeness (as, the house *requires* a fresh coat of paint).
lack′a·dai′si·cal (lăk′ȧ·dā′zĭ·kăl), *adj.* Affectedly languid; listless. — **lack′a·dai′si·cal·ly,** *adv.* — **lack′a·dai′si·cal·ness,** *n.*
lack′a·day′ (lăk′ȧ·dā′), *interj.* Short for ALACKADAY.
lack′er (lăk′ẽr). Var. of LACQUER.
lack′ey (lăk′ĭ), *n.; pl.* LACKEYS (-ĭz). [F. *laquais,* fr. Sp. *lacayo.*] A footman; a valet; figuratively, a servile follower; a toady. — *v. i. & t.* To attend as a lackey.
lack′lus′ter, lack′lus′tre (lăk′lŭs′tẽr), *n.* A lack of luster. — *adj.* Lacking luster or brightness.
la·con′ic (lȧ·kŏn′ĭk), *adj.* [L. *Laconicus* Laconian, fr. Gr. *Lakōnikos.*] Sparing of words; terse; brief and pithy. — **Syn.** See CONCISE. — **la·con′i·cal·ly** (-ĭ·kăl·ĭ), *adv.*
lac′o·nism (lăk′ō·nĭz′m), *n.* [Gr. *Lakōnismos,* fr. *Lakōnizein* to imitate Lacedaemonian manners, to speak laconically.] Vigorous, brief expression; laconic style or brevity.
lac′quer (lăk′ẽr), *n.* [MF. *lacre,* fr. Pg. *lacre* sealing wax, fr. or var. of Pg. *laca* lac.] **1.** **a** A spirit varnish, as shellac. **b** Any of certain natural varnishes, specif. that obtained in Japan and China (***Japanese or Chinese lacquer***) from the sap of a sumac (*Rhus verniciflua*). **c** Any of various artificial varnishes and varnish paints, opaque or colored, some of which are baked on. **2.** A decorative article made of wood coated with lacquer. — *v. t.* To coat with lacquer. — **lac′quer·er** (-ẽr), *n.*
lac′quey (lăk′ĭ). Var. of LACKEY.
lac′ri·mal, lac′ry·mal (lăk′rĭ·măl), **lac′ri·ma·to′ry, lac′ry·ma·to′ry, lac′ri·mose, lac′ry·mose.** Vars. of LACHRYMAL, LACHRYMATORY, LACHRYMOSE.
la·crosse′ (lȧ·krŏs′; 74), *n.* [F. *la crosse,* lit., the crosier, hooked stick.] A game of ball, originating among the North American Indians, played with a long-handled racket (*crosse*), with which the hard ball is caught, carried, or thrown.
lact-. = LACTO-.
lac′tam (lăk′tăm), *n.* [*lact*one + *am*ino.] *Chem.* An anhydride of an amino acid, formed by the loss of a molecule of water from the amino and carboxyl groups.
lac′ta·ry (lăk′tȧ·rĭ), *adj.* [L. *lactarius,* fr. *lac, lactis,* milk.] Of, pert. to, or connected with milk.
lac′tase (lăk′tās), *n.* [See LACTOSE; -ASE.] *Biochem.* An enzyme, found in certain yeasts and in the animal body, which decomposes lactose into dextrose and galactose.
lac′tate (-tāt), *n.* A salt or ester of lactic acid.
lac·ta′tion (lăk·tā′shŭn), *n.* The secretion and yielding of milk by the mammary gland; act of giving suck.
lac′te·al (lăk′tē·ăl), *adj.* [L. *lacteus* milky, fr. *lac, lactis,* milk.] **1.** Pertaining to, consisting of, or resembling milk; milky; as, the *lacteal* fluid. **2.** *Anat.* Conveying or containing chyle; as, the *lacteal* vessels. — *n. Anat.* One of the lymphatic vessels of the small intestine which convey the chyle from the intestine to the thoracic duct.
lac′te·ous (-ŭs), *adj.* Milky; resembling milk.
lac·tes′cence (lăk·tĕs′ĕns; -′ns), *n.* Also **lac·tes′cen·cy** (-ĕn·sĭ; -′n·sĭ). A becoming milky; milkiness.
lac·tes′cent (-ĕnt; -′nt), *adj.* [L. *lactescens,* pres. part., deriv. of *lac, lactis,* milk.] **1.** Having a milky look. **2.** Secreting, or concerned in the secretion of, milk.
lac′tic (lăk′tĭk), *adj.* [L. *lac, lactis,* milk.] Of or pert. to milk; procured from sour milk or whey; as, *lactic* acid.
lactic acid. A colorless sirupy acid, $CH_3CH(OH)CO_2H$.
lac·tif′er·ous (lăk·tĭf′ẽr·ŭs), *adj.* [L. *lac, lactis,* milk + *-ferous.*] Secreting or conveying milk.
lac′to- (lăk′tō-), **lact-.** [L. *lac, lactis.*] **1.** Combining form meaning *milk.* **2.** *Chem.* Combining form for *lactate, lactic.*
lac′to·ba·cil′lus (-bȧ·sĭl′ŭs), *n.* [NL., fr. *lacto-* + *bacillus.*] Any of a genus (*Lactobacillus*) of lactic-acid-forming bacteria.
lac′to·fla′vin (lăk′tō·flā′vĭn; 2), *n.* [*lacto-* + *flavin.*] Vitamin B_2 (see VITAMIN).
lac′tone (lăk′tōn), *n. Chem.* Any of a series of cyclic anhydrides of acids having one or more hydroxyl groups in addition to that in the acid group.
lac′to·pro′te·in (lăk′tō·prō′tē·ĭn; -tēn), *n.* Also **lac′to·pro′te·id** (-tē·ĭd). [*lacto-* + *protein.*] Any of the proteins in milk.
lac′to·scope (lăk′tō·skōp), *n.* [*lacto-* + *-scope.*] An instrument for estimating the amount of cream in milk.
lac′tose (-tōs), *n.* [L. *lac, lactis,* milk + *-ose.*] *Chem.* A sugar, $C_{12}H_{22}O_{11}$, present in milk, separable by evaporation as hard crystals containing a molecule of water; milk sugar.
la·cu′na (lȧ·kū′nȧ), *n.; pl.* -NAE (-nē), -NAS (-nȧz). [L., ditch, pit, lake.] **1.** A blank space, as in a manuscript; gap. **2.** Specif.: **a** *Anat.* One of the minute cavities in bone occupied by the bone cells. **b** *Biol.* Any space or cavity in or among cells.
la·cu′nal (-năl; -n′l), **la·cu′nar** (-nẽr), *adj.* Lacunary.

la·cu′nar (-nẽr), *n.; pl.* LACUNARS (-nẽrz), LACUNARIA (lăk′ū·nā′rĭ·ȧ; 6). [L.] *Arch.* A ceiling, esp. one of the ancient Roman type made up of sunk panels.

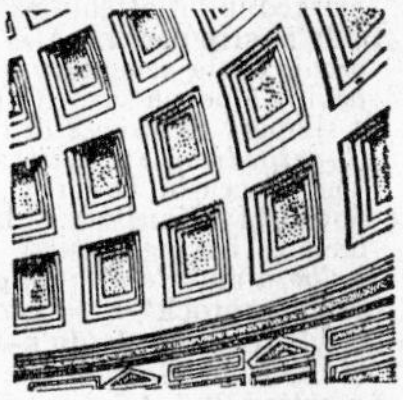
Lacunar in the Pantheon, Rome.

lac′u·nar′y (lăk′ū·nẽr′ĭ *or, esp. Brit.,* -nẽr·ĭ; lȧ·kū′nȧ·rĭ), *adj.* Of or pertaining to a lacuna; having lacunae.
la·cu′nose (lȧ·kū′nōs), *adj.* Having, or full of, lacunae.
la·cus′trine (lȧ·kŭs′trĭn), *adj.* [L. *lacus* lake.] Of or pertaining to, or growing in, lakes.
lac′y (lās′ĭ), *adj.;* LAC′I·ER (-ĭ·ẽr); LAC′I·EST. Resembling, or consisting of, lace. — **lac′i·ly,** *adv.* — **lac′i·ness,** *n.*
lad (lăd), *n.* [ME. *ladde.*] A boy; youth; often, in familiarity, a man of any age.
lad′a·num (lăd′ȧ·nŭm). Var. of LABDANUM.
lad′der (lăd′ẽr), *n.* [AS. *hlǣder, hlǣdder.*] **1.** An appliance consisting of two long sidepieces, usually parallel, joined at intervals by crosspieces on which a person may step in ascending or descending. **2.** Something resembling or likened to a ladder in form or use. **3.** A run, as in a stocking.
lad′der–back′ (-băk′), *adj.* Having a back consisting of two upright posts connected by horizontal slats; as, a *ladder-back* chair.
ladder stitch. An embroidery stitch with crossbars.
lad′die (lăd′ĭ), *n. Chiefly Scot.* A lad.
lade (lād), *v. t.;* LAD′ED (lād′ĕd; -ĭd); LAD′ED OR LAD′EN (lād′′n); LAD′ING (lād′ĭng). [AS. *hladan* to load, draw (water).] **1.** To load; to put a burden or freight on or in, or to put or place as a load or cargo; as, to *lade* a vessel; to *lade* goods on a vessel. **2.** To throw or lift in or out with a ladle, dipper, or the like; to dip; bail. — *v. i.* **1.** To load; take on cargoes. **2.** To draw water, etc., by dipping as with a ladle.
lad′en (lād′′n), *adj.* Loaded; freighted; burdened; as, a *laden* vessel.
lad′en, *v. t.* To lade.
la′dies′ man (lā′dĭz). = LADY'S MAN.
La·din′ (lȧ·dēn′), *n.* [L. *Latinus* Latin. See LATIN.] **a** Any of the Rhaeto-Romanic dialects spoken in parts of Switzerland and Tirol. See INDO-EUROPEAN LANGUAGES, *Table.* **b** One speaking Ladin as a mother tongue.
lad′ing (lād′ĭng), *n.* **1.** A loading; also, a bailing or ladling. **2.** That which lades; cargo; freight.
La·di′no (lä·dē′nō; *Sp.* lä·thē′nō), *n.; pl.* -NOS (-nōz; *Sp.* -nōs). [Sp. cunning, learned, lit., Latin, fr. L. *Latinus* Latin.] **1.** The mixed Spanish and Hebrew language spoken by Sephardim. **2.** In Spanish America and Spanish colonies, a mestizo. **3.** [*not cap.*] *Southeastern U. S.* A cunningly vicious horse. **4.** = LADIN **b.**
la′dle (lā′d′l), *n.* [AS. *hlædel,* fr. *hladan* to load, drain.] A cuplike spoon, often large, with a long handle, used in lading or dipping. — *v. t.;* LA′DLED (-d′ld); LA′DLING (-dlĭng). To take up and convey in a ladle. — **la′dler** (-dlẽr), *n.*
la·drone′ (lȧ·drōn′), *n.* [Sp. *ladrón,* fr. L. *latro* robber.] A thief; esp., a highwayman; — in Spanish-speaking regions.
la·dron′ism (lȧ·drōn′ĭz′m), *n. Chiefly Phil. I.* Robbery or intimidation by ladrones; brigandage.
la′dy (lā′dĭ), *n.; pl.* LADIES (-dĭz). [ME. *ladi, lavedi, lafdi,* fr. AS. *hlǣfdīge,* fr. *hlāf* loaf + a stem akin to *dǣge* maid.] **1.** *Obs.* The mistress of a household. **2.** A woman having proprietary rights, rule, or authority; — a feminine correlative of *lord.* **3.** [*cap.*] Specif., the Virgin Mary; — usually with *Our* (***Our Lady***). **4.** [*cap.*] In the British Empire, a title prefixed to the name of women of certain ranks, as to that of: (1) A marchioness, countess, viscountess, or baroness; (2) The daughter of a nobleman not lower than earl; (3) The wife of one who has *Lord* prefixed by courtesy to his Christian name; (4) The wife of a baronet or knight. **5.** Wife; — now applied to one of recognized social standing. **6.** A woman of social distinction or position; — now correlative of *gentleman.*
☞ In addressing women, the *sing., lady,* is now confined to poetic, rhetorical, or uneducated use, the ordinary form being *madam;* but in the *pl., ladies* is the ordinary term.
7. A woman to whom one is devoted or bound; a sweetheart. **8.** The triturating apparatus in the stomach of a lobster. — **Syn.** See FEMALE, *n.* — *adj.* **1.** Belonging or becoming to a lady or ladies; ladylike. **2.** Female; as, *lady* president.
— *v. t. Obs.* To make a lady of.
lady beetle. A ladybird.
la′dy·bird′ (lā′dĭ·bûrd′), *n.* [Equiv. to bird of Our Lady.] Any of a family (Coccinellidae) of small, often brightly colored beetles of temperate and tropical regions, feeding upon insects and their eggs. They are of great value to man in destroying plant lice and scale insects.
la′dy·bug′ (-bŭg′), *n. U. S. & Dial. Eng.* A ladybird.
Lady chapel. A chapel in a cathedral or parish church, dedicated to the Virgin Mary; hence, erroneously, any side chapel in a church.
Lady Day. Orig., any feast day of the Virgin Mary; now, Annunciation Day, March 25; — the present use in England where it is a quarter day.
la′dy·fin′ger (lā′dĭ·fĭng′gẽr), *n. Cookery.* A small finger-shaped spongecake.
lady in waiting. A lady of a queen's or a princess's household, appointed to wait upon or attend her.
la′dy–kill′er, *n. Slang.* A man who has the reputation of fascinating women. — **la′dy–kill′ing,** *adj. & n.*
la′dy·kin (lā′dĭ·kĭn), *n.* [*lady* + *-kin.*] A little lady.
la′dy·like′ (-līk′), *adj.* **1.** Like a lady; well-bred. **2.** Becoming or suitable to a lady. — **Syn.** See FEMALE, *adj.*
la′dy·love′ (-lŭv′; 2), *n.* A sweetheart or mistress.
la′dy's–fin′ger (lā′dĭz·fĭng′gẽr), *n. Cookery.* Var. of LADYFINGER.
la′dy·ship (lā′dĭ·shĭp), *n.* Rank, position, or personality of a lady; — used (when preceded by *her* or *your*) to designate or address one having the ranking title of *Lady.*
la′dy–slip′per, *n.* = LADY'S-SLIPPER.
lady's maid. A woman servant who cares for a lady's clothes and assists at her toilette.

lady's, *or* **ladies', man.** A man who affects the society of ladies, is marked in his attentions to them, etc.

la'dy's–slip'per, *n.* Also **la'dy–slip'per.** **a** Any orchid of the genera *Cypripedium* and *Fissipes,* having a pouch-shaped lip somewhat resembling a slipper. *Fissipes acaulis* and all species of *Cypripedium* are also called *moccasin flower.* The moccasin flower *C. reginae* is the State flower of Minnesota. **b** Any of certain other orchids having similar flowers, as *Cytherea bulbosa* and *Peramium giganteum.*

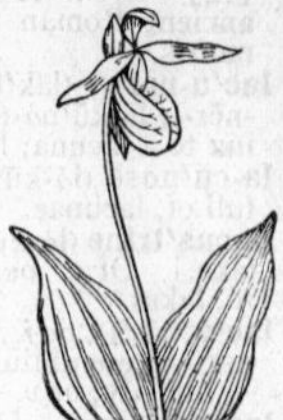

Lady's-slipper. (1/4)

la'dy's–smock', *n.* = CUCKOOFLOWER **a.**

la'dy's–tress'es, la'dy's–trac'es, *n.* Any orchid of the genus *Spiranthes.*

La·er'tes (lā·ûr'tēz), *n.* [L., fr. Gr. *Laertēs.*] **1.** In Greek legend, father of Odysseus. **2.** The impetuous son of Polonius, and brother of Ophelia, in Shakespeare's *Hamlet.*

Lae·ta're Sun'day (lē·tā'rē). The fourth Sunday of Lent; — from *Laetare* (rejoice), the first word of the Introit for that day.

lae'vo- (lē'vō-). Var. of LEVO-, as in **lae'vo·ro·ta'tion.** — **lae'vo** (-vō), *adj.*

lag (lăg), *adj.* **1.** *Now Dial.* Last; hindermost. **2.** *Obs. exc. Dial.* Belated; sluggish; tardy. — *v. i.;* LAGGED (lăgd); LAG'GING. **1.** To walk or move slowly; to stay or fall behind; to linger or loiter. **2.** *Marbles.* To toss one's taw toward a line (***lag line***) on the ground, to determine the order of play. — **Syn.** See DELAY. — *n.* **1.** *Now Rare.* One who lags; that which is last. **2.** *Obs.* The lowest class. **3. a** Act or condition of lagging; retardation, as in movement or development. **b** Amount of retardation. **4.** *Marbles.* Act of lagging.

lag, *v. t.* *Slang.* **a** To transport for crime; to send to penal servitude. **b** To arrest. — *n. Slang.* **a** Also **lag'ger.** One who has been transported or sentenced to penal servitude; a jailbird. **b** A term of transportation or penal servitude.

lag, *n.* A stave of a cask, drum, etc.; also, one of the narrow strips covering a boiler, a carding machine cylinder, or the like. — *v. t.;* LAGGED (lăgd); LAG'GING. To cover or provide with lags or lagging.

lag'an (lăg'ăn), **lag'end** (-ĕnd), *n.* [OF. *lagan, lagand.*] *Law.* Goods sunk in the sea with a buoy attached in order that they may be found again. Cf. FLOTSAM, JETSAM.

Lag b'O'mer (läg bō'mĕr). See JEWISH HOLIDAYS.

la'ger (lä'gẽr). Var. of LAAGER.

la'ger beer, *or* **la'ger** (lä'gẽr; lô'-), *n.* [G. *lager* bed, storehouse + *bier* beer.] A beer, made orig. in Germany, that is laid up or stored for some months before use.

lag'gard (lăg'ẽrd), *adj.* Slow; sluggish; loitering. — *n.* A loiterer. — **lag'gard·ly,** *adv.* — **lag'gard·ness,** *n.*

lag'ger (lăg'ẽr), *n.* One who lags.

lag'gin (lăg'ĭn), **lag'gen** (-ĕn), *n.* *Dial.* The inside angle between the side and bottom of a wooden dish.

lag'ging (lăg'ĭng), *n.* **a** Action of covering something, as a boiler, with lags, strips, or the like, or with a covering of nonconducting material. **b** The material so used.

La Gio·con'da (lä jō·kōn'dä). See MONA LISA.

la·gniappe' (lăn·yăp'), **la·gnappe'** (lăn·yăp'), *n.* [Creole, fr. F. *la* the + Sp. *ñapa, yapa,* in the same sense.] In Louisiana, a trifling present given to customers by tradesmen.

lag'o·morph (lăg'ō·môrf), *n.* [NL., fr. *lago-* (combining form, fr. Gr. *lagōs* hare) + *-morph.*] *Zool.* A member of an order (Lagomorpha) of gnawing mammals having two pairs of upper incisors one behind the other, comprising rabbits, hares, and pikas.

la·goon' (lȧ·gōōn'), *n.* Also **la·gune'.** [F. and It.; F. *lagune,* fr. It. *laguna,* fr. L. *lacuna* ditch, pool, pond, fr. *lacus* lake.] A shallow sound, pond, or lake, esp. one near, or communicating with, the sea; as, the *lagoons* of Venice. Cf. ATOLL.

la'ic (lā'ĭk), *adj.* [LL. *laicus.*] Of or pert. to a layman or the laity; lay; secular. — *n.* A layman. — **la'i·cal** (lā'ĭ·kăl), *adj.* — **la'i·cal·ly,** *adv.*

la'i·cize (lā'ĭ·sīz), *v. t.* To secularize; to put under the direction of, or to open to, laymen. — **la'i·ci·za'tion** (-sĭ·zā'shŭn; -sī·zā'shŭn), *n.*

laid (lād), *past & past part.* of LAY.

laid paper. Paper marked with parallel lines or watermarks, as if ribbed, from parallel wires. Cf. WOVE PAPER.

laigh (lāK), *adj. & adv.* *Scot.* Low. — *n.* *Scot.* A lowland, or bottom; a hollow.

lain (lān), *past part.* of LIE, to recline.

lair (lâr), *n.* [AS. *leger.*] A place in which to lie or rest; a bed or couch; esp., the bed of a wild beast. — *v. i.* To go to one's lair; to rest. — *v. t.* To provide with a lair.

lair, *v. i.* *Scot.* To stick or sink when wading in mud.

lair. Dial. var. of LORE, learning.

laird (lârd; *Scot.* lārd), *n.* [See LORD.] *Chiefly Scot.* A landed proprietor. — **laird'ly,** *adj.*

‖**lais'sez' faire** (lĕ'sā' fâr'). Also **lais'ser' faire** (lĕ'sā'). [F.] Literally, let (people) do, or make (what they choose); hence, noninterference; — a phrase used in economics, esp. by the physiocrats, deprecating governmental interference intended to foster or regulate labor, etc.

lais'sez'–faire', *adj.* Noninterfering; tolerant.

laith (lāth). Dial. var. of LOATH.

la'i·ty (lā'ĭ·tĭ), *n.; pl.* -TIES (-tĭz). [See LAY, *adj.*] **1.** The people, as distinguished from the clergy; laymen. **2.** Those not of a certain profession, as law or medicine, as distinguished from those belonging to it.

La'ius (lā'yŭs; lī'ŭs), *n.* See OEDIPUS.

lake (lāk), *n.* [F. *laque,* fr. Per. *lak.* See LAC resin.] **1.** A purplish-red pigment prepared from lac or cochineal; also, the color of this pigment. **2.** Any of many colored insoluble metallic compounds of dyes. — **lak'y** (lāk'ĭ), *adj.*

lake (lāk), *n.* [OF. *lac,* fr. L. *lacus.*] **1.** A considerable inland body of standing water. **2.** A pool of other liquid, as lava, oil, or pitch. — **lak'y** (lāk'ĭ), *adj.*

Lake District *or* **Country.** See *Gaz.*

lake dwelling. A dwelling built over a lake; specif., such a dwelling of prehistoric times. Cf. CRANNOG. — **lake dweller.**

lake herring. See CISCO.

Lake poets. Southey, Coleridge, and Wordsworth, who lived in the Lake District; — orig. so called in derision.

lak'er (lāk'ẽr), *n.* **1.** One who lives or works on a lake or on a lake steamer. **2.** A fish, esp. a lake trout, living in or taken from a lake. **3.** A vessel for lake navigation.

lake salmon. The namaycush.

lake trout. Any of certain trout and salmon found in lakes; esp., in America, the namaycush.

lakh (lăk). Var. of LAC, one hundred thousand.

la'kin (lā'kĭn). Obs. contraction of LADYKIN.

Lal'lan (lăl'ăn), *adj.* *Scot.* Of the Lowlands. — *n.* *Scot.* Lowland Scottish.

lal·la'tion (lă·lā'shŭn), *n.* [L. *lallare* to sing lalla, or lullaby.] Imperfect enunciation of the letter *r,* whereby it sounds like *l.*

lam (lăm), *v. t. & i.;* LAMMED (lămd); LAM'MING. *Now Slang.* To beat soundly; to thrash; whack.

lam, *v. i.* *Slang.* To flee, esp. from an officer of justice. — *n. Slang.* A getaway; escape. — ***on the lam.*** In precipitate flight. — ***take it on the lam.*** To flee precipitately. *Underworld Slang.*

la'ma (lä'mȧ), *n.; pl.* LAMAS (-mȧz). [Tibetan, written as *blama.*] In Tibet, etc., a priest of Lamaism; — so called by foreigners.

La'ma·ism (-ĭz'm), *n.* The Buddhism of Tibet and Mongolia, the tenets of which are those of Buddhism coupled with corrupted Sivaism and native shamanistic practices. Its elaborate hierarchy is headed by the ***Grand, or Dalai, Lama.*** — **La'ma·ist** (-ĭst), *n. & adj.* — **La'ma·is'tic** (-ĭs'tĭk), *adj.*

La·marck'i·an (lȧ·mär'kĭ·ăn), *adj.* Designating, or pertaining to, the theories of Lamarck. See LAMARCKISM. — *n.* A supporter of these theories.

La·marck'ism (lȧ·märk'ĭz'm), *n.* *Biol.* The theory of organic evolution proposed and maintained by the French naturalist Lamarck (1744–1829), that changes in environment cause changes in structure of animals and plants, and that acquired characters are transmitted to offspring.

la'ma·ser'y (lä'mȧ·sẽr'ĭ *or, Brit.,* -sẽr·ĭ; lȧ·mä'sẽr·ĭ), *n.; pl.* -SERIES (-ĭz). A monastery or convent of lamas in Tibet, Mongolia, etc.

lamb (lăm), *n.* [AS. *lamb.*] **1.** A young sheep. **2.** The flesh of a young sheep, when slaughtered and dressed for food. **3. a** Short for LAMBSKIN. **b** The fur or pelt of a lamb, esp. that obtained from the karakul lamb, as astrakhan or broadtail. **4.** A person innocent, gentle, or weak as a lamb. **5.** *Stock Exchange Cant.* One who speculates amateurishly. — *v. i.* To bring forth a lamb or lambs; to yean.

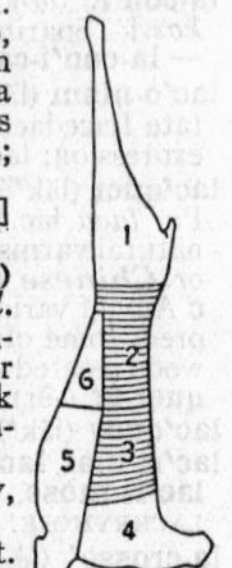

Cuts of Lamb. 1 Leg (Chops and Roast); 2 Loin (Chops or Roast); 3 Hotel Rack (Rib, or French, Chops); 4 Chuck (Roasts and Stews); 5 Breast (Stews or Rolled Roast); 6 Flank (Stews). Cf. SHEEP, *Illust.*

lam'baste' (lăm'bāst'), *v. t.* [*lam* + *baste* to beat.] *Slang.* To beat; thrash; also, to chide roughly.

lamb'da (lăm'dȧ), *n.* [Gr.] The eleventh letter (Λ, λ) of the Greek alphabet, corresponding to the English *L, l.*

lamb'doid (lăm'doid), *adj.* Also **lamb·doi'dal** (lăm·doi'dăl; -d'l). [Gr. *lambdoeidēs,* fr. *lambda* the letter lambda (Λ) + *eidos* shape.] Of the shape of the Greek lambda (Λ); hence, *Anat.,* designating the suture connecting the occipital and parietal bones.

lam'ben·cy (lăm'bĕn·sĭ), *n.; pl.* -CIES (-sĭz). Quality, state, or fact of being lambent; that which is lambent.

lam'bent (-bĕnt), *adj.* [L. *lambens, -entis,* pres. part. of *lambere* to lick.] **1.** Playing lightly over a surface; flickering; as, a *lambent* flame. **2.** Softly radiant; as, *lambent* eyes. **3.** Characterized by lightness of touch and brilliance; as, *lambent* humor. — **lam'bent·ly,** *adv.*

lam'bert (lăm'bẽrt), *n.* [After Johann H. *Lambert* (1728–77), Ger. physicist.] *Photom.* The C.G.S. unit of brightness, equal to the brightness of a surface which is radiating or reflecting one lumen per square centimeter.

Lam'beth Pal'ace (lăm'bĕth; -bĕth). The official London residence of the archbishop of Canterbury.

lamb'kill' (lăm'kĭl'), *n.* *U. S.* = SHEEP LAUREL.

lamb'kin (lăm'kĭn), *n.* **1.** A small or young lamb. **2.** A young or tender person; — chiefly in endearment.

lamb'like' (-līk'), *adj.* Like a lamb; gentle; meek.

Lamb of God, the Lamb. *Bib.* Christ, in allusion to the paschal lamb. *John* i. 29.

lam'boys (lăm'boiz), *n.* [Perh. fr. F. *lambeaux* flaps.] The steel skirt, from waist to knees, of armor of the 15th and 16th centuries.

lam'bre·quin (lăm'brĕ·kĭn; lăm'bẽr-), *n.* [F.] **1.** *Obs. exc. Hist.* A scarf attached to a helmet, to protect it from wet or heat. **2.** *U. S.* A piece of drapery hanging from a shelf or from the casing above a window.

lamb'skin' (lăm'skĭn'), *n.* A lamb's skin, or leather made from it; esp., a skin dressed with the wool on.

lame (lām), *adj.* [AS. *lama.*] **1.** Physically disabled; infirm. **2.** Disabled by reason of the imperfect action of a limb through injury or defect; specif., disabled in the leg or foot. **3.** Hence, hobbling; limping; also, unsatisfactory; as, a *lame* excuse. — *v. t.* To make lame; cripple. — *v. i.* To go or become lame. — **lame'ly,** *adv.* — **lame'ness,** *n.*

lame (lām; *F.* làm), *n.* [F., fr. L. *lamina, lamna.*] **a** A thin plate, as of metal. **b** *pl.* Small steel plates combined so as to slide one upon the other and form a piece of armor.

la·mé' (là·mā'), *n.* [F., lit., laminated, fr. *lame* gold or silver thread or wire.] A rich fabric woven from metal threads sometimes mixed with silk, wool, or cotton.

lame duck. A disabled person or thing; specif.: **a** *Stock Exchange.* A person unable to fulfill his engagements. **b** *U. S. Political Cant.* An officeholder who has failed of re-election, esp. one who is nearing the end of his term.

la·mel'la (lȧ·mĕl'ȧ), *n.; pl.* -LAE (-ē), -LAS (-ȧz). [L., dim. of *lamina* plate, leaf, layer.] A thin plate, leaf, or layer; a platelike organ, process, or part, as: **a** *Bot.* The layer (***middle lamella***) of intercellular material, composed chiefly of pectins, that cements together adjacent cells. **b** One of the thin plates forming the gills in bivalve mollusks. **c** A gill of a mushroom.

la·mel'lar (lȧ·mĕl'ẽr; lăm'ĕ·lẽr), *adj.* Lamellate.

lam'el·late (lăm'ĕ·lāt; lȧ·mĕl'āt), **lam'el·lat'ed** (lăm'ĕ·lāt'ĕd; -ĭd), *adj.* **a** Composed of, or furnished with, thin plates or lamellae. **b** Composed of a flat plate or leaf.

la·mel′li·branch (lȧ·mĕl′ĭ·brăngk), *n.* [See LAMELLA; BRANCHIA.] *Zool.* Any of a class (Lamellibranchia or Lamellibranchiata) of mollusks, including the clams, oysters, mussels, etc., distinguished by having the body bilaterally symmetrical, compressed, and enclosed within the mantle, which builds up a bivalved shell whose right and left parts are connected by a hinge over the animal's back. — **la·mel′li·bran′chi·ate** (-brăng′kĭ·āt), *adj. & n.*

la·mel′li·corn (-kôrn), *adj.* [*lamella* + L. *cornu* a horn.] *Zool.* **1.** Having or designating antennae ending in flattened plates. **2.** Belonging to a superfamily (Lamellicornia) of beetles having this form of antennae. — *n.* A lamellicorn beetle, as the dung beetle.

la·mel′li·ros′tral (-rŏs′trăl), **la·mel′li·ros′trate** (-trāt), *adj.* [See LAMELLA; ROSTRUM.] Belonging to a group (Lamellirostres) of birds including ducks, geese, and swans.

la·mel′lose (lȧ·mĕl′ōs; lăm′ĕ·lōs), *adj.* Lamellate.

la·ment′ (lȧ·mĕnt′), *v. i.* [F. *lamenter*, fr. L. *lamentari*, fr. *lamentum* a lament.] To express or feel sorrow; to mourn greatly. — *v. t.* To express deep sorrow for or about. — **Syn.** See DEPLORE. — *n.* **1.** Expression of grief or sorrow; lamentation; weeping. **2.** An expression of lamentation in a literary form, as an elegy or dirge.

lam′en·ta·ble (lăm′ĕn·tȧ·b'l), *adj.* **1.** Mournful; expressing grief. **2.** Fitted to awaken lament; sorrowful; pitiable; deplorable. — **lam′en·ta·bly**, *adv.*

lam′en·ta′tion (-tā′shŭn), *n.* Act of lamenting or bewailing; audible expression of sorrow; wailing; a lament.

Lam′en·ta′tions (-shŭnz), *n. pl., construed as sing.* A book of the Old Testament attributed to the prophet Jeremiah. See BIBLE.

la·ment′ed (lȧ·mĕn′tĕd; -tĭd), *adj.* Mourned for.

la′mi·a (lā′mĭ·ȧ), *n.* [L., fr. Gr. *lamia.*] **1.** *Class. Myth.* One of a class of man-devouring monsters, commonly represented with the head and breast of a woman and body of a serpent. **2.** Hence, a vampire; witch; sorceress.

la′mi·a′ceous (lā′mĭ·ā′shŭs), *adj.* [NL. *Lamium*, genus name (fr. L. *lamium* a dead nettle) + *-aceous.*] *Bot.* Belonging to the mint family (Lamiaceae, syn. Menthaceae). See 1st MINT.

lam′i·na (lăm′ĭ·nȧ), *n.; pl.* -NAE (-nē), -NAS (-nȧz). [L.] **1.** A thin plate or scale; a layer; a flake. See VERTEBRA, *Illust.* **2.** *Bot.* The blade or expanded part of a foliage leaf; — distinguished from *petiole*, or *leafstalk*. **3.** *Farriery.* One of the narrow thin parallel plates of soft sensitive tissue which cover the flesh inside the wall of the hoof.

lam′i·na·ble (lăm′ĭ·nȧ·b'l), *adj.* That may be formed into laminae.

lam′i·nar (-nēr), *adj.* Also **lam′i·nal** (-năl). Arranged in, consisting of, or like laminae.

laminar flow. Streamline flow in a viscous fluid near solid boundaries; — contrasted with *turbulent flow.*

lam′i·nar′i·a′ceous (-nâr′ĭ·ā′shŭs), *adj.* [NL. *Laminaria*, genus name (fr. L. *lamina* thin plate) + *-aceous.*] Belonging to a family (Laminariaceae) of brown algae, comprising many seaweeds, including the largest of the kelps (species of *Macrocystis*). See ALGA.

lam′i·nate (lăm′ĭ·nāt), *adj.* Shaped like, or consisting of, laminae. — (-nāt), *v. t.* **1.** To cause to separate into laminae. **2.** To form, as metal, into a thin plate, as by rolling. **3.** To cover or construct with laminae. **4.** To make (a material) by bonding together superposed layers of paper, fabric, or plywood, impregnated with a resinoid, by simultaneous application of heat and pressure, into a dense, tough, homogeneous solid. — (-nāt), *v. i.* To divide into laminae. — *n.* A laminated plastic.

lam′i·nat′ed (-nāt′ĕd; -ĭd), *adj.* Laminate.

lam′i·na′tion (-nā′shŭn), *n.* Process of laminating; state of being laminated; also, a laminated structure; a lamina.

lam′i·ni′tis (-nī′tĭs), *n.* [NL.] Inflammation of a lamina, esp. of the fleshy laminae of the horse's hoof.

lam′i·nose (lăm′ĭ·nōs), *adj.* Laminate.

lam′i·nous (-nŭs), *adj.* Laminate.

Lam′mas (lăm′ȧs), *n.* [AS. *hlāmmesse, hlāfmæsse*, loaf Mass, bread feast, fr. *hlāf* loaf + *mæsse* Mass.] The first day of August (**Lammas Day**) or the time of year (**Lam′mas·tide′** [-tīd′]) about that day.

lam′mer·gei′er, lam′mer·gey′er (lăm′ẽr·gī′ẽr), *n.* Also **lam′mer·geir′** (-gīr′). [G. *lämmergeier*, fr. *lamm*, pl. *lämmer*, lamb + *geier* vulture.] The largest European bird of prey (*Gypaëtus barbatus grandis*), found in mountainous regions from the Pyrenees to northern India, resembling both the eagles and the vultures.

lamp (lămp), *n.* [OF. *lampe*, fr. L. *lampas, -adis*, fr. Gr. *lampas, -ados*, torch, fr. *lampein* to shine.] **1.** A vessel with a wick for burning oil or other inflammable liquid to produce artificial light; hence, any of various vessels or devices for producing light or heat; as, an arc *lamp;* safety *lamp.* **2.** *Poetic.* **a** A torch. **b** A heavenly body, as the sun, moon, or a star; also, a flash.

lam′pad (lăm′păd), *n.* [Gr. *lampas, lampados.* See LAMP.] A lamp or candlestick; — from *Rev.* iv. 5.

lam′pas (lăm′pȧs), *n.* [F.] A decorative textile fabric, as a flowered silk.

lam′pas, *n.* [F.] In horses, congestion of the mucous membrane of the hard palate.

lamp′black′ (lămp′blăk′), *n.* [*lamp* + *black.*] Fine soot deposited by imperfectly burning carbonaceous materials. It is used esp. in paints, varnishes, and printer's ink.

lam′per eel (lăm′pẽr). Any lamprey.

lam′pi·on (lăm′pĭ·ŭn), *n.* [F.] A small lamp, as a pot of oil with a wick.

lamp′light′er (lămp′līt′ẽr), *n.* One who or that which lights a lamp, as a spill of paper or wood for lighting lamps.

lam·poon′ (lăm·po͞on′), *n.* [F. *lampon*, orig. a drinking song, fr. *lampons* let us drink.] A personal satire in writing, usually malicious or abusive. — *v. t.* To subject to abusive ridicule in writing. — **lam·poon′er**, *n.* — **lam·poon′er·y**, *n.* — **lam·poon′ist**, *n.*

lam′prey (lăm′prĭ), *n.* [OF. *lampreie*, fr. ML. *lampreda.*] Any of an order (Hyperoartia) of eellike aquatic vertebrates, widely distributed in temperate and subarctic regions in both fresh and salt water. The mouth is large, circular, jawless, and suctorial.

‖**la·na′i** (lä·nä′ē), *n.* [Hawaiian.] A veranda; porch.

la′nate (lā′nāt), *adj.* [L. *lanatus*, fr. *lana* wool, down.] Woolly; covered with fine, long hair.

Lan′cas·ter (lăng′kȧs·tẽr; *U. S. also* lăn[g]′kăs′tẽr), *n.* Name of an English royal house or family. See LANCASTRIAN, *n.*

Lan·cas′tri·an (lăng·kăs′trĭ·ăn), *adj.* Of or pertaining to the English royal house of Lancaster. — *n.* **a** *Eng. Hist.* A member or supporter of the English royal house of Lancaster, esp. in the Wars of the Roses in which its symbol was the red rose. Cf. YORKIST. **b** A native or citizen of Lancashire.

lance (lȧns; 9), *n.* [OF. *lance*, fr. L. *lancea.*] **1.** A weapon with a long shaft and a sharp steel head, carried by light cavalry. **2.** A soldier armed with a lance; a lancer. **3.** Any of various sharp objects suggestive of a soldier's lance, as a spear used by fishermen, a lancet, etc. — *v. t.;* LANCED (lȧnst); LANC′ING (lȧn′sĭng). [OF. *lancier.*] **1.** To pierce, as with a lance. **2.** To open with or as with a lancet.

lance. Var. of LAUNCE.

lance corporal. *Mil.* A private appointed acting corporal without change of pay.

lance′let (lȧns′lĕt; -lĭt), *n.* [*lance* + *-let.*] Any of certain small, translucent marine animals (constituting the subphylum Cephalochordata) most nearly related to the vertebrates.

Lan′ce·lot (lȧn′sĕ·lŏt; lȧns′lŏt), *n.* [F.] The most famous knight, called also **Lan′ce·lot du Lac** (dü lăk′), of King Arthur's Round Table, paramour of Guinevere.

lan′ce·o·late (lăn′sē·ō·lāt), *adj.* [LL. *lanceolatus*, fr. *lanceola* a little lance, dim. of *lancea* lance.] *Bot. & Zool.* Lance-shaped. See LEAF, *Illust.* (3).

lanc′er (lȧn′sẽr), *n.* **1.** One who carries a lance; specif., a light cavalry soldier armed with the lance. **2.** *pl.* Also **lan′ciers** (lȧn′sẽrz). A set of quadrilles of a certain arrangement; also, the music for these dances.

lance sergeant. *Mil.* A corporal appointed to perform temporarily the duties of a sergeant; an acting sergeant.

lan′cet (lȧn′sĕt; -sĭt; 9), *n.* [F. *lancette*, dim. of *lance* lance.] **1.** A surgical instrument, commonly sharp-pointed and two-edged, used to open boils, etc. **2.** *Arch.* A lancet arch or window.

lancet arch. An acutely pointed arch. See ARCH, *Illust.*

lan′cet·ed (lȧn′sĕ·tĕd; -sĭ·tĕd; -tĭd; 9), *adj.* Having a lancet arch or window.

lancet window. A high narrow window with an acutely pointed head and without tracery.

lance′wood′ (lȧns′wo͝od′), *n.* A tough, elastic wood, often used for shafts, fishing rods, cabinetwork, etc.; also, any of several trees (esp. *Oxandra lanceolata*) yielding this wood.

lan′ci·nate (lăn′sĭ·nāt), *v. t.* [L. *lancinatus*, past part. of *lancinare* to tear.] To pierce or stab. — **lan′ci·na′tion** (-nā′shŭn), *n.*

land (lănd), *n.* [AS. *land, lond.*] **1.** The solid part of the surface of the earth. **2.** Any portion of the surface of the earth, considered by itself, as a country, estate, farm, or tract; hence, a nation; a people. **3.** Ground, esp. in respect to its situation, nature, or quality; soil. **4.** Landed property; *pl.*, territorial possessions; as, to divide *lands* among heirs. **5.** In any surface prepared with indentations or grooves, a part not so treated, as the surface of the bore of a rifle between consecutive grooves. **6.** *Econ.* All those elements in the wealth of a nation supposed to be furnished by nature. **7** *Law.* **a** Any ground, soil, or earth whatsoever, regarded as the subject of ownership. **b** An interest or estate in land; loosely, any tenement or hereditament.

-land (-lȧnd; -lănd). A combining form of *land*, denoting: **a** *A kind of tract* or *soil*, as low*land.* **b** A *country* or *region*, as in Ire*land.* **c** *A realm of a* (specified) *class* or *type*, as in dream*land.* Corresponding nouns, denoting *inhabitants*, are formed in **-lander**, as in High*lander.*

land (lănd), *v. t.* **1.** To set or put on shore from a ship; to disembark. **2.** To set down after conveying; to cause to reach, or come to rest in, a particular place; also, *Slang*, to deliver squarely upon the spot aimed at, as a punch. **3.** To catch; as, to *land* a fish; also, *Colloq.*, to win, gain, or secure, usually as a result of artful effort; as, the detective *landed* the criminal. — *v. i.* **1. a** To go ashore from a ship; to disembark. **b** Of a ship or boat, to touch at a place on shore. **c** Of aircraft, to come to the ground or the surface of water. **2.** To come to the end of a course, to a stage in a journey, or to a particular position; to come to rest; to arrive.

lan′dau (lăn′dô; -dou), *n.* [From *Landau*, town in Germany.] A four-wheeled covered vehicle with a top divided so that the vehicle can be used opened or closed; also, a closed automobile body with provision for opening or folding the rear quarter.

lan′dau·let′ (lăn′dô·lĕt′), *n.* Also **lan′dau·lette′.** **1.** A small landau. **2.** An automobile body with an enclosed rear section containing one cross seat, the roof being collapsible and the driver's seat open.

land bank. **1.** A bank, such as any of the Federal Land Banks in the United States, whose chief function is the financing of transactions in real property. **2.** Formerly, in England, a bank which based its currency upon real property.

land′ed (lăn′dĕd; -dĭd), *adj.* Having an estate in land; consisting in land or real estate; as, *landed* men or property.

land′fall′ (lănd′fôl′), *n.* **a** *Naut.* A sighting or making land when at sea. **b** *Aeronautics.* A landing.

land grant. A grant of land by the government, esp. for roads or railroads, or for agricultural colleges.

land′-grant′ col′lege *or* **u′ni·ver′si·ty.** One of certain institutions for higher education in the United States, receiving federal aid under the Morrill Acts of 1862 and 1890 (**Land-Grant Acts**). They are so called because the original law granted public lands to each state for the support of at least one college teaching such branches of learning as are related to agriculture and the mechanic arts.

land′grave′ (lănd′grāv′), *n.* [G. *landgraf*, lit., land count.] A German count having a certain territorial jurisdiction; later, the title of certain German princes.

land·gra′vi·ate (lănd·grā′vĭ·āt), **land′gra·vate** (lănd′grȧ·vāt), *n.* Office, jurisdiction, or authority of a landgrave.

land′gra·vine (lănd′grȧ·vēn), *n.* [G. *landgräfin.*] The wife of a landgrave, or a woman of the rank and position of a landgrave.

land′hold′er (-hōl′dẽr), *n.* A holder or owner of land.

land′ing, *n.* **1.** A going or bringing on or to shore or land; act of alighting on the earth, as of an airplane. When made because of engine failure or bad weather it is called a ***forced landing.*** **2.** A place for discharging persons or things, as a platform, pier, dock, etc. **3.** *Arch.* The level part of a staircase, at the end of a flight of stairs.

landing craft. Any of numerous naval war vessels specially designed for putting ashore troops and/or equipment, esp. in amphibious beach assault, as the ocean-going 328 ft. Landing Ship, Tank (LST) displacing 5500 tons, the 157 ft. Landing Craft, Infantry (LCI) with bunks for 200 soldiers, the 36 ft. Landing Craft, Personnel (LCP) bearing 36 assault troops, and smaller control and support craft.

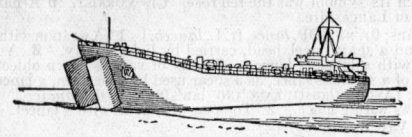

Landing Craft (LST).

landing field. A field where aircraft may land and take off.

landing gear. The under structure of an aircraft, designed to carry the load when in contact with the land or water. See AIRPLANE, *Illust.*

landing strip. See STRIP.

land'la·dy (lănd'lā'dĭ), *n.; pl.* -DIES (-dĭz). **1.** A woman having real estate which she leases. **2.** The mistress of an inn, lodginghouse, or boardinghouse.

land'less, *adj.* Having no property or estate in land.

land'locked' (lănd'lŏkt'), *adj.* **1.** Enclosed, or nearly enclosed, by land, as a harbor. **2.** Confined to fresh water by some barrier; cut off from the sea; — said of certain fish; as, the **landlocked salmon.**

land'lord' (-lôrd'), *n.* **1.** The owner or holder of land or houses which he leases. **2.** The master of an inn.

land'lord·ism, *n.* The system or doctrine of the ownership of the soil being vested in one who leases it to cultivators.

land'loup·er (lănd'loup'ēr; -loop'ēr), *n.* Also **land'lop'er** (-lŏp'ēr). [D. *landlooper,* lit., landrunner.] A vagrant.

land'lub'ber (-lŭb'ēr), *n.* [*land* + *lubber.*] *Naut.* One who passes his life on land; hence, anyone who is clumsy on shipboard; — a term used in ridicule.

land'man (-mǎn), *n.* A man who lives or serves on land.

land'mark' (-märk'), *n.* **1.** A mark to designate the boundary of land. **2.** Any conspicuous object on land that marks a locality. **3.** Any event which marks a turning point.

land measure. A system of square measure used for measuring land; also, a table of areas used in such measurement. See MEASURE, *Table 3;* METRIC SYSTEM, *Table 3.*

Land of Beu'lah (bū'là). In Bunyan's *Pilgrim's Progress,* a land of rest and quiet lying upon the hither side of the River of Death. The name occurs in Isaiah lxii. 4.

land office. A government office in which the entries upon, and sales of, public land are registered.

land'-of'fice busi'ness. *Colloq., U. S.* Extensive and rapid business.

Land of Promise. Canaan; — so called because promised to Abraham (*Gen.* xv. 18; xvii. 8); hence [*not caps.*], a better country or condition of which one has expectation.

land'own'er (lănd'ōn'ēr), *n.* An owner of land. — **land'own'er·ship,** *n.* — **land'own'ing,** *n. & adj.*

land'-poor' (-pōōr'; 2), *adj. Colloq.* Pecuniarily embarrassed by owning much unprofitable or encumbered land.

land power. a Military power. **b** A nation having military power, esp., formidable military power. Cf. SEA POWER.

land'scape (lănd'skāp; lăn'skāp; 25), *n.* Formerly also **land'skip** (-skĭp). [D. *landschap,* fr. *land* land + -*schap,* equiv. to E. -*ship.*] **1.** A portion of land which the eye can comprehend in a single view, esp. in its pictorial aspect. **2.** A picture representing inland natural scenery. — *v. t.* To improve by landscape architecture or gardening. — *v. i.* To engage in landscape gardening.

landscape architect. One whose profession is to so arrange the effects of natural scenery over a given tract as to produce the best aesthetic effect, considering the use to which the tract is to be put. — **landscape architecture.**

landscape gardener. A person who lays out or develops a garden, grounds, etc. — **landscape gardening.**

land'side' (lănd'sīd'), *n.* A sidepiece opposite the moldboard in a plow, guiding the plow and receiving the side pressure when the furrow is turned. See PLOW, *Illust.*

land'slide' (lănd'slīd'; 25), *n.* **1.** The slipping down of a mass of earth or rock on a mountain or slope or behind a sea cliff; also, the mass which slips down. **2.** A great majority of votes for one side, esp. in an election.

land'slip' (-slĭp'), *n. Chiefly Eng.* A landslide (sense 1).

lands'man (lăndz'mǎn), *n.* **1.** One who lives on the land. **2.** *Naut.* **a** *Obs.* A sailor on his first voyage. **b** A sailor of little experience rated below an ordinary seaman. See SEAMAN.

Lands'ting, Lands'thing (läns'tĭng), *n.* [Dan. *landsting, landsthing,* fr. *land* land + *ting, thing,* parliament.] *Denmark.* The upper house of the legislature.

Land'sturm' (länt'shtoorm'), *n.* [G. See LAND; STORM.] *Mil.* **a** A calling out of the militia; a general levy in time of war. **b** The force so summoned. In Japan and Switzerland and, before World War I, in Germany, Austria, etc., a force composed of all men liable to service not already in the army, navy, or reserves.

Land'tag (länt'täk'), *n.; pl.* -TAGE (-tä'gě). [G.] A diet, or legislative assembly, esp. in one of the German states.

land'ward (lănd'wĕrd), *adv.* Also **land'wards** (-wĕrdz). Toward the land.

land'ward, *adj.* Lying or being towards the land.

Land'wehr' (länt'vär'), *n.* [G., fr. *land* land, country + *wehr* defense.] *Mil.* That part of the armed forces in the former German and Austrian empires, Japan, Switzerland, etc., which has completed service with the colors.

lane (lān), *n.* [AS. *lane, lone.*] **1.** A narrow way between fences or hedges which is not traveled as a highroad; hence, in a general sense, any narrow way or track. **2. a** An ocean route prescribed for steamers traveling in the same direction, in order to avoid collisions. **b** A strip of roadway used for a single line of traffic. **c** *Sports.* Any of several parallel courses laid out on a running track, etc.

lane. Scot. var. of LONE, as in *his lane,* by himself.

lang (lăng). Scot & dial. Eng. var. of LONG.

lang'lauf' (läng'louf'), *n.* [G., lit., long course.] *Skiing.* Running or racing across country on skis.

lang'läu'fer (-loi'fēr), *n.* [G.] A cross-country skier.

lan'grage (lăng'grĭj), *n.* Also **lan'grel** (lăng'grĕl), **lan'gridge** (-grĭj). A type of shot formerly used in battle at sea, for tearing sails and rigging.

lang'syne' (lăng'sīn'; *Scot.* làng'-), *adv., adj., & n.* [Scot. *lang* long + *syne* since.] *Scot.* Long ago.

lan'guage (lăng'gwĭj), *n.* [With *u* after F. *langue,* fr. ME. *language,* fr. OF. *langage,* fr. *langue* tongue, language, fr. L. *lingua.*] **1.** The body of words and methods of combining words used and understood by a considerable community; a tongue.

THE CHIEF LANGUAGE FAMILIES OF THE WORLD*

I	AFRICAN	Negro	Bantu	
			Sudanic	
		Hamitic	Coptic	
			Berber	
			Cushitic	
II	SEMITIC (Arabia, Egypt, North Africa)		Phoenician	
			Hebrew	
			Arabic	
			Aramaic	
			Ethiopic	
III	INDO-EUROPEAN or ARYAN	(See INDO-EUROPEAN LANGUAGES, *Table*)		
IV	INDO-CHINESE	Chinese		
		Thai	Siamese	
			Shan	
		Tibetan		
		Burmese		
V	JAPANESE			
VI	URAL-ALTAIC	Finno-Ugric	Magyar	
			Finnish	
			Estonian	
		Turkic	Uigur	
			Turkish	
			Uzbek	
			Kirghiz	
		Mongolian		
VII	AUSTRONESIAN	Indonesian	Malay	
			Javanese	
			Tagala	
		Polynesian	Maori	
			Hawaiian	
		Melanesian		
VIII	INDIAN (North American)	Algonquian		
		Siouan		
		Uto-Aztecan		
IX	INDIAN (South American)	Arawakan		
		Cariban		
		Tupian	Tupi	
			Guarani	
		Quechua		
		Araucanian		

* Only the most important language names are given in this Table.

2. Any means, vocal or other, of expressing or communicating feeling or thought. **3.** *Specif.:* **a** The faculty of verbal expression and the use of words in human intercourse; also, the words themselves in their grammatical relationships. **b** The inarticulate sounds by which animals express their feelings. **4. a** Form or manner of expression; style. **b** The vocabulary and phraseology belonging to an art or department of knowledge. **c** The suggestion, by objects, actions, or conditions, of ideas associated therewith; as, the *language* of flowers. **5.** The study of language, a language, or languages.

||langue d'oc (läng' dôk'). [F., prop., language of yes, Pr. *oc* yes.] The Romance dialects of the southerly provinces of France; — so called from *oc* (yes) in contrast with the **langue d'o·ïl'** (dô'ēl') [OF. *oïl* yes, F. *oui*] of the basin of the Loire and north, and the **langue de si** (dě sē') [It. *si* yes] of Italy. See INDO-EUROPEAN LANGUAGES, *Table.*

lan'guet, lan'guette (lăng'gwĕt), *n.* [F. *languette,* dim. of *langue* tongue. See LANGUAGE.] Anything resembling the tongue in form or office; a tonguelike part. See FLUE PIPE, *Illust.*

lan'guid (lăng'gwĭd), *adj.* [F. or L.; F. *languide,* fr. L. *languidus,* fr. *languere* to be languid.] **1.** Drooping or flagging from exhaustion; weak. **2.** Sluggish; dull; listless. **3.** Slow; without force; as, a *languid* interest. — **lan'guid·ly,** *adv.* — **lan'guid·ness,** *n.*

lan'guish (lăng'gwĭsh), *v. i.* [OF. *languir,* fr. L. *languere.*] **1.** To become languid; to pine, wither, or fade; to lose force. **2.** To lose strength or vitality because of outward circumstances; as, he *languished* in prison. **3.** To assume an expression of weariness or emotion, appealing for sympathy. — *n.* A languishing, tender look or expression. — **lan'guish·er,** *n.*

lan'guish·ing, *adj.* That languishes; as: **a** Becoming languid and weak. **b** Amorously pensive. **c** Slow; without force or interest. **d** Lingering; as, a *languishing* illness. — **lan'guish·ing·ly,** *adv.*

lan'guish·ment (-mĕnt), *n.* **1.** Act or state of languishing; weakness; lassitude. **2.** Tenderness of look or mien.

lan'guor (lăng'gēr; lăng'ēr; -gwēr), *n.* [OF. *languor,* fr. L. *languor.*] **1.** A languid feeling; lassitude. **2.** Dullness; sluggishness; lack of vigor. — **Syn.** See LETHARGY.

lan'guor·ous (-ŭs), *adj.* Producing, or tending to produce, languor; characterized by languor. — **lan'guor·ous·ly,** *adv.*

lan·gur' (lŭng-gōor'), *n.* [Hind. *langur,* fr. Skr. *lāngūlin.*] Any of many species of Asiatic slender, long-tailed monkeys (genus *Presbytis*) with bushy eyebrows and a chin tuft.

lani-. [L. *lana*.] Combining form meaning *wool*, as in **la·nif'er·ous, la·nig'er·ous.**

lan'iard (lăn'yẽrd). Var. of LANYARD.

la'ni·ar'y (lā'nĭ·ĕr'ĭ; -ẽr·ĭ; lăn'ĭ-), *adj. & n.* [L. *laniarius*, fr. *lanius* butcher, fr. *laniare* to tear in pieces.] *Anat.* Canine; as, *laniary* teeth.

Lan'i·tal (lăn'ĭ·tăl), *n.* A trade-mark applied to threads and yarns made of artificial wool obtained from casein.

lank (lăngk), *adj.* [AS. *hlanc.*] **1.** Slender and thin; lean. **2.** Of hair, without curl or wave. — **Syn.** See LEAN. — **lank'ly**, *adv.* — **lank'ness**, *n.*

lank'y (lăngk'ĭ), *adj.*; LANK'I·ER (-ĭ·ẽr); LANK'I·EST. Lank; of a person, tall, spare, and, usually, loose-jointed. — **Syn.** See LEAN. — **lank'i·ly**, *adv.* — **lank'i·ness**, *n.*

lan'ner (lăn'ẽr), *n.* [F. *lanier*, ult. fr. L. *laniare* to tear in pieces.] **a** A falcon (*Falco biarmicus feldeggi*) of southern Europe. **b** *Falconry.* The female lanner, the male (which is smaller) being called **lan'ner·et** (-ĕt) [F. *laneret*].

lan'o·lin (lăn'ō·lĭn), **lan'o·line** (-lĭn; -lēn), *n.* [L. *lana* wool + *-ol*, 2 + *-in*.] Wool fat or grease, esp. when purified and incorporated with water, used in ointments, cosmetics, etc.

la'nose (lā'nōs), *adj.* Lanate; woolly.

lans'downe (lănz'doun), *n.* A fine, closely woven dress fabric of silk and wool.

lans'que·net (lăns'kĕ·nĕt), *n.* [F., fr. G. *landsknecht* a foot soldier, also a game of cards, fr. *land* country + *knecht* boy, servant.] **1.** A German foot soldier in foreign service, 15th to the 17th centuries. **2.** A gambling game at cards.

lan·ta'na (lăn·tā'nȧ; -tä'nȧ), *n.* [NL., viburnum.] *Bot.* Any of a genus (*Lantana*) of tropical shrubs of the verbena family (Verbenaceae).

lan'tern (lăn'tẽrn), *n.* [OF. *lanterne*, fr. L. *lanterna*, *laterna*, fr. Gr. *lamptēr* light, torch, fr. *lampein* to shine.] **1.** An enclosure for a light, protecting it from wind, rain, etc. **2.** A lighthouse; now, the chamber in a lighthouse containing the light. **3.** Short for MAGIC LANTERN. **4.** *Arch.* **a** A light open structure upon a roof, to give light and air to the interior. **b** A smaller cupola or towerlike member crowning a larger one, for ornament, or to admit light. **5.** *Fr. Hist.* [F. *lanterne.*] A street lamp, to the cords or chains of which many "aristocrats" were hanged in the French Revolution.

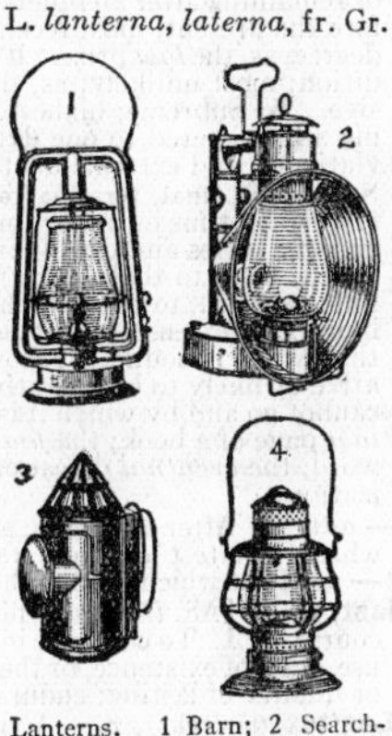

Lanterns. 1 Barn; 2 Searchlight; 3 Bull's-eye; 4 Railroad.

lantern fly. Any of several species of large, handsomely marked insects (*Laternaria, Fulgora,* and allied genera) having the front of the head prolonged into a hollow structure formerly supposed to be luminous.

lantern jaw. An undershot jaw; *pl.*, long, thin jaws; hence, a thin visage. — **lan'tern–jawed'** (-jôd'), *adj.*

lantern pinion. Also **lantern wheel.** *Mach.* A pinion or wheel having cylindrical trundles, instead of teeth.

lan'tha·num (lăn'thȧ·nŭm), *n.* [NL., fr. Gr. *lanthanein* to lie hid.] *Chem.* A rare-earth metallic element (see RARE-EARTH ELEMENT). Symbol, *La*; at. no., 57; at. wt., 138.92.

lant'horn (lănt'hôrn; lăn'tẽrn). Archaic var. of LANTERN.

la·nu'gi·nose (lȧ·nū'jĭ·nōs), *adj.* Lanuginous.

la·nu'gi·nous (-nŭs), *adj.* [L. *lanuginosus*, fr. *lanugo*, *-ginis*, down, fr. *lana* wool.] Covered with down; downy.

la·nu'go (lȧ·nū'gō), *n.* [L.] A dense cottony or downy growth; specif., *Anat.*, the soft woolly hair which covers the human fetus and that of some other mammals.

lan'yard, lan'iard (lăn'yẽrd), *n.* [F. *lanière*, fr. OF. *lasniere*, fr. *lasne* strap, thong, noose.] **1. a** *Naut.* A short piece of rope for fastening something in ships; esp., one of the pieces passing through deadeyes and used to extend shrouds, stays, etc. **b** A cord worn around the neck, as one worn by sailors to which is usually attached a knife (***knife lanyard***). **2.** *Mil.* A strong cord with a hook at one end used in firing certain kinds of cannon.

La·oc'o·ön (lā·ŏk'ō·ŏn), *n.* [L., fr. Gr. *Laokoōn.*] *Class. Myth.* A Trojan priest who distrusted the wooden horse and, with his two sons, was destroyed by two huge serpents, which Athena caused to come up out of the sea.

La·od'i·ce'an (lā·ŏd'ĭ·sē'ăn), *adj.* Lukewarm or indifferent, as were the Christians of ancient Laodicea, a city in Greater Phrygia. — **La·od'i·ce'an**, *n.*

lap (lăp), *n.* [AS. *læppa.*] **1.** A lower part of a garment that may be folded over; a skirt of a coat or of a gown. **2.** A fold of a garment used as a receptacle. **3.** The part of the clothing that lies on the knees, thighs, and lower part of the body when one sits; hence, that part of the person thus covered; figuratively, a place of rearing and fostering; as, the *lap* of luxury.

lap, *v. t.*; LAPPED (lăpt) or, *Rare*, LAPT; LAP'PING. [ME. *lappen* to fold.] **1.** To fold; to bend and lay (over or on something); as, to *lap* a piece of cloth. **2.** *Archaic.* To wrap up. **3.** To infold; to hold as in the lap. **4.** To lay together one partly over another; as, to *lap* weatherboards; also, to be partly over, or by the side of (something); as, the hinder boat *lapped* the foremost one. **5.** *Carp.* To unite, as beams or timbers, so as to preserve the same breadth and depth throughout, as in scarfing. **6.** *Mach.* To cut or polish with a lap (sense 2), as glass, gems, cutlery, etc. **7.** *Racing.* To get or be a lap in the lead of. — *v. i.* To be folded; to lie partly on or by the side of something, or of one another; to project (over, beyond, or into something); as, the cloth *laps* back; the edges *lap.*

— *n.* [From LAP, *v.*, to fold, wrap.] **1.** That part of anything that overlaps another part; also, the measure of such overlapping. **2.** *Mach.* A revolving disk of brass, lead, etc., used to hold an abrasive powder on its surface for cutting glass, gems, etc. **3.** *Racing.* One circuit around a race track, when such a circuit is a fraction of the distance to be traversed. **4.** *Roofing.* The distance one layer of shingle or slate extends over the second one below. Cf. COVER, *n.*, 7.

lap, *v. i.* [AS. *lapian.*] **1.** To take up liquid food with the tongue, in the manner of cats or dogs. **2.** To make a sound like that produced by taking up drink with the tongue. — *v. t.* **1.** To lick up with a quick motion of the tongue. **2.** Of water, waves, etc., to flow against, or wash, with a sound as of licking up liquid. — *n.* [From LAP to lick.] **1.** Act of lapping with or as with the tongue. **2.** A sound of or as of lapping. **3.** That which is lapped, as liquid food for dogs.

lap. Dial. past tense of LEAP.

lap'a·ro- (lăp'ȧ·rō-), **lapar-**. [Gr. *lapara.*] *Med. & Surg.* A combining form denoting *the flank*, or, loosely, *the abdominal wall*, as in **lap'a·rot'o·my, lap'a·rec'to·my** (see -TOMY, -ECTOMY).

lap'board' (lăp'bōrd'; 70), *n.* A board used on the lap as a substitute for a table, as by tailors, seamstresses, etc.

lap dog. A pet dog which may be held in the lap.

la·pel' (lȧ·pĕl'), *n.* [Dim. of LAP a fold.] That part of a garment which is turned back; specif., the fold of the front of a coat in continuation of the collar; — usually *pl.*

lap'ful (lăp'fo͝ol), *n.* As much as the lap can contain.

lap'i·dar'y (lăp'ĭ·dĕr'ĭ *or, esp. Brit.*, -dẽr·ĭ), *n.*; *pl.* -IES (-ĭz). [See LAPIDARY, *adj.*] An artificer who cuts, polishes, and engraves precious stones. — *adj.* [L. *lapidarius* pert. to stone, fr. *lapis* stone.] **1.** Of or pertaining to the art of cutting stones. **2.** Engraved upon stone.

lap'i·date (-dāt), *v. t.* [L. *lapidatus*, past part. of *lapidare*, fr. *lapis* stone.] To stone; to kill by stoning. — **lap'i·da'tion** (-dā'shŭn), *n.*

la·pid'i·fy (lȧ·pĭd'ĭ·fī), *v. t. & i.*; -FIED (-fīd); -FY'ING. [F. *lapidifier.* See LAPIS; -FY.] To turn to stone; to petrify. — **la·pid'i·fi·ca'tion** (-fĭ·kā'shŭn), *n.*

la·pil'lus (lȧ·pĭl'ŭs), *n.*; *pl.* LAPILLI (-ī). [L.] A small stone; *pl.*, small volcanic stony or glassy fragments.

‖**la'pin'** (lȧ'păN'; *Angl.* lăp'ĭn), *n.* [F.] A rabbit; also, rabbit fur.

‖**la'pis** (lā'pĭs; lăp'ĭs), *n.*; *pl.* LAPIDES (lăp'ĭ·dēz). [L. *lapis*, *lapidos.*] A stone; — chiefly in Latin phrases.

lap'is laz'u·li (lăp'ĭs, *or* lā'pĭs, lăz'ū·lī *or* -lĭ). [F. & NL.; ML. *lazulus* is fr. Ar. See AZURE.] A stone, a complex silicate containing sulfur, of a rich azure-blue color; also, the color of this stone.

lap joint. A joint made by one layer, part, or piece overlapping another. — **lap'–joint'**, *v. t.*

Lap'land·er (lăp'lăn·dẽr), *n.* A Lapp.

Lapp (lăp), *n.* [Sw.] **1.** One of a Mongoloid race of northern Scandinavia and parts of Russia, very short and brachycephalous. **2.** The language of these people.

lap'per (lăp'ẽr), *n.* One who or that which laps.

lap'per (lȧp'ẽr). Scot. & Ir. var. of LOPPER, to curdle.

lap'pet (lăp'ĕt; -ĭt), *n.* [Dim. of LAP a fold.] **1.** A loose fold or flap of a garment or headdress. See VESTMENT, *Illust.* **2.** Anything hanging or lying in a fold or loosely pendent, as a flap of flesh, a lobe of the ear, the wattle of a bird, etc.

lap·sa'tion (lăp·sā'shŭn), *n.* *U.S.* A lapsing.

lapse (lăps), *n.* [L. *lapsus*, fr. *labi*, past part. *lapsus*, to slide, fall.] **1.** A slip, as of the tongue or pen; slight error. **2.** A gliding, slipping, or gradual falling, esp. from a higher to a lower state, or in time. **3.** A falling into ruin or disuse; as, the *lapse* of a custom. **4.** *Law.* The termination or failure of a right or privilege through neglect to exercise it within some limit of time. **5.** *Meteorol.* Decrease of temperature, pressure, etc., as the height increases. **6.** *Theol.* A fall or apostasy. — **Syn.** See ERROR. — *v. i.* **1.** To pass or slip gradually and smoothly downward, backward, or away. **2.** To slide or slip from virtue. **3.** To fall into disuse or ruin. **4.** *Law.* To fall or pass from one to another by lapse.

lap'streak' (lăp'strēk'), *adj.* = CLINKER-BUILT. — *n.* A clinker-built boat.

‖**lap'sus** (lăp'sŭs), *n.* [L.] A slip; error; as in: **lap'sus ca'la·mi** (kăl'ȧ·mī), a slip of the pen; **lap'sus lin'guae** (lĭng'gwē), a slip of the tongue; **lap'sus me·mo'ri·ae** (mē·mō'rĭ·ē), a slip of the memory.

La·pu'ta (lȧ·pū'tȧ), *n.* In Swift's *Gulliver's Travels*, a flying island whose inhabitants are philosophers, devoted to mathematics and music.

lap'wing' (lăp'wĭng'), *n.* [AS. *hlēapewince.*] An abundant crested plover (*Vanellus vanellus*) of Europe, Asia, and northern Africa, noted for its slow irregular flapping flight and its shrill wailing cry.

lar (lär), *n.*; *pl.* LARES (lā'rēz; 6). [L.] See LARES.

lar'board (lär'bōrd; -bẽrd; 70), *n.* [With *r* after *starboard*, fr. ME. *ladeborde*, appar. the loading side.] *Naut.* The left-hand side of a ship to one on board facing toward the bow; port; — opposed to *starboard.* — **lar'board**, *adj. & adv.*

☞ *Larboard* has been, in actual use, superseded by *port.*

lar'ce·ner (lär'sĕ·nẽr), **lar'ce·nist** (-nĭst), *n.* One who commits larceny; a thief.

lar'ce·nous (-nŭs), *adj.* Having the character of larceny; committing larceny; thievish. — **lar'ce·nous·ly**, *adv.*

lar'ce·ny (-nĭ), *n.*; *pl.* -NIES (-nĭz). [F. *larcin*, fr. OF. *larrecin*, fr. L. *latrocinium*, fr. *latro* robber.] *Law.* The unlawful taking and carrying away of things personal with intent to deprive the rightful owner of the same; theft. Larceny at the common law was formerly distinguished as ***grand larceny*** and ***petit, or petty, larceny***, according to the value of the property stolen, but this distinction has been generally abolished.

larch (lärch), *n.* [G. *lärche*, fr. L. *larix*, *-icis.*] Any of a genus (*Larix*) of trees of the pine family, of graceful habit, distinguished by their short fascicled deciduous leaves; also, the tough durable wood of these trees.

lard (lärd), *n.* [OF., bacon, fr. L. *lardum*, *laridum.*] The melted and clarified fat of swine, esp. the internal fat of the abdomen. — *v. t.* **1.** To stuff or enrich with pork or bacon. **2.** To smear with lard, fat, or grease. **3.** To mix or garnish with something, as by way of improvement; to interlard. **4.** *Obs.* To fatten; to enrich with fat.

lard'er (lär'dẽr), *n.* [OF. *lardier*, fr. ML. *lardarium.*] A place where meat and other articles of food are kept. Cf. PANTRY.

lar'don (lär'dŏn), **lar·doon'** (lär·do͞on'), *n.* [F. *lardon*, fr. *lard* lard.] A strip of pork or bacon used in larding.

‖**la'res** (lā'rēz; 6), *n. pl.*; *sing.* LAR (lär). [L.] *Rom. Relig.* Tutelary gods or spirits, as of the house, etc.

la'res and pe·na'tes (lā'rēz *or* lär'ĕz; pē·nā'tēz). Household gods; hence, one's personal or household effects.

large (lärj), *adj.*; LARG'ER (lär'jẽr); LARG'EST. [OF., fr. L. *largus.*] **1.** *Obs.* Liberal; lavish. **2.** *Archaic.* Abundant; ample; also, broad; wide. **3.** Having more than usual power, capacity, range, or scope; comprehensive; magnanimous. **4.** Exceeding most other things of like kind in bulk, capacity, etc.; big; great; — opposed to *small*. **5.** *Archaic.* Full in statement; diffuse. **6.** *Archaic.* Lax; unrestrained; of speech or language, loose; licentious. **7.** *Naut.* Of the wind, free; fair; favorable. **8.** Handling or dealing with great numbers or quantities; as, a *large* exporter.

Syn. Large, big, great mean above the average of its kind in magnitude. Large is the preferred term when the dimensions, the extent, the capacity, the quantity, etc., is being considered (as, a *large* lot; a *large* hall; a *large* allowance); big is the preferred term when the emphasis is on bulk, weight, or volume (as, a *big* book; a *big* box; a *big* voice); great sometimes implies physical magnitude, then also connoting some impression such as wonder, surprise, awe, etc., but more often it implies magnitude in degree (as, *great* kindness; *great* haste). Figuratively, large suggests breadth, comprehensiveness, generosity; big, impressiveness rather than solidity; great, eminence, distinction, or supremacy.

— *adv.* **1.** *Obs.* Amply; liberally. **2.** *Naut.* With the wind free, or abaft the beam; as, to sail *large.*

— *n.* Liberty; freedom. *Obs.*, exc. in ***at large***, meaning: **a** Without restraint or confinement. **b** Diffusely; at length; as, to speak *at large.* **c** In general; altogether; as, society *at large.* **d** *U.S.* Of electors, representatives, etc., chosen to represent the whole of a state, county, or other division having subdivisions.

— **large′ly**, *adv.* — **large′ness**, *n.*

large′heart′ed (lärj′här′tĕd; -tĭd; 2), *adj.* Having a generous heart; liberal. — **large′heart′ed·ness**, *n.*

large′–mind′ed (-mīn′dĕd; -dĭd; 2), *adj.* Liberal in ideas; characterized by breadth of view; not narrow. — **large′–mind′ed·ly**, *adv.* — **large′–mind′ed·ness**, *n.*

large′–scale′, *adj.* That is on a large scale; of wide scope; also, drawn to a large scale.

lar′gess, lar′gesse (lär′jĕs), *n.* [OF. *largesse.* See LARGE, *adj.*] Liberal giving; also, a liberal gift.

lar·ghet′to (lär·gĕt′ō), *adj.* [It., dim. of *largo* largo.] *Music.* Somewhat slow, but less so than largo. — *n.* A larghetto movement. — *adv.* In larghetto tempo.

larg′ish (lär′jĭsh), *adj.* Rather large.

lar′go (lär′gō), *adj. & adv.* [It., fr. L. *largus.*] *Music.* Very slow; broad; stately; — used as a direction. — *n.* A largo movement or piece. — *adv.* In largo tempo.

lar′i·at (lăr′ĭ·ăt), *n.* [Sp. *la reata* the rope.] **a** A lasso; riata. **b** A rope for picketing animals while grazing.

lar′ine (lăr′ĭn; lā′rīn; 6), *adj.* [LL. *larus* gull, fr. Gr. *laros.*] Belonging to or designating a subfamily (Larinae, family Laridae) of birds, comprising the typical gulls, as disting. from the terns and jaegers.

la·rith′mics (lȧ·rĭth′mĭks), *n.*; see -ICS. [Gr. *laos* people + *arithmos* number.] The scientific study of the quantitative aspects of population. — **la·rith′mic** (-mĭk), *adj.*

lark (lärk), *n.* [AS. *lāwerce, lāferce.*] **1.** Any of numerous singing birds (family Alaudidae), esp. the skylark. They are found chiefly in Europe, Asia, and northern Africa. **2.** Any of many, usually ground-living, similar birds of other families; as, the meadow *larks*, tit*larks*, etc.

lark, *v. i.* *Colloq.* To sport; frolic; also, to ride across country or over obstacles. — *v. t. Colloq.* **a** To make sport of. **b** To jump, on horseback; as, to *lark* the hedge. — *n.* A frolic. — **lark′er**, *n.*

lark′spur (lärk′spûr), *n.* [*lark* bird + *spur.*] Any of a genus (*Delphinium*) of plants of the crowfoot family, many species of which are cultivated for their showy irregular flowers with spurred calyxes. The ***scarlet larkspur*** (*Delphinium cardinale*) is a native of southern California.

lar′ri·gan (lăr′ĭ·găn), *n.* *U.S. & Canada.* An oil-tanned moccasin with legs, used by lumbermen and trappers.

lar′ri·kin (lăr′ĭ·kĭn), *n.* [Cf. E. dial. *larrikin* a mischievous or frolicsome youth, *larrick* lively, careless, *larack* to frolic.] A rowdy street loafer. — *adj.* Rowdy; rough.

lar′rup (lăr′ŭp), *v. t.* *Colloq.* To beat or flog soundly. — *n. Colloq.* A blow.

lar′um (lăr′ŭm; lär′ŭm), *n.* *Archaic.* Short for ALARUM.

lar′va (lär′vȧ), *n.*; *pl.* -VAE (-vē). [L., ghost, mask.] **1.** The immature, wingless, and often wormlike form in which certain insects hatch from the egg, and in which they remain, with increase in size and other minor changes, until they assume the pupa or chrysalis stage. Various kinds are known as *caterpillars, grubs, maggots*, etc. See BOLL WEEVIL, SILKWORM, WIGGLER, *Illusts.* **2.** *Zool.* The early form of any animal which while immature is unlike its parent and must pass through a metamorphosis before assuming the adult characters. — **lar′val** (-văl), *adj.*

lar′vi·cide (lär′vĭ·sīd), *n.* [*larva* + *-cide.*] An agent or preparation for destroying larvae. — **lar′vi·cid′al** (-sīd′ăl; 2), *adj.*

la·ryn′gal (lȧ·rĭng′găl), *adj.* Produced in the larynx.

la·ryn′ge·al (lȧ·rĭn′jē·ăl; lăr′ĭn·jē′ăl), *adj.* [From LARYNX.] Of or pertaining to, or used on, the larynx.

lar′yn·gi′tis (lăr′ĭn·jī′tĭs), *n.* [NL., fr. *laryng-* + *-itis.*] Inflammation of the larynx. — **lar′yn·git′ic** (-jĭt′ĭk), *adj.*

la·ryn′go- (lȧ·rĭng′gō-), **laryng-.** [Gr. *larynx, -yngos.*] A combining form denoting: **a** *The larynx*, as in **lar′yn·got′o·my** (see -TOMY). **b** *Laryngeal and*, as in **la·ryn′go·pha·ryn′ge·al**, pertaining to both larynx and pharynx.

lar′yn·gol′o·gy (lăr′ĭng·gŏl′ō·jĭ), *n.* [*laryngo-* + *-logy.*] Systematized knowledge of the larynx; pathology of the larynx. — **la·ryn′go·log′i·cal** (lȧ·rĭng′gō·lŏj′ĭ·kăl), *adj.* — **lar′yn·gol′o·gist** (lăr′ĭng·gŏl′ō·jĭst), *n.*

la·ryn′go·scope (lȧ·rĭng′gō·skōp), *n.* [*laryngo-* + *-scope.*] An instrument for examining the interior of the larynx. — **la·ryn′go·scop′ic** (lȧ·rĭng′gō·skŏp′ĭk), **la·ryn′go·scop′i·cal** (-ĭ·kăl), *adj.* — **lar′yn·gos′co·pist** (lăr′ĭng·gŏs′kō·pĭst), *n.* — **lar′yn·gos′co·py** (-pĭ), *n.*

lar′ynx (lăr′ĭngks), *n.*; *pl.* LARYNGES (lȧ·rĭn′jēz), LARYNXES (lăr′ĭngk·sĕz; -sĭz). [NL., fr. Gr. *larynx, -yngos.*] *Anat. & Zool.* The modified upper part of the trachea. In man and other mammals, and in amphibians, it is the organ of voice. Cf. SYRINX, PHARYNX.

las′car (lăs′kẽr; lăs·kär′), *n.* [Hind. *lashkar* army, fr. Per. *lashkar*, fr. Ar. *al-'askar* the army.] An East Indian native sailor.

las·civ′i·ous (lȧ·sĭv′ĭ·ŭs), *adj.* [LL. *lasciviosus*, fr. L. *lascivia* wantonness, fr. *lascivus* wanton.] **1.** Wanton; lewd; lustful. **2.** Tending to produce lewd emotions. — **las·civ′i·ous·ly**, *adv.* — **las·civ′i·ous·ness**, *n.*

lash (lăsh), *n.* [ME. *lasche* a whiplash, a blow.] **1.** A stroke with a whip, or anything pliant and tough; hence, a sudden swinging blow. **2.** The flexible part of a whip; anything used for whipping. **3.** A stroke of satire, sarcasm, or the like. **4.** An eyelash. — *v. t.* **1.** To whip or scourge. **2.** To strike forcibly and quickly, as with a lash. **3.** To berate; as, to *lash* vice. **4.** To drive, as with a lash. **5.** To throw with a jerk or quickly. — *v. i.* **1.** To move suddenly; to dash; as, the rain *lashes* down. **2.** To ply the whip; to strike. — **lash′er**, *n.*

lash, *v. t.* [OF. *lachier*, dial. form of *lacier* to lace.] To bind with a rope, cord, or chain. — **lash′er**, *n.*

lash′ing, *pres. part. & verbal n.* of (either) LASH. Specif.: *n.* **1.** **a** Act of one who lashes or binds. **b** That used to bind anything, as the cord for a sailor's hammock. **2.** Act of one that lashes; castigation.

lass (lăs), *n.* [ME. *lasse, lasce.*] **1.** A young woman; also, sweetheart. **2.** *Scot. & Dial.* A maidservant.

las′sie (lăs′ĭ), *n.* Diminutive of LASS.

las′si·tude (lăs′ĭ·tūd), *n.* [F., fr. L. *lassitudo*, fr. *lassus* faint, weary.] Condition of weariness; a fact or instance of this; languor. — **Syn.** See LETHARGY.

las′so (lăs′ō; *sometimes* lă·sōō′), *n.*; *pl.* LASSOS (-ōz; -sōōz′), LASSOES (-ōz; -sōōz′). [Sp. *lazo*, fr. L. *laqueus.* See LACE.] A rope or long thong of leather with a running noose, used for catching horses, cattle, etc.; lariat; riata. — *v. t.*; LAS′SOED (lăs′ōd; lă·sōōd′); LAS′SO·ING. To catch with a lasso. — **las′so·er** (lăs′ō·ẽr; lă·sōō′ẽr), *n.*

last (låst; 9), *n.* [AS. *hlæst.*] A certain weight or measure, often estimated at 4000 lb., but varying for different articles and in different countries.

last, *n.* [AS. *lāst, lǣst*, trace, footstep.] A block or form shaped like a foot, over which shoe uppers are drawn and shaped. — *v. t.* To shape with a last. — **last′er**, *n.*

last, *adj.* [ME. *last, latst*, contr. of *latest*, superl. of *late.*] **1.** Being or remaining after all others; following all the rest; final. **2.** Next before the present; most recent; as, *last* week. **3.** **a** Lowest in rank or degree; as, the *last* prize. **b** Furthest of all from a given quality or condition; most unlikely; as, the *last* person to be accused. **4.** Conclusive. **5.** Supreme; highest in degree; utmost. **6.** *Eccl.* Final as being administered to one dying; — said of the sacraments of penance, viaticum, and extreme unction collectively.

Syn. Last, final, terminal, eventual, ultimate, mean following all others, esp. in time or importance. Last refers to that which comes at the end of a series and usually implies that no more will follow or have followed; final, to that which definitely closes a series, a process, or the like; terminal, to that which is at the end of something and marks the limit of its extension, of its growth, etc., or its completion; eventual, to that which is bound to follow as the final effect of causes already operative or likely to be operative; ultimate, to that beyond which a thing cannot go and by which it is definitely and forever terminated (as, the *last* page of a book; the *final* day of school; the *terminal* syllable of a word; the *eventual* defeat of the enemy; the *ultimate* collapse of civilization).

— *adv.* **1.** After all others; at the end. **2.** At a time or on an occasion which is latest or most recent. **3.** In conclusion; lastly; finally. — *n.* That which is last; the end.

last, *v. i.* [AS. *lǣstan* to perform, follow, last, fr. *lāst, lǣst*, footstep, course.] **1.** To continue in time; to endure. **2.** To endure in a given use, state of existence, or the like. — **Syn.** See CONTINUE. — *n.* Power or quality of lasting; endurance. — **last′er**, *n.*

Las′tex (lăs′tĕks), *n.* A trade-mark applied to an elastic yarn produced by winding a round filament made from latex with strands of inelastic cotton, silk, wool, or rayon.

last′ing, *n.* **1.** Endurance. **2.** A very durable woolen stuff, for women's shoes, for covering buttons, etc.

last′ing, *adj.* Existing or continuing a long while; enduring. — **last′ing·ly**, *adv.* — **last′ing·ness**, *n.*

Syn. Lasting, permanent, durable, stable mean enduring for so long as to seem fixed or established. Lasting, used sometimes in the sense of *everlasting*, more often implies a capacity for continuing indefinitely; permanent applies chiefly to things which are not temporary, tentative, or the like, but which continue indefinitely; durable implies power to resist destructive agencies; stable implies freedom from subjection to fluctuation, to variation, or the like.

Last Judgment. *Theol.* God's or Christ's final judgment or trial of mankind; also, the time of it.

last′ly, *adv.* In the last place; in conclusion.

Last Supper. The supper which was partaken of by Christ and his disciples on the night of his betrayal.

lat (lät), *n.*; *pl.* LATS (läts), LATU (lä′tōō). [Lett. *lats*, pl. *lati*, fr. *Latvia.*] The monetary unit of Latvia, representing .29 of a gram of gold; also, a coin of this value.

Lat′a·ki′a (lăt′ȧ·kē′ȧ), *n.* A superior kind of Turkish smoking tobacco; — from the Syrian port of Latakia.

latch (lăch), *n.* [ME. *lacche*, prob. fr. *lacchen* to seize, fr. AS. *læccan.*] A movable piece which holds anything in place by entering a notch or cavity; specif., the catch which holds a door or gate when closed, though it be not bolted. — *v. t. & i.* To catch or fasten by means of a latch.

latch′et (lăch′ĕt; -ĭt), *n.* [OF. *lachet*, dial. form of *lacet* plaited string, lace, dim. of *laz, lacs.* See LACE.] *Archaic.* The narrow thong by which a shoe or sandal is fastened upon the foot.

latch′key′ (lăch′kē′), *n.* A key used to lift or pull back a latch of a door; loosely, a front-door key.

latch′string′ (-strĭng′), *n.* A string on a latch, either hanging on the outside of the door so as to permit the raising of the latch from the outside, or drawn inside to prevent intrusion.

late (lāt), *adj.*; LAT′ER (lāt′ẽr), or LAT′TER (lăt′ẽr), LAT′EST (lāt′ĕst; -ĭst), or LAST (låst). [AS. *læt.*] **1.** Coming, or doing, after the due, usual, or proper time; tardy. **2.** Far advanced toward the end or close; as, a *late* hour of the day. **3.** Existing, or holding some position or relationship, recently, but not now; lately deceased, departed, or gone out of office; as, the *late* administration. **4.** Made, appearing, or happening just previous to the present time; recent. **5.** Continuing or doing until an advanced hour; as, *late* revels. — **Syn.** See DEAD. — *adv.* **1.** After the usual or proper time; after delay. **2.** Far in the night, day, week, or other period. **3.** Not long ago; lately; recently. — ***of late.*** During a time not long past.

lat′ed (lāt′ĕd; -ĭd), *adj.* *Poetic.* Belated.

la·teen′ (lă·tēn′), *adj.* [F. voile *latine* lateen sail, prop. *Latin* sail.] *Naut.* Designating, or pertaining to, a peculiar rig characteristically used in the Mediterranean. Cf. LATEEN SAIL.

lateen sail. *Naut.* A triangular sail, extended by a long yard, slung to the mast, which is usually low. It is chiefly used in the Mediterranean and by Arabs.

Lateen Sails.

Late Greek. See GREEK, *n.*, 4.
Late Latin. See LATIN, *n.*, 1.
late'ly (lāt'lĭ), *adv.* Not long ago; recently.
la'ten·cy (lā'tĕn·sĭ), *n.; pl.* -CIES (-sĭz). State or quality of being latent; concealed being or nature.
La Tène (lȧ tĕn'). *Archaeol.* Designating a period of civilization of the Iron Age in Europe following the Hallstatt epoch and assumed to date from 500 B.C. to A.D. 100.
late'ness (lāt'nĕs; -nĭs), *n.* State or quality of being late.
la'tent (lā'tĕnt), *adj.* [L. *latens, -entis,* pres. part. of *latere* to lie hid.] Not visible or apparent; hidden; dormant. — **la'tent·ly,** *adv.*
Syn. **Latent, dormant, quiescent, potential, abeyant** mean not now manifesting its existence. **Latent** stresses concealment as of that which is present without showing itself; **dormant** suggests inactivity or lack of activity as of a thing that is sleeping; **quiescent** suggests the cessation of action, usually for the time being; **potential** applies to that which does not yet exist but is bound to exist if the process of coming into being is not arrested; **abeyant** applies to being in abeyance, or state of suspended activity only.
latent period. **a** *Med.* The incubation period of a disease. **b** *Physiol.* The interval between stimulation and response.
lat'er·al (lăt'ẽr·ăl), *adj.* [L. *lateralis,* fr. *lătus, lateris,* side, flank.] Of or pertaining to the side; situated at, directed towards, or coming from, the side. — *n.* Anything having a lateral situation, growth, or extension; as: **a** *Football.* A lateral pass. **b** *Mining.* A drift to one side of, and parallel to, a main drift. — **lat'er·al·ly,** *adv.*
lateral pass. *Football.* A pass made in a direction approximately parallel with the goal line.
Lat'er·an (lăt'ẽr·ăn), *n.* [L. *Lateranus.* Named from the *Laterani* family, who possessed a palace on or near the spot where the church now stands.] **1.** The basilica of St. John Lateran, the cathedral church of Rome and highest in rank of all churches in the Catholic world. **2.** The Palazzo del Laterano, adjoining the basilica.
lat'er·ite (-īt), *n.* [L. *later* brick, tile.] *Geol.* A residual product of rock decay, red in color and having a high content in the oxides of iron and hydroxide of aluminum.
la·tes'cent (lȧ·tĕs'ĕnt; -'nt), *adj.* [L. *latescens, -entis,* pres. part of *latescere* to be concealed.] Becoming concealed, or latent, or hidden from view. — **la·tes'cence** (-ĕns; -'ns), *n.*
la'tex (lā'tĕks), *n.; pl.* LATICES (lăt'ĭ·sēz), LATEXES (lā'tĕk·sēz; -sĭz). [L., a fluid.] *Bot.* A milky, usually white, fluid found in certain cells in some families (as Asclepiadaceae, or milkweed family, also Apocynaceae, Sapotaceae, Euphorbiaceae, Moraceae, and Cichoriaceae) of seed plants. The latex contains various gum resins, fats, wax, and often a complex mixture of other substances. Rubber, gutta-percha, chicle, and balata are the chief commercial products. See RUBBER, 3.
lath (lȧth; 9), *n.; pl.* LATHS (lȧthz; lȧths). [AS. *lætt.*] *Building.* **a** Any of a number of thin narrow strips of wood, nailed to rafters, ceiling joists, etc., to make a groundwork for tiles, plastering, etc. **b** Metal in sheets, stiffened wire cloth, or the like, used as a substitute for wooden laths. **c** Laths collectively, or lathwork. — *v. t.* To cover or line with laths. — **lath'er** (lȧth'ẽr), *n.*
lathe (lāth), *n.* [Prob. of Scand. origin.] **1.** *Mach.* A machine in which the work is held and rotated while being shaped by a tool. **2.** A form of potter's wheel. — *v. t.* To cut, or shape, with a lathe. — **lath'er** (lāth'ẽr), *n.*
lathe, *n.* The movable swing frame of a loom, carrying the reed for separating the warp threads and driving the weft to its proper position.
lath'er (lăth'ẽr; *Brit. also* läth'ẽr), *n.* [AS. *lēathor* washing soda.] **1.** The foam or froth formed when soap is agitated in water. **2.** Foam, or condition of foaming, from profuse sweating. — *v. t.* **1.** To spread over with lather; as, to *lather* the face. **2.** *Colloq.* To beat severely, as with a strap. — *v. i. Colloq.* To form lather, or a froth like lather. — **lath'er·er,** *n.* — **lath'er·y,** *adj.*
lath'ing (lȧth'ĭng), *n.* Act or process of placing laths; also, laths, collectively; lathwork.
lathing hammer *or* **hatchet.** A hammer having a hatchet blade, used to trim and nail laths. See HATCHET, *Illust.*
lath'work' (lȧth'wûrk'), *n.* Lathing.
lat'i·ces (lăt'ĭ·sēz), *n., pl.* of LATEX.
lat'i·cif'er·ous (lăt'ĭ·sĭf'ẽr·ŭs), *adj.* [L. *latex, laticis,* a liquid + *-ferous.*] Containing, bearing, or secreting latex.
lat'i·fo'li·ate (-fō'lĭ·āt), **lat'i·fo'li·ous** (-ŭs), *adj.* [L. *latus* broad + *foliate, -folious.*] Broad-leaved.
lat'i·fun'di·um (-fŭn'dĭ·ŭm), *n.; pl.* -DIA (-ȧ). [L., fr. *latus* broad + *fundus* estate.] A large landed estate.
Lat'in (lăt'ĭn; -'n), *adj.* [L. *Latinus.*] **1.** Of or pertaining to Latium, or its people, the Latins, or the language used by the Romans, or Latins. **2.** Of or pertaining to the Latin Church (which see). **3.** Designating the peoples (French, Italian, Spanish, etc.) or countries whose languages and culture are descended from the Latin. — *n.* **1.** The language of ancient Latium and of Rome, and until modern times the dominant language of school, church, and state in western Europe. The language, from the end of the classical period (ab. A.D. 180), is often divided into ***Late Latin*** (2d–6th cent.; abbr. *LL.*), ***Medieval, or Middle, Latin*** (6th–16th cent.; abbr. *ML.*), and ***New Latin*** (abbr. *NL.*) ***or Modern Latin*** (used chiefly in scientific description and classification, and esp. in scientific names coined in Latin form from Latin or Greek or modern elements). Late Latin is sometimes used to include Medieval Latin as well; ***Low Latin*** is equivalent either to *Medieval Latin* or to *Late Latin* in this broader use. See VULGAR LATIN; INDO-EUROPEAN LANGUAGES, *Table.* **2.** One of the people of ancient Latium or Rome.
Latin Church *or* **Rite.** The portion of the Catholic Church which recognizes the pope as both pope and patriarch in distinction from such Eastern churches as recognize him only as pope. See PATRIARCH, 4 c; UNIAT; WESTERN CHURCH.
Latin cross. See CROSS, *Illust.* (1).
La·tin'i·an (lȧ·tĭn'ĭ·ăn), *adj.* Designating, or pertaining to, Latin; also, pertaining to certain dialects forming a branch of the Italic languages. See INDO-EUROPEAN LANGUAGES, *Table.*
Lat'in·ism (lăt'ĭn·ĭz'm), *n.* A Latin idiom or mode of speech.
Lat'in·ist (-ĭst), *n.* One skilled in Latin; a Latin scholar.
La·tin'i·ty (lȧ·tĭn'ĭ·tĭ), *n.* The use of the Latin tongue, style, or idiom.
Lat'in·ize (lăt'ĭn·īz), *v. t.* Also **lat'in·ize.** **1.** To translate into Latin; to give Latin terminations or forms to. **2.** To make like the Roman Catholic Church or diffuse Roman Catholic ideas in; as, to *Latinize* the Church of England. — *v. i.* To use Latinisms. — **Lat'in·i·za'tion** (-ĭ·zā'shŭn; -ī·zā'-), *n.*
Latin Quarter. [F. *Quartier Latin.*] The educational center of Paris, a district south of the Seine, containing the Sorbonne, Institute of France, and Luxembourg, and famous for its Bohemian life and revolutionary ideas.
lat'ish (lāt'ĭsh), *adj.* Somewhat late.
lat'i·tude (lăt'ĭ·tūd), *n.* [OF. or L.; OF., fr. L. *latitudo* breadth, fr. *latus* broad.] **1.** *Now Rare.* Breadth; also, scope. **2.** Freedom from narrow limits; as, great *latitude* of thought and speech. **3.** A region as marked by its latitude (sense 4). **4.** *Astron. & Geog.* Angular distance from some specific circle or plane of reference; as: **a** *Astron.* Angular distance of a celestial body from the ecliptic. **b** *Geog.* Angular distance measured on a meridian; now, distance measured in degrees (***degrees of latitude***) north and south, from the equator. Cf. LONGITUDE. **5.** *Photog.* The time range within which a film or plate may be overexposed or underexposed and still produce a good negative. — **lat'i·tu'di·nal** (-tū'dĭ·năl; -n'l), *adj.* — **lat'i·tu'di·nal·ly,** *adv.*
lat'i·tu'di·nar'i·an (-tū'dĭ·nâr'ĭ·ăn; 6), *adj.* Deviating from a standard of belief or opinion, esp. in matters of religion; tolerant of variations in opinion or doctrine; as, *latitudinarian* divines. — *n.* **1.** One who is broad and liberal in his standards of belief and conduct. **2.** *Ch. of Eng.* [*often cap.*] A churchman who favors freedom and difference of opinion respecting government, worship, or doctrine, within the church. — **lat'i·tu'di·nar'i·an·ism** (-ĭz'm), *n.*
la·tri'a (lȧ·trī'ȧ), *n.* [LL., fr. Gr. *latreia* service.] *R.C.Ch.* The highest kind of worship, or that paid to God only; — distinguished from *dulia* and *hyperdulia.*
la·trine' (lȧ·trēn'), *n.* [F. pl. *latrines,* fr. L. *latrina,* fr. *lavatrina,* fr. *lavare* to wash.] A privy, esp. in a camp.
la'tron (lā'trŭn), *n.* [L. *latro, latronis,* hireling.] A brigand.
-latry. [Gr. *latreia* service.] A combining form denoting *worship of* or *fanatical devotion to a* (specified) *object.*
lat·teen' (lă·tēn'). Var. of LATEEN.
lat'ten (lăt'ĕn; -'n), *n.* [OF. *laton.*] **1.** A kind of brass or brasslike alloy hammered into thin sheets, formerly much used for church utensils. **2.** Sheet tin; also, any metal in thin sheets.
lat'ter (lăt'ẽr), *adj.* [ME. *later, lætter* (fr. AS. *lætra*), compar. of *lat* late. See LATE.] **1.** Being more recent; later; specif., being, or belonging to, the end of a period of time. **2.** Of two things, being the one mentioned second; — opposed to *former.* **3.** *Obs.* Last; final.
lat'ter–day' (*see Pron.,* § 2), *adj.* Of present or recent times.
Latter–day Saint. A Mormon.
lat'ter·ly (lăt'ẽr·lĭ), *adv.* Lately; of late; recently.
lat'ter·most (-mōst; -mŭst), *adj.* Last; hindmost.
lat'tice (lăt'ĭs), *n.* [OF. *lattis* lathwork, fr. *latte* lath, of G. origin.] **1.** A framework or structure of crossed wood or metal strips; as, the *lattice* of a window; — called also *latticework;* hence, any window, door, gate, or the like, having a lattice. **2.** *Obs. exc. Hist.* A lattice (in sense 1) or an imitation of a lattice, used as the sign of an alehouse. — *v. t.;* LAT'TICED (-ĭst); LAT'TIC·ING (-ĭs·ĭng). **1.** To make a lattice of; to give the appearance of a lattice to. **2.** To close or enclose, as an opening, with latticework.
lattice girder. A girder, as of a bridge (***lattice bridge***), with top and bottom flanges connected by a latticework web.
lat'tice·work' (-wûrk'), *n.* A lattice, or work made of lattices; lattices collectively.
lat'tic·ing (lăt'ĭs·ĭng), *n.* **1.** Process of making a lattice. **2.** A lattice; latticework.
la'tu (lä'to͞o), *n., pl.* of LAT.
laud (lôd), *n.* [OF. *laude,* fr. L. *laus, laudis.*] **1.** High commendation; praise **2.** *pl.* [*often cap.*] *Eccl.* A religious service which constitutes the second (or, with matins, the first) of the canonical hours and which, in monastic houses, is usually sung at dawn. **3.** An ascription or hymn of praise to God. **4.** A song in praise of anyone. — *v. t.* To praise; extol.
laud'a·ble (lôd'ȧ·b'l), *adj.* **1.** Worthy of being lauded; praiseworthy. **2.** *Med.* Healthy; not noxious; as, *laudable* pus. — **laud'a·bil'i·ty** (-bĭl'ĭ·tĭ), **laud'a·ble·ness,** *n.* — **laud'a·bly,** *adv.*
lau'da·num (lô'dȧ·nŭm; lôd'nŭm), *n.* [NL., prob. fr. ML. *laudanum,* var. of *ladanum.*] Formerly, any of various preparations of opium; now, a tincture of opium.
lau·da'tion (lô·dā'shŭn), *n.* Act of lauding; praise.
laud'a·tive (lôd'ȧ·tĭv), *adj. & n.* Laudatory.
laud'a·to'ry (-tō'rĭ *or, esp. Brit.,* -tẽr·ĭ), *adj.* Pertaining to or expressing praise.
laud'er (lôd'ẽr), *n.* One who lauds.
laugh (läf; lȧf; 9), *v. i.* [AS. *hlehhan, hlyhhan, hliehhan.*] **1.** To show mirth, satisfaction, or derision, by an expression of the face and explosive or chuckling sounds from the throat. **2.** To be or appear gay, cheerful, etc. — *v. t.* **1.** To affect, influence (in a specified manner), or to effect, by means of laughter. **2.** To express by, or utter with, laughter. — ***laugh in one's sleeve.*** To laugh privately or secretly while appearing grave or serious. — *n.* Act of laughing; the sound heard in laughing.
laugh'a·ble (läf'ȧ·b'l; lȧf'-; 9), *adj.* Fitted to excite laughter. — **laugh'a·ble·ness,** *n.* — **laugh'a·bly,** *adv.*
Syn. **Laughable, ludicrous, ridiculous, comic, comical, farcical, risible, droll, funny** mean provoking or evoking laughter or mirth. **Laughable,** the general term, implies no more than this; **ludicrous** suggests also the absurdity, incongruity, or preposterousness of that which is laughable; **ridiculous** suggests its extreme absurdity, foolishness, or contemptibility; **comic** applies esp. to that which arouses thoughtful laughter or amused reflection; **comical** applies to that which arouses unrestrained laughter; **farcical** applies to that which is highly comical because extravagant, nonsensical, or the like; **risible** applies to that which evokes amusement of any sort or degree; **droll** usually imputes oddity, strangeness, quaintness, etc., to that which is laughable or risible; **funny,** the ordinary colloquial term, may be used in place of any term in the group, but frequently carries the implications of *droll.*

laugh'er (läf'ẽr; làf'-), *n.* One who laughs.
laugh'ing, *adj.* Fit to be treated or accompanied with laughter; — in phrases such as a *laughing matter.*
laughing gas. *Chem.* = NITROUS OXIDE.
laughing jackass. A kingfisher (*Dacelo gigas*), of Australia, with a call resembling loud laughter.
laugh'ing·ly, *adv.* With a laugh; with laughter.
laugh'ing·stock' (läf'ĭng·stŏk'; làf'-; 9), *n.* An object of ridicule; a butt.
laugh'ter (läf'tẽr; làf'-; 9), *n.* [AS. *hleahtor.*] **1.** A movement of the muscles of the face, esp. of the lips, indicating merriment, satisfaction, or derision, and attended by explosive sounds from the throat; also, an expression of the eyes or countenance indicative of amusement. **2.** A cause of, or subject for, laughter.
launce, lance (làns), *n.* [ME. *launce, lance,* lance.] One of a family (Ammodytidae) of teleost fishes; a sand launce.
launch (lônch; länch), *v. t.* [ONF. *lanchier* (OF. *lancier*). See LANCE, *v.*] **1.** To throw, as a lance. **2.** To cause to slide into the water; as, to *launch* a ship. **3. a** To shove or send off, esp. with force; as, to *launch* an airplane. **b** To plunge or start (a person) in a specified course. **c** To start or set in operation. — *v. i.* **1.** To move with force and swiftness like a ship sliding into the water. **2.** To set out, as upon the sea; — often with *forth* or *out.* — *n.* The movement of a vessel from the land into the water, esp. from the stocks on which it is built.
launch (lônch; länch), *n.* [Sp. & Pg. *lancha.*] *Naut.* **a** The boat of the largest size belonging to a ship of war. **b** An open, or largely undecked, power-driven boat.
launch'er (lôn'chẽr; län'-), *n.* One who or that which launches; specif.: **a** *Mil.* A rifle accessory with special sights for firing high-explosive or armor-piercing grenades. **b** Any device for launching a rocket or rocket shell; *Mil.*, a rocket launcher.
laun'der (lôn'dẽr; län'-), *n.* [ME. *lander,* fr. *lavender,* fr. OF. *lavandiere* laundress, fr. LL., fr. L. *lavandus* to be washed, fr. *lavare* to wash.] A trough; specif., *Ore Dressing,* a conduit conveying middlings or tailings suspended in water. — *v. t.* To wash, as clothes; to wash, and to smooth with a flatiron or mangle. — *v. i.* To launder clothes, etc. — **laun'der·er**, *n.*
laun'dress (-drĕs; -drĭs), *n.* A woman who launders.
laun'dry (-drĭ), *n.; pl.* -DRIES (-drĭz). **1.** Act of laundering; a washing. **2.** A place where laundering is done. **3.** Clothes or other articles sent to a laundry to be washed.
laun'dry·man (-măn), *n.* A male worker in a laundry. — **laun'dry·wom'an** (-wo͝om'ăn), *n.*
lau·ra'ceous (lô·rā'shŭs), *adj.* [L. *laurus* laurel.] Belonging to the laurel family (Lauraceae). See LAUREL.
lau're·ate (lô'rē·ăt; -ĭt), *adj.* [L. *laureatus,* fr. *laurea* laurel tree, fr. *laureus* of laurel, fr. *laurus* laurel.] Crowned, or decked, with laurel as a mark of honor; hence, distinguished; worthy of honor, esp. for poetic excellence. — *n.* One crowned with laurel; a poet laureate. — (-āt), *v. t.* **1.** To honor by crowning with a wreath of laurel. **2.** To appoint to the office of poet laureate. — **lau're·ate·ship'**, *n.* — **lau're·a'tion** (-ā'shŭn), *n.*
lau'rel (lô'rĕl; lŏr'ĕl), *n.* [OF. *lorier, laurier,* fr. *lor,* fr. L. *laurus.*] **1.** Any of a genus (*Laurus*) of trees or shrubs typifying a family (Lauraceae, the laurel family) including also sassafras, cinnamon, etc.; specif., the true laurel (*nobilis*), of southern Europe. See DAPHNE, 2. Its foliage was used by the ancient Greeks to crown victors in the Pythian games, and as a mark of distinction for certain offices. Later, a crown of laurel was used to indicate academic honors. **2.** Any of various trees or shrubs like the true laurel; as: *U. S.* Any of two genera (*Kalmia* and *Rhododendron*) of plants of the heath family. See KALMIA, MOUNTAIN LAUREL, RHODODENDRON. **3.** A crown of laurel; hence, honor; fame. — *v. t.;* LAU'RELED (-rĕld; -ĕld) or LAU'RELLED; LAU'REL·ING or LAU'REL·LING. To deck or crown with laurel.
lau'rus·tine (lô'rŭs·tĭn), *n.* [NL. *laurustinus,* fr. L. *laurus* the laurel + *tinus* laurustine.] A European shrub (*Viburnum tinus*) widely cultivated for its evergreen leaves and white or pink fragrant flowers.
‖**laus De'o** (lôs dē'ō; lous dā'ō). [L.] Praise (be) to God.
Lau'wine (lô'wĭn; *G.* lou·vē'nĕ). [G.] = LAWINE.
la'va (lä'vȧ; lăv'ȧ), *n.* [It., lava, orig. in Naples, a torrent of rain overflowing the streets, fr. It. & L. *lavare* to wash.] Fluid rock such as that which issues from a volcano; also, such rock solidified. According to its constituent material, lava is classed as basaltic, trachytic, etc.
la·va'bo (lȧ·vā'bō), *n.; pl.* LAVABOES (-bōz). [L., I will wash.] **1.** *R.C.Ch.* **a** [*cap.*] The verses 6–12 of Psalm xxv in the Vulgate (xxvi in A.V. and R.V.) beginning "Lavabo inter innocentes," recited by the priest in the Mass, after the Offertory, while washing his hands. **b** The liturgical act which this recitation accompanies. **c** [*cap.*] The towel used in this rite. **d** The basin used for this washing. **2.** A wash basin with its necessary fittings.
lav'age (lăv'ĭj; *F.* lȧ'vȧzh'), *n.* [F. See LAVE to wash.] A washing; esp., *Med.*, the washing out of an organ.
la'va–la'va (lä'vä·lä'vä), *n.* [Native word.] A printed calico waist cloth or kilt worn around the loins by natives of Samoa and Tonga.
lav'a·liere', lav'a·lier' (lăv'ȧ·lēr'; lä'vȧ-), *n.* Also **la'val'lière'** (*F.* lȧ'vȧ'lyâr'). [F. *la vallière, lavallière,* a sort of necktie, perh. from Louise de *La Vallière,* mistress of Louis XIV.] A pendent ornament made up of one or many gems, often on a chain.
lav'a·ret (lăv'ȧ·rĕt), *n.* [F.] A central European whitefish (*Coregonus lavaretus*), found in mountain lakes.
la·va'tion (lā·vā'shŭn), *n.* A washing or cleansing.
lav'a·to'ry (lăv'ȧ·tō'rĭ *or, esp. Brit.,* -tẽr·ĭ), *n.; pl.* -TORIES (-rĭz). [LL. *lavatorium.* See LAVE to wash.] **1.** A basin or other vessel for washing. **2.** A room with conveniences for washing. **3.** *Rare.* A laundry. **4.** *Eccl.* A ritual washing of the hands by a celebrant of the Eucharist: **a** During the service, at the Offertory. **b** *Obs.* After the cleansing of the vessels.
lave (lāv), *v. t. & i.* [From AS. *lafian* to lave, pour water on (perh. fr. L.) and fr. OF. *laver,* fr. L. *lavare.*] *Chiefly Poetic.* To wash; bathe; wash or flow along or against.
lave, *n.* [AS. *lāf.*] *Obs. exc. Dial.* The remainder.
la·veer' (lȧ·vēr'), *v. i.* [D. *laveren.*] *Archaic. Naut.* To beat against the wind; to tack.
lav'en·der (lăv'ĕn·dẽr; -ĭn·dẽr), *n.* [AF. *lavendre,* fr. ML. *lavendula, livendula.*] **1.** A European mint (*Lavandula officinalis*) with spikes of small lilac-purple flowers, cultivated for its aromatic oil, known as ***oil of lavender.*** **2.** The dried leaves and flowers of this plant, used to perfume clothing, bed linen, etc. **3.** A color, bluish blue-red in hue, of low saturation and medium brilliance; the color of lavender flowers. See COLOR. — *adj.* Of the color of lavender. — *v. t.* To sprinkle, or perfume, with lavender.
la'ver (lā'vẽr), *n.* [L., a water plant.] Any of several common purple seaweeds (genus *Porphyra,* as *P. laciniata* and *P. vulgaris*); — called also ***red laver.*** The fronds are eaten in Europe, either pickled or stewed.
la'ver, *n.* [OF. *laveoir,* fr. LL. *lavatorium* a washing place.] **1.** *Archaic.* A vessel for washing; a basin or bowl. **2.** *Jewish Antiq.* **a** A large brazen vessel where the priests washed their hands and feet. **b** One of several vessels in Solomon's Temple in which the offerings for burnt sacrifices were washed. **3.** That which cleanses; specif., baptismal water.
lav'er·ock (lăv'ẽr·ŭk; lăv'rŭk), **lav'rock** (lăv'rŭk), *n.* *Now Scot.* A lark.
lav'ish (lăv'ĭsh), *adj.* [OF. *lavasse, lavache,* a deluge of rain, fr. Pr. *lavaci,* fr. L. *lavatio* a washing, fr. *lavare* to wash.] **1.** Expending or bestowing profusely; prodigal. **2.** Expended or produced profusely; very abundant. — **Syn.** See PROFUSE. — **Ant.** Sparing. — *v. t.* To expend or bestow with profusion; to squander. — **lav'ish·er**, *n.* — **lav'ish·ly**, *adv.* — **lav'ish·ness**, *n.*
law (lô), *n.* [AS. *lagu,* fr. Scand.] **1.** The binding custom or practice of a community; rules of conduct enforced by a controlling authority; also, any single rule of conduct so enforced. **2.** A divine commandment or a revelation of the will of God; collectively, the whole body of God's commandments. **3.** In arts, works, games, etc.: The rules of construction, or of procedure; a principle, maxim, or usage; as, the *laws* of poetry. **4.** The whole body of rules relating to one subject; as, insurance *law.* **5.** *Bible.* The Jewish or Mosaic law, contained in the Hexateuch (Pentateuch and Joshua) and in Ezekiel xl–xlviii; also, this part of the Scriptures. Hence, in Christian usage, the Old Testament **6.** *Law & Polit. Science.* **a** A rule of conduct or action prescribed by the supreme governing authority and enforced by a sanction, as any edict, decree, order, ordinance, statute, judicial decision, etc. **b** The whole body of such rules; also, the control or regulation, or state of society, brought about by the existence and enforcement of such rules. See STATUTE LAW, COMMON LAW, CIVIL LAW, CANON LAW, NATURAL LAW (under NATURAL, *adj.*, 4). **c** Legal science; jurisprudence. **d** Trial or remedial justice under or by the laws of the land; judicial remedy; litigation; as, to go to *law.* **e** In England and many of her colonies, the system of rules expounded and remedies administered by the common-law courts. **f** The legal profession as a whole. **7.** *Math.* The rule or formula according to which anything proceeds or comes into being. **8.** *Philos. & Science.* A statement of an order or relation of phenomena which, so far as known, is invariable under the given conditions. **9.** *Sports.* An allowance of time or distance given to a weaker competitor, an animal in the chase, or the like.

Syn. (1) **Law, rule, regulation, precept, statute, ordinance, canon** mean a principle laid down or accepted as governing conduct, action, or procedure. **Law** usually implies imposition by a sovereign authority and the obligation of obedience on the part of those governed; **rule** may or may not imply prohibition but it usually suggests a desire for order, discipline, uniformity in method, or the like; **regulation** often equals *rule* but it carries a stronger implication of prescription by authority for the sake of controlling an organization or system; **precept** usually implies a law but one having a greater bearing on individual conduct than on government and communicated by teaching; **statute** implies a law enacted by a legislative body; **ordinance** implies, in America, a local law or, in England, a law or regulation enacted by a lesser body than parliament; **canon** implies, strictly, a law of the church but, also, any law having the sanction of authority that is enforced by conscience. (2) See HYPOTHESIS.
— *v. i. Colloq.* To go to law; to litigate.
— *adj.* Of or pert. to the law, the legal profession, or its procedure.
law (lô). Scot. & N. of Eng. var. of LOW.
law'–a·bid'ing, *adj.* Abiding by or obedient to the law.
law'break'er (lô'brāk'ẽr), *n.* One who violates the law. — **law'break'ing**, *n. & adj.*
law'ful (-fo͝ol; -f'l), *adj.* **1.** Conformable to law; legitimate. **2.** Constituted, authorized, or established by law; rightful. — **law'ful·ly**, *adv.* — **law'ful·ness**, *n.*

Syn. **Lawful, legal, legitimate, licit** mean in accordance with law. **Lawful** is distinguished by its reference to law of any sort, such as divine law, the law of the land, canon law, etc., and is often close in meaning to *allowable* or *permissible;* **legal** implies reference to the law as it appears on the statute books or is administered in the courts; **legitimate** implies, usually, a legal right establishing one's claim (as son, heir, king, etc.) but sometimes comes nearer to *rightful* in meaning; **licit** implies conformity to the provisions of the law respecting the way in which something should be carried on, executed, or the like (as, a *lawful* practice; *legal* interest; *legitimate* owner; a *legitimate* conclusion; a *licit* marriage).
law'giv'er (-gĭv'ẽr), *n.* A maker of laws; legislator.
law'–hand', *n.* *Eng.* The peculiar style of handwriting used in engrossing old legal documents.
‖**La·wi'ne** (lä·vē'nĕ), *n.; pl.* -NEN (-nĕn). [G.] Avalanche.
law'ing (lô'ĭng), *n.* *Scot.* A reckoning at a tavern.
law'less (lô'lĕs; -lĭs), *adj.* **1.** Without law; not regulated by law; having no laws; as, the *lawless* desert. **2.** Not restrained by law; unruly; licentious; also, illegal. — **law'less·ly**, *adv.* — **law'less·ness**, *n.* — **Syn.** See ANARCHY.
law'mak'ing (-māk'ĭng), *adj.* Enacting laws; legislative. — *n.* The enacting of laws; legislation. — **law'mak'er** (-ẽr), *n.*
law mer'chant (mûr'chănt). **a** Orig., the legal rules which were applied to cases arising in mercantile transactions. **b** Loosely, the legal rules dealing esp. with mercantile transactions; commercial law; mercantile law.
lawn (lôn), *n.* [Earlier *laune lynen,* i. e., *lawn linen,* fr. *Laon,* town in France.] A fine, sheer, plain-woven linen or cotton fabric, thinner than cambric, used for dresses, handkerchiefs, and the like. — **lawn'y** (-ĭ), *adj.*
lawn (lôn), *n.* [OF. *launde, lande,* moor, of Celt. origin.] **1.** *Archaic.* A glade. **2.** Ground covered with fine grass kept closely mown, esp. about a house. — **lawn'y**, *adj.*
lawn mower. A machine used to clip the grass on lawns.
lawn tennis. A variety of tennis, played on a court of turf or some even surface.
Law of Moses. The Pentateuch.

law of nations. International law.
law′suit′ (lô′sūt′), *n.* A suit in law; a case before a court.
law′yer (lô′yẽr), *n.* **1.** One versed in the laws, or a practitioner of law, comprehending attorneys, counselors, solicitors, barristers, sergeants, advocates, etc. **2.** *Dial. Eng.* A bramble, or the thorny stem of a brier.

Syn. **Lawyer, counselor, barrister, counsel, attorney, solicitor** mean one authorized to practice law. **Lawyer,** the general term, applies to anyone in the profession; **counselor** (more fully *counselor at law*) applies to one who accepts court cases or gives advice on legal problems; the corresponding British term is **barrister** but the emphasis is on court pleading; **counsel** is used in the United States sometimes for *counselor* but often collectively for its plural, and in England in the phrase "king's counsel" (abbr. *K.C.*) or "queen's counsel" (abbr. *Q.C.*) for a leading barrister; **attorney,** in the United States, and **solicitor,** in England, are strictly applied to a lawyer transacting legal business for his client.

lax (lăks), *adj.* [L. *laxus.*] **1.** Of the bowels, loose; open; also, having the bowels loose. **2.** Not tense, firm, or rigid; loose; slack. **3.** Not rigid, strict, or stringent; as, *lax* discipline. **4.** *Bot.* Loose; scattered; open; as, a *lax* panicle. **5.** *Phonet.* Of vowels, uttered with the tongue and associated muscles in a relatively relaxed state, as ĭ, ŏŏ, as contrasted with tense ē, ōō; wide. — **Syn.** See NEGLIGENT. — **lax′ly,** *adv.* — **lax′ness,** *n.*
lax·a′tion (lăks·ā′shŭn), *n.* [L. *laxatio.*] Act of loosening or relaxing; state of being loosened or relaxed.
lax′a·tive (lăk′sȧ·tĭv), *adj.* [F. *laxatif,* fr. L. *laxativus* mitigating, assuaging.] **1.** Having a tendency to loosen or relax, or, esp., to relieve from constipation. **2.** *Now Rare.* Free; loose; incontinent; as, a *laxative* tongue. — *n.* A laxative medicine.
lax′i·ty (lăk′sĭ·tĭ), *n.* [F. *laxité,* fr. L. *laxitas,* fr. *laxus* loose, slack.] State or quality of being lax; lack of tenseness, strictness, or precision.
lay (lā), *past* of LIE, to recline.
lay, *n.* [OF. *lai,* of Celt. origin.] **1.** A song; a simple lyric or short narrative poem. **2.** A melody.
lay, *adj.* [OF. *lai,* fr. LL. *laicus,* fr. Gr. *laïkos* of or from the people, lay, fr. *laos, leōs,* people.] **1.** Of or pertaining to the laity, as distinct from the clergy. **2.** Belonging to that class in a religious order occupied with domestic or manual work; as, a *lay* brother; — contrasted with *choir.* **3.** Not of or from a particular profession; as, a *lay* opinion.
lay, *v. t.;* LAID (lād); LAY′ING. [AS. *lecgan,* caus. fr. the root of *licgan* to lie.] **1.** To bring down, as with force; to beat down. **2.** To place in a recumbent or lower position resting on or in something; to deposit. **3.** To bring forth and deposit (an egg or eggs). **4.** To wager; bet. **5.** To calm; allay; suppress. **6.** *Obs.* To deposit as a pledge or hostage. **7.** To dispose over or as over a surface; as, to *lay* a pavement; also, to press down smooth or even; as, to *lay* nap on cloth. **8.** To impose as a duty, burden, punishment, etc. **9.** To set in order for a meal; as, to *lay* the table. **10.** To place or repose (something immaterial) in or on something or someone; to put; as, he *lays* stress on correct grammar. **11.** To place or put in position or in operation or action; as, he *laid* an ambush; he *laid* the ax to the tree. **12.** To put into, cause to be in, or place in, a given condition; as, to *lay* waste a region. **13.** To present, offer, or put forward as true or valid. **14.** To prefer or assert; as, he *laid* claim to the estate. **15.** To advance as an accusation; to impute; charge; ascribe. **16.** *Ropemaking.* To put (strands) in place and twist to form a rope, a cable, or the like. — *v. i.* **1.** To produce and deposit eggs. **2.** *Now Illit.* To lie (be prostrate, etc.). **3.** To lay a wager; to bet. **4.** *Now Dial.* To plan; prepare; scheme. **5.** To apply oneself vigorously; as, to *lay* to one's oars. **6.** *Naut.* To place oneself in a specified position; as, to *lay* aloft; to *lay* forward.
lay about, lay about one. To strike vigorously in all directions; to act vigorously. — ***lay by the heels.*** To put in the stocks; to fetter. — ***lay down.*** **a** To discard; to give up; as, to *lay down* one's arms, i. e., to surrender. **b** To stake, as a wager, pledge, or payment. **c** To construct or put in place the foundation of; to frame; hence, to establish; prescribe. **d** To assert, or command, dogmatically. **e** To store, esp. to store (wine, etc.) in a cellar; to store or pack as eggs in water glass. — ***lay hold of, or on.*** To seize; grasp. — ***lay off.*** **a** To cease to operate or employ; esp., to dismiss (a workman). **b** To cease (work). **c** *Slang.* To desist. — ***lay on.*** **a** To apply or spread on a surface; to lay; as, to *lay on* paint. **b** To strike; beat, attack. — ***lay out.*** **a** To spread out; to prepare (a corpse) for burial. **b** To expend. **c** To map out; to arrange, as grounds or plans. **d** To display; exhibit. **e** To exert; reflexively, *Colloq.,* to exert oneself greatly. **f** *Slang.* To knock unconscious. **g** To purpose; plan. — ***lay siege to.*** To besiege. — ***lay to.*** *Naut.* **a** To bring (a ship) into the wind and hold stationary except for drifting. **b** To lie to. — ***lay up.*** **a** To store up; deposit for future use. **b** To confine; disable, as with illness.
— *n.* **1.** *Slang.* A plan, or field, of operations or business; a job. **2.** A share of the profit of a venture, esp. on whaling and sealing vessels; hence, employment on shares. **3.** The way in which a thing lies or is laid in relation to something else; as, the *lay* of the land. **4.** *Ropemaking.* **a** The amount of advance of any point in a strand for one turn. **b** The nature of a fiber rope as determined by the amount of twist, the angle of the strands, and the angle of the threads in the strands.
lay day. **a** *pl.* The days allowed by the charter party for loading or unloading a vessel. **b** A day of delay in port.
lay′er (lā′ẽr), *n.* **1.** One who lays (in various senses); as, a hen that is a good *layer.* **2.** That which is laid; a stratum; one thickness, course, or fold laid over or under another; as, a *layer* of clay; a *layer* of bricks. **3.** *Hort.* A shoot which is bent down and covered with soil for propagation. — *v. t. & i. Hort.* To propagate by layers.
lay′er·age (-ĭj), *n.* *Hort.* Propagation by layers.
layer cake. A fancy cake made in thin layers, usually held together by a sweet filling.
lay·ette′ (lā·ĕt′), *n.* [F.] A complete outfit of clothing, blankets, etc., for a newborn infant.
lay figure. [For older *layman,* fr. D. *leeman,* fr. MD. *led, lit,* limb, member + *man* man.] **a** A jointed model of the human body, used by artists for showing the disposition of drapery, etc. **b** A puppet.
lay′man (lā′măn), *n.; pl.* -MEN (-mĕn). [*lay* + *man.*] One of the laity; also, one not belonging to some particular profession. — **lay′-wom′an** (-wŏŏm′ăn), *n.*
lay′off′ (-ôf′; 74), *n.* The act of laying off, esp. work or workmen; a period of being laid off work; a shutdown.
lay′out′ (-out′), *n.* **1.** Act or process of planning; the arrangement of something planned. **2.** That which is laid out; specif.: **a** An outfit or supply. **b** An outline usually with a diagram providing directions for work. **c** The make-up of a book, newspaper, etc. **3.** *Slang.* Something displayed; a spread; as, the dinner was a fine *layout.*
lay′o′ver (-ō′vẽr), *n.* A stay for a period in a place.
la′zar (lā′zẽr; lăz′ẽr), *n.* [ML. *lazarus,* fr. *Lazarus* the beggar (*Luke* xvi. 20).] A person, esp. a poor person, afflicted with some loathsome disease; specif., a leper.
laz′a·ret′, laz′a·rette′ (lăz′ȧ·rĕt′; *by seamen often* lăz′ȧ·rĕt′), *n.* [F. *lazaret,* fr. It.] A lazaretto.
laz′a·ret′to (-rĕt′ō), *n.; pl.* -TOS (-ōz). [It. *lazzaretto,* fr. Venetian *lazareto* (after It. *lazzaro* leper, fr. *Lazzaro* Lazarus), fr. *nazareto,* fr. the church Santa Maria di *Nazaret,* used in 15th cent. as a pesthouse.] **1.** A public hospital, esp. for lazars. **2.** *Naut.* A space between decks in some merchant vessels, used as a storeroom.
Laz′a·rus (lăz′ȧ·rŭs), *n.* [L., fr. Gr. *Lazaros,* fr. Heb.] **1.** *Bib.* **a** A brother of Mary and Martha, whom Jesus raised from the dead. **b** The beggar in the parable of the rich man and beggar. *Luke* xvi. **2.** [*sometimes not cap.*] A diseased, esp. a leprous, beggar.
laze (lāz), *v. i.* [From LAZY.] To be lazy; to act lazily. — *v. t.* To waste in sloth; to spend, as time, in idleness.
laz′u·li (lăz′ū·lī), *n.* = LAPIS LAZULI. — **laz′u·line** (-līn; -lĭn), *adj.*
laz′u·lite (lăz′ū·līt), *n.* [ML. *lazulum.* See AZURE.] *Mineral.* A native azure-blue hydrous phosphate of aluminum and magnesium, often occurring in crystals.
la′zy (lā′zĭ), *adj.;* LA′ZI·ER (-zĭ·ẽr); LA′ZI·EST. **1.** Disinclined to action or exertion; indolent; slothful. **2.** Slow; sluggish; as, a *lazy* stream. **3.** Of a livestock brand, lying on its side, as ш (a *lazy* E). — **la′zi·ly,** *adv.* — **la′zi·ness,** *n.*

Syn. **Lazy, indolent, slothful** mean not easily aroused to activity. **Lazy** suggests a disinclination or aversion to work; **indolent,** a habitual love of ease and a settled dislike of movement or activity; **slothful,** the temper of one who is inactive when he knows he should be active or who moves or acts with slowness when speed is essential.

la′zy·bones′ (-bōnz′), *n.* A lazy person.
Lazy Susan. **1.** A small three-tiered table for holding sandwiches, cakes, etc., at tea. **2.** A revolving tray placed on a dining table to hold condiments, relishes, etc.
lazy tongs. A system of jointed bars capable of great extension, sometimes with a device for picking up objects.

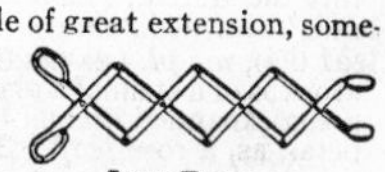
Lazy Tongs.

laz′za·ro′ne (läz′ȧ·rō′nā; *It.* läd′dzä·rō′nā), *n.; pl.* -RONI (*It.* -nē). [It., fr. *lazzaro.*] One of the homeless idlers of Naples.
L bar, L beam. An L-shaped steel bar or beam.
lea (lē), *n.* [AS. *lēah, lēa.*] Pasture or grassland; meadow.
lea, *n.* *Textile Manuf.* A varying measure of yarn; for linen, usually 300 yards; for cotton and silk, 120 yards.
leach (lēch), *v. t.* [From AS. *leccan* to moisten and ON. *leka* to leak, trickle.] **1.** To percolate (a liquid) through something, as ashes. **2.** To subject to the action of percolating liquid in order to remove the soluble parts. **3.** To dissolve out by a percolating liquid; as, to *leach* out alkali from ashes. — *v. i.* To part with soluble constituents under the effect of a percolating liquid. — *n.* A perforated vessel to hold wood ashes through which water is to be passed to extract the lye. — **leach′er** (-ẽr), *n.*
lead (lĕd), *n.* [AS. *lēad.*] **1.** A heavy, pliable, and inelastic metallic element. Symbol, *Pb* (L. *plumbum*); at. no., 82; at. wt., 207.21; sp. gr., 11.34. It is usually found in the form of the sulfide galena, its chief ore. Lead of at. wt. from 206 to 208 is formed in certain radioactive decompositions. **2.** An article made of lead or an alloy of lead; as: **a** A plummet for sounding at sea. See SOUNDING LINE, *Illust.* **b** *pl. Eng.* A flat roof which may be treated as a floor. **c** Lead framing for panes in windows. Cf. CAME, *n.* **3. a** Short for BLACK LEAD. **b** A thin cylinder of black lead, or plumbago, used in pencils. **c** White lead. **4.** Bullets; as, a shower of *lead.* **5.** *Print.* A thin strip of type metal, used to separate lines of type in printing. — *adj.* Pert. to or made of lead; containing lead. — *v. t.* **1.** To cover, or line the inside of, with lead; also, to weight with lead. **2.** To treat or mix with lead or a lead compound. **3.** *Building.* To fix (window glass) in position with leads. **4.** *Ceramics.* To glaze (pottery) with a glaze of which lead is the chief constituent. **5.** *Print.* To place leads between the lines of.
lead (lēd), *v. t.;* LED (lĕd); LEAD′ING. [AS. *lǣdan;* prop. caus. fr. the root of AS. *līthan* to go.] **1.** To guide or conduct; hence, to direct in action, thought, opinion, etc.; instruct. **2.** To precede and direct in movement; as, to *lead* an army; hence, to be foremost among; as, Demosthenes *leads* all orators. **3.** To follow the path or course of. **4.** To draw or direct by influence, good or bad; to allure; as, to *lead* one astray. **5.** To take the directing part in; as, to *lead* an orchestra. **6.** To aim a firearm in front of (a moving object); as, to *lead* a duck. **7.** *Boxing.* To direct (a blow) at the opponent. **8.** *Cards, Dominoes,* etc. To begin a game, round, or trick, with; as, to *lead* trumps. — **Syn.** See GUIDE. — *v. i.* **1.** To guide or conduct; — used in most of the corresponding senses of *lead,* v. t. **2.** To be led; to admit of being led. **3.** To tend or reach in a certain direction; to take its course. **4.** *Boxing.* To direct a blow at the opponent. **5.** *Cards.* To play the first card on any trick.
— *n.* **1. a** *Obs.* Action of one that leads; guidance; direction. **b** Position at the front; van. **c** Leadership. **2.** Precedence; also, the measure of precedence; as, a *lead* of a second. **3.** That which leads or acts as a guide, clue, etc. **4.** *Boxing.* A blow directed at the opponent. **5.** *Cards, Dominoes, etc.* Act or right of playing first in a game, round, or trick; also, the card, suit, or piece so played. **6.** *Elec.* An insulated conductor. **7.** *Journalism.* A brief summary introducing a newspaper article. **8.** *Mining.* **a** A lode. **b** An auriferous gravel deposit in an old river bed, esp. one buried under lava. **9.** *Naut.* The course of a rope from end to end. **10.** *Theat.* A role for a leading man or woman; one who plays such a role.
— *adj.* That acts as a leader.
lead acetate (lĕd). *Chem.* A colorless crystalline salt, $Pb(C_2H_3O_2)_2.3H_2O$, of sweet, astringent, metallic taste.
lead arsenate (lĕd). *Chem.* A white crystalline salt, $Pb_3(AsO_4)_2$, used as an insecticide.
lead′en (lĕd′'n), *adj.* **1.** Made of lead; of the nature of lead; — often used with special allusion to its qualities (as softness, heaviness, etc.); as, a *leaden* sleep. **2.** Hence: **a** Like lead in color; dull gray. **b** Base in quality; cheap. **c** Heavy or dull, as in action, feeling, understanding, etc.; sluggish. — **lead′en·ly,** *adv.* — **lead′en·ness,** *n.*

lead′er (lēd′ēr), *n.* One that leads; as: **1.** A guide; conductor. **2.** A chief; commander; also, the head of a group, sect, undertaking, etc. **3.** A horse placed in advance of others. **4.** A pipe for conducting fluid. **5.** *Angling.* **a** A net for leading fish into a pound, weir, etc. **b** A short line of transparent fiber, used to attach the end of a fishline to the lure. **6.** *Com.* A chief article of trade, esp. one sold at a low price to bring trade. **7.** *Journalism.* An editorial article; a leading article. **8.** *Music.* **a** = CONDUCTOR **d.** **b** The leading performer of a group. **9.** *Naut.* A metal fitting or block of hardwood pierced with suitable holes for leading ropes in their proper places. **10.** *pl. Print.* A row of dots or hyphens, used to lead the eye across a space to the right word or number. — **lead′er·ship,** *n.*

lead glass (lĕd). Glass containing lead.

lead′–in′ (lĕd′ĭn′), *adj.* That leads in; — used esp. of an electrical conductor; as, a *lead-in* wire.

lead′in′ (lĕd′ĭn′), *n. Radio.* The part of an antenna which runs to the transmitting or receiving set.

lead′ing (lĕd′ĭng), *n.* Lead, or articles of lead, collectively.

lead′ing (lēd′ĭng), *n.* **1.** Action of one who leads; guidance. **2.** Suggestion; hint. — *adj.* That leads; guiding; directing; foremost.

leading article. An editorial article; a leader.

leading edge. *Aeronautics.* The foremost edge of an airfoil or propeller blade. See AIRPLANE, *Illust.*

leading question. A question so framed as to guide the person questioned in making his reply.

leading strings. Strings by which infants learning to walk are sometimes supported. — *in leading strings.* Dependent on, or under the guidance of, others.

leading tone *or* **note.** *Music.* The seventh note or tone in the major and minor scales; — so called from its tendency to lead up to the tonic. Called also (rarely) the *subtonic.*

lead line (lĕd). *Naut.* A sounding line. See SOUNDING LINE, *Illust.*

lead′–off′ (lĕd′ŏf′; 74), *adj.* That leads off.

lead′off′ (lĕd′ŏf′), *n.* **a** A beginning or leading action. **b** A player who leads off, as, in baseball, the player who heads the batting order.

lead pencil (lĕd). A pencil of which the marking material is graphite.

lead poisoning. A diseased condition caused by the absorption of lead into the system; plumbism.

leads′man (lĕdz′mǎn), *n. Naut.* The man who heaves the lead.

leaf (lēf), *n.; pl.* LEAVES (lēvz). [AS. *lēaf.*] **1.** One of the lateral outgrowths of a stem of a plant; esp., in popular usage, one of the ordinary green expanded organs (*foliage leaves*) of plants. **2.** Popularly, a petal; as, a rose *leaf.* **3.** Collectively, the leaves of any plant as an article of commerce; specif., the leaves of the tea plant; also, tobacco leaves. **4.** Something suggestive of a leaf; as: **a** A part of a book or folded sheet containing two pages, one on each side. **b** A part that slides or is hinged, as of folding doors, gates, etc. **c** The movable part of a table top. **d** A thin sheet or plate of any substance; a lamina. **e** *Now Chiefly Dial.* One of the layers of fat (*leaf fat*) about the kidneys of a hog. See PORK, *Illust.* **5.** One of the plates of a leaf spring.

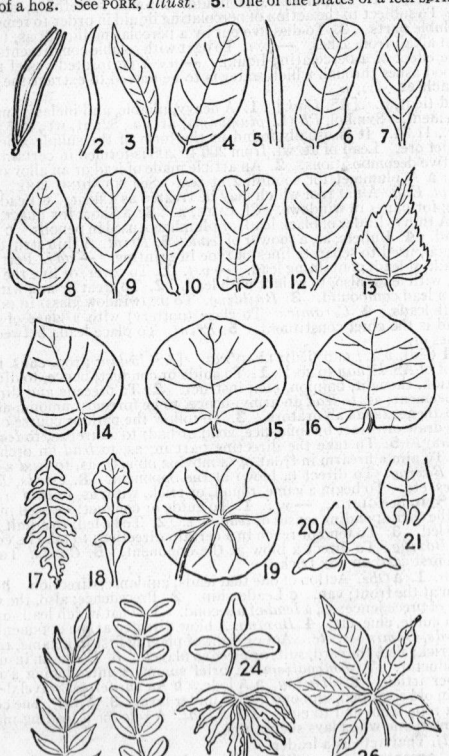

Forms of Leaves. 1 Acerose; 2 Linear; 3 Lanceolate; 4 Elliptic; 5 Ensiform; 6 Oblong; 7 Oblanceolate in form, with acuminate tip; 8 Ovate in form, with acute tip; 9 Obovate; 10 Spatulate; 11 Panduriform; 12 Cuneate; 13 Deltoid; 14 Cordate; 15 Reniform; 16 Orbiculate; 17 Runcinate; 18 Lyrate; 19 Peltate; 20 Hastate; 21 Sagittate; 22, 23 Pinnate (22 Odd-pinnate, 23 Abruptly Pinnate); 24–26 Palmate (24 Trifoliolate, 25 Pedate in form, with margin incised; 26 Quinquefoliolate). See also LOBATION, VENATION, *Illusts.*

— *adj.* Of or pertaining to, or in the form of, a leaf or leaves; as, *leaf* tobacco. — *v. i.* To shoot out or produce leaves; to leave. — *v. t.* To turn the leaves or pages of; as, to *leaf* a book.

leaf′age (lēf′ĭj), *n.* Foliage; leaves collectively.

leaf′hop′per (lēf′hŏp′ēr), *n.* Any of numerous leaping insects (family Cicadellidae) which suck the juices of plants.

leaf lard. Lard made from leaf fat (see LEAF, *n.,* 4 e), the highest quality lard.

leaf′less (lēf′lĕs; -lĭs), *adj.* Having no leaves.

leaf′let (-lĕt; -lĭt), *n.* **1.** *Bot.* One of the divisions of a compound (pinnate or palmate) leaf. **2.** Popularly, a small foliage leaf. **3.** A leaflike organ or part. **4.** **a** A small printed sheet, as for free distribution. **b** *Print.* A sheet of small pages folded, but not stitched; a folder.

leaf spring. A spring made of superposed strips, or leaves. See SPRING, *Illust.*

leaf′stalk′ (lēf′stôk′), *n.* A petiole.

leaf′y (lēf′ĭ), *adj.;* LEAF′I·ER (-ĭ-ēr); LEAF′I·EST. **1.** Furnished with, or abounding in, leaves. **2.** Having broad-bladed leaves. **3.** Made or consisting of leaves. **4.** Of the nature of a leaf; laminate.

league (lēg), *n.* [OF. *legue* (F. *lieue*), fr. LL. *leuga, leuca,* of Gaulish origin.] **1.** A measure of distance varying for different times and countries from about 2.4 to 4.6 miles (3.9–7.4 kilometers). See MEASURE, *Tables* 1 & 9. **2.** A measure of area; a square league (5760 acres for the English land league; about 4439 acres, or 1796 hectares, for the old Spanish land league).

league (lēg), *n.* [F. *ligue,* fr. It. *liga,* var. of *lega,* fr. *legare* to bind, fr. L. *ligare.*] An agreement or covenant between two or more nations, parties, or persons, for the accomplishment of some purpose by their co-operation, as for mutual defense; also, the alliance or combination so formed; a confederacy. — *v. i. & t.;* LEAGUED (lēgd); LEA′GUING (lē′gĭng). To unite in a league or confederacy. — **lea′guer** (lē′gēr), *n.*

League of Nations. An association of states for lessening the likelihood of war, encouraging adoption of the principle of arbitration, administering conquered or surrendered colonies (mandates), and promoting international co-operation on other world problems. It came into existence January 10, 1920 in accordance with a covenant inserted in the peace treaty (1919) following World War I. It was officially dissolved April 18, 1946, and many of its functions were taken over by the United Nations (which see).

lea′guer (lē′gēr), *n.* [D. *leger* camp, couch, lair.] **a** *Obs. exc. Hist.* The camp of a besieging army. **b** *Rare.* A siege or beleaguering. — *v. t.* To besiege; beleaguer.

leak (lēk), *n.* **1.** A crack or hole which (contrary to intention) admits fluid, or lets it escape; figuratively, anything which (contrary to intention) permits the admission, or escape or loss, of something; as, a *leak* in the treasury. **2.** Act of leaking; leakage. **3.** *Elec.* A loss of electricity through imperfect insulation; also, the point at which such loss occurs. — *v. i.* [ON. *leka.*] **1.** To let fluid in or out (contrary to what is intended) through a hole, crevice, etc. **2.** To enter or escape (contrary to what is intended), as a fluid, through a hole, crevice, etc.; figuratively, to be divulged gradually or clandestinely; as, the facts *leaked* out. — *v. t.* To permit to enter or escape through a leak.

leak′age (-ĭj), *n.* **1.** A leaking; an entering or escaping by a leak. **2.** *Elec.* A leak. **3.** That which, or the amount that, leaks in or out. **4.** Allowance made for leakage of fluid.

leak′y (-ĭ), *adj.;* LEAK′I·ER (-ĭ-ēr); LEAK′I·EST. **1.** Permitting leakage of fluid. **2.** *Colloq.* Apt to disclose secrets; tattling. — **leak′i·ness,** *n.*

leal (lēl), *adj.* [OF. *leial.* See LOYAL.] *Poetic exc. Scot.* Faithful; loyal. — **leal′ly** (lēl′lĭ), *adv.* — **le′al·ty** (lē′ăl-tĭ), *n.*

lean (lēn), *v. i.;* LEANED (lēnd), sometimes LEANT (lĕnt); LEAN′ING. [AS. *hlinian, hleonian,* v. i.] **1.** To incline, deviate, or bend from a vertical position. **2.** To incline or bend so as to receive support; as, he *leaned* on his staff. **3.** To rely for support, comfort, etc. **4.** To incline in opinion or desire; to conform in conduct. — *v. t.* To cause to lean; incline. — *n.* Act of leaning.

lean, *adj.* [AS. *hlǣne.*] **1.** Lacking flesh; deficient in fat; thin. **2.** Having little fat; — said of flesh. **3.** Wanting fullness, richness, or productiveness; slender; poor; mean. **4.** Of a mixture of air and gas or vapor, deficient in the combustible component; — opp. to *rich.* — *n.* That part of flesh which consists principally of muscle without the fat; lean meat. — **lean′ly,** *adv.* — **lean′ness,** *n.*

Syn. Lean, spare, lank, lanky, gaunt, rawboned, scrawny, skinny mean thin because of absence of superfluous flesh. Lean stresses lack of fat and of curving contours; spare, leanness from abstemious living or much exercise; lank, tallness as well as leanness; lanky, awkwardness and loose-jointedness as well as lankness; gaunt, a lankness that suggests overwork or undernourishment; rawboned, a gaunt, ungainly frame; scrawny and skinny, an extreme leanness that suggests deficient vitality.

Le·an′der (lē·ăn′dēr), *n.* See HERO AND LEANDER.

lean′ing (lēn′ĭng), *n.* Act or state of one that leans; inclination.

Syn. Leaning, propensity, proclivity, penchant, flair mean a strong instinct or liking for something that drives or leads one to it. Leaning implies a natural bent or the pull of that which attracts; propensity, an inherent or innate and, often, uncontrollable longing; proclivity, a proneness or natural inclination, often to something evil, heightened by habitual indulgence or constitutional peculiarities; penchant, a decided taste for in the person or an irresistible attraction in the thing; flair, an instinct comparable to that of a dog on the scent, that leads to success in following it.

lean′–to′ (lēn′tōō′), *adj. Arch.* Having only one slope or pitch; — said of a roof. — *n.; pl.* LEAN-TOS (-tōōz′). **1.** *Arch.* A wing or extension of a building having a lean-to roof. **2.** A rough shed with an inclined roof, built against posts or trees.

leap (lēp), *v. i.;* LEAPED (lēpt) or LEAPT (lĕpt; lēpt); LEAP′ING (lēp′ĭng). [AS. *hlēapan* to leap, jump, run.] **1.** To spring clear of the ground with the feet; to jump; vault. **2.** To spring or move suddenly as if by a jump; to bound; move swiftly. — *v. t.* **1.** To pass over by a leap or jump. **2.** To cause to leap; as, to *leap* a horse across a ditch. — *n.* **1.** Act of leaping; a jump. **2.** A place that is, or must be, leaped over; the distance covered by a leap.

leap′frog′ (-frŏg′), *n.* A child's game, in which one stoops down and another leaps over him. — *v. i.;* LEAP′FROGGED′ (-frŏgd′); LEAP′FROG′GING. To vault as in leapfrog. — *v. t.* **1.** To leapfrog over. **2.** *Mil.* To advance (two units) by keeping one in action and moving the other past it to a more advanced position.

leap year. **a** A year containing 366 days, February 29 being added as the extra day. Every year exactly divisible by 4 (for example, 1904 or 1940) is a leap year, except the years at the end of a century, which are leap years only when exactly divisible by 400. See MEASURE, *Table* 6. **b** A year (in any calendar) in which there is intercalation.

lear (lēr), *n.* *Now Scot.* Learning; lore.

lear (lēr). Var. of 1st LEER.

Lear (lēr). = KING LEAR.

lea rig (lē rĭg; lā). *Scot.* A ridge left unplowed.

learn (lûrn), *v. t.*; LEARNED (lûrnd), LEARNT (lûrnt); LEARN′ING. [AS. *leornian.*] **1.** To gain knowledge or understanding of, or skill in, by study, instruction, or investigation. **2.** To find out about; to ascertain. **3.** To teach; — now a vulgarism. — **Syn.** See DISCOVER. — *v. i.* To acquire knowledge or skill; to receive instruction. — **learn′er**, *n.*

learn′ed (lûr′nĕd; -nĭd), *adj.* Of or pert. to learning; characterized by learning; erudite. — **learn′ed·ly**, *adv.*

learn′ing, *n.* **1.** Acquisition of knowledge or skill. **2.** Knowledge or skill received by instruction or study.

lease (lēs), *v. t.* [OF. *laissier, lessier* (F. *laisser*), to leave, transmit, fr. L. *laxare* to loose, fr. *laxus* loose.] **1.** To grant by lease; to let. **2.** To hold under a lease; to take a lease of. — **Syn.** See HIRE. — *n.* [OF. *lais* (F. *legs* legacy), fr. the v.] **1.** A contract by which one conveys real estate for life, for a term of years, or at will, usually for a specified rent; also, the act of such conveyance, or the term for which it is made. **2.** A piece of leased land or property.

lease′hold′ (-hōld′), *adj.* Held by lease. — *n.* A tenure by lease, or the land held. — **lease′hold′er** (-hōl′dẽr), *n.*

leash (lēsh), *n.* [OF. *lesse, laisse,* fr. L. *laxa,* fem. of *laxus* loose.] **1.** A thong or cord, as for a hawk or dog. **2.** In sporting, a brace and a half; three, as of greyhounds, foxes, bucks, or hares. — *v. t.* To tie together, or hold, with a leash.

leas′ing (lēz′ĭng), *n.* [AS. *lēasung,* fr. *lēasian* to lie, fr. *lēas* false.] *Archaic & Dial.* Act of lying; a lie or lies.

least (lēst), *adj.* [AS. *lǣsast, lǣsest,* superl. of *lǣssa* less.] Used as the superlative of *little.* Smallest; shortest; slightest; most unimportant. — *n.* The smallest amount, quantity, price, etc. — *adv.* In the smallest or lowest degree.

least common multiple. See COMMON MULTIPLE.

least flycatcher. See FLYCATCHER.

least′ways′ (lēst′wāz′), *adv.* *Chiefly Dial.* Leastwise.

least′wise′ (-wīz′), *adv.* *Colloq.* At least.

leath′er (lĕth′ẽr), *n.* [AS. *lether.*] **1.** The skin of an animal, tanned or otherwise dressed for use. Cf. HIDE, *Illust.* **2.** An article or part made of leather. **3.** *Sporting.* The pendulous part of the ear of a dog, esp. of a bloodhound. See DOG, *Illust.* — *adj.* Pertaining to, made of, or like leather. — *v. t.* **1.** To cover with leather. **2.** *Colloq.* To beat with a strap; to thrash.

leath′er·back′ (-băk′), *n.* See TURTLE, 1.

Leath′er·ette′ (lĕth′ẽr·ĕt′), *n.* A trade-mark for a paper or cloth product imitating leather.

leath′ern (lĕth′ẽrn), *adj.* [AS. *letheren.*] **1.** Made of leather; consisting of leather. **2.** Of the nature of leather.

leath′er·neck′ (lĕth′ẽr·nĕk′), *n.* *Slang.* A marine.

leath′er·wood′ (-wŏŏd′), *n.* *U.S.* A small tree (*Dirca palustris*) with tough, pliant stems and yellow flowers.

leath′er·y (-ĭ), *adj.* Resembling leather in appearance or consistency; tough. — **leath′er·i·ness**, *n.*

leave (lēv), *n.* [AS. *lēaf.*] **1.** Permission; allowance; specif., leave of absence, as from military duty. **2.** A formal parting; farewell.

leave (lēv), *v. t.*; LEFT (lĕft); LEAV′ING. [AS. *lǣfan.*] **1.** To allow or cause to remain; as, he *left* a coin on the table; hence, to bequeath at death; as, he *left* a legacy to his sister. **2.** To let remain unremoved or undone; to let stay or continue, in distinction from what is removed or changed; as, seven from ten *leaves* three. **3.** To let be without interference; to commit; refer; as, to *leave* the decision to arbitrators; also, to suffer to be undisturbed in action; as, I *left* him alone. **4.** To put, place, deposit, deliver, or the like, so as to allow to remain. **5.** To take leave of or withdraw oneself from; to go away or depart from. **6.** To desert; forsake; hence, to give up; relinquish. **7.** To cease from; stop. — *v. i.* **1.** *Colloq.* To depart; to set out. **2.** To cease; to desist. — **Syn.** See GO.

leave in. *Bridge.* To refuse to take (one's partner) out of his declaration. — ***leave off.*** **a** To desist from; stop. **b** To cease wearing or using. **c** To forsake.

leave (lēv), *v. i.* [See LEAF.] To send out leaves; to leaf.

leaved (lēvd), *adj.* Having (such or so many) leaves; — chiefly in combination, as in broad-*leaved.*

leav′en (lĕv′ĕn), *n.* [OF. *levain,* fr. L. *levamen,* alleviation, taken in the sense of a raising, that which raises, fr. *levare* to raise.] **1.** Any substance used to produce fermentation, as in dough or liquids; esp., a portion of fermenting dough reserved for this use; also, specif., yeast; barm. **2.** Sometimes, any ferment. **3.** Anything which makes a general assimilating change in a mass or aggregate; as, a *leaven* of wit. — *v. t.* **1.** To cause to ferment, as dough; hence, to make light by a leavening agent. **2.** To mingle or permeate with a transforming element or admixture; to imbue, impregnate, alloy, or the like. — **Syn.** See INFUSE.

leav′en·ing (-ĕn·ĭng), *n.* **1.** Act of making light, or causing to ferment, by leaven. **2.** That which leavens, or makes light; leaven.

leaves (lēvz), *n., pl.* of LEAF.

leave′-tak′ing, *n.* Taking of leave; adieu.

leav′ing (lēv′ĭng), *n.* **1.** Thing left; remnant; residue; — usually in *pl.* **2.** *pl.* Refuse; offal.

leav′y (lēv′ĭ), *adj.*; LEAV′I·ER (-ĭ·ẽr); -I·EST. Leafy.

le′bens·raum′ (lā′bĕns·roum′), *n.* [G.] Space in which to live and grow; specif.: **a** Territory that is considered necessary for the existence of a state, as popularized in Nazism, for the economic self-sufficiency of a world power. **b** The area required for the life and growth of any community, organism, or individual.

lech′er (lĕch′ẽr), *n.* [OF. *lecheor, lecheur,* glutton, libertine, fr. *lechier* to lick.] A man given to lewdness.

lech′er·ous (-ŭs), *adj.* Addicted to lewdness or lust. — **lech′er·ous·ly**, *adv.* — **lech′er·ous·ness**, *n.*

lech′er·y (-ĭ), *n.* Free indulgence of lust; lewdness.

lec′i·thin (lĕs′ĭ·thĭn), *n.* [Gr. *lekithos* yolk of an egg + *-in.*] *Biochem.* Any of several complex nitrogenous substances found esp. in the brain and nerve tissue and in yolk of eggs. Lecithin is used in manufacture as an emulsifier.

lec′tern (lĕk′tẽrn) *n.* [OF. *leitrun, lettrun,* fr. LL. *lectrum,* fr. L. *legere, lectum,* to read.] A reading desk in some churches, from which the Scripture lessons are read.

lec′tion (lĕk′shŭn), *n.* [L. *lectio,* fr. *legere, lectum,* to read.] **1.** A reading; a variation in the text. **2.** *Eccl.* A selection, esp. of Scripture, read in divine service.

lec′tion·ar′y (-ẽr′ĭ *or, esp. Brit.,* -ẽr·ĭ), *n.*; *pl.* -IES (-ĭz). *Eccl.* A book, or a list, of lections, for divine service.

lec′tor (lĕk′tẽr; -tôr), *n.* [L.] *Eccl.* One whose chief duty is to read the lessons in the church service.

lec′ture (lĕk′tūr), *n.* [F., fr. L. *lectura,* fr. *legere, lectum,* to read.] **1.** A discourse delivered on any subject; esp., a formal discourse intended for instruction. **2.** A reprimand or formal reproof; admonition. — *v. i.* To deliver a lecture or lectures. — *v. t.* **a** To read or deliver a lecture or lectures to; to instruct by lectures. **b** To reprove formally; to reprimand. — **lec′tur·er** (-tūr·ẽr), *n.*

lec′ture·ship, *n.* Office or function of a lecturer.

led (lĕd), *past & past part.* of LEAD, to guide.

ledge (lĕj), *n.* [ME. *legge* a bar.] **1.** A projecting ridge or raised edge along a surface; a shelf. **2.** A ridge or reef, esp. one under water near the shore. **3.** A narrow flat surface or shelf, esp. one that projects, as from a wall of rock. **4.** *Mining.* A lode or vein.

ledg′er (lĕj′ẽr), *n.* [Earlier *lidger, legger,* appar. fr. ME. *liggen* to lie, *leggen* to lay.] **1.** **a** A large flat stone, esp. one laid over a tomb. **b** A horizontal piece of timber secured to the uprights supporting the putlogs in a scaffolding, or the like. **2.** *Angling.* A ledger bait, line, or tackle; as, to fish with a *ledger;* — sometimes spelled **leg′er.** **3.** *Bookkeeping.* The final book of record in business transactions, in which all debits and credits from the journal, etc., are placed under appropriate heads.

ledg′er, leg′er (lĕj′ẽr), *adj.* Lying or remaining in a place; hence, resident; stationary; — now only in certain phrases.

ledger bait. Fishing bait attached to a floating line fastened to the bank of a stream, pond, etc.

ledger board. A horizontal board forming the top rail of a simple fence, the handrail to a balustrade, or the like.

ledger line. **a** *Angling.* See LEDGER TACKLE. **b** *Music.* A line added above or below the staff to extend its compass.

ledger paper. A medium to heavy writing paper, with good erasing quality, used esp. in ledgers.

ledger tackle, line, etc. *Angling.* A tackle, line, etc., arranged so that the lead rests upon the bottom.

lee (lē), *n.* [AS. *hlēo,* for *hlēow,* shelter, protection.] **1.** Shelter or protection; also, a sheltered place or side, esp. one protected from the wind; as, the *lee* of a mountain. **2.** *Naut.* The quarter towards which the wind blows; that side, as of a ship, that is farthest from the point from which the wind blows. — *adj.* *Naut.* Of or pertaining to the lee; — opposed to *weather.*

lee (lē), *n.*; *pl.* LEES (lēz). [OF. *lie,* fr. ML. *lia.*] That which settles at the bottom, as of a cask of liquor, esp. wine; sediment; dregs; — used now only in *pl.*

lee′board′ (lē′bōrd′; 70), *n.* A device for preventing leeway in a sailing vessel, consisting of a plane of wood or metal attached to the outside of the hull and lowered or raised by a tackle.

leech (lēch), *n.* [Of LG. origin.] *Naut.* Either edge of a square sail; also, the after edge of any fore-and-aft sail.

leech, *n.* [AS. *lǣce.*] **1.** *Archaic.* A physician or surgeon. **2.** Any of numerous carnivorous or bloodsucking annelid worms (constituting a class (Hirudinea)). One order (Gnathobdellae) includes the ***medicinal leech*** (*Hirudo medicinalis*), a European fresh-water species two or three inches long formerly much used by physicians for bleeding patients. **3.** One who clings to another to draw gain from him. **4.** *Med.* An apparatus for drawing blood by suction. — *v. t.* **a** *Archaic.* To cure; heal; to treat as a physician. **b** To bleed by the use of leeches.

leek (lēk), *n.* [AS. *lēc, lēac.*] A cultivated biennial (*Allium porrum*), of the lily family, much like the closely related onion and having similar culinary uses, but distinguished from the onion by having smaller bulbs and flat, succulent leaves. It is the floral emblem of Wales.

leer, lear (lēr), *adj.* [ME. *lere.*] *Now Dial.* Empty; void.

leer (lēr), *v. i.* [Cf. ME. *lere* cheek, look.] To look askance; esp., to cast a sidelong lustful or malign look. — *n.* A gaze askance; a look conveying a sly, sinister, or immodest suggestion. — **leer′ing·ly**, *adv.*

leer′y (-ĭ), *adj.* *Dial.* Leer, or empty; faint with hunger.

leer′y, lear′y (lēr′ĭ), *adj.* *Slang.* Knowing; wary.

lees (lēz), *n. pl.* Dregs. See 2d LEE.

lee shore. A shore on the lee side of a vessel, — a danger in stormy weather. — ***on a lee shore.*** In difficulties.

leet (lēt), *n.* *Eng. Hist.* A kind of manor court, or its jurisdiction, or the day on which the court was held.

lee′ward (lē′wẽrd; *naut. & hist.* lū′ẽrd, lŏŏ′-), *adj.* Pert. to, or in the direction of, the lee part or side; — opp. to *windward.* — *n.* The lee side; the lee. — *adv.* Toward the lee.

lee′way′ (lē′wā′), *n.* **1.** **a** *Naut.* The lateral movement of a ship to the leeward of her course. **b** *Aeronautics.* The angle of drift due to cross currents of wind. **2.** *Colloq.* Margin or room for action or the like.

leeze me on (lēz′ mē ŏn′). *Scot.* I delight in; give me.

left (lĕft), *past & past part.* of LEAVE.

left (lĕft), *adj.* [ME. *left, lift, luft.*] **1.** Designating, or pertaining to, that side of the body on which in man the muscular action of the limbs is, with most individuals, weaker than on the other side; — opposed to *right;* as, the *left* hand. **2.** Situated so that the left side of the body is toward it; as, the *left* wing of an army is that to the left of the center to one facing an enemy. — *n.* **1.** That part of space toward which the left side of one's body is turned; the part on the left side. **2.** In games, etc., the person, place, or action, at or to the left side. **3.** *Politics.* [sometimes *cap.*, when used of a specific group.] In some legislative bodies of Europe, those members collectively who have seats to the left of the presiding officer; also, the liberal or radical groups which occupy these seats; hence, political liberals or radicals collectively.

left′-hand′, *adj.* **1.** Situated on the left. **2.** Left-handed.

left′-hand′ed (-hăn′dĕd; -dĭd; 2), *adj.* **1.** Using the left hand habitually or more easily than the right. **2.** Of, pert. to, adapted to, or done with the left hand. **3.** Morganatic. **4.** Clumsy; awkward; also, insincere; malicious; as, a *left-handed* compliment. **5.** **a** Having a direction contrary to that of the hands of a watch viewed from in front; counterclockwise; — said of a twist, rotary motion, or spiral curve as viewed from a given direction with respect to the axis of rotation. **b** Having a structure involving a counterclockwise direction; as, a *left-handed* screw. — **left′-hand′ed**, *adv.* — **left′-hand′ed·ly**, *adv.* — **left′-hand′ed·ness**, *n.*

left′ist (lĕf′tĭst), *n.* **1.** *Politics.* **a** A member of the left. See LEFT, *n.*, 3. **b** A member of a radical or revolutionary party; a radical. **2.** One who holds or advocates ultraliberal principles. — **left′ist**, *adj.*

left wing. [*usually caps.*] *Colloq.* The more liberal or radical element, as of a political party.

leg (lĕg), *n.* [ON. *leggr* leg, calf.] **1.** A limb of an animal used for supporting the body; specif.: **a** That part of the limb between the knee and foot. **b** The back half of a hindquarter of lamb, mutton, or veal. See LAMB, *Illust.* **2.** The part of an article of clothing which covers the leg. **3.** *Archaic.* A bow or obeisance; esp. in the phrase, *to make a leg.* **4.** That which resembles a leg in form or use; as: **a** A pole or bar serving as a support, as in a prop to a building. **b** One of the divisions of an object that is forked, as one of the branches of a pair of compasses. **c** One of the comparatively long supports of a piece of furniture. **5.** *Cricket.* That part of the on side of the field which lies between the rear boundary and the popping crease extended. See CREASE, *n.*, 2. **6.** *Math.* Either side of a triangle as distinguished from the base or hypotenuse. **7.** *Naut.* The course and distance made by a vessel on one tack. **8.** *Sports.* The first event won, when a second is still necessary to decide the contest. — *v. i.*; LEGGED (lĕgd); LEG′GING. To use the legs, as in walking (usually with *it*).

leg′a·cy (lĕg′ȧ·sĭ), *n.*; *pl.* -CIES (-sĭz). [OF. *legacie* the office of a legate, fr. ML. *legatia*, fr. L. *legatus* legate.] **1.** Something coming from an ancestor or predecessor. **2.** *Law.* A gift of property by will; a bequest.

le′gal (lē′găl), *adj.* [F. *légal*, fr. L. *legalis*, fr. *lex, legis*, law.] **1.** Of, pertaining to, based upon, or governed by law. **2.** In conformity with, or permitted by, law; lawful; — opposed to *illegal, unlawful.* **3.** Enforced, protected, or the like, in courts of law; — distinguished from *equitable.* **4.** Established by the constructions of law; as, a *legal* fiction. **5.** *Theol.* **a** According to the law of Moses. **b** According to the law of works as distinguished from free grace; resting on works for salvation. — **Syn.** See LAWFUL. — **Ant.** Illegal. — *n.* A class of securities in which savings banks, savings departments of commercial banks, and similarly regulated institutions of deposit, may legally invest. — **le′gal·ly**, *adv.*

legal cap. A folio writing paper, made for lawyers, in narrow sheets with the fold at the top.

legal holiday. A day set apart by law as exempt from official business, service of process, demand and protest of commercial paper, etc. See HOLIDAY, 3.

le′gal·ism (lē′găl·ĭz′m), *n.* Strictness, or the doctrine of strictness, in conforming to law, or, in theology, to a code of deeds and observances as a means of justification. — **le′gal·ist** (-ĭst), *n. & adj.* — **le′gal·is′tic** (-ĭs′tĭk), *adj.*

le·gal′i·ty (lē·găl′ĭ·tĭ), *n.*; *pl.* -TIES (-tĭz). **1.** Conformity to, or observance of, law. **2.** Quality or state of being legal; lawfulness.

le′gal·ize (lē′găl·īz), *v. t.* To make legal; to give legal sanction to. — **le′gal·i·za′tion** (-ĭ·zā′shŭn; -ī·zā′-), *n.*

legal reserve. *Banking.* The reserve required by statute to be held against deposits.

legal separation. *Law.* A divorce which leaves the parties husband and wife but discharges them from the duty of living together.

legal tender. *Law.* That currency, or money, which the law authorizes a debtor to tender and requires a creditor to receive in payment of money obligations.

leg′ate (lĕg′ĭt), *n.* [OF. *legat*, fr. L. *legatus*, fr. *legare* to send with a commission, depute, fr. *lex, legis*, law.] **1.** An ecclesiastic representing the pope and invested with the authority of the Holy See. **2.** Ambassador or envoy; a delegate. **3.** *Rom. Hist.* **a** An official assistant of a general or governor of a province. **b** Under the emperors, a governor sent to a province. — **leg′ate·ship**, *n.*

leg′a·tee′ (lĕg′ȧ·tē′), *n.* *Law.* One to whom a legacy is bequeathed.

leg′a·tine (lĕg′ȧ·tĭn; -tīn), *adj.* Of or pert. to a legate.

le·ga′tion (lē·gā′shŭn), *n.* [F. *légation*, fr. L. *legatio*.] **1.** The sending forth of one person to act for another; the errand on which one is sent. **2.** A legate and his associates; an embassy; deputation. **3.** The place of business or official residence of a diplomatic minister. **4.** The office and dignity of a legate.

le·ga′to (lā·gä′tō; lē-), *adj. & adv.* [It., tied.] *Music.* Smooth and connected with no breaks between tones.

leg bye. *Cricket.* A bye made on a ball that glances off the body (except the hand or wrist).

leg′end (lĕj′ĕnd; lē′jĕnd), *n.* [OF. *legende*, fr. ML., fr. L. *legendus* to be read, fr. *legere* to read.] **1.** *Obs. exc. Hist.* A story of life, as of a saint, or a collection of such stories. **2.** An inscription, motto, or title, as on a medal or coin. **3.** Any story coming down from the past, esp. one popularly taken as historical though not verifiable; also, such stories collectively. **4.** *Print.* A title or a brief description beneath an illustration.

leg′end·ar′y (lĕj′ĕn·dĕr′ĭ *or, esp. Brit.*, -dẽr·ĭ), *adj.* Of or pertaining to a legend or legends; like a legend; fabulous. — **Syn.** See FICTITIOUS.

leg′end·ry (lĕj′ĕn·drĭ), *n.* Legends collectively.

leg′er (lĕj′ẽr). Var. of LEDGER, *n. & adj.*

leg′er·de·main′ (lĕj′ẽr·dē·mān′), *n.* [F. *léger de main*, lit., light of hand.] **a** Sleight of hand. **b** Any artful trick. — **leg′er·de·main′ist** (-ĭst), *n.*

le·ger′i·ty (lē·jĕr′ĭ·tĭ), *n.* [F. *légèreté*.] Lightness; nimbleness. — **Syn.** See CELERITY.

‖**le′ges** (lē′jēz), *n.*, *pl.* of LEX.

legged (lĕgd; *in comb.*, -lĕg′ĕd; -ĭd, *or, esp. Brit.*, -lĕgd), *adj.* Having (such or so many) legs; — chiefly in combination.

leg′ging (lĕg′ĭng), *n.* [From LEG.] A cover for the leg, like a long gaiter; — chiefly in *pl.*

leg hit. *Cricket.* A hit sending the ball to leg.

leg′horn (lĕg′hôrn; lĕg′ẽrn; -ôrn; *Brit. also* lĕ·gôrn′), *n.* **1.** A plaiting made from straw grown in Tuscany, Italy; — from *Leghorn*, the seaport. **2.** A hat or bonnet of this plaiting. **3.** [*cap.*] One of a small hardy Mediterranean breed of fowls.

leg′i·ble (lĕj′ĭ·b'l), *adj.* [LL. *legibilis*, fr. *legere* to read.] **1.** Capable of being read or deciphered; plain. **2.** Easy to read. — **leg′i·bil′i·ty** (-bĭl′ĭ·tĭ), *n.* — **leg′i·bly**, *adv.*

le′gion (lē′jŭn), *n.* [OF. *legion*, fr. L. *legio*, fr. *legere* to gather, collect.] **1.** *Rom. Antiq.* A body of soldiers forming the principal army unit, varying from 3000 foot soldiers and 300 cavalrymen in early times to 5000–6000 foot soldiers under the empire. **2.** A military force; an army. **3.** A great number; a multitude.

le′gion·ar′y (-ĕr′ĭ *or, esp. Brit.*, -ẽr·ĭ), *adj.* Belonging to a legion; also, consisting of a legion or legions. — *n.*; *pl.* -IES (-ĭz). A member of a legion.

le′gion·naire′ (lē′jŭn·âr′), *n.* [F. *légionnaire.*] A member of a legion, esp. of a patriotic organization of military and naval veterans.

Legion of Honor. A French order, established by Napoleon in 1802 as a reward for either civil or military merit.

Legion of Merit. *Mil., U. S.* A decoration awarded for exceptionally meritorious conduct in the performance of outstanding services, awarded to foreigners in any of four degrees (chief commander, commander, officer, and legionnaire) but to U. S. personnel without degree.

leg′is·late (lĕj′ĭs·lāt), *v. i.* [See LEGISLATOR.] To make or enact a law or laws. — *v. t.* To cause to be, become, go, etc., by legislation.

leg′is·la′tion (-lā′shŭn), *n.* [L. *legis latio.* See LEGISLATOR.] **1.** Act of legislating; preparation and enactment of laws. **2.** Also, the laws that are so enacted.

leg′is·la′tive (lĕj′ĭs·lā′tĭv; -lȧ·tĭv), *adj.* **1.** Making laws; — disting. from *executive* or *administrative*, and *judicial.* **2.** Of or pertaining to the making of laws, or the body which makes the laws; suitable to, or involved in, legislation. — *n.* The legislative power, body, or department; the legislature. — **leg′is·la′tive·ly**, *adv.*

leg′is·la′tor (-lā′tẽr), *n.* [L. *legis lator*, prop., a proposer of a law, fr. *lex, legis*, law + *lator* a proposer.] A member of a legislative body; a lawgiver. — **leg′is·la·to′ri·al** (-lȧ·tō′rĭ·ăl; 70), *adj.* — **leg′is·la′tress** (lĕj′ĭs·lā′trĕs; -trĭs), **leg′is·la′trix** (-lā′trĭks), *n. fem.*

leg′is·la′ture (lĕj′ĭs·lā′tûr), *n.* The body of persons in a state invested with power to make, alter, and repeal laws.

le′gist (lē′jĭst), *n.* One skilled in the law.

le·git′ (lē·jĭt′), *n. Slang.* Short for LEGITIMATE DRAMA. — **le·git′**, *adj.*

le·git′i·ma·cy (lē·jĭt′ĭ·mȧ·sĭ), *n.* State or quality of being legitimate.

le·git′i·mate (-mĭt), *adj.* [ML. *legitimatus*, past part. of *legitimare* to legitimate, fr. L. *legitimus* legitimate. See LEGAL.] **1.** Lawfully begotten; born in wedlock. **2.** Real; genuine. **3.** Accordant with law; lawful; hence, existing or ruling by hereditary right; as, a *legitimate* monarch. **4.** Conforming to recognized principles or accepted standards; as, *legitimate* reasoning. — **Syn.** See LAWFUL. — (-māt), *v. t.* To make legitimate; to give legal force to. Hence, to authorize or justify. — **le·git′i·mate·ly**, *adv.* — **le·git′i·ma′tion** (-mā′shŭn), *n.*

legitimate drama, *or* **le·git′i·mate** (-mĭt), *n.* Orig., drama of literary value as opposed to farce and melodrama; later, spoken drama with plot, dialogue, and action.

le·git′i·ma·tize (lē·jĭt′ĭ·mȧ·tīz), *v. t.* To legitimate.

le·git′i·mist (-mĭst), *n.* One who supports legitimate authority, esp. a monarchy. — **le·git′i·mism** (-mĭz′m), *n.* — **le·git′i·mist**, *adj.* — **le·git′i·mis′tic** (-mĭs′tĭk), *adj.*

le·git′i·mize (-mīz), *v. t.* To legitimate. — **le·git′i·mi·za′tion** (-mĭ·zā′shŭn; -mī·zā′-), *n.*

leg′len (lĕg′lĕn), *n. Scot.* A milk pail.

leg′less (-lĕs; -lĭs), *adj.* Having no leg or legs.

leg′-of-mut′ton, *adj.* Having the general shape or outline of a leg of mutton; as, a ***leg-of-mutton sail***, a triangular sail with its apex at the masthead. See SHARPIE, *Illust.*

Le·gree′ (lē·grē′), **Simon.** In Mrs. Stowe's *Uncle Tom's Cabin*, a brutal slave dealer. Hence, a cruel taskmaster.

leg stump. *Cricket.* The stump on the leg, or "on," side.

leg′ume (lĕg′ūm; lē·gūm′), *n.* [F. *légume*, fr. L. *legumen*, prob. fr. *legere* to gather.] **1.** The fruit or seed of a pod-bearing plant, as peas, beans, etc., used for food; hence, any edible vegetable. **2.** A leguminous plant, esp. one grown as a forage crop, as clover, alfalfa, soybeans, etc. **3.** *Bot.* A superior one-celled monocarpellary fruit usually dehiscent into two valves, having the seeds attached along the ventral suture; — commonly called *pod*, and restricted to the pea family.

le·gu′min (lē·gū′mĭn), *n.* A globulin found in legumes.

le·gu′mi·nous (-mĭ·nŭs), *adj.* **1.** Pertaining to, or consisting of or of the nature of, peas or other legumes. **2.** *Bot.* Of or pert. to a group (Leguminosae) of dicotyledonous plants bearing legumes, or pods.

le·hu′a (lā·hōō′ä), *n.* [Hawaiian.] *Hawaii.* A common, showy tree (*Metrosideros polymorpha*) of the myrtle family, found on the Pacific islands and having bright-red corymbose flowers and a hard wood; also, its flower, the floral emblem of the island of Hawaii.

‖**le′i** (lā′ē; lā), *n.*; *pl.* LEIS (lā′ēz; lāz). [Hawaiian.] A wreath, garland, or ornamental headdress, as of leaves and flowers.

‖**lei** (lā), *n.*, *pl.* of LEU.

Leices′ter (lĕs′tẽr), *n.* [From *Leicester*, county seat of Leicestershire, Eng.] A breed of white-faced sheep originating in England, but now widely kept elsewhere.

leis′ter (lēs′tẽr), *n.* [ON. *ljōstr.*] A spear armed with three or more prongs, for striking fish. — *v. t.* To spear with a leister.

lei′sure (lē′zhẽr; lĕzh′ẽr), *n.* [OF. *leisir*, orig., permission, fr. L. *licere* to be permitted.] **1.** Freedom afforded by exemption from occupation or business; time free from employment. **2.** Time free from engagement; hence, convenience; ease. — *adj.* Unemployed; as, *leisure* hours.

lei′sure·ly, *adj.* Characterized by leisure, taking abundant time. — *adv.* In a leisurely manner. — **lei′sure·li·ness**, *n.*

leit′mo·tiv′, leit′mo·tif′ (līt′mō·tēf′), *n.* [G. *leitmotiv.*] *Music.* In Wagnerian music drama, a marked melodic phrase or short passage, expressive of, or associated with, a certain idea, person, or situation, and accompanying its reappearance.

lem′an (lĕm′ăn; lē′măn), *n.* [ME. *lemman*, *lefman*, fr. AS. *lēof* dear + *mann* man.] *Archaic.* A sweetheart or lover, of either sex; specif., a mistress.

lem′ma (lĕm′ȧ), *n.*; *pl.* -MAS (-ȧz); -MATA (-ȧ·tȧ). [L., fr. Gr. *lēmma* anything received, an assumption, fr. root of *lambanein* to take, assume.] A preliminary or auxiliary proposition accepted as true and used in a demonstration of some other proposition.

lem′ma (lĕm′ȧ), *n.*; *pl.* LEMMAS (-ȧz). [Gr.] The lower of the two bracts enclosing the flower in the spikelet of grasses.

lem′ming (lĕm′ĭng), *n.*; see PLURAL, *Note*, 3. [Dan. & Nor.] Any of several small rodents of circumpolar distribution (genera *Lemmus* and *Dicrostonyx*), four or five inches long, with a short tail, furry feet, and small ears. A European species (*L. lemmus*) is notable for making devastating migrations in enormous numbers at long and irregular intervals.

lem·nis′cus (lĕm·nĭs′kŭs), *n.; pl.* LEMNISCI (-ī). [NL., fr. L. *lemniscus* a ribbon hanging down.] *Anat.* Any band of fibers, esp. nerve fibers.

lem′on (lĕm′ŭn), *n.* [F. *limon*, fr. Ar. *laymūn*.] **1.** The acid fruit of a tree (*Citrus limonia*) related to the orange. The rind contains the fragrant essential ***oil of lemon***. **2.** The stout, thorny tree which bears this fruit. **3.** The color **lemon yellow**, the color of ripe lemons, reddish-yellow in hue, of high saturation, and very high brilliance. See COLOR. **4.** *Slang, U.S.* Something worthless; a flat failure. — *adj.* Lemon-colored.

lem′on·ade′ (lĕm′ŭn·ād′), *n.* [F. *limonade*.] A beverage of lemon juice mixed with water and sweetened.

lemon geranium. A common garden pelargonium, having lemon-scented foliage.

lemon squash. *Brit.* Lemonade.

lemon verbena. A small South American shrub (*Lippia citriodora*) of the verbena family, with narrow verticillate lemon-scented leaves.

lem·pi′ra (lĕm·pē′rä), *n.* [Amer.-Sp., after a native chief.] The gold monetary unit of Honduras, authorized by law in 1926, and under the International Monetary Fund made equivalent to the U. S. half dollar.

le′mur (lē′mẽr), *n.; pl.* LEMURS (-mẽrz). [L. *lemures* nocturnal spirits, ghosts. So named from its nocturnal habits.] Any of numerous arboreal, chiefly nocturnal mammals, allied to the monkeys but usually regarded as constituting a distinct suborder (Lemuroidea), found chiefly in Madagascar. Lemurs have a sharp foxlike muzzle, large eyes, and very soft woolly fur. See MACACO; cf. FLYING LEMUR. — **lem′u·roid** (lĕm′ū·roid), *adj.*

lem′u·res (lĕm′ū·rēz), *n. pl.* [L. See LEMUR.] *Rom. Relig.* Nocturnal spirits; souls of the dead.

lend (lĕnd), *v. t.;* LENT (lĕnt); LEND′ING. [AS. *lǣnan*, fr. *lǣn* loan.] **1.** To allow the use of, on condition of the return of the same; as, to *lend* a book; — opposed to *borrow*. **2.** To let out (money) for temporary use on condition of return with interest. **3.** To afford; furnish; as, to *lend* assistance. — *v. i.* To make a loan or loans. — **lend′er**, *n.*

Lend′-Lease′ Ad·min′is·tra′tion. In full **Office of Lend-Lease Administration.** *U. S.* An administrative unit established by executive order (Oct. 28, 1941) to exercise powers granted to the president by the **Lend-Lease Act** (March 11, 1941), known as H. R. 1776, for supplying any government whose defense the president deems vital to the defense of the U. S. with war requirements of tanks, aircraft, weapons, other munitions, metals, tools, raw materials, foodstuffs, and services, such as rental or repair of ships, supply bases, etc. — **lend′-lease′**, *adj. & v. t.*

length (lĕngth; lĕngkth; 68), *n.* [AS. *length*, fr. the stem of *lang, long*, long.] **1. a** The longest, or longer, dimension of any object, in distinction from *breadth* or *width;* extent from end to end. **b** A specific extent or distance in this dimension; as, a *length* of two feet. See MEASURE, METRIC SYSTEM, *Tables*. **2.** Extent in time, number, or quantity. **3.** Quality or state of being long, in space or time; extent; duration. **4.** A portion of space or of time, esp. when long; a long stretch. **5.** Prolongation in time; as, to pursue a subject to a great *length*. **6.** A single piece of a series of pieces which may be connected together; as, a *length* of pipe. **7.** *Phonet.* Of a vowel or consonant, duration in time as long or short; also, inaccurately, quality of vowels. **8.** *Pros.* Quantity, as of a vowel or syllable. **9.** *Racing.* The general measure of the thing competing, as a boat or horse, constituting a unit to describe the amount of space by which one wins. — ***at length***. **a** At or in the full extent; without abbreviation. **b** At the end or conclusion; after a long period.

length′en (lĕng′thĕn), *v. t. & i.* To make or become longer. — **Syn.** See EXTEND.

length′wise′ (lĕngth′wīz′), *adv.* In the direction of the length; longitudinally. — *adj.* Moving, placed, or directed lengthwise. — **length′ways′** (-wāz′), *adv.*

length′y (lĕng′thĭ), *adj.;* LENGTH′I·ER (-thĭ·ẽr); LENGTH′I·EST. Having length; specif.: **a** Rather long or too long; not brief; — said chiefly of discourses, etc. **b** *Colloq.* Of a person, tall. — **length′i·ly**, *adv.* — **length′i·ness**, *n.*

le′ni·en·cy (lē′nĭ·ĕn·sĭ; lēn′yĕn·sĭ), *n.* Also **le′ni·ence** (lē′nĭ·ĕns; lēn′yĕns). Quality or state of being lenient.

le′ni·ent (lē′nĭ·ĕnt; lēn′yĕnt), *adj.* [L. *leniens, -entis*, pres. part. of *lenire* to soften, fr. *lenis* soft, mild.] **1.** Relaxing; emollient; softening. **2.** Mild; clement; merciful; not rigorous or severe. — **Syn.** See SOFT. — **le′ni·ent·ly**, *adv.*

Len′i-Len′a·pe, Len′ni-Len′a·pe (lĕn′ĭ·lĕn′ȧ·pē), *n. pl.* The Delaware Indians.

Len′in·ism (lĕn′ĭn·ĭz′m), *n.* The doctrine, tactics, and practice of the Bolshevik (Communist) party as established and modified by Nikolai Lenin. Founded upon Marxism, it was transformed after 1928 into Stalinism. — **Len′in·ist** (-ĭst), *n. & adj.* — **Len′in·ite** (-īt), *n. & adj.*

len′i·tive (lĕn′ĭ·tĭv), *adj.* Having the quality of softening or mitigating; emollient. — *n.* **1.** *Med.* A medicine or application that eases pain. **2.** That which softens or mitigates; a palliative.

len′i·ty (lĕn′ĭ·tĭ), *n.; pl.* -TIES (-tĭz). [OF. *lenité*, fr. L. *lenitas*, fr. *lenis* soft, mild.] State or quality of being lenient; mildness; also, a lenient act or action; — opposed to *severity* and *rigor*. — **Syn.** See MERCY. — **Ant.** Severity.

lens (lĕnz), *n.* [L., lentil; — from the resemblance in shape of a double convex lens to the seed of a lentil.] **1.** A piece of glass, or other transparent substance, having two opposite regular surfaces, either both curved, or one curved and the other plane, and commonly used, either singly or combined, in an optical instrument for forming an image by changing the direction of rays of light. Of spherical lenses there are six varieties, as shown in section: viz., *a* plano-concave; *b* double-concave, or biconcave; *c* plano-convex; *d* double-convex, or biconvex; *e* converging concavo-convex, or converging meniscus; *f* diverging concavo-convex, or diverging meniscus. **2.** A combination of two or more simple lenses. **3.** *Anat. & Zool.* A highly transparent, biconvex, lens-shaped (or nearly spherical) body in the eye which serves to focus the rays of light, as upon the retina. See EYE, *Illust.*

a b c d e f

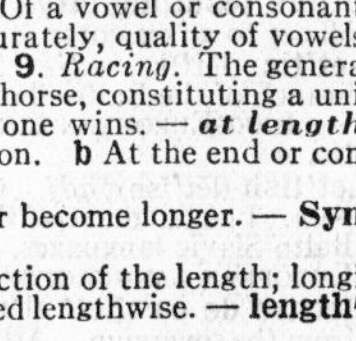

1

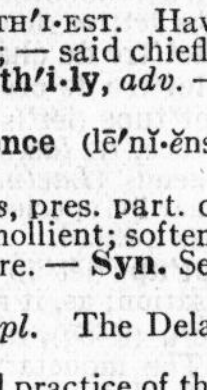

2

1 Lenses, 1; 2 Lens, 2. Cf. FOCUS, *Illust.*

lent (lĕnt), *past & past part.* of LEND.

Lent (lĕnt), *n.* [AS. *lengten, lencten*, spring, Lent.] **1.** *Eccl.* The spring period of fasting in preparation for Easter; in the Western Church, a penitential period extending from Ash Wednesday to Easter, 40 fast days (in the Western Church, 46 calendar days; in the Eastern Church, 56 calendar days). See EASTER, *Table*. **2.** A period of fasting, as, in the Middle Ages, ***St. Martin's Lent***, from Martinmas (Nov. 11) to Christmas.

‖**len′ta·men′te** (lĕn′tä·măn′tā), *adv.* [It.] *Music.* Slowly; — used as a direction.

‖**len·tan′do** (lĕn·tän′dō), *adj.* [It.] *Music.* Becoming slower; retarding; — used as a direction.

Lent′en (lĕn′tĕn), *adj.* [*often not cap.*] **1.** Of or pertaining to, or suitable to, Lent. **2.** Spare; meager; somber; as, *Lenten* fare, dress.

len′ti·cel (lĕn′tĭ·sĕl), *n.* [F. *lenticelle*, dim. fr. L. *lens, lentis*, a lentil.] *Bot.* One of the cortical pores in the stems of woody plants by means of which air penetrates to the interior.

len·tic′u·lar (lĕn·tĭk′ū·lẽr), *adj.* [L. *lenticularis*.] **1.** Like a lentil in size or form; having the form of a double-convex lens. **2.** Of or pertaining to a lens.

len·tig′i·nous (lĕn·tĭj′ĭ·nŭs), *adj.* Freckly.

len·ti′go (lĕn·tī′gō), *n.; pl.* -TIGINES (-tĭj′ĭ·nēz). [L., fr. *lens, lentis*, lentil.] A freckly pigmentation of the skin.

len′til (lĕn′tĭl; -t′l), *n.* [OF. *lentille*, fr. L. *lenticula*, dim. of *lens, lentis*, lentil.] **a** A Eurasian annual plant (*Lens culinaris*, syn. *esculenta*) of the pea family, grown for its edible, lens-shaped seeds. **b** The seed of this plant.

‖**len·tis′si·mo** (lĕn·tēs′sē·mō; lĕn·tĭs′ĭ·mō), *adj.* [It.] *Music.* Very slow; — a direction. — *adv.* Very slowly.

len′to (lĕn′tō), *adj.* [It.] *Music.* Slow; — used as a direction. — *adv.* Slowly.

len′toid (-toid), *adj.* [See LENS; -OID.] Lens-shaped.

l′en·voi′, l′en·voy′ (lĕn·voi′; *F.* läɴ′vwȧ′), *n.* [F. *le* the + *envoi* a sending.] = 1st ENVOY.

Le′o (lē′ō), *n.; gen.* LEONIS (lē·ō′nĭs). [L. See LION.] **a** A northern constellation east of Cancer. **b** The fifth sign [♌] of the zodiac. See ZODIAC.

Le′o·nar·desque′ (lē′ō·när·dĕsk′), *adj.* After the style of the painter Leonardo da Vinci (1452–1519), whose work is remarkable for its subtlety, mysticism, and draftsmanship.

Le′o·nid (lē′ō·nĭd), *n.; pl.* LEONIDS (-nĭdz), LEONIDES (lē·ŏn′ĭ·dēz). [From LEO.] *Astron.* One of the shooting stars which constitute the meteoric shower that recurs near the 14th of November.

le′o·nine (lē′ō·nīn), *adj.* [L. *leoninus*, fr. *leo, leonis*, lion.] Pertaining to, or characteristic of, the lion.

leop′ard (lĕp′ẽrd), *n.* [OF., fr. L., fr. Gr. *leopardos*, fr. *leōn* lion + *pardos* pard.] **1.** A large and ferocious spotted cat (*Felis pardus*) of southern Asia and Africa. Its color is tawny with black spots. A black phase is known, usually showing the spotted pattern in certain lights. Called also *panther*. **2.** *Her.* A lion represented as walking forward, with head facing to the front, as a lion of England. — **leop′ard·ess**, *n.*

leop′ard's-bane′ (lĕp′ẽrdz·bān′), *n.* See DORONICUM.

le′o·tard (lē′ō·tärd), *n.* [After *Léotard* (b. 1838), French aerial gymnast.] A short, close-fitting sleeveless garment worn by acrobats and aerial performers.

lep′er (lĕp′ẽr), *n.* [OF. *lepre*, fr. L. *lepra*, fr. Gr. *lepra*, fr. *lepros* scaly.] A person affected with leprosy; a lazar.

lep′i·do- (lĕp′ĭ·dō-), **lepid-.** [Gr. *lepis, lepidos*.] A combining form, meaning *scale, flake*, as in *lepidopterous*.

le·pid′o·lite (lē·pĭd′ō·līt; lĕp′ĭ·dō·līt), *n.* [*lepido-* + *-lite*.] *Mineral.* A species of mica containing lithia.

lep′i·dop′ter·on (lĕp′ĭ·dŏp′tẽr·ŏn), *n.; pl.* -TERA (-ȧ). *Zool.* A lepidopterous insect.

lep′i·dop′ter·ous (-ŭs), *adj.* [*lepido-* + Gr. *pteron* feather, wing.] Belonging to an order (Lepidoptera) of insects which consists of the butterflies and moths, which when adult have four broad wings usually covered with minute, overlapping, often brightly colored scales. — **lep′i·dop′ter·al** (-ăl), *adj.* — **lep′i·dop′ter·an** (-ăn), *adj. & n.*

lep′i·do·si′ren (lĕp′ĭ·dō·sī′rĕn), *n.* [*lepido-* + Gr. *seirēn* a siren.] *Zool.* One of a genus (*Lepidosiren*) of dipnoan eel-shaped fishes of the swamps of the Amazon and La Plata.

lep′i·dote (lĕp′ĭ·dōt), *adj.* [Gr. *lepidōtos* covered with scales, fr. *lepis, -idos*, a scale.] *Bot.* Covered with scurf.

lep′o·rid (lĕp′ō·rĭd), *n.* [NL., fr. L. *lepus, leporis*, hare + *-id*.] *Zool.* One of a family (Leporidae) consisting of the hares and rabbits, which with the pikas (Ochotonidae) constitute an order (Lagomorpha). — **lep′o·rid**, *adj.*

lep′o·rine (lĕp′ō·rīn; -rĭn), *adj.* [L. *leporinus*.] Of, pertaining to, or like a hare.

lep′re·chaun (lĕp′rĕ·kôn), *n.* [Ir. *lupracān, lugharcān*, MIr. *luchrupān*, fr. *lu* little + *corpān*, dim. of *corp* body, fr. L. *corpus*.] *Irish Folklore.* A little fairy usually conceived as a tricky old man, who if caught may reveal the hiding place of treasure.

lep′rose (lĕp′rōs), *adj.* *Nat. Hist.* Scurfy; scaly.

lep′ro·sy (lĕp′rō·sĭ), *n.* [See LEPROUS.] *Med.* A chronic endemic infectious disease, apparently caused by a microorganism (*Mycobacterium*, formerly *Bacillus, leprae*) and marked by the formation of nodules, ulcerations, and deformities, and by disturbances of sensation.

lep′rous (-rŭs), *adj.* [OF. *leprous, lepros*, fr. LL. *leprosus*, fr. *lepra* leprosy. See LEPER.] **1.** Infected with leprosy; pert. to or resembling leprosy. **2.** Leprose.

-lep′sy (-lĕp′sĭ), **-lep′si·a** (-lĕp′sĭ·ȧ). [NL. *-lepsia*, fr. Gr. *-lēpsia*, as in *epilēpsia* epilepsy.] Suffixes denoting *a seizing*, esp., in medicine, *a violent* or *paroxysmal attack*, as in *epilepsy*, etc.

lep′to- (lĕp′tō-), **lept-.** [Gr. *leptos*.] A combining form meaning *small, weak, thin, fine*, as in **lep′to·dac′ty·lous**, having slender toes, as some birds; **lep′to·phyl′lous**, having slender leaves.

lep′ton (lĕp′tŏn), *n.; pl.* -TA (-tȧ). [Gr.] A minor coin denomination of modern Greece, equivalent to $\frac{1}{100}$ drachma.

lep′tus (lĕp′tŭs), *n.* [NL., fr. Gr. *leptos* thin, small.] *Zool.* The six-legged larva of certain mites; — sometimes [*cap.*] used loosely as a generic name.

Le′pus (lē′pŭs), *n.* [L., a hare.] *Zool.* The genus (family Leporidae) including most of the hares and rabbits.

‖**le roi est mort, vive le roi!** (lẽ rwä ĕ mōr′, vēv′ lẽ rwä′). [F.] The king is dead, long live the king!

‖**le roi le veut** (lẽ rwä′ lẽ vû′). [F.] The king wills it.

Les′bi·an (lĕz′bĭ·ăn), *adj.* **1.** Of or pertaining to Lesbos (now Mytilene), one of the Aegean Islands. **2.** Erotic; — in allusion to the reputed sensuality of the people of Lesbos. **3.** Of or pertaining to Lesbianism. — *n.* **1.** An inhabitant of Lesbos. **2.** A homosexual woman.

Les′bi·an·ism (-ĭz′m), *n. Med.* Homosexual relations between women.

lese maj′es·ty (lēz măj′ĕs·tĭ; -ĭs·tĭ). Also ‖**lèse′-ma′jes′té′** (lĕz′-mȧ′zhĕs′tā′), *n.* Also **leze maj′es·ty** (lēz). [F. *lèse-majesté*, fr. L. *laesus*, fem. *laesa*, injured + *majestas* majesty.] *Law.* Any crime committed against the sovereign power; specif., any of various offenses violating the dignity of a ruler as representative of sovereign power.

le′sion (lē′zhŭn), *n.* [F. *lésion*, fr. L. *laesio*, fr. *laedere*, *laesum*, to injure.] **1.** A hurt; an injury. **2.** *Med., Veter., & Plant Pathol.* Any morbid change in the structure of organs or parts.

les′pe·de′za (lĕs′pē·dē′zȧ), *n.* [NL., erron. after V. M. de *Zespedes*, Spanish governor of East Florida.] Any bush clover; esp., Japan clover. See CLOVER, 2.

less (lĕs), *adj.* [AS. *lǣssa*.] Used as the comparative of *little*. **1.** Smaller; not so great, so much, so many, etc. **2.** In respect to age, rank, etc., secondary; inferior. *Obs.*, except as in the phrase "no *less* a person than." — *adv.* Not so much; in a smaller or lower degree. — *n.* **1.** A smaller portion or quantity. **2.** The inferior, younger, or smaller. — *prep.* Diminished by; minus; with the subtraction of; as, five dollars *less* interest; six *less* four.

-less (-lĕs; -lĭs; 30). [AS. *-lēas*, also separately *lēas* free from, without, false.] A privative adjective suffix, denoting: **a** With nouns, *without, destitute of, not having, free from*, as in child*less*. **b** *Beyond the range of*; — with nouns of action, as in count*less*. **c** With verbs, *unable* or *without power* (to be acted on, or to act, as indicated by the verb), as in resist*less*, not to be resisted.

les·see′ (lĕs·ē′), *n. Law.* A tenant under a lease.

less′en (lĕs′'n), *v. t. & i.* To make or become less; to decrease; diminish; reduce. — **Syn.** See DECREASE.

less′er (lĕs′ẽr), *adj.* [See -ER.] Less; smaller; inferior.

Lesser Bear. *Astron.* = URSA MINOR.

les′son (lĕs′'n), *n.* [OF. *leçon* lesson, reading, fr. L. *lectio* a reading, fr. *legere* to read.] **1.** Something which is learned or taught; instruction. **2.** A reading or exercise assigned to a pupil to be studied. **3.** A severe lecture; reproof. **4.** *Eccl.* A portion of Scripture read in divine service for instruction. — *v. t.* To give a lesson or lessons to; also, to lecture or rebuke; to punish.

les′sor (lĕs′ôr; lĕs·ôr′), *n. Law.* One who leases.

lest (lĕst), *conj.* [AS. *thȳ lǣs the* the less that.] **1.** For fear that; that . . . not. **2.** That; — after certain expressions denoting *fear* or *apprehension*.

‖**le style, c'est l'homme** (lē stēl′, sĕ lôm′). [F.] The style is the man, i. e., exhibits his character.

let (lĕt), *v. t.* [AS. *lettan* to delay, hinder; akin to AS. *læt* slow.] *Archaic.* To hinder; impede; prevent. — *n.* **1.** A retarding; hindrance; obstacle; — common in the phrase *without let or hindrance*. **2.** *Lawn Tennis, Rackets, etc.* An obstruction of the ball in some way specified as such in the rules, as a served ball otherwise good which touches the net. In such a case the ball is replayed.

let, *v. t.*; LET (*Obs.*, LET′TED); LET′TING. [AS. *lǣtan* (past tense *lēt*, past part. *lǣten*).] **1.** To leave; abandon. *Archaic*, except when followed by *alone* or *be*; as, *let* me *alone*; *let* me *be*. **2.** To lease; rent; hire out; also, to give or assign, as a work or contract. **3.** To permit; allow. An infinitive following *let* in this sense is commonly without the sign *to*; as, to *let* us walk, i. e., to permit or suffer us to walk. Sometimes there is entire omission of the verb; as, to *let* [to be or to go] loose. **4.** To cause; make. *Obs.*, except in *to let* (one) *know*. **5.** To make escape, as a fluid or sound; — now *Dial.*, except in "to *let* blood," to bleed. **6.** To permit to enter, pass, or leave. — *v. i.* To be let or leased; as, the farm *lets* for $500 a year.

Syn. (1) See HIRE.

(2) **Let, allow, permit** mean not to prevent or forbid. **Let** (always followed by an expressed or elliptical infinitive) sometimes implies inadvertence, negligence, or the like, and, sometimes, lack of power or authority; **allow** implies little more than forbearance of prohibition; **permit** implies willingness or acquiescence.

-let (-lĕt; -lĭt; 30). [From two French dim. endings *-el* (fr. L. *-ellus*) and *-et*, as in bracel*et*.] A noun suffix having a diminutive force, as in ring*let*, leaf*let*; denoting also *an article worn on*, as in arm*let*, wrist*let*.

‖**l'é′tat′, c'est moi** (lā′tȧ′, sĕ mwȧ′). [F.] The state, it is I; I am the state; — a saying wrongly attributed to Louis XIV, of France.

let′down′ (lĕt′doun′), *n.* **1.** A slackening, as of speed or effort. **2.** *Colloq.* A disappointment.

le′thal (lē′thăl), *adj.* [L. *lethalis*, better *letalis*, fr. *letum* death.] **1.** Deadly; fatal. **2.** Of or relating to death. — **Syn.** See DEADLY.

lethal factor *or* **gene.** Any gene which in certain (homozygous) conditions may prevent development or cause the death of an organism.

le·thar′gic (lē·thär′jĭk), *adj.* Also **le·thar′gi·cal** (-jĭ·kăl). Pertaining to, affected with, causing, or resembling, lethargy; morbidly drowsy; dull; heavy. — **le·thar′gi·cal·ly**, *adv.*

leth′ar·gize (lĕth′ẽr·jīz), *v. t.* To make lethargic.

leth′ar·gy (-jĭ), *n.*; *pl.* -GIES (-jĭz). [OF. *litargie*, fr. LL. *lethargia*, fr. Gr. *lēthargia*, fr. *lēthargos* forgetful, fr. *lēthē* forgetfulness.] **1.** Morbid drowsiness; profound sleep. **2.** A state of inaction or indifference.

Syn. Lethargy, languor, lassitude, stupor, torpor, torpidity mean physical or mental inertness. **Lethargy** implies aversion to activity induced by disease, fatigue, intemperance, or the like; **languor**, in current use, an inertia arising from soft living, an enervating climate, amorous emotion, or the like; **lassitude**, listlessness or seediness resulting from great strain, poor health, or intense worry; **stupor**, a deadening of the mind by extreme drowsiness, by coma, or by narcotics or intoxicants; **torpor** and **torpidity**, a state of suspended animation, as in some forms of physical or mental illness.

Le′the (lē′thē), *n.* [L., fr. Gr. *lēthē* forgetfulness.] **1.** *Gr. Myth.* A river of Hades whose water when drunk caused forgetfulness of the past. **2.** Oblivion; forgetfulness. — **Le·the′an** (lē·thē′ăn), *adj.*

le·thif′er·ous (lē·thĭf′ẽr·ŭs), *adj.* [L. *lethifer*, *letifer*, fr. *letum* death + *ferre* to bear.] Deadly; destructive.

Le′to (lē′tō), *n.* Mother of Apollo and Artemis by Zeus.

‖**l'é′toile′ du nord** (lā′twȧl′ dü nôr′). [F.] The star of the north; — motto of the State of Minnesota.

‖**le tout en′sem′ble** (lē tōō′-täN′säN′bl′). [F.] The whole taken or considered together.

Lett (lĕt), *n.* One of a people, closely related to the Lithuanians, dwelling chiefly in Latvia.

let′ter (lĕt′ẽr), *n.* One who lets or permits.

let′ter, *n.* [OF. *lettre*, fr. L. *littera*, *litera*, a letter, pl., an epistle, a writing, literature.] **1.** An alphabetic character; one of the symbols used in writing or print to represent speech sounds. **2.** A written or printed communication of a direct or personal nature. **3.** Usually *pl.* Literature; belles-lettres; hence, learning; erudition; as, a man of *letters*. **4.** Verbal expression; literal statement or meaning; as, the *letter* of the law. **5.** A size of paper, 10 in. × 16 in. **6.** *Print.* A single type; type, collectively; a style of type. — *v. t.* To mark with letters or words, as a book. — **let′ter·er**, *n.*

letter box. A box for letters, as for mailing.

letter carrier. *U. S.* A postman.

let′tered (lĕt′ẽrd), *adj.* **1.** Literate; educated. **2.** Of or pertaining to learning or literature; learned. **3.** Inscribed, stamped, or marked with or as with letters.

let′ter·gram (lĕt′ẽr·grăm), *n. Teleg.* A long telegram sent at special low rates in consideration of its being dispatched and delivered subject to priority of regular messages; — called also *day* or *night letter* or *lettergram*.

let′ter·head′ (-hĕd′), *n.* A heading printed or engraved on letter paper; also, paper having such heading.

let′ter·ing, *n.* **1.** Act or business of making, or marking with, letters. **2.** The letters made.

letter of advice. A letter, as from a consignor to a consignee, giving some special information; specif., the letter by which the drawer of a bill of exchange notifies the drawee that the bill has been issued.

letter of credit. *Com.* **a** A letter addressed by a banker to his correspondents certifying that the person named therein is entitled to draw on him or his credit up to a certain sum; — often called a *traveler's letter of credit*. **b** A letter addressed by a banker to the person to whom the credit is given authorizing him to draw on the maker up to a certain sum, and guaranteeing to accept the drafts if duly made.

letter, *or, usually,* **letters, of marque (and reprisal).** A license or commission granted by a government to a private person to fit out an armed vessel to cruise as a privateer and make prize of the enemy's ships and merchandise.

let′ter–per′fect (*see Pron.*, § 2), *adj.* Knowing the words or lines of a (player's) part, recitation, or the like, perfectly.

letter press. A press for copying letters.

let′ter·press′ (lĕt′ẽr·prĕs′), *n.* Print; — often used of the reading matter in distinction from illustrations.

letters of administration. *Law.* The instrument by which an administrator or administratrix is authorized to administer the goods or estate of a deceased person.

letters of credence. Also **letter of credence, letters credential.** *Internat. Law.* A formal document furnished a diplomatic agent for accrediting him to the government to which he is sent.

let′ters pat′ent (păt′ĕnt). *Chiefly Eng. Law.* A writing granting to a person power and authority to do some act or enjoy some right; — construed as both *sing. & pl.*

letters testamentary. *Law.* An instrument granted by the proper officer to an executor of a will, authorizing him to act as executor.

Let′tic (lĕt′ĭk), *adj.* **1.** Designating, or belonging to, the Baltic branch of the Balto-Slavic subfamily of the Indo-European languages. See INDO-EUROPEAN LANGUAGES, *Table*. **2.** = LETTISH, *adj.* — **Let′tic**, *n.*

Let′tish (lĕt′ĭsh), *adj.* Of or pertaining to the Letts or their language. — *n.* The language of the Letts, a member of the Baltic branch of the Balto-Slavic languages, closely related to the Lithuanian. See INDO-EUROPEAN LANGUAGES, *Table*.

‖**let′tre de ca′chet′** (lĕt′r' dē kȧ′shĕ′). [F.] A sealed letter, esp. from the sovereign. Arbitrary orders of imprisonment were often given by lettres de cachet in France before the Revolution.

‖**let′tre de change** (shäNzh′). [F.] A bill of exchange.

‖**let′tre de cré′ance′** (krā′äNs′). [F.] A letter of credit.

let′tuce (lĕt′ĭs; -ŭs), *n.* [OF. *laitues*, pl. of *laitue*, fr. L. *lactuca* lettuce, fr. *lac*, *lactis*, milk, on account of its milky juice.] Any of a genus (*Lactuca*) of plants of the chicory family; esp., the common garden species (*L. sativa*), the crisp, succulent leaves of which are used as a salad.

let′up′ (lĕt′ŭp′), *n.* [See LET to forbear.] *Colloq.* Abatement; cessation; as, it rained without *letup*.

le′u (lĕ′ōō), *n.*; *pl.* LEI (lā). Also **ley** (lā). [Romanian, lit., lion.] The monetary unit of Romania containing 100 bani. See MONEY, *Tables*.

leu′cine (lū′sēn; -sĭn), *n.* Also **leu′cin.** [Gr. *leukos* white.] *Biochem.* A white, crystalline, amino acid, $C_6H_{13}NO_2$, formed in the decomposition of protein by pancreatic digestion and otherwise.

leu′cite (-sīt), *n.* [G. *leucit*, fr. Gr. *leukos* white.] *Mineral.* A white or gray mineral found in igneous rocks. It is a potassium aluminum silicate, $KAl(SiO_3)_2$.

leu′co- (lū′kō-), **leuc-.** [Gr. *leukos* white.] A combining form meaning: **1.** *White, colorless*, as in *leuco*cyte. **2.** *Chem.* A *colorless* or *weakly colored* compound obtained by reduction of a dye, or closely related to a colored compound.

leu′co·cyte (lū′kō·sīt), *n.* [*leuco-* + *-cyte*.] *Anat.* A white or colorless blood corpuscle. See CORPUSCLE.

leu′co·cy·the′mi·a, leu′co·cy·thae′mi·a (-sī·thē′mĭ·ȧ), *n.* [NL., fr. *leucocyte* + *-hemia* (see -EMIA).] *Med.* Leukemia.

leu′co·cyt′ic (-sĭt′ĭk), *adj.* Of or pertaining to leucocytes; characterized by an excess of leucocytes.

leu′co·cy·to′sis (-sī·tō′sĭs), *n.* [NL., fr. *leucocyte* + *-osis*.] *Physiol. & Med.* An increase in the number of leucocytes in the blood. — **leu′co·cy·tot′ic** (-tŏt′ĭk), *adj.*

leu′co·der′ma (-dûr′mȧ), *n.* [NL. See LEUCO-; -DERM.] *Med.* Abnormal whiteness of the skin in spots.

leu·co′ma (lū·kō′mȧ), *n.* [NL., fr. Gr. *leukōma*, fr. *leukos* white.] *Med.* A dense, white opacity in the cornea of the eye.

leu·co′ma·ine (-mȧ·ēn; -ĭn), *n.* Also **leu·co′ma·in.** [*leuco-* + *-maine* as in pto*maine*.] *Biochem.* Any basic substance normally produced in the living animal body as a decomposition product of protein matter.

leu′co·me·lan′ic (lū′kō·mē·lăn′ĭk), *adj.* Leucomelanous.

leu′co·mel′a·nous (-mĕl′ȧ·nŭs), *adj.* [*leuco-* + Gr. *melas*, *-anos*, black.] Of a fair complexion with dark hair or dark hair and eyes.

leu′co·plast (lū′kō·plăst), **leu′co·plas′tid** (-plăs′tĭd), *n.* [*leuco-* + *-plast, plastid.*] *Bot.* One of the colorless plastids in the cytoplasm of plants in the interior of tissues where light cannot penetrate, as in tubers or roots. They serve as nuclei for starch grains.

leu′cor·rhe′a, -rhoe′a (lū′kŏ·rē′ȧ), *n.* [NL., fr. *leuco-* + *-rrhea.*] *Med.* A morbid discharge of a whitish viscid mucus from the vagina.

leu·co′sis (lū·kō′sĭs), *n.* [*leuc(o)-* + *-osis.*] **a** = LEUKEMIA. **b** *Veter.* Any of several diseases of poultry marked by disturbed blood formation and by paralysis, tumor formation, leukemia, or visual disturbances. — **leu·cot′ic** (-kŏt′ĭk), *adj.*

leu′co·tome (lū′kō·tōm), *n.* [Gr. *leukos* white + *-tome.*] A narrow rotating blade in a cannula for use in **leu·cot′o·my** (lū·kŏt′ō·mĭ), incision into the frontal lobe of the brain for severing nerve fibers for relief of certain mental disorders.

leud (lūd), *n.; pl.* LEUDS (lūdz), LEUDES (lū′dēz). [ML. *leudes,* of Teut. origin.] *Hist.* A feudal tenant or vassal.

leu·ke′mi·a, leu·kae′mi·a (lū·kē′mĭ·ȧ), *n.* [NL., fr. Gr. *leukos* white + *-emia.*] Derangement of the blood-making organs involving excess formation of leucocytes.

leu′ko-, leuk-. Vars. of LEUCO-, LEUC-.

lev (lĕf), *n.; pl.* LEVA (lĕ′vȧ). [Bulg. *lev* lion.] The gold monetary unit of Bulgaria, containing 100 stotinki. See MONEY, *Tables.*

Le·vant′ (lē·vănt′), *n.* [F. *levant,* lit., rising (of the sun), fr. *se lever* to rise.] **1.** The East; the Orient. *Obs.* except, specif., the countries washed by, or near to, the eastern Mediterranean. **2.** [*not cap.*] Levant morocco.

le·vant′ (lē·vănt′), *v. i.* [Sp. *levantar* to raise, go from one place to another.] *Eng.* To run away from debts; to decamp. — **le·vant′er,** *n.*

Levant dollar *or* **thaler.** See DOLLAR, *n.,* 1 **b.**

Le·vant′er (lē·văn′tẽr), *n.* [*usually not cap.*] A strong easterly wind peculiar to the Mediterranean.

Le·van′tine (lē·văn′tĭn; -tīn; lĕv′ăn·tĭn; -tīn), *adj.* [F. *levantin,* or It. *levantino.*] Of or pertaining to the Levant. — *n.* **1.** A native or inhabitant of the Levant. **2.** [*not cap.*] [F. *levantine.*] A stout twilled silk fabric formerly made in the Levant.

Levant morocco. A variety of morocco leather with large, irregular grain, highly prized for bookbinding.

le·va′tor (lē·vā′tẽr; -tôr), *n.; pl.* LEVATORES (lĕv′ȧ·tō′rēz; 70). [NL., fr. L. *levare* to raise.] **1.** *Anat.* A muscle that serves to raise some part. **2.** *Surg.* A surgical instrument used to raise a depressed part of the skull.

lev′ee (lĕv′ē), *n.* [F. *levée,* fr. *lever* to raise, fr. L. *levare.*] **1.** *U. S.* An embankment to prevent inundation; also, a landing place, pier, or quay. **2.** *Irrigation.* A small continuous dike or ridge of earth for confining the areas of land to be flooded. — *v. t. U. S.* To make levees on.

lev′ee (lĕv′ē; lĕ·vē′; -vā′), *n.* Also **lev′ée.** [F. *levé, lever,* fr. *lever* to raise, *se lever* to rise.] **1. a** A morning reception, esp. one held by a person of distinction. **b** In Great Britain and Ireland, a court assembly held (in the early afternoon) for men only. **c** Any miscellaneous gathering of guests, at any time of day; esp., *U. S.,* one of the president's receptions.

lev′el (lĕv′ĕl; -′l), *n.* [OF. *livel, nivel,* deriv. of L. *libella* level, water level, plumb level, dim. of *libra* pound, measure for liquids, level.] **1.** A device for establishing a horizontal line, the essential part being a glass tube nearly filled with alcohol or ether and enclosing a movable bubble which when centered indicates the tangent to the tube at the point or the line of sight to be truly horizontal. **2.** A measurement of the difference of altitude of two points by means of a level. **3.** Horizontal condition; equilibrium marked by a horizontal surface of even altitude; as, water seeks its own *level.* **4.** A horizontal line or surface taken as an index of altitude, or distance from sea level. **5.** A surface or an area practically horizontal. **6.** A certain position, rank, etc., conceived of as in one of several planes of different elevation; as, to find one's *level.* **7.** A line or surface that cuts perpendicularly all plumb lines that it meets; — strictly the *geoid,* or ***true level.*** **8.** *Mining.* A horizontal passage in a mine, intended for regular working and transportation.

— *adj.* **1.** Having no part higher than another; having, or conforming to, the curvature of the undisturbed liquid parts of the earth's surface. **2.** Parallel with the plane of the horizon; horizontal. **3.** Of the same rank, condition, etc.; specif.: **a** Even or equally advanced with anything else. **b** Even or uniform in quality, tone, style, pitch, stress, etc. **4.** *Colloq.* Well balanced; steady; as, a *level* head. **5.** *Physics.* Perpendicular to all lines of force in a field of force; equipotential.

Syn. **Level, flat, plane, even, smooth** mean having a surface comparable to that of a calm sea. **Level** usually describes a horizontal surface which throughout its extent lies on a line corresponding to that of the horizon; **flat** applies to any surface free or approximately free of prominences or depressions; **plane** applies to any flat surface, real or imaginary, in which a line drawn between any two points lies continuously in that surface; **even** implies a uniformity of all the points, not only of a plane surface but of a line, so that the surface's flatness or levelness or the line's straightness is clearly observable; **smooth** implies a perfect evenness of surface as though rolled, planed, or the like.

— *adv.* In a straight or level line; directly.

— *v. t.;* LEV′ELED (-ĕld; -′ld) or LEV′ELLED; LEV′EL·ING or LEV′EL·LING. **1.** To make level, flat, or even. **2.** To bring to a horizontal position, as a gun; hence, to aim. **3.** To bring to a common level or plane, esp. as to rank, privilege, etc.; also, to bring to a level with. **4.** To bring to a lower level; to overthrow; to lower. **5.** To make even, equal, or uniform, as in color. **6.** *Surv.* To find the heights of different points in (a piece of land), as with a surveyor's level. — *v. i.* **1.** To aim a gun, spear, etc.; hence, to aim or direct one's effort or comment. **2.** To bring persons or things to a level.

level off. **a** To make level, or flat or even; to flatten. **b** *Aviation.* To fly horizontally, near the ground, preparatory to landing.

level crossing. See GRADE CROSSING.

lev′el·er, lev′el·ler (lĕv′ĕl·ẽr; -′l·ẽr), *n.* **1.** One who or that which levels, or brings to a level. **2.** One who would remove social or political inequalities or distinctions.

lev′el·head′ed (lĕv′ĕl·hĕd′ĕd; -ĭd; lĕv′′l-; 2; 30), *adj.* Having sound judgment. — **lev′el·head′ed·ness,** *n.*

lev′el·ing rod *or* **staff.** *Surv.* A graduated rod used in measuring the vertical distance between given points and the line of sight of a leveling instrument.

lev′el·ly (lĕv′ĕl·lĭ; -′l·lĭ), *adv.* In a level manner.

lev′el·ness, *n.* State of being level.

le′ver (lē′vẽr; lĕv′ẽr), *n.* [OF. *leveor,* prop., a lifter, fr. *lever* to raise, fr. L. *levare.*] **1.** A bar used to pry or dislodge something firmly fixed; a pry. **2.** A piece to open or close the barrel of a breech-loading firearm. See GUNLOCK, *Illust.* **3.** *Mech.* A rigid piece capable of turning about one point, or axis (the fulcrum), and in which are two or more other points where forces are applied, used for transmitting and modifying force and motion; specif., a bar used to exert a pressure, or sustain a weight, at one point of its length, by the application of a force at a second, and turning at a third on a fixed point called a *fulcrum.* See SIMPLE MACHINE, *Illust.* — *v. t.* To pry up, raise, etc., as with a lever; also, to use as a lever.

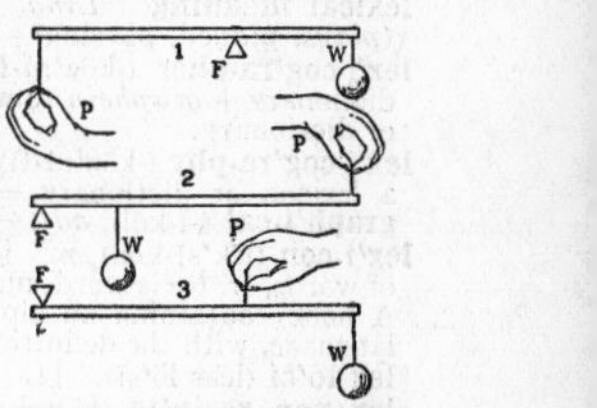

The Three Classes of Levers. *F* Fulcrum; *P* Power; *W* Weight.

le′ver·age (-ĭj), *n.* The action of a lever, or the mechanical advantage gained by the lever.

lev′er·et (lĕv′ẽr·ĕt; -ĭt), *n.* [Dim. fr. OF. *levre* hare, fr. L. *lepus, leporis.*] A hare in its first year.

Le′vi (lē′vī), *n.* [Heb. *Lēwī,* lit., joining.] *Bib.* See JACOB, LEVITE.

lev′i·a·ble (lĕv′ĭ·ȧ·b′l), *adj.* That may be levied or levied on.

le·vi′a·than (lē·vī′ȧ·thăn), *n.* [LL., fr. Heb. *liwyāthān.*] **1.** *Bib.* An aquatic monster interpreted variously as a crocodile (*Job* xli. 1–8, *Ps.* lxxiv. 14), a whale (*Ps.* civ. 26), as a dragon (*Job* iii. 8 R.V., *Is.* xxvii. 1). **2.** Something huge and formidable of its kind.

lev′i·er (lĕv′ĭ·ẽr), *n.* One who levies.

lev′i·gate (lĕv′ĭ·gāt), *v. t.* [L. *lēvigatus,* past part. of *lēvigare* to make smooth, fr. *lēvis* smooth.] To make smooth; as: **a** To free from grit; to reduce to powder or paste. **b** To mix thoroughly, as semiliquids. **c** To polish. — *adj.* Smooth, as if polished. — **lev′i·ga′tion** (-gā′shŭn), *n.*

lev′in (lĕv′ĭn), *n.* [ME. *levene.*] *Archaic.* Lightning.

lev′i·rate (lĕv′ĭ·rāt; lē′vĭ-), *n.* [L. *levir* a husband's brother.] A Jewish custom obliging the brother of a man who died leaving a widow but no children to marry the widow (*Deut.* xxv. 5–10). — **lev′i·rat′i·cal** (-răt′ĭ·kăl), *adj.*

Le′vi's (lē′vīz), *n.* A trade-mark applied to bibless overalls of heavy blue denim reinforced at strain points with copper rivets; — the possessive form of the first name of their manufacturer, Levi Strauss.

lev′i·tate (lĕv′ĭ·tāt), *v. i.* [See LEVITY.] To rise, or tend to rise, by or as if by lightness or buoyancy.

lev′i·ta′tion (-tā′shŭn), *n.* **1.** Act or process of levitating; also, buoyancy. **2.** The phenomenon or illusion of moving heavy objects, as the human body, in the air without support; also, the subjective illusion of rising into or moving through the air without support, as in dreams.

Le′vite (lē′vīt), *n.* *Bib. Hist.* One of the tribe or family of Levi, esp. one designated to aid the priests in the care of the tabernacle, sacred vessels, and temple.

Le·vit′i·cal (lē·vĭt′ĭ·kăl), *adj.* Of or pert. to a Levite or Levites or the law contained in the book of Leviticus.

Le·vit′i·cus (-kŭs), *n.* [LL.] The third book of the Pentateuch, containing the ceremonial laws for the priests and Levites. See BIBLE.

lev′i·ty (lĕv′ĭ·tĭ), *n.; pl.* -TIES (-tĭz). [L. *levitas,* fr. *levis* light in weight.] **1.** Lightness; buoyancy. **2.** Lack of gravity in deportment or character; trifling gaiety; unseemly frivolity or jocularity. **3.** Lack of constancy; fickleness. — **Syn.** See LIGHTNESS.

le′vo-, lae′vo- (lē′vō-). [L. *laevus* left.] A combining form meaning: **a** *Of, pertaining to,* or *toward the left.* **b** *Chem. Levorotatory,* as in **le′vo·tar·tar′ic** (acid). Abbr. *l-* (no period).

le′vo, lae′vo (lē′vō), *adj.* *Chem.* = LEVO- **b.** Abbr. *l* (no period).

le′vo·gy′rate, lae′vo·gy′rate (lē′vō·jī′rāt), **le′vo·gy′rous, lae′vo·gy′rous** (-jī′rŭs), *adj.* Levorotatory.

le′vo·ro·ta′tion, lae′vo·ro·ta′tion (-rō·tā′shŭn), *n.* [*levo-* + *rotation.*] *Physics & Chem.* Left-handed or counterclockwise rotation, esp. of the plane of polarization of light.

le′vo·ro′ta·to′ry, lae′vo·ro′ta·to′ry (-rō′tȧ·tō′rĭ *or, esp. Brit.,* -tẽr·ĭ), *adj.* Turning toward the left, or counterclockwise; esp., turning the plane of polarized light to the left; as, *levorotatory* crystals; — opp. to *dextrorotatory.*

lev′u·lin (lĕv′ū·lĭn), *n.* *Chem.* A substance resembling dextrin and yielding levulose on hydrolysis.

lev′u·lose (-lōs), *n.* [L. *laevus* left + *-ule* + *-ose.*] *Chem.* A levorotatory sugar, $C_6H_{12}O_6$, crystallizable with difficulty, occurring in honey and in most sweet fruits, and obtained, with dextrose, by inversion of sucrose; D-fructose; — called also *fruit sugar.* See FRUCTOSE.

lev′y (lĕv′ĭ), *n.; pl.* LEVIES (-ĭz). [F. *levée,* fr. *lever* to raise. See LEVER.] **1.** A collecting or exacting by authority or superior force. **2.** A mustering or calling into service of troops. **3.** That which is levied, as an army.

— *v. t.;* LEV′IED (-ĭd); LEV′Y·ING. **1.** To raise or collect, as by assessment or execution. **2.** To raise or collect (as troops) for service. **3.** To make or carry on (war); to wage. **4.** *Law.* In the phrase ***to levy a fine,*** to establish a fine, that is, a compromise, esp. of a suit for lands. — *v. i.* To seize property; to make a levy.

lev′y en masse (äN mȧs′). [See LEVY, *n.;* EN MASSE.] *Internat. Law.* The spontaneous taking of arms for self-defense by the people of a territory threatened by the approach of an enemy but not yet occupied, when the people lack time to organize under recognized rules of warfare.

lewd (lūd), *adj.* [ME. *lewed, lewd,* lay, ignorant, vile, fr. AS. *lǣwede* laical.] **1.** *Obs.* Wicked; worthless; base. **2.** Lustful; lascivious; unchaste. — **lewd′ly,** *adv.* — **lewd′ness,** *n.*

lew′is (lū′ĭs; lōō′-), *n.* Also **lew′is·son** (-ĭ·sŭn). An iron dovetailed tenon, made in sections, which can be fitted into a dovetail mortise, as to hoist stones.

lew′is·ite (lū′ĭs·īt; lōō′-), *n.* [After W. Lee *Lewis* (1878–1943), Am. chemist.] *Mil.* A colorless vesicant, produced by a reaction of acetylene with arsenic trichloride, developed as a poison gas for war use.

Lew′is ma·chine′ gun (lū′ĭs; lōō′-). A light gas-operated and air-cooled automatic rifle or machine gun, fed from circular magazines, invented by Col. I. N. Lewis, U. S. Army.

‖**lex** (lĕks), *n.; pl.* LEGES (lē′jēz). [L.] A law; the law.

lex'i·cal (lĕk'sĭ·kăl), *adj.* **1.** Of, pertaining to, or connected with words, or the vocabulary of a language, as distinguished from its grammar or construction. **2.** Of or pertaining to a lexicon or lexicography.

lexical meaning. *Ling.* The meaning of the base in a paradigm (*plays, played, playing*). Cf. GRAMMATICAL MEANING.

lex'i·cog'ra·pher (-kŏg'rȧ·fẽr), *n.* [Gr. *lexikographos*, fr. *lexikon* dictionary + *graphein* to write.] An author or compiler of a lexicon or dictionary.

lex'i·cog'ra·phy (-kŏg'rȧ·fĭ), *n.* Art, process, or occupation of making a lexicon or dictionary. — **lex'i·co·graph'ic** (-kō·grăf'ĭk), **lex'i·co·graph'i·cal** (-ĭ·kăl), *adj.* — **lex'i·co·graph'i·cal·ly,** *adv.*

lex'i·con (lĕk'sĭ·kŏn), *n.* [Gr. *lexikon* (sc. *biblion*), neut. of *lexikos* of words, fr. *lexis* word, phrase, diction; akin to Gr. *legein* to speak.] A book containing an alphabetical arrangement of the words in a language, with the definition of each; a dictionary.

‖**lex lo'ci** (lĕks lō'sī). [L.] The law of the place; — in legal phrases.

‖**lex non scrip'ta** (nŏn skrĭp'tȧ). [L.] Unwritten law; esp., the common law.

‖**lex scrip'ta.** [L.] Written law; the statute law.

‖**lex ta'li·o'nis** (tăl'ĭ·ō'nĭs). [L.] Law of retaliation.

ley (lā). Var. of LEU.

‖**ley de fu'ga** (lâ'ĕ thā fōō'gä). [Sp., lit., law of flight.] In Spanish America, the right of police to kill a prisoner trying to escape, often used as a pretext for killing a prisoner purposely set free.

Ley'den jar (lī'dĕn; -d'n). [From *Leiden*, Holland.] *Elec.* An electrical condenser consisting of a glass jar coated with tin foil, within and without, and surmounted by a brass knob which communicates with the inner coating.

leze maj'es·ty. Var. of LESE MAJESTY.

li (lē), *n. sing. & pl.* [Chin. (Pek.) *li*[3].] A Chinese unit of measure equal to about one third of a mile.

li'a·bil'i·ty (lī'ȧ·bĭl'ĭ·tĭ), *n.; pl.* -TIES (-tĭz). **1.** State or quality of being liable. **2.** That for which one is liable; specif., in the *pl.*, one's pecuniary obligations, or debts, collectively; — opposed to *assets.* **3.** *Accounting.* A debt; an amount which is owed, whether payable in money, other property, or services.

li'a·ble (lī'ȧ·b'l), *adj.* [F. *lier* to bind, fr. L. *ligare.*] **1.** Bound or obliged by law or submission to other forces; answerable; as, he is *liable* for the debt; men *liable* for military service. **2.** Exposed to the danger or risk of something undesired; as, *liable* to err; a disease to which man is *liable.*

Syn. (1) See RESPONSIBLE.
(2) **Liable, open, exposed, subject, prone, susceptible, sensitive, incident** mean such that something may be incurred. **Liable** implies that the possibility of incurrence depends on a person's or thing's position, state, nature, or the like; **open,** on its lack of barriers or on its ease of access; **exposed,** on its lack of protection or powers of resistance; **subject,** on its openness for any reason to something which must be suffered, borne, or undergone; **prone,** on its natural tendency or propensity; **susceptible,** on conditions existing in its nature or constitution that make it open or prone (*to*) or admit (*of*); **sensitive,** on physical or emotional conditions that make for susceptibility; **incident,** differing from the others, applies not to the person or thing which is liable or open but to the thing to which he or it is liable, open, etc. (as, life is *subject* to change; change is *incident* to life).

li'ai·son' (lē'ā·zôn'; lē'ȧ·zŏn; lē·ā'z'n, -zŏn), *n.* [F., fr. *lier* to bind. See LIABLE.] **1.** A bond or connecting link; a linking up; also, coordination of activities; as, close *liaison* between departments. **2.** An intimacy, esp. illicit, between a man and a woman. **3.** *Cookery.* A thickening of flour and butter, dextrin and butter, or egg yolk, for sauces, soups, etc. **4.** *Mil.* Intercommunication between a commander and subordinates or between units acting as neighbors. **5.** *Phonet.* In spoken French, the carrying over of the final consonant (otherwise silent) of one word to the beginning of the next word, when beginning with a vowel or an *h* not aspirated.

li·a'na (lē·ä'nȧ; lĭ·ăn'ȧ), **li·ane'** (lĭ·än'), *n.* [F. dial. *liane.*] Any climbing plant that roots in the ground. Woody lianas are characteristic of tropical rain forests.

liang (lyăng), *n. sing. & pl.* [Chin. (Pek.) *liang*[3].] A Chinese unit of weight, 1/16 of a catty. Since 1929, the official liang has been equivalent to the hectogram.

li'ar (lī'ẽr), *n.* A person who knowingly utters falsehood.

Li'as (lī'ăs), *n.* [OF. *liois* (F. *liais*) sort of limestone.] *Geol.* The oldest division of the European Jurassic system, being a series of clayey limestone rich in fossils.

li·ba'tion (lī·bā'shŭn), *n.* [L. *libatio*, fr. *libare* to pour out as an offering.] **1.** A pouring of a liquid, as wine, either on the ground or on a victim in sacrifice, in honor of a deity; also, the liquid poured. **2.** *Humorous.* A potation.

‖**li·bec'cio** (lē·bĕt'chō), *n.* Incorrectly **libecchio.** [It. *libeccio*, fr. Gr. *lips, libos.*] The southwest wind.

li'bel (lī'bĕl; -b'l), *n.* [OF., fr. L. *libellus*, dim. of *liber* book, inner bark of a tree (on which was written).] **1.** *Obs. exc. Hist.* A handbill, circular, or the like, defaming a person. **2.** Loosely, any defamatory statement, oral or in writing; as, this account of New York is a *libel.* **3.** *Law.* Any statement or representation, published without just cause or excuse, or by pictures, effigies, or other signs, tending to expose another to public hatred, contempt, or ridicule; also, the act, tort, or crime of publishing this. Cf. SLANDER. **4.** *Law.* In Civil-law practice and in that of admiralty and ecclesiastical courts, the plaintiff's written statement of his cause of action, and of the relief he seeks. — *v. t.*; LI'BELED (-bĕld; -b'ld) or LI'BELLED; LI'BEL·ING or LI'BEL·LING. **1.** To make or publish a libel against. **2.** *Law.* To proceed against by filing a libel, as against a ship or goods.

li'bel·ant, li'bel·lant (lī'bĕl·ănt; lī'b'l-), *n.* One who institutes a suit by a libel. See LIBEL, *n.*, 4.

li'bel·ee', li'bel·lee' (lī'bĕl·ē'), *n.* One against whom a libel is filed.

li'bel·er, li'bel·ler (lī'bĕl·ẽr; lī'b'l-), *n.* One who libels.

li'bel·ous, li'bel·lous (lī'bĕl·ŭs), *adj.* Involving a libel; defamatory. — **li'bel·ous·ly, li'bel·lous·ly,** *adv.*

lib'er·al (lĭb'ẽr·ăl), *adj.* [OF., fr. L. *liberalis*, fr. *liber* free.] **1.** Befitting a man of free birth; not restricted; as, a *liberal* manner or education. **2.** Bestowing in a large and noble way; generous; bounteous; openhanded. **3.** Bestowed in a large way; hence, abundant; bountiful; ample. **4.** *Archaic.* Free from restraint; unchecked; licentious; as, a *liberal* villain. **5.** Not confined or restricted to the literal sense; free; as, a *liberal* translation. **6.** Not narrow or contracted in mind; broad-minded. **7.** Not bound by orthodox tenets or established forms in political or religious philosophy; independent in opinion; not conservative; often, specif., having tendency toward democratic or republican, as distinguished from monarchical or aristocratic, forms; hence [*cap.*], designating one of the political parties, as in England. Cf. CONSERVATIVE. — *n.* One who is liberal in thought or principles; specif. [*cap.*], a member of the Liberal party. — **lib'er·al·ly,** *adv.*

Syn. Liberal, generous, bountiful, munificent mean giving freely or unstintedly. **Liberal** suggests openhandedness and largeness in the thing given; **generous,** warmhearted readiness to give, more than the size or importance of the gift; **bountiful,** unremitting liberality in giving or providing; **munificent,** splendid or princely liberality.

liberal arts. [Trans. of L. *artes liberales* the higher arts, which, among the Romans, only freemen (*liberi*) were permitted to pursue.] The languages, sciences, philosophy, history, etc., which compose the curriculum of academic or collegiate education, as distinguished from technical or professional education. The abbreviated term *arts* is also used; as, bachelor of *arts.*

lib'er·al·ism (lĭb'ẽr·ăl·ĭz'm), *n.* Liberal principles and theories; specif. [*often cap.*]: **a** The principles of the Liberal party. **b** A movement in contemporary Protestantism emphasizing intellectual liberty and the spiritual and ethical content of Christianity. — **lib'er·al·ist** (-ĭst), *n. & adj.* — **lib'er·al·is'tic** (-ĭs'tĭk), *adj.*

lib'er·al'i·ty (lĭb'ẽr·ăl'ĭ·tĭ), *n.; pl.* -TIES (-tĭz). **1.** Quality of being liberal in giving; generosity. **2.** A gift. **3.** Quality or state of being liberal in mind; broad-mindedness.

lib'er·al·ize (lĭb'ẽr·ăl·īz), *v. t. & i.* To make, or become, liberal. — **lib'er·al·i·za'tion** (-ĭ·zā'shŭn; -ī·zā'-), *n.* — **lib'er·al·iz'er** (-īz'ẽr), *n.*

lib'er·ate (lĭb'ẽr·āt), *v. t.* [L. *liberatus*, past part. of *liberare* to free, fr. *liber* free.] **1.** To release from restraint or bondage; to free. **2.** To disengage; free from combination, as gases. — **Syn.** See FREE. — **lib'er·a'tion** (-ā'shŭn), *n.* — **lib'er·a'tor** (-ā'tẽr), *n.*

lib'er·tar'i·an (lĭb'ẽr·târ'ĭ·ăn; 6), *n.* One who holds to the doctrine of free will; also, one who upholds the principles of liberty, esp. liberty of thought and action. — **lib'er·tar'i·an,** *adj.* — **lib'er·tar'i·an·ism** (-ĭz'm), *n.*

li·ber'ti·cide (lĭ·bûr'tĭ·sīd), *n.* [L. *libertas* liberty + *-cide.*] The destruction, or a destroyer, of liberty. — **li·ber'ti·cid'al** (-sīd'ăl; 2), **li·ber'ti·cide,** *adj.*

lib'er·tin·age (lĭb'ẽr·tĭn·ĭj), *n.* Libertinism in conduct.

lib'er·tine (lĭb'ẽr·tēn; -tĭn), *n.* [L. *libertinus* freedman, fr. *libertus* one made free, fr. *liber* free.] **1.** *Rom. Antiq.* A manumitted slave. **2.** A freethinker; — used derogatorily. **3.** One free from self-restraint; specif., a rake. — *adj.* **1.** Freethinking in religion; — used derogatorily. **2.** *Now Rare.* Uncontrolled. **3.** Dissolute; licentious; profligate; loose in morals.

lib'er·tin·ism (-tĭn·ĭz'm), *n.* Licentious conduct; debauchery; lewdness.

lib'er·ty (lĭb'ẽr·tĭ), *n.; pl.* -TIES (-tĭz). [OF. *liberté*, fr. L. *libertas*, fr. *liber* free.] **1.** Exemption from slavery, bondage, imprisonment, or control of another. **2.** Freedom from external restraint or compulsion; also, with *of* and *to*, leave or permission; as, the *liberty* of the air. **3.** Privilege; franchise; right or immunity by grant. **4.** The sum of the rights and immunities of all the citizens of an organized civil community concurrent with the guaranteed protection against interference with such rights and privileges (***civil liberty***), or the state or condition of those who have the right effectually to share in framing and conducting their government (***political liberty***), or of those who are free from external restraint in exercising rights without the province of a government to control (***individual liberty***). Individual liberty now generally involves freedom of the person in going and coming (***personal liberty***), equality before the courts, security of private property, freedom of opinion and its expression, and freedom of conscience. **5.** A privilege or license in violation of propriety; a familiarity; as, to take a *liberty.* **6.** A certain amount of freedom; also, the limits within which such freedom is exercised; as, the *liberty* of the dungeon. **7.** *U. S. Navy.* Permission for a sailor to go ashore off duty for a specified number of hours, longer absences being granted as *leave.* **8.** *Philos.* The power of choice; freedom from necessity. — **Syn.** See FREEDOM. — ***at liberty.*** **a** Unconfined. **b** At leisure; unoccupied. **c** Free or having the right (to do something).

liberty cap. A limp, close-fitting cap often used as a symbol of liberty.

li·bid'i·nous (lĭ·bĭd'ĭ·nŭs), *adj.* [F. or L.; F. *libidineux*, fr. L. *libidinosus*, fr. *libido, libidinis*, pleasure, desire, lust, fr. *libet, lubet*, it pleases.] Having lustful desires; lustful; lascivious. — **li·bid'i·nous·ly,** *adv.* — **li·bid'i·nous·ness,** *n.*

li·bi'do (lĭ·bī'dō; -bē'dō), *n.* [L.] **1.** Desire; esp., sexual desire. **2.** *Psychoanalysis.* Energy, motive force, desire, or striving, either as derived from the sex instinct or from the primal urge to live. — **li·bid'i·nal** (-bĭd'ĭ·năl; -n'l), *adj.*

li'bra (lī'brȧ), *n.; pl.* -BRAE (-brē). [L.] **1.** A weight of ancient Rome, equal to 0.718 lb. av. **2.** [Sp.] A former gold coin of Peru equal in value to 10 sols.

Li'bra (lī'brȧ), *n.; gen.* LIBRAE (-brē). [L., a balance.] **a** A southern zodiacal constellation between Virgo and Scorpio, represented as a pair of scales. **b** The seventh sign (♎) of the zodiac, which the sun enters at the autumnal equinox in September. See ZODIAC.

li·brar'i·an (lī·brâr'ĭ·ăn; 6), *n.* One who has the care or charge of a library.

li'brar'y (lī'brẽr'ĭ; lī'brĭ; -b[r]ẽr·ĭ), *n.; pl.* -IES (-ĭz). [OF. *librairie* library (F., bookseller's shop), fr. *libraire* copyist (F., bookseller), fr. L. *librarius*, fr. *liber* book.] **1.** An apartment or a building devoted to a collection of books, manuscripts, etc., kept for use but not for sale; also, an institution for the custody, circulation, or administration of such a collection. **2.** A collection of books, manuscripts, etc., kept for study or reading. **3.** A commercial establishment for the renting of books. **4.** A series of books of some similarity issued by the same publisher.

li'brate (lī'brāt), *v. i.* [L. *libratus*, past part. of *librare* to balance, fr. *libra* balance.] To vibrate as a balance does before coming to rest; hence, to be poised.

li·bra'tion (lī·brā'shŭn), *n.* **1.** Act or state of librating, or of being balanced or poised. **2.** *Astron.* A real or apparent oscillatory motion, like that of a balance.

li'bra·to'ry (lī'brȧ·tō'rĭ *or, esp. Brit.*, -tẽr·ĭ), *adj.* Balancing; moving like a balance as it tends to an equipoise.

li·bret'tist (lĭ·brĕt'ĭst), *n.* The writer of a libretto, as of an opera.

li·bret'to (lĭ·brĕt'ō), *n.; pl.* -TOS (-ōz), -TI (-tē). [It., dim. of *libro*

book.] *Music.* **a** The text, or words, of an opera or any extended choral composition. **b** The book containing such a text.
li′bri·form (lī′brĭ·fôrm), *adj.* [L. *liber* bast + *-form.*] *Bot.* Having the form of, or resembling, bast or fiber.
lice (līs), *n., pl.* of LOUSE.
li′cense, li′cence (lī′sĕns; -s′ns), *n.* [OF. *licence,* fr. L. *licentia,* fr. *licere* to be permitted.] **1.** Authority or liberty given to do or forbear any act; esp., a formal permission from the authorities to carry on a certain business otherwise illegal; also, the document embodying such permission. **2.** Excess of liberty; freedom abused; also, licentiousness. **3.** That deviation from strict fact, form, or rule by an artist or writer for the effect gained; as, poetic *license.* **4.** Any permitted unusual freedom of action. — **Syn.** See FREEDOM.
li′cense (lī′sĕns; -s′ns), *v. t.* Also **li′cence.** To permit or authorize, esp. by formal license; to give license to. — **li′cens·er, li′cenc·er** (-sĕn-sẽr; -s′n-), *n.*, in *Law,* **li′cen·sor** (-sẽr).
li′cen·see′, li′cen·cee′ (lī′sĕn·sē′; lī′s′n-ē′), *n.* *Law.* The person to whom a license is given.
li·cen′ti·ate (lī·sĕn′shĭ·āt), *n.* **1.** One who has a license to practice a profession, esp. one granted by a university; as, a *licentiate* in medicine. **2.** In Europe, a university degree intermediate between that of bachelor and that of doctor.
li·cen′tious (lī·sĕn′shŭs), *adj.* [F. *licencieux,* fr. L. *licentiosus.*] **1.** Characterized by license; lawless; now esp., dissolute; libertine; lewd. **2.** Unrestrained by strict rules of correctness, as verse. — **li·cen′tious·ly,** *adv.* — **li·cen′tious·ness,** *n.*
lich (lĭch), *n.* [AS. *līc* body.] *Scot. & Dial. Eng.* Corpse.
li′chee (lē′chē). Var. of LITCHI.
li′chen (lī′kĕn; -kĭn), *n.* [L., fr. Gr. *leichēn.*] Any of a group of thallophytic plants (Lichenes) growing as epiphytes on rocks, bark, etc. A lichen is a composite organism, consisting of an ascomycetous (rarely basidiomycetous) fungus (**lichen fungus**) living symbiotically with an alga. — *v. t.* To cover with lichens. — **li′chen·ose** (-ōs), **li′chen·ous** (-ŭs), *adj.*
li′chen·in (lī′kĕn·ĭn), *n.* *Chem.* A gelatinous polysaccharide, $(C_6H_{10}O_5)_x$, found in certain mosses, etc.
li′chen·ol′o·gy (-ŏl′ō·jĭ), *n.* The study of lichens.
lich gate (lĭch). [See LICH, *n.*] An opening or gate to a churchyard where a bier is placed to await the arrival of the clergyman, and which commonly is roofed.
licht (*Scot.* lĭkt), **licht′ly.** Scot. vars. of LIGHT, etc.
lic′it (lĭs′ĭt), *adj.* [F. *licite,* fr. L. *licitus* permitted, lawful, fr. *licere.*] In accordance with the law. — **Syn.** See LAWFUL. — **lic′it·ly,** *adv.*
lick (lĭk), *v. t.* [AS. *liccian.*] **1.** To draw or pass the tongue over; as, a dog *licks* his master's hand. **2.** To pass, or play, over or about, like a tongue; as, flames *licked* the woodwork. **3.** *Colloq.* To strike with repeated blows for punishment; to flog; also, to conquer, as in a fight. — **Syn.** See CONQUER. — ***lick the dust.*** **a** To be slain; to fall in battle. **b** To show abject servility. — *n.* **1.** A stroke of the tongue in licking. **2.** A small quantity such as might be taken upon the tongue. **3.** *Colloq.* A quick and careless application of anything, as by a stroke of the tongue; hence, a stroke (of work); also, a burst of energy; speed. **4.** A place where salt is found on the surface of the earth (***salt lick***), to which wild animals resort to lick it up. **5.** *Swing Music Cant.* A musical figure; often specif., an interpolated figure or phrase.
lick′er·ish, liq′uor·ish (lĭk′ẽr·ĭsh), *adj.* [From earlier *lickerous,* fr. ONF. form of OF. *lecheros.* See LECHEROUS.] **1.** Eager or craving; esp., eager to taste or enjoy. **2.** *Obs.* Tempting the appetite; dainty. **3.** Lecherous; lustful. — **lick′er·ish·ness,** *n.*
lick′ing (lĭk′ĭng), *n.* Act of one who licks; esp., *Colloq.*, a flogging or thrashing.
lick′spit′ (lĭk′spĭt′), **lick′spit′tle** (-spĭt′′l), *n.* An abject parasite or toady.
lic′o·rice, liq′uo·rice (lĭk′ō·rĭs; -rĭsh), *n.* [ME. *licoris,* through OF., fr. LL. *liquiritia,* corrupted fr. *glycyrrhiza,* fr. Gr. *glykyrrhiza,* fr. *glykys* sweet + *rhiza* root.] **1.** A European plant (*Glycyrrhiza glabra*) of the pea family, with pinnate leaves and spikes of blue flowers. **2.** Its dried root or an extract from it, used in medicine, brewing, flavoring tobacco, confectionery, etc.
lic′tor (lĭk′tẽr; -tôr), *n.* [L.] *Rom. Antiq.* An officer bearing the fasces as insignia, whose duty was to clear the way for the chief magistrates in public.
lid (lĭd), *n.* [AS. *hlid.*] **1.** That which covers the opening of a vessel, box, etc.; a movable cover; as, a stove *lid.* **2.** An eyelid. **3.** *Slang.* A hat. **4.** *Colloq.* A curb or check; as, the *lid* is on gambling. **5.** *Bot.* **a** In mosses, the operculum. **b** The cap of a pyxis. — **lid′ded** (lĭd′ĕd; -ĭd), *adj.*
lid′less, *adj.* Having no lid; not covered with the lids, as the eyes; hence, sleepless; watchful.
lie (lī), *n.* [AS. *lyge.*] **1.** A falsehood uttered or acted to deceive. **2.** Anything which deceives; as, his cordiality was a *lie.* **3.** A charge of lying; as, to take the *lie* from none. — *v. i.;* LIED (līd); LY′ING (lī′ĭng). [AS. *lēogan.*] To utter falsehood with intent to deceive; to tell or act a lie. — *v. t.* To affect by lying; as, he *lied* himself out of trouble.
Syn. Lie, prevaricate, equivocate, palter, fib mean to tell an untruth. **Lie** is the straightforward word, imputing dishonesty; **prevaricate** implies evasion of the truth, as by quibbling, dodging, etc.; **equivocate,** the use of words having more than one sense in the hope that a sense not intended will be accepted; **palter,** a playing fast and loose not only in statements but in dealings; **fib,** a telling of an untruth that is trivial in matter or in significance.
lie, *v. i.;* LAY (lā); LAIN (lān); LY′ING (lī′ĭng). [AS. *licgan.*] **1.** To have or assume a position as of rest extended on the ground or any support; to be prostrate; to recline. **2.** To be in a position implying helplessness. **3.** Of inanimate things, to be or remain in a flat or horizontal position upon any broad support. **4.** To have direction; to extend; as, the road *lies* before you. **5.** To occupy a certain relative place or position; as, Ireland *lies* west of England; to have its place in relation to other things; as, the difficulty *lies* here. **6.** To sojourn; lodge; specif., to be in camp or quarters or temporarily stationed. **7.** To be or exist; to consist; — with *in;* as, his greatness *lay* in his character. **8.** *Law.* To be sustainable or admissible.
lie by. To rest; to intermit labor, activity, etc. — ***lie in.*** To be in childbed. — ***lie low.*** **a** To lie prostrate. **b** *Colloq.* To remain in hiding. **c** *Slang.* To hide one's intentions. — ***lie to.*** *Naut.* To lie as nearly stationary as feasible with head to windward.
— *n.* **1.** The lay, as of land; slope. **2.** The haunt of an animal; covert. **3.** *Golf.* Position of a ball on the ground.
lied (lēt; *Angl.* lēd), *n.; pl.* LIEDER (lē′dẽr). [G.] *Music.* A German lyric or lay; a German song.
Lie′der·kranz′ (lē′dẽr·kränts′), *n.* A trade-mark applied to a cheese with the texture of Camembert but with a strong flavor and odor.
lief (lēf), *adj.* [AS. *lēof.*] *Archaic.* Dear; beloved; also, willing; glad. — *adv.* Gladly; willingly; freely; — now only in *had as lief, would as lief, had* or *would liefer,* etc.
liege (lēj), *adj.* [OF. *liege, lige,* liege, free, fr. LL. *laeticus,* fr. *letus, litus,* freedman.] **1.** *Feudalism.* Entitled or pertaining to, or bound to give, service and allegiance. **2.** Bound to loyalty or fidelity; hence, loyal; faithful. — *n.* **1.** A liege lord. **2.** A liege subject.
liege man, *or* **liege′man** (lēj′măn), *n.* A vassal; hence, a devoted adherent and follower.
li′en (lē′ĕn; lēn), *n.* [F., band, bond, tie, fr. L. *ligamen,* fr. *ligare* to bind.] *Law.* A charge upon real or personal property for the satisfaction of some debt or duty; a right in one to control or to enforce a charge against the property of another until some claim of the former is paid or satisfied.
li′en·ter′y (lī′ĕn·tẽr′ĭ; -tẽr·ĭ), *n.* [Through F. & ML., fr. Gr. *leienteria,* fr. *leios* smooth + *enteron* an intestine.] *Med.* Diarrhea in which the food is discharged imperfectly digested. — **li′en·ter′ic** (-tĕr′ĭk), *adj.*
li·erne′ (lĭ·ûrn′), *n.* [F.] *Arch.* In Gothic vaulting, any rib which does not spring from the impost and is not a ridge rib, but passes from one boss of the main ribs to another.
lieu (lū), *n.* [F., fr. L. *locus* place.] Place; stead; — chiefly in the phrase ***in lieu of,*** that is, instead of.
lieu·ten′an·cy (lū·tĕn′ăn·sĭ; *see* LIEUTENANT), *n.* Office, rank, or commission of a lieutenant.
lieu·ten′ant (lū·tĕn′ănt; *in Brit. use generally* lĕf·tĕn′ănt, lĭf-, *but sometimes* lōō- *in the navy*), *n.* [F., fr. *lieu* place + *tenant* holding, pres. part. of *tenir* to hold, fr. L. *tenere.*] **1.** An officer who supplies the place of a superior in his absence. **2.** Abbr. *Lieut.* or *Lt.* **a** *Mil.* A commissioned officer of a grade below a captain. There are two grades in the Army, Air Force, and Marine Corps, called ***first*** and ***second lieutenant,*** the former being higher in rank. **b** *Nav.* A commissioned officer ranking above an ensign and below a lieutenant commander, either a **lieutenant junior grade,** ranking next above an ensign, or a **lieutenant,** ranking above a lieutenant junior grade and next below a lieutenant commander.
lieutenant colonel. *Mil.* A commissioned officer who ranks above a major and below a colonel.
lieutenant commander. *Nav.* A commissioned officer ranking above a lieutenant and below a commander.
lieutenant general. A commissioned army officer next in rank below a general and next above a major general.
lieutenant governor. A deputy governor; specif.: **a** *U. S.* An officer of a state, next in rank to the governor. **b** *British.* An acting governor of a district or province under a governor general.
lieve (lēv), *adj. & adv.;* LIEV′ER (lēv′ẽr); LIEV′EST. Lief; — formerly standard literary written form but now used in writing chiefly to represent dialect and archaic usage.
life (līf), *n.; pl.* LIVES (līvz). [AS. *līf.*] **1.** The quality or character distinguishing an animal or a plant from inorganic or from dead organic bodies, which is especially manifested by metabolism, growth, reproduction, and internal powers of adaptation to environment. **2.** The vital force, whether regarded as physical or spiritual, the presence of which distinguishes organic from inorganic matter. **3.** The series of experiences, of body and mind, which make up the history of an animal from birth to death. **4.** Existence, esp. conscious existence, conceived as a quality of the soul or as the soul's nature and being. **5.** The state of that which is alive, or the fact of being a living being; specif.: **a** Exercise of vital activities; animate existence; as, to bring to *life.* **b** A vital or living being; esp., a person. **c** Living beings collectively or in the aggregate; as, marine *life.* **6.** The duration of a life. **7.** An individual human existence; as, each day of one's *life;* also, a biography. **8. a** Way or manner of living; hence, human affairs; also, lives, considered collectively, as a distinct class or type; as, low *life.* **b** The activities of a given sphere or time, and the participants in them; as, night *life.* **9.** That which imparts or excites spirit or vigor; as, he was the *life* of the company. **10.** The living form or semblance; as, a drawing from the *life;* also, animation spirit. **11.** The period of duration of anything; as, the *life* of a state, a machine. **12.** [*cap.*] *Christian Science.* A synonym for God.
life belt. A life preserver in the form of a buoyant belt.
life′blood′ (līf′blŭd′), *n.* **1.** The blood necessary to life. **2.** That which gives strength and energy.
life′boat′ (-bōt′), *n.* **1.** A strong, buoyant boat especially designed for use in saving shipwrecked people. **2.** One of the boats carried by a vessel for use in emergency.

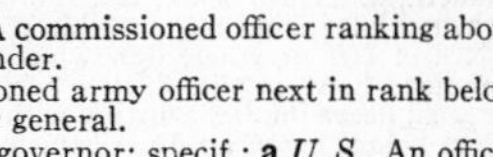
Lifeboat mounted on Wagon.

life buoy. A float, usually a ring of buoyant material, intended to support persons who have fallen into the water.
life cycle. *Biol.* The series of stages in form and mode of life which an organism exhibits between successive recurrences of a certain primary stage.
life′ful (līf′fōōl; -f′l), *adj.* Full of, or giving, vitality.
life′-giv′ing, *adj.* Giving life or spirit; invigorating.
life′guard′ (-gärd′), *n.* *U. S.* An expert swimmer employed at a bathing resort to safeguard bathers and to prevent drownings.
life history. *Biol.* The history of the changes which an organism passes through in its development from the egg, spore, or other primary stage until its natural death; also, one series of these changes, often constituting a life cycle.
life insurance *or* **assurance.** A contract of insurance based upon the life of a person, insuring one person against loss by the death of another or guaranteeing a stipulated sum to the insured if surviving at the end of a specified period.
life′less, *adj.* Destitute of life, or deprived of life; dead; not giving or sustaining life; hence, spiritless; powerless; dull. — **Syn.** See DEAD. — **life′less·ly,** *adv.* — **life′less·ness,** *n.*
life′like′ (līf′līk′), *adj.* Accurately representing or imitating real life. — **life′like′ness,** *n.*

life′line′ (līf′līn′), *n.* **1.** A line shot over a vessel in distress, by which a hawser can be taken aboard. **2.** Any of various anchored lines to be clung to, as one for surf bathers. **3.** That which may be depended on, as long as it remains intact, to save from complete loss or breakdown. **4.** A line attached to a diver's helmet, by which he is lowered and raised. **5.** An indispensable sea, land, or air route for moving vital supplies to and/or from a remote place, often a sea lane or transcontinental railroad joining parts of a far-flung commercial system or a military line of communication.
life′long′ (līf′lŏng′; 74), *adj.* Continuing through life.
life net. A strong net or blanket held by firemen or others to catch persons jumping from burning buildings.
life preserver. **1.** An apparatus for saving one from drowning by buoying up the body while in the water. **2.** A short, usually flexible, bludgeon loaded with lead at one end.
lif′er (līf′ẽr), *n. Slang.* One sentenced to imprisonment, or similar punishment, for life.
life raft. A very buoyant raft for use in lifesaving.
life′sav′er (līf′sāv′ẽr), *n.* **1.** One who saves a life. **2.** A member of the **Lifesaving Service**, a service which has many stations along the coasts equipped with lifesaving apparatus and manned by crews who patrol the beach. — **life′sav′ing** (-sāv′ĭng), *adj. & n.*
life′-sized′, -size′, *adj.* Of natural size; of the size of the original.
life table. = MORTALITY TABLE.
life′time′ (līf′tīm′), *n.* The time that a life continues. — **life′time′**, *adj.*
life′work′ (-wûrk′), *n.* The whole or chief work of one's life.
lift (lĭft), *n.* [AS. *lyft* air.] *Now Dial.* The sky.
lift (lĭft), *v. t.* [ON. *lypta* (Sw. *lyfta*, Dan. *löfte*), prop., to raise into the air.] **1.** To bring up from a lower place to a higher one; to raise; elevate. **2.** To exalt or improve in rank, estimation, spirits, etc.; to raise to a higher plane; as, to *lift* an issue out of petty politics; also, *Bib.*, to puff up. **3.** *Colloq.* To steal; to plagiarize. **4.** *Now Dial.* To collect, as moneys due. **5.** *U.S.* To pay and so take up (a mortgage bond). **6.** *Chiefly Dial.* To remove, esp. from the ground, as treasure. **7.** *Golf.* To pick up (a ball) from the ground. — *v. i.* **1.** To try to raise something. **2.** To rise; to become or appear raised or elevated.
Syn. **Lift, raise, rear, elevate, hoist, heave, boost** mean to move from a lower to a higher place. **Lift** usually implies effort exerted to overcome resistance of weight, but in figurative or poetic use it may be used of anything that rises; **raise** carries a stronger implication of bringing something to a vertical position or, in figurative use, of bringing up something as into being; **rear** is often used in place of *raise*, especially when the bringing up of children is implied; **elevate** is often used in place of *lift* or *raise*, esp. when exalting, enhancing, or the like is implied; **hoist** implies lifting something heavy, esp. by mechanical means; **heave** implies a lifting with strain or effort, as by an impulsion from below; **boost**, an Americanism, implies lifting by means of a push or the like.
— *n.* **1.** Act of lifting, or raising; also, the act of rising as if lifting something; upward movement; hence, elevated carriage, as of the head. **2.** That which is or may be lifted at one time, as a load. **3.** **a** A rise in position or condition; advance; promotion. **b** Assistance, as by lifting; aid towards attainment; help. **c** A ride along one's way in a vehicle. **d** Lifting power; hence, elevating influence or effect; elevation of spirit. **4.** That by means of which something lifts or is lifted; specif.: **a** *Chiefly Eng.* An elevator. **b** *Mining.* A set of pumps. **c** *Shoe Mfg.* One of the layers composing a heel. **5.** Extent to which a thing rises or is raised; degree of elevation; rise. **6.** The distance through which something is lifted. **7.** *Aeronautics.* That component of the total air force which is perpendicular to the relative wind and in the plane of symmetry. It is the force which is opposed to gravity. — **lift′er**, *n.*
lig′a·ment (lĭg′ȧ·mĕnt), *n.; pl.* LIGAMENTS (-mĕnts). [L. *ligamentum*, fr. *ligare* to bind.] **1.** Anything that ties one thing or part to another; a bandage; a bond. **2.** *Anat.* A tough band of tissue serving to connect the articular extremities of bones or to support an organ in place. — **lig′a·men′ta·ry** (-mĕn′tȧ·rĭ), **lig′a·men′tous** (-tŭs), *adj.*
lig′a·men′tum (lĭg′ȧ·mĕn′tŭm), *n.; pl.* LIGAMENTA (-tȧ). [L.] Ligament.
li′gan (lī′găn). Var. of LAGAN.
li′gate (lī′gāt), *v. t.* [L. *ligatus*, past part. of *ligare*.] To tie with a ligature, as a bleeding artery.
li·ga′tion (lī·gā′shŭn), *n.* [L. *ligatio*, fr. *ligare* to bind.] Act or process of binding, or state of being bound; also, that which binds; ligature; bond.
lig′a·ture (lĭg′ȧ·tūr; 118), *n.* [F., fr. LL. *ligatura*, fr. *ligare*, *ligatum*, to bind.] **1.** Act of binding or tying. **2.** Anything that binds; a bandage. **3.** *Music.* A curve or line connecting notes; a tie; a slur; also, a group of notes connected by a slur. **4.** *Print. & Writing.* **a** A character consisting of two or more letters or characters united, as *æ*, *fi*, *fl*; — distinguished from *logotype*. **b** A connecting line or stroke; a tie. **5.** *Surg.* **a** A thread or string for tying the blood vessels. **b** A thread or wire used to remove tumors and the like. — *v. t.* To bind or furnish with a ligature.
li′geance (lī′jăns; lē′-), *n.* [OF.] **1.** *Archaic.* Allegiance. **2.** *Law.* The jurisdiction of a liege lord or of a sovereign.
light (līt), *n.* [AS. *lēoht*.] **1.** The essential condition of vision; the opposite of darkness; hence: **a** An emanation from a light-giving body; as, flames give *light*. **b** The sensation aroused by stimulation of the visual centers in the brain. **2.** The sun's light; daylight; also, day; esp., the dawn of day. **3.** *Poetic.* The power of perception by vision; eyesight. **4.** Mental or spiritual illumination or enlightenment or its source; as, to throw *light* on a subject. **5.** Visible state or condition; hence, state of exposure to public observation; as, to bring, or come, to *light*. **6.** Appearance due to the particular facts presented to view; as, to put a person in a false *light*. **7.** That which furnishes, or is a source of, light, as the sun, a star, candle, lamp, etc. **8.** A particular or local illumination; a radiance; a brightness; as, the picture hung in a good *light*. **9.** *pl.* Natural or acquired means of informing one's mind; as, a good man according to his *lights*. **10.** One who is conspicuous or noteworthy; a model or example. **11.** The medium through which light is admitted, as a window, or pane in a window. **12.** That by which something, as a cigar, may be lighted. **13.** *Law.* The natural light unobstructed by erections, or a right to it. **14.** *Painting.* That part of a picture which represents those objects upon which the light is supposed to fall. **15.** *Physics.* **a** The radiant energy which, by its action upon the organs of vision, enables them to perform their function of sight; — more accurately called *luminous energy*. Light is transmitted by an undulatory, or vibrational, movement at a velocity of about 186,300 miles a second. **b** Radiant energy incapable of appreciably affecting the average normal retina (ultraviolet light or infrared light), but otherwise like luminous energy. **c** The rate of transfer of luminous energy. Its unit is the *lumen*. Called also *luminous flux*.
— *adj.* **1.** Having light; not dark or obscure; bright; as, a *light* room. **2.** **a** Somewhat resembling white; pale in color; as, a *light* complexion. **b** Of colors, of high or very high brilliance.
— *v. t.;* LIGHT′ED (līt′ĕd; -ĭd) or LIT (lĭt); LIGHT′ING. [AS. *lȳhtan*, *līhtan*, to shine.] **1.** To set fire to; to ignite; as, to *light* the gas. **2.** To illuminate; to fill with light or furnish with lights; as, *lighted* by electricity; hence, to animate; brighten; — often with *up;* as, joy *lighted* up his eyes. **3.** To attend with or as with a light. — *v. i.* **1.** To be illuminated; to brighten; — usually with *up*. **2.** To become ignited, as a match.
light, *adj.* [AS. *līgt*, *lēoht*.] **1.** Having comparatively little weight; not heavy. **2.** Not burdensome; easy to be endured, performed, or the like; not severe; as, *light* taxes. **3.** Hence: **a** Easy to be digested; hence, moderate; slight; as, a *light* lunch. **b** Slight; not important; as, held in *light* esteem. **4.** **a** Not heavy or violent in movement or pressure; as, a *light* touch. **b** *U.S. Weather Bureau.* Of a velocity up to 7 miles per hour; — of wind. Cf. BEAUFORT'S SCALE. **c** Active; nimble; swift; as, *light* of foot. **5.** Easily influenced by trifling considerations; volatile; fickle; as, a girl's *light* fancy. **6.** Not oppressed by care or suffering; buoyant; as, a *light* heart. **7.** Indulging in, inclined to, or marked by, levity; trifling; frivolous. **8.** Wanton; unchaste. **9.** Dizzy; giddy; flighty; delirious; as, *light* in the head. **10.** Designed merely to entertain; not serious in theme or mood; as, *light* opera. **11.** Having a relatively small percentage of alcohol. **12.** Loose; easily pulverized; as, a *light* soil. **13.** Having little weight in proportion to bulk. **14.** Not copious; not dense; as, a *light* snow. **15.** Below the legal or standard weight; — of coin. **16.** Not heavy or massive in construction or appearance; as, *light* tracery. **17.** Not heavily encumbered; carrying a relatively small load. **18.** *Cookery.* Well leavened; not soggy. **19.** *Mil.* Armed with light weapons or accouterments; as, *light* artillery, cavalry. **20.** *Phonet. & Pros.* Of a syllable, unaccented; of a vowel, unaccented and obscurely pronounced; of accent or stress, weak. — **Syn.** See EASY. — **Ant.** Heavy.
— *adv.* Lightly; as, she treads so *light*; *light*-armed.
— *v. i.;* LIGHT′ED (līt′ĕd; -ĭd) or LIT (lĭt); LIGHT′ING. **1.** To dismount; to alight; — with *from, off, on, upon, at, in*. **2.** To descend and rest, perch, or settle, as a bird or snow; as, a cat always *lights* on its feet. **3.** To come down suddenly and forcibly; to fall, as a blow. **4.** To come or arrive by chance; to happen.
light′en (līt′'n), *v. i.* **1.** To flash or shine brightly. **2.** To grow lighter; brighten. **3.** To shine with, or like, lightning. — *v. t.* **1.** To make light or clear; illuminate. **2.** To illuminate intellectually or spiritually; to enlighten. **3.** To disclose in or as in lightning.
light′en, *v. t.* [See LIGHT to alight.] **1.** To relieve of a load in whole or in part; to make lighter. **2.** To make less burdensome; to alleviate. **3.** To cheer; gladden. — **Syn.** See RELIEVE.
light′en·er (līt′'n·ẽr), *n.* One who or that which lightens.
light′er (līt′ẽr), *n.* One who or that which lights or ignites.
light′er, *n.* [D. *lichter*, fr. *lichten* to make light, unload.] *Naut.* A large boat used in unloading or loading vessels not lying at wharves, or in transporting freight about a harbor. — *v. t.* To convey by a lighter.
light′er·age (-ĭj), *n.* **a** Price paid for lightering. **b** Loading, unloading, or transportation by means of a lighter.
light′face′ (līt′fās′), *n. Print.* A type having light, thin lines. See TYPE. — **light′face′**, *adj.* — **light′-faced′** (-fāst′), *adj.*
light′-fin′gered (-fĭng′gẽrd; 2), *adj.* Dexterous in stealing, esp. by picking pockets; thievish; pilfering.
light′-foot′ed (-fo͝ot′ĕd; -ĭd; 2), *adj.* Also **light′-foot′**. Having a light, springy step; nimble-footed. — **light′-foot′ed·ly**, *adv.* — **light′-foot′ed·ness**, *n.*
light′head′ (līt′hĕd′), *n.* A lightheaded, or frivolous, person.
light′head′ed (-hĕd′ĕd; -ĭd; 2), *adj.* **1.** Dizzy; delirious. **2.** Thoughtless; heedless; frivolous; fickle. — **light′head′ed·ly**, *adv.* — **light′head′ed·ness**, *n.*
light′heart′ed (-här′tĕd; -tĭd; 2), *adj.* Free from grief or anxiety; gay; cheerful. — **Syn.** See GLAD. — **light′heart′ed·ly**, *adv.* — **light′heart′ed·ness**, *n.*
light heavyweight. *Boxing.* A man weighing not less than 161 or more than 175 pounds.
light′-horse′man (-hôrs′măn), *n.* A soldier of light cavalry.
light′house′ (līt′hous′), *n.* A tower with a powerful light at the top, for guiding navigators at night; a pharos.
light′ing (līt′ĭng), *n.* **1.** Illumination; ignition. **2.** Incidence or disposition of light, as in a painting. **3.** Artificial supply of light or the apparatus providing it. In ***direct lighting***, the greater part of the light goes directly from the fixture toward the area to be illuminated; in ***indirect lighting***, it is reflected from a ceiling or other object external to the fixture.

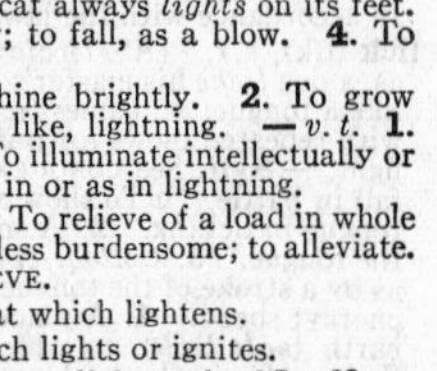

Lighthouses. 1 Stone Tower; 2 Steel Tower; 3 Steel Cylinder.

light′less, *adj.* Having no light.
light′ly (līt′lĭ), *adv.* **1.** With little weight or force; hence, gently. **2.** In a small degree or quantity; as, he ate *lightly*. **3.** Without reason, or for reasons of little weight. **4.** *Archaic.* Easily. **5.** Swiftly; nimbly. **6.** Without heed or care; slightingly. **7.** Without dejection; cheerfully; gaily. **8.** Not chastely; wantonly. — *v. t. Chiefly Scot.* To treat slightingly.
light′-mind′ed (līt′mīn′dĕd; -dĭd; 2), *adj.* Frivolous; volatile; trifling. — **light′-mind′ed·ly**, *adv.* — **light′-mind′ed·ness**, *n.*
light′ness (līt′nĕs; -nĭs), *n.* [AS. *līhtnes*.] **1.** State, quality, or degree of illumination. **2.** Absence of depth or of duskiness in color.
light′ness, *n.* [From LIGHT in weight.] State or quality of being light, or not heavy; hence, buoyancy; levity; fickleness; wantonness; nimbleness; delicacy; grace; etc.
Syn. **Lightness, levity, frivolity, flippancy, volatility, flightiness** mean indifference and gaiety, esp. when seriousness is expected. **Lightness** implies a lack of weight or seriousness in character, mood, or conduct;

levity, trifling or unseasonable gaiety; **frivolity**, indulgence in meaningless gaieties or in empty or idle speech or conduct; **flippancy**, an unbecoming levity, esp. in speaking of serious or sacred things; **volatility**, such lightness or fickleness of disposition as precludes long dwelling on any idea or plan; **flightiness**, extreme volatility that often implies loss of mental balance.

light′ning (līt′nĭng), *n.* [For *lightening*, fr. *lighten* to flash.] The flashing of light produced by a discharge of atmospheric electricity from one cloud to another or from a cloud to the earth; hence, the discharge itself.

lightning arrester. A device for protecting electrical apparatus or radio sets from injury by lightning, as by carrying the discharges to the ground.

lightning beetle *or* **bug.** A firefly.

lightning rod. A metallic rod connected with the earth or water, as on a house or vessel, to diminish the chances of destructive effect by lightning.

light′-o′-love′ (līt′ō̇-lŭv′), *n.* A fickle or wanton woman.

light quantum. = QUANTUM, 2.

lights (līts), *n. pl.* [So called from their lightness in weight.] The lungs of animals.

light′ship′ (līt′shĭp′), *n.* A vessel carrying a brilliant light or lights, moored off a shoal or place of danger to navigation.

light′some (-sŭm), *adj.* Lighted; luminous; bright.

light′some, *adj.* **1.** Airy; graceful; nimble. **2.** Gay; cheerful; merry. **3.** Frivolous; fickle. — **light′some·ly,** *adv.* — **light′some·ness,** *n.*

light′-struck′ (-strŭk′), *adj.* *Photog.* Fogged by light.

light′weight′ (-wāt′), *adj.* Light in weight; specif., that is a lightweight. — *n.* One of less than average weight; specif.: **a** In boxing, one weighing between 127 and 135 pounds. **b** *Colloq.* A person of little importance or ability.

light′wood′ (-wŏŏd′), *n.* *Southern U. S.* Pitchy pine wood.

light′-year′, *n.* *Astron.* The distance over which light can travel in a year's time; — used in expressing stellar distances. It is approximately 6,000,000,000,000 miles. Most of the stars are more than 100 light-years away from the earth.

lign′al′oes (līn′ăl′ōz; lĭg·năl′ōz), *n.* [OF., fr. L. *lignum aloës* wood of aloe.] **1.** The soft resinous wood of an East Indian tree (*Aquilaria agallocha*) of the mezereon family, burnt as a perfume. **2.** The drug aloes.

lig′ne·ous (lĭg′nē·ŭs), *adj.* [L. *ligneus*, fr. *lignum* wood.] Of, of the nature of, or like wood; woody.

lig′ni- (lĭg′nĭ-), **lig′no-** (lĭg′nō-), **lign-.** [L. *lignum.*] A combining form for *wood*, as in **lig′ni·form, lig·niv′o·rous, lig·nog′ra·phy** (wood engraving).

lig′ni·fy (lĭg′nĭ·fī), *v. t.;* -FIED (-fīd); -FY′ING. [*ligni-* + *-fy.*] *Bot.* To convert into wood. — *v. i.* To become wood or woody by conversion of constituents of the cell wall into lignin. — **lig′ni·fi·ca′tion** (-fĭ·kā′shŭn), *n.*

lig′nin (lĭg′nĭn), *n.* [*lign-* + *-in.*] *Bot. & Chem.* A substance related to cellulose and with it constituting the essential part of woody tissue.

lig′nite (-nīt), *n.* [F., fr. L. *lignum* wood.] *Mineral.* A noncaking, usually brownish-black, variety of coal intermediate between peat and bituminous coal, esp. one in which the texture of the original wood is distinct; — called also *brown coal.* — **lig·nit′ic** (lĭg·nĭt′ĭk), *adj.*

lig′no·cel′lu·lose (lĭg′nō·sĕl′ū·lōs), *n.* [*ligno-* + *cellulose.*] *Bot. & Chem.* Any of several closely related substances constituting the essential part of woody tissue, as jute fiber.

lig′nose (lĭg′nōs), *n.* [*lign-* + *-ose.*] **1.** *Bot. & Chem.* Lignin. **2.** An explosive consisting of wood fiber and nitroglycerin.

lig′num vi′tae (lĭg′nŭm vī′tē). [NL., wood of life, fr. L. *lignum* wood + *vita*, gen. *vitae*, life.] **1.** A tropical American tree (*Guaiacum officinale*) of the bean-caper family; also, its hard, heavy wood. **2.** A related tree (*G. sanctum*), the ***bastard lignum vitae.***

lig′ro·ine, lig′ro·in (lĭg′rō·ĭn), *n.* A volatile, inflammable petroleum distillate used as a solvent in chemistry and pharmacy.

lig′u·la (lĭg′ū·lȧ), *n.; pl.* -LAE (-lē), -LAS (-lȧz). [L. See LIGULE.] **1.** *Bot.* A ligule. **2.** *Zool.* The distal segment of part of the labium of insects. See HYMENOPTERON, *Illust.*

lig′u·late (lĭg′ū·lāt), *adj.* **1.** Strap-shaped; — applied esp. to the narrow flat corollas of the ray flowers in a composite plant. **2.** Furnished with ligules or with strap-shaped corollas.

lig′ule (lĭg′ūl), *n.* Also **lig′u·la** (-ū·lȧ), *n.; pl.* -LAE (-lē), -LAS (-lȧz). [L. *ligula* little tongue, projection, strap.] *Bot.* **a** A thin appendage of a leaf at the junction of blade and petiole, as in the leaves of grasses. **b** A ligulate corolla of a ray floret.

lig′ure (lĭg′ūr), *n.* [LL. *ligurius*, fr. LGr. *ligyrion.*] *Bib.* A variety of precious stone, perhaps the jacinth.

lik′a·ble, like′a·ble (līk′ȧ·b'l), *adj.* Such as can be liked or attracts liking. — **lik′a·ble·ness, like′a·ble·ness,** *n.*

like (līk), *adj.; formerly, but now infrequently,* LIK′ER (līk′ēr), LIK′EST (-ĕst; -ĭst). [AS. *gelīc*, fr. *ge-* + *līc* body, and orig. meaning, having the same body or shape, and hence, like.] **1.** Having the same, or nearly the same, appearance, qualities, or characteristics as another or others referred to as a basis of comparison. Specif.: **a** The same, or nearly the same, in character or degree; as, members of the cat family have *like* dispositions; fluids of *like* viscosity. **b** Indistinguishable; as, "almost as *like* as two eggs" (*Shak.*). **c** Equal, or nearly equal, in amount or extent; as, contributing a *like* sum. **d** Closely resembling its original; as, the sketch is not at all *like.* **e** *Now Rare.* Alike; as, no two were *like.* **2.** The same as; identical with; duplicating; indistinguishable from; closely corresponding to or resembling; similar to; suggesting; — in older English often followed by *to, unto, of, with, as;* as, "Wishing me *like* to one more rich in hope" (*Shak.*); "Wherefore in all things it behoved him to be made *like* unto his brethren" (*Heb.* ii. 17); "My father's brother, but no more *like* my father Than I to Hercules" (*Shak.*); "There is an El Greco hung there that is *liker* Tintoretto than himself" (*E. V. Lucas*); "Unchanging, yet so *like* our perishing earth" (*Wallace Stevens*); your reactions are not quite *like* mine. Hence: **a** Characteristic of; as, such behavior is just *like* him. **b** Indicative of; giving promise of; as, it looks *like* good fishing today. **c** Inclined toward; disposed to; as, to feel rather *like* taking a walk. **3.** *Colloq.* Likely; as, they're *like* to meet again. — *adv.* [AS. *gelīce.* See LIKE, *adj.*, above.] **1.** In a manner similar to or characteristic of; so as to equal in speed, skill, etc.; as, "You speak so *like* my dear old master" (*Dickens*); no one can recite quite *like* her. **2.** In the manner of one that is; — now chiefly in *like* mad. **3.** *Colloq.* Likely; probably; as, that was he, *like* enough; you'll *liker* find him in a bar; as *like* as not it'll rain. **4.** *Popular.* As it were; or at least somewhat so or seemingly so; as, his tone was condescending *like.*

— *prep.* **1.** Identical with; indistinguishable from; corresponding or similar to; (being) characteristic of; (seeming) indicative of; (feeling) inclined toward; as, your reactions are *like* mine. **2.** In the same manner as; so as to equal in speed, skill, etc.; as, to run *like* a deer. — *conj.* In the same manner or to the same extent or degree as; as, "They raven down scenery *like* children do sweetmeats" (*Keats*); he took to figures *like* a duck to water.

☞ *Like* introducing a clause, either a complete clause or one in which the predicate is to be supplied from the context, is common in popular usage but in the work of careful writers is usually replaced by *as.*

like (līk), *n.* That which is like another; counterpart.

-like (-līk). The adj. *like*, used as a suffix to form adjectives meaning: **a** *Having the characteristics of*, as in life*like.* **b** *Like that* or *those of*, as in tiger*like* ferocity.

☞ The suffix -LIKE usually forms a typographically solid word, but in *bell-like*, etc., it is hyphened.

like (līk), *v. i.* [AS. *līcian, gelīcian*, to please.] **1.** *Archaic.* To be suitable, pleasing, or agreeable; as, it *likes* me not. **2.** To choose; feel inclined; as, you may do as you *like.* — *v. t.* To be attracted towards; to have a liking for; to wish for; to enjoy. — *n.* A liking; a preference; a fancy; — usually *pl.*

like′a·ble, like′a·ble·ness. Vars. of LIKABLE, etc.

like′li·hood (līk′lĭ·hŏŏd), *n.* **1.** Probability; as, it will rain in all *likelihood.* **2.** A probability; also, an indication.

like′ly (līk′lĭ), *adj.;* LIKE′LI·ER (-lĭ·ēr); LIKE′LI·EST. **1.** Of such a nature or so circumstanced as to render something probable; as, the fate *likely* to befall them. **2.** Appearing like truth; probable; credible; as, a *likely* story. **3.** Suitable or qualified; as, a *likely* place to fish. **4.** Giving evidence of capability; promising. — **Syn.** See PROBABLE. — *adv.* In all probability.

lik′en (līk′ĕn), *v. t.* To represent as like; to compare.

like′ness (līk′nĕs; -nĭs), *n.* **1.** State or quality of being like. **2.** Appearance; guise; semblance. **3.** A copy; effigy; portrait.

Syn. **Likeness, similarity, resemblance, similitude, analogy, affinity** mean agreement or correspondence in details, qualities, or the like, brought out by comparison. **Likeness** commonly implies closer correspondence than **similarity,** which often implies that they are merely somewhat alike; **resemblance** implies similarity in appearance or in external qualities; **similitude** is sometimes preferred when an abstract term is desired; **analogy** implies likeness or parallelism in relations rather than in appearance or qualities; **affinity** adds to *resemblance* the implications of a relationship such as kinship, or common experiences or influences, responsible for the similarity.

like′wise′ (-wīz′), *adv.* [See WISE, *n.*] **1.** In like manner. **2.** Also; moreover; too.

li′kin′ (lē′kēn′), *n.* [Chin. (Pek.) *li*[4]*-chin*[1].] A Chinese provincial tax at inland stations on articles in transit.

lik′ing (līk′ĭng), *n.* [AS. *līcung.*] Favorable regard; fondness; one's taste or preference.

li′lac (lī′lăk; -lăk), *n.* [MF. (F. *lilas*), fr. Sp. *lilac*, fr. Ar. *laylak*, fr. Per. *nīlak* bluish, dim. fr. *nīl* blue, indigo.] **1.** A common garden shrub (*Syringa vulgaris*) with large panicles of pink-purple fragrant flowers which are the State emblem of New Hampshire. **2.** The color of lilac flowers, bluish blue-red in hue, of medium saturation and high brilliance. See COLOR. — *adj.* Of the color lilac.

lil′i·a′ceous (lĭl′ĭ·ā′shŭs), *adj.* [LL. *liliaceus*, fr. L. *lilium* lily.] **1.** Like, or pertaining to, lilies. **2.** *Bot.* Belonging to the lily family (Liliaceae). See LILY.

lil′ied (lĭl′ĭd), *adj.* **1.** Like a lily; fair as a lily. **2.** Covered or decorated with, or having many, lilies.

Lil′ith (lĭl′ĭth; lī′lĭth), *n.* [Heb. *Līlīth.*] *Semitic Myth.* A female evil spirit roaming in desolate places, attacking children. In Jewish and medieval popular belief, she was the first wife of Adam; in the demonology of the Middle Ages, she was a famous witch.

lil′li·bul·le′ro (lĭl′ĭ·bŭ·lēr′ō; -lâr′ō), *n.* Part of the refrain of a song, mocking the Irish Catholics, popular in England during the revolution of 1688; hence, the song itself.

Lil′li·pu′tian (-pū′shăn), *adj.* Of or pertaining to Lilliput, an imaginary island in Swift's *Gulliver's Travels*, the inhabitants of which were six inches tall; hence, diminutive; dwarfed. — *n.* One of these people; hence, a pygmy.

lilt (lĭlt), *n.* [See LILT, *v.*] **1.** A lively, buoyant, cheerful song or air. **2.** Rhythmical swing, flow, or cadence. **3.** A springy motion or movement. — *v. i. & t.* [ME. *lulten*, of obscure origin.] To sing rhythmically or cheerfully.

lil′y (lĭl′ĭ), *n.; pl.* -IES (-ĭz). [AS. *lilie*, fr. L. *lilium*, prob. fr. Gr. *leirion.*] **1.** Any of a genus (*Lilium*), typifying a family (Liliaceae, the lily family), of bulbous herbs with whorled or scattered leaves and showy flowers; also, a flower or bulb of such a plant. Common species are the ***golden-banded lily*** (*L. auratum*), the ***Madonna lily*** (*L. candidum*); ***Turk's-cap lily*** (garden species *L. martagon* or wild species *L. superbum*); ***wood lily*** (*L. philadelphicum*), ***meadow lily*** *or* ***Canada lily*** (*L. canadense*). See DAY LILY, MARIPOSA LILY, TIGER LILY. **2.** Any of numerous plants, flowers, or bulbs related to or like the lily. See CALLA, WATER LILY. **3.** The heraldic fleur-de-lis as the symbol of France. See FLEUR-DE-LIS, *Illust.*

lil′y, *adj.* Like a lily; hence, pure, white, pale, or delicate.

lily iron. A kind of harpoon with detachable head.

lil′y-liv′ered (lĭl′ĭ·lĭv′ērd), *adj.* White-livered; cowardly.

lily of the valley. A low perennial herb (*Convallaria majalis*), having a raceme of fragrant nodding bell-shaped white flowers. The lily of the valley typifies a family (Convallariaceae, the lily-of-the-valley family) of herbs resembling lilies but having fleshy baccate fruit and no bulb.

lily pad. *U. S.* One of the floating leaves of the water lily.

Li′ma bean (lī′mȧ). A common variety of bean (*Phaseolus limensis*); also, its flat seed, much used for food.

lim′a·cine (lĭm′ȧ·sĭn; -sīn; lī′mȧ-), *adj.* [L. *limax, limacis*, a slug.] *Zool.* Of, pertaining to, or like the slugs (genus *Limax* and its allies).

limb (lĭm), *n.* [AS. *lim.*] **1.** A leg or arm of a human being; a leg, arm, or wing of an animal. **2.** A large primary branch or bough of a tree. **3.** A thing or person regarded as a part or agent; as, a *limb* of the law. **4.** *Colloq.* A young scamp. **5.** A branch or arm of anything, as of the sea. — **Syn.** See SHOOT. — *v. t.* To dismember; to cut or tear off the limbs of.

limb (lĭm), *n.* [L. *limbus* border.] A border or edge, in certain special uses, as: **1.** The graduated margin of an arc or circle in an instrument for measuring angles. See SEXTANT, *Illust.* **2.** *Astron.* The outer edge (of a celestial body). **3.** *Bot.* The upper spreading portion of a gamopetalous corolla or of a gamosepalous calyx, as distinguished from the basal tube.

lim′bate (lĭm′bāt), *adj.* [LL. *limbatus*, fr. L. *limbus* border, edge.] *Bot. & Zool.* Bordered, as when one color is surrounded by an edging of another.

limbed (lĭmd), *adj.* Having limbs; esp., in combinations, having (such or so many) limbs; as, large-*limbed*.

lim′ber (lĭm′bẽr), *adj.* **1.** Pliant; yielding. **2.** Bending easily; supple; lithe. — *v. t.* To make limber. — **lim′ber·ly**, *adv.* — **lim′ber·ness**, *n.*

lim′ber, *n.* *Mil.* The detachable fore part of a gun carriage or caisson, consisting of two wheels, an axle, and a pole. — *v. t. & i.* *Mil.* To attach the limber to (the gun carriage).

lim′bers (lĭm′bẽrz), *n. pl.* [F. *lumière*, lit., light.] *Shipbuilding.* Gutters or conduits on each side of the keelson to afford a passage for water to the pump well.

lim′bic (lĭm′bĭk), *adj.* Of or forming a limbus.

limb′less (lĭm′lĕs; -lĭs), *adj.* Without limbs.

lim′bo (lĭm′bō), *n.; pl.* LIMBOES (-bōz). [L. *limbus* border, edge, *in limbo* on the border.] **1.** [*often cap.*] *Theol.* The abode of souls barred from heaven through no fault of their own, esp. of the souls of just men who died before the coming of Christ, or of the souls of unbaptized infants. **2.** Hence: A place of confinement, or a place or condition of neglect or oblivion.

Lim′burg·er (lĭm′bûrg·ẽr), *n.* A semihard unpressed cheese originally made in the Belgian province of Limburg (Limbourg), having a peculiar odor and a nutty flavor.

lim′bus (lĭm′bŭs), *n.* [L.] *Zool. & Bot.* A border distinguished by color or structure.

lime (līm), *n.* [AS. *līm.*] **1.** Birdlime. **2.** A caustic, highly infusible solid, white when pure, chemically CaO obtained by calcining limestone, shells, or other forms of calcium carbonate; — called also *quicklime, burnt lime, caustic lime.* Quicklime develops great heat when treated with water, forming a crumbly mass of ***slaked lime,*** *or* ***hydrated lime,*** which is calcium hydroxide, $Ca(OH)_2$. — *v. t.* **1.** To cement. **2.** To smear with a viscous substance, as birdlime. **3.** To ensnare, as if with birdlime. **4.** To treat with lime, as hides for removing the hair, or sails for whitening. — **lime,** *adj.*

lime, *n.* [Formerly *line*, for earlier *lind.*] The linden.

lime, *n.* [F., the fruit, fr. Pr. *limo*, fr. *limoun.* See LEMON.] An Asiatic tree (*Citrus aurantifolia*) of the rue family; also, its small, globose, greenish-yellow fruit, containing a juicy, very acid pulp of a characteristic flavor.

lime′kiln′ (līm′kĭl′; -kĭln′), *n.* A kiln or furnace in which limestone or shells are burned and reduced to lime.

lime′light′ (-līt′), *n.* **1.** An instrument for lighting a stage, producing a concentrated beam of light by directing an oxyhydrogen flame on a cylinder of lime; also, the light thus produced or cast. **2. a** *Theater.* That part of the stage upon which the limelight is cast, usually where the chief action is. **b** Conspicuous position before the public.

li′men (lī′mĕn), *n.* [L.] *Psychol. & Physiol.* = THRESHOLD, 3.

Lim′er·ick (lĭm′ẽr·ĭk), *n.* [From *Limerick*, Eire.] A nonsense poem of five anapaestic lines, of which lines 1, 2, and 5 are of three feet, and rhyme, and lines 3 and 4 are of two feet, and rhyme.

li′mes (lī′mēz), *n.; pl.* LIMITES (lĭm′ĭ·tēz). [L.] **1.** *Rom. Antiq.* A boundary; specif. [*cap.*], one of the fortified frontiers of the Roman Empire. **2.** [*cap.*] (*pron.* lī′mēz; *G.* lē′mĕs) A line of defensive fortifications built by Germany facing the Maginot line; — called also *Siegfried line.*

lime′stone′ (līm′stōn′), *n.* A rock consisting chiefly of calcium carbonate, usually an accumulation of organic remains such as shells, which yields lime when burned. Crystalline limestone is called *marble.* See CHALK, 1; FORAMINIFER.

lime tree. a The linden tree. **b** A tupelo, or sour gum (*Nyssa ogeche*), of the southern United States. See GUM, *n.*, 5.

lime twig. A twig covered with birdlime, hence, a snare.

lime′wa′ter (līm′wô′tẽr; -wŏt′ẽr), *n.* **1.** A water solution of slaked lime. **2.** Natural water containing considerable amounts of calcium carbonate or sulfate in solution.

lim′ey (lī′mĭ), *n.* [From *lime-juicer*, applied to a British ship or sailor because of the compulsory provision of lime juice on British ships to prevent scurvy.] *Slang.* An English sailor or soldier; by extension, an Englishman.

li·mic′o·line (lī·mĭk′ō·lĭn; -līn), *adj.* [LL. *limicolae* dwellers in the mud, fr. L. *limus* mud + *colere* to dwell.] Shore-inhabiting; belonging to a suborder (Charadrii) of wading birds, the shore birds, including the plovers, snipes, and sandpipers.

li·mic′o·lous (lī·mĭk′ō·lŭs), *adj.* Living in mud.

lim′i·nal (lĭm′ĭ·năl; -n′l; *in psychology usually* lī′mĭ-), *adj.* [L. *limen, liminis*, threshold.] Pertaining to, or at, the limen, or threshold.

lim′it (lĭm′ĭt), *n.* [L. *limes, limitis.*] **1.** A boundary or boundary line; *pl.*, bounds. **2.** That which terminates, circumscribes, or confines; the utmost extent; as, the *limits* of knowledge. **3.** *Archaic.* A region defined by bounds. **4.** *Games.* In betting, the sum agreed on as the greatest by which stakes may be increased at one time. **5.** *Math.* A fixed value or form which a varying value or form may approach indefinitely but cannot reach. — *v. t.* **1.** *Obs. exc. Law.* To assign to or within certain limits. **2.** To apply a limit to, or set a limit or bounds for. — **lim′it·a·ble**, *adj.*

Syn. **Limit, restrict, circumscribe, confine** mean to set bounds for. **Limit** implies a point in space, time, speed, or the like, beyond which a person or thing cannot go or is not permitted to go; **restrict** implies a boundary that encircles or encloses and often connotes a narrowing or tightening within those boundaries; **circumscribe** differs from *restrict* only in being clearer or more emphatic; **confine** may imply limitation, restriction, or circumscription, but it carries stronger connotations of cramping, hampering, bottling up, and the like.

lim′i·tar′y (lĭm′ĭ·tẽr′ĭ *or, esp. Brit.*, -tẽr·ĭ), *adj.* **1.** Limited, as an authority. **2.** Of or pertaining to a boundary; limiting.

lim′i·ta′tion (-tā′shŭn), *n.* **1.** Act or instance of limiting; state of being limited. **2.** That by which something is limited; restriction; qualification; as, his *limitations* as a writer. **3.** *Law.* A certain statutory period after which the claimant shall not enforce his claims by suit.

lim′i·ta′tive (lĭm′ĭ·tā′tĭv; -tȧ·tĭv), *adj.* Limiting; tending to limit or restrict; restrictive.

lim′it·ed (lĭm′ĭ·tĕd; -tĭd), *adj.* **1.** Confined within limits; narrow; circumscribed. **2.** *Railroads.* Accommodating a limited class of passengers, and usually requiring an extra fare. **3.** Conditioned by constitutional limitations upon the scope of action of one or more of its branches; as, a *limited* monarchy. **4.** *Eng.* Limiting the liability of each shareholder to the amount of his stock or shares or to an amount fixed by a guarantee; as, a *limited* (or *limited*-liability) company. Abbr. *Ltd.* — *n.* A limited train.

lim′it·er (lĭm′ĭ·tẽr), *n.* One who or that which limits.

lim′it·ing, *adj.* *Gram.* Restrictive; answering to the questions who, what, or which?, as in ***limiting adjectives*** (including pronominal and numeral adjectives, and the articles).

lim′it·less, *adj.* Having no limits; unbounded; boundless.

lim′mer (lĭm′ẽr), *n.* *Scot.* A hussy; also, a rascal.

limn (lĭm), *v. t.;* LIMNED (lĭmd); LIM′NING (lĭm′nĭng; lĭm′ĭng). [OF. *enluminer* to illuminate, limn, fr. L. *illuminare.*] To draw or paint, as a picture; to portray; delineate. — **lim′ner** (lĭm′nẽr), *n.*

lim·net′ic (lĭm·nĕt′ĭk), *adj.* [Gr. *limnē* pool, marsh.] Pertaining to, or living in, fresh water; as, *limnetic* organisms.

lim·nol′o·gy (lĭm·nŏl′ō·jĭ), *n.* [Gr. *limnē* pool + *-logy.*] The scientific study of fresh waters, esp. ponds and lakes, including physical, chemical, and biological conditions.

lim′o·nene (lĭm′ō·nēn), *n.* [NL. *Limonum* (fr. Citrus medica *limon*, the lemon) + *-ene.*] *Chem.* A widely distributed terpene, $C_{10}H_{16}$, occurring in three modifications, all liquids of agreeable lemonlike odor.

li′mo·nite (lī′mō·nīt), *n.* [Gr. *leimōn* meadow.] *Mineral.* Hydrous ferric oxide, $2Fe_2O_3.3H_2O$, an important ore of iron, occurring in mammillary or earthy forms as ochers, and as a yellowish-brown powder; — called also *brown hematite* (see HEMATITE). — **li′mo·nit′ic** (-nĭt′ĭk), *adj.*

lim′ou·sine′ (lĭm′ōō·zēn′; 2), *n.* [F., closed carriage, orig., a hood, cloak, fr. *Limousin*, old province in France.] A large luxurious chauffeur-driven sedan, often one used for bus service to and from an airport.

limp (lĭmp), *adj.* **1.** Lacking stiffness; flaccid; flexible; as, a *limp* cravat. **2.** Lacking firmness or strength.

Syn. **Limp, loppy, flaccid, flabby, flimsy, sleazy** mean wanting firmness in texture or substance. **Limp** implies a lack or loss of stiffness, with a tendency to droop; **loppy**, a hanging limply as if sagging; **flaccid**, a want or loss of resilience with loss of power to keep or return to shape; **flabby**, a hanging loosely from its own weight; **flimsy**, such looseness of structure or texture as to be without value or endurance; **sleazy**, a flimsiness that suggests carelessness or fraud.

— *v. i.* To halt; to walk lamely; also, to proceed with difficulty; as, a ship *limps* to port.

— *n.* A halt in one's walk; the act of limping.

— **limp′er**, *n.* — **limp′ly**, *adv.* — **limp′ness**, *n.*

lim′pet (lĭm′pĕt; -pĭt), *n.* [AS. *lempedu*, fr. ML. *lampreda* limpet, lamprey.] Any marine gastropod mollusk having a low conical shell, broadly open beneath and lacking any internal partition or shelf. It is usually found adhering to rocks or timbers.

lim′pid (lĭm′pĭd), *adj.* [F. *limpide*, fr. L. *limpidus*, fr. *limpa, lumpa*, water.] Characterized by clearness or transparency; pellucid; as, a *limpid* atmosphere. — **Syn.** See CLEAR. — **lim′pid·ly**, *adv.* — **lim′pid·ness**, *n.*

lim·pid′i·ty (lĭm·pĭd′ĭ·tĭ), *n.* Quality or state of being limpid.

limp′kin (lĭmp′kĭn), *n.* See COURLAN.

limp′sy (lĭmp′sĭ), *adj.* Also **lim′sy** (lĭm′-). *U.S. & Dial.* Limp; flimsy.

lim′u·loid (lĭm′ū·loid), *adj.* [*limulus* + *-oid.*] *Zool.* Like, or pertaining to, the king crabs. — *n.* A king crab.

lim′u·lus (-lŭs), *n.; pl.* LIMULI (-lī). [L., dim. of *limus* sidelong, askance.] A king crab.

lim′y (līm′ĭ), *adj.;* LIM′I·ER (-ĭ·ẽr); LIM′I·EST. **1.** Smeared with, or consisting of, lime; viscous. **2.** Containing, resembling, or having the qualities of lime.

lin′age (līn′ĭj), **line′age**, *n.* [*line* + *-age.*] **a** Alignment. **b** Number of lines of written or printed matter.

lin·al′o·öl (lĭn·ăl′ō·ōl; -ŏl; lĭn′ȧ·lōōl′), *n.* [*linaloa*, a Mexican perfume-yielding wood + *-ol*, 1.] *Chem.* An alcohol, $C_{10}H_{17}OH$, having an open-chain structure, but closely related to the terpenes. It is found in various essential oils.

linch′pin′ (lĭnch′pĭn′), *n.* A pin inserted in an axletree outside of the wheel to prevent the latter from slipping off.

Lin′coln (lĭng′kŭn), *n.* [From *Lincoln*, Eng.] An English breed of sheep similar to the Leicester, but heavier.

Lin′coln's Birth′day′ (lĭng′kŭnz). February 12, a holiday in many states of the United States.

Lincoln's Inn. See INN OF COURT.

Lind′bergh Act (lĭnd′bûrg). [After Charles A. *Lindbergh*, Am. aviator, whose son was kidnaped, March, 1932.] *Colloq.* A law (Patterson Act) passed by Congress (1932) providing a penalty of life imprisonment for transporting a kidnaped person across state boundaries, amended (Federal Crime Control Act, Number 232, 1934) to provide the death penalty unless the victim be returned unharmed or the jury recommend mercy.

lin′den (lĭn′dĕn), *n.* [Orig. an adj. fr. *lind* linden tree, fr. AS. *lind, linde.*] Any of a genus (*Tilia*, esp., in the United States, *T. glabra*) of fine-proportioned trees with large cordate leaves and cymose yellowish flowers which abound in honey; the basswood. The genus is typical of a family (Tiliaceae, the linden family) of herbs, shrubs, or trees distinguished mainly by the free stamens and 2-celled anthers.

line (līn), *n.* [AS. *līne* cord, rope, row, line; influenced by F. *ligne* line, fr. L. *linea.*] **1.** A thread, string, cord, or rope; esp., a comparatively slender and strong cord; as, a tow*line.* **2.** A cord, wire, steel tape, or the like, used in measuring, leveling, etc. **3.** *pl.* The boundary lines of an estate, inheritance, or the like; figuratively, fortune; lot. **4.** The piping for conveying a fluid, as steam or oil, from one location to another. **5.** The wire or pair of wires connecting one telegraph or telephone station with another, or the whole of a system of such wires. **6.** A fishing line. **7.** Something distinct and marked as if drawn by a pencil or graver, as a furrow or band; as, the *lines* in

stratified rock; any long mark or threadlike formation; as, a chalk *line*. **8**. A straight line; — used where no confusion with *curve* is possible. **9**. A straight line, as determined by the position of persons or things; also, agreement; harmony; as, recalcitrants were brought into *line*. **10**. A threadlike crease on the face or the hand. **11**. A mark of division or outline as on a map; hence, a boundary; often, any definite division or limitation; as, to overstep the *line* of good taste. **12**. Lineament; outline; contour. **13**. A plan of making or doing something; as, an epic on the *lines* of the *Iliad*. **14**. A row of letters, words, etc., written or printed; esp., a row of words extending across a page or column (abbr. *l*; pl. *ll*); specif.: **a** A verse. **b** A short letter or other writing; a note. **c** *pl. Colloq.* Marriage certificate. **15**. Course of conduct, thought, or policy; as, the *line* of duty. **16**. A series of ancestors or descendants of a given person; lineage. **17**. The course followed by anything regarded as in motion; hence, a road or route; as, out of the *line* of fire. **18**. A series or rank of objects counted as of the same kind; as, a *line* of type. **19**. A department of industry or trade. **20**. A number of public conveyances plying regularly under one management over a certain route; also, any system of transportation or the company owning or operating it. **21**. *Advertising.* One agate line one column wide. **22**. *Bridge.* In scoring, the horizontal line dividing trick scores (***below the line***) from honor scores (***above the line***). **23**. *pl. Drama.* The words of a part. **24**. *Fine Arts.* **a** A mark made by a pencil, brush, etc., forming a part of the formal design as distinguished from shading or coloring. **b** The general style of a composition with respect to the sequence or arrangement of its outlines and contours; — chiefly in *pl.* **25**. *Geog.* **a** On a map, a circle of latitude or of longitude. **b** The equator. **26**. *Math.* A locus of points whose co-ordinates depend on a single independent variable or parameter; a curve; the intersection of two surfaces. **27**. *Mil. & Nav.* **a** A trench or rampart. **b** *pl.* Dispositions made to cover extended positions and presenting a front to the enemy. **c** A formation of troops or ships in which the elements are abreast of each other. **d** The regular troops of an army, as distinguished from militia, guards, volunteers, etc.; also, the purely combatant forces as distinguished from the staff corps and supply departments. **e** *U.S. Navy.* The officers in military command, or in succession to military command, of combatant forces. **28**. *Music.* One of the horizontal parallel strokes of the staff. **29**. *Naut.* **a** A rope used in towing, in hauling, or in mooring. **b** Hose or pipe; as, an air *line*. **30**. *Railroads.* The track and roadbed. **31**. *Television.* A scanning line (see SCAN, *v. t.*, 3). **32**. *Trade.* A supply or stock of various qualities and values of the same general class of articles.
— *v. t.* **1**. To mark with a line or lines; to cover with lines. **2**. To represent by lines; portray, esp. in outline; hence, to outline. **3**. To place, be placed, or be, in a line along; as, wharves *line* the harbor. **4**. To bring into accurate adjustment to a line or into agreement with some standard; to align; as, to *line* troops. — *v. i.* To form a line.

Syn. **Line, align** (*or* **aline**), **range, array** mean to arrange in a line or lines. Literally, **line** (or, more often, *line up*) implies a setting in single file or in parallel rows; **align** implies a bringing of points or parts into a straight line; **range** implies a forming in parallel lines, but often also connotes a separation into groups or classes according to a plan; **array** implies esp. a setting in battle order and therefore suggests full equipment and readiness for action. Figuratively, **line** (or *line up*) suggests organization for unity or singleness of effort; **align**, falling into line or a line-up; **range**, a putting or falling into a group; **array**, arrangement in logical, or chronological, or merely impressive, order.

line (līn), *v. t.* [From ME. *lin* flax. See LINEN.] **1**. To cover the inner surface of, as a cloak. **2**. To put something in the inside of, as a purse. **3**. To serve as the lining of, as the walls. **4**. To strengthen (books) after sewing, by applying glue to the back and affixing super, leather, etc., and paper.

lin'e·age (lĭn'ē·ĭj), *n.* [OF. *lignage*, fr. L. *linea* line.] Descent in a line from a common progenitor; also, the line thus descending; race; family. — **Syn.** See ANCESTRY.

line'age (līn'ĭj). Var. of LINAGE.

lin'e·al (lĭn'ē·ăl), *adj.* [F. *linéal*, fr. L. *linealis* belonging to a line, fr. *linea* line.] **1**. Of or pert. to a line or lines; linear; as, *lineal* measure. **2**. Consisting of, or being in, a direct line of ancestry or descendants; — opp. to *collateral*. See CONSANGUINITY, *Illust.* **3**. Derived from ancestors in the direct line; hereditary. — **lin'e·al·ly**, *adv.*

lin'e·a·ment (lĭn'ē·ȧ·mĕnt), *n.* [F. *linéament*, fr. L. *lineamentum*, fr. *linea* line.] One of the outlines, features, or contours of a body or figure, esp. of the face.

lin'e·ar (lĭn'ē·ẽr; 39), *adj.* [L. *linearis, linearius*, fr. *linea* line.] **1**. Of, pert. to, or consisting of a line or lines; lineal. **2**. Like a line; long and uniform in width; as, a *linear* leaf. See LEAF, *Illust.* (2).

linear accelerator. A device in which charged particles are accelerated through a long vacuum tube by successive impulses from a series of electric fields.

linear equation. *Math.* An equation of the first degree between two variables.

linear measure. A measurement of length; also, a system for such measurement. See MEASURE, *Table* 1.

lin'e·ate (lĭn'ē·āt), *adj.* Also **lin'e·at'ed** (-āt'ĕd; -ĭd). [L. *lineatus*, fr. *linea* line.] Marked with lines or stripes.

lin'e·a'tion (-ā'shŭn), *n.* **1**. A marking with lines; an outlining; hence, an outline. **2**. An arrangement of lines; markings.

line breeding. Breeding or mating of successive generations among themselves to secure certain desired characters. — **line'-breed'**, *v. t.*

line drawing. A drawing done in solid lines or solid masses as copy for engravings, esp. with a pen, crayon, or other pointed instrument.

line engraving. Engraving in which the effects are produced by lines of different width and closeness, cut into copper or similar material; also, a plate so engraved, or a picture produced from such a plate.

line'man (līn'măn), *n.* **1**. *U.S.* One who carries the line in surveying, etc. **2**. A man employed to set up or repair telegraph, telephone, or electric-light or power lines. **3**. *Amer. Football.* A forward.

lin'en (lĭn'ĕn; -ĭn), *n.* [ME., fr. AS. *līnen* made of flax.] **1**. Thread or cloth made of flax or (rarely) of hemp, often including articles made of cambric, shirting, sheeting, etc. **2**. Clothing as shirts and collars, or house furnishings as sheets and tablecloths, made, or formerly made, of linen (sense 1). **3**. A high grade writing paper, originally made from linen rags only. — *adj.* Made of flax or linen.

line of force. A line in a field of force, whose tangent at any point gives the direction of the field at that point.

line of sight. **1**. The line or direction along which one looks when sighting an object. **2**. = LINE OF VISION.

line of vision. A straight line joining the fovea of the eye with the fixation point.

lin'e·o·late (lĭn'ē·ō·lāt), *adj.* [L. *lineola*, dim. of *linea* line.] *Zool. & Bot.* Marked with fine lines.

lin'er (līn'ẽr), *n.* **1**. One who lines. **2**. Something used to line or back up another part.

lin'er, *n.* **1**. One who makes or draws lines. **2**. Anything with which lines are made. **3**. A vessel or aircraft belonging to a regular line; as, a transatlantic *liner*. **4**. *Baseball.* A ball which, when struck, flies through the air in a nearly straight line not far from the ground.

lines'man (līnz'măn), *n.* **1**. A lineman. **2**. **a** *Lawn Tennis.* An official who decides whether a ball falls on one side or the other of the line or lines that he watches. **b** *Amer. Football.* An official who marks the distances gained or lost, marks the point where the ball goes out of bounds, and reports to the referee certain violations of the rules.

line squall *or* **thunderstorm.** *Meteorol.* A squall or thunderstorm occurring along a cold front.

line'-up', line'up' (līn'ŭp'), *n.* **1**. A line of persons arranged for inspection, esp. of suspects for identification. **2**. The formation or disposition of players before the start of a game or a restart of play; hence, any arrangement of persons having a common purpose.

ling (lĭng), *n.* [ON. *lyng*.] The common heather.

ling, *n.*; see PLURAL, *Note*, 5. [ME. *lenge*; — from its being *long*. See LONG, *adj.*] **a** A large gadoid marine fish (*Molva molva*), of northern Europe and Greenland, usually salted and dried. **b** See BURBOT.

-ling (-lĭng). [AS.] A noun suffix used: **a** To denote *one pertaining to* or *having the quality of*, as in world*ling*. **b** To convey a *diminutive* or a *depreciatory* force, as in prince*ling*.

-ling, -lings (-lĭngz). [AS. *-ling*; an adverbial *s*, orig. a genitive ending, sometimes added.] A suffix expressing direction, used chiefly to form adverbs of *state* or *manner*, as in dark*ling*, flat*ling*.

lin'ger (lĭng'gẽr), *v. i.* [Freq. of ME. *lengen* to tarry, fr. AS. *lengan* to prolong, put off, fr. stem of *lang* long.] **1**. To delay; tarry; to be slow in parting or in quitting anything. **2**. To procrastinate; dally; hesitate. **3**. To remain alive, although waning or dying; as, old customs *linger*. **4**. To move slowly; to saunter. — **Syn.** See STAY. — *v. t.* To spend or pass in a lingering manner. — **lin'ger·er**, *n.*

lin'ge·rie (län'zhē·rē; -rā; lăn'zhē·rē; *Fr.* lăNzh'rē'), *n.* [F.] Linen goods collectively; linen underwear, esp. of women; loosely, underwear of silk, rayon, etc. — **lin'ge·rie'**, *adj.*

lin'go (lĭng'gō), *n.*; *pl.* LINGOES (-gōz), *sometimes* LINGOS (-gōz). [Pr., fr. L. *lingua* tongue, language.] Language; dialect; often contemptuously, a foreign language or a strange speech. — **Syn.** See DIALECT.

lin'gua (lĭng'gwȧ), *n.*; *pl.* LINGUAE (-gwē). [L., the tongue.] A tongue or tonguelike organ; as, *Zool.*: **a** The glossa. **b** The proboscis of a butterfly or moth.

lin'gua fran'ca (frăng'kȧ). [It., prop., language of the Franks.] **a** A language, consisting of Italian mixed with French, Spanish, Greek, and Arabic, spoken in Mediterranean ports. **b** Any hybrid language used widely as a commercial tongue, such as pidgin English.

lin'gual (lĭng'gwăl), *adj.* [ML. *lingualis*, fr. L. *lingua* tongue.] Of or pertaining to the tongue or a tonguelike organ or part; glossal; *Phonet.*, formed with the aid of the tongue (as *t, d, n, s*). — *n.* A lingual sound or letter.

lin'gui·form (lĭng'gwĭ·fôrm), *adj.* [L. *lingua* tongue + *-form.*] Having the form of the tongue; tongue-shaped.

lin'guist (lĭng'gwĭst), *n.* [L. *lingua* tongue, language.] **1**. A person skilled in languages, esp. living languages. **2**. A person versed in linguistics.

lin·guis'tic (lĭng·gwĭs'tĭk), *adj.* Also **lin·guis'ti·cal** (-tĭ·kăl). Of or pertaining to language or the study of languages; relating to linguistics. — **lin·guis'ti·cal·ly**, *adv.*

linguistic atlas. Also **dialect atlas**. A set of maps on which are recorded dialectal variations of pronunciation, vocabulary, and idiom.

linguistic form. *Ling.* A meaningful unit of speech, whether a phoneme, a combination of phonemes, a word, phrase, or sentence; — called also *speech form.*

linguistic geography. = DIALECT GEOGRAPHY.

lin·guis'tics (-tĭks), *n.*; see -ICS. The study of human speech including the units, structure, and modification of language, or languages. It includes esp. phonetics, morphology, semantics, general or philosophical grammar; — called also **linguistic science**. Cf. PHILOLOGY.

lin'gu·late (lĭng'gū·lāt), *adj.* [L. *lingulatus*, fr. *lingula* a little tongue.] Shaped like the tongue; ligulate.

lin'i·ment (lĭn'ĭ·mĕnt), *n.* [LL. *linimentum*, fr. *linire, linere*, to besmear, anoint.] A preparation thinner than an ointment, rubbed on the skin, esp. as an anodyne or counterirritant; an embrocation.

li'nin (lī'nĭn), *n.* [L. *linum* flax.] **1**. *Chem.* A bitter, white purgative substance, derived from a European annual herb (*Cathartolinum catharticum*). **2**. *Biol.* The substance of the achromatic fibrous network of a cell nucleus. See CELL, 4, *Illust.*

lin'ing (līn'ĭng), *n.* [See LINE to cover the inside.] **1**. That which lines the inner surface of anything, as of a garment; also, the contents of anything. **2**. Act of providing or inserting a lining. **3**. *Bookbinding.* The material used in reinforcing the back (spine) of a book. **4**. *Elec.* An insulating part between live and other parts.

link (lĭngk), *n.* A torch made of tow and pitch, or the like.

link, *n.* [ME. *linke*, of Scand. origin.] **1**. A single ring or division of a chain; specif., one of the divisions of a surveyor's chain (see MEASURE, *Tables* 2 & 4) **2**. Anything analogous to a link of a chain in form or function; specif.: **a** *Chiefly Dial.* A sausage or pudding as a division of a chain. **b** *Scot.* A winding of a stream; also, the adjacent ground; — usually *pl.* **3**. Something which binds together or connects. **4**. *Chem.* = BOND. **5**. *Elec.* The fusible member of a fuse. **6**. *Mach.* Any intermediate rod or piece for transmitting force or motion. See GUNLOCK, *Illust.* — *v. t. & i.* To connect or unite with or as with a link. — **Syn.** See JOIN.

link, *v. i.* *Scot.* To trip or skip smartly along.

link'age (lĭngk'ĭj), *n.* **1**. Act of linking, or state of being linked; also, a system of links. **2**. *Biol.* The tendency of certain genes (or the corresponding characters) to remain associated in inheritance; the failure of segregation during maturation of such genes or characters. Linked genes (**linkage groups**) are considered to be located in the same chromosome. **3**. *Elec.* The product of the magnetic flux through a coil by its number of turns, the magnetic flux and the coil being connected like two links of a chain. **4**. *Mech.* Any system of links or bars joined together and more or less constrained by having a link or links fixed, by which straight lines, or other point paths, may be traced.

link′boy′ (lĭngk′boi′), **link′man** (-măn), *n.* *Hist.* An attendant who bears a link, or torch.

linked (lĭngkt), *adj.* *Biol.* Exhibiting linkage.

link motion. *Mach.* A variety of valve gear or reversing gear for a steam engine, in which the valve rod is connected to a block (called the **link block**) capable of sliding in a slotted link controlled by a system of links, two eccentrics, and a drag link.

links (lĭngks), *n. pl.* [AS. *hlinc* ridge, hill.] **a** *Scot.* Sand hills, esp. along the seashore. **b** Any golf course.

link, *or* **link′ing, verb.** *Gram.* A verb that subordinates its own meaning to the function of connecting the predicate idea with the subject (for example: *be, become, seem, appear, feel, grow*); — called also *copula* or *copulative verb.*

link′work′ (lĭngk′wûrk′), *n.* **1.** A fabric of links; a chain. **2.** *Mach.* Mechanism in which links are employed.

linn (lĭn), *n.* [From AS. *hlynn* and from Gael. *linne.*] *Chiefly Scot.* **1.** A pool, esp. one below a fall. **2.** A waterfall. **3.** A steep ravine.

Lin·nae′an, Lin·ne′an (lĭ·nē′ăn), *adj.* Pertaining to, or after the method of, Karl von Linne, Latinized *Linnaeus,* Swedish naturalist, who proposed (1735) a classification of plants based chiefly on the sporophylls, and who established the system of binomial nomenclature, in which each species receives two names, that of the genus to which it belongs and that of the species itself.

lin′net (lĭn′ĕt; -ĭt), *n.* [OF. *linette,* fr. L. *linum* flax; — because it feeds on the seeds of flax and hemp.] A common small finch (*Carduelis cannabina*), of the Old World, with plumage varyingly gray, red, pied, or nearly white.

lin′o·le′ic (lĭn′ō·lē′ĭk; lĭ·nō′lē·ĭk), *adj.* Pertaining to or designating an unsaturated acid, $C_{17}H_{31}.CO_2H$.

li·no′le·um (lĭ·nō′lē·ŭm; 58), *n.* [L. *linum* flax + *oleum* oil.] **1.** Linseed oil solidified by oxidation. **2.** A floor covering made by laying, on a burlap or canvas backing, a mixture of solidified linseed oil with gums, cork dust (or wood flour or both), and usually pigments.

Lin′o·type (lĭn′ō·tīp), *n.* *Print.* A trade-mark applied to a kind of typesetting machine which produces castings, or slugs, each of which corresponds to a line of separate types.

lin′sang (lĭn′săng), *n.* [Jav. (*w*)*linsan̄.*] A long-tailed mammal related to the civet, of catlike habits, of the East Indies.

lin′seed′ (lĭn′sēd′), *n.* [AS. *līnsǣd.*] Flaxseed.

linseed oil. A yellowish drying oil expressed or extracted from flaxseed, used in making oil paints, printer's ink, etc.

lin′sey-wool′sey (lĭn′zĭ·wŏŏl′zĭ), *n.; pl.* -WOOLSEYS (-zĭz). Also **lin′sey.** [From earlier *linsey* (fr. *Lindsey,* village in Suffolk, Eng.), taken as fr. *linen* + *woolsey,* fr. *wool.*] **1.** Coarse cloth made of linen and wool, or cotton and wool. **2.** *Obs.* Jargon; nonsense. *Shak.*

lin′stock (lĭn′stŏk), *n.* [Corrupt. fr. D. *lontstok,* fr. *lont* lunt + *stok* stock, stick.] *Hist.* A pointed forked staff, shod with iron, to hold a lighted match for firing cannon.

lint (lĭnt), *n.* [ME. *lynt,* prob. fr. LL. *linta,* L. *linteum* a linen cloth, linen, fr. *linteus* linen, adj., fr. *linum* flax, lint.] **1.** *Obs. exc. Scot.* Flax. **2.** Linen scraped or otherwise made into a soft, downy, or fleecy substance for dressing wounds; also, fine ravelings or fluff from yarn or fabrics.

lin′tel (lĭn′tĕl; -t'l), *n.* [OF., fr. a VL. dim. of L. *limes* limit.] A horizontal member spanning an opening to carry a superstructure.

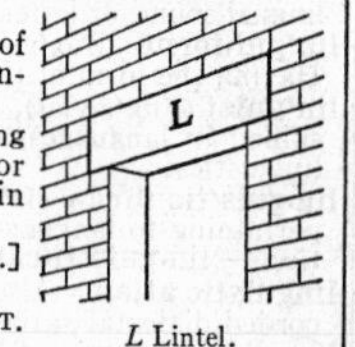

L Lintel.

lint′er (lĭn′tẽr), *n.* **1.** A machine for removing lint. **2.** *pl.* A mixture of long, usually soft or flaccid, fibers and fuzz escaping removal in ginning, used in making cotton batting.

lint′white′ (lĭnt′hwīt′), *n.* [AS. *līnetwige.*] = LINNET.

lint′y (lĭn′tĭ), *adj.;* LINT′I·ER (-tĭ·ẽr); LINT′I·EST. Like lint; full of, or covered with lint.

li′on (lī′ŭn), *n.* See PLURAL, *Note,* 3. [OF. *lion, leon,* fr. L. *leo, -onis,* fr. Gr. *leōn.*] **1.** A large carnivorous mammal (*Felis leo*) of the cat family, having tufted tail and, in the male, a shaggy mane, inhabiting Africa and southern Asia to western India. Cf. COUGAR. **2.** One like a lion either in courage or ravenous cruelty. **3.** An object of interest and curiosity, esp. a person who is so regarded; as, a social *lion.* **4.** [*cap.*] A member of any one of an association of service clubs (***International Association of Lions Clubs***), founded in 1917 and affiliated internationally. The objects are good government, citizenship, and fellowship, and community, national and international welfare. **5.** [*cap.*] The constellation Leo.

li′on·ess (lī′ŭn·ĕs; -ĭs), *n.* A female lion.

li′on·et (-ĕt), *n.* [OF.] A young or small lion.

li′on·heart′ (-härt′), *n.* A brave and magnanimous person; esp. [*cap.*], Richard I of England, called *Cœur de Lion.*

li′on·ize (lī′ŭn·īz), *v. t.* **1.** To treat or regard as an object of great interest; esp., to make a social "lion" of (a person). **2.** To visit the objects of interest of (a place). — **li′on·ism** (-ĭz'm), *n.* — **li′on·i·za′tion** (-ĭ·zā′shŭn; -ī·zā′-), *n.*

lip (lĭp), *n.* [AS. *lippa.*] **1.** Either of the two fleshy folds which surround the orifice of the mouth in man and many other animals. **2.** Talk; esp., saucy or impudent talk; back talk. **3.** The edge or margin of a hollow vessel or cavity, esp. where it shows a slight flare, as of a bell or crater. **4.** The sharp cutting edge on the end of an auger. **5.** *Bot. & Zool.* Any liplike part or structure; specif.: **a** A labium. **b** The labellum. **6.** *Music.* **a** An embouchure. **b** See FLUE PIPE, *Illust.* **7.** *Surg.* An edge of a wound. — *adj.* Belonging to the lips; specif.: **a** Coming from the lips only, and hence insincere. **b** *Phonet.* Formed or pronounced with the aid of the lips; labial. — *v. t.;* LIPPED (lĭpt); LIP′PING. **1.** To touch with the lips; to put the lips to. **2.** To utter, esp. in a murmuring voice. **3.** *Golf.* To strike the ball so that it hits the edge of (the cup) but fails to drop in.

lip′a·roid (lĭp′ȧ·roid), *adj.* [Gr. *liparos* oily + *-oid.*] *Med.* Resembling fat; fatty.

li′pase (lī′pās; lĭp′ās), *n.* [Gr. *lipos* fat.] *Biochem.* Any of a class of enzymes that accelerate the hydrolysis of fats to fatty acids and glycerol. Cf. ESTERASE.

lip′ide (lĭp′īd; -ĭd; lī′pīd; -pĭd), *n.* Also **lip′id.** [*lip-* + *-ide.*] *Biochem.* Any of a group of substances comprising the fats and other esters that possess analogous properties. They are characterized by solubility in fat solvents, by insolubility in water, and by their greasy feel.

lip′o- (lĭp′ō-), **lip-.** [Gr. *lipos* fat.] A combining form denoting: **a** *Med., Physiol., etc.* Fat, fatty, as in **lip′o·cyte,** a fat cell. **b** *Chem.* A lipide, as in *lip*ase.

lip′o·ca′ic (-kā′ĭk), *n.* [*lipo-* + Gr. *kaiein* to burn.] *Biochem.* A pancreas preparation said to influence the utilization of fat in the liver.

lip′oid (lĭp′oid; lī′poid), *adj.* [*lip-* + *-oid.*] *Biochem.* Fatlike. — *n.* A fatlike substance.

li·pol′y·sis (lĭ·pŏl′ĭ·sĭs), *n.* [NL., fr. *lipo-* + *-lysis.*] Decomposition of fat. — **lip′o·lyt′ic** (lĭp′ō·lĭt′ĭk), *adj.*

li·po′ma (lĭ·pō′mȧ), *n.; pl.* -MATA (-mȧ·tȧ), -MAS (-mȧz). [NL., fr. *lip-* + *-oma.*] *Med.* A tumor of fatty tissue.

lip′o·pro′te·in (lĭp′ō·prō′tē·ĭn; -tēn), *n.* [*lipo-* + *protein.*] *Biochem.* Any of a class of proteins containing a lipide group.

lip′o·trop′ic (-trŏp′ĭk), *adj.* [*lipo-* + *-tropic.*] *Biochem.* Promoting the utilization of fat.

lipped (lĭpt), *adj.* Having a lip or lips, or a raised edge like a lip; also, *Bot.,* labiate; — often used in combination.

lip′pen (lĭp′ĕn), *v. i. & t.* *Scot.* To trust; confide; also, to expect.

lip′per (lĭp′ẽr), *n.* *Naut.* A slight roughness of the sea.

lip reading. The catching of the words of a speaker by watching his lips. — **lip′-read′** (lĭp′rēd′), *v. t. & i.* — **lip reader.**

lip service. Commendation or avowal of allegiance that goes no further than expression in words; profession without implementation.

lip′stick′ (lĭp′stĭk′), *n.* A kind of pomade, a perfumed ointment, or a rouge, for the lips, put up in stick form.

li′quate (lī′kwāt), *v. t.* [L. *liquatus,* past part. of *liquare* to melt.] *Metal.* To separate (a more fusible substance) from one less fusible, by heat. — **li·qua′tion** (lī·kwā′shŭn), *n.*

liq′ue·fa′cient (lĭk′wē·fā′shĕnt), *n.* [L. *liquefaciens,* pres. part. of *liquefacere.*] That which serves to liquefy.

liq′ue·fac′tion (-făk′shŭn), *n.* Act or process of making or becoming liquid; esp., conversion of a solid into a liquid by heat.

liq′ue·fy (lĭk′wē·fī), *v. t. & i.;* -FIED (-fīd); -FY′ING. [F. *liquéfier,* fr. L. *liquere* to be liquid + *-ficare* (in comp.), to make.] To reduce to a liquid state; — said both of solids and of gases. — **liq′ue·fi′a·ble** (-fī′ȧ·b'l), *adj.* — **liq′ue·fi′er** (-ẽr), *n.*

li·ques′cent (lĭ·kwĕs′ĕnt; -'nt), *adj.* [L. *liquescens,* pres. part.] Becoming, or tending to become, liquid; melting. — **li·ques′cence** (-ĕns; -'ns), **li·ques′cen·cy** (-ĕn·sĭ; -'n·sĭ), *n.*

li·queur′ (lē·kûr′; lĭ·kûr′), *n.* [F.] A spirituous liquor flavored with aromatic substances.

liq′uid (lĭk′wĭd), *adj.* [OF. *liquide,* fr. L. *liquidus,* fr. *liquere* to be fluid.] **1.** Flowing freely like water; fluid. **2.** Fluid and transparent; as, the *liquid* air. **3.** Flowing or sounding smoothly; as, a *liquid* melody. **4.** Such as are cash, or as can be promptly converted into cash; as, **liquid assets.** **5.** *Phonet.* Of consonant sounds, smooth; flowing; vowellike, as the sounds of *l* and *r.* **6.** *Physics.* Characterized by free movement of the constituent molecules among themselves, but without the tendency to separate from one another characteristic of gases; neither solid nor gaseous; as, *liquid* mercury, state. — *n.* **1.** A substance in the liquid state. **2.** *Phonet.* A liquid consonant. — **liq′uid·ly,** *adv.* — **liq′uid·ness,** *n.*

Syn. **Liquid, fluid** mean flowing or not solid. **Liquid** implies the flow characteristic of water and suggests a substance that has definite volume but no definite form except such as is given by its container; **fluid** implies flowing of any sort and is applicable not only to all liquids but to any gas or gaseous substance which has neither independent volume nor shape, and is the preferred form in describing a viscous or melted substance.

liquid air. Air in the liquid state, prepared by subjecting air to great pressure and then cooling it by its own expansion to a temperature below the boiling point of its chief constituents. Its chief use is as a refrigerant.

liq′uid·am′bar (lĭk′wĭd·ăm′bẽr; *L.* -bär), *n.* [NL. See LIQUID; AMBER.] **1.** *Bot.* Any of a genus (*Liquidambar,* family Altingiaceae), of trees with small monoecious flowers and a globose fruit composed of many woody carpels. **2.** Also **liq′uid·am′ber** (-bẽr). Copalm, the balsam yielded by the sweet gum (*L. styraciflua*). See GUM, *n.,* 5 **a** (2).

liq′ui·date (lĭk′wĭ·dāt), *v. t.* [ML. *liquidatus,* past part. of *liquidare* to liquidate, fr. L. *liquidus* liquid, clear.] **1.** *Law.* To determine by agreement or by litigation the precise amount of (indebtedness or damages). **2.** To discharge; to pay off, as an indebtedness. **3.** To settle the accounts and distribute the assets of (a corporation or estate) in the process of winding up, esp. through a receiver or trustee. **4.** Figuratively, to clear up and dispose of as if by such a process; as, to *liquidate* illiteracy. **5.** To do away with as if by secret killing or to eradicate ruthlessly; — a euphemism. **6.** To do away with, get rid of, or destroy. — *v. i.* To liquidate one's debts or accounts.

liq′ui·da′tion (-dā′shŭn), *n.* Act or process of liquidating, or state of being liquidated. — ***to go into liquidation.*** Of a business concern, to give up business and effect a liquidation of assets for final distribution.

liq′ui·da′tor (lĭk′wĭ·dā′tẽr), *n.* One who liquidates; esp., one appointed to conduct the winding up of a company.

liquid crystal. A liquid having certain physical properties, esp. optical, shown by crystalline solids but not by ordinary liquids.

liquid fire. *Mil.* A burning liquid to be thrown from a flame projector.

li·quid′i·ty (lĭ·kwĭd′ĭ·tĭ), *n.* State or quality of being liquid.

liquid measure. The measurement of liquids, or a system for such measurement. See MEASURE, *Table* 11.

liq′uor (lĭk′ẽr), *n.* [OF. *licour, licur,* fr. L. *liquor.*] **1.** Any liquid substance, as water, milk, blood, sap, juice, etc. **2.** Specif., an alcoholic beverage; — often limited to such as are strong or distilled; as, beer, wines, and *liquors.* **3.** *Pharm.* A solution of a medicinal substance in water. — *v. t.* **1.** To cover or dress with oil or grease. **2.** To treat with a liquor or solution. **3.** *Slang.* To supply or ply with liquor; treat. — *v. i.* *Slang.* To drink liquor; — often with *up.*

liq′uo·rice (lĭk′ō·rĭs; -rĭsh). Var. of LICORICE.

liq′uor·ish (lĭk′ẽr·ĭsh). Var. of LICKERISH.

liq′uor·ish (lĭk′ẽr·ĭsh). Dial. var. of LICORICE.

li′ra (lē′rä), *n.; pl.* LIRE (-rā), LIRAS (-räz). [It., fr. L. *libra* pound.] **1.** A nickel coin and the monetary unit of Italy, containing 100 centesimi. See MONEY, *Tables.* **2.** A gold coin of Turkey, containing 100 piasters; the Turkish pound.

lir′i·o·den′dron (lĭr′ĭ·ō·dĕn′drŏn), *n.; pl.* -DRA (-drȧ). [NL., fr. Gr. *leirion* lily + *-dendron.*] *Bot.* Any of a genus (*Liriodendron*) of

North American and Asiatic trees of the magnolia family, as the tulip tree *L. tulipifera*.

lir'i·pipe (lĭr'ĭ·pīp), **lir'i·poop** (-po͞op), *n.* [ML. *liripipium.*] *Obs. exc. Hist.* A pendent part of the old clerical or academic tippet; afterwards, a tippet; scarf; hood.

lisle (līl; *F.* lēl), *n.* Short for **Lisle thread**, a hard twisted cotton thread, orig. made at Lille (form. Lisle); also, a fabric or article woven of Lisle thread. — **lisle**, *adj.*

lisp (lĭsp), *v. i.* [AS. *wlispian*, fr. *wlisp* stammering, lisping.] **1.** To pronounce the sibilants *s* and *z* imperfectly, as by giving them the sounds of *th*. **2.** Hence, to speak imperfectly or falteringly. — *v. t.* To pronounce or speak in a faltering manner; hence, to express by the use of simple, childlike language. — *n.* The habit or act of lisping; also, a lisping sound. — **lisp'er**, *n.*

‖**lis pen'dens** (lĭs pĕn'dĕnz). [L.] A pending suit; — used esp. with reference to the doctrines that a court has control over the property involved in a suit.

lis'some (lĭs'ŭm), *adj.* Also **lis'som.** [From LITHESOME.] Limber; supple; hence, nimble; agile. — **lis'some·ly**, *adv.* — **lis'some·ness**, *n.*

list (lĭst), *n.* [AS. *līste.*] **1.** A bordering strip. *Obs.*, exc. as a strip forming the selvage of cloth. **2.** A strip or band of material, esp. of cloth. **3. a** A stripe of color, as on an animal's body. **b** A division of the hair or beard, formed by parting. **4.** A limit or boundary; also, an enclosure. **5.** [From *list* border, merged with OF. *lice* the lists, enclosing barrier, of Teut. origin.] *pl.* **a** The barriers of a tilting field; hence, the field itself; the field or arena for a tournament. **b** Hence, a place of combat or contest; an arena; — esp. in ***to enter the lists***, to join in a contest. **6.** [F. *liste*, fr. OHG. *līsta.*] A roll or catalogue, as of names of items; a register. **7.** *Agric. N. Amer.* One of the ridges made in listing. **8.** *Arch.* A narrow fillet; a listel. **9.** *Carp.* A narrow strip of wood, esp. sapwood, cut from the edge of a plank or board. **10.** *Stock Exchange.* With *the*, the total register of securities admitted to trading on a stock exchange.
— *adj.* Made of selvage or other strips of cloth, usually woolen; as, *list* carpet.
— *v. t.* **1.** To put a list, or border, on; as, to *list* a garment; also, to put on as a list or border. **2.** Specif., to cover with list, or with strips of cloth. **3.** To enter or enroll in a list, catalogue, register, or the like; as, to *list* property for taxation; goods *listed* above the market price; also, to enlist. **4.** *Agric.* **a** *Southern U. S.* To prepare (land) for a crop by making alternating beds and furrows. **b** *N. Amer.* To put (land) in corn (maize) with a lister. **5.** *Carp.* To cut away a narrow strip, as of sapwood, from the edge of; as, to *list* a board. **6.** *Stock Exchange.* To enter (a stock or other security) in the list of those officially admitted to dealings on the exchange. — *v. i.* To enlist in the army or navy.

list, *v. i.*; LIST'ED, *Archaic* LIST; LIST'ED; LIST'ING. [AS. *lystan* to be pleasing, fr. the stem of AS. *lust* pleasure.] **1.** *Archaic.* To please; suit; like; wish; incline (*to*). **2.** [From LIST inclination.] *Naut.* **a** To careen; — said of a ship. **b** To heel. — *v. t. Naut.* To cause to list. — *n.* **1.** *Archaic.* Inclination; wish. **2.** An inclination to one side; — mostly nautical; as, the ship has a *list* to starboard.

list, *v. t. & i.* [See LISTEN.] *Archaic.* To hearken; attend.

lis'tel (lĭs'tĕl; -t'l), *n.* [F.] *Arch.* A list, or narrow fillet. See IONIC, *Illust.*

lis'ten (lĭs''n; 105), *v. i.* [AS. *hlystan*, fr. *hlyst* hearing.] **1.** To give ear; to hearken. **2.** To give heed; to yield to advice. — *v. t. Archaic.* To hearken to. — *n.* Act of listening. — **lis'ten·er** (lĭs''n·ẽr; lĭs'nẽr), *n.*

list'er (lĭs'tẽr), *n.* **1.** One who or that which lists. **2. a** *Agric. Mach.* A double moldboard plow which throws a furrow slice both ways. **b** Also **lister drill.** A machine in which such a plow is combined with a drill which sows as the furrow is opened.

Lis'ter·ine' (lĭs'tẽr·ēn'; lĭs'tẽr·ēn), *n.* A trade-mark for (originally) a chemical or medical preparation, an antiseptic.

list'less (lĭst'lĕs; -lĭs), *adj.* [*list* desire + *-less.*] Having no desire or inclination; indifferent; spiritless. — **list'less·ly**, *adv.* — **list'less·ness**, *n.*

lit (lĭt), *n.*; *pl.* LITS (lĭts). See LITAS.

lit (lĭt), *past & past part.* of LIGHT.

lit'a·ny (lĭt'ȧ·nĭ), *n.*; *pl.* LITANIES (-nĭz). [OF. *letanie*, fr. LL. *litania*, fr. Gr. *litaneia*; akin to Gr. *litaneuein* to pray.] **a** A form of liturgical prayer, consisting of a series of invocations and supplications with alternate responses in which clergy and congregation join. **b** [*cap.*, with *The*] The general supplication of this form contained in the Book of Common Prayer.

li'tas (lē'täs), *n.*; *pl.* LITAI (-tā), LITU (-to͞o); Angl. **lit** (lĭt), *pl.* LITS (lĭts). The former gold monetary unit of Lithuania, equivalent at par to $0.1693 U. S. currency.

li'tchi (lē'chē; *Chin.* lē'dzŭ'), *n.* [Chin. (Pek.) *li*[4]*-chih*[1].] **1.** The fruit of a tree (*Litchi chinensis*) of the soapberry family. The fruit is oval, the outer covering hard and scaly, and the seed small and hard. The flesh surrounding the seed when dried is firm, sweetish, and black, constituting the edible part of the so-called **litchi nuts** of commerce. **2.** The tree bearing this fruit.

‖**lit de jus'tice'** (lē' dē zhüs'tēs'). [F.] *Fr. Hist.* Bed of justice; the platform on which the king sat when he held a formal session of Parliament; also, the session itself.

-lite (-līt). [After F. *-lite*, for *-lithe.*] A combining form equivalent to *-lith*, denoting a *mineral*, *rock*, or the like.

li'ter, li'tre (lē'tẽr), *n.* [F. *litre*, fr. *litron* an old measure, fr. ML., fr. Gr. *litra* a silver coin, pound.] The unit of capacity in the metric system. Abbr. *l.* (*sing. & pl.*). See METRIC SYSTEM, *Table* 4.

lit'er·a·cy (lĭt'ẽr·ȧ·sĭ), *n.* State of being literate.

lit'er·al (lĭt'ẽr·ăl), *adj.* [OF., fr. LL. *litteralis*, *literalis*, fr. L. *littera*, *litera*, a letter.] **1.** According to the "letter," or the natural or usual construction and implication of a writing or expression. **2.** Hence: **a** True to the fact; not exaggerated. **b** Giving a strict construction; matter-of-fact; — applied to persons. **3.** Of, pertaining to, or expressed by letters or alphabetic characters; as, a *literal* error. **4.** Of senses of words, conveying the primary meaning; — opposed to *figurative*, *specific*, etc. **5.** Of translations, transcriptions, etc., representing or following the exact words. — **lit'er·al·ly**, *adv.* — **lit'er·al·ness**, *n.*

lit'er·al·ism (-ĭz'm), *n.* Practice or theory of following the letter, or literal sense, or the tendency to adopt literal interpretations; hence, *Fine Arts*, extreme realism in portrayal. — **lit'er·al·ist** (-ĭst), *n. & adj.* — **lit'er·al·is'tic** (-ĭs'tĭk), *adj.*

lit'er·al'i·ty (-ăl'ĭ·tĭ), *n.*; *pl.* -TIES (-tĭz). State or quality of being literal; also, a literal meaning or interpretation.

lit'er·al·ize (lĭt'ẽr·ăl·īz), *v. t.* To make literal; to interpret according to literal meaning. — **lit'er·al·i·za'tion** (-ĭ·zā'shŭn; -ī·zā'-), *n.*

lit'er·ar'y (lĭt'ẽr·ẽr'ĭ *or, esp. Brit.*, -ẽr·ĭ), *adj.* **1.** Of or pertaining to letters, or literature (often esp. belles-lettres). **2.** Versed in literature, connected with literature or with men of letters.

lit'er·ate (-ĭt), *adj.* [L. *litteratus*, *literatus*. See LETTER.] **1.** Instructed in letters; specif., able to read and write. **2.** Pertaining to, or learned in, literature; literary. — *n.* **1.** A learned or literary person. **2.** One who can read and write.

lit'e·ra'ti (lĭt'ĕ·rā'tī; -rä'tĭ), *n. pl.* [L.] Men of letters; also, *Colloq.*, well-educated persons.

‖**lit'e·ra'tim** (-rā'tĭm), *adv.* Formerly **lit'te·ra'tim.** [L., fr. *littera*, *litera*, letter.] Letter for letter; literally.

lit'er·a'tor (lĭt'ẽr·ā'tẽr), *n.* A literary man, esp. a critic.

lit'er·a·ture (lĭt'ẽr·ȧ·tůr), *n.* [F. *littérature*, fr. L. *litteratura*, *literatura*, learning, grammar, writing, fr. *littera*, *litera*, letter.] **1.** *Rare.* Literary culture. **2.** Production of literary work, esp. as an occupation. **3.** Literary productions as a collective body; as: **a** The total of preserved writings belonging to a given language or people. **b** Specif., that part of it which is notable for literary form or expression; belles-lettres. **c** The body of writings having to do with a given subject; as, the *literature* of magic. **4.** *Colloq.* Any kind of printed matter, as advertising.

lith (lĭth), *n.* [AS.] *Now Scot.* A joint or limb; a member.

lith-. = LITHO- (which see).

-lith (-lĭth). [F. *-lithe*, fr. Gr. *lithos* stone, calculus.] A combining form used to denote: **a** *Art & Archaeol. A structure, figure*, or *implement of stone*, as in mono*lith*. **b** *An artificial stone* or *cement*. **c** *Med. A calculus*, as in nephro*lith*. **d** *Mineral., Geol., & Paleontol.* = -LITE.

lith'arge (lĭth'ärj; lĭ·thärj'), *n.* [OF. *litarge*, fr. L. *lithargyrus*, fr. Gr. *lithargyros* the scum of silver, fr. *lithos* stone + *argyros* silver. Litharge is found in silver-bearing lead ore.] *Chem.* A fused form of lead monoxide; loosely, lead monoxide in any form. Cf. MASSICOT.

lithe (līth), *adj.* [AS. *līthe* tender, mild, gentle.] Capable of being easily bent; pliant; flexible; limber. — **lithe'ly**, *adv.* — **lithe'ness**, *n.*

li·the'mi·a, li·thae'mi·a (lĭ·thē'mĭ·ȧ), *n.* [NL., fr. *lith*ic + *-emia.*] *Med.* A condition in which uric acid is present in the blood in excess. — **li·the'mic, li·thae'mic** (-mĭk), *adj.*

lithe'some (līth'sŭm), *adj.* Pliant; limber; supple.

lith'i·a (lĭth'ĭ·ȧ), *n.* [NL., fr. Gr. *lithos* stone.] *Chem.* A white crystalline substance, lithium oxide, Li_2O.

li·thi'a·sis (lĭ·thī'ȧ·sĭs), *n.* [NL., fr. Gr. *lithiasis*, fr. *lithos* stone.] *Med.* The formation of stony concretions in the body, esp. in the urinary bladder and gall bladder.

lithia water. A mineral water characterized by the presence of lithium salts.

lith'ic (lĭth'ĭk), *adj.* *Chem.* Of or pertaining to lithium.

lith'ic, *adj.* [Gr. *lithikos* of stones, fr. *lithos* stone.] **1.** Of or pertaining to stone. **2.** *Med.* Pertaining to, or characterized by, formation of uric-acid concretions (stone), esp. in the bladder.

-lith'ic (-lĭth'ĭk). [Gr. *lithos* stone + *-ic.*] An adjective suffix denoting *pertaining to* or *characteristic of a* (specified) *stage in the use of stone*, as in neo*lithic*.

lith'i·um (lĭth'ĭ·ŭm), *n.* [NL., fr. Gr. *lithos* stone; — it was discovered in a mineral.] *Chem.* A soft, silver-white metallic element, the lightest metal known (sp. gr., 0.53). Symbol, *Li*; at. no., 3; at. wt., 6.940.

lith'o- (lĭth'ō-), **lith-.** [Gr. *lithos.*] A combining form meaning *stone*, *calculus*, as in **lith'o·ne·phrot'o·my.**

lith'o·graph (lĭth'ō·grăf; 9), *v. t.* [*litho-* + *-graph.*] To produce, copy, or portray by lithography. — *n.* A print made by lithography.

li·thog'ra·pher (lĭ·thŏg'rȧ·fẽr; lĭth'ō·grăf'ẽr), *n.* One who lithographs.

li·thog'ra·phy (lĭ·thŏg'rȧ·fĭ), *n.* [*litho-* + *-graphy.*] The art or process of putting writing or designs on stone with a greasy material, and of producing printed impressions therefrom; also, any process based on the same principle, as one using zinc, aluminum, or some other substance instead of stone. — **lith'o·graph'ic** (lĭth'ō·grăf'ĭk), **lith'o·graph'i·cal** (-ĭ·kăl), *adj.* — **lith'o·graph'i·cal·ly**, *adv.*

lith'oid (lĭth'oid), *adj.* Also **li·thoi'dal** (lĭ·thoi'dăl). [Gr. *lithoeidēs.*] Like a stone.

li·thol'o·gy (lĭ·thŏl'ō·jĭ), *n.* [*litho-* + *-logy.*] The study of rocks. — **lith'o·log'ic** (lĭth'ō·lŏj'ĭk), **lith'o·log'i·cal** (-ĭ·kăl), *adj.* — **li·thol'o·gist** (lĭ·thŏl'ō·jĭst), *n.*

lith'o·marge (lĭth'ō·märj), *n.* [*litho-* + L. *marga* marl.] *Mineral.* A smooth compact variety of common kaolin.

lith'o·phyte (-fīt), *n.* [*litho-* + *-phyte.*] **1.** *Rare.* A plant or plantlike organism having a stony structure, as corals. **2.** A plant which grows on the surface of rocks.

lith'o·pone (-pōn), *n.* [Prob. fr. *litho-* + L. *ponere* to place.] A white pigment containing zinc sulfide, used in linoleum, rubber goods, etc.

lith'o·print' (-prĭnt'), *v. t.* To lithograph. — *n.* A lithoprinted book. — **lith'o·print'er**, *n.*

lith'o·sphere (-sfēr), *n.* [*litho-* + *sphere.*] The solid part of the earth.

li·thot'o·my (lĭ·thŏt'ō·mĭ), *n.* [LL. *lithotomia*, fr. Gr. *lithotomia.* See LITHO-; -TOMY.] *Surg.* The operation or art of cutting for stone in the bladder. — **lith'o·tom'ic** (lĭth'ō·tŏm'ĭk), *adj.* — **lith'o·tom'i·cal** (-ĭ·kăl), *adj.*

li·thot'ri·ty (-rĭ·tĭ), *n.* [*litho-* + L. *terere*, *tritum*, to rub, grind.] *Surg.* The operation of breaking a stone in the bladder into pieces capable of being voided.

Lith'u·a'ni·an (lĭth'ů·ā'nĭ·ăn; 58), *adj.* Of or pertaining to Lithuania or the Lithuanians or their language. — *n.* **1.** A native of Lithuania. **2.** One of a branch of the Lettish and Lithuanian peoples in the Baltic area bordering on the Gulf of Riga. **3.** The language (archaic and highly inflected) of the Lithuanians. See INDO-EUROPEAN LANGUAGES, *Table.*

lit'i·ga·ble (lĭt'ĭ·gȧ·b'l), *adj.* Such as can be litigated.

lit'i·gant (-gănt), *adj.* [F., fr. L. *litigans*, *-antis*, pres. part.] Disposed to litigate; also, engaged in a lawsuit. — *n.* One engaged in a lawsuit.

lit'i·gate (-gāt), *v. t.* [L. *litigatus*, past part. of *litigare*, fr. *lis*, *litis*, dispute, lawsuit.] To make the subject of a lawsuit; to contest in law.

— *v. i.* To carry on a legal contest by judicial process. — **lit′i·ga′tor** (lĭt′ĭ·gā′tẽr), *n.*

lit′i·ga′tion (lĭt′ĭ·gā′shŭn), *n.* Act or process of litigating; a suit at law; also, figuratively, dispute; discussion.

li·ti′gious (lĭ·tĭj′ŭs), *adj.* [F. *litigieux*, fr. L. *litigiosus*, fr. *litigium* dispute quarrel, fr. *litigare*. See LITIGATE.] **1.** Inclined to judicial contest; contentious. **2.** Subject to, or involved in, dispute at law. **3.** Of or pertaining to litigation. — **Syn.** See BELLIGERENT. — **li·ti′gious·ly**, *adv.* — **li·ti′gious·ness**, *n.*

lit′mus (lĭt′mŭs), *n.* [ON. *litmose* lichen used in dyeing, fr. *litr* color, dye + *mosi* moss.] *Chem.* A dyestuff prepared from archil (a product of certain genera of lichens such as *Roccella* and *Lecanora*). It turns red in an acid and blue in a basic medium.

litmus paper. *Chem.* Unsized paper colored with litmus.

li′to·tes (lī′tō·tēz; lĭt′ō-), *n.* [NL., fr. Gr. *litotēs*, fr. *litos* plain, simple.] *Rhet.* Understatement to avoid censure or to increase the effect (a citizen of no mean city, that is, of an illustrious city).

li′tre (lē′tẽr). Var. of LITER.

lit′ten (lĭt′'n), *adj. Poetic.* Lighted.

lit′ter (lĭt′ẽr), *n.* [OF. *litiere*, deriv. of L. *lectus* bed.] **1. a** A couch with shafts, usually covered and provided with curtains, for carrying passengers. **b** A stretcher for carrying a sick or wounded person. **2.** The young brought forth at one time by a sow or other multiparous animal, taken collectively. **3.** Straw, hay, etc., used as bedding for animals, or for other uses, as for a covering for plants. **4. a** Things lying scattered about; scattered rubbish. **b** Disorder or untidiness. **5.** *Forestry.* The upper, only slightly decomposed, portion of the forest floor. — *v. t.* **1.** To supply with litter, as cattle; to cover with litter. **2.** To put into disorder, as a room. **3.** To bear a litter of; to give birth to; — esp. of animals. — *v. i.* To produce a litter, or young.

‖**lit′te·rae hu·ma′ni·o′res** (lĭt′ĕ·rē hū·măn′ĭ·ō′rēz). [L.] Humane letters; the ancient classics and belles-lettres.

lit′té′ra′teur′ (lē′tā′rà′tûr′), **lit′ter·a·teur′** (lĭt′ẽr·ȧ·tûr′), *n.* [F. *littérateur.*] A literary man.

lit′tle (lĭt′'l), *adj.;* LIT′TLER (-lẽr); LIT′TLEST; both chiefly dial. or familiar, comparison being regularly made by LESS or LESSER, LEAST, except in some special applications. [AS. *lȳtel.*] **1.** Small in size or extent; diminutive; — the opposite of *big, large*, or *great*; as, a *little* body. **2.** Short in duration; brief. **3.** Small in quantity, amount, or degree; not much. **4.** Small in dignity, power, importance, or scope. **5.** Small in force or efficiency; not strong; weak. **6. a** Pleasingly small or trifling; as, fascinating *little* ways. **b** Small in extent of view; narrow; illiberal; as, men of *little* natures. — **Syn.** See SMALL. — *adv.* **1.** In a small quantity or degree; slightly. **2.** When preceding a verb: Not at all; as, he *little* thought he was going to his doom. — *n.* **1.** That which is little; a small amount, time, distance, etc. **2.** A small degree or scale; miniature. — **lit′tle·ness**, *n.*

little auk. See DOVEKIE.

Little Bear. *Astron.* Ursa Minor. See URSA MINOR, *Illust.*

little hours. *R.C.Ch.* The offices of prime, tierce, sext, and none. Vespers and complin are sometimes included.

lit′tle·neck′ (lĭt′'l·nĕk′), *n., or* **littleneck clam.** See CLAM, 1.

little office. *R.C.Ch.* An office in honor of the Virgin Mary like, but shorter than, the Breviary.

Little Rhod′y (rōd′ĭ). Rhode Island; — a nickname alluding to its small size.

Little Russian. See RUSSIAN, *n.*, 1 & 2; INDO-EUROPEAN LANGUAGES, *Table.*

little theater. A small theater, esp. one in which a company, usually amateur, produces experimental dramas.

lit′to·ral (lĭt′ō·răl), *adj.* [L. *littoralis*, prop. *litoralis*, fr. *littus*, prop. *litus*, the seashore.] Of or pert. to a shore, esp. of the sea. — *n.* [It. *littorale.*] A coastal region.

li′tu (lē′to͞o), *n., pl.* of LITAS.

li·tur′gi·cal (lĭ·tûr′jĭ·kăl), *adj.* Also **li·tur′gic** (-jĭk). [Gr. *leitourgikos.*] Pert. to, or of the nature of, a liturgy; of or pert. to public prayer and worship. — **li·tur′gi·cal·ly**, *adv.*

li·tur′gics (lĭ·tûr′jĭks), *n.;* see -ICS. The science of worship; the history, doctrine, and interpretation of liturgies.

lit′ur·gist (lĭt′ẽr·jĭst), *n.* **a** One who favors or adheres to a liturgy. **b** A student or compiler of liturgies.

lit′ur·gy (-jĭ), *n.; pl.* -GIES (-jĭz). [F. *liturgie*, fr. ML. *liturgia*, fr. Gr. *leitourgia* a public service, public worship.] **1.** *Eccl.* The public rites and services of the Christian Church; specif.: **a** The Eucharistic rite, called the ***Liturgy*** (also ***Divine Liturgy***) in the Eastern, ***the Mass*** in the Western, Church. **b** The Eucharistic rite in any of its historical forms; as, the Roman *liturgy*. See RITE. **2.** A rite or body of rites prescribed for public worship.

liv′a·ble (lĭv′ȧ·b'l), *adj.* **1.** Such as can be lived; endurable. **2.** Such as is pleasant or suitable to live in or with.

live (lĭv), *v. i.* [AS. *libban, lifian.*] **1.** To be alive; to have life. **2.** To continue in life. **3.** To get a livelihood; subsist; also, to be nourished; feed. **4.** To pass life in a certain manner, as to habits or circumstances. **5.** To dwell; reside. **6.** To continue in human memory or record. **7.** To outlast danger; to float; — said chiefly of a vessel. **8.** To live a life rich in experience. — *v. t.* **1.** To experience, pass, or spend, as one's life. **2.** To act habitually in conformity with.

live (līv), *adj.* [From ALIVE.] **1.** Alive; not dead. **2.** Of or pertaining to the living state or a living being or beings. **3.** Of fire, fuels, etc.: Burning; glowing; hence, ardent; as, a *live* hatred; of a match, etc., not burned, exploded, or the like. **4.** Full of life; specif.: **a** Teeming with living beings. **b** *Chiefly U.S.* Full of, or characterized by, vigor or alert interest; also, of current interest; as, a *live* topic. **5.** Of color, bright; vivid; also, of timber, etc., of normal brightness; not "dead," or opaque. **6.** In its pure or native state; of rock, unwrought; not quarried. **7.** *Elec.* Electrically connected to a source of voltage, or electrically charged. **8.** *Engin.* Imparting power; driven; as, a *live* axle. **9.** *Gun.* Charged, as a shell, cartridge, etc. **10.** *Print.* Ready for use; not dead; as, *live* matter. **11.** *Radio & Television.* **a** Of, or involving the actual presence of, real people; as, a *live* performance or audience. **b** Broadcast directly at the time of its production instead of from recorded or filmed material; — esp. of a program; as, *live* television.

live′a·ble (lĭv′ȧ·b'l). Var. of LIVABLE.

live center (līv). *Mach.* A center that rotates with the spindle and work. Cf. DEAD CENTER.

lived (līvd), *adj.* Having life.

live′-for·ev′er (lĭv′-), *n.* A common Eurasian garden herb (*Sedum triphyllum*) of the orpine family, naturalized in eastern North America.

live′li·hood (līv′lĭ·ho͝od), *n.* [ME. *livelode, liflode*, prop., course of life, life's support, maintenance, fr. AS. *līf* life + *lād* way, maintenance.] Means of supporting life; living; subsistence.

live load (līv). *Arch. & Eng.* The load to which a structure is subjected in addition to its own weight.

live′long′ (lĭv′lŏng′; līv′-; 74), *adj.* [ME. (the) *lefe longe, leve longe.* See LIEF; LONG.] Whole; entire; long in passing; — used of time, esp. as tedious.

live′ly (līv′lĭ), *adj.;* -LI·ER (-lĭ·ẽr); -LI·EST. [AS. *līflīc* living. See LIFE; -LY.] **1.** Full of life; as: **a** Vigorous; brisk. **b** Animated; spirited. **c** Vivid; keen. **2.** *Rare.* Representing life; lifelike. **3.** Indicating or imparting activity; enlivening; as, a *lively* air. **4.** Responding quickly to outer forces; rebounding quickly; as, a *lively* ball. — *adv.* In a lively manner; briskly; vividly. — **live′li·ly**, *adv.* — **live′li·ness**, *n.*

Syn. **Lively, animated, vivacious, sprightly, gay** mean keenly alive. **Lively** suggests briskness, alertness, or energy; **animated**, spiritedness and brightness; **vivacious**, and especially **sprightly**, greater lightness of spirits or quickness of wit; **gay**, utter carefreeness and exuberant or overflowing spirits. — **Ant.** Dull.

liv′en (līv′ĕn), *v. t. & i. Colloq.* To enliven.

live oak (līv). Any of several evergreen oaks; esp., *Southeastern U. S.*, a timber tree (*Quercus virginiana*) much used in shipbuilding.

liv′er (lĭv′ẽr), *n.* **1.** One who or that which lives. **2.** A resident; a dweller; as, a *liver* in Brooklyn.

liv′er, *n.* [AS. *lifer.*] **1.** In vertebrates, a large glandular organ which secretes bile and causes important changes in the blood, esp. by converting sugars into glycogen, and in forming urea. **2.** In many invertebrates, a large compound gland discharging into the alimentary canal. **3.** The liver regarded as the seat of passion or desire. A *white liver* is traditionally the characteristic of a coward. **4.** The tissue of the liver of an animal used as food.

liver extract. An extract of the water-soluble constituents of fresh mammalian liver, used in anemia.

liv′er·ied (lĭv′ẽr·ĭd), *adj.* Wearing a livery.

liv′er·ish (-ĭsh), *adj. Colloq.* Having a disordered liver; hence, crabbed; testy.

liv′er·wort′ (lĭv′ẽr·wûrt′), *n.* **1.** Any bryophyte of a class (Hepaticae) related to and resembling the mosses, but differing in reproduction, development, and in the structure of the gametophyte. **2.** Any herb of the genus *Hepatica.*

liv′er·wurst′ (-wûrst′; -wo͝orst′), *n.* [Partial trans. of G. *leberwurst.*] A sausage containing a large proportion of liver.

liv′er·y (lĭv′ẽr·ĭ), *n.; pl.* -ERIES (-ĭz). [OF. *livree* a gift of clothes made by the master to his servants, prop., that handed over, fr. *livrer* to deliver, fr. ML. & L. *liberare.*] **1.** That which is delivered out formally; as: **a** *Now Rare.* An allowance of food, as to a family, to servants, to horses, etc. **b** The uniform clothing issued by feudal superiors to their retainers. **c** The peculiar dress by which the servants of a person of some fashion are often distinguished. **2.** Characteristic dress or outward appearance. **3. a** Persons in one's service; retainers; — used as a collective noun. **b** The peculiar garb appropriated by any association of persons to their own use; also, the whole company of persons wearing such a garb, and entitled to the privileges of the association; a livery company. **4.** Of horses: **a** The feeding, stabling, and care of horses for pay. **b** The keeping of horses, and hence of vehicles, boats, etc., in readiness to be hired. **c** *U. S.* A livery stable. **5.** *Law.* The act of delivering legal possession of property.

livery company. One of the guilds of London.

liv′er·y·man (lĭv′ẽr·ĭ·măn), *n.* **1.** *Archaic.* A liveried retainer. **2.** A freeman of the city in London, entitled to wear the livery of the company to which he belongs. **3.** One who keeps a livery stable.

livery stable. A stable where horses and vehicles are kept for hire, and where stabling is provided.

lives (līvz), *n., pl.* of LIFE.

live steam. Steam direct from the boiler, having its full power of expansion.

live′stock′ (līv′stŏk′), *n.* Domestic animals used or raised on a farm, esp. those kept for profit.

liv′id (lĭv′ĭd), *adj.* [F. or L.; F. *livide*, fr. L. *lividus;* akin to L. *livere* to be of a bluish color.] **1. a** Discolored, as flesh by contusion; black and blue. **b** Of the color lead. **2.** Ashy pale. — **li·vid′i·ty** (lĭ·vĭd′ĭ·tĭ), *n.* — **liv′id·ly**, *adv.* — **liv′id·ness**, *n.*

liv′ing (lĭv′ĭng), *n.* **1.** The state of one that lives. **2.** The passing of one's life (in a specified manner); as, riotous *living*. **3.** Means of living; livelihood. **4.** *Archaic.* Estate; property. **5.** *Eng. Eccl.* A benefice.

— *adj.* **1.** Alive; that lives; — opp. to *dead*. **2.** Active; operative; as, *living* ideas; a *living* faith. **3.** Ignited; burning; as, *living* coals. **4.** Of or pertaining to the living; as, within *living* memory. **5.** Producing life or vigor; enlivening. **6.** Full of, or true to, life; vivid. — ***the living.*** Those who are alive.

Syn. **Living, alive, quick, animate, animated, vital** mean endowed with or manifesting life. **Living** and **alive** are opposed to *dead* and are applied usually to organic bodies which have life as opposed to those from which life has departed; **quick** is applied usually to things which have life because it is their nature as distinguished from those incapable of life; **animate** presupposes life but is used in opposition to *inanimate*, which may be applied to bodies that are dead or to things incapable of life; **animated**, opposed to *lifeless* and *inert*, is applicable only to that which becomes alive; **vital**, opposed to *mechanical*, is applied chiefly to power, motion, energy, etc., which result from life. In figurative use, **living** implies continued activity, efficacy, and force; **alive** and **vital**, abundance, vigor, etc.; **animated**, qualities suggestive of life; **quick** and **animate**, newness, freshness, responsiveness.

living death. Life deprived of all that makes it worth living.

living room. A room in a residence designed for general use, and not for any special function; a sitting room.

living wage. *Econ.* A wage sufficient to live on, that is, generally, to meet the reasonable mental, moral, and physical needs of a person in his station in life.

li′vre (lē′vẽr; *F.* lē′vr′), *n.* [F., fr. L. *libra* a pound of twelve ounces.] A former French money of account, orig. the value of a pound of silver.

lix·iv′i·ate (lĭk·sĭv′ĭ·āt), *v. t.* [L. *lixivius*, fr. *lix* ashes, lye.] To separate by washing with some solvent; leach. — **lix·iv′i·a′tion** (-ā′shŭn), *n.* — **lix·iv′i·a′tor** (-ā′tẽr), *n.*

lix·iv′i·um (lĭk·sĭv′ĭ·ŭm), *n.* [L. *lixivium, lixivia.*] Any solution obtained by lixiviation, esp. lye.

liz′ard (lĭz′ẽrd), *n.* [OF. *laisard* (F. *lézard*), fr. VL. *lacertus*, for L. *lacerta.*] **a** Any of the numerous small, long-bodied, four-legged reptiles, with tapering tail, and scaly or tuberculated skin. The term is extended to similar reptiles, many of them of large size, as dinosaurs, crocodilians, etc., and, incorrectly, to similarly shaped amphibians, as salamanders and newts. **b** *Zool.* Any member of a division (Lacertilia) of reptiles including chameleons, geckos, and allied limbless forms.

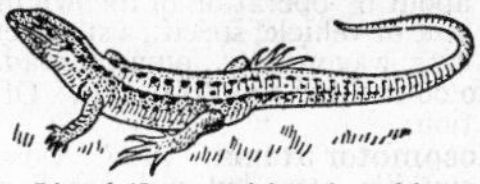

Lizard (*Lacerta vivipara*). (¼)

lizard fish. **a** Any of certain slender marine fishes constituting a family (Synodontidae) and having a scaly lizardlike head and large mouth. **b** The saury.

lla′ma (lä′mȧ), *n.;* see PLURAL, *Note,* 3. [Sp., fr. Quechua *llama.*] Any of several wild and domesticated South American ruminants allied to the camels, but smaller and without a hump; esp., the domesticated variety of the guanaco, used as a beast of burden in the Andes.

lla′no (lä′nō; *Sp.* [l]yä′nō), *n.; pl.* LLANOS (-nōz; *Sp.* -nōs). [Sp., plain, even, fr. L. *planus.*] *Sp. Amer.* An extensive plain.

Lloyd's (loidz), *n.* *Insurance.* **1.** A corporation of London, Eng., for conducting an insurance business, protecting the commercial and maritime interests of its members, and publishing shipping news. Marine insurance is the principal business. Lloyd's originated from the coffeehouse opened by Edward Lloyd, in 1688. **2.** A society in London, whose chief object is the establishment of a standard of construction for merchant vessels and yachts. It publishes annually **Lloyd's Register** of vessels, their age, build, tonnage, classification, etc.

lo (lō), *interj.* [ME. *lo,* fr. AS. *lā.*] Look! Behold!

loach (lōch), *n.; pl.* LOACHES (-ĕz; -ĭz). [F. *loche.*] Any of certain small Old World fresh-water carplike fishes (*Cobitis, Nemachilus,* and allied genera), constituting a family (Cobitidae).

load (lōd), *n.* [ME. *lode* load, way, prop. the same word as *lode,* but confused with *lade.*] **1.** That which is, or is to be, laid on or put in anything for conveyance; a burden; hence, a cargo; pack. **2.** A weight or quantity of anything resting upon something else regarded as its support. **3.** That which burdens or weighs down the mind or spirits. **4.** The charge of a firearm; as, a *load* of powder. **5.** *Colloq. pl.* A great deal; very much. **6.** The amount of work which an office or worker is expected to carry; as, a teaching *load* of twelve hours. **7.** *Elec.* The power delivered by a source of electric current. **8.** *Mech.* **a** Amount of pressure due to superimposed weight, whether stationary or moving. **b** External resistance overcome by a machine or prime mover. **9.** *Mech. & Elec. Engin.* The rate at which work is being done at any time by a plant or system; also, its output at any moment. — *v. t.* **1.** To lay a load or burden on or in; hence, to add weight to so as to oppress or embarrass. **2.** To place on or in something, as for carriage. **3.** To weigh down or oppress as does a burden. **4.** To supply abundantly; as, to *load* a man with honors. **5.** To increase in weight by addition of some heavy substance; as, to *load* sugar, sponges, etc.; *loaded* dice are weighted so as to influence their position on settling after a throw. **6.** To place a load or charge in (a firearm, etc.). **7.** To adulterate or drug; as, to *load* wine. **8.** *Insurance.* To add loading to (a premium). — *v. i.* **1.** To give or receive a load. **2.** To insert the charge or cartridge in a firearm.

load displacement. *Naut.* The displacement of a ship when loaded to the extent for which she was designed.

load′er (lōd′ẽr), *n.* One who or that which loads.

load factor. *Elec.* The ratio of average to maximum load, whether of production, use, or endurance.

load′ing, *n.* **a** *Aeronautics.* The wing loading. **b** *Insurance.* An amount added to the net premium to provide for business expenses, future contingencies, etc.

loading coil. *Elec.* A coil inserted in a circuit to increase its inductance.

load line. *Naut.* The line on a vessel indicating the depth to which she sinks in the water when properly loaded.

load′star′ (lōd′stär′). Var. of LODESTAR.

load′stone′, lode′stone′ (lōd′stōn′), *n.* [*load, lode* + *stone.*] Magnetite possessing polarity; hence, that which strongly attracts.

loaf (lōf), *n.; pl.* LOAVES (lōvz). [AS. *hlāf.*] **1. a** *Obs. exc. Dial.* Bread. **b** A regularly shaped or molded mass of bread; hence, a shaped mass of cake or sugar. **2.** *Cookery.* A dish, as of highly seasoned minced meat and vegetables, baked in the form of a loaf.

loaf, *v. i.* [Origin uncert.] To spend time in idleness.

loaf′er (lōf′ẽr), *n.* **1.** One who loafs; a lazy lounger. **2.** A man's or woman's low leather step-in shoe with upper resembling a moccasin but with broad flat heel and the outsole of a regular shoe.

loam (lōm; *Brit.* lōm *or* lo͞om; lo͞om *is common in the U. S., but not now in good usage*), *n.* [AS. *lām.*] **1.** *Archaic.* Any earth or soil. **2.** A soil consisting of a friable mixture of varying proportions of clay, sand, and organic matter. — *v. t.* To cover or fill with loam. — **loam′y** (-ĭ), *adj.*

loan (lōn), *n.* [ON. *lān.*] **1.** Act of lending; a lending; permission to use; as, the *loan* of a book. **2.** That lent or borrowed, esp. a sum of money lent at interest. **3.** Short for LOANWORD. — *v. t. & i.* To lend.

loan (lōn), **loan′in** (lōn′ĭn), *n.* *Scot.* A milking yard; also, a lane.

loan translation. A term indirectly borrowed by translation (*superman,* from German *Übermensch; normal school,* from French *école normale*).

loan′word′ (lōn′wûrd′), *n.* Also **loan word.** [After G. *lehnwort.*] A word taken from another language and at least partly naturalized.

loath, loth (lōth), *adj.* [AS. *lāth* hostile, odious.] **1.** *Obs.* Hateful; repulsive. **2.** Reluctant; averse. — **Syn.** See DISINCLINED.

loathe (lōth), *v. t.;* LOATHED (lōthd); LOATH′ING (lōth′ĭng). [AS. *lāthian* to be hateful.] To dislike greatly; now, esp., to have extreme disgust at; to abhor. — **Syn.** See HATE.

loath′ful (lōth′fo͝ol; -f'l), *adj.* Loathsome.

loath′ing (lōth′ĭng), *n.* Extreme disgust; detestation.

loath′ly (lōth′lĭ), *adj.* Loathsome. — (lōth′-; lōth′-), *adv.* Unwillingly.

loath′some (lōth′sŭm), *adj.* Fitted to cause loathing; disgusting; odious. — **loath′some·ly,** *adv.* — **loath′some·ness,** *n.*

loaves (lōvz), *n., pl.* of LOAF.

lob (lŏb), *n.* *Obs. exc. Dial.* A dull, heavy person.

lob, *v. t.;* LOBBED (lŏbd); LOB′BING. To throw, toss, or the like heavily or slowly; as: **a** *Cricket.* To bowl underhand. **b** *Lawn Tennis.* To return (a ball) in a high curve. — *v. i.* **1.** To go heavily or lumberingly. **2.** *Lawn Tennis.* To make a lob. — *n.* **a** *Cricket.* A slow underhand ball pitched well up in the air, usually with considerable spin. **b** *Tennis.* A ball returned in a high curve.

lo′bar (lō′bẽr), *adj.* Of or pertaining to a lobe or lobes; as, *lobar* pneumonia.

lo′bate (lō′bāt), *adj.* Also **lo′bat·ed** (-bāt·ĕd; -ĭd). [See LOBE.] Having lobes or rounded divisions. — **lo′bate·ly,** *adv.*

lo·ba′tion (lō·bā′shŭn), *n.* **a** State of being lobed; formation of lobes or lobules. **b** A lobe or lobule.

lob′ber (lŏb′ẽr), *n.* One who lobs.

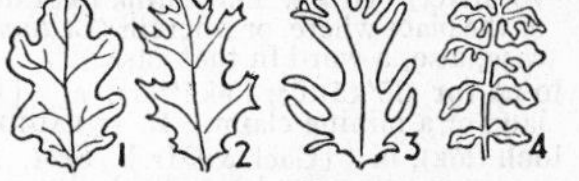

Lobation, *Bot.* 1 Lobed; 2 Cleft; 3 Parted; 4 Divided.

lob′by (lŏb′ĭ), *n.; pl.* -BIES (-ĭz). [ML. *lobium, lobia.* See LODGE.] **1.** A passage or hall, esp. when large enough to serve also as a waiting room, etc., as in the British House of Commons, and in the United States in capitols and large railroad stations. Hence, the foyer of a hotel. **2.** The persons, collectively, who frequent the lobbies of a legislative house to transact business with the legislators, esp. in the effort to influence proceedings by personal agency. — *v. i.;* -BIED (-ĭd); -BY·ING. *U. S.* To address or solicit members of a legislative body in the lobby or elsewhere, with intent to influence legislation. — *v. t.* To urge or procure passage of (a bill, etc.) by lobbying.

lob′by·ist (-ĭst), *n.* *U. S.* One who lobbies. — **lob′by·ism** (-ĭz′m), *n.*

lobe (lōb), *n.* [F. *lobe,* NL. *lobus,* fr. Gr. *lobos.*] **1.** A projection or division of a rounded form. **2.** *Anat.* A rounded projection of an organ or part, esp. one marked off by a fissure; as, the *lobes* of the brain, the lungs, etc. See EAR, *Illust.*

lobed (lōbd), *adj.* Having lobes; lobate; — specif. of leaves. See LOBATION, *Illust.* (1).

lo·be′li·a (lō·bē′lĭ·ȧ; -bēl′yȧ; 58), *n.* [NL., after Matthias de *Lobel* (1538–1616), Flemish botanist.] Any of a genus (*Lobelia,* family Lobeliaceae, the lobelia family) of herbaceous plants, of wide distribution. Many species are cultivated.

lob′lol′ly (lŏb′lŏl′ĭ), *n.; pl.* -LOLLIES (-ĭz). **1.** Thick gruel. **2.** Also **loblolly pine.** Any of several pines of the southern United States, esp. one (*Pinus taeda*) with thick, flaky bark, and spiny-tipped cones; also, the wood.

loblolly boy. A surgeon's attendant on shipboard.

lo′bo (lō′bō), *n.; pl.* LOBOS (-bōz). [Sp., fr. L. *lupus.*] *Western U. S.* The timber wolf. See WOLF, 1 **a.**

lo·bot′o·my (lō·bŏt′ō·mĭ), *n.* [*lobe* + *-tomy.*] Leucotomy.

lob′scouse′ (lŏb′skous′), *n.* Also **lob′scourse′** (-skōrs′; 70). *Naut.* A stew of meat, vegetables, ship biscuit, etc.

lob′ster (lŏb′stẽr), *n.;* see PLURAL, *Note,* 3. [AS. *loppestre, lopystre,* fr. L. *locusta* lobster, locust, perh. under the influence of AS. *loppe* a spider.] **1.** Any large marine macrural crustacean used as food. The common lobsters of Europe and North America, with stalked compound eyes, and five pairs of legs, of which the first pair is modified into enormous chelae, or pincers, are chiefly of the genus *Homarus,* sometimes regarded as type of a family (Homaridae). The ***spiny lobsters or sea crayfishes*** (constituting the family Palinuridae, type genus *Palinurus*) lack the large chelae. **2.** *Slang.* A gullible, awkward, bungling, or red-faced person.

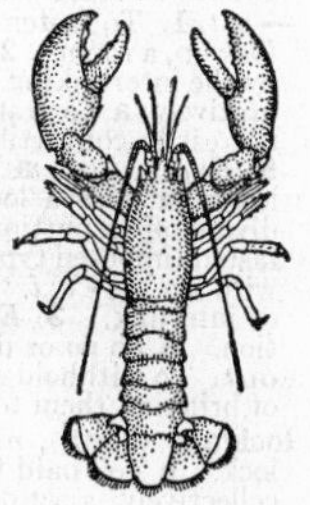

American Lobster (*H. americanus*). (1⁄10)

lobster pot. A trap for catching lobsters, commonly an oblong cage with slat sides and a funnel-shaped net, opening inward at each end.

lob′ster ther′mi·dor (thûr′mĭ·dôr). A mixture of lobster meat, mushrooms, and cream sauce, served in a lobster shell and browned.

lob′ule (lŏb′ūl), *n.* A small lobe; also, a subdivision of a lobe. See EAR, *Illust.* — **lob′u·lar** (-ū·lẽr), *adj.*

lob′worm′ (lŏb′wûrm′), *n.* A lugworm.

lo′ca (lō′kȧ), *n., pl.* of LOCUS.

lo′cal (lō′kăl), *adj.* [F., fr. LL. *localis,* fr. *locus* place.] **1.** Characterized by, or relating to, place, or position in space; as, a *local* body. **2.** Characterized by, relating to, or occupying a particular place or places; not general or widespread; as, *local* anesthesia; *local* celebrities. **3.** Hence, not broad or general; as, a *local* point of view. **4. a** Relating to, esp. confined to or dependent upon, a single transportation line, esp. a railroad; as, *local* traffic. **b** Of railway trains, accommodating a certain limited district; as, *local* service, rates; — opp. to *through.* **c** Of a public conveyance, making all the stops on its run; — opp. to *express.* — *n.* A local person or thing; as: **a** A local train, or other public conveyance. **b** A local branch, lodge, or chapter of a fraternal organization or the like, as a labor union or a college fraternity. **c** *Newspapers.* An item of news relating to the place where the paper is published. — **lo′cal·ly,** *adv.*

local color. *Literature.* Color derived from the presentation of the features and peculiarities of a particular locality and its inhabitants.

lo·cale′ (lō·kăl′; -käl′), *properly* **lo·cal′,** *n.* [F. *local.*] A locality, esp. with reference to some characteristic feature.

local government. *Polit. Sci.* Self-government in local affairs by a city or other limited area; also, the governing body or person of such a city or locality.

lo′cal·ism (lō′kăl·ĭz′m), *n.* State or quality of being local: **a** Concernment with local affairs; sectionalism; specif., tendency to place local interests above national. **b** A local idiom or peculiarity of speaking or acting.

lo·cal′i·ty (lō·kăl′ĭ·tĭ), *n.; pl.* -TIES (-tĭz). **1.** Fact or state of being local. **2.** Position; place; situation.

lo′cal·ize (lō′kăl·īz), *v. t.* [From LOCAL.] To make local; to fix in, or assign or confine to, a definite place or locality. — **lo′cal·i·za′tion** (-ĭ·zā′shŭn; -ī·zā′-), *n.*

local option. The right of determining by popular vote within certain districts, as in each county, city, or town, whether the sale of alcoholic beverages shall be allowed.

lo′cate (lō′kāt; lō·kāt′), *v. t.* [L. *locatus,* past part. of *locare* to place, fr. *locus* place.] **1.** *Chiefly U. S.* To designate the site of; as, to *locate* a public building, a mining claim. **2.** To set or establish in a particular spot. **3.** To search for and discover the position of; as, to *lo-*

cate an enemy. **4.** To assign a place to; as, to *locate* the reign of an Assyrian king. — *v. i. Colloq.* To take up one's residence; to settle.

lo·ca′tion (lō·kā′shŭn), *n.* **1.** Act or process of locating (in various senses). **2.** Situation; place; specif., locality of or for a residence, factory, store, etc. **3.** That which is located; esp., a tract of land designated in respect to place and purpose, as a mining claim (U. S.), a farm or station (Australia). **4.** *Civil Law.* A letting for hire; a contract for the use of a thing, or service of a person, for hire. **5.** *Motion Pictures.* A place outside of a studio where a picture or part of it is filmed; — chiefly in *on location.*

loc′a·tive (lŏk′ȧ·tĭv), *adj.* [From L. *locus* place, after L. *vocativus* vocative.] *Gram.* Pertaining to or designating a case denoting place, or the place where, or wherein (L. *domo,* at home). — *n.* The locative case; also, a word in that case.

lo′ca·tor (lō′kā·tẽr; lō·kā′tẽr), *n.* [L.] **1.** *U. S.* One who locates land or a mining claim. **2.** = RADIOLOCATOR.

loch (lŏĸ), *n.* [Gael. & OIr.] *Scot.* A lake; also, a bay or arm of the sea, esp. when nearly landlocked.

lo′chi·a (lō′kĭ·ȧ; lŏk′ĭ·ȧ), *n. pl., sometimes construed as sing.* [NL., fr. Gr. *lochia,* pl., fr. *lochios* of childbirth, fr. *lochos* a lying-in, childbirth.] *Med. & Veter.* The discharge from the uterus and vagina following delivery. — **lo′chi·al** (lō′kĭ·ăl), *adj.*

lo′ci (lō′sī), *n., pl.* of LOCUS.

lock (lŏk), *n.* [AS. *locc.*] **1.** A tuft, tress, or ringlet of hair; hence, *pl.,* the hair of the head. **2.** A naturally cohering bunch of wool, cotton, flax, or the like; a flock.

lock, *n.* [AS. *loc* enclosure, an enclosed place.] **1.** A fastening, as for a door, a trunk lid, a drawer, etc., operated by a key or a combination. **2.** An enclosure in a canal, river, dock, etc., with gates at each end, used in raising or lowering boats as they pass from level to level. **3.** A locking or fastening together; also, a state of being locked or fixed. **4.** *Engin.* A chamber with airtight doors connecting a compartment where the air is under pressure (as a ship's stokehole under forced draft) with places having normal air pressure. **5.** *Firearms.* The part or apparatus by which the charge is exploded; as, a match*lock.* **6.** *Vehicles.* A device to lock a wheel in descending a hill. **7.** *Wrestling.* Any of various holds; esp., one in which a limb of one contestant is twisted in some way around a limb of the other.

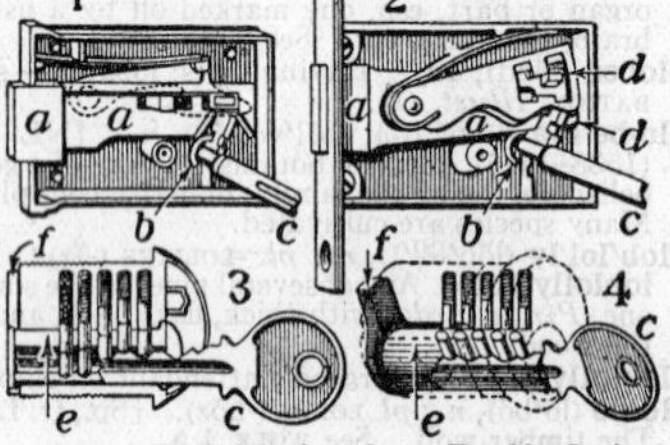

Locks. 1 Warded Lock; 2 Lever Tumbler Lock; 3 Cylinder Lock, with Key partly inserted, 4 with Key inserted and turned. *a* Bolt; *b* Ward; *c* Key; *d* Tumblers; *e* Revolving Plug; *f* Cam to operate Bolt.

— *v. t.* **1.** To fasten the lock or locks of; as, to *lock* a door; to *lock,* or *lock* up, a room. **2.** To confine, or to shut in or out. **3.** To make fast by the interlinking of parts; as, to *lock* arms; to *lock* wheels. **4.** Figuratively: **a** To grapple in combat. **b** To invest, as capital, where it is not easily convertible into money. **c** To hold inactive; to overcome. **5.** *Engin., etc.* **a** To move (a vessel) or permit it to pass, by raising or lowering it in a lock. **b** To provide with locks, as a canal. **c** To divide off (a portion of a river) by a lock; — with *off.* **6.** *Print.* To fasten (imposed type, etc.) securely in a chase by tightening the quoins; with *up.* — *v. i.* **1.** To become locked, as a door. **2.** To interlock or interlink. **3.** *Engin., etc.* **a** To build locks to facilitate navigation. **b** To go or pass by means of a lock, as of a canal, etc. — ***lock out.*** To withhold employment from (a body of employees) as a means of bringing them to accept the employers' terms.

lock′age (lŏk′ĭj), *n.* **a** Act or process of passing a vessel through a lock. **b** Toll paid for passing through a lock, as in a canal. **c** Locks collectively; a set or system of locks.

lock′er (-ẽr), *n.* **1.** One who or that which locks. **2.** A drawer, cupboard, compartment, or chest, that may be closed with a lock. **3.** A compartment for storing quick-frozen foods for long periods at constant subfreezing temperature and proper humidity. **4.** *Naut.* Any chest or compartment for stowing anything snugly; as, a chain *locker.*

lock′et (lŏk′ĕt; -ĭt), *n.* [F. *loquet* latch, dim. of OF. *loc* latch, lock.] A little case for a memento, as for a miniature, usually worn suspended as from a necklace.

lock′jaw′ (lŏk′jô′), *n. Med.* A variety of tetanus in which the jaws are locked rigidly together.

lock nut, *or* **lock′nut′** (lŏk′nŭt′), *n. Mech.* **a** A nut screwed down hard on another to prevent it from slacking back. See VALVE, *Illust.* **b** A nut so constructed that it locks itself when screwed up tight.

lock′out′ (lŏk′out′; 2), *n.* Act of locking out, specif. of locking out employees. See *lock out,* under LOCK, *v.*

lock′smith′ (lŏk′smĭth′), *n.* An artificer who makes or mends locks. — **lock′smith′er·y** (-ẽr·ĭ), **lock′smith′ing,** *n.*

lock step. A mode of marching in step by a body of men going one after another as closely as possible.

lock stitch. A stitch formed by the interlocking of two threads, as in the work done by some sewing machines.

lock′up′ (lŏk′ŭp′), *n.* **1.** A locking up or being locked up. **2.** A jail.

lo′co (lō′kō), *n.* [Sp. *loco* insane.] **a** = LOCOWEED. **b** = LOCO DISEASE. — *v. t.* To poison with locoweed; hence, *Colloq.,* to render insane or mad. — *adj.* [Sp.] *Slang.* Crazy; out of one's mind.

‖**lo′co ci·ta′to** (lō′kō sĭ·tā′tō). [L.] In the place cited; in the passage quoted. Abbr. *loc. cit.*

loco disease. [Sp. *loco* insane.] A chronic nervous affection of cattle, horses, and sheep, caused by eating locoweed.

lo′co·fo′co (lō′kō·fō′kō), *n.* **1.** *Obs. U. S.* A friction match. **2.** [*cap.*] *U. S. Hist.* A member of the antimonopolist wing of New York City Democrats (1835); — later applied for a time by the Whigs to any Democrat.

lo′co·mo′tion (lō′kō·mō′shŭn), *n.* [L. *locus* place + *motio* motion.] Act or power of moving from place to place; progressive movement; hence, travel.

lo′co·mo′tive (-mō′tĭv), *adj.* [See LOCOMOTION.] **1.** Of or pertaining to locomotion, or travel. **2.** Able to move from place to place. **3.** Of, pertaining to, or designating a machine, esp. an engine, that moves about by operation of its own mechanism. — *n.* A self-propelled engine or vehicle; specif., a steam engine or electric motor used for hauling cars, wagons, etc., on a railroad.

lo′co·mo′tor (-mō′tẽr), *adj.* Of or pertaining to movement or locomotion.

locomotor ataxia. *Med.* A disorder of the nervous system caused by syphilis, attended with peculiar disturbances of gait, difficulty in coordinating voluntary movements, etc.

lo′co·weed′ (lō′kō·wēd′), *n., or* **loco weed.** Any of a number of herbs (as *Astragalus mollissimus, A. bigelovii, Oxytropis macounii,* and *O. splendens*) of the western U. S., which poison cattle, sheep, and horses (see LOCO DISEASE); — called also *crazyweed.*

loc′u·lar (lŏk′ū·lẽr), *adj.* [See LOCULUS.] *Bot. & Zool.* Having or composed of cells or loculi; as, bi*locular.*

loc′u·late (-lāt), *adj.* [L. *loculatus.*] *Bot.* Having loculi.

loc′u·lat′ed (-lāt′ĕd; -ĭd), *adj. Bot.* Loculate.

loc′u·li·cid′al (lŏk′ū·lĭ·sīd′ăl; -′l; 2), *adj.* [L. *loculus* cell + *caedere* to cut.] *Bot.* Dehiscent along the dorsal suture of a carpel or loculus; — of capsular fruits. Cf. SEPTICIDAL.

loc′u·lus (lŏk′ū·lŭs), *n.; pl.* LOCULI (-lī). [L., little place, a compartment, dim. of *locus* place.] A small chamber or cavity; specif.: *Bot.* **a** One of the cells of a compound ovary. **b** The cavity of a pollen sac.

lo′cum (lō′kŭm), *n. Colloq.* A locum tenens.

lo′cum te′nens (tē′nĕnz). [L., holding the place, fr. *locus* place + *tenens,* pres. part. of *tenere* to hold. See LIEUTENANT.] A substitute; one temporarily taking the place of another, as esp. of a doctor or clergyman.

lo′cus (lō′kŭs), *n.; pl.* LOCI (-sī), LOCA (-kȧ). [L., place.] **1.** A place; locality. **2.** Short for LOCUS CLASSICUS. **3.** *Math.* The path of a point or curve moving according to some law; the assemblage of all possible positions of the moving or generating element.

‖**lo′cus clas′si·cus** (klăs′ĭ·kŭs); *pl.* LOCI CLASSICI (lō′sī klăs′ĭ·sī). [L.] A classical passage; a standard passage important for the elucidation of a word or subject.

‖**lo′cus si·gil′li** (sĭ·jĭl′ī). [L.] The place of the seal. Abbr. *L. S.*

lo′cust (lō′kŭst), *n.* [OF. or L.; OF. *locuste,* fr. L. *locusta* locust, grasshopper.] **1.** Any grasshopper of the family Acridiidae, esp. any of certain migratory species destructive to vegetation, as the ***migratory locust*** of Europe and Asia (*Pachytylus migratorius*), a South African species (*P. pardalina*), and the Rocky Mountain grasshopper of North America (*Melanoplus spretus*). See GRASSHOPPER. **2.** = CICADA. **3.** [The name of the insect was first applied to the carob bean.] Any of several trees: **a** In U. S. also called *acacia.* A North American tree (*Robinia pseudoacacia*) of the pea family, with pinnate leaves and drooping racemes of fragrant white flowers; also, its hard, durable wood. **b** The honey locust. **c** The carob tree.

lo·cus′ta (lō·kŭs′tȧ), *n.* [NL. See LOCUST.] *Bot.* A spikelet. See SPIKELET, *Illust.*

lo·cu′tion (lō·kū′shŭn), *n.* [L. *locutio,* fr. *loqui* to speak.] **1.** Style of discourse; phraseology. **2.** A particular form of expression; as, odd or figurative *locutions.*

lode (lōd), *n.* [AS. *lād* way, journey.] **1.** *Dial. Eng.* A waterway. **2.** *Mining.* **a** Strictly, a mineral deposit that fills a fissure in the native rock. **b** Any ore deposit occurring in its natural or original position within definite boundaries, separating it from adjoining rocks.

lode′star′, load′star′ (lōd′stär′), *n.* [*lode, load* + *star.* See LODE.] A star that leads; esp., the polestar.

lode′stone′ (lōd′stōn′). Var. of LOADSTONE.

lodge (lŏj), *n.* [OF. *loge,* fr. ML. *laubia, lobia,* porch, gallery, fr. OHG. *louba,* fr. *loub* foliage.] **1.** *Archaic & Dial.* A hut; hovel. **2.** **a** A house set apart for residence in the hunting or other special season. **b** A house on an estate, occupied by a gamekeeper, caretaker, porter, or the like. **c** At Cambridge, Eng., the residence of the head of a college. **3.** In Masonic and other orders or societies, esp. secret societies, the hall or meeting place of a local branch or the members composing such a branch. **4.** The den or lair of a wild animal or gregarious group of animals, esp. one requiring constructive work; as, a beaver's *lodge.* **5.** A cabin, hut, or tent of the North American Indians; a wigwam, tepee, or the like (cf. TEPEE, WICKIUP, WIGWAM); hence, the regular occupants of such a lodge; a family of Indians.
— *v. t.;* LODGED (lŏjd); LODG′ING (lŏj′ĭng). **1.** To provide quarters for, esp. temporarily; also, to serve as a shelter for. **2.** Hence, to receive as a guest or denizen; specif., to take as a paying guest. **3.** To establish or settle (oneself) in a place. **4.** To bring to a certain position, as by casting, discharging, thrusting; as, to *lodge* a sword in one. **5.** To throw or beat down, as growing grain; as, oats *lodged* by the rain. **6.** To place or vest as in an agent; as, to *lodge* powers in a commission. **7.** To place or deposit; as, to *lodge* records in a place of deposit. **8.** To lay or deposit, as a complaint, before a proper authority; as, to *lodge* information against a swindler. — *v. i.* **1.** To occupy a place temporarily; to have lodging; as, to *lodge* at a hotel. **2.** To reside as a paying guest, or lodger. **3.** To stop and remain; as, the bullet *lodged* in the bark of a tree.

lodg′er (lŏj′ẽr), *n.* One who or that which lodges; specif., one who occupies a hired room in another's house; a roomer.

lodg′ing (-ĭng), *n.* **1.** Dwelling; abode; esp., temporary abode; sleeping place; quarters. **2.** *pl.* A room or rooms in the house of another, as a place of residence.

lodg′ing·house′ (-hous′), *n.* A house where lodgings are provided and let.

lodg′ment, lodge′ment (lŏj′mĕnt), *n.* **1.** A lodging place; lodgings. **2.** Act, fact, or manner of lodging; esp., a placing, depositing, or coming to rest; as, the *lodgment* of a balloon in a tree. **3.** An accumulation of something deposited in a place or remaining at rest. **4.** *Mil.* The occupation and holding of a position in hostile or disputed territory; as, to effect a *lodgment.*

lod′i·cule (lŏd′ĭ·kūl), *n.* [L. *lodicula,* dim. of *lodix, lodicis,* a coverlet.] *Bot.* In the flowers of grasses, one of the two delicate membranous scales borne on the torus outside of the stamens, possibly representing a perianth or merely a bractlet.

loe, loo (lōō). Scot. var. of LOVE.

lo′ess (lō′ĕs; lûs), *n.* [G. *löss,* dial. fr. *lösen* to pour, dissolve.] *Geol.* An unstratified deposit of yellowish-brown loam covering areas in North America, Europe, and Asia, now generally thought to be chiefly an aeolian deposit.

loft (lŏft; 74), *n.* [ME., air, height, loft, fr. AS. *loft,* fr. ON. *lopt* air, heaven, loft.] **1.** An upper room or story; esp., an attic. **2.** Hence:

a A hayloft. **b** *U.S.* One of the upper floors of a warehouse or business building, especially when without partitions. **c** A gallery in a church, hall, etc.; as, the organ *loft*. **3.** *Golf.* **a** Backward slant of the face of a club. **b** Act of lofting, or a lofting stroke. — *v. t.* **1.** To make or furnish with a loft. **2.** To place or store in a loft; as, to *loft* pigeons. **3.** *Golf.* **a** To strike (the ball) so that it rises well. **b** To lay back the face of (a club). — *v. i. Golf.* To loft the ball.

loft'er (lŏf'tẽr), *n.* Also **loft'ing i'ron.** *Golf.* An iron club with the face laid back for use in lofting the ball.

loft'y (lŏf'tĭ), *adj.*; LOFT'I·ER (-tĭ·ẽr); -I·EST. [From LOFT.] **1.** Extending or rising high; esp., having imposing height; towering. **2.** Haughty; arrogant. **3.** Elevated in character, rank, spirit, language, etc.; exalted. — **Syn.** See HIGH. — **loft'i·ly,** *adv.* — **loft'i·ness,** *n.*

log (lŏg; 74), *n.* [ME. *logge*, prob. of Scand. origin.] **1.** A bulky piece or length of the trunk of a tree or of unshaped timber. **2.** Figuratively, something inert, heavy, or stupid. **3.** [Orig. an ordinary piece of wood.] An apparatus for measuring the rate of a ship's motion through the water, consisting of a block (**log chip**) fastened to a line (**log line**) and run out from a reel (**log reel**). **4.** Hence: **a** The record of the rate of a ship's speed or of her daily progress; also, the full nautical record of a ship's voyage. **b** The full record of a flight by an aircraft. **5.** Hence, any record of performance; specif.: **a** The record of an engine, boiler, or other test. **b** A record of the progress in drilling a well. — *adj.* Made from a log or built of logs; as, a *log* cabin. — *v. t.*; LOGGED (lŏgd); LOG'GING. **1.** To fell and lop (a tree); to cut (timber) into logs. **2.** To enter in a logbook; as, to *log* the miles run; also, to sail or move (a specified distance) as shown by the ship's log. — *v. i.* To engage in the business of cutting or transporting logs for timber.

lo'gan·ber'ry (lō'găn·bĕr'ĭ), *n.*; *pl.* LOGANBERRIES (-ĭz). [After Judge J. H. *Logan*, who found it in 1881.] A red-fruited upright-growing dewberry, variously regarded as a variety of the western dewberry (*Rubus ursinus*), or as a hybrid (*R. loganobaccus*) between it and the red raspberry (*R. idaeus*); also, the berry on this plant.

lo·ga'ni·a'ceous (lō·gā'nĭ·ā'shŭs), *adj.* [After James *Logan*, Ir. botanist.] *Bot.* Belonging to a family (Loganiaceae; order Gentianales) of herbs, shrubs, and trees distinguished from the gentian family by the presence of stipules. See BUDDLEIA, GELSEMIUM, STRYCHNOS.

log'a·oe'dic (lŏg'ȧ·ē'dĭk), *adj.* [Gr. *logaoidikos*, lit., prose-poetic (from the mixed rhythm), fr. *logos*, discourse, prose + *aoidē* song.] *Gr. & Lat. Pros.* Composed of dactyls and trochees, or of anapaests and iambi, combined in the same cola, or metrical series. — *n.* A logaoedic verse.

log'a·rithm (lŏg'ȧ·rĭth'm; -rĭth'm; 74), *n.* [NL. *logarithmus*, fr. Gr. *logos* word, proportion + *arithmos* number.] *Math.* The exponent of that power of a fixed number (called the *base*) which equals a given number (called the *antilogarithm*). Abbr. *log* (no period). Logarithms to the base 10 are called ***common, or Briggsian,*** and are universally used in computation.

log'a·rith'mic (-rĭth'mĭk; -rĭth'mĭk), *adj.* Also **log'a·rith'mi·cal** (-mĭ·kăl). *Math.* Of or connected with the logarithm. — **log'a·rith'mi·cal·ly,** *adv.*

log'book' (lŏg'bo͝ok'), *n.* A book in which is entered the daily progress of a ship at sea, as indicated by the log, with notes on the weather and incidents of the voyage.

log chip. *Naut.* See LOG, *n.*, 3.

loge (lōzh), *n.* [F. See LODGE.] A booth or stall; specif., a box or stall, as in a theater or opera house.

log'ger (lŏg'ẽr; 74), *n.* *Lumbering.* **a** One engaged in logging. **b** A machine for hauling and loading logs.

log'ger, *adj.* [Cf. LOGGERHEAD.] *Scot.* Heavy; stupid.

log'ger·head' (-hĕd'), *n.* [Dial. *logger* a log or block of wood + *head*.] **1.** A blockhead; numskull. **2.** A long-handled iron tool terminating in a ball or bulb used, when heated, to melt tar, to heat liquids, as flip, etc. **3.** In a whaleboat, an upright piece of round timber around which a turn of the line is taken when it is running out too fast. **4.** Also **loggerhead turtle.** See TURTLE, 1. **5.** Also **loggerhead shrike.** See SHRIKE. — ***to be at loggerheads.*** To quarrel.

log'gia (lŏj'ȧ; lô'jĭ·ȧ; *It.* lôd'jä), *n.*; *pl.* LOGGIAS (lŏj'ȧz; lô'jĭ·ȧz), LOGGIE (lôd'jā). [It., fr. OF. *loge*. See LODGE.] *Arch.* A roofed open gallery. It differs from a *veranda* or a *porch* in being more architectural and in forming more decidedly a part of the main edifice.

log'ging (lŏg'ĭng; 74), *n.* The business of felling trees, cutting them into logs, and transporting the logs to sawmills or to market.

log'i·a (lŏg'ĭ·ȧ), *n.*, *pl.* of LOGION (-ŏn). [Gr. pl., sayings, fr. *logos* word.] Sayings of a religious teacher; specif. [*often cap.*], sayings of Jesus; — applied esp. to early collections supposed to have been used by the evangelists, and to Agrapha.

log'ic (lŏj'ĭk), *n.* [OF. *logique*, fr. L. *logica*, fr. Gr. *logikē* (sc. *technē*), fr. *logikos* belonging to speaking or reason, fr. *logos* word, speech, reason, fr. *legein* to say.] **1.** The science that deals with the canons and criteria of validity in thought and demonstration; the science of the formal principles of reasoning. **2.** A treatise on this science; also, the methodology or formal principles of any branch of knowledge; as, the *logic* of art. **3.** Reasoning; esp., sound reasoning; also, ironically, whatever convinces or makes argument useless; as, artillery has been called the *logic* of kings. **4.** Connection, as of facts or events, in a rational way; as, by the *logic* of events, anarchy leads to tyranny.

log'i·cal (-ĭ·kăl), *adj.* **1.** Of or pertaining to logic; used in logic. **2.** According to the rules of logic; as, *logical* reasoning. **3.** Skilled in logic; as, he is a *logical* thinker. **4.** In accordance with the inferences reasonably to be drawn from events or circumstances; as, a *logical* candidate; the *logical* result. — **log'i·cal·ly,** *adv.*

log'i·cal'i·ty (lŏj'ĭ·kăl'ĭ·tĭ), *n.* Logical character.

lo·gi'cian (lō·jĭsh'ăn), *n.* One skilled in logic.

log'i·on (lŏg'ĭ·ŏn), *n.*, *sing.* of LOGIA.

lo·gis'tics (lō·jĭs'tĭks), *n.*; see -ICS. [F. *logistique*, fr. *logis* quarters, lodging, fr. *loger* to quarter.] *Mil.* That branch of the military art which embraces the details of the transport, quartering, and supply of troops. — **lo·gis'tic** (-tĭk), *adj.* — **lo·gis'ti·cal** (-tĭ·kăl), *adj.*

log line. *Naut.* See LOG, *n.*, 3.

log'o- (lŏg'ō-), **log-.** [Gr. *logos*.] A combining form meaning *word, thought, speech, discourse.*

log'o·gram (-grăm), *n.* [*logo-* + *-gram*.] A word letter; a phonogram representing a word. — **log'o·gram·mat'ic** (-grȧ·măt'ĭk), *adj.*

log'o·graph (-grăf; 9), *n.* A logogram.

lo·gog'ra·phy (lō·gŏg'rȧ·fĭ), *n.* [Gr. *logographia* a writing of speeches, fr. *logos* word, speech + *graphein* to write.] **1.** Use of logotypes in printing. **2.** A mode of reporting speeches in longhand, a number of reporters taking three or four words each in succession. — **log'o·graph'ic** (lŏg'ō·grăf'ĭk), **log'o·graph'i·cal** (-ĭ·kăl), *adj.*

log'o·griph (lŏg'ō·grĭf), *n.* [*logo-* + Gr. *griphos* a fishing net, a dark saying, a riddle.] **a** A sort of riddle in which it is required to discover a chosen word from various combinations of its letters; — thus, to discover the chosen word *chatter* from *cat, rat, hate, rate,* etc. **b** An anagram.

lo·gom'a·chy (lō·gŏm'ȧ·kĭ), *n.*; *pl.* -CHIES (-kĭz). [Gr. *logomachia*, fr. *logos* word + *machē* fight, contest.] **1.** Contention in or about words; a war of words. **2.** A game of wordmaking. — **lo·gom'a·chist** (-kĭst), *n.*

log'or·rhe'a (lŏg'ō·rē'ȧ), *n.* [NL., fr. *logo-* + *-rrhea*.] Excessive and often incoherent talkativeness.

log'os (lŏg'ŏs), *n.* [Gr., the word or form which expresses a thought, also, the thought.] **1.** *Philos.* [*often cap.*] The rational principle in the universe. **2.** [*cap.*] *Theol.* The Word (that is, the actively expressed, creative, and revelatory thought and will) of God, at once distinguished from and identified with him; — identified with Jesus Christ in the prologue to the Fourth Gospel (*John* i. 1–18).

log'o·type (lŏg'ō·tīp), *n.* [*logo-* + *-type*.] *Print.* A single type body containing two or more letters often associated, as *the, and;* — distinguished from *ligature* (which see). — **log'o·typ'y** (-tīp'ĭ), *n.*

log reel. See LOG, *n.*, 3.

log'roll'ing (lŏg'rōl'ĭng), *n.* *Chiefly U.S.* **1.** The rolling of logs in water by treading; also, a sport in which men treading logs try to dislodge one another. **2.** A combining to assist another in consideration of assistance in return, esp. among politicians for political ends. — **log'roll',** *v. t. & i.* — **log'roll'er,** *n.*

log ship. Var. of LOG CHIP. See LOG, *n.*, 3.

-logue (-lŏg; 74). [F., fr. L. *-logus*, fr. Gr. *-logos*. See -LOGY.] A combining form denoting *a* (specified) *type of discourse* or *discourser*, as in dia*logue*, trave*logue*.

log'way' (lŏg'wā'; 74), *n.* *Logging.* = GANGWAY, 2 **d.**

log'wood' (-wo͝od'), *n.* [So called from being imported in *logs*.] **a** The very hard brownish heartwood of a Central American and West Indian medium-sized tree (*Haematoxylon campechianum*) of the senna family. It is used in dyeing. **b** The tree itself.

lo'gy (lō'gĭ), *adj.*; LO'GI·ER (-gĭ·ẽr); LO'GI·EST. *U.S.* Heavy or dull, esp. in motion or thought.

-logy. [F. or L. or Gr.; F. *-logie*, fr. (Gr. or) L. *-logia*, fr. Gr. *-logia*, fr. *logos* word, discourse, *legein* to speak.] A combining form denoting: **a** A *speaking*, or *saying*, as in eu*logy*. **b** A *doctrine, theory,* or *science*, as in bio*logy*.

Lo'hen·grin (lō'ĕn·grĭn), *n.* [G.] The title and hero of a medieval German romance, and of a music drama (1850) by Richard Wagner.

loin (loin), *n.* [OF. *loigne*, deriv. of L. *lumbus* loin.] **1.** That part of a human being or quadruped on either side of the spinal column between the hip bone and the false ribs (see DOG, *Illust.*); — chiefly in *pl.* and often, in Biblical and poetic diction, denoting: **a** That part of the body to be clothed or girded. **b** The seat of generation or procreation. **2.** The front part of a hindquarter of beef, mutton, lamb, pork, or veal, with the flank removed. See BEEF, LAMB, PORK, *Illusts.*

loin'cloth' (-klŏth'; 74), *n.* A primitive garment consisting of a cloth worn about the loins.

loi'ter (loi'tẽr), *v. i.* [MD. *loteren* to shake, be loose (D. *leuteren* to loiter).] To be slow in moving; lag behind. — **Syn.** See DELAY. — **loi'ter·er,** *n.*

Lo'ki (lō'kē), *n.* [ON.] *Norse Myth.* A god, contriver of discord and mischief, sometimes classed with the Aesir, sometimes with the Jotunns.

loll (lŏl), *v. i.* [ME. *lollen, lullen*, of imitative origin.] **1.** To hang laxly; to droop; dangle. **2.** Of an animal, to let the tongue hang out, as when heated by labor. **3.** To move or recline in a lax, lazy, or indolent manner. — *v. t.* To let droop or dangle. — *n.* Act of lolling. — **loll'er,** *n.*

Lol'lard (lŏl'ẽrd), *n.* [MD. *lollaerd*, lit., a mumbler (of prayers or psalms), fr. *lollen* to mutter, doze.] One of the followers of Wycliffe in the 14th and 15th centuries.

lol'li·pop (lŏl'ĭ·pŏp), *n.* A variety of candy, often in the form of a lump on the end of a stick.

lol'lop (lŏl'ŭp), *v. i.* [From LOLL.] **1.** *Colloq. & Dial.* To loll; lounge. **2.** To go with bounds or leaps; also, to bound or bob up.

Lom'bard (lŏm'bärd; -bẽrd; lŭm'-), *n.* [F., fr. It. *Lombardo*.] **1.** One of a Teutonic tribe which invaded Italy in 568 and settled in the valley of the Po; hence, a person descended from the Teutonic Lombards, or a native of the part of Italy which derived its name from them. **2.** [*also not cap.*] A moneylender or banker; — from the famous bankers or moneylenders of Lombardy. — **Lom·bar'dic** (lŏm·bär'dĭk), *adj.*

Lombard Street. The principal street in London for banks and note brokers; the money market of London. Cf. WALL STREET.

Lom'bard·y pop'lar (lŏm'bẽr·dĭ; lŭm'-; -bär'dĭ). See POPLAR, 1 **a.**

lo'ment (lō'mĕnt), *n.* [L. *lomentum* bean meal, used as a cosmetic wash, fr. *lavare, lotum*, to wash.] *Bot.* An indehiscent legume which breaks at maturity into one-seeded joints. It is the characteristic fruit of the tick trefoils (genus *Desmodium*) and related plants of the pea family. — **lo'men·ta'ceous** (lō'mĕn·tā'shŭs), *adj.*

lo·men'tum (lō·mĕn'tŭm), *n.* [L.] *Bot.* A loment.

lone (lōn), *adj.* [From ALONE.] **1.** Without company; solitary; hence, lonesome. **2.** *Humorous.* Single; unmarried or widowed. **3.** Situated apart from other things of the kind; also, unfrequented; hence, lonely. — **Syn.** See ALONE.

lone'ly (lōn'lĭ), *adj.*; -LI·ER (-lĭ·ẽr); -LI·EST. **1.** Without company; lone; as, a *lonely* traveler. **2.** Sequestered from company; solitary. **3.** Not frequented by human beings; as, a *lonely* wood. **4.** Depressed at being alone; lonesome. **5.** Giving a feeling of loneliness; desolate; as, a *lonely* sky. — **Syn.** See ALONE. — **lone'li·ly,** *adv.* — **lone'li·ness,** *n.*

lone'some (-sŭm), *adj.* **1.** Secluded from society; solitary. **2.** Conscious of, and depressed by, solitude. — **Syn.** See ALONE. — **lone'some·ly,** *adv.* — **lone'some·ness,** *n.*

Lone'-Star' State. Texas; — a nickname alluding to the single star on its coat of arms.

long (lŏng; 74), *adj.*; LONG'ER (lŏng'gẽr); LONG'EST (lŏng'gĕst; -gĭst). [AS. *long, lang*.] **1.** Of considerable extent from end to end; as, a *long* road; *long* hair; specif.: **a** With reference to shape: Forming the chief linear dimensions; as, the *long* side of anything; hence, notably

greater in this dimension than in any other; as, a *long* boat. **b** Of great or unusual extent from base to top; tall; as, a *long* person. **2. a** Of time: Having great duration; not brief. **b** Hence, tiresomely long; tedious. **c** Of a series: Containing many items, counts, or members; as, a *long* list. **3.** Extended to a (specified) measure of length, in space or time or in any series; as, a mile *long;* a drama five acts *long.* **4.** Designating a measure of a greater length or quantity than the standard; as, a *long* mile. **5.** Extending or directed to what is distant in space, time, or accessibility; as, *long* sight (farsightedness); hence, involving more than ordinary liability to error; as, a *long* guess. **6.** Having a high percentage of some specific ingredient; as, *long* in oil. **7.** *Finance & Com.* Having a supply of stocks or goods; prepared for, or believing in, advance in prices; as, *long* of cotton. Hence: ***to be,*** or ***go, long of the market, to be on the long side of the market,*** to hold products or securities for a rise in price. **8. a** *Phonet.* Of relatively great duration; — said esp. of a vowel or consonant sound as compared with one called *short.* **b** *Pros.* Of a syllable or vowel, of relatively extended duration. **9.** *Gambling.* Of unusual degree of difference in related amounts; as, to give *long* odds of 30 to 1; also, of or pertaining to the greater amount in betting odds.
— *n.* **1.** *Com.* One who purchases or is on the long side of the market. **2.** *Phonet. & Pros.* A long sound or syllable. — ***the long and*** (***the***) ***short.*** The sum and substance.
— *adv.* [AS. *lange.*] **1.** For or during a long time. **2.** At a point of duration far distant. **3.** In the comparative: After or beyond the indicated time; as, to stay *longer;* to hold out *longer.* — ***as,*** *or* ***so, long as.*** On condition that; since; as, *so long as* you desire it, we will do it. — ***so long.*** *Slang.* Good-by.

long (lŏng; 74), *adv.* *Archaic & Dial.* Aphetic form of ALONG.

long (lŏng; 74), *v. i.;* LONGED (lŏngd); LONG'ING (lŏng'ĭng). [AS. *langian* to grow long, to long.] To feel a strong desire or craving; to yearn.
Syn. **Long, yearn, hanker, pine, hunger, thirst** mean to have an urgent desire for something. **Long** implies a wishing with one's whole heart and, often, a striving to attain; **yearn,** an eager, restless, often passionate, longing; **hanker,** an uneasy desire because of an unsatisfied appetite or passion; **pine,** a languishing or a fruitless longing; **hunger** and **thirst,** a compelling, insistent craving for something good or bad.

long, *v. i.* [AS. *gelang* belonging, dependent, consequent.] **1.** *Archaic.* To be suitable or meet. **2.** *Obs. exc. Dial.* To belong as property.

lon'ga·nim'i·ty (lŏng'gȧ·nĭm'ĭ·tĭ), *n.* [LL. *longanimitas,* fr. *longus* long + *animus* mind.] Disposition to bear injuries patiently; forbearance.

long'boat' (lŏng'bōt'), *n.* *Naut.* The largest boat carried by a merchant sailing vessel.

long'bow' (-bō'), *n.* A wooden bow drawn by hand, usually 5½ to 6 feet long. — ***to draw*** (***pull, use,*** etc.) ***the longbow.*** To tell large stories; to exaggerate.

long'-dis'tance (*see Pron.,* § 2), *adj.* Being a long distance away; also, covering a long distance; specif., *Telephony,* of, pertaining to, or designating communication with points connected with a distant exchange, esp. one in another city. — *n.* The operator or exchange that gives long-distance connections.

long dozen. One more than a dozen; thirteen.

longe (lŭnj), *n.* [F.] *Manège.* **a** A long rope used to lead or guide a horse in training. **b** The use of such a rope. — *v. t.;* LONGED (lŭnjd); LONGE'ING. To guide or exercise (a horse) by means of a longe.

‖**lon·ge·ron'** (lôNzh'rôN'), *n.* [F.] *Aeronautics.* A fore-and-aft framing member of an airplane fuselage.

lon·gev'i·ty (lŏn·jĕv'ĭ·tĭ), *n.* Length of life.

lon·ge'vous (-jē'vŭs), *adj.* [L. *longaevus.*] Long-lived.

long green. *Slang, U. S.* Paper money, esp. greenbacks.

long'hand' (lŏng'hănd'; 74), *n.* The characters used in ordinary writing; handwriting. Cf. SHORTHAND.

long'head' (lŏng'hĕd'), *n.* **1. a** A head with a low cephalic index. **b** A dolichocephalic person. **2.** Written **long head.** *Colloq.* Foresight; sagacity. — **long'head'ed** (-hĕd'ĕd; -ĭd; 2), *adj.* — **long'head'ed·ly,** *adv.* — **long'head'ed·ness,** *n.*

long'horn' (-hôrn'), *n.* A long-horned animal; specif., any of certain practically extinct long-horned cattle of Spanish derivation, often called ***Texas longhorns,*** formerly common in the southwestern U. S.

long house. The communal dwelling of the Iroquois.

long hundredweight. The British hundredweight of 112 lb. av. (50.8 kg.).

lon'gi- (lŏn'jĭ-). [L. *longus.*] A combining form meaning *long,* as in **lon'gi·cau'dal,** having a long tail.

lon'gi·corn (-kôrn), *adj.* [*longi-* + L. *cornu* horn.] *Zool.* Having long antennae. — *n.* A longicorn beetle.

long'ing (lŏng'ĭng; 74), *n.* An eager desire; craving.

long'ing·ly (-lĭ), *adv.* In a manner showing eager desire.

long'ish (lŏng'ĭsh), *adj.* Somewhat long; moderately long.

lon'gi·tude (lŏn'jĭ·tūd), *n.* [OF. or L.; OF., fr. L. *longitudo,* fr. *longus* long.] **1.** *Jocular.* Length. **2.** *Astron. & Geod.* Angular distance measured on a great circle of reference from the intersection of the adopted zero meridian with this reference circle to the similar intersection of the meridian passing through the object. **3.** *Geog.* The arc or portion of the equator intersected between the meridian of a given place and the prime meridian, as from Greenwich, England. The longitude of a place is expressed either in degrees (**longitude in arc**) or in time (**longitude in time**); as, the *longitude* of New York is 74° or 4 h. 56 min. west of Greenwich. Cf. LATITUDE; see MEASURE, *Table* 8.

lon'gi·tu'di·nal (-tū'dĭ·năl; -n'l), *adj.* **1.** Of or pertaining to length. **2.** Extending in length; placed or running lengthwise, as distinguished from *transverse.* **3.** Pertaining to the lengthwise dimension. — **lon'gi·tu'di·nal·ly,** *adv.*

long jump. *Athletics.* = BROAD JUMP.

long'leaf', long'-leaf' (lŏng'lēf'), *n.* Also **longleaf pine, longleaf yellow pine, long'-leaved' pine.** The Georgia pine (see PINE).

long'-lived' (-līvd'; *Brit. also* -lĭvd'; 2), *adj.* Having a long life; as, a *long-lived* tree. — **long'-lived'ness,** *n.*

long measure. = LINEAR MEASURE.

long moss. An epiphytic plant (*Tillandsia usneoides*) of the pineapple family, with threadlike stems, forming pendent tufts on trees in the southern U. S. and the West Indies.

Lon'go·bar'di (lŏng'gō·bär'dī), *n. pl.* [LL.] Lombards.

long pig. The human victim of a cannibal feast; — from the terms employed by Maori and Polynesian cannibals.

long'-play'ing (2), *adj.* Having a playing time commonly between twelve and thirty minutes, when played on a record player at 33⅓ revolutions per minute.

long run. The whole course of things; — in the phrase ***in*** (*or* ***at***) ***the long run,*** in the course of time; finally.

long'shore'man (lŏng'shōr'măn), *n.* [Abbr. fr. *alongshoreman.*] *U. S.* A laborer, as a stevedore or loader, who works about the wharves of a seaport.

long'-sight'ed (-sīt'ĕd; -ĭd; 2), *adj.* Able to see objects at a distance; hence, having foresight; sagacious; farsighted.

long'some (lŏng'sŭm), *adj.* [AS. *langsum.*] *Archaic & Dial.* Extended in length; hence, tediously long.

long'spur' (-spûr'), *n.* [From the length of the hind claw.] Any of several long-clawed fringilline birds (chiefly of the genus *Calcarius*) inhabiting the arctic regions and the Great Plains of North America.

long'-suf'fer·ance, *n.* *Archaic.* Long-suffering.

long'-suf'fer·ing, *n.* Long and patient endurance of offense. — **long'-suf'fer·ing** (*see Pron.,* § 2), *adj.*

long'-term' bond *or* **note.** *Finance.* An obligation, esp. of a government, that runs for at least two years.

Long Tom. **1.** *Naut.* **a** A long pivot gun, carried on deck. **b** Any large gun of long range, esp. when used ashore. **2.** [*not cap.*] *U. S.* A trough for washing gold-bearing earth.

long ton. See TON, 1 **a.**

‖**lon'gueur'** (lôN'gûr'), *n.* [F.] A dull or tedious passage in a book.

long'-wind'ed (lŏng'wĭn'dĕd; -dĭd; 2), *adj.* Tediously long in speaking. — **long'wind'ed·ly,** *adv.* — **long'wind'ed·ness,** *n.*

long'wise' (lŏng'wīz'), *adv.* Also **long'ways'** (-wāz'). Lengthwise.

loo (lōō), *n.* [From older *lanterloo,* fr. F. *lanturelu,* orig., the refrain of a vaudeville.] **1.** A game at cards. **2.** The money played for, or each stake, at loo. — *v. t.;* LOOED (lōōd); LOO'ING. To cause to deposit a new stake at loo, as for not winning a trick.

loo'by (lōō'bĭ), *n.; pl.* LOOBIES (-bĭz). An awkward, clumsy fellow.

loof (lōōf), *n.* *Scot.* The palm of the hand.

loof. Var. of LUFF.

look (lo͝ok), *v. i.* [AS. *lōcian.*] **1.** To have or exercise the visual sense; to see. **2.** To turn, direct, or hold the eyes as for viewing, noting, or ascertaining. **3.** To seem to a percipient; to appear; hence, with *like,* to show promise of; as, it *looks* like snow. **4.** To direct or pay attention; as, *look* to your laurels. **5.** To expect; to look forward (to). **6.** To have (an indicated) direction or outlook; as, the house *looks* to the east. **7.** To indicate; point; as, the evidence *looks* to acquittal. **8.** To appear or show oneself to see or as if to see; — usually with *out.* — **Syn.** See SEE: EXPECT. — *v. t.* **1.** To observe; inspect; examine. *Now Dial.,* except in *look over.* **2.** To look for; specif.: **a** To look forward to. **b** To search for. *Obs.,* except with *out* or *up;* as, to *look* up information. **c** To direct the vision in order to perceive or find out; as, *look* where you are going. **3.** To give a look to; as, to *look* a man in the eyes. **4.** To influence by looking; as, to *look* down opposition. **5.** To express by a look. **6.** To appear as accords with; as, to *look* one's age.
— *n.* **1.** Act of looking; a glance. **2.** Appearance or expression of the countenance. **3.** Appearance; aspect.

look'er (lo͝ok'ẽr), *n.* One who looks; specif., *Slang,* a person having features or an appearance of a specified kind.

look'er-on', *n.; pl.* LOOKERS-ON. A spectator; onlooker.

look'ing glass. A mirror.

look'out' (lo͝ok'out'), *n.* **1. a** A careful looking or watching for any object or event. **b** The place, esp. an elevated place, from which such observation is made. **c** A person engaged in watching. **2.** View; prospect. **3.** *Colloq.* Object of care or concern. **4.** *Naut.* A crow's-nest.

loom (lōōm), *n.* [See LOON the bird.] **a** A loon. **b** An auk, guillemot, or puffin.

loom, *v. i.* [Origin uncert.] **1.** To come into sight, esp. above the surface of sea or land, in enlarged, or distorted and indistinct form, often because of atmospheric conditions. **2.** Hence, figuratively, to appear in an exaggerated or an impressively great form. — *n.* An appearance of exaggerated height or size of anything, as of land or a ship seen in fog or darkness; also, a looming shadow, as of land.

loom, *n.* [AS. *gelōma* utensil, implement.] **1.** A frame or machine for interweaving yarn or threads into a fabric, the operation being performed by laying lengthwise a series called the *warp* and weaving in across this other threads called the *weft, woof,* or *filling.* **2.** *Naut.* That part of an oar which is inboard from the rowlock.

loon (lōōn), *n.* Also, *Obs. exc. Dial. & Scot.,* **loun, lown** (lōōn). [Scot. *loun, lown, loon.*] **1.** A lout; rascal. **2.** *Archaic.* A menial. *Shak.* **3.** *Scot.* A lad; also, a harlot.

loon, *n.* [From *loom,* of Scand. origin.] Any of several fish-eating diving birds (genus *Gavia*) of the northern part of the Northern Hemisphere. The common loon (*G. immer*) is nearly three feet long.

loon'y, lun'y (lōōn'ĭ), *adj.;* LOON'I·ER, LUN'I·ER (-ĭ·ẽr); LOON'I·EST, LUN'I·EST. [From *lunatic.*] *Slang.* Crazy; daft. — *n.; pl.* -IES (-ĭz). *Slang.* A loony person.

loop (lōōp), *n.* [ME. *loupe.*] *Archaic.* A small, narrow opening; a loophole.

loop, *n.* [ME. *loupe,* perh. of Celt. origin.] **1.** A fold or doubling of a thread, cord, rope, etc., through which another thread, cord, etc., can be passed; hence, a ring or fold forming a catch, often one of metal or wood; an eye, staple, etc. **2.** A loop-shaped figure, course, bend, or the like; as, the *loop* of the letter "h." **3.** *Aviation.* An aerial maneuver in which the airplane describes an approximately circular path in the plane of the longitudinal and normal axes, the lateral axis remaining horizontal and the upper side of the airplane remaining on the inside of the circle. In an ***outside loop*** the airplane remains on the outside of the circle. **4.** *Elec.* A complete electric circuit. **5.** *Needlework.* A stitch in crocheting, knitting, netting, and tatting. See STITCH, *Illust.* **6.** *Physics.* The part of a vibrating string, air column, etc., between two nodes; also, its middle point. See NODE, 8, *Illust.* — *v. t.* **1.** To make a loop or loops of or in. **2.** To make a loop or loops on or about. **3.** *Elec.* To connect (electric conductors) so as to complete a circuit in a loop. — *v. i.* **1.** To make a loop. **2.** To crawl after the manner of a measuring worm. **3.** *Aviation.* To execute a vertical loop; — also, ***loop the loop.***

loop, *n.* [F. *loupe.*] *Ironworks.* A mass of iron in a pasty condition gathered into a ball for the tilt hammer or rolls.

loop'er (lo͝op'ẽr), *n.* **1.** One who or that which loops, as a shuttle in a double-thread sewing machine. **2.** See GEOMETRID. **3.** One who performs a loop, as in aviation.
loop'hole' (-hōl'), *n.* [*loop* opening + *hole.*] **1.** *Mil.* A small opening, as in a parapet, through which small arms may be discharged. **2.** A hole that gives a passage, means of escape, etc. **— *v. t.*** To make loopholes in.
loop knot. See KNOT, *Illust.* (4).
loop stitch. = RAILWAY STITCH. See STITCH, *Illust.*
loop'y (lo͝op'ĭ), *adj.* **1.** Having loops. **2.** *Scot.* Sly.
loose (lo͞os), *adj.* [ON. *lauss.*] **1.** Not fastened so as to be fixed, rigid, firm, or tight. **2.** Free; unattached; — said esp. of things ordinarily confined. **3.** Hence, disconnected; detached; random; as, *loose* information. **4.** Not dense, close, or compact, in structure or arrangement. **5.** Composed of free particles; as, *loose* sand. **6.** Wanting in restraint, lax; open; as, a *loose* tongue. **7.** Wanting in moral restraint; as, a *loose* life; hence, immoral, unchaste. **8.** Wanting in precision; not strict, close, or rigid; as, *loose* reasoning.
— *adv.* Loosely; not so as unduly to bind or constrain.
— *v. t.* **1.** To make loose; to unbind, untie, undo, etc. **2.** To break up the firmness or coherence of; as, to *loose* the sod. **3.** To relax; to make less rigid, tight, or strict. **4.** To let or set loose; to free. **5.** To release from anything obligatory or burdensome; hence, to absolve; remit. **6.** *Chiefly Naut.* To cast loose; to let go. Hence, *Obs.*, ***loose the anchor***, to weigh anchor. **7.** To discharge (an arrow, a gun); hence, to send forth as a missile. **— *v. i.*** **1.** To become loose; to loosen. **2.** To discharge an arrow, gun, etc.; to shoot.
— **loose'ly**, *adv.* — **loose'ness**, *n.*
loose'-joint'ed, *adj.* Having joints apparently not closely articulated; hence, capable of unusually free movements.
loos'en (lo͞os''n), *v. t.* **1.** To set or let loose; to free. **2.** To free from binding, tightness, firmness, or fixedness; as, to *loosen* the earth around the roots of the tree. **3.** To relax (the bowels). **4.** To permit to become less strict; as, to *loosen* discipline. — **loos'en·er** (-ẽr), *n.*
loose sentence. *Rhet.* A sentence the latter part of which contains only inconsequential modifiers and unimportant ideas. Cf. PERIODIC SENTENCE.
loose'strife' (lo͞os'strīf'), *n.* [*loose*, v. + *strife;* as a trans. of the L. name *Lysimachia.*] **a** Any of a genus (*Lysimachia*) of plants of the primrose family, with leafy stems and yellow or white flowers. **b** Any of a genus (*Lythrum*, family Lythraceae, the loosestrife family) of herbs, esp. the ***purple loosestrife*** (*L. salicaria*) with a long spike of purple flowers.
loot (lo͞ot), *n.* [Hind. *lūt.*] **1.** Plunder; booty; esp., the booty taken in war, or the gains of corrupt officials. **2.** The action of looting; as, the *loot* of a bank. — **Syn.** See SPOIL. **— *v. t. & i.*** To plunder or sack, as a conquered city; to rob, esp. by corruption; as, to *loot* a city's funds. — **loot'er**, *n.*
loot. Scot. past of LET.
lop (lŏp), *v. t.;* LOPPED (lŏpt); LOP'PING. **1.** To hew or cut branches, twigs, etc., from (a tree, vine, etc.); to trim. **2.** To cut off, or remove, as superfluous parts. **— *n.*** A part or parts of a tree, etc., lopped off; esp., parts not measured for timber; trimmings.
lop, *v. i. & t.* To hang downward; to be pendent; hence, to flop about loosely. **— *adj.*** Hanging down; as, *lop* ears.
lope (lōp), *v. i.* [ON. *hlaupa.*] To go or move with a lope; as, a *loping* pony. **— *n.*** **1.** An easy gait, resembling a canter. **2.** Hence, an easy bounding gait capable of being sustained for a long time. — **lop'er** (lōp'ẽr), *n.*
lop'-eared', *adj.* Having ears that droop.
lo'pho·branch (lō'fō·brăngk; lŏf'ō-), *adj.* [Gr. *lophos* crest, tuft + *branchion* gill.] Of or pert. to a suborder of small teleost fishes including the sea horses and pipefishes. **— *n.*** A lophobranch fish. — **lo'pho·bran'chi·ate** (-brăng'kĭ·āt), *adj. & n.*
lop'per (lŏp'ẽr), *n.* One who lops.
lop'per, *v. i. & t.* *Now Dial.* To curdle. **— *n.*** Clabber.
lop'py (lŏp'ĭ), *adj.;* LOP'PI·ER (-ĭ·ẽr); LOP'PI·EST. Hanging loose; limp. — **Syn.** See LIMP.
lop'sid'ed (lŏp'sīd'ĕd; -ĭd; 2), *adj.* Leaning to one side, as from a defect of structure; as, a *lopsided* barn; hence, unsymmetrical. — **lop'sid'ed·ly**, *adv.* — **lop'sid'ed·ness**, *n.*
lo·qua'cious (lō·kwā'shŭs), *adj.* [L. *loquax, -acis*, talkative, fr. *loqui* to speak.] Given to talking; garrulous. — **Syn.** See TALKATIVE. — **lo·qua'cious·ly**, *adv.*
lo·quac'i·ty (lō·kwăs'ĭ·tĭ), *n.* Talkativeness; garrulity.
lo'quat (lō'kwŏt; lō·kwŏt'), *n.* [Cant. pron. of Chin. (Pek.) *lu² chü²*, lit., rush orange.] **a** An Asiatic evergreen tree (*Eriobotrya japonica*) often cultivated for its fruit. **b** The plumlike fruit of this tree, used for preserves, etc.
‖**lo'qui·tur** (lŏk'wĭ·tẽr), *v. i.* [L.] He (she, or it) speaks; — used esp. in stage directions.
lo'ran (lō'răn; lô'răn), *n.* [*long-range navigation.*] A system of long-range navigation in which pulsed signals sent out by two pairs of radio stations are utilized by a navigator to determine the geographical position of a ship or aircraft. Cf. SHORAN.
lord (lôrd), *n.* [AS. *hlāford*, for *hlāfweard*, i. e., bread keeper, fr. *hlāf* bread, loaf + *weard* keeper, guard.] **1.** One who has power and authority, as from headship or leadership; a master; ruler. **2.** [*cap.*] **a** The Supreme Being; Jehovah. **b** The Saviour; Jesus Christ. **3. a** A titled nobleman; — applied in England: (1) to a baron; (2) less formally, to any temporal peer from baron to marquis; (3) by courtesy, to the son of a duke or marquis, or the eldest son of an earl; (4) by right or courtesy, to a bishop; (5) as a judicial title, to a Scottish lord of session (one of the judges of the supreme civil court). **b** [*cap.*] *pl.* Usually with *the*, the House of Lords (***the Lords***). **4.** A title of reference or address prefixed to the names of titled noblemen and forming part of certain official titles; as, *Lord* Advocate, *Lord* Chamberlain, etc. Its use is now as follows: (1) in less formal use for "Marquis," "Earl," "Viscount," with *of* omitted when it occurs in the full title; thus, "the Earl of Derby," becomes *Lord* Derby. (2) A baron, whether actual or by courtesy, has *Lord* before his title of peerage, the Christian name, if mentioned, coming first; thus, Alfred, *Lord* Tennyson. (3) The younger sons of dukes and marquises have (by courtesy) *Lord* before their name and surname. **5.** *Astrol.* A planet having controlling power or influence. **6.** *Feudalism.* One of whom a fee or estate is held; the proprietor of feudal land. **7.** *Humorous.* A husband; as, her *lord* and master.
— *v. i.* To play the lord; to domineer; — often with *it.*

lord chancellor. In Great Britain, the first great officer of state, whose official title is Lord High Chancellor of Great Britain. He ranks next after the blood royal and the archbishop of Canterbury. He is keeper of the great seal, privy councilor, president and prolocutor of the House of Lords, and usually a member of the cabinet.
lord'ing, *n.* [*lord* + 1st *-ing.*] **1.** *Archaic.* A lord; — frequent as a form of address; esp., *pl.*, sirs; masters. **2.** A petty lord.
lord'ling (lôrd'lĭng), *n.* A little or insignificant lord.
lord'ly (-lĭ), *adj.;* LORD'LI·ER (-lĭ·ẽr); LORD'LI·EST. Suitable for a lord; of or pertaining to, or like, a lord; specif.: **a** Grand; noble. **b** Proud; haughty. — **Syn.** See PROUD. **— *adv.*** In a lordly manner. — **lord'li·ness**, *n.*
Lord of hosts. Jehovah as supreme over all.
lord of misrule. Formerly, in England, the master of revels, as at Christmas.
lor·do'sis (lôr·dō'sĭs), *n.* [NL., fr. Gr. *lordōsis*, fr. *lordos* bent so as to be convex in front.] *Med.* Curvature of the spine forward.
Lord's day, the. Sunday; — so called as that of the resurrection of Christ. *Luke* xxiv. 1, 6; *Rev.* i. 10.
lord'ship (lôrd'shĭp), *n.* **1.** The rank or position of a lord; hence (with *his* or *your*), a title applied to a lord (except an archbishop or duke, who is called *his* or *your Grace*) or a judge (in Great Britain), etc. **2.** Seigniory; the territory over which a lord holds jurisdiction. **3.** Dominion; authority.
Lord's Prayer, the. The prayer which Christ taught his disciples. *Matt.* vi. 9–13.
Lord's Supper, the. **a** The supper partaken of by Jesus the night before his crucifixion. **b** The sacrament of the Eucharist; the Holy Communion.
Lord's table, the. *Eccl.* The altar; the Communion table.
lore (lōr; 70), *n.* [L. *lorum* thong.] *Zool.* The space between the eye and bill in birds, and the corresponding region in reptiles and fishes.
lore, *n.* [AS. *lār.*] **1.** *Archaic.* Act of teaching, or that which is taught; hence, instruction; wisdom; counsel. **2.** Knowledge; learning; often, the whole body of knowledge possessed by a people or class, or pertaining to a particular subject, esp. when such knowledge is regarded as of a traditional description.
Lor'e·lei (lôr'ĕ·lī), *n.* Also **Lur'lei** (lo͞or'lī). [G.] In German legend, a siren who haunted a rock on the Rhine, and by her beauty and song lured sailors to destruction.
lor'gnette' (lôr'nyĕt'), *n.* [F.] An eyeglass or eyeglasses with a long handle; also, an opera glass.
‖**lor'gnon'** (lôr'nyôɴ'), *n.* [F.] Eyeglasses, esp. a pince-nez.
lo·ri'ca (lō·rī'kȧ), *n.; pl.* -CAE (-sē). [L., lit., a corselet of thongs, fr. *lorum* thong.] **1.** A Roman cuirass, orig. of leather. **2.** *Zool.* A hard protective case or shell.
lor'i·cate (lŏr'ĭ·kāt), *adj.* Also **lor'i·cat'ed** (-kāt'ĕd; -ĭd). *Zool.* Having a lorica; of the nature of a lorica.
lor'i·keet (lŏr'ĭ·kĕt; lŏr'ĭ·kēt'), *n.* [*lory* + para*keet.*] Any of numerous small, arboreal, usually brush-tongued parrots or lories, found mostly in Australasia.
lo'ris (lō'rĭs; 70), *n.* [F., fr. Flem. *lorrias* lazy, the sloth.] Either of two small nocturnal slow-moving lemurs, esp. the ***slender loris*** (*Loris gracilis*) of southern India.
lorn (lôrn), *adj.* [See FORLORN.] **1.** *Archaic.* Lost; ruined. **2.** Forsaken; desolate; bereft; forlorn.
Lor·raine' cross (lŏ·rān'; lō-). See CROSS, *Illust.* (5).
lor'ry (lŏr'ĭ), *n.; pl.* -RIES (-ĭz). [Prob. from dial. *lurry* to pull or lug.] **1.** A large, low horse or automobile truck. **2.** Any of various trucks or other vehicles running on rails.
lo'ry (lō'rĭ; 70), *n.; pl.* LORIES (-rĭz). [Malay *luri*, var. of *nuri.*] Any of numerous parrots (chiefly genera *Domicella*, *Trichoglossus*, *Chalcopsitta*, and *Eos*) generally having the tongue papillose or brushlike at the tip, found in Australia, New Guinea, and the adjacent islands.
los'a·ble (lo͞oz'ȧ·b'l), *adj.* That may be lost.
lose (lo͞oz), *v. t.;* LOST (lŏst; 74); LOS'ING (lo͞oz'ĭng). [AS. *losian* to become lost, perish.] **1.** To bring to destruction; to ruin; — now *Rare*, except in the passive; as, the ship was *lost* on the reef. **2.** To miss from one's possession, or from its customary place. **3.** To be deprived of, esp. in an unforeseen manner. **4.** To suffer loss through the death or removal of, or final separation from (a person); as, to *lose* a son; of a commander, to suffer loss through the killing, wounding, capture, or desertion, of (troops, etc.). **5.** To waste; squander. **6.** To fail to gain or win; as, to *lose* a prize, a game; hence, to fail to catch with the mind or senses; miss; as, I *lost* a part of what he said. **7.** To cause the loss of; as, this speech *lost* him the election. **8.** To fail to keep, sustain, or maintain (something precarious); as, to *lose* one's balance. **9. a** To cause or suffer (oneself, a person) to wander from his way; as, he *lost* himself in the maze of the city streets. **b** To suffer loss of identity, clearness of thought, etc.; as, to *lose* oneself in reverie. **10.** To wander from; to miss, so as not to be able to find; as, to *lose* one's way; also, to draw away from; to outstrip; as, the runner *lost* all his competitors. **11.** To fail to keep in sight or mind. **12.** To forget. **— *v. i.*** To suffer loss.
lose caste. To lose social position or consideration. — ***lose face.*** *Orig. China.* To undergo loss of prestige. — ***lose out.*** *Colloq.* To be defeated; to fail of success. — ***lose track of.*** To cease to keep in touch with.
lo'sel (lō'z'l; lo͞oz''l; *dial. also* lŏz''l), *n.* [ME.] *Archaic exc. Dial.* A worthless person. **— *adj.*** Worthless.
los'er (lo͞oz'ẽr), *n.* One who or that which loses.
los'ing (lo͞oz'ĭng), *n.* Act of one who loses; also, *pl.*, that which is lost, as stakes. **— *adj.*** That loses.
loss (lŏs; 74), *n.* [AS. *los* destruction.] **1.** State or fact of being lost or destroyed; ruin; destruction. **2. a** Act or fact of losing (in various senses); esp., unintentional parting with something of value; as, the *loss* of property; also, the deprivation, harm, etc., which ensues from such loss. **b** An instance of losing. **3.** That which is lost; specif., waste. **4. a** Act or fact of failing to win, gain, obtain, or utilize. **b** Decrease in amount or degree (without reference to its effect); — opposed to *gain.* **5.** *Elec.* The power diminution of a circuit element, corresponding to conversion of electric power into heat by some form of resistance. **6.** *Insurance.* Death, injury, destruction, or damage in such a manner as to charge the insurer with a liability under the terms of the policy; an instance of it; also, that which incurs it. **7.** *Mil.* The losing of soldiers in battle or by surrender; also, chiefly in *pl.*, killed, wounded, or captured soldiers. — ***at a loss.*** Puzzled; unable to determine; uncertain.

loss leader. *Com.* A popular article sold for less than its regular price, often below cost, to draw customers.

loss ratio. *Insurance.* The ratio between losses incurred and premiums earned during a given period.

lost (lŏst; 74), *past & past part.* of LOSE. Specif.: *adj.* **1.** Ruined or destroyed. **2.** **a** Parted with; gone out of one's possession. **b** That has ceased to be known or practiced; as, *lost* arts. **3.** Having wandered from, or unable to find, the way; as, a *lost* sheep; also, no longer visible. **4.** Absorbed; as, *lost* in thought. **5.** Not gained or won; also, wasted; as, a *lost* opportunity. **6.** With *to:* **a** Taken from the possession of, or denied to the efforts of; as, the victory was *lost* to them. **b** Of persons, hardened beyond sensibility or recovery; insensible; as, *lost* to shame.

lost tribes. Those members of the ten tribes of the ancient kingdom of Israel who were carried into captivity by Sargon after his capture of Samaria, 722 B.C., and who never returned in a body to Palestine.

lot (lŏt), *n.* [AS. *hlot.*] **1.** An object used as a counter or check in determining a question by chance. **2.** The use of such a counter as a means of deciding anything; as, to choose by *lot.* **3.** What comes to or befalls one upon whom a choice by lot has fallen; hence, a share; allotment. **4.** Hazard; fortune; esp., the fate which falls to one by the will of the powers overruling man's destiny, as, in Christian conception, by Divine Providence; as, a man content with his *lot.* **5.** *Chiefly Brit.* A tax, duty, or customs fee. **6.** A distinct portion or plot of land; specif.: **a** One of the smaller portions of land (as a division of a block) into which cities, towns, or villages are laid out. **b** A parcel of land in a cemetery, for burial of one or more persons. **7.** A number of associated persons or things taken collectively. **8.** *Colloq.* A considerable quantity or number. **9.** *Colloq.* Kind or sort (of person, etc.); as, he is a bad *lot.* **10.** *Motion Pictures.* A studio and its adjoining territory. — **Syn.** See FATE.

— *adv.* To a great extent or degree; a great deal; — used in phrases, as *a lot better, a lot worse, a lot more,* etc.

— *v. t.;* LOT′TED; LOT′TING. **1.** To form or divide into lots; as, to *lot* land. **2.** To allot; apportion. **3.** To choose or divide by lot. — *v. i.* To use or draw lots.

Lot (lŏt), *n.* [Heb. *Lōṭ.*] *Bib.* The nephew of Abraham, who escaped the destruction of Sodom. His wife was turned into a pillar of salt because she looked back when fleeing. *Gen.* xiii, xix.

lo′ta, lo′tah (lō′tȧ), *n.* [Hind. *loṭā.*] *India.* A small vessel for water, usually globular and made of brass or copper.

lote (lōt), *n. Archaic.* = LOTUS (in various senses).

loth, loth′ly, loth′some, etc. Vars. of LOATH, etc.

Lo·thar′i·o (lō·thâr′ĭ·ō; 6), *n.; pl.* LOTHARIOS (-ōz). In Rowe's drama *The Fair Penitent,* a gay and unscrupulous rake and seducer; hence, a gay seducer.

lo′tion (lō′shŭn), *n.* [L. *lotio,* fr. *lavare, lotum,* to wash.] **1.** *Obs.* Act of washing; ablution. **2.** A liquid medicinal preparation for washing; a wash.

lo′tos, lo′tos–eat′er. Vars. of LOTUS, LOTUS-EATER.

lot′ter·y (lŏt′ẽr·ĭ), *n.; pl.* -TERIES (-ĭz). [It. *lotteria,* fr. *lotto* lottery, lot, fr. F. *lot* share, lot, of Teut. origin.] **1.** A scheme for the distribution of prizes by lot; esp., such a scheme in which lots, or chances, are sold. **2.** Figuratively, an affair of chance.

lot′to (lŏt′ō), *n.* [It., prop., a lot.] A game of chance, played with numbered cards. Cf. KENO.

lo′tus (lō′tŭs), *n.* [L., fr. Gr. *lōtos.*] **1.** *Gr. Legend.* The fruit eaten by the lotus-eaters, causing indolence and dreamy contentment; also, the tree (*Zizyphus lotus*) of the buckthorn family, reputed to bear this fruit. **2.** Any of several flowering water plants represented in ancient Egyptian and Hindu art: **a** The ***Indian lotus,*** *or* ***sacred lotus*** (*Nelumbo nucifera*), with stately leaves and large pink flowers. **b** Either of two African water lilies (the white *Nymphaea lotus* and the blue *N. coerulea*), called specif. ***Egyptian lotus*** and used as the floral emblem of Egypt. **3.** Any of a genus (*Lotus*) of widely distributed herbs or subshrubs of the pea family.

lo′tus–eat′er, lo′tos–eat′er (lō′tŭs·ēt′ẽr), *n.* In the *Odyssey,* one of a people who subsisted on the lotus and lived in the dreamy indolence it induced.

loud (loud), *adj.* [AS. *hlūd.*] **1.** Of sound: Marked by intensity; not low, soft, or subdued. **2.** Giving or making a resounding sound or sounds; as, a *loud* trumpet; hence, noisy; as, *loud* streets. **3.** Figuratively: Striking or impressive as from clamor, emphasis, or the like. **4.** *Colloq.* Of other than auditory impressions, offensively vivid or strong; as, *loud* colors; showy; as, *loud* jewelry; hence, unrefined; as, *loud* manners. — *adv.* [AS. *hlūde.*] With loudness; loudly. — **loud′ly,** *adv.* — **loud′ness,** *n.*

loud′en (loud′'n), *v. i. & t.* To become, or make, loud.

loud′mouthed′ (-mouthd′; -moutht′; 2), *adj.* Having a loud voice; talking or sounding noisily; blatant.

loud′–speak′er, *n. Elec.* A form of telephone receiver for producing sounds loud enough to be readily heard some distance away.

lough (lŏk), *n.* [Gael. & Ir. *loch.*] **a** *Obs.* A lake; a pool; water; sea. **b** *Dial.* A loch.

lou′is d'or′ (lo͞o′ĭ dôr′). [F., gold louis.] **a** A French gold coin, 1640–1795, ranging in value from $3.84 to $5.79. **b** A former French gold coin, the 20-franc piece ($3.86).

Lou′is Treize′ (lo͞o′ĭ trâz′), **Lou′is Qua·torze′** (kȧ·tôrz′), **Lou′is Quinze′** (kăNz′), **Lou′is Seize′** (sâz′). [F.] Designating, resembling, or pertaining to, the French styles in architecture, furniture, etc., prevailing during the times of Louis XIII, XIV, XV, XVI, respectively.

lounge (lounj), *v. i.;* LOUNGED (lounjd); LOUNG′ING (loun′jĭng). To move or act in a lazy or listless way; also, to spend time lazily, whether lolling or idly sauntering. — *v. t.* To waste by lounging; to fritter (away), as time. — *n.* **1.** **a** Act or period of lounging. **b** An idle gait or stroll. **2.** A place of lounging; a room where one may lounge. **3.** An upholstered piece of furniture adapted for one reclining; a sofa; a couch. — **loung′er** (loun′jẽr), *n.*

loup (loup; lōp; lo͞op), *v. i.* [ON. *hlaupa.*] *Chiefly Scot.* To leap; to flee.

‖**loup** (lo͞o), *n.* [F.] A half mask, usually of silk.

loup′–cer′vier′ (lo͞o′sẽr′vyā′), *n.* [F.] See LYNX.

‖**loup′–ga′rou′** (lo͞o′gȧ′ro͞o′), *n.; pl.* LOUPS-GAROUS (lo͞o′gȧ′ro͞o′). [F., fr. *loup* wolf + a Teut. word akin to E. *werewolf.*] A werewolf; a lycanthrope.

lour (lour), **lour′ing, lour′y.** Vars. of LOWER, frown, etc.

louse (lous), *n.; pl.* LICE (līs). [AS. *lūs,* pl. *lȳs.*] **1.** Any of certain small, wingless, usually flattened insects, parasitic on warm-blooded animals. They constitute two groups: (1) The true lice, or ***sucking lice,*** forming an order (Anoplura), including the ***head louse*** (*Pediculus capitis*) and ***body louse*** (*P. vestimenti*). (2) The ***biting lice,*** *or* ***bird lice,*** forming an order (Mallophaga). **2.** Hence, any of various insects or small arachnids, crustaceans, etc., which live on animals or plants, sucking their blood or juices, including the ***plant louse*** (an aphid or related insect) and *scale insect* (which see); also, any of various similar forms that are not parasitic, as the *wood louse* (which see), and ***book louse*** (a wingless insect injurious to old books and papers).

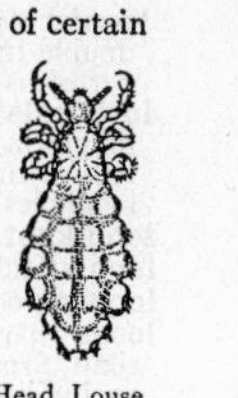

Head Louse, much enlarged.

louse′wort′ (-wûrt′), *n.* Any of a genus (*Pedicularis*) of plants of the figwort family, formerly reputed to cause sheep feeding upon them to be subject to vermin; wood betony.

lous′y (louz′ĭ), *adj.;* -I·ER (-ĭ·ẽr); -I·EST. Infested with or as if with lice. Hence, *Slang,* disgusting or contemptible. — **lous′i·ly,** *adv.* — **lous′i·ness,** *n.*

lout (lout), *v. i. & t.* [AS. *lūtan.*] *Dial. & Archaic.* To bend; bow; stoop.

lout, *n.* [ON. *lūtr* bent down, stooping.] A clownish, awkward fellow; a bumpkin. — *v. t. Obs.* To treat as a lout; to flout.

lout′ish (lout′ĭsh), *adj.* Clownish; rude; awkward. — **Syn.** See BOORISH. — **lout′ish·ly,** *adv.* — **lout′ish·ness,** *n.*

lou′ver (lo͞o′vẽr), *n.* [OF. *lover, lovier.*] **1.** *Medieval Arch.* A roof lantern, or turret, for the escape of smoke, or the admission of light and air. **2.** A louver board, or an aperture or frame with louver boards fitted in; a slatted panel, as in a ship's bulkhead or automobile hood, for ventilation. — **lou′vered** (-vẽrd), *adj.*

louver boards *or* **boarding.** The sloping boards set to shed rain water outward in openings which are to be left otherwise unfilled, as belfry windows.

Lou′vre (lo͞o′vr′), *n.* [F.] An ancient palace in Paris, now occupied by a museum of art and public offices.

lov′a·ble (lŭv′ȧ·b'l), *adj.* Having qualities that excite, or are fitted to excite, love; worthy of love. — **lov′a·bil′i·ty** (-bĭl′ĭ·tĭ), *n.* — **lov′a·ble·ness,** *n.* — **lov′a·bly,** *adv.*

Syn. Lovable, amiable mean worthy of liking. Lovable implies a definitely personal reaction; amiable, little more than an agreeable impression. — **Ant.** Hateful.

lov′age (lŭv′ĭj), *n.* [OF. *luvesche, leuesche,* fr. LL. *levisticum,* deriv. of L. *Ligusticus* Ligurian.] A European herb (*Levisticum officinale*) of the carrot family, cultivated in old gardens as a domestic remedy.

love (lŭv), *n.* [AS. *lufu.*] **1.** A feeling of strong personal attachment induced by sympathetic understanding, or by ties of kinship; ardent affection. **2.** The benevolence attributed to God as being like a father's affection for his children; also, men's adoration of God. **3.** Strong liking; fondness; good will; as, *love* of learning; *love* of country. **4.** Tender and passionate affection for one of the opposite sex. **5.** The object of affection; sweetheart. **6.** [*cap.*] Cupid, or Eros, as god of love; sometimes, Venus. **7.** [*cap.*] *Christian Science.* A synonym for God. **8.** *Tennis, etc.* Nothing; no points scored; — used in counting the score. — **Ant.** Hate. — *v. t.;* LOVED (lŭvd); LOV′ING (lŭv′ĭng). **1.** To have or manifest love for. **2.** To take delight or pleasure in; as, to *love* books. **3.** To show love for by caressing. — *v. i.* To have the feeling of love, esp. for one of the other sex; to be in love.

love′a·ble, love′a·bly, etc. Vars. of LOVABLE, etc.

love affair. An affair between lovers; an amour.

love apple. The tomato.

love′bird′ (lŭv′bûrd′), *n.* Any of numerous small parrots (esp. genera *Agapornis* of Africa and *Psittacula* of South America) that show great affection for their mates.

love feast. Among the primitive Christians, a meal taken together to signify the Christian affection existing between members of the church; hence, among some religious denominations, a religious service in imitation of this.

love game. *Tennis, etc.* A game won without loss of a point.

love′–in–a–mist′, *n.* A European garden plant (*Nigella damascena*) of the crowfoot family, having the flowers enveloped in a number of finely dissected bracts.

love′–in–i′dle·ness, *n.* The wild pansy. See PANSY.

love knot. A knot or bow of ribbon as a token of love.

love′less, *adj.* Without love; unloved or unloving. — **love′less·ly,** *adv.* — **love′less·ness,** *n.*

love′–lies–bleed′ing, *n.* Any cultivated amaranth.

love′lock′ (lŭv′lŏk′), *n.* A long lock of hair; esp., that worn by men of fashion in the reigns of Elizabeth and James I.

love′lorn′ (-lôrn′), *adj.* Forsaken by one's love.

love′ly (lŭv′lĭ), *adj.;* LOVE′LI·ER (-lĭ·ẽr); LOVE′LI·EST. **1.** *Archaic.* Loving; also, lovable. **2.** Beautiful; esp., having a delicate or exquisite beauty. **3.** Beautiful in refined moral or spiritual quality. **4.** *Colloq.* Very pleasing; as, a *lovely* view. — **Syn.** See BEAUTIFUL. — **love′li·ly,** *adv.* — **love′li·ness,** *n.*

love′–mak′ing (-māk′ĭng), *n.* Courtship.

lov′er (lŭv′ẽr), *n.* One who loves; specif.: **a** One held in affection by, or holding affection for, another; a friend. **b** One who is in love with one of the other sex; usually, *sing.,* a male lover; *pl.,* a pair in love with each other. **c** A paramour. **d** One who has a strong liking.

lov′er·ly (-lĭ), *adj. & adv.* Like or as a lover.

love seat. A double chair, or a settee or sofa for two persons.

love set. *Tennis, etc.* A set won without loss of a game.

love′sick′ (lŭv′sĭk′), *adj.* Languishing with love; expressive of languishing love. — **love′sick′ness,** *n.*

love′some (-sŭm), *adj. Archaic & Dial.* **1.** Lovely; lovable. **2.** Loving; amorous.

love vine. The dodder.

lov′ing (lŭv′ĭng), *adj.* Feeling or expressing love or kindness. — **lov′ing·ly,** *adv.* — **lov′ing·ness,** *n.*

loving cup. A large ornamental drinking vessel having two or more handles for convenience in passing.

lov′ing–kind′ness, *n.* Tender regard; mercy; favor.

low (lō), *v. i.* [AS. *hlōwan.*] To make the calling sound of cows; to moo. — *v. t.* To utter with a lowing sound. — *n.* The calling sound made by cattle.

low, lowe (lō), *n. & v. i.* [ON. *logi*, n., *loga*, v.] *Scot.* Flame; blaze; glow; light.

low (lō), *adj.* [ME. *low, louh, lah*, fr. ON. *lāgr.*] **1.** Having small elevation; extending upward relatively little. **2.** Situated below the normal level, surface, or base of measurement, or the mean elevation. **3.** Dead; — now only as predicate adj. **4.** Of a dress: Low-necked; décolleté. **5.** Not loud; as, a *low* voice. **6. a** Near, or not very distant from, the equator; as, in the *low* northern latitudes. **b** Near the horizon; as, the afternoon sun is *low*. **c** With reference to historic time: Comparatively recent; as, a coin of *low* date. **7.** Inferior; commonplace; specif., humble in rank or station. **8.** Deficient or inferior in strength, energy, or the like; specif.: **a** Deficient in vital energy. **b** Wanting animation; dejected. **9.** Deficient or unusually small in quantity, intensity, value, etc.; as, *low* pressure; a *low* fever; *low* wages. **10.** In an automotive vehicle, designating the least speed or gear ratio. **11.** Lacking elevation or high character; specif.: **a** Wanting dignity; as, a *low* comparison. **b** Mean; vulgar. **12.** Not rich, high-seasoned, or nourishing; plain; simple; as, a *low* diet. **13.** Not advanced in evolution, civilization, etc.; as, *low* organisms; the *low* races. **14.** *Eccl.* Holding Low Church doctrines. **15.** *Music & Acous.* Depressed in the scale of pitch; grave. **16.** *Phonet.* = BROAD, *adj.*, 10 **a**. — **Syn.** See BASE.

— *adv.* **1.** In or to a low position; in a low manner; not aloft. **2. a** In subjection, poverty, or disgrace. **b** Humbly; meanly. **3.** Cheaply; as, to sell wheat *low*. **4. a** With a low sound; not loudly. **b** With a low musical pitch or tone. **5.** *Astron.* Near the equator, or near the horizon.

— *n.* That which is low; specif.: **a** *Automobiles.* The low gear or speed. **b** *Card Playing.* The lowest trump. **c** *Meteorol.* An area of low barometric pressure. **d** *Sports, Games, etc.* The lowest number, score, etc.

low′born′ (lō′bôrn′), *adj.* Born in a low condition or rank.

low′boy′ (-boi′), *n.* A table with drawers, about three feet high.

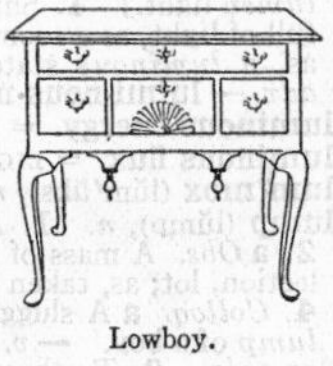
Lowboy.

low′bred′ (-brĕd′), *adj.* Vulgar; coarse; unrefined.

low′brow′ (-brou′), *n.* A person without intellectual interests or cultivation; often, one with low tastes. — **low′brow′**, *adj.*

Low Church. The party in the churches of the Anglican Communion holding evangelical views. — **Low′-Church′man**, *n.*

low comedy. Comedy bordering on farce, characterized by burlesque, horseplay, or the representation of low life.

low′-down′ (lō′doun′; 2), *adj.* *Colloq.* Very low, mean, or base.

low′-down′, *n.* *Slang.* The actual facts; inside information.

lowe (lō). Var. of LOW, flame.

low′er (lou′ẽr), **lour** (lour), *v. i.* [ME. *lowren, luren.*] **1.** To frown; to look sullen. **2.** To be dark and threatening, as clouds. — **Syn.** See FROWN. — *n.* A lowering look.

low′er (lō′ẽr), *adj.*, comparative of LOW.

low′er (lō′ẽr), *v. t.* [From LOWER, compar. of *low*, adj.] **1.** To let descend by its own weight; to let down. **2.** To reduce in value, amount, etc. **3.** To depress as to direction or object; as, to *lower* one's hopes. **4.** To bring down; humble. **5.** To reduce the degree, intensity, strength, etc., of. **6.** To reduce the height of; as, to *lower* a wall. — *v. i.* To become lower or less; to decrease.

lower case. *Print.* **a** See 2d CASE, *n.*, 6. **b** Print in small letters. Abbr. *l.c.*

low′er-case′ (lō′ẽr-kās′; 2), *adj.* *Print.* Pertaining to, or kept in, the lower case; small (not capital); as, *lower-case* letters. — *v. t.* To change to small letters.

low′er-class′man (lō′ẽr-klȧs′măn), *n.* A sophomore or freshman in a school or college.

lower criticism. Textual criticism, or criticism which aims to reconstruct the original texts of the Bible. Cf. HIGHER CRITICISM.

Lower House. [*often not cap.*] The popular, and usually the larger and more representative, branch of a legislature having two chambers.

low′er·ing (lou′ẽr-ĭng), **lour′ing** (lour′ĭng), *adj.* Frowning; gloomy. — **low′er·ing·ly, lour′ing·ly**, *adv.*

low′er·most (lō′ẽr-mōst), *adj.* Lowest.

Lower Silurian. *Geol.* The Ordovician.

lower world. **a** The earth. **b** The nether world.

low′er·y (lou′ẽr-ĭ), **lour′y** (lour′ĭ), *adj.* [From LOWER, LOUR, *n.*] Cloudy; gloomy; lowering; as, a *lowery* sky.

low′est com′mon mul′ti·ple (lō′ĕst; -ĭst). See COMMON MULTIPLE.

Low German. **a** The German dialects of the lowlands, esp. near the seashore. **b** Plattdeutsch. **c** The group of West Germanic languages including Dutch, English, etc. See INDO-EUROPEAN LANGUAGES, *Table.*

low′land (lō′lănd), *n.* Low or level country. — ***the Lowlands.*** The southern and eastern part of Scotland, or the speech of that district. — **low′land, Low′land**, *adj.*

low′land·er (-lăn-dẽr), *n.* A native or inhabitant of the lowlands, esp. [*cap.*] of Scotland.

Low Latin. See LATIN, *n.*, 1.

low′li·head (lō′lĭ-hĕd), *n.* *Archaic.* Lowly state.

low′ly (lō′lĭ), *adj.*; LOW′LI·ER (-lĭ-ẽr); LOW′LI·EST. **1.** Belonging to a low rank; hence, modest; humble; meek. **2.** Low in position or development; inferior, secondary; as, *lowly* organisms. — **Syn.** See HUMBLE. — *adv.* **1.** Humbly; meekly. **2.** In a low position, manner, or degree. — **low′li·ness**, *n.*

Low Mass. Mass said, not sung, in the simplest ceremonial form.

low′-mind′ed (lō′mīn′dĕd; -dĭd; 2), *adj.* Inclined in mind to low or unworthy things; showing a base mind. — **low′-mind′ed·ly**, *adv.* — **low′-mind′ed·ness**, *n.*

lown (loun), *adj., n., & v. t. & i.* [Of Scand. origin.] *Dial.* Calm; quiet.

lown (lo͞on). Var. of LOON.

low′-necked′ (lō′nĕkt′; 2), *adj.* Cut low in the neck; décolleté; — said of a woman's dress.

low′ness, *n.* Condition or quality of being low.

low′-pres′sure (-prĕsh′ẽr; 2), *adj.* Having, employing, exerting, or operating under a low degree of pressure.

low relief. See RELIEF, *n.*, 6.

lowse (*dial. adj.* lōs; *vb.* lōz). Scot. & dial. var. of LOOSE.

low′-spir′it·ed (*see Pron.*, § 2), *adj.* Dejected; depressed. — **low′-spir′it·ed·ly**, *adv.* — **low′-spir′it·ed·ness**, *n.*

Low Sunday. The Sunday following Easter.

low′-ten′sion (*see Pron.*, § 2), *adj.* **a** Having a low potential. **b** Constructed to be used at low tension, as certain apparatus.

low′-test′ (*see Pron.*, § 2), *adj.* Having a high boiling-point range; — said of gasoline, etc.

low tide. The farthest ebb of the tide.

low water. Low tide; a low stage of the water in a river, lake, etc. — **low′-wa′ter** (*see Pron.*, § 2), *adj.*

lox′o·drom′ic (lŏk′sō-drŏm′ĭk), *adj.* Also **lox′o·drom′i·cal** (-ĭ-kăl). [Gr. *loxos* oblique + *-drome.*] Pertaining to sailing on rhumb lines.

lox′o·drom′ics (-ĭks), *n.*; see -ICS. Also **lox·od′ro·my** (lŏks-ŏd′rō-mĭ). The art or method of sailing on rhumb lines.

loy′al (loi′ăl), *adj.* [F., fr. OF. *loial, leial*, fr. L. *legalis*, fr. *lex, legis*, law.] **1.** Faithful to the lawful government, or to the sovereign to whom one is subject. **2.** True to any person to whom one owes fidelity; constant. **3.** Of, pertaining to, or showing loyalty; as, *loyal* expressions. **4.** *Obs.* Lawful; legitimate. — **Syn.** See FAITHFUL. — **loy′al·ly**, *adv.*

loy′al·ist (-ĭst), *n.* A person who is loyal, esp. in times of revolt; specif., one who at the time of the American Revolution was opposed to separation from Great Britain. — **loy′al·ism** (-ĭz′m), *n.* — **loy′al·ist**, *adj.*

loy′al·ty (-tĭ), *n.*; *pl.* -TIES (-tĭz). State, quality, or instance of being loyal; fidelity. — **Syn.** See FIDELITY.

loz′enge (lŏz′ĕnj; -ĭnj), *n.* [OF. *losenge* (F. *losange*), fr. *losengié* rhombic.] **1.** A figure with four equal sides and two acute and two obtuse angles; diamond. **2.** Something having the general form of a lozenge (sense 1), as a small candy.

lub′ber (lŭb′ẽr), *n.* **1.** A big, clumsy fellow; a lout. **2.** *Naut.* A clumsy or unskilled seaman. — *adj.* Clumsy; lubberly.

lub′ber·ly (-lĭ), *adj. & adv.* Like a lubber. — **lub′ber·li·ness** (-lĭ-nĕs; 30), *n.*

lub′ber's hole (lŭb′ẽrz). *Naut.* A hole in the floor of the "top," next the mast, through which one may go farther aloft without going over the rim by the futtock shrouds.

lubber's line. Also **lubber line** *or* **lubber's point.** In a mariner's compass, a vertical line on the inner surface of the bowl from which the readings are made. The compass is set up with the lubber's line toward the ship's head.

lube (lūb; 114), *n.*, *or* **lube oil.** *Mach.* Short for **lu′bri·cat′ing oil**, oil distilled from petroleum and used for lubricating machinery.

lu′bric (lū′brĭk), **lu′bri·cal** (-brĭ-kăl), *adj.* [F. *lubrique*, fr. L. *lubricus* slippery.] *Now Rare.* Lubricous.

lu′bri·cant (-brĭ-kănt; 114), *adj.* Lubricating. — *n.* That which lubricates; specif., a substance, like oil or grease, which may be interposed between moving parts of machinery to make surfaces slippery, reduce friction, and prevent sticking between the lubricated surfaces.

lu′bri·cate (lū′brĭ-kāt), *v. t.*; LU′BRI·CAT′ED (-kāt′ĕd; -ĭd); LU′BRI·CAT′ING. [L. *lubricatus*, past part. of *lubricare* to lubricate, fr. *lubricus* slippery.] **1.** To make smooth or slippery. **2.** To apply a lubricant to, as oil, tallow, graphite, etc. — **lu′bri·ca′tive** (-kā′tĭv), *adj.*

lu′bri·ca′tion (-kā′shŭn), *n.* Act of lubricating, or state of being lubricated. — **lu′bri·ca′tion·al** (-ăl; -′l), *adj.*

lu′bri·ca′tor (lū′brĭ-kā′tẽr), *n.* One who or that which lubricates; a lubricant; specif., a device for lubricating.

lu·bric′i·ty (lū-brĭs′ĭ-tĭ), *n.*; *pl.* -TIES (-tĭz). [F. *lubricité*, fr. LL. *lubricitas* slipperiness.] **1.** Smoothness; also, property that diminishes friction; as, the *lubricity* of oil. **2.** Slipperiness; instability. **3.** Lasciviousness; lewdness.

lu′bri·cous (lū′brĭ-kŭs), *adj.* Rarely, **lu·bri′cious** (lū-brĭsh′ŭs). [L. *lubricus.*] **a** Having a smooth surface; slippery. **b** Unstable; elusive; tricky.

lu·carne′ (lū-kärn′), *n.* [F.] A dormer window.

luce (lūs), *n.* [OF. *lus*, fr. L. *lucius* a kind of fish.] A pike, esp. when full-grown.

lu′cent (lū′sĕnt; -s′nt), *adj.* [L. *lucens*, pres. part. of *lucere* to shine.] Shining; bright; also, clear; translucent. — **lu′cen·cy** (-sĕn-sĭ; -s′n-sĭ), *n.* — **lu′cent·ly**, *adv.*

lu·cerne′, lu·cern′ (lū-sûrn′), *n.* [F. *luzerne.*] A deep-rooted European herb (*Medicago sativa*) of the pea family, with trifoliolate leaves and bluish-purple cloverlike flowers; — in the U. S. called more often *alfalfa* (see ALFALFA, *Illust.*); in England called often *purple medic.*

lu′ces (lū′sēz), *n.*, *pl.* of LUX.

lu′cid (lū′sĭd; 114), *adj.* [L. *lucidus*; akin to L. *lucere* to shine.] **1.** Shining; bright. **2.** Clear; pellucid. **3.** Designating, or characterized by, a sane or normal state of the faculties; as, a *lucid* patient. **4.** Easily understood; clear. — **Syn.** See CLEAR. — **lu′cid·ly**, *adv.* — **lu′cid·ness**, *n.*

lu·cid′i·ty (lū-sĭd′ĭ-tĭ), *n.* Quality or state of being lucid.

Lu′ci·fer (lū′sĭ-fẽr; 114), *n.* [L., bringing light, the morning star, fr. *lux, lucis*, light + *ferre* to bring.] **1.** *Astron.* The planet Venus, when appearing as the morning star. **2.** Satan as identified with the rebel archangel before his fall. **3.** [*not cap.*] Also **lucifer match.** A type of friction match.

lu·cif′er·in (lū-sĭf′ẽr-ĭn), *n.* [*lucifer* + *-in.*] *Biochem.* A diffusible thermostable compound formed in the cells of luminescent organisms, as fireflies, giving practically heatless light in undergoing oxidation which is promoted by an enzyme, **lu·cif′er·ase** (-ās).

lu·cif′er·ous (-ŭs), *adj.* [See LUCIFER.] Giving light; affording mental illumination; illuminating.

Lu′cite (lū′sīt; 114), *n.* A trade-mark applied to a transparent synthetic resin, namely polymerized methyl methacrylate.

luck (lŭk), *n.* [MD. *gheluc, ghelucke* (D. *geluk, luk*).] **1.** That which happens to one seemingly by chance; hap; fate; fortune. **2.** Good luck; favorable fortune.

luck′less, *adj.* Being without luck; having ill fortune; unfortunate. — **luck′less·ly**, *adv.*

luck′y (lŭk′ĭ), *adj.*; LUCK′I·ER (-ĭ-ẽr); LUCK′I·EST. **1.** Favored by luck; fortunate. **2.** Producing or resulting in good, by chance or unexpectedly; favorable; fortunate. — **luck′i·ly**, *adv.* — **luck′i·ness**, *n.*

Syn. **Lucky, fortunate, happy, providential** mean meeting with or having a favorable issue. **Lucky** implies success by chance rather than as the result of merit; **fortunate**, less suggestive of a favorable accident, may carry a hint of being watched over by a higher power or of being blessed beyond one's deserts; **happy** combines the implications of *lucky* and *fortunate* with stress on being blessed; **providential** more definitely implies the help or intervention of Providence.

luck'y, luck'ie (lŭk'ĭ), *n.* *Scot.* Mistress; grandmother.

lu'cra·tive (lū'krȧ·tĭv), *adj.* [L. *lucrativus*, fr. *lucrari* to gain, fr. *lucrum* gain.] Yielding lucre; profitable. — **lu'cra·tive·ly**, *adv.* — **lu'cra·tive·ness**, *n.*

lu'cre (lū'kẽr; lōō'-), *n.* [L. *lucrum.*] Gain in money or goods; profit; riches; — now in a bad sense.

lu'cu·brate (lū'kū·brāt), *v. i.;* LU'CU·BRAT'ED (-brāt'ĕd; -ĭd); LU'CU·BRAT'ING. [L. *lucubrare* to work by lamplight; akin to L. *lucere* to shine.] To work, esp. to study, by artificial light; hence, to study laboriously.

lu'cu·bra'tion (-brā'shŭn), *n.* **1.** Laborious study. **2.** That which is produced by study in retirement; hence, any elaborate literary composition, esp. an overlabored work.

lu'cu·bra'tor (lū'kū·brā'tẽr), *n.* One who lucubrates.

lu'cu·lent (-kū·lĕnt), *adj.* [L. *luculentus.*] Lucid; clear.

Lu·cul'lan (lū·kŭl'ăn), **Lu·cul'li·an** (-ĭ·ăn), **Lu'cul·le'an** (lū'kŭ·lē'ăn), *adj.* Of, pertaining to, or like L. Licinius Lucullus, a wealthy Roman consul famous for his banquets.

Lud'dite (lŭd'īt), *n.* *Eng. Hist.* One of a band of workmen who (1811–16) tried to prevent the use of labor-saving machinery by breaking it, burning factories, etc.; — said to have been so called after Ned Lud, a half-witted man who about 1779 broke up stocking frames.

lu'di·crous (lū'dĭ·krŭs; 114), *adj.* [L. *ludicrus.*] Adapted to excite laughter, esp. from incongruity or exaggeration; ridiculous. — **Syn.** See LAUGHABLE. — **lu'di·crous·ly**, *adv.* — **lu'di·crous·ness**, *n.*

lu'es (lū'ēz), *n.* [L., plague.] Syphilis.

luff (lŭf), *n.* [Early ME. *lof, loof*, appar. a steering oar.] *Naut.* **a** The act of sailing a ship closer to the wind. **b** The forward or weather leech of a fore-and-aft sail. — *v. i. Naut.* To turn the head of a vessel toward the wind; to sail nearer the wind; — often with *up.*

‖**Luft'waf'fe** (lōōft'väf'ĕ), *n.; pl.* -WAFFEN (-ĕn). [G., lit., air weapon.] The air force of the Third Reich.

lug (lŭg), *n.* **1.** *Scot.* The ear. **2.** That which projects like an ear, esp. that by which anything is carried or grasped. **3.** The leather loop or ear on a harness saddle, through which the shaft passes. **4.** *Slang.* A lout; blockhead.

lug, *v. t. & i.;* LUGGED (lŭgd); LUG'GING. [ME. *luggen*, fr. Sw. & Nor. *lugga* to pull by the hair.] **1.** To pull with force; to haul; to drag along with difficulty, as something heavy. **2.** Hence, to bring in or introduce in a forced manner; as, to *lug* a story into conversation.

lug, *n.* **1.** *Colloq.* Act of lugging; also, that which is lugged. **2.** *Colloq., U.S. pl.* Airs; affectations; as, to put on *lugs;* also, showy clothes. **3.** *Naut.* = LUGSAIL.

lug, *n.* A lugworm.

lug'gage (lŭg'ĭj), *n.* [From LUG to drag.] That which is lugged; esp., a traveler's personal baggage; — the usual term in Great Britain, as *baggage* is in U. S. and Canada.

lug'ger (lŭg'ẽr), *n.* [From LUGSAIL.] *Naut.* A vessel carrying a lugsail or lugsails.

lug'gie (lŭg'ĭ; lōōg'ĭ; lōōg'ĭ), *n.* [See LUG ear.] *Chiefly Scot.* A small wooden pail or dish with a handle.

lug'sail' (lŭg'sāl'; *naut.* -s'l), *or* **lug**, *n.* [From LUG, *v.*] *Naut.* A four-sided sail bent to a yard which hangs obliquely on a mast, and is hoisted and lowered with the sail.

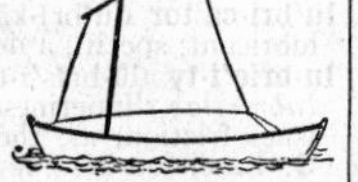
Lugsail.

lu·gu'bri·ous (lū·gū'brĭ·ŭs), *adj.* [L. *lugubris*, fr. *lugere* to mourn.] Mournful; indicating sorrow, often ridiculously or feignedly. — **lu·gu'bri·ous·ly**, *adv.* — **lu·gu'bri·ous·ness**, *n.*

lug'worm' (lŭg'wûrm'), *n.* Any of a genus (*Arenicola*) of marine polychaetous annelids having a row of tufted gills along the back. They are used for bait.

Luke (lūk), *n.* [L. *Lucas*, fr. Gr. *Loukas.*] **a** The Evangelist, a physician and companion of St. Paul, — probably a Gentile. **b** The Gospel of Luke in the New Testament. See BIBLE.

luke'warm' (lūk'wôrm'; 2), *adj.* Moderately warm; tepid; as, *lukewarm* water; not ardent; indifferent; as, *lukewarm* interest. — **luke'warm'ly**, *adv.* — **luke'warm'ness**, *n.*

lull (lŭl), *v. t.* [ME. *lullen*, of imitative origin.] To cause to rest by soothing influences; to calm; soothe. — *v. i.* To become gradually calm. — *n.* **1.** *Rare.* A lullaby. **2.** A temporary cessation of storm or confusion.

lull'a·by' (lŭl'ȧ·bī'), *n.; pl.* -BIES (-bīz'). **a** A song to quiet babes or lull them to sleep. Cf. BERCEUSE. **b** *Obs.* Hence, good night; good-by. — *v. t.;* LULL'A·BIED' (-bīd'); LULL'A·BY'ING. *Rare.* To soothe with a lullaby.

lum (lŭm; lōōm), *n.* *Dial.* A chimney.

lum·ba'go (lŭm·bā'gō), *n.* [L., fr. *lumbus* loin.] *Med.* Rheumatic pain in the loins and the lower back.

lum'bar (lŭm'bẽr), *adj.* [L. *lumbus* loin.] Of, pert. to, or near the loins. — *n.* A lumbar vertebra or nerve. See VERTEBRA, *Illust.*

lum'ber (lŭm'bẽr), *n.* [From *Lombard.* See LOMBARD, 2.] **1.** Old or refuse household stuff. **2.** *Chiefly U. S.* Timber, esp. that sawed or split into boards, planks, etc.; — in England called *timber.* — *adj.* Of lumber; dealing in lumber; as, a *lumber* merchant. — *v. t.* **1.** To heap together in disorder. **2.** To fill or encumber with lumber. **3.** To log and saw timber on (land). — *v. i. U. S. & Canada.* To cut logs in the forest, or to saw logs into lumber for the market. — **lum'ber·er, lum'ber·man** (-măn), *n.*

lum'ber, *v. i.* [Origin uncert.] **1.** To move clumsily or as if burdened. **2.** To rumble. — *n.* A lumbering noise.

lum'ber·ing, *n.* *U. S. & Canada.* The business of cutting or getting timber or logs from the forest for lumber.

lum'ber·ing, *adj.* That lumbers; clumsy; awkward; also, rumbling. — **lum'ber·ing·ly**, *adv.* — **lum'ber·ing·ness**, *n.*

lum'ber·jack' (lŭm'bẽr·jăk'), *n.* A lumberman.

lum'ber·yard' (-yärd'), *n.* *U. S. & Canada.* A yard where a stock of lumber is offered for sale.

lum'bo- (lŭm'bō-), **lumb-.** [L. *lumbus* loin.] A combining form denoting: **a** *The loin.* **b** *Lumbar and*, as in **lum'bo-ab·dom'i·nal.**

lum'bri·ca'lis (lŭm'brĭ·kā'lĭs), *n.; pl.* LUMBRICALES (-lēz). [NL., fr. L. *lumbricus* earthworm.] *Anat.* **a** Any of the four small muscles in the palm of the hand. **b** Any of four similar muscles in the sole of the foot. — **lum'bri·cal** (lŭm'brĭ·kăl), *adj. & n.*

lum'bri·coid (lŭm'brĭ·koid), *adj.* [L. *lumbricus* earthworm + *-oid.*] Like an earthworm; specif., designating a nematode worm (*Ascaris lumbricoides*) parasitic in the human intestine. — *n.* The worm *Ascaris lumbricoides.*

lu'men (lū'mĕn), *n.; pl.* LUMINA (-mĭ·nȧ), LUMENS (-mĕnz). [L., light, an opening for light.] **1.** A unit of light, being the light emitted in a unit solid angle by a uniform point source of one international candle. See CANDLE, *n.*, 3; FOOT-CANDLE. **2.** *Anat. & Zool.* The passageway of a tubular organ, as of a gland.

Lu'mi·nal (lū'mĭ·năl), *n.* *Pharm.* A trade-mark applied to phenobarbital.

lu'mi·nar'y (lū'mĭ·nĕr'ĭ *or, esp. Brit.*, -nẽr·ĭ; 114), *n.; pl.* -IES (-ĭz). [OF. *luminarie*, fr. L. *luminaria*, fr. *luminare*, fr. *lumen, luminis*, light.] **1.** A body that gives light, esp. one of the heavenly bodies. **2.** An artificial light. **3.** One who is a source of light in the world in which he moves. — *adj.* Pertaining to light.

lu'mine (lū'mĭn), *v. t.* *Now Rare.* To illumine.

lu'mi·nesce' (lū'mĭ·nĕs'), *v. i.* To exhibit luminescence.

lu'mi·nes'cence (-nĕs'ĕns; -'ns), *n.* *Physics.* Any emission of light not ascribable directly to incandescence, and therefore occurring at low temperatures. It may be produced by physiological processes, as in the firefly, or by chemical or electrical action.

lu'mi·nes'cent (lū'mĭ·nĕs'ĕnt; -'nt), *adj.* [L. *lumen* light + *-escent.*] *Physics.* Pertaining to, exhibiting, or adapted for the production of luminescence.

lu'mi·nif'er·ous (-nĭf'ẽr·ŭs), *adj.* [L. *lumen* light + *-ferous.*] Transmitting, producing, or yielding light.

lu'mi·nist (lū'mĭ·nĭst), *n.* *Painting.* A painter who especially studies and tries to depict the effects of light on colored objects. See IMPRESSIONISM.

lu'mi·nos'i·ty (-nŏs'ĭ·tĭ), *n.; pl.* -TIES (-tĭz). Quality or state of being luminous; also, a luminous thing.

lu'mi·nous (lū'mĭ·nŭs), *adj.* [F. *lumineux*, fr. L. *luminosus*, fr. *lumen* light.] **1.** Shining; emitting light; brilliant. **2.** Illuminated; full of light, as a room. **3.** Enlightened; intelligent; also, intelligible; as, a *luminous* statement. — **Syn.** See BRIGHT. — **lu'mi·nous·ly**, *adv.* — **lu'mi·nous·ness**, *n.*

luminous energy. = LIGHT, *n.*, 15 **a.**

luminous flux. = LIGHT, *n.*, 15 **c.**

lum'mox (lŭm'ŭks), *n.* *U. S.* A clumsy person; bungler.

lump (lŭmp), *n.* **1.** A piece or mass of indefinite or irregular shape. **2. a** *Obs.* A mass of things; cluster. **b** The whole aggregation, collection, lot; as, taken in the *lump.* **3.** A protuberance, as a swelling. **4.** *Colloq.* **a** A sluggish or dull person. **b** A thickset person; as, a *lump* of a boy. — *v. t.* **1.** To make into a lump; also, to make lumps on or in. **2.** To throw into a mass. **3.** To speak of collectively; also, to group together indiscriminately. — *v. i.* **1.** To form into a lump; become lumpy. **2.** To grow by accretion; bulk. **3.** To move or fall heavily.

lump, *v. t.* *Colloq.* To put up with (something distasteful); as, if you don't like it, you must *lump* it.

lump'er (lŭmp'ẽr), *n.* **1.** One who lumps things together. **2.** A laborer employed to handle freight, as in loading ships.

lump'fish' (lŭmp'fĭsh'), *n.; pl.*, see FISH. A soft, thick, clumsy, usually sea-green fish (*Cyclopterus lumpus*) of both coasts of the northern North Atlantic.

lump'ish, *adj.* Forming a lump; like a lump; hence, dull; stupid. — **lump'ish·ly**, *adv.* — **lump'ish·ness**, *n.*

lump'y (lŭmp'ĭ), *adj.;* LUMP'I·ER (-ĭ·ẽr); LUMP'I·EST. **1.** Covered with, or full of, lumps; hence, of water, rough; choppy. **2.** Like a lump. — **lump'i·ly**, *adv.* — **lump'i·ness**, *n.*

lumpy jaw. *Med. & Veter.* Actinomycosis.

lu'na (lū'nȧ; 114), *n.* [L., the moon.] **1.** [*cap.*] *Rom. Relig.* The moon-goddess. **2.** *Alchemy.* Silver.

lu'na·cy (lū'nȧ·sĭ), *n.; pl.* -CIES (-sĭz). [From LUNATIC.] **1. a** *Orig.*, a kind of insanity with lucid intervals, formerly supposed to be influenced by the changes of the moon. **b** *Now Chiefly Legal.* Insanity amounting to lack of responsibility in the eyes of the law. **2.** Wild foolishness. — **Syn.** See INSANITY.

Luna moth. A large American moth (*Tropaea luna*), having long tails to the hind wings.

lu'nar (lū'nẽr; 114), *adj.* [L. *lunaris*, fr. *luna* the moon.] **1.** Of or pertaining to the moon; orbed or crescent. **2.** Measured by the moon's revolutions; as, a *lunar* day. **3.** [See LUNA, 2.] Pertaining to or containing silver.

lunar caustic. *Med. Chem.* Silver nitrate, $AgNO_3$, fused and molded into sticks for use as a cautery.

lunar cycle. The Metonic cycle.

lu'nate (lū'nāt; 114), *adj.* Also **lu'nat·ed** (-nāt·ĕd; -ĭd). [L. *lunatus*, fr. *luna* the moon.] Crescent-shaped; as, a *lunate* spot. — **lu'nate·ly**, *adv.*

lu'na·tic (lū'nȧ·tĭk), *adj.* Also **lu·nat'i·cal** (lū·năt'ĭ·kăl). [LL. *lunaticus*, fr. *luna* the moon.] **1.** Affected with lunacy; now, insane; mad. **2.** Evincing insanity; crazy. **3.** [Attrib. use of the noun.] Appropriated to, or used by, insane persons; as, a *lunatic* asylum. — *n.* A person affected with lunacy; an insane person.

lu·na'tion (lū·nā'shŭn), *n.* The period of time, averaging 29 d., 12 h., 44 m., 2.8 s., between two successive new moons.

lunch (lŭnch), *n.* [See LUNCHEON.] **1.** A light meal, usually in the middle of the day; luncheon. **2.** A portion of food prepared for a lunch. — *v. i.* To take lunch. — *v. t.* To provide lunch for. — **lunch'er** (lŭn'chẽr), *n.*

lunch'eon (lŭn'chŭn), *n.* [E. dial. *luncheon, lunchion, lunshin*, a large lump of food, fr. dial. *lunch* a lump.] **a** A portion of food, or light repast, taken between meals or as an irregular meal. **b** = LUNCH, 1.

lunch'eon·ette' (-ĕt'), *n.* [See -ETTE.] A light lunch; also, a place where light lunches are sold.

lunch'room' (lŭnch'rōōm'), *n.* A restaurant specializing in food ready to serve or quickly prepared for light meals.

lune (lūn; 114), *n.* [F., fr. L. *luna* moon.] *Geom.* A crescent-shaped figure bounded by two intersecting arcs of circles, on a plane or a sphere.

lune, *n.* [OF. *loigne* leash.] A hawk's leash.

lunes (lūnz), *n. pl.* [See LUNATIC.] Fits of lunacy.

lu·nette' (lū·nĕt'), *n.* Also, formerly, **lu'net** (lū'nĕt; -nĭt). [F. *lunette*, dim. of *lune* moon.] **1.** *Arch.* That surface at the upper part of a wall which is partly surrounded by a vault which the wall intersects.

This space is often filled by windows or by mural painting. **2.** *Fort.* A fieldwork consisting of two faces, forming a salient angle, and two parallel flanks. **3.** *Ordn.* A ring in the plate at the rear of a gun carriage to receive the pintle.

lung (lŭng), *n.* [AS. *lungen.*] **1.** One of the (usually two) saclike organs forming the special respiratory organ of air-breathing vertebrates. Cf. BRONCHIAL TUBE, *Illust.* **2.** Any of various somewhat analogous saclike respiratory organs of certain air-breathing invertebrates, as pulmonate gastropods, spiders, and scorpions.

lunge (lŭnj), *n.* [From *allonge,* fr. F. *allonge,* fr. *allonger,* fr. *à* (L. *ad*) + *long* long.] **1.** A sudden thrust, as with a sword. **2.** Act of plunging forward; a plunge, pitch, or leap. — *v. i. & t.;* LUNGED (lŭnjd); LUNG'ING (lŭn'jĭng). **1.** To make, cause to make, or move with a lunge. **2.** *Manège.* To cause (a horse) to move in a circle while held by a long rein; to longe. — **lung'er** (lŭn'jẽr), *n.*

lun'geous (lŭn'jŭs), *adj.* [*lunge* a thrust + *-ous.*] *Dial. Eng.* Given to lunging, or thrusting; hence, mischievous.

lung'er (lŭng'ẽr), *n.* *Slang, U. S.* A tubercular person.

lung'fish' (lŭng'fĭsh'), *n.; pl.,* see FISH. Any of a group (Dipnoi) of fishes which breathe by lungs as well as gills; a dipnoan fish.

lun'gi, lun'gee (lo͝ong'gē), *n.* [Hind. & Per. *lungī.*] *India.* A long cloth worn as a scarf, loincloth, turban, etc.

lung'wort' (lŭng'wûrt'), *n.* A European herb (*Pulmonaria officinalis*), of the borage family, with blue flowers.

lu'ni- (lū'nĭ-). [L. *luna.*] A combining form meaning *moon,* as in **lu'ni·form,** and denoting also *lunar and,* as in **lu'ni·so'lar.**

‖**l'u'nion' fait la force** (lü'nyôN' fĕ lȧ fôrs'). [F.] Union makes strength; — motto of Belgium.

lu'ni·tid'al (lū'nĭ·tīd'ăl; -'l), *adj.* Pertaining to tidal movements dependent on the moon; as, the **lunitidal interval,** the interval between the transit of the moon and the time of the lunar high tide next following.

lunk'head' (lŭngk'hĕd'), *n.* *Colloq., U. S.* A blockhead.

lunt (lŭnt; lo͞ont), *n.* [D. *lont.*] *Chiefly Scot.* **a** A slow match; a torch. **b** Smoke. — *v. t. & i.* *Chiefly Scot.* To kindle; light; also, to smoke.

lu'nule (lū'nūl; 114), *n.* Also **lu'nu·la** (lū'nū·lȧ). [L. *lunula,* dim. of *luna* moon.] *Zool. & Anat.* A crescent-shaped part or marking, as the whitish mark at the base of the fingernails. — **lu'nu·lar** (lū'nū·lẽr), *adj.* — **lu'nu·late** (-lāt), **lu'nu·lat'ed** (-lāt'ĕd; -ĭd), *adj.*

lun'y (lo͞on'ĭ). Var. of LOONY.

Lu'per·ca'li·a (lū'pẽr·kā'lĭ·ȧ), *n. pl.,* or, *Now Rare,* **Lu'per·cal** (lū'pẽr·kăl), *n.* [L.] *Rom. Relig.* A ceremony, observed on Feb. 15, in which the priests of Faunus (**Lu·per'ci** [lū·pûr'sī]) made a circuit of the Palatine Hill, striking with goatskin thongs all women encountered, a rite believed to ensure fertility and easy delivery. — **Lu'per·ca'li·an** (-ăn), *adj.*

lu'pine (lū'pīn; 114), *adj.* [L. *lupinus,* fr. *lupus* wolf.] Wolfish; ravenous.

lu'pine (lū'pĭn), *n.* [L. *lupinus, lupinum.*] **a** Any of a genus (*Lupinus*) of herbs of the pea family, with white, yellow, or blue flowers. See BLUEBONNET, 2 **b.** **b** The seed of this plant, esp. of the white lupine of Europe (*L. albus*), used as food.

lu'pu·lin (lū'pū·lĭn), *n.* [NL. *lupulus* the hop, fr. L. *lupus* the hop.] The fine yellow resinous powder on the strobiles of hops. It is a sedative.

lu'pus (lū'pŭs), *n.* [L., a wolf.] *Med.* A tuberculous disease occurring in several forms, affecting the skin. **lu'pus er'y·them'a·to'sus** is characterized by scaly red patches, esp. in the region of the nose; **lu'pus vul·ga'ris** is marked by nodules esp. on the face, which often ulcerate and leave scars.

lurch (lûrch), *n.* [Origin obscure.] A sudden roll of a ship; hence, a swaying or staggering movement. — *v. i.* To roll or sway suddenly to one side, as a ship or a drunken man; to move with a lurch or lurches.

lurch, *n.* [F. *lourche* name of a game, as adj., deceived, embarrassed.] **1.** A conclusion of a game or set of games with one player far ahead or with one failing to score. **2.** Embarrassment; disadvantage; discomfiture. *Obs.,* except in the phrase *to leave one in the lurch.*

lurch, *v. i.* [Var. of LURK.] *Obs. exc. Dial.* To stay about a place furtively; to prowl; lurk. — *v. t. Archaic.* To get the start of (a person) so as to prevent his getting a fair share, as of food; hence, to cheat or rob (a person); to filch or steal (goods). — *n. Obs.* Act of lurching, or lurking, or a lurking place.

lurch'er (lûr'chẽr), *n.* **1.** One who lurches, or lies in wait; one who watches to pilfer, or to betray or entrap. **2.** *Brit.* A mongrel breed of dogs, often used by poachers.

lur'dan, lur'dane (lûr'dăn), *n.* [OF. *lourdin,* fr. *lourd* heavy, dull.] A lazy, stupid person. — *adj.* Stupid and lazy.

lure (lūr; 114), *n.* [F. *leurre,* of Teut. origin.] **1.** A bunch of feathers attached to a long cord, and often baited with raw meat, — used by falconers in recalling hawks. **2.** An allurement; enticement. **3.** A decoy or bait for fish or animals, specif., a tassellike structure on the head of pediculate fishes. Cf. ANGLER, *Illust.* — *v. t.* To draw to the lure; hence, to entice. — **lur'er** (lūr'ẽr), *n.*

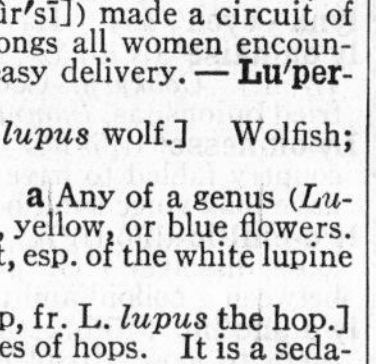

Lures, 3, for fishing. 1 Wiggler; 2 Plunker; 3 Minnow; 4 Spinner; 5 Spoon; 6 Bucktail.

Syn. **Lure, entice, inveigle, decoy, tempt, seduce** mean to draw one into danger or evil through attracting and deceiving. **Lure** implies an irresistible and, often, baleful attraction; **entice,** the exercise of artfulness and adroitness; **inveigle,** enticement by cajoling or beguiling; **decoy,** an entrapping or endangering by artifice or by false appearances; **tempt,** an attraction so strong that it overcomes the objections of conscience or better judgment; **seduce,** a leading astray from rectitude, propriety, or duty by overcoming one's scruples.

lu'rid (lū'rĭd), *adj.* [L. *luridus.*] **1.** Ghastly pale; wan; dismal. **2.** Appearing like glowing fire seen through cloud or smoke; as, *lurid* lightning. **3.** Harshly vivid or terrible; often, marked by violent passion or crime; as, a *lurid* story. — **Syn.** See GHASTLY. — **lu'rid·ly,** *adv.* — **lu'rid·ness,** *n.*

lurk (lûrk), *v. i.* [ME. *lurken, lorken.*] **1.** To lie hidden, as in ambush; to stay in or about a place secretly or furtively. **2.** To escape notice or to exist secretly; as, a *lurking* passion. **3.** To move furtively; to sneak or steal. — **lurk'er,** *n.* — **lurk'ing·ly,** *adv.*

Syn. **Lurk, couch, skulk, slink, sneak** mean to behave so as to escape attention. **Lurk** implies a lying in wait, usually stealthily and often for an evil intention; **couch,** a hiding from view, often with a malign intention; **skulk,** furtive movements, often sinister or cowardly; **slink,** stealthy or sly movements, often merely to escape attention; **sneak,** a getting into or out of a place by slinking, or out of a difficulty or the like by methods that are underhanded or not straightforward.

Lur'lei (lo͝or'lī). Var. of LORELEI.

lus'cious (lŭsh'ŭs), *adj.* **1.** Grateful to taste or smell, esp. from sweetness; delicious. **2.** Deliciously sensuous; often, cloying. — **lus'cious·ly,** *adv.* — **lus'cious·ness,** *n.*

lush (lŭsh), *adj.* **1.** Characterized by, or covered with, luxuriant growth. **2. a** Lavish; opulent; luscious; luxurious. **b** Extravagant; oversweet; too rich. **c** Richly profitable or prosperous. — **Syn.** See PROFUSE. — **lush'ness,** *n.*

lush, *n. Slang.* Liquor; also, a drunken person. — *v. i. & t. Slang.* To drink liquor, or to give drink to.

lust (lŭst), *n.* [AS., pleasure, longing.] **1.** *Obs.* **a** Pleasure; liking. **b** Inclination; desire. **2.** Sensuous desire; bodily appetite; commonly, sexual desire as a degrading passion. **3.** Longing or eagerness to enjoy. — *v. i.* To have an eager and, esp., an inordinate or sinful desire.

lus'ter, lus'tre (lŭs'tẽr), *n.* [F. *lustre,* fr. It. *lustro,* fr. *lustrare* to illuminate, fr. L. *lustrare.*] **1.** Fact or quality of shining with reflected light; shine or sheen; gloss. **2.** Brightness; glitter; as, the *luster* of the stars. **3.** Radiance of beauty or renown; splendor; distinction. **4.** A light-giving object; specif., a chandelier. **5. a** A substance which imparts luster to a surface, as plumbago. **b** A fabric of wool and cotton with a lustrous surface. **6.** *Mineral.* The appearance of the surface of a mineral as affected by, or dependent upon, its reflecting qualities. **7.** *Pottery.* A surface, ***metallic luster,*** sometimes iridescent and always metallic in appearance. — *v. t.* To make or finish with a lustrous gloss, as cotton by mercerizing, or pottery by adding a glaze. — *v. i.* To have luster; become lustrous.

lus'ter, lus'tre, *n.* [L. *lustrum.*] A lustrum.

lus'ter·ware', lus'tre·ware' (-wâr'), *n.* Earthenware decorated by applying to the glaze metallic oxides, which acquire brilliancy in the process of baking.

lust'ful (lŭst'fo͝ol; -f'l), *adj.* **1.** Full of, or excited by, lust; characterized by lust. **2.** *Obs.* Strong; lusty. — **lust'ful·ly,** *adv.* — **lust'ful·ness,** *n.*

lust'i·hood (lŭs'tĭ·ho͝od), *n.* Also **lust'i·head** (-hĕd). *Archaic.* State of being lusty; vigor of body.

lus'tral (lŭs'trăl), *adj.* [L. *lustralis,* fr. *lustrum.*] **1.** Of or pert. to, or used for, purification; as, *lustral* days. **2.** Of or pert. to a lustrum.

lus'trate (lŭs'trāt), *v. t.* [L. *lustratus,* past part. of *lustrare* to lustrate, fr. *lustrum.*] To make pure by means of a propitiatory offering; to purify. — **lus·tra'tion** (lŭs·trā'shŭn), *n.*

lus'tre (lŭs'tẽr). Var. of LUSTER.

lus'tring (lŭs'trĭng), *n.* [F. *lustrine,* fr. It. *lustrino.* See 1st LUSTER.] A plain, stout, lustrous silk fabric, used for dresses and for ribbon.

lus'trous (-trŭs), *adj.* Having luster; shining; hence, radiant; illustrious. — **Syn.** See BRIGHT. — **lus'trous·ly,** *adv.* — **lus'trous·ness,** *n.*

lus'trum (-trŭm), *n.; pl.* LUSTRUMS (-trŭmz), LUSTRA (-trȧ). [L.; akin to L. *lavare* to wash.] **1.** *Rom. Antiq.* **a** A purification of the whole Roman people made after the census every five years. **b** Hence, the census. **2.** A period of five years; a luster.

lust'y (lŭs'tĭ), *adj.;* LUST'I·ER (-tĭ·ẽr); LUST'I·EST. [From LUST, *n.*] **1.** *Archaic & Dial.* Merry; gay. **2.** Full of life and vigor; sturdy. **3.** *Obs.* **a** Pleasant; agreeable. **b** Lustful. **c** Courageous. — **Syn.** See VIGOROUS. — **lust'i·ly,** *adv.* — **lust'i·ness,** *n.*

‖**lu'sus na·tu'rae** (lū'sŭs nȧ·tū'rē). [L.] A sport or freak of nature.

lu'ta·nist (lū'tȧ·nĭst), *n.* Also **lu'te·nist.** [ML. *lutanista,* fr. *lutana* lute.] A lute player; hence, a poet.

lute (lūt; 114), *n.* [F. *lut,* fr. L. *lutum* mud, clay.] A substance, esp. a cement of clay, for packing a joint, coating a porous surface, etc., to produce imperviousness to gas or liquid. — *v. t.* To seal with lute.

lute, *n.* [OF. *leüt,* fr. Pr. *laut,* fr. Ar. *al-'ūd* the piece of wood.] *Music.* A stringed instrument with a large pear-shaped body, a long neck with a fretted finger board, and a head with screws for tuning. It is played by plucking the strings with the fingers. — *v. t. & i.* To play on, or to sound, a lute.

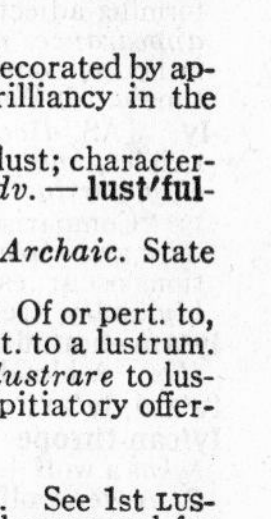

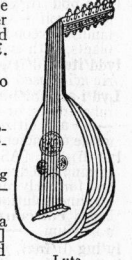

Lute.

lu'te·al (lū'tē·ăl; 114), *adj.* *Anat.* Of or pertaining to the corpus luteum.

lu·te'ci·um, *n.* See LUTETIUM.

lu'te·in (lū'tē·ĭn), *n.* [From corpus *luteum.*] *Biochem.* **a** = XANTHOPHYLL **a.** **b** A hormone from corpus luteum.

lu'te·o- (lū'tē·ō-). [L. *luteus* yellow.] A combining form signifying *orange yellow* or *brownish yellow.* — **lu'te·o** (-ō), *adj.*

lu'te·o·lin (-ō·lĭn), *n.* [F. *lutéoline,* fr. NL. Reseda *luteola,* fr. L. *luteolus* yellowish, fr. *luteus* yellow.] *Chem.* A yellow crystalline compound, $C_{15}H_{10}O_6$, used in dyeing.

lu'te·ous (-ŭs), *adj.* [L. *luteus,* fr. *lutum,* a plant used by dyers.] Of any of several colors averaging yellow in hue, of medium saturation and high brilliance. See COLOR.

lu·te'ti·um (lū·tē'shĭ·ŭm), *n.* Formerly **lu·te'ci·um** (-shĭ·ŭm; -sĭ·ŭm). [NL., fr. L. *Lutetia* a town in Gaul, now Paris.] *Chem.* A metallic element (see RARE-EARTH ELEMENT) separated from ytterbium in 1907. Symbol, *Lu;* at. no., 71; at. wt., 174.99.

Lu'ther·an (lū'thẽr·ăn; 114), *adj.* Of or pertaining to Martin Luther (1483–1546); adhering to the doctrines of Luther. — *n.* A member or adherent of a denomination of Christians that accepts the doctrines of Luther. The cardinal doctrine is that of justification by faith alone. — **Lu'ther·an·ism** (-ĭz'm), *n.*

Lu'tine bell (lo͞o'tēn). The bell of the British warship *Lutine,* wrecked in 1799, which was salvaged and hangs in the offices of Lloyd's (see LLOYD'S, 1). The bell is sounded before announcements of ships lost at sea or reports of overdue ships.

lut'ing (lūt'ĭng), *n.* *Chem.* = LUTE, cement.

lut'ist (-ĭst), *n.* A lute player; also, a maker of lutes.

lux (lŭks), *n.; pl.* LUXES (lŭk'sĕz; -sĭz), LUCES (lū'sēz). [L., light.] *Photom.* The international unit of illumination, being the direct illumination on a surface which is everywhere one meter from a uniform point source of one international candle. It is equal to one lumen per square meter, or 0.0929 foot-candle.

lux'ate (lŭk'sāt), *v. t.* [L. *luxatus*, past part. of *luxare* to dislocate.] To displace, as a joint; to put out of joint; to dislocate. — **lux·a'tion** (lŭks·ā'shŭn), *n.*

luxe (lo͝oks; lŭks; *F.* lüks), *n.* [F., fr. L. *luxus*.] Elegance; sumptuous quality or make; — usually preceded by *de* (of); as, articles *de luxe*.

lux·u'ri·ance (lŭks·ū'rĭ·ăns; lŭg·zho͝or'ĭ·ăns), *n.* Also **lux·u'ri·an·cy** (-ăn·sĭ). State or quality of being luxuriant; rank.

lux·u'ri·ant (-ănt), *adj.* [L. *luxurians*, pres. part. of *luxuriare*.] **1.** *Now Rare.* Exceedingly fertile. **2.** Exuberant in growth; rank; as, *luxuriant* foliage. **3.** Hence, characterized by profuse and intricate design, great fertility in invention, or vivid or florid figures. — **Syn.** See PROFUSE. — **lux·u'ri·ant·ly**, *adv.*

lux·u'ri·ate (-āt), *v. i.* [L. *luxuriari*, *-are*, to luxuriate.] **1.** To grow exuberantly. **2.** To feed or live in luxury. **3.** To indulge with unrestrained delight and freedom; as, to *luxuriate* in description. — **lux·u'ri·a'tion** (-ā'shŭn), *n.*

lux·u'ri·ous (-ŭs), *adj.* Of or pertaining to luxury; ministering to luxury. — **lux·u'ri·ous·ly**, *adv.* — **lux·u'ri·ous·ness**, *n.*

Syn. (1) See SENSUOUS. — **Ant.** Ascetic.

(2) **Luxurious, sumptuous, opulent** mean ostentatiously rich or magnificent. **Luxurious** applies to that which is exceedingly choice or costly; **sumptuous**, to that which overwhelms one with its grandeur, gorgeousness, luxuriousness, or the like; **opulent**, to that which seems to flaunt its luxuriousness, luxuriance, or in some cases, costliness.

lux'u·ry (lŭk'sho͞o·rĭ; lŭks'ū·rĭ), *n.*; *pl.* -RIES (-rĭz). [OF. *luxurie*, fr. L. *luxuria*; akin to L. *luxus* luxury.] **1.** A free indulgence in costly food, dress, or anything which gratifies the appetites or tastes; also, a mode of life characterized by material abundance. **2.** Anything which pleases the senses, and is also costly, or difficult to obtain; an expensive rarity; as, silks and jewels are *luxuries*.

-ly (-lĭ). [AS. *-līc*, *-lic*, orig., the same word as *līc* body.] A suffix forming adjectives, now mostly from nouns, and denoting: **a** *Like in appearance, manner,* or *nature; characteristic of;* as in queen*ly*, father*ly;* sometimes specif., in a good sense, *befitting*, as in man*ly*, time*ly*. **b** With nouns of time, *every* (so often), as in dai*ly*.

-ly. [AS. *-līce*, *-lice*.] A suffix forming adverbs from adjectives, participles, and (rarely) nouns, as in slow*ly*, bad*ly*, smiling*ly*, unexpected*ly*, part*ly*.

☞ Comparison is now made with *more* and *most*, but formerly by *-lier* and *-liest*, as in soft*lier*, tru*liest*. Before *-ly*, various contractions occur, esp. by dropping *l* or *le* or by changing *y* to *i*, as in capa*bly*, du*lly*, treb*ly*, happi*ly*.

ly'am–hound' (lī'ăm·hound'), **lyme'–hound'** (līm'-), *n.* *Obs. exc. Hist.* A bloodhound.

ly'ard, ly'art (lī'ẽrd, -ẽrt), *adj.* *Dial.* Gray, or streaked with gray.

ly'can·thrope (lī'kăn·thrōp; lī·kăn'-), *n.* [Gr. *lykanthrōpos*, fr. *lykos* a wolf + *anthrōpos* a man.] **1.** One affected with lycanthropy. **2.** A werewolf.

ly·can'thro·py (lī·kăn'thrō·pĭ), *n.* **1.** A form of insanity in which the patient imagines himself a wolf. **2.** *Folklore.* Assumption of the form and traits of a wolf by witchcraft or magic. — **ly'can·throp'ic** (lī'kăn·thrŏp'ĭk), *adj.*

‖**ly'cée'** (lē'sā'), *n.* [F.] A French public secondary school which prepares for the university.

ly·ce'um (lī·sē'ŭm), *n.* [L., fr. Gr. *lykeion*, after the neighboring temple of Apollo, fr. *Lykeios*, epithet of Apollo.] **1.** [*cap.*] A tract of ground near ancient Athens, the site of a gymnasium, but most famous as the place in whose shaded walks Aristotle taught. **2.** A house or apartment appropriated to instruction by lectures. **3.** *U.S.* An association providing inspirational lectures, concerts, entertainments, etc. **4.** = LYCÉE.

lych, lych gate. Vars. of LICH, LICH GATE.

lych'nis (lĭk'nĭs), *n.* [L., a kind of red flower, fr. Gr. *lychnis*.] *Bot.* Any of a genus (*Lychnis*) of herbs of the pink family, with terminal cymes of showy, mostly red or white flowers, as the ***scarlet lychnis*** (*L. chalcedonica*) and the ***rose campion*** (*L. coronaria*). See CAMPION.

ly'co·pod (lī'kō·pŏd), *n.* Also **ly'co·po'di·um** (-pō'dĭ·ŭm). [Gr. *lykos* wolf + *-pod*, *-podium*.] *Bot.* Any of a genus (*Lycopodium*, family Lycopodiaceae, the club-moss family) of erect or creeping plants, with evergreen leaves. See GROUND PINE **b**.

lydd'ite (lĭd'īt), *n.* [From *Lydd*, Eng.] A high explosive, chiefly picric acid, used as a shell explosive.

Lyd'i·an (lĭd'ĭ·ăn; 58), *adj.* **1.** Of or pertaining to ancient Lydia, its inhabitants, or its language. **2.** Soft or effeminate; also, voluptuous. — *n.* **a** A citizen or one of the people of ancient Lydia. **b** The language of ancient Lydia, showing certain affinities with the Hittite.

lye (lī), *n.* [AS. *lēah*.] **1.** Originally, a strong alkaline liquor (containing chiefly potassium carbonate), obtained by leaching wood ashes and formerly much used in soapmaking, washing, etc.; now, any strong alkaline solution. Solid sodium (or potassium) hydroxide is often called ***concentrated lye***. **2.** Any solution obtained by lixiviation; a lixivium. — *v. t.*; LYED (līd); LY'ING (lī'ĭng). To treat with lye.

ly'ing (lī'ĭng), *pres. part.* of LIE (either sense). — **Syn.** See DISHONEST.

ly'ing–in', *n.* The state attending, and consequent to, childbirth; confinement; also, act of bearing a child.

lymph (lĭmf; 89), *n.* [L. *lympha*, for earlier *limpa*, *lumpa*, water, goddess of water, fr. Gr. *nymphē* bride, nymph, goddess of moisture.] **1.** *Poetic.* A spring of water; hence, water. **2.** *Obs.* The sap of plants. **3.** *Anat. & Physiol.* A nearly colorless coagulable fluid, contained in the lymphatic vessels. It consists chiefly of blood plasma and colorless corpuscles. Cf. CHYLE.

lymph-. = LYMPHO-.

lym·phad'e·ni'tis (lĭm·făd'ē·nī'tĭs; lĭm'fȧ·dē-), *n.* [NL., fr. *lymph-* + *aden-* + *-itis*.] *Med.* Inflammation of lymphatic glands.

lym·phan'gi·al (lĭm·făn'jĭ·ăl), *adj.* *Anat.* Of or pertaining to the lymphatic vessels.

lym·phan'gi·o- (lĭm·făn'jĭ·ō-), **lymphangi-.** A combining form for *lymphangial*, as in **lym·phan'gi·i'tis, lym·phan'gi·ot'o·my** (see -ITIS, -TOMY).

lym·phat'ic (lĭm·făt'ĭk), *adj.* [L. *lymphaticus* distracted, frantic.] **1.** Of, pertaining to, containing, or conveying lymph; pertaining to lymph glands or lymphatics (which together constitute the ***lymphatic system***); also, caused by the condition of the lymphatic glands; as, *lymphatic* leukemia. **2.** Designating, or having, a temperament lacking energy or indisposed to exertion or excitement. — *n.* A vessel containing or conveying lymph.

lymphatic gland. = LYMPH GLAND.

lym'pha·to- (lĭm'fȧ·tō-). A combining form for *lymphatic*, as in **lym'pha·tol'y·sis** (see -LYSIS).

lymph cell. = LYMPHOCYTE.

lymph gland *or* **node.** One of the rounded masses of lymphoid tissue, surrounded by a capsule of connective tissue, which occur in the course of the lymphatic vessels. They are not true glands, but consist of a reticulum of connective tissue fibers in the meshes of which are contained numerous small round cells, the *lymphoid cells*, having a large, round, deeply staining nucleus. These cells, when carried off by the lymph flowing through the gland, become lymphocytes.

lym'pho- (lĭm'fō-), **lymph-.** [See LYMPH.] A combining form for *lymph* denoting: *Connection with*, or *relation to, lymph* or *the lymphatics.*

lym'pho·blast (lĭm'fō·blăst), *n.* [*lympho-* + *-blast*.] *Anat.* A cell destined to become a lymphocyte. — **lym'pho·blas'tic** (-blăs'tĭk), *adj.*

lym'pho·cyte (-sīt), *n.* [*lympho-* + *-cyte*.] A white or colorless amoeboid blood cell derived from lymphatic tissues. Cf. LEUCOCYTE.

lym'pho·cy·to'sis (-sī·tō'sĭs), *n.* [NL., fr. *lymphocyte* + *-osis*.] *Med.* A condition marked by increased number of lymphocytes in the blood. — **lym'pho·cy·tot'ic** (-sī·tŏt'ĭk), *adj.*

lym'pho·gran'u·lo'ma (-grăn'ū·lō'mȧ), *n.* [*lympho-* + *granuloma* (NL., fr. LL. *granulum* granule + *-oma*).] *Med.* A contagious venereal disease, caused by a filtrable virus, which is marked by swelling and ulceration of lymphatic tissues in the hip and groin regions.

lymph'oid (lĭm'foid), *adj.* [*lymph* + *-oid*.] *Anat.* **a** Like, pert. to, or resembling lymph. **b** Of, like, or pert. to **lymphoid tissue**, the tissue characteristic of the lymph glands. See ADENOID, *adj.*, **b**.

lymphoid cell. See LYMPH GLAND.

lyn·ce'an (lĭn·sē'ăn), *adj.* Of or pertaining to a lynx; sharp-sighted.

lynch (lĭnch), *v. t.* To inflict punishment, especially death, upon, without the forms of law, as when a mob captures and hangs a suspected person. — **lynch'er**, *n.*

lynch law. Formerly **Lynch's law** (lĭnch'ĭz). [Prob. after Charles *Lynch* (1736–96), planter and justice of the peace in Virginia, who employed extralegal methods of trial and punishment.] Act or practice by private persons of inflicting punishment for crimes or offenses, without due process of law.

lynx (lĭngks), *n.*; see PLURAL, *Note*, 3. [L. *lynx*, *lyncis*, fr. Gr. *lynx*.] Any of a genus (*Lynx*) of wildcats having long legs, a short stubby tail, and often tufted ears. There is a common lynx of northern Europe (*Lynx lynx*). The American lynxes include the ***Canada lynx*** *or* ***loup-cervier*** (*L. canadensis*) and the ***bay lynx*** of eastern United States (*L. rufus*) and allied varieties of western U. S. and northern Mexico. The bay lynx and allied varieties are called also ***bobcat***.

lynx'–eyed', *adj.* Having acute sight.

ly'on·naise' (lī'ŭ·nāz'; *F.* lē'ô'nâz'), *adj.* [F., fem. of *lyonnais* of Lyon.] *Cookery.* Cooked ***à la lyonnaise***, or with flaked or sliced fried onions; as, *lyonnaise* potatoes.

Ly'on·nesse' (lī'ŏ·nĕs'), *n.* [OF. *Leonois*.] In Arthurian legend, a country fabled to have been formerly contiguous to Cornwall, but to have long since sunk beneath the sea.

ly'o·phil'ic (lī'ō·fĭl'ĭk), *adj.* [*lyo-*, combining form (fr. Gr. *lyein* to loose, dissolve) + Gr. *philos* loving.] *Chem.* Denoting strong affinity between a colloid and the liquid in which it is dispersed.

ly'o·pho'bic (-fō'bĭk; -fŏb'ĭk), *adj.* [*lyo-*, combining form (fr. Gr. *lyein* to loose, dissolve) + *phobos* fear.] *Chem.* Denoting lack of strong affinity between a colloid and the liquid in which it is dispersed.

Ly'ra (lī'rȧ), *n.*; *gen.* LYRAE (-rē). [L. See LYRE.] A northern constellation, representing the lyre of Orpheus or Mercury; the Harp. It contains Vega, fourth brightest star in the heavens.

ly'rate (lī'rāt), *adj.* Also **ly'rat·ed** (-rāt·ĕd; -ĭd). **1.** *Bot.* Lyre-shaped, or spatulate and oblong, with small lobes toward the base. See LEAF, *Illust.* (18). **2.** Shaped like a lyre, as the tail of the lyre-bird. — **ly'rate·ly**, *adv.*

lyre (līr), *n.* [OF. *lire* (F. *lyre*), fr. L. *lyra*, fr. Gr. *lyra*.] **1.** *Music.* A stringed instrument of the harp class used by the ancient Greeks, esp. in accompanying song and recitation. **2.** [*cap.*] *Astron.* The constellation Lyra.

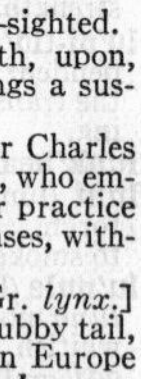
Lyre.

lyre'bird' (-bûrd'), *n.* Any of three species of Australian passerine birds (genera *Menura* and *Harriwhitea*), the males of which have very long tail feathers which are lyre-shaped when spread.

lyr'ic (lĭr'ĭk), *adj.* [F. or L.; F. *lyrique*, fr. L. *lyricus*, fr. Gr. *lyrikos*.] **1.** Of or pertaining to a lyre. **2.** Suited to be sung to the lyre; appropriate for song; as, *lyric* poetry. **lyric poetry**, whether actually sung or not, is generally composed in stanzas, is expressive of the poet's feeling rather than of outward incident or events, and may take a special form, as ode, sonnet, hymn, roundel, or any of numerous verse schemes. **3.** *Music.* **a** Of a quality especially adapted for singing songs; — contrasted with *dramatic* and *coloratura*, and said of voices. **b** Musical; operatic; as, the *lyric* drama. — *n.* **1.** A lyric poem or composition. **2.** The words of a song.

lyr'i·cal (lĭr'ĭ·kăl), *adj.* Lyric. — **lyr'i·cal·ly**, *adv.*

lyr'i·cism (lĭr'ĭ·sĭz'm), *n.* Quality of being lyric.

lyr'i·co- (lĭr'ĭ·kō-). A combining form for *lyric*, denoting *lyrical and*, as in **lyr'i·co–dra·mat'ic, lyr'i·co–ep'ic.**

lyr'ism (lĭr'ĭz'm; lĭr'ĭz'm), *n.* **a** Act of playing on a lyre or harp. **b** (*pron.* lĭr'ĭz'm) = LYRICISM.

lyr'ist (lĭr'ĭst; lĭr'-), *n.* A player on the lyre; hence (*pron.* lĭr'ĭst), a composer or singer of lyrical poetry.

lyse (līs), *v. t.* *Bacteriol. & Physiol.* To cause to undergo lysis. — *v. i.* *Bacteriol. & Physiol.* To undergo lysis.

-lyse (-līz). = -LYZE.

ly'si- (lī'sĭ-; lĭs'ĭ-), **lys-.** [Gr. *lysis*.] A combining form meaning *loosening*, used as equiv. to *-lysis*, as in *lysin*.

ly·sim'e·ter (lī·sĭm'ē·tẽr), *n.* [*lysi-* + *-meter*.] A device for measuring percolation of water through soils and determining the soluble constituents removed in drainage.

ly'sin (lī'sĭn), *n.* *Biochem.* Any of a class of substances capable of dissolving bacteria, blood corpuscles, etc.

ly'sine (lī'sēn; -sĭn), *n.* Also **ly'sin.** [Gr. *lysis* a loosing, dissolution.] A biologically important basic amino acid, $C_6H_{14}N_2O_2$, produced on hydrolysis of many proteins.

ly'sis (lī'sĭs), *n.* [NL., fr. Gr. *lysis*.] **1.** *Med.* The resolution or favorable termination of a disease, coming on gradually. Cf. CRISIS. **2.** *Biochem.* A process of disintegration or solution, as the action of a lysin; cell destruction.

-lysis. [Gr. *lysis* a loosing.] A combining form signifying: **1.** *A* *loosing, dissolving, solution, dissolution,* as in cata*lysis*, para*lysis*, pneumato*lysis*. **2.** *Chem.* **a** The *decomposition of a substance,* as in electro*lysis*, hydro*lysis*. **b** In biochemistry, *dissolution, destruction,* or *disintegration;* as in auto*lysis*.

ly′so·zyme (lī′sō·zīm; -zĭm), *n.* [*lys-* + en*zyme*.] *Biochem.* A bacteriolytic substance occurring in body secretions.

-lyte (-līt). [Gr. *-lytos*, corresponding to nouns in *-lysis*.] *Physical Chem.* A combining form denoting *a substance subjected to decomposition,* as in electro*lyte*.

-lyte (-līt). = -LITE.

lyt′ic (lĭt′ĭk), *adj.* Of or pertaining to lysis or a lysin; specif., *Biochem.,* productive of, or effecting, lysis, or cell destruction.

-lyt′ic (-lĭt′ĭk). [Gr. *-lytikos*, fr. *lytikos*, able to loose, loosing.] **1.** A suffix of adjectives corresponding to nouns ending in *-lysis*, as in ana*lytic*, para*lytic*. See -LYSIS. **2.** *Biochem.* A suffix denoting hydrolytic enzyme action on the substance to the name of which it is added.

lyt′ta (lĭt′ȧ), *n.; pl.* LYTTAE (-ē). [L., a worm said to grow under the tongue of dogs, and to cause canine madness, fr. Gr. *lytta*, *lyssa*, lit., madness.] A rod of cartilage lying along the tongue in many carnivores, as dogs.

-lyze, -lyse (-līz). [F. *-lyser*.] A combining form forming transitive verbs corresponding to nouns ending in *-lysis*, as in ana*lyze*, cata*lyze*, hydro*lyze*.

M

M, m (ĕm), *n.; pl.* M's, m's, Ms, ms (ĕmz). **1.** The thirteenth letter of the English alphabet. It comes through the Latin from the Greek M (mu), which in turn was derived from a Phoenician letter. **2.** The sound of this letter. Its sound is that of a voiced, or sonant, bilabial continuant. See *Pron.*, § 64. **3.** [*cap.*] In Roman numerals, 1,000, or, in the form $\overline{M}$, 1,000,000. **4.** As a *symbol*, the twelfth or (see K, 3) thirteenth in order or class.

m-. *Chem.* See META-.

ma′am (măm; mäm; *after "yes," also* ′m), *n.* Madam; — a colloquial contraction. At the English court it is used (*pron.* măm) in addressing the queen or a royal princess.

Mab (măb), *n.* See QUEEN MAB.

mac (măk), *n.* *Colloq., Brit.* Short for MACKINTOSH.

ma·ca′bre (mȧ·kä′b′r; *F.* mȧ′kȧ′br′), *adj.* Also **ma·ca′ber** (mȧ·kä′bẽr). [F. *macabre*, for OF. *Macabré, dance Macabré,* the dance of *Macabré*, where *Macabré* is a proper name.] Pertaining to, or suggestive of, the dance of death, a dance in which Death, as a skeleton, leads skeletons to the grave; hence, gruesome. — **Syn.** See GHASTLY.

ma·ca′co (mȧ·kā′kō), *n.* [Pg., fr. Tupi *macaca*, *macaco*, monkey. Cf. MACAQUE.] Any of several lemurs, as the black lemur (*Lemur macaco*) and the ring-tailed lemur (*L. catta*).

mac·ad′am (măk·ăd′ăm), *n.* [After John L. *McAdam* (1756–1836), Scot. engineer.] **a** Macadamized roadway or pavement. **b** The broken stone used in macadamizing.

Mac′a·da′mi·a (măk′ȧ·dā′mĭ·ȧ), *n.* [NL., after John *Macadam* (1827–65), Scottish scientist in Australia.] *Bot.* A small Australian genus of trees or shrubs (family Proteaceae) characterized by the 4-lobed disk and by the two pendulous ovules.

mac·ad′am·ize (măk·ăd′ăm·īz), *v. t.* To construct or finish (a road) by packing a layer of small broken stone on a convex well-drained earth roadbed. — **mac·ad′am·i·za′tion** (-ĭ·zā′shŭn; -ī·zā′-), *n.*

ma·caque′ (mȧ·käk′), *n.* [F., fr. Pg. *macaco*.] Any of certain short-tailed monkeys (genus *Macaca* and allied genera) of Asia and the East Indies.

mac′a·ro′ni (măk′ȧ·rō′nĭ), *n.; pl.* -NIS (-nĭz), esp. in sense 1, or -NIES (-nĭz), esp. in sense 2. [It. *maccheroni*, *maccaroni*, pl.] **1.** A paste, chiefly of wheat flour, dried in the form of slender tubes, and used, when cooked, as food. Cf. SPAGHETTI, VERMICELLI. **2.** *Hist.* One of a class of traveled young men affecting foreign ways; hence, a fop; a dandy.

mac′a·ron′ic (-rŏn′ĭk), *adj.* Also **mac′a·ron′i·cal** (-ĭ·kăl). **1.** Like or likened to macaroni; hence, mixed; confused. **2.** Of or pertaining to a burlesque composition (called a **macaronic**) in which vernacular words of one or more modern languages are intermixed with Latin words, and with hybrids.

mac′a·roon′ (măk′ȧ·ro͞on′; 2), *n.* [F. *macaron*, fr. It. *maccherone*.] A small cake, composed chiefly of the white of eggs, sugar, and pounded almonds, or, sometimes, filberts, coconut, or the like.

ma·caw′ (mȧ·kô′), *n.* [Pg. *macao*.] Any of numerous parrots (chiefly genus *Ara*) of South and Central America. They are among the largest of parrots, with brilliant plumage. See PARROT, *Illust.*

Mac·beth′ (măk·bĕth′), *n.* A tragedy by Shakespeare; also, its hero.

Mac′ca·be′an (măk′ȧ·bē′ăn), *adj.* Of or pert. to Judas Maccabeus or the Maccabees; as, the *Maccabean* princes.

Mac′ca·bees (măk′ȧ·bēz), *n. pl.* **1.** The name given in later times to the Hasmonaeans, a family of Jewish patriots, who headed a religious revolt in the reign of Antiochus IV, 175–164 B.C. **2.** (*n. pl., construed as sing.*) *Douay Bib.* **Mach′a·bees** (măk′ȧ·bēz). One of two historical books of the Apocrypha. See BIBLE.

mac′ca·boy (măk′ȧ·boi), **mac′co·boy** (măk′ō-), *n.* [From *Macouba*, district in Martinique where it is made.] A variety of snuff.

mac′ca·ro′ni, mac′ca·ron′ic. Vars. of MACARONI, etc.

Mc·Coy′, the (mȧ·koi′). Also, **the real McCoy.** *Slang, U.S.* The genuine person or article; the real thing.

mace (mās), *n.* [OF.] **1.** A heavy staff, often spiked, used esp. in the Middle Ages for breaking armor. Hence, a club used as a weapon. **2.** A staff borne by, or carried before, a dignitary as an ensign of his authority. **3.** One who carries a mace. **4.** *Billiards.* A rod with a flat wooden head, formerly sometimes used instead of a cue.

mace, *n.* [OF. *macis*.] An aromatic spice consisting of the dried external fibrous covering of the nutmeg.

mace′–bear′er, *n.* An officer who carries a mace.

mac′é·doine′ (măs′ā·dwän′; *F.* mȧ′sā′dwȧn′), *n.* [F.] A mixture of cut or small cooked vegetables served as a salad or cocktail or in a jellied dessert, or used in a sauce or as a garnish.

mac′er (măs′ẽr), *n.* [F. *massier*.] A mace-bearer.

mac′er·ate (măs′ẽr·āt), *v. t. & i.* [L. *maceratus*, past part. of *macerare* to soften.] **1.** To waste away; hence, to oppress; torment. **2.** To soften by steeping in a liquid; to separate the parts of (vegetable fibers) by steeping; also, to soften and wear away (food) by digestive or other physiological processes. — **mac′er·at′er** (-āt′ẽr), **mac′er·a′tor** (-ā′tẽr), *n.* — **mac′er·a′tion** (-ā′shŭn), *n.*

Mach, *n.* See MACH NUMBER.

Mach′a·bees, *n. pl.* See MACCABEES, 2.

ma·che′te (mä·chā′tā; *also* mȧ·shĕt′, mȧ·shēt′), *n.* [Sp.] A large heavy knife, used, esp. in South America and the West Indies, for cutting cane, clearing paths, etc.

Mach′i·a·vel′li·an (măk′ĭ·ȧ·vĕl′ĭ·ăn; -yăn; 58), *adj.* Also **Mach′i·a·vel′i·an.** **a** Of or pertaining to the Florentine statesman Niccolò Machiavelli (1469–1527), or relating to his political theories, esp. to the doctrine that any means, however unscrupulous, may be justifiably employed by a ruler in order to maintain a strong central government. **b** Hence, characterized by political cunning or bad faith. — **Mach′i·a·vel′li·an**, *n.* — **Mach′i·a·vel′lism** (-vĕl′ĭz′m), *n.*

ma·chic′o·late (mȧ·chĭk′ō·lāt), *v. t.* [ML. *machicolatus*, past part.] To furnish with machicolations, as a turret.

ma·chic′o·la′tion (-lā′shŭn), *n.* *Arch.* An opening between the corbels of a parapet, or in the floor of a gallery or the roof of a portal, for discharging missiles upon assailants; also, a gallery or parapet containing such openings. See BATTLEMENT, *Illust.*

mach′i·nate (măk′ĭ·nāt), *v. i. & t.* [L. *machinatus*, past part. of *machinari* to devise, plot. See MACHINE.] To plan; contrive; esp., to scheme to do harm; to plot.

mach′i·na′tion (-nā′shŭn), *n.* **1.** Act of machinating. **2.** An artful design or plot. — **Syn.** See PLOT.

mach′i·na′tor (măk′ĭ·nā′tẽr), *n.* A plotter.

ma·chine′ (mȧ·shēn′), *n.* [F., fr. L. *machina* machine, device, trick, fr. Gr. *mēchanē*, fr. *mēchos* means, expedient.] **1.** *Archaic.* A material construction, handiwork of a divine or supernatural power; specif., the bodily frame. **2.** Hence, a contrivance of a mechanical sort; specif., a vehicle or conveyance; — applied formerly to a coach, cart, etc., now variously to an automobile, airplane, bicycle, etc. **3.** **a** In the theater, an apparatus to produce stage effects; — chiefly in reference to the ancient stage. Cf. DEUS EX MACHINA. **b** Hence, in reference to literature, any contrivance for dramatic presentation; esp., a supernatural agency. **4.** Any device consisting of two or more resistant, relatively constrained parts, which may serve to transmit and modify force and motion so as to do some desired kind of work (see SIMPLE MACHINE, *Illust.*); popularly, a complex combination of such parts together with their framework, fastenings, etc. **5.** Any person or organization that acts like a machine. **6.** The working bodies, often under the power of a boss, in a political party, through which its policies and activities are directed; — used disparagingly. — *adj.* Of or pertaining to a machine or machinery; as, *machine* parts; characterized by the use of machinery; as, the *machine* age; also, produced by machinery; as, *machine* products; figuratively, stereotyped. — *v. t.* To plane, shape, turn, mill, etc., by a machine or machines.

machine gun. *Mil.* An automatic gun using small-arms ammunition for rapid continuous firing. See RIFLE, *Illust.*

ma·chin′er·y (mȧ·shēn′ẽr·ĭ; -shēn′rĭ), *n.* **1.** The assemblage of contrivances employed in the development of a plot, as of a poem. **2.** Machines, in general or collectively; also, the working parts of a machine. **3.** The means and appliances by which anything is kept in action or a desired result is obtained.

machine shop. A workshop in which work is machined to size and assembled. — **ma·chine′–shop′**, *adj.*

machine tool. A nonportable power-driven machine partly or wholly automatic in action for milling, planing, turning, grinding, boring, drilling, or otherwise changing the shape of material by removing metal in the form of blocks, fragments, spiral shavings, or the like; a machine for making machines or machinery, for example, a lathe.

ma·chin′ist (mȧ·shēn′ĭst), *n.* **1.** **a** A constructor of machines and engines. **b** One skilled in the use of machine tools. **c** One who works or runs a machine. **2.** One who constructs or controls theatrical machinery. **3.** *U. S. Navy.* A warrant officer assistant to the engineer officer.

Mach′ num′ber (mäk′). Also **Mach**, *n.* [After Ernst *Mach* (1838–1916), Austrian physicist.] *Aerodynamics.* A number representing the ratio of the speed of a body to the speed of sound in the surrounding atmosphere. For subsonic speeds the Mach number is less than one, as 0.80, and for supersonic speeds it is greater than one, as 1.31.

ma·chree′ (mȧ·krē′), *n.* [Ir. *mo* my + *croidhe*, OIr. *cride*, heart.] An Anglo-Irish term of endearment.

-machy. [Gr. *machē* battle.] A combining form denoting *contest between* or *by means of*, as in logo*machy*.

mac′in·tosh (măk′ĭn·tŏsh). Var. of MACKINTOSH.

Mc′In·tosh (măk′ĭn·tŏsh), *n.* Also **McIntosh Red.** [After John *McIntosh*, of Ontario, who discovered it.] *Hort.* A late-ripening fine variety of brilliant-red apple.

mack′er·el (măk′ẽr·ĕl), *n.;* see PLURAL, *Note*, 3. [OF. *maquerel*, fr. ML. *macarellus*.] An important North Atlantic spiny-finned food fish (*Scomber scombrus*, family Scombridae), about 18 inches long, green with blue bars above and silvery below; also, any of various related fishes of a superfamily (Scombroidea), as the ***frigate mackerel*** (*Auxis thazard* and *A. rochei*), and the ***Spanish mackerel*** (genus *Scomberomorus*, esp. *S. maculatus*) found off the American Atlantic coast from Cape Ann to Brazil. Cf. HORSE MACKEREL.

mackerel sky. A sky covered with rows of clouds, alto-cumulus or cirro-cumulus, resembling the patterns on a mackerel's back. See CLOUD, *Illust.*

Mack′i·naw (măk′ĭ·nô), *adj.* [Can. F. *Mackinac*, fr. *Michilimackinac*.] Pertaining to Mackinac, Michigan, where stores were formerly distributed to the Indians, or to the Straits of Mackinac.

Mackinaw blanket. A thick blanket formerly in common use in the western United States.

Mack'i·naw boat (măk'ĭ·nô). A flat-bottomed boat, used esp. on the upper Great Lakes and their tributaries.
Mackinaw coat, *or* **Mack'i·naw**, *n. U. S.* A short, heavy, plaid coat.
Mackinaw trout. The namaycush.
mack'in·tosh (măk'ĭn·tŏsh), *n.* [After Charles *Macintosh* (1766–1843), the inventor.] **a** A waterproof outer garment. **b** The cloth from which mackintoshes are made.
mack'le (măk''l), *n.* [F. *macule.*] A macule; specif., *Print.*, a blur or a double impression, as from a slipping of the paper. — *v. t. Print.* To blur or double (an impression from type).
ma'cle (măk''l), *n.* [F.] **a** A twin crystal; esp., a flat, twinned crystal of diamond. **b** A dark spot in a mineral.
mac'ra·mé (măk'rȧ·mā), *n.*, *or* **macramé lace.** [Turk. *maqramah* handkerchief, fr. Ar. *miqramah* embroidered veil.] A coarse, usually fringed, lace made by tying threads into knots (**macramé knots**) to form geometrical designs, used esp. for decorating furniture.

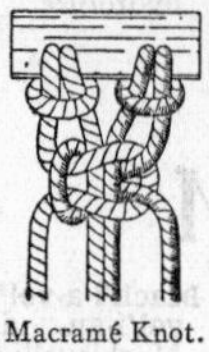
Macramé Knot.

mac'ro- (măk'rō-), **macr-.** [Gr. *makros* long.] A combining form meaning *long in extent* or *duration;* — opposed to *micro-*, as in *macro*cosm. Specif.: **a** *Anat. & Med. An enlargement* or *excessive development;* — chiefly in nouns, as in:
macrocephaly macrodactylism macrostomia
b *Bot. & Zool. Having* (a specified part) *unusually large*, esp. elongated; — in adjectives, as in:
macrocarpous macromandibular macrostomatous
c [Cf. MACROCOSM.] *An individual* or *unit of greater size in a* (specified) *type;* — chiefly in *Biol.* and *Measures*, as in:
macrobacterium macrococcus macrofarad
d *Denoting a kind visibly large; macroscopic.*
mac'ro·cli'mate (măk'rō·klī'mĭt; 2), *n.* [*macro-* + *climate.*] The over-all climate of a region, generally of a large geographic area, as opposed to a *microclimate.* — **mac'ro·cli·mat'ic** (-klī·măt'ĭk), *adj.*
mac'ro·cosm (măk'rō·kŏz'm), *n.* [F. *macrocosme*, fr. Gr. *makros* long, great + *kosmos* world.] The great world; the universe; — contrasted with *microcosm.* — **mac'ro·cos'mic** (-kŏz'mĭk), *adj.*
mac'ro·cyst (-sĭst), *n.* A large spore case or cyst; specif., *Biol.*, a very young encysted plasmodium.
mac'ro·cyte (-sīt), *n.* [*macro-* + *-cyte.*] *Med.* A very large red blood corpuscle, found especially in the blood in pernicious anemia.
mac'ro·dome (-dōm), *n. Cryst.* See DOME, *n.*, 4.
mac'ro·ga·mete' (măk'rō·gȧ·mēt'), *n. Biol.* The large (commonly the female) gamete of a heterogamous organism; — in botany the preferred term is *megagamete.* Cf. MICROGAMETE.
mac'ro·graph (măk'rō·grȧf; 9), *n.* A graphic reproduction of an object either unmagnified or slightly magnified. Cf. MICROGRAPH, 2.
ma·crog'ra·phy (mȧ·krŏg'rȧ·fĭ), *n.* Writing of great size, an indication of nervous disorder.
ma'cron (mā'krŏn; măk'rŏn), *n.* [Gr. *makron*, neut. of *makros* long.] A short, straight, horizontal mark [¯] placed over vowels to denote long quantity.
☞ In the respelling for pronunciation in this Dictionary the macron indicates the regular "long," or name, sounds of the vowels: *ā* in *dāme*, *ē* in *ēve*, *ī* in *īce*, *ō* in *ōld*, and *ū* in *ūse.*
mac'ro·scop'ic (măk'rō·skŏp'ĭk), *adj.* Large enough to be observed by the naked eye; — opposed to *microscopic.*
mac'ro·spore (măk'rō·spōr; 70), *n. Bot.* = MEGASPORE.
ma·cru'ral (mȧ·krōōr'ăl), *adj.* [*macr-* + Gr. *oura* tail.] *Zool.* Belonging to or designating a suborder (Macrura) or other division of decapod crustaceans, including the lobsters, prawns, shrimps, and many similar forms. — **ma·cru'ran** (-ăn), *n.* — **ma·cru'roid** (-oid), *adj.* — **ma·cru'rous** (-ŭs), *adj.*
mac'u·la (măk'ū·lȧ), *n.; pl.* MACULAE (-lē). [L., spot, stain.] A spot, blotch, or stain; a macule.
mac'u·late (-lāt), *v. t.* [L. *maculatus*, past part. of *maculare* to spot.] To spot; stain; defile. — (-lĭt), *adj.* Blotched; hence, defiled; impure.
mac'u·la'tion (-lā'shŭn), *n.* **a** A spotting; a spot; blemish. **b** The arrangement of spots on an animal or plant.
mac'ule (măk'ūl), *n.* [F., fr. L. *macula.*] A spot or blemish; a macula; a mackle. — *v. t. & i.* To blur; to spot; to mackle.
mad (măd), *adj.;* MAD'DER (-ẽr); MAD'DEST. [AS. *gemǣd*, past part. of a v. fr. *gemād* mad.] **1.** Crazy; insane. **2.** Proceeding from, or characterized by, delusion or want of reason; foolish; esp., rashly foolish; senseless. **3. a** Carried away by anger; enraged. **b** Frantic or distraught; as, *mad* with anxiety. **c** Carried away by desire; senselessly devoted. **d** Extravagant; esp., extravagantly gay; hilarious. **4.** Rabid; furious because of abnormal excitation. **5.** Affected with rabies; as, a *mad* dog. — *v. t. & i.;* MAD'DED; MAD'DING. To madden.
mad'am (măd'ăm), *n.* [See MADAME.] A form of polite address to a lady; — variously used. Cf. MA'AM.
mad'ame (măd'ăm; *F.* mȧ'dȧm'), *n.; pl.* MESDAMES (mā'dȧm'). [F., fr. *ma* my (fr. L. *mea*) + *dame* dame.] My lady; — a French title given to all married women. In English usage it is commonly applied to foreign married ladies of whatever nationality. Abbr. *Mme.;* pl. *Mmes.*
mad'cap' (măd'kăp'), *adj.* Inclined to wild sports; hence, wild; reckless. — *n.* A madcap person.
mad'den (măd''n), *v. t.* To make mad; to drive to madness; to craze; enrage. — *v. i.* To become mad; to act as if mad.
mad'den·ing, *adj.* That maddens; also, irritating; vexatious. — **mad'den·ing·ly**, *adv.*
mad'der (măd'ẽr), *n.* [AS. *mædere.*] **1.** A Eurasian herb (*Rubia tinctorum*) type of a family (Rubiaceae, the madder family), of mostly tropical plants, consisting of herbs, shrubs and trees, and including the trees yielding coffee and cinchona, the gardenias, houstonias, and the bedstraw. The madder has verticillate leaves and small yellowish panicled flowers succeeded by berries. Also, by extension, any other species of the genus *Rubia.* **2.** The root of this plant, used in dyeing; also, a dyestuff prepared from it. **3.** The color (Turkey red, etc.) imparted by madder. — *v. t.* To treat or dye with madder.
mad'ding (măd'ĭng), *adj.* Mad; raving; wild; furious.
mad'dish (-ĭsh), *adj.* Somewhat mad.
made (mād), *past & past part.* of MAKE, *v.*
Ma·dei'ra (mȧ·dēr'ȧ; mȧ·dā'rȧ), *n.* Wine made on the island of Madeira.
‖**ma'de·moi'selle'** (măd'mwȧ'zĕl'; măd'ĕ·mō·zĕl'; *colloq.* măm'zĕl'), *n.; pl.* MESDEMOISELLES (mād'mwȧ'zĕl'). [F., fr. *ma* my, fem. of *mon* + *demoiselle* a young lady.] A French title of courtesy given to an unmarried lady, equivalent to *Miss.* Abbr. *Mlle.;* pl. *Mlles.*
made'-up', *adj.* **a** Falsely devised; fabricated, as a story. **b** Artificial; as, a *made-up* complexion.
mad'house' (măd'hous'), *n.* A house where insane persons are detained and treated; also, a place of confusion.
mad'ly (-lĭ), *adv.* In a mad manner; wildly.
mad'man (-măn), *n.; pl.* -MEN (-mĕn). A lunatic; a crazy man.
mad'ness, *n.* Condition or instance of being mad; lunacy; also, extreme folly or rage.
Ma·don'na (mȧ·dŏn'ȧ), *n.* [It. *madonna* my lady.] **1.** [*not cap.*] My lady; — a term of address in Italian, formerly equivalent of *madame*, where *signora* is now substituted. **2. a** An Italian designation of the Virgin Mary. **b** A pictorial or carved representation of the Virgin Mary.
ma·dras' (mȧ·drăs'; -dräs'; măd'rȧs), *n.* [From *Madras*, India.] **1.** A large silk or cotton kerchief, usually of bright colors, such as is often used by Negroes for turbans. **2.** A fine cotton fabric used for dresses and shirts. — **ma·dras'**, *adj.*
‖**ma'dre** (*Sp.* mä'thrā; *It.* mä'drā), *n.* [Sp. & It.] Mother.
mad're·pore (măd'rē·pōr; 70), *n.* [F. *madrépore*, fr. It. *madrepora*, fr. *madre* mother + *poro* pore (see PORE, *n.*) or perh. Gr. *pōros* a soft stone.] Any of an order (Madreporaria) of stony anthozoan corals, often greatly branched, the chief reef-building corals of tropical seas.
mad'ri·gal (măd'rĭ·găl), *n.* [It. *madrigale*, *mandrigale*, fr. LL. *matricalis* (sc. *herba*) an everlasting.] **1.** A lyric, usually amorous and adapted to musical setting. **2.** *Music.* **a** An unaccompanied setting of such a poem in (usually) five or six parts. **b** Any part song or glee.
mad'ri·gal·ist (-ĭst), *n.* A composer of madrigals.
ma·dro'ña, ma·dro'ño (mȧ·drō'nyȧ, -nyō; *local U. S.* -nȧ *for both*), *n.* [Sp. *madroño.*] An evergreen tree or shrub (*Arbutus menziesii*), of the Pacific coast of North America, having a smooth bark and edible red berries (**madroña apples**).
ma·du'ro (mȧ·dōō'rō), *adj.* [Sp., mature.] Dark-colored and strong; — said of cigars. Cf. CLARO, COLORADO. — *n.* A maduro cigar.
mad'wom'an (măd'wŏŏm'ăn), *n.; pl.* -WOMEN (-wĭm'ĕn; -ĭn). An insane woman.
mad'wort' (-wûrt'), *n.* **a** Any cress of the genus *Lobularia.* **b** Gold-of-pleasure.
mae (mā). Scot. & dial. var. of MORE.
Mae·ce'nas (mē·sē'năs), *n.; pl.* -CENASES (-ĕz; -ĭz). [L., name of the patron of Horace and Vergil. See *Biog.*] A patron, esp. of literature and art.
Mael'strom (māl'strŏm), *n.* [D., now *maalstroom*, fr. *malen* to grind, whirl round + *stroom* stream.] A whirlpool off the west coast of Norway; hence [*not cap.*], any turmoil of wide-reaching influence; as, a *maelstrom* of vice.
mae'nad (mē'năd), *n.; pl.* MAENADS (-nădz), MAENADES (mĕn'ȧ·dēz). [L. *Maenas*, *-adis*, fr. Gr. *mainas*, *-ados*, fr. *mainesthai* to rave.] **1.** *Gr. Relig.* A nymph attendant upon Dionysus; a bacchante. **2.** Any frenzied or unnaturally excited woman. — **mae·nad'ic** (mē·năd'ĭk), *adj.*
‖**ma'es·to'so** (mä'ĕs·tō'sō), *adj.* [It.] *Music.* Majestic; stately; — used as a direction. — **ma'es·to'so**, *adv.*
ma·e'stro (mä·ĕ'strō; *almost* mīs'trō), *n.; pl.* -STROS (-strōz), -STRI (-strē). [It., fr. L. *magister.* See MASTER.] Master; a master in any art, esp. music; a composer, conductor, or teacher of eminence.
Mae West (mā' wĕst'). [After *Mae West* (b. 1892), Amer. actress.] **a** A yellow lifesaving jacket, inflatable by means of two cartridges of carbon dioxide, which is worn like a vest by pilots in flights over the sea. **b** *U. S. Army.* A twin-turreted combat tank.
maf'fi·a (mäf'fē·ä), **ma'fi·a** (mä'fē·ä), *n.* [It. *maffia.*] **1.** In Sicily, popular hostility to the law; also, the body of persons imbued with this sentiment which in time developed into a loosely organized secret society. **2.** [*cap.*] Hence, a supposed organization of Sicilians or Italians in foreign countries, as revealed by similar hostility to law and by acts of violence.
maf'fick (măf'ĭk), *v. i.* [From *Mafeking*, town in South Africa.] *Colloq. Brit.* To celebrate hilariously, as the English did after the relief of Mafeking, May 17, 1900.
‖**ma foi** (mȧ fwȧ'). [F.] My faith; indeed.
mag (măg), *n. Slang, Eng.* A halfpenny.
mag'a·zine' (măg'ȧ·zēn'; *in sense* 4, *often* măg'ȧ·zēn; 2), *n.* [F. *magasin*, through OF. & It., fr. Ar. *makhāzin*, pl. of *makhzan* storehouse, granary, cellar.] **1.** A warehouse, storehouse, or depot, esp. for military stores. **2. a** The room in which powder is kept in a fort or a ship. **b** A district rich in natural products. **c** A reservoir or supply chamber for a stove, battery, camera, or other apparatus. **d** A chamber in a gun for holding cartridges to be fed to the piece. **3.** The contents of a storehouse; as: **a** An accumulation of munitions of war. **b** A stock of provisions or goods. **4.** A periodical containing miscellaneous articles, stories, poems, etc. **5.** In France, a store, or shop.
magazine gun, rifle, *or* **pistol.** A rapid-firing small arm, as a rifle, with a reservoir of cartridges.
mag'a·zin'ist (măg'ȧ·zēn'ĭst), *n.* One who edits or writes for a magazine. — **mag'a·zin'ism** (-ĭz'm), *n.*
Mag'da·len (măg'dȧ·lĕn; *see note below*), **Mag'da·lene** (-lēn *or*, *esp. in* Mary Magdalene, măg'dȧ·lē'nē), *n.* [LL. *Magdalene*, fr. Gr. *Magdalēnē.*] **1.** Mary Magdalene; — used with *the.* **2.** [*not cap.*] **a** A reformed prostitute. **b** A house of refuge or reformatory for prostitutes.
☞ The pron. môd'lĭn (cf. MAUDLIN) is usual for *Magdalen* College, Oxford, and *Magdalene* College, Cambridge.
Mag'da·le'ni·an pe'ri·od (măg'dȧ·lē'nĭ·ăn; 58). *Archaeol.* A period representing the highest paleolithic culture in Europe; — from La Madeleine in France, where artifacts were discovered.
mage (māj), *n.* [F., fr. L. *magus.*] A magician.
Mag'el·lan'ic (măj'ĕ·lăn'ĭk; măg'-; *the name Magellan is commonly pron'd* mȧ·jĕl'ăn *in U. S.*, mȧ·gĕl'ăn *in Eng.*), *adj.* Of, pert. to, or named from Magellan, the navigator.
Magellanic Cloud. *Astron.* **a** Either of two nebulous appearances about 30° from the South Pole, resembling thin clouds. **b** A black space in the Milky Way, near the Southern Cross.

ma·gen′ta (mȧ·jĕn′tȧ), *n.* [From *Magenta*, Italy.] Fuchsin; also, the purplish shade of red produced by the dye.

mag′got (măg′ŭt), *n.* **1.** A soft-bodied, grublike, footless larva of an insect, as of the housefly; — applied esp. to forms living in decaying matter. **2.** A fantastic notion or caprice; as, a bigger *maggot* than usual in his head. — **mag′got·y** (-ĭ), *adj.*

Ma′gi (mā′jī), *n. pl.; sing.* MAGUS (-gŭs). [L., pl. of *Magus*, fr. Gr. *Magos*, fr. OPer. *Magu.*] **1.** A priestly caste or order of ancient Media and Persia. Their religion was very similar to that of Zoroaster. **2.** [*not cap.*] Pl. of MAGUS **b.** — **Ma′gi·an, ma′gi·an** (mā′jĭ·ăn), *adj. & n.*

mag′ic (măj′ĭk), *n.* [OF. *magique*, fr. L. *magice*, fr. Gr. *magikē* (sc. *technē*), fr. *magikos*. See MAGIC, *adj.*] **1.** The art which claims or is believed to produce effects by the assistance of supernatural beings or by a mastery of secret forces in nature. **2.** The power brought into play by magic; hence, any seemingly occult power.
— *adj.* Also **mag′i·cal** (-ĭ·kăl). [OF. *magique*, fr. L. *magicus*, fr. Gr. *magikos*, fr. *magos*. See MAGI.] **1.** Of or pertaining to magic. **2.** Hence: Seemingly requiring more than human power; startling in performance; producing effects which seem supernatural; as, a *magic* lantern; *magic* skill. **3.** Characterized by, or having the powers or effects of, magic; hence, enchanting; as, a *magic* land or scene. — **mag′i·cal·ly**, *adv.*

ma·gi′cian (mȧ·jĭsh′ăn), *n.* [F. *magicien.*] One skilled in magic; a necromancer; sorcerer; conjurer.

magic lantern. An optical instrument having lenses for throwing upon a screen magnified pictures from slides placed in the focus of the outer lens. See STEREOPTICON.

ma·gilp′ (mȧ·gĭlp′), **ma·gilph′** (-gĭlf′). Vars. of MEGILP.

Ma′gi·not line (măzh′ĭ·nō). [After André *Maginot* (1877–1932), Fr. minister of war.] A line of defensive fortifications built by France (1930–34) to protect her eastern border.

mag′is·te′ri·al (măj′ĭs·tēr′ĭ·ăl), *adj.* [ML. *magisterialis*, fr. LL. *magisterius.*] **1.** Of or pert. to a master; authoritative; hence, dictatorial. **2.** Of or pert. to a magistrate, his office, or his duties. — **Syn.** See DICTATORIAL. — **mag′is·te′ri·al·ly**, *adv.*

mag′is·ter′y (măj′ĭs·tĕr′ĭ; -tĕr·ĭ), *n.; pl.* -TERIES (-ĭz). [L. *magisterium* the office of a chief, president, director, tutor. See MAGISTRATE.] *Alchemy.* A principle of nature having transmuting or curative powers.

mag′is·tra·cy (-trȧ·sĭ), *n.; pl.* -CIES (-sĭz). **1.** State of being a magistrate. **2.** Office or dignity of a magistrate; also, the collective body of magistrates. **3.** District or jurisdiction of a magistrate.

mag′is·tral (-trăl), *adj.* [L. *magistralis.*] **1.** Magisterial; authoritative. **2.** Prescribed by a physician; hence, effectual. **3.** *Fort.* Guiding; principal; as, **magistral line**, a guiding line with reference to which the drawing for a work is made. **4.** *Pharm.* Formulated for a particular case; — opposed to *officinal* and said of prescriptions and medicines.

mag′is·trate (-trāt; -trĭt), *n.* [L. *magistratus*, fr. *magister* master.] A person clothed with power as a public civil officer; as: **a** The official first in rank in a government, the ***chief, or first, magistrate.*** **b** A public official of a class having summary, often criminal, jurisdiction, as, a police *magistrate.*

mag′is·tra·ture (-trā·tūr), *n.* Magistracy.

mag′ma (măg′mȧ), *n.; pl.* -MATA (-mȧ·tȧ), -MAS (-mȧz). [L., fr. Gr. *magma.*] **1.** Any crude mixture of mineral or organic matters in the state of a thin paste. **2.** *Geol.* Molten rock material within the earth from which an igneous rock results by cooling and crystallization. **3.** *Pharm.* A suspension of precipitated material in a watery vehicle; as, magnesia *magma* (milk of magnesia). — **mag·mat′ic** (măg·măt′ĭk), *adj.*

Mag′na Char′ta (măg′nȧ kär′tȧ), **Mag′na Car′ta.** [ML.] **1.** The Great Charter, so called, to which the English barons forced King John to affix his seal June 15, 1215, at Runnymede. **2.** A constitution guaranteeing rights and privileges.

‖**mag′na cum lau′de.** See CUM LAUDE.

‖**mag′na est ve′ri·tas, et prae′va·le′bit,** *or* **prae·va′let** (măg′nȧ ĕst vĕr′ĭ·tăs, ĕt prē′vȧ·lē′bĭt, prē·vā′lĕt). [L.] Truth is mighty and will prevail.

mag′na·nim′i·ty (măg′nȧ·nĭm′ĭ·tĭ), *n.; pl.* -TIES (-tĭz). **1.** Quality of being magnanimous; a loftiness of spirit enabling one to bear trouble calmly, to disdain meanness and revenge, and to make sacrifices for worthy ends. **2.** A magnanimous act.

mag·nan′i·mous (măg·năn′ĭ·mŭs), *adj.* [L. *magnanimus*, fr. *magnus* great + *animus* mind.] **1.** Great of mind; elevated above what is low, mean, or ungenerous. **2.** Dictated by or exhibiting nobleness of soul; honorable. — **mag·nan′i·mous·ly,** *adv.* — **mag·nan′i·mous·ness,** *n.*

mag′nate (măg′nāt), *n.* [LL. (pl.) *magnates, magnati*, fr. *magnus* great.] **1.** A person of rank or distinction. **2.** Formerly, one of the nobility, or certain high officers of state, of Hungary or of Poland. **3.** A person prominent in the management of a large industry; as, an oil *magnate.*

mag·ne′sia (măg·nē′shȧ; -zhȧ), *n.* [ML., fr. Gr. *hē Magnēsia lithos*, prop., the Magnesian stone.] *Chem.* Magnesium oxide, MgO, a light earthy white substance, slightly alkaline, used as a mild antacid laxative. It is also used in making firebricks and crucibles, as an insulator, etc. — **mag·ne′sian** (-shăn; -zhăn), *adj.* — **mag·ne′sic** (-sĭk), *adj.*

mag′ne·site (măg′nē·sīt), *n.* Native magnesium carbonate, $MgCO_3$.

mag·ne′si·um (măg·nē′shĭ·ŭm; -zhĭ·ŭm), *n.* [NL. See MAGNESIA.] *Chem.* A silver-white metallic element, malleable and ductile, and light (sp. gr., 1.74). Symbol, *Mg*; at. no., 12; at. wt., 24.32. It burns with a dazzling, strongly actinic light (**magnesium light**), used in signaling and in photography.

mag′net (măg′nĕt; -nĭt), *n.* [OF. *magnete*, fr. L. *magnes, -etis*, fr. Gr. *Magnētis lithos* a magnet, metal that looked like silver, prop., stone of *Magnesia.*] **1.** A loadstone; hence, something which attracts. **2.** Any body having the property of attracting iron; specif., a mass of iron or steel having this property artificially imparted and hence called an ***artificial magnet;*** — called also, according to its shape, a ***bar magnet, horseshoe magnet,*** etc. Cf. FIELD MAGNET; see MAGNETO, *Illust.* (1).

mag·net′ic (măg·nĕt′ĭk), *adj.* **1.** Of or pertaining to a substance that becomes magnetized when it is in a magnetic field; as, a *magnetic* needle. **2.** Of or pertaining to, or characterized by, the earth's magnetism; as, the *magnetic* meridian. **3.** Capable of being magnetized, as a piece of iron. **4.** Endowed with great personal attractiveness. **5.** Having, susceptible to, or induced by, hypnotism (formerly called *animal magnetism*); as, a *magnetic* sleep. — **mag·net′i·cal** (-ĭ·kăl), *adj.* — **mag·net′i·cal·ly**, *adv.*

magnetic declination *or* **variation.** = DECLINATION, *n.*, 5.

magnetic dip. = DIP, *n.*, 8.

magnetic equator. The aclinic line. See ACLINIC.

magnetic field. The portion of space near a magnetic body (or a body carrying a current) in which the forces (***magnetic forces***) due to the body (or current) can be detected.

magnetic flux. The total amount of magnetic induction across or through a given surface.

magnetic induction. See INDUCTION, 4.

magnetic mine. A naval mine which is detonated when the hull of a passing vesssel causes the deflection of a magnetic needle that closes an electric circuit.

magnetic moment. *Physics.* The product of the distance between the poles of a magnet and the strength of either pole.

magnetic needle. A slender bar of magnetized steel which, when suspended so as to be free to turn, is used to indicate the direction of the earth's magnetism. It constitutes the essential part of a compass.

magnetic north. The direction indicated by the north-seeking pole of the horizontal magnetic needle. See VARIATION, *Illust.*

magnetic pole. Either of the poles of a magnet; specif. [*caps.*], either of two spots on the earth's surface, toward which the compass needle points from any direction throughout adjacent regions. These spots are respectively the ***North Magnetic Pole*** (approximately 73° 35′ N. lat., 92° 20′ W. long.) and the ***South Magnetic Pole*** (approximately 70° S. lat., 148° E. long.). Cf. VARIATION, *Illust.*

magnetic recorder. A device for recording sound by magnetic means, as a tape or wire recorder.

magnetic storm. Any marked disturbance of the earth's magnetic conditions. A connection between sunspots and magnetic disturbances is established.

mag′net·ism (măg′nĕ·tĭz′m; -nĭ·tĭz′m), *n.* **1.** *Physics.* A property of the molecules of certain substances, as iron, in virtue of which they may be magnetized. **2.** Power to attract or gain the affections. **3.** The science which treats of magnetic phenomena. **4.** Mesmerism.

mag′net·ite (-tīt), *n.* *Mineral.* An iron oxide (Fe_3O_4) and important ore, sometimes possessing polarity, being then called *loadstone.*

mag′net·iz′a·ble (-tīz′ȧ·b'l), *adj.* Capable of being magnetized. — **mag′net·iz′a·bil′i·ty** (-bĭl′ĭ·tĭ), *n.*

mag′net·ize (măg′nĕ·tīz; -nĭ·tīz), *v. t.* **1.** To communicate magnetic properties to; to convert into a magnet; as, to *magnetize* a needle. **2.** To attract as a magnet attracts; to charm; captivate. **3.** To hypnotize. — **mag′net·i·za′tion** (măg′nĕ·tĭ·zā′shŭn; -tĭ·zā′-; măg′nĭ-), *n.*

mag·ne′to- (măg·nē′tō-). [See MAGNET.] A combining form for *magnetic*, denoting: **a** *Magnetic force*, as in *magneto*meter. **b** *Pertaining to* or *actuated by magnetism*, as in *magneto*electric. **c** *Magnetoelectric*, as in **mag·ne′to·ma·chine′, mag·ne′to·tel′e·graph, mag·ne′to·tel′e·phone.**

mag·ne′to (măg·nē′tō), *n.; pl.* -NETOS (-tōz). *Elec.* A magnetoelectric machine; esp., an alternator (**magneto alternator**) with permanent magnets, used to generate the current for the electric ignition in an internal-combustion engine and operated by the engine itself.

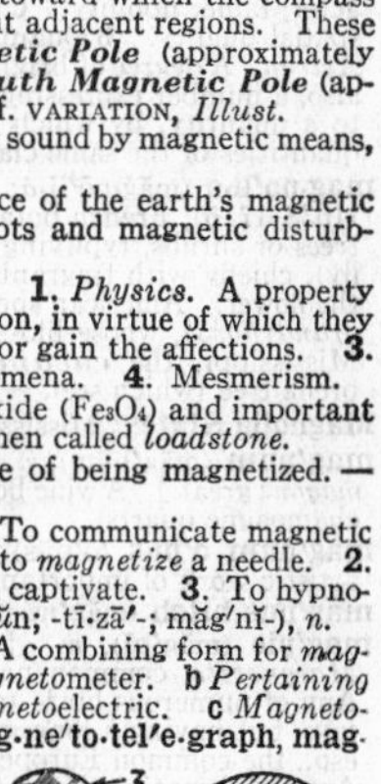

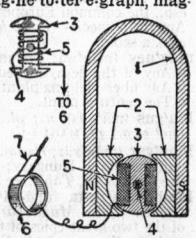

Magneto. 1 Permanent Magnet; 2 Pole Pieces; 3 Armature Core; 4 Armature Shaft; 5 Armature Winding, one end of which is in direct connection with the Armature Shaft, the other attached to the Slip Ring (6) which is fastened to and revolves with the Armature Shaft; 7 Collector Brush.

mag·ne′to·chem′is·try (măg·nē′tō·kĕm′ĭs·trĭ), *n.* The science which deals with the relation of magnetism to chemical phenomena. — **mag·ne′to·chem′i·cal** (-ĭ·kăl), *adj.*

mag·ne′to·dy′na·mo (-dī′nȧ·mō), *n.* A dynamo with permanent field magnets.

mag·ne′to·e·lec′tric (-ē·lĕk′trĭk), *adj.* Also **mag·ne′to·e·lec′tri·cal** (-trĭ·kăl). *Physics.* Pertaining to, or characterized by, electricity developed by magnets.

mag·ne′to·e·lec′tric′i·ty (-ē·lĕk′trĭs′ĭ·tĭ), *n.* Electricity developed by means of magnets; also, the science dealing with such electricity.

mag·ne′to·gen′er·a′tor (-jĕn′ēr·ā′tēr), *n.* A magneto.

mag′ne·tom′e·ter (măg′nē·tŏm′ē·tēr), *n.* [*magneto-* + *-meter.*] *Physics.* An instrument for measuring the intensity and direction of magnetic forces. — **mag′ne·tom′e·try** (-trĭ), *n.*

mag·ne′to·mo′tive (măg·nē′tō·mō′tĭv), *adj.* *Elec.* Pertaining to or designating a force (**magnetomotive force**), the cause of a flux of magnetic induction.

mag′ne·ton (măg′nē·tŏn), *n.* [NL. See MAGNET.] *Physics.* The natural unit of magnetic moment.

mag·ne′to·op′tics (măg·nē′tō·ŏp′tĭks), *n.;* see -ICS. [*magneto-* + *optics.*] A branch of physics dealing with the influence of the magnetic field upon light. — **mag·ne′to·op′tic** (-tĭk), **mag·ne′to·op′ti·cal** (-tĭ·kăl), *adj.*

mag·ne′to·scope (măg·nē′tō·skōp; măg·nĕt′ō-), *n.* *Physics.* An instrument for detecting magnetic force.

mag·ne′to·stric′tion (măg·nē′tō·strĭk′shŭn), *n* [*magneto-* + L. *strictio* a drawing together.] *Physics.* A change in the dimensions of a body when magnetized.

mag′ne·tron (măg′nē·trŏn), *n.* [*magnet* + elec*tron.*] A vacuum tube containing an anode and a heated cathode, the flow of electrons from cathode to anode being controlled by an externally applied magnetic field.

magni-. [L. *magnus.*] A combining form meaning *big, great*, as in *magni*ficent, *magni*loquent; **mag·nip′o·tence, mag·nip′o·tent, mag·nis′o·nant.** Specif., *Zool., long*, as in **mag′ni·cau′date, mag′ni·ros′trate.**

mag·nif′ic (măg·nĭf′ĭk), *adj.* Also **mag·nif′i·cal** (-ĭ·kăl). [F. *magnifique*, fr. L. *magnificus.*] **1.** Magnificent; sublime. **2.** Grandiloquent; also, eulogistic.

Mag·nif′i·cat (-ĭ·kăt), *n.* [L., it magnifies.] The Latin version of the song of the Virgin Mary, Luke i. 46–55.

mag′ni·fi·ca′tion (măg′nĭ·fĭ·kā′shŭn), *n.* A magnifying; specif.: **a** Laudation; exaltation, as by praise. **b** Apparent enlargement of an object by an optical instrument.

mag·nif′i·cence (măg·nĭf′ĭ·sĕns; -s'ns), *n.* [OF., fr. L. *magnificentia*, fr. *magnificus* magnificent, fr. *magnus* great + *facere* to make.] Splendor of surroundings; also, grandeur; spectacular beauty.

mag·nif′i·cent (-sĕnt; -s'nt), *adj.* [OF.] **1.** Exalted in place; — now only of former famous rulers; as, Lorenzo [de' Medici] the *Magnificent.* **2. a** Characterized by sensuous splendor or sumptuous adornment; also, characterized by grandeur or majestic beauty. **b** As applied to ideas, language, etc., exalted; noble. — **Syn.** See GRAND. — **Ant.** Modest. — **mag·nif′i·cent·ly**, *adv.*

mag·nif′i·co (măg·nĭf′ĭ·kō), *n.; pl.* -COES (-kōz). [It., magnific.] **1.** An honorary title denoting a grandee of Venice. **2.** Any person of high position.

mag′ni·fy (măg′nĭ·fī), *v. t.* [OF. and L.; OF. *magnifier*, fr. L. *magnificare.* See MAGNIFICENCE.] **1.** *Archaic.* **a** To praise highly. **b** To cause to be held in greater esteem or respect. **2.** To enlarge, either in fact or in appearance; as, the microscope *magnified* the object 100 diameters. **3.** To exaggerate; as, to *magnify* a loss. — *v. i.;* MAG′NI·FIED (-fīd); MAG′NI·FY′ING. To have the power of causing objects to appear larger than they are. — **mag′ni·fi′er** (-fī′ẽr), *n.*

mag·nil′o·quent (măg·nĭl′ō·kwĕnt), *adj.* [L. *magnus* great + *loquens, -entis,* pres. part. of *loqui* to speak.] Speaking pompously; bombastic; grandiloquent. — **mag·nil′o·quence** (-kwĕns), *n.* — **mag·nil′o·quent·ly**, *adv.*

mag′ni·tude (măg′nĭ·tūd), *n.* [L. *magnitudo*, fr. *magnus*, great.] **1.** Greatness; as: **a** Physical greatness. **b** *Obs.* Greatness of character; fame; nobility. **c** Greatness of influence or effect. **2. a** Size; spatial quality. **b** Quantity, capability of being greater or less. **3.** *Astron.* A degree of brightness of a celestial body, esp. of a fixed star; also, a number expressing brightness. **4.** *Math.* A number assigned to a quantity, by which the quantity may be compared with other quantities of the same class.

mag·no′li·a (măg·nō′lĭ·ȧ; -nōl′yȧ; 58), *n.* [NL., after Pierre *Magnol* (1638–1715), French botanist.] *Bot.* Any of a genus (*Magnolia*) of trees or shrubs, typifying a family (Magnoliaceae, the magnolia family), chiefly with fragrant, large, white, pink, or purple flowers; also, the flower. American species include the ***evergreen magnolia*** (*M. grandiflora*), whose blossom is the State flower of Louisiana and of Mississippi, the ***cucumber tree*** (*M. acuminata*), and the umbrella tree (which see). — **mag·no′li·a′ceous** (măg·nō′lĭ·ā′shŭs), *adj.*

Magnolia State. Mississippi; — a nickname.

mag′num (măg′nŭm), *n.; pl.* MAGNUMS (-nŭmz). [Neut. sing. of L. *magnus* great.] A wine bottle containing two quarts (usually 26-ounce champagne quarts).

mag′num o′pus (ō′pŭs). [L.] A great work; esp., a literary or artistic work of importance; one's greatest work.

mag′nus hitch (măg′nŭs). See KNOT, *Illust.* (24).

mag′pie (măg′pī), *n.* [*Mag, Maggot,* fr. F. *Margot,* old dim. of *Marguerite,* common name of the magpie. See PIE magpie.] **1.** Any of numerous birds (genus *Pica* and related genera) allied to the jays, but having a long graduated tail and black-and-white plumage; esp., the common European species (*P. pica*), and the closely similar American species (*P. p. hudsonia* and *P. nuttali*). **2.** A chatterer; also, a scold.

mag′uey (măg′wā; *Sp.* mä·gä′ē), *n.* [Sp., prob. of Taino origin.] **a** Any of the fleshy-leaved Mexican agaves, esp. one yielding pulque. **b** Any fiber-yielding plant of a genus (*Furcraea*) related to the agaves. **c** The century plant.

Ma′gus (mā′gŭs), *n.; pl.* MAGI (-jī). [L.] **a** One of the Magi. **b** [*not cap.*] *pl.* MAGI (-jī). A magician.

Mag′yar (măg′yär; *Hung.* mŏd′yŏr), *n.* [Hung.] One of the dominant people of Hungary; also, their language, a Finno-Ugric tongue. See LANGUAGE, *Table.* — **Mag′yar**, *adj.*

Ma·ha′bha′ra·ta (mȧ·hä′bä′rȧ·tȧ), *n.* Also **Ma·ha′bha′ra·tam** (-tȧm). [Skr. *Mahābhārata,* lit., the Great Bharata (Story).] One of the two great epics of the Hindus.

ma·ha′ra′ja, ma·ha′ra′jah (mȧ·hä′rä′jȧ; *Angl.* mä′hä·rä′jȧ), *n.* [Skr. *mahārāja,* fr. *mahat* great + *rājan* king.] **1.** Title of certain Hindu princes, esp. of the ruling chiefs of the principal native states, ranking above a raja. **2.** One bearing this title.

ma·ha′ra′ni, ma·ha′ra′nee (mȧ·hä′rä′nē; *Angl.* mä′hä·rä′nē), *n.* [Hind. *mahārānī* great queen.] **1.** Title of a queen or sovereign princess of an Indian state. **2.** One bearing this title.

ma·hat′ma (mȧ·hät′mȧ; *Angl.* mȧ·hăt′mȧ), *n.* [Skr. *mahātman,* lit., great-souled, wise.] **1.** Any individual regarded as high-minded or great-souled. **2.** *Theos.* One of a class of sages, reputed to have superior knowledge and powers. — **ma·hat′ma·ism** (-ĭz'm), *n.*

Mah′di (mä′dē), *n.* [Ar., the guided one.] Among Mohammedans, the last imam, or leader of the faithful. The title has been taken by several leaders of Moslem sects, notably by Mohammed Ahmed, who overran the Egyptian Sudan, and in 1885 captured Khartoum.

Ma·hi′can (mȧ·hē′kăn), *n.* Any of the Algonquian Indians formerly between the Hudson River and Narragansett Bay; specif.: **a** One of the Mohican, a confederacy on the upper Hudson. **b** One of the Mohegan, a tribe of Connecticut.

mah′–jongg′ (mä′jŏng′), **mah′jong′**, *n.* [From Cant. pron. of Chin. (Pek.) *ma²-ch'iao³,* lit., house sparrow.] A Chinese game played, usually, by four persons with 144 "tiles," similar to dominoes.

mahl′stick′ (mäl′stĭk′; môl′-). Var. of MAULSTICK.

ma·hog′a·ny (mȧ·hŏg′ȧ·nĭ), *n.; pl.* -NIES (-nĭz). [Obs. Sp. *mahogani,* formerly current in the W. Indies.] **1.** The tropical American tree (*Swietenia mahagoni*) typifying a family (Meliaceae, the mahogany family) of tropical trees and shrubs characterized chiefly by the monadelphous stamens; also, the valuable hardwood yielded by this tree. **2.** Any of various other trees yielding a wood resembling mahogany (sense 1). **3.** The average color of mahogany wood, reddish red-yellow in hue, of medium saturation and low brilliance. See COLOR. — *adj.* Of or pertaining to the mahogany.

Ma·hom′et·an (mȧ·hŏm′ĕ·tăn; -ĭ·tăn), **Ma·hom′et·an·ism**, etc. Vars. of MOHAMMEDAN, etc.

ma·ho′ni·a (mȧ·hō′nĭ·ȧ), *n.* [NL., after Bernard McMahon, American botanist.] Any of a genus of North American and Asiatic shrubs of the barberry family. See OREGON GRAPE.

Ma·hound′ (mȧ·hound′; -hōōnd′), *n.* [OF. *Mahon, Mahom;* influenced by E. *hound.*] **1.** *Archaic.* Mohammed. **2.** *Scot.* The Devil.

ma·hout′ (mȧ·hout′), *n.* [Hind. *mahāut.*] *East Indies.* The keeper and driver of an elephant.

Mah·rat′ta (mȧ·răt′ȧ), **Mah·rat′ti.** Vars. of MARATHA, MARATHI.

ma′hua (mä′hwä), *n.* [Hind. *mahuā,* fr. Skr. *madhūka,* fr. *madhu* sweet, honey.] An East Indian tree (genus *Madhuca*) of the sapodilla family whose honey-filled flowers yield food and an intoxicating drink and whose seeds yield a white or yellow butterlike fat, **mahua butter.**

maid (mād), *n.* [From MAIDEN.] **1.** An unmarried girl or woman; usually, a young unmarried woman; a maiden; esp., a virgin. **2.** A female servant.

maid′en (mād′'n), *n.* [AS. *mægden;* akin to AS. *mægth* maid.] **1.** A maid. **2.** An instrument like the guillotine, formerly used in Scotland for beheading. **3.** *Cricket.* A maiden over. **4.** *Horse Racing.* In trotting, a horse that has never won a race. — *adj.* **1.** Never having been married; virgin. **2.** Of or pertaining to a maiden; characteristic of a virgin. **3.** First; earliest; as, a *maiden* speech. **4.** Designating, or pertaining to, a horse that has never won a prize, soil that has never been plowed, etc.; fresh; untried; unused.

maid′en·hair′ (-hâr′), *n., or* **maidenhair fern.** Any of a genus (*Adiantum*) of ferns with delicate fronds.

maid′en·head (-hĕd), *n.* **1.** Maidenhood; virginity. **2.** The hymen, or virginal membrane.

maid′en·hood (-hōōd), *n.* **1.** State of being a maid or a virgin; virginity. **2.** Newness; freshness.

maid′en·ly (-lĭ), *adj.* Of or pertaining to a maiden or maidenhood; gentle; modest. — **maid′en·li·ness**, *n.*

maiden name. The surname of a woman before she is married.

maiden over. *Cricket.* An over from which no runs are scored from hits.

maid′hood (mād′hōōd), *n.* Maidenhood.

maid of honor. a An unmarried lady, usually of noble birth, whose duty it is to attend a queen or a princess. **b** The principal attendant on a bride at the wedding ceremony; — so called when unmarried; when married, called *matron of honor.*

maid′serv′ant (mād′sûr′vănt), *n.* A female servant.

ma·ieu′tic (mā·ū′tĭk), *adj.* [Gr. *maieutikos,* fr. *maia* midwife.] Designating, or pertaining to, the Socratic method (which see); — so called because Socrates held that teaching is eliciting memory. — **ma·ieu′ti·cal** (-tĭ·kăl), *adj.*

mai′gre (mā′gẽr; mā′gr′), *adj.* [F. See MEAGER.] Designating articles of diet free from flesh or the juices of flesh and hence appropriate for fast days.

mai′hem (mā′hĕm). Var. of MAIM, MAYHEM.

mail (māl), *n.* Also **maill.** [AS. *māl,* fr. ON. *māl* speech, agreement.] *Obs. exc. Scot.* Payment; rent.

mail, *n.* [OF. *maille,* fr. L. *macula* spot, a mesh of a net.] **1.** A flexible fabric of interlinked metal rings used as defensive armor; — called also ***chain mail.*** Cf. COAT OF MAIL, HAUBERK. **2.** The hard protective covering of various animals, as of a lobster. — *v. t.* To arm with mail.

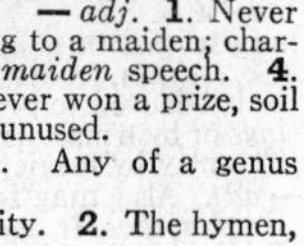

Mail, 1. Fragment of a Medieval Hauberk.

mail, *n.* [OF. *male,* fr. OHG. *malaha, malha,* wallet.] **1.** *Obs. exc. Scot.* A bag; a traveling bag. **2. a** The bag or bags, with the letters, papers, etc., conveyed under public authority from one post office to another. **b** The system of appliances used in the postal service. **3.** *Now Chiefly U. S.* That which comes in the mail; letters, etc., received through the post office. **4.** That which conveys mail, as a vehicle, boat, or person. — *adj.* Carrying or used in handling mail. — *v. t. Chiefly U. S.* To deliver into the custody of the post office for transmission; to post. — **mail′bag′** (-băg′), *n.* — **mail′box′** (-bŏks′), *n.*

mail′a·ble (māl′ȧ·b'l), *adj.* *U. S.* Lawful to mail, or post.

mailed (māld), *adj.* [See 2d MAIL.] Protected by mail; armed with mail; also, covered with maillike scales, etc.

mailed fist. Figuratively, threat of armed force.

mail′er (māl′ẽr), *n.* One who or that which mails; also, a machine (**mailing machine**) for addressing mail matter.

mail′ing (māl′ĭng), *n.* [See MAIL rent.] *Scot.* A rented farm, or the rent paid.

maill (māl). Var. of 1st MAIL.

‖**mail′lot′** (mȧ′yō′), *n.* [F., dim. See 2d MAIL.] A tight-fitting garment covering the torso, and used by dancers, acrobats, swimmers, etc.

mail′man′ (māl′măn′), *n; pl.* -MEN (-mĕn′). A postman.

mail order. An order for goods which is received and filled by mail. — **mail′–or′der**, *adj.* — **mail–order house.**

maim (mām), *v. t.* [OF. *mahaignier, meshaignier.*] **1.** To deprive of the use of a member, so as to render a person less able to defend himself. **2.** To mutilate; disable.

maim, *n.* In law language **may′hem** (mā′hĕm; -ĕm), and **mai′hem.** [ME. *maheym,* fr. OF. *mahaing.*] *Archaic.* Privation of the use of a member of the body; a serious physical injury; hence, a serious defect or blemish.

main (mān), *n.* [AS. *mægen* strength, power, force.] **1.** Physical strength; hence, force; power. *Archaic,* exc. in the phrase "with might and *main.*" **2.** A broad expanse; specif.: **a** *Archaic.* The mainland. **b** *Poetic.* The high sea. **c** [*cap.*] Short for SPANISH MAIN. **3.** [From MAIN, *adj.*] The chief part; the essential point. **4.** A principal line or conduit; specif.: **a** A principal duct or pipe, as from a reservoir. **b** A principal conductor in a system of electric distribution. **c** A trunk line of a railroad. **5.** *Naut.* Mainmast. — ***for, or in, the main.*** For the most part.

— *adj.* **1.** Powerful; forceful. **2.** Sheer; utter; as, by *main* force. **3.** Designating a great stretch of land, sea, or expanse of space. **4.** Principal; chief. **5.** *Obs.* Essential to results, momentous, exalted in rank, etc. **6.** *Gram.* Expressing the chief predication in a complex sentence (see SENTENCE). **7.** *Naut.* Attached to, or connected with, the mainmast.

main, *n.* **1.** In the game of hazard, a number which the caster calls before throwing; also, figuratively, a match at dice, a stake played for, etc. **2.** A match at cockfighting.

main′land′ (mān′lănd′; -lănd), *n.* The continent; the principal land; — in general, opp. to *island* or *peninsula.*

main′ly, *adv.* **1.** *Archaic.* Powerfully; forcibly; hence, abundantly. **2.** Principally; chiefly.

main′mast′ (mān′mȧst′; -mȧst), *n.* *Naut.* The mast regarded as the principal mast in a ship or other vessel. It is the second mast from the bow except in two-masted vessels where the aftermast is small, as in a yawl or ketch.

mains (mānz), *n.* [Scot., pl. of *main* for *domain.* *Oxf. E. D.*] *Scot.* The farm attached to a mansion.

main'sail' (mān'sāl'; *naut.* mān's'l), *n.* *Naut.* The principal sail on the mainmast. In a square-rigged vessel it is the **main course** and hangs from the main yard. See SAIL, SLOOP, *Illusts.*

main'sheet' (-shēt'), *n.* *Naut.* A rope or sheet by which the mainsail is trimmed and secured.

main'spring' (-sprĭng'), *n.* **a** The principal spring in a piece of mechanism. See GUNLOCK, *Illust.* **b** The chief motive, agent, or agency.

main'stay' (-stā'), *n.* **1.** *Naut.* The stay from the maintop forward, usually to the foot of the foremast. **2.** Main support.

main·tain' (mān·tān'; mĕn-), *v. t.* [OF. *maintenir*, fr. L. *manu tenere* to hold in the hand.] **1.** To continue or persevere in or with; to carry on. **2.** To keep possession of. **3.** To hold or keep in any condition, esp. in a state of efficiency or validity; to support, sustain, or uphold; to keep up. **4.** To uphold and defend. **5.** To affirm; esp., to assert as true or as subject to proof; also, to support or defend by argument. **6.** To bear the expense of; support. — **main·tain'a·ble,** *adj.* — **main·tain'er,** *n.*

Syn. Maintain, assert, defend, vindicate, justify mean to uphold as true, right, just, etc. Maintain implies firmness of conviction and is often used in place of *argue* for that reason; assert, determination to make others accept what one puts forward; defend, a maintaining in the face of attack; vindicate, a successful attempt at defending; justify, a showing conclusively to be true, valid, or the like.

main'te·nance (mān'tʼn·ăns; mānt'năns), *n.* **1.** Act of maintaining, or state of being maintained; support, defense, etc. **2.** That which maintains; means of sustenance. **3.** The upkeep of property, equipment, etc. **4.** *Crim. Law.* An officious or unlawful intermeddling in a cause depending between others, by assisting either party with money or means to carry it on.

maintenance of membership. A clause in certain labor-union contracts by which all who have previously joined the union or who join during the term of the contract must keep up payment of union dues or on failure must be discharged by the employer. Such a clause does not forbid employment of nonmembers of the union nor require a nonmember to join.

main'top' (mān'tŏp'), *n.* *Naut.* The platform about the head of the mainmast in square-rigged vessels.

main'-top'mast (-tŏp'mȧst), *n.* A mast next above the mainmast.

main yard. *Naut.* The yard of the mainsail.

mair (mâr), **maist** (māst). Dial. vars. of MORE, MOST.

‖**mai'son' de san'té'** (mā'zôɴ' dĕ säɴ'tā'). [F.] Private hospital, asylum, or sanatorium.

maî'tre d'hô'tel' (mâ'trĕ dô'tĕl'; māt' dô'tĕl'). [F., lit., master of the house.] **a** A chief officer or servant of a house, hotel, etc.; house steward; major-domo. **b** A kind of sauce, of melted butter, chopped parsley, salt, pepper, and lemon juice or vinegar.

maize (māz), *n.* [Sp. *maíz*, fr. Taino *mahiz*, *mayz.*] Indian corn (*Zea mays*). See CORN, *n.*, 3.

ma·jes'tic (mȧ·jĕs'tĭk), *adj.* Also **ma·jes'ti·cal** (-tĭ·kăl). Possessing or exhibiting majesty; of august dignity; noble; grand. — **Syn.** See GRAND. — **ma·jes'ti·cal·ly,** *adv.*

maj'es·ty (măj'ĕs·tĭ; -ĭs·tĭ), *n.; pl.* -TIES (-tĭz). [OF. *majesté*, fr. L. *majestas*, fr. an old compar. of *magnus* great.] **1.** Dignity or authority of sovereign power; also, the person of a sovereign. **2.** Hence [*cap.*], with a possessive, the title of an emperor, empress, king, queen, etc.; as, His Britannic *Majesty.* **3.** Grandeur; stateliness.

ma·jol'i·ca (mȧ·jŏl'ĭ·kȧ; mȧ·yŏl'-), *n.* [It.] A variety of Renaissance Italian pottery, glazed and richly colored and ornamented.

ma'jor (mā'jẽr), *adj.* [L., compar. of *magnus* great.] **1.** Greater in number, quantity, or extent. **2.** Greater in dignity, rank, or importance. **3.** Of full legal age. **4.** Constituting the majority; as, the *major* vote. **5.** *Educ., U. S.* Designating a principal subject of study, chosen by a student for a degree, in which he is required to take a certain number of courses or hours. Cf. MINOR, *adj.*, 4. **6.** *Music.* **a** Greater by a half step than the minor; — of an interval. **b** Based on the scale pattern of the major mode; as, the key of E *major.* **c** Distant by a major interval; — of a tone.

— *n.* **1.** One of superior rank in a given class. **2.** *Educ.* A major subject or course. **3.** *Law.* A person of full legal age. See AGE, *n.*, 3 & 4. **4.** *Logic.* The **major term,** that is, the predicate of the conclusion; also, the **major premise,** that is, that premise which contains the major term, — the first proposition of a regular syllogism. Cf. MINOR, *n.*, 3. **5.** *Mil.* A commissioned officer next in rank above a captain and next below a lieutenant colonel. Abbr. *Maj.*

— *v. i.* *Colloq.* To take a certain subject as one's major.

ma'jor-do'mo (-dō'mō), *n.; pl.* -DOMOS (-mōz). [Sp. *mayordomo*, fr. ML. *major domus*, fr. *major* the chief + *domus*, gen. of *domus* house.] A man having charge of a great household, esp. of a princely establishment; a head steward. Hence, jocularly, a butler or steward.

ma'jor·ette' (mā'jẽr·ĕt'), *n.* Short for DRUM MAJORETTE.

major general; *pl.* MAJOR GENERALS. *Mil.* A commissioned officer ranking next above a brigadier general and next below a lieutenant general, properly commanding a division. — **ma'jor-gen'er·al·cy** (mā'jẽr·jĕn'ẽr·ăl·sĭ), *n.* — **ma'jor-gen'er·al·ship',** *n.*

ma·jor'i·ty (mȧ·jŏr'ĭ·tĭ), *n.; pl.* -TIES (-tĭz). [F. *majorité.*] **1.** Quality or state of being major or greater; superiority; now, specif., the status of being of full legal age. **2.** The greater of two numbers regarded as parts of a whole; the number greater than half; also, the excess of this greater number, as of votes, over the remainder. Cf. PLURALITY, 4. **3.** The group or party whose votes preponderate. **4.** The military rank and office of a major. — ***to go over to, or to join, the majority or the great majority.*** To die.

major key. *Music.* A key or tonality in the major mode. Cf. MINOR KEY.

major league. *Baseball.* Either of the two principal leagues of professional baseball clubs in America. Cf. MINOR LEAGUE.

major mode. *Music.* The arrangement or grouping of tones as found in the major scale. Cf. MINOR MODE.

major scale. *Music.* One of the two standard scales of modern music. It consists of eight tones (the eighth being the octave of the first) with a major third between the first and third tones. The intervals between the scale tones are all whole steps except those between 3–4 and 7–8, which are half steps. Cf. MINOR SCALE.

major suit. *Bridge.* Either spades or hearts; — from their superior value in the count. Cf. MINOR SUIT.

ma·jus'cule (mȧ·jŭs'kūl), *n.* [F., fr. L. *majuscula* somewhat greater or great, fem. dim. of *major*, *majus.*] A large letter, capital or uncial; — a term used chiefly in paleography, often in contrast to *minuscule.* See UNCIAL, *Illust.* — **ma·jus'cule, ma·jus'cu·lar** (-kū·lẽr), *adj.*

make (māk), *n.* [AS. *gemaca.*] *Now Dial.* A companion or mate.

make (māk), *v. t.;* MADE (mād); MAK'ING (māk'ĭng). [AS. *macian.*] **1.** To form or constitute in external nature; primarily, to fashion or construct; secondarily, to enter into as parts or elements. **2.** To form by an assembling of individuals; as, twice one *makes* two; also, to enter in as, or count as; as, he *made* the thirteenth at the table. **3.** To compose, as parts or materials; as, the house is *made* of stone. **4.** To lay out or construct, as a road. **5.** To form the essential being of; as, one swallow does not *make* a summer. **6.** To be, or to be capable of being, changed or fashioned into; as, wool *makes* warm clothing. **7.** To frame or formulate in the mind. **8.** To treat in thought or feeling. **9.** To compute to be; as, he *made* the weight about fifty pounds. **10.** To signify; as, that *makes* no difference in my plans. **11.** To regard or consider as being. **12.** To understand; as, I could *make* nothing of his words; hence, ***to make neither head nor tail of,*** not to understand. **13.** To cause to exist, appear, or occur; as, God *made* the universe. **14.** To perform (the action indicated by the object); to do, act, work, commit, carry on, etc.; as, to *make* war. **15.** To so act that (one thing) appears in place (of another); as, to *make* a friend of an enemy. **16.** To constrain or compel (some action, or some person in respect to action). **17.** *Archaic.* To do; to be concerned in. **18.** To cause to be or become; as, to *make* known; to *make* fast. **19.** To cause (someone) to go or come (to some specified state); as, he was *made* to death; — now commonly in the intransitive form, *to make away with.* **20.** To perform in the appropriate manner; as, to *make* a note, a will. **21.** To cause or assure the success of. **22.** To deliver orally; as, to *make* a speech. **23.** To act or behave so as to produce or gain; as, to *make* friends. **24.** To gain; acquire; as, to *make* money. **25.** To go to, accomplish by going, traverse, etc.; as, to *make* ninety miles an hour; to *make* the rounds of a camp. **26.** *Colloq.* To acquire a place on; as, to *make* the team. **27.** *Card Playing.* **a** To take a trick with (a card). **b** To shuffle (the cards). **c** To name (the trump). **28.** *Elec.* To complete (a circuit); to effect (a contact). **29.** *Sports & Games.* To score or secure as a score.

Syn. Make, form, shape, fashion, fabricate, manufacture, forge mean to cause something to come into being, esp. material being. Make, the most general term, covers not only a producing by the hands, machinery, etc., but by the mind, by God, or the like; form implies that the thing produced has a definite outline, design, structure, or the like; shape suggests impressing a form upon some material; fashion suggests the use of inventive power or ingenuity; fabricate suggests a making of many parts into a whole, sometimes implying use of the imagination; manufacture, in current use, suggests a making by machinery; forge suggests a devising or concocting by physical or mental effort.

— *v. i.* **1.** To cause something to assume a designated condition or to perform a designated action; as, to *make* ready. **2.** *Archaic.* To behave, esp. with feigning; to pretend; as, he *made* as if he were angry. **3.** To proceed; move; go; also, to lie in the direction (*toward* or *through*); as, the road *makes* toward Rome. **4.** To act in a certain manner, as in ***make free; make merry.*** **5.** To increase, as in height, thickness, etc.; augment; as, the snow *makes* fast. **6.** To engage in a process of forming or constructing something. **7.** To start to do something; as, he *made* to go. **8.** To tend; to have effect; as, it *makes* for his advantage.

make a clean breast. To confess. — ***make as if or as though.*** To pretend that. — ***make believe.*** **a** To cause the belief. **b** To feign. — ***make head.*** **a** To advance. **b** To accumulate power, as steam in an engine boiler. — ***make heavy weather.*** *Naut.* To labor in a seaway. — ***make no bones.*** *Colloq.* To make no scruple; not to hesitate. — ***make out.*** **a** To draw up or write; as, to *make out* a bill. **b** To accomplish; achieve. **c** To discern or descry. **d** To find out; decipher. **e** To prove; to establish. **f** To make complete or exact. — ***make over.*** **a** To transfer the title of; as, he *made over* his estate in trust. **b** To refashion, as garments. — ***make sail.*** *Naut.* **a** To set or spread sail. **b** To set out on a voyage. — ***make sternway.*** To move with the stern foremost. — ***make up.*** **a** To compose, as from ingredients; to constitute. **b** To compose, as a document. **c** To invent or concoct, as a story. **d** To wrap or fasten up, as a parcel. **e** To form by an arranging of parts; as, to *make up* a train of cars. **f** To prepare; arrange; adjust; also, to assume a guise; to impersonate. **g** *Print.* To arrange set type in (pages, columns, etc.) for printing. **h** To bring up to; as, to *make up* a required sum. **i** To compensate for; to make good; as, to *make up* sleep. **j** To dress, paint, etc., for a part, as one to be acted on the stage; to apply cosmetics. **k** To reconcile or become reconciled; as, to *make up* a difference. **l** To settle or arrange mentally; to decide; as, to *make up* one's mind; also, in the passive, to be composed or prepared in mind. **m** To advance; go or come; as, a beggar *made up* to us. **n** To compensate or atone (*for*). **o** *Educ.* To remove (a deficiency in record), as by special study or examination.

make (māk), *n.* **1. a** The manner in which a thing is constructed; structure; form. Cf. BUILD, *n.* **b** Nature; character; kind. **2. a** Action or process of manufacture; — often referring to the quality or origin of an article; as, what *make* is your car? **b** Quantity manufactured; output. **3.** *Bridge.* The declaration; esp., the final declaration. **4.** *Elec.* The closing or completing of an electric circuit.

make and break. *Elec.* An apparatus for making and breaking an electric circuit.

make'bate' (māk'bāt'), *n.* [*make*, v. + obs. *bate* quarrel.] *Archaic.* One who excites contentions and quarrels.

make'-be·lieve', *n.* **1.** A feigning to believe; pretending. **2.** A pretender. — *adj.* Feigned; insincere.

make'fast' (māk'făst'; 9), *n.* *Naut.* Anything to which a boat is fastened, as a buoy or a post on a wharf.

make'less, *adj.* *Obs.* Having no mate.

make'-peace', *n.* A peacemaker.

mak'er (māk'ẽr), *n.* **1.** One who makes. **2.** Hence: **a** [*cap.*] The Creator; — with *the.* **b** *Archaic & Scot.* (*Scot. pron.* mȧk'ẽr). One who writes verses; a poet. **c** *Law.* The person who makes a promissory note. **3.** *Bridge.* The player who first names the winning declaration; the declarer.

make'-read'y, *n.* *Print.* The process of preparing a form, plate, or engraving to obtain the proper impression; also, the material used in the process.

make'shift' (māk'shĭft'), *n.* A temporary expedient; a shift; stopgap. — **Syn.** See RESOURCE. — *adj.* Also **make'shift'y** (-shĭf'tĭ). Serving as makeshift.

make'-up', *n.* **1.** The way in which the parts of anything are put together; also, the constitution or composition of anything. **2.** Material as cosmetics, wigs, etc., used for making up; as, theatrical *make-up*.

3. *Colloq., Educ.* A special examination in which a student may make up for absence or failure at a regular examination. 4. *Printing.* a Arrangement of type for printing. b The arrangement of articles, illustrations, headlines, etc., of a newspaper, periodical, or book. 5. *Theater.* The act, process or result of dressing up, painting, etc., as for a part.

make′weight′ (māk′wāt′), *n.* 1. That which is thrown into a scale to make weight. 2. A counterweight.

mak′ing (māk′ĭng), *n.* 1. Action of one who or that which makes (forming, causing, doing, etc.). 2. Process or means of advancement or success; as, misfortune was the *making* of him. 3. Composition or structure. 4. Something made; as, a *making* of bread. 5. a Material from which something can be developed; as, there is the *making* of a race horse in this colt. b *Colloq., U. S. pl.* The materials from which something, as a cigarette, may be made.

mak′luk (măk′lŭk), *n.* [Alaskan Esk. *makliak, muklok,* large seal.] A large seal.

mal- (măl-). [F. *mal,* fr. L. *male,* adv., fr. *malus* bad, ill.] A combining form denoting *ill, badly, bad, evil,* as in *mal*content, *mal*treat.

Ma·lac′ca cane (mȧ·lăk′ȧ). [From *Malacca.* See *Gaz.*] A cane, often mottled, from an Asiatic rattan palm (*Calamus rotang*).

ma·la′ceous (mȧ·lā′shŭs), *adj.* [L. *malus* apple tree, *malum* apple.] *Bot.* Belonging to the apple family (Malaceae). See APPLE.

Mal′a·chi (măl′ȧ·kī), *n. Douay Bib.* **Mal′a·chi′as** (-kī′ăs). [Heb. *Malākhī.*] a A Hebrew prophet, ascribed to the Persian period, about 464–424 B.C. b A book of the Old Testament. See BIBLE.

mal′a·chite (măl′ȧ·kīt), *n.* [F., fr. OF. *melochite,* fr. Gr. *malachē, molochē,* a mallow; — from its green color, like that of a mallow leaf.] *Mineral.* A native green basic carbonate of copper, $CuCO_3.Cu(OH)_2$.

mal′a·co- (măl′ȧ·kō-). [Gr. *malakos* soft.] A combining form meaning: a *Soft,* as in *malaco*pterygian. b *Mollusks,* as in *malaco*logy.

mal′a·col′o·gy (măl′ȧ·kŏl′ō·jĭ), *n.* [*malaco-* + *-logy.*] The branch of zoology which deals with mollusks.

mal′a·cop′ter·yg′i·an (-kŏp′tẽr·ĭj′ĭ·ăn), *adj.* [*malaco-* + Gr. *pteryx, pterygos,* wing, fin.] *Zool.* Of or pert. to a division (Malacopterygii) of teleost fishes having soft fin rays.

mal′a·cos′tra·can (-kŏs′trȧ·kăn), *adj.* [*malaco-* + Gr. *ostrakon* shell.] *Zool.* Belonging to a subclass (Malacostraca) of crustaceans, including crabs, lobsters, shrimps, pill bugs, sand fleas, etc. — **mal′a·cos′tra·can,** *n.* — **mal′a·cos′tra·cous** (-kŭs), *adj.*

mal′ad·ap·ta′tion (măl′ăd·ăp·tā′shŭn), *n.* Poor or inadequate adaptation.

mal′ad·just′ed (măl′ă·jŭs′tĕd; -tĭd), *adj.* Badly, or inadequately, adjusted; *Psychol.,* out of harmony with one's environment, from failure to reach a satisfactory adjustment between one's desires and one's conditions of life.

mal′ad·just′ment (măl′ă·jŭst′mĕnt), *n.* Poor or inadequate adjustment.

mal′ad·min′is·ter (-ăd·mĭn′ĭs·tẽr), *v. t.* To administer badly. — **mal′ad·min′is·tra′tion** (-trā′shŭn), *n.*

mal′a·droit′ (măl′ȧ·droit′; 2), *adj.* [F. See MAL-; ADROIT.] Of a quality opposed to adroitness; clumsy; awkward. — **Syn.** See AWKWARD. — **mal′a·droit′ly,** *adv.* — **mal′a·droit′ness,** *n.*

mal′a·dy (măl′ȧ·dĭ), *n.; pl.* -DIES (-dĭz). [OF. *maladie,* fr. *malade* ill, sick, fr. L. *male habitus,* i. e., ill-kept, not in good condition.] 1. Any disease of the human body. 2. A moral or mental defect or disorder.

ma′la fi′de (mā′lȧ fī′dē). [L.] In or with bad faith.

‖**ma′la fi′des** (fī′dēz). [L.] Bad faith.

Mal′a·ga (măl′ȧ·gȧ), *n.* [From *Málaga,* city and province of Spain.] 1. A white wine from Málaga. 2. A sweet, white, firm-fleshed grape of Spain and California.

Mal′a·gas′y (măl′ȧ·găs′ĭ), *n.* 1. *sing. & pl.* A native of Madagascar. 2. The Malay language of these natives.

ma·laise′ (mă·lāz′; *F.* mȧ′lâz′), *n.* [F., fr. *mal* ill + *aise* ease.] An indefinite feeling of bodily uneasiness or illness; also, generally, a feeling of discomfort.

Ma′la·mute (mä′lȧ·mūt). Var. of MALEMUTE.

mal·an·ders (măl′ăn·dẽrz), *n. pl.* [F. *malandres,* fr. L. *malandria* blisters or sores, esp. on horses.] A chronic eczema on the posterior surface of the foreleg in horses. Cf. SALLENDERS.

mal′a·pert (măl′ȧ·pûrt), *adj.* [OF. *mal apert* unskillful, ill-taught, ill-bred, fr. *mal* ill + *apert* adroit, intelligent.] Bold; impudent; saucy; pert. — *n.* A malapert person. — **mal′a·pert′ly,** *adv.* — **mal′a·pert′ness,** *n.*

Mal′a·prop, Mrs. (măl′ȧ·prŏp). [From MALAPROPOS.] A character in Sheridan's *Rivals,* noted for her blunders in the use of words. — **mal′a·prop·ism** (-ĭz′m), *n.*

mal′ap·ro·pos′ (măl′ăp·rō·pō′), *adj.* [F. *mal à propos,* fr. *mal* badly + *à propos* to the purpose.] Unseasonable; inopportune. — *adv.* Unseasonably; inappropriately. Cf. APROPOS.

ma′lar (mā′lẽr), *adj.* [L. *mala* the cheek.] Pert. to the cheek, or sides of the head. — *n.* The bone of the cheek.

ma·lar′i·a (mȧ·lâr′ĭ·ȧ), *n.* [It., contr. fr. *mala aria* bad air.] 1. *Obs.* Air infected with a noxious substance capable of engendering disease; esp., miasma. 2. *Med.* A serious febrile disease caused by a protozoan, the **malaria parasite** (genus *Plasmodium*), which multiplies in and destroys red blood cells. It occurs in three forms caused by separate species of the parasite which are transmitted to man by the bite of the anopheles mosquito. All are characterized by recurrent paroxysms marked by chill followed by high fever and sweating and by progressive anemia. — **ma·lar′i·al** (-ăl), **ma·lar′i·an** (-ăn), **ma·lar′i·ous** (-ŭs), *adj.*

mal′as·sim′i·la′tion (măl′ă·sĭm′ĭ·lā′shŭn), *n. Med.* Imperfect assimilation of nutritive material.

mal′ate (măl′āt; mā′lāt), *n.* [L. *malum* apple.] *Chem.* A salt or ester of malic acid.

Ma·lay′ (mȧ·lā′; mā′lā; 2), *adj.* Of or pertaining to the Malay Peninsula or Malaysia or their inhabitants. — *n.* 1. A member of the dominant brown race of the Malay Peninsula and Malaysia. 2. The agglutinative language spoken by the Malays, an Indonesian tongue. See LANGUAGE, *Table.* 3. An oriental breed of game fowls. — **Ma·lay′an** (mȧ·lā′ăn), *adj.*

Mal′a·ya′lam (măl′ȧ·yä′lȧm), *n.* The Dravidian language of the Malabar coast of India, an offshoot of Tamil.

Ma·lay′o- (mȧ·lā′ō-). A combining form for *Malay,* meaning *Malayan and,* as in **Ma·lay′o–In′do·ne′sian.**

Ma·lay′o–Pol′y·ne′sian, *adj.* Pertaining to both the Malays and the Polynesians; belonging to or designating the family of languages now usually called the Austronesian (which see).

Ma·lay′sian (mȧ·lā′shăn; -zhăn), *adj.* Of or pertaining to Malaysia, or the Malay Archipelago. — *n.* A native of Malaysia.

mal′con·tent′ (măl′kŏn·tĕnt′), *adj.* [F., fr. *mal* ill + *content.*] Discontented; esp., dissatisfied with the government; rebellious. — *n.* One discontented; esp., a discontented subject of a government; a political agitator.

‖**mal de mer** (mȧl′ dē mâr′). [F.] Seasickness.

‖**mal du pays** (dü pā′ē′). [F.] Homesickness.

male (māl), *adj.* [OF. *male, masle, mascle,* fr. L. *masculus* male, masculine, dim. of *mas* a male.] 1. Designating, or of or pertaining to, a human being or animal of the sex which begets young; — opposed to *female.* 2. Suitable to the male sex; characteristic of a male; masculine. 3. Denoting an intensity or superiority of the characteristic qualities of anything. 4. Consisting of males; as, a *male* choir. 5. *Bot.* Pertaining to or designating any organ or reproductive body accomplishing fertilization, or the plant bearing such organs; as, a *male* gamete. In seed plants, *male* is a popular equivalent of *staminate.* In *Zool. & Bot.* the male sex is indicated by the symbol of Mars (♂). 6. *Mach.* Adapted for fitting into a corresponding hollow piece; as, a *male* gauge.

Syn. **Male, masculine, manly, manlike, mannish, manful, virile** mean of or like a male. **Male** applies to animals and plants as well as to human beings and always indicates sex; **masculine** usually suggests qualities distinguishing men; **manly,** the finer qualities of a mature man, esp. as found in youth; **manlike,** the characteristic qualities of men, particularly their foibles; **mannish,** applied usually to women and boys, usually suggests imitation of the airs, manners, dress, etc., of a man; **manful** differs from *manly* in stressing sturdiness and resolution, **virile** in stressing aggressiveness, forcefulness, etc. — **Ant.** Female.

— *n.* A male human being; hence, any male organism.

mal′e·dict (măl′ē·dĭkt), *adj.* [L. *maledictus,* past part. of *maledicere.*] *Archaic.* Accursed; abominable.

mal′e·dic′tion (-dĭk′shŭn), *n.* [L. *maledictio,* fr. *maledicere* to speak ill, to curse, fr. *male* ill + *dicere* to say.] 1. A proclaiming of evil against someone; a curse; — opposed to *benediction.* 2. A speaking evil; slander. — **mal′e·dic′to·ry** (-dĭk′tō·rĭ), *adj.*

mal′e·fac′tion (-făk′shŭn), *n.* An evil deed; offense.

mal′e·fac′tor (măl′ē·făk′tẽr), *n.* [L., fr. *malefacere* to do evil, fr. *male* ill, evil + *facere* to do.] One guilty of a malefaction; a criminal. — **mal′e·fac′tress** (-trĕs; -trĭs), *n.*

ma·lef′ic (mȧ·lĕf′ĭk), *adj.* [L. *maleficus.*] Harmful.

ma·lef′i·cence (mȧ·lĕf′ĭ·sĕns; -s′ns), *n.* 1. Evil action; also, an evil deed. 2. Maleficent or malefic quality.

ma·lef′i·cent (-sĕnt; -s′nt), *adj.* [See MALEFIC.] Harmful.

Ma′le·mute (mä′lē·mūt), *n.* A dog of a breed originally bred and owned by natives of the arctic regions.

‖**mal′en′ten′du′** (mȧl′äɴ′täɴ′dü′), *adj.* [F.] Ill-conceived; ill-contrived. — *n.* Misunderstanding.

ma·lev′o·lent (mȧ·lĕv′ō·lĕnt), *adj.* [OF. *malivolent,* fr. L. *malevolens, -entis,* fr. *male* ill + *volens* wishing.] Wishing evil; arising from, or indicative of, ill will. — **ma·lev′o·lence** (-lĕns), *n.* — **Syn.** See MALICE. — **ma·lev′o·lent·ly,** *adv.*

mal·fea′sance (măl·fē′zăns), *n.* [F. *malfaisance,* fr. *malfaisant* doing ill, fr. *mal* ill, evil + *faisant* doing.] The doing of an act which a person ought not to do; an illegal deed; — often used of official misconduct.

mal·fea′sant (-zănt), *n.* A criminal.

mal′for·ma′tion (măl′fôr·mā′shŭn), *n.* Irregular, anomalous, abnormal, or wrong formation or structure.

mal·formed′ (măl·fôrmd′), *adj.* Characterized by malformation; ill-formed; abnormally formed.

‖**mal′gré′** (mȧl′grā′), *prep.* [F.] In spite of.

‖**mal′gré′ lui** (mȧl′grā′ lwē′). [F.] In spite of oneself; i. e., against one's intent or belief.

mal′ic (măl′ĭk; mā′lĭk), *adj.* [F. *malique,* fr. L. *malum* an apple.] *Chem.* Designating, or pertaining to, a crystallizable hydroxy diacid $C_2H_3OH(CO_2H)_2$ occurring in various plant juices, as in apples, grapes, etc.

mal′ice (măl′ĭs), *n.* [OF., fr. L. *malitia,* fr. *malus* ill, evil.] 1. Enmity of heart; ill will. 2. *Law.* The state of mind manifested by an intent to commit an unlawful act; esp., **malice aforethought,** a deliberate intention to commit the act.

Syn. **Malice, malevolence, ill will, spite, malignity, spleen, grudge** mean a wish for another's suffering. **Malice** usually implies a deep-seated and often unreasonable dislike that takes pleasure in seeing others suffer; **malevolence** and **ill will,** a mood born of hatred, resentment, or the like which has similar effects; **spite,** active malevolence or ill will colored by envy or meanness of spirit; **malignity,** the intensity of the malevolence and its driving force; **spleen,** deep-seated ill will combined with a choleric temper; **grudge,** a cherished feeling of ill will which seeks satisfaction.

ma·li′cious (mȧ·lĭsh′ŭs), *adj.* 1. Indulging or exercising malice. 2. Proceeding from ill will; dictated by malice. 3. *Law.* Done with wicked or mischievous intentions or motives. — **ma·li′cious·ly,** *adv.* — **ma·li′cious·ness,** *n.*

ma·lign′ (mȧ·līn′), *adj.* [OF. *maligne, malin,* fr. L. *malignus,* for *maligenus,* i. e., of a bad kind or nature, fr. *malus* bad + root of *genus* race, kind.] 1. Having an evil disposition toward others; malevolent; — opposed to *benign.* 2. Tending to injure; baleful. — **Syn.** See SINISTER. — *v. t.* To speak evil of; to traduce. — **ma·lign′ly,** *adv.*

Syn. **Malign, traduce, asperse, vilify, calumniate, defame, slander** mean to injure by speaking evil of regardless of truth. **Malign** and **traduce** both suggest bitter persecution, but *malign* does not always imply deliberate lying, and *traduce* stresses the resulting ignominy; **asperse** and **vilify** imply efforts to destroy one's good name, *asperse* by detracting from one's reputation, and *vilify* by open attempts to blacken it; **calumniate** imputes malice to the speaker as well as falsity to his assertions; **defame** and **slander** suggest the effects, *defame* stressing the actual injury to one's good name, and *slander* the suffering of the victim.

ma·lig′nan·cy (mȧ·lĭg′năn·sĭ), *n.* Also **ma·lig′nance** (-năns). State or quality of being malignant; specif.: a Evil, malign, or baleful nature. b Extreme malevolence; bitter enmity. c *Med.* Virulence; as, the *malignancy* of a tumor.

ma·lig′nant (mȧ·lĭg′nănt), *adj.* [L. *malignans, -antis,* pres. part. of *malignare, malignari,* to do or make maliciously.] **1.** Rebellious against God or against a government; malcontent. **2.** Having a baleful influence; malign. **3.** Disposed to do harm; malicious. **4.** *Med.* Tending or threatening to produce death; virulent; as, a *malignant* tumor; — opposed to *benign.* — *n.* A malcontent. — **ma·lig′nant·ly,** *adv.*

ma·lign′er (mȧ·līn′ẽr), *n.* One who maligns.

ma·lig′ni·ty (mȧ·lĭg′nĭ·tĭ), *n.; pl.* -TIES (-tĭz). **1.** State or quality of being malignant; malignancy. **2.** Usually in *pl.* A malignant act, feeling, event, etc.; as, "war, waste, plague, famine, all *malignities.*" — **Syn.** See MALICE.

ma·lines′ (mȧ·lēn′; *F.* mȧ′lēn′), *n.* [F.] **1.** = MECHLIN LACE. **2.** Also **ma·line′** (mȧ·lēn′). A fine silk net, rather stiff, used in millinery and dressmaking.

ma·lin′ger (mȧ·lĭng′gẽr), *v. i.* [F. *malingre* sickly, weakly.] To feign illness or inability in order to avoid doing one's duty; to shirk. — **ma·lin′ger·er** (-ẽr), *n.*

mal′i·son (măl′ĭ·z'n; -s'n), *n.* [OF. *maleïçon,* fr. L. *maledictio.* See MALEDICTION.] Malediction; curse.

mal′kin, maw′kin (mô′kĭn; mô′-), *n.* [Dim. of *Maud, Matilda.*] **1.** *Obs. exc. Dial.* A slattern; a drab; also, a scarecrow. **2.** *Scot. & Dial. Eng.* A hare; also, a cat; also [*cap.*], a cat personified as a specter or familiar spirit.

mall (môl; măl; *in Pall Mall,* mĕl *is the preferred pron.* Cf. PALL-MALL), *n.* [From ME. *malle* (see MAUL), but associated in 17th cent. with F. *mail.*] **1.** The mallet used in pall-mall. **2.** The game of pall-mall. **3.** A place for playing pall-mall. Hence: A shaded walk; as, *the mall,* a fashionable promenade in St. James's Park, London.

mall (môl). Var. of MAUL.

mal′lard (măl′ẽrd), *n.* [OF. *mallart.*] **1.** The drake of the common wild duck, or, *Obs.,* of any of its domesticated varieties. **2.** *pl.,* see PLURAL, *Note,* 3. Hence: The common wild duck (*Anas platyrhynchos*), of either sex, of the Northern Hemisphere. The domestic ducks are descended from it.

mal′le·a·bil′i·ty (măl′ē·ȧ·bĭl′ĭ·tĭ), *n.* Quality or state of being malleable.

mal′le·a·ble (măl′ē·ȧ·b'l; 58), *adj.* [OF., fr. L. *malleare* to hammer, fr. *malleus* a hammer.] **1.** Capable of being extended or shaped by beating with a hammer, or by the pressure of rollers. The so-called **malleable cast iron,** or, popularly, **malleable iron,** is cast iron made by a complex process from a certain variety of pig iron. **2.** Susceptible of being fashioned or molded. — **Syn.** See PLASTIC. — **mal′le·a·ble·ness,** *n.*

mal′lee (măl′ē), *n.* [Native name.] **a** Any of several low-growing Australian eucalypts (esp. *Eucalyptus dumosa* and *E. oleosa*). **b** *Australia.* The dense thicket formed by these eucalypts.

mal′le·muck (măl′ē·mŭk), *n.* [D. *mallemok,* fr. *mal* foolish, silly + *mok* mew, gull.] A large petrel, fulmar, albatross, or other oceanic bird.

mal·le′o·lar (mă·lē′ō·lẽr; măl′ē·ō·lẽr), *adj.* [See MALLEOLUS.] *Anat.* Of or pertaining to a malleolus.

mal·le′o·lus (mă·lē′ō·lŭs), *n.; pl.* -OLI (-lī). [L., dim. of *malleus* hammer.] *Anat.* The rounded lateral projection on each bone of the leg at the ankle.

mal′let (măl′ĕt; -ĭt), *n.* [F. *maillet,* dim. of *mail.* See MAUL.] **1.** A small maul with a short handle, used esp. for driving a chisel. **2.** Hence: **a** A long-handled stick with a cylindrical head, used in playing croquet. **b** A polo stick. See POLO, *n.*

mal′le·us (măl′ē·ŭs), *n.; pl.* MALLEI (-ī). [L., *hammer.* See MAUL.] *Anat. & Zool.* The outermost of the three small bones of the ear. See EAR, 1 *& Illust.*

mal′low (măl′ō), *n.* [AS. *mealwe,* fr. L. *malva.*] Any of a genus (*Malva*) typifying a family (Malvaceae, the mallow family) of herbs, shrubs, and trees, including the checkerbloom, cotton, okra, hollyhock, hibiscus, althea, etc. The genus *Malva* includes plants with palmately lobed or dissected leaves, including the common wild mallow (*M. sylvestris*) of Europe, or the dwarf mallow (*M. rotundifolia*). Cf. ROSE MALLOW.

mallow rose. = ROSE MALLOW **a.**

malm (mäm; *dial. also* môm), *n.* [AS. *mealm.*] *Petrog.* **a** A soft, grayish-white, friable limestone. **b** *Dial. Eng.* A rich clayey soil containing chalk; marl.

malm′sey (mäm′zĭ), *n.* [ML. *malmasia,* fr. Gr. *Monembasia,* or Malvasia, in the Morea.] A rich, sweet, aromatic wine, orig. produced in Cyprus, but now also in Spain, Italy, Madeira and elsewhere, from the malvasia grape.

mal′nu·tri′tion (măl′nū·trĭsh′ŭn), *n.* Faulty or imperfect nutrition.

mal·o′dor, mal·o′dour (măl·ō′dẽr), *n.* An offensive odor.

mal·o′dor·ous (-ŭs), *adj.* Ill-smelling. — **mal·o′dor·ous·ly,** *adv.* — **mal·o′dor·ous·ness,** *n.*

Syn. **Malodorous, stinking, fetid, noisome, putrid, rank, fusty, musty** mean evil-smelling. **Malodorous,** the general term, implies distinct offensiveness; **stinking,** and **fetid** (the literary term) imply also disgusting foulness; **noisome,** poisonous or unwholesome malodorousness; **putrid,** loathsome malodorousness as of decaying flesh; **rank,** a strong and unpleasing but not necessarily loathsome odor; **fusty** and **musty** suggest lack of air and sunlight, but *fusty* also implies prolonged uncleanliness, and *musty* moldiness or age.

ma·lo′nic (mȧ·lō′nĭk; -lŏn′ĭk), *adj.* [F. *malonique.*] *Chem.* Pertaining to or designating a white crystalline diacid, $CH_2(CO_2H)_2$, obtained esp. by oxidation of malic acid.

mal·pigh′i·a′ceous (măl·pĭg′ĭ·ā′shŭs), *adj.* [See MALPIGHIAN.] *Bot.* Belonging to a family (Malpighiaceae) of tropical herbs, shrubs, or trees (order Geraniales), having opposite leaves and yellow or red flowers.

Mal·pigh′i·an (măl·pĭg′ĭ·ăn), *adj.* Of, pert. to, or discovered by Marcello Malpighi (1628–94), Italian anatomist.

Malpighian body *or* **corpuscle.** *Anat.* A kidney corpuscle. See KIDNEY, 1.

Malpighian layer. *Anat.* The deeper portion of the epidermis, consisting of cells whose protoplasm has not yet changed into horny material.

Malpighian tubes *or* **vessels.** *Zool.* Tubular glands opening into the posterior portion of the alimentary canal in nearly all insects.

Malpighian tuft. See KIDNEY, 1.

mal′po·si′tion (măl′pō·zĭsh′ŭn), *n.* Wrong or faulty position, as of the fetus; misplacement.

mal′prac′tice (măl′prăk′tĭs), *n.* The treatment of a case by a surgeon or physician in a manner contrary to accepted rules and with injurious results to the patient; hence, any professional misconduct or unreasonable lack of skill in performing professional or fiduciary duties. — **mal′prac·ti′tion·er** (măl′prăk·tĭsh′ŭn·ẽr), *n.*

malt (môlt; mŏlt), *n.* [AS. *mealt.*] **1.** Grain, generally barley, softened by steeping in water and allowed to germinate. Malt is essential in brewing and distilling. Its large carbohydrate and protein content is responsible for its use as a nutrient, esp. in wasting diseases. **2.** *Colloq.* Malt liquor; beer. — *v. t.* **1.** To convert into malt, or maltlike material; as, to *malt* barley. **2.** To make or treat with malt or malt extract; as, *malted* milk. — *v. i.* To become malt or maltlike; also, to make grain into malt. — **malt,** *adj.*

Mal′ta fe′ver (môl′tȧ; mŏl′tȧ). [From *Malta.* See *Gaz.*] Undulant fever.

malt′ase (môl′tās; mŏl′-), *n.* [*malt* + *-ase.*] *Biochem.* An enzyme that accelerates the hydrolysis of maltose to dextrose. It is found in plants, animals, yeast, bacteria, etc.

Mal′tese′ (môl′tēz′; -tēs′; mŏl′-; 2), *adj.* Of or pertaining to Malta or its inhabitants. — *n.* **1.** *sing. & pl.* A native of Malta. **2.** The native language of the Maltese.

Maltese cat. A bluish-gray variety of the domestic cat.

Maltese cross. See CROSS, *Illust.* (8).

malt extract. A sugary mucilaginous substance obtained from wort.

mal′tha (măl′thȧ), *n.* [L., fr. Gr. *maltha.*] **1.** Any of various cements, some bituminous, others like mortar. **2. a** A black viscid substance intermediate between petroleum and asphalt; mineral tar. **b** A variety of ozocerite.

Mal·thu′sian (măl·thū′zhăn; -zĭ·ăn), *adj.* Of or pertaining to the political economist Rev. T. R. Malthus (1766–1834), or to his views; as, *Malthusian* theories. Malthus held that population tends to multiply faster than its means of subsistence can be made to do, and that, unless an increase of population be checked by prudential restraint, poverty is inevitable. — **Mal·thu′sian,** *n.*

malt liquor. A fermented liquor, as beer, made with malt.

malt′ose (môl′tōs; mŏl′-), *n.* [From MALT.] A crystalline sugar, $C_{12}H_{22}O_{11}$, formed esp. from starch by the action of amylase; — called also **malt sugar.** It is dextrorotatory and fermentable.

mal·treat′ (măl·trēt′), *v. t.* [F. *maltraiter.*] To treat ill; to abuse; to treat roughly. — **mal·treat′ment,** *n.*

malt′ster (môlt′stẽr; mŏlt′-), *n.* A maker of malt.

malt′y (môl′tĭ; mŏl′-), *adj.* **a** Containing, or like, malt. **b** *Humorous.* Addicted to malt liquor. **c** *Slang.* Drunk.

mal·va′ceous (măl·vā′shŭs), *adj.* [L. *malva* mallow.] *Bot.* Belonging to the mallow family (Malvaceae). See MALLOW.

mal′va·si′a (măl′vȧ·zē′ȧ; -sē′ȧ), *n.* [It. See MALMSEY.] A variety of grape which yields the wine known as malmsey; also, the wine itself. — **mal′va·si′an** (-ăn), *adj.*

mal′ver·sa′tion (măl′vẽr·sā′shŭn), *n.* [F., fr. *malverser* to be corrupt in office, fr. L. *male* ill + *versari* to occupy oneself.] Evil conduct; esp., misbehavior, corruption, or extortion in office.

mal′voi·sie (măl′voi·zĭ; măl′vȧ-), *n.* [F.] Malmsey.

ma′ma (mä′mȧ; mȧ·mä′; *Brit. usually* mȧ·mä′). Var. of MAMMA.

mam′ba (mäm′bä), *n.* [Zulu *im-amba,* for *in-amba.*] Any of several tropical and southern African venomous snakes (genus *Dendraspis*) allied to the cobras but with no hood; — called also *cobra* or *tree cobra.*

Mam′e·luke (măm′ĕ·lūk), *n.* [F. *mameluk,* fr. Ar. *mamlūk* a white (non-Negro) slave or captive.] **1.** One of a body of soldiers recruited from slaves converted to Islamism, who had great political power in Egypt (Mameluke sultans, 1250–1517) until exterminated or dispersed by Mehemet Ali in 1811. **2.** [*not cap.*] In Mohammedan countries a white or yellow slave. **3.** [*not cap.*] A fighting slave.

ma·mey′ (mȧ·mā′). Var. of MAMMEE.

mam′ma (mä′mȧ; mȧ·mä′; *cf.* MAMA), *n.* Also **ma′ma.** [Reduplicated from the infantine word *ma,* influenced in spelling by L. *mamma* breast.] Mother; — now usually a child's word.

mam′ma (măm′ȧ), *n.; pl.* -MAE (-ē). [L., breast.] *Anat. & Zool.* A glandular organ for secreting milk, characteristic of all mammals, but normally rudimentary in the male.

mam′mal (măm′ăl), *n.* A mammalian.

mam·ma′li·an (mă·mā′lĭ·ăn), *n.* [LL. *mammalis* of the breast, fr. *mamma* breast.] *Zool.* Any of the highest class (Mammalia) of vertebrates, including man and other animals that nourish their young with milk. — **mam·ma′li·an,** *adj.*

mam·mal′o·gy (mă·măl′ō·jĭ), *n.* [*Mammalia* + *-logy.*] The branch of zoology which deals with mammals.

mam′ma·ry (măm′ȧ·rĭ), *adj.* Of or pert. to the mammae; as, the *mammary* glands.

mam·ma′to-cu′mu·lus (mă·mā′tō·kū′mū·lŭs), *n.* *Meteorol.* A cumulus cloud having nipplelike protuberances below and indicating rain.

mam′mee (măm′ē; mă·mē′), *n.* Also **ma·mey′** (mȧ·mā′). [Sp. *mamey,* fr. Taino *mamey.*] Any one of three tropical American trees or their fruits: **a** Also **mammee apple.** One of a genus (*Mammea,* esp. *M. americana*) of trees with a valvate 2-parted calyx and a large drupaceous fruit. **b** The marmalade tree or its fruit, called also **mammee sa·po′ta** (sȧ·pō′tȧ) *or* **mammee col′o·ra′do** (kŏl′ō·rä′dō). **c** The sapodilla.

mam′mer (*dial.* măm′ẽr, mäm′ẽr), *v. t. & i.* *Dial.* To confuse or be confused; perplex; waver; stammer.

mam′met. *Dial. var.* of MAUMET.

mam·mif′er·ous (mă·mĭf′ẽr·ŭs), *adj.* [*mamma* breast + *-ferous.*] Having breasts, or mammae.

mam·mil′la (mă·mĭl′ȧ), *n.; pl.* -LAE (-ē). [L., better *mamilla,* dim. of *mamma* a breast.] *Anat.* A nipple.

mam′mil·lar′y (măm′ĭ·lĕr′ĭ *or, esp. Brit.,* -lẽr·ĭ), *adj.* Of, pertaining to, or resembling a mammilla.

mam′mil·late (măm′ĭ·lāt), **mam′mil·lat′ed** (-lāt′ĕd; -ĭd), *adj.* Having nipples.

mam′mock (măm′ŭk), *n.* *Dial.* A shapeless piece; scrap.

mam′mon (măm′ŭn), *n.* [LL. *mammona,* fr. Gr. *mamōnas,* fr. Aram. *māmōnā* riches.] In the New Testament, riches; hence [*cap.*], the demon of cupidity. — **mam′mon·ish,** *adj.*

mam′mon·ism (-ĭz'm), *n.* Devotion to the pursuit of wealth; the service of mammon; worldliness. — **mam′mon·ist** (-ĭst), **mam′mon·ite** (-īt), *n.*

mam′moth (măm′ŭth), *n.* [Russ. *mammot, mamant, mamont.*]

Any extinct elephant (family Elephantidae) distinguished by molars having cement filling the spaces between the ridges of enamel. The ***woolly, or northern, mammoth*** (*Mammonteus primigenius*) resembled the existing Indian elephant, but had very long, upwardly curving tusks, and a long thick hairy coat. The ***imperial mammoth*** (*Archidiskodon imperator*), of the American Pleistocene, is the largest known, reaching a height of nearly fourteen feet. — *adj.* Like a mammoth in size; very large. — **Syn.** See ENORMOUS.

mam'my (măm'ĭ), *n.*; *pl.* -MIES (-ĭz). **a** Mother; — a child's word. **b** *U.S.* A Negro woman who is a nurse or servant.

man (măn), *n.*; *pl.* MEN (mĕn). [AS. *mann, man, monn, mon.*] **1.** A human being; esp., a male human being; — now restricted to males except in general application; as, every *man*; few *men*. **2.** The human race; mankind. **3.** (with *a*) One, or anyone, indefinitely. **4.** Manly character; manliness. **5.** A married man; a husband; — correlative to *wife*. *Now Chiefly Dial.*, except in the phrase *man and wife.* **6.** An adult male servant, as a valet; also, an adult male employee; as, the *men* are on a strike. **7.** A term of familiar address often implying authority, impatience, or contempt; as, Come, *man*, we must go. **8.** One having manly excellence. **9.** *Anthropol.* An individual (genus *Homo*, family Hominidae, class Mammalia) of the highest type of animal existing or known to have existed, differing from other high types of animals, esp. in his extraordinary mental development. Only one human species (*Homo sapiens*) is generally recognized. But some anthropologists consider the extinct *Neanderthal man* (which see) as intermediate between the *Java man* (see PITHECANTHROPUS) and existing races. Cf. PEKING MAN, PILTDOWN MAN, HEIDELBERG MAN, CRO-MAGNON. **10.** *Christian Science.* The compound idea of infinite Spirit; the spiritual image and likeness of God; the full representation of Mind. *Mary Baker Eddy.* **11.** *Feudalism.* A vassal or liege man. **12.** *Games.* One of the pieces with which certain games, as chess or draughts, are played. — *v. t.*; MANNED (mănd); MAN'NING. **1.** To supply with men, as for service, defense, etc. **2.** To furnish with strength for action; to fortify; brace. **3.** *Falconry.* To accustom to man, as a hawk; to tame. **4.** *Naut.* To station men to take hold of and exert strength upon, as by pulling. — *adj.* Male; as, *man* cook.

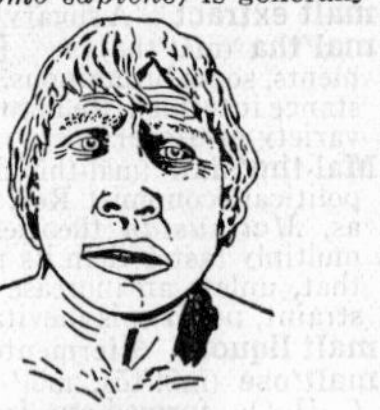

Right, Piltdown Man. *Below*, 1 Java Man; 2 Neanderthal Man; 3 Cro-Magnon type of *Homo sapiens*. After the restorations of J. H. McGregor.

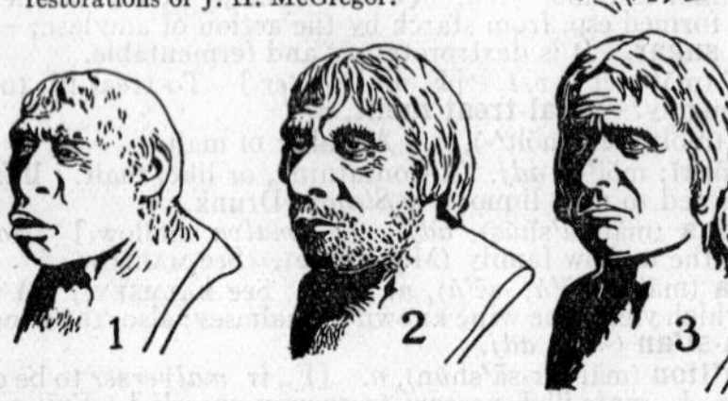

ma'na (mä'nä), *n.* [Polynesian.] *Polynesia & Australasia.* Extraphysical power immanent in and emanating from nature viewed as the embodiment of all elemental forces which produce and maintain the order of the universe. Mana is manifested physically by authority, prestige, magical powers, etc.

man'a·cle (măn'ȧ·k'l), *n.* [OF. *manicle*, fr. L. *manicula* a little hand, dim. of *manus* hand.] A handcuff; hence, a fetter; restraint; usually in *pl.* See HANDCUFF, *Illust.* — *v. t.*; MAN'A·CLED (-k'ld); MAN'A·CLING (-klĭng). To impede by, or as if by, putting handcuffs on. — **Syn.** See HAMPER.

man'age (măn'ĭj), *n.* [It. *maneggio*, fr. *maneggiare* to manage, fr. *mano* hand, fr. L. *manus*. In Eng. influenced by F. *ménage* housekeeping.] **1.** *Archaic.* Management. **2.** *Archaic.* The action and paces of a trained riding horse. **3.** A riding school; manège. — *v. t.*; MAN'AGED (-ĭjd); MAN'AG·ING (-ĭj·ĭng). **1.** To train (a horse) in the manège; to put through his paces. **2.** To control and direct; to conduct; guide; administer. **3.** To render and keep (one) submissive; to wield with address. **4.** To treat with care; to husband. **5.** To bring about by contriving; to contrive. — **Syn.** See CONDUCT. — *v. i.* **1.** To direct affairs; to carry on business or affairs. **2.** *Colloq.* To achieve one's purpose.

man'age·a·ble (măn'ĭj·ȧ·b'l), *adj.* Such as can be managed; submitting to control; tractable. — **man'age·a·bil'i·ty** (-bĭl'ĭ·tĭ), *n.* — **man'age·a·ble·ness**, *n.* — **man'age·a·bly**, *adv.*

man'aged cur'ren·cy (măn'ĭjd). Currency whose purchasing power is theoretically to be stabilized, as by variation of the gold content represented by the standard monetary unit.

man'age·ment (măn'ĭj·mĕnt), *n.* **1.** Act or art of managing; conduct; control; direction. **2.** Judicious use of means to accomplish an end; skillful treatment. **3.** Capacity for managing; executive skill. **4.** The collective body of those who manage any enterprise or interest.

man'ag·er (măn'ĭj·ẽr), *n.* **1.** One who manages; director. Abbr. *Mgr.* **2.** A person who conducts business or household affairs with economy. — **man'ag·er·ship'**, *n.*

man'ag·er·ess (-ĕs; -ĭs), *n.* A female manager.

man'a·ge'ri·al (măn'ȧ·jẽr'ĭ·ăl), *adj.* Of, pertaining to, or characteristic of a manager. — **man'a·ge'ri·al·ly**, *adv.*

man'a·kin (măn'ȧ·kĭn), *n.* [See MANIKIN.] **1.** Any of numerous small bright-colored clamatorial birds (family Pipridae) of Central and South America. **2.** Var. of MANIKIN.

‖**ma·ña'na** (mä·nyä'nä), *n.* [Sp.] Tomorrow. — *adv.* Tomorrow; before long.

Ma·nas'seh (mȧ·năs'ĕ), *n. Douay Bib.* **Ma·nas'ses** (-ēz). [Heb. *Měnaşşeh.*] **1.** See JACOB. **2.** A king of Judah. 2 *Kings* xxi.

man'-at-arms', *n.*; *pl.* MEN-AT-ARMS. A soldier; esp., a heavy-armed horse soldier.

man'a·tee' (măn'ȧ·tē'), *n.* [Sp. *manatí*, of Cariban origin.] Any of several aquatic herbivorous mammals (genus *Trichechus*), differing from the dugong in having the tail broad and rounded; a sea cow.

man'chet (măn'chĕt; -chĭt), *n. Archaic & Dial. Eng.* A loaf or roll of fine wheat bread.

man'chi·neel' (măn'chĭ·nēl'), *n.* [F. *mancenille*, fr. Sp. *manzanillo*, fr. *manzana* apple.] A poisonous tropical American tree (*Hippomane mancinella*) having a milky juice and apple-shaped fruit.

Man'chu (măn'choo; măn'choo'), *adj.* Of or pertaining to Manchuria or its inhabitants. — *n.* **1.** One of the native Mongolian race of Manchuria, which conquered China and established a dynasty there (***Manchu, or Ch'ing, dynasty***, 1644–1912). **2.** The language of the Manchus, a Ural-Altaic tongue. — **Man·chu'ri·an** (măn·choor'ĭ·ăn), *adj. & n.*

man'ci·ple (măn'sĭ·p'l), *n.* [OF. *manciple, mancipe*, slave, servant, fr. L. *mancipium*, fr. *mancipare* to sell.] A steward or purveyor, as for a college or Inn of Court.

-man'cy (-măn'sĭ). [OF. or LL.; OF. *-mancie*, fr. LL. *-mantia*, fr. Gr. *mantia* divination.] A combining form denoting *divination*, esp. *by means of a* (specified) *thing*, as in chiro*mancy*.

Man·dae'an (măn·dē'ăn), *n.* [Mandaean *mandayyā* having knowledge.] A dialect of Aramaic.

man·da'mus (măn·dā'mŭs), *n.* [L., we command, fr. *mandare* to command.] *Law.* **a** Orig., in England, any of various ancient prerogative writs; hence, the prerogative writ issued to enforce the performance of some public duty. **b** *U. S.* A common-law writ similarly issued and used. **c** By extension, any of various court orders similarly used. — *v. t. Colloq.* To serve or coerce with a mandamus.

man'da·rin (măn'dȧ·rĭn), *n.* [Pg. *mandarim*, fr. Malay *mantrī* minister of state.] **1.** Under the Chinese Empire, a public official of one of the nine grades entitled to wear a button on the hat. **2.** [*cap.*] **a** The dialect of Chinese used by the official classes, under the Empire. **b** More widely, the chief dialect of China (of which Pekingese is the standard form). See CHINESE, 2. **3.** Any of a group of Chinese oranges (derived from *Citrus reticulata*) or their reddish-yellow fruit, smaller than the common orange, with a loose rind and sweet pulp; — called also *tangerine*. **4.** An orange dye.

mandarin duck. A beautiful, crested Asiatic duck (*Aix galericulata*), often domesticated.

man'da·tar'y (măn'dȧ·tĕr'ĭ; -tẽr·ĭ), *n.*; *pl.* -TARIES (-ĭz). [LL. *mandatarius.*] One to whom a mandate is given (see MANDATE, *n.*, 4).

man'date (măn'dāt; -dĭt), *n.* [F. and L.; F. *mandat*, fr. L. *mandatum*, fr. *mandare* to commit to one's charge, to order, orig., to put into one's hand. See MANUAL.] **1.** An authoritative command; order. **2. a** A prescript from a superior court or official to an inferior one. **b** *Canon Law Hist.* A papal ordinance in an individual case, as preferment to a benefice. **c** *Roman Hist.* An order of the emperor to an imperial officer, esp. in the provinces. **d** In the Civil-law systems and often in law text writers, any contract of agency in which one undertakes to perform some act for another. **3.** *Political Science.* The instruction given by a constituency to the elected legislative body or one of its members. **4.** An order or commission, granted by the League of Nations as mandator to a member nation as its mandatary, for the establishment of a responsible government over former German colonies or other conquered territory; also, a mandated territory. — (-dāt), *v. t.* To administer or assign under a mandate.

man·da'tor (măn·dā'tẽr), *n.* One who gives a mandate.

man'da·to'ry (măn'dȧ·tō'rĭ *or, esp. Brit.*, -tẽr·ĭ), *adj.* **1.** Containing or of the nature of a mandate or command; hence, obligatory. **2.** Of or pertaining to a mandate as granted by the League of Nations; as, *mandatory* powers. — *n.* A mandatary; esp., one holding a mandate from the League of Nations.

man'di·ble (măn'dĭ·b'l), *n.* [OF., fr. LL. *mandibula*, fr. *mandere* to chew.] **1.** *Anat.* **a** = JAW, 1 **b**; — used esp. of the jaws of beaked animals, as birds. Cf. BILL, *Illust.* **b** See JAW, 1 **a**. **2.** *Zool.* In arthropods, either one of the anterior pair of mouth appendages which often form strong biting jaws. See HYMENOPTERON, *Illust.*

man·dib'u·lar (măn·dĭb'ū·lẽr), *adj.* Of, pertaining to, or like a mandible. — *n.* The mandible, or lower jawbone.

man·dib'u·late (-lāt), *adj.* **1.** Having jaws adapted for chewing, as certain insects. **2.** Having a lower jaw, as most vertebrate animals. — **man·dib'u·late**, *n.*

Man·din'go (măn·dĭng'gō), *n.*; *pl.* -GOS or -GOES (-gōz). Also **Man·din'ga** (-gȧ). **1.** A Negro of a linguistic stock of the western Sudan. **2.** The language, or languages, of the Mandingos. — **Man·din'gan** (-găn), *adj. & n.*

man'do·lin (măn'dō·lĭn; -lĭn'), *n.* [F. *mandoline*, fr. It. *mandolino*, dim. of *mandola*, fr. LL. *pandura*. See BANDORE.] *Music.* An instrument of the lute kind, having a deep pear-shaped body and fretted neck. — **man'do·lin·ist** (-ĭst), *n.*

man·drag'o·ra (măn·drăg'ō·rȧ), *n.* [L. *mandragoras.*] *Bot.* A plant of a genus (*Mandragora*) of Eurasian acaulescent herbs of the nightshade family; also, its root.

man'drake (măn'drāk), *n.* [AS. *mandragora*, fr. L. *mandragoras*, fr. Gr. *mandragoras.*] **1.** An herb (*Mandragora officinarum*) of southern Europe and northern Africa, with ovate leaves and whitish or violet-purple flowers; also, its large forked root, the subject of many superstitions, esp. that eating it is supposed to promote conception. **2.** *U. S.* The May apple.

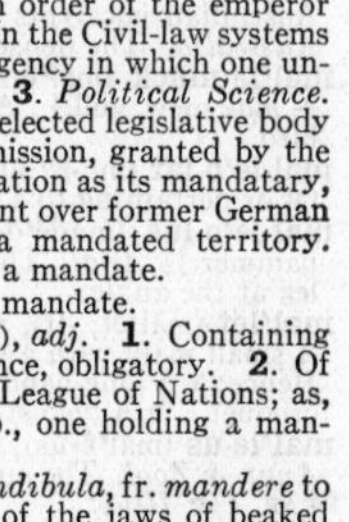

Mandrake (*M. officinarum*). (1/8)

man'drel (măn'drĕl), *n.* Also **man'dril** (-drĭl). [F. *mandrin.*] *Mach.* **a** An axle, spindle, or arbor, inserted forcibly into a piece of work to support it while the work is machined. **b** A metal bar, used as a core around which metal or other material may be cast, molded, or otherwise shaped.

man'drill (măn'drĭl), *n.* [*man* + earlier *drill* baboon.] A large, gregarious, ferocious West African baboon (*Papio mormon*).

man'du·cate (măn'dū·kāt), *v. t.* [L. *manducatus*, past part. of *manducare* to chew. See MANGER.] To masticate; chew; eat.

mane (mān), *n.* [AS. *manu.*] **1.** The long heavy hair growing on the upper side of, or about, the neck of some quadrupeds, as the horse, lion, etc. See HORSE, *Illust.* (12). **2.** Long heavy hair on a person's head. — **maned** (mānd), *adj.*

man'-eat'er, *n.* One that has, or is fancied to have, an appetite for human flesh; specif.: **a** A cannibal. **b** The man-eating shark (see

SHARK). **c** A lion or tiger that has acquired the habit of feeding on human flesh.

ma·nège′ (mȧ·nĕzh′; -nāzh′), *n.* Also **ma·nege′.** [F. *manège*, fr. It. See MANAGE, *n.*] **1.** A school for teaching horsemanship, and for training horses; a riding academy. **2.** Art of horsemanship; also, the paces of a trained horse.

ma′nes (mā′nēz), *n. pl.* [L.] **1.** [*often cap.*] *Rom. Relig.* The spirits of the dead and gods of the lower world. **2.** Hence, ancestral spirits worshiped as gods.

ma·neu′ver, ma·noeu′vre (mȧ·nōō′vẽr; -nū′vẽr), *n.* [F. *manœuvre*, fr. LL. *manuopera* handwork, manual labor, fr. L. *manu operari* to work by hand.] **1. a** A military or naval evolution. **b** Hence, *pl.*, extended field exercises of troops, or similar exercises in which ships and coast defenses participate. **2.** Management with artful design; adroit proceeding. — **Syn.** See TRICK. — *v. i.* **1.** To perform a movement in military or naval tactics for getting advantage in attack or defense. **2.** To manage with address or art; to scheme. — *v. t.* **1.** To cause to execute tactical movements. **2.** To put, get, make, draw, etc., by maneuvering. **3.** To manage, or bring about, with skill; to manipulate. — **ma·neu′ver·a·bil′i·ty** (-vẽr·ȧ·bĭl′ĭ·tĭ), **ma·neu′vra·bil′i·ty** (-vrȧ·bĭl′ĭ·tĭ), *n.* — **ma·neu′ver·a·ble, ma·neu′vra·ble,** *adj.* — **ma·neu′ver·er, ma·noeu′vrer,** *n.*

man Friday. A person wholly subservient to another, like Robinson Crusoe's servant Friday; a servile follower.

man′ful (măn′fŏŏl; -f'l), *adj.* Showing manliness; brave; resolute. — **Syn.** See MALE. — **man′ful·ly,** *adv.* — **man′ful·ness,** *n.*

man′ga·nate (măng′gȧ·nāt), *n.* A salt of manganic acid.

man′ga·nese (-nēs; -nēz), *n.* [F. *manganèse*, fr. It. *manganese*, corrupt. fr. ML. *magnesia*. See MAGNESIA.] *Chem.* A grayish-white metal with reddish tinge, soft when pure but ordinarily hard and brittle, like iron but not magnetic. Symbol, *Mn;* at. no., 25; at. wt., 54.93; sp. gr., 7.2.

manganese spar. Rhodonite.

manganese steel. Cast steel containing 12 to 14 per cent of manganese. It is very hard without becoming brittle.

man·gan′ic (măn·găn′ĭk), *adj. Chem.* Of, pertaining to, resembling, or containing manganese; specif., designating compounds in which manganese has a higher valence as contrasted with *manganous* compounds; as, **manganic acid,** an acid, H_2MnO_4, known only in the form of its salts.

man′ga·nite (măng′gȧ·nīt), *n.* [*manganese* + *-ite.*] **1.** *Mineral.* An ore of manganese, the hydrous oxide MnO(OH); — called also ***gray manganese ore.*** **2.** *Chem.* Any of various salts derived from certain hydroxides of manganese related to the dioxide, and regarded as acids (***manganous acids***).

man′ga·nous (măng′gȧ·nŭs; măn·găn′ŭs), *adj. Chem.* Of, pertaining to, or designating those compounds of manganese in which the element has a lower valence than in *manganic* compounds.

mange (mānj), *n.* [OF. *manjue, mangeue*, itching, eating, fr. *manjuer, mangier* (F. *manger*) to eat. See MANGER.] Any of various forms of skin disease affecting domestic animals and sometimes man, esp. those caused by parasites (**mange mites**). Cf. SCAB.

man′gel-wur′zel (măng′g'l·wûr′z'l), *n.* Also **man′gel.** [G., corrupt. fr. *mangoldwurzel*, fr. *mangold* beet + *wurzel* root.] A large coarse variety of beet (*Beta vulgaris macrorhiza*) grown, esp. in Europe, as food for cattle.

man′ger (mān′jẽr), *n.* [OF. *maingeure*, deriv. of L. *manducare* to eat, chew (whence F. *manger* to eat).] A trough or box holding fodder for horses or cattle to eat.

man′gle (măng′g'l), *v. t.;* MAN′GLED (-g'ld); MAN′GLING (-glĭng). [AF. *mangler, mahangler*, freq. of OF. *mahaignier*. See MAIM.] **1.** To cut, bruise, or hack with repeated blows. **2.** To spoil or injure in making or performing. — **man′gler** (-glẽr), *n.*

man′gle, *n.* [D. *mangel*, fr. *mangelen* to mangle.] A machine for smoothing cloth, as sheets, clothing, etc., by roller pressure. — **man′gle,** *v. t.* — **man′gler,** *n.*

man′go (măng′gō), *n.; pl.* -GOES or -GOS (-gōz). [Pg. *manga*, fr. Malay *mangga*, fr. Tamil *mān-kāy*.] An oblong, yellowish-red tropical fruit, with a thick rind, a fibrous, agreeably subacid juicy pulp, and a hard stone; also, the tree (*Mangifera indica*) of the sumac family, which bears this fruit.

man′go·nel (măng′gō·nĕl), *n.* [OF., deriv. of Gr. *manganon.*] A military engine formerly used for throwing stones, etc.

man′go·steen (măng′gō·stēn), *n.* [Malay *mangustan.*] An East Indian fruit, with a thick rind and juicy flesh; also, the tree (*Garcinia mangostana*) which bears it.

man′grove (măng′grōv), *n.* [Sp. *mangle* mangrove + E. *grove.*] **1.** Any of a genus (*Rhizophora*, esp. *R. mangle*) of tropical maritime trees or shrubs which throw out many prop roots. Mangrove swamps become active land builders. **2.** A tree (*Avicennia marina*) of the West Indies and southern Florida coast, forming dense thickets extending into the water; — called specif. ***black mangrove.***

man′gy (mān′jĭ), *adj.;* MAN′GI·ER (-jĭ·ẽr); MAN′GI·EST. **1.** Infected with, of the nature of, or caused by the mange. **2.** Shabby; squalid; formerly, mean; "lousy." — **man′gi·ly,** *adv.* — **man′gi·ness,** *n.*

man′han′dle (măn′hăn′d'l; măn·hăn′d'l), *v. t.;* -HAN′DLED (-d'ld); -HAN′DLING (-dlĭng). **1.** To move, or manage, by human force. **2.** To handle roughly.

man′hole′ (măn′hōl′), *n.* A hole through which a man may go, esp. to gain access to a drain, electric conduit, etc.

man′hood (măn′hŏŏd), *n.* **1.** State of being man (i. e., a human being), or a man as distinguished from a child or a woman. **2.** Manly quality; courage. **3.** Men collectively.

man′-hour′, *n.* A unit of work performed by one man in one hour, esp. as a basis of wages and cost finding.

ma′ni·a (mā′nĭ·ȧ; 58), *n.* [L., fr. Gr. *mania.*] **1.** Madness; specif., the excited phase of manic-depressive insanity, characterized by disordered speech and thinking, by impulsive movements, and by excessive emotion. **2.** Excessive enthusiasm; a craze; as, the sport *mania.* — **Syn.** See INSANITY.

-ma′ni·a (-mā′nĭ·ȧ; 58). [Gr. *mania* madness.] A combining form denoting: **a** *A* (specified) *type of madness* or *manic condition*, as in klepto*mania*. **b** *An infatuation* or *passion for; a craze;* as in Anglo*mania*. Corresponding adjectives, often used also as nouns, are formed in **-ma′ni·ac** (-ăk).

ma′ni·ac (mā′nĭ·ăk; 58), *n.* A raving lunatic; a madman. — **ma′ni·ac,** *adj.*

ma·ni′a·cal (mȧ·nī′ȧ·kăl), *adj.* Affected with, or characterized by, madness; maniac. — **ma·ni′a·cal·ly,** *adv.*

ma′nic (mā′nĭk; măn′ĭk), *adj.* [Gr. *manikos* mad.] *Med.* Affected with mania; pertaining to or like mania.

ma′nic-de·pres′sive, *adj.* Characterized by alternating mania and mental depression; — esp. in **manic-depressive insanity.**

Man′i·chae′an, Man′i·che′an (măn′ĭ·kē′ăn), *n.* [LL. *Manichaeus.*] A believer in the doctrines of Manes (216?–276?), a Persian who taught a system compounded of Zoroastrian dualism and Christian soteriology. According to it, man's soul, sprung from the Kingdom of Light, seeks escape from the Kingdom of Darkness, the body. — **Man′i·chae′an, Man′i·che′an,** *adj.* — **Man′i·chae′an·ism, Man′i·che′an·ism** (-ĭz'm), *n.* — **Man′i·chae′ism, Man′i·che′ism** (măn′ĭ·kē′ĭz'm), *n.*

Man′i·chee′ (măn′ĭ·kē′), *n.* A Manichaean.

man′i·cure (măn′ĭ·kūr; 114), *n.* [F., fr. L. *manus* hand + *cura* care.] **a** A person who makes a business of taking care of people's hands, especially their nails. **b** The care of the hands and nails; also, a single treatment of them. — *v. t. & i.* To do manicure work (on); to trim. — **man′i·cur′ist** (-kūr′ĭst), *n.*

man′i·fest (măn′ĭ·fĕst), *adj.* [F. or L.; F. *manifeste*, fr. L. *manifestus, manufestus*, orig., seized by the hand, hence, palpable.] Evident to the senses, esp. to the sight; hence, obvious to the understanding; not obscure. — **Syn.** See EVIDENT.

— *v. t.* **1.** To make to appear distinctly; to display; evidence. **2.** To exhibit the manifest of, as of a cargo. — **Syn.** See SHOW.

— *n.* **1.** *Obs.* A manifesto. **2.** A list or invoice of a ship's cargo, to be exhibited at the customhouse.

man′i·fes′tant (-fĕs′tănt), *n.* One who participates in a manifestation.

man′i·fes·ta′tion (-fĕs·tā′shŭn), *n.* **1.** Act of manifesting; also, that which manifests; display; disclosure. **2.** Specif., a public demonstration of power and purpose, as by a government or by a political party. **3.** *Spiritualism.* A materialization.

man′i·fest·ly (măn′ĭ·fĕst·lĭ), *adv.* In a manifest manner.

man′i·fes′to (-fĕs′tō), *n.; pl.* -TOES, *sometimes* -TOS (-tōz). [It.] **1.** A public declaration, usually of a sovereign or person claiming large powers, showing intentions and motives. **2.** A statement of policy or opinion issued by an organization, party, or school. — *v. i.;* MAN′I-FES′TOED (-tōd); MAN′I·FES′TO·ING. To issue a manifesto.

man′i·fold (măn′ĭ·fōld), *adj.* [AS. *manigfeald*. See MANY; -FOLD.] **1.** Numerous and varied; as, our *manifold* blessings. **2.** Comprehensive of various features. **3.** Being so in many ways; rightfully so called for many reasons; as, he is a *manifold* traitor. **4.** Consisting of or operating many of one kind combined; as, a *manifold* bell pull.

— *v. t.* **1.** To make manifold; to multiply. **2.** To make many or several copies of; as, to *manifold* a letter.

— *n.* **1.** That which is manifold. **2.** A copy made with a manifolder. **3.** *Mach.* A pipe fitting with several lateral outlets, for connecting one pipe with others. — **man′i·fold′ly,** *adv.* — **man′i·fold′ness,** *n.*

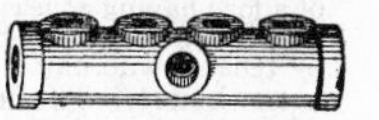
Manifold.

man′i·fold′er (-fōl′dẽr), *n.* One who or that which manifolds; esp., a contrivance for manifold writing.

man′i·hot (măn′ĭ·hŏt), *n.* [NL., fr. F. *manihot*, of Tupian origin.] Any of a genus (*Manihot*) of tropical economic plants. See CASSAVA.

man′i·kin (măn′ĭ·kĭn), *n.* [D. *manneken*, dim. of *man* man.] **1.** A little man; a dwarf. **2.** A mannequin. **3.** A model of the human body, commonly in detachable pieces, for exhibiting the parts and organs.

Ma·nil′a hemp (mȧ·nĭl′ȧ). The fiber obtained from the leaf stalk of a banana (*Musa textilis*), native to the Philippine Islands; — called also by the native name *abacá*.

Manila paper. A durable brown or buff paper made orig. of Manila hemp, used as a wrapping paper.

Manila rope. Rope made from Manila hemp.

ma·nil′la (mȧ·nĭl′ȧ), *n.* Also **ma·nille′** (mȧ·nĭl′). [F. and Sp.; F. *manille*, fr. Sp. *malilla* (sc. *carta* card), fr. *malillo*, dim. of *malo* bad.] In various card games, the second-best trump.

Ma·nil′la (mȧ·nĭl′ȧ). Var. of MANILA, as in phrases above.

man′i·oc (măn′ĭ·ŏk; mā′nĭ·ŏk), *n.* [F., of Tupian origin.] Cassava.

man′i·ple (măn′ĭ·p'l), *n.* [OF. *maniple, manipule*, fr. L. *manipulus* a handful, fr. *manus* hand + root of *plere* to fill.] **1.** A subdivision of the Roman legion, either 120 or 60 men. **2.** *Eccl.* A narrow band of the same material and color as the chasuble carried suspended from the left arm by the celebrant and ministers at Mass. See VESTMENT, *Illust.*

ma·nip′u·lar (mȧ·nĭp′ū·lẽr), *adj.* [L. *manipularis.*] **1.** Of or pert. to a Roman maniple. **2.** Manipulatory. — *n.* A soldier of a maniple.

ma·nip′u·late (mȧ·nĭp′ū·lāt), *v. t.* [See MANIPLE.] **1.** To treat or operate with the hands, or by mechanical means, esp. with skill. **2.** To treat or manage with the intellect. **3.** To control the action of, by management; as, to *manipulate* a convention; also, to manage artfully or fraudulently. **4.** *Exchanges.* To force (prices) up or down, as by matched orders, wash sales, etc.; to rig. — **Syn.** See HANDLE. — **ma·nip′u·lat′a·ble** (-lāt′ȧ·b'l), *adj.* — **ma·nip′u·la′tive** (-lā′tĭv; -lȧ·tĭv), *adj.* — **ma·nip′u·la′tor** (-lā′tẽr), *n.*

ma·nip′u·la′tion (-lā′shŭn), *n.* [F.] **1.** Act of manipulating or state of being manipulated. **2.** Skillful or dexterous management, sometimes for purposes of fraud.

ma·nip′u·la·to′ry (mȧ·nĭp′ū·lȧ·tō′rĭ; -tẽr·ĭ), *adj.* Of, pertaining to, or performed by manipulation; manipulative.

man′i·to (măn′ĭ·tō), **man′i·tou** (-tōō), **man′i·tu** (-tōō), *n.* [Of Algonquian origin.] Among the Algonquian Indians, one of the powers dominating the forces of nature.

man′kind′, *n.* **1.** (*pron.* măn′kīnd′; *formerly also* măn′kīnd′) The human race; man, taken collectively. **2.** (*pron.* măn′kīnd′) Men, as distinguished from women.

man′like′ (măn′līk′), *adj.* Like, becoming to, or belonging to a man or men; manly. — **Syn.** See MALE.

man′ly (-lĭ), *adj.;* MAN′LI·ER (-lĭ·ẽr); MAN′LI·EST. Having qualities becoming to a man; manlike; esp., brave; resolute; noble. — **Syn.** See MALE. — *adv.* In a manly manner; manfully. — **man′li·ness,** *n.*

man′na (măn′ȧ), *n.* [LL., fr. Gr. *manna*, neut., fr. Aram. *mannā*, fr. Heb. *mān.*] **1.** The food miraculously supplied to the Israelites in the wilderness (*Ex.* xvi); hence, divinely supplied spiritual nourishment. **2.** Something likened to the Biblical manna. **3.** The sweetish exudate of the European flowering ash (*Fraxinus ornus*) and of several related species, used as a mild laxative.

manna grass. = MEADOW GRASS b.

man'ne·quin (măn'ĕ·kĭn), *n.* [F. (fr. D.). See MANIKIN.] **1.** An artist's, tailor's, or dressmaker's lay figure. **2.** A woman hired to display gowns by wearing them, as at a costumer's or on the stage.

man'ner (măn'ẽr), *n.* [OF. *maniere*, fr. L. *manuarius* belonging to the hand, fr. *manus* hand.] **1.** A way of acting; a mode of procedure. **2.** A customary way of acting; normal behavior; habit; custom. **3.** Hence: Mode of living or acting; conduct; specif.: **a** *pl.* Social conduct or rules of conduct as shown in the prevalent customs; as, the novel is a study of *manners*. **b** *pl.* Habitual deportment; as, good *manners;* also, good or polite deportment. **c** Bearing; mien; as, the grand *manner*. **4.** Distinguished deportment. **5.** *Archaic.* **a** Species; kind; sort; as, all *manner* of goods. **b** Fashion; nature. — **Syn.** See METHOD: BEARING. — ***to the manner born.*** Born to follow a certain practice or custom; having lifelong acquaintance with given conditions, customs, etc.

man'nered (măn'ẽrd), *adj.* **1.** Having manners; as, a well-*mannered* child. **2.** Affected with mannerism or excessive peculiarity.

man'ner·ism (măn'ẽr·ĭz'm), *n.* Excessive adherence to a peculiar style, esp. in literature or art; a characteristic mode or peculiarity of action, bearing, speaking, etc. — **Syn.** See POSE. — **man'ner·ist** (-ĭst), *n.*

man'ner·less, *adj.* Destitute of manners; unmannerly.

man'ner·ly, *adj.* Showing good manners; civil; polite. — *adv.* Politely. — **man'ner·li·ness,** *n.*

man'ni·kin. Var. of MANIKIN.

man'nish (măn'ĭsh), *adj.* Resembling, suitable to, or characteristic of a man; manlike. — **Syn.** See MALE. — **man'nish·ly,** *adv.* — **man'nish·ness,** *n.*

man'nite (măn'īt), *n.* *Chem.* Mannitol. — **man·nit'ic** (mă·nĭt'ĭk), *adj.*

man'ni·tol (măn'ĭ·tōl; -tŏl), *n.* [*mannite* + *-ol*, 1.] *Chem.* A white crystalline alcohol, $C_6H_8(OH)_6$, occurring in three optically different modifications.

man'nose (măn'ōs), *n.* [*mannitol* + *-ose.*] *Chem.* A sugar, ($C_6H_{12}O_6$), obtained by oxidation of mannitol.

ma·noeu'vre, etc. Vars. of MANEUVER, etc.

man'-of-war', *n.; pl.* MEN-OF-WAR. A war vessel of a recognized navy, esp. one armed for active hostilities.

man'-of-war' bird *or* **hawk.** = FRIGATE BIRD.

ma·nom'e·ter (mȧ·nŏm'ē·tẽr), *n.* [Gr. *manos* thin, rare + *-meter.*] A gauge for measuring pressure of gases and vapors; a pressure gauge. — **man'o·met'ric** (măn'ō·mĕt'rĭk), **man'o·met'ri·cal** (-rĭ·kăl), *adj.*

man'or (măn'ẽr), *n.* [OF. *manoir* habitation, village, fr. inf. *manoir* to stay, dwell, fr. L. *manere.*] **1.** *Obs.* The house or hall of an estate; mansion. **2.** *Eng. Hist.* An estate administered as a unit, esp. a demesne of a lord for which a court-baron was held; later, the holding of a lord having at least the number of freehold tenants required to entitle it to hold a court-baron. **3.** *Amer. Hist.* In law, a tract occupied by tenants who pay a fixed rent to the proprietor.

manor house. The house of the lord of a manor.

ma·no'ri·al (mȧ·nō'rĭ·ăl; 70), *adj.* Of or belonging to, or like, a manor; as, *manorial* court; *manorial* accounts.

man power. Also **man'pow'er** (măn'pou'ẽr; 2), *n.* **a** Power available from or supplied by physical effort of man. **b** Usually *manpower.* The strength of a nation as expressed in terms of the number of men and women available for the armed services and/or civilian defense services.

‖**man'qué'** (mäɴ'kā'), *adj. masc.*, **man'quée'** (-kā'), *fem.* [F.] Literally, defective; that has not achieved the quality expected of its kind; short of fulfillment of one's aspiration.

man'rope' (măn'rōp'), *n.* *Naut.* A side rope to a gangway, ladder, etc., used as a handrail.

man'sard roof (măn'särd). *Arch.* A roof having on all sides two slopes, the lower one being steeper than the upper one.

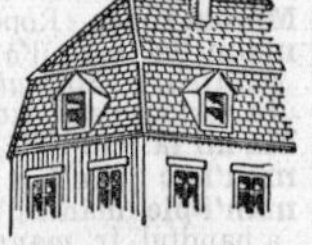

Mansard Roof.

manse (măns), *n.* [ML. *mansa* a farm, fr. L. *manere, mansum*, to stay, dwell.] **1.** *Archaic.* The dwelling of a householder. **2.** The residence of an ecclesiastic; esp., in Scotland, the house assigned to or occupied by a minister.

man'serv'ant (măn'sûr'vănt), *n.; pl.* MENSERVANTS (mĕn'sûr'vănts). A male servant.

man'sion (măn'shŭn), *n.* [OF., fr. L. *mansio* a dwelling, fr. *manere, mansum*, to dwell.] **1. a** *Obs.* Stay; sojourn. **b** *Archaic.* A dwelling place; abode. **2.** A separate lodging, apartment, etc.; — chiefly *pl.* **3.** Formerly, a manor house; hence, any house of some size or pretension. **4.** *Astrol.* **a** A house. **b** One of twenty-eight parts into which the moon's monthly course is divided.

man'slaugh'ter (măn'slô'tẽr), *n.* *Law.* The unlawful killing of a human being without malice express or implied.

man'slay'er (-slā'ẽr), *n.* One who commits manslaughter.

man'stop'ping (-stŏp'ĭng), *adj.* *Mil.* Designating a bullet (**man'stop'per**) that will cause a shock sufficient to stop a soldier advancing in a charge.

man'sue·tude (măn'swē·tūd), *n.* [L. *mansuetudo.*] Tameness; mildness.

man'ta (măn'tȧ; *Sp.* män'tä), *n.* [Sp.] **1.** A blanket or cloth, as for a horse or mule; also, a kind of cloak or wrap, worn esp. as a protection. **2.** *Mil.* A portable bulwark or shelter; a mantelet. **3.** *Zool.* A devilfish.

man'teau (măn'tō; *F.* mäɴ'tō'), *n.* [F.] **a** *Obs.* A mantua. **b** A loose robe; a negligee.

man'tel (măn't'l), *n.* [See MANTLE.] **1.** The beam, stone, or arch serving as a lintel to support the masonry above a fireplace; a manteltree. **2.** The framework or finish around a fireplace. **3.** The shelf above a fireplace, often forming part of the mantel (def. 2).

man'tel·et (măn't'l·ĕt; mănt'lĕt; -lĭt), *n.* [OF., dim. of *mantel.* See MANTLE.] **1.** A short mantle or cape. **2.** *Mil.* Often **mant'let** (mănt'lĕt; -lĭt). **a** A kind of movable shelter, formerly used by besiegers as a protection when attacking. **b** A bulletproof screen or shelter.

man'tel·let'ta (măn'tĕ·lĕt'ȧ), *n.* [It.] *R.C.Ch.* A short mantle of silk or wool with armholes but without sleeves, worn over the rochet by cardinals, bishops, and prelates of the first rank.

man'tel·piece' (măn't'l·pēs'), *n.* Also **man'tel·shelf'** (-shĕlf'). The shelf of a mantel.

man'tel·tree' (-trē'), *n.* *Arch.* A mantel, esp. of wood.

man'tic (măn'tĭk), *adj.* [Gr. *mantikos* prophetic, fr. *mantis* seer.] Of or pertaining to divination; also, gifted with prophetic powers.

man·til'la (măn·tĭl'ȧ), *n.* [Sp., fr. *manta.*] **1.** A woman's light cloak or cape. **2.** A kind of veil worn in Spain, Mexico, etc.

man'tis (măn'tĭs), *n.; pl.* -TES (-tēz), -TISES (-ĕz; -ĭz). [NL., fr. Gr. *mantis* prophet.] Any of certain insects (genus *Mantis* or allied genera), remarkable for their grotesque form, and for holding their stout anterior legs like hands folded in prayer; — hence often called ***praying mantis.***

mantis crab *or* **shrimp.** A squilla.

man·tis'sa (măn·tĭs'ȧ), *n.* [L., an addition, makeweight.] *Math.* The decimal part of common logarithms.

man'tle (măn't'l), *n.* [From AS. *mentel* (fr. L.) and fr. OF. *mantel* (F. *manteau*), fr. L. *mantellum, mantelum.*] **1.** A loose sleeveless garment worn over other garments; a cloak. **2.** Something that envelops, enfolds, or covers. **3.** A lacelike hood or envelope of some refractory material which, placed in position over a flame, gives light by incandescence. The common type is the ***Welsbach mantle,*** composed chiefly of thoria and ceria. **4.** *Mech.* The outer wall and casing of a blast furnace, above the hearth. **5.** *Zool.* **a** In mollusks and branchiopods, the fold, or lobe, or pair of lobes, of the body wall which in shell-bearing forms lines the shell, and bears the shell-secreting glands. See CLAM, OYSTER, *Illusts.* **b** In tunicates and barnacles, the soft external body wall which lines the test or the shell. **c** In birds, the back together with the folded wings. — *v. t.;* -TLED (-t'ld); -TLING (-tlĭng). To cover or envelop, as with a mantle; to cloak. — *v. i.* **1. a** To spread out the wings, one after the other, over the legs; — said of hawks. **b** To spread out; — said of wings. **2.** To gather or assume a covering, as froth or scum. **3.** To spread over the surface as a covering; as, a scum *mantled* the pool; to be or become suffused with blood; of the blood, to gather so as to produce a flush or blush; to blush; flush.

man'tle (măn't'l). Var. of MANTEL.

mant'let (mănt'lĕt; -lĭt). Var. of MANTELET.

Man'toux test (măn'tōō; *F.* mäɴ'tōō'). [After Charles *Mantoux* (b. 1877), Parisian physician.] *Med.* A type of tuberculin test that uses diluted old tuberculin in intracutaneous injection. See TUBERCULIN.

man'tu·a (măn'tū·ȧ), *n.* [From *Mantua*, Italy.] **1.** *Obs.* A rich fabric, prob. of silk. **2.** *Hist.* [From MANTEAU; confused with MANTUA.] A lady's loose-bodied robe, usually an overdress, resembling a mantle.

man'u·al (măn'ū·ăl), *adj.* [F. and L.; F. *manuel*, fr. L. *manualis*, fr. *manus* hand.] **1.** Of or pertaining to the hand or hands; done, made, or operated by hand; as, *manual* labor. **2.** Of the nature of, or designed for, a manual, as a text. — *n.* **1.** A small book; handbook. **2.** *Mil.* A prescribed exercise in the handling of a weapon; as, the *manual* of arms. **3.** *Music.* An organ keyboard for the fingers. — **man'u·al·ly,** *adv.*

manual training. Training in work done with the hands, as woodworking, metalworking, sewing, etc.

ma·nu'bri·um (mȧ·nū'brĭ·ŭm), *n.; pl.* -BRIA (-ȧ), -BRIUMS (-ŭmz). [L., handle, fr. *manus* hand.] *Anat.* A handlelike process or part; especially, in man and most mammals, the cephalic segment of the sternum.

man'u·fac'to·ry (măn'ū·făk'tō·rĭ), *n.; pl.* -RIES (-rĭz). A factory.

man'u·fac'ture (-tūr), *n.* [F., fr. ML. *manufactura*, fr. L. *manu*, abl. of *manus* hand + *factura* a making, fr. *facere* to make.] **1.** *Obs.* A making by hand. **2.** The process of making wares by hand, by machinery, or by other agency, often with division of labor and the use of machinery. **3.** Anything manufactured. **4.** By extension, the making of anything by any agency or process. — *v. t.* **1.** To make (wares) by hand, by machinery, or by other agency; to produce by labor, esp., now, with division of labor, and usually with machinery. **2.** To work into suitable forms for use; as, to *manufacture* wool, iron, etc. **3.** To fabricate; invent; as, to *manufacture* an excuse; also, to produce mechanically. — **Syn.** See MAKE. — **man'u·fac'tur·ing** (-tūr·ĭng), *n.* Abbr. *Mfg.*

man'u·fac'tur·er (-tūr·ẽr), *n.* One who manufactures; an employer of operatives in manufacturing. Abbr. *Mfr.*

man'u·mis'sion (-mĭsh'ŭn), *n.* Act of manumitting, or state of being manumitted; formal liberation of a slave.

man'u·mit' (-mĭt'), *v. t.;* -MIT'TED; -MIT'TING. [OF. *manumiter*, fr. L. *manumittere, manumissum*, fr. *manu*, abl. of *manus* the hand + *emittere* to send forth.] To release from slavery; to free, as a slave. — **Syn.** See FREE.

ma·nure' (mȧ·nūr'; 114), *v. t.* [OF. *manouvrer* to cultivate by manual labor. See MANEUVER.] To apply manure to; to enrich, as land, by application of a fertilizer. — *n.* A fertilizer; esp. refuse of stables and barnyards, consisting of animal excreta, with or without litter, the dung of birds, etc. — **ma·nur'er** (-nūr'ẽr), *n.*

ma'nus (mā'nŭs), *n.; pl.* MANUS. [L., the hand.] **1.** *Anat. & Zool.* The distal segment of the forelimb of a vertebrate, including the carpus and forefoot or hand. **2.** *Rom. Law.* The power or rights of a husband over his wife.

man'u·script (măn'ū·skrĭpt), *adj.* [L. *manu scriptus.* See MANUAL; SCRIBE.] Written with or by the hand. — *n.* **1.** A written composition, as an ancient book. **2.** An author's copy of his work in handwriting or typewriting; a written or typewritten document of any kind as distinguished from a printed copy. Abbr. *MS., Ms.*, or *ms.*, pl. *MSS., Mss.*, or *mss.*

man'ward (măn'wẽrd), **man'wards** (-wẽrdz), *adv.* Toward, or in relation to, man.

man'ward, *adj.* Directed toward man.

man'wise' (-wīz'), *adv.* After the manner of men.

Manx (măngks), *adj.* [For *Mansk, Manisk* fr. an (assumed) Scand. adj., fr. the Celtic name of the island.] Of or pertaining to the Isle of Man or its inhabitants. — *n.* **1.** The native language of the Manxmen, a Goidelic dialect of Celtic. See INDO-EUROPEAN LANGUAGES, *Table.* **2.** Manxmen.

Manx cat. One of a breed of domestic cats having a rudimentary tail, containing only about three vertebrae.

Manx'man (măngks'măn), *n.; pl.* -MEN (-mĕn). A native of the Isle of Man.

man'y (mĕn'ĭ), *adj.* The comparative and superlative are supplied by *more, most*, from a different root. [AS. *manig, maenig, monig.*] Consisting of a great number; numerous; not few.

☞ With a singular noun *many* is now used attributively only in

many a, and predicatively only in an inverted construction; as, *many* is the time I've warned him.
— *n.* A large number; as, a good *many* came; — considered elliptical for "a *many* of."
— *pron.* Many persons; as, *many* knew him.
man'y·plies' (mĕn'ĭ·plīz'), *n.* [*many*, adj. + *plies*, pl. of *ply* a fold.] The third stomach of a ruminant; the psalterium. See RUMINANT, *Illust.*
man'y-sid'ed (-sīd'ĕd; -ĭd; 2; 30), *adj.* Having many sides or aspects; hence, versatile. — **Syn.** See VERSATILE.
man'za·ni'ta (măn'zȧ·nē'tȧ; män'sä·nē'tä), *n.* [Sp., dim. of *manzana* apple.] Any of various Californian shrubs (genus *Arctostaphylos*) of the heath family.
Ma'o·ri (mä'ō·rĭ; mou'rĭ; mä'rĭ), *n.*; *pl.* MAORIS (-rĭz). **1.** One of the aborigines of New Zealand, a Polynesian people, tall, vigorous, and brave. **2.** The language of the Maoris. See LANGUAGE, *Table.* — **Ma'o·ri**, *adj.*
map (măp), *n.* [F. *mappe*, in *mappemonde* map of the world, fr. ML. *mappa mundi*, fr. L. *mappa* napkin.] **1.** A representation (usually flat) of the surface of the earth, or of part of it; also, such a representation of the celestial sphere, or of part of it. Cf. CHART. **2.** Anything suggestive of a map. — *v. t.*; MAPPED (măpt); MAP'PING. **1.** To delineate as on a map; also, to explore, survey, etc., in getting data for a map. **2.** To chart the course of; to plan in detail.
ma'ple (mā'p'l), *n.* [AS. *mapolder, mapulder, mapultrēow*, maple tree.] Any of a genus (*Acer*) of trees or shrubs with opposite leaves and a fruit of two united samaras (see SAMARA, *Illust.*), typifying a family (Aceraceae, the maple family); also, the hard, light-colored, close-grained wood of these trees, used for hardwood floors, house furnishings, etc. American species include the ***broad-leaved maple*** (*Acer macrophyllum*) of the Pacific coast; the ***striped maple*** *or* ***moosewood*** (*A. pennsylvanicum*) of eastern North America; the ***sugar maple*** *or* ***rock maple*** (*A. saccharum*) of eastern North America, yielding a sap which is the main source of *maple sugar*, and having gray bark, 3–5-lobed leaves (adopted as the floral emblem of Canada), and umbellike clusters of drooping yellow flowers; the ***silver maple*** (*A. saccharinum*) with deeply cut leaves, light green above and silvery white beneath; the ***red maple*** (*A. rubrum*) with crimson flowers produced before the leaves in early spring; the ***Norway maple*** (*A. platanoides*) introduced into United States and planted as a shade tree, with dark-green leaves; and the ***Schwedler's maple*** (*A. platanoides schwedleri*), a variety of the Norway maple, with bronze-red foliage in the spring turning later to green. Any species of maple having compound leaves is called *box elder* (which see). Cf. BIRD'S-EYE, *adj.*, 2; CURLY, 2.
maple sirup. Sirup made by concentrating the sap of certain maples, esp. the sugar maple. By further evaporation **maple sugar** is obtained, which consists largely of sucrose with some invert sugar, organic matter, and ash.
‖**ma'quis'** (mä'kē'), *n. sing. & pl.* [F., tough scrub.] A Corsican outlaw; hence, during World War II, a French guerrilla fighting the Germans.
mar (mär), *v. t.*; MARRED (märd); MAR'RING. [AS. *merran, myrran* (in comp.), to obstruct, impede, dissipate.] **1.** To damage greatly; impair. **2.** To do physical injury to; disfigure. — **Syn.** See INJURE.
mar'a·bou (măr'ȧ·bōō), **mar'a·bout** (-bōōt), *n.* [F.] **1. a** A large stork (genus *Leptoptilus*; esp., the African species *L. crumeniferus*). Also, the adjutant (*L. dubius*). **b** Collectively, the long soft tail or wing coverts of a marabou or adjutant, used in millinery. **2.** A kind of thrown raw silk; also, a thin fabric made from it.
ma·ra'ca (mä·rä'kä), *n.* [Pg. *maracá*.] A dried gourd or a gourdlike rattle containing pebbles, used as a percussion instrument.
mar'a·schi'no (măr'ȧ·skē'nō), *n.* [It., fr. *marasca, amarasca*, a sour cherry, fr. L. *amarus* bitter.] A liqueur distilled from the fermented juice of the **ma·ras'ca** (mȧ·răs'kȧ), a small bitter wild cherry (*Prunus cerasus marasca*).
maraschino cherries. Cherries preserved in maraschino.
ma·ras'mus (mȧ·răz'mŭs), *n.* [NL., fr. Gr. *marasmos*, fr. *marainein* to waste away.] *Med.* Progressive emaciation, esp. in infants. — **ma·ras'mic** (-mĭk), *adj.*
Ma·ra'tha (mȧ·rä'tȧ), **Mah·rat'ta** (-răt'ȧ), *n.* [Hind. *Marhaṭā*, fr. Skr. *Mahārāṣṭra*.] A member of a race of India of the western Deccan and Bombay province.
Ma·ra'thi (mȧ·rä'tē; -răt'ē), **Mah·rat'ti** (-răt'ē), *n.* A Sanskritic language spoken esp. by the Marathas. It has an extensive literature dating from the 13th century. See INDO-EUROPEAN LANGUAGES, *Table.*
mar'a·thon (măr'ȧ·thŏn; -thŭn), *n.* A long-distance running race (**marathon race**), now usually 26 miles, 385 yards in length, commemorating the reputed feat of the Greek who ran from Marathon to Athens bearing news of victory (490 B.C.); hence, any similar long-distance contest or an endurance contest.
ma·raud' (mȧ·rôd'), *v. i.* [F. *marauder*, fr. *maraud* vagabond.] To rove in quest of plunder; to raid. — *v. t.* To make a raid upon or into for plunder. — *n.* Act of marauding; plundering. — **ma·raud'er** (-ẽr), *n.*
mar'a·ve'di (măr'ȧ·vā'dĭ), *n.* [Sp., fr. Ar. *Murābiṭīn*, a Moorish dynasty.] **a** The dinar of the Moors in Spain and Morocco. **b** *Obs.* A Spanish copper coin unit, worth about ⅓ cent.
mar'ble (mär'b'l), *n.* [OF. *marbre*, fr. L. *marmor*, fr. Gr. *marmaros*, orig., stone, boulder.] **1.** Any limestone, granular to compact in texture, capable of taking a polish or of being used for fine architectural work. Marble (proper) differs from common limestone in being more or less crystallized by metamorphism. **2.** A piece, slab, etc., of marble; a work of art, record, etc., of marble. **3.** By transfer, something suggesting marble in coldness, smoothness, hardness, etc. **4.** A little ball, orig. of marble, used as a plaything by children. **5.** A mottled color or pattern like that of variegated marble; marbling. **6.** *Games.* **mar'bles** (-b'lz) (*pl. in form but used with singular verb*). A children's game played with marbles (sense 4).
— *adj.* **1.** Resembling or imitating marble; also, made of marble. **2.** Cold, hard, smooth, white, etc., as marble.
— *v. t.*; -BLED (-b'ld); -BLING (-blĭng). [From MARBLE, *n.*] To stain or vein like marble; as, to *marble* book edges.
marble cake. A loaf cake that is mottled by the use of alternate spoonfuls of light and dark batter.
mar'ble·ize (mär'b'l·īz), *v. t.* *U. S.* To make, stain, vein, or grain, in imitation of marble.
mar'bling (-blĭng), *n.* **a** Art or practice of variegating like marble **b** Markings, coloration, coating, etc., suggestive of the markings of marble, as an intermixture of fat and lean in meat. **c** *Bookbinding.* Decoration of surfaces, as book edges, to resemble certain marbles.
marc (märk; *F.* màr), *n.* [F., fr. *marcher* to trample.] **1.** The refuse matter remaining after pressing seeds, fruits, etc., esp. grapes. **2.** An insoluble residue left after extracting a substance with some solvent.
mar'ca·site (mär'kȧ·sīt), *n.* [F. *marcassite.*] **1.** *Mineral.* **a** Formerly, crystallized iron pyrites. **b** Iron disulfide, FeS_2, resembling iron pyrites, but of lower specific gravity. **2.** A piece of crystallized iron pyrites used for ornament and formerly for striking a light with steel.
mar·cel' (mär·sĕl'), *v. t.*; -CELLED' (-sĕld'); -CEL'LING. [After *Marcel* (b. 1852), French hairdresser.] To dress (the hair) with a marcel wave. — *n.* A marcel wave.
marcel wave. Also **mar·cel'**, *n.* *Hairdressing.* A deep-grooved wave made by a special curling iron.
mar·ces'cent (mär·sĕs'ĕnt; -'nt), *adj.* [L. *marcescens*, pres. part. of *marcescere* to wither, decay, fr. *marcere* to wither, droop.] *Bot.* Withering without falling off.
March (märch), *n.* [OF. *march, marz*, fr. L. *Martius* (sc. *mensis* month) of *Mars* Mars.] The third month of the year containing 31 days. Abbr. *Mar.*
march, *n.* [OF. *marche*, of Teut. origin.] A territorial border or frontier; esp., *Eng. Hist.*, *pl.*, the frontier borderlands between England and Scotland, and England and Wales. — *v. i.* To border.
march, *v. i.* [F. *marcher*, in OF. also, to tread, trample.] **1.** To advance in step or in military order, or in regular formation, or in an organized body. **2.** To walk in a grave or stately manner; hence, to proceed; progress; as, time *marches* on. — *v. t.* To cause to march, or move in military array. — *n.* **1.** Act of marching; military progress; advance of troops. **2.** Measured and regular advance or movement, like that of soldiers; hence, progress; course. **3.** A regular and uniform step, esp. by soldiers. **4.** *Mil.* The amount of marching done in one continuous advance; as, an hour's *march*. **5.** *Music.* A piece of strongly rhythmical music designed or fitted to accompany marching. A march in quick tempo is often called a *quickstep* (which see), or ***military march***; one in slow tempo, a ***processional march***.
‖**Mär'chen** (mâr'kĕn), *n. sing. & pl.* [G.] A story; fiction; esp., a fairy tale or folk tale.
march'er (mär'chẽr), *n.* [See MARCH border.] One who inhabits a march, or border region.
march'er, *n.* One who marches.
‖**mar·che'sa** (mär·kā'zä), *n.*; *pl.* -CHESE (-zā). [It.] In Italy, a woman of the rank of a marchese; a marchioness.
‖**mar·che'se** (-zā), *n.*; *pl.* -CHESI (-zē). [It. See MARQUIS.] In Italy, a noble in rank next above a count (*conte*), and next below a prince (*principe*).
mar'chion·ess (mär'shŭn·ĕs; -ĭs; 30), *n.* [ML. *marchionissa, marcionissa*, fr. *marchio*, fr. *marca* march.] Wife or widow of a marquis; a woman of the rank and dignity of a marquis.
march'pane' (märch'pān'), *n.* [It. *marzapane.*] A sweetmeat of a paste of pounded almonds, sugar, etc.
Mar·co'ni (mär·kō'nĭ), *adj.* [After Guglielmo *Marconi*, It. inventor.] Designating, or pertaining to, Marconi's system of wireless telegraphy.
mar·co'ni·gram (-grăm), *n.* A Marconi radio message.
mar·co'ni·graph (-grăf; 9), *n.* The apparatus used in Marconi wireless telegraphy. — **mar·co'ni·graph**, *v. t. & i.*
Marconi rig. A type of yachting rig introduced about 1920, characterized by a tall pole mast and relatively short boom, the triangular sail hoisting on a slide or jackstay on the mast with the foot laced to the boom.
Mar'di gras' (mär'dē grä'; 2). [F., lit., fat Tuesday.] Shrove Tuesday; — in some cities a day of carnival.
Mar'duk (mär'dŏŏk), *n.* [Bab.] *Babylon Relig.* The chief deity of the Babylonian pantheon, orig. a local sun deity.
mare (mâr), *n.* [AS. *mara* incubus.] *Obs.* A spirit or goblin popularly believed to produce nightmare.
mare, *n.* [AS. *mere, myre*, fem. to AS. *mearh* horse.] The female of the horse and other members of the horse kind, as the ass and the zebra.
ma're clau'sum (mā'rē klô'sŭm). [L.] Closed sea; a sea within the separate jurisdiction of one state.
‖**ma're li'be·rum** (lĭb'ẽ·rŭm). [L.] Open sea, as contrasted with *mare clausum*.
ma·rem'ma (mȧ·rĕm'ȧ), *n.*; *pl.* -ME (-ē). [It., in sense 1, fr. L. *maritimus.*] **1.** In Italy, low marshy maritime country. **2.** The miasma of such a region.
mare's'-nest' (mârz'nĕst'), *n.* Something believed to be wonderful, but turning out to be imaginary or a hoax.
mare's'-tail', *n.* **1.** A spreading cirrus cloud. **2. a** A common aquatic plant (*Hippuris vulgaris*) with elongated shoots clothed with dense whorls of subulate leaves. **b** = HORSETAIL, 2 **a**.
mar·gar'ic (mär·găr'ĭk; -gär'ĭk; mär'gȧ·rĭk), *adj.* [See MARGARITE.] *Chem.* Designating a white crystalline acid (margaric acid), $C_{16}H_{33}$-CO_2H, between palmitic and stearic acids.
mar'ga·rine (mär'jȧ·rēn; -rĭn; -gȧ-), *n.* [F.] A food product made from a blend of refined vegetable oils or of refined vegetable oils and meat fats, churned with ripened skim milk to a plastic consistency, used as a spread on bread and as a cooking fat. Other ingredients may be added, especially coloring matter, which is subject to legal restrictions, and salt. Margarine is generally fortified with a minimum of 15,000 U.S.P. units of vitamin A per pound.
mar'ga·rite (mär'gȧ·rīt), *n.* [OF., fr. L. *margarita*, fr. Gr. *margaritēs* a pearl, fr. *margaron* pearl, fr. *margaros* pearl oyster.] *Archaic.* A pearl.
mar'gay (mär'gā), *n.* [F. (& Sp.), fr. Pg. *maracajá*, fr. Tupi *maracaja.*] An American spotted cat (*Felis tigrina*) resembling the ocelot, ranging from Central America to Brazil.
marge (märj), *n.* [F.] *Poetic.* A margin.
mar'gent (mär'jĕnt), *n.* *Archaic.* A margin.
mar'gin (mär'jĭn), *n.* [L. *margo, -ginis.*] **1.** A border; edge. **2.** A condition approximately marking a limit; limit. **3.** An amount, as of time or money, which is allowed to meet conditions that cannot be foreseen. **4.** *Com.* The difference between the net sales and the cost of merchandise sold, taken as that from which expenses must be met, profit derived, etc. **5.** *Econ.* The minimum return or reward, barely covering the costs of production, and constituting a limit below which economic activity under existing conditions cannot be continued. **6.**

Print. That part of a page outside of the main body of printed or written matter. **7.** *Stock & Produce Exchanges.* **a** Cash or collateral deposited with a broker to secure him from loss on a contract. **b** A customer's equity if his account is terminated at prevailing market prices. **c** A speculative transaction in which the broker does part of the financing. **8.** *Psychol.* That part of the momentary field of consciousness which is felt only vaguely and dimly. — **Syn.** See BORDER.
— *v. t.* **1.** To enter or summarize in the margin of a page. **2.** To furnish with a margin; to form a margin to; to border. **3.** *Com. & Stock Exchange.* To deposit a margin upon; to keep secured by depositing or adding to a margin.

mar'gin·al (mär'jĭ·năl; -n'l), *adj.* [NL. *marginalis.*] **1.** Written or printed in the margin; as, a *marginal* note. **2.** Of, pertaining to, or situated at a margin or border. **3.** Occupying the borderland of any relatively stable territorial or cultural area or the margin of consciousness; as, *marginal* tribes or sensations. **4.** Close to the lower limit of qualification, acceptability, or worthwhile operation; as, *marginal* capacity. **5.** *Econ.* Producing or able to produce a supply of goods which, when sold at existing price levels, will barely cover cost of production; as, *marginal* land; of, pertaining to, or derived from goods produced and marketed with such result; as, *marginal* profits. **6.** *Sociol.* Incompletely assimilated and denied full social acceptance and participation by the dominant group or groups in a society because of racial or cultural conflict; as, a second-generation immigrant often becomes a *marginal* man because of color, racial, and other barriers. — **mar'gin·al'i·ty** (-năl'ĭ·tĭ), *n.* — **mar'gin·al·ly,** *adv.*

mar'gi·na'li·a (mär'jĭ·nā'lĭ·ȧ), *n. pl.* [NL.] Marginal notes.

marginal utility. The minimum degree of utility necessary for continued production or use of goods or services.

mar'gin·ate (mär'jĭ·nāt), *adj.* [L. *marginatus,* past part.] Having a margin distinct in appearance or structure. — *v. t.* To margin. — **mar'gin·a'tion** (-nā'shŭn), *n.*

mar'gin·at'ed (-nāt'ĕd; -ĭd), *adj.* Marginate.

mar'grave (mär'grāv), *n.* [MD. *marcgrave* (D. *markgraaf*).] **a** Orig., a military keeper of the marches, or borders, in Germany. **b** English equiv. of the German hereditary title of nobility *Markgraf.* — **mar·gra'vi·ate** (mär·grā'vĭ·āt), **mar'gra·vate** (mär'grȧ·vāt), *n.*

mar'gra·vine (-grȧ·vēn), *n.* The wife of a margrave.

mar'gue·rite' (mär'gĕ·rēt'), *n.* [F., pearl, daisy. See MARGARITE.] **a** The daisy (senses 1 & 2). **b** Any of various single-flowered chrysanthemums, esp. *Chrysanthemum frutescens* of the Canary Islands.

‖**ma'ri·age' de con've·nance'** (mȧ'ryȧzh' dĕ kôɴv'näɴs'). [F.] An advantageous and suitable marriage.

Mar'i·an (mâr'ĭ·ăn; măr'ĭ·ăn), *adj.* Of or pert. to Mary: as (1) the Virgin Mary; (2) Mary, Queen (1553–58) of England; (3) Mary, Queen of Scots (1542–87). — *n.* **1.** One who worships, or is devoted to, the Virgin Mary. **2.** A follower or defender of Mary, Queen of Scots.

Ma·ri'a The·re'sa dol'lar *or* **tha'ler** (mȧ·rē'ȧ tĕ·rē'sȧ; mȧ·rī'ȧ; tĕ·rē'zȧ). See DOLLAR, **1 b.**

mar'i·gold (măr'ĭ·gōld), *n.* [*Mary* + *gold.*] Any of several plants (as of the genus *Tagetes* [of the aster family], esp. *T. erecta,* the ***African marigold,*** and *T. patula,* the ***French marigold***), with yellow, red, or variegated heads of flowers. Cf. MARSH MARIGOLD, FIG MARIGOLD, POT MARIGOLD, BUR MARIGOLD.

mar'i·jua'na (măr'ĭ·wä'nȧ), *n.* Also **mar'i·hua'na.** [Am. Sp. *mariguana, marihuana.*] The hemp (*Cannabis sativa*); also, its dried leaves and flowers, which are smoked in cigarettes as a narcotic.

ma·rim'ba (mȧ·rĭm'bȧ), *n.* [Pl. (also *malimba*) of *limba,* name of various musical instruments in Bantu.] A kind of primitive xylophone, used in South Africa and Central America; also, a modern improved form of this instrument. Cf. XYLOPHONE, *Illust.*

mar'i·nade' (măr'ĭ·nād'), *n.* [F.] *Cookery.* A pickle in which meat or fish are soaked to enrich their flavor; also, the meat or fish pickled in it. — (măr'ĭ·nād), *v. t.* To marinate.

mar'i·nate (măr'ĭ·nāt), *v. t.* [See MARINE.] **1.** To let lie, as meat or fish, in a brine or pickle. **2.** To season, as lobster or chicken prepared for salad, with French dressing some hours before adding mayonnaise.

ma·rine' (mȧ·rēn'), *adj.* [F. *marin,* fr. L. *marinus,* fr. *mare* the sea.] **1.** Of or pert. to the sea or the ocean. **2.** Of or pert. to the navigation of the sea; nautical; as, a *marine* chart. **3.** Of or pert. to the commerce of the sea; maritime; as, *marine* insurance. **4.** Serving on shipboard; also, belonging or pertaining to the marines.
— *n.* **1.** One who serves on shipboard; esp., one of a class of soldiers serving on shipboard; specif., *U.S.,* a member of the ***Marine Corps,*** a corps of officers and men equipped and drilled much as land soldiers are, but associated with the naval service and often used as a landing force. **2.** The collective mercantile and naval shipping of a country; seagoing vessels collectively. **3.** In some European countries, the executive department having to do with naval matters. **4.** A picture of some marine subject.

mar'i·ner (măr'ĭ·nĕr), *n.* [OF. *marinier,* fr. ML. *marinarius.* See MARINE, *adj.*] One whose occupation is to navigate or assist in navigating ships; a seaman or sailor.

mar'i·ner's com'pass (măr'ĭ·nĕrz). A compass used for navigation, having magnetic needles attached to a card that is marked to indicate directions. See COMPASS CARD, *Illust.*

Mar'i·ol'a·try (mâr'ĭ·ŏl'ȧ·trĭ), *n.* [Gr. *Maria* Mary + *-latry.*] Worship of the Virgin Mary; — a term of opprobrium.

mar'i·o·nette' (măr'ĭ·ō·nĕt'), *n.* [F. *marionnette,* prop. a dim. of *Marion,* fr. *Marie* Mary.] A puppet.

Mar'i·po'sa lil'y *or* **tu'lip** (-ĭ·pō'sȧ; -zȧ). [Sp. *mariposa* a butterfly; — alluding to the gay appearance of the blossoms.] Any of a genus (*Calochortus*) of plants of the lily family, of western North America; as, the ***white mariposa*** (*C. venustus*) of California, with red-blotched white flowers.

mar'ish (măr'ĭsh), *n.* [OF. *marais.*] *Poetic.* A marsh.

mar'i·tal (măr'ĭ·tăl; mȧ·rī'tăl; -t'l), *adj.* [L. *maritalis,* fr. *maritus* of marriage, n., a husband.] Of or pertaining to a husband or marriage. — **Syn.** See MATRIMONIAL. — **mar'i·tal·ly,** *adv.*

mar'i·time (măr'ĭ·tīm; -tĭm; -tēm), *adj.* [F., fr. L. *maritimus,* fr. *mare* the sea.] **1.** Bordering on, or situated near, the ocean; as, the *Maritime* Provinces of Canada. **2.** Connected with the sea in respect to navigation, commerce, etc. **3.** Characteristic of a mariner; nautical.

mar'jo·ram (mär'jō·răm), *n.* [OF. *majoraine, -rane,* fr. ML. *majorana, majoraca.*] Any of two genera (*Origanum* and *Majorana*) of mints, esp. the common ***sweet marjoram*** (*M. hortensis*) used in cookery for flavoring.

mark (märk), *n.* [AS. *marc.*] **1.** An old weight for gold and silver, equal to about 8 oz. **2.** A money of account and coin, orig. of the value of a mark of silver. Specif.: **a** *Obs.* A Scottish silver coin, orig. worth 13s. 4d. **b** A silver coin and the gold monetary unit of the former German Empire, worth 23.8 cents. The mark, as the monetary unit, was superseded in 1924 by the *reichsmark* (which see). **3.** = MARKKA.

mark, *n.* [AS. *mearc, merc.*] **1.** *Archaic & Hist.* Boundary; march. **2.** A thing aimed at; a target; goal. **3.** An indication of character; characteristic; trait. **4.** Importance; distinction; as, a fellow of no *mark.* **5.** A brand, size, quality, or the like. **6.** Limit or standard of action or fact; as, to come up to the *mark.* **7.** *Obs.* A landmark. **8. a** A label, brand, seal, or the like, put on an article to show the maker or owner, to certify quality, etc.; trade-mark. **b** A visible sign assumed by, or put upon, a person, as a badge or sign of honor, stigma, etc. **c** A character (usually a cross) made as a substitute for a signature by one who cannot write. **d** A written or printed symbol; as, an interrogation *mark.* **e** A number or other character used in registering; hence, the unit of award in any system of registering the work or conduct of pupils, prisoners, examined candidates, etc.; also, the award made. **9.** A stamp, figure, stain, scar, etc. **10.** A conspicuous object of known position serving as a guide for travelers; as, a *mark* for pilots. **11.** Something, as a line, notch, or fixed object, designed to record position; as, a low-water *mark.* **12.** *Naut.* **a** One of the bits of leather or colored bunting placed on a sounding, or lead, line at intervals. Cf. DEEP, *n.,* 4; see SOUNDING LINE, *Illust.* **b** = PLIMSOLL MARK. **13.** *Sports.* **a** *Bowls.* The jack. **b** *Boxing.* The pit of the stomach. **c** *Track Athletics.* The position at the starting line assigned to a contestant. **14.** *Veter.* A hollow on a horse's incisor tooth indicative of the animal's age. — **Syn.** See SIGN.
— *v. t.* **1.** To put a mark on; specif.: **a** To fix or trace out the bounds or limits of. **b** To affix a significant identifying mark to, as a trade-mark, hallmark, etc. **2.** To designate as by a mark; as, his courage *marked* him for a leader. **3.** To indicate by marks or symbols; as, to *mark* an accent; also, to register, as a barometer. **4.** To form, as a figure, by making marks. **5.** To furnish with natural marks (of a specified kind). **6.** To notice or observe; to give attention to. **7.** To distinguish; as, stunted trees *mark* the higher peaks. **8.** To set apart by or as by a mark. **9.** To determine the value or correctness of; to grade. **10.** *Com.* To put price signs on (articles). **11.** *Games.* To keep account of (the points); to score. **12.** *London Stock Exchange.* To record a transaction so that it will appear on the official price list. — *v. i.* **1.** To make a mark, as with a pencil. **2.** To notice or observe critically. **3.** *Games.* To record points made.

Mark (märk), *n.* [L. *Marcus,* fr. *Mars, Martis.*] **1. a** The evangelist ***John Mark,*** traditionally regarded as author of the Gospel of Mark. **b** The Gospel of Mark in the New Testament. See BIBLE. **2.** See TRISTRAM.

Mark (märk), *n.* [G. *marke* label, brand.] *Mil.* A designation, used with a numeral, for a particular model of a weapon, machine, or article of equipment; as, a *Mark* IV tank; a *Mark* 18 sight. Abbr. *Mk.*

marked (märkt), *adj.* Having a mark; hence, emphasized; noticeable. — **mark'ed·ly** (mär'kĕd·lĭ; -kĭd·lĭ; 30), *adv.*

mark'er (mär'kĕr), *n.* **1.** One who marks, as a scorer at games, a monitor, etc. **2.** That which marks, as a bookmark, a device for marking lines on tennis courts, etc.

mar'ket (mär'kĕt; -kĭt), *n.* [ONF. *market,* fr. L. *mercatus* trade, market place, fr. *mercari,* past part. *mercatus,* to trade, traffic, fr. *merx, mercis,* merchandise.] **1.** A meeting of people for traffic by private purchase and sale, and, usually, not by auction; also, the people at such a meeting. **2.** A public place (as in a town), or a large building, where a market is held. **3.** The region in which any commodity can be sold. **4.** The course of commercial activity by which the exchange of commodities is effected; as, the *market* is active. **5.** A body or group of men associated in, or organized for, the buying and selling of goods; as, the stock *market;* the beef *market.* — ***at the market.*** *Stock Exc.* At the price obtainable when a broker executes a customer's order. — *v. i.* To deal in a market; to buy or sell. — *v. t.* To expose for sale in a market; by extension, to sell. — **mar'ket·er** (-ĕr), *n.*

mar'ket·a·ble (-ȧ·b'l), *adj.* **1.** Fit or qualified to be offered for sale. **2.** Pert. to buying or selling. — **mar'ket·a·bil'i·ty** (-bĭl'ĭ·tĭ), *n.*

market garden. A garden in which vegetables are raised for market. — **market gardener.** — **market gardening.**

mar'ket·ing, *n.* The aggregate of functions involved in transferring title and in moving goods from producer to consumer, including among others buying, selling, storing, transporting, standardizing, financing, risk bearing, and supplying market information.

market order. *Exchanges.* An order to buy or sell at the price prevailing in the market when the order is executed.

market place. An open place or square in a town where markets or public sales are held.

market price. *Econ.* The price given in current market dealings.

market value. *Econ.* The average value of a commodity in a given market during a short period.

mark'ing, *n.* Act of one who marks; also, the mark or marks made; arrangement or disposition of marks.

mark'ka (märk'kä), *n.; pl.* MARKKAA (-kä). [Finn., fr. Sw. *mark.*] A nickel coin and the monetary unit of Finland, containing 100 pennia. See MONEY, *Tables.*

marks'man (märks'măn), *n.* One who shoots at a mark; one skillful in hitting a mark. — **marks'man·ship,** *n.*

mark'up' (märk'ŭp'), *n.* **1.** Raising of price; an article raised in price. **2.** *Commerce.* The amount added to the cost price in figuring a selling price to cover overhead and profit.

marl (märl), *n.* [OF. *marle,* fr. LL. *margila,* dim. of L. *marga* marl.] **1.** An earthy, crumbling deposit consisting chiefly of clay mixed with calcium carbonate, used esp. as a fertilizer for soils deficient in lime. **2.** *Poetic.* Earth. — *v. t.* To overspread or fertilize with or as with marl. — **marl'y** (mär'lĭ), *adj.*

marl, *v. t.* [D. *marlen.*] To cover or fasten with marline.

marled (märld), *adj. Scot.* Marbled; variegated.

mar'lin (mär'lĭn), *n.* [From *marlinespike.*] **a** Any of several large oceanic game fishes (genus *Makaira*), related to sailfishes and spearfishes. One species (*M. ampla*) occurs in the Atlantic, and the ***black marlin*** (*M. marlina*), ***barred marlin*** (*M. mitsukurii*), and ***striped marlin*** (*M. holei*) are well-known Pacific species. **b** A spearfish.

mar'line (-lĭn), *n.* Also **mar'ling** (-lĭng). [From D. *marling* (fr. *marlen*) and D. *marlijn,* fr. *maren* to fasten + *lijn* line.] *Naut.* A small line of two strands twisted loosely left-handed, used for seizing.

mar′line·spike′ (mär′lĭn·spīk′), *n.* Also **mar′lin-** (-lĭn-), **mar′ling-** (-lĭng-). *Naut.* A pointed iron tool used in splicing and in marling.

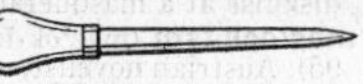

Marlinespike.

marl′ite (märl′īt), *n.* A variety of marl that is resistant to the action of air. — **mar·lit′ic** (mär·lĭt′ĭk), *adj.*

mar′ma·lade (mär′mȧ·lād; 2) *n.* [F. *marmelade*, fr. Sp., fr. Pg. *marmelada*, fr. *marmelo* quince, fr. L. *melimelum* honey apple, fr. Gr. *melimēlon*, fr. *meli* honey + *mēlon* apple.] A thick pulpy jam; as, orange *marmalade*.

marmalade tree. **a** A tropical American tree (*Calocarpum mammosum*) of the sapodilla family, with egg-shaped, single-seeded fruit, the **marmalade plum** *or* **fruit**, often called *mammee sapota*, which is used for preserves. **b** = MAMMEE **a**.

mar·mo′re·al (mär·mō′rē·ăl; 70), *adj.* Also **mar·mo′re·an** (-ăn). [L. *marmoreus*, fr. *marmor* marble.] Pertaining to, or like, marble, as in being cold, white, smooth, etc.

mar′mo·set (mär′mō·zĕt), *n.* [OF. *marmouset* grotesque carved image, later, ape.] Any of numerous South and Central American monkeys (family Callitrichidae), including the true marmosets (genus *Callithrix*) and the tamarins (genus *Midas*), the smallest of monkeys.

mar′mot (mär′mŭt), *n.* [F. *marmotte.*] Any of certain stout-bodied, short-legged rodents (genus *Marmota*) with coarse fur, a short bushy tail, and small ears. The American species are called *woodchucks* or *ground hogs.*

ma·roon′ (mȧ·ro͞on′), *n.* [F. *marron*, fr. Sp. *cimarrón* wild.] **1.** In the West Indies and Guiana, a fugitive slave, or one of a class of Negroes descended from fugitive slaves. **2.** A person who is marooned.

ma·roon′, *v. t.* [From 1st MAROON.] **1.** To put (a person) ashore on a desolate island or coast and leave him to his fate. **2.** To place or leave in helpless isolation.

ma·roon′, *n.* [F. *marron* chestnut-colored, fr. *marron* a large French chestnut, fr. It. *marrone.*] A color, yellowish-red in hue, of medium saturation and low brilliance. See COLOR. — **ma·roon′**, *adj.*

mar′plot′ (mär′plŏt′), *n.* One who, by his officious interference, mars or frustrates a design, plan, or plot.

marque (märk), *n.* [F., fr. Pr. *marca* seizure, reprisal, fr. *marcar* to seize as a pledge.] A seizing as a pledge or by way of retaliation. *Obs.*, exc. sometimes short for LETTER OF MARQUE.

mar·quee′ (mär·kē′), *n.* [F. *marquise*, misunderstood as a plural.] **1.** A large field tent common at outdoor entertainments. **2.** A canopy projecting over an entrance, as of a hotel or theater.

mar′quess (mär′kwĕs; -kwĭs; 30), **mar′quess·ate.** Vars. of MARQUIS, etc.

mar′que·try (mär′kĕ·trĭ), *n.; pl.* MARQUETRIES (-trĭz). Also **mar′que·te·rie** (mär′kĕ·trĭ). [F. *marqueterie*, fr. *marqueter* to inlay, fr. *marque* mark, sign.] Inlaid work, as in furniture; work inlaid with wood, shells, ivory, etc.

mar′quis (mär′kwĭs; *F.* màr′kē′), *n.* [OF. *marquis, markis*, fr. ML. *markensis*, fr. *marca* frontier, march, of Teut. origin.] In Europe, a nobleman of hereditary rank next above that of earl or count and below duke. — **mar′quis·ate** (mär′kwĭs·āt), *n.*

mar·quise′ (mär·kēz′; *F.* màr′kēz′), *n.* [F.] **1.** The wife of a marquis; a marchioness. **2.** = MARQUEE. **3.** *Jewelry.* A gem or a ring setting or bezel generally elliptical in shape but with pointed ends. See BRILLIANT, *Illust.*

mar′qui·sette′ (mär′kĭ·zĕt′; -kwĭ·zĕt′), *n.* [Dim. of F. *marquise* awning, marquise.] A sheer, somewhat lustrous cotton fabric; also, a sheer light silk fabric for dresses.

mar′riage (măr′ĭj), *n.* [OF. *mariage*, fr. *marier* to marry, fr. L. *maritare.*] **1.** State of being married; also, the mutual relation of husband and wife; wedlock; abstractly, the social institution whereby men and women are joined in a special kind of social and legal dependence for the purpose of founding and maintaining a family. **2.** Act of marrying, or rite used in marrying; often, the wedding ceremony and attendant festivities or formalities. **3.** Any intimate or close union.

mar′riage·a·ble (-ȧ·b'l), *adj.* Fit for or capable of marriage. — **mar′riage·a·bil′i·ty** (-bĭl′ĭ·tĭ), **mar′riage·a·ble·ness**, *n.*

mar′ried (măr′ĭd), *adj.* **a** United in marriage; wedded. **b** Of or pertaining to marriage; connubial.

mar′ri·er (măr′ĭ·ẽr), *n.* One who marries.

mar′ron (măr′ŏn; *F.* mȧ′rôɴ′), *n.* [F.] **a** The large sweet European chestnut. **b** *pl.* (*pron.* măr′ŏnz; *F.* mȧ′rôɴ′). Chestnuts preserved in sirup flavored with vanilla.

‖**mar′rons′ gla′cés′** (mȧ′rôɴ′ glȧ′sā′). [F.] Marrons preserved in sirup; sometimes, marrons glazed with sugar.

mar′row (măr′ō), *n.* [AS. *mearg, mearh.*] **1.** *Anat.* A highly vascular, soft tissue which fills the cavities of most bones; the medulla. The so-called ***spinal marrow*** is the spinal cord. **2.** The choicest part; as: **a** The choicest of food. **b** The source of animal vigor. **c** The inmost or essential part; as, he was chilled to the *marrow.* **3. a** *U. S.* **marrow squash**, any of several fine-grained, ovoid varieties of squash. **b** *Eng.* Vegetable marrow.

mar′row (măr′ō; *Scot.* mȧr′ō, -ŭ), *n.* [ME. *maru, maro.*] *Scot.* Match; mate.

mar′row·bone′ (măr′ō·bōn′), *n.* **1.** A bone containing marrow. **2.** *pl. Jocular.* Knee bones or knees.

mar′row·fat′ (-făt′), *n., or* **marrowfat pea.** Also **marrow pea.** One of a group of late varieties of pea having large, rich seeds; also, a plant or seed of this type.

mar′ry (măr′ĭ), *v. t.;* MAR′RIED (-ĭd); MAR′RY·ING. [OF. *marier*, fr. L. *maritare*, fr. *maritus* husband, married.] **1.** To unite in wedlock. **2.** To join (a man) to a woman as his wife, or (a woman) to a man as her husband. **3.** To give (a man or woman) in marriage; — said esp. of a parent. **4.** To take as husband or wife; to wed. **5.** To unite in close relation. — *v. i.* **1.** To enter into the conjugal state; to wed. **2.** To enter into close union.

mar′ry (măr′ĭ; *dial.* mȧr′ĭ), *interj.* [From name of the Virgin *Mary.*] *Archaic & Dial.* Indeed! in truth!

Mars (märz), *n.* [L.] **1.** *Rom. Relig.* The god of war, identified with the Greek *Ares*, and hence associated in cult with Venus. **2.** *Alchemy.* Iron. **3.** *Astron.* One of the planets of the solar system, conspicuous for the redness of its light. Symbol, ♂. It is the fourth in order from the sun, or the next beyond the earth, having a diameter of about 4,200 miles, a period of 687 days, and a mean distance of 141,000,000 miles from the sun. See PLANET, *Table.*

Mar′seil·laise′ (mär′sĕ·lāz′; *F.* màr′sĕ′yâz′), *n.* [F.] The national song of republican France, composed in 1792, by Rouget de l'Isle, and first sung by the band of men who came from Marseille to aid in the revolution of August 10, 1792. Cf. ÇA IRA; CARMAGNOLE, 3.

mar·seilles′ (mär·sālz′), *n.* A stout cotton fabric, similar to piqué.

marsh (märsh), *n.* [AS. *mersc, merisc.*] A tract of soft wet land; a fen; swamp; morass. — **marsh**, *adj.*

mar′shal (mär′shăl), *n.* [OF. *mareschal*, fr. LL., fr. OHG. *marahscalc*, fr. *marah* horse + *scalc* servant.] **1.** A high official in the household of a medieval king, prince, or noble, usually having charge of the military affairs. **2.** A military commander. *Obs.*, exc.: **a** Short for FIELD MARSHAL. **b** A general officer of the highest rank in various foreign armies; as, *Marshal* Foch. **3.** One who regulates rank and order at a feast or other assembly, directs the order of procession, and the like. **4.** *U. S. Law.* **a** A ministerial officer, appointed for each judicial district, to execute the process of the courts and perform various duties similar to those of a sheriff. **b** In some cities, a law officer intrusted with certain duties, such as serving the process of justices' courts, etc. **c** In some cities, the head of the police or fire department. — *v. t.;* -SHALED (-shăld) or -SHALLED; -SHAL·ING or -SHAL·LING. **1.** To dispose in order, esp. military order. **2.** To usher, guide, or lead. — **Syn.** See ORDER. — **mar′shal·cy** (-sĭ), *n.*

Mar′shall Plan (mär′shăl). A program for the economic rehabilitation of Europe with freedom intact, through mutual co-operation among the countries and financial aid from the United States; — after George C. Marshall, who as U. S. Secretary of State advanced the idea (June 5, 1947).

Mar′shal·sea (mär′shăl·sē), *n.* [OF. *mareschaucie.*] **a** A court in London (abolished 1849) for the king's domestic servants. **b** A prison in Southwark, long used as a debtors' prison (abolished 1842).

marsh cress. See CRESS.

marsh elder. **a** The guelder-rose. **b** *U. S.* Any of a genus (*Iva*) of salt-marsh shrubs of the ragweed family, esp. one species (*I. oraria*).

marsh gas. *Chem.* = METHANE.

marsh hawk. See 2d HARRIER, 2.

marsh hen. *U. S.* Any of various birds (family Rallidae), as the rail and the American coot (*Fulica americana*).

marsh mallow. [AS. *merscmealwe.* See MARSH; MALLOW.] A European perennial herb (*Althaea officinalis*) of the mallow family, naturalized in the eastern United States. The root is used in medicine as a demulcent. See FLOWER, *Illust.*

marsh′mal′low (märsh′măl′ō), *n.* Orig., a sweetened paste, made from the root of the marsh mallow; now, a confection made from corn sirup, sugar, starch, and gelatin, beaten to a creamy consistency.

marsh marigold. A perennial swamp plant (*Caltha palustris*) of the crowfoot family, native to Europe and North America, with bright-yellow flowers; — often called *cowslip* in the United States.

marsh′y (mär′shĭ), *adj.;* MARSH′I·ER (-shĭ·ẽr); MARSH′I·EST. **a** Resembling a marsh; boggy. **b** Pertaining to, or produced in, marshes; as, a *marshy* weed. — **marsh′i·ness**, *n.*

mar·su′pi·al (mär·sū′pĭ·ăl), *adj.* [L. *marsupium* a pouch, bag, fr. Gr. *marsypion*, dim. of *marsypos.*] **a** Having a pouch for carrying the young; of or pertaining to marsupials. **b** Of, pertaining to, or resembling a marsupium. — *n.* An animal of an order (Marsupialia) comprising the lowest existing mammals except the monotremes. It contains the kangaroos, wombats, bandicoots, opossums, etc. With few exceptions, they develop no placenta, and the females have an abdominal pouch (*marsupium*) for carrying the young.

mar·su′pi·um (-ŭm), *n.; pl.* -PIA (-ȧ). [L., a pouch.] *Anat. & Zool.* An abdominal pouch formed by a fold of the skin and enclosing the mammary glands of most marsupials; also, an analogous structure in lower animals, as fishes, crustaceans, etc.

mart (märt), *n.* [D. *markt.*] **a** *Archaic.* A fair. **b** *Obs.* Traffic; also, a bargain. **c** A market; an emporium.

mart, *n.* [Gael. & Ir.] *Scot. & N. of Eng.* A beef for slaughter; also, any meat salted down for winter.

Mar·tel′lo tow′er, *or* **mar·tel′lo** (mär·tĕl′ō), *n.* *Fort.* A circular masonry fort.

mar′ten (mär′tĕn; -tĭn), *n.;* see PLURAL, *Note*, 3. [OF. *martrine*, fr. *martrin*, adj., of the marten, fr. *martre*, of Teut. origin.] **1.** Any of several slender-bodied carnivorous mammals (genus *Martes*) considerably larger than the weasels, and of somewhat arboreal habits. The name belongs esp. to the ***pine marten*** (*M. martes*) and the ***stone***, or ***beech, marten*** (*M. foina*) of Europe and Asia, and to the ***American sable*** (*M. americana*), called also ***pine marten.*** **2.** The fur or pelt of a marten; — called often *sable.*

mar′tens·ite (mär′tĕnz·īt), *n.* [After A. *Martens*, Ger. metallurgist.] *Metal.* A hard brittle substance consisting of iron with 2 per cent or less of carbon, and forming the chief constituent of quenched steel.

Mar′tha (mär′thȧ), *n.* *Bib.* Sister of Lazarus and Mary, and friend of Jesus. *Luke* x. 40.

mar′tial (mär′shăl), *adj.* [L. *martialis* of *Mars*, the god of war.] **1.** Of, pertaining to, or suited for war; as, *martial* music. **2.** Belonging or pertaining to an army or to military life; — opp. to *civil. Rare*, exc. in *court-martial*, etc. **3.** Experienced in or inclined to war; warlike; brave. **4.** [*cap.*] *Astrol.* Under the baleful influence of Mars. **5.** *Old Chem.* Of, pertaining to, or like iron; chalybeate. — **mar′tial·ly**, *adv.*

Syn. **Martial, warlike, military** mean of, or characteristic of, war. **Martial** suggests esp. the pomp and circumstance of war; **warlike**, the feeling or temper which leads to or accompanies war; **military**, whatever pertains to a soldier or to the art or conduct of war, esp. on land.

martial law. The law administered by the military power of a government when it has superseded the civil authority.

Mar′ti·an (mär′shĭ·ăn; -shăn), *adj.* [L. *Martius.*] Of or pertaining to Mars, god of war, or the planet Mars or its hypothetical inhabitants. — *n.* One of the hypothetical inhabitants of Mars.

mar′tin (mär′tĭn), *n.* [F.] A small European swallow (*Delichon urbica*); by extension, any of various swallows, as the bank swallow, or ***sand martin*** (*Riparia riparia*), the ***purple martin*** (*Progne subis*), etc.

mar′ti·net′ (mär′tĭ·nĕt′; mär′tĭ·nĕt), *n.* A strict military disciplinarian; — commonly depreciatory.

mar′tin·gale (mär′tĭn·gāl; mär′tĭng-; mär′t'n-), *n.* Also **mar′tin·gal** (-găl). [F., fr. Pr. *martengalo, martegalo.*] **1.** A strap fastened to a horse's girth, passing between his forelegs, and fastened to the bit, intended to hold down the head of the horse, and prevent him from rearing. **2.** *Naut.* A lower stay for the jib boom or flying jib boom to sustain the strain of the head stays, fastened to, or rove through, the dolphin striker; also, rarely, the dolphin striker. **3.** Any system of betting which, in a series of bets, seeks to determine the amount to be wagered after each win or loss.

Mar′tin·mas (mär′tĭn·măs), *n.* [St. *Martin* + *-mas.*] *Eccl.* The feast of St. Martin, November 11th.

mart′let (märt′lĕt; -lĭt), *n.* [F. *martelet*, fr. *martinet.* See MARTIN the bird.] The common European martin.

mar′tyr (mär′tẽr), *n.* [AS., fr. LL. *martyr*, fr. Gr. *martyr, martys*, prop., a witness.] **1.** One who voluntarily suffered death for refusing to renounce his religion. **2.** One who sacrifices his life, station, etc., for the sake of principle. **3.** *Colloq.* A constant sufferer, as from disease. — *v. t.* **1.** To put to death for adhering to some belief, esp. Christianity. **2.** To torture.

mar′tyr·dom (mär′tẽr·dŭm), *n.* **1.** The suffering of death for adherence to the Christian faith, or to any cause. **2.** Affliction; torture.

mar′tyr·ize (-īz), *v. t. & i.* To make or become a martyr. — **mar′tyr·i·za′tion** (-ĭ·zā′shŭn; -ī·zā′-), *n.*

mar′tyr·ol′o·gy (-ŏl′ō·jĭ), *n.; pl.* -GIES (-jĭz). [ML. *martyrologium.* See MARTYR; -LOGY.] **1.** A history or a register of martyrs. **2.** Ecclesiastical history treating of the lives and sufferings of martyrs. — **mar′tyr·o·log′i·cal** (-ō·lŏj′ĭ·kăl), *adj.* — **mar′tyr·ol′o·gist** (-ŏl′ō·jĭst), *n.*

mar′tyr·y (mär′tẽr·ĭ), *n.; pl.* -TYRIES (-ĭz). [ML. *martyrium.*] A shrine erected in honor of a martyr.

mar′vel (mär′vĕl; -v'l), *n.* [OF. *merveille*, fr. L. *mirabilia* wonderful things, pl., fr. *mirabilis* wonderful, fr. *mirari* to wonder at.] **1.** That which causes wonder; a prodigy. **2.** Wonder; astonishment. — *v. i.;* -VELED (-vĕld) or -VELLED; -VEL·ING or -VEL·LING. **1.** To be struck with surprise; wonder. **2.** To have a wondering curiosity (about something); as, I *marveled* at what he told me.

mar′vel-of-Pe·ru′, *n.* The four o'clock *Mirabilis jalapa.*

mar′vel·ous, mar′vel·lous (mär′vĕl·ŭs), *adj.* **1.** Exciting marvel; astonishing. **2.** Partaking of the character of miracle; incredible. **3.** *Colloq.* Splendid. — **mar′vel·ous·ly, mar′vel·lous·ly,** *adv.* — **mar′vel·ous·ness, mar′vel·lous·ness,** *n.*

Marx′i·an (märk′sĭ·ăn), *adj.* Of or pertaining to Karl Marx (1818–83) or the socialist theories held by him. See SOCIALISM. — **Marx′i·an,** *n.*

Marx′ism (märk′sĭz′m), **Marx′i·an·ism** (-sĭ·ăn·ĭz′m), *n.* The socialism of Marx and Engels, which makes the class struggle the fundamental force in history. Cf. COMMUNISM. — **Marx′ist** (-sĭst), *n. & adj.*

Mar′y (mâr′ĭ; 6), *n.; pl.* MARYS (-ĭz), MARIES (-ĭz). [LL. *Maria*, fr. Gr. *Maria, Mariam*, fr. Heb. *Miryām* Miriam.] *Bib.* **a** The mother of Jesus; — often called the ***Blessed Virgin Mary*** or ***Saint Mary.*** **b** The sister of Martha. **c** Mary of Magdala, ***Mary Magdalene,*** who was healed of evil spirits by Jesus.

mar′zi·pan (mär′zĭ·păn; mär′zĭ·păn′). Var. of MARCHPANE.

-mas (-măs). Combining form of *Mass*, denoting *a feast day* or *festival* or *the time of its celebration*, as in Candle*mas*, Michael*mas.*

mas·car′a (măs·kăr′ȧ; măs·kär′ȧ; mäs·kär′ȧ), *n.* A preparation for coloring the eyelashes.

mas′cle (măs′k'l), *n.* [OF.] **1.** *Her.* A lozenge voided; formerly, a lozenge plain. **2.** A steel plate, esp. of lozenge shape, used in series on 13th-century armor.

mas′cot (măs′kŏt; -kŭt), *n.* Also **mas′cotte.** [F. *mascotte*, fr. Pr. *mascot* a little sorcerer, fr. *masco* sorceress.] Any person or thing supposed to bring good luck.

mas′cu·line (măs′kū·lĭn), *adj.* [OF. *masculin*, fr. L. *masculinus*, fr. *masculus* male, manly. See MALE.] **1.** *Now Rare.* Male. **2.** Belonging to, or consisting of, males; appropriated to, or used by, males. **3.** Suitable to, or characteristic of, a man; virile; robust; sometimes, of a woman, mannish. **4.** *Gram.* Conforming, or denoting conformity, to the class of words viewed as distinguished for males. See GENDER. Abbr. *masc.* — **Syn.** See MALE. — **Ant.** Feminine. — *n.* That which is masculine; as: **a** A male person. **b** *Gram.* A word or form of the masculine gender; also, the masculine gender. — **mas′cu·line·ly,** *adv.* — **mas′cu·line·ness,** *n.* — **mas′cu·lin′i·ty** (-lĭn′ĭ·tĭ), *n.*

masculine rhyme. *Pros.* A rhyme in which only final and accented syllables correspond, as *amend* and *pretend.* See FEMININE RHYME.

mash (măsh), *n.* [AS. *māsc-, māx-*, in comp.] **1.** *Brewing, etc.* Crushed malt, or meal of grain, steeped and stirred in hot water to produce wort. **2.** A mixture of ground feeds for feeding livestock. **3.** A soft, pulpy mass of anything. — *v. t.* **1.** *Brewing.* To subject (crushed malt, etc.) to the action of water, with heating and stirring, for preparing wort. **2.** To reduce to a soft pulpy state by beating or pressure. — **mash′er** (-ẽr), *n.*

mash, *v. t. Slang.* To affect so as to cause a sentimental regard. — *v. i.* To ogle; flirt. — *n. Slang.* A state of being sentimentally enamored; also, one who feels or is the cause of such a state. — **mash′er,** *n.*

mash′ie, mash′y (măsh′ĭ), *n.; pl.* MASHIES (-ĭz). *Golf.* An iron club with a rather wide blade well laid back; — in combination, any of certain other clubs for lofting; as, **mashie iron, mashie niblick.** See GOLF, *Illust.*

mask (måsk; 9), *n.* [F. *masque*, fr. It. *maschera, mascara*, fr. Ar. *maskharah* buffoon.] **1.** A cover for the face, used for disguise. **2.** A festive dance where all wear masks; a masquerade; hence, a revel; — now often spelled *masque.* **3.** That which disguises or conceals; as, the *mask* of night. **4.** A person wearing a mask; a masker. **5.** A grotesque false face worn at carnivals, etc. **6.** A sculptured face or face and neck, or a copy of a face made by means of a mold in plaster, wax, etc.; as, a death *mask.* **7.** The head or face of an animal, as a fox or dog. **8.** A protective covering, esp. for the face; as, a baseball *mask;* a gas *mask* (which see). **9.** A respirator to allow the inhalation of a gas or vapor; as, an oxygen *mask.* **10.** *Arch., etc.* A head or face, often grotesque, used as an adornment. **11.** *Mil.* A natural or artificial terrain feature which conceals or protects. **12.** *Theater.* **a** In classical antiquity, a figure of a head worn on the stage, serving to identify the character and project the voice. **b** Also **masque.** An old form of dramatic performance in which the actors wore masks; also, a dramatic composition for such a performance. — *v. t.* **1.** To cover, as the face, by way of concealment or defense. **2.** To disguise; cover. **3.** To conceal from the enemy's sight, as the position of a battery. — **Syn.** See DISGUISE.

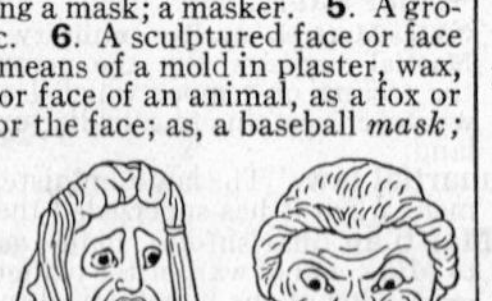

1 2

Ancient Greek Masks used in (1) Tragedy and (2) Comedy.

mas′ka·longe (măs′kȧ·lŏnj), **mas′ka·nonge** (-nŏnj). Vars. of MUSKELLUNGE.

mask′er (mås′kẽr; 9), *n.* One who wears a mask; one who appears in disguise at a masquerade.

mas′och·ism (măz′ŏk·ĭz′m), *n.* [After L. von Sacher-*Masoch* (1835–95), Austrian novelist, who described it.] *Med.* Abnormal sexual passion characterized by pleasure in being abused by one's associate; hence, any pleasure in being abused or dominated. Cf. SADISM. — **mas′och·ist** (-ĭst), *n.*

ma′son (mā′s'n), *n.* [OF. *masson, maçon*, fr. ML. *matio, macio, -onis.*] **1.** One who builds with stone, brick, or the like. **2.** [*cap.*] A Freemason. — *v. t.* To construct of masonry; to build stonework or brickwork about, under, etc.

Ma′son and Dix′on's line (mā′s'n, dĭk′s'nz), *also* **Ma′son-Dix′on Line** (-dĭk′s'n). The southern boundary line of Pennsylvania, run (except about thirty-six miles) by Charles Mason and Jeremiah Dixon, two English astronomers, between 1763 and 1767 to settle an old boundary dispute between proprietors of Pennsylvania and Maryland. It became famous in U. S. history as being in part the boundary between the free and the slave states.

mason bee. Any of numerous solitary bees (esp. *Chalicodoma muraria*) which construct nests of mud and sand.

ma·son′ic (mȧ·sŏn′ĭk; mā-), *adj.* [*usually cap.*] Of, pert. to, or characteristic of Freemasons or their mysteries.

Ma′son·ite (mā′s'n·īt), *n.* A trade-mark applied to various fiberboards made from steam-exploded wood fiber, and used variously, as for insulation and paneling.

Mason jar. [Patented by John L. *Mason*, of N. Y. City.] A glass jar for use in home canning.

ma′son·ry (mā′s'n·rĭ), *n.; pl.* -RIES (-rĭz). **1.** Art, trade, or occupation of a mason. **2.** The work of a mason. **3.** Anything constructed of the materials, as stone, brick, or tiles, used by masons. **4.** [*cap.*] Freemasonry.

Ma·so′ra, Ma·so′rah (mȧ·sō′rȧ), *n.* [NHeb. *māsōrāh* tradition, fr. Heb. *māsōreth.*] The early Hebrew tradition as to the correct form of the text of the Scriptures; also, in the written editions, the marginal notes, or the text and notes, embodying the results of this tradition.

Mas′o·rete (măs′ō·rēt), *n.* A Hebrew scholar learned in the Masora; esp., one of the scribes who wrote down the Masora.

Mas′o·ret′ic (-rĕt′ĭk), **Mas′o·ret′i·cal** (-ĭ·kăl), *adj.* Of or relating to the Masora or the Masoretes.

masque (måsk; 9). Var. of MASK, 2 & 12 **b.**

mas′quer·ade′ (mås′kẽr·ād′; 9), *n.* [F. *mascarade*, fr. It. *mascherata*, fr. *maschera* a mask. See MASK.] **1.** An assembly of persons wearing masks, as at a dance. **2.** A costume for wear at such an assembly. **3.** Acting or living under false pretenses. — *v. i.* **a** To take part in a masquerade. **b** To frolic in disguise; to make a show of being what one is not. — **mas′quer·ad′er** (-ād′ẽr), *n.*

Mass (măs; mås; 9), *n.* [AS. *mæsse*, fr. LL. *missa*, fr. *mittere, missum*, to send, dismiss.] **1. a** The Eucharistic rite of the Latin church; the sequence of prayers and ceremonies constituting the commemorative sacrifice of the Body and Blood of Christ under the appearances of bread and wine. **b** [*often not cap.*] A celebrating of the Mass. When sung, and when there are assisting ministers, it is called ***High Mass. Low Mass*** is the service without music. **2.** *Music.* The setting of portions of the Mass considered as a musical composition.

mass, *n.* [OF. *masse*, fr. L. *massa*, fr. Gr. *maza* a barley cake.] **1.** A quantity of matter, or the form of matter, cohering together in one body or quantity, usually of considerable size. **2.** A large quantity; a bulk. **3.** Magnitude; size. **4.** The principal part; as, the *mass* of imports. **5.** With *the*, the general body of mankind, a nation, etc.; hence, *pl.*, ***the masses*** (-ĕz; -ĭz), the great body of the people as contrasted with the classes; the populace. **6.** *Physics.* A measure of the quantity of matter in a body as determined by comparing the changes in the velocities that result when the body and a standard body impinge. Mass is the quotient obtained by dividing the weight of a body by the acceleration due to gravity. Cf. INERTIA, WEIGHT, SLUG. — **Syn.** See BULK. — *adj.* Of, pertaining to, or characteristic of a mass or the masses (see MASS, 5, above); as, *mass* education. — *v. t. & i.* [F. *masser.*] To form or collect into a mass.

mas′sa·cre (măs′ȧ·kẽr), *n.* [F., fr. OF. *maçacre, macecle*, shambles, slaughter.] The killing of a number of human beings under circumstances of atrocity or cruelty. — *v. t.;* -CRED (-kẽrd); -CRING (-krĭng). [F. *massacrer.*] To kill by massacre; slaughter. — **mas′sa·crer** (-krẽr), *n.*

mas·sage′ (mȧ·säzh′; *Brit. also* măs′äzh), *n.* [F.] A method of treating the body for remedial or hygienic purposes, consisting in rubbing, stroking, kneading, tapping, etc., with the hand or an instrument. — *v. t.;* -SAGED′ (mȧ·säzhd′); -SAG′ING (-säzh′ĭng). To treat by massage. — **mas·sag′er** (-säzh′ẽr), *n.* — **mas·sag′ist** (mȧ·säzh′ĭst), *n.*

mas′sa·sau′ga (măs′ȧ·sô′gȧ), *n.* [From *Missisauga* River, Ontario.] Any of several small rattlesnakes of the genus *Sistrurus.*

mass defect. *Physics & Chem.* The difference between the mass number of an isotope and its atomic weight.

mas·sé′ (mă·sā′ *or, esp. Brit.,* măs′ā), *n., or* **massé shot.** [F. *massé*, past part. of *masser* to make such a stroke, fr. *masse* cue, club.] *Billiards.* A stroke made by hitting the cue ball nearly vertically on the side so as to make it pass round an obstructing object ball.

mass′-en′er·gy e·qua′tion. *Physics & Chem.* An equation for the interconversion of mass and energy, developed by Albert Einstein in 1905. It may be written $E = MC^2$, where E is the energy in ergs, M is the mass in grams, and C is the velocity of light in centimeters per second. A loss of one ounce of mass, as by fission of uranium, means the liberation of about 700 million kilowatt hours of energy; — called also *Einstein equation.*

mas·se′ter (mă·sē′tẽr), *n.* [NL., fr. Gr. *masētēr* a chewer, *mys masētēr* a muscle of the lower jaw used in chewing, fr. *masasthai* to chew.] *Anat.* A large muscle which raises the lower jaw and assists in mastication. — **mas′se·ter′ic** (măs′ē·tĕr′ĭk), *adj.*

mas·seur′ (mă·sûr′), *n.; pl.* -SEURS (-sûrz′; *F.* -sûr′). [F.] A man practitioner of massage. — **mas·seuse′** (-sûz′), *n. fem.; pl.* -SEUSES (-sûz′ĕz; -ĭz; *F.* -sûz′).

mas′si·cot (măs′ĭ·kŏt), *n.* [F., fr. It., fr. Sp. *mazacote* potash, soda.] Unfused lead monoxide, PbO. Cf. LITHARGE.

mas′sif (măs′ĭf; *F.* mȧ′sēf′), *n.* [F.] *Geol.* **a** A principal mountain mass. **b** A block of the earth's crust bounded by faults and displaced as a unit without internal change.

mas′sive (măs′ĭv), *adj.* [F. *massif.*] **1.** Forming, or consisting of, a large mass; weighty; massy. **2.** Of the features, large and bold.

3. Of immaterial things, impressive as solid, imposing, or broad in scope, effect, or the like. **4.** Impressive for nonphysical solidity and strength, latent power, or accumulated momentum. **5.** Large in comparison to what is typical; — used esp. of medical dosage or infective agents. **6.** Extensive and severe; — of pathological conditions. **7.** *Mineral.* In mass, not necessarily without a crystalline structure, but having no regular form. — **mas′sive·ly**, *adv.* — **mas′sive·ness**, *n.*

mass meeting. A large or general assembly of people.

mass number. *Physics & Chem.* The integer which most closely expresses the mass of an isotope. Symbol, *A* See ATOMIC MASS.

mas′so·ther′a·py (măs′ō·thĕr′ȧ·pĭ), *n.* [Gr. *massein* to knead + *therapy.*] Treatment of disease by massage.

mass production. *Com.* Production of goods in quantity usually by machinery. — **mass′–pro·duce′**, *v. t.* — **mass′–pro·duced′**, *adj.*

mass spectrograph. *Physics.* An instrument for deflecting electrified particles into separate streams according to their respective masses, the resulting spectrum being called a **mass spectrum.**

mass′y (măs′ĭ; màs′ĭ), *adj.;* MASS′I·ER (-ĭ·ẽr); MASS′I·EST. Having bulk and weight or substance; massive. — **mass′i·ness**, *n.*

mast (màst; 9), *n.* [AS. *mæst*, fem.] Nuts collectively, esp. as food for hogs or other animals; specif., beechnuts.

mast, *n.* [AS. *mæst*, masc.] **1.** A long pole or spar rising from the keel of a vessel through the decks, if any, into the air to sustain the yards, booms, sails, and rigging generally. Masts of one length are called ***pole masts;*** masts made of several pieces bound together are called ***made, or built-up, masts.*** **2.** Any vertical pole, as an upright post in various cranes. See DERRICK, *Illust.* — *v. t.* To furnish with a mast or masts. — ***before the mast.*** *Naut.* Forward of the foremast; hence, as a common sailor, — because of the quartering of sailors in the forecastle.

mast-. = MASTO-, as in **mas·tec′to·my.**

mas′ta·ba (măs′tȧ·bȧ), *n.* Also **mas′ta·bah.** [Ar. *maṣṭabah.*] *Egypt. Archaeol.* A type of tomb, oblong with sloping sides and connected with a mummy chamber in the rock beneath.

mas′ter (màs′tẽr; 9), *n.* [From AS. *magister* and fr. OF. *maistre*, both fr. L. *magister*, orig. a double comparative from the root of *magnus* great.] **1.** A male person having another being subject to his will, as a teacher, an employer, an owner of a slave or a dog, an official in a school, etc.; often [*cap.*], with *the, our*, etc., Christ, as a leader and teacher of his disciples and followers. **2.** One who uses, or controls at will, anything inanimate; as, to be *master* of one's time. **3.** A victor, as in a contest. **4. a** A title of a man or youth, orig. used only of persons of high rank, later of men in general. As a courtesy title for men, *master* came to be pronounced mĭstẽr, and only the abbreviation *Mr.* and the spelling *Mister* are now so used. **b** A youth or boy too young to be called *mister.* **c** In Scotland, the title of the heir apparent of a viscount or a baron; as, the *Master* of Ballantrae. **5.** A presiding official in an institution or society, as a college, corporation, etc. **6.** A workman so proficient as to follow his trade independently and teach apprentices. **7. a** One, esp. an artist, who has attained great skill in the use of anything; as, a *master* of oratory. **b** A painting, statue, etc., by one of the great artists of former times; as, it was an old *master.* **8.** *Educ.* **a** A tutor or preceptor. **b** [*sometimes cap.*] A person holding an academic degree of an advanced character; also, the degree itself. It is now usually the second degree, ranking above *bachelor* and below *doctor.* **9.** *Law.* Any of various officers of court appointed to assist the judge, as by hearing and reporting upon matters referred to him. **10.** *Naut.* The commander of a merchant vessel.

— *v. t.* **1.** To become the master of; subdue. **2.** To become an adept in; as, to *master* a science. **3.** To rule or direct.

— *adj.* Being master, or characteristic of a master; principal; controlling; often specif., *Mach., etc.*, designating a device or mechanism that controls the operation of different mechanisms or establishes a standard; as, a *master* key. — **mas′ter·dom**, *n.* — **mas′ter·hood**, *n.* — **mas′ter·less**, *adj.*

mas′ter–at–arms′, *n.* *Nav.* A petty officer on a man-of-war charged with the maintenance of order, discipline, the custody of prisoners, etc.

master builder. One who has attained proficiency in one of the building crafts and is qualified to supervise building construction.

mas′ter·ful (màs′tẽr·fo͝ol; -f'l), *adj.* **1.** Domineering; arbitrary. **2.** Having the skill or power of a master; also, indicating or expressing power or mastery. — **mas′ter·ful·ly**, *adv.* — **mas′ter·ful·ness**, *n.*

Syn. **Masterful, domineering, imperious, peremptory, imperative** mean imposing one's will on another. **Masterful** implies a strong, virile personality and ability to deal commandingly with affairs; **domineering**, an overbearing or tyrannical manner and an obstinate endeavor to enforce one's will; **imperious**, more arrogance than *masterful* but less insolence than *domineering;* **peremptory**, an insistence on an immediate response to one's commands; **imperative**, peremptoriness more from the urgency of the situation than from one's temperament.

mas′ter·ly, *adj.* Suitable to, or characteristic of, a master; indicating superior skill and power; as, a *masterly* performance. — **mas′ter·ly**, *adv.* — **mas′ter·li·ness**, *n.*

master mason. **a** A mason thoroughly competent in his trade, usually one in business for himself. **b** [*caps.*] A Freemason raised to the third degree.

master mechanic. **1.** A foreman mechanic. **2.** A mechanic who is a thorough master of his trade.

master of ceremonies. **a** A person appointed to determine or supervise matters of formal procedure as on a public occasion. **b** A person who conducts a program, as on the radio, introducing numbers, interviewing speakers, and usually providing the continuity.

mas′ter·piece′ (màs′tẽr·pēs′; 9), *n.* Anything done or made with extraordinary skill; a chef-d'oeuvre.

mas′ter·ship, *n.* **1.** The authority of a master. **2.** Status, office, or function of a master. **3.** The proficiency of a master; mastery.

mas′ter·sing′er (-sĭng′ẽr), *n.* [Trans. of G. *meistersinger.*] = MEISTERSINGER.

master stroke. A capital performance; a masterly action.

mas′ter·work′ (màs′tẽr·wûrk′), *n.* The most important work by a skilled person, as in architecture, literature, etc.; also, a masterpiece.

master workman. One specially skilled in any art, handicraft, or trade, or who is an overseer, foreman, or employer.

mas′ter·y (màs′tẽr·ĭ), *n.; pl.* -IES (-ĭz). [OF. *maistrie.*] **1. a** The status, position, or authority of a master; mastership. **b** Superiority or ascendancy in war or competition. **2.** A mastering, or state of having mastered; skill or knowledge in, or intellectual command of, a subject.

mast′head′ (màst′hĕd′), *n.* **1.** *Naut.* The top of a mast, esp. of the lower mast. **2.** The matter printed in every issue of a newspaper or journal, stating the title, ownership, advertising rates, etc.

mast′head′ (màst′hĕd′; màst′hĕd′), *v. t.* *Naut.* **a** To send to the masthead as a punishment. **b** To hoist to the masthead, as a flag.

mas′tic (măs′tĭk), *n.* [OF., fr. LL. *mastichum*, fr. Gr. *mastichē* gum mastic.] **1.** A resin exuding from the **mastic tree** (*Pistacia lenticus*) of southern Europe, obtained by incision. It is used as an astringent and also as an ingredient in varnishes. **2.** Short for MASTIC TREE. **3.** Any of various pasty cements.

mas′ti·cate (măs′tĭ·kāt), *v. t. & i.* [LL. *masticatus*, past part. of *masticare* to chew, fr. Gr. *mastichan* to gnash the teeth, *mastax* mouth, morsel.] **1.** To grind or crush with or as if with the teeth and prepare for swallowing, as food; to chew. **2.** To reduce to pulp by crushing or kneading as rubber. — **mas′ti·ca′tion** (-kā′shŭn), *n.* — **mas′ti·ca′tor** (-kā′tẽr), *n.*

mas′ti·ca·to′ry (-kȧ·tō′rĭ *or, esp. Brit.*, -tẽr·ĭ *or* -kā′tō·rĭ), *adj.* **1.** Chewing; adapted to the chewing of food. **2.** Of or pert. to or affecting the masticating organs. — *n.; pl.* -RIES (-rĭz). A substance to be chewed to increase saliva.

mas′tiff (màs′tĭf; 9), *n.* [ME. *mastif* (with ending after OF. *mestif* mongrel), fr. OF. *mastin*, deriv. of L. *mansuetus* tame.] A giant smooth-coated dog of a very old breed, orig. used as a hunting dog.

mas·ti′tis (măs·tī′tĭs), *n.* [NL., fr. *mast-* + *-itis.*] *Med. & Veter.* Inflammation of the breast or of the mammary gland.

mas′to- (măs′tō-), **mast-.** [Gr. *mastos* breast.] A combining form denoting: **a** The *breast;* a *mammary gland*, as in **mas′to·car′ci·no′ma, mas·tot′o·my.** **b** *Mastoid* and, as in **mas′to·pa·ri′e·tal.**

mas′to·don (măs′tō·dŏn), *n.* [NL., fr. *mast-* + Gr. *odous, odontos*, tooth; — from the conical projections upon its molar teeth.] Any of numerous extinct elephantlike animals (families Mammutidae and Bunomastodontidae, esp. genus *Mammut*), differing from the mammoths and existing elephants chiefly in the molar teeth.

mas′toid (măs′toid), *adj.* [Gr. *mastoeidēs*, fr. *mastos* the breast + *eidos* form.] *Anat. & Zool.* **a** Naming a process of the temporal bone behind the ear, in many mammals. **b** Pertaining to, or in the region of, this process. — *n.* The mastoid process; *Colloq.*, mastoiditis.

mas′toid·ec′to·my (-ĕk′tō·mĭ), *n.* [*mastoid* + *-ectomy.*] Surgical removal of the bone surrounding the mastoid cells.

mas′toid·i′tis (-ī′tĭs), *n.* [NL., fr. *mastoid* + *-itis.*] *Med.* Inflammation of the mastoid, esp. of the mastoid cells.

mas′tur·bate (măs′tẽr·bāt), *v. i. & t.* To perform masturbation (of).

mas′tur·ba′tion (-bā′shŭn), *n.* [L. *masturbatus*, past part.] Production of an orgasm by excitation of the genital organs, as by manipulation or friction, without heterosexual intercourse.

ma·su′ri·um (mȧ·zo͞or′ĭ·ŭm), *n.* [NL., fr. *Masuria*, region in East Prussia.] *Chem.* The element of atomic number 43; — a former name. Symbol, *Ma* Cf. TECHNETIUM.

mat (măt), *n.* [AS. *matt, meatt*, fr. L. *matta* a mat made of rushes.] **1.** A piece of coarse fabric made by weaving or plaiting rushes, straw, hemp, or the like; hence, anything of similar form and use. **2.** A piece of material for use at a door to wipe the shoes on. **3.** Anything closely interwoven, so as to resemble a mat; as, a *mat* of hair. **4.** A piece of material, as of knitted work, used to support vases, dishes, etc., or for ornament. **5.** *Wrestling.* A cushion several inches thick and sixteen to twenty feet square, on which matches are contested. — *v. t. & i.;* MAT′TED (-ĕd; -ĭd); MAT′TING. To cover with or as with a mat or matting; hence, to twist or interweave into, or like, a mat.

mat, *adj.* [F. See MAT border.] Without luster or gloss; as, a *mat* surface; having a dulled but even surface. — *v. t.* To render mat, as metal or glass. — *n.* [F., a dull color, fr. *mat*, adj., dull-colored, without brilliancy, fr. OF. *mat* defeated, overcome, fr. Ar. *māt.*] **1.** A border with a gold surface, or of white or colored paper, serving as a frame of a picture. **2.** A dead or dull finish, or roughened surface, as in gilding or in painting. **3.** *Printing, etc.* A matrix.

mat. Var. of MATTE.

Mat′a·be′le (măt′ȧ·bē′lē) *or* **Mat′a·be′les** (-lēz), *n. pl.; sing.* MATABELE. A Zulu people driven out of the Transvaal by the Boers in 1837, and now in Matabeleland.

mat′a·dor (măt′ȧ·dōr; -dôr), *n.* [Sp., prop., a killer.] **1.** The man appointed to kill the bull in bullfights. **2.** *Card Playing.* In certain games, as solo, quadrille, or omber, one of the principal trumps.

match (măch), *n.* [OF. *mesche* (F. *mèche*).] **1.** A wick or cord prepared to burn at a uniform rate, as for firing a charge of powder. **2.** *Obs. exc. Hist.* A splint of wood or a piece of cord, paper, or cloth, dipped in melted sulfur to make it ignitible by tinder. **3.** A short, slender piece of wood, or other material, tipped with a mixture by means of which fire is produced, as by friction.

match, *n.* [AS. *gemæcca.*] **1.** A person or thing equal or similar to another. **2.** One able to mate or cope with another. **3.** An exact counterpart. **4.** A pair suitably associated; as, the carpet and curtains are a *match.* **5.** A bringing or coming together of two or more parties for a contest, or the like. **6.** A matrimonial union. **7.** A person to be gained in marriage. **8.** *Obs.* An equal or companion, as in age or rank; also, a rival. **9.** A contest under formal regulations between two persons, teams, etc.

— *v. t.* **1.** To marry; — with reference to the suitability of the parties. **2.** To encounter as an antagonist; now, to encounter successfully; also, to rival. **3.** To bring a match, or equal, against; to show an equal competitor to. **4.** To make or procure the equal of, or that which is exactly similar to; as, to *match* a vase, horses. **5.** To adapt, fit, or suit (one thing to another). **6.** To fit together, or make suitable for fitting together; as, to *match* boards. **7.** *Colloq.* To toss or flip (a coin) so that it falls with the same face up as a coin tossed by another; also, to toss coins with (a person) to decide something by their fall. — *v. i.* **1.** To be united in marriage; to mate. **2.** To be of equal or similar size, figure, color, or the like; to suit.

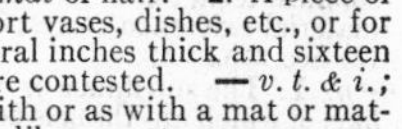

Matchboards.

match′board′ (măch′bōrd′; 70), *n.* *Carp.* A board, one of many cut for ceiling, etc., each having a groove in one edge and a tongue on the other.

matched or′der (măcht). *Exchanges.* An order to buy and to sell the same amount of a single stock or produce at the same price.

match′er (măch′ẽr), *n.* One who or that which matches.

match′less, *adj.* Having no equal; unequaled. — **match′less·ly**, *adv.* — **match′less·ness**, *n.*

match′lock′ (măch′lŏk′), *n.* An old form of gunlock with a match, usually of cord, for firing the priming; hence, a gun with such a lock.

match′mak′er (măch′māk′ẽr), *n.* One who makes matches for burning. — **match′mak′ing** (-ĭng), *n.* & *adj.*

match′mak′er, *n.* One who arranges a match; esp., one who schemes to bring about marriages. — **match′mak′ing,** *n.* & *adj.*

match play. **a** Play in a sporting match. **b** *Golf.* Play in which the score is reckoned by counting the holes won or lost by each side. Cf. MEDAL PLAY. — **match player.**

match point. The last point needed to win a match.

match′wood′ (măch′wŏŏd′), *n.* Wood suitable for matches; hence, splinters; small pieces.

mate (māt), *v. t.* & *i.*; MAT′ED (māt′ĕd; -ĭd); MAT′ING. [OF. *mater* to overcome, checkmate, fr. *mat.* See MAT border.] **1.** To checkmate. **2.** To overcome, as by prowess, terror, etc.; to confound; baffle. — *n.* & *interj. Chess.* Checkmate.

mate, *n.* [ME., appar. fr. MLG. *māt, mate,* companion.] **1.** A comrade. **2.** A husband or wife; also, one of a pair of creatures or objects, as of birds or gloves. **3.** *Archaic.* A suitable companion; a match. **4.** *Naut.* A deck officer in the merchant marine ranking below the captain. **5.** *Nav.* **a** A subordinate assistant to a warrant officer; as, a boatswain's *mate.* **b** In the U. S. Navy, a subordinate officer having no rank, but taking precedence of all other enlisted men. — *v. t.* **1.** To join as mates; to match; of animals, to pair for breeding. **2.** To couple or associate as mate, or equal. **3.** *Obs.* To oppose as equal; to match.

ma′té, ma′te (mä′tā; măt′ā), *n.* [Sp. *mate,* fr. Quechua.] **1.** An aromatic beverage prepared in South America from the leaves of the Paraguay tea (*Ilex paraguayensis*). **2.** The plant Paraguay tea.

mat′e·lote (măt′ĕ·lōt), **mat′e·lotte** (-lŏt), *n.* [F. *matelote,* fr. *matelot* sailor.] A dish, commonly of fish, served with a wine sauce containing onions, mushrooms, etc.

‖**ma′ter do′lo·ro′sa** (mā′tẽr dō′lō·rō′sȧ). [L.] Literally, sorrowful mother; — applied esp. to the Virgin Mary.

ma′ter·fa·mil′i·as (mā′tẽr·fȧ·mĭl′ĭ·ăs), *n.* [L., fr. *mater* mother + *familias,* gen. of *familia* family.] The mistress of a house; the mother of a family; a matron.

ma·te′ri·al (mȧ·tēr′ĭ·ăl), *adj.* [LL. *materialis,* fr. *materia* stuff, matter.] **1.** Of or pertaining to, or consisting of, matter; not spiritual; physical. **2.** **a** Of solid or weighty character; of consequence; important. **b** Relevant; pertinent. **3.** Relating to, or derived from, matter as the constituent of the physical universe; as, *material* forces. **4.** Pertaining to, or affecting, man's bodily wants, interests, or comforts. **5.** *Philos.* Pertaining to real significance rather than to form, logical manner, etc.

Syn. (1) **Material, physical, corporeal, phenomenal, sensible, objective** mean of or belonging to actuality. **Material** (opp. to *spiritual*) suggests formation out of matter, and substantiality; **physical** (opp. to *mental,* etc.), perception, identification, or the like (as, *material* objects; *physical* forces); **corporeal,** tangible physical existence (as, energy is a *physical* power found chiefly in *corporeal* things); **phenomenal,** existence known through the senses or experience rather than by intuition or the like; **sensible** is a more ordinary term describing anything that may be seen, heard, touched, or the like; **objective** is a philosophical term implying that the thing one hears, sees, touches, etc., has material existence corresponding to the image one has of it.
(2) See RELEVANT.

— *n.* **1.** The substance or substances, or the parts, goods, stock, or the like, of which anything is composed or may be made; as, raw *materials.* **2.** Data of any sort, such as notes, sketches, etc., which may be worked up into a more finished form. **3.** Matter viewed as the relatively formless basis of reality. **4.** *pl.* The implements necessary to the doing of anything; as, writing *materials.* **5.** A fabric; specif., woolen or cloth stuff.

ma·te′ri·al·ism (mȧ·tēr′ĭ·ăl·ĭz′m), *n.* **1.** **a** Any theory which considers the facts of the universe to be sufficiently explained by the existence and nature of matter. Cf. ATOMISM. **b** The ethical doctrine that consideration of material well-being, esp. of the individual himself, should rule in the determination of conduct. **2.** The tendency to give undue importance to material interests. — **ma·te′ri·al·ist** (-ĭst), *n.* & *adj.* — **ma·te′ri·al·is′tic** (-ĭs′tĭk), *adj.* — **-ti·cal·ly** (-tĭ·kăl·ĭ), *adv.*

ma·te′ri·al′i·ty (-ăl′ĭ·tĭ), *n.*; *pl.* -TIES (-tĭz). **1.** Quality or state of being material. **2.** That which is material; *pl.,* material things.

ma·te′ri·al·ize (mȧ·tēr′ĭ·ăl·īz), *v. t.* **1.** To invest with material characteristics; hence, to present to the mind through the medium of material objects. **2.** *Spiritualism.* To make visible in or as in a material form; — said of spirits. — *v. i.* **1.** To appear as a material form; to become a realized fact. **2.** *Spiritualism.* To assume visible or concrete form; — said of a spirit. — **ma·te′ri·al·i·za′tion** (-ĭ·zā′shŭn; -ī·zā′-), *n.* — **ma·te′ri·al·iz′er** (-īz′ẽr), *n.*

ma·te′ri·al·ly, *adv.* **1.** *Philos.* In respect to the matter, as disting. from the form; in respect to the material cause. **2.** With respect to physical substance; in a material state or manner. **3.** In an important regard; substantially. **4.** As regards material interests or comforts.

ma·te′ri·a med′i·ca (mȧ·tē′rĭ·ȧ mĕd′ĭ·kȧ). [ML. See MATTER; MEDICAL.] **a** Material or substance used in preparing remedies. **b** Medical science treating of the nature and properties of all the substances used in curing diseases.

ma·té′ri·el′ (mȧ·tē′rĭ·ĕl′), *n.* [F. See MATERIAL.] Material equipment, apparatus, and supplies of an organization or institution; — disting. from *personnel.*

ma·ter′nal (mȧ·tûr′năl; -n′l), *adj.* [F. *maternel,* fr. L. *maternus,* fr. *mater* mother.] **1.** Of or pertaining to a mother; motherly. **2.** Derived or received from one's mother. — **ma·ter′nal·ly,** *adv.*

ma·ter′ni·ty (-nĭ·tĭ), *n.*; *pl.* -TIES (-tĭz). **1.** State or quality of being a mother; the character or relation of a mother; motherliness. **2.** Short for **maternity hospital,** a lying-in hospital. — **ma·ter′ni·ty,** *adj.*

mate′y (māt′ĭ), *adj.* Companionable.

math (măth), *n.* [AS. *mǣth.*] *Now Dial.* A mowing.

math′e·mat′ic (măth′ē·măt′ĭk), *adj.* [F. or L.; F. *mathématique,* fr. L., fr. Gr. *mathēmatikos* disposed to learn, mathematical, fr. *mathēmata* things learned, fr. *manthanein* to learn.] *Now Rare.* Mathematical. — *n.* Mathematics.

math′e·mat′i·cal (-ĭ·kăl), *adj.* Of, pertaining to, or according to mathematics; hence, theoretically precise; accurate. — **-i·cal·ly,** *adv.*

mathematical logic. A system of formal logic using symbols, esp. for propositions, classes, and relations, designed to avoid the ambiguities of everyday language by constituting calculi governed by precise rules.

math′e·ma·ti′cian (măth′ē·mȧ·tĭsh′ăn), *n.* One versed in mathematics.

math′e·mat′ics (-măt′ĭks), *n.*; see -ICS. That science treating of the exact relations existing between quantities or magnitudes and operations, and of the methods by which, in accordance with these relations, quantities sought are deducible from others known or supposed.

mat′in (măt′ĭn), *n.* [OF. *matines,* fem. pl. fr. L. *matutinus* of the morning.] **1.** *pl.* [*often cap.*] *Eccl.* **a** A service or office which with lauds constitutes the first of the canonical hours. **b** In the churches of the Anglican Communion, the order for, or service of, Morning Prayer; — often spelled *mattins.* **2.** *Poetic.* A morning song or call. — *adj.* Of or pertaining to matins or morning. — **mat′in·al** (măt′ĭ·năl; -n′l), *adj.*

mat′i·nee′ (măt′ĭ·nā′ *or, esp. Brit.,* măt′ĭ·nā), *n.* [F. *matinée,* fr. *matin* morning.] A reception, or a musical or dramatic entertainment, held in the daytime, esp. in the afternoon. — **mat′i·nee′,** *adj.*

mat′ing (māt′ĭng), *n.* A pairing or matching.

mat′rass (măt′răs), *n.* [F. *matras,* fr. *matras* arrow, bolt.] **a** *Old Chem.* A round-bottomed glass flask having a long neck; a bolthead. **b** *Chem.* (Also **mattrass** in the trade). A small hard glass tube closed at one end, used in blowpipe analysis.

matri-. [L. *mater, matris.*] A combining form meaning *mother,* as in *matricide.*

ma′tri·arch (mā′trĭ·ärk), *n.* [L. *mater, matris,* mother + E. patri*arch.*] A woman who rules a family, a group, a state; specif., *Sociol.,* a mother who is head and ruler of her family and descendants. — **ma′tri·ar′chal** (-är′kăl), *adj.*

ma′tri·arch′ate (-är′kāt), *n.* **1.** A family, group, or state governed by a matriarch. **2.** *Sociol.* A theoretical stage or state in primitive society in which women, or mothers, held the chief authority.

ma′tri·arch′y (-är′kĭ), *n.* **1.** = MATRIARCHATE. **2.** *Sociol.* A state or stage in social evolution in which descent is traced in the female line, all children belonging to the mother's clan. Cf. PATRIARCHY. — **ma′tri·ar′chic** (-är′kĭk), *adj.*

ma′tri·ces (mā′trĭ·sēz; măt′rĭ-; *rarely,* mȧ·trī′sēz), *n., pl.* of MATRIX.

ma′tri·cide (mā′trĭ·sīd; măt′rĭ-), *n.* [L. *matricidium,* fr. *mater* mother + *caedere* to kill, slay.] **1.** Murder of a mother by her child. **2.** [L. *matricida.*] One who murders one's own mother. — **ma′tri·cid′al** (-sīd′ăl; -′l; 2), *adj.*

ma·tric′u·lant (mȧ·trĭk′ū·lănt), *n.* A matriculating student.

ma·tric′u·late (-lāt), *v. t.* & *i.* [LL. *matricula* a public roll, dim. of *matrix* a mother.] To enroll, esp. in a body or society, as a college or university, by entering the name in the register. — (-lăt), *n.* One who is matriculated. — **ma·tric′u·la′tion** (-lā′shŭn), *n.*

mat′ri·mo′ni·al (măt′rĭ·mō′nĭ·ăl; 58), *adj.* Of or pertaining to marriage. — **mat′ri·mo′ni·al·ly,** *adv.*

Syn. Matrimonial, marital, conjugal, connubial, nuptial mean of or characteristic of marriage. **Matrimonial** is applicable to that which has to do with matrimony or marriage in any of its senses; **marital,** strictly, implies reference to the husband and his part in marriage but is often used as equal to *matrimonial;* **conjugal** implies reference to persons who are married, **connubial** to the marriage state, but the terms are often interchanged; **nuptial** applies to rites, ceremonies, etc., attending marriage.

mat′ri·mo′ny (măt′rĭ·mō′nĭ *or, esp. Brit.,* -mŭn·ĭ), *n.*; *pl.* -NIES (-nĭz). [OF. *matrimoine, matremoigne,* fr. L. *matrimonium,* fr. *mater* mother.] **1.** The union of man and woman as husband and wife; the rite (see SACRAMENT, 1) or act of marrying; also, the married state; marriage; wedlock. **2.** *Card Playing.* **a** A game of cards. **b** Any king and queen in this game.

matrimony vine. The boxthorn.

ma′trix (mā′trĭks; măt′rĭks), *n.*; *pl.* MATRICES (mā′trĭ·sēz; măt′rĭ-; *rarely,* mȧ·trī′sēz); MATRIXES (mā′trĭk·sĕz; -sĭz; măt′rĭk-). [L.] **1.** The womb. **2.** A place or enveloping element within which something originates, takes form, or develops. **3.** **a** The natural material in which any metal, fossil, pebble, crystal, or gem is embedded. **b** Gangue; veinstone. **4.** That which gives form, origin, or foundation to something enclosed or embedded in it, as a mold for casting; specif., a plaster or papier-maché impression of type used in stereotypy or electrotypy. **5.** **a** *Anat.* & *Biol.* The intercellular substance of a tissue. **b** *Anat.* The part of the cutis beneath a nail. **6.** *Type Founding.* A metal plate, usually of copper, suitably formed to mold the face of a type.

ma′tron (mā′trŭn), *n.* [OF. *matrone,* fr. L. *matrona,* fr. *mater* mother.] **1.** A wife or a widow, esp. one who has borne children; a staid or motherly woman. **2.** **a** A housekeeper; esp., a woman who manages the domestic economy of a public institution. **b** A woman having supervisory charge of women and children, as in a dormitory, police station, etc. — **ma′tron·al** (mā′trŭn·ăl; -′l; măt′rŭn-), *adj.*

ma′tron·age (mā′trŭn·ĭj; măt′rŭn-), *n.* **1.** A body of matrons. **2.** Matronly care; also, matronly state.

ma′tron·ize (-īz), *v. t.* **1.** To make matronlike. **2.** To act the part of a matron toward; to chaperon.

ma′tron·ly (mā′trŭn·lĭ), *adj.* & *adv.* Like, or befitting, a matron. — **ma′tron·li·ness,** *n.*

matron of honor. See MAID OF HONOR **b.**

mat′ro·nym′ic (măt′rō·nĭm′ĭk), *adj.* & *n.* [L. *mater* mother + *-onymic* as in patr*onymic.*] Metronymic.

matte (măt), *n.* Also **mat.** [F.] **1.** *Metal.* A crude mixture of sulfides formed in smelting sulfide ores of certain metals, esp. copper, lead, and nickel. **2.** Mat or dull finish.

mat′ted (măt′ĕd; -ĭd), *adj.* Tangled closely together.

mat′ter (măt′ẽr), *n.* [OF. *matere* (F. *matière*), fr. L. *materia* matter, wood.] **1.** That of which any physical object is composed; material; constituents; also, a particular kind or portion of material; as, coloring *matter.* **2.** Specif., substance discharged by suppuration from living animal bodies; pus; purulent substance. **3.** Amount; quantity; — often indefinite. **4.** *Archaic.* That which pertains to a subject or sphere; as, this is not *matter* for dispute. **5.** Indefinitely, a thing or things; as, personal *matters.* **6.** **a** Formerly, an affair concerning a (specified) person; as, his *matter* shall be sped. **b** *pl.* Circumstances having reference to a particular occasion; as, carrying *matters* too far. **7.** Material treated or to be treated in a book, speech, etc. **8.** Affair worthy of account; importance; — in the phrases *what matter? no matter,* etc. **9.** *Obs.* Ground; reason; cause. **10.** *Christian Science.* Another name for mortal mind; illusion; the opposite of Spirit; that of which immortal Mind takes no cognizance; that which mortal mind sees, feels, hears, tastes, and smells only in belief. *Mary Baker Eddy.* **11.** *Law.* That which is to be proved; as: **a** By some record (***matter of record***). **b** By evidence of any kind except a record (***matter in deed***). **12.** *Philos.* The indeterminate subject of reality; the unorganized basis or stuff of experience which when combined with form (see FORM, *n.*, 17) gives phenomena, or real and individual objects. **13.** *Physics.* Whatever occupies space; that which is considered to constitute the substance of the physical universe, and, with energy, to form the basis of objective phenomena. **14.** *Post Office.* Mail matter. **15.** *Print.* Anything to be set in type; copy. — *v. i.* **1.** To be of importance; to import; signify. **2.** To form or discharge pus; to maturate.

mat′ter-of-course′, *adj.* Such as is or may be expected or depended upon as a matter of natural, logical result.

mat′ter-of-fact′, *adj.* Adhering to, or concerned with, fact; not fanciful or imaginative; commonplace.

Mat′thew (măth′ū), *n.* [F. *Mathieu*, fr. LL. *Matthaeus*, fr. Gr. *Matthaios*, fr. Heb. *Mattithyāh.*] *Bib.* **a** A collector of customs at Capernaum, one of the twelve apostles. **b** The Gospel of Matthew in the New Testament. See BIBLE.

mat′tins (măt′ĭnz). *Now Ch. of Eng.* Var. of *matins* (see MATIN, *n.*, 1).

mat′ting (măt′ĭng), *n.* **1.** An interweaving so as to make a mat. **2.** Materials for mats; also, mats collectively. **3.** A matlike fabric, as for covering floors, packing articles, etc.

mat′ting, *n.* [See MAT a dull finish.] A dull, lusterless surface in gilding, metalwork, glassmaking, etc.

mat′tock (măt′ŭk), *n.* [AS. *mattuc.*] An implement for digging and grubbing.

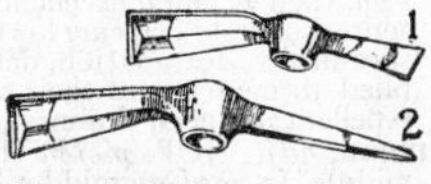

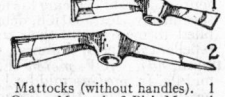

Mattocks (without handles). 1 Cutter Mattock; 2 Pick Mattock.

mat′toid (-oid), *n.* [It. *mattoide*, fr. *matto* mad.] A person of congenitally abnormal mind bordering on insanity or degeneracy.

mat′trass. Var. of MATRASS.

mat′tress (măt′rĕs; -rĭs), *n.* [OF. *materas*, fr. It. *materasso*, fr. Ar. *matrah* place where something is laid.] **1.** A bed stuffed with hair, moss, or other suitable material, and tufted or otherwise fastened. **2.** *Hydraul. Engin.* A mass of interwoven brush, poles, etc., to protect a bank from erosion.

mat′u·rate (măt′ū·rāt), *v. i.* [L. *maturatus*, past part. of *maturare* to make ripe, fr. *maturus* ripe, mature.] **1.** To mature; ripen. **2.** To generate pus; to suppurate; matter.

mat′u·ra′tion (-rā′shŭn), *n.* **1.** The formation of pus or matter. **2.** Process of bringing, or of coming, to full development. **3.** *Biol.* **a** The development of a germ cell subsequent to meiosis. **b** Meiosis (which see) and maturation (def. 3 **a**, above). **c** Final differentiation in the growth of cells. — **ma·tur′a·tive** (mȧ·tūr′ȧ·tĭv; măt′ū·rā′tĭv), *adj.*

ma·ture′ (mȧ·tūr′; 114), *adj.* [L. *maturus* ripe, seasonable.] **1.** Brought by natural process to completeness of growth and development; full-grown; ripe. **2.** Completely worked out; perfected; as, a *mature* plan. **3.** Of or pertaining to a condition of full development; as, a man of *mature* years. **4.** Having run to the limit of its time; due, as a note. **5.** *Phys. Geog.* **a** Designating the topography of surface well dissected by the erosion of running water so that slopes predominate greatly over flats. **b** Adjusted to rock structure; — said of streams. — *v. t. & i.* To bring or hasten to maturity; to complete; hence, to become due, as a note. — **ma·ture′ly**, *adv.* — **ma·ture′ness**, *n.*

ma·tu′ri·ty (mȧ·tū′rĭ·tĭ), *n.* **1.** State or quality of being mature; ripeness; full development. **2.** A becoming due; termination of the period a note, or other obligation, has to run; as, to hold bonds until *maturity.*

ma·tu′ti·nal (mȧ·tū′tĭ·năl; măt′ū·tī′năl; -n′l), *adj.* [L. *matutinalis*, fr. *matutinus.*] Of or pert. to the morning; early. — **-nal·ly**, *adv.*

matz′oth (mät′sōth), **matz′os** (-sōs), *n. pl.*; *sing.* MATZO (-sō). [Heb. *matstsōth*, pl. of *matstsāh* unleavened.] Unleavened bread eaten at the Passover.

maud (môd), *n.* A gray plaid used by shepherds in the south of Scotland; hence, a rug or shawl of such plaid.

maud′lin (môd′lĭn), *adj.* [From *Maudlin*, fr. OF. *Maudelene*, *Madeleine*, Magdalen, who is often depicted with eyes swollen and red with weeping.] **1.** Effusively sentimental; as, a *maudlin* poet; *maudlin* eloquence. **2.** Drunk enough to be emotionally silly; fuddled.

mau′ger, mau′gre (mô′gẽr), *prep.* [OF. *maugré*, *malgré*, prop., ill will.] *Archaic.* In spite of.

mau′kin (mô′kĭn). Scot. var. of MALKIN.

maul, mall (môl), *n.* [OF. *mail*, fr. L. *malleus.*] **1.** *Archaic.* A heavy mallet, staff, or mace. **2.** Any of various heavy hammers, as one for driving wedges or piles. — *v. t.* **1.** To beat and bruise or mangle; hence, to handle roughly. **2.** *U. S.* To split, as a rail, with a maul and wedge. — **maul′er** (-ẽr), *n.*

maul′stick′ (môl′stĭk′), *n.* [D. *maalstok*, fr. *malen* to paint + *stok* stick.] A stick used by painters as a rest for the hand while working.

mau′met (mô′mĕt; -mĭt), *n.* [Contr. fr. *Mahomet.*] **1.** *Obs.* A false god or idol. **2.** *Now Dial.* A puppet; doll; image. — **mau′met·ry** (-rĭ), *n.*; *pl.* MAUMETRIES (-rĭz).

maun (mŏn; môn), **man** (măn), *v. i. or auxiliary.* [Of Scand. origin.] *Scot. & N. of Eng.* Must.

maund (mônd), *n.* [Hind. & Per. *man.*] A greatly varying weight of India; also, a corresponding weight of Persia, Turkey, etc. In Madras a maund is about 25 lb.

maun′der (môn′dẽr; män′-), *v. i.* **1.** *Obs.* To grumble; growl. **2.** To move languidly or idly. **3.** To speak indistinctly or disconnectedly; mutter. — **maun′der·er**, *n.*

Maun′dy Thurs′day (môn′dĭ). [OF. *mandé*, fr. L. *mandatum*, fr. *mandare* to command; — from the old custom of washing the feet of the poor on this day as a fulfillment of the "new commandment," *John* xiii, 5, 34.] *Eccl.* The Thursday in Holy Week.

Mau′ser (mou′zẽr), *n.* A trade-mark applied to a certain kind of firearm of the repeating type or for parts therefor.

mau′so·le′um (mô′sō·lē′ŭm), *n.*; *pl.* -LEUMS (-ŭmz), -LEA (-ȧ). [L., fr. Gr. *mausōleion*, fr. *Mausōlos* Mausolus, king of Caria, whose tomb was one of the Seven Wonders of the World.] **1.** A magnificent tomb. **2.** *Chiefly Humorous.* A large, gloomy building, room, or structure.

‖**mau′vaise′ honte** (mô′vāz′ ôɴt′). [F.] Literally, bad shame; bashfulness.

mauve (mōv), *n.* [F., mallow; — from the purplish petals.] A delicate purple, violet, or lilac color; technically, a color, bluish blue-red in hue, of saturation varying from high to very high and of brilliance varying from brilliant to low.

mav′er·ick (măv′ẽr·ĭk), *n.* [After S. A. *Maverick* (1803–1870), a Texas cattle owner who did not brand his calves.] *U. S.* **1.** An unbranded animal, esp. a motherless calf, formerly customarily claimed by the one first branding it. **2.** *Colloq.* A refractory or recalcitrant individual who bolts his party or group and initiates an independent course.

ma′vis (mā′vĭs), *n.* [F. *mauvis.*] The song thrush (*Turdus musicus*) of Europe. See THRUSH.

ma·vour′nin, ma·vour′neen (mȧ·vōōr′nēn), *n.* [Ir. *mo muirnīn.*] My darling; — an Anglo-Irish term of endearment.

maw (mô), *n.* [AS. *maga* stomach.] **1.** A stomach; in birds, the craw. **2.** The stomach as the seat or symbol of voracious appetite. **3.** The throat, gullet, or jaws.

mawk′ish (môk′ĭsh), *adj.* [Orig., maggoty.] **1.** Apt to cause satiety; nauseous. **2.** Marked by sickly sentimentality; weakly sentimental. — **mawk′ish·ly**, *adv.* — **mawk′ish·ness**, *n.*

max·il′la (măk·sĭl′ȧ), *n.*; *pl.* -LAE (-ē). [L.] **1. a** *Anat.* A jaw, esp. an upper jaw; — now used chiefly of man and higher mammals in which the bones of the upper jaw are closely fused together. **b** Either of two membrane bone elements of the upper jaw located lateral to the premaxillae. In higher vertebrates and man they bear most of the upper teeth. **2.** *Zool.* In most arthropods, one of the paired appendages immediately behind the mandibles. See HYMENOPTERON, *Illust.*

max′il·lar′y (măk′sĭ·lẽr′ĭ *or, esp. Brit.*, măks·ĭl′ȧ·rĭ), *adj. Anat. & Zool.* Of, pertaining to, or designating a maxilla. — *n.*; *pl.* -LARIES (-ĭz). A maxillary bone.

max·il′lo- (măk·sĭl′ō-). A combining form for *maxilla*, denoting *maxillary and*, as in **max·il′lo·pal′a·tal**, pertaining to the maxilla and palatine bones.

max′im (măk′sĭm), *n.* [F. *maxime*, fr. L. *maxima* (sc. *sententia*, or a similar noun) the greatest sentence or axiom, i. e., of the greatest authority, fem. fr. *maximus* greatest, superl. of *magnus* great.] A general truth or a rule of conduct expressed in sententious form; esp., a saying of a proverbial nature. — **Syn.** Adage, proverb, saw.

max′i·mal (măk′sĭ·măl), *adj.* Highest; greatest.

Max′i·mal·ist (măk′sĭ·măl·ĭst), *n.* [*maximal* + *-ist.*] A member of the extreme radical group of the former Russian Social Revolutionary party. Cf. MINIMALIST.

Max′im gun (măk′sĭm). *Ordn.* A recoil-operated machine gun, named after its inventor, Hiram S. Maxim.

max′im·ite (măk′sĭm·īt), *n.* [After Hudson *Maxim*, its inventor.] A high explosive of the picric acid class, formerly used in armor-piercing shells.

max′i·mize (măk′sĭ·mīz), *v. t.* [L. *maximus* greatest.] To increase to the highest degree; — opposite of *minimize.* — *v. i.* To interpret a doctrine, duty, etc., in the broadest sense.

max′i·mum (-mŭm), *n.*; *pl.* -MA (-mȧ), -MUMS (-mŭmz). [L., neut. fr. *maximus* the greatest. See MAXIM.] **1.** The greatest quantity or value attainable in a given case; or, the greatest value attained by a quantity which first increases and then begins to decrease; the highest point or degree; — opposed to *minimum.* **2.** An upper limit allowed by law or other authority. — *adj.* **1.** Greatest in quantity or highest in degree attainable or attained. **2.** Pertaining to, marking, or determining a maximum.

ma·xi′xe (mȧ·shē′shȧ; mȧk′sĕks′), *n.* A round dance of Brazilian origin somewhat like the two-step.

max′well (măks′wĕl; -wĕl), *n.* [After James Clerk *Maxwell*, Scot. physicist.] *Elec.* The C.G.S. unit of magnetic flux. It is equal to one gauss—cm^2.

may (mā), *n.* [AS. *mæg.*] *Archaic & Poetic.* A maiden.

may (mā; 4), *v.*; *pres., sing., 1st & 3d pers.* MAY, *2d* MAY′EST (mā′ĕst; -ĭst), MAYST (māst), *pl.* MAY; *past tense* MIGHT (mīt). Infinitive and participles lacking in present use. [AS. pres. *mæg* I am able, pret. *meahte*, *mihte.*] **1.** *v. i. Obs.* To be able. **2.** As an auxiliary verb (see CAN, *Note*), followed by the infinitive without *to*, adding the sense of: **a** *Archaic.* Ability; — now expressed by *can.* **b** Liberty; opportunity; permission; possibility; as, he *may* go. **c** Desire or wish, as in prayer; as, *may* you be happy. **d** Contingency; — used, esp. in clauses of purpose, result, concession, etc.; as, he flatters so that he *may* win favor.

May (mā), *n.* [OF. *mai*, fr. L. *Maius*, fr. (*deus*) *Maius* Jupiter, prop., the great (god).] **1.** The fifth month of the year, having 31 days. Abbr. *My.* **2.** The springtime of life; prime; heyday. **3.** [*not cap.*] The hawthorn or its blossoms; also, any spring-blooming spiraea. **4.** The merrymaking of May Day.

Ma′ya (mä′yȧ; mī′ȧ), *n.* **1.** An Indian of the most important of the Mayan tribes, now inhabiting Yucatán, northern Guatemala, and British Honduras. When discovered, shortly after 1500, the Mayan peoples had a high culture. **2.** The language of the Mayas.

Ma′yan (mä′yăn; mī′ăn), *adj.* Pertaining to or designating an American Indian linguistic family, the Mayas. — *n.* An Indian of the Mayan stock.

May apple, *or* **may′ap′ple** (mā′ăp′'l), *n.* A North American herb (*Podophyllum peltatum*) bearing a single large white flower; also, its yellow, egg-shaped fruit, edible, but of mawkish flavor.

may′be (mā′bē; -bĭ), *adv.* [For *it may be.*] Perhaps.

May Day. The first day of May, often celebrated by the crowning of a May queen with a garland, and by dancing about a Maypole. In Germany, Russia, and other European countries and in the Philippine Islands May Day is observed as Labor Day. — **May′–day′**, *adj.*

May′fair′ (mā′fâr′; mā′fâr′), *n.* A fashionable district in London; — from an annual fair formerly held there in May.

May′flow′er (mā′flou′ẽr), *n.* **1.** *Eng.* Any of several plants whose flowers appear in May, as the hawthorn, the marsh marigold, etc. **2.** *U. S.* Any of several spring-blooming plants: **a** The trailing arbutus, State flower of Massachusetts. **b** The hepatica. **c** Various species of anemone. **3.** The ship which brought the Pilgrims to America in 1620.

May fly. a A fragile, short-lived insect (order Ephemerida); an ephemerid; drake fly. **b** *Angling.* An artificial fly imitating this insect.

may′hap′ (mā′hăp′; mā′hăp), **may′hap′pen** (-hăp′ĕn), *adv.* Also **may′haps′** (-hăps′). [For *it may hap.*] *Archaic & Dial.* Perhaps.

may′hem (mā′hĕm; -ĕm), *n.* [The same as MAIM.] *Law.* The maiming of a person by depriving him of the use of any of his members necessary for him in defending himself; — often extended by statute to cover all willful disfigurings of the body.

May′ing (mā′ĭng), *n.* The celebrating of May Day.

may′on·naise′ (mā′ŏ-nāz′; *F.* mȧ′yô′nâz′), *n.* [F.] A thick sauce of egg yolk beaten up with edible vegetable oil and seasoned; — used in dressing salads, fish, etc.
may′or (mā′ẽr; mâr), *n.* [OF. *maire*, fr. L. *major* greater, higher.] The chief magistrate of a city or borough.
may′or·al·ty (-ăl·tĭ), *n.* Office or term of office of a mayor.
may′or·ess (mā′ẽr-ĕs; mâr′ĕs; -ĭs; 30), *n.* **a** The wife of a mayor. **b** A woman holding the office of mayor.
May′pole′ (mā′pōl′), *n.* A tall pole in an open place and wreathed with flowers, forming a center for May-day sports.
may′pop′ (-pŏp′), *n.* [Corrupt. of *maracock*, an Amer. Indian word.] The insipid, yellow, applelike fruit of a passionflower (*Passiflora incarnata*) of the southern U. S.; also, the plant itself. The blossom was formerly the State flower of Tennessee.
May queen. A girl crowned queen in May-day sports.
May′tide′ (mā′tīd′), **May′time′** (-tīm′), *n.* The month of May.
may′weed′ (-wēd′), *n.* [For *maythe-weed.*] A strong-scented European weed (*Anthemis cotula*) of the aster family, naturalized in the U. S. It has flowers with a yellow disk and white rays.
maz′ard, maz′zard (măz′ẽrd), *n.* *Obs.* **a** A cup or bowl. **b** The head.
Maz′da (măz′dȧ), *n.* A trade-mark applied to certain electric lamps.
Maz′da·ism, Maz′de·ism (măz′dȧ·ĭz′m), *n.* The religion of the ancient Persians. See ORMAZD, ZOROASTRIANISM.
maze (māz), *n.* [ME. *maze, mase.*] **1.** *Now Colloq.* A state of bewilderment. **2.** A confusing and baffling network, as of paths; labyrinth. — *v. t. Now Rare or Archaic.* **a** To make dizzy; daze. **b** To bewilder.
ma′zer (mā′zẽr), *n.* [ME. *maser.*] A large drinking bowl, orig. of a hard wood.
ma·zur′ka (mȧ·zûr′kȧ; mȧ·zōōr′kȧ), **ma·zour′ka** (mȧ·zōōr′kȧ), *n.* [Pol. *mazurka* a woman of the province Mazovia.] **a** A Polish dance in moderate triple measure. **b** Music for this dance, usually in 3/4 or 3/8 measure, slower than the waltz.
ma′zy (mā′zĭ), *adj.*; MA′ZI·ER (-zĭ·ẽr); MA′ZI·EST. [From MAZE.] Perplexed with or as if with turns and windings; winding; intricate. — **ma′zi·ly,** *adv.* — **ma′zi·ness,** *n.*
maz′zard (măz′ẽrd), *n.* [Earlier *mazer.*] The wild sweet cherry (*Prunus avium*), used as rootstocks for improved varieties. See CHERRY, 1.
maz′zard. Var. of MAZARD.
M day (ĕm). Mobilization day, or the day of initial outbreak of active hostilities commencing a war.
me (mē; *weak forms* mĕ, mĭ; 4), *pers. pron.* [AS. *mē*, dat. & acc.] The objective case of *I*, used either as a dative of indirect object, or as the direct object of a verb, etc.
☞ *Me* used predicatively with forms of the verb *be* is acceptable in spoken and informal English instead of *I*; thus, it's *me.*
mead (mēd), *n.* [AS. *meodu.*] A fermented drink of water and honey with malt, yeast, etc.; also, one made from manna. See HYDROMEL.
mead, *n.* [AS. *mǣd.*] *Poetic.* A meadow.
mead′ow (mĕd′ō), *n.* [AS. *mǣdwe*, an inflectional form of *mǣd.*] Grassland, esp. a field on which grass is grown for hay; often, a tract of low or level grassland.
meadow crowfoot. See CROWFOOT, 1.
meadow fescue. A tall European fescue grass (*Festuca elatior*) widely cultivated in Europe and America for permanent pasture and hay. It is sometimes divided into two species, *F. elatior* and *F. pratensis*, the former then being called ***tall fescue***, the latter ***meadow fescue***. See SPIKELET, *Illust.*
meadow grass. **a** Any pasture grass of the genus *Poa*, esp. *P. pratensis*, so called in England, but better known as *Kentucky bluegrass* or *June grass* in the United States. **b** *U. S.* Any grass of the genus *Glyceria;* manna grass.
meadow lark. Any of several North American birds (genus *Sturnella*, family Icteridae), about the size of a robin, with brown and buff upper parts and yellow breast.
meadow mouse. See VOLE.
meadow mushroom. See MUSHROOM.
meadow rue. Any of a genus (*Thalictrum*) of plants of the crowfoot family, with leaves resembling those of rue.
mead′ow·sweet′ (mĕd′ō·swēt′), *n.* **a** Any spiraea; esp., an Asiatic shrub (*Spiraea salicifolia*), with white flowers in terminal panicles, and a common American species (*S. latifolia*). See SPIRAEA. **b** Any plant of a closely related genus (*Filipendula*).
mea′ger, mea′gre (mē′gẽr), *adj.* [OF. *megre, maigre*, fr. L. *macer.*] **1.** Destitute of, or having little, flesh; thin. **2.** Destitute of richness, strength, or the like. — **mea′ger·ly, mea′gre·ly,** *adv.* — **mea′ger·ness, mea′gre·ness,** *n.*
Syn. **Meager, scanty, scant, exiguous, spare, sparse** mean falling short of that which is normal or necessary. **Meager** implies thinness, esp. in substance, quality, or the like; **scanty,** insufficiency in amount, quantity, extent; **scant,** deficiency in amount, quantity, etc., of that which is desired or desirable; **exiguous,** a marked deficiency in number or measure; **spare,** a falling short of that which is enough or ample; **sparse,** a thin scattering of units, esp. where density or the like is desirable (as, a *meager* diet; a *scanty* supply; *scant* weight; an *exiguous* navy; *spare* vegetation; *sparse* population).
meal (mēl), *n.* [AS. *melu, melo.*] **1. a** Coarsely ground and unbolted grain, esp. cereal grain; specif., *U. S.*, Indian meal. **b** Hence, a similar product made by grinding other seeds, or nuts. **2.** Any substance resembling meal (sense 1 **a**).
meal, *n.* [AS. *mǣl* measure, mark, sign, appointed time, a meal.] The portion of food taken at one time to satisfy appetite; also, act or time of eating a meal.
-meal (-mēl). [AS. *-mǣlum*, orig. dat. pl. of *mǣl* measure. See MEAL repast.] A suffix used formerly in forming adverbs, and signifying the *measure* or *portion taken at one time*, as in piece*meal.*
meal′ies (mēl′ĭz), *n. pl.; sing.* MEALIE (-ĭ), MEALY (-ĭ). [S. Afr. D. *milje*, fr. Pg. *milho* maize, millet, fr. L. *milium* millet.] *S. Africa.* Maize, or Indian corn. In *sing.*, an ear of maize.
meal′time′ (mēl′tīm′), *n.* The usual time for eating.
meal worm. The larva of certain beetles (family Tenebrionidae) that infests granaries, bakeries, etc., and is injurious to flour and meal.
meal′y (mēl′ĭ), *adj.*; MEAL′I·ER (-ĭ·ẽr); MEAL′I·EST. **1.** Soft, dry, and friable, like meal. **2.** Containing meal; farinaceous. **3.** Overspread with or as with meal. **4.** Soft-spoken; mealymouthed. **5.** Flecked with white or gray; spotty; also, pale; floury. — **meal′i·ness,** *n.*

meal′y-mouthed′ (-mouthd′; -moutht′; 2), *adj.* Smooth, plausible, and insincere; as, a *mealymouthed* orator.
mean (mēn), *v. t.*; MEANT (mĕnt); MEAN′ING. [AS. *mǣnan* to recite, tell, intend, wish.] **1.** To have in the mind as a purpose; to intend. **2.** To have in mind as the object, signification, or the like, of any expression or symbol; hence, to signify; denote; as, the words do not *mean* that. **3.** To have in mind a particular reference or destination for (a remark, gift, or the like); as, his criticism is not *meant* for me. — *v. i.* **1.** To have a purpose or intention. *Rare*, except in *to mean well*, or *ill.* **2.** To be of a (specified) degree of importance in influence or effect; as, environment *means* much to a child.
mean, *adj.* [AS. *gemǣne* common, general.] **1.** Destitute of distinction; common; humble. **2.** Destitute of power or acumen; ordinary; as, a man of *mean* intelligence. **3.** Of little value; of poor quality; shabby; contemptible. **4.** Ignoble; base. **5.** Penurious; stingy. **6.** *Colloq., U. S.* **a** Characterized by petty selfishness or malice; contemptibly ill-tempered. **b** Ashamed; "small"; as, to feel *mean;* also, indisposed.
Syn. **Mean, ignoble, abject, sordid** mean below standards of human behavior or dignity. **Mean** usually suggests repellent antisocial characteristics such as small-mindedness, malevolence, or cupidity; **ignoble** suggests loss or lack of some essential high quality of mind or soul, such as moral excellence or elevation; **abject,** in its most inclusive sense, suggests extreme lowness in station, degree, or scale, but often, specifically, degradation, debasement, servility, etc.; **sordid,** seldom applied to men but to their surroundings, circumstances, etc., suggests repellent dullness, drabness, drudgery, or the like.
mean, *adj.* [OF. *meien* (F. *moyen*), fr. L. *medianus* that is in the middle, fr. *medius* middle.] **1.** Occupying a middle position; intermediate in place, time, order, etc. **2.** *Math.* Average; having an intermediate value between two extremes; as, *mean* distance; *mean* motion.
— *n.* **1.** *Obs.* Something intermediate. **2.** The middle point, or that which is at or near it; as, the golden *mean;* hence, medium; moderation. **3.** That through which, or by the help of which, an end is attained; — now always in the pl. form, *means*, with either sing. or pl. sense and construction. **4.** *pl.* Resources; property, revenue, or the like. **5.** *Math.* A quantity having an intermediate value between several others from which it is derived and of which it expresses the mean value. Usually, it is the one simple average (***arithmetical mean***) formed by adding the quantities together and dividing by their number. The ***geometric mean*** of two quantities is the square root of the product of the quantities.
Syn. (1) See AVERAGE.
(2) In plural form *means.* **Means, instrument, agent, agency, medium** mean a person or thing through or by which an end is effected. **Means** may be used abstractedly or with definite reference to a person or a thing of any sort; **instrument** always implies someone or something definite used as a means (often suggesting a tool) of carrying out one's intentions; **agent** implies a person, or sometimes a thing, acting to achieve the ends conceived by another's **agency,** the activity or operation of a person or thing which serves as a cause producing an effect; **medium** implies the means by which something is conveyed, transmitted, communicated, or the like.
me·an′der (mē-ăn′dẽr), *n.* [L. *maeander*, fr. Gr. *maiandros*, fr. *Maiandros*, a river in Phrygia proverbial for its windings (now the Menderes).] A turn or winding, as of a stream; hence, a winding path or course; a labyrinth. — *v. i. & t.* **1.** To wind or turn in a course; to follow a meander or intricate course. **2.** To wander aimlessly or listlessly.
mean distance (of a planet from the sun). *Astron.* The mean of the perihelion and aphelion distances, which is equivalent to half the major axis of the orbit.
me·an′drous (mē-ăn′drŭs), *adj.* Winding; flexuous.
mean′ing (mēn′ĭng), *n.* **1.** That which is meant; intent; aim; object. **2.** That which one intends to convey by an act or, esp., by language; also, sense in which a statement, or the like, is understood. **3.** Hence, sense; significance; as, a look full of *meaning.* — **mean′ing·ful,** *adj.*
Syn. **Meaning, sense, acceptation, signification, significance, import** denote the idea conveyed to the mind. **Meaning,** the general term, is used of anything requiring interpretation, such as a word, a sign, a poem; **sense,** of the meaning (or one of the meanings) of a word or phrase; **acceptation,** of a sense of a word or phrase as accepted by a large number of writers and speakers; **signification,** of the meaning of a term, symbol, character, or the like, esp. as established; **significance,** of the covert as distinguished from the ostensible meaning (or lack of meaning) of a speech, a book, or the like; **import,** of the meaning a person wishes to convey, esp. through language.
— *adj.* Intending; also, significant; as, a *meaning* look. — **mean′ing·ly,** *adv.*
mean′ing·less, *adj.* Without meaning. — **mean′ing·less·ly,** *adv.* — **mean′ing·less·ness,** *n.*
mean′ly, *adv.* [From MEAN common.] In a mean manner; specif.: **a** Poorly; humbly. **b** In an inferior manner; badly. **c** Ungenerously; stingily; shabbily.
mean′ly, *adv.* [From MEAN middle.] *Obs.* Moderately.
mean′ness, *n.* **1.** Condition or quality of being mean (in various senses). **2.** A mean act; as, to be guilty of a *meanness.*
means (mēnz), *n., pl.* of MEAN (see esp. defs. 3 & 4).
means test. *Brit.* The test made of an unemployed person's means, at the cessation of his unemployment insurance payments, to determine his eligibility to receive further payments from noninsurance funds.
mean sun. *Astron.* A fictitious sun supposed (for purposes of calculation) to move uniformly in the equator. When the mean sun is on the meridian it is **mean noon.**
meant (mĕnt), *past & past part.* of MEAN.
mean′time′ (mēn′tīm′; 2), *adv.* Also **mean′while′** (-hwīl′). In the intervening time; at the same time. — *n.* The intervening time.
mean time, *or* **mean solar time.** Time as measured by the apparent westward motion of the mean sun, but actually due to the uniform eastward turning of the earth on its axis.
mean′while′ (mēn′hwīl′), *adv.* See MEANTIME.
mea′sled (mē′z′ld), *adj.* Infected with measles, as pork.
mea′sles (mē′z′lz), *n.; pl. in form, but used as singular in senses* 1 & 2 **a.** [ME. *masel*, pl. *maseles, mesel.*] **1.** *Med.* **a** A contagious febrile disease, marked by the appearance of round red spots on the skin. **b** With qualifier, any of various other eruptive diseases; as, German *measles* (see RUBELLA). **2.** [Prob. fr. ME. *mesel* leprous.]

Veter. **a** A disease of cattle and swine caused by the larvae of certain tapeworms (genus *Taenia*). **b** *pl.* The larvae causing this disease.

mea′sly (mē′zlĭ), *adj.*; MEA′SLI·ER (-zlĭ-ĕr); MEA′SLI·EST. **1.** Infected with measles. **2.** Containing larval tapeworms; — said of meat. **3.** *Slang.* Contemptible; mean.

meas′ur·a·ble (mĕzh′ẽr·å·b'l), *adj.* Capable of being measured. — **meas′ur·a·bil′i·ty** (-bĭl′ĭ·tĭ), **meas′ur·a·ble·ness**, *n.* — **meas′ur·a·bly**, *adv.*

meas′ure (mĕzh′ẽr), *n.* [OF. *mesure*, fr. LL. *mensura*, fr. *metiri*, *mensus*, to measure.] **1.** Due or given extent, degree, or quantity; specif.: **a** Extent or degree not excessive; due limitation; — esp. in: *in measure; without, or beyond, measure;* etc. **b** Determined extent; prescribed limit. **2.** An instrument for measuring, as a yardstick, a graduated tape, or a vessel of known capacity. **3.** The dimensions, capacity, or quantity of anything, determined by measuring. **4.** *Poetic.* A tune; melody. **5.** Act or process of ascertaining the extent, dimensions, quantity, degree, capacity, or the like, of a thing. **6.** A system of measurement; as, long *measure;* board *measure.* See also *Tables* at METRIC SYSTEM and WEIGHT.

TABLES
(with metric equivalents)
1. Linear Measure or Long Measure

12 inches (in., *pl.* in. *or* ins.; *symbol* ″)	= 1 foot (ft., *sing. & pl.; symbol* ′)
3 feet	= 1 yard (yd., *pl. yd. or* yds.)
5½ yards or 16½ feet	= 1 rod (rd.) or pole (p.) or perch (p.)
40 rods	= 1 furlong (fur.)
8 furlongs or 1760 yards or 5280 feet	= 1 mile (m. *or* mi.) (English *statute* mile)
3 miles	= 1 (land) league

Metric Equivalents: 1 in. = 2.54 cm.; 1 ft. = 0.3048 m.; 1 yd. = 0.9144 m.; 1 rd. = 5.029 m.; 1 fur. = 201.17 m.; 1 mi. = 1.6093 km. or 1609.3 m.; 1 league = 4.83 km.

2. Chain Measure

7.92 inches	= 1 link (li.)
100 links or 66 feet	= 1 chain (ch.)
10 chains	= 1 furlong (fur.)
80 chains	= 1 mile (mi.)

The *engineer's chain* is 100 feet long, with links one foot long (52.8 chains = 1 mile). *Metric Equivalents:* 1 link = 20.12 cm.; 1 chain = 20.12 m.

3. Square Measure (Area)

144 square inches (sq. in.)	= 1 square foot (sq. ft.)
9 square feet	= 1 square yard (sq. yd.)
30¼ square yards	= 1 square rod (sq. rd.) or square pole or square perch (sq. p.)
160 square rods or 4840 square yards or 43,560 square feet	= 1 acre (A.)

Metric equivalents: 1 sq. in. = 6.452 sq. cm.; 1 sq. ft. = 929 sq. cm. (0.0929 sq. m.); 1 sq. yd. = 0.8361 sq. m.; 1 sq. rd. = 25.29 sq. m.; 1 acre = 40.4687 ares (0.4047 ha.).

4. Surveyor's Measure (Area)

625 square links (sq. li.)	= 1 square pole (sq. p.)
16 square poles	= 1 square chain (sq. ch.)
10 square chains	= 1 acre (A.)
640 acres	= 1 square mile (sq. mi.) or 1 section (sec.)
36 square miles	= 1 township (tp.)

Metric Equivalents: 1 sq. mi. = 259 ha. (2.59 sq. km.); 1 tp. = 9324.0 ha. (93.24 sq. km.).

5. Cubic Measure (Volume)

1728 cubic inches (cu. in.)	= 1 cubic foot (cu. ft.)
27 cubic feet	= 1 cubic yard (cu. yd.)
(for measuring cordwood, etc.)	
16 cubic feet	= 1 cord foot (cd. ft.) or 4′ × 4′ × 1′
8 cord feet or 128 cubic feet	= 1 cord (cd.) or 4′ × 4′ × 8′

Metric Equivalents: 1 cu. in. = 16.387 cu. cm.; 1 cu. ft. = 0.0283 cu. m.; 1 cu. yd. = 0.7646 cu. m. = 3.625 cu. m.

6. Time Measure

60 seconds (sec. *or* s.; *symbol* ″)	= 1 minute (min. *or* m.; *symbol* ′)
60 minutes	= 1 hour (hr.)
24 hours	= 1 day (da. *or* d.)
7 days	= 1 week (wk.)
30 days (commonly)	= 1 calendar month (mo.)
365 days or 12 calendar months	= 1 common year (yr.)
366 days	= 1 leap year
100 years	= 1 century

The length of the *astronomical year* is about 365¼ days, or 365 days, 5 hours, 48 minutes, 45.51 seconds. As the *common year* is 365 days, it becomes necessary once in every four years to add a day to the year, making the *leap year* of 366 days. See LEAP YEAR, in *Vocab.* For *sidereal day, hour, minute, second,* see SIDEREAL, *adj.*, in *Vocab.*

7. Circular Measure

60 seconds (″)	= 1 minute (′)
60 minutes	= 1 degree (°)
90 degrees	= 1 quadrant
4 quadrants or 360 degrees	= 1 circle

8. Longitude and Time

1 second of longitude (″)	= ¹⁄₁₅ sec. of time
1 minute " " (′)	= 4 sec. of time
1 degree " " (°)	= 4 min. of time
15 degrees " "	= 1 hour
360 degrees " "	= 24 hours

9. Nautical Measure

6 feet	= 1 fathom (f. or fm.)
100 fathoms	= 1 cable's length (ordinary). A cable's length, however, is taken variously as: 608 ft. (Br.), 720 ft. or 120 fathoms (U. S. Navy).
10 cables' lengths	= 1 nautical mile of 6080 ft. (Br., the *Admiralty mile*) or 6080.20 ft. (former U. S.). A nautical, or geographical or sea, mile is the length of a minute of arc, or ¹⁄₂₁₆₀₀, of a great circle of the earth. Because the earth is not a perfect sphere several different values are in use. The international nautical mile of 6076.1033 ft. was adopted officially in the U. S. on July 1, 1954.
3 nautical miles	= 1 (marine) league
60 nautical miles	= 1 degree (of a great circle of the earth)

Metric Equivalents: 1 fathom = 1.829 m.; 1 nautical mile of 6080 ft. = 1853.2 m., of 6080.20 ft. = 1853.248 m., of 6076.1033 ft. = 1852 m.

10. Dry Measure (Grain, Fruit, etc.)

2 pints (pt.)	= 1 quart (qt.)	= 67.20 cu. in.	= 1.1012 l.
8 quarts	= 1 peck (pk.)	= 537.61 cu. in.	= 8.8096 l.
4 pecks	= 1 bushel (bu.)	= 2150.42 cu. in.	= 35.2383 l.

The British dry quart = 1.0320 U. S. dry quarts, as given above. The weight of a bushel of wheat, as fixed by the United States government, is 60 lb. avoirdupois; of barley, 48 lb.; of oats, 32 lb.; of rye, 56 lb.; and of Indian corn, 56 lb. In the various states, a bushel of corn varies in weight from 52 to 56 lb., and of barley from 32 to 50 lb. The customary legal weight of a bushel of potatoes is 60 lb., but in North Carolina and West Virginia it is 56 lb.

11. Liquid Measure

4 gills (gi.)	= 1 pint (pt.)	= 28.875 cu. in.	= 0.4732 l.
2 pints	= 1 quart (qt.)	= 57.75 cu. in.	= 0.9463 l.
4 quarts	= 1 gallon (gal.)	= 231 cu. in.	= 3.7853 l.

A *gill* = 0.118 l. The *imperial gallon* of Great Britain (= 277.420 cu. in.) contains 4 *imperial quarts* each of which = 1.20095 U. S. liquid quarts. The *barrel* is usually 31½ gallons in U. S., or 36 imperial gallons in Great Britain. See also in *Vocab.* HOGSHEAD; 1st BUTT; PIPE, 7; TUN, 2.

12. Apothecaries' Fluid Measure (Drugs, etc.)

60 minims or drops (♏)	= 1 fluid dram (f℈)
8 fluid drams	= 1 fluid ounce (f℥)
16 (in U. S.; in Britain 20) fluid ounces	= 1 pint (O. or o.)
8 pints	= 1 gallon (C. or c.)

Metric Equivalents: 1 minim = 0.062 ml. (U. S.); 1 fluid ounce = 0.2976 dl. or 0.0297 l.

7. A unit of measurement, esp. a unit of length, area, or volume. **8.** Any standard with reference to which something is valued or estimated; a criterion. **9.** Regulated division of movement; rhythm. **10.** An extent, degree, or quantity (of something); as, a *measure* of indulgence is due to children. **11.** A step or definite part of a progressive course or policy; specif., a legislative enactment. **12.** *Arith.* A number contained in a given number a number of times without a remainder. **13.** *Dancing.* A dance; esp., a slow and stately dance. **14.** *Geol. pl.* Beds or strata, esp. of coal. **15.** *Music.* The group of beats made by the regular recurrence of primary, or heavy, accents, the position of which is marked on the staff by bars just before them. Hence, the notes or rests between two adjacent bars. **16.** *Pros.* Measured rhythm in verse; meter.
— *v. t.* [OF. *mesurer*, fr. LL. *mensurare.* See MEASURE, *n.*] **1.** To ascertain the extent, degree, or capacity of, by a standard; hence, to estimate. **2.** *Archaic.* To allot by measure. **3.** To determine or lay off in measuring, as a distance. **4.** To pass through or over in journeying. **5.** To mark the bounds or limits of; — with *out.* **6.** To serve as the measure of; as, the thermometer *measures* changes of temperature. **7.** To bring into comparison or competition (with); as, to *measure* one's skill against a rival. — *v. i.* **1.** To take or make a measurement; to measure something. **2.** To result, or turn out, on being measured, esp. in respect of length, breadth, etc.; as, the cloth *measured* three yards. — **meas′ur·er** (mĕzh′ẽr·ẽr), *n.*

meas′ured (mĕzh′ẽrd), *adj.* **1.** Regulated by a standard; hence, uniform; graduated; also, calculated; deliberated. **2.** Metrical; rhythmical. — **meas′ured·ly**, *adv.*

meas′ure·less, *adj.* Without measure; immeasurable.

meas′ure·ment (mĕzh′ẽr·mĕnt), *n.* **1.** Act or result of measuring something; mensuration. **2.** The extent, capacity, or amount ascertained by measuring. **3.** A system of measures.

meas′ur·ing worm (mĕzh′ẽr·ĭng). The larva of any geometrid moth. See GEOMETRID.

meat (mēt), *n.* [AS. *mete.*] **1.** Food in general; esp., solid food; hence, the edible part of anything; as, the *meat* of a lobster, a nut, an egg. **2.** The flesh of animals used as food; specif., = FLESH, *n.*, 2. **3.** A meal; specif., dinner; the chief meal; — esp. in the phrases *at, before,* or *after, meat,* etc. — **meat′less**, *adj.*

meat′man′ (mēt′măn′), *n.* A butcher; one who vends meat.

me·a′tus (mē·ā′tŭs), *n.; pl.* -TUSES (-ĕz; -ĭz), -TUS. [L., a passage, fr. *meare* to go.] *Anat.* **a** A natural passage or canal. **b** The opening of such a passage.

meat′y (mēt′ĭ), *adj.*; MEAT′I·ER (-ĭ·ẽr); MEAT′I·EST. Abounding in, or resembling, meat; hence, full of matter for thought; pithy; also, solid; substantial.

Mec′ca (mĕk′å), *n.* An Arabian city, birthplace of Mohammed and holy city of the Moslems (cf. KAABA); hence [*often not cap.*], any place sought by numbers of people as a goal. — **Mec′can** (-ăn), *adj.*

me·chan′ic (mē·kăn′ĭk), *adj.* [L. *mechanicus,* fr. Gr. *mēchanikos,* fr. *mēchanē* machine. See MACHINE.] **1.** Pert. to manual labor; involving manual skill; as, the *mechanic* arts. **2.** Of or pert. to a mechanic or artisan, or the artisan class. **3.** Of the nature of, relating to, or derived from, a machine or machines; mechanical; as, *mechanic* devices. — *n.* One who practices any mechanic art; an artisan.

me·chan′i·cal (-ĭ·kăl), *adj.* **1.** Of, pertaining to, or concerned with, machinery or manual operations; made by a machine or with tools; as, *mechanical* employment. **2.** Of, pertaining to, or concerned with, manual labor; of the artisan class. **3.** Done as if by a machine; proceeding automatically; as, *mechanical* singing. **4.** Pert. to, governed by, or in accordance with, mechanics; as, *mechanical* work, principles.

5. Explaining phenomena in terms of mechanics; as, *mechanical* physiologists. — **Syn.** See SPONTANEOUS. — **me·chan′i·cal·ly,** *adv.*

mechanical advantage. *Mech.* The ratio of the force which performs useful work of a machine to the force which is applied to the machine; — called also ***actual mechanical advantage.*** The ***theoretical mechanical advantage*** is the ratio of the distance which the applied force moves to the distance which the resisting force moves.

mech′a·ni′cian (mĕk′ȧ·nĭsh′ăn), *n.* One skilled in the theory or construction of machines; a mechanic.

me·chan′ics (mē·kăn′ĭks), *n.; see* -ICS. **1.** That part of physical science which treats of the action of forces on bodies. Cf. DYNAMICS, STATICS, KINETICS, KINEMATICS. **2.** The practical application of the principles of physics, esp. the laws of motion, and of the effect of forces upon the properties of bodies, to the working of machines. **3.** Mechanical details; as, the *mechanics* of play writing.

mech′a·nism (mĕk′ȧ·nĭz′m), *n.* **1.** The parts of a machine, taken collectively; the arrangement or relation of the parts of anything as adapted to produce an effect. **2.** Mechanical operation or action. **3.** *Philos. & Biol.* **a** A natural process conceived as being machine-like or mechanically necessitated. **b** The doctrine that natural processes are mechanically determined and capable of explanation by the laws of physics and chemistry. Cf. TELEOLOGY, 2. **4.** *Psychol.* **a** The combination of mental processes by which a result is obtained; as, the *mechanism* of invention. **b** The means unconsciously adopted to gratify a desire; as, a ***defense mechanism,*** one adopted to conceal a person's weaknesses.

mech′a·nist (-nĭst), *n.* **1.** *Rare.* One skilled in mechanics. **2.** *Philos.* One who holds the doctrine of mechanism.

mech′a·nis′tic (-nĭs′tĭk), *adj.* **1.** Mechanically determined; as, a concept of a *mechanistic* universe. **2.** Of or pert. to the theory of philosophical mechanism. **3.** Mechanical.

mech′a·nize (mĕk′ȧ·nīz), *v. t.* **1.** To make mechanical or machine-like; esp., to replace personnel with machinery wherever possible. **2.** *Mil.* To equip with mechanical aids for the efficiency and protection of personnel, esp. armed and armored self-propelling motor vehicles from which to fight. — **mech′a·ni·za′tion** (-nĭ·zā′shŭn; -nī·zā′-), *n.*

mech′a·no·mor′phism (mĕk′ȧ·nō·môr′fĭz′m), *n.* The conception of deity as a force or energy, operating mechanically or according to the laws of physics or chemistry. — **mech′a·no·mor′phic** (-fĭk), *adj.*

mech′a·no·ther′a·py (-thĕr′ȧ·pĭ), *n.* *Med.* Treatment of disease by mechanical means, esp. by forced movements.

Mech′lin lace (mĕk′lĭn). Orig., any Flemish lace; now, a dainty bobbin lace made in Malines (Mechlin), Belgium.

med′al (mĕd′'l), *n.* [F. *médaille,* fr. It. *medaglia,* deriv. of L. *metallum* metal.] A piece of metal, cast or struck with a device, etc., intended to preserve the remembrance of a notable event or person, or to serve as a reward. See SERVICE MEDAL. — *v. t.;* -ALED or -ALLED (-'ld); -AL·ING or -AL·LING. To honor or reward with a medal.

Medal for Merit. *U.S.* A decoration awarded to civilians for exceptionally meritorious conduct in the performance of outstanding services.

med′al·ist, med′al·list (mĕd′'l·ĭst), *n.* **a** A designer, engraver, or maker of medals. **b** One who has gained a medal as a reward.

me·dal′lion (mē·dăl′yŭn), *n.* [F. *médaillon,* fr. It. *medaglione,* augm. of *medaglia.* See MEDAL.] **1.** A large medal. **2.** Something resembling a large medal, as a tablet bearing a figure in relief, a portrait, or a design in lace.

Medal of Honor. *Mil., U. S.* A decoration awarded in the name of the Congress for conspicuous gallantry and intrepidity at the risk of life above and beyond the call of duty in action with an enemy.

medal play. *Golf.* Play in which the score is reckoned by counting the total strokes for the round of the course. Cf. MATCH PLAY **b.**

med′dle (mĕd′'l), *v. i.;* MED′DLED (-'ld); MED′DLING (-lĭng). [OF. *medler, mesler,* deriv. of a dim. of L. *miscere* to mix.] **1.** *Obs.* To mix; mingle; also, to fight. **2.** To interest oneself unnecessarily or impertinently; interfere. — **med′dler** (-lẽr), *n.*

med′dle·some (-sŭm), *adj.* Given to meddling; officiously intrusive. — **Syn.** See IMPERTINENT. — **med′dle·some·ness,** *n.*

Mede (mēd), *n.* One of the people of ancient Media, a kingdom in what is now northwestern Persia, which attained its greatest power 700–500 B.C.

Me·de′a (mē·dē′ȧ), *n.* [L., fr. Gr. *Mēdeia.*] An enchantress, daughter of Aeëtes, King of Colchis. She helped Jason to win the Golden Fleece and returned with him to Iolcus, retarding her father's pursuit by strewing the sea with the limbs of her brother. She restored Jason's father to youth, and brought about the death of Pelias. When Jason deserted her, she sent her rival a poisoned robe, killed her own children, set fire to the palace, and fled.

me′di·a (mē′dĭ·ȧ), *n.; pl.* MEDIAE (-ē). [NL., fr. L. *medius* middle.] **1.** *Phonet.* One of the sonant mutes (voiced stops), β, δ, γ (*b, d, g*), in Greek, or their equivalents in other languages, so named as intermediate between the *tenues,* π, τ, κ (*p, t, k*), and the *aspirates* φ, θ, χ (*ph* or *f, th, ch*). **2.** *Anat.* The middle coat of the wall of a blood vessel.

me′di·a, *n., pl.* of MEDIUM.

me′di·a·cy (mē′dĭ·ȧ·sĭ), *n.* Mediate state or quality; also, intermediate agency.

me′di·ae′val, -ae′val·ism, etc. Vars. of MEDIEVAL, etc.

me′di·al (mē′dĭ·ăl; 58), *adj.* [LL. *medialis,* fr. *medius* middle.] **1.** Being, situated, or occurring, in the middle; median. **2.** *Phonet.* Situated within a word, as *g* in *aged, eagle.* **3.** Of or pertaining to a mean or average; mean; average. — *n. Gram.* A medial letter; also, a form of a letter used medially. — **me′di·al·ly,** *adv.*

me′di·an (-ăn), *adj.* [L. *medianus.*] **1.** Being in the middle; medial; middle. **2.** *Statistics.* Designating a point so chosen in a series that half of the individuals in the series are on one side of it, and half on the other. To illustrate the distinction between *median* and *average,* suppose five persons have wages respectively of $3, $4, $5, $7, and $11. The *average* wage is $6; the *median* wage is $5. **3.** *Zool.* Lying in a plane dividing a bilateral animal into right and left halves. — *n.* A median line, point, or number. — **Syn.** See AVERAGE.

me′di·ant (mē′dĭ·ănt), *n.* *Music.* The third note above the keynote, dividing the interval between the tonic and dominant into two thirds.

me′di·as·ti′num (mē′dĭ·ăs·tī′nŭm), *n.; pl.* -TINA (-nȧ). [NL., fr. ML. *mediastinus* medial, fr. *medius* middle.] *Anat.* The space containing the heart and all the viscera of the chest except the lungs.

me′di·ate (mē′dĭ·ĭt), *adj.* [LL. *mediatus,* past part. of *mediare,* v. t., to halve, v. i., to be in the middle.] **1.** *Rare.* Intermediate. **2.** Acting by an intervening cause or instrument; not direct. **3.** Gained or effected through an intermediate agency or condition. — (-āt), *v. i.* To interpose between parties as the equal friend of each, esp. to effect a reconciliation. — *v. t.* **1.** To effect or settle by mediation. **2.** To act as the intermediary or medium in effecting, bringing about, transferring, or the like. — **Syn.** See INTERPOSE.

me′di·ate·ly (mē′dĭ·ĭt·lĭ), *adv.* In a mediate manner; by or through an intervening cause or agent; — opposed to *immediately.*

me′di·a′tion (-ā′shŭn), *n.* **1.** Act of mediating; specif., intervention. **2.** *Internat. Law.* Intercession of one power between other powers on their invitation or consent to arrange amicably differences between them.

me′di·a′tive (mē′dĭ·ā′tĭv), *adj.* Mediating; used in mediation.

me′di·a·tize (-ȧ·tīz), *v. t.* [From F. *mediatiser,* or G. *mediatisieren.*] **1.** Under the Holy Roman Empire, to cause (a prince or state) to hold mediately instead of immediately of the empire; hence, to annex (a state, etc.) to another, the former sovereign being allowed to retain his title and usually some governmental rights. **2.** To render mediate; to cause to be mediate in position. — **me′di·a·ti·za′tion** (-tĭ·zā′shŭn; -tī·zā′-), *n.*

me′di·a′tor (-ā′tẽr), *n.* One who mediates; esp., one who interposes between parties at variance to reconcile them.

me′di·a·to′ry (-ȧ·tō′rĭ; -tẽr·ĭ), *adj.* Of, pertaining to, or of the nature of mediation. — **me′di·a·to′ri·al** (-tō′rĭ·ăl; 70), *adj.*

me′di·a′tress (mē′dĭ·ā′trĕs; -trĭs), *n.* Also **me′di·a′trice** (-ā′trĭs), **me′di·a′trix** (-ā′trĭks). A female mediator.

med′ic (mĕd′ĭk), *n.* [L. *medica,* fr. Gr. *mēdikē* (sc. *poa*) a kind of clover from *Media,* fr. *Medikos* Median.] Any of a genus (*Medicago*) of cloverlike herbs, esp. the alfalfa. The ***black medic*** is *M. lupulina.* See SHAMROCK, *Illust.*

med′ic, *n.* **a** A physician. **b** *Colloq.* A medical student.

med′i·ca·ble (mĕd′ĭ·kȧ·b'l), *adj.* [L. *medicabilis,* fr. *medicare, medicari,* to heal, fr. *medicus* physician.] Capable of being medicated, cured, or healed.

med′i·cal (mĕd′ĭ·kăl), *adj.* [F. *médical,* fr. LL. *medicalis,* fr. L. *medicus* physician.] Of, pertaining to, or dealing with the healing art or the science of medicine. — **med′i·cal·ly,** *adv.*

medical examiner. *Law.* A governmental official whose functions are to make post-mortem examination of bodies dead from violence, suicide, crime, etc., and to investigate the circumstances of the death. Cf. CORONER.

me·dic′a·ment (mē·dĭk′ȧ·mĕnt; mĕd′ĭ·kȧ-), *n.* [L. *medicamentum.*] A medicine; a healing application.

med′i·cate (mĕd′ĭ·kāt), *v. t.* [L. *medicatus,* past part. of *medicare, medicari,* to heal.] **1.** To treat with medicine; to cure. **2.** To impregnate with anything medicinal; to drug.

med′i·ca′tion (-kā′shŭn), *n.* Act or process of medicating; medical treatment; also, a medicament.

med′i·ca′tive (mĕd′ĭ·kā′tĭv; -kȧ·tĭv), *adj.* Medicinal; curative.

Med′i·ce′an (mĕd′ĭ·sē′ăn), *adj.* Of or pert. to a Florentine family, the Medici, of the 14th, 15th, and 16th centuries.

me·dic′i·na·ble (mē·dĭs′ĭ·nȧ·b'l; *older pron.* mĕd′sĭn·ȧ·b'l), *adj.* *Archaic.* Medicinal; healing.

me·dic′i·nal (mē·dĭs′ĭ·năl; -n'l; *form.* mĕd′sĭ·năl *or* mĕd′ĭ·sī′năl), *adj.* [OF.] Curative or alleviative. — **me·dic′i·nal·ly,** *adv.*

med′i·cine (mĕd′ĭ·sĭn; -s'n; *Brit., except in Scotland, usually* mĕd′sĭn *or, esp. in sense* 2, mĕd′ĭ·sĭn), *n.* [OF. *medicine, medecine,* fr. L. *medicina,* fr. *medicus.* See MEDICAL.] **1.** Any preparation used in treating disease. **2. a** The science and art dealing with the prevention, cure, or alleviation of disease. **b** In a narrower sense, that part of this science and art which is the province of the physician as distinguished from the surgeon and obstetrician. **3.** *Obs.* A drug or the like used for a purpose not curative, as a love potion, a poison, etc. **4.** Among the North American Indians, any object supposed to give control over natural or magical forces; also, magical power or a magical rite. — *v. t.* To give medicine to.

medicine ball. A large, stuffed, leather-covered ball weighing several pounds, tossed and caught for exercise.

medicine lodge. Among the North American Indians, a lodge for ceremonial dances, initiations, etc.

medicine man. Among the North American Indians and other primitive peoples, a person who professes to cure sickness by drugs, charms, and fetishes; a shaman; magician.

med′i·co (mĕd′ĭ·kō), *n.; pl.* -COS (-kōz). [Sp. *médico* physician, or It. *medico.*] *Colloq.* A physician, surgeon, or medical student.

med′i·co- (mĕd′ĭ·kō-). [L. *medicus.*] A combining form signifying: **a** *Medical,* as in **med′i·co·ma′ni·a, med′i·co·psy·chol′o·gy.** **b** *Medical and,* as in **med′i·co·le′gal.**

me′di·e′val, me′di·ae′val (mē′dĭ·ē′văl *or, esp. Brit.,* mĕd′ĭ-), *adj.* [L. *medius* middle + *aevum* age.] Of, pertaining to, or characteristic of the Middle Ages; as, *medieval* architecture; like the literature, art, etc., of the Middle Ages. — **me′di·e′val·ly, me′di·ae′val·ly,** *adv.*

me′di·e′val·ism, me′di·ae′val·ism (-ĭz′m), *n.* Medieval belief or practice; the method or spirit of the Middle Ages; devotion to the institutions, arts, and practices of the Middle Ages; also, a survival from the Middle Ages. — **me′di·e′val·ist, me′di·ae′val·ist** (-ĭst), *n.*

Medieval Latin. See LATIN, *n.,* 1. Abbr. *ML.*

me′di·o- (mē′dĭ·ō-), **me′di-** (mē′dĭ-). [L. *medius.*] A combining form meaning *middle.*

me′di·o′cre (mē′dĭ·ō′kẽr; mē′dĭ·ō′kẽr; 2), *adj.* [F. *médiocre,* fr. L. *mediocris,* fr. *medius* middle + *ocris* peak.] Of but moderate excellence; ordinary.

me′di·oc′ri·ty (-ŏk′rĭ·tĭ), *n.; pl.* -TIES (-tĭz). **1** Quality or state of being mediocre; moderate ability, skill, etc. **2.** A mediocre person.

med′i·tate (mĕd′ĭ·tāt), *v. t.* [L. *meditatus,* past part. of *meditari* to meditate.] **1.** *Rare.* To contemplate; ponder. **2.** To intend; plan. — *v. i.* To dwell in thought; to muse; reflect; cogitate. — **Syn.** See PONDER. — **med′i·ta′tor** (-tā′tẽr), *n.*

med′i·ta′tion (-tā′shŭn), *n.* **1.** Act of meditating; thought; esp., close or continued thought. **2.** A form of private devotion consisting of deep, continued reflection on some religious theme. **3.** A treatise or discourse treating a theme meditatively.

med′i·ta′tive (mĕd′ĭ·tā′tĭv), *adj.* Disposed or given to meditate, or to meditation. — **med′i·ta′tive·ly,** *adv.*

med′i·ter·ra′ne·an (mĕd′ĭ·tĕ·rā′nē·ăn; 58), *adj.* [L. *mediterraneus* fr. *medius* middle + *terra* land.] **1.** Enclosed, or nearly enclosed, with land; as, the *Mediterranean* Sea. **2.** [*cap.*] Of or pertaining to the Mediterranean Sea.

Mediterranean fever. *Med.* See UNDULANT FEVER.

Mediterranean race. *Ethnol.* A division of the white race dwelling about the shores of the Mediterranean Sea and comprising the ancient Iberian, Ligurian, Pelasgian, and certain Hamitic peoples, together with their descendants.

me′di·um (mē′dĭ·ŭm; 58), *n.; pl.*, in general sense and of persons, MEDIUMS (-ŭmz); in scientific use, MEDIA (-ȧ). [L., the middle, fr. *medius* middle.] **1.** That which lies in the middle; hence, middle condition or degree; mean. **2.** A substance through which a force acts or an effect is transmitted; surrounding or enveloping substance; environment. **3.** That through or by which anything is accomplished; as, an advertising *medium.* **4.** A person supposed to be susceptible to supernormal agencies and able to impart knowledge derived from them or to perform actions impossible without their aid; as, a spiritualistic *medium.* **5.** *Biol.* **a** A nutritive mixture or substance, as broth, gelatin, agar, for cultivating bacteria, fungi, etc. **b** A fluid or solid used to preserve, mount, etc., organic structures. **6.** *Paints.* A liquid, as oil or water, with which pigment is mixed in preparing it for application; a vehicle. — **Syn.** See MEAN. — *adj.* Intermediate in amount, quality, position, or degree.

me′di·um·is′tic (-ĭs′tĭk), *adj.* Of or pertaining to, or having the qualities of a medium (sense 4).

medium of exchange. See MONEY, *n.*, 5.

med′lar (mĕd′lẽr), *n.* [OF. *medler, meslier*, fr. OF. *mesle, mesple*, the fruit, fr. L. *mespilum*, fr. Gr. *mespilon.*] A small Eurasian tree (*Mespilus germanica*); also, its fruit, which resembles a crab apple, and is used for preserves.

med′ley (mĕd′lĭ), *n.* [OF. *meslee, medlee*, fr. *mesler*, v. See MEDDLE.] **1.** *Archaic.* A melee. **2.** A mixture; esp., a hodgepodge. **3.** *Music.* A composition of passages or scraps, esp. disjointed or incongruous ones, from several different pieces; a potpourri. — *adj.* Mingled; motley.

Me·doc′, Mé·doc′ (mā·dŏk′; mā′dŏk; *F.* mā′dôk′), *n.* [F. *Médoc.*] Wine from Médoc, France.

me·dul′la (mē·dŭl′ȧ), *n.; pl.* MEDULLAE (-ē). [L.] **1.** *Anat.* **a** The marrow of bones. **b** The deep or inner substance or tissue of an organ or part, as of the kidney or of a hair. **c** The medulla oblongata. **2.** *Bot.* The pith or central portion of parenchyma when enclosed by a definite vascular cylinder, as in the stems of dicotyledons and gymnosperms.

me·dul′la ob′lon·ga′ta (ŏb′lŏng·gā′tȧ; -gä′tȧ); *pl.* MEDULLAE OBLONGATAE (mē·dŭl′ē ŏb′lŏng·gā′tē; -gä′tē). [NL., oblong medulla.] *Anat.* The lowest or posterior part of the brain, tapering off into the spinal cord. See HINDBRAIN; BRAIN, *Illust.*

med′ul·lar′y (mĕd′ŭ·lẽr′ĭ; mē·dŭl′ȧ·rĭ; mĕd′ŭ·lẽr·ĭ), *adj.* *Anat.* Pertaining to, containing, consisting of, or resembling, the medulla or medulla oblongata.

medullary ray. *Bot.* One of the radial plates of parenchymatous tissue, usually separating the vascular bundles in stems of gymnosperms and woody dicotyledons; — more correctly called *wood ray* or *xylary ray.*

medullary sheath. *Anat. & Biochem.* See MYELIN.

med′ul·lat′ed (mĕd′ŭ·lāt′ĕd; mē·dŭl′āt·ĕd· -ĭd), *adj.* *Anat.* Having a medullary sheath.

Me·du′sa (mē·dū′sȧ; -zȧ), *n.* [L., fr. Gr. *Medousa.*] **1.** *Gr. Myth.* A Gorgon slain by Perseus, who gave her head to Athena. **2.** [*not cap.*] [*pl.* MEDUSAE (-sē; -zē).] *Zool.* A jellyfish. — **me·du′san** (-săn; -s′n; -zăn; -z′n), *adj.* — **me·du′soid** (-soid; -zoid), *adj.*

meed (mēd), *n* [AS. *mēd.*] **1.** That which is bestowed for merit; reward; recompense. **2.** *Obs.* **a** A gift; also, a bribe. **b** Merit or desert; worth.

meek (mēk), *adj.* [ON *mjūkr* mild, soft.] **1.** Mild of temper; patient under injuries; long-suffering. **2.** In an unfavorable sense, spiritless. **3.** *Obs.* Gentle; kind. — **Syn.** See HUMBLE. — *adv.* In a meek, patient, long-suffering manner. — **meek′ly**, *adv.* — **meek′ness**, *n.*

meer′schaum (mẽr′shŭm), *n.* [G., lit., sea foam.] **1.** A fine white claylike mineral, mined chiefly in Asia Minor and used esp. for tobacco pipes, cigar holders, etc.; sepiolite. H., 2–2.5; sp. gr., 2. It is a hydrous magnesium silicate, $H_4Mg_2Si_3O_{10}$. **2.** A tobacco pipe made of this mineral.

meet (mēt), *v. t.;* MET (mĕt); MEET′ING. [AS. *mētan;* akin to AS. *mōt, gemōt*, a meeting.] **1.** To come upon or across. **2.** To come into contact or proximity with; also, to go to the place of arrival of; as, to *meet* a train. **3.** To encounter hostilely; to fight with. **4.** To come into connection with; to join or intersect; as, where one road *meets* another. **5.** To come into the presence of, or association with; as, an appointment to *meet* the president. **6.** To encounter; experience; as, he *met* his fate. **7.** To come within the perception or recognition of; as, the sounds that *met* his ear. **8.** To conform to; to match; to discharge or pay, as a debt. — *v. i.* **1.** To come together by mutual approach; to come into contact or proximity. **2.** *Archaic.* **a** To conflict. **b** To come to, or be at, a meeting. **c** To agree. **3.** To come together for a common purpose; to assemble; as, Congress *meets* on Tuesday. — *n.* **1.** Act of meeting. **2.** An assembling together; esp., an assembling of huntsmen for the hunt, or of contestants in athletic sport; also, the persons who so assemble, or the place of meeting.

meet, *adj.* [ME. *mete*, fr. AS. *gemǣte.*] Suitable; fit. — **Syn.** See FIT. — *adv. Obs.* Suitably. — **meet′ly**, *adv.*

meet′ing, *n.* **1.** Act of persons or things that meet; specif.: **a** A duel. **b** A gathering; assembly. **c** An assembly for worship. **d** A gathering for holding races; a race meeting. **2.** A junction, intersection, or confluence.

meet′ing·house′ (mēt′ĭng·hous′), *n.* A building used for worship; a church; in England, only a house so used by dissenters.

meg′a- (mĕg′ȧ-), **meg-** (mĕg-). [Gr. *megas, megalou.*] A combining form meaning *great, mighty*, signifying: **a** *Great, extended, powerful*, as in *mega*scope. **b** In the metric system, electricity, mechanics, etc., *a million times; a million of;* as in **meg′a·far′ad**, a million farads, **meg′a·me′ter, meg′a·me′tre**, a million meters, **meg′a·volt′, meg′erg′, meg′ohm′**, etc.

meg′a·ce·phal′ic (-sē·făl′ĭk), *adj.* Also **meg′a·ceph′a·lous** (-sĕf′ȧ·lŭs). [*mega-* + Gr. *kephalē* head.] Large-headed. Specif., *Craniom.*, having a cranial capacity in excess of the mean (which for modern Europeans and Asiatics ranges from 1500 to 1600 cubic centimeters).

meg′a·cy′cle (mĕg′ȧ·sī′k'l), *n.* *Radio.* A million cycles.

meg′a·ga·mete′ (-gȧ·mēt′), *n.* [*mega-* + *gamete.*] *Biol.* See MACROGAMETE.

meg′a·lith (mĕg′ȧ·lĭth), *n.* [*mega-* + *-lith.*] *Archaeol.* One of the huge stones or boulders used in various types of prehistoric monuments. — **meg′a·lith′ic** (-lĭth′ĭk), *adj.*

meg′a·lo- (mĕg′ȧ·lō-), **megal-.** [Gr. *megas, megalou.*] A combining form meaning *large, great*, as in **meg′a·lo·ce·pha′li·a, meg′a·lo·ceph′a·ly**, the condition of having an abnormally large head; specif., *Med., abnormal enlargement*, as in **meg′a·lo·car′di·a**, abnormal enlargement of the heart.

meg′a·lo·ma′ni·a (-mā′nĭ·ȧ), *n.* [NL., fr. *megalo-* + *-mania.*] A disordered mental condition in which the patient has grandiose delusions. — **meg′a·lo·ma′ni·ac** (-ăk), *n.* — **meg′a·lo·ma·ni′a·cal** (-mȧ·nī′ȧ·kăl), *adj.*

meg′a·lop′o·lis (mĕg′ȧ·lŏp′ō·lĭs), *n.* A very large city.

meg′a·lo·saur′ (mĕg′ȧ·lō·sôr′), *n.* [*megalo-* + Gr. *sauros* lizard.] *Paleontol.* One of a genus (*Megalosaurus*) of gigantic carnivorous dinosaurs (group Theropoda). — **meg′a·lo·sau′ri·an** (-sô′rĭ·ăn), *adj. & n.*

meg′a·phone (mĕg′ȧ·fōn), *n.* [*mega-* + *-phone.*] A device to magnify sound, or direct it in a greater volume, as a very large funnel used as a speaking trumpet. — *v. t. & i.* To speak or address through or as if through a megaphone.

meg′a·pod (mĕg′ȧ·pŏd), *adj.* Large-footed.

meg′a·scope (-skōp), *n.* [*mega-* + *-scope.*] A type of magic lantern for throwing a magnified image on a screen. — **meg′a·scop′ic** (-skŏp′ĭk), *adj.* — **meg′a·scop′i·cal·ly** (-ĭ·kăl·ĭ), *adv.*

meg′a·spo·ran′gi·um (-spō·răn′jĭ·ŭm), *n.; pl.* -GIA (-ȧ). [NL.] A sporangium which develops only megaspores.

meg′a·spore′ (mĕg′ȧ·spōr′), *n.* A variety of asexual spore produced by seed plants and some ferns, which always gives rise to the female prothallium or gametophyte. The embryo sac in seed plants is a megaspore.

meg′a·spo′ro·phyll (mĕg′ȧ·spō′rō·fĭl), *n.* *Bot.* A sporophyll which develops only megasporangia.

me·gass′ (mē·găs′), **me·gasse′.** Vars. of BAGASSE.

meg′a·there (mĕg′ȧ·thẽr), *n.* [*mega-* + Gr. *thērion* beast.] Any of a genus (*Megatherium*) of ground sloths, allied to the sloths and the anteaters, found in the Pleistocene of America. Some of them, as *M. americanum*, were of gigantic size.

meg′a·ton′ (mĕg′ȧ·tŭn′), *n.* [*mega-* + *ton.*] A million tons.

me·gilp′ (mē·gĭlp′), **me·gilph′** (-gĭlf′), *n.* Also **ma·gilp′** (mȧ·gĭlp′), **me·guilp′**, etc. [Origin unknown.] A gelatinous preparation commonly of linseed oil and mastic varnish, used by artists as a vehicle for colors.

me′grim (mē′grĭm), *n.* [OF. *migraine.*] **1.** Migraine. **2.** A fancy; whim; esp. in *pl.*, lowness of spirits; "the blues"; hypochondria.

Mei′ji (mā′jĭ), *n.* [Jap., lit., enlightened rule.] *Japanese Hist.* The name of the period of the reign (1868–1912) of Emperor Mutsuhito.

mein′ie, mein′y (mān′ĭ), *n.* [OF. *meisniée, maisnie.* See MENIAL.] **1.** *Archaic.* A body of feudal retainers or, later, of attendants; retinue. **2.** *Scot.* A multitude.

mei·o′sis (mī·ō′sĭs), *n.* [NL., fr. Gr. *meiōsis*, fr. *meioun* to make smaller, fr. *meiōn* smaller.] *Biol.* The complex nuclear changes resulting in cells (usually gametes) with half the number of chromosomes present in the original cell; — called also *reduction division.* Typically the process involves two nuclear divisions: one in which the chromosomes, without undergoing prior splitting (cf. MITOSIS), separate so that half the original (diploid) number enters each of the two nuclei, and a second essentially mitotic in character. The two divisions thus produce four haploid cells. — **mei·ot′ic** (-ŏt′ĭk), *adj.*

Meis′ter·sing′er (mīs′tẽr·sĭng′ẽr; -zĭng′ẽr), *n. sing. & pl.* [G. See MASTER; SINGER.] A member of one of certain guilds, chiefly of workingmen, established between about 1300 and 1500 in certain German cities, for the cultivation of poetry and music.

mel (mĕl), *n.* [L.] *Pharm.* Honey.

mel′a·mine (mĕl′ȧ·mēn; mĕl′ȧ·mēn′; -mĭn), *n.* Also **-min.** [From *mel*am (arbitrarily formed name of a chemical compound) + *amine.*] *Chem.* A white crystalline compound, $C_3H_6N_6$, produced commercially from calcium cyanamide, $CaCN_2$. It condenses with formaldehyde to form **mel′a·mine–form·al′de·hyde res′ins**, thermosetting resins used for surface coatings, insulators, molded articles, etc.

mel′an·cho′li·a (mĕl′ăn·kō′lĭ·ȧ), *n.* [LL. See MELANCHOLY.] A disordered mental condition characterized by extreme depression of spirits, painful delusions, and brooding. — **Syn.** See SADNESS. — **mel′an·cho′li·ac** (-ăk), *adj. & n.*

mel′an·chol′ic (-kŏl′ĭk), *adj.* **1.** Given to or having melancholy; depressed; unhappy. **2.** Affected with, like, or pert. to melancholia. — **mel′an·chol′i·cal·ly** (-ĭ·kăl·ĭ), *adv.*

mel′an·chol′y (mĕl′ăn·kŏl′ĭ *or, esp. Brit.*, -kŭl·ĭ), *n.; pl.* -CHOLIES (-ĭz). [OF. *melancolie*, fr. LL., fr. Gr. *melancholia*, fr. *melas, -anos*, black + *cholē* gall, bile.] **1.** *Archaic & Hist.* A thick, dark, acrid bile formerly imagined to be a secretion of the kidneys or spleen, and the cause of gloominess, irascibility, or mental dejection; later, melancholia. **2. a** Depression of spirits; dejection. **b** Pensive meditation. — **Syn.** See SADNESS. — *adj.* **1.** Suggestive or expressive of melancholy or dejection; dismal; depressing. **2.** Producing sadness; lamentable; as, a *melancholy* event. **3.** Seriously thoughtful or meditative; pensive.

Mel′a·ne′sian (mĕl′ȧ·nē′shăn; -zhăn), *adj.* [Gr. *melas, -anos*, black + *nēsos* island.] Of or pertaining to Melanesia or Melanesians, or their Austronesian language. — *n.* **1.** A member of the dominant native race of Melanesia, a dark-skinned people with thick beards and frizzly hair. **2.** The language spoken by the dominant native race on the islands of Micronesia and Melanesia, forming a subfamily of the Austronesian languages. See LANGUAGE, *Table.*

mé′lange′ (mā′länzh′), *n.* [F.] A mixture; medley.

me·lan′ic (mē·lăn′ĭk), *adj.* [Gr. *melas, -anos*, black.] **1.** Melanotic. **2.** *Ethnol.* Exhibiting melanism.

mel′a·nin (mĕl′ȧ·nĭn), *n.* *Biochem.* Any of the various dark pigments of animal origin, as that of the skin of dark-complexioned peoples.

mel′a·nism (-nĭz'm), *n.* [Gr. *melas, -anos*, black.] **1.** *Physiol. & Zool.* An unusual development of black or nearly black color in the skin or in the plumage or pelage. **2.** *Ethnol.* The character of having a high degree of pigmentation, as shown in dark skin, eyes, and hair. — **mel′a·nis′tic** (-nĭs′tĭk), *adj.*

mel'a·nite (mĕl'ȧ·nīt), *n.* [Gr. *melas, -anos,* black.] *Mineral.* A black kind of garnet.
mel'a·no- (mĕl'ȧ·nō-), **melan-.** [Gr. *melas, melanos.*] A combining form meaning *black, dark.*
Mel'a·noch'ro·i (mĕl'ȧ·nŏk'rō·ī), *n. pl.* [NL., fr. *melan-* + Gr. *ōchros* pale.] Caucasians having dark hair and pale complexion. — **Mel'a·noch'roid** (-roid), *adj.*
mel'a·noid (mĕl'ȧ·noid), *adj.* Blackish; like melanin; also, pertaining to or like melanosis.
mel'a·no'ma (-nō'mȧ), *n.; pl.* -NOMATA (-mȧ·tȧ), -NOMAS (-mȧz). [NL., fr. *melan-* + *-oma.*] *Med.* A tumor containing dark pigment.
mel'a·no'sis (-nō'sĭs), *n.* [NL., fr. Gr. *melanōsis* a growing black.] *Med.* A condition of morbid deposition of melanin in the tissues. — **mel'a·not'ic** (-nŏt'ĭk), *adj.*
mel'a·nous (mĕl'ȧ·nŭs), *adj.* [Gr. *melas, -anos,* black.] *Ethnol.* Having black hair and dark skin; melanic.
mel'an·tha'ceous (mĕl'ăn·thā'shŭs), *adj.* [Gr. *melas, -anos,* black + *anthos* flower.] *Bot.* Belonging to the bunchflower family (Melanthaceae). See BUNCHFLOWER.
mel'a·phyre (mĕl'ȧ·fīr), *n.* [F., fr. Gr. *melas, -anos,* black + *porphyre* porphyry.] *Petrog.* A porphyritic igneous rock with dark-colored aphanitic groundmass.
Mel'ba toast (mĕl'bȧ). [After Madame *Melba.*] Very thin bread toasted till crisp.
Mel·chiz'e·dek (mĕl·kĭz'ĕ·dĕk), *n.* [Heb. *Malkī-Tsedheq.*] *Bib.* A pre-Aaronic and pre-Levitical priest-king, to whom Abraham paid tithes (*Gen.* xiv. 18).
meld (mĕld), *v. t. & i.* [G. *melden* to announce.] *Card Playing.* In pinochle, to declare or announce for a score; as, to *meld* four kings. — *n.* Act of melding; a combination which is or may be melded.
meld (mĕld), *v. t. & i.* [Blend of *melt* and *weld.*] To merge.
mel'der (mĕl'dẽr), *n.* [ON. *meldr.*] *Scot. & Dial. Eng.* The quantity of meal, esp. of oats, ground at one time; hence, a large quantity.
Mel'e·a'ger (mĕl'ē·ā'jẽr), *n.* [L., fr. Gr. *Meleagros.*] *Gr. Myth.* A hero at whose birth it was foretold that his life would last no longer than the brand then burning on the hearth. His mother quenched it, and hid it. At the Calydonian boar hunt, Meleager gave Atalanta the trophies. In the quarrel which this caused with his uncles he slew them. His mother, enraged, thrust the fatal brand into the fire, so causing Meleager's death.
me·lee' (mā·lā'; mā'lā; mĕl'ā; *F.* mâ'lā'), *n.* [F. *mêlée.* See MEDLEY.] A fight between combatants mingled in a confused mass; an affray.
me'li·a'ceous (mē'lĭ·ā'shŭs), *adj.* [Gr. *melia* the ash tree.] *Bot.* Belonging to the mahogany family (Meliaceae, order Geraniales). See MAHOGANY.
mel'ic (mĕl'ĭk), *adj.* [Gr. *melikos,* fr. *melos* song.] Of or pertaining to song; designed to be sung; lyric; — of poetry, esp. Greek lyrical poetry of a form developed in the 7th and 6th centuries B.C.
mel'i·lot (mĕl'ĭ·lŏt), *n.* Sweet clover (see CLOVER, 2).
mel'i·nite (mĕl'ĭ·nīt), *n.* [F. *mélinite,* fr. Gr. *mēlinos* quince-yellow.] A high explosive similar to lyddite.
mel'io·rate (mēl'yō·rāt), *v. t. & i.* [LL. *melioratus,* past part. of *meliorare* to meliorate, fr. L. *melior* better.] To make or become better; to improve; to make more tolerable. — **mel'io·ra·ble** (-rȧ·b'l), *adj.* — **mel'io·ra'tion** (-rā'shŭn), *n.* — **mel'io·ra'tive** (-rā'tĭv), *adj.* — **mel'io·ra'tor** (-tẽr), *n.*
mel'io·rism (-rĭz'm), *n.* [L. *melior* better.] *Ethics.* The belief or doctrine that the world tends to become better and that man has the power of aiding its betterment; — contrasted with *pessimism* and *optimism.* — **mel'io·rist** (-rĭst), *n. & adj.* — **mel'io·ris'tic** (-rĭs'tĭk), *adj.*
mel·ior'i·ty (mēl·yŏr'ĭ·tĭ), *n.* Superiority.
mell (mĕl), *v. t. & i.* [OF. *meller, mesler.* See MEDDLE.] *Archaic & Dial.* To mix; mingle; meddle.
mel·lif'er·ous (mĕ·lĭf'ẽr·ŭs), *adj.* [L. *mellifer,* fr. *mel, mellis,* honey + *ferre* to bear.] Producing honey.
mel·lif'lu·ent (-lōō·ĕnt), *adj.* [LL. *mellifluens.*] Mellifluous. — **mel·lif'lu·ence** (-ĕns), *n.* — **mel·lif'lu·ent·ly,** *adv.*
mel·lif'lu·ous (-ŭs), *adj.* [LL. *mellifluus,* fr. *mel, mellis,* honey + *fluere* to flow.] Flowing or sweetened with or as with honey; flowing smoothly; as, a *mellifluous* voice. — **mel·lif'lu·ous·ly,** *adv.*
mel'low (mĕl'ō), *adj.* [ME. *melwe.*] **1.** Soft or tender by reason of ripeness; having a tender pulp. **2.** Easily worked; loamy; — of soil. **3.** Mature; fully developed; also, made sweet or gentle by maturity. **4.** Not coarse, rough, or harsh; full and pure; — of sound, color, etc. **5.** Well-matured; not harsh or acid; — of wine. — *v. t. & i.* To make or become mellow. — **mel'low·ly,** *adv.* — **mel'low·ness,** *n.*
me·lo'de·on (mē·lō'dē·ŭn), *n.* [See MELODY.] A variety of small reed organ in which a suction bellows draws air inward through the reeds.
me·lo'di·a (-dĭ·ȧ), *n.* [LL.] *Music.* An 8-foot labial organ stop with wood pipes, and tone of soft flute quality. See STOP, *n.*
me·lod'ic (mē·lŏd'ĭk), *adj.* Of the nature of melody; relating to or made up of melody. — **me·lod'i·cal·ly** (-ĭ·kăl·ĭ), *adv.*
me·lod'ics (-ĭks), *n.;* see -ICS. The theory of melody and its construction.
me·lo'di·ous (mē·lō'dĭ·ŭs; 58), *adj.* Containing, producing, characterized by, or of the nature of, melody; agreeable to the ear by a sweet succession of sounds. — **me·lo'di·ous·ly,** *adv.* — **me·lo'di·ous·ness,** *n.*
mel'o·dist (mĕl'ō·dĭst), *n.* A composer or singer of melodies.
mel'o·dize (-dīz), *v. t.* To form into, or set to, melody. — *v. i.* To make melody; to compose melodies.
mel'o·dra'ma (mĕl'ō·drä'mȧ; mĕl'ō·drä'mȧ; -drăm'ȧ), *n.* [F. *mélodrame,* fr. Gr. *melos* song + *drama* drama.] A variety of drama, commonly romantic and sensational, with both song and instrumental music interspersed; hence, any romantic and sensational drama, typically with a happy ending. — **mel'o·dram'a·tist** (-drăm'ȧ·tĭst), *n.*
mel'o·dra·mat'ic (mĕl'ō·drȧ·măt'ĭk), *adj.* Of, pertaining to, or characteristic of melodrama; sensational in situation or action. — **Syn.** See DRAMATIC. — **mel'o·dra·mat'i·cal·ly** (-ĭ·kăl·ĭ), *adv.*
mel'o·dra·mat'ics (-ĭks), *n. pl.;* see -ICS. Melodramatic conduct.
mel'o·dy (mĕl'ō·dĭ), *n.; pl.* -DIES (-dĭz). [OF. *melodie,* fr. LL. *melodia,* fr. Gr. *melōidia* a singing, choral song, fr. *melōidos* melodious, fr. *melos* song + *aoidos* singer.] **1.** A sweet or agreeable succession or arrangement of sounds; tunefulness. **2.** *Music.* **a** A succession of single tones, having the relationship of a given mode or key and of a rhythmical structure; also, a symmetrical whole so formed; an air or tune. **b** The succession of single tones, one of the three vital elements (*melody, harmony, rhythm*) of music. **c** The chief voice part in a harmonic composition; the air. **3.** A poem composed for singing to some melody or tune.
mel'oid (mĕl'oid), *n.* [NL. *meloe* oil beetle.] *Zool.* Any of a family (Meloidae) of insects including the blister beetles and oil beetles. — **mel'oid,** *adj.*
mel'o·lon'thine (mĕl'ō·lŏn'thīn; -thĭn), *adj.* [Gr. *mēlolonthē* the cockchafer.] *Zool.* Of or pertaining to a large subfamily (Melolonthinae) of scarabaeoid beetles, including the June bugs and rose bugs. — **mel'o·lon'thine,** *n.*
mel'on (mĕl'ŭn), *n.* [OF., fr. LL. *melo,* for *melopepo* an apple-shaped melon, fr. Gr. *mēlopepōn,* fr. *mēlon* apple + *pepōn* a species of melon.] **1. a** The muskmelon. **b** The watermelon. **2.** *Slang, U. S.* A surplus of profits available for distribution to stockholders; as, to cut a *melon.*
Mel·pom'e·ne (mĕl·pŏm'ē·nē), *n.* [L., fr. Gr. *Melpomenē,* lit., the songstress.] *Gr. Myth.* The Muse of tragedy.
melt (mĕlt), *v. i.;* MELT'ED; MELT'ING. *Archaic past part.* MOL'TEN. [AS. *meltan,* v. i., *mieltan, myltan,* v. t.] **1.** To be changed from a solid to a liquid state, usually by heat. **2.** To dissolve or disintegrate, as sugar in the mouth. **3.** *Obs.* To be crushed or fail, as the heart. **4.** To dwindle rapidly, as funds or one's supporters; to disappear by being dispersed or dissipated, as clouds; to vanish. **5.** To be or become softened; to become tender or gentle. **6.** To lose distinct form; to blend; as, outlines *melting* into each other. — *v. t.* **1.** To liquefy; fuse; as, to *melt* wax. **2.** To cause to vanish; as, the sun *melted* the morning mist. **3.** To soften; to render gentle or susceptible to mild influences. **4.** To cause to pass or merge insensibly; to blend. — *n.* **1.** Act of melting; state of being melted. **2.** A melted substance; also, the quantity melted at a single operation or during a certain period. — **melt'a·bil'i·ty,** *n.* — **melt'a·ble,** *adj.* — **melt'er,** *n.*
melt'ing point. The temperature at which a solid substance begins to melt, specif. when under standard pressure; as, the *melting point* of ice is 0° C. or 32° F.
melting pot. a A vessel in which anything is melted; a crucible. **b** The United States as a place of the amalgamation of races and of mores.
mel'ton (mĕl'tŭn; -t'n), *n.* [From *Melton* Mowbray, Eng.] A stout smooth woolen cloth with short nap.
mem'ber (mĕm'bẽr), *n.* [OF. *membre,* fr. L. *membrum.*] **1.** *Archaic.* A bodily part or organ, esp., a limb. **2.** One of the persons composing a society, community, or party. **3.** Short for: **a** *Eng.* Member of Parliament (i. e. of the House of Commons). **b** *U. S.* Member of Congress (i. e. of the House of Representatives). **4.** A part of a whole; an independent constituent of a body, structure, or any organized thing, or a unit in a series, as one of the sides of an algebraic equation or one of the propositions of a syllogism; as, a species is a *member* of a certain genus. **5.** *Bot.* A unit of structure in a plant body. — **Syn.** See PART.
mem'ber·ship, *n.* **1.** State or status of being a member. **2.** The collective body of members, as of a society.
mem'bra·na'ceous (mĕm'brȧ·nā'shŭs), *adj.* Membranous.
mem'brane (mĕm'brān), *n.* [L. *membrana* skin covering the separate members of the body, parchment, fr. L. *membrum* member.] **1.** Any thin, soft, pliable sheet or layer, esp. of animal or vegetable origin. **2.** *Paleog.* A piece of parchment forming part of a roll.
membrane bone. *Anat.* A bone which ossifies in connective tissue, instead of in a cartilage.
mem'bra·nous (mĕm'brȧ·nŭs), *adj.* **1.** Consisting of, resembling, or of the nature of, membrane. **2.** *Med.* Characterized by, or formed of, a membrane.
me·men'to (mē·mĕn'tō), *n.; pl.* -TOS, -TOES (-tōz). [L., remember, be mindful, imper. of *meminisse* to remember.] **1.** [*cap.*] In the Canon of the Mass (Roman rite), either of two prayers, one for the living and one for the dead, beginning "Memento." **2.** Something to awaken memory, as a token, warning, or memorial.
‖**me·men'to mo'ri** (mō'rī; 70). [L., remember that you must die.] An object, as a death's-head, used as a reminder of death.
Mem'non (mĕm'nŏn), *n.* [L., fr. Gr. *Memnōn.*] *Gr. Myth.* King of the Ethiopians made immortal by Zeus. — **Mem·no'ni·an** (mĕm·nō'nĭ·ăn), *adj.*
mem'oir (mĕm'wär; -wôr), *n.* [F. *mémoire,* m., memorandum, fr. *mémoire,* f., memory, fr. L. *memoria.*] **1.** *pl.* A history or narrative composed from personal experience and memory; often, esp., an account of one's life, or of episodes in it, written by oneself. **2.** A biography, esp. one written without special regard for completeness. **3.** An essay or dissertation; a record of investigations of any subject.
mem'o·ra·bil'i·a (mĕm'ō·rȧ·bĭl'ĭ·ȧ), *n. pl.; sing.* -RABILE (-răb'ĭ·lē). [L.] Things remarkable and worthy of remembrance or record; also, the record of these.
mem'o·ra·ble (mĕm'ō·rȧ·b'l), *adj.* [L. *memorabilis,* fr. *memorare* to bring to remembrance, fr. *memor* mindful.] Worthy of being remembered or noted. — **mem'o·ra·bil'i·ty** (-bĭl'ĭ·tĭ), *n.* — **mem'o·ra·bly,** *adv.*
mem'o·ran'dum (mĕm'ō·răn'dŭm), *n.; pl.* -DUMS (-dŭmz) or (sense 1) -DA (-dȧ). [L., something to be remembered.] **1.** An informal record of something; a note to help or jog the memory. Colloquially **mem'o** (mĕm'ō) and abbr. *memo.* **2.** *Com.* A statement of the terms of a shipment sent with the privilege of return if not sold; hence, the goods are sent ***on memorandum.*** **3.** *Diplomacy.* An informal summary or statement of grounds for or against an action, issue, etc.
me·mo'ri·al (mē·mō'rĭ·ăl; 70), *adj.* [OF., fr. L. *memorialis,* fr. *memoria.*] **1.** Serving to preserve remembrance; commemorative; as, a *memorial* arch; *Memorial* Day. **2.** Of or pertaining to memory. — *n.* **1.** Anything, as a monument, intended to preserve the memory of a person or event. **2.** A statement of facts, addressed to the government, to a society, etc., often with a petition. **3.** *Diplomacy.* An informal state paper, as one presented by the ambassador of one state to the representative of another in the course of negotiations.
Memorial Day. *U. S.* A day appointed for commemorating dead soldiers and sailors, in most of the states a legal holiday, May 30. Confederate Memorial Day is variously Apr. 26, May 10, May 30, June 3.
me·mo'ri·al·ist (mē·mō'rĭ·ăl·ĭst), *n.* **1.** One who writes or signs a memorial. **2.** A writer of memorials, or memoirs.

me·mo′ri·al·ize (mē·mō′rĭ·ăl·īz), *v. t.* To address or petition by a memorial; to present a memorial to; also, to commemorate. — **me·mo′ri·al·i·za′tion** (-ĭ·zā′shŭn; -ī·zā′-), *n.*

‖**me·mo′ri·ter** (mē·mŏr′ĭ·tẽr), *adv.* [L.] By, or from, memory; by heart.

mem′o·rize (mĕm′ō·rīz), *v. t.* [From MEMORY.] To commit to memory; to learn by heart. — **mem′o·ri·za′tion** (-rĭ·zā′shŭn; -rī·zā′-), *n.* — **mem′o·riz′er** (-rīz′ẽr), *n.*

mem′o·ry (mĕm′ō·rĭ), *n.; pl.* -RIES (-rĭz). [OF. *memoire, memorie,* fr. L. *memoria,* fr. *memor* mindful.] **1.** The power, function, or act of reproducing and identifying what has been learned or experienced; the faculty of remembering. **2.** Commemoration; remembrance; as, in *memory* of youth. **3.** The sum of what one can remember; as, a richly stored *memory.* **4.** A character or conduct, etc., as preserved in remembrance, history, or tradition; as, the war became only a *memory.* **5.** The time within which past events can be or are remembered. **6.** Any particular act or experience of remembering; as, absorbed in *memories* of childhood; also, the thing or things remembered.

Syn. **Memory, remembrance, recollection, reminiscence** mean a re-membering or being remembered. **Memory** applies chiefly to the power or function of remembering, esp. what has been experienced or learned; **remembrance,** to the act or process of remembering or to the fact of being remembered; **recollection** adds the implication of bringing back to mind that which is not clear in all of its details; **reminiscence,** of remembering incidents, experiences, etc., from a remote past, such as of one's childhood, in old age.

Mem′phi·an (mĕm′fĭ·ăn), *adj.* Of or pertaining to the ancient city of Memphis in Egypt; hence, Egyptian.

‖**mem′-sa′hib** (mĕm′sä′ĭb), *n.* [Hind. *mem-sāhib,* fr. *mem,* fr. E. *ma'am.*] *India.* Lady; mistress; — used in addressing European women.

men (mĕn), *n., pl. of* MAN.

men′ace (mĕn′ĭs; -ăs), *n.* [OF., fr. L. *minacia,* fr. *minax, -acis,* projecting, threatening, fr. *minari* to threaten.] **1.** The show of an intention to inflict evil; a threat. **2.** That which threatens. — *v. t.;* MEN′ACED (-ĭst; -ăst); MEN′AC·ING (-ĭs·ĭng). To express or show intention to inflict evil or injury upon; to threaten. — *v. i.* To act threateningly; to utter threats. — **Syn.** See THREATEN. — **men′ac·ing·ly,** *adv.*

me′nad, me·nad′ic. Vars. of MAENAD, MAENADIC.

mé·nage′ (mā·näzh′), **me·nage′** (mĕ·näzh′), *n.* [F. *ménage.*] **1.** A household. **2.** Domestic management; housekeeping.

me·nag′er·ie (mē·năj′ẽr·ĭ; mē·năzh′ẽr·ĭ), *n.* [F. *ménagerie,* fr. *ménage* household, fr. LL. *mansionaticus* pert. to the house, fr. L. *mansio* a dwelling.] **1.** A place where animals are kept and trained, esp. for exhibition. **2.** A collection of wild animals in cages, esp. for exhibition.

mend (mĕnd), *v. t.* [From AMEND.] **1.** To free from faults or defects; — as in *to mend one's manners* or *ways;* to correct; as, to *mend* a fault; also, to repair; to put in shape again; as, to *mend* clothes, shoes. **2.** To make amends for; — now only in *least said, soonest mended.* **3.** To improve, better, or ameliorate; as, to *mend* conditions. — *v. i.* To improve, esp. in health. — **mend′er,** *n.*

Syn. **Mend, repair, patch, rebuild, remodel** mean to make something damaged fit for use. **Mend** now implies a making whole or sound something broken, torn, worn, etc.; **repair,** often used in place of *mend,* is the preferred term when the thing has become dilapidated, or the like; **patch** implies mending of a hole, a rent, a breach, or the like by the insertion or application of the same or similar material; **rebuild** is often preferred to *repair* when the intent is to suggest a making like new; **remodel** is preferred when there are changes in structure or design.

— *n.* Act of mending, or repairing; also, a mended place. — ***on the mend.*** Growing better, as in health; improving.

men·da′cious (mĕn·dā′shŭs), *adj.* [L. *mendax, -acis,* lying.] Given to falsehood; lying. — **Syn.** See DISHONEST. — **men·da′cious·ly,** *adv.*

men·dac′i·ty (-dăs′ĭ·tĭ), *n.; pl.* -TIES (-tĭz). Quality or state of being mendacious; a lie.

Men·de′li·an (mĕn·dē′lĭ·ăn; -dēl′yăn; 58), *adj.* [See MENDEL'S LAW.] *Biol.* Of or pertaining to Mendel; pertaining to or following Mendel's law. — **Men·de′li·an·ism** (-ĭz′m), **Men′del·ism** (mĕn′dĕl·ĭz′m), *n.*

Men′del's law (mĕn′dĕlz). The law observed in the inheritance of many characters in animals and plants, discovered by Gregor J. Mendel (Austrian Augustinian abbot, 1822–84) in breeding experiments with peas. He showed that the height, color, and other characters depend on the presence of determining factors (***genes***) which behave as units, and that the second and later generations of crossbreeds exhibit these characters in all possible combinations, each combination in a definite proportion of individuals.

Men′de·lye′ev's, *or* **Men′de·le′ev's, law** (mĕn′dĕ·lā′(y)ĕfs; *Russ.* myĕn·dyĭ·lyā′yĕfs). *Chem.* = PERIODIC LAW.

men′di·cant (mĕn′dĭ·kănt), *adj.* [L. *mendicans, -antis,* pres. part. of *mendicare* to beg, fr. *mendicus* beggar.] Practicing beggary; living by alms (as the Franciscans, Dominicans, Carmelites, and Augustinians). — *n.* A beggar; specif., a member of a mendicant order. — **men′di·can·cy** (-kăn·sĭ), *n.*

men·dic′i·ty (mĕn·dĭs′ĭ·tĭ), *n.* [F. *mendicité,* fr. L. *mendicitas.*] Mendicancy.

Men′e·la′us (mĕn′ĕ·lā′ŭs), *n.* [L., fr. Gr. *Menelaos.*] A king of Sparta, son of Atreus and younger brother of Agamemnon, and husband of Helen. See APPLE OF DISCORD, ATREUS.

men·ha′den (mĕn·hā′d'n), *n.,* see PLURAL, *Note,* 4. [Of Algonquian origin.] A marine clupeoid fish (*Brevoortia tyrannus*), abundant along the Atlantic coast of the United States, used for bait or converted into oil and fertilizer.

men′hir (mĕn′hĭr), *n.* [F., fr. Bret. *men* stone + *hir* long.] *Archaeol.* An upright rough stone, a monolith standing either alone or as one in an avenue or circle.

me′ni·al (mē′nĭ·ăl; mēn′yăl; 58), *adj.* [ME. *meyneal,* fr. *meinie, mayne,* household, fr. OF. *meisniée, maisnie.*] Pertaining or appropriate to servants, esp. domestic servants; low; mean. — **Syn.** See SUBSERVIENT. — *n.* **1.** A domestic servant or retainer. **2.** A person of a servile character. — **me′ni·al·ly,** *adv.*

me·nin′ges (mē·nĭn′jēz), *n. pl.; sing.* MENINX (mē′nĭngks). [NL., fr. Gr. *mēninx, -ingos,* membrane.] *Anat.* The three membranes (the dura mater, arachnoid, and pia mater) which envelop the brain and spinal cord. — **me·nin′ge·al** (-jē·ăl), *adj.*

men′in·gi′tis (mĕn′ĭn·jī′tĭs), *n.; pl.* -GITIDES (-jĭt′ĭ·dēz). [NL. See MENINGES; -ITIS.] *Med.* Inflammation of the meninges, esp. the pia mater and the arachnoid; also, any disease in which it occurs, caused by any of various bacteria (as *Neisseria intracellularis*). — **men′in·git′ic** (mĕn′ĭn·jĭt′ĭk), *adj.*

me·nin′go·coc′cus (mē·nĭng′gō·kŏk′ŭs), *n.; pl.* -COCCI (-sī). *Bacteriol.* The bacterium *Neisseria intracellularis* (syn. *Diplococcus,* or *Micrococcus, intracellularis meningitidis*) which causes cerebrospinal meningitis. — **me·nin′go·coc′cal** (-ăl), *adj.* — **me·nin′go·coc′cic** (-sĭk), *adj.*

me·nis′cus (mē·nĭs′kŭs), *n.; pl.* -CI (-nĭs′ī), -CUSES (-kŭs·ĕz; -ĭz). [NL., fr. Gr. *mēniskos,* dim. of *mēnē* the moon.] **1.** A crescent or crescent-shaped body. **2.** *Optics.* A concavo-convex lens. See LENS, *Illust.* **3.** *Physics.* The curved upper surface of a liquid column, concave when the containing walls are wetted by the liquid and convex when not. Cf. CAPILLARITY, 2.

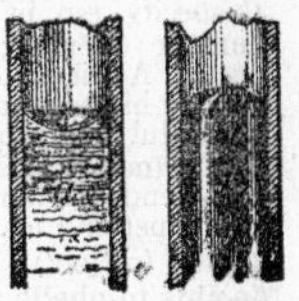

a Concave Meniscus of Water; *b* Convex Meniscus of Mercury.

men′i·sper·ma′ceous (mĕn′ĭ·spẽr·mā′shŭs), *adj.* [Gr. *mēnē* the moon + *sperma* seed.] *Bot.* Belonging to the moonseed family (Menispermaceae). See MOONSEED.

Men′non·ite (mĕn′ŏn·īt), *n.* One of a denomination of evangelical Protestant Christians, so called from Menno Simons (1492–1559) of Friesland, who have stood for nonresistance, plainness of dress, restriction of marriage to members of the group, and the rite of foot washing.

‖**me′no** (mā′nō), *adv.* [It.] *Music.* Less; — in directions; as, ‖**me′no mos′so** (môs′sō), less rapid.

me·nol′o·gy (mē·nŏl′ō·jĭ), *n.; pl.* -GIES (-jĭz). [NL. *menologium,* fr. LGr., fr. Gr. *mēn* month + *logos* discourse.] A calendar of months; specif., a collection of short lives of saints arranged in calendar order for liturgical use.

men′o·pause (mĕn′ō·pôz), *n.* [Gr. *mēn, mēnos,* month + *pauein* to cause to cease.] *Physiol.* The period of natural cessation of menstruation, occurring usually between the ages of forty-five and fifty. — **men′o·paus′al** (-pôz′ăl; -'l), *adj.*

men′or·rha′gi·a (mĕn′ō·rā′jĭ·ȧ), *n.* [NL., fr. Gr. *mēn, mēnos,* month, denoting *relation to menstruation* + *-rrhagia.*] *Med.* Excessive menstrual discharge.

men′sal (mĕn′săl; -s'l), *adj.* [LL. *mensalis,* fr. *mensa* table.] Belonging to, or used or done at, the table.

men′sal, *adj.* [L. *mensis* month.] Monthly.

mense (mĕns), *n.* [For *mensk,* fr. ME. *menske,* fr. ON. *mennska* humanity.] *Scot.* Propriety or grace in behavior; discretion. — **mense′ful,** *adj.* — **mense′less,** *adj.*

men′ses (mĕn′sēz), *n. pl.* [L. *mensis* month, pl. *menses,* lit., months.] *Physiol.* Flow of bloody fluid from the uterus, occurring normally every four weeks.

Men′she·vik, men′she·vik (mĕn′shĕ·vĭk), *n.; pl.* MENSHEVIKI, MEN- (mĕn′shĕ·vē′kē), -SHEVIKS (-vĭks). [Russ., lit., the littler; — because orig. the minority group of the party.] In Russian politics, a member of the less radical wing of the Social Democratic party. Cf. BOLSHEVIK. — **Men′she·vism, men′she·vism** (-vĭz′m), *n.* — **Men′she·vist, men′she·vist** (-vĭst), *adj.*

‖**mens sa′na in cor′po·re sa′no** (mĕnz sā′nȧ ĭn kôr′pō·rē sā′no). [L.] A sound mind in a sound body.

men′stru·al (mĕn′stro͞o·ăl), *adj.* [L. *menstrualis.*] **1.** Recurring once a month. **2.** Pertaining to the menses.

men′stru·ate (-āt), *v. i.* To discharge the menses. — **men′stru·a′tion** (-ā′shŭn), *n.*

men′stru·ous (-ŭs), *adj.* [L. *menstruus,* fr. *mensis* month.] **1.** Having the menses. **2.** Menstrual.

men′stru·um (-ŭm), *n.; pl.* -UMS (-ŭmz), -STRUA (-ȧ). [L., neut. of *menstruus.*] Any substance which dissolves a solid body; a solvent.

men′sur·a·ble (mĕn′sho͝or·ȧ·b'l), *adj.* [LL. *mensurabilis,* fr. *mensurare* to measure, fr. *mensura* measure.] That can be measured; measurable. — **men′sur·a·bil′i·ty** (-bĭl′ĭ·tĭ), *n.*

men′su·ral (mĕn′sho͝o·răl), *adj.* Of or pert. to measure.

men′su·ra′tion (mĕn′sho͝o·rā′shŭn), *n.* [LL. *mensuratio,* fr. *mensuratus,* past part. See MEASURE.] **1.** Act, process, or art of measuring. **2.** The branch of applied geometry concerned with finding length of lines, areas of surfaces, and volumes of solids, from certain simple data of lines and angles.

men′su·ra′tive (mĕn′sho͝o·rā′tĭv), *adj.* Adapted for measuring.

-ment (-mĕnt). [F., fr. L. *-mentum.*] A suffix forming nouns chiefly from verbs, and meaning: **1. a** *Concrete result* or *thing;* as in entanglements (objects that entangle). **b** *Concrete means* or *instrument,* as in nutri*ment,* orna*ment.* **2.** *Action;* as in abridg*ment;* — often implying *process, continuance, manner, art, amount,* or other modification; as in develop*ment,* the fact or process of developing. **3.** *State* or *quality; state, condition, quality* or *degree;* as in amaze*ment.*

men′tal (mĕn′tăl; -t'l), *adj.* [L. *mentum* the chin.] *Anat. & Zool.* Of or pertaining to the chin; genial.

men′tal, *adj.* [F., fr. LL. *mentalis,* fr. *mens, mentis,* the mind.] **1.** Of or pertaining to mind; — in the broadest sense referring to the integrated activity of the organism; as, *mental* life; *mental* hygiene; — often with emphasis on intellectual activity; as, *mental* deficiency, or on internal as against overt motor activity or sensory processes; as, *mental* arithmetic, image. **2.** Affected with mental deficiency or disorder; as, a *mental* patient; intended for care of the insane; as, a *mental* hospital.

mental deficiency. *Psychol.* Lack of intelligence such as to disqualify an individual from parity with his fellows in school or in later life; feeble-mindedness. *Idiocy* (the most extreme degree), *imbecility,* and *moronity* (the mildest degree) are forms of mental deficiency.

mental healing. The act, practice, or process of healing ailments of any kind through the instrumentality of the mind. — **mental healer.**

men·tal′i·ty (mĕn·tăl′ĭ·tĭ), *n.* **1.** Mental endowment or acumen; mental power. **2.** Mind considered as a characteristic; as, the *mentality* of the lower animals.

men′tal·ly (mĕn′tăl·ĭ), *adv.* In the mind; intellectually.

men·tha′ceous (mĕn·thā′shŭs), *adj.* [L. *mentha* mint. See MINT the plant.] Lamiaceous.

men′thene (mĕn′thēn), *n.* [menth*ol* + *-ene.*] *Chem.* A colorless oily hydrocarbon, $C_{10}H_{18}$, obtained from menthol by dehydration.

men′thol (-thōl; -thŏl), *n.* [L. *mentha* mint + *-ol,* 1.] *Chem.* A white anodyne crystalline alcohol, $C_{10}H_{19}OH$, the principal constituent of oil of peppermint. It is an anodyne, used, esp. locally, in neuralgia and rhinitis.

men'tho·lat'ed (mĕn'thō·lāt'ĕd; -ĭd), *adj.* **a** Treated with menthol. **b** Containing or impregnated with menthol.

men'tion (mĕn'shŭn), *n.* [OF. *mention*, fr. L. *mentio.*] A speaking or notice, esp. in a brief or cursory manner; a specification, usually by name. — *v. t.* To make mention of; to refer to or discuss casually; to specify, esp. by name. — **men'tion·a·ble**, *adj.* — **men'tion·er**, *n.*

men'tor (mĕn'tĕr; -tôr), *n.* [Gr. *Mentōr*, prop., counselor.] **1.** [*cap.*] A friend to whom Odysseus, when setting out for Troy, entrusted his house and the education of Telemachus. **2.** [F.] Hence, a faithful counselor.

men'u (mĕn'ū; mā'nū; *F.* mē·nü'), *n.; pl.* MENUS (-ūz; *F.* mē·nü'). [F., slender, minute, detailed, fr. L. *minutus* small.] The details of a banquet or a meal; a bill of fare; also, the dishes served.

me·ow' (mē·ou'). Var. of MIAOW.

Me·phis'to·phe'le·an (mē·fĭs'tō·fē'lē·ăn; mĕf'ĭ·stŏf'ĕ·lē'ăn; 58), **-phe'li·an** (mē·fĭs'tō·fē'lĭ·ăn; -fēl'yăn; 58), *adj.* Pertaining to, or resembling, the devil Mephistopheles, esp. as portrayed in Goethe's *Faust;* devilish; crafty.

Meph'i·stoph'e·les (mĕf'ĭ·stŏf'ĕ·lēz), *n.* Often **Me·phis'to** (mē·fĭs'tō). [G.] One of the seven chief devils in medieval demonology; — best known to modern readers as the cold, scoffing, relentless fiend of Goethe's *Faust.*

me·phit'ic (mē·fĭt'ĭk), *adj.* Of, pertaining to, or due to mephitis; offensive to the smell; noxious.

me·phi'tis (mē·fī'tĭs), *n.* [L.] A noxious, pestilential, or foul exhalation from the earth; also, a stench.

mer'can·tile (mûr'kăn·tĭl; -tēl), *adj.* [F., fr. It. *mercantile*, fr. L. *mercans, -antis*, pres. part. of *mercari* to traffic.] **1.** Of or pertaining to merchants or trade; commercial. **2.** Of or pert. to the mercantile system.

mercantile paper. Negotiable paper given by merchants for goods bought or received on consignment.

mercantile system. *Econ.* The system of public economy developed in Europe upon the decay of the feudal systems, the policy of which was to secure a favorable balance of trade, to develop agriculture and manufactures, to create a merchant marine, and establish foreign trading monopolies.

mer'can·til·ism (mûr'kăn·tĭl·ĭz'm; -tēl·ĭz'm), *n.* **1.** The spirit, theory, or practice of mercantile pursuits; commercialism. **2.** Theory or practice of the mercantile system. — **mer'can·til·ist** (-ĭst), *adj. & n.*

mer·cap'tan (mẽr·kăp'tăn; mûr'kăp·tăn'), *n.* [G., fr. ML. *mercurium captans* seizing mercury (*captans*, pres. part. of L. *captare* to seize).] *Chem.* Any of a series of compounds of the general formula RSH, analogous to the alcohols and phenols, but containing sulfur in place of oxygen; specif., ***ethyl mercaptan***, C_2H_5SH.

Mer·ca'tor's pro·jec'tion (mûr·kā'tẽrz; mĕr·kä'tôrz). [After Gerhard *Mercator*, Flemish geographer.] A method of map making in which the meridians are drawn parallel to each other, and the parallels of latitude are straight lines whose distance from each other increases with their distance from the equator.

mer'ce·nar'y (mûr'sē·nĕr'ĭ *or, esp. Brit.*, -nẽr·ĭ), *adj.* [L. *mercenarius*, fr. *merces* wages, reward.] **1.** Acting merely for reward; serving or done solely for pay; hireling; venal. **2.** Hired for service in an army not of his own country. — *n.; pl.* -IES (-ĭz). A hireling; — now only a soldier hired into a foreign service.

mer'cer (mûr'sẽr), *n.* [OF. *mercier*, fr. L. *merx, mercis*, wares.] *Eng.* A dealer in textile fabrics.

mer'cer·ize (-īz), *v. t.* [After John *Mercer* (1791–1866), Eng. calico printer.] To treat (cotton fiber or fabrics) with a solution of caustic alkali, to make the fiber stronger and more receptive of dyes, often in a way to give a silky luster.

mer'cer·y (-ĭ), *n.; pl.* -IES (-ĭz). [OF. *mercerie.*] *Eng.* Wares or goods to be found in a mercer's shop; also, a mercer's shop.

mer'chan·dise (mûr'chăn·dīz; -dīs), *n.* [OF. *marchandise.*] **1.** The objects of commerce; wares; goods. Abbr. *mdse.* **2.** *Archaic.* Trade. — (-dīz), *v. i. & t.* To trade or traffic (in); specif., to seek to further sales or use (of merchandise or services) by attractive presentation and publicity.

mer'chant (mûr'chănt), *n.* [OF. *marcheant, marchant*, deriv. of *mercari* to traffic, fr. *merx, mercis*, wares.] **1.** Originally, a trafficker; a trader; now esp., one who traffics on a large scale, esp. with foreign countries. **2.** One who carries on a retail business; a storekeeper or shopkeeper. — *adj.* **1.** Pertaining to, or used in, trade; of the merchant marine; commercial. **2.** Being, or of the character of, a merchant; as, a *merchant* prince.

mer'chant·a·ble (mûr'chăn·tȧ·b'l), *adj.* Marketable.

mer'chant·man (mûr'chănt·măn), *n.; pl.* -MEN (-mĕn). **1.** *Archaic.* A merchant. **2.** A trading vessel.

merchant marine. The commercial vessels of a nation; also, the personnel of these vessels.

mer'ci·ful (mûr'sĭ·fo͝ol; -f'l), *adj.* Full of mercy; exercising mercy; compassionate. — **mer'ci·ful·ly**, *adv.* — **mer'ci·ful·ness**, *n.*

mer'ci·less, *adj.* Destitute of mercy; pitiless; unsparing. — **mer'ci·less·ly**, *adv.* — **mer'ci·less·ness**, *n.*

mer'cu·rate (mûr'kū·rāt), *v. t.* *Chem.* To combine or treat with mercury or a mercury salt.

mer·cu'ri·al (mûr·kū'rĭ·ăl; 114), *adj.* [L. *mercurialis* of Mercury, fr. *Mercurius* Mercury.] **1.** Having qualities supposed to come from being born under the planet Mercury, or supposedly inspired by the god Mercury, or likened to the properties of the metal mercury; as: swift; eloquent; clever; commercial; thievish; volatile. **2.** *Med.* Caused by, or exhibiting the effect of, the use of mercury. — **Syn.** See INCONSTANT. — *n. Pharm.* A preparation containing mercury. — **mer·cu'ri·al·ly**, *adv.* — **mer·cu'ri·al·ness**, *n.*

mer·cu'ri·al·ism (-ĭz'm), *n.* *Med.* Chronic mercury poisoning.

mer·cu'ri·al·ize (-īz), *v. t.* **1.** To make mercurial. **2.** *Med.* To treat with mercury.

mer·cu'ric (mûr·kū'rĭk; 114), *adj.* *Chem.* Of, pertaining to, or containing mercury; — specif. of compounds in which this element has a valence of two.

mercuric chloride. See MERCURY CHLORIDE.

Mer·cu'ro·chrome' (mûr·kū'rō·krōm'), *n.* A trade-mark applied to a red organic mercury-containing dye used as an antiseptic and germicide.

mer·cu'rous (mûr·kū'rŭs; mûr'kū·rŭs), *adj.* *Chem.* Of, pertaining to, or derived from mercury; — used specif. of compounds in which this element is univalent.

Mer'cu·ry (mûr'kū·rĭ), *n.; pl.* -RIES (-rĭz). [L. *Mercurius*, the god and the planet.] **1.** *Rom. Relig.* A god identified with the Greek Hermes. **2.** [*not cap.*] A carrier of tidings; a messenger; a guide. **3.** [*not cap.*] A heavy silver-white metallic element, the only metal that is liquid at ordinary temperatures; — called also, popularly, *quicksilver.* Symbol, *Hg* (*hydrargyrum*); at. no., 80; at. wt., 200.61. **4.** [*not cap.*] The mercury in a thermometer or barometer. Cf. ALTIMETER, THERMOMETER, *Illusts.* **5.** *Astron.* The smallest planet of the solar system (diameter 3,000 miles) being the nearest known one to the sun, from which its mean distance is about 36,000,000 miles. See PLANET, *Table.* **6.** *Bot.* [*not cap.*] A poisonous European plant (*M. perennis*) of the spurge family.

mercury, *or* **mercuric, chloride.** A heavy crystalline salt, $HgCl_2$; — called also *corrosive sublimate* and (loosely) *bichloride of mercury.* It is a virulent poison, a powerful antiseptic and preservative, and an antisyphilitic, and is useful in dyeing and photography.

mer'cu·ry–va'por lamp. A lamp in which an electric discharge through mercury vapor in a vacuum tube (***mercury arc***) emits a light rich in actinic and ultraviolet rays.

mer'cy (mûr'sĭ), *n.; pl.* MERCIES (-sĭz). [OF. *merci*, fr. L. *merces, mercedis*, hire, pay, reward, LL., equiv. to *misericordia* pity, mercy.] **1.** Forbearance from inflicting harm, esp. as punishment, under provocation; compassionate treatment of an offender or adversary. **2.** Disposition to exercise compassion or forgiveness; willingness to spare or to help. **3.** The power to be merciful; clemency; as, to throw oneself on the *mercy* of the court. **4.** Any circumstance felt to be providential. **5.** Compassionate treatment of the unfortunate.

Syn. Mercy, charity, grace, clemency, lenity mean a showing compassion or kindness in dealing with others. Mercy implies compassion so great as to enable one to forbear punishing even when justice demands it; charity stresses benevolence and good will as manifest not only in giving but in broad understanding of others and kindly tolerance; grace implies benignancy and helpfulness to those dependent on one, especially on God; clemency implies a mild or merciful disposition, esp. in a judge; lenity implies a lack of severity in punishing.

— *adj.* Administered, or acting, out of mercy, esp. for putting a victim out of misery; as, a *mercy* slaying or slayer.

mercy seat. **a** *Jewish Antiq.* The gold plate resting on the Ark on which the blood of sacrificial animals was sprinkled. **b** Figuratively, the throne of God or of Christ.

mere (mēr), *n.* [AS. *mǣre, gemǣre.*] A boundary.

mere, *n.* [AS. *mere* sea.] *Archaic.* A small lake; a pond or pool.

mere (mēr), *adj.; superl.* MER'EST (mēr'ĕst; -ĭst). [OF. and L.; OF. *mier*, fr. L. *merus.*] **1.** *Obs.* Nothing less than; absolute; sheer; unqualified. **2.** Only this, and nothing else; nothing more than; such and no more; as, a *mere* form.

-mere (-mēr). [Gr. *meros.*] A combining form meaning *part, portion*, as in blasto*mere.*

mere'ly (mēr'lĭ), *adv.* **1.** *Obs.* Purely; absolutely. **2.** Not otherwise than; simply; barely; only.

mer'e·tri'cious (mĕr'ē·trĭsh'ŭs), *adj.* [L. *meretricius*, fr. *meretrix, -icis*, a prostitute, fr. *merere* to earn.] **1.** Of, pertaining to, characteristic of, or being a prostitute. **2.** Alluring by false show; gaudily and deceitfully ornamental. — **Syn.** See GAUDY. — **mer'e·tri'cious·ly**, *adv.* — **mer'e·tri'cious·ness**, *n.*

mer·gan'ser (mẽr·găn'sẽr), *n.; see* PLURAL, *Note*, 3. [NL., fr. L. *mergus* diver (bird, fr. *mergere* to plunge) + *anser* goose.] Any of a subfamily (Merginae) of fish-eating ducks, expert divers, having a slender bill, hooked at the end, and the head usually crested. See BILL, *Illust.* The ***hooded merganser*** (*Lophodytes cucullatus*) is a small North American variety, with a high round crest on the head of the adult male. The ***red-breasted merganser*** (*Mergus serrator*) is an allied form found both in Europe and America.

merge (mûrj), *v. t.;* MERGED (mûrjd); MERG'ING (mûr'jĭng). [L. *mergere, mersum.*] **1.** To cause to be swallowed up; to immerse; sink. **2.** To cause to combine or coalesce. — *v. i.* To be swallowed up; to lose identity by absorption or immersion in something else. — **Syn.** See MIX.

mer'gence (mûr'jĕns), *n.* A merging; state of being merged.

merg'er (mûr'jẽr), *n.* *Law.* **a** An absorption of one estate, or of one contract or interest, in another, or of a minor offense in a greater. **b** Specif., of corporations, the vesting of the control of different corporations in a single one by the issue of stock of the controlling corporation in place of a majority of the stock of the others, without dissolution of the consolidating companies as, strictly, in *consolidation.*

me·rid'i·an (mē·rĭd'ĭ·ăn; mē-), *adj.* [OF. *meridien*, fr. L. *meridianus*, fr. *meridies* noon, for older *medidies*, fr. *medius* middle + *dies* day.] **1.** Being at, or pertaining to, midday; belonging to, or passing through, the highest point attained by a heavenly body in its diurnal course. **2.** Of or pertaining to a meridian. **3.** Pertaining to, or characteristic of, the highest point or culmination.

— *n.* **1.** *Obs.* Midday; noon. **2.** Of a star or the sun, its highest apparent point. **3.** The highest point, as of success, prosperity, or the like; culmination, as the prime of a man's life. **4.** *Astron.* A great circle of the celestial sphere passing through its poles and the zenith of a given place. **5.** *Geog.* **a** A great circle on the surface of the earth, passing through the poles and any given place; also, and now usually, the half of such a circle included between the poles. See PRIME MERIDIAN. **b** The representation of such a circle or half circle, as by means of a line, the series of such lines being numbered according to the degrees of longitude. — **Syn.** See SUMMIT.

me·rid'i·o·nal (-ō·năl; -n'l), *adj.* [F. *méridional*, fr. LL. *meridionalis*, fr. *meridies* midday, south. See MERIDIAN.] **1.** Of, pert. to, or located in the south; southern; southerly. **2.** Of, pert. to, or characteristic of, people living in the south, as of Europe, esp. France. **3.** Of, pert. to, or suggestive of a meridian. — *n.* [*cap.*] One who lives in the south, as of Europe, esp. France. — **me·rid'i·o·nal·ly**, *adv.*

me·ringue' (mē·răng'; *F.* -răng'), *n.* [F.] A delicate mixture of the beaten whites of eggs and powdered sugar, used as an icing or made into small cakes and quickly browned; also, a cake or shell made of this.

me·ri'no (mĕ·rē'nō; mē-), *n.; pl.* -NOS (-nōz). [Sp.] **1.** A fine-wooled white sheep of a hardy gregarious breed (**Merino**) with heavy twisted horns in the male. **2.** A fine soft fabric resembling cashmere, orig. of merino wool. **3.** A fine wool yarn used in hosiery, knit underwear, etc. — **me·ri'no**, *adj.*

mer'i·stem (mĕr'ĭ·stĕm), *n.* [Gr. *meristos* divided, divisible, fr.

merizein to divide, fr. *meros* part.] *Bot.* Embryonic or undifferentiated tissue the cells of which are capable of active division. ***apical meristem*** is located at the tips of the axes, etc.; ***intercalary meristem*** lies at nodal regions separating portions of permanent tissue; ***lateral meristem*** has a layered distribution. — **mer′i·ste·mat′ic** (mĕr′ĭ·stē·măt′ĭk), *adj.*

mer′it (mĕr′ĭt), *n.* [OF. *merite*, fr. L. *meritum*, fr. *merere, mereri*, to deserve.] **1.** Due reward or punishment; usually, reward deserved; a mark or token of excellence or approbation. **2.** Quality, state, or fact of deserving well or ill; desert; as, each according to his *merit.* **3.** Worth; excellence. **4.** That which is counted to one as a cause or reason of deserving well; a praiseworthy quality, act, etc. — *v. t. & i.* To earn by service or performance; deserve.

mer′it·ed, *adj.* Deserved. — **mer′it·ed·ly**, *adv.*

mer′i·to′ri·ous (mĕr′ĭ·tō′rĭ·ŭs), *adj.* [L. *meritorius* that brings in money.] Deserving of reward or honor; well-deserving. — **mer′i·to′ri·ous·ly**, *adv.* — **mer′i·to′ri·ous·ness**, *n.*

merit system. The system of appointing employees to the civil service, and of promoting them, for competence only. Cf. SPOILS SYSTEM.

merl, merle (mûrl), *n.* [F. *merle*, fr. L. *merulus, merula.*] The European blackbird (*Turdus merula*).

mer′lin (mûr′lĭn), *n.* [OF. *esmerillon.*] A small European falcon (*Falco aesalon*) resembling the American pigeon hawk (*F. columbarius*) to which the name has been extended. See HAWK.

Mer′lin, *n.* [ML. *Merlinus*, W. *Myrddin.*] In medieval romance, a prophet and magician of the 5th century. Cf. VIVIAN.

mer′lon (-lŏn), *n.* [F., fr. It. *merlone*, augm. of *merlo.*] *Fort.* One of the solid intervals between crenels of a battlemented parapet. See BATTLEMENT, *Illust.*

mer′maid′ (mûr′mād′), *n.* [See MERE lake; MAID.] A fabled marine creature, typically represented with a woman's body and a fish's tail. The corresponding male is called **mer′man′** (-măn′); *pl.* -MEN (-mĕn′).

mer′o·blas′tic (mĕr′ō·blăs′tĭk), *adj.* [Gr. *meros* part + *-blast* + *-ic.*] *Embryol.* Undergoing partial or incomplete cleavage; — said of eggs that contain considerable accumulations of food yolk, and opp. to *holoblastic.*

-merous. [Gr. *meros* part.] *Bot.* A suffix meaning *partite*, denoting *of* (so many or such) *parts*, as in *dimerous, trimerous,* tetra*merous,* penta*merous,* etc. (Often written 2-*merous*, etc.)

Mer′o·vin′gi·an (mĕr′ō·vĭn′jĭ·ăn), *adj.* Of or designating the first Frankish dynasty in Gaul or France, founded by Clovis I about A.D. 500. Cf. CAROLINGIAN.

mer′ri·ment (mĕr′ĭ·mĕnt), *n.* Act of merrymaking; gaiety; mirth; hilarity; fun.

mer′ry (mĕr′ĭ), *adj.*; -RI·ER (-ĭ·ĕr); -RI·EST. [AS. *myrge, myrige,* pleasant.] **1.** *Archaic.* Pleasant; delightful; of sounds, etc., sweet; of a wind, favorable. **2.** Laughingly gay; mirthful. **3.** Amusing; funny. **4.** Marked by gaiety or festivity. **5.** *Archaic.* Facetious; jocular. — **mer′ri·ly**, *adv.* — **mer′ri·ness**, *n.*

Syn. **Merry, blithe, jocund, jovial, jolly** mean exhibiting high spirits or lightness of heart. **Merry** implies uninhibited enjoyment of frolic, festivity, or fun; **blithe** stresses, in addition, freshness and buoyancy as manifest in singing, leaping, and dancing; **jocund** stresses exhilaration of spirits and elation; **jovial** stresses the stimulation of good fellowship or conviviality; **jolly** stresses extremely high spirits as manifest in jesting, bantering, and the like.

mer′ry–an′drew (-ăn′drōō), *n.* One whose business is to make sport for others; a buffoon; a clown; a zany.

mer′ry–go–round′, *n.* **1.** A revolving contrivance for children, as a ring of wooden horses on a revolving platform; a carrousel. **2.** Figuratively, a rapid round; a whirl.

mer′ry·mak′ing (mĕr′ĭ·māk′ĭng), *adj.* Festive; jolly. — *n.* Act of making merry; festivity. — **mer′ry·mak′er** (-ĕr), *n.*

mer′ry·thought′ (-thôt′), *n.* The wishbone.

Mer·thi′o·late (mûr·thī′ō·lāt), *n.* A trade-mark applied to a mercurial antiseptic and germicide used in medicine and surgery, and as a biological preservative.

mes-. = MESO-, as in *mes*encephalon.

me′sa (mā′sȧ), *n.* [Sp.] A flat-topped rocky hill with steeply sloping sides, common in southwestern U. S.

‖**mé′sal′liance′** (mā′zȧ′lyäns′; mā·zăl′ĭ·ăns), *n.* [F.] A marriage with a person of inferior social position.

mes·cal′ (mĕs·kăl′), *n.* [Sp. *mezcal*, fr. Nahuatl *mexcalli* a drink.] **1.** A small cactus (*Lophophora williamsii*), having rounded stems or joints covered with ribbed tubercles, the tops being called *mescal buttons.* The plant is used as a stimulant and antispasmodic, esp. among the Mexican Indians. **2.** A colorless liquor distilled from pulque; also, any plant which yields the liquor, esp. maguey.

mes′dames′ (mā′dȧm′), *n., pl.* of MADAM, MADAME.

‖**mes′de·moi′selles′** (mād′mwȧ′zĕl′), *n., pl.* of MADEMOISELLE.

me·seems′ (mē·sēmz′), *v. impers.; past tense* ME·SEEMED′ (-sēmd′). *Chiefly Archaic.* It seems to me.

mes′en·ceph′a·lon (mĕs′ĕn·sĕf′ȧ·lŏn), *n.* See MIDBRAIN. — **mes′en·ce·phal′ic** (-sē·făl′ĭk), *adj.*

mes′en·chyme (mĕs′ĕng·kīm), *n.* [*mes-* + Gr. *en* in + *chein* to pour.] *Embryol.* A mesoblastic tissue, comprising all the mesoblast except the mesothelium and the structures derived from it, which gives rise to the connective tissues, blood lymphatics, bone, cartilage, etc. — **mes·en′chy·mal** (mĕs·ĕng′kĭ·măl), *adj.*

mes·en′ter·on (mĕs·ĕn′tĕr·ŏn), *n.*; *pl.* -TERA (-ȧ). [NL., fr. *mes-* + *enteron.*] *Anat. & Zool.* All that part of the alimentary canal developed from the archenteron and lined with hypoblast; — disting. from *proctodaeum* and *stomodaeum.* See GASTRULA. — **mes·en′ter·on′ic** (-ŏn′ĭk), *adj.*

mes′en·ter′y (mĕs′ĕn·tĕr′ĭ *or, esp. Brit.,* -tĕr·ĭ), *n.*; *pl.* -TERIES (-ĭz). [From ML., fr. Gr. *mesenterion*, fr. *mesos* middle + *enteron* intestine.] *Anat. & Zool.* The membranes or one of the membranes that invest the intestines and connect them with the dorsal wall of the abdominal cavity; also, in various invertebrates, a similar membranous fold. — **mes′en·ter′ic** (-tĕr′ĭk), *adj.* — **mes·en′ter·i′tis** (mĕs·ĕn′tĕr·ī′tĭs), *n.* (see -ITIS).

mesh (mĕsh), *n.* **1.** One of the spaces enclosed by the threads of a net between knot and knot; also, one of the similar spaces of any network, as a sieve. The coarseness or fineness of screens is expressed as the number of such openings per linear inch; as, a 60-*mesh* screen. **2.** *pl.* The threads enclosing such a space. **3.** Network; a net. **4.** *Mach.* Engagement, or working contact, of the teeth of wheels or of a wheel and rack; — chiefly in *in mesh.* — *v. t.* **1.** To catch in meshes as of a net; to entangle. **2.** *Mach.* To cause to engage; put in mesh. **3.** To put into close adjustment; — often with *into* or *with.* — *v. i.* **1.** To become entangled in or as in meshes. **2.** *Mach.* To engage with each other, as the teeth of wheels. **3.** To fit together in close adjustment.

mesh′work′ (mĕsh′wûrk′), *n.* Meshes; network.

me′si·al (mē′zĭ·ăl; mĕs′ĭ·ăl), *adj.* [Gr. *mesos* middle.] Middle; dividing an animal into right and left halves. — **me′si·al·ly**, *adv.*

me·sit′y·lene (mē·sĭt′ĭ·lēn; mĕs′ĭ·tĭ·lēn′), *n.* [*mesityl* (Gr. *mesitēs* mediator, fr. *mesos* middle) + *-ene.*] *Chem.* A colorless oily hydrocarbon, $C_6H_3(CH_3)_3$, prepared by distilling acetone with sulfuric acid.

mes·mer′ic (mĕz·mĕr′ĭk; mĕs-), *adj.* Of, pert. to, or induced by mesmerism. — **mes·mer′i·cal·ly** (-ĭ·kăl·ĭ), *adv.*

mes′mer·ism (mĕz′mĕr·ĭz′m; mĕs′-), *n.* [After F. A. *Mesmer* (1734–1815), Viennese physician.] Hypnotism. — **mes′mer·ist** (-ĭst), *n.*

mes′mer·ize (mĕz′mĕr·īz; mĕs′-), *v. t. & i.* To hypnotize. — **mes′mer·iz′er** (-īz′ĕr), *n.*

mesne (mēn), *adj.* [Law F. form of AF. *meen.* See MEAN intermediate.] *Law.* Middle; intervening; as, a **mesne lord**, one *tenant* to a superior but *lord* to his own tenant.

mes′o- (mĕs′ō-; mē′sō-), **mes-.** [Gr. *mesos* middle.] A combining form meaning: **1.** *In the middle*, as in **mes′o·seis′mal**, pert. to the center of an earthquake disturbance; *intermediate in position, size, time,* or *degree,* as in **mes′o·dont**, having medium-sized teeth. **2.** *Anat.* **a** *An intermediate connective part,* as in **mes′o·cae′cum**, the fold of peritoneum attached to the caecum; **mes′o·rec′tum.** **b** *A mesentery,* as in **mes′o·co′lon**, a mesentery joining the abdominal wall; **mes′o·ap·pen′dix; mes′o·va′ri·um.**

mes′o·blast (mĕs′ō·blăst; mē′sō-), *n.* [*meso-* + *-blast.*] *Embryol. & Zool.* The middle germ layer of the embryo. — **mes′o·blas′tic** (-blăs′tĭk), *adj.*

mes′o·carp (-kärp), *n.* [*meso-* + *-carp.*] *Bot.* The middle layer of a pericarp. See ENDOCARP, *Illust.*

mes′o·ce·phal′ic (-sē·făl′ĭk), *adj.* Having the cranial cavity of medium capacity.

mes′o·derm (mĕs′ō·dûrm; mē′sō-), *n.* [*meso-* + *-derm.*] *Embryol. & Zool.* The mesoblast; also, the tissues subsequently developed from it. — **mes′o·der′mal** (-dûr′măl), *adj.*

mes′o·gas′tri·um (-găs′trĭ·ŭm), *n.* [NL., fr. *meso-* + Gr. *gastēr* belly.] *Anat.* **a** In the embryo, either of the two mesenteries of the stomach. **b** The umbilical region. — **mes′o·gas′tric** (-trĭk), *adj.*

mes′o·gloe′a, mes′o·gle′a (-glē′ȧ), *n.* [NL., fr. *meso-* + Gr. *gloios* a glutinous substance.] *Zool.* In coelenterates, a jellylike interstitial material which takes the place of the mesoblastic layer of higher animals. — **mes′o·gloe′al, mes′o·gle′al** (-ăl), *adj.*

me·sog′na·thous (mē·sŏg′nȧ·thŭs; mē-), *adj.* [*meso-* + *-gnathous.*] *Anthropom.* Having the jaws of medium size and slightly projecting; also, having a facial profile angle of 80° to 85°. — **me·sog′na·thism** (-thĭz′m), **me·sog′na·thy** (-thĭ).

mes′o·mor′phic (mĕs′ō·môr′fĭk; mē′sō-), *adj.* [*meso*derm + *-morphic.*] *Anthropol.* Characterized by predominance of the structures developed from the mesodermal layer of the embryo, that is, bone, muscle, and connective tissue; hence, of the athletic type of body build. Cf. ECTOMORPHIC, ENDOMORPHIC. — **mes′o·mor′phy** (mĕs′ō·môr′fĭ; mē′sō-), *n.* — **mes′o·morph** (-môrf), *n.*

mes′on (mĕs′ŏn; mē′sŏn), *n.* [NL., fr. *meso-* + electr*on.*] *Physics & Chem.* A particle of approximately 200 times the mass of the electron, having either a positive or a negative charge. It has been detected in cosmic rays and in the rays from vacuum tubes producing high-energy X rays. It is unstable and has a half life of a few microseconds. Called also *mesotron.*

mes′o·neph′ros (mĕs′ō·nĕf′rŏs; mē′sō-), *n.* [NL., fr. *meso-* + Gr. *nephros* kidney.] *Embryol.* One of the middle of the three pairs of embryonic renal organs of typical vertebrates; the Wolffian body. — **mes′o·neph′ric** (-rĭk), *adj.*

mes′o·phyll (mĕs′ō·fĭl; mē′sō-), *n.* *Bot.* The green parenchyma between the epidermal layers of a foliage leaf.

mes′o·phyte (-fīt), *n.* A plant that grows under medium conditions of moisture. — **mes′o·phyt′ic** (-fĭt′ĭk), *adj.*

mes′o·plast (-plăst), *n.* [*meso-* + *-plast.*] *Biol.* The nucleus of a cell. — **mes′o·plas′tic** (-plăs′tĭk), *adj.*

mes′o·the′li·um (mĕs′ō·thē′lĭ·ŭm; mē′sō-), *n.* [NL., fr. *meso-* + epi*thelium.*] *Anat. & Embryol.* **a** Epithelium of mesoblastic origin. **b** That part of the mesoblast which lines the primitive coelom, and is distinguished from the mesenchyme by its epithelial character. — **mes′o·the′li·al** (-ăl), *adj.*

mes′o·tho′rax (-thō′răks), *n.* *Zool.* The middle of the three segments of the thorax of an insect. See INSECT, *Illust.*

mes′o·tho′ri·um (mĕs′ō·thō′rĭ·ŭm; mĕz′ō-), *n.* [NL., fr. *meso-* + *thorium.*] *Chem.* Either of two radioactive products intermediate between thorium and radiothorium; specif., **mesothorium 1** (at. no., 88, an isotope of radium), disintegrating to give **mesothorium 2** (at. no., 89).

mes′o·tron (mĕs′ō·trŏn; mē′sō-), *n.* [NL., fr. *meso-* + elec*tron.*] = MESON.

Mes′o·zo′ic (mĕs′ō·zō′ĭk; mē′sō-), *adj.* [*meso-* + Gr. *zōē* life.] Of, pertaining to, or designating an era of geological history between the Paleozoic and the Cenozoic, or the group of rocks formed in this era. It is the age of dinosaurs, of marine and flying reptiles, and of ganoid fishes. — **Mes′o·zo′ic**, *n.*

mes·quite′ (mĕs·kēt′; mĕs′kēt), *n.* [Sp. *mezquite*, fr. Nahuatl *mizquitl.*] **a** A spiny, deep-rooted tree or shrub (*Prosopis juliflora*) of the mimosa family, of southwestern U. S. and Mexico, bearing beanlike pods rich in sugar. **b** The screw bean.

mess (mĕs), *n.* [OF. *mes*, fr. L. *missus* course at a meal, prop., past part. of *mittere* to put, place (e.g., on the table), fr. L. *mittere* to send.] **1.** A quantity of food; specif.: **a** A prepared dish or a portion or kind of soft food, as milk or porridge. **b** A sufficient quantity (of a specified kind of food) for a dish or meal. **2.** A group of persons who regularly eat together; also, the meal so taken; as, absent from *mess.* **3. a** A confused or disagreeable mixture of things; a hodgepodge. **b** A muddle; botch. — *v. t.* **1.** To supply with messes, or meals. **2.** *Colloq.* To make a mess of; to muddle. — *v. i.* **1.** To take meals with a mess. **2.** To make a mess; hence, to putter; meddle.

mes′sage (mĕs′ĭj), *n.* [OF., fr. ML. *missaticum*, fr. L. *mittere, missum,* to send.] **1.** Any notice or communication sent from one person to another. **2.** A messenger's errand or function. **3.** A divinely inspired communication, as of a prophet; divine tidings.

mes′sa·line′ (mĕs′ȧ·lēn′; mĕs′ȧ·lēn), *n.* [F.] A soft, twilled, usually silk, fabric.

mes′san (mĕs′ăn), **mes′sin** (mĕs′′n), *n.* [Gael. *measan.*] *Scot. & Dial.* A lap dog; a cur.

mes′sei·gneurs′ (mĕs′ā·nyûrz′; *F.* mā′sĕ′nyûr′), *n., pl.* of MONSEIGNEUR.

mes′sen·ger (mĕs′ĕn·jẽr; -ĭn·jẽr), *n.* [With intrusive *n*, fr. OF. *messagier.* See MESSAGE.] **1.** One who bears a message or does an errand; as: **a** A government dispatch bearer; courier. **b** An employee who bears messages; a runner. **2.** A forerunner; herald.

Mes·si′ah (mĕ·sī′ȧ), *n.* [Aram. *mĕshīḥā*, Heb. *māhsīaḥ*, anointed.] The expected king and deliverer of the Hebrews; the Christ. — **mes·si′ah·ship**, *n.* — **Mes′si·an′ic** (mĕs′ĭ·ăn′ĭk), *adj.*

Mes·si′as (mĕ·sī′ăs), *n.* [LL., fr. Gr.] The Messiah.

‖Mes′si′dor′ (mĕ′sē′dôr′), *n.* [F., fr. L. *messis* harvest + Gr. *dōron* gift.] See REVOLUTIONARY CALENDAR.

mes′sieurs (mĕs′ẽrz; -yẽrz; *F.* mā′syû′), *n., pl.* of MONSIEUR; — used [*cap.*] as *pl.* of E. *Mister* (*Mr.*) and abbreviated to *Messrs.*

mess jacket. *Mil. & Nav.* A short tailless uniform jacket open in front, worn on semiformal evening occasions.

mess kit. The cooking and table utensils of a mess, with the container in which they are packed for transportation; also, a soldier's or a camper's kit for cooking or holding food at mess.

mess′mate′ (mĕs′māt′), *n.* An associate in a mess, esp. in a sailors' mess.

mes′suage (mĕs′wĭj), *n.* [AF. *mesuage*, prob. for *mesnage.* See MÉNAGE.] *Law.* A dwelling house, with the adjacent buildings and curtilage, and the adjoining lands; a toft.

mess′y (mĕs′ĭ), *adj.*; MESS′I·ER (-ĭ·ẽr); MESS′I·EST. Like a mess; disordered, untidy. — **mess′i·ness**, *n.*

mes·tee′ (mĕs·tē′), *n.* [From MESTIZO.] A mustee.

mes·ti′zo (mĕs·tē′zō), *n.*; *pl.* -ZOS (-zōz). [Sp., fr. LL. *misticius*, *mixticius*, fr. L. *mixtus* mixed.] Esp. in Spanish America and the Philippines, a person of mixed blood; esp., the offspring of a European and an (East) Indian, Negro, or Malay; often, *Phil. I.*, a person of Chinese and native blood. — **mes·ti′za** (-zȧ), *n. fem.*

met (mĕt), *past & past part.* of MEET.

met′a- (mĕt′ȧ-), **met-.** [Gr. *meta* between, with, after.] A prefix meaning in general *along with, after*, denoting: **1. a** *Posteriority* or *succession*, as in *meta*genesis; also, *Anat.*, *dorso-*. **b** *Change; transposition; transfer; trans-*; as in *meta*morphosis. **c** [From *meta*physics.] *Beyond; transcending; higher;* as in *meta*psychosis. **2.** *Chem.* **a** A substance *isomeric with*, or *otherwise closely related to* (the one to whose name the prefix is attached). **b** Denoting certain inorganic acids and hydroxides *derived from the ortho*, or ordinary, *form by loss of water* (*usually of one molecule of water from each molecule of acid or hydroxide*), as in *meta*phosphoric acid, HPO_3. Cf. PYRO-. **c** Any of certain benzene derivatives or compounds analogous to them in structure. Abbr. *m-*. See BENZENE RING. **3.** *Med. Occurring subsequently; post-*; as in ***met′a·in·fec′tive***, occurring after infection.

met′a (mĕt′ȧ), *adj. Chem.* = META-, 2; as, *meta* position.

met′a·bol′ic (mĕt′ȧ·bŏl′ĭk), *adj.* [Gr. *metabolikos*, fr. *metabolē* change, fr. *meta* beyond + *ballein* to throw.] **1.** *Biol. & Physiol.* Of, pertaining to, or characterized by metabolism. **2.** *Zool.* Undergoing, or pertaining to, a metamorphosis.

me·tab′o·lism (mĕ·tăb′ō·lĭz′m), *n.* **1.** *Biol. & Physiol.* The sum of the processes concerned in the building up (*anabolism*) of protoplasm and its destruction (*catabolism*) incidental to life; the chemical changes in living cells, by which the energy is provided for the vital processes and activities, and new material is assimilated to repair the waste. **2.** *Zool.* Metamorphosis; — esp. that in insects.

me·tab′o·lite (-līt), *n.* Any product of metabolism.

me·tab′o·lize (-līz), *v. t. & i. Physiol.* To subject to or perform metabolism.

met′a·car′pus (mĕt′ȧ·kär′pŭs), *n.* [NL., fr. Gr. *metakarpion*, fr. *meta* beyond, between + *karpos* the wrist.] *Anat. & Zool.* The part of the hand or forefoot (esp. of its skeleton) between the carpus and the phalanges. — **met′a·car′pal** (-păl), *adj. & n.*

met′a·cen′ter, met′a·cen′tre (mĕt′ȧ·sĕn′tẽr; mĕt′ȧ·sĕn′tẽr), *n.* [See META-; CENTER.] *Hydros. & Shipbuilding.* The point of intersection (*M* in *Illust.*) of the vertical through the center of buoyancy (*B*) of a floating body with the vertical through the new center of buoyancy (*B′*) when the body is displaced however little. When *M* is above the center of gravity (*G*) of the floating body the position of the body is stable; when below it, unstable; when coincident with it, neutral. — **met′a·cen′tric** (mĕt′ȧ·sĕn′trĭk), *adj.*

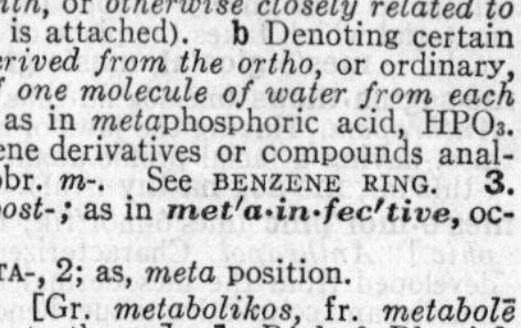

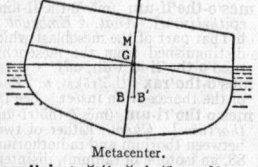

Metacenter.

met′a·chro′ma·tism (mĕt′ȧ·krō′mȧ·tĭz′m), *n.* [*meta-* + Gr. *chrōma*, *chrōmatos*, color.] Change of color; specif., *Physical Chem.*, such a change, due to a change in physical conditions, esp. in the temperature of a body.

met′a·cy′mene (-sī′mēn), *n.* See CYMENE.

met′a·gal′ax·y (mĕt′ȧ·găl′ăk·sĭ; 2), *n.* [*meta-* + *galaxy.*] *Astron.* The entire system of galaxies external to our own Galaxy; the universe. — **met′a·ga·lac′tic** (-gȧ·lăk′tĭk), *adj.*

met′age (mēt′ĭj), *n.* [From METE, *v.*] Official measurement of contents or weight; also, the charge for it.

met′a·gen′e·sis (mĕt′ȧ·jĕn′ĕ·sĭs), *n. Biol.* Alternation of generations. — **met′a·ge·net′ic** (-jĕ·nĕt′ĭk), *adj.*

me·tag′na·thous (mĕ·tăg′nȧ·thŭs), *adj.* [*meta-* + *gnathous.*] Having the tips of the mandibles crossed, as the crossbills. — **me·tag′na·thism** (-thĭz′m), *n.*

met′al (mĕt′′l), *n.* [OF. *metal, metail*, fr. L. *metallum* metal, mine, fr. Gr. *metallon* mine.] **1.** Any of a class of substances which typically show a peculiar luster, are good conductors of electricity and heat, are opaque, and may be fused; also, any such substance without reference to special character; as, a piece of *metal*. **2.** Material; substance; stuff; hence, spirit; mettle. **3.** *Chem.* An elementary metal (sense 1), as distinguished from a mixed metal, or *alloy*. **4.** *Glass Mfg.* Glass in a state of fusion. **5.** *Her.* Or (gold) or argent (silver) used as a tincture. **6.** *Naval.* The effective power of guns on a war vessel, expressed in terms of the weight of projectiles fired in a broadside; as, a ship with more *metal* in its main battery. **7.** *Print.* Type metal; hence, state of being in type. **8.** *Roads, Railroads, etc.* Crushed stone, cinders, etc., used in making roads, ballasting roadbeds, or the like. — *v. t.*; MET′ALED (-′ld) or MET′ALLED; MET′AL·ING or MET′AL·LING. To cover or furnish with metal.

met′al·ize, met′al·lize (-īz), *v. t.* To coat with or impregnate with a metal or metallic compound.

me·tal′lic (mĕ·tăl′ĭk), *adj.* **1.** Of, pertaining to, or made of a metal; of the nature of metal; being, or characteristic of, a metal in the free state. **2.** Resembling metal, as in sound under percussion, or in hard, inflexible quality. **3.** Yielding metal; metalliferous.

met′al·lif′er·ous (mĕt′′l·ĭf′ẽr·ŭs), *adj.* [L. *metallifer*, fr. *metallum* metal + *ferre* to bear.] Producing or containing metal.

met′al·line (mĕt′′l·ĭn; -īn), *adj.* **1.** Metallic. **2.** Impregnated with metallic salts.

met′al·log′ra·phy (-ŏg′rȧ·fĭ), *n.* Microscopic study of metal structure and alloys. — **me·tal′lo·graph′ic** (mĕ·tăl′ō·grăf′ĭk), *adj.*

met′al·loid (mĕt′′l·oid), *n. Chem.* **a** A nonmetal. See NONMETAL. **b** An element, as arsenic, antimony, or tellurium, resembling the typical metals in certain properties only. — *adj.* **1.** Having the appearance of a metal. **2.** *Chem.* Of, pertaining to, or of the nature of a metalloid.

me·tal′lo·ther′a·py (mĕ·tăl′ō·thĕr′ȧ·pĭ), *n.* [Gr. *metallon* metal + *therapy.*] *Med.* Treatment of disease by administration of metals, or esp., of their salts.

met′al·lur′gy (mĕt′′l·ûr′jĭ; mĕ·tăl′ẽr·jĭ), *n.* [NL. *metallurgia*, fr. Gr. *metallourgos*, fr. *metallon* metal + *-ergos* worker.] The science and art of extracting metals from their ores, refining them, and preparing them for use. — **met′al·lur′gic** (mĕt′′l·ûr′jĭk), **met′al·lur′gi·cal** (-jĭ·kăl), *adj.* — **met′al·lur′gist** (mĕt′′l·ûr′jĭst; mĕ·tăl′ẽr·jĭst), *n.*

met′al·ware′ (mĕt′′l·wâr′), *n.* Work or ware of metal; esp., artistic work in metal.

met′al·work′ing (mĕt′′l·wûr′kĭng), *n.* The process or occupation of shaping things out of metal. — **met′al·work′** (-wûrk′), *n. & v.* — **met′al·work′er** (-wûr′kẽr), *n.*

met′a·mere (mĕt′ȧ·mēr), *n.* [*meta-* + *-mere.*] *Zool.* One of the more or less similar segments arranged in a longitudinal series composing the body of many animals. — **met′a·mer′ic** (-mĕr′ĭk), *adj.* — **me·tam′er·ism** (mĕ·tăm′ẽr·ĭz′m), *n.*

met′a·mor′phic (mĕt′ȧ·môr′fĭk), *adj.* **1.** Involving physical transformation; as, a *metamorphic* potion. **2.** Pertaining to metamorphosis. **3.** *Geol.* Of, pert. to, produced by, or exhibiting metamorphism; — esp. of rocks.

met′a·mor′phism (-fĭz′m), *n.* **1.** Metamorphosis. **2.** *Geol.* Change in the constitution of any rock; esp., a pronounced change effected by pressure, heat, and water, resulting in a more compact and crystalline condition.

met′a·mor′phose (-fōz; -fōs), *v. t.* **1.** To change into a different form; to transform; transmute. **2.** To cause to undergo metamorphosis or (*Geol.*) metamorphism. — **Syn.** See TRANSFORM.

met′a·mor′pho·sis (mĕt′ȧ·môr′fō·sĭs; -môr·fō′sĭs), *n.*; *pl.* -PHOSES (-sēz). [L., fr. Gr. *metamorphōsis*, fr. *metamorphoun* to transform, fr. *meta* beyond, over + *morphē* form.] **1.** Change of form, structure, or substance, esp. by witchcraft or magic; also, the form resulting from such a change. **2.** A striking alteration in appearance, character, or circumstances. **3.** *Med.* A form of degeneration marked by conversion of certain tissues or structures into other material. **4.** *Zool.* A marked and more or less abrupt change in the form or structure (and usually also in the habits, food, etc.) of an animal during postembryonic development, as when the larva of an insect becomes a pupa, or a tadpole changes to a frog.

met′a·neph′ros (-nĕf′rŏs), *n.* [NL., fr. *meta-* + Gr. *nephros* kidney.] *Embryol.* One of the posterior of the three pairs of embryonic renal organs developed in typical vertebrates.

met′a·phase (mĕt′ȧ·fāz), *n.* [*meta-* + *phase.*] *Biol.* A stage in mitosis following the prophase, in which the split chromosomes are grouped in the equatorial plane of the spindle. Cf. ANAPHASE.

Met′a·phen (mĕt′ȧ·fĕn), *n.* A trade-mark applied to a mercurial antiseptic used in skin sterilization, treatment of urogenital infection, and diseases of the eye, ear, nose, and throat.

met′a·phor (mĕt′ȧ·fẽr; -fôr), *n.* [F. *métaphore*, fr. L., fr. Gr. *metaphora*, fr. *metapherein* to carry over, transfer, fr. *meta* beyond, over + *pherein* to bring, bear.] *Rhet.* A figure of speech in which a word or phrase literally denoting one kind of object or idea is used in place of another by way of suggesting a likeness or analogy between them (the ship *plows* the sea; a *volley* of oaths). Cf. COMPARISON, 3; SIMILE; TROPE, 3.

met′a·phor′i·cal (-fŏr′ĭ·kăl), *adj.* Also **met′a·phor′ic** (-ĭk). Of, pertaining to, or comprising a metaphor. — **met′a·phor′i·cal·ly**, *adv.*

met′a·phos′phate (mĕt′ȧ·fŏs′fāt), *n. Chem.* A salt of metaphosphoric acid.

met′a·phos·phor′ic ac′id (mĕt′ȧ·fŏs·fŏr′ĭk; -fŏr′ĭk). See PHOSPHORIC ACID.

met′a·phrase (mĕt′ȧ·frāz), *n.* [Gr. *metaphrasis*, fr. *metaphrazein* to paraphrase.] A translation from one language into another. — *v. t.* **a** To make a metaphrase of. **b** To alter the wording of.

met′a·phrast (-frăst), *n.* One who metaphrases, as by rendering verse into a different meter, or prose into verse.

met′a·phys′ic (-fĭz′ĭk), *adj.* Metaphysical. — *n.* Metaphysics.

met′a·phys′i·cal (-fĭz′ĭ·kăl), *adj.* **1.** Of or pert. to metaphysics; hence, abstract or abstruse; as, *metaphysical* reasoning. **2.** Having, or pert. to, real being or essential nature of reality; as, *metaphysical* truth. **3.** *Obs.* Preternatural or supernatural. **4.** Designating or pertaining to a school of 17th-century poets, whose works abound in elaborate subtleties of thought and expression, including Donne, Cowley, and Herbert. — **met′a·phys′i·cal·ly**, *adv.*

met′a·phy·si′cian (-fĭ·zĭsh′ăn), *n.* A person versed in metaphysics.

met′a·phys′ics (-fĭz′ĭks), *n.*; see -ICS. [Gr. *meta ta physika* after physics, fr. *meta* beyond, after + *physikos* relating to external nature, natural, fr. *physis* nature.] That division of philosophy which includes ontology, or the science of being, and cosmology, or the science of the fundamental causes and processes in things; in a looser sense, all of the more abstruse philosophical disciplines; in a narrower sense, ontology alone.

met′a·pla′si·a (mĕt′ȧ·plā′zhĭ·ȧ), *n.* [NL. See META-; -PLASIA.] *Physiol.* Direct transformation of one form of tissue into another form, as of cartilage into bone.

met'a·plasm (mĕt'ȧ·plăz'm), *n.* [L. *metaplasmus*, fr. Gr. *metaplasmos*, fr. *meta* beyond, over + *plassein* to mold.] **1.** *Biol.* That part of the contents of a cell consisting of lifeless matter or inclusions, as certain carbohydrates. See CELL, 4, *Illust.* **2.** *Gram.* A change in the letters or syllables of a word. — **met'a·plas'mic** (-plăz'mĭk), *adj.*

met'a·pro'te·in (-prō'tē·ĭn; -tēn), *n.* [*meta-* + *protein.*] *Biochem.* Any of a class of products derived from proteins through the action of acids (***acid metaprotein***) or alkalies (***alkali metaprotein***), by which the solubility and sometimes the composition is changed.

met'a·psy·chol'o·gy (-sī·kŏl'ō·jĭ), *n.* Psychology which supplements empiricism by speculations on the connection of mental and physical processes or on the place of mind in the universe. — **met'a·psy'cho·log'i·cal** (-sī'kō·lŏj'ĭ·kăl), *adj.*

me·tap'sy·cho'sis (mĕ·tăp'sĭ·kō'sĭs), *n.* [NL.] The action of mind on mind without known physical agency.

met'a·so'ma·tism (mĕt'ȧ·sō'mȧ·tĭz'm), *n.* *Geol.* Metasomatosis.

met'a·so'ma·to'sis (-tō'sĭs), *n.* [NL., fr. *meta-* + Gr. *sōma*, *sōmatos*, body.] *Geol.* Metamorphism developed by chemical transformation and partial replacement of the constituent minerals.

met'a·sta'ble (mĕt'ȧ·stā'b'l), *adj.* *Physics & Chem.* Designating or pertaining to a condition of comparative stability, as in **metastable state**, a peculiar state of pseudoequilibrium in which the energy content of the system is either more or less than that required for its most stable state, as in supercooled water or in an excited atom that needs further stimulus before radiating its energy.

me·tas'ta·sis (mē·tăs'tȧ·sĭs), *n.; pl.* -SES (-sēz). [LL., transition, fr. Gr. *metastasis*, fr. *methistanai* to place in another way, fr. *meta* after + *histanai* to place.] **1.** Change of state, substance or form. **2.** *Biol.* Metabolism. **3.** *Med.* The transfer of disease from one part of the body to another with development of the characteristic lesion in the new location, as in cancer. **4.** *Rhet.* Change of subject; esp., sudden transition. — **met'a·stat'ic** (mĕt'ȧ·stăt'ĭk), *adj.*

me·tas'ta·size (-sīz), *v. i.* *Med.* To spread by metastasis.

met'a·tar'sal (mĕt'ȧ·tär'săl; -s'l), *adj.* *Anat.* Of or pertaining to the metatarsus. — *n.* A metatarsal bone.

met'a·tar'sus (mĕt'ȧ·tär'sŭs), *n.; pl.* -SI (-sī). [NL.] *Anat. & Zool.* The part of the foot (in quadrupeds, of the hind foot), or of its skeleton, between the tarsus and phalanges.

me·tath'e·sis (mē·tăth'ē·sĭs), *n.; pl.* -SES (-sēz). [LL., fr. Gr. *metathesis*, fr. *metatithenai* to place differently, fr. *meta* + *tithenai* to set.] **1.** Change of place, condition, etc.; specif., transposition, as of the letters, sounds, or syllables of a word, as in Anglo-Saxon *ascian*, *axian* (cs = x). **2.** *Chem.* A reaction between polar compounds in which the positive radical of one reacts with the negative radical of the other and vice versa. — **met'a·thet'ic** (mĕt'ȧ·thĕt'ĭk), **met'a·thet'i·cal** (-ĭ·kăl), *adj.*

met'a·tho'rax (mĕt'ȧ·thō'răks; 70), *n.* [NL.] The posterior segment of the thorax in insects. See INSECT, *Illust.*

met'a·xy'lem (mĕt'ȧ·zī'lĕm), *n.* *Bot.* The primary xylem (see XYLEM) which differentiates from the procambium subsequent to differentiation of the protoxylem (which see). By some botanists, metaxylem is regarded as the primary xylem which differentiates from the procambium during elongation of an organ.

mé'ta'yer' (*F.* mā'tĕ'yā'; *E.* mĕ·tā'yẽr), *n.* [F.] One who cultivates land for a share (usually one half) of its yield, receiving stock, tools, and seed from the landlord.

met'a·zo'an (mĕt'ȧ·zō'ăn), *n.* [*meta-* + Gr. *zōion* animal.] *Zool.* Any of a group (Metazoa) comprising all animals except the protozoans. They have the body when adult composed of numerous cells differentiated into tissues and organs. Reproduction is chiefly sexual, each individual beginning its existence as a single cell (see EGG) and generally passing through an embryonic stage known as a gastrula. — **met'a·zo'an**, *adj.* — **met'a·zo'ic** (-ĭk), *adj.*

mete (mēt), *v. t.* [AS. *metan.*] **1.** To find the quantity, dimensions, or capacity of, by any rule or standard; to measure. **2.** To assign by measure; to allot.

mete, *n.* [OF., fr. L. *meta.*] Boundary.

met'em·pir'ics (mĕt'ĕm·pĭr'ĭks), *n.;* see -ICS. The science or study of concepts and relations which are conceived as beyond, and yet as related to, the knowledge gained empirically. — **met'em·pir'ic** (-ĭk), **met'em·pir'i·cal** (-ĭ·kăl), *adj.*

me·temp'sy·cho'sis (mĕ·tĕmp'sĭ·kō'sĭs; mĕt'ĕm·sī-), *n.; pl.* -CHOSES (-sēz). [LL., fr. Gr. *metempsychōsis*, fr. *meta* beyond, over + *empsychoun* to animate, fr. *en* in + *psychē* soul.] The passing of the soul at death into another body; transmigration of souls.

met'en·ceph'a·lon (mĕt'ĕn·sĕf'ȧ·lŏn), *n.; pl.* -LA (-lȧ). [NL., fr. *met-* + *encephalon.*] See HINDBRAIN. — **met'en·ce·phal'ic** (-sē·făl'ĭk), *adj.*

me'te·or (mē'tē·ẽr; 58), *n.* [OF. or ML.; OF. *meteore*, fr. ML. *meteorum*, fr. Gr. *meteōron*, pl. *meteōra* things in the air, fr. *meteōros* high in air, fr. *meta* beyond + *eōra*, *aiōra*, a suspension.] **1.** Any phenomenon in the atmosphere, as whirlwinds, hail, rainbows, halos, shooting stars, etc. **2.** *Astron.* A transient celestial body that enters the earth's atmosphere with great velocity, incandescent with heat generated by the resistance of the air.

me'te·or'ic (-ŏr'ĭk), *adj.* **1.** Of or pert. to a meteor or meteors. **2.** Like a meteor in appearance, flight, etc.; transiently brilliant.

meteoric shower. *Astron.* A large number of meteors appearing on the same night or on successive nights, due to swarms of meteoric bodies connected with comets or remnants of disintegrated comets moving around the sun in definite orbits. Meteoric showers are named for apparent points of origin from constellations or stars, or from comets.

me'te·or·ite (mē'tē·ẽr·īt; 58), *n.* A stony or metallic body that has fallen to the earth from outer space; an aerolite; loosely, a meteor. — **me'te·or·it'ic** (-ĭt'ĭk), *adj.*

me'te·or·it'ics (-ĭt'ĭks), *n.;* see -ICS. *Astron.* The science which treats of meteorites.

me'te·or·o·graph' (mē'tē·ŏr·ō·grȧf'; mē'tē·ŏr'-), *n.* *Meteorol.* An autographic apparatus for recording simultaneously several meteorologic elements, as temperature, moisture, etc.

me'te·or·oid' (mē'tē·ẽr·oid'), *n.* *Astron.* One of the countless small solid bodies in the solar system, which become meteors on entering the earth's atmosphere.

me'te·or·o·log'ic (mē'tē·ŏr·ō·lŏj'ĭk; mē'tē·ŏr'-), **me'te·or·o·log'i·cal** (-ĭ·kăl), *adj.* Of or pert. to the atmosphere and its phenomena, or meteorology. — **me'te·or·o·log'i·cal·ly**, *adv.*

me'te·or·ol'o·gist (mē'tē·ẽr·ŏl'ō·jĭst), *n.* A specialist in meteorology.

me'te·or·ol'o·gy (-jĭ), *n.* [Gr. *meteōrologia*, fr. *meteōros* high in the air + *logos* discourse.] The branch of physics treating of the atmosphere and its phenomena, esp. of its variations of heat and moisture, of its winds, etc.

me'ter, me'tre (mē'tẽr), *n.* [OF. *metre* (F. *mètre*), fr. L. *metrum*, fr. Gr. *metron.*] **1.** Systematically arranged and measured rhythm in verse; specif.: **a** The property of a verse that is divided into feet or syllabic groups. **b** The pattern of a verse marked by the prevailing foot and the number of feet. **c** The metrical pattern of a stanza or strophe, esp. in hymns; as, common *meter*. **2.** *Music.* Rhythmical structure as concerned with the division into measures consisting of a uniform number of beats or time units. **3.** [F. *mètre*, fr. Gr. *metron.*] A measure of length, the basis of the *metric system*, equal to 39.37 inches. Abbr. *m.* See METRIC SYSTEM, *Tables* 1, 2, 3, & 6.

me'ter (mē'tẽr), *n.* [From METE to measure.] **1.** One that measures; esp., an official measurer of commodities. **2.** An instrument for measuring, usually for recording automatically the quantity measured; as, a gas *meter*. — *v. t.* To measure by means of a meter or meters.

-meter. [NL. *-metrum* or F. *-mètre*, both fr. Gr. *metron* measure. See 1st METER.] A combining form denoting an *instrument* or *means for measuring some* (specified) *thing*, as in baro*meter*, volt*meter*.

me'ter·age (mē'tẽr·ĭj), *n.* Act, result, or cost of measuring.

me'tered mail (mē'tẽrd). *Post Office.* Prepaid mail matter requiring no postage stamps but marked by an electrical machine, controlled by the post office.

meth-. = METHO-.

meth·ac'ry·late (mĕth·ăk'rĭ·lāt), *n.* *Chem.* A salt or ester of methacrylic acid. See ACRYLIC RESIN.

meth'a·cryl'ic ac'id (mĕth'ȧ·krĭl'ĭk). [*meth-* + *acrylic.*] See ACRYLIC RESIN.

meth'ane (mĕth'ān), *n.* [*methyl* + *-ane.*] *Chem.* A gaseous hydrocarbon, CH_4, odorless and inflammable, a product of decomposition of organic matter in marshes and mines, and of dry distillation of organic substances. It is the type of the **methane series**, a homologous series of saturated open-chain hydrocarbons of the general formula C_nH_{2n+2}.

meth'a·nol (mĕth'ȧ·nōl; -nŏl), *n.* [*methane* + *-ol*, 1.] *Chem.* A light, volatile, inflammable liquid, CH_3OH, obtained by the distillation of wood or by synthesis from carbon monoxide and hydrogen and used as a solvent, as a fuel, but chiefly in the manufacture of formaldehyde and other organic chemicals; — called also *wood alcohol*.

me·theg'lin (mē·thĕg'lĭn), *n.* [W. *meddyglyn*, fr. *meddyg* physician (fr. L. *medicus*) + *llyn* liquor, juice.] A beverage made of fermented honey and water; mead.

met·he'mo·glo'bin (mĕt·hē'mō·glō'bĭn; mĕt·hĕm'ō-; mĕth·ē'mō-), *n.* Also **met·hae'mo·glo'bin.** [*met-* + *hemoglobin.*] *Biochem.* A soluble, brownish-red, crystalline compound, formed by the spontaneous decomposition of blood and by the action of oxidizing reagents, as ozone.

me·the'na·mine (mĕ·thē'nȧ·mēn; -mĭn), *n.* Also **-min.** [*methene* (*methyl* + *-ene*) + *amine.*] *Pharm.* Hexamethylenetetramine, used as a diuretic and as a solvent for uric acid.

me·thinks' (mē·thĭngks'), *v. impers.; past* -THOUGHT' (-thôt'). [AS. *thyncan* to seem, *mē thync(e)th*, *mē thūhte*, ME. *me think(e)th, me thoughte.*] *Now Only Poetic.* It seems to me.

me·thi'o·nine (mĕ·thī'ō·nēn; -nĭn), *n.* [*methyl* + *thio-* + *-ine.*] *Biochem.* A sulfur-containing amino acid, $C_5H_{11}NO_2S$, found in certain proteins, as casein, egg albumin, and yeast.

meth'o- (mĕth'ō-), **meth-.** A combining form for *methyl*.

meth'od (mĕth'ŭd), *n.* [F. *méthode*, fr. L. *methodus*, fr. Gr. *methodos* method, investigation following after, fr. *meta* after + *hodos* way.] **1.** An orderly procedure or process; regular way or manner of doing anything; hence, a set form of procedure, as in investigation or instruction. **2.** Orderly arrangement, elucidation, development, or classification; more generally, orderliness and regularity or habitual practice of them in action.

Syn. Method, mode, manner, way, fashion, system denote the means taken or the procedure followed in achieving an end. **Method**, often used abstractly, implies orderly, logical, or effective arrangement, usually in steps; **mode** implies the order or course pursued by custom, tradition, or personal preference; **manner** implies a procedure or method which is individual or distinctive; **way** and **fashion**, less explicit than *method* or *manner*, often replace them when individuality is connoted, *way* being more poignant and *fashion* far less suggestive of formality; **system**, very much like *method*, often suggests a more fully developed or carefully formulated plan of procedure.

me·thod'ic (mē·thŏd'ĭk), *adj.* Methodical; systematic.

me·thod'i·cal (-ĭ·kăl), *adj.* **1.** Arranged with or characterized by method or orderliness. **2.** Habitually proceeding according to method; systematic. — **me·thod'i·cal·ly**, *adv.* — **me·thod'i·cal·ness**, *n.*

Meth'od·ism (mĕth'ŭd·ĭz'm), *n.* **1.** The doctrines, polity, and worship of Methodists. **2.** [*not cap.*] Methodical procedure.

Meth'od·ist (-ĭst), *n.* [See METHOD.] **1.** One of a denomination of Protestant Christians, the outgrowth of a small religious club formed at Oxford University, in 1729, by John and Charles Wesley and others, the parent body being known as ***Wesleyan Methodists***. The name *Methodist* was originally applied derisively by Oxford students to members of the club in allusion of their methodical habits of study and religious observance. **2.** [*not cap.*] One who lays great stress on method. — **Meth'od·ist**, *adj.* — **Meth'od·is'tic** (-ĭs'tĭk), *adj.*

meth'od·ize (-īz), *v. t.* To reduce to method. — **Syn.** See ORDER.

meth'od·ol'o·gy (-ŏl'ō·jĭ), *n.* [Gr. *methodos* method + *-logy.*] The science of method or arrangement; hence: **a** A branch of logic dealing with principles of procedure. **b** *Educ.* The science which describes and evaluates arrangements of materials of instruction. — **meth'od·o·log'i·cal** (-ō·lŏj'ĭ·kăl), *adj.*

me·thought' (mē·thôt'), *past of* METHINKS.

Me·thu'se·lah (mē·thū'zĕ·lȧ; -sĕ·lȧ), *n.* [Heb. *Mĕthushā'ĕl.*] *Bib.* A patriarch, said (*Gen.* v. 27) to have lived 969 years; hence, an aged man.

meth'yl (mĕth'ĭl), *n.* [From METHYLENE.] *Chem.* The univalent hydrocarbon radical CH_3, of which methane is the hydride.

meth'yl·al' (mĕth'ĭl·ăl'; mĕth'ĭl·ăl), *n.* [*methylene* + *aldehyde.*] *Chem.* A light, volatile liquid, $H_2C(OCH_3)_2$, of a pleasant ethereal odor, obtained by partial oxidation of methanol and used in medicine as a hypnotic.

methyl alcohol. *Chem.* Methanol.

meth′yl·a·mine′ (mĕth′ĭl·*ȧ*·mēn′; -ăm′ĭn), *n.* Also **meth′yl·am′in.** *Chem.* A colorless, inflammable gas, CH_3NH_2, of strong ammoniacal odor, obtained by distillation of bones, wood, etc., and otherwise.

meth′yl·ate (mĕth′ĭ·lāt), *n.* [*methyl* + 1st *-ate*, 3.] *Chem.* A compound derived from methanol by the replacement of the hydroxyl hydrogen by a metal. — *v. t.* **a** To impregnate or mix with methanol. **b** To introduce the radical methyl (CH_3) into.

meth′yl·at′ed spir′it (-lāt′ĕd; -ĭd). Ordinary, or ethyl, alcohol denatured with methanol.

meth′yl·ene (-lēn), *n.* [F. *méthylène*, fr. Gr. *methy* wine + *hylē* wood; — a word coined to correspond to the name *wood spirit.*] **a** *Chem.* A bivalent hydrocarbon radical, CH_2, not known in the free state, but conveniently regarded as a component of various compounds; as, *methylene* bromide, CH_2Br_2. **b** *Com.* Methanol.

me·thyl′ic (mē·thĭl′ĭk), *adj.* *Chem.* Of, pertaining to, or derived from methyl; as, *methylic* amine.

methyl methacrylate. *Chem.* The methyl ester of methacrylic acid. This substance polymerizes to form a light strong transparent plastic, used esp. as a substitute for glass.

me·tic′u·lous (mē·tĭk′ū·lŭs), *adj.* [F. *méticuleux*, fr. L. *meticulosus*, fr. *metus* fear.] Unduly or excessively careful of small details; finically scrupulous. — **Syn.** See CAREFUL. — **me·tic′u·los′i·ty** (-lŏs′ĭ·tĭ), *n.* — **me·tic′u·lous·ly**, *adv.*

mé·tier′ (mā·tyā′; mā′tyā), *n.* [F.] One's calling or profession; occupation to which one is specially adapted; line. — **Syn.** See WORK.

mé′tis′ (mā′tēs′), *n. masc.*, **mé′tisse′** (mā′tēs′), *fem.* [F.] A person of mixed blood; specif., *Canada*, a half-breed; locally, *U. S.*, an octoroon.

Me′tol (mē′tōl), *n.* A trade-mark applied to a whitish soluble powder (chemically, the sulfate of methyl-*p*-aminophenol) used as a photographic developer.

Me·ton′ic cy′cle (mē·tŏn′ĭk). [After *Meton*, Athenian astronomer of the 5th century B.C.] A period of 19 years, after the lapse of which the new and full moon returns to the same days of the year. It was the basis of the Greek calendar.

met′o·nym (mĕt′ō·nĭm), *n.* A word used in metonymy.

met′o·nym′i·cal (-nĭm′ĭ·kăl), *adj.* Also **met′o·nym′ic** (-ĭk). Pertaining to, involving, or used in metonymy.

me·ton′y·my (mē·tŏn′ĭ·mĭ), *n.* [L. *metonymia*, fr. Gr. *metōnymia*, fr. *meta*, indicating change + *onyma*, *onoma*, name.] *Rhet.* Use of one word for another that it suggests, as the effect for the cause, the cause for the effect, the sign for the thing signified, the container for the thing contained, etc. (a man keeps a good *table*, instead of good *food*). Cf. SYNECDOCHE.

met′o·pe (mĕt′ō·pē; mĕt′ōp), *n.* [L. *metopa*, fr. Gr. *metopē*, fr. *meta* with, between + *opē* opening, hole.] *Arch.* The space between two triglyphs of the Doric frieze, often adorned with carved work.

me·top′ic (mē·tŏp′ĭk), *adj.* [Gr. *metōpon* the forehead.] *Anat.* Of the forehead; frontal; as, **metopic suture**, a suture uniting the frontal bones in the fetus.

me·tral′gi·a (mē·trăl′jĭ·*ȧ*), *n.* [NL., fr. Gr. *mētra* uterus + *-algia.*] Pain in the uterus.

Met′ra·zol (mĕt′r*ȧ*·zōl; -zŏl), *n.* A trade-mark applied to a drug, $C_6H_{10}N_4$, used as a respiratory and circulatory stimulant and also to produce a state of convulsion in the treatment of certain mental disorders.

me′tre (mē′tẽr). Var. of METER.

met′ric (mĕt′rĭk), *adj.* [L. *metricus*, fr. Gr. *metrikos.*] **1.** Relating to measurement; involving, or proceeding by, measurement. **2.** [F. *métrique.*] Of or pertaining to the meter (measure) or the metric system. **3.** = METRICAL, 1.

met′ri·cal (-rĭ·kăl), *adj.* **1.** Of or pertaining to meter; arranged in meter. **2.** = METRIC, 1 & 2.

met′ri·cal·ly, *adv.* of METRIC, METRICAL.

metric hundredweight. A metric weight of 50 kilograms.

me·tri′cian (mē·trĭsh′ăn), *n.* A composer in, or student of, meter.

met′rics (mĕt′rĭks), *n.*; see -ICS. The part of prosody dealing with metrical composition.

metric system. A decimal system of measures and weights, with the meter and the gram as bases. The unit of length, the meter, was intended to be, and is very nearly, one ten-millionth part of the distance measured on a meridian from the equator to the pole, or 39.37 U. S. inches. Upon the meter are based the other primary units of measure: the *square meter*, the *cubic meter*, or *stere*, the *are* (100 square meters), the *liter* (the volume of a kilogram of distilled water at 4° C., equal to 1.000027 cubic decimeters), and the *gram* (the weight, very nearly, of distilled water at 4° C. contained in a cube whose edge is one hundredth of a meter). The Greek prefix *deca-*, or *deka-*, before a unit means ten; *hecto-*, one hundred; *kilo-*, one thousand; *myria-*, ten thousand; *mega-*, one million; thus, a *hecto*meter is 100 meters. Similarly, the Latin prefix *deci-* before a unit means one tenth; *centi-*, one hundredth; *milli-*, one thousandth; and *micro-*, one millionth; thus, a *centi*gram is one hundredth of a gram. See also *Tables* at MEASURE and WEIGHT.

METRIC TABLES

The most commonly used names are printed in italics.

1. Measures of Length

10 *millimeters* (mm.)	= 1 *centimeter* (cm.)	=	0.3937 in.
10 centimeters	= 1 decimeter (dm.)	=	3.937 in.
10 decimeters	= 1 *meter* (m.)	=	39.37 in. or 3.28 ft.
10 meters	= 1 decameter (dkm.)	=	393.7 in.
10 decameters	= 1 hectometer (hm.)	=	328 ft. 1 in.
10 hectometers	= 1 *kilometer* (km.)	=	0.62137 mi.
10 kilometers	= 1 myriameter (mym.)	=	6.2137 mi.

The *micron* (μ) is one millionth of a meter or one thousandth of a millimeter.

2. Measures of Surface

100 *sq. millimeters* (mm².)	= 1 *sq. centimeter* (cm².)
100 sq. centimeters	= 1 sq. decimeter (dm².)
100 sq. decimeters	= 1 *sq. meter* (m².)
100 sq. meters	= 1 sq. decameter (dkm².)
100 sq. decameters	= 1 sq. hectometer (hm².)
100 sq. hectometers	= 1 *sq. kilometer* (km².)

3. Land Measure

1 sq. meter (m².)	= 1 centiare (ca.)	=	1550 sq. in.
100 centiares or 100 m².	= 1 *are* (a.)	=	119.6 sq. yd.
100 ares or 10,000 m².	= 1 *hectare* (ha.)	=	2.471 acres
1 sq. kilometer (km².)	= 1,000,000 sq. meters	=	.3861 sq. mi.

The *square kilometer* is used in surveys on a large scale, or in maps or charts that show roads, plans of towns, contour lines, etc. The *hectare* is used for field measurements, like our *acre*. For city lots and the like, the *are* is generally used.

4. Measures of Capacity

The standard unit of capacity is the *liter*, equal to 1 cubic decimeter or 0.9081 dry quart or 1.0567 liquid quarts.

10 milliliters (ml.)	= 1 *centiliter* (cl.)	=	0.338 fl. oz.
10 centiliters	= 1 deciliter (dl.)	=	6.1025 cu. in.
10 deciliters	= 1 *liter* (l.)	=	0.9081 dry qt. or 1.0567 liquid qts.
10 liters	= 1 decaliter (dkl.)	=	0.284 bu. or 2.64 gal.
10 decaliters	= 1 *hectoliter* (hl.)	=	2.838 bu. or 26.418 gal.
10 hectoliters	= 1 kiloliter (kl.)	=	35.315 cu. ft. or 264.18 gal.

5. Weights

The standard unit of weight is the *gram*, equal to 15.432 grains.

10 *milligrams* (mg.)	= 1 *centigram* (cg.)	=	0.1543 gr.
10 centigrams	= 1 decigram (dg.)	=	1.5432 gr.
10 decigrams	= 1 *gram* (g.)	=	15.432 gr.
10 grams	= 1 decagram (dkg.)	=	0.3527 oz.
10 decagrams	= 1 hectogram (hg.)	=	3.5274 oz.
10 hectograms	= 1 *kilogram* or *kilo* (kg.)	=	2.2046 lb.
10 kilograms	= 1 myriagram (myg.)	=	22.046 lb.
10 myriagrams	= 1 quintal (q.)	=	220.46 lb.
10 quintals or 1000 kg.	= 1 *metric ton* (M.T.)	=	2204.6 lb.

6. Measures of Volume

The standard unit of volume is the *cubic meter*, equal to 1.308 cubic yards.

1000 *cu. millimeters* (mm³.)	= 1 *cu. centimeter* (cm³.)
1000 cu. centimeters	= 1 *cu. decimeter* (dm³.)
1000 cu. decimeters	= 1 *cu. meter* (m³.), or 1 stere (st.)

The *stere* is used for firewood. 1 stere = 0.2759 cord; 1 decistere = ⅒ stere; 1 decastere = 10 steres.

metric ton. See METRIC SYSTEM, *Table* 5.

met′ri·fy (mĕt′rĭ·fī), *v. t.*; -FIED (-fīd); -FY′ING. [F. *métrifier.* See -FY.] To compose in, or put into, meter; to make a metrical version of. — **met′ri·fi′er** (-fī′ẽr), *n.*

me′trist (mē′trĭst; mĕt′rĭst), *n.* [ML. *metrista.*] A maker of verses; also, one skillful in handling meter.

me·tri′tis (mē·trī′tĭs), *n.* [NL., fr. Gr. *mētra* uterus + *-itis.*] *Med.* Inflammation of the uterus.

Met′ro (mĕt′rō), *n.* Also **met′ro.** Orig., short for *Metropolitan District Railway*, one of the underground and suburban railways of London; hence, any underground railway, as in Paris, Madrid, etc.

me·trol′o·gy (mē·trŏl′ō·jĭ), *n.* [Gr. *metron* measure + *-logy.*] The science of, or a system of, weights and measures. — **met′ro·log′i·cal** (mĕt′rō·lŏj′ĭ·kăl), *adj.* — **me·trol′o·gist** (mē·trŏl′ō·jĭst), *n.*

met′ro·nome (mĕt′rō·nōm), *n.* [Gr. *metron* measure + *nomos* law.] An instrument for marking exact time, esp. in music, usually a clockwork pendulum. — **met′ro·nom′ic** (-nŏm′ĭk), *adj.*

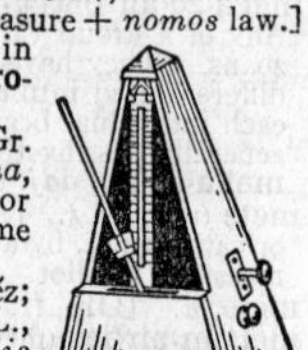

Metronome.

me′tro·nym′ic (mē′trō·nĭm′ĭk; mĕt′rō-), *adj.* [Gr. *mētrōnymikos*, fr. *mētēr* mother + *onyma*, *onoma*, name.] Derived from the name of the mother or other female ancestor. — *n.* A metronymic name or appellation.

me·trop′o·lis (mē·trŏp′ō·lĭs), *n.*; *pl.* -LISES (-ĕz; -ĭz), -LEIS (-līs), *or, incorrectly*, -LES (-lēz). [LL., fr. Gr. *mētropolis*, fr. *mētēr* mother + *polis* city.] **1.** The mother or parent city or state of a colony; — orig. used of Greek cities or states. **2.** The chief or capital city of a country, state, region, etc. **3.** A principal seat or center, as of religion. **4.** *Eccl.* The seat, or see, of a metropolitan (sense 1).

met′ro·pol′i·tan (mĕt′rō·pŏl′ĭ·tăn), *adj.* **1.** *Eccl.* Pertaining to or designating a metropolis or metropolitan. **2.** Of, pertaining to, or being a metropolis. — *n.* **1.** *Eccl.* The head of an ecclesiastical province. **2.** One who lives in or has the manners or ideas of a metropolis (sense 2). **3.** *Gr. Hist.* A citizen of a metropolis (sense 1).

me′tror·rha′gi·a (mē′trō·rā′jĭ·*ȧ*; mĕt′rō-), *n.* [NL., fr. Gr. *mētra* uterus + *-rrhagia.*] Profuse bleeding from the uterus, esp. such as is not menstrual.

met′ro·style (mĕt′rō·stīl), *n.* [Gr. *metron* measure + *style.*] A speed-regulating device for player pianos.

-metry. [See -METER.] A combining form denoting *an art, process, or science of measuring*, as in acidi*metry*.

met′tle (mĕt′'l), *n.* [E. *metal*, used in allusion to the temper of the metal of a sword blade.] Quality of temperament or disposition; spirit, esp. as regards honor, fortitude, ardor, etc. — **Syn.** See COURAGE. — ***on one's mettle.*** Incited to the use of one's best efforts.

met′tle·some (mĕt′'l·sŭm), *adj.* Also **met′tled** (-'ld). Full of mettle, or spirit; spirited.

‖**me′um** (mē′ŭm), *n.* [L.] Literally, mine; — used in **me′um et tu′um** (ĕt tū′ŭm); as, to confound *meum et tuum*, to fail to distinguish one's own property from that of others.

mew (mū), *n.* [AS. *mǣw.*] A gull (see 2d GULL **b**); esp., the common European gull (*Larus canus*).

mew, *v. t. & i.* [OF. *muer* to molt, change, fr. L. *mutare* to change.] *Archaic.* To shed, cast, or change (feathers); to molt; — of birds.

mew, *n.* [OF. *mue* change of feathers, scales, skin, fr. *muer* to molt, mew.] **1.** A cage for hawks, esp. while mewing. **2.** *Dial. Eng.* A breeding cage, as for canaries. **3.** Concealment; also, hiding place; den. **4.** *pl. construed as a sing.* **a** The royal stables in London, built on the site of the king's mews for hawks. **b** A range of stables, with coach houses, round an open space or area. **c** A row of garages. — *v. t.* **1.** To put or keep (a hawk) in a mew, esp. when molting. **2.** To shut up; to enclose; to conceal, as in a cage; as, to *mew* oneself up from the world.

mew (mū), *v. i.* [Imitative.] To utter a cry sounding like *mew*, as a cat; miaow. — *n.* The common cry of the cat.

mewl (mūl), *v. i. & t.* To cry weakly, as a young child.

Mex'i·can bean beetle (mĕk'sĭ·kăn). A spotted ladybird (*Epilachna corrupta*) which feeds on the leaves of beans.

Mexican hairless dog. A dog, about the size of a fox terrier, of a breed of unknown origin found in Mexico. It is hairless except for a tuft on the skull and fuzz along the lower half of its long tail.

Mexican poppy. See PRICKLY POPPY.

me·ze're·on (mē·zē'rē·ŏn), *n.* [ML., fr. Ar. *māzariyūn*.] **a** A small European shrub (*Daphne mezereum*), with fragrant lilac-purple flowers, type of a family (Thymelaeaceae, the mezereon family) of tough-barked trees, shrubs, and herbs. **b** = MEZEREUM **b**.

me·ze're·um (-ŭm), *n.* [NL.] **a** = MEZEREON **a**. **b** *Pharm. & Med.* The dried acrid bark of mezereon, used in liniments and internally as a diuretic, diaphoretic, and stimulant.

me·zu'zah, me·zu'za (mĕ·zōō'zä), *n.; Heb. pl.* -ZOTH (-zōth). [Heb. *mĕzūzāh* doorpost.] Among the orthodox Hebrews, a piece of parchment bearing the passages Deut. vi. 4–9 and xi. 13–21 written in twenty-two lines. It is rolled up in a wooden, metal, or glass case or tube and attached to the doorpost as both the passages command.

mez'za·nine (mĕz'ȧ·nēn; -nĭn), *n.* [F., fr. It. *mezzanino*, fr. *mezzano* middle, fr. L. *medianus*.] An intermediate or fractional story between the floor and ceiling of a main story, usually just above the ground or main floor and extending over only part of a main floor, as, in a theater, projecting between the main floor and the first balcony.

mez'zo (mĕd'zō), *adj. masc.*, **mez'za** (-zä), *fem.* [It., fr. L. *medius* middle, half.] *Music.* Mean; not extreme.

mez'zo-re·lie'vo (mĕd'zō·rē·lē'vō), ‖**mez'zo-ri·lie'vo** (mĕd'dzō·rē·lyâ'vō), *n.; pl.* -VOS (-vōz), MEZZI-RILIEVI (mĕd'dzē·rē·lyâ'vē). [It. *mezzo rilievo*.] See RELIEF, *n.*, 6.

mez'zo-so·pra'no (mĕd'zō·sō·prä'nō; -prăn'ō), *n.; pl.* -NOS (-nōz), -NI (-nē). [It.] *Music.* **a** A woman's voice having full, deep quality between that of the soprano and contralto. **b** A singer having such a voice. — **mez'zo-so·pra'no,** *adj.*

mez'zo·tint (mĕd'zō·tĭnt; mĕz'ō-), *n.* Also **mez'zo·tin'to** (-tĭn'tō). [It. *mezzo* half + *tinto* tinted, past part.] **a** A manner of engraving on copper or steel by scraping or burnishing a roughened surface to produce light and shade. **b** An engraving so produced. — *v. t.* To engrave in, or represent by, mezzotint.

MGB (ĕm'jē'bē'). [From the initials of the Russ. *M*inisterstvo *G*osudarstvennoi *B*ezopasnosti.] The Soviet Ministry of State Security, charged with investigating cases involving treason against the Soviet state.

mho (mō), *n.* [Anagram of *ohm*.] *Elec.* A unit of conductance, being the reciprocal of the ohm.

mi (mē), *n.* [It.] *Music.* A syllable applied to the third tone of the diatonic scale in solmization.

Mi·am'i (mī·ăm'ĭ; mē·ä'mĭ; *locally often* -ȧ, -mȧ), *n.; pl.* MIAMI, MIAMIS (-ĭz). An Indian of an Algonquian tribe, formerly of the region about Indiana.

mi·aow', mi·aou' (mē·ou'; myou), *interj. & n.* [Imitative.] The mew of a cat. — *v. t. & i.;* MI·AOWED', MI·AOUED' (mē·oud'; myoud); MI·AOW'ING, MI·AOU'ING. To mew.

mi·as'ma (mī·ăz'mȧ; mĭ-), *n.; pl.* -MATA (-mȧ·tȧ), -MAS (-mȧz). [NL., fr. Gr. *miasma* defilement.] **a** Noxious effluvium formerly supposed to emanate from putrescent matter, swamps, etc., and to float in the air, esp. in night mists. **b** Figuratively, noxious influence or atmosphere. — **mi·as'mal** (-măl), *adj.* — **mi'as·mat'ic** (mī'ăz·măt'ĭk), **mi'as·mat'i·cal** (-ĭ·kăl), *adj.* — **mi·as'mic** (mī·ăz'mĭk; mĭ-), *adj.*

mi·aul' (mĭ·ôl'; mĭ·oul'), *v. i. & t.* To cry as a cat; to mew; caterwaul. — *n.* The crying of a cat.

mib (mĭb), *n. Dial.* A marble; *pl.*, the game of marbles.

mi'ca (mī'kȧ), *n.* [L. *mica* crumb, grain.] *Mineral.* Any of a group of mineral silicates crystallizing in monoclinic forms that readily separate into very thin leaves. The transparent forms are popularly called *isinglass.* — **mi'ca,** *adj.* — **mi·ca'ceous** (mī·kā'shē·ŭs), *adj.*

Mi'cah (mī'kȧ), *n.* [Heb.] **a** A Hebrew prophet of the 8th century B.C. **b** A book of the Old Testament. See BIBLE.

mice (mīs), *n., pl.* of MOUSE.

mi·celle' (mĭ·sĕl'), *n.* Also **mi·cel'la** (mĭ·sĕl'ȧ; mī-), **mi·cell'.** [NL., *micella*, dim. fr. L. *mica* morsel, grain.] *Biol. & Chem.* A unit of structure built up from complex molecules in colloids. It may have crystalline properties and is capable of change in size without chemical change.

Mi'chael (mī'kĕl; -k'l; *Bib.* mī'kā·ĕl), *n. Bib.* One of the archangels.

Mich'ael·mas (mĭk'ĕl·mȧs; -'l·mȧs), *n., or* **Michaelmas Day.** [*Michael* + *-mas*.] The feast of the archangel Michael, September 29, one of the four quarter days in England.

Michaelmas daisy. **a** A wild aster, esp. one blooming about Michaelmas. **b** Any of various hybrid asters.

miche (mĭch), *v. i.* [Prob. fr. OF. *muchier, musser*, to conceal, lurk (of Celt. origin).] *Now Dial.* To skulk; sneak; also, to play truant. — **mich'er** (mĭch'ẽr), *n.*

Mi·che'as (mī·kē'ăs). *Douay Bib.* Micah.

Mick'ey Finn, mick'ey finn (mĭk'ĭ fĭn'). *Slang, U. S.* A drugged drink of liquor.

mick'le (mĭk''l), *adj.* [AS. *micel, mycel*.] *Archaic & Dial.* Great; much. — **mick'le,** *adv.*

Mic'mac (mĭk'măk), *n.* One of a tribe of Algonquian Indians of Newfoundland and eastern Canada.

mi'cra (mī'krȧ), *n., pl.* of MICRON.

mi'cri·fy (mī'krĭ·fī), *v. t.;* -FIED (-fīd); -FY'ING. To make small or insignificant.

mi'cro- (mī'krō-; *occas.* mĭk'rō-), **micr-.** [Gr. *mikros*.] A combining form (opposed to *macro-* and *mega-*), meaning: **1.** *Small, petty,* as in *micro*cosm, *micro*logy; used also to denote specif.: **a** *Enlarging as does the microscope;* — in names of instruments, as in *micro*phone. **b** In the metric system and in various terms in electricity, etc., *one millionth part of a* (specified) *unit,* as in:

microampere, microerg, microliter
microinch, microfarad, microphot
microcoulomb, microhenry, microsecond
microcurie, microhm, microvolt

2. *Microscopic,* as in **mi'cro·nu'cle·us,** a lesser nucleus; esp., *dealing with* or *used in microscopy,* as in:

microbiology, micromechanics, micropetrography
microchemistry, micrometallography, micropetrology
microcrystallography, micrometallurgy, microphysics
microcrystalloscopy, micromineralogy, microphysiography
microgeology, micropathology, microzoology

3. *Bot. & Zool.* **a** *Very small in a* (specified) *feature;* — in adjectives, as in *micro*phyllous. **b** *A variety of a* (specified) *type relatively small in size* or *extent;* — in nouns, as in *micro*gamete, *micro*spore. **4.** *Chem. Of or pertaining to, or for, very small or minute amounts of material; microanalytical;* as in **mi'cro·bal'ance, mi'cro·dis'til·la'tion, mi'cro·re·a'gent. 5.** *Med. Abnormally small,* as in **mi'cro·ce·phal'ic, mi'cro·ceph'a·lous,** having a small head or small cranial capacity. **6.** *Petrog.* **a** *Of very fine grain.* **b** *Visible only under the microscope.*

mi'cro·a·nal'y·sis (-ȧ·năl'ĭ·sĭs), *n. Chem.* Analysis of minute quantities of material. — **mi'cro·an'a·lyt'i·cal** (-ăn'ȧ·lĭt'ĭ·kăl), *adj.*

mi'cro·bar'o·graph (-băr'ō·grăf; 9), *n.* A barograph for recording small and rapid changes.

mi'crobe (mī'krōb), *n.* [F., fr. Gr. *mikros* small + *bios* life.] A very minute organism; a microorganism; a germ; — popularly, a bacterium, esp. a pathogenic form. — **mi·cro'bi·al** (mī·krō'bĭ·ăl), *adj.* — **mi·cro'bic** (-krō'bĭk; -krŏb'ĭk), *adj.*

mi·cro'bi·cide (mī·krō'bĭ·sīd), *n.* [*microbe* + *-cide*.] Any agent that kills microbes. — **mi·cro'bi·cid'al** (-sīd'ăl), *adj.*

mi'cro·cli'ma·tol'o·gy (mī'krō·klī'mȧ·tŏl'ō·jĭ), *n.* [*micro-* + *climatology*.] Climatology that deals with **mi'cro·cli'mate** (mī'krō·klī'mĭt; 2), that is, the climate of an area, usually small, over which weather conditions are substantially the same. Differences of soil, soil covering, and elevation sometimes are responsible for different climates in areas only a few hundred feet apart. Cf. MACROCLIMATE. — **mi'cro·cli'ma·to·log'i·cal** (-tō·lŏj'ĭ·kăl), *adj.*

mi'cro·cline (mī'krō·klīn), *n.* [*micro-* + Gr. *klinein* to incline.] *Mineral.* A mineral of the feldspar group, like orthoclase or common feldspar in composition, but triclinic in form. It is white to pale yellow, red, or green.

mi'cro·coc'cus (-kŏk'ŭs), *n.; pl.* -COCCI (-sī). [NL., fr. *micro-* + *-coccus*.] Any of a genus (*Micrococcus*) of spherical bacteria occurring in plates or irregular groups and living on dead matter or as parasites. — **mi'cro·coc'cal** (-ăl), *adj.* — **mi'cro·coc'cic** (-sĭk), *adj.*

mi'cro·cosm (mī'krō·kŏz'm), *n.* [F. *microcosme*, fr. LL. *microcosmus*, fr. Gr. *mikros kosmos*, lit., little world. The Gr. phrase = man.] **1.** A little world; esp., man as a supposed epitome of the exterior universe; — contr. with *macrocosm.* **2.** A community, institution, town, etc., regarded as an epitome of the world or as a little world. — **mi'cro·cos'mic, mi'cro·cos'mi·cal** (-kŏz'mĭk, -mĭ·kăl), *adj.*

mi'cro·cos'mic salt (-kŏz'mĭk). *Chem.* A white crystalline salt, $NaNH_4HPO_4.4H_2O$, originally obtained from human urine. It is used as a blowpipe reagent in testing for metallic oxides.

mi'cro·crys'tal·line (-krĭs'tăl·ĭn; -īn), *adj. Petrog.* Having its constituent crystalline grains visible by microscope.

mi'cro·cyte (mī'krō·sīt), *n.* [*micro-* + *-cyte*.] *Med.* An abnormally small red blood corpuscle characteristic of certain anemias. — **mi'cro·cyt'ic** (-sĭt'ĭk), *adj.*

mi'cro·de·tec'tor (-dē·tĕk'tẽr), *n.* A device for detecting small amounts or changes, as in electric current.

mi'cro·dis·sec'tion (-dĭ·sĕk'shŭn), *n.* Dissection under the microscope.

mi'cro·dont (mī'krō·dŏnt), *adj.* [*micr-* + *-odont*.] Having small teeth. — **mi'cro·don'tous** (-dŏn'tŭs), *adj.*

mi'cro·el'e·ment (mī'krō·ĕl'ē·mĕnt; 2), *n. Chem.* An element occurring in minute quantities only.

mi'cro·film' (mī'krō·fĭlm'), *n.* [*micro-* + *film*.] A film of small size; specif., a strip of film of standard motion-picture film size or smaller, used for keeping a photographic record of printed matter, manuscripts, etc., in a small space. — *v. t. & i.* To photograph on microfilm.

mi'cro·ga·mete' (-gȧ·mēt'), *n.* [*micro-* + *gamete*.] *Biol.* The smaller (commonly the male) gamete of a heterogamous organism. Cf. MACROGAMETE.

mi'cro·gram, mi'cro·gramme (mī'krō·grăm), *n.* [*micro-* + *gram*.] *Physics.* One millionth of a gram. Symbol μg.

mi'cro·graph (-grăf; 9), *n.* **1.** Instrument for executing minute writing or engraving. **2.** A graphic reproduction of an object as seen through the microscope. Cf. MACROGRAPH. **3.** *Physics.* An instrument for measuring minute movements by the magnified record of movements of a diaphragm.

mi·crog'ra·phy (mī·krŏg'rȧ·fĭ), *n.* [*micro-* + *-graphy*.] **1.** Description of microscopic objects. **2.** Art or practice of minute handwriting. **3.** Examination or study with the microscope. — **mi'cro·graph'ic** (mī'krō·grăf'ĭk), *adj.*

mi'cro·groove' (mī'krō·grōōv'), *n.* [*micro-* + *groove*.] A narrow V-shaped groove used on phonograph records intended to play at speeds of 33⅓ or 45 revolutions per minute.

mi·crol'o·gy (mī·krŏl'ō·jĭ), *n.* [Gr. *mikrologia*. See MICRO-; -LOGY.] Attention to petty items or differences.

mi·crom'e·ter (mī·krŏm'ē·tẽr), *n.* [F. *micromètre*. See MICRO-; -METER.] **a** An instrument, used with a telescope or microscope, for measuring minute distances. **b** Short for MICROMETER CALIPER, etc.

micrometer caliper. *Mach.* A caliper with micrometer screw attached, used for very exact measurement.

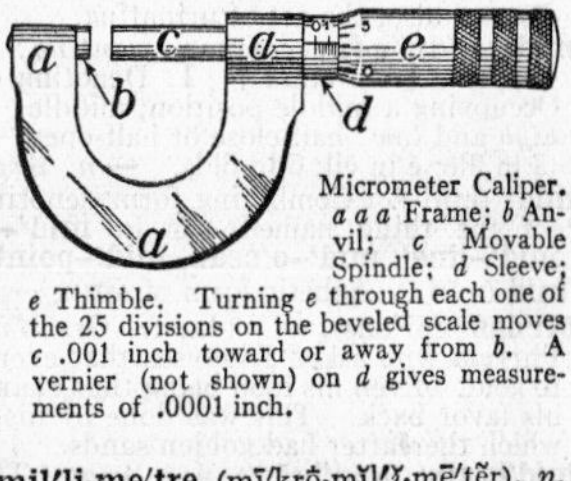

Micrometer Caliper. *a a a* Frame; *b* Anvil; *c* Movable Spindle; *d* Sleeve; *e* Thimble. Turning *e* through each one of the 25 divisions on the beveled scale moves *c* .001 inch toward or away from *b*. A vernier (not shown) on *d* gives measurements of .0001 inch.

micrometer screw. A screw with a graduated head (**micrometer head**) and fine threads, used in micrometers, etc.

mi·crom'e·try (mī·krŏm'ē·trĭ), *n.* Art of measuring with a micrometer.

mi'cro·mil'li·me'ter, mi'cro·mil'li·me'tre (mī'krō·mĭl'ĭ·mē'tẽr), *n.* The millionth part of a millimeter, or a millimicron; also, as in *Biol.*, a micron. Symbol, $m\mu$.

mi'cron (mī'krŏn), *n.; pl.* MICRONS (-krŏnz), MICRA (-krȧ). [NL., fr.

Gr. *mikros* small.] **1.** A unit of length, the thousandth part of one millimeter. Symbol, μ. See METRIC SYSTEM, *Table* 1. **2.** *Physical Chem.* A particle of diameter between 0.01 and 0.0001 millimeter.

Mi′cro·ne′sian (mī′krō·nē′shăn; -zhăn), *adj.* [From *Micronesia*, fr. Gr. *mikros* small + *nēsos* island.] Of or pertaining to Micronesia or the Micronesians, peoples mostly of mixed Melanesian, Polynesian, and Malaysian stocks, or to their Melanesian languages. — *n.* A native of Micronesia.

mi′cro·or′gan·ism (mī′krō·ôr′găn·ĭz′m), *n.* *Biol.* Any organism of microscopic (also, in a broad sense, ultramicroscopic) size; — applied esp. to bacteria and protozoa.

mi′cro·par′a·site (-păr′ȧ·sīt), *n.* A parasitic microorganism. — **mi′cro·par′a·sit′ic** (-sĭt′ĭk), *adj.*

mi′cro·phone (mī′krō·fōn), *n.* [*micro-* + *-phone.*] *Physics.* An instrument for intensifying feeble sounds or for transmitting sounds. The transmitter of the modern telephone is essentially a microphone, the pressure of the sound waves being communicated to the conductors by means of a diaphragm. The more sensitive forms, as radiomicrophones, are devices for converting sound into electrical waves. — **mi′cro·phon′ic** (-fŏn′ĭk), *adj.*

mi′cro·pho′to·graph (-fō′tō·grȧf; 9), *n.* **a** A microscopically small photograph. **b** Loosely, a photomicrograph. — **mi′cro·pho′to·graph′ic** (-grăf′ĭk), *adj.* — **mi′cro·pho·tog′ra·phy** (-fō·tŏg′rȧ·fĭ), *n.*

mi′cro·phyte (mī′krō·fīt), *n.* *Bot.* A minute plant, esp. one of the bacteria. — **mi′cro·phyt′ic** (-fĭt′ĭk), *adj.*

mi′cro·print′ (-prĭnt′), *n.* A graphic image of reduced size on an opaque surface, produced by a photographic or photomechanical process, viewed with an enlarging device.

mi′cro·pyle (-pīl), *n.* [F., fr. *micro-* + Gr. *pylē* gate.] **1.** *Zool.* A minute opening, as that in the investing membranes of an egg, by which spermatozoa may enter. **2.** *Bot.* The minute orifice in the integuments of an ovule through which the pollen tube penetrates to the embryo sac. — **mi′cro·py′lar** (-pī′lẽr), *adj.*

mi′cro·py·rom′e·ter (-pī·rŏm′ē·tẽr), *n.* *Physics.* An instrument for the optical determination of the temperature or emissivity of microscopic glowing bodies.

mi′cro·scope (mī′krō·skōp), *n.* [NL. *microscopium.* See MICRO-; -SCOPE.] An optical instrument, consisting of lens, or combination of lenses, for making enlarged or magnified images of minute objects. The ***simple microscope*** consists merely of a single lens or magnifying glass set in a frame; the ***compound microscope*** requires an *objective* and an *eyepiece,* usually mounted in a sliding tube.

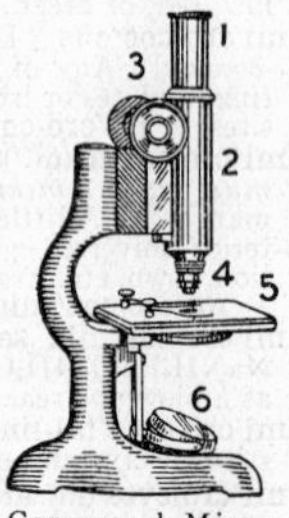

Compound Microscope. 1 Eyepiece; 2 Tube; 3 Adjusting Screw; 4 Objective Lens; 5 Table, or Stage; 6 Illuminating Mirror.

mi′cro·scop′ic (-skŏp′ĭk), *adj.* Also **mi′cro·scop′i·cal** (-ĭ·kăl). **1.** Of, pertaining to, or conducted with the microscope or microscopy; as, a *microscopic* examination. **2.** Like a microscope; able to see very minute objects. **3.** So small or fine as to be invisible or not clearly distinguished without the use of a microscope. Hence, loosely, very small. — **mi′cro·scop′i·cal·ly,** *adv.*

mi·cros′co·py (mī·krŏs′kō·pĭ; mī′krō·skō′pĭ), *n.* Use of the microscope; investigation with the microscope. — **mi·cros′co·pist** (-pĭst), *n.*

mi′cro·seism (mī′krō·sīz′m; -sīs′m), *n.* [*micro-* + Gr. *seismos* earthquake.] A feeble earth tremor. — **mi′cro·seis′mic** (-sīz′mĭk; -sīs′-), **mi′cro·seis′mi·cal** (-mĭ·kăl), *adj.*

mi′cro·some (-sōm), *n.* [*micro-* + 2d *-some.*] *Biol.* One of the minute granules embedded in the ground substance of protoplasm.

mi′cro·spo·ran′gi·um (-spō·răn′jĭ·ŭm), *n.; pl.* -GIA (-ȧ). [NL.] *Bot.* A sporangium with microspores, as, in seed plants, the pollen sac of the anther.

mi′cro·spore (mī′krō·spōr; 70), *n.* [*micro-* + *-spore.*] *Bot.* One of the smaller of the two kinds of asexual spores produced by heterosporous plants, giving rise to the male prothallium, as the pollen grain of seed plants.

mi′cro·spo′ro·phyll (mī′krō·spō′rō·fĭl), *n.* *Bot.* A sporophyll bearing microsporangia.

mi′cro·stom′a·tous (-stŏm′ȧ·tŭs; -stō′mȧ-), *adj.* Also **mi·cros′to·mous** (mī·krŏs′tō·mŭs). [*micro-* + Gr. *stoma, -atos,* mouth.] Having a small mouth.

mi′cro·tome (mī′krō·tōm), *n.* [*micro-* + *-tome.*] An instrument for cutting sections, as of organic tissues, for microscopic examination.

mi·crot′o·my (mī·krŏt′ō·mĭ), *n.* Art of using the microtome, or of preparing, with its aid, objects for microscopic study. — **mi′cro·tom′ic** (mī′krō·tŏm′ĭk), **mi′cro·tom′i·cal** (-ĭ·kăl), *adj.* — **mi·crot′o·mist** (mī·krŏt′ō·mĭst), *n.*

mi′cro·wave′ (mī′krō·wāv′), *n.* *Radio.* A very short electromagnetic wave; formerly any wave of less than 10 meters, more recently any wave between 100 centimeters and 1 centimeter, in wave length.

mic′tu·rate (mĭk′tū·rāt), *v. i.* [See MICTURITION.] To urinate.

mic′tu·ri′tion (-rĭsh′ŭn), *n.* [L. *micturire* to desire to make water, desiderative verb fr. *mingere, mictum,* to make water.] Orig., desire to urinate; hence, excessively frequent passage of urine, due to disease; also, the act of urinating.

mid (mĭd), *adj.; compar. wanting; superl.* MID′MOST (mĭd′mōst; -mŭst). [AS. *midd.*] **1.** Denoting or being the middle part. **2.** Occupying a middle position; middle. **3.** *Phonet.* Midway between *high* and *low;* half-close or half-open; — said of certain vowel sounds (ā in āle; ĕ in ĕll; ō in ōld). — *n.* *Archaic.* Middle.

mid- (mĭd-). Combining form denoting the *middle* or *middle part* (of the thing named), as in **mid′–chan′nel, mid′–con′ti·nent, mid′–line′, mid′–o′cean, mid′–point′.**

′mid (mĭd). Aphetic form of AMID; — often written *mid.*

Mi′das (mī′dȧs), *n.* [L., fr. Gr. *Midas.*] *Gr. Myth.* A king of Phrygia who asked Dionysus that everything he touched might turn to gold. Even his food being thus changed, he begged the god to take his favor back. This was done by his bathing in the river Pactolus, which thereafter had golden sands.

mid′brain′ (mĭd′brān′), *n.* *Anat.* The middle of the three primary divisions of the brain of vertebrates; — called also *mesencephalon.* Cf. FOREBRAIN, HINDBRAIN.

mid′day′ (mĭd′dā′; 2), *n.* [AS. *middæg.*] The middle part of the day; noon. — *adj.* Of or pertaining to midday.

mid′den (mĭd′′n), *n.* [ME. *midding,* of Scand. origin.] **1.** *Chiefly Dial.* A dunghill. **2.** An accumulation of refuse about a dwelling place; as, a ***kitchen midden,*** a refuse heap marking the site of a primitive habitation.

mid′dle (mĭd′′l), *adj.* [AS. *middel.*] **1.** Equally distant from given extremes; mean; medial. **2.** Intermediate; intervening; rarely, intermediary; formerly, taking a middle course. **3.** [*cap.*] Denoting a division intermediate to those prior and later, upper and lower, etc.; as, the *Middle* Ages. **4.** *Philol.* Pertaining to or designating a form or voice of the Greek verb by which its subject is represented as both the agent and the object of action. **5.** [*cap.*] Designating a period of a language or literature intermediate between periods called *Old* and *New* or *Modern;* as, *Middle* English, *Middle* French, *Middle* High German, *Middle* Persian (see ENGLISH, FRENCH, GERMAN, PERSIAN). **6.** *Phonet.* Medial. — *n.* **1.** A middle point, part, or position; midst; central portion; specif., the waist. **2.** *Now Rare.* Something intermediate between extremes. — *v. t. & i.;* MID′DLED (mĭd′′ld); MID′DLING (-lĭng). *Chiefly Naut.* To fold in the middle; to double.

middle age. **a** The middle period of life; middle life. **b** [*caps.*] Usually in *pl.* The period between ancient and modern times, as between the fall of the Roman Empire and the revival of letters; also, the period from about A.D. 400 to 1400. The term ***Dark Ages*** is applied to the whole or, more often, to the earlier part of this period because of its intellectual stagnation.

mid′dle–aged′ (mĭd′′l·ājd′; 2), *adj.* Being about the middle of the ordinary age of man, between youth and age; also, pertaining to or characteristic of people of this age.

mid′dle·break′er (-brāk′ẽr), *n.* Also **mid′dle·bust′er** (-bŭs′tẽr). *Agric. Mach.* = LISTER, 2 **a.**

middle C. The note designated by the first ledger line below the treble staff and the first above the bass staff. See PITCH, *Illust.*

middle class. [often in *pl.*] In England, people who have an intermediate position between the nobility or leisured class and the working class. It includes professional men, bankers, merchants, and small landed proprietors. Hence, a similar class elsewhere. Cf. BOURGEOISIE. — **mid′dle–class′** (-klȧs′; 2), *adj.*

middle distance. **1.** *Painting.* In a picture, that part between the foreground and the background. **2.** *Running.* Any distance from 880 yards to (but not including) one mile.

middle ear. *Anat.* The tympanum.

Middle East. The southwestern part of Asia and the northeastern part of Africa; — a term indefinite in its application, sometimes covering only the region, or part of the region, from Egypt and Turkey in the west to Afghanistan in the east, sometimes including countries from Tunisia to Burma. Cf. FAR EAST, NEAR EAST. — **Middle Eastern,** *adj.*

Middle Kingdom. **a** Also **Middle Empire.** In ancient Egypt, the kingdom with Heracleopolis, and later Thebes, as its capital, from about 2400 B.C. to 1580 B.C. **b** [Transl. of Chin. (Pek.) *Chung*[1] *kuo*[2].] China; — a name given by the natives: (1) to the eighteen provinces, or China proper; or (2) to the Chinese empire as occupying the center of the earth.

middle lamella. *Bot.* See LAMELLA.

mid′dle·man′ (mĭd′′l·măn′; -măn), *n.; pl.* -MEN (-mĕn′; -mĕn). An agent between two parties; specif., *Com.,* any agent between the producer and the consumer, esp. between the producer and a retail merchant, as a jobber, or commission merchant.

mid′dle·most (-mōst; -mŭst), *adj.* Midmost.

Middle Temple. See INN OF COURT.

middle term. *Logic.* That term of a syllogism which occurs in both premises.

mid′dle·weight′ (mĭd′′l·wāt′), *n.* One of average weight; specif., in wrestling, boxing, etc., one of a class heavier than a welterweight and lighter than a heavyweight, the middleweight limit being 160 pounds.

Middle West. Also **Mid′west′** (mĭd′wĕst′), *n.* [*also not cap.*] That part of the United States from the Rocky Mountains to the Alleghenies, north of the Ohio River and the southern boundaries of Missouri and Kansas. — **Middle Western,** *adj.* — **Middle Westerner,** *n.*

mid′dling (mĭd′lĭng), *adj.* Of middle or medium rank, state, size, or quality; medium; ordinary. — *adv. Dial.* Moderately; rather.

mid′dling, *n.* *Usually pl.* Any of various commodities of intermediate position or quality, as the medium-sized particles separated in the sifting of ground grain used in producing the finest flour.

mid′dy (mĭd′ĭ), *n.; pl.* -DIES (-ĭz). *Colloq.* A midshipman.

middy blouse. A loose blouse with sailor collar, worn by women and children; — often called simply **mid′dy.**

Mid′gard (mĭd′gärd), *n.* Also **Mid′garth** (-gärth), **Mith′gar′thr** (mĭth′gär′thẽr). [ON. *mithgarthr.*] *Teut. Myth.* The middle space between heaven and hell, the abode of human beings; the earth.

midge (mĭj), *n.* [AS. *mycge, mycg.*] **1.** Any very small gnat or fly (esp. of the family Chironomidae, genus *Culicoides*). **2.** A diminutive person.

midg′et (mĭj′ĕt; -ĭt), *n.* A very diminutive person. — *adj.* Like a midget in size; very diminutive.

mid′–gut′, *n.* *Embryol. & Zool.* The middle part of the alimentary canal between the fore-gut and hind-gut.

‖**Mi′di′** (mē′dē′), *n.* [F.] The south, esp. of France.

Mid′i·an·ite (mĭd′ĭ·ăn·īt), *n.* *Bib.* One of a north-Arabian tribe, descendants of Abraham's son **Mid′i·an** (mĭd′ĭ·ăn). *Gen.* xxv. 2.

mid′i·nette′ (mĭd′ĭ·nĕt′; *F.* mē′dē′nĕt′), *n.* [F.] *Colloq.* A Parisian shopgirl; — so called because these girls come out of the shops in great numbers at noon.

mid′i′ron (mĭd′ī′ẽrn), *n.* *Golf.* An iron club having more loft than a cleek and less than a mashie. See GOLF, *Illust.*

mid′land (mĭd′lănd), *n.* The central region of a country; — usually in *pl.;* specif. [*cap.*], the central counties of England. — *adj.* **1.** Being in the interior country; inland. **2.** [*cap.*] Of or pertaining to the English Midlands.

mid mashie. See GOLF, *Illust.*

mid′most (mĭd′mōst; -mŭst), *adj.* **1.** In the exact middle. **2.** Partitively, being the middle of. **3.** Most intimate.

mid′night′ (-nīt′), *n.* The middle of the night; twelve o'clock at night. — **mid′night′,** *adj.*

midnight sun. The sun shining at midnight in the arctic or antarctic summer.

mid′noon′ (mĭd′nōōn′; 2), *n.* Midday; noon.

mid′rash (mĭd′răsh), *n.; pl.* MIDRASHIM (mĭd·rä′shēm), MIDRASHOTH (-shōth), or -SHOT (-shōt). [Heb., explanation.] An exposition of the

Hebrew Scriptures, esp. [*cap.*] that made during a period of about 1500 years after the Exile. Cf. HAGGADA, HALAKAH.

mid′rib′ (mĭd′rĭb′), *n.* Central vein of a leaf. See VENATION, *Illust.*

mid′riff (mĭd′rĭf), *n.* [AS. *midhrif*, fr. *midd* mid, middle + *hrif* bowels, womb.] **1.** The diaphragm (of the body). **2. a** The part of a woman's garment, usually an inset, made to fit snugly over the diaphragm. **b** A woman's garment, usually in two pieces, which exposes part of the diaphragm section of the body.

mid′ship′ (mĭd′shĭp′), *adj.* Of, pert. to, or in, the middle of a ship.

mid′ship′man (-măn), *n.; pl.* -MEN (-mĕn). **1.** In the British Navy, a subordinate officer, usually a minor, who is receiving on shipboard his education for promotion to the grade of sublieutenant. **2.** In the United States Navy, one of the rank next below a commissioned officer, composed of the students of the Naval Academy. Cf. CADET, 3.

mid′ship·mite (mĭd′shĭp·mīt), *n. Now Humorous.* Midshipman.

mid′ships′ (mĭd′shĭps′), *adv.* Amidships.

midst (mĭdst), *n.* [From *middest, in the middest,* for older *in middes,* where *-s* is adverbial.] **1.** The interior or central part or place; middle. *Now Rare,* exc. as governed by *in, from,* etc.; as, in the *midst* of the forest.

☞ The construction *in our* (*your, their*) *midst* for *in the midst of us* (*you, them*) is common only in recent use, and its propriety has been much disputed.

2. Hence: **a** The position or condition of being beset; as, in the *midst* of duties. **b** Environment; setting.

midst, *prep.* In the midst of; amidst.

mid′sum′mer (mĭd′sŭm′ẽr; 2), *n.* The middle of summer; the period about the summer solstice. — **mid′sum′mer** (*see Pron.,* § 2), *adj.*

mid′way′ (-wā′), *n.; pl.* MIDWAYS (-wāz′). [AS. *midweg.*] **1.** *Obs.* A middle way or course. **2.** At a fair or exposition, a central avenue for exhibition of curiosities, fantastic amusements, etc. — (-wā′; 2), *adv. & adj.* In the middle of the way or distance.

mid′week′ (-wēk′), *n.* The middle of the week; among the Friends, [*cap.*], Wednesday. — **mid′week′,** *adj.* — **mid′week′ly,** *adv. & adj.*

Mid′west′ (mĭd′wĕst′; 2), *n.* = MIDDLE WEST. — **Mid′west′,** *adj.* — **Mid′west′ern** (-wĕs′tẽrn), *adj. U.S.* — **Mid′west′ern·er** (-tẽr·nẽr), *n.*

mid′wife′ (mĭd′wīf′), *n.; pl.* -WIVES (-wīvz′). [AS. *mid* with + *wīf* woman, wife.] A woman who assists women in childbirth.

mid′wife′ry (mĭd′wīf′rĭ; -ẽr·ĭ; *esp. Brit.,* -wĭf·rĭ), *n.* Art, practice, act, or fact of assisting at childbirth; obstetrics.

mid′win′ter (mĭd′wĭn′tẽr; 2), *n.* [AS.] The middle of winter; specif., the winter solstice.

mid′year′ (-yēr′; 2), *adj.* Occurring in the middle of a year, esp. an academic year. — *n. Colloq.* A midyear examination; *pl.,* the period of midyear examinations.

mien (mēn), *n.* [Prob. fr. *demean,* n.; influenced by F. *mine,* fr. Bret. *min* beak, muzzle.] Air; demeanor; bearing; as, a man of haughty *mien;* formerly, aspect; appearance. — **Syn.** See BEARING.

miff (mĭf), *n. Slang.* A petty quarrel; tiff. — *v. t. & i. Slang.* To offend or take offense. — **miff′y** (-ĭ), *adj.*

mig, migg (mĭg), *n.* A marble.

might (mīt), *past of* MAY.

might, *n.* [AS. *meaht, miht.*] Power to do something; force or power of any kind. — **Syn.** See POWER.

might′y (mīt′ĭ), *adj.;* MIGHT′I·ER (-ĭ·ẽr); MIGHT′I·EST. **1.** Possessing might; potent. **2.** Accomplished or characterized by might; hence, extraordinary; wonderful. — **might′i·ly,** *adv.* — **might′i·ness,** *n.* — **might′y,** *adv.*

mi′gnon (mĭn′yŏn; *F.* mē′nyôN′), *adj. masc.,* **mi′gnonne** (mĭn′yŏn; *F.* mē′nyŏn′), *fem.* [F.] Delicate and graceful; dainty; daintily small; petite.

mi′gnon·ette′ (mĭn′yŭn·ĕt′), *n.* [F. *mignonnette,* dim. of *mignon.*] Any of a genus (*Reseda*) of herbs typifying a family (Resedaceae, the mignonette family); esp., a garden annual (*R. odorata*) bearing racemes of greenish-white flowers. See RESEDA.

mi′graine (mī′grān; mĭ·grān′; mē′grān), *n.* [F., fr. LL., fr. Gr. *hēmikrania,* fr. *hēmi-* half + *kranion* skull.] A variety of nervous headache, usually periodical and confined to one side of the head.

mi′grant (mī′grănt), *adj.* [L. *migrans,* pres. part.] Migrating. — *n.* One that migrates, as a plant or animal.

mi′grate (mī′grāt), *v. i.* [L. *migratus,* past part. of *migrare* to migrate.] **1.** To move from one country or place of abode to another, with a view to residence. **2.** To pass periodically from one region or climate to another for feeding or breeding, as various birds and other animals.

mi·gra′tion (mī·grā′shŭn), *n.* [L. *migratio.*] **1.** Act or instance of migrating; also, collectively, the individuals taking part in a migratory movement. **2.** *Chem.* **a** A shifting of an atom or atoms from one part of the molecule to another. **b** A movement or drift of ions toward one or the other electrode under the influence of electromotive force. — **mi·gra′tion·al** (-ăl; -′l), *adj.*

mi′gra·to′ry (mī′grȧ·tō′rĭ *or, esp. Brit.,* -tẽr·ĭ), *adj.* **1.** Making a migration. **2.** Roving; nomadic; as, *migratory* habits. **3.** Of or pertaining to migration.

mi·ka′do (mĭ·kä′dō), *n.* [Jap. *mi,* a term of respect + *kado* door.] [*often cap.*] The title used by foreigners for the emperor of Japan.

mike (mīk), *n. Slang.* Short for MICROPHONE.

mi′kron (mī′krŏn). Var. of MICRON.

mil (mĭl), *n.* [L. *mille* thousand.] **1.** A unit used in measuring the diameter of wires, being 0.001 inch. **2.** *Mil.* A unit of angular measurement, equal to $\frac{1}{6400}$ of 360 degrees, used for figuring fire data. **3.** The one-thousandth part of the Israeli pound; also, a bronze coin of this value. See MONEY, *Tables.*

mi·la′dy (mĭ·lā′dĭ), *n.* [F., fr. E. *my lady.*] An English noblewoman or gentlewoman; a woman of fashion. Cf. MILORD.

mil′age (mīl′ĭj). Var. of MILEAGE.

milch (mĭlch; *now often* mĭlk), *adj.* Giving milk; as, a *milch* cow.

mild (mīld), *adj.* [AS. *milde.*] **1.** Gentle in nature or behavior; expressing gentleness. **2.** Moderate in action or effect; clement. **3.** Soft; malleable; as, *mild* steel. — **Syn.** See SOFT. — **mild′ly,** *adv.* — **mild′ness,** *n.*

mild′en (mīl′dĕn; -d′n), *v. t. & i.* To make or become mild.

mil′dew (mĭl′dū), *n.* [AS. *meledēaw, mildēaw,* honeydew.] **1. a** A thin, whitish growth produced on organic matter and on plants by fungi (as of the families Erysiphaceae and Peronosporaceae). **b** Any fungus producing mildew. **2.** Popularly, any discoloration caused by parasitic fungi on vegetable matter or on other substances. — *v. t. & i.* To affect, or be affected, with mildew. — **mil′dew·y** (-ĭ), *adj.*

mile (mīl), *n.* [AS. *mīl,* fr. L. *milia, millia,* pl. of *mille* a thousand, i. e., *milia passuum* a thousand paces, the ancient Roman mile being about 1620 English yards or 1482 meters.] A measure of distance. Abbr. *m., mi.* See MEASURE, *Tables* 1, 2, 4, & 9.

mile′age (mīl′ĭj), *n.* **1.** An allowance for traveling expenses at a certain rate per mile. **2.** Aggregate length or distance in miles. **3.** *Railroads.* A charge per mile, as for the use of the cars of a road; also, loosely, a book of **mileage tickets,** tickets issued in a collective form as in a **mileage book,** each ticket entitling the bearer to travel one or more miles.

mile′post′ (mīl′pōst′), *n.* A post indicating the distance in miles from a given point.

mil′er (mīl′ẽr), *n. Racing Slang.* A man or a horse specially qualified or trained to run or go a mile.

‖**mi′les glo′ri·o′sus** (mī′lēz glō′rĭ·ō′sŭs); *pl.* MILITES GLORIOSI (mĭl′ĭ-tēz glō′rĭ·ō′sī). [L.] Boastful soldier; esp. [*caps.*], the title of a comedy by Plautus.

mile′stone′ (mīl′stōn′), *n.* A stone serving as a milepost; hence, a significant point in any course.

mil′foil (mĭl′foil), *n.* [OF. *milfoil,* fr. L. *millefolium,* fr. *mille* thousand + *folium* leaf.] The yarrow.

mil′i·ar′i·a (mĭl′ĭ·âr′ĭ·ȧ; 6), *n.* [NL. See MILIARY.] An inflammatory disease of the skin characterized esp. by an eruption, burning and itching, and, usually, excessive perspiration.

mil′i·ar′y (mĭl′ĭ·ĕr′ĭ; -ẽr·ĭ; mĭl′yȧ·rĭ), *adj.* [L. *miliarius,* fr. *milium* millet.] **1.** Resembling millet seeds. **2.** *Med.* Accompanied with an eruption of spots resembling millet seeds.

miliary tuberculosis. Tuberculosis in which one or several organs contain minute tubercles developed from a tubercle bacillus carried in the blood from another focus.

mi′lieu′ (mē′lyû′), *n.* [F., fr. OF. *mi* middle (fr. L. *medius*) + *lieu* place.] Environment; setting.

mil′i·tant (mĭl′ĭ·tănt), *adj.* [F., fr. L. *militans, -antis,* pres. part. of *militare* to be a soldier.] Engaged in warfare; fighting; also, combative; aggressively active. — **Syn.** See AGGRESSIVE. — *n.* A militant person. — **mil′i·tan·cy** (-tăn·sĭ), *n.* — **mil′i·tant·ly,** *adv.*

mil′i·ta·rism (-tȧ·rĭz′m), *n.* Predominance of the military class or prevalence of their ideals; the spirit which exalts military virtues and ideals; the policy of aggressive military preparedness.

mil′i·ta·rist (-rĭst), *n.* An expert in military matters; also, one imbued with militarism. — **mil′i·ta·ris′tic** (-rĭs′tĭk), *adj.* — **mil′i·ta·ris′ti·cal·ly** (-tĭ·kăl·ĭ), *adv.*

mil′i·ta·rize (-rīz), *v. t.* To imbue with militarism. — **mil′i·ta·ri·za′tion** (-rĭ·zā′shŭn; -rī·zā′-), *n.*

mil′i·tar′y (mĭl′ĭ·tĕr′ĭ *or, esp. Brit.,* -tẽr·ĭ), *adj.* [F. *militaire,* fr. L. *militaris,* fr. *miles, militis,* soldier.] **1.** Of or pertaining to soldiers, arms, or war; according to the methods and customs of war or of armies. **2.** Performed or made by soldiers; supported by armed force. — **Syn.** See MARTIAL. — *n.* Soldiery; troops; the army. — **mil′i·tar′i·ly,** *adv.*

☞ As a label in this Dictionary, *military* (abbr. *Mil.*) is often used to include all branches of the armed services.

military attaché. An army officer on duty with the diplomatic representative of his country at a foreign capital.

military police. *Mil.* An organized part of an army or command, which exercises the functions of police among the soldiers and those attached to the troops. Abbr. *MP* or *M.P.*

mil′i·tate (mĭl′ĭ·tāt), *v. i.* [L. *militare, militatum,* to be a soldier.] **1.** *Rare.* To serve as a soldier. **2.** Of things, to have weight or effect; to make (for or against); — used esp. with *against;* as, his age *militated* against him.

mi·li′tia (mĭ·lĭsh′ȧ), *n.* [L., military service, soldiery.] A body of citizens enrolled as a regular military force for periodical instruction, discipline, and drill, but not called into active service except in emergencies. In the United States, it includes all able-bodied male citizens between eighteen and forty-five and is divided into two classes, the ***organized militia*** of the individual states, and the ***reserve militia,*** the organized militia being now called the ***National Guard.*** — **mi·li′tia·man** (-măn), *n.*

milk (mĭlk), *n.* [AS. *meoluc, meoloc, meolc, milc.*] **1.** A fluid secreted by the mammary glands of female mammals for the nourishment of their young. **2.** A liquid resembling milk in appearance, as the latex of a plant, the juice of the coconut, etc. — *v. t.* **1.** To press or draw milk from the breasts or udder of; to withdraw the milk of. **2.** To draw from the breast or udder; to extract, as milk. **3.** To draw anything from as if by milking; to exploit. **4.** To draw (out); to drain, as something away. **5.** To draw out the sap, venom, etc., from. **6.** To subject to an action suggestive of that practiced in milking an animal. — *v. i.* To draw or to yield milk.

milk adder. The milk snake.

milk′-and-wa′ter (*see Pron.,* § 2), *adj.* Weak; insipid; wishy-washy.

milk′er (mĭl′kẽr), *n.* **1.** One who or that which milks. **2.** One that gives milk, or a fluid likened to milk.

milk fever. A slight fever attending first lactation.

milk leg. A painful general swelling of the leg, at childbirth, caused by inflammation and clotting in the veins.

milk′-liv′ered, *adj.* Cowardly; timorous.

milk′maid′ (mĭlk′mād′), *n.* A woman who milks cows or is employed in a dairy.

milk′man′ (-măn′; -măn), *n.; pl.* -MEN (-mĕn′; -mĕn). A man who sells or delivers milk.

milk of magnesia. *Pharm.* A milk-white suspension of magnesium hydroxide, $Mg(OH)_2$, in water, used as an antacid and laxative.

milk punch. A punch made with spirit, milk, sugar, etc.

milk shake. *Colloq., U.S.* A beverage of milk, or milk and egg, and usually ice cream, flavored, and shaken or beaten thoroughly.

milk sickness. A disease characterized by vomiting, constipation, and muscular tremors, and caused by eating the dairy products or meat of cattle poisoned by certain plants.

milk snake. A common harmless snake (*Lampropeltis triangulum*), gray with black-bordered blotches and an arrow-shaped occipital spot; — called also *checkered, milk,* or *spotted adder.*

milk′sop′ (mĭlk′sŏp′), *n.* An unmanly man; a mollycoddle.

milk sugar. = LACTOSE.

milk tooth. One of the temporary deciduous teeth of a mammal. In man there are twenty in all.

milk vetch. **a** An Old World herb (*Astragalus glycyphyllos*) supposed to increase the yield of milk in goats. **b** Hence, any of various related plants.

milk′weed′ (mĭlk′wēd′), *n*. **a** Any of a genus (*Asclepias*) of plants, so called from the milk, or latex, and typifying a vast family (Asclepiadaceae, the milkweed family) of herbs and shrubs mostly with milky juice and umbellate flowers. Cf. BUTTERFLY WEED **a**. **b** Hence, any of various related plants.

milk′wort′ (mĭlk′wûrt′), *n*. Any of a genus (*Polygala*) of plants with showy flowers, typifying a family (Polygalaceae, the milkwort family); esp., a European species (*P. vulgaris*), formerly reputed to promote lactation, and the ***orange milkwort*** (*P. lutea*) of the southeastern United States.

milk′y (mĭl′kĭ), *adj.*; MILK′I·ER (-kĭ·ẽr); MILK′I·EST. **1**. Like, or suggestive of, milk, as in color or consistency. **2**. Mild; gentle; timorous. **3**. Consisting of, containing, or abounding in milk. — **milk′i·ness**, *n*.

Milky Way, *or* **Galaxy**, *n*. *Astron*. **1**. [usually with "the."] The faintly luminous tract seen at night stretching across the heavens, composed chiefly of distant stars. **2**. [*usually not caps.*] By extension, any of the numerous similar star aggregations. See ISLAND UNIVERSE.

mill (mĭl), *n*. [L. *mille* a thousand.] A money of account of the United States having the value of 1/10 of a cent. See MONEY OF ACCOUNT.

mill, *n*. [AS. *myln*, *mylen*, fr. LL. *molina*, *molinum*, fr. L. *mola* millstone.] **1**. A building provided with machinery for grinding grain into flour; hence, a machine for grinding grain and other material. **2**. Any of various machines which produce a manufactured product by the continuous repetition of some simple action; as, a saw*mill*. **3**. A building or collection of buildings with machinery by which the processes of manufacturing are carried on; as, a powder *mill*; a steel *mill*. **4**. Any of various machines, as: **a** A machine for stamping coins. **b** A machine for expelling juice, sap, etc., from vegetable tissues by pressure, grinding, etc.; as, a cider *mill*. **c** A machine for polishing; as, a lapidary *mill*. **5**. *Cant*. [From the v.] A pugilistic encounter. **6**. *Scot*. A snuffbox. **7**. *Mach*. A rotary cutter for shaping and dressing metal surfaces. — *v. t.* **1**. To subject, as grain, cloth, timber, metal, etc., to some operation or process in a mill; to shape, finish, transform, etc., by means of a mill or machine. **2**. To make a raised border around, or to cut fine grooves around the edge of; as, to *mill* coins. **3**. *Cant*. To beat, as with the fists; to thrash. **4**. To make frothy, as by churning or whipping; as, to *mill* chocolate. — *v. i.* **1**. *Slang*. To take part in a pugilistic encounter; to box. **2**. **a** To move in a circle, as cattle upon a plain. **b** To move in a riotous, esp. eddying, mass.

mill′board′ (mĭl′bōrd′; 70), *n*. A board made of wood pulp or wastepaper, used esp. in bookbinding.

mill′dam′ (-dăm′), *n*. A dam to make a millpond; also, the millpond itself.

milled (mĭld), *adj*. Having been subjected to milling; as, a silver dollar with *milled* edge.

mil′le·nar′i·an (mĭl′ĕ·nâr′ĭ·ăn; 6), *adj*. Of or pertaining to a thousand (years); of or pertaining to the millennium or the millenarians. — *n*. A believer in the millennium.

mil′le·nar′y (mĭl′ĕ·nĕr′ĭ *or, esp. Brit.*, -nẽr·ĭ), *adj*. [LL. *millenarius*, fr. *milleni* a thousand each, fr. *mille* a thousand.] **1**. Pertaining to, or consisting of, a thousand, esp. a thousand years. **2**. Pertaining to the millennium or the millenarians; millennial. — *n*. **1**. A thousand; a period of a thousand years; millennium. **2**. A millenarian. **3**. A thousandth anniversary or its celebration.

mil·len′ni·al (mĭ·lĕn′ĭ·ăl), *adj*. Of or pert. to a millennium, esp. the millennium of Christian prophecy.

Millennial Church. See SHAKER, 2.

mil·len′ni·um (-ŭm), *n.*; *pl*. -NIUMS (-ŭmz), -NIA (-ȧ). [NL., fr. L. *mille* a thousand + *annus* a year.] **1**. A thousand years; also, a thousandth anniversary; a millenary. **2**. Specif., the thousand years mentioned in Revelation xx, during which holiness is to be triumphant. Some believe that during this period Christ will reign on earth. **3**. Hence, a period of great happiness, good government, freedom from wickedness, etc.

mil′le·pede (mĭl′ĕ·pēd), **mil′li·pede** (mĭl′ĭ-), *n*. [L. *millepeda*, fr. *mille* a thousand + *pes*, *pedis*, foot.] Any of numerous myriapods (division Diplopoda), chiefly with a round body of numerous segments covered with hard integument.

mil′le·pore (-pōr; 70), *n*. [F. *millépore*, fr. *mille* thousand + *pore* a pore. Cf. MADREPORE.] Any of an order (Milleporina) comprising a single genus (*Millepora*) of stony hydrozoan corals which form incrusting, branching, or leaflike masses, often of large size. Cf. CORAL, 1.

mill′er (mĭl′ẽr), *n*. **1**. One who operates, keeps, or attends a mill. **2**. Any of various moths; — so called because their wings appear as if covered with dust, like a miller's clothes. **3**. A milling machine, or a tool for use in one.

mill′er·ite (-īt), *n*. [After W. H. *Miller*, Eng. mineralogist.] *Mineral*. Native nickel sulfide, NiS, a brass-yellow mineral occurring in crystals and incrustations.

Mill′er·ite, *n*. A believer in the doctrine of William Miller (1782–1849), an American preacher who taught that the end of the world and the second coming of Christ were at hand.

mill′er's–thumb′ (mĭl′ẽrz·thŭm′), *n*. Any of certain small fresh-water spiny-finned fishes (genus *Cottus*, family Cottidae).

mil·les′i·mal (mĭ·lĕs′ĭ·măl), *adj*. [L. *millesimus*, fr. *mille* a thousand.] Thousandth; consisting of thousandth parts; also, of or pert. to a thousandth; as, *millesimal* fractions. — *n*. A thousandth.

mil′let (mĭl′ĕt; -ĭt), *n*. [F., dim. of *mil*, fr. L. *milium*.] **1**. Any of various small-seeded cereal and forage grasses; as, ***pearl millet*** (*Pennisetum glaucum*), ***Italian millet*** (*Setaria italica*); specif., an annual grass (*Panicum miliaceum*) cultivated for its grain, which is used esp. in Europe and Asia for food. **2**. The grain or seed of any of these grasses.

mil′li- (mĭl′ĭ-). [L. *mille* thousand.] A combining form denoting: **a** *A thousand*, as in **mil′li·fold′**, **mil′li·form′**, **mil′li·grade′**. See -FOLD, -FORM, -GRADE. **b** *A thousandth*; — in units of the metric system (see METRIC SYSTEM, *Tables*), electricity, etc., as in **mil′li·am′pere**, **mil′li·are**, **mil′li·far′ad**, **mil′li·gram** *or* **mil′li·gramme**, **mil′li·lam′bert**, **mil′li·li′ter** *or* **mil′li·li′tre**, **mil′li·phot**, **mil′li·stere**, **mil′li·volt**, etc.

mil′li·ard (mĭl′ĭ·ärd; -yärd; *F.* mē′lyȧr′), *n*. [F., fr. Pr. *milhar* a thousand.] In the French, German, and English system of numeration, a thousand millions; — usually called *billion* in America. See NUMERATION, *Table*.

mil′li·ar′y (mĭl′ĭ·ĕr′ĭ *or, esp. Brit.*, -ẽr·ĭ), *adj*. [L. *milliarius* containing a thousand, fr. *mille* thousand. See MILE.] Of or pertaining to the ancient Roman mile.

mil′li·bar (mĭl′ĭ·bär), *n*. [*milli-* + Gr. *baros* weight.] One thousand dynes per square centimeter; — used in measuring atmospheric pressure.

mil′lième′ (mē′lyĕm′), *n*. [F.] The thousandth part of a monetary unit; esp. in Egypt, the thousandth of the pound.

‖**mil′lier′** (mē′lyā′), *n*. [F.] A metric ton. See METRIC SYSTEM, *Table* 5.

mil′li·me′ter, **mil′li·me′tre** (mĭl′ĭ·mē′tẽr), *n*. [F. *millimètre*.] One thousandth of a meter. Abbr. *mm*. See METRIC SYSTEM, *Tables* 1, 2, & 6.

mil′li·mi′cron (mĭl′ĭ·mī′krŏn), *n*. [*milli-* + *micron*.] The thousandth part of a micron, or the millionth part of a millimeter; a micromillimeter; — used in measuring light waves, etc. Symbol, mμ.

mil′line′ (mĭl′līn′), *n*. [*million* + *line*.] A unit of space and circulation, equivalent to one agate line, a column wide, appearing in one million copies of a publication.

mil′li·ner (mĭl′ĭ·nẽr), *n*. [From *Milaner* an inhabitant of *Milan*, in Italy; hence, a man from *Milan* who imported women's finery.] **1**. *Obs*. An importer or vendor of miscellaneous fancy articles, esp. from Milan. **2**. A person, usually a woman, who makes, trims, or deals in hats, bonnets, headdresses, etc., for women.

mil′li·ner′y (-nĕr′ĭ; -nẽr·ĭ), *n*. **1**. The articles made or sold by milliners. **2**. The business or work of a milliner.

mill′ing ma·chine′ (mĭl′ĭng). A metal-cutting machine tool in which the surface of the work is shaped or dressed by being fed past revolving toothed cutters of various shapes and sizes.

mil′lion (mĭl′yŭn), *n*. [OF., fr. It. *millione* (now *milione*), aug. fr. *mille* thousand, fr. L. *mille*.] **1**. The number of ten hundred thousand, or a thousand thousand; — written 1,000,000. See NUMBER, *Table*; NUMERATION, *Table*. **2**. An indefinitely large number. **3**. **a** A million monetary units of some understood kind, as dollars or pounds. **b** The mass of common people; — with *the*. — **mil′lion**, *adj*. — **mil′lionth** (-yŭnth), *n*. & *adj*.

mil′lion·aire′ (mĭl′yŭn·âr′), *n*. Also **mil′lion·naire′**. [F. *millionnaire*.] One whose wealth is estimated at a million or in millions of dollars, pounds, francs, etc.

mil′lion·fold′ (mĭl′yŭn·fōld′), *adj*. & *adv*. See -FOLD.

mil′li·pede (-ĭ·pēd), **mil′li·ped** (-pĕd). Vars. of MILLEPEDE.

mill′pond′ (mĭl′pŏnd′), *n*. **1**. A pond that supplies the water for a mill. **2**. *Jocose*. The Atlantic Ocean.

mill′race′ (-rās′), *n*. The canal in which water goes to a mill wheel, or the current which drives the wheel. Cf. RACE.

Mills grenade (mĭlz). [After (Sir) Wm. *Mills* (1856–1932), Brit. inventor.] A time hand grenade filled with high explosive.

mill′stone′ (mĭl′stōn′), *n*. **1**. Either of two circular stones used for grinding grain or other substance; also, the material of which the stones are composed. **2**. **a** Something that grinds or crushes. **b** A heavy burden. *Matt*. xviii. 6.

mill′stream′ (-strēm′), *n*. The stream in a millrace.

mill wheel. The water wheel that drives a mill.

mill′wright′ (-rīt′), *n*. One whose occupation is to build mills, or to set up their machinery; now, usually, a workman who erects the shafting, cares for belting, etc.

mi·lord′ (mĭ·lôrd′; -lôr′), *n*. [F., fr. E. *my lord*.] Literally, my lord; hence (as used on the Continent), an English nobleman or gentleman. Cf. MILADY.

mil′pa (mĭl′pä), *n*. In Central America, a small jungle clearing cropped for a few seasons and then abandoned for a fresh clearing. This method of primitive native agriculture is known as the **milpa system**.

mil′reis′ (mĭl′rās′), *n. sing.* & *pl*. [Pg. *mil reis*, i. e., one thousand reis. See REIS.] **a** A Portuguese money of account and coin, superseded in 1911 by the escudo. **b** A Brazilian money of account, chiefly in paper currency, superseded 1942 by the cruzeiro.

milt (mĭlt), *n*. [AS. *milte*.] The spleen.

milt, *n*. The male reproductive glands of fishes when filled with secretion, or the secretion itself. Also used attributively of male breeding fishes; as, a *milt* shad. — *v. t.* To impregnate (the roe of a fish) with milt.

milt′er (mĭl′tẽr), *n*. A male fish in breeding time.

Mil·ton′ic (mĭl·tŏn′ĭk), *adj*. Also **Mil·to′ni·an** (-tō′nĭ·ăn; 58). Characteristic of or pert. to John Milton (1608–74) or his work, characterized by imaginative power and sublimity of style.

mim (mĭm), *adj*. *Dial*. Affectedly shy or modest.

mime (mīm), *n*. [L. *mimus*, fr. Gr. *mimos*.] **1**. *Antiq*. A type of drama in which scenes from life were imitated and generally travestied; also, a dialogue for such drama. **2**. An actor in such drama. **3**. A mimic; buffoon. — *v. t.* **1**. To act out in the manner of a mime. **2**. To mimic; imitate. — *v.i.* To act as a mime; to play a part with mimic action and usually without words. — **mim′er** (mīm′ẽr), *n*.

mim′e·o·graph′ (mĭm′ĕ·ō·grȧf′; 9), *n*. A stencil duplicator for making many copies. — *v. t.* & *i.* To print by means of a mimeograph.

mi·me′sis (mĭ·mē′sĭs; mī·mē′sĭs), *n*. [NL., fr. Gr. *mimēsis* imitation.] *Rhet., Biol.,* & *Med*. Imitation; mimicry.

mi·met′ic (mĭ·mĕt′ĭk; mī-), *adj*. [Gr. *mimētikos*.] **1**. Apt to imitate; imitative. **2**. Pert. to, of the nature of, or characterized by imitation. **3**. = MIMIC, *adj.*, 2. **4**. *Biol*. Characterized by mimicry. — **mi·met′i·cal·ly** (-ĭ·kăl·ĭ), *adv*.

mim′ic (mĭm′ĭk), *adj*. [L. *mimicus*, fr. Gr. *mimikos*, fr. *mimos* mime.] **1**. Imitative; mimetic. **2**. Copying or imitating (the thing or person denoted by the noun limited); as, a *mimic* battle. — *n*. **1**. *Obs*. A mime, or actor in mimes. **2**. One that imitates or mimics, esp. to make sport; also, one that servilely imitates. — *v. t.*; MIM′ICKED (-ĭkt); MIM′ICK·ING. **1**. To ridicule by copying or imitating. **2**. To imitate closely; to ape; also, to simulate. **3**. *Biol*. To have or assume a resemblance to (some other organism or some object), in form, color, or the like. See MIMICRY, 2. — **Syn**. See COPY.

mim′i·cal (mĭm′ĭ·kăl), *adj*. *Now Rare*. Mimic.

mim′ick·er (mĭm′ĭk·ẽr), *n*. One that mimics.

mim′ic·ry (-ĭk·rĭ), *n*. **1**. Act, practice, or art of one who mimics;

also, an instance of mimicking; a thing that mimics. **2.** *Zool.* The superficial resemblance which some animals exhibit to other animals or to the natural objects among which they live, thereby securing concealment, protection, or the like.

Mi'mir (mē'mĕr), *n.* [ON. *Mīmir.*] *Norse Myth.* A giant whose abode is by the well at the root of Yggdrasill. Drinking the waters of the spring, he knows the past and future.

mi·mo'sa (mĭ·mō'sȧ; -zȧ), *n.* [NL., fr. L. *mimus* actor, mime.] Any of a large genus (*Mimosa*) of trees, shrubs, and herbs, natives of warm regions, typifying a family (Mimosaceae, the mimosa family). They have usually bipinnate, often prickly, leaves and globular heads of small white or pink flowers. In many species, as the sensitive plant (*M. pudica*), the leaves are sensitive to touch. Also, the flower of any of these plants. — **mim'o·sa'ceous** (mĭm'ō·sā'shŭs; mī'mō-), *adj.*

mi'na (mī'nȧ), *n.; pl.* MINAE (-nē), MINAS (-nȧz). [L. *mina*, fr. Gr. *mna*, of Sem. origin.] An ancient weight and money unit of varying value; 1/60 talent.

mi·na'cious (mĭ·nā'shŭs), *adj.* [L. *minax*, *-acis.* See MENACE.] Threatening; menacing. — **mi·na'cious·ly**, *adv.* — **mi·na'cious·ness**, *n.* — **mi·nac'i·ty** (-năs'ĭ·tĭ), *n.*

min'a·ret' (mĭn'ȧ·rĕt' *or, esp. Brit.*, mĭn'ȧ·rĕt), *n.* [F. *minaret*, or Sp. *minarete*, fr. Turk. *manārat*, fr. Ar. *manārah* lamp, lighthouse.] *Arch.* A slender, lofty tower attached to a mosque and surrounded by one or more balconies, from which the summons to prayer is cried by the muezzin.

min'a·to·ry (mĭn'ȧ·tō'rĭ *or, esp. Brit.*, -tĕr·ĭ), *adj.* [OF. *minatoire*, fr. LL. *minatorius*, fr. *minari* to threaten. See MENACE.] Threatening; menacing. — **min'a·to'ri·ly**, *adv.*

mince (mĭns), *v. t.;* MINCED (mĭnst); MINC'ING (mĭn'sĭng). [OF. *mincier* (F. *mincer*).] **1.** To cut or chop into very small pieces; to hash; hence, to subdivide minutely. **2.** To suppress or weaken the force of; as, a *minced* oath; he *minced* no words in his accusation; also, to utter or pronounce with affected daintiness. — *v. i.* **1.** To walk with short steps or in a prim, affected manner; to affect delicacy of manner. **2.** To talk or speak with affected nicety. — *n.* The small bits into which something is chopped; specif., minced meat; mincemeat.

mince'meat' (mĭns'mēt'), *n.* **1.** Minced meat; meat chopped very fine. **2.** A finely chopped, cooked mixture of raisins, apples, suet, spices, etc., with or without meat.

mince pie. A pie of mincemeat (def. 2).

minc'er (mĭn'sĕr), *n.* One that minces.

minc'ing (mĭn'sĭng), *adj.* That minces; esp., affectedly nice. — **minc'ing·ly**, *adv.*

mind (mīnd), *n.* [AS. *gemynd.*] **1.** Memory; now, specif.: **a** Recollection; as, to call to *mind.* **b** Power of remembering; scope of memory; as, time out of *mind.* **c** Retention in memory; heed; as, out of sight, out of *mind.* **2.** Commemoration; specif., a commemorative mass for a deceased person one month after (***month's mind***), or on the anniversary of, his death. **3.** That which one thinks; opinion; as, to speak one's *mind.* **4.** Intention or wish; purpose; desire; — in phrases; as, to change one's *mind.* **5. a** *Obs.* Sentiment; disposition. **b** Choice; liking; inclination. **6.** The subject of consciousness; that which feels, perceives, wills, thinks, etc. **7.** The perceptive and thinking part of consciousness, exclusive of will and emotion. **8.** [*cap.*] *Christian Science.* Specif., Divine Mind; — a synonym for God. **9.** *Philos.* The conscious element or factor in the universe; spirit; intelligence; — contrasted with *matter.* **10.** *Psychol.* **a** The total of the conscious states of an individual. **b** One's capacity for mental activity.

— *v. t.* **1.** To remember; to call to mind. **2.** *Now Dial.* To remind. **3.** To turn the mind or attention to; specif.: **a** To perceive; notice. **b** To regard with attention; to heed. **c** To obey; as, to *mind* parents. **d** To attend strictly or closely to. **4.** *Now Dial.* To purpose; intend. **5.** To be concerned about; to care about; hence, to object to; to dislike; as, I don't *mind* the change. **6.** To be careful or wary about; as, *mind* what you are doing. **7.** To take care or charge of; to tend; as, to *mind* a baby. — *v. i.* **1.** To be careful or wary; to look out. **2.** To be concerned; to care; as, never *mind.* **3.** To pay heed, esp. in order to obey; hence, to obey; as, the dog *minds* well.

mind cure. A method or act of healing disease, esp. the neuroses, by mental procedures; psychotherapy.

mind'er (mīn'dĕr), *n.* **1.** One who minds, tends, or watches something. **2.** One to be attended; specif., *Eng.*, a pauper child entrusted to the care of a private person.

mind'ful (mīnd'fo͝ol; -f'l), *adj.* Bearing in mind; regardful. — **mind'ful·ly**, *adv.* — **mind'ful·ness**, *n.*

mind'less (-lĕs; -lĭs), *adj.* Destitute of mind; stupid; unintelligent; also, inattentive. — **mind'less·ly**, *adv.*

mind reading. The perceiving of another's thought without normal means of communication. — **mind reader.**

mind's eye (mīndz). An imaginary sight or view, as opposed to one actually seen.

mine (mīn), *pron.* [AS. *mīn* my, of me.] The possessive case of I, used absolutely: **a** In a predicative construction; as, vengeance is *mine.* **b** By ellipsis of the noun denoting that which is possessed; also, my kindred or family; as, he honored me and *mine.* **c** After *of;* as, this brother of *mine.* — *adj. Chiefly Archaic & Poetic.* My; — now used only before a vowel or *h*, except when it follows its noun; as, mother *mine.* Specif.: **1.** Of or belonging to me; associated with me; as, *mine* hostess. **2.** Of or relating to me as object of an action; as, *mine* undoing.

mine, *n.* [OF., of Celt. origin.] **1. a** A pit or excavation from which ores, precious stones, coal, etc., are taken by digging. Cf. QUARRY. **b** Loosely, an ore deposit. **2.** A rich or abundant source or store. **3.** A subterranean passage. **4.** *Fireworks.* A piece comprising various small fireworks which are scattered into the air with a loud report. **5.** *Mil.* An explosive charge designed to destroy enemy vessels, installations, equipment, or personnel; orig., one placed in an excavation in the earth, now usually one contained in a case and placed in the water (***naval mine***) or buried in the ground (***land mine***) or dropped from an airplane (***aerial mine***). — *v. i.* **1.** To dig a mine; to get ore, metals, coal, or precious stones, out of the earth. **2.** To form a burrow; to burrow; also, to lay a mine, as to destroy enemy works. — *v. t.* **1.** To dig below the surface of; to dig away the foundation of; to lay or make a military mine under; to sap; hence, to ruin by slow degrees or secret means. **2.** To make by burrowing, esp. underground. **3.** To get (ore, metal, etc.) from the earth by digging, blasting, etc. **4.** To dig into, for ore or metal.

mine field. *Mil.* The whole space occupied or commanded by mines either on land or in the water.

mine layer. A naval vessel especially equipped for, or engaged in, the laying of underwater mines.

‖**Mi'nen·wer'fer** (mē'nĕn·vĕr'fĕr), *n.* [G., lit., mine thrower.] A German muzzle-loading rifled trench gun, mounted on wheels to accompany advancing infantry.

min'er (mīn'ĕr), *n.* One who mines; esp., a worker in a mine.

min'er·al (mĭn'ĕr·ăl), *n.* [OF., fr. ML. *minerale.* See MINERAL, *adj.*] **1.** Any chemical element or compound occurring naturally as a product of inorganic processes. Rocks, except certain glassy forms, are either simple minerals or aggregates of two or more minerals. Such substances as coal and amber are not true minerals. **2. a** *Obs.* A mine. **b** *Colloq. Mining.* Ore. **3.** Anything which is neither animal nor vegetable, as in the old general classification of things into three kingdoms (animal, vegetable, and mineral). **4.** = MINERAL WATER. — *adj.* [F. *minéral*, fr. ML. *mineralis*, fr. *minera* ore, mine, fr. OF. *miniere.*] **1.** Of or pert to, or of the nature of, a mineral or minerals; inorganic. **2.** Impregnated with minerals.

min'er·al·ize (-īz), *v. t.* **1.** To transform (a metal) into an ore. **2.** To petrify; as, *mineralized* leaves or bones. **3.** To impregnate or supply with minerals or any inorganic compound; to convert into mineral form. — *v. i.* To go on an excursion for collecting minerals. — **min'er·al·i·za'tion** (-ĭ·zā'shŭn; -ī·zā'-), *n.* — **min'er·al·iz'er** (-īz'ĕr), *n.*

mineral jelly. A semisolid substance from petroleum used as a stabilizer in explosives.

min'er·al'o·gist (mĭn'ĕr·ăl'ō·jĭst), *n.* Specialist in mineralogy.

min'er·al'o·gy (-jĭ), *n.; pl.* -GIES (-jĭz). [*mineral* + *-logy;* cf. F. *minéralogie.*] The science of minerals, dealing with their physical and chemical properties, their classification, and the ways of distinguishing them; also, the materials of the science, or a treatise on it. — **min'er·al·og'i·cal** (-ăl·ŏj'ĭ·kăl), *adj.* — **min'er·al·og'i·cal·ly**, *adv.*

mineral oil. Any oil of mineral origin, as petroleum.

mineral pitch. = ASPHALT, *n.*, 1.

mineral tar. = MALTHA, 2 **a.**

mineral water. Any water naturally or artificially impregnated with mineral salts or gases.

mineral wax. Ozocerite.

mineral wool. A fibrous woollike material made from melted slag. It is a poor conductor of heat.

Mi·ner'va (mĭ·nûr'vȧ), *n.* [L.] *Rom. Relig.* A goddess identified with the Greek Athena.

‖**mi·ne·stro'ne** (mē·nā·strō'nā), *n.* [It.] A rich thick soup, with barley, vermicelli, or the like, and vegetables.

mine sweeping. *Mil. & Nav.* Act of dragging a body of water to free it from submarine or floating mines. — **mine sweeper.**

Ming (mĭng), *n.* [Chin. (Pek.) *Ming*², lit., luminous.] A dynasty in Chinese history (A.D. 1368–1644) noted for its works of art, paintings, porcelains, textiles, etc.

min'gle (mĭng'g'l), *v. t.;* MIN'GLED (-g'ld); MIN'GLING (-glĭng). [Freq. of ME. *mengen*, fr. AS. *mengan.*] **1.** To combine or join in a mixed mass; to intermix. **2.** To associate or unite, as things by interspersion or persons by ties of relationship; to join in company. **3.** To concoct. — *v. i.* To become mingled; to mix. — **Syn.** See MIX. — **min'gler** (-glĕr), *n.*

ming' tree' (mĭng'). [See MING.] An artificial plant made by attaching irregular pads of alpine buckwheat (*Eriogonum ovalifolium*), left natural gray or painted, to one or more branches, commonly of manzanita.

min'i·a·ture (mĭn'ĭ·ȧ·tūr; mĭn'yȧ-; mĭn'ĭ·tūr), *n.* [It. *miniatura*, fr. ML. *miniatura*, fr. *miniare* to color with minium.] **1.** A painting in colors, as in medieval manuscripts; an illumination. **2.** Any very small painting, esp. a portrait, as an ivory; also, the art of painting such works. **3.** A representation on a much reduced scale; a small copy. — *adj.* Being, or represented, on a small scale. — **Syn.** See SMALL.

miniature camera. A camera using film 35 mm. wide or smaller, used esp. in candid photography. — **miniature photography.**

min'i·cam' (mĭn'ĭ·kăm'), **min'i·cam'er·a** (-kăm'ĕr·ȧ), *n.* Short for MINIATURE CAMERA.

Min'i·é ball (mĭn'ĭ·ā; *popularly* mĭn'ĭ). [After the inventor, Capt. C. E. *Minié* (1814–1879), of France.] A type of conical rifle bullet, much used in the middle of the 19th century.

min'i·fy (mĭn'ĭ·fī), *v. t.;* -FIED (-fīd); -FY'ING. [L. *minor* less + *-fy.*] To make small or smaller; to lessen.

min'i·kin (-kĭn), *n.* [Obs. D. *minneken* a darling, dim. of *minne* love.] *Obs.* Anything delicate or diminutive. — *adj.* **1.** Delicate; hence, affected; mincing. **2.** Very small; tiny.

min'im (mĭn'ĭm), *n.* [L. *minimus* smallest, a superl. fr. the root of *minor.*] **1.** *Music.* A half note, formerly the shortest in use. See NOTE *n.* **2.** Anything very minute; a jot. **3.** The smallest liquid measure, about a drop. Symbol ♏. See MEASURE, *Table* 12. **4.** *Penmanship.* A single down stroke, as any of the three in the letter *m.* — *adj.* Smallest; minute.

min'i·mal (-ĭ·măl), *adj.* Constituting a minim; hence, lowest or least attainable, possible, usual, etc.

Min'i·mal·ist (mĭn'ĭ·măl·ĭst), *n.* [*minimal* + *-ist.*] A member of the less radical wing of the former Russian Social Revolutionary party. Cf. MAXIMALIST.

min'i·mize (-mīz), *v. t.* To reduce to the smallest part or proportion possible; to reduce to, or to estimate at, a minimum. — **Syn.** See DECRY. — **min'i·mi·za'tion** (-mĭ·zā'shŭn; -mī·zā'-), *n.* — **min'i·miz'er** (-mīz'ĕr), *n.*

min'i·mum (-mŭm), *n.; pl.* MINIMA (-mȧ), -MUMS (-mŭmz). [L., neut. of *minimus.* See MINIM.] **1.** The least quantity or amount assignable, admissible, possible, etc.; — opposed to *maximum.* **2.** The lowest point or amount registered; — used of something that varies, as temperature. — *adj.* Being a minimum; lowest or least attainable, possible, usual, etc.

minimum wage. **a** = LIVING WAGE. **b** A wage agreed upon or fixed by legally conferred authority as the smallest wage payable to an employee of a specified class.

min'ing (mīn'ĭng), *n.* Act or business of working mines.

min'ion (mĭn'yŭn), *n.* [F. *mignon*, fem. *mignonne*, dainty, a darling.] **1. a** *Now Rare.* A ladylove or lover; usually, a mistress; a paramour. **b** One highly favored; a favorite; idol; — now used only derogatorily. **c** Esp., a servile dependent or agent; a creature. **2.**

[F. *mignonne.*] A size of type (7 points). See TYPE. — *adj.* Delicate; dainty.

min'ish (mĭn'ĭsh), *v. t. & i.* [OF. *menuisier* to make small.] *Now Rare & Archaic.* To diminish; lessen.

min'is·ter (mĭn'ĭs·tẽr), *n.* [OF. *ministre*, fr. L. *minister* (after *magister*; cf. MASTER), fr. root of *minor* less.] **1. a** *Archaic.* A servant; attendant. **b** *Now Rare.* An agent. **2.** One duly authorized to conduct Christian worship, preach the gospel, administer the sacraments, etc.; esp., a priest; pastor; clergyman. **3.** One to whom the sovereign or executive head of a government entrusts the management of affairs of state, or some department of such affairs. **4.** A representative of a government sent to a foreign nation to transact diplomatic business. Cf. AMBASSADOR. — *v. t.* **1.** *Archaic.* To furnish; supply. **2.** *Now Rare.* To administer; to dispense, as a sacrament; to apply. — *v. i.* **1.** To act as an attendant or agent; to attend. **2.** To do things needful or helpful; to aid.

min'is·te'ri·al (-tẽr'ĭ·ăl), *adj.* **1.** Of or pert. to ministry or service. **2.** Of or pert. to the office of minister or the ministry as a body, whether civil or sacerdotal. **3.** Of the nature of those acts or duties belonging to the administration of the executive function or done by a person in a manner prescribed by the nature of his official position; — opposed to *judicial.* **4.** Acting or active as an agent. — **min'is·te'ri·al·ly**, *adv.*

min'is·te'ri·al·ist (-ĭst), *n.* A supporter of the ministry, or of the party in power.

minister plenipotentiary; *pl.* MINISTERS PLENIPOTENTIARY. A principal diplomatic agent with full authority. Cf. AMBASSADOR.

min'is·trant (mĭn'ĭs·trănt), *adj.* [L. *ministrans, -antis*, pres. part.] Ministering. — *n.* One who ministers.

min'is·tra'tion (-trā'shŭn), *n.* Act of ministering, esp. in religion; ministry. — **min'is·tra'tive** (mĭn'ĭs·trā'tĭv; -trȧ·tĭv), *adj.*

min'is·try (mĭn'ĭs·trĭ), *n.; pl.* -TRIES (-trĭz). [L. *ministerium*, fr. *minister.*] **1.** Act of ministering; ministration. **2.** The office, duties, or functions of a minister; ecclesiastical, executive, or ambassadorial function or profession. **3.** Ministers of religion, collectively; the clergy. **4.** Agency; instrumentality. **5.** An incumbent's period of ministration. **6. a** The body of ministers of a state; sometimes, loosely, the body consisting of those ministers who, as in Great Britain, acting together, with the prime minister, form the cabinet. **b** In many countries of Europe, a government department presided over by a minister; also, the building in which such a department transacts its business.

min'i·um (mĭn'ĭ·ŭm), *n.* [L., an Iberian word, the Romans getting all their cinnabar from Spain.] **1.** The color vermilion. **2.** Red oxide of lead, Pb_3O_4.

min'i·ver (mĭn'ĭ·vẽr), *n.* [OF. *menu vair* a grayish fur, fr. *menu* small + *vair* a kind of fur.] A fur esteemed in the Middle Ages as a part of costume; — officially, in England, recently used to mean a plain white fur.

mink (mĭngk), *n.;* see PLURAL, *Note*, 3. **1.** A slender-bodied semiaquatic weasellike mammal (genus *Mustela*, esp. *M. vison* of North America), larger than most weasels, with partly webbed feet and a somewhat bushy tail. Its thick soft fur is usually dark brown in color with a few white spots on the chin and breast. A related species (*M. siberica*) occurs in eastern Asia. **2.** The fur of the mink.

min'ne·sing'er (mĭn'ĕ·sĭng'ẽr), *n.* [G., fr. *minne* love + *singen* to sing.] One of a class of German lyric poets and musicians who flourished from about 1150 to about 1350.

min'nie (mĭn'ĭ), *n.* *Scot.* Mother; — a child's word.

min'nie (mĭn'ĭ), *n.* *Slang.* Short for MINENWERFER.

min'now (mĭn'ō), *n.;* see PLURAL, *Note*, 3. [AS. *myne.*] **a** A small European fish (*Phoxinus phoxinus*) of the carp family. **b** In America, any small fish of the carp family (Cyprinidae), or any of the killifishes (family Cyprinodontidae); also, loosely, any of various other small fishes.

Mi·no'an (mĭ·nō'ăn), *adj.* [L. *Minous*, fr. *Minos.*] *Archaeol., Arch., etc.* Designating or pertaining to the prehistoric culture of Crete, later than neolithic. It dates from about 3000 to about 1100 B.C.

mi'nor (mī'nẽr), *adj.* [L.] **1.** Inferior in bulk, degree, importance, etc.; less; smaller. **2.** Not having reached the age of majority. **3.** Constituting the minority; as, the *minor* vote. **4.** *Educ. U. S.* **a** Designating a subject in which a student is required to take a certain number of courses or hours, fewer than required for a *major* subject. **b** Designating a course in which the number of class hours is less than for a major course. Cf. MAJOR, *adj.*, 5. **5.** *Music.* **a** Less by a half step than the corresponding major interval. **b** Based on the scale pattern of the minor mode; as, the key A *minor.* **c** Distant by a minor (def. 5 **a**) interval; — of a tone; as, E-flat is the *minor* third of C. — *n.* **1.** A person under full age or majority. **2.** *Educ., U. S.* A minor subject or course. **3.** *Logic.* The *minor term*, that is, the subject of the conclusion; also, the *minor premise*, that is, that premise which contains the minor term, — the second proposition of a regular syllogism. Cf. MAJOR, *n.*, 4. **4.** *Music.* A minor chord, key, or mode. **5.** *U. S. Sports.* A minor league; — usually in *pl.* with *the.*

Mi·nor'ca (mĭ·nôr'kȧ), *n.* [From *Minorca*, Balearic Islands, fr. Sp. *Menorca.*] A domestic fowl of a Mediterranean breed resembling the Leghorns, but larger.

Mi'nor·ite (mī'nẽr·īt), *n.* A Franciscan friar.

mi·nor'i·ty (mĭ·nŏr'ĭ·tĭ; mī-), *n.; pl.* -TIES (-tĭz). **1.** State or period of being a minor, or under age. **2.** The smaller number; esp., in a political body, the group having less than the number of votes necessary to control; — opposed to *majority.* — **mi·nor'i·ty**, *adj.*

minor key. *Music.* A key or tonality in the minor mode; hence, figuratively, a tone or mood of melancholy or pathos.

minor league. *U. S. & Can.* Any league of professional clubs in a sport, as baseball or ice hockey, other than the recognized major league or leagues. — **mi'nor-lea'guer**, *n.*

minor mode. *Music.* The arrangement or grouping of tones as found in the minor scale. It often gives an effect of somberness or weirdness. Cf. MAJOR MODE.

minor scale. *Music.* A scale of eight tones (the eighth being the octave of the first) with a minor third between the first and third tones. In the original form the intervals are whole steps except those between 2–3 and 5–6, which are half steps. Cf. MAJOR SCALE.

minor sentence. *Gram.* See SENTENCE.

minor suit. *Bridge.* Either clubs or diamonds. Cf. MAJOR SUIT.

Mi'nos (mī'nŏs), *n.* [Gr. *Minōs.*] *Gr. Myth.* A king and lawgiver of Crete, son of Zeus and Europa, after death a judge in Hades, or his grandson, the husband of Pasiphaë and father of Ariadne. See MINOTAUR.

Min'o·taur (mĭn'ō·tôr), *n.* [OF. *Minotaur*, fr. L. *Minotaurus*, fr. Gr. *Minōtauros*, fr. *Minōs* Minos + *tauros* a bull.] *Gr. Myth.* A monster, half man and half bull, confined in the labyrinth built by Daedalus for Minos, where it devoured the periodical tribute of seven youths and seven maidens sent by Athens, until slain by Theseus. See ARIADNE, PASIPHAË.

min'ster (mĭn'stẽr), *n.* [AS. *mynster*, fr. LL. *monasterium.*] A church of a monastery. The name is often retained and applied to the church after the monastery has ceased to exist and is also often used for any large church.

min'strel (mĭn'strĕl), *n.* [OF. *ministral, menestrel*, minstrel, fr. LL. *ministerialis* an official, fr. *ministerium* office, service.] **1.** One of a medieval class of musical entertainers, esp. such as sang to the accompaniment of a harp. **2.** *Poetic.* A poet; a musician. **3.** One of a troupe of comedians, typically giving Negro melodies, jokes, etc., and usually blacked in imitation of Negroes; hence: **minstrel show.**

min'strel·sy (-sĭ), *n.* **1.** The art, singing, and playing, of a minstrel. **2. a** A body of minstrels. **b** A body of songs, orig. of minstrels' songs.

mint (mĭnt), *n.* [AS. *minte*, fr. L. *menta, mentha*, fr. Gr. *mintha.*] Any of a genus (*Mentha*) of aromatic herbs, typifying a family (Lamiaceae, the mint family), and used for flavoring, condiments, etc.; by extension, any related plant.

mint, *n.* [AS. *mynet* money, coin, fr. L. *moneta* the mint, coined money, fr. *Moneta*, a surname of Juno, in whose temple money was coined.] **1.** *Obs.* A coin; money. **2.** A place where money is coined. **3.** A great supply of money, such as issues from a mint; a vast sum or amount. **4.** A place where anything is manufactured; as, nature's *mint.* — *adj.* In the original condition, as if fresh from a mint; as, *mint* specimens of postage stamps. — *v. t.* **1.** To make by stamping, as money; to coin. **2.** To fabricate; invent. — **mint'er**, *n.*

mint, *v. t. & i.* *Now Scot.* To intend; hint at.

mint'age (mĭn'tĭj), *n.* **1.** Act or process of minting coin; coinage. **2.** The cost of coining. **3.** The stamp impressed upon a coin in minting.

mint julep. See JULEP, 2.

min'u·end (mĭn'ū·ĕnd), *n.* [L. *minuendus* to be diminished, fr. *minuere* to lessen.] *Math.* The number or quantity from which another (the *subtrahend*) is to be subtracted. See REMAINDER, 5.

min'u·et' (mĭn'ū·ĕt'; mĭn'ū·ĕt), *n.* [F. *menuet*, fr. *menu* small; — from the short steps of the dance.] **1.** A slow graceful dance, consisting of a shift from one foot to the other, a high step, and a balance. **2.** Music for this dance.

mi'nus (mī'nŭs), *prep.* [L., adj., neut. of *minor* less. See MINOR, *adj.*] Diminished by; with the subtraction of; less; as, seven *minus* four. — *adj.* **1.** Indicating subtraction; as, the *minus* sign [−]; also negative (in mode of reckoning); not positive; as, a *minus* quantity or value. Symbol [−]. **2.** *Colloq.* Deprived of; without; as, he was *minus* his hat. **3.** *Bot.* Pertaining to a physiological sexlike differentiation comparable to *female*, in certain plants, as fungi; as, a *minus* strain or mycelium. — *n.* **a** The minus sign; also, a minus quantity. **b** Hence, a lack; defect; deficiency.

mi·nus'cule (mĭ·nŭs'kūl), *n.* [F., fr. L. *minusculus* rather small, fr. *minus* less.] **1.** *Paleog.* Any of several styles of ancient and medieval writing developed from the cursive hand distinguished by simplified and relatively small letters; also, a letter of this style. Cf. MAJUSCULE. **2.** *Print.* A lower-case letter. — *adj.* **1.** In, or of the size or style of, minuscules. **2.** Very small.

minus sign. *Math.* The sign − (opposed to +, or *plus sign*), indicating subtraction or a negative quantity.

min'ute (mĭn'ĭt; *occas. in Brit. use, esp. in sense* 4, *also* mĭn'ūt), *n.* [F. and ML.; F., fr. ML. *minuta*, fr. L. *minutus* small. See MINUTE, *adj.*] **1.** The sixtieth part of an hour of time or of a degree. Abbr. *m.*, or *min.* See MEASURE, *Tables* 6, 7, & 8. **2.** The distance one can traverse in a minute. **3.** A short space of time; moment. **4. a** A memorandum or draft, as of instructions; as, to take *minutes* of a debate. **b** Specif.: *pl.* The official record made of proceedings at a meeting. — *v. t.* To make a minute or a summary of.

mi·nute' (mĭ·nūt'; mī·nūt'), *adj.* [L. *minutus*, past part. of *minuere* to lessen.] **1.** Very small; little. **2.** Of small importance; trifling. **3.** Marked by, or paying, attention to small things or details. — **Syn.** See SMALL; CIRCUMSTANTIAL. — **mi·nute'ly**, *adv.* — **mi·nute'ness**, *n.*

min'ute gun (mĭn'ĭt). A discharge of a cannon repeated at intervals of a minute, usually as a sign of distress or mourning.

min'ute hand. The long hand of a watch or clock, which makes the circuit in an hour, and marks the minutes.

min'ute·ly (mĭn'ĭt·lĭ), *adj.* Happening every minute; continual. — *adv.* Every minute; from minute to minute.

min'ute·man' (-măn'), *n.* *Amer. Hist.* One of a class of armed citizens who pledged themselves to take the field at a minute's notice, during, and just previous to, the War of Independence.

min'ute steak (mĭn'ĭt). A small thin steak that can be quickly cooked.

mi·nu'ti·a (mĭ·nū'shĭ·ȧ; mī-), *n.; pl.* -TIAE (-ē). [L., fr. *minutus* small, minute.] A minute, precise, or minor detail; — used chiefly in *pl.*

minx (mĭngks), *n.; pl.* MINXES (-ĕz; -ĭz). **1.** *Obs.* A wanton woman. **2.** A pert girl; — now used playfully.

Mi'o·cene (mī'ō·sēn), *adj.* [Gr. *meiōn* less + *kainos* new, recent.] *Geol.* Of, pertaining to, or designating the period of the Tertiary division of the Cenozoic era between the Oligocene and the Pliocene periods, or the system of rocks formed during this period. — **mi'o·cene**, *n.*

mi·o'sis (mī·ō'sĭs), **mi·ot'ic** (-ŏt'ĭk). Vars of MEIOSIS, MYOSIS; MEIOTIC, MYOTIC.

miq'ue·let (mĭk'ĕ·lĕt), *n.* [F., fr. Sp. *miquelete.*] *Mil.* **a** An irregular or partisan soldier during the Peninsular War. **b** A soldier of certain Spanish local infantry regiments, much used as escorts.

mir (mẽr), *n.* [Russ.] *Russia.* = VILLAGE COMMUNITY.

‖**mi·ra'bi·le dic'tu** (mĭ·răb'ĭ·lē dĭk'tū). [L.] Wonderful to relate.

mir'a·cle (mĭr'ȧ·k'l; -ĭ·k'l), *n.* [OF., fr. L. *miraculum*, fr. *mirari* to wonder.] **1.** An event or effect in the physical world deviating from the known laws of nature, or transcending our knowledge of these laws; an extraordinary, anomalous, or abnormal event brought about by superhuman agency. **2.** A wonder or wonderful thing; a marvel. **3.** A miracle play. **4.** *Christian Science.* That which is divinely natural, but must be learned humanly; a phenomenon of Science. *Mary Baker Eddy.*

miracle play. One of a medieval type of dramatic representation showing episodes from the life of some wonder-working saint; also, the type itself. In England the term was used for both this type and the *mystery.*

mi·rac′u·lous (mĭ·răk′ū·lŭs), *adj.* [F. *miraculeux.* See MIRACLE.] **1.** Of the nature of a miracle. **2.** Like a miracle; marvelous. **3.** Working, or able to work, miracles. — **mi·rac′u·lous·ly,** *adv.* — **mi·rac′u·lous·ness,** *n.*

mir′a·dor′ (mĭr′ȧ·dōr′; -dôr′), *n.* [Sp., fr. *mirar* to behold, view.] *Arch.* A turret, or often a bay window, oriel window, or the like, designed to command a wide outlook; — used in Spanish architecture.

mi·rage′ (mĭ·räzh′), *n.* [F., fr. *mirer* to look at carefully, aim, *se mirer* to look at oneself in a glass, reflect, be reflected, fr. VL. *mirare* to look at.] **1.** An optical phenomenon produced by a stratum of hot air of varying density across which the observer sees reflections, usually inverted, of some distant object or objects. **2.** Something illusory like a mirage (sense 1). — **Syn.** See DELUSION.

mire (mīr), *n.* [ON. *mýrr* swamp.] **1.** Wet, spongy earth; bog. **2.** Soft or deep mud, slush, or the like. — *v. t.* **a** To cause to stick fast in or as in mire; hence, to entangle or involve. **b** To soil with mud or foul matter. — *v. i.* To sink or stick in mire. — **mir′y** (mīr′ĭ), *adj.*

mirk (mûrk), **mirk′y,** etc. Vars. of MURK, etc.

mir′ror (mĭr′ẽr), *n.* [OF. *mirour, mireor* (F. *miroir*), fr. VL. *mirare* to look at, L. *mirari* to wonder.] **1.** Any glass or polished or smooth substance that forms images by reflection; a looking glass; speculum. **2.** *Archaic.* A crystal or similar device used by diviners, sorcerers, etc. **3.** That which gives a true likeness or image; hence, a pattern. — *v. t.* To reflect, as in a mirror.

mirth (mûrth), *n.* [AS. *myrth, myrgth, mirhth.* See MERRY.] Gladness or gaiety, as shown by, or accompanied with, laughter; merriment; jollity. — **mirth′less,** *adj.* — **mirth′less·ly,** *adv.*

Syn. **Mirth, glee, jollity, hilarity** mean the mood or temper of a person in high spirits. **Mirth** implies lightness of heart, a love of gaiety, and, often, great amusement; **glee,** applicable to an individual or group, suggests exultancy manifested in laughter, cries of joy, or, sometimes, malicious delight; **jollity** suggests exuberance or lack of restraint in mirth or glee; **hilarity** suggests exhilaration of spirits and, sometimes, boisterousness.

mirth′ful (-fo͝ol; -f′l), *adj.* Full of, expressing, or indicating mirth. — **mirth′ful·ly,** *adv.* — **mirth′ful·ness,** *n.*

mir′za (mēr′zä), *n.* [Per. *mīrza,* abbr. fr. *mīrzādah,* fr. Ar. *amīr* commander + Per. *zādah* son of.] The common title of honor in Persia, prefixed to the surname.

mis- (mĭs-). [In words of Teut. origin, fr. AS. *mis-;* in words from French, fr. OF. *mes-* (F. *mé-, més-*), fr. L. *minus* less; but the two prefixes are commonly confounded.] A prefix meaning *amiss, wrong, ill, wrongly,* used: **a** With adverbial force, before verbs, and participial and other adjectives, as in *mis*lead, *mis*construe, *mis*spent. **b** With attributive force before verbal and other nouns, *bad,* as in *mis*giving, *mis*conduct, *mis*deed.

☞ COMBINATIONS are:

misadvise	misgauge	mispunctuation
misbestow	misinfer	misqualify
mischoose	misinstruct	misrecite
mis-citation	misintend	misregulate
mis-cite	mislabel	misrelate
misclassify	mislocate	mis-send
miscounsel	misnumber	mistaught
misdate	mispage	misterm
misderive	misplant	misthrow
misdescribe	mispronounce	mistranscribe
misemploy	mispronunciation	mistranslate
misform	misproportion	mistranslation
misformation	mispunctuate	misword

mis-. = MISS-.

mis′ad·ven′ture (mĭs′ăd·vĕn′tūr), *n.* Mischance; esp., a mishap.

mis′al·li′ance (-ȧ·lī′ăns), *n.* [After F. *mésalliance.*] An improper alliance, esp. in marriage; a mésalliance.

mis′al·ly′ (-ȧ·lī′), *v. t.;* see ALLY. To ally unsuitably.

mis′an·thrope (mĭs′ăn·thrōp; mĭz′-), *n.* [Gr. *misanthrōpos,* fr. *misein* to hate + *anthrōpos* a man.] A hater of mankind.

mis′an·throp′ic (-thrŏp′ĭk), *adj.* Also **mis′an·throp′i·cal** (-ĭ·kăl). Of, pertaining to, like, or characteristic of a misanthrope; hating or disliking mankind. — **Syn.** See CYNICAL. — **mis′an·throp′i·cal·ly,** *adv.*

mis·an′thro·pist (mĭs·ăn′thrō·pĭst; mĭ·zăn′-), *n.* A misanthrope.

mis·an′thro·py (-pĭ), *n.* Hatred of mankind; — opposed to *philanthropy.*

mis′ap·ply′ (mĭs′ă·plī′), *v. t.;* see APPLY. To apply wrongly; as, to *misapply* public money. — **mis′ap·pli·ca′tion** (mĭs′ăp·lĭ·kā′shŭn), *n.*

mis′ap·pre·hend′ (mĭs′ăp·rē·hĕnd′), *v. t.* To apprehend wrongly; to misunderstand.

mis′ap·pre·hen′sion (-hĕn′shŭn), *n.* A misapprehending; misunderstanding.

mis′ap·pro′pri·ate (mĭs′ă·prō′prĭ·āt), *v. t.* To appropriate wrongly; to misapply. — **mis′ap·pro′pri·a′tion** (-ā′shŭn), *n.*

mis′ar·range′ (mĭs′ă·rānj′), *v. t.;* see ARRANGE. To arrange wrongly. — **mis′ar·range′ment,** *n.*

mis′be·come′ (-bē·kŭm′), *v. t.;* see BECOME. Not to befit; to suit ill.

mis′be·com′ing (-kŭm′ĭng), *adj.* Unbecoming.

mis′be·got′ten (mĭs′bē·gŏt′’n), **mis′be·got′** (-gŏt′), *adj.* Unlawfully or irregularly begotten; illegitimate.

mis′be·have′ (-bē·hāv′), *v. t. & i.* To behave improperly. — **mis′be·hav′ior, mis′be·hav′iour** (-hāv′yẽr), *n.*

mis′be·lief′ (-lēf′), *n.* Erroneous or false belief.

mis′be·lieve′ (-lēv′), *v. i.* To believe erroneously, or in a false religion. — **mis′be·liev′er** (-lēv′ẽr), *n.*

mis·brand′ (mĭs·brănd′), *v. t. Com.* To brand falsely.

mis·cal′cu·late (mĭs·kăl′kū·lāt), *v. t. & i.* To calculate erroneously. — **mis′cal·cu·la′tion** (mĭs′kăl·kū·lā′shŭn), *n.*

mis·call′ (mĭs·kôl′), *v. t.* **1.** To call by a wrong name; to misname. **2.** *Obs. exc. Dial.* To abuse; revile.

mis·car′riage (-kăr′ĭj), *n.* **1.** Mismanagement; failure. **2. a** Failure (of something sent) to arrive. **b** Failure to carry properly; as, *miscarriage* of goods. **3.** Premature expulsion of a fetus; abortion.

mis·car′ry (-ĭ), *v. i.;* see CARRY. **1.** To undergo mishap or go wrong; to go astray. **2.** To suffer miscarriage or be delivered prematurely. **3.** To fail of the intended effect or of one's object; as, the project *miscarried.*

mis′ce·ge·na′tion (mĭs′ē·jē·nā′shŭn), *n.* [L. *miscere* to mix + *genus* race.] **1.** An interbreeding of races. **2.** *Law.* Intermarriage or interbreeding of whites and other races; — used chiefly, in the U. S., of marriage with Negroes.

mis′cel·la′ne·a (mĭs′ĕ·lā′nē·ȧ), *n. pl.* [L.] A collection of miscellaneous matters; esp., a literary miscellany.

mis′cel·la′ne·ous (mĭs′ĕ·lā′nē·ŭs), *adj.* [L. *miscellaneus,* fr. *miscellus* mixed, fr. *miscere* to mix.] **1.** Consisting of diverse things or members; heterogeneous. **2.** Having various qualities; dealing with, or interested in, diverse subjects. — **mis′cel·la′ne·ous·ly,** *adv.* — **mis′cel·la′ne·ous·ness,** *n.*

mis′cel·la′nist (mĭs′ĕ·lā′nĭst; -lȧ·nĭst; mĭ·sĕl′ȧ-), *n.* A writer of miscellanies.

mis′cel·la′ny (mĭs′ĕ·lā′nĭ *or, esp. Brit.,* -lȧ·nĭ; *Brit. also* mĭ·sĕl′ȧ·nĭ; 3), *n.; pl.* -NIES (-nĭz). [F. *miscellanée,* fr. L. *miscellanea,* neut. pl. of *miscellaneus.*] **1.** A mixture of various things; esp., a collection of writings on various subjects. **2.** *pl.* Miscellaneous treatises collected into one book.

mis·chance′ (mĭs·châns′; 9), *n.* [OF. *mescheance.*] Ill luck; a mishap; misadventure. — **Syn.** See MISFORTUNE.

mis′chief (mĭs′chĭf), *n.* [ME. *meschef* bad result, fr. OF. *meschief,* fr. *meschever* to be unfortunate, fr. *mes-* (fr. L. *minus* less) + *chief* end, head.] **1.** Harm; damage; esp., trouble or vexation caused by human agency. **2.** Harmful quality or character; mischievousness. **3.** A cause or source of harm, trouble, or vexation; esp., a person who causes mischief or annoyance. **4.** Action that annoys or vexes; esp., such as may cause trivial trouble to others.

mis′chief-mak′er (mĭs′chĭf·māk′ẽr), *n.* A maker of mischief; an inciter of quarrels. — **mis′chief-mak′ing,** *adj. & n.*

mis′chie·vous (mĭs′chĭ·vŭs), *adj.* Causing mischief; full of mischief; specif.: **a** Injurious; harmful. **b** Causing, or inclined to cause, petty injury, trouble, or annoyance to others, as from carelessness or in sport. — **mis′chie·vous·ly,** *adv.* — **mis′chie·vous·ness,** *n.*

mis′ci·ble (mĭs′ĭ·b’l), *adj.* [L. *miscere* to mix.] Capable of being mixed. — **mis′ci·bil′i·ty** (-bĭl′ĭ·tĭ), *n.*

mis·col′or, mis·col′our (mĭs·kŭl′ẽr), *v. t.* To give a wrong color to; figuratively, to misrepresent, as facts.

mis′con·ceive′ (mĭs′kŏn·sēv′), *v. t. & i.* To conceive wrongly; interpret incorrectly. — **mis′con·ceiv′er** (-sēv′ẽr), *n.*

mis′con·cep′tion (-sĕp′shŭn), *n.* Act or result of misconceiving; an inaccurate or erroneous conception.

mis′con·duct′ (mĭs′kŏn·dŭkt′), *v. t.* To conduct amiss; to mismanage.

mis·con′duct (mĭs·kŏn′dŭkt), *n.* Wrong or improper conduct; unlawful behavior; specif., malfeasance or adultery.

mis′con·struc′tion (mĭs′kŏn·strŭk′shŭn), *n.* A misconstruing; erroneous interpretation.

mis′con·strue′ (mĭs′kŏn·stro͞o′; mĭs·kŏn′stro͞o), *v. t.;* MIS′CON·STRUED′ (-stro͞od′; -stro͞od); MIS′CON·STRU′ING. To construe wrongly; interpret erroneously; misinterpret.

mis·count′ (mĭs·kount′), *v. t. & i.* To count erroneously; miscalculate. — *n.* A wrong computation.

mis′cre·ance (mĭs′krē·ăns), *n. Archaic.* Adherence to false faith; unbelief.

mis′cre·an·cy (-ăn·sĭ), *n.* **1.** *Archaic.* Miscreance. **2.** Villainy; turpitude.

mis′cre·ant (mĭs′krē·ănt), *adj.* [OF. *mescreant,* pres. part. of *mescroire* to disbelieve, fr. *mes-* (fr. L. *minus* less) + *croire* to believe, fr. L. *credere.*] **1.** *Archaic.* Infidel; heretical; unbelieving. **2.** Destitute of conscience; unscrupulous; villainous. — *n.* **1.** *Archaic.* An infidel or heretic. **2.** A base villain; a vile wretch; a rascal.

mis′cre·ate′ (mĭs′krē·āt′), *v. t. & i.* To create misshapen or amiss. — *adj.* Miscreated. — **mis′cre·a′tion** (-ā′shŭn), *n.*

mis·cue′ (mĭs·kū′), *n.* **a** *Billiards & Pool.* A stroke in which the cue slips. **b** *Slang.* A mistake; a slip. — *v. i.;* MIS·CUED′ (-kūd′); MIS·CU′ING (-kū′ĭng). **a** To make a miscue. **b** *Theater.* To miss one's cue; to answer a wrong cue.

mis·deal′ (-dēl′), *v. t. & i.* To deal or distribute wrongly. — *n.* A misdealing. — **mis·deal′er** (-ẽr), *n.*

mis·deed′ (-dēd′), *n.* A gravely wrongful deed.

mis·deem′ (-dēm′), *v. t. & i.* To deem wrongly.

mis′de·mean′ (mĭs′dē·mēn′), *v. t. & i.* To misbehave.

mis′de·mean′ant (-ănt), *n.* One convicted of a misdemeanor; also, one guilty of misconduct.

mis′de·mean′or, mis′de·mean′our (-ẽr), *n.* **1.** *Now Rare.* Misbehavior. **2.** *Law.* A crime less than a felony. The distinction between *felonies* and *misdemeanors* is now arbitrary.

mis′di·rect′ (mĭs′dĭ·rĕkt′; mĭs′dī-), *v. t.* To give a wrong direction to.

mis′di·rec′tion (-rĕk′shŭn), *n.* **1.** A misdirecting. **2.** *Law.* An error of a judge in charging the jury on a matter of law.

mis·do′ (mĭs·do͞o′), *v. t. & i.;* see DO. [AS. *misdōn.*] To do wrongly or improperly; to do amiss. — **mis·do′er** (-do͞o′ẽr), *n.* — **mis·do′ing** (-ĭng), *n.*

mis·doubt′ (-dout′), *v. t. & i.* **1.** To have doubts or suspicion (of). **2.** To fear. — *n.* Suspicion; mistrust.

mise (mēz; mīz), *n.* [F., a putting, setting, fr. *mettre* to put, lay, fr. L. *mittere* to send.] **1.** An agreement; as, the *mise* of Amiens and the *mise* of Lewes, two agreements in 1264 between Henry III of England and rebellious barons. **2.** *Law.* The (general) issue in a proceeding upon a writ of right.

mis·ease′ (mĭs·ēz′), *n.* Discomfort; distress; uneasiness.

‖**mise en scène** (mē′-zäN sân′). [F.] **a** Scenery, properties, etc., for presenting a play; also, the arrangement of scenery and players in a scene. **b** Hence, setting; milieu.

mi′ser (mī′zẽr), *n.* [L. *miser* wretched.] **1.** *Obs.* A wretched person. **2.** A covetous, grasping person; esp., one who lives miserably to increase his hoard.

mis′er·a·ble (mĭz′ẽr·ȧ·b’l), *adj.* [F. *misérable,* fr. L. *miserabilis,* fr. *miserari* to lament, pity, fr. *miser* wretched.] **1.** Being in a state of misery; wretched; — often hyperbolical. **2.** Causing misery, unhappiness, or great discomfort; as, a *miserable* cold. **3.** Pitiable; lamentable; now esp., mean; paltry; sorry; as, a *miserable* dinner. — *n.* One who is miserable, or in misery. — **Syn.** Wretched. — **Ant.** Comfortable. — **mis′er·a·ble·ness,** *n.* — **mis′er·a·bly,** *adv.*

Mis′e·re′re (mĭz′ē·rē′rē; -rā′-), *n.* [L., have mercy, fr. *misereri* to have mercy, fr. *miser* wretched.] **1.** The 50th Psalm in the Vulgate (51st in *A.V.*); — from its first word. **2.** A musical setting of this

Psalm. **3.** [*not cap.*] A bracket on the under side of the seat of a church stall, usable as a rest by one standing when the seat is turned up.

mis′er·i·cord′, mis′er·i·corde′ (mĭz′ẽr·ĭ·kôrd′; mĭ·zẽr′ĭ·kôrd), *n.* [F. *miséricorde*, fr. L. *misericordia* mercy, compassion, fr. *misereri* to feel pity + *cor, cordis*, heart.] **1.** A thin-bladed medieval dagger for giving the death, or "mercy," stroke. **2.** *Eccl.* **a** A dispensation, as from fasting, granted to a religious. **b** A room which monks, dispensed from fasting, used as a refectory. **3.** *Eccl. Arch.* = MISERERE, 3.

mi′ser·ly (mī′zẽr·lĭ), *adj.* Pertaining to, like, or characteristic of a miser; sordidly avaricious. — **Syn.** See STINGY. — **mi′ser·li·ness,** *n.*

mis′er·y (mĭz′ẽr·ĭ), *n.; pl.* -IES (-ĭz). [OF. *miserie, misere*, fr. L. *miseria*, fr. *miser* wretched.] **1.** A state of great distress; wretchedness; distress due esp. to privation, poverty, or affliction. **2.** A wretched circumstance; a cause of misery. — **Syn.** See DISTRESS.

mis′es·teem′ (mĭs′ĕs·tēm′), *v. t.* To esteem amiss or too low.

mis·es′ti·mate (mĭs·ĕs′tĭ·māt), *v. t.* To estimate erroneously. — (-māt), *n.* A wrong estimate. — **mis·es′ti·ma′tion** (-mā′shŭn), *n.*

mis·faith′ (mĭs·fāth′), *n.* Want of faith; disbelief; distrust.

mis·fea′sance (-fē′zăns), *n.* [OF. *mesfaisance*, fr. *mesfaire* to do wrong, fr. *mes-* (fr. L. *minus* less) + *faire* to do, fr. L. *facere*.] *Law.* A trespass; now, specif., the doing wrongfully and injuriously of an act which one might do in a lawful manner; — disting. from *nonfeasance* and *malfeasance*. — **mis·fea′sor** (-zẽr), *n.*

mis·fea′ture (-fē′tūr), *n.* An ill, distorted, or bad feature. — *v. t.* To distort the features of.

mis·fire′ (-fīr′), *v. i.* **1.** *Mach.* To have its explosive charge fail to ignite at the proper time; — of an internal-combustion engine. **2.** To fail to be fired; — of a gun, mine, etc. — *n.* Act of misfiring; also, an instance of misfiring.

mis·fit′ (mĭs·fĭt′), *v. t. & i.;* see FIT. To fit badly. — *n.* **1.** Act or state of fitting badly. **2.** Something that fits badly, as a coat. **3.** A person poorly adjusted to his environment.

mis·for′tune (-fôr′tūn), *n.* Bad fortune or luck; calamity; an evil accident; disaster; mischance; mishap.

Syn. **Misfortune, mischance, adversity** mean bad luck or adverse fortune. **Misfortune** and **mischance** both refer to an incident or conjunction of events that involves a change of fortune, but *misfortune* implies the mental or physical distress caused by it, and *mischance* the resulting inconvenience, disruption of plans, etc.; **adversity** implies grave and continued misfortune.

mis·give′ (mĭs·gĭv′), *v. t.;* see GIVE. To give or suggest doubt and apprehension to; make apprehensive or suspicious; — usually of the mind or heart; as, my mind *misgives* me. — *v. i.* To be fearful or apprehensive.

mis·giv′ing (-gĭv′ĭng), *n.* A premonition of evil; a sense of distrust or apprehension; foreboding; presentiment.

mis·gov′ern (-gŭv′ẽrn), *v. t.* To govern ill; rule badly. — **mis·gov′ern·ment,** *n.*

mis·guide′ (-gīd′), *v. t.* To guide wrongly; lead astray. — **mis·guid′ance** (-gīd′ăns), *n.* — **mis·guid′er** (-ẽr), *n.*

mis·han′dle (-hăn′d'l), *v. t.;* MIS·HAN′DLED (-d'ld); MIS·HAN′DLING (-dlĭng). To handle roughly; maltreat.

mi·shan′ter (mĭ·shăn′tẽr), *n.* *Chiefly Scot.* Misfortune.

mis·hap′ (mĭs·hăp′; mĭs′hăp), *n.* **1.** Ill luck; misfortune. **2.** An injurious or unfortunate accident.

mish′mash′ (mĭsh′măsh′), *n. & v. t.* Jumble; medley.

Mish′nah, Mish′na (mĭsh′nȧ), *n.; pl.* MISHNAYOTH (mĭsh′nä·yōth′). [NHeb. *mishnāh*, i. e., instruction, oral law, fr. Heb. *shānāh* to repeat, in post-Biblical Heb. to teach, learn.] **a** The traditional doctrine of the Jews as developed chiefly in the decisions of the rabbis before the 3d century A.D. **b** A single tenet; a view of a rabbi. **c** Any collection of such tenets. **d** The collection of Halakoth, which is the basis of the Talmud. — **Mish·na′ic** (mĭsh·nā′ĭk), **Mish′nic** (mĭsh′nĭk), **Mish′ni·cal** (-nĭ·kăl), *adj.*

mis′in·form′ (mĭs′ĭn·fôrm′), *v. t. & i.* To give untrue or misleading information (to). — **mis′in·form′ant** (-fôr′mănt), *n.* — **mis′in·for·ma′tion** (mĭs′ĭn·fŏr·mā′shŭn), *n.* — **mis′in·form′er,** *n.*

mis′in·ter′pret (-ĭn·tûr′prĕt; -prĭt), *v. t. & i.* To interpret erroneously; understand or explain in a wrong sense. — **mis′in·ter′pre·ta′tion** (-prē·tā′shŭn), *n.*

mis·join′der (mĭs·join′dẽr), *n.* *Law.* An incorrect union of parties or of causes of action in procedure.

mis·judge′ (-jŭj′), *v. t. & i.;* see JUDGE. To judge erroneously or unjustly; to misconstrue. — **mis·judg′ment, mis·judge′ment** (-jŭj′mĕnt), *n.*

mis·know′ (-nō′), *v. t.;* see KNOW. **1.** To fail to recognize. **2.** To misunderstand. — **mis·knowl′edge** (-nŏl′ĕj; -ĭj), *n.*

mis·lay′ (-lā′), *v. t.;* see LAY. To lay in a place not recollected; lose. — **mis·lay′er** (-lā′ẽr), *n.*

mis·lead′ (-lēd′), *v. t.;* see LEAD. To lead into a wrong way; lead astray; deceive. — **Syn.** See DECEIVE.

mis·lead′ing, *adj.* Deceptive; delusive. — **mis·lead′ing·ly,** *adv.*

mis·leared′ (mĭs·lērd′), *adj.* *Scot.* Mischievous; ill-bred.

mis·like′ (-līk′), *v. t.* **1.** To displease. **2.** To dislike. — *n.* Dislike; aversion; distaste. — **mis·lik′er** (-līk′ẽr), *n.*

mis·made′ (-mād′), *adj.* Badly or improperly made.

mis·make′ (-māk′), *v. t.;* see MAKE. To form amiss; spoil in making.

mis·man′age (-măn′ĭj), *v. t. & i.* To manage ill or improperly. — **mis·man′age·ment,** *n.*

mis·mar′riage (-măr′ĭj), *n.* An unsuitable marriage.

mis·match′ (-măch′), *v. t.* To match unsuitably or ill, as in marriage. — **mis·match′,** *n.*

mis·mate′ (-māt′), *v. t. & i.* To mate unsuitably.

mis·move′ (-mōōv′), *n.* A wrong move; also, *U. S.*, a mistaken step.

mis·name′ (-nām′), *v. t.* To call by the wrong name.

mis·no′mer (-nō′mẽr), *n.* [OF. *mesnommer* to misname, infin. used as n., fr. *mes-* amiss, wrong (fr. L. *minus* less) + *nommer* to name, fr. L. *nominare*, fr. *nomen* name.] **1.** The misnaming of a person in a legal instrument. **2.** A wrong name; an incorrect designation.

mis′o- (mĭs′ō-; mī′sō-), **mis-.** [Gr. *misein* to hate, *misos* hatred.] A combining form denoting *hating, hatred;* — opp. to *philo-*, as in **mis′o·the′ism, mis′o·tyr′an·ny.**

mi·sog′a·my (mĭ·sŏg′ȧ·mĭ; mī-), *n.* [*miso-* + *-gamy*.] Hatred of marriage. — **mi·sog′a·mist** (-mĭst), *n. & adj.*

mis′o·gyn′ic (mĭs′ō·jĭn′ĭk; mī′sō-), *adj.* Also **mi·sog′y·nous** (mĭ·sŏj′ĭ·nŭs; mī-). Woman-hating. — **Syn.** See CYNICAL.

mi·sog′y·ny (mĭ·sŏj′ĭ·nĭ; mī-), *n.* [Gr. *misogynia*.] Hatred of women; — opposed to *philogyny*. — **mi·sog′y·nist** (-nĭst), *n.*

mi·sol′o·gy (mĭ·sŏl′ō·jĭ; mī-), *n.* [Gr. *misologia*, fr. *misein* to hate + *logos* discourse.] Hatred of argument or discussion or of enlightenment. — **mi·sol′o·gist** (-jĭst), *n.*

mis′o·ne′ism (mĭs′ō·nē′ĭz'm; mī′sō-), *n.* [*miso-* + Gr. *neos* new + *-ism*.] A hatred or intolerance of anything new or changed. — **mis′o·ne′ist** (-ĭst), *n.*

mis′pick′el (mĭs′pĭk′ĕl), *n.* [G.] *Mineral.* Arsenopyrite.

mis·place′ (mĭs·plās′), *v. t.* To put in a wrong place; to place upon an unworthy object; as, *misplaced* confidence. — **mis·place′ment,** *n.*

mis·play′ (-plā′), *n.* A wrong play; a mismove. — *v. t. & i.* To play wrongly.

mis·plead′ing (-plēd′ĭng), *n.* *Chiefly Law.* An error in pleading; a wrong pleading. — **mis·plead′,** *v. t. & i.*

mis·print′ (mĭs·prĭnt′), *v. t.* To print wrong or incorrectly. — (mĭs·prĭnt′; 2), *n.* A mistake in printing.

mis·pri′sion (mĭs·prĭzh′ŭn), *n.* [OF. *mesprison, mesprision*, mistake, fr. *mesprendre* to do wrong, prop., to mistake, fr. *mes-* amiss (fr. L. *minus*) + *prendre* to take.] **1.** Misconduct, esp. in office or in neglect of duty. **2.** *Archaic.* Misunderstanding; mistake.

mis·pri′sion, *n.* *Archaic.* Contempt; scorn.

mis·prize′ (-prīz′), *v. t.* Also **mis·prise′.** [OF. *mesprisier* (for orig. *mespreisier*) to despise, fr. *mes-* amiss, wrong (fr. L. *minus* less) + LL. *pretiare* to value, fr. L. *pretium* price.] To scorn; despise; slight or undervalue.

mis·proud′ (-proud′), *adj.* *Archaic.* Wickedly proud.

mis·quote′ (mĭs·kwōt′), *v. t. & i.* To quote erroneously. — **mis′quo·ta′tion** (mĭs′kwō·tā′shŭn), *n.*

mis·read′ (-rēd′), *v. t.;* see READ. To read amiss; to misinterpret in reading.

mis·reck′on (-rĕk′ŭn), *v. t. & i.* To miscalculate; miscount.

mis′re·mem′ber (mĭs′rē·mĕm′bẽr), *v. t. & i.* To mistake in remembering; not to remember correctly.

mis′re·port′ (-rē·pōrt′; 70), *n.* Erroneous report. — *v. t. & i.* To report erroneously. — **mis′re·port′er** (-pōr′tẽr), *n.*

mis′rep·re·sent′ (-rĕp·rē·zĕnt′), *v. t. & i.* To represent incorrectly or improperly; as: **a** To give a false, improper, or imperfect representation (of). **b** To fail to represent adequately as an agent or representative. — **mis′rep·re·sen·ta′tion** (-zĕn·tā′shŭn), *n.*

mis·rule′ (mĭs·rōōl′), *v. t.* To rule badly; misgovern. — *n.* Bad rule; misgovernment; hence, disorder; confusion.

miss (mĭs), *n.; pl.* MISSES (mĭs′ĕz; -ĭz). [Contr. fr. MISTRESS.] **1.** [*cap.*] A title of courtesy prefixed to the name of an unmarried girl or woman. **2.** A young unmarried woman or a girl; — now sportive or in trade use.

miss, *v. t.* [AS. *missan*.] **1.** To fail of hitting, meeting, finding, attaining, getting, receiving, seeing, hearing, perceiving, etc. **2.** To escape; avoid; — now *Dial.* or with adverbs; as, he barely or just *missed* being killed. **3.** To omit; fail or neglect to have, do, keep, attend, etc.; as, to *miss* one's classes. **4.** To discover or feel the absence or loss of; want. — *v. i.* **1.** To fail to hit; fly wide. **2.** To fail; not to succeed. **3.** *Archaic.* To fail to obtain, receive, do, find, see, profit, etc.; — with *of*.

miss fire. To fail to discharge; — of firearms; hence, to fail in discharging a function.

— *n.* **1.** *Now Chiefly Dial.* Loss; lack. **2.** Failure to hit. **3.** Failure to reach, find, obtain, achieve, attend, etc.

mis′sal (mĭs′ăl; -'l), *n.* [ML. *missale*, liber *missalis*, fr. *missa* Mass.] **a** The book containing that which is said or sung at Mass for each and every day of the year. **b** Loosely, a book of devotions.

mis·say′ (mĭs·sā′), *v. t. & i.;* see SAY. *Archaic.* **a** To speak evil (of); slander. **b** To say amiss, or wrongly. — **mis·say′er** (-sā′ẽr), *n.*

mis·seem′ (mĭs·sēm′), *v. t.* *Now Rare.* To misbecome.

mis′sel (mĭs′ĕl; -'l), *n.* Also **missel thrush.** See THRUSH.

mis·shape′ (mĭs·shāp′), *v. t.* To shape ill; distort; deform. — **mis·shap′en** (-shāp′ĕn), *adj.*

mis′sile (mĭs′ĭl; -'l; 56), *adj.* [L. *missilis*, fr. *mittere, missum*, to cause to go, send, throw.] Capable of being thrown, hurled, or projected, so as to strike a distant object. — *n.* A missile weapon or object, as a spear, arrow, or bullet; also, a self-propelling pilotless weapon, as a rocket or a robot bomb.

miss′ing (mĭs′ĭng), *adj.* Absent; lost; not present when called or looked for.

missing link. **a** A member needed to complete a series. **b** A hypothetical intermediate form between man and his presumed simian progenitors. Cf. PITHECANTHROPUS.

mis′sion (mĭsh′ŭn), *n.* [L. *missio*, fr. *mittere, missum*, to send.] **1.** A sending forth; now, *Eccl.*, a sending forth of men with authority to preach, and administer the sacraments. **2.** Persons sent somewhere to perform a stipulated service, esp. sent by one country to a foreign country to carry on negotiations, establish relations, etc.; a body of envoys; a special, or *U. S.*, a permanent, embassy. **3.** That with which a messenger or agent is charged; errand; commission. **4.** A body of missionaries; also, esp. *pl.*, organized missionary work. **5.** A station of missionaries; a missionary field or post. **6.** A course of sermons and services designed to quicken the faith and zeal of Christians, or to convert unbelievers. **7.** That which one is destined or fitted to do; calling. **8.** An organization for doing religious and charitable work among the needy, outcast, etc. **9.** A village or outlying district ministered to by the pastor or priests of a neighboring parish church. **10.** *Mil. & Naval.* A definite task or errand, usually calling for performance in a combat area or enemy territory, assigned to an individual or unit, as a flight operation of a single airplane or a group of airplanes. — *v. t.* **1.** To commission. **2.** To carry on a mission among or in. — *adj.* Of or pertaining to missions, a mission, or, specif., the early Spanish missions in and near California; as, **mission furniture,** a type of plain, dark, heavy furniture. — **mis′sion·al** (-ăl; -'l), *adj.* — **mis′sion·er** (-ẽr), *n.*

mis′sion·ar′y (-ĕr′ĭ *or, esp. Brit.*, -ẽr·ĭ, -'n·rĭ), *adj.* Of or pertaining to missions; engaged in, or devoted to, missions, esp. church missions; as, a *missionary* society; *missionary* zeal. — *n.; pl.* -IES (-ĭz). One sent on a mission; now, esp., one sent to propagate religion.

mis′sis (mĭs′ĭs; -ĭz), *n.* *Illiterate.* Mistress; wife.

Mis′sis·sip′pi·an (mĭs′ĭ·sĭp′ĭ·ăn), *adj.* **1.** Of or pertaining to Mississippi or the Mississippi River. **2.** *Geol.* See CARBONIFEROUS, 2. — **Mis′sis·sip′pi·an,** *n.*

mis′sive (mĭs′ĭv), *n.* [F. See MISSION, *n.*] A letter. — *adj.* Specially sent or prepared to be sent.

mis·spell′ (mĭs·spĕl′), *v. t. & i.;* see SPELL. To spell incorrectly.

mis·spend′ (mĭs·spĕnd′), *v. t.;* see SPEND. To spend amiss; to squander.

mis·state′ (-stāt′), *v. t.* To state wrongly. — **mis·state′ment,** *n.*

mis·step′ (-stĕp′), *n.* A false step; slip, as in conduct.

mis′sus (mĭs′ŭs; -ŭz). Var. of MISSIS.

mist (mĭst), *n.* [AS.] **1.** Water in the form of particles suspended in the atmosphere at or near the surface of the earth; small water droplets, floating or falling and approaching the form of rain. Cf. FOG. **2.** Anything which obscures, blurs, or intercepts vision, physical or mental. **3.** Dimness of vision; a film before the eyes. **4.** A cloud of smoke, dust, or the like; a haze. **5.** A suspension of any finely divided liquid in any gas. — **Syn.** See HAZE. — *v. i. & t.* To be, become, or cause to become, misty; dim or blur with or as with mist.

mis·tak′a·ble (mĭs·tāk′ȧ·b'l), *adj.* Liable to be mistaken or misunderstood; capable of being misconceived.

mis·take′ (-tāk′), *v. t.;* see TAKE. [ON. *mistaka.* See MIS-; TAKE.] **1.** To misapprehend, misunderstand, or misconceive. **2.** To substitute erroneously in thought or perception; as, to *mistake* James for John. **3.** To err in recognizing, estimating, etc. — *v. i.* To make a mistake. — *n.* **1.** An apprehending wrongly; a misunderstanding. **2.** An unintentional error. — **Syn.** See ERROR.

mis·tak′en (-tāk′ĕn), *adj.* **1.** In error; judging wrongly; as, he is *mistaken.* **2.** Erroneous; as, a *mistaken* notion. — **mis·tak′en·ly,** *adv.*

mis·teach′ (mĭs·tēch′), *v. t.;* see TEACH. To teach wrongly; to instruct imperfectly. — **mis·teach′er** (-ēr), *n.*

Mis′ter (mĭs′tēr), *n.* [See MASTER.] A title of courtesy prefixed to the name of a man and to a designation of occupation or office; — usually in abbreviated form *Mr.* (*pl.* MESSRS.); as, *Mr.* Smith; *Mr.* President.

mist′flow′er (mĭst′flou′ēr), *n.* A cultivated herb (***Eupatorium coelestinum***) of the aster family, with violet heads.

mis·think′ (mĭs·thĭngk′), *v. i. & t.;* see THINK. To think wrongly or unfavorably; think erroneously or ill (of).

mis·time′ (-tīm′), *v. t.* To time wrongly.

mis′tle·toe (mĭs′'l·tō; mĭz′-), *n.* [AS. *misteltān,* fr. *mistel* mistletoe + *tān* twig.] **1.** A European semiparasitic green shrub (*Viscum album*), with thick leaves, small yellowish flowers, and waxy-white glutinous berries. It is typical of a family (Loranthaceae, the mistletoe family). **2.** A related American plant (*Phoradendron flavescens*), which grows on certain deciduous trees, esp. the tupelo and the red maple. The mistletoe is the State emblem of Oklahoma.

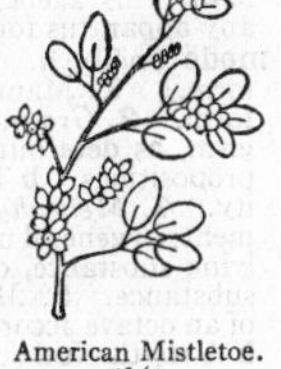

American Mistletoe. (⅙)

mis·took′ (mĭs·to͝ok′), *past & obs. past part.* of MISTAKE.

mis′tral (mĭs′trăl; mĭs·träl′), *n.* [F., fr. Pr., fr. L. *magistralis,* adj.] A violent, cold, and dry northerly wind of the Mediterranean provinces of France, etc.

mis·treat′ (mĭs·trēt′), *v. t.* To treat ill; abuse. — **mis·treat′ment,** *n.*

mis′tress (mĭs′trĕs; -trĭs), *n.* [OF. *maistresse,* fem. of *maistre.* See MASTER.] **1.** A woman having authority or ownership; the female head of a family, a school, etc. **2. a** A woman paramour. **b** A sweetheart; lady love. **3.** *Archaic & Dial.* for MADAM. **4.** A woman teacher. **5.** A woman having the mastery of something. **6.** [*cap.*] A title of courtesy prefixed to the name of a woman, married or unmarried; — now superseded, exc. *Dial.,* by the contracted forms, *Mrs.* (pronounced mĭs′ĭz *or* -ĭs), for a married, and *Miss,* for an unmarried, woman.

mis·tri′al (mĭs·trī′ăl), *n.* *Law.* A trial legally of no effect by reason of some error in the proceedings.

mis·trust′ (-trŭst′), *n.* Lack of confidence or trust. — **Syn.** See UNCERTAINTY. — *v. t. & i.* **a** To regard with suspicion; have no confidence (in). **b** To doubt the integrity, truth, validity, or the like (of). **c** *Now Rare.* To forebode; surmise. — **mis·trust′er,** *n.* — **mis·trust′ing·ly,** *adv.*

mis·trust′ful (-fo͝ol; -f'l), *adj.* Full of mistrust or forebodings; suspicious. — **mis·trust′ful·ly,** *adv.* — **mis·trust′ful·ness,** *n.*

mis·tryst′ (mĭs·trĭst′), *v. t.* *Scot.* **a** To fail to keep a tryst with. **b** To perplex; — in the passive.

mist′y (mĭs′tĭ), *adj.;* MIST′I·ER (-tĭ·ēr); MIST′I·EST. [AS. *mistig.*] **1.** Accompanied or characterized by mist; blurred by, or as by, mist. **2.** Vague; indistinct; shadowy; hazy. — **mist′i·ly,** *adv.* — **mist′i·ness,** *n.*

mis′un·der·stand′ (mĭs′ŭn·dēr·stănd′), *v. t. & i.* To fail to understand; misconceive; miscomprehend.

mis′un·der·stand′ing, *n.* **1.** Mistake of meaning; misinterpretation. **2.** Disagreement; quarrel.

mis′un·der·stood′ (mĭs′ŭn·dēr·sto͝od′), *adj.* **a** Wrongly or inadequately understood. **b** Not sympathetically appreciated.

mis·us′age (mĭs·ūs′ĭj; -ūz′ĭj), *n.* **1.** Ill usage; abuse. **2.** Wrong or improper use, as of words.

mis·use′ (-ūs′), *n.* **1.** Wrong use; misapplication; misappropriation. **2.** *Obs.* **a** Improper conduct. **b** Maltreatment.

mis·use′ (-ūz′), *v. t.* To subject to misuse; misapply; maltreat. — **mis·us′er** (-ūz′ēr), *n.*

mis·val′ue (mĭs·văl′ū), *v. t.* To value wrongly; misesteem.

mis·ven′ture (mĭs·vĕn′tūr), *n.* A misadventure.

mis·wor′ship (-wûr′shĭp; -shĭp), *n.* Wrong or false worship.

mis·write′ (-rīt′), *v. t.;* MIS·WROTE′ (-rōt′); MIS·WRIT′TEN (-rĭt′'n); MIS·WRIT′ING (-rīt′ĭng). To write incorrectly.

mite (mīt), *n.* [AS. *mīte* mite (in sense 1).] **1.** Any of numerous small, often very minute, arachnids (order Acarina), often infesting animals, plants, stored foods, etc. **2.** [MD. *mite* (D. *mijt*), perh. through OF. Same word as MITE, 1.] A small coin or sum of money; — translating the New Testament *lepton;* specif., half a farthing (see *Mark* xii. 42). **3.** *Now Colloq.* A minute object or creature; a particle; bit; jot.

mi′ter, mi′tre (mī′tēr), *n.* [OF. *mitre,* fr. L. *mitra* headband, turban, fr. Gr. *mitra.*] **1.** *Hist.* A headband or fillet worn by women. **2.** A liturgical headdress worn by bishops and abbots; hence, a bishop's office or dignity; bishopric. See VESTMENT, *Illust.* **3.** [Perh. a different word.] *Carpentry.* **a** The surface forming the beveled end or edge of a piece where a **miter joint,** or joint formed by pieces matched and united upon a line bisecting the angle of junction, is made. **b** A miter joint. **c** A miter square. **4.** *Jewish Antiq.* The official headdress of the high priest. — *v. t.;* MI′TERED OR MI′TRED (-tērd); MI′TER·ING (-tēr·ĭng) OR MI′TRING (-trĭng). **1.** To invest with a miter; — chiefly in *past part.;* as, *mitered* abbot. **2.** To match or fit together in a miter joint. — **mi′ter·er** (-ēr), *n.*

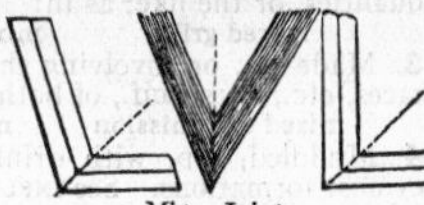

Miter Joints.

miter box. *Carp., etc.* An apparatus for guiding a handsaw at the proper angle in making a miter joint in wood.

miter gear. A bevel gear in which the wheels are of equal diameter with axes at right angles. See BEVEL GEAR, *Illust.*

miter square. *Carp.* A bevel with an immovable arm at an angle of 45°; also, a square with an arm adjustable to any angle.

mi′ter·wort′, mi′tre·wort′ (mī′tēr·wûrt′), *n.* **a** Any of a genus (*Mitella*) of plants of the saxifrage family, whose capsule resembles a bishop's miter. **b** An annual loganiaceous herb (*Cynoctonum mitreola*) of the southern U. S.

Mith′gar′thr (mĭth′gär′thēr). Var. of MIDGARD.

Mith′ras (mĭth′răs; mī′thrăs), *n.* Also **Mith′ra** (mĭth′rȧ; mī′thrȧ). [L. & Gr. *Mithras,* fr. OPer. *Mithra.*] A Persian god of light, defender of truth, and enemy of the powers of darkness. — **Mith·ra′ic** (mĭth·rā′ĭk), *adj.* — **Mith·ra′i·cism** (-ĭ·sĭz'm), *n.* — **Mith′ra·ism** (mĭth′rȧ·ĭz'm), **Mith′ra·ist** (-ĭst), *n.* — **Mith′ra·is′tic** (-ĭs′tĭk), *adj.*

mith′ri·date (mĭth′rĭ·dāt), *n.* [ML. *mithridatum,* fr. LL. *mithridatium.*] *Hist.* An antidote against poison; esp., an electuary, supposed to be a remedy for poison.

mith′ri·da′tism (-dā′tĭz'm), *n.* Immunity from a poison, produced by administration of gradually increased doses of it; — from Mithridates VI, King of Pontus (d. 63 B.C.), who is said to have produced this condition in himself. — **mith′ri·dat′ic** (-dăt′ĭk), *adj.*

mit′i·ga·ble (mĭt′ĭ·gȧ·b'l), *adj.* That can be mitigated.

mit′i·gant (-gănt), *adj.* Mitigative; alleviating; soothing.

mit′i·gate (-gāt), *v. t. & i.* [L. *mitigatus,* past part. of *mitigare* to soften, fr. *mitis* mild, soft.] **1.** *Now Rare.* To render or become mild or milder; mollify. **2.** To make or become less severe, harsh, etc.; meliorate; temper; as, to *mitigate* grief. — **Syn.** See RELIEVE. — **Ant.** Intensify. — **mit′i·ga′tion** (-gā′shŭn), *n.* — **mit′i·ga′tive** (-gā′tĭv), *adj. & n.* — **mit′i·ga′tor** (-gā′tēr), *n.*

mit′i·ga·to′ry (-gȧ·tō′rĭ; -gā′tō·rĭ), *adj. & n.* Serving to mitigate; palliative.

mi′tis cast′ing (mī′tĭs; mē′tĭs). A process for producing malleable iron castings (**mitis,** *or* **mitis metal**); also, a casting made by this process.

mi·to′sis (mī·tō′sĭs), *n.* [NL., fr. Gr. *mitos* a thread.] *Biol.* Cell division in which complex nuclear processes precede the dividing of the cytoplasm; indirect cell division; — called also *karyokinesis* and opposed to *amitosis.* It typically involves four successive stages: (1) the ***prophase,*** in which the chromatin condenses into a threadlike ***spireme*** (or several spiremes) which splits longitudinally and rearranges into paired chromosomes (see CHROMOSOME); (2) the ***metaphase,*** during which the chromosomes orient at the median transverse plane of the spindle (see SPINDLE, 2 **b**); (3) the ***anaphase,*** in which a chromosome of each pair moves to an opposite pole of the spindle; (4) the ***telophase,*** during which each polar set of chromosomes forms a new nucleus containing the original (diploid) number of chromosomes. Cf. MEIOSIS. — **mi·tot′ic** (-tŏt′ĭk), *adj.* — **mi·tot′i·cal·ly** (-ĭ·kăl·ĭ), *adv.*

‖**mi′trail′leur′** (mē′trȧ′yûr′), *n.* [F.] *Mil.* **a** An artilleryman who serves a mitrailleuse. **b** A mitrailleuse.

mi′trail·leuse′ (mē′trā·ūz′; *F.* mē′trȧ′yûz′), *n.* [F., fr. *mitrailler* to fire grapeshot.] *Mil.* A breech-loading machine gun firing small projectiles rapidly from a number of barrels.

mi′tral (mī′trăl), *adj.* Pertaining to, or resembling, a miter or the mitral valve.

mitral valve. *Anat.* The cardiac valve guarding the opening between the left auricle and the left ventricle, and preventing the return of blood to the auricle.

mi′tre (mī′tēr), etc. Vars. of MITER, etc.

mitt (mĭt), *n.* [Abbr. fr. *mitten.*] **1.** A kind of glove with or without short finger and thumb sheaths; specif., *Baseball,* a kind of glove protected on the palm side by a large mitten-shaped pad. **2.** A mitten.

mit′ten (mĭt′'n), *n.* [OF. *mitaine.*] **1.** A covering for the hand having a separate sheath only for the thumb. Cf. GLOVE. **2.** *pl. Slang.* Boxing gloves. — ***to get,*** *or* ***give, the mitten.*** To be refused, or to refuse, as a lover.

mit′ti·mus (mĭt′ĭ·mŭs), *n.* [L., we send, fr. *mittere* to send.] *Law.* A warrant of commitment to prison.

mitz′vah, mits′vah (mĭts′vä), *n.; pl.* MITZVOTH (-vōth). [Heb. *mitswāh* commandment.] *Jewish Relig.* **a** A Biblical or rabbinic commandment. **b** An act of charity performed in the interests of Jewish religion or law, or of any individual.

mix (mĭks), *v. t. & i.;* MIXED (mĭkst) or MIXT; MIX′ING. [From earlier *mixt,* past part., fr. F. *mixte,* fr. L. *mixtus,* past part. of *miscere.*] **1.** To unite or blend into one mass or compound, as by stirring together; mingle. **2.** To unite with in company; associate; hold intercourse. **3.** To form by mingling; compound. **4.** *Breeding.* To cross. — **mix′er** (mĭk′sēr), *n.*

Syn. **Mix, mingle, commingle, blend, merge, coalesce, amalgamate, fuse** mean to combine so as to form a more or less homogeneous whole. **Mix** may or may not imply complete loss of each element's identity; **mingle** usually suggests that the elements are somewhat distinguishable; **commingle,** that they form a close, intimate union; **blend,** that though losing or obscuring their individual qualities, the mixture resulting is enhanced; **merge,** a combining that causes the loss of one or more elements in the whole; **coalesce,** a natural affinity in the things merging and, usually, a resulting organic unity; **amalgamate,** an effective, harmonious union rather than a complete loss of identities; **fuse,** a bringing into an indissoluble union by or as by being melted.

mix, *n.* **1.** Act or result of mixing; also, state of being mixed or confused. **2.** A mixture; *Colloq.,* a muddle. **3.** A commercial preparation of mixed ingredients; as, an ice-cream *mix.*

mixed (mĭkst), *adj.* [For *mixt,* fr. F. *mixte,* fr. L. *mixtus.* See

MIX, *v.*] **1.** Mingled; blended. **2.** Made up of dissimilar parts, qualities, or the like; as in:

mixed grill **mixed metaphor** **mixed nerve**

3. Made up, or involving the action, of persons of different types, races, etc., or, specif., of both sexes, sides, etc., as in:

mixed commission **mixed foursome** **mixed marriage**

4. Muddled, esp. with drink. **5.** *Bot.* Combining racemose and cymose formations. See INFLORESCENCE, *Illust.* **6.** *Law.* Involving relations with two or more classes of property rights, etc.; as, a *mixed* action. **7.** *Phonet.* Of a vowel, having a tongue position intermediate between front and back, as the *a* in *sofa*; central.

mixed number. *Math.* Sum of an integer and a fraction.

mix′ture (mĭks′tūr; 118), *n.* [F., fr. L. *mixtura*, fr. *miscere, mixtum*, to mix.] **1.** A mixing. **2.** Addition or presence of a foreign element, ingredient, etc.; admixture; as, English ancestry without *mixture*. **3.** Something mixed; as: **a** A fabric woven of variously colored threads. **b** A preparation consisting of two or more ingredients, kinds, etc.; as, a smoking *mixture*. **4.** *Physics & Chem.* A complex of two or more ingredients which do not bear a fixed proportion to one another and which, however thoroughly commingled, are conceived as retaining a separate existence. Cf. COMPOUND.

mix′–up′, *n.* *Colloq.* A confusion; also, a conflict or melee.

Mi′zar (mī′zär), *n.* A star of the second magnitude in the handle of the Big Dipper. See URSA MAJOR, *Illust.*

miz′zen, miz′en (mĭz′'n), *adj.* [F. *misaine* foresail, fr. It. *mezzana*, fr. *mezzano* middle. See MEZZANINE.] *Naut.* Of or pertaining to the mizzenmast. — *n.* **a** A fore-and-aft sail set on the mizzenmast. **b** A mizzenmast; — often used in hyphened names of sails, as **miz′zen–roy′al, miz′zen–top′gal′lant.** See SAIL, *Illust.*

miz′zen·mast′, miz′en·mast′ (-mȧst′; *naut.* -măst), *n.* *Naut.* The aftermost mast in a two-masted vessel (yawl or ketch), and in a three-masted vessel (ship, bark, barkentine, and schooner), and the third mast in a vessel having four or more masts.

miz′zle (mĭz′'l), *v. t. & i. & n.* *Dial.* Drizzle; mist.

miz′zle, *v. i.* *Slang.* To take oneself off; decamp.

mne·mon′ic (nē·mŏn′ĭk), *adj.* [Gr. *mnēmonikos*, fr. *mnēmōn* mindful, fr. *mnasthai* to remember.] Assisting, or intended to assist, memory. — *n.* **1.** A mnemonic device. **2.** Mnemonics.

mne·mon′ics (-ĭks), *n.*; see -ICS. **1.** The art of improving the efficiency of the memory. **2.** *pl.* Mnemonic figures or characters.

Mne·mos′y·ne (nē·mŏs′ĭ·nē; nē·mŏz′-), *n.* [L., fr. Gr. *mnēmosynē* remembrance, memory.] *Gr. Myth.* A Titaness, goddess of memory, and mother of the Muses by Zeus.

-mo (-mō). A suffix added to certain numerals, or their names, to indicate number of leaves made by folding a sheet of paper, as in sixteen*mo* or 16*mo*. Symbol °; as, 16°.

mo′a (mō′ȧ), *n.* [Native name.] Any of numerous extinct flightless ratite birds confined to New Zealand and constituting a family (Dinornithidae). The largest (*Dinornis robustus*) was about 12 feet in height. Cf. APTERYX, *Illust.*

Mo′ab·ite (mō′ăb·īt), *n.* One of an ancient Semitic people related to the Hebrews. *Gen.* xix. 37. — **Mo′ab·ite, Mo′ab·it′ish** (-īt′ĭsh), *adj.* — **Mo′ab·it′ess** (-ĕs; -ĭs), *n.*

moan (mōn), *n.* [ME. *mone, mon, mane.*] Lamentation; complaint; now, a low prolonged sound, indicative of pain or of grief; also, a sound like a moan. — *v. t. & i.* **1.** To bewail audibly; to emit moans; lament; bemoan. **2.** To utter with moans. — **-ing·ly**, *adv.*

moat (mōt), *n.* [OF. *mote* hill, dike, bank.] A deep wide trench around the rampart of a castle or other fortified place, usually filled with water; a ditch. — *v. t.* To surround with or as with a moat.

mob (mŏb), *n.* [L. *mobile vulgus*, the movable common people. See MOBILE, *adj.*] **1.** The populace; the masses. **2.** The, or a, disorderly element of the populace; the rabble; hence, a promiscuous collection of people; a crowd. **3.** *Slang.* A criminal gang. — **Syn.** See CROWD. — *v. t.*; MOBBED (mŏbd); MOB′BING. To crowd about, as a mob, and attack or annoy. — **mob′bish**, *adj.*

mob′cap′ (mŏb′kăp′), *n.* *Chiefly Hist.* A woman's cap; esp., one having a full crown and frills, and fastened under the chin.

mo′bile (mō′bĭl; -bēl; 56), *adj.* [F., fr. L. *mobilis*, fr. *movere* to move.] **1.** Movable. **2.** Characterized by extreme fluidity, as mercury or ether. **3.** Characterized by ease of movement; as: **a** Readily expressing changes, esp. in feeling; as, *mobile* features. **b** Quickly responding to any stimulus; easily moved; hence, changeable; also, versatile. **4.** *Mil.* Capable of being readily moved about; as, *mobile* artillery. — **mo·bil′i·ty** (mō·bĭl′ĭ·tĭ), *n.*

mo′bile (mō′bēl; -bīl; -bĭl), *n.* A sculpture, as of paper or wire, having movable parts which can be easily set in motion, as by a current of air.

mo′bi·lize (mō′bĭ·līz), *v. t.* [F. *mobiliser.*] **1.** To render mobile. **2.** *Mil. & Nav.* To assemble and put in a state of readiness for active service in war, as an army or a fleet. **3.** To assemble and make ready for use, as resources. — *v. i.* To be mobilized. — **mo′bi·li·za′tion** (mō′bĭ·lĭ·zā′shŭn; mŏb′ĭ-; -lī·zā′shŭn), *n.*

mo′ble (mŏb′'l), *v. t.* *Obs. exc. Dial.* To wrap or muffle the head of, as in a hood.

mob·oc′ra·cy (mŏb·ŏk′rȧ·sĭ), *n.*; *pl.* -CIES (-sĭz). [*mob* + *-cracy.*] **1.** Rule of the mob. **2.** The mob as a ruling class. — **mob′o·crat′ic** (mŏb′ō·krăt′ĭk), **mob′o·crat′i·cal** (-ĭ·kăl), *adj.*

moc′ca·sin (mŏk′ȧ·sĭn), *n.* [Of Algonquian origin.] **1.** A soft-leather heelless shoe having its sole and sides made of one piece whose edges are joined with a puckered seam to a U-shaped piece lying on top of the foot. **2.** Any pit viper (see VIPER, 1 **b**) of the genus *Agkistrodon*, esp. the ***water moccasin, or cottonmouth*** (*A. piscivorus*) of the southern United States, which reaches a length of over four feet and feeds largely on fish, and the *copperhead* (which see). Certain harmless water snakes of the genus *Natrix* resemble the moccasins in color, are commonly mistaken for them, and are sometimes called ***water moccasins.***

moccasin flower. See LADY'S-SLIPPER **a.**

Mo′cha (mō′kȧ), *n.* **1.** A variety of coffee from Mocha or the Yemen district, Arabia. **2.** A soft pliable leather for gloves, esp. one made from the skin of an Arabian goat. — *adj.* [*not cap.*] Designating a rich icing made with butter and chocolate and flavored with coffee, or a cake iced with it.

mock (mŏk; 74), *v. t.* [OF. *mocquer.*] **1.** To treat with scorn or contempt; deride; ridicule. **2.** To deceive; delude. **3.** To defy; disregard. **4.** To imitate; counterfeit; esp., to mimic in sport; to deride by mimicry. — *v. i.* To make sport in contempt or jest; scoff; jeer. — **Syn.** See RIDICULE; COPY. — *n.* **1.** A mocking; a sneer; a jibe. **2.** An object of, or worthy of, ridicule. **3.** Mockery; derision. **4.** Imitation. — *adj.* Imitating reality or the real thing; not real; sham. — **mock′er**, *n.* — **mock′ing·ly**, *adv.*

mock′er·y (mŏk′ẽr·ĭ), *n.*; *pl.* -ERIES (-ĭz). **1.** Insulting or contemptuous action or speech; derision. **2.** A subject of laughter or derision. **3.** Mimicry; imitation; now, an insincere, contemptible, or impertinent imitation. **4.** That which is ridiculously or impudently unsuitable.

mock′–he·ro′ic, *adj.* Ridiculing or burlesquing the heroic style, character, or action; as, a *mock-heroic* poem.

mock′ing·bird′ (mŏk′ĭng·bûrd′; 74), *n.* A common bird (*Mimus polyglottos*) of the southern United States, remarkable for its exact imitations of the notes of other birds.

mock orange. *U. S.* Any of a genus (*Philadelphus*) of shrubs of the hydrangea family.

mock turtle soup. A soup of calf's head, veal, or other meat, and condiments, in imitation of green turtle soup.

mock′–up′ (mŏk′ŭp′), *n.* [From MOCK, *v. t.*, 4.] A full-sized dummy or structural model, built accurately to scale out of plywood, cardboard, canvas, clay, etc., chiefly for instructional purposes and for perfecting details of designing for the test model, as of an airplane fuselage.

mod′al (mōd′ăl; -'l), *adj.* [ML. *modalis*, fr. L. *modus.*] **1.** Of or pertaining to mode; specif.: **a** *Law.* Containing provisions as to the mode or manner of taking effect; — said of a will, contract, etc. **b** *Logic.* Indicating or expressing modality. **c** *Music.* Written in one of the old church modes, as the Gregorian chant. **2.** *Gram.* Pertaining to some particular attitude (as wish, possibility, supposal, etc.) toward the fulfillment of the action or state predicated, which may be conveyed by inflectional mood, use of auxiliary verb, word order, etc.; also, expressive of such an attitude; as, a *modal* auxiliary or link verb (go lest he *should* be angry); a *modal* adverb (she *doubtless* smiled). **3.** *Philos.* Of, pertaining to, or consisting in form as opposed to substance; relating to the mode, or manifestation; as, a *modal* distinction between things. — **mod′al·ly**, *adv.*

mo·dal′i·ty (mō·dăl′ĭ·tĭ), *n.*; *pl.* -TIES (-tĭz). **1.** Modal quality; also, mode; method. **2.** *Logic.* That qualification of propositions according to which they are distinguished as asserting (or denying) the possibility, impossibility, contingency, or necessity, of their content. **3.** *Med.* Any agency used in physical therapy, such as diathermy; also, any apparatus for applying such agency.

mode (mōd), *n.* [L. and F.; F., fr. L. *modus* a measure, manner, form.] **1.** Manner of doing or being; method; fashion; particular form. **2.** *Gram.* = 1st MOOD. **3.** *Logic.* **a** The form of the syllogism, as determined by the quantity and quality of the constituent propositions. **b** The form of a proposition with reference to its modality. **4.** *Metaphysics.* A manifestation, form, or manner of arrangement; in general use, a particular form or manifestation of some underlying substance, or of some permanent aspect or attribute of such a substance. **5.** *Music.* **a** An arrangement of the eight diatonic tones of an octave according to one of certain fixed schemes of their intervals. **b** A rhythmical scheme. **6.** *Petrog.* The actual mineral composition of a rock as distinguished from the hypothetical. **7.** *Statistics.* The item, in a series of statistical data, which occurs oftenest. — **Syn.** See METHOD.

mode, *n.* [F., fr. L. *modus* manner.] A prevailing popular custom or style; fashion, etc. — **Syn.** See FASHION.

mod′el (mŏd′'l), *n.* [F. *modèle*, fr. It. *modello*, fr. L. *modulus* a small measure, dim. of *modus.* See MODE.] **1.** *Obs.* A set of plans for a building. **2.** *Dial.* A copy. **3.** A miniature representation of a thing; sometimes, a facsimile. **4.** Style of structure; design. **5.** An archetype. **6.** An example for imitation; as, a *model* of virtue. **7.** A pattern of something to be made; as, the clay *model*. **8.** A person or thing that serves as an artist's pattern; specif., a person who poses for an artist. **9.** A woman employed to display gowns, hats, etc., to customers; a mannequin.

Syn. **Model, example, pattern, exemplar, ideal** mean something held up before one for imitation or guidance. **Model** may or may not carry a further implication of a person or thing eminently worthy of imitation; **example** stresses the prominence, authoritativeness, etc., of the person or thing that challenges imitation, but apart from the context carries no implication of its worth; **pattern** suggests someone or something to be followed as rigidly as a pattern, or carefully worked-out plan or design; **exemplar** suggests a person or thing that sums up the qualities (usually but not invariably good qualities) that distinguish the type; **ideal** suggests a person or thing, whether real or conceived, that represents the perfection one hopes to attain.

— *v. t.*; MOD′ELED (-'ld) or MOD′ELLED; MOD′EL·ING or MOD′EL·LING. To plan or form after a pattern; form in model; shape; mold. — *v. i.* **1.** To make a model or models. **2.** To assume the appearance of natural relief; — said of parts of drawing when being drawn. **3.** To act, pose, or serve as a model (senses 8 & 9). — *adj.* Serving, or suitable, for a model or pattern. — **mod′el·er, mod′el·ler** (-ẽr), *n.*

mod′er·ate (mŏd′ẽr·ĭt), *adj.* [L. *moderatus*, past part. of *moderare, moderari*, to moderate, regulate.] Kept within due bounds; observing reasonable limits; not excessive; restrained; as: **a** Sparing; temperate; abstemious. **b** Reasonable; calm; tempered. **c** Not extreme in opinion, in partisanship, etc.; as, *moderate* views. **d** Of the wind, according to Beaufort's scale (which see) and the wind scale of the U. S. Weather Bureau, designating a velocity of 13 to 18 miles per hour. **e** Fair; mediocre; as, *moderate* abilities.

Syn. **Moderate, temperate** mean neither too much nor too little. **Moderate** implies absence or avoidance of excess; **temperate**, restraint or restriction.

— *n.* A holder of moderate views, as in politics; hence [*usually cap.*], a member of any party designated "Moderate."

— (-āt), *v. t. & i.* **1.** To render or become moderate; to diminish or become diminished in force, violence, etc.; abate. **2.** To preside (over); serve as moderator (of). — **mod′er·ate·ly**, *adv.* — **mod′er·ate·ness**, *n.* — **mod′er·a′tion** (-ā′shŭn), *n.*

mod′e·ra′to (mŏd′ĕ·rä′tō), *adj.* [It.] *Music.* Moderate; — used as a direction indicating tempo.

mod′er·a′tor (mŏd′ẽr·ā′tẽr), *n.* **1.** One who moderates; esp., the presiding officer, as of a town meeting or of a presbytery, synod, or other court of the Presbyterian church. **2.** *Physics & Chem.* A substance, as graphite, deuterium (in heavy water), or beryllium, used for slowing down neutrons in an atomic pile. — **mod′er·a′tor·ship**, *n.*

mod′ern (mŏd′ẽrn), *adj.* [F. *moderne*, fr. LL. *modernus*, fr. *modo* just now, orig. abl. of *modus* measure, hence, by measure, just now.]

1. Of or characteristic of the present or recent time; hence, new-fashioned. 2. [*cap.*] Designating the most recent period of a language or literature, in contrast with its earlier periods, usually termed *Old* and *Middle;* as, *Modern* English, *Modern* French (see ENGLISH, FRENCH); — sometimes replaced by *New* (see NEW, adj., 7). — **Syn.** See NEW. — *n.* 1. A person of modern times or views. 2. *Print.* A style of type distinguished from the *old style* by greater regularity of shape, more precise curves, straight hairline serifs, and heavy strokes. See TYPE. — **mod′ern·ly**, *adv.* — **mod′ern·ness**, *n.*

mod′ern·ism (mŏd′ẽr·nĭz′m), *n.* 1. Modern practice; esp., a modern usage, expression, characteristic, etc. 2. [*often cap.*] A current Protestant movement which applies modern critical methods to the study of the Bible, and places less emphasis on historic dogmas and creeds. 3. [*cap.*] *R.C.Ch.* A body of methods and tendencies in the fields of Scripture, apologetics, dogma, history, and ethics, seeking to adapt Church teachings to the conclusions of modern scientific and critical research. Pius X condemned it as substituting purely subjective criteria in matters of faith and morals for the authority of the Church. — **mod′ern·ist** (-nĭst), *n. & adj.* — **mod′ern·is′tic** (-nĭs′tĭk), *adj.*

mo·der′ni·ty (mō·dûr′nĭ·tĭ), *n.; pl.* -TIES (-tĭz). Modernness; something modern; — opposed to *antiquity.*

mod′ern·ize (mŏd′ẽr·nīz), *v. t.* To render modern; make conform to present usage, style, taste, etc. — **mod′ern·i·za′tion** (-nĭ·zā′shŭn; -nī·zā′-), *n.* — **mod′ern·iz′er** (-nīz′ẽr), *n.*

mod′est (mŏd′ĕst; -ĭst), *adj.* [F. *modeste,* fr. L. *modestus.*] 1. Placing a moderate or low estimate on one's own merits; not forward or boastful. 2. Evincing, or arising from, lack of boldness, presumption, display, etc.; moderate; unpretentious; as, a *modest* request or home. 3. Observing the proprieties of sex; chaste; decent. — **Syn.** See HUMBLE: SHY: CHASTE (**Ant.** immodest). — **mod′est·ly**, *adv.*

mod′es·ty (-ĕs·tĭ; -ĭs·tĭ), *n.* Quality or state of being modest; also, the temper resulting from a modest estimate of oneself; absence of self-assertion, arrogance, or presumption.

mod′i·cum (mŏd′ĭ·kŭm), *n.; pl.* -CUMS (-kŭmz). [L., neut. of *modicus* moderate, fr. *modus* measure.] A little; a small quantity or portion.

mod′i·fi′a·ble (mŏd′ĭ·fī′ȧ·b'l), *adj.* That may be modified.

mod′i·fi·ca′tion (-fĭ·kā′shŭn), *n.* Act of modifying, or state of being modified; specif.: **a** Limitation or qualification. **b** Partial alteration; state or result of being so altered; also, a modified form. **c** *Biol.* A noninheritable change in an organism caused by the influence of its environment.

mod′i·fi·ca′to·ry (mŏd′ĭ·fĭ·kā′tō·rĭ), *adj.* Tending to modify.

mod′i·fi′er (mŏd′ĭ·fī′ẽr), *n.* 1. One who or that which modifies. 2. *Gram.* = QUALIFIER, 2.

mod′i·fy (mŏd′ĭ·fī), *v. t.;* -FIED (-fīd); -FY′ING. [OF. *modifier,* fr. L. *modificare, modificari,* fr. *modus* limit + *-ficare* (in comp.) to make.] 1. To reduce in extent or degree; moderate. 2. To change somewhat the form or qualities of; as, to *modify* the terms of a contract. 3. *Gram.* To limit or restrict the meaning of; qualify. 4. *Philol.* To change by umlaut. — *v. i.* To undergo or make a modification. — **Syn.** See CHANGE.

mo·dil′lion (mō·dĭl′yŭn), *n.* [It. *modiglione.*] *Arch.* An ornamental block or bracket under the corona of the cornice in the Corinthian and other orders.

mo·di′o·lus (mō·dī′ō·lŭs), *n.; pl.* -OLI (-lī). [L., a small measure, dim. of *modius* the Roman corn measure.] *Anat.* The central bony column in the cochlea of the ear.

mod′ish (mōd′ĭsh), *adj.* In the mode; fashionable. — **mod′ish·ly**, *adv.* — **mod′ish·ness**, *n.*

mo·diste′ (mō·dēst′), *n.* [F.] A dressmaker.

Mo′dred (mō′drĕd), *n.* A knight of the Round Table, the rebellious nephew of King Arthur.

mod′u·lar (mŏd′ū·lẽr), *adj.* Of or pertaining to a module or modulus.

mod′u·late (-lāt), *v. t.* [L. *modulatus,* past part. of *modulari* to measure, modulate, fr. *modulus.* See MODULE.] 1. To adjust to, or regulate by, a certain proportion; temper; soften. 2. To tune to a certain key or pitch; vary or inflect in tone, as the voice. 3. To intone; as, to *modulate* a prayer. 4. *Elec.* To change the frequency of (as electrical waves) by imposing upon them others of another, usually a lower, frequency. — *v. i.* 1. To modulate the tones, as in singing. 2. *Music.* To pass by regular chord or melodic progression, as from one key to another. 3. *Radio.* To produce modulation. — **mod′u·la′tor** (-lā′tẽr), *n.* — **mod′u·la·to′ry** (-lȧ·tō′rĭ *or, esp. Brit.,* -lā·tẽr·ĭ), *adj.*

mod′u·la′tion (-lā′shŭn), *n.* 1. A modulating; also, extent or degree of being modulated. 2. *Ling.* The use of stress or pitch to convey meaning; also, an instance of this. 3. *Music.* Act or process of changing from one key to another, esp. without a break in the melody or chord succession. 4. *Radio.* Alteration of the amplitude or frequency of a wave in accordance with speech or a signal.

mod′ule (mŏd′ūl), *n.* [F. and L.; F., fr. L. *modulus* a small measure. See MODEL.] 1. A standard or unit of measurement. 2. *Arch.* The size of some one part, as the semidiameter of the base of a shaft, taken as a unit of measure for regulating proportions.

mod′u·lus (mŏd′ū·lŭs), *n.; pl.* -LI (-lī). [L., a small measure. See MODULE.] A real positive quantity, numerical or physical, that expresses the measure of some function, property, or effect, as of elasticity, strength, efficiency, etc., esp. under unit conditions; — often denoted by μ or M; as, the *modulus* of elasticity.

‖**mo′dus o′pe·ran′di** (mō′dŭs ŏp′ĕ·răn′dī). [L.] Manner or mode of operating or working.

mo′dus vi·ven′di (vĭ·vĕn′dī). [L.] Mode of living; hence, a temporary arrangement pending settlement of a dispute.

mo·fette′ (mō·fĕt′), *n.* Also **mof·fette′**. [F. *mofette.*] *Geol.* A vent in the earth from which carbon dioxide and other gases issue.

mog (mŏg), *v. i. & t.* *Dial.* To depart; move slowly; jog.

Mo·gul′ (mō·gŭl′; mō′gŭl; 2), *n.* [Per. *Mughul* a Mongolian, the Great Mogul.] 1. A person of the Mongolian race; specif., one of the Mongol conquerors of India or their descendants. 2. Hence [*not cap.*]: **a** A great personage; magnate; autocrat. **b** A type of locomotive.

mo′hair′ (mō′hâr′), *n.* [It. *moccaiaro,* fr. Ar. *mukhayyar.*] 1. A fine camlet made from the hair of the Angora goat; also, such hair or the yarn made from it. 2. A lustrous fabric imitating true mohair, usually of cotton and wool mixed. 3. A garment of this fabric.

Mo·ham′med·an (mō·hăm′ĕ·dăn; -ĭ·dăn), *adj.* [From *Mohammed,* fr. Ar. *muhammad* praiseworthy, highly praised.] Of or pertaining to Mohammed, or the religion and institutions founded by Mohammed. — *n.* A follower of Mohammed, the founder of Islam; a Moslem.

Mohammedan calendar. A lunar calendar reckoning from the year of the hegira (Anno Hegirae, abbr. A.H.), A.D. 622. Thirty of its years constitute a cycle, of which the 2d, 5th, 7th, 10th, 13th, 16th, 18th, 21st, 24th, 26th, and 29th are leap years, having 355 days; the others are common, having 354 days. By the following tables any Mohammedan date may be changed into the Christian date, or vice versa, for the years 1945–64.

MONTHS OF THE MOHAMMEDAN YEAR

1 **Muharram**...30	5 **Jumada I**....30	9 **Ramadan**...30
2 **Safar**........29	6 **Jumada II**...29	10 **Shawwal**...29
3 **Rabia I**......30	7 **Rajab**........30	11 **Zu'lkadah**..30
4 **Rabia II**.....29	8 **Shaban**.......29	12 **Zu'lhijjah**..29*

* In leap year, 30 days.

A.H.	A.D.	A.H.	A.D.
1365 begins	Dec. 6, 1945	1375 begins	Aug. 20, 1955
1366*	Nov. 25, 1946	1376*	Aug. 8, 1956
1367	Nov. 15, 1947	1377	July 29, 1957
1368*	Nov. 3, 1948	1378	July 18, 1958
1369	Oct. 24, 1949	1379*	July 7, 1959
1370	Oct. 13, 1950	1380	June 26, 1960
1371*	Oct. 2, 1951	1381†	June 15, 1961
1372	Sept. 21, 1952	1382*	June 4, 1962
1373	Sept. 10, 1953	1383	May 25, 1963
1374*	Aug. 30, 1954	1384	May 13, 1964

* Leap Year. † First year of the 47th cycle.

The following general rule for finding the date of commencement of any Mohammedan year has a maximum error of a day. Multiply 970,224 by the Mohammedan year, point off six decimal places, and add 621.5774. The whole number will be the year A.D., and the decimal multiplied by 365 will give the day of the year.

Mo·ham′med·an·ism (mō·hăm′ĕ·dăn·ĭz′m; -ĭ·dăn-), *n.* The religion of Mohammed; Islam. — **Mo·ham′med·an·ize** (-īz), *v. t.*

Mo′hawk (mō′hôk), *n.; pl.* MOHAWK, MOHAWKS (-hôks). [Of Algonquian origin.] An Indian of a tribe of the Iroquois Confederacy, formerly occupying the Mohawk Valley, New York; also, their language.

Mo·he′gan (mō·hē′găn), *n.* See MAHICAN **b**.

Mo·hi′can (mō·hē′kăn; *Brit. usually* mō′ĭ·kăn), *n.* See MAHICAN **a**.

Mo′hock (mō′hŏk), *n.* 1. *Obs.* Var. of MOHAWK. 2. One of certain ruffians, often aristocrats, who in gangs committed outrages in London early in the 18th century.

mo′hur (mō′hẽr), *n.* [Hind. *muhur, muhr,* a gold coin, seal, fr. Per.] A former gold coin of India and Persia equal to 15 rupees.

moi′dore (moi′dōr), *n.* [Pg. *moeda d'ouro,* lit., coin of gold.] A former Portuguese gold coin worth about $3.27.

moi′e·ty (moi′ĕ·tĭ), *n.; pl.* -TIES (-tĭz). [F. *moitié,* fr. L. *medietas,* fr. *medius* middle, half.] 1. A half. 2. About a half; a part or portion. 3. *Anthrop.* Either of two basic, complementary tribal subdivisions.

moil (moil), *v. t.* [OF. *moillier, muiller,* fr. L. *mollis* soft.] *Archaic & Dial.* To moisten or wet; daub; dirty. — *v. i.* To work hard, often in the mire or wet; drudge. — *n.* 1. Hard work; drudgery; toil. 2. Confusion; turmoil. — **moil′er**, *n.* — **moil′ing·ly**, *adv.*

moire (mwär; mōr), *n.* [F., fr. E. MOHAIR.] Orig., a kind of watered mohair; later, any textile fabric, esp. silk, to which a watered appearance is given in calendering.

‖**moi·ré′** (mwȧ′rā′; mō′rā), *adj.* [F.] 1. Watered; having a watered or clouded appearance, as silk, paper, etc. 2. *Philately.* Having a fine network of wavy lines printed on the back, as a protection against forgery. — *n.* 1. A watered, clouded, or frosted appearance on textile fabrics or metallic surfaces. 2. Erroneously, moire.

moist (moist), *adj.* [OF. *moiste,* fr. LL. *muccidus,* for L. *mucidus* moldy, musty.] 1. Slightly wet; damp; of the eyes, tearful; of a climate, season, etc., rainy. 2. Connected or accompanied with, or characterized by, moisture. — **Syn.** See WET. — **moist′ness**, *n.*

mois′ten (mois′'n), *v. t. & i.* To make or become moist.

mois′ture (mois′tūr), *n.* Liquid, usually water, diffused or condensed in relatively small quantity.

moke (mōk), *n.* *Slang.* A donkey; a dolt.

mol (mōl), *n.* *Chem.* Var. of MOLE.

mo′lar (mō′lẽr), *adj.* [L. *moles* mass.] 1. *Mech.* Of or pertaining to a mass of matter, as disting. from the properties or motions of molecules or atoms. 2. *Chem.* Also **mo′lal** (-lăl). Of, pertaining to, or containing a mole, or gram molecule.

☞ According to best modern usage regarding solutions, *molar* refers to moles per liter of solution, while *molal* refers to moles per 1000 grams of solvent.

mo′lar (mō′lẽr), *adj.* [L. *molaris,* fr. *mola* mill.] 1. Having power to grind; grinding. 2. Of or pert. to the molar teeth. — *n.* Also **molar tooth**. A tooth with a broad rounded or flattened surface adapted for grinding; specif., one of the cheek teeth behind the incisors and canines. See TOOTH, *Illust.*

mo·las′ses (mō·lăs′ĕz; -ĭz), *n., sing. & pl.* [Pg. *melaço,* fr. LL. *mellaceus* honeylike, fr. *mel, mellis,* honey.] The thick, brown or dark-colored, viscid sirup which drains from sugar in the process of manufacture. See TREACLE, 3.

mold, mould (mōld), *n.* [ME. *moul,* prob. confused with *mold* earth.] **a** A growth, often woolly, produced on various forms of organic matter, esp. when damp or decaying, by saprophytic fungi; as, ***black mold***, a cottony substance covered with black dots, found on bread; ***blue mold***, a blue-green surface on jelly and cheese. Cf. MILDEW, PENICILLIN. **b** Also **mold**, *or* **mould, fungus**. Any mold-producing fungus; esp. any fungus of the order Mucorales. — *v. i. & t.* To become, or cause to be, moldy.

mold, mould, *n.* [AS. *molde.*] 1. Soft, friable earth; esp., earth containing the remains or constituents of organic matter, and suited to plants; humus. 2. *Archaic & Dial.* The ground; earth; hence, a grave. 3. Earthy material; constituent matter; material.

mold, mould, *n.* [OF. *modle, molle,* fr. L. *modulus.* See MODULE.] 1. The matrix, or cavity, in which anything is shaped; also, the body containing the cavity; as, a sand *mold* for casting metals. 2. A frame or body on or about which something is made; as a button *mold.* 3. Distinctive character or nature; cast. 4. Form; shape; also, body or corporeal form. 5. That which is molded; material for molding. 6. *Arch.* **a** A molding. **b** A group of moldings. — *v. t.* 1. To mix or knead (esp. dough) to a required consistency or shape. 2. To shape in or as in a mold; also, shape; model. **3.** To ornament by molding or carving. **4.** *Founding.* To form a mold of, as in sand. — **mold′a·ble, mould′a·ble,** *adj.* — **mold′er, mould′er,** *n.*

mold′board′, mould′board′ (mōld′bōrd′; *dial.* mŭl′bōrd′; 70), *n.* **1.** A curved iron plate attached to a plowshare which lifts, turns, and pulverizes the soil. See PLOW, *Illust.* **2.** One of the boards forming a mold for concrete.

mold′er, mould′er (mōl′dẽr), *v. i.* [From MOLD soil.] To crumble into particles; to turn to dust by natural decay.

mold′ing, mould′ing, *n.* **1.** Act or process of shaping in or on a mold, or of making molds. **2.** Anything cast in a mold, or which ap-

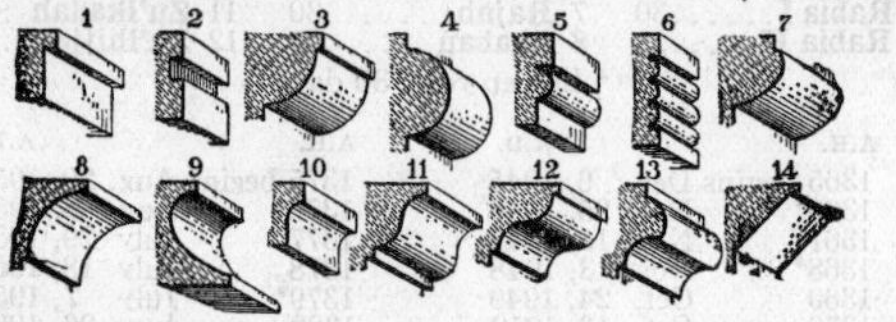

Moldings, 3. 1 Fillet and Fascia; 2 Sunk Fillet; 3 Quarter Round, sometimes called Ovolo; 4 Torus (when large and combined with other moldings); 5 Bead or Astragal; 6 Reed or Reeding; 7 Ovolo, or Thumb; 8 Cavetto; 9 Scotia; 10 Congé; 11 Cyma Recta; 12 Cyma Reversa; 13 Beak; 14 Splay.

pears to be so cast. **3.** *Arch.* **a** A plane, or curved, narrow surface, either sunk or projecting, used for decoration. **b** A strip of material having such a surface.

mold′warp′, mould′warp′ (mōld′wôrp′), *n.* [AS. *molde* soil + *weorpan* to throw up.] *Local, Eng.* The European mole (*Talpa europaea*).

mold′y, mould′y (mōl′dĭ), *adj.*; -I·ER (-dĭ·ẽr); -I·EST. [From 1st MOLD.] Overgrown with, or containing, mold; musty. — **mold′i·ness, mould′i·ness,** *n.*

mole (mōl), *n.* [F. *môle*, fr. L. *mola* mill, cake, and (after Gr. *mylē*) mola.] A mass of fleshy or other more or less solid matter generated in the uterus.

mole, *n.* [AS. *māl.*] A congenital spot, mark, or small permanent protuberance on the human body.

mole, *n.* [ME. *molle.*] **1.** Any of numerous burrowing insectivores (chiefly of the family Talpidae) with minute eyes, concealed ears, and soft fur. **2.** One who works in a dark place or in the dark. **3.** Moleskin; *pl.*, moleskins.

mole (mōl), *n.* [F. *môle*, fr. MGr. *mōlos*, fr. L. *moles* mass, burden.] A massive work of masonry or of large stones, laid in the sea, often as a breakwater.

mole, *n.* [See MOLECULE.] *Chem.* A gram molecule.

Mo′lech (mō′lĕk). Var. of MOLOCH.

mo·lec′u·lar (mō·lĕk′ū·lẽr), *adj.* [See MOLECULE.] *Physics & Chem.* Pertaining to, connected with, produced by, or consisting of molecules; as, *molecular* grouping, etc.

molecular film. *Physical Chem.* A monomolecular layer. See MONOMOLECULAR.

molecular weight. *Chem.* The weight of any molecule, being the sum of the weights of its constituent atoms.

mol′e·cule (mŏl′ē·kūl; mō′lē·kūl), *n.* [F. *molécule*, fr. L. *moles* mass. See 4th MOLE.] **1.** Any minute particle. **2.** *Chem. & Physics.* **a** A unit of matter, the smallest portion of an element or compound that retains chemical identity with the substance in mass. **b** A quantity proportional to the molecular weight; specif., a gram molecule.

mole′hill′ (mōl′hĭl′), *n.* A little ridge thrown up by moles; hence, an insignificant obstacle, difficulty, etc.

mole′skin′ (-skĭn′), *n.* **1.** The skin of the mole used as fur, or some skin cut to look like it. **2.** A fabric resembling moleskin, as velveteen. **3.** *pl.* Garments, esp. trousers, made of this fabric.

mo·lest′ (mō·lĕst′), *v. t.* [OF. *molester*, fr. L. *molestare*, fr. *molestus* troublesome.] To interfere with or meddle with unwarrantably so as to injure or disturb. — **mo·lest′er,** *n.*

mo′les·ta′tion (mō′lĕs·tā′shŭn; mŏl′ĕs-), *n.* Act of molesting, or state of being molested; annoyance.

mo′line (mō′lĭn; mō·lĭn′), *adj.* *Her.* Resembling the rynd of a millstone in shape; — said of a cross. See CROSS, *Illust.* (15).

Moll (mŏl), *n.* **1.** A diminutive of MARY. **2.** [*often not cap.*] *Slang & Dial.* **a** A wench; prostitute. **b** A gangster's mistress.

mol·les′cent (mŏ·lĕs′ĕnt; -′nt), *adj.* [L. *mollescens.*] Tending to soften; softening. — **mol·les′cence** (-ĕns; -′ns), *n.*

mol′li·fi·ca′tion (mŏl′ĭ·fĭ·kā′shŭn), *n.* Act of mollifying, or state of being mollified; mitigation.

mol′li·fy (mŏl′ĭ·fī), *v. t.*; -FIED (-fīd); -FY′ING. [F. *mollifier*, fr. LL. *mollificare*, fr. *mollis* soft + *-ficare* (in comp.) to make.] **1.** *Rare.* To soften. **2.** To allay, as rage; appease; mitigate; calm. — **Syn.** See PACIFY. — *v. i.* **1.** *Obs.* To become soft or tender. **2.** To become softened. — **mol′li·fi′er** (-fī′ẽr), *n.* — **mol′li·fy′ing·ly,** *adv.*

mol·li′ti·es (mŏ·lĭsh′ĭ·ēz), *n.* [L., softness.] Softness.

mol·lus′coid (mŏ·lŭs′koid), *adj.* Also **mol′lus·coi′dal** (mŏl′ŭs·koi′dăl; -d′l). Like a mollusk. — *n.* A molluscoid animal.

mol·lus′cous (-kŭs), *adj.* Molluscan.

mol′lusk (mŏl′ŭsk), *n.* Also **mol′lusc.** [F. *mollusque*, fr. L. *molluscus* soft, fr. *mollis* soft.] One of a large phylum (Mollusca) containing most of the animals popularly called *shellfish* except the crustaceans. It comprises the slugs, snails, mussels, clams, oysters, whelks, limpets, cuttlefishes, etc., all of which have a soft unsegmented body, protected in most instances by a calcareous shell. — **mol·lus′can** (mŏ·lŭs′kăn), *adj. & n.*

Moll′wei′de pro·jec′tion (môl′vī′dĕ). [After Karl B. *Mollweide* (1774–1825), Ger. mathematician and astronomer.] An equal-area representation of the surface of the earth as a plane in the form of an ellipse, with the equator and central meridian as straight lines and the scales along the equator and parallels of latitude constant and equal. Meridians are equally spaced ellipses and all outer areas are progressively distorted. It was first used by Mollweide in 1805.

mol′ly·cod′dle (mŏl′ĭ·kŏd′′l), *n.* A person who coddles himself or is coddled; an effeminate man or boy. — *v. t. & i.* To coddle; pamper. — **Syn.** See INDULGE. — **mol′ly·cod′dler** (-lẽr), *n.*

Mo′loch (mō′lŏk), *n.* [LL., fr. Gr. *Moloch*, fr. Heb. *Mōlekh.*] *Bib.* A Semitic deity, whose worship was accompanied by human sacrifice, esp. of first-born children.

Mol′o·tov bread′bas′ket (mŏl′ŭ·tŏf; mô′lŭ·tŭf). [After V. M. *Molotov* (b. 1890).] A torpedolike rack that, on being dropped from an airplane, rotates as it falls, scattering one by one by centrifugal force its load of dozens of incendiary bombs, and in some types releasing also a demolition bomb with delayed-action fuse.

Molotov cocktail. [After V. M. *Molotov.*] A crude hand grenade made of a bottle filled with an inflammable liquid, chiefly gasoline, and fitted with a wick or saturated rag taped to the bottom, which is ignited at the moment of hurling.

molt, moult (mōlt), *v. i.* [AS. *mūtian*, in *bimūtian* to exchange for, fr. L. *mutare.*] To shed or cast off the hair, feathers, outer layer of the skin, horns, or the like, the castoff parts being replaced by new growth. — *v. t.* To cast off and renew by molting. — *n.* A molting; also, the castoff covering. — **molt′er, moult′er,** *n.*

mol′ten (mōl′tĕn; -t′n). Archaic past part. of MELT. Hence: *adj.* **1.** Melted; in fusion, esp. from intense heat. **2.** Made by melting and casting; as, a *molten* image.

‖mol′to (mōl′tō), *adv.* [It.] *Music.* Much; very; — in directions; as in **‖mol′to a·da′gio** (ä·dä′jō), very slowly.

mo′ly (mō′lĭ), *n.*; *pl.* MOLIES (-lĭz). [L., fr. Gr. *mōly.*] A fabulous herb of occult power, mentioned by Homer, Milton, and others.

mo·lyb′de·nite (mō·lĭb′dē·nīt; mŏl′ĭb·dē′nīt), *n.* [See MOLYBDENUM.] *Mineral.* Molybdenum disulfide, MoS_2, occurring in foliated masses or scales resembling graphite.

mo·lyb′de·num (mō·lĭb′dē·nŭm; mŏl′ĭb·dē′nŭm), *n.* [NL., fr. L. *molybdaena* galena, fr. Gr. *molybdaina*, fr. *molybdos* lead.] A metallic element of the chromium group, resembling iron in its white color, malleability, difficult fusibility, and its capacity for forming steellike alloys with carbon. Sp. gr., 10.2. Symbol, *Mo*; at. no., 42; at. wt., 95.95.

mo·lyb′dic (mō·lĭb′dĭk), *adj.* *Chem.* Of, pert. to, or containing molybdenum, esp. in a higher valence. Cf. MOLYBDOUS.

mo·lyb′dous (-dŭs), *adj.* Of, pert. to, or containing molybdenum, esp. in a lower valence. Cf. MOLYBDIC.

mome (mōm), *n.* *Archaic.* A blockhead.

mo′ment (mō′mĕnt), *n.* [OF., fr. L. *momentum*, for *movimentum*, movement, motion, moment, fr. *movere* to move.] **1.** A minute portion of time; an instant. **2.** Importance, as in influence or effect; consequence; as, affairs of *moment.* **3.** A definite period or point; specif., *Chiefly Philos.*, a stage in development, as in the history of thought, a social institution, etc.; esp., a stage in logical development, in cognition, etc. **4.** An essential or constituent element. **5.** *Mech.* Tendency, or measure of tendency, to produce motion, esp. about a point or axis. — **Syn.** See IMPORTANCE.

mo′men·tar′y (mō′mĕn·tẽr′ĭ *or, esp. Brit.*, -tẽr·ĭ), *adj.* Continuing only a moment; transitory; ephemeral. — **Syn.** See TRANSIENT. — **mo′men·tar′i·ly,** *adv.* — **mo′men·tar′i·ness,** *n.*

mo′ment·ly (mō′mĕnt·lĭ), *adv.* **1.** From moment to moment; every moment; as, increasing *momently.* **2.** At any moment; instantly. **3.** For a, or the, moment; as, *momently* hidden.

mo·men′tous (mō·mĕn′tŭs), *adj.* Of moment or consequence; very important; as, *momentous* decisions. — **mo·men′tous·ly,** *adv.* — **mo·men′tous·ness,** *n.*

mo·men′tum (-tŭm), *n.*; *pl.* -TA (-tȧ), -TUMS (-tŭmz). [L.] **1.** *Mech.* Quantity of motion; the property of a moving body which determines the length of time required to bring it to rest when under the action of a constant force or moment. **2.** Popularly, impetus. **3.** = MOMENT, 5.

Mo′mus (mō′mŭs), *n.* [L., fr. Gr. *mōmos* blame, ridicule, Momus.] **1.** *Gr. Myth.* Ridicule personified as a mocking and censorious god. **2.** Hence, a carping critic.

mon (mŏn). *Scot. & Dial.* Var. of MAN.

mon- (mŏn-). = MONO- (which see), as in *mon*androus.

mon′a·chal (mŏn′ȧ·kăl), *adj.* [ML. *monachalis*, fr. *monachus* a monk.] Monastic.

mon′a·chism (-kĭz′m), *n.* Monasticism.

mon·ac′id (mŏn·ăs′ĭd). Var. of MONOACID.

mon′ad (mŏn′ăd; mō′năd), *n.* [LL. *monas, -adis*, a unit, fr. Gr. *monas, -ados*, fr. *monos* alone.] **1.** *Philos.* **a** A unit; individual; atom. **b** An individual elementary being, psychical or spiritual in nature, reflecting within itself the whole universe. **2.** *Biol.* Any minute simple organism or organic unit. **3.** *Zool.* A flagellate protozoan. — *adj.* Of the nature of a monad. — **mo·nad′ic** (mō·năd′ĭk), **mo·nad′i·cal** (-ĭ·kăl), *adj.*

mon′a·del′phous (mŏn′ȧ·dĕl′fŭs), *adj.* [*mon-* + Gr. *adelphos* brother.] *Bot.* Having the filaments united into a single tube around the gynoecium, as in flowers of the mallow family.

mon′ad·ism (mŏn′ăd·ĭz′m; mō′năd-), *n.* The theory that the universe is a composite of monads.

mo·nad′nock (mō·năd′nŏk), *n.* [From Mt. *Monadnock*, N. H., a typical example.] *Phys. Geog.* A hill or mountain of resistant rock surmounting a peneplain.

Mo′na Li′sa (mō′nȧ lē′zȧ; mŏn′ȧ). [It. *Mona, Monna* madam.] Leonardo da Vinci's portrait of Lisa, wife of a Florentine, Francesco del Giocondo, which is famous for its subtle smile; — called also *La Gioconda.*

mo·nan′drous (mō·năn′drŭs), *adj.* [*mon-* + *-androus.*] **1.** Having flowers with a single stamen, as many orchids. **2.** [Gr. *monandros.*] Of or pertaining to monandry.

mo·nan′dry (-drĭ), *n.* [Gr. *monandros* having one husband.] **1.** State or custom of having only one husband at a time. Cf. POLYANDRY. **2.** *Bot.* Condition of being monandrous.

mo·nan′thous (-thŭs), *adj.* *Bot.* One-flowered.

mon′arch (mŏn′ẽrk), *n.* [LL. *monarcha*, fr. Gr. *monarchēs, monarchos*, fr. *monos* alone + *archein* to be first, rule.] **1.** A sole supreme ruler; also, the hereditary chief of a limited or constitutional monarchy. **2.** One likened to a sole ruler in position, dignity, power, etc.; as, an oak is called the *monarch* of the forest. **3.** A large butterfly (*Danaüs archippus*) with black-veined and black-bordered orange-brown wings, the larva of which feeds on milkweed. — **mo·nar′chal** (mō·när′kăl), **mo·nar′chi·al** (-kĭ·ăl), *adj.*

mo·nar′chi·an·ism (mō·när′kĭ·ăn·ĭz′m), *n.* *Eccl. Hist. & Theol.* Any of several anti-Trinitarian doctrines current in the church of the 2d and 3d centuries, the common principle of which was that God is one in person as well as in nature. — **mo·nar′chi·an·ist** (-ĭst), *n.*

mo·nar′chic (-kĭk), *adj.* Also **mo·nar′chi·cal** (-kĭ·kăl). Of or pert. to, or of the nature of, a monarch or monarchy; favoring a monarchy. — **mo·nar′chi·cal·ly,** *adv.*

mon′arch·ism (mŏn′ẽr·kĭz′m), *n.* Monarchic government or prin-

ciples, or advocacy of them. — **mon′arch·ist** (mŏn′ẽr·kĭst), *n. & adj.*
— **mon′arch·is′tic** (-kĭs′tĭk), *adj.*

mon′arch·y (mŏn′ẽr·kĭ), *n.; pl.* -IES (-kĭz). [OF. *monarchie*, fr. LL. *monarchia*, fr. Gr. *monarchia*. See MONARCH.] **1.** *Now Rare.* Sovereignty of a single person. **2.** A state ruled over by a monarch; also, the rule exercised by such a person. A monarchy is called an *absolute monarchy* when there are no constitutional limitations on the monarch's powers; a *limited, or constitutional, monarchy*, when there are such limitations. **3.** Government in which a single person is sovereign.

mon′as (mŏn′ăs; mō′năs), *n.; pl.* MONADES (mŏn′á-dēz). [LL.] A monad.

mon′as·ter·y (mŏn′ăs·tĕr′ĭ or, esp. Brit., -trĭ), *n.; pl.* -TERIES (-ĭz). [LL. *monasterium*, fr. Gr. *monastērion*, fr. *monastēs* a solitary, a monk, fr. *monazein* to be alone, live in solitude, fr. *monos* alone.] A house of religious retirement, or of seclusion from the world for persons under religious vows, esp. monks; a convent. — **Syn.** See CLOISTER. — **mon′as·te′ri·al** (-tĕr′ĭ·ăl), *adj.*

mo·nas′tic (mō·năs′tĭk), *adj.* [ML. *monasticus*.] Of or pert. to monasteries or their occupants; also, secluded from temporal concerns and devoted to religion. — *n.* A monk. — **mo·nas′ti·cal** (-tĭ·kăl), *adj.* — **mo·nas′ti·cal·ly**, *adv.*

mo·nas′ti·cism (mō·năs′tĭ·sĭz′m), *n.* The monastic life, system, or condition; specif., organized asceticism.

mon′a·tom′ic (mŏn′á·tŏm′ĭk), *adj.* [*mon-* + *atomic*.] *Chem.* **a** Consisting of one atom; having one atom in the molecule. **b** Univalent. **c** Having one replaceable atom or radical.

mon·ax′i·al (mŏn·ăk′sĭ·ăl), *adj.* [*mon-* + *axial*.] Having a single axis; uniaxial; specif., *Bot.*, developing inflorescence directly on the primary axis. Cf. PLURIAXIAL.

mon′a·zite (mŏn′á·zīt), *n.* [Gr. *monazein* to be solitary; in allusion to its isolated crystals.] A mineral occurring often in sand deposits, especially in the Carolinas, Brazil, and India. It is a phosphate of certain rare earths, essentially (Ca, La, Nd, Pr)PO₄, usually also containing thorium.

‖**mon cher** (môN shâr′), *masc.;* ‖**ma chère** (má shâr′), *fem.* [F.] My dear.

Mon′day (mŭn′dĭ), *n.* [AS. *mōnandæg*, i. e., day of (sacred to) the moon; a translation of L. *lunae dies.*] The second day of the week; the day following Sunday. Abbr. *Mon.*

‖**monde** (môNd; *E.* mŏnd), *n.* [F.] The world of fashion; society; one's coterie or circle.

mo·ne′cious (mō·nē′shŭs). Var. of MONOECIOUS.

Mo·nel′ (mō·nĕl′), *n.,* **Monel metal.** A trade-mark for an alloy of nickel, copper, and other elements, chiefly iron and manganese, in certain proportions, made by direct reduction from ore in which the constituent metals occur in these proportions. It resembles nickel.

mon′e·tar′y (mŏn′ê·tĕr′ĭ; mŭn′-; *or, esp. Brit.*, -tĕr·ĭ), *adj.* [L. *monetarius* belonging to a mint.] **1.** Of or pertaining to the coinage or currency. **2.** Of or having to do with money; pecuniary. — **Syn.** See FINANCIAL. — **mon′e·tar′i·ly**, *adv.*

monetary unit. The standard unit of value of a national currency. See *Tables,* below.

mon′e·tize (mŏn′ê·tīz; mŭn′-), *v. t.* To convert or coin into money; give a standard value to in a national currency; as, to *monetize* silver. — **mon′e·ti·za′tion** (-tĭ·zā′shŭn; -tĭ·zā′-), *n.*

mon′ey (mŭn′ĭ), *n.; pl.* MONEYS (-ĭz). The irregular plural *monies* occurs, esp. in the sense of "sums of money." [OF. *moneie*, fr. L. *moneta.* See 2d MINT.] **1.** Metal, as gold, silver, or copper, coined, or stamped, and issued as a medium of exchange. See *Tables,* below. **2.** A sum (definite or indefinite) of money. **3.** Wealth reckoned in terms of money. **4.** Any form or denomination of coin or paper lawfully current as money; — chiefly *pl.* **5.** Anything customarily used as a medium of exchange and measure of value, as sheep, wampum, gold dust, etc. **6.** Written or stamped promises or certificates, which pass current as a means of payment; paper money (which see).

☞ COMBINATIONS are:

money-changer	moneylender	money-mad

mon′ey-bag′ (-băg′), *n.* **1.** A bag for containing money. **2.** *pl. Colloq.* **a** Wealth. **b** A rich person.

mon′eyed (mŭn′ĭd), *adj.* **1.** Supplied with money; wealthy. **2.** Consisting in, derived from, or due to money.

mon′ey·er (mŭn′ĭ·ẽr), *n.* **1.** An authorized coiner of money; a minter. **2.** *Rare.* A banker.

mon′ey-mak′ing (-māk′ĭng), *n.* Act or process of making or acquiring money. — *adj.* **1.** Lucrative. **2.** Engaged in money-making. — **mon′ey-mak′er** (-ẽr), *n.*

money of account. A denominator of value, or basis of exchange, used in keeping accounts, for which there may, or may not, be an equivalent coin; thus, the mill is a *money of account* in the United States, but not a coin.

money order. An order issued by a post office or express or telegraph office for payment of a specified sum of money at another named office.

mon′ey-wort′ (mŭn′ĭ-wûrt′), *n.* A trailing herb (*Lysimachia nummularia*) of the primrose family, with rounded opposite leaves and solitary yellow flowers in their axils.

mon′ger (mŭng′gẽr), *n.* [AS. *mangere,* fr. *mangian* to trade.] A trader; a dealer; — now often implying petty or discreditable dealing or traffic.

mon′ger·ing (mŭng′gẽr·ĭng), *n. & adj.* Dealing; trafficking; trading; — chiefly in combination, as in news*mongering.*

Mon′gol (mŏng′gŏl), *adj.* Mongolian. — *n.* **1.** One of the native tribes of Mongolia, mostly nomadic tent dwellers. **2.** = MONGOLIAN, *n.,* 2. **3.** A member of the Mongolian race.

Mon·go′lian (mŏng·gō′lyăn; -gō′lĭ·ăn; mŏn-), *adj.* **1.** Of or pertaining to Mongolia, the Mongols, or their language. **2.** Designating, or belonging or relating to, the division of mankind named the **Mongolian race,** and comprising the peoples of nearly all of Asia excepting Hindustan and the Mohammedan countries of the southwest. **3.** *Med.* Pertaining to or afflicted with Mongolism. — *n.* **1.** A member of the Mongolian race; also, a Mongol (sense 1). **2.** The language of the Mongols (sense 1), which comprises various dialects written in an alphabet derived from the Uigur. See LANGUAGE, *Table.* **3.** *Med.* One affected with Mongolism.

Mon·gol′ic (-gŏl′ĭk), *adj.* Mongolian. — *n.* The Mongolian language.

TABLES OF MONETARY UNITS AND DENOMINATIONS

WITH VALUES OF FOREIGN UNITS IN U. S. CURRENCY

NOTE. In the following tables the monetary units are indicated (in column two) by italic type and their par values in terms of United States currency are given (in column three). For many of the monetary units the par values have been determined by agreement between the particular countries concerned and the International Monetary Fund, established as an agency of the United Nations in July 1944; such values are indicated by an asterisk. These par values are not always the same as the actual exchange rates, which may change from day to day and which may vary considerably over a given period of time. For the current effective exchange value of any particular unit the daily newspapers should be consulted. By law the gold content of the U. S. dollar was fixed Jan. 31, 1934, at 15.238 grains of gold, or $35.00 to a fine ounce; the British sovereign contains 113 grains. Because gold is held in reserve by the chief governments of the world, few gold coins have in recent years actually been minted or remain in circulation. Paper money and silver are most widely used for the higher denominations, aluminum-bronze and nickel for coins of smaller value, and bronze, copper, and alloys for the coins of lowest value.

United States of America
100 cents (*c., ¢*) = 1 *dollar* ($)
Minor coins are the nickel (5 cents), dime (10 cents), quarter (25 cents), half dollar (50 cents). The ten-dollar gold piece, formerly coined, was known as the eagle. The silver dollar contains (since 1837) 412.5 grains of silver .900 fine.

Afghanistan
100 puls	= 1 *afghani* (rupee)	$0.0595

Argentina
100 centavos	= 1 *peso* (p., $)	$0.0555 *

Australia
20 shillings	= 1 *Australian pound* (£A)	$2.240 *

(Same system of coinage as in GREAT BRITAIN.)

Austria
100 groschen	= 1 *schilling* (s.)	$0.0385 *

Belgium
100 centimes	= 1 *franc* (fr.)	$0.0200 *

Bolivia
100 centavos	= 1 *boliviano* (b.)	$0.0053 *

Brazil
100 centavos	= 1 *cruzeiro* (Cr.$)	$0.0541 *
1000 cruzeiros	= 1 conto	

Bulgaria
100 stotinki	= 1 *lev* (l.)	$0.00348

Burma
100 pyas	= 1 *kyat* (K.)	$0.21

Canada
100 cents	= 1 *dollar* ($)	$0.9091

Ceylon
100 cents	= 1 *rupee*	$0.2100 *

Chile
100 centavos	= 1 *peso* (p., $)	$0.0091 *

China
100 cents	= 1 *yuan* ($)	

Colombia
100 centavos	= 1 *peso* (p., $)	$0.5128 *

Costa Rica
100 centimos	= 1 *colon* (¢)	$0.1781 *

Cuba
100 centavos	= 1 *peso* (p., $)	$1.00 *

Czechoslovakia
100 heller	= 1 *koruna* (Kč)	$0.1389

Denmark
100 öre	= 1 *krone* (k.)	$0.1448 *

Dominican Republic
100 centavos = 1 peso (p., $) ... $1.00 *

Ecuador
100 centavos = 1 sucre (s/.) ... $0.0667 *

Egypt
10 millièmes = 1 piaster (Pi., pias.)
100 piasters = 1 Egyptian pound (£E) ... $2.8716 *

El Salvador
100 centavos = 1 colon (¢) ... $0.40 *

Ethiopia
100 centimes = 1 dollar ($E) ... $0.4025 *

Finland
100 pennia = 1 markka (mk.) ... $0.0031 *

France
100 centimes = 1 franc (fr.) ... $0.0024

Germany (Western)
100 pfennig = 1 Deutsche mark (DM, Dm.) ... $0.2381 *

Great Britain
4 farthings = 1 penny (d.)
12 pence = 1 shilling (s.)
20 shillings = 1 pound (£) ... $2.800 *
21 shillings = 1 guinea
Additional coins in the British system are threepence, sixpence, florin, half crown, crown, half sovereign, sovereign. (See these in *Vocab.*)

Greece
100 lepta = 1 drachma (dr., d.) ... $0.0334

Guatemala
100 centavos = 1 quetzal (q.) ... $1.00 *

Haiti
100 centimes = 1 gourde (g., gde.) ... $0.20 *

Honduras
100 centavos = 1 lempira (l.) ... $0.50 *

Hong Kong
100 cents = 1 dollar (HK$) ... $0.1750 *

Hungary
100 fillér = 1 forint ... $0.0852

Iceland
100 aurar = 1 króna (kr.) ... $0.0614 *

India, Republic of
3 pies = 1 pice
4 pice = 1 anna
16 annas = 1 rupee (R., Re.) ... $0.2100 *
13⅓ rupees (Rs.) = 1 pound sterling (£1)
100,000 rupees = 1 lac

Iran
100 dinars = 1 rial ... $0.0132 *
100 rials = 1 pahlavi

Iraq
1000 fils = 1 Iraqi dinar (I.D.) ... $2.80 *

Ireland, Republic of
Same system as Great Britain.

Israel
1000 prutoth = 1 Israeli pound (£I) ... $0.5556 *

Italy
100 centesimi = 1 lira (l.) ... $0.0016

Japan
10 rin = 1 sen
100 sen = 1 yen (¥) ... $0.0028 *

Lebanon
100 piasters = 1 Lebanese pound (£Leb.) ... $0.4563 *

Luxembourg: Same system as Belgium.

Mexico
100 centavos = 1 peso (p., $) ... $0.0800 *

Netherlands
100 cents = 1 gulden or guilder (gld.) ... $0.2632 *

New Zealand
Same system as Great Britain.

Nicaragua
100 centavos = 1 cordoba (C$) ... $0.1429 *

Norway
100 öre = 1 krone (k.) ... $0.1400 *

Pakistan
16 annas = 1 rupee ... $0.2100 *
(Same system of coinage as in India.)

Panama
100 centesimos = 1 balboa (b.) ... $1.00 *

Paraguay
100 centimos = 1 guarani ... $0.0167 *

Peru
100 centavos = 1 sol (s/.)

Philippines
100 centavos = 1 peso (₱) ... $0.500 *

Poland
100 groszy = 1 zloty (zl.) ... $0.25

Portugal
100 centavos = 1 escudo ... $0.03478
1000 escudos = 1 conto

Romania
100 bani = 1 leu (l.) ... $0.1667

Spain
100 centimos = 1 peseta (p., pta.) ... $0.0913

Sweden
100 öre = 1 krona (k.) ... $0.1933 *

Switzerland
100 centimes = 1 franc (fr.) ... $0.234

Syria
100 piasters = 1 Syrian pound (£Syr.) ... $0.4563 *

Thailand
100 satang = 1 baht (or tical) ... $0.0800

Turkey
40 paras = 1 kuruş (Krş) or piaster (Pi., pias.)
100 kuruş = 1 Turkish pound (£T), or lira ... $0.3571 *

Union of South Africa
Same system as Great Britain.

Union of Soviet Socialist Republics
100 kopecks (kop.) = 1 ruble (rub.) ... $0.25
10 rubles = 1 chervonets (ch.)

Uruguay
100 centesimos = 1 peso (p., $) ... $0.6583

Venezuela
100 centimos = 1 bolivar (b.) ... $0.2985 *

Yugoslavia
100 paras = 1 dinar (d., din.) ... $0.0333 *

Mon'gol·ism (mŏng'gŏl-ĭz'm), n. Med. A congenital malformation, in which the child has slanting eyes, a large tongue, and a broad, short skull. Such children are often imbeciles.

Mon'gol·oid (-oid), adj. Resembling a Mongol or the Mongols; specif., designating or pertaining to, the peoples of the Himalaya regions and the peninsula of Indochina in which Mongolian traits appear in a modified or inconstant form. — **Mon'gol·oid**, n.

mon'goose (mŏng'gōōs), n.; pl. MONGOOSES (-ĕz; -ĭz). [Marathi muṅgūs.] A viverrine mammal of India (Herpestes nyula) about the size of a ferret. It fearlessly attacks and kills the most poisonous snakes. See ICHNEUMON, 1.

mon'grel (mŭng'grĕl; mŏng'-), n. 1. The progeny resulting from the crossing, originally of two, now of several, breeds, as of dogs; anything of mixed breed; — often disparaging. 2. A cross between types of persons or things. — adj. 1. Of or pertaining to an impure or mixed breed or race. 2. Of mixed origin or character; of no definite type.

'mongst (mŭngst), prep. Aphetic form of AMONGST.

mon'i·ker, mon'ick·er (mŏn'ĭ-kẽr), n. a A tramp's identifying sign or mark. b Slang. A name; a nickname.

mo·nil'i·form (mō-nĭl'ĭ-fôrm), adj. [L. monile necklace + -form.] Bot. & Zool. Jointed or constricted at regular intervals, so as to resemble a string of beads.

mon'ish (mŏn'ĭsh), v. t. Archaic. To admonish.

mon'ism (mŏn'ĭz'm; mō'nĭz'm), n. [NL. monismus, fr. Gr. monos single.] Philos. a The doctrine that there is only one kind of substance or ultimate reality, as mind or matter. b The doctrine that reality is one unitary, organic whole, with no independent parts. Cf. DUALISM, PLURALISM. — **mon'ist** (mŏn'ĭst; mō'nĭst), n. — **mo·nis'tic** (mō-nĭs'tĭk), **mo·nis'ti·cal** (-tĭ-kǎl), adj.

mo·ni'tion (mō-nĭsh'ŭn), n. [OF., fr. L. monitio, fr. monere to warn, bring to mind.] 1. An admonition; warning; caution. 2. An intimation or notice, as of something impending. 3. Law. A summons or citation to appear and answer, or to appear and answer in default of performing some certain act.

mon'i·tor (mŏn'ĭ·tẽr), *n.* [L., fr. *monere* to warn.] **1.** One who admonishes, esp. in reproof or caution. **2.** A pupil or student selected for special duties, often disciplinary. **3.** A warning; a reminder. **4.** Any of certain large pleurodont lizards constituting a genus (*Varanus*) and a family (Varanidae) of Africa, southern Asia, and Australia. **5.** [So called from the name given by Captain Ericsson, its designer, to the first ship of the kind.] A heavily armored war vessel, with low freeboard, having one or more revolving turrets, carrying heavy guns. **6.** One who monitors or an instrument used for monitoring. — *v. i. & t.* **1.** To check by means of a receiver (the operation of a telegraph, telephone, radio, television, or similar transmitter) to ascertain the quality of transmission, fidelity to a frequency band, etc., or (the matter transmitted by telephone, radio, television, etc.), as for military or political significance. **2.** *Physics.* To test (a surface, beam, etc.) for intensity of radiations, especially those due to radioactivity, to determine whether the intensity comes within specified limits. — **mon'i·to'ri·al** (-tō'rĭ·ăl; 70), *adj.* — **mon'i·tor·ship'**, **mon'i·tress**, *n.*

mon'i·to'ry (mŏn'ĭ·tō'rĭ *or, esp. Brit.*, -tẽr·ĭ), *adj.* [L. *monitorius.*] Admonishing; warning. — *n.* Also **monitory letter.** A papal letter containing an admonition.

monk (mŭngk), *n.* [AS. *munuc*, fr. VL. *monicus*, fr. LL. *monachus*, fr. Gr. *monachos*, fr. *monos* alone.] Orig., a man who retired from the world and devoted himself to asceticism as a solitary or cenobite; now, specif., a member of a religious order, as the Benedictines or Cistercians, devoted primarily to contemplation and solemn liturgical observances. Monks are cloistered and carry on all their activities within the limits of a monastic establishment. — **Syn.** See RELIGIOUS.

monk'er·y (mŭngk'ẽr·ĭ), *n.; pl.* -ERIES (-ĭz). **1.** Monastic state, life, or profession; *pl.*, monastic usages, practices, etc.; — often disparaging. **2.** A community of monks.

mon'key (mŭng'kĭ), *n.; pl.* -KEYS (-kĭz). [Prob. fr. MLG. *moneke*, a word of Romanic origin, and ult. fr. Turk.] **1.** a Broadly, any member of the highest order of mammals (*Primates*) except man, and, usually, the lemurs. b Narrowly, one of the smaller, longer-tailed forms as contrasted with the *apes*. **2.** The fur or skin of certain long-haired monkeys, used esp. as trimming. **3.** A person likened to a monkey; esp., a mischievous child. **4.** Any of various machines, implements, vessels, etc., as a falling weight of a pile driver. — *v. i.;* MON'KEYED (-kĭd); MON'KEY·ING. To act as a monkey acts; to meddle; trifle; fool. — *v. t.* To treat as a monkey does; to ape; mimic. — **mon'key·ish,** *adj.*

monkey bread. The fruit of the baobab; also, the tree.

monkey flower. Any of a genus (*Mimulus*) of plants of the figwort family, with a gaping or ringed corolla; esp., the ***scarlet monkey flower*** (*M. cardinalis*).

monkey jacket. A short tight jacket, worn by sailors, etc.

mon'key·nut' (mŭng'kĭ·nŭt'), *n.* The peanut.

mon'key·pot' (mŭng'kĭ·pŏt'), *n.* a The urn-shaped fruit of various trees (genus *Lecythis*, family Lecythidaceae) of Brazil. It is a large woody capsule with numerous nuts. b The tree bearing this fruit.

mon'key·shine' (mŭng'kĭ·shīn'), *n.* *Slang, U. S.* A monkeyish trick, antic, or prank.

monkey wrench. A wrench having a straight handle, one fixed jaw at right angles to the handle, and one adjustable jaw. See WRENCH, *Illust.*

Mon'–Khmer' (mōn'k'mĕr'), *adj.* Designating a division of primitive monosyllabic languages of southeastern Asia.

monk'hood (mŭngk'hŏŏd), *n.* **1.** The condition or profession of a monk. **2.** Monks collectively.

monk'ish (mŭngk'ĭsh), *adj.* **1.** Of or pert. to monks; monastic. **2.** Characteristic of monks or monasticism; — often derogatory; as, *monkish* manners. — **monk'ish·ly,** *adv.* — **monk'ish·ness,** *n.*

monk's cloth (mŭngks). A coarse, heavy fabric in basket weave, orig. of worsted and used for monks' habits, but now chiefly of cotton or linen and used for draperies, etc.

monks'hood' (mŭngks'hŏŏd'), *n.* Any of a genus (*Aconitum*, esp. *A. napellus*) of plants of the crowfoot family; — so called from the shape of the flower.

mon'o- (mŏn'ō-), **mon-.** [Gr. *monos.*] **1.** A combining form meaning *one; single; alone;* as in *mono*plane, *mono*gamy, *mono*graph. **2.** (*pron.* mŏn'ō-; mō'nō-). *Chem.* Indicating that a compound contains *one atom* or *group* of that to the name of which it is united, as in *mon*oxide, an oxide containing one oxygen atom in the molecule. **3.** *Physical Chem.* Short for MONOMOLECULAR as in **mon'o·film',** **mon'o·lay'er.**

mon'o·ac'id (mŏn'ō·ăs'ĭd; mō'nō-), *adj.* Also **mon'o·a·cid'ic** (-ă·sĭd'ĭk). *Chem.* a Capable of reacting with but one equivalent of an acid to form a salt or ester; characterized by one hydroxyl group; — said of bases and alcohols. b Having but one acid hydrogen atom in the molecule. — *n.* *Chem.* An acid having but one replaceable hydrogen atom.

mon'o·bas'ic (-bās'ĭk), *adj.* **1.** *Chem.* a Having but one hydrogen atom replaceable by a metal or basic radical; — said of acids. b Having but one basic hydroxyl group. c Containing a metal or basic radical replacing one acid hydrogen atom. **2.** *Biol.* Based upon a single species; — said of genera.

mon'o·car'pel·lar'y (mŏn'ō·kär'pĕ·lĕr'ĭ *or, esp. Brit.*, -lẽr·ĭ), *adj.* *Bot.* Consisting of a single carpel, as a legume.

mon'o·car'pic (-kär'pĭk), *adj.* [*mono-* + Gr. *karpos* fruit.] *Bot.* Bearing fruit but once, and dying, as all annuals and biennials and certain other plants, as the century plant. Such plants are called **mon'o·carps** (mŏn'ō·kärps).

mon'o·car'pous (-kär'pŭs), *adj.* *Bot.* Having a gynoecium forming a single ovary.

mon'o·cha'si·um (-kā'zhĭ·ŭm; -zĭ·ŭm), *n.; pl.* -SIA (-ȧ). [NL., fr. *mono-* + Gr. *chasis* division.] *Bot.* A cymose inflorescence which produces only one main axis. Cf. DICHASIUM, POLYCHASIUM. — **mon'o·cha'si·al** (-ăl), *adj.*

mon'o·chlo'ride (mŏn'ō·klō'rīd; -rĭd; mō'nō-), *n.* *Chem.* A chloride containing one chlorine atom in the molecule.

mon'o·chord (mŏn'ō·kôrd), *n.* [From LL., fr. Gr. deriv. of *monos* only, single + *chordē* string.] **1.** *Music & Acous.* A one-stringed instrument for measuring the mathematical relations of musical sounds. The string is stretched over a sounding board and a movable bridge set on a graduated scale so that the string can be divided into separate vibrating parts which can be measured. **2.** *Rare.* Concord; agreement.

mon'o·chro'ic (-krō'ĭk), *adj.* [Gr. *monochroos*, fr. *monos* single + *chrōs, chroos*, color.] Monochromatic.

mon'o·chro·mat'ic (-krō·măt'ĭk), *adj.* Having, or consisting of, one color or hue. — **mon'o·chro·mat'i·cal·ly** (-ĭ·kăl·ĭ), *adv.*

mon'o·chrome (mŏn'ō·krōm), *n.* [Gr. *monochrōmos* of one color, fr. *monos* single + *chrōma* color.] A painting or drawing in a single hue; also, the art or process of producing such a picture. — **mon'o·chro'mic** (-krō'mĭk), **mon'o·chro'mi·cal** (-mĭ·kăl), *adj.* — **mon'o·chrom'ist** (mŏn'ō·krōm'ĭst), *n.*

mon'o·cle (mŏn'ō·k'l), *n.* [F., fr. L. *monoculus.*] An eyeglass for one eye. — **mon'o·cled** (-k'ld), *adj.*

mon'o·cli'nal (-klī'năl; -n'l), *adj.* *Geol.* Having, or pert. to, a single oblique inclination. — *n.* *Geol.* A monocline.

mon'o·cline (mŏn'ō·klīn), *n.* *Geol.* A monoclinal fold.

mon'o·clin'ic (-klĭn'ĭk), *adj.* [*mono-* + Gr. *klinein* to incline.] *Cryst.* Having one oblique intersection of the axes.

mon'o·cli'nous (mŏn'ō·klī'nŭs; mŏn'ō·klī'nŭs), *adj.* [*mono-* + Gr. *klinē* couch.] *Bot.* Having both androecium and gynoecium in the same flower. Cf. DICLINOUS.

mon'o·cot (mŏn'ō·kŏt), **mon'o·cot'yl** (-kŏt'ĭl), *n.* *Bot.* A monocotyledon.

mon'o·cot'y·le'don (mŏn'ō·kŏt'ĭ·lē'dŭn), *n.* *Bot.* Any seed plant having a single cotyledon; a member of one (Monocotyledones) of the two subclasses of angiospermous plants (Angiospermae), co-ordinate with the dicotyledons, and including all that produce a single cotyledon. The grasses, lilies, orchids, palms, etc., are monocotyledons. — **mon'o·cot'y·le'don·ous** (-lē'dŭn·ŭs; -lĕd'ŭn·ŭs), *adj.*

mo·noc'ra·cy (mō·nŏk'rȧ·sĭ), *n.* [*mono-* + *-cracy.*] Government by one autocrat, or **mon'o·crat** (mŏn'ō·krăt).

mo·noc'u·lar (mō·nŏk'ū·lẽr; mŏn·ŏk'-), *adj.* [L. *monoculus*, fr. Gr. *monos* single + L. *oculus* eye.] a Having only one eye. b Pertaining, or adapted, to the use of only one eye.

mon'o·cul'ture (mŏn'ō·kŭl'tūr), *n.* *Agric.* Cultivation of a single product, as wheat or wool, to the exclusion of other possible uses of the land.

mon'o·cy'cle (-sī'k'l), *n.* A one-wheeled vehicle propelled by its rider.

mon'o·cy'clic (mŏn'ō·sī'klĭk; -sĭk'lĭk), *adj.* Having a single cycle; specif.: a *Bot. & Zool.* Arranged in or consisting of one whorl or cycle. b (*pron.* mŏn'ō-; mō'nō-). *Chem.* Containing one ring.

mon'o·dac'ty·lous (mŏn'ō·dăk'tĭ·lŭs), *adj.* [Gr. *monodaktylos*, fr. *monos* single + *daktylos* finger.] Having but one digit or claw.

mo·nod'ic (mō·nŏd'ĭk), *adj.* Also **mo·nod'i·cal** (-ĭ·kăl). [Gr. *monōidikos.*] Of, pert. to, or of the nature of monody.

mon'o·dra'ma (mŏn'ō·drä'mȧ; -drăm'ȧ), *n.* [*mono-* + Gr. *drama* drama.] A drama acted, or designed to be acted, by one person.

mon'o·dy (mŏn'ō·dĭ), *n.; pl.* -DIES (-dĭz). [LL. *monodia*, fr. Gr. *monōidia*, fr. *monōidos* singing alone, fr. *monos* single + *ōidē* song.] **1.** *Gr. Lit.* An ode sung by one voice, as in a tragedy; a funeral song; a dirge. **2.** A species of poem in which a single mourner laments. **3.** *Music.* a The style of composition in which but one voice part carries a melody; homophony, as opposed to *polyphony.* b A monodic composition. — **mon'o·dist** (-dĭst), *n.*

mo·noe'cious (mō·nē'shŭs), *adj.* [*mon-* + Gr. *oikos* house.] *Biol.* Having both male and female reproductive organs in the same individual; specif., *Bot.*, having staminate and pistillate flowers on the same plant, as in the hazel, oak, walnut, etc.

mon'o·gam'ic (mŏn'ō·găm'ĭk), *adj.* Monogamous.

mo·nog'a·mist (mō·nŏg'ȧ·mĭst), *n.* One who practices or upholds monogamy. — **mo·nog'a·mist,** *adj.*

mo·nog'a·mous (-mŭs), *adj.* [LL. *monogamus*, fr. Gr. *monogamos*, fr. *monos* single + *gamos* marriage.] Of or pert. to monogamy; upholding or practicing monogamy.

mo·nog'a·my (-mĭ), *n.* Single marriage; specif.: a One marriage only during life. Cf. DEUTEROGAMY, DIGAMY. b Marriage with but one person at a time; — opposed to *bigamy* and *polygamy.*

mon'o·gen'e·sis (mŏn'ō·jĕn'ē·sĭs), *n.* [NL., fr. *mono-* + *-genesis.*] **1.** Oneness of origin; specif.: *Biol.* a The theory of the development of all living things from a single cell; — opposed to *polygenesis.* b Monogenism. **2.** *Biol.* a Asexual reproduction. b Direct development without metamorphosis.

mon'o·ge·net'ic (-jē·nĕt'ĭk), *adj.* **1.** *Biol.* Relating to, or involving monogenesis. **2.** *Geol.* Resulting from one process of formation; — used of a mountain range.

mon'o·gen'ic (-jĕn'ĭk), *adj.* **1.** Having a single or a common origin; specif., *Biol.*, monogenetic. **2.** *Zool.* Reproducing in one way only.

mo·nog'e·nism (mō·nŏj'ē·nĭz'm), *n.* The theory or doctrine that all human races have descended from a single created pair, or from a common ancestral type. — **mo·nog'e·nist** (-nĭst), *n.*

mo·nog'e·ny (-nĭ), *n.* **1.** *Biol.* Monogenesis (sense 2 a). **2.** Monogenism.

mon'o·gram (mŏn'ō·grăm), *n.* [L. *monogramma*, fr. Gr. *monos* single + *gramma* letter.] A character or cipher composed of two or more letters interwoven or combined, commonly so as to represent a name. — **mon'o·gram·mat'ic** (-grȧ·măt'ĭk), *adj.*

mon'o·graph (-grȧf; 9), *n.* A written account of a single thing, or class; a special treatise on a particular subject. — **mon'o·graph,** *v. t.* — **mo·nog'ra·pher** (mō·nŏg'rȧ·fẽr), *n.* — **mon'o·graph'ic** (mŏn'ō·grăf'ĭk), *adj.*

mo·nog'y·ny (mō·nŏj'ĭ·nĭ), *n.* [*mono-* + Gr. *gynē* woman, female.] State or custom of having only one wife at a time. Cf. POLYGYNY.

mon'o·hy'drate (mŏn'ō·hī'drāt; mō'nō-), *n.* *Chem.* A hydrate containing one molecule of water.

mon'o·hy'dric (-drĭk), *adj.* *Chem.* a Containing one hydroxyl group. b Having one replaceable hydrogen atom.

mo·noi'cous (mō·noi'kŭs), *adj.* *Bot.* Monoecious.

mo·nol'a·try (mō·nŏl'ȧ·trĭ), *n.* [*mono-* + Gr. *latreia* worship.] Worship of but one god, although more than one may be recognized as existing. — **mo·nol'a·ter** (-tẽr), **mo·nol'a·trist** (-trĭst), *n.*

mon'o·lith (mŏn'ō·lĭth), *n.* [F. *monolithe*, fr. L. *monolithus*, fr. Gr. *monolithos*, fr. *monos* single + *lithos* stone.] A single stone or block of stone, esp. one of large size, shaped into a pillar, statue, or monument.

mon'o·lith'ic (-lĭth'ĭk), *adj.* **1.** Consisting of, pertaining to, or of the nature of a monolith. **2.** Constituting one massive undifferentiated whole, exhibiting solid uniformity and one harmonious pattern whole; as, a *monolithic* party or culture.

mon'o·logue (mŏn'ō·lŏg; 74), *n.* Also **mon'o·log.** [F. *monologue*, fr. Gr. *monologos* speaking alone, fr. *monos* alone, single + *logos* discourse.] **1.** Literary composition, or a poem, of the nature of, or in the form of, a soliloquy. **2.** A long speech uttered by one person; soliloquy. — **mon′o·log′ic** (mŏn′ō·lŏj′ĭk), **mon′o·log′i·cal** (-ĭ·kăl), *adj.* — **mo·nol′o·gist** (mō·nŏl′ō·jĭst; mŏn′ō·lŏg′ĭst), **mon′o·logu′ist** (mŏn′ō·lŏg′ĭst; 74), *n.*

mon′o·ma′ni·a (mŏn′ō·mā′nĭ·ȧ), *n.* [NL., fr. *mono-* + *mania.*] Mental derangement (orig., insanity) restricted to one idea or group of ideas. — **mon′o·ma′ni·ac** (-ăk), *n.* — **mon′o·ma·ni′a·cal** (-mȧ·nī′ȧ·kăl), *adj.*

mon′o·mer (mŏn′ō·mẽr; mō′nō-), *n.* [*mono-* + Gr. *meros* part.] *Chem.* The simple unpolymerized form of a compound, as distinguished from *polymer.* — **mon′o·mer′ic** (mŏn′ō·mĕr′ĭk), *adj.*

mo·nom′er·ous (mō·nŏm′ẽr·ŭs), *adj.* [Gr. *monomerēs* single, fr. *monos* alone + *meros* part.] *Bot.* Having a single member in each whorl; — applied to flowers, and often written *1-merous.*

mon′o·me·tal′lic (mŏn′ō·mē·tăl′ĭk), *adj.* Consisting of, or employing, one metal; of or pertaining to monometallism.

mon′o·met′al·lism (-mĕt′ăl·ĭz′m), *n.* The legalized use of one metal only, as gold or silver, in the standard currency of a country, or as the standard of money values; also, the theory or practice favoring such a standard. Cf. BIMETALLISM.

mo·no′mi·al (mō·nō′mĭ·ăl), *adj.* [*mono-* + *-nomial* as in bi*nomial.*] **1.** *Alg.* Consisting of but a single term. **2.** *Biol.* Consisting of a single word or term. — *n.* A monomial name or expression.

mon′o·mo·lec′u·lar (mŏn′ō·mō·lĕk′ū·lẽr; mō′nō-), *adj.* Designating or consisting of a layer one molecule in thickness.

mon′o·mor′phic (mŏn′ō·môr′fĭk), **mon′o·mor′phous** (-fŭs), *adj.* [*mono-* + *-morphic, -morphous.*] *Biol.* Having but a single form; exhibiting the same or an essentially similar type of structure. Cf. DIMORPHIC, HETEROMORPHIC, POLYMORPHIC.

mon′o·pet′al·ous (-pĕt′ăl·ŭs), *adj.* [*mono-* + *petalous.*] *Bot.* **a** Gamopetalous. **b** Having a solitary petal.

mon′o·pho′bi·a (mŏn′ō·fō′bĭ·ȧ), *n.* [NL. See MONO-; -PHOBIA.] *Med.* Morbid dread of being alone.

mon′o·phon′ic (-fŏn′ĭk), *adj.* *Music.* = MONODIC.

mon′oph·thong (mŏn′ŏf·thŏng; 74), *n.* [Gr. *monophthongos* with one sound, fr. *monos* alone + *phthongos* sound, voice.] *Phonet.* A single, simple vowel sound, formed with the superglottal speech organs in a fixed position. — **mon′oph·thon′gal** (-thŏng′găl), *adj.*

mon′o·phy·let′ic (mŏn′ō·fī·lĕt′ĭk), *adj.* [See MONO-; PHYLETIC.] Of or pertaining to a single stock; developed from a single common parent form. Cf. POLYPHYLETIC.

mon′o·phyl′lous (-fĭl′ŭs), *adj.* [Gr. *monophyllos,* fr. *monos* alone + *phyllon* leaf.] *Bot.* Composed of a single leaf; as, a *monophyllous* calyx.

Mo·noph′y·site (mō·nŏf′ĭ·sīt), *n.* [Gr. *monophysitēs,* fr. *monos* single + *physis* nature.] *Eccl.* One of those who maintain that there was but a single nature in Christ or that the human and divine in Jesus Christ constituted but one composite nature. — **Mon′o·phy·sit′ic** (mŏn′ō·fĭ·sĭt′ĭk), *adj.*

mon′o·plane (mŏn′ō·plān), *n.* An airplane with only one main supporting surface. — **mon′o·plan′ist** (-plān′ĭst), *n.*

mon′o·ple′gi·a (-plē′jĭ·ȧ), *n.* [NL., fr. *mono-* + Gr. *plēgē* a stroke.] *Med.* Paralysis affecting a single limb or part of the body. — **mon′o·pleg′ic** (-plĕj′ĭk; -plē′jĭk), *adj.*

mon′o·pode (mŏn′ō·pōd), *n.* [L. *monopodius.*] **1.** A one-footed creature. **2.** *Bot.* A monopodium.

mon′o·po′di·um (-pō′dĭ·ŭm), *n.; pl.* -DIA (-ȧ). [NL. See MONO-; -PODIUM.] *Bot.* A main axis that continues its original line of growth, giving off axes or lateral branches, as in the excurrent trunks of certain coniferous trees. Cf. SYMPODIUM. — **mon′o·po′di·al** (-ăl), *adj.*

mo·nop′o·lize (mō·nŏp′ō·līz), *v. t.* To acquire a monopoly of. — **mo·nop′o·li·za′tion** (-lĭ·zā′shŭn; -lī·zā′-), *n.* — **mo·nop′o·liz′er** (-līz′ẽr), *n.*

mo·nop′o·ly (-lĭ), *n.; pl.* -LIES (-lĭz). [L. *monopolium,* fr. Gr. *monopōlia, monopōlion,* fr. *monos* alone + *pōlein* to sell.] **1.** Exclusive control of the supply of any commodity or service in a given market; hence, in popular use, any such control in a given market as enables the one having this control to raise the price of a commodity or service materially above the price fixed by free competition. **2.** A grant or charter of a monopoly (sense 1). **3.** Exclusive possession of anything, as of learning. **4.** The commodity to which the monopoly relates. **5.** A company or combination having a monopoly. — **mo·nop′o·lism** (-lĭz′m), *n.* — **mo·nop′o·list** (-lĭst), *n.* & *adj.* — **mo·nop′o·lis′tic** (-lĭs′tĭk), *adj.*

Syn. **Monopoly, corner, pool, syndicate, trust, cartel,** though not strictly synonyms, are often confused. **Monopoly** implies exclusive control, as of a public service, or, now esp., of exclusive power to buy or sell a commodity or the like in a given market; **corner,** a temporary monopoly of something sold on stock or produce exchanges, thereby compelling the buyer to pay the price asked; **pool,** a joint undertaking, esp. by competing companies, to manipulate prices, to regulate output, etc.; **syndicate,** orig. an organization of financiers to profit by a monopoly, but now more often of corporations, etc., to carry on a temporary enterprise such as marketing an issue of bonds; **trust,** a merger of corporations by which control is given to trustees and the individual owners are compensated by shares of stock; **cartel** commonly implies an international combination (in Europe, often a local state-fostered combination) of firms for controlling production and sale of their products.

mon′o·rail′ (mŏn′ō·rāl′), *n.* A single rail serving as a track for a wheeled carriage, truck, etc.

mon′o·sac′cha·ride (mŏn′ō·săk′ȧ·rīd; -rĭd; mō′nō-), *n.* [*mono-* + *saccharide.*] *Chem.* A simple sugar, not decomposable by hydrolysis.

mon′o·sep′al·ous (mŏn′ō·sĕp′ăl·ŭs), *adj.* [*mono-* + *-sepalous.*] *Bot.* **a** Gamosepalous. **b** Having a single sepal.

mon′o·sper′mous (-spûr′mŭs), *adj.* Also **mon′o·sper′mal** (-măl), *adj.* [*mono-* + Gr. *sperma* seed.] *Bot.* Having only one seed.

mon′o·stich (mŏn′ō·stĭk), *n.* [Gr. *monostichon,* deriv. of *monos* single + *stichos* line, verse.] *Pros.* A single verse, or a poem of one verse.

mo·nos′to·mous (mō·nŏs′tō·mŭs), **mon′o·stome** (mŏn′ō·stōm), *adj.* [*mono-* + *-stomous.*] Having one mouth or sucker.

mo·nos′tro·phe (mō·nŏs′trō·fē; mŏn′ō·strōf), *n.* [NL., fr. Gr. *monostrophos,* fr. *monos* single + *strophē* strophe.] *Pros.* A poem in which all the strophes or stanzas are of the same metric form. — **mon′o·stroph′ic** (mŏn′ō·strŏf′ĭk), *adj.*

mon′o·sty′lous (mŏn′ō·stī′lŭs), *adj.* *Bot.* Having a single style.

mon′o·syl′la·bize (-sĭl′ȧ·bīz), *v. t.* & *i.* To make, or be, monosyllabic. — **mon′o·syl′la·bism** (-bĭz′m), *n.*

mon′o·syl′la·ble (mŏn′ō·sĭl′ȧ·b′l), *n.* [L. *monosyllabus* of one syllable, fr. Gr. *monosyllabos.*] A word of one syllable. — **mon′o·syl·lab′ic** (-sĭ·lăb′ĭk), *adj.* — **mon′o·syl·lab′i·cal·ly** (-ĭ·kăl·ĭ), *adv.*

mon′o·sym·met′ric (mŏn′ō·sĭ·mĕt′rĭk), **mon′o·sym·met′ri·cal** (-rĭ·kăl), *adj.* **1.** *Cryst.* Monoclinic. **2.** *Biol.* Bilaterally symmetrical; specif., *Bot.,* see SYMMETRICAL, 2 **a.**

mon′o·the·ism (mŏn′ō·thē·ĭz′m), *n.* [*mono-* + Gr. *theos* god.] The doctrine or belief that there is but one God. Cf. POLYTHEISM, THEISM. — **mon′o·the·ist** (-ĭst), *n.* & *adj.* — **mon′o·the·is′tic** (-ĭs′tĭk), **mon′o·the·is′ti·cal** (-tĭ·kăl), *adj.* — **mon′o·the·is′ti·cal·ly,** *adv.*

mon′o·tint (mŏn′ō·tĭnt), *n.* Monochrome.

mon′o·tone (mŏn′ō·tōn), *n.* [See MONOTONOUS.] **1.** Succession of syllables, words, or sentences on one unvaried key or pitch. **2.** Monotony or sameness of tone or style. **3.** *Music.* **a** A single unvaried tone. **b** Recitation in such a tone, esp. of liturgy; intoning.

mo·not′o·nous (mō·nŏt′ō·nŭs), *adj.* [Gr. *monotonos,* fr. *monos* single + *tonos* tone.] **1.** Uttered in one unvarying tone. **2.** Without change or variety; wearisomely uniform. — **mo·not′o·nous·ly,** *adv.* — **mo·not′o·nous·ness,** *n.*

mo·not′o·ny (-nĭ), *n.* **1.** Sameness of tone or sound; use or continuity of one unvarying tone or sound. **2.** Sameness or want of variety, esp. wearisome sameness.

mon′o·trem′a·tous (mŏn′ō·trĕm′ȧ·tŭs; -trē′mȧ·tŭs), *adj.* [*mono-* + Gr. *trēma* hole.] *Zool.* Of the lowest order (Monotremata) of mammals, consisting of the duckbills and the echidnas.

mon′o·treme (mŏn′ō·trēm), *n.* A monotrematous animal.

mo·not′ri·chous (mō·nŏt′rĭ·kŭs), *adj.* Also **mon′o·trich′ic** (mŏn′ō·trĭk′ĭk). [*mono-* + Gr. *thrix, trichos,* hair.] *Biol.* Having a single flagellum at one pole, as certain bacteria.

mon′o·type (mŏn′ō·tīp), *n.* [*mono-* + *-type.*] *Biol.* The only representative of its group, as a single species constituting a genus.

Mon′o·type, *n.* A trade-mark for either of two machines for setting type, one a keyboard machine, the other a casting machine.

mon′o·typ′ic (-tĭp′ĭk), *adj.* *Biol.* **1.** Having a single type or representative, as a genus with only one species; — opp. to *polytypic.* **2.** Of the nature of a monotype.

mon′o·va′lent (mŏn′ō·vā′lĕnt; mō·nŏv′ȧ·lĕnt; 2), *adj.* [*mono-* + L. *valens,* pres. part. See VALENCE.] **a** *Bacteriol.* Containing antibodies specific for, or antigens of, one strain of a given species. **b** *Chem.* Univalent. — **mon′o·va′lence** (-lĕns), **mon′o·va′len·cy** (mŏn′ō·vā′lĕn·sĭ), *n.*

mon·ox′ide (mŏn·ŏk′sīd; mō·nŏk′-; -sĭd), *n.* *Chem.* An oxide containing but one oxygen atom in the molecule.

Mon·roe′ Doc′trine (mŭn·rō′). *U. S. Hist.* The unilateral statement, now generally accepted, made by President Monroe (Dec. 2, 1823), that the United States will regard as an unfriendly act any attempt on the part of European powers to extend their systems or their control in the Western Hemisphere.

‖**mons** (mŏnz), *n.* [L. See MOUNT.] Mountain; eminence. The **mons pu′bis** (pū′bĭs) is the rounded eminence at the lower point of the abdomen (at the pubic symphysis); in the female it is often called the **mons Ve′ne·ris** (vĕn′ĕ·rĭs).

mon′sei·gneur′ (mŏn′sā·nyûr′; *F.* môɴ′sĕ′nyûr′), *n.; pl.* MESSEIGNEURS (mĕs′ā·nyûrz′; *F.* mā′sĕ′nyûr′). [F., fr. *mon* my + *seigneur* lord, fr. L. *senior* older.] My lord; — a title [*cap.*] given in France esp. to princes and church and court dignitaries, and used before titles of office or rank; as, *Monseigneur* the Archbishop. Abbr. *Mgr.*

mon·sieur′ (mē·syû′), *n.; pl.* MESSIEURS (mā′syû′). [F., fr. *mon* my + *sieur,* abbr. of *seigneur* lord.] **1.** Literally, my lord; sir; — title [*cap.*] of civility in France corresponding to the English *Mr.* Abbr. *M.;* pl. *MM.* or *Messrs.* **2.** [*cap.*] *Hist.* The oldest brother of the King of France; — a title.

mon·si′gnor (mŏn·sē′nyôr; *It.* môn′sē·nyôr′), ‖**mon′si·gno′re** (môn′sē·nyō′rā), *n.; pl.* MONSIGNORI (môn′sē·nyō′rē). [It., my lord.] [*usually cap.*] A title of honor borne by some prelates. Abbrs. *Mgr., Msgr.*

mon·soon′ (mŏn·sōōn′), *n.* [Obs. D. *monssoen,* fr. Pg. *monção,* fr. Ar. *mausim* a time, a season.] A periodic wind, esp. in the Indian Ocean and southern Asia. Also, the rainy season of the southwest monsoon in India.

mon′ster (mŏn′stẽr), *n.* [OF. *monstre,* fr. L. *monstrum,* orig., a divine omen, indicating misfortune.] **1.** An animal or plant departing greatly in form or structure from the usual type of the species; a monstrosity. **2.** A fabulous or actually existing animal of strange, grotesque, or horrible form. **3.** Any enormous animal or thing. **4.** Anything monstrous, esp. a person of unnatural ugliness, cruelty, etc. — *adj.* Enormous in size, extent, or numbers.

mon′strance (mŏn′străns), *n.* [OF., fr. ML. *monstrantia,* fr. L. *monstrare* to show.] *R.C.Ch.* A vessel in which the consecrated Host is exposed to receive the veneration of the faithful.

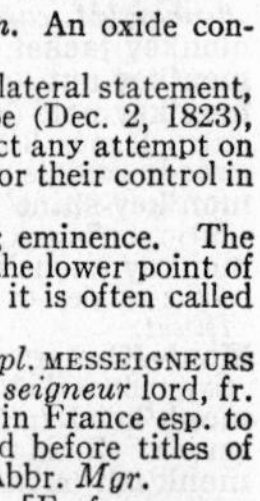
Monstrance.

mon·stros′i·ty (mŏn·strŏs′ĭ·tĭ), *n.; pl.* -TIES (-tĭz). [L. *monstrositas.*] Quality or state of being monstrous; also, a monster.

mon′strous (mŏn′strŭs), *adj.* [OF. *monstreux,* fr. L. *monstrosus,* fr. *monstrum.* See MONSTER.] **1.** Extraordinary in a way to excite wonder; esp., huge. **2.** Having the qualities or appearance of a monster. **3.** Deviating greatly from the natural form or character; malformed. **4.** Shockingly wrong or ridiculous. — **mon′strous·ly,** *adv.* — **mon′strous·ness,** *n.*

Syn. (1) **Monstrous, prodigious, tremendous, stupendous** mean astonishingly impressive, esp. in size. **Monstrous** further implies ugliness, fabulousness, or the like; **prodigious,** a marvelousness exceeding belief; **tremendous,** in strict use, a power to terrify or inspire awe; **stupendous,** a power to stun or astound.
(2) See OUTRAGEOUS.

mon·tage′ (mŏn·täzh′; mŏn-; *F.* môɴ′täzh′), *n.* [F., mounting, assembling, fr. *monter.* See MOUNT, *v.*] **1. a** The act or process of producing a composite picture by combining several distinct pictures, often so that they blend with or into each other. **b** Such a composite picture. **2.** Any literary, musical, or artistic composite combining and blending more or less heterogeneous elements usually superimposed or overlapping each other, as in radio often a quick succession of snatches of dialogue, music, and sound effects. **3.** *Motion Pictures.* **a** The production of a rapid succession of images to illustrate an association of ideas. **b** The process of producing several images that revolve around each other or that rush one after the other to a sharp focus in the foreground, as newspaper headlines. **c** A portion of a motion picture using montage. — *v. t.* To combine into or depict in a montage.

Mon′ta·gue (mŏn′tȧ·gū), *n.* See ROMEO.

mon′tane (mŏn′tān), *adj.* [L. *montanus.*] Pertaining to or living in mountains; — said esp. of flora and fauna.

‖**mon·ta′ni sem′per li′be·ri** (mŏn·tā′nī sĕm′pĕr lĭb′ĕ·rī). [L.] Mountaineers (are) always free men; — motto of West Virginia.

mon′tan wax (mŏn′tăn). [L. *montanus* of a mountain, fr. *mons, montis,* mountain.] A wax of varying composition obtained by extraction of certain lignites, peat, etc. It is used in making candles and phonograph records.

‖**mont′-de-pié′té′** (môɴ′dē-pyā′tā′), *n.; pl.* MONTS-DE-PIÉTÉ (môɴ′-). [F., fr. It. *monte di pietà* bank (prop., mount) of pity or piety.] One of certain public pawnbroking establishments to lend money at a low rate to poor people.

mon′te (mŏn′tā; mŏn′tȧ), *n.* Fully, **monte bank**. [Sp., lit., mountain, hence, the cards remaining after laying out a certain number.] *Cards.* A Spanish and Spanish-American gambling game, played with a Spanish pack of cards.

mon·teith′ (mŏn·tēth′), *n.* A large 17th-century punch bowl, usually of silver; — from the name of the inventor.

‖**mon·te′ro** (môn·tā′rō), *n.; pl.* -ROS (-rōs; *E.* -rōz). [Sp. *montera* hunting cap, *montero* huntsman, fr. *monte* mountain.] A round cap with a flap, worn by huntsmen.

Mon′tes·so′ri meth′od *or* **sys′tem** (mŏn′tĕ·sō′rē; *It.* mōn·tās·sô′rē). *Educ.* A system of training and instruction for children from three to six years of age, devised by Dr. Maria Montessori (b. 1870), of Rome, Italy.

mont·gol′fi·er (mŏnt·gŏl′fĭ·ẽr; *F.* môɴ′gôl′fyā′), *n.* A balloon raised by the buoyancy of air heated by a fire in the lower part; — so called from Jacques and Joseph Montgolfier, who first made one.

month (mŭnth), *n.* [AS. *mōnath;* akin to *mōna* moon.] **1. a** One of the twelve portions (***calendar month***) into which the year is divided; the twelfth part of a year, corresponding nearly to the length of a synodical revolution of the moon; popularly, a period of four weeks or of thirty days. See MEASURE, *Table* 6. Abbr. *mo.;* pl. *mo,* or *mos.* **b** *Astron.* More fully ***lunar month.*** The period of a complete revolution of the moon, esp. of a synodical revolution, mean length 29 days, 12 hours, 44 minutes, and 2.8 seconds. **2.** The twelfth part of the solar year; — called also ***solar month.***

month′ly (mŭnth′lĭ), *adj.* **1.** Continued, or in, a month; as, the *monthly* revolution of the moon. **2.** Done, happening, payable, published, etc., once a month, or every month. **3.** Of or pertaining to the menses. — *n.; pl.* -LIES (-lĭz). **1.** *pl.* The menses. **2.** A publication appearing once a month. — *adv.* Once a month; in every month.

month's mind (mŭnths). *R.C.Ch.* A requiem Mass for a person a month after his death.

mon′ti·cule (mŏn′tĭ·kūl), *n.* [F., fr. LL. *monticulus,* dim. of *mons, montis,* mountain.] A little mount; specif., a subordinate cone of a volcano.

mon′u·ment (mŏn′ū·mĕnt), *n.* [OF., fr. L. *monumentum,* fr. *monere* to remind.] **1.** *Obs.* A tomb or burial vault. **2.** A written memorial. **3.** A building, pillar, stone, or the like, erected in memory of the dead or of a person, event, etc. **4.** A statue; effigy. **5.** A work, saying, deed, etc., worthy of record or of enduring. **6.** A stone or other permanent object to mark a boundary. **7.** Any natural feature, as a mountain canyon, natural bridge, etc., reserved by the government as public property (***national monument***).

mon′u·men′tal (-mĕn′tăl; -t′l), *adj.* **1.** Of, pertaining to, suitable for, or occurring on a monument. **2.** Serving as a monument. **3.** Of the nature of a monument; hence, massive and lasting; impressive. **4.** Colossal; notable. — **mon′u·men′tal·ly,** *adv.*

mon′u·men′tal·ize (-īz), *v. t.* To record or memorialize lastingly as by a monument.

-mony. [F. or L.; F. *-monie, -moine,* fr. L. *-monia, -monium.*] A suffix in nouns denoting *resulting thing* or *abstract condition; -ment;* as in acri*mony,* cere*mony.*

mon′zo·nite (mŏn′zō·nīt), *n.* [From Mt. *Monzoni,* Tirol.] *Petrog.* A granular igneous rock composed of augite, plagioclase, and orthoclase in about equal quantities together with a little biotite. — **mon′zo·nit′ic** (-nĭt′ĭk), *adj.*

moo (mōō), *v. i.;* MOOED (mōōd); MOO′ING. [Imitative.] To make the characteristic noise of a cow; to low. — *n.* The lowing of a cow.

mooch (mōōch), *v. t. & i. Slang.* To steal; pilfer; also, to sponge; beg; live as a vagrant. — **mooch′er** (-ẽr), *n.*

mood (mōōd), *n.* [From *mode,* after *mood* temper. See MODE.] *Gram.* Distinction of form in a verb to express the manner in which the action or state it denotes is conceived, whether as fact, or as a matter of supposal, wish, possibility, etc.; a set of forms expressive of one of these modal forces. English has the *indicative, subjunctive,* and *imperative* moods; verbal phrases with modal force (as with *would, should,* etc.) are also loosely called moods, as *conditional, potential,* etc.

mood, *n.* [AS. *mōd* mind, feeling, heart, courage.] **1.** *Obs.* Anger; temper. **2. a** Temper of mind; humor; particular state of mind, esp. as affected by emotion; as, to be in the *mood* to work. **b** *pl.* A morose state of mind.

Syn. **Mood, humor, temper, vein** mean a mental state in which an emotion or set of emotions gains ascendancy. **Mood** implies pervasiveness and compelling power; **humor,** a mood which results from one's peculiar temperament or one's physical or mental condition; **temper,** a mood dominated by a towering emotion, esp. anger; **vein,** a transitory mood or humor.

mood′y (mōōd′ĭ), *adj.;* MOOD′I·ER (-ĭ·ẽr); MOOD′I·EST. **1.** Affected by a mood; subject or given to moods, or fits of depression or bad temper. **2.** Expressing, or characteristic of, a mood. — **mood′i·ly,** *adv.* — **mood′i·ness,** *n.*

mool (mōōl), *n. Scot.* **a** Mold; soil. **b** A grave; — often *pl.*

moon (mōōn), *n.* [AS. *mōna.*] **1.** The satellite of the earth, revolving about the latter from west to east in a little less than a calendar month and accompanying it in the annual revolution about the sun. The moon's diameter is 2,160 miles; mean distance from the earth, about 238,857 miles; mass, about one eightieth that of the earth, and volume, about one forty-ninth. See MONTH, TIDE, etc.

Symbols: ● New ☽ First quarter ○ Full ☾ Last quarter

2. A month; also, the moon during that period. **3.** The light of the moon; moonlight. **4.** Something shaped like the moon, esp. like a crescent moon. **5.** Any satellite, or secondary planet. — *v. i.* **1.** *Rare.* To revolve or emit light as a moon. **2.** To act as if moonstruck; to wander, idle, or gaze, about in an abstracted manner.

moon′beam′ (mōōn′bēm′), *n.* A ray of moonlight.

moon′-blind′ (-blīnd′), *adj.* Afflicted with moon blindness.

moon blindness. **1.** *Veter.* An inflammation of the eye of the horse, recurring at periodic intervals. **2.** *Med.* Nyctalopia, improperly attributed to moonlight.

moon′calf′ (mōōn′käf′; -kȧf′; 9), *n.; pl.* MOONCALVES (-kävz′; -kȧvz′). **1.** *Archaic.* A monster; a monstrosity. **2.** A dolt; a born fool; also, one who moons.

mooned (mōōnd *or, esp. poet.,* mōōn′ĕd), *adj.* Of or like the moon; symbolized by, or identified with, the moon.

moon′eye′ (mōōn′ī′), *n.* **a** An eye affected with moon blindness. **b** = MOON BLINDNESS.

moon′-eyed′ (-īd′), *adj.* **1.** Moon-blind. **2.** Round-eyed, as in wonder, terror, or dismay.

moon′fish′ (-fĭsh′), *n.; pl.,* see FISH. **1.** Any of a number of compressed, short, deep-bodied, silvery or yellowish marine fishes, as any species of two carangoid genera (*Vomer* and *Argyreiosus*), esp. one (*V. setapinnis* or *A. vomer*) of the southern coasts of North America. **2.** Any of various other fishes, as a Mexican top minnow (*Platypoecilus maculatus,* family Poeciliidae).

moon′flow′er (-flou′ẽr), *n.* **1.** *Eng.* The oxeye daisy (see DAISY, 2). **2.** *U.S.* A tropical American morning-glory (*Calonyction aculeatum*); also, any of several species of related genera.

moon′ish (-ĭsh), *adj.* Like the moon; hence, capricious.

moon′light′ (-līt′), *n.* The light of the moon. — *adj.* Of or pertaining to moonlight; occurring during or done by moonlight; moonlit.

moon′lit′ (-lĭt′), *or, Poetic,* **moon′lit′ten** (-lĭt′′n), *adj.* Lighted or illuminated by the moon.

moon′rise′ (mōōn′rīz′), *n.* The rising of the moon.

moon′seed′ (-sēd′), *n.* Any of a genus (*Menispermum*) of plants with crescent-shaped seeds, type of a family (Menispermaceae, the moonseed family) of herbaceous or woody climbers having small 3-parted dioecious flowers and narcotic properties.

moon′set′ (-sĕt′), *n.* The setting of the moon.

moon′shine′ (-shīn′), *n.* **1.** The light of the moon. **2.** Hence, show without substance or reality; empty show. **3.** *Slang.* Liquor, esp. whisky, illicitly distilled.

moon′shin′er (-shīn′ẽr), *n. Slang.* A person engaged by night in an illicit trade, as illicit distilling.

moon′stone′ (mōōn′stōn′), *n.* A transparent or translucent feldspar of pearly or opaline luster, used as a gem.

moon′-struck′, *adj.* Also **moon′-strick′en,** *adj.* Having a derangement attributed to an influence of the moon; lunatic.

moon′wort′ (mōōn′wûrt′), *n.* **a** Any fern of the genus *Botrychium,* esp. *B. lunaria.* **b** The plant honesty.

moon′y (mōōn′ĭ), *adj.;* MOON′I·ER (-ĭ·ẽr); MOON′I·EST. **1.** Resembling a moon; esp., crescent-shaped; round. **2.** Pertaining to, or like, moonlight. **3.** Illuminated by the moon. **4.** *Colloq.* Given to mooning; dreamy.

moor (mōōr; 84), *n.* [AS. *mōr.*] An extensive area of waste ground overlaid with peat, and usually more or less wet. Cf. HEATH, 1. — **moor′ish,** *adj.* — **moor′land′,** *n.* — **moor′y,** *adj.*

moor, *v. t.* [Late ME. *moren.*] *Naut.* To secure (a vessel) in a place by fastening with cables and anchors or with lines. — *v. i.* **1.** To secure a vessel by mooring; to anchor. **2.** To be secured by being moored.

Moor (mōōr; 84), *n.* [F. *More, Maure,* fr. L. *Maurus,* fr. Gr. *Mauros.*] **1.** A native of Morocco, or North African states. **2.** A Moslem of one of the native North African races or of the Arabs settled in North Africa; esp., one of the Saracenic invaders of Spain or their descendants.

moor′age (mōōr′ĭj), *n.* Act of mooring or a place for mooring; also, a charge for mooring.

moor cock. The male of the moorfowl.

moor′fowl′ (-foul′), *n.* The red grouse (*Lagopus scoticus*).

moor hen. **a** The female of the moorfowl. **b** A gallinule, esp. the common European species (*Gallinula chloropus*).

moor′ing (mōōr′ĭng), *n.* **1.** That which moors a vessel, as anchors, cables, etc.; — usually *pl.* **2.** *pl.* The place or position of a moored vessel.

mooring mast *or* **tower.** A mast with a fitting at the top to receive the mooring device of a rigid dirigible airship.

Moor′ish (mōōr′ĭsh; 84), *adj.* Of, pert. to, or in the style of the Moors.

moor′wort′ (mōōr′wûrt′), *n.* A small bog or moor shrub (*Andromeda polifolia*) of the heath family, of the North Temperate Zone.

moose (mōōs), *n. sing. & pl.* [Of Algonquian origin.] **a** A large mammal of the deer family (*Alces americana*), inhabiting forested parts of Canada and the northern United States. The male is called a *bull,* the female a *cow.* **b** The European elk.

moose′wood′ (-wŏŏd′), *n.* The striped maple (see MAPLE).

moot (mōōt), *n.* [AS. *mōt* (in comp.), *gemōt,* a meeting.] **1.** *Eng. Hist.* A deliberative meeting, esp. of the freemen of a village, town, hundred, shire, etc. The term *moot* was applied to any assembly met to administer justice or for administrative purposes. **2.** Discussion, debate, or argument; now, a discussion of fictitious causes by way of practice, as by law students. — *v. t. & i.* [AS. *mōtian* to meet or assemble for conversation, to discuss.] To argue for and against; to debate; discuss; esp., *Archaic,* to discuss by way of exercise; to argue for practice. — *adj.* Subjected or subject to argument or discussion. — **moot′er** (mōōt′ẽr), *n.*

moot court. A mock court, such as is held by students of law for practicing the conduct of hypothetical law cases.

mop (mŏp), *n.* [ME. *mappe,* fr. *mapple.*] **1.** An implement for washing floors, or the like, made of a piece of cloth, or a collection of thrums, coarse yarn, or rags, fastened to a handle. **2.** Something likened to a mop, as a kind of dredge for collecting starfish, a tangled mass of hair, etc. — *v. t.;* MOPPED (mŏpt); MOP′PING. To rub or wipe with or as with a mop.

mop, *v. i.* To make a wry mouth. — *n.* A pout; grimace.

mop′board′ (mŏp′bōrd′; 70), *n. U.S.* The baseboard around the bottom of the walls of a room.

mope (mōp), *v. i.* To be dull and spiritless. — *v. t.* To make spiritless or dejected. — *n.* **1.** A dull, spiritless person. **2.** *pl.* Low spirits; dumps. — **mop'er** (mōp'ẽr), *n.*

mop'ish (mōp'ĭsh), *adj.* Given to, or characterized by, moping. — **mop'ish·ly**, *adv.* — **mop'ish·ness**, *n.*

mop'pet (mŏp'ĕt; -ĭt), *n.* [Dim. fr. ME. *mop, moppe*, rag doll, baby.] **1.** *Archaic.* Baby; darling. **2.** *Colloq.* Child; youngster.

mo·quette' (mō·kĕt'), *n.* [F.] A variety of carpet or upholstery fabric having a velvety pile.

mo'ra (mō'rȧ; 70), *n.; pl.* MORAE (-rē), MORAS (-rȧz). [L.] *Pros.* The unit of quantitative meter, a common short syllable; — represented by ⏑ or by the eighth note ♪.

mo·ra'ceous (mō·rā'shŭs), *adj.* [L. *morus* the mulberry tree.] Belonging to the mulberry family (Moraceae). See MULBERRY.

mo·raine' (mō·rān'), *n.* [F.] *Geol.* An accumulation of earth, stones, etc., deposited by a glacier. There are various types, as terminal, lateral, medial, etc.

mor'al (mŏr'ăl; 74), *adj.* [OF., fr. L. *moralis*, fr. *mos, moris*, manner, custom, habit.] **1.** Characterized by excellence in what pertains to practice or conduct; right and proper. **2.** Dealing or concerned with establishing principles of right and wrong in behavior; ethical; as, *moral* philosophy. **3.** Serving to teach or convey a moral; as, a *moral* lesson. **4.** Pertaining to character, conduct, intentions, social relations, etc., viewed ethically; as, *moral* ideas; *moral* convictions. **5.** Conforming to a standard of what is good and right; virtuous; as, a *moral* life. **6.** Pertaining to or affecting morality, morals, or morale; as, a *moral* force. **7.** Sanctioned by, or operative upon, one's conscience or ethical judgment; as, a *moral* obligation. **8.** Capable of right and wrong action; as, a *moral* agent. **9.** Virtual, rather than actual, immediate, or completely demonstrable; as, to have *moral* certainty of B's guilt.

Syn. Moral, ethical, virtuous, righteous, noble mean conforming to a standard of what is right or good. **Moral** sometimes means just this, esp. as applied to conduct or character, but sometimes, esp. as applied to goodness, value, etc., implies an opposition to *spiritual, intellectual, aesthetic*, etc.; **ethical** implies a relation to or dependence upon the principles of morality; **virtuous**, the possession or manifestation of moral excellence in character; **righteous**, guiltlessness or blamelessness; **noble**, eminence in virtuousness.

— *n.* **1.** Moral conduct or teachings; — usually *pl.* **2.** The inner meaning or practical lesson of a fable, an experience, etc. **3.** A maxim. **4.** (*pron.* mō·răl') = MORALE.

mo·rale' (mō·răl'; -räl'), *n.* [F. *moral*. See MORAL, *adj.*] **1.** Formerly, moral principles, teachings, or conduct. **2.** Prevailing mood and spirit conducive to willing and dependable performance, steady self-control, and courageous, determined conduct despite danger and privations, based upon a conviction of being in the right and on the way to success and upon faith in the cause or program and in the leadership, usually connoting, esp. when qualified by the adjective *high*, a confident, aggressive, resolute, often buoyant, spirit of wholehearted co-operation in a common effort, often attended particularly by zeal, self-sacrifice, or indomitableness.

moral hazard. *Insurance.* The hazard arising from the uncertainty of the honesty of the insured.

mor'al·ism (mŏr'ăl·ĭz'm), *n.* **1.** Moral teaching or counsel; moralizing. **2.** A maxim embodying a moral truth. **3.** Practice of morality as distinct from religion; leading a moral life as distinguished from a religious life.

mor'al·ist (-ĭst), *n.* **1.** One who moralizes; a teacher or student of morals. **2.** One who leads a moral life. — **mor'al·is'tic** (-ĭs'tĭk), *adj.*

mo·ral'i·ty (mō·răl'ĭ·tĭ), *n.; pl.* -TIES (-tĭz). **1.** Moral character; virtue. **2.** That which instills moral lessons; moral inference, meaning, or lesson. **3.** The science, or a system, of morals. **4.** Moral practice or action. **5.** The quality of that which conforms to right ideals or principles of human conduct. **6.** A type of allegorical play, with actors representing Charity, Faith, Vice, etc.

mor'al·ize (mŏr'ăl·īz), *v. t.* **1.** To explain in a moral sense; to draw a moral from. **2.** *Archaic.* To furnish with moral lessons. **3.** To render morally better; as, efforts to *moralize* business. — *v. i.* To make moral reflections. — **mor'al·i·za'tion** (-ĭ·zā'shŭn; -ī·zā'-), *n.* — **mor'al·iz'er** (-īz'ẽr), *n.*

mor'al·ly (mŏr'ăl·ĭ), *adv.* In a moral sense, manner, etc.

moral philosophy. Ethics.

mor'als (mŏr'ălz), *n. pl.* **1.** Science or doctrine of conduct, esp. as to the sense of duty; ethics. **2.** Moral principles and practice.

mo·rass' (mō·răs'), *n.* [D. *moeras*, fr. OF. *marais*, fr. ML. *mariscus*.] A marsh; swamp.

mor'a·to'ri·um (mŏr'ȧ·tō'rĭ·ŭm; 70), *n.; pl.* -RIA (-ȧ), -RIUMS (-ŭmz). [NL. See MORATORY.] A period of permissive or obligatory delay; specif., *Law*, a period during which an obligor has a legal right to delay meeting an obligation, esp. such a period granted in an emergency, as to a bank or debtors generally, by a moratory law.

mor'a·to'ry (mŏr'ȧ·tō'rĭ *or, esp. Brit.*, -tẽr·ĭ), *adj.* [LL. *moratorius* delaying, fr. *morari* to delay.] Of or pertaining to delay; esp., designating a law granting a moratorium.

Mo·ra'vi·an (mō·rā'vĭ·ăn; 58), *adj.* Of or pertaining to Moravia, Moravians, or the Moravian sect. — *n.* **1. a** A native or inhabitant of Moravia, a part of Czechoslovakia. **b** The speech of the Moravians; — a group of dialects transitional between Slovak and Czech. **2.** *Eccl.* One of a Protestant Christian sect established in Bohemia as the *Bohemian Brethren* in 1467 and reconstituted as *Moravians* in 1722. See BOHEMIAN BRETHREN.

mo·ray' (mō·rā'; mō'rā; 70), *n.* Any of a number of voracious, savage, and often brightly colored eels, constituting a family (Muraenidae). They occur in all warm seas, esp. in crevices about coral reefs. A Mediterranean species (*Muraena helena*) is a valued food fish. See EEL.

mor'bid (môr'bĭd), *adj.* [L. *morbidus*, fr. *morbus* disease.] **1.** Not sound and healthful; diseased; hence, abnormally impressionable, esp. by ideas of a gloomy nature. **2.** Relating to disease; as, *morbid* anatomy. **3.** Grisly; gruesome; as, *morbid* details. — **mor'bid·ly**, *adv.* — **mor'bid·ness**, *n.*

‖**mor·bi·dez'za** (môr·bē·dāt'tsä), *n.* [It.] In the fine arts, delicacy or softness, esp., *Painting*, in representation of flesh.

mor·bid'i·ty (môr·bĭd'ĭ·tĭ), *n.* Morbid state or character.

mor·bif'ic (-bĭf'ĭk), **mor·bif'i·cal** (-ĭ·kăl), *adj.* [L. *morbus* disease + *-ficus*. See -FIC.] Causing sickness.

mor·bil'li (môr·bĭl'ī), *n. pl.* [ML.] *Med.* Measles.

‖**mor'ceau'** (môr'sō'), *n.* [F.] A bit; a morsel; — applied esp. to a short literary or musical piece.

mor·da'cious (môr·dā'shŭs), *adj.* [L. *mordax, -acis*, fr. *mordere, morsum*, to bite.] Biting or given to biting; acrid; hence, now of language, caustic. — **mor·dac'i·ty** (-dăs'ĭ·tĭ), *n.*

mor'dan·cy (môr'dăn·sĭ), *n.* Biting or caustic quality or tendency; mordacity.

mor'dant (-dănt), *adj.* [F., pres. part. of *mordre* to bite, fr. L. *mordere*.] **1.** Biting; caustic; sarcastic; keen. **2.** *Dyeing & Calico Printing.* Acting as a mordant. — *n.* **1.** Any corroding substance used in etching. **2.** *Dyeing.* Any substance which, by combining with a dyestuff to form an insoluble compound or lake, serves to produce a fixed color in a textile fiber, in leather, etc. — *v. t.* To subject to the action of, or imbue with, a mordant.

Mor'de·cai (môr'dē·kī; -kā'ī), *n.* *Bib.* In the book of Esther, the cousin of Esther, who saved the Jews from the destruction planned by Haman.

mor'dent (môr'dĕnt), *n.* [G., fr. It. *mordente*.] *Music.* A grace made by a quick alternation of a principal tone with an auxiliary tone usually a half step lower. It is either *single* or *double* (*long*). The name ***inverted mordent*** is sometimes applied to the pralltriller (which see).

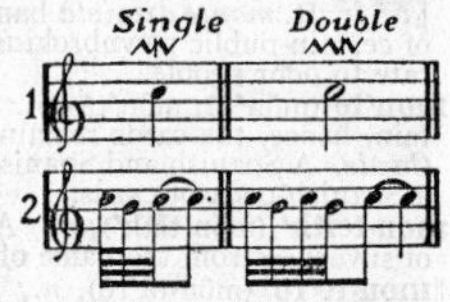

Mordents. 1 As written; 2 As performed.

more (mōr; 70), *adj.; now often used as compar. of* MUCH, MANY; *positive wanting; superl.* MOST (mōst). [AS. *māra, mā*.] **1.** Greater, as in size, number, power, degree, etc. **2.** Additional; other; as, no *more* worlds to conquer. — *n.* **1.** A greater quantity, amount, or number. **2.** That which is in addition; an additional amount; as, no *more;* much *more.* — *adv.* **1.** In or to a greater extent or degree. **2.** In addition; moreover.

mo·reen' (mō·rēn'), *n.* A coarse, stout woolen or woolen-and-cotton fabric, usually watered or embossed.

mo·rel' (mō·rĕl'), *n.* [F. *morelle*, fr. LL. *maurella*.] Any of various nightshades, esp. the black nightshade. See NIGHTSHADE; cf. GREAT MOREL.

mo·rel' (mō·rĕl'; mŏr'ĕl), *n.* [F. *morille*, fr. D. *morilje*, fr. OHG.] Any edible fungus of the genus *Morchella*, esp. *M. esculenta.* See FUNGUS, *Illust.*

mo·rel'lo (mō·rĕl'ō), *n.* [Flem. *marelle*, fr. *amarelle*, fr. It., deriv. of L. *amarus* bitter.] A cultivated sour cherry of any of several types distinguished from the amarelles by their dark-colored skin and juice. See CHERRY, 1; KIRSCH.

more·o'ver (mōr·ō'vẽr; 70), *adv.* Beyond what has been said; further.

mo'res (mō'rēz), *n. pl.* [L.] Customs; specif., fixed customs or folkways imbued with an ethical significance; customs or conventions which have the force of law.

Mo·resque' (mō·rĕsk'), *adj.* [F., fr. It. *moresco*, fr. *Moro*.] Moorish. — *n.* Moorish style of architecture or decoration.

Mor'gain, *or, commonly,* **Mor'gan, le Fay** (môr'găn; -găn lē fā). [OF. *Morgain la fée* Morgan the fairy; *Morgain* is of Celtic origin.] A fairy, sister of King Arthur.

Mor'gan (môr'găn), *n.* [After Justin *Morgan* (1747–1798) an Amer. horse breeder.] One of a celebrated American breed of light horses which originated in Vermont.

mor'ga·nat'ic (môr'gȧ·năt'ĭk), *adj.* [ML. *matrimonium ad morganaticum*, fr. *morganatica* a morning gift, fr. OHG. *morgan* morning, in *morgengeba* morning gift.] Of the nature of a form of marriage which members of various royal families in Europe may contract with persons of inferior rank, and wherein the wife, if inferior, does not acquire the husband's rank, and the children do not succeed to the titles, fiefs, or entailed property of the parent of higher rank. — **mor'ga·nat'i·cal·ly** (-ĭ·kăl·ĭ), *adv.*

mor'gan·ite (môr'găn·īt), *n.* [After J. P. *Morgan*, Am. financier.] A rose-colored gem variety of beryl.

mor'gen (môr'gĕn), *n.; pl.* MORGEN *or* MORGENS (-gĕnz). [D. & G.] A land measure of varying value in different countries. The old Dutch *morgen* was about 2.1 acres.

morgue (môrg), *n.* [F.] **1.** A place where the bodies of persons found dead are exposed for identification. **2.** *Journalism.* A department of a newspaper office where miscellaneous material for reference is filed.

mor'i·bund (mŏr'ĭ·bŭnd), *adj.* [L. *moribundus*, fr. *moriri* to die.] In a dying state; near death. — **mor'i·bun'di·ty** (-bŭn'dĭ·tĭ), *n.* — **mor'i·bund·ly**, *adv.*

mo'ri·on (mō'rĭ·ŏn; 70), *n.* [F., fr. Sp. *morrión*, fr. *morra* the upper part of the head.] A foot soldier's visorless high-crested helmet, of Spanish origin, with edge turned up. See HELMET, *Illust.* (12).

mo'ri·on, *n.* [G.] A dark, nearly black variety of cairngorm (smoky quartz).

Mo·ris'co (mō·rĭs'kō), *adj.* [Sp., fr. *Moro* Moor.] Moorish. — *n.; pl.* -COS *or* -COES (-kōz). A Moor, esp. of Spain.

‖**mo'ri·tu'ri te sa'lu·ta'mus** (mŏr'ĭ·tū'rī tē săl'ū·tā'mŭs). [L.] We (who are) about to die, salute thee; — cry of the Roman gladiators to the emperor.

Mor'mon (môr'mŭn), *n.* A member of the Church of Jesus Christ of Latter-day Saints (unofficially but generally called **Mormon Church**). — **Mor'mon,** *adj.* — **Mor'mon·ism** (-ĭz'm), *n.*

morn (môrn), *n.* [ME. *morn, morwen, morgen*, fr. AS. *morgen.*] *Chiefly Poetic.* Morning.

morn'ing (môr'nĭng), *n.* [ME. *morning, morwening*, with *-ing* after *evening*. See MORN.] **1.** The first or early part of the day. **2.** The first or early part; as, the *morning* of life. **3. a** The dawn. **b** [*cap.*] The goddess Aurora or Eos. — *adj.* Pertaining to the morning; being, used, occurring, or the like, in the morning.

morn'ing-glo'ry (-glō'rĭ; 70), *n.; pl.* -RIES (-rĭz). **a** Any vine of the genus *Ipomoea* with trumpet-shaped flowers of various colors, including the common cultivated species (*I. purpurea*) and the ***Japanese morning-glory*** (descended from *I. nil*) with crested, frilled, and double flowers; also, the flower. **b** Any vine, herb, shrub, or tree of related genera of the same family (Convolvulaceae, the morning-glory family), having alternate leaves and regular pentamerous flowers, typified by the convolvulus (which see). See PLUMULE, *Illust.*

morning gun. A gun fired at the first note of reveille or of a preceding march at military posts or on naval vessels.

morning sickness. *Med.* Nausea and vomiting on rising in the morning; — a common sign of pregnancy.

morning star. **a** Any of the planets Venus, Jupiter, Mars, Mercury, and Saturn, when it precedes the sun in rising, esp. Venus. **b** An annual Californian herb (*Mentzelia aurea*) having handsome yellow flowers.

Mo'ro (mō'rō), *n.; pl.* MOROS (-rōz). [Sp., Moor.] A member of any of the Moslem tribes of the southern Philippine Islands, of mixed Malayan stock; also, their language. — **Mo'ro**, *adj.*

mo·roc'co (mō·rŏk'ō), *n.* Also **morocco leather**. A fine variety of leather from goatskin tanned with sumac; — said to have been first made by the Moors.

mo'ron (mō'rŏn), *n.* [Gr. *mōron*, neut. of *mōros* sluggish, dull.] A moderately feeble-minded person. Most morons can be happy with tasks too simple and monotonous to satisfy an intelligent person. See MENTAL DEFICIENCY. — **Syn.** See FOOL. — **mo·ron'ic** (mō·rŏn'ĭk), *adj.* — **mo'ron·ism** (mō'rŏn·ĭz'm), *n.* — **mo·ron'i·ty** (mō·rŏn'ĭ·tĭ), *n.*

mo·rose' (mō·rōs'), *adj.* [L. *morosus*, fr. *mos, moris*, manner, habit, way of life.] Of a sour or gloomy temper; glum; sullen. — **Syn.** See SULLEN. — **mo·rose'ly**, *adv.* — **mo·rose'ness**, *n.*

-morph (-môrf). [Gr. *morphē* form.] A combining form denoting *one characterized by a* (specified) *form;* — in nouns, usually corresponding to adjectives ending in *-morphic*, or *-morphous*.

mor'pheme (môr'fēm), *n.* [F. *morphème*, fr. Gr. *morphē*.] *Linguistics.* **a** An element or property of language showing grammatical relations. It may be an affix (John'*s*), a preposition (*of* John), a conjunction, a relation adverb (*more* blessed), an auxiliary or copulative verb, intonation, accentuation, ablaut variation, or an order of words. Cf. SEMANTEME. **b** A meaningful linguistic unit, whether a *free form* (*pin, child, load, pray*) or a *bound form* (pins, child*hood*, *un*loader, pray*ed*), which contains no smaller meaningful parts.

Mor'pheus (môr'fūs; *popularly* môr'fē·ŭs), *n.* [L., as if fr. Gr. *Morpheus*, prop., the fashioner, because of the shapes he calls up before the sleeper, fr. *morphē* form, shape.] *Gr. Myth.* The god of dreams; hence, popularly, the god of sleep.

mor'phi·a (môr'fĭ·ȧ), *n.* [NL.] Morphine.

-mor'phic (-môr'fĭk). [Gr. *morphē* form + *-ic.*] A combining form meaning *characterized by a* (specified) *type of formation.*

mor'phine (môr'fēn; -fĭn), *n.* Also **mor'phin**. [F. *morphine*, G. *morphin*, fr. MORPHEUS.] *Chem.* A bitter, white, crystalline, narcotic base, $C_{17}H_{19}NO_3$, the principal alkaloid of opium.

mor'phin·ism (môr'fĭn·ĭz'm), *n. Med.* A morbid condition produced by the habitual use of morphine.

mor'pho·gen'e·sis (môr'fō·jĕn'ē·sĭs), *n.* [NL., fr. Gr. *morphē* form + *-genesis.*] *Biol.* Production or evolution of morphological characters. — **mor'pho·gen'ic** (-jĕn'ĭk), *adj.*

morphologic construction. *Ling.* See CONSTRUCTION.

mor·phol'o·gy (môr·fŏl'ō·jĭ), *n.* [Gr. *morphē* form + *-logy.*] **1. a** The branch of biology dealing with the form and structure of animals and plants; the science of structural organic types. **b** The features, collectively, comprised in the form and structure of an organism or any of its parts. **2.** The branch of linguistic study which deals with the history and functions of inflections and derivational forms. **3.** *Geol.* The external structure of rocks in relation to the development of forms or topographic features produced by erosion. — **mor'pho·log'ic** (môr'fō·lŏj'ĭk), **mor'pho·log'i·cal** (-ĭ·kăl), *adj.* — **mor'pho·log'i·cal·ly**, *adv.* — **mor·phol'o·gist** (môr·fŏl'ō·jĭst), *n.*

-mor'phous (-môr'fŭs). [Gr. *morphē* form.] A combining form meaning *formed* or *shaped of* or *like*, denoting *of a* (specified) *form* or *shape.*

mor'ris (mŏr'ĭs), *n.* More fully **morris dance**. [From earlier *morys, morish*, Moorish. See MOOR.] A spectacular, often mumming dance, once common in England in pageants and May-day games.

Mor'ris chair. [After William *Morris*, Eng. artist, but in use before his time.] An easy chair, with adjustable back and removable cushions.

Morris Plan bank. *U. S.* An industrial bank organized to extend loans in small amounts to wage earners.

‖**mor'ro** (môr'rō; *Angl.* mŏr'ō), *n.* [Sp.] A round hill or point of land; hence, **morro castle**, a castle on a hill.

mor'row (mŏr'ō), *n.* [ME. *morwe, morwen*, fr. AS. *morgen.*] **1.** *Archaic.* Morning. **2. a** The day subsequent to any day specified or understood. **b** Tomorrow.

Mors (môrz), *n.* [L.] *Rom. Relig.* Death, as a deity.

Morse (môrs), *adj.* Of or pert. to a Morse telegraph system or code; also, loosely, of any similar system or code. — *n. Colloq.* Morse alphabet, or telegraph, or the like.

Morse code *or* **alphabet**. *Teleg.* The telegraphic alphabet or code, consisting of dots, dashes, and spaces, invented by Samuel F. B. Morse. A modified form, differing in eleven letters, is called ***continental code, continental Morse code,*** *or* ***international code.***

mor'sel (môr'sĕl; -s'l), *n.* [OF. (F. *morceau*), fr. *mors*, fr. L. *morsus* a bite, fr. *mordere* to bite.] **1.** *Orig.*, a little bite or bit of food; now, a small quantity; a little piece. **2.** A tasty dish. — *v. t.;* MOR'SELED or MOR'SELLED (-sĕld; -s'ld); MOR'SEL·ING or MOR'SEL·LING. To divide into or apportion in small parts.

Morse telegraph. A form of electric telegraph first used publicly in 1844 and still the form in most common use.

mort (môrt), *n.* [F., death, fr. L. *mors, mortis.*] **1.** *Obs.* Death. **2.** *Hunting.* The note sounded on the horn at a kill.

mort, *n.* A salmon in its third year.

mort, *n. Dial.* A great quantity or number.

mor'tal (môr'tăl; -t'l), *adj.* [OF. *mortal, mortel*, fr. L. *mortalis*, fr. *mors, mortis*, death.] **1.** Subject to death; destined to die. **2. a** Destructive to life; deadly; fatal; specif., exposing to or deserving spiritual death; as, *mortal* sin. **b** So severe as to be thought of as threatening death. **c** Wishing, or involving a wish, to kill; deadly; as, a *mortal* enemy. **3.** Human; belonging to man; as, *mortal* wit. **4.** Of or pertaining to death or its occasion; deathly; as, the *mortal* place, a vital spot. **5.** *Colloq.* Extreme; very great; esp., very tedious; as, a sermon lasting two *mortal* hours. — **Syn.** See DEADLY. — *adv.* Mortally; — now rare except, *Chiefly Dial.*, in the sense of "extremely"; as, so *mortal* cold. — *n.* A being subject to death; a human being.

mor·tal'i·ty (môr·tăl'ĭ·tĭ), *n.* **1.** Condition or quality of being mortal. **2.** The death of large numbers, esp. by war or disease. **3.** The proportion of deaths to population; death rate; as, a time of great, or of low, *mortality.* **4.** Quality of being deadly or, of sin, mortal. **5.** The human race; humanity. **6.** *Obs.* Death.

mortality table. *Ins.* A table giving the number, l_x, of people out of an arbitrarily selected number of births who have been found to reach the age of x years. It may be constructed from two sources: population statistics and statistics of insured lives.

mor'tal·ly (môr'tăl·ĭ; -t'l·ĭ), *adv.* of MORTAL. **a** Fatally; deadly. **b** Very severely; as, *mortally* offended. **c** In the manner of a mortal. **d** Extremely; as, he was *mortally* jealous.

mortal mind. *Christian Science.* Nothing claiming to be something, for Mind is immortal; a belief that life, substance, and intelligence are in and of matter; the opposite of Spirit, and therefore the opposite of God, or good; the belief that man is the offspring of mortals; the belief that there can be more than one creator. *Mary Baker Eddy.*

mor'tar (môr'tẽr), *n.* [AS. *mortere* (fr. L.), and fr. OF. *mortier*, fr. L. *mortarium.*] **1. a** A strong vessel in which substances are pounded or rubbed with a pestle. **b** Hence, any similar mechanical device. **2.** [F. *mortier.*] **a** *Mil.* A cannon with a tube short in relation to its caliber, used to throw projectiles with low muzzle velocities at high angles. **b** A similar cannon used to throw a lifeline. **c** Any of various contrivances for throwing pyrotechnic bombs.

mor'tar, *n.* [OF. *mortier*, fr. L. *mortarium* mortar, a trough in which mortar is made.] A plastic building material, as that made by mixing lime, cement, or the like with sand, water, and sometimes other materials. — *v. t.* To plaster or make fast with mortar.

mor'tar·board' (môr'tẽr·bōrd'; 70), *n.* **a** A board about 30″ × 30″ used by masons and plasterers for holding mortar. **b** An academic cap with a broad, projecting, square top.

mort'gage (môr'gĭj), *n.* [OF., fr. *mort* dead (fr. L. *mortuus*) + *gage* pledge.] **1.** *Law.* At the common law, a conveyance of property, upon condition, as security for the payment of a debt or the performance of a duty, and to become void upon payment or performance according to the stipulated terms. **2.** The instrument by which a mortgage conveyance is made, the state of the property so conveyed, or the interest of the mortgagee therein. — *v. t.;* -GAGED (-gĭjd); -GAG·ING (-gĭj·ĭng). **1.** *Law.* At common law, to grant or convey by a mortgage. **2.** To pledge; to subject to a claim or obligation.

mort'ga·gee' (môr'gĭ·jē'), *n. Law.* A person to whom property is mortgaged.

mort'ga·gor' (môr'gĭ·jôr'; môr'gĭj·ẽr), *n.* Also **mort'gag·er** (môr'gĭj·ẽr). *Law.* One who gives a mortgage.

mor'tice (môr'tĭs). Var. of MORTISE.

mor·ti'cian (môr·tĭsh'ăn), *n.* [L. *mors, mortis*, death + *physician.*] A professional undertaker.

mor·tif'er·ous (môr·tĭf'ẽr·ŭs), *adj. Rare.* Deadly; fatal.

mor'ti·fi·ca'tion (môr'tĭ·fĭ·kā'shŭn), *n.* **1** A mortifying, or state of being mortified; as: **a** Subjection of the passions and appetites, by penance, abstinence, etc. **b** Humiliation and chagrin caused esp. by something which wounds one's pride, as a slight. **2.** That which mortifies; the cause of humiliation, chagrin, or vexation. **3.** *Med.* Gangrene; necrosis.

mor'ti·fy (môr'tĭ·fī), *v. t.;* -FIED (-fīd); -FY'ING. [OF. *mortifier*, fr. LL. *mortificare*, fr. L. *mors, mortis*, death + *-ficare* (in comp.) to make.] **1.** *Obs.* To destroy the vigor, strength, or the like, of. **2.** To deaden by religious or other discipline, as the carnal affections, bodily appetites, or worldly desires; to abase; humble. **3.** To affect with vexation, chagrin, or humiliation. **4.** To cause (a part of the body) to become gangrenous. — *v. i.* **1.** To practice mortification (sense 1 **a**). **2.** To lose vitality and organic structure; to gangrene.

mor'tise, mor'tice (môr'tĭs), *n.* [F. *mortaise*, fr. OF. *mortoise*, fr. Ar. *murtazz* fastened, fixed in.] A cavity, hole, or the like, into or through which some other part fits or passes; specif., a cavity cut into a piece of timber, or other material, to receive a tenon. See DOVETAIL, *Illust.* — *v. t.* **1.** To join or fasten securely; specif., to join or fasten by a tenon and mortise. **2.** To cut or make a mortise in.

mort'main (môrt'mān), *n.* [OF. *mortemain* (F. *mainmorte*), fr. ML. *murtua manus.* See MORTAL; MANUAL.] *Law.* Literally, dead hand; hence, the hand or possession of ecclesiastical corporations, ecclesiastics being in the early law deemed civilly dead; later, the possession of, or tenure by, any corporation which, by reason of the nature of corporations, may be perpetual.

mor'tu·ar'y (môr'tū̇·ẽr'ĭ *or, esp. Brit.*, -ẽr·ĭ), *n.; pl.* -IES (-ĭz). [ML. *mortuarium.*] **1.** *Hist.* A gift to the priest of a parish from the personal estate of a person dying in the parish or to a priest's superior from the estate of a priest. **2.** A place where dead bodies are kept for a time before burial. — *adj.* [L. *mortuarius*, fr. *mortuus* dead.] Of or pert. to the burial of the dead; also, of, pert. to, or connected with death or mourning.

mor'u·la (mŏr'ū·lȧ; -ōō·lȧ), *n.; pl.* -LAE (-lē). [NL., dim. of L. *morum* a mulberry.] *Embryol.* The globular mass of cells (*blastomeres*) formed by cleavage of the egg of many animals in its early development.

Mo·sa'ic (mō·zā'ĭk), *adj.* Also **Mo·sa'i·cal** (-ĭ·kăl). Of or pert. to Moses, or the institutions or writings attributed to him; as, the *Mosaic* law.

mo·sa'ic, *n.* [F. *mosaïque*, through It. and ML., fr. Gr. *Mouseios* of the Muses.] **1.** *Fine Arts.* A surface decoration made by inlaying in patterns small pieces of colored glass, stone, or other material; also, the process of making it. **2.** A picture or design made in mosaic. **3.** Something likened to mosaic, as a literary composition. **4.** Also **mosaic disease**. *Plant Pathol.* Any of certain virus diseases of plants characterized by mottling of the foliage. — **mo·sa'ic**, *adj.*

mosaic gold. **a** Stannic sulfide, SnS_2, used as a pigment. **b** Ormolu.

mo·sa'i·cist (mō·zā'ĭ·sĭst), *n.* A designer of mosaics, or a workman who makes them; also, a dealer in mosaics.

mosaic vision. *Zool.* A type of vision characteristic of insects in which, because of the presence of compound eyes made up of many simple independent visual units, the object viewed resembles a mosaic.

mos'cha·tel' (mŏs'kȧ·tĕl'; mŏs'kȧ·tĕl), *n.* [F. *moscatelle*, fr. It. *moscatella.* See MUSCATEL.] A small herb (*Adoxa moschatellina*) of the North Temperate Zone, with greenish-white musk-scented flowers.

Mo·selle' (mō·zĕl'), *n.* Wine made in the valley of the Moselle from Trier to Coblenz.

Mo'ses (mō'zĭz; -zĭs), *n.* [L. *Moses, Moyses*, fr. Gr. *Mōsēs, Mōysēs*, fr. Heb. *Mōsheh*, perh. of Egypt. origin.] **1.** *Bib.* The great Hebrew prophet and lawgiver who led the Israelites out of Egypt. **2.** Figuratively, a leader; also, a meek man.

mo′sey (mō′zĭ), *v. i.;* MO′SEYED (-zĭd); MO′SEY·ING. *Slang.* To go or move in a strolling, shuffling manner; esp., to depart.

Mos′lem (mŏz′lĕm; -lĕm; mŏs′-), *n.; pl.* MOSLEMS (-lĕmz; -lĕmz) *or collectively* MOSLEM. [Ar. *muslim* a believer in the faith established by Mohammed, fr. *aslama* to surrender (to God).] A Mussulman; an orthodox Mohammedan. — **Mos′lem**, *adj.*

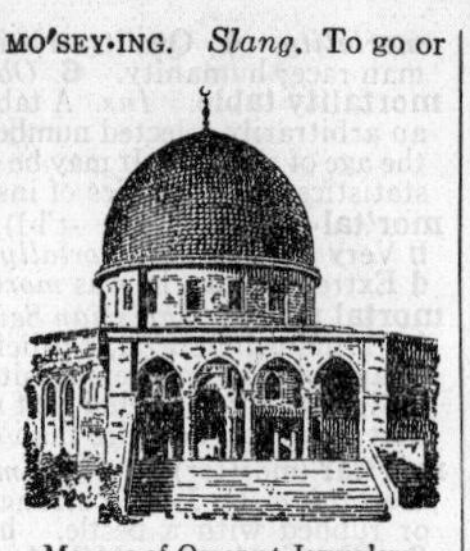

Mosque of Omar at Jerusalem.

Mos′lem·ism (mŏz′lĕm·ĭz′m; mŏs′-), *n.* Mohammedanism.

mosque (mŏsk), *n.* Also **mosk** [F. *mosquée*, fr. It., fr. Ar. *masjid*, fr. *sajada* to bow down, adore.] An Islamic place of public religious worship.

mos·qui′to (mŭs·kē′tō), *n.; pl.* -TOES (-tōz). [Sp., fr. *mosca* fly, fr. L. *musca*.] **1.** Any of certain insects (order Diptera, family Culicidae), having, in the females, needlelike organs in the proboscis with which they puncture the skin of animals to suck their blood. Certain mosquitoes are the only transmitting agents of various diseases, as malaria and yellow fever. See AËDES, ANOPHELES, CULEX, WIGGLER, WRIGGLER. **2.** [*pl.* -TOES or -TOS] A light, speedy British twin-engined long-range bomber.

mosquito boat. = MOTOR TORPEDO BOAT. See PT BOAT, *Illust.*

mosquito net. A net, screen, or curtain for excluding mosquitoes. — **mosquito netting.**

moss (mŏs; 74), *n.* [AS. *mos* a marshy place.] **1.** *Chiefly Scot.* A bog; swamp; esp., a peat bog. **2. a** Any bryophytic plant (class Musci) characterized by the small, leafy, often tufted stems bearing sex organs at the tips. **b** A clump of these plants. **3.** Hence: **a** Any of numerous mosslike lichens, as Iceland *moss*, rock *moss*, etc. See ICELAND MOSS. **b** Any of several pteridophytic plants of a mosslike habit, as club mosses (genus *Lycopodium*). See CLUB MOSS. — *v. t.* To cover or overgrow with moss.

moss agate. *Mineral.* A variety of agate, containing brown, black, or green mosslike markings.

moss′back′ (mŏs′băk′; 74), *n.* *Slang, Chiefly U.S.* An ultraconservative person; a fogy.

moss′bunk′er (-bŭngk′ẽr), *n.* [D. *marsbanker.*] The menhaden.

moss′-grown′, *adj.* Overgrown with moss; antiquated.

moss hag. *Scot.* A pit or slough in a peat bog.

‖**mos′so** (môs′sō), *adj.* [It., past part. of *muovere* to move.] *Music.* Literally, moved; rapid; — in directions; as, ***meno mosso***, less rapid.

moss pink. A low, tufted plant (*Phlox subulata*) of the phlox family, of the eastern United States, with pink or white flowers.

moss rose. A variety (*Rosa centifolia muscosa*) of rose having a mossy calyx and flower stalk.

moss′troop′er (mŏs′trōōp′ẽr), *n.* One of a class of 17th-century freebooters who infested the border country between England and Scotland, called ***the mosses*** from its mossy or boggy character; hence, a freebooter. — **moss′troop′er·y**, *n.* — **moss′troop′ing**, *n. & adj.*

moss′y (mŏs′ĭ; 74), *adj.;* MOSS′I·ER (-ĭ·ẽr); MOSS′I·EST. **1.** Overgrown or edged with moss or something like moss; as, *mossy* trees. **2.** Resembling moss; as, *mossy* green. — **moss′i·ness**, *n.*

most (mōst), *adj.; superl.* of MORE. [AS. *mǣst.*] **1.** Greatest in number, quantity, size, or extent; — often as superlative of *many*, *much*. **2.** Greatest in degree. **3.** Nearly all; as, *most* men. — *adv.* **1.** In the greatest degree or to the greatest extent; — used with an adjective or adverb to form the superlative degree; as, *most* wicked; *most* rapidly. **2.** [Short for *almost.*] *Colloq. & Dial.* Almost; nearly. — *n.* **1.** The greatest or largest quantity, amount, etc. **2. a** The greatest number or part; preponderating portion. **b** Most persons; as, cleverer than *most*. **3.** The utmost value, degree, result, etc.

-most (-mōst; *in familiar words also* -mŭst). [AS. *-mest.*] A suffix forming superlatives of adjectives and adverbs, as in hind*most*, fore*most*, etc.

most′ly (mōst′lĭ), *adv.* For the greatest part; chiefly.

mot, *n.* [F. See MOTTO.] **1.** (*pron.* mō) A pithy or witty saying. **2.** (*pron.* mŏt) *Archaic.* A note of a bugle.

mote (mōt), *v. i.; past tense* MOSTE (mōst). [See MUST, *v.*] *Archaic.* May; might.

mote, *n.* [AS. *mot.*] A small particle, as of floating dust.

mo·tel′ (mō·tĕl′), *n.* [From *mo*torists′ ho*tel.*] An inn or group of cabins along a highway, in which motorists may spend the night.

mo·tet′ (mō·tĕt′), *n.* [F., dim. of *mot* word. See MOTTO.] *Music.* A polyphonic choral composition on a sacred text, usually without instrumental accompaniment.

moth (mŏth; 74), *n.; pl.* MOTHS (mŏthz; mŏths). [AS. *moththe.*] **1.** Any of several small yellowish or buff tineid insects (esp. *Tinea pellionella*) whose larvae eat woolen goods, furs, feathers, etc.; — called also CLOTHES MOTH. **2.** Any of certain insects (order Lepidoptera), distinguished from butterflies by generally stouter bodies, smaller wings, less brilliant coloring, and usually nocturnal habits. In the larval or caterpillar state most moths feed upon plants, many being destructive (see GYPSY MOTH, BROWN-TAIL MOTH, etc.), and few (see SILKWORM) of any direct use to man. See PUPA, SILKWORM, *Illusts.*

moth ball. A ball, formerly of camphor, now of naphthalene, for keeping moths from clothing.

moth′-eat′en, *part. adj.* Eaten into by moths; like moth-eaten cloth. — **moth′-eat′**, *v. t.*

moth′er (mŭth′ẽr), *n.* [Prob. after *mother* parent, fr. MD. *modder* filth, mud.] A slimy membrane composed of yeast cells and bacteria which develops on the surface of alcoholic liquids undergoing acetous fermentation. It is added to wine or cider to produce vinegar. Called also **mother of vinegar.**

moth′er, *n.* [AS. *mōdor.*] **1. a** A female parent, esp. one of the human race. **b** Ancestress. **2.** That which has produced or nurtured anything; source of birth or origin. **3. a** A woman in authority or dignity like a mother's; — used specif. as a title of a woman head of a religious house; as, a *mother* superior. **b** An old or elderly woman, esp. of humble station; as, *Mother* Hubbard. **4.** Maternal tenderness or affection. — *v. t.* **1.** To adopt or care for as a child. **2.** To acknowledge that one is the mother of. — *adj.* **1. a** That is a mother or a mother's; as, *mother* love. **b** Bearing the relation of a mother; as, a *mother* church. **2.** Derived from or as from one's mother; native; as, one's *mother* tongue.

Moth′er Car′ey's chick′en (kâr′ĭz). Any of several species of small petrels, esp. the stormy petrel (which see).

Mother Goose. **1.** The feigned narrator of a volume of fairy tales by Charles Perrault, first published in 1697. **2.** The pretended writer of the ancient nursery rhymes known orig. as *Mother Goose's Melodies* but usually entitled in modern editions **Mother Goose's Nursery Rhymes**, first published in London about 1760.

moth′er·hood (mŭth′ẽr·hŏŏd), *n.* **1.** State of being a mother; character, qualities, or spirit of a mother. **2.** A body of mothers; as, the *motherhood* of the nation.

Moth′er Hub′bard (hŭb′ẽrd). **1.** The subject of a well-known nursery rhyme. **2.** A type of loose full gown worn by women.

moth′er-in-law′, *n.; pl.* MOTHERS-IN-LAW. **a** Mother of one's husband or wife. **b** A stepmother; — now not in standard use.

moth′er·land′ (mŭth′ẽr·lănd′), *n.* **a** A country regarded as a place of origin. **b** = FATHERLAND.

moth′er·less, *adj.* Destitute of a mother.

moth′er·ly (mŭth′ẽr·lĭ), *adj.* Like, suitable for, or characteristic of a mother. — **moth′er·li·ness**, *n.*

Mother of God. *Eccl.* The title of the Virgin Mary, sanctioned by the Council of Ephesus (A.D. 431), in opposition to the Nestorians.

moth′er-of-pearl′, *n.* The hard pearly internal layer of several kinds of shells, esp. of pearl oysters, river mussels, and the abalone shells; nacre. — **moth′er-of-pearl′**, *adj.*

Moth′er's Day (mŭth′ẽrz). *U.S. & Can.* A day appointed for the honoring of motherhood and the loving remembrance of one's mother, — observed on the second Sunday in May, or in schools the preceding Friday.

mother tongue. **1.** One's native language. **2.** A language from which another language originates.

mother wit. Natural or native wit or intelligence.

moth′er·wort′ (mŭth′ẽr·wûrt′), *n.* A bitter Old World mint (*Leonurus cardiaca*) with dentate, wedge-shaped leaves and axillary whorls of small purple flowers.

moth′y (mŏth′ĭ), *adj.;* MOTH′I·ER (-ĭ·ẽr); MOTH′I·EST. Full of moths.

mo·tif′ (mō·tēf′), *n.* [F.] **1.** In literature and the fine arts, a salient feature of a work; esp., the theme, or dominant feature. **2.** *Music.* = MOTIVE, *n.*, 3.

mo′tile (mō′tĭl; 56), *adj.* [See MOTIVE.] *Biol.* Exhibiting, or capable of, spontaneous movement. — *n.* *Psychol.* One whose mental imagery takes the form of inner feelings of action, as muscular movements, etc. Cf. AUDILE, VISUALIZER. — **mo·til′i·ty** (mō·tĭl′ĭ·tĭ), *n.*

mo′tion (mō′shŭn), *n.* [OF., fr. L. *motio*, fr. *movere*, *motum* to move.] **1.** Act, process, or instance of changing place or position; movement; — opp. to *rest*. **2.** Action of a machine with respect to the relative movement of its parts. **3.** Mental act, or impulse to any action; inclination. **4.** A proposal looking to action; esp., a formal proposal made in a deliberative assembly. **5.** *pl.* Movements; actions. **6.** *Obs.* A puppet show or puppet. **7.** *Law.* An application made to a court or judge to obtain an order, ruling, direction, or the like. **8.** *Mach.* A mechanism; as, a straight-line *motion*. **9.** *Music.* Melodic progression, as a change of pitch in the successive tones of a voice part. — *v. i.* To make a significant movement or gesture, as with the hand. — *v. t.* To direct or invite by a motion.

mo′tion·less, *adj.* Without motion; unable to move. — **mo′tion·less·ly**, *adv.* — **mo′tion·less·ness**, *n.*

motion picture. **a** A series of pictures, usually photographs taken with a **mo′tion-pic′ture cam′er·a** presented in very rapid succession, with objects represented in successive positions slightly changed, and producing, because of the persistence of vision, the optical effect of a continuous picture in which the objects move. **b** Specif., a photoplay. A machine for projecting motion pictures on a screen is a **mo′tion-pic′ture pro·jec′tor** (or *cinematograph*). — **mo′tion-pic′ture**, *adj.*

motion sickness. Nausea, dizziness, etc., caused by motion, as of an airplane, automobile, or ship.

mo′ti·vate (mō′tĭ·vāt), *v. t.* To provide with a motive; to impel; incite. — **mo′ti·va′tion** (-vā′shŭn), *n.*

mo′tive (mō′tĭv), *n.* [OF. *motif*, fr. ML. *motivus* moving, fr. L. *movere*, *motum*, to move.] **1.** That within the individual, rather than without, which incites him to action; any idea, need, emotion, or organic state that prompts to an action. **2.** A theme or dominant feature, as of a literary composition; a motif. **3.** *Music.* The theme or subject; a leading phrase or passage which is reproduced and varied through the course of a composition or a movement.

Syn. **Motive, spring, impulse, incentive, inducement, spur, goad** mean a stimulus to action. **Motive** implies any emotion or desire operating on one's will and driving it to action; **spring** (or more commonly *springs*), the basic motive, often unrecognized; **impulse**, an impetus or driving power either as given by another or arising in oneself; **incentive**, a motive developed through extraneous influences; **inducement**, one prompted by enticements or allurements; **spur**, one that stimulates the mind or increases energy or ardor; **goad**, one that keeps one going even in spite of drawbacks.

— *adj.* **a** *Now Rare.* Moving or tending to move to action. **b** Relating to motion or the causing of motion; as, *motive* power. **c** Pertaining to a motive or motives.

— *v. t.* **1.** To prompt or incite by or as by a motive or motives. **2.** To connect with the guiding or controlling idea of a work, as in art, literature, etc.

motive power. Any power, as water, steam, wind, electricity, etc., used to impart motion to machinery.

mo·tiv′i·ty (mō·tĭv′ĭ·tĭ), *n.* The power of moving or producing motion; available energy.

‖**mot juste** (mō′ zhüst′). [F.] The exactly right word; precisely expressive phrasing.

mot′ley (mŏt′lĭ), *adj.;* MOT′LEY·ER; MOT′LEY·EST. [ME. *motteley.*] **1.** Variegated in color; parti-colored. **2.** Hence: **a** Diverse; heterogeneous. **b** Composed of varying parts; discordantly composite. **3.** Wearing motley. — *n.* **1.** A woolen fabric of mixed colors, made in England between the 14th and 17th centuries. **2.** A garment of such cloth; the characteristic dress of the professional fool. **3.** *Obs.* A jester; fool. **4.** Any mixture, esp. an incongruous mixture, as of colors.

mot′mot (mŏt′mŏt), *n.* Any of numerous jaylike nonpasserine birds (subfamily Momotinae) confined to tropical forests from Mexico to Brazil. The color is chiefly green and the tail is long and peculiarly shaped.

mo'to·car' (mō'tō·kär'), **mo'to·cy'cle**, etc. Vars. of MOTORCAR, etc.
mo'tor (mō'tēr), *n.* [L., fr. *movere, motum*, to move.] **1.** One who or that which imparts motion. **2.** A prime mover, as a steam engine, a windmill, etc. **3. a** Short for MOTORCAR. **b** Any automotive vehicle. **4.** *Elec.* A rotating machine, as a dynamo, which transforms electrical energy into mechanical energy. **5.** *Mach.* Any internal-combustion engine, esp. a gasoline engine, as for an automotive vehicle, motorboat, etc. **6.** *Stock Exchange. pl.* Securities issued by automobile manufacturing companies. — *adj.* **1.** Causing, setting up, or imparting motion. **2. a** Equipped with or driven by a motor or motors. **b** Of or pertaining to automotive vehicles. **3.** *Anat. & Physiol.* Designating or pertaining to a nerve or nerve fiber which passes from the central nervous system or a ganglion to a muscle and by the impulse (***motor impulse***) which it transmits causes movement. The term is often loosely applied to any efferent nerve as opposed to a *sensory* or *afferent* nerve. **4.** *Psychol.* Involving, or pertaining to, muscular movement. — *v. i.* To ride in, travel by, or drive, a motor-propelled vehicle, as an automobile.
mo'tor·boat' (mō'tēr·bōt'), *n.* A boat propelled by an internal-combustion engine or an electric motor.
mo'tor·bus' (-bŭs'), *n.* Also **motor coach.** An automotive omnibus.
mo'tor·cade (-kād), *n.* [*motor* + *-cade.*] A procession of automobiles.
mo'tor·car' (mō'tēr·kär'), *n.* An automobile.
motor coach. See COACH, 2 **b.**
motor court. = MOTEL.
mo'tor·cy'cle (-sī'k'l), *n.* A two-wheeled automotive vehicle having one or two riding saddles and sometimes having a third wheel for the

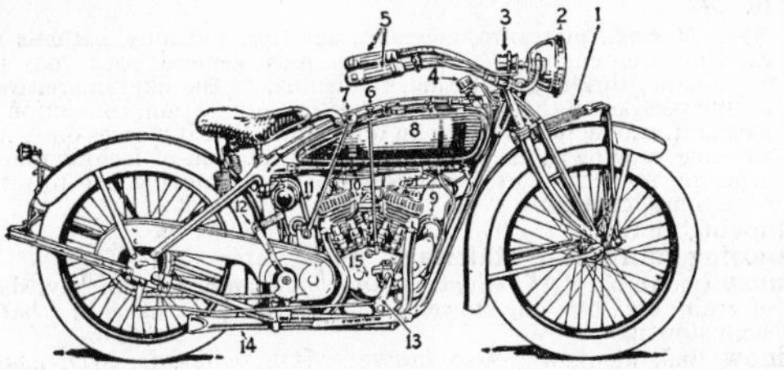

Motorcycle. 1 Spring Fork; 2 Headlight; 3 Horn; 4 Ammeter; 5 Handle-bar Controls; 6 Valve Release; 7 Gear Lever; 8 Gasoline and Oil Tanks; 9 Magneto; 10 Carburetor; 11 Generator; 12 Kick Starter; 13 Brake Lever; 14 Muffler; 15 Cam Case.

support of a sidecar. — *v. i.* To ride a motorcycle. — **mo'tor·cy'clist** (-klĭst), *n.*
motor drive. An electric motor and auxiliaries for driving a machine or group of machines. — **mo'tor–driv'en** (-drĭv'ĕn), *adj.*
mo'tor·drome' (mō'tēr·drōm'), *n.* [*motor* + *-drome.*] A track or course for races, tests, etc., of automobile vehicles.
mo'tored (mō'tērd), *adj.* Equipped with a motor
motor generator, motor generator set. *Elec.* One or more motors mechanically coupled to one or more generators for transforming electric currents.
mo'tor·ing (mō'tēr·ĭng), *n.* Act or recreation of riding in or driving a motorcar, or automobile.
mo'tor·ist (-ĭst), *n.* One who motors, esp. habitually.
mo'tor·ize (-īz), *v. t.* **1.** To equip with a motor or motors, specif. in substituting motor-driven vehicles for others; as, to *motorize* a fire department. **2.** *Mil.* To equip (ground-fighting infantry) with motor-driven vehicles for transportation; — dist. from *mechanize.* — **mo'tor·i·za'tion** (-ĭ·zā'shŭn; -ī·zā'-), *n.*
mo'tor·man (-măn), *n.; pl.* -MEN (-mĕn). A man who drives a motor; esp., the driver of an electric car or locomotive.
motor ship. A seagoing vessel propelled by a motor, esp. by an internal-combustion engine or engines, as a Diesel engine.
motor torpedo boat. A high-speed motorboat 60–100 ft. long, mounting two or four torpedo tubes, antiaircraft and machine guns, and equipped with depth charges and smokemaking apparatus; — called also *mosquito boat, PT boat* (see illust. at that entry), and by the British *E-boat.*
mot'tle (mŏt''l), *v. t.;* MOT'TLED (-'ld); MOT'TLING (-lĭng). [From MOTTLED.] To mark with spots or blotches of different color, or shades of color, as if stained. — *n.* **1.** A colored spot. **2.** An appearance like that of a surface having colored blotches or cloudy markings, as in many kinds of marble. — **mot'tler** (-lēr), *n.*
mot'tled (-'ld), *adj.* [From MOTLEY.] Marked with spots of different colors; dappled; spotted; as, *mottled* wood.
mottled enamel. Spotted enamel of teeth caused by drinking water having excessive amounts of fluorides during time the teeth are developing.
mot'to (mŏt'ō), *n.; pl.* MOTTOES, MOTTOS (-ōz). [It., word, saying, fr. F. *mot*, fr. L. *muttum* a mutter, grunt.] **a** A sentence or word inscribed on anything as appropriate to, or indicative of, its character or use. **b** A maxim.
‖**mo'tu pro'pri·o** (mō'tū prō'prĭ·ō). [L.] By one's own motion; of one's own impulse.
mouch (mōōch). Var. of MOOCH.
‖**mou'choir'** (mōō'shwär'), *n.* [F.] A handkerchief.
mou'di·warp' (mou'dĭ·wôrp'; mō'-; mōō'-). Var. of MOLDWARP.
‖**moue** (mōō), *n.* [F.] A grimace expressive of petulance, dissatisfaction, or the like.
mouf'lon, mouf'flon (mōōf'lŏn), *n.; pl.*, see PLURAL, *Note*, 3. [F. *mouflon*, fr. It. *muffolo* (dial.), *muffione*, fr. LL. dial. *mufro.*] A wild sheep (*Ovis musimon*), of Sardinia and Corsica, with large curving horns in the male.
mouil'lé' (mōō'yā'), *adj.* [F., lit., wet.] *Phonet.* Softened in sound; given a palatal quality, as *l* or *n* modified by a following *y* sound (*million, minion*).
mou·jik' (mōō·zhĭk'; mōō'zhĭk), *n.* A muzhik.
‖**mou'lage'** (mōō'läzh'), *n.* [F.] Molding; specif., *Criminology*, the making of plastic molds of objects for future use as evidence; also, a mold of such an object.
mould (mōld), **mould'board', mould'er, mould'y**, etc. Vars. of MOLD, etc.

mou'lin' (mōō'lăN'), *n.* [F., lit., a mill, fr. LL. *molinum.*] A nearly vertical shaft in a glacier into which a stream of water pours.
moult (mōlt), **moult'er.** Vars. of MOLT, etc.
mound (mound), *n.* = GLOBE, *n.*, 4.
mound, *n.* **1.** An artificial hill of earth; a raised bank; also, a natural elevation appearing as if thrown up artificially; a hill or knoll. **2.** *Baseball Cant.* The slightly elevated ground on which the pitcher stands when pitching. — *v. t.* **a** To enclose, fortify, or bound with a fence, mound, or rampart. **b** To form into, or heap up like, a mound.
mound builder. One who builds a mound; specif. [*cap.*], usually *pl.*, the builders of the earthworks, known as Indian mounds, found in the Mississippi Valley, the Gulf States, and the region of the Great Lakes.
mount (mount), *n.* [AS. *munt* and OF. *mont*, both fr. L. *mons, montis.*] **1.** A mountain; a high hill; — used instead of *mountain* before a proper name; as, *Mount* Sinai. Abbr. *Mt.* **2.** *Obs. exc. Hist.* A mound or raised work, as for military operations. **3.** *Palmistry.* One of the regions on the palm of the hand, supposed to indicate temperament or traits of character.
mount, *v. i.* [OF. *monter*, fr. L. *mons, montis*, mountain.] **1.** To rise or ascend; — often with *up.* **2.** To get up (on something, as a platform); esp. to seat oneself on a horse for riding. **3.** To rise or increase in amount; as, debts *mount* fast. — *v. t.* **1. a** To ascend; to climb. **b** To place or seat oneself on; as, to *mount* a horse. **2.** *Obs.* To cause to rise. **3.** To cause to get on horseback; to furnish with animals for riding. **4.** To put or place upon something elevated; as, to *mount* a statue on its pedestal. **5.** To put or fasten upon anything that sustains and fits for use, as a gun on a carriage, a map on paper, a jewel in a setting, etc. **6.** To prepare or set up (a skin, skeleton, etc.) for view, esp. in a natural position. **7.** To furnish with the necessary appurtenances, esp. for representation; as, to *mount* a play, that is, to furnish the scenery, properties, etc. **8.** To put on or show oneself in (an article of clothing). **9.** *Micros.* To place (an object) upon a slide or prepare for microscopic examination. **10.** *Mil. & Nav.* **a** To place or have in position, as cannon. **b** To be armed or equipped with. **c** To post as a means of defense or observation; as, to *mount* a guard. — **Syn.** See ASCEND.
— *n.* **1.** Act or manner of mounting. **2.** That upon which a thing is mounted, as a horse or bicycle for riding, the mounting of a picture, the structure supporting a cannon, etc. **3.** *Colloq.* An opportunity to ride, esp. to ride a horse in a race. **4.** *Microscopy.* The glass slide, with its accessories, on which objects are placed for examination with a microscope. **5.** *Philately.* A hinge.
mount'a·ble (moun'tȧ·b'l), *adj.* That may be mounted.
moun'tain (moun'tĭn; -tĕn), *n.* [OF. *montaigne*, fr. L. *mons, montis*, a mountain.] **1.** Any part of a land mass which projects conspicuously above its surroundings; *pl.*, a row or group of such elevations; as, the Rocky *Mountains.* Abbr. *Mt.*, pl. *Mts.* **2.** A great mass; a vast amount or quantity. — **moun'tain,** *adj.* — **moun'tain·side'** (-sīd'), *n.* — ***the Mountain.*** [F. *la Montagne.*] *Fr. Hist.* In the National Convention during the French Revolution, the benches (the highest) occupied by the deputies of the extreme revolutionary faction; hence, these deputies or their party.
mountain ash. Any of several trees (as of genus *Sorbus*, of the apple family) having ashlike leaves, white flowers, and bright-red fruits, as, in the U. S., *Sorbus americana* and *S. decora*, the latter often called ***western mountain ash.***
mountain avens. An arctic or alpine plant (*Dryas octopetala*) of the rose family.
mountain cat. a = COUGAR. **b** = BOBCAT (see LYNX).
mountain cranberry. See CRANBERRY, 2 **b.**
mountain dew. *Colloq.* Whisky, esp. Scotch whisky, illicitly distilled in the mountains.
moun'tain·eer' (moun'tĭ·nēr'), *n.* **1.** An inhabitant or native of a mountain region. **2.** A mountain climber. — *v. i.* To climb mountains.
mountain goat. A goatlike mammal (*Oreamnos montanus*) of the mountains of northwestern North America.
mountain laurel. A North American evergreen shrub (*Kalmia latifolia*) of the heath family, with glossy leaves and umbels of rose-colored or white flowers. The foliage is poisonous if eaten. It is the State flower of Connecticut and Pennsylvania.
mountain lion. The cougar.
moun'tain·ous (moun'tĭ·nŭs), *adj.* **1.** Containing, or abounding in, mountains. **2.** Resembling a mountain, esp. in size; huge. — **moun'tain·ous·ly,** *adv.*
mountain sheep. Any of various wild sheep inhabiting high mountains, esp. the ***bighorn,*** or ***Rocky Mountain sheep*** (*Ovis canadensis*), which ranges from northern Mexico to northern British Columbia. See BIGHORN.
mountain sickness. *Med.* A feeling of illness experienced by those ascending to extreme altitudes, and marked by difficulty of breathing, fatigue etc.
Mountain standard time, Mountain time. See STANDARD TIME.
Mountain State. Montana; — a nickname.
moun'te·bank (moun'tē·băngk), *n.* [It. *montimbanco, montambanco*, fr. *montare* to mount + *in* in, upon + *banco* bench.] **1.** One who mounts a bench in a public place and sells quack medicines. **2.** Any boastful and unscrupulous pretender; a charlatan. — *v. i.* To play the mountebank.
mount'ed (moun'tĕd; -tĭd), *adj.* **1.** Seated, serving, or performed on horseback; as, *mounted* police. **2.** Placed on a suitable support, fixed in a setting, etc.; as, a *mounted* gun; a *mounted* gem.
mount'er (moun'tēr), *n.* One who or that which mounts.
mount'ing, *n.* **1.** Act of one who mounts. **2.** That which serves as a mount; equipment; setting, standard, or support.
mourn (mōrn; 70), *v. i.* [AS. *murnan.*] **1.** To express or to feel grief or sorrow; to grieve; lament. **2.** To show the customary tokens of grief for the death of someone. **3.** To make a low continued sound likened to mourning; — said esp. of doves. — *v. t.* **1.** To grieve or express grief for. **2.** To utter in a mournful manner. — **mourn'er,** *n.*
mourn'ful (-fŏŏl; -f'l), *adj.* **1.** Full of sorrow; also, denoting or expressing sorrow; sorrowful. **2.** Causing sorrow; saddening. — **mourn'ful·ly,** *adv.* — **mourn'ful·ness,** *n.*
mourn'ing, *n.* **1.** Act of sorrowing, esp. for a person's death; lamentation. **2.** The customary exhibition of grief for the death of a person; also, the period of so doing. **3.** Garb or emblems indicative of grief, as black clothing. — **mourn'ing,** *adj.* — **mourn'ing·ly,** *adv.*
mourning cloak. A purplish-brown butterfly (*Euvanessa antiopa*)

with a broad yellow border to the wings, found both in Europe and America.
mourning dove. A wild dove (*Zenaidura macroura carolinensis*), of the United States, named from its plaintive note.
mouse (mous), *n.; pl.* MICE (mīs). [AS. *mūs*, pl. *mȳs*.] **1.** Any of numerous species of small rodents, esp. the ***house mouse*** (*Mus musculus*), now found in human habitations throughout most of the world. Cf. VOLE. **2.** A person, as a woman, so called by way of endearment. **3.** *Slang.* **a** A dark-colored swelling caused by a blow. **b** A person without spirit or courage. **4.** *Naut.* **a** A knob made on a rope with spun yarn parceling, or the like, as to prevent a running eye from slipping. **b** = MOUSING.
mouse (mouz), *v. i.;* MOUSED (mouzd); MOUS′ING (mouz′ĭng). **1.** To hunt for and catch mice. **2.** To watch for or pursue anything in a sly manner. — *v. t.* **1.** *Obs.* To handle as a cat does a mouse; hence, to pull about roughly in sport; to toy or play with wantonly. **2.** To hunt as a cat hunts a mouse.
mouse′–ear′ (mous′ēr′), *n.* **a** Also **mouse′–ear′ hawk′weed′.** A European hawkweed (*Hieracium pilosella*); — from its soft hairy leaves. **b** The forget-me-not (*Myosotis*).
mouse–ear chickweed. Either of two common hairy chickweeds (*Cerastium vulgatum* and *C. viscosum*).
mous′er (mouz′ẽr), *n.* **1.** A cat or, sometimes, other animal that catches mice. **2.** One who pries about looking for something.
mouse′tail′ (mous′tāl′), *n.* Any of a genus (*Myosurus*, esp. *M. minimus*) of plants of the crowfoot family; — so called from the taillike torus of the flower.
mous′ing (mouz′ĭng), *n.* *Naut.* A turn or lashing of spun yarn or small stuff, or a metallic clasp or fastening, uniting the point and shank of a hook.
mous′que·taire′ (mōōs′kĕ·târ′), *n.* [F.] A musketeer; esp. [*cap.*], one of the French royal musketeers of the 17th and 18th centuries conspicuous both for their daring and their dandified dress. The term is used adjectively of articles of dress regarded as like theirs.
mousse (mōōs), *n.* [F., froth, foam.] *Cookery.* A frozen dessert of sweetened and flavored whipped cream or thin cream and gelatin, frozen without stirring.
‖**mousse′line′** (mōōs′lēn′), *n.* [F.] Muslin.
‖**mousse′line′ de laine** (dĕ lĕn′). [F., muslin of wool.] = DELAINE.
‖**mousse′line′ de soie** (swȧ′). [F., muslin of silk.] A soft thin silk fabric with a weave like that of muslin.
mous·tache′, mous·ta′chio, etc. Vars. of MUSTACHE, etc.
Mous·te′ri·an, Mous·tie′ri·an (mōōs·tēr′ĭ·ăn), *adj.* [F. *moustérien.*] Of, pertaining to, or designating a period of paleolithic culture named after the type station of Le Moustier cave, on the bank of the Vézère, in France. This period marks the culmination of the Neanderthal race.
mous′y (mous′ĭ; mouz′ĭ), *adj.;* MOUS′I·ER (-ĭ·ẽr); MOUS′I·EST. **a** Of or resembling a mouse. **b** Quiet, like a mouse. **c** Infested with mice.
mouth (mouth), *n.; pl.* MOUTHS (mouthz). [AS. *mūth.*] **1.** The opening through which an animal receives food; also, the cavity containing the tongue and teeth (when present) or the structures enclosing this cavity. **2.** **a** The mouth as the means of eating, tasting, etc.; hence, a person as a consumer of food; as, hungry *mouths.* **b** The mouth as a means of speech or voice; hence, speech; utterance. **3.** An opening resembling or likened to a mouth, as one affording entrance or exit; orifice; aperture; as, the *mouth* of a jar, tube, cave, volcano, etc.; the *mouth* of a river where it empties into the sea. **4.** A wry face; a grimace. **5.** *Music.* The opening between the lips of an organ pipe (see FLUE PIPE, *Illust.*); also, an opening, as in a flute, across which the performer blows.
mouth (mouth), *v. t.* **1.** To utter; now usually, to speak in a strained or unnaturally sonorous manner; to declaim. **2.** To take into, or put in, the mouth; to mumble; lick. — *v. i.* **1.** To speak; talk; now only, to declaim; rant. **2.** To make mouths or grimaces, esp. in contempt. — **mouth′er** (mouth′ẽr), *n.*
mouth′breed′er (mouth′brēd′ẽr), *n.* **a** Any small fish (family Cichlidae) which carries its eggs and young in the mouth, as a brightly marked African species (*Haplochromis multicolor*) often kept in aquariums. **b** Any of several marine catfishes with similar habits.
mouth′ful (mouth′fōōl), *n.; pl.* MOUTHFULS (-fōōlz). **1.** **a** As much as the mouth will hold. **b** As much as is usually put into the mouth at one time. **2.** A small quantity.
mouth organ. *Music.* **a** = PANPIPE. **b** = HARMONICA **c**.
mouth′piece′ (mouth′pēs′), *n.* **1.** Something placed at or forming a mouth. **2.** The part of a horse's bit that passes through the mouth. See BIT, *Illust.* **3.** The part of a musical instrument to which the mouth is applied. See REED, *Illust.* **4.** One who delivers the opinion of others; a spokesman. **5.** *Slang.* A criminal lawyer.
mouth′y (mouth′ĭ; mouth′ĭ), *adj.;* MOUTH′I·ER (-ĭ·ẽr); MOUTH′I·EST. Emptily loquacious; bombastic. — **mouth′i·ly,** *adv.* — **mouth′i·ness,** *n.*
mou′ton·née′ (mōō′tō·nā′), *adj.* Also **mou′ton·néed′** (-nād′). [F. *moutonnée.*] *Phys. Geog.* Rounded like a sheep's back.
mov′a·ble (mōōv′ȧ·b'l), *adj.* Also **move′a·ble.** **1.** Capable of being moved; not fixed or stationary. **2.** Changing from one date to another; as, *movable* feasts, the dates of which vary from year to year. — *n.* **1.** A thing capable of being moved. **2.** An article of wares or goods; esp., and now only, an article of furniture; — usually in *pl.* **3.** *Law. Usually pl.* A subject of property of such a nature as to permit of its being moved from place to place without injury; — opposed to *immovable.* — **mov′a·bil′i·ty, move′a·bil′i·ty** (-bĭl′ĭ·tĭ), *n.* — **mov′a·ble·ness, move′a·ble·ness,** *n.* — **mov′a·bly, move′a·bly,** *adv.*
move (mōōv), *v. t.* [OF. *moveir* (3d pl. pres. *muevent*), fr. L. *movere.*] **1.** To change the place or position of; to shift. **2.** To set in motion; to stir; actuate. **3.** To rouse by appeal to the mind or desires; to influence; impel. **4.** To arouse the feelings or passions of; esp., to affect with any emotion; as, the pitiful tale deeply *moved* them. **5.** To propose; recommend; specif., to propose formally for consideration in a deliberative assembly; to submit, as a resolution. **6.** *Com.* To cause to move, or be sold. **7.** *Med.* To cause to operate; as, to *move* the bowels.
Syn. **Move, actuate, drive, impel** mean to set or keep going or in motion. **Move** is so general that the direction or nature of the motion can be gathered only from the context; **actuate** implies communication of power to work or set in motion; **drive,** forward, and usually continuous, motion, often emphasizing the effect produced rather than the impetus; **impel,** greater force in the impetus and more headlong action.
— *v. i.* **1.** To change place, position, or posture; to stir; proceed; also, of a door, machine, etc., to turn; work; revolve. **2.** **a** To progress; advance. **b** *Colloq.* To show marked activity. **3.** To carry on one's mode of life or activities; as, to *move* in select circles. **4.** To take action; to begin to act; as, to *move* in a matter. **5.** *Colloq.* To depart; betake oneself off; — often with *on.* **6.** To make an appeal, application, or the like; — used with *for;* as, the plaintiff *moved* for a rehearing. **7.** To change residence. **8.** Of the bowels, to have an evacuation. **9.** *Com.* To be sold or exchanged; — said of commodities.
— *n.* Act of moving; a movement; specif.: **a** An act for the attainment of an object; a device; as, a shrewd *move.* **b** A change of place or habitation.
move′ment (mōōv′mĕnt), *n.* **1.** Act of moving; change of place, position, or posture; a particular act or manner of moving. **2.** An act of evacuation of the bowels; also, the matter evacuated. **3.** A series of acts and events tending toward some definite end; as, the prohibition *movement; pl.* activities of a person or group of persons. **4.** An effect as of motion; hence, in literature and other art, action; incident. **5.** *Mech.* A system of mechanism for transmitting or transforming motion; esp., a delicate train of wheelwork, as in a watch. **6.** *Mil. & Nav.* A component part of a maneuver. **7.** *Music.* **a** = MOTION, *n.*, 9. **b** Rhythm; as, a dance *movement.* **c** Time. **d** = TEMPO. **e** A structural division of an extended composition, as a symphony. **8.** *Pros.* Particular rhythmical flow.
mov′er (mōōv′ẽr), *n.* A person or thing that moves.
mov′ie (mōōv′ĭ), *n.* A motion picture. — **mov′ie,** *adj.*
mov′ing (mōōv′ĭng), *adj.* **a** Changing place or posture; causing motion or action. **b** Adapted to move the sympathies, etc. — **mov′ing·ly,** *adv.*
Syn. **Moving, impressive, poignant, affecting, touching, pathetic** mean exciting deep emotion. **Moving,** the most general word, may imply entrancing, thrilling, agitating, saddening, or the like; **impressive,** imposing itself upon the mind by compelling admiration, conviction, etc.; **poignant,** producing so sharp an impression that it pierces one's heart; **affecting,** moving to tears or similar manifestation of feeling; **touching,** arousing tenderness or compassion; **pathetic,** moving one to pity or, sometimes, contempt.
moving picture. *Colloq.* A motion picture.
moving staircase *or* **stairway.** An escalator.
mow (mou), *n.* [AS. *mūga, mūha.*] A heap or mass of hay, sheaves of grain, etc., esp. one stowed in a barn; also, the place in a barn for such stowing.
mow (mō; mou), *n.* Also **mowe.** [OF. *moue*, fr. MD. *mouwe.*] *Archaic.* A grimace. — *v. i.* To make grimaces; to mock.
mow (mō), *v. t.;* MOWED (mōd); MOWED *or* MOWN (mōn); MOW′ING. [AS. *māwan.*] **1.** **a** To cut down, as grass, with a scythe or machine. **b** To cut the grass, grain, etc., from; as, to *mow* a lawn. **2.** To cut down; to cause to fall in rows or masses; as, the machine guns *mowed* down the men. — *v. i.* To cut grass, etc., with a scythe or machine.
mow′er (mō′ẽr), *n.* One that mows; a mowing machine.
mow′ing ma·chine′ (mō′ĭng). *Agric. Mach.* An implement with cutting blades for cutting standing grass, etc.
mox′a (mŏk′sȧ), *n.* [Corrupt. of Jap. *mogusa* (pronounced *mongsa*), a caustic.] **1.** *Med.* A soft woolly mass prepared from the young leaves of a Chinese wormwood (*Artemisia moxa*), and used as a cautery by burning it on the skin; hence, any substance similarly used. **2.** The plant from which this substance is obtained.
‖**moy′en′ âge** (mwȧ′yĕ′-näzh′). [F.] The Middle Ages.
moz·zet′ta (mō·zĕt′ȧ; *It.* mōt·tsăt′tä), **mo·zet′ta** (mō·zĕt′ȧ), *n.* [It. *mozzetta.*] A short cape with a small ornamental hood, worn, ordinarily, over the rochet by the pope, cardinals, bishops, abbots and canons.
mpret (′m·prĕt′), *n.* The title of the ruler of Albania (1913–14).
Mr. (mĭs′tẽr). The written form of the title Mister.
Mrs. (mĭs′ĭz; -ĭs). The form of Mistress used as a title.
mu (mū; mōō; mü), *n.* [Gr. *my.*] The twelfth letter (M, μ) of the Greek alphabet, equivalent to English *m.*
muc-. = MUCO-.
much (mŭch), *adj.; compar.* MORE (mōr; 70); *superl.* MOST (mōst); — both from another root. [ME. *moche, muche*, fr. *mochel, muchel*, fr. AS. *mycel, micel.*] **1.** *Archaic.* Many in number. **2.** Great in quantity, extent, or duration. — *n.* **1.** A great quantity; also, an indefinite quantity. **2.** A thing uncommon, wonderful, or noticeable.
☞*Much* can be regarded as an adjective qualifying a word unexpressed, and may often, therefore, be modified by *as, so, too, very.*
— *adv.* **1.** To a great extent; greatly. **2.** Nearly; almost.
much′ness (mŭch′nĕs; -nĭs), *n.* Greatness.
mu′cic (mū′sĭk), *adj.* [F. *mucique*, fr. L. *mucus* mucus.] *Chem.* Pertaining to or designating a white crystalline diacid, $(CHOH)_4(CO_2H)_2$, obtained by the oxidation of gums, lactose, etc.
mu′cid (-sĭd), *adj.* [L. *mucidus*, fr. *mucus* mucus.] Musty; slimy; mucous. — **mu′cid·ness,** *n.*
mu′ci·lage (mū′sĭ·lĭj), *n.* [F., fr. LL. *mucilago* a musty juice, fr. L. *mucus.*] **1.** *Bot.* Any of certain gelatinous substances found in plants, as in fucoid seaweeds, etc. Chemically, they are mixtures from which have been isolated complex carbohydrates. **2.** An aqueous solution of gum, or the like, used as an adhesive.
mu′ci·lag′i·nous (-lăj′ĭ·nŭs), *adj.* **1.** Moist and viscid, or sticky. **2.** Of, pert. to, or secreting mucilage, as a cell.
mu′cin (mū′sĭn), *n.* [From MUCUS.] *Biochem.* Any of certain mucoproteins originating from mucous membranes. — **mu′cin·ous** (-sĭ·nŭs), *adj.*
muck (mŭk), *n.* [ME. *muk*, of Scand. origin.] **1.** Dung in a moist state; manure. **2.** Any impure or decayed peat or black swamp earth, esp. when used as a manure. **3.** That which befouls; filth. — *v. t.* **1.** To manure with muck. **2.** *Colloq.* To defile with muck or filth.
muck′er (-ẽr), *n.* *Slang, U. S.* A coarse, vulgar person.
muck′le (mŭk′'l), *n.* *Dial., U. S.* A club for killing fish.
muck′luck (mŭk′lŭk). Var. of MUKLUK.
muck rake. A rake for scraping up muck or dung.
muck′rake′ (mŭk′rāk′), *v. i.* [Orig., an allusion to a character in Bunyan's *Pilgrim's Progress;* used in 1906 by Pres. Theodore Roosevelt.] To seek for, expose, or charge, esp. habitually, corruption, real or alleged, on the part of public men and corporations. — **muck′rak′er** (-rāk′ẽr), *n.*
muck′worm′ (-wûrm′), *n.* **1.** A larva or grub that lives in muck or manure. **2.** A miser.
muc′luc (mŭk′lŭk). Var. of MUKLUK.

mu′co- (mū′kō-), **muc-**. A combining form for *mucus* or *mucous membrane*, as in **mu′co·pu′ru·lent**, containing mucus and pus.

mu′coid (mū′koid), *n.* [*mucin* + *-oid.*] *Biochem.* Any of a group of glycoproteins resembling mucin. They occur in the vitreous humor and the cornea, in cysts, in tissues, etc.

mu′co·pro′te·in (mū′kō·prō′tē·ĭn; -prō′tēn), *n.* [*muco-* + *protein.*] *Biochem.* Any of a class of viscous glycoproteins found in mucous secretions and elsewhere.

mu′cor (mū′kŏr), *n.* *Bot.* A mold of a genus (*Mucor*) containing some of the commonest molds, as those on bread, jam, etc.

mu·co′sa (mū·kō′sȧ), *n.; pl.* -SAE (-sē). [NL.] *Anat.* A mucous membrane.

mu′cous (mū′kŭs), *adj.* [L. *mucosus*, fr. *mucus* mucus.] **1.** Of, pertaining to, or resembling mucus. **2.** Secreting or containing mucus. **3.** Covered with mucus, or the like; slimy. — **mu·cos′i·ty** (mū·kŏs′ĭ·tĭ), *n.*

mucous membrane. The lining membrane of those cavities of the body which communicate directly or indirectly with the exterior.

mu′cro (mū′krō), *n.; pl.* MUCRONES (mū·krō′nēz). [L.] *Bot. & Zool.* Any abrupt point, tip, or process, as that which terminates some leaves.

mu′cro·nate (mū′krō·nāt), *adj.* Also **mu′cro·nat′ed** (-nāt′ĕd; -ĭd). [L. *mucronatus.*] Ending in a sharp point, as some leaves.

mu′cus (mū′kŭs), *n.* [L.] A viscid, slippery secretion produced by mucous membranes, which it moistens and protects.

mud (mŭd), *n.* [ME. *mode, mudde.*] **1.** A slimy, sticky mixture of solid material with water. **2.** Abusive and malicious remarks or charges; as, to throw *mud* at a rival. — *v. t.* To make muddy or turbid.

mud dauber. Any of numerous wasps (family Sphecidae) which construct mud cells in each of which the female places an egg, with spiders or insects, paralyzed by a sting, as food for the larva.

mud′dle (mŭd′'l), *v. t.;* -DLED (-'ld); -DLING (-lĭng). [From MUD.] To confuse; specif.: **a** To cloud or fog, as one's brain. **b** To render stupid with liquor. **c** To mix confusedly. **d** To make a mess of; to bungle. — *n.* Confusion; a jumbled mess. — **mud′dler** (-lẽr), *n.*

mud′dle·head′ (-hĕd′), *n.* A dolt; blockhead. — **mud′dle·head′ed** (-hĕd′ĕd; -ĭd; 2; 30), *adj.*

mud′dy (mŭd′ĭ), *adj.;* MUD′DI·ER (-ĭ·ẽr); MUD′DI·EST. **1.** Of or formed from mud. **2.** Abounding in mud; besmeared with mud; also, turbid with sediment; as, *muddy* coffee. **3.** Not clear or bright; dull or cloudy in color; murky. **4.** Clouded or confused; muddled. — **Syn.** See TURBID. — *v. t.;* MUD′DIED (-ĭd); MUD′DY·ING. **1.** To soil with mud; to dirty; to render turbid. **2.** To cloud or fog. — **mud′di·ly**, *adv.* — **mud′di·ness**, *n.*

mud′fish′ (mŭd′fĭsh′), *n.; pl.,* see FISH. Any of several fishes which frequent muddy water or burrow in mud, as a loach, bowfin, and killifish.

mud′guard′ (-gärd′), *n.* A guard over a cycle or vehicle wheel to catch or deflect mud.

mud hen. A coot, gallinule, or large rail; a marsh hen.

mud puppy. Any of various, mostly large, American salamanders; esp., the hellbender.

mud′sill′ (mŭd′sĭl′), *n.* The lowest sill of a structure, as of a house, bridge, or dam, usually embedded in soil.

mud′sling′ing (-slĭng′ĭng), *n.* Use of offensive epithets and personalities, as in political campaigns. — **mud′sling′ing**, *adj.* — **mud′sling′er** (-ẽr), *n.*

mud′stone′ (-stōn′), *n.* *Petrog.* A hardened shale, produced by the consolidation of mud.

mud turtle. See TURTLE, 1.

mu·ez′zin (mū·ĕz′ĭn; moo-), *n.* [Ar. *mu'adhdhin.*] A Mohammedan crier of the hour of prayer.

muff (mŭf), *n.* [D. *mof*, fr. Walloon *mouffe*, fr. F. *moufle* mitten.] **1.** A soft, thick cover to protect the hands from cold. **2.** A bungling performance; in games, a failure to hold a ball in trying to catch it. **3.** *Colloq.* = DUFFER, 2. — *v. t. & i.* To handle awkwardly; to bungle; in games, to fail to hold (a ball) when trying to catch it.

muf′fin (mŭf′ĭn), *n.* A quick bread made of batter containing egg and baked in a cup-shaped pan; also, a similarly shaped biscuit (***English muffin***) made from yeast dough.

muf′fin·eer′ (mŭf′ĭ·nēr′), *n.* A dish for keeping muffins hot; also, a vessel with a perforated top for sprinkling muffins with sugar, spice, salt, or the like.

muf′fle (mŭf′'l), *v. t.;* -FLED (-'ld); -FLING (-lĭng). [OF. en*moufler*. See MUFFLE, *n.*] **1.** To wrap up so as to conceal or protect; hence, to conceal or cover the face of. **2.** To wrap or pad with something to deaden or dull the sound of; as, to *muffle* oars; hence, to deaden the sound of; as, to *muffle* a cry, a drum. — *n.* [F. *moufle* mitten. See MUFF.] **1.** Anything with which another thing is muffled. **2.** An oven used in a furnace in firing certain wares which must be protected from flame. **3.** In mammals, the end of the muzzle.

muf′fler (mŭf′lẽr), *n.* **1.** A scarf for the throat. **2.** Hence: **a** A covering, as a veil or scarf, worn as a protection or as a disguise. **b** A mitten with a thumb. **3.** *Mach.* Any of various devices to deaden noise.

muf′ti (mŭf′tĭ), *n.; pl.* -TIS (-tĭz). [Ar.] An official expounder of Moslem law, often an assessor to a court.

muf′ti, *n.* *Colloq.* Civilian dress, esp. when worn by a naval or military officer; ordinary dress.

mug (mŭg), *n.* **1.** A kind of earthen or metal drinking cup, with a handle, — usually cylindrical, with no lip. **2.** The quantity a mug holds. **3.** [Perh. a different word.] *Slang.* **a** The face or mouth. **b** A grimace. **c** *Brit.* A dupe. — *v. t. & i.;* MUGGED (mŭgd); MUG′GING. **1.** *Slang.* To grimace; make faces (at). **2.** To photograph; — esp. used of photographing criminals.

mug, mugg (mŭg), *v. t. & i.* *Slang, U. S.* To assault, esp. by garroting, for robbery.

mug′ger (mŭg′ẽr), *n.* One who mugs (in any sense).

mug′ger (mŭg′ẽr), *n.* Also **mug′gar, mug′gur** (-ŭr). [Hind. *magar*, fr. Skr. *makara* sea monster.] The common crocodile (*Crocodilus palustris*) of India, the East Indies, etc.

mug′gins (mŭg′ĭnz), *n.* **1.** A simpleton. **2.** One form of a game of dominoes. **3.** A game at cards.

mug′gy (mŭg′ĭ), *adj.;* MUG′GI·ER (-ĭ·ẽr); MUG′GI·EST. [From dial. *mug* a mist, of Scand. origin.] Warm, damp, and close; as, *muggy* weather. — **mug′gi·ness**, *n.*

mug′wump′ (mŭg′wŭmp′), *n.* [Of Algonquian origin.] *Polit. Cant, U. S.* A bolter from the Republican party in 1884; hence, an independent in politics.

Mu·ham′mad·an (mo͝o·hăm′ȧ·dăn), **Mu·ham′med·an, Mu·ham′mad·an·ism**, etc. Vars. of MOHAMMEDAN, etc.

Mu·har′ram (mo͝o·hăr′ăm), *n.* [Ar. *muharram* sacred, forbidden, the first month of the lunar year.] The first month of the Mohammedan year. See MOHAMMEDAN CALENDAR.

mu·jik′ (mo͞o·zhĭk′; mo͞o′zhĭk). Var. of MUZHIK.

muk′luk (mŭk′lŭk), *n.* Also **muk′lek** (-lĕk). [See MAKLUK.] A type of sealskin boot worn by Eskimos.

mu·lat′to (mū·lăt′ō), *n.; pl.* MULATTOES (-ōz). [Pg. & Sp. *mulato*, masc., *mulata*, fem., of mixed breed, fr. *mulo* mule, fr. L. *mulus.*] The first generation offspring of a pure Negro and a white; in popular use, any person of mixed Caucasian and Negro blood. — *adj.* Of the yellowish-brown color of a mulatto.

mul′ber′ry (mŭl′bĕr′ĭ; -bẽr·ĭ), *n.; pl.* MULBERRIES (-ĭz). [ME. *mulberie, murberie* (see BERRY), fr. OF. *mure, moure*, fr. VL. *mora*, fr. L. *morum* mulberry, fr. Gr. *mōron, moron.*] **1.** Any of a genus (*Morus*) of trees, typifying a family (Moraceae, the mulberry family) and including the ***white mulberry*** (*M. alba*), grown esp. for its leaves, which serve as food for silkworms. **2.** The edible, usually purple, berrylike fruit of these trees. **3.** The color of this fruit, reddish-blue in hue, of very low saturation and very low brilliance. See COLOR.

mulch (mŭlch), *n.* [ME. *molsh*, adj.] *Agric.* Any substance, as straw, spread upon the ground to protect the roots of plants from heat, cold, or drought, or to keep fruit clean. — *v. t.* To cover with mulch.

mulct (mŭlkt), *n.* [MF. *mulcte*, fr. L. *mulcta, multa.*] A fine or penalty. — *v. t.* To punish for an offense by imposing a fine; hence, to deprive of, as by deceit.

mule (mūl), *n.* [OF. *mul*, masc., *mule*, fem., fr. L. *mulus, mula.*] **1.** A hybrid between the horse and the ass; esp., the offspring of a male ass and a mare. Cf. HINNY. **2.** *Colloq.* A very stubborn person. **3.** *Biol.* A hybrid, esp. a sterile one; — used of hybrids between the canary and related birds. **4.** *Spinning.* A machine for simultaneously drawing and twisting (spinning) cotton, wool, etc., into yarn or thread and winding it into cops.

mule, *n.* [F., fr. D. *muil*, fr. L. *mulleus* a shoe of red leather.] A variety of slipper without quarter.

mule deer. A long-eared deer (*Odocoileus hemionus*) of western North America, larger than the Virginia deer. Cf. DEER.

mule skinner. *Colloq., U. S.* A mule driver.

mu′le·teer′ (mū′lĕ·tēr′), *n.* [F. *muletier*, fr. *mulet* a mule, dim. fr. L. *mulus.*] One who drives mules.

mu′ley (mū′lĭ; mo͝ol′ĭ; mo͞ol′ĭ). Var. of MULLEY.

muley saw. A stiff, long saw guided at the ends but not stretched in a gate.

mu′li·eb′ri·ty (mū′lĭ·ĕb′rĭ·tĭ), *n.* [LL. *muliebritas*, fr. *muliebris* of a woman, fr. *mulier* woman.] **1.** State of being a woman; womanhood; — correlative of *virility*. **2.** Womanliness; femininity.

mul′ish (mūl′ĭsh), *adj.* Like a mule; specif.: **a** Sullen; stubborn. **b** Hybrid; sterile. — **Syn.** See OBSTINATE. — **mul′ish·ly**, *adv.* — **mul′ish·ness**, *n.*

mull (mŭl), *n.* [Hind. & Per. *malmal.*] A thin, soft muslin.

mull, *v. i. & t.* [ME. *mullen* to pulverize.] *Colloq.* To ponder mentally; to cogitate.

mull, *v. t.* To heat, sweeten, and spice, as wine.

mul′lah (mŭl′ȧ; mo͝ol′ȧ), *n.* Also **mul′la**. [Turk., Per., & Hind. *mulla*, fr. Ar. *mawla.*] In Mohammedan use, a teacher or expounder of the law and dogmas of Islam.

mul′lein (mŭl′ĭn), *n.* Also **mul′len** (-ĕn; -ĭn). [OF. *moleine.*] Any of a genus (*Verbascum*) of herbs of the figwort family, including the woolly-leaved ***great mullein*** (*V. thapsus*) and the ***moth mullein*** (*V. blattaria*).

mull′er (mŭl′ẽr), *n.* [ME. *mullen* to pulverize, fr. *mul, mol*, dust.] A stone or thick lump of glass or metal used as a pestle for grinding grains, pigments, drugs, or ore.

mul′let (mŭl′ĕt; -ĭt), *n.;* see PLURAL, *Note*, 3. [OF. *mulet*, prob. dim. fr. L. *mullus* red mullet, fr. Gr. *myllos.*] **1.** Any of a family (Mugilidae) of valuable food fishes, the ***gray mullets***, occurring in streams and most seas. **2.** Any of a family (Mullidae) of moderate-sized fishes, the ***red mullets or surmullets***, usually red or golden in color, with two barbels on the chin.

mul′ley (mo͝ol′ĭ; mo͞ol′ĭ), *n.; pl.* MULLEYS (-ĭz). [Also *muley, mooley, moiley*, of Celt. origin.] **1.** *U. S.* A polled animal. **2.** *Dial. Eng.* A cow; — in the United States, a child's word. — *adj.* Hornless; polled; — said of beef cattle.

mul′li·gan (mŭl′ĭ·găn), *n.* *Slang, U. S.* A stew of vegetables, meat, etc.; — used orig. by tramps.

mul′li·ga·taw′ny (mŭl′ĭ·gȧ·tô′nĭ), *n.; pl.* MULLIGATAWNIES (-nĭz). [Tamil *milagutanni*, or Malayalam *mulagu-tanni*, pepper water.] An East Indian curry soup, made of chicken or other meat.

mul′li·grubs (mŭl′ĭ·grŭbz), *n. pl.* *Slang.* A griping of the intestines; colic; hence, the sulks; the blues.

mul′lion (mŭl′yŭn), *n.* [OF. *moienel, meienel*, medial, fr. L. *medianus.*] *Arch.* A slender bar or pier between lights of windows, screens, etc. — *v. t.* To furnish with or divide by mullions.

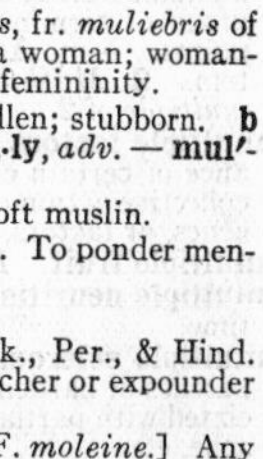

a, a, a, a Mullions; *b, b, b* Transoms.

mul′lock (mŭl′ŭk), *n.* *Australasia. Mining.* Refuse earth or rock from a mine; also, earth or rock bearing no gold. — **mul′lock·y**, *adj.*

Mul·read′y (mŭl·rĕd′ĭ; mŭl′rĕd·ĭ), *n.; pl.* MULREADIES (-ĭz). The first postal envelope (1d. and 2d.) ever used, issued by Great Britain in 1840, designed by William Mulready, British artist.

mult-. = MULTI- (which see), as in **mul·tan′gu·lar**, having many angles.

mul′ti- (mŭl′tĭ-). [L. *multus.*] A combining form meaning *many, much*. Specif.: **a** *Consisting of, containing,* or *having many*, as in *multi*cellular, *multi*phase. **b** *Many times over; in many respects;* as in *multi*millionaire. **c** Often restrictedly, *more than two*. **d** *Med. Affecting many parts.*

☞ The meanings of the following words can be understood from the definitions of their elements.

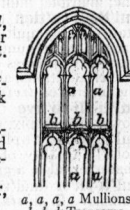

multiangular
multiaxial
multicellular
multicoil
multicostate
multicuspid
multicylinder
multidentate
multielectrode
multiflorous
multifoliolate
multiganglionic
multijugate
multilaminar
multilaminate
multilineal
multilinear
multilingual
multilobar
multilobate
multilobular
multilocular
multiloculated
multimolecular
multimotor
multimotored
multinominal
multinuclear
multinucleate
multinucleolar
multinucleolate
multinucleolated
multiovular
multiovulate
multipinnate
multipolar
multipurpose
multiradial
multiradiate
multirooted
multisegmented
multiseptate
multisonous
multispeed
multispermous
multispiculate
multispinous
multispiral
multistaminate
multistoried
multistriate
multitoed
multitoned
multituberculate
multitubular
multivalved
multivalvular
multivocal
multivoiced
multivolumed

mul′ti·far′i·ous (mŭl′tĭ·fâr′ĭ·ŭs; 6), *adj.* [L. *multifarius*, fr. *multus* much, many. Cf. BIFARIOUS.] Having great diversity; of various kinds; manifold. — **mul′ti·far′i·ous·ly**, *adv.* — **mul′ti·far′i·ous·ness**, *n.*

mul′ti·fid (mŭl′tĭ·fĭd), *adj.* [L. *multifidus*, fr. *multus* much, many + *findere* to split.] Cleft into many parts; as, a *multifid* leaf.

mul′ti·fold (-fōld), *adj.* Many times doubled; manifold.

mul′ti·form (-fôrm), *adj.* [F. or L.; F. *multiforme*, fr. L. *multiformis.*] Having many forms. — **mul′ti·for′mi·ty** (-fôr′mĭ·tĭ), *n.*

Mul′ti·graph (mŭl′tĭ·gráf; 9), *n.* A trade-mark for a small printing press, used esp. for printing circulars, and the like.

mul′ti·lat′er·al (-lăt′ẽr·ăl), *adj.* **1.** Having many sides. **2.** Participated in by more than two states; as, a *multilateral* treaty. — **mul′ti·lat′er·al·ly**, *adv.*

mul′ti·mil′lion·aire′ (-mĭl′yŭn·âr′), *n.* One having two or more million (dollars, pounds, francs, or the like).

mul·tip′a·ra (mŭl·tĭp′ȧ·rȧ), *n.; pl.* -RAE (-rē). [NL.] *Med.* A woman who has borne more than one child. Cf. PRIMIPARA, NULLIPARA.

mul·tip′a·rous (-rŭs), *adj.* [NL. *multiparus.* See MULTI-; -PAROUS.] **a** Of or pertaining to a multipara. **b** *Zool.* Producing many, or more than one, at a birth.

mul′ti·par′tite (mŭl′tĭ·pär′tīt), *adj.* [L. *multipartitus.*] Divided into many parts; having several parts.

mul′ti·ped (mŭl′tĭ·pĕd), **mul′ti·pede** (-pēd), *adj.* [L. *multipes, multipeda*, fr. *multus* many + *pes, pedis*, foot.] Having many feet. — *n. Rare.* A multiped animal.

mul′ti·phase (-fāz), *adj.* Having many phases; specif., *Elec.*, polyphase.

mul′ti·ple (mŭl′tĭ·p'l), *adj.* [F., fr. L. *multiplex.*] **1.** Containing more than once, or more than one; manifold. **2.** *Elec.* **a** Designating a circuit having a number of conductors in parallel. **b** Designating a group of terminals which make a circuit available at a number of points. — *n.* **1.** *Elec.* A multiple arrangement of an electrical system. **2.** *Math.* The product of a quantity by an integer; as, 4 is a *multiple* of 2.

multiple factors. *Biol.* In genetics, the hypothesis that the inheritance of certain characters, as size, skin color, etc., depends upon the collective action of a group of two or more similarly acting but distinct genes, or factors, the effect being apparently cumulative.

multiple fruit. *Bot.* = COLLECTIVE FRUIT.

multiple neuritis. *Med.* Neuritis affecting several nerves at the same time.

multiple sclerosis. *Med.* A diseased condition in which there are patches of hardened tissue in the brain or the spinal cord. It is associated with partial or complete paralysis, jerking muscle tremor, headache, etc.

multiple star. *Astron.* Several stars in close proximity, which appear to form a single system.

mul′ti·plet (mŭl′tĭ·plĕt; -plĭt), *n.* [From MULTIPLE.] *Physics.* A spectrum line having several components.

multiple voting. Voting by the same individual at the same election in various places in each of which he possesses the legal qualifications, as was possible under the British franchise law prior to 1918.

mul′ti·plex (mŭl′tĭ·plĕks), *adj.* [L. *multiplex, -plicis.*] **1.** Manifold; multiple. **2. a** *Teleg. & Teleph.* Pertaining to or designating a system of transmitting several simultaneous messages on the same circuit. **b** *Radio & Television.* Pertaining to or designating simultaneous transmission of two or more independent signals on the same carrier wave. — *v. t. & i.* **a** *Teleg. & Teleph.* To send (several messages) simultaneously over the same circuit. **b** *Radio & Television.* To send (several signals) simultaneously on the same carrier wave.

mul′ti·pli·ca·ble (mŭl′tĭ·plĭ·kȧ·b'l), *adj.* Also **mul′ti·pli′a·ble** (-plī′ȧ·b'l). Capable of being multiplied.

mul′ti·pli·cand′ (mŭl′tĭ·plĭ·kănd′), *n.* [L. *multiplicandus* to be multiplied.] *Math.* The number or quantity that is to be multiplied by another (called the *multiplier*). See PRODUCT, 4.

mul′ti·pli·cate (mŭl′tĭ·plĭ·kāt), *adj.* [L. *multiplicatus*, past part. of *multiplicare.* See MULTIPLY.] Consisting of many, or of more than one; multiple; multifold.

mul′ti·pli·ca′tion (-kā′shŭn), *n.* **1.** Act or process of multiplying; state of being multiplied. **2.** *Math.* The process of repeating or adding any given number or quantity a certain number of times; commonly, the process of ascertaining by a briefer computation the result of such additions; also, the rule by which the operation is performed; — the inverse of *division.* Sign, $\times$.

mul′ti·pli·ca′tive (mŭl′tĭ·plĭ·kā′tĭv), *adj.* Tending or having the power to multiply, or increase, numbers.

mul′ti·plic′i·ty (-plĭs′ĭ·tĭ), *n.* [LL. *multiplicitas*, fr. *multiplex* manifold.] Quality of being multiple, manifold, or various; multiform character; also, a great number.

mul′ti·pli′er (mŭl′tĭ·plī′ẽr), *n.* **1.** One that multiplies or increases in number. **2.** *Math.* The number or quantity by which another (the *multiplicand*) is multiplied. See PRODUCT, 4. **3.** *Physics.* A device for multiplying or intensifying some effect, as of heat.

mul′ti·ply (mŭl′tĭ·plī), *v. t.;* -PLIED (-plīd); -PLY′ING. [OF. *multiplier*, fr. L. *multiplicare*, fr. *multiplex* manifold.] **1.** To increase in number; to add quantity to. **2.** *Math.* To take by addition a certain number of times; to find the product of by multiplication. — *v. i.* **1.** To become greater in number. **2.** To increase in extent and influence. **3.** To perform the operation of multiplication. — **Syn.** See INCREASE.

mul′ti·tude (-tūd), *n.* [OF., fr. L. *multitudo, multitudinis*, fr. *multus* much, many.] **1.** A crowd; throng. **2.** A great number of persons or things, regarded collectively. **3.** The state of being many; numerousness.

mul′ti·tu′di·nous (-tū′dĭ·nŭs), *adj.* **1.** Comprising, or existing in, a great multitude; myriad. **2.** Issuing from or as from, or resembling, a vast host. **3.** *Rare.* Of or pertaining to the multitude. — **mul′ti·tu′di·nous·ly**, *adv.* — **mul′ti·tu′di·nous·ness**, *n.*

mul′ti·va′lent (mŭl′tĭ·vā′lĕnt; mŭl·tĭv′ȧ·lĕnt), *adj.* [*multi-* + L. *valens*, pres. part. See VALENCE.] *Chem.* **a** Having a valence of several units. **b** Having more than one valence, as sulfur. — **mul′ti·va′lence** (-lĕns), *n.*

mul′ti·valve′ (mŭl′tĭ·vălv′), *adj.* Having many valves.

‖**mul′tum in par′vo** (mŭl′tŭm ĭn pär′vō). [L.] Much in little.

mul′ture (mŭl′tūr), *n.* [OF. *moulture*, fr. ML. *molitura* a grinding, fr. *molere* to grind.] *Archaic & Dial.* A toll for the grinding of grain at a mill.

mum (mŭm), *interj.* [Imitative.] Be silent; hush; — an exclamation enjoining silence. — *adj.* Silent; not speaking.

mum, mumm (mŭm), *v. i.;* MUMMED (mŭmd); MUM′MING. [Cf. OF. *momer, mommer*, MD. *mommen.*] To play in a dumb show, mask, or disguise; specif., *Eng.*, to go about in disguise at Christmastide making merry.

mum, *n.* [G. *mumme.*] A strong ale or beer.

mum′ble (mŭm′b'l), *v. i. & t.;* MUM′BLED (-b'ld); MUM′BLING (-blĭng). [ME. *momelen.*] **1.** To speak with the lips partly closed; to mutter. **2.** To chew gently with closed lips, or with little use of the teeth. — *n.* A low, confused utterance. — **mum′bler** (-blẽr), *n.* — **mum′bling·ly**, *adv.*

Mum′bo Jum′bo (mŭm′bō jŭm′bō). [From *mama dyambo*, in the language of a Mandingo tribe on the Senegal.] **1.** Among Negroes of the western Sudan, the tutelary genius of a village, represented by a masked man who wards off evil and keeps the women in awe and subjection. **2.** [*also not cap.*] A fetish; bugaboo. **3.** [*not cap.*] Meaningless incantation; mummery.

mum′mer (mŭm′ẽr), *n.* [MF. *mommeur.*] **a** One who mums, as in merrymaking at Christmastide; a buffoon. **b** Hence, any theatrical performer; an actor.

mum′mer·y (-ĭ), *n.; pl.* -MERIES (-ĭz). [MF. *mommerie.*] **1.** Masking, as by mummers. **2.** Ceremonies regarded as ridiculous, hypocritical, or pretentious.

mum′mi·fy (mŭm′ĭ·fī), *v. t.;* -FIED (-fīd); -FY′ING. To embalm and dry as a mummy. — *v. i.* To dry up like a mummy, as tissue. — **mum′mi·fi·ca′tion** (-fĭ·kā′shŭn), *n.*

mum′my (mŭm′ĭ), *n.; pl.* -MIES (-ĭz). [F. *momie*, fr. ML. *mumia*, fr. Ar. *mūmiya* mummy, bitumen, fr. Per. *mūm* wax.] **1.** *Obs.* Part of a mummified body, probably powdered, used as a drug. **2.** *Rare.* Lifeless flesh. *Shak.* **3.** A body embalmed or treated for burial with preservatives after the manner of the ancient Egyptians; hence, any body unusually well preserved, owing to the manner of its burial or to some special preparation for burial; as, a Peruvian *mummy.* **4.** A brown pigment prepared from bitumen, bones, etc.; also, a brown color. — *v. t.;* -MIED (-ĭd); -MY·ING. To mummify.

mump (mŭmp), *v. t. & i. Now Chiefly Dial.* **1.** To mumble. **2.** To beg mumblingly; hence, to cheat; also, to be sulky.

mumps (mŭmps), *n. pl., construed as sing.* An infectious disease marked by fever, and swelling and inflammation of the parotid gland and sometimes other salivary glands in the lower cheeks; parotitis.

munch (mŭnch), *v. t. & i.* [ME. *monchen, manchen.*] To chew with a crunching sound. — **munch′er**, *n.*

Mun·chau′sen, Baron (mŭn·chô′z'n; -chou′-; mŭn-; mŭn′chô′; mŭn′-chou′-). The pretended author of a book of travels (by Rudolph Eric Raspe, 1785) filled with extravagant fictions.

mun′dane (mŭn′dān), *adj.* [F. *mondain*, fr. L. *mundanus*, fr. *mundus* the world, universe, heavens.] Of or pertaining to the world; worldly; earthly; as, *mundane* affairs. — **Syn.** See EARTHLY. — **mun′dane·ly**, *adv.*

mun·dun′gus (mŭn·dŭng′gŭs), *n.* Also **mun·dun′go** (-gō). [Sp. *mondongo* paunch, tripe.] *Archaic.* Offensive-smelling tobacco.

mun′go (mŭng′gō), *n.* A reclaimed wool of an inferior quality. Cf. SHODDY.

mu·nic′i·pal (mū·nĭs′ĭ·păl), *adj.* [L. *municipalis*, fr. *municeps* an inhabitant of a *municipium*, or town possessing the right of Roman citizenship, fr. *munia* official duties + the root of *capere* to take.] **1. a** Enjoying local self-government; — said of a town, city, etc. **b** Of or pert. to, or characteristic of, a municipality. **2.** Of or pert. to the internal or government affairs of a state, kingdom, or nation; — used chiefly in the phrase **municipal law.**

mu·nic′i·pal·ism (mū·nĭs′ĭ·păl·ĭz'm), *n.* Municipal government; also, a theory that government by municipalities should be extended. — **mu·nic′i·pal·ist** (-ĭst), *n.*

mu·nic′i·pal′i·ty (-păl′ĭ·tĭ), *n.; pl.* -TIES (-tĭz). **1.** A town, city, or other district having powers of local self-government; a municipal corporation; also, the community under the jurisdiction of a municipal government. **2.** *Phil. I.* The administrative area into which provinces are divided, comprising a number of barrios.

mu·nic′i·pal·ize (mū·nĭs′ĭ·păl·īz), *v. t.* To make municipal; to bring under municipal oversight, ownership, or control.

mu·nif′i·cence (mū·nĭf′ĭ·sĕns; -s'ns), *n.* Quality or state of being munificent; lavish generosity.

mu·nif′i·cent (-sĕnt; -s'nt), *adj.* [L. *munificus*, fr. *munus* service, gift + *-ficus.* See -FIC.] Very liberal in giving; lavish; also, characterized by great liberality. — **Syn.** See LIBERAL. — **mu·nif′i·cent·ly**, *adv.*

mu′ni·ment (mū′nĭ·mĕnt), *n.* [OF., fr. L. *munimentum*, fr. *munire* to fortify.] **1.** *pl. Law.* The evidences or writings whereby one is enabled to defend the title to property. **2.** A means of defense.

mu·ni′tion (mū·nĭsh′ŭn), *n.* [F., munition of war, fr. L. *munitio* fortification, fr. *munire* to fortify.] Ammunition; also, military stores of all kinds; hence, necessary equipment; — usually in *pl.* — *v. t.* To provide with munitions.

mun′nion (mŭn′yŭn), *n.* A mullion.

munt′jac, munt′jak (mŭnt′jăk), *n.* [Malay & Jav. *mĕnjaṅan.*] Any of several species of small deer (genus *Muntiacus*) of southeastern Asia and the East Indies; esp., a species (*M. muntjak*) of Java and adjacent regions.

mu·rae′na (mū·rē′nȧ), *n.* [L., fr. Gr. *myraina.*] A moray.
mu′ral (mū′răl), *adj.* [F., fr. L. *muralis*, fr. *murus* wall.] **1.** Of or pertaining to a wall; on or in a wall; as, *mural* paintings. **2.** Like a wall, as in being steep; as, a *mural* precipice. — *n.* A mural painting.
mur′der (mûr′dẽr), *n.* [ME. *morder* (influenced by OF. *mordre*, of Teut. origin), *morther*, fr. AS. *morthor.*] *Law.* The offense of unlawfully killing a human being with malice aforethought, express or implied. — *v. t.* **1.** To kill (a human being) unlawfully and with premeditated malice. **2.** To mutilate, spoil, or deform by wretched performance; to mangle; butcher. — *v. i.* To commit murder. — **Syn.** See KILL. — **mur′der·er**, *n.* — **mur′der·ess**, *n.*
mur′der·ous (-ŭs), *adj.* Of or pertaining to murder; characterized by, or causing, murder or bloodshed; bloody. — **mur′der·ous·ly**, *adv.*
mure (mūr), *n.* [F. *mur*, fr. L. *murus.*] *Obs.* A wall. — *v. t.* To enclose within walls; to immure.
mu′rex (mū′rĕks), *n.; pl.* -RICES (-rĭ·sēz), -REXES (-rĕk·sĕz; -sĭz). [L., the purple fish.] Any mollusk of a genus (*Murex*) of marine gastropods having a rough shell. A secretion of the animal is used as a purple dye.
mur′geon (mûr′jŭn), *n. & v. Now Scot.* Grimace; grumble.
mu′ri·ate (mū′rĭ·āt), *n. Chem.* A salt of hydrochloric acid; a chloride; specif., *Fertilizers*, potassium chloride.
mu′ri·at′ed (-āt′ĕd; -ĭd), *adj.* Containing much salt; briny; as, *muriated* waters.
mu′ri·at′ic (-ăt′ĭk), *adj.* [L. *muriaticus* pickled, fr. *muria* brine.] Hydrochloric; — a commercial term; as, *muriatic* acid.
mu′ri·cate (mū′rĭ·kāt), *adj.* Also **mu′ri·cat′ed** (-kāt′ĕd; -ĭd). [L. *muricatus*, fr. *murex* a pointed rock or stone.] Having sharp points; prickly.
mu′rine (mū′rīn; -rĭn; 56), *adj.* [L. *murinus*, fr. *mus, muris*, mouse.] *Zool.* Belonging to a family (Muridae) of rodents, including the true rats and mice and their allies. — **mu′rine**, *n.*
murk, mirk (mûrk), *adj.* [AS. *mirce*, or fr. ON. *myrkr.*] *Poetic & Dial.* Dark; hence, obscure; also, gloomy. — *n. Chiefly Dial.* Darkness; gloom.
murk′y, mirk′y (mûr′kĭ), *adj.;* -I·ER (-kĭ·ẽr); -I·EST. Dark; obscure; gloomy. — **Syn.** See DARK. — **murk′i·ly**, *adv.* — **murk′i·ness**, *n.*
mur′mur (mûr′mẽr), *n.* [OF. *murmure.*] **1.** A low, confused, and indistinct sound, like that of running water; as, the *murmur* of conversation. **2.** A low, muttered complaint or repining; grumbling. **3.** *Med.* An abnormal sound, heard on auscultation of the heart, as in leaking heart valves. — *v. i. & t.* [OF. *murmurer*, fr. L. *murmurare*, fr. *murmur* murmur.] To make, or utter in or with, a murmur. — **mur′mur·er**, *n.* — **mur′mur·ing**, *adj.*
mur′mur·ous (-ŭs), *adj.* Attended with, or making, murmurs; low and indistinct. — **mur′mur·ous·ly**, *adv.*
mur′phy (mûr′fĭ), *n.; pl.* MURPHIES (-fĭz). [From proper name.] *Jocose.* A potato.
mur′rain (mûr′ĭn), *n.* [OF. *morine*, fr. *morir* to die, fr. L. *mori, moriri.*] A pestilence or plague, now only one affecting domestic animals, as anthrax or Texas fever; — formerly sometimes used in imprecations; as, a *murrain* take you, a plague take you.
murre (mûr), *n.* **a** Any of several guillemots (genus *Uria*); specif., the foolish guillemot. **b** The razor-billed auk.
mur′rey (mûr′ĭ), *n.* [OF. *moree* a dark-red color, fr. ML. *morata*, fr. L. *morum* mulberry.] A color, red in hue, of high saturation and low brilliance. See COLOR. — *adj.* Of a dark-red color.
mur′rhine (mûr′ĭn; -īn), *adj.* [L. *murr(h)inus*, fr. *murr(h)a.*] *Rom. Antiq.* Made of **mur′ra**, *or* **mur′rha** (mûr′ȧ), a semiprecious stone (perhaps fluorite) of which beautiful and costly vases were made. — *n.* A murrhine vase.
murrhine glass. Glassware in which the body is transparent and shows embedded pieces of colored glass.
mur′ther (mûr′thẽr). *Now Dial.* Var. of MURDER.
mu·sa′ceous (mū·zā′shŭs), *adj.* [NL. *Musa* (type genus, fr. Ar. *mawzah* banana) + *-aceous.*] Belonging to the banana family (Musaceae). See BANANA.
mus′ca·del′ (mŭs′kȧ·dĕl′; mŭs′kȧ·dĕl), *n.* = MUSCATEL.
mus′ca·dine (mŭs′kȧ·dĭn; -dīn), *n.* **1.** *Obs. exc. Hist.* Muscatel, the wine. **2.** A grape (*Muscadinia rotundifolia*) of the southern United States.
‖**mus′cae vo′li·tan′tes** (mŭs′sē vŏl′ĭ·tăn′tēz). [L., flying flies.] Figures, as dots, in the field of vision, due to cells and fragments in the vitreous humor and lens.
mus′cat (mŭs′kăt; -kăt), *n.* [F., n. & adj., fr. Pr. *muscat*, prop., smelling like musk, fr. LL. *muscus* musk.] **1.** Muscatel, the wine. **2.** Any of several cultivated varieties of the European grape.
mus′ca·tel′ (mŭs′kȧ·tĕl′; mŭs′kȧ·tĕl), *n.* [MF. *muscatel, muscadel*, fr. Pr. *muscat.* See MUSCAT.] **1.** A rich sweet wine produced in France, Italy, and other countries from muscat grapes. **2.** The muscat grape.
mus′cid (mŭs′ĭd), *adj.* [L. *musca* a fly.] Belonging to a family (Muscidae) of dipterous insects, of which the housefly is the type. — **mus′cid**, *n.*
mus′cle (mŭs′'l), *n.* [F., fr. L. *musculus* muscle, little mouse, dim. of *mus* mouse.] **1.** An organ whose special function is the production of motion; also, the tissue of which such an organ is made, consisting of modified, usually greatly elongated, cells (called **muscle fibers**), which contract when stimulated. **2.** Muscular strength or development. — *v. i.;* MUS′CLED (-'ld); MUS′CLING (-lĭng). *Colloq.* To make one's way by brute strength; as, to *muscle* through a crowd.
mus′cle-bound′, *adj. Med.* Having some of the muscles tense and enlarged and of impaired elasticity — a condition sometimes produced by excessive athletic exercise.
muscle sense. *Psychol. & Physiol.* The sense whose end organs lie in the muscles.
mus′co·va′do (mŭs′kō·vā′dō), *n.* [Sp. *mascabado* or Pg. *mascavado* unrefined, for *mascabado*, past part. of *mascabar* to depreciate, for *menoscabar*, fr. *menos* less + *cabo* head, end.] Raw sugar, obtained from the juice of the sugar cane by evaporation and draining off the molasses.
Mus′co·vite (mŭs′kō·vīt), *n.* **1.** A native or inhabitant of Muscovy, or ancient Russia; hence, a Russian. **2.** [*not cap.*] *Mineral.* Common, or potash, mica, essentially $(H,K)AlSiO_4$. — **Mus′co·vite**, *adj.*
mus′co·vy duck (mŭs′kō·vĭ). [A corruption of *musk duck.*] A duck (*Cairina moschata*), native from Mexico to southern Brazil, but widely kept in domestication.
mus′cu·lar (mŭs′kū·lẽr), *adj.* **1.** Of or pert. to a muscle or a system of muscles; consisting of a muscle or muscles. **2.** Performed by a muscle or the muscles; also, affecting the muscles. **3.** Having well-developed muscles; brawny; strong. — **mus′cu·lar′i·ty** (-lăr′ĭ·tĭ), *n.*
muscular dystrophy. *Med.* A hereditary disease characterized by progressive wasting of muscles.
mus′cu·la·ture (mŭs′kū·lȧ·tūr), *n.* [F.] The muscles of an animal or of any part of it considered with reference to their arrangement of relations or functions.
mus′cu·lo- (mŭs′kū·lō-), **muscul-.** [L. *musculus.*] A combining form meaning *muscle.*
muse (mūz), *v. i. & t.* [OF. *muser* to loiter, trifle, to muse, reflect.] To meditate; ponder. — **Syn.** See PONDER. — *n.* A state of profound meditation. — **mus′er** (mūz′ẽr), *n.*
Muse, *n.* [OF., fr. L. *Musa*, fr. Gr. *Mousa.*] **1.** *Gr. Myth.* One of the nine goddesses of song and poetry and also the arts and sciences; — often in *pl.* They are Calliope, Clio, Erato, Euterpe, Melpomene, Polyhymnia or Polymnia, Terpsichore, Thalia, and Urania. **2.** [*often not cap.*] The inspiring goddess of a poet.
muse′ful (mūz′fo͝ol; -f'l), *adj.* Meditative.
mu·sette′ (mū·zĕt′), *n.* [F.] **1.** A small bagpipe formerly popular in France, having a soft and sweet tone. **2.** Also **musette bag.** A canvas or leather case or wallet suspended from a belt worn over the shoulder, used esp. by soldiers for carrying provisions.
mu·se′um (mū·zē′ŭm), *n.* [L., a temple of the Muses, hence, a place of study, fr. Gr. *mouseion*, fr. *Mousa* a Muse.] A building, or part of one, in which are preserved and exhibited objects of permanent interest in one or more of the arts and sciences.
mush (mŭsh), *n.* [E. dial. *mush* a mash, crumbled matter.] **1.** *U. S.* Meal (esp. Indian meal) boiled in water. **2.** Anything soft and thick, like mush. **3.** *Colloq.* Sickly sentimentality. — *v. t. & i. Dial.* To reduce to mush; to crumble.
mush, *n.* [Prob. short for *mush on*, a corrupt. of F. *marchons*, the cry of voyageurs and trappers to their dogs.] *Northwestern America.* A march on foot, esp. across snow with dogs. — *interj.* A call to urge dog teams on. — *v. i.* To travel on foot, esp. across snow with dogs. — **mush′er** (-ẽr), *n.*
mush′room (mŭsh′ro͞om), *n.* [OF. *moisseron, mouscheron.*] **1.** Any fleshy fungus of a large class (Basidiomycetes) including also the rusts, smuts, puffballs, etc.; popularly, any edible fungus (orders Agaricales or Lycoperdales), esp. the ***meadow, or field, mushroom*** (*Agaricus campestris*). Cf. AGARIC, CHAMPIGNON, CHANTERELLE; see FUNGUS, *Illust.* **2.** A parvenu; upstart. **3.** Anything like, or likened to, a mushroom in shape. — *adj.* **1.** Of or pertaining to mushrooms. **2.** Mushroomlike in its quick growth and decay; hence, upstart; also, shaped like a mushroom. — *v. i.* **1.** To rise or grow rapidly, like a mushroom. **2.** To spread at the end so as to resemble a mushroom.
mush′y (mŭsh′ĭ), *adj.;* MUSH′I·ER (-ĭ·ẽr); MUSH′I·EST. Soft like mush; esp., good-naturedly weak and effusive; weakly sentimental.
mu′sic (mū′zĭk), *n.* [OF. *musique*, fr. L. *musica*, fr. Gr. *mousikē* (sc. *technē*), any art over which the Muses presided, esp. music, lyric poetry set and sung to music.] **1.** The science or art of pleasing, expressive, or intelligible combination of tones; the art of making such combinations, esp. into compositions of definite structure and significance; the art of inventing or writing, or of rendering, such compositions. **2.** **a** *Obs.* A composition so made. **b** Tones arranged into such a composition; as, to set to *music.* **c** Such compositions collectively. **d** Musical composition. **3.** Sounds having rhythm and melody. **4.** Figuratively: **a** *Obs. exc. Mil.* A band of musical performers; as, the *music* of a regiment. **b** Responsiveness to music.
mu′si·cal (mū′zĭ·kăl), *adj.* **1.** Of or pert. to music or the notation or performance of music. **2.** Having the pleasing qualities of music; melodious; harmonious. **3.** Fond of, or intelligently appreciative of, music. **4.** Set to music; accompanied by music. — *n.* **1.** *Colloq.* A musicale. **2.** A musical comedy. — **mu′si·cal·ly**, *adv.* — **mu′si·cal·ness**, *n.*
musical comedy. A type of theatrical performance, typically whimsical or picturesque, consisting of musical numbers and of dialogue, with a slender plot.
mu′si·cale′ (mū′zĭ·kăl′), *n.* [F. *soirée musicale.*] A social entertainment, with music as the leading feature.
music box. A box or case containing apparatus moved by clockwork so as to play certain tunes automatically.
music drama. An opera in which the text and action are not interrupted by set arias, duets, etc., the music being determined throughout by dramatic appropriateness.
music hall. A place for public musical entertainments; specif., esp. *Eng.*, a hall for vaudeville performances.
mu·si′cian (mū·zĭsh′ăn), *n.* One skilled in music; esp., a composer or professional performer. — **mu·si′cian·ly**, *adj.*
music of the spheres. An ethereal harmony supposed by Pythagoras to be produced by the planetary motions.
mus′ing (mūz′ĭng), *adj.* Meditative. — *n.* Meditation. — **mus′ing·ly**, *adv.*
musk (mŭsk), *n.* [OF. *musc*, fr. LL. *muscus*, ML. *moschus*, fr. Gr. *moskos, moschos*, fr. Per. *mushk.*] **1.** A substance obtained from a sac (**musk bag**) under the skin of the abdomen of the male musk deer. It is used as the basis for many perfumes. **2.** The musk deer; also, any animal resembling the musk deer, esp. in having a musky odor. **3.** Any of various plants with musk-scented foliage or flowers, as the grape hyacinth. **4.** The perfume emitted by musk or any like perfume.
mus′kal·longe (mŭs′kȧ·lŏnj), **mus′kal·lunge.** Vars. of MUSKELLUNGE.
musk deer. A small ungulate (*Moschus moschiferus*) inhabiting high altitudes of central Asia, constituting a subfamily of Cervidae (see DEER).
mus′keg (mŭs′kĕg), *n.* [Of Algonquian origin.] **a** *Northern U. S. & Canada.* A bog characterized by an abundance of sphagnum moss and by tussocks. **b** Any of various mosses of the genera *Sphagnum, Hypnum*, etc.
mus′kel·lunge (mŭs′kĕ·lŭnj), *n. sing. & pl.* [Ojibway *mashkinoje*, lit., great pike.] A large North American pike (*Esox masquinongy*), valued as a game fish, sometimes weighing 60 to 80 pounds.
mus′ket (mŭs′kĕt; -kĭt), *n.* [F. *mousquet*, fr. It. *moschetto*, formerly, a kind of hawk, fr. L. *musca* a fly.] A hand firearm formerly carried by soldiers, esp. infantry; loosely, any piece carried by infantry.
mus′ket·eer′ (mŭs′kĕ·tēr′; -kĭ·tēr′), *n.* [F. *mousquetaire.*] A soldier armed with a musket.
mus′ket·ry (mŭs′kĕt·rĭ; -kĭt·rĭ), *n.; pl.* MUSKETRIES (-rĭz). **1.** Mus-

kets; also, musketeers. **2.** The fire of muskets, or the art of firing muskets.

Mus·kho′ge·an (mŭs·kō′gē·ăn), *adj.* Pertaining to or designating one of the chief linguistic families of North American Indians, formerly dwelling in southeastern United States. They include the Creeks, Choctaws, Chickasaws, and Seminoles (of the Five Civilized Nations), now chiefly in Oklahoma.

musk′mel′on (mŭsk′mĕl′ŭn), *n.* [*musk* + *melon*.] The fruit of a plant (*Cucumis melo*, or esp. *C. m. reticulatus*, also known as ***nutmeg melon***) of the gourd family; also, the plant. Broadly, muskmelons are of three general types specified as *muskmelons, cantaloupes*, and *winter melons*. In the United States there is no clear distinction between the first two types, although the varieties having skins with a netlike pattern are generally known as *cantaloupes*.

musk ox. A hollow-horned ungulate (*Ovibos moschatus*), now confined to Greenland and the barren grounds of North America.

musk′rat′ (mŭsk′răt′), *n.*; see PLURAL, *Note*, 3. **1.** An aquatic rodent (*Ondatra zibethicus*) of the United States and Canada. It has the tail long, scaly, and laterally compressed, the hind feet webbed, and the fur dark glossy brown. Cf. RODENT, *Illust.* **2.** The fur or pelt of this animal.

musk rose. A rose (*Rosa moschata*) of the Mediterranean region, with fragrant flowers.

musk′y (mŭs′kĭ), *adj.*; MUSK′I·ER (-kĭ·ĕr); MUSK′I·EST. Having an odor of or like musk.

Mus′lem (mŭz′lĕm; mŭs′-), **Mus′lim** (-lĭm). Vars. of MOSLEM.

mus′lin (mŭz′lĭn), *n.* [F. *mousseline*, fr. It. *mussolino*, through Ar., fr. *Mosul*, a city of Mesopotamia.] Any of various cotton cloths; as: **a** A very thin, fine, and soft plain cloth made in India, or an imitation of it. **b** A stouter fabric, plain, printed, dyed, or dotted. **c** *U. S.* Any of various coarser and heavier cotton goods.

muslin delaine. = DELAINE.

muslin kail (kāl). *Scot.* Broth of barley and greens.

mus′quash (mŭs′kwŏsh), *n.* [Of Algonquian origin.] = MUSKRAT, 1.

muss (mŭs), *n.* **1.** *Obs.* A scramble. **2.** *Chiefly Dial. & Colloq.* **a** A state of disorder. **b** That which makes disorder, as rubbish. **3.** *Slang, U. S.* A row; squabble. — *v. t. Chiefly Dial. & Colloq.* **a** To disarrange, as clothing; rumple. **b** To soil; to mess. — **muss′y** (mŭs′ĭ), *adj.*

mus′sel (mŭs′'l), *n.* Also **mus′cle.** [AS. *musle*, fr. L. *musculus* mussel, muscle.] **1.** Any of certain marine bivalve mollusks (genus *Mytilus* and related genera). The common mussel (*Mytilus edulis*) is much used as food. **2.** Any of numerous fresh-water bivalve mollusks (*Unio, Anodonta*, and related genera) found esp. in the central United States. Their shells are used in making buttons, etc.

Mus′sul·man (mŭs′ŭl·măn), *n.*; *pl.* -MANS (-mănz), sometimes -MEN (-mĕn). [Per. & Turk. *musulmān*, fr. Ar. *muslim*, pl. *muslimūn*. See MOSLEM.] A Moslem.

must (mŭst), *n.* [AS., fr. L. *mustum* (sc. *vinum*), fr. *mustus* young, fresh.] The expressed juice of the grape, or other fruit, before fermentation; new wine.

must, *n.* Mustiness; mold.

must (mŭst; 4), *v.* Used, without inflection, as *present*, and (sometimes) *past, tense.* Infinitive and participles lacking. [ME. *moste*, a pret., could, was free to, had to, pres. *mot, moot*, fr. AS. *mōste*, pret., *mōt*, pres.] An auxiliary of predication used before the infinitive without *to*, denoting am (or is, are, etc.) obliged, required, compelled, etc. — *adj.* Of a nature to demand doing, reading, visiting, adoption, etc., without fail; as, a *must* book; designated as mandatory; as, items on the editor's *must* list. — *n.* A must, or obligatory, action or item.

must (mŭst), *n. Scot.* Musk; also, hair powder. — *v. t. Scot.* To powder (the hair).

must, *adj.* Also **musth.** [Hind. *mast* ruttish, intoxicated, fr. Per. *mast.*] Being in a condition of dangerous frenzy, usually connected with sexual excitement; — said of adult male elephants. — *n.* **a** The condition of frenzy. **b** An elephant in such a condition.

mus·tache′, mous·tache′ (mŭs·tăsh′; mŭs′tăsh; *or, esp. Brit.*, mo͞os·tăsh′; 9), *n.* [F. *moustache*, fr. It. *mostaccio, -chio*, fr. ML. *mustacia*, fr. Gr. *mystax* mustache, upper lip.] **1.** The hair growing on man's upper lip or that on either side of the upper lip. **2.** *A Gallicism.* A soldier; — in phrase *old mustache.* **3.** *Zool.* Hair or bristles round the mouth of an animal.

mus·ta′chio (mŭs·tä′shō), *n.*; *pl.* -CHIOS (-shōz). A mustache. — **mus·ta′chioed** (-shōd), *adj.*

mus′tang (mŭs′tăng), *n.* [Sp. *mesteño* belonging to the graziers, strayed, wild.] The small, hardy, half-wild horse of Texas, New Mexico, etc. Cf. BRONCO.

mus′tard (mŭs′tẽrd), *n.* [OF. *moustarde*, fr. L. *mustum* must; — mustard was prepared for use by being mixed with *must.*] **1.** Any of a genus (*Brassica*) of plants typifying a family (Brassicaceae, the mustard, cabbage, or cress family) and having lyrately lobed leaves, yellow flowers, and linear beaked pods. The ***white mustard*** (*B. hirta*) and the ***black mustard*** (*B. nigra*) are cultivated, esp. in Europe, for their seeds. Cf. HEDGE GARLIC. **2.** A yellow powder of mustard seed mixed with liquid for use as a condiment and as a rubefacient or counterirritant. **3.** The sharp pungent flour of mustard seed.

mustard gas. *Chem.* An oily liquid, $(ClCH_2CH_2)_2S$, used as a shell filling in World War I because of its violent irritant and blistering properties.

mustard oil. An oil from mustard; esp., a fixed semidrying oil of unpleasant odor used in soapmaking, etc.

mustard plaster. A counterirritant and rubefacient plaster containing powdered mustard.

mus·tee′ (mŭs·tē′; mŭs′tē), *n.* [From MESTIZO.] *West Indies & India.* An octoroon; loosely, any half-breed.

mus′te·line (mŭs′tē·līn; -lĭn; 56), *adj.* [L. *mustelinus*, fr. *mustela* weasel.] Belonging to or designating a family (Mustelidae) containing the weasels, badgers, otters, minks, skunks, etc. — **mus′te·line,** *n.*

mus′ter (mŭs′tẽr), *v. t.* [ME. *mustren*, prop., to show, fr. OF. *mostrer, mustrer, monstrer*, fr. L. *monstrare* to show.] **1.** To assemble, as troops, for a muster. **2.** *Obs.* To enroll. **3.** Hence: To summon together; to collect and display. — **Syn.** See SUMMON. — *v. i.* To be gathered together for a muster; to come together as parts of a force or body. — *n.* **1.** *Now Rare.* A sample; pattern. **2.** An assembly of troops or a ship's company, as for parade; in the army and navy, such an assembling for roll call. **3.** The sum total of a company assembled for muster; also, the roll of the men. **4.** An assemblage.

mus′ty (mŭs′tĭ), *adj.*; MUS′TI·ER (-tĭ·ĕr); MUS′TI·EST. [Perh. for earlier *moisty.* See MOIST.] **1.** Having the disagreeable odor and taste of substances that have spoiled in close, muggy weather; sour and fetid; moldy; as, *musty* corn, wine, books. **2.** Spoiled by age; stale; trite. **3.** Dull and spiritless. — **Syn.** See MALODOROUS. — **mus′ti·ly,** *adv.* — **mus′ti·ness,** *n.*

mus′ty, *n.* A former cheap snuff of a musty flavor.

mu′ta·ble (mū′tȧ·b'l), *adj.* [L. *mutabilis*, fr. *mutare* to change.] **1.** Capable of change or being changed in form or nature. **2.** Given to constant or frequent change; changeable; changeful; fickle. — **mu′ta·bil′i·ty** (-bĭl′ĭ·tĭ), **mu′ta·ble·ness,** *n.* — **mu′ta·bly,** *adv.*

mu′tant (mū′tănt), *adj. & n.* [L. *mutans, -antis*, pres. part. of *mutare* to change.] (One) that undergoes mutation.

mu′tate (mū′tāt *or, esp. Brit.*, mū·tāt′), *v. t. & i.* To alter; to undergo mutation. See MUTATION, 3.

mu·ta′tion (mū·tā′shŭn), *n.* [F., fr. L. *mutatio*, fr. *mutare* to change.] **1.** Change; alteration in form or qualities. **2.** *Biol.* **a** A sudden variation, the offspring differing from its parents in some well-marked character or characters, due to changes within the chromosomes or genes. **b** The result of the above process; a suddenly produced variation. **3.** *Philol.* Umlaut. — **Syn.** See CHANGE. — **mu·ta′tion·al** (-ăl; -'l), *adj.* — **mu′ta·tive** (mū′tȧ·tĭv), *adj.*

‖**mu·ta′tis mu·tan′dis** (mū·tā′tĭs mū·tăn′dĭs). [L.] Necessary changes having been made.

‖**mu·ta′to no′mi·ne** (mū·tā′tō nŏm′ĭ·nē). [L.] The name being changed.

mutch (mŭch), *n.* [MD. *mutse.*] *Dial.* A woman's linen cap.

mutch′kin (mŭch′kĭn), *n.* [Obs. D. *mudseken.*] *Scot.* An old English pint, equal to ¾ imperial pint.

mute (mūt), *adj.* [L. *mutus.*] **1.** Not speaking; silent. **2.** *Law.* Of a prisoner, refusing to plead. He is then said to *stand mute.* **3.** *Phonet.* **a** Not uttered; unpronounced. **b** Produced with a complete momentary closure of the breath passage. — *n.* **1.** One who does not speak. Specif.: **a** A deaf-mute. **b** Among the Turks, an attendant selected for his place because he cannot speak. **c** A person employed by undertakers to attend a funeral as a hired mourner. **2.** *Music.* Any device on a musical instrument serving to deaden, soften, or muffle its tone. **3.** *Phonet.* **a** A letter representing no sound; a silent letter. **b** A consonant formed with complete momentary stoppage of the breath, as *p, b, t, d, k, g.* See STOP, *n.* — *v. t.* To muffle or deaden the sound of, as by a mute. — **mute′ly,** *adv.* — **mute′ness,** *n.*

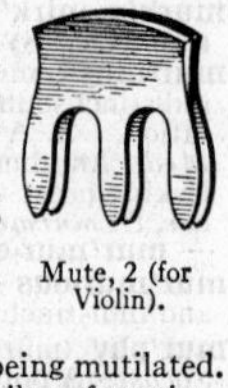

Mute, 2 (for Violin).

mu′ti·late (mū′tĭ·lāt), *v. t.* [L. *mutilatus*, past part. of *mutilare* to mutilate, fr. *mutilus* maimed.] **1.** To cut off or remove a limb or essential part of; to maim; sometimes, to castrate. **2.** To destroy or remove a material part of, so as to render imperfect. — **mu′ti·la′tive** (-lā′tĭv), *adj.* — **mu′ti·la′tor** (-lā′tẽr), *n.*

mu′ti·la′tion (-lā′shŭn), *n.* A mutilating, or state of being mutilated.

mu′ti·neer′ (mū′tĭ·nēr′), *n.* [F. *mutinier.*] One guilty of mutiny. — *v. i.* To mutiny.

mu′ti·nous (mū′tĭ·nŭs), *adj.* Disposed to or indicating mutiny; seditious; rebellious; hence, unruly; as, *mutinous* passions. — **mu′ti·nous·ly,** *adv.* — **mu′ti·nous·ness,** *n.*

mu′ti·ny (-nĭ), *n.*; *pl.* -NIES (-nĭz). [From *mutine* to mutiny, fr. F. *se mutiner*, fr. *mutin* stubborn, mutinous, fr. OF. *muete* riot, fr. L. *movere* to move.] **1.** *Obs.* Tumult; strife. **2.** Insurrection against, or refusal to obey, constituted authority, esp. military or naval authority; insubordination. — **Syn.** See REBELLION. — *v. i.*; -NIED (-nĭd); -NY·ING. To excite, or to be guilty of, mutiny.

mut′ism (mūt′ĭz'm), *n.* Condition or state of being muted, or without power of speech.

mutt (mŭt), *n.* Also **mut.** [From *muttonhead* a stupid person.] *Slang.* **a** A commonplace or stupid person. **b** A mongrel dog; cur.

mut′ter (mŭt′ẽr), *v. i.* [ME. *muteren, moteren.*] **1.** To utter words indistinctly, esp. in expressing complaint or anger; to grumble. **2.** To sound with a low, rumbling noise. — *v. t.* To utter with imperfect articulations, or with a low voice. — *n.* Repressed or obscure utterance; murmur. — **mut′ter·er,** *n.* — **mut′ter·ing·ly,** *adv.*

mut′ton (mŭt′'n), *n.* [OF. *moton, molton*, a ram (F. *mouton* sheep), fr. ML. *multo.*] **1.** The flesh of a sheep. Cf. LAMB. **2.** *Now Rare.* A sheep. — **mut′ton·y** (-'n·ĭ), *adj.*

mut′ton·chop′ (-chŏp′), *adj.* Having a form suggestive of a mutton chop, or roundish at one end and narrow and prolonged at the other; — said esp. of side whiskers (**mutton chops**).

mu′tu·al (mū′tū·ăl), *adj.* [F. *mutuel*, fr. L. *mutuus*, orig., exchanged, lent.] **1.** Entertained, proffered, or exerted by each with respect to the other of two, or each of the others of a group; reciprocally given and received. Also, having the same relation to each other; as, *mutual* foes. **2.** Common; joint; as, *mutual* effort. This use is now avoided by careful writers. **3.** *Insurance.* Designating, or pertaining to, the method or plan (**mutual plan**) in which the policyholders constitute the members of the insuring company, electing their own managers or directors and sharing the profits. — **Syn.** See RECIPROCAL. — **mu′tu·al·ly,** *adv.*

mu′tu·al′i·ty (mū′tū·ăl′ĭ·tĭ), *n.*; *pl.* -TIES (-tĭz). State or quality of being mutual; interaction; interdependence.

mu′tu·al·ize (mū′tū·ăl·īz), *v. t. & i.* **1.** To make or become mutual. **2.** *Colloq. Finance.* To organize or reorganize (a corporation) so as to place a substantial amount of the common stock in the hands of its employees or customers. — **mu′tu·al·i·za′tion** (-ĭ·zā′shŭn; -ī·zā′-), *n.*

mutual savings bank. A savings bank without capital, the depositors of which share in the profits.

mu′tule (mū′tūl), *n.* [F., fr. L. *mutulus.*] *Arch.* A flat block projecting under the corona of the Doric cornice.

mu·zhik′, mu·zjik′ (mo͞o·zhĭk′; mo͞o′zhĭk), *n.* [Russ. *muzhik.*] A Russian peasant.

muzz (mŭz), *v. i. Slang, Eng.* **a** To study; "grind." **b** To idle. — *v. t. Slang, Eng.* To make muzzy, or muddled.

muz′zle (mŭz′'l), *n.* [OF. *musel* muzzle or snout, fr. ML. *musellum*, dim. of *musus.*] **1.** The projecting jaws and nose of an animal (see DOG, SHEEP, *Illusts.*); hence, jocosely, the human mouth or face. **2.** A fastening or covering for the mouth of an animal, to prevent eating, vicious biting, etc. **3.** The mouth of a thing; the end for entrance or discharge; as, the *muzzle* of a gun. **4.** A respirator; a gas mask. — *v. t.*; MUZ′ZLED (-'ld); MUZ′ZLING (-lĭng). To bind the muzzle of; to fasten the mouth of, so as to prevent biting or eating; hence, to restrain from speech or action; gag. — **muz′zler** (-lẽr), *n.*

muz'zle-load'er (mŭz'’l·lōd'ẽr), *n.* A gun that is loaded through the muzzle. — **muz'zle-load'ing** (-lōd'ĭng; 2), *adj.*

muz'zy (mŭz'ĭ), *adj.;* MUZ'ZI·ER (-ĭ·ẽr); MUZ'ZI·EST. Dull-spirited; muddled.

MVD (ĕm'vē'dē'). [From the initials of the Russ. *M*inisterstvo *V*nutrennikh *D*el.] The Soviet Ministry of Internal Affairs, charged with preserving internal order, administering the fire and highway departments, police, border guards, labor camps, etc.

my (mī; 4), *pron.* [ME. *mi,* fr. *min.* See MINE.] Possessive case of *I.* Cf. MINE. — *adj.* Of, belonging to, or relating to me. Cf. MINE.

my-. = MYO- (which see), as in **my·al'gi·a, my'as·the'ni·a.**

my·ce'li·um (mī·sē'lĭ·ŭm), *n.; pl.* -LIA (-ȧ). [NL., fr. Gr. *mykēs* mushroom.] *Bot.* The mass of interwoven threadlike filaments forming the vegetative portion of the thallus in fungi; also, the similar mass formed by certain of the higher bacteria. Cf. HYPHA. — **my·ce'li·al** (-ăl), *adj.* — **my·ce'li·an** (-ăn), *adj.* — **my·ce'li·oid** (-oid), *adj.* — **my'ce·loid** (mī'sē·loid), *adj.*

My'ce·nae'an (mī'sē·nē'ăn), *adj.* Of or pert. to the ancient city of Mycenae in Argolis or designating the civilization in the Mediterranean area (c. 1400 B.C.–1100 B.C.) which preceded the Greek.

-my·ce'tes (-mī·sē'tēz). [NL., fr. Gr. *mykēs, mykētos.*] *Bot.* A combining form meaning *fungus;* — used in names of large classes, as in Asco*mycetes.* For a member of the class **-my·cete'** (-mī·sēt') is used. Derivative adjectives are formed in **-my·ce'tous** (-mī·sē'tŭs), **-my·ce'tic** (-tĭk).

my·ce'to·zo'an (mī·sē'tō·zō'ăn), *adj.* Myxomycetous.

my'co- (mī'kō-), **myc-.** [Gr. *mykēs.*] A combining form meaning *fungus,* as in *myco*logy.

my'co·bac·te'ri·um (-băk·tēr'ĭ·ŭm), *n.* [NL., fr. *myco-* + *bacterium.*] *Bacteriol.* Any of a genus (*Mycobacterium*) of nonmotile, aerobic bacteria difficult to stain. One species (*M. tuberculosis hominis*) causes tuberculosis in man, one (*M. t. bovis*) causes tuberculosis in cattle and man, and another (*M. leprae*) causes leprosy.

my·col'o·gy (mī·kŏl'ō·jĭ), *n.* [*myco-* + *-logy.*] The branch of botany dealing with fungi. Hence, fungal life, as of a region; also, the life phenomena exhibited by a fungus; as, the *mycology* of a mold. — **my·col'o·gist** (-jĭst), *n.*

my'cor·rhi'za, my'co·rhi'za (mī'kō·rī'zȧ), *n.* [NL., fr. *myco-* + *-rrhiza.*] *Bot.* The association, usually symbiotic, of the mycelium of various fungi and the roots of seed plants. — **my'cor·rhi'zal, my'co·rhi'zal** (-zăl), *adj.* — **my'cor·rhi'zic, my'co·rhi'zic** (-zĭk), *adj.*

my·co'sis (mī·kō'sĭs), *n.; pl.* -COSES (-sēz). [NL., fr. *myc-* + *-osis.*] *Med.* **a** The infesting of any part of the body by fungi. **b** A disease due to such infestation. — **my·cot'ic** (-kŏt'ĭk), *adj.*

my·dri'a·sis (mĭ·drī'ȧ·sĭs; mī-), *n.* [L., fr. Gr. *mydriasis.*] *Physiol. & Med.* A long-continued or excessive dilatation of the pupil of the eye.

myd'ri·at'ic (mĭd'rĭ·ăt'ĭk), *adj.* Causing dilatation of the pupil. — *n.* A mydriatic medicine or agent, as belladonna.

my'e·len·ceph'a·lon (mī'ĕ·lĕn·sĕf'ȧ·lŏn), *n.* See HINDBRAIN.

my'e·lin (mī'ĕ·lĭn), *n.* Also **my'e·line** (-lĭn; -lēn). [G. *myelin,* fr. Gr. *myelos* marrow.] *Anat. & Biochem.* A soft, white, somewhat fatty material which, in certain nerve fibers, forms a thick sheath (the ***myelin,*** *or* ***medullary, sheath***) about the axis cylinder.

my'e·lo- (mī'ĕ·lō-), **myel-.** [Gr. *myelos* marrow.] *Med.* A combining form meaning *marrow; the spinal cord;* as in **my'e·li'tis,** inflammation of the spinal cord or bone marrow.

my'e·loid (mī'ĕ·loid), *adj.* [*myel-* + *-oid.*] *Anat.* **a** Of or pert. to the spinal cord. **b** Of, pert. to, arising from, or like the bone marrow.

my'ia·sis (mī'yȧ·sĭs), *n.* [NL., fr. Gr. *myia* fly.] *Med.* Any disease due to presence of larvae of flies in or on the body.

my'na, my'nah (mī'nȧ), *n.* [Hind. *mainā.*] A common bird (*Acridotheres tristis*) of southeastern Asia, allied to the starlings.

Myn·heer' (mĭ·nār'; mīn·hēr'), *n.* [D. *mijnheer.*] Dutch equiv. of *Mr.* or *Sir;* hence [*not cap.*], a Dutchman.

my'o- (mī'ō-), **my-.** [Gr. *mys, myos.*] A combining form meaning *muscle,* as in **my·ol'o·gy,** the science that treats of muscles, and in:

myoatrophy	**myogenetic**	**myopathia**
myoclonus	**myoneural**	**myoscope**
myodegeneration	**myoneuralgia**	**myotomy**

my'o·car'di·o·graph' (mī'ō·kär'dĭ·ō·grăf'; 9), *n.* [*myo-* + *cardiograph.*] *Physiol.* A recording instrument for making a tracing (**my'o·car'di·o·gram'** [-grăm']) of the action of the heart.

my'o·car·di'tis (-kär·dī'tĭs), *n.* [NL., fr. *myocardium* + *-itis.*] Inflammation of the muscular part (**my'o·car'di·um** [-kär'dĭ·ŭm]) of the heart wall; carditis. Cf. ENDOCARDITIS, PERICARDITIS.

my'o·graph (mī'ō·grăf; 9), *n.* [*myo-* + *-graph.*] *Physiol.* An instrument for making a record (**my'o·gram** [-grăm]) of intensity, velocity, etc., of a muscular contraction.

my·ol'o·gy (mī·ŏl'ō·jĭ), *n.* The branch of science that treats of muscles. — **my·ol'o·gist** (-jĭst), *n.*

my·o'ma (mī·ō'mȧ), *n.; pl.* -MATA (-mȧ·tȧ). [NL., fr. *my-* + *-oma.*] *Med.* A tumor consisting of muscular tissue. — **my·om'a·tous** (-ŏm'ȧ·tŭs; -ō'mȧ·tŭs), *adj.*

my·o'pi·a (mī·ō'pĭ·ȧ), *n.* [NL., fr. Gr. *myōps, myōpos,* fr. *myein* to shut the eyes + *ōps, ōpos,* the eye.] *Med.* Nearsightedness; a condition of the eye in which the rays from distant objects are brought to a focus before reaching the retina; hence, figuratively, shortsightedness. — **my·op'ic** (-ŏp'ĭk), *adj.*

my'o·sin (mī'ō·sĭn), *n.* [Gr. *mys, myos,* a muscle.] *Biochem.* A globulin of muscle held to be the protein of rigor mortis and to give a clot of insoluble protein.

my·o'sis (mī·ō'sĭs), *n.* [NL., fr. Gr. *myein* to close the eyes or lips.] *Med.* Abnormal contraction of the pupil of the eye.

my'o·so'tis (mī'ō·sō'tĭs), *n.* Also **my'o·sote** (mī'ō·sōt). [NL., fr. Gr. *myosōtis,* lit., mouse ear.] *Bot.* One of a genus (*Myosotis*) of herbs of the borage family, including the common forget-me-not (*M. palustris*).

my·ot'ic (mī·ŏt'ĭk), *adj. Med.* Of or pertaining to myosis; producing myosis, as opium, etc.; affected with myosis. — *n.* A myotic drug.

myr'i·a- (mĭr'ĭ·ȧ-), **myri-.** [Gr. *myrias* a myriad.] A combining form, used esp. in the metric system (see METRIC SYSTEM, *Tables*), denoting *ten thousand* (times), as in: **myr'i·a·gram',** 10 kilograms, or 10,000 grams; **myr'i·a·li'ter; myr'i·a·me'ter.**

myr'i·ad (mĭr'ĭ·ăd), *n.* [Gr. *myrias, myriados,* fr. *myrios* numberless, pl. *myrioi* ten thousand.] **1.** The number of ten thousand; ten thousand persons or things. **2.** An indefinitely large number. — *adj.* Consisting of a very great, but indefinite, number.

myr'i·a·pod' (mĭr'ĭ·ȧ·pŏd'), *n.* [NL., fr. *myria-* + *-pod.*] *Zool.* Any of a group (Myriapoda) of arthropods having the body made up of numerous similar segments, nearly all of which bear true jointed legs. The group includes the millepedes (class Diplopoda) and the centipedes (class Chilopoda). — **myr'i·a·pod',** *adj.* — **myr'i·ap'o·dan** (-ăp'ō·dăn), *adj. & n.* — **myr'i·ap'o·dous** (-dŭs), *adj.*

myr'me·co- (mûr'mē·kō-). [Gr. *myrmēx, myrmēkos.*] A combining form meaning *an ant,* as in: **myr'me·coph'a·gous,** feeding on ants; **myr'me·coph'i·lous,** fond of or benefited by ants, as certain insects.

myr'me·col'o·gy (-kŏl'ō·jĭ), *n.* [*myrmeco-* + *-logy.*] *Zool.* The scientific study of ants. — **myr'me·co·log'i·cal** (-kō·lŏj'ĭ·kăl), *adj.* — **myr'me·col'o·gist** (-kŏl'ō·jĭst), *n.*

Myr'mi·don (mûr'mĭ·dŏn; -dŭn), *n.; pl.* -DONS (-dŏnz; -dŭnz), -DONES (mûr·mĭd'ō·nēz). [L. *Myrmidones,* pl., fr. Gr. *Myrmidones.*] **1.** *Gr. Myth.* One of a Thessalian tribe or troop who accompanied Achilles, their king, to the Trojan War. **2.** [*not cap.*] A subordinate who executes orders without protest or pity; — sometimes applied to bailiffs, policemen, etc.; as, the *myrmidons* of the law.

my·rob'a·lan (mī·rŏb'ȧ·lăn; mĭ-), *n.* [F. or L.; F. *myrobolan,* fr. L. *myrobalanum* fruit of a palm tree from which a balsam was made, fr. Gr. *myrobalanos,* fr. *myron* any sweet juice distilling from plants + *balanos* an acorn.] A dried astringent fruit much like a prune, yielded by a tropical tree (genus *Terminalia*). It contains tannin, and is now used in tanning and dyeing.

myrrh (mûr), *n.* [From AS. *myrra, myrre* (fr. L.), and fr. OF. *mirre,* fr. L. *myrrha, murra,* fr. Gr. *myrrha,* of Sem. origin.] A yellowish-brown to reddish-brown aromatic gum resin with a bitter, slightly pungent taste. True myrrh is obtained from a tree (*Commiphora abyssinica*) of east Africa and Arabia. The myrrh of the Bible is supposed to have been a mixture of myrrh and labdanum.

myr·ta'ceous (mûr·tā'shŭs), *adj.* [L. *myrtus* myrtle + *-aceous.*] *Bot.* Belonging to the myrtle family (Myrtaceae). See MYRTLE.

myr'tle (mûr't'l), *n.* [F. *myrtille* bilberry, OF., myrtleberry, fr. ML. *myrtillus,* fr. L. *myrtus* myrtle, fr. Gr. *myrtos.*] **1.** Any of a genus (*Myrtus*) of shrubs typifying a family (*Myrtaceae,* the myrtle family) of trees and shrubs including many gum-producing and timber trees, as the eucalypts and many plants yielding spices (cloves, pimento, allspice, etc.); esp., a European species (*M. communis*) which has ovate or lanceolate evergreen leaves and solitary, axillary, white or rosy flowers, followed by black berries. The ancients considered it sacred to Venus. **2.** *U. S.* **a** The common trailing periwinkle (*Vinca minor*). **b** The California laurel (*Umbellularia californica*).

my·self' (mī·sĕlf'; 4), *pron.; pl.* OURSELVES (our·sĕlvz'). An emphasized form of the pronoun for the 1st person singular; as I *myself* was there; I brought one for *myself.*

mys'ta·gogue (mĭs'tȧ·gŏg; 74), *n.* [L. *mystagogus,* fr. Gr. *mystagōgos,* fr. *mystēs* one initiated in mysteries + *agōgos* leading, n., a leader, fr. *agein* to lead.] One who initiates into or interprets mysteries, orig., the Eleusinian mysteries. — **mys'ta·go'gy** (mĭs'tȧ·gō'jĭ), *n.*

mys·te'ri·ous (mĭs·tēr'ĭ·ŭs), *adj.* [L. *mysterium* mystery.] Of or pertaining to mystery; containing, conveying, or implying, a mystery; enigmatical. — **mys·te'ri·ous·ly,** *adv.* — **mys·te'ri·ous·ness,** *n.*

Syn. **Mysterious, inscrutable** mean beyond one's power to discover or explain. **Mysterious** applies to that which excites wonder, curiosity, or surprise, yet baffles all attempts to explain; **inscrutable,** to that which defies one's efforts to understand and leaves one feeling hopeless or defeated.

mys'ter·y (mĭs'tẽr·ĭ), *n.; pl.* -TERIES (-ĭz). [L. *mysterium,* fr. Gr. *mystērion;* akin to Gr. *mystēs* one initiated in mysteries (prop., close-mouthed), fr. *myein* to close, be shut.] **1.** Something that has not been, or cannot be, explained; hence, something beyond human comprehension. **2.** A profound secret; an enigma. **3.** *pl.* Rites, practices, or doctrine revealed only to initiates. **4.** Profound and inexplicable quality or character. **5.** *Class Relig.* **a** A secret religious rite to which none but duly initiated worshipers were admitted. **b** [*often cap.*] A cult characterized by such rites; as, the Eleusinian *mysteries.* **6.** [After F. *mystère.*] *Drama.* One of a class of medieval religious dramas based on Scriptural incidents, and usually centering in the life, death, and resurrection of Christ; also, this type of drama. **7.** *R.C. & Eastern Churches.* **a** The Mass or Divine Liturgy. **b** The Eucharist. **8.** *Theol.* An article of faith beyond human comprehension, as the doctrine of the Trinity.

Syn. **Mystery, problem, enigma, riddle, puzzle, conundrum** mean anything which baffles and seeks solution. **Mystery,** in strictest use, implies the thing's incapacity for comprehension by human reason, but in loose use, only its extremely mystifying quality; **problem,** a demand for a solution which, if not found, will put one into a predicament; **enigma,** a meaning extremely difficult to find; **riddle,** an enigma involving a paradox or a contradiction that can be solved only by guessing; **puzzle,** an enigma or problem that tests one's ingenuity; **conundrum,** a riddle phrased as a question and, usually, involving speculation, often endless.

mys'ter·y, *n.* [ML. *misterium* (after *mysterium;* cf. 1st MYSTERY), fr. L. *ministerium* service, office.] *Archaic.* A trade; craft; also, a body of persons engaged in a particular trade; a guild.

mys'tic (mĭs'tĭk), *adj.* [L. *mysticus,* fr. Gr. *mystikos* belonging to secret rites, fr. *mystēs* one initiated.] **1.** *Now Rare.* = MYSTICAL, 1. **2.** Of or pertaining to ancient mysteries, as the Eleusinian; hence, designating or pertaining to any occult or esoteric rite, religion, etc. **3.** Of or pertaining to mysticism, mystics, the mystical experience, or the like; as, *mystic* state; the *mystic* way. **4.** Loosely, mysterious; enigmatic. — *n.* One having frequent mystical experiences; a follower, often an expounder, of a mystical way of life.

mys'ti·cal (-tĭ·kăl), *adj.* **1.** Having a spiritual meaning, reality, or the like, neither apparent to the senses nor obvious to the intelligence; symbolical; as, the church is the *mystical* body of Christ. **2.** Of, resulting from, or manifesting an individual's direct communion with God through contemplation, vision, an inner light, or the like; as, *mystical* rapture. **3.** *Now Rare.* Unintelligible; cryptic. — **mys'ti·cal·ly,** *adv.* — **mys'ti·cal·ness,** *n.*

mys'ti·cism (mĭs'tĭ·sĭz'm), *n.* **1.** The doctrine or belief that direct knowledge of God, of spiritual truth, etc., is attainable through immediate intuition or insight and in a way differing from ordinary sense perception or the use of logical reasoning; as, nature *mysticism.* **2.** Any type of theory asserting the possibility of attaining knowledge or power through faith or spiritual insight. **3.** Hence, vague speculation.

mys'ti·fy (mĭs'tĭ·fī), *v. t.;* -FIED (-fīd); -FY'ING. [F. *mystifier.* See MYSTIC; -FY.] **1.** To involve in mystery; to make difficult to understand; as, to *mystify* a passage of Scripture. **2.** To puzzle; bewilder. — **mys'ti·fi·ca'tion** (mĭs'tĭ-fĭ-kā'shŭn), *n.* — **mys'ti·fy'ing·ly,** *adv.*

myth (mĭth; *Brit. also* mīth), *n.* [Gr. *mythos* myth, fable, tale, talk, speech.] **1.** A story, the origin of which is forgotten, ostensibly historical but usually such as to explain some practice, belief, institution, or natural phenomenon. Myths are especially associated with religious rites and beliefs. **2.** A person or thing existing only in imagination. **3.** Such legends collectively; legendary or mythical matter.

myth'i·cal (mĭth'ĭ-kăl), *adj.* Also **myth'ic** (-ĭk). Based on, or described in, a myth or myths; of the nature of a myth; also, arbitrarily invented; imaginary. — **Syn.** See FICTITIOUS. — **myth'i·cal·ly,** *adv.*

myth'i·cize (mĭth'ĭ-sīz), *v. t.* To turn into myth or envelop in myths. — **myth'i·cism** (-sĭz'm), *n.*

myth'i·co- (mĭth'ĭ-kô-). A combining form for *mythic,* denoting *mythical and,* as in **myth'i·co-his·tor'i·cal.**

myth'o- (mĭth'ô-). [Gr. *mythos* fable, legend.] A combining form: a *Myth, myths,* as in **my·thog'ra·pher,** a maker of, or writer about, myths. **b** *Mythical and,* as in **myth'o·his·tor'ic.**

myth'o·log'i·cal (mĭth'ô-lŏj'ĭ-kăl), *adj.* Also **myth'o·log'ic** (-ĭk). Of or pertaining to mythology or myths; mythical; legendary. — **myth'o·log'i·cal·ly,** *adv.*

my·thol'o·gist (mĭ-thŏl'ô-jĭst; mĭ-), *n.* One versed in mythology or myths; also, a maker of myths.

my·thol'o·gize (-jīz), *v. i.* To relate, classify, and explain myths; to write about myths. — **my·thol'o·giz'er** (-jĭz'ẽr), *n.*

my·thol'o·gy (mĭ-thŏl'ô-jĭ), *n.; pl.* -GIES (-jĭz). [F. or LL.; F. *mythologie,* fr. LL., fr. Gr. *mythologia,* fr. *mythos* fable, myth + *logos* speech, discourse.] **1.** A body of myths; esp., the collective myths

describing the gods of a people, esp. demigods and legendary human beings in stories which involve supernatural elements. **2.** The science which treats of myths; also, a treatise on myths.

myth'o·ma'ni·a (mĭth'ô-mā'nĭ·ȧ), *n.* [NL., fr. *mytho-* + *-mania.*] *Psychopathol.* An abnormal propensity for lying and exaggerating. — **myth'o·ma'ni·ac** (-ăk), *n.* & *adj.*

myth'o·poe'ic, myth'o·pe'ic (-pē'ĭk), *adj.* [Gr. *mythopoios* making myths, fr. *mythos* myth + *poiein* to make.] Making or giving rise to myths. — **myth'o·poe'ism** (-ĭz'm), *n.* — **myth'o·poe'ist, myth'o·pe'ist** (-ĭst), *n.*

myx-. = MYXO-.

myx'e·de'ma, myx'oe·de'ma (mĭk'sē-dē'mȧ), *n.* [NL. See MYXO- EDEMA.] *Med.* A diseased condition of the skin, characterized by dryness and swelling. It is due to insufficiency of thyroid function. — **myx'e·dem'a·tous, myx'oe·dem'a·tous** (-dĕm'ȧ-tŭs; -dē'mȧ-tŭs), **-dem'ic** (-dĕm'ĭk), *adj.*

myx'o- (mĭk'sô-), **myx-.** [Gr. *myxa.*] A combining form meaning *mucus, slime,* as in *myxomycetous.*

myx'o·my·cete' (-mĭ-sēt'), *n.* A myxomycetous organism; a slime mold.

myx'o·my·ce'tous (-mĭ-sē'tŭs), *adj.* [*myxo-* + Gr. *mykēs, mykētos,* fungus.] *Bot.* Of or belonging to a class (Myxomycetes) of peculiar organisms, the slime molds, sometimes considered to be animals (Mycetozoa), but commonly regarded as plants and included by some botanists in the phylum Thallophyta, by others separated as a distinct phylum (Myxophyta). Except for a few parasitic species, they are found on damp earth and decaying vegetable matter, and consist of naked masses of protoplasm.

N

N, n (ĕn), *n.; pl.* N's, N's, Ns, NS (ĕnz). **1.** The fourteenth letter of the English alphabet. N comes through the Latin from the Greek N (nu), which took it from the Phoenician. **2.** The sound of this letter. See *Pron.,* § 66. **3.** *Math.* [*not cap.*] An indefinite number. See NTH. **4.** As a *symbol,* the thirteenth or (cf. K, 3) fourteenth in order or class.

na (nä; nȧ), *adv.* [See NO, *adv.*] *Scot. & Dial.* No. — *conj. Scot. & Dial.* Nor.

nab (năb), *v. t.; NABBED* (năbd); NAB'BING. *Slang.* **a** To catch or seize in arrest. **b** To seize suddenly; snatch away.

na'bob (nā'bŏb), *n.* [Hind. *navvāb, navāb,* colloq. *nabāb,* fr. Ar. *nuwwāb,* pl. of *nā'ib* vicegerent, governor.] **1.** A native deputy or viceroy in India; a Mogul provincial governor. **2.** A man of great wealth. — **na'bob·er·y** (nā'bŏb'ẽr-ĭ; nā'bŏb'ẽr-ĭ), *n.; pl.* NABOBERIES (-ĭz). — **na'bob·ism** (nā'bŏb-ĭz'm), *n.*

Na'both (nā'bŏth; -bôth), *n. Bib.* Owner of a vineyard which Ahab coveted and seized. 1 *Kings* xxi.

na·celle' (nȧ-sĕl'), *n.* [F.] An enclosed shelter on an aircraft for passengers or for a power plant.

na'cre (nā'kẽr), *n.* [F.] **1.** A shellfish, as any of certain oysters, river mussels, and abalones, that yields mother-of-pearl. See ABALONE, *Illust.* **2.** Mother-of-pearl. — **na'cre·ous** (nā'krē-ŭs), *adj.*

na'dir (nā'dẽr; *also, Brit.,* nā'dẽr), *n.* [OF., fr. Ar. *nazīr* (*al-samt*) opposite (the zenith).] **1.** That point of the celestial sphere directly under the place where one stands, and directly opposite to the zenith; the inferior pole of the horizon. **2.** The lowest point; time of greatest depression; as, the *nadir* of his fortunes.

nae (nā), *adj. & adv.* Dial. var. of NO, NOT.

nae'void (nē'void), **nae'vus.** Vars. of NEVOID, NEVUS.

nag (năg), *n.* [ME. *nagge.*] A pony; hence, any horse; — now used in a derogatory sense.

nag, *v. t. & i.; NAGGED* (năgd); NAG'GING. [Of Scand. origin.] To annoy by faultfinding; to irritate by persistent scolding or urging. — **nag'ger,** *n.* — **nag'ging·ly,** *adv.*

na·ga'na (nä-gä'nä), *n.* [Zulu u(lu)-*nakane.*] *S. Africa.* A disease of livestock caused by certain parasitic protozoans (genus *Trypanosoma*) transmitted by the tsetse fly.

Na'hua·tl (nä'wä·t'l), *n.* The language of an American Indian linguistic stock, related to the Shoshonean, comprising the Aztec and other civilized tribes of central Mexico and parts of Central America. — **Na'hua·tl, Na'hua·tlan** (-tlăn), *adj.*

Na'hum (nā'(h)ŭm; -hŭm), *n.* [Heb. *Naḥūm.*] *Bib.* **a** A Hebrew prophet of the 7th century B.C. **b** A book of the Old Testament. See BIBLE.

nai'ad (nā'ăd; nī'ăd), *n.; pl.* NAIADS (-ădz), NAIADES (nā'ȧ-dēz; nī'ȧ-). [L. *naias, -adis, nais, -idis,* a water nymph, fr. Gr. *naias, nais.*] *Gr. & Rom. Myth.* One of the nymphs believed to live in, and give life and perpetuity to, lakes, rivers, springs, and fountains. Cf. DRYAD.

na·if' (nä-ēf'), *adj.* [F.] See NAÏVE. Naïve.

nail (nāl), *n.* [AS. *nægel.*] **1.** The horny scale or plate on the upper surface of the end of a finger or toe. The fingers and toes of man, apes, and other animals. **2.** A slender, usually pointed and headed, piece of metal used for driving into or through wood. **3.** One sixteenth of a yard, or 2¼ inches (5.715 cm.). — *on the nail* **a** On the spot; immediately. **b** Of immediate interest.

— *v. t.* **1.** To fasten, stud, or boss with or as with nails; also, to close up or secure by means of nails. **2.** To secure; to bind, pin, or hold, as to a bargain; hence, to catch; trap; as, to *nail* a thief. **3.** To fix in steady attention, as the eyes. **4.** To detect and expose, and keep from spreading, as a lie. — **nail'er** (-ẽr), *n.*

Nails, 2. 1 Common Wire; 2 Flooring; 3 Finishing (wire); 4, 5 Boat; 6 Hinge (with Countersunk Head); 7 Horseshoe; 8 Chair; 9 Finishing (cut); 10, 11 Upholsterer's; 12 Clout; 13 Headless Wire.

nain'sook (nān'sŏŏk; nān'-), *n.* [Hind. *nainsukh,* lit., eye delight.] A variety of muslin, plain or striped.

na·ive' (nä-ēv'), *adj.* Also **na·ïve'.** [F. *naïf,* fem. *naïve,* fr. L.

nativus innate, native.] Having unaffected simplicity; ingenuous; artless; unsophisticated. — **Syn.** See NATURAL. — **na·ive'ly,** *adv.* — **na·ive'ness,** *n.*

na·ive·té' (nä-ēv'tā'), *n.* Also **na·ive·te'.** [F.] The quality or an instance of being naïve; artlessness.

na'ked (nā'kĕd; -kĭd), *adj.* [AS. *nacod.*] **1.** Having on no clothes; nude. **2.** Destitute of customary or natural covering; as: **a** Out of, or not provided with, a sheath or case; as, a *naked* sword. **b** Stripped or barren of leaves, grass, etc.; as, *naked* trees. **c** Bare of furnishings; as, *naked* rooms. **d** *Bot.* Without pubescence, as a stem; also, destitute of enveloping parts or subtending leaves; as, a *naked* bud. **e** *Zool.* Destitute of hair, feathers, shell, etc. **3.** Without additions that strengthen, embellish, dignify, etc.; plain; simple; as, to tell the *naked* truth; *naked* history. **4.** Without concealment or disguise; as, facts *naked* and glaring. **5.** Defenseless; unprotected. **6.** *Bot.* **a** Without pubescence. **b** Destitute of enveloping parts or subtending leaves, as a flower without a perianth or buds without scales. **7.** *Law.* Having nothing to confirm or support it; as, a *naked* title. — **Syn.** See BARE. — **na'ked·ly,** *adv.* — **na'ked·ness,** *n.*

nam'a·ble, name'a·ble (nām'ȧ·b'l), *adj.* **a** Capable of being named. **b** Worthy of being named; memorable.

nam'ay·cush (năm'ȧ-kŭsh), *n.* [Of Algonquian origin.] A large trout (*Christivomer namaycush*) of the lakes of North America from New Brunswick to Alaska. See TROUT, 1.

nam'by-pam'by (năm'bĭ-păm'bĭ), *adj.* [From *Ambrose Philips,* ridiculing his verses.] Affectedly pretty; weakly sentimental; insipid. — *n.* Namby-pamby talk, writing, etc.

name (nām), *n.* [AS. *nama.*] **1.** The title by which any person or thing is known or designated. **2.** A descriptive or qualifying appellation; an epithet, often disparaging in nature; as, to call one *names.* **3.** Reputed character; reputation; esp., illustrious fame; honorable reputation; as, he has made a *name* for himself as a writer. **4.** A noted or notorious figure or individual; as, the great *names* of past ages. **5.** Mere appellation or designation in distinction from reality; semblance; as, there was only the *name* of friendship between them. **6.** Those of a certain name; a family; clan. **7.** *Logic.* A term; any word or phrase designating a logical concept.

— *adj.* Bearing or known by a name; hence, *Colloq.,* recognized as of front rank; as, a *name* band.

— *v. t.* **1.** To give a distinctive name to; entitle; style; term. **2.** To refer to by name; mention. **3.** To select and designate; nominate; appoint; as, to *name* a day for a wedding. **4.** To call by name; to identify or specify by class or proper names; as, to *name* the cities of a state. **5.** To cite; state; as, to *name* a price. — **nam'er** (nām'ẽr), *n.*

name'less, *adj.* **1.** Undistinguished; obscure. **2.** Not known by name; anonymous. **3.** Having no legal right to a name; illegitimate; bastard. **4.** Not having been given a name; unnamed. **5.** Not marked with any name; as, a *nameless* grave. **6.** Unnamable; indescribable; also, unmentionable. — **name'less·ly,** *adv.* — **name'less·ness,** *n.*

name'ly, *adv.* That is to say; to wit; videlicet.

name'sake (-sāk'), *n.* [For *name's sake;* i. e., one named for the sake of another's name.] One that has the same name as another; esp., one named after another.

nan·keen' (năn-kēn'), *n.* Also **nan·kin'.** [From *Nanking,* China.] **1.** Brownish-yellow cloth of firm texture and great durability, originally brought from China. **2.** *pl.* Nankeen trousers. **3.** [*cap.*] In full **Nankeen porcelain.** Chinese porcelain painted in blue on white.

nan'ny goat (năn'ĭ). *Colloq.* A female goat.

Na·o'mi (nā-ō'mĭ; nā'ô-mĭ; -mĭ), *n.* [Heb. *Nā'omī.*] *Bib.* The mother-in-law of Ruth.

na'os (nā'ŏs), *n.* [NL., fr. Gr. *naos.*] *Arch.* = CELLA.

nap (năp), *v. i.; NAPPED* (năpt); NAP'PING. [AS. *hnæppian.*] To have a short sleep; doze; hence, figuratively, to be off one's guard. — *n.* A short sleep; a doze.

nap, *n.* [MD. *noppe* (D. *nop*).] A hairy or downy surface found on some fabrics, of wool, and now raised by teaseling, brushing, etc.; — disting. from *pile.* — *v. t. & i.* To raise a nap (on).

nap, *n.* = NAPOLEON, 1 & 2.

na'palm (nā'päm), *n.* [From names of aluminum salts of *naphthenic* and *palmitic* acids.] A thickener (chemically a mixture of aluminum soaps of certain fatty acids, etc.) used in gelling gasoline for incendiary bombs and flame throwers; also, the gelled fuel made with it.

nape (nāp; *colloq. or dial.* năp), *n.* The back of the neck.

na′per·y (nā′pĕr·ĭ), *n.; pl.* NAPERIES (-ĭz). [OF. *naperie,* fr. *nape.* See NAPKIN.] Household linen; esp., table linen.

Naph′ta·li (năf′tȧ·lī), *n. Bib.* See JACOB.

naph′tha (năf′thȧ), *n.* [L., fr. Gr. *naphtha.*] **1.** Petroleum. **2.** Any of several volatile inflammable liquids obtained by distilling certain carbonaceous materials and used as solvents in dry cleaning, varnish making, etc., and as fuels.

naph′tha·lene (năf′thȧ·lēn), *n.* Also **naph′tha·lin** (-lĭn), **naph′tha·line** (-lĭn; -lēn). [From NAPHTHA.] *Chem.* A hydrocarbon, $C_{10}H_8$, an important constituent of coal tar, forming brilliant white flakelike crystals of peculiar odor.

naph′thene (năf′thēn), *n. Chem.* Any of a series of saturated cyclic hydrocarbons of the general formula C_nH_{2n}; — applied esp. to those members occurring in certain kinds of petroleum, in shale, tar oil, etc.

naph′thol (năf′thōl; năf·thōl′; năf′thŏl), *n.* Also **naph′tol** (-tōl; -tŏl). [*naphth*alene + *-ol.*] *Chem.* **a** Either of two white, crystalline hydroxyl derivatives of napththalene, $C_{10}H_7OH$, distinguished as alpha-naphthol and beta-naphthol; specif., in the United States Pharmacopoeia, beta-naphthol. Both are used as antiseptics and in manufacture of dyes. **b** Any of various hydroxy derivatives containing the naphthalene nucleus.

na′pi·form (nā′pĭ·fôrm), *adj.* [L. *napus* turnip + *-form.*] *Bot.* Turnip-shaped; — of roots.

nap′kin (năp′kĭn), *n.* [Dim. of OF. *nape, nappe,* fr. L. *mappa.* See MAP.] A small cloth or towel; specif., one used at table for wiping the lips or fingers; a serviette; also, a baby's diaper.

na·po′le·on (nȧ·pō′lē·ŭn), *n.* [After *Napoleon* I.] **1.** A former French gold coin of 20 francs ($3.86). **2.** Usually *nap.* **a** A game at cards. **b** A bid to win all five tricks in this game. **3.** An oblong French pastry having cream filling between its layers.

Na·po′le·on′ic (-ŏn′ĭk), *adj.* Of, pertaining to, or characteristic of Napoleon I or his family.

nap′per (năp′ẽr), *n.* A machine for raising the nap on cloth.

nap′per, *n.* One who naps, or sleeps lightly.

nap′py (năp′ĭ), *adj.* Strong; heady; — said of liquors.

nap′py (năp′ĭ; nȧp′ĭ), *n. Scot. & Dial.* Liquor; esp., ale.

na·prap′a·thy (nȧ·prăp′ȧ·thĭ), *n.* [Czech *naprava* correction + *-pathy.*] A therapeutic system using manipulation and based on the theory that diseases result from strained or contracted ligaments in pelvis, spine, or thorax. — **nap′ra·path** (năp′rȧ·păth), *n.*

nar′ce·ine (när′sē·ēn; -ĭn), *n.* Also **nar′ce·in** (-ĭn). [L. *narce* numbness, fr. Gr. *narkē.*] *Chem.* A bitter, white, crystalline alkaloid, $C_{23}H_{27}NO_8$, found in small quantities in opium.

nar′cism (när′sĭz′m), **nar′cist** (-sĭst), etc. = NARCISSISM, etc.

nar·cis′sism (när·sĭs′ĭz′m), *n.* [See NARCISSUS, 1; -ISM.] *Psychoanalysis.* Erotic feeling aroused by one's own body and personality. — **nar·cis′sist** (-ĭst), *n.* — **nar′cis·sis′tic** (när′sĭ·sĭs′tĭk), *adj.*

Nar·cis′sus (när·sĭs′ŭs), *n.* [L., fr. Gr. *Narkissos.*] **1.** *Gr. Myth.* A beautiful youth for vain love of whom Echo died. Nemesis caused him to fall in love with his own reflection in a fountain. He pined away in desire for it and was changed into the narcissus. **2.** [*not cap.; pl.* -CISSUSES (-ĕz; -ĭz), -CISSI (-sĭs′ī).] Any of a genus (*Narcissus*) of Old World bulbous herbs of the amaryllis family, including the daffodils and the jonquils. The ***paper-white narcissus*** (*N. tazetta*) bears clusters of small, very fragrant, pure-white blossoms.

nar′co·lep′sy (när′kō·lĕp′sĭ), *n.* [Gr. *narkē* stupor, torpor + *-lepsy.*] *Med.* A condition characterized by brief attacks of deep sleep. — **nar′co·lep′tic** (-lĕp′tĭk), *adj.*

nar·co′sis (när·kō′sĭs), *n.* [NL., fr. Gr. *narkōsis.* See NARCOTIC.] A state of stupor or arrested activity, produced by narcotics, or, as in living tissues or cells, by concentrations of alcohols, ethers, etc.; also, narcotization.

nar′co·syn′the·sis (när′kō·sĭn′thē·sĭs), *n.* [*narcosis* + *synthesis.*] *Psychiatry.* Mental treatment intended to make a person under narcosis recollect and talk of repressed painful memories, thereby relieving his emotional conflicts and enabling him to integrate, or synthesize, these memories into his consciousness.

nar·cot′ic (när·kŏt′ĭk), *adj.* [From F. or ML., fr. Gr. *narkōtikos,* deriv. of *narkē* torpor.] **1.** Having the properties of a narcotic; yielding a narcotic; of or inducing narcosis; hence, inducing mental lethargy; as, a *narcotic* speech. **2.** Of, induced by, or concerned with narcotics or their use. **3.** Of, involving, or for narcotic addicts or their care. — *n.* **1.** A drug, as opium, which in moderate doses allays sensibility, relieves pain, and produces profound sleep, but in poisonous doses produces stupor, coma, or convulsions. **2.** Figuratively, something that soothes, relieves, or lulls. **3.** One who is addicted to the use of a narcotic.

nar′co·tism (när′kō·tĭz′m), *n.* **a** Narcosis. **b** Tendency to narcosis; a narcotic influence. **c** Addiction to narcotics.

nar′co·tize (-tīz), *v. t.* To subject to the influence of a narcotic; also, figuratively, to soothe to unconsciousness. — **nar′co·ti·za′tion** (-tĭ·zā′shŭn; -tī·zā′-), *n.*

nard (närd), *n.* [OF. or L.; OF. *narde,* fr. L. *nardus,* fr. Gr. *nardos.*] A fragrant ointment, esp. one of the ancients, believed to have been derived from the plant *Nardostachys jatamansi;* also, this plant; spikenard.

na′res (nā′rēz), *n. pl.; sing.* NARIS (-rĭs). [L., pl. of *naris* nostril.] The nostrils. — **nar′i·al** (nâr′ĭ·ăl; 6), **nar′ine** (-ĭn; -īn), *adj.*

nar′ghi·le, nar′gi·le (när′gĭ·lē), *n.* Also **nar′gi·leh.** [Per. *nārgīleh,* fr. *nārgīl* coconut (of which orig. made).] An Oriental apparatus for smoking tobacco. See *Illust.* The smoke is drawn through water. Cf. HOOKAH.

nark (närk), *n.* [Romany *nāk* nose.] *Slang.* A spy employed by the police; an informer.

nar·rate′ (nă·rāt′), *v. t. & i.* [L. *narratus,* past part. of *narrare* to narrate.] To tell, as a story; give an account (of); relate. — **nar·ra′tor** (-rā′tẽr), **nar·rat′er** (-rāt′ẽr), *n.*

nar·ra′tion (nă·rā′shŭn), *n.* **1.** A narrating. **2.** A narrative; a story. **3.** Discourse, or an example of it, designed to represent a connected succession of happenings; esp., such discourse involving plot, setting, and characterization.

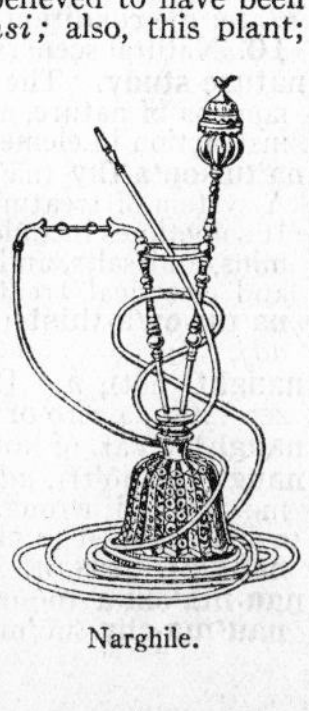

Narghile.

nar′ra·tive (năr′ȧ·tĭv), *n.* **1.** That which is narrated; an account; a tale; a story. **2.** Act, art, or practice of narrating; as, a master of *narrative.* — **nar′ra·tive,** *adj.* — **nar′ra·tive·ly,** *adv.*

nar′row (năr′ō), *adj.* [AS. *nearu.*] **1.** Of little breadth; not wide or broad. **2.** Limited, as in scope or amount; restricted; circumscribed. **3.** Close; accurate; exact; as, to make a *narrow* search. **4.** *Now Chiefly Dial.* Parsimonious; niggardly. **5.** Having but a little margin; having barely sufficient space, time, etc.; near; as, a *narrow* escape. **6.** Illiberal; bigoted; — often in combination, as in *narrow-minded.* **7.** *Agric.* Containing a relatively large amount of protein as compared with the carbohydrates and fats; — of feed rations. Cf. WIDE, *adj.,* 9. **8.** *Phonet.* Tense. **9.** *Textiles.* Woven in widths suitable for ribbons, neckties, and the like; as, *narrow* cloth. — *v. t. & i.* To lessen in breadth or compass; restrict. — *n.* **1.** A narrow part, place, or thing. **2.** A narrow passage; a strait; — usually in *pl.* — **nar′row·ly,** *adv.* — **nar′row·ness,** *n.*

nar′row-gauge′ (-gāj′; 2), *adj.* **1.** Having a narrow gauge (see GAUGE, *n.,* 9 **a**); — of a railroad. **2.** Narrow-minded.

nar′row-mind′ed (-mīn′dĕd; -dĭd; 2), *adj.* Not liberal; bigoted. — **nar′row-mind′ed·ly,** *adv.* — **nar′row-mind′ed·ness,** *n.*

nar′thex (när′thĕks), *n.* [L., giant fennel, fr. Gr. *narthēx.*] *Arch.* The portico of ancient churches; — now used of any vestibule leading to the nave.

nar′whal (när′hwăl), *n.* Also **nar′wal** (-wăl), **nar′whale** (-hwāl). [Sw. or Dan. *narhval.*] An arctic cetacean (*Monodon monoceros,* family Delphinidae), which becomes about 20 feet long. The male has a long tusk which furnishes ivory of commercial value.

nar′y (nâr′ĭ; nā′rĭ), *adj. Dial.* Not one; never a.

na′sal (nā′zăl; -z′l), *adj.* [L. *nasus* the nose.] **1.** Of or pertaining to the nose. **2.** *Phonet.* **a** Uttered through the nose only, as *m, n, ng.* **b** Uttered through both nose and mouth, with velum fully lowered, as the French nasal vowels. **c** Characterized by such utterance. — *n.* **1.** *Anat. & Zool.* A nasal bone, plate, or scale. **2.** [OF. *nasel, nasal.*] *Armor.* The nosepiece of a helmet. **3.** [From NASAL, *adj.*] *Phonet.* A nasal sound, as *m, n, ng.* — **na·sal′i·ty** (nā·zăl′ĭ·tĭ), *n.* — **na′sal·ly,** *adv.*

nasal index. *Craniom.* The ratio of the greatest breadth of the anterior opening of the nasal cavities in the skull to the height from the projection below to the middle point of the suture of the bones above. It is usually expressed in hundredths of the height.

na′sal·ize (nā′zăl·īz; nā′z′l-), *v. t.* To pronounce as a nasal or nasally. — *v. i.* To speak in a nasal manner. — **na′sal·i·za′tion** (-ĭ·zā′shŭn; -ī·zā′-), *n.*

nas′cent (năs′ĕnt; -′nt; nā′sĕnt; -s′nt), *adj.* [L. *nascens, -entis,* pres. part. of *nasci* to be born.] Being born; coming into existence; beginning to exist, grow, or develop. — **nas′cen·cy** (năs′ĕn·sĭ; -′n·sĭ; nā′sĕn·sĭ; -s′n·sĭ), **nas′cence** (-ĕns; -′ns; -sĕns; -s′ns), *n.*

nascent state *or* **condition.** *Chem.* The condition of an element at the moment of liberation from a compound.

nase′ber′ry (nāz′bĕr′ĭ; -bẽr·ĭ), *n.; pl.* NASEBERRIES (-ĭz). [Sp. *níspero* medlar.] The sapodilla plum.

na′si·on (nā′zĭ·ŏn), *n.* [NL., fr. L. *nasus* nose.] *Craniom.* The middle point of the nasofrontal suture. See GNATHIC INDEX. — **na′si·al** (-ăl), *adj.*

na′so- (nā′zō-). [L. *nasus* nose.] A combining form denoting: **a** *The nose;* — in nouns, as in **na·sol′o·gy, na′so·scope** (see -LOGY, -SCOPE). **b** *Nasal and;* — in adjectives, as in **na′so·bron′chi·al, na′so·fron′tal, na′so·lach′ry·mal, na′so·pal′a·tine.**

na′so·phar′ynx (nā′zō·făr′ĭngks), *n.* [NL.] The upper part of the pharynx, continuous with the nasal passages.

-nas′tic (-năs′tĭk). A combining form denoting *change in position in a* (specified) *direction* or *by a* (specified) *agency.* Corresponding nouns are formed in **-nas′ty** (-tĭ).

nas·tur′tium (năs·tûr′shŭm), *n.* [L., a cress, prop., nose twist, in allusion to its pungency, fr. *nasus* nose + *torquere, tortum,* to twist.] *Hort.* Any of a genus (*Tropaeolum*) of herbs bearing showy spurred red and yellow flowers and having pungent seeds and flower buds, and typifying a family (Tropaeolaceae, the nasturtium family).

nas′ty (nȧs′tĭ; 9), *adj.;* NAS′TI·ER (-tĭ·ẽr); -TI·EST. **1.** Disgustingly filthy. **2.** Obscene; indecent. **3.** Nauseous; nauseating. **4. a** *Colloq.* Very disagreeable or objectionable. **b** Mean; ill-natured. **5.** Seriously harmful or dangerous; as, a *nasty* fall. — **Syn.** See DIRTY. — **nas′ti·ly,** *adv.* — **nas′ti·ness,** *n.*

-nas′ty (-năs′tĭ). See -NASTIC.

na′tal (nā′tăl; -t′l), *adj.* [L. *natalis,* fr. *natus,* past part. of *nasci* to be born.] **1.** Native; as, names from their *natal* places. **2.** Pertaining to one's birth; dating from one's birth.

na·tal′i·ty (nā·tăl′ĭ·tĭ), *n.* [*natal* pertaining to birth + *-ity* as in mortal*ity.*] **a** Birth. **b** Birth rate.

na′tant (nā′tănt; -t′nt), *adj.* [L. *natans, -antis,* fr. *natare* to swim, float; akin to L. *nare* to swim.] Swimming; floating; specif., *Bot.,* floating in water, as lily pads.

na·ta′tion (nā·tā′shŭn), *n.* [L. *natatio,* fr. *natare* to swim.] Act or art of swimming or floating.

na′ta·to′ri·um (nā′tȧ·tō′rĭ·ŭm; 70), *n.; pl.* -TORIUMS (-ŭmz), -TORIA (-ȧ). [LL.] A place for swimming; esp., an indoor swimming pool.

na′ta·to′ry (nā′tȧ·tō′rĭ *or, esp. Brit.,* -tẽr·ĭ), *adj.* Also **na′ta·to′ri·al** (-tō′rĭ·ăl; 70). [LL. *natatorius.*] **1.** Of or pert. to swimming. **2.** Adapted for, or used in, swimming.

Natch′ez (năch′ĕz; -ĭz), *n. sing. & pl.* An Indian of a Muskhogean tribe formerly living on the lower Mississippi.

na′tes (nā′tēz), *n. pl.* [L., pl.] *Anat.* The buttocks.

nathe′less (nāth′lĕs; năth′-; 30), **nath′less** (năth′-), *adv.* [ME. *natheles, na the les,* not the less, fr. AS. *nā* never.] *Archaic.* Nevertheless; notwithstanding.

na′tion (nā′shŭn), *n.* [OF. *nacion,* fr. L. *natio* nation, race, orig., a being born, fr. *natus,* past part. of *nasci* to be born.] **1.** A people connected by supposed ties of blood generally manifested by community of language, religion, customs, etc. **2.** Any aggregation of people having like institutions and customs and a sense of social homogeneity and mutual interest. **3.** The body of inhabitants of a country united under a single independent government; a state. **4.** A multitude; host. **5.** One of a group of Indian tribes; as, the Six *Nations.*

na′tion·al (năsh′ŭn·ăl; -′l), *adj.* **1.** Of or pertaining to a (or the) nation. **2.** Devoted to one's country's interests; patriotic. — *n.* A member of a nation; loosely, a fellow countryman. — **Syn.** See CITIZEN. — **na′tion·al·ly,** *adv.*

national bank. a A bank having association with the finances of a nation, as the Reichsbank of Germany. b *U. S.* A commercial bank organized under the National Bank Act, and chartered by the federal government.
National Guard. *U. S.* A militia force controlled and partly maintained by the several states but subject to the call either of the state government or of the federal government.
National Heroes' Day. *Phil. I.* See HOLIDAY, 3.
National Industrial Recovery Act. An act of Congress (passed June 13, 1933; declared unconstitutional by the Supreme Court May 27, 1935) recognizing "a national emergency" and vesting in the president of the U. S. authority to approve or establish codes of fair competition for various trades and industries, regulate wages, hours of labor, output of goods, imports, etc. The **National Recovery Administration** (abbr. *NRA*) was established to administer the act. See BLUE EAGLE.
na'tion·al·ism (năsh'ŭn·ăl·ĭz'm; -'l·ĭz'm), *n.* 1. National character; nationality. 2. An idiom, trait, or character peculiar to any nation. 3. Devotion to, or advocacy of, national interests or national unity and independence. 4. *Chiefly U. S.* Socialism advocating the nationalizing of industries.
na'tion·al·ist (-ĭst), *n.* 1. An advocate of national independence, unity, etc. 2. One who favors the nationalizing of industries. — **na'tion·al·ist,** *adj.* — **na'tion·al·is'tic** (-ĭs'tĭk), *adj.* — **na'tion·al·is'ti·cal·ly** (-tĭ·kăl·ĭ), *adv.*
na'tion·al'i·ty (năsh'ŭn·ăl'ĭ·tĭ), *n.; pl.* -TIES (-tĭz). 1. State or quality of being a nation or national; national character or existence. 2. State, quality, or fact of belonging to a nation, as by nativity or allegiance. 3. A people united by common institutions, language, etc.; a nation.
na'tion·al·ize (năsh'ŭn·ăl·īz), *v. t.* 1. To make national; make a nation of. 2. To vest in the national government the control, ownership, or the like, of; as, to *nationalize* industries. — **na'tion·al·i·za'tion** (-ĭ·zā'shŭn; -ī·zā'-), *n.* — **na'tion·al·iz'er** (-īz'ẽr), *n.*
National Labor Relations Act. = WAGNER ACT.
National Labor Relations Board. *U. S.* A government agency, created July 9, 1934, and re-established under the Wagner and Taft-Hartley acts, with power to investigate labor controversies, to safeguard employees' right to self-organization and collective bargaining, to prevent unfair labor practice, etc. Abbr. *NLRB*
national monument. See MONUMENT, 7.
national park. An area of enduring scenic, historical, or biological or other scientific interest, permanently maintained by a national government especially for the recreational use of the public.
National Socialist German Workers' party. A German Fascist party, formerly the ***National Socialist party***. See NAZISM.
National War Labor Board. *U. S.* A board, established by executive order Jan. 12, 1942, amended Oct. 3, 1942, for adjusting and settling all labor disputes in which negotiations and procedures otherwise provided have failed, and for controlling wage rates. Terminated Dec. 1945. Abbr. *NWLB, WLB*
na'tive (nā'tĭv), *adj.* [F. *natif*, fr. L. *nativus*, fr. *nasei*, past part. *natus*.] 1. Born with one; inborn; not acquired; as, *native* cheerfulness. 2. *Archaic.* Closely related, as by birth. 3. Born in a particular place, region, or country; as, a city's *native* sons; specif., of the non-Caucasian people or peoples inhabiting a colony, dependency, or the like; as, to use *native* troops in India. 4. Of, pertaining to, or belonging to one as the place of one's birth, or because of the place or the circumstances of one's birth; as, *native* land, language, etc. 5. Natural; naïve; unaffected. 6. Grown, produced, or originating in a particular place, region, or country; as, *native* art; specif., *Biol.*, indigenous; as, a *native* species. *Native* is applied by colonists, as in Australia, to indigenous plants and animals related to, or resembling, those of the mother country. 7. Constituting the original substance, source, or condition; original; as, salt in its *native* state. 8. Of, pert. to, or characteristic of natives; as, *native* customs. 9. Occurring naturally; not combined with other elements or artificially prepared.
Syn. **Native, indigenous, endemic, aboriginal** mean of the locality in question. **Native,** said of individuals, implies birth or origin there; **indigenous,** said of species and races, adds to *native* the implication of not having been introduced; **endemic,** said of diseases, plants, etc., implies peculiarity to the region; **aboriginal,** said chiefly of races, implies an absence of any known predecessor.
— *n.* 1. One born in a place or country referred to; specif.: a An indigenous animal, fruit, or vegetable. b One of a race inhabiting a country when it was discovered, colonized, etc. 2. a An inhabitant, as disting. from a visitor or temporary resident. b A product from nearby rather than from distant regions; as, *native* peaches. 3. *Astrol.* a One born under a particular sign. b The subject of a nativity. — **na'tive·ly,** *adv.* — **na'tive·ness,** *n.*
native cod. See COD.
na'tiv·ism (nā'tĭv·ĭz'm), *n.* 1. Policy of favoring the native inhabitants of a country as against immigrants. 2. *Philos.* The doctrine of innate ideas. — **na'tiv·ist** (-ĭst), *n.* — **na'tiv·is'tic** (-ĭs'tĭk), *adj.*
na·tiv'i·ty (nā·tĭv'ĭ·tĭ), *n.; pl.* -TIES (-tĭz). [OF. *nativité*, fr. LL. *nativitas*.] 1. Birth, or the circumstances attending it. 2. [*cap.*, usually with *the*.] The birth of Christ; also, Christmas Day. 3. *Astrol.* A horoscope at or of the time of one's birth.
na'tri·um (nā'trĭ·ŭm), *n.* Sodium. Symbol, *Na* (no period).
nat'ro·lite (năt'rō·līt; nā'trō-), *n.* [*natron* + *-lite*.] *Mineral.* Native sodium aluminum silicate $Na_2Al_2Si_3O_{10}.2H_2O$.
na'tron (nā'trŏn), *n.* [F., fr. Sp. *natrón*, fr. Ar. *naṭrūn*, fr. Gr. *nitron*.] *Mineral.* Native sodium carbonate, $Na_2CO_3.10H_2O$.
nat'ty (năt'ĭ), *adj.;* -TI·ER (-ĭ·ẽr); -TI·EST. *Colloq.* Trimly neat and tidy; spruce. — **nat'ti·ly,** *adv.* — **nat'ti·ness,** *n.*
nat'u·ral (năt'ū·răl; 118), *adj.* [OF., fr. L. *naturalis*, fr. *natura*. See NATURE.] 1. Of, from, or by, birth; innate; inborn; as, *natural* instincts; also, being such in character, gift, etc., by birth; as, a *natural* fool. 2. Born out of wedlock; illegitimate. 3. In accordance with the nature of its kind; normal to the species; as, parental love is *natural;* the *natural* food of dogs; also, of men, human; not brutal or bestial. 4. Pertaining to, in accordance with, or determined by, nature; specif.: a Designating law (***natural law***) discernible to reason, as disting. from law laid down in codes by state, church, etc.; hence, deriving its validity from natural law; as, ***natural rights,*** the rights to life, liberty, and the pursuit of happiness. b Characteristic of or explainable by the operations of the physical world; as, the *natural* cause of a seeming miracle. 5. Of or pertaining to the physical universe or the study of it; physical; — often in old names of science or the sciences; as, *natural* history or philosophy. 6. Being or found in its native state; specif.: a Not regenerate, enlightened, etc.; as, passions of the *natural* man. b Not artificial, synthetic, processed, acquired by external means, etc.; as, *natural* rubber. 7. Truly representing or expressing one's nature, appearance, sentiment, etc.; as, a *natural* gesture or portrait. 8. *Math.* Starting from, or referred to, 1 as the base; as, *natural* number, an integer as 1, 2, or 3; *natural* sine, cosine, etc., a sine, cosine, etc., taken in a circle with radius 1. 9. *Music.* a Having neither flats nor sharps, as a key or scale. b Neither sharped nor flatted; — of notes and tones. c Having the pitch modified by the natural sign (♮).
Syn. (1) See REGULAR.
(2) **Natural, ingenuous, naïve, unsophisticated, artless** mean free from all pretense. **Natural** implies lack of artificiality, and an ease or spontaneousness suggestive of nature; **ingenuous,** inability to disguise or conceal one's thoughts or feelings; **naïve,** freedom from all that is conventional, artificial, or worldly-wise; **unsophisticated,** lack of experience or training necessary for ease and adroitness, esp. in social relations; **artless,** naturalness that results from unawareness of the impression one is producing.
— *n.* 1. One that is natural; esp., a natural fool; an idiot. 2. a Anyone who is naturally expert. b *Slang.* Anything that is immediately successful. 3. *Music.* a In full **natural sign.** A character (♮) placed on any degree of the staff to annul, or to remove the effect of, a sharp or flat preceding it. b A note or tone affected by this sign. c A white key, as of a piano. — **Syn.** See FOOL.
— **nat'u·ral·ly,** *adv.* — **nat'u·ral·ness,** *n.*
natural gas. A gas issuing from the earth's crust through natural openings or bored walls and often accompanied by petroleum.
natural history. Formerly, zoology, botany, mineralogy, etc.; — now commonly restricted to a study of these subjects in a more or less unsystematic way.
nat'u·ral·ism (năt'ū·răl·ĭz'm), *n.* 1. Action, inclination, or thought based on natural desires and instincts alone. 2. Realism in art or literature; specif., a type of realism, represented by Zola, Maupassant, and others, emphasizing scientific methods of observation and experiment in the treatment of character. 3. *Philos.* The doctrine denying that anything in reality has a supernatural significance; specif., the doctrine that scientific laws account for all phenomena, and that teleological conceptions of nature are invalid; loosely, materialism and positivism. 4. *Theol.* The denial of the miraculous and supernatural in religion, and the rejection of revelation as a means of attaining truth.
nat'u·ral·ist (năt'ū·răl·ĭst), *n.* 1. One versed in natural science; esp., a student of animals or plants. 2. An adherent of naturalism, as in art or literature. — **nat'u·ral·is'tic** (-ĭs'tĭk), *adj.*
nat'u·ral·ize (-īz), *v. t.* 1. To bring into, or treat as in, accord with nature; give a natural aspect to or explanation of; as, to *naturalize* so-called miracles. 2. To confer the rights and privileges of a native subject or citizen on; to adopt as a subject or citizen. 3. To receive or adopt as native, natural, or vernacular; as, to *naturalize* foreign words. 4. To cause to grow, as something not indigenous; acclimate; as, to *naturalize* a fruit. — *v. i.* 1. To become as if native. 2. To explain phenomena by natural facts, agencies, or laws, to the exclusion of the supernatural. 3. To carry on investigations in natural history. — **nat'u·ral·i·za'tion** (-ĭ·zā'shŭn; -ī·zā'-), *n.*
natural law. See NATURAL, *adj.*, 4.
natural philosophy. a The study of the physical universe. b Physics. — **natural philosopher.**
natural resources. Capacities, as native wit, or materials, as mineral deposits or water power, supplied by nature.
natural rights. See NATURAL, *adj.*, 4.
natural science. The branches of knowledge collectively which deal directly with natural objects, thus including biology in all its branches, mineralogy, geology, chemistry, physics, etc., but not abstract mathematics or philosophy.
natural selection. The natural process tending to cause the "survival of the fittest" (that is, the survival of those forms of animals and plants best adjusted to the conditions under which they live), and extinction of poorly adapted forms. Darwin considered natural selection as the most important factor in organic evolution.
‖**na·tu'ra non fa'cit sal'tum** (nȧ·tū'rȧ nŏn fā'sĭt săl'tŭm). [L.] Nature makes no leap; — implying the uniformity and continuity of natural phenomena.
na'ture (nā'tūr; 118), *n.* [OF., fr. L. *natura*, fr. *natus* born, produced, past part. of *nasci* to be born.] 1. Essential character or constitution; distinguishing quality or qualities; essence; as, the *nature* of steel, or of love. 2. Substance or essence of a distinct species or kind; as, one's physical or spiritual *nature;* hence, kind, sort, type; as, events of this *nature.* 3. Innate or inherent character, disposition, or temperament; as, contrary to one's *nature.* 4. The vital functions, processes, organs, or the like; — now chiefly a euphemism; as, interference with *nature.* 5. The system of all phenomena in space and time; the physical universe; as, the study of *nature.* 6. [*sometimes cap.*] An agent, force, or principle, or set of such forces or principles, viewed as creating, controlling, or guiding the universe; as, by provision of *nature.* 7. In an individual, any of the natural instincts, desires, or appetites, or all collectively; as, to control *nature* by grace. 8. Natural feeling, esp. kindliness or affection. 9. Man's native, or original, state; the condition of simple, primitive man; as, a return to *nature.* 10. Natural scenery; as, wild *nature.* — **Syn.** See TYPE.
nature study. The objective study of any or all the objects and phenomena of nature, as birds, flowers, weather, etc., esp. as a subject of instruction in elementary schools.
na'tur·op'a·thy (nā'tūr·ŏp'ȧ·thĭ), *n.* [L. *natura* nature + *-pathy*.] A system of treatment of disease which emphasizes assisting nature. It sometimes includes the use of certain medicines such as herbs, vitamins, and salts, and of certain physical means such as manipulation and electrical treatment. — **na'tur·o·path'** (nā'tūr·ō·păth'), *n.* — **na'tur·op'a·thist** (-ŏp'ȧ·thĭst), *n.* — **na'tur·o·path'ic** (-ō·păth'ĭk), *adj.*
naught (nôt), *n.* [See NOUGHT.] 1. The arithmetical character 0; zero; also, a zero or cipher. 2. Var. of NOUGHT.
naught. Var. of NOUGHT, *adj.* & *adv.*
naugh'ty (nô'tĭ), *adj.;* -TI·ER (-tĭ·ẽr); -TI·EST. 1. *Archaic.* Wicked; morally bad; wrong. 2. Mischievous; wayward; disobedient; — now chiefly applied to children. — **Syn.** See BAD. — **naugh'ti·ly,** *adv.* — **naugh'ti·ness,** *n.*
nau·ma'chi·a (nô·mā'kĭ·ȧ), *n.; pl.* -CHIAE (-ē), -CHIAS (-ȧz). Also **nau'ma·chy** (nô'mȧ·kĭ); *pl.* -CHIES (-kĭz). [L., fr. Gr. *naumachia,*

fr. *naus* ship + *machē* battle.] *Rom. Antiq.* **a** A mock sea fight or a spectacle representing a naval battle. **b** A place for such exhibitions.

nau'pli·us (nô'plĭ·ŭs), *n.; pl.* -PLII (-ī). [L., a kind of shellfish.] In many crustaceans, a larval form (usually the first stage after leaving the egg) with three pairs of appendages, a median eye, and little or no segmentation.

nau'se·a (nô'shē·ȧ; -sē·ȧ; -shȧ), *n.* [L., fr. Gr. *nausia*, fr. *naus* ship.] **1.** Any sickness of the stomach, like seasickness, with a desire to vomit; qualm. **2.** Extreme disgust.

nau'se·ate (nô'shē·āt; -sē·āt), *v. t. & i.* [L. *nauseare, nauseatum*, fr. *nausea*.] To affect or become affected with nausea; disgust; sicken. — **nau'se·a'tion** (-ā'shŭn), *n.*

nau'seous (nô'shŭs; -shē·ŭs), *adj.* [L. *nauseosus*.] Causing, or fitted to cause, nausea; disgusting. — **nau'seous·ly**, *adv.* — **nau'seous·ness**, *n.*

nautch (nôch), *n.* [Hind. *nāc*, fr. Prakrit *nacca*, fr. Skr. *nṛtya* dancing.] *India.* An entertainment chiefly of dancing by professional dancing girls (**nautch girls**).

nau'ti·cal (nô'tĭ·kăl), *adj.* [F. *nautique*, fr. L. *nauticus*, fr. Gr. *nautikos*, fr. *nautēs* a seaman, sailor, fr. *naus* ship.] Of or pertaining to seamen, navigation, or ships; as, **nautical measure** (see MEASURE, *Table* 9). — **nau'ti·cal·ly**, *adv.*

nau'ti·lus (nô'tĭ·lŭs), *n.; pl.* -LUSES (-ĕz; -ĭz), NAUTILI (-lī). [L., fr. Gr. *nautilos* a sailor, a shellfish supposed to have a membrane which served as a sail, fr. *naus* ship.] **1.** Any of a genus (*Nautilus*) of cephalopod mollusks of the South Pacific and Indian oceans, having a spiral chambered shell, pearly on the inside, whence the name ***pearly nautilus***. The animal has four gills and four auricles. **2.** An eight-armed cephalopod (genus *Argonauta*) related to the octopus, the female having a fragile, papery, unchambered shell; — called also ***paper nautilus***.

Nav'a·ho, Nav'a·jo (năv'ȧ·hō), *n.; pl.* -HOS, -JOS (-hōz), or -HOES, -JOES (-hōz). [Sp. Apaches de *Navajó*.] One of a tribe of Indians mostly living on a reservation in Arizona, New Mexico, and Utah.

na'val (nā'văl), *adj.* [L. *navalis*, fr. *navis* ship.] **1.** *Obs.* Of or pertaining to ships or shipping. **2.** Of, pert. to, possessing, or characteristic of vessels of war or a navy.

nave (nāv), *n.* [AS. *nafu*.] **1.** The hub of a wheel. See WHEEL, *Illust.* **2.** *Rare.* The navel.

nave, *n.* [L. *navis* ship, to which the church was often likened.] In basilican and cruciform churches, the part that rises higher than the aisles flanking it and has, usually, a clerestory. See GOTHIC, *Illust.*

na'vel (nā'vĕl), *n.* [AS. *nafela*.] **1.** A depression in the middle of the abdomen; umbilicus. **2.** Center; the middle. **3.** *Her.* See ESCUTCHEON, *Illust.*

navel orange. A type of orange in which the fruit encloses a small secondary fruit, the rind showing externally a navellike pit. They are usually seedless.

na'vel·wort' (nā'vĕl·wûrt'), *n.* See PENNYWORT.

nav'i·cert (năv'ĭ·sûrt), *n.* [From *navigation certificate*.] A certificate issued by authorized British officials, such as consular officers, exempting a noncontraband consignment from seizure or search by patrols maintaining a British blockade.

na·vic'u·lar (nȧ·vĭk'ū·lẽr), *adj.* [L. *navicularius*, fr. *navicula*, dim. of *navis* ship.] Boat-shaped; scaphoid. — *n.* Also **na·vic'u·la're** (-lā'rē). A bone having a fancied resemblance to a boat, as the lateral bone on the radial side of the proximal row of the carpus.

nav'i·ga·ble (năv'ĭ·gȧ·b'l), *adj.* Capable of being navigated; specif.: **a** Deep enough and wide enough to afford passage to vessels; as, a *navigable* river. **b** Dirigible, as a balloon. — **nav'i·ga·bil'i·ty** (-bĭl'ĭ·tĭ), **nav'i·ga·ble·ness**, *n.* — **nav'i·ga·bly**, *adv.*

nav'i·gate (năv'ĭ·gāt), *v. i.* [L. *navigatus*, past part. of *navigare*, fr. *navis* ship + *agere* to move, direct.] **1.** To journey by water; sail or manage a vessel. **2.** To direct one's course; steer; esp., to operate an airplane or airship. — *v. t.* **1.** To pass over in vessels; to sail over or on; hence, to direct one's course through. **2.** To conduct (a vessel) upon the water by the art or skill of seamen; hence, to operate, steer, control the course of (an airplane or airship).

nav'i·ga'tion (-gā'shŭn), *n.* Act or art of navigating; esp., the science of navigating ships, airplanes, etc., through the use of calculations as to position and direction, etc. — **nav'i·ga'tion·al** (-ăl; -'l), *adj.*

nav'i·ga'tor (năv'ĭ·gā'tẽr), *n.* [L.] **1.** One who navigates or is skilled in navigation; on war vessels, an officer charged with the navigation of the ship; on aircraft, one who handles its controls or directs its operations (see WINGS, *Illust.*). **2.** *Eng.* A navvy.

nav'vy (năv'ĭ), *n.; pl.* NAVVIES (-ĭz). [Abbr. fr. *navigator*.] *Eng.* An unskilled or common laborer.

na'vy (nā'vĭ), *n.; pl.* NAVIES (-vĭz). [OF. *navie* ship, fleet, deriv. of L. *navis* ship.] **1.** *Archaic.* A fleet of ships. **2.** The war vessels belonging to a nation, considered collectively. **3.** [*usually cap.*] The naval establishment of a nation, including yards, shops, stations, men, ships, offices and officers, etc.; the complete organization for naval warfare. **4.** In full, **navy blue**. A color, reddish-blue in hue, of low saturation and low brilliance, lower than indigo. See COLOR.

navy bean. A white-seeded variety of the common kidney bean, grown esp. for its nutritious seeds.

Navy Cross. *U. S.* A decoration awarded for extraordinary heroism in operations against an armed enemy.

navy yard. A shore station for the navy, with facilities for building, equipping, and repairing war vessels.

na·wab' (nȧ·wôb'), *n.* [Hind. *navāb*. See NABOB.] *India.* **a** A viceroy under the Mogul government; also [*cap.*], the title of a Moslem prince. **b** A rich, retired Anglo-Indian; a nabob.

nay (nā), *adv.* [ME. *nay, nei*, fr. ON. *nei*, fr. *ne* not + *ei* ever.] **1.** *Archaic.* No; — a negative answer. **2.** Not this merely, but also; not only so, but. — *n.* **1.** A denial or refusal; also, a prohibition. **2.** A negative reply, vote, or voter.

Naz'a·rene' (năz'ȧ·rēn'), *adj.* [LL. *Nazarenus*, fr. Gr. *Nazarēnos*.] Of or pertaining to Nazareth, or, usually, the Nazarenes. — *n.* **1.** A native or inhabitant of Nazareth; — applied esp. to Jesus Christ. **2.** A Christian. **3.** One of a denomination of Protestant Christians organized in 1908 from Methodist backgrounds and built chiefly on the doctrines of regeneration and sanctification.

Naz'a·rite (năz'ȧ·rīt), *n.* Also **Naz'i·rite** (năz'ĭ-). [LL. *Nazaraeus*, fr. Gr. *Nazēraios*, fr. Heb. *nāzar* to dedicate.] **1.** Among ancient Hebrews, a consecrated person, forbidden to use wine, cut the hair, or touch a corpse. **2.** *Now Rare.* A (or the) Nazarene.

Na'zi (nä'tsē; năt'sē), *n.; pl.* NAZIS (-tsēz; -sēz). [G., abbr. representing pron. of first two syllables of *Nati*onalsozialistische (Partei).] **1.** A member of the former National Socialist German Workers' party, founded on fascist principles in 1919, headed by Hitler from 1921. **2.** [*also not cap.*] An adherent of Nazism in another country. — **Na'zi, na'zi**, *adj.* — **Na'zi·fy, na'zi·fy** (nä'tsē·fī; năt'sē-), *v. t.*

Na'zism (nä'tsĭz'm; năt'sĭz'm), **Na'zi·ism** (nä'tsē·ĭz'm; năt'sē-), *n.* The body of political and economic doctrines held and put into effect by the National Socialist German Workers' party in the Third German Reich, including the totalitarian principle of government, state control of all industry, predominance of groups assumed to be racially superior, and supremacy of the Führer; German fascism.

Ne·an'der·thal' (nē·ăn'dẽr·täl'; *Ger.* nā·än'dẽr·täl'), *adj.* *Anthropol.* Of or pertaining to the Neanderthal, a valley in the Rhine Province, in which were found parts of a skeleton of an early type of man; hence, designating a species (*Homo neanderthalensis*), the **Neanderthal race,** *or* **man** (see MAN, *Illust.*), known from other remains to have been widespread in paleolithic Europe.

neap (nēp), *adj.* [AS. *nēpflōd* neap flood.] Designating certain tides (**neap tides**), the least in the lunar month. — *n.* A neap tide. See TIDE, *Illust.*

neap, *n.* *U. S.* The pole of a vehicle drawn by two animals.

Ne'a·pol'i·tan ice cream (nē'ȧ·pŏl'ĭ·tăn). A mold of from two to four kinds of ice cream and, often, water ice, arranged in lengthwise layers.

near (nēr), *adv.* [AS. *nēar*, compar. of *nēah* nigh.] **1.** At, within, or to a little distance (in place or time). **2.** Within little; almost; nearly; — denoting proximity in degree. **3.** Closely; as, they are *near* related. **4.** Thriftily.

— *adj.* **1.** Closely akin or related. **2.** Close to one's interests, affection, etc.; intimate; as, one's *near* friends. **3.** Not far distant; not remote; nigh. **4.** Close; narrow; as, a *near* escape. **5.** Of animals, vehicles, etc., left; as, the *near* ox; the *near* wheel. **6.** Direct; short. **7.** Closefisted; parsimonious. **8.** Close to anything followed or imitated; also, approximating the genuine; as, *near* silk. — **Syn.** See CLOSE.

— *prep.* At or within little distance from; close to or upon.

— *v. t. & i.* To draw near (to); approach.

— **near'ly**, *adv.* — **near'ness**, *n.*

near'by', near by, near'-by' (nēr'bī'), *adv.* Close at hand. — **near'by', near'-by'**, *adj.*

Near East. **a** Formerly, the Balkan States. **b** The countries at or near the east end of the Mediterranean Sea. **c** The Middle East. Cf. FAR EAST.

near'est (nēr'ĕst; -ĭst), *adj., superl.* of NEAR.

near'-hand', *adv.* *Scot.* **a** Near at hand. **b** Almost; nearly.

near'sight'ed (nēr'sīt'ĕd; -ĭd; 2), *adj.* Seeing distinctly at short distances only; shortsighted. — **near'-sight'**, *n.* — **near'sight'ed·ly**, *adv.* — **near'sight'ed·ness**, *n.*

neat (nēt), *n. sing. & pl.* [AS. *nēat*.] Cattle of the ox kind, as distinguished from horses, sheep, and goats. — **neat**, *adj.*

neat, *adj.* [F. *net*, fr. L. *nitidus* brilliant, elegant, LL., clean, pure, fr. *nitere* to shine.] **1.** Free from admixture or adulteration; as, *neat* silk; of liquors, undiluted; straight. **2.** Free from what is unbecoming, inappropriate, or tawdry; tasteful. **3.** Free from bungling; adroit; as, a *neat* retort. **4.** Orderly and cleanly; tidy. **5.** Clear; net; as, he made a *neat* profit on the transaction. — **neat'ly**, *adv.* — **neat'ness**, *n.*

Syn. **Neat, tidy, trim, trig** mean showing care and orderliness. **Neat** stresses perfect cleanliness or freedom from that which clutters; **tidy**, orderliness, careful arrangement, and a place for everything; **trim**, smartness or spruceness in appearance; **trig**, compactness, neatness, and jauntiness in appearance.

'neath (nēth; nēth), *prep.* *Poetic.* Contr. of BENEATH.

neat'herd' (nēt'hûrd'), *n.* A herdsman; a cowherd.

neat's'-foot' oil (nēts'fo͝ot'). A pale-yellow fixed oil made by boiling the feet and shin bones of neat cattle, used chiefly as a leather dressing and fine lubricant.

neb (nĕb), *n.* [AS. *nebb*.] **1.** The beak of a bird or tortoise; bill; hence: **a** The face. **b** The nose; a snout. **c** A person's mouth. **2.** The tip or nib, as of a pen.

Ne'bi·im' (nĕb'ē·ēm'; *Heb.* nĕ·vē'ēm'), *n. pl.* [Heb. *nebī'īm*, pl. of *nābī* prophet.] The books of the Hebrew Bible placed between the Torah and the Hagiographa, and generally called the *Prophets.*

Neb'u·chad·nez'zar (nĕb'ū·kăd·nĕz'ẽr), *or, more properly,* **Neb'u·chad·rez'zar** (-rĕz'ẽr), *n.* *Bib.* King of Babylon from 605 to 562 B.C., who captured Jerusalem.

neb'u·la (nĕb'ū·lȧ), *n.; pl.* -LAE (-lē), -LAS (-lȧz). [L., mist, cloud.] **1.** *Astron.* One of a large class of celestial structures, of great extension and extreme tenuity, composed of matter in a gaseous or finely divided state. **2.** *Med.* **a** A slight cloudlike opacity of the cornea. **b** A cloudy appearance in the urine. — **neb'u·lar** (-lẽr), *adj.*

neb'u·lar hy·poth'e·sis. A hypothesis that the stars and planets were formed out of primal nebular matter, esp., as in the hypothesis of Laplace, by the throwing off of successive rings from a vast, rotating, gradually cooling and contracting nebular mass.

neb'u·lize (nĕb'ū·līz), *v. t.* To reduce to a fine spray; atomize. — **neb'u·li·za'tion** (-lĭ·zā'shŭn; -lī·zā'-), *n.* — **neb'u·liz'er** (-līz'ẽr), *n.*

neb'u·lose (nĕb'ū·lōs), *adj.* Nebulous. — **neb'u·los'i·ty** (-lŏs'ĭ·tĭ), *n.*

neb'u·lous (-lŭs), *adj.* [L. *nebulosus*.] **1.** Cloudy; hazy; misty; vague; also, cloudlike; clouded. **2.** *Astron.* Of, pertaining to, or like a nebula; nebular. — **neb'u·lous·ly**, *adv.* — **neb'u·lous·ness**, *n.*

nec'es·sar'i·an (nĕs'ĕ·sâr'ĭ·ăn; 6), *adj. & n.* Necessitarian.

nec'es·sar'y (nĕs'ĕ·sĕr'ĭ *or, esp. Brit.,* -sẽr·ĭ; 3), *adj.* [L. *necessarius*, fr. *necesse* necessary, fr. *ne-* not + *cedere* to go away.] **1.** Essential to an end or condition; indispensable. **2.** Resulting from necessity; inevitable. **3.** Resulting from, or acting under, compulsion; not voluntary. **4.** Rendering service, esp. of an essential and intimate kind; — now only in phrase **necessary woman**. **5.** *Logic.* **a** Logically unavoidable; as, a *necessary* consequence. **b** Impossible of denial without contradiction; as, a *necessary* truth. — *n.; pl.* -IES (-ĭz). **1.** A necessary thing; a requisite; esp., *pl., Law,* such things as are requisite for support of an incompetent or dependent in his station of life. **2.** *Now Dial.* A privy; a water closet. — **nec'es·sar'i·ly** (nĕs'ĕ·sĕr'ĭ·lĭ; *emphatic also* nĕs'ĕ·sâr'ĭ·lĭ), *adv.*

ne·ces'si·tar'i·an (nē·sĕs'ĭ·târ'ĭ·ăn; 6), *adj.* Of or pert. to necessitarianism. — *n.* An adherent of necessitarianism.

ne·ces'si·tar'i·an·ism (-ĭz'm), *n.* The doctrine that results follow by invariable sequence from causes, and esp. that the will is not free. Cf. DETERMINISM.

ne·ces′si·tate (nē·sĕs′ĭ·tāt), *v. t.* **1.** To make necessary, or indispensable, unavoidable, or inevitable. **2.** To force; compel; constrain. — **ne·ces′si·ta′tion** (-tā′shŭn), *n.*

ne·ces′si·tous (-tŭs), *adj.* **1.** Needy; indigent. **2.** Narrow; destitute; pinching; pinched. **3.** Necessitated; forced; as, *necessitous* selling forced prices down. — **ne·ces′si·tous·ly**, *adv.* — **ne·ces′si·tous·ness**, *n.*

ne·ces′si·ty (-tĭ), *n.* [OF. *necessité*, fr. L. *necessitas*, fr. *necesse.*] **1.** Necessary character or quality. **2.** That which is necessary; as: **a** That which is unavoidable because compelled, inevitable, or the like; as, to submit to *necessity.* **b** A requisite; an indispensable; as, *necessities* of life. **3.** Urgent need; as, telephone in case of *necessity;* also, want; poverty. **4.** A compelling force or principle; specif., fate. **5.** *Philos.* **a** The relation of that which must be to the grounds of its being; inevitable connection. **b** The principle of universal and uniform causation; — contrasted with *chance.* **c** The negation of freedom in voluntary action. — **Syn.** See NEED.

neck (nĕk), *n.* [AS. *hnecca.*] **1.** The part of an animal connecting the head and the trunk. **2.** The part of a garment covering, or nearest to, the neck. **3.** Something suggestive of a neck; as: **a** The slender part of a bottle, a gourd, etc. **b** An isthmus, cape, or other narrow stretch of land. **c** A strait. **d** *Anat.* A constricted part of an organ; as, the *neck* of the uterus; the *neck* of a tooth (see TOOTH, *Illust.*). **e** *Music.* The part of a violin, guitar, or the like, extending from head to body. **f** *Print.* The beard of a type. See TYPE, *Illust.*
— *v. t.* **1.** To kill, as a fowl, by striking or stretching the neck. **2.** Also *v. i. Colloq.* To embrace about the neck; to caress; pet.
— *adj.* Of, pert. to, or for use at or round the neck; as in:

neckband	**neckguard**	**neckpiece**
neckcloth	**neckline**	**neckwear**

neck′er·chief (nĕk′ẽr·chĭf), *n.* [For *neck kerchief.*] A kerchief for the neck.

neck′ing, *n. Arch.* Any small molding near the top of a column. See IONIC, *Illust.*

neck′lace (nĕk′lĭs), *n.* A string of jewels or beads, or a chain of gold or other metal, worn around the neck.

neck′tie′ (-tī′), *n.* **a** A band of material, as silk, passing round the neck and tied in front; a cravat. Cf. FOUR-IN-HAND, 2; SCARF, 2 **c.** **b** A bow fastened at the front of the neck.

nec′ro- (nĕk′rō-), **necr-**. [Gr. *nekros* dead body.] A combining form meaning: **a** *A dead body; the dead;* as in:

necrolatry	**necrophile**	**necrophilic**
necrophagous	**necrophilia**	**necrophobia**

b *Necrosis; gangrene;* as in:

necremia	**necrobiosis**	**necropathy**

c *Dead tissue*, as in **nec·rec′to·my.**

ne·crol′o·gy (nĕ·krŏl′ō·jĭ), *n.; pl.* -GIES (-jĭz). [*necro-* + *-logy.*] **1.** A register of deaths; a roll of the dead. **2.** An obituary notice. — **nec′ro·log′i·cal** (nĕk′rō·lŏj′ĭ·kăl), *adj.* — **nec′ro·log′i·cal·ly**, *adv.* — **ne·crol′o·gist** (nĕ·krŏl′ō·jĭst), *n.*

nec′ro·man′cy (nĕk′rō·măn′sĭ), *n.* [OF. *nigromance*, fr. L. *necromantia*, fr. Gr. *nekromanteia*, fr. *nekros* a dead body + *manteia* divination. The old spelling is due to confusion with L. *niger* black. Hence the name *black art.*] The art of, or a device for, revealing the future by pretended communication with the spirits of the dead; hence, magic in general; conjuration. — **nec′ro·man′cer** (-sẽr), *n.* — **nec′ro·man′tic** (-măn′tĭk), *adj.*

ne·crop′o·lis (nĕ·krŏp′ō·lĭs; nē-), *n.; pl.* -LISES (-lĭs·ĕz; -ĭz), NECROPOLEIS (-līs). [Gr. *nekropolis*, fr. *nekros* a dead body + *polis* city.] A cemetery, esp. one of large size.

nec′rop·sy (nĕk′rŏp·sĭ), *n.* Also **ne·cros′co·py** (nĕ·krŏs′kō·pĭ). [*necr-* + Gr. *opsis* sight.] A post-mortem examination; autopsy.

ne·crose′ (nĕ·krōs′; nĕk′rōs), *v. t. & i.* To affect with, or undergo, necrosis.

ne·cro′sis (nĕ·krō′sĭs), *n.; pl.* -SES (-sēz). [NL., fr. Gr. *nekrōsis*, fr. *nekroun* to make dead, mortify, fr. *nekros* dead body.] Death of tissue; esp. mortification of bodily tissue, as from loss of blood supply, burning, etc.

ne·crot′ic (nĕ·krŏt′ĭk), *adj.* Necrosed; also, characterized by, or producing, necrosis, as in **necrotic enteritis.**

ne·crot′o·my (nĕ·krŏt′ō·mĭ), *n.* [*necro-* + *-tomy.*] **a** The dissection of dead bodies. **b** The surgical removal of necrosed bone. — **nec′ro·tom′ic** (nĕk′rō·tŏm′ĭk), *adj.* — **ne·crot′o·mist** (nĕ·krŏt′ō·mĭst), *n.*

nec′tar (nĕk′tẽr), *n.* [L., fr. Gr. *nektar.*] **1.** *Gr. Myth. & Poetic.* The drink (sometimes, less properly, the food) of the gods; hence, any delicious or inspiring beverage. **2.** *Bot.* A sweet liquid secreted by certain glands (*nectaries*) of a plant. — **nec·tar′e·an** (nĕk·târ′ē·ăn), **nec·tar′e·ous** (-ŭs), *adj.*

nec′tar·ine′ (nĕk′tẽr·ēn′; nĕk′tẽr·ĭn, -ēn), *n.* [See NECTAR.] A smooth-skinned variety of peach.

nec′ta·ry (nĕk′tȧ·rĭ), *n.; pl.* -RIES (-rĭz). **1.** *Bot.* A gland that secretes nectar; also, sometimes, the organ or part containing the gland. **2.** *Zool.* The honey tube of an aphid.

nee, née (nā), *adj. fem.* [F. *née*, fr. L. *nata*, fem. of *natus*, past part. of *nasci* to be born.] Born; — used in introducing the maiden family name of a married woman.

need (nēd), *n.* [AS. *nēad, nīed, nēd, nēod, nȳd.*] **1.** A condition requiring supply or relief; urgent exigency; as, no *need* exists for haste. **2.** The lack of anything requisite, desired, or useful; as, he felt the *need* of a better education. **3.** Want; poverty; as, to live in *need.* **4.** Anything needed or felt to be needed; as, our daily *needs.*

Syn. **Need, necessity, exigency** mean a pressing lack of something. **Need** implies urgency; **necessity** implies an imperative demand or a compelling cause; **exigency** adds the implication of circumstances imposing restrictions, strain, or the like.

— *v. t.* To be in need of; require; — often used as an auxiliary before an infinitive without *to;* as, he *need* not fear. — **Syn.** See LACK.
— *v. i.* **1.** To be needful; to be necessary; — now chiefly in various impersonal constructions; as, it *needs* not that your stay be long. **2.** To be in need or want. — **need′er**, *n.*

need′ful (-fo͝ol; -f′l), *adj.* **1.** Full of needs; needy. **2.** Necessary; requisite. — *n.* Something needed. — ***the needful.*** *Slang.* Money. — **need′ful·ly**, *adv.* — **need′ful·ness**, *n.*

need′i·ness (-ĭ·nĕs; -nĭs), *n.* Indigence; poverty.

nee′dle (nē′d′l), *n.* [AS. *nǣdl.*] **1.** A small instrument for sewing, usually of steel, sharp at one end, with an eyehole for thread. **2.** A slender rod, usually of steel, wood, or plastic, with bluntly pointed ends, used in knitting by hand (in full, ***knitting needles***); also, one with a hook for netting or crocheting. **3.** Any needlelike object, as a pointed crystal, a sharp rock, an obelisk, etc. **4.** A slender, sharp-pointed piece, as of steel or wood, used in a phonograph to transmit vibrations. **5.** A magnetic needle. **6.** *Bot.* Any needle-shaped leaf, specif. that of the pine. **7.** *Mach.* A slender pointed rod controlling a fine inlet or outlet, as in a valve (**needle valve**) capable of fine adjustment. **8.** *Med.* A sharp-pointed, slender instrument for sewing or puncturing tissues. — *v. t.;* NEE′DLED (nē′d′ld); NEE′DLING (-dlĭng). **1.** To sew, pierce, etc., with a needle. **2.** *Colloq.* To strengthen (beer, ale, etc.) by adding raw alcohol. **3.** *Colloq.* To tease or annoy or, often, to incite to a desired action by repeated sharp prods, gibes, etc.

nee′dle-bar′ cam. See CAM, *Illust.*

nee′dle·fish′ (nē′d′l·fĭsh′), *n.;* see FISH. **1.** Any of a family (Belonidae), of voracious elongate teleost fishes (called also *billfishes, garfishes*, and *gars*), resembling, but not related to, the fresh-water gars. **2.** A pipefish.

nee′dle-point′, *adj.* Designating a type of lace (**needle-point lace**) made with a needle on a parchment or paper pattern; — disting. esp. from *bobbin lace.*

needle point. **1.** Needle-point lace. **2.** Embroidery done in cross-stitch, tent stitch, etc., on canvas.

need′less (nēd′lĕs; -lĭs), *adj.* Not needed; unnecessary. — **need′less·ly**, *adv.* — **need′less·ness**, *n.*

nee′dle·wom′an (nē′d′l·wo͝om′ăn), *n.; pl.* -WOMEN (-wĭm′ĕn; -ĭn). A woman adept in needlework; a seamstress.

nee′dle·work′ (-wûrk′), *n.* Work done with a needle; sewing; embroidery; also, the occupation of one who sews.

needs (nēdz), *adv.* [Orig. a gen. of *need*, AS. *nēdes.*] Of necessity; necessarily; — now chiefly with *must.*

need′y (nēd′ĭ), *adj.;* NEED′I·ER (-ĭ·ẽr); NEED′I·EST. Distressed by lack of the means of living; poverty-stricken.

neep (nēp), *n.* [AS. *nǣp.*] *Scot. & Dial.* A turnip.

ne′er (nâr; năr; 6). *Chiefly Poet.* Contraction of NEVER.

ne′er-do-well′, *n. & adj.* (One) hopelessly incompetent or incorrigible.

ne·far′i·ous (nē·fâr′ĭ·ŭs; 6), *adj.* [L. *nefarius*, fr. *nefas* crime, wrong, fr. *ne-* not + *fas* divine law.] Heinously or impiously wicked; iniquitous. — **Syn.** See VICIOUS. — **ne·far′i·ous·ly**, *adv.* — **ne·far′i·ous·ness**, *n.*

ne·gate′ (nē·gāt′; nē′gāt), *v. t.* [See NEGATION.] **a** To deny; nullify. **b** To declare or prove nonexistent. — **Syn.** See NULLIFY.

ne·ga′tion (nē·gā′shŭn), *n.* [F. or L.; F. *négation*, fr. L. *negatio*, fr. *negare* to say no, deny.] **1.** Act or instance of denying; a negative answer, assertion, etc. **2.** State of being negated; variously, annihilation, nullity, etc.; specif., *Philos.*, privation or nonexistence.

neg′a·tive (nĕg′ȧ·tĭv), *adj.* [F. or L.; F. *négatif*, fr. L. *negativus*, fr. *negare* to deny.] **1.** Expressing, implying, or containing a negation; as, a *negative* answer; — opp. to *affirmative.* **2.** Not positive; without affirmative statement, demonstration, character, etc.; as, a *negative* argument; also, privative. **3.** **a** *Bacteriol., etc.* Not affirming the presence of the organism or condition in question. **b** *Biol.* Directed or moving away from a source of stimulation. **4.** *Elec.* **a** Designating or pertaining to a kind of electricity. See ELECTRICITY, 2. **b** Specif.: (1) Charged with negative electricity. (2) Tending to gain electrons, and thus become negative [in sense (1)]. **5.** *Logic.* Denying a predicate of a subject, or of a part of a subject; — opposed to *affirmative.* **6.** *Math., Physics, etc.* **a** Designating a quantity to be subtracted; minus. **b** Reckoned or proceeding oppositely to an ordinary or arbitrary positive direction. **c** Falling on the side of a line or plane opposite to an arbitrary positive side. **7.** *Photog.* Having the lights and shades in approximately inverse order to those of the original subject. **8.** *Psychol.* Characterized by resistance or retreat to suggestion or stimulus.
— *n.* **1.** A negative proposition, term, particle, as *not, no*, etc. Abbr. *neg.* **2.** A negative reply or vote; a refusal; also, veto. **3.** That side of a question which denies or refuses. **4.** *Elec.* The negative plate of a voltaic or electrolytic cell. **5.** *Math.* A negative quantity or symbol. **6.** *Photog.* A negative image; the film or plate used in printing positive pictures.
— *v. t.* **1.** To refuse assent to; veto. **2.** To pronounce against; specif., to reject by vote. **3.** To disprove. **4.** To contradict; deny. **5.** To neutralize; counteract. — **Syn.** See DENY.
— **neg′a·tiv′i·ty** (-tĭv′ĭ·tĭ), **neg′a·tive·ness**, *n.* — **neg′a·tive·ly**, *adv.*

neg′a·tiv·ism (nĕg′ȧ·tĭv·ĭz′m), *n.* **1.** The doctrines of one who holds sceptical or agnostic views, or who denies reality, esp. of the phenomenal universe. **2.** *Psychol.* A peculiarity of behavior, esp. in children, consisting either in not performing acts which are commanded or suggested (***passive negativism***) or in doing the opposite (***active negativism***). — **neg′a·tiv·ist** (-ĭst), *n. & adj.* — **neg′a·tiv·is′tic** (-ĭs′tĭk), *adj.*

neg′a·to′ry (-tō′rĭ; -tẽr·ĭ), *adj.* Expressing, or of the nature of, negation.

neg′a·tron (nĕg′ȧ·trŏn), *n.* [*negative* + *electron.*] *Physics & Chem.* An electron.

neg·lect′ (nĕg·lĕkt′), *v. t.* [L. *neglectus*, past part. of *negligere, neglegere*, fr. *neg-* not + *legere* to pick up, gather.] To disregard; esp.: **a** To omit to notice; slight. **b** To be remiss in attending to; fail to do, care for, etc.

Syn. **Neglect, omit, disregard, ignore, overlook, slight, forget** mean to pass over without giving due attention. **Neglect** implies lack of sufficient attention; **omit**, absence of all attention; **disregard**, inattention, often voluntary; **ignore**, an intention to disregard or a failure to regard something obvious; **overlook**, a disregarding or ignoring, usually through haste or lack of care; **slight**, a neglect, omission, or disregarding, often through arrogance; **forget**, a willful ignoring or a failure to impress on one's mind.

— *n.* **1.** A neglecting; state or fact of being neglected; also, formerly, indifference or lack of consideration; as, to treat an offer with *neglect.* **2.** An act or instance of negligence or carelessness.
— **neg·lect′er**, *n.* — **neg·lect′ful**, *adj.* — **Syn.** See NEGLIGENT. — **neg·lect′ful·ly**, *adv.* — **neg·lect′ful·ness**, *n.*

neg′li·gee′ (nĕg′lĭ·zhā′; nĕg′lĭ·zhā′), ‖**né′gli′gé′** (nā′glē′zhā′), *n.* [F. *négligé*, past part. of *négliger* to neglect.] A type of easy robe or dressing gown worn by women; hence, easy, unceremonious attire; undress.

neg′li·gence (nĕg′lĭ·jĕns), *n.* **1.** Quality or state of being negligent; neglect. **2.** *Law.* Failure to exercise the care that the circumstances justly demand; omission of duty in doing or forbearing. **3.** An act or instance of negligence or carelessness.

neg′li·gent (nĕg′lĭ·jĕnt), *adj.* [OF. or L.; OF., fr. L. *negligens*, pres. part. of *negligere*. See NEGLECT.] Guilty of, or given to, neglect or disregard; culpably careless, inattentive, indifferent, etc. — **neg′li·gent·ly**, *adv.*

Syn. **Negligent, neglectful, lax, slack, remiss** mean culpably careless. **Negligent** implies inattention to one's duty or business; **neglectful** adds the implication of laziness or blameworthiness; **lax** implies want of strictness, severity, or precision; **slack** implies want of proper or necessary diligence, expedition, and care; **remiss** implies culpable carelessness that shows itself in slackness, forgetfulness, or neglect.

neg′li·gi·ble (-jĭ·b'l), *adj.* That may be neglected or disregarded. — **neg′li·gi·bil′i·ty** (-bĭl′ĭ·tĭ), *n.* — **neg′li·gi·bly**, *adv.*

ne·go′ti·a·ble (nē·gō′shĭ·à·b'l), *adj.* Capable of being negotiated; transferable in the ordinary course of business; specif., transferable by delivery, with or without endorsement; as, *negotiable* instruments; *negotiable* bonds. — **ne·go′ti·a·bil′i·ty** (-bĭl′ĭ·tĭ), *n.*

ne·go′ti·ant (-ănt), *n.* A negotiator.

ne·go′ti·ate (nē·gō′shĭ·āt), *v. i.* [L. *negotiatus*, past part. of *negotiari*, fr. *negotium* business, fr. *neg-* not + *otium* leisure.] To hold intercourse with a view to coming to terms; to confer regarding a basis of agreement; as, to *negotiate* for the purchase of a house. — *v. t.* **1.** To transfer for a valuable consideration; to sell, pass, or the like, as commercial paper, bills of exchange, etc. **2.** To negotiate concerning; to procure, or arrange for, by negotiation; as, to *negotiate* peace; to *negotiate* a loan. **3.** *Colloq.* To surmount or traverse; accomplish; to deal with as desired. — **ne·go′ti·a′tor** (-ā′tēr), *n.*

ne·go′ti·a′tion (-ā′shŭn), *n.* A negotiating; a parley or conference regarding terms.

Ne·gril′lo (nē·grĭl′ō), *n.; pl.* -LOS (-ōz). [Sp., dim. of *negro* black.] A Negrito; a Pygmy or Bushman.

Ne·gri′to (nē·grē′tō), *n.; pl.* -TOS or -TOES (-tōz). [Sp., dim. of *negro* black.] A member of any of a number of dwarfish Negroid peoples, found esp. in central and southern Africa and in Oceania.

Ne′gro (nē′grō), *n.; pl.* NEGROES (-grōz). [Sp. *negro*, fr. *negro* black, fr. L. *niger*.] **1.** A person of the typical African branch of the black race (formerly called the Ethiopian) inhabiting the Sudan, or loosely, of any of the black races of Africa, including, besides the Negroes proper, Bantus, Pygmies, Hottentots, and Bushmen. See LANGUAGE, *Table*. **2.** A black man; esp., a person having more or less Negro blood. — **Ne′gro**, *adj.*

Ne′groid (-groid), *adj.* Characteristic of, or like, the Negro or Negroes. — *n.* A member of a race perceptibly sharing Negro blood or displaying Negro traits; esp., a Bantu.

Ne′gro·phile (nē′grō·fīl; -fĭl), *n.* Also **Ne′gro·phil** (-fĭl). [*Negro* + *-phile, -phil*.] One friendly to the Negro.

Ne′gro·pho′bi·a (-fō′bĭ·à), *n.* Dread of, or strong aversion to, the Negro. — **Ne′gro·phobe** (nē′grō·fōb), *n.*

Ne′gus (nē′gŭs), *n.* [Amharic (fr. Eth.) *nĕgūš* king.] The title of the sovereign of Ethiopia.

ne′gus (nē′gŭs), *n.* [After Col. Francis *Negus* (d. 1732), its first maker.] A beverage of wine, hot water, sugar, nutmeg, and lemon juice.

Ne′he·mi′ah (nē′hē·mī′à; nē′ĕ-), *n.* *Douay Bib.* **Ne′he·mi′as** (-ăs). [Heb. *Nĕhemyāh*.] *Bib.* **a** A famous Jewish leader of the 5th century B.C. **b** A book of the Old Testament. See BIBLE.

neigh (nā), *v. i.* [AS. *hnǣgan*.] To utter the loud and prolonged cry of the horse. — *n.* Sound of neighing.

neigh′bor, neigh′bour (nā′bēr), *n.* [AS. *nēahgebūr*, lit., nigh-dweller.] **1.** A person who lives near another. **2.** A person or thing near another. **3.** A fellow man. — *adj.* Neighboring; nearby. — *v. t.* **1.** To adjoin; border on; be near to. **2.** To bring near; hence, to draw into close association. — *v. i.* **1.** To dwell or be situated in the vicinity. **2.** To be or associate on neighborly terms.

neigh′bor·hood, neigh′bour·hood (-hŏŏd), *n.* **1.** *Now Rare.* Neighborliness. **2.** Quality or condition of being neighbors; proximity. **3.** Vicinity; a place or region near; — usually with *of*. **4.** The people living near one, or near one another; community. **5.** A district or section, esp. with reference to the condition or type of its inhabitants.

neigh′bor·ing, neigh′bour·ing, *adj.* Living or being near; adjacent.

neigh′bor·ly, neigh′bour·ly, *adj.* Appropriate to the relation of neighbors; friendly. — **Syn.** See AMICABLE. — **-li·ness**, *n.*

neist (nēst). Scot. & dial. var. of NEXT.

nei′ther (nē′thēr; nī′thēr), *adj.* [AS. *nāwther*, *nāhwæther*, *nōhwæther*, *nōwther*, fr. *nā*, *nō*, not + *hwæther* whether.] Not either; as, *neither* one of us. — *pron.* Not the one or the other; as, *neither* is a man of substance; — sometimes construed as plural. — *conj.* **1.** Not either; — usually introducing the first of two or more coordinate words or clauses joined by *nor* or, formerly, *neither*. **2.** Nor yet; also not; as, do not eat it, *neither* touch it. — *adv.* *Now Chiefly Dial.* Any more so; — used at the end of a clause to enforce a foregoing negative (*nor, not, no*); as, very tall but not too tall *neither*.

nek′ton (nĕk′tŏn), *n.* [NL., fr. Gr. *nēkton*, neut. of *nēktos* swimming.] *Zool.* The actively swimming pelagic organisms. Cf. PLANKTON. — **nek·ton′ic** (nĕk·tŏn′ĭk), *adj.*

ne·lum′bo (nē·lŭm′bō), *n.* [NL., fr. Singhalese *nelumbu*.] Any of a genus (*Nelumbo*) of large water lilies, esp. the Indian lotus, and the water chinquapin; — called also **ne·lum′bi·um** (nē·lŭm′bĭ·ŭm).

nem′a·thel′minth (nĕm′à·thĕl′mĭnth), *n.* Also **nem′a·tel′minth** (-tĕl′mĭnth). [Gr. *nēma*, *nēmatos*, thread + *helmins*, *helminthos*, worm.] Any of a phylum (Nemathelminthes) of worms including the roundworms or nematodes, having a cylindrical unsegmented body.

nem′a·to- (nĕm′à·tō-), **nemat-**. [Gr. *nēma*, *nēmatos*.] *Bot. & Zool.* A combining form meaning: **a** *A thread*, as in **nem′a·to·blast′**. **b** *Nematode*, as in **nem′a·tol′o·gy**.

nem′a·to·cyst′ (-sĭst′), *n.* [*nemato-* + *-cyst*.] *Zool.* One of the stinging organs of hydrozoans, scyphozoans, and anthozoans, or of various protozoans, mollusks, worms, etc. — **nem′a·to·cys′tic** (-sĭs′tĭk), *adj.*

nem′a·tode (nĕm′à·tōd), *n.* [Gr. *nēma*, *nēmatos*, thread.] Any of a class (Nematoda) of worms, including the pinworm, trichina, and Guinea worm; a roundworm. Cf. NEMATHELMINTH. — **nem′a·tode**, *adj.*

Nem′bu·tal (nĕm′bū·tōl; -tăl), *n.* A trade-mark applied to a sedative, hypnotic, and antispasmodic, chemically sodium ethyl-(1-methylbutyl) barbiturate.

Ne·me′an (nē·mē′ăn; nē′mē·ăn), *adj.* Of or pertaining to Nemea, a valley in Argolis. The biennial **Nemean games** constituted one of the four chief Panhellenic festivals.

Nemean lion. *Gr. Myth.* A fierce lion of Nemea the strangling of which was one of the twelve labors of Hercules.

ne·mer′te·an (nē·mûr′tē·ăn), **ne·mer′ti·an** (-tĭ·ăn), *n.* [Gr. *Nēmertēs*, name of a Nereid.] Any of a class (Nemertinea) of often vividly colored, marine worms, most of which burrow in the mud or sand along seacoasts. — **ne·mer′te·an, ne·mer′ti·an**, *adj.* — **nem′er·tin′e·an** (nĕm′ēr·tĭn′ē·ăn), *adj. & n.*

Nem′e·sis (nĕm′ē·sĭs), *n.* [Gr., prop., imputation, distribution, fr. *nemein* to deal out.] **1.** *Gr. Relig.* Goddess of retributive justice. **2.** [*often not cap.; pl.* NEMESES (-sēz)] One who inflicts retribution; also, an act of retribution.

‖**ne′mi·ne con′tra·di·cen′te** (nĕm′ĭ·nē kŏn′trà·dĭ·sĕn′tē). [L.] Without a dissenting vote; unanimously. Abbr. *nem. con.*

‖**ne′mi·ne dis·sen′ti·en′te** (dĭ·sĕn′shĭ·ĕn′tē). [L.] Without a dissenting vote; unanimously. Abbr. *nem. diss.*

‖**ne′mo me im·pu′ne la·ces′sit** (nē′mō mē ĭm·pū′nē là·sĕs′ĭt). [L.] No one attacks me with impunity; — motto of Scotland.

ne′o- (nē′ō-). [Gr. *neos* new.] A combining form meaning: **1.** *New, recent;* esp., *a new and different period* or *form* of a faith, school, language, etc., as in:

neo-Catholic	**neo-Egyptian**	**neo-Hellenic**
neo-Christianity	**neoformation**	**neo-Latin**
neoclassic	**neo-Gothic**	**neopaganism**

2. *Geol. The latest subdivision of a period*, as in **Ne′o·pa′le·o·zo′ic.**

ne′o·ars·phen′a·mine (-ärs·fĕn′à·mēn; -à·mĭn), *n.* Also **ne′o·ars′·phen·am′in.** *Pharm.* A synthetic organic compound of arsenic, essentially $C_{12}H_{11}N_2O_2As_2(CH_2O)SONa$.

Ne′o·cene (nē′ō·sēn), *adj.* [*neo* + Gr. *kainos* new.] *Geol.* Pertaining to or designating the later portion of the Tertiary, including both the Miocene and Pliocene. See TERTIARY, *adj.* — **Ne′o·cene**, *n.*

Ne′o–Dar′win·ism, *n.* The theory which holds natural selection, as explained by Darwin, to be the chief factor in the evolution of plants and animals, and denies the inheritance of acquired characters. Cf. NEO-LAMARCKISM, WEISMANNISM. — **Ne′o–Dar·win′i·an**, *adj. & n.* — **Ne′o–Dar′win·ist**, *n.*

ne′o·dym′i·um (nē′ō·dĭm′ĭ·ŭm), *n.* [NL. See NEO-; DIDYMIUM.] A rare metallic element. Symbol, *Nd;* at. no., 60; at. wt., 144.27.

Ne′o·gae′a (nē′ō·jē′à), *n.* [NL., fr. *neo-* + Gr. *gaia* earth.] *Biogeog.* The Neotropical region regarded as one of three primary divisions. — **Ne′o·gae′an, Ne′o·ge′an** (-jē′ăn), *adj.*

Ne′o–He·bra′ic, *n.* The modern Hebrew language. — **Ne′o–He·bra′ic**, *adj.*

ne′o·im·pres′sion·ism (nē′ō·ĭm·prĕsh′ŭn·ĭz′m), *n.* *Painting.* A development, on more rigorously scientific lines, of the theory and practice of impressionism, originated by Georges Seurat. Its characteristic method is *pointillism*. See IMPRESSIONISM, POINTILLISM. — **ne′o·im·pres′sion·ist** (-ĭst), *n. & adj.*

Ne′o–La·marck′ism, *n.* *Biol.* Lamarckism as revived, modified, and expounded by recent biologists, esp. as maintaining that the offspring inherits acquired characters. Cf. NEO-DARWINISM. — **Ne′o–La·marck′i·an**, *adj. & n.* — **Ne′o–La·marck′ist**, *n.*

ne′o·lith (nē′ō·lĭth), *n.* A neolithic stone implement.

ne′o·lith′ic (nē′ō·lĭth′ĭk), *adj.* [*neo-* + *-lith* + *-ic*.] Designating or pertaining to a stage (**Neolithic period**) of culture following the paleolithic and characterized by the use of polished stone implements, and many cultural advances, as pottery making, domestication of animals, cultivation of grain and fruit trees, linen weaving, etc.

ne·ol′o·gism (nē·ŏl′ō·jĭz′m), *n.* A new word, usage, or expression; the use of a new word or of an old word in a new or different sense. — **ne·ol′o·gist** (-jĭst), *n.* — **ne·ol′o·gis′tic** (-jĭs′tĭk), **ne·ol′o·gis′ti·cal** (-tĭ·kăl), *adj.*

ne·ol′o·gy (nē·ŏl′ō·jĭ), *n.; pl.* -GIES (-jĭz). [F. *néologie*. See NEO-; -LOGY.] Neologism. — **ne′o·log′i·cal** (nē′ō·lŏj′ĭ·kăl), *adj.*

ne′on (nē′ŏn), *n.* [NL., fr. Gr. *neos* new.] *Chem.* A colorless inert gaseous element found in the atmosphere. Symbol, *Ne;* at. no., 10; at. wt., 20.183. It gives a reddish glow in a vacuum tube and is used with other gases in a type of electric lamp (**neon lamp**).

ne′o·phyte (nē′ō·fīt), *n.* [LL. *neophytus*, fr. Gr. *neophytos*, prop., newly planted, fr. *neos* new + *phytos* grown, fr. *phyein* to grow.] **1.** A new convert; esp., a newly baptized Christian. **2.** *R.C.Ch.* **a** A newly ordained priest. **b** A novice in a convent. **3.** A beginner; tyro.

ne′o·plasm (-plăz′m), *n.; pl.* -PLASMS (-plăz′mz). *Med.* Any abnormal formation; any morbid growth, as a tumor.

ne′o·plas′tic (-plăs′tĭk), *adj.* *Med.* Of or pertaining to a neoplasm or to neoplasty.

ne′o·plas′ti·cism (-plăs′tĭ·sĭz′m), *n.* A school of abstract painting founded by the Dutch painter Pieter Mondriaan, characterized by asymmetrical, straight-line designs. — **ne′o·plas′ti·cist** (-sĭst), *n.*

ne′o·plas′ty (nē′ō·plăs′tĭ), *n.* *Surg.* Restoration of a part by a plastic operation.

Ne′o·pla′to·nism, Ne′o–Pla′to·nism (nē′ō·plā′tō·nĭz′m), *n.* The philosophy of a group of thinkers of the early Christian Era who endeavored to reconcile the teachings of Plato and Aristotle with Oriental conceptions; also, teachings and doctrines, similar to those of the ancient Neoplatonists, promulgated in medieval and modern times. — **Ne′o·pla·ton′ic, Ne′o–Pla·ton′ic** (-plà·tŏn′ĭk; -plā-), *adj.* — **Ne′o·pla′to·nist, Ne′o–Pla′to·nist** (-plā′tō·nĭst), *n.*

ne′o·prene (nē′ō·prēn), *n.* [*neo-* + chloro*prene*.] A synthetic rubberlike plastic formed by the polymerization of chloroprene.

Ne′o·sal′var·san (-săl′vēr·săn), *n.* A trade-mark for neoarsphenamine.

Ne′o–Scho·las′ti·cism, *n.* A current philosophy which aims to restate and expound scholasticism in modern terms and to extend its scope by using the findings of modern research. — **Ne′o–Scho·las′tic**, *adj.*

ne′o·style (nē′ō·stīl), *n.* [*neo-* + *style*.] A type of manifolding device. — *v. t.* To duplicate by neostyle.

ne′o·ter′ic (nē′ō·tĕr′ĭk), *adj.* [L. *neotericus*, fr. Gr. *neōterikos*, fr. *neōteros*, compar. of *neos* young, new.] Modern; new. — **ne′o·ter′ic**, *n.* — **ne′o·ter′i·cal·ly** (-ĭ·kăl·ĭ), *adv.*

Ne′o·trop′i·cal (-trŏp′ĭ·kăl), *adj.* Also **Ne′o·trop′ic** (-ĭk). *Geog. & Biogeog.* Of, pertaining to, or designating a terrestrial region comprising South America, the West Indies, and tropical North America.

ne′o·yt·ter′bi·um (-ĭ·tûr′bĭ·ŭm), *n.* = YTTERBIUM.

Ne′o·zo′ic (nē′ō·zō′ĭk), *adj. & n.* [*neo-* + Gr. *zōē* life.] *Geol.* **a** Pertaining to or designating the entire period from the end of the Mesozoic to the present time. **b** = CENOZOIC, *adj. & n.* **c** = TERTIARY, *adj.*, 4, & *n.*, 2.

Nep, NEP (nĕp), *n.* Short for NEW ECONOMIC POLICY.

ne·pen′the (nē·pĕn′thē), *n.* Also **ne·pen′thes** (-thēz). [From L., fr. Gr. *nēpenthes*, neut. of *nēpenthēs* removing sorrow, an epithet of an Egyptian drug, fr. *nē-* not + *penthos* sorrow.] A potion or drug used by the ancients to drown pain and sorrow; hence, anything causing oblivion.

neph′e·lin·ite (nĕf′ĕ·lĭn·īt), *n.* *Petrog.* A dark, heavy, volcanic rock which may be regarded as basalt containing no olivine and with nephelite replacing the feldspar.

neph′e·lite (nĕf′ĕ·līt), **neph′e·line** (-lĭn), *n.* [Gr. *nephelē* cloud.] A native silicate of sodium, potassium, and aluminum, $K_2Na_6Al_8Si_9O_{34}$ occurring in various igneous rocks.

neph′e·lom′e·ter (-lŏm′ē·tẽr), *n.* [Gr. *nephelē* cloud + *-meter.*] **1.** *Bacteriol.* A set of barium chloride standards used for estimating turbidity of a fluid and thereby the approximate number of bacteria in suspension. **2.** *Physical Chem.* An instrument for studying the character of suspensions by means of diffuse transmitted or reflected light.

neph′ew (nĕf′ū *or, esp. Brit.*, nĕv′ū), *n.* [OF. *neveu, nevou*, fr. L. *nepos.*] **1.** The son of a brother or a sister, or, loosely, of a brother-in-law or sister-in-law. Cf. CONSANGUINITY, *Illust.* **2.** *Obs.* A grandson, or remoter lineal descendant.

neph′o- (nĕf′ō-). [Gr. *nephos.*] A combining form meaning *cloud*, as in **neph′o·gram, neph′o·graph, ne·phol′o·gy, neph′o·scope.**

nephr-. = NEPHRO-, as in **ne·phral′gi·a, ne·phrec′to·my.**

neph′ric (nĕf′rĭk), *adj.* [Gr. *nephros* kidney.] Renal.

ne·phrid′i·um (nē·frĭd′ĭ·ŭm; nĕ-), *n.; pl.* -IA (-ȧ). [NL., fr. Gr. *nephridios* of the kidneys.] *Zool. & Anat.* An excretory organ of the type found in annulate worms, mollusks, certain arthropods, etc. — **ne·phrid′i·al** (-ăl), *adj.*

neph′rism (nĕf′rĭz′m), *n.* [*nephr-* + *-ism.*] *Med.* The morbid condition caused by chronic disease of the kidney.

neph′rite (-rīt), *n.* [G. *nephrit*, fr. Gr. *nephros* kidney. See NEPHRITIC.] *Mineral.* A compact variety of amphibole, constituting the less valuable kind of jade, and formerly worn as a remedy for kidney diseases.

ne·phrit′ic (nē·frĭt′ĭk; nĕ-), *adj.* [LL. *nephriticus*, fr. Gr. *nephritikos*, fr. *nephros* a kidney.] **1.** Renal. **2.** *Med.* Of, pertaining to, or affected with nephritis.

ne·phri′tis (-frī′tĭs), *n.* [LL., fr. Gr. *nephritis.*] *Med.* Inflammation of the kidneys. Nephritis occurs in acute and chronic forms, certain types of which are known as acute and chronic *Bright's disease.*

neph′ro- (nĕf′rō-), **nephr-.** [Gr. *nephros.*] A combining form meaning: **1.** *Kidney*, as in:

nephrocele	nephrolithotomy	nephropathy
nephrogenous	nephrology	nephrotomy
nephrolith	nephrolysis	nephrotoxic

2. In adjectives, *nephric and*, as in **neph′ro·car′di·ac, neph′ro·gas′tric.**

Neph′ta·li (nĕf′tȧ·lī), *n.* *Douay Bib.* Naphtali. See JACOB.

‖**ne plus ul′tra** (nē plŭs ŭl′trȧ). [L., no further, fr. *ne* no not + *plus* more + *ultra* beyond.] The uttermost point to which one can go; hence, the summit of achievement.

nep′man (nĕp′măn), *n.* In Russia, one who engages in private trade as permitted by the New Economic Policy (Nep).

nep′o·tism (nĕp′ō·tĭz′m), *n.* [Through F. & It., fr. L. *nepos, nepotis.*] Favoritism shown to nephews and other relatives; bestowal of patronage by reason of relationship rather than merit. — **nep′o·tist** (-tĭst), *n.*

Nep′tune (nĕp′tūn), *n.* [L. *Neptunus.*] **1.** *Rom. Relig.* A god identified with the Greek Poseidon, god of the sea. **2.** *Astron.* The third largest of the planets. Its diameter is about 33,000 miles, its mean distance from the sun, about 2,793,000,000 miles, and its period of revolution, 164.79 years. It is invisible to the naked eye. Symbol, ♆ or ♆. See PLANET, *Table.* — **Nep·tu′ni·an** (nĕp·tū′nĭ·ăn; 58), *adj.*

nep·tu′ni·um (nĕp·tū′nĭ·ŭm), *n.* [NL., fr. *Neptune* the planet.] *Chem.* A short-lived radioactive element artificially produced by neutron bombardment of the uranium isotope of atomic weight 238. Symbol, *Np;* at. no., 93. The disintegration of neptunium 239 proceeds with the emission of an electron and the formation of plutonium.

Ne′re·id (nē′rē·ĭd), *n.* [L. *Nereis, -idis*, fr. Gr. *Nēreis, -idos.*] *Gr. Myth.* A sea nymph, one of the daughters of **Ne′reus** (nē′rūs), a sea-god.

Ne′re·is (nē′rē·ĭs), *n.; pl.* NEREIDES (nē·rē′ĭ·dēz). [L.] *Gr. Myth.* A Nereid.

ner′o·li oil (nĕr′ō·lĭ; nē′rō-). [F. *néroli*, fr. It. *neroli*, said to be from the name of an Italian princess.] A yellowish essential oil obtained from orange flowers, chiefly by distillation, and used in cologne and other perfumes, in liqueurs, etc.

nerv′al (nûr′văl), *adj.* [F., or L. *nervalis.*] Neural.

nerv′ate (nûr′vāt), *adj.* *Bot.* Having nerves.

ner·va′tion (nûr·vā′shŭn), *n.* The arrangement of nerves, esp. those of leaves; neuration; venation.

nerve (nûrv), *n.* [L. *nervus.*] **1.** A sinew or tendon; — now rare exc. in phrase ***to strain every nerve***, to put forth the utmost exertion. **2.** One of the cordlike or filamentous bands of tissue that connect parts of the nervous system with the other organs, and conduct impulses. **3.** Constitutional vigor; energy; strength. **4.** Power of endurance; pluck; resolution; as, to work on one's *nerve.* **5.** *Slang.* Audacity. **6.** *pl.* **a** Nervous system as an index of health, endurance, etc.; as, he has *nerves* of steel. **b** Nervousness; often, hysteria; as, an attack of *nerves.* **7.** *Bot. & Zool.* A vein; nervure. **8.** *Dent.* The sensitive pulp of a tooth. — **Syn.** See TEMERITY. — *v. t.* To give strength, vigor, or courage to.

nerve center. *Anat. & Physiol.* A group of associated nerve cells controlling those impulses concerned with or regulating any bodily function, as respiration.

nerve fiber. *Anat.* A protoplasmic process of a nerve cell.

nerve′less, *adj.* **1.** Destitute of strength or of courage; powerless; inert; unnerved. **2.** Without nerves. — **nerve′less·ly**, *adv.* — **nerve′less·ness**, *n.*

nerve′-rack′ing, *adj.* Also **nerve′-wrack′ing.** Extremely trying on the nerves.

nerv′ine (nûr′vēn; -vīn), *adj.* [NL. *nervinus.*] *Med.* Affecting the nerves; soothing. — *n.* A nerve tonic.

nerv′ous (nûr′vŭs), *adj.* [L. *nervosus* sinewy, vigorous. See NERVE.] **1.** Sinewy; strong. **2.** Manifesting vigor of mind; forcible in thought, feeling, or style; spirited. **3.** Composed of, or abounding in, nerves. **4.** Of or pertaining to the nerves; affected by or affecting the nerves; as, *nervous* excitement. **5.** Easily excited, agitated, or annoyed; excitable; hence, fearful; apprehensive. — **Syn.** See VIGOROUS. — **nerv′ous·ly**, *adv.* — **nerv′ous·ness**, *n.*

nervous system. The nerve cells and associated cells, collectively, which among higher forms are organized into nerves and nerve centers, co-ordinating and regulating excitation of effectors, as muscles, and directly conditioning behavior and consciousness. In all higher, and some lower, animals they form a *central* nervous system with *peripheral* connections. In vertebrates the nervous system comprises two major parts, the *cerebrospinal* and the *autonomic.*

ner′vure (nûr′vūr), *n.* [F.] **a** *Bot.* A vein. **b** *Zool.* One of the ribs in an insect's wings.

nerv′y (nûr′vĭ), *adj.;* NERV′I·ER (-vĭ·ẽr); NERV′I·EST. **1.** Strong; sinewy. **2.** *Colloq.* Characterized by assurance; bold. **3.** *Chiefly Brit.* Nervous; excitable.

nes′ci·ence (nĕsh′ĭ·ĕns; nĕsh′ĕns), *n.* [LL. *nescentia*, fr. L. *nesciens, -entis*, pres. part. of *nescire* not to know, fr. *ne* not + *scire* to know.] Lack of knowledge; complete ignorance; specif., *Philos.*, the doctrine that God, and all that goes beyond natural phenomena, are incapable of being known. — **nes′ci·ent** (-ĕnt), *adj.* — **Syn.** See IGNORANT.

ness (nĕs), *n.* [AS. *næs, nes.*] A promontory; cape; headland; — often a suffix in place names; as, Sheer*ness.*

-ness (-nĕs; -nĭs; 30). [AS. *-ness, -nyss, -nys.*] **1.** A suffix used primarily to form nouns denoting *state, condition, quality*, or *degree*, as in good*ness*, quality or state of being good. **2.** Hence, denoting: **a** *A particular instance of the quality or state;* as, to show them many kind*nesses.* **b** *Something exhibiting or causing the quality or state;* as, to rub off the dim*ness* from a glass.

Nes′sel·rode pud′ding (nĕs′ĕl·rōd). [After Count K. R. *Nesselrode*, Russ. diplomat.] **1.** A gelatin pudding containing chestnuts. **2.** A rich ice cream containing chestnuts, candied fruit, and maraschino.

Nes′sus (nĕs′ŭs), *n.* [L., fr. Gr. *Nessos.*] *Gr. Myth.* A centaur shot with a poisoned arrow by Hercules for trying to ravish his wife, Deianira. Following the advice of the dying Nessus, Deianira steeped her husband's shirt in the centaur's blood as a love charm, but it poisoned Hercules, causing such agony that he killed himself.

nest (nĕst), *n.* [AS.] **1.** The bed or receptacle prepared by a bird for its eggs and young. **2.** The place where the eggs of insects, fishes, turtles, etc., are laid and hatched. **3.** Any snug retreat or abode. **4.** A haunt; den. **5.** The occupants or frequenters of a nest, collectively; swarm. **6.** A set or group of similar things; esp., a graduated series of boxes, bowls, or the like, each put within the one next larger. — *v. t.* To form a nest for; to settle or place in or as in a nest. — *v. i.* To build or occupy a nest.

‖**n'est-ce pas?** (nĕs·pä′). [F.] Isn't it so?

nest egg. An egg left in the nest to induce the hen to lay more in the same place; hence, something laid up as the beginning of a fund or collection, or as a reserve.

nes′tle (nĕs′'l), *v. i.;* NES′TLED (-'ld); NES′TLING (-lĭng). [AS. *nestlian.*] **1.** *Now Rare.* To nest. **2.** To lie close and snug, as a bird in her nest; cuddle up; to settle as in a nest. — *v. t.* **1.** To settle, shelter, or house, as in a nest. **2.** To move (a part of the body) against or into something as if nestling. — **nes′tler** (-lẽr), *n.*

nest′ling (nĕst′lĭng; nĕs′lĭng), *n.* A young bird which has not abandoned the nest; hence, a very young child.

Nes′tor (nĕs′tôr; -tẽr), *n.* [L., fr. Gr. *Nestōr.*] An aged and wise counselor of the Greeks in the Trojan War; hence, figuratively, a wise old counselor.

Nes·to′ri·an (nĕs·tō′rĭ·ăn; 70), *n.* *Eccl. Hist.* An adherent of Nestorius, patriarch of Constantinople, condemned as a heretic by the Council of Ephesus in 431. He maintained that in Jesus Christ a divine person (the Logos) and a human person were joined in perfect harmony of action but not in the unity of a single individual. — **Nes·to′ri·an**, *adj.* — **Nes·to′ri·an·ism** (-ĭz′m), *n.*

net (nĕt), *n.* [AS.] **1.** A fabric wrought or woven into meshes, and used for catching fish, birds, etc. **2.** Anything fitted to entrap or catch; a snare. **3.** Anything wrought or woven in meshes; as, a tennis *net.* **4.** A network, as of lines. **5.** *Tennis, etc.* A ball hit into the net. — *v. t.;* NET′TED (-ĕd; -ĭd); NET′TING. **1.** To cover or enclose with or as with a net or nets. **2.** To take in or as in a net; to capture by stratagem. **3.** To make into a net. **4.** *Lawn Tennis, etc.* To hit (the ball) into the net. — *adj.* Netted; also, of net (fabric).

net, *adj.* Also **nett.** [F. See NEAT clean.] Clear of, or free from, all charges, deductions, etc.; specif.: **a** Remaining after the deduction of all charges, outlay, loss, etc.; as, *net* profit; *net* income; — opposed to *gross.* **b** Clear of or excluding all tare, tret, or the like; as, *net* weight. — *n.* A net amount, profit, weight, etc. — *v. t.* To produce or gain as clear profit.

neth′er (nĕth′ẽr), *adj.* [AS. *nithera*, fr. the adv. *nither, nithor*, downward.] Situated down or below; lower; under.

neth′er·most (-mōst; -mŭst), *adj.* Lowest.

nether world. World of the dead or of future punishment.

net′ting, *n.* **a** Act or process of making nets or network, or of forming meshes. **b** Act, process, or right of fishing with a net or nets. **c** A piece of network.

net′tle (nĕt′'l), *n.* [AS. *netele, netle.*] **1.** Any of a genus (*Urtica*) of plants, chiefly coarse herbs armed with stinging hairs, typifying a family (Urticaceae, the nettle family). **2.** Any of many other prickly or stinging plants. — *v. t.;* NET′TLED (-'ld); NET′TLING (-lĭng). **1.** To whip with nettles. **2.** To fret or sting as with nettles; hence, to irritate; vex. — **Syn.** See IRRITATE.

nettle rash. *Med.* An eruption on the skin resembling the condition produced by stinging with nettles; urticaria.

net ton. A short ton. See TON.

net′work′ (nĕt′wûrk′), *n.* **1.** A fabric or structure of threads, cords, wires, or the like, crossing each other at certain intervals, and knotted or secured at the crossings. **2.** Any system of lines or channels interlacing like the fabric of a net. **3.** *Radio.* A chain of radio stations.

Neuf′châ′tel′ (nū′shä′tĕl′), *n.*, *or* **Neufchâtel cheese.** A variety of soft white cheese; — from Neufchâtel in France.

neuk (*Scot.* nūk). Scot. & dial. var. of NOOK.

neur-. = NEURO-.

neu′ral (nū′răl), *adj.* [Gr. *neuron* nerve.] *Anat. & Zool.* **a** Of or pertaining to a nerve or to the nervous system. **b** In vertebrate anatomy, situated in the region of, or on the same side of the body as, the brain and spinal cord; as, *neural* arch (see VERTEBRA, *Illust.*).

neu·ral′gia (nū̇·răl′jȧ; -jĭ·ȧ), *n.* [NL., fr. *neur-* + *-algia.*] *Med.* An acute pain, radiating along the course of a nerve and its branches; also, the morbid condition characterized by such pain. — **neu·ral′gic** (-jĭk), *adj.*

neu′ras·the′ni·a (nū′răs·thē′nĭ·ȧ; 114), *n.* [NL., fr. *neur-* + Gr. *astheneia* weakness.] *Psychopathol.* A neurotic condition characterized by worry, disturbances of digestion and circulation, etc. It is attributed to emotional conflict, feeling of inferiority, etc. — **neu′ras·then′ic** (-thĕn′ĭk; -thē′nĭk), *adj.* & *n.*

neu·ra′tion (nū̇·rā′shŭn), *n.* The arrangement of nerves, esp. the nervures of the wings of insects.

neu′ri·lem′ma (nū′rĭ·lĕm′ȧ), *n.* [NL. (also *neurilema*), fr. Gr. *neuron* nerve + *eilēma* covering.] *Anat.* The delicate outer sheath of a nerve fiber.

neu′rite (nū′rīt), *n.* = AXON.

neu·ri′tis (nū̇·rī′tĭs), *n.* [NL., fr. *neur-* + *-itis.*] *Med.* Inflammation of a nerve or nerves; also, the resultant morbid condition. — **neu·rit′ic** (-rĭt′ĭk), *adj.*

neu′ro- (nū′rō-), **neur-.** [Gr. *neuron.*] A combining form, meaning *nerve*, as in **neu·rec′to·my** (see -ECTOMY); **neu′ro·blast**, one of the embryonic cells from which nerve cells develop; **neu′ro·coele**, the cavity in the interior of the central nervous system; **neu′ro·pa·thol′o·gy**, **neu′ro·psy·chi′a·try**, **neu·rot′o·my** (see -TOMY), **neu′ro·trop′ic**.

neu·rog′li·a (nū̇·rŏg′lĭ·ȧ), *n.* [NL., fr. *neuro-* + Gr. *glia* glue.] *Anat.* The supporting tissue which fills the interstices and supports the essential elements of nervous tissue, esp. in the brain, spinal cord, and ganglia.

neu·rol′o·gist (nū̇·rŏl′ō·jĭst), *n.* **a** One versed in neurology. **b** One skilled in the treatment of nervous diseases.

neu·rol′o·gy (-jĭ), *n.* [*neuro-* + *-logy.*] The science dealing with the nervous system, specif. with diseases of the nervous system. — **neu′ro·log′i·cal** (nū′rō·lŏj′ĭ·kăl), *adj.*

neu·ro′ma (nū̇·rō′mȧ), *n.; pl.* -MATA (-mȧ·tȧ), -MAS (-mȧz). [NL. See NEURO-; -OMA.] A tumor developed from a nerve.

neu′ron (nū′rŏn; -rōn), **neu′rone** (-rōn), *n.* [NL. *neuron*, fr. Gr. *neuron* nerve.] *Anat.* A nerve cell with all of its processes. — **neu·ron′ic** (nū̇·rŏn′ĭk), *adj.*

neu′ro·path (nū′rō·păth), *n.* *Med.* A person liable to nervous disease.

neu·rop′a·thist (nū̇·rŏp′ȧ·thĭst), *n.* A specialist in nervous diseases.

neu·rop′a·thy (-thĭ), *n.* [*neuro-* + *-pathy.*] *Med.* An abnormal condition of the nervous system or of a nerve. — **neu′ro·path′ic** (nū′rō·păth′ĭk), **-path′i·cal** (-ĭ·kăl), *adj.* — **neu′ro·path′i·cal·ly**, *adv.*

neu′ro·psy·cho′sis (nū′rō·sī·kō′sĭs), *n.* [NL., fr. *neuro-* + *psychosis.*] *Med.* Mental disorder closely connected with, or caused by, nerve disease.

neu·rop′ter·ous (nū̇·rŏp′tẽr·ŭs), *adj.* [*neuro-* + Gr. *pteron* a wing.] Belonging to an order (Neuroptera) of insects with four net-veined wings and jaws adapted for chewing, including the lacewings, ant lions, and allied forms. — **neu·rop′ter·an** (-ăn), **neu·rop′ter·oid** (-oid), *adj.* — **neu·rop′ter·on** (-ŏn), *n.*

neu·ro′sis (nū̇·rō′sĭs), *n.; pl.* -SES (-sēz). [NL., fr. Gr. *neuron* nerve.] **1.** *Physiol.* Any activity of the nervous system. **2.** *Psychiatry.* A functional nervous disorder, without demonstrable physical lesion. Cf. PSYCHOSIS.

neu·rot′ic (-rŏt′ĭk), *adj.* [Gr. *neuron* nerve.] *Med.* **a** Of, pert. to, or affecting the nerves; nervous. **b** Affected with neurosis. — *n.* *Med.* **a** Any toxic agent affecting the nervous system. **b** A disease in the nerves. **c** A neurotic person.

neu′ter (nū′tẽr), *adj.* [F. or L.; F. *neutre*, fr. L. *neuter*, fr. *ne-* not + *uter* either, one of two.] **1.** *Gram.* Neither masculine nor feminine; as, the *neuter* gender; a *neuter* noun. **2.** *Archaic.* Taking no side; neutral. **3.** *Biol.* **a** Having no generative organs; sexless. **b** Having imperfectly developed generative organs, as a worker bee. — *n.* **1.** *Gram.* A noun, pronoun, adjective, or inflectional form or class of the neuter gender; also, the gender thus distinguished. **2.** A person who is neutral. **3.** One of the imperfectly developed females of certain social insects, as ants and honeybees, that do the work of the community. **4.** A castrated animal.

neu′tral (nū′trăl), *adj.* [L. *neutralis*, fr. *neuter.*] **1.** Not engaged on either side; specif., of a state or power, lending no active assistance to either or any belligerent. **2.** Of or pertaining to a neutral state or power; not involved in hostilities. **3.** Neither one thing nor the other; indifferent. **4. a** Not decided in color; quiet in tone. **b** Free from tinges of other colors; as, a *neutral* blue. **5.** *Bot.* Without stamens or pistils, as the ray florets of many composites. **6.** *Biol.* Neuter. **7.** *Chem.* Neither acid nor basic. **8.** *Elec.* Neither positive nor negative. — *n.* **1.** A person, party, vessel, or nation that takes, or belongs to one who takes, no part in a contest between others; one that is neutral. **2.** A neutral tone or color. **3.** *Mach.* A position of disengagement, as of gears, from the motive power. — **neu′tral·ly**, *adv.*

neu·tral′i·ty (nū̇·trăl′ĭ·tĭ), *n.* **1.** Quality or state of being neutral. **2.** The character of a neutral thing, place, or the like, during hostilities; as, to respect the *neutrality* of a port. **3.** *Internat. Law.* The condition of a state or government which refrains from taking part, directly or indirectly, in a war between other powers; also, a condition of immunity from invasion or use by belligerents.

neu′tral·ize (nū′trăl·īz), *v. t.* **1.** *Chem.* To render neutral; to destroy the peculiar properties or effect of; as, to *neutralize* an acid with a base. **2.** To destroy the peculiar properties or opposite dispositions of; as, to *neutralize* efforts, opposition, etc. **3.** *Elec.* To make void of electricity, or electrically inert, by combining equal positive and negative quantities. **4.** *Internat. Law.* To invest with conventional or obligatory neutrality conferring inviolability by belligerents. — **neu′tral·i·za′tion** (-ĭ·zā′shŭn; -ī·zā′-), *n.* — **neu′tral·iz′er** (-īz′ẽr), *n.*

neu·tri′no (nū̇·trē′nō), *n.* [See NEUTRON; 2d -INE.] *Physics & Chem.* A hypothetical uncharged particle of smaller mass than the neutron.

neu′tron (nū′trŏn), *n.* [NL., fr. L. *neuter* neither; — from having neither positive nor negative charge.] *Physics & Chem.* An uncharged particle of slightly greater mass (1.00893 atomic mass units or 1.675×10^{-24} gm.) than the proton. Neutrons are constituents of atomic nuclei (except those of ordinary hydrogen). Being uncharged, neutrons are able to penetrate nuclei and are therefore used for bombarding in nuclear disintegration experiments. Symbol *n* (no period).

né′vé′ (nā′vā′), *n.* [F., ult. fr. L. *nix, nivis*, snow.] The partially compacted granular snow at the upper end of a glacier; by extension, any field of granular snow; firn.

nev′er (nĕv′ẽr), *adv.* [AS. *nǣfre*, fr. *ne* not, no + *ǣfre* ever.] **1.** Not ever; at no time. **2.** Not in any degree, way, or condition.

nev′er·more′ (-mōr′; 70), *adv.* Never again.

nev′er·the·less′ (-thē·lĕs′), *adv.* Not the less; notwithstanding; yet.

ne′vus, nae′vus (nē′vŭs), *n.; pl.* -VI (-vī). [L.] *Med.* A pigmented place on the skin, usually congenital; a birthmark; esp., a vascular tumor. — **ne′void, nae′void** (-void), *adj.*

new (nū; 114), *adj.* [AS. *nīwe, nēowe.*] **1.** Having existed, or having been made, but a short time; recent; modern; — opposed to *old.* **2. a** Recently manifested, recognized, or experienced; hence, strange; unfamiliar; as, *new* lands. **b** Other than the former, or old; as, a *new* teacher. **3.** Not habituated; unaccustomed; as, *new* to the plow. **4.** Beginning or appearing as the recurrence, resumption, or repetition of some previous act or thing; as, a *new* year; also, renovated or recreated; as, rest had made him a *new* man. **5.** Different or distinguished from a person, place, or thing of the same kind or name that has longer existed; as, the *new* reservoir. **6.** Not of ancient lineage; recently acquiring rank, distinction, or the like; as, a *new* family. **7.** [*cap.*] In names of languages, modern; esp., in use since medieval times; as, *New* Greek, *New* Latin (see GREEK, LATIN).

Syn. **New, novel, modern, original, fresh** mean having recently come into existence or use. **New** applies to that never until recently known, experienced, manufactured, or the like; **novel**, to that which is not only new but strange, unusual, or unfamiliar; **modern**, to that which belongs to the present time or is characteristic of it; **original**, to one who produces, or to a thing that is, something new or novel and, at the same time, the first of its kind; **fresh**, to that which is or seems so new that it has not lost signs of newness. — **Ant.** Old.

— *n.* That which is new; something new.

— *adv.* Newly; recently; anew.

new′born′ (nū′bôrn′; 2), *adj.* Recently born.

New Church. See NEW JERUSALEM CHURCH.

new′com′er (nū′kŭm′ẽr), *n.* One who has lately come.

New Deal. A number of measures of President F. D. Roosevelt designed to promote economic recovery and social security.

New Economic Policy. The policy of the Russian Soviet government (1921) by which the smaller industrial plants were returned to private ownership, private trading was legitimized, and the wage system restored. Often called *Nep.* or *NEP.*

new′el (nū′ĕl), *n.* [OF. *nouel, noiel*, stone of a fruit, newel, fr. LL. *nucale*, deriv. of L. *nux, nucis*, nut.] *Arch.* The upright about which the steps of a circular staircase wind; hence, in stairways with straight flights, the main post at the foot, or a secondary one at a landing.

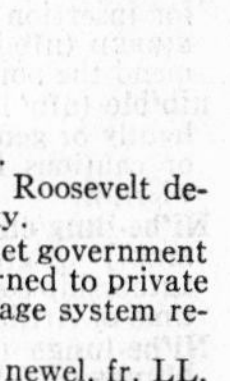
Newel.

New Eng′land as′ter. See ASTER, 1.

new′fan′gled (nū′făng′g'ld; nū′făng′g'ld; 2), *adj.* **1.** Inclined to novelties; given to new theories or fashions. **2.** Newly made; novel.

new′-fash′ioned (nū′făsh′ŭnd; 2), *adj.* Made in a new fashion or form, or lately come into fashion.

New·found′land dog (nū·foun(d)′lănd; *see in Gaz. for pron. of place name*). A large, intelligent, usually black-coated dog of a breed native to North America.

New′gate (nū′gāt; -gĭt), *n.* A famous old prison in London, razed in 1902.

New Ionic. See GREEK, *n.*, 4.

New Jerusalem. The Heavenly, or Celestial, City; the abode of the redeemed. *Rev.* xxi 2.

New Jerusalem Church, New Church, *or* **Church of the New Jerusalem.** The church holding the doctrines taught by Emanuel Swedenborg. See SWEDENBORGIAN.

New Learning. English learning of the 16th century based on the study, then introduced into England, of the Bible and the classics in the original; also, the learning or doctrines of the English Reformation.

new′ly (nū′lĭ), *adv.* **1.** Lately; recently. **2.** Afresh.

new′mar′ket (nū′mär′kĕt; -kĭt), *n.* [From *Newmarket*, England.] **1.** A long, closely fitting coat or cloak; — called also **Newmarket coat.** **2.** A game at cards.

new′ness (nū′nĕs; -nĭs), *n.* Quality or state of being new.

news (nūz; 114), *n.; plural in form but construed as sing.* [From NEW.] **1.** A report of a recent event; tidings. **2.** Matter of interest to newspaper readers.

news′boy′ (-boi′), *n.* A boy who distributes or sells newspapers.

news′cast′ (-kȧst′; 9), *n.* *Radio.* A broadcast of a program of news.

news′cast′er (-kȧs′tẽr; 9), *n.* *Radio.* One who is engaged to edit and broadcast news; sometimes, a commentator. — **news′cast′ing**, *n.*

news′let′ter (-lĕt′ẽr), *n.* A circular letter written or printed for the dissemination of news.

news′man (-măn), *n.; pl.* -MEN (-mĕn). **a** A newspaperman. **b** A man who distributes or sells newspapers.

news′mon′ger (-mŭng′gẽr), *n.* A gossip; one active in spreading news. — **news′mon′ger·ing**, *n.*

news′pa′per (nūz′pā′pẽr; nūs′-), *n.* A paper printed and distributed, at stated intervals, usually daily or weekly, to convey news, advocate opinions, etc.

news′pa′per·man′ (-măn′), *n.; pl.* -MEN (-mĕn′). One who writes for, or one who owns or conducts, a newspaper.

news′print′ (nūz′prĭnt′), *n.* Cheap machine-finished paper, chiefly from wood pulp, and used mostly for newspapers.

news′reel′ (-rēl′), *n.* A reel of motion pictures of current events.

news′stand′ (-stănd′), *n.* A place, esp. an open-air stall, for the sale of newspapers, periodicals, etc.

New Style. The style or method of reckoning time as fixed by the Gregorian calendar (which see). Abbr. *N. S.*

news′y (nūz′ĭ), *adj.*; NEWS′I·ER (-ĭ·ẽr); NEWS′I·EST. *Colloq.* Abounding in news.

newt (nūt), *n.* [ME. *newte*, for *ewte, evete*, fr. AS. *efete; an ewt* being taken for *a newt.*] Any of various small salamanders of semiaquatic habits, esp. those of the genus *Triturus;* an eft or triton.

New Testament. The covenant of God with man embodied in the coming of Christ and the teaching of Christ and his followers as set forth in the Bible; hence, usually, that portion of the Bible in which this covenant is contained. Abbr. *N.T.*, *New Test.* See BIBLE, TESTAMENT, 1.

New Thought. Any form of modern belief in and practice of mental healing other than those associated with traditional Christianity, Christian Science, and hypnotism and psychotherapy.

New·to′ni·an (nū·tō′nĭ·ăn; 58), *adj.* Of, pertaining to, or following Sir Isaac Newton (1642–1727), his discoveries, or doctrines. — *n.* A follower of Newton.

New World. The land of the Western Hemisphere.

new year. The year approaching or just begun; also, the first days of a year; also, New Year's Day.

New Year's Day, *or Colloq.,* **New Year's.** The first day of a calendar year; the first day of January. See HOLIDAY, 3.

next (nĕkst), *adj., superl. of* NIGH. [AS. *nēhst, nīehst, nȳhst,* superl. of *nēah* nigh.] Nearest; immediately preceding or following. — *adv.* **1.** In the time, place, or order nearest or immediately succeeding. **2.** On the first occasion to come; as, when *next* we meet.

next friend. *Law.* One who, not being regularly appointed a guardian, acts for the benefit of an infant, a married woman, or any person not sui juris, as in a suit at law.

next of kin. *Law.* Literally, the nearest blood relatives; hence, those blood relatives of a person who in case of his death intestate will be entitled to share his estate.

nex′us (nĕk′sŭs), *n.; pl.* NEXUSES (-ĕz; -ĭz), NEXUS. [L.] Connection or interconnection; tie; link.

Nez′ Per′cé′ (nā′ pĕr′sā′; *Angl.* nĕz′ pûrs′); *pl.* NEZ PERCÉS (-sā′). [F., lit., pierced nose.] An Indian of the chief Shahaptian tribe, formerly occupying central Idaho, eastern Oregon, and Washington.

ni′a·cin (nī′ȧ·sĭn), *n.* [*nicotinic acid* + *-in.*] A member of the vitamin-B complex. See VITAMIN.

nib (nĭb), *n.* [Cf. NEB.] **1.** *Zool.* A bill or beak. See BILL, *Illust.* **2.** The point of a pen; also, the whole pen, as of steel or gold, intended for insertion into a holder. **3.** A pointed part; a prong. — *v. t.;* NIBBED (nĭbd); NIB′BING. **a** To furnish with a nib; to point. **b** To mend the point of (a pen).

nib′ble (nĭb′'l), *v. t. & i.;* NIB′BLED (-'ld); NIB′BLING (-lĭng). To bite lightly or gently; to eat in small bits. — *n.* Act of nibbling; a small or cautious bite, or the amount taken in such a bite. — **nib′bler** (-lẽr), *n.*

Ni′be·lung′en·lied′ (nē′bĕ·lo͝ong′ĕn·lēt′), *n.* [G. See NIBELUNGS; LIED.] A great medieval German late 12th-century epic of unknown authorship containing traditions which refer to the Burgundians at the time of Attila and mythological elements pointing to heathen times.

Ni′be·lungs (-lo͝ongz), *n. pl.; sing.* NIBELUNG (-lo͝ong). Also **Ni′blungs** (nē′blo͝ongz). In German mythology, the children of the mist, a race of dwarfs or demonic beings, the original possessors of the famous hoard and ring won by Siegfried; also, the Burgundian kings in the Nibelungenlied.

nib′lick (nĭb′lĭk), *n.* A golf club with an iron head, having a wide face laid back at an angle of 45 degrees or more. See GOLF, *Illust.*

Ni·cae′an (nī·sē′ăn), *adj.* Nicene.

nic′co·lite (nĭk′ō·līt), *n.* [NL. *niccolum* nickel. See NICKEL.] *Mineral.* A mineral of a pale copper-red color and metallic luster, usually occurring massive. It is essentially a nickel arsenide, NiAs.

nice (nīs), *adj.;* NIC′ER (nīs′ẽr); NIC′EST. [OF., ignorant, fool, fr. L. *nescius* ignorant, fr. *nescire* to be ignorant, fr. *ne-* not + *scire* to know.] **1.** *Obs.* **a** Foolish; silly. **b** Lewd; wanton. **2.** *Archaic.* Affecting coy reserve; shy. **3.** Fastidious; hence, finical; also, refined; discriminating. **4.** Demanding close discrimination, delicate handling, or the like. **5.** Displaying, or characterized by, close discrimination, delicate treatment, etc.; subtle; as, a *nice* distinction. **6.** Susceptible to fine distinctions, or able to make them; delicately discriminative; hence, of instruments, methods, etc., minutely accurate. **7.** Scrupulous; punctilious. **8.** Pleasing; agreeable. **9.** Properly modest; well-mannered. — **nice′ly,** *adv.* — **nice′ness,** *n.*

Syn. (1) **Nice, dainty, fastidious, finical, particular, squeamish** mean exacting, as in selection, judgment, or workmanship. **Nice** implies power of discriminating the very good from the good; **dainty,** a tendency to select or to reject that which does or does not satisfy one's delicate taste or sensibility; **fastidious,** the possession of ethical, artistic, or social standards so high as to impose strain on the selector or the selected; **finical,** an overnice fastidiousness; **particular,** insistence that one's standards should be met; **squeamish,** disgust for or an aversion to that which does not satisfy one's standards.
(2) See CORRECT.

Ni·cene′ (nī·sēn′; nī′sēn; 2), **Ni·cae′an** (nī·sē′ăn), *adj.* [LL. *Nicaenus,* fr. *Nicaea* Nice, fr. Gr. *Nikaia.*] Of or pertaining to Nicaea, or Nice, an ancient city of Asia Minor; also, designating, or pertaining to, the Nicene Creed.

Nicene Creed. *Eccl.* **a** A confession formulated and decreed by the First Council of Nicaea, A.D. 325. **b** An expanded form of the foregoing read at the Council of Chalcedon (A.D. 451) as the creed of the Council of Constantinople; — hence called also ***Ni·ce′no-Con·stan′ti·no·pol′i·tan*** (*or* ***Constantinopolitan***) ***Creed.*** **c** A form now in use in the Western Church identical with the preceding except for one extra clause inserted at a church council in A.D. 589. Cf. CREDO.

ni′ce·ty (nī′sĕ·tĭ; -sĭ·tĭ), *n.; pl.* -TIES (-tĭz). [OF. *niceté* foolishness.] **1.** Quality or state of being nice; specif.: *Obs.* **a** Excessive elegance. **b** Modesty; reserve; also, prudishness. **2.** A dainty or elegant thing or feature; as, the *niceties* of life. **3.** An expression, act, etc., involving delicacy or subtlety; a minute distinction, point, or detail; as, *niceties* of workmanship. **4.** Delicacy or exactness of perception or discrimination; precision; accuracy. **5.** The quality of demanding delicacy of treatment; as, a question of great *nicety.* **6.** Delicacy of taste or feeling; fastidiousness; often, squeamishness.

niche (nĭch), *n.* [F., fr. OF. *nichier* to nestle, deriv. of L. *nidus* nest.] **1.** A recess in a wall, esp. one for a bust, etc. **2.** A place, condition of life or work, position, or the like, suitable for the abilities or merits of a person, or for the qualities of a thing; as, his poetry fills a *niche* of its own. — *v. t.* To place in, or as in, a niche.

nich′er (*Scot.* nĭk′ẽr), *v. & n. Scot.* = NICKER, neigh.

‖**nicht wahr?** (nĭкt vär′). [G.] Not true? Isn't that so?

nick (nĭk), *n.* **1.** A notch; slit. **2.** A broken or indented place in any edge or surface; as, *nicks* in china. **3.** A particular point considered as marked by a nick; hence, the precise time of any occurrence; as, he arrived at the *nick* of time. **4.** *Print.* A notch on the body of a type. See TYPE, *Illust.* — *v. t.* **1.** To make a nick or nicks in; to chip. **2.** *Colloq.* To keep track of, as by making a nick on a stick; hence, to jot down; to record. **3.** To cut; to cut through, into, or out; to cut short. Specif., to make a cut or cuts across the under side of (the tail of a horse, in order to make him carry it higher); to cut under the tail of (a horse). **4.** To hit, strike, catch, or grasp at the precise and proper point or time. **5.** *Slang.* To catch off guard; also, to cheat; as, he *nicked* his partner for a thousand dollars.

Nick (nĭk), *n.* [Dim. of *Nicholas.*] The Devil; — usually *Old Nick.*

nick′el (nĭk′ĕl; -'l), *n.* [G., abbr. fr. *kupfernickel,* fr. *kupfer* copper + prob. *nickel* demon (the ore seeming to contain copper, but yielding none).] **1.** *Chem.* A hard, malleable, ductile, metallic element, nearly silver-white, capable of a high polish, and resistant to oxidation. Sp. gr., about 8.8; symbol, *Ni;* at. no., 28; at. wt., 58.69. Nickel occurs native in meteorites. **2.** *Colloq., U. S. & Canada.* The five-cent piece. See MONEY, *Tables.* — *v. t.* To plate with nickel.

nick′el·ic (nĭk′ĕl·ĭk; nĭ·kĕl′-), *adj. Chem.* Pertaining to or containing nickel, esp. trivalent nickel.

nick′el·if′er·ous (nĭk′ĕl·ĭf′ẽr·ŭs), *adj.* [*nickel* + *-ferous.*] Containing nickel; as, *nickeliferous* iron.

nick′el·o′de·on (-ō′dē·ŭn), *n.* [See NICKEL; cf. ODEUM.] **1.** *U. S.* A theater affording a motion-picture exhibition, variety show, or the like, for a nickel. **2.** A juke box.

nick′el·ous (nĭk′ĕl·ŭs), *adj. Chem.* Pertaining to or containing nickel, esp. bivalent nickel.

nick′el-plate′, *v. t.* To electroplate with nickel.

nickel silver. See GERMAN SILVER.

nick′er (nĭk′ẽr), *n.* One who or that which nicks; specif., one of the 18th-century night brawlers of London noted for breaking windows with halfpence.

nick′er, *n. & v. i.* [Imitative.] *Dial.* Neigh; laugh.

nick′nack′ (nĭk′năk′). Var. of KNICKKNACK.

nick′name′ (nĭk′nām′), *n.* [ME. *ekename* surname, hence, a nickname, *an ekename* being understood as *a nekename.* See EKE; NAME.] **1.** A name given instead of the one belonging to a person, place, or thing, usually descriptive and given in sport. **2.** A familiar form of a proper name, as "Bill." — *v. t.* **1.** To misname. **2.** To give a nickname to; to call by a nickname.

ni·co′ti·a′na (nĭ·kō′shĭ·ā′nȧ), *n.* [NL., after Jean *Nicot.* See NICOTINE.] See TOBACCO, 1.

nic′o·tin′a·mide (nĭk′ō·tĭn′ȧ·mīd; -mĭd), *n.* Also **-mid.** One of the members of the vitamin-B complex. See VITAMIN.

nic′o·tine (nĭk′ō·tēn; -tĭn), *n.* Also **-tin.** [F. *nicotine,* after Jean *Nicot,* who introduced tobacco into France in 1560.] *Chem.* A poisonous alkaloid, $C_{10}H_{14}N_2$, the active principle of tobacco. It is a colorless, oily, acrid liquid. The natural alkaloid is levorotatory. In aqueous solution it is used as an insecticide.

nic′o·tin′ic ac′id (nĭk′ō·tĭn′ĭk). A member of the vitamin-B complex. See VITAMIN.

nic′o·tin·ism (nĭk′ō·tēn·ĭz′m; -tĭn·ĭz′m), *n.* The morbid condition induced by excessive use of tobacco.

nic′ti·tate (nĭk′tĭ·tāt), *v. i.* Also **nic′tate** (nĭk′tāt). [*nictitate,* freq. of *nictate,* fr. L. *nictare, nictatum,* to wink.] To wink. — **nic′ti·ta′tion** (nĭk′tĭ·tā′shŭn), **nic·ta′tion** (nĭk·tā′shŭn), *n.*

nic′ti·tat′ing (nĭk′tĭ·tāt′ĭng), *or* **nic′tat·ing** (-tāt·ĭng), **mem′brane.** A thin membrane, found in many animals at the inner angle, or beneath the lower lid, of the eye, and capable of being drawn across the eyeball.

nid′der·ing (nĭd′ẽr·ĭng), *n.* Also **nid′er·ing.** *Pseudoarchaic.* Coward. — *adj.* Infamous; base; cowardly.

nide (nīd), *n.* [F. or L.; F. *nid,* fr. L. *nidus* a nest.] *Chiefly Eng.* A nest or brood of pheasants.

nid′i·fi·cate (nĭd′ĭ·fĭ·kāt), *v. i.* [L. *nidificare, -catum,* fr. *nidus* nest + *-ficare* (in comp.) to make.] To build a nest; to nidify. — **nid′i·fi·ca′tion** (-kā′shŭn), *n.*

nid′i·fy (nĭd′ĭ·fī), *v. i.;* NID′I·FIED (-fīd); NID′I·FY′ING. To build a nest.

ni′dus (nī′dŭs), *n.; pl.* NIDI (-dī), NIDUSES (-dŭs·ĕz; -ĭz). [L.] **1.** A nest, esp. for the eggs of insects, spiders, etc. **2.** A breeding place; esp., the place in an animal or plant where disease germs or other organisms lodge or develop.

niece (nēs), *n.* [OF. *niece,* fr. VL. *neptia,* fr. L. *neptis* a granddaughter, niece.] A daughter of one's brother or sister, or, loosely, of one's brother-in-law or sister-in-law. Cf. CONSANGUINITY, *Illust.*

ni·el′lo (nĭ·ĕl′ō), *n.; pl.* NIELLI (-ē), NIELLOS (-ōz). [It., fr. L. *nigellus,* dim. of *niger* black.] **1.** Any of several metallic alloys of sulfur, with silver, copper, lead, or the like, having a deep-black color. **2.** Art, process, or method of decorating metal with incised designs filled with the black alloy; work of this kind. **3.** A piece of metal, or any object, so decorated. — *v. t.;* NI·EL′LOED (-ōd); NI·EL′LO·ING. To inlay, or ornament, with niello. — **ni·el′list,** *n.*

Nier′stein·er (nēr′stīn·ẽr; -shtīn·ẽr), *n.* [G., fr. *Nierstein,* Hesse, Ger.] A white, still, Rhine wine.

Nie′tzsche·ism (nē′chĕ·ĭz′m), *n.* The philosophical doctrines of Friedrich Wilhelm Nietzsche (German philosopher, 1844–1900) and his followers, esp. that of the perfectibility of man through forcible self-assertion, leading to glorification of the superman. — **Nie′tzsche·an** (-ăn), *n. & adj.* — **Nie′tzsche·an·ism** (-ĭz′m), *n.*

nieve (nēv), **neif** (nēf), *n.* [ME. *neve, nefe,* fr. ON. *hnefi.*] *Archaic & Dial.* The fist; the hand.

nif′fer (nĭf′ẽr), *n. & v. Scot.* Exchange; bargain.

Ni′fl·heim, Ni′fel·heim (nĭv′'l·hām), *n.* Also **Ni′fl·heimr** (-hām′ẽr). [ON. *Niflheimr.*] *Norse Myth.* The northern region of cold and darkness.

nif′ty (nĭf′tĭ), *adj.;* NIF′TI·ER (-tĭ·ẽr); NIF′TI·EST. *Slang, Chiefly U. S.* Very good; esp., attractively stylish.

nig′gard (nĭg′ẽrd), *n.* [ME. *nig* a niggard + *-ard.*] A person meanly close and covetous; a miser. — *adj.* Niggardly. — *v. t. & i. Obs.* To treat or act niggardly.

nig′gard·ly (-lĭ), *adv.* In the manner of a niggard. — *adj.* **1.** Meanly parsimonious. **2.** Characteristic of a niggard; scanty; as, *niggardly* gifts. — **Syn.** See STINGY. — **Ant.** Bountiful. — **nig′gard·li·ness,** *n.*

nig′ger (nĭg′ẽr), *n.* [Earlier *neger,* fr. F. *nègre,* fr. Sp. *negro.* See NEGRO.] (*A substandard term.*) **1.** A Negro; — often used familiarly, now chiefly contemptuously. **2.** Loosely, a member of any very dark-skinned race. — **nig′ger·ish,** *adj.* — **nig′ger·y,** *adj.*

nig′ger-fish′ (nĭg′ẽr-fĭsh′), *n.; pl.* -FISH, -FISHES (-fĭsh′ĕz; -ĭz). A grouper (*Cephalopolis fulvus*) of the West Indies and southern Florida, with blue or black spots.

nig′gle (nĭg′'l), *v. i.;* NIG′GLED (-'ld); NIG′GLING (-lĭng). To trifle; to potter. — **nig′gler** (-lẽr), *n.*

nig′gling (-lĭng), *n.* Pottering work, esp. on unimportant detail. — *adj.* That niggles. — **nig′gling·ly,** *adv.*

nigh (nī), *adv.* [AS. *nēah, nēh.*] *Now Archaic & Dial.* **1.** Near, esp. in place, time, relationship, likeness, or in the course of events; close. **2.** Almost; nearly; — often, *Dial.,* with *about, by, on, upon,* etc. — *adj.;* NIGH'ER (nī'ẽr); NIGH'EST or NEXT (nĕkst). *Now Archaic & Dial.* **1.** Near; close. **2.** Direct; short. **3.** Of domestic animals, vehicles, etc., on the left; near. — **Syn.** See CLOSE. — *prep.* Close upon; near to; as, "The bridge that stood *nigh* it." *Samuel Woodworth.* — *v. t. & i. Now Rare.* To approach.

night (nīt), *n.* [AS. *neaht, niht.*] **1.** The time from dusk to dawn, when no light of the sun is visible. **2.** Nightfall. **3.** The darkness of night; hence: **a** Concealment. **b** Intellectual or moral darkness. **c** A period of affliction. **d** The period after life; death. — **night,** *adj.*

night blindness. Nyctalopia. — **night'-blind',** *adj.*

night'-bloom'ing ce're·us. **a** A cereus (*Selenicereus grandiflorus*) with climbing, angled branches and large, fragrant, white flowers opening about midnight. **b** Any of several other species of night-blooming cacti (esp. *Peniocereus greggii* and *Hylocereus undatus*).

night'cap' (nīt'kăp'), *n.* **1.** A cap worn in bed or, formerly, in undress. **2.** Something soporific taken at bedtime, esp. a drink of spirits. **3.** The final contest in a day's sports.

night clothes. Garments worn in bed.

night club. A commercial establishment operating at night to supply food and entertainment to its customers.

night crawler. *Colloq., U. S.* = NIGHTWALKER **b.**

night'dress' (nīt'drĕs'), *n.* A nightgown; night clothes.

night'fall' (-fôl'), *n.* The close of the day; dusk.

night'gown' (-goun'), *n.* **1.** *Obs.* A dressing gown worn esp. at night. **2.** A long, loose garment worn in bed.

night'hawk' (-hôk'), *n.* **1.** **a** Any of several North American goatsuckers (genus *Chordeiles*) related to the whippoorwill. Cf. BULLBAT. **b** The European nightjar (*Caprimulgus europaeus*). **2.** One who is habitually up or abroad at night.

night heron. Any of certain herons (of *Nycticorax* and allied genera) active at night or at twilight, esp. one (*N. nycticorax*) which ranges from southern Europe to India and northern Africa. The American variety is the ***black-crowned night heron*** (*N. n. hoactli*).

night'in·gale (nīt'ĭn·gāl; nīt'ĭng-), *n.* [AS. *nihtegale,* prop., night singer.] Any of several Old World birds (genus *Luscinia*) of the thrush family (Turdidae). The common species of Great Britain (*L. megarhyncha*) is about six inches long and is noted for the sweet song of the male, heard at night during the breeding season.

night'jar' (nīt'jär'), *n.* [See JAR to sound.] A goatsucker, especially the common European species (*Caprimulgus europaeus*).

night latch. A kind of door latch or lock having a spring bolt (called the **night bolt**) operated from the outside by a key (**night key**) and from the inside by a knob.

night letter, night lettergram. See LETTERGRAM.

night'long' (nīt'lŏng'; 74), *adj. & adv.* Lasting all night.

night'ly, *adj.* **1.** Of or pertaining to the night or every night; happening, done, or used by night or every night. **2.** Characteristic of, or resembling, night. — *adv.* Every night; also, at or by night.

night'mare' (nīt'mâr'), *n.* [*night* + *mare* incubus.] **1.** A fiend or incubus formerly supposed to oppress people during sleep. **2.** A condition brought on in sleep, commonly by digestive or nervous disorders, and characterized by a sense of extreme discomfort or by frightful dreams. **3.** Any impression or experience having a similar effect.

night owl. **a** An owl of especially nocturnal habits. **b** *Colloq.* One who keeps late hours at night.

night raven. A bird that cries at night; esp., a night heron.

night rider. *Chiefly U. S.* One of a secret band who ride masked at night doing acts of violence to punish or terrorize.

night robe. A nightgown.

nights (nīts), *adv. Now Dial. exc. U. S.* At or by night.

night'shade' (nīt'shād'), *n.* [AS. *nihtscada.*] **a** Any of a genus (*Solanum*) typifying a family (Solanaceae, the nightshade family) of strong-scented, often narcotic, herbs, shrubs, and trees including the ***black nightshade*** (*S. nigrum*), a weed with poisonous leaves, white flowers, and edible black berries, and the potato, eggplant, etc. **b** The belladonna; — called also ***deadly nightshade.*** **c** The henbane.

night'shirt' (-shûrt'), *n.* Nightgown for a man or boy.

night soil. The excrement collected at night for manure.

night stick. A policeman's club carried by night.

night'tide' (nīt'tīd'), *n.* Nighttime.

night'time' (-tīm'), *n.* The time from dusk to dawn.

night'walk'er (-wôk'ẽr), *n.* One who or that which roves about at night; specif.: **a** *Now Rare.* A footpad. **b** Any large angleworm crawling about at night.

night watch. **a** A watch or guard during the night. **b** A chronological division of the night; — usually in *pl.*

night'wear' (nīt'wâr'), *n.* Night clothes.

ni·gres'cent (nī·grĕs'ĕnt; -'nt), *adj.* [L. *nigrescens,* pres. part. of *nigrescere* to grow black, fr. *niger* black.] Approaching to blackness; blackish. — **ni·gres'cence** (-ĕns; -'ns), *n.*

nig'ri·tude (nĭg'rĭ·tūd), *n.* [L. *nigritudo,* fr. *niger* black.] Blackness; intense darkness; also, anything black.

ni'gro·sine (nī'grō·sēn; -sĭn), *n.* Also **ni'gro·sin.** [From L. *niger* black.] *Chem.* **a** Any of several dyes closely related to the indulines. **b** A bluish-black dye obtained by heating aniline and iron with certain chemicals, used in coloring varnish, leather, etc.

‖**ni'hil** (nī'hĭl), *n.* [L.] Nothing; a thing of no value.

ni'hil·ism (nī'ĭ·lĭz'm; nī'hĭ-), *n.* [L. *nihil* nothing.] **1.** *Philos.* **a** A doctrine which denies any objective or real ground of truth. **b** The doctrine which denies any objective ground of moral principles; — called also ***ethical nihilism.*** **2.** **a** The doctrine that conditions in the social organization are so bad as to make destruction desirable for its own sake, independent of any constructive program; esp. [*cap.*], the program or doctrine of a Russian party of the 19th and 20th centuries, who proposed various schemes of revolutionary reform and resorted to terrorism. **b** In loose usage, revolutionary propaganda; terrorism.

ni'hil·ist (-lĭst), *n.* One who advocates a doctrine of nihilism; esp. [*cap.*], a member of a Russian nihilistic party resorting to terrorism. — **ni'hil·ist, ni'hil·is'tic** (-lĭs'tĭk), *adj.*

ni·hil'i·ty (nī·hĭl'ĭ·tĭ), *n.; pl.* -TIES (-tĭz). Nothingness.

‖**ni'hil ob'stat** (nī'hĭl ŏb'stăt). [L.] *R.C.Ch.* Nothing hinders; — a formula on title pages signifying the imprimatur of the official censor, whose name follows.

Ni'ke (nī'kē; nē'kā), *n.* [Gr. *Nikē.*] *Gr. Relig.* **a** The goddess of victory, represented as winged and as carrying a wreath and a palm branch. **b** Athena, as giver of victory.

nil (nĭl), *n.* [L., a contr. of *nihil.* See NIHIL.] Nothing.

‖**nil ad'mi·ra'ri** (ăd'mĭ·rā'rī). [L.] To be excited by nothing; to wonder at nothing.

‖**nil de'spe·ran'dum** (dĕs'pĕ·răn'dŭm). [L.] Nothing must be despaired of; never despair.

Nile green (nīl). A color, yellow-green in hue, of low saturation and high brilliance. See COLOR.

nil'gai (nĭl'gī), *n.;* see PLURAL, *Note,* 3. [Hind. & Per. *nīlgāw,* prop., a blue cow.] A large antelope (*Boselaphus tragocamelus*) of India.

nill (nĭl), *v. t. & i.* [AS. *nyllan, nellan,* fr. *ne* not + *willan* to will.] *Archaic.* Not to will; to be unwilling.

‖**nil ni'si bo'num.** Short for DE MORTUIS NIL NISI BONUM.

Ni·lom'e·ter (nī·lŏm'ē·tẽr), *n.* [Gr. *Neilometrion,* fr. *Neilos* the Nile + *metron* measure.] Instrument for measuring the height of water in the Nile, esp. during flood.

Ni·lot'ic (nī·lŏt'ĭk), *adj.* [L. *Niloticus.*] Of or pertaining to the Nile or the peoples of the Nile basin.

‖**nil si'ne nu'mi·ne** (nĭl sī'nē nū'mĭ·nē). [L.] Nothing without the divine will; — motto of Colorado.

nim (nĭm), *v. t.; past* NAM (näm; năm) or NIMMED (nĭmd); *past part.* NO'MEN (nō'mĕn) or NOME (nōm); *pres. part.* NIM'MING. [AS. *niman.*] *Archaic.* To take; specif., to filch.

nim'ble (nĭm'b'l), *adj.* [ME. *nimel, nemel.*] **1.** Quick and light in motion; agile. **2.** **a** Alert; as, a *nimble* wit; also, quick-witted; adroit; as, a *nimble* thinker. **b** Revealing mental quickness; as, a *nimble* jest. — **Syn.** See AGILE. — **nim'ble·ness,** *n.* — **nim'bly** (-blĭ), *adv.*

nim'bo- (nĭm'bō-). A combining form for *nimbus,* denoting *nimbus and,* as in **nim'bo-stra'tus.** See CLOUD, *Illust.*

nim'bus (nĭm'bŭs), *n.; pl.* NIMBI (-bī), NIMBUSES (-bŭs·ĕz; -ĭz). [L., rainstorm, cloud.] **1.** A luminous vapor or cloud about a god or goddess when on earth; hence, a cloud, as of romance, about a person or thing. **2.** *Art.* A circle or any indication of radiant light around the heads of divinities, saints, and sovereigns, on medals, pictures, etc. **3.** *Meteorol.* The rain cloud, uniformly gray and extending over the entire sky; in general, any cloud from which rain is falling. Cf. CLOUD, *Illust.*

ni·mi'e·ty (nĭ·mī'ē·tĭ), *n.* [L. *nimietas,* fr. *nimius,* adj., *nimis,* adv., too much.] Excess; redundancy.

nim'i·ny-pim'i·ny (nĭm'ĭ·nĭ·pĭm'ĭ·nĭ), *adj.* Affectedly refined; mincing; effeminate.

‖**n'im'porte'** (năN'pôrt'). [F.] It doesn't matter; it's no matter.

Nim'rod (nĭm'rŏd), *n.* **1.** *Bib.* A son of Cush, described in Gen. x. 8–10 as a mighty hunter and ruler. **2.** A hunter.

nin'com·poop (nĭn'kŏm·pōōp; 2), *n.* A fool; simpleton.

nine (nīn), *n.* **1.** [AS. *nigon, nigan.*] See NUMBER, *Table.* **2.** Something having as an essential feature nine units or members, as a playing card with nine pips, a baseball team of nine players, etc. — **nine,** *adj.* — ***the Nine.*** The Muses.

nine'fold' (nīn'fōld'; 2), *adj. & adv.* See -FOLD.

nine'pence (-pĕns), *n.; pl.* -PENCES (-pĕn·sĕz; -sĭz). The sum of nine pence, or a coin of this value.

nine'pin' (-pĭn'), *n.* One of the pins used in ninepins.

nine'pins' (-pĭnz'), *n.; pl. in form, but construed as sing.* **a** A bowling game played with nine wooden pins set on end. **b** Tenpins without the head pin.

nine'teen' (nīn'tēn'; 2), *n. & adj.* [AS. *nigontȳne, nigontēne.*] See NUMBER, *Table.* — **nine'teenth'** (-tēnth'; 2), *n. & adj.*

nine'ty (nīn'tĭ), *n. & adj.* [AS. *nigontig.*] See NUMBER, *Table.* — **nine'ti·eth** (-tĭ·ĕth; -ĭth), *n. & adj.*

nine'ty·fold' (-fōld'; 2), *adj. & adv.* See -FOLD.

nin'ny (nĭn'ĭ), *n.; pl.* -NIES (-ĭz). A fool; a simpleton.

nin'ny·ham'mer (-hăm'ẽr), *n.* A simpleton; a silly person.

ni'non' (nē'nôN'), *n.* [F.] Any of various fabrics, as a silk voile.

ninth (nīnth; 106), *n. & adj.* See NUMBER, *Table.* — **ninth'ly,** *adv.*

Ni'o·be (nī'ō·bē), *n.* [L. *Nioba, Niobe,* Gr. *Niobē.*] *Gr. Myth.* Daughter of Tantalus, and wife of Amphion. Her pride in her numerous children led her to compare herself to Leto, who had only two; to punish her, Apollo and Artemis, Leto's children, slew Niobe's children. Niobe, changed by Zeus into stone, continued to weep her loss.

ni·o'bi·um (nī·ō'bĭ·ŭm), *n.* [NL., fr. L. & E. *Niobe.*] *Chem.* Columbium. *Niobium* is now the preferred name. See COLUMBIUM.

nip (nĭp), *v. t.;* NIPPED (nĭpt); NIP'PING. [ME. *nippen.*] **1.** To catch hold or squeeze tightly between two surfaces, edges, or points; to pinch; clamp. **2.** *Chiefly Hort.* To sever, esp. by pinching or clipping with shears, as a shoot. **3.** To benumb (cheeks, fingers, etc.) as by severe cold; hence, to blight. **4.** To check sharply and, sometimes, to destroy the growth, progress, or fulfillment of; — now often with *in the bud, head,* or the like. **5.** To seize suddenly; snatch. — *v. i.* To move nimbly; to hurry.

— *n.* **1.** The act of nipping; a peck. **2.** Something that nips; as: **a** A stinging remark. **b** A check to the growth of vegetation due to cold or frost; hence, sudden, sharp cold. **c** A sting in a cold wind. **d** A tang in cheese.

nip, *n.* Formerly, a half pint of ale; now, a sip or small draft; a dram. — *v. t. & i.* To take (liquor) in nips; esp., to tipple.

Nip (nĭp), *n. & adj. Colloq.* Nipponese; Japanese.

ni'pa (nē'pȧ; nī'pȧ), *n.* [Sp., fr. Malay *nipah.*] **a** An East Indian palm (*Nipa fruticans*). **b** An alcoholic drink made from its juice. **c** A thatch made of its leaves.

nip and tuck. *U. S.* With rapid alternation of favorable and unfavorable prospects.

nip'per (nĭp'ẽr), *n.* **1.** One who or that which nips. **2.** Usually in *pl.* Any of various devices for nipping, as pincers. See PINCERS, *Illust.* **3.** *Colloq.* Handcuffs or leg irons. **4.** **a** In horses, an incisor, esp. one of the middle four. **b** One of the large claws or pincers of a crab or lobster. **5.** *Slang, Eng.* A young boy; lad.

nip'ping (nĭp'ĭng), *adj.* That nips; as, a *nipping* frost. — **nip'ping·ly,** *adv.*

nip'ple (nĭp''l), *n.* **1.** The protuberance of a breast, or mamma, upon which, in the female, the ducts open; teat; pap. **2.** **a** An artificial device resembling a teat and used for sucking. **b** A similarly constructed device with an orifice through which the discharge of a fluid can be regulated, as in a stopcock. **3.** Any protuberance resembling or suggesting the nipple of a breast; esp., a projection on metal or glass.

Nip′pon·ese′ (nĭp′ŏ·nēz′; -nēs′; 2), *n. sing. & pl.* [From *Nippon*, the Japanese name for Japan.] A Japanese; also, the Japanese. — *adj.* Japanese.

nip′py (nĭp′ĭ), *adj.;* -PI·ER (-ĭ·ẽr); -PI·EST. Disposed or tending to nip; nipping; biting; hence, active; brisk; as, a *nippy* wind.

nir·va′na (nĭr·vä′nȧ; *popularly* nûr·vä′nȧ, -văn′ȧ), *n.* [Skr. *nirvāṇa.*] **1.** *Hinduism.* Extinction of the flame of life; final emancipation; reunion with Brahma. **2.** *Buddhism.* The dying out in the heart of passion, hatred, and delusion. This emancipation involves a beatific spiritual condition, and freedom from the necessity of future transmigration. **3.** Oblivion to care, pain, or external reality.

Ni′san (nī′săn; *Heb.* nē·sän′), *n.* [Heb. *Nīsān.*] The first month of the Jewish ecclesiastical calendar, corresponding to March–April. See JEWISH CALENDAR.

ni′sei′ (nē′sā′), *n.; pl.* NISEI, NISEIS (-sāz′). [Jap. *ni* second + *sei* generation.] A native-born resident of America, esp. U. S. or Canada, having Japanese immigrant parents, who is in the U. S. a citizen by right of birth. Cf. ISSEI.

‖**ni′si** (nī′sī), *conj.* [L.] Unless; if not; — used in *Law* after the word of *decree* or *order* to denote that it shall take effect at a given time, *unless* before then it is modified or avoided by cause shown or further proceedings.

ni′si pri′us (nī′sī prī′ŭs). [L.] *Law.* Lit., unless before; — used of certain causes, writs, actions, or trials.

Nis′sen hut (nĭs′'n). [After its British designer, Lieut. Col. P. N. *Nissen* (1871–1930).] *Mil.* A barrel-shaped prefabricated shelter of corrugated iron, with cement floor.

ni′sus (nī′sŭs), *n.; pl.* NISUS. [L., fr. *niti*, past part. *nisus*, to strive.] **1.** A striving; conative state or character. **2.** *Physiol.* The periodic procreative desire manifested in the spring by birds, etc.

nit (nĭt), *n.* [AS. *hnitu.*] The egg of a louse or other parasitic insect; also, the insect itself when young.

ni′ter, ni′tre (nī′tẽr), *n.* [F. *nitre*, fr. L. *nitrum* native soda, natron, fr. Gr. *nitron.*] **1.** *Obs.* Natron. **2.** *Chem.* **a** Potassium nitrate (saltpeter). **b** Sodium nitrate (Chile saltpeter).

nit′id (nĭt′ĭd), *adj.* [L. *nitidus.*] *Rare.* Bright; lustrous.

ni′ton (nī′tŏn), *n.* [L. *nitere* to shine.] = RADON. Symbol *Nt*

ni′trate (nī′trāt), *n.* **1.** *Chem.* A salt or ester of nitric acid. **2.** Potassium nitrate or sodium nitrate, as a fertilizer. — *v. t.* To treat or combine with nitric acid or a nitrate; specif., *Org. Chem.*, to convert into a nitro compound or a nitrate.

ni′tric (nī′trĭk), *adj.* [F. *nitrique.*] *Chem.* Of, pertaining to, or containing nitrogen; specif., designating compounds in its higher valence.

nitric acid. A colorless, fuming, corrosive liquid, HNO_3, made esp. by the action of sulfuric acid on nitrates, used in making explosives, dyes, celluloid, etc.

nitric bacteria. See NITROBACTERIA.

nitric oxide. A colorless poisonous gas, NO, obtained by oxidation of nitrogen or ammonia.

ni′tride (nī′trīd; -trĭd), *n.* Also **ni′trid.** [From NITROGEN.] *Chem.* A binary compound of nitrogen with a more positive element, as boron, silicon, and many metals.

ni′tri·fi·ca′tion (nī′trĭ·fĭ·kā′shŭn), *n. Chem. & Bacteriol.* Act or process of nitrifying; specif., the oxidation, esp. by bacteria, of ammonium salts to nitrites and the further oxidation of nitrites to nitrates. See NITROBACTERIA.

ni′tri·fy (nī′trĭ·fī), *v. t.;* -FIED (-fīd); -FY′ING. [F. *nitrifier.* See NITER; -FY.] *Chem.* **a** To combine or impregnate with nitrogen or a nitrogen compound. **b** To convert, by oxidation, into nitrous or nitric acid or their salts.

ni′trile (nī′trĭl; -trēl; -trīl; *in compounds often* -nĭ·trĭl′, -nĭ·trēl′), *n.* Also **ni′tril.** [See NITRO-.] *Chem.* An organic cyanide, characterized by the univalent group CN, which on hydrolysis yields an acid with elimination of ammonia.

ni′trite (nī′trīt), *n. Chem.* A salt or ester of nitrous acid.

ni′tro- (nī′trō-), **nitr-.** [L. *nitrum* native soda, natron, fr. Gr. *nitron.* See NITER.] A combining form denoting: **1.** Niter, as in *nitro*bacteria. **2.** *Chem.* **a** *Certain compounds of nitrogen* or *of its acids.* **b** The *group* or *radical* NO_2, or *its compounds*, as in *nitro*benzene. — **ni′tro** (-trō), *adj.*

ni′tro·bac·te′ri·a (-băk·tẽr′ĭ·ȧ), *n. pl.* [NL.] *Bacteriol.* The soil bacteria concerned in nitrification. They are of two classes: the ***nitric bacteria*** which oxidize nitrites to nitrates, and the ***nitrous bacteria*** which oxidize ammonia compounds to nitrites.

ni′tro·ben′zene (-bĕn′zēn; -bĕn·zēn′), *n. Chem.* Any nitro derivative of benzene; specif., the compound, $C_6H_5NO_2$, produced by action of nitric acid on benzene. It is used in making explosives, dyes, perfumes, etc.

ni′tro·cel′lu·lose, ni′tro–cel′lu·lose (-sĕl′ū·lōs), *n.* Nitrated cellulose.

ni′tro·gen (nī′trō·jĕn), *n.* [F. *nitrogène.* See NITRO-; -GEN.] *Chem.* A colorless gaseous element, tasteless and odorless, constituting about four fifths (78.03 per cent) of the atmosphere by volume, and a constituent of all living tissues. Symbol, *N;* at. no., 7; at. wt., 14.008.

nitrogen cycle. *Chem.* The fixation of atmospheric nitrogen, as by the aid of bacteria, and its passage into the soil, into plant tissue or into plant and then animal tissue, and back to the soil, where it is converted by bacteria into forms suitable for plant growth or into gaseous nitrogen.

nitrogen fixation. **a** The conversion of free nitrogen into combined form so as to render it useful for fertilizers, explosives, etc. **b** The assimilation of atmospheric nitrogen by certain soil organisms, called **nitrogen fixers,** as those living symbiotically on roots of various leguminous plants. Upon the death of the bacteria and plants, the nitrogen unites with elements in the soil, becoming available as plant food. — **ni′tro·gen–fix′ing,** *adj.*

ni′tro·gen·ize (nī′trō·jĕn·īz), *v. t.* To combine, or impregnate, with nitrogen or its compounds. — **ni′tro·gen·i·za′tion** (nī′trō·jĕn·ĭ·zā′shŭn; -ī·zā′-), *n.*

nitrogen mustard. *Chem.* Any of a group of toxic, blistering compounds analogous in composition to mustard gas but with nitrogen replacing sulfur.

ni·trog′e·nous (nī·trŏj′ē·nŭs), *adj. Chem.* Of, pertaining to, or containing nitrogen.

ni′tro·glyc′er·in, ni′tro·glyc′er·ine (nī′trō·glĭs′ẽr·ĭn), *n.* [*nitro-* + *glycerin.*] Any nitrate of glycerol; specif., a colorless, heavy, oily, explosive liquid, $C_3H_5(NO_3)_3$, obtained by treating glycerol with a mixture of nitric and sulfuric acids, used esp. in making dynamite (which see).

ni·trol′ic (nī·trŏl′ĭk), *adj. Chem.* Pertaining to or designating any of a series of acids of the general formula $RC(:NOH)NO_2$, formed by action of nitrous acid on nitroparaffins.

ni·trom′e·ter (nī·trŏm′ē·tẽr), *n.* [*nitro-* + *-meter.*] *Chem.* An apparatus for determining the amount of nitrogen or some of its compounds in any substance analyzed.

ni′tro·par′af·fin (nī′trō·păr′ă·fĭn), *n. Chem.* A nitro derivative of any member of the paraffin series.

ni′tros·a·mine′ (nī′trōs·ȧ·mēn′; -ăm′ĭn), *n.* Also **ni′tros·am′in.** [*nitroso-* + *amine.*] *Chem.* Any of a class of neutral compounds characterized by the grouping >N.NO.

ni·tro′so- (nī·trō′sō-). [L. *nitrosus* nitrous.] *Chem.* A combining form denoting the group or radical NO (called the **nitroso group,** or **ni·tro′syl** [nī·trō′sĭl; nī′trō·sēl′; nī′trō·sĭl]) or its compounds, as in **ni·tro′so·ben′zene,** C_6H_5NO. — **ni·tro′so** (-sō), *adj.*

ni′trous (nī′trŭs), *adj.* [L. *nitrosus* full of natron. See NITER.] **1.** Of, pertaining to, containing, or impregnated with niter; of the nature of, or like, niter. **2.** *Chem.* Pertaining to or designating any compound in which nitrogen is lower in valence than in *nitric* compounds.

nitrous acid. *Chem.* An acid, HNO_2, forming a series of salts, the *nitrites*, but itself known only in solution.

nitrous bacteria. See NITROBACTERIA.

nitrous oxide. *Chem.* A colorless gas, N_2O, which when inhaled produces loss of sensibility to pain, preceded by laughter. It is used as an anesthetic in dentistry; — called also *laughing gas.*

nit′wit′ (nĭt′wĭt′), *n. Slang.* A stupid person.

‖**Ni′vôse′** (nē′vōz′), *n.* [F.] See REVOLUTIONARY CALENDAR.

nix (nĭks), *n.; fem.* **nix′e** (nĭk′sĕ); *pl.* NIXES (nĭk′sĕz; -sĭz); *G. pl.* NIXE (nĭk′sĕ) or NIXEN (-sĕn). [G.] *Teut. Myth.* A water sprite, in the form sometimes of a woman, sometimes of a man, or part man, part fish.

nix, *n.* [G. *nichts* nothing.] *Slang.* Nothing; no one; also, no; I don't agree, allow, permit, etc.

nix′ie (nĭk′sĭ), *n.* A female water sprite. See 1st NIX.

Ni·zam′ (nĭ·zäm′; -zăm′), *n.* [Hind. & Per. *niẓām* ruler, fr. Ar. *niẓām* order, arrangement.] **1.** The title in use since 1713 by the native sovereigns of Hyderabad, India. **2.** [*not cap.*] [Turk. (fr. Ar.) *niẓām.*] *pl.* NIZAM. A regular soldier of the Turkish army.

ni·zam′ate (-āt), *n.* The territory of the Nizam.

Njorth (nyôrth), *n.* Also **Njord** (nyôrd). [ON. *Njörthr.*] One of the Vanir, Scandinavian gods of fertility.

NKVD, N.K.V.D. (ĕn′kā′vē′dē′). [Russ., from the initial letters of the words for People's Commissariat for Internal Affairs.] The Soviet secret police, succeeding the Ogpu. See GAY-PAY-OO.

no (nō; 4), *adv.* [AS. *nā*, fr. *ne* not + *ā* ever.] **1.** Not; — now only *Scot.* or in expressions of alternative or opposing courses of action, judgments, or the like. **2.** Not any; not at all. **3.** Not so; — the opposite of *yes.* — *n.; pl.* NOES (nōz). **1.** Act of uttering *no;* a refusal by use of *no;* a denial. **2.** A negative vote or decision; *pl.*, those who vote in the negative; as, the *noes* have it. — *adj.* Not any; not a; as, I have *no* great regard for him.

no (nō), *n. sing. & pl.* Also **no′–ga′ku** (nō′gä′kōō). [Jap. *nō.*] *Japanese Drama.* A type of drama, originating in an ancient religious dance accompanied with choric songs.

No·a′chi·an (nō·ā′kĭ·ăn), *adj.* Also **No·ach′ic** (nō·ăk′ĭk; -ā′kĭk). Of or pertaining to the patriarch Noah or his time; figuratively, ancient or antique.

No′ah (nō′ȧ), *n.* [Heb. *Nōaḥ.*] *Bib.* A patriarch who at God's command built an ark to save his family and a number of individuals of all living creatures in the time of the Deluge, or Flood. *Gen.* v. 28–x. Cf. DEUCALION AND PYRRHA.

nob (nŏb), *n. Slang.* **1.** The head. **2.** *Cribbage.* A knave, or jack, of the same suit as the card turned up, held in a hand. It counts one to the holder.

nob, *n. Slang.* One in a superior position in life.

no′–ball′, *n. Cricket.* A ball unfairly bowled. A no-ball counts one run to the batting side and cannot take a wicket.

nob′ble (nŏb′'l), *v. t.;* NOB′BLED (-'ld); NOB′BLING (-lĭng). **a** *Racing Cant, Eng.* To incapacitate (a horse), as by drugging. **b** *Slang, Brit.* (1) To win over to one's side or interest, as by bribery. (2) To steal. (3) To swindle. (4) To catch; "nab." — **nob′bler** (-lẽr), *n.*

nob′by (nŏb′ĭ), *adj.;* -BI·ER (-ĭ·ẽr); -BI·EST. [From NOB a swell.] *Slang.* Of, pert. to, or befitting "nobs"; stylish.

No·bel′ prizes (nō·bĕl′). Prizes for the encouragement of persons who work for the interests of humanity, established by the will of Alfred Nobel (1833–96), Swedish inventor of dynamite, who left his estate for this purpose.

no·bil′i·ar′y (nō·bĭl′ĭ·ĕr′ĭ; -yȧ·rĭ; 58), *adj.* [F. *nobiliarie.* See NOBLE.] Of or pertaining to the nobility.

no·bil′i·ty (nō·bĭl′ĭ·tĭ), *n.; pl.* -TIES (-tĭz). [OF. *nobilité*, fr. L. *nobilitas.*] **1.** Quality or state of being noble in character, ability, rank, etc. **2.** Collectively: Usually with *the*, those who are noble; the body of titled persons in a state; in Great Britain, the peerage.

no′ble (nō′b'l), *adj.* [OF., fr. L. *nobilis* well-known, highborn, noble.] **1.** Of persons, possessing eminence, dignity, or the like; illustrious; of deeds or acts, famous. **2.** Of high birth or exalted rank or station; aristocratic; as, *noble* blood, birth. **3.** **a** Possessing excellent qualities; as, *noble* hawks. **b** Broadly, very good or excellent; as, a *noble* estate. **4.** Grand, esp. in appearance; stately; as, a *noble* edifice. **5.** Possessing, characterized by, or indicating, superiority of mind or character; magnanimous; lofty. **6.** *Chem.* Resisting chemical action; inert. **7.** Designating a metal or alloy, as gold or silver, of high value or superior qualities, esp. resistance to corrosion; — opposed to *base.* — **Syn.** See GRAND: MORAL.

— *n.* **1.** A person of noble rank or birth; a nobleman; peer. **2.** An English gold coin, current, till 1461, at 6s. 8d. **3.** *Labor Union Slang.* A captain of strikebreakers ("finks"), or an overseer in charge of strikebreaking operations.

no′ble·man (nō′b'l·măn), *n.; pl.* -MEN (-mĕn). One of the nobility; a peer. — **no′ble·wom′an** (-wŏŏm′ăn), *n.; pl.* -WOMEN (-wĭm′ĕn; -ĭn).

no′ble·ness, *n.* Quality or state of being noble.

no·blesse′ (nō·blĕs′), *n.* [OF. *noblece*, fr. F. *noblesse.* See NOBLE.] **1.** *Rare.* Noble birth or condition; nobility. **2.** The nobility, esp. of France.

‖no'blesse' o'blige' (nô'blĕs' ô'blēzh'). [F.] Nobility obligates; — used to denote the obligation of honorable and generous behavior associated with high rank or birth.

no'bly (nō'blĭ), *adv.* **a** With greatness of soul; gallantly. **b** Magnificently. **c** Of noble extraction; as, *nobly* born.

no'bod·y (nō'bŏd·ĭ; -bŭd·ĭ), *pron.* Not anybody. — *n.; pl.* -BODIES (-ĭz). A person of no influence, standing, etc.

no'cent (nō'sĕnt; -s'nt), *adj.* [L. *nocens*, pres. part. of *nocere* to hurt.] *Now Rare.* Doing hurt or harm; harmful.

no'ci·as·so'ci·a'tion (nō'sĭ·ă·sō'sĭ·ā'shŭn; -shĭ·ā'shŭn), *n.* [L. *nocere* to hurt + E. *association.*] *Med.* Nervous energy discharge as manifested in shock, trauma, etc.

nock (nŏk), *n.* *Archery.* A notch, as at either end of a bow for the string, or in an arrow for taking the string. See ARROW, *Illust.* — *v. t.* To make a notch in, as in a bow or in an arrow; also, to fit (an arrow) on the string.

noc·tam'bu·la'tion (nŏk·tăm'bū·lā'shŭn), *n.* [L. *nox, noctis,* night + *ambulare* to walk.] Also **noc·tam'bu·lism** (-tăm'bū·lĭz'm). Somnambulism. — **noc·tam'bu·list** (-lĭst), *n.*

nocti-. [L. *nox, noctis.*] A combining form meaning *night.*

noc'ti·lu'ca (nŏk'tĭ·lū'kȧ), *n.* [L., something that shines by night, fr. *nox, noctis,* night + *lucere* to shine, fr. *lux* light.] Any of a genus (*Noctiluca*) of marine bioluminescent flagellates (order Dinoflagellata). The phosphorescence of the sea is often due to these organisms.

noc'tu·id (nŏk'tū̇·ĭd), *n.* [L. *noctua* a night owl.] *Zool.* Any of a family (Noctuidae) of moths comprising a great variety of forms, including the cutworm moths, army-worm moth, and their allies, and containing a majority of the moths that fly into houses at night. Their larvae are in most cases naked; many of them are well-known pests to agriculture. — **noc'tu·id,** *adj.*

noc'tule (nŏk'tūl), *n.* [F.] A large Old World brown bat (*Nyctalus noctula*).

noc·tur'nal (nŏk·tûr'năl; -n'l), *adj.* [LL. *nocturnalis*, fr. L. *nocturnus*, fr. *nox, noctis,* night.] **1.** Of, pert. to, done, or occurring in the night; — opposed to *diurnal.* **2.** Moving about at night; as, *nocturnal* birds and insects. — **noc·tur'nal·ly,** *adv.*

nocturnal arc. See ARC, 2.

noc'turne (nŏk'tûrn; nŏk·tûrn'), *n.* [F.] **1.** *Music.* A composition dealing with or referring to night; a serenade; esp., a dreamy, pensive instrumental composition. **2.** *Painting.* A night scene.

noc'u·ous (nŏk'ū·ŭs), *adj.* [L. *nocuus*, fr. *nocere* to hurt.] Hurtful; noxious. — **noc'u·ous·ly,** *adv.* — **noc'u·ous·ness,** *n.*

nod (nŏd), *v. i. & t.;* NOD'DED; NOD'DING. [ME. *nodden.*] **1.** To make a quick downward motion of the head as a sign of assent, salutation, or command, or involuntarily because of drowsiness. **2.** To bend or incline the upper part downward or forward with a quick motion; as, *nodding* plumes. **3.** To be for the moment inattentive; to make a slip or error. — *n.* Act of one who nods. — **nod'der,** *n.*

nod'al (nōd'ăl; -'l), *adj.* Of the nature of, or pert. to, a node.

nod'dle (nŏd''l), *n.* *Chiefly Jocose.* The head; pate.

nod'dle, *v. t. & i.;* NOD'DLED (-'ld); NOD'DLING (-lĭng). [Freq. of NOD.] To nod quickly or slightly.

nod'dy (nŏd'ĭ), *n.; pl.* -DIES (-ĭz). **1.** A simpleton; fool. **2.** Any of several stout-bodied terns (genera *Anoüs* and *Micranous*) so called from their tameness and stupidity.

node (nōd), *n.* [L. *nodus.*] **1.** A knot or complication, as in a drama. **2.** A knot, knob, protuberance, or swelling. **3.** A point at which subsidiary parts center. **4.** *Anat. & Zool.* A swelling; some part likened to a knot. **5.** *Astron.* Either of the two points where the orbit of a planet or comet intersects the ecliptic, or where the orbit of a satellite intersects the plane of the orbit of its primary. The node passed as the body goes north is called the ***ascending node*** (☊), that passed in going south, the ***descending node*** (☋). See DRAGON'S HEAD, 2. **6.** *Bot.* The joint of a stem; also, the point of insertion of a leaf or leaves. **7.** *Geom.* A double point, which in regard to intersections counts as more than one point; the coincidence of two nonconsecutive points of a curve regarded as a system of points. **8.** *Physics.* A point, line, or surface of a vibrating body marked by absolute or relative freedom from vibratory motion.

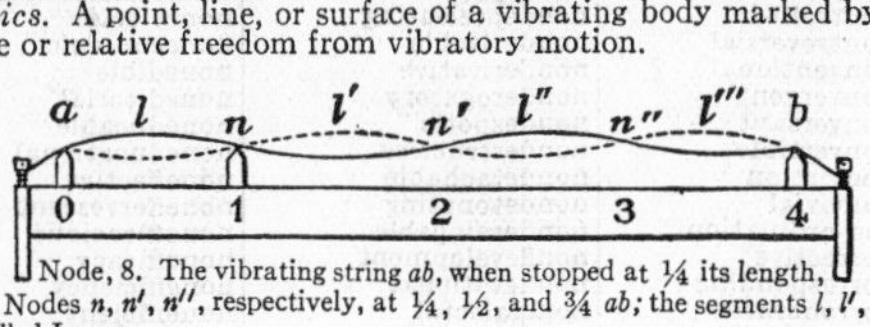

Node, 8. The vibrating string *ab*, when stopped at ¼ its length, forms Nodes *n, n', n''*, respectively, at ¼, ½, and ¾ *ab;* the segments *l, l'*, etc., are called Loops.

nod'i·cal (nŏd'ĭ·kăl; nō'dĭ-), *adj.* *Astron.* Of or pert. to the nodes; as, the *nodical* revolution of the moon.

no'dose (nō'dōs; nō·dōs'), *adj.* [L. *nodosus*, fr. *nodus* knot.] Knotty; having numerous or conspicuous nodes, or protuberances. — **no·dos'i·ty** (nō·dŏs'ĭ·tĭ), *n.*

no'dous (nō'dŭs), *adj.* [L. *nodosus.* See NODE.] Knotty.

nod'u·lar (nŏd'ū̇·lẽr), *adj.* Pert. to, characterized by, having, or in the form of nodules; as, *nodular* structure.

nod'ule (nŏd'ūl), *n.* [L. *nodulus*, dim. of *nodus* knot.] **1.** A rounded mass of irregular shape; a little lump. **2.** *Bot.* A tubercle, as on the roots of certain legumes.

nod'u·lose (nŏd'ū̇·lōs; nŏd'ū̇·lōs'), *adj.* Also **nod'u·lous** (nŏd'ū̇·lŭs). Having nodules, or small knots or knobs.

no'dus (nō'dŭs), *n.; pl.* -DI (-dī). [L., knot.] Knot; node; specif., a complication, or difficulty.

no·el' (nō·ĕl'), *n.* [F. *noël*, fr. L. *natalis* birthday, fr. *natalis* natal. See NATAL.] **1.** A Christmas carol; also, the shout of *noel*, made as a sign of joy. **2.** [*cap.*] (*pron.* nō'ĕl; -ĕl) Christmas.

‖no·e'sis (nō·ē'sĭs), *n.* [Gr. *noēsis*, fr. *noein* to perceive, fr. *nous* mind.] **1.** *Philos.* Purely intellectual apprehension. **2.** *Psychol.* Cognition, esp. through direct and self-evident knowledge. — **no·et'ic** (-ĕt'ĭk), *adj.*

nog, nogg (nŏg), *n.* **1.** *Dial. Eng.* A kind of strong ale, formerly brewed in Norfolk. **2.** Short for EGGNOG. **3.** *U.S.* Loosely, any mixed drink containing an egg beaten with (usually) spirits; as, a brandy *nog.*

nog (nŏg), *n.* A wooden peg, pin, or block of the size of a brick, as in a wall to serve as a hold for nails.

nog'gin (nŏg'ĭn), *n.* A small mug; also, a small quantity of drink, usually a gill; as, a *noggin* of milk.

nog'ging (-ĭng), *n.* Rough brick masonry used to fill in the open spaces of a wooden frame.

no'how' (nō'hou'), *adv.* *Dial.* In no way; not at all.

noil (noil), *n.* A piece or knot of short hair or fiber, as of wool combed from the longer staple, or a similar piece of waste silk; also, such pieces collectively.

noise (noiz), *n.* [OF., noisy strife, brawl.] **1.** Loud, confused, or senseless shouting; clamor. **2.** *Obs.* General or common talk; rumor; specif., slander. **3.** Sound or a sound of any sort; esp., sound without agreeable musical quality. — *v. t.* To report; to rumor. — *v. i.* **1.** To talk much or loudly. **2.** To make a noise.

noise'less, *adj.* Making, or causing, no noise or stir; without noise; silent; quiet; as, the *noiseless* foot of time. — **noise'less·ly,** *adv.* — **noise'less·ness,** *n.*

noise'mak'er (noiz'māk'ẽr), *n.* One who or that which makes noise; specif., any of several devices, as a horn, a clapper, for making noise at celebrations, etc. — **noise'mak'ing,** *n. & adj.*

noi'some (noi'sŭm), *adj.* [For *noysome*, fr. *noy* for *annoy.* See ANNOY.] **1.** Noxious; harmful. **2.** Offensive to the smell or other senses; disgusting. — **Syn.** See MALODOROUS. — **noi'some·ly,** *adv.* — **noi'some·ness,** *n.*

nois'y (noiz'ĭ), *adj.;* NOIS'I·ER (-ĭ·ẽr); NOIS'I·EST. **1.** Making a noise, esp. a loud sound. **2.** Characterized by noise; as, the *noisy* town. — **nois'i·ly,** *adv.* — **nois'i·ness,** *n.*

‖no'lens vo'lens (nō'lĕnz vō'lĕnz). [L.] Unwilling (or) willing; willy-nilly.

‖no'li me tan'ge·re, *or* **no'li–me–tan'ge·re** (nō'lī·mē·tăn'jē·rē), *n.* [L., touch me not.] **1.** A warning against touching or interference. **2.** A painting representing Christ's appearance to Mary Magdalene after the Resurrection. *John* xx. 17.

nol'le pros'e·qui (nŏl'ē prŏs'ē·kwī). [L., to be unwilling to prosecute.] *Law.* An entry on the record denoting that the prosecutor or plaintiff will proceed no further in his action or suit, either as a whole, or as to some count. Abbr. *nol pros.*

‖no'lo con·ten'de·re (nō'lō kŏn·tĕn'dĕ·rē). [L., I do not wish to contend.] *Law.* A plea by the defendant in a criminal prosecution, which, without admitting guilt, subjects him to conviction, but does not preclude him from denying the truth of the charges in a collateral proceeding.

nol'–pros' (nŏl'prŏs'), *v. t.;* -PROSSED' (-prŏst'); -PROS'SING. To discontinue by entering a nolle prosequi.

no'ma (nō'mȧ), *n.* [NL., fr. Gr. *nomē*, lit., a feeding.] *Med.* Gangrenous stomatitis, occurring oftenest in debilitated children, esp. after exhausting diseases.

no'mad (nō'măd *or, esp. Brit.,* nŏm'ăd), *n.* [L. *nomas, -adis,* fr. Gr. *nomas, -ados,* pasturing, roaming about for pasture.] One of a race or tribe that has no fixed location, but wanders from place to place. — *adj.* Roving; nomadic. — **no'mad·ism** (-ĭz'm), *n.*

no·mad'ic (nō·măd'ĭk), *adj.* Also, *Rare,* **no·mad'i·cal** (-ĭ·kăl). Of or pertaining to, or characteristic of, nomads or their way of life; wandering. — **no·mad'i·cal·ly,** *adv.*

no man's land. **a** A strip of unowned land, as at a border. **b** In warfare, a belt of ground between the most advanced trenches of opposing armies.

nom'arch (nŏm'ärk), *n.* [Gr. *nomos* a district + *-arch.*] The chief magistrate of a nome, or nomarchy.

nom'arch·y (-är·kĭ), *n.; pl.* -ARCHIES (-kĭz). A province of modern Greece; a nome or department.

nom'bles (nŭm'b'lz). Var. of NUMBLES.

nom'bril (nŏm'brĭl), *n.* *Her.* See ESCUTCHEON, *Illust.*

‖nom de guerre (nôɴ' dĕ gâr'). [F.] Literally, war name; hence, a fictitious name; pseudonym.

nom de plume (nŏm' dē plōōm'; *F.* nôɴ' dĕ plüm'). [An English formation from French.] Literally, pen name; a name assumed by an author; a pseudonym.

nome (nōm), *n.* In Greek form **no'mos** (nō'mŏs). [Gr. *nomos.*] A province of modern Greece or of ancient Egypt.

‖no'men (nō'mĕn), *n.; pl.* NOMINA (nŏm'ĭ·nȧ). [L.] The name of the gens, the second of the three names (*praenomen, nomen, cognomen*) of a person among the ancient Romans.

no'men·cla'tor (nō'mĕn·klā'tẽr), *n.* [L., fr. *nomen* name + *calare* to call.] **1.** One who calls persons or things by their names; in modern use, one who announces the names of guests or of persons generally. **2.** One who gives names to things; a classifier of objects under appropriate names.

no'men·cla'ture (nō'mĕn·klā'tū̇r; nō·mĕn'klȧ·tū̇r), *n.* The system of names used in a particular branch of knowledge or art, or by any school or individual; esp., the names used in classifications, as disting. from other technical terms. Cf. TERMINOLOGY.

nom'i·nal (nŏm'ĭ·năl; -n'l), *adj.* [L. *nominalis*, fr. *nomen, nominis,* name.] **1.** Of, pertaining to, of the nature of, or consisting in, a name or names. **2.** Existing in name only; not real or actual; hence, so small, slight, or the like, as to be hardly worth the name; as, a *nominal* price. **3.** Consisting of, containing, or giving names; bearing the name of a person, as shares. **4.** *Gram.* Of, pertaining to, or of the nature of a noun or nouns. — **nom'i·nal·ly,** *adv.*

nom'i·nal·ism (-ĭz'm), *n.* *Philos.* The doctrine that there are no universal essences in reality, and that the mind can frame no single concept or image corresponding to any general term; — opposed to (logical) *realism.* — **nom'i·nal·ist** (-ĭst), *n. & adj.* — **nom'i·nal·is'tic** (-ĭs'tĭk), *adj.*

nominal sentence. *Gram.* = EQUATIONAL SENTENCE.

nominal value. Value stated, as on the face of a certificate of stock.

nominal wages. See REAL WAGES.

nom'i·nate (nŏm'ĭ·nāt), *v. t.* [L. *nominatus*, past part. of *nominare* to nominate, fr. *nomen* name.] **1.** Formerly: **a** To call; entitle; name. **b** To specify. **2.** To name as a candidate for an election, choice, etc.; to propose for office. — (-năt), *adj.* Having a special or certain name.

nom'i·na'tion (-nā'shŭn), *n.* A nominating, or state of being nominated, esp. of a candidate for office.

nom'i·na·tive (nŏm'ĭ·nȧ·tĭv; -nā'tĭv), *adj.* [F. or L.; F. *nominatif*, fr. L. *nominativus* of a name, nominative.] **1.** (*pron. usually* nŏm'ĭ·nā'tĭv) Named for an office; nominated. **2.** Bearing a person's name; nominal, as shares. **3.** *Gram.* Designating or pert. to the case denoting the subject of a finite verb, a predicate noun referring to the subject, a noun word in apposition with either, or one in certain absolute constructions; also, designating or pertaining to the relation of subject, etc., denoted by this case. — *n.* The nominative case, or a word in it. Abbr. *nom.*

nom′i·na′tor (nŏm′ĭ·nā′tẽr), *n.* [LL.] One who nominates.

nom′i·nee′ (nŏm′ĭ·nē′), *n.* [See NOMINATE; -EE.] A person named for any office, duty, or position.

no′mism (nō′mĭz′m), *n.* [Gr. *nomos* law.] Ethical or religious basing of conduct on the observance of moral law. — **no·mis′tic** (nō·mĭs′tĭk), *adj.*

nom′o·gram (nŏm′ō·grăm), *n.* Also **nom′o·graph** (-grăf; 9). **a** A graph that enables one by the aid of a straightedge to read off the value of a dependent variable when the value of the independent variable is given. **b** A graphic representation of numerical relations by any of various systems. **c** A treatise on the drafting of laws.

no·mog′ra·phy (nō·mŏg′rȧ·fĭ), *n.* [Gr. *nomographia*, fr. *nomos* law + *graphein* to write.] **a** The art of, or a treatise on, drafting laws. **b** The making of nomograms.

no·mol′o·gy (nō·mŏl′ō·jĭ), *n.* [Gr. *nomos* law + *-logy.*] **a** The science of law and legislation. **b** The science of the laws of the mind. — **nom′o·log′i·cal** (nŏm′ō·lŏj′ĭ·kăl), *adj.*

nom′o·thet′ic (nŏm′ō·thĕt′ĭk), **nom′o·thet′i·cal** (-ĭ·kăl), *adj.* [Gr. *nomothetikos.*] Giving or enacting laws; legislative.

-nomy. [Gr. *nomos* law.] A combining form denoting *a system of laws governing a* (specified) *field* or *the sum of knowledge regarding them*, as in astro*nomy*.

non- (nŏn-; *accent varies according to emphasis or sentence rhythm*). [F. and L.; OF. *non-*, fr. L. *non.*] A prefix in common use in the sense of *not, un-, in-*. *Non-* is generally less emphatic than *in-* or *un-*, being merely negative, while *in-* and *un-* are positive, often implying an opposite thing or quality. Cf. *non*religious, *ir*religious; *non*moral, *im*moral; *non*-Christian, *un*christian.

☞ The meanings of the words in the list beginning at the foot of this page can be understood from the definitions of the terms with which *non-* is combined.

non′age (nŏn′ĭj; nōn′ĭj), *n.* [OF. See NON-; AGE.] State of not being of age; legal minority; immaturity.

non′a·ge·nar′i·an (nŏn′ȧ·jē·nâr′ĭ·ăn *or, esp. Brit.*, nō′nȧ-), *adj.* [L. *nonagenarius* containing ninety, fr. *nonageni* ninety each.] Ninety, or between ninety and one hundred, years old. — *n.* A person of such age.

non′a·gon (nŏn′ȧ·gŏn), *n.* [L. *nonus* ninth + Gr. *gōnia* angle.] *Math.* A polygon having nine angles and therefore nine sides.

no′na·ry (nō′nȧ·rĭ), *adj.* [L. *nonus* ninth.] **1.** Consisting of nine; ninefold. **2.** *Math.* Using nine as a base; — said of a system of numeration.

nonce (nŏns), *n.* [For the *nonce*, fr. ME. for the *nones*, fr. for then *ones*, where *n* in *then* is a relic of AS. *m* in *tham*, dat. of *the*. See THE.] Literally, the one, particular, or present (occasion, use, or purpose); — chiefly in the phrase ***for the nonce***.

nonce word. A word formed and used for one particular occasion, but not adopted into general use.

non′cha·lance (nŏn′shȧ·lăns; -läns), *n.* [F.] State of being nonchalant; lack of enthusiasm or interest; also, *Colloq.*, jaunty carelessness; gay imperturbability.

non′cha·lant (-lănt; -länt), *adj.* [F., fr. *non* not (fr. L. *non*) + *chaloir* to concern (oneself) for, fr. L. *calere* to be warm.] Lacking in warmth of feeling, enthusiasm, or interest; indifferent; also, *Colloq.*, casual and imperturbable. — **Syn.** See COOL. — **non′cha·lant·ly**, *adv.*

non′com′ (nŏn′kŏm′), *adj. & n. Mil.* Noncommissioned (officer).

non·com′bat·ant (nŏn·kŏm′bȧ·tănt; nŏn′kŏm·băt′'nt; nŏn·kŭm′bȧ·tănt), *n. Mil.* A person whose military or naval duties do not include fighting, as a chaplain; also, any civilian.

non′com·mis′sioned (nŏn′kŏ·mĭsh′ŭnd), *adj.* Not having a commission; as, **noncommissioned officer**, a subordinate officer, as a corporal or sergeant, appointed from the enlisted personnel of an army by a warrant issued by an appointing officer, as a regimental commander, named by law. See WARRANT OFFICER **a**, COMMISSIONED OFFICER.

non′com·mit′tal (-mĭt′ăl; -'l), *adj.* Characterized by forbearance or refusal to commit oneself; indicating neither consent nor dissent. — **non′com·mit′tal·ly**, *adv.*

‖**non com′pos men′tis** (nŏn kŏm′pŏs mĕn′tĭs). [L.] *Law.* Not of sound mind; — a term including all mental unsoundness. Often shortened to *non compos*. Cf. COMPOS MENTIS.

non′con·duc′tor (nŏn′kŏn·dŭk′tẽr), *n. Physics & Elec.* A substance that does not conduct (convey or transmit) heat, electricity, sound, or the like; — opp. to *conductor*. Cf. INSULATOR.

non′con·form′ist (-fôr′mĭst), *n.* One who does not conform to an established church; esp. [*often cap.*], one who does not conform to the established Church of England. Cf. CONFORMIST.

non′con·form′i·ty (-fôr′mĭ·tĭ), *n.* Neglect, failure, or refusal to conform, as to a rule or practice; specif., refusal to conform to an established church, esp. [*often cap.*], the Church of England.

non′–co–op′er·a′tion, *n.* Failure or refusal to co-operate; specif., refusal, through civil disobedience, of a people to co-operate with the government of a country, esp. by nonpayment of taxes. — **non′–co–op′er·a′tion·ist**, *n.* — **non′–co–op′er·a′tive**, *adj.* — **-er·a′tor**, *n.*

non′de·script (nŏn′dē·skrĭpt), *adj.* [*non-* + L. *descriptus* described.] Not easily described; belonging, or apparently belonging, to no particular class or kind. — *n.* A person or thing of no particular class or kind; — usually applied disparagingly.

non′dis·tinc′tive (nŏn′dĭs·tĭngk′tĭv), *adj.* Not distinctive; specif., *Phonet.*, not capable of differentiating meaning; — applied to a speech sound. Cf. DISTINCTIVE.

none (nŭn), *pron.* [AS. *nān*, fr. *ne* not + *ān* one.] **1.** Not any. As subject, *none* with a plural verb is the commoner construction. **2.** No one; not one. **3.** Not any such thing or person; as, half a loaf is better than *none*. — *adv.* Not at all; in no way; to no extent.

none, None (nōn), *n.* [F., fr. L. *nona*. See NOON.] = NONES, 2.

non·e′go (nŏn·ē′gō; -ĕg′ō), *n.; pl.* -GOS (-gōz). *Philos.* The external world or object of knowledge as contrasted with the subject or ego.

non·en′ti·ty (nŏn·ĕn′tĭ·tĭ), *n.; pl.* -TIES (-tĭz). **1.** Nonexistence; negation of being. **2.** A thing not existing, or existing only in the imagination. **3.** A person or thing of little or no account.

nones (nōnz), *n. pl.* [F., fr. L. *nonae*, fr. *nonus* ninth.] **1.** The ninth day before the ides (counting the ides) in the Roman calendar.

☞ See NON-, *Note.*
nonabsorbent
nonabstainer
nonaccent
nonacceptance
nonacid
nonactinic
nonactive
nonadhesive
nonadjacent
nonadjectival
nonadministrative
nonadmission
nonadvantageous
nonadverbial
nonaesthetic
non-African
nonaggression
nonaggressive
nonagricultural
nonalcoholic
nonalienating
nonalliterative
non-American
non-Anglican
nonannexation
nonantagonistic
nonapologetic
nonapostolic
nonappearance
nonappearing
nonapprehension
nonaquatic
non-Arab
non-Arabic
nonaristocratic
nonarithmetical
non-Aryan
non-Asiatic
nonassertive
nonassessable
nonassignable
nonassimilable
nonassimilation
nonassociable
nonatmospheric
nonattendance
non-Attic
nonattributive
nonaugmentative
nonauricular
nonauriferous
nonauthoritative
nonautomatic
nonautomotive
nonbacterial
nonbasic
nonbeliever
nonbelieving
nonbelligerent
nonbenevolent
non-Biblical
nonblooming
non-Bolshevik
non-Bolshevist
non-Brahmanical
nonbreakable
non-British
non-Buddhist
nonbudding
nonbureaucratic
nonbusiness
noncaffeine
noncaking
noncalcareous
non-Calvinist
noncannibalistic
noncanonical
noncapitalistic
noncarnivorous
noncategorical
non-Catholic
non-Caucasian
noncelestial
noncellular
non-Celtic
noncentral
noncereal
noncerebral
nonceremonial
noncertified
nonchargeable
non-Chinese
non-Christian
nonchurch
nonciliate
noncivilized
nonclassifiable
noncleistogamic
nonclerical
nonclinical
nonclotting
noncoagulable
noncoalescing
noncoercive
noncognition
noncognitive
noncoherent
noncollaborative
noncollapsible
noncollectable
noncollegiate
noncolloid
noncollusive
noncombat
noncombining
noncombustible
noncombustion
noncommendable
noncommercial
noncommunicable
noncommunicant
noncommunicating
noncommunication
noncommunist
noncommunistic
noncompensating
noncompensation
noncompetency
noncompetent
noncompeting
noncompetitive
noncompetitively
noncomplaisance
noncompletion
noncompliance
noncomplying
noncompressible
noncompression
noncompulsion
nonconcealment
nonconcentration
nonconciliating
nonconcordant
nonconcurrence
nonconcurrency
nonconcurrent
noncondensable
noncondensation
noncondensible
nonconditioned
nonconducive
nonconductibility
nonconductible
nonconducting
nonconductive
nonconferrable
nonconfidential
nonconfiscable
nonconflicting
nonconformance
nonconforming
noncongealing
noncongenital
noncongestion
non-Congressional
nonconjugate
nonconnective
nonconnivance
nonconnubial
nonconscious
nonconsecutive
nonconsent
nonconsenting
nonconservative
nonconsistorial
nonconspiring
nonconstitutional
nonconstructive
nonconsular
nonconsultative
noncontagious
noncontemplative
noncontemporary
noncontentious
noncontentiously
noncontiguous
noncontinental
noncontinuance
noncontinuous
noncontraband
noncontradictory
noncontributing
noncontributory
noncontrolled
noncontroversial
nonconventional
nonconvergent
nonconversant
nonconvertible
nonconviction
nonconvivial
non-co-ordination
noncorrective
noncorresponding
noncorroborative
noncorrodible
noncorroding
noncorrosive
noncosmic
noncotyledonous
noncreative
noncredible
noncreditor
noncriminal
noncrinoid
noncritical
noncrucial
noncrystalline
noncrystallizable
noncrystallized
noncrystallizing
nonculpable
noncultivated
noncultivation
noncumulative
non-Czech
nondamageable
non-Darwinian
nondecaying
nondeceptive
nondeciduous
nondefamatory
nondefensive
nondeferable
nondeferential
nondeferrable
nondefilement
nondefining
nondefinitive
nondegeneration
nondehiscent
nondelineation
nondeliquescent
nondelirious
nondelivery
nondemand
nondemocratic
nondepartmental
nondeparture
nondependence
nondepletion
nondeportation
nondepositor
nondepreciating
nonderivable
nonderivative
nonderogatory
nondespotic
nondestructive
nondetachable
nondetonating
nondevelopable
nondevelopment
nondevotional
nondialectal
nondiatomaceous
nondichotomous
nondictatorial
nondidactic
nondifferentiable
nondifferentiation
nondiffractive
nondiffusing
nondilatable
nondiphtheritic
nondiplomatic
nondirectional
nondirigible
nondisappearing
nondischarging
nondisciplinary
nondiscontinuance
nondiscountable
nondiscovery
nondiscrimination
nondiscriminatory
nondisfranchised
nondisinterested
nondisparaging
nondisparate
nondispersion
nondisposal
nondisqualifying
nondissenting
nondistribution
nondistributive
nondivergence
nondivergent
nondiversification
nondivisibility
nondivisible
nondivision
nondivisional
nondoctrinal
nondocumentary
nondogmatic
nondomesticated
nondramatic
nondrying
nondutiable
nondynastic
nonearning
nonecclesiastical
noneclectic
noneconomic
nonedible
noneditorial
noneducable
noneducational
noneffective
noneffervescent
nonefficacious
nonefficacy
nonefficiency
nonefficient
non-Egyptian
nonelastic
nonelect
nonelection
nonelective
nonelectric
nonelectrical
nonelectrified
nonelementary
nonelimination
nonembryonic
nonemotional
nonemphatic
nonempirical
nonemulative
nonencyclopedic
nonendemic
nonenforceable
nonenforcement
non-English
nonentailed
nonenteric
nonephemeral
nonepicurean
nonepiscopal
nonepithelial
nonequal
nonequatorial
nonequilateral
nonequivalent
nonequivocating
nonerasure
nonerotic
nonerudite

2. Often **Nones** [orig. an error for NONE.] *Eccl.* One of the canonical hours, being the ninth hour (according to the ancient Roman and Eastern reckoning), or 3 P.M.; hence, an office recited, formerly at 3 P.M., but now in the Roman Catholic Church often somewhat earlier.

‖**non est** (nŏn ĕst). [L.] It is not; it is wanting.

none′such′ (nŭn′sŭch′), *n.* A person or thing that no other approaches in likeness; esp., a paragon.

non·fea′sance (nŏn-fē′zăns), *n. Law.* Omission to do something, esp. what ought to have been done.

non·fer′rous (-fĕr′ŭs), *adj.* Not containing, including, or pertaining to iron; relating to metals other than iron.

non·flam′ma·ble (nŏn-flăm′á·b'l), *adj.* Not flammable.

no·nil′lion (nō-nĭl′yŭn), *n. & adj.* [F., fr. L. *nonus* ninth, after *million.*] See NUMERATION, *Table.* — **no·nil′lionth** (-yŭnth), *n.*

non′in·duc′tive (nŏn′ĭn-dŭk′tĭv), *adj.* Not inductive, as an electrical resistance.

non′in·flam′ma·ble (-ĭn-flăm′á·b'l), *adj.* Not inflammable.

non′in·ter·ven′tion (nŏn′ĭn-tẽr-vĕn′shŭn), *n.* State or habit of not intervening; failure or refusal to intervene.

non·join′der (nŏn-join′dẽr), *n. Law.* The omission of some person who ought to have been made a party to a suit, or of some cause of action which ought to be joined.

non·ju′ror (nŏn-jŏŏr′ẽr), *n. Eng. Hist.* One who refused to take a certain oath (esp. of allegiance, supremacy, or abjuration); specif. [*often cap.*], one of those beneficed clergy in Great Britain who refused to take the oath of allegiance to William and Mary, or to their successors, after the revolution of 1688.

non′met′al (nŏn′mĕt′'l), *n. Chem.* An element not a metal; any of several elements, as carbon, phosphorus, nitrogen, oxygen, sulfur, bromine, etc., which do not form basic oxides or basic hydroxides.

non′me·tal′lic (nŏn′mě·tăl′ĭk), *adj.* **1.** Not metallic. **2.** *Chem.* Of, pert. to, or of the nature of a nonmetal.

non·mod′al (nŏn·mōd′ăl; -'l), *adj.* Not modal; specif., *Gram.,* not predicative, as gerunds and participles.

non·ni·trog′e·nous (nŏn′nī·trŏj′ē·nŭs), *adj.* Devoid of nitrogen; as, a *nonnitrogenous* principle.

‖**non ob·stan′te** (nŏn ŏb·stăn′tē). [L.] Notwithstanding.

non′pa·reil′ (nŏn′pá·rĕl′), *adj.* [F., fr. *non* not + *pareil* equal, fr. LL. dim. of L. *par* equal.] Having no equal; peerless. — *n.* **1.** Something of unequaled excellence; a paragon. **2.** The painted bun-

ting. **3.** [F. *nonpareille*.] *Print.* A size of type (6 point). See TYPE.

non·par′ous (nŏn·păr′ŭs), *adj.* Not having borne children.

non·par·tic′i·pat′ing (nŏn′pär·tĭs′ĭ·pāt′ĭng; nŏn′pĕr-), *adj.* See NON-; specif., *Insurance,* not participating, or giving the right to participate, in surplus or profit.

non·par′ti·san (nŏn·pär′tĭ·zăn), *adj.* Not partisan; of, pert. to, or consisting of persons appointed or elected without regard to political affiliations; not controlled by parties or party spirit or interests; as, a *nonpartisan* board.

non·pas′ser·ine (-păs′ẽr·ĭn; -ĭn), *adj. Zool.* Not passerine; — often designating esp. birds of the order Coraciiformes (see CORACIIFORM).

‖**non pla′cet** (nŏn plā′sĕt). [L.] It does not please; — used in giving a negative vote.

non′plus (nŏn′plŭs), *n.* [L. *non* not + *plus* more, further.] A state in which no more can be said or done, or which baffles reason or confounds judgment; quandary. — *v. t.;* -PLUSED (-plŭst) or -PLUSSED; -PLUS·ING or -PLUS·SING. To bring, put, reduce, etc., to a nonplus. — **Syn.** See PUZZLE.

‖**non pos′su·mus** (nŏn pŏs′ū·mŭs). [L.] Literally, we cannot; — used to express the impossibility of acting or moving in a matter.

non′pro·duc′tive (nŏn′prŏ·dŭk′tĭv), *adj.* Unproductive; also, not directly productive; — applied specif. to: **a** Labor not directly concerned with production, as clerks, inspectors, etc. **b** *Cost Accounting.* Sometimes, general or overhead expenditures. — **non′pro·duc′tive·ness,** *n.*

non′-pros′ (nŏn′prŏs′), *v. t.;* NON′-PROSSED (-prŏst′); NON′-PROS′SING. To enter a non prosequitur against.

‖**non pro·se′qui·tur** (nŏn prō·sĕk′wĭ·tẽr). [L., he does not prosecute.] *Law.* A judgment entered against the plaintiff in a suit where he does not appear to prosecute; — usually abbreviated to **non pros.** See NOLLE PROSEQUI.

non′rep·re·sen·ta′tion·al (nŏn′rĕp·rē·zĕn·tā′shŭn·ăl), *adj. Art.* Representing no recognizable object in nature; nonimitative. Cf. ABSTRACT, *adj.,* 4.

non·res′i·dence (nŏn·rĕz′ĭ·dĕns), *n.* Also **non·res′i·den·cy** (-dĕn·sĭ). State or fact of being nonresident.

non·res′i·dent (-dĕnt), *adj.* Not residing in a particular place, on one's own estate, or in one's proper place; absent from one's benefice, charge, or estate. — *n.* A nonresident person.

☞ See NON-, *Note.*

nonessential	nonflowering	nonindividual	nonmagnetizable	nonodorous	nonprehensile
nonesthetic	nonfluctuating	nonindividualistic	non-Magyar	nonoffensive	nonprejudicial
noneternal	nonflying	non-Indo-European	nonmaintenance	nonofficial	nonprepositional
nonethereal	nonfocal	nonindustrial	non-Malay	nonofficially	non-Presbyterian
nonethical	nonforfeitable	noninfallible	non-Malayan	nonoperating	nonprescriptive
nonethnological	nonforfeiting	noninfected	nonmalicious	nonoperative	nonpreservation
non-Euclidean	nonforfeiture	noninfection	nonmalignant	nonoptional	nonpresidential
noneugenic	nonformal	noninfectious	nonmalleable	nonorganic	nonprevalent
non-European	nonfortuitous	noninfinite	nonmarital	nonoriental	nonpriestly
nonevacuation	nonfossiliferous	noninflammatory	nonmaritime	nonorthodox	nonproducer
nonevanescent	nonfraudulent	noninflectional	nonmarriageable	nonoxidizable	nonproducing
nonevangelical	nonfreezing	noninformative	nonmarrying	nonoxidizing	nonprofane
nonevasive	non-French	noninheritable	nonmartial	nonoxygenated	nonprofessional
noneviction	nonfricative	noninjurious	nonmaterial	nonpacific	nonprofessorial
nonevolutionary	nonfulfillment	noninquiring	nonmaterialistic	nonpagan	nonproficiency
nonexcessive	nonfunctional	noninstructional	nonmateriality	nonpalatal	nonproficient
nonexchangeable	nonfundamental	noninstrumental	nonmaternal	nonpalatalization	nonprofit
nonexciting	nonganglionic	noninsurance	nonmathematical	nonpapal	nonprofiteering
nonexclusive	nongaseous	nonintellectual	nonmatrimonial	nonpapist	nonprogressive
nonexcusable	nongelatinous	nonintelligent	nonmechanical	nonpar	nonprohibitive
nonexecution	nongenealogical	noninterchangeable	nonmechanistic	nonparallel	nonprolific
nonexecutive	nongenerative	nonintercourse	nonmedicinal	nonparalytic	nonpromiscuous
nonexemplary	nongenetic	noninterference	nonmelodious	nonparasitic	nonprophetic
nonexempt	nongentile	noninterfering	nonmember	nonparental	nonpropitiation
nonexercise	non-German	nonintermittent	nonmercantile	nonparishioner	nonproportional
nonexistence	non-Germanic	noninternational	nonmetalliferous	nonparliamentary	nonproprietary
nonexistent	non-Government	noninterrupted	nonmetaphysical	nonparochial	nonproscriptive
nonexisting	nongovernmental	nonintersecting	nonmeteoric	nonparticipant	nonprotective
nonexotic	nongranular	nonintoxicant	nonmetropolitan	nonparticipation	non-Protestant
nonexpansive	non-Greek	nonintoxicating	nonmigratory	nonpartisanship	non-Prussian
nonexpansively	nongregarious	nonintrospective	nonmilitant	nonpathogenic	nonpsychic
nonexperienced	nonhabitable	nonintuitive	nonmilitary	nonpaying	nonpulmonary
nonexperimental	nonhabitual	noninverted	nonmimetic	nonpayment	nonpuncturable
nonexploitation	nonharmonious	noninvidious	nonmineral	nonpelagic	nonpunishable
nonexplosive	nonhazardous	noniodized	nonministerial	nonpenalized	nonpurulent
nonexportable	nonheading	nonionized	nonmiraculous	nonpensionable	nonputrescent
nonexportation	nonheathen	non-Irish	nonmischievous	nonperceptual	nonputrescible
nonextended	nonhedonistic	nonirradiated	nonmobile	nonperforated	nonracial
nonextensile	non-Hellenic	nonirrigable	non-Mohammedan	nonperforating	nonradiating
nonextension	nonhereditary	nonirrigated	non-Mongolian	nonperformance	nonradical
nonexternal	noninheritable	nonirrigating	nonmoral	nonperformer	nonratable
nonextinction	nonheritor	nonirrigation	non-Mormon	nonperforming	nonrated
nonextortion	non-Hibernian	nonirritant	nonmortal	nonperiodical	nonrational
nonextraditable	nonhistoric	nonirritating	non-Moslem	nonperishable	nonrationalized
nonextradition	nonhistorical	non-Islamic	nonmotile	nonperishing	nonreactive
nonextraneous	non-Homeric	non-Israelite	nonmunicipal	nonpermanent	nonreality
nonfacetious	nonhomogeneous	non-Italian	nonmuscular	nonpermeability	nonreasonable
nonfactual	nonhostile	non-Japanese	nonmystical	nonpermeable	nonreceiving
nonfading	nonhouseholder	non-Jew	nonmythical	nonpermissible	nonreciprocal
nonfanatical	nonhuman	non-Jewish	nonnational	nonperpendicular	nonreciprocating
nonfanciful	nonhumorous	nonjudicial	nonnative	nonperpetual	nonrecognition
non-Fascist	nonidentical	nonjurable	nonnautical	nonpersecution	nonrecourse
nonfastidious	nonidentity	nonjuristic	nonnaval	nonperseverance	nonrecoverable
nonfatal	nonidiomatic	nonlaminated	nonnavigable	nonpersistence	nonrecurrent
nonfatalistic	nonidolatrous	non-Latin	nonnegotiable	nonpersistent	nonrecurring
nonfederal	nonignitible	nonlegal	nonnegotiation	nonphilanthropic	nonrefillable
nonfederated	nonimaginary	nonlicensed	non-Negro	nonphilosophical	nonrefueling
nonfermentable	nonimitative	nonlicentiate	nonneutral	nonphysical	nonregenerating
nonfermentation	nonimmune	nonlimiting	Syn-Norman	nonphysiological	nonregenerative
nonfermentative	nonimmunity	nonliquefying	non-Norse	nonplanetary	nonregimented
nonfertile	nonimmunized	nonliquidating	nonnotional	nonplastic	nonregistered
nonfertility	nonimpairment	nonliquidation	nonnucleated	nonplausible	nonregistrable
nonfestive	nonimperative	nonliterary	nonnutrient	nonplutocratic	nonrelative
nonfeudal	nonimperial	nonlitigious	nonnutritious	nonpoetic	nonreligious
nonfiction	nonimportation	nonliturgical	nonnutritive	nonpoisonous	nonremission
nonfictional	nonimporting	nonliving	nonobedience	nonpolarizable	nonremunerative
nonfiduciary	nonimpregnated	nonlocal	nonobedient	non-Polish	nonrenewable
nonfigurative	nonincandescent	nonloving	nonobligatory	nonpolitical	nonrepatriable
nonfilamentous	noninclusive	nonluminescent	nonobservable	nonporous	nonrepayable
nonfimbriate	nonincrease	nonluminosity	nonobservance	non-Portuguese	nonrepentance
nonfinancial	nonindependent	nonluminous	nonobservant	nonpractical	nonrepetition
nonfireproof	non-Indian	nonlustrous	nonobstructive	nonpredatory	nonreprehensible
nonfiscal	nonindictable	non-Lutheran	nonoccupational	nonpredicative	nonrepresentative
nonfissile	nonindictment	nonmagnetic	nonoccurrence	nonpredictable	nonreproductive
					nonrequital

non′re·stric′tive (nŏn′rē·strĭk′tĭv), *adj.* Not restrictive; specif., *Gram.*, = DESCRIPTIVE, 2 **b**.

non·rig′id (nŏn·rĭj′ĭd), *adj.* Not rigid. See AIRSHIP.

‖**non sans droict** (nŏn′ sänz′ droit′). [OF.] Not without right; — motto on Shakespeare's coat of arms.

non′sense (nŏn′sĕns *or, esp. Brit.*, -sĕns; -s'ns), *n.* [*non-* + *sense.*] **1.** That which is not sense, or has no sense; words or language having no meaning; also, senseless action or behavior; absurdity. **2.** Trifles; things of no importance or value. **3.** Humbug; also, evasive treatment or conduct; as, to stand no *nonsense.* — **non·sen′si·cal** (nŏn·sĕn′sĭ-kăl), *adj.* — **non·sen′si·cal·ly**, *adv.*

‖**non se′qui·tur** (nŏn sĕk′wĭ·tẽr). [L., it does not follow.] *Logic.* An inference that does not follow from the premises; specif., any fallacy resulting from a simple conversion of a universal affirmative proposition or from the transposition of a condition and its consequent.

non′skid′ (nŏn′skĭd′; 2), **non′skid′ding** (nŏn′skĭd′ĭng), *adj.* Having the tread corrugated or otherwise specially constructed to resist skidding; — said esp. of automobile tires.

non·stand′ard (nŏn·stăn′dẽrd), *adj.* **1.** Not standard. **2.** *Ling.* = SUBSTANDARD **b**.

non′stop′ (nŏn′stŏp′; 2), *adj. & adv.* Without a stop.

non′such′ (nŭn′sŭch′). Var. of NONESUCH.

non′suit′ (nŏn′sūt′), *v. t.* **1.** *Law.* To determine, adjudge, or record (a plaintiff) as having terminated his suit by default or failure to establish a good cause of action. **2.** Hence, to deny the suit of. — *n. Law.* A judgment given against a plaintiff because of his failure to prosecute his case or his inability to establish a prima-facie case at the trial.

non′sup·port′ (nŏn′sŭ·pōrt′; 70), *n.* *Law.* Failure to provide maintenance on the part of one under obligation to provide such support.

‖**non trop′po** (nŏn trôp′pō). [It.] *Music.* Not excessively; — used in directions; as, ‖**non trop′po pre′sto** (prĕs′tō), not too fast.

non·un′ion (nŏn·ūn′yŭn), *n.* Lack of union; failure to unite; specif., *Med.*, failure of parts of a broken bone to knit.

non·un′ion, *adj.* **a** Not belonging to, or affiliated with, or according with the requirements of a union; as, *nonunion* carpenters, labor. **b** Not recognizing any union as representing the eligible employees and excluding union affiliates; as, a *nonunion* shop or plant.

non·un′ion·ism (-ĭz'm), *n.* The theories, opinions, or practices of those who do not support or favor trade-unions. — **non·un′ion·ist** (-ĭst), *n. & adj.*

noo′dle (nōō′d'l), *n.* *Slang.* = NODDLE, the head.

noo′dle (nōō′d'l), *n.* [Cf. NODDY.] A simpleton; blockhead.

noo′dle, *n.* [G. *nudel* vermicelli.] An alimentary paste, shaped in ribbon form, and usually made with egg.

nook (nŏŏk), *n.* [ME. *nok.*] A space formed by an angle; a corner; specif.: **a** *Now Chiefly Scot.* A corner of cloth, paper, etc. **b** A corner piece or angular portion of land. **c** An interior angle or corner formed by the meeting of two walls or the like. **d** A sheltered corner or place.

noon (nōōn), *n.* [AS. *nōn*, orig., the ninth hour, fr. L. *nona* (sc. *hora*) the ninth hour, or the church services (called *nones*) at that hour, later at noon.] **1.** The middle of the day; midday. **2. a** Midnight; — chiefly in *noon of night.* **b** *Poetic.* The moon's position in the sky at midnight. **3.** The highest point. — **noon**, *adj.*

noon′day′ (nōōn′dā′), *n. & adj.* Midday.

no one, *or* **no′-one′** (nō′wŭn′), *pron.* No person; nobody.

noon′ing (nōōn′ĭng), *n.* *Dial., U.S.* **a** Noontime. **b** A meal or drink taken at noon. **c** A midday intermission, as for food.

noon′tide′ (-tīd′), *n.* **1.** Noon; midday. **2.** Midnight; the moon's place at midnight. **3.** Highest or culminating point.

noon′time′ (-tīm′), *n.* Midday; noontide.

noose (nōōs), *n.* [Pr. *nous*, fr. L. *nodus.*] **1.** A loop with a running knot, as in a lasso, which binds closer the more it is drawn. **2.** Figuratively, a tie, bond, or snare. — *v. t.* **1.** To secure by or as by a noose; to entrap. **2.** To make a noose in or of; as, to *noose* a rope.

no′pal (nō′păl), *n.* [Sp., fr. Nahuatl *nopalli.*] **a** Any of a genus (*Nopalea*) of cacti. **b** Hence, any prickly pear.

no′-par′ (nō′pär′; 2), *adj.* Having no face value; as, *no-par* share; *no-par* value. Cf. PAR, 2.

nor (nôr; 4), *conj.* [ME., contr. fr. *nother.* See NEITHER.] Likewise not; and not; or not; — introducing the second (and each following) member of an alternative proposition or of a negative proposition expressing reciprocation, and indicating the continuation of the force of a negative.

nor (nôr), *conj.* *Dial.* Than.

nor′ (nôr). Also **nor.** Abbr. of *north*, esp. in compounds, as in **nor′′-east′, nor′′east′er, nor′′west′er.**

nor-. [From *nor*mal.] *Chem.* A prefix denoting: **a** A parent compound. **b** A normal compound.

Nor′dic (nôr′dĭk), *adj.* [NL. *nordicus* of the north.] Of or pertaining to the Germanic peoples of northern Europe, esp. the Scandinavians. — *n.* A Nordic individual.

Nor′folk jack′et *or* **coat** (nôr′fŭk). A loose-fitting, single-breasted jacket, box-plaited and belted.

no′ri·a (nō′rĭ·ȧ), *n.* [Sp., fr. Ar. *nā′ūrah.*] An undershot water wheel of the bucket type.

nor′land (nôr′lănd), *n.* [For *northland.*] [*often cap.*] *Chiefly Poetic.* The land in the north; north country.

norm (nôrm), *n.* [L. *norma* a rule.] **1.** A rule or authoritative standard; model; type; pattern. **2.** *Educ.* A set standard of development or achievement, usually the average or median achievement of a large group. — **Syn.** See AVERAGE.

nor′mal (nôr′măl), *adj.* [L. *normalis*, fr. *norma* rule, pattern, carpenter's square.] **1.** According to, constituting, or not deviating from, an established norm, rule, or principle; standard; regular; natural. **2.** *Biol., Immunol., etc.* **a** Unaffected by, or not exposed to, any particular infection or experimental treatment; as, a *normal* animal. **b** Occurring naturally. **3.** *Chem.* **a** *Anal. Chem.* Denoting a solution of such strength that one liter contains one gram atom of replaceable hydrogen or its equivalent. **b** *Physical Chem.* Not associated; as, *normal* molecules. **c** *Org. Chem.* Pertaining to or designating aliphatic hydrocarbons or hydrocarbon derivatives in which no carbon atom is united with more than two other carbon atoms. **4.** *Psychol.* **a** Of or indicating average intelligence or development. **b** Free from mental disorder; not insane or neurotic. — **Syn.** See REGULAR. — *n.* **1.** One who or that which is normal. **2.** The usual condition, degree, quantity, or the like; average; mean. **3.** *Geom.* **a** Any perpendicular; specif., a line or plane perpendicular to the tangent line (or plane) to a curve (or surface) at a point of the curve (or surface). **b** The intercept (on the normal line) between the curve and the *x* axis. — **nor′mal·ly**, *adv.* — **nor′mal·ness**, *n.*

nor′mal·cy (nôr′măl·sĭ), *n.* State, condition, or fact of being normal; normality; as, a return to *normalcy.*

nor·mal′i·ty (nôr·măl′ĭ·tĭ), *n.* Normal state or quality.

nor′mal·ize (nôr′măl·īz), *v. t.* To make normal; to make conform to, or reduce to, a norm or standard. — **nor′mal·i·za′tion** (-ĭ·zā′shŭn; -ī·zā′-), *n.* — **nor′mal·iz′er** (-īz′ẽr), *n.*

normal school. [After F. *école normale.*] A school offering a professional course for the training of persons, usually secondary-school graduates, to become teachers.

Nor′man (nôr′măn), *adj.* [OF. *normant* (F. *normand*); of Scand. origin.] Of or pertaining to Normandy or the Normans. — *n.* **1.** A native or inhabitant of Normandy; orig., one of the Northmen or Scandinavians who conquered Normandy in the 10th century; later, one of the mixed (Norman-French) race which, in 1066, conquered England. **2.** = NORMAN-FRENCH.

Norman architecture *or* **style.** **a** The peculiar type of Romanesque first appearing in and near Normandy about A.D. 950. **b** The Romanesque style as introduced, under Norman influence, into England.

Norman Conquest. The conquest of England by the Normans under Duke William (William I of Eng.), 1066.

Nor′man-French′, *adj.* Anglo-French. — *n.* The French language as used by the Normans; Anglo-French.

Nor′man·ize (nôr′măn·īz), *v. i. & t.* To render or become Norman, as in character. — **Nor′man·i·za′tion** (-ĭ·zā′shŭn; -ī·zā′-), *n.*

nor′ma·tive (nôr′mȧ·tĭv), *adj.* **1.** Relating to or establishing a norm. **2.** *Gram.* Concerned with norms or standards of usage; as, *normative* grammar.

nor′mo·ten′sive (nôr′mō·tĕn′sĭv), *adj.* *Med.* Characterized by normal blood pressure.

Norn (nôrn), *n.* [ON. *norn*, pl. *nornir.*] *Teut. Myth. & Folklore.* One of the demigoddesses or divine giantesses who preside over and determine the fates of men and gods.

Norse (nôrs), *adj.* [D. *Noorsch* Norwegian, fr. *noord* north.] **1.** Of or pertaining to ancient Scandinavia or the language of its inhabitants. **2.** Of or pertaining to Norway or the Norwegians. — *n.* **1.** Col-

---

☞ See NON-, *Note.*

nonresidential
nonresidual
nonresistance
nonresistant
nonresisting
nonresistive
nonresolvable
nonresonant
nonrespirable
nonrestraint
nonrestricted
nonretention
nonretentive
nonretinal
nonretiring
nonretraceable
nonretractile
nonretrenchment
nonretroactive
nonreturnable
nonrevealing
nonreversible
nonrevertible
nonreviewable
nonrevival
nonrevolting
nonrevolving
nonrhetorical
nonrhymed
nonrhyming
nonrhythmic
nonritualistic
nonrival
non-Roman
nonromantic
nonrotatable
nonrotating
nonroyal
nonruminant
nonrural
non-Russian
nonsacerdotal
nonsacramental
nonsacred
nonsacrificial
nonsalable
nonsalaried
nonsalutary
nonsaturated
non-Scandinavian
nonschismatic
nonscholastic
nonscientific
nonscoring
nonseasonal
nonsecret
nonsecretarial
nonsecretive
nonsecretory
nonsectarian
nonsectional
nonsecular
nonsedentary
nonseditious
nonsegmented
nonselective
non-Semite
non-Semitic
nonsenatorial
nonsensitive
nonsensitized
nonsensuous
nonsentient
nonserous
nonservile
non-Shakespearean
nonsharing
nonshatter
nonshrinkable
nonsiliceous
nonsilver
nonsimplification
nonsinkable
nonslaveholding
non-Slavic
nonsmoker
nonsmoking
nonsocial
nonsocialist
nonsocialistic
nonsolid
nonsolvent
nonsovereign
non-Spanish
nonsparing
non-Spartan
nonspecialized
nonspecific
nonspectacular
nonspectral
nonspeculative
nonspherical
nonspillable
nonspiritual
nonspirituous
nonspontaneous
nonsporting
nonspottable
nonstainable
nonstaining
nonstandardized
nonstarter
nonstarting
nonstatic
nonstationary
nonstatistical
nonstatutory
non-Stoic
nonstrategic
nonstretchable
nonstriated
nonstriker
nonstriking
nonstructural
nonsubmissive
nonsubscriber
nonsubscribing
nonsubstantial
nonsuccess
nonsuccessful
nonsuccessive
nonsuctorial
nonsulfurous
nonsupporter
nonsupporting
nonsuppurative
nonsustaining
non-Swedish
non-Swiss
nonsymbolic
nonsymmetrical
nonsympathetic
nonsympathizer
nonsymphonic
nonsymptomatic
nonsynchronous
nonsyntactic
nonsyntactical
nonsynthesized
nonsystematic
nontarnishable
nontaxability
nontaxable
nonteachable
nontechnical
nonteleological
nontemporal
nontemporizing
nonterrestrial
nonterritorial
nontestamentary
nontheatrical
nontheological
nontheosophical
nontherapeutic
nonthinking
nontitular
nontoxic
nontraditional
nontransferability
nontransferable
nontransitional
nontransparent
nontransposing
nontransposition
nontreasonable
nontributary
nontropical
nontuberculous
non-Turkish
non-Tuscan
nontypical
nontypographical
nontyrannical
nonubiquitous
nonulcerous
nonunderstandable
nonunderstanding
non-Unitarian
nonuniversal
non-Universalist
nonuniversity
nonuser
nonusing
nonuterine
nonutilitarian
nonutilized
nonvascular
nonvegetative
nonvenereal
nonvenomous
nonvenous
nonvernacular
nonvertical
nonvesicular
nonvibratory
nonvicarious
nonviolation
nonviolence
nonvirulent
nonviscous
nonvisiting
nonvisual
nonvisualized
nonvitreous
nonvocal
nonvocalic
nonvocational
nonvolatile
nonvolcanic
nonvoluntary
nonvortical
nonvoter
nonvoting
nonworker
nonworking
nonyielding

lectively: **a** Scandinavians. **b** Norwegians. **2.** The Scandinavian branch of Germanic; specif., the language of Norway. See OLD NORSE.
Norse'man (nôrs'măn), *n.* One of the ancient Scandinavians.
north (nôrth; *see note below*), *n.* [AS.] **1.** That one of the four cardinal points of the compass which lies in the plane of the true meridian, and on the left hand of a person facing due east; the direction opposite south. See COMPASS CARD, *Illust.* **2.** Any country or region north of another. **3.** [*cap.*] **a** That part of the United States lying in general north of Mason and Dixon's line and the Ohio River. **b** That part of Britain north of the Humber. **4.** *Poetic.* The north wind.
— *adj.* **1.** [*cap.*] Designating the northern division of a race or nation, the northern part of a country, etc.; as, *North* Germany. **2.** Northern; specif.: **a** Situated at or toward the north. **b** Proceeding or facing north. **c** Blowing or coming from the north.
— *adv.* To or toward, or in, the north; northward.
☞ In compounds, as *northeast, northwest*, etc., the pron. nôr-, chiefly nautical, is an accepted colloquialism.
North American, *adj.* Of or pertaining to North America or its people. — *n.* An inhabitant of North America.
north by east. *Navig. & Surv.* One point, or 11° 15′, east of due north; N. 11° 15′ E. See COMPASS CARD, *Illust.*
north by west. *Navig. & Surv.* One point, or 11° 15′, west of due north; N. 11° 15′ W. See COMPASS CARD, *Illust.*
north'east' (nôrth'ēst'; *see* NORTH), *n.* The point of the horizon or direction between the north and east; the northeast part or region. See COMPASS CARD, *Illust.* — *adj.* Of or pert. to the northeast; situated in or toward the northeast; proceeding northeast; blowing from northeast. — *adv.* Toward the northeast. — **north'east'ern**, *adj.* — **north'east'ward**, *adv., adj., & n.* — **north'east'ward·ly**, *adj. & adv.* — **north'east'wards**, *adv.*
northeast by east. *Navig. & Surv.* One point, or 11° 15′, east of due northeast; N. 56° 15′ E. See COMPASS CARD, *Illust.*
northeast by north. *Navig. & Surv.* One point, or 11° 15′, north of due northeast; N. 33° 45′ E. See COMPASS CARD, *Illust.*
north'east'er (-ēs'tẽr; *see* NORTH), *n.* A storm, strong wind, or gale, coming from the northeast.
north'east'er·ly, *adj.* Pertaining to, or situated toward, the northeast; of the wind, blowing from the northeast.
— *adv.* Toward or from the northeast.
north'er (nôr'thẽr), *n.* A north wind; specif., *Chiefly U. S.*, a sudden strong north wind over the Plains, or in Texas, or on the Gulf of Mexico and the western Caribbean Sea.
north'er·ly, *adj.* Of or pertaining to, or situated toward, the north; of the wind, blowing from the north. — *adv.* Toward the north. — **north'er·li·ness** (-lĭ·nĕs; -nĭs), *n.*
north'ern (nôr'thẽrn), *adj.* [AS. *northerne.*] **1.** Of, pertaining to, or living or originating in the north; being in the north. **2.** [*cap.*] *U. S.* Of or pertaining to the North (sense 3 **a**). **3.** Directed toward, or coming or blowing from, the north. — *n.* **a** A native or inhabitant of the north. **b** A north wind. — **north'ern·most**, *adj.*
Northern Cross. *Astron.* A cross formed by six stars in Cygnus.
Northern Crown. Corona Borealis.
north'ern·er (nôr'thẽr·nẽr), *n.* A native or inhabitant of the north, esp. [*cap.*], *U.S.*, of the North (sense 3 **a**).
northern lights. Aurora borealis.
Northern Spy. An American variety of yellowish-red winter apple.
north'ing (nôr'thĭng; -thĭng), *n.* **1.** *Surv. & Navig.* Difference of latitude to the north from the last preceding point of reckoning. **2.** *Astron.* North declination. See DECLINATION, 6.
north'land (nôrth'lănd), *n.* [AS. *northland.*] Land in the north; the north of a country, etc. — **north'land·er**, *n.*
North'man (-măn), *n.; pl.* -MEN (-mĕn). One of the inhabitants of the north of Europe; esp., a Norseman.
north'-north'east', north'-north'west', *adj.* Lying or leading to a direction or point halfway between north and northeast (northwest); blowing or coming from that direction. — *adv.* Toward or from a point in that direction. — *n.* A direction or point halfway between north and northeast (northwest); two points, or 22° 30′, east (west) of due north; N. 22° 30′ E. (W.). See COMPASS CARD, *Illust.*
North Pole. The northernmost point of the earth; the northern extremity of the earth's axis. Its zenith is the ***north pole of the heavens***, which is slightly more than 1°, or less than 2 moon breadths, from Polaris.
North Star. The star of the Northern Hemisphere toward which the axis of the earth points; the polestar. See URSA MINOR, *Illust.*
North·um'bri·an (nôr·thŭm'brĭ·ăn), *adj. & n.* from NORTHUMBERLAND, *Gaz.* — *n.* The modern English dialect of Northumberland.
North·um'bri·an, *adj. & n.* from NORTHUMBRIA, *Gaz.* — *n.* The Anglo-Saxon dialect spoken in Northumbria.
north'ward (nôrth'wẽrd; *naut.* nôr'thẽrd), *adv.* Toward the north. — *adj.* Situated, directed, looking, or extending northward. — *n.* The northward direction, point, or part. — **north'ward·ly**, *adj. & adv.* — **north'wards** (-wẽrdz), *adv.*
north'west' (nôrth'wĕst'; *see* NORTH), *n.* The point or direction halfway between the north and west; the northwest part or region. See COMPASS CARD, *Illust.* — *adj.* Of, pertaining to, or situated in or toward the northwest; proceeding toward the northwest; of the wind, blowing from the northwest. — *adv.* Toward, in, or from the northwest. — **north'west'ern**, *adj.* — **north'west'ward**, *adv., adj., & n.* — **north'west'ward·ly**, *adj. & adv.* — **north'west'wards**, *adv.*
northwest by north. *Navig. & Surv.* One point, or 11° 15′, north of due northwest; N. 33° 45′ W. See COMPASS CARD, *Illust.*
northwest by west. *Navig. & Surv.* One point, or 11° 15′, west of due northwest; N. 56° 15′ W. See COMPASS CARD, *Illust.*
north'west'er (-wĕs'tẽr; *see* NORTH), *n.* A storm or gale from the northwest; a strong northwest wind.
north'west'er·ly, *adj.* That is toward the northwest; blowing from the northwest. — **north'west'er·ly**, *adv.*
Nor·we'gian (nôr·wē'jăn), *adj.* Of or pertaining to Norway, its inhabitants, or its language. — *n.* **1.** A native or inhabitant of Norway. **2.** The Scandinavian language of the Norwegians, closely resembling the Danish. See INDO-EUROPEAN LANGUAGES, *Table.*
nose (nōz), *n.* [AS. *nosu.*] **1.** In man, the part of the face which bears the nostrils. **2.** This part regarded as an organ, as of smell. **3.** Sense or faculty of smelling; hence, scent. **4.** Something suggestive of, or associated with, the nose, as a projecting point, edge, etc., at the front of an object; nozzle; spout. **5.** *Slang, Eng.* An informer; a spy, as of the police. **6.** *Aeronautics.* The forward end of an aircraft. **7.** *Anat. & Zool.* The olfactory organ of vertebrates. **8.** *Naut.* The stem; the piece protecting the stem. — *v. t.* **1.** To smell or scent; hence, to detect by or as by smell; to scent. **2.** To touch or rub with the nose. **3.** To make by advancing the nose or front end; as, the train *nosed* its way into the station. — *v. i.* **1.** To use the nose in smelling or examining; to smell; to sniff. **2.** To pry or search, esp. into what does not concern one. **3.** To push or move with the nose or front forward. **4.** *Thieves' Slang.* To act as an informer.
nose bag. A bag, fastening on top of the head and fitting over nose and mouth, for feeding grain, mash, etc., to a horse or other animal.
nose'band' (nōz'bănd'), *n.* That part of the headstall which passes over a horse's nose. — **nose'band'ed**, *adj.*
nose'bleed' (-blēd'), *n.* Bleeding at the nose; epistaxis.
nose dive. A head-on dive in an airplane; hence, a sharp sudden drop, as in security prices. — **nose'-dive'**, *v. i.*
nose'gay' (nōz'gā'), *n.* [*nose* + *gay* in the sense of a gay or showy thing.] A bunch of flowers or herbs; posy.
nose'piece' (-pēs'), *n.* **1.** A piece of armor, a covering, etc., for the nose (see HELMET, *Illust.*); also, a piece like or forming a nose. **2.** The nozzle of a hose, pipe, bellows, etc.
nose'y (nōz'ĭ). Var. of NOSY.
no'-show' (nō'shō'), *n.* A passenger who, after reserving space on an airplane, fails to show up to claim it and has made no cancellation.
nos'ing (nōz'ĭng), *n.* That part of the tread of a stair which projects over the riser, or any like projection.
nos'o- (nŏs'ō-), **nos-**. [Gr. *nosos.*] A combining form meaning *disease*, as in **no·sog'ra·phy**, a description of diseases.
no·sol'o·gy (nō·sŏl'ō·jĭ), *n.* [*noso-* + *-logy.*] *Med.* **a** A classification, or list, of diseases. **b** The science which treats of diseases, or of the classification of diseases. **c** Diagnostic character of a disease. — **nos'o·log'i·cal** (nŏs'ō·lŏj'ĭ·kăl), *adj.* — **no·sol'o·gist** (nō·sŏl'ō·jĭst), *n.*
nos·tal'gi·a (nŏs·tăl'jĭ·ȧ; -jȧ), *n.* [NL., fr. Gr. *nostos* a return home + *-algia.*] **1. a** Orig., *Med.*, a severe melancholia caused by protracted absence from home, as of military recruits. **b** Homesickness; esp., a brooding or poignant, enervating homesickness. **2.** Any wistful or excessively sentimental, sometimes morbid, yearning for return to or of some past period or irrecoverable condition. — **nos·tal'gic** (-jĭk), *adj.*
nos'toc (nŏs'tŏk), *n.* [NL. Coined by Paracelsus.] *Bot.* Any blue-green alga of the genus *Nostoc*, found in moist places and made up of filaments united into a jellylike spherical or lobed colony.
nos·tol'o·gy (nŏs·tŏl'ō·jĭ), *n.* [Gr. *nostos* a return home + *-logy.*] *Biol.* The study of the senile stages of an organism or race of organisms. — **nos'to·log'ic** (nŏs'tō·lŏj'ĭk), *adj.*
Nos'tra·da'mus (nŏs'trȧ·dā'mŭs), *n.* A prophet; seer; — from *Nostradamus* (1503–1566), a French astrologer.
nos'tril (nŏs'trĭl), *n.* [AS. *nosthyrl*, fr. *nos* for *nosu* nose + *thyrel* opening, hole.] An external opening of the nose.
nos'trum (nŏs'trŭm), *n.* [Neut. sing. of L. *noster* our.] **1.** A medicine recommended by its preparer; esp., a quack medicine. **2.** A favorite remedy, as a scheme proposed to allay some social unrest.
nos'y (nōz'ĭ), *adj.;* NOS'I·ER (-ĭ·ẽr); NOS'I·EST. *Colloq.* Given to nosing; inquisitive.
nos'y, *or* **nose'y, Par'ker** (nōz'ĭ pär'kẽr). *Colloq., Brit.* A prying or offensively inquisitive person.
not (nŏt; 4), *adv.* [ME. *not, noht, nought*, the same word as E. NOUGHT.] An adverbial particle expressing negation.
not-. = NOTO- (which see).
‖**no'ta be'ne** (nō'tȧ bē'nē). [L.] Note particularly; take notice. Abbr. *N. B.*
no'ta·bil'i·ty (nō'tȧ·bĭl'ĭ·tĭ), *n.; pl.* -TIES (-tĭz). **1.** A person of note. **2.** Quality of being notable.
no'ta·ble (nō'tȧ·b'l), *adj.* [OF., fr. L. *notabilis*, fr. *notare* to mark.] **1.** Worthy of note or notice; remarkable; distinguished. **2.** (*the older pron.* nŏt'ȧ·b'l *for this sense is still usual among those who observe the distinction in meaning*) Efficient; capable; — of women and in reference to household management. — *n.* **1.** A person of note or distinction. **2.** [*cap.*] *Fr. Hist.* One of a number of persons, chiefly of the higher orders, summoned by the king in emergencies as a deliberative body. — **no'ta·ble·ness**, *n.* — **no'ta·bly**, *adv.*
no·tar'i·al (nō·târ'ĭ·ăl; 6), *adj.* Of, pert. to, or characteristic of a notary; done, executed, etc., by a notary.
no'ta·rize (nō'tȧ·rīz), *v. t.* To acknowledge or attest (a document) as a notary public.
no'ta·ry (nō'tȧ·rĭ), *n.; pl.* -RIES (-rĭz). [L. *notarius* a shorthand writer, fr. *notare* to note.] *Law.* A public officer who attests or certifies deeds and other writings to make them authentic, and takes affidavits, depositions, and protests of negotiable paper; — generally called a **notary public** (*pl.* NOTARIES PUBLIC).
no·ta'tion (nō·tā'shŭn), *n.* [L. *notatio* a marking, etymology, fr. *notare* to mark, fr. *nota* mark.] **1.** Act, process, or method of representing by a system or set of marks, signs, figures, or characters; also, any system of symbols or abbreviated expressions used in an art or science to express technical facts, quantities, etc.; as, musical *notation;* mathematical *notation.* **2.** Act of noting; observation; also, an annotation; note. — **no·ta'tion·al** (-ăl; -'l), *adj.*
notch (nŏch), *n.* **1.** A V-shaped indentation; a nick, as one cut in a tally stick. **2.** *U. S.* A deep, close pass; a defile; gap. **3.** *Colloq.* Figuratively, a degree; step; peg. — *v. t.* To cut or make a notch or notches in; also, to score, mark, record, or tally by or as if by notches.
note (nōt), *n.* [OF., fr. L. *nota* a mark, sign.] **1.** A mark by which a thing may be known; distinctive mark or feature. **2.** A musical sound; as: **a** A melody; tune. **b** The musical call of a bird. **c** A tone of definite pitch, as of a musical instrument or the voice. **3.** A cry, call, or sound; as, the raven's *note.* **4.** A sign or character, excluding letters, used in printing or writing, as ! (**note of exclamation**) or ? (**note of interrogation**). **5.** Reputation; distinction; as, a family of *note.* **6. a** A memorandum. **b** Usually in *pl.*, a record of impressions, incidents, etc. **7.** A comment or explanation, as in the margin of a page. **8.** Observation; notice; heed; as, take no *note* of it. **9.** A written communication; specif.: **a** A short informal letter. **b** A list of items. **c** A written or printed paper acknowledging a debt, and promising payment; as, a promissory *note;* a bank *note;* a treasury *note* (*note* often being used alone for any such phrase). Cf. 3d BILL, *n.*, 6 **b**. **d** A formal diplomatic or official missive. **10.** Notification; information. **11.** *Music.* **a** A character indicating the relative duration of a tone by its

shape, and the pitch by its position on the staff. See BREVE, *n.*, 4; PITCH, *Illust.*; cf. REST, *Illust.* The notes in present general use are:

whole note, or *semibreve,*	𝅝;	*half note,* or *minim,*	𝅗𝅥;
quarter note, or *crotchet,*	♩;	*eighth note,* or *quaver,*	♪;
sixteenth note, or *semiquaver,*	𝅘𝅥𝅯;	*thirty-second note,* or *demisemiquaver,*	𝅘𝅥𝅰;
sixty-fourth note, or *hemidemisemiquaver,*	𝅘𝅥𝅱.		

b Inaccurately, a key of a pianoforte or similar instrument. — **Syn.** See SIGN.

— *v. t.* **1.** To notice or observe with care; to observe; heed. **2.** To make a special mention of. **3.** To record or set (down) in writing; to make a note of. — **not′er** (nōt′ẽr), *n.*

note′book′ (nōt′bo͝ok′), *n.* **1.** A book for memoranda. **2.** A book in which promissory notes are registered.

note′case′ (-kās′), *n. Brit.* A billfold.

not′ed (nōt′ĕd; -ĭd), *adj.* Specially marked; hence, well known by reputation; eminent; celebrated. — **Syn.** See FAMOUS. — **not′ed·ly,** *adv.* — **not′ed·ness,** *n.*

note′less (nōt′lĕs; -lĭs), *adj.* **1.** Not noted or not noticed; undistinguished. **2.** Unmusical; voiceless.

note of hand. A promissory note.

note paper. Paper for social notes.

note′wor′thy (nōt′wûr′thĭ), *adj.* Worthy of observation or notice; remarkable. — **note′wor′thi·ly** (-thĭ·lĭ), *adv.*

noth′ing (nŭth′ĭng), *n.* [From *no*, adj. + *thing*.] **1.** Not any thing; nought; — opposed to *anything* and *something*. **2.** That which does not exist; a nonentity. **3.** A thing, event, or remark of no account, value, note, or the like. **4.** *Arith.* Absence of all magnitude or quantity; a zero. — *adv.* In no degree; not at all; in no wise.

noth′ing·ness, *n.* **1.** Quality or state of being nothing; as: **a** Nonexistence. **b** Utter insignificance. **c** Unconsciousness. **2.** A thing that is, or is as if, nonexistent or valueless.

no′tice (nō′tĭs), *n.* [F., fr. L. *notitia* a being known, knowledge, fr. *notus* known, fr. *noscere* to know.] **1.** Information, esp. of a formal nature; announcement. **2.** Notification by one of the parties to an agreement or relation of intention of terminating it at a specified time. **3.** Act of remarking or observing; observation; heed. **4.** Polite or favorable attention; favor; civility. **5.** A written or printed sign, or the like, communicating information or warning. **6.** An announcement or written mention. — *v. t.*; -TICED (-tĭst); -TIC·ING (-tĭs·ĭng). **1.** To make mention of; remark upon; also, to review briefly, as a book. **2.** To take notice or note of; to observe; pay attention to. **3.** To give a formal notice to; to serve a notice on, as a tenant.

no′tice·a·ble (-*ȧ*·b'l), *adj.* Capable of being observed; worthy of notice; conspicuous. — **no′tice·a·bly,** *adv.*

Syn. **Noticeable, remarkable, prominent, outstanding, conspicuous, salient, signal, striking** mean attracting notice or attention. **Noticeable** implies an inability to escape attention; **remarkable,** a demanding attention; **prominent,** noticeability because of protuberance (literally or figuratively); **outstanding,** remarkability because of comparison with others of the kind; **conspicuous,** an obviousness or patency to the sight or mind; **salient,** an emphatic quality that thrusts itself into attention; **signal,** remarkability because of its unusual or extraordinary character; **striking,** a character that deeply impresses itself on mind or vision.

no′ti·fi·ca′tion (nō′tĭ·fĭ·kā′shŭn), *n.* **1.** A notifying; an intimation or notice. **2.** A written or printed matter which gives notice.

no′ti·fy (nō′tĭ·fī), *v. t.*; NO′TI·FIED (-fīd); NO′TI·FY′ING. [OF. *notifier*, fr. L. *notificare*, fr. *notus* known + *-ficare* (in comp.) to make.] **1.** To give notice of; to make known; as, to *notify* a fact to a person. **2.** To give notice to; to inform. — **Syn.** See INFORM. — **no′ti·fi′er** (-fī′ẽr), *n.*

no′tion (nō′shŭn), *n.* [L. *notio*, fr. *noscere*, *notum*, to know.] **1.** A mental apprehension of whatever may be known or imagined; an idea; a conception; properly, a general conception. **2.** A theory, belief, or opinion. **3.** An inclination; whim; as, a *notion* to do it. **4.** *Colloq.* An ingenious device; knickknack; any of various small useful articles. — **Syn.** See IDEA.

no′tion·al (-*ă*l; -'l), *adj.* **1.** Consisting of, or conveying, ideas; expressing abstract conceptions; as, the *notional* sciences. **2.** Existing in idea only; imaginary; unreal. **3.** *U. S.* Given to foolish or visionary fancies or moods. **4.** *Gram.* Carrying a full meaning of its own. Cf. RELATIONAL, 3. — **no′tion·al·ly,** *adv.*

no′to- (nō′tō-), **not-.** [Gr. *nōton*.] A combining form, meaning *the back, the back part*, as in *noto*chord.

no′to·chord (-kôrd), *n.* [*noto-* + *chord*.] *Anat. & Zool.* A longitudinal elastic rod of cells which in the lowest vertebrates (as amphiorus and the lampreys), and in the embryos of the higher vertebrates, forms the supporting axis of the body. It represents the backbone of higher forms.

no′to·ri′e·ty (nō′tō·rī′ĕ·tĭ), *n.*; *pl.* -TIES (-tĭz). **1.** Quality or state of being notorious. **2.** A well-known person.

no·to′ri·ous (nō·tō′rĭ·*ŭ*s; 70), *adj.* [ML. *notorius*, fr. *notus* known.] Generally known and talked of; widely known; — now usually unfavorable in sense. — **Syn.** See FAMOUS. — **no·to′ri·ous·ly,** *adv.* — **no·to′ri·ous·ness,** *n.*

no·tor′nis (nō·tôr′nĭs), *n.* [NL., fr. Gr. *notos* the south + *ornis* bird.] *Zool.* Any of a genus (*Notornis*) of flightless birds allied to the gallinules.

no′-trump′, *adj.* Without trumps; *Bridge*, denoting a declaration to play, or a hand suitable to play, without any suit being trumps. — *n.* At bridge, play or a declaration to play without any suit being trumps.

no′-trump′er, *n. Bridge.* A no-trump hand.

no·tun′gu·late (nō·tŭng′gū·lāt), *adj. Paleontol.* Belonging to an order (Notungulata) of extinct herbivorous mammals. — **no·tun′gu·late,** *n.*

not′with·stand′ing (nŏt′wĭth·stăn′dĭng; -wĭth-), *prep.* In spite of. — *adv.* Nevertheless; however; yet. — *conj.* Also **notwithstanding that.** Although.

nou′gat (no͞o′găt; no͞o′gä), *n.* [F., fr. Pr. *nogat*, fr. *noga* nut, fr. L. *nux*.] A candy made usually with almonds, pistachio, or other nuts, stirred into a sugar paste.

nought (nôt), *n.* [AS. *nāwiht*, *nōwiht*, fr. *ne* not + *ā* ever + *wiht* thing, whit; hence, not ever a whit.] **1.** Nothing; naught. **2.** A worthless thing or person. **3.** = NAUGHT, 1. — *adj.* Of no account; bad; useless; also, *Obs.*, harmful. — *adv. Archaic.* Not at all.

nou′me·non (no͞o′mē·nŏn; nou′-), *n.*; *pl.* -NA (-n*ȧ*). [NL., fr. Gr. *nooumenon* thing perceived, passive pres. part. of *noein* to perceive.] *Metaph.* An object of purely rational apprehension; specif., with Kant, a nonempirical concept; — opp. to *phenomenon* (sense 1). — **nou′me·nal** (-n*ă*l; -n'l), *adj.* — **nou′me·nal·ism** (-ĭz'm), *n.*

noun (noun), *n.* [OF. *nun, non, nom* (F. *nom*), fr. L. *nomen* name.] *Gram.* A word that is the name of a subject of discourse, as a person, place, thing, quality, idea, action. A ***common noun*** is one that names any of a class of beings or things or, specif. in English, in a classification based on form, one that may take a limiting modifier (*man, whip, American*); one that names a group of beings or things of the same kind (*jury, flock*) is usually called a ***collective noun***; one that names a quality, activity, or state considered apart from any particular being or thing (*weight, belief, peace*) is usually called an ***abstract noun.*** Abstract nouns may form plurals having the concrete meaning of *acts* or *instances* of the quality or state named (*falsities*, acts or instances of falsity). A ***proper noun*** is one that names a particular being or thing or, specif. in English, in a classification based on form, one that does not regularly take a limiting modifier (*Shakespeare, America*) or one that regularly takes *the* (the *Mississippi*, a river; the *Missouri*, a battleship). Abbr. *n.* See PART OF SPEECH; FORM CLASS. — **noun, noun′al** (-*ă*l; -'l), *adj.* — **noun′al·ly,** *adv.*

nour′ish (nûr′ĭsh), *v. t.* [OF. *nurir, norir*, fr. L. *nutrire*.] To furnish or sustain with nutriment; to feed; foster; maintain; support. — **nour′ish·er,** *n.*

nour′ish·ing, *adj.* Nutritious. — **nour′ish·ing·ly,** *adv.*

nour′ish·ment (-mĕnt), *n.* **1.** Act of nourishing, or state of being nourished. **2.** That which nourishes; nutriment. — **Syn.** See FOOD.

nous (no͞os; nous), *n.* [Gr. *nous, noos*, mind.] *Philos.* Mind, esp. the mind as rational; the reason; the highest intellect; God regarded as the World Reason.

‖**nou′veau′ riche′** (no͞o′vō′ rēsh′); *pl.* NOUVEAUX RICHES (no͞o′vō′ rēsh′). [F.] A person newly rich; a parvenu.

‖**nou′veau′té′** (no͞o′vō′tā′), *n.* [F.] Something new; — in commercial use, in *pl.* form **nou′veau′tés′** (-tā′; *Angl.* -tāz′), novelties.

no′va (nō′v*ȧ*), *n.*; *pl.* NOVAE (-vē), NOVAS (-v*ȧ*z). [L., fem. sing. of *novus* new.] A star which suddenly increases its light and energy output tremendously, and then sinks back to relative obscurity.

No′va·chord (nō′v*ȧ*·kôrd), *n.* A trade-mark for a polyphonic pianolike musical instrument electrically producing and controlling by means of vacuum tubes musical tones ranging in quality from those of the piano and organ to those of stringed and woodwind instruments, — invented by Laurens Hammond.

no·vac′u·lite (nō·văk′ū·līt), *n.* [L. *novacula* a sharp knife, razor.] *Petrog.* A hard, fine-grained siliceous rock used for whetstones. It is thought to be of sedimentary origin.

no·va′tion (nō·vā′shŭn), *n.* **1.** *Now Rare.* Innovation. **2.** *Law.* Substitution of a new obligation for an old one.

nov′el (nŏv′ĕl; -'l), *adj.* [OF. (F. *nouvel, nouveau*), fr. L. *novellus*, dim. of *novus* new.] New; not formerly known; of a new kind; hence, unusual; strange. — **Syn.** See NEW. — *n.* **1.** [It. *novella*.] A novella; — usually in *pl.* **2.** [F. *nouvelle* a short story, or It. *novella*.] A fictitious prose tale of considerable length, in which characters and actions professing to represent those of real life are portrayed in a plot; also, now generically with *the*, the type of prose fiction constituted or exemplified by such tales. **3.** *pl.* [*cap.*] *Rom. Law.* Certain statutes of Justinian subsequent to the Justinian Code, now the fourth part of the Corpus Juris Civilis.

nov′el·ette′ (nŏv′ĕl·ĕt′), *n.* A short novel.

nov′el·ist (nŏv′ĕl·ĭst; nŏv′'l-), *n.* A writer of novels.

nov′el·ize (-īz), *v. t.* To put into the form of a novel. — **nov′el·i·za′tion** (-ĭ·zā′shŭn; -ī·zā′-), *n.*

‖**no·vel′la** (nō·vĕl′lä), *n.*; *pl.* NOVELLE (-lā). [It.] A tale, narrative, or story, with a compact plot and a point. The stories of Boccaccio's *Decameron* are typical novelle.

nov′el·ty (nŏv′'l·tĭ), *n.*; *pl.* -TIES (-tĭz). [OF. *novelté*, fr. L. *novellitas*.] **1.** Quality or state of being novel; newness. **2.** Something novel; an innovation. **3.** *Chiefly pl.* In the trade, any of a group of small manufactured articles used largely in personal or household adornment.

No·vem′ber (nō·vĕm′bẽr), *n.* [L. *November*, or *Novembris* (sc. *mensis*), the ninth month of the old Roman year, fr. *novem* nine.] The eleventh month of the year, having 30 days. Abbr. *Nov.*

no′vem·de·cil′lion (nō′vĕm·dē·sĭl′yŭn), *n.* See NUMERATION, *Table.*

no·ve′na (nō·vē′n*ȧ*), *n.*; *pl.* -NAE (-nē). [ML., fr. L. *novem* nine.] *R.C.Ch.* A nine days' devotion for any religious object.

no·ver′cal (nō·vûr′k*ă*l), *adj.* [L. *novercalis*, fr. *noverca* a stepmother.] Pert. to, or like or suitable to, a stepmother.

nov′ice (nŏv′ĭs), *n.* [OF., fr. L. *novicius, novitius*, new, fr. *novus* new.] **1.** *Eccl.* One who has entered a religious house and is on probation. **2.** One newly received into the church, or one newly converted to the Christian faith. **3.** A beginner; tyro. — **nov′ice·hood,** *n.*

no·vi′ti·ate, no·vi′ci·ate (nō·vĭsh′ĭ·āt), *n.* [ML. *novitiatus*.] **1.** *Eccl.* State or time of being a novice; apprenticeship; a place where novices are trained. **2.** A novice (in senses 1 and 3).

No′vo·cain (nō′vō·kān), *n. Pharm.* A trade-mark applied to the local anesthetic procaine.

‖**no′vus or′do se·clo′rum** (nō′vŭs ôr′dō sē·klō′rŭm). [L.] A new order of the ages; — a motto on the reverse of the Great Seal of the United States and appearing on the Federal $1.00 silver certificates of 1935. It was adapted from Vergil, *Eclogues* IV. 5, in reference to the beginning of a new American era.

now (nou), *adv.* [AS. *nū*.] **1.** At the present time; also, in or under the present circumstances. **2.** Hence: **a** In the time immediately to follow; forthwith. **b** Very lately; a moment ago. **c** At the time spoken of or referred to; as, peace *now* ensued. **3.** With the sense of present time weakened or lost, simply marking transition of thought; as, come *now*, we must plan. — *conj.* Since, at, or by this time; seeing that; — often with *that*; as, *now* that the snow was melting. — *n.* The present time or moment; the present. — *interj.* An exclamation of admonition. — **now and then** (*or* **again**). At one time and another.

now′a·days′ (nou′*ȧ*·dāz′), *adv.* [*now* + *a*, prep. + *day* + *-s*. See 2d -s.] In these days; at the present time.

no′way (nō′wā), **no′ways** (-wāz), *adv.* Nowise. See -WAYS.

now·el′ (nō·ĕl′; nō′ĕl), *n.* [See NOEL.] *Archaic.* Noel.

no′where (nō′hwâr), *adv.* [AS. *nāhwǣr.*] Not anywhere; not in, to, or at any place. — **no′where,** *n.*
no′wheres (-hwârz), *adv. Dial., U. S.* Nowhere.
no′whith′er (nō′hwĭth′ẽr), *adv.* [*no,* adv. + *whither;* AS. *nāhwider.*] To or toward no place; nowhere.
no′wise (-wīz), *adv.* In no manner or degree; not at all.
nowt (nout), *n. Scot.* **a** *pl.* Neat cattle. **b** An ox.
Nox (nŏks), *n.* [L.] *Rom. Myth.* Goddess of night.
nox′ious (nŏk′shŭs), *adj.* [L. *noxius,* fr. *noxa* harm.] Hurtful; unwholesome; also, corrupting to morals. — **Syn.** See PERNICIOUS. — **nox′ious·ly,** *adv.* — **nox′ious·ness,** *n.*
no·yade′ (nwä·yäd′; *F.* nwȧ′yȧd′), *n.* [F., fr. *noyer* to drown, fr. L. *necare* to kill.] Drowning; specif. [*usually cap.*], a drowning of many persons at once, as at Nantes during the Reign of Terror. — **no·yade′** (nwä·yäd′), *v. t.*
noz′zle (nŏz′'l), *n.* [Dim. of NOSE.] **1.** The projecting vent of anything; a small spout, as of a hose, pipe, teapot, etc. **2.** *Slang.* The nose; the snout.

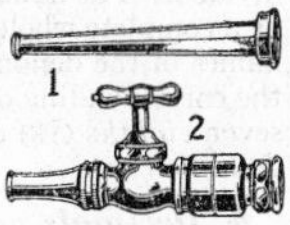

1 Ordinary Nozzle; 2 Chemical Engine Nozzle.

nth (ĕnth), *adj.* Denoting an ordinal corresponding to *n.* Hence, of any required size; indefinitely large or little.
nth degree. *Math.* An indefinite power. — ***to the nth degree.*** To an extreme.
nu (nū; nü), *n.* [Gr. *ny.*] The thirteenth letter (Ν, ν) of the Greek alphabet, equivalent to English *n.*
nu·ance′ (nū·äns′, nū′äns; *F.* nü′äɴs′), *n.; pl.* NUANCES (nū·än′sĕz, -sĭz; *F.* nü′äɴs′). [F.] A shade of difference; a delicate gradation; a subtle variation.
nub (nŭb), *n.* **1.** A knob or knot; a lump. **2.** *Colloq., U. S.* The point or gist, as of a story.
nub′bin (nŭb′ĭn), *n.* [From NUB.] *Chiefly U. S.* **a** Any small or imperfect ear of Indian corn. **b** Any small projecting bit.
nub′ble (nŭb′'l), *n.* [Dim. of NUB.] A small knob or lump.
nub′bly (nŭb′lĭ), *adj.* Having or like nubbles; knobby.
nu′bile (nū′bĭl), *adj.* [F. or L.; F., fr. L. *nubilis,* fr. *nubere* to marry.] Marriageable; — used esp. of age. — **nu·bil′i·ty** (nū·bĭl′ĭ·tĭ), *n.*
nu′bi·lous (nū′bĭ·lŭs), *adj.* [L. *nubilus,* fr. *nubes* cloud.] Cloudy; foggy; misty; figuratively, obscure; vague.
nu·cel′lus (nū·sĕl′ŭs), *n.; pl.* -LI (-ī). [NL., fr. L. *nucella,* dim. of *nux, nucis,* a nut.] *Bot.* The central and chief part of the body of an ovule, containing the embryo sac. — **nu·cel′lar** (-ẽr), *adj.*
nu′cha (nū′kȧ), *n.; pl.* NUCHAE (-kē). [ML., fr. Ar. *nukhā'* spinal marrow.] Nape of the neck. — **nu′chal** (-kăl), *adj.*
nuci-. [L. *nux, nucis.*] A combining form meaning *nut,* as in **nu·cif′er·ous** (nū·sĭf′ẽr·ŭs), **nu′ci·form** (nū′sĭ·fôrm).
nu′cle·ar (nū′klē·ẽr), *adj.* Of, pertaining to, constituting, or like a nucleus; as, *nuclear* membrane (see CELL, 4, *Illust.*); specif., *Chem. & Physics,* of or pert. to: (1) the atomic nucleus; as, *nuclear* physics; (2) atomic energy; as, *nuclear* power.
nuclear energy. = ATOMIC ENERGY.
nuclear fission. *Chem. & Physics.* = FISSION, 3.
nuclear physics. The branch of physics that deals with the atomic nucleus.
nu′cle·ase (nū′klē·ās), *n.* [*nuclein* + *-ase.*] *Biochem.* Any of the enzymes found in plants and animals that accelerate hydrolysis of nucleins and nucleic acids.
nu′cle·ate (nū′klē·āt), *adj.* [L. *nucleatus* having a kernel.] Nucleated. — (-āt), *v. t. & i.* To form (into), or gather as, a nucleus. — **nu′cle·a′tion** (-ā′shŭn), *n.* — **nu′cle·a′tor** (-ā′tẽr), *n.*
nu·cle′ic ac′id (nū·klē′ĭk). *Biochem.* Any of a group of acids, combinations of a sugar or a derivative of a sugar with phosphoric acid and a base, found in nuclear material.
nu′cle·in (nū′klē·ĭn), *n. Biochem.* Any of a group of amorphous substances obtained from cell nuclei, composed of mixtures of nucleic acid and proteins rich in phosphorus.
nu·cle′o·lar (nū·klē′ō·lẽr), *adj. Biol.* Of or pertaining to, or of the nature of, a nucleolus.
nu′cle·o·lat′ed (nū′klē·ō·lāt′ĕd; -ĭd), *adj.* Also **nu′cle·o·late** (-lāt). Having a nucleolus or nucleoli.
nu′cle·ole (nū′klē·ōl), *n.* A nucleolus.
nu·cle′o·lus (nū·klē′ō·lŭs), *n.; pl.* -LI (-lī). [LL., a little nut.] A comparatively large and conspicuous and usually rounded body, found in the nucleus of most cells. See CELL, 4, *Illust.;* OVUM, *Illust.*
nu′cle·on (nū′klē·ŏn), *n.* [From *nucleus.*] *Physics & Chem.* A proton or neutron, especially in the atomic nucleus.
nu′cle·on′ics (-ŏn′ĭks), *n.;* see -ICS. [From *nucle*us, *nucle*ar + electr*onics.*] That branch of physical science which deals with nucleons, or, more widely, with all phenomena of the nucleus.
nu′cle·o·plasm (nū′klē·ō·plăz′m), *n.* The ground substance of a cell nucleus. — **nu′cle·o·plas′mic** (-plăz′mĭk), *adj.*
nu′cle·o·pro′te·in (-prō′tē·ĭn; -prō′tēn), *n.* Also **nu′cle·o·pro′te·id** (-tē·ĭd). [*nucleo-,* a combining form for *nucleus* + *protein, proteid.*] *Biochem.* Any of a class of proteins found in nearly all cell nuclei.
nu′cle·us (nū′klē·ŭs), *n.; pl.* NUCLEI (-ī), NUCLEUSES (-ĕz; -ĭz). [L., a kernel, dim. fr. *nux, nucis,* nut.] **1.** A kernel, as of a nut or seed. **2.** A central mass or point about which matter is gathered; the central or focal portion; core. **3.** *Anat.* A mass of gray matter, or group of nerve cells in the central nervous system, esp. in the brain. **4.** *Astron.* The small, brighter, and denser portion of the head of a comet. **5.** *Biol.* A specialized portion of the protoplasm of most cells, regarded as of crucial importance to cell physiology and heredity. It typically consists of nucleoplasm bounded by a nuclear membrane and containing linin, chromatin, and differentiated structures, as nucleoli. See CELL, 4, *Illust.;* OVUM, *Illust.* **6.** *Org. Chem.* A characteristic and stable complex (specif., a ring) of atoms to which other atoms may be variously attached. **7.** *Physics & Chem.* The central part of an atom, containing most of its mass and having a positive charge equal to the atomic number of the element. The nucleus of ordinary or light hydrogen is the proton; according to present theory, all other nuclei are combinations of protons and neutrons. Cf. ATOM, 3.
nude (nūd; 114), *adj.* [L. *nudus.*] **1.** *Law.* Naked; without consideration; as, a *nude* pact. **2.** Bare; devoid of covering; naked; unclothed. — **Syn.** See BARE. — *n.* **1.** A nude or undraped figure. **2.** With *the.* The undraped human figure, or a representation of it in art; also, the state of being unclothed. — **nude′ly,** *adv.* — **nude′ness,** *n.*

nudge (nŭj), *v. t.;* NUDGED (nŭjd); NUDG′ING (nŭj′ĭng). To touch or push gently, as with the elbow, in order to call attention. — *n.* A gentle push or jog, as with the elbow.
nu′di- (nū′dĭ-). [L. *nudus.*] A combining form meaning *naked, bare.*
nu′di·bran′chi·ate (-brăng′kĭ·āt), *n.* [*nudi-* + *branchia.*] *Zool.* Any of a suborder (Nudibranchia or Nudibranchiata) comprising a great variety of marine gastropod mollusks (order Opisthobranchia) without shell in the adult state and without true gills. — **nu′di·bran′chi·ate,** *adj.*
nu′di·caul (nū′dĭ·kôl), **nu′di·cau′lous** (-kô′lŭs), *adj.* [*nudi-* + L. *caulis* stem.] *Bot.* Having leafless stems.
nud′ism (nūd′ĭz'm; 114), *n.* The cult or practice of living in a nude state. — **nud′ist** (-ĭst), *n. & adj.*
nu′di·ty (nū′dĭ·tĭ), *n.; pl.* -TIES (-tĭz). **1.** Quality, state, or fact of being nude; nakedness. **2.** That which is nude.
‖**nu′dum pac′tum** (nū′dŭm păk′tŭm). [L.] Literally, a nude pact; hence, loosely, a contract without consideration.
nu′ga·to′ry (nū′gȧ·tō′rĭ *or, esp. Brit.,* -tẽr·ĭ), *adj.* [L. *nugatorius,* fr. *nugari* to trifle, fr. *nugae* jests, trifles.] **1.** Trifling; of little account; worthless. **2.** Of no force; ineffectual. — **Syn.** See VAIN.
nug′get (nŭg′ĕt; -ĭt), *n.* A lump; a mass, esp. a native lump of a precious metal; as, a *nugget* of gold.
nui′sance (nū′săns; -s'ns), *n.* [OF., fr. *nuire* to harm, hurt, fr. L. *nocere.*] **1.** Injury; annoyance. **2.** *Law.* An annoying, unpleasant, or obnoxious thing or practice.
nuisance tax. A small tax which is a nuisance because passed on for collection in small amounts from the consumer.
null (nŭl), *adj.* [F. or L.; F. *nul,* fr. L. *nullus* not any, none, fr. *ne-* not + *ullus* any, dim. of *unus* one.] **1.** Of no legal or binding force; invalid; void. **2.** Amounting to nothing. **3.** Of no consequence; insignificant.
nul′lah (nŭl′ȧ), *n.* [Hind. *nallā.*] *Anglo-Ind.* A gully.
null and void. Of no force, binding power, or validity.
nul′li·fi·ca′tion (nŭl′ĭ·fĭ·kā′shŭn), *n.* A nullifying, or state of being nullified; specif. [*often cap.*], *U. S. Hist.,* action of a state impeding or attempting to prevent the operation and enforcement within its territory of a law of the United States. — **nul′li·fi·ca′tion·ist,** *n.*
nul′li·fid′i·an (nŭl′ĭ·fĭd′ĭ·ăn), *n.* [L. *nullus* none + *fides* faith.] A person of no faith or religion; a skeptic.
nul′li·fy (nŭl′ĭ·fī), *v. t.;* NUL′LI·FIED (-fīd); NUL′LI·FY′ING. [LL. *nullificare,* fr. *nullus* none + *-ficare* (in comp.) to make.] **1.** To make null, esp. legally. **2.** To make or render of no value. — **nul′li·fi′er** (-fī′ẽr), *n.*
Syn. Nullify, negate, annul, abrogate, invalidate mean to deprive of effective or continued existence. One thing **nullifies** another that reduces it to ineffectualness; one thing **negates** another when each one is destructive of the other; one thing **annuls** another by neutralizing its power to act or to work; one thing **abrogates** another when the former dispenses with or abolishes the latter; one thing **invalidates** another when it deprives the latter of force or legality.
nul·lip′a·ra (nŭ·lĭp′ȧ·rȧ), *n.; pl.* NULLIPARAE (-rē). [NL., fr. L. *nullus* none + *parere* to bring forth.] *Med.* A woman who has never borne a child. Cf. PRIMIPARA, MULTIPARA. — **nul·lip′a·rous** (-rŭs), *adj.*
nul′li·pore (nŭl′ĭ·pōr; 70), *n.* [L. *nullus* none + *porus* pore.] Any of several lime-secreting coralline algae formerly thought to be animals.
nul′li·ty (nŭl′ĭ·tĭ), *n.; pl.* -TIES (-tĭz). [F. or ML.; F. *nullité,* fr. ML. *nullitas,* fr. L. *nullus* none.] **1.** Quality or state of being null; esp., legal invalidity. **2.** That which is null; an act void of legal effect.
numb (nŭm), *adj.* [ME. *nume, nome,* prop., seized, taken, past part. of *nimen* to take, fr. AS. *niman,* past part. *numen.*] Deprived, or partially deprived, of feeling and motion, esp. from cold; benumbed. — *v. t.* To make numb. — **numb′ly,** *adv.* — **numb′ness,** *n.*
num′ber (nŭm′bẽr), *n.* [OF. *nombre,* fr. L. *numerus.*] **1.** The, or a total, aggregate, or amount of units. Abbr. *No.* or *no.* Symbol #. **2.** A figure or word, or a group of figures or words, representing graphically an arithmetical sum; a numeral; as, the *number* 45. See *Table of Numbers,* p. 576. **3.** *pl.* Arithmetic; as, skill in *numbers.* **4.** A numeral by which a thing or person is designated in a series; as, a house *number.* **5.** The full count or complement (of a company or class of persons); an aggregate or company; an assemblage; a considerable number; many. When *number* is used collectively, it is regularly followed by the singular verb (a limited *number* of cars is available); when used distributively, it is regularly followed by the plural verb (a *number* of accidents always occur on slippery pavements). **6. a** Quantity, as made up of units; as, the difference between the notions "many" and "few" is one of *number.* **b** Possibility of numbering; as, times without *number.* **7.** A single member of a series designated by consecutive numerals; as, the May *number* of the periodical; hence, one of a collection, as of vaudeville acts; a distinct part. **8.** *Gram.* Distinction of word form to denote reference to one, or to more than one; also, the distinctive form itself. See DUAL, *adj.,* 1; PLURAL, *adj.,* 1; SINGULAR, *adj.,* 5. **9.** *pl. Poetry & Music.* Metrical, esp. syllabic, verses or measures; hence, verses or verse. **10.** *Colloq.* A thing or person singled out from a collection or aggregate; as, the saleswoman exhibited a smart little *number* in black crepe; specif., ***opposite number,*** counterpart or complement corresponding in class, service, grade, department, etc.; as, his *opposite number* in the navy. — **Syn.** See SUM. — *v. t.* **1.** To count; enumerate. **2.** To distinguish by a number. **3.** To reckon as one of a collection, company, or multitude. **4.** To fix the number or duration of. **5.** *Archaic.* To appoint, allot, or destine. **6.** To amount to; to equal in number. **7.** *Obs.* To levy up to a fixed number. — *v. i.* To make an enumeration; to count. — **num′ber·er,** *n.*
num′ber·less, *adj.* Innumerable; countless.
Num′bers (nŭm′bẽrz), *n. pl., construed as sing. Bib.* The fourth book of the Pentateuch, containing the census of the Hebrews. See BIBLE.
numbers pool. A daily lottery, illegally conducted, in which small bets, as low as a few cents, may be wagered on the appearance of a particular number, as the last digits in the pari-mutuel racing totals for the day or other unpredictable figures.
numb′fish′ (nŭm′fĭsh′), *n.; pl.,* see FISH. See 1st RAY.
numb′ing (nŭm′ĭng), *adj.* That numbs. — **numb′ing·ly,** *adv.*
num′bles, nom′bles (nŭm′b'lz), *n. pl.* [OF., fr. L. *lumbulus,* dim. of *lumbus* a loin.] *Archaic.* Certain entrails, esp. of a deer, used for food, as the heart, lights, liver.
numb′skull′ (nŭm′skŭl′). Var. of NUMSKULL.

TABLE OF NUMBERS

1. Cardinal numbers are shown in the first three columns of the *Table*. First the names of the cardinal numbers are given; then the Arabic symbols (*Arabic numerals*) for them, as commonly used in arithmetic; next the Roman symbols (*Roman numerals*), used for dates, for introductory pages in books, upon the dials of timepieces, etc.; as in: the year MCMLIII (1953); page lxvi. The cardinal numbers are used in simple counting, or in answer to the question, "How many?" They give no information about the kind of things counted, or about the order in which they are counted, or about any relation they may have to each other.

The words for these numbers may be used as nouns (he counted to *twelve*) or as adjectives (*twelve* boys). A number word is often used for a thing that is made up of the number of parts shown by the number word used, or that is marked with the figure or with the number of spots, marks, etc., shown by this word. Thus, a *seven* is sometimes used for a billiard ball with a 7 on it or for a playing card with seven spots, a *five* is used for a basketball team (which has five men), an *eight* for a racing crew in rowing, a *nine* for a baseball team, and so on.

2. Ordinal numbers are shown in the fourth and fifth columns of the *Table*. These names are formed usually by adding the suffix *-th* or *-eth* to the name of the corresponding cardinal number. The names of the ordinal numbers for 1 and 2, however, come from different words, and those for 3, 5, 8, 9, 12, 20, etc., have become more or less changed. The ordinal numbers are used (as adjectives or as nouns) to show the order or succession in which names, objects, periods of time, or the like,

are considered; as, the *twelfth* month; the *fourth* in a row of seats; the *18th* century.

3. Fractions (not shown in the *Table*). A fraction is one or more of the equal parts into which a unit, or an object or group of objects, may be divided. When written, a simple fraction consists of two numbers divided by a line ($\frac{1}{3}$ or $\frac{1}{3}$, $\frac{3}{4}$ or $\frac{3}{4}$). The figure below the line (*denominator*) shows the total number of equal parts into which a unit is divided, the figure above the line (*numerator*) shows how many of these equal parts of the fraction are taken. Thus, the fraction $\frac{3}{4}$ (read "three fourths") indicates 3 of the 4 equal parts into which the unit is divided. The number *one* is unity or a complete whole. The fraction of a complete whole divided into two equal parts is one *half* ($\frac{1}{2}$); the names of the denominators of other fractions are the same as those of the corresponding ordinal numbers; as, one *third* ($\frac{1}{3}$); one *fourth* ($\frac{1}{4}$); seven *eighths* ($\frac{7}{8}$) of the people present; a dime is one *tenth* ($\frac{1}{10}$) of a dollar.

4. Decimals or *decimal fractions* (not shown in the *Table*). A decimal or decimal fraction is a proper fraction in which the denominator is some power of 10, usually not expressed, but signified by a point (*decimal point*) placed at the left of the numerator; as, $.2 = \frac{2}{10}$, $.25 = \frac{25}{100}$, $.025 = \frac{25}{1000}$. There are as many places to the right of the decimal point as there are ciphers in the denominator; as, $\frac{88}{10,000}$ is written .0088. The decimal .25 may also be expressed by the fraction $\frac{1}{4}$ or by 25% (see PER CENT).

	CARDINAL NUMBERS		ORDINAL NUMBERS	
NAME	ARABIC (SYMBOLS)	ROMAN *	NAME	ABBREVIATION
naught, zero	0			
one	1	I	first	1st
two	2	II	second	2d or 2nd
three	3	III	third	3d or 3rd
four	4	IV *or* IIII	fourth	4th
five	5	V	fifth	5th
six	6	VI	sixth	6th
seven	7	VII	seventh	7th
eight	8	VIII	eighth	8th
nine	9	IX *or* VIIII	ninth	9th
ten	10	X	tenth	10th
eleven	11	XI	eleventh	11th
twelve	12	XII	twelfth	12th
thirteen	13	XIII	thirteenth	13th
fourteen	14	XIV *or* XIIII	fourteenth	14th
fifteen	15	XV	fifteenth	15th
sixteen	16	XVI	sixteenth	16th
seventeen	17	XVII	seventeenth	17th
eighteen	18	XVIII	eighteenth	18th
nineteen	19	XIX *or* XVIIII	nineteenth	19th
twenty	20	XX	twentieth	20th
twenty-one	21	XXI	twenty-first	21st
twenty-two	22	XXII	twenty-second	22d or 22nd
twenty-three	23	XXIII	twenty-third	23d or 23rd
twenty-four	24	XXIV	twenty-fourth	24th
twenty-five	25	XXV	twenty-fifth	25th
twenty-six	26	XXVI	twenty-sixth	26th
twenty-seven	27	XXVII	twenty-seventh	27th
twenty-eight	28	XXVIII	twenty-eighth	28th
twenty-nine	29	XXIX	twenty-ninth	29th
thirty	30	XXX	thirtieth	30th
thirty-one	31	XXXI	thirty-first	31st
thirty-two, etc.	32	XXXII	thirty-second	32d or 32nd
forty	40	XL *or* XXXX	fortieth	40th
forty-one	41	XLI	forty-first	41st
forty-two, etc.	42	XLII	forty-second	42d or 42nd
fifty	50	L	fiftieth	50th
sixty	60	LX	sixtieth	60th
seventy	70	LXX	seventieth	70th
eighty	80	LXXX *or* XXC	eightieth	80th
ninety	90	XC *or* LXXXX	ninetieth	90th
one hundred	100	C	(one) hundredth	100th
one hundred and one	101	CI	(one) hundred and first	101st
one hundred and two	102	CII	(one) hundred and second	102d or 102nd
one hundred and fifty	150	CL	(one) hundred and fiftieth	150th
two hundred	200	CC	two hundredth	200th
three hundred	300	CCC	three hundredth	300th
four hundred	400	CD *or* CCCC	four hundredth	400th
five hundred	500	D *or* IↃ	five hundredth	500th
six hundred	600	DC *or* IↃC	six hundredth	600th
seven hundred	700	DCC *or* IↃCC	seven hundredth	700th
eight hundred	800	DCCC	eight hundredth	800th
nine hundred	900	CM	nine hundredth	900th
one thousand	1000	M *or* CIↃ	(one) thousandth	1000th
two thousand	2000	MM	two thousandth	2000th
ten thousand	10,000	X̄	ten thousandth	10,000th
one hundred thousand	100,000	C̄	(one) hundred thousandth	100,000th
one million	1,000,000	M̄	(one) millionth	1,000,000th

* The Roman symbols are written either in capitals (XXVIII, XLI, DCC) or in lower-case letters (xxviii, xli, dcc). The more usual forms are given first in the list; the others are rare.

nu·men (nū′mĕn), *n.; pl.* NUMINA (-mǐ·nà). [L.] *Rom. Relig.* A divine or presiding spirit.

nu·mer·a·ble (nū′mĕr·à·b'l; 114), *adj.* [L. *numerabilis.*] Capable of being numbered or counted.

nu·mer·al (nū′mĕr·ăl), *adj.* [LL. *numeralis,* fr. *numerus* number.] **1.** Expressing, denoting, or representing number. **2.** Of or pert. to number; consisting of number or numerals. — *n.* **1.** A word expressing a number. **2.** A figure or character, or group of either, used to express a number. **3.** *pl.* The numbers designating by year a school or college class, worn as a badge of distinction in an extracurricular activity, as athletics.

nu·mer·ar·y (-ĕr′ĭ or, *esp. Brit.,* -ĕr·ĭ), *adj.* Of or pertaining to a number or numbers.

nu·mer·ate (-āt), *v. t.* [L. *numeratus,* past part. of *numerare* to count.] To enumerate; to read according to numeration.

nu·mer·a′tion (-ā′shŭn), *n.* **1.** Act, process, or art of numbering; specif.: **a** A method of numbering or computing. **b** Calculation; applying of a number or numbers to something. **c** Enumeration; census. **2.** *Math.* Act or art of reading numbers when expressed by means of numerals.

☞ According to the British and the German system, the billion is a million of millions, a trillion a million of billions, and each higher denomination is a million times the one preceding. According to the French and United States systems, the billion (or *milliard* in France) is a thousand millions, and each higher denomination is a thousand times the preceding.

	EQUIVALENTS			
NAME	French & U.S. systems	No. of zeros	British & German systems	No. of zeros
million	1000 thousands	6	1000 thousands	6
milliard	1000 millions [F. *mil′liard′* (mē′-lyär′)]	9	1000 millions [G. *Mil·liar′de* (mǐl·yär′dě)]	9
billion	1000 millions (usual U. S. term)	9	1,000,000 millions (1,000,000,000,000)	12
trillion	1000 billions *or* 1,000,000 millions (1,000,000,000,000)	12	1,000,000 billions *or* 1,000,000 million millions (1,000,000,000,000,000,000)	18
quadrillion	1000 trillions	15	1,000,000 trillions	24
quintillion	1000 quadrillions	18	1,000,000 quadrillions	30
sextillion	1000 quintillions	21	1,000,000 quintillions	36
septillion	1000 sextillions	24	1,000,000 sextillions	42
octillion	1000 septillions	27	1,000,000 septillions	48
nonillion	1000 octillions	30	1,000,000 octillions	54
decillion	1000 nonillions	33	1,000,000 nonillions	60
undecillion	1000 decillions	36	1,000,000 decillions	66
duodecillion	1000 undecillions	39	1,000,000 undecillions	72
tredecillion	1000 duodecillions	42	1,000,000 duodecillions	78
quattuordecillion	1000 tredecillions	45	1,000,000 tredecillions	84
quindecillion	1000 quattuordecillions	48	1,000,000 quattuordecillions	90
sexdecillion	1000 quindecillions	51	1,000,000 quindecillions	96
septendecillion	1000 sexdecillions	54	1,000,000 sexdecillions	102
octodecillion	1000 septendecillions	57	1,000,000 septendecillions	108
novemdecillion	1000 octodecillions	60	1,000,000 octodecillions	114
vigintillion	1000 novemdecillions	63	1,000,000 novemdecillions	120

Billion, trillion, etc., are also used adjectively. The ordinal forms, *noun & adj.,* are **billionth, trillionth,** etc. (see 3d -TH). Cf. NUMBER, *Table.* A vigintillion in figures (French & U.S. systems) is 1,000,000,000,000,000,000,000,000,000,000,000,000,000,000,000,000,000,000,000,000,000,000,000,000,000,000.

nu′mer·a′tor (nū′mĕr·ā′tĕr; 114), *n.* [LL., in sense 2.] **1.** *Math.* The term in a fraction which indicates the number of fractional units taken. In a common fraction the numerator is written above the line. **2.** One who or that which numbers.

nu·mer′i·cal (nů·mĕr′ĭ·kăl), *adj.* Belonging to, pert. to, or of the nature of number; denoting number or a number; expressed by numbers. — **nu·mer′i·cal·ly,** *adv.*

nu′mer·ol′o·gy (nū′mĕr·ŏl′ō·jĭ), *n.* [L. *numerus* number + *-logy.*] The study of the occult significance of numbers.

nu′mer·ous (nū′mĕr·ŭs), *adj.* [L. *numerosus.*] **1.** Consisting of or containing a great number of units; plentiful. **2.** Being many; of or pertaining to great number. — **nu′mer·ous·ly,** *adv.* — **nu′mer·ous·ness,** *n.*

nu·mis·mat′ic (nū′mĭz·măt′ĭk; nů′mĭs-), *adj.* Also **nu·mis·mat′i·cal** (-ĭ·kăl). [F. *numismatique,* fr. L. *numisma* coin, fr. Gr. *nomisma* the current coin.] Of, pertaining to, or consisting of coins; relating to numismatics.

nu·mis·mat′ics (-ĭks), *n.; see* -ICS. The science of coins, tokens, medals, paper money, and objects closely resembling them in form or purpose; — construed as *sing.* — **nu·mis′ma·tist** (nů·mĭz′mà·tĭst; nů·mĭs′-), *n.* — **nu·mis′ma·tol′o·gy** (nů·mĭz′mà·tŏl′ō·jĭ; nů·mĭs′-), *n.* Numismatics. — **nu·mis′ma·tol′o·gist** (-jĭst), *n.*

num′mu·lar (nŭm′ů·lẽr), *adj.* [L. *nummularius,* fr. *nummulus,* dim. of *nummus* a coin.] *Med.* Coin-shaped.

num′mu·lite (nŭm′ů·līt), *n.* [L. *nummus* a coin + *-lite.*] *Zool.* Any member of a family (Camerinidae) of foraminifers (which see), mostly extinct, having a shell with spirally arranged chambers. — **num′mu·lit′ic** (-lĭt′ĭk), *adj.*

num′skull′, numb′skull′ (nŭm′skŭl′), *n.* [*numb* + *skull.*] *Colloq.* A dunce; dolt; also, the head or skull of such a one.

nun (nŭn), *n.* [AS. *nunne,* fr. LL. *nonna* nun, child's nurse.] A woman under certain religious vows; commonly, a woman in a convent, under vows of poverty, chastity, and obedience. — **Syn.** See RELIGIOUS.

nun buoy. See BUOY, 1.

Nunc Di·mit′tis (nŭngk dĭ·mĭt′ĭs). [L. *nunc* now + *dimittis* thou lettest depart.] **1.** *Eccl.* The song of Simeon (*Luke* ii. 29–32), used as a hymn or canticle. **2.** [*not caps.*] Permission to depart; dismissal.

nun′ci·a·ture (nŭn′shǐ·à·tūr), *n.* [It. *nunziatura.* See NUNCIO.] The office or period of office of a nuncio.

nun′ci·o (nŭn′shĭ·ō), *n.; pl.* NUNCIOS (-ōz). [It. *nunzio, nuncio,* fr. L. *nuncius, nuntius,* messenger.] The permanent official representative of the pope at a foreign court or seat of government.

nun′cle (nŭng′k'l; *dial. also* nŏong′k'l), *n.* *Now Dial.* Uncle; — from combination with a preceding *n* sound, as of *mine.*

nun′cu·pa′tive (nŭng′ků·pā′tĭv; nŭng·kū′pà·tĭv), *adj.* [LL. *nuncupativus* nominal.] Oral; not written; — of wills.

nun·na′tion (nŭn·ā′shŭn), *n.* [NL. *nunnatio,* fr. *nūn,* Arabic name of letter *n.*] *Gram.* Addition of a final *n* in declension of nouns, as in Arabic.

nun′ner·y (nŭn′ẽr·ĭ), *n.; pl.* -IES (-ĭz). A convent of or for nuns. — **Syn.** See CLOISTER.

nun's′ veil′ing (nŭnz′ vāl′ĭng). A soft, fine, untwilled woolen fabric.

nup′tial (nŭp′shăl), *adj.* [F. or L.; F., fr. L. *nuptialis,* fr. *nuptiae* marriage, wedding, fr. *nubere, nuptum,* to marry.] Of or pert. to marriage, or the wedding ceremony. — **Syn.** See MATRIMONIAL. — *n.* Marriage; wedding; — usually *pl.*

nurl (nûrl). Var. of KNURL.

nurse (nûrs), *n.* [OF. *nurrice, norrice,* fr. L. *nutricia* nurse, prop., fem. of *nutricius* that nourishes, fr. *nutrix, -icis,* nurse.] **1.** A woman (*wet nurse*) who suckles and takes care of an infant not her own; now, more usually, a woman (*dry nurse*) who has the care of a young child or children. **2.** One who or that which rears, furnishes nutriment, fosters, etc. **3.** A person trained to care for and wait upon the sick or infirm and assist doctors, surgeons, etc. **4.** *Billiards.* Act of nursing the balls; as, the rail nurse. **5.** *Zool.* A worker ant or bee that cares for the young. — *v. t.* **1.** To act as a nurse for: **a** To nourish at the breast; suckle (an infant). **b** To take care of (a child). **c** To take care of or tend, as an invalid. **2.** To care or provide for tenderly or sedulously; to cherish; foster. **3.** To use, handle, drive, or the like, with especial care to conserve the energy of or avoid injury to; as, to *nurse* a weak ankle; also, to cherish or brood over in one's mind; as, to *nurse* a grudge. **4.** To give curative care to (an ailment or ailing part of oneself); as, to *nurse* a cold. **5.** To clasp in one's hands, as the knees; to fondle. **6.** *Billiards.* To keep (the balls) close together and in good position during a series of caroms. — *v. i.* **1.** To suckle; of a child, to take the breast. **2.** To act, serve, or be employed as a nurse. — **nurs′er** (nûr′sẽr), *n.*

nurse′maid′ (nûrs′mād′), *n.* A girl employed to tend children.

nurs′er·y (nûr′sẽr·ĭ), *n.; pl.* -ERIES (-ĭz). **1.** The place where nursing is carried on; as: **a** A room or a place appropriated to the care of children. **b** A place for training, educating, or the like. **2.** That which fosters or educates; as, commerce is the *nursery* of seamen. **3.** *Obs.* A nursing; fosterage. **4.** *Hort.* A place where trees, shrubs, vines, etc., are propagated for transplanting or for use as stocks for grafting.

nurs′er·y·maid′ (-măd′), *n.* A nursemaid.

nurs′er·y·man (-măn), *n.; pl.* -MEN (-mĕn). One who conducts or cultivates a nursery, as for plants.

nursery rhyme. A tale in rhymed verse for children.

nursery school. *Educ.* A training and socializing center for children usually under five years of age.

nurs′ing bottle (nûr′sĭng). A bottle with a rubber nipple, used in supplying food to infants.

nursing home. *Chiefly Brit.* A private hospital.

nurs′ling (nûrs′lĭng), *n.* Also **nurse′ling.** A child that is nursed; hence, one solicitously cared for.

nur′ture (nûr′tůr), *n.* [OF. *norriture, norreture,* fr. LL. *nutritura* a nursing.] **1.** Breeding; education; training. **2.** That which nourishes; food. — *v. t.* **1.** To feed or rear; to foster. **2.** To educate; to bring up or train. — **nur′tur·er** (-tůr·ẽr), *n.*

nut (nŭt), *n.* [AS. *hnutu.*] **1.** A dry fruit or seed having a separable rind or shell and interior kernel or meat; also, the kernel or meat itself. **2.** Something likened to a nut (sense 1) in the difficulty it presents, as a problem; as, a hard *nut* to crack. **3.** A perforated block (usually of metal) with an internal, or female, screw thread, used on a bolt or screw for tightening or holding something. Cf. BOLT, *Illust.* **4.** *Slang.* **a** The head. **b** Fellow; used disparagingly. **c** One whose thinking or conduct is eccentric. **d** A crank. **5.** *Bot.* An indehiscent, polycarpellary, one-seeded fruit, with a woody pericarp, as the acorn, hazelnut, chestnut, etc. **6.** *Music.* In stringed instruments, the ridge on the upper end of the finger board over which the strings pass. See VIOLIN, *Illust.* — *v. i.; -* NUT′TED; NUT′TING. To gather or seek nuts.

nu′tant (nū′tănt), *adj.* Nodding; drooping.

nu·ta′tion (nů·tā′shŭn), *n.* [L. *nutatio,* fr. *nutare* to nod, freq. of *nuere* (in comp.) to nod.] **1.** Act of nodding, esp. the head. **2.** *Astron.* A small inequality in the motion of precession; a libratory motion of the earth's axis, like the nodding of a top. **3.** *Plant Physiol.* A spontaneous more or less rhythmical change in the position of growing organs. Cf. CIRCUMNUTATION. — **nu·ta′tion·al** (-ăl, -'l), *adj.*

nut'crack'er (nŭt'krăk'ẽr), n. 1. Also **nut'crack'ers** (-ẽrz). An instrument for cracking nuts. 2. **a** A European bird (*Nucifraga caryocatactes*) of the crow family. It is dark brown, spotted with white. **b** A grayish-white related bird (*N. columbiana*) of western North America; — called also *Clark's nutcracker*. **c** A nuthatch.

nut'gall' (-gôl'), n. Any nutlike gall, esp. on the oak.

nut'hatch' (-hăch'), n. [ME. *notehach*, *nuthake*.] Any of certain birds (family Sittidae) intermediate in character and habits between the titmice and creepers.

nut'let (-lĕt), n. 1. *Bot.* Any small nutlike fruit or seed, as of plants of the borage family. 2. The stone of a drupe.

nut'meg (nŭt'mĕg), n. [ME. *notemuge*, fr. *note* nut + OF. *mugue* musk.] The aromatic seed of a tree (*Myristica fragrans*), native to the Moluccas; also, the tree itself. The seed is much used as a spice.

nutmeg melon. See MUSKMELON.

Nutmeg State. Connecticut; — a nickname alluding to the alleged trick of selling wooden nutmegs as genuine.

nut'pick' (nŭt'pĭk'), n. A small sharp-pointed table implement for extracting the kernels from nuts.

nu'tri-a (nū'trĭ-à), n. [Sp., otter, fr. L. *lutra*.] **a** The coypu. **b** The plucked fur of the coypu. It is a light-brown durable fur, and is blended to imitate beaver.

nu'tri-ent (nū'trĭ-ĕnt), adj. [L. *nutriens*, pres. part. of *nutrire*. See NOURISH.] Nutritious. — n. A nutritious substance; a nutritive ingredient (of food).

nu'tri-ment (nū'trĭ-mĕnt), n. [L. *nutrimentum*.] 1. That which nourishes; nourishment; food. 2. That which promotes development. — **Syn.** See FOOD.

nu-tri'tion (nū-trĭsh'ŭn), n. 1. Act or process of nourishing or being nourished; specif., *Physiol. & Biol.*, the sum of the processes by which an animal or plant absorbs, or takes in and utilizes, food substances. 2. That which nourishes; nourishment; nutriment; food. — **nu-tri'tion-al** (-ăl, -'l), adj. — **nu-tri'tion-al-ly**, adv.

nu-tri'tion-ist (-ĭst), n. One professionally engaged in investigating and solving problems of nutrition.

nu-tri'tious (nū-trĭsh'ŭs), adj. [L. *nutricius*, *nutritius*, fr. *nutrix*, *-icis*, a nurse.] Nourishing; promoting growth and repairing natural waste. — **nu-tri'tious-ly**, adv. — **nu-tri'tious-ness**, n.

nu'tri-tive (nū'trĭ-tĭv), adj. Of, pertaining to, or concerned in nutrition; nutritious; as, *nutritive* food. — **nu'tri-tive-ly**, adv. — **nu'tri-tive-ness**, n.

nut'shell' (nŭt'shĕl'), n. 1. The shell, or hard external covering, in which the kernel of a nut is enclosed. 2. Hence, a thing of little or small compass, size, etc. — *in a nutshell*. In or within a small compass or limit.

nut'ter (nŭt'ẽr), n. A gatherer of nuts.

nut'ting (nŭt'ĭng), n. Gathering of nuts.

nut'ty (nŭt'ĭ), adj.; NUT'TI-ER (-ĭ-ẽr); NUT'TI-EST. 1. Abounding in, or producing, nuts. 2. Having a flavor like that of nuts; hence, pleasant; *Slang*, spicy; piquant. 3. *Slang.* Crackbrained; queer. — **nut'-ti-ness**, n.

nux vom'i-ca (nŭks vŏm'ĭ-kà). [ML., fr. L. *nux* a nut + *vomere* to vomit.] 1. The poisonous seed of an Asiatic tree (*Strychnos nux-vomica*), containing several alkaloids, chiefly strychnine and brucine. See STRYCHNOS. 2. The tree that yields these seeds.

nuz'zle (nŭz''l), v. t. *Now Rare.* To foster; nurse; cherish.

nuz'zle, v. i. & t. [Freq. fr. NOSE.] 1. To work with the nose, as a swine does in the mud; to root, thrust, poke, or snuff with the nose. 2. To nestle; to lie close or snug.

ny-an'za (nĭ-ăn'zà; nĭ-), n. [Bantu.] In Central Africa, any large body of water; a lake or river; — chiefly in proper names.

nyc'ta-gi-na'ceous (nĭk'tà-jĭ-nā'shŭs), adj. [From *Nyctago*, former genus name, deriv. of Gr. *nyx*, *nyktos*, night.] Belonging to the four-o'clock family (Nyctaginaceae). See FOUR-O'CLOCK.

nyc'ta-lo'pi-a (-lō'pĭ-à), n. [LL., fr. L., fr. Gr. *nyktalōps*, fr. *nyx*, *nyktos*, night + *alaos* blind + *ōps*, *ōpos*, eye.] A condition of the eyes in which one can see well only by day or in a strong light. — **nyc'ta-lop'ic** (-lŏp'ĭk), adj.

nyc'ti- (nĭk'tĭ-), **nyc'to-** (-tō-), **nyct-**. [Gr. *nyx*, *nyktos*.] A combining form meaning *night*, as in **nyc-tit'ro-pism** (nĭk-tĭt'rō-pĭz'm), tendency of certain plant organs, as the leaflets of clover, to assume special "sleeping" positions at night; **nyc'ti-trop'ic** (-trŏp'ĭk), adj.

nyl'ghai (nĭl'gī), **nyl'ghaie** (-gī), **nyl'ghau** (-gô). Vars. of NILGAI.

ny'lon (nī'lŏn), n. **a** A synthetic material, of proteinlike structure, derivable from coal, air, and water, which is adapted for fashioning into filaments of extreme toughness, strength, and elasticity, used in knitting hosiery and the like, or into bristles or sheets. **b** *pl.* Stockings made of nylon.

nymph (nĭmf; 89), n. [OF. *nimphe*, fr. L. *nympha* nymph, bride, young woman, fr. Gr. *nymphē*.] 1. *Gr. & Rom. Myth.* One of the inferior divinities of nature represented as beautiful maidens dwelling in the mountains, forests, meadows, waters, etc. 2. *Poetic.* A nymphlike maiden. 3. Also **nym'pha** (nĭm'fà). *Zool.* Any of certain insects in an immature form, esp. that characteristic of a preadult stage in insects with incomplete metamorphosis. — **nymph'al** (nĭm'făl), adj.

nym'phae-a'ceous (nĭm'fē-ā'shŭs), adj. [L. *nymphaea* the water lily, fr. Gr. *nymphaia*.] Belonging to the water-lily family (Nymphaeaceae). See WATER LILY.

nym'pha-lid (nĭm'fà-lĭd), n. [*Nymphalis*, type genus, fr. Gr. *nymphē* nymph.] *Zool.* Any of a large family (Nymphalidae) of butterflies having greatly reduced forelegs, including the monarch, admirals, etc. — **nym'pha-lid**, adj.

nym'pho-lep'sy (nĭm'fō-lĕp'sĭ), n. Also **nym'pho-lep'si-a** (-lĕp'sĭ-à). [See NYMPH; -LEPSY.] A species of demoniac enthusiasm supposed to seize one bewitched by a nymph; hence, a frenzy of emotion, as for some unattainable ideal. — **nym'pho-lept** (-lĕpt), n. — **nym'pho-lep'tic** (-lĕp'tĭk), adj.

nym'pho-ma'ni-a (-mā'nĭ-à), n. [NL., fr. Gr. *nymphē* a bride + *-mania*.] *Med.* Morbid and uncontrollable sexual desire in a female. — **nym'pho-ma'ni-ac** (-ăk), adj. & n.

nys-tag'mus (nĭs-tăg'mŭs), n. [NL., fr. Gr. *nystagmos* drowsiness, fr. *nystazein* to nod in sleep.] *Med.* A rapid involuntary oscillation of the eyeballs. — **nys-tag'mic** (-mĭk), adj.

O

O, o (ō), n.; pl. O's, o's, Os, os, OES (ōz). 1. The fifteenth letter of the English alphabet. It comes through the Latin from the Greek, which took it from the Phoenician. O stands for various sounds in English. See Pron., § 69. 2. The sound of the letter O. 3. A cipher; zero. 4. As a *symbol*, the fourteenth or (see K, 3) fifteenth in order or class.

O' [Ir. ō a descendant.] A prefix to Irish family names, meaning *a descendant of.* The apostrophe is due to the mistaken notion that *O* stands for "of."

O (ō), *interj.* An exclamation used in direct address or invocation or, less often than *oh*, in expressing pain, grief, surprise, etc.; as, *O* Lord, help us. — n.; pl. O's (ōz). An utterance of pain, lamentation, or the like.

o' (ō; ŏ), *prep.* Formerly **o**. *Colloq. & Dial.* A shortened form of *of* or *on*.

o-. *Chem.* See ORTHO-.

oaf (ōf), n.; pl. OAFS (ōfs), *sometimes* OAVES (ōvz). [Also *auf*, fr. ON. *alfr* elf.] Orig., an elf's child; changeling; hence, a deformed or foolish child; a simpleton; dolt; blockhead; idiot; also, a lubberly person. — **oaf'ish**, adj. — **oaf'ish-ly**, adv. — **oaf'ish-ness**, n.

oak (ōk), n. [AS. ác.] 1. **a** Any of a genus (*Quercus*) or of its related genus (*Lithocarpus*) of hardwood fagaceous trees and shrubs, the fruit of which is a rounded nut (*acorn*). See BLACKJACK, 5; BLACK OAK; BLUEJACK, 2; CORK, 1; DURMAST; ENCINA; HOLM OAK; KERMES, 2; LIVE OAK; QUERCITRON; RED OAK; ROBLE; WATER OAK; WHITE OAK. **b** The wood of these trees. The best oak timber is hard, tough, and durable, with a handsome grain. In North America, oak lumber is sold as *white oak*, derived mostly from *Q. alba*, *stellata*, bicolor, and *macrocarpa*, and *red oak*, derived from *Q. borealis*, *velutina*, *palustris*, and *phellos*. 2. Any of various plants suggestive of the oak, as

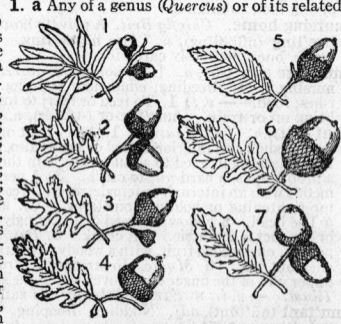

Leaves and Acorns of Oaks. 1 Willow Oak (*Q. phellos*); 2 White Oak (*Q. alba*); 3 Black Oak, or Quercitron (*Q. velutina*); 4 Red Oak (*Q. borealis*); 5 Chestnut Oak (*Q. prinus*); 6 Bur Oak (*Q. macrocarpa*); 7 Swamp White Oak (*Q. bicolor*). All reduced.

in foliage; as, poison *oak*. 3. Oak leaves worn in a wreath. 4. *Eng. University Slang.* A stout door, often made of oak; hence, *to sport one's oak*, to close one's outer door, signifying that one is out or does not desire callers. 5. Woodwork, furniture, or the like, of oak.

oak apple. Any of several applelike galls on oak leaves, produced by certain gallflies (genera *Amphibolips* and *Diplolepis*).

oak'en (ōk'ĕn), adj. Made of or pert. to oak or oaks.

oak'-leaf' clus'ter. *U.S.* An addition to certain military decorations, in the form of a bronze or (for five such additions) silver cluster of oak leaves and acorns, to signify a second or subsequent award of the basic decoration.

oa'kum (ō'kŭm), n. [AS. *ācumba*, fr. *ā-* out + *cemban* to comb, *camb* comb.] Loose fiber obtained by untwisting and picking old hemp ropes, and used esp. for calking the seams of ships.

oar (ōr; 70), n. [AS. *ār*.] 1. A long, slender, broad-bladed wooden implement for propelling or steering a boat. 2. A thing resembling an oar in shape or use. 3. An oarsman; a rower. — v. t. & i. 1. To propel with or as with oars; row. 2. **a** To make or accomplish by rowing or a rowing motion. **b** To move with a rowing motion.

oar'fish' (-fĭsh'), n.; *plural*, see FISH. Any of a genus (*Regalecus*) of narrow fishes 20 to 30 feet long, with a dorsal fin that runs the length of the body, its anterior rays, which are tipped with red, rising like a mane above the head; — called also *ribbonfish*.

oar'lock' (-lŏk'), n. [AS. *ārloc*.] A rowlock, esp. one in which a steering oar is worked.

oars'man (ōrz'mån; 70), n.; pl. -MEN (-mĕn). A rower. — **oars'man-ship**, n.

o-a'sis (ō-ā'sĭs; ō'à-sĭs), n.; pl. OASES (-sēz). [L., fr. Gr. *oasis*.] A fertile or green spot in a waste or desert.

oast (ōst), n. [AS. *āst*.] A hop, malt, or tobacco kiln.

oat (ōt), n. [AS. *āte*, pl. *ātan*.] 1. **a** The grain of a cereal grass (*Avena sativa*), or the plant itself; — commonly in *pl.* **b** Any other species of *Avena*, esp. the wild oat *A. fatua*. 2. A crude reed instrument made of an oat straw.

oat'cake' (ōt'kāk'), n. A thin, flat oatmeal cake.

oat'en (ōt''n), adj. Of or made of oats, oatmeal, oat straw, etc.

oat grass. **a** Any wild oat. **b** Any of several oatlike grasses.

oath (ōth), n.; pl. OATHS (ōthz). [AS. *āth*.] 1. A solemn appeal to God, or to a sacred or revered person or sanction (as the Bible, the temple, the altar) by way of attesting the truth of one's word, the inviolability of a promise, etc.; also, the affirmation or promise supported by the oath, or its form of expression. 2. Any solemn attestation of the truth or inviolability of what is stated. 3. A careless or blasphemous use of the name of the divine Being, or anything divine or sacred.

oat'meal' (ōt'mēl'; 2), n. Meal made of oats, or porridge made of such meal, esp. in the form of rolled oats.

ob- (ŏb-). [L. *ob*, prep.] A prefix signifying: **a** *To, toward, before, facing.* **b** *Against, in opposition to.* **c** *Upon* or *over;* also, *down.* **d** *Completely.* **e** In modern scientific Latin and English, *reversely, in an opposite direction;* — with adjectives, as in:

obclavate **obconical** **obcuneate**

O'ba·di'ah (ō'bȧ·dī'ȧ), *n.* **a** A Hebrew prophet of uncertain date. **b** A book of the Old Testament. See BIBLE.

ob'bli·ga'to (ŏb'lĭ·gä'tō), *adj.* [It. lit., bound.] *Music.* Required; indispensable; — applied to voices, instruments, or esp. accompaniments, necessary to the just performance of a composition; — opposed to *ad libitum.* — *n.; pl.* -TOS (-tōz), -TI (-tē). **a** *Music.* An accompanying part usually played by a single instrument; as, a violin *obbligato.* **b** An accompaniment of any sort.

ob·cor'date (ŏb·kôr'dāt), *adj.* *Bot.* Heart-shaped, with the broad end toward the apex, as the leaflets of the wood sorrel.

ob'du·ra·cy (ŏb'dū·rȧ·sĭ; ŏb·dū'rȧ·sĭ), *n.* Quality, state, or instance of being obdurate; stubbornness; hardheartedness.

ob'du·rate (ŏb'dū·rāt; *also, esp. in poetry,* ŏb·dū'rāt), *adj.* [L. *obduratus*, past part. of *obdurare* to harden, fr. *ob-* + *durare* to harden, fr. *durus* hard.] **1.** Hardened in feeling; unyielding; hardhearted; also, stubbornly wicked. **2.** Hard; harsh; intractable. — **Syn.** See INFLEXIBLE. — **ob'du·rate·ly**, *adv.* — **ob'du·rate·ness**, *n.*

o'be·ah (ō'bē·ȧ), *n.* [Of African origin.] **a** [*often cap.*] A form of sorcery and magic formerly practiced by Negroes, chiefly of the British West Indies, the Guianas, and the southeastern United States. **b** *Colloq.* A charm or fetish used in, or the influence of, obeah. — **o'be·ah·ism** (-ĭz'm), *n.*

o·be'di·ence (ō·bē'dĭ·ĕns; 58), *n.* **1.** Act or fact of obeying, or state of being obedient. **2.** *Now Chiefly R.C.Ch.* Jurisdiction; control. **3.** *Archaic & Dial.* An obeisance.

o·be'di·ent (-ĕnt), *adj.* [OF., fr. L. *obediens, oboediens, -entis*, pres. part. of *obedire, oboedire.* See OBEY.] Obeying; willing to obey; submissive to restraint, control, or command. — **o·be'di·ent·ly**, *adv.*

Syn. **Obedient, docile, tractable, amenable** mean submissive to the control or guidance of another. **Obedient** implies compliance with the demands or requests of one in authority; **docile** implies a predisposition to submit to control or an indisposition to resist authority; **tractable**, applicable to things also, implies success or ease in handling or managing; **amenable** implies a temperamental willingness or readiness to submit.

o·bei'sance (ō·bā'săns; -s'ns; ō·bē'-), *n.* [OF. *obeissance* obedience.] A bow, curtsy, genuflection, etc., in token of respect, submission, or reverence; also, deference; homage. — **Syn.** See HONOR. — **o·bei'sant** (-sănt; -s'nt), *adj.*

ob'e·lisk (ŏb'ĕ·lĭsk), *n.* [L. *obeliscus*, fr. Gr. *obeliskos*, dim. of *obelos* a spit, pointed pillar.] **1.** A four-sided, usually monolithic, pillar, tapering as it rises, and terminating in a pyramid. **2. a** An obelus (— or ÷). **b** The mark of reference †; a dagger. — **ob'e·lis'cal** (-lĭs'kăl), *adj.*

ob'e·lize (-līz), *v. t.* To designate with an obelus or obelisk.

ob'e·lus (-lŭs), *n.; pl.* -LI (-lī). [LL., fr. Gr. *obelos*, prop., a spit.] The mark — or ÷, used in old mss. to mark a doubtful or spurious passage or reading.

O'ber·on (ō'bĕr·ŏn; ŏb'ĕr-; -ŭn), *n.* [F., fr. OF. *Auberon.*] In medieval folklore, king of the fairies and husband of Titania.

o·bese' (ō·bēs'), *adj.* [L. *obesus* that has eaten itself fat, stout, past part. of *obedere* to devour, fr. *ob-* + *edere* to eat.] Excessively corpulent; very fat. — **o·bese'ly**, *adv.* — **o·bes'i·ty** (ō·bĕs'ĭ·tĭ; ō·bēs'-), *n.*

o·bey' (ō·bā'), *v. t.;* O·BEYED' (ō·bād'); O·BEY'ING. [OF. *obeir*, fr. L. *obedire, oboedire*, fr. *ob-* + *audire* to hear.] **1.** To be obedient to; execute the commands of; also, to execute, as an order. **2.** To be ruled or controlled by; to follow the guidance, operation, etc., of; as, to *obey* reason; to *obey* the law of gravitation. — *v. i.* To yield obedience. — **o·bey'er** (-ẽr), *n.*

ob·fus'cate (ŏb·fŭs'kāt; ŏb'fŭs·kāt), *v. t.* [LL. *obfuscatus*, past part. of *obfuscare* to darken, fr. *ob-* + *fuscare* to darken, fr. *fuscus* dark.] To darken by or as by depriving of light; obscure; hence, to confuse; bewilder. — **ob'fus·ca'tion** (ŏb'fŭs·kā'shŭn), *n.*

o'bi (ō'bĭ), *n.* [Jap.] A broad sash worn with a kimono.

o'bi (ō'bĭ), **o'bi·ism.** Vars. of OBEAH, etc.

||**ob'i·it** (ŏb'ĭ·ĭt; ō'bĭ·ĭt). [L.] He (or she) died. Abbr. *ob.*

o'bit (ō'bĭt; ŏb'ĭt), *n.* [OF., fr. L. *obitus*, fr. *obire* to go to meet, (sc. *mortem*) to die, fr. *ob* + *ire* to go.] **1.** *Obs.* **a** A person's death. **b** A funeral ceremony. **2.** A service for the soul of a deceased person on the anniversary of his death. **3.** A notice of a person's death; esp., an obituary in a newspaper.

ob'i·ter dic'tum (ŏb'ĭ·tẽr dĭk'tŭm); *pl.* OBITER DICTA (-tȧ). [L.] **a** *Law.* An incidental and collateral opinion uttered by a judge. **b** Any incidental remark or observation.

o·bit'u·ar'y (ō·bĭt'ū·ĕr'ĭ *or, esp. Brit.,* -ẽr·ĭ), *n.; pl.* -IES (-ĭz). [ML. *obituarius*, fr. L. *obitus.* See OBIT.] A notice of a death, esp. with a biographical sketch. — **o·bit'u·ar'y**, *adj.*

ob·ject' (ŏb·jĕkt'), *v. t.* [L. *objectus*, past part. of *objicere, obicere*, to throw before, oppose, fr. *ob-* + *jacere* to throw.] **1.** *Archaic.* To oppose, interpose, or expose; hence, adduce. **2.** To offer in opposition; adduce in opposing or dissenting. — *v. i.* To state or declare opposition; often, to feel averse; disapprove.

Syn. **Object, protest, remonstrate, expostulate, kick** mean to oppose by arguing against. **Object** stresses dislike or aversion; **protest**, the presentation of objections in speech or in writing; **remonstrate**, an attempt to convince as by warning, reproving, etc.; **expostulate**, a firm, earnest, but friendly insistence on the merits of one's arguments; **kick**, now a colloquialism, strenuous protestation.

ob'ject (ŏb'jĕkt; -jĭkt), *n.* **1.** Something put, or regarded as put, in the way of some of the senses; something visible or tangible; a concrete thing. **2.** A sight which arouses feelings as of pity or disgust; a spectacle. **3.** Aim; motive. **4.** *Gram.* A noun or noun equivalent denoting that on or toward which the action of a verb is directed, or that, in a prepositional phrase, to which the preposition bears the relation expressed. The ***direct object*** of a verb denotes that which is immediately acted on, as *ball* in "he threw the *ball*"; the ***indirect object*** of a verb denotes that which the action affects less immediately or indispensably, as *John* in "throw *John* the ball." The ***cognate object*** repeats the idea of the governing verb (to live one's *life*); the ***secondary object*** is complementary after verbs of asking, teaching, etc., which take a direct object (ask me no *questions*); the ***retained object*** preserves its object relation in the passive construction (a book was given *me*). **5.** *Philos.* That of which the mind by any of its activities takes cognizance, whether a thing external in space or a conception formed by the mind itself. — **Syn.** See INTENTION.

object ball. *Billiards & Pool.* The ball first struck, or any ball that may be hit, by the cue ball. Cf. CUE BALL.

object glass *or* **lens.** *Optics.* The objective of a microscope, etc.

ob·jec'ti·fy (ŏb·jĕk'tĭ·fī), *v. t.;* -FIED (-fīd); -FY'ING. [*object* + *-fy.*] To cause to become, or assume the character of, an object; render objective; externalize. — **ob·jec'ti·fi·ca'tion** (-fĭ·kā'shŭn), *n.*

ob·jec'tion (ŏb·jĕk'shŭn), *n.* **1.** An objecting. **2.** That which is presented in objecting; adverse reason or argument; also, a feeling of disapproval.

ob·jec'tion·a·ble (-ȧ·b'l), *adj.* Open to objection; offensive.

ob·jec'tive (ŏb·jĕk'tĭv), *adj.* **1.** Of or pertaining to an object, esp. to the object, or end; as, to reach our *objective* point. **2.** Exhibiting or characterized by emphasis upon or the tendency to view events, phenomena, ideas, etc., as external and apart from self-consciousness; not subjective; hence, detached; impersonal; unprejudiced; as, an *objective* discussion; *objective* criteria. **3.** *Gram.* Pertaining to or designating the case of the object of a verb or preposition. **4.** *Med.* Perceptible to persons other than the patient; — of symptoms. **5.** *Perspective.* Belonging or relating to the object to be delineated; as, an *objective* line, plane, or point. **6. a** *Philos.* Contained in, or having the nature or status of, an object, or something cognized or cognizable; as, to render an abstraction *objective.* **b** Existing independent of mind; pertaining to an object as it is in itself or as distinguished from consciousness or the subject; as, to deny the *objective* reality of things. Cf. SUBJECTIVE. — **Syn.** See FAIR: MATERIAL. — *n.* **1.** An aim or end of action; point to be hit, reached, etc. **2.** That which is objective, or external to the mind. **3.** *Gram.* The objective case, or a word in it. Abbr. *obj.* **4.** *Optics.* The lens or system of lenses, as in a camera or microscope, which forms an image of the object. — **Syn.** See INTENTION. — **ob·jec'tive·ly**, *adv.* — **ob·jec'tive·ness**, *n.*

ob·jec'tiv·ism (-tĭv·ĭz'm), *n.* **1.** *Philos.* Any of certain theories stressing the objective reality, esp. as distinguished from the purely subjective existence, of the phenomenal world, of moral good, or the like. **2.** *Aesthetics.* Theory or practice of objective art or literature. See OBJECTIVE, *adj.,* 2. — **ob·jec'tiv·ist** (-ĭst), *n. & adj.* — **ob·jec'ti·vis'tic** (-tĭ·vĭs'tĭk), *adj.*

ob'jec·tiv'i·ty (ŏb'jĕk·tĭv'ĭ·tĭ), *n.* State, quality, or relation of being objective; also, objective reality.

object lens. = OBJECT GLASS.

ob'ject·less, *adj.* Having no object or purpose.

object lesson. A lesson in which a material object is made the basis of instruction; figuratively, something that teaches by a concrete example.

ob·jec'tor (ŏb·jĕk'tẽr), *n.* One who objects.

||**ob'jet' d'art** (ôb'zhĕ' dȧr'); *pl.* OBJETS D'ART (ôb'zhĕ'). [F.] An article of artistic worth.

ob'jur·gate (ŏb'jẽr·gāt; ŏb·jûr'gāt), *v. t.* [L. *objurgatus*, past part. of *objurgare* to chide, fr. *ob-* + *jurgare* to scold.] To denounce or reprove strongly. — **Syn.** See EXECRATE. — **ob'jur·ga'tion** (ŏb'jẽr·gā'shŭn), *n.* — **ob'jur·ga'tor** (ŏb'jẽr·gā'tẽr; ŏb·jûr'gȧ·tẽr), *n.* — **ob·jur'ga·to'ry** (ŏb·jûr'gȧ·tō'rĭ *or, esp. Brit.,* -tẽr·ĭ; ŏb'jẽr·gā'tō·rĭ), *adj.*

ob·lan'ce·o·late (ŏb·lăn'sē·ō·lāt), *adj.* *Bot.* Inversely lanceolate. See LEAF, *Illust.* (7).

ob'late (ŏb'lāt; ŏb·lāt'), *adj.* [L. *oblatus* offered; in sense **b** taken as the opposite of *prolate.*] **a** Offered up; devoted; dedicated; — used chiefly in titles of religious orders. **b** *Geom.* Flattened or depressed at the poles; as, an *oblate* spheroid. Cf. PROLATE. — **ob'late**, *n.* — **ob'late·ly**, *adv.*

ob·la'tion (ŏb·lā'shŭn), *n.* [OF., fr. LL. *oblatio*, fr. *oblatus*, used as past part. of *offerre* to offer.] A religious or ritualistic offering, usually of something inanimate in contrast with a sacrifice of living things; also, that which is offered; hence, any offering to a church, charity, etc. — **ob'la·to'ry** (ŏb'lȧ·tō'rĭ *or, esp. Brit.,* -tẽr·ĭ), *adj.*

ob'li·gate (ŏb'lĭ·gāt), *adj.* [L. *obligatus*, past part. of *obligare.* See OBLIGE.] **1.** Bound; under obligation; restricted. **2.** *Biol.* Limited to a single life condition; — opp. to *facultative;* as, an *obligate* parasite. — (-gāt), *v. t.* To bring or place under moral or legal duty or constraint; to bind by an obligation.

ob'li·ga'tion (-gā'shŭn), *n.* **1.** An obligating; state of being obligated. **2.** The agreement, promise, contract, oath, or the like, by which one is bound. **3.** Any duty imposed by law, promise, or contract, by social relations, etc. **4.** That which obligates; the binding power of a promise, contract, vow, etc. **5.** Indebtedness for an act of favor or kindness; also, the debt so incurred. **6.** *Law.* A conditional bond with a penalty for nonfulfillment; in a larger sense, a formal and binding agreement or acknowledgment of a liability. — **ob'li·ga'tor** (ŏb'lĭ·gā'tẽr), *n.*

Syn. **Obligation, duty** mean that which one person is bound to do or not to do as a responsible person. **Obligation** implies constraint under immediate circumstances; **duty**, impulsion from within on moral grounds.

ob'li·ga'to (ŏb'lĭ·gä'tō). Var. of OBBLIGATO.

ob·lig'a·to'ry (ŏb·lĭg'ȧ·tō'rĭ, -tẽr·ĭ; ŏb'lĭ·gȧ·tō'rĭ, -gā'tō·rĭ), *adj.* [LL. *obligatorius.*] **1.** Binding in law or conscience; imposing, or of the nature of, duty or obligation. **2.** That must be done; required. — **ob·lig'a·to'ri·ly**, *adv.*

o·blige' (ō·blīj'), *v. t.;* O·BLIGED' (-blījd'); O·BLIG'ING (-blīj'ĭng). [OF. *obligier, obliger*, fr. L. *obligare*, fr. *ob-* + *ligare* to bind.] **1.** To constrain; put under obligation to do or forbear something. **2.** To bind by some favor rendered; obligate, esp. by gratitude; hence, to do a favor for. **3.** *Obs.* To please; gratify. — **Syn.** See FORCE.

ob'li·gee' (ŏb'lĭ·jē'), *n.* **1.** *Law.* One to whom another is obligated; — opposed to *obligor.* **2.** One who is obliged; — opposed to *obliger.*

o·blig'er (ō·blīj'ẽr), *n.* One who obligates or obliges.

o·blig'ing (ō·blīj'ĭng), *adj.* **a** *Now Rare.* Obligating; obligatory. **b** Disposed to do favors; hence, helpful; accommodating. — **Syn.** See AMIABLE. — **o·blig'ing·ly**, *adv.* — **o·blig'ing·ness**, *n.*

ob'li·gor' (ŏb'lĭ·gôr'; ŏb'lĭ·gôr), *n.* *Law.* One who places himself under a legal obligation; — correlative to *obligee.*

o·blique' (ŏb·lēk'; *mil.* -līk'), *adj.* [F. or L.; F., fr. L. *obliquus*, fr. *ob-* + stem of *liquis* oblique.] **1. a** Neither perpendicular nor horizontal; slanting; inclined. **b** Of solids, having the axis not perpendicular to the base. **2.** Not straightforward; indirect; hence, disingenuous; underhand; as, *oblique* accusations. **3.** Not direct in descent; collateral. **4.** *Anat.* Designating specif. certain obliquely placed muscles, esp.: **a** The thin flat muscles forming the outer and middle layers of the lateral walls of the abdomen. **b** Either of two muscles of the eyeball. — **Syn.** See CROOKED. — *v. i.* **1.** To deviate from the perpendicular. **2.** *Mil.* To march or advance obliquely. — **ob·lique′ly**, *adv.* — **ob·lique′ness**, *n.*

oblique angle. An acute or obtuse angle; — opp. to *right angle.*

oblique case. *Gram.* Any case except the nominative and vocative.

oblique sailing. The movement of a vessel when she sails upon a course making an oblique angle with the meridian.

ob·liq′ui·tous (ŏb·lĭk′wĭ·tŭs), *adj.* Having obliquity.

ob·liq′ui·ty (-tĭ), *n.; pl.* -TIES (-tĭz). **1.** State of being oblique; deviation from a right line, or from parallelism or perpendicularity; the amount of such deviation; divergence. **2.** Deviation from moral rectitude or sound thinking. **3.** *Astron.* Of the ecliptic, the angle between the planes of the earth's equator and orbit (ecliptic).

ob·lit′er·ate (ŏb·lĭt′ẽr·āt), *v. t.* [L. *obliteratus*, past part. of *obliterare* to obliterate, fr. *ob-* + *litera, littera*, letter.] **1.** To erase or blot out; efface; cancel. **2.** To destroy, as if by effacing; render imperceptible. — **Syn.** See ERASE. — **ob·lit′er·a′tion** (-ā′shŭn), *n.* — **ob·lit′er·a′tor** (-ā′tẽr), *n.*

ob·liv′i·on (ŏb·lĭv′ĭ·ŭn), *n.* [OF., fr. L. *oblivio*, fr. *oblivisci* to forget, prop., to smooth.] **1.** Act of forgetting, or fact of having forgotten; forgetfulness. **2.** State or fact of being forgotten. **3.** Official ignoring of offenses; pardon.

ob·liv′i·ous (-ŭs), *adj.* [L. *obliviosus.*] **1.** Forgetful; not mindful; — often with *of.* **2.** Promoting oblivion; causing forgetfulness. — **Syn.** See FORGETFUL. — **ob·liv′i·ous·ly**, *adv.* — **ob·liv′i·ous·ness**, *n.*

ob′long (ŏb′lŏng; 74), *adj.* [L. *oblongus*, fr. *ob-* + *longus* long.] Elongated, esp. as deviating from a square or circular form; longer in one direction than in another, with sides parallel or nearly so; specif.: **a** *Geom.* Rectangular, with adjacent sides unequal. **b** *Bot.* Broadly elliptical. See LEAF, *Illust.* (6). — *n.* An oblong figure.

ob′lo·quy (ŏb′lō·kwĭ), *n.; pl.* -QUIES (-kwĭz). [LL. *obloquium*, fr. *obloqui* to speak against, blame, fr. *ob-* + *loqui* to speak.] **1.** Censorious speech; defamatory language; calumny. **2.** State of being spoken ill of; bad repute. — **Syn.** See ABUSE; DISGRACE.

ob·nox′ious (ŏb·nŏk′shŭs), *adj.* [L. *obnoxiosus*, fr. *obnoxius*, fr. *ob-* + *noxa* harm.] **1.** Subject, liable, or open, as to harm, injury, or evil; also, *Now Rare*, censurable; punishable. **2.** *Now Chiefly Legal.* Answerable; amenable; dependent; — usually with *to.* **3.** Offensive; objectionable. — **Syn.** See REPUGNANT. — **ob·nox′ious·ly**, *adv.* — **ob·nox′ious·ness**, *n.*

o′boe (ō′bō; ō′boi), *n.* [It., fr. F. *hautbois.* See HAUTBOY.] *Music.* **a** A slender, slightly conical wood-wind instrument with a double reed and a thin, penetrating, plaintive tone; a hautboy. **b** An organ reed stop giving an oboelike tone.

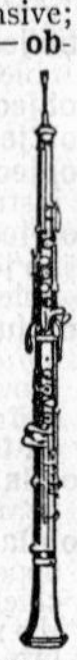

Oboe.

o′bo·ist (ō′bō·ĭst), *n.* A performer on the oboe.

ob′ol (ŏb′ŏl; ō′bŏl), *n.* [See OBOLUS.] An ancient Greek coin (originally a weight), 1/6 drachma.

ob′o·lus (ŏb′ō·lŭs), *n.; pl.* OBOLI (-lī). [L., fr. Gr. *obolos.*] An Attic weight of 11¼ grains; also, an obol.

ob·o′vate (ŏb·ō′vāt), *adj.* Inversely ovate. See LEAF, *Illust.* (9).

ob·o′void (-void), *adj. Bot.* Ovoid, with the broad end toward the apex, as some fruits, etc.

ob·scene′ (ŏb·sēn′; 2), *adj.* [F. *obscène*, fr. L. *obscenus, obscaenus, obscoenus*, ill-looking, filthy, obscene.] **1.** Foul; disgusting. **2.** Offensive to chastity or to modesty; lewd. — **Syn.** See COARSE. — **ob·scene′ly**, *adv.* — **ob·scene′ness**, *n.*

ob·scen′i·ty (ŏb·sĕn′ĭ·tĭ; -sē′nĭ·tĭ), *n.; pl.* -TIES (-tĭz). Obscene quality, language, or acts.

ob·scur′ant (ŏb·skūr′ănt), *n.* [L. *obscurans*, pres. part.] One who obscures; one who strives to hinder the progress or spread of knowledge. — **ob·scur′ant**, *adj.* — **ob·scur′ant·ism** (ŏb·skūr′ăn·tĭz′m; ŏb′skū·răn′tĭz′m), *n.* — **ob·scur′ant·ist** (-tĭst), *n. & adj.*

ob′scu·ra′tion (ŏb′skū·rā′shŭn), *n.* Act of obscuring, or state of being obscured.

ob·scure′ (ŏb·skūr′), *adj.* [F. *obscur*, fr. L. *obscurus*, orig., covered.] **1.** Destitute of light; hence, dark; dusky; gloomy. **2.** Not readily seen; as: **a** Retired or remote; hidden. **b** Not easily understood or clearly expressed; abstruse; vague. **c** Not noticeable; inconspicuous; mean. **d** Not distinct; faint; undefined.

Syn. (1) See DARK.
(2) **Obscure, dark, vague, enigmatic, cryptic, ambiguous, equivocal** mean not clearly understood. **Obscure** implies a hiding or veiling of the meaning through some fault in the thing or in the person who would understand; **dark**, an imperfect or clouded revelation; **vague**, a lack of clear formulation, often because not fully thought out; **enigmatic**, a puzzling, mystifying quality; **cryptic**, a dark and enigmatic statement; **ambiguous** and **equivocal**, use of the same word in different senses, *ambiguous*, however, implying inadvertence, and *equivocal* an attempt to confuse.

— *v. t.* **1.** To make obscure, or dark, dim, vague, indistinct. **2.** *Phonet.* To reduce (a vowel) to a sound of neutral or indefinite quality; thus, the *o* of the noun "object" is, in the verb, *obscured.*
— *n.* Obscurity; an obscure part, as in a picture.
— **ob·scure′ly**, *adv.* — **ob·scure′ness**, *n.*

ob·scu′ri·ty (ŏb·skū′rĭ·tĭ), *n.; pl.* -TIES (-tĭz). **1.** Quality or state of being obscure. **2.** Someone or something obscure.

ob′se·crate (ŏb′sē·krāt), *v. t.* [L. *obsecratus*, past part. of *obsecrare*, prop., to ask on religious grounds, fr. *ob-* + *sacrare* to declare as sacred, fr. *sacer* sacred.] To beseech; supplicate. — **ob′se·cra′tion** (-krā′shŭn), *n.*

ob·se′qui·ous (ŏb·sē′kwĭ·ŭs), *adj.* [F. *obséquieux*, fr. L. *obsequiosus*, fr. *obsequium* compliance, fr. *obsequi* to comply with, fr. *ob-* + *sequi* to follow.] **1.** *Now Rare.* Compliant; devoted. **2.** Servilely attentive; fawning. — **Syn.** See SUBSERVIENT. — **ob·se′qui·ous·ly**, *adv.* — **ob·se′qui·ous·ness**, *n.*

ob′se·quy (ŏb′sē·kwĭ), *n.; pl.* -QUIES (-kwĭz). [From OF., fr. ML. *obsequiae*, pl., funeral rites.] Now only in *pl.* Funeral rites; burial ceremonies.

ob·serv′a·ble (ŏb·zûr′vȧ·b'l), *adj.* **1.** That must or may be observed. **2.** Capable of being observed; discernible; noticeable. — **ob·serv′a·bly**, *adv.*

ob·serv′ance (-văns), *n.* **1.** Act or practice of observing a rule, law, custom, etc.; a heeding with care. **2.** A customary act; as: **a** A particular religious rite or ceremony. **b** A form; practice; custom. **3.** *Archaic.* Respectful attention; deference. **4.** Observation. **5.** *R.C.Ch.* **a** A rule or ordinance for religious. **b** An order or convent observing such rules.

ob·serv′ant (ŏb·zûr′vănt), *adj.* [F., pres. part. of *observer.* See OBSERVE.] **1.** Taking careful notice; attentive. **2.** Attentive in observing; regardful; mindful; — with *of.* **3.** Careful; heedful. — (ŏb·zûr′vănt; ŏb′zẽr-; ŏb′sẽr-), *n.* **1.** *Obs.* An obsequious servant or attendant. **2.** [*cap.*] One of a branch of Franciscans who observe the primitive rules, esp. of poverty. — **ob·serv′ant·ly** (ŏb·zûr′vănt·lĭ), *adv.*

ob′ser·va′tion (ŏb′zẽr·vā′shŭn; -sẽr-), *n.* **1.** *Now Rare.* Observance, as of rules. **2.** Act or faculty of observing, or taking notice; also, that which is observed, or noted; specif.: **a** The gathering of data, as for scientific studies, by recognizing and noting facts or occurrences; also, *chiefly pl.*, the information or data so obtained. **b** *Naut.* The ascertaining of the altitude of a heavenly body to find a vessel's position at sea. **3.** An inference drawn from observations or something observed; hence, a comment; judgment; a remark. **4.** Fact of being observed; as, in danger of *observation.* — *adj.* Used or for use in viewing scenery, or the like, or in making observations; as, an *observation* car, platform, post. — **ob′ser·va′tion·al** (-ăl; -'l), *adj.*

ob·serv′a·to′ry (ŏb·zûr′vȧ·tō′rĭ *or, esp. Brit.*, -tẽr·ĭ, -trĭ), *n.* **1.** A building equipped for observation of natural phenomena, as in meteorology, magnetism, or astronomy; also, an institution whose primary purpose is making such observations. **2.** A position or place commanding a wide view.

ob·serve′ (ŏb·zûrv′), *v. t.* [OF. *observer*, fr. L. *observare, observatum*, fr. *ob-* + *servare* to save, keep, observe.] **1.** To conform one's action or practice to; comply with; as, to *observe* the rules. **2.** To inspect or take note of as an augury or omen. **3.** To celebrate or solemnize in customary form; as, to *observe* the Sabbath. **4.** To pay attention to; watch. **5.** To perceive or notice; remark; also, to utter as an observation; say casually. **6.** To make an observation (sense 2 **a**) of; to ascertain by scientific observation. — **Syn.** See KEEP. — *v. i.* **1. a** To take notice. **b** To make observations. **2.** To remark; comment; — generally with *on* or *upon.* — **ob·serv′ing·ly**, *adv.*

ob·serv′er (ŏb·zûr′vẽr), *n.* One who observes; specif.: **a** A representative sent to observe and listen, but not to participate officially in a gathering. **b** *Aeronautics.* One who accompanies the pilot of an airplane in order to make observations during flight.

ob·sess′ (ŏb·sĕs′), *v. t.* [L. *obsessus*, past part. of *obsidēre* to besiege, fr. *ob-* + *sedere* to sit.] To beset; haunt; — of evil spirits; hence, to harass; to influence, as by a fixed idea, to an unreasonable degree. — **ob·ses′sive** (-sĕs′ĭv), *adj.* — **ob·ses′sor** (-ẽr), *n.*

ob·ses′sion (ŏb·sĕsh′ŭn), *n.* **1.** Act of an evil spirit in besetting a person, or impelling him to action, from without; the fact of being so beset or impelled. Cf. POSSESSION. **2.** Persistent and inescapable preoccupation with an idea or emotion; also, the emotion or idea.

ob·sid′i·an (ŏb·sĭd′ĭ·ăn), *n.* [From a Lat. prop. name.] *Petrog.* Volcanic glass; specif., except as limited by the attributive (as in basalt *obsidian*), such glass having the same composition as rhyolite.

ob′so·les′cent (ŏb′sō·lĕs′ĕnt; -'nt), *adj.* [L. *obsolescens, -entis*, pres. part. of *obsolescere* to wear out, fall into disuse.] Going out of use; becoming obsolete. — **ob′so·les′cence** (-ĕns; -'ns), *n.* — **ob′so·les′cent·ly**, *adv.*

ob′so·lete (ŏb′sō·lēt), *adj.* [L. *obsoletus*, past part. of *obsolescere.* See OBSOLESCENT.] **1.** No longer in use; disused; as, an *obsolete* word, law, or tax. Abbr. *obs.* **2.** Of a type or fashion no longer current; out of date; as, an *obsolete* machine. **3.** *Biol.* Indistinct or absent; — of an organ or the like which has a functional counterpart in a related species or in an earlier stage. — **Syn.** See OLD. — **ob′so·lete·ly**, *adv.* — **ob′so·lete·ness**, *n.*

ob′sta·cle (ŏb′stȧ·k'l; -stĭ·k'l), *n.* [OF., fr. L. *obstaculum*, fr. *obstare* to withstand, fr. *ob-* + *stare* to stand.] That which stands in the way, or opposes; a hindrance; an impediment; an obstruction.

ob·stet′ric (ŏb·stĕt′rĭk), **ob·stet′ri·cal** (-rĭ·kăl), *adj.* [L. *obstetricius*, fr. *obstetrix, -icis*, a midwife, fr. *obstare* to stand before. See OBSTACLE.] Of or pert. to obstetrics.

ob′ste·tri′cian (ŏb′stē·trĭsh′ăn), *n. Med.* A physician specializing in obstetrics.

ob·stet′rics (ŏb·stĕt′rĭks), *n.;* see -ICS. Science or art of assisting women in parturition; midwifery; the management of pregnancy and labor.

ob′sti·na·cy (ŏb′stĭ·nȧ·sĭ), *n.; pl.* -CIES (-sĭz). **1.** Quality or state of being obstinate; as: **a** Firm and usually unreasonable adherence to an opinion, purpose, or system; stubbornness. **b** Persistency in spite of efforts to remedy, relieve, or subdue; as, the *obstinacy* of evil. **2.** An instance of being obstinate; an obstinate action.

ob′sti·nate (-nĭt), *adj.* [L. *obstinatus*, past part. of *obstinare* to set about a thing with firmness, persist in.] **1.** Pertinaciously adhering to an opinion, purpose, or course; not yielding to reason or arguments. **2.** Not yielding to treatment, force, etc.; not easily subdued or removed. — **ob′sti·nate·ly**, *adv.* — **ob′sti·nate·ness**, *n.*

Syn. Obstinate, dogged, stubborn, pertinacious, mulish mean fixed and unyielding in purpose or course. **Obstinate** implies persistent, often perverse, adherence; **dogged**, downright, tenacious and, sometimes, sullen persistence; **stubborn**, sturdiness in resisting attempts to change purpose, course, opinion; **pertinacious**, a persistence that is annoying or irksome; **mulish**, an obstinacy as unreasonable as that of a mule. — **Ant.** Pliant.

ob·strep′er·ous (ŏb·strĕp′ẽr·ŭs), *adj.* [L. *obstreperus*, fr. *obstrepere* to make a noise at, fr. *ob-* + *strepere* to make a noise.] Uncontrollably noisy; unruly. — **Syn.** See VOCIFEROUS. — **ob·strep′er·ous·ly**, *adv.* — **ob·strep′er·ous·ness**, *n.*

ob·struct′ (ŏb·strŭkt′), *v. t.* [L. *obstructus*, past part. of *obstruere* to build up before or against, obstruct, fr. *ob* + *struere* to pile up.] **1.** To block up; stop up or close, as a way; to place an obstacle in, or fill with obstacles. **2** To be, or come, in the way of; to hinder from a passing, action, or operation; impede; retard; as, clouds *obstruct* the light. **3.** To cut off the sight of (an object). — **Syn.** See HINDER. — **ob·struct′er, ob·struc′tor**, *n.* — **ob·struc′tive**, *adj. & n.*

ob·struc′tion (ŏb·strŭk′shŭn), *n.* **1.** An obstructing; state of being obstructed. **2.** The delay, or attempted delay, of business by dilatory parliamentary tactics in a deliberative body. **3.** A thing that obstructs; an obstacle, impediment, or hindrance.

ob·struc′tion·ist (-ĭst), *n.* One who hinders progress; esp., one hampering legislation by obstruction. — **ob·struc′tion·ism** (-ĭz′m), *n.* — **ob·struc′tion·ist**, *adj.*

ob′stru·ent (ŏb′strōō·ĕnt; 114), *n. & adj.* [L. *obstruens*, pres. part.] *Chiefly Med.* (Something) causing obstruction or blocking up.

ob·tain′ (ŏb·tān′), *v. t.* [F. *obtenir*, fr. L. *obtinere*, fr. *ob-* + *tenere* to hold.] **1.** To get hold of by effort; gain possession of; procure. **2.** *Archaic.* To arrive at; attain. — **Syn.** See GET. — *v. i.* **1.** *Archaic.*

To prevail; succeed. **2.** To be recognized or established; to be prevalent or general; as, the custom *obtains* of taking vacations in summer. — **ob·tain′a·ble,** *adj.* — **ob·tain′er,** *n.*

ob·tect′ed (ŏb·tĕk′tĕd; -tĭd), *adj.* [L. *obtectus*, past part. of *obtegere* to cover over.] *Zool.* Covered with a hard horny case, as the pupa of certain flies.

ob·test′ (ŏb·tĕst′), *v. t.* [L. *obtestari*, fr. *ob-* + *testari* to witness, fr. *testis* a witness.] **1.** To beseech. **2.** To call to witness; to invoke as a witness. — **ob′tes·ta′tion** (ŏb′tĕs·tā′shŭn), *n.*

ob·trude′ (ŏb·trōōd′; 114), *v. t.* [L. *obtrudere, obtrusum*, fr. *ob-* + *trudere* to thrust.] **1.** To thrust out; eject; expel. **2.** To thrust forward or present without warrant or request. — *v. i.* To thrust oneself upon attention; to intrude. — **Syn.** See INTRUDE. — **ob·trud′er** (-trōōd′ẽr), *n.*

ob·tru′sion (ŏb·trōō′zhŭn; 114), *n.* Act of obtruding; also, that which is obtruded.

ob·tru′sive (-sĭv), *adj.* **1.** *Rare.* Protruding. **2.** Disposed to obtrude; forward; pushing; intrusive. — **Syn.** See IMPERTINENT. — **ob·tru′sive·ly,** *adv.* — **ob·tru′sive·ness,** *n.*

ob·tund′ (ŏb·tŭnd′), *v. t.* [L. *obtundere, obtusum*, fr. *ob-* + *tundere* to strike.] To reduce the edge, pungency, or violence of; to dull, as the senses. — **ob·tund′ent** (-tŭn′dĕnt), *adj.* & *n.*

ob′tu·rate (ŏb′tū·rāt), *v. t.* [L. *obturatus*, past part. of *obturare.*] To stop or close, as an opening; specif., *Ordn.*, to stop (a gun breech) so as to prevent the escape of gas in firing. — **ob′tu·ra′tion** (-rā′shŭn), *n.* — **ob′tu·ra′tor** (-rā′tẽr), *n.*

ob·tuse′ (ŏb·tūs′; 2), *adj.* [L. *obtusus*, past part. of *obtundere.* See OBTUND.] **1.** Not pointed or acute; blunt; specif.: **a** Greater than a right angle and less than two right angles; — of an angle. See ANGLE, *Illust.* **b** Having one or more obtuse angles. See TRIANGLE, *Illust.* **2.** Not having acute sensibility or perceptions; insensitive; stupid; as, he was too *obtuse* to understand. **3.** Not causing an acute impression; dull; as, *obtuse* sound. — **Syn.** See DULL. — **ob·tuse′ly,** *adv.* — **ob·tuse′ness,** *n.*

ob·tu′si- (ŏb·tū′sĭ-). [L. *obtusus.*] A combining form meaning *obtuse*, as in: **ob·tu′si·fid, ob·tu′si·lin′gual, ob·tu′si·pen′nate.**

ob·verse′ (ŏb·vûrs′; ŏb′vûrs; 2), *adj.* [L. *obversus*, past part. of *obvertere.* See OBVERT.] **1.** Facing the observer or opponent; — opposite of *reverse.* **2.** Having the base narrower than the top; as, an *obverse* leaf. — **ob·verse′ly,** *adv.*

ob′verse (ŏb′vûrs), *n.* **1.** As the opposite of *reverse:* **a** The side of a coin bearing the principal image or inscription, or, in those of the United States, the date. **b** The front or principal surface of anything. **2.** A counterpart; that which answers to, complements, or corresponds with, something else. **3.** *Logic.* A proposition inferred immediately from another by denying the opposite of that which the given proposition affirms; as, (given) All A is B; (*obverse*) No A is not-B.

ob·ver′sion (ŏb·vûr′shŭn), *n.* **1.** An obverting. **2.** *Logic.* The operation of inferring the obverse.

ob·vert′ (ŏb·vûrt′), *v. t.* [L. *obvertere*, fr. *ob-* + *vertere* to turn.] **1.** To turn (something) so as to present a different surface or aspect. **2.** *Logic.* To subject (a proposition) to obversion.

ob′vi·ate (ŏb′vĭ·āt), *v. t.* [L. *obviare*, fr. *ob-* + *via* way.] To meet or anticipate and dispose of; make unnecessary. — **Syn.** See PREVENT. — **ob′vi·a′tion** (-ā′shŭn), *n.* — **ob′vi·a′tor** (-ā′tẽr), *n.*

ob′vi·ous (-ŭs), *adj.* [L. *obvius.*] **1.** *Archaic.* That is in the way or in front; opposite; fronting. **2.** Easily discovered, seen, or understood; plain; evident. — **Syn.** See EVIDENT. — **ob′vi·ous·ly,** *adv.* — **ob′vi·ous·ness,** *n.*

ob′vo·lute (ŏb′vō·lūt), *adj.* [L. *obvolutus*, past part. of *obvolvere* to wrap round, fr. *ob-* + *volvere* to roll.] Overlapping; convolute; — specif., *Bot.*, applied to overlapping vernation, as in the sage. — **ob′vo·lu′tion** (-lū′shŭn), *n.* — **ob′vo·lu′tive** (-lū′tĭv), *adj.*

oc′a·ri′na (ŏk′ȧ·rē′nȧ), *n.* [Dim. of It. *oca* goose; named fr. the shape.] *Music.* A simple wind instrument or toy having a terra-cotta body, with mouthpiece and finger holes, and giving soft whistlelike tones.

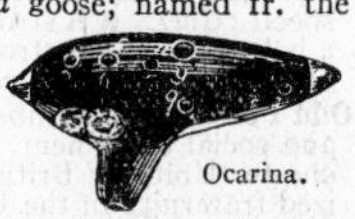
Ocarina.

oc·ca′sion (ŏ·kā′zhŭn), *n.* [OF., fr. L. *occasio*, fr. *occidere, occasum*, to fall down, fr. *ob-* + *cadere* to fall.] **1.** A favorable opportunity; a timely chance or juncture. **2.** A juncture affording ground or reason for something; as, to avoid *occasions* of sin. **3.** An occurrence, or a condition of affairs, that brings something about; cause; esp., the immediate inciting circumstances as distinguished from the real, or fundamental, cause. **4.** A happening; occurrence; now usually, time of happening; as, on the *occasion* of his reappearance. **5.** A special event, ceremony, or function. **6.** A juncture entailing need; an exigency; hence: *Obs.* **a** *pl.* Needs; requirements. **b** *pl.* Business affairs. — **Syn.** See CAUSE. — *v. t.* To give occasion to; to cause, esp. incidentally.

oc·ca′sion·al (-ăl; -'l), *adj.* **1.** Of or pertaining to an occasion or occasions; acting, met with, or occurring now and then; casual; incidental; also, infrequent. **2.** Suitable or designed for, or acting on, a special occasion or particular occasions; as, an *occasional* speaker. **3.** Acting as the occasion or contributory cause. — **oc·ca′sion·al·ly,** *adv.*

oc′ci·dent (ŏk′sĭ·dĕnt), *n.* [OF., fr. L. *occidens, -dentis*, fr. *occidens*, pres. part. of *occidere* to fall, go down.] The west; — opposed to *orient;* specif. [*cap.*], orig., Europe as opposed to Asia and the Orient; now, also, the Western Hemisphere.

oc′ci·den′tal (-dĕn′tăl; -t'l), *adj.* [F., fr. L. *occidentalis.*] Of, pertaining to, or situated in the occident, or west; western; — opposed to *oriental;* specif. [*cap.*], of or pertaining to the Occident. — *n.* An inhabitant of an occidental region or [*cap.*] of the Occident. — **oc′ci·den′tal·ly,** *adv.*

Oc′ci·den′tal·ism (-ĭz'm), *n.* The character, institutions, and culture of Occidental peoples. — **Oc′ci·den′tal·ist** (-ĭst), *n.* & *adj.*

Oc′ci·den′tal·ize (-īz), *v. t.* To render Occidental; to imbue with Occidentalism. — **Oc′ci·den′tal·i·za′tion** (-ĭ·zā′shŭn; -ī·zā′-), *n.*

oc·cip′i·tal (ŏk·sĭp′ĭ·tăl), *adj.* [ML. *occipitalis.*] *Anat.* Of or pertaining to the occiput or the compound bone, **occipital bone,** which forms the posterior part of the skull. — *n.* The occipital bone.

oc·cip′i·to- (ŏk·sĭp′ĭ·tō-). [See OCCIPUT.] *Anat.* A combining form denoting *occipital and.*

oc′ci·put (ŏk′sĭ·pŭt; -pŭt), *n.;* *pl.* OCCIPITA (ŏk·sĭp′ĭ·tȧ). [L., fr. *ob-* + *caput* head.] *Anat.* The back part of the skull. See DOG, *Illust.*

oc·clude′ (ŏ·klōōd′; 114), *v. t.* [L. *occludere, occlusum*, fr. *ob-* + *claudere* to shut.] **1.** To close; obstruct. **2.** To shut in or out by or as by closing a passage. **3.** *Chem.* To absorb; — said esp. of the absorbing of gases by certain substances; as, iron *occludes* hydrogen. — *v. i.* *Dent.* To close with the cusps fitting together, as upper and lower teeth. — **oc·clud′ent** (ŏ·klōōd′ĕnt), *n.* & *adj.* — **oc·clu′sion** (-klōō′zhŭn), *n.* — **oc·clu′sive** (-sĭv), *adj.*

oc·cult′ (ŏ·kŭlt′; ŏk′ŭlt; 2), *adj.* [L. *occultus*, past part. of *occulere* to cover up, hide.] **1.** *Now Rare.* Hidden from sight; obscure. **2.** Of, pertaining to, concerned with, or designating alchemy, magic, astrology and other arts and practices involving use of divination, incantation, magical formulae, etc. **3.** Beyond the scope of the understanding; mysterious. — *n.* That which is occult; esp., the occult arts, or sciences. — (ŏ·kŭlt′), *v. t.* & *i.* To hide or become hidden from sight; specif., *Astron.*, to conceal by occultation.

oc′cul·ta′tion (ŏk′ŭl·tā′shŭn), *n.* **1.** Concealment; state of being hidden from view or lost to notice. **2.** *Astron.* Shutting off of the light of one celestial body by the intervention of another; — applied esp. to eclipses of stars and planets by the moon.

oc·cult′er (ŏ·kŭl′tẽr), *n.* An occulting screen.

oc·cult′ism (ŏ·kŭl′tĭz'm), *n.* Occult theory or practice; belief in hidden or mysterious powers and the possibility of human control of them. — **oc·cult′ist** (-tĭst), *n.* & *adj.*

oc′cu·pan·cy (ŏk′ū·păn·sĭ), *n.* **1.** Occupation; a taking or holding possession. **2.** *Law.* Act of taking possession of an unowned thing, as a derelict, thus acquiring title thereto.

oc′cu·pant (-pănt), *n.* [F. or L.; F., fr. L. *occupans*, pres. part.] One who occupies; as, the *occupant* of the house; esp., *Law*, one who acquires a title by occupancy.

oc′cu·pa′tion (-pā′shŭn), *n.* [OF., fr. L. *occupatio.*] **1.** Act or process of occupying; state of being occupied; occupancy. **2.** That which occupies, or engages, the time and attention; one's principal business; vocation. — **Syn.** See WORK.

oc′cu·pa′tion·al (ŏk′ū·pā′shŭn·ăl; -'l), *adj.* Of or pertaining to, or resulting from (a particular) occupation; as, *occupational* diseases. — **oc′cu·pa′tion·al·ly,** *adv.*

occupational therapy. The science or art of treating disease or injury by prescribing regulated work of a sort suitable for promoting recovery or rehabilitation.

Occupation Day. July 25, the anniversary of the landing of American troops in 1898 at Guanica, Puerto Rico, celebrated as a holiday.

oc′cu·py (ŏk′ū·pī), *v. t.;* OC′CU·PIED (-pīd); OC′CU·PY′ING. [OF. *occuper*, fr. L. *occupare.*] **1.** To take or enter upon possession of, as a place by settling in it or conquering it. **2.** To take up, or have place in, the extent (in space or time) of; fill; as, the camp *occupies* five acres. **3.** To be in possession of on tenure; hold, as an office; dwell in, as a tenant. **4.** To employ; busy; keep engaged; as, to *occupy* oneself in reading. — *v. i.* *Now Rare.* To take or hold possession. — **oc′cu·pi′er** (-pī′ẽr), *n.*

oc·cur′ (ŏ·kûr′), *v. i.;* -CURRED′ (-kûrd′); -CUR′RING. [L. *occurrere, occursum*, fr. *ob-* + *currere* to run.] **1.** To be found or met with; present itself; appear; hence, to happen. **2.** To come to the mind; suggest itself. — **Syn.** See HAPPEN.

oc·cur′rence (ŏ·kûr′ĕns), *n.* **1.** Appearance or happening. **2.** Any incident or event; esp., an unexpected happening.

Syn. Occurrence, event, incident, episode, circumstance mean something that happens or takes place. **Occurrence,** the general term, suggests no more than this; **event** implies a more or less important occurrence, frequently one that has antecedents; **incident,** an occurrence of subordinate character, of secondary importance, or a single event as in a play; **episode,** an incident marked by distinctiveness or apartness; **circumstance,** an incident thought of as a detail.

oc·cur′rent (-ĕnt), *adj.* *Now Rare.* Occurring. — *n.* *Obs.* An occurrence.

o′cean (ō′shăn), *n.* [OF., fr. L. *oceanus*, fr. Gr. *ōkeanos* ocean, in Homer, the great river supposed to encompass the earth.] **1.** The whole body of salt water which covers nearly three fourths of the surface of the globe. **2.** One of the large bodies of water into which the great ocean is regarded as divided; as, the Atlantic *Ocean.* **3.** An immense expanse; any unlimited space or quantity.

o′ce·an′ic (ō′shē·ăn′ĭk), *adj.* Of, pertaining to, found in or about, or produced by the ocean.

O·ce′a·nid (ō·sē′ȧ·nĭd), *n.* [Gr. *Ōkeanis, -idos.*] *Gr. Myth.* An ocean nymph, one of the 3000 daughters of Oceanus and Tethys.

o′ce·a·nog′ra·phy (ō′shē·ȧ·nŏg′rȧ·fĭ; ō′shăn·ŏg′-), *n.* Geography that deals with the ocean and its phenomena. — **o′ce·a·nog′ra·pher** (-fẽr), *n.* — **o′ce·a·no·graph′ic** (-nō·grăf′ĭk), **o′ce·a·no·graph′i·cal** (-ĭ·kăl), *adj.* — **o′ce·a·no·graph′i·cal·ly,** *adv.*

O·ce′a·nus (ō·sē′ȧ·nŭs), *n.* [L., fr. Gr. *Ōkeanos.*] *Gr. Myth.* **a** The great outer sea encircling the earth. **b** The god of this sea, and the father of the Oceanids.

o·cel′lar (ō·sĕl′ẽr), *adj.* *Zool.* Of or pert. to an ocellus or ocelli.

oc′el·lat′ed (ŏs′ĕ·lāt′ĕd; ō·sĕl′āt·ĕd; -ĭd), *adj.* Also **oc′el·late** (ŏs′ĕ·lāt; ō·sĕl′āt). [L. *ocellatus*, fr. *ocellus.*] **a** Having ocelli. Cf. BLENNY, *Illust.* **b** Like an eye or ocellus. — **oc′el·la′tion** (ŏs′ĕ·lā′shŭn), *n.*

o·cel′lus (ō·sĕl′ŭs), *n.;* *pl.* OCELLI (-ī). [L., dim. of *oculus* an eye.] *Zool.* **a** A little eye; a minute simple eye or eyespot found in many invertebrates. See HYMENOPTERON, *Illust.* **b** An eyelike spot.

o′ce·lot (ō′sĕ·lŏt; ŏs′ĕ-), *n.;* see PLURAL, *Note*, 3. [F., abbr. of Nahuatl *thalocelotl*, lit., field jaguar.] A large American cat (*Felis pardalis*), ranging from Texas to Patagonia, tawny yellow or gray with markings of black.

o′cher, o′chre (ō′kẽr), *n.* [F. *ocre*, fr. L. *ochra*, fr. Gr. *ōchra*, fr. *ōchros* pale yellow.] **1.** An earthy, often impure ore of iron, usually red (hematite) or yellow (limonite), used as a pigment in paints, etc. **2.** The color of ocher, esp. of yellow ocher. — *v. t.;* O′CHERED, O′CHRED (-kẽrd); O′CHER·ING (-kẽr·ĭng), O′CHRING (-krĭng). To color with ocher. — **o′cher·ous** (ō′kẽr·ŭs), **o′chre·ous** (ō′kẽr·ŭs; ō′krē·ŭs), *adj.* — **o′cher·y** (ō′kẽr·ĭ), **o′chry** (ō′krĭ), *adj.*

och·loc′ra·cy (ŏk·lŏk′rȧ·sĭ), *n.* [From F., fr. Gr. *ochlokratia*, fr. *ochlos* populace + *kratos* strength.] Government by the mob; mob rule. — **och′lo·crat** (ŏk′lō·krăt), *n.* — **och′lo·crat′ic** (-krăt′ĭk), **och′lo·crat′i·cal** (-ĭ·kăl), *adj.*

och′lo·pho′bi·a (ŏk′lō·fō′bĭ·ȧ), *n.* [NL., fr. Gr. *ochlos* crowd + *-phobia.*] Morbid fear of crowds.

och·one′ (ŭĸ·ōn′), *interj.* [Ir. *ochon.*] *Ir. & Scot.* Alas!

och′re·a (ŏk′rē·ȧ). Erroneous for *ocrea.*

o′chroid (ō′kroid), *adj.* [Gr. *ōchroeidēs*, fr. *ōchros* pale yellow + *eidos* form.] Like ocher in color.

-ock (-ŭk). [AS. *-uc, -oc.*] A suffix forming *diminutives.*

o'clock' (ō·klŏk'; 4). Of the clock. See CLOCK, *n., Note.*

o'co·til'lo (ō'kō·tēl'yō; -tē'yō), *n.* [Sp., dim. of *ocote* a Mexican pine.] A thorny, scarlet-flowered candlewood (*Fouquieria splendens*) of the southwestern U. S. and Mexico.

oc're·a (ŏk'rē·ȧ; ō'krē·ȧ), *n.; pl.* OCREAE (-ē). [L., greave, legging.] **1.** *Bot.* A tubular sheath around the base of a leafstalk. **2.** *Zool.* A sheath, as of a booted tarsus of a bird. — **oc're·ate** (-āt), *adj.*

oc'ta- (ŏk'tȧ-), **oct-**. [Gr. *oktō.*] A prefix meaning *eight,* as in **oc'ta·va'lent,** having a valence of eight.

oc'ta·chord (ŏk'tȧ·kôrd), *n.* [Gr. *oktachordos* with eight strings. See OCTO-; CHORD.] *Music.* **a** An instrument of eight strings. **b** A system of eight tones, as the diatonic octave. — **oc'ta·chor'dal** (-kôr'dăl; -d'l), *adj.*

oc'tad (ŏk'tăd), *n.* [Gr. *oktas, -ados,* the number eight.] A group of eight, as, in ancient notation, a group of eight figures representing consecutive powers of ten. — **oc·tad'ic** (ŏk·tăd'ĭk), *adj.*

oc'ta·gon (ŏk'tȧ·gŏn; -gŭn), *n.* [L. *octogonos,* adj., fr. Gr. *oktagōnos* eight-cornered, fr. *okta-* (for *oktō* eight) + *gōnia* an angle.] A (plane) polygon having eight angles, and therefore eight sides.

oc·tag'o·nal (ŏk·tăg'ō·năl; -n'l), *adj.* Having eight angles and eight sides. — **oc·tag'o·nal·ly,** *adv.*

oc'ta·he'dral (ŏk'tȧ·hē'drăl), *adj.* Having eight plane faces; of, pert. to, or formed in octahedra; as, *octahedral* crystals.

oc'ta·he'drite (-drīt), *n.* *Mineral.* A tetragonal form of titanium dioxide, TiO_2.

oc'ta·he'dron (-drŭn), *n.; pl.* -DRA (-drȧ). [Gr. *oktaedron,* fr. *oktaedros* eight-sided, fr. *okta-* (for *oktō* eight) + *hedra* base.] *Geom.* A solid formed by eight faces.

oc·tam'er·ous (ŏk·tăm'ẽr·ŭs), *adj.* [*octa-* + *-merous.*] *Bot. & Zool.* Having or designating organs or parts arranged in eights. Often written 8-*merous.* — **oc·tam'er·ism** (-ĭz'm), *n.*

oc·tam'e·ter (-ē·tẽr), *adj.* [LL., in eight feet, fr. Gr. *oktametros.*] *Pros.* Containing eight measures or feet. — *n.* A verse containing eight feet.

oc'tane (ŏk'tān), *n.* [*oct-* + *-ane* as in meth*ane.*] *Chem.* Any of a group of isomeric hydrocarbons, C_8H_{18}, of the methane series.

octane number *or* **rating.** A number used to measure the antiknock properties of a liquid motor fuel. It is the percentage by volume of a certain octane ("iso-octane," 2, 2, 4-trimethyl-pentane) in a mixture of this octane and another hydrocarbon ("heptane," C_7H_{16}) that matches the fuel being tested in the property of knocking. The higher the octane number the less is the likelihood of knocking. Cf. CETANE NUMBER.

oc'tan·gle (ŏk'tăng·g'l), *adj.* Octangular. — *n.* An octagon.

oc·tan'gu·lar (ŏk·tăng'gū·lẽr), *adj.* [L. *octangulus* eight-cornered, fr. *octo* eight + *angulus* angle.] Octagonal.

oc'tant (ŏk'tănt), *n.* [L. *octans, -antis,* fr. *octo* eight.] **1.** *Geom.* The eighth part of a circle; an arc or angle of 45 degrees. **2.** **a** *Astron. & Astrol.* The position or aspect of a celestial body, as the moon or a planet, when distant from another body by 45 degrees. **b** A type of instrument for measuring angles, similar to a sextant. **3.** *Math. & Cryst.* Any of the eight parts into which a space is divided by three co-ordinate planes. — **oc·tan'tal** (ŏk·tăn'tăl; -t'l), *adj.*

oc'tarch·y (ŏk'tär·kĭ), *n.; pl.* -IES (-kĭz). [*oct-* + *-archy.*] **1.** A government by eight rulers. **2.** A group of eight governments; — used esp. of Anglo-Saxon Britain by those who consider "heptarchy" inaccurate.

oc'tave (ŏk'tāv; -tĭv), *n.* [F., fr. L. *octava* an eighth, fr. *octavus* eighth, fr. *octo* eight.] **1.** The eighth day (counting the festival day) after a church festival; also, the week after the festival. **2.** Any group of eight. **3.** *Music.* **a** An interval embracing eight diatonic degrees. **b** A tone or note at this interval, or of successive like intervals above or below. **c** The harmonic combination of two tones an octave apart. **d** The whole series of notes, tones, or keys comprised within this interval; one of several such series or tone groups reckoned from a standard tone. See PITCH, *Illust.* **e** An organ stop giving tones an octave above those corresponding to the digitals. **4.** *Pros.* The first two quatrains, or first eight verses, of a sonnet; a stanza of eight lines. — *adj.* Consisting of an octave; eight; *Music,* producing sounds an octave higher; as, an *octave* instrument. — **oc·ta'val** (ŏk·tā'văl; ŏk'tȧ-), *adj.*

oc·ta'vo (ŏk·tā'vō; ŏk·tä'-), *n.; pl.* -VOS (-vōz). [L. *in octavo,* fr. *in* in + *octavo,* abl. of *octavus.* See OCTAVE.] A book of sheets folded each into eight leaves; hence, a more or less definite size of book so made; — usually written 8vo or 8°. — **oc·ta'vo,** *adj.*

oc·ten'ni·al (ŏk·tĕn'ĭ·ăl; 58), *adj.* [LL. *octennium* period of eight years, fr. *octo* + *annus* year.] Happening every eighth year; also, lasting eight years. — **oc·ten'ni·al·ly,** *adv.*

oc·tet' (ŏk·tĕt'), *n.* Also **oc·tette'.** [From L. *octo* eight, after E. *duet.*] **1.** *Music.* A composition for eight parts, usually for eight soloists; also, the eight performers of such a composition. **2.** Any group of eight; specif., the first eight lines of a sonnet.

oc·til'lion (ŏk·tĭl'yŭn), *n. & adj.* [F.] See NUMERATION, *Table.* — **oc·til'lionth** (-yŭnth), *n. & adj.*

oc'to- (ŏk'tō-), **oct-.** [Gr. *oktō.*] A combining form meaning *eight.*

Oc·to'ber (ŏk·tō'bẽr), *n.* [L., the eighth month of the primitive Roman year, which began in March, fr. *octo* eight.] **1.** The tenth month of the year, containing 31 days. Abbr. *Oct.* **2.** Ale made in the month of October.

October Revolution. *Russ. Hist.* The revolution, starting Oct. 25, 1917, O.S. (Nov. 7, N.S.), by which the Kerenski provisional government in Russia was overthrown and, ultimately, the Bolsheviks gained power.

oc'to·de·cil'lion (ŏk'tō·dē·sĭl'yŭn), *n.* See NUMERATION, *Table.*

oc'to·dec'i·mo (-dĕs'ĭ·mō), *n.; pl.* -MOS (-mōz). [L. *octodecimus* eighteenth.] A size of book resulting from folding each sheet into eighteen leaves, measuring about 4 by 6½ inches; also, a book of such size; — usually written 18mo or 18°, and called *eighteenmo.* — **oc'to·dec'i·mo,** *adj.*

oc'to·ge·nar'i·an (-jē·nâr'ĭ·ăn; 6), *adj.* [See OCTOGENARY.] Eighty, or between eighty and eighty-nine, years old; of or pert. to such age. — *n.* An octogenarian person.

oc·tog'e·nar'y (ŏk·tŏj'ē·nĕr'ĭ; -nẽr·ĭ), *adj.* [L. *octogenarius,* fr. *octogeni* eighty each, fr. *octoginta* eighty.] Octogenarian. — *n.; pl.* -IES (-ĭz). An octogenarian.

oc'to·nar'y (ŏk'tō·nĕr'ĭ; -nẽr·ĭ), *adj.* [L. *octonarius,* fr. *octoni* eight each, fr. *octo* eight.] Of or pertaining to the number eight. — *n.; pl.* -IES (-ĭz). **a** A group or set of eight; an ogdoad. **b** *Pros.* An octave.

oc'to·pus (ŏk'tō·pŭs; *L.* ŏk·tō'pŭs), *n.; pl.* OCTOPUSES (ŏk'tō·pŭs·ĕz; -ĭz); OCTOPODES (ŏk·tŏp'ō·dēz; -tō'pō·dēz); OCTOPI (ŏk·tō'pī). [NL., fr. Gr. *oktōpous* eight-footed, fr. *oktō* eight + *pous, podos,* foot.] **1.** A member of the typical genus (*Octopus*) of an order (Octopoda) of eight-armed dibranchiate cephalopods, or, in a broader sense, any member of that order except the argonauts. Most species are rather small and, usually, timid and inoffensive. **2.** Something suggestive of an octopus; esp., an organization with many branches through which it maintains a hold on others.

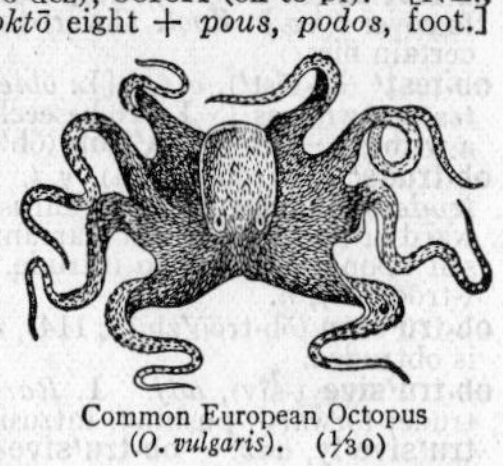

Common European Octopus (*O. vulgaris*). (1/30)

oc'to·roon' (ŏk'tō·rōōn'), *n.* [*octo-* + *-roon* as in quad*roon.*] The offspring of a quadroon and a white person.

oc'to·syl'la·ble (ŏk'tō·sĭl'ȧ·b'l; ŏk'tō·sĭl'-), *n.* A line or a word of eight syllables. — **oc'to·syl'la·ble,** *adj.* — **oc'to·syl·lab'ic** (-sĭ·lăb'ĭk), *adj.*

oc·troi' (ŏk·trwä'; *F.* ôk'trwȧ'), *n.; pl.* OCTROIS (ŏk·trwäz'; *F.* ôk'trwȧ'). [F.] **a** A tax on commodities being brought into a town. **b** The boundary where, or the officials by whom, this tax is collected.

oc'tu·ple (ŏk'tū·p'l; ŏk·tū'-), *adj.* [L. *octuplus.*] Eightfold. — *v. t.;* OC'TU·PLED (-p'ld); OC'TU·PLING (-plĭng). To multiply by eight.

oc'u·lar (ŏk'ū·lẽr), *adj.* [L. *ocularis,* fr. *oculus* the eye.] **1.** Of, pertaining to, connected with, or used for or by the eye; also, eyelike. **2.** Obtained, or received, by the sight; visual; as, *ocular* proof. — *n.* *Optics.* The eyepiece of an optical instrument.

oc'u·list (-lĭst), *n.* [F. *oculiste,* fr. L. *oculus* the eye.] A specialist in diseases of the eye; an ophthalmologist.

oc'u·lo- (ŏk'ū·lō-), **ocul-.** [L. *oculus.*] A combining form meaning *the eye; ocular and.*

oc'u·lo·mo'tor (-mō'tẽr), *adj.* [*oculo-* + *motor.*] *Anat.* Designating or pertaining to a motor nerve (**oculomotor nerve**), one of a pair of cranial nerves that originate in the midbrain and are distributed to nearly all the muscles of the eye. — *n.* The oculomotor nerve.

Od *or* **'Od** (ŏd). Also **Odd.** [*often not cap.*] *Archaic & Dial.* A minced form of *God,* used euphemistically.

od (ŏd; ōd), *n.* [G.; coined by Reichenbach, Ger. naturalist.] A theoretical force or natural power, supposed to produce the phenomena of hypnotism, and to be developed by magnets, heat, light, chemical or vital action, etc.

o'da·lisque, o'da·lisk (ō'dȧ·lĭsk), *n.* [F. *odalisque,* fr. Turk. *ōdahliq* chambermaid, fr. *ōdah* chamber.] A female slave or concubine in a harem, esp. of a Turkish sultan.

odd (ŏd; 73), *adj.* In sense 6 compared: ODD'ER (-ẽr); ODD'EST. [ON. *oddi* tongue of land, triangle, odd number, orig., a point, tip.] **1.** Not paired with another; without a mate; as, an *odd* shoe. **2.** Not divisible by 2 without leaving a remainder; — opposed to *even;* hence, designated by an odd number; as, an *odd* year. **3.** Left over after a definite round number has been taken or mentioned; a few more; as, a thousand and *odd* years ago. **4.** Designating an inconsiderable surplus of a smaller denomination; — as in the phrase *and odd money,* now shortened to *odd;* as, it cost ten pounds *odd.* **5.** Being in addition to what is usual, regular, found in a set, accounted for, etc.; extra; as, *odd* minutes or jobs; an *odd* chair; also, *Com.,* being other (commonly, less) than the usual unit in transactions; as, to buy shares in *odd* lots. **6.** **a** Unusual; singular; strange. **b** *Colloq.* Marked by oddities; eccentric. **7.** Doing odd jobs or hired for an odd job; as, an *odd* man. — **Syn.** See STRANGE. — *n.* Something odd, or additional; specif.: *Golf.* **a** A stroke more than the last played by an opponent at a hole. **b** *Eng.* A stroke taken from a player's total at a hole, to give him odds. — **odd'ly,** *adv.* — **odd'ness,** *n.*

Odd Fellow. A member of a secret order, or fraternity, for mutual aid and social enjoyment, the Independent Order of Odd Fellows, Manchester Unity, of British origin; also, a member of a separately organized fraternity in the United States.

odd'i·ty (ŏd'ĭ·tĭ; 73), *n.; pl.* -TIES (-tĭz). **1.** State or quality of being odd; singularity. **2.** That which is odd; as, a collection of *oddities;* an odd person, trait, etc.

odd'ment (ŏd'mĕnt), *n.* **1.** An odd thing; something left over; a scrap, etc. **2.** *Printing.* Any of the separate small parts in a book, other than the text, as the title page, contents page, etc.

odd'-pin'nate, *adj.* *Bot.* Pinnate with a single terminal leaflet; imparipinnate. See LEAF, *Illust.* (22).

odds (ŏdz; 73), *n. pl. & sing.* **1.** Unequal things or conditions; as, to make *odds* even, to level unequal things to equality. **2.** Difference or amount of difference; now, difference with respect to disadvantage, or more commonly advantage; excess of chances; as, the *odds* lie on our side. **3.** An equalizing allowance to the competing part that is at a disadvantage; as, to give or take *odds* in betting. **4.** Quarrel; dispute; variance; — chiefly in *at odds.*

odds and ends. Remnants; scraps; oddments.

ode (ōd), *n.* [F., fr. LL. *ode, oda,* fr. Gr. *ōidē* a song, esp. a lyric song, contr. fr. *aoidē,* fr. *aeidein* to sing.] A poem suited to be set to music and sung or chanted orig. by a chorus moving rhythmically; esp., such a poem characterized by nobility of sentiment and dignity of style. In metrical form, odes are of the following types: (1) the ***regular,*** *or* ***Pindaric, ode,*** such as Gray's *Bard,* divided into sections, each having a strophe and an antistrophe of identical form and an epode of contrasting form; (2) the ***irregular,*** *or* ***Pseudo-Pindaric, ode,*** such as the so-called *Pindaric Odes* of Cowley marked by lack of design in verse and stanzaic structure, and of correspondences between parts; (3) the ***Lesbian,*** *or* ***Horatian, ode,*** such as Keats's *To Autumn,* having uniform lyric stanzas.

-ode (-ōd). [Gr. *-ōdēs, -odes,* fr. *-o-* + *-eidēs* like, fr. *eidos* form.] A suffix denoting *like, thing that is like,* as in *geode.*

-ode. [Gr. *hodos.*] A suffix meaning *way, path,* as in cath*ode,* an*ode,* electr*ode.*

o·de'um (ō·dē'ŭm), *n.; pl.* ODEA (-ȧ). [L., fr. Gr. *ōideion,* fr. *ōidē.* See ODE.] In ancient Greece and Rome, a small, roofed theater; hence, a hall, gallery, etc., for musical or dramatic performances.

od'ic (ōd'ĭk), *adj.* Pertaining to, or forming, an ode.

od'ic (ŏd'ĭk; ōd'ĭk), *adj.* Of or pertaining to od.

O'din (ō'dĭn), **O'thin** (ō'thĭn), *n.* [Dan. *Odin*, ON. *Ōthinn.* See WODEN.] *Norse Myth.* The chief god of the mythology of the Eddas. He was god of war, of those slain in battle, of wisdom, and also of poetry. His wife was Frigg.

o'di·ous (ō'dĭ·ŭs *or, esp. Brit.*, ōd'yŭs; 58), *adj.* [OF. *odieus*, fr. L. *odiosus*, fr. *odium* hatred.] Deserving of or provoking hatred or repugnance; exciting odium. — **Syn.** See HATEFUL. — **o'di·ous·ly**, *adv.* — **o'di·ous·ness**, *n.*

o'di·um (ō'dĭ·ŭm), *n.* [L.; akin to L. *odi* I hate.] **1.** Hatred; now, usually, state or fact of being hated. **2.** The stigma attaching to what is hateful; opprobrium. — **Syn.** See DISGRACE.

o'do·graph (ō'dō·grăf; 9), *n.* [Gr. *hodos* way + *-graph.*] **1.** A machine for registering the distance traversed by a vehicle or pedestrian. **2.** A device for recording the length and rapidity of stride and number of steps taken by a walker. **3.** An automatic device for plotting the course and distance traveled by a vehicle.

o·dom'e·ter (ō·dŏm'ē·tẽr), *n.* [Gr. *hodometron, -tros*, an instrument for measuring distances, fr. *hodos* way + *metron* measure.] An instrument to measure the distance traversed, as by a vehicle. — **o·dom'e·try** (-trĭ), *n.*

-o·dont (-ō·dŏnt). [Gr. *odōn, odontos.*] A combining form meaning *tooth.*

o·don'to- (ō·dŏn'tō-), **odont-**. [Gr. *odōn, odontos.*] A combining form meaning *tooth*, as in **o'don·tal'gi·a, o'don·tal'gic, o'don·ti'a·sis.**

o·don'to·blast (-blăst), *n.* [*odonto-* + *-blast.*] *Anat.* One of the cells on the outer surface of the pulp of a tooth which secrete the dentine. — **o·don'to·blas'tic** (-blăs'tĭk), *adj.*

o·don'to·glos'sum (-glŏs'ŭm), *n.* [NL., fr. *odonto-* + Gr. *glōssa* tongue.] Any of a genus (*Odontoglossum*) of widely cultivated tropical American epiphytic orchids.

o·don'to·graph (ō·dŏn'tō·grăf; 9), *n.* An instrument for marking or laying off the outlines of gear teeth.

o·don'toid (-toid), *adj.* [Gr. *odontoeidēs*, fr. *odōn, odontos*, a tooth + *eidos* form.] *Anat. & Zool.* **a** Toothlike. **b** Designating or pertaining to a toothlike process (**odontoid process** *or* **peg**) projecting from the anterior end of the centrum of the axis vertebra on which the atlas vertebra rotates. — **o·don'toid**, *n.*

o'don·tol'o·gy (ō'dŏn·tŏl'ō·jĭ; ŏd'ŏn-), *n.* [*odonto-* + *-logy.*] The science which treats of the teeth, their structure and development, and their diseases. — **o·don'to·log'i·cal** (ō·dŏn'tō·lŏj'ĭ·kăl), *adj.* — **o'don·tol'o·gist** (ō'dŏn·tŏl'ō·jĭst; ŏd'ŏn-), *n.*

o·don'to·phore (ō·dŏn'tō·fōr; 70), *n.* [*odonto-* + *-phore.*] *Zool.* **a** A structure, usually protrusible, in the mouth of most mollusks except the bivalves, supporting the radula. **b** The radula. — **o'don·toph'o·ral** (ō'dŏn·tŏf'ō·răl), **o'don·toph'o·rine** (-rīn; -rĭn), **o'don·toph'o·rous** (-rŭs), *adj.*

o'dor, o'dour (ō'dẽr), *n.* [OF., fr. L. *odor.*] **1.** That property of a substance which affects the sense of smell; any smell; scent; fragrance. **2.** A perfume. **3.** Repute; estimation; as, to be in bad *odor.* — **Syn.** See SMELL.

o'dor·if'er·ous (ō'dẽr·ĭf'ẽr·ŭs), *adj.* [L. *odorifer*, fr. *odor* odor + *ferre* to bear.] Yielding an odor; usually fragrant. — **o'dor·if'er·ous·ly**, *adv.* — **o'dor·if'er·ous·ness**, *n.*

o'dor·less (ō'dẽr·lĕs; -lĭs), *adj.* Free from odor.

o'dor·ous (ō'dẽr·ŭs), *adj.* [L. *odorus.*] Having an odor, esp. a sweet odor; odoriferous; fragrant. — **o'dor·ous·ly**, *adv.* — **o'dor·ous·ness**, *n.*

od'yl, od'yle (ŏd'ĭl; ŏd'-), *n.* [*od* + Gr. *hylē* matter, material.] = OD. — **o·dyl'ic** (ō·dĭl'ĭk), *adj.*

-o·dy'ni·a (-ō·dĭn'ĭ·ȧ; -ō·dī'nĭ·ȧ). [NL., fr. Gr. *odynē* pain.] A combining form denoting *state of pain, morbid pain in a certain* (specified) *part.*

O·dys'seus (ō·dĭs'ūs; -dĭs'ē·ŭs), *n.* [Gr.] A king of Ithaca, one of the Greek chieftains in the Trojan War, famed for his craft, wisdom, and eloquence. See ODYSSEY.

Od'ys·sey (ŏd'ĭ·sĭ), *n.* [L. *Odyssea*, fr. Gr. *Odysseia*, fr. *Odysseus* Ulysses.] **1.** An epic attributed to Homer, which describes the ten years' wanderings of Odysseus in returning home after the siege of Troy. **2.** [*often not cap.; pl.* -SEYS (-sĭz).] A long wandering or series of travels. — **Od'ys·se'an** (-sē'ăn), *adj.*

oe-. For many words beginning with *oe-* (as **oe·col'o·gy, oec'u·men'i·cal, oe·de'ma**), see the preferred form in *e-*.

Oed'i·pus (ĕd'ĭ·pŭs; ē'dĭ·pŭs), *n.* [L., fr. Gr. *Oidipous.*] Son of Laius and Jocasta, king and queen of Thebes who, because of an oracle foretelling that he would kill his father, was given at birth to a herdsman to expose. His life was spared and eventually he was adopted by the king of Corinth. When grown he left Corinth, an oracle having warned him that he would kill his father and marry his mother. This prophecy was fulfilled. Cf. SEVEN AGAINST THEBES.

Oedipus complex. See COMPLEX, *n.*, 2.

‖**œil-de-bœuf** (û'y'·dē·bûf'), *n.; pl.* ŒILS-DE-BŒUF (û'y'-). [F., lit., eye of an ox.] *Arch.* A circular or oval window; — of architecture of the 17th and 18th centuries.

‖**œil'lade'** (û'yȧd'), *n.* [F., fr. *œil* eye.] A glance of the eye; an amorous look; an ogle.

oe·nol'o·gy (ē·nŏl'ō·jĭ), *n.* [Gr. *oinos* wine + *-logy.*] Knowledge or study of wines. — **oe'no·log'i·cal** (ē'nō·lŏj'ĭ·kăl), *adj.* — **oe·nol'o·gist** (ē·nŏl'ō·jĭst), *n.*

oe'no·mel (ē'nō·mĕl; ĕn'ō-), *n.* [LL. *oenomeli*, fr. Gr. *oinomeli*, fr. *oinos* wine + *meli* honey.] **1.** *Gr. Antiq.* A beverage consisting of wine and honey. **2.** *Poetic.* A strong, sweet draught, as of language or thought.

Oe·no'ne (ē·nō'nē), *n.* *Greek Myth.* A nymph of Mount Ida and wife of Paris, who abandoned her for Helen of Troy. See APPLE OF DISCORD.

o'er (ōr; 70), *prep., adv. & prefix.* Over; — a contraction.

oer'sted (ûr'stĕd), *n.* [After Hans Christian *Oersted* (1777–1851), Dan. physicist.] *Elec.* **a** The C.G.S. unit of intensity of a magnetic field which unit equals the intensity in a vacuum at a distance of one centimeter from a unit magnetic pole. **b** Formerly, a unit of reluctance which equaled one gilbert per maxwell.

oesophag-. For variant forms beginning *oesophag-*, see forms in *esophag-*.

oes'tra·di'ol (ĕs'trȧ·dī'ōl; -ŏl; ēs'-), **oes'tri·ol** (ĕs'trī·ōl; -ŏl; ēs'-; ēs·trī'-; ĕs-), **oes'tro·gen** (ĕs'trō·jĕn; ēs'-). Vars. of ESTRADIOL, ESTRIOL, ESTROGEN.

oes'trin (ĕs'trĭn; ēs'-), *n.* *Biochem.* Estrone.

oes'trous (ĕs'trŭs; ēs'-), *adj.* Of or pertaining to the oestrus.

oestrous, *or* **oestrus, cycle.** The entire sequence of changes, esp. in the reproductive organs, involved in the onset and subsidence of oestrus.

oes'trum (ĕs'trŭm; ēs'-), *n.* [NL.] **1.** = OESTRUS, 2. **2.** Oestrus; esp., the period of sexual heat. — **oes'tru·al** (ĕs'trōō·ăl), *adj.*

oes'trus (ĕs'trŭs; ēs'-), *n.* [L., a gadfly, frenzy, fr. Gr. *oistros* gadfly, hence, sting, frenzy.] **1.** A vehement desire or impulse; stimulus; frenzy. **2.** The sexual heat of animals, esp. female mammals; rut; also, the whole oestrous cycle.

of (ŏv; ŭv; 4), *prep.* [AS. *of* of, from, off.] **1.** From; — indicating derivation, separation, source, etc.; as, born *of* noble blood; north *of* Paris. **2.** From, as a cause, motive, or reason; because of; as, to die *of* shame. **3.** By; as, the plays *of* Shaw. **4.** With, as a means or material; as, make it *of* gold. **5.** Made, filled, formed, etc., with; having as its material, parts, elements, extent, etc.; as, a throne *of* gold; a distance *of* five miles. **6.** That is; specified as; as, the city *of* Rome. **7.** About; relating to; with reference to; as, to boast *of* one's achievement. **8.** Having for its object, aim, terminus, etc.; — chiefly after a noun denoting an action or agent; as, a commission *of* a crime; a drinker *of* wine; also, after some verbs and adjectives in idiomatic constructions; as, to smell *of* a flower; astride *of* a horse. **9.** In; in respect to; as, slow *of* speech. **10.** Distinguished by, as in quality, quantity, size, age, etc.; as, a man *of* courage; a time *of* drought. **11.** Belonging to, or separated from (a specified aggregate, whole, number, etc.); from amongst; out of; as, most *of* the company; to give *of* one's energy. **12.** Belonging or pertaining to; connected with (a place, time, person, or thing); as, the right *of* the possessor; the gate *of* heaven; the cube *of* a number. **13.** During; on; as, *of* late years. **14.** *Chiefly Colloq.* Before (an hour by the clock); as, a quarter *of* ten.

o'fay (ō'fā), *n.* [From *ole fay*, i. e., old fay.] *Negro Dial., U. S.* A white person.

off (ŏf; 74), *adv.* [ME. *of*, orig. the same word as E. *of*, prep.] In a general sense, denoting *from*, or *away from*, something. Specifically used: **1.** So as to move away, to a distance, out from a place or position; as, march *off*; push *off*. **2.** So as to be no longer supported, attached, or united; as, to take *off* the hat. **3.** To a state or point of discontinuance, exhaustion, or completion; to a finish; as, the pain passed *off*; also, so as to decrease, esp. in amount; as, profits fell *off*. **4.** In absence from or suspension of regular work; as, to take a day *off*. **5.** At a distance or remove as to place or time; as, he stood ten paces *off*.
— *prep.* **1.** Away from; so as no longer to be on. **2.** *Now Chiefly Dial.* From; of; as, to dine *off* roast beef. **3.** Relieved or released from; on vacation or absence from; as, *off* duty; also, *Slang*, abstaining from; as, to be *off* candy. **4.** Below the standard, mark, etc., of; as, *off* his game. **5.** Diverging or branching from; as, a street *off* Fifth Avenue. **6.** *Naut.* To seaward of; as, two miles *off* shore.
— *adj.* **1.** Being out or away, removed, absent, discontinued, disconnected, inaccurate, below standard, or the like; as, his coat is *off*; he is *off* to war; *off* in his reckoning. **2.** More removed or distant; further; as, on the *off* side; specif.: **a** Of horses, vehicles, etc., right. **b** *Cricket.* Designating the side of the field or the wicket opposite to that on which the batsman stands. **c** *Naut.* Farther from the shore; seaward. **3.** Characterized by being off standard, off duty, etc.; hence, inferior; as, an *off* grade; slack; free; as, an *off* season. **4.** Conditioned or circumstanced, esp. as to material welfare; as, he is badly *off*.
— *n.* **1.** State or condition of being off. **2.** *Cricket.* The off side of the wicket.
— *interj.* Stand off! away! begone!

of'fal (ŏf'ăl), *n.* [*off* + *fall.*] **1.** That which falls, or is removed, from a thing as worthless or unsuitable for the immediate purpose; specif.: **a** The extreme side and end pieces of a hide of leather. **b** *construed as sing. or pl.* The parts, esp. inedible parts, removed in dressing a butchered animal. **2.** Refuse in general; rubbish; garbage.

off and on. Not constantly; intermittently.

off'cast' (ŏf'kȧst'), *adj. & n.* Also **off'-cast'.** Castoff.

off'-chance', *n.* A remote or unlikely chance.

off'-col'or, off'-col'our (-kŭl'ẽr; 2), *adj.* **1.** Not of the proper or natural color; below standard. **2.** Dubious; of doubtful propriety; risqué; as, an *off-color* story.

of·fence', of·fence'less, etc. Vars. of OFFENSE, etc.

of·fend' (ŏ·fĕnd'), *v. i.* [OF. *offendre*, fr. L. *offendere, offensum*, fr. *ob-* + *fendere* (in comp.) to thrust, dash.] **1.** To transgress the moral or divine law; sin. **2.** To cause dislike, anger, or vexation; displease. — *v. t.* **1.** *Obs.* **a** To transgress; violate. **b** To oppose or obstruct in duty; cause to sin or to fall. **2.** To cause to feel hurt or resentful; wound; annoy. — **of·fend'er**, *n.*

Syn. **Offend, outrage, affront, insult** mean to cause hurt feelings or deep annoyance. **Offend** carries no clear implication of intent and often suggests a violation of the victim's sense of what is proper or fitting: **outrage** implies offending beyond endurance, as one's sense of pride, honor, or justice; **affront** implies an offending that humiliates one and arouses resentment; **insult**, a wanton and insolent affront or offense.

of·fense', of·fence' (ŏ·fĕns'), *n.* **1.** *Obs.* **a** Stumbling. **b** Injury; hurt; damage. **2.** An occasion of sin; a stumbling block. **3.** Act of attacking; assault; as, weapons of *offense.* **4.** Act of offending, or affronting; state of being offended. **5.** A breach of conduct; an infraction of law; crime; sin; transgression; misdeed. — **of·fense'less, of·fence'less,** *adj.*

Syn. (1) **Offense, resentment, umbrage, pique, dudgeon, huff** mean one's emotional reaction to a slight or indignity. **Offense** implies displeasure or wounded feelings; **resentment**, more or less prolonged dwelling upon an offense as a grievance; **umbrage**, a feeling of being slighted or ignored; **pique**, a more transient word, suggests wounded vanity; **dudgeon** implies a fit of angry resentment, esp. when opposed, refused, etc.; **huff**, a fit of angry petulance and refusal to have more to do with those who have offended.
(2) **Offense, sin, vice, crime, scandal** mean a transgression of law. **Offense**, the widest term, covers an infraction of any law, as of the state, church, or society; **sin** applies to an offense against the moral law; **vice** more often applies to a habit or a practice that corrupts, degrades, etc.; **crime** applies to an offense, often a great offense, punishable by the law, esp. of the state; **scandal** applies to an offense against the law that offends the public conscience or puts a stumbling block in the way of those needing a good example.

of·fen'sive (ŏ·fĕn'sĭv), *adj.* **1.** Making attack; pert. to, or characterized by, offense or attack; aggressive; hence, fitted for, or used in, attacking; — opposed to *defensive.* **2.** Obnoxious; revolting; as, an *offensive* smell. **3.** Giving offense; causing displeasure or resentment; insulting. — *n.* State or posture of one who offends or makes attack; aggressive attitude or action; — opposed to *defensive*; as, to be on the *offensive*; the army launched an *offensive* against the enemy. — **of·fen'sive·ly**, *adv.* — **of·fen'sive·ness**, *n.*

of′fer (ŏf′ẽr; 74), *v. t.* [AS. *offrian* to sacrifice, fr. L. *offerre*, fr. *ob-* + *ferre* to bear, bring.] **1.** To present, as an act of worship; make an oblation of; sacrifice; — often with *up.* **2.** To present for acceptance or rejection; tender; proffer. **3.** To present for action or consideration; propose; suggest. **4.** To attempt to inflict, make, or do; hence, to do, make, or give; as, to *offer* resistance. **5.** To try; — with the infinitive. "All that *offer* to defend him." *Shak.* **6. a** To present, bring forward, or expose for sale. **b** To bid, as a price; make an offer to give or to pay. **— *v. i.* 1.** To make a sacrifice or oblation in worship. **2.** *Archaic.* To make an attempt; — with *at.* **3.** To present itself. **4.** To propose. **— *n.* 1.** An offering; a proffer; a proposal; an advance; a bid. **2.** Attempt; endeavor. — **of′fer·er, of′fer·or,** *n.*

of′fer·ing, *n.* Act of one who offers; also, that which is offered; specif.: **a** Anything ceremonially offered to God or a god. **b** A gift; esp., money given a church for its support or activities.

of′fer·to′ry (ŏf′ẽr·tō′rĭ *or, esp. Brit.,* -tẽr·ĭ; 74), *n.; pl.* OFFERTORIES (-rĭz). [LL. *offertorium* the place to which offerings were brought.] **1.** [*usually cap.*] *Eccl.* **a** That part of the Eucharistic service in which bread and wine are offered to God before they are consecrated. In the Roman rite it follows the Credo of the Mass; in the Anglican rite it follows the Creed and includes offerings of money, if any. **b** The prayers said by the priest when making the offerings. **c** An antiphon or anthem sung by the choir at this time. **2.** The collection of money taken at a religious service.

off′hand′ (ŏf′hănd′), *adv.* Without previous study or preparation; extempore. — (ŏf′hănd′; 2), *adj.* Done or made offhand; hence, casual; as, an *offhand* manner.

of′fice (ŏf′ĭs; 74), *n.* [OF., fr. L. *officium.*] **1.** Something done for another or others; a service. **2.** Special, proper, or assigned service, duty, or function; specif., one's task or part in an occupation or position. **3.** Position of trust, ministration, or authority; esp., a position of trust or authority conferred by an act of governmental power, for a certain term, with specified duties, and with emoluments; also, an executive position with a corporation, institution, etc. **4.** A ceremonial observance, religious or social; a rite; esp., *pl.* obsequies. **5.** The place where a particular kind of business or service for others is transacted; esp.: **a** The building, room, or department in which the clerical work of an establishment is done. **b** The building, room, etc., for an (or the) executive and his assistants, for the work of administration, or for an administrative department. **c** *pl.* The apartments, buildings, etc., in which the domestics discharge the duties attached to the service of a house. **6.** The company, or persons collectively, whose place of business is an office; specif., the body of administrative or executive officers, as of a government; as, the War *Office.* **7.** *Eccl.* Any prescribed service or form of worship; as, the *Office* of the Dead; specif.: **a** The daily service of the breviary (the ***Divine Office***); the canonical hours; as, to say one's *office.* **b** The daily rites as contained in the missal; as, to begin the *office* of the Mass. **c** The Communion service. **d** The Morning or Evening Prayer. — **Syn.** See FUNCTION; POSITION.

office boy. A boy employed, esp. for odd jobs, in a business office.

of′fice·hold′er (ŏf′ĭs·hōl′dẽr), *n.* One holding a government office.

Office of Civilian Defense. *U. S.* A war agency established by executive order May 20, 1941, charged with the protection of civilian life and property against hazards of war, as air raids, gas attack, fire, or sabotage, and promotion of civilian participation in the defense program. Terminated June 1945. Abbr. *OCD*

Office of Defense Transportation. *U. S.* A war agency established by executive order Dec. 18, 1941, amended May 2, 1942, to regulate and control all rail, motor, inland waterway, and coastal and intercoastal transport, and pipe lines. Abbr. *ODT*

Office of Price Administration. *U. S.* A government agency established by executive order April 11 and August 28, 1941, duly authorized by Congress Jan. 30, 1942, for stabilizing prices and rents and controlling the rationing of products for sale or transfer during national emergency. Terminated June 1947. Abbr. *OPA*

Office of War Information. *U. S.* A government agency established by executive order June 13, 1942, for disseminating information at home and abroad on the progress of the war effort and of the war policies and aims of the government. Terminated Dec. 1945. Abbr. *OWI*

of′fi·cer (ŏf′ĭ·sẽr; 74), *n.* [OF. *officier*, fr. ML. *officiarius.*] **1.** *Obs.* An agent; a minister. **2.** One who holds an office, whether civil, military, or ecclesiastical, and whether under the state or a private corporation or the like. **3. a** *Mil. & Nav.* One who holds a position of authority or command in an army or navy; specif., a commissioned officer. **b** On a merchant or pleasure vessel, the master or any of the mates. **4.** A policeman, constable, bailiff, or the like. **5.** In some honorary orders, a member in some grade above the lowest; as, an *officer* of the Legion of Honor. **— *v. t.* 1.** To furnish with officers. **2.** To command or direct as an officer. **3.** To direct; conduct; manage.

of·fi′cial (ŏ·fĭsh′ăl), *adj.* [LL. *officialis.*] **1.** Of, pertaining to, holding, or derived from an office, position, or trust. **2.** Authorized; authoritative; as, an *official* messenger or statement. **3.** Befitting to, or characteristic of, a person in office or a person when acting in this official capacity; formal. **4.** *Pharm.* Sanctioned by an authoritative pharmacopoeia. **— *n.*** One holding or invested with an office; esp., one having subordinate executive powers. — **of·fi′cial·dom,** *n.* — **of·fi′cial·ly,** *adv.*

of·fi′cial·ism (-ĭz′m), *n.* Action characteristic of an official; esp., strict adherence to office routine.

of·fi′ci·ant (ŏ·fĭsh′ĭ·ănt), *n.* [ML. *officians*, pres. part. See OFFICIATE.] *Eccl.* An officiating priest or minister.

of·fi′ci·ar′y (-ẽr′ĭ *or, esp. Brit.,* -ẽr·ĭ), *adj.* Connected with, derived from, or having a title or rank in virtue of holding, an office.

of·fi′ci·ate (ŏ·fĭsh′ĭ·āt), *v. i.* [ML. *officiare.* See OFFICE.] **1.** To perform an office, or prescribed religious service. **2.** Hence, to act as an officer in performing a duty. **3.** To carry through a prescribed or traditional ceremony; as, to *officiate* as toastmaster. — **of·fi′ci·a′tion** (-ā′shŭn), **of·fi′ci·a′tor** (-ā′tẽr), *n.*

of·fic′i·nal (ŏ·fĭs′ĭ·năl; -n′l), *adj.* [ML. *officinalis*, fr. L. *officina* a workshop, contr. fr. *opificina*, fr. *opifex* a workman.] *Pharm.* Kept in stock by apothecaries; — of drugs. Cf. MAGISTRAL, 4. **— *n.*** An officinal drug or medicine.

of·fi′cious (ŏ·fĭsh′ŭs), *adj.* [F. or L.; F. *officieux*, fr. L. *officiosus.*] **1.** *Obs.* Kind; obliging; dutiful. **2.** Volunteering one's services where they are neither asked nor needed; meddlesome. **3.** *Diplomacy.* Of an informal or unauthorized nature; unofficial; as, an *officious* conversation. — **Syn.** See IMPERTINENT. — **of·fi′cious·ly,** *adv.* — **of·fi′cious·ness,** *n.*

off′ing (ŏf′ĭng; 74), *n.* [From OFF.] That part of the visible sea where there is deep water and no need of a pilot; also, distance, or position at a distance, from the shore; hence, somewhat remote distance or future.

off′ish (-ĭsh), *adj. Colloq.* Inclined to stand aloof.

off′-peak′, *adj.* Not at a peak, or maximum.

off′print′ (ŏf′prĭnt′; 74), *n.* An excerpt, as a magazine article, separately printed. **— *v. t.*** To reprint, as an excerpt.

off′scour′ing (-skour′ĭng), *n.* That which is scoured off; hence, refuse; also, a vile worthless wretch.

off′set′ (-sĕt′), *n.* [*off* + *set.*] **1.** In general, that which sets off, springs from, or is derived or set off from something; as: **a** A lateral or collateral branch; an offshoot. **b** A spur from a range of hills. **c** Something that serves to counterbalance or to compensate for something else. **2.** *Arch.* A horizontal ledge on a wall, formed by a diminution of its thickness above. **3.** *Elec.* A conductor leading from a main. **4.** *Hort.* A short prostrate lateral shoot used for propagation. **5.** *Lithog.* An impression taken for the purpose of transferring a design. **6.** *Mach.* An abrupt bend in an object, as a pipe or rod, by which one part is turned aside out of line. **7.** *Print.* **a** A transfer of type impression or pictures to the back of the next sheet. **b** Offset process or printing. See OFFSET, *adj.* **8.** *Surv.* A short distance measured at right angles from a line, as to avoid an obstruction.

off′set′ (ŏf′sĕt′; ŏf′sĕt′; 2; 74), *v. t.;* OFF′SET′; OFF′SET′TING. **1.** To set off; to place over against; to balance; also, to counterbalance. **2.** To form an offset in. — **Syn.** See COMPENSATE. **— *v. i.* 1.** To proceed or project as an offset. **2.** (*pron.* ŏf′sĕt′) *Print.* To make an offset.

off′set′, *adj.* Designating a process of printing from a flat surface in which the impression is first received by a rubber-surfaced cylinder, from which it is transferred to the paper.

offset lithography. See PHOTO-OFFSET.

off′shoot′ (ŏf′shōōt′; 74), *n.* [*off* + *shoot.*] **1.** *Bot.* A branch of a main stem; a lateral shoot. **2.** Hence, a lateral branch, as of a mountain range; a collateral or derived branch, descendant, or member.

off′shore′ (ŏf′shōr′; 70), *adj.* **1.** Coming, moving, or directed away, from the shore. **2.** Situated or done offshore.

off′shore′ (ŏf′shōr′; 2), *adv.* Away from the shore.

off side. In football and other games, said of or involving a player in such a position with respect to the ball that he is temporarily barred by the rules from participation in the play. — **off′side′** (ŏf′sīd′; 2), *adj.*

off′spring′ (ŏf′sprĭng′), *n.* [AS. *ofspring.*] **1.** Progeny; a child or children. **2.** Result; issue; fruit.

off′-the-rec′ord, *adj.* That is off the record. See under RECORD, *n.*

off′-white′ (ŏf′hwīt′; 2), *adj.* Falling short of white; — often with a suggestion of yellowish.

oft (ŏft; 74), *adv.* [AS.] *Archaic & Poetic.* Often.

of′ten (ŏf′ĕn; -′n; *see note below*), *adv.;* OF′TEN·ER (-ẽr); OF′TEN·EST. [Formerly also *ofte*, fr. *oft.*] Many times; frequently. **— *adj.*** Frequent.

☞ The pronunciation ŏf′tĕn is not uncommon among the educated in some sections, and is often used in singing.

of′ten·times′ (-tīmz′), *adv.* Also, **oft′times′.** Often.

og′am, og′ham (ŏg′ăm; ō′ăm), *n.* [Ir. *ogham.*] A system of writing peculiar to the early Irish (chiefly 5th and 6th centuries) in which an alphabet of 20 letters is represented by notches (for vowels) and lines (for consonants) cut on the edges of rough, standing tombstones.

og′do·ad (ŏg′dō·ăd), *n.* [Gr. *ogdoas, -ados*, fr. *oktō* eight.] **a** The number eight. **b** A group or set of eight.

o·gee′ (ō·jē′; ō′jē), *n.* [F. *ogive.*] **1.** A molding with an S-shaped profile; a cyma recta or cyma reversa. See MOLDING, PANTILE, *Illusts.* **2.** In full, **ogee arch.** A pointed arch having on each side a reversed curve near the apex. See ARCH, *Illust.*

o′give (ō′jīv; ō·jīv′), *n.* [F. *ogive*, OF. also *orgive, augive.*] *Arch.* **a** The arch or rib crossing a Gothic vault diagonally. **b** A pointed arch. — **o·gi′val** (ō·jī′văl), *adj.*

o′gle (ō′g'l), *v. i. & t.;* O′GLED (ō′g'ld); O′GLING (ō′glĭng). [Of LG. origin.] To cast coquettish glances designed to invite advances; to stare or eye amorously. **— *n.*** An amorous stare or coquettish glance. — **o′gler** (ō′glẽr), *n.*

Og′pu (ŏg′pōō), *n.* [Russ., fr. the initials of its name. See GAY-PAY-OO.] The Soviet secret service; the Gay-Pay-Oo.

o′gre (ō′gẽr), *n.* [F.] A monster or hideous giant of fairy tales and folklore, who lives on human beings; hence, a hideous or cruel man. — **o′gress** (ō′grĕs; -grĭs), *n. fem.*

o′gre·ish (ō′gẽr·ĭsh), **o′grish** (ō′grĭsh), *adj.* Resembling an ogre; suitable to or befitting an ogre.

oh (ō), *interj.* An exclamation expressing surprise, grief, a wish, etc. **— *n.; pl.*** OH'S, OHS (ōz). The exclamation *oh!*

ohm (ōm), *n.* [After the German electrician G. S. *Ohm.*] *Elec.* The practical unit of electrical resistance, being the resistance of a circuit in which a potential difference of one volt produces a current of one ampere. — **ohm′ic** (ōm′ĭk), *adj.* — **ohm′me′ter** (-mē′tẽr), *n.*

ohm′age (ōm′ĭj), *n.* The ohmic resistance of a conductor.

-oid (-oid; *in Greek and Latin the* o *and* i *are pronounced separately*). [Gr. *-o-eidēs*, fr. *eidos* form.] A suffix meaning *like, in the form of,* as in coll*oid*, spher*oid*.

-oi′de·a (-oi′dē·ȧ; *see* -OID). [NL. See -OID.] *Zool.* A combining form used to denote a *class* or, esp. in entomology, a *superfamily.*

oil (oil), *n.* [OF. *oile, oille*, fr. L. *oleum*, fr. Gr. *elaion* olive oil.] **1. a** Any of a large class of unctuous combustible substances which are liquid, or at least easily liquefiable on warming, and soluble in ether, but not in water. They leave a greasy stain on paper, cloth, etc. **b** Specif., petroleum. **2.** Any substance of an oily consistency; as, *oil* of vitriol. **3.** *Art.* Oil color; as, to paint in *oils.* **— *v. t.*** To smear, rub over, or lubricate with oil. **— *adj.*** Of or like oil; having to do with oil or the production or distribution of oil; produced by the burning of oil; yielding oil; as, *oil* shale; using oil; as, an *oil* lamp, furnace. — **oil′er** (oil′ẽr), *n.*

oil beetle. Any beetle of the genus *Meloe.* These beetles when disturbed emit from the joints of their legs an oily liquid.

oil′bird′ (oil′bûrd′), *n.* The guacharo.

oil cake. The solid residue after extracting the oil from seeds of cotton, hemp, flax, soybeans, etc., or coconut meat.

oil′cloth′ (oil′klŏth′; 74), *n.* Cloth treated with oil or paint, and used for garments, table and shelf covering, etc.

oil color. a Any pigment used for oil paint. **b** Oil paint.

oil field. A district containing a subterranean store of petroleum of economic value.

oil of vitriol. Concentrated sulfuric acid.
oil paint. Paint in which oil is the vehicle.
oil painting. **1.** Act or art of painting in oil colors. **2.** Any kind of painting of which the pigments are originally ground in oil.
oil palm. An African pinnate-leaved palm (*Elaeis guineensis*), cultivated in Africa and Brazil, bearing drupaceous fruit in large clusters, the fleshy part and the seeds yielding palm oil.
oil′skin′ (oil′skĭn′), *n.* Cloth made waterproof by oil; also, a piece or garment, or *pl.*, a suit of this material.
oil slick. A slick formed by putting oil on the water.
oil′stone′ (oil′stōn′), *n.* A whetstone used with oil.
oil well. A dug or drilled well from which petroleum is obtained as a commercial product.
oil′y (oil′ĭ), *adj.*; OIL′I·ER (-ĭ·ẽr); OIL′I·EST. **1.** Of, pertaining to, consisting of, or containing oil; unctuous; oleaginous. **2.** Covered or soaked with oil. **3.** Smoothly subservient; compliant; unctuous; bland; as, an *oily* rascal. — **oil′i·ly,** *adv.* — **oil′i·ness,** *n.*
oint′ment (oint′mĕnt), *n.* [OF. *oignement*, deriv. of L. *unguentum*. The first *t* in the E. word is due to the influence of *anoint*.] That which serves to anoint; an unguent; salve.
Oir′each·tas (ĕr′ĕк·thȧs), *n.* [Ir. assembly.] The legislature of the Republic of Ireland. Cf. DAIL EIREANN.
oi′ti·ci′ca (oi′tĭ·sē′kȧ), *n.* [Pg., fr. Tupi *oity-cica, uiti-cica*.] Any of several South American trees, esp. a Brazilian species (*Licania rigida*) whose seeds yield an oil used in paints and varnishes.
O·jib′way, O·jib′wa (ō·jĭb′wā), *n. sing. & pl.*; also, *pl.* -WAYS, -WAS (-wāz). One of a large tribe of Algonquian Indians of the Lake Superior region.
O.K., *or* **OK.** (ō′kā′). [From the *O. K.* Club, a Democratic organization supporting (1840) President Van Buren for re-election, fr. *Old Kinderhook*, N. Y., his birthplace. See *Saturday Review of Literature*, July 19, 1941.] *Colloq.*, exc. in endorsing documents. Correct; all right.
O.K. (ō′kā′), *v. t.*; O.K.′D (ō′kād′); O.K.′ING (ō′kā′ĭng). To put or endorse "O.K." on; to approve.
o′ka (ō′kȧ), **oke** (ōk), *n.* [Turk. *ōqah*, fr. Ar. *ūqīyah*, fr. Gr. *oungia, ounkia*, ounce, fr. L. *uncia*.] A weight of Turkey, Bulgaria, Egypt, etc., of about 2¾ lbs.; also, a liquid measure, about 1⅓ quarts.
o·ka′pi (ō·kä′pĭ), *n.*; *pl.* OKAPIS (-pĭz). See PLURAL, *Note*, 3. [Native name.] A rare African mammal (*Okapia johnstoni*) closely related to the giraffe.
o′kay′, o′keh′ (ō′kā′; ō′kā′). Vars. of O.K.
O′kie (ō′kĭ), *n.* *U.S.* An itinerant agricultural worker from Oklahoma; also, any migratory agricultural worker.
o′kra (ō′krȧ; ŏk′rȧ), *n.* [Corrupt. of Tshi *nkruman*.] **1.** A tall annual (*Abelmoschus esculentus*) of the mallow family, cultivated for its mucilaginous green pods, used as the basis of soups, stews, etc.; also, the pod, or pods, of this plant. **2.** A dish prepared of this vegetable; gumbo.
-ol (-ōl; -ŏl). **1.** [From alcoh*ol*.] *Chem.* A suffix denoting an *alcohol* or *phenol*, as in glycer*ol*, cres*ol*. **2.** [L. *oleum* oil.] *Chem.* Var. of -OLE, as in benz*ol*.
old (ōld), *adj.*; OLD′ER (ōl′dẽr) or ELD′ER; OLD′EST or ELD′EST. [AS. *ald, eald*.] **1.** Having existed long; advanced far in years or life; having lost the vigor of youth. **2.** Having (a certain) age or length of existence; as, she was eight years *old*. **3. a** Not new; not recently made. **b** Worn out; weakened or exhausted from age or by use. **4.** Quondam; former. **5.** Belonging to the distant past; ancient or medieval; antiquated; famous in or from antiquity. **6.** Designating that one of two or more things of the same kind, or periods or stages of the same thing, which precedes the other or others; as, the *Old* Testament; the *Old* World; *Old* English, *Old* French, *Old* High German, *Old* Icelandic, *Old* Persian (see ENGLISH, FRENCH, GERMAN, ICELANDIC, PERSIAN). See INDO-EUROPEAN LANGUAGES, *Table*. **7.** Dating from the remote past; of long standing; as, an *old* custom. **8.** Long practiced; as, an *old* offender. **9.** *Colloq.* Long familiar; — expressing cordiality or affection; as, *old* chap. **10.** Of, pertaining to, or characteristic of old persons or advanced life. **11.** *Colloq.* Plentiful; "grand"; — an intensive; as, a high *old* time. **12.** *Phys. Geog.* Well advanced toward reduction to base level; — of topographic features. — **old′ness,** *n.*
Syn. **Old, ancient, venerable, antique, antiquated, archaic, obsolete** mean of advanced age or having passed the period of greatest usefulness. **Old** may imply actual or relative length of existence, use, etc.; **ancient** implies occurrence, existence, or use in the distant past; **venerable**, the hoariness and dignity of old age; **antique**, a coming down from ancient or old times; **antiquated**, a having gone out of vogue or fashion; **archaic**, a having the character or characteristics of a much earlier period; **obsolete**, a having gone out of use or currency. — **Ant.** New.
— *n.* Old time or a former time; as, days of *old*.
Old Bulgarian; *also* **Old Church Slavic** *or* **Slavonic.** = CHURCH SLAVIC.
old country. The country of origin of an immigrant; — applied esp. to European countries, originally to the British Isles.
Old Dominion. Virginia; — a nickname.
old′en (ōl′dĕn; -d'n), *adj.* *Poetic.* Of or from old times.
Ol′den·burg (ōl′dĕn·bûrg), *n.* [In full, *Duchess of Oldenburg* (Germany).] A hardy, early-ripening apple.
Old English. a See ENGLISH, *n.*, 2. **b** *Print.* A style of black letter. See TYPE.
old′fan′gled (ōld′făng′g'ld; 2), *adj.* Old-fashioned.
old′-fash′ioned (ōld′făsh′ŭnd; 2), *adj.* Formed or done according to, or adhering to, obsolete fashion; antiquated; adhering to old customs or ideas.
old′-fo′gy·ish, old′-fo′gey·ish, *adj.* Characteristic of or appropriate to old fogies.
Old Glory. *Colloq., U. S.* The flag of the United States.
old gold. A color, reddish-yellow in hue, of low saturation and medium brilliance. — **old′-gold′,** *adj.* See COLOR.
Old Guard. [F. *Vieille Garde*.] **1.** The original imperial guard created by Napoleon I in 1804. **2.** [*often not caps.*] **a** Any old group of supporters of a belief, style, etc. **b** The older and more conservative element of a community.
Old Ionic. See GREEK, *n.*, 4.
old′ish, *adj.* Somewhat old.
old′-line′ (ōld′līn′; 2), *adj.* **1.** Belonging to or descended from an old line. **2.** Following or adhering to old lines, as in business or politics; conservative.
old maid. 1. An elderly or confirmed spinster. **2.** *Colloq.* A fussy, nervous, timid person. **3.** A simple game of cards, played by matching them. — **old′-maid′ish,** *adj.*
old man. 1. *Familiar.* **a** The head of a household; one's father or, sometimes, one's husband. **b** Hence, a commanding officer, an employer, the principal of a school, or other person of chief authority. **2.** An affectionate form of address or reference to an old or intimate friend.
old master. 1. One of the distinguished painters who lived before the modern period (i. e., before the 18th century). **2.** A painting by one of these painters.
Old Nick. The Devil. *Colloq.*
Old Norse. Old Scandinavian, best represented in literary form by Old Icelandic (see ICELANDIC). The oldest forms known are found in runic inscriptions. With its descendants, it forms the Scandinavian branch of the Teutonic family. See INDO-EUROPEAN LANGUAGES, *Table*.
Old North French. The northern dialects of Old French (see FRENCH, *n.*, 2), including especially those of Normandy and Picardy.
old rose. A color, red in hue, of low saturation and medium brilliance. See COLOR. — **old′-rose′,** *adj.*
Old Saxon. The language of the original Saxon tribes of northwest Germany. See SAXON, *n.*, 2.
old school. A school or party belonging to a former time, or preserving the character, manner, or opinions of a former time; as, a gentleman of the *old school*. — **old′-school′** (ōld′skōōl′; 2), *adj.*
old sledge. *Card Games.* = SEVEN-UP.
old squaw. A common sea duck (*Clangula hyemalis*) of the more northern parts of the Northern Hemisphere.
old′ster (ōld′stẽr), *n.* [After *youngster*.] *Colloq.* An old or elderly person.
old style. a [*caps.*] A style of reckoning time used before the adoption of the present calendar. Abbr. *O. S.* See GREGORIAN CALENDAR. **b** *Print.* [*often cap.*] A style of type distinguished from *modern* by irregularity among individual letters, oblique serifs, and slight contrast between light and heavy elements of the letter design. See TYPE. — **old′-style′,** *adj.*
Old Testament. The covenant of God with the Hebrews as set forth in the Bible; also, the books of the Bible in which this covenant is given, the canonical books including the Law, Prophets, and Hagiographia, and, *R.C.Ch.*, the books except two of the Apocrypha of Protestants. Abbr. *O.T.*, *Old Test.* See BIBLE, TESTAMENT, 1.
old′-time′, *adj.* Also **old′-times′.** Of, pertaining to, or characteristic of old or former times.
old′-tim′er (ōld′tīm′ẽr), *n.* *Colloq.* One who has lived long in a place or held the same position for a long time; one whose experience reaches far back; an old-fashioned person or thing.
old′wife′ (ōld′wīf′), *n.*; *pl.* OLDWIVES (-wīvz′). Also **old wife. 1.** Any of several, esp. West Indian, fishes, including the alewife, menhaden, and various triggerfishes. **2.** The old squaw (duck).
old wives′ tale (wīvz). A tale, or bit of lore, or a notion, esp. a superstitious traditional notion, characteristic of old women.
old′-world′ (ōld′wûrld′; 2), *adj.* **1.** Of the old, or ancient, world or state of things. **2.** [written *Old World*.] Of or characteristic of the Eastern Hemisphere.
-ole (-ōl). Also **-ol** (-ōl; -ŏl). [L. *oleum* oil.] *Chem.* **a** A suffix denoting the presence of a five-membered ring. **b** A suffix used in the names of certain ethers and aldehydes.
o′le·a′ceous (ō′lē·ā′shŭs), *adj.* [L. *olea* olive + *-aceous*.] *Bot.* Belonging to the olive family (Oleaceae). See OLIVE.
o′le·ag′i·nous (-ăj′ĭ·nŭs), *adj.* [F. *oléagineux*, fr. L. *oleaginus* of the olive, fr. *olea* olive.] Of the nature of or producing oil; oily; unctuous. — **o′le·ag′i·nous·ness,** *n.*
o′le·an′der (ō′lē·ăn′dẽr; ō′lē·ăn′dẽr), *n.* [ML. (whence F. *oléandre*).] A poisonous evergreen shrub (*Nerium oleander*) of the dogbane family, with fragrant white-to-red flowers.
o′le·as′ter (ō′lē·ăs′tẽr), *n.* [L., fr. *olea* olive, olive tree.] A shrub or small tree (*Elaeagnus angustifolia*) of southern Europe, with fragrant yellow flowers and bitter olive-shaped fruit.
o′le·ate (ō′lē·āt), *n.* *Chem.* A salt or ester of oleic acid.
o·lec′ra·non (ō·lĕk′rȧ·nŏn; ō′lē·krā′nŏn), *n.* [NL., fr. Gr. *ōlekranon*, fr. *ōlenē* elbow + *kranion* the head.] *Anat.* The process of the ulna projecting behind the elbow joint.
o′le·fin (ō′lē·fĭn), **o′le·fine** (-fĭn; -fēn), *n.* [From F. *oléfiant*, fr. L. *oleum* oil + *-ficare* (in comp.) to make.] *Chem.* Any open-chain hydrocarbon having one or more double bonds. — **o′le·fin′ic** (-fĭn′ĭk), *adj.*
o·le′ic (ō·lē′ĭk; ō′lē·ĭk), *adj.* [L. *oleum* oil.] *Chem.* Pertaining to, derived from, or contained in oil.
oleic acid. *Chem.* An oily acid, $C_{17}H_{33}CO_2H$, found in the form of olein in fats and oils.
o′le·in (ō′lē·ĭn), *n.* [L. *oleum* oil.] **1.** *Chem.* A fat, the glyceryl ester of oleic acid, liquid at ordinary temperatures. **2.** Often **o′le·ine** (-ĭn; -ēn). **a** The liquid part of any fat; — distinguished from *stearin*. **b** Commercial oleic acid.
o′le·o- (ō′lē·ō-). [L. *oleum* oil.] A combining form meaning: **a** Oil, as in *ole*in. **b** Olein, oleic, as in *oleo*margarine.
o′le·o (ō′lē·ō), *n.* Short for: **a** OLEOMARGARINE. **b** OLEO OIL.
o′le·o·graph′ (-grăf′; 9), *n.* [*oleo-* + *-graph*.] A type of chromolithograph imitative of an oil painting. — **o′le·o·graph′ic** (-grăf′ĭk), *adj.* — **o′le·og′ra·phy** (-ŏg′rȧ·fĭ), *n.*
o′le·o·mar′ga·rine (ō′lē·ō·mär′jȧ·rēn; -rĭn; -gȧ-), *n.* Also **-rin.** [*oleo-* + *margarine*.] Margarine; — in the U. S. extended by statute to include butter substitutes made from fats and oils derived from certain animals and plants.
oleo oil. A yellow oil of buttery consistency expressed from certain animal fats and used in making oleomargarine.
o′le·o·res′in (ō′lē·ō·rĕz′ĭn; -'n), *n.* [*oleo-* + *resin*.] **1.** A natural product, as copaiba, containing essential oil and resin. **2.** *Pharm.* A preparation of fixed or volatile oil and resin.
o′le·o·res′in·ous (-ĭ·nŭs), *adj.* **1.** Of, pertaining to, or containing

oleoresin. **2.** Made of or containing drying oils and resins, usually cooked; — said esp. of varnish.

oleo strut. [See OLEO- **a.**] *Airplanes.* A cylindrical strut with a built-in telescopic shock absorber, an **oleo gear,** that damps or absorbs rectilinear shock, esp. in landing gear, by forcing oil up through an orifice in the bottom of a hollow piston into an air-compression chamber.

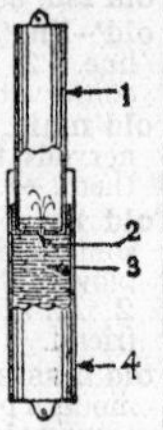

Oleo Strut. 1 Inner Cylinder; 2 Orifice; 3 Oil; 4 Outer Cylinder.

ol'er·i·cul'ture (ŏl'ẽr·ĭ·kŭl'tụ̄r), *n.* [L. *olus, oleris* potherb + E. *culture.*] Culture of edible vegetables. — **ol'er·i·cul'tur·al** (-kŭl'tụ̄r·ăl), *adj.* — **ol'er·i·cul'tur·ist** (-ĭst), *n.*

ol·fac'tion (ŏl·făk'shŭn), *n.* [See OLFACTORY.] *Physiol.* The sense of smell; act, process, or faculty of smelling.

ol·fac'to·ry (-tō·rĭ), *adj.* [L. *olfactus,* past part. of *olfacere* to smell, fr. *odefacere,* fr. *odere* to have a smell + *facere* to make.] Of, pert. to, or connected with the sense of smell; as, *olfactory* nerve. — *n.; pl.* -RIES (-rĭz). An olfactory organ; also, sense of smell; — usually *pl.*

o·lib'a·num (ō·lĭb'ȧ·nŭm), *n.* [ML.] The fragrant gum resin frankincense.

ol'i·garch (ŏl'ĭ·gärk), *n.* A member of an oligarchy.

ol'i·gar'chic (-gär'kĭk), **ol'i·gar'chi·cal** (-kĭ·kăl), *adj.* Of, pertaining to, or supporting oligarchy.

ol'i·garch'y (ŏl'ĭ·gär'kĭ), *n.; pl.* -IES (-kĭz). [Gr. *oligarchia,* fr. *oligos* few, little + *archein* to rule.] A form of government in which the power is vested in a few, or a state so governed; also, those who form the ruling few.

ol'i·go- (ŏl'ĭ·gō-), **olig-.** [Gr. *oligos* small.] A combining form meaning *few, but a little, scant,* as in **ol'i·go·don'tous,** having few teeth; specif., *Med., deficiency.*

Ol'i·go·cene (-sēn), *adj.* [*oligo-* + Gr. *kainos* new, recent.] *Geol.* Of, pertaining to, or designating the period of the Tertiary division of the Cenozoic era between the Eocene and Miocene periods, or the system of rocks formed during this period. — **Ol'i·go·cene,** *n.*

ol'i·go·chae'tous (-kē'tŭs), *adj.* [*oligo-* + Gr. *chaitē* hair.] Pertaining to or designating members of an order (Oligochaeta) of hermaphrodite worms having no distinct head, including the earthworms and related species. — **ol'i·go·chaete'** (ŏl'ĭ·gō·kēt'), *n.*

ol'i·go·clase (ŏl'ĭ·gō·klās), *n.* [*oligo-* + Gr. *klasis* fracture.] *Mineral.* A soda-lime feldspar.

ol'i·go·cy·the'mi·a, ol'i·go·cy·thae'mi·a (-sī·thē'mĭ·ȧ), *n.* [NL. See OLIGO-; -CYTE; -EMIA.] *Med.* Anemia in which the blood is deficient in red corpuscles.

ol'i·gop'o·ly (ŏl'ĭ·gŏp'ō·lĭ), *n.* [*oligo-* + mono*poly.*] Control by a few competing sellers of the amount and price of a given product or service to a large number of buyers. — **ol'i·gop'o·lis'tic** (-gŏp'ō·lĭs'tĭk), *adj.*

ol'i·go·sac'cha·ride (ŏl'ĭ·gō·săk'ȧ·rīd; -rĭd), *n.* [*oligo-* + *saccharide.*] *Chem.* A carbohydrate decomposable into a few (specif., 2 to 6) monosaccharide molecules. Cf. POLYSACCHARIDE.

ol'i·gu·re'sis (ŏl'ĭ·gū·rē'sĭs), *n.* [NL., fr. *olig-* + Gr. *ourēsis* urination.] *Med.* Deficiency in the excretion of urine.

o'li·o (ō'lĭ·ō; 58), *n.; pl.* -OS (-ōz). [Sp. *olla* earthen pot, a dish of stewed meat, fr. L. *olla* a pot, dish.] **1.** An olla (sense 2). **2.** Any mixture; hodgepodge. **3.** A miscellaneous collection; a medley.

ol'i·va'ceous (ŏl'ĭ·vā'shŭs), *adj.* [L. *oliva* olive.] Resembling the olive; of the color olive; olive-green.

ol'i·var'y (ŏl'ĭ·vẽr'ĭ *or, esp. Brit.,* -vẽr·ĭ), *adj.* [L. *olivarius* belonging to olives, fr. *oliva* an olive.] *Anat.* **a** Shaped like an olive. **b** Of or pertaining to the **olivary body,** *Anat.,* an oval prominence on each side of the anterior surface of the medulla oblongata.

ol'ive (ŏl'ĭv), *n.* [OF., fr. L. *oliva,* fr. Gr. *elai(w)a.*] **1.** A tree (*Olea europaea*), the type of a family (Oleaceae, the olive family) including also the ashes, lilacs, jasmine, forsythias, etc. The olive is cultivated for its fruit, which is an important source of oil, and is eaten as a pickle or relish esp. when green, or its hard, yellow wood, used in turnery. Also, the fruit of this tree. **2.** An olive branch or wreath. **3.** Also **olive green.** The color of the olive, greenish-yellow in hue, of low saturation and low brilliance. See COLOR. — *adj.* **a** Of the color olive. **b** Of a color approaching olive, as a complexion.

olive branch. A branch of the olive tree, considered an emblem of peace; hence, anything offered as a sign of peace.

olive drab. A color, greenish-yellow in hue, of low saturation and low brilliance. See COLOR. — **ol'ive-drab',** *adj.*

o·liv'en·ite (ō·lĭv'ĕn·īt; ŏl'ĭ·vĕn-), *n.* [G. *olivenerz* + *-ite.*] *Mineral.* A native basic copper arsenate, $Cu_3(AsO_4)_2.Cu(OH)_2$, olive-green, brown, or yellowish.

olive oil. A pale-yellow nondrying oil from olives, used as a salad oil and in cooking, in soaps, etc.

Ol'i·ver (ŏl'ĭ·vẽr), *n.* [F. *Olivier.*] One of the twelve peers of Charlemagne (see *Biog.*), the companion-in-arms of Roland. See ROLAND.

ol'i·vine (ŏl'ĭ·vēn; ŏl'ĭ·vēn'; ŏl'ĭ·vĭn), *n.* [*olive* + 3d *-ine.*] **a** *Mineral.* Chrysolite. **b** Green garnet.

ol'la (ŏl'ȧ; *Sp.* ō(l)'yä), *n.; pl.* OLLAS (ŏl'ȧz; *Sp.* ō(l)'yäs). [Sp. See OLIO.] **1.** In Spain, Spanish America, etc., a bulging widemouthed pot or jar. **2.** A highly seasoned dish of meat and vegetables cooked in such a pot.

ol'la-po·dri'da (ŏl'ȧ·pō·drē'dȧ), *n.* [Sp., lit., a rotten pot. See OLIO.] **1.** An olla (sense 2). **2.** An olio; hodgepodge.

ol'o·gy (ŏl'ō·jĭ), *n.; pl.* -GIES (-jĭz). [See -LOGY.] *Humorous.* A science or branch of knowledge.

O·lym'pi·ad (ō·lĭm'pĭ·ăd), *n.* [F. *olympiade,* fr. L., fr. Gr. *Olympias, -ados,* fr. *Olympos* Olympus.] **1.** *Gr. Antiq.* A period of four (or, in the inclusive reckoning of the Greeks, five) years from one Olympian festival to the next. **2.** The quadrennial celebration of the modern Olympics.

O·lym'pi·an (-ăn), *adj.* **1.** Of or dwelling on Olympus; celestial; also, godlike; as, *Olympian* dignitaries. **2.** Of or pertaining to Olympia in ancient Elis, in the Peloponnesus; as, the **Olympian games,** held every fourth year, from the year 776 B.C., the date adopted by the Greeks as the primary date of their chronology, which was reckoned in Olympiads. A modified revival (always called **Olympic games**), of the ancient Olympian games, consisting of international athletic games, races, etc., is now held once in four years, the first having been at Athens in 1896. — *n.* **1.** *Gr. Relig.* One of the deities of highest rank (generally twelve), supposed to dwell upon Olympus, under the direct oversight of Zeus. **2.** A native of Olympia; a participator in the Olympian games or the Olympic games.

O·lym'pic (ō·lĭm'pĭk), *adj.* Olympian. — *n.* An Olympian game or an Olympic game; — usually *pl.*

O·lym'pus (ō·lĭm'pŭs), *n.* [L., fr. Gr. *Olympos.*] **1.** A mountain in Macedonia, mythical abode of the Greek gods. **2.** Any abode or circle of godlike beings.

-o'ma (-ō'mȧ), *pl.* -OMATA (-ō'mȧ·tȧ), -OMAS (-ō'mȧz). [Gr. *-ōma, -ōmatos.*] *Med.* A suffix used to denote a *morbid affection* of some part, usually a tumor, as in sarc*oma.*

O'ma·ha (ō'mȧ·hô), *n.* A member of an important tribe of Siouan Indians of Nebraska.

o·ma'sum (ō·mā'sŭm), *n.; pl.* OMASA (-sȧ). [L., bullock's tripe.] *Zool.* The third division in the stomach of ruminants; the psalterium or manyplies. See RUMINANT, *Illust.*

om'ber, om'bre (ŏm'bẽr), *n.* [F. *ombre, hombre,* fr. Sp. *hombre,* lit., a man, fr. L. *homo.*] An old card game of Spanish origin; also, the player who attempts to win the pool in this game.

o·me'ga (ō·mē'gȧ; ō'mĕ·gȧ; ō·mĕg'ȧ), *n.* [Gr. *ō mega,* lit., great *o.*] **1.** The long *o,* the last letter (Ω, ω) of the Greek alphabet. **2.** The last; the end.

om'e·let, om'e·lette (ŏm'ĕ·lĕt; ŏm'lĕt; -lĭt), *n.* [F. *omelette.*] Eggs beaten up with milk or water and cooked in a frying pan.

o'men (ō'mĕn; -mĕn), *n.; pl.* OMENS (-mĕnz; -mĕnz), OMINA (ŏm'ĭ·nȧ). [L.] An occurrence or phenomenon supposed to portend some future event; a foretoken; also, a foreboding. — *v. t. & i.* To foreshow by signs or portents; to presage.

o·men'tum (ō·mĕn'tŭm), *n.; pl.* -TA (-tȧ). [L.] *Anat.* A free fold of the peritoneum, or one serving to connect viscera, support blood vessels, etc. The ***great omentum*** is attached to the stomach and transverse colon. The ***lesser omentum*** connects the stomach and the liver. — **o·men'tal** (-tăl; -t'l), *adj.*

o'mer (ō'mẽr), *n.* [Heb. *'ōmer.*] A Hebrew measure, the tenth of an ephah.

om'i·cron (ŏm'ĭ·krŏn; ō·mī'krŏn), *n.* [Gr. *o mikron,* lit., little *o.*] The short *o,* the fifteenth letter (Ο, ο) of the Greek alphabet.

om'i·nous (ŏm'ĭ·nŭs), *adj.* [L. *ominosus,* fr. *omen.*] Being or exhibiting an omen; portentous; esp., foreboding or foreshowing evil; inauspicious; as, an *ominous* dread. — **om'i·nous·ly,** *adv.* — **om'i·nous·ness,** *n.*

Syn. **Ominous, portentous, fateful** mean having a menacing character. **Ominous** now implies a frightening or alarming quality but rarely connotes, as earlier, a foreboding of disaster; **portentous** also has lost its implication of a portent, or forewarning of calamity, and means little more than frighteningly big or marvelous; **fateful** now usually implies momentousness, decisiveness, or the like (as, an *ominous* noise; *portentous* gravity; a *fateful* occasion).

o·mis'si·ble (ō·mĭs'ĭ·b'l), *adj.* That may be omitted.

o·mis'sion (ō·mĭsh'ŭn), *n.* [LL. *omissio.* See OMIT.] **1.** Act or instance of omitting; also, state of being omitted. **2.** A thing which is omitted.

o·mis'sive (ō·mĭs'ĭv), *adj.* Leaving out; omitting.

o·mit' (ō·mĭt'), *v. t.;* O·MIT'TED; O·MIT'TING. [L. *omittere, omissum,* fr. *ob-* + *mittere* to send.] **1.** To leave out or unmentioned; to abstain from inserting or naming. **2.** To forbear to perform or to make use of; neglect. — **Syn.** See NEGLECT.

om'ma·tid'i·um (ŏm'ȧ·tĭd'ĭ·ŭm), *n.; pl.* -TIDIA (-ȧ). [NL., dim. of Gr. *omma, -atos,* the eye.] *Zool.* One of the elements (each corresponding to a small simple eye or ocellus) of which the compound eye (**om'ma·te'um** [-tē'ŭm]) of an arthropod is built up. — **om'ma·tid'i·al** (-ăl), *adj.*

om·mat'o·phore (ŏ·măt'ō·fōr; 70), *n.* [Gr. *omma, -atos,* eye + *-phore.*] *Zool.* A movable peduncle bearing an eye, as of a snail. — **om'ma·toph'o·rous** (ŏm'ȧ·tŏf'ō·rŭs), *adj.*

Om·mi'ad (ō·mī'ăd), *n.; pl.* -ADS, -ADES (-ădz; -ȧ·dēz). Any member of a dynasty (661–750) of caliphs which was succeeded by the Abbassides; also, any member of an offshoot of this dynasty established in Spain (756–1031). — **Om·mi'ad,** *adj.*

om'ni- (ŏm'nĭ-). [L. *omnis.*] A combining form meaning *all,* as in *omni*potent, *omni*vorous.

‖**om'ni·a mu·tan'tur, nos et mu·ta'mur in il'lis** (ŏm'nĭ·ȧ mū·tăn'tẽr, nōs ĕt mū·tā'mẽr ĭn ĭl'ĭs). [L.] All things are changing, and we are changing with them.

‖**om'ni·a vin'cit a'mor** (vĭn'sĭt ā'môr). [L.] Love conquers all things.

om'ni·bus (ŏm'nĭ·bŭs; -bŭs), *n.; pl.* -BUSES (-bŭs'ĕz; -bŭs·ĕz; -ĭz). [F., fr. L. *omnibus* for all, dat. pl. fr. *omnis* all.] **1.** A public vehicle, usually four-wheeled, designed to carry a large number of passengers; a bus. **2.** A book containing reprints of a number of works, as of a single author, bound together. — *adj.* Pert. to, or providing for, many things or classes at once.

omnibus bill. *Colloq.* A legislative bill which makes a number of miscellaneous provisions or appropriations.

om'ni·far'i·ous (ŏm'nĭ·fâr'ĭ·ŭs; 6), *adj.* [L. *omnifarius.*] Of all varieties, forms, or kinds. — **om'ni·far'i·ous·ness,** *n.*

om·nif'ic (ŏm·nĭf'ĭk), *adj.* [*omni-* + *-fic.*] All-creating.

om·nip'o·tence (ŏm·nĭp'ō·tĕns), *n.* Quality of being omnipotent; unlimited power; hence [*cap.*], the Deity.

om·nip'o·tent (-tĕnt), *adj.* [OF., fr. L. *omnipotens, -entis,* fr. *omnis* all + *potens* powerful.] Unlimited in power, ability, or authority; almighty. — *n.* One who is omnipotent; [*cap.*] with *the,* God. — **om·nip'o·tent·ly,** *adv.*

om'ni·pres'ent (ŏm'nĭ·prĕz'ĕnt; -'nt), *adj.* [ML. *omnipraesens.* See OMNI-; PRESENT.] Present everywhere at once. — **om'ni·pres'ence** (-ĕns; -'ns), *n.*

Syn. **Omnipresent, ubiquitous** mean present or existent everywhere. **Omnipresent** strictly implies being present everywhere at the same time but, in looser use, a never being absent; **ubiquitous,** a being present everywhere but not necessarily at the same time or in the same region. *Omnipresent* in its strict sense is applicable only to the Supreme Being.

om·nis'cience (ŏm·nĭsh'ĕns *or, esp. Brit.,* -nĭs'ĭ·ĕns), *n.* Quality of being omniscient; infinite knowledge; hence, the omniscient being; God.

om·nis'cient (ŏm·nĭsh'ĕnt *or, esp. Brit.,* -nĭs'ĭ·ĕnt), *adj.* [*omni-* + L. *sciens, -entis,* pres. part. of *scire* to know.] Having universal knowledge; infinitely wise. — *n.* One who is omniscient; hence [*cap.*], with *the,* God. — **om·nis'cient·ly,** *adv.*

om'ni·um-gath'er·um (ŏm'nĭ·ŭm·găth'ẽr·ŭm), *n.* [L. *omnium* (gen. pl. of *omnis* all) + E. *gather.*] A miscellaneous collection of all sorts of things or persons; a medley.

om′ni·vore (ŏm′nĭ·vōr; 70), *n.* An omnivorous animal; esp., *Zool.*, any of a group (**Om·niv′o·ra** [ŏm·nĭv′ō·rȧ]) of animals which eat both animal and vegetable food.

om·niv′o·rous (ŏm·nĭv′ō·rŭs), *adj.* [L. *omnivorus*, fr. *omnis* all + *vorare* to eat greedily.] Eating everything; esp., eating both animal and vegetable food. — **om·niv′o·rous·ly**, *adv.* — **om·niv′o·rous·ness**, *n.*

o·moph′a·gous (ō·mŏf′ȧ·gŭs), *adj.* Also **o′mo·phag′ic** (ō′mō·făj′ĭk). [Gr. *ōmophagos*, fr. *ōmos* raw + *phagein* to eat.] Eating raw flesh.

om′pha·lo- (ŏm′fȧ·lō-). [Gr. *omphalos*.] A combining form meaning *the navel, umbilicus.*

om′pha·los (ŏm′fȧ·lŏs), *n.; pl.* OMPHALI (-lī). [LL., fr. Gr.] **1.** *Anat.* The navel. **2.** A central part or point; center.

om′pha·lo·skep′sis (ŏm′fȧ·lō·skĕp′sĭs), *n.* [NL., fr. *omphalo-* + Gr. *skepsis* a looking at.] Meditation while gazing at the navel, as practiced by some mystics.

on (ŏn; 4), *prep.* [AS. *on, an.*] Primarily, indicating position of contact with or against a supporting surface (see AT, *Note*); as: **1.** Over and in contact with; as, the book lies *on* the table. **2.** In contact or juxtaposition with; as, a fly *on* the ceiling. **3.** In connection or activity with or in respect of; as, *on* duty; engaged in making; as, *on* a tour. **4.** With, as a basis or ground of action, award, opinion, reliance, etc.; as, stated *on* authority; by reason of. **5.** At; in the region that is toward; as, the town lies *on* the east; hence, in phrases, as *on one's behalf, on the contrary.* **6.** Within; during; as, *on* Monday. **7.** Upon the occasion of; following the time of, often as a result of; as, cash *on* delivery. **8.** In a state or process of; as, *on* fire, tap, sale. **9.** To or against; as, rain falls *on* the earth; hence, toward; to the account of; as, she smiled *on* him. **10.** In relation to; with respect to; as, to agree *on* a price. **11.** With, through, or over as means or instrument; as, to cut *on* a knife; to hear one *on* the radio. **12.** In addition to; besides; as, heaps *on* heaps. **13.** *Colloq.* To the disadvantage of; as, a joke *on* me.
— (ŏn; 73), *adv.* **1.** In or into the position of being supported by, attached to, or covering, something; as, put *on* the plates; put boots *on.* **2.** With direction toward something; as, to look *on;* head *on.* **3.** Forward; onward; — often with verb omitted; as, time glides *on; on* with the show. **4.** In continuance or succession; as, and so *on;* sleep *on.* **5.** Into action; so as to flow, shine, etc.; as, to bring *on* pneumonia; to turn *on* the heat.
— *adj.* **1.** Used predicatively: **a** Assigned to play a part; as, he is *on* as Macbeth. **b** In progress; as, the game is *on.* **c** Open; unobstructed; as, the draft or a switch is *on.* **d** Of a braking device, in application. **2.** *Cricket.* Designating the side of the field on which the batsman stands.

-on (-ŏn). [NL., fr. Gr.] A suffix in nouns, denoting *an ultimate particle*, as in prot*on;* — used specif. in *Chem.* in naming the inert gases, as in rad*on.*

on′a·ger (ŏn′ȧ·jĕr), *n.; pl.* -GRI (-grī), -GERS (-jĕrz). [L. *onager, onagrus*, fr. Gr. *onagros*.] **1.** A wild ass (*Equus onager*) of Asia, probably only a variety of the kiang and differing from it in being smaller and lighter-colored. **2.** *Mil.* A type of catapult.

on′a·gra′ceous (ŏn′ȧ·grā′shŭs), *adj.* Belonging to the evening-primrose family (Onagraceae). See EVENING PRIMROSE.

o′nan·ism (ō′năn·ĭz′m), *n.* [*Onan* (*Gen.* xxxviii. 9).] **a** Uncompleted coition. **b** Masturbation.

once (wŭns; 106), *adv.* [ME. *ones, anes*, an adverbial form fr. *one, on, an*, one.] **1.** One time and no more. **2.** At any one time; ever. **3.** At some one time; esp., formerly. — *conj.* If ever; whenever; as soon as; as, *once* that is accomplished, all will be well. — *adj.* That once was; former; quondam. — *n.* One or the sole time; — used in *at once, for once, this once.* — **at once. a** Simultaneously. **b** Equally. **c** Immediately.

on·col′o·gy (ŏng·kŏl′ō·jĭ), *n.* [Gr. *onkos* bulk, also tumor + *-logy.*] *Med.* The study of tumors.

on′com′ing (ŏn′kŭm′ĭng), *adj.* Approaching.

on′-ding′, *n.* [*on*, adv. + E. dial. *ding* to drive.] *Scot. & Dial.* A heavy fall, as of snow.

‖on dit (ôN′ dē′). [F.] They say, or it is said.

on′do·graph (ŏn′dō·grăf; 9), *n.* [F. *onde* wave (L. *unda*) + *-graph.*] *Elec.* An instrument for making an autographic record (**on′do·gram** [-grăm]) of the wave forms of varying currents, esp. rapidly varying alternating currents.

one (wŭn; 4), *adj.* [ME. *one, on, an*, fr. AS. *ān.*] **1** Being a single unit, being, or thing. See NUMBER, *Table.* **2.** Undivided; united; as, with *one* voice. **3.** Denoting a particular thing or person; — often in antithesis to *another, other.* **4.** Denoting a person or thing indefinitely; a certain. **5.** Single in kind; the same. — *n.* **1.** The number denoting unity; unity. See NUMBER, *Table.* **2.** A single person or thing. — *pron.* **1.** (*pl.* ONES [wŭnz]) A certain person or thing not specified, some person or thing. **2.** Any person or thing whatever; anybody, indefinitely.

-one (-ōn). [From Gr. *-ōnē* female descendant.] *Chem.* A suffix indicating a *ketone*, as in acet*one.*

one′-horse′ (wŭn′hôrs′; 2), *adj.* **1.** Drawn or operated by one horse. **2.** *Colloq.* Second-rate; inferior; petty.

O·nei′da (ō·nī′dȧ), *n.* [Iroquois *Onĕñiute′.*] See IROQUOIAN, IROQUOIS.

o·nei′ro·crit′ic (ō·nī′rō·krĭt′ĭk), *n.* An interpreter of dreams.

o·nei′ro·crit′i·cal (-ĭ·kăl), *adj.* [Gr. *oneirokritikos*, fr. *oneiros* a dream + *kritikos* critical, fr. *krinein* to discern.] Of, pert. to, or skilled in the interpretation of dreams.

o·nei′ro·man′cy (ō·nī′rō·măn′sĭ), *n.* [Gr. *oneiros* dream + *-mancy.*] Divination by dreams.

one′ness (wŭn′nĕs; -nĭs), *n.* **1.** Singleness; unity. **2.** Identity; singleness in mind, purpose, or feeling.

on′er·ous (ŏn′ĕr·ŭs), *adj.* [OF. *onereus*, fr. L. *onerosus*, fr. *onus, oneris*, a load.] **1.** Burdensome; oppressive. **2.** *Law.* Imposing or constituting a legal burden. — **on′er·ous·ly**, *adv.* — **on′er·ous·ness**, *n.*

Syn. Onerous, burdensome, oppressive, exacting mean imposing great hardships. **Onerous** stresses laboriousness and heaviness, esp. because of distastefulness; **burdensome** stresses the causing of mental as well as of physical strain; **oppressive** implies extreme harshness or severity either in that imposed or the one imposing; **exacting** implies rigor or sternness, rather than tyranny, in the demands or in the one demanding.

one·self′ (wŭn·sĕlf′; 4), *pron.*, *or* **one's self.** The reflexive and emphatic form of the indefinite pronoun *one.*

one′-sid′ed (wŭn′sīd′ĕd; -ĭd; 2), *adj.* **1.** Having, or occurring on, one side only; having one side prominent or more developed; hence, limited to one side; partial. **2.** *Law.* Unilateral; as, a *one-sided* contract.

one′-step′, *n.* A ballroom dance adapted from the turkey trot; also, music for this dance.

one′time′ (wŭn′tīm′), *adj.* Former; quondam. — *adv.* Formerly.

one′-track′ (wŭn′trăk′; 2), *adj.* Having but one track, as a stretch of railroad; hence, narrow or undiversified; as, a *one-track* mind.

one′-way′ (-wā′; 2), *adj.* Moving, or permitting of motion or traffic, in one direction.

on′ion (ŭn′yŭn), *n.* [OF. *oignon*, fr. L. *unio* oneness.] **1.** An Asiatic plant (*Allium cepa*) of the lily family; also, its edible bulb of pungent taste and odor. **2.** Any wild species of the same genus.

on′ion·skin′ (-skĭn′), *n.* A kind of thin, translucent paper with a glossy finish.

on′look′er (ŏn′lo͝ok′ĕr), *n.* A looker-on; spectator. — **on′look′ing**, *adj. & n.*

on′ly (ōn′lĭ), *adj.; dial. & poetic intensive superl.* ON′LI·EST (-lĭ·ĕst; -ĭst). [AS. *ānlīc*, fr. *ān* one + *-līc.* See ONE; -LY.] **1.** Alone in its or their class; sole. **2.** Alone, by reason of superiority; pre-eminent; chief. — *adv.* **1.** Exclusively; solely; merely. **2.** Singly; as the only one; — in **on′ly-be·got′ten.** — *conj.* Were it not for this one condition, namely; except that.

on′o·mas′tic (ŏn′ō·măs′tĭk), *adj.* [Gr. *onomastikos* of naming, fr. *onomazein* to name, fr. *onoma* name.] **1.** Of or pertaining to, or consisting of, names or a name. **2.** Designating an autograph signature, as to a document the body of which is written by another. Cf. HOLOGRAPH.

on′o·mat′o·poe′ia (ŏn′ō·măt′ō·pē′yȧ; ō·nŏm′ȧ·tō-), *n.* [LL., fr. Gr. *onomatopoiia*, fr. *onoma, onomatos*, a name + *poiein* to make.] **1.** *Philol.* Formation of words in imitation of natural sounds (*buzz; hiss*). **2.** *Rhet.* Use of words whose sound suggests the sense. — **on′o·mat′o·poe′ic** (-ĭk), *adj.* — **on′o·mat′o·po·et′ic** (-pō·ĕt′ĭk), *adj.* — **on′o·mat′o·po·et′i·cal·ly** (-ĭ·kăl·ĭ), *adv.*

On′on·da′ga (ŏn′ŏn·dô′gȧ), *n.* [Iroquois *Onontą′ge‘.*] See IROQUOIAN, IROQUOIS.

on′rush′ (ŏn′rŭsh′), *n.* A rushing onward.

on′set′ (-sĕt′), *n.* [*on* + *set.*] **1.** A setting upon; attack; assault. **2.** A setting about; beginning; start.

on′shore′ (ŏn′shōr′), *adj.* That moves or is directed toward the shore; also, being on the shore. — **on′shore′** (-shōr′; 2), *adv.*

on side. *Football, etc.* Not off side. See OFF SIDE. — **on′side′** (ŏn′sīd′; 2), *adj.*

on′slaught′ (ŏn′slôt′), *n.* A furious attack or assault.

on′to (ŏn′to͞o; 4), *prep., or* **on to. 1.** To a position on or against; upon. **2.** *Slang, U.S.* Aware of or familiar with; as, he is *onto* your tricks.

on·tog′e·ny (ŏn·tŏj′ē·nĭ), *n.* Also **on′to·gen′e·sis** (ŏn′tō·jĕn′ē·sĭs). [See ONTOLOGY; GENESIS.] *Biol.* The life history or development of an individual organism. Cf. PHYLOGENY. — **on′to·ge·net′ic** (ŏn′tō·jē·nĕt′ĭk), *adj.* — **on·tog′e·nist** (ŏn·tŏj′ē·nĭst), *n.*

on·tol′o·gy (ŏn·tŏl′ō·jĭ), *n.* [Gr. *onta* the things which exist + *-logy.*] The science of being or reality; the branch of knowledge that investigates the nature, essential properties, and relations of being. — **on′to·log′i·cal** (ŏn′tō·lŏj′ĭ·kăl), *adj.* — **on·tol′o·gist** (ŏn·tŏl′ō·jĭst), *n.*

o′nus (ō′nŭs), *n.* [L.] A burden; obligation; charge.

‖o′nus pro·ban′di (prō·băn′dī). [L.] Burden of proof.

on′ward (ŏn′wĕrd), *adv.* [*on* + *-ward.*] **1.** Toward a point before or in front; forward. **2.** In an advanced position; in front; on. — *adj.* Moving or directed forward.

on′wards (ŏn′wĕrdz), *adv.* [See -WARDS.] Onward.

on′yx (ŏn′ĭks; ō′nĭks), *n.; pl.* ONYXES (-ĕz; -ĭz). [L., fr. Gr. *onyx* a claw, fingernail, veined gem.] Chalcedony in parallel layers of different shades of color, used esp. in making cameos. See SARDONYX.

o′ö- (ō′ō-). [Gr. *ōion.*] A combining form meaning *an egg, eggs*, as in oölogy; *Biol., an ovum*, as in oögonium.

o′ö·cyte (ō′ō·sīt), *n.* [*oö-* + *-cyte.*] *Embryol. & Zool.* An egg before maturation (formation of the polar bodies); or, in certain protozoans, a female gamete before undergoing changes believed to correspond to maturation.

oo′dles (o͞o′d′lz), *n. pl. Colloq.* An abundance; a great quantity; a lot.

o·ög′a·mous (ō·ŏg′ȧ·mŭs), *adj. Biol.* Having gametes exhibiting distinctions of sex; heterogamous.

o′ö·gen′e·sis (ō′ō·jĕn′ē·sĭs), *n.* [NL.] *Biol.* Formation of the egg and its preparation for fertilization and development.

o′ö·go′ni·um (-gō′nĭ·ŭm), *n.; pl.* -NIA (-ȧ), -NIUMS (-ŭmz). [NL., fr. *oö-* + Gr. *gonos* offspring.] **1.** *Bot.* The female sexual organ in oögamous thallophytic plants, containing one or more eggs, or oöspheres, which develop after fertilization into oöspores. **2.** *Embryol.* One of the descendants of a primordial germ cell which give rise to the oöcytes.

o′ö·lite (ō′ō·līt), *n.* [*oö-* + *-lite.*] *Petrog.* A rock consisting of small round grains, usually carbonate of lime, cemented together. — **o′ö·lit′ic** (-lĭt′ĭk), *adj.*

o·öl′o·gist (ō·ŏl′ō·jĭst), *n.* One versed in oölogy.

o·öl′o·gy (-jĭ), *n.* The branch of ornithology treating of birds' eggs. — **o′ö·log′i·cal** (ō′ō·lŏj′ĭ·kăl), *adj.*

oo′long (o͞o′lŏng; *Chin.* oo′lông′), *n.* [Cant. pron. of Chin. (Pek.) *wu*[1]*-lung*[2], lit., black dragon.] See TEA, 1 **b.**

oo′mi·ac, oo′mi·ak. Vars. of UMIAK.

o′ö·phore (ō′ō·fōr; 70), *n.* [*oö-* + *-phore.*] *Bot.* An oöphyte. — **o′ö·phor′ic** (-fŏr′ĭk), *adj.*

o·öph′o·ro- (ō·ŏf′ō·rō-), **oöphor-**. [NL. *oöphoron* ovary, fr. Gr. *ōion* egg + *-phoros*, fr. *pherein* to bear.] A combining form denoting *an ovary, ovarian*, as in **o′ö·pho·rec′to·my, o′ö·pho·ri′tis** (see -ECTOMY, -ITIS).

o′ö·phyte (ō′ō·fīt), *n.* [*oö-* + *-phyte.*] *Bot.* That generation in the life history of an archegoniate plant, as a moss, fern, or liverwort, in which sexual organs are developed. — **o′ö·phyt′ic** (-fĭt′ĭk), *adj.*

oo·ra′li (o͞o·rä′lē), *n.* Curare.

o′ö·sperm (ō′ō·spûrm), *n.* [*oö-* + Gr. *sperma* seed.] **a** *Zool.* A fertilized egg; a zygote. **b** *Bot.* = OÖSPORE.

o′ö·sphere (-sfēr), *n.* [*oö-* + Gr. *sphaira* sphere, ball.] *Biol.* An unfertilized egg; a female gamete.

o′ö·spore (ō′ō·spōr; 70), *n.* [oö- + *spore*.] *Bot.* The spore resulting from the fertilization of an oösphere by a sperm cell. Cf. ZYGOSPORE. — **o′ö·spor′ic** (-spŏr′ĭk), **o·ös′po·rous** (ō·ŏs′pō·rŭs; ō′ō·spō′rŭs), *adj.*

o′ö·the′ca (ō′ō·thē′kȧ), *n.; pl.* -CAE (-sē). [NL., fr. *oö-* + Gr. *thēkē* a case.] *Zool.* An egg case, esp. that of many varieties of mollusks, and of some insects, as cockroaches.

ooze (ōōz), *n.* [AS. *wōs* juice, sap.] **1.** A decoction of oak bark, sumac, catechu, etc., used for tanning leather. **2.** Act of oozing; also, that which oozes. — *v. i.* **1.** To percolate, as a liquid through the pores of a substance. **2.** To escape slowly and quietly; as, his courage *oozed* away. **3.** To exude moisture. — *v. t.* To exude.

ooze, *n.* [AS. *wāse* mud, mire.] **1.** Soft mud or slime, as in a river bed. **2.** A piece of muddy ground; a marsh; a bog. **3.** *Oceanography.* A soft deposit covering large areas of the ocean bottom, composed largely of the shells of minute organisms, as radiolarians.

ooze leather. Leather made from sheepskins or calfskins by forcing ooze through them; esp., such leather with a soft, finely granulated finish put on the flesh side.

o·pac′i·ty (ō·păs′ĭ·tĭ), *n.; pl.* -TIES (-tĭz). [F. *opacité*, fr. L. *opacitas*.] Quality or state of a body which renders it impervious to rays of light; opaqueness; hence, specif.: **a** Obscurity of sense. **b** Mental obtuseness.

o′pah (ō′pȧ), *n.* [West African *úbà*.] A large brilliantly colored fish (*Lampris regius*) of the Atlantic Ocean, constituting a family (Lampridae).

o′pal (ō′păl), *n.* [L. *opalus*, fr. Gr. *opalios*, fr. Skr. *upala* a stone, precious stone.] *Mineral.* An amorphous form of silica, softer and lighter than quartz. H., 5.5–6.5. The ***precious, or noble, opal,*** esteemed as a gem, is iridescent; the ***common opal*** has a milky or resinous appearance; the ***black opal*** combines iridescence with a deep-black background. See also GIRASOL, 2.

o′pal·es′cent (ō′păl·ĕs′ĕnt; -′nt), *adj.* [*opal* + *-escent*.] Reflecting an iridescent light; having a milky iridescence. — **o′pal·es′cence** (-ĕns; -′ns), *n.*

o′pal·ine (ō′păl·ĭn; -īn), *adj.* Of or like opal; opalescent.

o·paque′ (ō·pāk′), *adj.* [F. and L.; F., fr. L. *opacus* shady, dark.] **1.** Not reflecting or giving out light. **2.** Impervious to the rays of light. **3.** Impervious to radiant heat, electric waves, or other form of radiant energy. **4.** Obscure; unintelligible; also, obtuse. — *n.* **1.** That which is opaque. **2.** *Photog.* An opaque paint for blotting out portions of a negative. — **o·paque′ly,** *adv.* — **o·paque′ness,** *n.*

ope (ōp), *adj. & v. Now Poetic.* Open.

o′pen (ō′pĕn), *adj.* [AS.] **1.** Not impeding or preventing passage; not shut up; affording free ingress or egress; not covered over; not clogged. **2.** Hence: Free to be entered, visited, or used; without restrictions as to the participants; also, free to avail oneself of; as, the invitation is still *open;* specif., disengaged; as, an *open* date. **3.** Empty, or nearly so, of obstruction to passage or view; as, an *open* field; specif., not frosty or inclement; as, an *open* winter. **4.** Uncovered or unprotected; exposed; not enclosed; as, an *open* motor; hence, with *to*, liable; as, *open* to temptation; specif., *Mil.*, of a city or town, unoccupied and undefended by military forces and divested of any military installation; hence, when so proclaimed and acknowledged, immune under international law from enemy bombardment or sack. **5.** Not secret or disguised; revealed; public. **6.** Expanded; spread out. **7.** Without reserve or pretense; frank. **8.** Having openings, interstices, or the like; as, *open* ranks; also, perforated; porous. **9.** Yet to be decided; as, an *open* question. **10.** Not closed against appeals, proposals, etc.; accessible; also, responsive; amenable; as, to keep one's mind *open;* hence, generous. **11.** *Colloq., U. S.* Having no effective restrictions as to operation of drinking or gambling places or the like. **12.** *Music.* **a** Not stopped, as a string by the finger or a horn by the hand; not closed, as the top of an organ pipe. **b** Produced by an open string, pipe, etc.; natural. **13.** *Naut.* Not foggy. **14.** *Phonet.* **a** Of a vowel, low. See BROAD, *adj.*, 10 **a**. **b** Of a consonant, formed with the articulating organs narrowed without contact or with loose contact, as *s;* spirant; fricative. **15.** *Printing.* **a** More or less widely spaced or leaded. **b** Of type, made in outline. **16.** *Sports.* Legally available for hunting or fishing. — **Syn.** See LIABLE: FRANK.
— *v. t.* **1.** To move (a gate, lid, etc.) from its shut position. **2.** To spread out; expand; unroll. **3.** To make one or more openings or apertures in. **4.** To disclose; reveal; divulge. **5.** To enlighten, expand, or enlarge, as the understanding. **6.** To render clear for ingress or egress; to turn back or remove a door, covering, etc., from. **7.** To render accessible, as for settlement, trade, etc.; to declare (as a park) to be open to the public. **8.** To loosen or make less compact. **9.** To enter upon; begin; start. **10.** *Law.* To restore or recall, as an order, rule, judgment, etc., from a finally determined state to a state in which the parties are free to prosecute or oppose it. — *v. i.* **1.** To become open, as a door, wound, store. **2.** To expand; spread out or apart; hence, to become enlightened. **3.** To become or be disclosed, as to view. **4.** To give access. **5.** To begin. **6.** *Hunt.* To bark on finding the scent.
— *n.* Open or unobstructed space, as land without trees; also, open ocean or air; — with *the.* — **o′pen·ly,** *adv.* — **o′pen·ness,** *n.*

open air. The air out of doors.

o′pen–air′ (ō′pĕn·âr′; 2), *adj.* Outdoor; *Painting*, plein-air.

o′pen–and–shut′, *adj. Colloq.* Quite simple; obvious.

open chain. *Chem.* An arrangement of atoms represented in the structural formula by a chain whose ends are open, that is, not joined so as to form a ring (cf. RING, *n.*, 11); — opposed to *closed chain.*

open door. **a** Open or free admission to all. **b** In modern diplomacy, opportunity for intercourse, esp. commercial, open to all upon equal terms. — **o′pen–door′** (-dōr′; 2), *adj.*

o′pen·er (ō′pĕn·ẽr), *n.* **1.** One who or that which opens; as, a can *opener.* **2.** *Poker.* **a** One who opens a jack pot. **b** *pl.* Cards entitling one to open a jack pot.

o′pen–eyed′ (-īd′; 2), *adj.* Watchful; discerning; receptive.

o′pen·hand′ed (-hăn′dĕd; -dĭd; 2), *adj.* Generous; liberal. — **o′pen·hand′ed·ly,** *adv.* — **o′pen·hand′ed·ness,** *n.*

o′pen·heart′ed (-här′tĕd; -tĭd; 2), *adj.* Frank; generous. — **o′pen·heart′ed·ly,** *adv.* — **o′pen·heart′ed·ness,** *n.*

o′pen–hearth′ (-härth′; 2), *adj.* *Metal.* Designating or pert. to a process (**open–hearth process**) of making steel in a furnace of the regenerative reverberatory type. The open-hearth process (either *acid* or *basic:* see these terms) is the leading method of making steel.

open house. Hospitality or entertainment for all comers.

o′pen·ing (ō′pĕn·ĭng; ōp′nĭng), *n.* **1.** A making or becoming open. **2.** A place or part which is open; a breach; aperture; a gap. **3.** *U. S.* A thinly wooded space in the midst of a forest. **4.** Act of beginning; commencement. **5.** An opportunity. **6.** *Games.* A series of moves beginning a game.

open letter. A letter of protest or appeal, addressed to an individual, but intended for the general public and printed in a newspaper or periodical. — **o′pen–let′ter** (*see Pron.*, § 2), *adj.*

o′pen–mind′ed (ō′pĕn·mīn′dĕd; -dĭd; 2), *adj.* Receptive of arguments or ideas. — **o′pen–mind′ed·ly,** *adv.* — **o′pen–mind′ed·ness,** *n.*

o′pen·mouthed′ (-mouthd′; -moutht′; 2), *adj.* Gaping; hence, greedy; clamorous; vociferous.

open order. *Mil. & Nav.* A formation in which the units are separated by considerable intervals; extended order.

open policy. *Insurance.* A policy covering goods of a class subject to change in volume, the premium being computed periodically.

Open sesame! The magical command which opened the door of the robbers' den in the *Arabian Nights'* tale of *Ali Baba and the Forty Thieves;* hence (often **o′pen–ses′a·me**), something that unfailingly opens or admits; a magical key.

open shop. An establishment in which eligibility for employment and retention on the payroll are not determined by membership or nonmembership in a labor union, though there may be an agreement by which a union is recognized as sole bargaining agent. — **o′pen–shop′** (-shŏp′; 2), *adj.*

open sight. A rear sight on a firearm having an open notch instead of a peephole. See SIGHT, *Illust.*

open syllable. A syllable ending in a vowel or diphthong.

o′pen·work′ (ō′pĕn·wûrk′), *n.* Any work so made as to show openings through its substance. — **o′pen·work′,** *adj.*

op′er·a (ŏp′ẽr·ȧ), *n.; pl.* OPERAS (-ȧz). [It., fr. *opera* work, composition, fr. L. *opera* pains, work, fr. *opus, operis,* work.] **1.** A drama wholly or mostly sung, consisting of recitative, arias, choruses, duets, etc., with orchestral accompaniment and appropriate costumes, scenery, and action. ***comic opera,*** as disting. from *grand opera* (which see), has spoken, often farcical, dialogue between the musical numbers. See also OPERETTA. **2.** The score or performance of a musical drama. **3.** Musical drama as a form of art.

op′e·ra (ŏp′ĕ·rȧ), *n., pl.* of OPUS.

op′er·a·ble (ŏp′ẽr·ȧ·b′l), *adj.* Practicable; specif., *Med.*, admitting of treatment by operation.

‖**o′pé′ra′ bouffe** (ō′pā′rȧ′ bōōf′). [F., fr. *opéra* opera + *bouffe* comic, fr. It. *buffo.*] Farcical comic opera.

‖**o′pé′ra′ co′mique′** (kō′mēk′). [F.] Comic opera.

opera glass *or* **glasses.** A small telescope, usually binocular, adapted for use at the opera.

opera hat. A man's collapsible top hat made on a steel frame with spring attached.

opera house. **a** A theater devoted principally to the performance of operas. **b** Loosely, in small towns, a theater.

op′er·ant (ŏp′ẽr·ănt), *n. & adj.* Operative.

op′er·ate (-āt), *v. i.* [L. *operatus*, past part. of *operari* to work, fr. *opus, operis,* work, labor.] **1.** To perform a work or labor; to act; to produce an effect; to work; function. **2.** To produce an appropriate effect, as a drug. **3.** To perform an operation or series of operations. **4.** To carry on a military or naval action or mission. See OPERATION, 6. **5.** *Colloq.* To deal in stocks, esp. speculatively. — *v. t.* **1.** To produce as an effect. **2.** To put into, or to continue in, operation.

op′er·at′ic (-ăt′ĭk), *adj.* Of, pertaining to, or like opera; adapted for opera. — **op′er·at′i·cal·ly** (-ĭ·kăl·ĭ), *adv.*

op′er·a′tion (ŏp′ẽr·ā′shŭn), *n.* **1.** The act, process, or effect of operating. **2.** Agency; exertion of power or influence; as, by the *operation* of law. **3.** Method or way of operating or functioning. **4.** State of being operative. **5.** An action done as a part of practical work; as, the manual *operations* in painting. **6.** A military and/or naval action or mission including movement, supply, attack, defense, and all requisite maneuvers, often designated from its inception as a detailed plan by a code word; for example, *Operation* Torch, the invasion of French North Africa, *Operation* Overlord, the invasion of Normandy, *Operation* Crossroads, the test at Bikini atoll. **7.** *Com.* A transaction, esp. a speculative one. **8.** *Math.* Some transformation, indicated by rules or symbols, to be made upon quantities. **9.** *Surg.* A procedure on the living body, usually with instruments, esp. for restoring health.

op′er·a′tion·al (-ăl; -′l), *adj.* **1.** Of, pertaining to, or connected with operations or an operation, specif. operations in a campaign or battle as distinguished from training, testing, reconnaissance, etc. **2.** Of an aircraft, serviced in readiness for action.

op′er·a′tive (ŏp′ẽr·ā′tĭv; -ȧ·tĭv), *adj.* **1.** Exerting force or influence; operating; as, an *operative* motive. **2.** Producing the appropriate effect; efficacious; as, an *operative* dose. **3.** Having to do with physical or mechanical operations. **4.** *Surg.* Based upon, or consisting of, an operation or operations; as, *operative* surgery. **5.** Engaged in, or doing, work. — (-ȧ·tĭv; -ā′tĭv), *n.* A worker, esp. one employed in a mechanical industry.

op′er·a′tor (-ā′tẽr), *n.* **1.** One who operates, as in transmitting or receiving telegraph or radio messages, handling telephone calls at a switchboard, dealing in stocks, or performing surgical operations; one who operates a (specified) thing; as, a linotype *operator.* **2.** One who owns, leases, or manages mining property.

o·per′cu·late (ō·pûr′kū·lāt), **o·per′cu·lat′ed** (-lāt′ĕd; -ĭd), *adj.* Having a lid, or operculum.

o·per′cu·lum (-lŭm), *n.; pl.* -LA (-lȧ), -LUMS (-lŭmz). [L., a cover or lid, fr. *operire* to cover.] **1.** *Bot.* **a** A lid, or covering flap, as of a moss capsule or of a pyxidium in seed plants. **b** The calyx limb in eucalypti. **2.** *Zool.* A lidlike process or part, as: **a** The plate of horn or shell on the foot of many gastropod mollusks which serves to close the shell when the animal is retracted. See KING CRAB, GASTROPOD, *Illusts.* **b** The protective covering of the gills of fishes. — **o·per′cu·lar** (-lẽr), *adj.*

‖**op′e·re ci·ta′to** (ŏp′ĕ·rē sĭ·tā′tō). [L.] In the work quoted. Abbr. *op. cit.*

op′er·et′ta (ŏp′ẽr·ĕt′ȧ), *n.; pl.* -TAS (-ȧz), -TE (-ē). [It., dim. of *opera.*] *Music.* A musical-dramatic work with slight plot, cheerful music, and spoken dialogue.

op′er·ose (ŏp′ẽr·ōs), *adj.* [L. *operosus*, fr. *opera* pains, labor.] Laborious; diligent. — **op′er·ose′ly,** *adv.* — **op′er·ose′ness,** *n.*

O·phe′lia (ō·fēl′yȧ; 58), *n.* The daughter of Polonius in Shakespeare's *Hamlet.* She goes mad and is drowned.

o·phid′i·an (ō·fĭd′ĭ·ăn), *n.* [Dim. fr. Gr. *ophis* snake.] Any of a division (Ophidia) of reptiles consisting of the snakes or serpents. — *adj.* Of or pert. to this division.

oph′i·ol′a·try (ŏf′ĭ·ŏl′ȧ·trĭ; ō′fĭ-), *n.* [Gr. *ophis* snake + *-latry.*] Serpent worship. — **oph′i·ol′a·trous** (-trŭs), *adj.*

oph′i·ol′o·gy (-ŏl′ō·jĭ), *n.* The branch of zoology that treats of the ophidians. — **oph′i·o·log′i·cal** (-ō·lŏj′ĭ·kăl), *adj.* — **oph′i·ol′o·gist** (-ŏl′ō·jĭst), *n.*

O′phir (ō′fẽr), *n.* [Heb. *Ōphīr.*] A region mentioned in the Old Testament as the source of gold. 1 *Kings* x. 11.

oph′ite (ŏf′īt; ō′fīt), *n.* [L. *ophites*, fr. Gr. *ophitēs* (sc. *lithos*), a marble spotted like a serpent.] *Petrog.* A variety of green diabase whose augite is altered to uralite.

o·phit′ic (ō·fĭt′ĭk), *adj. Petrog.* Of the nature of, or pert. to, ophite; having a rock fabric in which plagioclase crystals are enclosed in later-formed augite, as in diabase.

oph·thal′mi·a (ŏf·thăl′mĭ·ȧ), *n.* [LL., fr. Gr. *ophthalmia*, fr. *ophthalmos* the eye.] *Med.* An inflammation of the conjunctiva or of the eyeball.

oph·thal′mic (-mĭk), *adj.* Of, or in the region of, the eye.

oph′thal·mi′tis (ŏf′thăl·mī′tĭs), *n.* [NL.] *Med.* Ophthalmia.

oph·thal′mo- (ŏf·thăl′mō-), **ophthalm-**. [Gr. *ophthalmos* eye.] A combining form meaning *the eye* or *eyes*, as in **oph′thal·mot′o·my.**

oph′thal·mol′o·gist (ŏf′thăl·mŏl′ō·jĭst), *n. Med.* A physician specializing in the study and treatment of defects and diseases of the eye.

oph′thal·mol′o·gy (ŏf′thăl·mŏl′ō·jĭ), *n.* [*ophthalmo-* + *-logy.*] The science which treats of the structure, functions, and diseases of the eye. — **oph·thal′mo·log′i·cal** (ŏf·thăl′mō·lŏj′ĭ·kăl), *adj.*

oph·thal′mo·scope (ŏf·thăl′mō·skōp), *n.* [*ophthalmo-* + *-scope.*] *Physiol.* An instrument with a mirror centrally perforated for viewing the interior of the eye, esp. the retina. — **oph·thal′mo·scop′ic** (-skŏp′ĭk), **oph·thal′mo·scop′i·cal** (-ĭ·kăl), *adj.* — **oph′thal·mos′co·py** (ŏf′thăl·mŏs′kō·pĭ), *n.*

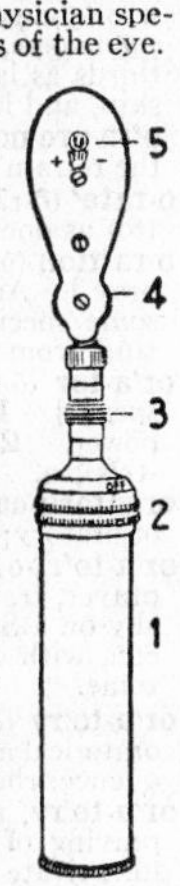

Ophthalmoscope. 1 Handle containing dry-cell battery; 2 Rheostat; 3 Focusing Ferrule; 4 Gear Wheel for rotating lenses; 5 Sight Hole.

-o′pi·a (-ō′pĭ·ȧ), **-opy.** [Gr. *ōps, ōpos*, eye.] A combining form denoting *a* (specified) *kind* or *defect of eye*, as in *myopia.*

o′pi·ate (ō′pĭ·āt; -ĭt), *n.* [ML. *opiatus*, adj. See OPIUM.] **1.** Any medicine containing, or derived from, opium; a narcotic. **2.** Anything restful or soothing. Cf. ANODYNE. — *adj.* Containing, or mixed with, opium; inducing sleep; narcotic. — (-āt), *v. t.* To subject to an opiate.

o·pine′ (ō·pīn′), *v. t. & i.* [F. *opiner*, fr. L. *opinari*, past part. *opinatus.*] *Now Often Humorous.* To have or express an opinion or as one's opinion; think; suppose.

o·pin′ion (ō·pĭn′yŭn), *n.* [OF., fr. L. *opinio.* See OPINE.] **1.** Belief stronger than impression, less strong than positive knowledge; a belief; view; judgment. **2.** The judgment or sentiment which the mind forms of persons or things; estimation; sometimes, favorable estimation; esteem. **3.** A formal expression by an expert; as, to get the doctor's *opinion.* **4.** *Law.* The formal expression by a judge, court, referee, or the like, of the legal reasons and principles upon which the decision is based.

Syn. Opinion, view, belief, conviction, persuasion, sentiment mean a judgment one holds as true. Opinion implies a having been thought out yet open to dispute; view, an opinion more or less colored by bias; belief, acceptance and intellectual assent; conviction, a belief held firmly; persuasion, a belief grounded on assurance of its truth; sentiment, a more or less settled opinion.

o·pin′ion·at′ed (-āt′ĕd; -ĭd), *adj.* Unduly attached or adhering to one's own opinion; obstinate; opinionative. — **o·pin′ion·at′ed·ness**, *n.*

o·pin′ion·a′tive (-ā′tĭv), *adj.* **1.** Of, pertaining to, or consisting in opinion; doctrinal. **2.** Opinionated. — **o·pin′ion·a′tive·ly**, *adv.* — **o·pin′ion·a′tive·ness**, *n.*

op′is·thog′na·thous (ŏp′ĭs·thŏg′nȧ·thŭs), *adj.* [Gr. *opisthen* behind + *-gnathous.*] Having retreating jaws; — opposed to *prognathous.* — **op′is·thog′na·thism** (-thĭz′m), *n.*

o′pi·um (ō′pĭ·ŭm; 58), *n.* [L., fr. Gr. *opion* poppy juice, dim. of *opos* vegetable juice.] A narcotic drug consisting of the dried juice of the **opium poppy** (see POPPY).

o′pi·um·ism (-ĭz′m), *n. Med.* The habitual use of opium, or the state resulting from its habitual overuse.

op′o·del′doc (ŏp′ō·dĕl′dŏk), *n.* Camphorated soap liniment.

o·pos′sum (ō·pŏs′ŭm), *n.; pl.* -SUMS (-ŭmz). See PLURAL, *Note*, 3. [Of Algonquian origin.] Any of a family (Didelphidae; esp., *Didelphis virginiana*) of American marsupials, chiefly nocturnal, largely arboreal, and almost omnivorous. When caught it feigns death.

op′pi·dan (ŏp′ĭ·dăn), *adj.* [L. *oppidanus*, fr. *oppidum* town.] Of or pertaining to a town. — *n.* **1.** A townsman. **2.** At Eton, a student who boards in the town.

op·po′nen·cy (ŏ·pō′nĕn·sĭ), *n.* Opposition; antagonism.

op·po′nent (-nĕnt), *adj.* [L. *opponens, -entis*, pres. part. of *opponere* to set or place against, oppose, fr. *ob-* + *ponere* to place.] **1.** Situated in front; opposite; also, adverse; antagonistic. **2.** *Anat.* Bringing into opposition, as a muscle. — *n.* One who opposes; an adversary; foe.

Syn. Opponent, antagonist, adversary mean one showing opposition. Opponent implies position on another side, as in a debate, an election, or a conflict; antagonist implies sharper opposition, esp. in a struggle for supremacy; adversary may imply opposition only, but usually it suggests active hostility.

op′por·tune′ (ŏp′ŏr·tūn′; ŏp′ŏr·tūn; 2), *adj.* [F. *opportun*, fr. L. *opportunus*, fr. *ob-* + *portus* port, harbor.] Fit; ready; hence, seasonable; timely. — **Syn.** See SEASONABLE. — **op′por·tune′ly**, *adv.* — **op′por·tune′ness**, *n.*

op′por·tun′ism (-tūn′ĭz′m), *n.* A taking advantage, as in politics, of opportunities or circumstances, with little regard for principles or ultimate consequences. — **op′por·tun′ist** (-ĭst), *n. & adj.* — **op′por·tun·is′tic** (-tūn·ĭs′tĭk), *adj.*

op′por·tu′ni·ty (-tū′nĭ·tĭ), *n.; pl.* -TIES (-tĭz). Fit time; a favorable juncture of circumstances; a good chance.

op·pos′a·ble (ŏ·pōz′ȧ·b′l), *adj.* **1.** Capable of being opposed; as, *opposable* arguments. **2.** Capable of being placed opposite something else; apposable. — **op·pos′a·bil′i·ty** (-bĭl′ĭ·tĭ), *n.*

op·pose′ (ŏ·pōz′), *v. t.* [OF. *opposer.* See OB-; POSE to place.] **1.** To put in opposition, with a view to counterbalance; to set against, by way of contrast or resistance. **2.** To place in front of, or over against. **3.** To resist by physical means or by arguments; to contend against; withstand. — **op·pos′er** (ŏ·pōz′ẽr), *n.*

Syn. Oppose, combat, resist, withstand, antagonize mean to set one against. Oppose implies anything between mere objection and intense hostility or warfare; combat, an actual conflict with that which one opposes; resist and withstand, an answer to an offensive action, by using counter force, *withstand* often adding a hint of a successful outcome; antagonize, an invitation to resistance or hostility.

op′po·site (ŏp′ō·zĭt), *adj.* [OF., fr. L. *oppositus*, past part. of *opponere.* See OPPONENT.] Abbr. *opp.* **1.** Set over against; facing; — often with *to.* **2.** Contrarily turned or moving. **3.** Opposed or hostile; as, the *opposite* sides of the question. **4.** Diametrically different; contrary; repugnant; antagonistic. **5.** *Bot.* **a** Situated in pairs on an axis, each being separated from the other by half the circumference of the axis, as certain leaves. **b** Of floral parts, = SUPERPOSED.

Syn. Opposite, contradictory, contrary, antithetical (*or* antithetic), antonymous mean so far apart as to seem irreconcilable. Opposite implies a setting against each other so as to bring out sharply the contrast, conflict, or antagonism between them; contradictory, a setting against so as to bring out their denial of each other (esp. terms, propositions, etc.) so that if one is true, the other must be false; contrary, extreme divergence, often diametrical opposition; antithetical, clear and unequivocal diametrical opposition; antonymous, applicable only to words, implies an opposition in meaning so great that each one negates or nullifies every one of the implications in the other.

— *n.* **1.** *Archaic.* An opponent. **2.** That which is opposed, or contrary. **3.** An antonym. — *adv.* On opposite sides. — *prep.* Across from and facing or on the same level with. — **op′po·site·ly**, *adv.* — **op′po·site·ness**, *n.*

opposite number. A person of corresponding or comparable rank in another government, organization, system, subdivision, or the like.

op′po·si′tion (ŏp′ō·zĭsh′ŭn), *n.* [OF., fr. L. *oppositio.* See OPPOSITE.] **1.** Act of setting opposite, or the state of being so set. **2.** Hostile or contrary action or condition; resistance. **3.** That which opposes; an obstacle; the aggregate of those opposing; [*often cap.*], in politics, the party opposed to the party in power. **4.** [The earliest sense in English.] *Astron. & Astrol.* The situation of a celestial body with respect to another when differing from it in longitude by 180°; esp., such position of a planet or satellite with respect to the sun; — signified by the symbol ☍; as, ☍ ♃ ☉, opposition of Jupiter to the sun. **5.** *Logic.* The relation between two propositions when, having the same subject and predicate, they differ in quantity, quality, or both.

op·press′ (ŏ·prĕs′), *v. t.* [OF. *oppresser*, fr. ML. *oppressare*, fr. L. *opprimere, oppressum*, fr. *ob-* + *premere* to press.] **1.** *Obs.* To crush; trample; hence, *Poetic*, to overpower. **2.** To burden spiritually as if with weight; to weigh down. **3.** To crush, burden, or trample down by abuse of power or authority; to treat with unjust rigor or with cruelty. — **Syn.** See DEPRESS: WRONG.

op·pres′sion (ŏ·prĕsh′ŭn), *n.* **1.** Unjust or cruel exercise of authority or power, esp. by the imposition of burdens; also, that which so oppresses. **2.** A sense of heaviness or obstruction in the body or mind; depression; lassitude.

op·pres′sive (ŏ·prĕs′ĭv), *adj.* **1.** Unreasonably burdensome; unjustly severe. **2.** Tyrannical. **3.** Overpowering to spirit or senses. — **Syn.** See ONEROUS. — **op·pres′sive·ly**, *adv.* — **op·pres′sive·ness**, *n.*

op·pres′sor (ŏ·prĕs′ẽr), *n.* One who oppresses.

op·pro′bri·ous (ŏ·prō′brĭ·ŭs), *adj.* [OF. or L.; OF. *opprobrieux*, fr. L. *opprobriosus*, fr. *opprobrium.* See OPPROBRIUM.] **1.** Expressive of opprobrium; attaching disgrace; reproachful; scurrilous. **2.** Infamous; involving or bringing opprobrium. — **op·pro′bri·ous·ly**, *adv.* — **op·pro′bri·ous·ness**, *n.*

op·pro′bri·um (-ŭm), *n.* [L., fr. *opprobrare* to taunt, fr. *ob-* + *probrum* reproach, infamy.] The disgrace that follows shameful conduct; infamy; also, a cause of such disgrace. — **Syn.** See DISGRACE.

op·pugn′ (ŏ·pūn′), *v. t.* [L. *oppugnare*, fr. *ob-* + *pugnare* to fight.] To assail or call in question; controvert.

op·pug′nant (ŏ·pŭg′nănt), *adj.* Hostile; opposing; antagonistic. — **op·pug′nan·cy** (-năn·sĭ), *n.*

op·pugn′er (ŏ·pūn′ẽr), *n.* One who oppugns.

Ops (ŏps), *n.* [L.] Italian goddess of the harvest.

-op′sis (-ŏp′sĭs). [Gr. *opsis.*] A combining form meaning *appearance, sight*, used in botany and zoology.

op·son′ic (ŏp·sŏn′ĭk), *adj.* Of or affected by opsonin.

opsonic index. The ratio of the phagocytic index of a tested serum to that of normal serum.

op·son′i·fi·ca′tion (ŏp·sŏn′ĭ·fĭ·kā′shŭn), *n. Immunol.* The action or the effect of opsonins in rendering bacteria more readily consumed by phagocytosis. — **op·son′i·fy** (-sŏn′ĭ·fī), *v. t.;* OP·SON′I·FIED (-fīd); OP·SON′I·FY′ING.

op′so·nin (ŏp′sō·nĭn), *n.* [Gr. *opsōnein* to buy victuals, to cater.] *Bacteriol.* A constituent of blood serum which renders cells, as invading pathogenic bacteria, more susceptible to the action of the phagocytes.

op′so·nize (-nīz), *v. t. Immunol.* To form opsonins in.

opt (ŏpt), *v. i.* [F. *opter*, fr. L. *optare.*] To make choice.

op′ta·tive (ŏp′tȧ·tĭv; *Brit. also* ŏp·tā′tĭv), *adj.* [F. *optatif*, fr. LL. *optativus*, fr. *optare* to wish.] Expressive of wish or desire; — chiefly of grammatical mood. — *n. Gram.* The optative mood, or a verbal form denoting it. Abbr. *opt.*

op′tic (ŏp′tĭk), *adj.* [F. *optique*, fr. ML. *opticus*, fr. Gr. *optikos.*] Of or pertaining to vision or the eye. — *n. Humorous.* An eye.

op′ti·cal (ŏp′tĭ·kăl), *adj.* **1.** Relating to the science of optics. **2.** Relating to vision; ocular; as, an *optical* illusion. — **op′ti·cal·ly**, *adv.*

optic axis. *Mineral.* The line in a doubly refracting crystal in the direction of which no double refraction occurs. A uniaxial crystal has one such line, a biaxial crystal has two.

op·ti′cian (ŏp·tĭsh′ăn), *n.* [F. *opticien.*] One who makes, or who deals in, optical glasses and instruments.

optic nerve. The special nerve of sight, connecting the eye and the optic centers of the brain. See EYE, *Illust.*

op′tics (ŏp′tĭks), *n.;* see -ICS. [From *optic*, adj., after ML. *optica.*] The science treating of light (sense 15 **a**), its genesis and propagation, the effects which it suffers and produces, and other phenomena, as those of vision. Cf. PHOTICS.

optic thalamus. *Anat.* The thalamus of either side, containing optic centers which are large in man.
op′ti·me (ŏp′tĭ·mē), *n.* [L., adv. fr. *optimus* the best.] In Cambridge University, an honor man ranking below the wranglers and called either ***senior optime*** (second class) or ***junior optime*** (third class).
op′ti·mism (ŏp′tĭ·mĭz'm), *n.* [F. *optimisme*, fr. L. *optimus* the best.] **1.** *Philos.* **a** The doctrine that the world is the best possible world. **b** The doctrine that reality is essentially good. **c** The doctrine that the good of life overbalances the pain and evil of it. **2.** An inclination to put the most favorable construction upon actions and happenings, or anticipate the best possible outcome.
op′ti·mist (-mĭst), *n.* One given to optimism; specif., an adherent of philosophical optimism; — opposite of *pessimist.*
op′ti·mis′tic (-mĭs′tĭk), *adj.* Also **op′ti·mis′ti·cal** (-tĭ·kăl). **1.** Of or pertaining to or characterized by optimism. **2.** Hopeful; sanguine. — **op′ti·mis′ti·cal·ly,** *adv.*
op′ti·mum (ŏp′tĭ·mŭm), *n.; pl.* -MA (-mȧ), -MUMS (-mŭmz). [L., prop. neut. of *optimus* best.] **1.** The best or most favorable degree, quantity, number, etc. **2.** *Biol.* The most favorable condition as to temperature, light, moisture, etc., for the growth and reproduction of an organism. — *adj.* Most favorable or conducive to a given end.
op′tion (ŏp′shŭn), *n.* [F., fr. L. *optio.*] **1.** The exercise of the power of choice. **2.** Power of choosing; the right of choice; an alternative. **3.** That which is offered for choice, or which is chosen. **4.** *Com. & Fin.* A stipulated privilege of buying or selling a stated property, security, or commodity at a given price within a specified time. **5.** *Insurance.* The right of an insured person to choose the form in which payments due him on a policy shall be made or applied. — **Syn.** See CHOICE.
op′tion·al (-ăl; -'l), *adj.* Involving an option; left to one's discretion; not compulsory. — **op′tion·al·ly,** *adv.*
op·tom′e·ter (ŏp·tŏm′ē·tēr), *n.* [*optic* + *-meter.*] *Physiol.* An instrument for measuring the distance of distinct vision, or the scope of the automatic adjustment of the eye, as in selecting eyeglasses.
op·tom′e·try (-trĭ), *n.* **1.** Measurement of the range of vision. **2.** Scientific examination of the eye to detect diseases or defects, prescription of correctional lenses or exercises but not of the use of drugs, and supplying of lenses. — **op·tom′e·trist** (-trĭst), *n.*
op′u·lence (ŏp′ū·lĕns), *n.* Also **op′u·len·cy** (-lĕn·sĭ). Wealth; affluence; hence, plenty; profusion.
op′u·lent (-lĕnt), *adj.* [L. *opulens, opulentus*, fr. *ops, opis*, power, wealth, riches.] Having a large estate or property; wealthy; hence, amply or plentifully provided or fashioned; luxuriant; profuse. — **Syn.** See RICH; LUXURIOUS.
o·pun′ti·a (ō·pŭn′shĭ·ȧ), *n.* [NL., fr. L. *Opuntia* (*herba*), a plant, fr. *Opus*, city in Locris, Greece.] *Bot.* Any of a large genus (*Opuntia*) of cacti, the prickly pears, having flat or terete joints usually studded with tubercles bearing sharp spines or prickly hairs or both and bearing yellow flowers succeeded by edible pulpy fruits.
o′pus (ō′pŭs *or, esp. Brit.,* ŏp′ŭs), *n.; pl.* OPERA (ŏp′ē·rȧ). [L. See OPERA.] A work; esp., a musical composition. Abbr. *op.* See MAGNUM OPUS.
o·pus′cule (ō·pŭs′kūl), *n.* [F. *opuscule*, fr. L. *opusculum*, dim. of *opus* work.] A small or petty work.
o·quas′sa (ō·kwăs′ȧ), *n.* [From *Oquassa* Lake, Maine.] *Zool.* A small, rather slender trout (*Salvelinus oquassa*) of the Rangeley Lakes in Maine. See TROUT, 1; 2d CHAR.
or (ôr), *conj. & prep.* [From ON. *ār*, adv., early, formerly.] *Archaic & Dial.* Ere; before. — ***or ever, or ere.*** *Archaic.* Before.
or (ôr; 4), *conj.* [ME. *or*, fr. *outher, other, auther*, either, or, fr. AS. *āwther*, contr. fr. *āhwæther*, fr. *ā* aye + *hwæther* whether; or ME. *other, or*, may be fr. AS. *oththe.*] A co-ordinating particle that marks an alternative; as, you may telephone *or* you may write.
or (ôr), *n.* [F., fr. L. *aurum* gold.] *Her.* The color gold or the color yellow, — represented in drawing or engraving by small dots.
-or (*see note below*). A noun suffix denoting: **1.** [OF. *-or, -ur, -our* (F. *-eur*), fr. L. *-or.*] *State* or *quality*, as in error, fervor, candor. **2.** [From OF., fr. L. *-or* or fr. L. *-ator.*] *Agent* or *doer*, as in auditor, one who hears; donor, one who gives; elevator, creditor, executor; — appended to words of Latin, as *-er* to those of English, origin.
☞ *-or* is generally pronounced -ēr, the same as *-er*, as in such common words as *ardor, labor*, etc., but often -ôr in learned or technical words, as *obligor, rigor mortis.*
or′ach, or′ache (ŏr′ăch), *n.* [F. *arroche*, fr. L. *atriplex*, fr. Gr. *atraphaxys.*] Any of a genus (*Atriplex*) of herbs of the goosefoot family, esp. a red ornamental variety (*A. hortensis*).
or′a·cle (ŏr′ȧ·k'l; -ĭ·k'l), *n.* [OF., fr. L. *oraculum*, fr. *orare* to speak, utter, pray.] **1.** *Gr. & Rom. Antiq.* The medium by which a god reveals hidden knowledge or makes known the divine purpose; also, the place where the revelation is given. **2.** The response of an oracle to a question or petition. **3. a** A place of communication from God, as the holy of holies of the Jewish temple; also, an inspired prophet. **b** The revelation received from such a place or medium; *pl.*, the Scriptures. **4.** A thing or person supposed to give divine or authoritative decisions. **5.** An authoritative or wise expression; a wise answer.
o·rac′u·lar (ō·răk′ū·lēr), *adj.* **1.** Of or pertaining to an oracle; forecasting the future. **2.** Resembling an oracle, as in solemnity, wisdom, obscurity, ambiguity, dogmatism. — **Syn.** See DICTATORIAL. — **o·rac′u·lar′i·ty** (-lăr′ĭ·tĭ), *n.* — **o·rac′u·lar·ly,** *adv.*
o′ral (ō′răl; 70), *adj.* [L. *os, oris*, mouth, face.] **1.** Uttered by the mouth; spoken. **2.** Using speech or the lips, esp. in teaching the deaf. **3.** Of or pertaining to or surrounding the mouth; as, *oral* cilia; also, done by the mouth. **4.** *Zool.* On, or pertaining to, the same side as the mouth; actinal. — **o′ral·ly,** *adv.*
Syn. **Oral, verbal** are frequently confused. **Oral** applies to that which is uttered or spoken; **verbal**, to that which uses words and which therefore may be either written or spoken.
or′ange (ŏr′ĕnj; -ĭnj), *n.* [OF. *orenge* (F. *orange*), fr. Pr. *auranja* (after *aur* gold, F. *or*), fr. earlier (*n*)*aranja* (with loss of *n* due to confusion with indef. art.), Sp. *naranja*, fr. Ar. *nāranj*, fr. Per. *nārang.*] **1.** The nearly globose fruit, botanically a berry, of an evergreen tree (genus *Citrus*) of the rue family, of several varieties, as the ***sweet orange*** (*C. sinensis*), the ***bitter orange*** (*C. aurantium*), the bergamot, the mandarin. **2.** The tree bearing this fruit, with oval unifoliolate leaves and fragrant white flowers. The **orange blossom** is the State flower of Florida. **3.** Any of several trees or fruits more or less resembling the orange, as the Osage orange. **4.** Any of the colors resembling those of oranges, varying in hue from reddish red-yellow to red-yellow, in saturation from high to very high, and in brilliance from medium to high. See COLOR. — *adj.* Of or pertaining to an orange; of the color orange.
or′ange·ade′ (-ād′), *n.* [F.] A beverage made of orange juice mixed with water and sweetened.
Or′ange·ism (ŏr′ĕn·jĭz'm; -ĭn·jĭz'm), *n.* The tenets or practices of the Orangemen. — **Or′ange·ist** (-jĭst), *n.*
Or′ange·man (ŏr′ĕnj·măn; ŏr′ĭnj-), *n.; pl.* -MEN (-mĕn). One of a secret society organized in the north of Ireland in 1795 for the support of the Protestant religion; — so called in honor of William, Prince of Orange (William III of England).
Or′ange·men's Day (-mĕnz). July 12, celebrated in Northern Ireland in commemoration of the Battle of the Boyne (July 1, 1690) and the Battle of Aughrim (July 12, 1691). See HOLIDAY, *n.*, 3.
orange pekoe. See PEKOE.
or′ange·ry (ŏr′ĕnj·rĭ; ŏr′ĭnj-), *n.; pl.* -RIES (-rĭz). [F. *orangerie*, fr. *orange.*] A house or other protected place for raising oranges in cool climates.
or′ange·wood′ (-wŏŏd′), *n.* The wood of the orange used in turnery and for dental work. — **or′ange·wood′,** *adj.*
o·rang′u·tan′ (ō·răng′ōō·tăn′; ō′răng·ōō′tăn), **o·rang′ou·tang′** (-tăng′), *n.* [Malay *orań utan* wild man, savage (fr. *orań* man + *utan* wild), wrongly used by Europeans for the ape.] An anthropoid ape (*Pongo pygmaeus*, syn. *Simia satyrus*) of Borneo and Sumatra, about two thirds as large as the gorilla, and distinguished by small ears, brown skin, and long, sparse, reddish-brown hair.
‖**o′ra pro no′bis** (ō′rȧ prō nō′bĭs). [L.] Pray for us; specif., *R.C.Ch.*, the refrain of a litany to the Virgin in the liturgy.
o·rate′ (ō·rāt′; ō′rāt), *v. t. & i.* [See ORATION.] *Humorous.* To speak (to) as one pronouncing an oration; harangue.
o·ra′tion (ō·rā′shŭn), *n.* [F. or L.; F., fr. L. *oratio*, fr. *orare* to speak, pray.] An elaborate and dignified discourse, esp. one delivered on some special occasion, as a funeral or anniversary; a speech; — disting. from a sermon or lecture.
or′a·tor (ŏr′ȧ·tēr; 74), *n.* [OF. *oratour*, fr. L. *orator*, fr. *orare* to speak.] **1.** A public speaker; esp., one distinguished for skill and power. **2.** *Law.* The petitioner or plaintiff. — **or′a·tress** (-trĕs; -trĭs), *n.*
or′a·tor′i·cal (ŏr′ȧ·tŏr′ĭ·kăl; 74), *adj.* Of or characteristic of an orator or oratory; rhetorical; becoming to an orator. — **or′a·tor′i·cal·ly,** *adv.*
or′a·to′ri·o (ŏr′ȧ·tō′rĭ·ō; 70), *n.; pl.* -RIOS (-ōz). [It., orig., place of prayer, fr. LL. *oratorium.*] *Music.* A dramatic text or poem, usually on a Scripture theme, set to music, in recitative, arias, choruses, etc., with orchestral accompaniment, but no action, scenery, or costume.
or′a·to′ry (ŏr′ȧ·tō′rĭ *or, esp. Brit.,* -tēr·ĭ), *n.* [L. *oratoria* (sc. *ars*) oratorical art.] Art of speaking in public eloquently or effectively; eloquence; rhetorical language.
or′a·to′ry, *n.; pl.* -RIES (-rĭz). [LL. *oratorium*, fr. L. *oratorius* of praying, of an orator.] **1.** A place of orisons, or prayer; esp., a chapel for private devotions. **2.** *R.C.Ch.* One of certain societies of priests who without vows live in communities.
orb (ôrb), *n.* [F. or L.; F. *orbe*, fr. L. *orbis* circle, disk.] **1.** A spherical body; esp., a celestial sphere (sun, moon, planet, or star); *Obs.*, the earth. **2.** *Poetic.* The eye; eyeball. **3.** *Now Rare.* A sphere of action. **4.** A collective whole; a world; as, an *orb* of witnesses. **5.** A sphere surmounted by a cross, symbolizing kingly power and justice. **6.** *Poetic.* A circle; anything circular. **7.** *Obs. Astron.* The orbit, or the plane of the orbit, of a heavenly body. — *v. t.* **1.** To form into a globe. **2.** *Poetic.* To encircle; enclose. — *v. i.* **1.** *Rare.* To move in an orbit. **2.** *Poetic.* To become round like an orb.
or·bic′u·lar (ôr·bĭk′ū·lēr), *adj.* [LL. *orbicularis*, fr. *orbiculus*, dim. of *orbis* orb.] Resembling, or having the form of, an orb; spherical; circular. — **or·bic′u·lar′i·ty** (-lăr′ĭ·tĭ), *n.* — **or·bic′u·lar·ly,** *adv.*
or·bic′u·late (-lāt), **or·bic′u·lat′ed** (-lāt′ĕd; -ĭd), *adj.* [L. *orbiculatus.*] Circular, or nearly circular, in outline; as, an *orbiculate* leaf. See LEAF, *Illust.* (16).
‖**or′bis sci·en′ti·a′rum** (ôr′bĭs sī·ĕn′shĭ·ā′rŭm). [L.] Circle of the sciences; hence, total of scientific knowledge.
or′bit (ôr′bĭt), *n.* [F. or L.; F. *orbite*, fr. L. *orbita* a track made by a wheel, course, circuit. See ORB.] **1.** *Anat.* The eye socket. **2.** The path described by one body in its revolution about another, as by the earth about the sun or by an electron about a nucleus. **3.** Region or scope of activity, influence, etc. **4.** *Zool.* The border around the eye of a bird, insect, etc. — **or′bit·al,** *adj.*
or′bit·al in′dex (ôr′bĭ·tăl; -t'l). *Craniom.* The ratio of the length of the orbital cavity to its greatest height, usually expressed in hundredths of the length.
orc (ôrk), *n.* [F. *orque*, fr. L. *orca* a kind of whale.] The grampus or a supposedly similar sea animal.
or′ce·in (ôr′sē·ĭn), *n.* [From *orcin.*] *Chem.* A purple nitrogenous dyestuff, got from orcinol by action of ammonia and oxygen.
or′chard (ôr′chērd), *n.* [AS. *orceard, ortgeard.*] A large enclosure containing fruit trees, nut-bearing trees, sugar maples, etc.; also, the trees collectively.
or′chard·ist (ôr′chēr·dĭst), *n.* Also **or′chard·man** (ôr′chērd·măn). One skilled in the cultivation of orchards.
orchard oriole. See ORIOLE, 2.
or′ches·tra (ôr′kĕs·trȧ; -kĭs·trȧ), *n.* [L., fr. Gr. *orchēstra*, orig., the place for the chorus of dancers, fr. *orcheisthai* to dance.] **1.** In ancient Greek theaters, the circular space used by the chorus, in front of the proscenium; in Roman theaters, a corresponding space used for seating persons of distinction. **2.** In a modern theater or other public hall, the space used by a band of instrumental performers, just in front of the stage; by extension, the forward part, sometimes all, of the main floor in a theater. Cf. STALL, *n.*, 7. **3.** *Music.* A band of performers on various instruments, including esp. those of the viol class, adapted for rendering symphonies, overtures, etc.
or·ches′tral (ôr·kĕs′trăl), *adj.* Of or pertaining to an orchestra; suitable for, or performed in or by, an orchestra. — **or·ches′tral·ly,** *adv.*
or′ches·trate (ôr′kĕs·trāt; ôr′kĭs-), *v. t. & i.* To compose or arrange (music) for an orchestra; to provide with instrumentation. — **or′ches·tra′tion** (-trā′shŭn), *n.*
or·ches′tri·on (ôr·kĕs′trĭ·ŏn), *n.* Also **or·ches′tri·na** (ôr′kĕs·trē′nȧ). A large music box like an elaborate barrel organ, with stops, imitating orchestral instruments.

or′chid (ôr′kĭd), *n.* [L. *orchis*, wrongly inflected *orchidis*, etc. See ORCHIS.] **1.** Any plant or flower of a large family (Orchidaceae, the orchid family) of perennial epiphytic or terrestrial plants having, usually, showy flowers with a corolla of three petals, one (the *labellum* or *lip*) differing greatly from the others and often spurred. See ORCHIS, LADY'S-SLIPPER, *Illust.* **2.** A color, blue-red in hue, of medium saturation and medium brilliance. See COLOR. — **or′chi·da′ceous** (ôr′kĭ·dā′shŭs), *adj.*

or′chi·do- (ôr′kĭ·dō-). Also **or′chi-** (ôr′kĭ-), **or′chi·o-** (ôr′kĭ·ō-). [From *orchidos*, erron. gen. for Gr. *orchis* testicle.] A combining form meaning *testicle*, as in **or·chi′tis, or·chit′ic, or′chi·dot′o·my** (see -ITIS, -TOMY).

or′chil (ôr′kĭl; -chĭl), **or′chal** (ôr′kăl), *n.* Archil.

or′chis (ôr′kĭs), *n.; pl.* ORCHISES (-ĕz; -ĭz). [L., fr. Gr. *orchis* testicle, orchis.] An orchid; specif., one of the type genus (*Orchis*); one of a related genus, as the ***fringed orchis*** (*Blephariglottis*), distinguished by a fringed lip, or the North American ***showy orchis*** (*Galeorchis spectabilis*) with a spike of handsome flowers, violet-purple mixed with white.

or′cin·ol (ôr′sĭ·nōl; -nŏl), *n.* Also **or′cin** (ôr′sĭn). [It. *orcello* archil. See ARCHIL.] *Chem.* A colorless crystalline phenol, $C_6H_3CH_3(OH)_2$, obtained from certain lichens, from extract of aloes, and from derivatives of toluene.

or·dain′ (ôr·dān′), *v. t.;* OR·DAINED′ (-dānd′); OR·DAIN′ING. [OF. *ordener*, fr. L. *ordinare*, fr. *ordo, ordinis*, order.] **1.** To establish by appointment, decree, or law; to enact; esp., of the Deity, fate, etc., to destine; predestine. **2.** *Obs.* To appoint to a duty or office. *Shak.* **3.** *Eccl.* To invest with ministerial or sacerdotal functions; to introduce into the office of the Christian ministry. — **or·dain′er,** *n.* — **or·dain′ment,** *n.*

or·deal′ (ôr·dēl′; ôr′dēl; ôr·dē′ăl), *n.* [AS. *ordāl, ordǣl*, a judgment.] **1.** A primitive means used to determine guilt or innocence by submitting the accused to dangerous or painful tests supposed to be under superhuman control. **2.** Any severe trial or experience.

or′der (ôr′dẽr), *n.* [OF. *ordre*, fr. L. *ordo, ordinis*, line, order.] **1.** A society of persons united by some common rule of obligation or honorary distinction. Specif.: **a** A monastic brotherhood or society. **b** One of certain knightly fraternities, typically one of those originating in the era of the crusades, as the Knights Templars. **c** A society patterned on these orders of chivalry; also, its insignia or badge. **2.** In medieval angelology, any of the nine grades of angels. **3.** A rank or class in society; as, men of the higher *orders;* the military *order.* **4.** Regular arrangement; any methodical or established succession or harmonious relation; method; system. **5.** Customary mode of procedure in debate; as, to raise a point of *order.* **6.** Conformity to law or decorum; public quiet; as, police to maintain *order.* **7.** Condition in general; normal state. **8.** The prevailing mode of a period. **9.** A rule or regulation made by competent authority; also, a mandate. **10.** An amount ordered as a purchase. **11.** *Arch.* **a** A style of building. **b** *Classical Arch.* A type of column and entablature, viewed as the unit of a style. The Greeks used three orders, the Doric, Ionic, and Corinthian, to which the Romans added the Tuscan and the Composite.

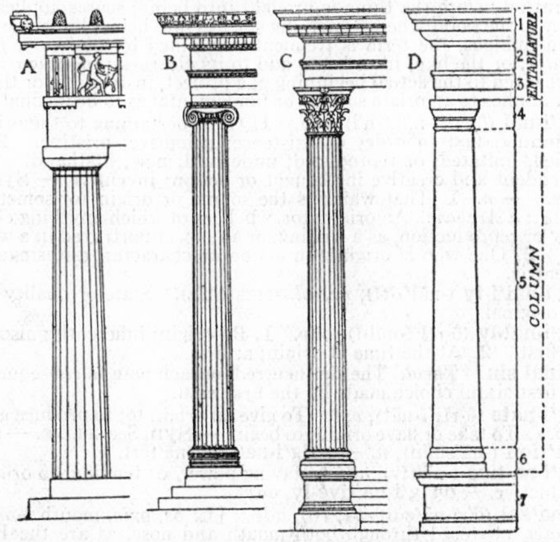

Order, 11 b. *A* Doric; *B* Ionic; *C* Corinthian; *D* Tuscan. 1 Cornice; 2 Frieze; 3 Architrave; 4 Capital (see also IONIC, *Illust.*); 5 Shaft; 6 Base (see also BASE, DADO, *Illusts.*); 7 Stylobate.

12. *Biol.* A category of classification ranking above the family and below the class. **13.** *Com.* **a** The direction by which the payee or holder of negotiable paper prescribes to whom payment shall be made. **b** A commission to purchase, sell, or supply goods; a direction, in writing, to furnish supplies; as, *orders* for blankets are large. **14.** *Eccl.* **a** Any of the several grades or ranks of the Christian ministry; as ***major, or holy, orders*** (which see) and ***minor orders*** (acolyte, exorcist, lector, doorkeeper). **b** The office or status of a person in the Christian ministry; as, to take *orders*, or *holy orders;* also, the conferment of such office; ordination. **c** A prescribed form of service. **15.** *Gram.* The sequence of constituents as a device for conveying meaning (*Cain* [subject] *killed* [predicate] *Abel* [object]). **16.** *Law.* **a** Any command or direction of a court. **b** Usually, any direction of a judge or court entered in writing and not included in a judgment or decree. **17.** *Math.* Degree. **18.** *Mil.* ORDER ARMS.
— ***in order.*** In due course as the next proceeding; as, it is *in order* to adjourn. — ***in order to.*** For the purpose of. — ***to order.*** In fulfillment of an order given.

— *v. t.* **1.** *Archaic.* To put in order or in battle array. **2.** To regulate; dispose. **3.** To give an order to; command. **4.** To give an order for.

Syn. (1) **Order, arrange, marshal, organize, systematize, methodize** mean to put persons or things into their proper places, esp. in relation to each other. **Order** now usually suggests a straightening out so as to eliminate confusion; **arrange**, a setting in sequence, relationship, or adjustment; **marshal**, an arrangement for advantage in managing; **organize**, an arranging so that the whole works as a unit, each person or thing having a proper function, duty, or the like; **systematize**, an arranging according to a definite, predetermined scheme; **methodize**, an imposition of orderly procedure rather than a fixed scheme.
(2) See COMMAND.

order arms. Of a soldier, to bring his rifle to a vertical position at his side, with the butt on the ground; also, this position.

or′der·ly (ôr′dẽr·lĭ), *adj.* **1.** Conformed to order; in order; regular. **2.** Observant of order, authority, or rule; hence, peaceable. **3.** Performed in good or established order. **4.** Pertaining to, or charged with the transmission or execution of, military orders. — **Syn.** Methodical, systematic. — *n.; pl.* -LIES (-lĭz). **1.** *Mil.* A noncommissioned officer or soldier who attends a superior officer to carry his orders. **2.** A hospital attendant who does general work. — *adv. Now Rare.* Regularly; methodically. — **or′der·li·ness,** *n.*

or′di·nal (ôr′dĭ·năl; -n'l), *adj.* [LL. *ordinalis*, fr. *ordo, ordinis*, order.] **1.** Indicating order or succession; as, the *ordinal* numbers, first, second, etc. See NUMBER, *Table.* **2.** Of or pert. to an order. — *n.* An ordinal number.

or′di·nal (ôr′dĭ·năl; -n'l), *n.* **a** [*often cap.*] *Anglican Ch.* The book of forms used in ordination. **b** [*usually cap.*] *R.C.Ch.* A book containing directions for the services every day in the year.

or′di·nance (ôr′dĭ·năns), *n.* [OF. *ordenance.* See ORDAIN.] **1. a** That which is decreed or ordained, as by God or Fate. **b** A prescribed practice or usage. **2.** An authoritative decree or direction, esp. one promulgated by governmental authority; specif., *Chiefly U. S.*, a local law or regulation enacted by a municipal government. Cf. BYLAW. **3.** *Eccl.* An established rite for the administration of a sacrament; hence, a sacrament, esp. the Communion. — **Syn.** See LAW.

or′di·nar′y (ôr′dĭ·nĕr′ĭ *or, esp. Brit.,* -nẽr·ĭ, -d'n·rĭ), *adj.* [L. *ordinarius*, fr. *ordo, ordinis*, order.] **1.** Having or taking its place according to customary occurrence or procedure; usual; normal. **2.** Of common rank, quality, or ability; not distinguished by superiority of any kind; commonplace. **3.** *Law.* Having or designating immediate or original jurisdiction, as opposed to that which is delegated; also, belonging to such jurisdiction. — **Syn.** See COMMON. — **Ant.** Extraordinary.

— *n.; pl.* -IES (-ĭz). **1.** An officer who has original jurisdiction in his own right, and not by deputation; specif., *Eng. Eccl. Law*, the archbishop of a province, or a bishop or his deputy in a diocese; *Law*, in some states of the U. S., a judge of probate. **2.** Formerly, in England, a clergyman appointed to prepare criminals for the death penalty. **3.** A meal served to all comers at a fixed price; a table-d'hôte meal. **4.** A tavern or eating house; orig. and esp., one that serves regular meals. **5.** A bicycle of the early type, with a very large and a very small wheel. **6.** *Eccl.* An order of service; specif. [*sometimes cap.*], the parts of the Mass which do not vary from day to day, or the book containing this. **7.** *Her.* A charge or bearing of simple form and in constant use, as the *bend, chevron, chief, cross, fess, pale,* and *saltier.* — ***in ordinary.*** In actual and constant service.
— **or′di·nar′i·ly,** *adv.* — **or′di·nar′i·ness,** *n.*

ordinary seaman. See SEAMAN, 2.

or′di·nate (ôr′dĭ·nāt), *n.* [L. *ordinatus*, past part. of *ordinare.* See ORDAIN.] *Math.* That one of the co-ordinates (of a point) which is drawn parallel to a line (called the ***axis of ordinates***) to the point from the other axis (called ***axis of abscissas***) or from the plane of the other axes of co-ordinates, assumed as the base of reference. See CO-ORDINATE, *n.*, 2.

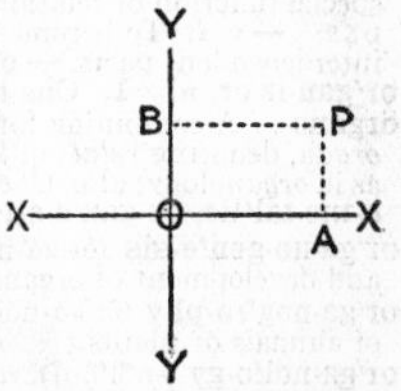

Ordinate. *P* Any Point; *XX* Axis of Abscissas; *YY* Axis of Ordinates; *PA* or *BO* Ordinate of *P; PB* or *AO* Abscissa of *P.*

or′di·na′tion (-nā′shŭn), *n.* [L. *ordinatio.*] **1.** Act of ordaining, or state of being ordained; specif., *Eccl.*, the conferring of holy orders. **2.** Arrangement; disposition.

ord′nance (ôrd′năns), *n.* [See ORDINANCE.] **1.** Military supplies; — usually in the phrase "ordnance and ordnance stores," which includes all artillery with mounts, carriages, and ammunition, small arms, machinery and material for making or repairing these. **2.** Cannon; artillery.

‖**or′do** (ôr′dō), *n.; pl.* ORDINES (-dĭ·nēz). [L.] Order; hence [*cap.*], *R.C.Ch.*, an annual calendar of offices and feasts.

or′don·nance (ôr′dŏ·năns; *F.* ôr′dô′näɴs′), *n.* [F.] **1.** Arrangement; specif., disposition of the parts of a composition with regard to one another and the whole. **2.** In Europe, a decree; an ordinance.

Or′do·vi′cian (ôr′dō·vĭsh′ăn), *adj.* [L. *Ordovices*, a Celtic people in Wales.] *Geol.* Pertaining to or designating the period of the Paleozoic era between the Cambrian and the Silurian, or the system of rocks formed during this period; — sometimes called *Lower Silurian.* It is marked by the emergence of great areas of land in North America and by the largest development of trilobites and cystoids. — **Or′do·vi′cian,** *n.*

or′dure (ôr′dūr), *n.* [OF., fr. *ord* filthy, foul, fr. L. *horridus* horrid.] Dung; excrement; feces.

ö′re (û′rĕ), *n. sing. & pl.* [Dan., Sw., & Nor.] A bronze coin and money of account of Denmark and Norway, 1/100 of a krone; in Sweden, 1/100 of a krona.

ore (ōr; 70), *n.* [AS. *ār* brass, copper.] Any material containing valuable metallic constituents for the sake of which it is mined and worked; — often loosely applied to nonmetalliferous material, as sulfur.

o′re·ad (ō′rē·ăd; 70), *n.* [L. *Oreas, -adis*, fr. Gr. *Oreias, -ados*, fr. *oros* mountain.] *Gr. Myth.* One of the nymphs of mountains and hills.

ore dressing. Treatment of ore involving physical, not chemical, change, as crushing, concentrating, sampling, etc. — **ore′-dress′ing,** *adj.*

Or′e·gon fir *or* **pine** (ŏr′ē·gŭn; -gŏn; 74). The Douglas fir.

Oregon grape. An evergreen shrub (*Mahonia aquifolia*) of the barberry family, of Oregon and California; also, its small blue-black berry. It is the State flower of Oregon.

‖**o′re ro·tun′do** (ō′rē rō·tŭn′dō). [L.] Literally, with round mouth; hence, with well-turned speech; loud and plain.

O·res′tes (ō·rĕs′tēz), *n.* [L., fr. Gr. *Orestēs.*] A son of Agamemnon and Clytemnestra, who, abetted by his sister Electra, avenged his father's murder by slaying his mother and Aegisthus. Cf. COMPLEX, *n.*, 2.

or′gan (ôr′găn), *n.* [OF. and L.; OF. *organe*, fr. L. *organum*, pl. *organa*, fr. Gr. *organon*.] **1. a** *Chiefly Bib.* One of various wind instruments. **b** A wind instrument, in its complete modern form the largest, most powerful, and most varied in resources of musical instruments, consisting of from one to many sets of pipes, sounded by compressed air, and played by means of one or more keyboards; — called specif. a ***pipe organ***, as distinguished from a *reed organ* (which see). See FLUE PIPE, *Illust.* **c** A reed organ. **d** A barrel organ. **2.** A part or structure in an animal or plant adapted for the performance of some specific function or functions, as the heart, kidney, etc. **3.** An instrument or medium by which an important action is performed or end accomplished; as, legislatures are *organs* of government. **4.** A medium of communication; as, a newspaper is the *organ* of a party.

or′gan·dy, or′gan·die (ôr′găn·dĭ; *Brit. also* ôr·găn′dĭ), *n.*; *pl.* -DIES (-dĭz). [F. *organdi.*] Fine thin, plain or figured muslin, usually having a permanent stiff finish, and used for dresses.

or′gan–grind′er, *n.* One who grinds, or cranks, a hand organ; esp., an itinerant street musician who grinds a barrel organ.

or·gan′ic (ôr·găn′ĭk), *adj.* [L. *organicus*, fr. Gr. *organikos.*] **1.** Of or pertaining to an organ or a system of organs; specif., pertaining to the internal organs of the body; as, *organic* changes in emotion. **2. a** Having systematic co-ordination; organized; as, they formed an *organic* whole. **b** Pertaining to, or inherent in, a certain organization; constitutional; not secondary or accidental. **3.** *Biol.* Pertaining to, or derived from, living organisms; exhibiting characters peculiar to living organisms. **4.** *Chem.* Pertaining to or designating that branch of chemistry which treats of the compounds of carbon. See CHEMISTRY, 1. **5.** *Law.* Designating, or pertaining to, the law or laws by virtue of which a government or organization exists as such. **6.** *Med.* Affecting the structure of the organism. Cf. FUNCTIONAL, 3. **7.** *Philos.* Possessed of a complex structure comparable to that of living beings. — **or·gan′i·cal·ly** (-ĭ·kăl·ĭ), *adv.*

organic disease. *Med.* A disease attended with morbid changes in the structure of the affected organs.

or·gan′i·cism (ôr·găn′ĭ·sĭz′m), *n.* *Philos. & Biol.* The doctrine that life and living processes are the manifestation of an activity possible only in virtue of the state of autonomous organization of the system, rather than because of its individual components; — opposed to *mechanism* and to *vitalism.*

or′gan·ism (ôr′găn·ĭz′m), *n.* **1.** *Biol.* An individual constituted to carry on the activities of life by means of organs separate in function but mutually dependent; any living being. **2.** *Philos.* Any highly complex thing or structure with parts so integrated that their relation to one another is governed by their relation to the whole.

or′gan·ist (-ĭst), *n.* A player on an organ.

or′gan·i·za′tion (-ĭ·zā′shŭn; -ī·zā′shŭn), *n.* **1.** Act or process of organizing. **2.** State or manner of being organized; organic structure. **3.** An organism; any vitally or systematically organic whole; an association or society. **4.** The executive structure of a business; the personnel of management. **5.** *Politics.* The entire body of the officials and committees, national, state, or local, of a political party.

or′gan·ize (ôr′găn·īz), *v. t.* **1.** To give an organic structure to. **2.** To arrange or constitute in interdependent parts, each having a special function or relation with respect to the whole. — **Syn.** See ORDER. — *v. i.* To become systematized or constituted into a whole of interdependent parts. — **or′gan·iz′a·ble** (-īz′à·b′l), *adj.*

or′gan·iz′er, *n.* **1.** One that organizes. **2.** *Biol.* = INDUCTOR, 2.

organo-. A combining form, Greek *organo-*, from *organon*, meaning *organ*, denoting *relation to*, or *connection with, an organ or organs*, as in *organology*; also, *Chem.* (*pron.* ôr·găn′ō-), *organic*, as in **or·gan′o·me·tal′lic, or·gan′o·sil′i·con.**

or′ga·no·gen′e·sis (ôr′gȧ·nō·jĕn′ē·sĭs), *n.* [NL.] *Biol.* The origin and development of organs in plants and animals.

or′ga·nog′ra·phy (ôr′gȧ·nŏg′rȧ·fĭ), *n.* *Biol.* Description of the organs of animals or plants.

or′ga·nol′o·gy (-nŏl′ō·jĭ), *n.* The science of organs or of organic structure; also, study of the viscera; splanchnology.

or′ga·non (ôr′gȧ·nŏn), *n.*; *pl.* -NA (-nȧ), -NONS (-nŏnz). [Gr. See ORGAN.] **1.** Any instrumentality for acquisition of knowledge. **2.** *Philos.* A method for scientific or philosophic procedure or investigation.

or′ga·no·ther′a·py (ôr′gȧ·nō·thĕr′ȧ·pĭ), *n.* Also **or′ga·no·ther′a·peu′tics** (-pū′tĭks); see -ICS. *Med.* Treatment of disease by administration of extracts of certain animal organs.

or′ga·num (ôr′gȧ·nŭm), *n.*; *pl.* -NA (-nȧ), -NUMS (-nŭmz). [L.] **1.** An organon. **2.** *Medieval Music.* **a** A voice part accompanying the melody, usually at a fourth, fifth, or octave above or below. **b** Part singing of this nature.

or·gan′za (ôr·găn′zȧ), *n.* [Cf. ORGANDY.] A sheer cotton fabric resembling organdy.

or′gan·zine (ôr′găn·zēn), *n.* [F. *organsin.*] A fine kind of silk used for the warp in silk weaving.

or′gasm (ôr′găz′m), *n.* [F. *orgasme*, fr. Gr. *orgasmos.*] *Physiol.* Eager or immoderate excitement or action; esp., the culmination of coition. — **or·gas′tic** (ôr·găs′tĭk), *adj.*

or′geat (ôr′zhăt; *F.* ôr′zhȧ′), *n.* [F., fr. Pr. *orjat*, fr. *ordi, orge*, barley, fr. L. *hordeum.*] A flavoring sirup prepared with an emulsion of almonds, or formerly with a decoction of barley.

or′gi·as′tic (ôr′jĭ·ăs′tĭk), *adj.* [Gr. *orgiastikos.* See ORGY.] Pertaining to or of the nature of orgies.

or′gy (ôr′jĭ), *n.*; *pl.* ORGIES (-jĭz). [F. *orgie, orgies*, fr. L. *orgia*, pl., fr. Gr. *orgia.*] **1.** *Chiefly pl.* Among the Greeks and Romans, secret ceremonial rites in honor of a deity, esp. those of the worship of Dionysus, or Bacchus, characterized by ecstatic singing and dancing, and often by revelry. **2.** Drunken revelry; carousal. **3.** Excessive indulgence in some activity, as speechmaking.

or′i·bi (ŏr′ĭ·bĭ), *n.* [S. Afr. D.] Any of several small tawny African antelopes (genus *Ourebia*).

o′ri·el (ō′rĭ·ĕl; 70), *n.* [OF. *oriol* gallery, corridor, fr. ML. *oriolum* portico, hall.] *Arch.* A large bay window, usually supported by a corbel or bracket.

o′ri·ent (ō′rĭ·ĕnt; -ĕnt; 70), *n.* [OF., fr. L. *oriens.* See ORIENT, *adj.*] **1.** *Now Poetic.* The east. **2.** [*now usually cap.*] The East; esp., the countries east of the Mediterranean; also, the countries of Asia generally; sometimes, eastern Asiatic countries. **3.** A pearl of great luster. — (-ĕnt), *adj.* [L. *oriens, -entis*, pres. part. of *oriri* to rise.] **1.** *Now Poetic.* Eastern; oriental. **2.** Bright; lustrous; pellucid; — originally of superior pearls and precious stones. **3.** Rising, as the sun. — (-ĕnt), *v. t.* **1.** To cause to face or point toward the east; specif., to build, as a church, with its longitudinal axis pointing eastward, and its chief altar at the eastern end; also, to set in any certain position in relation to the points of the compass, as a map with its east side to the east, north to north, etc.; hence, to ascertain the bearings of. **2.** To set right by adjusting to facts or principles; to put (esp. oneself) into correct position or relation; to acquaint (esp. oneself) with the existing situation. **3.** To arrange in order or place so as to show the relations of parts among themselves.

o′ri·en′tal (ō′rĭ·ĕn′tăl; -t′l), *adj.* [OF., fr. L. *orientalis.*] **1.** Eastern. **2.** [*usually cap.*] Pertaining to, situated in, or characteristic of the Orient; Eastern; esp., Asiatic. **3.** *Biogeog.* Designating a realm or region including Asia south of the Himalayas, the Philippine Islands, and part of the Indo-Malayan Archipelago. **4.** *Gems.* [*sometimes cap.*] Precious; of highest quality or grade; — often used specif. [*usually cap.*] with the name of a gem (as *amethyst* or *emerald*) to designate a variety of sapphire of the same color as the named gem. See SAPPHIRE, 1 **b.** — *n.* [*cap.*] A member of one of the indigenous races of the Orient; esp., a person reared in one of the three great civilizations of Asia (the Mohammedan, Indian, and Chinese-Japanese).

o′ri·en′tal·ism (ō′rĭ·ĕn′tăl·ĭz′m), *n.* [*often cap.*] **1.** Any trait, expression, etc., peculiar to Oriental people. **2.** Knowledge of Oriental languages, literature, history, etc. — **o′ri·en′tal·ist** (-ĭst), *n.*

o′ri·en′tal·ize (-īz), *v. t. & i.* To make or become Oriental.

Oriental rug *or* **carpet.** Any hand-woven or hand-knotted one-piece rug or carpet made in the Orient.

o′ri·en·tate′ (ō′rĭ·ĕn·tāt′; ō′rĭ·ĕn′tāt; 70), *v. t.* To orient. — *v. i.* To face east; to have orientation.

o′ri·en·ta′tion (ō′rĭ·ĕn·tā′shŭn), *n.* **1.** Act or process of orienting. **2.** Position, state, or fact of being oriented. **3.** Determination or sense of one's position with relation to environment or to some particular person, thing, field of knowledge, etc. **4.** *Psychol.* Awareness of the existing situation, with reference to time, place, and identity of persons.

or′i·fice (ŏr′ĭ·fĭs), *n.* [F., fr. L. *orificium*, fr. *os, oris*, a mouth + *facere* to make.] A mouthlike aperture, as of a tube, pipe, etc.; an opening; vent. — **Syn.** See APERTURE.

or′i·flamme (ŏr′ĭ·flăm), *n.* [F. *oriflamme*, fr. OF. *orieflambe*, fr. L. *aurea flamma* golden flame.] **1.** The ancient banner of St. Denis, a red silk banderole on a lance, carried into battle by early French kings. **2.** Anything suggestive of the historic oriflamme because of color, etc.

or′i·gan (ŏr′ĭ·găn), *n.* [F., fr. L. *origanum*, fr. Gr. *origanon, oreiganon.*] A marjoram.

or′i·gin (ŏr′ĭ·jĭn), *n.* [F. *origine*, fr. L. *origo, -iginis*, fr. *orior* I rise, become visible.] **1.** The fact or process of coming into being from a source; derivation. **2. a** Parentage; ancestry. **b** That from which anything primarily proceeds; source; spring; cause. **3.** *Anat.* The more fixed, central, or larger attachment of a muscle. Cf. INSERTION.

Syn. **Origin, source, inception, root** mean that at which something begins its course. **Origin** applies to the things (sometimes, persons) from which something is ultimately derived, and often to the causes in operation before the thing is brought into being; **source** applies more often to the point where something springs into being, but since this is often dubious, the term is frequently modified by *ultimate, fundamental*, or the like, in order to add to its clearness; **inception** applies more often to the actual beginning of a project, institution, or the like; **root** applies to an origin so deep or fundamental as to be its final cause.

o·rig′i·nal (ō·rĭj′ĭ·năl; -n′l), *adj.* **1.** Of or pertaining to the origin or beginning; first in order or existence; primitive; pristine. **2.** Not copied, imitated, or reproduced; underived; new; firsthand. **3.** Independent and creative in thought or action; inventive. — **Syn.** See NEW. — *n.* **1.** That which is the source or origin (of something); specif.: **a** *Archaic.* An originator. **b** That of which anything else is a copy or reproduction, as a writing, or an object portrayed in a work of art. **2.** One who is original in action or character, esp. singular or eccentric.

o·rig′i·nal′i·ty (-năl′ĭ·tĭ), *n.*; *pl.* -TIES (-tĭz). State or quality of being original.

o·rig′i·nal·ly (ō·rĭj′ĭ·năl·ĭ), *adv.* **1.** By origin; inherently; also, from the first. **2.** At the time of origin; at first.

original sin. *Theol.* The sin incurred by each man in consequence of the first sinful choice made by the first man.

o·rig′i·nate (ō·rĭj′ĭ·nāt), *v. t.* To give an origin to; to produce as new. — *v. i.* To take or have origin; to begin. — **Syn.** See SPRING. — **o·rig′i·na′tion** (-nā′shŭn), *n.* — **o·rig′i·na′tor** (-nā′tēr), *n.*

o·rig′i·na′tive (-nā′tĭv), *adj.* Having power, or tending, to originate; productive. — **o·rig′i·na′tive·ly**, *adv.*

o′ri·na′sal (ō′rĭ·nā′zăl; -z′l; 70), *adj.* [L. *os, oris*, mouth + *nasal.*] *Phonet.* Uttered through both mouth and nose, as are the French nasal vowels. — *n.* An orinasal sound.

o′ri·ole (ō′rĭ·ōl; 70), *n.* [OF. *oriol*, fr. L. *aureolus* golden, dim. of *aureus* golden. See AUREOLE.] **1.** In Europe, any of a family (Oriolidae) of passerine birds related to the crows; esp., the ***golden oriole*** (*Oriolus oriolus*) which is bright yellow, with wings and tail black. **2.** In America any of various oscine birds of a family (Icteridae), not closely related to the Old World orioles, the males being usually bright black and yellow or orange, the females chiefly greenish or yellowish, as the ***Baltimore oriole*** (*Icterus galbula*) and the ***orchard oriole*** (*I. spurius*).

O·ri′on (ō·rī′ŏn), *n.*; *gen.* ORIONIS (ō·rī′ō·nĭs; ŏr′ĭ·ō′nĭs). A constellation on the equator east of Taurus, represented on charts by the figure of a hunter with belt and sword.

or′i·son (ŏr′ĭ·zŭn; -z'n), *n.* [OF. *orison, oreison*, fr. L. *oratio.* See *oration.*] A prayer.

O·ri′ya (ō·rē′yä), *n.* One of the chief Sanskritic languages of India, closely related to Bengali. See INDO-EUROPEAN LANGUAGES, *Table.*

Or·lan′do (ôr·lăn′dō; *It.* ōr·län′dō), *n.* = ROLAND.

orle (ôrl), *n.* [F., fr. OF. *ourle*, fr. a dim. fr. L. *ora* border, margin.] *Her.* A bearing within the shield but at some distance from the border; more correctly, a voided escutcheon.

Or′le·an·ist (ôr′lē·ăn·ĭst), *n.* An adherent of the Orleans family which claims the throne of France by descent from a younger brother of Louis XIV.

or′lop (ôr′lŏp), *n.* [D. *overloop* a covering, lit., a running over.] *Naut.* The lowest deck of a vessel, esp. of a ship of war. See DECK, *Illust.*

Or′mazd (ôr′măzd), **Or′muzd** (-mŭzd), *n.* [Per. *Ormazd, Ormuzd,*

OPer. *Auramazda.*] *Zoroastrianism.* The supreme deity, principle of good, creator of the world, and guardian of mankind. Cf. AHRIMAN.

or′mer (ôr′mẽr), *n.* [F. *ormier.*] An ear shell, or abalone; esp. *Haliotis tuberculata*, used as food in Guernsey. See ABALONE, *Illust.*

or′mo·lu (ôr′mō·lo͞o), *n.* [F. *or moulu*, fr. *or* gold + *moulu*, past part. of *moudre* to grind, fr. L. *molere.*] A variety of brass made to imitate gold in appearance.

or′na·ment (ôr′nȧ·mĕnt), *n.* [OF. *ornement*, fr. L. *ornamentum*, fr. *ornare* to adorn.] **1.** *Now Eccl.* An article of equipment; an adjunct. **2. a** That which is added to embellish or adorn; an embellishment; a decoration. **b** A quality which serves to adorn. **3.** One whose qualities confer luster on those about him. **4.** Addition of anything that beautifies; ornamentation. **5.** *Music.* An embellishing note or notes not belonging to the essential harmony or melody. — (-mĕnt), *v. t.* To provide with ornament; decorate; embellish. — **Syn.** See ADORN.

or′na·men′tal (-mĕn′tăl; -t'l), *adj.* Serving to ornament; decorative. — *n. Hort.* A plant cultivated essentially for decorative purposes. — **or′na·men′tal·ly**, *adv.*

or′na·men·ta′tion (-mĕn·tā′shŭn), *n.* **1.** Act of ornamenting; state of being ornamented. **2.** That which ornaments.

or·nate′ (ôr·nāt′; 2), *adj.* [L. *ornatus*, past part. of *ornare* to adorn, equip.] **1.** Adorned; now, adorned elaborately, esp. in excess. **2.** Of style, embellished with figures of speech. — **or·nate′ly**, *adv.* — **or·nate′ness**, *n.*

or′ner·y (ôr′nẽr·ĭ). Dial. var. of ORDINARY. Esp., *U. S.*, of bad disposition; hard to manage. — **or′ner·i·ness**, *n.*

or′nis (ôr′nĭs), *n.* [G., fr. Gr. *ornis* bird.] The bird life of a region; an avifauna.

or·nith′ic (ôr·nĭth′ĭk), *adj.* [Gr. *ornithikos*, fr. *ornis, ornithos*, a bird.] Of or characteristic of birds.

or′ni·tho- (ôr′nĭ·thō-; ôr·nī′thō-), **ornith-**. [Gr. *ornis, ornithos.*] A combining form meaning *bird.*

or′ni·thol′o·gy (ôr′nĭ·thŏl′ō·jĭ), *n.* [*ornitho-* + *-logy.*] That branch of zoology which treats of birds; also, a treatise on birds. — **or′ni·tho·log′i·cal** (-thō·lŏj′ĭ·kăl), *adj.* — **or′ni·thol′o·gist** (-thŏl′ō·jĭst), *n.*

or′ni·tho·pod′ (ôr′nĭ·thō·pŏd′; ôr·nī′thō·pŏd), *adj.* [*ornitho-* + *-pod.*] *Paleontol.* Of or pertaining to a group of dinosaurs (order Ornithischia) having digitigrade hind limbs. — *n.* One of this group.

or′ni·thop′ter (ôr′nĭ·thŏp′tẽr), *n. Aeronautics.* = ORTHOPTER.

or′ni·tho·rhyn′chus (ôr′nĭ·thō·rĭng′kŭs; ôr·nī′thō-), *n.* [NL., fr. *ornitho-* + Gr. *rhynchos* beak.] A duckbill.

or′o- (ŏr′ō-). [Gr. *oros.*] A combining form meaning *mountain*, as in *orogeny.*

o′ro- (ō′rō-). [L. *os, oris.*] *Anat.* A combining form meaning *mouth*, as in **o′ro·phar′ynx**, the lower pharynx, also *oral and*, as in **o′ro·na′sal**.

or′o·ban·cha′ceous (ŏr′ō·băng·kā′shŭs), *adj.* [L. *orobanche* broomrape.] Belonging to the broomrape family (Orobanchaceae). See BROOMRAPE.

o·rog′e·ny (ō·rŏj′ē·nĭ), **or′o·gen′e·sis** (ŏr′ō·jĕn′ē·sĭs), *n.* [1st *oro-* + *-geny, -genesis.*] *Geol.* Process of mountain making, esp. by folding of the crust. — **or′o·gen′ic** (ŏr′ō·jĕn′ĭk), *adj.*

o·rog′ra·phy (ō·rŏg′rȧ·fĭ), *n.* That branch of physical geography which treats of mountains; orology. — **or′o·graph′ic** (ŏr′ō·grăf′ĭk), **or′o·graph′i·cal** (-ĭ·kăl), *adj.*

o′ro·ide (ō′rō·īd; -ĭd; 70), *n.* [F. *or* gold + Gr. *eidos* form.] An alloy, chiefly of copper and zinc or tin, like gold in color and brilliancy, used in making cheap jewelry.

o·rol′o·gy (ō·rŏl′ō·jĭ), *n.* The science of mountains; orography. — **or′o·log′i·cal** (ŏr′ō·lŏj′ĭ·kăl), *adj.* — **o·rol′o·gist** (ō·rŏl′ō·jĭst), *n.*

o′ro·tund (ō′rō·tŭnd; ŏr′ō-; 70), *adj.* [L. *ore rotundo*, lit., with round mouth.] Full, clear, strong, and smooth; ringing and musical; — of the voice or vocal delivery; also, pompous; bombastic; — of style.

‖**o′ro y pla′ta** (ō′rō ē plä′tä). [Sp.] Gold and silver; — motto of Montana.

or′phan (ôr′făn), *n.* [LL. *orphanus*, fr. Gr. *orphanos.*] A child bereaved by death of both father and mother, or, less commonly, of either parent. — *adj.* That is an orphan. — *v. t.* To cause to become an orphan; to deprive of parents. — **or′phan·hood** (-ho͝od), *n.*

or′phan·age (-ĭj), *n.* **1.** State of being an orphan; orphans, collectively. **2.** An institution for the care of orphans.

Or′pheus (ôr′fūs; *commonly* ôr′fē·ŭs), *n.* [L., fr. Gr. *Orpheus.*] *Gr. Myth.* A Thracian poet and musician, son of Apollo and Calliope. When his wife, Eurydice, died, he descended to Hades, and so pleased Pluto by his music that the god allowed him to lead her back to earth on the condition that he should not look behind him, but he looked back, and Eurydice vanished among the shades. — **Or·phe′an** (ôr·fē′ăn), *adj.*

Or′phic (ôr′fĭk), *adj.* **1.** Designating, characteristic of, or pertaining to Orpheus or the mysteries or secret rites and doctrines ascribed to him. **2.** [*also not cap.*] Mystic; esoteric in diction; oracular. **3.** Like the music ascribed to Orpheus; entrancing.

Or′phism (ôr′fĭz′m), *n.* The religion of the Orphic mysteries.

or′phrey (ôr′frĭ), *n.; pl.* ORPHREYS (-frĭz). [OF. *orfreis* (F. *orfroi*), fr. L. *aurum* gold + *Phrygius* Phrygian.] **a** *Obs. exc. Hist.* Elaborate embroidery, esp. of gold. **b** A band, usually of rich embroidery, wholly or in part of gold, affixed to ecclesiastical vestments.

or′pi·ment (ôr′pĭ·mĕnt), *n.* [OF., fr. L. *auripigmentum*, fr. *aurum* gold + *pigmentum* pigment.] Arsenic trisulfide, As_2S_3, a crystalline mineral or produced artificially as a lemon-yellow amorphous powder and used as a pigment.

or′pine (ôr′pĭn), **or′pin**, *n.* [F. *orpin* a kind of stonecrop; — from the yellow blossoms of a common species (*Sedum acre*).] A species of stonecrop (*Sedum telephium*) with fleshy leaves and pink or purple flowers, formerly used as a vulnerary. It belongs to a family (Crassulaceae, the orpine family) of succulent herbs, including the sedum, stonecrop, houseleek, etc.

Or′ping·ton (ôr′pĭng·tŭn), *n.* [From *Orpington*, Kent, Eng.] A large, deep-breasted domestic fowl of an English breed.

or′ra (ŏr′ȧ), *adj. Scot.* Odd; not matched; extra.

or′rer·y (ŏr′ẽr·ĭ), *n.; pl.* -ERIES (-ĭz). [After Charles Boyle, 4th Earl of *Orrery* (1676–1731).] An apparatus showing the positions and motions of bodies in the solar system by balls moved by wheelwork; a planetarium.

or′ris (ŏr′ĭs), *n.* Also **or′rice**. A European species of iris (*Iris florentina*), or its fragrant rootstock (**or′ris·root′**) which is powdered for use in perfume, medicine, sachet powder, etc.

ort (ôrt), *n.* A morsel left at a meal; *pl.*, scraps; bits.

or′thi·con′ (ôr′thĭ·kŏn′), *n. Television.* A pickup or camera tube, representing a refinement upon the iconoscope, in which the storage electrode is scanned by low-impact-velocity electrons.

or′tho- (ôr′thō-), **orth-**. [Gr. *orthos* straight.] **1.** A combining form meaning: **a** *Straight*, as in *ortho*pteran. **b** *Upright*, as in *ortho*gnathous. **c** *Right; correct; proper;* as in *ortho*dox. **d** *In correct relation*, as in *ortho*chromatic. **e** *A right angle*, as in *ortho*clase. **f** *Med. Correction of deformity*, as in *ortho*pedics. **2.** *Chem.* A prefix denoting: **a** Certain higher forms of hydration, esp. in the case of acids; thus, *ortho*phosphoric acid, $OP(OH)_3$, disting. from *meta*phosphoric acid, $O_2P(OH)$. **b** Certain benzene derivatives, as in **or′tho·xy′lene**. Abbr. *o-*. See BENZENE RING.

or′tho (ôr′thō), *adj. Chem.* = ORTHO-, 2 **b**; as, the *ortho* position.

or′tho·ce·phal′ic (ôr′thō·sē·făl′ĭk), **or′tho·ceph′a·lous** (-sĕf′ȧ·lŭs), *adj.* [*ortho-* + *-cephalic, -cephalous.*] *Craniom.* Having the relation of the height to the length or breadth of the skull medium. — **or′tho·ceph′a·ly** (-sĕf′ȧ·lĭ), *n.*

or′tho·chro·mat′ic (-krō·măt′ĭk), *adj. Photog.* **a** Of, pert. to, or producing tone values (of light and shade) in a black and white photograph, corresponding to the various colored tones of nature. **b** Sensitive to green but not to red.

or′tho·clase (ôr′thō·klās; -klāz), *n.* [*ortho-* + Gr. *klan* to break.] *Mineral.* Common or potash feldspar, which is monoclinic and orthoclastic. H., 6. Sp. gr., 2.57.

or′tho·clas′tic (-klăs′tĭk), *adj. Cryst.* Cleaving in directions at right angles to each other; — of monoclinic feldspars.

or′tho·cy′mene (-sī′mēn), *n.* See CYMENE.

or′tho·don′tics (ôr′thō·dŏn′tĭks), *n.* Also **or′tho·don′ti·a** (-dŏn′shĭ·ȧ; -tĭ·ȧ). [NL., fr. *orth-* + *-odont* + *-ics, -ia.*] Dentistry dealing with irregularities of the teeth and their correction, esp. by mechanical aids; dental orthopedics. — **or′tho·don′tic** (-tĭk), *adj.* — **or′tho·don′tist** (-tĭst), *n.*

or′tho·dox (ôr′thō·dŏks), *adj.* [F. or L.; F. *orthodoxe*, fr. LL. *orthodoxus*, fr. Gr. *orthodoxos*, fr. *orthos* right, true + *doxa* opinion.] **1.** Sound in opinion or doctrine, esp. in religious doctrine; hence, specif., holding the Christian faith as formulated in the great church creeds and confessions. **2.** [*cap.*] Of, pertaining to, or designating a church (**Orthodox Church**), the dominant Christian communion in Eastern Europe, Asia, and Egypt. It is composed of several bodies, usually national churches, nearly all recognizing the headship of the Patriarch of Constantinople. **3.** *U. S.* Maintaining the doctrine of the Trinity; — as distinguished from those who reject this doctrine. **4.** According to, or congruous with, the creed of a church, the decree of a council, or the like; as, an *orthodox* opinion. **5.** Approved; conforming to a standardized doctrine; as, an *orthodox* Marxian; also, conventional. — **or′tho·dox·ly**, *adv.*

or′tho·dox′y (-dŏk′sĭ), *n.; pl.* -DOXIES (-sĭz). Orthodox character; orthodox belief, practice, etc.

or′tho·ëp′y (ôr′thō·ĕp′ĭ; ôr·thō′ē·pĭ), *n.* [Gr. *orthoepeia*, fr. *orthos* right + *epos* a word.] **a** The art of pronouncing words correctly; correct or accepted pronunciation. **b** That part of grammar which treats of pronunciation; phonology. — **or′tho·ëp′ic** (ôr′thō·ĕp′ĭk), *adj.* — **or′tho·ëp′ist** (ôr′thō·ĕp′ĭst; ôr·thō′ē·pĭst), *n.*

or·thog′a·my (ôr·thŏg′ȧ·mĭ), *n.* = AUTOGAMY. — **or·thog′a·mous** (-mŭs), *adj.*

or′tho·gen′e·sis (ôr′thō·jĕn′ē·sĭs), *n.* [NL., fr. *ortho-* + *-genesis.*] **1.** *Biol.* Variation which in successive generations of an organism follows some particular line, evolving some new type irrespective of natural selection or other external factor; determinate variation or evolution. **2.** *Sociol.* The theory that social evolution always follows the same direction and passes through the same stages in each culture despite differing external conditions. — **or′tho·ge·net′ic** (-jē·nĕt′ĭk), *adj.*

or′tho·gen′ic (-jĕn′ĭk), *adj.* Of, pertaining to, or designating that branch of educational, medical, and surgical treatment which aims to correct mental and nervous defects in children.

or·thog′na·thous (ôr·thŏg′nȧ·thŭs), *adj.* Also **or′thog·nath′ic** (ôr′thŏg·năth′ĭk). [*ortho-* + Gr. *gnathos* jaw.] *Craniom.* Having straight jaws; not having the lower parts of the face projecting. See FACIAL ANGLE, *Illust.* — **or·thog′na·thism** (-thĭz′m), **or·thog′na·thy** (-thĭ), *n.*

or·thog′o·nal (ôr·thŏg′ō·năl; -n'l), *adj.* [From L. *orthogonium*, neut. See ORTHO-; POLYGON.] Right-angled; rectangular. — **or·thog′o·nal·ly**, *adv.*

or·thog′ra·pher (ôr·thŏg′rȧ·fẽr), *n.* One versed in orthography; one who spells correctly.

or′tho·graph′ic (ôr′thō·grăf′ĭk), **or′tho·graph′i·cal** (-ĭ·kăl), *adj.* **1.** Of or pert. to orthography; also, correct in spelling. **2.** *Geom.* Of or pert. to perpendicular lines or right angles. — **-i·cal·ly**, *adv.*

orthographic projection. Projection in which the projecting lines are perpendicular to the plane of projection.

or·thog′ra·phy (ôr·thŏg′rȧ·fĭ), *n.; pl.* -PHIES (-fĭz). [OF. *ortographie*, fr. L., fr. Gr. *orthographia*, deriv. of *orthos* right + *graphein* to write.] **1.** Art of writing words with the proper letters, according to standard usage; correct spelling; also, mode of spelling. **2.** Grammar treating of letters and spelling. **3.** A drawing in correct projection.

or′tho·pe′dic, or′tho·pae′dic (ôr′thō·pē′dĭk), *adj. Med.* Pertaining or relating to, or employed in, orthopedics.

or′tho·pe′dics, or′tho·pae′dics (-dĭks), *n.*; see -ICS. Also **or′tho·pe′dy** (ôr′thō·pē′dĭ). [*ortho-* + Gr. *pais, paidos*, a child.] Correction or prevention of deformities, esp. in children. — **or′tho·pe′dist, or′tho·pae′dist** (-dĭst), *n.*

or′tho·phos·phor′ic ac′id (ôr′thō·fŏs·fŏr′ĭk). A siruplike or deliquescent crystalline acid, H_3PO_4, obtained by oxidation of phosphorus or decomposition of phosphates, which forms two soluble acid phosphates used in fertilizers.

or′tho·psy·chi′a·try (-sī·kī′ȧ·trĭ; -psī-), *n.* Prophylactic psychiatry, esp. of incipient mental disorders in youth.

or·thop′ter (ôr·thŏp′tẽr), *n.* [Gr. *orthos* straight + *pteron* wing.] **1.** [From F. *orthoptère.*] *Aeronautics.* A flying machine propelled by flapping of wings; a mechanical bird. **2.** *Zool.* An orthopterous insect.

or·thop′ter·ous (ôr·thŏp′tẽr·ŭs), *adj.* [*ortho-* + Gr. *pteron* feather, wing.] Belonging to an order (Orthoptera) of insects including the grasshoppers, locusts, and crickets which have biting mouth parts, and typically two pairs of wings, the membranous hind wings folding fanwise under the front pair. See INSECT, *Illust.* — **or·thop′ter·an** (-ăn), *adj. & n.* — **or·thop′ter·on** (-ŏn), *n.*

or·thop′tic (ôr·thŏp′tĭk), *adj.* [*orth-* + *optic.*] *Med.* Pert. to, characterized by, or securing normal binocular vision; as, **orthoptic exercises**, in which ocular muscles are exercised by means of prisms to correct deviation.

or′tho·rhom′bic (ôr′thō·rŏm′bĭk), *adj.* *Cryst.* Having three unequal axes at right angles to each other.

or′tho·scop′ic (-skŏp′ĭk), *adj.* *Optics.* Giving an image in correct or normal proportions; giving a flat field of view.

or·thos′ti·chy (ôr·thŏs′tĭ·kĭ), *n.; pl.* -CHIES (-kĭz). [*ortho-* + Gr. *stichos* row.] *Bot.* In phyllotaxy, the vertical line along a stem axis connecting those leaves directly above one another, or the row of leaves along such a line. Cf. PARASTICHY. — **or·thos′ti·chous** (-kŭs), *adj.*

or·thot′ro·pism (ôr·thŏt′rō·pĭz′m), *n.* [*ortho-* + *-tropism.*] *Plant Physiol.* Vertical growth; the tendency to elongate vertically, as most primary stems and roots. Cf. PLAGIOTROPISM. — **or′tho·trop′ic** (ôr′thō·trŏp′ĭk), *adj.*

or·thot′ro·pous (ôr·thŏt′rō·pŭs), *adj.* [*ortho-* + Gr. *trepein* to turn.] *Bot.* Having the nucellus straight.

or′to·lan (ôr′tō·lăn), *n.* [F., fr. Pr. *ortolan* ortolan, gardener, fr. L. *hortulanus* gardener.] **1.** A European bunting (*Emberiza hortulana*) about six inches long, valued as a table delicacy. **2. a** The sora. **b** *U. S.* The bobolink.

-ory. [F. or L.; ONF. *-ori, -orie,* OF. *-oir, -oire,* fr. L. *-orius, -oria, -orium.*] An adjective suffix meaning *of* or *pertaining to, serving for,* as in auditory, prohibitory.

-ory. [L. *-orium.*] A noun suffix denoting *place of* or *for,* or *that which pertains to* or *serves for,* as in offertory.

o′ryx (ō′rĭks; ŏr′ĭks; 70), *n.;* see PLURAL, *Note,* 3. [L., fr. Gr. *oryx.*] Any of a genus (*Oryx*) of large straight-horned African antelopes. See GEMSBOK.

‖**os** (ŏs), *n.; pl.* OSSA (ŏs′ȧ). [L.] *Anat. & Zool.* A bone.

‖**os** (ŏs), *n.; pl.* ORA (ō′rȧ). [L.] *Anat.* A mouth; an opening.

os (ōs), *n.; pl.* OSAR (ō′sär). [Sw. *ås* ridge, chain of hills, pl. *åsar.*] *Geol.* Esker.

O′sage or′ange (ō′sāj). An ornamental American tree (*Maclura pomifera*) of the mulberry family, having hard, bright-orange wood; also, its yellowish apple-shaped fruit.

Os′can (ŏs′kăn), *n.* One of a people of ancient Italy occupying Campania; also, their language, originally that of the Samnites, preserved in various inscriptions. See INDO-EUROPEAN LANGUAGES, *Table.* — **Os′can,** *adj.*

os′cil·late (ŏs′ĭ·lāt), *v. i.* [L. *oscillare* to swing.] **1.** To swing backward and forward; to vibrate like a pendulum. **2.** To fluctuate between fixed limits or between opposing beliefs or opinions. **3.** *Physics, Math., etc.* To vibrate above and below a mean value. — **Syn.** See SWING.

os′cil·la′tion (-lā′shŭn), *n.* **1.** Act or fact of oscillating; vibration. **2.** Fluctuation; variation. **3.** *Elec. pl.* Fluctuations in a system or circuit, esp. those consisting of the flow of charges of electricity alternately in opposite directions. **4.** *Physics.* A single swing from one extreme limit to the other of an oscillating body.

os′cil·la′tor (ŏs′ĭ·lā′tẽr), *n.* One who or that which oscillates; *Elec.,* any device for producing electric oscillations; specif., *Radio,* a radio-frequency generator.

os′cil·la·to′ry (-lȧ·tō′rĭ *or, esp. Brit.,* -lā′tẽr·ĭ, -lȧ·tẽr·ĭ), *adj.* Characterized by oscillation; oscillating; vibratory.

os·cil′lo·gram (ŏ·sĭl′ō·grăm), *n.* [L. *oscillare* + *-gram.*] An autographic record made by an oscillograph.

os·cil′lo·graph (-grȧf; 9), *n.* [L. *oscillare* to swing + *-graph.*] *Elec.* An apparatus for recording or indicating alternating-current wave forms or other electrical oscillations, usually a galvanometer with strong field or a vacuum tube utilizing the deflection of a beam of cathode rays.

os·cil′lo·scope (ŏ·sĭl′ō·skōp), *n.* [L. *oscillare* to swing + *-scope.*] *Elec.* An instrument for showing visually the changes in a varying current, esp. by means of the wavy line made on a fluorescent screen by the deflection of a beam of cathode rays.

os′cine (ŏs′ĭn; -īn), *n.* [L. *oscen, -inis,* a singing bird.] Any of a suborder (Oscines) of passerine birds comprising those with the most highly specialized vocal apparatus; — commonly referred to as ***singing birds,*** though many among them do not sing. — **os′cine,** *adj.*

os′ci·tan·cy (ŏs′ĭ·tăn·sĭ), **os′ci·tance** (-tăns), *n.* [L. *oscitare* to yawn.] Drowsiness; hence, dullness; sluggishness.

Os′co-Um′bri·an (ŏs′kō·ŭm′brĭ·ăn), *adj.* Of, pertaining to, or designating the language group comprising Oscan and Umbrian. See INDO-EUROPEAN LANGUAGES, *Table.*

os′cu·lant (ŏs′kū·lănt), *adj.* [L. *osculans, -antis,* pres. part. of *osculari* to kiss. See OSCULATE.] *Biol.* Intermediate in character; forming a connecting link between two groups.

os′cu·lar (-lẽr), *adj.* [L. *osculum* little mouth, a kiss.] Of or pertaining to the mouth or a kiss.

os′cu·late (-lāt), *v. t. & i.* [L. *osculatus,* past part. of *osculari* to kiss, fr. *osculum* a kiss, a little mouth.] **1.** To kiss. **2.** *Biol.* To have characters in common with two groups. **3.** *Geom.* To touch closely so as to have three or more points in common at the point of contact. — **os′cu·la·to′ry** (-lȧ·tō′rĭ *or, esp. Brit.,* -tẽr·ĭ), *adj.*

os′cu·la′tion (-lā′shŭn), *n.* **1.** Kissing; a kiss. **2.** *Geom.* The contact of a curve or surface with an osculating curve or surface.

os′cu·lum (ŏs′kū·lŭm), *n.; pl.* OSCULA (-lȧ). [L., a little mouth.] *Zool.* One of the excurrent orifices of a sponge.

-ose (-ōs). [L. *-osus.*] A suffix equivalent to *-ous,* esp., in technical words, as in comatose, globose. Corresponding nouns usually end in **-os′i·ty** (-ŏs′ĭ·tĭ).

-ose (-ōs). [F. *-ose,* fr. glucose. See GLUCOSE.] *Chem.* A suffix indicating that the substance to the name of which it is affixed is: **a** A carbohydrate, as in cellulose, fructose. **b** A primary alteration, or hydrolysis, product of a protein, as in proteose.

O′see (ō′zē; ō′sē), *n.* *Douay Bib.* Hosea. See BIBLE.

O·set′i·an, O·set′ic. Vars. of OSSETIAN, OSSETIC.

o′sier (ō′zhẽr), *n.* [OF., fr. ML. *ausaria* osier bed.] **1.** Any of various willows (esp. *Salix viminalis*) whose pliable twigs are used for furniture, basketry, etc. **2.** A willow rod used in basketry. **3.** Any of several American dogwoods (genus *Cornus*). — *adj.* Made of, covered with, or containing osiers.

O·si′ris (ō·sī′rĭs), *n.* [L., fr. Gr. *Osiris,* fr. Egypt. *Ȧs-ȧr* or *Us-ȧr.*] *Egypt. Relig.* The god of the underworld and judge of the dead, brother and husband of Isis.

-o′sis (-ō′sĭs); *pl.* -OSES (-ō′sēz). [L. or Gr.; L. *-osis,* fr. Gr. *-ōsis,* as in *metamorphōsis* metamorphosis.] A suffix signifying: **a** *Condition, state, process,* and the like, as in psychosis, osmosis; specif., in pathology, *abnormal* or *diseased condition,* as in melanosis, varicosis. **b** *A physiological increase* or *formation,* as in chylosis.

-os′i·ty (-ŏs′ĭ·tĭ). [F. or L.; F. *-osité,* fr. L. *-ositas.*] A suffix of nouns corresponding to adjectives in *-ose* and *-ous.*

Os·man′li (ŏs·măn′lĭ; ŏz-), *n.; pl.* -LIS (-lĭz). [Turk. *‘Osmānli* belonging to *‘Osmān,* Ar. *‘Uthmān.* See OTTOMAN.] A Turk of the Western branch of the Turkish peoples; also, the dominant Turkic language of Turkey; Ottoman Turkish. — **Os·man′li,** *adj.*

os′mic (ŏz′mĭk; ŏs′-), *adj.* *Chem.* Of or pertaining to osmium, esp. in a relatively high valence.

os′mi·ous (ŏz′mĭ·ŭs; ŏs′-), *adj.* *Chem.* Of or pertaining to osmium, esp. in a relatively low valence.

os′mi·rid′i·um (ŏs′mĭ·rĭd′ĭ·ŭm; ŏz′-), *n.* Also **os′mi-i·rid′i·um** (-ĭ·rĭd′ĭ·ŭm; -ī·rĭd′-). [NL., fr. *osmium* + *iridium.*] *Mineral.* = IRIDOSMINE.

os′mi·um (ŏz′mĭ·ŭm; ŏs′-), *n.* [NL., fr. Gr. *osmē* a smell; — from the chlorinelike odor of osmium tetroxide.] *Chem.* A hard, bluish-white or grayish-white metallic element of the platinum group, the heaviest substance known (sp. gr. in crystalline form, 22.48). Symbol, *Os;* at. no., 76; at. wt., 190.2; melting point about 2700° C.

os′mose (ŏs′mōs; ŏz′-), *v. t.* *Chem.* To subject to osmosis.

os·mo′sis (ŏs·mō′sĭs; ŏz-), *n.* Also **os′mose** (ŏs′mōs; ŏz′-). [NL. *osmosis,* deriv. of Gr. *ōsmos* impulse + *-ose.*] *Physical Chem. & Physiol.* The diffusion which proceeds through a semipermeable membrane, typically separating two solutions, or a solvent and a solution, and tending to equalize their concentrations. The net movement in osmosis is diffusion of solvent into the more concentrated solution, whether by vaporization, adsorption, or otherwise is not clear. Living cells characteristically have semipermeable membranes and depend for much of their activity upon osmosis. — **os·mot′ic** (-mŏt′ĭk), *adj.* — **os·mot′i·cal·ly** (-ĭ·kăl·ĭ), *adv.*

os′mund (ŏs′mŭnd; ŏz′-), *n.* [F. *osmonde.*] Any of a genus (*Osmunda*) of ferns, esp. the ***royal fern*** (*O. regalis*), having pinnate or bipinnate circinate fronds and bearing sporangia on modified pinnae.

os′prey (ŏs′prĭ), *n.; pl.* OSPREYS (-prĭz). [Prob. through OF. fr. L. *ossifraga* (orig., the bonebreaker). See OSSIFRAGE.] **1.** A large hawk (*Pandion haliaëtus*) which feeds on fish; fish hawk. **2.** A type of feather trimming used in millinery.

Os′sa (ŏs′ȧ), *n.* [L., fr. Gr. *Ossa.*] A Thessalian mountain. In Greek mythology, the giants, striving to attack the Olympians, piled Mount Pelion on Ossa.

os′se·in (ŏs′ē·ĭn), *n.* [L. *osseus* bony.] *Biochem.* The organic basis of bone tissue, supposed to be identical with collagen.

os′se·ous (-ŭs), *adj.* [L. *osseus,* fr. *os, ossis,* bone.] Composed of, or resembling, bone; bony. — **os′se·ous·ly,** *adv.*

Os′set (ŏs′ĕt), *n.* Also **Os′sete** (ŏs′ēt; ŏ·sĕt′). One of a people of central Caucasus, possibly immigrants from Persia and of Aryan descent and speech. They dwell in the North Ossetian A.S.S.R. and in the South Ossetian Autonomous Region, Soviet Russia, Europe, and speak Ossetic.

Os·se′tian (ŏ·sē′shăn), *adj.* Also **O·se′tian.** Ossetic. — *n.* An Osset.

Os·set′ic (-ĭk), *adj.* Also **O·set′ic.** Of or pertaining to the Ossets. — *n.* The Iranian language of the Ossets, descendant of ancient Scythian (which see). See INDO-EUROPEAN LANGUAGES, *Table.*

Os′si·an′ic (ŏsh′ĭ·ăn′ĭk; ŏs′ĭ-), *adj.* **a** Of or pertaining to **Os′sian** (ŏsh′ăn; ŏs′ĭ·ăn; *Ir.* ŭsh·ēn′), an Irish hero of the 3d century. **b** Pert. to the poetry or rhythmic prose employed by James Macpherson in *The Poems of Ossian* (pub. 1760, 1762), which he claimed to be translations of poems of Ossian.

os′si·cle (ŏs′ĭ·k′l), *n.* [L. *ossiculum,* dim. of *os, ossis,* a bone.] *Anat. & Zool.* A little bone or bonelike part.

os′si·fi·ca′tion (ŏs′ĭ·fĭ·kā′shŭn), *n.* **1.** State or process of being ossified. **2.** A mass or point of ossified tissue.

os′si·frage (ŏs′ĭ·frĭj), *n.* [L. *ossifraga, ossifragus,* fr. *ossifragus* bone-breaking, fr. *os, ossis,* a bone + *frangere, fractum,* to break.] **a** The lammergeier. **b** The osprey.

os′si·fy (ŏs′ĭ·fī), *v. i. & t.;* OS′SI·FIED (-fīd); OS′SI·FY′ING. [L. *os, ossis,* bone + *-fy.*] **1.** *Physiol.* To change into or form bone. **2.** Figuratively, to harden; to set or become set in a conventional form.

os′su·ar′y (ŏs′ū·ĕr′ĭ; -ẽr·ĭ; ŏsh′ū-), *n.; pl.* -IES (-ĭz). [LL. *ossuarium,* fr. *ossuarius* of or for bones, fr. L. *os, ossis,* bone.] A depository for the bones of the dead.

os′te- (ŏs′tē-). = OSTEO-, as in **os′te·ec′to·my, os′te·i′tis.**

os′te·al (ŏs′tē·ăl), *adj.* [Gr. *osteon* a bone.] Osseous.

os·ten′si·ble (ŏs·tĕn′sĭ·b′l), *adj.* [F., fr. L. *ostendere, ostensum, -tum,* to show, prop., to stretch out before, fr. *obs-* (fr. *ob-*) + *tendere* to stretch.] Avowed; professed; apparent; — often used as if opposed to *real* or *actual;* as, an *ostensible* motive. — **Syn.** See APPARENT. — **os·ten′si·bly** (-blĭ), *adv.*

os·ten′sive (-sĭv), *adj.* Manifestly demonstrative; also, exhibiting; ostensible. — **os·ten′sive·ly,** *adv.*

os′ten·ta′tion (ŏs′tĕn·tā′shŭn), *n.* [F., fr. L. *ostentatio.*] **1.** Unnecessary show; pretentious parade. **2.** *Archaic.* Act of displaying; display.

os′ten·ta′tious (-shŭs), *adj.* Characterized by, fond of, or evincing ostentation; pretentious. — **Syn.** See SHOWY. — **os′ten·ta′tious·ly,** *adv.*

os′te·o- (ŏs′tē·ō-), **os′te-** (ŏs′tē-). [Gr. *osteon.*] A combining form meaning *bone,* as in **os′te·o·ar·thri′tis, os′te·o·gen′e·sis, os′te·og′e·ny, os′te·om′e·try, os′te·o·my′e·li′tis.**

os′te·o·blast′ (-blăst′), *n.* *Anat.* A bone-forming cell.

os′te·oc′la·sis (ŏs′tē·ŏk′lȧ·sĭs), *n.* [NL.] *Surg.* The operation of breaking a bone to correct deformity.

os′te·o·clast′ (ŏs′tē·ō·klăst′), *n.* [*osteo-* + Gr. *klastos* broken.] **1.** *Anat.* One of the large multinuclear cells in developing bone which absorb the bony tissue in the formation of the canals, marrow cavity, etc. **2.** *Surg.* An instrument for performing osteoclasis.

os′te·oid (ŏs′tē·oid), *adj.* [*oste-* + *-oid.*] Like bone.

os′te·ol′o·gy (ŏs′tē·ŏl′ō·jĭ), *n.* [*osteo-* + *-logy.*] **1.** The science dealing with the bones of vertebrates. **2.** The bony structure of an organism; as, the *osteology* of the head. — **os′te·o·log′i·cal** (-ō·lŏj′ĭ·kăl), *adj.* — **os′te·ol′o·gist** (-ŏl′ō·jĭst), *n.*

os′te·o′ma (ŏs′tē·ō′mȧ), *n.; pl.* -MAS (-mȧz), -MATA (-mȧ·tȧ). [NL.] *Med.* A benign tumor composed of bone.

os′te·o·path (ŏs′tē·ō·păth), *n.* Also **os′te·op′a·thist** (-ŏp′ȧ·thĭst). A practitioner of osteopathy.

os′te·op′a·thy (ŏs′tē·ŏp′ȧ·thĭ), *n.* [*osteo-* + *-pathy.*] A system of medical practice based on the theory that disease is due chiefly to mechanical derangement in tissues, placing emphasis on restoration of structural integrity by manipulation of the parts. The use of medicines, surgery, proper diet, psychotherapy, and other measures are included in osteopathy. — **os′te·o·path′ic** (-ō·păth′ĭk), *adj.*

os′te·o·phyte′ (ŏs′tē·ō·fīt′), *n.* [*osteo-* + *-phyte.*] *Med.* A bony outgrowth. — **os′te·o·phyt′ic** (-fĭt′ĭk), *adj.*

os′te·o·plas′tic (-plăs′tĭk), *adj.* **1.** *Physiol.* Producing bone. **2.** *Surg.* Of or pert. to the replacement of bone.

os′te·o·plas′ty (ŏs′tē·ō·plăs′tĭ), *n.* [*osteo-* + *-plasty.*] *Surg.* A plastic operation to remedy a defect or loss of bone.

os′te·o·tome′ (ŏs′tē·ō·tōm′), *n.* [*osteo-* + *-tome.*] *Surg.* Strong nippers or a chisel for dividing bone.

os′te·ot′o·my (-ŏt′ō·mĭ), *n.* [*osteo-* + *-tomy.*] *Surg.* The operation of dividing a bone or of cutting a piece out of it.

os′ti·ar′y (ŏs′tĭ·ĕr′ĭ *or, esp. Brit.,* -ẽr·ĭ), *n.; pl.* -IES (-ĭz). [L. *ostiarius* doorkeeper, fr. *ostium* door.] A doorkeeper, esp. of a church; *R.C.Ch.*, a member of the lowest of the minor orders.

os′ti·ole (ŏs′tĭ·ōl), *n.* [L. *ostiolum*, dim. of *ostium* a door.] A small aperture; an orifice or pore. — **os′ti·o·lar** (ŏs′tĭ·ō·lẽr; ŏs·tī′-), *adj.*

ost′ler (ŏs′lẽr), *n.* [For *hostler.*] Var. of HOSTLER.

os·to′sis (ŏs·tō′sĭs), *n.* [NL., fr. *osteo-* + *-osis.*] *Physiol.* Bone formation; ossification.

os′tra·cism (ŏs′trȧ·sĭz′m), *n.* [See OSTRACIZE.] **1.** *Gr. Antiq.* A method of temporary banishment by popular vote (with ballots of potsherds or tiles, and without a trial or special accusation). **2.** Exclusion by general consent from common privileges, favor, etc.; as, social *ostracism.*

os′tra·cize (-sīz), *v. t.* [Gr. *ostrakizein*, fr. *ostrakon* a tile, a tablet used in voting, a shell.] **1.** *Gr. Antiq.* To exile by ostracism. **2.** To banish from social or political favor or fellowship.

os′trich (ŏs′trĭch; *formerly often, & still occas.,* -trĭj; 74), *n.;* see PLURAL, *Note,* 3. [OF. *ostruche*, fr. L. *avis struthio*, fr. *avis* bird + *struthio* ostrich.] **a** A very swift-footed two-toed ratite bird (genus *Struthio*, esp., *S. camelus* of northern Africa), with small useless wings, the largest of existing birds, often weighing 300 lbs. **b** A rhea.

Os′tro·goth (ŏs′trō·gŏth), *n.* [LL. *Ostrogothae*, pl.] One of the East Goths. See GOTH, *n.* — **Os′tro·goth′ic** (-gŏth′ĭk), *adj.*

Os·we′go tea (ŏs·wē′gō). See BALM, *n.*, 4.

o·tal′gi·a (ō·tăl′jĭ·ȧ), *n.* [NL., fr. Gr. *ōtalgia*, fr. *ous, ōtos*, the ear + *algos* pain.] *Med.* Earache. — **o·tal′gic** (-jĭk), *adj.*

‖**O tem′po·ra! O mo′res!** (ō tĕm′pō·rȧ ō mō′rēz). [L.] O the times! O the manners!

O·thel′lo (ō·thĕl′ō), *n.* In Shakespeare's tragedy *Othello, the Moor of Venice,* a noble-spirited Moor who has won honor in the military service of Venice, and marries a senator's daughter, Desdemona. He is led by Iago to believe her unfaithful, and smothers her before learning of her innocence, after which he kills himself.

oth′er (ŭth′ẽr), *adj.* [AS. *ōther* one of two, either, other.] **1.** Being the one of two (or more) distinct from the one already mentioned or understood; (the) remaining; as, the *other* sons. **2. a** Additional; as, without *other* resources. **b** Not the same; different; as, *other* than what he is. **3. a** Second. *Obs.*, exc. in ***every other,*** every alternate. **b** That precedes. *Obs.*, exc. in the ***other day,*** a recent, unspecified day. — *pron.* **1.** (*pl.* formerly OTHER, now OTHERS [-ẽrz]) One or ones remaining; part remaining; as, better than the *others.* **2.** (*pl.* OTHER, *Archaic;* OTHERS) A different or additional one; as, some person or *other* will be there. — *adv.* Otherwise.

oth′er·guess′ (-gĕs′), *adj. & adv.* [Corrupt. of dial. *othergates* in another way.] Of another kind; in another way.

oth′er·ness (-nĕs; -nĭs), *n.* Quality or state of being other, or different; also, something other, or different.

oth′er·where′ (-hwâr′), *adv.* Elsewhere.

oth′er·while′ (-hwīl′), *adv.* Also **oth′er·whiles′** (-hwīlz′). *Archaic & Dial.* At another time, or other times.

oth′er·wise′ (-wīz′), *adv.* [*other* + *wise* manner.] **1.** In a different manner; in other ways; contrarily. **2.** In different circumstances. **3.** In other respects. — *adj.* Different.

other world. The supposed world beyond death.

oth′er·world′ly (ŭth′ẽr·wûrld′lĭ), *adj.* **1. a** Transmundane; transcendental. **b** Devoted to the prospect of a world to come, often to the exclusion of interest in the affairs of this world. **2.** Devoted to the pursuit of intellectual or imaginative concerns. — **oth′er·world′li·ness** (-wûrld′lĭ·nĕs; -nĭs), *n.*

O′thin (ō′thĭn). Var. of ODIN.

Oth′man (ŏth′măn), *n.; pl.* -MANS (-mănz). Var. of OTTOMAN.

o′tic (ō′tĭk; ŏt′ĭk), *adj.* [Gr. *ōtikos*, fr. *ous, ōtos*, the ear.] Pertaining to, or in the region of, the ear; auricular.

o′ti·ose (ō′shĭ·ōs), *adj.* [L. *otiosus*, fr. *otium* ease.] **1.** Being at leisure; indolent. **2.** Sterile; futile. **3.** Useless; without function. — **Syn.** See VAIN. — **o′ti·ose·ly**, *adv.* — **o′ti·os′i·ty** (-ŏs′ĭ·tĭ), *n.*

‖**o′ti·um cum dig′ni·ta′te** (ō′shĭ·ŭm kŭm dĭg′nĭ·tā′tē). [L.] Leisure with dignity; dignified leisure.

o′to- (ō′tō-), **ot-.** [Gr. *ous, ōtos.*] A combining form meaning *the ear,* as in:

otitis	otoplasty	otoscopic
otologist	otorrhea	otoscopy
otology	otoscope	ototomy

o′to·cyst (-sĭst), *n.* *Zool.* In invertebrates, one of the supposed auditory organs, containing a fluid and otoliths.

o′to·lar′yn·gol′o·gy (ō′tō·lăr′ĭng·gŏl′ō·jĭ), *n.* [*oto-* + *laryngology.*] The branch of medicine which treats of diseases of the ear and larynx. — **o′to·lar′yn·gol′o·gist** (-jĭst), *n.*

o′to·lith (ō′tō·lĭth), *n.* [*oto-* + *-lith.*] *Anat. & Zool.* A calcareous concretion in the internal ear of a vertebrate or in the otocyst of an invertebrate. In many teleost fishes, otoliths form hard bodies, called *ear stones.*

ot′tar (ŏt′ẽr), *n.* Attar.

‖**ot·ta′va** (ōt·tä′vä), *n.; pl.* OTTAVE (-vā). [It., eighth, octave.] *Music.* An octave. Cf. ALL'OTTAVA.

ot·ta′va ri′ma (rē′mä). [It. See OCTAVE; RHYME.] *Pros.* A stanza of eight lines of heroic verse, with three rhymes, the first six lines rhyming alternately and the last two forming a couplet: thus, *abababcc.* It was used by Byron in *Don Juan.*

Ot′ta·wa (ŏt′ȧ·wȧ; -wŏ; -wä), *n.* [Can. F. *Otaua, Otawa,* of Algonquian origin.] One of a tribe of Algonquian Indians driven by the Iroquois to the Lake Superior region.

ot′ter (ŏt′ẽr), *n.;* see PLURAL, *Note,* 3. [AS. *otor.*] Any of several aquatic fish-eating mammals (chiefly subfamily Lutrinae, genus *Lutra*) related to the weasels, badgers, minks, and skunks, and having webbed and clawed feet and dark-brown fur; also, the fur of this animal.

ot′to (ŏt′ō), *n.* Attar.

Ot′to·man (ŏt′ō·măn), *adj.* [F. *ottoman*, through It. & ML., fr. Ar. *'Uthmānī* belonging to Osman. Cf. OSMANLI.] Of or pertaining to the Turks or Turkey; Osmanli. — *n.; pl.* -MANS (-mănz). **1.** A Turk. **2.** [*not cap.*] An upholstered seat without a back; also, a flat overstuffed couch with or without a back. **3.** [*not cap.*] A stuffed, usually overstuffed, footstool.

oua·ba′in (wä·bä′ĭn), *n.* [*ouabaio* either of two South African trees + *-in.*] *Chem.* A poisonous glucoside, $C_{29}H_{44}O_{12}$, in the seeds of certain African trees, used as an arrow poison and in medicine as a local anesthetic and cardiac stimulant.

oua′na′niche′ (wȧ′nȧ′nēsh′), *n. sing. & pl.* [Can. F.] A small landlocked salmon (*Salmo ouananiche*) of eastern Canada.

ou′bli·ette′ (ōō′blē·ĕt′), *n.* [F., fr. *oublier* to forget.] A dungeon with an opening only at the top.

ouch (ouch), *n.* [ME. *ouche, nouche* (*a nouch* being taken for *an ouch*), fr. OF. *nusche, nosche,* necklace, collar, of Teut. origin.] *Archaic.* A clasp or brooch; also, a setting for a precious stone; hence, a jewel or ornament. — *v. t. Archaic.* To adorn with or as with ouches.

ought (ôt), *v.* Orig. *past tense,* later also *past part.,* of OWE. [ME. *oughte, aughte, ahte,* fr. AS. *āhte.* See OWE.] **1.** *Obs.* **a** Owned. **b** Owed. **2.** As an auxiliary verb followed by an infinitive, usually with *to,* specif.: **a** To be bound, as by practical duty, by moral laws, or by conscience, hence, by ideal right. **b** To be necessary, becoming, or expedient. **c** To be a natural or logical consequence. **d** To require; as, this shoe *ought* to be mended.

☞ A past sense with *ought* is made clear by putting the following infinitive in the perfect tense; as, you *ought* to have gone.

ought (ôt), *n.* Aught; anything. — *adv.* Aught; at all.

ought, *n.* Erroneous for NOUGHT; zero; cipher.

ought′lins (ôKT′lĭnz), *adv.* [*ought* aught + *-lings* (= 2d *ling*).] *Scot.* In any degree.

Oui′ja (wē′jȧ), *n.* [F. *oui* yes + G. *ja* yes.] A trade-mark for a board, marked with the alphabet and various signs, used with a planchette to obtain mediumistic messages.

ounce (ouns; 106), *n.* [OF. *unce* (F. *once*), fr. L. *uncia* a twelfth, twelfth part of a pound or foot.] **1.** A weight of various values. See WEIGHT, *Tables* 1, 2, 3, & 4. **2.** A fluid ounce. See MEASURE, *Table* 12. **3.** A small portion or quantity.

ounce (ouns), *n.* [OF. *once*, fr. *lonce*, taken as *l'once,* for L. *lyncea,* fr. *lynx* lynx.] A large, beautiful, leopardlike cat (*Felis uncia*), grayish white spotted with black, of Tibet and southern Siberia.

ouphe (ouf; ōōf), *n.* [See OAF.] An elf or goblin.

our (our), *pron.* [AS. *ūre* our, of us.] The possessive plural form of the personal pronoun I, pl. we: Of us; as, in *our* midst; in *our* despite. — *adj.* [Possessive case of *we.*] **1.** Of or belonging or relating to us; due to us; inherent in us; effected by us; experienced by us as subjects or as objects; that we have to do with. **2.** Hence, that we (royal or editorial *we;* cf. WE) have in mind or are speaking of.

ou·ra′ri (ōō·rä′rē). Var. of CURARI.

ou′rie (*Scot.* ōō′rĭ), *adj. Scot.* Dingy; dreary; also, cold.

ou·rol′o·gy, ou·ros′co·py. Vars. of UROLOGY, UROSCOPY.

ours (ourz), *pron.* The form of the possessive *our* used with no noun following; as, this world of *ours.*

our·self′ (our·sĕlf′), *pron.* Equiv. of OURSELVES; — used to denote a single person, as in regal or editorial style. Cf. OUR, *adj.*, 2.

our·selves′ (-sĕlvz′), *pron.* An emphasized form of the pronoun of the first person plural; as, we *ourselves* know.

-ous (-ŭs). [F. or L.; OF. *-ous, -us, -os, -eus* (F. *-eux*), fr. L. *-osus.*] **1.** An adjective suffix meaning *full of, abounding in, having, possessing the qualities of, like,* as in graci*ous,* abounding in grace; bulb*ous;* riot*ous;* poison*ous;* also used in adapting Latin adjectives, as in vari*ous,* -fer*ous,* polygam*ous.* **2.** *Chem.* A suffix denoting a valence lower than that denoted by *-ic,* as in nitr*ous,* as contrasted with nitr*ic.* **3.** *Zool.* Used to form adjectives corresponding to nouns of classification, as in amphibi*ous.*

ou′sel (ōō′z'l). Var. of OUZEL.

‖**ou·si′a** (ōō·sē′ä), *n.* [Gr.] Nature; substance; essence.

oust (oust), *v. t.* [AF. *ouster*, OF. *oster.*] To eject or dispossess from; to turn out; expel. — **Syn.** See EJECT.

oust′er (ous′tẽr), *n.* [AF., infin. used as n.] One that ousts; specif., *Law,* a putting out of possession; esp., a wrongful dispossession.

out (out), *adv.* [ME. *out, ut, oute,* fr. AS. *ūt.*] Away from within a space; from the interior, or beyond the limits or boundary, of something; specif.: **1.** In a direction away from the inside or center; hence, from a container; from indoors; away from a normal or usual place, as from home; from among others; at or into domestic service; as, to empty, send, or pick something *out;* a woman works *out.* **2.** Beyond possession, control, or occupation; hence, in or into a state of loss or deprivation, as of office; into a perplexed state of mind; as, to vote *out* the Whigs; put *out* about books. **3.** Beyond the limit of existence, continuance, or supply; hence, to extinction, exhaustion, completion; to the fullest degree; as, to burn *out;* talked *out;* thresh *out;* decked *out.* **4.** Beyond the limits of concealment, constraint, etc., actual or figurative; hence, in or into a state of freedom, disclosure, publicity; into application or manifestation; with a considerable volume of sound; as, disease breaks *out;* to draw *out* students; to cry *out.* **5.** From agreement or harmony; as, friends fall *out.* **6.** *Baseball, Cricket, etc.* At the end of a turn at batting. — ***out of.*** **a** From within or among; beyond the limits or range of; as, to squeeze juice *out of* the pulp. **b** From (material or constituents); because of; as, built *out of* old lumber; *out of* curiosity; also, born of; as, a colt *out of* Cleopatra (dam). **c** Into or in a condition of deprivation of, or release or divergence from; as, swindled *out of* his savings; *out of* alignment.

— *prep.* From a position within; — now only in *from out.*

— *adj.* Used only predicatively (except senses 6 & 7): **1.** In a condition of absence or removal; as, a ship three days *out* from port. **2.** In a condition of loss or deprivation or of being beyond control; as, *out* a hundred dollars; land *out* at rent. **3.** In a condition of completion or exhaustion; as, before the week is *out;* extinguished; not in vogue. **4.**

In a condition of issuance from concealment or of disclosure; unfolded; as, the secret is *out;* the latest edition, *out* today; having made a debut; also, openly competing or striving; as, *out* to win. **5.** In a condition of exceeding the bounds of what is true, reasonable, correct, proper, seasonable, etc.; specif.: Erring; as, but a few thousandths *out;* at odds; as, *out* with his friends; fallen away from perfect skill; as, my hand is *out;* deranged in mind. **6.** Out of the ordinary; as, *out* sizes. **7.** Outlying. **8.** *Games.* Not having its innings; retired.
— *n.* **1.** *Generally pl.* **a** One who is out of office. **b** A sum expended or paid out. **c** A place or space outside of something; an angle projecting outward. **d** An inharmonious relationship; as, at *outs,* or on the *outs,* that is, at odds. **2.** That which is opposed; a drawback. **3.** *Baseball.* **a** A put-out. **b** An outcurve. **4.** *Lawn Tennis.* A return of the ball that, untouched by opponent, goes out of court. **5.** *Print.* A word or words omitted by the compositor in setting type.
— *interj.* Expressing impatience, anger, or abhorrence; begone; — often in *out upon* or *on* (archaic equivalent of "shame upon," "away with").
— *v. t.* To put out; eject. — *v. i.* To become public.

out- (out-). A combining form of the adverb *out* meaning: **1.** (Forming mostly nouns, with primary accent usually on *out-*) *Situated* or *placed near* or *beyond the boundaries,* or *belonging to that which is so situated; external; outside of;* as in *out*door; *remote from the center; distant; residing, journeying,* or *employed outside; foreign;* as in:

outcity	**outkitchen**	**outquarters**
outclerk	**outmerchant**	**outsentry**
outdistrict	**outoffice**	**outservant**
outdweller	**outparish**	**outsettlement**
outdwelling	**outpupil**	**outsettler**

2. (Forming adjectives and nouns, with varying accent) *Away from the center* or *source; forth; outward; leading, opening, projecting,* or *inclining outward,* as in:

outbound	**outglare**	**outpath**
outbowed	**outjet**	**outrush**
outbranching	**outlipped**	**outvoyage**

3. (Forming verbs, with primary accent usually on verbal element): **a** *Forth; away; out of place* or *being;* as in **out·wrench′**; *forth into manifestation,* as in **out·shape′**; *to the full extent; completely,* as in *out*wear; *to the elimination of,* as in **out·jest′**.

☞ Further examples follow; also, see ☞ under 3 **b.**

outawe	**outlaunch**	**outslide**
outban	**outlengthen**	**outspill**

b *A going* or *passing beyond in a* (specified) *quality* or *action; an exceeding, excelling, surpassing,* often with reference to a competitor; as in:

outact	**outjump**	**outsnore**
outargue	**outmarch**	**outstare**
outbargain	**outnumber**	**outstrive**
outbox	**outpreach**	**outsulk**
outbrag	**outrank**	**outswear**
outbribe	**outroar**	**outswim**
outchatter	**outrow**	**outtalk**
outchide	**outrun**	**outtrot**
outclimb	**outsail**	**outvote**
outdare	**outscorn**	**outwait**
outguess	**outshriek**	**outwalk**
outjockey	**outsleep**	**outwatch**

☞ Many compounds have both senses 3 **a** and 3 **b**; as:

outfly	**outpass**	**outstrain**
outleap	**outring**	**outweep**

out′age (out′ĭj), *n.* [*out* + *-age.*] **1.** State of being out of commission; disuse, as for repairs. **2.** *Elec.* A period of interruption of electric current.

out′-and-out′, *adj.* Thoroughgoing; complete; outright.

out·bal′ance (out·băl′ăns), *v. t.* To outweigh; to exceed in weight or effect.

out·bid′ (-bĭd′), *v. t.;* see BID. To offer a higher price than; in card playing, to bid more than.

out′board′ (out′bōrd′; 70), *adv.* *Naut.* Outside of a vessel's bulwarks; in a lateral direction from the hull. — *adj.* **1.** *Naut.* Situated outboard. **2.** *Mach.* Designating a bearing, center, or other support, used in conjunction with, and outside of, a main bearing.

outboard motor. A small internal-combustion engine with propeller attached, temporarily fastened to the stern of a small boat.

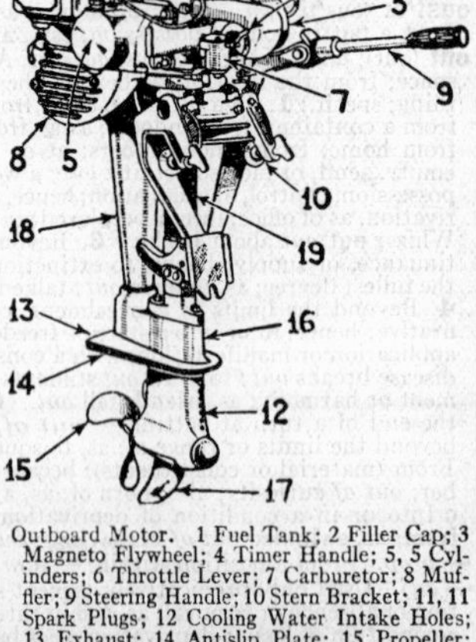

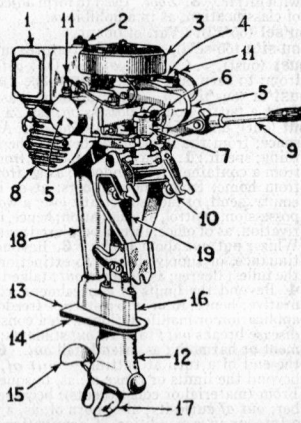

Outboard Motor. 1 Fuel Tank; 2 Filler Cap; 3 Magneto Flywheel; 4 Timer Handle; 5, 5 Cylinders; 6 Throttle Lever; 7 Carburetor; 8 Muffler; 9 Steering Handle; 10 Stern Bracket; 11, 11 Spark Plugs; 12 Cooling Water Intake Holes; 13 Exhaust; 14 Antislip Plate; 15 Propeller; 16 Gear Housing; 17 Propeller Skeg; 18 Exhaust Tube; 19 Drive Housing.

out·brave′ (out·brāv′), *v. t.* **1.** To face or resist defiantly; also, to excel in bravery. **2.** To excel in dress, or finery.

out′break′ (out′brāk′), *n.* A bursting forth; insurrection.

out·breed′ (out·brēd′), *v. t.;* see BREED. To subject to outbreeding.

out′breed′ing (out′brēd′ĭng), *n.* Breeding or mating of individuals, stocks, etc., which are relatively unrelated. Cf. INBREEDING.

out′build′ing (out′bĭl′dĭng), *n.* A building separate from, and subordinate to, the main house; an outhouse.

out′burst′ (-bûrst′), *n.* A bursting forth; eruption.

out′by′, out′bye′ (out′bī′), *adv.* *Scot.* At a distance; outside; outdoors.

out′cast′ (out′kȧst′; 9), *adj.* **1.** Cast out; degraded. **2.** Rejected; thrown aside or away. — *n.* **1.** One who is cast out or expelled; an exile; one driven from home, society, or country; hence, often, a degraded person; a vagabond. **2.** That which is cast out or forth; specif., refuse; waste. **3.** *Scot.* A quarrel.

out′caste′ (-kȧst′; 9), *n.* In India, one who has been ejected from his caste for violation of its customs or rules. The outcastes are denied all ordinary social rights.

out·class′ (out·klȧs′; 9), *v. t.* To excel or surpass so decisively as to appear of a higher class.

out′come′ (out′kŭm′), *n.* Issue; result; consequence; upshot; as, the *outcome* of an election. — **Syn.** See EFFECT.

out′crop′ (out′krŏp′), *n.* *Geol. & Mining.* **a** The coming out of a stratum to the surface of the ground. **b** That part of a stratum which appears at the surface. — (out·krŏp′; 2), *v. i.;* see CROP. *Geol.* To come out to the surface of the ground, as strata.

out′cross′ing (out′krŏs′ĭng), *n.* Breeding or mating of individuals of different strains but, in livestock, of the same breed. — **out·cross′** (out·krŏs′; 2), *v. t.* — **out′cross′** (out′krŏs′), *n.*

out′cry′ (out′krī′), *n.; pl.* -CRIES (-krīz′). **1.** A loud cry; a cry of distress or alarm. **2.** Sale at public auction.

out·cry′ (out·krī′), *v. t.;* see CRY. To exceed in clamor.

out′curve′ (out′kûrv′), *n.* A ball that curves away from a right-handed batter.

out·dis′tance (out·dĭs′tăns), *v. t.* To outstrip; to surpass greatly.

out·do′ (-dōō′), *v. t.;* see DO. To excel; surpass. — **Syn.** See EXCEED.

out′door′ (out′dōr′; 70), *adj.* **1.** Being, belonging, or done out of doors. **2.** Belonging or arising outside the walls of an institution such as a hospital.

out′doors′ (out′dōrz′; 2), *adv.* [*out,* as prep. = out of.] Out of the house; out of doors. — (out′dōrz′), *adj.* Outdoor.

out′doors′ (out′dōrz′), *n.* The world out of doors.

out′er (out′ẽr), *adj.* [Compar. of OUT.] Being on the outside; external; farthest or farther from the interior; — opposed to *inner.*

out′er·most (-mōst; -mŭst), *adj.* [From OUTER.] Being on the extreme external part; farthest outward. — **out′er·most,** *adv.*

out·face′ (out·fās′), *v. t.* To face or look (one) out of countenance; to resist by effrontery; also, to defy.

out′fall′ (out′fôl′), *n.* The vent of a river, drain, etc.

out′field′ (-fēld′), *n.* **1.** An outlying field of a farm. **2.** *Baseball.* **a** The part of the field beyond the diamond, or infield. **b** The players in the outfield. **3.** *Cricket.* The part of the field farthest from the batsman. — **out′field′er** (-fēl′dẽr), *n.*

out′fit (out′fĭt), *n.* **1.** A fitting out; an equipping; also, cost of equipment. **2.** The articles or instruments forming an equipment; as, a gambling *outfit;* hence, figuratively, mental or moral endowments. **3.** The persons constituting a party engaged in exploring, herding, building, etc. — (out′fĭt′), *v. t. & i.;* OUT′FIT′TED (-ĕd; -ĭd); OUT′FIT′TING. To furnish with an outfit; to fit out. — **Syn.** See FURNISH.

out′fit′ter (-fĭt′ẽr), *n.* **1.** One who furnishes outfits. **2.** A retail dealer in clothing, haberdashery, etc.

out·flank′ (out·flăngk′), *v. t.* *Mil.* To go, extend, or be beyond the flank or flanks of; to turn the flank of.

out′flow′ (out′flō′), *n.* A flowing out; efflux.

out·foot′ (out·fŏŏt′), *v. t.* To outstrip in pace; of a vessel, to outsail.

out·frown′ (-froun′), *v. t.* To overbear by frowning.

out·gen′er·al (-jĕn′ẽr·ăl), *v. t.;* -ALED (-ăld) or -ALLED; -AL·ING or -AL·LING. To exceed in generalship; outmaneuver.

out·go′ (out·gō′), *v. t.;* see GO. To go beyond; to surpass; outdo. — (out′gō′), *n.; pl.* OUTGOES (-gōz′). **1.** That which goes out; specif., outlay. **2.** The efflux; outflow.

out′go′ing (out′gō′ĭng), *adj.* Going out; as, the *outgoing* tide; departing; as, an *outgoing* steamer; retiring; as, the *outgoing* administration. — *n.* Outgo; specif.: **a** Act or fact of going out. **b** Outlay.

out·grow′ (out·grō′), *v. t.;* see GROW. **1.** To surpass in growing. **2.** To grow out of or away from; to grow too large for; as, to *outgrow* clothing.

out′growth′ (out′grōth′), *n.* **1.** That which grows out of, or proceeds from, anything. **2.** A result; consequence; product; also, esp., a by-product.

out′haul′ (out′hôl′), *n.* *Naut.* A rope used for hauling, as for hauling out a sail upon a spar.

out-Her′od (out·hĕr′ŭd), *v. t.* To outdo (Herod) in violence; — in allusion to *Hamlet,* act III, scene ii, which refers to the blustering role of Herod in the mystery plays.

out′house′ (out′hous′), *n.* An outbuilding; specif., a privy.

out′ing (out′ĭng), *n.* **1.** A trip or stay in the open; an excursion. **2.** Distance out at sea; seaward distance. — *adj.* Pertaining to, or suitable for, an outing or outdoor wear.

outing flannel. See FLANNEL.

out′land′ (out′lănd′), *n.* [AS. *ūtland.*] A foreign land. — *adj.* **1.** Foreign. **2.** Outlying.

out′land′er (-lăn′dẽr), *n.* A foreigner; alien; stranger.

out·land′ish (out·lăn′dĭsh), *adj.* **1.** *Archaic.* Foreign. **2.** Of foreign appearance or manner; hence, bizarre; barbarous; uncouth. **3.** Remote from civilization. — **Syn.** See STRANGE. — **out·land′ish·ly,** *adv.* — **out·land′ish·ness,** *n.*

out·last′ (out·lȧst′; 9), *v. t.* To last longer than; to survive. — **Syn.** See OUTLIVE.

out′law′ (out′lô′), *n.* [AS. *ūtlaga, ūtlah,* fr. ON. *ūtlagi,* n., *utlagr,* adj.] **1.** A person excluded from the benefit or protection of the law. **2.** Hence, a lawless person, or a fugitive from the law. — *v. t.* [AS. *ūtlagian.*] **1.** To deprive of the benefit and protection of law; to proscribe. **2.** *Colloq., U. S.* To remove from legal jurisdiction or enforcement. **3. a** To place under a ban or disability. **b** To stigmatize as irregular or illegitimate. **c** To put in the status of an outlaw; to make illegal; as, to *outlaw* war.

out′law′ry (-rĭ), *n.; pl.* -RIES (-rĭz). The act or process of outlawing; the state of being outlawed.

out·lay′ (out·lā′), *v. t.;* see LAY. To spend (money).

out′lay′ (out′lā′), *n.* **1.** Act of laying out, or expending. **2.** An expenditure.

out′let (out′lĕt; -lĭt), *n.* **1. a** The opening by which anything is let out; an exit; a vent. **b** A means or way of escape or issue; as, an *outlet* for the emotions. **2.** A stream flowing out of a lake, a larger stream, or the like. **3.** *Com.* A market for a commodity.

outlet box. *Elec.* A box for electric wiring or fittings at which the wires terminate for connection to electric fixtures.

out′li′er (out′lī′ẽr), *n.* **1.** One who does not live where his office, or business, or estate is. **2.** That which lies, dwells, or is situated or classed away from the main body.

out′line′ (out′līn′), *n.* **1. a** The line which marks the outer limits of an object or figure; contour; — commonly *pl.* **b** The style of drawing in which contours are figured without shading. **c** A sketch drawn in outline. **2.** A preliminary or general sketch of a plan, system, etc. **3.** A short summary, often in the form of heads and subheads; hence, a compendious presentation of the most significant features of a general subject; as, an *outline* of history.

Syn. **Outline, contour, profile, silhouette** mean the boundary line that defines the shape of a thing. **Outline** implies that which defines the outer edges or limits of a body or mass; **contour** suggests merely an outline but stresses its quality, such as grace, beauty, or softness, or their contraries; **profile** suggests a varied and sharply defined outline against a background (usually monotoned); **silhouette** suggests an outline, esp. of a person, originally formed by cutting out his shadow as thrown on paper, but now often seen as if in shadow with other details blotted out.

— *v. t.* **1.** To draw or trace the outline or contour of. **2.** To indicate by, or as by, an outline.

out·live′ (out·lĭv′), *v. t.* **1.** To live beyond, or longer than; to survive. **2.** To outgrow; as, he *outlived* the disgrace.

Syn. **Outlive, outlast, survive** mean to exist longer than or after a person or thing. **Outlive** stresses a capacity for enduring, often suggesting competition, struggle, etc. (as, to *outlive* one's brother or one's shame); **outlast,** greater length of existence (as, the custom *outlasted* its usefulness); **survive,** a living after another, as a relative, a precarious event, etc. (as, to *survive* many grievous experiences).

out′look′ (out′lo͝ok′), *n.* **1.** A careful watching; a lookout. **2.** The view obtained by one looking out; prospect; hence, the scope of mental vision. **3.** Prospect for the future. — **Syn.** See PROSPECT.

out′ly′ing (out′lī′ĭng), *adj.* Lying, or being at a distance from, the central part, or the main body; frontier; remote.

out′ma·neu′ver, out′ma·noeu′vre (out′mȧ·no͞o′vẽr), *v. t.* To surpass, or get an advantage of, in maneuvering.

out·mode′ (out·mōd′), *v. t.* To make obsolete or unfashionable.

out·mod′ed (-mōd′ĕd; -ĭd), *adj.* Left behind by change of fashion; also, no longer accepted or approved; as, *outmoded* doctrines.

out′most (out′mōst), *adj.* Farthest outward; outermost.

out of commission. Not in working order; laid up.

out′-of-date′, *adj.* Obsolete; unfashionable.

out′-of-door′ (*see Pron.*, § 2), *adj.* Also **out′-of-doors′.** Outdoor.

out′-of-the-way′, *adj.* Out of the beaten path; secluded.

out′pa′tient (out′pā′shĕnt), *n.* A patient who is not an inmate of a hospital, but receives treatment from it.

out·play′ (out·plā′), *v. t.* To excel or defeat in a game.

out·point′ (out·point′), *v. t.* **1.** To excel (a competitor) in number of points scored. **2.** *Naut.* To sail closer to the wind than.

out′post′ (out′pōst′), *n.* **1.** *Mil.* **a** A security detachment thrown out by a halted command to protect against enemy enterprises. **b** The post or station of such detachment. **2.** An outlying or frontier settlement.

out·pour′ (out·pōr′; 70), *v. t. & i.* To pour out.

out·pour′ (out′pōr′), *n.* **1.** Act of pouring out. **2.** That which pours out; outburst; outflow.

out′put′ (out′po͝ot′), *n.* **1.** The total product of one or more mines, furnaces, or mills during a given time. **2.** Hence, yield of any commodity; also, the amount which a man, machine, factory, or industry produces or is able to produce in a given time. **3.** Power or energy delivered by a machine, electric storage battery, etc.

out′rage (out′rāj), *n.* [OF., fr. *outrer* to overdo, fr. *outre* beyond, fr. L. *ultra.*] **1.** Extravagant or violent misdoing; wrong done to persons or things. **2.** *Archaic.* Passionate violence of expression. — *v. t.;* OUT′RAGED (-rājd); OUT′RAG·ING (-rāj·ĭng). **1.** To subject to violent injury; to treat with violence or abuse. **2.** To ravish (a female). — **Syn.** See OFFEND.

out·ra′geous (out·rā′jŭs), *adj.* **1.** Of the nature of outrage or of an outrage. **2.** Violent in action or emotion. **3.** Involving or doing violent injury; atrocious. **4.** Extremely offensive. — **out·ra′geous·ly,** *adv.* — **out·ra′geous·ness,** *n.*

Syn. **Outrageous, monstrous, heinous, atrocious** mean enormously bad or horrible. **Outrageous** implies exceeding one's power to bear or endure; **monstrous,** shocking in its wrongness, absurdity, or the like; **heinous,** such flagrant conspicuousness that it excites hatred or horror; **atrocious,** such savagery or barbarity or, in loose use, such badness, that it excites condemnation.

‖**ou′trance′** (o͞o′träɴs′), *n.* [F.] The utmost or last extremity.

out·range′ (out·rānj′), *v. t.* To exceed in range.

‖**ou′tré′** (o͞o′trā′; o͞o′trā), *adj.* [F., past part. of *outrer* to exaggerate. See OUTRAGE.] Out of the common course or limits; extravagant; bizarre; as, an *outré* costume.

out·reach′ (out·rēch′), *v. t. & i.* To reach or extend beyond; to surpass.

out′reach′ (out′rēch′), *n.* Act or process of reaching out.

ou′tre·mer′ (o͞o′trē·mâr′), *n.* [F., beyond the sea.] The region beyond the sea; foreign parts.

out·ride′ (out·rīd′), *v. t.* **1.** To ride better, faster, or farther than. **2.** To ride out (a storm); — of a ship.

out′ride′ (out′rīd′), *n.* **1.** A riding forth; an excursion; raid. **2.** *Pros.* One, two, or three syllables added to the slack of a foot in sprung rhythm but not counted in the scansion because of their lack of effect upon the rhythmical movement.

out′rid′er (out′rīd′ẽr), *n.* One who rides out; specif., a servant on horseback attending a carriage.

out′rig′ger (out′rĭg′ẽr), *n.* **1.** Any spar or projecting timber, beam, or the like, run out for temporary use, as from a ship's mast to extend a rope or a sail, from a building to support hoisting tackle, from a carriage to enable a second horse to be driven outside the shafts, etc. **2.** *Naut.* **a** A projecting support for a rowlock. **b** A boat equipped with such supports. **c** A projecting contrivance at the side, or sides, of a boat to prevent upsetting, as light projecting spars with a shaped log at the end. **3.** *Aeronautics.* A projecting frame to support the elevator or tail planes, etc.

out′right′ (out′rīt′; out′rīt′), *adv.* **1.** *Now Rare.* Straight ahead. **2.** Completely; wholly; esp., completely in one act or transaction; as, to sell *outright.*

out′right′ (out′rīt′; out′rīt′; 2), *adj.* **1.** Proceeding directly onward. **2.** Straightforward. **3.** Complete; whole.

out·root′ (out·ro͞ot′; 85), *v. t.* To eradicate; extirpate.

out′run′ner (out′rŭn′ẽr), *n.* One who or that which runs out; esp., an attendant running with or before a carriage; also, a leader of a team of dogs on a dog sledge.

out·sell′ (out·sĕl′), *v. t.;* see SELL. **1.** To exceed in amount of sales; to sell more than. **2.** To exceed in the price of selling; to exceed in value.

out′sert (out′sûrt), *n.* [*out* + *-sert* as in *insert.*] A section, as of a magazine, so imposed and printed that it can be placed outside another signature.

out′set′ (out′sĕt′), *n.* Act or instance of setting out; beginning; start.

out·shine′ (out·shīn′), *v. i.;* see SHINE. To shine forth. — *v. t.* To shine brighter than; hence, to excel.

out·shoot′ (-sho͞ot′), *v. t.;* see SHOOT. To exceed or excel in shooting. — *v. i.* To shoot out; to protrude.

out′shoot′ (out′sho͞ot′), *n.* **1.** Act of shooting out; also, that which shoots out. **2.** *Baseball.* A pitched ball that curves suddenly away from a right-handed batter.

out′side′ (out′sīd′; 2), *n.* **1.** The external part; hence, that which appears; also, that which is superficial. **2.** The outer side, as of a door, walk, or boundary. **3.** The furthest limit, as to number, quantity, extent, etc. — *adj.* **1.** Of, on, or pertaining to the outside; external; superficial. **2.** *Colloq.* Reaching the extreme or farthest limit, as to extent, quantity, etc.; as, an *outside* estimate. **3.** Situated or done beyond certain limits; also, coming from or living outside of a given area; as, *outside* labor. **4.** Not included in a society, movement, organization, etc.; as, an *outside* broker. **5.** Of, from, or for outsiders; as, *outside* interference. **6.** Placed on or toward the outer side of any curve or turn; as, stemming with the *outside* ski. — *adv.* On or to the outside or outer side; in or into the open; without an enclosure or certain limits.

out′side′ (out′sīd′; out′sīd′), *prep.* On or to the outside or exterior of; without or beyond the limits of.

out′sid′er (out′sīd′ẽr), *n.* One who is outside; esp., one not belonging to the institution, party, clique, etc., spoken of.

out sister. A nun, especially in a cloistered order, who attends to the outside affairs of the convent.

out·sit′ (out·sĭt′), *v. t.;* see SIT. To remain sitting, or in session, longer than, or beyond the time of.

out′size′ (out′sīz′), *n.* An unusual size; esp., a size larger than or varying from the standard size. — **out′size′** (-sīz′), **out′sized′** (-sīzd′), *adj.*

out′skirt′ (out′skûrt′), *n.* A part remote from the center; edge; border; — usually in *pl.*; as, the *outskirts* of a town.

out·smart′ (out·smärt′), *v. t.* *Colloq., U. S.* To outwit.

out·soar′ (out·sōr′; 70), *v. t.* To soar beyond or above.

out′sole′ (out′sōl′), *n.* The outside sole of a boot or shoe. See SHOE, *Illust.*

out′span′ (out′spăn′), *v. t. & i.;* OUT′SPANNED′ (-spănd′); OUT′SPAN′NING. [D. *uitspannen.*] *S. Africa.* To unyoke, as oxen from a wagon. — *n.* *S. Africa.* Act of outspanning; also, a place for outspanning.

out·speak′ (out·spēk′), *v. t.;* see SPEAK. **1.** To excel in speaking. **2.** To speak openly or boldly.

out′spent′ (out′spĕnt′; out·spĕnt′; 2), *adj.* Exhausted.

out′spo′ken (out′spō′kĕn; 2), *adj.* Speaking or spoken freely, openly, or boldly. — **out′spo′ken·ness,** *n.*

out·spread′ (out·sprĕd′), *v. t. & i.;* see SPREAD. To spread out; expand; also, to exceed in expanse or spread.

out′spread′ (out′sprĕd′), *n.* A spreading out; expansion. — (out-sprĕd′; 2), *adj.* **a** Extended. **b** Diffused.

out·stand′ (out·stănd′), *v. t.;* see STAND. To resist effectually; to withstand; also, to endure beyond. — *v. i.* **1.** To stand out distinctly. **2.** To sail outward; — said of ships.

out·stand′ing (out·stăn′dĭng; 2), *adj.* That stands out; specif.: **a** Projecting; conspicuous. **b** Resisting. **c** Undischarged; uncollected or unpaid; unsettled. — **Syn.** See NOTICEABLE.

out′sta′tion (out′stā′shŭn), *n.* An outlying station, as on the outskirts or in the bush. — **out′sta′tion,** *adj.*

out·stay′ (out·stā′), *v. t.;* see STAY. To stay beyond or longer than; also, to surpass in staying power.

out·stretch′ (-strĕch′), *v. t.* To stretch out; expand.

out·strip′ (-strĭp′), *v. t.;* see STRIP. [*out-* + *strip* to pass, outstrip.] **1.** To go faster than; to leave behind. **2.** Hence, to excel; surpass. — **Syn.** See EXCEED.

out·tell′ (-tĕl′), *v. t.;* see TELL. To declare openly.

out′turn′ (out′tûrn′), *n.* **1.** Yield, as of a crop; product or output, as of a manufacture. **2.** *Com.* A turning out, or proving to be, with respect to quantity, quality, etc.

out′ward (out′wẽrd), *adv.* [See OUTWARD, *adj.*] **a** On the outside; hence, visibly; publicly. **b** Toward the outside; from the interior toward the exterior. — *adj.* [AS. *ūteweard, ūtweard.* See OUT; -WARD, -WARDS.] **1.** Out; outer; exterior; external; specif.: turning or moving toward the outside or away from the center; as, an *outward* train; situated or done on the outside; as, an *outward* apartment; relating to, or forming, the outer surface; as, the *outward* appearance. **2. a** Of or pertaining to the physical, as distinguished from the mental or spiritual, character; *Theol.*, designating body in contrast to soul. **b** Hence, extrinsic; superficial. **3.** External to a given interest, office, or sphere of activity. — *n.* **a** That which is outward, as an outer part; external form or appearance. **b** (*Usually pl.*) The material world, regarded as external to the mind.

out′ward·ly, *adv.* **1.** On or toward the outside; externally. **2.** In regard to external or physical character or action; in respect of appearance.

out′wards (out′wẽrdz), *adv.* Outward.

out·wear′ (out·wâr′), *v. t.;* see WEAR. **1.** To wear out; hence, to destroy the value of by constant use; to exhaust; as, an *outworn* quotation. **2.** To last longer than; to outlast. **3.** To outlive or outgrow; as, *outworn* creeds.

out·weigh′ (-wā′), *v. t.* To exceed in weight or value.

out·wind′ (-wĭnd′), *v. t.* To exhaust the breath of.

out·wit′ (-wĭt′), *v. t.;* -WIT′TED; -WIT′TING. **1.** *Archaic.* To surpass in wisdom. **2.** To surpass in ingenuity or cunning; to overreach. — **Syn.** See FRUSTRATE.

out·work′ (out·wûrk′), *v. t.;* see WORK. **1.** To work out; to produce. **2.** To exceed in working; to work more than.

out′work′ (out′wûrk′), *n.* *Fort.* A minor defense beyond the main body of a work, as a ravelin, rifle pits, etc.
out′worn′ (out′wōrn′; 2; 70), *past part.* of OUTWEAR.
out·write′ (out·rīt′), *v. t.*; see WRITE. To excel in writing.
ou′zel, ou′sel (ōō′z'l), *n.* [AS. *ōsle.*] **a** The European blackbird (*Turdus merula*). **b** Any of certain other thrushes or allied birds. See RING OUZEL, WATER OUZEL.
o′va (ō′vȧ), *n., pl.* of OVUM.
o′val (ō′văl; -v'l), *adj.* [F. *oval, ovale,* fr. L. *ovum* egg.] Having the figure of an egg; popularly, elliptical or ellipsoidal. — *n.* An object of oval or ellipsoidal shape. — **o′val·ly**, *adv.* — **o′val·ness**, *n.*

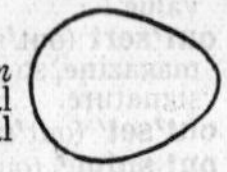

Oval.

o·var′i·ot′o·my (ō·vâr′ĭ·ŏt′ō·mĭ), *n.* [L. *ovarium* ovary + *-tomy.*] *Surg.* **a** Literally, the cutting of an ovary. **b** Loosely, but commonly, the surgical removal of one or both ovaries.
o′va·ri′tis (ō′vȧ·rī′tĭs), *n.* [NL., fr. *ovary* + *-itis.*] *Med.* Inflammation of the ovaries.
o·var′i·um (ō·vâr′ĭ·ŭm), *n.*; *pl.* -IA (-ȧ). [NL.] An ovary.
o′va·ry (ō′vȧ·rĭ), *n.*; *pl.* -RIES (-rĭz). [NL. *ovarium,* fr. L. *ovum* egg.] **1.** *Anat. & Zool.* The essential female reproductive organ; the organ in which the eggs are produced. **2.** *Bot.* In angiospermous plants, an enlarged (usually the basal) portion of the pistil or gynoecium, containing ovules. — **o·var′i·an** (ō·vâr′ĭ·ăn; 6), *adj.*
o′vate (ō′vāt), *adj.* [L. *ovatus,* fr. *ovum* egg.] **1.** Shaped like an egg; oval. **2.** *Bot.* Having the shape of the longitudinal section of an egg, with the broader end basal. See LEAF, *Illust.* (8).
o·va′tion (ō·vā′shŭn), *n.* [L. *ovatio,* fr. *ovare* to exult, rejoice, triumph in an ovation.] **1.** *Rom. Antiq.* Ceremony tendered a general who had won a victory of less importance than that for which a triumph was granted. **2.** Enthusiastic popular homage or tribute.
ov′en (ŭv′ĕn), *n.* [AS. *ofen, ofn.*] A chamber for baking, heating, or drying, esp. in a stove.
ov′en·bird′ (-bûrd′), *n.* **1.** Any of certain South American passerine birds of the genus *Furnarius,* family Furnariidae. **2.** An American warbler (*Seiurus aurocapillus*) which builds its dome-shaped nest on the ground.
o′ver (ō′vẽr), *adv.* [AS. *ofer,* adv. & prep.] **1.** Above. **2.** To the other side; across. **3.** Specif.: **a** Beyond or away from the perpendicular; as, to fall *over.* **b** So as to face oppositely. **c** From side to side; across. **d** Across the brim; as, full and running *over.* **4.** Beyond or above, or in excess of, a certain quantity or limit; as, boys of twelve years and *over.* **5.** From beginning to end; as, to look *over* accounts. **6.** Again; as, to do the work *over.* — ***over again.*** Once more; afresh; anew. — ***over against.*** Opposite to; in contrast with. — ***over and above.*** Besides; in addition. — ***over and over.*** Repeatedly; again and again.
— *prep.* **1.** Above, often in a way to cover; — opposed to *under.* **2.** Above, in authority, power, dignity, value, etc. **3.** More than or better than, in quality, degree, or measure. **4. a** Upon the surface of; throughout; as, to wander *over* the earth. **b** Along the length or course of; as, to motor *over* a new route. **c** By way of; as, *over* the air. **5.** Across; as, to leap *over* a stream. **6.** Throughout or during; as, to keep anything *over* night. **7.** During occupation with; with respect to; as, merry *over* their wine.
— *adj.* **1.** Upper; superior; also, excessive; surplus. **2.** Used predicatively: **a** Having reached the opposite side; as, the ferryboat is *over.* **b** Ended; finished. **c** *Colloq.* Having an excess; as, to find the cashier several dollars *over.*
— *n.* **1.** A thing made or given in addition to a set number; as, the *overs,* or extra impressions, of a printed job. **2.** *Cricket.* The series of balls (usually six) bowled from each wicket alternately. **3.** *Mil.* A shot which falls beyond the target.
— *v. t.* To leap over or to go over.
o′ver- (ō′vẽr-; *the accent varies according to meaning, rhythm, or sense stress and emphasis*). A combining form denoting: **1.** *Above,* in place, quality, station, etc., as in *over*look, *over*grown, *over*lord. **2.** *Across; beyond;* as in *over*sea, *over*stay, *over*leap. **3.** *Above* or *beyond in degree; to a great* or *excessive degree; too much;* as in *over*time, *over*do, *over*confident. **4.** *So as to fall* or *become inverted,* as in *over*balance, *over*throw, *over*turn.
☞ The compounds in the list beginning at the foot of this page contain *over-* in sense 3. Most of the adjectives have derivatives in *-ly* and *-ness.*
o′ver·act′ (ō′vẽr·ăkt′), *v. t.* To exaggerate in acting.
o′ver·age (ō′vẽr·ĭj), *n.* *Com.* Surplus goods.
o′ver·age′ (ō′vẽr·āj′; 2), *adj.* Beyond the normal age, or a specified age.
o′ver–all′, *adj.* Including everything.
o′ver·alls′ (ō′vẽr·ôlz′), *n. pl.* A type of loose trousers worn over others as a protection from soiling, wear, or weather.
o′ver·arm′ (ō′vẽr·ärm′), *adj.* *Cricket, etc.* Done (as bowling or pitching) with the arm raised above the shoulder.
o′ver·awe′ (ō′vẽr·ô′), *v. t.* To restrain by awe or fear.
o′ver·bal′ance (-băl′ăns), *v. t.* **1.** To outweigh. **2.** To cause to lose balance or equilibrium. — *n.* Excess of weight or value; a thing more than an equivalent.
o′ver·bear′ (ō′vẽr·bâr′), *v. t.*; see BEAR. **1.** To bear down or carry down, as by excess of weight, force, etc. **2.** To domineer over. — *v. i.* To bear fruit or offspring to excess.
o′ver·bear′ing, *adj.* Aggressively haughty or arrogant. — **Syn.** See PROUD.
o′ver·bid′ (ō′vẽr·bĭd′), *v. t. & i.*; see BID. To outbid; also, to bid too much (for). — **o′ver·bid′** (ō′vẽr·bĭd′), *n.*
o′ver·blow′ (-blō′), *v. t.*; see BLOW. **1.** To blow away, over, or down. **2.** To cover, as with snow, by blowing.
o′ver·blown′ (ō′vẽr·blōn′; 2), *adj.* Blown or blossomed to excess.
o′ver·board′ (ō′vẽr·bōrd′; 70), *adv.* [AS. *ofer bord.*] Over the side of a ship; hence, from a ship into the water.
o′ver·borne′ (ō′vẽr·bōrn′; 70), *past part.* of OVERBEAR.
o′ver·build′ (-bĭld′), *v. t.*; see BUILD. **1.** To build over. **2.** To build beyond the demand; to put too many buildings in or on. — **o′ver·built′** (ō′vẽr·bĭlt′; 2), *adj.*
o′ver·bur′den (ō′vẽr·bûr′d'n), *v. t.* To load to excess. — **o′ver·bur′·den** (ō′vẽr·bûr′d'n), *n.*
o′ver·buy′ (-bī′), *v. t. & i.*; see BUY. To buy in quantities exceeding the demand; *Exchanges,* to make purchases which are large in relation to the floating supply, esp. purchases beyond what one can provide additional margin for in case of a decline in prices. — *v. i.* To buy to excess, esp. beyond one's means.
o′ver·call′ (ō′vẽr·kôl′), *v. t.* At cards, to outbid. — **o′ver·call′** (ō′vẽr·kôl′), *n.*
o′ver·cap′i·tal·ize (-kăp′ĭ·tăl·īz; *see* CAPITALIZE), *v. t.* **1.** To put a nominal value on the capital of a corporation higher than its actual cost or its fair market value. **2.** To capitalize beyond what the business or the profit-making prospects warrant. — **o′ver·cap′i·tal·i·za′·tion** (-ĭ·zā′shŭn; -ī·zā′-), *n.*
o′ver·cast′ (-kȧst′; 9), *v. t.*; see CAST. **1.** To overspread; specif., to cloud; darken; overshadow. **2.** (*pron. usually* ō′vẽr·kȧst′) *Sewing.* To take long slanting stitches over (raw edges of a seam) to prevent raveling. — (ō′vẽr·kȧst′), *adj.* **a** Clouded over; gloomy; — of weather and moods. **b** *Sewing.* Made with overcasting.
o′ver·cast′ing (ō′vẽr·kȧs′tĭng; ō′vẽr·kȧs′tĭng), *n.* **a** Act or process of giving a rough coat of plaster to masonry. **b** *Sewing.* A slanting stitch over the edge of cloth to prevent raveling.
o′ver·cast′ stitch. *Embroidery.* A small, close stitch, sometimes over a foundation thread, used to form outlines. See STITCH, *Illust.*
o′ver·cer′ti·fy (ō′vẽr·sûr′tĭ·fī), *v. t.* *Banking.* To certify a check for an amount in excess of the balance of the deposit account of the drawer. — **o′ver·cer′ti·fi·ca′tion** (-fĭ·kā′shŭn), *n.*
o′ver·charge′ (-chärj′), *v. t. & i.*; see CHARGE. **1.** To load too heavily; burden; hence, to fill too full; crowd. **2.** To charge excessively. **3.** To exaggerate; overdraw.
o′ver·charge′ (ō′vẽr·chärj′), *n.* [Cf. SUPERCARGO, SUPERCHARGE.] **1.** An excessive burden. **2.** A charge in an account, either in excess of the agreed amount, or exorbitant.
o′ver·check′ (-chĕk′), *n., or* **overcheck rein.** A checkrein passing between the ears of a horse. — **o′ver·check′**, *adj*
o′ver·clothes′ (-klōthz′; *cf.* CLOTHES), *n. pl.* Outer garments.
o′ver·cloud′ (-kloud′), *v. t. & i.* To overspread with clouds.
o′ver·coat′ (ō′vẽr·kōt′), *n.* A coat worn over a suit, esp. in cold weather; a greatcoat; a topcoat.
o′ver·come′ (-kŭm′), *v. t.*; see COME. [AS. *ofercuman.*] **1.** To get the better of; to conquer; hence (usually in the passive), to render helpless or exhausted; as, to be *overcome* by illness. **2.** *Now Rare.* To spread or flow over. — *v. i.* To gain the superiority; to win. — **Syn.** See CONQUER. — **o′ver·com′er** (-kŭm′ẽr), *n.*
o′ver·crop′ (ō′vẽr·krŏp′), *v. t.*; see CROP. To exhaust the fertility of by excessive production.
o′ver·de·vel′op (-dē·vĕl′ŭp), *v. t.* To develop excessively; *Photog.,* to subject (a plate, film, etc.) too long to the developing process. — **o′ver·de·vel′op·ment** (-mĕnt), *n.*
o′ver·do′ (-dōō′), *v. t.*; see DO. [AS. *oferdōn.*] **1.** To do too much; to exaggerate; to carry too far. **2.** To cook too much; as, to *overdo* meat. **3.** To overtask, or overtax; as, to *overdo* one's strength. — *v. i.* To do too much.
o′ver·dose′ (ō′vẽr·dōs′), *n.* An excessive dose.
o′ver·dose′ (ō′vẽr·dōs′), *v. t.* To dose to excess.
o′ver·draft′, o′ver·draught′ (ō′vẽr·drȧft′; 9), *n.* **1.** A draft or current of air passing over a fire, kiln, etc. **2.** *Banking.* Act of overdrawing, or state of being overdrawn; also, the sum overdrawn.
o′ver·draw′ (ō′vẽr·drô′), *v. t.*; see DRAW. **1.** To draw too much or too far; hence, to exaggerate. **2.** *Banking.* To make drafts upon in excess of the proper amount, esp. in excess of the amount to the credit of the drawer.
o′ver·due′ (ō′vẽr·dū′; 2), *adj.* Delayed or unpaid beyond the proper time of arrival or payment, etc.
o′ver·dye′ (ō′vẽr·dī′), *v. t.*; see DYE. To put one color over (another).
o′ver·ex·pose′ (-ĕks·pōz′), *v. t.* *Photog.* To expose for a longer time than is needed. — **o′ver·ex·po′sure** (-ĕks·pō′zhẽr; -ĭks-), *n.*
o′ver·flow′ (ō′vẽr·flō′), *v. t.* [AS. *oferflōwan.*] **1.** To flow over; to inundate. **2.** To flow over the brim of; also, to cause to overflow. — *v. i.* **1.** To flow over the bounds, as water; hence, of a crowd, to more than fill some space. **2.** To be filled to running over; hence, to superabound.
o′ver·flow′ (ō′vẽr·flō′), *n.* **1.** A flowing over; an inundation. **2.** That which flows over; as, the *overflow* of the Nile River; a superfluous portion. **3.** An outlet or receptacle for surplus liquid.
o′ver·gar′ment (-gär′mĕnt), *n.* An outer garment.

☞ See OVER-, *Note.*

overabound	overburdensome	overconfident	overdainty	overemotional	overfastidious
overabundance	overbusy	overconscientious	overdear	overemphasize	overfat
overabundant	overcapacity	overconscious	overdecorate	overemphatic	overfatigue
overaccentuate	overcaptious	overconsciousness	overdeliberate	overenthusiastic	overfearful
overactive	overcaptiousness	overconservative	overdelicate	overestimate	overfeed
overambitious	overcareful	overconsiderate	overdemand	overestimation	overfluent
overanxious	overcareless	overcontribute	overdesirous	overexcitable	overfond
overapprehensive	overcaution	overcook	overdignified	overexcite	overfoolish
overarch	overcautious	overcool	overdiligence	overexcitement	overfrail
overassertive	overcharitable	overcorrupt	overdiligent	overexercise	overfrank
overassessment	overcheap	overcourteous	overdress	overexert	overfraught
overattentive	overchildish	overcovetous	overdrive	overexertion	overfree
overbashful	overcivil	overcredulous	overeager	overexpansion	overfreely
overboastful	overclean	overcritical	overearnest	overexpectation	overfrequency
overbold	overclever	overcrowd	overeat	overexuberant	overfrequent
overbrilliant	overcomplex	overcultivate	overeducate	overfacile	overfruitful
overbrutal	overcompliant	overcunning	overelaborate	overfamiliar	overfull
	overconfidence	overcurious	overembellish	overfanciful	overfullness

o'ver·gild' (ō'vĕr-gĭld'), v. t.; see GILD. To gild over.

o'ver·glance' (-gláns'; 9), v. t. To glance over.

o'ver·glaze' (-glāz'), v. t. To glaze over. — o'ver·glaze' (ō'vĕr-glāz'), n.

o'ver·grow' (-grō'), v. t.; see GROW. 1. To grow over; to cover with growth or herbage, esp. that which is rank. 2. To grow beyond; outgrow; as, to overgrow childish prejudices. — v. i. 1. To grow beyond the fit size. 2. To grow in too great plenty or luxuriance. — o'ver·grown' (-grōn'; 2), adj. — o'ver·growth' (ō'vĕr-grōth'), n.

o'ver·hand' (-hǎnd'), adj. 1. Down from above, as a blow. 2. Grasping with the palm downward, or inward toward the body; playing, or played, with the hand in this position; as, an overhand stroke. 3. Cricket, etc. = OVERARM, adj. 4. Sewing. Over and over; — applied to a style of sewing, or to a seam, in which two edges, usually selvages, are sewed together by passing each stitch over both.

o'ver·hand' (-hǎnd'; 2), adv. In an overhand manner.

o'ver·hand' (-hǎnd'), n. Mastery of, or style in, the execution of overhand strokes, as in tennis.

o'ver·hand' (-hǎnd'), v. t. Sewing. To sew over and over.

o'ver·hand·ed (-hǎn'dĕd; -dĭd; 2), adj. Oversupplied with workmen, or hands.

overhand knot. See KNOT, Illust. (1).

overhand stitch. A small, close stitch used to join two finished edges, as selvages.

o'ver·hang' (ō'vĕr·hǎng'), v. t.; see HANG. 1. To hang over; to jut or project over (something); esp., to hang over threateningly; to impend. 2. To adorn with hangings. — v. i. To project so as to be over something.

o'ver·hang' (ō'vĕr·hǎng'), n. 1. A projection; also, the measure of the projection. 2. Specif.: a Aeronautics. One half the difference in span of any two main supporting surfaces of an airplane. b Arch. A projection of an upper part (as a roof, upper story) of a building beyond the lower part. c Naut. The part of the bow or stern of a vessel that projects over the water beyond the water line.

o'ver·haul' (ō'vĕr·hôl'), v. t. 1. To haul or drag over; hence, to examine thoroughly, as for repair. 2. To gain upon in a chase; to overtake; — said esp. of ships; hence, in general, to overtake; to come up with. — (ō'vĕr·hôl'), n. An overhauling.

o'ver·haul'ing, n. Also o'ver·haul'. An examination with a view to repairs.

o'ver·head' (-hĕd'), adv. Above one's head; aloft; above.

o'ver·head' (ō'vĕr·hĕd'; 2), adj. 1. Operating or situated above or overhead. 2. Passing over the head. 3. Com. General, indirect, undistributed, as distinct from particular and direct; — said of business costs, etc. — (ō'vĕr·hĕd'), n. Accounting. Those general charges, collectively, in any business which cannot be charged up to any particular part of the work or product, as rent, taxes, insurance, lighting, heating, accounting and other office expenses, and depreciation.

o'ver·hear' (ō'vĕr·hēr'), v. t.; see HEAR. [AS. oferhīeran.] To hear (something uttered) beyond the intended range of the speaker's voice. — o'ver·hear'er, n.

o'ver·is'sue (ō'vĕr·ĭsh'ū; -ōō), n. An excessive issue; an issue, as of bonds, exceeding the limit of capital, credit, or authority.

o'ver·laid' (-lād'), past & past part. of OVERLAY.

o'ver·land' (ō'vĕr·lǎnd'; ō'vĕr·lǎnd'), adv. By, upon, or across land. — (-lǎnd'), adj. Going, or accomplished, over the land, instead of by sea.

o'ver·lap' (ō'vĕr·lǎp'), v. t. & i.; see LAP. To lap over; to extend over and beyond.

o'ver·lap' (ō'vĕr·lǎp'), n. Act, instance, or extent of overlapping; also, an overlapping part.

o'ver·lay' (-lā'), past & past part. of OVERLIE.

o'ver·lay' (-lā'), v. t.; see LAY. 1. To lay or spread over or across; to superimpose or cover. 2. To oppress as with a weight; to weigh down. 3. To lie over; overlie, as an infant. 4. Print. To put an overlay or overlays on.

o'ver·lay' (ō'vĕr·lā'), n. 1. Scot. A cravat. 2. A covering, esp. of a temporary sort. 3. Ornamental work formed by overlaying, as with veneer. 4. Print. A piece of material pasted on the tympan sheet to make a stronger impression.

o'ver·leap' (-lēp'), v. t.; see LEAP. 1. To leap over or across; hence, to omit; ignore. 2. To leap beyond (one's mark or aim); defeat by leaping too far.

o'ver·lie' (-lī'), v. t.; see LIE. To lie over or upon; specif., to suffocate by lying upon; as, to overlie an infant.

o'ver·live' (-lĭv'), v. t. & i. To outlive; survive.

o'ver·look' (-lŏŏk'), v. t. 1. To look over or view from a higher position; hence, to rise above; to overtop. 2. To inspect; survey. 3. To supervise; to watch over. 4. To look over and beyond (anything) without seeing it; to miss in looking; hence, to neglect; to pass over without censure or punishment. 5. To bewitch by looking on. — Syn. See NEGLECT.

o'ver·lord' (ō'vĕr·lôrd'), n. One who is lord over another.

o'ver·ly (ō'vĕr·lĭ), adv. Chiefly Scot. & U. S. Excessively.

o'ver·ly'ing (ō'vĕr·lī'ĭng), pres. part. of OVERLIE.

o'ver·man (ō'vĕr·mǎn), n. 1. An overseer or foreman. 2. An arbiter. 3. (pron. ō'vĕr·mǎn') [Trans. of G. übermensch. Cf. SUPERMAN.] A superman; — used in early translations of Nietzsche.

o'ver·man' (-mǎn'), v. t.; o'ver·manned' (-mǎnd') ; o'ver·man'ning. To have or get too many men for the needs of; as, to overman a ship.

o'ver·mas'ter (-más'tēr; 9), v. t. To overpower; subdue. — o'ver·mas'ter·ing, adj.

o'ver·match' (-mǎch'), v. t. To be more than a match for; hence, to vanquish.

o'ver·much' (ō'vĕr·mŭch'; 2), adj. Too much. — adv. In too great a degree; too much. — n. An excess; a surplus.

o'ver·night' (ō'vĕr·nīt'; 2), adv. In the fore part of the previous night; in the evening before; also, during the night.

o'ver·night' (ō'vĕr·nīt'), n. The previous evening. — adj. 1. Done or lasting during the night; also, of or relating to the previous evening. 2. Of the duration of one night; staying one night; as, overnight guests. 3. For use on short journeys; as, an overnight case.

o'ver·pass' (ō'vĕr·pás'; 9), v. t. & i. 1. To traverse; hence, to pass through; also, to overcome. 2. To pass across, over, or beyond; hence, to transgress. 3. To surpass, excel, or exceed. 4. To overlook or disregard.

o'ver·pass' (ō'vĕr·pás'; 9), n. A bridge, road, or culvert for highway traffic above a railway, canal, or other road. Cf. UNDERPASS, GRADE CROSSING.

o'ver·per·suade' (-pẽr·swād'), v. t.; see PERSUADE. To persuade to adopt one's side or view. — o'ver·per·sua'sion (-swā'zhŭn), n.

o'ver·play' (-plā'), v. t. 1. To surpass in playing. 2. Golf. To strike (the ball) beyond the putting green.

o'ver·plus (ō'vĕr·plŭs), n. [over + L. plus.] A surplus.

o'ver·pow'er (-pou'ĕr), v. t. 1. To excel or exceed in power; to vanquish; subdue. 2. To affect intensely or overwhelmingly. 3. To supply with more power than is needed.

o'ver·pow'er·ing, adj. That overpowers. — o'ver·pow'er·ing·ly, adv.

o'ver·print' (ō'vĕr·prĭnt'), v. t. Print. To impress, as a printed surface, with other print.

o'ver·print' (ō'vĕr·prĭnt'), n. 1. Anything overprinted. 2. Philately. Any word, denomination, or device, printed across the surface of a stamp, altering its value, use, etc.

o'ver·prize' (-prīz'), v. t. To prize excessively; overvalue.

o'ver·pro·duc'tion (ō'vĕr·prō·dŭk'shŭn), n. Excessive production; supply beyond the demand at remunerative prices.

o'ver·proof' (-proof'; 2), adj. Containing more alcohol than proof spirit (which see).

o'ver·pro·por'tion (ō'vĕr·prō·pōr'shŭn; 70), n. Proportion in excess of the norm. — v. t. To make of too great proportion. — o'ver·pro·por'tion·ate (-ĭt), adj. — o'ver·pro·por'tion·ate·ly, adv. — o'ver·pro·por'tioned (-shŭnd), adj.

o'ver·rate' (ō'vĕr·rāt'), v. t. To rate, or estimate, too highly.

o'ver·reach' (-rēch'), v. t. 1. To reach above or beyond; also, to spread over. 2. Now Dial. To overtake. 3. a To miss by reaching too far. b To strain (oneself) or defeat (one's purposes) by overdoing. 4. To get the better of, esp. by artifice or cunning; to outwit; cheat. — Syn. See CHEAT. — v. i. 1. To reach too far. 2. To cheat. 3. To strike the toe of the hind foot against the heel or quarter of the forefoot; — said of horses.

o'ver·ride' (-rīd'), v. t.; see RIDE. [AS. oferrīdan.] 1. To ride over or across; to ride upon; to trample down. 2. To ride too much, as a horse. 3. To set aside; annul; as, to override a veto; also, to disregard the wishes of; to domineer over. 4. To pass over; esp., chiefly Med., to overlap; as, to override of the ends of a fractured bone.

o'ver·rule' (-rool'; 114), v. t. a To rule or determine in a contrary way; to decide against. b To reverse a previous decision or ruling; as, the appellate court overruled the action of the trial judge. 2. To prevail over; to overcome. — o'ver·rul'ing (-rool'ĭng), adj. — o'ver·rul'ing·ly, adv.

o'ver·run' (-rŭn'), v. t.; see RUN. 1. To run over; as: a To run across or athwart. b To run over as a fluid or as a rapid growth; to overspread. 2. Hence: a To run over harmfully; either, to trample or bear down; or, to grow or spread over in excess; to infest; also, to run over as a hostile army; to ravage. b Obs. To crush; destroy. 3. To pass over rapidly, esp. in thought or speech. 4. To exceed or excel in running. 5. To go, extend, or lie beyond. 6. Print. To readjust, as lines, columns, or pages, by shifting letters or words from one line into another. — v. i. To run, pass, spread, or flow over or by something; to be in excess.

o'ver·run' (ō'vĕr·rŭn'), n. Act or instance of overrunning; also, amount by which something overruns.

o'ver·sea' (ō'vĕr·sē'; 2), adv. & adj. Over the sea; foreign.

o'ver·seas' (-sēz'; 2), adv. & adj. Oversea.

o'ver·see' (ō'vĕr·sē'), v. t.; see SEE. [AS. ofersēon to survey, despise.] 1. To survey; watch. 2. To inspect; examine; also, to superintend; supervise.

o'ver·se'er (ō'vĕr·sē'ĕr), n. 1. One who oversees; a superintendent; supervisor. 2. In England, a parish administrative officer (called in full **overseer of the poor.**

---

o′ver·sell′ (ō′vẽr·sĕl′), *v. t.;* see SELL. **1.** *Com.* To sell more than can be advantageously purchased. **2.** *Brokers' Cant.* To sell beyond means of delivery, or, sometimes, beyond what one can margin in case of an advance in prices.

o′ver·set′ (-sĕt′), *v. t.;* see SET. **1.** To overcome mentally or physically; upset. **2.** To tip over; upset. **3.** To cause to fall, or to fail; as, to *overset* a plot. **4.** *Print.* To set too much type for, or to set too wide; as, to *overset* a line. — *v. i.* To turn over; to upset.

o′ver·set′ (ō′vẽr·sĕt′), *n.* An upsetting; overturn.

o′ver·sew′; (ō′vẽr·sō′; ō′vẽr·sō′), *v. t.;* see SEW. To sew over and over; to overhand.

o′ver·shade′ (ō′vẽr·shād′), *v. t. & i.* To overshadow.

o′ver·shad′ow (-shăd′ō), *v. t.* **1.** To throw a shadow, or shade, over; to darken; obscure. **2.** Figuratively, to tower above as if to cast a shadow over; to dominate; to be more important than.

o′ver·shine′ (-shīn′), *v. t.;* see SHINE. To shine over or upon; illumine; also, to excel in shining; outshine.

o′ver·shoe′ (ō′vẽr·shōō′), *n.* A shoe that is worn over another for protection from wet or cold; esp., a rubber shoe.

o′ver·shoot′ (-shōōt′), *v. t.;* see SHOOT. **1.** To pass swiftly beyond. **2.** **a** To shoot over or beyond; to miss by shooting too far or too high. **b** Hence, to excel in shooting. — *v. i.* To fly or shoot above or beyond the mark.

o′ver·shot′ (ō′vẽr·shŏt′; 2), *adj.* **1.** Of the mouth or jaw, having the upper jaw extending beyond the lower, as in some dogs. **2.** Actuated by water shooting over from above; as, an *overshot* (water) wheel. Cf. UNDERSHOT, 2.

o′ver·sight′ (ō′vẽr·sīt′), *n.* **1.** Watchful care or supervision. **2.** An overlooking or something overlooked; omission or error due to inadvertence.

o′ver·size′ (ō′vẽr·sīz′), *n.* A size larger than the nominal or normal size, as of a book, a shoe, or a tire. — **o′ver·sized′** (-sīzd′; 2), *adj.*

o′ver·skirt′ (-skûrt′), *n.* An upper skirt.

o′ver·slaugh′ (ō′vẽr·slô′), *n.* [D. *overslag.*] *Military, England.* Exemption from a duty because detailed on a superior duty.

o′ver·slaugh′ (ō′vẽr·slô′), *v. t.* [D. *overslaan.*] *U.S.* To pass over, as for an appointment, in favor of another.

o′ver·sleep′ (ō′vẽr·slēp′), *v. i.;* see SLEEP. To sleep beyond the time for waking.

o′ver·slip′ (-slĭp′), *v. t.;* see SLIP. **1.** To slip or slide over; omit; neglect. **2.** To slip away from, past, or by.

o′ver·soul′ (ō′vẽr·sōl′), *n.* According to the New England transcendentalists, the absolute reality, conceived as a spiritual being in which the ideal nature is perfectly realized.

o′ver·spend′ (-spĕnd′), *v. t.;* see SPEND. **1.** To spend or use to excess; to exhaust. **2.** To spend more than; also, to spend extravagantly. — *v. i.* To spend beyond one's means.

o′ver·spread′ (-sprĕd′), *v. t. & i.;* see SPREAD. To spread over or above; to extend over.

o′ver·state′ (-stāt′), *v. t.* To state in too strong terms; to exaggerate. — **o′ver·state′ment** (-mĕnt), *n.*

o′ver·stay′ (-stā′), *v. t.* **1.** To stay beyond the time or the limits of. **2.** *Colloq., Com.* To carry a transaction in (a market) beyond the point of greatest profit.

o′ver·step′ (-stĕp′), *v. t. & i.;* see STEP. To step over or beyond; to transgress; as, to *overstep* the bounds of good taste.

o′ver·stride′ (-strīd′), *v. t.;* see STRIDE. To stride over, across, or beyond; hence, to exceed; surpass.

o′ver·strung′ (ō′vẽr·strŭng′; 2), *adj.* Too highly strung; too sensitive; as, *overstrung* nerves.

o′ver·stuff′ (-stŭf′), *v. t.* **a** To stuff to excess. **b** *Furniture.* To cover completely and deeply with upholstery.

o′ver·sub·scribe′ (-sŭb·skrīb′), *v. t. & i.* To subscribe for more (of) than is offered for sale; as, to *oversubscribe* an issue of bonds. — **o′ver·sub·scrip′tion** (-skrĭp′shŭn), *n.*

o′ver·sup·ply′ (-sŭ·plī′), *v. t.;* see SUPPLY. To supply in excess. — *n.* An excess supply.

o′vert (ō′vûrt), *adj.* [OF. *overt,* past part. of *ovrir* to open.] Open to view; public; apparent; manifest.

o′ver·take′ (ō′vẽr·tāk′), *v. t.;* see TAKE. **1.** To come or catch up with in a course or motion. **2.** To catch up with in the course of a task or game, or in a press of business. **3.** To come upon suddenly; as, *overtaken* by disaster.

o′ver–the–count′er, *adj.* Of stocks, bonds, etc., sold in any other way than through the market of an exchange.

o′ver·throw′ (ō′vẽr·thrō′), *v. t.;* see THROW. **1.** To overturn; upset. **2.** To cause to fall or to fail; subvert; defeat. **3.** To bring to disorder; to derange. — **Syn.** See CONQUER.

o′ver·throw′ (ō′vẽr·thrō′), *n.* Act of overthrowing, or state of being overthrown; defeat; ruin; subversion.

o′ver·time′ (-tīm′), *n.* Time beyond, or in excess of, a set limit; esp., extra working time. — (-tīm′; 2), *adv. & adj.* During, at, or for overtime.

o′ver·time′ (-tīm′), *v. t.* To exceed the proper limit in timing; as, to *overtime* a photographic exposure.

o′vert·ly (ō′vûrt·lĭ), *adv.* Publicly; openly.

o′ver·tone′ (ō′vẽr·tōn′), *n.* [After G. *oberton.*] **1.** *Music & Acoustics.* One of the higher tones, or upper partials, which, with the fundamental, make up a complex musical tone. **2.** The color of the light reflected, as by a paint film. Cf. UNDERTONE, 2 **b.** **3.** *Chiefly pl.* Richness of suggestion, associations, and connotation; — used esp. of language.

o′ver·top′ (-tŏp′), *v. t.;* see TOP. **1.** To rise above the top of; to tower above. **2.** To transcend; surpass.

o′ver·trade′ (-trād′), *v. i.* To trade beyond one's capital; to buy goods beyond the means of paying for or selling them.

o′ver·trick′ (ō′vẽr·trĭk′), *n.* *Card Games.* A trick won in excess of the number bid or needed to win the game.

o′ver·trump′ (-trŭmp′), *v. t. & i.* *Card Games.* To outdo in trumping by playing a higher trump.

o′ver·ture (ō′vẽr·tūr), *n.* [OF. (F. *ouverture*), fr. L. *apertura.* See OVERT.] **1.** A proposal; a proposition formally submitted, as of peace. **2.** In American Presbyterian churches, the submission of a question of doctrine or polity by the highest court to the presbyteries for their judgment on it before formal determination by the court; also, the question thus submitted. **3.** *Music.* An orchestral composition introductory to an oratorio, opera, etc. — *v. t.* To put forward as an overture; also, to introduce with an overture.

o′ver·turn′ (ō′vẽr·tûrn′), *v. t.* **1.** To turn over; upset. **2.** To subvert; overthrow; as, to *overturn* a ministry. — *v. i.* To turn over; esp., to upset or capsize.

o′ver·turn′ (ō′vẽr·tûrn′), *n.* **1.** Act of overturning. **2.** A reversal; also, a turning over, as of goods in trade.

o′ver·watch′ (-wŏch′), *v. t.* **1.** To weary or exhaust by watching. **2.** To watch over.

o′ver·wear′ (ō′vẽr·wâr′), *v. t.;* see WEAR. **1.** To wear out; to use up or exhaust by wearing. **2.** To outwear or outgrow.

o′ver·wea′ry (ō′vẽr·wẽr′ĭ; *see* OVER-), *adj.* Wearied to excess. — *v. t.;* see WEARY. To weary too much.

o′ver·ween′ (-wēn′), *v. i.* To think too highly or arrogantly; hence, to be egotistic, arrogant, or rash, in opinion.

o′ver·ween′ing (-wēn′ĭng), *n.* Excessive self-importance. — *adj.* Unduly confident; arrogant; also, of an opinion, purpose, etc., too pretentious; exaggerated. — **o′ver·ween′ing·ly,** *adv.*

o′ver·weigh′ (-wā′), *v. t.* To exceed in weight; to overbalance; hence, to weigh down; to oppress.

o′ver·weight′ (ō′vẽr·wāt′), *n.* Weight over and above what is required; also, excessive or burdensome weight. — *adj.* Exceeding normal or proper weight.

o′ver·whelm′ (-hwĕlm′), *v. t.* **1.** To overturn, upset, or overthrow. **2.** To cover over completely, as by a great wave; to submerge; hence, to overpower; crush.

o′ver·whelm′ing, *adj.* That overwhelms. — **o′ver·whelm′ing·ly,** *adv.*

o′ver·wind′ (ō′vẽr·wīnd′), *v. t.;* see WIND. **1.** To wind too tightly or too far, as a spring. **2.** *Elec.* To wind (a magnet, as in a series motor) so that magnetic saturation requires less than normal current.

o′ver·word′ (ō′vẽr·wûrd′), *n.* A repeated word; refrain.

o′ver·work′ (-wûrk′), *v. t.;* see WORK. **1.** To decorate all over; — only in *past part.* **2.** **a** To cause to labor too much or too long. **b** To work upon the mind or feelings of to excess, or so as to excite or confuse. **3.** To overdo or overelaborate. **4.** To fill too full of work. — *v. i.* To work too much; to overdo.

o′ver·work′ (ō′vẽr·wûrk′), *n.* **a** Excessively severe work. **b** (*pron.* ō′vẽr·wûrk′) Work in excess of the usual or stipulated time or quantity; extra work.

o′ver·wrought′ (ō′vẽr·rôt′; 2), *past & past part.* of OVERWORK. Hence: *adj.* **a** Wrought upon excessively; overexcited. **b** Worked to excess. **c** Elaborated to excess.

o′vi- (ō′vĭ-). [L. *ovum.*] A combining form meaning *egg,* as in **o·vif′er·ous,** serving to hold or carry eggs.

o′vi·bos (ō′vĭ·bŏs), *n.* [NL., fr. L. *ovis* sheep + *bos* ox.] = MUSK OX.

o′vi·duct (ō′vĭ·dŭkt), *n.* [See OVUM; DUCT.] *Anat. & Zool.* A tube or duct serving for the passage of the eggs out from the ovary.

o′vi·form (-fôrm), *adj.* [*ovi-* + *-form.*] Egg-shaped.

o′vine (ō′vīn; -vĭn), *adj.* [LL. *ovinus,* fr. *ovis* sheep.] Designating, or pertaining to, sheep; sheeplike.

o·vip′a·ra (ō·vĭp′ȧ·rȧ), *n. pl.* [NL.] Oviparous animals.

o·vip′a·rous (-rŭs), *adj.* [L. *oviparus,* fr. *ovum* egg + *parere* to bring forth.] *Zool.* Producing eggs that hatch after exclusion from the body; also, designating this form of reproduction; — contrasted with *viviparous.* — **o′vi·par′i·ty** (ō′vĭ·păr′ĭ·tĭ), *n.*

o′vi·pos′it (ō′vĭ·pŏz′ĭt), *v. i.* [See OVUM; POSIT.] To lay eggs; — esp. of insects. — **o′vi·po·si′tion** (-pō·zĭsh′ŭn), *n.*

o′vi·pos′i·tor (-pŏz′ĭ·tẽr), *n.* [*ovi-* + L. *positor* a placer, fr. *ponere* to place.] *Zool.* A specialized organ, as of insects, for depositing eggs.

o′vi·sac (ō′vĭ·săk), *n.* **a** *Zool.* An egg case, or oötheca. **b** *Anat.* A Graafian follicle.

o′void (ō′void), *adj.* [L. *ovum* egg + *-oid.*] Egglike; egg-shaped. — *n.* An ovoid body.

o′vo·lo (ō′vō·lō), *n.; pl.* OVOLI (-lē). [It., fr. L. *ovum* an egg.] A rounded, convex molding. See MOLDING, *Illust.*

o′vo·vi·vip′a·rous (ō′vō·vī·vĭp′ȧ·rŭs), *adj.* [See OVUM; VIVIPAROUS.] *Zool.* Producing eggs that have a well-developed shell as in oviparous animals, but which hatch within the body of the parent, as in the case of many reptiles and elasmobranch fishes. — **o′vo·vi·vip′a·rous·ly,** *adv.* — **o′vo·vi·vip′a·rous·ness,** *n.*

o′vu·lar (ō′vū·lẽr), *adj.* Also **o′vu·lar′y** (-lẽr′ĭ *or, esp. Brit.,* -lẽr·ĭ). *Bot. & Zool.* Pertaining to, or of the nature of, an ovule.

o′vu·late (ō′vū·lāt), *v. i.* *Biol.* To produce eggs, or discharge them from an ovary. — **o′vu·la′tion** (-lā′shŭn), *n.*

o′vule (ō′vūl), *n.* [F., dim. fr. L. *ovum* egg.] **1.** *Bot.* The megasporangium of a seed plant; popularly, an immature seed. See FLOWER, *Illust.* **2.** A small egg; an egg in an early stage of growth.

☞ See OVER-, *Note.*	oversimplicity	overstimulate	oversufficient	overtechnical	overuse
oversensitive	oversimplify	overstimulation	oversure	overtedious	overvaluation
oversentimental	overskeptical	overstock	oversusceptible	overtenacious	overvalue
overserious	overslow	overstrain	oversuspicious	overtender	overvehement
overservile	oversolemn	overstress	oversweet	overthrifty	overventilate
oversevere	oversolicitous	overstretch	oversystematic	overthrust	overventuresome
overseverity	oversophisticated	overstrict	oversystematize	overtimid	overventurous
oversharp	overspecialize	overstrident	overtalkative	overtimorous	overwealthy
overshort	overspeculate	overstudious	overtame	overtire	overwet
overshorten	overspeculation	overstudy	overtask	overtrain	overwide
oversilent	oversqueamish	oversubtle	overtax	overtrustful	overwise
oversimple	overstiff	oversubtlety	overtaxation	overunionized	overzealous

o'vum (ō'vŭm), *n.; pl.* OVA (ō'vȧ). [L., egg.] *Biol.* A female germ cell; an egg cell, or egg, in the biological sense of that word.

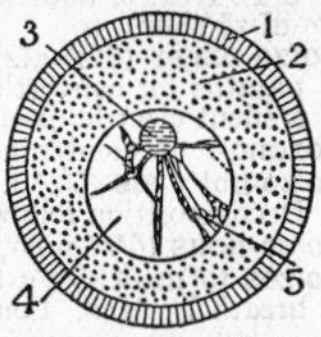

Ovum of a Sea Urchin, greatly magnified. 1 Cell Wall; 2 Cytoplasm; 3 Nucleolus; 4 Nucleus; 5 Chromatin.

owe (ō), *v. t.;* OWED (ōd), formerly OUGHT (ôt); OW'ING. [ME. *owen, awan, aghen,* to have, own, have (to do), hence, owe, fr. AS. *āgan* to have.] **1.** *Obs.* To own; possess. **2.** To have or bear (a feeling, involving a certain type of conduct); as, to *owe* a grudge. **3.** To be under an obligation to render (something) in return for something received; to be indebted in the sum of. **4.** To have an obligation to (someone) on account of something done or received; to be indebted to. **5.** To have or possess, as something derived or bestowed; as, he *owed* his wealth to his father. — *v. i.* To be in debt.

ow'ing (ō'ĭng), *adj.* [Used in a passive sense for *owed.* See OWE.] **1. a** *Rare.* Indebted; beholden. **b** Due to be paid; owed. **2.** Had or experienced as a result, issue, etc.

owl (oul), *n.* [AS. *ūle.*] Any member of a group, now usually considered as constituting a separate order (Strigiformes) of birds of prey distinguished by their large head and eyes, short, hooked bill, strong talons and more or less nocturnal habits. Cf. RAPTORIAL, *Illust.* Among North American owls are the ***barn owl*** (*Tyto alba pratincola*), the ***great horned owl*** (*Bubo virginianus*), the ***screech owl*** (*Otus,* esp. *O. asio* of the East), and the ***snowy owl*** (*Nyctea nyctea*) of the arctic regions.

owl'et (-ĕt; -ĭt), *n.* [Dim. of *owl.*] **a** A European owl (*Athene noctua*). **b** A young or small owl.

owl'ish, *adj.* Resembling, or characteristic of, an owl.

owl's'–clo'ver, *n.* A Californian herb (genus *Orthocarpus,* esp. *O. erianthus*) of the figwort family.

own (ōn), *adj.* [ME. *owen, awan,* fr. AS. *āgen,* past part. of *āgan* to possess. See OWE.] Belonging to oneself or itself; — often following a possessive adjective or pronoun.

own, *v. t.* [ME. *ohnien, ahnien,* fr. AS. *āgnian,* fr. *āgen* own, adj. See OWN, *adj.*] **1.** To possess; to have or hold as property. **2.** To acknowledge; admit; as, to *own* a fault, a debt. — *v. i.* To confess; — with *to.* — **Syn.** See HAVE: ACKNOWLEDGE.

own'er (ōn'ẽr), *n.* One who owns; a proprietor.

own'er·ship (ōn'ẽr·shĭp), *n.* State, relation, or fact of being an owner; lawful claim or title; proprietorship.

owse (ous), **ow'sen** (ou'sĕn; -zĕn). Scot. var. of OX, OXEN.

ox (ŏks), *n.; pl.* OXEN (ŏk'sĕn; -s'n), *rarely* OX. [AS. *oxa.*] **1.** The domestic bovine quadruped (*Bos taurus*), esp. an adult castrated male; a steer. **2.** Any bovine quadruped.

oxa-. *Chem.* A combining form denoting the *presence of oxygen replacing carbon, esp. in a ring.*

ox'a·late (ŏk'sȧ·lāt), *n.* [F.] *Chem.* A salt or ester of oxalic acid.

ox·al'ic (ŏks·ăl'ĭk), *adj.* [F. *oxalique,* fr. L. *oxalis.* See OXALIS.] *Chem.* Pertaining to or designating an acid (**oxalic acid**), $C_2H_2O_4$, or $(COOH)_2$, existing in oxalis as acid potassium oxalate, and in many plant tissues as calcium oxalate. It is used in dyeing, calico printing, etc.

ox'a·lis (ŏk'sȧ·lĭs), *n.* [L., a kind of sorrel, fr. Gr. *oxalis,* fr. *oxys* sharp, acid.] = WOOD SORREL **a.**

ox'a·zine (ŏk'sȧ·zēn; -zĭn), *n.* Also **ox'a·zin.** [*oxygen* + *azine.*] *Chem.* Any of several parent compounds, C_4H_5NO, containing a ring of four carbon atoms, one oxygen atom and one nitrogen atom.

ox'bow' (ŏks'bō'), *n.* **1.** A U-shaped frame, embracing an ox's neck as a kind of collar. **2.** Anything shaped like an oxbow; specif., *Phys. Geog.,* a river bend such that only a neck of land is left between two parts of the stream.

ox'eye' (ŏks'ī'), *n.* [*ox* + *eye.*] Any of several composite plants having heads with a conspicuous disk and marginal rays, as the oxeye daisy.

oxeye daisy. See DAISY, 2.

Ox'ford (ŏks'fẽrd), *n.* Also **Oxford shoe** *or* **tie.** A low shoe laced or tied over the instep, — named from Oxford, Eng.

Oxford Down. A large hornless sheep of a breed developed by crossing Cotswolds and Hampshire Downs.

Oxford gray. A neutral gray of medium brilliance.

Oxford Group movement. A religious movement or cult, founded 1921 at Oxford, Eng., by Frank Buchman, which professes a return to primitive Christianity, stressing the confession of sin.

Oxford movement. See TRACTARIANISM.

ox'heart' (ŏks'härt'), *n. Hort.* Any of certain varieties of the sweet cherry (*Prunus avium*). See CHERRY, 1.

ox'i·dase (ŏk'sĭ·dās; -dāz), *n.* [*oxidation* + *-ase.*] *Biochem.* Any of a group of enzymes that promote the oxidation of various substances.

ox'i·date (ŏk'sĭ·dāt), *v. t. & i.* To oxidize. — **ox'i·da'tion** (-dā'shŭn), *n.* — **ox'i·da'tive** (-dā'tĭv), *adj.*

ox'ide (ŏk'sīd; -sĭd), *n.* Also **ox'id.** [F. *oxide, oxyde,* fr. *oxygène* oxygen + *acide* acid.] *Chem.* A binary compound of oxygen with an element or radical.

☞ In Lavoisier's nomenclature, *oxides* included all compounds of *oxygen* which had no acid properties, as contrasted with the acids.

ox'i·dize (ŏk'sĭ·dīz), *v. t. Chem.* **a** To combine with oxygen. **b** To deprive (a compound) of hydrogen, as by the action of oxygen. **c** By extension, to change (a compound) by increasing the proportion of the electronegative part, or to change (an element) from a lower to a higher positive valence. — *v. i. Chem.* To become oxidized. — **ox'i·diz'a·ble** (-dīz'ȧ·b'l), *adj.* — **ox'i·diz'er,** *n.*

ox'ime (ŏk'sēm; -sĭm), *n.* Also **ox'im.** [*oxygen* + *imide.*] *Chem.* Any of a series of compounds obtained chiefly by the action of hydroxylamine on aldehydes and ketones, in which the oxygen of the carbonyl group is replaced by the group :NOH (the **oxime group**).

ox'lip' (ŏks'lĭp'), *n.* [AS. *oxanslyppe.* See OX; cf. COWSLIP.] **a** Orig., a hybrid primrose. **b** A Eurasian primula (*Primula elatior*) differing from the cowslip *P. veris* chiefly in the flat corolla limb; — called also *polyanthus.*

Ox·o'ni·an (ŏks·ō'nĭ·ăn), *adj.* [ML. *Oxonia* Oxford.] Of or pertaining to the city of Oxford or the university of Oxford, England. — *n.* A native or resident of Oxford; usually, a student or a graduate of Oxford University.

ox'tail' (ŏks'tāl'), *n.* The tail of an ox, esp. the skinned tail, used for soup. — **ox'tail',** *adj.*

ox'ter (ŏk'stẽr), *n.* [AS. *ōhsta.*] *Scot. & Dial.* The armpit. — *v. t. & i. Scot. & Dial.* To hold up with the arm or under the arms.

ox'tongue' (ŏks'tŭng'), *n.* Any of several plants having rough, tongue-shaped leaves, as the bugloss.

ox'y- (ŏk'sĭ-). [Gr. *oxys.*] A combining form meaning *sharp, keen, acid, shrill, quick.* Specif., *acid,* as in *oxygen.*

ox'y-. [From OXYGEN.] A prefix denoting: **a** *Presence* or *addition of oxygen;* specif., in organic chemistry, *an oxygen atom united to two different atoms,* as in **ox'y·di'a·ce'tic ac'id,** $O(CH_2CO_2H)_2$. **b** *The presence of the hydroxyl group* (in this sense more properly *hydroxy-*), as in **ox'y·al'de·hyde,** a hydroxy derivative of an aldehyde.

ox'y·a·cet'y·lene (-ȧ·sĕt'ĭ·lēn), *adj.* Of, pertaining to, or consisting of a mixture of oxygen and acetylene.

oxyacetylene blowpipe *or* **torch.** A welding blowpipe using oxygen and acetylene.

ox'y·ac'id (ŏk'sĭ·ăs'ĭd), *n.* See OXYGEN ACID.

ox'y·cal'ci·um (ŏk'sĭ·kăl'sĭ·ŭm), *adj.* Of or pertaining to oxygen and calcium; as, the *oxycalcium* light or limelight.

ox'y·gen (ŏk'sĭ·jĕn), *n.* [F. *oxygène,* fr. Gr. *oxys* sharp, acid + root of *gignesthai* to be born. So called by Lavoisier because supposed by him to be an essential part of every *acid.*] *Chem.* An element occurring free as a colorless, tasteless, odorless gas (ordinary oxygen) in the atmosphere, of which it forms about 23 per cent by weight and about 21 per cent by volume, being slightly heavier than nitrogen. Symbol, *O;* at. no., 8; at. wt., 16.0000. Oxygen is the most abundant of all the elements on the earth's surface, for it forms, in combination, eight ninths by weight of water and nearly one half by weight of the rocks composing the earth's crust. It is also a constituent of a large proportion of organic compounds. It is indispensable in respiration.

oxygen acid. Also **ox'y·ac'id** (ŏk'sĭ·ăs'ĭd). *Chem.* An acid containing oxygen, as chloric acid, sulfuric acid.

ox'y·gen·ate (ŏk'sĭ·jĕn·āt), *v. t. Chem.* To impregnate or combine with oxygen; to oxidize. — **ox'y·gen·a'tion** (-ā'shŭn), *n.*

ox'y·gen–hy'dro·gen weld'ing. Gas welding with oxygen and hydrogen, producing heat estimated at over 5,000° F.

ox'y·gen·ize (ŏk'sĭ·jĕn·īz), *v. t.* To oxidize; to oxygenate.

ox'y·he'mo·glo'bin, ox'y·hae'mo- (ŏk'sĭ·hē'mō·glō'bĭn; -hĕm'ō-), *n.* [2d *oxy-* + *hemoglobin.*] See HEMOGLOBIN.

ox'y·hy'dro·gen (ŏk'sĭ·hī'drō·jĕn), *adj. Chem.* Of, pertaining to, or consisting of a mixture of oxygen and hydrogen. — *n.* Oxyhydrogen gas.

oxyhydrogen blowpipe *or* **torch.** A welding blowpipe using oxygen and hydrogen.

ox'y·mo'ron (ŏk'sĭ·mō'rŏn; 70), *n.; pl.* -RA (-rȧ). [NL., fr. Gr. *oxymōron,* deriv. of *oxys* sharp + *mōros* foolish.] *Rhet.* A combination for epigrammatic effect of contradictory or incongruous words (*cruel kindness*).

ox'y·salt' (ŏk'sĭ·sôlt'), *n.* [2d *oxy-* + *salt.*] *Chem.* A salt of an oxyacid (oxygen acid), as a sulfate.

ox'y·sul'fide (-sŭl'fīd; -fĭd), *n.* Also **-fid, -phide, -phid.** *Chem.* A compound of oxygen and sulfur with an element or radical. Oxysulfides may be regarded as sulfides in which part of the sulfur is replaced by oxygen.

ox'y·to'cic (-tō'sĭk; -tŏs'ĭk), *adj.* [1st *oxy-* + Gr. *tokos* birth.] *Med.* **a** Pertaining to or designating the hastening of parturition. **b** Loosely, stimulating any nonstriated muscle.

ox'y·tone (ŏk'sĭ·tōn), *adj.* [Gr. *oxytonos,* fr. *oxys* sharp + *tonos* tone.] *Gram.* Having an acute accent on the last syllable. — *n. Gram.* An oxytone word.

oy, oye, oe (oi), *n. Scot.* A grandchild.

o'yer (ō'yẽr; oi'ẽr), *n.* [AF., a hearing, infin. as n., fr. OF. *oïr* to hear, fr. L. *audire.*] *Law.* **a** Short for OYER AND TERMINER. **b** *Common Law. Pleading.* A hearing or an inspection in open court which a party might demand of any instrument of which the opposite party was bound to make profert; also, the demand for this.

oyer and terminer. Literally, to hear and determine; hence, a hearing and determining; — used in England in commissions to judges of assize, and in the U. S. in designations of various superior courts of similar jurisdiction.

o'yez' (ō'yĕs'), *interj.* Also **o'yes'.** [AF. *oyez* hear ye. See OYER.] Hear; attend; — a cry used by criers of courts to secure silence before a proclamation. — **o'yez',** *n.*

oys'ter (ois'tẽr), *n.* [OF. *oistre,* fr. L. *ostrea, ostreum,* fr. Gr. *ostreon.*] **1.** Any of a genus (*Ostrea*) or family (Ostreidae) of marine bivalve mollusks. The American oyster (*O. virginica*) of the Atlantic and Gulf coasts, the European oyster (*O. edulis*), and the native species (*O. lurida*) of the Pacific coast of North America, are esteemed as food. **2.** Any of various other bivalve mollusks more or less resembling the true oyster, as the ***pearl oysters*** (genera *Avicula* and *Pinctada*). **3.** The piece of meat contained in a concavity of the pelvic bone on each side of the lower part of the back of a fowl, turkey, etc. **4.** *Slang.* An extremely taciturn person.

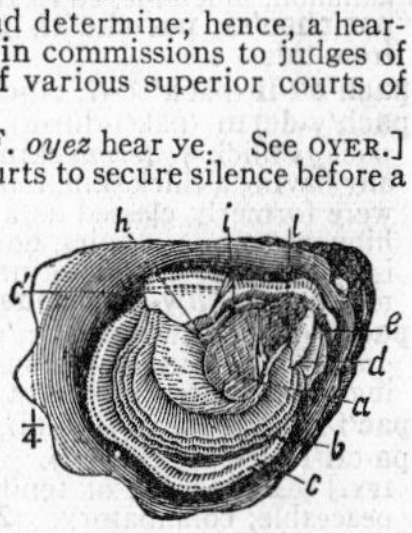

Oyster (cut away). *a* Muscle; *b* Gills; *c c'* Mantle; *d* Palpi; *e* Mouth; *h* Anus; *i* Intestine; *l* Liver.

oyster bed. A place where oysters grow or are cultivated.

oyster catcher. Any of a genus (*Haematopus*) of wading birds, from 16 to 20 inches long, with stout legs and heavy wedge-shaped bill. The plumage of the common species of the American Atlantic coast (*H. palliatus*) is chiefly black and white.

oyster crab. A crab (*Pinnotheres ostreum*) which lives as a commensal in the gill cavity of the oyster.

oyster cracker. A small salted cracker for serving with oyster stew, soups, etc.

oys'ter·man (ois'tẽr·măn), *n.; pl.* -MEN (-mĕn). **a** A gatherer, breeder, or seller of oysters. **b** A vessel used for gathering oysters.

oyster plant. a Salsify. **b** The sea lungwort.

oyster rake. A long-handled rake, usually with curved teeth, for gathering oysters in water of moderate depth.

oys'ter·root' (ois'tẽr·rōōt'; 85), *n.* Salsify.

oys'ter·wom'an (-wŏŏm'ăn), *n.* A woman who sells oysters.

ozo-. 1. A combining form, Greek *ozo-,* from *ozein,* to smell, meaning *a bad smell,* as in *ozocerite.* **2.** *Chem.* = OZONO-.

o·zo'ce·rite (ō·zō'kē·rīt; -sē·rīt; ō'zō·sē'rīt), *n.* [Gr. *ozein* to smell +

kēros wax.] A waxlike mineral, colorless or white when pure. It is a mixture of hydrocarbons and is used in making candles, etc.

o'zone (ō'zōn; ō·zōn'), *n.* [Gr. *ozein* to smell.] **1.** *Chem.* A faintly blue, gaseous, allotropic form of oxygen, obtained (usually much diluted) by the silent discharge of electricity in ordinary oxygen or in air, and by other methods; — so called from its peculiar odor, which recalls that of weak chlorine. Ozone is used commercially for sterilizing water, purifying air, bleaching, etc. **2.** *Colloq.* Hence, pure and refreshing air. — **o·zon'ic** (ō·zŏn'ĭk; ō·zō'nĭk), *adj.*

o·zon'ic e'ther. A solution of hydrogen peroxide in ether.

o'zo·nide (ō'zō·nīd), *n.* Also **o'zo·nid** (-nĭd). *Chem.* A compound of ozone.

o'zo·nize (ō'zō·nīz), *v. t.* *Chem.* **a** To convert into ozone, as oxygen. **b** To treat or impregnate with ozone. — **o'zo·ni·za'tion** (-nĭ·zā'shŭn; -nī·zā'shŭn), *n.*

o'zo·niz'er (ō'zō·nīz'ẽr), *n.* *Chem.* One that ozonizes; esp., an apparatus for converting ordinary oxygen into ozone, usually by passing a silent electric discharge through a current of oxygen or air.

ozono-. A combining form for *ozone.*

o'zo·nol'y·sis (ō'zō·nŏl'ĭ·sĭs), *n.* [NL., fr. *ozone* + *-lysis.*] *Chem.* Decomposition following ozonization.

o'zo·nous (ō'zō·nŭs), *adj.* Pertaining to or containing ozone.

o'zos·to'mi·a (ō'zŏs·tō'mĭ·ȧ), *n.* [NL., fr. Gr. *ozostomos* having foul breath.] *Med.* Foulness of breath.

P

P, p (pē), *n.; pl.* P's, p's, Ps, ps (pēz). **1.** The sixteenth letter of the English alphabet. It comes through the Latin from the Greek (*pi*), which borrowed it from the Phoenician (Hebrew *pe*), where it represented the sound which it has ever since retained. **2.** The sound of the letter P, that of a voiceless bilabial stopped consonant (English *pet*), corresponding to the voiced *b* (*bet*). See *Pron.*, § 88. **3.** As a *symbol*, used to denote: **a** The fifteenth or (see K, 3) the sixteenth in order or class. **b** In Mendelian inheritance, the parental generation. Cf. F.

p-. *Chem.* See 1st PARA-, 2 **b.**

pab'u·lum (păb'ū·lŭm), *n.* [L.] The means of sustenance; food; nourishment. — **Syn.** See FOOD.

pa'ca (pä'kȧ; păk'ȧ), *n.* [Pg. & Sp., of Tupian origin.] Any of a genus (*Cumiculus*, esp. *C. paca*) of large South American and Central American rodents.

pace (pās), *n.* [OF. *pas*, fr. L. *passus* a step, pace.] **1.** A step. **2.** The length of a step in walking. Ordinarily the pace is estimated at 2.5 feet; but in measuring distances, it is taken as 3 feet or 3.3 feet (= ⅕ rod). The ***geometrical pace, or great pace,*** is 5 feet. The regulation pace in the United States Army is 30 inches for quick time, and 36 inches for double time. The ***Roman pace*** (*passus*) was from the heel of one foot to the heel of the same foot when it next touched the ground, 5 Roman feet. **3.** Manner of stepping or moving; gait. **4.** Specif., a gait of the horse in which the legs move in lateral pairs, the animal being supported alternately on the right and left legs. **5.** Rate of movement; speed; as, to set the *pace.* **6.** *Lit. & Motion Pictures.* Rate of tempo and timing in the presentation; specif., appropriately rapid and timed presentation to maintain or heighten narrative or dramatic effect. — *v. i.;* PACED (pāst); PAC'ING (pās'ĭng). **1.** To move with slow or measured steps. **2.** To move at a pace, as a horse. — *v. t.* **1.** To walk over with measured tread. **2.** To measure by paces. **3.** To develop, guide, or control the pace of. **4.** *Racing.* To set the pace for.

‖**pa'ce** (pā'sē), *adv. & prep.* [L.] By or with the favor, or leave (of); — usually to express polite disagreement.

paced (pāst), *adj.* **1.** Having, or trained in, a certain pace; as, slow-*paced.* **2.** Measured by pacing. **3.** *Racing.* Having the pace set by a pacemaker; as, a *paced* mile.

pace'mak'er (pās'māk'ẽr), *n.* *Racing.* One who makes or sets the pace for another. — **pace'mak'ing,** *n.*

pac'er (pās'ẽr), *n.* One who or that which paces; esp., a horse that paces; also, one that acts as pacemaker.

pa·cha', pa·cha'lic. Vars. of PASHA, PASHALIK.

pa·chi'si (pä·chē'zĭ), *n.* [Hind. *pacīsī*, fr. *pacīs* twenty-five, the highest throw in the game.] **1.** A game, somewhat resembling backgammon, much played in India. **2.** *U.S. & Eng.* Commonly spelled **par·chee'si, par·che'si, par·chi'si** (pär·chē'zĭ). A game adapted from this.

pach'ou·li (păch'ōō·lĭ; pȧ·chōō'lĭ). Var. of PATCHOULI.

pach'y·derm (păk'ĭ·dûrm), *n.* [Gr. *pachydermos* thick-skinned, fr. *pachys* thick + *derma* skin.] **1.** Any of various hoofed animals, usually having a thick skin, esp. an elephant or rhinoceros. These animals were formerly classed as a group (Pachydermata) including also the hippopotamuses, tapirs, horses, pigs, and others. **2.** Hence, one who is insensitive; a thick-skinned person. — **pach'y·der'ma·tous** (-dûr'mȧ·tŭs), **pach'y·der'mous** (-dûr'mŭs), *adj.*

pach'y·san'dra (păk'ĭ·săn'drȧ), *n.* [NL., fr. Gr. *pachys* thick + *androus.*] Any of a genus (*Pachysandra*) of evergreen woody trailing plants, often used as a ground cover.

pac'i·fi'a·ble (păs'ĭ·fī'ȧ·b'l), *adj.* Capable of being pacified.

pa·cif'ic (pȧ·sĭf'ĭk), *adj.* [F. *pacifique*, fr. L. *pacificus.* See PACIFY.] **1.** Making or tending to make peace; of peaceful character; peaceable; conciliatory. **2.** [*cap.*] Of or pert. to the Pacific Ocean. — **pa·cif'i·cal** (-ĭ·kăl), *adj.* — **pa·cif'i·cal·ly,** *adv.*

pa·cif'i·cate (-ĭ·kāt), *v. t.* [L. *pacificatus*, past part. of *pacificare.*] To render peaceable; to pacify.

pac'i·fi·ca'tion (păs'ĭ·fĭ·kā'shŭn; pȧ·sĭf'ĭ·kā'-), *n.* **1.** Act or process of pacifying, or state of being pacified; appeasement. **2.** A treaty of peace; as, the *Pacification* of Ghent.

pa·cif'i·ca'tor (pȧ·sĭf'ĭ·kā'tẽr), *n.* A peacemaker.

pa·cif'i·ca·to'ry (-kȧ·tō'rĭ *or, esp. Brit.*, -tẽr·ĭ), *adj.* Conciliatory.

pa·cif'i·cism (pȧ·sĭf'ĭ·sĭz'm), *n.* = PACIFISM. — **pa·cif'i·cist** (-sĭst), *n.*

pa·ci'fi·co (pä·sē'fē·kō; *Angl.* pȧ·sĭf'ĭ·kō), *n.; pl.* -COS (-kōs; *Angl.* -kōz). [Sp. *pacífico.* See PACIFIC.] A peaceable person; — applied specif. by the Spaniards to the natives in Cuba and the Philippine Islands who did not oppose the Spanish arms.

Pacific standard time, Pacific time. See STANDARD TIME.

pac'i·fi'er (păs'ĭ·fī'ẽr), *n.* **1.** One who pacifies. **2.** A nipplelike device, or a ring, for babies to suck or bite upon.

pac'i·fism (-fĭz'm), *n.* Opposition to war or to the use of military force for any purpose; esp., an attitude of mind opposing all war and advocating settlement of international disputes entirely by arbitration. — **pac'i·fist** (-fĭst), *n. & adj.* — **pac'i·fis'tic** (-fĭs'tĭk), *adj.*

pac'i·fy (păs'ĭ·fī), *v. t.;* -FIED (-fīd); -FY'ING. [F. *pacifier*, fr. L. *pacificare*, fr. *pax, pacis*, peace + *-ficare* (in comp.) to make.] To make to be at peace; as, to *pacify* a country; to allay the agitation, excitement, or resentment of; to tranquilize; calm.

Syn. **Pacify, appease, placate, mollify, propitiate, conciliate** mean to allay disturbance or excitement. **Pacify** implies a disturbance of the peace quieted; **appease,** agitating and exacting demands pacified by satisfying or contenting; **placate,** bitterness or resentment changed to good will; **mollify,** rising anger or hurt feelings softened or soothed; **propitiate,** an offending or affronting placated for the sake of gaining active good will; **conciliate,** an estranging ended by persuasion or settlement of differences.

pack (păk), *n.* [ME. *pakke*, of LG. *origin.*] **1.** A bundle prepared to be carried; package; packet; parcel; as, a *pack* of cigarettes; esp., a bundle to be carried on the back; as, a peddler's *pack.* **2.** *Archaic.* A low or worthless person; — usually with *naughty.* **3.** A number or quantity of associated or similar persons or things; as: **a** A gang; as, a *pack* of thieves. **b** A great collection (of things); multitude; "lot." **c** A number of hounds hunting or kept together. **d** A number of wild animals of the same kind, as wolves. **e** A full set of playing cards. **4.** In full ***ice pack.*** A large area of floating ice driven closely together. **5.** Amount packed, as of fish or fruit in a year. **6.** A cosmetic paste composed chiefly of fuller's earth, bleaches, and astringents, to be applied to the face and left until dry. **7.** *Med.* In hydropathic practice, a wrapping of blankets or sheets called ***dry pack, wet pack, cold pack, hot pack,*** etc., according to the condition of the blankets or sheets used, put about a patient to give him treatment.

— *v. t.* **1.** To make a pack of; to place as in a pack; to put up for preservation or transportation. **2.** To crowd together. **3.** To fill closely or to repletion; to cram. **4.** To load with a pack; hence, to load; encumber. **5.** To form into a pack, as hounds, cards, or ice. **6.** To cover or protect tightly with something; specif., to render impervious or airtight, as by filling or surrounding with suitable material; as, to *pack* a joint in a pipe. **7.** *Western U.S.* To transport in a pack, or in the manner of a pack. **8.** To send away suddenly; — often with *off.* **9.** *Boxing Slang.* To be capable of delivering (a punch, wallop, etc.) with force. **10.** *Med.* To envelop in a pack (sense 7), within numerous coverings.

— *v. i.* **1.** To make up packs, bales, or bundles. **2.** To gather into packs; to crowd together. **3.** To admit of stowage, or of making up for transportation or storage. **4.** To depart, esp. in haste; — generally with *off* or *away.*

— *adj.* **1. a** Used in or suitable for packing. **b** Forming or formed into a pack; packed; as, *pack* ice. **2. a** Carrying, or used for carrying, a pack; as, *pack* animals. **b** Hence, composed of pack animals; as, a *pack* train.

pack, *v. t.* **1.** To bring together or make up fraudulently, to secure a certain result; as, to *pack* a jury. **2.** *Archaic.* To arrange (the cards in a pack) so as to cheat.

pack (pȧk), *adj.* *Chiefly Scot.* Intimate; also, tame.

pack'age (păk'ĭj), *n.* **1.** Act or process of packing. **2.** Something that is packed or prepared in compact form: **a** A bundle or parcel wrapped or made up for storage or transportation, esp. one of small or moderate size; as, a *package* of manuscript; a load of Christmas *packages.* **b** One unit of a product uniformly processed, wrapped or sealed in a sheath or container, and labeled for marketing, esp. large-scale marketing, for example, a *package* of prunes or of asbestos. **c** Any finished product which has been made ready for immediate operation, installation, or use by preassembling all essential elements into a self-contained unit, for example, a power unit, an air-conditioning apparatus, a prefabricated building. **d** A fully constructed and integrated program or plan, such as a radio show or a tour, prearranged in full detail and made ready for immediate operation as a unit, and usually offered for sale at a flat sum. **3.** That in which anything is packed; a box, case, barrel, crate, bale, can, etc., in which goods are packed. Abbr. *pkg.* — *v. t.;* -AGED (-ĭjd); -AG·ING (-ĭj·ĭng). To make up into a package or packages; as, to *package* yarn or tobacco; a *packaged* bale of synthetic rubber; also, to enclose in a package or packages; as, *packaged* poultry ready for the oven; airplanes *packaged* with a spray of plastic solution.

package store. A store where intoxicating liquors are sold only by the bottle, jug, or other container, and may not be drunk on the premises.

pack animal. An animal used in carrying packs.

pack'er (păk'ẽr), *n.* One who packs; esp., a person who makes up bundles; specif., *Chiefly U.S.,* a wholesale dealer in provisions who packs his wares for transportation and for market.

pack'et (păk'ĕt; -ĭt), *n.* [AF. *pacquet*, dim. of ME. *pakke.* See PACK, *n.*] **1.** A small pack or package; a little parcel. **2.** *Naut.* **a** A vessel conveying dispatches, mails, passengers, and goods, and having fixed sailing days. **b** Loosely, a ship. — *v. t.* To make up into, or wrap or put up in, a packet; to package.

pack'ing, *n.* **1.** Act or process of one who or that which packs; esp., the putting up of meat, fruit, etc., for future sale. **2.** Any material used to pack, as a layer of material put between the surfaces of a flange joint. See STUFFING BOX, *Illust.*

packing house. A factory where meats, and sometimes other foodstuffs, are prepared for transportation, preservation, etc., as by packing in sealed cans for the market.

pack'man (păk'măn), *n.; pl.* -MEN (-mĕn). One who bears a pack; a peddler.

pack rat. A wood rat, esp. a large bushy-tailed species (*Neotoma cinerea*) of the Rocky Mountain area.

pack′sack′ (păk′săk′), *n.* A sack, as of canvas or leather, to hold blankets, clothing, etc., when traveling.

pack′sad′dle (-săd′'l), *n.* A saddle made for supporting the load on a pack animal. — **pack′sad′dle,** *v. t.*

pack′thread′ (-thrĕd′), *n.* Strong thread or small twine, such as that used for sewing or tying packs or parcels.

pact (păkt), *n.* [OF. *pact*, fr. L. *pactum*, fr. *paciscere* to covenant.] An agreement; compact.

pad (păd), *n.* [D. or LG. See PATH.] **1.** *Now Dial. Eng.* A path. **2.** *Now Rare.* A highway robber. **3.** An easy-paced horse. — *v. i. & t.;* PAD′DED; PAD′DING. **1.** To travel on foot; to trudge. **2.** To walk or run with steady dull footfalls; — said esp. of animals.

pad, *n.* [Imitative.] The dull sound made by repeated footfalls or impacts of a staff.

pad, *n.* [Origin uncert.] **1.** A cushion. **2.** A cushion used as a saddle. **3.** Something of the nature of a cushion used to lessen the effect of jarring, impact, or friction. **4.** A block of many sheets of writing paper; a tablet. **5.** A type of cushion of absorbent material saturated with ink for inking the surface of a rubber stamp. **6.** The foot of certain animals, as the fox, hare, wolf, otter. **7.** *U. S.* A floating leaf of a water plant, esp. a water lily. **8.** *Zool.* **a** A cushionlike thickening of the skin on the soles or under part of the toes of certain animals. **b** The pulvillus of an insect's foot. — *v. t.;* PAD′DED (păd′ĕd; -ĭd); PAD′DING. **1.** To stuff; to furnish with padding. **2.** To fill out or expand with needless matter.

pad′ding (păd′ĭng), *n.* **1.** Act or process of one that pads. **2.** The material with which anything is padded.

pad′dle (păd′'l), *n.* **1.** *Dial. Eng. & Scot.* A kind of long-handled spud for rooting up weeds, cleaning a plowshare, etc. **2.** An implement with a broad blade, used without a fixed fulcrum to propel and steer canoes and other boats. **3.** One of the broad boards, or floats, at the circumference of a water wheel, or paddle wheel. **4.** Short for PADDLE WHEEL. **5.** A broad-bladed implement for stirring or mixing, as in puddling iron, beating clothes in washing, etc.
— *v. i.;* -DLED (-'ld); -DLING (-lĭng). **1.** To use a paddle for propelling one on or through the water. **2.** To row easily or gently. — *v. t.* **1.** To propel or move with or as with a paddle. **2.** To beat or stir as with a paddle; also, *Colloq., U. S.*, to beat or punish as with a paddle.

pad′dle, *v. i.* **1.** To move the feet or wade about in shallow water. **2.** To use the hands or fingers in toying or caressing. **3.** To toddle.

paddle box. The structure enclosing the upper part of a paddle wheel of a vessel.

pad′dle·fish′ (păd′'l·fĭsh′), *n.; see* FISH. Any of a family (Polyodontidae) of ganoid fishes, esp. one (*Polyodon spathula*) of the Mississippi Valley, about four feet long, with a spatula-shaped snout.

pad′dler (păd′lẽr), *n.* One who or that which paddles.

paddle wheel. *Naut.* A wheel with paddles, floats, or boards around its circumference used to propel a vessel.

pad′dock (păd′ŭk), *n.* [ME. *paddok*, fr. *padde* toad + *-ock*.] **1.** *Obs. exc. Scot.* A frog. **2.** *Archaic.* A toad.

pad′dock (păd′ŭk), *n.* [For E. dial. *parrock*, fr. AS. *pearruc* enclosure, fence.] **1.** A small enclosure, esp. one for pasture, adjoining a stable or house. **2.** An enclosure near the stables, esp. at a racecourse, in which horses are exercised, etc. **3.** In Australia, any field or subdivision of arable land or grassland enclosed by a fence. — *v. t.* To confine in or as in a paddock.

pad′dy, pad′i (păd′ĭ), *n.* [Malay *padi*.] Unmilled or rough rice, growing or cut; also, rice in general, or a field in which rice is grown.

Pad′dy (păd′ĭ), *n.; pl.* PADDIES (-ĭz). [Dim. fr. Ir. *Pādraig* Patrick, Christian name, after St. Patrick, the tutelar saint of Ireland.] An Irishman; — a nickname.

pad′dy·whack′ (păd′ĭ·hwăk′), **pad′dy·wack′** (-wăk′), *n.* *Dial. Eng.* A rage, passion, or temper.

pa′di·shah (pä′dĭ·shä), *n.* [Per. *pādshāh*.] Chief ruler; great king; — [*often cap.*] a title, esp. of the shah of Persia, and, until 1947, of the sovereign of Great Britain as emperor of India.

pa′dle (pā′d'l), *n. & v. t.* *Scot.* Hoe.

pad′lock′ (păd′lŏk′), *n.* A detachable, portable lock having a shackle adapted to be opened for engagement through a staple or chain. — *v. t.* To fasten as with a padlock.

pad′nag′ (păd′năg′), *n.* [*pad* path + *nag*.] An ambling nag.

pa′dre (pä′drĭ; *Sp.* pä′thrā; *It.* -drā), *n.; pl.* PADRES (-drĭz); Sp. PADRES (-thrās); It. PADRI (-drē). [Sp., Pg., & It., fr. L. *pater* father.] **1.** A monk or priest; — esp. as used in Italy, Spain, Portugal, and Spanish America. **2.** *Soldiers' & Sailors' Slang.* Chaplain.

‖**pa·dro′ne** (pä·drō′nā), *n.; pl.* -NI (-nē). [It., fr. L. *patronus*.] **1.** A patron; a master. **2.** The master of a small coaster in the Mediterranean. **3.** In Italy, an innkeeper. **4.** (*pron.* pȧ·drō′nĭ) *pl.* PADRONES (-nĭz). An Italian employment agent, as in America. — **pa·dro′nism** (pȧ·drō′nĭz'm), *n.*

pad′u·a·soy (păd′ū·ȧ·soi), *n.* [F. *pou-de-soie*, influenced by *Padua*, city in Italy.] A rich and heavy corded silk stuff; also, a garment made of it. — **pad′u·a·soy,** *adj.*

pae′an (pē′ăn), *n.* Also **pe′an.** [L. *paean*, fr. Gr. *paian*, fr. *Paian* the physician of the gods, later, Apollo.] **1.** *Gr. Antiq.* A hymn of praise, joy, or triumph, associated esp. with the cult of Apollo and Artemis. **2.** A song of joy, praise, triumph, or the like.

pae′do- (pē′dō-), **paed-.** Var. of PEDO-, PED-, as in: **pae′da·gog′ic, pae′di·at′ric** (see PEDAGOGIC, PEDIATRIC) and in **pae′do·gen′e·sis** (-jĕn′ē·sĭs), reproduction by young or larval animals, esp. by parthenogenesis in certain gall midges.

pae′on (pē′ŏn), *n.* [L. *paeon*, fr. Gr. *paiōn* a solemn song, also, a paeon, equiv. to *paian*. See PAEAN.] *Gr. & Lat. Pros.* A foot of four syllables, one long and three short.

pa′gan (pā′găn), *n.* [LL. *paganus* heathen, fr. L. *paganus* civilian, also, peasant, fr. *pagus* village, district.] **1.** Formerly, one not of a Christian people; now, one who is neither a Christian, a Mohammedan, nor a Jew; a heathen. **2.** An irreligious person. — *adj.* **1.** Of or pertaining to pagans or their worship; heathen; idolatrous. **2.** Irreligious; heathen. — **pa′gan·ish,** *adj.*

pa′gan·ism (-ĭz'm), *n.* **1.** State of being pagan; esp., the religion and worship of pagans; heathenism. **2.** Pagan character or morals.

pa′gan·ize (-īz), *v. t. & i.* To render or become pagan.

page (pāj), *n.* [OF., fr. It. *paggio*.] **1.** Formerly, a youth undergoing training for knighthood, who acted as attendant of his master and mistress, or a youth attending a person of high degree, esp. at courts, as a service of honor and education. **2.** Now, a youth employed for doing errands, carrying messages, etc., as in a hotel; also, *U. S.*, a boy employed to wait upon the members of a legislative body, or a uniformed attendant at a theater. — *v. t. & i.* **1.** To attend (one) as a page; to act as page. **2.** To seek out (a person) by calling his name aloud, as pages do in a hotel.

page, *n.* [F., fr. L. *pagina*.] **1.** One side of a leaf of a book, manuscript, letter, etc. Abbr. *p.;* pl. *pp.* **2.** Figuratively: **a** A record; writing; as, the *page* of history. **b** An event or circumstance which might fill a written page. **3.** *Print.* The type set for printing a page. — *v. t.;* PAGED (pājd); PAG′ING (pāj′ĭng). To mark or number the pages of; to furnish with folios.

pag′eant (păj′ĕnt; *formerly, & still occas., also* pā′jĕnt), *n.* [ME. *pagent, pagen*, a movable scaffold or stage, also, what was exhibited on it, fr. Anglo-Lat. *pagina*.] **1.** *Hist.* **a** One of a series of (usually) movable structures, on which the scenes of the mysteries were performed in the open air. **b** A theatrical exhibition. **c** Any show, tableau, or temporary decoration on a fixed stage or a carriage in a public celebration. **2.** A specious display; unsubstantial pomp. **3.** An elaborate exhibition, esp. a parade, often with floats, for public entertainment; also, a stately funeral procession. **4.** A type of community drama based on local history, given by local actors, out of doors.

pag′eant·ry (-rĭ), *n.; pl.* -RIES (-rĭz). **1.** Pageants or scenic spectacles, taken collectively; also, a pageant, or play. **2.** Elaborate display; pomp.

pag′i·nal (păj′ĭ·năl; -n'l), *adj.* [LL. *paginalis*.] Consisting of pages; of or pertaining to a page or pages.

pag′i·nate (-nāt), *v. t.* To page, as a book.

pag′i·na′tion (-nā′shŭn), *n.* Act or process of paging a book, etc.; the characters indicating the sequence of the pages; page numbering; also, the number of pages.

pa·go′da (pȧ·gō′dȧ), *n.* *Archaic,* **pag′od** (păg′ŏd; pȧ·gŏd′). [Pg. *pagode*, fr. Tamil *pagavadi*.] A towerlike storied structure, usually a temple or a memorial, such as is frequent in India, China, Indochina, and Japan. Cf. 3d TOPE.

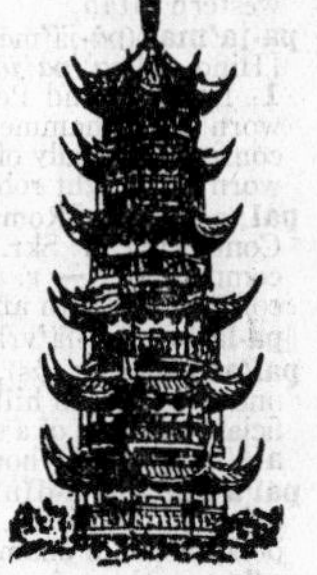
Pagoda at Shanghai.

pa·gu′ri·an (pȧ·gū′rĭ·ăn), *adj.* [L. *pagurus*, a kind of crab, fr. Gr. *pagouros*.] *Zool.* Belonging to the family (Paguridae) containing the typical hermit crabs. — **pa·gu′ri·an,** *n.* — **pa·gu′rid** (pȧ·gū′rĭd; păg′ū·rĭd), *n.*

Pah′la·vi (pä′lȧ·vē), *n.* Also **Peh′le·vi** (pā′lĕ·vē). [Per. *Pahlavi*, fr. OPer. *Parthava* Parthia.] The chief Persian language from the 3d to the 9th century A.D., employing a Semitic alphabet related to that of the Avesta.

pah′la·vi (pä′lȧ·vē; pȧ′-), *n. sing. & pl.* [Per., pert. to Riza Khan *Pahlavi*, Shah of Persia.] A gold coin of Iran introduced in 1927. See MONEY, *Tables*.

paid (pād), *past & past part.* of 2d PAY.

paid′-in′ sur′plus. *Accounting.* Surplus resulting from sale of shares at a premium.

pai′do- (pā′dō-; pī′dō-), **paid-.** Var. of PEDO-, PED-, as in **pai·dol′o·gy.**

paik (pāk), *n.* *Scot.* A thump. — *v. t.* *Scot.* To strike.

pail (pāl), *n.* [ME. *payle*, appar. fr. AS. *pægel* a wine vessel, gill.] A vessel, commonly circular in section, having an arched handle and often fitted with a cover; a bucket. — **pail′ful** (-fŏŏl), *n.*

pail·lasse′ (păl·yăs′; păl′yăs), *n.* [F., fr. It. *pagliaccio*, fr. L. *palea* chaff.] An under bed or mattress of straw.

pail·lette′ (păl·yĕt′), *n.* [F., dim. of *paille* straw. See PALLET bed.] A spangle; specif., a piece of paillon.

‖**pail′lon′** (pȧ′yôN′), *n.; pl.* -LONS (*F.* -yôN′). [F., fr. *paille* straw.] A thin leaf of metal, as for use in gilding.

pain (pān), *n.* [OF. *peine*, fr. L. *poena* penalty, punishment, fr. Gr. *poinē* penalty.] **1.** Punishment; penalty. *Obs.* exc. in phrases, esp. *on*, or *under, pain of.* **2.** A distressing feeling due to disease, bodily injury, or organic disorders. **3.** Distressing uneasiness of mind; grief. **4.** *pl.* The throes of childbirth. **5.** *Chiefly pl.* Labor; care or trouble; as, to take *pains*. — **Syn.** See EFFORT. — *v. t.* **1.** To put to bodily uneasiness or anguish; to distress. **2.** To render mentally distressed; grieve. — *v. i.* To give pain.

painch (*dial.* pänsh). Dial. var. of PAUNCH.

pain′ful (pān′fŏŏl; -f'l), *adj.* **1.** Full of pain; inflicting pain. **2.** Requiring labor or toil. **3.** *Archaic.* Careful; industrious. **4.** Of the body or a bodily part, affected with pain. — **pain′ful·ly,** *adv.* — **pain′ful·ness,** *n.*

pain′less, *adj.* Free from pain; without pain. — **pain′less·ly,** *adv.*

pains′tak′ing (pānz′tāk′ĭng), *n.* Act of taking pains. — *adj.* Taking pains; assiduous. — **pains′tak′ing·ly,** *adv.*

paint (pānt), *v. t.* [OF. *peint*, past part. of *peindre* to paint, fr. L. *pingere, pictum*.] **1. a** To form a representation of, as on a canvas, by applying paints. **b** To make or create (a picture or design) by means of pigments. **2.** To cover with coloring matter; to apply paint to; to color. **3.** To ornament by painting. **4.** To tinge; to adorn with or as with colors. **5.** To represent vividly to the mind as if by painting; to depict. **6.** To put on or apply like paint. — *v. i.* **1.** To practice the art of painting; also, to describe vividly. **2.** To color one's face in an attempt to beautify it.
— *n.* **1.** A mixture of a pigment with some suitable liquid to form a solid adherent covering when spread on a surface in thin coats for decoration, protection, etc.; also, the pigment in the form of a cake. **2.** The dried film of paint on a surface. **3.** Pigment, as rouge, etc., for the face. **4.** Act of painting; a coloring.

paint′brush′ (pānt′brŭsh′), *n.* **1.** A brush for applying paint. **2.** The painted cup (which see).

paint′ed bun′ting (pān′tĕd; -tĭd). A beautifully colored finch (*Passerina ciris*), of the southern United States.

painted cup. Any of a genus (*Castilleja*) of plants of the figwort family, with brightly colored bracts, including *C. linariaefolia*, the State flower of Wyoming; — called also *Indian paintbrush*.

paint′er (pān′tẽr), *n.* [Var. of PANTHER.] The cougar.

paint′er, *n.* [OF. *pentoir* suspensory cordage, fr. L. *pendēre* to hang.] A rope for making a boat fast.

paint′er, *n.* [OF. *peintour*.] One who paints; esp.: **a** An artist who paints pictures. **b** One who covers buildings, ships, or the like, with paint.

paint'er's col'ic (pān'tẽrz). Violent intestinal colic, caused by chronic lead poisoning.

paint'ing, *n.* **1.** Act of laying on, or adorning with, paints; also, that which is painted. **2.** *Fine Arts.* The work of the painter; also, any work of art so produced.

pair (pâr), *n.; pl.* PAIRS; after a numeral, formerly, and now sometimes, PAIR. [OF. *paire,* fr. L. *paria,* neut. pl. of *par* equal.] **1.** Two things of a kind, suited to each other, and intended to be used together. Abbr. *pr.* **2.** A single thing composed of two corresponding pieces; as, a *pair* of scissors, *pair* of compasses. **3.** Two of a sort; a couple; a brace. **4.** Two persons or animals of opposite sexes associated together. **5.** *Now Chiefly Dial.* A set; as, a *pair* of stairs. **6.** Two members of opposite parties or opinion in a deliberative body, who mutually agree not to vote on a given question, or on issues of a party nature, during a specified time; also, the arrangement thus made. **7.** *Card Playing.* **a** A set of two cards of the same value or denomination. See POKER, *Illust.* **b** *pl.* Partners who continue playing against different opponents, as at duplicate bridge. **8.** *Kinematics.* A combination of two parts, called *elements,* which are so applied to each other as mutually to constrain relative motion.
— *v. t.* To unite or arrange in a pair or couple. — *v. i.* **1.** To form a pair; to match; suit. **2.** To unite in a pair; to couple; to mate. **3.** To agree with one of the opposite party or opinion to abstain from voting. See PAIR, *n.,* 6.

pair'-oar', *n.* A boat rowed by two men, each pulling one oar and seated one abaft the other. — **pair'-oar',** *adj.*

pair production. The simultaneous and complete transformation of a quantum of radiant energy into an electron and a positron when the quantum of radiant energy interacts with the intense electric field of the nucleus.

Pais'ley shawl (pāz'lĭ). A type of woolen shawl imitating a Cashmere shawl, formerly made at Paisley, Scotland.

Pai·ute' (pī·ūt'; 2), *n.* An Indian of a small Shoshonean tribe of southwestern Utah.

pa·ja'ma (pȧ·jä'mȧ; -jăm'ȧ), **py·ja'ma** (pĭ·jä'mȧ; pī-; -jăm'ȧ), *n.* [Hind. colloq. *paijāmā, pājāmā,* fr. Per. *pā(i)* leg + *jāmah* garment.] **1.** In India and Persia, thin loose trousers or drawers such as those worn by Mohammedan men and women. **2.** *Chiefly pl.* A garment consisting usually of jacket and trousers of silk, cotton, or the like, and worn as a night robe, dressing gown, or costume.

pal (păl), *n.* [Romany (in England) *pal* brother, mate, *pral* (on the Continent), fr. Skr. *bhrātṛ* brother.] *Slang.* A partner; also, a boon companion. — *v. i.;* PALLED (păld); PAL'LING. *Slang.* To be or become a pal (with another).

‖**pa·la'bra** (pä·lä'vrä; 17), *n.* [Sp.] A word; hence, palaver.

pal'ace (păl'ĭs; -ȧs), *n.* [OF. *palais,* fr. L. *palatium,* fr. *Palatium* one of the seven hills of Rome, where Augustus resided.] **1.** The official residence of a sovereign or, *Eng.,* of an archbishop or bishop. **2. a** A large stately house. **b** A large public building, as for a legislature.

pal'a·din (păl'ȧ·dĭn), *n.* [F., fr. It. *paladino,* fr. L. *palatinus* an officer of the palace.] In the Charlemagne romances, one of the douzepers; hence, a champion; a legendary hero.

pa'lae-. Var. of PALE- (see PALEO-), as in **pa'lae·eth·nol'o·gy.**

pa'lae·o- (pā'lē·ō-; păl'ē·ō-). Var. of PALEO-.

pa·laes'tra, pa·les'tra (pȧ·lĕs'trȧ), *n.; pl.* -TRAE (-trē), -TRAS (-trȧz). [L. *palaestra,* fr. Gr. *palaistra,* fr. *palaiein* to wrestle.] *Antiq.* A wrestling school; hence, a gymnasium.

pal'an·quin', pal'an·keen' (păl'ăn·kēn'), *n.* [Pg. *palanquim,* fr. Jav. *pĕlaṅki,* fr. Skr. *palyaṅka,* var. of *paryaṅka* palanquin, bed.] A conveyance, usually for one person, consisting of an enclosed litter borne on the shoulders of men by means of poles. It is used in India, China, etc.

pal'at·a·ble (păl'ĭt·ȧ·b'l), *adj.* Agreeable to the taste; savory; hence, acceptable; pleasing. — **pal'at·a·bil'i·ty** (-bĭl'ĭ·tĭ), *n.* — **pal'at·a·ble·ness,** *n.* — **pal'at·a·bly,** *adv.*

pal'a·tal (păl'ȧ·tăl; -t'l), *adj.* [F., fr. L. *palatum.*] **1.** Of or pertaining to the palate. **2.** *Phonet.* **a** Formed with the front of the tongue, behind the tip (which is lowered), near or touching the hard palate, as in the voiceless fricative *ch* of Germ. *ich,* or the nonfricative Eng. *y* (*yield*); in the Fr. nasal *gn* (*agneau*); and in the vowels ĭ and ē; — distinguished from *palatalized* and contrasted with *velar.* **b** More inclusively: (1) Formed with the blade of the tongue near the hard palate, as *ch* (*chin*), *j* (*jug*), *sh* (*she*), *zh* (*vision*). (2) Of a vowel, front. — *n. Phonet.* A palatal sound or its symbol.

pal'a·tal·ize (-īz), *v. t. Phonet.* To pronounce as a palatal or front sound; specif., to modify the utterance of (a nonpalatal sound) by simultaneously bringing the front of the tongue to or near the hard palate. — **pal'a·tal·i·za'tion** (-ĭ·zā'shŭn; -ī·zā'-), *n.*

pal'ate (păl'ĭt; -ȧt), *n.* [L. *palatum.*] **1.** The roof of the mouth. In man the portion supported by the maxillary and palatine bones is called the ***hard palate,*** and the fold suspended from the posterior margin of the hard palate is called the ***soft palate,*** *or* ***velum.*** **2.** Taste; — from the mistaken notion that the palate is the organ of taste. **3.** Mental relish; intellectual taste. — **Syn.** See TASTE.

pa·la'tial (pȧ·lā'shăl), *adj.* [L. *palatium* palace.] Of, befitting, or pert. to a palace; magnificent. — **pa·la'tial·ly,** *adv.*

pa·lat'i·nate (pȧ·lăt'ĭ·nāt), *n.* **1.** The territory of a palatine. **2.** [*cap.*] A native or inhabitant of the Palatinate (see *Gaz.*).

pal'a·tine (păl'ȧ·tīn; -tĭn), *adj.* [F. *palatin,* fr. L. *palatum.*] *Anat.* Of or pertaining to the palate. — *n. Anat.* A palatine bone.

pal'a·tine, *adj.* [F. *palatin,* fr. L. *palatinus,* fr. *palatium.* See PALACE.] **1.** Of or pertaining to a palace; palatial. **2.** Possessing royal privileges; as, a count *palatine;* of or pertaining to such a count, earl, or county. **3.** [*cap.*] Of or pertaining to the Palatinate. — *n.* **1.** An officer of an imperial palace: **a** Orig., the mayor of the palace. **b** Hence, esp. in medieval Europe, a vassal lord invested with royal rights in his domains. **2.** [*cap.*] **a** A native or inhabitant of the Palatinate. **b** One of the seven hills of Rome. See SEVEN HILLS. **3.** A fur piece covering the neck and shoulders.

pa·lav'er (pȧ·lăv'ẽr; pȧ·lä'vẽr), *n.* [Pg. *palavra,* fr. L. *parabola* a comparison, parable, ML., tale, word. See PARABLE.] **1.** In Africa, a parley, usually a long one among or with the natives; hence, a conference; a debate. **2.** Talk; esp., profuse talk; flattery. — *v. i.* To talk profusely; to parley; to talk idly or so as to beguile.

pale (pāl), *adj.* [OF., fr. L. *pallidus.*] **1.** Wanting in color or in intensity of color; dusky white; ashen; pallid; wan. **2.** Not bright or brilliant; faint; dim. **3.** Of colors, wanting in chroma; as, a *pale* pink. — *v. i. & t.* To turn or make pale; to lose color. — **pale'ly,** *adv.* — **pale'ness,** *n.*

pale (pāl), *n.* [OF. *pal,* fr. L. *palus.*] **1.** A stake; a pointed slat, as for fencing; a picket. **2.** *Now Rare.* A fence or enclosure of or as of pales; barrier. **3.** An enclosure; also, limits; bounds; as, in the cloister's *pale.* **4.** A territory or district within certain bounds; specif., *Hist.,* short for ***English Pale,*** the territory of Calais, in France, under English control, or the country (also called simply ***the Pale***) around Dublin within which alone the English conquerors of Ireland held dominion before Cromwell. **5.** *Her.* A perpendicular stripe in an escutcheon. — ***beyond, outside,*** *or* ***out of, the pale.*** Beyond the limits, privileges, or protection, as of the church. — *v. t.* To enclose with or as with pales; to fence.

pa'le- (pā'lē-; păl'ē-). = PALEO- (which see).

pa'le·a (pā'lē·ȧ), *n.; pl.* PALEAE (-ē). [L., chaff.] *Bot.* **a** One of the chaffy scales on the receptacle in many composite plants, esp. sunflowers. **b** The upper bract, which, with the lemma, encloses the flower in grasses. See SPIKELET, *Illust.* — **pa'le·a'ceous** (pā'lē·ā'shŭs), *adj.*

pa'le·eth·nol'o·gy, pa'lae·eth·nol'o·gy (pā'lē·ĕth·nŏl'ō·jĭ; păl'ē-), *n.* [*pale-* + *ethnology.*] Ethnology of early prehistoric man. — **pa'le·eth'no·log'ic, pa'lae-** (-ĕth'nō·lŏj'ĭk), **pa'le·eth'no·log'i·cal, pa'lae-** (-ĭ·kăl), *adj.* — **pa'le·eth·nol'o·gist, pa'lae-** (-ĕth·nŏl'ō·jĭst), *n.*

pale'face' (pāl'fās'), *n.* A white person; — so called, as alleged, by the American Indians.

pa'le·o-, pa'lae·o- (pā'lē·ō-; păl'ē·ō-). Before vowels usually **pa'le-, pa'lae-.** [Gr. *palaios.*] A combining form meaning *old, ancient,* used to denote: **a** *Remote in the past,* as in *paleo*graphy, *paleo*ntology; also, short for *paleontological,* as in *paleo*botany. **b** Early; primitive; archaic; as in *paleo*lithic; also, short for *paleolithic.*

pa'le·o·bot'a·ny, pa'lae·o·bot'a·ny (-bŏt'ȧ·nĭ), *n.* The paleontology of plants. — **pa'le·o·bo·tan'ic, pa'lae·o-** (-bō·tăn'ĭk), **pa'le·o·bo·tan'i·cal, pa'lae·o-** (-ĭ·kăl), *adj.* — **pa'le·o·bot'a·nist, pa'lae·o-** (-bŏt'ȧ·nĭst), *n.*

pa'le·og'ra·phy, pa'lae·og'ra·phy (pā'lē·ŏg'rȧ·fĭ; păl'ē-), *n.* **1.** An ancient manner of writing; ancient writings, collectively. **2.** The study or science of deciphering ancient writings, determining their origin, period, etc. — **pa'le·og'ra·pher, pa'lae·og'ra·pher** (-fẽr), *n.* — **pa'le·o·graph'ic, pa'lae·o-** (-ō·grăf'ĭk), *adj.* — **pa'le·o·graph'i·cal, pa'lae·o-** (-ĭ·kăl), *adj.*

pa'le·o·lith'ic (-ō·lĭth'ĭk), *adj.* Also **pa'lae·o·lith'ic.** [*paleo-* + *-lith* + *-ic.*] Of or pertaining to the early human culture characterized by rough or chipped stone implements; also, designating the period of this culture.

paleolithic man. *Anthropol.* Any type of man of, or peculiar to, the Paleolithic period, as the Heidelberg, Peking, Neanderthal, or Cro-Magnon man.

pa'le·on·tog'ra·phy, pa'lae·on·tog'ra·phy (pā'lē·ŏn·tŏg'rȧ·fĭ; păl'ē-), *n.* [*paleo-* + Gr. *onta* existing things + *-graphy.*] The description of fossils. — **pa'le·on'to·graph'ic, pa'lae-** (-ŏn'tō·grăf'ĭk), *adj.* — **pa'le·on'to·graph'i·cal, pa'lae-** (-ĭ·kăl), *adj.*

pa'le·on·tol'o·gy, pa'lae·on·tol'o·gy (-tŏl'ō·jĭ), *n.* [*paleo-* + Gr. *onta* existing things + *-logy.*] **1.** The science that deals with the life of past geological periods. It is based on the study of fossils. **2.** A treatise on this science. — **pa'le·on'to·log'ic, pa'lae-** (-ŏn'tō·lŏj'ĭk), *adj.* — **pa'le·on'to·log'i·cal, pa'lae-** (-ĭ·kăl), *adj.* — **pa'le·on'to·log'i·cal·ly, pa'lae-,** *adv.* — **pa'le·on·tol'o·gist, pa'lae-** (-ŏn·tŏl'ō·jĭst), *n.*

pa'le·o·pe·dol'o·gy, pa'lae·o·pe·dol'o·gy (pā'lē·ō·pē·dŏl'ō·jĭ; păl'ē·ō-), *n.* [*paleo-* + *pedology.*] The science which treats of the soils of past geological ages.

Pa'le·o·zo'ic, Pa'lae·o·zo'ic (pā'lē·ō·zō'ĭk; păl'ē-), *adj.* [*paleo-* + Gr. *zōē* life.] *Geol.* Of or pertaining to, or designating, an era of geological history from the Proterozoic to the Mesozoic, or the group of rocks formed during this era. In its later epochs land plants, amphibians, and reptiles first appeared. — **Pa'le·o·zo'ic, Pa'lae·o·zo'ic,** *n.*

pa'le·o·zo·ol'o·gy, pa'lae·o·zo·ol'o·gy (-zō·ŏl'ō·jĭ), *n.* The paleontology of animals. — **pa'le·o·zo'o·log'i·cal, pa'lae-** (-zō'ō·lŏj'ĭ·kăl), *adj.* — **pa'le·o·zo·ol'o·gist, pa'lae·o-** (-zō·ŏl'ō·jĭst), *n.*

pa·les'tra (pȧ·lĕs'trȧ). Var. of PALAESTRA.

pal'e·tot (păl'ē·tō; păl'tō), *n.* [F.] **a** A type of loose overcoat. **b** A woman's outer garment of varying fashion.

pal'ette (păl'ĕt; -ĭt), *n.* [F. See PALLET a thin board.] **a** A thin board or tablet, with a thumb hole at one end for holding it, on which a painter lays and mixes his pigments. **b** The set of colors put on the palette.

palette knife. A knife, having a very flexible steel blade and no cutting edge, used by painters to mix colors. See KNIFE, *Illust.* (8).

pal'frey (pôl'frĭ), *n.; pl.* -FREYS (-frĭz). [OF. *palefrei,* fr. LL. *palefredus,* fr. *paraveredus* an extra post horse, fr. Gr. *para* along + L. *veredus* post horse.] A saddle horse; esp., a small horse for ladies.

Pa'li (pä'lē), *n.* [Skr. *pāli* row, line.] A dialect descended from Vedic Aryan, used in Buddhist sacred writings. See INDO-EUROPEAN LANGUAGES, *Table.*

pal'i·kar (păl'ĭ·kär), *n.* [NGr. *palikari, pallēkari,* young man.] A soldier of the Greek militia in the war (1821–28) against Turkey.

pal'imp·sest (păl'ĭmp·sĕst), *n.* [From L., fr. Gr. *palimpsēstos* scraped again, *palimpsēston* a palimpsest, fr. *palin* again + *psēn* to rub.] A parchment, tablet, etc., which has been used twice or three times (***double palimpsest***), the earlier writing having been erased.

pal'in·drome (păl'ĭn·drōm), *n.* [Gr. *palindromos* running back again, fr. *palin* again + *dramein* to run.] A word, verse, or sentence, that is the same when read backward or forward (*madam; Hannah*).

pal'ing (pāl'ĭng), *n.* **1.** Act of building, or of enclosing with, a fence. **2.** Wood for making pales; pales collectively; a fence.

pal'in·gen'e·sis (păl'ĭn·jĕn'ē·sĭs), *n.* [NL., fr. Gr. *palin* again + *-genesis.*] **1.** A new birth; regeneration; specif., Christian baptism. **2.** The doctrine of continued rebirths; metempsychosis. **3.** *Biol.* **a** The processes in the development of an individual which repeat the race history (phylogeny) of its group; — opposed to *cenogenesis.* **b** *Obs.* Spontaneous generation. **c** Abrupt metamorphosis.

pal'i·node (păl'ĭ·nōd), *n.* [MF. *palinod,* fr. LL. *palinodia,* fr. Gr. *palinōidia,* fr. *palin* again + *ōidē* a song.] **1.** An ode or song retracting something in a former one. **2.** A formal retraction; recantation.

pal'i·sade' (păl'ĭ·sād'), *n.* [F. *palissade,* fr. Pr., deriv. of L. *palus* a stake, pale.] **1.** A fence of pales or stakes, as for defense. **2.** A long, pointed stake, set with others in a close row as a defense. **3.** A line of bold cliffs; — usually *pl.* — *v. t.* To surround or fortify with palisades.

pal'ish (păl'ĭsh), *adj.* Somewhat or rather pale.

pall (pôl), *n.* [AS. *pæl*, fr. L. *pallium* cover, mantle, pall.] **1.** A fine cloth spread over something (*Archaic in general sense*); esp., a heavy cloth, as of black velvet, thrown over a coffin; hence, figuratively, a coffin. **2.** A covering or concealing thing; formerly, a cloak; now, esp., an overspreading mass which produces a gloomy effect; as, a *pall* of smoke. **3.** *Archaic.* An outer garment; a cloak. **4.** *Eccl.* **a** *Archaic.* An altar cloth. **b** A linen cloth for covering the chalice; now, esp., a square piece of cardboard, covered with linen and usually embroidered on the upper side. — *v. t.* To cover with or as with a pall; to cloak.

pall, *v. i.* [From APPALL.] **1.** To become vapid, dull, or insipid. **2.** To become satiated or cloyed, as the stomach. — *v. t.* **1.** *Rare.* To make vapid or insipid; stale. **2.** To satiate; cloy. — **Syn.** See SATIATE.

Pal·la'di·an (pă·lā'dĭ·ăn; 58), *adj.* Of or pertaining to Pallas Athena, goddess of wisdom; hence, of or pert. to wisdom or learning.

Pal·la'di·an, *adj.* *Arch.* Of, pert. to, or designating a variety of the revived classic style, founded on the works of the Italian Andrea Palladio (see *Biog.*).

pal·lad'ic (pă·lăd'ĭk; pă·lā'dĭk), *adj.* *Chem.* Of or pert. to palladium; — used specif. of quadrivalent compounds.

Pal·la'di·um (pă·lā'dĭ·ŭm), *n.; pl.* -DIA (-*ȧ*). **1.** *Class. Antiq.* A statue of Pallas Athena, esp. the famous one on the preservation of which was supposed to depend the safety of Troy. **2.** [*not cap.*] That which affords security; a safeguard.

pal·la'di·um, *n.* [NL., fr. the asteroid *Pallas.*] *Chem.* A rare metallic element of the platinum group, silver-white, ductile, malleable, and permanent in the air, but lighter (sp. gr., 12.0) and more easily fusible than platinum. Symbol, *Pd*; at. no., 46; at. wt., 106.7.

pal·la'dous (pă·lā'dŭs; păl'*ȧ*-), *adj.* *Chem.* Of or pert. to palladium; — used specif. of bivalent compounds.

Pal'las (păl'*ȧ*s), *n.* [L., fr. Gr. *Pallas, -ados.*] **1.** *Gr. Myth.* **a** A giant slain by Athena in the war between the Olympians and the giants. **b** An epithet of Athena. Cf. 1st PALLADIAN. **2.** *Astron.* One of the asteroids.

pall'bear'er (pôl'bâr'ẽr), *n.* One of those who attend the coffin at a funeral.

pal'let (păl'ĕt; -ĭt), *n.* [ME. *paillet*, fr. OF. *paille* straw, fr. L. *palea* chaff.] **1.** A small and mean bed; a bed of straw. **2.** *Chiefly Southern U. S.* A quilt or blanket spread on the floor for a bed.

pal'let, *n.* [F. *palette*, dim. fr. L. *pala* shovel.] **1.** A wooden, flat-bladed implement such as used by potters, crucible makers, etc., for forming, beating, and rounding their works. **2.** An artist's palette. **3.** A portable, shallow, double-faced wooden or metal platform, commonly about four feet square, for holding material for storage or transportation, as in a warehouse. **4.** *Gilding.* A flat brush used in manipulating gold leaves. **5.** *Horol.* Any of the clicks or detents connected with the piece which transmits impulses from the escapement wheel to the balance, and checks the escape wheel until the return movement of the balance. See ESCAPEMENT, *Illust.* **6.** *Mach.* A click or pawl driving a ratchet wheel.

pal'let·ize (-īz), *v. t.* To place on a pallet (def. 3).

pal'lette (păl'ĕt; -ĭt), *n.* [See PALETTE.] *Armor.* One of the plates at the armpits. See ARMOR, *Illust.*

pal·liasse' (păl·yăs'; păl'yăs; păl'ĭ·ăs', păl'ĭ·ăs), *n.* Var. of PAILLASSE.

pal'li·ate (păl'ĭ·āt), *v. t.* [L. *palliatus* cloaked, fr. *pallium.* See PALL cloak.] **1.** *Obs.* To cloak; shelter; hide. **2.** To mitigate; to ease without curing; as, to *palliate* a disease. **3.** To cover with excuses; to extenuate; as, to *palliate* faults. — **pal'li·a'tor** (-ā'tẽr), *n.*

pal'li·a'tion (-ā'shŭn), *n.* [F.] A palliating; as: **a** Extenuation; excuse. **b** Mitigation; alleviation.

pal'li·a'tive (păl'ĭ·ā'tĭv; -*ȧ*·tĭv; 58), *adj.* Serving to palliate. — *n.* A palliative agent, as a drug.

pal'lid (păl'ĭd), *adj.* [L. *pallidus.*] Deficient in color; pale; wan. — **pal'lid·ly,** *adv.* — **pal'lid·ness,** *n.*

‖**pal'li·da Mors** (păl'ĭ·d*ȧ* môrz). [L.] Pale Death.

pal'li·um (păl'ĭ·ŭm), *n.; pl.* -LIA (-*ȧ*), -LIUMS (-ŭmz). [L. See PALL cloak.] **1.** *Anc. Costume.* A himation; — the Roman name. **2.** *Anat.* The cerebral cortex as a whole. **3.** *Eccl.* **a** *R.C.Ch.* A circular band of white wool with pendants, worn by archbishops over the chasuble on certain occasions. See VESTMENT, *Illust.* **b** An altar cloth; a pall. **4.** *Zool.* The mantle of a mollusk, brachiopod, or bird.

pall'-mall' (pĕl'mĕl'), *n.* [Obs. F. *palemail*, fr. It. *pallamaglio*, fr. *palla* ball + *maglio*, fr. L. *malleus* mallet.] **1.** A game, once common, in which a wooden ball was driven with a mallet; also, the alley in which it was played. **2.** Written **Pall Mall** (*pron. also* păl'măl'). In London, a street on the site of a former pall-mall alley, the center of club life.

pal'lor (păl'ẽr), *n.* [L.] Deficiency of color, as in the face; a wan appearance; paleness.

palm (päm), *n.* [ME. and L.; ME. *paume*, fr. OF. *paume*, fr. L. *palma.*] **1.** The somewhat concave part of the hand between the bases of the fingers and the wrist. **2.** The part of a glove covering the palm. **3.** A lineal measure equal either to the breadth of the hand (3–4 inches) or to its length from the wrist to the ends of the fingers (7–10 inches). **4.** A flat expanding part at the end of an armlike projection; specif., the blade of an oar or paddle. **5.** The broad flattened part of an antler, as of the moose. **6.** *Naut.* **a** The flat inner face of an anchor fluke; also, the fluke itself. See ANCHOR, *Illust.* **b** *Sailmaking.* A metal disk worn on the palm of the hand, used to push the needle through canvas in sewing sails.
— *v. t.* **1.** To stroke with the palm or hand; also, to shake hands with. **2.** In sleight of hand, to conceal about the hand. **3. a** To impose by fraud; — usually with *on* or *upon.* **b** To pass or put by trickery; — usually with *off.*

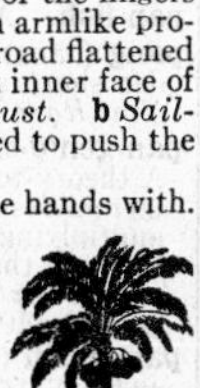

Date Palm (*Phoenix dactylifera*). (1/1000)

palm, *n.* [AS. *palm, palma*, fr. L. *palma*; — from the resemblance of the leaf to a hand.] **1.** Any of a family (Arecaceae, the palm family) of mostly tropical or subtropical monocotyledonous trees marked commonly by a simple stem and terminal crown of large leaves, pinnate in some species (*feather palms*) and fan-shaped in others (*fan palms*). Cf. ROYAL PALM. Certain species are of great economic importance, as the *betel coconut, date, gomuti, nipa, oil, piassava, rattan,* and *wax palms.* **2.** A leaf of the palm, borne as a symbol of victory or rejoicing. **3.** Any symbol of success or triumph; also, victory; triumph. **4.** *Mil.* An addition to a military decoration, specif. the French *Croix de guerre*, in the form of a palm frond, to indicate a second award of the basic decoration. — **pal·ma'ceous** (păl·mā'shŭs), *adj.*

pal'mar (păl'mẽr), *adj.* [L. *palmaris.*] *Anat.* Pert. to, corresponding to, or situated in the palm of the hand.

pal'mate (păl'māt), *adj.* Also **pal'mat·ed** (-māt·ĕd; -ĭd). [L. *palmatus.*] Hand-shaped; resembling a hand with the fingers spread; specif.: **a** *Bot.* Having lobes radiating from a common point; — said esp. of leaf blades. See LEAF, *Illust.* (24, 25, 26); VENATION, *Illust.* **b** *Zool.* Having the anterior toes united by a web, as in most swimming birds. — **pal'mate·ly,** *adv.*

pal·ma'tion (păl·mā'shŭn), *n.* State or quality of being palmate; palmate lobation; also, a palmate part.

palm cabbage. **a** The cabbage palmetto. **b** = CABBAGE, *n.*, 2.

palm crab. = PURSE CRAB.

palm'er (päm'ẽr), *n.* [OF. *paumier, palmier*, fr. ML. *palmarius.*] A pilgrim who wore two leaves of palm crosswise in token that he had visited the Holy Land.

palm'er, *v. i.* *Scot.* To wander about like a palmer.

palmer worm. [From *palmer* pilgrim.] Any caterpillar which suddenly appears in great numbers, devouring herbage. In America, esp. the larva of a moth (*Dichomeris ligulellus*) which is destructive to fruit trees.

pal·met'to (păl·mĕt'ō), *n.; pl.* -TOS, -TOES (-ōz). [Sp. *palmito*, dim. of *palma* palm tree.] **1.** Any of various fan palms (see 2d PALM, *n.*, 1), esp. of southern U. S. and the West Indies, as the ***cabbage palmetto*** (*Sabal palmetto*) and palms of the genera *Thrinax* and *Coccothrinax.* **2.** Strips of palmetto leaves, used in weaving.

Palmetto State. South Carolina; — a nickname alluding to the state arms, which contain a representation of a palmetto.

palm'ist (päm'ĭst; *formerly also* păl'mĭst), *n.* One who practices palmistry.

palm'is·try (päm'ĭs·trĭ; *formerly also* păl'mĭs-), *n.* [ME. *pawmestry*, fr. *paume* palm of the hand + (prob.) *maistrie* mastery, skill, fr. OF. *maistrie.*] Art or practice of telling fortunes or of judging of character, aptitudes, etc., by study of the palm of the hand; chiromancy.

pal'mi·tate (păl'mĭ·tāt), *n.* A salt or ester of palmitic acid.

pal·mit'ic (păl·mĭt'ĭk), *adj.* *Chem.* Designating a white, crystalline fatty acid (**palmitic acid,** $CH_3(CH_2)_{14}CO_2H$) occurring free in palm oil, and as the glyceryl ester (palmitin) in many fats.

pal'mi·tin (păl'mĭ·tĭn), *n.* [G. *palmitin*säure, trans. of F. *acide palmitique.*] *Chem.* A solid crystalline fat, a glyceryl ester of palmitic acid, associated with stearin and olein in animal fats.

palm oil. A solid yellow or reddish fat or butter obtained from the flesh of the fruit of several species of palms, esp. the oil palm, used in soap and candles, in greases, etc.

palm sugar. Sugar yielded by the sap of certain palms.

Palm Sunday. *Eccl.* The Sunday preceding Easter, commemorating Christ's entry into Jerusalem.

palm'y (päm'ĭ), *adj.;* PALM'I·ER (-ĭ·ẽr); PALM'I·EST. **1.** Bearing palms; abounding in palms. **2.** Flourishing; prosperous.

pal·my'ra (păl·mī'r*ȧ*), *n., or* **palmyra palm** *or* **tree.** [Pg. *palmeira* palm tree.] A tall, African palm (*Borassus flabelliformis*) with large fan-shaped leaves.

pal'o·mi'no (păl'ō·mē'nō), *n.* [Am. Sp., fr. Sp. *palomilla.*] *U. S.* **1.** A slender-legged short-coupled horse of a light tan or cream color, with flaxen or white mane and tail, from ancestry largely of Arabian stock. **2.** A color like that of this horse.

palp (pălp), *n.* [F. *palpe.*] A palpus.

pal'pa·ble (păl'p*ȧ*·b'l), *adj.* [OF., fr. LL. *palpabilis*, fr. *palpare* to feel, stroke.] **1.** Capable of being touched or felt; tangible. **2.** Easily perceptible by the senses; readily visible, audible, etc. **3.** Easily perceptible intellectually; plain; obvious. — **Syn.** See PERCEPTIBLE. — **Ant.** Impalpable. — **pal'pa·bil'i·ty** (-bĭl'ĭ·tĭ), *n.* — **pal'pa·bly,** *adv.*

pal'pate (păl'pāt), *adj.* *Zool.* Having a palpus or palpi.

pal'pate (-pāt), *v. t.* [L. *palpare, palpatum*, to feel.] To examine by touch, esp. medically. — **pal·pa'tion** (păl·pā'shŭn), *n.*

pal'pe·bral (păl'pē·brăl), *adj.* [LL. *palpebralis*, fr. *palpebra.*] Of or pertaining to the eyelids.

pal'pi (păl'pī), *n., pl.* of PALPUS.

pal'pi·tant (păl'pĭ·tănt), *adj.* [L. *palpitans*, pres. part.] Palpitating; throbbing.

pal'pi·tate (-tāt), *v. i.* [L. *palpitare, palpitatum*, v. intens. fr. *palpare.* See PALPABLE.] To beat rapidly and strongly; to flutter; throb; — of the heart.

pal'pi·ta'tion (-tā'shŭn), *n.* A rapid pulsation; esp., an abnormal, rapid beating of the heart.

pal'pus (păl'pŭs), *n.; pl.* -PI (-pī). [NL., a feeler, L., the soft palm of the hand.] *Zool.* In arthropods, a segmented process attached to a mouth part, usually having a tactile or gustatory function. See HYMENOPTERON, OYSTER, *Illusts.*

pals'grave' (pôlz'grāv'; pălz'-), *n.* [D. *paltsgrave*, now *paltsgraaf*, fr. *palts* palace + *graaf* count.] *Ger. Hist.* A count palatine. — **pals'gra·vine'** (-gr*ȧ*·vēn'), *n.*

pal'sy (pôl'zĭ), *n.; pl.* -SIES (-zĭz). [ME. *palesie*, fr. OF. *paralysie*, fr. L. *paralysis.* See PARALYSIS.] Paralysis. — *v. t.;* -SIED (-zĭd); -SY·ING. To affect with or as with palsy; to paralyze. — **pal'sied** (-zĭd), *adj.*

pal'ter (pôl'tẽr), *v. i.* **1.** To act insincerely; to equivocate. **2.** To haggle; chaffer. — **Syn.** See LIE.

pal'try (pôl'trĭ), *adj.* Rubbishy; trashy; worthless; contemptible. — **pal'tri·ly,** *adv.* — **pal'tri·ness,** *n.*

pa·lu'dal (p*ȧ*·lū'dăl; păl'ū·dăl; -d'l), *adj.* Also **pal'u·dine** (păl'ū·dĭn; -dīn). [L. *palus, -udis*, a marsh.] Of or pertaining to marshes or fens; marshy.

pal'u·dism (păl'ū·dĭz'm), *n.* *Med.* Malarial disease.

pal'u·drine (păl'ū·drēn; -drĭn), *n.* Also **pal'u·drin.** [*paludi-*, a combining form from L. *palus* marsh + *-ine.*] *Chem. & Pharm.* A colorless synthetic antimalarial drug, $C_{11}H_{16}ClN_5$.

pal'y (pāl'ĭ), *adj.;* PAL'I·ER (-ĭ·ẽr); PAL'I·EST. *Chiefly Poetic.* Pale; wan; pallid.

pal'y, *adj.* [F. *palé.* See PALE a stake.] *Her.* Divided into four or more equal parts by perpendicular lines, and of two different tinctures disposed alternately.

pam (păm), *n.* [F. *pamphile*, fr. Gr. personal name *Pamphilos.*]

Card Playing. **a** The knave of clubs in the game of loo. **b** A game like napoleon in which pam is the highest trump.

pam′pas (păm′pȧz; *attrib.* -pȧs; *Sp.* päm′päs), *n. pl.* [Sp., pl. of *pampa*, fr. Quechua *pampa* a plain.] Vast treeless plains, esp. those of Argentina.

pampas grass. A South American grass (*Cortaderia argentea*) with ample, silky white panicles.

pam·pe′an (păm·pē′ăn; păm′pē·ăn), *adj.* Of or pertaining to the pampas of South America or their Indian inhabitants. — *n.* An Indian of the pampas.

pam′per (păm′pẽr), *v. t.* **1.** *Obs.* To feed to the full; to glut. **2.** To indulge to excess. — **Syn.** See INDULGE. — **pam′per·er** (-ẽr), *n.*

pam·pe′ro (päm·pā′rō), *n.; pl.* -ROS (-rōz; *Sp.* -rôs). [Sp., fr. *pampa* a plain.] A strong, cold wind from the west or southwest, which sweeps over the pampas.

pam′phlet (păm′flĕt; -flĭt), *n.* [ME. *pamflet, pamfilet*, prob. a dim., through OF., fr. *Pamphilus*, a Latin poem of the 12th c.] A book of a few sheets of printed matter, commonly with a paper cover.

pam′phlet·eer′ (-ẽr′), *v. i.* To write and publish pamphlets. — *n.* A writer of pamphlets; — often contemptuous.

pan (păn), *n.* [AS. *panne.*] **1.** A dish or vessel for domestic uses, commonly broad, shallow, and open. **2. a** Either of the receptacles in a pair of scales. **b** A vessel for evaporating, as salt brine. **c** A vessel for grinding and amalgamating ores; also, a vessel for separating gold, tin, etc., from gravel, crushed rock, etc. **3. a** In old guns or pistols, the hollow part of the lock to receive the priming. **b** A natural depression, esp. one containing standing water or mud. **4.** Hardpan. — *v. t.;* PANNED (pănd); PAN′NING. **1.** To cook, wash, or otherwise treat in a pan; as, to *pan* gravel for gold. **2.** *Slang.* To criticize severely. — *v. i.* **1.** *Mining.* **a** To wash earth, gravel, etc., in a pan in searching for gold. **b** To yield gold in the process of panning. **2.** *Colloq.* To turn out (profitably or unprofitably); to result; — used with *out.*

pan (pän), *n.* [Hind. *pān*, fr. Skr. *parṇa* leaf.] The betel leaf; also, the masticatory made of it.

pan (păn), *v. t. & i.;* PANNED (pănd); PAN′NING. [Short for *panorama.*] *Motion Pictures.* To move in both the vertical and horizontal planes so as to keep an object in the picture or secure a panoramic effect; as to *pan* a camera; the camera *pans* to pick up the group.

Pan (păn), *n.* [L., fr. Gr. *Pan.*] *Gr. Relig.* A god of flocks and pastures, forests and their wild life, patron of shepherds, hunters, etc. Pan was represented as having the legs and sometimes the ears and horns of a goat. Cf. FAUNUS.

pan-, pan– (păn-). [Gr. *pas*, m., *pan*, neut., gen. *pantos*, all.] A combining form meaning *all, every*, used to denote: **a** Adverbially with adjectives, *all-*, as in *pansophic.* **b** [*cap.*] *The entirety of a diversified group;* — with the names of countries, or with adjectives formed therefrom, to imply a common bond or union, as in:

Pan-Asiatic	Pan-Hispanic	Pan-Scandinavian
Pan-British	Pan-Islam	Pan-Slav
Pan-European	Pan-Islamic	Pan-Slavic
Pan-German	Pan-Mongolian	Pan-Slavism
Pan-Germanic	Pan-Moslemism	Pan-Slavonic
Pan-Germanism	Pan-Pacific	Pan-Slavonism
Panhellenic	Pan-Russian	Pan-Teutonism
Panhellenism		

c *A type*, esp. of instrument or theory, *covering* or *superseding more limited forms*, as in *pangenesis.* **d** *Extending throughout an implied group* or *field.* **e** *Med. Affecting all* or *several parts; general*, as in:

panatrophy	panneuritic	panplegia

pan′a·ce′a (păn′ȧ·sē′ȧ), *n.* [L., fr. Gr. *panakeia*, fr. *panakēs* all-healing, fr. *pas, pan*, all + *akeisthai* to heal.] A remedy for all diseases; a cure-all. — **pan′a·ce′an** (-ăn), *adj.*

pa·nache′ (pȧ·nȧsh′), *n.* [F., fr. It. *pennacchio*, fr. *penna* feather.] A plume or bunch of feathers, esp. on a helmet.

pa·na′da (pȧ·nä′dȧ; -nā′dȧ), *n.* [Sp., fr. L. *panis* bread.] A prepared dish containing soaked bread crumbs; as, chicken *panada.*

Pan′a·ma hat (păn′ȧ·mô; -mä). Also **pan′a·ma**, *n.* [From *Panama* (city).] A fine hand-plaited hat, made in Ecuador of leaves of the jipijapa.

Pan′–A·mer′i·can, *adj.* [See PAN-.] Of or pertaining to both North America and South America or all Americans.

Pan′–A·mer′i·can·ism, *n.* **a** Advocacy of a political alliance of all the states of America. **b** Co-operation among the American republics in political and economic matters.

pan′a·tel′a (păn′ȧ·tĕl′ȧ), *n.* [Sp. *panetela.*] A cigar of a shape shorter, slenderer, and more tapering than the belvedere. See CIGAR.

pan′cake′ (păn′kāk′), *n.* **1.** A griddlecake. **2.** *Aviation.* A landing made abruptly and with little or no forward movement, as in pancaking. — *v. i. Aviation.* To "level off" an airplane higher than for a normal landing, causing it to stall and descend with the wings at a very large angle of attack, on a steeply inclined path.

pan′chro·mat′ic (păn′krō·măt′ĭk), *adj.* [*pan-* + *chromatic.*] *Photog.* Sensitive, as a plate, to light of all colors. — **pan·chro′ma·tism** (păn·krō′mȧ·tĭz′m), *n.*

pan·cra′ti·um (păn·krā′shĭ·ŭm), *n.* [L., fr. Gr. *pankration* a complete contest, fr. *pas, pan*, all + *kratos* strength.] *Gr. Antiq.* An athletic contest involving both boxing and wrestling. — **pan·crat′ic** (-krăt′ĭk), *adj.*

pan′cre·as (păn′krē·ăs; păng′-), *n.* [NL., fr. Gr. *pankreas*, fr. *pas, pan*, all + *kreas* flesh, meat.] *Anat. & Zool.* A large racemose gland discharging into the intestine, present in most vertebrates. It is called *sweetbread* when used as food. — **pan′cre·at′ic** (păng′krē·ăt′ĭk; păn′-), *adj.*

pan′cre·at′ic juice. *Physiol.* The clear alkaline secretion of the pancreas which is poured into the duodenum, and acts on the food already acted on by the gastric juice.

pan′cre·a·tin (păng′krē·ȧ·tĭn; păn′-), *n. Biochem.* **a** Any enzyme of the pancreatic juice; also, a mixture of these enzymes. **b** A preparation made from the pancreas of animals, used as a digestive.

pan′cre·a·to- (păng′krē·ȧ·tō-; păn′-), **pancreat-.** [From the stem of Gr. *pankreas.*] A combining form used to indicate *connection with,* or *relation to, the pancreas;* as in **pan′cre·a·tec′to·my, pan′cre·a·tot′o·my** (see -ECTOMY, -TOMY).

pan′da (păn′dȧ), *n.* **1.** A plantigrade carnivorous mammal (*Ailurus fulgens*) of the Himalayas, related to the raccoons. **2.** Short for **giant panda**, a large black-and-white bearlike mammal (*Ailuropoda*, syn. *Pandarctos, melanoleuca*) of Tibet.

pan·da′nus (păn·dā′nŭs), *n.* [NL., fr. Malay *pandan.*] Any of a genus (*Pandanus*) of tropical Old World plants, the screw pines. See SCREW PINE.

Pan′da·rus (păn′dȧ·rŭs), *n.* [L., fr. Gr. *Pandaros.*] A leader of the Lycians in the Trojan War. In medieval romances, and by Chaucer and Shakespeare, he is represented as procuring Cressida for Troilus.

Pan·de′an (păn·dē′ăn), *adj.* Of or pert. to the god Pan.

Pandean pipes. = PANPIPE.

pan′dect (păn′dĕkt), *n.* [F. *pandecte*, fr. L. *pandecta, pandectes*, fr. Gr. *pandektēs* all-receiving, fr. *pas, pan*, all + *dechesthai* to receive.] **1.** *pl.* [*cap.*] The digest of the decisions, writings, and opinions of the old Roman jurists, — the leading compilation of the Roman civil law. **2.** Any complete code of laws. **3.** A complete digest.

pan·dem′ic (păn·dĕm′ĭk), *adj.* [LL. *pandemus*, fr. Gr. *pandēmos, pandēmios*, fr. *pas, pan*, all + *dēmos* the people.] Of or pert. to all the people; general; universal; specif., *Med.*, affecting the majority of people in a country or a number of countries; everywhere epidemic. — *n.* A pandemic disease.

Pan′de·mo′ni·um (păn′dē·mō′nĭ·ŭm; 58), *n.* [NL., fr. *pan-* + Gr. *daimōn* a demon.] **1.** The abode of demons; in Milton, the capital of Hell or palace of Satan; loosely, hell. **2.** [*not cap.*] A wild tumult.

pan′der (păn′dẽr), *n.* [See PANDARUS.] **1.** A go-between in love intrigues; a pimp. **2.** A minister to the evil passions of others. — *v. t.* To play the pander for. — *v. i.* To act the part of a pander. — **pan′der·er** (-ẽr), *n.*

Pan·do′ra (păn·dō′rȧ; 70), *n.* [L., fr. Gr. *Pandōra*, fr. *pas, pan*, all + *dōron* a gift.] *Gr. Myth.* A woman sent by Zeus as punishment for the human race because Prometheus had stolen fire from heaven. Zeus gave her a box (**Pandora's box**) enclosing all human ills, which escaped when she opened the box. Hope, also in the box, remained.

pan·do′ra (păn·dō′rȧ; 70), **pan·dore′** (păn·dōr′; păn′dōr), *n.* [It. *pandora.* See BANDORE.] A bandore.

pan′dour (păn′do͝or), *n.* [F., fr. G. *pandur*, fr. Croatian *pandur* constable, mounted policeman.] One of a local Croatian constabulary or military force organized chiefly to repress brigands.

pan·dow′dy (păn·dou′dĭ), *n.; pl.* PANDOWDIES (-dĭz). *U.S.* A deep pie or pudding of apples, often sweetened with molasses.

pan·du′ri·form (păn·dū′rĭ·fôrm), *adj.* Also **pan′du·rate** (păn′dū·rāt). [LL. *pandura* a pandora + *-form.*] Obovate, with a concavity in each side, like a violin. See LEAF, *Illust.* (11).

pan′dy (păn′dĭ), *n.; pl.* -DIES (-dĭz). [L. *pande* hold out (your hand), imper. of *pandere* to extend.] *Scot. & Dial.* A stroke on the palm, as with a cane. — *v. t. & i.* To strike (the hand), as with a cane.

pane (pān), *n.* [OF. *pan*, fr. L. *pannus* a cloth, rag.] **1.** A piece, section, or side of something; specif.: **a** A star facet. **b** One of the sides of a nut or bolthead. **2.** *Arch.* A panel; hence: **a** One of the compartments of a window, door, etc., consisting of one sheet of glass in a frame. **b** In modern use, the glass, or substitute for it, in one compartment of a window sash, door, etc. **3.** *Obs.* A counterpane. **4.** One of the divisions (usually two or four) of a sheet of stamps.

pan′e·gyr′ic (păn′ē·jĭr′ĭk), *n.* [L. *panegyricus*, fr. Gr. *panēgyrikos*, fr. *panēgyris* an assembly of the people, fr. *pas, pan*, all + *agyris, agora*, an assembly.] A eulogistic oration or writing; also, formal eulogizing. — **Syn.** See ENCOMIUM. — **pan′e·gyr′i·cal** (-ĭ·kăl), *adj.* — **pan′e·gyr′i·cal·ly**, *adv.*

pan′e·gyr′ist (păn′ē·jĭr′ĭst; păn′ē·jĭr′ĭst), *n.* A eulogist.

pan′e·gy·rize (păn′ē·jĭ·rīz), *v. t. & i.* To write or deliver a panegyric on; to eulogize.

pan′el (păn′ĕl; -'l), *n.* [OF., fr. L. *panis* panel.] **1.** A pad or cushion serving as a saddle. **2.** *Arch., etc.* A compartment, portion, or section of a wall, ceiling, or other surface; specif.: **a** Of a fence or railing, a section between two posts. **b** A portion of a framed structure, as of a bridge truss, between adjacent posts or struts. **c** A thin, usually rectangular, board or the like, set in a frame, as in a door. **d** Of or in a window, a compartment or pane. **3.** Something resembling a door or wainscot panel, as a thin flat piece of wood on which, instead of canvas, a picture is painted; also, a painting on such a surface. **4. a** Any of several units of construction of a wing surface of an airplane. **b** In rigid airships, the area bounded by two adjacent longerons and two adjacent transverses. **5.** An ornamental strip placed lengthwise on a dress or skirt. **6.** *Elec.* A section of a switchboard. **7.** *Law.* A document containing the names of persons summoned as jurors by the sheriff; hence, generally, the whole jury. **8.** *Mining.* A division of a mine in one system of mining. **9.** A list or group of persons appointed for some service; as, an advisory *panel;* a *panel* on a television quiz program. — *v. t.;* -ELED (-ĕld; -'ld) or -ELLED; -EL·ING or -EL·LING. **1.** *Law.* **a** To impanel (a jury). **b** *Scots Law.* To indict. **2.** To furnish, fit, or adorn with paneling.

panel discussion. Discussion, as of public issues, in which a selected list, or panel, of speakers engage.

panel heating. The heating of a house, room, etc., by heat radiated from large warmed surfaces, as floors, ceilings, or panels; — called also *radiant heating.*

pan′el·ing, pan′el·ling (păn′ĕl·ĭng), *n.* Wood, etc., made into panels.

pan′el·ist (-ĭst), *n.* A member of a panel for discussion or entertainment.

pan′e·tel′a, pan′e·tel′la (păn′ē·tĕl′ȧ). Vars. of PANATELA.

pan fish. A small fish suitable for frying whole.

pang (păng), *n.* **1.** A paroxysm of extreme pain; a throe. **2.** A sudden sharp attack of any emotion; as, the *pangs* of remorse. — *v. t. Now Rare.* To cause to have a pang or pangs.

pan·gen′e·sis (păn·jĕn′ē·sĭs), *n.* [NL., fr. *pan-* + *-genesis.*] *Biol.* A theory to explain heredity that the cells throw off minute granules (gemmules), which, circulating freely throughout the system, and multiplying by subdivision, collect in the reproductive products, or in buds, so that the egg or bud contains gemmules from all parts of the parent or parents; — opposed to *blastogenesis.* — **pan′ge·net′ic** (păn′jē·nĕt′ĭk), *adj.*

pan·go′lin (păng·gō′lĭn), *n.* [Malay *pĕngulin* roller, fr. *gulin* to roll; — from its rolling itself into a ball.] Any of several Asiatic and African edentate mammals (*Manis* and allied genera, order Pholidota); a scaly anteater.

pan′han′dle (păn′hăn′d'l), *n.* The handle of a pan; hence, any arm or projection of land like the handle of a pan, such as the northwestern part of Oklahoma.

pan′han′dle, *v. t. & i.* [From *panhandler*, fr. *pan* bowl or cup for alms + *handler.*] *Slang.* To accost and beg (from). — **pan′han′dler** (-dlẽr), *n.*

Pan′hel·len′ic (păn′hĕ·lĕn′ĭk; -lē′nĭk), *adj.* **1.** Of or pertaining to all Greece or Panhellenism. **2.** Of or pertaining to all Greek-letter fraternities or sororities in the United States or an organization representing them.

Pan·hel′len·ism (păn·hĕl′ĕn·ĭz′m), *n.* The idea of, or movement or sympathy for, political union of all Greeks; Panhellenic spirit, policies, etc. — **Pan·hel′len·ist** (-ĭst), *n.*

pan′ic (păn′ĭk), *n.* [L. *panicum,* fr. *panus* ear of millet, tuft.] Panic grass; also, the edible grain of some species.

pan′ic, *adj.* [F. *panique,* fr. Gr. *panikos,* fr. *Pan* Pan.] **1.** Literally, of or pert. to Pan; — used of sudden, extreme, and groundless fear, such as Pan was supposed to cause; as, *panic* terror. **2.** Of, pert. to, or coming from such fear. — *n.* **1.** A sudden, overpowering fright, esp. when groundless. **2.** A sudden widespread fright concerning financial affairs, resulting in an artificial depression in values caused by violent measures for protection or for the sale of securities or other property. — *v. t.;* PAN′ICKED (-ĭkt); PAN′ICK·ING (-ĭk·ĭng). **1.** To affect with panic. **2.** *Slang.* To produce demonstrative appreciation on the part of; as, to *panic* an audience with a new act. — **Syn.** See FEAR. — **pan′ick·y** (păn′ĭk·ĭ), *adj.* — **pan′ic–strick′en, pan′ic–struck′,** *adj.*

panic grass. Any of a genus (*Panicum*) of grasses, or of several closely related genera (as *Echinochloa*).

pan′i·cle (păn′ĭ·k'l), *n.* [L. *panicula* tuft on plants, dim. of *panus* tuft, ear of millet.] *Bot.* A compound racemose inflorescence; popularly, any pyramidal loosely branched flower cluster. See INFLORESCENCE, *Illust.* (8).

pa·nic′u·late (pȧ·nĭk′ū·lāt), *adj.* *Bot.* Arranged in panicles; branching like a panicle. — **pa·nic′u·lat′ed** (-lāt′ĕd; -ĭd), *adj.* — **pa·nic′u·late·ly,** *adv.*

Pan·ja′bi (pŭn·jä′bē), *n.* The language of the Punjab, a Sanskritic language with Arabic and Persian loanwords. See INDO-EUROPEAN LANGUAGES, *Table.*

pan·jan′drum (păn·jăn′drŭm), *n.* [Coined in imitation of words from Gr. beginning with *pan-,* and of L. endings.] A burlesque title for a powerful or pretentious official.

panne (păn), *n.* [F.] A soft fabric resembling velvet, but with a longer, looser nap and a smooth, lustrous finish.

pan′nier (păn′yẽr; -ĭ·ẽr; 58), *n.* [OF. *panier,* fr. L. *panarium* breadbasket, fr. *panis* bread.] **1.** A rather large basket; esp., a wicker basket carried on the back of a horse or on the shoulder of a person. **2.** A framework formerly worn by women to expand their skirts at the hips; also, an overskirt puffed full at the sides.

pan′ni·kin (păn′ĭ·kĭn), *n.* A small pan or cup.

pan′nose (păn′ōs), *adj.* [L. *pannosus,* fr. *pannus* cloth.] *Bot.* Like felt or woolen cloth in texture or look.

pa·no′cha (pä·nō′chä), *n.* [Sp. *panocha, panoja.*] **a** A Mexican raw sugar. **b** Also **pa·no′che** (pȧ·nō′chĭ), **pa·nou′chi** (pȧ·nōō′chĭ), **pe·nu′che** (pē·nōō′chē), **pe·nu′chi** (pē·nōō′chĭ). A sweetmeat usually of brown sugar, cream, and nuts.

pan′o·ply (păn′ō·plĭ), *n.; pl.* -PLIES (-plĭz). [Gr. *panoplia,* fr. *pas, pan,* all + *hoplon* tool, in pl., armor, arms.] **1.** A full suit of armor. **2.** Anything protecting completely or forming a magnificent covering. — **pan′o·plied** (-plĭd), *adj.*

pan′o·ra′ma (păn′ō·rä′mȧ; -răm′ȧ), *n.* [Gr. *pas, pan,* all + *horama* that which is seen, fr. *horan* to see.] **1.** A picture exhibited a part at a time, by being unrolled before the spectator. **2.** An unobstructed or complete view of a region in every direction; hence, a comprehensive presentation of a subject. **3.** A mental picture of a series of images or events, etc. — **pan′o·ram′ic** (-răm′ĭk), *adj.*

pan′o·ram′ic sight. A form of periscopic sight for use by marksmen, etc.

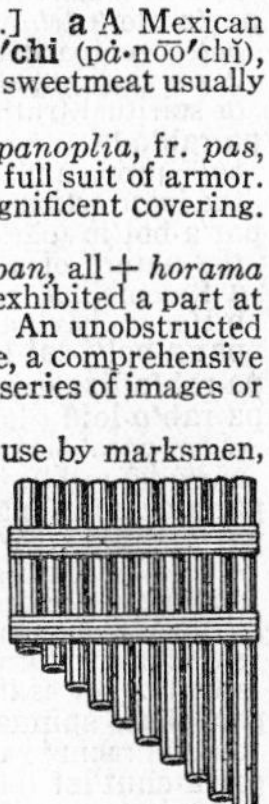
Panpipe.

Pan′pipe′ (păn′pīp′), *n.* *Music.* A primitive wind instrument, consisting of a series of short hollow reeds bound together side by side, the lower ends being stopped.

pan′so·phism (păn′sō·fĭz′m), *n.* [Gr. *pansophos* all-wise.] Pretension to universal knowledge. — **pan′so·phist** (-fĭst), *n.*

pan′so·phy (-fĭ), *n.* Universal wisdom or encyclopedic knowledge. — **pan·soph′ic** (păn·sŏf′ĭk), **pan·soph′i·cal** (-ĭ·kăl), *adj.*

pan′sy (păn′zĭ), *n.; pl.* -SIES (-zĭz). [F. *pensée* thought, pansy, fr. *penser* to think, fr. L. *pensare* to weigh, ponder.] **1.** A garden violet (*Viola tricolor hortensis*), derived from the ***wild pansy*** (*Viola tricolor*) of Europe; also, its flower. **2.** *Slang.* **a** An effeminate young man. **b** A male homosexual.

pant (pănt), *v. i.* [OF. *pantaisier* to be breathless.] **1.** To breathe quickly, or in a labored manner, as from exertion. **2.** Hence: To long eagerly; to yearn. **3.** To throb; to pulsate; — said of the heart, blood, etc. — *v. t.* To breathe or utter quickly or laboriously; gasp; — with *out* or *forth.* — *n.* **1.** One of a series of short spasmodic breaths, as after exertion; a gasp. Also, a throb or puff of an engine. **2.** A palpitation, or throb, as of the heart.

pant-. [Gr. *pas, pantos.*] A combining form meaning *all,* equivalent to *pan-.*

pan′ta-. Erron. var. of PANTO- (which see).

Pan·tag′ru·el (păn·tăg′rōō·ĕl; *F.* päɴ′tȧ′grü′ĕl′), *n.* [F.] The giant son of Gargantua in Rabelais's *Pantagruel.* He is a jolly drunkard, whose unrestrained humor has a serious satirical purpose. — **Pan′ta·gru·el′i·an** (păn′tȧ·grōō·ĕl′ĭ·ăn), *adj.* — **Pan′ta·gru′el·ism** (păn′tȧ·grōō′ĕl·ĭz′m; păn·tăg′rōō·ĕl·ĭz′m), *n.* — **Pan′ta·gru′el·ist** (-ĭst), *n.*

pan′ta·lets′, pan′ta·lettes′ (păn′tȧ·lĕts′), *n. pl.; sing., Rare,* PANTALET, PANTALETTE. [Dim., fr. PANTALOON.] In women's and girls' costume of about 1830–50, long loose drawers with a frill or ruffle at the bottom of each leg; also, a detachable frill or ruffle showing below the skirt.

pan′ta·loon′ (păn′tȧ·lōōn′), *n.* [F. *pantalon,* fr. It. *Pantalone,* a masked character in comedy, fr. *Pantaleone,* the patron saint of Venice.] **1.** [*cap.*] In Italian comedy, a character, usually a lean old dotard, with a kind of tight-fitting combination of trousers and stockings; also, in pantomimes, a buffoon. **2.** *Usually pl.* Trousers.

pan·tech′ni·con (păn·tĕk′nĭ·kŏn; -kŭn), *n.* [NL. See PAN-; TECHNIC.] *Eng.* A furniture van.

pan′the·ism (păn′thē·ĭz′m), *n.* [*pan-* + *theism.*] **1.** The doctrine that the universe, taken or conceived of as a whole, is God; the doctrine that there is no God but the combined forces and laws which are manifested in the existing universe. **2.** The worship of gods of different creeds, cults, or peoples indifferently. — **pan′the·ist** (-ĭst), *n.* — **pan′the·is′tic** (-ĭs′tĭk), **pan′the·is′ti·cal** (-tĭ·kăl), *adj.* — **pan′the·is′ti·cal·ly,** *adv.*

pan′the·on (păn′thē·ŏn; -ŭn; păn·thē′ŏn), *n.* [L., fr. Gr. *pantheion* (sc. *hieron*), fr. *pantheios* of all gods, fr. *pas, pan,* all + *theios* of the god, fr. *theos* a god.] **1.** A temple dedicated to all the gods; esp. [*cap.*], the building so called at Rome. **2.** A building resembling or likened to the Roman Pantheon; esp., a building where rest the famous dead of a nation. **3.** The aggregate gods of a people.

pan′ther (păn′thẽr), *n.* See PLURAL, *Note,* 3. [OF. *pantere* (F. *panthère*), fr. L. *panthera,* fr. Gr. *panthēr.*] **a** The leopard; esp., a supposed robust and fierce variety, or the black variety. **b** In America, the cougar, or, less often, the jaguar. — **pan′ther·ess** (-ĕs; -ĭs), *n.*

pant′ie, pant′ies. See PANTY.

pan′tile′ (păn′tīl′), *n.* [*pan* dish + *tile.*] **a** A roofing tile whose cross section is a dissymmetrical ogee curve. **b** A longitudinally curved roofing tile, laid alternately with convex covering tiles; a gutter tile.

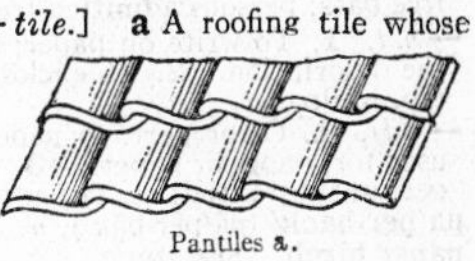
Pantiles a.

pant′ing, *adj.* That pants. — **pant′ing·ly,** *adv.*

pan′to- (păn′tō-). [Gr. *pas, pan,* gen. *pantos.*] A combining form meaning *all,* as in *panto*mime.

pan′to·fle, pan′tof·fle (păn′tō·f'l; păn·tŏf′'l; -tōō′f'l), *n.* [F. *pantoufle.*] A slipper.

pan′to·graph (păn′tō·grȧf; 9), *n.* [*panto-* + *-graph.*] **1.** An instrument, essentially of four light rigid links jointed in parallelogram form, to copy maps, plans, or the like on any predetermined scale. **2.** *Elec.* A trolley or current-collecting device carried by a light collapsible frame. — **pan′to·graph′ic** (-grăf′ĭk), *adj.* — **pan·tog′ra·phy** (păn·tŏg′rȧ·fĭ), *n.*

pan·tol′o·gy (păn·tŏl′ō·jĭ), *n.* A systematic view of all knowledge. — **pan′to·log′ic** (păn′tō·lŏj′ĭk), **pan′to·log′i·cal** (-ĭ·kăl), *adj.* — **pan·tol′o·gist** (păn·tŏl′ō·jĭst), *n.*

pan′to·mime (păn′tō·mīm), *n.* [F., fr. L. *pantomimus,* fr. Gr. *pantomimos,* lit., all-imitating, fr. *pas, pantos,* all + *mimos* mimic, mime.] **1.** An actor in a dumb-show performance, esp. in ancient Rome. **2.** A dramatic performance by actors using only, or chiefly, dumb show. **3.** Hence, dumb show of any sort. — *v. t. & i.* To represent by pantomime. — **pan′to·mim′ic** (-mĭm′ĭk), *adj.* — **pan′to·mim′ic·ry** (-rĭ), *n.*

pan′to·mim′ist (păn′tō·mīm′ĭst), *n.* An actor in pantomime; also, a composer of pantomimes.

pan′to·scope (păn′tō·skōp), *n.* [*panto-* + *-scope.*] *Photog.* A form of wide-angle lens.

pan′to·scop′ic (-skŏp′ĭk), *adj.* Having a wide field of view.

pan′to·then′ic ac′id (păn′tō·thĕn′ĭk). [Gr. *pantothen* from every side.] A member of the vitamin-B complex. See VITAMIN.

pan·toum′ (păn·tōōm′), *n.* [F. See PANTUN.] *Pros.* A series of quatrains rhyming ABAB, BCBC, CDCD, etc., with A as the final rhyme. See PANTUN.

pan′try (păn′trĭ), *n.; pl.* -TRIES (-trĭz). [OF. *paneterie,* fr. *panetier* pantler, fr. *pain* bread, fr. L. *panis.*] A room or closet where bread and other provisions are kept; also, a room near a dining room for glassware, chinaware, etc.

pants (pănts), *n. pl.* [Contr. *pantaloons.*] Trousers; (*Brit.*) drawers.

pan·tun′ (păn·tōōn′), *n.* [Malay.] *Pros.* The Malay verse form imitated under the name *pantoum* (which see).

pant′y (păn′tĭ), *n.* Also **pant′ie** (-tĭ). *Usually in pl.* **pant′ies** (-tĭz). A child's or woman's undergarment covering the lower trunk, with closed crotch and very short legs.

pant′y gir′dle (păn′tĭ). A woman's girdle with a closed crotch and usually without garters.

pant′y·waist′ (păn′tĭ·wāst′), *n.* A child's garment consisting of short pants buttoned to a waist; hence, *Slang,* a sissy. — *adj.* Childish; infantile; also, *Slang,* sissified.

Pan′urge (păn′ûrj; *F.* pȧ′nürzh′), *n.* [F., fr. Gr. *panourgos* ready to do anything, a rogue.] In Rabelais's *Pantagruel,* Pantagruel's favorite, a witty spendthrift, tippler, libertine, coward, and rogue.

Pan′za, Sancho. See SANCHO PANZA.

‖**Pan′zer** (pän′tsẽr; *Angl.* păn′zẽr), *n.* [G.] *Mil.* Literally, armor; — equivalent in combination with nouns to an adjective meaning *armored,* specif. in **Panzer division** [G. *Panzerdivision* (pän′tsẽr·dē·vē·zyōn′); *pl.* -DIVISIONEN (-dē·vē·zyō′nĕn)], a mechanized armored offense unit. Hence, **panzer,** *n.* Any mechanized armored force.

pap (păp), *n.* [ME. *pap, pappe.*] **1.** *Archaic.* A nipple; teat. **2.** Anything shaped like a nipple.

pap, *n.* **1.** A soft food for infants or invalids. **2.** *Colloq.* Support from official patronage; as, treasury *pap.*

pa′pa (pä′pȧ; pȧ·pä′; *Brit. usually* pȧ·pä′), *n.* [F., orig. a child's word.] Father; — a child's word.

pa′pa (pä′pä), *n.* [L., father, bishop, fr. Gr. *papas, pappas.*] *Eccl.* **a** The pope. **b** *Eastern Ch.* (1) The patriarch of Alexandria. (2) One of the lower clergy.

pa′pa·cy (pā′pȧ·sĭ), *n.; pl.* PAPACIES (-sĭz). [ML. *papatia,* fr. L. *papa.* See POPE.] **1.** The office and dignity of the pope; papal jurisdiction. **2.** The succession of popes; the papal line. **3.** The period of time a pope reigns. **4.** [*cap.*] The system of government in the Roman Catholic Church of which the pope is the supreme head.

pa·pa′in (pȧ·pā′ĭn; pā′pȧ·ĭn), *n.* [See PAPAW.] *Biochem.* A proteolytic enzyme in the juice of the green fruit of the papaya, and apparently intermediate in action between pepsin and trypsin. It is used as a digestive.

pa′pal (pā′păl), *adj.* [OF.] **1.** Of or pert. to the pope of Rome; ordered or uttered by the pope. **2.** Of or pertaining to the Roman Catholic Church.

papal cross. See CROSS, *Illust.* (4).

pa·pa′ver·a′ceous (pȧ·păv′ẽr·ā′shŭs), *adj.* [L. *papaver* poppy.] *Bot.* Belonging to the poppy family (Papaveraceae). See POPPY.

pa·pav′er·ine (pȧ·păv′ẽr·ēn; -ĭn; pȧ·pā′vẽr-), *n.* Also **pa·pav′er·in.** A crystalline alkaloid, $C_{20}H_{21}NO_4$, constituting about one per cent of opium. It relaxes nonstriated muscle and has a weak analgesic and local anesthetic action.

pa·paw′, paw·paw′ (pȧ·pô′, *less often* pô·pô′, *in sense* **1**; pô′pô′ *in sense* 2). [Sp. *papayo* papaw tree, *papaya* its fruit.] **1.** The papaya. **2.** The oblong yellowish fruit of a tree (*Asimina triloba*) of the central and southern United States; also, the tree.

pa·pay′a (pȧ·pī′ȧ), *n.* [Sp., prop., fruit of the papaw.] The large, oblong, yellow, edible fruit of a tropical American tree (*Carica papaya*, family Caricaceae); also, the tree.

pa′per (pā′pẽr), *n.* [OF. *papier*, fr. L. *papyrus* paper, papyrus, from which the Egyptians made a kind of paper, fr. Gr. *papyros*.] **1.** A substance made in thin sheets or leaves from rags, straw, bark, wood, or other fibrous material, for various uses. **2.** A sheet, leaf, or piece of such substance. **3.** Something resembling such sheets or leaves, as the papyrus of the ancients; also, papier-mâché. **4.** A sheet or leaf containing (usually) a definite quantity; as, a *paper* of pins. **5.** A document; a writing, as a note, or essay; specif., *pl.*, documents proving identity, validity, etc.; as, an officer's *papers*. Hence: **a** Negotiable paper. **b** (*pl.*) = SHIP'S PAPERS. **6.** A newspaper; journal. **7.** Decorated coverings for walls, made of paper (sense 1). **8.** *Slang.* A free pass; persons admitted free, as to a dramatic presentation. — *v. t.* **1.** To write on paper; also, to describe on paper and publish the description. **2.** To enclose in paper. **3.** To furnish with paper, esp. wallpaper. — *adj.* **1.** Of or pert. to paper; made of paper. **2.** Dealing in, or used for, paper or papers. **3.** Resembling paper; existing only on paper; unsubstantial; as, *paper* profit.

pa′per·back′ (pā′pẽr·băk′), *n.* *Colloq.* A paper-covered book.

paper birch. See BIRCH.

pa′per·board′ (pā′pẽr·bōrd′), *n.* Cardboard, pasteboard, etc. — **pa′per·board′**, *adj.*

paper chase. Hare and hounds. — **pa′per–chas′ing**, *adj. & n.*

paper cutter. A device fitted with a knife for cutting many sheets of paper simultaneously; also, a paper knife.

pa′per·er (pā′pẽr·ẽr), *n.* One who puts on paper, as a paper hanger; also, one who sandpapers.

paper hanger. One who covers walls, etc., with wallpaper. — **paper hanging.** — **pa′per–hang′ing**, *adj.*

paper hangings. Wallpaper.

paper knife. An implement with a thin blade, and often an ornamental handle, for slitting envelopes, the leaves of a book, etc.

paper money. Paper documents that circulate instead of metallic money; strictly, those forms issued for such circulation, as government notes, bank notes, etc.; loosely, all instruments, such as checks and drafts, that have the effect of replacing money in circulation.

paper nautilus. See NAUTILUS, 2.

paper profit. A prospective unrealized profit on a transaction not concluded.

pa′per·weight′ (pā′pẽr·wāt′), *n.* Any object designed to hold down loose papers by its weight.

paper work. The writing or reviewing of papers, specif., of records, army reports, school compositions or examinations, etc.

pa′per·y (pā′pẽr·ĭ), *adj.* Like paper; of the thinness or consistency of paper.

pap′e·terie (păp′ĕ·trĭ; *F.* pȧp′trē′), *n.* [F., fr. *papetier* maker or seller of paper, fr. *papier* paper.] A case or box with paper and writing materials.

Pa′phi·an (pā′fĭ·ăn), *adj.* Of or pertaining to Paphos, an ancient city of Cyprus with a famous temple of Aphrodite; hence, pertaining to love, esp. illicit love. — *n.* A prostitute.

‖**pa′pier′ col′lé′** (pȧ′pyā′ kô′lā′); *pl.* PAPIERS COLLÉS (pȧ′pyā′ kô′lā′). [F., lit., pasted paper.] *Cubism.* An agglomeration of bits of paper and odds and ends pasted flat on a board or canvas in a grouping directed by a subconscious impulse of the artist, to form a composition.

pa′pier–mâ·ché′ (pā′pẽr·mă·shā′; *F.* pȧ′pyā′mä′shā′), *n.* [F., chewed paper.] A hard and strong substance made of a paper pulp mixed with size, rosin, etc. — **pa′pier–mâ·ché′**, *adj.*

pa·pil′i·o·na′ceous (pȧ·pĭl′ĭ·ō·nā′shŭs), *adj.* [L. *papilio* a butterfly + *-aceous*.] Like a butterfly; specif.: *Bot.* **a** Belonging to the pea family (Fabaceae). **b** Having an irregular zygomorphic corolla somewhat resembling a butterfly.

pa·pil′la (pȧ·pĭl′ȧ), *n.; pl.* -LAE (-ē). [L., nipple.] **1.** The nipple; any small nipplelike projection or part. **2.** *Anat. & Zool.* **a** A process of connective tissue extending into and nourishing the root of a hair, feather, or developing tooth. **b** One of the vascular protuberances of the dermal layer of the skin. **c** One of the small protuberances over the upper surface of the tongue. **3.** *Bot.* An epidermal cell forming a conical protuberance like a minute hair.

pap′il·lar′y (păp′ĭ·lĕr′ĭ; -lẽr·ĭ; pȧ·pĭl′ȧ·rĭ), *adj.* Of, pertaining to, or resembling a papilla or papillae; papillose.

pap′il·lo′ma (păp′ĭ·lō′mȧ), *n.; pl.* -LOMATA (-tȧ), -LOMAS (-mȧz). [NL., fr. *papilla* + *-oma*.] *Med.* An epithelial tumor, such as a corn or a wart, formed by hypertrophy of the papillae of the skin or mucous membrane.

pap′il·lon (păp′ĭ·lŏn; *F.* pȧ′pē′yôɴ′), *n.* [F., lit. butterfly; — from the shape of its ears.] A tiny dog of a European breed kept almost solely as a pet.

pap′il·lose (păp′ĭ·lōs), *adj.* Covered with, or bearing, papillae; resembling papillae. — **pap′il·los′i·ty** (-lŏs′ĭ·tĭ), *n.*

pap′il·lote (-lōt), *n.* [F.] **1.** A curlpaper. **2.** A paper wrapper in which cutlets are sometimes served.

pa′pist, Pa′pist (pā′pĭst), *n.* A Roman Catholic regarded as a partisan of the pope; — used disparagingly. — **pa′pist, Pa′pist**, *adj.*

pa·pis′tic (pȧ·pĭs′tĭk), *adj.* Also **pa·pis′ti·cal** (-tĭ·kăl). Of or pertaining to the Roman Catholic Church and its doctrines, ceremonies, or government; — used disparagingly.

pa·poose′ (pă·po͞os′), *n.* [Amer. Ind. *papoos* suckling.] A young child of North American Indian parents.

pap′pose (păp′ōs; 2), *adj.* Also **pap′pous** (păp′ŭs). *Bot.* Furnished with a pappus; of the nature of a pappus.

pap′pus (păp′ŭs), *n.; pl.* PAPPI (-ī). [L., an old man, pappus, fr. Gr. *pappos*.] *Bot.* Any appendage or tuft of appendages crowning the ovary or fruit in certain seed plants, notably the composites.

pa·pri′ka (pă·prē′kȧ; păp′rĭ·kȧ), *n.* Also **pa·pri′ca**. [G. *paprika*, fr. Hung. *paprika* Turkish pepper.] **a** The ripe fruit of the bonnet pepper (*Capsicum tetragonum*) and possibly of other species of *Capsicum* (see PEPPER, *n.*, 3). **b** The mildly pungent spice prepared from these fruits.

Pap′u·an (păp′ū·ăn), *n.* [Malay *papuwa* frizzled.] **1.** One of the native race of Papua, or New Guinea, having sooty brown to black complexions and frizzly hair. **2.** One of any of the darker races of Oceania. — **Pap′u·an**, *adj.*

pap′ule (păp′ūl), *n.* [L. *papula* pimple.] *Med.* A pimple.

pa·py′rus (pȧ·pī′rŭs), *n.; pl.* PAPYRI (-rī). [L. See PAPER.] **1.** A tall sedge (*Cyperus papyrus*), native to the Nile region. **2.** The pith of this plant, sliced and pressed into a writing material by the ancient Egyptians, Greeks, and Romans. **3.** A writing on papyrus; esp., *pl.*, written scrolls of papyrus.

par (pär), *n.* [L., equal, an equal, equality.] **1.** The established value of the monetary unit of one country expressed in terms of the monetary unit of another using the same metal as the standard of value; — called in full the ***mint par of exchange***. **2.** The nominal value of securities or certificates of value. A security is said to be *at par* when the market price equals the par value. **3.** Equality as to value, condition, or circumstances; common level; — usually with *on* or *upon*; as, his ability is on a *par* with his rank. **4.** *Golf.* The number of strokes required for a hole or a round played perfectly. It is computed on the basis of the length of the hole, two strokes being allowed on each hole for putting. — ***above, below, under,*** *or* ***up to, par.*** Above, below, etc., the particular value or price taken as the par; hence, *Colloq.*, above, below, etc., an accepted standard or normal level, specif., of health. — **par**, *adj.*

par- (păr-). = 1st PARA-.

pa·ra′ (pä·rä′; pä′rä), *n.* [Turk. *pārah*, fr. Per. *pārah* a piece.] A minor coin of: **a** Turkey, 1/40 piaster. **b** Yugoslavia, 1/100 dinar.

Pa·rá′ (pä·rä′; *Pg.* pȧ·rȧ′), *n.* Short for PARÁ RUBBER.

par′a- (păr′ȧ-), **par-**. [Gr. *para-*, *par-*, fr. *para* beside.] A prefix meaning *beside*, in its senses: **1.** *Beside, alongside of, beyond, aside from, amiss*, as in *parallel, paragraph, paraphrase, parody*. **2.** *Chem.* A prefix (also, adjectively, **par′a**) designating: **a** A variety of a substance, or a substance in some way related to the one to whose name the prefix is attached, as an isomer, a modification, a derivative, etc.; as, *paraldehyde*. **b** Certain benzene derivatives, or compounds of analogous structure. Abbr. *p-*. See BENZENE RING. **3.** *Med.* **a** A *faulty* or *disordered condition; abnormal*; as in *paranoia*. **b** *Associated in a subsidiary* or *accessory capacity*, as in *parasympathetic*. **c** *Closely resembling the true form*; as in *paratyphoid*.

par′a-. [F., fr. It. imper. of *parare* to shield, defend.] **1.** A combining form meaning *that which shields* or *protects from*, as in *parachute, parasol*. **2.** *Mil.* A combining form for *parachute*, n., 1, meaning: **a** *Specially trained and equipped for descent by parachute from aircraft*, as in:

parabomb	**paramarine**	**paratroop**
paraengineer	**parasaboteur**	**paratrooper**

b *Of, by*, or *in defense against, armed parachutists*, as in **par′a·op′er·a′tion, par′a·spot′ter.**

par′a–a·mi′no·ben·zo′ic ac′id (păr′ȧ·ȧ·mē′nō·bĕn·zō′ĭk; -ăm′ĭ·nō-). A member of the vitamin-B complex. See VITAMIN.

par′a·blast (păr′ȧ·blăst), *n.* [See PARA-; -BLAST.] *Embryol.* The yolk of a meroblastic ovum. — **par′a·blas′tic** (-blăs′tĭk), *adj.*

par′a·ble (păr′ȧ·b'l), *n.* [OF. *parabole*, fr. L. *parabola*, fr. Gr. *parabolē* a comparing, a parable, deriv. of *para* beside + *ballein* to throw.] A comparison; specif., a short fictitious narrative from which a moral or spiritual truth is drawn; as, the *parables* of Christ.

pa·rab′o·la (pȧ·răb′ō·lȧ), *n.; pl.* -OLAS (-lȧz). [NL., fr. Gr. *parabolē*, prop., a placing beside. See PARABLE.] *Geom.* A conic section, the intersection of a cone with a plane parallel to its side.

par′a·bol′ic (păr′ȧ·bŏl′ĭk), *adj.* Also **par′a·bol′i·cal** (-ĭ·kăl). **1.** Of the nature of a parable; allegoric. **2.** [From PARABOLA.] *Geom.* **a** Resembling, relating to, or generated or directed by, a parabola. **b** Hence, having the form of a parabola; as, a *parabolic* course. — **par′a·bol′i·cal·ly**, *adv.*

pa·rab′o·lize (pȧ·răb′ō·līz), *v. t.* To express in, or explain as, parables.

pa·rab′o·loid (-loid), *n.* *Geom.* The surface generated by the rotation of a parabola about its axis. — **pa·rab′o·loi′dal** (pȧ·răb′ō·loi′dăl; păr′ȧ·bō-; -d'l), *adj.*

par′a·ca′se·in (păr′ȧ·kā′sē·ĭn), *n.* See CASEIN, 2.

par′a·chute (păr′ȧ·sho͞ot), *n.* [F., fr. 2d *para-* + *chute* a fall.] **1.** A folding, umbrellalike contrivance, usually of light fabric, used for making a safe descent through the air, esp. from an aircraft. **2.** The patagium of a mammal or reptile. **3.** Any contrivance suggestive of a parachute in form, use, or operation. — *v. t. & i.* To convey or to descend by, or as if by, means of a parachute.

parachute spinnaker. *Naut.* An exceptionally large spinnaker, used esp. on racing yachts.

par′a·chut′ist (păr′ȧ·sho͞ot′ĭst), *n.* One who descends by means of a parachute; specif., a soldier trained and equipped to descend by parachute from a transportation plane behind enemy lines, for attacking communications, obstructing bridges and railways, and the like.

par′a·clete (păr′ȧ·klēt), *n.* [OF. *paraclet*, fr. LL. *paracletus*, fr. Gr. *paraklētos*, fr. *parakalein* to call to aid, exhort, fr. *para-* + *kalein* to call.] An advocate; one called to aid or support; hence [*cap.*], the Comforter, Helper, or Intercessor; — applied to the Holy Spirit.

par′a·cy′mene (-sī′mēn), *n.* See CYMENE.

pa·rade′ (pȧ·rād′), *n.* [F., fr. Sp. *parada* stopping, an assembling for exercise, place where troops are assembled to exercise, fr. *parar* to stop, prepare.] **1.** Pompous show. **2.** *Mil.* **a** The ceremonial formation of a body of troops for the display of its condition, numbers, equipment, and proficiency. **b** The area upon which troops regularly assemble in such formation. **3.** Any march or procession; esp., a formal public procession. **4.** Place where people promenade; a public walk; also, those who parade. — *v. t.* **1.** To exhibit in a showy manner. **2.** To cause to march ceremoniously. — **Syn.** See SHOW. — *v. i.* **1.** To walk in public with some circumstance of show. **2.** To assemble in military order for evolutions and inspection. — **pa·rad′er** (-rād′ẽr), *n.*

par′a·di·chlo′ro·ben′zene (păr′ȧ·dī·klō′rō·bĕn′zēn; -bĕn·zēn′), *n.* Also **par′a·di·chlor·ben′zene** (-klōr·bĕn′zēn; -bĕn·zēn′). *Chem.* A colorless crystalline compound, $C_6H_4Cl_2$, used for the destruction of grubs, borers, etc.

par′a·digm (păr′ȧ·dĭm *or, esp. Brit.*, -dīm), *n.* [F. *paradigme*, fr. LL., fr. Gr. *paradeigma*, fr. *paradeiknynai* to set up as an example, fr. *para-* + *deiknynai* to show.] **1.** A model or pattern. **2.** *Gram.* An example of a conjugation or declension, showing a word in all its inflectional forms.

par′a·dig·mat′ic (păr′ȧ·dĭg·măt′ĭk), **par′a·dig·mat′i·cal** (-ĭ·kăl), *adj.* [Gr. *paradeigmatikos*.] **1.** Exemplary; typical. **2.** *Gram.* **a** Pertaining to a paradigm; as, a *paradigmatic* arrangement of forms. **b** Specif., of an affix, inflectional; — distinguished from *derivational*. — **par′a·dig·mat′i·cal·ly**, *adv.*

par′a·di·sa′ic (-dĭ·sā′ĭk), **par′a·di·sa′i·cal** (-ĭ·kăl), *adj.* Paradisiacal. — **par′a·di·sa′i·cal·ly**, *adv.*

par′a·dise (păr′ȧ·dīs; -dīz), *n.* [OF. *paradis,* fr. L., fr. Gr. *paradeisos* park, paradise, of Per. origin.] **1.** [*cap.*] The garden of Eden. **2. a** The abode of sanctified souls after death; either heaven, or, as some hold, an intermediate Elysium for the souls of the righteous during the interval between death and final judgment. **b** The Mohammedan heaven. **3.** A place of bliss; hence, a state of happiness.

par′a·di·si′a·cal (-dĭ·sī′ȧ·kăl), *adj.* Also **par′a·dis′i·ac** (-dĭs′ĭ·ăk). [LL. *paradisiacus.*] Of, pertaining to, or resembling paradise. — **par′a·di·si′a·cal·ly,** *adv.*

par′a·dox (păr′ȧ·dŏks), *n.* [F. *paradoxe,* fr. L., fr. Gr. *paradoxon,* neut. of *paradoxos,* adj., fr. *para* beside, contrary to + *doxa* opinion.] **1.** A tenet contrary to received opinion; also, an assertion or sentiment seemingly contradictory, or opposed to common sense, but that yet may be true in fact. **2.** A statement actually self-contradictory or false. — **par′a·dox′i·cal** (-dŏk′sĭ·kăl), *adj.* — **par′a·dox′i·cal·ly,** *adv.* — **par′a·dox′i·cal·ness,** *n.*

par′aes·the′si·a, par′aes·thet′ic, etc. Vars. of PARESTHESIA, etc.

par′af·fin (păr′ă·fĭn), **par′af·fine** (-fĭn; -fēn), *n.* [G. *paraffin,* fr. L. *parum* too little + *affinis* akin; — in allusion to its chemical inactivity.] **1. a** An inflammable waxy substance produced in distilling wood, shale, coal, etc., and occurring also in the earth as a constituent of petroleum or as a solid deposit. **b** By extension, any of a wide range of hydrocarbon mixtures. **2.** *Chem.* Any hydrocarbon of the methane series, esp. any of the solid members boiling above 300° C., of which commercial paraffin is essentially composed. **3.** *Brit.* Kerosene; — in full **paraffin oil.** — *v. t.* To treat or saturate with paraffin.

paraffin series. = METHANE SERIES.

paraffin wax. Solid paraffin.

par′a·gen′e·sis (păr′ȧ·jĕn′ē·sĭs), *n.* Also **par′a·ge·ne′si·a** (-jē·nē′sĭ·ȧ). [NL., fr. *para-* + *-genesis.*] *Geol.* The formation of minerals in contact, so as to affect one another's development. — **par′a·ge·net′ic** (-jē·nĕt′ĭk), *adj.*

par′a·glos′sa (-glŏs′ȧ), *n.; pl.* -GLOSSAE (-ē). [NL., fr. *para-* + Gr. *glōssa* tongue.] *Zool.* One of a pair of small lobes which, with the glossae, make up the ligula, or distal segment of the labium of certain insects. See HYMENOPTERON, *Illust.*

par′a·go′ge (păr′ȧ·gō′jē), *n.* [LL., fr. Gr. *paragōgē,* fr. *paragein* to protract.] *Gram.* Addition of a sound or syllable to the end of a word. — **par′a·gog′ic** (-gŏj′ĭk), *adj.*

par′a·gon (păr′ȧ·gŏn; -gŭn), *n.* [F. (now *parangon*), fr. It. *paragone,* prob. fr. Gr. *parakonan* to rub against, fr. *para-* + *akonē* whetstone.] **1.** A model; a type of perfection; as, a *paragon* of beauty. **2. a** A perfect diamond of 100 carats or more. **b** *Print.* A size of type (20 points). — *v. t.* **1.** To compare or compare with; to match. **2.** To serve as a model of; also, to present as a paragon. **3.** To surpass; as, to *paragon* description.

pa·rag′o·nite (pȧ·răg′ō·nīt), *n.* [From Gr. *paragōn,* pres. part. of *paragein* to mislead.] *Mineral.* A form of mica corresponding to muscovite, but with sodium instead of potassium.

par′a·graph (păr′ȧ·grȧf; 9), *n.* [F. *paragraphe,* fr. LL. *paragraphus,* fr. Gr. *paragraphos* (sc. *grammē*) a line or stroke drawn in the margin, deriv. of *para-* + *graphein* to write.] **1.** A character used in manuscripts and printing, now usually having the form ¶ or ⁋, used to indicate a paragraph in sense 2 (below), and as a reference mark. **2.** A distinct subdivision of a discourse, chapter, or writing. Abbr. *par.* **3.** A composition complete in one typographical section. — *v. t.* **1.** To express in the compass of a paragraph; also, to write paragraphs about. **2.** To divide into paragraphs. — *v. i.* To work as a paragrapher.

par′a·graph′er (-grȧf′ẽr), *n.* Also **par′a·graph′ist** (-ĭst). A writer of paragraphs, specif. of newspaper editorial paragraphs.

par′a·graph′i·a (-grăf′ĭ·ȧ), *n.* [NL., fr. *para-* + Gr. *graphein* to write.] A condition, in mental disorder, in which words or letters other than those intended are written.

par′a·graph′ic (-grăf′ĭk), **par′a·graph′i·cal** (-ĭ·kăl), *adj.* Pertaining to, or consisting of, a paragraph or paragraphs.

Par′a·guay tea (păr′ȧ·gwā; -gwī; *Sp.* pä′rä·gwī′). Maté. See MATÉ, 1 & 2.

par′a·keet (păr′ȧ·kēt), *n.* [OF. *paroquet,* fr. *perrot* parrot, dim. fr. *Pierre* Peter, fr. L. *Petrus.*] Any of certain parrots, esp. those of small size and slender form with a long graduated tail.

par·al′de·hyde (păr·ăl′dē·hīd), *n.* [*par-* + *aldehyde.*] *Chem.* A polymeric modification, $C_6H_{12}O_3$, of ordinary aldehyde. It is a colorless liquid used as a hypnotic.

par′a·leip′sis (păr′ȧ·līp′sĭs), **par′a·lep′sis** (-lĕp′sĭs), **par′a·lip′sis** (-lĭp′sĭs), *n.; pl.* -SES (-sēz). [Gr. *paraleipsis,* deriv. of *para-* + *leipein* to leave.] *Rhet.* A passing over with brief mention so as to emphasize the suggestiveness of what is omitted.

Par′a·li·pom′e·non (păr′ȧ·lĭ·pŏm′ē·nŏn; -lī-), *n.* [LL., fr. Gr. *paraleipomenōn* of things omitted, passive pres. part. (neut. genitive pl.) fr. *paraleipein* to omit.] *Douay Bib.* The two books of the Chronicles. See BIBLE.

par′al·lax (păr′ă·lăks), *n.* [F. *parallaxe,* fr. Gr. *parallaxis* alternation, mutual inclination of two lines forming an angle, fr. *parallassein* to change a little, deviate, fr. *para* beside, beyond + *allassein* to change.] The apparent displacement (or the difference in apparent direction) of an object, as seen from two different points. Specif., *Astron.,* the difference in direction of a heavenly body as seen from some point on the earth's surface, and as seen from some other conventional point, as the center of the earth or the sun. The word *parallax,* when not qualified, means ***diurnal,*** *or* ***geocentric, parallax,*** or the parallax with reference to the earth's center. The ***annual,*** *or* ***heliocentric, parallax*** is that with reference to the sun. — **par′al·lac′tic** (-lăk′tĭk), *adj.*

par′al·lel (păr′ă·lĕl), *adj.* [F. *parallèle,* fr. L. *parallelus,* fr. Gr. *parallēlos,* fr. *para-* + *allēlōn* of one another, fr. *allos* other.] **1.** *Geom.* Lying evenly everywhere in the same direction, but never meeting, however far extended; as, *parallel* lines or planes. This is the Euclidean notion; in projective geometry such parallel lines (or planes) are thought of as having only one point (or line) at infinity and that in common, and are said to meet at infinity. **2.** With like direction or tendency; like in essential parts; as, *parallel* passages. **3.** *Mach., etc.* Having parallel sides; as, a *parallel* file, reamer, etc. **4.** *Music.* Keeping at the same distance, in pitch, apart; as, *parallel* voice parts, fifths, octaves. — **Syn.** See SIMILAR.

— *n.* **1.** A parallel line, curve, or surface. **2.** Conformity in many particulars or in all essential points; similarity. **3.** A comparison to show resemblance; a tracing of similarity. **4.** Anything equal to or resembling another in all essential particulars; a counterpart. **5.** *Elec.* That arrangement of an electrical system, as of the cells of a battery, in which all positive poles, terminals, etc., are joined to one conductor, and all negative poles, etc., to another conductor, so that each unit is practically on a parallel branch, or shunt; — called also *multiple.* Opposed to *series.* **6.** *Fort.* One of a series of long trenches constructed as a cover for troops supporting an attack upon a besieged place. **7.** *Geog.* One of the imaginary circles on the surface of the earth, parallel to the equator, marking the latitude; also, the corresponding line on a globe or map. **8.** *pl. Print.* A character (‖) used in the text to direct attention to a similarly marked note.

— *v. t.;* -LELED (-lĕld); -LEL′ING (-lĕl′ĭng). **1.** To compare; also, to match; to correspond to; as, to *parallel* his wit with Sheridan's. **2.** To make to conform to something else in character, motive, aim, or the like. **3.** To place so as to be parallel to, or to conform in direction with, something else. **4.** *Chiefly Colloq.* To extend, run, or move in a direction parallel to; as, a canal *parallels* the railroad.

parallel bars. A pair of bars raised about five feet above the floor or ground, and parallel to each other, — used for gymnastic exercises.

par′al·lel′e·pi′ped (păr′ă·lĕl′ē·pī′pĕd; -pĭp′ĕd; -lĕl·ĕp′ĭ·pĕd), **par′al·lel′e·pip′e·don** (-lĕl′ē·pĭp′ē·dŏn), *n.* Commonly, but incorrectly, written *parallelopipedon, paralelopiped.* [Gr. *parallēlepipedon* a body with parallel surfaces, fr. *parallēlos* parallel + *epipedon* a plane surface.] *Geom.* A six-sided prism whose faces are parallelograms.

parallel forces. *Mech.* Forces acting in parallel directions.

par′al·lel·ism (păr′ă·lĕl·ĭz′m), *n.* **1.** Quality or state of being parallel. **2.** Resemblance; correspondence; similarity. **3.** *Philos.* The theory that mind and matter accompany one another but are not causally related.

parallel of latitude. *Geog.* = PARALLEL, *n.,* 7.

par′al·lel′o·gram (păr′ă·lĕl′ō·grăm), *n.* [Through F. & L., fr. Gr. *parallēlogrammon,* prop. neut. adj., fr. *parallēlos* parallel + *grammē* line.] *Geom.* A quadrilateral with opposite sides parallel, and therefore equal; — sometimes erroneously restricted to an oblong. Cf. *gnomon, Illust.*

parallel sailing. See SAILING.

pa·ral′o·gism (pȧ·răl′ō·jĭz′m), *n.* [Through F. & L., fr. Gr. *paralogismos,* deriv. of *para-* + *logizesthai* to reason.] *Logic.* A reasoning false in point of form, that is, contrary to logical rules or formulas. — **pa·ral′o·gist** (-jĭst), *n.* — **pa·ral′o·gis′tic** (-jĭs′tĭk), *adj.* — **pa·ral′o·gize** (pȧ·răl′ō·jīz), *v. i.*

pa·ral′y·sis (pȧ·răl′ĭ·sĭs), *n.; pl.* -SES (-sēz). [L., fr. Gr. *paralysis,* fr. *paralyein* to loosen or disable at the side, fr. *para-* + *lyein* to loosen.] *Med.* Abolition of function, complete or partial; esp., the loss of the power of voluntary motion or sensation; palsy. See GENERAL PARALYSIS.

par′a·lyt′ic (păr′ȧ·lĭt′ĭk), *adj.* **1.** Of, pert. to, or like paralysis. **2.** Affected with paralysis. **3.** Inclined or tending to paralysis. — *n.* One affected with paralysis.

par′a·lyze (păr′ȧ·līz), *v. t.* **1.** To affect or strike with paralysis, or palsy. **2.** Hence to unnerve; to render ineffective; as, war *paralyzes* trade. — **par′a·ly·za′tion** (-lĭ·zā′shŭn; -lī·zā′-), *n.*

par′a·mag′net (păr′ȧ·măg′nĕt; -nĭt), *n.* A magnet; a paramagnetic substance.

par′a·mag·net′ic (-măg·nĕt′ĭk), *adj.* [*para-* + *magnetic.*] *Magnetism.* Having, or capable of, a greater magnetization than a vacuum; having a permeability greater than unity; magnetic; — opposed to *diamagnetic.* Cf. FERROMAGNETIC. — **par′a·mag′net·ism** (-măg′nē·tĭz′m; -nĭ·tĭz′m), *n.*

par′a·mat′ta *or* **par′ra·mat′ta** (păr′ȧ·măt′ȧ), *n.* [From *Parramatta,* Australia.] A light dress fabric, resembling bombazine or merino.

par′a·me′ci·um (păr′ȧ·mē′shĭ·ŭm; -sĭ·ŭm), *n.; pl.* -CIA (-ȧ). [NL., fr. Gr. *paramēkēs* oblong, fr. *para-* + *mēkos* length.] *Zool.* Any of a genus (*Paramecium*) of ciliate infusorians. The body is elongate, rounded at the anterior end, and has on the oral surface an oblique funnel-shaped buccal groove with the mouth at the extremity.

pa·ram′e·ter (pȧ·răm′ē·tẽr), *n.* [NL. See PARA-; -METER.] *Math.* A quantity to which the operator may assign arbitrary values, as distinguished from a variable, which can assume only those values that the form of the function makes possible.

par′am·ne′si·a (păr′ăm·nē′zhĭ·ȧ; -zĭ·ȧ), *n.* [NL., fr. *par-* + *amnesia.*] *Med.* **a** A condition in which the proper medium of words cannot be remembered. **b** The illusion of remembering scenes and events experienced for the first time.

pa′ra·mo (pä′rȧ·mō; păr′ȧ-), *n.; pl.* -MOS (-mōz). [Sp. *páramo.*] A high, bleak plateau or district, as in the Andes.

par′a·mor′phism (păr′ȧ·môr′fĭz′m), *n.* [*para-* + Gr. *morphē* form.] *Mineral.* The change of one mineral species to another, involving a change in physical characters without change of chemical composition. — **par′a·mor′phic** (-fĭk), *adj.*

par′a·mount (păr′ȧ·mount), *adj.* [OF. *par amont* above, fr. *par* through, by + *amont* above, fr. *a* (fr. L. *ad*) to + *mont* mountain.] Highest in rank or jurisdiction; chief; pre-eminent; supreme. — **Syn.** See DOMINANT. — *n.* A lord paramount; supreme ruler.

par′a·mount·cy (-sĭ), *n.* State or quality of being paramount.

par′a·mour (păr′ȧ·mo͝or; 84), *n.* [OF. *par amour,* lit., by or with love.] A lover; now, esp., one who loves or is loved illicitly.

par′a·neph′ros (-nĕf′rŏs), *n.* [NL., fr. *para-* + Gr. *nephros* kidney.] *Anat.* A suprarenal gland. — **par′a·neph′ric** (-rĭk), *adj.*

pa·rang′ (pä·räng′), *n.* [Malay. See BARONG.] A short sword or knife characteristic of the Dyak.

par′a·noe′a (păr′ȧ·nē′ȧ), **par′a·noe′ac.** Vars. of PARANOIA, PARANOIAC.

par′a·noi′a (păr′ȧ·noi′ȧ), *n.* [NL., fr. Gr. *paranoia.* See PARA-; NOUS.] *Psychiatry.* A chronic mental disorder characterized by systematized delusions of persecution and of one's own greatness, sometimes with hallucinations. — **par′a·noi′ac** (-ăk), *adj. & n.*

par′a·nymph (păr′ȧ·nĭmf), *n.* [LL. *paranymphus,* fr. Gr. *paranymphos,* fr. *para* beside, near + *nymphē* a bride.] **1.** *Gr. Antiq.* **a** A friend who went with a bridegroom to fetch home the bride. **b** The bridesmaid who conducted the bride to the bridegroom. **2.** A best man or a bridesmaid.

par′a·pet (păr′ȧ·pĕt; 30), *n.* [F., fr. It. *parapetto,* fr. *parare,* to ward off, guard + *petto* the breast, fr. L. *pectus.*] **1.** *Fort.* A wall, rampart, or elevation to protect soldiers; a breastwork. Cf. BATTLEMENT, *Illust.* **2.** A low wall or protecting railing at the edge of a platform, bridge, etc. See GOTHIC, *Illust.* — **par′a·pet′ed** (-pĕt′ĕd; -ĭd), *adj.*

par′aph (păr′ăf), *n.* [F. *paraphe,* contr. fr. *paragraphe.* See PARA-

GRAPH.] A flourish at the end of a signature, used orig. as a safeguard against forgery.

par′a·pher·na′li·a (păr′ȧ·fẽr·nā′lĭ·ȧ; -nāl′yȧ; 58), *n. pl.* [ML. *paraphernalia bona*, fr. LL. *parapherna*, pl., fr. Gr. *parapherna*, fr. *para-* + *phernē* a bride's dowry.] **1.** *Law.* Formerly, the property (other than dower, marriage settlement, etc.) which at common law remained under the control of a married woman. **2.** Personal belongings, such as equipments, finery, etc. **3.** Furnishings or apparatus; as, the *paraphernalia* of a circus.

par′a·phrase (păr′ȧ·frāz), *n.* [F., fr. L., fr. Gr. *paraphrasis*, fr. *paraphrazein* to say the same thing in other words, fr. *para-* + *phrazein* to speak.] A restatement of a text, passage, or work, giving the meaning in another form; hence, the use or process of paraphrasing as a literary or educational method. — *v. t. & i.* To express, interpret, or translate with latitude; to give the meaning of (a passage) in other language. — **par′a·phras′er** (-frāz′ẽr) *or* **par′a·phrast** (-frăst), *n.*

par′a·phras′tic (-frăs′tĭk), *adj.* Paraphrasing; of the nature of paraphrase. — **par′a·phras′ti·cal·ly** (-tĭ·kăl·ĭ), *adv.*

pa·raph′y·sis (pȧ·răf′ĭ·sĭs), *n.; pl.* -YSES (-sēz). [NL., fr. *para-* + Gr. *physis* growth.] *Bot.* One of the slender sterile filaments commonly borne among the sporogenous organs in many ferns, mosses, etc.

par′a·ple′gi·a (păr′ȧ·plē′jĭ·ȧ), *n.* [NL., fr. Gr. *paraplēgia* hemiplegia, deriv. of *para* at the side + *plēssein* to strike.] *Med.* Paralysis of the lower half of the body on both sides. — **par′a·pleg′ic** (-plĕj′ĭk; -plē′jĭk), *adj. & n.*

par′a·psy·chol′o·gy (păr′ȧ·sī·kŏl′ō·jĭ; păr′ȧ·psī-; 2), *n.* [See PARA-, 3.] A branch of psychology concerned with the investigation of evidence for telepathy, clairvoyance, thought transference, and the like, and with experimentation in the field of extrasensory perception.

par′a·quet (păr′ȧ·kĕt). Var. of PARAKEET.

Pa·rá′ rub′ber (pä·rä′; *Pg.* pȧ·rȧ′). Native rubber from a South American tree (genus *Hevea*, esp. *H. brasiliensis*) of the spurge family.

par′a·sang (păr′ȧ·săng), *n.* [L. *parasanga*, fr. Gr. *parasangēs*, fr. OPer.] A Persian measure of length, anciently of about 30 stadia (2.8 to 4.2 miles).

par′a·se·le′ne (-sē·lē′nē), *n.; pl.* -NAE (-nē). [NL., fr. *para-* + Gr. *selēnē* the moon.] *Meteorol.* A mock moon, or luminous appearance seen in connection with lunar halos.

par′a·shah (păr′ȧ·shä), *n.; pl.* -SHOTH (-shōth) or -SHIOTH (-shē′ōth). [Heb. *pārāshāh*.] A lesson from the Torah, or Law, from which at least one section is read in the Jewish synagogue on every Sabbath and festival. See HAPHTARAH.

par′a·site (păr′ȧ·sīt), *n.* [F., fr. L. *parasitus*, fr. Gr. *parasitos*, lit., eating beside another, fr. *para-* + *sitos* food.] **1.** *Gr. Antiq.* **a** One who eats at the table of another, repaying him with flattery. **b** One of a class of assistants in religious rites who dined with the priests after a sacrifice. **2.** A hanger-on; toady; sycophant. **3.** *Biol.* A plant or animal living in, on, or with some other living organism (its *host*) at whose expense it obtains food, shelter, etc. Cf. SYMBIONT, COMMENSAL.

par′a·sit′ic (-sĭt′ĭk), **par′a·sit′i·cal** (-ĭ·kăl), *adj.* **1.** Of the nature of a parasite; sycophantic. **2.** *Biol.* In this sense generally *parasitic*. Pert. to, or with the habit of, a parasite; living on other organisms. — **par′a·sit′i·cal·ly**, *adv.*

par′a·sit′i·cide (-ĭ·sīd), *adj.* [See -CIDE.] Destructive to parasites. — *n.* Any agent used to destroy parasites.

par′a·sit·ism (păr′ȧ·sīt·ĭz′m), *n.* **1.** The act or practice of a parasite. **2.** *Biol.* State of being parasitic; antagonistic symbiosis. **3.** *Med.* Diseased state, esp. of the skin, due to parasites.

par′a·si·tol′o·gy (păr′ȧ·sī·tŏl′ō·jĭ), *n.* [Gr. *parasitos* + *-logy*.] The scientific study of parasites. — **par′a·si′to·log′i·cal** (-sī′tō·lŏj′ĭ·kăl), *adj.* — **par′a·si·tol′o·gist** (-sī·tŏl′ō·jĭst), *n.*

par′a·sol (păr′ȧ·sŏl; 74), *n.* [F., fr. It. *parasole*, fr. *parare* to ward off + *sole* sun.] A light portable sunshade.

pa·ras′ti·chy (pȧ·răs′tĭ·kĭ), *n.; pl.* -TICHIES (-kĭz). [*para-* + Gr. *stichos* a row.] *Bot.* In phyllotaxy, the helical line which would connect all successive leaves on a stem axis, or the arrangement of leaves on such a line. Cf. ORTHOSTICHY.

par′a·sym′pa·thet′ic (păr′ȧ·sĭm′pȧ·thĕt′ĭk), *adj.* *Anat. & Physiol.* Pert. to or designating that part of the autonomic nervous system which is made up of two groups of nerves arising in the cranial and sacral regions respectively, and their auxiliaries, and which has among its functions the constricting of the pupils, dilating of blood vessels, slowing of the heart, and increasing of the activity of the glands and digestive and reproductive organs. Cf. SYMPATHETIC. — *n.* A parasympathetic nerve.

par′a·syn·ap′sis (-sĭ·năp′sĭs), *n.* [NL., fr. *para-* + Gr. *synapsis* union.] *Biol.* Side-to-side union of chromosomes in synapsis.

par′a·syn′the·sis (-sĭn′thē·sĭs), *n.* [NL., fr. Gr. *parasynthesis*, fr. *para-* + *synthesis* composition.] The formation of words by derivation and composition jointly, as in *denationalize*. — **par′a·syn·thet′ic** (-sĭn·thĕt′ĭk), *adj.*

par′a·tax′is (-tăk′sĭs), *n.* [NL., fr. Gr. *parataxis* a placing beside, fr. *paratassein* to place beside.] *Gram.* Co-ordinative ranging of propositions one after another, without other expression of their syntactic relation (he laughed; she cried); — opposed to *hypotaxis*. — **par′a·tac′tic** (-tăk′tĭk), **par′a·tac′ti·cal** (-tĭ·kăl), *adj.* — **par′a·tac′ti·cal·ly**, *adv.*

par′a·thy′roid (-thī′roid), *adj.* [*para-* + *thyroid*.] *Anat.* Adjacent to the thyroid gland; specif., designating or pertaining to several (usually four) small ovoid glands near, or embedded in, the thyroid gland. — **par′a·thy′roid**, *n.*

par′a·troop′ (păr′ȧ·trōōp′), **par′a·troop′er.** See 2d PARA-, 2.

par′a·ty′phoid (-tī′foid), *adj.* Of, pertaining to, or designating a bacterial disease (**paratyphoid fever**) resembling typhoid fever in some of its symptoms. — **par′a·ty′phoid**, *n.*

‖**par a′vance′** (pȧr ȧ′väɴs′). [F.] In advance; by anticipation.

par′a·vane (păr′ȧ·vān), *n.* [*para-* + *vane*.] *Nav.* **a** A torpedo-shaped underwater protective device with sawlike teeth in its forward end, for use by vessels in mined areas to sever the moorings of mines. **b** A similar device, carrying a large charge of trinitrotoluene (TNT), detonated by an electric current passed through a core in the towing wire, for use against submarines.

‖**par a′vi·on′** (pȧr ȧ′vyôɴ′). [F.] By airplane; — French official label for mail matter intended for air mail.

par′boil′ (pär′boil′), *v. t.* [OF. *parboillir* to cook well, fr. LL. *perbullire*. Influenced in sense by E. *part*.] To boil partially; figuratively, to overheat.

par′buck′le (pär′bŭk′'l), *n.* [Earlier *parbunkel*, of unknown origin.] **a** A form of purchase for hoisting or lowering a cylindrical burden, as a cask. The middle of a long rope is made fast aloft and both parts are looped around the object, which rests in the loops, and rolls in them as the ends are hauled up or paid out. **b** A double sling made of a single rope, for slinging a cask, gun, etc. — *v. t.;* -BUCK′LED (-'ld); -BUCK′LING (-lĭng). To hoist or lower by a parbuckle.

Par′cae (pär′sē), *n. pl.* [L.] *Rom. Relig.* The three Fates.

par′cel (pär′sĕl; -s'l), *n.* [OF. *parcelle*, fr. VL. *particella*, for L. *particula*. See PARTICLE.] **1.** *Archaic.* A portion; fragment. **2.** An indefinite number or quantity; a collection. **3.** A bundle; package; pack. **4.** A collection of articles put up in lots for marketing; as, a *parcel* of diamonds. **5.** *Law.* A part; piece; as, a certain piece of land is part and *parcel* of another piece. — *v. t.;* -CELED (-sĕld; -s'ld), or -CELLED; -CEL·ING or -CEL·LING. **1.** To divide and distribute by parts. **2.** To make up into a parcel. **3.** [Perh. a different word.] *Naut.* To cover with strips of canvas. — *adj. & adv.* Part or half; in part; partly.

par′cel·ing, par′cel·ling, *n.* **1.** Act of dividing and distributing in portions or parts. **2.** *Naut.* Long, narrow slips of canvas wound about a rope to exclude moisture.

parcel post. Also, unofficially, **parcels post.** That branch of the post office having to do with the collection, transmission, and delivery of parcels.

par′ce·nar′y (pär′sē·nĕr′ĭ *or, esp. Brit.,* -nẽr·ĭ), *n.* Joint heirship; coparcenary.

par′ce·ner (-nẽr), *n.* [OF. *parçonier*, fr. ML. *partionarius*, for *partitionarius*, fr. *partitio* division.] *Law.* A joint heir in an estate; coheir; coparcener.

parch (pärch), *v. t.* [ME. *parchen*, *perchen*.] **1.** To burn the surface of; scorch; roast over the fire, as dry grain. **2.** To dry to extremity; to shrivel with heat. **3.** To shrivel or dry up by exposure to cold. — *v. i.* To become dry and hot.

par·chee′si, par·che′si, par·chi′si (pär·chē′zĭ). Vars. of PACHISI.

parch′ment (pärch′mĕnt), *n.* [OF. *parchemin*, fr. L. *Pergamenus* of or belonging to *Pergamum*, ancient city of Mysia in Asia Minor.] **a** The skin of a sheep, goat, or other animal, prepared for writing on. **b** Any of various superior papers made in imitation of the above. **c** Hence, a document on parchment.

pard (pärd), *n.* [OF., fr. L. *pardus*, fr. Gr. *pardos*, *pardalis*.] *Archaic.* A leopard.

pard (pärd), *n.* [From *pardner*, for *partner*.] *Slang.* Partner; chum; pal.

par·die′ (pär·dē′), *adv.* or *interj.* Also **par·di′, par·dy′, per·die′** (pẽr·dē′), etc. [OF. *par dé* (F. *pardieu, pardi*) by God.] *Archaic.* Surely; verily; — orig. an oath.

par′don (pär′d'n), *v. t.* [OF. *pardoner*, fr. LL. *perdonare*, fr. L. *per* through, thoroughly + *donare* to give.] **1.** To absolve from the penalty for a fault or crime; to free from penalty, as a person. **2.** To remit the penalty of; to forgive; — applied to offenses. **3.** To excuse; — often used in the phrase *Pardon me* to offer apology for an unintentional discourtesy. — **Syn.** See EXCUSE. — *n.* **1.** Act of pardoning; forgiveness. **2.** State of being pardoned or forgiven. **3.** *Eccl.* An indulgence. **4.** An official warrant of remission of penalty. **5.** Excuse or toleration of a fault, defect, or annoyance; — often used in apologizing for an unintentional discourtesy, oversight, etc. **6.** *Law.* Official release from the legal penalties or consequences of an offense. — **par′don·a·ble** (-ȧ·b'l), *adj.* — **par′don·a·bly**, *adv.*

par′don·er (pär′dŭn·ẽr; pär′d'n-), *n.* **1.** In the Middle Ages, a preacher delegated to raise money for certain religious works, by soliciting offerings to which indulgences were attached. Abuses by pardoners led to the abolition of the practice of granting indulgences for offerings, by the Council of Trent (1545–1563). **2.** [See PARDON, *v.*] One who pardons.

pare (pâr), *v. t.* [OF. *parer* to make ready, adorn (F., to deck, dress), fr. L. *parare* to prepare.] **1.** To cut off, or shave off, the superficial substance or extremities of; as, to *pare* an apple. **2.** To cut or shave, as the skin, rind, or outside part, from anything. **3.** To diminish the bulk of by or as by paring; to reduce; as, to *pare* down expenditures.

par′e·gor′ic (păr′ē·gŏr′ĭk), *adj.* Also **par′e·gor′i·cal** (-ĭ·kăl). [LL. *paregoricus*, fr. Gr. *parēgorikos*, fr. *parēgoros* addressing, soothing, fr. *para-* + *agora* assembly.] Mitigating; assuaging or soothing pain. — *n.* *Pharm.* A medicine that mitigates pain; an anodyne; specif., camphorated tincture of opium.

pa·rei′ra bra′va (pȧ·rā′rȧ brä′vȧ; brā′vȧ), *or* **pa·rei′ra**, *n.* [Pg. *parreira brava* wild vine.] *Pharm.* The root of a South American vine (*Chondrodendron tomentosum*) of the moonseed family, used as a diuretic.

pa·ren′chy·ma (pȧ·rĕng′kĭ·mȧ), *n.* [NL., fr. Gr. *parenchyma*, deriv. of *para-* + *en* in + *chein* to pour.] **1.** *Bot.* In higher plants, a tissue composed of living, thin-walled cells which makes up the bulk of the pulp of fruits, the pith of stems, etc., and is present, as meristem, in all growing regions. See PROSENCHYMA. **2.** *Anat. & Zool.* **a** The essential and proper tissue of an organ, esp. a gland; also, *Med.*, the essential tissue of an abnormal growth, as a tumor. **b** The soft jellylike connective tissue in the flatworms. **c** The endoplasm of a protozoan. — **par′en·chym′a·tous** (păr′ĕng·kĭm′ȧ·tŭs), *adj.*

par′ent (pâr′ĕnt; 6), *n.* [OF., fr. L. *parens*, *-entis*, fr. *parere* to bring forth.] **1.** One who begets or brings forth offspring; a father or a mother. **2.** That which produces, as a plant; also, a cause; source. — **par′ent**, *adj.*

par′ent·age (pâr′ĕn·tĭj), *n.* **1.** Descent from parents or ancestors; extraction; birth. **2.** The fact or condition of being a parent; parenthood.

pa·ren′tal (pȧ·rĕn′tăl; -t'l), *adj.* **1.** Of, pertaining to, or characteristic of a parent or parents. **2.** *Biol.* In genetics, being the generation made up of individuals of distinguishable genotypes crossed to produce hybrids. Symbol *P.* Cf. FILIAL. — **pa·ren′tal·ly**, *adv.*

par·en′ter·al (păr·ĕn′tẽr·ăl), *adj.* [*par-* + Gr. *enteron* intestine.] *Anat., Med., & Physiol.* Not intestinal; other than by way of the intestines.

pa·ren′the·sis (pȧ·rĕn′thē·sĭs), *n.; pl.* -SES (-sēz). [ML., fr. Gr. *parenthesis*, fr. *parentithenai* to put in beside, insert, fr. *para-* + *en* in + *tithenai* to put, place.] **1.** A word, phrase, or sentence, by way of comment or explanation, inserted in, or attached to, a sentence grammatically complete without it. It is usually marked off with curved lines (see sense 2, below), commas, or dashes. Abbr. *paren.* **2.** One of the curved marks ( ) used to enclose a parenthetic word, phrase, etc.; also, these marks collectively. The expression *in parentheses* is more usual than *in parenthesis.* **3.** An interval or interlude.

pa·ren′the·size (pȧ·rĕn′thē·sīz), *v. t.* To make a parenthesis of; to include within parenthetical marks.

par′en·thet′ic (păr′ĕn·thĕt′ĭk), **par′en·thet′i·cal** (-ĭ·kăl), *adj.* **1.** Of the nature of a parenthesis; pertaining to, or expressed in or as in, a parenthesis. **2.** Containing parentheses; also, using or given to using parenthesis. — **par′en·thet′i·cal·ly**, *adv.*

par′ent·hood (pâr′ĕnt·ho͝od), *n.* State or relation of a parent; the office or character of a parent.

pa·re′sis (pȧ·rē′sĭs; păr′ē·sĭs), *n.* [NL., fr. Gr. *paresis*, fr. *parienai* to let go, fr. *para* from + *hienai* to send.] *Med.* Incomplete paralysis. ***general paresis***, often called simply *paresis*, is general paralysis (which see).

par′es·the′si·a, par′aes·the′si·a (păr′ĕs·thē′zhĭ·ȧ; -zhȧ; -zĭ·ȧ), *n.* [NL. See PARA-; ESTHESIA.] *Med. & Physiol.* A sensation as of pricking, tingling, or creeping, on the skin, without objective cause. — **par′es·thet′ic, par′aes·thet′ic** (-thĕt′ĭk), *adj.*

pa·ret′ic (pȧ·rĕt′ĭk; pȧ·rē′tĭk), *adj.* Of, pertaining to, or affected with paresis. — *n.* A person having paresis.

‖**pa′re·u** (pä′rā·o͞o), *n.* [Tahitian.] *Polynesia.* A rectangular cotton skirt or loincloth printed with colored conventionalized leaf and flower designs.

par ex′cel·lence (pär ĕk′sĕ·läns; *F.* pȧr ĕk′sĕ′läɴs′). [F.] Pre-eminently.

‖**par ex′em′ple** (pȧr ĕg′zäɴ′pl′). [F.] For example; for instance.

par·fait′ (pär·fā′), *n.* [F., lit., perfect.] A frozen dessert of whipped cream, eggs cooked with sirup, and flavoring.

par′fleche (pär′flĕsh; pär·flĕsh′), *n.* [Can. F.] A rawhide, soaked in lye to remove the hair, and dried; also, a box or saddlebag of this material.

par′get (pär′jĕt; -jĭt), *v. t.*; -GET·ED or -GET·TED; -GET·ING or -GET·TING. [OF. *pargeter, parjeter*, to throw all over (a surface), fr. *par* + *jeter* to throw.] To coat, or plaster, esp. ornamentally. — *n.* Plaster, whitewash, or roughcast for coating a wall; also, ornamental pargeting on walls.

par′get·ing, par′get·ting (pär′jĕ·tĭng; -jĭ·tĭng), *n.* Plasterwork, esp. in raised ornamental figures.

par·he′lic (pär·hē′lĭk; -hĕl′ĭk), **par′he·li′a·cal** (pär′hē·lī′ȧ·kăl), *adj.* Or or pertaining to a parhelion or parhelia.

parhelic circle *or* **ring**. A luminous circle or halo parallel to the horizon at the altitude of the sun.

par·he′li·on (pär·hē′lĭ·ŏn; -hēl′yŏn; 58), *n.*; *pl.* -LIA (-lĭ·ȧ; -hēl′yȧ). [L. *parelion*, fr. Gr. *parēlion, parēlios*, fr. *para-* + *hēlios* the sun.] A mock sun, any one of several bright spots, often tinged with color, at the altitude of the sun.

par′i- (păr′ĭ-). [L. *par, paris.*] *Bot. & Zool.* A combining form meaning *equal*, as in **par′i·dig′i·tate.**

pa·ri′ah (pȧ·rī′ȧ; pä′rĭ·ȧ; păr′ĭ·ȧ; pâr′ĭ·ȧ), *n.* [Tamil *paraiyan*, lit., drummer, fr. *parai* a drum.] **1.** A member of a low caste of southern India and Burma. **2.** An outcast; one despised by society.

Par′i·an (pâr′ĭ·ăn), *adj.* [L. *Parius.*] **1.** Of or pert. to Paros, one of the Cyclades, noted for its beautiful marble. **2.** Resembling the marble of Paros; as, **Parian ware**, a cream-colored soft china used, unglazed, for making statuettes, etc. — *n.* **a** A native of Paros. **b** Parian ware.

pa′ri·es (pā′rĭ·ēz), *n.*; *pl.* PARIETES (pȧ·rī′ĕ·tēz). [L., a wall.] *Biol.* A wall; specif., the wall of a cavity or hollow organ; — usually in *pl.*

pa·ri′e·tal (pȧ·rī′ĕ·tăl; -t'l), *adj.* [F. *pariétal*, fr. LL. *parietalis*, fr. *paries, -ietis*, a wall.] **1.** *Anat. & Zool.* Of or pert. to the parietes, or walls, of a part or cavity. **2.** *Bot.* Attached to the main wall of the ovary, instead of to the axis; — said of ovules or a placenta. **3.** *U. S.* Resident within, or pert. to life within, the buildings of a college. — *n. Anat. & Zool.* One of the parietal bones.

parietal bones. *Anat.* A pair of membrane bones of the roof of the skull between the frontals and occipitals.

parietal lobe. *Anat.* The middle division of each cerebral hemisphere.

pa·ri′e·to- (pȧ·rī′ĕ·tō-). *Anat.* A combining form for the adjective and noun *parietal*, denoting *parietal and*, as in **pa·ri′e·to·mas′toid, pa·ri′e·to·vis′cer·al.**

par′i mu′tu·el (păr′ĭ mū′tū·ĕl; *F.* pȧ′rē′ mü′twĕl′). [F., lit., mutual stake or wager.] A form of betting on horses in which those who bet on the winning horse share the total stakes, less a small per cent to the management. The bets are registered on a machine called a **par′i-mu′tu·el** (păr′ĭ-mū′tū·ĕl) (also called *totalizator*).

par′ing (pâr′ĭng), *n.* **a** Act of one who pares. **b** That which is pared off; as, potato *parings.*

‖**pa′ri pas′su** (pā′rī păs′ū; păr′ĭ păs′o͞o). [L.] With or at equal pace; in or to an equal proportion, degree, etc.

par′i·pin′nate (păr′ĭ·pĭn′āt), *adj.* *Bot.* Abruptly pinnate (see PINNATE).

Par′is (păr′ĭs), *n.* [L., fr. Gr.] See APPLE OF DISCORD.

Paris green. An insecticide and pigment prepared as a very poisonous bright-green powder from arsenic trioxide and acetate of copper.

par′ish (păr′ĭsh), *n.* [OF. *parroche, paroisse*, fr. LL. *parochia*, for *paroecia*, fr. Gr. *paroikia* sojourning, a diocese, fr. *paroikos* dwelling beside, also, a sojourner, fr. *para-* + *oikos* a house.] **1.** *Brit.* Orig., the ecclesiastical unit of area committed to one pastor. **2.** *Brit.* The subdivision of a county often coinciding with an original ecclesiastical parish (see sense 1), constituting the unit of local government. **3.** **a** A portion of a diocese committed to the spiritual care of a priest or minister, called *rector* or *pastor.* **b** In various Protestant churches, a local ecclesiastical society composed of persons who choose to unite under one minister. **c** = SOCIETY, 6. **d** Loosely, the territory in which the members of a congregation live. **4.** In Louisiana, a civil division corresponding to a *county* in other states. **5.** The inhabitants or members of a parish, collectively.

pa·rish′ion·er (pȧ·rĭsh′ŭn·ẽr), *n.* [ME. *parishen* (fr. OF. *paroissien*) + *-er.*] One who belongs to, or dwells in, a parish.

par′i·ty (păr′ĭ·tĭ), *n.* [LL. *paritas*, fr. *par, paris*, equal.] **1.** Quality or condition of being equal or equivalent; equality; close analogy; as, naval *parity.* **2.** **a** Equality in purchasing power between different kinds of money at a given ratio. **b** Equivalence in a foreign currency. **3.** *Econ.* Balance between the prices received by the farmer for his products and the prices he has to pay for labor and for equipment, necessities, and comforts. In computing the farmer's purchasing power and for legislative purposes such a balance is assumed for the period August, 1909–July, 1914 in U. S. Hence, **parity price**, that price for a given amount of a farm commodity which will pay for as much in factory goods, taxes, etc., as the same amount of this commodity paid for in the 1909–1914 period.

par′i·ty, *n.* [L. *parere* to bear.] *Med.* State or fact of having borne offspring.

park (pärk), *n.* [OF. *parc*, fr. early ML. *parricus.*] **1.** *Eng. Law.* An enclosed piece of ground stocked with beasts of the chase, held by prescription or the king's grant. Cf. 1st CHASE, *n.*, 3; FOREST, 2. **2.** A tract of ground kept in its natural state, as for game, for walking, riding, or the like. **3.** A piece of ground, in or near a city or town, kept for ornament and recreation; also, an area maintained in its natural state as a public property; as, Yellowstone National *Park.* **4.** *U. S.* A level valley between mountain ranges; also, any open space surrounded by woodland. **5.** **a** A space occupied by military animals, wagons, supplies, etc.; also, the objects themselves; as, a *park* of artillery. **b** Hence, any place where vehicles, as automobiles, are assembled.
— *v. t.* **1.** To enclose in a park, or as in a park. **2.** To stop and keep (a vehicle, esp. a motor vehicle) standing for a time on a public way. **3.** *Slang, U. S.* Hence, to set and leave in a particular place; as, he *parked* his bag at the club. **4.** *Mil.* To bring together in a park, or compact body. — *v. i.* To park a motor vehicle.

par′ka (pär′kȧ), *n.* A Siberian and Alaskan outer garment, orig. of skins, now popularized as an elongated woolen shirt with a hood.

park′way′ (pärk′wā′), *n.* A broad thoroughfare beautified with trees and turf.

par′lance (pär′lăns), *n.* [OF., fr. *parler* to speak. See PARLEY.] Conversation; discourse; esp., debate or parley; also, manner of speech; diction; as, in legal *parlance.*

par·lan′do (pär·län′dō), *adj.* *Music.* Speaking, delivered or performed in a declamatory manner; — used as a direction in instrumental and vocal music.

par′lay (pär′lā), *v. t. & i.* [F. *paroli*, fr. It. *paroli*, fr. *paro* equal.] *U. S.* To apply an original stake and its winnings on a further stake, as on another horse in a later race. — **par′lay**, *n.*

parle (pärl), *n. & v. i. & t.* *Archaic & Dial.* Talk; parley.

par′le·ment. Var. of PARLIAMENT.

par′ley (pär′lĭ), *n.* [OF. *parlée*, fr. past part. of *parler* to speak, fr. L. *parabola* comparison, parable. See PARABLE.] Mutual discourse or conversation; esp., an oral conference with an enemy, as with regard to a truce. — *v. i.* To speak with another; specif., to confer orally with an enemy, as on an exchange of prisoners.

par′lia·ment (pär′lĭ·mĕnt; *esp. non-British*, pärl′yȧ·mĕnt), *n.* [OF. *parlement*, fr. *parler* to speak. See PARLEY.] **1.** A formal conference on public affairs; esp., *Hist.*, any of various councils. **2.** [*often cap.*, esp. as a permanent institution.] The assembly of the three estates of Great Britain and Northern Ireland, viz., the lords spiritual (bishops and archbishops) and lords temporal, constituting the House of Lords, and the representatives of the counties, boroughs, and universities, constituting the House of Commons, the two houses with the king (or queen) together constituting the legislature. **3.** Any of various legislative assemblies modeled upon the British parliament; as: **a** That of certain British dominions and their subdivisions. **b** The French Chambers, the legislature of Italy, Switzerland, etc. **4.** In France, before 1789, one of the several principal judicial courts.

par′lia·men·tar′i·an (pär′lĭ·mĕn·târ′ĭ·ăn; 6), *n.* **1.** [*cap.*] *Eng. Hist.* An adherent of Parliament in opposition to King Charles I. **2.** One versed in the rules and usages of parliament.

par′lia·men·tar′i·an·ism (-ĭz'm), *n.* The doctrine, or the system, of government by parliament.

par′lia·men′ta·ry (-mĕn′tȧ·rĭ), *adj.* **1.** Of or pert. to parliament; of the nature of a parliament. **2.** Enacted or ratified by parliament. **3.** According to the usages of parliament or of deliberative bodies. **4.** Having a parliament; established on the basis of government by a parliament; as, *parliamentary* states.

par′lor, par′lour (pär′lẽr), *n.* [OF. *parleor* for *parleoir*, fr. ML. *parlatorium.* See PARLEY.] **1.** A room primarily for conversation, for the reception of guests, etc. **2.** A room in an inn, hotel, or club, fitted for conversation, rest, or semiprivacy; often *pl.*, the suite of rooms devoted to the reception of guests or members. **3.** *U. S.* A room fitted up for the reception of customers in a business establishment; as, billiard *parlors.* — *adj.* **1.** Used in or suitable for a parlor; as, *parlor* furniture; also, resembling a parlor; as, a *parlor* car. **2.** Expounded or advocated, or expounding or advocating opinions, doctrines, or the like in comfortable seclusion without consequent action or application; as, *parlor* radicals or radicalism.

parlor car. *U. S.* A railroad car of superior type, furnished with individual chairs, on which extra fare is charged. See CHAIR CAR, CLUB CAR.

par′lor·maid′ (pär′lẽr·mād′), *n.* A maid whose chief duties are to attend to the parlor, the table, and the door.

par′lous (pär′lŭs), *adj.* [For *perlous*, a contr. fr. *perilous.*] **1.** *Archaic.* Attended with peril; risky. **2.** Dangerously clever or mischievous; hence, keen; shrewd. **3.** *Colloq.* Very bad; surprising; shocking; as, *parlous* housing conditions. — *adv.* Exceedingly; excessively.

Par′me·san′ (pär′mē·zăn′; 2), *adj.* [F. *parmesan*, fr. It. *parmigiano.*] Of or pertaining to Parma in Italy.

Parmesan cheese. A large, hard, dry Italian pressed cheese of sweetish flavor, made from skimmed milk.

Par·nas′si·an (pär·năs′ĭ·ăn; 58), *adj.* Of or pertaining to Parnassus or the Parnassians. — *n.* [F. *parnassien.*] One of a school of French poets of the middle of the 19th century, who emphasized metrical form; — from the name (*Parnasse-contemporain*) of their first collection (1866).

Par·nas′sus (-năs′ŭs), *n.* [L., fr. Gr. *Parnasos.*] **1.** *Anc. Geog. & Gr. Myth.* A mountain in Greece (in ancient Phocis) sacred to Apollo and the Muses. **2.** A once common title for a collection of poems.

pa·ro′chi·al (pȧ·rō′kĭ·ăl), *adj.* [OF., fr. LL. *parochialis*, fr. *parochia.* See PARISH.] **1.** Of or pertaining to a parish; as, *parochial* clergy. **2.** Confined or restricted to a parish; hence, limited in range or scope; narrow; as, a *parochial* opinion. — **pa·ro′chi·al·ly**, *adv.*

pa·ro′chi·al·ism (-ĭz'm), *n.* Quality or state of being parochial; hence, narrowness of interests or opinions.

parochial school. A school, usually for elementary instruction, maintained by a parish or by a religious body.

par′o·dy (păr′ō·dĭ), *n.*; *pl.* -DIES (-dĭz). [F. or L.; F. *parodie*, fr. L. *parodia*, fr. Gr. *parōidia*, fr. *para-* + *ōidē* a song.] **1.** A writing in which the language and style of an author is imitated or mimicked, esp. for comic effect or in ridicule. **2.** A burlesque musical composition.

3. Loosely, a feeble or ridiculous imitation. — **Syn.** See CARICATURE. — *v. t.*; -DIED (-dĭd); -DY·ING. To write a parody upon. — **par′o·dist** (păr′ō·dĭst), *n.*

pa·rol′ (pȧ·rōl′; păr′ŏl), *n.* Also **pa·role′**. [OF. *parole* word, speech. See PAROLE.] A word; — now seldom used except in ***by parol, Law,*** by word of mouth. — *adj.* Given or done by word of mouth; oral; as, a *parol* contract.

pa·role′ (pȧ·rōl′), *n.* [F., word, promise, fr. VL. *paraula* word, speech, fr. L. *parabola*. See PARLEY.] **1.** = PAROL, *n.* **2.** Word of promise; word of honor; plighted faith; esp., *Mil.*, promise of a prisoner of war upon his faith and honor to fulfill stated conditions, as not to bear arms against his captors, in consideration of special privileges, usually release from captivity; also, the condition of being upon parole. **3.** *Mil.* A watchword given only to officers of the guard and of the day; — distinguished from *countersign*. **4.** *Penol.* A conditional release of a prisoner with indeterminate or unexpired sentence; also, the state or period of such freedom. — *v. t.* To release on parole. — **pa·role′**, *adj.*

pa·rol′ee′ (pȧ·rōl′ē′), *n.* A person released on parole.

par′o·no·ma′si·a (păr′ō·nō·mā′zhĭ·ȧ; -zĭ·ȧ), *n.* [L., fr. Gr. *paronomasia*, fr. *paronomazein* to form a word by a slight change, fr. *para-* + *onomazein* to name, fr. *onomia* a name.] *Rhet.* A play upon words; a pun; also, punning. — **par′o·no·mas′tic** (-măs′tĭk), *adj.*

par′o·nym (păr′ō·nĭm), *n.* A paronymous word.

pa·ron′y·mous (pȧ·rŏn′ĭ·mŭs), *adj.* [Gr. *parōnymos*, fr. *para-* + *onoma*, *onyma*, a name.] Having the same derivation; allied in root; — said of words.

par′o·quet (păr′ō·kĕt). Var. of PARAKEET.

pa·ro′tic (pȧ·rō′tĭk; -rŏt′ĭk), *adj.* *Zool.* Near the ear.

pa·rot′id (pȧ·rŏt′ĭd), *adj.* [F. or L.; F. *parotide*, fr. L. *parotis*, *-idis*, a tumor near the ear, fr. Gr. *parōtis*, *-idos*, fr. *para* beside, near + *ous*, *ōtos*, the ear.] *Anat.* Designating, pert. to, or in the region of, a salivary gland below and in front of the ear. — *n.* The parotid gland.

par′o·ti′tis (păr′ō·tī′tĭs), *n.* [NL. See PAROTID; -ITIS.] *Med.* Inflammation of the parotid glands, as in mumps.

pa·ro′toid (pȧ·rō′toid), *adj.* [*parotid* + *-oid*.] *Zool.* Resembling the parotid gland; — applied esp. to cutaneous glandular elevations above the ear in toads, frogs, and salamanders. — *n.* A parotoid gland.

-parous. [L. *parere* to bear, beget.] A combining form used to signify *giving birth to, bearing, producing, secreting*.

par′ox·ysm (păr′ŏk·sĭz′m), *n.* [F. *paroxysme*, fr. Gr. *paroxysmos*, fr. *paroxynein* to sharpen, fr. *para* beyond + *oxynein* to sharpen, fr. *oxys* sharp.] **1.** *Med.* A fit, attack, or sharp increase in intensity, of a disease, occurring at intervals. **2.** Any sudden, violent action or emotion; a convulsion or fit. — **par′ox·ys′mal** (-sĭz′măl), *adj.*

par·ox′y·tone (păr·ŏk′sĭ·tōn), *n.* [Gr. *paroxytonos*, adj. See PARA-; OXYTONE.] *Gram.* A word having an acute accent on the penultimate syllable. — **par·ox′y·tone,** *adj.*

par·quet′ (pär·kā′; -kĕt′; 2), *n.* [F., dim. of *parc* an enclosure.] **1.** A flooring, esp. of parquetry. **2.** The lower floor of a theater, esp. that part from the orchestra to the parquet circle; — called also (esp. U. S.) *orchestra*. — *v. t.*; -QUETED′ (-kād′; -kĕt′ĕd, -ĭd); -QUET′ING. [F. *parqueter*.] To furnish with a parquetry floor; to make of parquetry.

parquet circle. That part of the lower floor of a theater with seats at the rear of the parquet beneath the galleries; parterre.

par′quet·ry (pär′kĕt·rĭ; -kĭt·rĭ), *n.*; *pl.* PARQUETRIES (-rĭz). [F. *parqueterie*. See PARQUET.] An inlay of geometric or other patterns in wood, used esp. for floors.

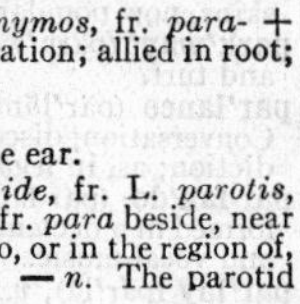
Parquetry.

parr (pär), *n.*; see PLURAL, *Note*, 3. A young salmon; also, the young of any of certain other fish, as of the coalfish, or pollack.

par′ra·keet (păr′ȧ·kēt). Var. of PARAKEET.

par′ra·mat′ta (păr′ȧ·măt′ȧ). Var. of PARAMATTA.

par′rel (păr′ĕl), **par′ral** (păr′ăl), *n.* [F. *appareil*.] *Naut.* The rope loop or sliding collar by means of which a yard or spar is held to the mast in such a way that it may be raised or lowered at will. Cf. JACKSTAY.

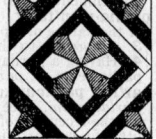

par′ri·cide (păr′ĭ·sīd), *n.* [F., fr. L. *parricida*, fr. *paricida*. See -CIDE.] **1.** One who murders a person to whom he stands in a sacred relation, as a parent. **2.** [F., fr. L. *parricidium*.] Act or crime of murdering one's own parent. — **par′ri·cid′al** (-sīd′ăl; -′l; 2), *adj.*

par′ridge (păr′ĭj), **par′ritch** (-ĭch). Scot. & N. of Eng. vars. of PORRIDGE.

par′ro·ket, par′ro·quet (păr′ō·kĕt). Vars. of PARAKEET.

par′rot (păr′ŭt), *n.* [F. *perrot*. See PARAKEET.] **1.** Broadly, any bird of an order (Psittaciformes) including the *parakeet*, *cockatoo*, *cockateel*, *kea*, *lorikeet*, *lory*, *lovebird*, *macaw*, and their allies, distinguished esp. by a stout, curved, hooked bill and zygodactyl feet; restrictedly, any of the genus *Psittacus*, having a short square tail, as the African ***gray parrot*** (*P. erithacus*) with gray plumage, red tail, and whitish face. Some parrots learn to simulate laughter, crying, etc., and to enunciate words and phrases. **2.** Hence, a person who repeats words mechanically and without understanding. — *v. t.* To repeat by rote like a parrot.

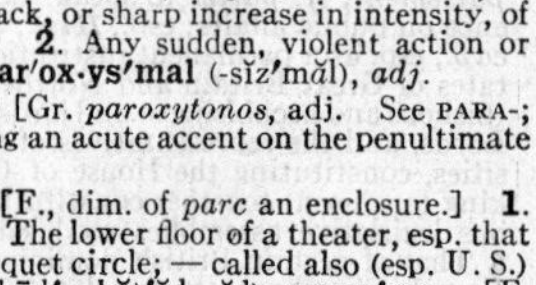
Bill and Foot of one of the Parrot Family (a Macaw).

parrot disease *or* **fever.** = PSITTACOSIS.

parrot fish. **a** Any marine fish of a family (Scaridae) resembling the wrasse family, esp., herbivorous fishes (genera *Sparisoma*, *Scarus*, and *Pseudoscarus*) of warm seas; — from their coloration or parrotlike jaws. **b** Any of various brightly colored labroid fishes, as the **parrot perch** (*Labrichthys psittacula*) of Australasia.

par′ry (păr′ĭ), *v. t.*; -RIED (-ĭd); -RY·ING. [F. *parez*, imper. of *parer*, fr. It. *parare* to parry, prevent, prepare, fr. L. *parare* to prepare.] **1.** To ward off, as a blow. **2.** To avoid; evade. — *v. i.* To ward off, evade, or turn aside something. — *n.*; *pl.* -RIES (-ĭz). A warding off of a thrust or blow, as in swordplay or boxing.

parse (pärs; *Brit. now usually* pärz), *v. t.* [From L. *pars* a part, *pars orationis* a part of speech.] *Gram.* To resolve into its elements, as a sentence, pointing out the several parts of speech, and their interrelation; to analyze and describe grammatically, as a word. — **pars′er.** *n.*

par′sec′ (pär′sĕk′), *n.* [*parallax* + *second*.] *Astron.* A unit of measure for interstellar space equal to a distance having a heliocentric parallax of one second, equal to 206,265 times the semimajor axis of the earth's orbit, or 3.26 light years, or 19.2 trillion miles.

Par′si, Par′see (pär′sē; pär·sē′), *n.* [Per. *Pārsī* Persian, fr. *Pars* Persia.] **1.** A Zoroastrian descended from Persian refugees settled in India, mostly at Bombay. Cf. GHEBER. **2.** See PERSIAN, *n.*, 2.

Par′si·fal (pär′zĕ·fäl), *n.* [G.] In Wagner's music drama *Parsifal*, a knight, who, seeing Amfortas suffering, recovers from Klingsor the sacred spear by which alone Amfortas's wound may be healed.

Par′si·ism, Par′see·ism (pär′sē·ĭz′m; pär·sē′-), *n.* The religious teachings and customs of the Parsis.

par′si·mo′ni·ous (pär′sĭ·mō′nĭ·ŭs; 58), *adj.* Exhibiting parsimony; frugal to excess; penurious. — **Syn.** See STINGY. — **par′si·mo′ni·ous·ly**, *adv.*

par′si·mo′ny (pär′sĭ·mō′nĭ *or, esp. Brit.*, -mŭn·ĭ), *n.* [L. *parsimonia*, *parcimonia*, fr. *parcere*, *parsum*, to spare, save.] Closeness in expenditure; niggardliness.

pars′ley (pärs′lĭ), *n.*; *pl.* PARSLEYS (-lĭz). [From AS. *petersilie* (fr. LL.), and fr. OF. *peresil* (F. *persil*), fr. LL. *petrosilium*, fr. L. *petroselinum* rock parsley, fr. Gr. *petroselinon*, fr. *petros* stone + *selinon* parsley.] **1.** A European aromatic garden herb (*Petroselinum crispum*) of the carrot family, whose leaves are used to flavor soups, stews, etc., or as a garnish. **2.** With qualifying word, any of various related plants.

pars′nip (pärs′nĭp), *n.* [ME. *pasnepe*, fr. OF. *pasnaie*, fr. L. *pastinaca*; but influenced by ME. *nepe* turnip.] **1.** A European biennial herb (*Pastinaca sativa*) of the carrot family, with large pinnate leaves and yellow flowers; also, its long, tapered root, poisonous in the wild state, but through cultivation made palatable and nutritious. **2.** Any of various related or similar plants, as the white-flowered ***cow parsnip*** *or* ***giant parsnip*** (genus *Heracleum*) and the yellow-flowered ***meadow parsnip*** (genus *Thaspium*), both of the carrot family.

par′son (pär′s′n), *n.* [ME. *persone* parson, person. See PERSON.] **1.** *Eccl.* The rector or incumbent of a parochial church. **2.** *Colloq.* Any clergyman.

par′son·age (-ĭj), *n.* **1.** *Eng. Eccl. Law.* A certain portion of lands, tithes, and offerings, to support a parson. **2.** The glebe and house, or the house only, appropriated by a parish for its pastor.

parson bird. = TUI.

part (pärt), *n.* [From AS. *part* (fr. L.), and fr. OF. *part* fr. L. *pars*, *partis*.] **1.** One of the portions into which anything is divided, or regarded as divided; a piece, fragment, fraction, member, or constituent. **2.** Specif.: **a** A formal or distinctive division; as, a *part* of speech. **b** An equal constituent portion; one of several or many like quantities, numbers, etc., into which anything is divided. **c** A spare piece or member of a machine or the like. **d** A constituent of character or capacity; esp., *pl.*, talent; as, a man of *parts*. **3.** Share; portion. **4.** Quarter; region; district; — usually in *pl.* **5.** One of the opposing parties in a conflict. **6.** *U. S.* The parting or dividing of the hair. **7.** *Math.* **a** An aliquot part. **b** *pl.* = PARTIAL FRACTIONS (see FRACTION). **8.** *Music.* **a** A melody or voice part, in concerted music or in harmony, for a particular voice or instrument. **b** A particular voice or instrument in concerted music; also the individual score for it. **9.** *Theater.* A character in a drama; also, the language, actions, and influence of a character in a play, or figuratively, in real life.

Syn. **Part, portion, piece, member, division, section, segment, fragment** mean something less than the whole. **Part**, the general term, may be used in place of any of the other words; **portion** definitely implies a part assigned, allotted, etc.; **piece**, a part separated or detached, not only from a whole but from a collection; **member**, a part of a body in any sense, that constitutes one of its units; **division** and **section**, a part made by or as if by cutting, *division* sometimes suggesting a diversity like that of the whole, and *section* a sharp distinction in character; **segment** usually applies to a part following natural lines of cleavage; **fragment**, to a more or less small part that is detached by breaking.

— ***in good part.*** Without offense; graciously; as, he received the warning *in good part*. — ***in part.*** In some degree; partly. — ***part and parcel.*** An essential or constituent portion; — a reduplicative phrase.

— *v. t.* [OF. *partir*, fr. L. *partire*, *partiri*, past part. *partitus*, fr. *pars*, *partis*, a part.] **1.** To divide or separate into distinct parts; also, to separate in thought; to analyze; specif., *Naut.*, to break or suffer the breaking of (a rope, anchor chain, etc.). **2.** To disunite; to sunder. **3.** To hold apart; to intervene betwixt, as combatants. **4.** To separate by a process of extraction, elimination, or secretion; as, to *part* gold from silver. **5.** *Obs.* To leave; quit. **6.** To apportion: share. — *v. i.* **1.** To be broken or divided into parts or pieces; to break. **2.** To go away; to depart; hence, to die. **3.** To perform an act of parting; to relinquish a connection of any kind; — followed by *with* or *from*. — **Syn.** See SEPARATE.

par·take′ (pär·tāk′; pẽr-), *v. i.*; see TAKE. [From *partaking*, *partaker*, fr. *part-taking*, *part-taker*, after L. *participare* to participate.] **1.** To have a share or part; to participate; share. **2.** Hence, to take or receive a portion (*of*). **3.** To have something of the properties or office (*of*). — *v. t.* To take a part or share in; to share. — **Syn.** See SHARE. — **par·tak′er** (-tāk′ẽr), *n.*

par′tan (pär′tăn), *n.* [Gael. *partan*, Ir. *partān*.] *Scot.* A European crab (*Cancer pagurus*) often used as food.

part′ed (pär′tĕd; -tĭd), *adj.* Separated; cleft; hence: **a** *Bot.* Cleft so that the divisions reach nearly, but not quite, to the base, as a leaf; — used chiefly in composition; as, 3-*parted*; 5-*parted*. See LOBATION, *Illust.* (3). **b** *Archaic.* Deceased.

par·terre′ (pär·târ′), *n.* [F., fr. *par* on, by + *terre* earth, ground, fr. L. *terra*.] **1.** *Hort.* An ornamental arrangement of flower plots. **2.** The part of the floor of a theater behind the orchestra, esp., in U. S., the part beneath the galleries.

par′the·no·gen′e·sis (pär′thē·nō·jĕn′ē·sĭs), *n.* Also **par′the·nog′e·ny** (pär′thē·nŏj′ē·nĭ). [NL., fr. Gr. *parthenos* maiden + *-genesis*.] **1.** *Biol.* Reproduction by the development of an unfertilized egg. *Natural* parthenogenesis typically involves the development of eggs from virgin females without fertilization by spermatozoa. It occurs chiefly in certain insects, crustaceans, and worms. **2.** *Bot.* The form of apogamy in which an embryo develops from an unfertilized egg, as among certain algae and fungi. — **par′the·no·ge·net′ic** (-jē·nĕt′ĭk), *adj.*

Par′the·non (pär′thē·nŏn; -nŭn), *n.* [L., fr. Gr. *Parthenōn*, fr. *parthenos* a virgin, i. e., the goddess Athena.] A celebrated Doric temple of Athena, on the Acropolis at Athens, built in the 5th century B.C.

Par′thi·an (pär′thĭ·ăn), *adj.* Of or pertaining to Parthia (see *Gaz.*) or its warlike people, as in **Parthian shot**, a parting shot, alluding to a method of fighting on horseback in which the rider turned his horse as if in flight after each discharge of an arrow. — **Par′thi·an**, *n.*

par′tial (pär′shăl), *adj.* [F., fr. LL. *partialis*, fr. L. *pars, partis*, a part.] **1.** Inclined to favor one party more than the other; biased. **2.** Having a predilection or fondness for a certain person or thing; esp., foolishly fond. **3.** Of, pertaining to, or affecting a part only; not general or total; as, a *partial* eclipse. — **par′tial·ly**, *adv.*

partial fractions. See FRACTION.

par′ti·al′i·ty (pär′shĭ·ăl′ĭ·tĭ; pär·shăl′ĭ·tĭ), *n.; pl.* -TIES (-tĭz). **1.** Quality or state of being partial; bias. **2.** A special taste or liking; as, a *partiality* for poetry.

partial tone, *or* **par′tial**, *n.* *Music & Acoustics.* One of the tones in the complex that forms an ordinary tone. An ***upper partial tone*** is an overtone or harmonic.

par′ti·ble (pär′tĭ·b'l), *adj.* Admitting of being parted; divisible, as an inheritance.

‖**par′ti·ceps cri′mi·nis** (pär′tĭ·sĕps krĭm′ĭ·nĭs). [L.] An accomplice.

par·tic′i·pance (pär·tĭs′ĭ·păns; pẽr-), **par·tic′i·pan·cy** (-păn·sĭ), *n.* Participation.

par·tic′i·pant (-pănt), *adj.* Sharing; participating. — *n.* A participator; sharer.

par·tic′i·pate (-pāt), *v. i.* [L. *participatus*, past part. of *participare* to participate, fr. *particeps* partaking, fr. *pars, partis*, part + *capere* to take.] To have a share in common with others; to partake; share. — *v. t.* To partake of; to share in. — **Syn.** See SHARE.

par·tic′i·pa′tion (pär·tĭs′ĭ·pā′shŭn; pẽr-), *n.* Act or state of participating, or sharing in common with others.

par·tic′i·pa′tor (pär·tĭs′ĭ·pā′tẽr; pẽr-), *n.* One who participates; a partaker; sharer

par′ti·cip′i·al (pär′tĭ·sĭp′ĭ·ăl), *adj.* [L. *participialis.*] *Gram.* Having the nature and use of a participle; formed from or with a participle. — **par′ti·cip′i·al·ly**, *adv.*

par′ti·ci·ple (pär′tĭ·sĭ·p'l), *n.* [F. *participe*, OF. also *-ciple*, fr. L. *participium*, fr. *particeps* sharing.] *Gram.* An adjective form of the verb, modifying a noun and at the same time taking objects and qualifiers like a verb (hastily *writing* it down, he left). The English verb has two participles: (1) the *present*, ending in *-ing*, as *writing;* (2) the *past*, or *perfect*, ending for the most part in *-ed, -d, -t, -en*, or *-n*, as *posted, kept, written*, etc. When a participle is not properly connected with the substantive which it modifies, it is called a ***dangling participle*** (*leaping* to the saddle, his horse bolted). Abbr. *part.*

par′ti·cle (pär′tĭ·k'l), *n.* [L. *particula*, dim. of *pars, partis*, a part.] **1.** A minute part of matter; atom; any small portion. **2.** A clause or article of a composition or document. **3.** *Gram.* **a** A unit of speech ranked as an uninflected word but serving almost as a loose affix, expressing some general aspect of meaning or some connective or other relation. Particles include the articles, most prepositions and conjunctions, various pronominal adverbs, etc. **b** A wordlike element that cannot be used except in composition; a derivational affix (*un*fair; back-*ward*). **4.** *Mech.* A mass conceived as being without extension, but retaining the other properties of matter, as inertia. **5.** *R.C.Ch.* **a** A little piece of consecrated Host. **b** The smaller Hosts distributed in the communion of the laity.

par′ti–col′ored, par′ty–col′ored (pär′tĭ·kŭl′ẽrd), *adj.* Also **–col′oured.** [F. *parti* divided.] Colored with different tints; variegated.

par·tic′u·lar (pẽr·tĭk′ū·lẽr; pär-), *adj.* [OF. *particuler*, fr. L. *particularis.* See PARTICLE.] **1.** Relating to a portion of anything; separate; specific. **2.** Of or pertaining to a single person, class, or thing; not general; hence, personal. **3.** Noteworthy; special; as, he had no *particular* news. **4.** Concerned with, or attentive to, details; hence, nice; fastidious; as, *particular* in dress. **5.** *Law.* **a** Containing a part only; as, a *particular* estate. **b** Holding, or relating to, a particular estate; as, a *particular* tenant. **6.** *Logic.* **a** Having the character of an individual, or of a specific subclass, which falls under some general concept. **b** Affirming or denying a predicate to some part of the subject; — opposed to *universal*, and applied to propositions; thus, "Some men are wise" is a *particular* affirmative. — **Syn.** See SINGLE: SPECIAL: CIRCUMSTANTIAL: NICE. — *n.* **1.** A separate member of a class, or part of a whole; an individual fact or item. **2.** Specif.: An item of information; a detail of news. **3.** *Logic.* **a** An individual, or a specific subclass, falling under some general concept or term. **b** A particular proposition. — **Syn.** See ITEM.

par·tic′u·lar·ism (-ĭz'm), *n.* **1.** Exclusive or special devotion to a particular interest, subject, party, sect, etc. **2.** *Theol.* The doctrine that redemption through Christ is provided only for the elect. **3.** The political theory which leaves each state in a federation free to promote its own interests without regard for the whole. — **par·tic′u·lar·ist**, *n.*

par·tic′u·lar′i·ty (-lăr′ĭ·tĭ), *n.; pl.* -TIES (-tĭz). **1.** State, quality, or fact of being particular; as: **a** Relation to a member or members of a class; individuality. **b** Attentiveness to detail; circumstantiality. **c** Preciseness in behavior or expression; fastidiousness. **2.** That which is particular; as: **a** Individual characteristic; peculiarity. **b** Special circumstance; minute detail.

par·tic′u·lar·ize (pẽr·tĭk′ū·lẽr·īz; pär-), *v. t.* To state in detail. — *v. i.* To mention or attend to particulars; to be circumstantial. — **-i·za′tion**, *n.*

par·tic′u·lar·ly, *adv.* **1.** In a particular manner; expressly. **2.** Especially; unusually.

par·tic′u·late (pär·tĭk′ū·lāt), *adj.* Pert. to or existing as minute separate particles.

part′ing (pär′tĭng), *adj.* [From PART, *v.*] **1.** Departing; figuratively, dying. **2.** Serving to part; dividing; separating. **3.** [From PARTING, *verbal n.*] Given, etc., when departing; farewell; as, a *parting* salute. — *n.* **1.** Act of parting, or state of being parted; division; separation; breaking or breaking up; sundering. **2.** *Archaic.* A departure; figuratively, dying; death. **3.** A part or place where a division or separation occurs; as, the *parting* of the ways. **4.** A leave-taking. **5.** Something serving to separate objects.

parting strip. *Arch.* Any thin piece for separating two adjoining members.

‖**par′ti′ pris** (pȧr′tē′ prē′). [F.] A preconceived opinion; prejudice; partiality.

par′ti·san (pär′tĭ·zăn), *n.* [F. *partisane.*] A kind of halberd or pike; also, a truncheon; staff.

par′ti·san, par′ti·zan (pär′tĭ·zăn; *Brit. now usually* pär′tĭ·zăn′), *n.* [F. *partisan*, fr. It. *partigiano*, deriv. of L. *pars, partis.*] **1.** A person who takes the part of another; esp., a devoted adherent. **2.** *Mil.* Any member of a body of detached light troops engaged in harassing an enemy. **3.** *Orig. Russia.* A member of a guerrilla band within enemy lines engaged in demolition, incendiarism, diversionary attacks, and teaching sabotage. — **Syn.** See FOLLOWER. — *adj.* **1.** Adherent to a party or faction, esp. unreasoningly. **2.** *Mil.* Of or pertaining to partisans or their operations. — **par′ti·san·ship′**, *n.*

par′tite (pär′tīt), *adj.* [L. *partitus*, past part.] Parted.

par·ti′tion (pär·tĭsh′ŭn; pẽr-), *n.* [F., fr. L. *partitio.* See PART, *v.*] **1.** A parting; separation; division. **2.** That which separates; specif., an interior wall dividing one part of a house, enclosure, etc., from another. **3.** A portion; a section or division. **4. a** *Law.* The severance of common or undivided interests, particularly in real estate; a division into severalty of property held jointly or in common. **b** *Logic.* Analysis of a class into constituent subclasses. **c** *Math.* Resolution of an integer into a set of integers. — *v. t.* **1.** To divide into parts or shares; *Law*, to divide into severalty; as, to *partition* an estate. **2.** To divide into distinct parts by lines, walls, etc. — **par·ti′tion·er**, *n.* — **par·ti′tion·ment**, *n.*

par′ti·tive (pär′tĭ·tĭv), *adj.* Serving to part or divide into parts; specif., *Gram.*, denoting a part; as, a **partitive genitive**, a genitive denoting the whole of which a part is spoken of. — *n.* *Gram.* A word expressing partition or denoting a part. — **par′ti·tive·ly**, *adv.*

part′let (pärt′lĕt; -lĭt), *n.* [From older *patelet*, fr. OF. *patelete* a band of stuff.] In 16th-century costume, a chemisette with a band or collar, often richly embroidered.

part′ly, *adv.* In part; in some measure; partially.

part music. *Music.* Vocal music for several voices in independent parts, generally without accompaniment; concerted or harmonized music, esp. vocal.

part′ner (pärt′nẽr), *n.* [ME. *partener*, for older *parcener*, influenced by *part.*] **1.** An associate; sharer; participant. **2. a** A husband or a wife. **b** Either of a couple who dance together. **3.** *Games.* One who plays with another or others against an opposing team, side, or the like. **4.** *Law.* One of two or more associated as joint principals in carrying on any business with a view to joint profit; a member of a partnership. **5.** *Naut.* One of the timbers forming a framework for an opening in a deck, to strengthen it for the support of a mast, capstan, or the like; — usually in *pl.* — *v. t.* **1.** To join as partners. **2.** To be the partner of; to provide with a partner.

part′ner·ship (-shĭp), *n.* **1.** State of being a partner; participation. **2.** The contract by which a partnership relation is created; also, the association of persons joined together for business; a firm. **3.** *Law.* The relation existing between two or more competent persons who have contracted to join in business and share the profits.

part of speech. *Gram.* One of the form classes which collectively embrace all the words of a language, class membership being determined by form, order, or function of words. The English vocabulary is traditionally divided into these parts of speech: noun, adjective, pronoun, verb, adverb, preposition, conjunction, interjection. See FORM CLASS.

par·took′ (pär·to͝ok′; pẽr-), *past* of PARTAKE.

par′tridge (pär′trĭj), *n.; see* PLURAL, *Note*, 3. [ME. *partriche, pertriche*, fr. OF. *pertris, perdriz*, fr. L. *perdix, -icis*, fr. Gr. *perdix.*] **a** Any of certain Old World stout-bodied gallinaceous game birds (*Perdix, Alectoris*, and allied genera). Cf. FRANCOLIN. **b** Any of a great variety of gallinaceous birds more or less like the above in size, habits or value as game, as (in northeastern U. S.) the ruffed grouse and (in southern and parts of western U. S.) the bobwhite. See BOBWHITE, *Illust.* **c** In South America, any of certain tinamous. — *adj.* Designating a color pattern resembling that of the partridge.

par′tridge·ber′ry (-bĕr′ĭ), *n.; pl.* PARTRIDGEBERRIES (-ĭz). **1. a** An American trailing plant (*Mitchella repens*) of the madder family, with evergreen leaves, and edible but insipid scarlet berries. **b** The berry of this plant. **2.** Incorrectly: **a** The American wintergreen (= WINTERGREEN, 2). **b** The fruit of this plant, the checkerberry.

part song. *Music.* A harmonized song melody, usually in four parts and often unaccompanied. — **part singing.**

par·tu′ri·ent (pär·tū′rĭ·ĕnt), *adj.* [L. *parturiens*, pres. part. of *parturire* to desire to bring forth, fr. *parere, partum*, to bring forth.] Bringing forth, or about to bring forth, young; figuratively, about to produce an idea, discovery, or the like. — **par·tu′ri·en·cy** (-ĕn·sĭ), *n.*

par·tu′ri·fa′cient (-fā′shĕnt), *n.* [L. *parturire* to desire to bring forth + *facere* to make.] A medicine tending to induce parturition or to give relief in childbirth.

par′tu·ri′tion (pär′tū̍·rĭsh′ŭn), *n.* Act of bringing forth young; act of giving birth; delivery; childbirth.

par′ty (pär′tĭ), *n.; pl.* -TIES (-tĭz). [OF. *partie* and in some senses *parti*, fr. *partir* to part, divide, fr. L. *partire, partiri.* See PART, *v.*] **1.** *Obs.* A part or share. **2.** A body of persons forming one side in a contest, etc.; a body of partisans; esp., one of the sections into which a people is divided on public questions; specif., *U. S. Politics*, an organized group of the electorate that attempts to control government through the election of its candidates to office. **3.** The practice or system of forming sides on public questions; partisanship. **4.** A detachment, as of troops. **5.** A company or association of persons, as for social enjoyment; also, the entertainment or gathering itself; as, to give a *party.* **6.** One of the persons who compose, or a body of persons constituting, one or other of the two sides in an action or affair. **7.** Specif., the plaintiff or the defendant in a lawsuit. **8.** *Slang.* A person. — *adj.* [F. *parti* divided, fr. *partir* to divide.] **1.** Pert. to or associated with a political party or parties. **2.** *Her.* Parted or divided; — said of an escutcheon, etc.

par′ty–col′ored, *or* **–col′oured.** Var. of PARTI-COLORED.

party line. **1. a** A single telephone circuit connecting several subscribers with the exchange. **b** The bounding line between the properties of two or more parties. **2.** *U. S.* A line of demarcation distinguishing the two main political parties in policy or practice, or limiting the action of all loyal members of one of the parties; as, to cross the *party line* in making appointments; the vote was strictly along *party lines.* **3.** The course of policy adopted by the Communist party. — **party liner.**

party wall. *Law & Arch.* A wall which divides two adjoining properties and in which each of the owners of the adjoining properties has rights of enjoyment.

pa·rure′ (pȧ·ro͞or′; *F.* pȧ′rür′), *n.* [F., fr. *parer* to prepare. See PARE.] A set of ornaments, esp. jeweled.

par value. Nominal value; face value.

par′ve·nu (pär′vē·nū), *n.* [F., prop. past part. of *parvenir* to attain to, succeed, rise to high station, fr. L. *pervenire* to come to, fr. *per* through + *venire* to come.] A person who has risen, as by the acquisition of wealth, above the social station in which he was born; usually, in a bad sense, such a person when unaccustomed to his new station; an upstart. — *adj.* Like or characteristic of a parvenu; upstart.

par′vis (pär′vĭs), *n.* [OF., paradise, also parvis, fr. L. *paradisus* paradise. See PARADISE.] *Rare.* A court or enclosed space before a building, esp. a church; sometimes, a single portico or colonnade before a church.

par′vo·line (pär′vō·lēn; -lĭn), *n.* Also **par′vo·lin.** [From L. *parvus* small, after quin*oline;* — from its low volatility.] *Chem.* Any of several isomeric liquid bases, $C_9H_{13}N$, derived from pyridine.

‖**pas** (pä), *n.* [F. See PACE.] **1.** Right of precedence. **2.** A dance step or combination of steps; also, a dance.

Pasch (păsk; 9), *n.* [OF. *pasche, pasque,* fr. LL. & LGr. *pascha,* fr. Heb. *pesaḥ,* fr. *pāsaḥ* to pass over.] *Chiefly Hist.* The Passover; hence, Easter.

pas′chal (păs′kăl; 9), *adj.* [F. *pascal,* fr. L. *paschalis.* See PASCH.] Of or pertaining to Passover or Easter.

paschal flower. Var. of PASQUEFLOWER.

paschal lamb. **a** The lamb slain and eaten at the Passover; hence [*caps.*], Christ. **b** [*caps.*] = AGNUS DEI, 1, 2 **a** & **b**.

‖**pas d'ac′tion′** (pä′ dȧk′syôɴ′). [F.] A ballet dance with mimetic elements, representing a dramatic scene.

‖**pas de deux, de trois** (dē dû′, trwȧ′), etc. [F.] A dance or figure for two, for three, etc., performers.

pash (păsh), *v. t. & i.* *Dial.* To smash; dash in pieces.

pash (pȧsh), *n.* *Obs. exc. Dial.* The head or poll.

pa·sha′, pa·cha′ (pȧ·shä′; pä′shȧ; păsh′ȧ; *Turk.* pä·shä′), *n.* [Turk. *pāshā, bāshā.*] Formerly, an honorary title, placed after the name, given to officers of high rank in Turkey. Cf. BASHAW.

pa·sha′lik (pȧ·shä′lĭk), *n.* Also **pa·sha′lic, pa·cha′lic.** [Turk. *pāshālik.*] The jurisdiction of a pasha.

Pash′to (pŭsh′tō), *n.* The chief language of southern and eastern Afghanistan and parts of India and Baluchistan. See INDO-EUROPEAN LANGUAGES, *Table.*

Pa·siph′a·ë (pȧ·sĭf′ȧ·ē), *n.* [L., fr. Gr. *Pasiphaē.*] *Gr. Myth.* Wife of Minos. She became enamored of a white bull belonging to Minos, and gave birth to the Minotaur.

pasque′flow′er (păsk′flou′ẽr), *n.* [OF. *pasque* Easter. See PASCH.] Any of a genus (*Pulsatilla*) of plants or flowers of the crowfoot family, low perennials with large white or purple flowers. The American pasqueflower (*P. ludoviciana*) is the State flower of South Dakota.

pas′quil (păs′kwĭl), *n.* [F.] A pasquinade.

pas′quin·ade′ (păs′kwĭ·nād′), *n.* [F., fr. It. *pasquinata,* fr. *Pasquino,* name of a statue in Rome on which lampoons were affixed.] A lampoon posted in a public place; a squib. — *v. t.* To lampoon; to satirize. — **pas′quin·ad′er** (-nād′ẽr), *n.*

pass (pȧs; 9), *n.* [OF. & F. *pas;* but influenced by the Eng. verb *pass.*] An opening, road, or track available for passing; esp., a defile between mountains.

pass, *n.* [F. *passe,* fr. *passer* to pass; but influenced by the English verb *pass.*] **1.** Act of passing; passage. **2.** Accomplishment; — now only in archaic phrases; as, to come to *pass.* **3.** State of things; condition; juncture. **4. a** Permission or license to pass, or to go and come. **b** A permit, ticket, or order, allowing one free transportation, admission, etc. **5. a** Transference of objects by sleight of hand or the like; also, a trick. **b** A movement of the hand over or along anything, as by a mesmerist. **6. a** *Rare.* A sally (of wit). *Shak.* **b** *Slang.* A short thrusting blow, esp. one that fails to land. **7.** *Cards.* A refusal to bid or raise. **8.** *Educ.* **a** Act of passing an examination. **b** The mark or certification of such passing. **9.** *Mil.* **a** A written permit allowing one to pass through the lines of an army, post, or the like. **b** Written leave of absence for a brief period given to a soldier. **10.** *Sports.* **a** *Fencing.* A thrust or lunge. **b** In football, hockey, etc., a transfer of the ball, etc., to another player of one's side. — **Syn.** See JUNCTURE.

— *v. i.; past* PASSED (pȧst) or, *Rare,* PAST; *past part.* PASSED, PAST; *pres. part.* PASS′ING. [OF. *passer,* fr. L. *passus* step.] **1.** To go; move; proceed. **2.** To be transferred from one place or condition to another; to change possession, condition, or circumstances. **3. a** To go by or move past. **b** To go by or glide by, as time; to elapse. **c** To go away; depart; specif., to depart from life; die. **4. a** To have passage; to force or make one's way. **b** To go unheeded, uncensured, or unchallenged; as, he let the remark *pass.* **5. a** To advance through all the steps necessary to validity or effectiveness; as, the bill *passed.* **b** To go through any inspection or test successfully; to attain the required standard. **6.** To take place; occur; happen. **7.** To be mutually exchanged; as, few words *passed.* **8. a** To go from one person to another; to circulate, as money. **b** To be held or regarded; — followed by *for, as,* or *by;* as, he *passes* easily for a German. **9.** *Cards.* **a** In poker, primero, etc., to decline to play a round or hand. **b** In bridge, euchre, napoleon, etc., to decline a privilege, as of bidding. **10.** *Law.* **a** To sit in inquest or adjudication; — said of a jury, inquest, etc., and used with *on* or *upon, between,* or *for* or *against.* **b** To adjudicate in a cause or proceeding; — used with *on* or *upon, for,* etc. **c** To be conveyed or transferred, as by will, deed, etc., so as to vest the title or interest in another. **11.** *Magic.* In sleight of hand, etc., to transfer an object, as if by magic. **12.** *Sports.* **a** *U.S.* To throw and catch a ball, as a baseball. **b** *Fencing.* To make a pass or lunge. **c** In football, hockey, etc., to make a pass.

— *v. t.* **1. a** To go by, beyond, over, through, or the like; to cross; traverse. **b** *Now Rare.* To go from one limit to the other of; to undergo. **c** *Now Rare.* To go by without noticing; to disregard. **d** To go successfully through, as an examination, trial, test, etc.; to be accepted or approved by; as, the bill *passed* the senate. **e** To transcend; surpass; excel. **2. a** To cause, let, or enable to go, move, or proceed; to transmit, send, transport, etc. **b** Specif.: To take a turn with (a rope, string, etc.) around anything, as a tree. **c** To cause to go, pass, or march by; as, to *pass* an author's works in review. **d** To cause to, or let, go past or through; as, to *pass* a person into a theater. **e** To cause to, or let, pass, go by, or elapse; to spend; as, to *pass* the winter at Rome. **f** To cause or allow to advance by stages of progress; to cause or allow to pass an examination; to let or get through; specif., to ratify; enact. **g** To transfer from one person to another; specif., to put in circulation; as, to *pass* counterfeit money. **h** To promise; pledge. **i** To emit or discharge from the bowels or other part of the body; to evacuate. **j** To utter; pronounce; specif., to utter or pronounce judicially; as, to *pass* judgment. **3.** *Cards.* In card tricks, to make or perform the pass on. **4.** *Sports.* In football, hockey, etc., to transfer (the ball, etc.) to another player of one's own side. **5.** *Law.* To transfer the right or property in; to make over, as the title to an estate. — ***pass a dividend.*** To omit the declaration and payment of a dividend at the time when due or regularly paid.

pass′a·ble (pȧs′ȧ·b'l; 9), *adj.* [OF.; F. only in sense 3.] **1.** Capable of being passed, traveled, penetrated, or the like; as, the roads are not *passable.* **2.** Capable of being freely circulated or disseminated; acceptable; current. **3.** Tolerable; admissible; moderate; mediocre. **4.** Capable of passing or being sanctioned or enacted.

pass′a·bly (-blĭ), *adv.* Moderately; tolerably.

pas·sade′ (pȧ·sād′), *n.* [F., fr. Pr. *passada,* or It. *passata.* See PASS, *v.*] **1.** *Manège.* A turn or course of a horse backward or forward on the same spot. **2.** *Obs.* = PASSADO.

pas·sa′do (pȧ·sä′dō), *n.; pl.* -DOS, -DOES (-dōz). [F. *passade,* fr. Pr. or It.] *Obs. Fencing.* A thrust, with the advance of one foot.

pas′sage (păs′ĭj), *v. i. & t.;* -SAGED (-ĭjd); -SAG·ING (-ĭj·ĭng). [F. *passager,* fr. *passéger,* fr. It. *passeggiare.*] To sidle, or walk or move sidewise, as a horse. — *n.* *Manège.* A sidewise movement of a horse.

pas′sage, *n.* [OF., fr. *passer.* See PASS, *v.*] **1.** Act of passing; transit from one place to another. **2. a** A means of passing; a way, channel or course. **b** A common avenue to various apartments, as a hall, lobby, vestibule, or entry. **3.** A journey, now only one by water; a voyage. **4.** Right, liberty, or permission to pass. **5.** Transition; course; progress; as, the *passage* of a bill through Congress. **6.** Of a measure or law: Act of passing; enactment. **7.** *Archaic.* Something that passes, or happens; an incident; act or deed. **8.** A mutual transaction; an interchange of vows, or the like, or an encounter; altercation. **9.** A particular portion constituting a part of something, as, esp., of a discourse or literary composition. **10.** *Obs.* Exit from life; decease; death. **11.** *Med.* A movement or an evacuation of the bowels. **12.** *Music.* **a** A scalelike or arpeggiolike series of tones; a run or flourish. **b** A phrase or other section of a piece. — *v. i.* **1.** To make a passage; to journey; voyage; cross. **2.** To engage in a passage at arms; to fence verbally.

pas′sage·way′ (păs′ĭj·wā′), *n.* A way for passage.

pas′sant (păs′ănt), *adj.* [OF., pres. part. of *passer.*] *Her.* Walking; — of any animal represented as walking with the dexter forepaw raised.

pass′book′ (pȧs′bo͝ok′), *n.* **a** *Banking.* A depositor's book in which a bank enters his deposits and (sometimes) withdrawals. **b** *Com.* A customer's book in which a dealer enters articles bought on credit.

pass degree. *Educ.* A degree without honors.

pas·sé′ (pȧ·sā′; păs′ā; *F.* pȧ′sā′), *adj.* [F.] Past; antiquated; past one's prime.

passed (pȧst), *adj.* **a** Having passed a test; esp., *Nav.,* having passed a promotion examination and awaiting a vacancy in a higher grade; as, *passed* assistant engineer. **b** *Finance.* Left unpaid; — said of dividends.

passed ball. *Baseball.* A pitched ball, not hit by the batsman, that passes the catcher when he should have stopped it, and allows a base runner to advance a base.

passe·men′terie (păs·mĕn′trĭ; *F.* päs′mäɴ′trē′), *n.* [F.] Trimmings, esp. of braids, cords, gimps, beads, or tinsel.

pas′sen·ger (păs′ĕn·jẽr; -ĭn·jẽr), *n.* [With intrusive *n,* fr. ME. *passager,* fr. OF. *passagier, passager.*] **1.** A passer-by; wayfarer; — now chiefly in *foot passenger.* **2.** A traveler by some public conveyance, as a boat, train, etc.

passenger pigeon. A North American wild pigeon (*Ectopistes migratorius*), formerly abundant, esp. in the Mississippi Valley, but now extinct.

‖**passe par′tout′** (päs′ pȧr′to͞o′). [F., fr. *passer* to pass + *partout* everywhere.] **1.** That which passes, or by which one can pass, everywhere; specif., a master key. **2.** [as an English word] (*pron.* păs′-pär·to͞o′; päs′-; -pẽr-) In picture framing: **a** A mat. **b** A form of framing in which picture, mat, glass, and back are held together by strips pasted over the edges. **3.** (*pron.* păs′pär·to͞o′; päs′-; -pẽr-) A strong, gummed paper, used esp. for mounting pictures.

pass′er (pȧs′ẽr), *n.* One who passes.

pass′er–by′, *n.; pl.* PASSERS-BY. One who passes by.

pas′ser·ine (păs′ẽr·ĭn; -īn), *adj.* [L. *passerinus,* fr. *passer* a sparrow.] Belonging to an order (Passeriformes) or its equivalent group (Passeres) of birds comprising chiefly songbirds of perching habits that range from the titmice to the ravens and birds of paradise, and including more than half of all birds. — *n.* A passerine bird.

‖**pas seul** (pä′ sûl′). [F.] A solo dance.

pas′si·ble (păs′ĭ·b'l), *adj.* [OF., fr. LL. *passibilis,* fr. *pati* to suffer.] Susceptible of feeling or suffering; sensible. — **pas′si·bil′i·ty** (-bĭl′ĭ·tĭ), *n.*

pas′si·flo·ra′ceous (păs′ĭ·flō·rā′shŭs), *adj.* [L. *passio* passion + *flos, floris,* flower.] Belonging to the passionflower family (Passifloraceae). See PASSIONFLOWER.

‖**pas′sim** (păs′ĭm), *adj.* [L.] Here and there.

pass′ing (pȧs′ĭng), *adj.* **1.** Going by, beyond, through, or away. **2.** Gliding by; transitory; fleeting; as, a *passing* fancy. **3.** Made, given, etc., in passing; casual; as, a *passing* remark. **4.** *Obs.* Surpassing. **5.** That passes upon, as candidates; examining. **6.** [From PASSING, *n.*] Of, pertaining to, used in or for, or indicating a passing, as of an examination or from life; as, a *passing* grade; a *passing* bell. — *adv.* Surpassingly; exceedingly; as, *passing* fair. — *n.* **1.** Act of one that passes. **2.** A means of passing; ford.

passing note. *Music.* A note, foreign to the harmony and usually unaccented, interposed for melodic smoothness.

pas′sion (păsh′ŭn), *n.* [OF., fr. LL. *passio,* fr. *pati, passus,* to suffer.] **1.** The enduring of inflicted pain, tortures, or the like; — now only specif.: **a** [*usually cap.*] The suffering of Christ on the cross, or his sufferings between the night of the Last Supper and his death. **b** The sufferings of a martyr; martyrdom. **2.** [*cap.*] One of the gospel narratives of the passion of Christ. **3.** *Now Chiefly Philos.* State or capacity of being affected by external agents or forces. **4.** Feeling; emotion; specif., one of the feelings natural to all men, as fear, hate, love, joy; *pl.,* these emotions collectively. **5.** Violent or intense emotion; emotional excitement or agitation. **6. a** Rage; wrath. **b** Ardent affection for one of the opposite sex; love. **c** *Often pl.* Sexual desire; lust. **7.** An object of love, deep interest, or zeal.

Syn. (1) See FEELING.

(2) **Passion, fervor** (*or* **fervour**), **ardor** (*or* **ardour**), **enthusiasm, zeal** mean intense emotion compelling action. **Passion** often implies an emotion that stirs one to the depths, as love or hate, but it may also be used more abstractly; **fervor** implies an emotion that burns with a glow and shows itself in prayer, preaching, etc.; **ardor,** an emotion like leap-

ing flames, intense but not always persistent; **enthusiasm** comes close to *ardor*, but always implies an objective or cause that is pursued with devotion; **zeal**, even more than *enthusiasm*, implies energetic and unflagging activity that manifests one's devotion to a cause or an end.

pas'sion·al (păsh'ŭn·ăl; -'l), *n.* A lectionary containing accounts of passions (sense 1 **b**) for use on saints' days. — *adj.* Of or pertaining to passion or passions.

pas'sion·ate (-ĭt), *adj.* [ML. *passionatus.*] **1.** Capable or susceptible of passion; easily moved, excited, or agitated; specif., irascible; quick-tempered. **2.** Affected with, or characterized by, passion; ardent; impassioned. — **Syn.** See IMPASSIONED. — **pas'sion·ate·ly**, *adv.* — **pas'sion·ate·ness**, *n.*

pas'sion·flow'er (păsh'ŭn·flou'ẽr), *n.* Any of a genus (*Passiflora*) of flowers and plants typifying a family (Passifloraceae, the passionflower family) of tropical woody tendril-climbing vines or erect herbs; — so called from a fancied resemblance of parts of the flower to the instruments of Christ's crucifixion, the corona representing the crown of thorns, the stamens and pistil the nails of the cross and the sepals and petals the ten faithful apostles. See MAYPOP; VERSATILE, *Illust.*

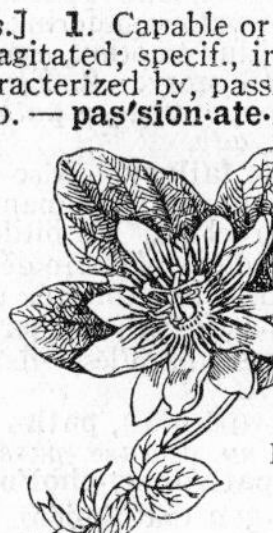

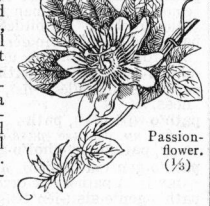

Passion-flower. (1/3)

pas'sion·less, *adj.* Void of passion; unemotional; calm.

Passion play. A mystery play representing the Passion of Christ; esp., one given every ten years by the villagers of Oberammergau, Bavaria.

Passion Sunday. The fifth Sunday in Lent.

Passion Week. Orig., the week before Easter; Holy Week; now, commonly, the week between Passion Sunday and Palm Sunday.

pas'sive (păs'ĭv), *adj.* [OF. or L.; OF. *passif*, fr. L. *passivus.* See PASSION.] **1.** Not active, but acted upon; affected by outside force or agency. **2.** Receiving or enduring without resistance or emotional reaction; submissive; patient. **3.** Inactive; inert. **4.** *Aeronautics.* Lacking or performed without motive power; as, a *passive* balloon or flight. **5.** *Chem.* Designating or characterized by a state of inactivity; not reacting readily. **6.** *Gram.* Designating, or pertaining to the voice, or a voice form, of a verb which represents the subject as the receiver of the action; — distinguished from *active*. In English, the passive voice is made up of forms of *be*, also *become* or *get*, and the past participle of the principal verb (the hunter *was killed* by a bear; "Charlotte also *became engaged* as a governess" [*Mrs. Gaskell*]; "a man *gets driven* into work" [*H. G. Wells*]). **7.** *Law & Finance.* Bearing no interest; — of various bonds, shares, etc., which, though bearing no interest, entitle the holder to a profit. **8.** *Med.* Pertaining to certain morbid conditions characterized by deficient vitality and reaction. — **Syn.** See INACTIVE.
— *n.* **1.** A passive thing, quality, etc.; — now usually *pl.* **2.** *Gram.* The passive voice, or a passive voice form. Abbr. *pass.*
— **pas'sive·ly**, *adv.* — **pas'sive·ness, pas·siv'i·ty** (pă·sĭv'ĭ·tĭ), *n.*

passive noun. *Gram.* A noun indicating the recipient of action.

passive resistance. Resistance, esp. to governmental authority, without resort to violence or to active opposition, as by not doing something required.

pas'siv·ism (păs'ĭv·ĭz'm), *n.* Passive character or behavior.

pass'key' (pås'kē'), *n.* A master key; also, a private key; a latchkey.

pass'o'ver (pås'ō'vẽr), *n.* [*pass* + *over.*] **1.** [*cap.*] An annual feast of the Jews, instituted (*Exodus* xii) to commemorate the sparing of the Hebrews in Egypt when God smote the first-born of the Egyptians. It is celebrated on the evening of the 14th day of Nisan, and by extension includes the eight days following. **2.** The sacrifice at the feast of the Passover; the paschal lamb. *Ex.* xii.

pass'port (pås'pōrt; 70), *n.* [F. *passeport*, fr. *passer* to pass + *port* a port, harbor.] **1.** A letter or document permitting free and unmolested travel, exit, entry, etc.; specif.: **a** A safe-conduct. **b** A formal document issued by a state officer to a citizen of the state, certifying his citizenship, authorizing him to leave that state and requesting protection for him abroad. **c** A document granting permission to a vessel to leave port, and requesting the privilege of free entry and exit to and from the territorial waters of foreign states. **2.** Any permission or authorization to pass about freely; also, anything which secures admission or acceptance.

pas'sus (păs'ŭs), *n.; pl.* -SUS, -SUSES (-ĕz; -ĭz). [L., step, pace. See PACE.] **1.** Of a poem or story, a division or part; a canto. **2.** A Roman pace. See PACE, *n.*, 2.

pass'word' (pås'wûrd'), *n.* A word to be uttered by one before he is allowed to pass; watchword; countersign. Cf. PAROLE, *n.*, 3.

past (påst; 9). See PASS, *v.* Hence, *adj.* **1.** Of or pertaining to a former time; also, just gone by or elapsed; just preceding; as, during the *past* year. **2.** Ex-; no longer serving as; as, a *past* president. **3.** *Gram.* Expressive of time gone by, either simply as bygone without implication as to duration, called also *preterit* or **past absolute** (On arriving I *wrote* to him), or as in progress, habitually done, or recurring, called also *imperfect* or **past descriptive** (I *was writing* while he slept; they *loved* fishing). — *n.* **1.** A former time or state; events of past time. **2.** Past life, history, or course of action; esp., a past career unknown or kept secret; as, a man with a *past.* **3.** *Gram.* The past tense, or a verb in it. Abbr. *p.* — *adv.* By; close in passing. — *prep.* Beyond, as in time, age, power, etc.

paste (pāst), *n.* [OF., fr. LL. *pasta*, fr. Gr. *pastē* barley broth.] **1.** Dough; specif.: **a** Dough containing a large proportion of fat for the crust of pies, tarts, etc. **b** Any shaped and dried dough prepared from semolina, farina, or wheat flour, or a mixture of these with water (as in macaroni, spaghetti, vermicelli), milk, or egg. **2.** A smooth food product made by evaporation, grinding, etc.; as, almond *paste.* **3.** A soft gumlike confection. **4.** A preparation of flour, starch, or the like, and water, used as an adhesive or a vehicle for mordant. **5.** The moistened clay, etc., used in making pottery or porcelain. **6.** A lead-glass composition of great brilliancy, used in imitation stones. — *v. t.* **1.** To unite or fasten; to cause to adhere by or as by paste. **2.** To cover by or as by pasting.

paste (pāst), *v. t.* [From BASTE to beat.] *Slang.* To hit or punch hard; to defeat. — **paste**, *n.*

paste'board' (-bōrd'; 70), *n.* **1.** A stiff material made by pasting together sheets of paper; loosely, any kind of paper board. **2.** *Slang.* **a** A visiting card. **b** A playing card. **c** A ticket. — *adj.* Of or like pasteboard; hence, unsubstantial; sham.

pas'tel (păs'tĕl), *n.* [F., fr. Pr. *pastel.*] Woad.

pas·tel' (păs·tĕl'; păs'tĕl), *n.* [F., fr. It. *pastello*, dim. fr. L. *pasta* paste.] **1.** A type of paste made of ground color or colors, etc., and used for making crayons; also, a crayon or crayons so made. **2.** A drawing made with such crayons; also, the art of drawing with these crayons. **3.** A light literary sketch. **4.** Any of various pale colors of very high brilliance and low or medium saturation. See COLOR. — **pas·tel'**, *adj.* — **pas'tel·ist, pas'tel·list** (păs'tĕl·ĭst; păs·tĕl'ĭst), *n.*

past'er (pās'tẽr), *n.* **1.** One who pastes. **2.** A gummed paper, to be pasted on or over something, as a name on a ballot.

pas'tern (păs'tẽrn), *n.* [OF. *pasturon*, fr. *pasture*, fr. LL., fr. L. *pastorius* pertaining to shepherds or herdsmen, fr. *pastor.* See PASTOR.] That part of the foot of the horse and allied animals, between the fetlock and the coffin joint, of which the upper bone is the ***great pastern bone***, the second, the ***small pastern bone***, and the joint between, the ***pastern joint***. See DOG, HORSE, *Illusts.*

pas'teur·ism (păs'tẽr·ĭz'm), *n.* [After Louis *Pasteur.*] The theory or practice of the chemist Louis Pasteur (see *Biog.*); specif.: **a** Treatment of rabies by inoculations with virus of gradually increasing strength. **b** Pasteurization.

pas'teur·i·za'tion (-ĭ·zā'shŭn; -ī·zā'shŭn), *n.* The partial sterilization of a fluid at a temperature (131°–158° F.) which destroys certain pathogenic organisms and undesirable bacteria.

pas'teur·ize (păs'tẽr·īz; *popularly also* păs'tūr·īz; 9), *v. t.* To subject to pasteurization; also, to treat by pasteurism (sense **a**).

‖**pas·tic'cio** (päs·tēt'chō), *n.; pl.* -CI (-chē). [It., fr. L. *pasta.* See PASTE.] A medley; a patchwork, esp. musical, literary, or artistic.

pas·tiche' (păs·tēsh'; päs·tēsh'), *n.* [F.] A literary or artistic composition imitating, often caricaturing, previous writings or paintings.

pas·tille' (păs·tēl'; -tĭl'), *n.* Also **pas'til** (păs'tĭl). [F. *pastille*, fr. L. *pastillus* a little loaf, a lozenge, dim. of *panis* bread, or a kindred word.] **1.** A small mass of aromatic paste for fumigating or deodorizing the air of a room. **2.** An aromatic or medicated lozenge; a troche.

pas'time' (pås'tīm'; 9), *n.* [*pass* + *time.*] That which amuses or makes time pass agreeably; diversion; recreation.

past'i·ness (pās'tĭ·nĕs; -nĭs), *n.* Quality of being pasty; pasty consistency or appearance.

past master. **a** A former master, as of a lodge of Freemasons. **b** An adept. — **past mistress.**

pas'tor (pås'tẽr; 9), *n.* [OF., fr. L. *pastor*, fr. *pascere, pastum*, to pasture, feed.] **1.** *Now Rare.* A shepherd. **2.** A spiritual overseer; specif., the minister or priest in charge of a church or parish. — **pas'tor·ship**, *n.*

pas'tor·age (-ĭj), *n.* = PASTORATE.

pas'to·ral (pås'tō·răl), *adj.* [L. *pastoralis.*] **1.** Of or pertaining to shepherds; hence: **a** Relating to rural life and scenes. **b** Of the nature of a pastoral; pert. to pastorals; as, *pastoral* poetry. **2.** Relating to the care of souls, or to the pastor of a church; as, *pastoral* duties. — **Syn.** See RURAL. — *n.* **1.** A poem, drama, romance, etc., of pastoral life or manners; esp., an idyllic poem in which the speakers assume the character of shepherds; also, pastoral poetry, drama, etc., as a literary form. **2.** A rural picture or scene. **3.** *Eccl.* **a** A book on the duties of pastors. **b** A letter of a pastor to his charge; specif., an episcopal letter to pastors and their churches. **c** In full, **pastoral staff.** A crosier. See VESTMENT, *Illust.* **4.** *Music.* A pastorale. — **pas'to·ral·ism** (-ĭz'm), *n.* — **pas'to·ral·ist** (-ĭst), *n.* — **pas'to·ral·ly**, *adv.*

pas'to·ra'le (pås'tō·rä'lā; -lē; pås'tō·răl'), *n.; pl.* -RALI (-rä'lē), -RALES (-rä'lāz; -rä'lēz; -rălz'). [It.] *Music.* **a** A lyric cantata relating to rural life. **b** An instrumental piece of idyllic or rustic simplicity and sentiment.

pas'tor·ate (pås'tẽr·ĭt), *n.* **1.** Office, state, jurisdiction, or tenure of office of a pastor; also, a body of pastors. **2.** A pastor's house; a parsonage.

pas·to'ri·um (pås·tō'rĭ·ŭm; 9; 70), *n.* [NL. See PASTOR.] *Southern U.S.* A Protestant parsonage.

past participle. See PARTICIPLE. Abbr. *past part.*

past perfect. *Gram.* Expressing the action or state as completed at or before a past time spoken of (by noon I *had left*); also, the past perfect tense, or a verb in it.

pas·tra'mi (pås·trä'mĭ), *n.* [Yiddish, fr. Romanian.] Beef, esp. from shoulder cuts, highly seasoned and smoked.

pas'try (pās'trĭ), *n.; pl.* -TRIES (-trĭz). [From *paste*, or perh. fr. OF. *pastaierie*, fr. *pastaier* pastry cook.] Articles of food made of or having a crust made of dough paste, as pies.

pas'tur·a·ble (pås'tūr·ȧ·b'l), *adj.* Fit for, or affording, pasture.

pas'tur·age (-ĭj), *n.* [OF.] **1.** Pasture. **2.** The right of pasturing cattle.

pas'ture (pås'tūr; 9), *n.* [OF. *pasture*, fr. LL. *pastura*, fr. *pascere, pastum*, to pasture, feed.] **1.** The right to pasture animals; — esp. in *common of pasture* (see COMMON, *n.*, 4). **2.** Grass or other plants grown for feeding grazing animals; also, land used for grazing. — *v. i. & t.* **1.** To feed on growing grass; to graze. **2.** To put cattle or flocks to graze (on). **3.** To supply with pasture. — **pas'tur·er**, *n.*

past'y (păs'tĭ; *see note below*), *n.; pl.* PASTIES (-tĭz). [OF. *pasté.*] A pie; often specif., a meat pie.

☞ In America, *pasty* is largely a literary word only, and is often read pās'tĭ; in Brit. use it is pronounced păs'tĭ, päs'tĭ, or, sometimes, pās'tĭ.

past'y (pās'tĭ), *adj.;* PAST'I·ER (-tĭ·ẽr); PAST'I·EST. Like paste, as in color.

PA, P.A., *or* **p.a., sys'tem** (pē'ā'). See PUBLIC-ADDRESS SYSTEM.

pat (păt), *n.* **1.** A light blow or stroke, as with a flat instrument or with the fingers. **2.** The sound made in patting. **3.** Something shaped by patting, esp. a mass of butter. — *v. t.;* PAT'TED; PAT'TING. **1.** To flatten, smooth, or shape, etc., by a pat or pats. **2.** To stroke, caress, or soothe with pats. **3.** To tap with light steps. — *v. i.* To fall, strike, walk, etc., so as to make a light beating sound.

pat, *adj.* **1.** Pertinent; opportune; timely. **2.** *Colloq.* Fixed or firm; incapable of being forgotten, moved, etc.; as, to have a lesson *pat;* to stand *pat.* — **Syn.** See SEASONABLE. — **pat**, *adv.*

pa·ta'gi·um (pȧ·tā'jĭ·ŭm), *n.; pl.* PATAGIA (-ȧ). [NL., fr. L., a gold edging.] A wing membrane, as of a bat; specif.: **a** The fold of skin connecting the forelimbs and hind limbs of flying squirrels and other leaping arboreal animals. **b** The fold of skin in front of the humeral and radio-ulnar parts of a bird's wing.

Pat'a·go'nian (păt'ȧ·gō'nyăn; -gō'nĭ·ăn), *n.* A native of Patagonia (see *Gaz.*), esp. one of the aboriginal Indian stock. — **Pat'a·go'nian**, *adj.*

patch (păch), *n.* *Colloq. & Dial.* Fool; ninny.

patch (păch), *n.* [ME. *pacche.*] **1.** Something like the original material used to mend, fill up, or cover a hole, rent, breach, or weak spot. **2.** A small piece of black silk or court plaster stuck on the face, esp. to heighten beauty. **3.** Hence: **a** A small piece; bit; scrap. **b** A passage; excerpt. **c** A spot or blotch differing in color from the ground. **d** A small area or plot distinguished from its surroundings; as, a *patch* of trees. — *v. t.* **1.** To mend, repair, strengthen, etc., with a patch or patches. **2.** To make out of patches, scraps, etc.; hence, to put together hastily or clumsily. **3.** To settle; adjust; as, to *patch* up a quarrel. — **Syn.** See MEND. — **patch'er,** *n.*

patch'ou·li, patch'ou·ly (păch'ōō·lĭ; pȧ·chōō'lĭ), *n.* [Tamil *paccilai* green leaf.] **1.** An East Indian mint (*Pogostemon patchouly*) yielding a fragrant essential oil. **2.** The perfume made from this plant.

patch pocket. A flat pocket applied to the outside of a garment.

patch test. *Med.* A test for determining a person's susceptibility, made by applying to the unbroken surface of the skin small pads soaked with the allergy-producing substance in question.

patch'work' (păch'wûrk'), *n.* **1.** Something made of incongruous, unrelated scraps or parts; a jumble. **2.** A cover (as for a quilt) or other piece of work made by sewing together pieces of cloth of various sizes, shapes, and colors. Cf. CRAZY QUILT. **3.** A variegated or checkered appearance, design, or scene; as, a *patchwork* of fields.

patch'y (păch'ĭ), *adj.*; PATCH'I·ER (-ĭ·ẽr); PATCH'I·EST. Marked by or diversified with patches; resembling patchwork; spotty.

pate (pāt), *n.* [ME., of unknown origin.] The head or crown of the head; hence, brain or brains; — now generally contemptuous and often in combination.

‖**pâte** (pät), *n.* [F.] Paste; specif., *Ceramics*, the paste or plastic material for pottery or porcelain.

‖**pâ'té'** (pä'tā'), *n.* [F.] **1.** A pie. **2.** A delicate meat paste, as in ‖**pâ'té' de foie gras** (dē fwä' grä'), a paste of fattened goose liver and truffles.

pa·tel'la (pȧ·tĕl'ȧ), *n.; pl.* -LAE (-ē). [L., a small pan, dim. of *patina*, *patena*, a pan.] *Anat.* A thick, flat, triangular, movable bone, forming the anterior point of the knee; the kneepan or kneecap. — **pa·tel'lar** (-ẽr), **pa·tel'late** (-āt), *adj.*

pa·tel'li·form (-ĭ·fôrm), *adj.* [*patella* + *-form.*] **1.** *Zool.* Shaped like a limpet shell. **2.** *Bot.* Disk-shaped.

pat'en (păt'ĕn), *n.* [OF. *patène*, fr. L. *patena*, *patina*, a shallow vessel, fr. Gr. *patanē.*] **1.** A plate; specif., a plate of precious metal used in the Eucharistic service for the bread or Host. **2.** A thin metal disk, or something like or likened to such a disk.

pa'ten·cy (pā'tĕn·sĭ; păt'ĕn-; *cf.* PATENT, *adj.*), *n.* **1.** State of being patent, or evident. **2.** *Chiefly Med.* State of being unobstructed.

pat'ent (păt'ĕnt; pā'tĕnt; *see note below*), *adj.* [L. *patens*, *-entis*, pres. part. of *patere* to be open; sense 1 is fr. F. *patent*, fr. L.] **1.** Open to public perusal; — said of a document conferring some right, privilege, etc.; as, letters *patent*. **2.** Open; not closed, shut, or hidden. Specif.: **a** Available or accessible. **b** Evident; obvious. **c** Affording unobstructed passage, as a tube, intestine, etc. **3.** Conferred, endowed with a right or privilege, or appointed, by letters patent. **4.** Of, pert. to, or concerned with the granting of patents, esp. for inventions; as, the United States *Patent* Office. **5.** Patented; made by a patented process or equipped with a patented device; as, a *patent* lock; also, proprietary; trade-marked; as, *patent* medicines. **6.** *Bot. & Zool.* Patulous; spreading. **7.** *Law.* Appropriated or protected by letters patent. **8.** *Milling.* Of a high grade; — applied to flour. — **Syn.** See EVIDENT.

☞ In all senses except 2 and 6, above, păt'ĕnt is the usual pronunciation in the U. S., while for senses 2 and 6, pā'tĕnt is usual. In British use, pā'tĕnt is usual except in *letters patent* and *Patent Office.*

— *n.* **1.** Letters patent; an official document conferring a right or privilege. **2.** A writing securing to an inventor, for a term of years, the exclusive right to make, use, and vend his invention; also, the monopoly or right so granted, or the thing patented. Patent rights rest entirely upon statute and, under international conventions, are recognized by the principal countries of the world. Cf. COPYRIGHT; ROYALTY, 6 **b**. **3.** Hence, a right, privilege, or license. **4.** An instrument making a conveyance or grant of public lands; also, the land so conveyed. — *v. t.* **1.** *Rare.* To grant to by patent; also, grant a patent for. **2.** To secure by letters patent exclusive right to make, use, and vend (an invention).

— **pat'ent·a·bil'i·ty,** *n.* — **pat'ent·a·ble,** *adj.*

pat'ent·ee' (păt'ĕn·tē'; pā'tĕn·tē'; *cf.* PATENT, *adj.*), *n.* One to whom a grant is made, or a privilege secured, by patent.

patent leather. A kind of leather, with a hard, smooth, glossy, usually black, surface finish.

pa'tent·ly (pā'tĕnt·lĭ; păt'ĕnt-), *adv.* In a patent manner; obviously; evidently.

pat'en·tor (păt'ĕn·tẽr; pā'tĕn-; *cf.* PATENT, *adj.*), *n.* **1.** One who grants a patent. **2.** Erroneous for PATENTEE.

patent right. A right granted by letters patent, esp. the exclusive right to an invention.

pa'ter (pā'tẽr; pä'tẽr), *n.* [L., father.] **1.** Short for PATERNOSTER, 1. **2.** *Familiar.* Father.

pa'ter·fa·mil'i·as (pā'tẽr·fȧ·mĭl'ĭ·ăs), *n.; pl.* PATRESFAMILIAS (pā'trēz-). [L., fr. *pater* father + *familias*, gen. of *familia* family.] **1.** *Rom. Law.* The head of a household; in a larger sense, anyone who is his own master. **2.** The father of a family.

pa·ter'nal (pȧ·tûr'năl; -n'l), *adj.* [L. *paternus*, fr. *pater* father.] **1.** Of or pert. to a father; fatherly. **2.** Received or inherited from a father or the male line. **3.** Related on one's father's side. — **pa·ter'nal·ly,** *adv.*

pa·ter'nal·ism (-ĭz'm), *n.* A relation between the governed and the government, the employed and the employer, etc., involving care and control suggestive of those followed by a father; also, the principles or practices so involved. — **pa·ter'nal·is'tic** (-ĭs'tĭk), *adj.* — **pa·ter'nal·is'ti·cal·ly** (-tĭ·kăl·ĭ), *adv.*

pa·ter'ni·ty (pȧ·tûr'nĭ·tĭ), *n.* [F. *paternité*, fr. LL. *paternitas.*] **1.** Quality or state of being a father; fatherhood. **2.** Derivation or descent from a father.

pa'ter·nos'ter (pā'tẽr·nŏs'tẽr; păt'ẽr-; 2), *n.* [L., our father.] **1.** *Often* **Pa'ter Nos'ter.** The Lord's Prayer; — from the opening words of its Latin form. **2.** One of the large beads of a rosary on which the Lord's Prayer is said. **3.** A spell, usually one muttered; as, the ***white paternoster***, or prayer for protection against evil spirits; the ***black paternoster***, or incantation addressed to evil spirits.

‖**Pa'ter Pa'tri·ae** (pā'tẽr pā'trĭ·ē). [L.] Father of his country.

path (pȧth; 9), *n.; pl.* PATHS (pȧthz). [AS. *pæth*, *path.*] **1.** A trodden way; a footway; more generally, any way or road. **2.** A track, roadway, or the like, specially constructed as for racing or riding. **3.** A route or course.

Pa·than' (pȧ·tän'; pȧt·hän'), *n.* [Hind. *Paṭhān.*] A member of the principal race (Indo-Iranian) of Afghanistan.

pa·thet'ic (pȧ·thĕt'ĭk), *adj.* Also (*Rare*) **pa·thet'i·cal** (-ĭ·kăl). [LL. *patheticus*, fr. Gr. *pathētikos*, fr. *pathētos* subject to suffering, fr. the root of *pathos* suffering, *pathein*, *paschein*, to suffer.] **1.** Affecting or exciting emotion, esp. the tender emotions, as pity or sorrow; as, a *pathetic* story. **2.** Expressing or intended to express pathos, strong emotion, etc.; as, a *pathetic* style. — **Syn.** See MOVING. — **pa·thet'i·cal·ly,** *adv.*

pathetic fallacy. A so-called fallacy of authors who, under stress of emotion, ascribe human traits or feelings to inanimate nature, as in "the cruel sea," "a pitiless storm."

path'find'er (pȧth'fīn'dẽr), *n.* One who discovers a way or, esp., a new route by exploring untraversed regions.

-path'i·a (-păth'ĭ·ȧ), **-path'ic** (-ĭk). See -PATHY.

path'less (pȧth'lĕs; -lĭs), *adj.* Untrodden; trackless. — **path'less·ness,** *n.*

path'o- (păth'ō-), **path-.** [Gr. *pathos.*] A combining form meaning *suffering, disease, passion;* also, *pathological*, as in: **path'o·bi·ol'o·gy, path'o·psy·chol'o·gy.**

path'o·gen (păth'ō·jĕn), *n.* Also **path'o·gene** (-jēn). [See PATHOS; -GEN.] A pathogenic organism or virus.

path'o·gen'e·sis (-jĕn'ē·sĭs), *n.* [NL.] The genesis of a pathological process or disease. — **path'o·ge·net'ic** (-jē·nĕt'ĭk), *adj.*

path'o·gen'ic (-jĕn'ĭk), *adj.* Pathogenetic; also, causing disease.

pa·thog'e·ny (pȧ·thŏj'ē·nĭ), *n.* Pathogenesis.

path'o·log'i·cal (păth'ō·lŏj'ĭ·kăl), *adj.* Also **path'o·log'ic** (-ĭk). **a** Of or pertaining to pathology. **b** Morbid; due to disease; as, *pathological* tissue. — **path'o·log'i·cal·ly,** *adv.*

pa·thol'o·gist (pȧ·thŏl'ō·jĭst), *n.* *Med.* A specialist in pathology; specif., one who makes post-mortem examinations, diagnoses morbid changes in tissues removed at operation, etc.

pa·thol'o·gy (-jĭ), *n.; pl.* -GIES (-jĭz). **1.** The science treating of diseases, their nature, causes, etc. **2.** The condition, as of an organ or fluid, produced by disease.

pa'thos (pā'thŏs), *n.* [Gr., a suffering, passion; akin to Gr. *penthos* grief, *pathein*, *paschein*, to suffer.] **1.** That quality of human or animal experience or of its representation in art which awakens feelings of pity, sympathy, and tender sorrow. **2.** *Rare.* **a** A pathetic passage or speech. **b** Suffering; affliction. **3.** *Aesthetics.* The quality or character of those emotions, traits, or experiences which are personal, and therefore restricted and evanescent. Cf. ETHOS, 1.

path'way' (pȧth'wā'), *n.; pl.* PATHWAYS (-wāz'). A footpath; any path or course.

-pathy. Also **-path'i·a** (-păth'ĭ·ȧ). [See PATHOS.] A combining form meaning: **a** *Feeling, suffering, affection*, as in a*pathy*. **b** *A disease of a* (specified) *part or type*, as in psycho*pathy*. See PSYCHO-. **c** *Treatment of ailments of a* (specified) *mode*, as in osteo*pathy*. Derivative adjectives are formed in **-path'ic** (-păth'ĭk).

pa'tience (pā'shĕns), *n.* **1.** State, quality, power, or fact of being patient; forbearance. **2.** *Obs.* Sufferance; permission. **3.** A card game, usually a form of solitaire.

pa'tient (-shĕnt), *adj.* [OF. *pacient* (F. *patient*), fr. L. *patiens*, *-entis*, pres. part. of *pati* to suffer.] **1.** Bearing or enduring pains, trials, or the like, without complaint or with equanimity. **2.** Exercising forbearance under provocation; long-suffering. **3.** Expectant with calmness or without discontent; also, undisturbed by obstacles, delays, failures, etc.; persevering. **4.** Marked by or manifesting patience; as, *patient* waiting. **5.** With *of:* **a** Able to bear strain, stress, etc.; as, *patient* of toil. **b** Susceptible; admitting. **6.** Acted upon; passive; — opposed to *agent*. — *n.* **1.** *Rare.* One who endures. **2.** A person under treatment or care, as by a physician or surgeon, or in a hospital. **3.** One affected; the object or recipient of an action; — distinguished from *agent*. — **pa'tient·ly,** *adv.*

pat'i·na (păt'ĭ·nȧ), *n.; pl.* PATINAE (-nē). [L., a dish, pan.] A paten.

pat'i·na, *n.* [It., of uncert. origin.] **1.** A film formed on copper and bronze by exposure or by treatment with acids, etc. A fine natural patina has artistic value. **2.** A surface mellowing or softening, as in color, with age or use.

pat·i·o (păt'ĭ·ō; pä'tĭ·ō), *n.; pl.* PATIOS. [Sp., a court.] **1.** In Spain, Spanish America, etc., a courtyard. **2.** A paved area adjoining a dwelling, used especially for recreation.

pat'ois (păt'wä; *F.* pȧ'twȧ'), *n.; pl.* PATOIS (păt'wäz; *F.* pȧ'twȧ'). [F.] A dialect; hence, illiterate or provincial speech; jargon; cant.

‖**Pa'tres con·scrip'ti** (pā'trēz kŏn·skrĭp'tī). [L.] Conscript fathers (which see); specif., Roman senators.

patri-. [L. *pater*, *patris.*] A combining form meaning *father*, as in **pat'ri·lin'e·al** (păt'rĭ·lĭn'ē·ăl; pā'trĭ-).

pa'tri·arch (pā'trĭ·ärk), *n.* [OF. *patriarche*, fr. LL., fr. Gr. *patriarchēs*, fr. *patria* lineage, race (fr. *patēr* father) + *archos* a leader, chief.] **1.** The father and ruler of a family or tribe, esp. in Biblical history before Moses. **2.** A person regarded as father or founder, as of a race, science, religion, etc. **3.** A venerable old man; veteran. **4.** *Eccl.* **a** In the early church, orig., a bishop; later, a metropolitan. **b** *Eastern Church.* (1) Any of the bishops of the five ancient sees of Rome, Constantinople, Alexandria, Antioch, and Jerusalem; — sometimes extended to bishops of other chief cities. The patriarch of Constantinople, the highest dignitary in the Orthodox Church, is entitled ***Ecumenical Patriarch.*** (2) The head of any of the separated (non-Orthodox) churches, as the Coptic Church. **c** *R.C.Ch.* An ecclesiastical dignitary next in rank to the pope but without patriarchal jurisdiction, except in the cases of the patriarchs of the various Uniat bodies, and of the pope himself, in his capacity as patriarch of the West, or the Latin Church. Certain differences in discipline between Uniat churches and the Latin Church such as those respecting celibacy of the clergy, result from such differences in jurisdiction. **d** *Mormon Church.* One of the higher order of priesthood, especially empowered to invoke and pronounce blessings within a prescribed jurisdiction. — **pa'tri·ar'chal** (pā'trĭ·är'kăl; 2), *adj.*

pa'tri·ar'chal cross. See CROSS, *Illust.* (3).

pa'tri·arch'ate (pā'trĭ·är'kāt), *n.* **1.** Office, dignity, province, see, etc., of a patriarch. **2.** A patriarchy.

pa'tri·arch'y (-är'kĭ), *n.; pl.* -ARCHIES (-kĭz). A state of social development characterized by the supremacy of the father in the clan or family. Cf. MATRIARCHY.

pa·tri′cian (pȧ·trĭsh′ăn), *adj.* [F. *patricien,* fr. L. *patricius,* fr. *patres* fathers or senators, pl. of *pater.*] **1.** *Hist.* Of, pertaining to, or consisting of patricians. **2.** Appropriate to or characteristic of a person of high birth or breeding; noble; aristocratic. — *n.* **1.** *Hist.* **a** *Rom. Antiq.* Orig., one of any of the families forming the *populus Romanus,* or body of Roman citizens, before the growth of the plebeian order; later, a noble by right of birth or privilege. **b** In the Roman Empire, one of an order of nobility founded by Constantine. **c** A hereditary noble of a medieval Italian city republic. **d** One of an order of citizens eligible for the senate or council in the German free cities and towns. **2.** A person distinguished by superior breeding and a high degree of cultivation; an aristocrat.

pa·tri′ci·ate (-ĭ·āt), *n.* Patrician dignity, rank, or class.

pat′ri·cide (păt′rĭ·sīd; pā′trĭ-), *n.* [L. *pater* father + *caedere* to kill.] Parricide. — **pat′ri·cid′al** (-sīd′ăl; -′l; 2), *adj.*

pat′ri·mo′ny (păt′rĭ·mō′nĭ *or, esp. Brit.,* -mŭn·ĭ), *n.; pl.* -NIES (-nĭz). [OF. *patrimoine,* fr. L. *patrimonium,* fr. *pater* father.] **1.** An estate inherited from one's father or other ancestor. **2.** An ancient endowment, as of a church. **3.** Any heritage. — **Syn.** See HERITAGE. — **pat′ri·mo′ni·al** (-mō′nĭ·ăl), *adj.*

pa′tri·ot (pā′trĭ·ŭt; păt′rĭ-: *the first pron. distinctly prevails in the U.S.*), *n.* [F. *patriote,* fr. LL. *patriota* a fellow countryman, fr. Gr. *patriōtēs,* fr. *patrios* established by forefathers, fr. *patēr* father.] One who loves his country and zealously supports its authority and interests. — **pa′tri·ot,** *adj.*

pa′tri·ot′ic (pā′trĭ·ŏt′ĭk *or, esp. Brit.,* păt′rĭ-), *adj.* Inspired by patriotism; fitting a patriot. — **pa′tri·ot′i·cal·ly** (-ĭ·kăl·ĭ), *adv.*

pa′tri·ot·ism (pā′trĭ·ŭt·ĭz′m; păt′rĭ-), *n.* Love of country; devotion to the welfare of one's country.

Pa′tri·ots′ Day. A legal holiday in Massachusetts and Maine, April 19, anniversary of the battles of Lexington and Concord.

pa·tris′tic (pȧ·trĭs′tĭk), **pa·tris′ti·cal** (-tĭ·kăl), *adj.* Of or pert. to the study of the writings or doctrines of the early Christian Fathers; loosely, of or pert. to the Fathers themselves. — **pa·tris′ti·cal·ly,** *adv.*

Pa·tro′clus (pȧ·trō′klŭs; pȧ·trŏk′lŭs; păt′rō·klŭs), *n.* [L., fr. Gr. *Patroklos.*] In the *Iliad,* a Greek whose slaying by Hector was avenged by his friend Achilles.

pa·trol′ (pȧ·trōl′), *v. i. & t.;* -TROLLED′ (-trōld′); -TROL′LING. [F. *patrouiller,* prop., to go through puddles, fr. *patouiller* to paddle.] To go the rounds (of), or traverse, for watching or protecting. — *n.* **1.** A patrolling. **2.** The man or men assigned to the duty of patrolling; the guard going the rounds. **3.** A subdivision of a troop of boy scouts, consisting of eight scouts. — **pa·trol′ler** (-trōl′ẽr), *n.*

pa·trol′man (-măn), *n.; pl.* -MEN (-mĕn). One who patrols; esp., a policeman assigned to a beat.

patrol wagon. *U. S.* **a** A wagon used by policemen to convey prisoners. **b** A light wagon used by an underwriter's fire patrol, salvage corps, or protective association.

pa′tron (pā′trŭn), *n.* [OF. *patrun, patron,* fr. L. *patronus,* fr. *pater* father.] **1.** One chosen, named, or honored as a special guardian, protector, supporter, or the like; as: **a** In full **patron saint.** A saint to whose care and intercession a person, church, place, etc., is dedicated. **b** *Hist.* A person to whom a book is dedicated, or whose portrait is included in a painting, by a writer or artist seeking his support or assistance. **c** A person named as a sponsor of a social or charitable affair. **2.** A supporter; specif.: **a** A benefactor. **b** A champion or advocate. **c** *Colloq.* A customer or client. **3.** *Eng.* One who has the right of presentation to a benefice; the owner of the advowson. **4.** *Rom. Law.* A master who had freed his slave, but still retained some rights over him. — **pa′tron·al** (pā′trŭn·ăl; păt′rŭn·ăl; -′l; *still occas.* pȧ·trō′năl; -n′l), *adj.*

pa′tron·age (pā′trŭn·ĭj; păt′rŭn-), *n.* **1.** Office, function, or status of a patron. **2.** Support, encouragement, etc. given by, or asked from, a patron. **3.** Condescension; as, an air of *patronage.* **4.** Patrons collectively; clientele; also, custom. **5.** The right of presentation to a church or ecclesiastical benefice; advowson. **6.** The right or control of nomination to political office; also, the offices, contracts, honors, etc., which an official may bestow by favor.

pa′tron·ess (pā′trŭn·ĕs; păt′rŭn-; -ĭs), *n.* A woman patron.

pa′tron·ize (pā′trŭn·īz; păt′rŭn-), *v. t.* **1.** To act as patron toward or of; to give one's protection, support, or countenance to. **2.** To treat with condescension. **3.** *Colloq.* To trade with. — **pa′tron·iz′er** (-īz′ẽr), *n.* — **pa′tron·iz′ing·ly,** *adv.*

pat′ro·nym′ic (păt′rō·nĭm′ĭk), *adj.* [LL. *patronymicus,* fr. Gr. *patrōnymikos,* fr. *patēr* father + *onoma* name.] Of or pertaining to a patronymic. — *n.* **1.** A name formed by the addition of a prefix or suffix indicating relationship to the name of one's father or paternal ancestor, as *Johnson,* son of John. **2.** Loosely, a patrilineal surname.

pa·troon′ (pȧ·trōōn′), *n.* [F. *patron;* in sense 2 fr. D. *patroon* a patron.] **1.** *Obs.* A patron. **2.** A proprietor of any of certain tracts of land with manorial privileges granted under the old Dutch governments of New York and New Jersey.

pat·tée′, pat·té′ (pȧ·tā′; păt′ē), **pat′y** (păt′ĭ), *adj. Her.* Having arms narrow at the center and expanding toward the ends; — said of a cross. See CROSS, *Illust.* (13).

pat′ten (păt′ĕn; -′n), *n.* [OF. *patin,* fr. *patte* paw, foot.] Any of various kinds of footgear worn at different periods or in various countries; specif., a type of overshoe with a high wooden sole, worn to raise the feet from the wet or the mud.

pat′ter (păt′ẽr), *v. i. & t.* [From *pater* in *paternoster.*] **1.** To recite paternosters or other prayers in rapid succession; hence, to say rapidly, mechanically, or mumblingly, as prayers. **2.** To talk glibly or volubly. — *n.* **1.** The cant of thieves, vagabonds, etc., or of any class or profession; jargon or lingo. **2.** A kind of rapid, voluble speech or harangue such as used by fakers or tricksters, or by comedians. — **pat′ter·er,** *n.*

pat′ter, *v. i. & t.* [Freq. of *pat* to strike gently.] To strike or cause to strike with quick pats. — *n.* A pattering; as, the *patter* of rain on the roof.

pat′tern (păt′ẽrn), *n.* [OF. *patron* patron, also, pattern. See PATRON.] **1.** Anything proposed for or worthy of imitation; exemplar; as, a *pattern* for men. **2.** Anything designed as a guide or model for making things; as, a dressmaker's *pattern.* **3.** *Archaic.* A representation or copy; a likeness. **4.** A specimen; sample. **5.** Design; specif.: **a** Form; shape; outline; as, vases in many *patterns.* **b** A decorative figure or motive; as, a chintz with a small *pattern.* **c** An arrangement or composition that suggests or reveals a design; a configuration; as, a poem with a *pattern.* **6.** *U. S.* A length of cloth sufficient for a garment. **7.** *Founding.* A model for making the mold into which molten metal is poured to form a casting. **8.** *Gun.* Distribution of shot from a shotgun or bullets from an exploded shrapnel. — **Syn.** See MODEL.
— *v. t.* **1.** To fashion with reference to a pattern; — usually with *after, on, upon.* **2.** *Rare.* **a** To foreshadow. **b** To match. **c** To imitate. **3.** To furnish with a pattern.

pat′tle (păt′′l), *n. Scot. & N. of Eng.* = PADDLE, 1.

pat′ty (păt′ĭ), *n.; pl.* PATTIES (-ĭz). [F. *pâté.*] A little pie or pasty baked in a small pan (**pat′ty·pan′**).

patty shell. A puff paste case for creamed meat, fish, etc.

pat′u·lous (păt′ū·lŭs), *adj.* [L. *patulus.*] **1.** Open; expanded; distended. **2.** *Bot.* Spreading, as branches of a tree. — **pat′u·lous·ly,** *adv.* — **pat′u·lous·ness,** *n.*

pat′y. Variant of PATTÉE.

‖**pau′cis ver′bis** (pô′sĭs vûr′bĭs). [L.] In or with few words.

pau′ci·ty (pô′sĭ·tĭ), *n.* [F. or L.; F. *paucité,* fr. L. *paucitas,* fr. *paucus* few, little.] **1.** Fewness; small number. **2.** Insufficiency; dearth; as, *paucity* of food, of evidence.

paugh′ty (*Scot.* pô′tĭ, päk′-, pôk′-; *dial.* pô′tĭ, päf′tĭ), *adj. Scot. & N. of Eng.* Haughty; also, pert; saucy.

Paul (pôl), *n.* [L. *Paulus,* or Gr. *Paulos.*] One of the apostles (see APOSTLE, 1) and writer of certain New Testament epistles. — **Paul′ine** (pôl′īn; -ēn), *adj.*

Paul Bun′yan (bŭn′yăn). In American folklore, esp. of the Northwest lumber camps, a mythical lumberjack, a superhero who performs prodigious feats.

Paul′ist (pôl′ĭst), *n. R.C.Ch.* **a** In India, a Jesuit. **b** A member of the Congregation of the Missionary Priests of St. Paul the Apostle, founded in 1858 at New York.

pau·low′ni·a (pô·lō′nĭ·ȧ), *n.* [NL., after the Russian princess Anna *Pavlovna,* daughter of Paul I.] Any of a genus (*Paulownia*) of Chinese trees of the figwort family; esp., one species (*P. tomentosa*) with purple foxglovelike flowers.

paunch (pônch; pänch), *n.* [OF. *panche, pance,* fr. L. *pantex, panticis.*] The belly and its contents; now, usually, a potbelly. — **paunch′y** (pôn′chĭ; pän′-), *adj.* — **paunch′i·ness,** *n.*

pau′per (pô′pẽr), *n.* [L. See POOR.] **1.** One without means except such as are derived from charity, esp. public poor funds. **2.** A very poor person. — **pau′per,** *adj.* — **pau′per·ism** (-ĭz′m), *n.* — **pau′per·ize** (-īz), *v. t.*

pause (pôz), *n.* [F., fr. L. *pausa,* fr. Gr. *pausis.*] **1.** A temporary stop or rest. **2.** Temporary inaction; hesitation. **3.** Reason or cause for pausing; as, a thought that gives one *pause.* **4.** In technical uses: **a** *Elocution.* A brief suspension of the voice. **b** In writing and printing, a punctuation point. **c** A break or paragraph in writing. **d** *Music.* A symbol (𝄐 or 𝄑) placed over or under a note or rest to indicate that it is to be prolonged. **e** *Pros.* A break in a verse, as a caesura. — *v. i.* **1.** To cease for a time; to intermit speaking or acting; hesitate. **2.** To remain fixed for a time; to linger; dwell (*on* or *upon*); as, to *pause* upon the last note. — **paus′er** (pôz′ẽr), *n.*

pav′an (păv′ăn), *n.* Also **pav′ane** (păv′ăn; *F.* pȧ′vän′). [F. *pavane,* fr. Sp. *pavana.*] A stately ceremonial old dance by couples; also, music for this dance.

pave (pāv), *v. t.* [OF. *paver* to pave, fr. L. *pavire* to beat, ram, or tread down.] **1.** To lay or cover with stone, asphalt, or the like, to make a firm, level surface for travel. **2.** To form the pavement, or flooring of. **3.** To cover compactly. — ***pave the way.*** To prepare a smooth, easy way or means; to overcome initial difficulties. — **pav′er** (pāv′ẽr), *n.*

‖**pa′vé′** (pȧ′vā′), *n.* [F., prop., past part. of *paver* to pave. See PAVE.] **1.** The pavement. **2.** *Jewelry.* A setting for jewels laid close together so as to cover the metal.

pave′ment (pāv′mĕnt), *n.* [OF., fr. L. *pavimentum.*] **a** That with which anything is paved. **b** A paved surface for travel; the artificial covering of a road, street, or sidewalk.

pav′id (păv′ĭd), *adj.* Timid; fearful.

pa·vil′ion (pȧ·vĭl′yŭn), *n.* [OF. *paveillon,* fr. L. *papilio* a butterfly, in ML., also a tent.] **1.** A tent; esp., a large tent with a peaked or rounded top. **2.** A tentlike covering; a canopy. **3.** The lower faceted part of a brilliant, between the girdle and the culet. See BRILLIANT, *Illust.* **4.** *Anat.* The auricle of the ear. **5.** *Arch.* **a** A light, ornamented building in a park, garden, or the like. **b** A body or mass of building projecting from a main mass. **c** Any of several detached or semidetached blocks or units into which a building, esp. a hospital (**pavilion hospital**), is sometimes divided. — *v. t.* To furnish or cover with, or put in or as in, a pavilion or pavilions.

pav′in (păv′ĭn). Var. of PAVAN.

pav′ing (pāv′ĭng), *n.* A pavement or material for it.

pav′ior, pav′iour (pāv′yẽr), *n.* One that paves; paver.

pav′o·nine (păv′ō·nīn; -nĭn), *adj.* [L. *pavoninus,* fr. *pavo* peacock.] Of or like a peacock; esp., colored like a peacock's tail or neck; iridescent.

paw (pô), *n.* [OF. *powe, poue, poe.*] **1.** The foot of a quadruped having claws, as the lion, dog, cat, etc.; also, the foot of any animal. **2.** A clutching or ungainly hand; jocosely, a hand. — *v. t. & i.* **1.** *Colloq.* To strike or touch with or as with the paw; hence, to handle clumsily, fondly, or rudely. **2.** To scrape or beat with the forefoot. **3.** To strike wildly with the hands; as, to *paw* the air. — **paw′er,** *n.*

pawk′y (pôk′ĭ), *adj.;* PAWK′I·ER (-ĭ·ẽr); PAWK′I·EST. **1.** *Chiefly Scot.* Arch; cunning; sly. **2.** *Dial.* Saucy; forward.

pawl (pôl), *n.* A pivoted tongue or sliding bolt on one part of a machine, adapted to fall into notches or interdental spaces on another part, as a ratchet wheel, so as to permit motion in only one direction. See JACK, RATCHET WHEEL, *Illusts.*

pawn (pôn), *n.* [OF. *paon, peon,* pawn, foot soldier, fr. LL. *pedo, pedonis,* fr. L. *pes, pedis,* foot.] *Chess.* The chessman of least value, moving only directly forward and but one square at a time (or at option two on its first move). Also, figuratively, an insignificant factor; as, a *pawn* in the political game.

pawn, *n.* [OF. *pand, pan,* pledge, surety.] **1.** Anything delivered to, or deposited with, another as security; a pledge; also, a hostage. **2.** A guaranty; an earnest. **3.** State of being pledged. **4.** A pawning, or pledging. — *v. t.* **1.** To deposit in pledge, or as security; to put in pawn. **2.** To stake; hazard. — **pawn′age** (-ĭj), *n.*

pawn′bro′ker (-brō′kẽr), *n.* One who loans money on the security of personal property pledged in his keeping. — **pawn′bro′king,** *n.*

Paw·nee′ (pô·nē′), *n.* An Indian of a tribe ranging between the Platte and Arkansas rivers, now citizens of Oklahoma.

pawn'er (pôn'ẽr), **pawn'or** (pôn'ẽr; pôn·ôr'), *n.* *Law.* One who pawns or pledges anything as security.
pawn'shop' (pôn'shŏp'), *n.* A pawnbroker's shop.
paw·paw' (*see* PAPAW), *n.* Var. of PAPAW.
pax (păks), *n.* [L.] **1.** Peace; — deified by the Romans. **2.** *R.C.Ch.* A tablet bearing a figure or symbol of Christ, the Virgin Mary, or a saint, which in medieval times was kissed by the priest and the people, before the Communion.
‖**pax vo·bis'cum** (vō·bĭs'kŭm). [L.] Peace (be) with you.
pax'wax' (păks'wăks'), *n.* [For *faxwax*, fr. AS. *feax* hair + a word akin to *weaxan* to grow.] In many mammals, the median ligament of the back of the neck, composed of yellow elastic tissue and used in supporting the head.
pay (pā), *v. t.;* PAYED (pād); PAY'ING. [OF. *peier, poier*, fr. L. *picare* to pitch, fr. *pix* pitch.] To smear or coat, as a vessel's bottom, a seam, etc., with a waterproof composition, as of tallow, resin, etc.
pay (pā), *v. t.;* PAID (pād) or, *Obs.* exc. in sense 6, PAYED; PAY'ING. [OF. *paier*, fr. L. *pacare* to pacify, appease, fr. *pax, pacis*, peace.] **1.** To satisfy (one) for service rendered, property delivered, etc.; remunerate. **2.** To give (something due) in return, satisfaction, or requital; also, to discharge indebtedness for; settle, as a bill. **3.** To make compensation or retaliation for. **4.** To give, offer, or make, freely or as fitting; as, to *pay* court or a visit. **5.** To be profitable to; also, bring in as a return. **6.** To pass out, as a rope; — now with *out* or *away.* — *v. i.* **1.** To give a recompense; make payment. **2.** To be profitable; to be worth the expense, effort, or the like.
Syn. **Pay, compensate, remunerate, satisfy, reimburse, indemnify, repay, recompense, requite** mean to give money or its equivalent in return for something. **Pay** implies the discharge of an obligation incurred; **compensate**, as here considered, a making up for services rendered or help given; **remunerate**, more clearly, a paying for services rendered; **satisfy**, paying a person that which is asked or required by law; **reimburse**, a return of money that has been expended; **indemnify**, a reimbursing for loss suffered through fire, accident, damage by war, or the like; **repay**, a paying back in kind or amount; **recompense**, often, a compensating for services rendered but, sometimes, for losses or injuries sustained; **requite**, a reciprocating or retaliation, often but not necessarily in kind.
pay off. **1.** To pay; specif., to pay in full and discharge. **2.** To requite. **3.** To allow to run off, as a thread or cord. **4.** *Colloq.* To yield full return, either to one's advantage or disadvantage; also, to attain full effectiveness. **5.** *Naut.* To turn (a vessel) to leeward.
— *n.* **1.** Act of paying; payment. **2.** State or status of being paid, or esp., of being on a payroll. **3.** Return; retributive punishment. **4.** That which is paid; remuneration; wages; salary. **5.** A person with reference to his ability to pay or record in paying. — **Syn.** See WAGE.
— *adj.* **1.** Containing or leading to something precious or valuable, as gold, oil, etc. **2.** Equipped with a device for receiving the toll or fee for use; as, a *pay* telephone.
pay'a·ble (pā'ȧ·b'l), *adj.* **1.** That may, can, or should be paid. **2.** Likely or able to yield a profit; profitable. **3.** *Law.* **a** That may be discharged or settled by delivery of value. **b** That is to be paid (by any particular person); also matured or maturing; due.
pay'ee' (pā'ē'), *n.* One to whom money is or is to be paid.
pay'er (pā'ẽr), *n.* One who pays; specif., the person by whom a bill or note has been, or should be, paid.
pay'mas'ter (pā'mȧs'tẽr; 9), *n.* One who regularly pays, esp. as an officer or agent of a government, corporation, etc.
pay'ment (pā'mĕnt), *n.* **1.** Act of paying. **2.** That which is paid; pay. Abbr. *payt.* **3.** Punishment; chastisement.
pay'nim (pā'nĭm), *n.* [OF. *paienisme* heathendom, fr. LL. *paganismus* paganism.] *Archaic.* Pagans or pagan countries; also, a pagan; an infidel, esp. a Mohammedan.
pay'off' (pā'ôf'), *n.* *Chiefly Colloq.* **1.** Act or time of paying employees' wages. **2.** Repayment or accrual for settlement at the outcome of an enterprise; reward or retribution. **3.** Climax of an incident or enterprise; specif., the denouement of a narrative. **4.** Decisive fact or factor resolving a situation, bringing about a definitive conclusion; as, the opinion of the Tax Court on taxability is the *payoff.* — *adj.* *Colloq.* Yielding results in the final test; rewarding or decisive.
pay'roll' (pā'rōl'), *n.* A paymaster's list of persons entitled to pay, with the amounts due to each; also, the amount necessary, or the money, for distribution to those on such a list.
‖**pay'sage'** (pā'ē·zȧzh'), *n.* [F.] A landscape or a landscape picture.
PC (pē'sē'). [patrol craft.] *U. S. Navy.* A fast patrol craft equipped with submarine-detection devices, 3-inch gun, machine guns, antiaircraft guns, and depth charges.
pea (pē), *n.; pl.* PEAS (pēz) or PEASE (pēz) (see *Note* below). [AS. *pise*, pl. *pisan*, fr. LL. *pisa*, fr. L. *pisum*, pl. *pisa*, fr. Gr. *pison, pisos.* The vowel may have been influenced by OF. *peis*, fr. L. *pisum.* The final *s* was misunderstood in English as a plural ending.] **1.** Any plant of a family (Fabaceae, the pea family) of herbs, shrubs, and trees, the fruit of which is a true pod or legume. **2.** The round, smooth or wrinkled, edible seed borne severally in dehiscent pods by a vine (*Pisum sativum*) of this family; also, the similar angular seed of a related plant (*P. arvense*). **3.** Any of various leguminous plants or their seeds, resembling the common pea; as, the sweet *pea*, cow*pea*, etc. **4.** Something like a pea, as in size.
☞ The plural *peas* was formerly used to indicate a definite number, as contrasted with the collective plural *pease;* the tendency now is to use *peas* as plural in all senses.
peace (pēs), *n.* [OF. *pais, paiz* (F. *paix*), fr. L. *pax, pacis.*] **1.** A pact or agreement to end hostilities, between those who have been at war or in a state of hostility. **2.** A state of tranquillity or quiet; esp.: **a** Freedom from civil disturbance or war. **b** Public order or security, as provided by law; as, a breach of the *peace.* **3.** Harmony in personal relations; mutual concord. **4.** Freedom from fears, agitating passions, moral conflict, etc. **5.** One who or that which makes or maintains peace. — *v. i.* To become quiet; be silent; — *Obs.*, except in the imperative.
peace'a·ble (pēs'ȧ·b'l), *adj.* Being in or at peace; not disposed to war, disorder, etc.; pacific. — **peace'a·ble·ness**, *n.* — **peace'a·bly**, *adv.*
peace'ful (-fŏŏl; -f'l), *adj.* **1.** *Now Rare.* Pacific; peaceable. **2.** Possessing, enjoying, or marked by, peace; tranquil; also, of or pert. to peace. — **Syn.** See CALM. — **Ant.** Turbulent. — **peace'ful·ly**, *adv.* — **peace'ful·ness**, *n.*
peace'mak'er (-māk'ẽr), *n.* One who makes peace or reconciles parties at variance. — **peace'mak'ing**, *n.* & *adj.*
peace offering. A propitiatory gift; esp., *Bib.*, a ceremonial propitiatory sacrifice.
peace officer. A civil officer whose duty it is to preserve the public peace, as a sheriff, constable, or policeman.
peace pipe. The calumet.
peach (pēch), *v. t.* [ME. *apechen*, fr. AF.] *Obs.* To impeach; indict. — *v. i.* *Obs. exc. Slang.* To turn informer; to blab.
peach, *n.* [OF. *peche, pesche*, fr. LL. *persica*, fr. L. *Persicum* (sc. *malum*) Persian apple, peach.] **1.** Any of a family (Amygdalaceae, the peach family) of trees and shrubs distinguished by the single pistil with united carpels, and the drupe, or stone fruit. **2.** The sweet, juicy fruit of a tree (*Amygdalus persica*), of this family, botanically a drupe, with a pulpy white or yellow mesocarp. **3.** The sessile pink flower (**peach blossom**) of this tree, borne on the naked twigs in early spring. It is the State flower of Delaware. **4.** One likened to a peach, as in beauty. **5.** A color, reddish red-yellow in hue, of low saturation and very high brilliance. See COLOR. — *adj.* Of the color peach.
peach'blow' (pēch'blō'), *n.* [*peach* + *blow* a flower.] A glaze of a delicate purplish-pink color likened to that of peach blooms; — applied esp. to a Chinese porcelain.
pea'cock' (pē'kŏk'), *n.;* see PLURAL, *Note*, 3. [ME. *pecok*, fr. AS. *pēa* peacock (fr. L. *pavo*) + E. *cock* the bird.] The male, or, in common usage, any individual, of a genus (*Pavo*) of large gallinaceous birds; esp., the common one (*P. cristatus*), domesticated since ancient times. The male has loosely webbed and greatly elongated upper tail coverts covered with ocellate spots. These are spread at will, displaying iridescent golden and green colors. — *v. t.* & *i.* To strut, pose, or display (oneself) vaingloriously. — **pea'cock'ish**, *adj.* — **pea'cock'y**, *adj.*

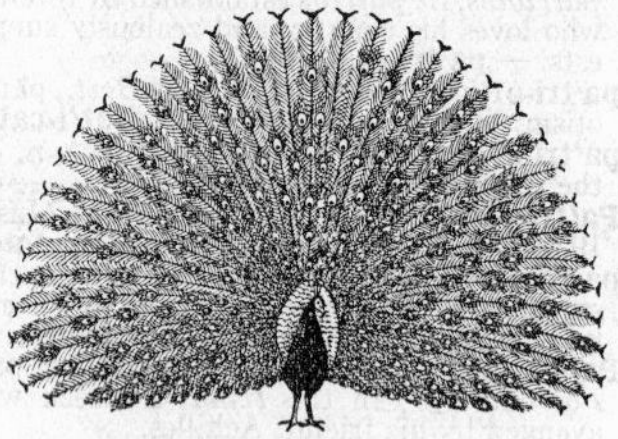

Peacock.

peacock blue. A color, bluish green-blue in hue, of medium saturation and low brilliance. See COLOR. — **pea'cock'-blue'**, *adj.*
pea'fowl' (pē'foul'), *n.* The peacock or peahen.
peag (pēg), *n.* Also **peage** (pēg). Wampum.
pea green. A color, yellowish yellow-green in hue, of low saturation and medium brilliance. See COLOR. — **pea'-green'**, *adj.*
pea'hen' (pē'hĕn'), *n.* The female of the peacock.
pea jacket. [Prob. fr. D. *pij, pije*, coat of a coarse woolen stuff.] A sailor's thick loose woolen double-breasted coat.
peak (pēk), *v. i.* To grow thin and sickly.
peak, *n.* [Var. of 1st PIKE.] **1.** The sharp or pointed end of anything. **2.** [For earlier *pike*, fr. Sp. & Pg. *pico.*] Specif.: **a** *Now Local.* A headland or promontory. **b** The top of a hill or mountain ending in a point; one of the crests of a range; often, the whole mountain, esp. when isolated. **c** The projecting front part of a cap or the like. **3.** The topmost point; summit; also, the highest point, as in a graph; maximum. **4.** *Naut.* **a** The upper aftermost corner of a fore-and-aft sail. **b** The narrow part of a vessel's bow or stern, or the part of the hold in it. **5.** A point formed by the hair on the forehead; — chiefly in ***widow's peak***, orig. such a point on a woman's forehead, now often a similar point on a man's forehead. — **Syn.** See SUMMIT. — *v. t.* To cause to come to a peak; specif., *Naut.*, to raise to a position perpendicular, or more nearly so, as a gaff.
peaked (pēkt; pēk'ĕd; -ĭd), *adj.* **1.** Pointed; having a peak. **2.** (*pron. usually* pēk'ĕd; -ĭd) [From PEAK to grow thin.] *Chiefly Colloq.* Thin; emaciated.
peal (pēl), *n.* [Shortened fr. APPEAL.] **1.** *Bell Ringing.* **a** Loosely, a set of bells tuned to the tones of the major scale for change ringing. **b** A complete set of changes on a given number of bells; esp., the series on seven bells. **c** Any shorter performance than a full set of changes; as, a wedding *peal.* **2.** A loud sound, or a succession of loud sounds, as of bells or thunder. — *v. i.* To give out peals; resound. — *v. t.* **1.** *Obs.* To assail or din, as with noise or loud sounds. **2.** To sound forth in or as in a peal or peals; noise abroad.
pe'an (pē'ăn). Var. of PAEAN.
pea'nut' (pē'nŭt'; -nŭt), *n.* A Brazilian herb (*Arachis hypogaea*) of the pea family, of erect habit, whose peduncles bend after fertilization and push the pods into the ground, where they ripen; also, the nutlike seed of this plant. **peanut oil** is expressed from these seeds; **peanut butter** is made from these seeds roasted, ground, and moistened.
pear (pâr), *n.* [AS. *pere, peru*, fr. LL. *pera, pira*, fr. L. *pirum*, pl. *pira.*] **a** The fleshy pome fruit of a tree (genus *Pyrus*, esp. *P. communis*) of the apple family. **b** The tree bearing this fruit.
pearl (pûrl), *n.* [OF. *perle*, fr. ML. *perla, perula.*] **1.** A dense concretion, lustrous and varying in color, formed as an abnormal growth within the shell of some mollusks, and used as a gem. **2.** Something resembling a pearl in shape, size, color, beauty, or value. **3.** **a** Mother-of-pearl; nacre. **b** In full **pearl blue.** The color of mother-of-pearl, a nearly neutral gray (slightly bluish) of high brilliance. See COLOR. **4.** *Print.* A size of type (5 point). See TYPE. — *v. t.* **1.** To adorn with pearls. **2.** To form into small round grains, as barley. **3.** To give to or suffuse with a pearly luster. — *v. i.* To fish or search for pearls. — *adj.* **1.** Of, like, or set with pearls. **2.** Formed into small round grains; as, **pearl barley; pearl tapioca.** — **pearl'er**, *n.*
pearl. Var. of PURL.
pearl'ash' (pûrl'ăsh'), *n.* Purified potash. See POTASH, 1.
pearl gray. The color of a fine pearl, a nearly neutral gray of high brilliance. See COLOR. — **pearl'-gray'** (-grā'; 2), *adj.*
pearl'ite (pûrl'īt), *n.* [*pearl* + *-ite.*] **1.** *Metal.* The readily fusible alloy of carbon and iron, containing 0.85 per cent carbon. **2.** *Petrog.* = PERLITE. — **pearl·it'ic** (pûrl·ĭt'ĭk), *adj.*
pearl'y (pûr'lĭ), *adj.;* PEARL'I·ER (-lĭ·ẽr); -I·EST. Of or like pearl or mother-of-pearl; adorned with or abounding in pearls.
pearly nautilus. See NAUTILUS, 1.
pear'main (pâr'mān), *n.* [OF. *permain, parmain.*] An apple of one of several different varieties.
peart (pērt; pyērt), **peart'ly.** Dial. vars. of PERT, etc.
peas'ant (pĕz'ănt; -'nt), *n.* [OF. *païsant, paisent*, fr. *païs, pays*, land, country, fr. LL. *pagensis*, fr. L. *pagus* country district. See

PAGAN.] **1.** A rustic; esp., in European countries, a tiller of the soil either as a small proprietor or as a laborer. **2.** *Obs.* A base fellow; knave.

peas'ant·ry (pĕz'ănt·rĭ; -'nt·rĭ), *n.* **1.** Peasants, collectively; a body of peasants. **2.** State, position, or rank of a peasant; rusticity.

pease (pēz), *n.; obs. pls.* PEASES (-ĕz; -ĭz), PEASEN (-'n). [See PEA.] **1.** *Obs.* A pea. **2.** Pl. of PEA. See PEA, *Note.*

pease'cod' (pēz'kŏd'), *n.* Also **peas'cod'** (pēz'-). The pod of the pea.

peat (pēt), *n. Archaic.* Pet; favorite; minion.

peat, *n.* [ME. *pete,* Anglo-Lat. *peta.*] **1.** A piece of turf cut for use as fuel. **2.** Semicarbonized vegetable tissue formed by partial decomposition in water of various plants, esp. mosses of the genus *Sphagnum.* — **peat'y** (pēt'ĭ), *adj.*

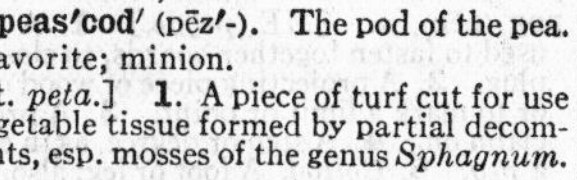

Peavey.

pea'vey, pea'vy (pē'vĭ), *n.; pl.* PEAVEYS; PEAVIES (pē'vĭz). [After Joseph *Peavey,* the inventor.] *Lumbering.* A stout lever having a hinged metal hook and armed with a strong and sharp spike.

peb'ble (pĕb''l), *n.* [AS. *papol* in *papolstān* pebblestone.] **1.** A small roundish stone, smaller than a cobblestone (which see), esp. one worn and rounded by the action of water. **2.** Transparent and colorless quartz; rock crystal; also, a lens of it. **3.** Pebbled leather; also, the surface produced by pebbling. — *v. t.;* -BLED (-'ld); -BLING (-lĭng). **1.** To pelt, pave, etc., with or as with pebbles. **2.** To grain (leather, paper, etc.) so as to produce a rough and irregularly indented surface. — **peb'bly** (-lĭ), *adj.*

pe·can' (pē·kăn'; -kän'), *n.* [Earlier *paccan,* of Algonquian origin.] A hickory (*Carya illinoensis*) of the south central U. S., or its oblong, thin-shelled nut.

pec'ca·ble (pĕk'ȧ·b'l), *adj.* [See PECCANT.] Liable or prone to sin; susceptible to temptation. — **pec'ca·bil'i·ty** (-bĭl'ĭ·tĭ), *n.*

pec'ca·dil'lo (-dĭl'ō), *n.; pl.* -LOES, -LOS (-ōz). [Sp. *pecadillo,* dim. of *pecado* a sin, fr. L. *peccatum.* See PECCANT.] A slight offense; a petty fault.

pec'cant (pĕk'ănt), *adj.* [L. *peccans, -antis,* pres. of *peccare* to sin.] **1.** Sinning; guilty of transgression. **2.** Violating a principle or rule, as of taste or propriety. **3.** [OF.] Morbid; inducing disease. — **pec'can·cy** (-ăn·sĭ), *n.* — **pec'cant·ly,** *adv.*

pec'ca·ry (pĕk'ȧ·rĭ), *n.;* see PLURAL, *Note,* 3. [Sp. *pecari,* of Cariban origin.] An American piglike mammal of either of two species: **a** The ***collared peccary*** (*Pecari angulatus*), about three feet long and grizzled, with an indistinct white collar. **b** The ***white-lipped peccary*** (*Tayassu pecari*), larger and blackish with whitish cheeks.

pec·ca'vi (pĕ·kā'vī; pĕ·kä'vē). [L.] I have sinned. Hence: *n.; pl.* -VIS (-vīz; -vēz). A confession or acknowledgment of sin.

pech (pĕĸ), *n.* [Imitative.] *Scot.* A breath; pant; heavy sigh. — *v. i.* To pant.

pech'an (pĕĸ'ăn), *n. Scot.* The stomach; also, the gullet.

peck (pĕk), *n.* [OF. *pek.*] **1.** A dry measure. See MEASURE, *Table* 10. Abbr. *pk.* **2.** A large quantity or number; as, a *peck* of troubles.

peck, *v. t.* [A collat. form of PICK to pierce.] **1.** To strike with the beak, with a pick, or the like, esp. repeatedly and quickly; also, to make (a hole, a design on stone, etc.) by such pecking. **2.** To pick up with or as with the beak; — often with *up.* **3.** *Colloq.* To eat or bite daintily or sparingly. — *v. i.* To strike, break, pick up, puncture, etc., something with or as with a beak. — *n.* **1.** A pecking; a quick, sharp stroke of a beak, a pointed instrument, etc. **2.** The impression made by pecking. — **peck'er** (pĕk'ẽr), *n.*

Peck·sniff'i·an (pĕk·snĭf'ĭ·ăn; 58), *adj.* Resembling the hypocrisy or unctuous insincerity of **Peck'sniff** (pĕk'snĭf), a canting rascal in Dickens's *Martin Chuzzlewit.*

pec'tase (pĕk'tās), *n.* [*pectin* + diastase.] *Biochem.* An enzyme hydrolyzing pectin to pectic acid and methanol.

pec'tate (-tāt), *n. Chem.* A salt or ester of pectic acid.

pec'ten (pĕk'tĕn), *n.; pl.* PECTINES (-tĭ·nēz). [L., a comb.] *Zool. & Anat.* In the eye of most birds and many reptiles, a membrane suggesting the teeth of a comb, projecting into the vitreous humor.

pec'tic (-tĭk), *adj.* [Gr. *pēktos* curdled.] *Chem.* Of, pertaining to, or derived from pectin.

pectic acid. Any of certain water-insoluble substances formed by hydrolyzing the methyl ester groups of pectins.

pec'tin (pĕk'tĭn), *n.* [Gr. *pēktos* curdled, congealed, fr. *pēgnynai* to make fast or stiff.] *Biochem.* Any of certain water-soluble substances in plant tissues, yielding a jelly which is the basis of fruit jellies.

pec'ti·nate (pĕk'tĭ·nāt), *adj.* Also **pec'ti·nat'ed** (-nāt'ĕd; -ĭd). [L. *pectinatus,* past part. of *pectinare* to comb, fr. *pecten, -inis,* a comb.] Having teethlike projections or divisions; as, a *pectinate* frond of a fern. — **pec'ti·na'tion** (-nā'shŭn), *n.*

pec'to·ral (pĕk'tō·răl), *adj.* [F. or L.; F., fr. L. *pectoralis,* fr. *pectus, -oris,* the breast.] **1.** Of, pertaining to, situated or occurring in or on, or worn on, the breast, or chest. **2.** Relating to, or good for, diseases of the chest or lungs; as, a *pectoral* medicine. **3.** Derived from one's personal experiences or feelings; subjective. — *n.* **1.** Something worn on the breast; specif.: **a** A breastplate (sense 2). **b** In full **pectoral cross.** A cross worn on the breast by bishops and abbots. **2.** A pectoral medicine.

pectoral arch *or* **girdle.** *Anat. & Zool.* The bony or cartilaginous arch supporting the forelimbs of a vertebrate.

pectoral sandpiper. A small migrating sandpiper (*Pisobia melanotos*) with a thickly streaked breast. It breeds in Arctic America.

pec'u·late (pĕk'ū·lāt), *v. i. & t.* [L. *peculatus,* past part. of *peculari* to peculate.] To steal or misappropriate moneys, esp. public moneys, entrusted to one's care; to embezzle. — **pec'u·la'tion** (-lā'shŭn), *n.* — **pec'u·la'tor** (-lā'tẽr), *n.*

pe·cul'iar (pē·kūl'yẽr), *adj.* [Obs. F. *peculier,* fr. L. *peculiaris,* fr. *peculium* private property.] **1.** Belonging to an individual; privately owned; not common. **2.** Characteristic of one only, as a person, place, class, race, or nation; distinctive; as, a custom *peculiar* to England. **3.** Different from the usual or normal; singular; hence: **a** Special; particular. **b** *Colloq.* Queer; eccentric. — **Syn.** See CHARACTERISTIC: STRANGE. — *n.* **1.** That which is peculiar; a peculiar possession, privilege, concern, etc. **2.** *Eng.* A church or parish within the jurisdiction of another than the ordinary in whose territory it is. — **pe·cul'iar·ize,** *v. t.* — **pe·cul'iar·ly,** *adv.*

pe·cu'li·ar'i·ty (pē·kū'lĭ·ăr'ĭ·tĭ; pē·kūl'yăr'ĭ·tĭ), *n.; pl.* -ITIES (-tĭz). **1.** Quality or state of being peculiar; distinctiveness; singularity. **2.** A peculiar trait, feature, etc.

peculiar people. *Eccl.* Jehovah's own people; the people of Israel; — used of themselves by many Christian bodies.

pe·cu'li·um (pē·kū'lĭ·ŭm), *n.* [L. See PECULIAR.] *Rom. Law.* The private property of a wife, child, or slave.

pe·cu'ni·ar'y (pē·kū'nĭ·ĕr'ĭ *or, esp. Brit.,* -kū'nyẽr·ĭ; -nĭ·ẽr·ĭ; 58), *adj.; pl.* PECUNIARIES (-ĭz). [L. *pecuniarius,* fr. *pecunia* money, orig., property in cattle, fr. *pecus* cattle.] **1.** Consisting of money; exacted or given in money; as, a *pecuniary* reward; also, entailing a money penalty. **2.** Relating to money; monetary; as, his *pecuniary* policy. — **Syn.** See FINANCIAL.

ped-. **a** = PEDO-. **b** = PEDI-.

-ped (-pĕd). Var. of -PEDE.

ped'a·gog'ic (pĕd'ȧ·gŏj'ĭk; -gŏ'jĭk), **ped'a·gog'i·cal** (-ĭ·kăl; -jĭ·kăl), *adj.* [Gr. *paidagōgikos.*] Of or pertaining to a pedagogue or pedagogy; concerned with or treating of pedagogy. — **ped'a·gog'i·cal·ly,** *adv.*

ped'a·gog'ics (-gŏj'ĭks), *n.;* see -ICS. Pedagogy.

ped'a·gog·ism (pĕd'ȧ·gŏg·ĭz'm; -gŏ·jĭz'm), **ped'a·gogu·ism** (-gŏg-ĭz'm), *n.* Occupation, character, principles, etc., of pedagogues.

ped'a·gogue (pĕd'ȧ·gŏg; 74), *n.* Also **ped'a·gog.** [OF., fr. L. *paedagogus,* fr. Gr. *paidagōgos,* fr. *pais, paidos,* a boy + *agōgos* leading.] A teacher of children or youth; a schoolmaster; sometimes, a teacher who is a pedant.

ped'a·go'gy (pĕd'ȧ·gō'jĭ; -gŏj'ĭ; *or, esp. Brit.,* -gŏg'ĭ), *n.* The art, practice, or profession of teaching; esp., systematized learning or instruction concerning principles and methods of teaching.

ped'al (pĕd'ăl, -'l; pē'dăl, -d'l; *the second pron. is usual only in technical* [*Anat. & Zool.*] *use*), *adj.* [L. *pedalis,* fr. *pes, pedis,* foot.] **1.** (*pron., see* NOTE, *above*) Of or pertaining to the foot, or feet. **2.** (*pron.* pĕd'ăl; -'l) Of or pertaining to a pedal.

ped'al (pĕd'ăl; -'l), *n.* [F. *pédale,* fr. It. *pedale,* fr. L. *pedalis,* adj.] A lever acted on by the foot, as in a lathe, bicycle (see BICYCLE, *Illust.*), or piano; a treadle (see TREADLE); specif., *Organs,* one of the keys of the keyboard operated with the feet (**pedal keyboard**). — *v. t. & i.;* -ALED (-ăld; -'ld), -ALLED; -AL·ING, -AL·LING. To use or work the pedals (of); to propel (oneself) by use of pedals, as on a bicycle.

pedal point. *Music.* A single tone, usually the tonic or dominant, sustained by one voice part while the others move in independent harmonies.

ped'ant (pĕd'ănt), *n.* [F. *pédant,* fr. It. *pedante.*] **1.** *Obs.* A schoolmaster. **2.** One who makes a display of learning either in ostentation or in unduly emphasizing minutiae; a formalist or precisionist in teaching or scholarship. — **pe·dan'tic** (pē·dăn'tĭk), *Rare* **pe·dan'ti·cal** (-tĭ·kăl), *adj.* — **pe·dan'ti·cal·ly,** *adv.*

ped'ant·ry (pĕd'ănt·rĭ), *n.; pl.* -RIES (-rĭz). **1.** Ostentatiousness, formalism, didacticism, or the like, in the presentation or application of knowledge or learning. **2.** A pedantic expression, act, method, etc.

ped'ate (pĕd'āt), *adj.* [L. *pedatus* having feet, fr. *pes, pedis,* a foot.] **1.** Having a foot or feet; specif., *Zool.,* having flexible tubular tentaclelike processes likened to feet, as many holothurians. **2.** Footlike; specif., *Bot.,* of leaves, palmate, with the lateral lobes cleft. See LEAF, *Illust.* (25). — **ped'ate·ly,** *adv.*

pe·dat'i- (pē·dăt'ĭ-; pē·dā'tĭ-). [L. *pedatus* pedate.] *Bot.* A combining form meaning *pedately,* as in: **pe·dat'i·fid, pe·dat'i·lobed'.**

ped'dle (pĕd''l), *v. i.;* -DLED (-'ld); -DLING (-lĭng). [From PEDDLER.] **1.** To travel about with wares for sale. **2.** [Cf. PIDDLE.] To do a small business; to be busy about trifles; piddle. — *v. t.* To sell from place to place; to hawk; hence, to retail in small quantities.

ped'dler, ped'lar (pĕd'lẽr), *n.* [ME. *pedlere.*] One who peddles; hawker. — **ped'dler·y, ped'lar·y** (-ĭ), *n.*

ped'dling (pĕd'lĭng), *adj.* Petty; insignificant; piddling.

-pede (-pēd). [F. or L.; F. *-pède,* fr. L. *-pes, -pedis,* fr. *pes, pedis, foot.*] A combining form denoting *-foot, -footed,* as in centi*pede,* veloci*pede.*

ped'es·tal (pĕd'ĕs·tăl; pĕd'ĭs-; -t'l), *n.* [F. *piédestal,* fr. It. *piedestallo,* fr. *piè* (*piede*) *de stallo* foot of a stall, seat, place for standing, fr. L. *pes, pedis,* foot, *de* of, and OHG. *stal* station, place.] **1.** In late classic and neoclassic art, the support or foot of a column and hence of a statue, vase, etc. **2.** Any base or foundation; a support. **3.** An elevated or superior plane, as in estimation. — *v. t.;* PED'ES·TALED or PED'ES·TALLED (-tăld; -t'ld); PED'ES·TAL·ING or PED'ES·TAL·LING. To place on a pedestal; to exalt.

pe·des'tri·an (pē·dĕs'trĭ·ăn), *adj.* [L. *pedester, -estris,* fr. *pes, pedis,* foot.] **1.** Going or performed on foot. **2.** Of or pertaining to walking; hence, slow, plodding or commonplace. — *n.* A walker; a foot traveler.

pe·des'tri·an·ism (-ĭz'm), *n.* Pedestrian exercise or addiction to it; also, a pedestrian quality or style.

ped'i- (pĕd'ĭ-), **ped-.** [L. *pes, pedis.*] A combining form meaning *foot.*

pe'di·a·tri'cian, pae'di·a·tri'cian (pē'dĭ·ȧ·trĭsh'ăn; pĕd'ĭ-), *n.* A physician specializing in pediatrics; a pediatrist.

pe'di·at'rics, pae'di·at'rics (pē'dĭ·ăt'rĭks; pĕd'ĭ-), *n.;* see -ICS. [Gr. *pais, paidos,* child + *-iatric.*] Medical science which treats of the hygiene and diseases of children. — **pe'di·at'ric, pae'di·at'ric** (-rĭk), *adj.* — **pe'di·at'rist** (-rĭst; pē·dī'ȧ·trĭst), *n.*

ped'i·cel (pĕd'ĭ·sĕl; -s'l), *n.* [NL. *pedicellus,* dim. fr. L. *pediculus.* See PEDICLE.] **1.** *Bot.* **a** Any slender stalk, esp. one that supports a fruiting or spore-bearing organ. See CORYMB, *Illust.* **b** In seed plants, one of the ultimate divisions of a common peduncle, bearing a single flower. **2.** *Anat. & Zool.* **a** A small stem or stalk; a peduncle; a narrow basal part by which a larger part or body is attached. **b** A small foot or footlike organ, as of an echinoderm. — **ped'i·cel'lar** (pĕd'ĭ·sĕl'ẽr), *adj.*

ped'i·cel·late (pĕd'ĭ·sĕ·lāt), *adj.* Having, or attached by, a pedicel.

ped'i·cle (pĕd'ĭ·k'l), *n.* [L. *pediculus* footstalk, little foot, dim. of *pes* foot.] A pedicel. See VERTEBRA, *Illust.*

pe·dic'u·lar (pē·dĭk'ū·lẽr), *adj.* [L. *pedicularis,* fr. *pediculus* a louse.] Of or pertaining to lice; lousy.

pe·dic'u·late (-lāt), *adj.* [See PEDICLE.] Of or pertaining to a group (Pediculati) of teleost fishes that have jugular ventral fins, bear the pectoral fins at the end of an armlike process, and have a portion of the dorsal fin modified into a lure. — *n.* A pediculate fish.

pe·dic'u·lo'sis (-lō'sĭs), *n.* [NL., fr. L. *pediculus* louse + *-osis.*] *Med.* Infestation with lice; lousiness. — **pe·dic'u·lous** (-dĭk'ū·lŭs), *adj.*

ped'i·cure (pĕd'ĭ·kūr), *n.* [*pedi-* + L. *cura* care.] Chiropody; also, a chiropodist. — **ped'i·cur'ist** (-kūr'ĭst), *n.*

ped'i·form (pĕd'ĭ·fôrm), *adj.* [*pedi-* + *-form.*] Foot-shaped.
ped'i·gree (pĕd'ĭ·grē), *n.* [ME. *pedegru*, fr. OF. *pié de grue* (F. *pied de grue*) crane's foot, fr. L. *pes, pedis*, foot, and *grus* a crane; — from a three-line mark used to indicate descent.] **1.** A table presenting a line of ancestors; a genealogical tree. **2.** An ancestral line; lineage; hence, derivation and development; as, words with the same *pedigree.* **3.** Distinguished ancestry; also, recorded, known, or notable descent. — **Syn.** See ANCESTRY. — *v. t.* **1.** To breed (an animal) so that descent is known and can be recorded. **2.** To provide with a pedigree. — **ped'i·greed** (-grēd), *adj.*

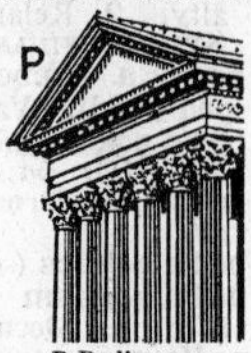
P Pediment.

ped'i·ment (pĕd'ĭ·mĕnt), *n.* Orig., in classical architecture, the triangular space forming the gable of a two-pitched roof; hence, a similar form used as a decoration over porticoes, doors, windows, etc. — **ped'i·men'tal** (-mĕn'tăl; -t'l), *adj.*
ped'lar *or* **ped'ler** (pĕd'lẽr), **ped'lar·y.** Vars. of PEDDLER, PEDDLERY.
pe'do- (pē'dō-), **ped-.** [Gr. *pais, paidos.*] A combining form, meaning *boy, child*, as in: **pe'do·bap'tism, pe·dol'o·gy.**
pe·dol'o·gy (pē·dŏl'ō·jĭ), *n.* [Gr. *pedon* ground + *-logy.*] The science which treats of soils. — **pe·dol'o·gist** (-jĭst), *n.*
pe·dom'e·ter (pē·dŏm'ē·tẽr), *n.* [F. *pédomètre.* See 1st PEDAL; -METER.] An instrument for measuring the distance one covers in walking, typically resembling a watch and operated by an oscillating weight which causes the index to advance a certain distance at each step.
pe'dro (pē'drō), *n.* [Sp. *Pedro* Peter, fr. LL. *Petrus.* See PETER.] *Card Games.* **a** In certain varieties of auction pitch and in cinch, the five of trumps. **b** A variety of auction pitch in which the five of trumps counts five.
pe·dun'cle (pē·dŭng'k'l), *n.* [NL. *pedunculus*, dim. of L. *pes, pedis*, a foot.] **1.** *Bot.* **a** A flower stalk. See CORYMB, *Illust.* **b** The stalk supporting the fructification in some thallophytes. **2.** *Zool.* A stem or stalk; a pedicel. **3.** *Anat.* A band of white matter joining different parts of the brain. — **pe·dun'cled** (-k'ld), *adj.* — **pe·dun'cu·lar** (-kū-lẽr), *adj.*
pe·dun'cu·late (-kū·lāt), *adj.* Also **pe·dun'cu·lat'ed** (-lāt'ĕd; -ĭd). Having, or growing on, a peduncle.
peek (pēk), *v. i.* [ME. *piken.*] To look slyly, esp. with the eyes half closed; peep; pry. — *n.* A glance; a peep.
peel (pēl), *n.* [ME. *pel* a stake, palisade, castle, fr. OF. *pel* a stake, fr. L. *palus.*] **1.** *Obs.* A stake; also, a stockade. **2.** A small, massive tower or fortified residence of a type common in the 16th century in the border counties of England and Scotland.
peel, *n.* [OF. *pele*, fr. L. *pala* shovel.] A spadelike implement, variously used, as for removing loaves of bread, etc., from a baker's oven.
peel, *v. t.* [ME. *pelen*, also *pilen.*] **1.** To strip off the skin, bark, or rind of. **2.** To strip or tear off. **3.** *Colloq.* To free from covering; — esp. in *to keep one's eye peeled*, to keep one's eye open. — *v. i.* To lose the skin, bark, or rind; to come off, as the skin, bark, or rind does. ***peel off.*** *Aviation.* To veer away in a wing over to the outside of a flight formation, esp. from the bottom of an echelon, for a steep dive upon a target or for a landing. Hence (of an escort vessel), to veer away from a convoy, as for an attack upon a submarine. — *n.* Skin or rind of a fruit.
peel'er (pēl'ẽr), *n.* **1.** One who or that which peels or strips. **2.** A log of softwood, esp. Douglas fir, suitable for cutting into rotary veneer which is "peeled" from the log by a lathe.
peel'er (pēl'ẽr), *n.* *Colloq.* A policeman; — so called from Sir Robert Peel, organizer of the Irish constabulary.
peen (pēn), *n.* The hemispherical, round-edged, sharp or thin end of the head of a hammer or sledge opposite to the face. See HAMMER, *Illust.* — *v. t.* To draw, bend, or flatten by hammering with the peen.
peenge (pēnj), *v. i.* *Scot. & N. of Eng.* To complain.
peep (pēp), *v. i.* [ME. *pepen*, of imitative origin.] **1.** To make a feeble shrill sound, as a bird newly hatched; chirp; cheep. **2.** To speak with a small weak voice; hence, to utter the slightest sound; as, he never dared *peep* again. — *n.* **1.** A peeping sound; chirp; cheep. **2.** See JEEP, 1 **a.**
peep, *v. i.* **1.** To peer through or as through a crevice; look cautiously or slyly; pry. **2.** To begin to emerge as if from concealment; show slightly; as, crocuses *peeping* through the grass. — *v. t.* To cause to protrude slightly. — *n.* **1.** A brief look; esp., a furtive, peering glance. **2.** The first appearance; as, the *peep* of dawn.
peep'er (pēp'ẽr), *n.* **1.** One that peeps, or chirps, as a young bird. **2.** Any of certain frogs (family Hylidae) that make peeping sounds.
peep'er, *n.* **1.** One who peeps; a prying person; a Peeping Tom. **2.** *Colloq.* **a** The eye. **b** A thing to peep into or through, as spectacles.
peep'hole' (pēp'hōl'), *n.* A hole or crevice to peep through.
Peep'ing Tom. **a** A tailor of Coventry who peeped at Lady Godiva (see GODIVA). **b** A pruriently prying person.
peep show. A small show or object exhibited, which is viewed through an orifice or a magnifying glass.
peep sight. An adjustable piece, with a small hole to peep through in aiming, attached to a rifle or other firearm near the breech. See SIGHT, *Illust.*
peer (pēr), *v. i.* **1.** To look narrowly, curiously, intently, or searchingly. **2.** *Poetic.* To come in sight; to appear. **3.** To emerge partly; peep out. — **Syn.** See GAZE.
peer, *n.* [OF. *per* (F. *pair*), fr. L. *par* equal.] **1.** One of the same rank, quality, etc.; an equal; match. **2.** *Archaic.* A comrade; fellow; associate. **3.** A nobleman; a member of one of the five degrees of the British nobility, namely, duke, marquis, earl, viscount, baron. A **peer of the realm** *or* **of the United Kingdom** has a right to a seat in the House of Lords. — *v. t.* **1.** To rival; to match. **2.** To raise to the peerage.
peer'age (pēr'ĭj), *n.* **1.** The body of peers; also, the rank or dignity of a peer. **2.** A list or record of peers; as, Burke's *Peerage.*
peer'ess (-ĕs; -ĭs), *n.* The wife of a peer; a woman ennobled in her own right or by right of marriage.
peer'ie, peer'y (pēr'ĭ), *n.* *Chiefly Scot.* A peg top.
peer'less (pēr'lĕs; -lĭs), *adj.* Having no peer, or equal; matchless. — **peer'less·ly,** *adv.* — **peer'less·ness,** *n.*
peet'weet (pēt'wēt), *n.* [Imitative.] The spotted sandpiper. See SANDPIPER.
peeve (pēv), *v. t. & i.* *Colloq.* To make or become peevish, resentful, or irritated. — **Syn.** See IRRITATE.
pee'vish (pē'vĭsh), *adj.* [ME. *pevische, peivesshe.*] **1.** Stubborn. **2.** Querulous in temperament or mood; fretful. **3.** Showing ill nature or ill temper, as actions or words. — **pee'vish·ly,** *adv.* — **pee'vish·ness,** *n.*
pee'wee (pē'wē), *n.* [Massachuset *pewe, peawe*, little, small.] Something diminutive or tiny.
pee'wit (pē'wĭt). Var. of PEWIT.
peg (pĕg), *n.* [ME. *pegge.*] **1.** A small pointed piece, as of wood, used to fasten together boards, to close the vent of a cask, etc.; a pin or plug. **2.** A projecting piece of wood or metal to hold things, as a coat, or to mark a limit or point. **3.** A pretext; reason; as, a *peg* to hang a claim on. **4.** A step or degree, as in estimation; as, to bring him down a *peg.* **5.** *Colloq.* A foot or leg; also, a tooth. **6.** A pointed prong or claw for catching or tearing. **7.** *Brit.* A small drink, as of spirits. **8.** In a stringed instrument, one of the wooden or metal pins, by turning which the pitch is adjusted. See VIOLIN, *Illust.* — *v. t.;* PEGGED (pĕgd); PEG'GING. **1.** To put a peg or pegs in; to fasten, keep fixed, etc., with or as with pegs. **2.** To indicate or mark by pegs. **3.** To strike or pierce with a thrown peg. — *v. i.* **1.** To work diligently; — usually with *away, at*, or *on.* **2.** To count and score with pegs, as in cribbage; also, to hit a peg in croquet.
Peg'a·sus (pĕg'ȧ·sŭs), *n.* [L., fr. Gr. *Pēgasos.*] **1.** *Gr. Myth.* A winged horse sprung from Medusa at her death. With a blow of his hoof, he caused Hippocrene, the fountain of the Muses, to spring from Mount Helicon. **2.** Hence, poetic inspiration. **3.** *gen.* -SI (-sī). A northern constellation near the vernal equinoctial point.
peg'ma·tite (pĕg'mȧ·tīt), *n.* [Gr. *pēgma* something fastened together; — in allusion to the quartz and feldspar in graphic granite.] *Petrog.* **a** Graphic granite. **b** A coarse variety of granite occurring in dikes or veins; also, the same formation in other rocks; as, syenite *pegmatite.*
peg top. **1.** A conical top, with a sharp metal peg, spun with a string by throwing it from the hand. **2.** *pl.* Trousers (**peg'–top' trou'sers** full at the hips and narrow at the ankles).
Peh'le·vi (pā'lĕ·vē). Var. of PAHLAVI.
peign·oir' (pān·wär'; pān'wär), *n.* [F., fr. *peigner* to comb, fr. L. *pectinare.* See PECTINATE.] A woman's loose dressing sack; hence, a loose morning dress; a negligee.
pein (pēn). Var. of PEEN.
‖**peine forte et dure** (pĕn' fôr'-tā dür'). [F.] Literally, strong and hard punishment; punishment formerly inflicted on a prisoner who refused to plead, by pressing him under heavy weights until he pleaded or was crushed to death.
peise (pāz; pēz), *v. t.* **1.** *Obs.* To weigh, as in a balance; also, to weigh mentally. **2.** *Obs.* To weigh down; oppress.
pe'jo·ra'tive (pē'jō·rā'tĭv; pĕj'ō-; pē·jŏr'ȧ·tĭv), *adj.* [LL. *pejorare* to render worse, fr. *pejor* worse.] Tending to make or become worse; depreciatory; esp., *Philol.*, used of words whose basic meaning is depreciated, as by a suffix (poet*aster*). — *n.* A depreciatory word. — **pe'jo·ra'tive·ly,** *adv.*
pek'an (pĕk'ăn), *n.* [Can. F. *pekan, pécan*, of Algonquian origin.] = FISHER, 2.
pe'kin' (pē'kĭn'), *n.* [F. *pékin*, fr. *Pékin* Peking.] A silk material, usually striped or flowered, orig. from China.
Pe'king' (pē'kĭng'; 2), *n.*, *or* **Peking duck.** [From *Peking.*] A large, active, creamy-white duck of a breed originating in China.
Pe'king·ese' (pē'kĭng·ēz'; -ēs'; 2), **Pe'kin·ese'** (pē'kĭn-), *adj.* Of or pertaining to Peking (now Peiping). — *n. sing. & pl.* **1.** **a** A native of Peking. **b** The dialect of Peking, the accepted standard form of Mandarin (see MANDARIN, 2 **b**). **2.** A very small pet dog, with short legs, pug nose, and long soft coat.
Peking man. An extinct species of man represented by skeletal and cultural remains found (1929 and various subsequent years) in Choukoutien, China. See MAN, *n.*, 9.
pe'koe (pē'kō *or, esp. Brit.*, pĕk'ō), *n.* [From southeastern pron. of Chin. (Pek.) *pai²-hao²*, lit., white down.] Formerly, tea made from the first three leaves of the spray or (***orange pekoe***) from the tiny leaf and end bud of the spray; now, a black tea (see TEA, 1 **b**) of India and Ceylon, with leaves of approximately the same sizes, obtained by screening fired tea.
pel'age (pĕl'ĭj), *n.* [F., fr. OF. *pel, peil*, hair, fr. L. *pilus.*] The coat of a mammal, as of wool, fur, or hair.
Pe·la'gi·an (pē·lā'jĭ·ăn), *n.* *Eccl. Hist.* A follower of Pelagius, a British monk, who denied original sin and held that man has perfect freedom of the will. — **Pe·la'gi·an,** *adj.* — **Pe·la'gi·an·ism** (-ĭz'm), *n.*
pe·lag'ic (pē·lăj'ĭk), *adj.* [L. *pelagicus*, fr. *pelagus* sea, fr. Gr. *pelagos.*] **a** Of or pert. to the ocean; oceanic. **b** Conducting operations upon the open sea; as, *pelagic* sealing.
pel'ar·gon'ic (pĕl'är·gŏn'ĭk; -gō'nĭk), *adj.* [*pelargonium* + *-ic.*] *Chem.* Pertaining to or designating an acid, $CH_3(CH_2)_7CO_2H$, of the formic acid series, found in the leaves of the geranium (*Pelargonium*), and obtained artificially.
pel'ar·go'ni·um (-gō'nĭ·ŭm), *n.* [NL., fr. Gr. *pelargos* stork.] Any of a genus (*Pelargonium*) of South African geraniaceous herbs. All garden geraniums (see GERANIUM, 2) belong to this genus.
Pe·las'gi·an (pē·lăz'jĭ·ăn), *n.* One of an early people or group of peoples mentioned by classical writers as the primitive dwellers in Greece and the eastern islands of the Mediterranean. — **Pe·las'gi·an, Pe·las'gic** (-jĭk), *adj.*
pel'er·ine' (pĕl'ẽr·ēn'), *n.* [F. *pèlerine* a tippet, fr. *pèlerin* pilgrim. See PILGRIM.] A woman's cape; esp., a fur cape with long ends hanging down in front.
pelf (pĕlf), *n.* [OF. *pelfre, peufre, peuffe.*] **1.** Stolen property; spoil. **2.** Money; lucre; gain.
Pe'li·as (pē'lĭ·ăs; pĕl'ĭ-), *n.* See JASON, MEDEA.
pel'i·can (pĕl'ĭ·kăn), *n.* [LL. *pelicanus, pelecanus*, fr. Gr. *pelekon.*] Any of a genus (*Pelecanus*) of large, web-footed birds with a very large bill and distensible gular pouch in which the food (fish) is caught. See BILL, *Illust.*
Pelican State. Louisiana; — a nickname from the device on its seal.
Pe·li'des (pē·lī'dēz), *n.* [L., fr. Gr. *Pēleidēs.*] A son of Peleus; esp., Achilles.
Pe'li·on (pē'lĭ·ŏn), *n.* [Gr. *Pēlion.*] *Gr. Geog.* A mountain in Thessaly. Cf. OSSA.
pe·lisse' (pĕ·lēs'), *n.* [F., fr. VL. *pellicia*, fr. L. *pelliceus, pellicius*, made of skins, fr. *pellis* a skin.] A long outer garment, originally of fur or fur-lined.

pel·la′gra (pĕ·lā′grȧ; -lăg′rȧ), *n.* [It.] *Med.* A chronic disease characterized by skin lesions, gastrointestinal disturbance, and nervous symptoms. It is believed to be caused by a faulty diet. — **pel·la′grous** (-lā′grŭs; -lăg′rŭs), *adj.*

pel′let (pĕl′ĕt; -ĭt), *n.* [OF. *pelote*, fr. ML., fr. L. *pila* a ball.] **1.** A little ball, esp. of food, medicine, or the like. **2.** A ball, usually stone, used as a missile in the Middle Ages; later, a bullet; esp., one of a charge of small shot. **3.** An imitation bullet, as of paper. — *v. t.* **a** To form into pellets. **b** To strike with pellets.

pel′li·cle (pĕl′ĭ·k'l), *n.* [L. *pellicula*, dim. of *pellis* skin.] A thin skin or film. — **pel·lic′u·lar** (pĕ·lĭk′ū·lẽr), *adj.*

pel′li·to′ry (pĕl′ĭ·tō′rĭ *or, esp. Brit.*, -tẽr·ĭ), *n.; pl.* -RIES (-rĭz). [OF. *paritoire, -taire*, fr. L. *parietaria*, fr. *paries, parietis*, a wall.] **1.** Any of a genus (*Parietaria*) of plants of the nettle family, as the ***wall pellitory*** (*P. officinalis*) of Europe. **2.** [OF. *peritre, piretre*, ult. fr. Gr. *pyrethron* feverfew.] Also **pellitory of Spain.** A southern European plant (*Anacyclus pyrethrum*) of the aster family, resembling yarrow. **3.** Any of various similar plants, as the feverfew, yarrow, etc.

pell′–mell′, pell′mell′ (pĕl′mĕl′; 2), *adv.* [F. *pêlemêle*, fr. OF. *pesle*, redup. fr. *mesler* to mix.] **1.** In mingled confusion or disorder as troops in flight. **2.** In furious haste; vehemently. — **pell′–mell′, pell′mell′**, *adj. & n.*

pel·lu′cid (pĕ·lū′sĭd), *adj.* [L. *pellucidus*, fr. *per-* + *lucidus* clear, bright.] Being transparent; limpid; hence, easy to understand. — **Syn.** See CLEAR. — **pel′lu·cid′i·ty** (pĕl′ū·sĭd′ĭ·tĭ), **pel·lu′cid·ness**, *n.* — **pel·lu′cid·ly**, *adv.*

Pe′lops (pē′lŏps), *n. Gr. Myth.* Son of Tantalus. His father served him up to the gods for food, but they restored his life.

pe·lo′ri·a (pē·lō′rĭ·ȧ; 70), *n.* [NL., fr. Gr. *pelōros* monstrous.] *Bot.* An abnormal regularity of structure occurring in normally irregular flowers. — **pe·lor′ic** (pē·lŏr′ĭk; -lō′rĭk), *adj.*

pe·lo′rus (pē·lō′rŭs; 70), *n.* [After *Pelorus*, said to have been Hannibal's pilot when he left Italy.] A navigational instrument for taking bearings. It consists of a sighting device at the center of a compass card about which is fixed a rim calibrated in degrees.

pe·lo′ta (pĕ·lō′tȧ), *n.* [Sp., lit., ball.] A Basque, Spanish, or Spanish American game played in a court with a ball and a wickerwork racket.

pelt (pĕlt), *n.* [Prob. fr. PELTRY.] **1.** A skin, esp. of a sheep, goat, or fur-bearing animal; — usually applied to the undressed skin with its hair, wool, or fur. Cf. 2d HIDE. **2.** A skin used as a garment; apparel of skins. **3.** *Humorous.* The human skin.

pelt, *v. t. & i.* **1.** To strike with a succession of blows, or missiles, or words as missiles. **2.** To hurl or throw; to dash; to beat or pound. — *n.* An act or instance of pelting; a blow. — **pelt′er**, *n.*

pel′tast (pĕl′tăst), *n.* [Gr. *peltastēs.*] *Gr. Antiq.* A soldier armed with a **pel′ta** (pĕl′tȧ), or light shield.

pel′tate (-tāt), *adj.* [L. *pelta* shield.] Shield-shaped; scutiform; specif., *Bot.*, having the stem or support attached to the lower surface, instead of at the base or margin. See LEAF, *Illust.* (19). — **pel′tate·ly**, *adv.*

pelt′ing, *adj. Archaic.* Mean; paltry.

pelt′ry (pĕl′trĭ), *n.; pl.* PELTRIES (-trĭz). [OF. *peleterie* peltry, furriery, fr. *peletier* furrier, fr. OF. *pel* skin, fr. L. *pellis.*] Pelts, or skins, collectively; skins with the fur on them; furs; also, a pelt; a skin with fur.

pel′vic (pĕl′vĭk), *adj.* Pert. to, or in the region of, the pelvis; as, the **pelvic arch** *or* **girdle**, the bony arch supporting the skeleton of the hind limbs of vertebrates.

pel′vis (-vĭs), *n.; pl.* PELVES (-vēz). [L., a basin.] **a** *Anat. & Zool.* The basinlike structure in the skeleton of many vertebrates, formed by the pelvic arch and adjoining bones. **b** *Anat.* The funnel-shaped expansion of the upper end of the ureter leaving the kidney.

pem′mi·can (pĕm′ĭ·kăn), *n.* Also **pem′i·can.** [Cree *pemikkân*, fr. *pimiy* grease, fat.] **1.** Among the North American Indians, lean meat, dried and pounded fine, packed in sacks of hide. **2.** A preparation, as of dried beef, suet, raisins, and sugar, used by explorers, etc.

pem′phi·gus (pĕm′fĭ·gŭs; pĕm·fī′-), *n.* [NL., fr. Gr. *pemphix, -igos*, a bubble.] *Med.* An inflammatory disease characterized by blobs on the skin or mucous membranes.

pen (pĕn), *n.* [AS. *penn.*] **1.** A small enclosure for animals; also, the animals in one such enclosure. **2.** Any small place of confinement or storage. **3.** A dock or slip for reconditioning submarines, esp. one protected by a superstructure of thick concrete against aerial bombs. — *v. t.;* PENNED (pĕnd) or PENT (pĕnt); PEN′NING (pĕn′ĭng). To shut in or as in a pen.

pen, *n.* [OF. *penne*, fr. L. *penna* pen, feather.] **1.** *Archaic.* A feather or quill. **2.** Anything resembling a feather or its stock; as, *Dial. Eng.*, the midrib of a leaf. **3.** A pinfeather. **4. a** An instrument with a point, usually split, for writing, drawing lines, etc., formerly made of a reed, or quill, but now usually of steel, gold, etc. **b** Such a pen and its holder together. **5. a** The writing instrument regarded as a means of expression; as, to live by one's *pen.* **b** A manner of expression; style. **c** A writer. **6.** *Zool.* The internal horny shell of a squid. — *v. t.;* PENNED; PEN′NING. To write; to indite.

pen, *n.* A female swan. Cf. COB, 2; CYGNET.

pe′nal (pē′năl; -n'l), *adj.* [F. *pénal*, fr. L. *poenalis*, fr. *poena* punishment.] Of or pert. to punishment or penalties.

penal code. *Law.* A code of laws concerning crimes and offenses and their punishment.

pe′nal·ize (pē′năl·īz; pĕn′ăl-), *v. t.* To impose a penalty on; as, to *penalize* a team 15 yards for holding. — **pe′nal·i·za′tion** (-ĭ·zā′shŭn; -ī·zā′-), *n.*

pen′al·ty (pĕn′ăl·tĭ; pĕn′'l-), *n.; pl.* -TIES (-tĭz). [F. *pénalité.*] **1.** Punishment for crime or offense. **2.** The suffering, or the forfeit, to which a person subjects himself by agreement for nonfulfillment of stipulation; fine. **3.** Loss due to some action, as violation of rules.

pen′ance (pĕn′ăns), *n.* [OF. *penance, peneance*, fr. L. *paenitentia* repentance.] *Eccl.* **a** [*often cap.*] In certain churches, the sacrament consisting in repentance or contrition for sin, confession to a priest, satisfaction as imposed by the confessor, and absolution. **b** An act of self-abasement, mortification, piety, or devotion, performed to show sorrow or repentance for sin. — *v. t.;* -ANCED (-ănst); -ANC·ING (-ăn·sĭng). To impose penance on; to punish.

pe·na′tes (pē·nā′tēz), *n. pl.* [L.] *Rom. Relig.* The gods of the household, worshiped in connection with Vesta, and with the lares and household genius.

pence (pĕns), *n., pl.* of PENNY.

pen′cel (pĕn′sĕl; -s'l), *n.* [OF. *penoncel*, dim. of *penon.*] *Archaic.* A small narrow flag or streamer; specif., such a flag carried at the lance head.

pen′chant (pĕn′chănt; päN′shäN′), *n.* [F., fr. *pencher* to bend, fr. L. *pendēre* to hang down. See PENDANT.] A strong leaning or attraction; strong inclination. — **Syn.** See LEANING.

pen′cil (pĕn′sĭl; -s'l), *n.* [OF. *pincel*, fr. L. *penicillum, penicillus*, dim. of *penis* tail.] **1.** A brush of hair or bristles used by artists to lay on colors. **2.** An artist's individual skill or manner; artistic style. **3.** A slender cylinder or strip of black lead, colored chalk, etc., usually incased in wood, for writing or drawing. **4.** Any of various objects suggesting a pencil; as: **a** A stick or crayon of rouge or other cosmetic; as, an eyebrow *pencil.* **b** *Optics & Math.* An aggregate or system of rays, or the like, as of rays of light, esp. when diverging from, or converging to, a point. **5.** *Med.* A small medicated stick, as of caustic. — *v. t.;* -CILED (-sĭld; -s'ld) or -CILLED; -CIL·ING or -CIL·LING. To paint, draw, or mark with or as with a pencil or brush; esp., now, to sketch or outline with a lead pencil, crayon, etc.; also, to write down with a lead pencil. — **pen′cil·er, pen′cil·ler**, *n.*

pen·cil′i·form (pĕn·sĭl′ĭ·fôrm; pĕn′sĭl-), *adj.* Pencil-shaped; — said specif. of a beam of light with well-defined boundaries, also of a group of parallel or slightly convergent lines which present an appearance suggesting a pencil.

pen′cil·ing, pen′cil·ling (pĕn′sĭ·lĭng), *n.* The work of the pencil or brush, or a product of this; as, delicate *penciling* in a picture.

pend (pĕnd), *v. i.* [F. *pendre.* See PENDANT.] **1.** *Chiefly Dial.* To depend. **2.** To be undecided, or in process of adjustment; as, the decision is still *pending.*

pend′ant (pĕn′dănt) *n.* [OF., orig. pres. part. of *pendre* to hang, fr. L. *pendēre*, v. i.] **1.** Something that hangs or depends, esp. as an ornament. **2.** That by which something is suspended; specif., the stem and ring of a watch. **3.** One of a pair; a companion piece; a match. **4.** *Arch.* A hanging ornament of roofs, ceilings, etc., much used in the later styles of Gothic architecture. **5.** *Elec.* A fitting, as a lamp holder or push button, suspended from a ceiling by a flexible cord or other means. **6.** *Naut.* = PENNANT, *n.*, 1; — an earlier spelling still official in the British Navy although pronounced pĕn′ănt.

pend′ant. Var. of PENDENT, *adj.*

pend′en·cy (pĕn′dĕn·sĭ), *n.* **a** State of being pendent, or suspended. **b** State of being undetermined, or not yet decided; as, the *pendency* of a suit.

pend′ent (-dĕnt), *adj.* [From F. *pendant*, after L. *pendens, -entis*, pres. part. of *pendēre* to hang.] **1.** Supported from above; suspended. **2.** Jutting over; overhanging. **3.** Remaining undetermined or not yet decided, as a suit at law; pending. — **pend′ent·ly**, *adv.*

pend′ent. Var. of PENDANT, *n.*

‖**pen·den′te li′te** (pĕn·dĕn′tē lī′tē). [L.] *Law.* Pending the suit; while litigation continues.

pen·den′tive (pĕn·dĕn′tĭv), *n.* [F. *pendentif.*] *Arch.* **a** One of the triangular pieces of vaulting which spring from the corners of a rectangular ground plan and serve to allow the room enclosing it to be covered by a cupola of rounded or polygonal plan. **b** That part of a groined vault which springs from a single pier or corbel.

pend′ing, *adj.* [See PENDENT.] **a** Hanging; overhanging; hence, imminent. **b** Not yet decided; as, a *pending* suit. — *prep.* **a** During; through the continuance of. **b** Until.

pen·drag′on (pĕn·drăg′ŭn), *n.* [W. fr. *pen* head + *dragon* a leader.] [*often cap.*] A chief leader or king; — an ancient British title. — **pen·drag′on·ship**, *n.*

pen′du·lous (pĕn′dû·lŭs), *adj.* [L. *pendulus*, fr. *pendēre* to hang.] Suspended or pendent; hanging; also, swinging or oscillating. — **pen′du·lous·ly**, *adv.* — **pen′du·lous·ness**, *n.*

pen′du·lum (-lŭm), *n.; pl.* -LUMS (-lŭmz). [NL., fr. L. *pendulus* hanging, swinging.] A body so suspended from a fixed point as to swing freely to and fro under the combined action of gravity and momentum. It is used to regulate the movements of clockwork and other machinery.

Pe·nel′o·pe (pē·nĕl′ō·pē), *n.* [L., fr. Gr. *Pēnelopē.*] The wife of Odysseus. During his absence, being importuned by suitors, she postponed decision until she finished weaving a funeral pall for her father-in-law, Laertes. Every night she unraveled what she had woven by day.

pe′ne·plain′, pe′ne·plane′ (pē′nē·plān′), *n.* [L. *paene* almost + E. *plain.*] *Geol.* A land surface worn down by erosion nearly to a plain. — *v. t.* To erode to a peneplain.

pen′e·tra·ble (pĕn′ē·trȧ·b'l), *adj.* [F. or L.; F. *pénétrable*, fr. L. *penetrabilis.*] Capable of being penetrated. — **pen′e·tra·bil′i·ty** (-bĭl′ĭ·tĭ), *n.* — **pen′e·tra·bly**, *adv.*

pen′e·tra′li·a (-trā′lĭ·ȧ), *n. pl.* [L., neut. pl. of *penetralis* internal.] **1.** The innermost parts, esp. of a temple or palace. **2.** Hidden things or secrets; privacy.

pen′e·trant (pĕn′ē·trănt), *adj.* Penetrating; sharp.

pen′e·trate (-trāt), *v. t.* [L. *penetratus*, past part. of *penetrare* to penetrate.] **1.** To enter into; to enter and pass through; to pierce. **2.** To diffuse itself through; to permeate. **3.** To affect profoundly; to move deeply. **4.** To recognize the precise nature of; to understand. — *v. i.* **1.** To pass into or through something; to pierce. **2.** To affect deeply the senses or feelings. — **Syn.** See ENTER.

pen′e·trat′ing (-trāt′ĭng), *adj.* **1.** Having the power of entering, piercing, or pervading; sharp; subtle. **2.** Acute; discerning. — **pen′e·trat′ing·ly**, *adv.*

pen′e·tra′tion (-trā′shŭn), *n.* **1.** Act or process of penetrating. **2.** Acuteness; sharp discernment; sagacity. **3.** *Gun.* The depth to which a projectile sinks into any substance. **4.** *Politics & Econ.* The act of entering a country, esp. by diplomatic or commercial bodies, so that actual establishment of influence is accomplished. — **Syn.** See DISCERNMENT.

pen′e·tra′tive (pĕn′ē·trā′tĭv; -trȧ·tĭv), *adj.* **1.** Tending to penetrate; piercing; also, acute; sagacious. **2.** Affecting; impressive. — **pen′e·tra′tive·ly**, *adv.*

pen′e·trom′e·ter (-trŏm′ē·tẽr), *n.* Also **pen′e·tram′e·ter** (-trăm′ē·tẽr). [L. *penetrare* to penetrate + *-meter.*] **1.** An instrument for measuring the consistency of pitch, grease, etc., from the depth to which a needle penetrates. **2.** An instrument for estimating the ability of X rays to penetrate a material.

pen′gö′ (pĕn′gû′), *n.; pl.* PENGÖ, PENGÖS (-gûz′). [Hung.] The monetary unit of Hungary from 1925 to 1946, replaced by the forint.

pen′guin (pĕn′gwĭn; pĕng′-), *n.* [Prob. orig. the great auk, fr. W. *pen* head + *gwyn* white.] **1.** *Obs.* The great auk. See AUK. **2.** Any of certain short-legged flightless aquatic birds (family Spheniscidae) of the Southern Hemisphere. **3.** A low-powered, small-winged airplane, incapable of leaving the ground, for use in aviation training.

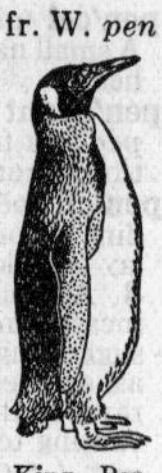

King Penguin (*Aptenodytes patagonica*). (1/36)

pen′hold′er (pĕn′hōl′dẽr), *n.* A holder for a pen.

pen′i·cil′late (pĕn′ĭ·sĭl′āt), *adj.* [See PENCIL.] *Bot. & Zool.* Ending in a tuft of hairs like a camel's-hair brush, as the stigmas of some grasses. — **pen′i·cil′late·ly**, *adv.* — **pen′i·cil·la′tion** (-sĭ·lā′shŭn), *n.*

pen′i·cil′lin (pĕn′ĭ·sĭl′ĭn), *n.* [*Penicill*ium + *-in.*] *Biochem.* A strongly antibacterial, relatively nontoxic acid substance extracted from a green mold (*Penicillium notatum*) and having a powerful bacteriostatic effect against staphylococci, gonococci, pneumococci, hemolytic streptococci, and certain meningococci.

pen′i·cil′li·um (pĕn′ĭ·sĭl′ĭ·ŭm), *n.* [NL., fr. L. *penicillus, penicillum*, pencil; — in allusion to the tufts at the ends of the conidiophores.] Any of a genus (*Penicillium*) of fungi (class Ascomycetes) typified by the mold (*P. crustaceum*) found on decaying or preserved fruit, cheese, etc.

pen·in′su·la (pĕn·ĭn′sū·lȧ), *n.* [L. *paeninsula*, fr. *paene* almost + *insula* an island.] A portion of land nearly surrounded by water, and connected with a larger body by a neck, or isthmus; also, any piece of land jutting out into the water; a promontory. — **pen·in′su·lar** (-lẽr), *adj.*

Pen·in′su·lar State. Florida; — a nickname.

pe′nis (pē′nĭs), *n.; pl.* PENES (-nēz), PENISES (-nĭs·ĕz; -ĭz). [L.] *Anat. & Zool.* The male organ of copulation.

pen′i·tence (pĕn′ĭ·tĕns), *n.* State of being penitent; sorrow for sins or faults.

Syn. **Penitence, repentance, contrition, compunction, remorse** mean regret for sin or wrongdoing. **Penitence** implies little more than sorrow or genuine regret; **repentance**, an awareness of one's shortcomings morally or spiritually and a change of heart; **contrition**, deep sorrow and purpose of amendment; **compunction**, a painful sting of conscience; **remorse**, prolonged and insistent self-reproach and, often, intense suffering for consequences that cannot be escaped.

pen′i·tent (-tĕnt), *adj.* [OF., fr. L. *paenitens, -entis, poenitens*, pres. part. of *paenitere, poenitere*, to repent.] Feeling pain or sorrow for sins or offenses; repentant. — *n.* **1.** One who repents of sin. **2.** One under church censure, but admitted to penance, esp. under the direction of a confessor. — **pen′i·tent·ly**, *adv.*

pen′i·ten′tial (-tĕn′shăl), *adj.* Of or pertaining to penitence or penance; of the nature of penance. — *n.* [ML. *poenitentiale, liber poenitentialis.*] **1.** *Eccl.* A manual of rules for the imposition of penances. **2.** A penitent. — **pen′i·ten′tial·ly**, *adv.*

pen′i·ten′tia·ry (pĕn′ĭ·tĕn′shȧ·rĭ), *n.; pl.* -RIES (-rĭz). **1.** *R.C.Ch.* **a** An officer in some dioceses vested with power from the bishop to absolve in cases reserved to him. **b** A tribunal of the Roman Curia which examines cases of conscience, confession, absolution from vows, etc. Its chief is a cardinal, called the ***grand penitentiary***. **2.** A house of correction, in which offenders are confined, usually at hard labor. — *adj.* **1.** Of or pertaining to penance. **2.** Used for punishment, discipline, and reformation. **3.** *U.S.* Making one liable to a term in a penitentiary; as, a *penitentiary* offense.

pen′knife′ (pĕn′nīf′), *n.; pl.* -KNIVES (-nīvz′). A small pocketknife, orig. for making and mending quill pens.

pen′man (-măn), *n.; pl.* -MEN (-mĕn). **1.** One who uses the pen; a writer. **2.** One expert in penmanship. **3.** An author.

pen′man·ship, *n.* Art or practice of writing with the pen; style or manner of writing.

pen′na (pĕn′ȧ), *n.; pl.* PENNAE (-ē). [L.] *Zool.* A normal contour feather, as distinguished from downs, plumes, etc.

pen name. An author's pseudonym; a nom de plume.

pen′nant (pĕn′ănt), *n.* [An alteration of *pennon*, fr. OF. *penon*, fr. L. *penna* feather.] **1.** *Naut.* **a** A flag usually with fly much longer than the hoist. **b** Any small flag used for signaling, etc.; also, a flag emblematic of a championship, as in a sport. **2.** *Music.* = HOOK, *n.*, 8.

pen′nate (-āt), *adj.* [L. *pennatus*, fr. *penna* feather, wing.] *Bot. & Zool.* Winged; feathered.

pen′ni (pĕn′ĭ), *n.; pl.* PENNIA (-ĭ·ȧ). [Finn., fr. G. *pfennig.*] A coin denomination and money of account of Finland, equal to 1/100 markka.

pen′ni- (pĕn′ĭ-). [L. *penna.*] A combining form meaning *feather*, as in **pen·nif′er·ous, pen′ni·form, pen·nig′er·ous** (see -FEROUS, etc.); also, *Bot., pinnately*, as in **pen′ni·nerv′ate, pen′ni·nerved′, pen′ni·veined′.**

pen′ni·less (pĕn′ĭ·lĕs; -lĭs), *adj.* Without a penny; destitute of money; impecunious.

pen′non (pĕn′ŭn), *n.* [See PENNANT.] **1.** A long triangular flag, esp. one used as the ensign of a knight in the Middle Ages, or of a regiment of lancers. **2.** Any flag or banner. **3.** A wing; pinion. **4.** *Naut.* A pennant.

pen′non·cel, pen′non·celle (pĕn′ŭn·sĕl). = PENCEL.

Penn′syl·va′nia Dutch (pĕn′sĭl·vān′yȧ; -vā′nĭ·ȧ; 58). Also **Pennsylvania German.** **1.** A dialect of High German with a mixture of English words, spoken in parts of Pennsylvania. **2.** Collectively, the descendants of immigrants to Pennsylvania in the 17th and 18th centuries from southwestern Germany and Switzerland.

Penn′syl·va′nian (-vān′yăn; -vā′nĭ·ăn), *adj.* **1.** Of or pert. to Pennsylvania. **2.** *Geol.* See CARBONIFEROUS, 2. — *n.* **1.** A native or inhabitant of Pennsylvania. **2.** *Geol.* The Pennsylvanian period.

pen′ny (pĕn′ĭ), *n.; pl.* PENNIES (-ĭz) or, usually collective, PENCE (pĕns). [AS. *penig, pening, pending.*] **1.** An English coin, now of bronze, worth 1/2 of a shilling. See MONEY, *Tables*. Abbr. *d.* (initial of *denarius*). **2.** *Colloq., U.S.* A cent. **3.** Money; a piece or sum of money; as, to earn an honest *penny*.

-pen′ny. A combining form of the noun *penny*, used with a numeral to indicate a price; as, a ten*penny* supper. As applied to nails (ten*penny*, 10-*penny*) it orig. indicated price per hundred, but now indicates length.

pen′ny-a-line′, *adj.* Getting low pay, as a penny for each line; hence, cheap; inferior. — **pen′ny-a-lin′er** (-ȧ·līn′ẽr), *n.*

penny ante. Poker in which the ante is one cent.

penny fee. *Scot.* Small pay; wages.

pen′ny·roy′al (pĕn′ĭ·roi′ăl), *n.* [Altered form of earlier *puliall royal*, in which *puliall* is fr. OF. *poliol, pouliol*, fr. L. *pulegium, puleium.*] **a** A European perennial mint (*Mentha pulegium*) with small pungently aromatic leaves. **b** A similar American plant (*Hedeoma pulegioides*) which yields an oil used to drive away mosquitoes.

pen′ny·weight′ (pĕn′ĭ·wāt′), *n.* A troy weight, originally the weight of a silver penny. See WEIGHT, *Table* 2.

pen′ny wheep (pĕn′ĭ hwēp). *Chiefly Scot.* Small beer.

pen′ny-wise′ (pĕn′ĭ·wīz′; 2), *adj.* Wise only in small matters; — used chiefly in *penny-wise and pound-foolish*.

pen′ny·wort′ (-wûrt′), *n.* Any of several round-leaved plants; as, the ***wall pennywort, or navelwort*** (*Cotyledon umbilicus*) and the ***marsh pennywort*** (genera *Hydrocotyle* and *Centella*).

pen′ny·worth′ (pĕn′ĭ·wûrth′; *colloq., Brit.*, pĕn′ẽrth), *n.* A penny's worth; hence: **a** A bargain. **b** A small quantity.

Pe·nob′scot (pē·nŏb′skŏt; -skŭt), *n.* An Indian of an Algonquian tribe dwelling on the Penobscot River.

pe·nol′o·gy (pē·nŏl′ō·jĭ), *n.* [Gr. *poinē*, or L. *poena*, punishment + *-logy.*] The branch of criminology dealing with prison management and the reformatory treatment of criminals. — **pe′no·log′i·cal** (pē′nō·lŏj′ĭ·kăl), *adj.* — **pe·nol′o·gist** (pē·nŏl′ō·jĭst), *n.*

pen′on·cel (pĕn′ŭn·sĕl). = PENCEL.

pen′sil, pen′sile. Vars. of PENCEL.

pen′sile (pĕn′sĭl; 56), *adj.* [L. *pensilis*, fr. *pendēre* to hang.] **1.** Hanging; pendent. **2.** Having or building a hanging nest, as some birds.

pen′sion (pĕn′shŭn), *n.* [OF., fr. L. *pensio* payment, fr. *pendĕre, pensum*, to weigh, pay.] **1.** A payment regularly made to any person, as by way of subsidy, gratuity, etc. **2.** A stated allowance to one retired from service, as to a retired soldier. **3.** (*pron. F.* päɴ′syôɴ′, *G.* pän·syōn′) A boardinghouse or boarding school, esp. one in continental Europe. — *v. t.* To grant or pay a pension to. — **pen′sion·a·ble**, *adj.*

pen′sion·ar′y (-ĕr′ĭ *or, esp. Brit.*, -ẽr·ĭ), *adj.* **1.** Receiving a pension; hence, hireling. **2.** Consisting of a pension. — *n.; pl.* -IES (-ĭz). A pensioner; often, a hireling.

pen′sion·er (-ẽr), *n.* **1.** One in receipt of pension; hence, a dependent. **2.** *Obs. exc. Hist.* **a** A gentleman-at-arms. **b** A mercenary. **c** A retainer; servant. **3.** In the University of Cambridge, England, one who pays for his living in commons; — corresponding to *commoner* at Oxford.

pen′sive (pĕn′sĭv), *adj.* [OF. *pensif*, fr. *penser* to think, fr. L. *pensare* to weigh, ponder, v. intens. fr. *pendĕre* to weigh.] **1.** Musingly or dreamily thoughtful. **2.** Expressing or suggesting thoughtfulness with sadness. — **pen′sive·ly**, *adv.* — **pen′sive·ness**, *n.*

pen·ste′mon (pĕn·stē′mŏn; pĕn′stē′mŏn). Var. of PENTSTEMON.

pen′stock′ (pĕn′stŏk′), *n.* [*pen* enclosure + *stock.*] **1.** A sluice for regulating flow of water, sewage, etc. **2.** *U. S.* A conduit for conducting water, as to a water wheel.

pent (pĕnt), *past & past part.* of PEN, to shut in. Hence, *adj.*, penned or shut up; confined.

pen′ta- (pĕn′tȧ-), **pent-.** [Gr. *pente.*] A combining form meaning *five*, as in **pen′ta·dac′tyl**, having five digits to the hand or foot.

pen′ta·cle (pĕn′tȧ·k'l), *n.* [MF., fr. ML. *pentaculum.*] A certain figure formerly used as a magic symbol, as a five-pointed, or a six-pointed, star.

pen′tad (pĕn′tăd), *n.* [Gr. *pentas, -ados*, a body of five, fr. *pente* five.] A group of five, esp. of five consecutive years.

pen′ta·gon (pĕn′tȧ·gŏn; -gŭn), *n.* [LL. *pentagonum*, fr. Gr. *pentagōnon*, fr. *pente* five + *gōnia* angle.] *Geom.* A polygon having five angles and therefore five sides.

pen·tag′o·nal (pĕn·tăg′ō·năl; -n'l), *adj.* Having five corners or angles. — **pen·tag′o·nal·ly**, *adv.*

pen′ta·gram (pĕn′tȧ·grăm), *n.* [Gr. *pentagrammon*, neut. of *pentagrammos* having five lines. See PENTA-; -GRAM.] **1.** A pentacle, or a five-pointed star. **2.** *Math.* A figure determined by five line segments joining five points.

pen′ta·he′dron (-hē′drŭn), *n.; pl.* -DRONS (-drŭnz), -DRA (-drȧ). [See PENTA-; -HEDRON.] A solid bounded by five faces. — **pen′ta·he′dral** (-drăl), *adj.*

pen·tam′er·ous (pĕn·tăm′ẽr·ŭs), *adj.* [*penta-* + *-merous.*] *Bot. & Zool.* Divided into, or consisting of, five parts, or arranged in five sets of parts; specif., *Bot.*, having each floral whorl consisting of five, or a multiple of five members, as the flax flower; — often written 5-*merous*. — **pen·tam′er·ism** (-ĭz'm), *n.*

pen·tam′e·ter (-ĕ·tẽr), *n.* [L., fr. Gr. *pentametros*, fr. *penta-* + *metron* measure.] *Pros.* A verse of five feet. Specif.: **a** The elegiac pentameter. **b** The iambic pentameter in English; heroic verse. — *adj.* Having five metrical feet.

pen′tane (pĕn′tān), *n.* [See PENTA-.] *Chem.* Any of three isomeric hydrocarbons, C_5H_{12}, of the methane series, occurring in petroleum. Two are colorless volatile liquids, one a gas.

pen′tan′gle (pĕn′tăng′g'l), *n.* A pentagram.

pen′tarch·y (pĕn′tär·kĭ), *n.; pl.* PENTARCHIES (-kĭz). [Gr. *pentarchia*. See PENTA-; -ARCHY.] A government by five persons; also, a union of five powers.

pen′ta·stich (pĕn′tȧ·stĭk), *n.* [Gr. *pentastichos* of five verses, fr. *penta-* + *stichos* line, verse.] A poem, stanza, or strophe consisting of five verses.

Pen′ta·teuch (pĕn′tȧ·tūk), *n.* [From LL., fr. Gr. *pentateuchos*, fr. *penta-* + *teuchos* tool, book.] The first five books of the Old Testament, collectively. See BIBLE.

pen·tath′lon (pĕn·tăth′lŏn), *n.* [Gr., fr. *penta-* + *athlon* a contest.] An athletic contest in which each contestant participates in five events, as, in the modern Olympic games, running broad jump, javelin throw, 200-meter race, discus throw, and 1500-meter flat race.

pen′ta·va′lent (pĕn′tȧ·vā′lĕnt; pĕn·tăv′ȧ·lĕnt), *adj.* Quinquevalent.

Pen′te·cost (pĕn′tē·kŏst; 74), *n.* [LL. *pentecoste*, fr. Gr. *pentēkostē* (sc. *hēmera*) the fiftieth day, Pentecost, fr. *pentēkostos* fiftieth, fr. *pentēkonta* fifty, fr. *pente* five.] **1.** A solemn festival of the Jews, celebrated on the fiftieth day (seven weeks) after the second day of the Passover. **2.** A Christian festival commemorating on the seventh Sunday after Easter the descent of the Holy Spirit on the Apostles; hence, Whitsunday. — **Pen′te·cos′tal** (-kŏs′tăl; -t'l), *adj.*

pent′house′ (pĕnt′hous′), *n.* [Corrupt. of *pentice*, fr. OF. *apentis*, fr. L. *appendēre* to belong to.] **1. a** A shed or roof attached to and sloping from a wall or building; hence, any smaller structure joined to a building; an annex. **b** An apartment or dwelling built on a roof. **2.** Anything likened to a penthouse, esp. in having a sloping top or roof, as a window awning, a shed to protect besiegers, etc.

pen'to·san (pĕn'tō·săn), *n.* Also **pen'to·sane** (-sān). [From PENTOSE.] *Chem.* One of a class of complex carbohydrates, found in plants, yielding pentoses on hydrolysis.

pen'tose (pĕn'tōs), *n.* [*pent-* + *-ose.*] *Chem.* Any of a group of simple sugars containing five oxygen atoms, not fermented by yeast, occurring in plants as pentosans, and also formed in the animal body.

Pen'to·thal So'di·um (pĕn'tō·thăl sō'dĭ·ŭm). A trade-mark applied to an intravenous anesthetic and hypnotic, chemically sodium ethyl-(1-methylbutyl)-thiobarbiturate.

pent·ox'ide (pĕnt·ŏk'sīd; -sĭd), *n.* Also **pent·ox'id.** [*pent-* + *oxide.*] *Chem.* A compound of an element or radical with five atoms of oxygen; as, phosphorus *pentoxide*, P_2O_5.

pent·ste'mon (pĕnt·stē'mŏn; pĕnt'stē'mŏn), *n.* [NL., fr. Gr. *pente* five + *stēmōn* warp. See STAMEN.] Any of a genus (*Pentstemon*) of chiefly American herbs of the figwort family, having showy blue, purple, red, yellow, or white flowers.

pe·nu'che (pē·nōō'chē), **pe·nu'chi** (pē·nōō'chĭ). Vars. of PANOCHA **b.**

pe'nuch'le, pe'nuck'le (pē'nŭk''l). Vars. of PINOCHLE.

pe'nult (pē'nŭlt; pē·nŭlt'), *n.* Also **pe·nul'ti·ma** (pē·nŭl'tĭ·mȧ). [L. *paenultima* (sc. *syllaba*), fem. of *paenultimus* last but one, fr. *paene* almost + *ultimus* the last.] The last but one; specif., *Gram. & Pros.*, the last syllable but one of a word.

pe·nul'ti·mate (pē·nŭl'tĭ·mĭt), *adj.* **1.** Last but one. **2.** Of or belonging to the penult. — *n.* The penult.

pe·num'bra (pē·nŭm'brȧ), *n.; pl.* PENUMBRAE (-brē), -BRAS (-brȧz). [NL., fr. L. *pene, paene*, almost + *umbra* shade.] **1.** The space of partial illumination, as in an eclipse, between the umbra, or perfect shadow, on all sides, and the full light. **2.** The shaded region around the dark central portion of a sunspot. — **pe·num'bral** (-brăl), *adj.*

pe·nu'ri·ous (pē·nū'rĭ·ŭs), *adj.* **1. a** *Obs.* Poverty-stricken. **b** *Now Rare.* Lacking richness; barren; poor; as, *penurious* soil. **2.** Excessively sparing in the use of money; stingy; miserly. — **Syn.** See STINGY. — **pe·nu'ri·ous·ly,** *adv.* — **pe·nu'ri·ous·ness,** *n.*

pen'u·ry (pĕn'ū·rĭ), *n.* [F. *pénurie*, fr. L. *penuria*, want, need.] Absence of resources; want; destitution. — **Syn.** See POVERTY.

pe'on (pē'ŏn), *n.* [Sp. *peón*, or Pg. *peão*, a foot traveler, foot soldier, pawn. See PAWN in chess.] **1.** In India: **a** A foot soldier. **b** A native policeman. **c** An attendant. **2.** In Spanish America, a member of the laboring class, orig. one forced to serve virtually in bondage to creditors. **3.** In southwestern states formerly part of Mexico, a person bound to service for payment of a debt.

pe'on·age (-ĭj), *n.* **1.** The state of being a peon. **2.** The use of peons for service. **3.** *Southeastern U.S.* The system of convict labor by which convicts are leased to contractors.

pe'on·ism (-ĭz'm), *n.* Peonage.

pe'o·ny (pē'ō·nĭ), *n.; pl.* PEONIES (-nĭz). [OF. *pione, peoine*, fr. L. *paeonia*, fr. Gr. *paiōnia*, fr. *Paiōn, Paian*, the god of healing.] Any of a genus (*Paeonia*) of plants of the crowfoot family, with large, usually double flowers of red and pink, or pure white; also, the flower. See CARPEL, *Illust.*

peo'ple (pē'p'l), *n. sing. & pl.*; and, in sense of a particular body of persons, *pl.* PEOPLES. [OF. *poeple, pueple* (F. *peuple*), fr. L. *populus.*] **1.** A body of persons united by a common character, culture, or sentiment; the individuals collectively of any characteristic group, conceived apart from the unity of the group as subject to a common government (that is, as a *state*) or as issued from a common stock (that is, as a *race* or *tribe*). **2.** A race, tribe, or nation; as, the *peoples* of Europe. **3.** Men or persons regarded merely as forming part of the aggregate of human beings; as, all sorts of *people.* **4. a** Human beings, as distinguished from animals. **b** Living creatures, esp. animals, of a certain kind; as, the bee *people.* **5.** The persons of a particular group; as, the *people* of New York. **6.** Members of a family or kindred; relatives; often, ancestry; as, my *people* were English. **7.** The mass of a community as distinguished from a special class; the populace; as, nobles and *people.* **8.** The body of enfranchised citizens of a state; the electorate. **9.** Persons regarded indefinitely (cf. French *on* and German *man*); as, so *people* say.
— *v. t.*; PEO'PLED (pē'p'ld); PEO'PLING (-plĭng). To supply, stock, or fill with or as with people. — **peo'pler** (-plẽr), *n.*

peo'ple's front (pē'p'lz). = POPULAR FRONT.

People's party. *U.S. Politics.* A party formed in 1891, advocating an increase of the currency, free coinage of silver, an income tax, etc. Its members were called *Populists.*

pep (pĕp), *n.* [Abbr. fr. *pepper.*] *Slang.* Brisk energy or initiative. — *v. t.*; PEPPED (pĕpt); PEP'PING. *Slang.* To inject pep into; to stimulate. — **pep'pi·ness,** *n.* — **pep'py,** *adj.*

pep'los (pĕp'lŏs), *n.* Also **pep'lus** (-lŭs). [L. *peplus*, fr. Gr. *peplos.*] *Gr. Antiq.* A shawllike, often costly, upper garment worn by women.

pep'lum (pĕp'lŭm), *n.; pl.* -LUMS (-lŭmz), -LA (-lȧ). [L.] **a** A peplos. **b** A short skirt attached to a waist or coat.

pe'po (pē'pō), *n.* [L., a kind of melon.] *Bot.* The characteristic fruit of the gourd family (Cucurbitaceae), a fleshy, many-seeded berry, usually with a hard rind, as the pumpkin, squash, melon, and cucumber.

pep'per (pĕp'ẽr), *n.* [AS. *pipor*, fr. L. *piper*, fr. Gr. *peperi, piperi*, ult. fr. Skr.] **1. a** A pungent condiment obtained from the fruit of an East Indian climbing shrub (*Piper nigrum*) with ovate leaves and spicate flowers succeeded by red berries. The dried berries yield the condiment ***black pepper***; the dried ripe seeds divested of their coatings yield ***white pepper.*** **b** A similar product obtained from several other species of the same genus. **2.** Any plant of the genus *Piper*, mostly climbing jointed shrubs, typifying a family (Piperaceae, the pepper family) of tropical plants having aromatic herbage and one-celled ovary. See BETEL, CUBEB. **3.** Any plant of the genus *Capsicum* (see CAPSICUM) or its fruit; also, the reddish condiment obtained from the fruits or seeds. The ***goat pepper,*** or chili (*C. frutescens*) and ***Guinea pepper*** (*C. annum*) are the chief sources of the hot and pungent condiment known as *cayenne pepper* or *red pepper*; the mild ***bonnet pepper*** (*C. tetragonum*) is the source of *paprika* (which see). Other species include the ***red pepper*** (*C. grossum*) whose unripe fruit, called ***green pepper*** or ***sweet pepper,*** is eaten as a vegetable, and the strong ***bird pepper*** (*C. baccatum*). — *v. t.* **1.** To sprinkle or season with or as if with pepper. **2.** To sprinkle as pepper is sprinkled; also, to strew in or as in grains. **3.** To shower shot or other missiles on; also, to thrash.

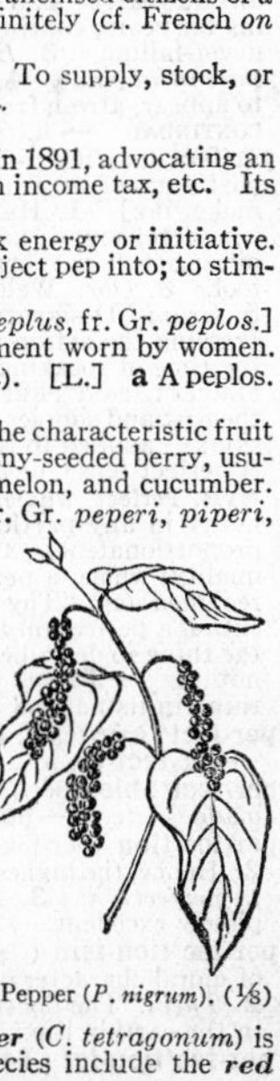

Pepper (*P. nigrum*). (⅛)

pep'per-and-salt', *adj.* Having black and white intermingled in small spots; hence, of a dull or neutral gray.

pep'per·box' (pĕp'ẽr·bŏks'), *n.* A small box or bottle, with a perforated top, used for sprinkling pepper.

pep'per·corn' (-kôrn'), *n.* [AS. *piporcorn.*] A dried berry of the black pepper, formerly stipulated in deeds, etc., as a nominal rent; hence, a trifling return.

pep'per·grass' (-gràs'; 9), *n.* Any of a genus (*Lepidium*) of cresses, as the ***garden peppergrass*** (*L. sativum*).

pep'per·idge (pĕp'ẽr·ĭj), *n.* See GUM, *n.*, 5 **a** (1).

pep'per·mint (-mĭnt), *n.* **1.** A pungent mint (*Mentha piperita*); also, its volatile oil (**peppermint oil**) or essence. **2.** A lozenge of sugar flavored with peppermint.

pepper pot. 1. = PEPPERBOX. **2. a** A West Indian stew of vegetables, meat or fish, and a preparation from the boiled sap of the cassava. **b** A highly seasoned stew of tripe, meat, dumplings, and vegetables; — called also ***Philadelphia pepper pot.*** **3.** A meat and vegetable soup seasoned with cayenne pepper, chilies, or the like.

pepper tree *or* **shrub.** A tropical American tree (*Schinus molle*), with graceful pinnate leaves and panicles of greenish flowers succeeded by red berrylike drupes.

pep'per·wort' (pĕp'ẽr·wûrt'), *n.* Peppergrass.

pep'per·y (-ĭ), *adj.* **1.** Of or pertaining to pepper; pungent. **2.** Hot-tempered; choleric. **3.** Of words, fiery; stinging. — **pep'per·i·ness,** *n.*

pep'sin (pĕp'sĭn), *n.* Also **pep'sine.** [G. *pepsin*, fr. Gr. *pepsis* digestion, fr. *peptein, pessein*, to cook, digest.] *Biochem.* A proteolytic enzyme secreted in the stomach of higher animals; also, a preparation of this enzyme from the stomachs of pigs, sheep, or calves, used as a digestive.

pep'sin·ate (pĕp'sĭ·nāt), *v. t.* To treat, mix, or impregnate with pepsin.

pep·sin'o·gen (pĕp·sĭn'ō·jĕn), *n.* [See PEPSIN; -GEN.] *Biochem.* A zymogen contained in the form of granules in the peptic cells of the gastric glands, and readily converted into pepsin.

pep'tic (pĕp'tĭk), *adj.* [Gr. *peptikos.* See PEPSIN.] **1.** Pertaining to digestion; aiding digestion. **2.** Able to digest. **3.** Of, pertaining to, or resembling pepsin. **4.** Connected with, or caused by, digestive juices; as, a *peptic* ulcer. — *n.* An agent that promotes digestion.

pep'tide (-tīd; -tĭd), *n.* Also **pep'tid** (-tĭd). [*peptone* + *-ide.*] *Biochem.* Any combination of amino acids in which the amino group of one acid is united with the carboxyl group of another.

pep'tize (-tīz), *v. t.* *Physical Chem.* To bring into colloidal solution; to convert into a sol.

pep'tone (-tōn), *n.* [G. *pepton*, fr. Gr. *pepton*, neut. of *peptos* cooked, digested.] *Biochem.* Any of a class of soluble and diffusible substances produced from proteins by peptic digestion, by the action of acids and alkalies, by putrefaction, etc. — **pep·ton'ic** (pĕp·tŏn'ĭk), *adj.*

pep'to·nize (-tō·nīz), *v. t.* To convert into peptone; to digest or dissolve by a proteolytic ferment. — **pep'to·ni·za'tion** (-nĭ·zā'shŭn; -nī·zā'-), *n.*

Pe'quot (pē'kwŏt), *n.* One of a warlike tribe of Algonquian Indians once dominant in eastern Connecticut.

per (pûr; pẽr), *prep.* [L.] **1.** Through; by means of. **2.** With equality, uniformity, or regularity on a basis of (a unit); as, *per* annum, yearly; *per* capita, by heads.

per-. [See PER, *prep.*] **1.** A prefix used to signify: **a** *Throughout in space* or *time*, as in *perennial.* **b** *Away* or *over*, as in *persuade.* **c** *Completely, thoroughly, perfectly*, as in *perfect*; also, *extremely, very*, as in *perfervid.* **2.** (*pron.* pûr-) *Chem.* A prefix denoting the presence of the largest possible, or a relatively large, proportion of some element, or the presence of an atom having its highest, or a relatively high, valence.

per·ac'id (pûr·ăs'ĭd), *n.* [*per-* + *acid.*] *Chem.* An acid which contains a large proportion of oxygen compared with the acid from which it is named.

per'ad·ven'ture (pûr'ăd·vĕn'tûr), *adv.* [OF. *par aventure.*] *Archaic.* Perhaps; it may be; possibly. — *n.* Chance; hap; hence, doubt; uncertainty.

per·am'bu·late (pẽr·ăm'bū·lāt), *v. t.* [L. *perambulatus*, past part. of *perambulare* to perambulate, fr. *per-* + *ambulare* to walk.] To walk through or over; traverse; esp., to travel over in order to inspect. — *v. i.* To walk about; stroll. — **per·am'bu·la'tion** (-lā'shŭn), *n.* — **per·am'bu·la·to'ry** (-lȧ·tō'rĭ *or, esp. Brit.*, -tẽr·ĭ), *adj.*

per·am'bu·la'tor (pẽr·ăm'bū·lā'tẽr *or, esp. Brit. and in sense* 3, prăm'bū-), *n.* **1.** One who perambulates. **2.** A surveyor's instrument for measuring distances. Cf. ODOMETER. **3.** A low carriage for a child, propelled by pushing; sometimes, any baby carriage.

per an'num (pẽr ăn'ŭm). [L.] By the year; each year.

per·bo'rate (pûr·bō'rāt), *n.* [See 1st -ATE, 3.] *Chem.* A salt of perboric acid; specif., *Com.*, sodium perborate (**per·bo'rax**), $NaBO_3.4H_2O$, used in washing and bleaching.

per·bo'ric ac'id (pûr·bō'rĭk). *Chem.* A hypothetical acid, HBO_3, salts of which are formed by hydrogen peroxide acting on borates.

Per·bu'nan (pûr·bū'năn), *n.* A registered trade-mark applied to a type of synthetic rubber.

per·cale' (pẽr·kāl'), *n.* [F., fr. Per. *pargālah.*] A fine, closely woven cotton fabric, usually printed on one side.

per'ca·line' (pûr'kȧ·lēn'), *n.* [F.] A fine cotton fabric, used for linings, bookbindings, etc.

per cap'i·ta (pẽr kăp'ĭ·tȧ). [L.] By heads; for each individual; in *Civil Law*, as individual; share and share alike.

per·ceiv'a·ble (pẽr·sēv'ȧ·b'l), *adj.* Perceptible; intelligible. — **per·ceiv'a·bly,** *adv.*

per·ceive' (pẽr·sēv'), *v. t. & i.* [OF. *parceivre, perceveir* (3d pl. pres. *perceivent, parceivent*), fr. L. *percipere, perceptum*, fr. *per-* + *capere* to take, receive.] **1.** To obtain knowledge (of) through the senses; to see, hear, etc. **2.** To apprehend with the mind; to understand.

per cent, per cen'tum (pẽr sĕn'tŭm). Also **per cent.** (with period). [L. *per centum.*] By the hundred; in the hundred; — used of proportions, rate of interest, etc. Symbol %.

per cent, *or* **per·cent'** (pẽr·sĕnt'), *n.* **1.** Parts, or a specified number of parts, in or to every hundred; amount or quantity measured by the

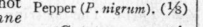

number of units in proportion to one hundred, as by volume or weight; as, ten *per cent* of the population; interest at four *per cent.* **2.** [*pl.*] Investments, esp. public securities, of a (specified) rate of interest; as, money in the three *per cents.*

per·cent′age (pẽr·sĕn′tĭj), *n.* [*per cent* + *-age* as in average.] **1.** A certain rate per cent; the allowance, rate of interest, discount, etc., on a hundred. **2. a** Loosely, a proportion or part of a whole. **b** *Slang.* A share of the winnings or profits; a rake-off.

per·cen′tile (pẽr·sĕn′tĭl; -tīl), *adj.* Expressed, or expressing values, in per cent terms; specif., based upon division into 100 equal consecutive groups, of a series of items arranged in order of magnitude in respect to a certain attribute; as, a *percentile* curve or graph; of rank, indicating the individual's superiority over the specified number of such groups of a distribution and inferiority to the remaining groups; as, his *percentile* rank is 40. — *n.* Any of the values of an attribute which separate the entire distribution into one hundred groups of equal frequency.

per cen′tum (pẽr sĕn′tŭm). See PER CENT.

per′cept (pûr′sĕpt), *n.* [L. *perceptum*, neut. past part. of *percipere.* See PERCEIVE.] An impression of an object obtained solely by use of the senses.

per·cep′ti·ble (pẽr·sĕp′tĭ·b'l), *adj.* Capable of being perceived; discernible; perceivable. — **per·cep′ti·bly**, *adv.*

Syn. Perceptible, sensible, palpable, tangible, appreciable, ponderable mean apprehensible as real or existent. **Perceptible** and **sensible** may refer to anything that comes within the range of any sense, but *perceptible* usually applies to that which is on the borderline or just above, and *sensible* to that which is clearly, though not markedly, seen, heard, smelled, etc.; **palpable** and **tangible** are applied to anything that may be known by touch, but *palpable* more often applies to that which makes its presence known as if by touching, and *tangible* to that which may be handled or grasped both physically and mentally; **appreciable** is applied to that which may be estimated as by a sensitive instrument; **ponderable**, to that which may be weighed physically or mentally, esp. as distinguished from that which eludes such determination.

per·cep′tion (pẽr·sĕp′shŭn), *n.* [OF. and L.; OF., fr. L. *perceptio.*] **1.** Awareness of objects; consciousness. **2. a** Direct acquaintance with anything through the senses. Cf. SENSATION, 1 **a**. **b** The process of perceiving. **c** The result of this process; what is known of an object by seeing or hearing it, etc. **3.** An immediate or intuitive cognition or judgment, often implying nice observation or subtle discrimination. Also, the power of having or exercising such perceptions. — **Syn.** See DISCERNMENT. — **per·cep′tion·al** (-ăl; -'l), *adj.*

per·cep′tive (-tĭv), *adj.* Of or pertaining to the act or power of perceiving; having the faculty of perception; hence, discerning. — **per·cep′tive·ness**, *n.*

per·cep′tu·al (-tū·ăl), *adj.* Pertaining to perception; involving perception. — **per·cep′tu·al·ly**, *adv.*

Per′ce·val. Var. of PERCIVAL.

perch (pûrch), *n.*; see PLURAL, *Note*, 6. [OF. *perche*, fr. L. *perca*, fr. Gr. *perkē.*] **1.** A rather small European fresh-water spiny-finned fish (*Perca fluviatilis*) typifying a family (Percidae); also, in the United States, a similar species (*P. flavescens*), the ***yellow perch.*** **2.** Any of numerous spiny-finned fishes, many of them marine.

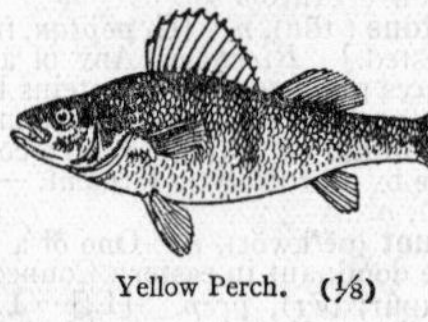

Yellow Perch. (1/8)

perch, *n.* [OF. *perche*, fr. L. *pertica.*] **1.** A pole, bar, or the like, placed horizontally above the ground for birds to roost on; hence, any elevated seat, station, or position. **2. a** A measure of length or surface. See MEASURE, *Tables* 1 & 3. **b** In measuring masonry, usually 24¾ cubic feet. **3.** *Vehicles.* A pole connecting the front gear and hind gear of a spring carriage. — *v. i.* To alight or settle, as a bird; to rest on or as on a perch. — *v. t.* To place or set on or as on a perch. — **perch′er**, *n.*

per·chance′ (pẽr·chȧns′; 9), *adv.* [F. *par* by + *chance.*] *Poetic or Archaic.* **1.** By chance. **2.** Perhaps; possibly.

Per′che·ron (pûr′chĕ·rŏn; pûr′shĕ-), *n.* [F.] A draft horse of a breed originating in Perche, an ancient division of France; — called also **Percheron Norman.**

per·chlo′rate (pûr·klō′rāt; 70), *n.* *Chem.* A salt of perchloric acid.

per·chlo′ric (-rĭk), *adj.* [*per-* + *chloric.*] *Chem.* Pert. to or designating the highest oxygen acid ($HClO_4$) of chlorine. It is a colorless, oily, fuming liquid.

per·chlo′ride (-rīd; -rĭd), *n.* Also **per·chlo′rid.** *Chem.* A chloride containing a relatively high proportion of chlorine.

per·chlo′rin·ate (pûr·klō′rĭ·nāt), *v. t.* To combine with a maximum amount of chlorine. — **per·chlo′rin·a′tion** (-nā′shŭn), *n.*

per·chlo′ro- (pûr·klō′rō-), **perchlor-.** *Chem.* A combining form, *per-* + *chloro-*, denoting the *presence of a relatively large amount of chlorine*, esp. replacing all the hydrogen in an organic compound.

per·chro′mate (pûr·krō′māt), *n.* [See 1st -ATE, 3.] *Chem.* A salt of perchromic acid.

per·chro′mic (-krō′mĭk), *adj.* [*per-* + *chromic.*] *Chem.* Pertaining to or designating an acid, H_3CrO_8 or $H_3CrO_8.2H_2O$, obtained as a blue crystalline mass.

per·cip′i·ence (pẽr·sĭp′ĭ·ĕns; 58), **per·cip′i·en·cy** (-ĕn·sĭ), *n.* Faculty, act, or power of perceiving; perception.

per·cip′i·ent (-ĕnt), *adj.* [L. *percipiens, -entis*, pres. part. of *percipere.* See PERCEIVE.] Capable of perception; perceiving, esp. keenly or quickly. — *n.* One who perceives.

Per′ci·vale (pûr′sĭ·văl), *n.* Also **Per′ce·val** (-sĕ-), **Per′ci·val**, etc. [OF. *Perceval.*] An Arthurian knight who, after many adventures, finally wins a sight of the Holy Grail.

per′coid (pûr′koid), **per·coi′de·an** (pẽr·koi′dē·ăn), *adj.* [L. *perca* a perch + *-oid.*] *Zool.* Belonging to an extensive superfamily (Percoidea) of spiny-finned fishes including the true perches, the sunfishes (family Centrarchidae), the serranoids, sparoids, and several related families. — *n.* A percoid fish.

per′co·late (pûr′kō·lāt), *v. t. & i.* [L. *percolatus*, past part. of *percolare* to percolate, fr. *per-* + *colare* to strain.] **1.** To cause (a liquid) to pass through interstices, as of a porous substance; to filter. **2.** Specif., to cause hot water to filter through (coffee) to extract its essence. **3.** To ooze through (some porous substance); to permeate. — (-lāt), *n.* *Pharm.* A liquid obtained by percolation. — **per′co·la′tion** (-lā′shŭn), *n.*

per′co·la′tor (pûr′kō·lā′tẽr), *n.* One that percolates; specif., a form of coffeepot in which heated water filters repeatedly through the coffee.

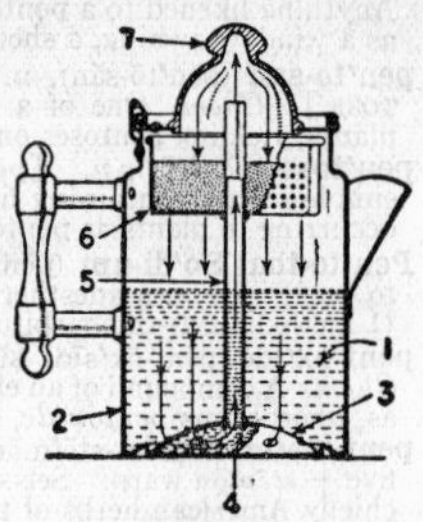

One form of Percolator. Water (1) in Container (2) passes under domed Base (3) into Chamber (4) and up Tube (5). Heat forces the water up against glass Dome (7), from which it falls downward, percolating through coffee in perforated Cup (6).

per con′tra (pẽr kŏn′trȧ). [L.] On the contrary; as an offset; on the other side.

per·cuss′ (pẽr·kŭs′), *v. t. & i.* [L. *percussus*, past part. of *percutere*, fr. *per-* + *quatere* to strike.] To tap sharply.

per·cus′sion (-kŭsh′ŭn), *n.* **1.** Act of percussing; esp., the striking of a percussion cap so as to set off the charge in a firearm. **2.** The striking or beating of sound on the ear. **3.** *Med.* Act of tapping the surface, as of the chest or abdomen, to learn the condition of the parts beneath by the sound emitted.

percussion cap. *Firearms.* A small metallic cap or cup, containing fulminating powder, used with a percussion lock.

percussion instrument. *Music.* Any instrument, as the piano, on which the tone is produced by percussing, or striking; more narrowly, an instrument of the percussion family of instruments, as disting. from the *strings* and *winds*, as esp. the drum, cymbals, tambourine, castanets, xylophone, etc.

percussion lock. The lock of a gun fired by percussion.

per·cus′sive (pẽr·kŭs′ĭv), *adj.* Of or pertaining to percussion; operative or operated by striking.

per·die′ (pẽr·dē′). Var. of PARDIE.

per di′em (pẽr dī′ĕm). [L.] By the day.

per·di′tion (pẽr·dĭsh′ŭn), *n.* [OF. *perdicion*, fr. LL. *perditio*, fr. *perdere, perditum*, to ruin, lose.] Entire loss; ruin; esp., utter loss of the soul, or of final happiness in a future state; damnation.

per·du′, per·due′ (pẽr·dū′; *F.* pĕr′dü′), *adj.* [F. *perdu*, fem. *perdue*, lost.] Lost to view; in concealment or hiding. — *n.* [See PERDU, *adj.*] *Obs.* A soldier or body of soldiers doing very hazardous duty.

per·dur′a·ble (pûr·dūr′ȧ·b'l), *adj.* [OF.] Very durable; lasting; eternal. — **per·dur′a·bly** (-blĭ), *adv.*

‖**père** (pâr), *n.* [F.] Father; — used: (1) after French proper names to distinguish a father from his son; (2) as a title for a priest.

per′e·gri·nate (pĕr′ē·grĭ·nāt), *v. i. & t.* [L. *peregrinatus*, past part. of *peregrinari* to travel. See PILGRIM.] To travel; to journey from place to place. — **per′e·gri·na′tor** (-nā′tẽr), *n.*

per′e·gri·na′tion (-nā′shŭn), *n.* A traveling or going about; a wandering.

per′e·grine (pĕr′ē·grĭn; -grīn; -grēn), **per′e·grin** (-grĭn), *adj.* [L. *peregrinus.*] Foreign; alien; hence, strange; exotic. — *n.* The peregrine falcon. See FALCON.

pe·rei′ra bark, *or* **pe·rei′ra** (pĕ·rā′rȧ), *n.* [NL. *Pereira*, obs. genus name, after Jonathan *Pereira* (1804–53) of London.] The bark of a Brazilian tree (*Geissospermum vellosii*) of the dogbane family, used as a tonic and febrifuge; also, the tree.

pe·rei′rine (-rēn; -rĭn), *n.* Also **pe·rei′rin.** *Chem.* An alkaloid, $C_{19}H_{24}N_2O$, occurring in pereira bark and extracted as a powder. It is used as an antiperiodic and tonic.

per·emp′to·ry (pẽr·ĕmp′tō·rĭ; pĕr′ĕmp·tō′rĭ, -tẽr·ĭ), *adj.* [L. *peremptorius* destructive, decisive, fr. *perimere* to take away entirely, destroy, fr. *per-* + *emere, emptum*, to buy, orig., to take.] **1. a** *Law.* Taking away a right of action, debate, etc.; as, a **peremptory exception** *or* **plea**, one which, if sustained, bars the action. **b** Hence, conclusive or absolute; decisive; as, a *peremptory* writ, a *peremptory* challenge (see CHALLENGE, *n.*, 5), etc. **2.** Leaving no chance for denial or refusal; incontrovertible. **3.** Positive, esp. in the expression of opinion; dogmatic; also, arrogant. — **Syn.** See MASTERFUL. — **per·emp′to·ri·ly**, *adv.* — **per·emp′to·ri·ness**, *n.*

per·en′ni·al (pẽr·ĕn′ĭ·ăl; 58), *adj.* [L. *perennis*, fr. *per* through + *annus* year.] **1.** Lasting or continuing through the year. **2.** Lasting for years; continuing without cessation or interruption; unceasing; never-failing. **3.** *Bot.* Continuing to live from year to year; as, a *perennial* plant. **4.** Recurring over a long period; appearing, or likely to appear, afresh from time to time; as, a *perennial* joke. — **Syn.** See CONTINUAL. — *n.* A perennial plant. — **per·en′ni·al·ly**, *adv.*

per′fect (pûr′fĕkt; -fĭkt), *adj.* [OF. *parfit, parfait*, fr. L. *perfectus*, past part. of *perficere* to perform, finish, perfect, fr. *per-* + *facere* to make, do.] **1.** Having all the properties naturally belonging to it; complete; sound; flawless. **2.** Exact; precise; as, a *perfect* hexagon; pure; utter; as, *perfect* red; also, *Colloq.*, unmitigated; as, a *perfect* fool. **3.** *Obs.* Well-informed; certain; sure. **4.** *Bot.* Monoclinous. **5.** *Gram.* Designating or pertaining to a form or forms of verb expressing the action or state as completed at a time denoted as either the time of speaking or a time spoken of. Abbr. *perf.* See PRESENT PERFECT, PAST PERFECT, FUTURE PERFECT. **6.** *Music.* Belonging to the first and simpler consonances which retain their character on inversion; — applied to the unison, octave, fifth, and fourth. — *n.* *Gram.* A perfect tense, or a verb in it.

Syn. Perfect, whole, entire, intact mean not deficient, defective, or faulty in any particular. **Perfect** further implies the soundness, the proportionateness, and excellence of every part, every element, or every quality; **whole**, a perfection that can be sought and gained and even regained (as, "Thy faith hath made thee *whole*" —*Matt.* ix. 22); **entire**, a perfection that derives from the integrity, soundness, etc., of the thing so described (as, "that ye may be *perfect* and *entire*, wanting nothing" —*James* i. 4); **intact** implies retention of perfection of a thing in its natural or original state.

per·fect′ (pẽr·fĕkt′; pûr′fĕkt, -fĭkt), *v. t.* To make perfect; complete. — **per·fect′er**, *n.*

per·fect′i·ble (pẽr·fĕk′tĭ·b'l), *adj.* Capable of becoming, or being made, perfect. — **per·fect′i·bil′i·ty** (-bĭl′ĭ·tĭ), *n.*

per·fec′tion (pẽr·fĕk′shŭn), *n.* **1.** Quality or state of being perfect. **2.** Hence, the highest possible degree of excellence; as, to do something to *perfection.* **3.** Act or process of perfecting. **4.** A quality completely excellent.

per·fec′tion·ism (-ĭz'm), *n.* **1.** *Ethics.* The doctrine that perfection of moral character or of man's ideal nature is the supreme ethical end. **2.** *Theol.* The doctrine that a state of freedom from sin is attainable in the earthly life.

per·fec′tion·ist (-ĭst), *n.* **1.** One who believes in or professes any theory of perfection; specif., an adherent of perfectionism. **2.** One who will not accept or be content with anything short of perfection. — **per·fec′tion·ist,** *adj.*

per·fec′tive (pẽr·fĕk′tĭv), *adj.* Tending or conducing to make perfect. — **per·fec′tive·ly,** *adv.* — **per·fec′tive·ness,** *n.*

per′fect·ly (pûr′fĕkt·lĭ; -fĭkt·lĭ), *adv.* In a perfect manner.

per·fec′to (pẽr·fĕk′tō), *n.; pl.* -TOS (-tōz). [Sp., perfect.] A large cigar, thick in the middle part and tapering down almost to a point at each end. See CIGAR.

perfect participle. *Gram.* See PARTICIPLE.

perfect rhyme. *Pros.* A rhyme between two words of identical form but different meaning.

perfect year. See JEWISH CALENDAR.

per·fer′vid (pûr·fûr′vĭd), *adj.* Very fervid; ardent. — **Syn.** See IMPASSIONED.

‖**per′fide′ Al′bi·on′** (pĕr′fēd′ ăl′byôɴ′). [F.] Perfidious Albion (England); — so called by Napoleon I.

per·fid′i·ous (pẽr·fĭd′ĭ·ŭs), *adj.* [L. *perfidiosus.*] **1.** Guilty of perfidy; esp., basely false to trust. **2.** Involving or of the nature of perfidy. — **Syn.** See FAITHLESS. — **per·fid′i·ous·ly,** *adv.* — **per·fid′i·ous·ness,** *n.*

per′fi·dy (pûr′fĭ·dĭ), *n.; pl.* -DIES (-dĭz). [F. *perfidie,* fr. L. *perfidia,* fr. *perfidus* faithless, fr. *per-* + *fides* faith.] Act of violating faith, or one's vow or promise, or a trust; faithlessness; treachery.

per·fo′li·ate (pẽr·fō′lĭ·āt), *adj.* [*per-* + L. *folium* leaf.] *Bot.* Having the basal part congenitally united around the stem; — said of leaves. — **per·fo′li·a′tion** (-ā′shŭn), *n.*

per′fo·rate (pûr′fō·rāt), *v. t. & i.* [L. *perforatus,* past part. of *perforare* to perforate, fr. *per-* + *forare* to bore.] To bore through; to pierce the surface of; specif., to make rows of small holes through or in, as for dress patterns, in sheets of stamps, etc. — **per′fo·ra′tive** (-rā′tĭv), *adj.* — **per′fo·ra′tor** (-rā′tẽr), *n.*

per′fo·rate (-rāt), **per′fo·rat′ed** (-rāt′ĕd; -ĭd), *adj.* Pierced with a hole or holes, or with pores. Abbr. *perf.*

per′fo·ra′tion (-rā′shŭn), *n.* **1.** Act of perforating, or state or process of being perforated. **2. a** A hole made by or as if by boring. **b** Specif., *Philately,* one of such a series of holes in which a part of the paper is removed. Abbr. *perf.*

per·force′ (pẽr·fōrs′; 70), *adv.* [F. *par* + *force.*] By force of circumstances; of necessity. — *n.* Compulsion.

per·form′ (pẽr·fôrm′), *v. t.* [OF. *parfornir, parfournir,* to finish, complete, fr. *par* + *fournir* to furnish, complete; — influenced by E. *form.*] **1.** To carry on to the finish; to accomplish; also, loosely, to do or make. **2.** To go through with or execute. **3.** *Obs.* **a** To make complete by adding what is wanting, as a story or sum. **b** To make, build, or manufacture. — *v. i.* To carry out or execute some action, engagement, or the like; to do something with special skill; also, to show off; as, to *perform* on the piano. — **per·form′a·ble,** *adj.* — **per·form′er,** *n.*

Syn. **Perform, execute, discharge, accomplish, achieve, effect, fulfill** mean to carry out completely. **Perform** usually refers to processes that are lengthy, exacting, or ceremonial, or to deeds that are striking; **execute** implies the carrying out of that which exists in plan or in intent; **discharge** implies a completion of a round of duties or tasks; **accomplish** implies a completion of a process rather than the means by which it is carried out; **achieve** adds to *accomplish* the implication of conquered difficulties; **effect** also implies obstacles to be surmounted, but it suggests inherent force in the agent; **fulfill,** often loosely used, strictly implies full realization of the ends or possibilities of a thing.

per·form′ance (pẽr·fôr′măns), *n.* **1.** The act of performing; specif., the execution of the functions required of one; often, effective operation, as of a motor. **2.** A deed; feat; hence, a public entertainment or exhibition of skill; a presentation of a play.

per·fume′ (pẽr·fūm′), *v. t.* [F. *parfumer,* fr. It., fr. L. *fumare* to smoke, fr. *fumus* smoke.] To fill or impregnate with an agreeable odor, as that of flowers; to scent.

per′fume (pûr′fūm; *formerly also and still occas.* pẽr·fūm′), *n.* [F. *parfum.*] **1.** The scent emitted from a sweet-smelling substance; a pleasant fragrance. **2.** A substance that emits an agreeable odor; specif., a fluid preparation, as of the essence of flowers, used for scenting. — **Syn.** See FRAGRANCE.

per·fum′er (pẽr·fūm′ẽr), *n.* **1.** One that perfumes. **2.** One whose trade is to make or sell perfumes.

per·fum′er·y (pẽr·fūm′ẽr·ĭ), *n.* **1.** A perfume or perfumes in general. **2.** A place for making or selling perfume.

per·func′to·ry (pẽr·fŭngk′tō·rĭ), *adj.* [LL. *perfunctorius,* fr. L. *perfunctus* dispatched, past part. of *perfungi* to discharge, fr. *per-* + *fungi* to perform.] **1.** Done mechanically and by way of routine or carelessly and superficially. **2.** Hence, mechanical; indifferent; without interest or zeal. — **per·func′to·ri·ly,** *adv.* — **per·func′to·ri·ness,** *n.*

per·fuse′ (pẽr·fūz′), *v. t.* [L. *perfusus,* past part. of *perfundere* to pour over, fr. *per-* + *fundere* to pour.] **1.** To cover, sprinkle, or suffuse with or as with a liquid. **2.** To spread, as a fluid, through or over something. — **per·fu′sion** (-fū′zhŭn), *n.* — **per·fu′sive** (-sĭv), *adj.*

per′go·la (pûr′gō·lȧ), *n.* [It., fr. L. *pergula* shed, shop, vine arbor.] Literally, an arbor or bower; specif., *Italian Art,* an arbor or trellis treated architecturally.

per·haps′ (pẽr·hăps′; *colloq., Amer., also* pẽr·ăps′, *Brit.* prăps), *adv.* [*per* + *pl.* of *hap* chance.] **1.** Possibly but uncertainly; maybe. **2.** By some chance; as may be the case; — used in a conditional or concessive clause.

pe′ri (pē′rĭ), *n.* [Per. *pari* fairy, genius.] **1.** *Persian Myth.* An imaginary being, like an elf or fairy, descended from fallen angels, excluded from paradise till penance is accomplished. **2.** A fairylike or elflike creature.

per′i- (pĕr′ĭ-). [Gr. *peri.*] A prefix meaning *all round, about, beyond,* used: **a** Adverbially, to signify: (1) *Around, about, round,* as in *perimeter, periphery.* (2) *Near,* as in *perigee.* **b** In anatomical and pathological terms, to signify *around, enclosing, surrounding a* (specified) *part,* in terms in *-itis* to signify *of* or *affecting the tissue surrounding a* (specified) *part,* as in **per′i·rec′tal, per′i·tho·rac′ic, per′i·vis′cer·al.**

per′i·anth (pĕr′ĭ·ănth), *n.* [Through F. fr. NL., fr. Gr. *peri* about + *anthos* flower.] *Bot.* The external envelope of a flower; the floral leaves collectively, esp. when not differentiated into *calyx* (external floral leaves) and *corolla* (internal floral leaves), as in monocotyledons. See CALYX, COROLLA.

per′i·apt (-ăpt), *n.* [F. *périapte,* fr. Gr. *periapton,* deriv. of *peri* about + *haptein* to tie.] A charm worn as a protection against disease or mischief; an amulet.

per′i·car′di·al (-kär′dĭ·ăl), **per′i·car′di·ac** (-ăk), *adj.* *Anat. & Zool.* Of or pertaining to the pericardium.

per′i·car·di′tis (-kär·dī′tĭs), *n.* [NL., fr. *pericardium* + *-itis.*] *Med.* Inflammation of the conical sac of serous membrane (**per′i·car′di·um** [-kär′dĭ·ŭm]) which encloses the heart. Cf. MYOCARDITIS.

per′i·carp (pĕr′ĭ·kärp), *n.* [Gr. *perikarpion,* fr. *peri* around + *karpos* fruit.] *Bot.* The ripened and variously modified walls of the ovary, sometimes exhibiting three distinct structural layers, the *endocarp, mesocarp,* and *epicarp.* See ENDOCARP, *Illust.* — **per′i·car′pi·al** (-kär′pĭ·ăl), *adj.*

per′i·chon′dri·um (-kŏn′drĭ·ŭm), *n.; pl.* -DRIA (-ȧ). [NL., fr. *peri-* + Gr. *chondros* cartilage.] *Anat.* The membrane of fibrous connective tissue that invests a cartilage except at joints. — **per′i·chon′dri·al** (-ăl), *adj.*

Per′i·cle′an (pĕr′ĭ·klē′ăn), *adj.* Of or pertaining to Pericles; designating, or pertaining to, his age, when Athens was at her highest material and intellectual state.

per′i·cline (pĕr′ĭ·klīn), *n.* [Gr. *periklinēs* sloping on all sides, fr. *peri* around + *klinein* to incline.] *Mineral.* A variety of albite occurring in white opaque crystals.

per′i·cra′ni·um (-krā′nĭ·ŭm), *n.; pl.* -NIA (-ȧ). [NL., fr. Gr. *perikranion,* neut. adj., round the skull.] *Anat.* The external periosteum of the skull. — **per′i·cra′ni·al** (-ăl), *adj.*

per′i·cy′cle (pĕr′ĭ·sī′k'l), *n.* [Gr. *perikyklos* spherical. See PERI-; CYCLE.] *Bot.* A thin layer of parenchymatous or sclerenchymatous cells surrounding the stele in most plants.

per′i·den′tal (pĕr′ĭ·dĕn′tăl; -t'l), *adj.* [*peri-* + *dental.*] *Anat.* = PERIODONTAL.

per′i·derm (pĕr′ĭ·dûrm), *n.* [*peri-* + *-derm.*] *Bot.* The cortical tissue derived from growth of the phellogen.

pe·rid′i·um (pē·rĭd′ĭ·ŭm), *n.; pl.* -IA (-ȧ). [NL., fr. Gr. *pēridion,* dim. of *pēra* leathern pouch, wallet.] *Bot.* The outer coating of the sporophore in many fungi. — **pe·rid′i·al** (-ăl), *adj.*

per′i·dot (pĕr′ĭ·dŏt), *n.* [F. *péridot.*] A deep yellowish-green variety of chrysolite. — **per′i·dot′ic** (-dŏt′ĭk), *adj.*

per′i·do′tite (-dō′tīt), *n.* *Petrog.* Any of a group of granitoid igneous rocks, composed of chrysolite and other ferromagnesian minerals, but little or no feldspar.

per′i·gee (pĕr′ĭ·jē), *n.* [F. and NL.; F. *périgée,* fr. NL. *perigium,* fr. Gr. *perigeios* around the earth, fr. *peri* near + *gē* the earth.] *Astron.* That point in the orbit of the moon nearest to the earth; — opposed to *apogee.* — **per′i·ge′al** (-jē′ăl), **per′i·ge′an** (-ăn), *adj.*

pe·rig′y·nous (pē·rĭj′ĭ·nŭs), *adj.* [NL. *perigynus.* See PERI-; -GYNOUS.] *Bot.* Borne on a ring or cup of the torus surrounding the pistil, as the stamens or petals; having stamens and petals so situated. — **pe·rig′y·ny** (-nĭ), *n.*

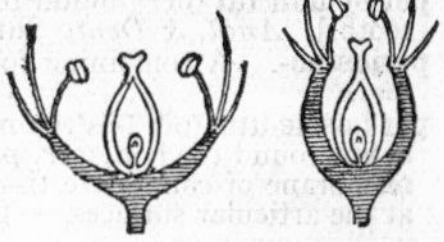

Perigynous Flowers (in section).

per′i·he′li·on (pĕr′ĭ·hē′lĭ·ŏn), *n.; pl.* -HELIA (-ȧ). [NL., fr. *peri-* + Gr. *hēlios* the sun.] *Astron.* That point of the orbit of a planet or comet which is nearest to the sun; — opposed to *aphelion.*

per′il (pĕr′ĭl), *n.* [OF., fr. L. *periculum, periclum.*] Exposure to the risk of being injured, destroyed, or lost; a position of jeopardy; danger. — *v. t.;* -ILED (-ĭld) or -ILLED; -IL·ING or -IL·LING. To expose to danger; to hazard; risk.

pe·ril′la (pē·rĭl′ȧ), *n.* [NL., appar. fr. Sp. *perilla,* dim. of *pera* pear.] Any of a small genus (*Perilla*) of Asiatic mints, the seeds of certain species (esp. *P. frutescens*) of which provide an oil used in paints and varnishes.

per′il·ous (pĕr′ĭ·lŭs), *adj.* [OF. *perillous, perilleus,* fr. L. *periculosus.*] Full of, or involving, peril; hazardous; dangerous. — **Syn.** See DANGEROUS. — **per′il·ous·ly,** *adv.* — **per′il·ous·ness,** *n.*

pe·rim′e·ter (pē·rĭm′ē·tẽr), *n.* [L. *perimetros,* fr. Gr. *perimetros,* fr. *peri* around + *metron* measure.] **1.** *Geom.* The whole outer boundary of a body or figure, or the measure of the same. **2.** *Mil.* The outer boundary formed by advanced posts encircling a position. **3.** *Optics.* An instrument for examining the discriminative powers of different parts of the retina. — **Syn.** See CIRCUMFERENCE. — **per′i·met′ric** (pĕr′ĭ·mĕt′rĭk), **per′i·met′ri·cal** (-rĭ·kăl), *adj.* — **per′i·met′ri·cal·ly,** *adv.*

per′i·morph (pĕr′ĭ·môrf), *n.* [*peri-* + *-morph.*] *Mineral.* A crystal of one species enclosing one of another species. Cf. ENDOMORPH. — **per′i·mor′phic** (-môr′fĭk), **per′i·mor′phous** (-fŭs), *adj.*

per′i·neph′ri·um (-nĕf′rĭ·ŭm), *n.* [NL.] *Anat.* The capsule of connective and fatty tissue about the kidney.

per′i·ne′um (-nē′ŭm), *n.; pl.* -NEA (-ȧ). [NL., fr. Gr. *perinaion, perineos.*] *Anat.* **a** The region included in the outlet of the pelvis, and traversed by the urinogenital passages and the rectum. **b** The superficial region between the thighs, including the anus and more or less of the genitals. — **per′i·ne′al** (-ăl), *adj.*

per′i·neu′ri·um (-nū′rĭ·ŭm), *n.; pl.* -RIA (-ȧ). [NL., fr. *peri-* + Gr. *neuron* a nerve.] *Anat.* The connective-tissue sheath that surrounds a bundle, or funiculus, of nerve fibers. — **per′i·neu·ri′tis** (-nū·rī′tĭs), *n.*

pe′ri·od (pē′rĭ·ŭd), *n.* [F. *période,* fr. L. *periodus,* fr. Gr. *periodos* a going round, way round, circumference, period, fr. *peri* round, about + *hodos* a way.] **1.** A point of time marking an end. **2.** The termination or completion of a revolution, cycle, series of events, or act; hence, a limit; bound. **3. a** A portion of time determined by some recurring phenomenon, as by the completion of a revolution of a heavenly body; as, the annual *period* of Uranus. **b** One of the chronological divisions as of a course, a development, a life; a stage; as, the *periods* of Shakespeare's career, of civilization, etc. **4.** *Educ.* One of the divisions of the academic day; a class hour. **5.** *Games.* A distinct portion of the duration of play. **6.** *Geol.* A division of geologic time longer than an epoch and included in an era; as, the Devonian *period.* **7.** *Music.* A complete musical sentence, usually of eight or sixteen measures, consisting of two or more contrasting or complementary phrases, and ending with a cadence. **8.** *Physics & Elec.* The interval of time required for a periodic motion or phenomenon to complete a cycle and begin to repeat itself. **9.** *Physiol.* Menses; — usually in *pl.* **10.** *Greek Pros.* A rhythmical division composed of two or more cola. **11.** *Punctuation.* **a** The full pause with which the enunciation of a complete sentence closes. **b** The point [.] that marks the end of a complete declarative sentence, or of an abbreviated word. **12.** *Rhet.* A complete sentence.

Syn. Period, epoch, era, age mean a portion or division of time. **Period,** the general term, may be applied to any extent of time, regardless of length; **epoch** is properly applied to the starting point of a new period as marked by a change or event, and **era** to the period which follows, but they are often used without distinction; **age** is usually applied to a period dominated by a central figure or clearly marked feature.

— *adj.* **1.** Of or pert. to a period or periods; of, fashioned after, or bearing upon, the style prevalent in a particular period or periods; as, *period* novel. **2.** Representing realistically a particular historical period; as, a *period* novel.

per·i′o·date (pûr′ĭ·ō·dāt), *n. Chem.* A salt of periodic acid.

pe′ri·od′ic (pēr′ĭ·ŏd′ĭk), *adj.* **1.** Of, pertaining to, or performed in a period, or regular revolution, of a heavenly body. **2.** Occurring at regular stated times; loosely, recurring; intermittent. **3.** *Rhet.* Expressed in, or characterized by, periods. — **Syn.** See INTERMITTENT.

per′i·od′ic (pûr′ĭ·ŏd′ĭk), *adj.* [*per-* + *iodic.*] *Chem.* Pert. to or designating the highest oxygen acid of iodine.

pe′ri·od′i·cal (pēr′ĭ·ŏd′ĭ·kăl), *adj.* **1.** Periodic. **2.** Published with a fixed interval (more than one day) between the issues or numbers; — said of magazines, reviews, etc.; also, publishing in, writing for, or connected with, such publications. — *n.* A publication which appears at regular intervals. — **pe′ri·od′i·cal·ly,** *adv.*

pe′ri·o·dic′i·ty (-ō·dĭs′ĭ·tĭ), *n.; pl.* -TIES (-tĭz). Quality or state of being periodical, or regularly recurrent; specif.: **a** *Chem.* The position of an element in the periodic table. **b** *Elec.* Frequency.

periodic law. *Chem.* The law that the elements, when arranged in the order of their atomic numbers, show a periodic variation in most of their properties.

periodic sentence. *Rhet.* A sentence the latter part of which contains salient grammatical elements and important ideas. Cf. LOOSE SENTENCE.

periodic system. *Chem.* The system of elements in their relationship as expressed by the periodic law.

periodic table. *Chem.* A table (see below) of the elements arranged according to the periodic law. Atomic numbers are in boldface type; atomic weights (in round numbers) are in lightface type following the symbols of the elements. The periodic variation in properties is shown in the *series* (horizontal rows) and *periods*. The *groups* (columns) include elements of related character; the subgroups or *families* of more closely related elements constitute vertical lines within the groups. The formulas at the top show the close connection between the valence of an element and the group to which it belongs.

per·i′o·dide (pûr·ĭ′ō·dīd; -dĭd), *n. Chem.* An iodide containing a relatively high proportion of iodine.

per′i·o·don′tal (pĕr′ĭ·ō·dŏn′tăl; -t'l), *adj.* [*peri-* + Gr. *odōn, odontos,* tooth.] *Anat. & Dent.* Surrounding a tooth; peridental.

periosteo-. A combining form for *periosteum,* denoting *periosteal* and.

per′i·os′te·um (pĕr′ĭ·ŏs′tē·ŭm), *n.; pl.* -TEA (-á). [NL., fr. Gr. *peri-osteos* round the bones, fr. *peri* around + *osteon* bone.] *Anat.* The membrane of connective tissue which closely invests all bones except at the articular surfaces. — **per′i·os′te·al** (-ăl), *adj.*

per′i·os·ti′tis (pĕr′ĭ·ŏs·tī′tĭs), *n.* [NL., fr. *periosteum* + *-itis.*] Inflammation of the periosteum. — **per′i·os·tit′ic** (-tĭt′ĭk), *adj.*

per′i·o′tic (-ō′tĭk; -ŏt′ĭk), *adj.* [*peri-* + Gr. *ous, ōtos,* the ear.] *Zool.* Around the ear; designating, pertaining to, or composed of the bony elements which surround the internal ear and form or help to form its capsule.

per′i·pa·tet′ic (-pá·tĕt′ĭk), *adj.* [Through F. & L., fr. Gr. *peripatēti-kos,* fr. *peripatein* to walk about, fr. *peri-* + *patein* to walk.] **1.** [*cap.*] Of or pertaining to the philosophy or the followers of Aristotle (**Peripatetics**). **2.** Performed or performing while moving about; as, a *peripatetic* preacher.

pe·riph′er·al (pĕ·rĭf′ĕr·ăl), *adj.* Of, pert. to, or constituting a periphery; hence, *Anat.,* external; away from the central nervous system; as, the *peripheral* termination of a nerve (see NERVOUS SYSTEM). — **pe·riph′er·al·ly,** *adv.*

pe·riph′er·y (-ĭ), *n.; pl.* -IES (-ĭz). [Through F. & LL., fr. Gr. *pc-riphereia,* fr. *peri* around + *pherein* to bear, carry.] **1.** The line bounding a rounded surface; more generally, the surface of any body. **2.** *Anat.* The region in which nerves terminate. **3.** *Geom.* The circumference or perimeter of a circle, ellipse, or other closed curvilinear figure. — **Syn.** See CIRCUMFERENCE.

per′i·phrase (pĕr′ĭ·frāz), *n.* Periphrasis.

pe·riph′ra·sis (pĕ·rĭf′rá·sĭs), *n.; pl.* -RASES (-sēz). [L., fr. Gr. *peri-phrasis,* fr. *peri-* + *phrazein* to speak.] *Rhet.* Circumlocution. Cf. TAUTOLOGY.

per′i·phras′tic (pĕr′ĭ·frăs′tĭk), *adj.* **1.** Characterized by periphrasis. **2.** *Gram.* Formed by the use of particles or auxiliaries instead of by inflection; as, *periphrastic* conjugation (he *does go* for he *goes*). — **per′i·phras′ti·cal·ly** (-tĭ·kăl·ĭ), *adv.*

pe·rip′ter·y (pĕ·rĭp′tĕr·ĭ), *n.; pl.* -IES (-ĭz). [Gr. *peripteros* flying round about, fr. *peri* around + *pteron* feather.] The region surrounding a moving body, as the wing of a bird or a gliding airplane, within which cyclic or vortical motions of the air occur.

pe·rique′ (pĕ·rēk′), *n.* [Louisiana F.] A strong-flavored tobacco, raised in Louisiana.

per′i·sarc (pĕr′ĭ·särk), *n.* [*peri-* + Gr. *sarx, sarkos,* flesh.] The outer, usually horny, integument of a hydroid.

per′i·scope (-skōp), *n.* [*peri-* + *-scope.*] **1.** A periscopic lens. **2.** An optical instrument used on submarines when submerged to a small depth, in battlefield trenches, etc., to enable an observer to obtain a field of view that otherwise would be impossible to get.

per′i·scop′ic (-skŏp′ĭk), *adj.* Also **per′i·scop′i·cal** (-ĭ·kăl). Viewing all around, or on all sides; — applied specif. to certain compound lenses for the microscope, camera, etc.

per′ish (pĕr′ĭsh), *v. i.* [OF. *perir,* fr. L. *perire* to go through, come to nothing, perish, fr. *per-* + *ire* to go.] To be destroyed or ruined; to pass away; to die.

per′ish·a·ble (-á·b'l), *adj.* Liable to perish; subject to destruction or deterioration; as, *perishable* goods. — *n.* Something subject to death, deterioration, etc.; esp., *pl.,* perishable goods. — **per′ish·a·bil′i·ty** (-bĭl′ĭ·tĭ), *n.* — **per′ish·a·ble·ness,** *n.*

pe·ris′so·dac′tyl, pe·ris′so·dac′tyle (pĕ·rĭs′ō·dăk′tĭl), *adj.* [Gr. *perissos* odd (fr. *peri* over) + *daktylos* finger.] Having toes in odd numbers, or unevenly disposed in relation to the axis of the foot, as the tapir, horse, etc. — *n.* A perissodactyl hoofed mammal (order

PERIODIC TABLE

		Group 0	Group I	Group II	Group III	Group IV	Group V	Group VI	Group VII	Group VIII	
Highest oxide (E = element)			E_2O	EO	E_2O_3	EO_2	E_2O_5	EO_3	E_2O_7	EO_4	
Highest hydride				EH	EH_2	EH_3	EH_4	EH_3	EH_2	EH	
Family →		A	B	A	B	A	B	A	B	A	B	A	B	A	B	A	B
Period	Series										
1	1		**1** H 1.0080								
2	2	**2** He 4	**3** Li 7	**4** Be 9	**5** B 11	**6** C 12	**7** N 14	**8** O 16	**9** F 19		
3	3	**10** Ne 20	**11** Na 23	**12** Mg 24	**13** Al 27	**14** Si 28	**15** P 31	**16** S 32	**17** Cl 35.5		
4	4	**18** A 40	**19** K 39	**20** Ca 40	**21** Sc 45	**22** Ti 48	**23** V 51	**24** Cr 52	**25** Mn 55	**26** Fe 55.8 **27** Co 58.9 **28** Ni 58.7	
	5		**29** Cu 64	**30** Zn 65	**31** Ga 70	**32** Ge 73	**33** As 75	**34** Se 79	**35** Br 80		
5	6	**36** Kr 84	**37** Rb 85	**38** Sr 88	**39** Y 89	**40** Zr 91	**41** Nb 93	**42** Mo 96	**43** Tc	**44** Ru 102 **45** Rh 103 **46** Pd 107	
	7		**47** Ag 108	**48** Cd 112	**49** In 115	**50** Sn 119	**51** Sb 122	**52** Te 128	**53** I 127		
6	8	**54** Xe 131	**55** Cs 133	**56** Ba 137	**57 La 58–71** Rare-earth Metals *	**72** Hf 179	**73** Ta 181	**74** W 184	**75** Re 186	**76** Os 190 **77** Ir 193 **78** Pt 195	
	9		**79** Au 197	**80** Hg 201	**81** Tl 204	**82** Pb 207	**83** Bi 209	**84** Po 210	**85** At		
7	10	**86** Rn 222	**87** Fr	**88** Ra 226	**89** Ac 227	**90** Th 232	**91** Pa 231	**92** U 238 †			

* 57 La 139, 58 Ce 140, 59 Pr 141, 60 Nd 144, 61 Pm, 62 Sm 150, 63 Eu 152, 64 Gd 157, 65 Tb 159, 66 Dy 162, 67 Ho 165, 68 Er 167, 69 Tm 169, 70 Yb 173, 71 Lu 175.
† Transuranian elements: 93 Np, 94 Pu, 95 Am, 96 Cm, 97 Bk, 98 Cf

Perissodactyla). Cf. ARTIODACTYL. — **pe·ris′so·dac′ty·lous** (pē·rĭs′-ō·dăk′tĭ·lŭs), *adj.*

per′i·stal′sis (pĕr′ĭ·stăl′sĭs), *n.; pl.* -SES (-sēz). [NL.] *Physiol.* Peristaltic contraction or action.

per′i·stal′tic (-tĭk), *adj.* [Gr. *peristaltikos* clasping and compressing, fr. *peristellein* to surround, fr. *peri* round + *stellein* to place.] *Physiol.* Designating, or pertaining to, the peculiar wormlike wave motion of the intestines and other hollow muscular structures, produced by the successive contraction of the muscular fibers of their walls, forcing their contents onward.

per′i·stome (pĕr′ĭ·stōm), *n.* [*peri-* + Gr. *stoma* mouth.] **1.** Also **pe·ris′to·ma** (pē·rĭs′tō·mȧ). *Bot.* In mosses, the fringe of teeth surrounding the orifice of the capsule. **2.** *Zool.* The region around the mouth in various invertebrates.

per′i·style (-stīl), *n.* [L. *peristylum*, fr. Gr. *peristylon, peristylos*, fr. *peri* about + *stylos* a column.] *Arch.* **a** A range of columns with their entablature, etc.; specif., a complete system of roof-supporting columns on all sides of a court or of a building. **b** By extension, the space so enclosed. — **per′i·sty′lar** (-stī′lẽr), *adj.*

per′i·the′ci·um (-thē′shĭ·ŭm; -sĭ·ŭm), *n.; pl.* -CIA (-ȧ). [NL., fr. *peri-* + Gr. *thēkē* box.] *Bot.* In certain fungi, a spherical or flask-shaped hollow structure, which contains the asci and usually opens by a terminal pore.

per′i·to·ne′o- (pĕr′ĭ·tō·nē′ō-), **per′i·to′ne-**. A combining form for *peritoneum.*

per′i·to·ne′um, per′i·to·nae′um (pĕr′ĭ·tō·nē′ŭm), *n.; pl.* -NEA, -NAEA (-ȧ). [LL., fr. Gr. *peritonaion*, fr. *peritonos* stretched round or over. See PERI-; TONE.] *Anat. & Zool.* In vertebrates, the smooth transparent serous membrane that lines the cavity containing the digestive organs and other viscera and also encloses these organs. — **per′i·to·ne′al, per′i·to·nae′al** (-ăl), *adj.*

per′i·to·ni′tis (-nī′tĭs), *n.* [NL., fr. *peritoneum* + *-itis.*] *Med.* Inflammation of the peritoneum.

per′i·wig (pĕr′ĭ·wĭg), *n.* [Formerly *perewyke, perwyke*, corrupt. fr. F. *perruque.* See PERUKE.] A wig; esp., one, often of white or powdered hair, dressed in the pompadour style fashionable in the 18th century.

per′i·win′kle (pĕr′ĭ·wĭng′k'l), *n.* [Prob. fr. AS. *pinewincle* (a doubtful spelling) a shellfish.] **a** Any of a genus (*Litorina*) of small marine snails; also, the shell of such a snail. **b** Any of various other small marine univalve shells, as certain American species of *Thais.* **c** *Chiefly U. S.* A winkle (sense **b**).

per′i·win′kle, *n.* [From AS. *pervince* (fr. L.), and fr. ONF. *pervenke* (OF. & F. *pervenche*), fr. L. *pervinca.*] **a** A trailing evergreen herb (*Vinca minor*) with solitary blue or white flowers; — in the U. S. commonly called *myrtle.* **b** A related herb (*Vinca major*), often called ***large periwinkle.*** **c** A related tropical woody plant (*Vinca rosea*) with large white or pinkish-purple flowers, called specif. ***red,*** *or* ***Cape,*** *or* ***Madagascar periwinkle.***

per′jure (pûr′jẽr), *v. t.* [OF. *parjurer*, fr. L. *perjurare*, fr. *per* through, over + *jurare* to swear.] To make a perjurer of (oneself), esp. by telling what is false when sworn to tell the truth; also, in passive, to be involved in, or proven guilty of, perjury. — **per′jur·er** (-jẽr·ẽr), *n.*

per′ju·ry (pûr′jẽr·ĭ), *n.; pl.* -RIES (-ĭz). [OF. *parjurie*, fr. L. *perjurium.*] False swearing; voluntary violation of an oath, either by swearing to what is untrue or by omission to do what has been promised under oath.

perk (pûrk), *v. i.* [ME. *perken.*] **1.** To lift up or stretch oneself or one's body or head, esp. in order to see or be seen; also, to smarten one's appearance; to prink. **2.** To be or become lively or animated. — *v. t.* **1.** To lift or thrust quickly, boldly, or the like; as, to *perk* the ears. **2.** To make (esp. oneself) trim or spruce in appearance; — often with *up* or *out.* — *adj.* Proud or jaunty in bearing; cocky. — **perk′y,** *adj.*

per′lite (pûr′līt), *n.* [F., fr. *perle* pearl.] *Petrog.* Volcanic glass with a concentric shelly structure. — **per·lit′ic** (pẽr·lĭt′ĭk), *adj.*

per′ma·nence (pûr′mȧ·nĕns), *n.* **1.** The fact or condition of being permanent; continued existence, operation, tenure, etc. **2.** The quality of being permanent, enduring, or fixed.

per′ma·nen·cy (-nĕn·sĭ), *n.; pl.* -CIES (-sĭz). **1.** Permanence (sense 2); duration. **2.** One that is permanent.

per′ma·nent (-nĕnt), *adj.* [F. or L.; F., fr. L. *permanens, -entis*, pres. part. of *permanere* to stay to the end, fr. *per-* + *manere* to remain.] Continuing or enduring in the same state, place, or the like, without marked change; not subject to alteration; lasting; abiding. — **Syn.** See LASTING. — **Ant.** Temporary. — **per′ma·nent·ly,** *adv.*

permanent magnetism. Magnetism which remains after the exciting force has been removed. Cf. HYSTERESIS. — **permanent magnet.**

permanent wave. A long-lasting hair wave produced by a combination of mechanical and chemical means.

per·man′ga·nate (pẽr·măng′gȧ·nāt; pûr-), *n.* *Chem.* A salt of permanganic acid. The permanganates are dark-purple crystalline compounds. See POTASSIUM PERMANGANATE.

per′man·gan′ic (pûr′măn·găn′ĭk), *adj.* [*per-* + *manganic.*] *Chem.* Pert. to or designating an unstable acid, $HMnO_4$, whose aqueous solution is strongly oxidizing.

per′me·a·bil′i·ty (pûr′mē·ȧ·bĭl′ĭ·tĭ), *n.* **1.** Quality or state of being permeable. **2.** *Aeronautics.* The measure of the rate of diffusion of gas through intact balloon fabric, usually expressed in liters per square meter of fabric per 24 hours, under standard conditions. **3.** *Magnetism.* Specific conductivity for magnetic flux. It is usually represented by the Greek letter μ.

per′me·a·ble (pûr′mē·ȧ·b'l), *adj.* [LL. *permeabilis.*] Capable of being permeated; penetrable; — used esp. of substances that allow the passage of fluids; as, wood is *permeable* to oil.

per′me·ance (pûr′mē·ăns), *n.* Permeation; specif., *Magnetism*, the reciprocal of reluctance.

per′me·ant (-ănt), *adj.* Permeating.

per′me·ate (-āt), *v. t. & i.* [L. *permeatus*, past part. of *permeare* to permeate, fr. *per-* + *meare* to go, pass.] **1.** To pass through the pores or interstices of; — esp. of fluids that pass through substances of loose texture; as, water *permeates* sand. **2.** To spread or diffuse itself through; to pervade. — **per′me·a′tion** (-ā′shŭn), *n.*

per′me·a′tive (-ā′tĭv; -ȧ·tĭv), *adj.* Permeating.

‖**per men′sem** (pûr mĕn′sĕm). [L.] By the month; monthly.

Per′mi·an (pûr′mĭ·ăn; 58), *adj.* [From the former province of *Perm*, eastern Russia, where the formation exists.] *Geol.* Designating or pertaining to the last period of the Paleozoic era following the Carboniferous, or the system of rocks formed during this period. It was marked by extensive glaciation in India, South Africa, South America, and Australia. — **Per′mi·an,** *n.*

per mill *or* **per mil.** By or in the thousand. Cf. PER CENT.

per·mil′lage (pẽr·mĭl′ĭj), *n.* Rate or proportion per thousand.

per·mis′si·ble (pẽr·mĭs′ĭ·b'l), *adj.* That may be permitted; allowable. — **per·mis′si·bil′i·ty** (-bĭl′ĭ·tĭ), *n.* — **per·mis′si·bly,** *adv.*

per·mis′sion (pẽr·mĭsh′ŭn), *n.* [L. *permissio.*] Act of permitting; formal consent; authorization; leave.

per·mis′sive (-mĭs′ĭv), *adj.* **1.** Permitting; granting permission. **2.** *Now Rare.* Permitted; tolerated. **3.** Allowable; not prohibited. — **per·mis′sive·ly,** *adv.*

per·mit′ (pẽr·mĭt′), *v. t.;* -MIT′TED; -MIT′TING. [L. *permittere, permissum*, to allow, permit, fr. *per-* + *mittere* to let go, send. See PER-; MISSION.] **1.** To tolerate; to consent to. **2.** To grant (one) license or liberty; to authorize. **3.** *Obs.* To give over; commit. — *v. i.* To allow; to make possible. — **Syn.** See LET. — **Ant.** Prohibit, forbid. — **per·mit′ter,** *n.*

per′mit (pûr′mĭt; pẽr·mĭt′), *n.* Warrant; permission; written license given by one having authority.

per·mut′a·ble (pẽr·mūt′ȧ·b'l), *adj.* Capable of being changed, exchanged, or interchanged.

per′mu·ta′tion (pûr′mū·tā′shŭn), *n.* **1.** A thorough change in character, condition, or the like; transformation. **2.** Any of the total number of changes in position or order possible within a group; hence, a change in grouping; as, the *permutations* of the alphabet. — **Syn.** See CHANGE.

per·mute′ (pẽr·mūt′), *v. t.* [F. *permuter*, fr. L. *permutare, permutatum*, fr. *per-* + *mutare* to change.] To subject to permutation, esp. to change in order or arrangement.

per·ni′cious (pẽr·nĭsh′ŭs), *adj.* [F. *pernicieux*, fr. L. *perniciosus*, fr. *pernicies* destruction, fr. *per-* + *nex, necis*, death.] **1.** Highly injurious or destructive in character; deadly. **2.** Intending or doing evil; wicked. — **per·ni′cious·ly,** *adv.* — **per·ni′cious·ness,** *n.*

Syn. **Pernicious, baneful, noxious, deleterious, detrimental** mean exceedingly harmful. **Pernicious** and **baneful** imply irreparability but the former applies to that which corrupts or undermines, and the latter to that which poisons or destroys; **noxious** implies injury to health of body or mind; **deleterious** implies injury when eaten, drunk, inhaled, or the like; **detrimental** implies obvious harmfulness to something stated. — **Ant.** Innocuous.

pernicious anemia. *Med.* A severe, often fatal, form of anemia, characterized by a progressive decrease in the number of red blood corpuscles, muscular weakness, and disturbances of the gastrointestinal and nervous systems, etc.

per·nick′et·y (pẽr·nĭk′ĕ·tĭ), *adj.* *Colloq.* **a** Finical or fussy. **b** Indicating or requiring great precision. — **per·nick′et·i·ness** (-tĭ·nĕs; -nĭs), *n.*

per′o·ne′al (pĕr′ō·nē′ăl), *adj.* [Gr. *peronē* the fibula.] *Anat.* Of or pertaining to the fibula; near the fibula.

per′o·rate (pĕr′ō·rāt), *v. i.* [See PERORATION.] To speak at length; to harangue; also, to conclude or sum up a speech.

per′o·ra′tion (-rā′shŭn), *n.* [L. *peroratio*, fr. *perorare, -ratum*, to speak from beginning to end, fr. *per-* + *orare* to speak.] The concluding part of a discourse, esp. of an oration; specif., a final summing up of an argument. Cf. EXORDIUM.

per·ox′ide (pẽr·ŏk′sīd; pûr-), *n.* Also **per·ox′id.** *Chem.* **a** An oxide containing a high proportion of oxygen. **b** Specif., hydrogen peroxide. — *v. t.* To bleach (hair) with peroxide.

per′pend (pûr′pĕnd), *n.* [F. *parpaing*, pierre *parpaigne.*] *Masonry.* A large stone reaching through a wall so as to appear on both sides of it, and acting as a binder.

per·pend′ (pẽr·pĕnd′), *v. t. & i.* [L. *perpendere, perpensum*, fr. *per-* + *pendere* to weigh.] *Archaic.* To ponder carefully.

per′pen·dic′u·lar (pûr′pĕn·dĭk′ū·lẽr), *adj.* [From OF., fr. L. *perpendicularis*, fr. *perpendiculum* plumb line, fr. *per-* + *pendere* to hang.] **1.** Exactly upright or vertical; at right angles to the plane of the horizontal; hence, *Geom.*, at right angles to a given line or surface. See ANGLE, *Illust.* **2.** Extremely steep; precipitous. **3.** [*cap.*] *Arch.* Of, pert. to, or in the **Perpendicular style,** the latest variety of English Gothic, in which vertical lines predominate. — **Syn.** See VERTICAL. — *n.* **1.** An appliance or instrument to indicate the vertical line from any point. **2.** A line at right angles to the plane of the horizon, or, *Geom.*, to another line or surface. **3.** Hence, upright position; also, rectitude. **4.** An extremely steep face, as of a cliff or mountain. — **per′pen·dic′u·lar′i·ty** (-lăr′ĭ·tĭ), *n.* — **per′pen·dic′u·lar·ly,** *adv.*

per′pent (pûr′pĕnt). Var. of PERPEND, *n.*

per′pe·trate (pûr′pē·trāt), *v. t.* [L. *perpetratus*, past part. of *perpetrare*, fr. *per-* + *patrare* to perform.] To do or perform; to commit (as an offense). — **per′pe·tra′tor** (-trā′tẽr), *n.*

per′pe·tra′tion (-trā′shŭn), *n.* A doing, esp. of something bad morally, artistically, etc.; also, an offensive action.

per·pet′u·al (pẽr·pĕt′ū·ăl), *adj.* [OF. *perpetuel*, fr. L. *perpetualis*, fr. *perpetuus*, continuing throughout, continuous, fr. *perpes, -etis*, lasting throughout.] **1.** Continuing forever; everlasting; also, continuous or indefinitely long-continued in use, service, action, etc.; permanent; as, a *perpetual* officer (opposed to *dative;* see DATIVE, *adj.*, 2 **b**). **2.** *Bot. & Hort.* Blooming more or less continuously throughout the season; as, a hybrid *perpetual* rose. — **Syn.** See CONTINUAL. — *n. Bot. & Hort.* **a** A perennial. **b** A hybrid perpetual rose. — **per·pet′u·al·ly,** *adv.*

perpetual calendar. A calendar that can be used perpetually or over a wide range of years. One method is as follows: To find the day of the week for any date in the Julian or Gregorian calendars to 2299: (1) Take the last two figures of the year date and add to them one quarter of the number formed by them, ignoring the remainder. (2) For the century: *Gregorian calendar*, if the first two figures are 17 (since 1752), add 4; 2 for 18; 0 for 19; 6 for 20; 4 for 21; 2 for 22; *Julian*, if the century figures (the first figure up to 999, the first two figures from 1000) are divisible by 7, add 0; if not, add the difference between the figures and the next multiple of 7 above it. (3) For the months, add as follows: *Gregorian*, 0 for Apr. or July; 1 for Jan. or Oct.; 2 for May; 3 for Aug.; 4 for Feb., Mar., or Nov.; 5 for June; 6 for Sept. or Dec.; if a leap year, add 0 for Jan. and 3 for Feb.; *Julian*, 0 for Aug.; 1 for Feb., Mar., or Nov.; 2 for June; 3 for Sept. or Dec.; 4 for Apr. or July; 5 for Jan. or Oct.; 6 for May; if a leap year, add 4 for Jan. and 0 for Feb. (4) Add the day of the month. (5) Divide the sum of (1) to (4) by 7 and the remainder will be the day of the week, Sunday being the first day. If there is no remainder, the day will be Saturday. Examples: 1. What day of the week was Feb. 28, 1930? (1) $30 + 7$; + (2) 0; + (3) 4; + (4) $28 = 69$. $69 \div 7 = 9 + 6$.

The sixth day of the week is Friday. 2. What day was Jan. 16, 1600? (1) 00 + 0; + (2) 5; + (3) 4 (leap year); + (4) 16 = 25. 25 ÷ 7 = 3 + 4. The fourth day is Wednesday.

per·pet′u·ance (pẽr·pĕt′ū·ăns), *n.* Perpetuity; perpetuation.

per·pet′u·ate (-āt), *v. t.* [L. *perpetuatus*, past part. of *perpetuare* to perpetuate. See PERPETUAL.] To make perpetual; to give an enduring character or existence to. — **per·pet′u·a′tor** (-ā′tẽr), *n.*

per·pet′u·a′tion (-ā′shŭn), *n.* A making perpetual.

per′pe·tu′i·ty (pûr′pē·tū′ĭ·tĭ), *n.; pl.* -TIES (-tĭz). [L. *perpetuitas*.] 1. Perpetual existence, duration, validity, etc. 2. Something perpetual or perpetually held or maintained. 3. Endless time. 4. *Law.* Quality or condition of an estate limited so that it will not take effect or vest within the period fixed by law; also, the estate itself so limited. 5. *Annuities.* An annuity payable forever.

per·plex′ (pẽr·plĕks′), *v. t.* [OF. *perplex*, *perplexe*, fr. L. *perplexus* involved, confused, fr. *per-* + *plexus*, past part. of *plectere* to plait.] 1. To disturb mentally; to confuse; puzzle. 2. To make complicated or involved, as a problem, situation, etc. — **Syn.** See PUZZLE.

per·plexed′ (-plĕkst′), *adj.* 1. Filled with uncertainty; puzzled. 2. Entangled; involved. — **per·plex′ed·ly** (pẽr·plĕk′sĕd·lĭ; -sĭd·lĭ), *adv.*

per·plex′ing, *adj.* That perplexes. — **per·plex′ing·ly**, *adv.*

per·plex′i·ty (pẽr·plĕk′sĭ·tĭ), *n.; pl.* -ITIES (-tĭz). 1. The state of being perplexed; bewilderment; distracting uncertainty. 2. Something that perplexes or may perplex one. 3. Complication; an involved state of affairs.

per′qui·site (pûr′kwĭ·zĭt), *n.* [L. *perquisitum*, neut. of *perquisitus*, past part. of *perquirere* to ask for diligently, fr. *per-* + *quaerere* to seek.] 1. A gain or profit incidentally made from employment in addition to regular salary or wages, esp. one of a kind expected or promised; also, pay for work; income. 2. A gratuity or tip.

per′ron (pĕr′ŏn; *F.* pĕ′rôɴ′), *n.* [OF., fr. L. *petra* stone.] *Arch.* An out-of-door flight of steps, as in a garden, leading to a terrace or upper story.

‖**per′ru′quier′** (pĕ′rü′kyā′; *E.* pĕ·rōō′kĭ·ẽr), *n.* [F.] A maker of, or dealer in, perukes; wigmaker.

per′ry (pĕr′ĭ), *n.* [OF. *peré*, fr. L. *pirum* pear.] A fermented liquor made from pears.

per′salt′ (pûr′sôlt′), *n.* *Chem.* A salt of a peracid.

perse (pûrs), *adj.* [F. *pers*.] Blue; esp., dark blue.

per se (pûr sē). [L.] By [or of] itself; intrinsically.

per second per second. Per second every second; — said of the rate of acceleration over an indefinite period; as, the rate of acceleration is 60 feet *per second per second;* that is, the velocity changes 60 feet per second every second.

per′se·cute (pûr′sē·kūt), *v. t.* [F. *persécuter*, fr. LL., fr. L. *persequi*, *persecutus*, to pursue, prosecute, fr. *per-* + *sequi* to follow.] 1. To pursue in a manner to injure; specif., to cause to suffer because of belief, esp. religious belief. 2. To afflict, harass, or annoy with urgent attacks, pleas, or the like. — **Syn.** See WRONG. — **per′se·cu′tive** (-kū′tĭv), **per′se·cu′to·ry** (-kū′tō·rĭ; pûr′sē·kū′tō·rĭ), *adj.*

per′se·cu′tion (-kū′shŭn), *n.* 1. The act or practice of persecuting; as, the *persecution* of the early Christians. 2. State or condition of being persecuted or harassed.

per′se·cu′tor (pûr′sē·kū′tẽr), *n.* One who persecutes.

Per′se·id (pûr′sē·ĭd), *n.* [From PERSEUS.] One of a group of shooting stars appearing annually about Aug. 11th.

Per·seph′o·ne (pẽr·sĕf′ō·nē), *n.* [L., fr. Gr. *Persephonē*.] *Gr. Myth.* The daughter of Zeus and Demeter, wife of Hades (Pluto), and queen of the infernal regions. The Romans called her *Proserpina.*

Per′seus (pûr′sūs; pûr′sē·ŭs), *n.* [L., fr. Gr. *Perseus*.] 1. *Gr. Myth.* A son of Zeus and Danaë, who slew the Gorgon Medusa. See ANDROMEDA, 1; MEDUSA, 1. 2. *genitive* -SEI (-sē·ī). A northern constellation between Taurus and Cassiopeia.

per′se·ver′ance (pûr′sē·vẽr′ăns), *n.* 1. The act or quality of persevering; persistence; steadfast pursuit of an undertaking or aim; steadfastness. 2. *Theol.* Continuance in a state of grace until it is succeeded by a state of glory.

per′se·vere′ (-vēr′), *v. i.* [OF. *perseverer*, fr. L. *perseverare*, fr. *perseverus* very strict, fr. *per-* + *severus* strict, severe.] To persist in any enterprise undertaken, in spite of counter influences, opposition, etc.

per′se·ver′ing (pûr′sē·vẽr′ĭng), *adj.* Of or characterized by perseverance; persistent. — **per′se·ver′ing·ly**, *adv.*

Per′sian (pûr′zhăn; -shăn), *n.* 1. One of the people of Persia (modern Iran); specif.: **a** One of the ancient Iranian Caucasians who under Cyrus and his successors became the dominant Asiatic race. **b** A member of one of the races forming the modern Persian (Iranian) nationality. 2. The principal language of the Iranian branch of the Indo-European family. It is divided into: ***Old Persian***, the language of ancient Persia, written in cuneiform characters, and closely akin to the language of the Avesta; ***Middle Persian***, including chiefly ***Pahlavi*** (which see) and ***Parsi***, the Iranian dialect of the Parsi religious literature; and ***Modern Persian*** (*or* ***Iranian***) dating from about the 9th century, in which the greatest of Persian literature is written; it contains many Arabic loan words and is written in the Arabic script. See INDO-EUROPEAN LANGUAGES, *Table.* 3. A thin silk fabric, used formerly for linings. 4. *pl.* Persiennes; Persian blinds. — **Per′sian**, *adj.*

Persian blinds. Persiennes.

Persian lamb. 1. The young of certain Asiatic sheep, esp. of Bokhara, which furnish the karakul or astrakhan skins used in furriery. 2. The finest grade of astrakhan. Cf. ASTRAKHAN, BROADTAIL, KARAKUL, KRIMMER.

Persian rug *or* **carpet.** An Oriental rug made in Persia.

per′si·car′y (pûr′sĭ·kĕr′ĭ; -kẽr·ĭ), *n.* [ML. *persicarius* peach tree, fr. L. *persicum* peach.] Any of a genus (*Persicaria*) of plants of the buckwheat family, esp., the common one (*P. mitis*).

per′si·ennes′ (pûr′zĭ·ĕnz′; *F.* pĕr′syĕn′), *n. pl.* [F.] Window blinds having movable slats, similar to Venetian blinds.

per′si·flage (pûr′sĭ·fläzh; pĕr′sĭ·fläzh′; *F.* pĕr′sē′fläzh′), *n.* [F., fr. *persifler* to quiz, fr. L. *per* + F. *siffler* to whistle, fr. L. *sifilare*.] Light raillery. — **Syn.** See BADINAGE.

per·sim′mon (pẽr·sĭm′ŭn), *n.* [Of Algonquian origin.] **a** Any of a genus (*Diospyros*) of trees of the ebony family, with hard fine wood, oblong leaves, small bell-shaped white flowers, and plumlike fruit; esp., an American species (*D. virginiana*) and the ***Japanese persimmon*** (*D. kaki*). **b** The fruit of this tree, sweet and palatable when fully ripe.

per·sist′ (pẽr·sĭst′; -zĭst′), *v. i.* [F. *persister*, fr. L. *persistere*, fr. *per-* + *sistere* to stand or be fixed, fr. *stare* to stand.] 1. To go on resolutely in spite of opposition, importunity, or warning; to persevere. 2. *Obs.* To remain fixed in a (specified) character, position, etc. 3. To be insistent in the repetition of a question, opinion, etc. 4. To continue to exist; to recur constantly. — **Syn.** See CONTINUE.

per·sist′ence (pẽr·sĭs′tĕns; -zĭs′tĕns), *n.* Also **per·sist′en·cy** (-tĕn·sĭ). 1. The action or fact of persisting. 2. The quality of being persistent; doggedness; perseverance.

per·sist′ent (-tĕnt), *adj.* 1. Persisting; inclined to persist; tenacious; also, enduring; constantly recurring. 2. Existing continuously; enduring; as: **a** *Bot.* Remaining long attached; as, *persistent* leaves, which cling all winter even though withered, as those of certain oaks; — opposed to *deciduous, caducous, fugacious.* **b** *Zool.* Continuing without change in function or structure; as, *persistent* teeth or gills; — opposed to *deciduous.* — **per·sist′ent·ly**, *adv.*

per′son (pûr′s′n), *n.* [OF. *persone* (F. *personne*), fr. L. *persona* a mask (used by actors), a personage, part, person.] 1. *Archaic.* A character or part, as in a play. 2. A human being; a particular individual. 3. **a** One spoken of indefinitely; as, any *person* present. **b** A human being as distinguished from things or animals. **c** One spoken of slightingly. 4. **a** The bodily form of a human being; also, outward appearance; as, of comely *person.* **b** Bodily presence; — in the phrase *in person.* 5. The real self of a human being; individual personality. 6. *Gram.* Any one of the three relations (that of the speaker, that of one spoken to, and that of another person or thing spoken of, called respectively the ***first, second,*** and ***third person***) underlying discourse, distinguished by certain pronouns and, in many languages, by inflected forms of the verb (*I go, thou goest, he goes*). 7. *Law.* A human being (natural person), or a body of persons, or, in a wider sense, an aggregate of property (***artificial, conventional, or juristic person***), that is recognized by law as the subject of rights and duties. 8. *Theol.* [*sometimes cap.*] Among Trinitarians, one of the three modes of being in the Godhead (the Father, the Son, and the Holy Ghost); a hypostasis. — ***in person.*** By oneself; with bodily presence.

per·so′na (pẽr·sō′nȧ), *n.; pl.* PERSONAE (-nē). [L.] Person; specif., *pl.*, the characters of a novel, play, etc.; as, dramatis *personae.*

per′son·a·ble (pûr′sŭn·ȧ·b′l), *adj.* Well-favored, esp. in body, or person; comely; shapely; attractive.

per′son·age (-ĭj), *n.* [OF. (F. *personnage*).] 1. *Now Humorous.* Physical form or bearing. 2. A person of rank or distinction; an eminent man or woman. 3. A dramatic, fictional, or historical character; also, an impersonation. 4. A person; a character; as, a very singular *personage.*

‖**per·so′na gra′ta** (pẽr·sō′nȧ grā′tȧ). [L.] An acceptable person. Cf. PERSONA NON GRATA.

per′son·al (pûr′sŭn·ăl), *adj.* [OF. *personel*, *personal*, fr. LL. *personalis*.] 1. Of or pertaining to a particular person; private; not public or general. 2. Done in person, without the intervention of another; direct from one person to another. 3. Pertaining to the person, or body; as, *personal* charms. 4. Relating to an individual, his character, conduct, motives, or private affairs, esp. in an offensive manner; as, *personal* remarks. 5. Rational and self-conscious; as, a *personal* God. 6. *Law.* Designating, or of or pertaining to, personal property; as, *personal* estate. See PERSONAL PROPERTY. 7. *Gram.* Denoting person; as, a *personal* suffix, a *personal* pronoun (see PRONOUN). Abbr. *pers.* — *n.* *U. S.* A short newspaper paragraph relating to a person or persons or to personal matters.

personal effects. Effects of a personal character; esp., as used in wills, tariff laws, etc., such property especially appertaining to one's person.

personal equation. See EQUATION, 2.

per′son·al′i·ty (pûr′sŭ·năl′ĭ·tĭ), *n.; pl.* -TIES (-tĭz). 1. Quality or state of being personal, or of being a person; personal existence or identity. 2. **a** Quality of referring directly to an individual, esp. disparagingly. **b** A disparaging or offensive remark or observation; as, to indulge in *personalities.* 3. Distinctive personal character; individuality. 4. Distinction or excellence of personal and social traits; magnetic personal quality. 5. A personal being; a person. 6. *Psychol.* **a** The totality of an individual's characteristics. **b** An integrated group of emotional trends, behavior tendencies, etc. ***alternating, double, or dual personality*** is a condition of mental dissociation in which one individual shows in alternation two different characters (*personalities*). In ***multiple personality*** there are three or more such states. — **Syn.** See DISPOSITION.

per′son·al·ize (pûr′sŭn·ăl·īz), *v. t.* 1. To personify; also, to invest or endow with personality, or individuality. 2. To make personal; to take, as a remark, personally.

per′son·al·ly, *adv.* In a personal manner or relation.

personal property. *Law.* Estate or property that is not real, consisting of things temporary or movable; chattels.

per′son·al·ty (pûr′sŭn·ăl·tĭ), *n.; pl.* -TIES (-tĭz). *Law.* Personal property.

‖**per·so′na non gra′ta** (pẽr·sō′nȧ nŏn grā′tȧ). [L.] A person who is not acceptable. Cf. PERSONA GRATA.

per′son·ate (pûr′sŭn·āt), *adj.* [L. *personatus* masked.] *Bot.* Of a bilabiate corolla, having the throat nearly closed by a projection of the base of the lower lip.

per′son·ate (-āt), *v. t.* [L. *personatus* masked, in an assumed character, fictitious, fr. *persona* mask. See PERSON.] 1. To impersonate or represent as an actor, pretender, or masquerader; to pretend or represent oneself to be. 2. In art, poetry, etc., to invest with personal characteristics. 3. *Law.* To assume without authority some character or capacity when done with fraudulent intent; as, to *personate* an officer of the law. — **per′son·a′tive** (-ā′tĭv), *adj.* — **per′son·a′tor** (-ā′tẽr), *n.*

per′son·a′tion (pûr′sŭ·nā′shŭn), *n.* Impersonation.

per·son′i·fi·ca′tion (pẽr·sŏn′ĭ·fĭ·kā′shŭn), *n.* Act of personifying or that which personifies; as: **a** Attribution of personal form, character, etc.; esp., *Rhet.*, representation of an inanimate object or abstract idea as endowed with personal attributes (the floods clap their hands). **b** A divinity or imaginary being thought of as representing a thing or abstraction; as, Aeolus is the *personification* of wind. **c** Embodiment; incarnation; as, the *personification* of pride.

per·son′i·fy (pẽr·sŏn′ĭ·fī), *v. t.; -*FIED (-fīd); -FY′ING. [F. *personnifier.* See PERSON; -FY.] 1. To conceive of or represent as a person; as, to *personify* nature. 2. To be the personification of; to incarnate; as, he *personifies* the law. — **per·son′i·fi′er** (-fī′ẽr), *n.*

per′son·nel′ (pûr′sŏ·nĕl′), *n.* [F.] The body of persons employed in some service, esp. a public service; — distinguished from *matériel.* — *adj.* Of, pertaining to, or having charge of personnel.

per·spec′tive (pẽr·spĕk′tĭv), *n.* [ML. *perspectiva* (sc. *ars*). See PERSPECTIVE, *adj.*] **1.** *Obs.* An optical glass, as a telescope. **2.** The art or science of representing, on a plane or curved surface, natural objects as they appear to the eye. The ***aerial perspective*** of painters is the expression of space by the gradations of color, distinctness, etc. ***linear perspective*** is perspective by which a true picture is produced upon a surface anywhere in space from the actual dimensions of the object, as given in a suitably chosen orthographic projection. **3.** The aspect of an object of thought from a particular standpoint; as, historical *perspective*. **4. a** A visible scene, esp. one giving a distinctive impression of distance; a vista; hence, a mental prospect. **b** A picture in linear perspective. **5.** The appearance to the eye of objects in respect to their relative distance and positions.
— *adj.* [LL. *perspectivus*, fr. *perspicere, perspectum*, to look through, fr. *per-* + *specere* to look.] **1.** *Obs.* Of an optical glass, aiding the vision. **2.** Of or pert. to perspective, esp. as an art; executed in perspective; as, *perspective* drawing. — **per·spec′tive·ly**, *adv.*

per′spi·ca′cious (pûr′spĭ·kā′shŭs), *adj.* [L. *perspicax, -acis*, fr. *perspicere* to look through.] **1.** *Now Rare.* Clear-sighted. **2.** Of acute mental vision or discernment. — **Syn.** See SHREWD. — **per′spi·ca′cious·ly**, *adv.*

per′spi·cac′i·ty (-kăs′ĭ·tĭ), *n.* Quality or state of being perspicacious; acuteness of sight or discernment.

per′spi·cu′i·ty (-kū′ĭ·tĭ), *n.* Quality of being clear to the understanding; lucidity in expression or development of ideas.

per·spic′u·ous (pẽr·spĭk′ū·ŭs), *adj.* [L. *perspicuus*, fr. *perspicere* to look through. See PERSPECTIVE.] Plain to the understanding; not obscure or ambiguous. — **Syn.** See CLEAR. — **per·spic′u·ous·ly**, *adv.* — **per·spic′u·ous·ness**, *n.*

per′spi·ra′tion (pûr′spĭ·rā′shŭn), *n.* **1.** Act of perspiring. **2.** The saline fluid secreted by the sweat glands; sweat. See TRANSPIRATION.

per·spir′a·to′ry (pẽr·spīr′*ȧ*·tō′rĭ *or, esp. Brit.*, -tẽr·ĭ), *adj.* Of, pertaining to, or inducing perspiration.

per·spire′ (pẽr·spīr′), *v. i. & t.* [L. *perspirare* to breathe everywhere, fr. *per* through + *spirare* to breathe.] To excrete (matter, esp. fluids) through the pores of the skin; to sweat.

per·suade′ (pẽr·swād′), *v. t.* [F. *persuader*, fr. L. *persuadere, -suasum*, fr. *per-* + *suadere* to advise, persuade.] **1.** To induce (one) to believe or do something; to argue into an opinion or procedure. **2.** To plead with; urge. — **Syn.** See INDUCE. — **per·suad′a·ble** (-swād′*ȧ*·b′l), *adj.* — **per·suad′er**, *n.*

per·sua′si·ble (-swā′sĭ·b′l; -zĭ·b′l), *adj.* Capable of being persuaded.

per·sua′sion (-swā′zhŭn), *n.* [F., fr. L. *persuasio*.] **1.** Act of persuading; act of influencing the mind by arguments and reasons. **2.** Power or quality of persuading; persuasiveness. **3.** State of being persuaded; induced opinion or conviction. **4.** A creed or belief, esp. religious; as, men of the same *persuasion;* also, a sect or party adhering to a certain creed; as, all *persuasions* are agreed. **5.** *Jocular.* Kind; sort; as, the male *persuasion.* — **Syn.** See OPINION.

per·sua′sive (-sĭv), *adj.* Tending to persuade. **— *n.*** That which persuades. — **per·sua′sive·ly**, *adv.* — **per·sua′sive·ness**, *n.*

pert (pûrt), *adj.* [An aphetic form of ME. & OF. *apert* open, known, true, free.] **1.** *Obs.* Expert; skillful; hence, keen; clever. **2.** Saucily free in speech or actions; bold. **3.** Lively; sprightly; — chiefly in dialect form *peart.* — **pert′ly**, *adv.* — **pert′ness**, *n.*

per·tain′ (pẽr·tān′), *v. i.* [OF. *partenir*, fr. L. *pertinere* to reach, pertain, fr. *per-* + *tenere* to hold, keep.] **1.** To belong or be attached as a part or accessory, to belong as a property, function, or proper concern; to appertain; as, duties that *pertain* to motherhood. Often with extended signification in the phrase **per·tain′ing to**, belonging to in any attendant relationship; characteristic of; peculiar to; connected with; relating to. **2.** To have reference; as, the letter does not *pertain* to politics.

per′ti·na′cious (pûr′tĭ·nā′shŭs), *adj.* [L. *pertinax, -acis*, fr. *per-* + *tenax* tenacious.] **1.** Adhering resolutely to an opinion, purpose, or design; often, perversely persistent; obstinate. **2.** Unyielding; tenacious; persistent; as, a *pertinacious* fever. — **Syn.** See OBSTINATE. — **per′ti·na′cious·ly**, *adv.* — **per′ti·na′cious·ness**, *n.*

per′ti·nac′i·ty (-năs′ĭ·tĭ), *n.* Quality or state of being pertinacious; obstinacy; persistency.

per′ti·nence (pûr′tĭ·nĕns), *n.* Also **per′ti·nen·cy** (-nĕn·sĭ). Quality or fact of being pertinent; relevancy.

per′ti·nent (-nĕnt), *adj.* [F., fr. L. *pertinens, -entis*, pres. part. of *pertinere.* See PERTAIN.] Related to the matter in hand; relevant. — **Syn.** See RELEVANT. — **per′ti·nent·ly**, *adv.*

per·turb′ (pẽr·tûrb′), *v. t.* [OF. *pertourber, perturber*, fr. L. *perturbare, -batum*, fr. *per-* + *turbare* to disturb.] To disturb greatly; to trouble profoundly; to agitate. — **Syn.** See DISCOMPOSE. — **per·turb′a·ble**, *adj.*

per′tur·ba′tion (pûr′tẽr·bā′shŭn), *n.* **1.** A perturbing, or state of being perturbed. **2.** Something perturbing or disquieting. **3.** *Astron.* A disturbance of the regular elliptic or other motion of a celestial body, produced by some force additional to that which causes its regular motion.

per·tus′sis (pẽr·tŭs′ĭs), *n.* [NL., fr. L. *per* (see PER-, 1 **c**) + *tussis* cough.] *Med.* Whooping cough. — **per·tus′sal** (-*ă*l), *adj.*

pe·ruke′ (pĕ·ro͞ok′), *n.* [F. *perruque*, fr. Pr. *perucat* with dressed hair.] A wig; periwig.

pe·rus′al (pē·ro͞oz′*ă*l; -′l), *n.* A perusing; a careful reading.

pe·ruse′ (pē·ro͞oz′), *v. t.* [*per-* + *use.*] **1.** *Now Rare.* To go through (a series), dealing with each unit; to inspect in detail. **2.** To read carefully or critically; loosely, to read. — **pe·rus′a·ble** (-ro͞oz′*ȧ*·b′l), *adj.* — **pe·rus′er**, *n.*

Pe·ru′vi·an bark (pē·ro͞o′vĭ·*ă*n; pĕ-). Cinchona.

per·vade′ (pẽr·vād′), *v. t.* [L. *pervadere, -vasum*, fr. *per-* + *vadere* to go, walk.] To pass or spread through or as through the pores or tissues of; permeate; hence, to be diffused throughout. — **per·va′sion** (-vā′zhŭn), *n.* — **per·va′sive** (-sĭv), *adj.* — **per·va′sive·ly**, *adv.* — **per·va′sive·ness**, *n.*

per·verse′ (pẽr·vûrs′), *adj.* [OF. *pervers*, fr. L. *perversus* turned the wrong way, past part. of *pervertere.* See PERVERT.] **1.** Deviating from the right, true, correct, etc.; erring. **2.** Obstinate in the wrong; willful. **3.** Petulant; cranky. — **Syn.** See CONTRARY. — **per·verse′ly**, *adv.* — **per·verse′ness**, *n.*

per·ver′sion (pẽr·vûr′zhŭn; -shŭn), *n.* **1.** Act of perverting, or process of being perverted; diversion to a wrong end or use; also, a perverted or corrupted form of something. **2.** *Psychopathol.* A maladjustment of the sexual life, such that satisfaction is sought in aberrant ways.

per·ver′si·ty (-sĭ·tĭ), *n.; pl.* -TIES (-tĭz). Quality, state, or an instance of being perverse.

per·ver′sive (-sĭv), *adj.* Tending to pervert.

per·vert′ (pẽr·vûrt′), *v. t.* [OF. *pervertir*, fr. L. *pervertere, -versum*, fr. *per-* + *vertere* to turn.] **1.** To turn aside; specif.: **a** To cause deviation from the right, true, or regular course in, of, or to; to derange. **b** To misinterpret or misapply. **2.** To lead astray; to corrupt. — **Syn.** See DEBASE. — **per·vert′er**, *n.* — **per·vert′i·ble**, *adj.*

per′vert (pûr′vûrt), *n.* One perverted; specif.: **a** One who has turned to error, esp. in religion. **b** *Psychol.* One who shows some form of sexual perversion.

per·vert′ed (pẽr·vûr′tĕd; -tĭd), *adj.* **1.** Turned from a right course; misdirected; as, a *perverted* sense of humor; a *perverted* taste in music. **2.** Willfully wicked; vicious. — **per·vert′ed·ly**, *adv.*

per′vi·ca′cious (pûr′vĭ·kā′shŭs), *adj.* Very obstinate; willful.

per′vi·ous (pûr′vĭ·ŭs), *adj.* [L. *pervius*, fr. *per-* + *via* a way.] **1.** Admitting passage; permeable. **2.** That penetrates, pervades, or permeates. — **per′vi·ous·ness**, *n.*

Pe′sach (pā′säk), **Pe′sah**, *n.* [See PASCH.] See JEWISH HOLIDAYS.

pe·se′ta (pĕ·sā′tä), *n.* [Sp.] A Spanish gold monetary unit containing 100 centimos; also, a silver coin nominally of the same value but actually considerably less. See MONEY, *Tables.*

Pe·shit′ta (pĕ·shēt′tä), **Pe·shi′to** (pĕ·shē′tō), *n.* [Syr. *peshīṭṭo.*] The standard Syriac version of the Bible.

pes′ky (pĕs′kĭ), *adj.;* PES′KI·ER (-kĭ·ẽr); PES′KI·EST. *Colloq., U.S.* Vexatious.

pe′so (pā′sō; *Sp.* -sō), *n.; pl.* -SOS (-sōz; *Sp.* -sōs). [Sp.] *In English often called* **dollar**. **1. a** An obsolete silver coin once used in Spain and Spanish America, equal to eight reals and hence called a *piece of eight.* **b** A current silver coin in Cuba, Mexico, the Philippines; in Chile a nickel-copper coin. **2.** The monetary unit in several Spanish-speaking countries; also, a paper currency note of the same value. See MONEY, *Tables.*

pes′sa·ry (pĕs′*ȧ*·rĭ), *n.; pl.* -RIES (-rĭz). [ML. *pessarium*, fr. L. *pessum, pessus*, fr. Gr. *pessos.*] *Med.* **a** A device to be worn in the vagina, as to support the uterus, or remedy a malposition. **b** A vaginal suppository.

pes′si·mism (pĕs′ĭ·mĭz′m), *n.* [L. *pessimus* worst, superl. of *pejor* worse.] Opposed to *optimism.* **1.** *Philos.* **a** The doctrine or opinion that reality is essentially evil. **b** The doctrine that the evils of life overbalance the happiness it affords. **2.** An inclination to put the least favorable construction upon actions and happenings.

pes′si·mist (pĕs′ĭ·mĭst), *n.* One given to pessimism; specif., an adherent of philosophical pessimism; — opposed to *optimist.*

pes′si·mis′tic (-mĭs′tĭk), *adj.* Of, pert. to, or characterized by pessimism; gloomy. — **Syn.** See CYNICAL. — **Ant.** Optimistic. — **pes′si·mis′ti·cal·ly** (-tĭ·k*ă*l·ĭ), *adv.*

pest (pĕst), *n.* [F. *peste*, fr. L. *pestis.*] **1.** A fatal epidemic disease; specif., the plague. **2.** Anything resembling such a disease in destructiveness, noxiousness, etc.; plague; now, esp., one who annoys. **3.** Any destructive insect.

pes′ter (pĕs′tẽr), *v. t.* **1.** *Obs.* To crowd thickly (a place). **2.** To harass with petty vexations; to annoy. — **Syn.** See WORRY.

pest′hole′ (pĕst′hōl′), *n.* [*pest* + *hole.*] A place subject or liable to epidemic disease.

pest′house′ (-hous′), *n.* A house or hospital for those infected with any pestilential disease.

pes′ti·cide (pĕs′tĭ·sīd), *n.* [L. *pestis* pest + *-cide*, 1.] Any substance used to kill rats, insects, bacteria, fungi, protozoans, minute forms of plant life, etc.

pes·tif′er·ous (pĕs·tĭf′ẽr·ŭs), *adj.* [L. *pestiferus, pestifer*, fr. *pestis* pest + *ferre* to bear.] **1.** Pestilential; carrying infection; also, infected with a pestilential disease. **2.** Noxious to peace, morals, or society; spreading vicious or harmful ideas, practices, etc.; also, *Colloq.*, troublesome; plaguy. — **pes·tif′er·ous·ly**, *adv.*

pes′ti·lence (pĕs′tĭ·lĕns), *n.* Any contagious or infectious epidemic disease that is virulent and devastating; specif., the bubonic plague; the pest.

pes′ti·lent (-lĕnt), *adj.* [L. *pestilens, -entis*, fr. *pestis* pest.] **1.** Deadly; poisonous. **2.** *Now Rare.* Infectious; also, pestiferous. **3.** Injuring peace, morals, etc.; pernicious. **4.** Pestering; troublesome. — **pes′ti·lent·ly**, *adv.*

pes′ti·len′tial (-lĕn′sh*ă*l), *adj.* **1.** Of, pertaining to, causing, or likely to cause pestilence. **2.** Morally noxious.

pes′tle (pĕs′′l; -t′l), *n.* [OF. *pestel*, fr. L. *pistillum, pistillus.*] **1.** An implement for pounding or braying substances in a mortar. **2.** Any of various instruments for pounding or stamping, as a stamp in a stamp mill. **— *v. t. & i.;*** PES′TLED (-′ld; -t′ld); PES′TLING (-lĭng; -tlĭng). To pound, pulverize, bray, or mix with or as with a pestle.

pet (pĕt), *n.* [Origin uncert.] **1.** A domesticated animal kept to fondle and play with. **2.** A person specially cherished and indulged; a darling. **— *adj.*** **1.** Especially liked, fondled, humored, etc. **2.** Expressive of fondness, indulgent sympathy, or endearment; as, a *pet* name. **— *v. t.;*** PET′TED; PET′TING. To treat as a pet; to fondle; caress. — **Syn.** See CARESS. **— *v. i.*** To indulge in fondling or, esp., in amorous caresses.

pet, *n.* A fit of peevishness, ill-humor, or annoyance. **— *v. i.*** To be in a pet; to sulk.

pet′al (pĕt′′l), *n.* [NL. *petalum*, fr. Gr. *petalon* a leaf, fr. *petalos* outspread, flat.] *Bot.* One of the leaves of a corolla. See COROLLA; FLOWER, *Illust.;* CARPEL, *Illust.* — **pet′aled, pet′alled** (-′ld), *adj.*

-petal. [NL. *-petus*, fr. L. *petere* to seek.] A combining form meaning *seeking*, as in acro*petal.*

pet′al·if′er·ous (pĕt′*ă*l·ĭf′ẽr·ŭs), *adj.* Bearing petals.

pet′al·ine (pĕt′*ă*l·ĭn; -īn), *adj.* *Bot.* Pertaining to a petal; attached to or resembling a petal.

pet′al·oid (-oid), *adj.* *Bot.* Having the form, appearance, or texture of a petal.

pet′al·ous (-ŭs), *adj.* Having petals; petaled; — usually in combination, as in platy*petalous.*

pe·tard′ (pē·tärd′), *n.* [F. *pétard*, fr. *péter* to explode, break wind, fr. *pet*, n., fr. L. *peditum*, fr. *pedere, peditum.*] **1.** *Mil.* A case containing an explosive, to be detonated against, and break in or down, gates, barricades, etc. **2.** A variety of firecracker. — ***hoist with his own petard.*** Blown up by his own bomb. Cf. HOISE.

pet′a·sos (pĕt′*ȧ*·sŏs), *n.* Also **pet′a·sus** (-sŭs). [L. *petasus*, fr. Gr. *petasos.*] *Antiq.* **a** A broad-brimmed, low-crowned hat. **b** Sometimes, the winged cap of Hermes.

pet cock, *or* **pet′cock′** (pĕt′kŏk′), *n.* *Mach.* A small cock, faucet, or valve, set (1) in a water pipe or pump to let air out, (2) at the end of a steam cylinder, in a radiator, or water jacket, to drain it, (3) at the end of an internal-combustion-engine cylinder to release compression, etc.

pete′man (pēt′măn), *n.* *Slang, U. S.* A cracksman; safeblower.

Pe′ter (pē′tẽr), *n.* [LL. *Petrus,* fr. Gr. *Petros,* fr. *petra* rock, *petros* stone.] **1.** *Bib.* **a** One of the twelve apostles, called also *Simon, Simon Peter,* or *Saint Peter,* a fisherman of Galilee and head of the apostolic band. He is the reputed author of the *First* and *Second Epistles of Peter.* **b** Either of the two Epistles of Peter. See BIBLE. **2.** [*not cap.*] *Naut.* = BLUE PETER.

pe′ter (pē′tẽr), *v. i.* *Colloq.* To become exhausted; to run out; to fail; — used generally with *out.*

Pe′ter Pan′ (păn′). The title and boy hero of a play (1904) by Sir James Barrie. Peter Pan is the boy who never grew up, the immortal spirit of youth.

pe′ter·sham (pē′tẽr·shăm), *n.* [After Lord *Petersham.*] A rough, knotted woolen cloth, or a coat of that material.

Pe′ter's pence (pē′tẽrz). Also **Pe′ter pence** *or, in sing.,* **Pe′ter,** *or* **Pe′ter's, pen′ny.** **1.** A former tax of a penny payable by each householder in England to the papal see. **2.** Since 1860, a voluntary annual contribution made by Roman Catholics to the Holy See.

pet′i·ol′ar (pĕt′ĭ·ōl′ẽr), *adj.* *Bot.* Pertaining to, or proceeding from, a petiole; as, a *petiolar* tendril.

pet′i·o·late (pĕt′ĭ·ō·lāt), *adj.* Also **pet′i·o·lat′ed** (-lāt′ĕd; -ĭd). *Bot. & Zool.* Having a stalk or petiole.

pet′i·ole (pĕt′ĭ·ōl), *n.* [NL. *petiolus,* fr. L. *petiolus* a little foot, fruit stalk.] **1.** *Bot.* The slender stem that supports the blade of a foliage leaf; a leafstalk; — disting. from *lamina.* **2.** *Zool.* A stalk or peduncle, as the slender abdominal segment or segments in certain insects, as wasps and ants.

pet′i·o·lule (pĕt′ĭ·ō·lūl; pĕt′ĭ·ŏl′ūl), *n.* [Dim. of *petiole.*] *Bot.* The petiole of a leaflet or other segment of a compound leaf.

pet′it (pĕt′ĭ; *F.* pē·tē′; *see note below*), *adj.* [F. See PETTY.] *Now Rare exc. Law.* Small; insignificant; — same as PETTY, as in *petit,* or *petty,* larceny (see LARCENY).

☞ The usual pron., at least in the U. S., in current legal phrases is pĕt′ĭ. When the word was in general English use, the final *t* was sounded, the accent being variable.

pe·tite′ (pē·tēt′), *adj.* [F., fem. of *petit.*] Small; little; of a woman or girl, small and trim. — **Syn.** See SMALL.

pe·ti′tion (pē·tĭsh′ŭn), *n.* [OF. *peticion* (F. *pétition*), fr. L. *petitio,* fr. *petere, petitum,* to beg, ask, seek.] **1.** A formal written request, esp. one addressed to a sovereign or political superior for a particular grace or right; also, the document. **2.** Any formal asking or begging; a prayer; entreaty; esp., a solemn request; a prayer to the Supreme Being; also, a single clause in such a prayer. **3.** That which is asked or supplicated. **4.** *Eng. Hist.* The bill in the form of a request by which Parliament formerly presented measures for the king's granting. **5.** *Law.* A written application to a court requesting its action upon some matter therein laid before it. — *v. t.* **1.** To make a prayer or request to; to entreat. **2.** To solicit; to plead for. — *v. i.* To make a petition. — **pe·ti′tion·er** (-ẽr), *n.*

pe·ti′tion·ar′y (-ĕr′ĭ *or, esp. Brit.,* -ẽr·ĭ), *adj.* **1.** Containing or of the nature of a petition. **2.** *Rare.* Supplicating.

‖**pe·ti′ti·o prin·ci′pi·i** (pē·tĭsh′ĭ·ō prĭn·sĭp′ĭ·ī). [L.] *Logic.* Begging of the question; a fallacy in which a premise is assumed to be true without warrant, or in which that which is to be proved is implicitly taken for granted.

pet′it ju′ry (pĕt′ĭ). A jury of twelve persons (**pet′it ju′rors**), impaneled to try, and decide upon the facts at issue in, causes for trial in a court; a trial jury; — disting. from the *grand jury.*

‖**pe·tit′-maî′tre** (pē·tē′mâ′tr′), *n.; pl.* PETITS-MAÎTRES (pē·tē′mâ′tr′). [F.] A dandy; fop; lady's man.

‖**pe·tit′ mal** (pē·tē′ măl′; *formerly* pĕt′ĭt). *Med.* A comparatively mild form of epilepsy, characterized by momentary dizziness or loss of consciousness. Cf. GRAND MAL.

pet′it point (pĕt′ĭ point). = TENT STITCH.

‖**pe·tits′ fours** (pē·tē′ fōōr′). [F.] Little spongecakes or poundcakes, usually ornamentally iced.

‖**pe·tits′ pois** (pwȧ′). [F.] Little peas; green peas.

pe′to (pā′tō), *n.* A tropical marine food fish (genus *Acanthorybium*), esp. a large dark-blue species (*A. petus*) of the West Indies.

pet′rel (pĕt′rĕl), *n.* [Prob. a dim. of the name *Peter;* — in allusion to St. Peter's walking on the sea (*Matt.* xiv. 29).] **1.** Any of numerous sea birds (order Procellariiformes and family Hydrobatidae) usually restricted to the small and medium-sized members of the group. They are long-winged birds, which fly far from land. See STORMY PETREL **a.** **2.** = STORMY PETREL **b.**

Pe′tri, *or* **pe′tri, dish** (pā′trē). [After R. J. *Petri,* Ger. scientist.] A small shallow dish of thin glass, with a loose cover, used for cultures in bacteriology.

pet′ri·fac′tion (pĕt′rĭ·făk′shŭn), *n.* **1.** *Petrog.* The process of petrifying. **2.** State of being petrified. **3.** That which is petrified.

pet′ri·fac′tive (-tĭv), *adj.* Having the quality of converting organic matter into stone; petrifying.

pet′ri·fi·ca′tion (pĕt′rĭ·fĭ·kā′shŭn), *n.* Petrifaction.

pet′ri·fy (pĕt′rĭ·fī), *v. t.;* -FIED (-fīd); -FY′ING. [F. *pétrifier,* fr. L. *petra* rock, stone. See -FY.] **1.** *Petrog.* To convert (organic matter) into stone or stony substance. **2.** To make rigid, like stone. Specif.: **a** To render lifeless, inactive, or the like; to benumb or harden. **b** To stupefy, paralyze, or confound with fear, amazement, awe, etc. — *v. i.* To become stone, or of a stony hardness or rigidity.

Pe′trine (pē′trīn; -trĭn), *adj.* Of, pert. to, or characteristic of the apostle Peter or his teachings and doctrines.

pet′ro- (pĕt′rō-), **petr-.** [Gr. *petra* rock or *petros* stone.] A combining form meaning *stone,* as in *petrology.*

pet′ro·glyph (-glĭf), *n.* [F. *pétroglyphe.* See PETRO-; GLYPH.] A carving upon a rock, esp. a prehistoric one.

pe·trog′ra·phy (pē·trŏg′rȧ·fĭ), *n.* [*petro-* + *-graphy.*] The description and systematic classification of rocks. Cf. PETROLOGY. — **pe·trog′ra·pher** (-fẽr), *n.* — **pet′ro·graph′ic** (pĕt′rō·grăf′ĭk), **pet′ro·graph′i·cal** (-ĭ·kăl), *adj.*

pet′rol (pĕt′rŏl; -rŭl), *n.* [F. *petrole,* fr. NL. *petroleum.*] **1.** *Obs.* Petroleum. **2.** *Brit.* Gasoline.

pet′ro·la′tum (pĕt′rō·lā′tŭm), *n.* [NL.] *Pharm.* A neutral unctuous substance, without taste or odor, derived from petroleum and used in ointments, etc. It is marketed under trade-marks, as *Vaseline,* etc.

pe·tro′le·um (pē·trō′lē·ŭm; 58), *n.* [ML., fr. L. *petra* a rock + *oleum* oil.] An oily, inflammable liquid, almost colorless to black, consisting of a complex mixture of hydrocarbons with small quantities of other materials and existing at many places in the upper strata of the earth. It is prepared for use by fractional distillation into gasoline, naphthas, kerosene, lubricating oils and waxes, coke, fuel oils, asphalts, etc. Cf. COAL OIL.

pe·trol′o·gy (pē·trŏl′ō·jĭ), *n.; pl.* -GIES (-jĭz). [*petro-* + *-logy.*] **1.** The science of rocks in its broad aspects. It treats of their origin, constitution, etc. Cf. PETROGRAPHY. **2.** A book or treatise dealing with this science. — **pet′ro·log′ic** (pĕt′rō·lŏj′ĭk), **pet′ro·log′i·cal** (-ĭ·kăl), *adj.* — **pet′ro·log′i·cal·ly,** *adv.* — **pe·trol′o·gist** (pē·trŏl′ō·jĭst), *n.*

pet′ro·nel (pĕt′rō·nĕl), *n.* *Hist.* A portable firearm of the 15th century, resembling a carbine of large caliber.

pe·tro′sal (pē·trō′săl; -s'l), *adj.* [See PETROUS.] Petrous; hard; stony; specif., *Anat. & Zool.,* pert. to, or in the region of, the petrous portion of the temporal bone or capsule of the internal ear. — *n.* *Zool.* A petrosal bone.

pet′rous (pĕt′rŭs; pē′trŭs), *adj.* [L. *petrosus,* fr. *petra* a stone, rock, fr. Gr. *petra.*] Like stone; hard; stony; rocky. Specif., *Anat.,* designating or pertaining to the exceptionally hard and dense portion of the temporal bone containing the internal auditory organs.

pet′ti·coat (pĕt′ĭ·kōt), *n.* [*petty* + *coat.*] **1.** A skirt worn by women, girls, or young children; esp., now an underskirt. **2.** The garment that betokens womanhood; hence, a woman or girl. **3.** Something suggestive of a woman's skirt, as a valance for a table. **4.** *Elec.* Any of the cups of a petticoat insulator; also, the insulator itself. — *adj.* **a** Womanlike; womanish. **b** Of, pertaining to, exercised by, or wielded by women; as, *petticoat* government.

petticoat insulator. An insulator in the form of superposed inverted cups, for high insulation. See INSULATOR, *Illust.*

pet′ti·fog (pĕt′ĭ·fŏg), *v. i.;* -FOGGED (-fŏgd); -FOG′GING. To do a petty law business; also, to do law business in a petty or tricky way. — **pet′ti·fog′ger** (-fŏg′ẽr), *n.* — **pet′ti·fog′ger·y,** *n.*

pet′ti·fog′ging (-fŏg′ĭng), *adj.* Petty; trivial.

pet′tish (pĕt′ĭsh), *adj.* [From PET peevishness.] Fretful; peevish. — **pet′tish·ly,** *adv.*

pet′ti·toes (pĕt′ĭ·tōz), *n. pl.* **1.** The feet of a pig, often used as food. **2.** Toes or feet, esp. those of a child.

pet′tle (pĕt′'l), *v. t.* *Scot.* To cherish; indulge; pet.

pet′tle. *Scot.* Var. of PADDLE (a spud).

‖**pet′to** (pĕt′tō), *n.; pl.* PETTI (-tē). [It., fr. L. *pectus.*] The breast; — used in the phrase ***in petto*** (which see).

pet′ty (pĕt′ĭ), *adj.;* PET′TI·ER (-ĭ·ẽr); PET′TI·EST. [OF. *petit,* prob. of Celt. origin.] Small in nature; trifling; as, *petty* affairs; mean or ungenerous; as, *petty* jealousy; inferior; subordinate; as, a *petty* prince. — **pet′ti·ly,** *adv.* — **pet′ti·ness,** *n.*

petty cash. *Accounting.* A cash fund kept on hand for the payment of minor items.

petty larceny. See LARCENY.

petty officer. A lesser officer or official; specif., *Nav.,* an enlisted man who roughly corresponds in rank to an army noncommissioned officer.

pet′u·lance (pĕt′ū·lăns), *n.* Also **pet′u·lan·cy** (-lăn·sĭ). Quality or state of being petulant: **a** *Now Rare.* Pertness. **b** Temporary peevishness; capricious ill humor.

pet′u·lant (-lănt), *adj.* [F. *pétulant,* fr. L. *petulans, -antis,* prop., making slight attacks upon, from a lost dim. of *petere* to attack.] **1.** *Now Rare.* Forward; also, saucy; pert. **2.** Capriciously fretful; peevish; querulous. — **pet′u·lant·ly,** *adv.*

pe·tu′ni·a (pē·tū′nĭ·ȧ; 58), *n.* [NL., fr. F. *petun* tobacco, fr. Pg., fr. Tupi *putûma, petûm.*] *Bot.* Any of a genus (*Petunia*) of tropical American herbs of the nightshade family, with funnel-shaped corollas.

pe·tun′tse (pē·tōōn′tsĕ; *Chin.* bĭ·dŭn′dzŭ), *n.* Also **pe·tun′se** (-sĕ), **pe·tun′tze,** etc. [Chin. (Pek.) *pai*^{2} *tun*^{1}*-tzŭ*^{3}, lit., white briquettes.] A partly decomposed granite, esp. as used in China in the manufacture of porcelain.

‖**peu à peu** (pû′ ȧ pû′). [F.] Little by little; by degrees.

‖**peu de chose** (pûd′shōz′). [F.] A very unimportant thing or person; a trifle.

pew (pū), *n.* [OF. *puie* parapet, balcony, fr. L. *podia,* pl. of *podium* an elevated place, a balcony, fr. Gr. *podion,* dim. of *pous, podos,* foot.] **a** A compartment in the auditorium of a church, providing seats for several persons. **b** One of the benches with backs and, sometimes, doors, fixed in rows in modern churches.

pe′wee (pē′wē), *n.* [From its note.] A phoebe or other small olive-green flycatcher, esp. the ***wood pewee*** (*Myiochanes virens*) of eastern North America.

pe′wit (pē′wĭt; pū′ĭt), *n.* [From its cry.] **a** The lapwing. **b** A small black-headed gull (*Larus ridibundus*) of Europe. **c** A pewee.

pew′ter (pū′tẽr), *n.* [OF. *peutre, peautre.*] **1.** Any of various alloys having tin as chief constituent, as one of tin and copper. **2.** Utensils of pewter, as dishes, pots, etc. — **pew′ter,** *adj.*

pew′ter·er (-ẽr), *n.* One who makes pewter utensils.

-pex′y (-pĕk′sĭ). Also **-pex′i·a** (-sĭ·ȧ), **-pex′is** (-sĭs). [NL. *-pexia, -pexis,* fr. Gr. *pēxis* a fixing, fr. *pēgnynai* to fasten.] *Surg.* A combining form denoting *a making fast, fixation of a* (specified) *part.*

pe·yo′tl (pā·yō′t'l; -tā), **pe·yo′te** (pā·yō′tā), *n.* [Sp. *peyote, pejote,* fr. Nahuatl *peyotl,* lit., caterpillar (with reference to the downy center of the button).] **a** A mescal; — applied also to other cacti. **b** A stimulant drug from mescal buttons.

pfen′nig (pfĕn′ĭg), *n.; pl.* -NIGS (-ĭgz), -NIGE (-ĭ·gĕ). [G.] A minor bronze coin and money of account of Germany, worth 1/100 mark. See MONEY, *Tables.*

***p*H.** *Chem.* A symbol denoting the negative logarithm of the concentration of the hydrogen ion in gram atoms per liter, used in expressing both acidity and alkalinity. *p*H values run from 0 to 14, 7 indicating neutrality, numbers less than 7 increasing acidity, and numbers greater than 7 increasing alkalinity. Thus, a *p*H of 6 means a concentration of 10^{-6}, or .000001 and indicates slight acidity.

Phae′dra (fē′drȧ), *n.* *Gr. Myth.* See HIPPOLYTUS.

Pha′ë·thon (fā′ĕ·thŏn), *n.* [L., fr. Gr. *Phaethōn,* fr. *phaethein, phaein,* to shine.] *Class. Myth.* The son of Helios. Permitted for a day to drive the chariot of the sun, he would have set the world on fire, had he not been struck down with a thunderbolt by Zeus.

pha′e·ton (fā′ĕ·t′n; *Brit., in sense* 1, *also* fā′t′n), *n.* [F. *phaéton.*] **1.** A type of light four-wheeled carriage having no sidepieces in front of the seat or (two) seats. **2.** An open automobile (body) with two cross seats.

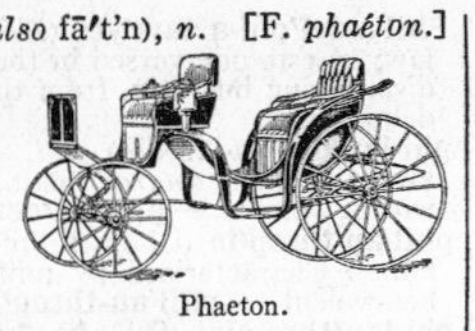
Phaeton.

-phage (-fāj). Also **-phag.** [See -PHAGOUS.] A combining form denoting *one that eats;* specif., *Biol., a cell,* esp. *a phagocyte, that destroys cells,* as in bacterio*phage.*

phag′e·de′na, phag′e·dae′na (făj′ē·dē′nȧ), *n.* [L. *phagedaena,* fr. Gr. *phagedaina,* fr. *phagein* to eat.] *Med.* **a** Rapidly spreading ulceration. **b** Gangrene.

phag′o- (făg′ō-), **phag-.** [Gr. *phagein* to eat.] A combining form used to denote: **a** *Eating; feeding.* **b** *Phagocyte,* as in **pha·gol′y·sis,** destruction of phagocytes.

phag′o·cyte (-sīt), *n.* [*phago-* + *-cyte.*] Any leucocyte active in ingesting and destroying waste and harmful material. See CORPUSCLE, 2. — **phag′o·cyt′ic** (-sĭt′ĭk), *adj.*

phag′o·cyt′ic in′dex. The average number of bacteria ingested by each leucocyte after incubation of a mixture of leucocytes, serum, and bacteria.

phag′o·cy·to′sis (-sī·tō′sĭs), *n.* [NL., fr. *phagocyte* + *-osis.*] The engulfing and, usually, destruction of microorganisms or other foreign bodies by phagocytes.

-phagous. [Gr. *phagein* to eat.] A combining form used to denote *eating, feeding on, consuming.*

-phagy. Also **-pha′gi·a** (-fā′jĭ·ȧ). [NL. *-phagia,* fr. Gr. *phagein* to eat.] A combining form denoting *eating of a* (specified) *type* or *substance.*

phal′ange (făl′ănj; fā′lănj; fȧ·lănj′), *n.* [F.] *Anat.* A phalanx.

pha·lan′ge·al (fȧ·lăn′jē·ăl), *adj.* Also **pha·lan′gal** (-lăng′găl). Of or pertaining to a phalanx or the phalanges.

pha·lan′ger (-jẽr), *n.* [NL., fr. Gr. *phalanx* bone of the finger or toe; — from the form of the phalanges.] Any of numerous marsupials (family Phalangeridae) of the Australian region, ranging in size from that of a mouse to that of a cat. The ***flying phalangers*** (esp. of the genera *Petaurus, Petauroides,* and *Acrobates*) have a parachutelike membrane like that of the flying squirrels. The smallest form (*A. pygmaeus*) is called ***flying mouse.***

pha·lan′ges (fȧ·lăn′jēz), *n., pl.* of PHALANX.

phal′ang·es (făl′ăn·jĕz; -jĭz; fā′lăn-; fȧ·lăn′-), *n., pl.* of PHALANGE.

phal′an·ster′y (făl′ăn·stĕr′ĭ *or, esp. Brit.,* -stẽr·ĭ), *n.; pl.* -STERIES (-ĭz). [F. *phalanstère,* fr. *phalange* a Fourierist community, lit., phalanx + monas*tère* monastery.] **1.** A Fourierist community; also, its dwelling or buildings. **2.** A group or association of persons, or their dwelling. — **phal′an·ste′ri·an** (-stē̆r′ĭ·ăn), *adj. & n.*

pha′lanx (fā′lăngks; făl′ăngks), *n.; pl.* PHALANXES (-lăngk·sĕz; -sĭz), PHALANGES (fȧ·lăn′jēz) (in scientific senses). [L., fr. Gr. *phalanx.*] **1. a** *Gr. Antiq.* A body of heavy-armed infantry formed in ranks close and deep. **b** Any body of troops in close array. **2.** A massed arrangement of persons, animals, or things; hence, an organized body of persons. **3.** A Fourierist community. **4.** *Anat. & Zool.* In vertebrates, one of the digital bones of the hand or foot.

phal′a·rope (făl′ȧ·rōp), *n.* [F., fr. NL. *phalaropus,* type genus, fr. Gr. *phalaris* coot + *pous* foot.] Any of certain small shore birds (family Phalaropodidae) which resemble sandpipers, but have lobate toes, and are good swimmers.

phal′lic (făl′ĭk), *adj.* Also **phal′li·cal** (-ĭ·kăl). [Gr. *phallikos.*] Of or pertaining to the phallus or phallicism.

phal′li·cism (-ĭ·sĭz′m), *n.* The worship of the phallus, or of the generative principle. — **phal′li·cist** (-sĭst), *n.*

phal′lus (făl′ŭs), *n.; pl.* -LI (-ī). [L., a phallus (in sense 1), fr. Gr. *phallos.*] **1.** A symbol of the male organ of generation, esp. as used in the Dionysiac mysteries. **2.** *Anat.* The penis or clitoris.

-phane (-fān). [Gr. *phainein* to appear.] A combining form denoting *a substance appearing like,* as in hydro*phane.*

phan′er·o·gam′ (făn′ẽr·ō·găm′), *n.* [Gr. *phaneros* visible + *gamos* marriage.] *Bot.* A seed plant or flowering plant; a spermatophyte; — opposed to *cryptogam.* — **phan′er·o·gam′ic** (-găm′ĭk), *adj.* — **phan′er·og′a·mous** (-ŏg′ȧ·mŭs), *adj.*

phan′tasm (făn′tăz′m), *n.* [OF. *fantasme,* fr. L. *phantasma.* See PHANTOM.] **1.** A product of phantasy; as: **a** *Archaic.* Delusive appearance; illusion. **b** A figment of the fancy or disordered mind; a fantasy. **c** A specter. **2.** A mental image of a real object. **3.** A deceptive or illusory appearance (of something); as, to follow *phantasms* of truth.

phan·tas′ma (făn·tăz′mȧ), *n.; pl.* -TASMATA (-mȧ·tȧ). [L.] A phantasm (sense 1).

phan·tas′ma·go′ri·a (-gō′rĭ·ȧ; 70), *n.* [NL., fr. Gr. *phantasma* a phantasm + (prob.) *agora* an assembly.] **1.** An optical effect by which figures on a screen appear to dwindle into the distance, or to rush toward the observer with enormous increase of size. **2.** A shifting succession of things seen, imagined, or evoked in the imagination, as by a fever; a changing medley. — **phan·tas′ma·go′ri·al** (-ăl), *adj.* — **phan·tas′ma·gor′ic** (-gŏr′ĭk), *adj.*

phan·tas′ma·go′ry (făn·tăz′mȧ·gō′rĭ), *n.* A phantasmagoria.

phan·tas′mal (-măl), *adj.* Of, pertaining to, of the nature of, or like a phantasm; spectral; illusive.

phan·tas′mic (-mĭk), *adj.* Phantasmal.

phan′ta·sy (făn′tȧ·sĭ; -zĭ), *n.; pl.* -SIES (-sĭz; -zĭz). [See FANTASY.] **1.** The power of receiving and reproducing external impressions. **2.** Creative imaginative activity or the product of this activity, esp. a fictive creation or an imagined fulfillment of desire.

phan′tom (făn′tŭm), *n.* [OF. *fantosme,* fr. L. *phantasma,* fr. Gr. *phantasma,* fr. *phainein* to show.] **1. a** *Obs.* Mere seeming; illusion. **b** A delusion. **2.** An immaterial semblance, as a specter; a phantasm; apparition. **3. a** One that is something in appearance but not in reality; as, only a *phantom* of a king. **b** A representation of something abstract, ideal, incorporeal, etc.; as, she was a *phantom* of delight. — *adj.* Being, of the nature of, or suggesting a phantom.

-phany. [Gr. *phainein* to show.] A combining form denoting *an appearance,* as in epi*phany.*

Phar′aoh (fâr′ō; fā′rō), *n.* [LL. *Pharao,* fr. Gr. *Pharaō,* fr. Heb. *Par'ōh,* fr. Egypt. *pr-'o* great house.] A title of the sovereigns of ancient Egypt; — used in the Bible as a proper name. — **Phar′a·on′ic** (fâr′ā·ŏn′ĭk), *adj.*

phar′i·sa′i·cal (făr′ĭ·sā′ĭ·kăl), *adj.* Also **phar′i·sa′ic** (-ĭk). Resembling the Pharisees; outwardly but not inwardly religious; hypocritical; self-righteous and censorious of others' manners and morals. — **phar′i·sa′i·cal·ly,** *adv.* — **phar′i·sa′i·cal·ness,** *n.*

Phar′i·sa·ism (făr′ĭ·sā·ĭz′m), *n.* The doctrines, ceremonies, etc., of the Pharisees; hence [*not cap.*], a pharisaical attitude, temper, or spirit.

Phar′i·see (făr′ĭ·sē), *n.* [OF. *pharisé,* fr. LL. *Pharisaeus,* fr. Gr. *Pharisaios,* fr. Aram. *pĕrīshaiyā* separated.] **1.** One of a sect among the ancient Jews, noted for strict observance of rites and ceremonies of the written law and for insistence on the validity of the traditions of the elders. **2.** [*not cap.*] A pharisaical person.

Phar′i·see·ism (-ĭz′m), *n.* Pharisaism.

phar′ma·ceu′tic (fär′mȧ·sū′tĭk), *adj.* Pharmaceutical.

phar′ma·ceu′ti·cal (-tĭ·kăl), *adj.* [LL. *pharmaceuticus,* fr. Gr. *pharmakeutikos,* fr. *pharmakeuein.* See PHARMACY.] Of or pertaining to pharmacy or pharmacists. — **phar′ma·ceu′ti·cal·ly,** *adv.*

phar′ma·ceu′tics (-tĭks), *n.;* see -ICS. The science of preparing, using, or dispensing medicines; pharmacy.

phar′ma·ceu′tist (-tĭst), **phar′ma·cist** (fär′mȧ·sĭst), *n.* One skilled in pharmacy; pharmaceutical chemist. — **Syn.** See DRUGGIST.

phar′ma·co- (fär′mȧ·kō-). [Gr. *pharmakon.*] A combining form meaning drug, medicine, poison, as in *pharmacology.*

phar′ma·co·dy·nam′ics (-dī·năm′ĭks; -dĭ-), *n.;* see -ICS. [*pharmaco-* + *dynamics.*] That branch of pharmacology which deals with the reactions between drugs and living structures; often specif., the experimental study of the action and fate of drugs in the animal organism. — **phar′ma·co·dy·nam′ic** (-ĭk), *adj.*

phar′ma·cog′no·sy (fär′mȧ·kŏg′nō·sĭ), *n.* [*pharmaco-* + Gr. *gnosis* a knowing.] The science of drugs; specif., descriptive pharmacology dealing with the characteristics of crude drugs and simples.

phar′ma·col′o·gy (-kŏl′ō·jĭ), *n.* [*pharmaco-* + *-logy.*] The science of drugs, including materia medica and therapeutics. — **phar′ma·co·log′i·cal** (-kō·lŏj′ĭ·kăl), *adj.* — **phar′ma·col′o·gist** (-kŏl′ō·jĭst), *n.*

phar′ma·co·poe′ia (-kō·pē′ȧ), *n.* [NL., fr. Gr. *pharmakopoiïa* preparation of medicines, fr. *pharmakon* medicine + *poiein* to make.] **1.** A book describing drugs, chemicals, and medicinal preparations, esp. one issued by official authority and recognized as a standard. **2.** A collection or stock of drugs. — **phar′ma·co·poe′ial** (-ăl), *adj.*

phar′ma·cy (fär′mȧ·sĭ), *n.; pl.* -CIES (-sĭz). [OF. *farmacie,* fr. ML., fr. Gr. *pharmakeia,* fr. *pharmakeuein,* to administer medicines, fr. *pharmakon* remedy, drug.] **1.** Art or practice of preparing and preserving drugs, and of compounding and dispensing medicines. **2.** A place where medicines are compounded or dispensed; a drugstore; apothecary's shop. **3.** = PHARMACOPOEIA, 2.

pha′ros (fā′rŏs; fâr′ŏs), *n.* [L., fr. Gr. *pharos,* fr. *Pharos* an island in Alexandria harbor, where Ptolemy Philadelphus built a lighthouse.] A lighthouse or beacon. See LIGHTHOUSE, *Illust.*

pha·ryn′ge·al (fȧ·rĭn′jē·ăl; făr′ĭn·jē′ăl), *adj.* Also **pha·ryn′gal** (fȧ·rĭng′găl). Pertaining to, or in the region of, the pharynx.

phar′yn·gi′tis (făr′ĭn·jī′tĭs), *n.* [NL., fr. *pharyng-* + *-itis.*] *Med.* Inflammation of the pharynx.

pha·ryn′go- (fȧ·rĭng′gō-), **pharyng-.** [Gr. *pharynx, pharyngos.*] A combining form meaning the *pharynx,* as in **phar′yn·gec′to·my, phar′yn·got′o·my** (see -ECTOMY, -TOMY); also, *pharyngeal and,* as in **pha·ryn′go·na′sal.**

phar′yn·gol′o·gy (făr′ĭng·gŏl′ō·jĭ), *n.* [*pharyngo-* + *-logy.*] That branch of medical science treating of the pharynx and its diseases.

pha·ryn′go·scope (fȧ·rĭng′gō·skōp), *n.* [*pharyngo-* + *-scope.*] *Med.* An instrument for inspecting the pharynx. — **phar′yn·gos′co·py** (făr′ĭng·gŏs′kō·pĭ), *n.*

phar′ynx (făr′ĭngks), *n.; pl.* PHARYNGES (fȧ·rĭn′jēz), PHARYNXES (făr′ĭngk·sĕz; -sĭz). [NL., fr. Gr. *pharynx, -yngos.*] *Anat. & Zool.* The part of the alimentary canal between the cavity of the mouth and the esophagus. Cf. LARYNX.

phase (fāz), *n.* [NL. *phasis,* fr. Gr. *phasis,* fr. *phainein* to make to appear.] **1.** *Astron.* A particular appearance or state in a recurring cycle of changes; as, the *phases* of the moon. **2.** A transitory state between changes in appearance, structure, character, etc.; as, to follow the *phases* of a man's career. **3.** Any aspect or side, as of situation or question, with reference to which such a situation, etc., may be considered. **4.** *Biol.* A stage in meiosis or mitosis. **5.** *Physical Chem.* A homogeneous, physically distinct portion of matter in a system which is not homogeneous; as, the three *phases* ice, water, and aqueous vapor. **6.** *Physics.* In uniform circular motion, simple harmonic motion, or in the periodic changes of any magnitude varying according to a simple harmonic law (as sound vibrations, alternating electric currents, etc.), the point or stage in the period to which the rotation, oscillation, or variation has advanced, considered in its relation to a standard position or assumed instant of starting. **7.** *Zool.* A color phase.

Syn. **Phase, aspect, side, facet, angle** mean one of the possible ways of viewing or of being presented to view. **Phase** implies a change in appearance, often without clear reference to an observer; **aspect,** usually, stresses the point of view of an observer and its limitation of that seen or considered; **side** stresses one of several aspects from which something may be viewed; **facet** stresses one of a multiplicity of sides each of which manifests the central quality of a thing; **angle** stresses an aspect seen from a very restricted point of view.

-pha′si·a (-fā′zhĭ·ȧ). [NL., fr. Gr. *phanai* to speak.] *Med.* A combining form used to denote *speech of a* (specified) *disordered type,* as in dys*phasia.*

pha′sis (fā′sĭs), *n.; pl.* PHASES (-sēz). [NL.] An aspect; a phase; a mode or manner of being.

-phasy. = -PHASIA.

pheas′ant (fĕz′ănt; -′nt), *n.;* see PLURAL, *Note,* 3. [OF. *faisant, faisan,* fr. Pr. *faisan,* fr. L. *phasianus,* fr. Gr. *phasianos* (sc. *ornis*), fr. *Phasis,* a river in Colchis.] **1.** Any of numerous large, long-tailed, brilliantly colored gallinaceous birds (genus *Phasianus,* family Phasianidae) natives of Asia, but widely bred as a game bird. **2.** Any of various birds having real or fancied resemblance to a pheasant; esp., *Southern U.S.,* the ruffed grouse. A brilliantly colored bird

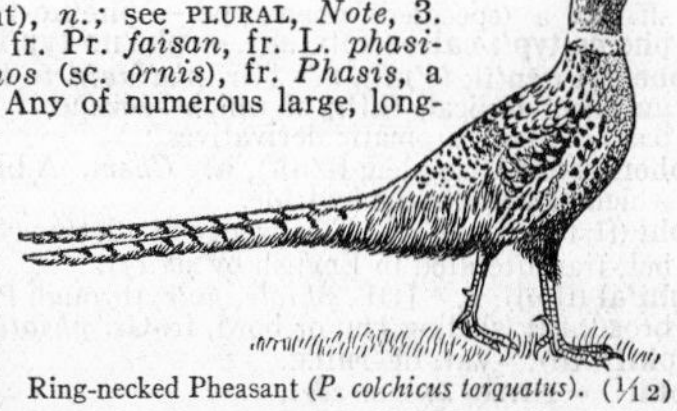
Ring-necked Pheasant (*P. colchicus torquatus*). (1/12)

(*Chrysolophus pictus*) of China and Tibet is known as the ***golden pheasant.***

phel′lo·derm (fĕl′ō·dûrm), *n.* [Gr. *phellos* cork + *-derm.*] *Bot.* A secondary cortical tissue, usually of ordinary green parenchyma, developed from the phellogen on the inner side of the cork. — **phel′lo·der′mal** (-dûr′măl), *adj.*

phel′lo·gen (-jĕn), *n.* [Gr. *phellos* cork + *-gen.*] *Bot.* In dicotyledonous stems, a secondary meristem giving rise externally to the characteristic cork tissue and phelloderm. — **phel′lo·ge·net′ic** (-jē·nĕt′ĭk), **phel′lo·gen′ic** (-jĕn′ĭk), *adj.*

phen-, phe′no- (fē′nō-; fĕn′ō-). [From PHENYL.] *Chem.* A combining form denoting *relation to*, or *derivation from, benzene* (*phene*) as in *phen*acetin.

phe′na·caine (fē′nȧ·kān; fĕn′ȧ-), *n.* [*phen-* + *cocaine.*] *Pharm.* A colorless, crystalline base, $C_{18}H_{22}N_2O_2$; also, its hydrochloride, used as a local anesthetic.

phe·nac′e·tin, phe·nac′e·tine (fē·năs′ē·tĭn), *n.* *Pharm.* A white, crystalline compound, $C_{10}H_{13}NO_2$, used in medicine principally as an antipyretic.

phen′a·cite (fĕn′ȧ·sīt), *n.* [Gr. *phenax, -akos*, deceiver.] *Mineral.* A glassy silicate of beryllium, occurring in rhombohedral crystals and sometimes used as a gem.

phe·nan′threne (fē·năn′thrēn), *n.* [*phenyl* + *anthracene.*] *Chem.* A colorless crystalline hydrocarbon, $C_{14}H_{10}$, occurring in coal tar.

phen′a·zine (fĕn′ȧ·zēn; -zĭn), *n.* Also **phen′a·zin.** [*phenyl* + *az-* + *-ine.*] *Chem.* A yellowish crystalline base, $C_6H_4N_2C_6H_4$, the parent substance of many important dyes.

phe·net′i·dine (fē·nĕt′ĭ·dēn; -dĭn), *n.* Also **phe·net′i·din.** [*phen*ol + *ethyl* + *amido.*] *Chem.* Any of three liquid basic amino derivatives, $C_6H_4(NH_2)OC_2H_5$, of phenetole, used in manufacturing dyestuffs.

phen′e·tole (fĕn′ē·tōl; -tŏl), *n.* Also **phen′e·tol.** [*phenyl* + *ethyl* + *-ole.*] *Chem.* A colorless aromatic liquid, $C_6H_5OC_2H_5$, the ethyl ether of phenol.

phe′nix (fē′nĭks). Var. of PHOENIX.

phe′no·bar′bi·tal (fē′nō·bär′bĭ·tôl; fĕn′ō-; -tăl), *n.* [*pheno-*, a combining form from *phenyl*, denoting relation to, or derivation from, benzene + *barbital.*] A white crystalline powder (chemically phenyl-ethyl-barbituric acid, $C_{12}H_{12}N_2O_3$) used as a hypnotic and sedative.

phe′no·cryst (fē′nō·krĭst; fĕn′ō-), *n.* [F. *phénocryste*, fr. Gr. *phainein* to show + *krystallos* crystal.] *Petrog.* One of the prominent embedded crystals of a porphyry.

phe′nol (fē′nōl; -nŏl; fē·nōl′), *n.* [*phen-* + *-ol.*] *Chem.* **1.** A crystalline compound, C_6H_5OH, produced by distillation of many organic substances, as wood, coal, etc., and obtained from coal tar; — popularly called *carbolic acid.* It is a caustic poison, and in solution is used as an antiseptic. **2.** By extension, any of the series of aromatic hydroxyl derivatives of which phenol proper is the type. — **phe·no′lic** (fē·nō′lĭk; -nŏl′ĭk), *adj.*

phe′no·late (fē′nō·lāt), *n.* *Chem.* A salt of phenol, in its capacity as a weak acid.

phe·nol′ic (fē·nŏl′ĭk), *n.* A synthetic phenolic resin, usually one made by reaction of phenol with an aldehyde. Phenolics are thermosetting and are used for molding, for insulating, in varnishes, etc.

phe·nol′o·gy (fē·nŏl′ō·jĭ), *n.* [Contr. fr. PHENOMENOLOGY.] *Biol.* The science of the relations between climate and periodic biological phenomena, as the migrations and breeding of birds, the fruiting of plants, etc. — **phe′no·log′i·cal** (fē′nō·lŏj′ĭ·kăl), *adj.* — **phe·nol′o·gist** (fē·nŏl′ō·jĭst), *n.*

phe′nol·phthal′ein, phe′nol–phthal′ein (fē′nōl·thăl′ēn; -fthăl′ē·ĭn; fē′nŏl-), *n.* *Chem.* A white or yellowish-white crystalline compound, $C_{20}H_{14}O_4$, used as an indicator, since its solution is red in alkalies and is decolorized by acids, and as a laxative.

phe·nom′e·na (fē·nŏm′ē·nȧ), *n., pl.* of PHENOMENON.

phe·nom′e·nal (-năl; -n′l), *adj.* Of, pert. to, or of the nature of a phenomenon; specif.: **a** Known through the senses rather than through thought or intuition. **b** Concerned with observed data rather than with hypotheses; as, *phenomenal* science. **c** Extraordinary; unusual. — **Syn.** See MATERIAL. — **phe·nom′e·nal·ly,** *adv.*

phe·nom′e·nal·ism (-ĭz′m), *n.* *Philos.* **a** The theory that limits knowledge to phenomena only. **b** The theory that we know only phenomena and that there is no existence except the phenomenal. — **phe·nom′e·nal·ist** (-ĭst), *n.* — **phe·nom′e·nal·is′tic** (-ĭs′tĭk), *adj.*

phe·nom′e·nol′o·gy (fē·nŏm′ē·nŏl′ō·jĭ), *n.* [*phenomenon* + *-logy.*] **1.** The branch of a science dealing with the description and classification of phenomena. **2.** Scientific description of actual phenomena, with avoidance of all interpretation, explanation, and evaluation.

phe·nom′e·non (fē·nŏm′ē·nŏn *or, esp. Brit.,* -nŭn), *n.; pl.* -ENA (-nȧ). [LL. *phaenomenon*, fr. Gr. *phainomenon*, neut. pres. part. of *phainesthai* to appear, pass. of *phainein* to show.] **1.** *Philos.* Any object known through the senses rather than through thought or intuition; specif., with Kant, the object of experience. Cf. NOUMENON. **2.** Any observable fact or event; specif.: **a** In scientific usage, any fact or event of scientific interest susceptible of scientific description and explanation. **b** In a secondary use in science, a rare fact or event, or one of unique significance. **3.** *pl.* PHENOMENONS (-nŏnz; -nŭnz). An exceptional or abnormal person, thing, or occurrence; prodigy.

phe′no·thi′a·zine (fē′nō·thī′ȧ·zēn; -zĭn), *n.* Also **phe′no·thi′a·zin.** [*pheno-* + *thiazine.*] *Chem.* A yellowish crystalline compound, $C_{12}H_9NS$, made from diphenylamine and sulfur. It is the parent of many dyes, and is used as a fungicide and insecticide and as an anthelmintic for cattle, sheep, swine, and horses.

phe′no·type (fē′nō·tīp), *n.* [Gr. *phainein* to show + *-type.*] *Biol.* **a** The physical make-up of an individual resulting from the interaction of genotypic characters and environment. **b** A group of individuals sharing a (specified) phenotype. — **phe′no·typ′ic** (-tĭp′ĭk), *adj.* — **phe′no·typ′i·cal** (-ĭ·kăl), *adj.* — **phe′no·typ′i·cal·ly,** *adv.*

phen′yl (fĕn′ĭl; fē′nĭl), *n.* [Gr. *phainein* to show + *-yl.*] *Chem.* A univalent radical, C_6H_5, of which benzene is the hydride. It is the basis of many aromatic derivatives.

phen′yl·ene (fĕn′ĭ·lēn; fē′nĭ-), *n.* *Chem.* A bivalent radical, C_6H_4, of which benzene is the hydride.

phi (fī; fē), *n.* [Gr.] The twenty-first letter (Φ, φ) of the Greek alphabet, transliterated in English by *ph* (*f*).

phi′al (fī′ăl), *n.* [OF. *phiole, fiole*, through Pr. & LL. fr. L. *phiala* a broad, flat, shallow cup or bowl, fr. Gr. *phialē.*] A vial.

-phil (-fĭl). Var. of -PHILE.

phil-. = PHILO- (which see).

phil′a·beg (fĭl′ȧ·bĕg), *n.* *Chiefly Scot.* A kilt. Cf. FILIBEG.

Phil′a·del′phi·a law′yer (fĭl′ȧ·dĕl′fĭ·ȧ; -dĕl′fyȧ; 58). A very shrewd lawyer, esp. one versed in the intricacies of legal phraseology; — now disparaging but orig. from the high colonial reputation of the Philadelphia bar.

phi·lan′der (fĭ·lăn′dẽr), *v. i.* [Gr. *philandros* loving men, fr. *philos* loving + *anēr, andros*, man.] To make love, esp. triflingly; to flirt with a woman. — **phi·lan′der·er,** *n.*

phil′an·throp′ic (fĭl′ăn·thrŏp′ĭk), *adj.* Also **phil′an·throp′i·cal** (-ĭ·kăl). Characterized by philanthropy; loving or helping mankind; benevolent. — **phil′an·throp′i·cal·ly,** *adv.*

phi·lan′thro·pist (fĭ·lăn′thrō·pĭst), *n.* [*philanthropy* + *-ist.*] One who practices philanthropy.

phi·lan′thro·pize (-pīz), *v. t.* To treat philanthropically.

phi·lan′thro·py (-pĭ), *n.; pl.* -PIES (-pĭz). [From LL., fr. Gr. *philanthrōpia*, fr. *philanthrōpos*, fr. *philos* loving + *anthrōpos* man.] **1.** Love for mankind; good will to all men; — opposed to *misanthropy.* **2.** A philanthropic act, institution, gift, or the like.

phi·lat′e·ly (fĭ·lăt′ē·lĭ), *n.* [F. *philatélie*, fr. Gr. *philos* loving + *ateleia* exemption from tax (*telos*).] The collection and study of postage stamps, stamped envelopes, etc., of various issues; stamp collecting. — **phil′a·tel′ic** (fĭl′ȧ·tĕl′ĭk), **phil′a·tel′i·cal** (-ĭ·kăl), *adj.* — **phil′a·tel′i·cal·ly,** *adv.* — **phi·lat′e·list** (fĭ·lăt′ē·lĭst), *n.*

Phi·la′the·a (fĭ·lā′thē·ȧ), *n.* [Gr. *philos* loving + *alētheia* truth.] An international organization of young women's Bible classes. Cf. BARACA.

-phile (-fīl; -fĭl), **-phil** (-fĭl). [Gr. *philos* loving.] A combining form used in adjectives and nouns to denote (*one*) *having a fondness* or *affinity* for, as in biblio*phile.*

Phi·le′mon (fĭ·lē′mŏn), *n.* The New Testament Epistle to Philemon. See BIBLE. Philemon was a friend and probable convert of Paul.

phil′har·mon′ic (fĭl′ẽr·mŏn′ĭk; -(h)är·mŏn′ĭk), *adj.* [Gr. *philos* loving + *harmonia* harmony.] Loving harmony or music; — often used [*cap.*] in names of musical societies.

phil′hel·len′ic (fĭl′hĕ·lĕn′ĭk; -lē′nĭk), *adj.* Friendly to, or aiding, the Greek cause, esp. in recovering independence. — **phil·hel′len·ism** (fĭl·hĕl′ĕn·ĭz′m), *n.* — **phil·hel′len·ist** (fĭl·hĕl′ĕn·ĭst; fĭl′hĕ·lē′nĭst), *n.*

-phil′i·a (-fĭl′ĭ·ȧ). *Med.* A combining form from Greek *philia*, affection, from *philos*, loving, used to denote: **a** *A tendency toward*, as in hemo*philia.* **b** *A morbid appetite* or *craving for*, as in necro*philia.* Corresponding adjectives end in *-philic*, as necro*philic.*

phil′i·beg (fĭl′ĭ·bĕg). Var. of PHILABEG.

Phi·lip′pi·ans (fĭ·lĭp′ĭ·ănz), *n. pl., construed as sing.* The Epistle to the Philippians, in the New Testament. See BIBLE.

Phi·lip′pic (-ĭk), *n.* [L. *Philippicus* pert. to Philip, ult. fr. Gr. *Philippos* Philip (of Macedon).] **1.** Any of the series of famous orations of Demosthenes, the Grecian orator, denouncing Philip, King of Macedon. **2.** [*not cap.*] Any discourse or declamation abounding in acrimonious invective.

-philism. A combining form [*-phil*e, *-phil*ia, *-phil*ic, or *-phil*ous + *-ism*], denoting *state* or *habit resulting from tendency toward* or *addiction to*, as in biblio*philism.*

-philist. A combining form [*-phil*ism + *-ist*], as in biblio*philist.*

Phi·lis′tine (fĭ·lĭs′tĭn; fĭl′ĭs·tĭn; -tēn; *Brit.* fĭl′ĭs·tīn, -tĭn), *n.* [F. *Philistin*, fr. LL. (*pl.*), fr. Gr. *Philistinoi*, fr. Heb. *Pĕlishtīm.*] **1.** A native or an inhabitant of ancient Philistia. **2.** A person regarded as antagonistic to those of artistic or poetic temperament; a prosaic person. **3.** An active or passive opponent of progress or progressive ideas. — *adj.* Of or pertaining to Philistines, or to the temper of a Philistine; specif., uncultured; unenlightened; prosaic. — **Phi·lis′tin·ism** (fĭ·lĭs′tĭn·ĭz′m; fĭl′ĭs-), *n.*

Phil′lis (fĭl′ĭs). Var. of PHYLLIS.

phil′o- (fĭl′ō-), **phil-.** [Gr. *philos* loving.] A combining form meaning: **1.** *Loving, fond of*, as in *philo*sophy, *phil*harmonic. **2.** *Loving* or *favorably disposed toward a* (specified) *people*, as in **phil′o–French′.** **3.** *Manifesting a proclivity* or *humane benevolence toward*, as in *philo*progenitive.

phil′o·den′dron (fĭl′ō·dĕn′drŏn), *n.* [NL., fr. Gr. *philodendros* loving trees. See PHILO-; -DENDRON.] **a** An ornamental plant (genus *Philodendron*) having heart-shaped leaves and sheathing leafstalks, grown commonly as a house plant, often in water alone. **b** Any plant of certain other genera also called philodendron, as *Monstera deliciosa.*

phi·log′y·ny (fĭ·lŏj′ĭ·nĭ), *n.* [Gr. *philogynia*, fr. *philos* loving + *gynē* woman.] Fondness for women; — opp. to *misogyny.* — **phi·log′y·nist** (-nĭst), *n.* — **phi·log′y·nous** (-nŭs), *adj.*

phi·lol′o·gy (fĭ·lŏl′ō·jĭ), *n.* [F. *philologie*, fr. L. *philologia* love of learning, interpretation, philology, fr. Gr. *philologia*, fr. *philologos* fond of learning, fr. *philos* loving + *logos* speech, discourse.] **1.** Orig., love of learning or literature; hence, the study of literature, in a wide sense including etymology, grammar, criticism, literary and linguistic history, etc. **2.** Linguistic science; linguistics. **3.** The study of the cultures of civilized peoples as revealed in their languages, literatures, and religions, including study of languages as such and comparatively by families, grammar, etymology, phonology, morphology, semantics, textual criticism, etc. — **phi·lol′o·ger** (-jẽr), *n.* — **phil′o·lo′gi·an** (fĭl′ō·lō′jĭ·ăn), *n.* — **phil′o·log′ic** (fĭl′ō·lŏj′ĭk), **phil′o·log′i·cal** (-ĭ·kăl), *adj.* — **phi·lol′o·gist** (fĭ·lŏl′ō·jĭst), *n.*

phil′o·mel (fĭl′ō·mĕl), *n.* [F. *philomèle.*] *Poetic.* The nightingale. See PHILOMELA.

Phil′o·me′la (fĭl′ō·mē′lȧ), *n.* [L., fr. Gr. *Philomēla.*] **1.** *Gr. Myth.* The daughter of a king of Athens who was violated and deprived of her tongue by Tereus, husband of her sister Procne. The sisters in revenge served up Tereus's own son to him as a meal and then fled. He pursued them, and all three were transformed into birds, Philomela into a swallow, Procne into a nightingale, and Tereus into a hoopoe or a hawk. According to Ovid it was Philomela who was transformed into a nightingale. **2.** *Poetic.* The nightingale; — as a proper name.

phil′o·pro·gen′i·tive (fĭl′ō·prō·jĕn′ĭ·tĭv), *adj.* [See PHILO-; PROGENITOR.] **1.** Prolific. **2.** Having or pertaining to the love of offspring. — **phil′o·pro·gen′i·tive·ness,** *n.*

phi·los′o·pher (fĭ·lŏs′ō·fẽr), *n.* [OF. *philosophe*, fr. L. *philosophus*, fr. Gr. *philosophos*, fr. *philos* loving + *sophos* wise.] **1.** One versed in, or devoted to, philosophy. **2.** One who reduces the principles of philosophy to practice in the conduct of life; hence, loosely, one who meets or regards all vicissitudes with calmness.

phi·los′o·phers′ stone (-fẽrz). Also **philosopher's stone.** An imaginary stone, substance, or chemical preparation, believed to have the power of transmuting the baser metals into gold and much sought for by the alchemists.

phil′o·soph′i·cal (fĭl′ō·sŏf′ĭ·kăl), **phil′o·soph′ic** (-ĭk), *adj.* Of or pert.

to philosophy; versed in the principles of philosophy; hence, characterizing a philosopher; rational; wise; temperate; unruffled. — **phil'o·soph'i·cal·ly**, *adv.*

phil'o·soph'i·co- (fĭl'ō·sŏf'ĭ·kō-). A combining form for *philosophic*, used to denote *philosophical and*, as in **phil'o·soph'i·co·re·li'gious**.

phi·los'o·phism (fĭ·lŏs'ō·fĭz'm), *n.* Spurious philosophizing; sophistry; also, a sophism.

phi·los'o·phize (fĭ·lŏs'ō·fīz), *v. i.* To reason like a philosopher; to search into the reason and nature of things. — **phi·los'o·phiz'er** (-fīz'ẽr), *n.*

phi·los'o·phy (-fĭ), *n.; pl.* -PHIES (-fĭz). [OF. *philosophie, filosofie*, fr. L. *philosophia*, fr. Gr. *philosophia*, lit., the love of wisdom.] **1.** Literally, the love of wisdom; in actual usage, the science which investigates the facts and principles of reality and of human nature and conduct; specif., and now usually, the science which comprises logic, ethics, aesthetics, metaphysics, and the theory of knowledge. **2.** A body of philosophical principles; esp., the body of principles underlying a given branch of learning, or major discipline, a religious system, a human activity, or the like; as, the *philosophy* of history, Christianity, or of business. **3.** Practical or moral wisdom; ethics. **4.** Calmness of temper and judgment befitting a philosopher; mental serenity. **5.** A treatise on philosophy.

-philous. [Gr. *philos.*] A combining form meaning *loving, having a fondness for.*

phil'ter, phil'tre (fĭl'tẽr), *n.* [F. *philtre*, fr. L. *philtrum*, fr. Gr. *philtron*, fr. *philein* to love.] A potion, drug, or charm supposed to be able to excite love; loosely, a potion to produce any magic effect.

phiz (fĭz), *n.; pl.* PHIZES (-ĕz; -ĭz). *Slang.* Short for PHYSIOGNOMY, 2.

phleb'o- (flĕb'ō-), **phleb-.** [Gr. *phleps, phlebos.*] *Med. & Surg.* A combining form meaning *vein*, as in **phle·bi'tis, phleb'o·scle·ro'sis** (see -ITIS, etc.).

phle·bot'o·my (flē·bŏt'ō·mĭ), *n.* [OF. *flebothomie*, fr. LL., fr. Gr. *phlebotomia*, fr. *phleps, phlebos*, a vein + *temnein* to cut.] *Med.* The act or practice of opening a vein for letting blood; venesection. — **phle·bot'o·mize** (-mīz), *v. t. & i.* — **phle·bot'o·mist** (-mĭst), *n.*

Phleg'e·thon (flĕg'ē·thŏn; flĕj'-), *n.* [L., fr. Gr. *Phlegethōn*, prop. pres. part. of *phlegethein* to blaze.] *Gr. Myth.* A river of Hades, containing fire instead of water.

phlegm (flĕm), *n.* [OF. *fleume, flemme*, fr. LL., fr. Gr. *phlegma* flame, inflammation, phlegm.] **1.** One of the four "humors" of early physiology. It was supposed to be cold and moist, and to cause sluggishness. **2.** Mucus; now, morbid or viscid mucus secreted in abnormal quantity, esp. in the respiratory passages; — a popular term used only of mucus discharged through the mouth. **3.** Sluggishness of temperament; apathy; also, calmness; equanimity. — **Syn.** See EQUANIMITY. — **phlegm'y** (flĕm'ĭ), *adj.*

phleg·mat'ic (flĕg·măt'ĭk), *adj.* Also **phleg·mat'i·cal** (-ĭ·kăl). [OF. *fleumatique* (F. *flegmatique*), fr. LL., fr. Gr. *phlegmatikos.*] **1.** *Chiefly Hist.* Of the nature of, abounding in, or generating, phlegm (the humor). **2.** Sluggish; not easily aroused or moved; apathetic; calm; composed. — **Syn.** See IMPASSIVE. — **phleg·mat'i·cal·ly**, *adv.*

phlo'em (flō'ĕm), *n.* [G., fr. Gr. *phloos* bark.] *Bot.* A complex tissue in higher plants, which consists of sieve tubes with adjacent cells and parenchyma, serving for conduction of food materials; bast; — disting. from *xylem.*

phlo·gis'tic (flō·jĭs'tĭk), *adj.* **1.** *Obs.* **a** Fiery; burning. **b** Impassioned; heated. **2.** *Med.* Inflammatory; pert. to inflammation. **3.** *Old Chem.* Pert. to phlogiston.

phlo·gis'ton (-tŏn; -tŭn), *n.* [NL., fr. Gr. *phlogistos* burnt, inflammable. See PHLOX.] *Old Chem.* The hypothetical principle of fire, regarded as a material substance.

phlog'o·pite (flŏg'ō·pīt), *n.* [Gr. *phlogōpos* firelike, fr. *phlox* flame + *ōps, ōpos*, face.] A species of mica.

phlo·go'sis (flō·gō'sĭs), *n.* [NL., fr. Gr. *phlogōsis* burning heat.] *Med.* Inflammation, esp. of external parts of the body; erysipelatous inflammation. — **phlo·got'ic** (-gŏt'ĭk), *adj.*

phlor'i·zin (flŏr'ĭ·zĭn; flō·rī'zĭn), **phlo·rhi'zin** (flō·rē'zĭn), *n.* Also **phlo·rid'zin** (flō·rĭd'zĭn). [Gr. *phloios, phloos*, bark + *rhiza* root.] *Chem.* A white, crystalline glucoside, $C_{21}H_{24}O_{10}$, extracted from the root bark of the apple, pear, etc. It is used as a tonic and antiperiodic.

phlox (flŏks), *n.* [L., a kind of flower, fr. Gr. *phlox* flame, name of a plant, fr. *phlegein* to burn.] *Bot.* Any of a genus (*Phlox*) of handsome American herbs having red, purple, white, or variegated flowers; also, its flower. The genus typifies a family (Polemoniaceae, the phlox family).

phlyc·te'na, phlyc·tae'na (flĭk·tē'nȧ), *n.; pl.* -NAE (-nē). [NL., fr. Gr. *phlyktaina.*] A small vesicle or pustule.

-phobe (-fōb). [Gr. *phobos* fear.] A combining form meaning *fearing*, used to denote *one having a phobia.*

pho'bi·a (fō'bĭ·ȧ), *n.* [NL., fr. Gr. *phobos* fear.] *Psychol.* An irrational, persistent fear of a particular object or class of objects. — **pho'bic** (fō'bĭk; fŏb'ĭk), *adj.*

-pho'bi·a (-fō'bĭ·ȧ; 58). [See PHOBIA.] A combining form denoting *fear, dread*, and often implying *dislike* or *aversion;* — used esp. in *Med. & Psychol.* with names of things toward which phobias are directed, as in Anglo*phobia.*

pho'cine (fō'sīn; -sĭn), *adj.* [L. *phoca* a seal.] *Zool.* Of or pertaining to the seals, esp. those of a subfamily (Phocinae) which contains the typical seals.

Phoe'be (fē'bē), *n.* [L., fr. Gr. *Phoibē*, fem. of *Phoibos* Phoebus.] **1.** *Gr. Myth.* Artemis. **2.** *Poetic.* The moon personified.

phoe'be, *n.* [See PEWEE, PEWIT.] Any of several American flycatchers (genus *Sayornis*), esp. one (*S. phoebe*) of the eastern United States. It has a slight crest, and is plain grayish brown above and yellowish white below.

Phoe'bus (fē'bŭs), *n.* [L., fr. Gr. *Phoibos*, fr. *phoibos* bright.] **1.** *Gr. Relig.* Apollo; — an epithet. **2.** *Poetic.* The sun personified.

Phoe·ni'cian (fē·nĭsh'ăn), *adj.* From PHOENICIA, *Gaz.* — *n.* **1.** One of the people of Phoenicia. **2.** The Phoenician language, a Semitic tongue. See LANGUAGE, *Table.*

phoe'nix, phe'nix (fē'nĭks), *n.* [L. *phoenix*, fr. Gr. *phoinix.*] In Egyptian religion, a miraculous bird, the embodiment of the sun-god. The bird was fabled to live for 500 years, to be consumed in fire by its own act, and to rise in youthful freshness from its own ashes. Hence it is often an emblem of immortality.

phon-. = PHONO-.

pho'nate (fō'nāt), *v. i.* [Gr. *phōnē* voice.] To produce vocal sounds; to utter voice. — **pho·na'tion** (fō·nā'shŭn), *n.*

phon·au'to·graph (fōn·ô'tō·grăf; 9), *n.* [*phon-* + *auto-* + *-graph.*] *Physics.* An instrument by which a sound can be made to produce a visible record of itself. — **phon·au'to·graph'ic** (-grăf'ĭk), *adj.*

phone (fōn), *n.* [Gr. *phōnē* sound, voice.] *Phonet.* A speech sound. See PHONEME.

phone, *n.* [Gr. *phōnē* sound; or an abbr. of E. *telephone.*] *Colloq.* Short for TELEPHONE, TELEPHONE RECEIVER, etc. — *v. t. & i. Colloq.* Short for TELEPHONE.

-phone (-fōn). [Gr. *phōnē.*] A combining form meaning *a sound, voice*, used: **a** In names of musical instruments, as in saxo*phone*, xylo*phone.* **b** In names of scientific apparatus transmitting sound, as in mega*phone.*

pho'neme (fō'nēm), *n.* [F. *phonème*, fr. Gr. *phōnēma* a sound.] *Phonet.* **1.** The smallest unit of speech that in any given language distinguishes one utterance from another, as the *p* in *pin* and the *f* in *fin*, by which these two English words are distinguished from each other. See ALLOPHONE. **2.** *Now Rare.* A speech sound; a phone.

pho·ne'mics (fō·nē'mĭks; -nĕm'ĭks), *n.;* see -ICS. [See PHONEME.] The branch of linguistic science that deals with phonemes.

pho·net'ic (fō·nĕt'ĭk), *adj.* [Gr. *phōnētikos*, fr. *phōnētos* to be spoken, fr. *phōnein* to produce a sound, fr. *phōnē* a sound, tone.] **1.** Of or pert. to the voice, or its use; of, relating to, or consisting of speech sounds; of or pert. to the science of phonetics. **2.** Representing sounds, esp. speech sounds; as, *phonetic* symbols; specif., made according to or designating a system of spelling in which each letter represents always the same speech sound. — **pho·net'i·cal** (-ĭ·kăl), *adj.* — **pho·net'i·cal·ly**, *adv.*

pho'ne·ti'cian (fō'nē·tĭsh'ăn; fŏn'ē-), *n.* One versed in phonetics; a phonetist.

pho·net'ics (fō·nĕt'ĭks), *n.;* see -ICS. The science of speech sounds considered as elements of language; esp., the study of their formation by the speech organs and apprehension by the ear, their attributes, and their relation to other aspects of language; also, the application of this science to the understanding and speaking of languages.

☞ *Phonetics* is usually construed as a singular noun.

pho'ne·tist (fō'nē·tĭst), *n.* **a** One versed in phonetics; a phonetician. **b** One who advocates, or uses, phonetic spelling.

pho'ney (fō'nĭ). Var. of PHONY.

phon'ic (fŏn'ĭk; fō'nĭk), *adj.* [Gr. *phōnē* sound.] **a** Of, pert. to, or of the nature of sound; specif., of or pert. to vocal sounds; phonetic. **b** Uttered with vocal tone; voiced.

phon'ics (fŏn'ĭks; fō'nĭks), *n.;* see -ICS. The science of sound; acoustics; phonetics; specif., the study and application of elementary phonetics as a method of teaching beginners to read or enunciate.

pho'no- (fō'nō-), **phon-.** [Gr. *phōnē.*] A combining form meaning *sound, voice, speech, tone*, as in *phono*graph.

pho'no·gram (-grăm), *n.* [*phono-* + *-gram.*] **1.** A character or symbol used to represent a word, syllable, or single speech sound. Cf. IDEOGRAM, 1. **2.** A phonograph record. — **pho'no·gram'mic, pho'no·gram'ic** (-grăm'ĭk), *adj.*

pho'no·graph (-grăf; 9), *n.* [*phono-* + *-graph.*] An instrument for recording, for reproducing, or for recording and reproducing speech, music, and other sounds. — **pho'no·graph'ic** (-grăf'ĭk), *adj.* — **pho'no·graph'i·cal·ly** (-ĭ·kăl·ĭ), *adv.*

pho·nog'ra·phy (fō·nŏg'rȧ·fĭ), *n.* [*phono-* + *-graphy.*] **1.** A description of the human voice, or of speech sounds, with reference esp. to their phonetic representation. **2.** Art of writing according to sound; specif., the shorthand system invented by Isaac Pitman (1813–97), or a modification of it. — **pho·nog'ra·pher** (-fẽr), *n.*

pho'no·lite (fō'nō·līt), *n.* [*phono-* + *-lite.*] *Petrog.* A gray or green volcanic rock, consisting essentially of orthoclase and nephelite, that gives a ringing sound when struck. Called also *clinkstone.* — **pho'no·lit'ic** (-lĭt'ĭk), *adj.*

pho·nol'o·gist (fō·nŏl'ō·jĭst), *n.* One versed in phonology.

pho·nol'o·gy (-jĭ), *n.* [*phono-* + *-logy.*] **a** The science of speech sounds, including especially the history and theory of sound changes. **b** That part of the grammar of a language which describes its sounds and sound changes; also, the sound system of a language. **c** Phonemics. — **pho'no·log'ic** (fō'nō·lŏj'ĭk), **pho'no·log'i·cal** (-ĭ·kăl), *adj.* — **pho'no·log'i·cal·ly**, *adv.*

pho·nom'e·ter (fō·nŏm'ē·tẽr), *n.* [*phono-* + *-meter.*] *Physics.* An instrument for measuring sounds, as to intensity, or as to frequency of vibrations. — **pho·nom'e·try** (-trĭ), *n.*

pho'no·phore (fō'nō·fōr; 70), *n.* Also **pho'no·pore** (-pōr). [*phono-* + *-phore.*] *Elec.* A device which enables telephone messages to be sent over a telegraph line simultaneously with the use of ordinary currents operating Morse instruments; also, a system using this apparatus.

pho'no·scope (-skōp), *n.* [*phono-* + *-scope.*] *Physics.* An instrument for observing or exhibiting motions or properties of sounding bodies; esp., a device for testing the qualities of musical strings.

pho'no·type (-tīp), *n.* A phonetic character used in phonotypy; phonetic type. — **pho'no·typ'ic** (-tĭp'ĭk), **pho'no·typ'i·cal** (-ĭ·kăl), *adj.* — **pho'no·typ'i·cal·ly**, *adv.*

pho'no·typ'y (-tīp'ĭ), *n.* A method of phonetic printing, esp. that devised by Isaac Pitman (1813–97) for printing English. — **pho'no·typ'ist** (-ĭst), *n.*

pho'ny (fō'nĭ), *adj.;* PHO'NI·ER (-nĭ·ẽr); -NI·EST. *Slang, U. S.* Not genuine; fake. — *n.; pl.* PHONIES (-nĭz). *Slang, U. S.* A fake.

-phony. Also **-pho'ni·a** (-fō'nĭ·ȧ). [Gr. *phōnē.*] A combining form meaning *sound, voice*, used to denote *a* (specified) *type of sound.*

-phore (-fōr; 70). [See -PHOROUS.] A combining form meaning *bearer, one that bears.*

-phorous. [Gr. *-phoros*, fr. *pherein* to bear.] A combining form meaning *bearing;* — in adjectives.

phos'gene (fŏz'jēn), *n.* [Gr. *phōs* light + *-gene* (= *-gen*).] *Chem.* A colorless gas, $COCl_2$, of unpleasant odor. It was used in World War I, in gas attacks and in shells and bombs. It is a severe respiratory irritant.

phos'ge·nite (-jē·nīt), *n.* *Mineral.* A mineral, $Pb_2Cl_2CO_3$, consisting of carbonate of lead and chloride of lead, occurring in tetragonal crystals.

phosph-. = PHOSPHO-.

phos'phate (fŏs'fāt), *n.* [F. See PHOSPHORUS.] **1.** *Chem.* A salt or ester of phosphoric acid; as, ***calcium phosphate***, $Ca_3(PO_4)_2$, a compound derived from phosphoric acid and occurring in bones, in certain rock, etc., used as a fertilizer, in medicine, etc. **2.** An effervescent drink of carbonated water, with a small amount of phosphoric acid (H₂PO₄) and flavored with fruit sirup. **3.** *Agric.* Any phosphatic material used for fertilizers.

phosphate rock. *Petrog.* A rock consisting of calcium phosphate, usually together with calcium carbonate and other minerals, used in making fertilizers.

phos·phat′ic (fŏs·făt′ĭk), *adj.* Pertaining to, or containing, phosphoric acid or phosphates.

phos′pha·tize (fŏs′fà·tīz), *v. t.* **1.** To change to a phosphate or phosphates. **2.** To treat with phosphoric acid or a phosphate. — **phos′pha·ti·za′tion** (-tĭ·zȧ·zā′shŭn; -tī·zā′-), *n.*

phos′pha·tu′ri·a (fŏs′fȧ·tū′rĭ·à), *n.* [NL. See PHOSPHATE; -URIA.] *Med.* The excessive discharge of phosphates in the urine. — **phos′pha·tu′ric** (-rĭk), *adj.*

phos′phene (fŏs′fēn), *n.* [Gr. *phōs* light + *phainein* to show.] *Physiol.* A luminous impression due to excitation of the retina, as by pressure on the eyeball when the lids are closed. Cf. AFTERIMAGE.

phos′phide (-fīd; -fĭd), *n.* Also **phos′phid.** *Chem.* A binary compound of phosphorus with an element or radical.

phos′phine (-fēn; -fĭn), *n.* Also **phos′phin.** **1.** *Chem.* A hydride of phosphorus, PH₃, a colorless and poisonous gas with a disagreeable garliclike odor. **2.** An acridine dye.

phos′phite (-fīt), *n.* A salt or ester of phosphorous acid.

phos′pho- (fŏs′fō-), **phosph-.** [From PHOSPHORUS.] A combining form used for *phosphoric, phosphorous, phosphorus.*

phos′pho·cre′a·tine (-krē′à·tēn; -tĭn), *n.* Also **phos′pho·cre′a·tin.** *Biochem.* A compound, C₄H₁₀N₃O₅P, of equal proportions of creatine and phosphoric acid, found in vertebrate muscle.

phos′pho·lip′ide (-lĭp′īd, -ĭd; -lĭ″pĭd, -pĭd), *n.* Also **phos′pho·lip′id.** *Biochem.* Any of a class of complex lipides which on hydrolysis yield phosphorus as phosphoric acid, nitrogen as the amino radical, and fatty acids. Phospholipides are found in all cells and, with cholesterol, constitute most of the so-called fat of certain tissues.

phos·pho′ni·um (fŏs·fō′nĭ·ŭm), *n.* [NL., fr. *phospho-* + *ammonium.*] *Chem.* The univalent radical PH₄, analogous to ammonium.

phos′pho·pro′te·in (fŏs′fō·prō′tē·ĭn; -prō′tēn), *n.* *Biochem.* Any of a class of proteins, as caseinogen, in which the protein molecule is combined with some phosphorus-containing substance other than nucleic acid or lecithin.

phos′phor (fŏs′fŏr), *n.* [See PHOSPHORUS.] **1.** [*cap.*] The morning star; specif., Venus, as morning star. **2.** Also **phos′phore** (-fōr). *Poetic.* A phosphorescent substance. **3.** *Physics.* A substance that emits light when excited by radiation, as in a fluorescent lamp.

phos′phor, *adj.* *Now Rare.* Phosphorescent.

Phosphor bronze. A trade-mark for a kind of bronze of great hardness, elasticity, and toughness, that contains a small amount of phosphorus.

phos′pho·resce′ (fŏs′fō·rĕs′), *v. i.* To exhibit phosphorescence; to gleam, esp. in the dark.

phos′pho·res′cence (-rĕs′ĕns; -′ns), *n.* **1.** State or property of emitting light without sensible heat, as shown by phosphorus; also, light so produced. **2.** *Physics.* Luminescence caused by the absorption of radiations, such as X rays or ultraviolet light, and continuing for a noticeable time after these radiations have stopped. Cf. FLUORESCENCE.

phos′pho·res′cent (-ĕnt; -′nt), *adj.* Exhibiting phosphorescence.

phos′pho·ret′ed, phos′pho·ret′ted (fŏs′fō·rĕt′ĕd; -ĭd), *adj.* *Chem.* Impregnated or combined with phosphorus; as, *phosphoreted* hydrogen.

phos·phor′ic (fŏs·fŏr′ĭk; -fōr′ĭk), *adj.* *Chem.* Of, pert. to, or like phosphorus, esp. in its higher valences.

phosphoric acid. *Chem.* Any of three oxygen acids of phosphorus: ordinary or **orthophosphoric acid,** H₃PO₄, **pyrophosphoric acid,** H₄P₂O₇, and **metaphosphoric acid,** HPO₃.

phos′pho·rism (fŏs′fō·rĭz′m), *n.* *Med.* Poisoning, esp. chronic poisoning, by phosphorus.

phos′pho·rite (-rīt), *n.* *Mineral. & Petrog.* A fibrous concretionary variety of apatite; also, often, phosphate rock.

phos′pho·ro- (fŏs′fō·rō-), **phosphor-.** A combining form for *phosphorus* and *phosphoric,* as in *phosphorescence;* denoting also *phosphorescence.*

phos·phor′o·scope (fŏs·fŏr′ō·skōp), *n.* [*phosphoro-* + *-scope.*] *Physics.* An apparatus for observing phosphorescence produced by action of light.

phos′pho·rous (fŏs′fō·rŭs; fŏs·fō′rŭs), *adj.* **1.** *Rare.* Phosphorescent. **2.** *Chem.* Of, pert. to, resembling, or containing phosphorus, esp. in its lowest valence.

phosphorous acid. A colorless crystalline acid, H₃PO₃, obtained by the oxidation of phosphorus, and otherwise. Its salts are called *phosphites.*

phos′pho·rus (fŏs′fō·rŭs), *n.; pl.* PHOSPHORI (-rī). **1.** *cap.* The morning star, fr. Gr. *phōsphoros,* lit., light bringer.] **1.** A phosphorescent substance or body, esp. one that shines in the dark. **2.** *Chem.* A nonmetallic, poisonous, active element of the nitrogen group, usually obtained as a waxy crystalline solid with a disagreeable smell. Symbol, *P;* at. no., 15; at. wt., 30.975.

phos·phor′yl·ase (fŏs·fŏr′ĭ·lās), *n.* [*phosphoryl,* the radical PO + *-ase.*] *Biochem.* An enzyme, found in animal tissues, which catalyzes the conversion of glycogen into glucose (in the form of phosphate).

phos′pho·ryl·a′tion (fŏs′fō·rĭ·lā′shŭn), *n.* [*phosphor-,* a combining form for phosphorus + *-yl* + *-ation.*] *Chem.* The act or process of converting into a compound of phosphorus, as a sugar into a phosphoric acid ester. — **phos·phor′yl·ate** (fŏs·fŏr′ĭ·lāt), *v. t.*

phos′phu·ret′ed, phos′phu·ret′ted (fŏs′fū·rĕt′ĕd; -ĭd), *n.* Vars. of PHOSPHORETED.

phot (fōt; fŏt), *n.* [Gr. *phōs, phōtos,* light.] *Photom.* A C.G.S. unit of illumination, being the direct illumination on a surface which is everywhere one centimeter from a uniform point source of one international foot-candle.

pho′tic (fō′tĭk), *adj.* [Gr. *phōs, phōtos,* light.] Of or pertaining to light; specif., *Biol.,* relating to the stimulation by or production of light by organisms.

pho′tics (-tĭks), *n.; see* -ICS. The science of light; — a general term sometimes used when the term *optics* is restricted to light as exciting vision.

photo-. [Gr. *phōs, phōtos,* light.] A combining form meaning: **1.** *Light,* as in *photography.* **2.** *Photograph* or *photographic,* as in

pho′to·film′. 3. *Produced by,* or *relating to, the action of light.* **4.** *Photoelectric,* as in *photocell.*

pho′to (fō′tō), *n.; pl.* PHOTOS (-tōz). A photograph. — *v. t. & i.;* PHO′TOED (-tōd); PHO′TO·ING. To photograph.

pho′to·ac·tin′ic (fō′tō·ăk·tĭn′ĭk), *adj.* [*photo-* + *actinic.*] Capable of producing actinic effect; — said esp. of blue or ultraviolet light.

pho′to·bi·ot′ic (-bī·ŏt′ĭk), *adj.* *Biol.* Requiring light in order to live or flourish.

pho′to·cell′ (fō′tō·sĕl′), *n.* = PHOTOELECTRIC CELL.

pho′to·chem′is·try (-kĕm′ĭs·trĭ), *n.* *Chem.* The branch of chemistry relating to the effect of radiant energy (esp. light) in causing chemical changes, as in photography. — **pho′to·chem′i·cal** (-ĭ·kăl), *adj.*

pho′to·chro′my (fō′tō·krō′mĭ), *n.* [*photo-* + Gr. *chrōma* color.] Color photography.

pho′to·chron′o·graph (-krŏn′ō·gráf; 9), *n.* **1.** An apparatus for photographing a moving object at regular minute intervals; also, one of the photographs thus taken. **2.** *Astron.* An instrument for the photographic recording of star transits. **3.** *Physics.* An instrument for recording minute intervals of time.

pho′to·con′duc·tiv′i·ty (-kŏn′dŭk·tĭv′ĭ·tĭ), *n.* [*photo-* + *conductivity.*] *Elec.* Conductivity, as that of certain minerals, which varies with the illumination.

pho′to·cur′rent (fō′tō·kûr′ĕnt), *n.* *Physics.* A stream of electrons (photoelectrons) produced by photoelectric or photovoltaic effects; — called also **photoelectric current.**

pho′to·dis·in′te·gra′tion (-dĭs·ĭn′tē·grā′shŭn), *n.* *Physics.* Disintegration of the nucleus of an atom produced by absorption of radiant energy.

pho′to·dra′ma (fō′tō·drä′mà; -drăm′à), *n.* A photoplay.

pho′to·dy·nam′ics (-dī·năm′ĭks; -dĭ-), *n.; see* -ICS. The effect of light on organisms, esp. in inducing phototropism in plants; the kinetics of this effect. — **pho′to·dy·nam′ic** (-ĭk), *adj.*

pho′to·e·lec′tric (-ē·lĕk′trĭk), **pho′to·e·lec′tri·cal** (-trĭ·kăl), *adj.* *Physics.* Pertaining to or descriptive of: (1) the emission of electrons from solid, liquid, or gaseous bodies when exposed to light or other radiation of suitable wave lengths; or (2) the decrease in electrical resistance of certain substances when exposed to light of certain wave lengths.

photoelectric cell. *Physics.* A cell or a vacuum tube whose electrical properties are modified by the action of light.

pho′to·e·lec′tron (fō′tō·ē·lĕk′trŏn), *n.* [*photo-* + *electron.*] *Physical Chem.* An electron emitted from a substance under the action of light or other radiation. See PHOTOELECTRIC.

pho′to·e·lec′tro·type (-ē·lĕk′trō·tīp), *n.* An electrotype produced by photographic means.

pho′to·e·mis′sive (-ē·mĭs′ĭv), *adj.* [*photo-* + *emissive.*] *Physics.* **a** Emitting or capable of emitting electrons when exposed to light or other radiation of suitable wave lengths. **b** Designating a photoelectric cell in which light causes the emission of electrons from the cathode. — **pho′to·e·mis′sion** (-mĭsh″ŭn), *n.*

pho′to·en·grave′ (-ĕn·grāv′), *v. t.* To make a photoengraving of. — **pho′to·en·grav′er** (-grāv′ẽr), *n.*

pho′to·en·grav′ing (fō′tō·ĕn·grāv′ĭng), *n.* **a** Engraving by the aid of photography; specif. and usually, any photomechanical process for reproducing pictures, etc., in which the printing surface is in relief, as contrasted with photolithography and photogravure. **b** A print made by such a process.

photo finish. *Racing.* A finish in which contestants are so close that a photograph of them as they cross the finish line has to be examined to determine the winner. — **pho′to-fin′ish** (see *Pron.,* § 2), *adj.*

pho′to·flash′ lamp (fō′tō·flăsh′). An electrically fired lamp having a clear glass bulb originally containing aluminum sheet foil and oxygen, for making flashlight photographs.

pho′to·flood′ lamp (-flŭd′). An electric lamp using excess voltage to give sustained brilliant illumination, for taking pictures.

pho′to·gel′a·tin (-jĕl′à·tĭn), *n.* Pert. to, designating, or made by a photographic process in which prints are made directly from a hardened film of gelatin or other colloid.

pho′to·gen (fō′tō·jĕn), *n.* [*photo-* + *-gen.*] **1.** Also **pho′to·gene** (-jēn). A light oil obtained by distilling bituminous shale, coal, peat, etc., and used for burning and as a solvent. **2.** *Biol.* A photogenic substance or organism.

pho′to·gene (-jēn), *n.* [See PHOTO-; -GEN.] Orig., a photograph; now, an afterimage.

pho′to·gen′ic (-jĕn′ĭk), *adj.* **1.** *Rare.* Due to light. **2.** Eminently suitable for being photographed, esp. from the aesthetic point of view. **3.** *Biol.* Producing or generating light; phosphorescent; as, *photogenic* bacteria. — **pho′to·gen′i·cal·ly** (-ĭ·kăl·ĭ), *adv.*

pho′to·gram′me·try (-grăm′ē·trĭ), *n.* [*photo-* + *-gram* + *-metry.*] *Photog.* The science or art of obtaining surveys by means of photography; specif., the process of making maps from photographs, esp. aerial photographs.

pho′to·graph (fō′tō·gráf; 9), *n.* [*photo-* + *-graph.*] A picture or likeness obtained by photography. — *v. t. & i.* To take a picture or copy (of) or as if by photography.

pho·tog′ra·pher (fō·tŏg′rà·fẽr), *n.* One who practices, or is skilled in, photography.

pho′to·graph′ic (fō′tō·grăf′ĭk), **pho′to·graph′i·cal** (-ĭ·kăl), *adj.* **1.** Of or pertaining to photography; obtained by, or used in, photography.

2. Of art, representing nature and human beings with the exactness of a photograph; as, the *photographic* realism of Zola. — **pho′to·graph′i·cal·ly**, *adv.*

pho·tog′ra·phy (fō·tŏg′rȧ·fĭ), *n.* The art or process of producing images on sensitized surfaces by the action of light.

pho′to·gra·vure′ (fō′tō·grȧ·vūr′; -grā′vūr), *n.* [F.] A process for making prints from an intaglio plate prepared by photographic methods; also, a print so made.

pho′to·he′li·o·graph′ (-hē′lĭ·ō·grȧf′; 9), *n.* *Astron.* A telescope specially adapted to photographing the sun.

pho′to·ki·ne′sis (-kĭ·nē′sĭs; -kī-), *n.* [NL.] *Physiol.* Motion or activity induced by light. — **pho′to·ki·net′ic** (-nĕt′ĭk), *adj.*

pho′to·lith′o (-lĭth′ō), *n.* Short for PHOTOLITHOGRAPH, PHOTOLITHOPRINT, etc.

pho′to·lith′o·graph (-lĭth′ō·grȧf; 9), *v. t.* To print by photolithography. — *n.* A print made by photolithography.

pho′to·li·thog′ra·phy (-lĭ·thŏg′rȧ·fĭ), *n.* A photomechanical, planographic process of printing in which an impression from printer's type or a design or picture, often with a halftone screen interposed, is first photographically transferred to a sensitized sheet of thin, flexible zinc or aluminum (or a special paper), then developed, made ink-receptive with a greasy chemical, and inked for printing upon paper. See PHOTO-OFFSET. — **pho′to·lith′o·graph′ic** (-lĭth′ō·grăf′ĭk), *adj.*

pho′to·lith′o·print′ (-lĭth′ō·prĭnt′), *n.* A photolithograph.

pho·tol′y·sis (fō·tŏl′ĭ·sĭs), *n.* [NL., fr. *photo-* + *-lysis.*] **1.** *Bot.* The arrangement of chlorophyll grains as affected by light. **2.** *Physical Chem.* Chemical decomposition by the action of radiant energy, esp. light. — **pho′to·lyt′ic** (fō′tō·lĭt′ĭk), *adj.*

pho′to·map′ (fō′tō·măp′), *n.* A map constructed by matching together a series of photographs taken vertically from an airplane. — **pho′to·map′**, *v. t. & i.*

pho′to·me·chan′i·cal (fō′tō·mē·kăn′ĭ·kăl), *adj.* Pertaining to or designating any process of producing pictures or copies by mechanical printing from a photographically prepared plate. — **pho′to·me·chan′i·cal·ly**, *adv.*

pho·tom′e·ter (fō·tŏm′ē·tẽr), *n.* *Physics.* An instrument for measuring luminous intensity, luminous flux, etc.

pho·tom′e·try (-trĭ), *n.* That branch of science which treats of the measurement of the intensity of light; also, the art of making such measurements. — **pho′to·met′ric** (fō′tō·mĕt′rĭk), **pho′to·met′ri·cal** (-rĭ·kăl), *adj.* — **pho·tom′e·trist** (fō·tŏm′ē·trĭst), *n.*

pho′to·mi′cro·graph (fō′tō·mī′krō·grȧf; 9), *n.* [*photo-* + *micro-* + *-graph.*] **1.** An enlarged photograph of a microscopic object. **2.** = MICROPHOTOGRAPH **a.** — **pho′to·mi·crog′ra·phy** (-mī·krŏg′rȧ·fĭ), *n.*

pho′to·mi′cro·scope (-mī′krō·skōp), *n.* *Photog.* A combined microscope, camera, and suitable light source, usually attached, adjustably, to a support.

pho′to·mon·tage′ (fō′tō·mŏn·täzh′; -môn·täzh′), *n.* [*photo-* + *montage.*] Montage using photographs; also, a picture produced by such montage.

pho′to·mu′ral (fō′tō·mū′răl; 2; 114), *n.* [*photo-* + *mural.*] An enlarged photograph, usually several yards long, used on a wall, esp. as decoration.

pho′ton (fō′tŏn), *n.* [*photo-* + Gr. *-on* (neut. suff.), denoting an ultimate particle.] **1.** *Optics.* A unit of intensity of light at the retina, equal to the illumination received per square millimeter of pupillary area from a surface having a brightness of one candle per square meter or 0.4 π millilambert. **2.** *Physics.* A quantum of radiant energy.

pho′to–off′set′ (fō′tō·ôf′sĕt′), *n.* *Graphic Arts.* A process of indirect, or offset, printing, in which an impression of printer's type or a design or picture, often with a halftone screen interposed, is first photographically transferred to a properly grained and sensitized sheet of thin, flexible zinc or aluminum (or a special paper), then developed and made ink-receptive and water-repellent with a coating of a greasy chemical for printing on a rubber-blanketed cylinder, from which it is impressed (that is, offset) upon a smooth or rough surface, whether of paper, tin, or the like. Called also *offset lithography.*

pho′to–off′set′, *v. t.*; -OFF′SET′; -OFF′SET′TING. To produce by photo-offset.

pho′to·pe′ri·od (fō′tō·pēr′ĭ·ŭd), *n.* [*photo-* + *period.*] *Plant Physiol.* The optimum length of day or period of daily illumination required for the normal growth and maturity of a plant. — **pho′to·pe′ri·od′ic** (-pēr′ĭ·ŏd′ĭk), *adj.*

pho′to·pe′ri·od·ism (-pēr′ĭ·ŭd·ĭz′m), *n.* **1.** *Physiol.* The response of an organism, as by growth, to the relative length of day; photoperiodic reactivity. **2.** *Plant Physiol.* The response of a plant to its photoperiod.

pho·toph′i·lous (fō·tŏf′ĭ·lŭs), *adj.* *Biol.* Light-loving. — **pho·toph′i·ly** (fō·tŏf′ĭ·lĭ), *n.*

pho′to·pho′bi·a (fō′tō·fō′bĭ·ȧ; 58), *n.* [NL.] Morbid dislike of light.

pho·to′pi·a (fō·tō′pĭ·ȧ), *n.* [*photo-* + *-opia* (fr. Gr. ōps, ōpos, eye).] *Physiol.* Vision in bright light, with light-adapted eyes. — **pho·top′ic** (fō·tŏp′ĭk; -tō′pĭk), *adj.*

pho′to·play′ (fō′tō·plā′), *n.* A motion-picture representation of a play; also, sometimes, a screenplay.

pho′to·print′ (-prĭnt′), *n.* Any print made by a photomechanical process.

pho′to·sen′si·tive (-sĕn′sĭ·tĭv), *adj.* *Physics.* Sensitive to the action of radiant energy, esp. light. — **pho′to·sen′si·tiv′i·ty** (-tĭv′ĭ·tĭ), *n.*

pho′to·spec′tro·scope (-spĕk′trō·skōp), *n.* An instrument recording spectra by photography. — **pho′to·spec′tro·scop′ic** (-skŏp′ĭk), *adj.*

pho′to·sphere (fō′tō·sfēr), *n.* **a** A sphere of light. **b** *Astron.* The luminous envelope of the sun. — **pho′to·spher′ic** (-sfĕr′ĭk), *adj.*

Pho′to·stat (fō′tō·stăt), *n.* A trade-mark applied to a device, largely automatic in its action, for making photographic copies of drawings, manuscripts, maps, etc., directly upon the surface of prepared paper, with the image in correct position and not reversed as in a negative.

pho′to·syn′the·sis (-sĭn′thē·sĭs), *n.* [NL.] *Chem. & Physiol.* Synthesis of chemical compounds effected with the aid of radiant energy, esp. light; specif., *Plant Physiol.*, formation of carbohydrates in the chlorophyll-containing tissues of plants exposed to light. Cf. RESPIRATION, 2. — **pho′to·syn·thet′ic** (-sĭn·thĕt′ĭk), *adj.*

pho′to·tax′is (-tăk′sĭs), *n.* Also **pho′to·tax′y** (fō′tō·tăk′sĭ). [NL., fr. *photo-* + *-taxis.*] *Biol.* A taxis in which light is the directive factor, as in the movement of an infusorian toward the lighted side of a vessel. — **pho′to·tac′tic** (-tăk′tĭk), *adj.*

pho′to·tech′nic (-tĕk′nĭk), *adj.* That involves one or more photographic processes in a technical method; as, *phototechnic* lithography.

pho′to·tel′e·graph (-tĕl′ē·grȧf; -tĕl′ĕ·grȧf; 9), *v. t. & i.* To transmit by phototelegraphy. — *n.* A picture so transmitted.

pho′to·te·leg′ra·phy (-tē·lĕg′rȧ·fĭ), *n.* **1.** Telegraphy by means of light, as by the heliograph. **2.** The transmission of photographs by telegraphy. — **pho′to·tel′e·graph′ic** (-tĕl′ē·grăf′ĭk; -tĕl′ĕ-), *adj.* — **pho′to·tel′e·graph′i·cal·ly** (-ĭ·kăl·ĭ), *adv.*

pho′to·tel′e·scope (-tĕl′ē·skōp; -tĕl′ĕ-), *n.* *Astron.* A telescope adapted for taking photographs of the heavenly bodies.

pho′to·ther′a·peu′tics (-thĕr′ȧ·pū′tĭks), *n.*; see -ICS. Phototherapy. — **pho′to·ther′a·peu′tic** (-tĭk), *adj.*

pho′to·ther′a·py (-thĕr′ȧ·pĭ), *n.* *Med.* The application of light for therapeutic purposes, esp. for treating skin diseases.

pho′to·ther′mic (-thûr′mĭk), *adj.* Of or pertaining to both light and heat.

pho·tot′o·nus (fō·tŏt′ō·nŭs), *n.* [NL. See PHOTO-; TONE.] *Physiol.* State of sensitiveness to light. — **pho′to·ton′ic** (fō′tō·tŏn′ĭk), *adj.*

pho′to·to·pog′ra·phy (fō′tō·tō·pŏg′rȧ·fĭ), *n.* Photogrammetry. — **pho′to·top′o·graph′ic** (-tŏp′ō·grăf′ĭk), *adj.*

pho·tot′ro·pism (fō·tŏt′rō·pĭz′m), *n.* [*photo-* + *-tropism.*] *Biol.* A tropism in which light is the orienting stimulus, as in the turning toward a light of a plant shoot. Cf. HELIOTROPISM. — **pho′to·trop′ic** (fō′tō·trŏp′ĭk), *adj.* — **pho′to·trop′i·cal·ly** (-ĭ·kăl·ĭ), *adv.*

pho′to·tube′ (fō′tō·tūb′), *n.* = PHOTOELECTRIC CELL.

pho′to·type (fō′tō·tīp), *n.* A block with a printing surface obtained from a photograph; also, any process by which such a surface is obtained. — **pho′to·typ′ic** (-tĭp′ĭk), *adj.*

pho′to·ty·pog′ra·phy (-tī·pŏg′rȧ·fĭ), *n.* Any photomechanical process in which the printing surface is in relief, so as to be used with type. — **pho′to·ty′po·graph′ic** (-tī′pō·grăf′ĭk; -tĭp′ō-), *adj.*

pho′to·typ′y (fō′tō·tīp′ĭ; fō·tŏt′ĭ·pĭ), *n.* Art or process of making phototypes.

pho′to·vol·ta′ic (fō′tō·vŏl·tā′ĭk), *adj.* *Physics.* **a** Photoelectric. **b** Designating a photoelectric cell in which light causes the generation of an electromotive force.

pho′to·zin·cog′ra·phy (-zĭng·kŏg′rȧ·fĭ), *n.* A process for reproducing pictures, etc., by using a zinc plate on which the design has been photographically produced.

phras′al (frāz′ăl; -'l), *adj.* Of, consisting of, or constituting a phrase or phrases; as, *phrasal* felicity.

phrase (frāz), *n.* [F., fr. L. *phrasis* phraseology, fr. Gr. *phrasis*, fr. *phrazein* to tell.] **1.** A short pithy expression, esp. one often used. **2.** A mode of speech; diction; phraseology. **3.** *Dances.* A series of movements comprising a pattern. **4.** *Gram.* Any group of two or more words that form a sense unit, either expressing a thought fragmentarily or as a sentence element not containing a predication but having the force of a single part of speech. Chief types of phrases are: ***prepositional phrase*** (*through the night*); ***participial phrase, infinitive phrase, or gerund phrase***, when containing a participle, infinitive, or gerund with its qualifiers and objects; ***verb phrase*** (*should have gained*). **5.** *Music.* A short musical thought at least two, but typically four, measures in length, closing with a cadence.

— *v. t. & i.* **1.** To express in words, esp. in appropriate words. **2.** *Music.* To divide (notes or tones) into melodic phrases.

phra′se·o·gram′ (frā′zē·ō·grăm′), *n.* [Gr. *phrasis* a phrase + *-gram.*] A symbol for a phrase.

phra′se·o·graph′ (-grȧf′; 9), *n.* A phrase having a phraseogram.

phra′se·ol′o·gist (-ŏl′ō·jĭst), *n.* One who deals with phraseology; also, one skilled in coining phrases.

phra′se·ol′o·gy (-jĭ), *n.* [See PHRASE; -LOGY.] Manner of expression; idiomatic or peculiar phrasing; diction; style. — **phra′se·o·log′i·cal** (-ō·lŏj′ĭ·kăl), *adj.*

phras′ing (frāz′ĭng), *n.* **a** Method of expression; phraseology; wording. **b** *Music.* Act, method, or result, of grouping the notes so as to form distinct musical phrases.

phra′try (frā′trĭ), *n.*; *pl.* -TRIES (-trĭz). [Gr. *phratria.*] A group of related families; in ancient Athens, a subdivision of the phyle. — **phra′tral** (frā′trăl), *adj.*

phre·net′ic (frē·nĕt′ĭk), *adj.* Also **phre·net′i·cal** (-ĭ·kăl). [OF. *frenetique.* See FRANTIC.] **1.** Insane; violent. **2.** Moved by extreme excitement; fanatic. — *n.* One who is phrenetic; a madman. — **phre·net′i·cal·ly**, *adv.*

phren′ic (frĕn′ĭk), *adj.* [Gr. *phrēn, phrenos*, the diaphragm, the heart, the mind.] **1.** *Anat.* Of or pertaining to the diaphragm. **2.** Of or pert. to the mind; mental.

phre·ni′tis (frē·nī′tĭs), *n.* [L., fr. Gr. *phrenitis.*] *Med.* Delirium; brain fever. — **phre·nit′ic** (-nĭt′ĭk), *adj.*

phren′o- (frĕn′ō-), **phren-**. [Gr. *phrēn, phrenos*, midriff, heart, mind.] A combining form denoting: **a** *The diaphragm.* **b** *Phrenic.*

phre·nol′o·gy (frē·nŏl′ō·jĭ), *n.* [*phreno-* + *-logy.*] The study of the conformation of the skull as indicative of mental faculties. — **phren′o·log′ic** (frĕn′ō·lŏj′ĭk), **phren′o·log′i·cal** (-ĭ·kăl), *adj.* — **phre·nol′o·gist** (frē·nŏl′ō·jĭst), *n.*

phren′sy (frĕn′zĭ). Var. of FRENZY.

Phryg′i·an (frĭj′ĭ·ăn), *n.* **1.** A native or inhabitant of ancient Phrygia. **2.** The language of the Phrygians, probably of Thracian origin, but little known. See INDO-EUROPEAN LANGUAGES, *Table.* — **Phryg′i·an**, *adj.*

phthal′ein (thăl′ēn; -ē·ĭn; fthăl′-; 90), *n.* [See PHTHALIC.] *Chem.* Any of a series of artificial organic dyes, as eosin, made by condensation of phenols with phthalic acid.

phthal′ic (thăl′ĭk; fthăl′ĭk), *adj.* [naphthalene + *-ic.*] *Chem.* Pertaining to or designating any of three isomeric diacids, $C_6H_4(CO_2H)_2$, obtained by oxidation of various benzene derivatives; specif., a white crystalline compound produced by oxidizing naphthalene and allied compounds.

phthal′in (-ĭn), *n.* *Chem.* Any of a series of colorless compounds obtained by reduction from the phthaleins.

phthis′ic (tĭz′ĭk), *n.* [OF. *tisique*, orig. fem. adj., fr. L. *phthisicus* phthisical, fr. Gr. *phthisikos.* See PHTHISIS.] Phthisis. — **phthis′i·cal** (-ĭ·kăl), *adj.*

phthi′sis (thī′sĭs; fthī′sĭs), *n.* [L., fr. Gr. *phthisis.*] *Med.* A wasting or consumption of the tissue; usually, pulmonary tuberculosis (see TUBERCULOSIS).

-phy′ce·ae (-fī′sē·ē; -fĭs′ē·ē). [NL., fr. Gr. *phykos.*] *Bot.* Combining form meaning *seaweed*, used in names of classes and orders of algae. Derivative adjectives are formed in **-phy′ceous** (-fĭsh′ŭs).

phy·col′o·gy (fī·kŏl′ō·jĭ), *n.* [Gr. *phykos* seaweed + *-logy.*] Algology.

phy′co·my·ce′tous (fī′kō·mī·sē′tŭs), *adj.* [Gr. *phykos* seaweed + *mykēs, mykētos,* fungus.] *Bot.* Belonging to a large class (Phycomycetes) of parasitic or saprophytic fungi, the algal or algalike fungi. — **phy′co·my·cete′** (-sēt′), *n.*

phy·lac′ter·y (fĭ·lăk′tẽr·ĭ), *n.; pl.* -TERIES (-ĭz). [LL. *phylacterium,* fr. Gr. *phylaktērion,* deriv. of *phylassein* to watch, guard.] **1.** A square leathern box, containing slips on which are written certain Scriptural passages. Two such boxes are worn by Jews, one on the head and one on the left arm, during prayer. **2.** A reminder; also, an indication of Pharisaism or hypocrisy; — in allusion to Matt. xxiii. 5. **3.** Anything worn as a charm; an amulet.

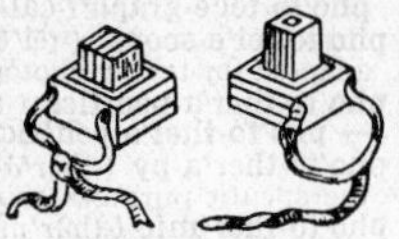

Phylacteries, 1.

phy′le (fī′lē), *n.; pl.* PHYLAE (-lē). [NL., fr. Gr. *phylē.*] *Gr. Hist.* The largest political subdivision among the ancient Athenians, corresponding to the Roman *tribe.*

phy·let′ic (fī·lĕt′ĭk), *adj.* [Gr. *phyletikos.*] *Biol.* Of or pertaining to a phylum, or line of descent; racial.

-phyll (-fĭl). [Gr. *phyllon.*] *Bot.* A combining form meaning *leaf,* as in chloro*phyll.*

Phyl′lis (fĭl′ĭs), *n.* A country girl in Vergil's *Eclogues.* Hence, often **Phil′lis,** pretty rustic maid or a sweetheart.

phyl′lo- (fĭl′ō-), **phyll-.** [Gr. *phyllon.*] A combining form meaning *leaf.*

phyl′lo·clade (-klăd), *n.* Also **phyl′lo·clad** (-klăd). [*phyllo-* + Gr. *klados* sprout.] *Bot.* Any flattened stem or branch performing the functions of leaves, as the joints of cacti. Also, erroneously, a cladophyll.

phyl′lode (fĭl′ōd), *n.* [F., fr. NL. *phyllodium,* fr. Gr. *phyllōdēs* leaflike, fr. *phyllon* leaf + *eidos* form.] *Bot.* A flat expanded petiole replacing the blade of a foliage leaf and fulfilling the same functions.

phyl′loid (-oid), *adj.* Resembling a leaf.

phyl′lome (fĭl′ōm), *n.* [Gr. *phyllōma* foliage.] *Bot.* A foliar organ; a leaf and its appendages or modifications, in the abstract. — **phyl·lom′ic** (fĭ·lŏm′ĭk; -lō′mĭk), *adj.*

phyl′lo·pod (fĭl′ō·pŏd), *n.* [*phyllo-* + *-pod.*] *Zool.* Any of a group (Phyllopoda) of crustaceans (Entomostraca) typically having leaflike swimming feet which also serve as gills. — **phyl′lo·pod,** *adj.* — **phyl·lop′o·dan** (fĭ·lŏp′ō·dăn), *adj. & n.*

phyl′lo·tax′y (-tăk′sĭ), *n.* Also **phyl′lo·tax′is** (-tăk′sĭs). [*phyllo-* + Gr. *taxis* arrangement.] *Bot.* The system or order of leaf arrangement on a stem.

-phyl′lous (-fĭl′ŭs). [See PHYLLO-.] *Bot.* A combining form meaning *having* (such or so many) *leaves,* or *leaflike parts.*

phyl′lox·e′ra (fĭl′ŏk·sē′rȧ; fĭ·lŏk′sē·rȧ), *n.* [NL., fr. *phyllo-* + Gr. *xēros* dry.] *Zool.* Any of a genus (*Phylloxera*) of plant lice differing from aphids in wing structure, in being continuously oviparous, and in lacking honey tubes.

phy′lo- (fī′lō-), **phyl-.** [Gr. *phylon.*] A combining form meaning *a tribe* or *race,* used also for *phylum.*

phy·log′e·ny (fī·lŏj′ē·nĭ), *n.; pl.* -NIES (-nĭz). Also **phy′lo·gen′e·sis** (fī′lō·jĕn′ē·sĭs). [*phylo-* + *-geny.*] The race history of an animal or vegetable type; — distinguished from *ontogeny.* — **phy′lo·gen′ic** (fī′lō·jĕn′ĭk), **phy′lo·ge·net′ic** (-jē·nĕt′ĭk), *adj.* — **phy′lo·ge·net′i·cal·ly** (-ĭ·kăl·ĭ), *adv.*

phy′lon (fī′lŏn), *n.; pl.* PHYLA (-lȧ). [NL., fr. Gr. *phylon* race, tribe.] *Biol.* A tribe or race; a genetically related group.

phy′lum (-lŭm), *n.; pl.* PHYLA (-lȧ). [NL. See PHYLON.] *Biol.* One of the primary divisions of the animal or vegetable kingdom; — so called because the members are assumed to have a common descent.

-phyre (-fīr). [F. *-phyre,* fr. *porphyre* (see PORPHYRY).] *Petrog.* A combining form denoting a *porphyritic rock.*

phys′i- (fĭz′ĭ-). = PHYSIO-.

phys′ic (fĭz′ĭk), *n.* [OF. *fisique, phisique,* fr. L., fr. Gr. *physikē,* fr. *physikos* natural, fr. *physis* nature.] **1.** *Now Rare.* Natural science; physics (sense 1). **2. a** *Archaic.* Medical science. **b** The art of healing diseases; the practice or profession of medicine. **3. a** A remedy for disease; medicine. **b** Specif., a cathartic. — *v. t.;* PHYS′ICKED (-ĭkt); PHYS′ICK·ING. **1.** To treat with physic or medicine, esp. a cathartic; to purge. **2.** To relieve; heal; cure.

phys′i·cal (fĭz′ĭ·kăl), *adj.* **1.** Of or pertaining to nature (as including all created existences) or the laws of nature; also, of or relating to natural or material things; material; natural. **2.** Of, pertaining to, or concerned with natural science or natural philosophy. **3.** Of or pertaining to physics; produced by the forces and operations of physics; as, *physical* changes; *physical* combinations. **4.** Of or pertaining to the body (as contrasted with the mind); bodily; as, *physical* strength. Cf. PSYCHICAL. — **Syn.** See MATERIAL: BODILY. — **phys′i·cal·ly,** *adv.*

physical education. Education in its application to the development and care of the body, esp. with reference to instruction in hygiene and systematic exercises.

physical geography. Geography which treats of the exterior physical features and changes of the earth.

physical science. Physics, or an allied science, as chemistry, mineralogy, petrology, geology, astronomy, meteorology, etc.; also, such sciences collectively.

physical therapy. Treatment of disease by physical and mechanical means, as by massage, electricity, etc.

phy·si′cian (fĭ·zĭsh′ăn), *n.* [OF. *fisicien, physicien.*] **1.** A person skilled in physic or the art of healing; a doctor of medicine; — often distinguished from a *surgeon.* **2.** A healer or restorer; as, a *physician* of the soul.

phys′i·cist (fĭz′ĭ·sĭst), *n.* A specialist in physics; also, one versed in natural science.

phys′i·co- (fĭz′ĭ·kō-). [Gr. *physikos* physical.] A combining form denoting: **a** *Physical; physical and,* as in **phys′i·co·men′tal. b** *Pertaining to physics and,* as in **phys′i·co·chem′i·cal, phys′i·co·math′e·mat′i·cal.**

phys′ics (fĭz′ĭks), *n.;* see -ICS. [See PHYSIC, *n.*] **1.** Orig., that branch of knowledge treating of the material world and its phenomena; natural philosophy. **2.** The science which deals with those phenomena of inanimate matter involving no changes in chemical composition; more specifically, the science of matter and motion. *Physics* includes mechanics, heat, electricity, light, and sound, and the branches of sciences devoted to the study of radiations (X rays, gamma rays, cosmic rays) and of atomic structure. **3.** A treatise on physics. **4.** The physical composition and properties of a substance; as, the *physics* of soils; physical processes collectively, as of an organism; as, the *physics* of a cell, of osmosis.

phys′i·o- (fĭz′ĭ·ō-), **phys′i-** (fĭz′ĭ-). [Gr. *physis.*] A combining form meaning *nature.*

phys′i·o·crat (-krăt), *n.* [F. *physiocrate.* See PHYSIO-; -CRAT.] One of the followers of Quesnay, a Frenchman, who, in the 18th century, founded a system of political and economic doctrines based on the supremacy of natural order, and emphasizing the powers of nature as the source of public wealth and national prosperity and the only proper source of public revenue. — **phys′i·o·crat′ic** (-krăt′ĭk), *adj.*

phys′i·og′no·my (fĭz′ĭ·ŏg′nō·mĭ; -ŏn′ō·mĭ), *n.* [OF. *phisonomie, fizonomie,* through ML., fr. Gr. *physiognōmonia,* fr. *physis* nature + *gnōmōn* a judge.] **1.** Art of discovering temperament and character from outward appearance, esp. from facial features. **2.** Face or countenance. **3.** External aspect; hence, inner character as revealed outwardly. — **Syn.** See FACE. — **phys′i·og·nom′ic** (-ŏg·nŏm′ĭk; -ō·nŏm′ĭk), **phys′i·og·nom′i·cal** (-ĭ·kăl), *adj.* — **phys′i·og·nom′i·cal·ly,** *adv.* — **phys′i·og′no·mist** (-ŏg′nō·mĭst; -ŏn′ō·mĭst), *n.*

phys′i·og′ra·phy (-ŏg′rȧ·fĭ), *n.* [*physio-* + *-graphy.*] **1.** A description of nature or natural phenomena in general. **2.** Physical geography. — **phys′i·og′ra·pher** (-fẽr), *n.* — **phys′i·o·graph′ic** (-ō·grăf′ĭk), **phys′i·o·graph′i·cal** (-ĭ·kăl), *adj.*

phys′i·o·log′i·cal (-ō·lŏj′ĭ·kăl), *adj.* Also **phys′i·o·log′ic** (-ĭk). **1.** Of or pertaining to physiology. **2.** Characteristic of or appropriate to an organism's healthy functioning. — **phys′i·o·log′i·cal·ly,** *adv.*

phys′i·ol′o·gist (fĭz′ĭ·ŏl′ō·jĭst), *n.* One versed in physiology.

phys′i·ol′o·gy (-jĭ), *n.* [F. or L.; F. *physiologie,* fr. L., fr. Gr. *physiologia,* fr. *physis* nature + *logos* discourse.] **1.** The branch of biology dealing with the processes, activities, and phenomena of life and living organisms; the study of the functions of the organs and parts during life, as distinct from *anatomy.* **2.** The organic processes and phenomena, collectively, of an organism or part. **3.** A treatise on physiology.

phys′i·o·ther′a·py (fĭz′ĭ·ō·thĕr′ȧ·pĭ), *n.* *Med.* Physical therapy.

phy·sique′ (fĭ·zēk′), *n.* [F. See PHYSIC, *n.*] One's body or a type of body with reference to its structure, constitution, appearance, or strength; as, a muscular *physique.*

phy′so·stig′mine (fī′sō·stĭg′mēn; -mĭn), *n.* Also **phy′so·stig′min.** [From *Physostigma,* generic name of the Calabar bean, fr. Gr. *physan* to inflate + *stigma.*] *Chem.* A colorless, crystalline, tasteless alkaloid, $C_{15}H_{21}N_3O_2$, the chief alkaloid of the Calabar bean. It is used as a myotic.

phy·sos′to·mous (fī·sŏs′tō·mŭs), *adj.* [Gr. *physa* bellows + *-stomous.*] *Zool.* **a** Having a duct to the air bladder. **b** Of or pertaining to a former order (Physostomi) of teleost fishes, in which the air bladder, if present, is joined with the esophagus by an open duct.

-phyte (-fīt). [Gr. *phyton* plant.] A combining form denoting *a plant having a* (specified) *characteristic* or *habitat,* as in bryo*phyte,* sapro*phyte.*

phy′tin (fī′tĭn), *n.* [Gr. *phyton* a plant + *-in.*] *Biochem. & Pharm.* A calcium-magnesium salt occurring as a reserve material in seeds, tubers, etc., used as a stimulant.

phy′to- (fī′tō-), **phyt-.** [Gr. *phyton.*] A combining form, meaning *a plant* or *plants,* as in *phyto*geography.

phy′to·cid′al (-sīd′ăl; -′l), *adj.* [See PHYTO-; -CIDE, 1.] Plant-killing.

phy′to·gen′e·sis (-jĕn′ē·sĭs), *n.* Also **phy·tog′e·ny** (fī·tŏj′ē·nĭ). [NL., fr. *phyto-* + *-genesis.*] The origin and developmental history of plants. — **phy′to·ge·net′ic** (-jē·nĕt′ĭk), **phy′to·ge·net′i·cal** (-ĭ·kăl), *adj.* — **phy′to·ge·net′i·cal·ly,** *adv.*

phy′to·gen′ic (fī′tō·jĕn′ĭk), **phy·tog′e·nous** (fī·tŏj′ē·nŭs), *adj.* Of, or chiefly of, vegetable origin.

phy′to·ge·og′ra·phy (-jē·ŏg′rȧ·fĭ), *n.* Geography treating of plants.

phy·tog′ra·phy (fī·tŏg′rȧ·fĭ), *n.* [NL. *phytographia.* See PHYTO-; -GRAPHY.] Taxonomic or descriptive botany.

phy′to·hor′mone (fī′tō·hôr′mōn), *n.* *Bot. & Chem.* An auxin.

phy·tol′o·gy (fī·tŏl′ō·jĭ), *n.* The science of plants; botany. — **phy′to·log′ic** (fī′tō·lŏj′ĭk), **phy′to·log′i·cal** (-ĭ·kăl), *adj.*

phy·toph′a·gous (fī·tŏf′ȧ·gŭs), *adj.* [*phyto-* + *-phagous.*] *Zool.* Feeding on plants; herbivorous.

phy′to·so′ci·ol′o·gy (fī′tō·sō′sĭ·ŏl′ō·jĭ; -sō′shĭ-), *n.* The study of the components of and interrelations among the flora of particular areas. — **phy′to·so′ci·o·log′ic** (-ō·lŏj′ĭk), **phy′to·so′ci·o·log′i·cal** (-ĭ·kăl), *adj.* — **phy′to·so′ci·ol′o·gist** (-ŏl′ō·jĭst), *n.*

phy·tos′ter·ol (fī·tŏs′tẽr·ōl; -ŏl), *n.* [*phyto-* + chole*sterol.*] *Chem.* Any of certain crystalline alcohols obtained from plants and having the properties of sterols, as ergosterol.

pi (pī; pē), *n.* [Gr.] **1.** The 16th letter (Π, π) of the Greek alphabet, corresponding to English *p.* **2.** *Math.* The letter Π, π denoting the ratio of the circumference of a circle to its diameter; also, the ratio itself. The value of this π, to eight decimal places, is 3.14159265.

pi (pī), *n. & v.* *Print.* See 4th PIE.

pi·ac′u·lar (pī·ăk′ū·lẽr), *adj.* [L. *piacularis.*] **a** Of the nature of expiation; expiatory. **b** Requiring expiation; sinful.

piaf′fer (pyăf′ẽr), *n.* [F., inf. taken as n.] *Manège.* A movement in which the horse lifts together one forefoot and the hind foot of the opposite side without advancing or receding. — **piaffe** (pyăf), *v. i.*

pi′al (pī′ăl), *adj.* [From *pia* mater.] *Anat.* Of or pertaining to the pia mater; as, a *pial* artery.

pi′a ma′ter (pī′ȧ mā′tẽr). [ML., fr. L., tender mother.] *Anat.* The vascular membrane investing the brain and spinal cord, internal to the arachnoid and dura mater.

pi′a·nis′si·mo (pē′ȧ·nĭs′ĭ·mō; *It.* pyä·nēs′sē·mō), *adj.* [It., superl. of *piano.*] *Music.* Very soft; — a direction. Abbr. *pp* — *adv.* *Music.* Very softly. — *n.* *Music.* A passage or movement so executed.

pi·an′ist (pĭ·ăn′ĭst; pē′ȧ·nĭst), *n.* A performer, esp. a skilled performer, on the piano.

pi·an′o (pĭ·ăn′ō; -ä′nō), *n.; pl.* PIANOS (-ōz). [It., fr. *piano* soft, fr. L. *planus* even, smooth.] *Music.* A stringed instrument of percussion, giving its tones from steel wires struck by felt-covered hammers operated from a keyboard. According to the shape of the case and the resulting disposition of the mechanism, pianos are classed as ***grand*** (of which the largest is *concert grand* and the smallest the *baby grand*), ***square,*** and ***upright.***

pi·a′no (pĭ·ä′nō), *adj.* [It., even, smooth, soft, fr. L. *planus* even, level.] *Music.* Soft; — a direction. Abbr. *p*

pi·an′o·for′te (pĭ·ăn′ō·fōr′tē; -ăn′ō·fōrt), *n.* [*piano* + It. *forte* strong, fr. L. *fortis*.] A piano.

pi′as·sa′va (pē′ȧ·sä′vȧ), *n.* Also **pi′as·sa′ba, pi′a·sa′va, pi′a·sa′ba.** [Pg. *piassaba, piaçaba*, fr. Tupi *piaçába*.] **a** A coarse brown fiber of a Brazilian pinnate-leaved palm (*Attalea funifera*), used in making ropes, brushes, etc.; also, the tree itself, which yields the coquilla nut (which see). **b** A Brazilian palm (*Leopoldinia piassaba*) which yields a similar but inferior fiber; also, the fiber. **c** The stiff coarse bast fiber of an African palm (*Raphia vinifera*).

pi·as′ter, pi·as′tre (pĭ·ăs′tẽr), *n.* [F. *piastre*, fr. It., fr. L. *emplastrum*. See PLASTER.] A coin of various countries, as Egypt and Syria; esp., a nickel coin of Turkey now known as the kuruş. See MONEY, *Tables*.

pi·az′za (pĭ·ăz′ȧ; *Brit. also* pĭ·ăt′sȧ, -ăd′zȧ; *It.* pyät′tsä), *n.; pl.* PIAZZAS (-ăz); It. PIAZZE (pyät′tsā). [It., place, square, fr. L. *platea* street, courtyard.] **1.** An open square in an Italian town. **2.** By extension, an arcaded and roofed gallery; hence, esp. *U. S. & Can.*, a veranda; porch.

pi′broch (pē′brŏk), *n.* [Gael. *piobaireachd* pipe music, fr. *piobair* a piper, fr. *piob* pipe, bagpipe, fr. English. See PIPE, *n.*] *Music.* A set of variations for the Scottish Highland bagpipe, usually martial or mournful.

pi′ca (pī′kȧ), *n.* [ML., a collection of rules (see 3d PIE).] *Print.* A size of type (12 points or, ***small pica***, 11 points). See TYPE.

pi′ca, *n.* [L., a pie, magpie.] *Med. & Veter.* Craving for unnatural food, as chalk, ashes, etc. Cf. GEOPHAGY.

pic′a·dor (pĭk′ȧ·dōr; 70), *n.* [Sp.] **1.** A horseman with a lance, who in a bullfight excites the bull by prodding without trying to kill him. **2.** Hence, an agile, clever debater, jester, or wit.

pic′a·resque′ (pĭk′ȧ·rĕsk′), *adj.* [Sp. *picaresco*, fr. Sp. *pícaro* rogue.] Of, pertaining to, or characteristic of rogues or rascals; specif., designating a type of fiction, of Spanish origin, having a rogue as a hero.

pic′a·ro (pĭk′ȧ·rō; *Sp.* pē′kä·rō), *n.*, *fem.* **pic′a·ra** (-rä). [Sp. *pícaro*, fem. *pícara*.] A rogue; knave; vagabond. Cf. PICARESQUE.

pic′a·roon′ (pĭk′ȧ·rōōn′), *n.* [Sp. *picarón*.] **1.** A rogue. **2.** A pirate; corsair. — *v. i.* To act as a pirate.

pic′a·yune′ (pĭk′ȧ·yōōn′; pĭk′ĭ·ūn′), *n.* [F. *picaillon* an old copper coin of Piedmont.] **1.** *Southern U. S.* A small coin, as a five-cent piece. **2.** *U. S.* Hence, something of small value.

pic′a·yune′, pic′a·yun′ish (-yōōn′ĭsh), *adj.* *U. S.* Of little value; petty; mean; as, a *picayunish* business.

Pic′ca·dil′ly (pĭk′ȧ·dĭl′ĭ; pĭk′ȧ·dĭl′ĭ), *n.* A famous London street of fine houses, clubs, and shops. **Piccadilly Circus** (see CIRCUS, 4) is near its eastern end.

pic′ca·lil′li (pĭk′ȧ·lĭl′ĭ), *n.* A pickle, orig. East Indian, of chopped vegetables and pungent spices.

pic′co·lo (pĭk′ō·lō), *n.; pl.* -LOS (-lōz). [It., small.] *Music.* A small, shrill flute, pitched an octave higher than the ordinary flute. — **pic′co·lo·ist** (-lō·ĭst), *n.*

pice (pīs), *n. sing. & pl.* [Hind. *paisā*.] A bronze coin of India. See MONEY, *Tables*.

pic′e·ous (pĭs′ē·ŭs; pī′sē-), *adj.* [L. *piceus*, fr. *pix, picis*, pitch.] Of, pertaining to, or like pitch; inflammable; esp., *Zool.*, resembling pitch in color.

pich′i·ci·a′go (pĭch′ĭ·sĭ·ä′gō; -ā′gō), *n.* [Cf. Sp. *pichiciego*.] A small burrowing South American armadillo (*Chlamyphorus truncatus*).

pick (pĭk), *n.* [Var. of 1st PIKE.] **1.** A heavy, pointed iron or steel tool, wielded by means of a wooden handle inserted in an eye between the ends; pickax. **2.** A pointed instrument for picking; — often in combination, as in tooth*pick;* specif., a plectrum, as for a mandolin.

pick, *v. t.* [ME. *piken*, fr. OF. *piquer*, and fr. the verb of AS. *picung* a pricking.] **1.** To use a pointed instrument on; to pierce, indent, break up, or the like, by striking with a pointed implement. **2.** To clear of, or free from, matter of some kind with the fingers, or the like; as, to *pick* a fowl, that is, to clear it of feathers; to *pick* a bone, that is, to clear it of flesh. **3.** To pull away, esp. with the fingers; to pluck; gather, as fruit from a tree; also, to pull apart or into small pieces; as, to *pick* rags. **4.** To choose; select. **5.** To rob; — now only in *to pick one's pocket, purse*, etc. **6.** To seek and find occasion for; to provoke; as, to *pick* a quarrel. **7.** To open (a lock) by or as by a wire. **8.** *Music. U. S.* To pull or pluck (the strings); hence, to play (as the banjo). — *v. i.* **1.** To work with a pick, pickax, etc. **2.** To gather flowers, fruit, cotton, etc. **3.** To search carefully; to choose with care. **4.** To pilfer. **5.** To eat sparingly or daintily. — **Syn.** See CHOOSE.

pick up. **a** To take up, as with the fingers. **b** To get by bits; to acquire casually; as, to *pick up* a habit. **c** To take up, in, or along; as, the bus *picked up* passengers. **d** To bring within range of sight, hearing, etc. **e** To recover, as health or strength; improve gradually. **f** To gather steam, speed, power, etc.

— *n.* **1.** Act of picking; specif.: **a** A blow with a pointed instrument. **b** Act of choosing; choice; also, the choicest or best. **2.** The portion or quantity of a crop gathered at one time, as of hops, fruit, or the like.

pick, *v. t.* [Collat. form of PITCH to throw.] **1.** *Now Dial.* To throw; fling; also, to pitch, as hay. **2.** *Weaving.* To throw (a shuttle). — *n.* **1.** *Chiefly N. of Eng.* Act of pitching or throwing; a pitch. **2.** *Weaving.* **a** The blow which drives the shuttle by which speed of a loom is reckoned; as, so many *picks* per minute. **b** Hence, in describing the fineness of a fabric, one of the weft threads; as, so many *picks* to an inch.

pick′a·back′ (pĭk′ȧ·băk′), *adv.* On the back or shoulders; as, to ride *pickaback*.

pickaback plane. An airplane designed for long-distance flights. It is heavily loaded with fuel, attached to the top of a larger airplane, carried aloft, and released in mid-air.

pick′a·nin′ny (pĭk′ȧ·nĭn′ĭ), *n.; pl.* -NIES (-ĭz). [Dim. of Sp. *pequeño* little, young or Pg. *pequeno*.] A small child; — applied in the United States to a colored child.

pick′ax′, pick′axe′ (pĭk′ăks′), *n.* [Corrupt. of ME. *pikois, pikeis*, fr. OF. *picois*.] A pick or mattock. — *v. t. & i.* To work or remove with a pickax.

pick′ed (pĭk′ĕd; -ĭd; pĭkt), *adj.* *Archaic & Dial.* Pointed; peaked; spiny.

picked (pĭkt; *see* -ED), *adj.* [From PICK to pierce.] **1.** Cleared with or as with a pick; stripped. **2.** That has been plucked; as, a *picked* chicken. **3.** That has been selected, etc.; choice; as, all *picked* men.

pick·eer′ (pĭk·ēr′), *v. i.* To skirmish; reconnoiter; scout.

pick′er (pĭk′ẽr), *n.* [From PICK to throw.] *Weaving.* The piece that impels the shuttle through the warp.

pick′er, *n.* [From PICK to pierce.] **1.** One who or that which picks, in any sense. **2.** *Mach.* A machine for picking fibrous materials to pieces so as to loosen and separate the fiber; also, its operator.

pick′er·el (pĭk′ẽr·ĕl), *n.; see* PLURAL, *Note*, 6. [Dim. of PIKE fish.] In America, sometimes, the pike; specif., any of several smaller species of the pike family, esp. one (*Esox niger*), a food fish about two feet long, of the eastern and southern states.

pick′er·el·weed′ (-wēd′), *n.* **a** An American aquatic herb (*Pontederia cordata*) growing in shallow water of streams and ponds. **b** Any of various species of the same genus (*Pontederia*) growing in still water.

pick′et (pĭk′ĕt; -ĭt), *n.* [F. *piquet*, dim. fr. *piquer* to pierce, prick. See PIKE a weapon.] **1.** A pointed or sharpened stake, peg, or pale; as: **a** A pale used in making fences. **b** A stake used for tethering horses. **2.** *Mil.* **a** A detached body of soldiers serving to guard an army from surprise. **b** A detachment kept ready in camp for such duty. **c** A sentinel. **3.** A person posted by a labor organization at a place of work affected by a strike. — *v. i.* **1.** To enclose, fasten, fence, or fortify with pickets. **2.** *Mil.* **a** To guard, as a camp, by an outlying picket. **b** To post as a picket. **3.** To tether to or as to a picket. **4. a** To post pickets (sense 3, above) at (a place of employment). **b** To walk or stand in front of (such a place) as a picket. — **pick′et·er,** *n.*

pick′ing (pĭk′ĭng), *n.* **1.** Act of one that picks. **2.** *pl.* A thing or amount picked; as: **a** A fragment or amount that may be picked, eaten, etc., esp. from refuse; a scrap. **b** Perquisites; share of spoils.

pick′le (pĭk′′l), *n.* *Scot.* A grain or kernel; little.

pick′le, *n.* [ME. *pykyl, pekille*.] **1. a** A salt-and-water solution for preserving or corning fish, meat, etc.; brine. **b** Vinegar, plain or spiced, for preserving vegetables, fish, eggs, oysters, etc. **2.** A predicament. **3.** Any article of food, esp. cucumbers, preserved in brine or in vinegar. **4.** *Metalwork.* A bath of acid, etc., to cleanse the surface of castings. — **Syn.** See PREDICAMENT. — *v. t.;* PICK′LED (-′ld); PICK′LING (-lĭng). To preserve in a pickle of any kind.

pick′lock′ (pĭk′lŏk′), *n.* One who picks locks; specif., a thief; also, a tool for picking locks.

pick′pock′et (-pŏk′ĕt; -ĭt), *n.* One who steals valuables from pockets.

pick′thank′ (-thăngk′), *n.* *Archaic.* One who curries favor with another, as by flattery or, esp., talebearing.

pick′up′ (-ŭp′), *n.* **1.** Act, process, or habit of picking up, in any sense. **2.** Improvement; revival of commercial activity. **3.** *Automobiles.* **a** Acceleration. **b** A light commercial truck for quick collection and delivery of goods. **4.** *Elec.* An attachment on a phonograph for converting the sound recorded on the disk into electrical current. **5.** *Games.* The fielding or hitting of a ball just after it strikes the ground. **6.** *Radio.* **a** The reception of sound in the transmitting apparatus for conversion into electrical energy. **b** The primary apparatus used for this process. **c** The place where a broadcast originates. **d** The electrical system for connecting to a broadcasting station a program produced outside the studio. **7.** *Television.* **a** The conversion of the image of a scene into electrical energy in the transmitting apparatus. **b** An apparatus used for this process. **8.** *Slang.* Something or a person picked up, as a bargain, a lost article, a passenger or hitchhiker, or an impromptu meal.

Pick·wick′i·an (pĭk·wĭk′ĭ·ăn), *adj.* Of, pertaining to, or characteristic of **Mr. Pick′wick** (pĭk′wĭk), the simple, goodhearted hero of Dickens's *Pickwick Papers*.

Pickwickian sense. A special or esoteric sense (of a word), suitable to a particular occasion or person.

pic′nic (pĭk′nĭk), *n.* [F. *piquenique*.] **1.** A pleasure party the food for which is usually provided by members of the group and is eaten in the open air. **2.** *Slang.* An easy, pleasant, or amusing time or experience. **3.** A shoulder of pork with much of the butt removed. See PORK, *Illust.* — *v. i.;* PIC′NICKED (-nĭkt); PIC′NICK·ING. To go on, or hold, a picnic; to eat in picnic fashion. — **pic′nick·er,** *n.*

pic′o·line (pĭk′ō·lēn; -lĭn), **pic′o·lin,** *n.* [L. *pix, picis*, pitch + *-ol*, 2 + *-ine*.] *Chem.* Any of three isomeric bases, C_6H_7N, occurring in oil from bones and in coal tar, as colorless mobile liquids of strong odor.

pi′cot (pē′kō), *n.; pl.* -COTS (-kōz). [F., dim. of *pic* a point.] One of many small loops forming a border or edging, as on ribbon, lace, etc. — **pi′cot,** *v. i. & t.;* PI′COTED (-kōd); PI′COT·ING (-kō·ĭng).

pic′o·tee′ (pĭk′ō·tē′), *n.* [F. *picoté* dotted, pricked.] *Hort.* One of a race of carnations having petals of a uniform ground color, with a marginal band of another color.

pi′cot stitch (pē′kō). = RAILWAY STITCH. See STITCH, *Illust.*

pic′rate (pĭk′rāt), *n.* *Chem.* A salt or ester of picric acid.

pic′ric (-rĭk), *adj.* [Gr. *pikros* bitter.] *Chem.* Pert. to or designating a yellow crystalline monoacid, $C_6H_2(NO_2)_3OH$, used in manufacturing high explosives, as a dye, etc.

pic′rite (-rīt), *n.* [Gr. *pikros* bitter; — so called from its large per cent of magnesia.] *Petrog.* A variety of peridotite, composed of augite and olivine.

pic′ro- (pĭk′rō-), **picr-.** [Gr. *pikros*.] Combining form meaning *bitter*.

pic′ro·tox′in (-tŏk′sĭn), *n.* [*picro-* + *toxic*.] *Chem.* A bitter colorless crystalline substance, $C_{30}H_{34}O_{13}$, resembling strychnine in its action as a violent poison.

Pict (pĭkt), *n.* [LL. *Picti*, pl.] One of a mixed race of aborigines and Aryan invaders, who once occupied Great Britain. About the 9th century they amalgamated with the Scots. — **Pict′ish** (pĭk′tĭsh), *adj. & n.*

pic′to·graph (pĭk′tō·grăf; 9), *n.* [See PICTURE; -GRAPH.] A picture or hieroglyph representing and expressing an idea; a writing in such symbols. Cf. IDEOGRAM. — **pic′to·graph′ic** (-grăf′ĭk), *adj.*

pic·tog′ra·phy (pĭk·tŏg′rȧ·fĭ), *n.* [L. *pictus* painted + *-graphy*.] Picture writing, or use of pictographs.

pic·to′ri·al (pĭk·tō′rĭ·ăl; 70), *adj.* [L. *pictorius*, fr. *pictor* a painter, fr. *pingere* to paint.] **1.** Of or pertaining to a painter or painting. **2. a** Consisting of pictures; in the form of a picture. **b** Illustrated by pictures; as, a *pictorial* weekly. **3.** Having the qualities of a picture; suggesting pictures; as, a *pictorial* style. — **Syn.** See GRAPHIC. — *n.* A pictorial journal or paper. — **pic·to′ri·al·ly,** *adv.*

pic′ture (pĭk′tūr), *n.* [L. *pictura*, fr. *pingere, pictum*, to paint.] **1.** A representation, as of a person or landscape, produced by painting, drawing, photography, etc. **2.** A description so vivid as to suggest a mental image (of the thing described). **3.** An image, likeness, or copy. **4.** A transitory visible image, as an image made by the lens of the eye or a telescope. **5.** A tableau; — more fully ***living picture*** (*tableau vivant*). **6.** = MOTION PICTURE. — *v. t.* **1.** To draw, paint, etc., a representation, image, or conception of; to depict. **2.** To represent visibly; to figure forth. **3.** To describe graphically; portray in words. **4.** To form a mental image of.

picture hat. A woman's broad-brimmed hat, usually black and adorned with ostrich plumes, modeled on hats seen in famous pictures.

pic′tur·esque′ (pĭk′tū̍r·ĕsk′; 2), *adj.* [F. *pittoresque*, fr. It. *pittoresco*.] **1.** Like a picture in coloring, design, technique, or the like; also, evoking a mental picture. **2.** Representing the charming in scenes, ideas, etc., without attaining beauty or sublimity; as, the *picturesque* school of poets. — **Syn.** See GRAPHIC. — *n.* With *the*, that which is picturesque; pictorial quality, esp. such as characterized 17th-century and 18th-century painting. — **pic′tur·esque′ly**, *adv.* — **pic′tur·esque′ness**, *n.*

picture window. An outsize window, usually one in a living room, framing a desirable exterior view.

picture writing. **a** Art of recording events or expressing messages by pictures representing the actions or facts. **b** The record or message so represented. Cf. PICTOGRAPHY.

pic′ul (pĭk′ŭl), *n.; pl.* PICUL or PICULS (-ŭlz). [Jav. & Malay *pikul*, fr. *pikul* to carry on the back; n., a man's burden.] A varying Oriental commercial weight of 100 catties. See CATTY.

pid′dle (pĭd′'l), *v. i.;* PID′DLED (-'ld); PID′DLING (-lĭng). To deal or work in a trifling or petty way.

pid′dling (-lĭng), *adj.* Trifling; trivial; paltry.

pid′dock (pĭd′ŭk), *n.* Any of a genus (*Pholas*) of bivalve mollusks which bore holes in wood, clay, and soft rocks.

pidg′in, pi′geon (pĭj′ĭn; -ŭn), *n.* Chinese corruption of *business;* — chiefly in **pidgin English**, the jargon used as a lingua franca between foreigners and the Chinese; sometimes, any similar jargon. Cf. BÊCHE-DE-MER, CHINOOK.

pie (pī), *n.* [OF., fr. L. *pica*.] A magpie.

pie, *n.* [ME. *pie, pye*.] An article of food consisting of a pastry crust with any of various kinds of filling; also, a kind of layer cake spread with jam or cream; as, Washington *pie*.

pie, pye (pī), *n.* [Prob. same word as *pie* magpie.] *Eccl.* A table used in England before the Reformation to ascertain the proper service or office for the day. This is probably the *pie* of the obsolete oath "By cock and *pie*."

pie (pī), *n.* Also **pi.** [Origin uncert.; perh. fr. *pie* (for food).] **a** *Print.* Type confusedly mixed or disarranged. **b** Hence, a jumble; mess. — *v. t.* **a** *Print.* To put into a mixed and disordered condition, as type. **b** Hence, to throw into disorder; to make a mess of.

pie (pī), *n.* [Hind. *pāī*.] A bronze coin of India. See MONEY, *Tables*.

pie′bald′ (pī′bôld′), *adj.* [*pie* the magpie + *bald*.] Of different colors, esp. white and black; mottled; pied. — *n.* A piebald animal, esp. a horse.

piece (pēs), *n.* [OF. *pece* (F. *pièce*), of Celt. origin.] **1.** A fragment or part separated from the whole in any manner. **2.** Any single object or individual (of a class or group): **a** *Archaic & Dial.* A person; individual. **b** *Now Dial.* (1) A short while. (2) A short distance. **c** A definite quantity regarded as distinct; as, a *piece* of land. **d** A single instance or example; as, a *piece* of news. **3.** A quantity, as a length, weight, or size, usually fixed, in which various articles are made or put up for sale or use; as, a *piece*, or roll (8–16 yards, in England usually 12), of wallpaper. Cf. PIECE GOODS. **4.** Short for *piece of work:* **a** A literary composition. **b** A picture; painting. **c** A play or drama. **d** A musical composition. **e** A passage to be recited or declaimed. **5.** A firearm, as a cannon; as, a battery of six *pieces*. **6.** A piece of money; a coin; as, *pieces* of silver. **7.** *Games.* **a** *Chess.* A superior man, as distinguished from a pawn; also, loosely, any man. **b** *Checkers, etc.* A man. — **Syn.** See PART. — ***of a piece.*** Uniform; alike. — *v. t.;* PIECED (pēst); PIEC′ING (pēs′ĭng). **1.** To repair, complete, or extend by adding pieces; as, to *piece* a garment. **2.** To join the pieces of; to mend by joining pieces; hence, to unite into a whole; as, to *piece* together accounts. — *adj.* **1.** Made of pieces; as, a *piece* quilt. **2.** Of or pert. to piecework; as, a *piece* price or wage.

‖**pièce de ré′sis′tance′** (pyĕs′ dĕ rā′zēs′täɴs′). [F.] Literally, piece of resistance; the main dish of a meal; hence, the chief article of any collection or series.

‖**pièce d'oc′ca′sion′** (pyĕs′ dô′kä′zyôɴ′). [F.] A piece for a special occasion; also, a bargain.

piece′–dyed′ (pēs′dīd′), *adj.* Dyed after being woven or knitted.

piece goods. Fabric or goods usually woven in and sold by pieces or fixed lengths, as shirtings, calicoes, etc.

piece′meal′ (pēs′mēl′), *adv.* [ME. *pecemele*, fr. *pece* a piece + AS. *mǣlum*, dat. pl. of *mǣl* measure.] **1.** Piece by piece; by degrees. **2.** In pieces; in fragments.

piece of eight. The Spanish and Spanish American peso of eight reals. See PESO, 1 **a**.

piec′er (pēs′ẽr), *n.* One who pieces; a patcher; one who joins pieces; esp. a textile worker who pieces threads.

piece′work′ (pēs′wûrk′), *n.* Work done by the piece; work paid for at a rate (**piece rate**) based on the amount done rather than on the time employed. — **piece′work′er** (-wûr′kẽr), *n.*

pied (pīd), *adj.* [From PIE magpie.] Of two or more colors in blotches; piebald; variegated.

‖**pied–à–terre** (pyā′tà·târ′), *n.* [F.] A temporary lodging.

pied′mont (pēd′mŏnt), *adj.* [From *Piedmont*, in Italy; cf. It. *Piemonte*.] *Phys. Geog.* Lying or formed at the base of mountains. — *n.* A piedmont district, plain, etc.

pie′plant′ (pī′plănt′; 9), *n.* *U. S.* The garden rhubarb.

pier (pēr), *n.* [ME. *pere, per*, fr. ML. *pera*.] **1.** An intermediate support for the adjacent ends of two bridge spans; — disting. from *abutment*. **2.** A breakwater or mole; hence, a structure built out into the water with piles for use as a landing place, pleasure resort, etc. **3.** *Arch.* **a** Either of the pillars supporting an arch or lintel. See GOTHIC, *Illust.* **b** A piece of wall between two openings. **c** An auxiliary mass of masonry used to stiffen a wall.

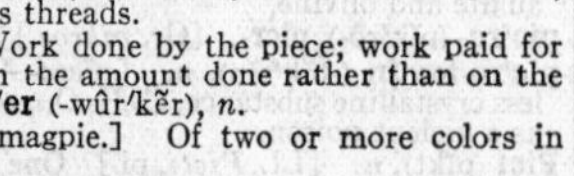

P, P Piers of a Bridge.

pierce (pērs), *v. t. & i.;* PIERCED (pērst); PIERC′ING (pēr′sĭng). [OF. *percer, percier*, fr. L. *pertundere, pertusum*, to beat.] **1.** To run into or through as a pointed instrument or weapon does; to stab; hence, to penetrate sharply and painfully. **2.** To bore or tunnel; to perforate. **3.** To force or wedge a way into or through; as, to *pierce* the enemy's line. **4.** To penetrate with the eye or mind; to discern. — **Syn.** See ENTER. — **pierc′er** (pēr′sẽr), *n.* — **pierc′ing·ly**, *adv.*

pier glass. A large high mirror, as, orig., a narrow one designed to occupy the pier or wall space between windows.

Pi·e′ri·an (pī·ēr′ĭ·ăn), *adj.* [L. *Pierius*.] Of or pert. to Pieria, a region of ancient Macedonia, one of the earliest seats of the worship of the Muses.

Pierian spring. A fountain in Pieria, sacred to the Muses, and believed to communicate poetic inspiration.

pi·er′i·dine (pī·ĕr′ĭ·dīn; -dĭn), *adj.* [From *Pieris*, type genus, fr. Gr. *Pieris*, a Muse.] *Zool.* Belonging to a family (Pieridae) of butterflies (type genus *Pieris*) having three pairs of well-developed legs.

Pi′er·rot (pē′ĕr·ō; *F.* pyĕ′rō′), *n.* [F., little Peter, fr. *Pierre* Peter.] In Old French pantomime, a jesting character (from old Italian comedy) in the role of a simple valet. He wore white pantaloons and a large white jacket with big buttons, and often had his face painted white.

pier table. A table for a pier (sense 3 **b**), esp. under a pier glass.

pi′et (pī′ĕt), *n.* [Dim. of PIE a magpie.] **a** The magpie. **b** *Scot.* Water ouzel.

‖**Pie·tà′** (pyā·tä′), *n.* [It., lit., pity, fr. L. *pietas* piety.] *Fine Arts.* A representation of the Virgin Mary mourning over the dead body of Christ.

pi′e·tism (pī′ĕ·tĭz'm), *n.* [G. *pietismus*.] **1.** The principles or practices of one who seeks to substitute the devotional for the intellectual ideal in Christian experience; also, affectation of devotion. **2.** [*cap.*] The principles and practice of a class of religious persons (**Pietists**) in Germany in the 17th century. They emphasized repentance, faith as an attitude of heart, and regeneration and sanctification as experiential facts. — **pi′e·tist** (-tĭst), *n. & adj.* — **pi′e·tis′tic** (-tĭs′tĭk), *adj.* — **Syn.** See DEVOUT.

pi′e·ty (pī′ĕ·tĭ), *n.; pl.* -TIES (-tĭz). [OF. *pieté*, fr. L. *pietas*.] **1.** Pity. **2.** Quality or state of being pious; as: **a** Loyal devotion to parents, family, race, etc. **b** Dutifulness in religion; devoutness. **3.** A pious act, expression, etc. — **Syn.** See FIDELITY.

pi·e′zo·e·lec′tric′i·ty (pī·ē′zō·ē·lĕk′trĭs′ĭ·tĭ; -ĕl′ĕk-), *n.* [Gr. *piezein* to press + *electricity*.] Electricity or electric polarity due to pressure, esp. in a crystallized substance, as quartz. — **pi·e′zo·e·lec′tric** (-ē·lĕk′trĭk), *adj.* — **pi·e′zo·e·lec′tri·cal·ly** (-trĭ·kăl·ĭ), *adv.*

pi′e·zom′e·try (pī′ē·zŏm′ē·trĭ), *n.* *Physics.* Measurement of the compressibility of liquids. — **pi′e·zom′e·ter** (-tẽr), *n.* — **pi·e′zo·met′ric** (pī·ē′zō·mĕt′rĭk), **pi·e′zo·met′ri·cal** (-rĭ·kăl), *adj.*

pif′fle (pĭf′'l), *n.* *Slang.* Trifling talk or action.

pig (pĭg), *n.* [Origin uncert.] *Scot.* **a** An earthenware vessel; a crock. **b** A hot-water bottle.

pig, *n.;* see PLURAL, *Note*, 3. [ME. *pigge*, of uncert. origin.] **1.** A young swine; also, a swine of any age. See SWINE, 1; HOG; BOAR; SOW; SHOAT. **2.** *Humorous.* Pig's flesh as food; pork. **3.** *Colloq.* A person or animal likened to a pig, as in greed or filth. **4.** *Metal.* **a** A crude casting of metal (now esp. of iron or lead) in size and shape convenient for transportation or storage, run directly from the smelting furnace; — from its size as disting. from a *sow*. See SOW, 2 **b**. **b** Any of the molds or channels in the pig bed. **c** Collectively, pig iron, pig lead, or the like. — *v. i.;* PIGGED (pĭgd); PIG′GING. To farrow; also, esp. with *it*, to live like pigs.

pig bed. A bed of sand in which iron is cast into pigs.

pig′boat′ (pĭg′bōt′), *n.* *U. S. Navy Slang.* A submarine; — from the likeness of submarines nosed against a tender to suckling pigs.

pi′geon (pĭj′ŭn; -ĭn), *n.;* see PLURAL, *Note*, 3. [OF. *pijon* (F. *pigeon*), fr. LL. *pipio, -onis*, a young chirping bird, fr. *pipire* to peep.] **1.** Any bird of a widely distributed family (Columbidae, order Columbiformes); a dove; esp., one of the domesticated varieties, as the carrier, fantail, homer, jacobin, pouter, trumpeter, tumbler, and turbit, derived from the ***rock pigeon*** (*Columba livia*) of Europe. Cf. PASSENGER PIGEON, WOOD PIGEON; see BILL, *Illust.* **2.** *Slang.* A gull; dupe. **3.** *Colloq.* Affair; business; as, that is your *pigeon*.

pi′geon. Var. of PIDGIN (English).

pigeon breast. *Med.* A deformity of the chest marked by sharp projection of the sternum, occurring esp. in rickets. — **pi′geon–breast′ed** (*see Pron.*, § 2), *adj.* — **pi′geon–breast′ed·ness**, *n.*

pi′geon·heart′ed (pĭj′ŭn·här′tĕd; -tĭd; pĭj′ĭn-; 2), *adj.* Timid; cowardly; chicken-hearted.

pi′geon·hole′ (pĭj′ŭn·hōl′; pĭj′ĭn-), *n.* **1.** A small recess for pigeons to nest. **2.** A small open compartment in a desk, cabinet, or the like, for letters, documents, etc. — *v. t.* **1.** To place in, or as in, the pigeonhole of a desk, cabinet, etc.; hence, to put away, as if in a place readily accessible, but in fact to lay aside indefinitely. **2.** To arrange (data) according to a logical scheme; to classify. — **Syn.** See ASSORT.

pi′geon–liv′ered (-lĭv′ẽrd; 2), *adj.* Meek; gentle. *Shak.*

pigeon pea. The small nutritious seed of a tropical woody herb (*Cajanus cajan*) with trifoliolate leaves, yellow flowers, and flattish pods; also, the plant.

pi′geon–toed′ (-tōd′), *adj.* Having the toes turned in.

pi′geon·wing′ (-wĭng′), *n.* **1.** *Dancing. U. S.* A fancy step executed by jumping and striking the legs together. **2.** *U. S.* A certain fancy figure in skating.

pig′fish′ (pĭg′fĭsh′), *n.; pl.*, see FISH. **a** Any of several salt-water grunts of the genus *Orthopristis*, esp. *O. chrysapterus*, a U. S. food fish from Long Island southward. **b** = SAILOR'S-CHOICE **a**.

pig′ger·y (pĭg′ẽr·ĭ), *n.; pl.* -IES (-ĭz). Place where swine are kept; a pigsty; also, pigs collectively.

pig′gin (pĭg′ĭn), *n.* *Dial.* A small wooden pail with an upright stave as a handle.

pig′gish (pĭg′ĭsh), *adj.* Like a pig; greedy; mean; filthy. — **pig′gish·ly**, *adv.* — **pig′gish·ness**, *n.*

pig′gy bank (pĭg′ĭ). A small receptacle for coins to be accumulated as savings, esp. by a child; — from a common type shaped like a pig.

pig′head′ed (pĭg′hĕd′ĕd; -ĭd; 2), *adj.* Obstinate; stubborn.

pig iron. Crude iron, the direct product of the blast furnace; — so called because usually cast into pigs.

pig lead. Lead cast in pigs.

pig′ment (pĭg′mĕnt), *n.* [L. *pigmentum*, fr. root of *pingere* to paint.] **1.** A coloring matter. **2.** Any powdered substance mixed with a suitable liquid, in which it is relatively insoluble, to form paints, enamels, etc. **3.** *Biol.* Any of various coloring matters in animals and plants, esp. in cells or tissues.

pig′men·tar′y (pĭg′mĕn·tĕr′ĭ *or, esp. Brit.*, -tẽr·ĭ), *adj.* Of, pertaining to, or containing pigment.

pig′men·ta′tion (pĭg′mĕn·tā′shŭn), *n.* Coloration with, or deposition of, pigment; in *Med.*, esp., an excessive deposition of pigment.
Pig′my (pĭg′mĭ). Var. of PYGMY.
pig′nus (pĭg′nŭs), *n.; pl.* PIGNORA (-nō·rȧ). [L.] *Rom. & Civil Law.* A pledge or pawn.
pig′nut′ (pĭg′nŭt′), *n.* **1.** A species (*Conopodium denudatum*) of earthnut of southern Europe; also, its edible tuber. **2.** The thin-shelled, somewhat bitter nut of a species of hickory (*Carya glabra*); also, the tree.
pig′pen′ (-pĕn′), *n.* A pen, or sty, for pigs.
pig′skin′ (-skĭn′), *n.* The skin of a pig or hog, or leather made of it; hence, *Colloq.:* **a** A jockey's saddle. **b** A football.
pig′stick′ (-stĭk′), *v. i.* To hunt the wild boar with a spear. — **pig′-stick′er**, *n.* — **pig′stick′ing**, *n.*
pig′sty′ (-stī′), *n.; pl.* -STIES (-stīz′). A pigpen.
pig′tail′ (-tāl′), *n.* **1.** Tobacco in small twisted ropes or rolls. **2. a** A tight braid of hair hanging down in back; a queue. **b** One who wears a pigtail; a Chinese.
pig′weed′ (-wēd′), *n.* **a** Any of the goosefoot family (Chenopodiaceae, esp. genus *Chenopodium*) of plants; esp., the ***white pigweed*** (*C. album*). **b** Any of several weedy herbs of the amaranth family, as *Amaranthus hybridus* and *A. retroflexus*.
pi′ka (pī′kȧ), *n.* [Tungusic *peeka*.] Any of certain small short-eared harelike mammals (family Ochotonidae), technically lagomorphs, of Asia and western North America; — called also *cony* and *rock rabbit*. See LEPORID.
pike (pīk), *n.* [From OF. *pic*, and fr. AS. *pīc*.] A point or spike, as in the center of a shield or buckler.
pike, *n.* [Prob. of Norse origin.] *N. of Eng.* A peaked mountain or hilltop; a peak; — used esp. in place names.
pike, *n.; see* PLURAL, *Note*, 6. [From PIKE a sharp point; — in ref. to the shape of its head.] An elongate, voracious, spiny-finned food fish (genus *Esox*, family Esocidae), often four feet long; also, any of various other fishes; as, the gar *pike* and the walleyed *pike*.
pike, *n.* [F. *pique*, fr. *piquer* to pierce, prick, fr. *pic* pick, pickax.] *Mil.* A foot soldier's weapon consisting of a long wooden shaft with a pointed steel head, now superseded by the bayonet. — *v. t.* To pierce, kill, or wound with or as with a pike. — **pike′man** (pīk′măn), *n.*
pike, *v. i. Colloq.* To go; to make one's way.
pike, *n.* Short for TURNPIKE (sense 2); hence, any main road or highway; also, the toll paid on a turnpike.
pike perch. Any of several fishes of the perch family, but like a pike, as the sauger, walleyed pike, and zander.
pik′er (pīk′ẽr), *n. Slang.* **a** A gambler or speculator in a small way. **b** One who does things in a small way; also, a niggard; a shirker; a quitter.
pike′staff′ (pīk′ståf′; 9), *n.; pl.* -STAVES (-stāvz′). **1.** *Rare.* A staff with a spike at the end, to guard the user from slipping. **2.** The staff of a pike (the weapon).
pi·laf′, pi·laff′ (pĭ·läf′; -lăf′). Vars. of PILAU.
pi·las′ter (pĭ·lăs′tẽr), *n.* [F. *pilastre*, fr. It. *pilastro*, fr. L. *pila* pillar.] *Arch.* An upright architectural member, rectangular in plan, structurally a pier, but architecturally treated as a column, with capital, shaft, and base.

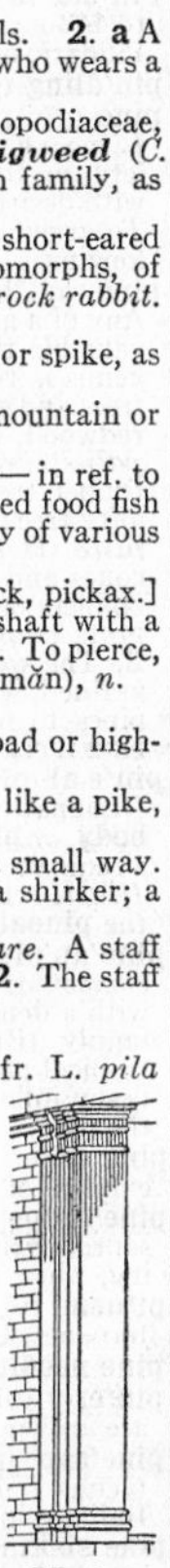

Pilaster.

Pi′late (pī′lȧt), *n. Bib.* Cognomen of the Roman procurator of Judea who gave Jesus up to be crucified.
pi·lau′ (pĭ·lō′; -lou′; -lô′), **pi·law′** (pĭ·lô′; -lou′; -läf′; -lăf′), *n.* [Per. & Turk. *pilāw*.] An Oriental dish made of rice (or cracked wheat) boiled with meat, fowl, or fish, spices, etc.
pil′chard (pĭl′chẽrd), *n.* A herringlike food fish (*Sardinia pilchardus*) occurring in great schools along European coasts. The young are called *sardines*.
pil′cher (pĭl′chẽr), *n.* Also **pil′cherd.** *Obs.* Pilchard.
pile (pīl), *n.* [L. *pilus* a hair.] **1.** Hair; esp., short fine hair like fur. **2. a** A velvety surface produced by an extra set of filling yarns that form raised loops which are cut and sheared; — distinguished from *nap*. **b** One of the filaments of such a surface.
pile, *n.* [F., fr. L. *pila* a pillar, pier or mole of stone.] **1.** A mass of things heaped together; a heap. **2. a** *Colloq.* A large number, quantity, or the like; a lot. **b** A heap of wood for burning a corpse or a sacrifice. **c** A large building, or mass of buildings. **d** *Slang.* A fortune; — short for *pile of money*. **3.** *Elec.* **a** Orig., a vertical series of alternate disks of two dissimilar metals, as copper and zinc, laid up with disks moistened with acid between them, for producing a current of electricity; — commonly called ***Volta's pile, voltaic pile***, or ***galvanic pile***. **b** Hence, any similar arrangement for generating an electric current; a battery. **4.** *Iron Mfg.* = FAGOT, *n.*, 2. **5.** *Physics & Chem.* An arrangement of fissionable material, with a moderator (as carbon or heavy water, for slowing down neutrons) and regulating devices, designed for producing and controlling a chain reaction, as for making plutonium from uranium or producing atomic energy, by the action of neutrons; — called specif. ***atomic pile, chain-reacting pile***. — *v. t.* **1.** To lay or throw in a pile; to heap up. **2.** To cover with heaps; to load; as, to *pile* a table with food. — *v. i.* **1.** To form a pile or piles; accumulate. **2.** To move or press forward in or as in a mass; to crowd; as, to *pile* into a car.
pile (pīl), *n.* [AS. *pīl* stake, dart, fr. L. *pilum* javelin.] **1.** A blade (of grass). **2.** *Civil Eng.* A long slender timber, stake, etc., driven into the ground to carry a vertical load. **3.** *Her.* A wedge-shaped charge, usually placed like a pale, with the broad end up. **4.** *Obs. Rom. Antiq.* The foot soldier's heavy javelin.
pile, *v. t.* To drive piles into; to support with piles.
pile, *n. Med.* A hemorrhoid. See PILES.
pi′le·ate (pī′lē·ăt; pĭl′ē-), *adj.* Also **pi′le·at′ed** (-āt′ĕd; -ĭd). [L. *pileatus*, fr. *pileus* felt cap.] **a** Having a pileus, or cap. **b** *Zool.* Having a crest covering the pileum; as, the *pileated* woodpecker (see WOODPECKER).
piled (pīld), *adj.* Having a pile; — said of textiles.
pile driver *or* **engine.** A machine for driving down piles, usually a high frame with appliances for raising a heavy mass of iron (**pile hammer**) which falls on the pile.
pi′le·ous (pī′lē·ŭs), *adj.* [See PILOSE.] Hairy; pilose.
piles (pīlz), *n. pl.* [L. *pila* a ball.] *Med.* Hemorrhoids.
pi′le·um (pī′lē·ŭm; pĭl′ē-), *n.; pl.* PILEA (-ȧ). [NL., fr. L. *pileum* cap.] *Zool.* The top of the head of a bird from the bill to the nape. See BIRD, *Illust.*
pi′le·us (-ŭs), *n.; pl.* PILEI (-ī). [L. *pileus*, better *pilleus*, felt cap.] **1.** *Rom. Antiq.* A cap. **2.** The umbrella-shaped part of a mushroom. See FUNGUS, *Illust.*
pile′wort′ (pīl′wûrt′), *n.* A European herb (*Ficaria verna*) with yellow flowers resembling buttercups; — called also *celandine* or *lesser celandine*. Its tuberous roots have been used in poultices as a specific for piles.
pil′fer (pĭl′fẽr), *v. i. & t.* [OF. *pelfrer*.] To steal, now esp. by taking small amounts or articles of little value. — **Syn.** See STEAL. — **pil′fer·age** (-ĭj), *n.* — **pil′fer·er** (-ẽr), *n.*
pil·gar′lic (pĭl·gär′lĭk), *n.* [Prop., a peeled head of garlic.] A bald-headed man; now, a man looked upon with humorous contempt or mock pity.
pil′grim (pĭl′grĭm), *n.* [L. *peregrinus* foreign, foreigner (LL. *pelegrinus*), fr. *peregre* abroad, fr. *per* through + *ager* field, country, land.] **1.** A wanderer; wayfarer. **2.** Specif., one who travels to some holy place as a devotee. **3.** [*cap.*] One of the Pilgrim Fathers.
pil′grim·age (pĭl′grĭ·mĭj), *n.* [OF. *pelrimage, pelerinage*.] The action of journeying, esp. as a devotee seeking a shrine; a long, weary journey, as to a shrine.
Pilgrim Fathers. The English colonists, led by a minority of separatists from the Church of England, who sailed to America in 1620 aboard the Mayflower and founded Plymouth colony, the first permanent settlement in New England.
Pil′grim's Prog′ress (pĭl′grĭmz). An allegory (1678; second part 1684) by John Bunyan.
pi·li′ (pē·lē′), *n.* [Tag.] The edible and (after roasting) very delicious nut (**pili nut**) of a Philippine tree (*Canarium ovatum*) of the torchwood family; also, the tree itself.
pili-. [L. *pilus*.] A combining form meaning *hair*, as in **pi·lif′er·ous, pil′i·form, pi·lig′er·ous.** See -FEROUS, etc.
pil′ing (pīl′ĭng), *n.* **1.** Act of supplying with piles. **2.** Piles, collectively; a structure of piles.
pill (pĭl), *n.* [OF. *pile*, fr. L. *pila* a ball.] **1.** A medicine in the form of a little ball, to be taken whole. **2.** Something unpleasant which must be endured. **3.** *Slang.* **a** A ball, esp. a baseball or golf ball. **b** A cigarette. **c** *pl. Eng.* Billiards. **d** A tiresome person. — *v. t.* **1.** To dose with pills. **2.** *Slang.* To blackball.
pill, *v. t.* [ME. *pillen, pilen*, fr. AS. *pilian* to peel, and fr. F. *piller* to plunder.] **1.** *Archaic.* To pillage. **2. a** *Archaic & Dial.* To peel; to pare off. **b** *Obs.* To deprive of hair; to remove (hair). — *v. i.* To pillage; plunder.
pil′lage (pĭl′ĭj), *n.* [F., fr. *piller* to plunder.] **1.** Act of pillaging or plundering, esp. in war; plunder. **2.** That which is pillaged; spoil. — **Syn.** See SPOIL. — *v. t. & i.;* -LAGED (-ĭjd); -LAG·ING (-ĭj·ĭng). **1.** To strip of money or goods by open violence; to spoil; loot. **2.** To seize as booty. — **Syn.** See RAVAGE. — **pil′lag·er** (-ĭj·ẽr), *n.*
pil′lar (pĭl′ẽr), *n.* [OF. *piler*, fr. L. *pila* pillar.] **1.** A firm, upright, insulated support, narrow compared to its height, for a superstructure; more widely, any vertical support; also, a shaft standing alone, as for a monument. **2.** Something resembling or suggesting a column; a main support; as, he is a *pillar* of the church. — ***from pillar to post.*** From one place, refuge, etc., to another. — *v. t.* To support or strengthen with or as with pillars.
pillar box *or* **post.** *Eng.* A pillar-shaped box in which postal matter may be deposited by the public.
Pillars of Hercules. The two promontories at eastern end of Strait of Gibraltar. It is fabled that Hercules set them there. See *Gaz.*
pill′box′ (pĭl′bŏks′), *n.* **1.** A box for pills, esp. a shallow round pasteboard one. **2.** A woman's small shallow hat with flat, usually round, top and no brim. **3.** *Mil.* A low round concrete-and-steel shelter, containing one or more machine guns.
pill bug. Any wood louse (family Armadillididae) that rolls into a ball when disturbed. See WOOD LOUSE.
pil′lion (pĭl′yŭn), *n.* [Gael. *pillean*, Ir. *pillīn*, fr. Gael. & Ir. *peall* a covering, hide, fr. L. *pellis* skin.] **1.** A form of saddle, as a light one for women; also, a pad or cushion put on behind a man's saddle, as for a woman to ride on. **2.** A motorcycle riding saddle for a passenger.
pil′lo·ry (pĭl′ō·rĭ), *n.; pl.* -RIES (-rĭz). [OF. *pilori*.] **1.** A device for publicly punishing offenders, consisting of a frame having holes through which the head and hands of the offender were thrust. **2.** Figuratively, any means for exposing to public scorn or ridicule. — *v. t.;* -RIED (-rĭd); -RY·ING. **1.** To set in, or punish with, the pillory. **2.** Hence, to expose to public scorn or ridicule.
pil′low (pĭl′ō), *n.* [AS. *pyle, pylu*, fr. L. *pulvinus*.] **1.** Anything used to support the head of a person when reposing; esp., a sack or case filled with feathers, down, or other soft material. **2.** A block or support likened to a pillow, as a block under a bowsprit, etc. **3.** Any of various padded things likened to a pillow, as a cushion used as a support or ground in making lace with bobbins (**pillow lace**). — *v. t. & i.* To rest or lay on or as on a pillow; also, to serve as a pillow for.
pillow block. *Mach.* A block or standard to support a journal, as of a shaft; a bearing.
pil′low·case′ (pĭl′ō·kās′), *n.*, *or* **pillow slip.** A removable covering for a pillow, usually of white linen or cotton.
pillow lace. = BOBBIN LACE. See BOBBIN, 1.
pillow sham. An ornamental covering for a bed pillow.
pi′lo·car′pine (pī′lō·kär′pēn; -pĭn; pĭl′ō-), *n.* Also **pi′lo·car′pin.** [*Pilocarpus*, type genus, fr. Gr. *pilos* felt + *karpos* fruit.] *Chem.* An alkaloid, $C_{11}H_{16}N_2O_2$, obtained from the leaves of jaborandi. It is a diuretic.
pi′lose (pī′lōs), *adj.* [L. *pilosus*, fr. *pilus* hair.] Covered with hair, esp. soft hair; hairy. — **pi·los′i·ty** (pī·lŏs′ĭ·tĭ), *n.*
pi′lot (pī′lŭt), *n.* [F. *pilote*, fr. It. *pilota, pedota*.] **1.** *Naut.* One employed to steer a vessel; a helmsman. **2.** Specif., a person duly qualified, and usually licensed, to conduct vessels into and out of a port, or in certain waters, often for fixed fees. **3.** A guide; a director or leader. **4.** *U. S.* The cowcatcher of a locomotive. **5.** *Aeronautics.* One who flies, or is qualified to fly, a balloon, an airship, or an airplane. See WINGS, *Illust.* **6.** *Mach.* A bar or simple element acting as a guide or relay for another element. — *adj.* That serves on a small scale as a guiding or tracing device, an activating or auxiliary unit of a full-scale contrivance, or as a trial unit in experimenting or in testing apparatus, or in checking technique or cost, etc., preparatory to full-scale activity; as, a *pilot* dye, a *pilot* parachute, a *pilot* plant, *pilot* production. — *v. t.* **1.** To serve as a pilot on, for, or over. **2.** To guide, direct, or lead in a straight or safe course. **3.** *Aeronautics.* To fly or act as pilot of (an aircraft). — **Syn.** See GUIDE.

pi'lot·age (pī'lŭt·ĭj), *n.* [F.] **1.** Act or business of piloting. **2.** The compensation made to a pilot.

pilot balloon. *Aeronautics.* A small unmanned balloon sent up to show the direction and speed of the wind.

pilot biscuit *or* **bread.** Ship biscuit.

pilot burner. A small burner kept lighted to rekindle a principal burner when desired, as in a gas stove.

pilot engine. A locomotive going in advance of a train to make sure that the way is clear.

pilot fish. A carangoid pelagic fish (*Naucrates ductor*); — so named because often seen with a shark.

pi'lot·house' (pī'lŭt·hous'), *n.* *Naut.* An enclosed place forward on the upper deck of a vessel, sheltering the steering gear and helmsman; — called also *wheelhouse.*

pilot lamp. An electric lamp indicating the position of a switch or circuit breaker, that a motor is in operation, that the power is on, etc.

pilot light. **1.** A pilot lamp. **2.** A pilot burner.

pi'lous (pī'lŭs), *adj.* Pilose.

Pilt'down' man (pĭlt'doun'). A supposedly very early primitive modern man based on skeletal remains that were uncovered in a gravel pit at Piltdown, Sussex, England and that are now known to have been at least in part deliberately faked.

pil'u·lar (pĭl'ū·lẽr), *adj.* Of, pert. to, or like a pill.

pil'ule (pĭl'ūl), *n.* [F.] A little pill.

Pi'man (pē'măn), *adj.* Pertaining to or designating a linguistic stock of North American Indians occupying southern Arizona and northwestern Mexico.

pi·men'to (pĭ·mĕn'tō), *n.; pl.* PIMENTOS (-tōz), PIMENTO. [Sp. *pimienta,* fr. L. *pigmentum* a pigment, juice of plants, hence, something spicy.] **1.** The Spanish paprika, or pimiento. **2.** Allspice; also, the allspice tree.

pimento cheese. A processed cheese made by adding pimentos to Neufchâtel curd.

pi·mien'to (pē·myĕn'tō), *n.* [Sp.] The fruit of the Spanish paprika, used as a vegetable, for stuffing olives, etc.

pim·o'la (pĭm·ō'lȧ), *n.* An olive stuffed with pimiento.

pimp (pĭmp), *n.* A pander. — *v. i.* To act the pimp.

pim'per·nel (pĭm'pẽr·nĕl; -n'l), *n.* [F. *pimprenelle.*] Any of a genus (*Anagallis*) of herbs of the primrose family, esp. the ***scarlet pimpernel*** (*A. arvensis*) whose scarlet, white, or purplish flowers close at the approach of rainy or cloudy weather.

pimp'ing (pĭmp'ĭng), *adj.* Petty; also, *Dial.,* puny.

pim'ple (pĭm'p'l), *n.* *Med.* Any small pointed elevation of the skin; a papule or pustule. — **pim'pled** (-p'ld), *adj.* — **pim'ply** (-plĭ), *adj.*

pin (pĭn), *n.* [AS. *pinn* a pin.] **1.** A piece of wood, metal, etc., used for fastening separate articles together, or as a support by which one article may be suspended from another; a peg; bolt. **2.** **a** A small pointed and headed piece of wire for fastening clothes, attaching papers, etc.; hence, a thing of small value; a trifle. **b** A larger and often ornamental pointed instrument for securing the hair or some article of dress. **c** Short for *clothespin, linchpin, rolling pin,* etc. **3.** Something that resembles, or is likened to, a pin. **4.** *Colloq. Chiefly pl.* The leg; as, to knock one off his *pins.* **5.** An ornament, as a brooch or badge, fastened to the clothing by a pin; as, a Masonic *pin.* **6.** *Obs.* A peg or the like in the center of a target; hence, the center. **7.** *Bowling, Skittles, etc.* One of the wooden pieces to be bowled at. **8.** *Golf.* The staff of the flag marking a hole. **9.** *Locks.* The part of the stem of a key which enters the lock. See KEY, *Illust.* **10.** *Music.* A peg for regulating the tension of the strings. **11.** *Naut.* **a** A tholepin. **b** A belaying pin.

— *v. t.;* PINNED (pĭnd); PIN'NING. **1.** To fasten, join, secure, transfix, by or with a pin. **2.** To fasten or hold as by thrusting a pin through; to seize and hold fast.

pi'ña (pē'nyä), *n.* [Sp., orig., pineapple, pine cone.] Throughout Latin America, the pineapple.

pi·na'ceous (pĭ·nā'shŭs), *adj.* [L. *pinus* a pine tree + *-aceous.*] Of or belonging to the pine family (Pinaceae). See PINE.

pi'ña cloth (pē'nyä). [See PIÑA.] A fine fabric woven from the fiber of the sterile pineapple plant.

pin'a·fore' (pĭn'ȧ·fōr'; 70), *n.* [*pin* + *afore.*] An apron, usually low-necked and sleeveless, worn esp. by children.

pin and web. Two concurrent symptoms of eye disease, or a single disease of the eye; — an old term.

pi·nas'ter (pĭ·năs'tẽr; pī-), *n.* [F., fr. *pinus* a pine.] A pine (*Pinus pinaster*) of the Mediterranean region.

pin'ball' (pĭn'bôl'), *n.* **1.** Formerly, a game somewhat like bagatelle. **2.** Usually **pinball machine.** A slot machine in which a ball projected up a sloping board by a plunger operated from outside the cabinet is made to rebound and roll downward amid electric-light bulbs that light up on being touched, thus scoring an indicated number of points.

pince'-nez' (păns'nā'; *F.* păɴs'nā'), *n.* [F., fr. *pincer* to pinch + *nez* nose.] Eyeglasses clipped to the nose by a spring.

pin'cers (pĭn'sẽrz), *n. pl.* [ME. *pynsours,* fr. OF. *pincier* to pinch.] **1.** An instrument having two handles and two grasping jaws used for gripping things; — often called a *pair of pincers.* **2.** *Zool.* A pincerlike claw, as of the lobster; a chela. **3.** *Mil.* A movement in which two columns are driven, one on each side of an enemy stronghold, so as to be able to converge like the jaws of pincers to isolate and crush the stronghold. — **pin'cer** (pĭn'sẽr), *adj.*

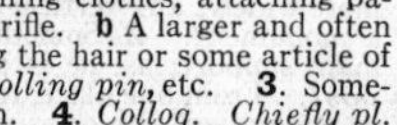

Pincers, 1.

pinch (pĭnch), *v. t.* [ME. *pinchen,* deriv. of OF. *pincier.*] **1.** To squeeze between the ends of the finger and thumb, between teeth or claws, or between the jaws of an instrument. **2.** To squeeze or compress painfully; as, a new shoe *pinches* the foot. **3.** To afflict; distress; as, *pinching* want. Also, to cramp, contract, etc., as by pain. **4.** To straiten; to stint; as, to be *pinched* for money. **5.** *Slang.* **a** To steal; rob. **b** To arrest; raid. **6.** *Naut.* To sail too close to the wind. — *v. i.* **1.** To compress; squeeze. **2.** To be miserly. **3.** *Mining & Petroleum.* Of a vein or deposit, to narrow or taper. Hence, ***pinch out,*** to terminate. — *n.* **1.** An emergency; special need; as, he could do it at a *pinch.* **2.** Pressure; pain; stress. **3.** **a** Act of pinching; a nip. **b** As much as may be taken between the finger and thumb; any small quantity; as, a *pinch* of snuff. **4.** *Slang.* A theft; arrest; raid. — **Syn.** See JUNCTURE.

pinch bar. A lever having a pointed projection at one end, used esp. to roll heavy wheels, etc.

pinch'beck (pĭnch'bĕk), *n.* [From the inventor's name.] **a** An alloy of copper and zinc, used to imitate gold in cheap jewelry, etc. **b** Hence, that which is spurious. — *adj.* Made of pinchbeck; hence, sham; cheap.

pinch'cock' (pĭnch'kŏk'), *n.* A clamp used on a flexible tube to regulate the flow of a fluid through the tube.

pinch'er (pĭn'chẽr), *n.* One that pinches; *pl.,* pincers.

pin cherry. See CHERRY.

pinch hitter. **1.** *Baseball Cant.* A player who is sent in to bat in the place of another in a pinch, as when a hit is particularly needed. **2.** Loosely, one who does another's work in an emergency. — **pinch'-hit',** *v. i.*

pin'cush'ion (pĭn'ko͝osh'ŭn; -ĭn), *n.* A small cushion in which pins may be stuck ready for use.

Pin·dar'ic (pĭn·dăr'ĭk), *adj.* Of, or after the manner of, Pindar (522? to 443 B.C.), Greek lyric poet, famous for grandeur of style. — *n.* A Pindaric ode. See ODE.

pin'dling (pĭn'dlĭng; -lĭn), *adj.* *Colloq., U. S.* Puny.

pine (pīn), *v. i.* [AS. *pīnian* to torment, fr. (assumed) *pīn* pain, fr. L. *poena.*] **1.** To languish; to lose vigor or flesh through grief, anxiety, or the like; hence, to wear away; to dwindle. **2.** To languish with desire or longing; to yearn. — **Syn.** See LONG. — *v. t. Archaic.* To grieve or mourn for. — *n. Archaic.* Suffering; difficulty; want; longing.

pine, *n.* [From AS. *pīn* (fr. L.) and fr. OF. *pin,* fr. L. *pinus.*] **1.** Any of a genus (*Pinus*) of coniferous trees, including some of the most valuable timber trees, as well as many ornamental evergreens. The genus is typical of a family (Pinaceae, the pine family) of coniferous trees and shrubs, including also the spruce, hemlock, fir, cypress, cedar, redwood, etc. Among the valuable pines are the ***Georgia pine*** (*P. palustris*), also known as ***yellow pine or longleaf pine,*** a valuable timber tree of southern U. S.; the ***sugar pine*** (*P. lambertiana*), a lofty tree of California and Oregon, having immense cones; the ***white pine*** (*P. strobus*) of eastern North America, with long-stalked green cones and leaves in clusters of five (the cone and tassel are the State emblem of Maine), and with valuable soft light wood. See also HUON PINE, LOBLOLLY, PIÑON, DOUGLAS FIR, ARAUCARIA. Cf. CONE, *Illust.* **2.** The wood of any of these trees. It is usually durable, straight-grained, white or yellow, and varies from extreme softness in the white pines to hardness in the Georgia pine and its allies. **3.** Short for PINEAPPLE.

pin'e·al (pĭn'ē·ăl; pī'nē·ăl), *adj.* [F. *pinéal,* fr. L. *pinea* a pine cone.] Designating, or pertaining to, an appendage of the brain, the **pineal body,** *or* **pineal gland,** present in all craniate vertebrates and evidently a remnant of an important sense organ in ancestral forms. See BRAIN, *Illust.* In some reptiles, it has the structure of an eye and is called the **pineal eye.**

pine'ap'ple (pīn'ăp''l), *n.* **1.** **a** An agavelike tropical plant (*Ananas comosus*), with rigid, spiny-margined, recurved leaves and a short stalk with a dense oblong head of small abortive flowers. It is typical of a family (Bromeliaceae, the pineapple family) of monocotyledonous tropical plants. **b** The fruit of this plant, consisting of the succulent fleshy inflorescence. **2.** *Slang.* A dynamite bomb, hand grenade, or the like.

pine cone. = CONE, *n.,* 1 **a.** The pine cone and tassel form the floral emblem of Maine.

pine'drops' (pīn'drŏps'), *n. sing. & pl.* **a** A purplish-brown, leafless saprophytic plant (*Pterospora andromedea*) with racemose, drooping, white flowers. **b** = BEECHDROPS **a.**

pi'nene (pī'nēn), *n.* [L. *pinus* pine + *-ene.*] *Chem.* Either of two terpenes, $C_{10}H_{16}$, found in oil of turpentine.

pine needle. One of the needle-shaped leaves of a pine tree.

pin'er·y (pīn'ẽr·ĭ), *n.; pl.* -ERIES (-ĭz). **1.** A place where pineapples are grown. **2.** A grove of pines.

pine'sap' (pīn'săp'), *n.* Any of several parasitic or saprophytic herbs (genus *Hypopitys*) of the North Temperate Zone, resembling the Indian pipe, but yellowish or reddish.

pine siskin *or* **finch.** A North American finch (*Spinus pinus*) with streaked plumage.

pine tar. Tar obtained by destructive distillation of pine wood, used in the treatment of skin diseases and colds.

Pine Tree State. Maine; — a nickname alluding to the pine tree in its coat of arms.

pi·ne'tum (pī·nē'tŭm), *n.; pl.* -TA (-tȧ). [L., a pine grove.] A plantation of pine trees; esp., a scientific collection of living coniferous trees.

pin'feath'er (pĭn'fĕth'ẽr), *n.* A feather not fully developed; esp., a young feather just emerging through the skin.

pin'fold' (pĭn'fōld'), *n.* A pound for animals; hence, a place of restraint; a confine. — *v. t.* To confine in or as in a pinfold.

ping (pĭng), *n.* [Of imitative origin.] A sharp sound such as that made by a bullet striking a wall, a tree, or other obstruction. — *v. i. & t.* To sound or strike with a ping.

Ping'-pong' (pĭng'pŏng'), *n.* A trade-mark for a kind of table tennis.

pin'guid (pĭng'gwĭd), *adj.* [L. *pinguis* fat.] Fat; oily; of soil, rich. — **pin·guid'i·ty** (pĭng·gwĭd'ĭ·tĭ), *n.*

pin'head' (pĭn'hĕd'), *n.* **1.** The head of a pin; hence, anything very small or insignificant. **2.** A person of small intelligence. **3.** A small minnow.

pin'hole' (-hōl'), *n.* A small hole made by or as by a pin.

pin'ion (pĭn'yŭn), *n.* [F. *pignon.*] A gear with a small number of teeth designed to mesh with a larger wheel, or rack; the smallest of a train of gear wheels. See RACK, SELF-STARTER, *Illusts.*

pin'ion, *n.* [OF. *pignon.*] **1.** *Zool.* The terminal section of a bird's wing, including the carpus, metacarpus, and phalanges. **2.** A wing. **3.** A feather; a quill; also, the flight feathers collectively. **4.** The anterior border of an insect's wing. — *v. t.* **1.** To cut off the pinion of a wing of (a bird) so as to prevent flying. **2.** To disable or restrain by binding the wings or arms, esp. to the body; to bind or confine the wings or arms of. **3.** To confine; shackle.

pin'ite (pĭn'īt; pī'nīt), *n.* [G. *pinit;* — from the *Pini* mine in Saxony.] *Mineral.* An amorphous mineral, essentially a hydrous silicate of aluminum and potassium.

pi'ni·tol (pī'nĭ·tōl; pĭn'ĭ·tōl), *n.* Also **pi'nite** (pī'nīt; pĭn'īt). [*pinite* (fr. L. *pinus* pine tree) + *-ol,* 1.] *Chem.* A sweet colorless crystalline compound, $C_6H_6(OH)_5OCH_3$, found in the resin of a species of pine (*Pinus lambertiana*) and in other plants.

pink (pĭngk), *n.* [D.] A vessel with a narrow stern.

pink, *v. t.* [Prob. a nasalized form of *pick.*] **1.** To perforate (cloth, paper, etc.) in an ornamental pattern; now usually, to cut the border or edge of in small scallops with indented edges. **2.** To stab; pierce, as with a sword. **3.** To adorn; decorate.

pink (pĭngk), *v. i.* *Now Dial.* **a** To wink or blink. **b** To gleam faintly, as dying light. — *adj.* Winking; blinking.

pink, *n.* [Origin uncert.] **1.** Any of a genus (*Dianthus*) of herbs typifying a family (Caryophyllaceae, the pink family) including also campions and babies'-breath; also, the flower of a plant of this genus; esp., the common ***garden pink*** (*D. plumarius*), the ***China pink*** (*D. chinensis*), the ***clove pink*** (*D. caryophyllus*) or its cultivated double-flowered forms, the carnation. **2.** Highest or most excellent example, state, or degree; as, in the *pink* of condition; also, a dandy; fop; exquisite. **3.** Any of a group of colors, averaging red in hue, of low saturation and high brilliance. See COLOR. **4.** The scarlet of a fox hunter's coat; hence, the fox hunter's coat or a fox hunter. **5.** [*often cap.*] A mild red (sense 4), or radical; one inclined to Bolshevism. — *adj.* **1.** Fashionable; smart; — now only in **pink tea**. **2.** Of the color pink. **3.** Mildly or partly red, or radical. See RED, *adj.*, 3. — **pink'ish**, *adj.*

pink'eye' (pĭngk'ī'), *n.* Also **pink eye**. An acute, highly contagious variety of conjunctivitis.

pink'ie (pĭngk'ĭ), *n.* *Naut.* A pink; esp., a fishing pink.

pink rhododendron. See RHODODENDRON.

pink'root' (pĭngk'rōōt'; 85), *n.* Any of several loganiaceous herbs (genus *Spigelia*), esp. the American wormroot (*S. marilandica*) with showy red flowers, or a South American species (*S. anthelmia*), used as anthelmintics.

Pink'ster (pĭngk'stẽr), *n.* Also **Pinx'ter** (pĭngks'tẽr). [D. *pinkster*, ult. fr. Gr. *pentēkostē*. See PENTECOST.] *Local, U. S.* Whitsuntide.

pinkster, *or* **pinxter, flower.** A pink azalea. See AZALEA.

pin money. Money allowed by a man to his wife for her own use; also, money for the purchase of incidentals.

pin'na (pĭn'ȧ), *n.; pl.* PINNAE (-ē), PINNAS (-ȧz). [L., a feather, prop., a sharp point.] **1.** *Bot.* A leaflet or primary division of a pinnate leaf. See FERN, *Illust.* **2.** *Anat. & Zool.* **a** A feather, wing, fin, or the like. **b** The auricle of the ear. See EAR, *Illust.* — **pin'nal** (-ăl), *adj.*

pin'nace (pĭn'ĭs; -ȧs), *n.* [F. *pinasse*, *pinace*, fr. It. *pinaccia* or Sp. *pinaza*.] **1.** *Hist. & Poetic.* A light sailing vessel used largely as a tender. **2.** Any of various ships' boats, as a man-of-war's steam launch.

pin'na·cle (pĭn'ȧ·k'l; -ĭ·k'l), *n.* [OF. *pinacle*, fr. LL. *pinnaculum*, fr. L. *pinna*.] **1.** *Arch.* An upright architectural member, generally ending in a small spire, on a buttress or an angle pier. See GOTHIC, *Illust.* **2.** A tall, slender, pointed mass; esp. a lofty peak. **3.** The summit, or highest point, of anything; acme. — **Syn.** See SUMMIT. — *v. t.;* -CLED (-k'ld); -CLING (-klĭng). **1.** To surmount with a pinnacle. **2.** To raise or rear on or as on a pinnacle.

pin'nate (pĭn'āt), *adj.* [L. *pinnatus* feathered, fr. *pinna* a feather.] Featherlike; having parts arranged along two sides of an axis; specif., *Bot.*, having the leaflets or primary divisions arranged on each side of a common petiole or rachis; — applied to compound leaves. Pinnate leaves may be either ***abruptly pinnate*** (*or* ***paripinnate***), without, *or* ***odd-pinnate*** (*or* ***imparipinnate***), with, a single terminal leaflet. See LEAF, *Illust.* (22, 23); VENATION, *Illust.* — **pin'nate·ly**, *adv.* — **pin·na'tion** (pĭ·nā'shŭn), *n.*

pin·nat'i- (pĭ·năt'ĭ-). [L. *pinnatus*.] Combining form meaning *pinnately*, as in:

pinnatilobate	pinnatipartite	pinnatisect
pinnatilobed	pinnatiped	pinnatisected

pin·nat'i·fid (-fĭd), *adj.* [*pinnati-* + *-fid*.] *Bot.* Cleft pinnately with narrow lobes not reaching to the midrib.

pin'ner (pĭn'ẽr), *n.* **1.** One who or that which pins. **2.** *Hist.* A headdress like a cap, with long lappets.

pin'ni·ped (pĭn'ĭ·pĕd), *adj.* [L. *pinna* feather, fin + *pes*, *pedis*, foot.] Belonging to a suborder (Pinnipedia) of aquatic carnivorous mammals including the seals and walruses. — **pin'ni·ped**, *n.* — **pin'ni·pe'di·an** (-pē'dĭ·ăn; 58), *adj. & n.*

pin'nu·la (pĭn'ū·lȧ), *n.; pl.* -LAE (-lē). [L., dim. of *pinna* feather.] **a** *Bot. & Zool.* A pinnule. **b** *Zool.* A barb of a feather. — **pin'nu·lar** (-lẽr), *adj.* — **pin'nu·late** (-lāt), **pin'nu·lat'ed** (-lāt'ĕd; -ĭd), *adj.*

pin'nule (pĭn'ūl), *n.* [L. *pinnula*, dim. of *pinna* feather.] **1.** *Zool.* **a** One of the secondary branches of a plumelike organ; specif., one of the lateral parts of the arm of a crinoid. **b** In fishes, a small detached fin, as in the mackerel. **2.** *Bot.* One of the ultimate divisions of a bipinnate leaf. See FERN, *Illust.*

pin oak. An oak (*Quercus palustris*) of eastern U. S. with persistent dead branches (resembling pins) and deeply pinnatifid leaves.

pi'noch'le, pi'noc'le (pē'nŭk''l), *n.* A game at cards using all cards above the eight in two decks; also, a meld in this game consisting of the queen of spades and knave of diamonds counting 40 points.

pi·no'le (pē·nō'lā), *n.* [Sp., fr. Nahuatl *pinolli*.] A meal made from parched seeds of various native plants of the southwestern U. S.

pi'ñon (pē'nyŏn; pĭn'yŭn; *Sp.* pē·nyôn'), *n.* [Sp. *piñón* pine nut.] Any of various low-growing pines (*Pinus parryana*, *P. edulis*, etc.) of western North America and Mexico; also, their edible seeds.

pin'point' (pĭn'point'), *v. t.* **1.** To locate with precision as if on a pin's point. **2.** To fix, determine, or identify with precision. **3.** To make to stand out conspicuously like points marked with pins on a map. **4.** To single out and bring into sharp focus. — *adj.* Directed with extreme precision; as, *pinpoint* bombing.

pin'scher (pĭn'shẽr), *n.* [G.] = DOBERMAN PINSCHER.

pint (pīnt), *n.* [OF. *pinte*.] **1.** A measure of capacity. See MEASURE, *Tables* 10, 11, & 12. **2.** A vessel or measure containing a pint. Apothecaries' symbol, *O* (fr. L. *octarius*). Abbr. *pt.*

pin'ta (pĭn'tȧ; *Sp.* pēn'tä), *n.* [Sp., lit., spot.] A tropical disease characterized by colored blotches on the skin.

pin·ta'do (pĭn·tä'dō), *n.; pl.* -DOS (-dōz) or -DOES. [Pg., painted, fr. *pintar* to paint.] A large mackerellike fish (*Scomberomorus regalis*) with elongated spots, common about Florida and the West Indies; — called also *cero*, *spotted cero*, or *sierra*.

pin'tail' (pĭn'tāl'), *n.;* see PLURAL, *Note*, 3. Any of several birds having elongated central tail feathers: **a** Also **pintail duck**. A river duck (*Dafila acuta*). **b** *Local, U. S.* (1) The ruddy duck. (2) A large grouse (*Pedioecetes phasianellus*). (3) The sand grouse *Pterocles alchata*.

pin·ta'no (pĭn·tä'nō), *n.* A black-banded green fish (*Abudefduf marginatus*) living along coral reefs.

pin'tle (pĭn't'l), *n.* [AS. *pintel* penis.] **1.** A (usually upright) pivot pin, as of a hinge or a rudder. **2.** *Ordn.* A hook at the rear of a limber to receive the lunette of the gun trail.

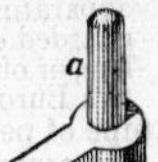

Pintle, 1.

pin'to (pĭn'tō; pēn'tō), *adj.* [Sp.] Literally, painted; hence, piebald; mottled; pied. — *n.; pl.* -TOS (-tōz). *Western U. S.* A piebald horse or pony.

pinto bean. Also **pin'to**, *n.* *Western U. S.* A variety of mottled field bean of the same species as the kidney bean.

Pintsch gas (pĭnch). [After Richard *Pintsch*, Ger. inventor.] A gas made by destructive distillation of oil, used for lighting railroad cars and buoys.

pin'-up' (pĭn'ŭp'), *adj.* Suitable because of companionable, intimate, or striking qualities, esp. sex appeal, for pinning up on an admirer's wall; also, popular as subject of pin-up pictures. — **pin'-up'**, *n.*

pin'weed' (pĭn'wēd'), *n.* Any of a genus (*Lechea*) of herbs of the rock-rose family, having slender stems and leaves.

pin wheel, *or* **pin'wheel'** (-hwēl'), *n.* **a** A toy having vanes of colored paper pinned to a stick. **b** *Fireworks.* A device which revolves on a pin and makes a wheel of colored fire.

pin'work' (pĭn'wûrk'), *n.* Fine stitches raised from the surface of a design in needle-point lace to add lightness to the effect.

pin'worm' (pĭn'wûrm'), *n.* A small nematode worm (*Enterobius vermicularis*) parasitic chiefly in the caecum of man.

pin wrench. A kind of wrench having a projecting pin to enter a hole in a nut, cylinder, etc., to make a hold.

‖**pinx'it** (pĭngk'sĭt). [L.] Literally, he (or she) painted (it).

Pinx'ter. Var. of PINKSTER.

pi'o·neer' (pī'ō·nēr'), *n.* [F. *pionnier*, orig., a foot soldier, fr. OF. *peonier*, fr. OF. *peon* foot soldier (F. *pion*). See PAWN chessman.] **1.** *Mil.* A member of a unit, usually of engineers, engaged in road building, bridging, etc. **2.** *Obs.* A digger; miner. **3.** One who goes before, preparing the way for others to follow; as, *pioneers* of reform; a *pioneer* in science; also, an early settler; a colonist; as, *pioneers* of the American West. — *adj.* Pioneering; hence, preparatory; earliest; first of its kind; as, in the *pioneer* stage; to do *pioneer* work in a field. — *v. t.* **1.** To open up (a way or the like) for others to follow; also, to discover or explore in advance of others. **2.** To act as a pioneer to, for, or in; as, to *pioneer* a cause. — *v. i.* To act as a pioneer; to open a way.

pi'ous (pī'ŭs), *adj.* [F. or L.; F. *pieux*, fr. L. *pius*.] **1.** *Archaic.* Dutiful or loyal to parents, family, race, etc. **2.** Manifesting devotion to God or the gods; zealous in prayer or acts of worship. **3.** Proceeding from or practiced by the religious or devout; — sometimes with implications of hypocrisy; as, *pious* frauds. **4.** Sacred; not profane or secular; as, *pious* uses. **5.** *Colloq.* Worthy; excellent; deserving commendation; as, to make a *pious* effort. — **Syn.** See DEVOUT. — **pi'ous·ly**, *adv.* — **pi'ous·ness**, *n.*

pip (pĭp), *n.* [MD. *pippe* (D. *pip*), fr. VL. *pipita*, fr. L. *pituita* slime, phlegm, the pip.] **1.** A disease of fowls marked by a "scale" formed on the tongue; also, this scale. **2.** *Colloq.* An illness such as dyspepsia or a cold; now usually, a slight indisposition.

pip, *n.* [From PIPPIN.] **1.** A small seed, as of an apple. **2.** *Slang.* An admired or admirable person or thing; a pippin.

pip, *n.* [Earlier *peep*, of unknown origin.] **1.** One of the conventional figures, or "spots," on playing cards, dominoes, etc. Cf. POKER, *Illust.* **2.** One of the segments of a pineapple's surface. **3.** *Hort.* The individual rootstock of the lily of the valley; also, any of various other dormant roots or rootstocks, as of peonies, anemones, etc.

pip, *n.* On a radarscope, the indication of the return of radar waves reflected from an object. It may be in the form of an inverted V or a spot of light.

pip (pĭp), *v. i.;* PIPPED (pĭpt); PIP'PING. [Var. of PEEP.] To peep, or chirp. — *v. t.* To break through (the shell); — of a hatching bird.

pip'age (pīp'ĭj), *n.* Transportation by pipes; such pipes collectively; also, the charge for such transportation.

pi'pal (pē'păl), *n.*, *or* **pipal tree.** [Hind. *pīpal*, fr. Skr. *pippala*.] A fig (*Ficus religiosa*) of India, distinguished from the banyan by the absence of prop roots.

pipe (pīp), *n.* [AS. *pīpe*, fr. L. *pipare* to chirp.] **1.** A wind instrument, consisting of a tube or tubes of straw, reed, wood, or metal; any tube which produces musical sounds; specif., more fully ***organ pipe***, one of the wooden or metal tubes of an organ, either: (1) a ***flue pipe***, in which the tone is produced by a current of air striking against a sharp edge (see FLUE PIPE, *Illust.*); or (2) a ***reed pipe*** in which the tone is produced by the vibration of a reed in a current of air; also, a bagpipe. **2.** The voice, esp. the singing voice; the peeping whistle, call, or note of a bird, insect, etc. **3.** Any long tube or hollow body of wood, metal, earthenware, or the like, as to conduct water, steam, etc. **4.** *Chiefly Dial.* A canal, or vessel of the body, esp. of the respiratory organs; — usually *pl.* **5.** Any of several things of pipelike or tubular form, as the stem of a plant. **6.** A slender tube with a small bowl at one end, used for smoking tobacco, opium, or the like. **7.** [OF., also, a wind instrument.] A large cask of varying capacity, now used esp. for wine and oil; also, such a cask with its contents; also, the volume of this cask as a liquid measure, in U. S. and English measure reckoned as two hogsheads. Cf. 1st BUTT; TUN, 2. **8.** *Slang.* An easy task or course, as of study; a certainty. **9.** *Naut.* A peculiar whistle used by boatswains or the signal given by it.
— *v. i.;* PIPED (pīpt); PIP'ING (pīp'ĭng). **1.** To play on a pipe; hence, to speak in a piping voice. **2.** To make a shrill or whistling sound. **3.** To become pipelike; to develop pipelike cavities, as solidifying steel. **4.** *Naut.* To convey orders, etc., by pipes, or signals. — *v. t.* **1.** To play on a pipe, etc.; hence, to utter shrilly. **2.** To affect, effect, bring, etc., by or as by piping; as, to *pipe* one into good spirits. **3.** To convey by means of pipes; as, to *pipe* oil. **4.** To put (liquor) into a pipe, or cask. **5.** To furnish with pipes. **6.** To ornament with piping. — ***pipe down.*** To be or become quiet; to stop talking, shouting, or the like. — ***pipe up.*** To begin to sing or speak. — **pip'er** (pīp'ẽr), *n.*

pipe clay. Highly plastic grayish-white clay, used in making pipes, in calico printing, in whitening, etc.

pipe'-clay', *v. t.* To whiten or clean with pipe clay.

pipe dream. A plan, hope, or story as illusory or fantastic as a dream caused by smoking opium.

pipe'fish' (pīp'fĭsh'), *n.;* see FISH. Any of certain slender lophobranch fishes (family Syngnathidae) having an elongate snout and an angular body covered with bony plates.

pipe′line′ (pīp′līn′), *n.* **1.** A line of pipe with pumping machinery and apparatus for conveying liquids, esp. petroleum. **2.** A direct, guarded channel conveying a continuous flow of supplies, music, or the like, or of information from an inside source; as, the lend-lease *pipeline* to a European country; to have a news *pipeline* to a cabinet member.

pipe of peace. The calumet.

pipe organ. *Music.* See ORGAN.

pip′er·a′ceous (pĭp′ẽr·ā′shŭs; pī′pẽr-), *adj.* [L. *piper* pepper + *-aceous.*] Belonging to the pepper family (Piperaceae). See PEPPER, *n.*, 2.

pi·per′a·zine (pĭ·pĕr′ȧ·zēn; pĭp′ẽr·ȧ·zēn; -zĭn), *n.* Also **pi·per′a·zin.** [*piperine* + *azote* + *-ine.*] *Chem.* A strongly basic crystalline substance, $(C_2H_4NH)_2$, used as an antirheumatic.

pi·per′i·dine (pĭ·pĕr′ĭ·dēn; pĭp′ẽr·ĭ·dēn; -dĭn), *n.* [F., fr. *piper*ine. Cf. *-ide, -ine,* in chemistry.] *Chem.* A liquid base, $C_5H_{11}N$, having a peppery, ammoniacal odor. It is obtained from piperine.

pip′er·ine (pĭp′ẽr·ēn; -ĭn), *n.* Also **pip′er·in.** [L. *piper* pepper.] *Chem.* A white crystalline alkaloid, $C_{17}H_{19}NO_3$, the chief active constituent of pepper.

pip′er·o·nal (pĭp′ẽr·ō·năl), *n.* [G., fr. *piperin* piperine.] *Chem.* A white crystalline aldehyde, $(CH_2O_2)C_6H_3CHO$, having the odor of heliotrope and used in perfumery.

pipe′stone′ (pīp′stōn′), *n.* *Petrog.* A pink clayey stone, carved by the Indians into tobacco pipes.

pi·pette′ (pĭ·pĕt′), *n.* Also **pi·pet′.** [F., dim. of *pipe* tube, cask.] A small piece of apparatus with which fluids are transferred, measured, etc., as in chemical operations. The simplest form is a narrow glass tube, the liquid being drawn up into it by suction and retained by closing the upper end.

pip′ing (pīp′ĭng), *n.* **1.** Act of one that pipes; also, the sounds produced. **2.** Pipes collectively; material in, or suggestive of, the form of a pipe or pipes. **3.** *Cookery.* Decorative pipelike lines of icing. **4.** *Dressmaking, etc.* A narrow bias fold used to decorate edges or seams; trimming by means of such folds. — *adj.* **1.** Playing on a musical pipe. **2.** Characterized by the music of the pipe rather than of the martial drum and fife; hence, soft; tranquil; as, the *piping* times of peace. **3.** Emitting a high, shrill sound; also, shrill. — *adv.* So as to pipe, or sizzle; as, *piping* hot.

pip′it (pĭp′ĭt), *n.* [From its call note.] Any of various small singing birds (family Motacillidae) resembling the lark; esp., one of the genus *Anthus.*

pip′kin (pĭp′kĭn), *n.* **1.** A small earthen pot. **2.** *Dial.* A piggin.

pip′pin (pĭp′ĭn), *n.* [ME. *pipin, pepin,* a seed, fr. OF. *pepin.*] **1.** *Now Dial.* A seed; pip. **2.** An apple of one of numerous varieties; as, the ***Fall Pippin,*** a rich-flavored variety of yellow apple, and the commercially important yellow winter apple ***Newtown Pippin.*** **3.** *Slang.* A highly admired or very admirable person or thing.

pip·sis′se·wa (pĭp·sĭs′ē·wȧ), *n.* [Of Algonquian origin.] Any of a genus (*Chimaphila,* esp. *C. corymbosa*) of evergreen herbs with astringent leaves used as a tonic and diuretic.

pi′quan·cy (pē′kăn·sĭ), *n.* Piquant character, flavor, etc.

pi′quant (pē′kănt), *adj.* [F., pres. part. of *piquer* to prick, sting.] **1.** *Archaic.* Stinging; disagreeably sharp. **2.** Agreeably stimulating to the palate; pleasantly tart, sharp, or biting; pungent. **3.** Engagingly provocative; also, having a lively arch charm; as, a *piquant* face. — **Syn.** See PUNGENT. — **pi′quant·ly,** *adv.*

pique (pēk), *n.* [F., fr. *piquer* to prick.] Offense taken by one slighted or disdained; also, a fit of resentment; dudgeon. — **Syn.** See OFFENSE. — *v. t.* **1.** To arouse anger or resentment in; nettle; offend by slighting. **2.** To excite or arouse by a provocation; challenge, rebuff, or the like; goad. **3.** To pride (oneself), — usually with *on* or *upon.* **4.** *Aeronautics.* To charge or attack, as by driving downward at. — **Syn.** See PROVOKE.

pi·qué′ (pē·kā′), *n.* [F., past part. of *piquer* to prick.] A ribbed cotton fabric, white, plain-colored, or printed, for dresses, waistcoats, etc.

pi·quet′ (pē·kā′; pē·kĕt′), *n.* [F.] A game at cards.

pi′ra·cy (pī′rȧ·sĭ), *n.; pl.* -CIES (-sĭz). [ML. *piratia,* fr. Gr. *peirateia.*] **1.** Robbery on the high seas. **2.** Any unauthorized appropriation and reproduction of another's production, invention, or conception; literary or artistic theft.

pi·ra′gua (pĭ·rä′gwȧ; -răg′wȧ), *n.* [Sp.] *Naut.* **a** A canoe made by hollowing out a large log; a dugout. **b** A dugout widened by cutting in two and inserting planks. **c** A two-masted, flat-bottomed boat.

pi·ra′nha (pĭ·rän′yȧ), *n.* [Pg., fr. Tupi.] = CARIBE.

pi′rate (pī′rĭt), *n.* [L. *pirata,* fr. Gr. *peiratēs,* fr. *peiran* to attempt, attack.] **1.** One who commits piracy; esp., a robber on the high seas. **2.** An armed vessel employed in piracy. — *v. i. & t.* **1.** To commit piracy (upon). **2.** To publish without proper authorization, esp. in infringement of copyright. **3.** To take over and use in violation of exclusive assignment to another, as a wave length. — **pi·rat′i·cal** (pī·răt′ĭ·kăl), **pi·rat′ic** (-ĭk), *adj.* — **pi·rat′i·cal·ly,** *adv.*

pirn (pûrn; *Scot. also* pĭrn), *n.* **1.** The reed or guide bobbin of a weaver's shuttle. **2.** *Scot.* The reel on a fishing rod.

pi·rogue′ (pĭ·rōg′), *n.* [F., fr. Sp. *piragua,* of Cariban and Arawakan origin.] A dugout canoe; any canoelike boat.

pir′ou·ette′ (pĭr′ōō·ĕt′), *n.* [F.] *Dancing.* A whirling on the toes of one or both feet. — **pir′ou·ette′,** *v. i.*

‖**pis al′ler′** (pē′-zȧ′lā′). [F.] Literally, to go worst; hence, the only course possible; a last resource.

pis′ca·ry (pĭs′kȧ·rĭ), *n.; pl.* -RIES (-rĭz). [L. *piscarius* relating to fishes or to fishing, fr. *piscis* a fish.] **1.** *Law.* The right or privilege of fishing in another man's waters; — now in phrase *common of piscary.* **2.** A fishing place; a fishery.

pis′ca·to′ri·al (pĭs′kȧ·tō′rĭ·ăl; 70), *adj.* Of or pertaining to fishes or fishing. — **pis′ca·to′ri·al·ly,** *adv.*

pis′ca·to′ry (pĭs′kȧ·tō′rĭ *or, esp. Brit.,* -tẽr·ĭ), *adj.* [L. *piscatorius,* deriv. of *piscis* a fish.] Piscatorial.

Pis′ces (pĭs′ēz), *n. pl.; gen.* PISCIUM (pĭsh′ĭ·ŭm). [L., fishes.] *Astron.* **a** A zodiacal constellation directly south of Andromeda; the Fish or Fishes. **b** The twelfth sign [♓ or ♓] of the zodiac. See ZODIAC.

pisci-. [L. *piscis.*] A combining form meaning *fish,* as in **pis′ci·cul′ture** (pĭs′ĭ·kŭl′tūr), **pis′ci·form, pis·civ′o·rous.**

pis·ci′na (pĭ·sī′nȧ; pĭ·sē′-), *n.* [L., a cistern, tank, fishpond, fr. *piscis* a fish.] *Eccl.* A basin with a drain for the disposal of water from liturgical ablutions and the washing of altar linens. — **pis′ci·nal** (pĭs′ĭ·năl; -n'l), *adj.*

pis′cine (pĭs′īn; -ĭn), *adj.* [L. *piscis* a fish.] *Zool.* Of or pertaining to, or like, a fish or fishes.

pi′si·form (pī′sĭ·fôrm), *adj.* [L. *pisum* pea + *-form.*] **1.** Like a pea in size and shape. **2.** *Anat. & Zool.* Designating a bone on the ulnar side of the carpus.

pis′mire′ (pĭs′mīr′), *n.* An ant.

pi′so·lite (pī′sō·līt; pĭz′ō-), *n.* [Gr. *pison* pea + *-lite.*] *Petrog.* A limestone composed of pisiform concretions. — **pi′so·lit′ic** (-lĭt′ĭk), *adj.*

pis·tach′i·o (pĭs·tăsh′ĭ·ō; pĭs·tä′shĭ-; pĭs·tā′-), *n.; pl.* -CHIOS (-ōz). Also **pis·tache′** (pĭs·tăsh′; *F.* pēs′tăsh′). [It. *pistacchio,* fr. L., fr. Gr. *pistakion,* fr. *pistakē,* the tree, fr. Per. *pistah,* the nut.] **1. a** A small tree (*Pistacia vera*) of the sumac family, whose drupaceous fruit contains a greenish seed (**pistachio nut**) used in cookery. **b** The seed of this tree. **2.** In full **pistachio green.** A color, yellow-green in hue, of low saturation and high brilliance. See COLOR. **3.** *Cookery.* The flavor of the pistachio nut.

pis′ta·reen′ (pĭs′tȧ·rēn′), *n.* A debased two-real piece of Spain, once current in America. — *adj.* Of small value.

pis′til (pĭs′tĭl; -t'l), *n.* [F., fr. L. *pistillum, pistillus,* a pestle.] *Bot.* The ovule-bearing organ of a seed plant; the ovary with its appendages. See SPIKELET, *Illust.*

pis′til·late (pĭs′tĭ·lāt), *adj.* *Bot.* Furnished with a pistil or pistils; specif., of diclinous flowers, having pistils but no stamens. See AMENT, *Illust.*; cf. STAMINATE.

pis′tol (pĭs′t'l), *n.* [F. *pistole,* fr. G. *pistole,* fr. Czech *pišt′al,* prop., a pipe.] A short firearm intended to be aimed and fired from one hand. Pistols are now usually either revolvers, or automatic, or semiautomatic, magazine pistols. — *v. t.;* -TOLED (-t'ld) or -TOLLED; -TOL·ING or -TOL·LING. To shoot with a pistol.

pis·tole′ (pĭs·tōl′), *n.* [F.] The old quarter doubloon of Spain, worth about $4; also, any of similar obsolete gold coins.

pis′to·leer′ (pĭs′tō·lēr′), *n.* Also **pis′to·lier′.** [F. *pistolier.*] One who uses, or is armed with, a pistol.

pis′ton (pĭs′tŭn; -t'n), *n.* [F., through It. & LL., fr. L. *pinsere, pistum,* to pound.] **1.** *Mach.* A sliding piece moved by, or moving against, fluid pressure, usually a short cylinder moving within a cylindrical vessel. See HYDRAULIC, *Illust.* **2.** *Music.* In certain brass-wind instruments, a sliding valve moving in a cylinder like an engine piston and serving, when depressed by a finger knob, to lower the pitch. See TRUMPET, *Illust.*

piston pin. *Mach.* = WRIST PIN.

piston ring. *Mach.* A yielding ring, usually metal, which surrounds a piston and maintains a tight fit inside a cylinder.

piston rod. *Mach.* A rod by which a piston is moved, or by which it communicates motion. See STUFFING BOX, *Illust.*

pit (pĭt), *n.* [D., kernel, pith.] *U. S.* The stone of a drupaceous fruit. — *v. t.* To remove the pit from.

pit, *n.* [AS. *pytt* pit, hole, prob. fr. L. *puteus* well, pit.] **1.** A cavity or hole in the ground. **2.** A pitfall for wild beasts; hence, a trap; a snare. **3.** A deep place; an abyss. **4.** Hades; hell, or a part of it; as, in the *pit* of hell. **5.** A surface depression or hollow, as on the human body; as, the arm*pit;* also, a scar, esp. one left by a pustule; as, smallpox *pits.* **6.** An enclosed hole or area for wild beasts, for cockfighting, etc. **7.** *U. S.* That part of the floor of some exchanges devoted to a special branch of business; as, wheat *pit.* **8.** *Eng.* **a** That part of a theater below the level of the stage and behind the orchestra; now, the cheaper part behind the stalls. **b** The spectators in this part of the theater.

— *v. t.;* PIT′TED (pĭt′ĕd; -ĭd); PIT′TING. **1.** To place, cast, bury, or store in a pit. **2.** To form pits in; to mark with pustule scars. **3.** To set in a pit to fight, as cocks; hence, to put in competition, rivalry, or antagonism; — with *against;* as, to *pit* A against B. — *v. i.* **1.** To excavate. **2.** To become marked with pits; specif., *Med.,* to preserve for a time an indentation made by pressure, as in edema.

pi′ta (pē′tȧ), *n.* [Sp.] **a** A fiber used for cordage, etc., obtained from the century plant (*Agave americana*); also, the plant itself. **b** Istle fiber. **c** The similar fiber of several other plants, as various species of yucca.

pit′a·pat′ (pĭt′ȧ·păt′), *adv.* With quick succession of beats; in a flutter; as, her heart went *pitapat.* — *v. i.* To move or beat pitapat. — *n.* A light, repeated sound; a pattering; as, the *pitapat* of little feet.

pitch (pĭch), *n.* [ME. *pich,* fr. AS. *pic,* fr. L. *pix, picis.*] **1.** A black or dark viscous substance obtained as a residue in distilling tar, wood tar, petroleum, etc., and occurring naturally as *asphalt.* Artificial pitch, like asphalt, consists chiefly of hydrocarbons, but varies much in composition and consistency according to the way it is produced. Thus, that from wood tar is hard and brittle; that from coal tar may be either hard or soft. Pitch is used in varnishes, for calking, street paving, etc. **2.** Any of various bituminous substances; — often with a qualifying word; as, mineral *pitch.* **3.** The resin, often medicinal, from certain conifers. — *v. t.* To cover over, smear, or soil, with or as with pitch.

pitch (pĭch), *v. t.* [ME. *picchen.*] **1.** To place and set up or erect; as, to *pitch* a tent. **2.** To throw, fling, hurl, or toss, usually with a definite aim or purpose; as, to *pitch* a quoit; to *pitch* hay. **3.** To set in order or arrange; — *Archaic,* except in *pitched battle.* **4.** To fix or set at a particular pitch or level; as, to *pitch* the voice high. **5.** *Baseball.* To throw (the ball) to the batsman. **6.** *Cards.* To lead (a card of a certain suit) and thereby establish trumps; to establish (the trump) in this way. — **Syn.** See THROW. — *v. i.* **1.** To encamp; locate. **2.** To plunge or fall; esp., to fall forward; also, to decline or slope. **3.** To pitch something as hay, a ball, etc. **4.** To fix one's choice; also, to select at random; — with *on* or *upon.* **5.** Of a ship, to plunge so that the bow and stern alternately rise and fall in the water; hence, to lurch. Cf. SCEND.

— *n.* **1.** Act or manner of pitching; as: **a** A throw; toss; cast. **b** A plunging forward and downward, esp. of a vessel in a head sea. **2.** That which is pitched; amount pitched. **3.** A point or peak; the extreme top or bottom; hence, the extreme reach. **4.** A slope or a degree of slope; inclination; specif., in technical uses: **a** *Aeronautics.* The distance advanced by a propeller in one revolution. **b** *Arch.* Of an arch or roof, the slope of the sides expressed by the ratio of the height to the span. **c** *Geol. & Mining.* Dip or inclination of a vein or bed. **d** *Mech. & Mach.* (1) Distance between one point on a gear tooth and the corresponding point on the next tooth. (2) Distance from any point on the thread of a screw to the corresponding point on an adjacent thread measured parallel to the axis. Cf. GAUGE, *Illust.* (6). **5.** *Cards.* A variety of seven-up in which the first card pitched is the trump. 6. *Music & Acous.* **a** That property of a musical tone which is determined by the frequency of vibration of the sound waves which strike the ear. The larger the number of vibrations per second the higher the pitch. **b** A standard of pitch used in tuning instruments; specif.: (1) The ***concert, or high, pitch,*** with a vibration number of about 450 for the first *a* above middle C (*a'*); (2) The ***diapason normal,*** called ***French, international,*** or ***low pitch,*** which gives *a'* 435; (3) The present standard pitch, called ***philharmonic pitch,*** which gives *a'* 440. 7. *Cricket.* The specially prepared part of the playing grounds between the bowling creases; the wicket (def. 4 **b**). Cf. CREASE, *n.*, 2.

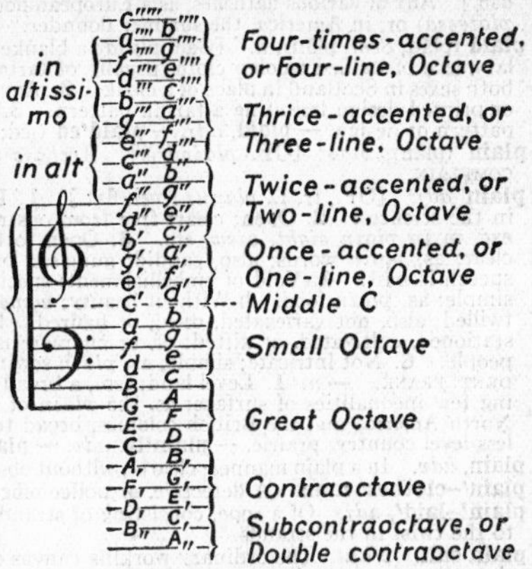
in altissimo
in alt
Four-times-accented, or Four-line, Octave
Thrice-accented, or Three-line, Octave
Twice-accented, or Two-line, Octave
Once-accented, or One-line, Octave
Middle C
Small Octave
Great Octave
Contraoctave
Subcontraoctave, or Double contraoctave
Staff Notation of Pitch, 6, showing the equivalent of each line and space in Letter Notation for Absolute Pitch. The notes of the accented octaves are also written with lines above the letter, as $\bar{c}$, $\bar{\bar{c}}$, $\bar{\bar{\bar{c}}}$, $\bar{\bar{\bar{\bar{c}}}}$, or with numerals, as a^1, a^2, a^3, a^4. Those of the contraoctave are also written with one line below the letter, as $\underline{C}$, with two letters, as CC, or with a numeral, as C_1; those of the subcontraoctave with two lines below, as $\underline{\underline{A}}$, three letters, as AAA, or a numeral, as A_2.

pitch′–black′ *or* **pitch′–dark′** (2), *adj.* As black or dark as pitch.

pitch′blende′ (pĭch′blĕnd′), *n.* [G. *pechblende.*] *Mineral.* A brown to black massive mineral with pitchlike luster occurring in certain metalliferous veins. It is a source of uranium and radium.

pitch′er (pĭch′ẽr), *n.* [OF. *pichier*, through Teut., fr. LL. *becarium.*] 1. A vessel, usually with a handle and lip or spout, for holding and pouring out liquids. 2. *Bot.* A tubular or cuplike appendage or modification of the leaves in certain plants; an ascidium.

pitch′er, *n.* 1. One who pitches; as, a baseball *pitcher.* 2. *Golf.* A light iron club with face laid far back. See GOLF, *Illust.*

pitcher plant. Any plant with leaves modified into pitchers, or ascidia; specif., the huntsman's-cup. Some pitchers contain water in which captured insects are macerated and dissolved; others digest their prey by acid secretions. See SARRACENIA.

pitch′fork′ (pĭch′fôrk′), *n.* A fork, usually long-handled, used in pitching hay, grain, etc. — *v. t.* To pitch with or as with a pitchfork.

pitch′ing nib′lick. See GOLF, *Illust.*

pitch′out′ (pĭch′out′), *n.* **a** *Baseball.* A pitch out of reach of the batter delivered on signal from the catcher in an attempt to throw out a base runner. **b** *Football.* A lateral pass made between two backs behind the scrimmage line.

pitch pipe. A small flue pipe or reed pipe, giving one or several tones, blown with the breath, for regulating the pitch, esp. of singers.

pitch′stone′ (pĭch′stōn′), *n.* [1st *pitch* + *stone*, after G. *pechstein.*] *Petrog.* A glassy rock with a resinous luster, containing more water than obsidian.

pitch′y (pĭch′ĭ), *adj.*; PITCH′I·ER (-ĭ·ẽr); PITCH′I·EST. 1. Of the quality or nature of pitch; resembling pitch. 2. Abounding in or smeared with pitch. 3. Black as pitch. — **pitch′i·ness,** *n.*

pit′e·ous (pĭt′ē·ŭs; 39), *adj.* [OF. *pitous.*] 1. *Obs.* Pitying; compassionate. 2. Exciting pity or compassion; pitiful. 3. *Now Dial.* Pitiable; paltry. — **Syn.** See PITIFUL. — **-ly,** *adv.* — **-ness,** *n.*

pit′fall′ (pĭt′fôl′), *n.* 1. A trap or snare; esp., a pit with the opening masked, into which animals or men may fall. 2. A danger, difficulty, or error into which one may fall unsuspectingly.

pith (pĭth), *n.* [AS. *pitha.*] 1. The loose spongy tissue occupying the center of the stem in dicotyledonous plants. 2. The soft or spongy interior of a bone, a feather, etc. 3. That which contains the strength or life; vigor; substance. — *v. t.* 1. To kill, as cattle, by piercing or severing the spinal cord. 2. To destroy the central nervous system of (an animal, as a frog), as by passing a wire up and down the vertebral canal. 3. To remove the pith from (the stem of a plant).

Pith′e·can·thro′pus (pĭth′ē·kăn·thrō′pŭs; -kăn′thrō·pŭs), *n.* [NL., fr. Gr. *pithēkos* ape + *anthrōpos* man.] **a** A genus of extinct primitive man comprising the apelike species *P. erectus* (called also ***Java man***) and possibly Peking man. See MAN, *Illust.* **b** [*not cap.*] *pl.* -THROPI (-pī). Also **pith′e·can′thrope** (-kăn′thrōp). A member of this genus.

pith′y (pĭth′ĭ), *adj.*; PITH′I·ER (-ĭ·ẽr); PITH′I·EST. 1. Consisting of or abounding in pith. 2. Having substance and point; tersely cogent. — **Syn.** See CONCISE. — **pith′i·ly,** *adv.* — **pith′i·ness,** *n.*

pit′i·a·ble (pĭt′ĭ·ȧ·b′l; 58), *adj.* 1. Deserving or exciting pity; lamentable. 2. Lamentably insignificant or mean; despicable; as, *pitiable* makeshifts. — **Syn.** See PITIFUL: CONTEMPTIBLE. — **pit′i·a·ble·ness,** *n.* — **pit′i·a·bly,** *adv.*

pit′i·ful (pĭt′ĭ·fo͝ol; -f′l), *adj.* 1. *Archaic.* Full of pity; compassionate. 2. Arousing pity; eliciting compassion. 3. Pitiable; worthy of contempt. — **pit′i·ful·ly,** *adv.* — **pit′i·ful·ness,** *n.*

Syn. **Pitiful, piteous, pitiable** mean calling for pity. **Pitiful** implies excitement of pity or commiseration by that which is felt to be pathetic; **piteous,** a character in that appealing, rather than an effect upon that impressed; **pitiable,** commiseration with some contempt.

pit′i·less, *adj.* Merciless; ruthless. — **pit′i·less·ly,** *adv.* — **-ness,** *n.*

pit′man (pĭt′măn), *n.* 1. *pl.* -MEN (-mĕn). One who works in a pit, as in mining. 2. *pl.* -MANS (-mănz). *Mach.* A connecting rod.

‖**pi′ton′** (pē′tôN′), *n.* [F.] 1. A sharp peak. 2. *Mountain Climbing.* An iron peg or stanchion, often with a circular head for attaching a rope.

Pi′tot′–stat′ic tube (pē′tō′stăt′ĭk). *Aeronautics.* A combination of a Pitot tube and a static tube used in connection with a manometer to determine the relative speed of the air. See AIRPLANE, *Illust.*

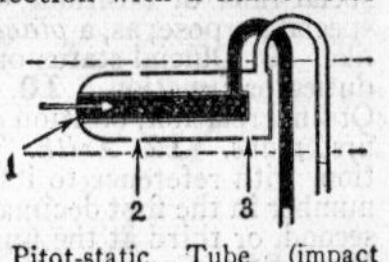
1
2
3
Pitot-static Tube (impact pressure black, static pressure white). 1 Pitot Opening; 2 Static Opening; 3 Drain Holes.

Pi′tot′, *or* **Pi′tot's′, tube** (pē′tō′, -tōz′). [After Henri *Pitot* (1695–1771), French physicist and engineer.] *Hydraulics.* A tube with a short right-angled bend, placed vertically in a moving body of fluid with the bent part lowermost and its mouth normal to the direction of flow, to measure the velocity of the fluid.

pit saw, *or* **pit′saw′** (pĭt′sô′), *n.* A saw worked by two men, one on the log, and one beneath it, often in a pit.

pit′tance (pĭt′ăns), *n.* [OF. *pitance.*] A small portion, quantity, allowance, or wage; a dole.

pit′ter–pat′ter (pĭt′ẽr·păt′ẽr), *n.* A rapid succession of light sounds or beats; a patter. — **pit′ter–pat′ter,** *adv.*

pi·tu′i·tar′y (pĭ·tū′ĭ·tĕr′ĭ *or, esp. Brit.,* -tẽr·ĭ; 114), *adj.* [L. *pituita* phlegm.] 1. *Anat.* Secreting mucus. 2. *Anat. & Zool.* Pert. to or designating a gland (**pituitary body** *or* **gland**), a small oval two-lobed vascular body attached to the infundibulum of the brain. See BRAIN, *Illust.* 3. Designating a type of obese, long-boned physique believed due to excessive secretion of this gland. — *n.* 1. The pituitary body or gland. 2. *Med.* A preparation made from either lobe of this gland. Extracts (**pituitary extracts**) of the anterior lobe promote skeletal growth, etc.; those of the posterior lobe cause increased blood pressure, contraction of nonstriated muscle, etc.

pi·tu′i·tous (-tŭs), *adj.* [L. *pituitosus.*] Full of, resembling, or due to mucus; discharging mucus.

pit′y (pĭt′ĭ), *n.*; *pl.* PITIES (-ĭz). [OF. *pite, pitie*, fr. L. *pietas* piety, kindness, pity, fr. *pius* pious.] 1. A feeling for the sufferings of others; sympathy; compassion. 2. A reason or cause of pity, grief, or regret; a thing to be regretted.

Syn. **Pity, compassion, commiseration, ruth, condolence, sympathy** mean feeling for another's suffering or misery. **Pity** implies tender or, sometimes, slightly contemptuous sorrow; **compassion,** pity coupled with an urgent desire to aid or to spare; **commiseration,** pity expressed outwardly in tears, words, etc.; **ruth,** pity with mercy, often implying a change of heart; **condolence,** grieving with another who has suffered loss, or an expression of such grief; **sympathy** is often used in place of *pity* or *compassion*, but strictly implies a power to enter into another's emotional experiences of any sort.

— *v. t.*; PIT′IED (-ĭd); PIT′Y·ING. To feel pity for; have sympathy with. — *v. i.* To feel pity. — **pit′y·ing·ly,** *adv.*

pit′y·ri′a·sis (pĭt′ĭ·rī′ȧ·sĭs), *n.* [NL., fr. Gr. *pityriasis*, fr. *pityron*, lit., bran.] 1. *Med.* A superficial affection of the skin, characterized by irregular patches of thin scales. 2. *Veter.* A disease of domestic animals characterized by dry epithelial scales.

‖**più** (pyo͞o), *adv.* [It., fr. L. *plus.*] *Music.* More; as, *più* allegro, more lively.

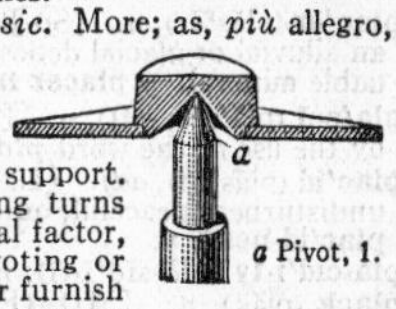
a
a Pivot, 1.

piv′ot (pĭv′ŭt), *n.* [F.] 1. A point, fixed pin, or short axis, on the end of which something turns. 2. The end of a shaft or arbor which rests and turns in a support. 3. That upon or around which something turns or depends; the central, cardinal, or crucial factor, member, part, person, etc. — *adj.* Pivoting or pivoted; pivotal. — *v. t.* To mount on, or furnish with, a pivot or pivots. — *v. i.* 1. To turn or swing on or as on a pivot. 2. *Cards.* To rotate about the table at intervals, one player sitting still and the others moving to the right. 3. *Dancing.* To turn as if on a pivot.

piv′ot·al (-ăl; -'l), *adj.* Of, pert. to, or constituting a pivot. — **piv′ot·al·ly,** *adv.*

pix (pĭks). Var. of PYX.

pix′i·lat′ed (pĭk′sĭ·lāt′ĕd; -ĭd), *adj.* *Colloq.* Slightly unbalanced mentally; balmy; daffy; hence, of an amusingly daffy nature; as, a *pixilated* comedy. — **pix′i·la′tion** (-lā′shŭn), *n.*

pix′y, pix′ie (pĭk′sĭ), *n.*; *pl.* PIXIES (-sĭz). In local English folklore, a mischievous sprite or fairy.

piz′za (pēt′sȧ; *Ital.* pĕt′tsä), *n.*; *pl.* PIZZAS (-sȧz), *It.* PIZZE (pĕt′tsā). [It.] A large flat tart made of bread dough spread with tomato pulp and strips of cheese and often shreds of meat, anchovies, or the like, highly flavored with savory herbs, and baked thoroughly.

piz′ze·ri′a (pēt′sẽ·rē′ȧ; *Ital.* pĕt·tsā·rē′ä), *n.* [It.] A bakery where pizzas are sold.

piz′zi·ca′to (pĭt′sē·kä′tō; pēt′-), *adj.* [It., pinched.] *Music.* Plucked; — a direction to players of bowed instruments to pluck the string instead of bowing. Abbr. *pizz.* — *n.*; *pl.* -TI (-tē). A tone so produced; a plucking.

pla′ca·ble (plā′kȧ·b′l; plăk′ȧ-), *adj.* [OF., fr. L. *placabilis*, fr. *placare* to quiet.] Capable of being, or ready to be, placated; disposed to forgive. — **pla′ca·bil′i·ty** (-bĭl′ĭ·tĭ), **pla′ca·ble·ness,** *n.* — **pla′ca·bly** (-blĭ), *adv.*

plac′ard (plăk′ärd), *n.* [F., fr. Pr. *placa* plaque.] A notice posted in a public place; a poster; bill.

pla·card′ (plȧ·kärd′; plăk′ärd), *v. t.* 1. To post placards upon or in. 2. To announce by placards. 3. To post as a placard. — *v. i.* To affix placards. — **pla·card′er** (plȧ·kär′dẽr; plăk′är·dẽr), *n.*

pla′cate (plā′kāt; plăk′āt; *or, esp. Brit.,* plȧ·kāt′), *v. t.* [L. *placatus*, past part. of *placare* to placate.] To appease; pacify. — **Syn.** See PACIFY. — **pla′cat·er** (plā′kāt·ẽr; plăk′āt·ẽr), *n.* — **pla·ca′tion** (plā·kā′shŭn), *n.* — **pla′ca·tive** (plā′kȧ·tĭv; plăk′ȧ-), *adj.*

pla′ca·to′ry (plā′kȧ·tō′rĭ; plăk′ȧ-; *or, esp. Brit.,* -tẽr·ĭ), *adj.* [LL. *placatorius.*] Designed to placate; conciliatory.

place (plās), *n.* [OF., fr. L. *platea* a street, area, courtyard, fr. Gr. *plateia* a street, prop. fem. of *platys* flat, broad.] 1. *Now Rare.* An open space, or square, in a city or town. Cf. 2d PLACE. 2. Space; specif.: **a** Room; as, make *place* for the ladies. **b** A region; locality. **c** A village, town, or city; as, one's native *place.* **d** A locality or spot occupied as a dwelling place or the like; as, to own a fine *place.* **e** A portion of space reserved for occupancy, as a seat in a theater. 3. A portion of space occupied by a body; hence, proper or assigned position, time, or character; as, everything is in its *place.* 4. Vacated or relinquished space; stead; lieu; as, to rule in *place* of the king; also, situation; state, as of mind or of affairs; as, if I were in his *place.* 5. A particular or specifiable spot, passage, or the like. **6.** Station; esp., social rank or position. **7.** A building, or the like, set apart for a special purpose; as, a *place* of worship. **8.** A short street, court, or the like. **9.** Official status or position; an office or employment; also, its duties or function. **10.** Space, esp. as contrasted with time. **11.** Ordinal relation; position or point in an ordered series; as, to say in the first *place.* **12.** *Arith.* The position of a figure, or a figure in position, with reference to its relation to others of a row or series; as, a number in the first decimal *place.* **13.** *Racing.* The position of first, second, or third at the finish, esp. the second position. Cf. SHOW, *n.*, 12. — **Syn.** See POSITION.

— *v. t.*; PLACED (plāst); PLAC'ING (plās'ĭng). **1.** To put in a particular place; to set, arrange, or establish, in a certain relative position, as in rank, order, condition, etc. **2.** To dispose of in a desired or selected way, as for investment, attention, adoption, etc.; as, to *place* an order. **3.** To identify by assigning to, or connecting with, some place, time, or the like; as, I cannot *place* him. **4.** In singing or speaking, to produce or cause to produce tones of (voice) with reference to the vocal organs and resonance cavities involved. **5.** *Racing.* To determine or announce the place of at the finish.

‖**place** (plȧs), *n.* [F.] Place; open place or square in a city or town. Cf. 1st PLACE, *n.*, 1; PLAZA.

‖**place aux dames** (plȧ'-sō dȧm'). [F.] Room for, or make way for, the ladies.

pla·ce'bo (plȧ·sē'bō), *n.; pl.* -BOS, -BOES (-bōz). [L., I shall please.] **1.** *R.C.Ch.* The first antiphon (Psalm cxiv. 9. Vulgate) of the Vespers for the dead; — from its first word. **2.** *Med.* A medicine, esp. an inactive one, given merely to satisfy a patient. **3.** A soothing or ingratiating remark, act, etc.

place kick. *Football.* Act of kicking the ball after it has been placed on the ground, or an instance of this. — **place'-kick'**, *v. t. & i.*

place'man (plās'măn), *n.* One who holds or occupies a place, esp. a public office; — usually contemptuous.

place'ment (-mĕnt), *n.* Act of placing, or fact of being placed; specif.: **a** The finding of employment for a worker. **b** *Amer. Football.* The placing of the ball on the ground for a place kick; also, the position of the placed ball; a place kick.

pla·cen'ta (plȧ·sĕn'tȧ), *n.; pl.* -TAE (-tē), -TAS (-tȧz). [L., a cake, fr. Gr. *plakous* a flat cake, fr. *plax, plakos,* anything flat and broad.] **1.** *Anat. & Zool.* In mammals (except monotremes and most marsupials), the vascular structure by which the fetus is nourished in the uterus. It consists of a modified part of the chorion. The fetus is attached to the placenta by the umbilical cord. Cf. AFTERBIRTH. **2.** *Bot.* Any sporangia-bearing surface; specif., that part of the carpel bearing ovules. — **pla·cen'tal** (-tăl; -t'l), **plac'en·tar'y** (plăs'ĕn·tĕr'ĭ; -tĕr·ĭ; plȧ·sĕn'tȧ·rĭ), *adj.*

pla·cen'tate (plȧ·sĕn'tāt), *adj.* Having a placenta.

plac'en·ta'tion (plăs'ĕn·tā'shŭn), *n.* **1.** *Anat. & Zool.* Mode of attachment of placenta. **2.** *Bot.* Placental arrangement or structure.

plac'er (plăs'ẽr), *n.* [Sp.] A place where gold is obtained by washing; an alluvial or glacial deposit, containing particles of gold or other valuable mineral. — **placer mining.** — **placer miner.**

pla'cet (plā'sĕt; -sĭt), *n.* [L., it pleases.] A vote of assent manifested by the use of the word *placet.*

plac'id (plăs'ĭd), *adj.* [L. *placidus,* fr. *placere* to please.] Unruffled; undisturbed; peaceful; quiet. — **Syn.** See CALM. — **plac'id·ly,** *adv.* — **plac'id·ness,** *n.*

pla·cid'i·ty (plȧ·sĭd'ĭ·tĭ), *n.* Calmness; serenity.

plack (plăk), *n.* [MD. (Flem.) *placke.*] *Scot.* A small copper coin used in Scotland in the 15th century; hence, anything of little value.

plack'et (plăk'ĕt; -ĭt), *n.* **1.** *Archaic.* A petticoat; figuratively, a woman. **2.** A slit or opening in a garment, esp. a skirt, for convenience in putting it on; — called also **placket hole.** **3.** A pocket, esp. one in a skirt.

plac'oid (plăk'oid), *adj.* [Gr. *plax, plakos,* tablet, flat plate.] *Zool.* Designating, or having the form of scales characteristic of, the elasmobranchs. These scales resemble teeth, bearing projecting spines. Cf. GANOID. — *n.* An elasmobranch.

‖**pla'fond'** (plȧ'fôɴ'), *n.* [F.] *Arch.* A ceiling formed by the underside of a floor, esp. when of elaborate design.

pla'gal (plā'găl), *adj.* [ML. *plagalis,* fr. *plaga* plagal mode, fr. Gr. *plagios* sidewise.] *Music.* Of a mode or melody, having its keynote in the middle of its compass.

‖**plage** (plȧzh), *n.* [F.] A beach.

pla'gi·a·rism (plā'jĭ·ȧ·rĭz'm; plā'jȧ-), *n.* Act of plagiarizing; also, something plagiarized. — **pla'gi·a·rist** (-rĭst), *n.* — **pla'gi·a·ris'tic** (-rĭs'tĭk), *adj.*

pla'gi·a·rize (-rīz), *v. t. & i.* To steal or purloin and pass off as one's own (ideas, writings, etc., of another). — **pla'gi·a·riz'er** (-rīz'ẽr), *n.*

pla'gi·ar'y (plā'jĭ·ĕr'ĭ; plā'jȧ·rĭ), *n.; pl.* -IES (-ĭz). [L. *plagiarius* kidnaper, plagiarist, fr. *plagium* kidnaping, fr. Gr. *plagios* oblique, crooked.] **1.** A plagiarist. **2.** Plagiarism.

pla'gi·o- (plā'jĭ·ō-), **pla'gi-** (plā'jĭ-). [Gr. *plagios.*] A combining form meaning *oblique, aslant,* as in **pla'gi·he'dral, pla'gi·o·ce·phal'ic.**

pla'gi·o·clase' (-klās'), *n.* [G. *plagioklas,* fr. Gr. *plagios* oblique + *klasis* a breaking.] *Mineral. & Petrog.* Triclinic feldspar in general; hence, esp., the soda-lime group. — **pla'gi·o·clas'tic** (-klăs'tĭk), *adj.*

pla'gi·o·trop'ic (-trŏp'ĭk), *adj.* [*plagio-* + *-tropic.*] *Plant Physiol.* Having the longer axis inclined away from the vertical line, as most roots and lateral branches. — **pla'gi·o·trop'i·cal·ly** (-ĭ·kăl·ĭ), *adv.* — **pla'gi·ot'ro·pism** (-ŏt'rō·pĭz'm), *n.*

plague (plāg; *colloq. or dial.* plĕg), *n.* [L. *plāga* a blow, plague, prob. fr. Gr. *plaga, plēgē.*] **1.** That which smites or troubles; any afflictive evil; scourge; infestation. **2.** *Colloq.* A nuisance. **3. a** Any malignant, esp. contagious, disease or pestilence. **b** An acute virulent disease caused by a bacterium (*Pasteurella pestis*). Several forms occur, of which ***bubonic plague*** is transmitted by the bite of fleas from infected rats and ***pneumonic, or pulmonary, plague*** is commonly spread from person to person by contact, droplets, etc. The *Black Death* of the Middle Ages is believed to have been the plague. — *v. t.*; PLAGUED (plāgd; plĕgd); PLA'GUING (plā'gĭng; plĕg'ĭng). **1.** To smite, infest, or afflict, as with disease, calamity, or natural evil. **2.** To pester; harass; torment. — **Syn.** See WORRY. — **pla'guer** (plā'gẽr; plĕg'ẽr), *n.*

pla'guy (plā'gĭ; *colloq. or dial.* plĕg'ĭ), *adj.* Also **pla'guey.** *Chiefly Colloq.* Of, pertaining to, or of the nature of a plague; harassing; — often used as a mere intensive; as, a *plaguy* nuisance. — **pla'gui·ly, pla'guy, pla'guey,** *adv.*

plaice (plās), *n. sing. & pl.* [OF. *plaïs, plaïz,* fr. LL. *platessa* flatfish.] Any of various flatfishes, as a European flounder (*Pleuronectes platessa*) or, in America, the summer flounder. See FLOUNDER.

plaid (plăd; *Scot.* plād), *n.* [Gael *plaide* a blanket.] **1.** A rectangular piece of twilled woolen cloth, usually of tartan pattern, worn by both sexes in Scotland in place of a cloak. **2.** Any fabric with a woven or printed design imitating a tartan pattern. **3.** A tartan or similar pattern or design. — **plaid,** *adj.* — **plaid'ed** (-ĕd; -ĭd), *adj.*

plain (plān), *v. i.* [OF. *plaindre.*] *Archaic & Dial.* Short for COMPLAIN.

plain, *adj.* [OF., fr. L. *planus* level, flat.] **1.** Plane; — rarely used in the sciences. **2.** Open; clear; free from obstructions; now *Dial.,* exc. in *in plain sight, view,* etc. **3.** Open to the mind; manifest; clear; as, *plain* words; also, candid; guileless; outspoken; as, *plain* speech is best. **4.** Void of embellishment; specif.: **a** Not luxurious; simple; as, *plain* food. **b** Without beauty; homely. **c** Of cloth, untwilled; also, not variegated, dyed, or figured. **5.** Not highly born, stationed, cultivated, or gifted; of, or characteristic of, the common people. **6.** Not intricate; simple; as, *plain* sewing. — **Syn.** See EVIDENT: FRANK. — *n.* **1.** Level land; esp., a broad stretch of land having few inequalities of surface; as, the *plain* of Jordan. **2.** *pl.* In North America and the British colonies, broad tracts of almost treeless level country; prairie. — **plain'ly,** *adv.* — **plain'ness,** *n.*

plain, *adv.* In a plain manner; clearly; without obscurity or ambiguity.

plain'-clothes' man. A detective, or police officer, not in uniform.

plain'-laid', *adj.* Of a rope, consisting of strands twisted oppositely to the twist in the strands.

plain sail. *Naut.* The ordinary working canvas of a vessel, or one of the sails composing it.

plain sailing. Sailing on an easy course, without obstacles; hence, any simple, easy line of action or progress.

plains'man (plānz'măn), *n.; pl.* -MEN (-mĕn). One who lives on the plains.

plain song *or* **plain chant. a** The ancient unisonous, nonmetrical chant melody of the church service. **b** Such a melody used as a cantus firmus; hence, any cantus firmus.

plain'stones' (plān'stōnz'), **plain'stanes'** (-stānz'), *n. pl. Scot.* Flagstones.

plaint (plānt), *n.* [OF. *plaint,* fr. L. *planctus,* fr. *plangere, planctum,* to beat, beat the breast, lament.] **1.** *Poetic.* Lamentation; a lament. **2.** A complaint or protest.

plain'tiff (plān'tĭf), *n.* [OF. *plaintif.*] *Law.* **a** One who commences a personal action or suit to obtain a remedy for an injury to his rights; — opposed to *defendant.* **b** The complaining party in any litigation.

plain'tive (-tĭv), *adj.* [OF. *plaintif.*] Expressive of sorrow or melancholy. — **plain'tive·ly,** *adv.* — **plain'tive·ness,** *n.*

plais'ter (plās'tẽr). Var. of PLASTER.

plait (plāt; plĕt; *Brit. usually, and in sense* 2 *of n.,* & 2, 3 *of v., often in the U. S.,* plăt), *n.* [OF. *pleit,* fr. L. *plicitum,* past part. of *plicare* to fold.] **1.** A flat fold; a doubling back, as of cloth on itself; a pleat. **2.** A braid, as of hair; a plat. — *v. t.* **1.** To fold, esp. in pleats. **2.** To interweave the strands or locks of; braid. **3.** To make by plaiting, or braiding.

plait'ing (plāt'ĭng; plĕt'-; plăt'-; *cf.* PLAIT), *n.* An arrangement of plaits, as in a skirt or blouse. In ***accordion plaiting*** and ***sunburst plaiting,*** the fabric is pressed so that creases pointing outward and inward alternate as in the bellows of an accordion. In sunburst plaiting, the folds gradually increase in depth. In ***knife plaiting*** and ***box plaiting,*** the folds are doubled over the cloth so that they lie flat with only one crease showing. In knife plaiting, the edges formed by these creases all point in the same direction; in box plaiting, the folds are in pairs, one edge pointing right, the other left.

plan (plăn), *n.* [F. *plan, plant,* fr. It. *piano* (fr. L. *planum* flat surface), and fr. It. *pianta,* fr. L. *planta* sole of the foot.] **1.** A draft or form, properly, one drawn on a plane, as a map; esp., a top view or the representation of a horizontal section; an orthographic projection on a horizontal plane; graphic representation; diagram. **2.** Method or scheme of action, procedure, or arrangement; project, program, outline or schedule. **3.** In perspective, one of a number of planes conceived as perpendicular to the line of vision, and interposed between the eye and the pictured objects.

Syn. **Plan, design, plot, scheme, project** mean a method devised for making, doing, etc. **Plan** always implies mental formulation and, sometimes, graphic representation; **design** often suggests a particular pattern; **plot** suggests a laying out in clearly distinguished sections with attention to their relations and their due proportions; **scheme** stresses calculation of the end in view; **project** more often suggests imaginative scope and vision.

— *v. t. & i.*; PLANNED (plănd); PLAN'NING. To form a plan (of or for); esp.: **a** To represent graphically. **b** To devise or project a method or course of action (of).

plan-. = 1st PLANO-.

pla·nar'i·an (plȧ·nâr'ĭ·ăn), *n.* [LL. *planarius* level.] *Zool.* Any of a class (Turbellaria) of mostly aquatic small, soft-bodied, leaf-shaped, completely ciliated flatworms.

planch, planche (plȧnch; 9), *n.* [OF. *planche.*] *Now Dial.* A plank, board, or slab; a floor.

planch'et (plăn'chĕt; -chĭt), *n.* [See PLANCHETTE.] A disk of metal ready to be stamped as a coin.

plan·chette' (plȧn·shĕt'; 9), *n.* [F., dim. of *planche* plank.] A small board supported on casters at two points and a vertical pencil at a third point, said, when lightly touched by fingers, to move of itself, the pencil thereby tracing words.

plane (plān), *n., or* **plane tree.** [F., fr. L. *platanus,* fr. Gr. *platanos,* fr. *platys* broad; — on account of its broad leaves and spreading form.] Any tree of a family (Platanaceae, the plane-tree family), consisting of one genus (*Platanus*), with large palmately lobed leaves and flowers in globose heads; — in U. S. called also *sycamore* and *buttonwood, button tree,* or *buttonball.*

plane, *adj.* [L. *planus.*] **1.** Without elevations or depressions; even; level; flat. **2.** *Math.* Involving only plane surfaces; as, *plane* geometry. Cf. SOLID, *adj.,* 2. — **Syn.** See LEVEL. — *n.* [L. *planum,* fr. *planus* level, flat.] **1.** A surface in which if any two points are taken, the straight line that joins them lies wholly in that surface. **2.** A flat or level material surface. **3.** A level as in development, existence, or a scale of values; as, to live on a low *plane.* **4. a** An airplane. See AIRPLANE, *Illust.* **b** One of the main supporting surfaces of an airplane or a wing; — now only in bi*plane*, tri*plane*, etc. — **plane′ness**, *n.*

plane (plān), *n.* [F., fr. *planer* to plane.] **1.** A kind of trowel to smooth or surface sand, clay, etc. **2.** *Joinery.* A tool for smoothing wood, forming moldings, etc. — *v. t.* **1.** To make smooth or even; level with or as with a plane. **2.** To efface or remove with or as with a plane. — *v. i.* To work with a plane; also, to do the work of a plane; as, this tool *planes* well. — **plan′er** (plān′ẽr), *n.*

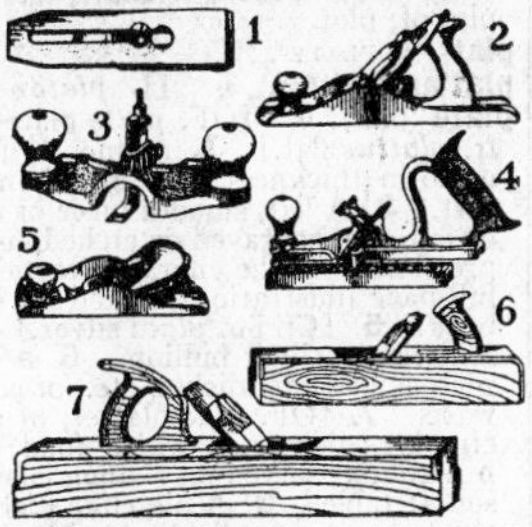

Planes, 2. 1 Plane Iron; 2 Steel Jack Plane; 3 Routing Plane; 4 Tonguing and Grooving Plane; 5 Block Plane; 6 Wooden Jack Plane; 7 Wooden Trying Plane.

plane, *v. i.* **1.** To soar; specif., of a boat, to lift more or less out of the water while in motion, as a hydroplane does. **2.** *Colloq.* To travel in an airplane.

plane angle. An angle formed by two straight lines lying in the same plane.

plane geometry. That branch of geometry which deals with the properties and relations of the plane figures that can be drawn with a ruler and compass.

plane iron. The blade of a plane. See 3d PLANE, *n.*, 2.

plan′er tree (plăn′ẽr). A tree (*Planera aquatica*) of the elm family, of the southeastern United States, somewhat like the hackberry, but with an oval, ribbed, nutlike fruit.

plane sailing. See SAILING.

plane′–shear′ (plān′shēr′), *n.* = PLANK-SHEER.

plan′et (plăn′ĕt; -ĭt), *n.* [OF. *planete*, fr. LL. *planeta*, fr. Gr. *planētēs*, prop., wandering.] **1.** *Astron.* **a** Anciently, any of the seven seemingly "wandering" celestial bodies (sun, moon, Venus, Jupiter, Mars, Mercury, and Saturn), as disting. from the *fixed stars.* **b** Now, any body, except a comet or a meteor, that revolves about the sun of our solar system. The ***inferior planets*** (nearer to the sun than is the earth) are Mercury and Venus; the ***superior planets*** (more distant than the earth) are Mars, the asteroids (planetoids, or ***minor planets***), Jupiter, Saturn, Uranus, Neptune, and Pluto.

PLANETS

Symbol	Name	Mean distance from the sun, that of the earth being unity	Period in days or years	Diameter in miles
☿	**Mercury**	.3871	87.97 d.	3,000
♀	**Venus**	.7233	224.70 d.	7,600
⊕	**Earth**	1.0000	365.26 d.	7,918
♂	**Mars**	1.5237	686.98 d.	4,200
♃	**Jupiter**	5.2028	11.86 y.	87,000
♄	**Saturn**	9.5388	29.46 y.	72,000
⛢	**Uranus**	19.1910	84.02 y.	31,000
♆	**Neptune**	30.0707	164.79 y.	33,000
♇	**Pluto**	39.5	248 y.	4,000?

2. a *Astrol.* A star, as influencing man's fate. **b** Anything to which is imputed such influence.

plane table. *Surv.* An instrument consisting essentially of a drawing board on a tripod with a ruler pointed at the object observed, used for plotting the lines of a survey directly from the observation.

plan′e·tar′i·um (plăn′ē·târ′ĭ·ŭm; 6), *n.; pl.* -IA (-ȧ). [NL.] **1.** A model or representation of the planetary system, esp. one (***Zeiss planetarium***) using projectors to display the movements of celestial bodies on a hemispherical ceiling. **2.** A room or building containing such a planetarium.

plan′e·tar′y (plăn′ē·tĕr′ĭ; plăn′ĭ-; *or, esp. Brit.*, -tẽr·ĭ), *adj.* **1.** Of or pert. to a planet or the planets. **2.** Erratic, wandering. **3.** Terrestrial; world-wide. **4.** *Astrol.* Under the dominion or influence of a planet. **5.** *Mach.* Designating or pertaining to an epicyclic train of gear wheels, esp. one constituting an automobile transmission gear. **6.** *Physics.* Having a motion like that of a planet; as, *planetary* electrons.

plan′e·tes′i·mal (plăn′ē·tĕs′ĭ·măl), *adj.* [From PLANET; cf. INFINITESIMAL.] *Astron.* Of or pertaining to the exceedingly small bodies of space. — *n.* A small solid body, probably similar to a meteorite in composition, revolving around a central gaseous nucleus in the manner of planets around the sun.

planetesimal hypothesis. A hypothesis postulating the growth of the planets by aggregation from planetesimals.

plan′et·oid (plăn′ĕt·oid; plăn′ĭt-), *n.* A body resembling a planet; asteroid. — **plan′et·oi′dal** (-oi′dăl; -d'l), *adj.*

plan′et–strick′en, plan′et–struck′, *adj.* Affected by the influence of planets; blasted; hence, panic-stricken.

planet wheel. *Mach.* A gear wheel which revolves around the wheel with which it meshes, in an epicyclic train. Cf. EPICYCLIC TRAIN, *Illust.*

plan′gent (plăn′jĕnt), *adj.* [L. *plangens, -entis*, fr. *plangere* to beat.] Sounding with deep or loud reverberation, as breaking waves or clanging or tolling bells; clangorous. — **plan′gen·cy** (-jĕn·sĭ), *n.* — **plan′gent·ly**, *adv.*

pla′ni- (plā′nĭ-; plăn′ĭ-). [L. *planus.*] A combining form meaning *flat, level, plane*, as in **pla·nim′e·try**, mensuration of plane surfaces, or in the adjectives:

planicaudate	**planipetalous**	**planirostrate**

pla·nim′e·ter (plă·nĭm′ē·tẽr), *n.* [F. *planimètre.* See PLANI-; -METER.] An instrument for measuring the area of any plane figure by passing a tracer around the boundary line.

plan′ish (plăn′ĭsh), *v. t.* [MF. *planir, aplanir.*] To make smooth, as sheet metal; to toughen and polish by hammering lightly.

plan′i·sphere (plăn′ĭ·sfēr), *n.* [See PLANI-; SPHERE.] The representation of the circles of the sphere on a plane; esp., a projection of the celestial sphere and the stars on a plane with adjustable parts for showing the position of the heavens, the time of rising and setting of stars, etc., for any given moment.

plank (plăngk), *n.* [ONF. *planke*, fr. LL. *planca.*] **1.** A heavy thick board. **2.** Timber in planks; planking; as, 1000 feet of *plank.* **3.** That which supports, as a plank does a swimmer. **4.** One of the separate articles in a platform of a political party. — *v. t.* **1.** To cover, floor, or lay with planks. **2.** *Colloq.* To lay (down), as money, forcibly or with emphasis; hence, to pay; — often with *down, out.* **3.** To cook and serve on a board, usually with an elaborate garnish of vegetables; as, a *planked* steak.

plank′ing, *n.* Act of laying planks; also, planks collectively.

plank′–sheer′ (plăngk′shēr′), *n.* The heavy plank forming the outer edge of a vessel's deck.

plank′ton (plăngk′tŏn), *n.* [G., fr. Gr. *plankton*, neut. of *planktos* wandering, fr. *plazesthai* to wander.] *Biol.* The passively floating or weakly swimming animal and plant life of a body of water. Cf. BENTHOS, NEKTON. — **plank·ton′ic** (plăngk·tŏn′ĭk), *adj.*

plan′ner (plăn′ẽr), *n.* One who plans; a projector; designer.

plan′o- (plăn′ō-), **plan-**. [Gr. *planos.*] A combining form meaning *roaming*, as in **plan′o·ga·mete′, plan′o·spore.**

pla′no- (plā′nō-). [L. *planus* plane.] A combining form meaning: **a** *Plane*, as in **pla·nom′e·ter, pla·nom′e·try.** **b** *Flatly*, as in **pla′no-ro·tund′.** **c** *Plane and*, as in **pla′no–con′cave, pla′no–con′vex.**

plan′o·blast (plăn′ō·blăst), *n.* [1st *plano-* + *-blast.*] The medusa, or jellyfish, form of a hydroid.

pla′no·graph (plā′nō·grȧf; 9), *v. t.* To print from a flat surface. — *n.* A planographic impression.

plan·og′ra·phy (plăn·ŏg′rȧ·fĭ), *n.* [From L. *planum* flat surface + *-graphy.*] A process of printing from a flat or plane surface, as a lithographic stone, a metal plate, or a collotype plate, which is based on the inability of a water-wet surface to take ink, as in lithography, photolithography, offset printing, and photo-offset. — **pla′no·graph′ic** (plā′nō·grăf′ĭk), *adj.* — **plan·og′ra·phist** (plăn·ŏg′rȧ·fĭst), *n.*

plan position indicator. = PPI.

plant (plȧnt; 9), *n.* [AS. *plante*, fr. L. *planta* sprout, shoot, slip.] **1.** A young tree, shrub, or herb, planted or ready to plant; a slip, cutting, or sapling. **2.** Any of a group of living organisms which typically do not exhibit voluntary motion or possess sensory or nervous organs; a vegetable, as distinguished from an animal. See CLASSIFICATION, 2. **3. a** The machinery, apparatus, fixtures, etc., sometimes also the real estate, employed in carrying on a trade or a mechanical or other industrial business; as, an electric-light *plant.* **b** A factory, workshop or apparatus complete, for the manufacture of a particular product; as, a bicycle *plant.* **c** The equipment of any institution, as a college. **4.** *Slang.* **a** [Cf. obs. F. *plant*, and E. PLAN.] A swindling plot or artifice. **b** Something deliberately placed or planned so as to entrap wrongdoers, give a false clue or impression, etc. — *v. t.* **1** To put or set in the ground for growth. **2.** To set firmly, as, or as if, in or on the ground; attach or fix in place. **3.** To implant or engender, as a passion, idea, or the like; to introduce and establish, as a religion. **4.** To stock or provide with something, as a river with fish. **5.** To colonize or settle. **6.** To establish (an animal) in a place in order to stock the locality; as, to *plant* oysters in beds. **7.** *Slang.* **a** To land, as a blow. **b** To place (something) as a plant, or false clue, or deception.

Plan·tag′e·net (plăn·tăj′ē·nĕt; -nĭt), *n.* [Orig. a nickname of Geoffrey; ult. fr. L. *planta* sprig + *genesta*, or *genista*, broom plant.] A member of the English royal house founded by Geoffrey, Count of Anjou, father of Henry II. The English kings from Henry II through Richard III were Plantagenets.

plan′tain (plăn′tĭn), *n.* [OF., fr. L. *plantago, -ginis.*] Any of a genus (*Plantago*, family Plantaginaceae, the plantain family) of short-stemmed, elliptic-leaved herbs with spikes of minute greenish flowers; esp., either of the common weeds *P. major* and *P. rugelii.*

plan′tain, *n.* [Sp. *plántano, plátano*, of Arawakan or Cariban origin.] A variety of banana (*Musa paradisiaca*) with fruit larger, less sweet, and more starchy than the ordinary banana.

plantain lily. = DAY LILY, 2.

plan′tar (plăn′tẽr), *adj.* [L. *plantaris*, fr. *planta* the sole of the foot.] Of or pertaining to the sole of the foot.

plan·ta′tion (plăn·tā′shŭn), *n.* [L. *plantatio.*] **1.** A planting; that which is planted; esp., *Hist.*, a colony. **2.** A grove or wood of planted trees. **3.** A place planted; esp., in the southern United States, West Indies, etc., a sizable estate cultivated by resident laborers.

plant′er (plȧn′tẽr), *n.* One who or that which plants; specif.: **a** A pioneer colonist. **b** An owner of a plantation.

plan′ti·grade (plăn′tĭ·grād), *adj.* [F., fr. L. *planta* sole + *-grade.*] *Zool.* Walking on the sole with the heel touching the ground, as the bears and man. Cf. DIGITIGRADE. — *n.* A plantigrade animal.

plant louse. An aphid or related insect.

plan′u·la (plăn′ū·lȧ), *n.; pl.* -LAE (-lē). [NL., dim. fr. L. *planus* flat.] *Zool.* The very young, free-swimming larva of coelenterates, usually of flattened oval or oblong form. — **plan′u·lar** (-lẽr), **plan′u·late** (-lāt), *adj.*

plaque (plăk; pläk), *n.* [F., fr. D. *plak* flat piece of wood, MD. *placke* piece, patch.] **1.** Any flat, thin piece of metal, ivory, or the like, used, as on a wall, for ornament, inserted in furniture, etc. **2.** An ornamental brooch or the like, as the badge of an honorary order.

plash (plăsh), *v. t.* [OF. *plaissier, plessier*, fr. L. *plectere* to weave.] To cut partly, bend, and intertwine (branches, stems, etc.) into a hedge; make or trim (a hedge) by so doing; pleach. — **plash′er**, *n.*

plash, *n.* [AS. *plæsc.*] A pool; puddle. — **plash′y**, *adj.*

plash, *v. t. & i. & n.* Splash.

-pla′si·a (-plā′zhĭ·ȧ; -zĭ·ȧ), **-plasis, -plasy.** [NL., fr. Gr. *plasis* a molding, fr. *plassein* to mold.] Combining forms denoting *development, formation*, as in cata*plasia.*

plasm (plăz'm), *n.* [LL. *plasma.* See PLASMA.] = PLASMA.

-plasm. [Gr. *plasma* form, thing molded.] A combining form used, esp. *Biol.*, to denote: **a** The *viscous material of an animal or vegetable cell.* **b** *Protoplasm.* Derivative adjectives are formed in **-plas′mic** (-plăz′mĭk).

plasm-. = PLASMO-.

plas′ma (plăz′mȧ), *n.* [LL., anything formed or molded, fr. Gr. *plasma, -atos*, fr. *plassein* to form, mold.] **1.** *Mineral.* A variety of quartz, green and faintly translucent. **2.** *Anat. & Physiol.* The fluid part of blood, lymph, or milk; also, the juice that can be expressed from muscle. **3.** *Biol.* Protoplasm. — **plas·mat'ic** (plăz·măt'ĭk), **plas'mic** (plăz'mĭk), *adj.*

plas'mo- (plăz'mō-), **plasm-.** A combining form for *plasma*, as in **plas'mo·cyte, plas·mo'ma, plas'mo·some.**

Plas'mo·chin (plăz'mō·kĭn), *n.* A trade-mark applied to an antimalarial drug ($C_{19}H_{29}N_3O$).

plas·mo'di·um (plăz·mō'dĭ·ŭm), *n.; pl.* -DIA (-*ȧ*). [NL. See PLASMA; 1st -ODE.] **1.** *Biol.* A multinucleate mass of naked protoplasm formed by the union of a number of amoebalike organisms. **2.** *Zool.* Any microorganism of a genus (*Plasmodium*) of protozoans that includes the parasites causing malaria.

plas·mol'y·sis (plăz·mŏl'ĭ·sĭs), *n.* [NL., fr. *plasmo-* + *-lysis.*] *Physiol.* Contraction or shrinking of the cytoplasm in a living cell, due to loss of water by exosmosis. — **plas'mo·lyze** (plăz'mō·līz), *v. t. & i.*

-plast (-plăst). [Gr. *plastos* formed, fr. *plassein* to form.] A combining form denoting *an organized particle* or *granule, cell*, as in chromo*plast*. Cf. PLASTID.

plas'ter (plȧs'tẽr; 9), *n.* Formerly also **plais'ter.** [AS., a plaster (in sense 1), fr. L., fr. Gr. *emplastron*, fr. *emplassein* to daub on.] **1.** *Pharm.* A preparation harder than ointment, spread on linen, leather, silk, or the like, and applied to the body; hence, anything applied to heal and soothe. **2.** A pasty composition, as of lime, water, and sand, that hardens on drying, used for coating walls, ceilings, and partitions. **3.** In full **plaster of Paris.** A white powdery substance, calcium sulfate, $CaSO_4.\frac{1}{2}H_2O$, formed by calcining gypsum. With water, it forms a quickly setting paste used for casts, moldings, etc. **4.** Short for COURT PLASTER, STICKING PLASTER, etc. — *v. t.* **1.** To overlay or cover with plaster or a similar material, as walls or ceilings. **2.** To smear or bedaub as if with plaster. **3.** To apply a medicinal plaster to, as a wound. **4.** To affix in the manner of a plaster; hence, to paste a notice, label, or the like upon. — **plas'ter·er**, *n.* — **plas'ter·y**, *adj.*

plas'ter·board' (plȧs'tẽr·bōrd'), *n.* A board consisting of a gypsum plaster core and surfaces of fibrous felt pressed together in sheets of various thicknesses from ¼ in. to ½ in. and used as a plaster base. — **plas'ter·board'**, *adj.*

plaster cast. **1.** A sculptor's model in plaster of Paris. **2.** *Surg.* A rigid dressing of gauze impregnated with plaster of Paris.

plas'tic (plăs'tĭk), *adj.* [L. *plasticus*, fr. Gr. *plastikos*, fr. *plassein* to form.] **1.** Formative; fashioning; creative; as, the *plastic* force of nature. **2.** Capable of being molded or modeled, as clay or plaster; hence, pliable; impressionable. **3.** Characterized by or using modeling; as, the *plastic* arts; hence, sculptural in form or effect. **4.** Made or consisting of a plastic. **5.** *Biol. & Surg.* Capable of undergoing metabolic transformation. **6.** *Physics.* Capable of being deformed continuously and permanently in any direction without rupture.

Syn. **Plastic, pliable, pliant, ductile, malleable, adaptable** mean susceptible of being modified in form or nature. **Plastic** suggests qualities, such as those of wax or clay, soft enough to be molded yet capable of hardening into desired form; **pliable** and **pliant**, the quality of willow twigs, supple enough to be easily manipulated and, therefore, yielding and compliant; **ductile**, the quality of that which can be drawn out at will and therefore responding to influences upon it; **malleable**, the quality of some metals after being heated, of being readily beaten or hammered into shape or form; **adaptable**, that of being easily modified to suit other conditions, needs, or uses.

— *n.* A plastic substance; specif., any of a large group of organic synthetic or processed materials that are molded or cast and used for making many kinds of small articles, cabinets, airplane bodies, etc., in varnishes, etc., and as a substitute for glass. Some are cellulose derivatives, some proteins, and many are resins formed by chemical condensation or polymerization. Rubber and similar materials (as neoprene) are sometimes included among plastics. Plastics are commonly known by their trade-mark names.

☞ The form *plastics* is preferred by some technical authorities for use as the singular (as, there is no one *plastics* that will meet all these requirements) to distinguish it from *plastic* meaning any substance capable of being molded.

-plas'tic. [Gr. *plastikos* fit for molding, plastic.] A combining form meaning *developing, forming, growing;* — also in adjectives corresponding to nouns ending in -PLAST or -PLASTY.

plas'ti·cal·ly (plăs'tĭ·kăl·ĭ), *adv.* In plastic or pliable fashion; pliably; also, sculpturally.

plas·tic'i·ty (plăs·tĭs'ĭ·tĭ), *n.* **1.** Plastic quality or state. **2.** The ability to retain a shape attained by pressure deformation (see PLASTIC, *adj.*, 6); specif., *Physical Chem.*, the ability of particles to be displaced without being removed from their sphere of attraction.

plas'ti·ciz'er (plăs'tĭ·sīz'ẽr), *n.* That which renders plastic; specif., an agent added to certain plastics and protective coatings to impart softness and flexibility. — **plas'ti·cize** (-sīz), *v. t.*

plas'tics (plăs'tĭks), *adj.* Of or made of a plastic or plastics; as, *plastics* uses; a *plastics* house.

plastic surgery. Surgery concerned with the repair or restoration of lost, injured, or deformed parts of the body, chiefly by transfer of tissue. — **plastic operation.**

plas'tid (plăs'tĭd), *n.* [G. *plastiden*, pl., fr. Gr. *plastides*, pl. of *plastis*, fem. of *plastēs* one who forms or molds.] *Biol.* **1.** A unit of protoplasmic matter; a cell. **2.** Any of certain small bodies of specialized protoplasm lying in the cytoplasm of some cells, esp. plant cells and certain protozoans. See CELL, 4, *Illust.*

plas·tom'e·ter (plăs·tŏm'ē·tẽr), *n.* [*plasto-* (fr. Gr. *plastos* molded) + *-meter.*] An instrument for measuring plasticity.

plas'tral (plăs'trăl), *adj.* *Zool.* Of or pert. to a plastron.

plas'tron (plăs'trŏn), *n.* [F., fr. It. *piastrone.*] **1. a** A metal breastplate. **b** A protection for the breast of a fencer. **2.** Also **plas'trum** (-trŭm). *Zool.* The ventral part of the shell of a turtle. **3. a** A trimming for the front of a woman's dress narrowing from the shoulders to the waist. **b** The starched front of a man's shirt.

-plas'ty (-plăs'tĭ). [Gr. *-plastia.* See -PLAST.] A combining form meaning: **1.** *Act* or *process of forming.* **2.** *Surg. Plastic surgery applied to a* (specified) *bodily part*, as in osteo*plasty*, or *from a* (specified) *source of material*, as in auto*plasty*, or *for a* (specified) *purpose.*

-plasy. = PLASIA.

plat (plăt), *v. t.;* PLAT'TED; PLAT'TING. [A var. of *plait.*] To interweave; form by braiding; plait. — *n.* *Now Dial.* A braid; plait.

plat, *n.* [ME. *plat, platte.*] **1.** A small plot of ground. **2.** *Chiefly U. S.* A plan, map, or chart, esp. of a town site. — *v. t.* To make a plat of; plot.

plat-. = PLATY-.

plat'an (plăt'ăn), *n.* [L. *platanus.*] The plane tree.

plate (plāt), *n.* [OF. *plate* plate of metal, fr. (assumed) VL. *platta*, fr. *plattus* flat.] **1.** A smooth, flat piece of any material, thin or of uniform thickness. **2.** Metal in sheets, whether beaten, rolled, or cast. **3.** A flat, smooth piece of metal on or from which anything is, or is to be, engraved or etched, as for printing. **4.** Hence: **a** An impression from the engraved metal; or, loosely, from a woodcut. **b** A full-page illustration printed on different paper from the rest of the book. **5.** [Cf. Sp. *plata* silver.] *Obs.* A coin, usually of silver; also, sometimes, silver bullion. **6. a** Domestic vessels, utensils, etc., esp. such as platters, dishes, etc., of gold or silver. **b** Silver-plated metalware. **7.** [OF. *plat* platter, orig., flat object.] A shallow, usually circular, dish from which food is eaten. **8.** Hence: **a** A plateful. **b** A course, served on a single plate. **c** Food and service for one person at table. **9.** A platelike dish used in churches for taking collections; hence, a collection. **10.** The thin under portion of the forequarter of beef. See BEEF, *Illust.* **11.** *Anat. & Zool.* A lamina; a scute. **12.** *Arch.* A horizontal timber for carrying the trusses of a roof or the rafters directly. See ROOF, *Illust.* **13.** *Armor.* One of the broad metal pieces used in armor; hence (also **plate armor**), armor of such plates. **14.** *Baseball.* A small five-sided area, enveloping a diamond-shaped area one foot square, beside which the batter stands and which must be touched by some part of a player on completing a run. **15.** *Dent.* That part of an artificial set of teeth which fits to the mouth. **16.** *Elec.* In an electron tube, the anode or electrode to which the electrons flow. It is usually a thin metal plate. **17.** *Photog.* A sensitized sheet of glass, metal, etc. **18.** *Print.* A page of stereotype, electrotype, or the like, to be printed from. **19.** *Railroads.* A rail; orig. a primitive type of flat rail with raised outer edge (**plate rail**). **20.** *Sports.* A prize given to a winner in a contest; hence, loosely, a contest, esp. a horse race (**plate race**), for a prize. — *v. t.* **1.** To cover or overlay with gold, silver, or other metal, mechanically, chemically, or electrically. **2.** To arm with armor plate. **3.** *Paper Mfg.* To impart a very high gloss to by pressing between polished metal plates. **4.** *Print.* To make a stereotype or electrotype plate of.

pla·teau' (plă·tō'; *Brit. also* plăt'ō), *n.; pl.* -TEAUS (-tōz'), -TEAUX (-tōz'). [F., fr. OF. *plat* a flat thing.] An elevated tract of land; a tableland.

plate'ful (plāt'fo͝ol), *n.; pl.* -FULS (-fo͝olz). Enough to fill a plate.

plate glass. Fine rolled, ground, and polished sheet glass.

plate'lay'er (plāt'lā'ẽr), *n.* *Railroads.* One who lays and maintains rails; a tracklayer.

plate'let (plāt'lĕt; -lĭt), *n.* [*plate* + *-let.*] A minute platelike body; specif., *Anat.*, a ***blood platelet***, any of certain colorless disks readily disintegrated, occurring in the blood of mammals.

plat'en (plăt''n), *n.* [F. *platine*, fr. OF. *plate* plate of metal.] **1.** A flat plate of metal, esp. one that exerts or receives pressure, as the part of a printing press which presses the paper against the type. **2.** The roller of a typewriter.

plat'er (plāt'ẽr), *n.* **1.** One who or that which plates. **2.** *Horse Racing.* A horse that runs chiefly in plate races; hence, an inferior race horse. See PLATE, *n.*, 20.

plate rail. **1.** See PLATE, *n.*, 19. **2.** A rail or narrow shelf along the upper part of a wall to hold plates, etc.

plat'form' (plăt'fôrm'), *n.* [F. *plateforme.*] **1.** *Obs.* A plan; design. **2.** A plan of ecclesiastical or religious polity or principles; as, the Cambridge *platform.* **3.** A horizontal, generally flat and raised, surface; as, a streetcar *platform;* a gun *platform;* esp., a raised flooring, stage, or dais, for speakers, performers, etc. **4.** A declaration of the principles for which a group of persons stand; esp., a declaration of principles and policies adopted by a political party. **5.** An outsole a half inch or more thick, made of wood, cork, etc., and usually covered with leather, used on a type of shoe (**platform shoes**).

platform car. *Railroads.* A car without permanent raised sides or covering; a flatcar.

plat'i·na (plăt'ĭ·nȧ; plȧ·tē'nȧ), *n.* [Sp. or NL.] *Chem.* Platinum; esp., crude native platinum.

plat'ing (plāt'ĭng), *n.* **1.** Act or process of one that plates. **2.** A coating of metal plates. **3.** A thin coating of metal.

pla·tin'ic (plȧ·tĭn'ĭk), *adj.* *Chem.* Of, pertaining to, or containing platinum; specif., designating compounds in which the element has a higher valence. Cf. PLATINOUS.

plat'in·i·rid'i·um (plăt'ĭn·ĭ·rĭd'ĭ·ŭm), *n.* [NL.] A natural alloy of iridium with platinum and other allied metals, occurring in silver-white or grayish metallic grains.

plat'i·nize (plăt'ĭ·nīz), *v. t.* To cover, treat, or combine with platinum.

plat'i·no·cy·an'ic (plăt'ĭ·nō·sī·ăn'ĭk), *adj.* [*platinum* + *cyanic.*] Pert. to or designating an acid, $H_2Pt(CN)_4$, obtained by decomposing certain salts of the acid.

plat'i·no·cy'a·nide (-sī'ȧ·nīd; -nĭd), *n.* Also **plat'i·no·cy'a·nid.** *Chem.* A salt of platinocyanic acid.

plat'i·noid (plăt'ĭ·noid), *adj.* [*platinum* + *-oid.*] Resembling platinum. — *n.* **a** An alloy chiefly of copper, nickel, and zinc, used for forming electrical resistance coils and standards. **b** Any metal allied to platinum.

plat'i·no·type' (-nō·tīp'), *n.* *Photog.* A permanent print in platinum black obtained by use of a platinum salt in the sensitizing solution or developer; also, the process.

plat'i·nous (plăt'ĭ·nŭs), *adj.* *Chem.* Of, pertaining to, or containing, platinum; specif., designating compounds in which the element has a lower valence. Cf. PLATINIC.

plat'i·num (plăt'ĭ·nŭm; -'n·ŭm), *n.* [NL., fr. earlier *platina*, fr. Sp. *platina*, fr. *plata* silver.] **1.** A heavy, grayish-white noncorroding precious metallic element, malleable and ductile but fusible with difficulty, and resistant to most chemicals (dissolves slowly in aqua regia); — formerly called also *platina.* Symbol, *Pt;* at. no., 78; at. wt., 195.23; sp. gr., 21.45. Melting point, 1755° C., 3191° F. It has a high electric resistance, expands slightly on heating, and is used for chemical apparatus, as a catalyst, for dental fillings, for jewelry, etc. **2.** A nearly neutral gray, slightly bluish, of medium brilliance. See COLOR.

platinum black. *Chem.* A soft, dull-black powder of metallic platinum obtained by reduction and precipitation from solutions of its salts. It is used as a catalyst.

plat′i·tude (plăt′ĭ·tūd), *n.* [F. (after *rectitude*, etc.), fr. *plat* flat.] **1.** Quality or state of being dull or insipid; triteness; commonplaceness. **2.** A flat, trite, or weak utterance; a dull or stale truism; a commonplace. — **plat′i·tu′di·nous** (-tū′dĭ·nŭs), *adj.*

plat′i·tu′di·nize (-tū′dĭ·nīz), *v. i.* To utter platitudes.

Pla·ton′ic (plȧ·tŏn′ĭk; plā-), *adj.* Also **Pla·ton′i·cal** (-ĭ·kăl). **1.** Of or pert. to Plato or his philosophy. **2.** Experiencing or professing Platonic love. — **Pla·ton′i·cal·ly**, *adv.*

Platonic love. **a** Love, according to Plato, ascending from passion for the individual to contemplation of the ideal. **b** A spiritual comradeship or love, esp. between persons of opposite sex, in which there is assumed to be no element of sexual desire; — a use originating with late Renaissance writers.

Platonic year. See PRECESSION OF THE EQUINOXES.

Pla′to·nism (plā′tō·nĭz′m), *n.* **1.** The philosophy of Plato; esp., his doctrine that actual things are but copies of the ideas (see IDEA, 1 **b**), that these ideas are the objects of true knowledge, and that they can be apprehended by an innate power of the soul, called *reminiscence.* **2.** = PLATONIC LOVE **a.** — **Pla′to·nist** (-nĭst), *n. & adj.*

Pla′to·nize (-nīz), *v. i. & t.* To make Platonic in character; to conform to Platonism; also, to idealize.

pla·toon′ (plă·tōōn′), *n.* [F. *peloton* ball of thread, group of men, platoon, fr. *pelote.* See PELLET.] **1.** A subdivision of a military tactical unit such as a company, troop, etc., normally commanded by a lieutenant. **2.** A set; a coterie. **3.** A subdivision of police.

Platt′deutsch′ (plät′doich′), *n.* [G., fr. *platt* flat + *deutsch* German.] The language of North Germany, a Low German tongue now spoken chiefly by the less educated. See INDO-EUROPEAN LANGUAGES, *Table.*

plat′ter (plăt′ẽr), *n.* [ME. & AF. *plater*, fr. OF. *plat.* See PLATE, 7.] **1.** A large plate or dish for serving meat, etc. **2.** A phonograph record or an electrical transcription record.

plat′y- (plăt′ĭ-), **plat-.** [Gr. *platys.*] A combining form meaning *wide, flat,* as in **plat′y·ceph′a·lous, plat′y·pet′al·ous, plat′y·pod.**

plat′y·hel′minth (-hĕl′mĭnth), *n.* [*platy-* + Gr. *helmins, helminthos,* worm.] Any of a phylum (Platyhelminthes) of soft-bodied, usually much flattened worms, comprising the planarians, flukes, tapeworms, etc.; a flatworm.

plat′y·pus (plăt′ĭ·pŭs), *n.; pl.* -PUSES (-pŭs·ĕz; -ĭz), -PI (-pī). [NL., fr. *platy-* + Gr. *pous* foot.] The duckbill.

plat′yr·rhin′i·an (plăt′ĭ·rĭn′ĭ·ăn), *adj.* [*platy-* + Gr. *rhis, rhinos,* nose.] Having a short broad nose or a high nasal index. — *n.* A platyrrhinian person.

plau′dit (plô′dĭt), *n.* [From L. *plaudite* (said by players at the end of a performance), 2d pers. pl. imper. *plaudere* to applaud.] An applauding, esp. by clapping; a round of applause; figuratively, approval.

plau′si·ble (plô′zĭ·b′l), *adj.* [L. *plausibilis* praiseworthy.] **a** Superficially fair, reasonable, or valuable; specious. **b** Of persons, apparently trustworthy, or fair; using specious arguments. — **plau′si·bil′i·ty** (-bĭl′ĭ·tĭ), **plau′si·ble·ness**, *n.* — **plau′si·bly**, *adv.*

Syn. **Plausible, credible, colorable, specious** mean outwardly acceptable as true or genuine. **Plausible** implies reasonableness at first sight or hearing, though it often adds a hint of a possibility of being deceived; **credible**, though often suggesting plausibility, stresses more clearly worthiness of belief; **colorable** stresses credibility on merely outward grounds; **specious** stresses colorability with always a clear suggestion of dissimulation or fraud.

plau′sive (-sĭv), *adj.* **1.** Manifesting praise or approval; applauding. **2.** *Obs.* Plausible.

play (plā), *v. i.* [AS. *plegian, plegan.*] **1.** To move swiftly, erratically or intermittently; to dart to and fro; flutter; vibrate; as, grasses *play* in the wind. **2.** To engage in sport or lively recreation; to amuse or divert oneself; frolic. **3.** To trifle; toy; touch lightly; finger; — often followed by *with.* **4.** To perform on an instrument of music; hence, of the instrument, to respond to the performer's fingering, bowing, etc.; sound. **5.** To contend, or take part, in a game; hence, to gamble. **6.** To act; to behave (as specified); as, to *play* fair. **7.** To act on or as on the stage; perform. **8. a** To move or function freely, esp. within prescribed limits. **b** To discharge, eject, or fire something, or to be discharged, ejected, or fired, repeatedly or so as to make a stream; as, the fountain *plays* daily. — *v. t.* **1. a** To engage in (a game, contest, or the like); as, to *play* baseball. **b** To pretend to be engaged in or as, esp. for amusement; as, to *play* policeman. **2.** To do or execute esp. for amusement, profit or edification; as, to *play* a part or a prank. **3.** To bring about; work; effect; as, to *play* havoc. **4.** To act or perform (a play); also, to act in the character or part of. **5. a** To contend against in or as in a game; also, to use as a contestant in a game. **b** To wager in a game; stake; also, to wager on; as, to *play* the races. **6. a** To perform or execute (music). **b** To perform music upon. **7.** To put in action or motion; actuate; operate; work; ply; also, to keep in action, operation, motion, etc. **8.** To act or perform in; as, to *play* the leading theaters.
— *n.* **1. a** Brisk handling, using, or plying; — chiefly in combination; as, sword*play.* **b** Brisk or nimble motion, alternation, intermittence, or the like; as, a *play* of light. **2.** The stage representation of a drama; also, a drama. **3.** Exercise or action for amusement or diversion; sport; frolic; also, a game; a particular amusement. **4.** Fun; jest; as, he said it in *play.* **5.** Gambling; as, to lose a fortune in *play.* **6.** The conduct or carrying on of a game; playing or manner of playing. **7. a** A particular act, maneuver, or point in play. **b** Turn to play. **8.** Method or manner of doing, esp. dealing; — *Obs.*, except in *fair play* and *foul play.* **9.** Action; activity; operation; as, *play* of wit. **10.** Freedom, room, or scope for motion or action; as, sleeves too tight for *play* of the arms. **11.** Abstinence or freedom from work; as, all work and no *play.* — **Syn.** See FUN. — ***in play.*** *Games.* In position or condition to be legitimately played; — of the ball, etc.

☞ COMBINATIONS are:

playbill	playfolk	playmaking
playbook	playgoer	playmonger
playbroker	playgoing	playwriting

pla′ya (plä′yȧ), *n.; pl.* PLAYAS (-yȧz). [Sp.] *Geol.* The flat-floored bottom of an undrained desert basin.

play′a·ble (plā′ȧ·b′l), *adj.* That can be played.

play′back′ ma·chine′, *or* **play′back′** (plā′băk′), *n.* = TURNTABLE, 2.

play′boy′ (plā′boi′), *n.* *Colloq.* **a** *U. S.* A pleasure-seeking profligate. **b** *Ir.* A buffoon; a tricky person.

play′down′ (plā′doun′), *n.* *Sports, Canada.* One of a series of playoffs, as among the winning teams from different leagues or localities.

played out (plād). Performed to the end; also, exhausted; used up.

play′er (plā′ẽr), *n.* One who plays; as: **a** An idler. **b** One who plays some (specified) game. **c** A gambler. **d** An actor, musician, etc. **e** A mechanical device for playing a musical instrument; esp., one for a piano, called specif. a ***piano player*** (a piano containing such a device being known as a **player piano**).

play′fel′low (plā′fĕl′ō), *n.* A playmate.

play′ful (-fōōl; -f′l), *adj.* Full of play; sportive; also, humorous. — **play′ful·ly**, *adv.* — **play′ful·ness**, *n.*

play′ground′ (-ground′), *n.* A piece of ground used for recreation, esp. by children under supervision.

play′house′ (-hous′), *n.* [AS. *pleghūs.*] **1.** A theater. **2.** A house for children to play in; also, a place built for play.

play′ing card. A card used in playing games; specif., any of the cards composing a pack of four suits (hearts, diamonds, clubs, and spades).

playing field. A field for various games as football, cricket, tennis, etc.; in the United States, esp. that part of the field officially marked off for play.

play′mate′ (plā′māt′), *n.* A companion in play; playfellow.

play′-off′ (-ôf′; 74), *n.* *Sports.* A final contest to determine the winner among competitors, teams, etc., that have previously tied.

play′room′ (-rōōm′), *n.* = RUMPUS ROOM.

play′thing′ (-thĭng′), *n.* A thing to play with; a toy.

play′time′ (-tīm′), *n.* Time for play or diversion.

play (up)on words. Use of a word or words in a double sense, in a sense different from one already used, or the like; also, an instance of this; a pun.

play′wright′ (plā′rīt′), *n.* A writer of plays; a dramatist.

pla′za (plä′zȧ; plăz′ȧ; *Sp.* plä′thä, -sä), *n.* [Sp.] A public square in a city or town; a market place. Cf. 2d PLACE.

plea (plē), *n.* [OF. *plait, plaid, plet,* fr. L. *placitum* that which is pleasing, an opinion, decision, orig. past part. neut. of *placere* to please.] **1.** *Obs. exc. Scot. Law.* An action or cause in court; a lawsuit. **2.** That which is alleged or pleaded, in defense, excuse, or justification; an excuse; apology. **3.** A prayer, appeal, or pleading; as, a *plea* for mercy. **4.** *Law.* An allegation; pleading; specif.: **a** An allegation of fact, as disting. from a *demurrer.* **b** In common-law practice, a defendant's answer to the plaintiff's declaration and demand, or, in criminal practice, the accused person's answer to the charge or indictment against him. **c** In equity practice, a special answer (***special plea***) showing cause why the suit should be either dismissed, delayed, or barred. — **Syn.** See APOLOGY.

pleach (plēch), *v. t.* [ONF. *plechier,* corresponding to OF. *plessier, plaissier,* to weave.] To plait; interlace.

plead (plēd), *v. i.; past & past part.* PLEAD′ED (-ĕd; -ĭd), *Colloq.* PLEAD (plĕd) OR PLED; *pres. part.* PLEAD′ING (plēd′ĭng). [OF. *plaidier,* fr. L. *placitum.* See PLEA.] **1.** *Law.* To make a plea, or conduct a cause in a court. **2.** To argue for or against a claim; hence, to entreat or appeal earnestly; beg; implore. — *v. t.* **1.** *Law.* To discuss, defend, and attempt to maintain by arguments or reasons; to argue at the bar. **2.** To allege or cite in, or by way of, a legal plea; as, to *plead* not guilty. **3.** To allege in support, defense, apology, or excuse; as, to *plead* self-defense.

plead′a·ble (-ȧ·b′l), *adj.* Capable of being lawfully maintained, or of being alleged in defense or excuse.

plead′er (-ẽr), *n.* **1.** *Law.* One who conducts legal pleas, esp. in court; an advocate. **2.** An intercessor.

plead′ing, *n.* **1.** *Law.* **a** The acting as an advocate or pleader in a cause; also, the science or art of drawing pleas or of conducting causes as an advocate. **b** *pl.* The successive statements, now usually written, by which the plaintiff sets forth his cause and claim, and the defendant his defense, until issue is joined. **2.** Advocacy; intercession; entreaty.

pleas′ance (plĕz′ăns), *n.* [OF. *plaisance.*] **1.** *Archaic & Poetic.* Pleasure; delight. **2.** A pleasure ground, typically one attached to a mansion.

pleas′ant (-ănt; -′nt), *adj.* [OF. *plaisant,* prop., pres. part. See PLEASE.] **1.** That gives pleasure; pleasing; agreeable; as, *pleasant* weather. **2.** Having, or characterized by, pleasing manners, behavior, or appearance; as, a *pleasant* fellow. — **pleas′ant·ly**, *adv.* — **pleas′ant·ness**, *n.*

Syn. **Pleasant, pleasing, agreeable, grateful, gratifying, welcome** mean highly acceptable to the mind or senses. **Pleasant** usually imputes this quality to an object; **pleasing** suggests its effect upon one; **agreeable** implies harmony with one's taste or likings; **grateful** implies the satisfaction or relief afforded by what is pleasing or agreeable; **gratifying** implies the mental pleasure afforded by satisfaction of one's desires, hopes, etc.; **welcome** implies the pleasure given by that which satisfies one's longings.

pleas′ant·ry (plĕz′ănt·rĭ; plĕz′′nt-), *n.; pl.* -RIES (-rĭz). **1.** An agreeable playfulness in conversation; good-humored banter. **2.** A humorous act or speech; a jest.

please (plēz), *v. i.* [OF. *plaisir,* fr. L. *placere.*] **1.** To afford pleasure or satisfaction; to be agreeable. **2.** To have the pleasure, will, desire, kindness, or humor; to be willing; choose; as, do as you *please.* — *v. t.* **1.** To give pleasure to; make glad; gratify; — orig. an intransitive use with dative object; as, ***to please oneself***, to gratify oneself; *Colloq.*, to do as one likes. **2.** To be the will or pleasure of; — used impersonally; as, so *please* you.

pleas′ing (plēz′ĭng), *adj.* Giving pleasure; agreeable. — **Syn.** See PLEASANT. — **pleas′ing·ly**, *adv.*

pleas′ur·a·ble (plĕzh′ẽr·ȧ·b′l), *adj.* Pleasant; gratifying. — **pleas′ur·a·ble·ness**, *n.* — **pleas′ur·a·bly**, *adv.*

pleas′ure (plĕzh′ẽr), *n.* [OF. *plesir, plaisir.*] **1.** State of gratification; delight; enjoyment; joy. **2.** What the will dictates or prefers as gratifying; hence, will; choice; as, what is your *pleasure?* **3.** A delight; joy; gratification. **4.** Sport; diversion; frivolous or dissipating enjoyment; sensual gratification; — opposed to *self-denial,* etc.

Syn. **Pleasure, delight, joy, delectation, enjoyment, fruition** mean the agreeable feeling accompanying the possession or acquisition of what is desired. **Pleasure** more often stresses satisfaction or gratification than visible happiness; **delight** usually reverses this stress; **joy** implies a more deep-rooted, rapturous emotion than either; **delectation** and **enjoyment** imply rather the state of mind of one who takes pleasure, delight, or joy in something, *delectation* more often suggesting amusement or diversion, and *enjoyment* gratification or happiness; **fruition** properly implies pleasure in possession or enjoyment in attainment (the common use of the term as meaning fulfillment or realization is not approved).

— *v. t.* To afford pleasure to; to please; gratify. — *v. i.* To take pleasure; delight; *Colloq.*, to seek pleasure.

pleat (plēt; *cf.* PLAIT), *n.* [ME. *pleten*, v.] A fold (of cloth, etc.); a plait (sense 1). — *v. t.* To fold (cloth, etc.); to plait (sense 1). — **pleat′er** (-ẽr), *n.*
pleb (plĕb), *n.* *Slang.* **a** A plebeian. **b** = PLEBE, 2.
plebe (plēb), *n.* [F. *plèbe*, fr. L. *plebs*.] **1.** *Obs.* The Roman plebs; the common people. **2.** A member of the lowest class in the military academy at West Point, and in the naval academy at Annapolis.
ple·be′ian (plē·bē′yăn; -ăn), *adj.* [L. *plebeius*, fr. *plebs, plebis*, the common people.] Of or pertaining to the Roman plebs; hence, of or pertaining to the common people; vulgar; common. — *n.* One of the plebs; a plebeian person. — **ple·be′ian·ism** (-ĭz′m), *n.*
pleb′i·scite (plĕb′ĭ·sĭt; -sīt; plē′bĭ·sĭt), *n.* [F. *plébiscite*, fr. L. *plebiscitum* vote, decree.] A vote or decree of the people on some measure submitted to them by some person or body having the initiative or authority; specif., a vote of the people of some region as to choice of sovereignty.
plebs (plĕbz), *n.; pl.* PLEBES (plē′bēz). [L.] **1.** *Rom. Hist.* The plebeians as a whole; the lower or secondary class of the people of ancient Rome, originally probably clients of the patrician gentes but later having practically equal political rights. **2.** The common people; the populace.
plec′tog·nath (plĕk′tŏg·năth), *adj.* [Gr. *plektos* twisted + *gnathos* jaw.] *Zool.* Of or pert. to a group of fishes (Plectognathi) that includes the filefishes, puffers, triggerfishes, and related kinds, usually having the body covered with bony plates, spines, etc. — **plec′tog·nath**, *n.*
plec′tron (plĕk′trŏn), *n.* = PLECTRUM.
plec′trum (-trŭm), *n.; pl.* -TRA (-trȧ), -TRUMS (-trŭmz). [L., fr. Gr. *plēktron* thing to strike with, fr. *plēssein* to strike.] A small thin piece of ivory, metal, etc., used in playing on the lyre and other plucked stringed instruments.
pled (plĕd). Colloq. & dial. past & past part. of PLEAD.
pledge (plĕj), *n.* [OF. *plege, pleige*, pledge, guaranty, fr. ML. *plebium, plevium*.] **1.** *Law.* **a** In early English law, a bail; hostage. **b** A bailment of a chattel, or object of personal property as security for the satisfaction of a debt or other obligation; also, the contract incidental to such a bailment; as, to give in *pledge*. **2.** Something given as a security for the performance of an act and, usually, liable to forfeiture in case of nonperformance; a guaranty. **3.** State of being given or held as a guaranty; pawn; — in phrases; as, in *pledge*. **4.** An assurance of good will or favor given by drinking one's health; a toast; a health. **5.** A promise or agreement by which one binds oneself to do or forbear something; a promise; specif., *Colloq., U.S.:* **a** (with *the*). A promise to abstain from intoxicants. **b** A promise to join a fraternity or society; also, the person who so promises.
— *v. t.;* PLEDGED (plĕjd); PLEDG′ING. **1.** To give as a pledge; to deposit, as a chattel, in pledge or pawn. Specif., to assign as security for the repayment of a loan. **2.** To bind by or as by a pledge; to plight. **3.** To give assurance of good will, favor, or the like, by or in drinking; to toast.
pledg′ee′ (plĕj′ē′), *n.* The one to whom a pledge is given.
pledge′or′, pledg′or′ (plĕj′ôr′), *n.* *Law.* A pledger.
pledg′er (plĕj′ẽr), *n.* One who pledges anything or anyone.
pledg′et (plĕj′ĕt; -ĭt), *n.* *Med.* A compress for a wound, ulcer, or the like, as to absorb pus.
-ple′gi·a (-plē′jĭ·ȧ). Also **-ple′gy** (-plē′jĭ). [Gr. *plēgē* stroke.] *Med.* A combining form used to signify *stroke* (of paralysis), *paralysis, palsy*, as in hemi*plegia*.
Ple′iad (plē′yăd; -ăd; plī′ăd), *n.* Any of the Pleiades.
Ple′ia·des (plē′yȧ·dēz; plē′ȧ-; plī′ȧ-), *n. pl.* [L., fr. Gr. *Pleiades*.] **1.** *Gr. Myth.* The seven daughters of Atlas, (Alcyone, Celaeno, Electra, Maia, Merope, Sterope or Asterope, and Taygeta). They were transformed into the group of stars so named, the invisible seventh, or "lost," one (Merope) concealing herself out of shame for having loved a mortal. **2.** [*gen.* PLEIADUM.] *Astron.* A conspicuous loose cluster of stars in the constellation Taurus. Six stars (for names see sense 1) are visible to the average eye, but the telescope reveals many hundreds more.
plein′-air′ (plăn′âr′), *adj.* [F.] Designating or pert. to certain schools of painting devoted esp. to representing effects of outdoor life, esp. of air and light, not observable in the studio. See IMPRESSIONISM. — **plein′-air′ist**, *n.*
Plei′o·cene (plī′ō·sēn). Var. of PLIOCENE.
Pleis′to·cene (plīs′tō·sēn), *adj.* [Gr. *pleistos* most + *kainos* new.] *Geol.* Of, pertaining to, or designating the earlier period (cf. RECENT, 3) of the Quaternary division of the Cenozoic era, or the system of rocks formed during this period; — called also *Glacial*. During this period Canada and northern U. S., northern Europe, and northern Asia were largely covered with ice. — **Pleis′to·cene**, *n.*
ple′na·ry (plē′nȧ·rĭ; plĕn′ȧ·rĭ), *adj.* [LL. *plenarius*, fr. L. *plenus*.] **1.** Full; entire; complete; as, *plenary* authority. **2.** Fully attended or constituted; including all entitled to be present; — said of an assembly, meeting, etc. — **Syn.** See FULL. — **ple′na·ri·ly**, *adv.*
plenary indulgence. *R.C.Ch.* The remission of the entire temporal punishment due to sin. See INDULGENCE.
ple·nip′o·tent (plē·nĭp′ō·tĕnt), *adj. & n.* [LL. *plenipotens*, fr. L. *plenus* full + *potens, -entis*, potent.] *Rare.* Plenipotentiary.
plen′i·po·ten′ti·ar′y (plĕn′ĭ·pō·tĕn′shĭ·ĕr′ĭ; -ẽr·ĭ; -shȧ·rĭ), *n.; pl.* -IES (-ĭz). [ML. *plenipotentiarius*.] A person invested with full power to transact any business; esp., a diplomatic agent having such power. — *adj.* Containing or conferring full power; invested with full power.
plen′ish (plĕn′ĭsh), *v. t.* *Scot. & Dial.* To fill up; stock.
plen′i·tude (plĕn′ĭ·tūd), *n.* [OF., fr. L. *plenitudo*.] **1.** State of being filled; fullness. **2.** An abundance; a sufficiency.
plen′te·ous (plĕn′tē·ŭs; 58), *adj.* **1.** Abundant; copious; plentiful. **2.** Yielding abundance; fruitful. — **plen′te·ous·ly**, *adv.* — **plen′te·ous·ness**, *n.*
plen′ti·ful (plĕn′tĭ·fōōl; -f'l), *adj.* **1.** Yielding or containing plenty; opulent. **2.** Constituting, characterized by, or existing in plenty; copious; ample; as, a *plentiful* harvest. — **plen′ti·ful·ly**, *adv.* — **plen′ti·ful·ness**, *n.*
Syn. **Plentiful, ample, abundant, copious** mean more than sufficient yet not in excess. **Plentiful** implies a great or rich supply; **ample**, a generous sufficiency to satisfy a definite requirement; **abundant**, an unusually large supply; **copious**, abundance or profusion in the quantity or number of things produced, yielded, used, etc.
plen′ty (plĕn′tĭ), *n.; pl.* -TIES (-tĭz). [OF. *plenté*, fr. L. *plenitas*, fr. *plenus* full.] **1.** Full supply; abundance. **2.** Copiousness or abundance. — *adj.;* PLEN′TI·ER (-tĭ·ẽr), PLEN′TI·EST. Plentiful; abundant; — used predicatively.
ple′num (plē′nŭm), *n.; pl.* PLENUMS (-nŭmz), PLENA (-nȧ). [L., prop., neut. of *plenus* full.] **1.** A space or all space every part of which is full of matter; — opposed to *vacuum*. **2.** Condition of being filled; fullness. **3.** A condition in which the pressure of the air in an enclosed space is greater than that of the outside atmosphere. **4.** A general or full assembly, esp. a joint assembly of all parts of a legislative or other body. — **ple′num**, *adj.*
ple′o·mor′phic (plē′ō·môr′fĭk), *adj.* [*pleo-* (fr. Gr. *pleiōn* more) + *-morphic*.] Pertaining to, or characterized by, occurrence of more than one distinct form, as in the life cycle of certain bacteria and fungi. — **ple′o·mor′phism** (-môr′fĭz′m), *n.*
ple′o·nasm (plē′ō·năz′m), *n.* [LL. *pleonasmus*, fr. Gr. *pleonasmos*, fr. *pleonazein* to be more than enough, abound, fr. *pleon*, neut. of *pleōn, pleiōn*, more, compar. of *polys* much.] *Gram. & Rhet.* Redundancy of language in speaking or writing; also, a case of this, or the redundant word or expression. — **ple′o·nas′tic** (-năs′tĭk), *adj.* — **ple′o·nas′ti·cal·ly** (-tĭ·kăl·ĭ), *adv.*
ple′o·pod (plē′ō·pŏd), *n.* [Gr. *pleōn*, pres. part. of *plein* to swim + *-pod*.] *Zool.* One of the abdominal limbs of a crustacean.
ple′si·o·saur′ (plē′sĭ·ō·sôr′), *n.* [Gr. *plēsios* near, close + *sauros* a lizard.] *Paleontol.* One of a suborder (Plesiosauria or Plesiosauri) of marine reptiles of the Mesozoic.
ple′si·o·sau′rus (-sô′rŭs), *n.* [NL.] *Paleontol.* Any of a genus (*Plesiosaurus*) of plesiosaurs, having a very long neck, a small head, and all four limbs developed as paddles for swimming.
pleth′o·ra (plĕth′ō·rȧ; *seldom* plē·thō′rȧ), *n.* [ML., fr. Gr. *plēthōrē*, fr. *plēthein* to be full.] **1.** *Med.* A morbid condition characterized by excess of blood in the body. **2.** State of being overfull; excess; superabundance.
ple·thor′ic (plē·thŏr′ĭk; plĕth′ō·rĭk), *adj.* **1.** Characterized by plethora; as, a *plethoric* constitution. **2.** Overfull; turgid; bombastic; as, *plethoric* phrases. — **ple·thor′i·cal·ly** (plē·thŏr′ĭ·kăl·ĭ), *adv.*
pleu′ra (plōōr′ȧ; 114), *n.; pl.* PLEURAE (-ē). [ML., fr. Gr. *pleura* a rib, the side.] *Anat. & Zool.* The delicate serous membrane lining each half of the thorax of mammals and folded back over the surface of the lung of the same side. — **pleu′ral** (-ăl), *adj.*
pleu′ri·sy (plōōr′ĭ·sĭ; 114), *n.* [OF. *pleurisie*, fr. LL., fr. Gr. *pleuritis*, fr. *pleura* rib, side.] *Med.* Inflammation of the pleura, usually accompanied with fever, painful and difficult respiration, cough, and exudation into the pleural cavity. — **pleu·rit′ic** (plōō·rĭt′ĭk), *adj.*
pleurisy root. The butterfly weed *Asclepias tuberosa;* also, its root, used as a remedy for pleuritic affections.
pleu′ro- (*pron. varies between* plōō′rō- *and* plōōr′ō-; 114), **pleur-**. [Gr. *pleura* rib, side.] A combining form used to denote *relation to a side;* specif., *connection with*, or *situation in* or *near, the pleura*, as in **pleu·rec′to·my, pleu·rot′o·my.** *Pleuro-* denotes also *pleural and* as in **pleu′ro·per′i·car′di·al, pleu′ro·per′i·to·ne′al.**
pleu′ro·dont (plōōr′ō·dŏnt; 114), *adj.* [*pleur-* + *-odont.*] *Zool.* **a** Consolidated with the inner surface of the alveolar ridge without sockets; — said of teeth. **b** Having pleurodont teeth; — opposed to *acrodont*. — *n.* A pleurodont animal.
pleu′ro·pneu·mo′ni·a (-nū·mō′nĭ·ȧ; 58), *n.* [NL.] *Med.* A combination of pleurisy and pneumonia.
plex′i·form (plĕk′sĭ·fôrm), *adj.* [*plexus* + *-form*.] Like a network, or plexus; complicated.
plex·im′e·ter (plĕks·ĭm′ē·tẽr), *n.* [Gr. *plēxis* stroke + *-meter*.] *Med.* A small, hard, flat plate, as of ivory, placed on the body to receive the blow, in percussion.
plex′us (plĕk′sŭs), *n.; pl.* PLEXUSES (-ĕz; -ĭz), PLEXUS. [L., a twining, braid, fr. *plectere, plexum*, to twine, braid.] **1.** *Anat.* A network, esp. of interlacing blood vessels or nerves. Cf. SOLAR PLEXUS. **2.** An interwoven combination of parts in a structure; a network; as, a *plexus* of mutual rights.
pli′a·ble (plī′ȧ·b'l), *adj.* [F., fr. *plier* to bend.] **1.** Flexible; pliant. **2.** Flexible in disposition or character; easily influenced. — **Syn.** See PLASTIC. — **pli′a·bil′i·ty** (-bĭl′ĭ·tĭ), *n.* — **pli′a·ble·ness**, *n.* — **pli′a·bly**, *adv.*
pli′ant (plī′ănt), *adj.* [OF., pres. part. of *plier* to bend. See PLY.] **1.** Bending; flexible; pliable. Also, easily influenced; compliant. **2.** Favorable to yielding; as, Othello chose "a *pliant* hour" to woo Desdemona. **3.** Capable of adaptation; as, a *pliant* style. — **Syn.** See PLASTIC. — **pli′an·cy** (-ăn·sĭ), *n.* — **pli′ant·ly**, *adv.* — **pli′ant·ness**, *n.*
pli′ca (plī′kȧ), *n.; pl.* -CAE (-sē). [ML., a fold, fr. L. *plicare* to fold.] **1.** *Med.* A disease (called also **pli′ca po·lon′i·ca** [pō·lŏn′ĭ·kȧ]) of the hair in which it becomes twisted and matted together. **2.** A fold or folded part; a bend, as a fold of skin.
pli′cate (plī′kāt), **pli′cat·ed** (-kāt·ĕd; -ĭd), *adj.* [L. *plicatus*, past part. of *plicare* to fold.] Plaited; folded like a fan; as, a *plicate* leaf. — **pli′cate·ly**, *adv.* — **pli′cate·ness**, *n.*
pli·ca′tion (plĭ·kā′shŭn; plī-), *n.* Also **plic′a·ture** (plĭk′ȧ·tūr). **1.** Act of folding, or state of being folded. **2.** A fold.
pli′er (plī′ẽr), *n.* **1.** One who or that which plies. **2.** *pl., sometimes construed as sing.* Small pincers with long jaws, used for bending or cutting wire, for handling small objects, etc.

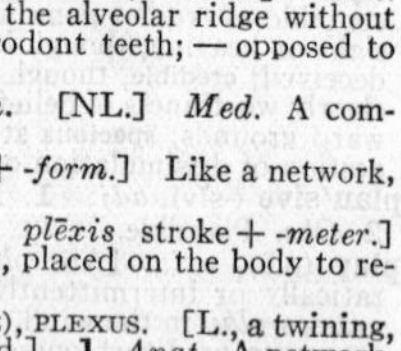

Pliers, 2.

plight (plīt), *n.* [ME. *plit* condition, state, prop., a folding, for *plet*, fr. OF. *ploit*, earlier *pleit*.] Condition; state; — now usually qualified as bad. — **Syn.** See PREDICAMENT.
plight, *n.* [AS. *pliht* danger.] *Now Rare.* Pledge (under penalty); engagement. — *v. t.* **1.** To put in danger of forfeiture; to engage; as, to *plight* faith. **2.** To bind by a pledge; promise; betroth. — **plight′er**, *n.*
Plim′soll, *or* **Plim′soll's, mark** (plĭm′s'l, -sŏl; -s'lz, -sŏlz). *Naut.* The load line (see LOAD LINE) on the sides of all British merchant vessels, to indicate the limit of submergence allowed by law; — from Samuel Plimsoll by whose efforts the act of Parliament to prevent overloading was procured.
plinth (plĭnth), *n.* [L. *plinthus*, fr. Gr. *plinthos* brick, plinth.] **1.** *Arch.* **a** The lowest member of a base; a block upon which the moldings of an architrave or trim are stopped at the bottom. See BASE, *Illust.* **b** A course of stones forming a continuous plinth; — called also **plinth course**. **2.** A block serving as a base for a statue, vase, etc.

Pli′o·cene (plī′ō·sēn), *adj.* [Gr. *pleiōn* more + *kainos* recent.] *Geol.* Of, pert. to, or designating the latest period of the Tertiary division of the Cenozoic era, or the system of rocks formed during this period. — **Pli′o·cene,** *n.*

Pli′o·film′ (plī′ō·fĭlm′), *n.* A trade-mark applied to a glossy, moisture-proof membrane made of rubber hydrochloride and used for making raincoats, packaging material, fruit wrapping, and the like.

plis′kie, plis′ky (plĭs′kĭ), *n. Scot.* A trick. — *adj.* Mischievous.

plod (plŏd), *v. i.;* PLOD′DED; PLOD′DING. **1.** To walk heavily; to trudge. **2.** To work laboriously and monotonously; to toil; drudge. — *v. t.* To walk slowly or heavily along; to make (one's way) thus. — *n.* Act or period of plodding. — **plod′der** (-ẽr), *n.* — **plod′ding·ly,** *adv.*

-ploid (-ploid). *Biol.* A combining form, Greek *-ploos,* meaning *-fold* + *-oid,* used in cytology and genetics to denote, in adjectives and nouns, *possessing the basic* (haploid) *number of chromosomes characteristic of a given group* (plant or animal), as in dip*loid,* trip*loid,* etc. Corresponding nouns denoting the *condition* are formed in **-ploi′dy** (-ploi′dĭ).

plop (plŏp), *v. i. & t.;* PLOPPED (plŏpt); PLOP′PING. [Imitative.] To fall, drop, or move suddenly, as on water, with a sound suggestive of the word *plop.* — **plop,** *n.*

plo′sion (plō′zhŭn), *n. Phonet.* Explosion.

plo′sive (plō′sĭv), *adj. & n. Phonet.* Explosive.

plot (plŏt), *n.* [ME. *plot, plotte,* patch, a piece of ground, prob. fr. *plat, platte.*] **1.** A small area of ground; a plat. **2.** *Chiefly U. S.* A ground plan, as of a building or area; a diagram. **3.** Any secret scheme or plan, usually evil; a conspiracy; intrigue. **4.** The plan or main story of a literary composition, as a play, novel, or poem.

Syn. (1) See PLAN.

(2) **Plot, intrigue, machination, conspiracy, cabal** mean a plan devised to entrap others. **Plot** implies careful planning of details and an evil or treacherous intent; **intrigue,** an attempt to gain one's ends by maneuvering and clandestine means; **machination,** a contriving of annoyances, injuries, or evils; **conspiracy,** a plot involving many devisers or agents and, usually, a treasonable intent; **cabal,** an intrigue that is also a conspiracy.

— *v. t.;* PLOT′TED; PLOT′TING. **1.** To make a plot, map, or plan, of (something). **2.** Specif.: To locate and mark (a point), as on paper ruled into small squares (**plot′ting pa′per,** or graph paper), by means of its co-ordinates; to make (a curve) by marking out a number of points in this way; hence, to represent graphically (a mathematical equation) by means of a curve so constructed. **3.** To scheme; contrive, esp. secretly. — *v. i.* To form a plot; to conspire.

plot′tage (plŏt′ĭj), *n.* The area included in a plot of land.

plot′ter (plŏt′ẽr), *n.* One who plots; esp., a conspirator.

plough (plou), **plough′er,** etc. Vars. of PLOW, etc.

plov′er (plŭv′ẽr; *in U. S. also* plō′vẽr), *n.;* see PLURAL, *Note,* 3. [OF. *plovier,* prop., the rain bird, fr. L. *pluvia* rain.] **1.** Any of certain shore-inhabiting birds (family Charadriidae) which differ from the sandpipers in the short bill and in their usually stouter build. See KILLDEER. **2.** Any of various other allied birds, as the turnstone, called ***chicken plover,*** and various sandpipers.

plow, plough (plou), *n.* [Late AS. *plōh.*] **1.** An implement used to cut, lift, invert, and partly pulverize soil. See *Illust.* **2.** Any of various devices operating like a plow. **3.** [*cap.*] *Astron.* Charles's Wain, or the Dipper; sometimes, the constellation Ursa Major. See URSA MAJOR, *Illust.*

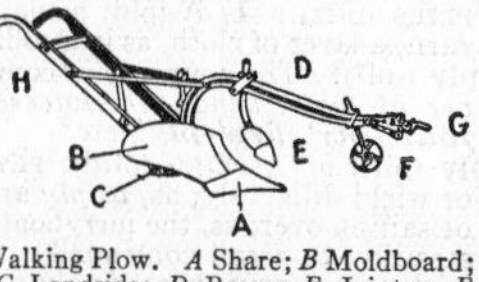

Walking Plow. *A* Share; *B* Moldboard; *C* Landside; *D* Beam; *E* Jointer; *F* Gauge Wheel; *G* Clevis; *H* Handles.

— *v. t.* **1.** To turn up, break up, or trench, with a plow; to till with or as with a plow. **2.** To make grooves or ridges in; to furrow. **3.** To move, cut, or cleave through; as, ships that *plow* the sea; to *plow* one's way through a crowd. **4.** [spelled **plough**] *Eng. Univ. Slang.* To pluck (sense 6). — *v. i.* **1.** To use a plow; to till with a plow; also, to admit of plowing; as, the field *plows* hard. **2.** To go, move, or cut, as through water or snow, as a plow does through soil; to proceed laboriously. — **plow′er, plough′er** (-ẽr), *n.* — **plow′boy′, plough′boy′** (-boi′), *n.* — **plow′man, plough′man** (-măn), *n.*

plow′share′, plough′share′ (-shâr′), *n. Agric. Mach.* That part of a moldboard plow which cuts the furrow. See PLOW, *Illust.*

ploy (ploi), *v. i. Mil.* To diminish front; esp., to form a column from a line. — **ploy′ment,** *n.*

ploy, *n. Chiefly Scot.* A pastime; sport; escapade.

pluck (plŭk), *v. t.* [AS. *pluccian.*] **1.** To pull or pick off or out; to pick. **2.** To pull off the feathers, hair, etc., of; as, to *pluck* a fowl. **3.** To pull; drag; — with *out, off, from, down, asunder,* etc. **4.** To jerk; twitch; hence, to make (a musical string) sound by such action; to twang. **5.** *Slang.* To rob; fleece. **6.** *Orig. Eng. Univ. Slang.* To reject (esp. a candidate for a degree) as for failure to pass in an examination. — *v. i.* To make a motion of sharp pulling or twitching; to tug; — usually with *at.* — *n.* **1.** A pull, twitch, tug, etc. **2.** The heart, liver, lungs, and windpipe of an animal killed for food. **3.** Spirit; courage; resolution. — **Syn.** See FORTITUDE. — **pluck′er** (-ẽr), *n.*

pluck′y (-ĭ), *adj.;* PLUCK′I·ER (-ĭ·ẽr); PLUCK′I·EST. Having or marked by pluck or courage; courageous; brave. — **pluck′i·ly,** *adv.* — **pluck′i·ness,** *n.*

plug (plŭg), *n.* [MD. *plugge* (D. *plug*).] **1.** Any piece used to stop or fill a hole; a stopple. **2.** *Slang.* Something inferior; as: **a** *U. S.* A worn-out horse; a jade. **b** A plugged coin. **c** An inferior operator. **3.** Short for PLUG HAT, etc. **4. a** A male fitting for making electrical connections by insertion in a receptacle or body. **b** A spark plug. **c** A device for connecting electric wires to a jack. **5.** The discharge pipe with a valve and spout at which water may be drawn from water mains (called specif. ***fireplug,*** or ***water plug***). **6.** In a cylinder lock, the cylindrical piece containing the keyhole and rotated by the key. See LOCK, *Illust.* **7.** A flat oblong cake of tobacco. **8.** *Chiefly Colloq.* **a** Insistent advertisement or favorable publicity. **b** *Radio.* A bit of advertising material inserted into a radio program.

— *v. t.;* PLUGGED (plŭgd); PLUG′GING. **1.** To stop, make tight, or secure by means of a plug; to insert a plug in; — often with *up.* **2.** *Slang.* **a** To hit with a bullet; shoot. **b** To strike with the fist; to punch. **3.** *Chiefly Colloq.* To advertise or publicize insistently. — *v. i. Slang.* **a** To keep doggedly at work or in action; to plod. **b** To fire shots; to shoot. — ***plug in.*** *Elec.* To establish a circuit by inserting a plug. — **plug′ger,** *n.*

plug hat. *Slang.* A top hat.

plug′-ug′ly (plŭg′ŭg′lĭ; 2), *n. Slang, U. S.* A type of city rowdy, ruffian, or disorderly tough.

plum (plŭm), *n.* [AS. *plūme,* fr. LL., fr. L. *prunum,* pl. *pruna,* fr. Gr. *prounon,* fr. *proumnon.*] **1.** The fruit of any of various species of trees (genus *Prunus*) of the peach family and allied to the cherries; also, the tree which bears this fruit. The plum is a drupe, larger than the cherry and with an oblong stone. **2.** Any of various unrelated trees having an edible plumlike fruit; also, the fruit itself. **3. a** A raisin, when used in puddings, etc. **b** Something like a plum, as in shape or sweetness; as, a sugar*plum;* also, short for SUGARPLUM. **4.** *Slang, Eng.* The sum of £100,000 sterling; also, formerly, a person possessing it. **5.** A color like that of some plums, blue-red in hue, of low saturation and very low brilliance. See COLOR. **6.** A good or choice thing of its kind.

plum′age (plōōm′ĭj; 114), *n.* [OF., fr. *plume,* a feather.] The entire clothing of feathers of a bird.

plu′mate (plōō′māt), *adj.* [L. *plumatus* feathered.] *Zool.* Like plumage; — said of hairs, antennae, etc.

plumb (plŭm), *n.* [F. *plomb,* fr. L. *plumbum* lead.] **1.** A weight of lead, attached to a line and used by builders, etc., to indicate a vertical direction; a plummet. **2.** A weighting lead, or plummet, as a mariner's sounding lead, etc. See SOUNDING LINE, *Illust.* — ***out of, or off, plumb.*** Not vertical or true.

— *adj.* Also **plum. 1.** Conforming to the direction of a line attached to a plumb; vertical; as, the wall is *plumb.* **2.** *Colloq.* Downright; absolute. — **Syn.** See VERTICAL.

— *adv.* Also **plum. 1.** In a plumb direction; vertically. **2.** Directly; exactly; also, immediately. **3.** *Colloq., U. S.* Completely; absolutely; as, he is *plumb* crazy.

— *v. t.* **1.** To sound with a plumb; hence, to ascertain the depth, quality, dimension, etc., of; fathom. **2.** To seal with lead. **3.** To test by a plumb line; as, to *plumb* a wall. **4.** To work upon (something) as a plumber.

plum·bag′i·nous (plŭm·băj′ĭ·nŭs), *adj.* Resembling, consisting of, or containing plumbago.

plum·ba′go (plŭm·bā′gō), *n.; pl.* -GOS (-gōz). [L., a kind of lead ore, fr. *plumbum* lead.] **1.** Graphite. **2.** Any of a genus (*Plumbago*) of woody plants, widely distributed in the tropics, having alternate leaves and blue and white flowers in spikes.

plumb bob. The bob, or weight, of a plumb line.

plum′be·ous (plŭm′bē·ŭs), *adj.* [L. *plumbeus.*] Consisting of, or resembling, lead; leaden.

plumb′er (plŭm′ẽr), *n.* [F. *plombier.* See PLUMB.] Orig., a worker in lead; now, an artisan who works in lead, zinc, tin, etc.; esp., one who fits and repairs water and gas pipes, cisterns, water closets, etc.

plumb′er·y (-ĭ), *n.; pl.* -ERIES (-ĭz). The business or work of a plumber; plumbing.

plum′bic (plŭm′bĭk), *adj.* [From PLUMBUM.] Pertaining to, or containing, lead; specif., *Chem.,* designating compounds in which lead has a relatively high valence.

plum·bif′er·ous (plŭm·bĭf′ẽr·ŭs), *adj.* [*plumbum* + *-ferous.*] Producing or containing lead.

plumb′ing (plŭm′ĭng), *n.* **1.** Act of using a plumb. **2.** A plumber's occupation or trade; also, plumber's work.

plum′bism (plŭm′bĭz′m), *n.* [From PLUMBUM.] *Med.* Lead poisoning.

plumb line. a A line or cord having at one end a weight (*plumb bob*) used to determine verticality. **b** A vertical line. **c** A sounding line.

plum′bous (plŭm′bŭs), *adj.* [L. *plumbosus* full of lead.] Pertaining to, or containing, lead; specif., *Chem.,* designating compounds in which lead has a low valence.

plumb rule. A narrow board with a plumb line and bob, used by builders and carpenters.

plum′bum (plŭm′bŭm), *n.* [L. See PLUMB.] Lead.

plum duff. A plain flour pudding containing raisins or currants, boiled in a bag.

plume (plōōm; 114), *n.* [OF., fr. L. *pluma.*] **1.** A feather; — now chiefly *Poetic,* exc. specif.: A long handsome feather; also, an ornamental tuft of feathers. **2.** Plumage, esp. downy feathers. **3.** A feather, tuft of hair or the like, esp. when worn as an ornament, as on a helmet. **4.** A token of honor or prowess; a prize. **5.** *Bot.* Any plumose appendage, as the pappus of a dandelion. — *v. t.* **1.** To provide or adorn with plumes or plumage. **2. a** To dress the feathers of (itself); — said of a bird. **b** To adorn (oneself) with or as with plumes; hence, to pride or congratulate; — used reflexively; as, he *plumes* himself on his skill. **3.** To preen.

plume′let (plōōm′lĕt; -lĭt), *n.* A small plume.

plum′met (plŭm′ĕt; -ĭt), *n.* [OF. *plommet,* fr. *plom* lead.] **1.** A plumb bob; also, a plumb rule; hence, a test or criterion. **2.** Something that weighs down or depresses; a weight. — *v. i.* To drop or plunge straight down.

plu′mose (plōō′mōs), *adj.* [L. *plumosus,* fr. *pluma* feather.] **1.** Having feathers or plumes; feathered. **2.** Feathery; plumelike. — **plu′mose·ly,** *adv.* — **plu·mos′i·ty** (plōō·mŏs′ĭ·tĭ; 114), *n.*

plump (plŭmp), *n. Archaic & Dial.* A cluster; flock.

plump, *adj.* [MD. *plomp,* MLG. *plump,* orig., falling, heavy, clumsy.] Well rounded or filled out; esp., chubby; fat. — *v. t. & i.* To make or become plump. — **plump′ly,** *adv.* — **plump′ness,** *n.*

plump, *v. i.* [MD. *plompen,* MLG. *plumpen,* of imitative origin.] To drop, fall, sink, or come in contact, suddenly or heavily; to come or go plump. — *v. t.* **1.** To drop, cast, or plunge all at once or suddenly and heavily. **2.** To blurt (out), as an opinion. — *n. Colloq.* A sudden plunge or heavy fall; also, the sound made by such a fall. — *adv.* **1.** With a sudden or heavy drop. **2.** Straight down; vertically. **3.** Directly; bluntly. — *adj.* Blunt; direct; unqualified.

plump′er (plŭmp′ẽr), *n.* One that swells out something; esp., something carried in the mouth to fill out the cheeks.

plump′er, *n.* **1.** A sudden heavy fall. **2.** A vote or votes given to one candidate only, when the voter might vote for more than one for the same office. **3.** *Slang.* **a** A heavy blow. **b** A downright lie.

plum pudding. A pudding containing plums; specif., a pudding of flour or bread crumbs, raisins, currants, and other fruits, suet, eggs, spices, etc., often boiled in a bag or cloth.

plu′mule (plo͞o′mūl; 114), *n.* [L. *plumula*, dim. of *pluma* a feather.] **1.** *Bot.* The primary bud of an embryo or germinating seed plant. **2.** *Zool.* A down feather.

plun′der (plŭn′dẽr), *v. t.* [G. *plündern*.] To pillage; spoil; sack. Hence, to take by force or wrongfully. — *v. i.* To commit robbery or looting. — *n.* **1.** Act of plundering, as in war; pillaging; hence, spoliation by extortion. **2.** Spoil; booty; loot. **3.** *Colloq., U. S.* Personal or household effects. — **Syn.** See SPOIL. — **plun′der·er,** *n.*

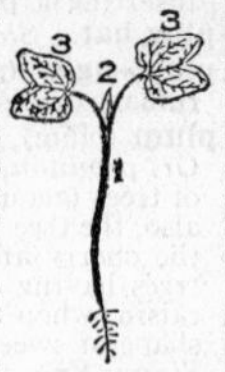

2 Plumule, of Morning-glory Seedling; 1 Hypocotyl; 3, 3 Cotyledon. See also EMBRYO, *Illust.*

plun′der·age (-ĭj), *n.* A plundering; specif., *Mar. Law,* embezzlement of goods on shipboard; also, the plunder so got.

plunge (plŭnj; 46), *v. t.;* PLUNGED (plŭnjd); PLUNG′ING (plŭn′jĭng). [OF. *plongier*, deriv. of L. *plumbum* lead.] To cause to penetrate or enter quickly and forcibly; to thrust or force (into or in liquid, a penetrable substance, or a cavity); to immerse; submerge; — also figuratively; as, to *plunge* a nation into war. — *v. i.* **1.** To thrust or cast oneself, as into water; to submerge oneself; — also figuratively; as, to *plunge* into debt. **2. a** To pitch or throw oneself violently forward and downward, as a horse or ship. **b** Hence, to act with reckless haste. **3.** *Slang.* To gamble heavily and with seeming recklessness. — *n.* **1.** A place for plunging or diving; a deep pool. **2.** A dive, leap, rush, or pitch into, or as into, water. **3.** *Slang.* Act or instance of engaging in heavy and reckless speculation.

plung′er (plŭn′jẽr), *n.* **1.** One who plunges; as: **a** A diver. **b** *Slang.* A reckless speculator. **2.** That which plunges; as: **a** *Automobiles.* The rod carrying the valves in the inner assembly of a tire valve unit. **b** *Mach.* A sliding reciprocating piece driven by or against fluid pressure; a piston; also, a piece or part with a similar motion.

plung′ing fire (plŭn′jĭng). *Gun.* Direct fire on a target from a superior elevation.

plunk (plŭngk), *v. i. & t.* [Imitative.] **1.** To make or cause to make a quick, hollow, metallic, or harsh sound. **2.** To drop or put down suddenly or heavily; to plump. — *n. Colloq.* Act or sound of plunking; a blow. — *adv.* With a plunking sound; plump.

plunk′er (plŭngk′ẽr), *n. Angling.* A type of casting lure making a plunking sound, which is used with a short line, esp. from a boat. See LURE, *Illust.*

plu′per′fect (plo͞o′pûr′fĕkt; plo͞o′pûr′fĕkt; -fĭkt; 2), *adj. & n.* [L. *plus-quam-perfectum* (sc. *tempus* tense) more than perfect.] *Gram.* Past perfect. Abbr. *plup.*

plu′ral (plo͝or′ăl; 114), *adj.* [OF. or L.; OF. *plurel*, fr. L. *pluralis*, fr. *plus, pluris*, more.] **1.** *Gram.* Designating or pert. to the form of a word denoting more than one; applying to more than one, as in the **plural number** of nouns, pronouns, and verbs (*oxen, them, were*). **2.** More than one; consisting of, or equal to, more than one. — *n. Gram.* The plural number, a form denoting it, or a word in that form. The plurals of English nouns are regularly formed by adding *-s;* when the singular ends with a sound with which the sound of *s* cannot unite in pronunciation, by adding *es* (or *s* after mute *e*), as *ashes, edges, boxes, mazes;* also, the plural of some nouns ending in *-o* preceded by a consonant ends in *-es*, as *echoes, embargoes, potatoes*, some in either *-s* or *-es*, as *cargoes, cargos, mottoes, mottos.* The three chief exceptions to this regular practice are: **a** Common nouns ending in *-y* preceded by a consonant form the plural by changing *y* to *i* and adding *-es*, as *fly, flies; colloquy, colloquies.* **b** Most monosyllabic nouns ending in *-f* or *-fe* form the plural by changing *f* or *fe* to *ves*, as *elf, elves; life, lives.* **c** Certain nouns form the plural by a change of vowel sound, as in *man, men; foot, feet; louse, lice; mouse, mice.* A plural in *-s* or *-es* is in general to be assumed as appropriate for use with common English nouns for which no plural form is specified in the Vocabulary. Compound nouns in the Vocabulary without a plural form may be assumed to have a plural corresponding to the plural of the final constituent element, as in *crosstree, crosstrees; huckleberry, huckleberries; iceman, icemen.* A few abbreviations double the final consonant to form a plural (*pp.*, pages). See *Orthography* §§ 12–14.

NOTE. — Some nouns have the same form in the plural as in the singular, as many names of tribes, as *Bantu, Iroquois,* and certain names of peoples, as *Siamese.* Certain names of fishes, birds, and mammals use varyingly a plural form differing from the singular and one identical with the singular, as follows:
(1) Always a differing plural form, as *bird* (and its compounds), *mongoose, osprey, wren.*
(2) A differing plural form except sometimes when qualified as by *wild, native, sea, mountain;* as, two *musk ox.*
(3) Usually a differing plural form but commonly, esp. in the language of those who hunt or fish, an identical plural form, as *beaver, buffalo, fox, partridge, seal, smelt, turtle, yak, zebu.*
(4) Always an identical plural form, as *bison, deer, grouse, moose, sheep.*
(5) Either a differing or an identical plural form, as *barracuda, tuna.*
(6) A differing plural form only to signify different kinds or species, as *eland, fish* (and its compounds, as *bluefish*), *haddock, springbok.*

plu′ral·ism (plo͝or′ăl·ĭz′m; 114), *n.* **1.** Quality, state, or instance of being plural. **2.** The holding by one person, as a clergyman, of two or more benefices or offices at one time. **3.** *Philos.* The doctrine that there is more than one kind of ultimate reality; — contrasted with *monism* (and, usually, with *dualism*). — **plu′ral·ist** (-ĭst), *n. & adj.* — **plu′ral·is′tic** (-ĭs′tĭk), *adj.*

plu·ral′i·ty (plo͞o·răl′ĭ·tĭ; 114), *n.; pl.* -TIES (-tĭz). **1.** State of being plural; also, state of being numerous; a multitude. **2.** *Eccl.* **a** The holding by one person of two or more benefices or livings at one time. **b** Any of the benefices or livings so held. **3.** The majority. **4.** *U. S. Politics.* In an election, an excess of votes over those for any other candidate for the same office, esp. over the number for the next opponent. Cf. MAJORITY, 2.

plu′ral·ize (plo͝or′ăl·īz; 114), *v. t.* To make plural by using the plural termination; to express in the plural form.

plu′ral·ly, *adv.* In a plural manner.

plu′ri- (plo͝or′ĭ-; *see* PLEURO-; 114). [L. *plus, pluris.*] A combining form meaning *several*, as in **plu′ri·ax′i·al,** having more than one axis, as certain plants on which the flowers are developed on secondary shoots.

plus (plŭs), *prep.* [L., more.] Increased by; with the addition of; as, four *plus* five (or 4 + 5); the debt *plus* interest; — opposed to *minus.* — *adj.* **1.** Indicating addition; positive; not negative; as, the *plus* sign [+]; a *plus* quantity; — used orally to render the sign +. Opposed to *minus.* **2.** Hence: **a** *Colloq.* In predicate use, having as an addition or gain; as, he was *plus* a coat. **b** Additional; extra. **3.** *Colloq.* Denoting a greater value than usual in the (specified) grade; as, A *plus.* **4.** *Bot.* Pertaining to or designating a physiological, sexlike differentiation comparable to *male*, in certain plants, as fungi; as, a *plus* strain. **5.** *Elec.* Positively electrified; positive. — *n.* **1.** The plus sign; — opposed to *minus.* Symbol + (no period). **2.** An added quantity; something extra. **3.** A positive quantity, also, surplus.

plus fours. A style of loose knickerbockers, very long and baggy at the knees, worn esp. in sports, as golf.

plush (plŭsh), *n.* [F. *pluche*, fr. *peluche*, fr. OF. *peluchier* to pluck, pick.] A textile fabric with a pile longer and softer than that of velvet.

plus sign. The sign + (orig. a contraction of Latin *et* meaning *and*) denoting addition or a positive quantity.

Plu′to (plo͞o′tō), *n.* [L., fr. Gr. *Ploutōn.*] **1.** *Class. Myth.* The god of the lower world, also called *Hades* by the Greeks and *Dis* by the Romans. **2.** *Astron.* The most remote known planet of the solar system, invisible to the naked eye. Its mean distance from the sun is about 3,680,000,000 miles, its period of revolution, 248 years, and its estimated diameter probably not greater than 4,000 miles. Symbol, ♇. See PLANET, *Table.*

plu·toc′ra·cy (plo͞o·tŏk′rȧ·sĭ), *n.; pl.* -CIES (-sĭz). [Gr. *ploutokratia*, fr. *ploutos* wealth. See DEMOCRACY.] Government by the wealthy; also, a controlling class of rich men.

plu′to·crat (plo͞o′tō·krăt; 114), *n.* One who has power or influence due to his wealth; one of the plutocracy.

plu′to·crat′ic (-krăt′ĭk), *adj.* Also **plu′to·crat′i·cal** (-ĭ·kăl). Of, pertaining to, or characterized by plutocrats or plutocracy. — **plu′to·crat′i·cal·ly,** *adv.*

Plu·to′ni·an (plo͞o·tō′nĭ·ăn; 58), *adj.* Of, pertaining to, or characteristic of Pluto or the lower world; infernal.

plu·ton′ic (-tŏn′ĭk), *adj.* **1.** *Geol.* Formed by solidification of a molten magma deep within the earth and crystalline throughout; as, *plutonic* rock. **2.** [*cap.*] Plutonian.

plu·to′ni·um (plo͞o·tō′nĭ·ŭm), *n.* [NL., fr. *Pluto* the planet. See PLUTO.] *Chem.* A radioactive element formed by the decay of neptunium, also found in minute quantities in pitchblende. Symbol, *Pu;* at. no., 94. Disintegration of plutonium 239 proceeds with the emission of a helium nucleus and the formation of uranium 235.

Plu′tus (plo͞o′tŭs), *n.* [L.] *Gr. Myth.* God of wealth.

plu′vi·al (-vĭ·ăl), *adj.* [L. *pluvialis*, fr. *pluvia* rain.] **1.** Of or pertaining to rain; characterized by abundant rain. **2.** *Geol.* Due to the action of rain.

plu′vi·om′e·ter (plo͞o′vĭ·ŏm′ē·tẽr), *n.* [L. *pluvia* rain + *-meter.*] A rain gauge. — **plu′vi·o·met′ric** (-ō·mĕt′rĭk), **plu′vi·o·met′ri·cal,** (-rĭ·kăl), *adj.* — **plu′vi·om′e·try** (-ŏm′ē·trĭ), *n.*

‖**Plu′viôse′** (plü′vyōz′; *Angl.* plo͞o′vĭ·ōs), *n.* [F.] See REVOLUTIONARY CALENDAR.

plu′vi·ous (plo͞o′vĭ·ŭs; 114), *adj.* Also **plu′vi·ose** (-ōs). [L. *pluviosus*, fr. *pluvia* rain.] Of or pert. to rain; rainy.

ply (plī), *v. t.;* PLIED (plīd); PLY′ING. [OF. *plier* (F. *plier*), fr. *ploier*, fr. L. *plicare* to fold.] To bend; fold; double, as silk in spinning. — *v. i. Obs.* To bend; yield; also, to comply; be pliant. — *n.; pl.* PLIES (plīz). **1.** A fold; a plait; one of the twists or strands, as in yarn; a layer of cloth, as in a collar. **2.** Figuratively, bend; twist; bias.

-ply (-plī). The noun *ply* in combination, denoting *a* (specified) *number of folds, bends, thicknesses, strands*, etc., as in ***three′-ply′, four′-ply′, five′-ply′***, etc.

ply (plī), *v. t.;* PLIED (plīd); PLY′ING. [From APPLY.] **1. a** To use or wield diligently; as, to *ply* an ax. **b** To make a practice of rowing or sailing over; as, the ferryboat *plies* the river. **2.** To do or work at steadily; to assail continually; to urge importunately; as, to *ply* one with questions; to keep supplying; as, to *ply* a man with liquor. — *v. i.* **1.** To work diligently; to apply oneself. **2.** To go or travel regularly (*between*); as, the steamer *plies* between two cities. **3.** *Now Poetic.* To direct one's course; to steer.

ply′er (plī′ẽr), *n.* **1.** One who or that which plies. **2.** *pl.* = PLIER, 2.

Plym′outh Breth′ren (plĭm′ŭth). Members of a religious sect originating at Plymouth, Eng., about 1830, taking the Scriptures as their sole guide, and rejecting all creeds, rituals, an ordained ministry, and ecclesiastical organization.

Plymouth Rock. One of an American breed of medium-sized single combed domestic fowls; esp., a variety (called also ***barred Rock***) whose grayish-white feathers are evenly barred with bluish black.

ply′wood′ (plī′wo͝od′), *n.* Wood made up of an odd number of veneer sheets glued together, the grains of the layers being (usually) at right angles to one another.

pneu′ma (nū′mȧ; p′nū′-; 88), *n.* [Gr.] Soul; spirit.

pneu·mat′ic (nū·măt′ĭk), *adj.* [From L., fr. Gr. *pneumatikos*, fr. *pneuma, pneumatos*, wind, air.] **1.** Of, pertaining to, or using air or wind. **2.** Specif.: **a** Moved or worked, as a tool, by pressure of air; as, a *pneumatic* drill. **b** Adapted for holding compressed air; inflated with air; as, a *pneumatic* tire. **3.** Fitted with pneumatic tires. — *n.* A pneumatic tire. — **pneu·mat′i·cal·ly** (-ĭ·kăl·ĭ), *adv.*

pneu·mat′ics (-ĭks), *n.;* see -ICS. That branch of physics treating of the mechanical properties of air and other gases, as of their weight, pressure, elasticity, etc.

pneu′ma·to- (nū′mȧ·tō-; p′nū′mȧ·tō-; 88). [See PNEUMATIC.] A combining form denoting: **a** *Wind, air*, as in *pneumato*lytic; hence, *respiration*, as in *pneumato*meter; also, *an air cavity*, as in *pneumato*phore. **b** *Spirit* or *spirits*, as in *pneumato*logy.

pneu′ma·tol′o·gy (nū′mȧ·tŏl′ō·jĭ; p′nū′mȧ-), *n.* **1.** Pneumatics. **2.** The doctrine of spiritual beings or spiritual phenomena; esp., the doctrine of spirits intermediate between God and man.

pneu′ma·tol′y·sis (-tŏl′ĭ·sĭs), *n.* [NL.] *Petrog.* Action by which pneumatolytic minerals are formed.

pneu′ma·to·lyt′ic, pneu′ma·to·lit′ic (-tō·lĭt′ĭk), *adj.* [*pneumato-* + *-lytic.*] *Petrog.* Formed or forming by hot vapors (or superheated liquids under pressure); — applied to minerals and ores.

pneu′ma·tom′e·ter (-tŏm′ē·tẽr), *n. Physiol.* An instrument for measuring the amount of force exerted by the lungs in respiration.

pneu′ma·to·phore′ (nū′mȧ·tō·fōr′; nū·măt′ō·fōr; p′nū′-; p′nū-; 70; 88), *n.* [*pneumato-* + Gr. *pherein* to bear.] *Bot.* A special root developed by various swamp or marsh plants. It often functions as a respiratory organ.

pneu·mec′to·my (nū·mĕk′tō·mĭ; p′nū-), *n.* [*pneumo-* + *-ectomy.*] The surgical removal of a part of a lung.

pneu′mo- (nū′mō-; p′nū′mō-; 88). = PNEUMONO-.
pneu′mo·ba·cil′lus (-bȧ·sĭl′ŭs), *n.; pl.* -LI (-ī). [NL., fr. *pneumo-* + *bacillus.*] *Bacteriol.* A bacterium associated with pneumonia and other respiratory inflammations.
pneu′mo·coc′cus (-kŏk′ŭs), *n.; pl.* -COCCI (-sī). [NL. See PNEUMO-; COCCUS.] *Bacteriol.* The bacterium (*Diplococcus pneumoniae*, syn. *Streptococcus lanceolatus*) which causes lobar pneumonia. — **pneu′mo·coc′cal** (-kŏk′ăl), **pneu′mo·coc′cic** (-sĭk), **pneu′mo·coc′cous** (-ŭs), *adj.*
pneu′mo·co′ni·o′sis (-kō′nĭ·ō′sĭs), *n.; pl.* -OSES (-sēz). [NL., fr. *pneumo-* + Gr. *konia* dust + *-osis.*] *Med.* Disease of the lungs caused by the habitual inhaling of minute mineral or metallic particles.
pneu′mo·dy·nam′ics (-dī·năm′ĭks; -dĭ-), *n.;* see -ICS. Pneumatics.
pneu′mo·gas′tric (-găs′trĭk), *adj. Anat.* Of or pertaining to the lungs and the stomach; designating or pertaining to the vagus. — *n.* The vagus.
pneu′mo·graph (nū′mō·grȧf; p′nū′-; 9), *n.* [*pneumo-* + *-graph.*] *Physiol.* An instrument for recording the movements of the thorax in respiration.
pneu·mo′ni·a (nū·mō′nĭ·ȧ; 58), *n.* [NL., fr. Gr. *pneumonia*, fr. *pneumōn*, pl. *pneumones* the lungs.] *Med.* Inflammation of the lungs with exudation of fluid into the lung spaces and resultant solidification of lung tissue. ***lobar pneumonia***, usually caused by a certain pneumococcus (*Diplococcus pneumoniae*), involves all or the greater part of the lobe of a lung. ***bronchial, catarrhal***, or ***lobular pneumonia***, or ***bronchopneumonia***, involves multiple and relatively small areas of the lung.
pneu·mon′ic (-mŏn′ĭk), *adj.* **a** Of or pertaining to the lungs; pulmonic. **b** Of or pertaining to pneumonia.
pneu′mo·no- (nū′mō·nō-; p′nū′mō·nō-; 88), **pneumon-**. [Gr. *pneumōn.* See PNEUMONIA.] A combining form denoting *lung*, as in **pneu′mo·not′o·my** (see -TOMY).
pneu′mo·tho′rax (nū′mō·thō′răks; p′nū′-), *n. Med.* A state in which air or other gas is present in the pleural cavity. When occurring naturally, it is called ***spontaneous pneumothorax;*** when induced therapeutically to collapse the lung, as in tuberculosis, ***artificial pneumothorax.***
po·a′ceous (pō·ā′shŭs), *adj.* [Gr. *poa* grass.] *Bot.* Belonging to the grass family (Poaceae). See GRASS.
poach (pōch), *v. t.* [OF. *pochier* to place in a pocket, hence, to poach eggs, fr. *poche* pocket, pouch.] To cook in boiling water, or the like, until coated; as, a *poached* egg.
poach, *v. t.* [MF. *pocher* to thrust or dig out with the fingers, fr. LG. *poken* to poke.] **1.** To stamp down, trample, or cut (up), as with hoofs; to make holes in (soft ground) by trampling. **2.** To reduce to a uniform consistency, as clay, by mixing thoroughly with water. **3.** To trespass on, esp. for game or fish; to take, as game or fish, by illegal methods. — *v. i.* **1.** To sink into mud or mire while walking. **2.** To become soft or muddy and full of holes when trampled on; as, the ground *poaches* badly. **3.** To trespass for something, esp. game or fish; to kill or destroy game illegally.
poach′er (pōch′ẽr), *n.* One who poaches for game.
po′chard (pō′chẽrd; *also* pō′kẽrd, pŏch′ẽrd, pŏk′-), *n.;* see PLURAL, *Note*, 3. A common Old World duck (*Nyroca ferina*) related to the redhead of America.
pock (pŏk), *n.* [AS. *pocc, poc.*] *Med.* A pustule or spot on the skin, as in smallpox; a pockmark.
pock. Scot. var. of POKE, a bag.
pock′et (pŏk′ĕt; -ĭt), *n.* [AF. *pokete*, dim. of ONF. *poke, poque*, bag, pouch.] **1.** A bag or pouch carried by a person; esp., a small bag inserted in a garment for carrying small articles, as money; hence, purse; money. **2.** Any place suggestive of a pocket; specif.: **a** A bin for storing coal, grain, etc. **b** An air pocket. **c** A cavity where foreign substance has collected or can collect. **3.** *Billiards & Pool.* Any of the bags or pouches at the corners or sides of the table. **4.** *Mining.* A cavity containing gold or other mineral or water; also, a small body of ore. **5.** *Naut.* A place for a spar or the like, made by sewing a strip of canvas on a sail. **6.** *Racing Slang.* The position of a contestant hemmed in by others.
— *v. t.* **1.** To put, enclose, confine, or conceal, in or as in a pocket. **2.** To receive (an affront, rebuff, etc.) without open resentment; to conceal or suppress, as pride or anger. **3.** To take (money, etc.), esp. secretly or fraudulently. **4.** *Billiards.* To drive (a ball) into a pocket of the table. **5.** *Politics. U.S.* To retain (a bill) unsigned until after Congress or the Legislature has adjourned; — said of the president and some state governors. **6.** *Racing Slang.* To put (a contestant) into a pocket.
— *adj.* **1.** Suitable, as in size, shape, etc., for carrying in the pocket; as, a *pocket* edition. **2.** Carried in or paid from one's own pocket or pocketbook, esp. for incidentals; as, *pocket* money.
pocket battleship. A small battleship built so as to come within treaty limitations of tonnage and armament.
pock′et·book′ (pŏk′ĕt·bo͝ok′; pŏk′ĭt-), *n.* A small case for carrying papers, money, etc., in the pocket; sometimes, a purse; hence, money; financial resources.
pocket borough. *Chiefly Brit.* A borough whose right of representation is controlled by a single person or family.
pock′et·knife′ (-nīf′), *n.; pl.* -KNIVES (-nīvz′). A knife with folding blades, to be carried in the pocket; a jackknife, penknife, or clasp knife. See KNIFE, *Illust.*
pocket money. Money for small personal expenses.
pocket veto. The retention by the president of the United States of a bill unsigned under such conditions that it does not become a law.
pock′mark′ (pŏk′märk′), *n.* A mark or pit due to smallpox. — **pock′–marked′** (-märkt′), *adj.*
‖**po′co** (pō′kō), *adj.* [It.] Little. — *adv.* Somewhat; slightly; — chiefly, *Music*, in directions. — *n.* A little.
‖**po′co a po′co** (ä pō′kō). [It.] Little by little.
po′co·cu·ran′te (pō′kō·ko͞o·rän′tä; -kū·răn′tē), *adj.* [It. *poco curante.*] Literally, caring little; hence, careless; indifferent; nonchalant. — *n.* A pococurante person; a trifler. — **po′co·cu·ran′te·ism** (-ĭz′m), **po′co·cu·ran′tism** (-kū·răn′tĭz′m), *n.*
pod (pŏd), *n.* A number of animals clustered together; a school, as of seals and whales; of birds, a flock.
pod, *n. Mech.* **a** The bit socket in a brace. **b** The straight groove or channel in the barrel of a certain kind (**pod auger**) of auger. See AUGER, *Illust.*
pod, *n.* [Origin uncert.] *Bot.* Any dry dehiscent seed vessel; specif., a legume, as of the pea or bean. — *v. i.;* POD′DED; POD′DING. **1.** To produce pods. **2.** To swell or fill out like a pod.
-pod (-pŏd). Also **-pode** (-pōd). [Gr. *pous, podos*, foot.] A combining form meaning *footed*, used to denote in adjectives and nouns (*one*) *having* (such or so many) *feet.*
-poda. [NL. See -POD.] *Zool.* A combining form denoting *creatures having* (so many or such) *feet*, used in names of phyla, orders, classes, etc., as in Arthro*poda*, which correspond to adjectives ending in *-podous.*
po·dag′ra (pō·dăg′rȧ; pŏd′ȧ·grȧ), *n.* [L., fr. Gr. *podagra*, fr. *pous, podos*, foot + *agra* a catching.] *Med.* Gout.
po′des·ta′ (pō′dĕs·tä′; pō·dĕs′tȧ), *n.* [It. *podestà*, fr. L. *potestas* power, magistracy.] In Italy, any of several public officers; specif.: **a** *Hist.* A chief magistrate in medieval times, with wide powers. **b** A subordinate magistrate in some towns. **c** Under the Fascist government, a chief executive of a commune (except Rome and Naples).
podg′y (pŏj′ĭ), *adj.;* PODG′I·ER (-ĭ·ẽr); PODG′I·EST. Fat and short; pudgy. — **podg′i·ness**, *n.*
po·di′a·try (pō·dī′ȧ·trĭ), *n.* [Gr. *pous, podos*, foot + *-iatry.*] *Med.* The study and treatment of disorders of the foot. — **po·di′a·trist** (-trĭst), *n.*
po′di·um (pō′dĭ·ŭm), *n.; pl.* PODIA (-ȧ). [L., fr. Gr. *podion*, dim. of *pous, podos*, foot.] **1.** *Arch.* A low wall serving as a foundation or terrace wall. In *Archaeol.*, esp.: **a** The dwarf wall around the arena of an amphitheater, from the top of which the seats began. **b** The masonry under the stylobate of a temple. **2.** A dais, as for an orchestra conductor.
-po′di·um (-pō′dĭ·ŭm). [NL. See PODIUM.] A combining form meaning *a footlike part*, as in mono*podium.*
pod′o·phyl′lin (pŏd′ō·fĭl′ĭn), *n.* [From *Podophyllum*, generic name of the May apple, fr. Gr. *pous, podos*, foot + *phyllon* leaf.] A bitter purgative resin extracted from the rootstalk of the May apple.
-podous. [Gr. *pous, podos*, foot.] A combining form meaning *footed*, used chiefly in adjectives corresponding to nouns ending in *-poda.*
pod′sol (pŏd′sŏl), **pod′zol** (-zŏl), *n.* [Russ., salting, saltness, ult. fr. *sol′* salt.] White or gray ashlike soil, typically occurring in northern Russia. — **pod·sol′ic** (pŏd·sŏl′ĭk), **pod·zol′ic** (-zŏl′ĭk), *adj.*
Po′dunk (pō′dŭngk), *n. U.S.* An imaginary small town taken as typical of placid dullness and lack of contact with the progress of the world.
po′em (pō′ĕm; -ĭm), *n.* [F. *poème*, fr. L. *poëma*, fr. Gr. *poēma, poiēma*, fr. *poiein, poein*, to make, compose, write, especially in verse.] **1.** A composition in verse, characterized by imagination and poetic diction; a piece of poetry; — opposed to *prose.* **2.** Any composition marked by qualities ascribed to poetry, as elevation or beauty.
poe·nol′o·gy (pē·nŏl′ō·jĭ). Var. of PENOLOGY.
po′e·sy (pō′ē·sĭ; -zĭ), *n.* [OF. *poësie*, fr. L. *poesis*, fr. Gr. *poiēsis.*] **1.** *Poetic.* Poetic works collectively; also, a poem. **2.** *Archaic.* Poetry as one of the arts; poetic writing in theory or in practice. **3.** *Hist.* A short motto, as on a ring.
po′et (pō′ĕt; -ĭt), *n.* [OF. *poëte*, fr. L. *poëta*, fr. Gr. *poiētēs.*] **1.** One who makes or composes verses; specif., a composer of poetry; a writer of poems. **2.** One endowed with great imaginative, emotional, or intuitive power and capable of expressing his conceptions, passion, or intuitions in appropriate language. — **po′et·ess**, *n.*
‖**po·e′ta na′sci·tur, non fit** (pō·ē′tȧ năs′ĭ·tẽr, nŏn fĭt). [L.] The poet is born, not made.
po′et·as′ter (pō′ĕt·ăs′tẽr; pō′ĕt·ăs′tẽr; -ĭt-), *n.* [NL. See 2d -ASTER.] A versifier rather than a true poet.
po·et′ic (pō·ĕt′ĭk), *adj.* **1.** Of, pertaining to, or according to the practice of a poet or poets; befitting a poet; as, *poetic* inspiration. **2.** Of, pertaining to, peculiar or proper to, or in the nature or manner of poetry; as, *poetic* diction. **3.** Written or composed in verse; as, *poetic* works.
po·et′i·cal (-ĭ·kăl), *adj.* **1.** Poetic. **2.** Beyond or above the truth of history or nature; fictitious; idealized; also, of writers, fanciful; highly imaginative.
po·et′i·cal·ly, *adv.* of POETIC, POETICAL.
poetic, *or* **poetical, justice.** The effective operation of justice with due punishing of vice and due reward of virtue; — so named by Thomas Rymer (1678) who held that the poet should observe the constant order or law of nature and of Providence.
poetic license. See LICENSE, *n.*, 3.
po·et′ics (pō·ĕt′ĭks), *n.;* see -ICS. Also **po·et′ic** (-ĭk). A treatise on poetry as an art; a theory of poetry; sometimes, specif., versification as a subject of study.
po′et·ize (pō′ĕt·īz; pō′ĭt-), *v. i.* To make or compose poetry. — *v. t.* To make poetical; to give a poetic character to. — **po′et·iz′er** (-īz′ẽr), *n.*
poet laureate; *pl.* POETS LAUREATE. **1.** Orig., a poet worthy of bearing the Muses' crown of laurel. **2.** In England, a title given to a poet appointed by the sovereign to be a member of the royal household, his duty being to compose odes, etc., for court and national occasions. **3.** One popularly regarded by a locality or country as its most eminent poet.
po′et·ry (pō′ĕt·rĭ; pō′ĭt-), *n.* [OF. *poëterie, poëtrie*, fr. ML. *poetria.* See POET.] **1.** The art or work of poets; the embodiment in appropriate language of beautiful or high thought, imagination, or emotion, the language being rhythmical, usually metrical, and adapted to arouse the feelings and imagination; metrical composition; also, poetical writings; poems collectively; verse. **2.** Something poetical; poetical quality, spirit, etc.
pog′a·mog′gan (pŏg′ȧ·mŏg′ăn), *n.* [Of Algonquian origin.] A club, used by Indians of the Great Lakes and Plains regions as a weapon or for ceremonial purposes.
po·go′ni·a (pō·gō′nĭ·ȧ; 58), *n.* [NL., fr. Gr. *pōgōn* beard.] *Bot.* Any of a genus (*Pogonia*) of terrestrial orchids of the North Temperate Zone, including the snakemouth. They have terminal solitary flowers with a crested lip.
pog′o·nip (pŏg′ō·nĭp), *n.* [Paiute.] *Western U.S.* A dense winter fog, containing frozen particles, formed in the deep valleys of the Sierra Nevadas.
po·grom′ (pō·grŏm′; pō′grŭm; pŏg′rŭm), *n.* [Russ., devastation.] An organized massacre of helpless people, as orig. of Jews in Russia.
po′gy (pō′gĭ; pŏg′ĭ), *n.; pl.* -GIES (-gĭz). The menhaden.
po′i (pō′ē; poi), *n.* [Hawaiian.] A native Hawaiian food prepared from the taro root pounded to a paste and allowed to ferment.

-poi·et'ic (-poi·ĕt'ĭk). [Gr. *poiētikos*, fr. *poiein* to make.] A combining form meaning *making*, used to denote *productive*, *formative*, as in hemato*poietic*.

poign'an·cy (poin'yăn·sĭ; -ăn·sĭ), *n.; pl.* -CIES (-sĭz). Quality or state of being poignant; a poignant instance.

poign'ant (-yănt; -ănt), *adj.* [OF., pres. part. of *poindre* to sting, fr. L. *pungere*.] **1.** Keen; piercingly effective; also, pungent. **2.** Painfully moving; affecting; touching. — **Syn.** See PUNGENT: MOVING. — **poign'ant·ly**, *adv.*

poi'ki·lo·ther'mic (poi'kĭ·lō·thûr'mĭk), *adj.* [Fr. Gr. *poikilos* many-colored.] Also **poi'ki·lo·ther'mal** (-măl). = COLD-BLOODED, 1.

poi'lu' (pwä'lü'; pwä'lōō), *n.* [F., lit., hairy, hence, physical man, fr. *poil* hair, fr. L. *pilus;* — as slang in World War I perh. suggested by the uncut hair of men at the front.] Strictly, a first-line French soldier of World War I; loosely, any French soldier.

poin'ci·an'a (poin'sĭ·ăn'*ȧ*; pwôN'-; pŏn'-), *n.* [NL., after M. de *Poinci*, a governor of the French West Indies.] **1.** *Bot.* Any of a small genus (*Poinciana*) of ornamental tropical trees or shrubs of the senna family, having bright-orange or red flowers. **2.** The ***royal poinciana*** (*Delonix regia*), a tropical tree, with immense racemes of scarlet and orange flowers, flat woody pods, and twice-pinnate leaves.

poind (poind; *Scot. also* pünd; pĭnd), *v. t.* [AS. *pyndan* to pen up.] *Scot.* **a** To distrain. **b** To impound. — *n. Scot.* Distraint.

poin·set'ti·a (poin·sĕt'ĭ·*ȧ*; -sĕt'*ȧ*), *n.* [NL., after J. R. *Poinsett* (1779–1851), of South Carolina.] *Bot.* Any of a genus (*Poinsettia*) of chiefly tropical American herbs or woody plants of the spurge family, having alternate leaves, and cymose inconspicuous green flowers, subtended by bright-colored involucral leaves.

point (point), *n.* [From OF. *point* a prick, place, moment, and fr. OF. *pointe* a sharp point, a pointed object (fr. LL. *puncta*); both fr. L. *pungere, punctum*, to prick.] **1.** The tapering end of anything pointed. Specif.: **a** The tapering end of a tract of land. **b** *pl.* Of a horse, the extremities. **2.** Hence, anything having a tapering end, as a dagger, a needle. **3. a** A separate part; item. **b** A physical characteristic of an animal, esp. one used as a standard in judging its breeding. **4.** Of immaterial things, the most prominent feature; as, the *point* of a story; (with *the*) the essential matter; the precise thing; — hence, ***in point***, pertinent; aptly illustrating; as, a case *in point*. **5.** A unit, as in the scoring of a game or test; specif., a unit in a rationing system. **6.** A place having definite position but no extent in space; a spot. **7.** *Archaic.* A state, as of body or health. **8.** A thing aimed at or striven for; end; object. **9.** A position or condition attained; a step; stage; as, boiling *point*. Specif.: **a** *Rare.* A crisis in affairs. **b** The exact time of occurring; as, the *point* of death. **c** Culmination. **d** End; conclusion. **e** A decision; resolution. **10.** A dot used in writing or printing. **11.** *Costume.* A tie or string ending with an aglet and used in the 16th and 17th centuries to join parts of a costume, as doublet and hose. **12.** *Educ.* A unit of academic credit. **13.** *Elec.* Either of two platinum or tungsten pieces of a distributor, through which the circuit is made or broken. **14.** *Exchanges.* A recognized unit in quoting prices of stocks, shares, and various commodities, varying with the commodity. In stocks, in the United States, one point ordinarily means $1 a share. **15.** *Games & Sports.* **a** In various games, a position of a certain player, or, by extension, the player himself. **b** In boxing, the tip of the chin. **16.** *Hunting.* **a** The attitude assumed by a pointer or setter dog when he finds game. **b** *Colloq.* A spot to which a straight run is made; hence, a cross-country run. **17.** *Lacemaking.* **a** Strictly, needle-point lace. **b** Loosely, any handmade lace. **18.** *Math.* An undefined geometric element concerning which it is postulated that at least two exist and that two suffice to determine a line. **19.** *Mil.* A small group of men thrown out before an advance guard or behind a rear guard on the march. **20.** *Music.* A short strain, phrase, or tune; a signal consisting of such. **21.** *Naut.* One of 32 points of the compass; also, the difference, of 11¼ degrees, between two points of the compass. See COMPASS CARD, *Illust.* **22.** *Philol.* = VOWEL POINT. **23.** *Punctuation.* A stop, as a comma, colon; or, esp., a period. **24.** *Railroads.* **a** *Brit.* A switch. **b** The tip of the angle between two rails in a frog. **25.** *Type Founding.* See POINT SYSTEM, 2. — ***to the point.*** Pertinent; apt; also, concise.

— *v. t.* **1.** To furnish with a point or points; as, to *point* a dart; also, to give point or piquancy to, as to a remark. **2.** To indicate the position of, as with the finger; — esp. with *out*. **3.** To direct (at, to, or upon); to aim; to turn; as, to *point* a gun. **4.** To mark or divide into periods or groups, or to separate by points or dots, as figures, or esp. the decimal fraction from the integral part; — with *off*. **5.** *Furriery.* To insert white hairs into (certain furs, as fox). **6.** *Hunting.* To indicate the presence and place of (game) by a fixed look and position; — said of setters or pointers. **7.** *Masonry.* To scratch out the old mortar from the joints of (a wall) and fill in with new material. **8.** *Philol.* To mark (as Hebrew) with vowel points. **9.** *Punctuation.* To supply with or as with punctuation marks. — *v. i.* **1.** To direct the point of something, as of a finger, to designate an object; also, to hint (at); allude (to); — with *at* or *to*. **2.** To point game. **3.** To face or look; also, to aim; tend. **4.** *Naut.* Of a sailing vessel, to sail more or less close to the wind.

point'-blank', *adv.* [Prob. fr. OF. *de pointe en blanc* directly, *blanc* prob. orig. referring to the white of the target.] In a point-blank manner.

point'-blank' (*see Pron.*, § 2), *adj.* **1.** Aimed directly toward the mark; specif., in gunnery, not having, or not allowing for, an appreciable curve in the trajectory; as, a *point-blank* shot. **2.** Direct; unqualified; blunt; as, a *point-blank* refusal.

‖**point d'ap'pui'** (pwăN' dȧ'pwē'). [F.] Point of support; basis; fulcrum; specif., *Mil.*, a basis of operations.

point'-de·vice' (point'dē·vīs'), *adj.* Also **point'-de·vise'**, **point'-de·vyse'**, etc. [ME. *at point devis*, fr. *at* + *point* point, condition + *devis* exact, careful, OF. *devis* fixed, set.] **1.** *Archaic.* Perfectly correct; very precise or particular. **2.** Dressed, equipped, or constructed to perfection. — *adv. Archaic.* Perfectly; completely.

point duty (point). The duty of a police constable stationed at a particular point, as a street corner or crossing, to regulate traffic.

‖**pointe** (pwăNt), *n.* [F.] *Dancing.* A position of balance on the extreme tip of the toe.

point'ed (poin'tĕd; -tĭd), *adj.* **1.** Having a point or points. **2. a** To the point; pertinent; terse. **b** Aimed at a particular person or persons; hence, very noticeable; conspicuous; marked. — **point'ed·ly**, *adv.* — **point'ed·ness**, *n.*

pointed arch. *Arch.* An arch with a pointed crown, which characterizes the Gothic style, or **pointed style.**

pointed fox. *Furriery.* Red fox dyed and treated to imitate silver fox. See FOX, 1 **a**; cf. POINT, *v. t.*, 5.

point'er (poin'tẽr), *n.* **1.** One who or that which points out; specif.: **a** A rod used to direct attention to something, as an index on a balance. **b** One who aims a gun. **c** A large gun dog of a lean, smooth-haired breed originating in Spain, that hunts by scent. **d** *U. S.* A hint or tip. **2.** *pl.* [*cap.*] *Astron.* The two stars in the Great Bear a line through which points to the North Star. See URSA MAJOR, *Illust.*

Point Four. A United States program of technical aid to the people of underdeveloped areas of the world and encouragement of private investment in business in these areas for raising the standard of living, which was the fourth point proposed in President Truman's inaugural, 1949.

poin'til·lism (pwăn'tĭ·lĭz'm), *n.* [F. *pointillisme.*] *Painting.* A form of divisionism (which see) in which the colors are applied in dots on a white ground and according to a severely systematic plan. See NEOIMPRESSIONISM. — **poin'til·list** (-lĭst), *n.*

point lace (point). Needle point. — **point'-laced'** (-lāst'; 2), *adj.*

point'less (point'lĕs; -lĭs), *adj.* Without a point; wanting point, keenness, or meaning. — **point'less·ly**, *adv.* — **point'less·ness**, *n.*

point of honor. A matter seriously affecting one's honor.

point of order. In parliamentary practice, a question of order or propriety under the rules.

point of view. Relative position or angle from which a thing is seen, a question considered, etc.

points of the compass. The thirty-two points of division in the compass card; the corresponding points by which the circle of the horizon is supposed to be divided, of which the four marking the directions of east, west, north, and south, are called *cardinal points*, and the rest are named from their respective directions, as N. by E., N.N.E., N.E. by N., N.E., etc.

point system. **1.** *Educ.* In some schools and colleges, the system of advancing students in individual subjects by points of credit for each piece of work. **2.** *Type Founding.* A system according to which the various sizes of type bodies, leads, etc., bear a fixed and simple relation to one another. The point system is based upon the pica, or 12-point, body, which when set solid makes 6 vertical lines (or 72 points) to the inch. This body is divided into twelfths, called *points*. The point size of any type may be determined by dividing 72 by the number of lines per column inch. Thus, type making 12 lines per column inch is 6 point; 9 lines, 8 point. The value of the point is .013837 inch, or nearly 1/72 inch. See TYPE.

poise (poiz), *v. t.* [OF. *peser* to weigh, balance, il *peise*, il *poise*, he weighs, fr. L. *pensare*, v. intens. fr. *pendere* to weigh.] **1.** *Now Rare.* To weigh. **2. a** To steady by weighting; to ballast. **b** To distribute the weight of properly; to balance exactly. **3.** To carry, maintain, or support in equilibrium; to suspend; — often reflexive. — *v. i.* To hang in equilibrium; to be balanced or suspended.

— *n.* [OF. *pois*, fr. earlier *peis*, fr. L. *pensum* a portion weighed out.] **1.** *Obs.* **a** Heaviness; weight; figuratively, importance. **b** A weight. **2.** Balance; equilibrium; stability. **3.** The bearing of the body or head; carriage. **4.** Suspension of motion due to an exact balance; hence, suspense; indecision. — **Syn.** See TACT.

poi'son (poi'z'n), *n.* [OF., fr. L. *potio* a drink, potion, a poisonous draft, fr. *potare* to drink.] **1.** Any agent which, introduced into an organism, may chemically produce an injurious or deadly effect; as, the *poison*, or venom, of a snake. **2.** That which taints or destroys moral purity, character, or the public welfare. — *v. t. & i.* **1.** To infect or impregnate with poison; as, to *poison* food. **2.** To injure or kill by poison. **3.** To exert a baneful influence on; to corrupt; pervert. — *adj.* That poisons or envenoms; venomous.

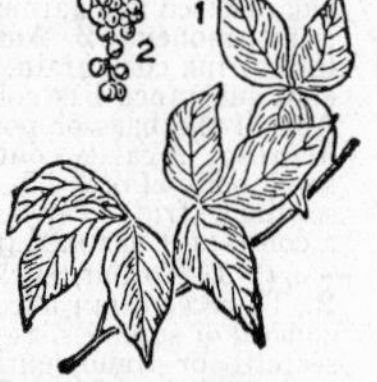

Poison Ivy. 1 Leaves; 2 Berries. (1/6)

poison dogwood *or* **elder.** Poison sumac.

poi'son·er (poi'z'n·ẽr), *n.* One who or that which poisons.

poison gas. A poisonous gas. See GAS, *n.*, 3.

poison hemlock. See HEMLOCK, 1.

poison ivy. Any of several American sumacs (genus *Toxicodendron*, esp. *T. radicans* and *T. pubescens*) of somewhat vinelike habit, with herbage poisonous to touch.

poison oak. **a** Poison sumac. **b** Any poison ivy of bushy habit.

poi'son·ous (poi'z'n·ŭs), *adj.* Having the properties or effects of poison; venomous. — **poi'son·ous·ly**, *adv.*

poison sumac. An American sumac (*Toxicodendron vernix*) containing an oil which renders the herbage very poisonous to touch. It is a smooth shrub growing in swamps, with greenish-white berries.

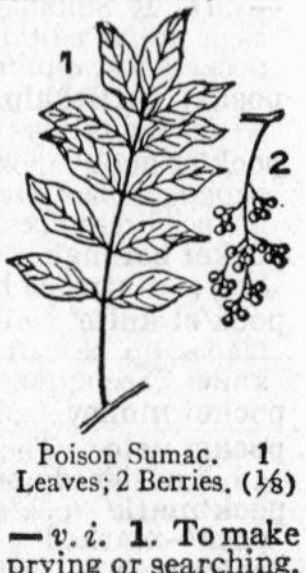

Poison Sumac. 1 Leaves; 2 Berries. (1/8)

poke (pōk), *n.* [Abbr. fr. *pocan*, of Amer. Indian origin.] Pokeweed.

poke (pōk), *n.* [ME., fr. OF. *poke; poque.*] **1.** *Now Local or Dial.* A bag; a sack. **2. a** *Scot.* A beggar's wallet. **b** *Archaic & Dial.* A pocket.

poke, *n.* [From POKE, *v.*] **1.** A projecting brim or front of a woman's bonnet. **2.** Short for POKE BONNET.

poke, *v. t.* [ME. *poken.*] **1.** To thrust or prod, as with one's arm, a stick, etc.; stir or arouse by or as by such action; as, to *poke* a dying fire. **2.** To thrust forward obtrusively or in annoying familiarity; to stick out. Hence, to ***poke one's nose into others' affairs***, to act the busybody. — *v. i.* **1.** To make thrusts with a stick, sword, or the like. **2.** To go prying or searching. **3.** To live pokily; to potter; dawdle. **4.** To project or stand out. — ***poke fun*** (***at***). To ridicule or banter. — *n.* A poking; a jog; nudge.

poke'ber'ry (pōk'bĕr'ĭ; -bẽr·ĭ), *n.* [See 1st POKE.] The berry of the pokeweed; also, the plant.

poke bonnet. A bonnet with a projecting brim or front.

pok'er (pōk'ẽr), *n.* That which is used in poking, as a metal rod for stirring a fire.

po'ker (pō'kẽr), *n.* Any of various card games in which players bet on the value of their hands to win a pool. In ***draw poker***, the principal game, each player, after contributing his ante, may discard any of his cards and receive (***draw***) from the dealer an equal number. In ***stud poker*** all cards but the first round are dealt face up and the betting usually begins after the second round. The rank of the usual poker hands, in ascending sequence, is as follows: pair, two pairs, three of a

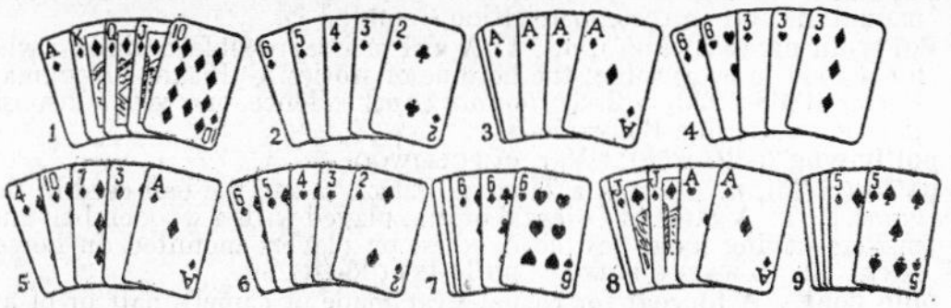

Poker Hands, in descending value: 1 Royal Flush; 2 Straight Flush; 3 Four of a Kind; 4 Full House; 5 Flush; 6 Straight; 7 Three of a Kind; 8 Two Pairs; 9 One Pair.

kind, straight, flush, full house, four of a kind, straight flush, royal flush.

po′ker face. *Colloq., U.S.* An immobile, inscrutable face or facial expression characteristic of an expert poker player.

poke′root′ (pōk′rōōt′; 85), *n.* The pokeweed.

poke′weed′ (-wēd′), *n.* [See 1st POKE.] A coarse American perennial herb (*Phytolacca americana*) with racemose white flowers and dark purple juicy berries. The root is poisonous but the young shoots are sometimes eaten.

pok′y, poke′y (pōk′ĭ), *adj.;* POK′I·ER (-ĭ·ẽr); POK′I·EST. **a** Small and cramped; as, a *poky* little room. **b** Shabby; mean; also, dull; tedious; dowdy.

Po′lack (pō′lăk), *n.* A Pole. *Shak.* (*Hamlet* I. i. 63).

Po′land Chi′na (pō′lănd). An animal of an American breed of large swine.

po′lar (pō′lẽr), *adj.* [ML. *polaris*, fr. L. *polus*.] **1.** Of or pertaining to a pole, as of a sphere, magnet, etc. **2.** Of, pertaining to, or coming from a geographical pole or poles; as, *polar* regions. **3.** Of, pert. to, or like a polestar; guiding; as, a *polar* principle. **4.** *Chem.* Designating, pert. to, or characterized by a union of atoms in which the chemical bond is electrostatic attraction between oppositely charged particles.

polar bear. See 2d BEAR, 1.

polar body, cell, *or* **globule.** *Biol.* One of the minute cells which separate from the egg during its maturation.

polar circle. *Astron. & Geog.* Either the Arctic or the Antarctic Circle. See ARCTIC CIRCLE; ANTARCTIC CIRCLE.

polar distance. See CODECLINATION.

po′lar·im′e·ter (pō′lẽr·ĭm′ē·tẽr), *n.* [L. *polaris* polar + *-meter*.] *Optics.* **a** An instrument for determining the amount of polarization of light, or the proportion of polarized light, in a partially polarized ray. **b** A polariscope for measuring the amount of rotation of the plane of polarization, esp. by liquids. See POLARIZATION, 2.

Po·la′ris (pō·lā′rĭs; -lăr′ĭs), *n.* [NL.] *Astron.* The star Alpha (α) Ursae Minoris; the North Star. See URSA MINOR, *Illust.*

po·lar′i·scope (pō·lăr′ĭ·skōp), *n.* *Optics.* An instrument for studying the properties of, or examining substances in, polarized light.

po·lar′i·ty (-tĭ), *n.* **1.** The quality or condition inherent in a body which exhibits opposite, or contrasted, properties or powers, in opposite, or contrasted, parts or directions; the having of poles; polarization. **2.** Particular state (positive or negative) with reference to the two poles or to polarization.

po′lar·i·za′tion (pō′lẽr·ĭ·zā′shŭn; -ī·zā′shŭn), *n.* **1.** Act of polarizing; state of being polarized, or of having poles. **2.** *Optics.* The act or process of affecting light or other radiation in such a way that the vibrations assume a definite form; also, the state of light so affected. In ordinary light the vibrations are supposed to be in all directions perpendicular to the ray; in polarized light, the paths of the vibrations (all in a plane perpendicular to the ray) may be straight lines, circles, or ellipses. The light is then said to be ***plane-polarized, circularly polarized,*** or ***elliptically polarized*** and the phenomenon is called ***plane polarization, circular polarization,*** or ***elliptical*** (*or* ***elliptic***) ***polarization,*** respectively. The ***angle of polarization,*** *or* ***polarizing angle,*** is that angle at which light reflected from a transparent substance is almost completely plane-polarized. **3.** *Elec.* An effect produced on the electrodes of a cell by the deposition on them of the gases liberated by the current.

po′lar·ize (pō′lẽr·īz), *v. t.* [F. *polariser*.] **1.** To give polarity to; to bring into a state of polarization. **2.** To fix the significance of. — **po′lar·iz′a·ble** (-īz′á·b'l), *adj.* — **po′lar·iz′er** (-īz′ẽr), *n.*

polar lights. The aurora borealis, or aurora australis.

po·lar′o·graph (pō·lăr′ō·grăf; pō′lẽr-), *n.* [*polarization* + *-graph*.] *Physical Chem.* An instrument for making records (**po·lar′o·grams** [-grămz]) of the degree of electrical polarization in electrolytes, used esp. in microanalysis. — **po·lar′o·graph′ic** (-grăf′ĭk), *adj.*

Po′lar·oid (pō′lẽr·oid), *n.* A trade-mark applied to light-polarizing material, comprising in one form oriented suspensions of dichroic particles in a light-transmitting medium, used esp. in eyeglasses and lamps to prevent glare, and in various optical devices.

polar valence. *Physical Chem.* = ELECTROVALENCE.

pol′der (pŏl′dẽr), *n.* [D.] A tract of low land reclaimed from the sea, or other body of water, by dikes, dams, etc.

pole (pōl), *n.* [AS. *pāl*, fr. L. *palus*.] **1.** A long slender piece of wood or timber, or, by extension, of metal; as, a telegraph *pole*. **2.** A wooden shaft extending from the front axle of a vehicle between the wheel horses, by which the vehicle is held back; a tongue. **3.** A measuring stick; also, a measure of length or surface (see MEASURE, *Tables* 1, 3, & 4). — *v. t.* To act upon with a pole; impel or push by a pole or poles, as a boat.

pole (pōl), *n.* [OF. *pole*, fr. L. *polus*, fr. Gr. *polos* a pivot, pole.] **1.** Either extremity of an axis of a sphere, esp. of the earth's axis. The two opposite points of the celestial sphere where it is pierced by the earth's axis extended are called the ***celestial poles.*** **2.** *Biol.* **a** In organisms or cells, esp. egg cells, either of two morphologically or physiologically differentiated areas at opposite ends of an axis. **b** A point on a cell where an axis is regarded as ending, as at the origin of a nerve cell process. **3.** *Elec.* **a** One of the two terminals of an electric cell, battery, or dynamo. **b** One of the points of a magnet at which its magnetic attraction for iron filings seems to be concentrated.

Pole, *n.* [G. *Pole, Polen* Poland.] A native or inhabitant of Poland.

pole′ax′, pole′axe′ (pōl′ăks′), *n.* [ME. *pollax, polax.* See POLL head; AX.] A battle-ax, originally long-handled, often with a hook or spike opposite the blade; also, a similar ax used in slaughtering cattle. — *v. t.* To attack, strike, or fell with or as with a poleax.

pole bean. Any long-stemmed variety of bean usually trained on poles, as the scarlet runner.

pole′cat′ (-kăt′), *n.;* see PLURAL, *Note,* 3. [ME. *polcat*, lit., poultry cat (it preys on poultry), fr. OF. *pole, poule,* fowl, hen.] **a** A European carnivorous mammal (*Mustela putorius*), of which the ferret is considered a domesticated variety. **b** *U.S.* A skunk.

pole horse. A horse harnessed beside the pole.

pole jump. = POLE VAULT. — **pole′-jump′,** *v. i.* — **pole jumper.**

po·lem′ic (pō·lĕm′ĭk), *adj.* Also **po·lem′i·cal** (-ĭ·kăl). [Gr *polemikos* warlike, fr. *polemos* war.] Of the nature of, pertaining to, or involving controversy; controversial. — *n.* **1.** A polemic argument. **2.** An aggressive controversialist; disputant. — **po·lem′i·cal·ly,** *adv.*

po·lem′i·cist (-ĭ·sĭst), **pol′e·mist** (pŏl′ē·mĭst), *n.* One skilled in or given to polemics.

po·lem′ics (pō·lĕm′ĭks), *n.;* see -ICS. Art or practice of disputation or controversy; specif., polemic theology, which has for its object refutation of errors.

pol′e·mo′ni·a′ceous (pŏl′ē·mō′nĭ·ā′shŭs), *adj.* [Gr. *polemōnion*, a kind of plant.] *Bot.* Belonging to the phlox family (Polemoniaceae). See PHLOX.

pole plate. *Arch.* A horizontal timber on the tie beams of a roof and receiving the ends of the rafters. It differs from the *plate* in not resting on the wall. See ROOF, *Illust.*

pol′er (pōl′ẽr), *n.* One who or that which poles; specif.: **a** A pole horse; a wheeler. **b** One who poles a boat.

poles of cold. In meteorology, places where the winter cold is the most intense, usually in the interior of a continent, as Verkhoyansk (a minimum of −90° registered) or Oimyakon in Soviet Russia in Asia, or Fort Conger on Ellesmere Island.

pole′star′ (pōl′stär′), *n.* **1.** The North Star. See URSA MINOR, *Illust.* **2.** Figuratively: **a** A directing principle. **b** A lodestar.

pole vault. A vault or vaulting with the aid of a pole; specif., *Athletics,* a field event in which such vaulting is performed for height. — **pole′-vault′,** *v. i.* — **pole vaulter.** — **pole vaulting.**

po·lice′ (pō·lēs′; *dial. or humorous* pō′lēs, -lĭs), *n.* [F., fr. L. *politia* government, administration, fr. Gr. *politeia*, fr. *politēs* citizen, fr. *polis* city.] **1.** The internal organization or regulation of a state; esp. such regulation with respect to matters affecting the comfort, health, morals, safety, or prosperity of the public. **2. a** The department of government charged with enforcing law and order, now esp. with respect to the prevention, detection, and prosecution of public nuisances, crimes, etc. **b** The organized force of civil officials in this department, esp., as a collective *pl.*, the police officers or constabulary of a town, city, etc. **3.** *Mil.* **a** In the U. S. Army, the soldiers detailed for police duty. **b** The act or process of putting in order a camp or garrison. — (pō·lēs′), *v. t.* **1.** To maintain law and order in (a country). **2.** To guard or keep in order by policemen, police boats, etc. **3.** To make clean and put in order, as a military camp.

police court. A court of record having jurisdiction over various minor offenses and power to bind over for trial in a superior court or for the grand jury persons accused of more serious offenses.

police dog. A dog, specif. one of wolflike appearance, trained to assist police in their work.

po·lice′man (pō·lēs′măn), *n.* A member of a body of police.

police power. The power of the state to protect the public against the abuse of individual liberty.

pol′i·clin′ic (pŏl′ĭ·klĭn′ĭk), *n.* [G. *poliklinik*.] *Med.* A dispensary or department of a hospital treating outpatients. Cf. POLYCLINIC.

pol′i·cy (pŏl′ĭ·sĭ), *n.; pl.* POLICIES (-sĭz). [OF. *policie*, fr. L. *politia*, fr. Gr. *politeia.* See POLICE.] **1.** *Now Rare.* Government; the science of government. **2.** Prudence or wisdom in the management of affairs; sagacity; shrewdness. **3.** Management or procedure based primarily on material interest, rather than on higher principles; hence, worldly wisdom. **4.** A settled course adopted and followed by a government, institution, body, or individual.

pol′i·cy, *n.* [F. *police*, fr. It. *polizza*, fr. ML. *apodixa* a receipt, fr. Gr. *apodeixis* a showing forth.] **1.** A certificate of insurance; any writing whereby a contract of insurance is made. **2.** A method of gambling by betting that certain numbers will be drawn in a lottery.

pol′i·cy·hold′er (-hōl′dẽr), *n.* A person to whom an insurance policy has been granted.

policy racket. [See 2d POLICY, 2.] = NUMBERS POOL.

po′li·o (pō′lĭ·ō; pŏl′ĭ·ō), *n.* Short for *acute anterior poliomyelitis*, or infantile paralysis. See POLIOMYELITIS.

po′li·o·my′e·li′tis (pō′lĭ·ō·mī′ĕ·lī′tĭs; pŏl′ĭ·ō-), *n.* [NL., fr. Gr. *polios* gray + *myelitis*.] *Med.* Inflammation of the gray matter of the spinal cord. It occurs esp. in children, and the anterior columns of gray matter are usually affected. ***acute anterior poliomyelitis*** is known as *infantile paralysis* (which see).

-polis. A combining form, Greek *-polis*, from *polis*, meaning *city*, as in cosmo*polis*.

pol′ish (pŏl′ĭsh), *n.* **1.** Act or process of polishing. **2.** A smooth, glossy surface; a gloss or luster. **3. a** Refinement; culture. **b** Finish; perfecting touches. **4.** A preparation used to produce a gloss; as, shoe *polish*. — *v. t.* [OF. *polir*, fr. L. *polire*.] **1.** To make smooth and glossy, usually by friction; to give luster to. **2.** To smooth, soften, or refine in manners, style, etc. **3.** To transform or eliminate by polishing; — with *away, into, out,* etc. — *v. i.* To become smooth or glossy, as from or through friction. — **pol′ish·er** (-ẽr), *n.*

Pol′ish (pōl′ĭsh), *adj.* Of or pert. to Poland, its inhabitants, or their language. — *n.* The language of the Poles, a western Slavic tongue using the Roman alphabet. See INDO-EUROPEAN LANGUAGES, *Table.*

Po·lit′bu·ro, *n.* Also **Po·lit′bu·reau** (pō·lĭt′bū·rō). [Russ. *politicheskoe* political + *byuro* bureau.] The inner executive committee or controlling body of the Russian Communist party, and the bureau of foreign Communist propaganda.

po·lite′ (pō·līt′), *adj.* [L. *politus*, past part. of *polire* to polish.] **1.** Polished, refined, or cultivated. Specif.: **a** Of, pertaining to, or characteristic of highly cultivated persons, classes, or races; — now chiefly in phrases, as: **polite society,** the **polite languages** *or* **arts, polite learning, polite letters. b** Of a person, cultivated; urbane; polished; courteous; versed in usages of polite society. **2.** Marked by courtesy, good breeding, or tact. — **Syn.** See CIVIL. — **po·lite′ly,** *adv.* — **po·lite′ness,** *n.*

pol′i·tesse′ (pŏl′ĭ·tĕs′; *F.* pō′lē′tĕs′), *n.* [F.] Formal politeness; decorousness.

pol′i·tic (pŏl′ĭ·tĭk), *adj.* [OF. *politique*, fr. L. *politicus* political, fr. Gr. *politikos* of the citizens, fr. *politēs* citizen.] **1.** Of or pertaining to civil government; political; — now *Rare*, except in the *body politic* (which see). **2.** Sagacious in promoting a policy; ingenious in statecraft; also, of measures, plans, etc., shrewdly contrived, esp. with regard to self-interest; expedient. **3.** Artful in address or procedure; worldly-wise. — **Syn.** See EXPEDIENT; SUAVE.

po·lit′i·cal (pō·lĭt′ĭ·kăl), *adj.* **1.** Of or pertaining to polity, or politics, or the conduct of government; as, *political* theories. **2.** Having, or conforming to, a polity, or settled system of administration. **3.** Of or pertaining to the organization or action of individuals, parties, or interests that seek to control the appointment or action of those who manage the affairs of a state. **4.** Of or pertaining to politicians in their partisan activities. — **po·lit′i·cal·ly**, *adv.*

political economist. One who is versed in, or a student of, political economy; esp., a teacher of, or writer on, economics.

political economy Economics (which see).

political science. That branch of the social sciences dealing with the organization and government of states. — **political scientist.**

pol′i·ti′cian (pŏl′ĭ·tĭsh′ăn), *n.* **1.** One versed or experienced in the science of government. **2.** One addicted to, or actively engaged in, politics as managed by parties; often, one primarily interested in political offices or the profits from them as a source of private gain.

po·lit′i·cize (pō·lĭt′ĭ·sīz), *v. i.* To discuss or take part in politics. — *v. t.* To bring within the sphere of politics.

pol′i·tic·ly (pŏl′ĭ·tĭk·lĭ), *adv.* In a politic manner.

po·lit′i·co (pō·lĭt′ĭ·kō), *n.; pl.* POLITICOS (-kōz), *sometimes* POLITICOES. [It. *politico* or Sp. *político*.] A politician.

po·lit′i·co- (pō·lĭt′ĭ·kō-). [Gr. *politikos* civic, political.] A combining form meaning *politically, political and*, as in:

politico-economic · politico-geographical · politico-scientific
politico-economical · politico-religious · politico-social

pol′i·tics (pŏl′ĭ·tĭks), *n.;* see -ICS. **1.** The science and art of government; political science. **2.** The theory or practice of managing affairs of public policy or of political parties; hence, political affairs, principles, or the like; in a bad sense, dishonest management to secure the success of political candidates or parties. **3.** Political affairs viewed as a profession, interest, or the like; as, to enter *politics*.

pol′i·ty (pŏl′ĭ·tĭ), *n.; pl.* -TIES (-tĭz). [OF. *politie*, fr. L. *politia*. See 1st POLICY.] **1.** Form or constitution of the government of a state, or of any institution or organization similarly administered. **2.** A politically organized community; a state.

pol′ka (pō(l)′kȧ; *Brit.* pŏl′kȧ), *n.* [F., prob. ult. fr. Pol. *Polka* a Polish woman.] A vivacious hopping dance of Bohemian origin performed by two persons; the dance tune in 2/4 measure, with the third eighth note (second beat) accented. — *v. i.* To dance the polka.

polka dot. In textile fabrics, a pattern of many round dots regularly distributed.

poll (pōl), *n.* [Gr. *hoi polloi* the many, the rabble.] *Camb. Univ., Eng.* With *the*, the students who "go up" for, or obtain a **poll degree**, that is, a degree without honors.

poll (pōl), *n.* [ME. *pol, polle*, fr. MD. *polle*.] **1.** The head; the skull; esp., the back, or back and top, of the head; also, the nape of the neck. **2.** The broad or flat end of a hammer or similar tool. Cf. HAMMER, *Illust.* **3. a** The casting or recording of the votes of a body of persons. **b** The result of the counting of such votes; the number of such votes cast. **c** The place where the votes are cast or recorded; — in U. S. *pl.* **d** A register or list of the electors. **4.** = POLL TAX. **5.** A questioning or canvassing of persons, usually selected at random or by quota from various groups, for obtaining information or opinions, esp. to be analyzed, as for reporting trends in public opinion. — *v. t.* **1.** To cut off or cut short the hair, wool, or the like of; to shear; clip; also, to cut off or cut short (the hair, etc.). **2. a** To cut off the head or top of, as a tree or plant; to pollard. **b** To cut off or cut short the horns of (cattle). **3.** To enter, as polls or persons, in a list or register; to enroll, as in order to count; specif., to receive and register the votes of; as, the county was *polled* on the question. **4.** To register or deposit, as a vote; also, to elicit, as votes or voters. **5.** To canvass in a poll. — *v. i.* To cast one's vote at a poll.

pol′lack (pŏl′ăk), **pol′lock** (-ŭk), *n.;* see PLURAL, *Note*, 6. Any of several gadoid fishes (genera *Pollachius* and *Theragra*), valued as food, including the true pollack (*Pollachius pollachius*) of the Atlantic coast of Europe, an allied species (*P. virens*) called *coalfish*, and the ***Alaska pollack*** (*T. chalcogramma*) of the North Pacific.

pol′lard (pŏl′ērd), *n.* [See POLL, *v.*, POLL head.] **1.** A hornless stag, ox, sheep, goat, or the like. **2.** A tree cut back to the trunk to promote the growth of a dense head of foliage. — **pol′lard**, *v. t.*

polled (pōld), *adj.* **a** Shaved; shorn. **b** Hornless.

poll′ee′ (pōl′ē′), *n.* One who is questioned in a poll.

pol′len (pŏl′ĕn), *n.* [L. *pollen, pollinis*, fine flour, dust.] *Bot.* The mass of microspores in seed plants, usually a fine yellow dust.

pol′lex (pŏl′ĕks), *n.; pl.* POLLICES (-ĭ·sēz). [L., the thumb.] *Anat. & Zool.* The first (preaxial) digit of the forelimb; the thumb.

‖**pol′li·ce ver′so** (pŏl′ĭ·sē vûr′sō). [L.] With thumb turned (down); — the sign by which spectators at Roman gladiatorial combats condemned a vanquished gladiator to death.

pol′li·nate (pŏl′ĭ·nāt), *v. t.* *Bot.* To perform pollination on.

pol′li·na′tion (-nā′shŭn), *n.* *Bot.* The transfer of pollen from the androecium to the gynoecium. See SELF-POLLINATED, CROSS-POLLINATION.

poll′ing (pōl′ĭng), *adj.* **a** That polls. **b** Of or pertaining to the registering or casting of votes; as, a *polling* booth, *polling* clerk.

pol′li·nif′er·ous (pŏl′ĭ·nĭf′ēr·ŭs), *adj.* [L. *pollen, -inis*, pollen + *-ferous*.] **1.** *Bot.* Bearing or producing pollen. **2.** *Zool.* Adapted for the purpose of carrying pollen.

pol·lin′i·um (pŏ·lĭn′ĭ·ŭm), *n.; pl.* -IA (-ȧ). [NL.] *Bot.* A coherent mass of pollen grains, as in the orchid.

pol′li·nize (pŏl′ĭ·nīz), *v. t.* To pollinate.

pol′li·no′sis (pŏl′ĭ·nō′sĭs), *n.* [NL., fr. L. *pollen, -inis*, pollen + *-osis*.] Hay fever.

pol′li·wog (pŏl′ĭ·wŏg), *n.* [ME. *polwigle*.] A tadpole.

pol′lock (pŏl′ŭk). Var. of POLLACK.

poll′ster (pōl′stēr), *n.* One who conducts polls, esp. professionally.

poll tax (pōl). A tax of so much per head, levied usually on every male person over a given age.

pol·lute′ (pŏ·lūt′), *v. t.* [L. *pollutus*, past part. of *polluere* to pollute.] To make or render unclean; to defile; desecrate; profane. — **Syn.** See CONTAMINATE.

pol·lu′tion (pŏ·lū′shŭn), *n.* Act of polluting, or state of being polluted; defilement; impurity.

Pol′lux (pŏl′ŭks), *n.* [L.] **1.** *Gr. Myth.* See DIOSCURI. **2.** A first magnitude star in the constellation Gemini.

Pol′ly·an′na (pŏl′ĭ·ăn′ȧ), *n.* **1.** A girl of irrepressible optimism who finds good in everything, the heroine of stories by Eleanor Hodgman Porter (1868–1920). **2.** [*often not cap.*] Hence, one with a disposition or nature like Pollyanna's.

pol′ly·wog (pŏl′ĭ·wŏg). Var. of POLLIWOG.

po′lo (pō′lō), *n.* [From a Tibetan dialect, prop., the ball used in the game.] **1.** A game of Oriental origin, played with a wooden ball and mallets having long, flexible handles, by players mounted on horseback. **2.** = WATER POLO. — **po′lo·ist** (-lō·ĭst), *n.*

polo coat. A topcoat for casual wear made of camel's hair or of an imitation.

pol′o·naise′ (pŏl′ō·nāz′; pō′lō·nāz′), *n.* **1.** [F., prop. fem. of *polonais* Polish.] A woman's garment, consisting of a waist and drapery in one piece worn over a separate skirt. **2.** A stately Polish dance developed from the promenade, or the music for it in 3/4 measure.

po·lo′ni·um (pŏ·lō′nĭ·ŭm), *n.* [NL., fr. ML. *Polonia* Poland; — from the nationality of Mme. Curie.] *Chem.* A radioelement discovered, by M. and Mme. Curie, in pitchblende, identical with radium F. Symbol, *Po;* at. no., 84; at. wt., 210.

Po·lo′ni·us (-ŭs), *n.* A garrulous old courtier, father of Ophelia and Laertes, in Shakespeare's *Hamlet*.

po′lo shirt (pō′lō). A close-fitting pull-over jersey or shirt of cotton knitwear, with very short sleeves and either folding collar or round collarless neck, originally patterned after the jerseys worn by polo players. Sometimes, also, a T shirt for outer wear; sometimes, also, a sport shirt.

pol′ter·geist′ (pôl′tēr·gīst′), *n.* [G., fr. *polter* noise + *geist* ghost.] A noisy ghost; a spirit assumed as the explanation of rappings and other unexplained noises.

pol·troon′ (pŏl·trōōn′), *n.* [F. *poltron*, fr. It. *poltrone* sluggard, coward, also, idle, lazy, fr. *poltro* bed.] An arrant coward; a craven. — *adj.* Cowardly. — **Syn.** See COWARDLY.

pol·troon′er·y (-ēr·ĭ), *n.* Cowardice; mean pusillanimity.

pol′y- (pŏl′ĭ-). [Gr. *polys*.] A combining form meaning many or much; having or consisting of many; several; sometimes, more than the normal or usual number, as in *poly*dactyl; specif.: **a** *Chem.* (1) An indefinite number more than one, as in *poly*atomic; (2) a polymer of a (specified) compound. **b** *Med.* Affecting many parts, as in *poly*arthritis; also, excessive, as in *poly*phagia.

polyangular	polyconic	polynuclear
polyarchy	polydaemonism	polyphyllous
polyarthritis	polyethnic	polypseudonymous
polyarticular	polylinguist	polyrhythmic
polyatomic	polyneural	polysepalous
polycarpellary	polyneuritis	polyzonal

pol′y·am′ide (-ăm′ĭd; -ĭd), *n.* Also **pol′y·am′id**. *Chem.* A compound characterized by more than one amide group; specif., a polymeric amide, as nylon or a protein.

pol′y·an′drous (-ăn′drŭs), *adj.* **1.** *Bot.* Having 20 or more free hypogynous stamens. **2.** Of or practicing polyandry.

pol′y·an′dry (pŏl′ĭ·ăn′drĭ; pŏl′ĭ·ăn′drĭ), *n.* [Gr. *polyandria*, deriv. of *polys* many + *anēr, andros*, man, male.] **1.** The possession by a woman of more than one husband at the same time. Cf. MONANDRY, 1; POLYGYNY, 1. **2.** *Bot.* State of being polyandrous.

pol′y·an′thus (pŏl′ĭ·ăn′thŭs), *n.* [NL., fr. Gr. *polyanthos* rich in flowers, fr. *polys* many + *anthos* flower.] **a** The oxlip. **b** A narcissus (*Narcissus tazetta*) or a variety of it, having rather small umbeled white or yellow flowers.

pol′y·bas′ic (-bās′ĭk), *adj.* *Chem.* Having more than one hydrogen atom replaceable by basic atoms or radicals; — said of acids.

pol′y·bas′ite (pŏl′ĭ·bās′īt; pō·lĭb′ȧ·sīt), *n.* [G. *polybasit*.] *Mineral.* An iron-colored, metallic-looking ore of silver, consisting chiefly of silver, sulfur, and antimony, Ag_9SbS_6.

pol′y·chae′tous (pŏl′ĭ·kē′tŭs), *adj.* [*poly-* + Gr. *chaitē* hair.] *Zool.* Belonging to an order (Polychaeta) of annelid worms comprising most of the common marine worms having unsegmented, stumplike limbs. — **pol′y·chaete** (pŏl′ĭ·kēt), *adj. & n.*

pol′y·cha′si·um (-kā′zhĭ·ŭm; -zĭ·ŭm), *n.; pl.* -SIA (-ȧ). [NL., fr. *poly-* + Gr. *chasis* division.] *Bot.* A cymose inflorescence in which each relative main axis produces more than two branches. Cf. MONOCHASIUM, DICHASIUM.

pol′y·chro·mat′ic (-krō·măt′ĭk), *adj.* Also **pol′y·chro′mic** (-krō′mĭk). Showing a variety, or a change, of colors; multicolored.

pol′y·chrome (pŏl′ĭ·krōm), *adj.* [F., fr. Gr. *polychrōmos*. See POLY-; CHROMATIC.] Many-colored; specif., printed or painted on a background of various colors.

pol′y·chro′my (-krō′mĭ), *n.* Art of combining different colors, esp. brilliant ones, in an artistic way.

pol′y·clin′ic (-klĭn′ĭk), *n.* *Med.* A clinic treating diseases of many sorts, or a hospital for all kinds of diseases.

pol′y·con′ic pro·jec′tion (-kŏn′ĭk). *Map Making.* A projection of the earth's surface, or a part of it, in which each narrow section is projected on a cone touching the sphere along this zone, the cone surfaces being then unrolled.

pol′y·cot′y·le′don (-kŏt′ĭ·lē′dŭn), *n.* Also **pol′y·cot′yl** (-kŏt′ĭl). [NL.] *Bot.* A plant having more than two cotyledons, as the pine and other conifers. — **pol′y·cot′y·le′don·ous** (-lē′dŭn·ŭs; -lĕd′ŭn·ŭs), *adj.*

pol′y·dac′tyl, pol′y·dac′tyle (-dăk′tĭl), *adj.* Having several or many digits, esp. more than usual. — *n.* A polydactyl animal. — **pol′y·dac′tyl·ism** (-tĭ·lĭz′m), *n.*

pol′y·dac′ty·lous (-dăk′tĭ·lŭs), *adj.* Polydactyl.

pol′y·eth′yl·ene (-ĕth′ĭ·lēn), *n.* *Chem.* A polymer of ethylene; specif., any of a group of light thermoplastic synthetic resins used for insulating, etc.

po·lyg′a·la (pō·lĭg′ȧ·lȧ), *n.* [L., milkwort, fr. Gr. *polygalon*, fr. *polys* much + *gala* milk.] Any of a genus (*Polygala*) of herbs and shrubs, the milkworts, having many-colored flowers with the three petals united below into a tube. — **pol′y·ga·la′ceous** (pŏl′ĭ·gȧ·lā′shŭs; pō·lĭg′ȧ-), *adj.*

po·lyg′a·mist (-mĭst), *n.* One who practices polygamy.

po·lyg′a·mous (-mŭs), *adj.* [Gr. *polygamos* living in polygamy, fr. *polys* many + *gamos* marriage.] **1.** Of, pertaining to, or characterized by polygamy; — opposed to *monogamous*. **2.** *Bot.* Bearing both monoclinous and diclinous flowers on the same plant. **3.** *Zool.*

Having more than one mate at the same time. — **po·lyg′a·mous·ly**, *adv.*

po·lyg′a·my (pō·lĭg′ȧ·mĭ), *n.* State or fact of having a plurality of wives or (rarely) of husbands, at the same time; — opposed to *monogamy.*

pol′y·gen′e·sis (pŏl′ĭ·jĕn′ē·sĭs), *n.* [NL.] **1.** Plurality of origin. **2.** *Anthropol.* The theory that two or more branches of the human race evolved independently.

pol′y·ge·net′ic (-jē·nĕt′ĭk), *adj.* **1.** Having many distinct sources; originating at various places or times. Cf. MONOGENETIC. **2.** *Biol.* Of or pertaining to polygenesis.

pol′y·glot (pŏl′ĭ·glŏt), *adj.* [Gr. *polyglōttos* many-tongued, fr. *polys* many + *glōtta* tongue.] **1.** Speaking, or writing, many languages. **2.** Containing, or made up of, several languages. — *n.* **1.** One who speaks or writes several languages. **2.** A book containing versions of the same text in several languages, esp. the Scriptures in several languages. **3.** A confusion of languages; a polyglot jargon.

pol′y·gon (pŏl′ĭ·gŏn *or, esp. Brit.,* -gŭn), *n.* [LL. *polygonum,* fr. Gr. *polygōnos* polygonal, fr. *polys* many + *gōnia* angle.] *Geom.* A figure, generally plane and closed, having many angles, and hence many sides; esp., one of more than four angles. — **po·lyg′o·nal** (pō·lĭg′ō·năl; -n′l), *adj.* — **po·lyg′o·nal·ly**, *adv.*

pol′y·go·na′ceous (pŏl′ĭ·gō·nā′shŭs), *adj.* [See POLYGONUM.] *Bot.* Belonging to the buckwheat family (Polygonaceae). See BUCKWHEAT.

po·lyg′o·num (pō·lĭg′ō·nŭm), *n.* Also **po·lyg′o·ny** (-nĭ). [NL. *polygonum,* fr. L. *polygonos, -on,* a kind of plant, fr. Gr. *polygonon,* fr. *polys* many + *gony* knee; — in allusion to the numerous joints.] *Bot.* Any of a large genus (*Polygonum*) of herbs, the knotgrasses.

pol′y·graph (pŏl′ĭ·grăf; 9), *n.* [Gr. *polygraphos* writing much.] **1.** A manifold writer; copying machine. **2.** *Med.* An instrument for recording tracings of several different pulsations simultaneously, as of the heart and one or more of the arteries. — **pol′y·graph′ic** (-grăf′ĭk), *adj.*

po·lyg′y·nous (pō·lĭj′ĭ·nŭs), *adj.* **1.** Pertaining to, practicing, or characterized by polygyny. **2.** *Bot.* Having many styles.

po·lyg′y·ny (-nĭ), *n.* [*poly-* + Gr. *gynē* woman, wife.] **1.** Plurality of wives or concubines. Cf. MONOGYNY, POLYANDRY, POLYGAMY. **2.** The mating of one male animal with several females.

pol′y·he′dron (pŏl′ĭ·hē′drŭn), *n.; pl.* -DRONS (-drŭnz), -DRA (-drȧ). [NL., fr. Gr. *polyedros* with many sides, fr. *polys* many + *hedra* seat, side.] *Geom.* A figure or solid formed by many plane faces, esp. by more than six. — **pol′y·he′dral** (-drăl), *adj.*

pol′y·his′tor (-hĭs′tŏr), *or* **pol′y·his·to′ri·an** (-hĭs·tō′rĭ·ăn), *n.* [Gr. *polyistōr* very learned.] One of encyclopedic learning.

Pol′y·hym′ni·a (-hĭm′nĭ·ȧ), *n.* Also **Po·lym′ni·a** (pō·lĭm′nĭ·ȧ). [L., fr. Gr. *Polymnia,* fr. *polys* many + *hymnos* hymn.] Muse of the sacred lyric.

pol′y·mer (pŏl′ĭ·mẽr), *n.* [See POLYMERIC.] *Chem.* Any of two or more polymeric compounds; specif., one of higher molecular weight, esp. one produced by polymerization.

pol′y·mer′ic (-mĕr′ĭk), *adj.* [*poly-* + Gr. *meros* part.] *Chem.* Consisting of the same elements in the same proportions by weight, but differing in molecular weight; as, cyanic acid (CNOH) and cyanuric acid ($C_3N_3O_3H_3$) are *polymeric* with each other.

pol′y·mer·ize (pŏl′ĭ·mẽr·īz; pō·lĭm′ẽr·īz), *v. t. & i.* *Chem.* To change (by union of two or more molecules of the same kind) into another compound having the same elements in the same proportions, but a higher molecular weight and different physical properties. — **po·lym′er·ism** (pō·lĭm′ẽr·ĭz′m; pŏl′ĭ·mẽr·ĭz′m), *n.* — **pol′y·mer·i·za′tion** (-ĭ·zā′shŭn; -ī·zā′-), *n.*

po·lym′er·ous (pō·lĭm′ẽr·ŭs), *adj.* *Bot.* Having many parts or members in a whorl.

pol′y·morph (pŏl′ĭ·môrf), *n.* [Gr. *polymorphos* multiform, fr. *polys* many + *morphē* form.] **1.** *Biol.* A polymorphous organism, or one of its several forms. **2.** *Cryst.* A substance crystallizable in several distinct forms, or one of these forms.

pol′y·mor′phic (-môr′fĭk), **pol′y·mor′phous** (-môr′fŭs), *adj.* [*poly-* + *-morphic, -morphous.*] Having, assuming, or occurring in, various forms, characters, or styles. Cf. DIMORPHIC, HETEROMORPHIC, MONOMORPHIC. — **pol′y·mor′phism** (-fĭz′m), *n.*

Pol′y·ne′sian (pŏl′ĭ·nē′shăn; -zhăn), *adj.* [From NL. *Polynesia,* fr. Gr. *polys* many + *nēsos* island.] Of or pertaining to Polynesia or the Polynesians. — *n.* **1.** A member of any of the brown races of Oceania. **2.** The agglutinative Polynesian language or languages. See LANGUAGE, *Table.*

Pol′y·ni′ces (pŏl′ĭ·nī′sēz), *n.* [L. *Polynices,* fr. Gr. *Polyneikēs.*] See ANTIGONE, SEVEN AGAINST THEBES.

pol′y·no′mi·al (pŏl′ĭ·nō′mĭ·ăl; 58), *n.* [*poly-* + *-nomial* as in *binomial.*] *Alg.* An expression of two or more terms, as $a^2 - 2ab + b^2$. — **pol′y·no′mi·al**, *adj.*

pol′yp (pŏl′ĭp), *n.* [F. *polype,* fr. L. *polypus,* fr. Gr. *polypous, polypodos,* fr. *polys* many + *pous, podos,* foot.] **1.** *Zool.* A coelenterate, having typically a hollow cylindrical body, closed and attached at one end, and opening at the other by a central mouth surrounded by tentacles armed with nematocysts, as the hydra, sea anemone, coral, etc. **2.** *Med.* A projecting mass of swollen and hypertrophied mucous membrane, as in the nasal cavity.

pol′y·par′y (pŏl′ĭ·pĕr′ĭ; -pẽr·ĭ), *n.; pl.* -IES (-ĭz). *Zool.* The common investing structure or tissue in which the polyps of corals and other compound forms are embedded.

pol′y·pep′tide (pŏl′ĭ·pĕp′tīd; -tĭd), *n.* Also **pol′y·pep′tid.** [G. *polypeptide.*] *Biochem.* Any of the simple nonprotein combinations of several amino-acid molecules.

pol′y·pet′al·ous (-pĕt′ăl·ŭs), *adj.* *Bot.* Having the petals separate; choripetalous; — opp. to *gamopetalous.*

pol′y·pha′gi·a (-fā′jĭ·ȧ), *n.* [NL., fr. Gr. *polyphagia* excess in eating.] **a** *Med.* Excessive eating. **b** *Zool.* Ability to subsist on various kinds of food. — **po·lyph′a·gous** (pō·lĭf′ȧ·gŭs), *adj.*

pol′y·phase (pŏl′ĭ·fāz), *adj.* Having or producing two or more phases; multiphase; as, a *polyphase* electric current.

Pol′y·phe′mus (-fē′mŭs), *n.* [L., fr. Gr. *Polyphēmos.*] *Gr. Myth.* A Cyclops who imprisoned Odysseus and his companions in a cavern and devoured two of the company daily until Odysseus made him drunk and blinded him.

Polyphemus moth. A very large American silkworm moth (*Telea polyphemus*) of a yellowish or brownish color, with a large eyelike spot in each hind wing.

pol′y·phon′ic (pŏl′ĭ·fŏn′ĭk; -fō′nĭk), *adj.* [Gr. *polyphōnos,* fr. *polys* many + *phōnē* sound.] **1.** Having, or consisting of, many sounds or voices. **2.** *Music.* **a** Pertaining to polyphony; consisting of two or more melodies combined; contrapuntal. **b** Capable of giving more than one tone at a time, as the harp. **3.** *Phonet.* Having more than one phonetic value.

polyphonic prose. A poetic form of expression which is printed as prose but makes use of rhythm, rhyme, assonance, etc., with many changes from one form to another.

po·lyph′o·ny (pō·lĭf′ō·nĭ; pŏl′ĭ·fō′nĭ), *n.* [Gr. *polyphōnia.*] **1.** Multiplicity of sounds, as in reverberations of an echo. **2.** *Music.* Composition in simultaneous and harmonizing but melodically independent and individual parts or voices; contrapuntal composition. **3.** *Phonet.* Representation of more than one sound by means of the same written character. — **po·lyph′o·nous** (pō·lĭf′ō·nŭs), *adj.*

pol′y·phy·let′ic (pŏl′ĭ·fī·lĕt′ĭk), *adj.* [*poly-* + Gr. *phylē* clan, *phyletēs* one of the same clan.] Derived from more than one original or ancestral type, race, or family. Cf. MONOPHYLETIC.

po·lyp′i·dom (pō·lĭp′ĭ·dŭm; pŏl′ĭ·pĭ·dŭm), *n.* [*polypus* + Gr. *domos* house.] A polypary.

pol′y·ploid (pŏl′ĭ·ploid), *adj.* Manifold in appearance or arrangement; specif., *Biol.,* having or designating a chromosome number which is a multiple of a basic haploid number. — **pol′y·ploi′dic** (-ploi′dĭk), *adj.* — **pol′y·ploid,** *n.*

pol′y·ploi′dy (pŏl′ĭ·ploi′dĭ), *n.* A polyploid condition; specif., *Hort.,* such a condition frequently induced by means of chemicals or hormones in order to develop plants of unusual size or vigor.

pol′y·po′dy (-pō′dĭ), *n.; pl.* -DIES (-dĭz). [L. *polypodium,* fr. Gr. *polypodion,* dim. of *polypous.* See POLYP.] Any of a genus (*Polypodium*) of ferns with naked sori.

pol′y·pous (-pŭs), *adj.* Pert. to or of the nature of a polyp.

pol′yp·tych (pŏl′ĭp·tĭk), *n.* An arrangement of panels or pieces hinged or folding together, having more parts than a triptych.

pol′y·pus (pŏl′ĭ·pŭs), *n.; pl.* -PI (-pī), -PUSES (-pŭs·ĕz; -ĭz). [L.] A polyp.

pol′y·sac′cha·ride (pŏl′ĭ·săk′ȧ·rīd; -rĭd), *n.* Also **pol′y·sac′cha·rid.** *Chem.* Any carbohydrate decomposable by hydrolysis into two or more molecules of simple sugars or monosaccharides; specif., one decomposable into more than six monosaccharide molecules. Cf. OLIGOSACCHARIDE.

pol′y·sty′rene (-stī′rēn; -stĭr′ēn), *n.* *Chem.* A polymer of styrene; specif., a colorless, transparent plastic used for molding various articles, for insulation, for transparent sheets, for radio parts, etc.

pol′y·sul′fide (-sŭl′fīd; -fĭd), *n.* Also **-fid, -phide, -phid.** *Chem.* A compound of more than one atom of sulfur with an element or radical.

pol′y·syl·lab′ic (-sĭ·lăb′ĭk), *adj.* Also **pol′y·syl·lab′i·cal** (-ĭ·kăl). [From ML., fr. Gr. *polysyllabos,* fr. *polys* many + *syllabē* syllable.] Having, or characterized by, many syllables; of a word, having more than three syllables.

pol′y·syl′la·ble (pŏl′ĭ·sĭl′ȧ·b′l), *n.* A polysyllabic word.

pol′y·syn′de·ton (-sĭn′dē·tŏn), *n.* [NL., fr. *poly-* + Gr. *syndetos* bound together.] *Rhet.* Repetition of conjunctions in close succession. Cf. ASYNDETON.

pol′y·tech′nic (-tĕk′nĭk), *adj.* [F. *polytechnique,* fr. Gr. *polytechnos,* fr. *polys* many + *technē* an art.] Of or devoted to instruction in many technical arts or applied sciences; — esp. designating schools or institutions. — *n.* A polytechnic school.

pol′y·the·ism (pŏl′ĭ·thē·ĭz′m), *n.* [F. *polythéisme,* fr. Gr. *polys* many + *theos* god.] The doctrine of, or belief in, a plurality of gods. Cf. MONOTHEISM. — **pol′y·the·ist** (-ĭst), *n. & adj.* — **pol′y·the·is′tic** (-ĭs′tĭk), **pol′y·the·is′ti·cal** (-tĭ·kăl), *adj.*

pol′y·to·nal′i·ty (pŏl′ĭ·tō·năl′ĭ·tĭ), *n.* *Music.* The simultaneous use of two or more keys or tonalities; also, the effect so produced.

pol′y·troph′ic (-trŏf′ĭk), *adj.* [Gr. *polytrophos* nutritious.] *Bacteriol.* Deriving nourishment from more than one organic substance, as pathogenic bacteria.

pol′y·typ′ic (-tĭp′ĭk), **pol′y·typ′i·cal** (-ĭ·kăl), *adj.* Having several or many types or representatives; — opposed to *monotypic.*

pol′y·u′ri·a (-ū′rĭ·ȧ), *n.* [NL., fr. *poly-* + *-uria.*] *Med.* Excessive secretion of urine. — **pol′y·u′ric** (-rĭk), *adj.*

pol′y·va′lent (pŏl′ĭ·vā′lĕnt; pō·lĭv′ȧ·lĕnt; 2), *adj.* [*poly-* + L. *valens,* pres. part. See VALENT.] **1.** *Bacteriol.* Containing antibodies specific for, or antigens of, more than one species or strain of microorganism. **2.** *Chem.* Multivalent. — **pol′y·va′lence** (-lĕns), *n.*

pol′y·vi′nyl (pŏl′ĭ·vī′nĭl; -vĭn′ĭl), *adj.* *Chem.* Pertaining to or designating a compound made by polymerizing a compound or compounds containing the vinyl radical, CH_2:CH–. Polyvinyl compounds important as thermoplastic resins include: **polyvinyl acetal,** polymerized from vinyl alcohol and aldehyde, used in molding, etc.; **polyvinyl acetate,** made from acetylene and acetic acid, used for adhesives, etc.; **polyvinyl alcohol,** $(CH_2{:}CHOH)_x$, used like polyvinyl acetal; **polyvinyl butyral,** polymerized from butyraldehyde, C_3H_7CHO, and vinyl alcohol, used for the interlayer in safety glass, for waterproofing fabrics, etc.; **polyvinyl chloride,** used for insulating, etc.; **polyvinyl resin** = VINYL RESIN.

pol′y·vi·nyl′i·dene chlo′ride, res′in (-vī·nĭl′ĭ·dēn). = *vinylidene chloride, resin,* under VINYLIDENE.

pol′y·zo′an (pŏl′ĭ·zō′ăn), *adj. & n.* [*poly-* + *-zoa* + *-an.*] *Zool.* Bryozoan.

pol′y·zo·ar′i·um (-zō·âr′ĭ·ŭm), *n.; pl.* -IA (-ȧ). [NL.] *Zool.* A bryozoan colony or its supporting skeleton.

pol′y·zo′ic (-zō′ĭk), *adj.* *Zool.* **a** Composed of many zooids. **b** Designating a spore that produces many sporozoites.

pom′ace (pŭm′ĭs; -ȧs), *n.* [OF. *pomat,* fr. L. *pomum* apple.] **1.** The substance of apples, etc., crushed by grinding, as in making cider. **2.** The substance of anything crushed to a pulpy mass, as of fish or the castor bean.

po·ma′ceous (pō·mā′shŭs), *adj.* [L. *pomum* apple.] **1.** *Bot.* **a** Belonging to the apple family (Pomaceae). **b** Of the nature of or resembling a pome. **2.** *Poetic.* Of or pertaining to apples.

po·made′ (pō·măd′; pō·mäd′), *n.* [F. *pommade,* fr. It., fr. L. *pomum* apple.] A perfumed ointment; esp., an unguent for the hair; pomatum. — *v. t.* To anoint with pomade.

po′man·der (pō′măn·dẽr; pō·măn′dẽr), *n.* [Formerly also *pomamber, pomeamber* (*Oxf. E. D.*). See POME; AMBER.] A perfume or mixture of perfumes, enclosed in a perforated box or bag, and carried on the person, as to guard against infection.

po·ma′tum (pō·mā′tŭm; -mä′tŭm), *n.* [NL.] Pomade.

pome (pōm), *n.* [OF., apple (F. *pomme*), fr. L. *pomum* a fruit, later, an apple.] The characteristic fleshy carpellate fruit of trees and shrubs of the apple family.

pome′gran′ate (pŏm′grăn′ĭt; pŭm′-; pŏm·grăn′ĭt; pŭm-), *n.* [ME. *pomgarnet*, fr. OF. *pome grenate.* See POME; GRENADE.] A thick-skinned several-celled reddish berry, of the size of an orange, having many seeds in a crimson pulp of agreeable acid flavor, borne on a tropical African and Asiatic tree (*Punica granatum*); also, the tree.

pom′e·lo (pŏm′ĕ·lō), *n.; pl.* -LOS (-lōz). **a** The shaddock. **b** The grapefruit.

Pom′er·a′nian (pŏm′ēr·ā′nĭ·ăn; -ā′nĭ·ăn; 58), *adj.* from POMERANIA, *Gaz.* — *n.* **1.** A native or inhabitant of Pomerania. **2.** A small long-haired dog of a breed with a foxlike head, erect ears, tail turned over the back, and a double coat of which the outer is very abundant round the neck.

po′mi·cul′ture (pō′mĭ·kŭl′tūr), *n.* [L. *pomum* fruit + *cultura* culture.] Fruit culture. — **po′mi·cul′tur·ist** (-kŭl′tūr·ĭst), *n.*

po·mif′er·ous (pō·mĭf′ēr·ŭs), *adj.* [L. *pomifer*, fr. *pomum* fruit + *ferre* to bear.] Bearing pomes or applelike fruits.

pom′mée′, pom′mé′ (pô′mā′), *adj.* *Her.* Having the ends terminating in round knobs or single balls; — said of a cross. See CROSS, *Illust.* (11).

pom′mel (pŭm′ĕl; -′l; pŏm′-), *n.* Also **pum′mel** (pŭm′-). [OF. *pomel*, fr. L. *pomum* apple. See POME.] **1.** A rounded knob, as on the hilt of a sword. **2.** The knoblike protuberance at the front and top of a saddlebow. Cf. CANTLE. — *v. t.*; -MELED (-ĕld; -′ld) *or* -MELLED; -MEL·ING *or* -MEL·LING. Often **pum′mel.** To beat soundly, as with the pommel of a sword or with the fists.

po·mol′o·gy (pō·mŏl′ō·jĭ), *n.* [L. *pomum* fruit + *-logy.*] Science and practice of fruit growing. — **po′mo·log′i·cal** (pō′mō·lŏj′ĭ·kăl), *adj.* — **po·mol′o·gist** (pō·mŏl′ō·jĭst), *n.*

Po·mo′na (pō·mō′nȧ), *n.* [L., fr. *pomum* fruit.] *Rom. Relig.* The old Italian goddess of the fruit of trees.

pomp (pŏmp), *n.* [OF. *pompe*, fr. L. *pompa*, fr. Gr. *pompē* a sending, a solemn procession, pomp, fr. *pempein* to send.] **1.** Formerly, a pageant. **2.** A show of magnificence; brilliant display; splendor. **3.** Ostentatious display or an instance of it.

pom′pa·dour (pŏm′pȧ·dōr; -dōōr), *n.* [After the Marquise de *Pompadour.*] A style of dressing the hair high over the forehead, either by drawing long hair over a roll, or by brushing short hair back so that it stands erect; also, the hair dressed in this style.

pom′pa·no (pŏm′pȧ·nō), *n.; pl.* -PANOS (-nōz). [Sp. *pámpano.*] *Zool.* **a** A carangoid fish (*Trachinotus carolinus*) of the southern Atlantic and Gulf coasts of North America, one of the best of food fishes. **b** A California coast fish (*Palometa simillima*) which resembles the pompano.

pom′-pom′ (pŏm′pŏm′), *n.* [Imitative.] A one-pounder automatic machine cannon; — from its drumming sound.

pom′pon (pŏm′pŏn; *F.* pôɴ′pôɴ′), *n.* [F.] **1.** An ornamental ball, as of silk or feathers, for women's costume. **2.** A hardy garden chrysanthemum having close buttonlike heads of flowers. **3.** *Mil.* A tuft or ball as of wool, worn on the front of the hat, shako, etc.

pom·pos′i·ty (pŏm·pŏs′ĭ·tĭ), *n.; pl.* -TIES (-tĭz). Pompous demeanor, speech, or action.

pomp′ous (pŏmp′ŭs), *adj.* [F. *pompeux*, fr. LL. *pomposus.* See POMP.] **1.** Of the nature of a pomp, or spectacle; magnificent. **2.** Characterized by ostentation; of persons, self-important. — **Syn.** See SHOWY. — **pomp′ous·ly,** *adv.* — **pomp′ous·ness,** *n.*

pon′cho (pŏn′chō), *n.; pl.* -CHOS (-chōz). [Sp., fr. Araucan *poncho, pontho.*] A Spanish-American cloak like a blanket with a slit in the middle for the head; also, a similar garment, as of rubber or oiled cloth, worn elsewhere, chiefly as a raincoat.

pond (pŏnd), *n.* [ME. *ponde*, orig. an enclosed body of water, and same word as *pound* an enclosure.] A body of water, usually smaller than a lake.

pon′der (pŏn′dēr), *v. t. & i.* [OF. *ponderer*, fr. L. *ponderare*, fr. *pondus, ponderis* a weight.] To weigh in the mind; to meditate; deliberate.

Syn. **Ponder, meditate, muse, ruminate** mean to consider with deliberation. **Ponder** implies a careful weighing of a problem or the like so that nothing important escapes attention; **meditate,** a definite focusing of one's thoughts upon something so as to understand it deeply; **muse,** though suggesting focused attention, implies absorption as in a dream; **ruminate,** a going over the same problem or subject again and again, as in speculation.

pon′der·a·ble (-ȧ·b′l), *adj.* Having weight; appreciable. — **Syn.** See PERCEPTIBLE. — **pon′der·a·bil′i·ty** (-bĭl′ĭ·tĭ), *n.*

pon′der·ous (-ŭs), *adj.* [F. *pondéreux*, fr. L. *ponderosus*, fr. *pondus, -eris*, a weight.] **1.** Of very great weight; extremely heavy. **2.** Heavy; dull; wanting lightness or spirit; as, a *ponderous* style. — **Syn.** See HEAVY. — **pon′der·os′i·ty** (-ŏs′ĭ·tĭ), *n.* — **pon′der·ous·ly,** *adv.* — **pon′der·ous·ness,** *n.*

pond lily. The water lily.

pond scum. A spirogyra or alga of a related genus; also, the mass of tangled filaments formed by these on stagnant waters.

pond′weed′ (pŏnd′wēd′), *n.* Any of a genus (*Potamogeton*, family Zannichelliaceae, the pondweed family) of aquatic plants, growing in quiet waters.

pone (pōn), *n.* [Of Algonquian origin.] = CORN PONE.

pon·gee′ (pŏn·jē′; pŭn-), *n.* [Chin. (Pek.) *pen³-chi⁴* home loom.] A thin soft fabric made of the brownish undyed silk of the silkworm of China; any similar dyed silk fabric.

pon′iard (pŏn′yērd), *n.* [F. *poignard*, fr. *poing* fist, fr. L. *pugnus.*] A dagger, usually slender with a triangular or square blade. — *v. t.* To pierce with a poniard.

‖**pons** (pŏnz), *n.; pl.* PONTES (pŏn′tēz). [L., a bridge.] *Anat. & Zool.* **a** A bridge. **b** Also ‖**pons Va·ro′li·i** (vȧ·rō′lĭ·ī). A broad mass of transverse nerve fibers on the ventral surface of the brain of man and mammals, at the anterior end of the medulla oblongata. See HINDBRAIN; BRAIN, *Illust.*

pons as′i·no′rum (ăs′ĭ·nō′rŭm; 70). [L.] = ASSES' BRIDGE.

Pon′tic (pŏn′tĭk), *adj.* [L. *Ponticus*, fr. Gr. *Pontikos*, fr. *pontos* the sea, esp., the Black Sea.] Of or pertaining to Pontus, or the Black Sea or its region.

pon′ti·fex (pŏn′tĭ·fĕks), *n.; pl.* PONTIFICES (pŏn·tĭf′ĭ·sēz). [L. See PONTIFF.] **1.** *Rom. Antiq.* A member of the Pontifical College; = PONTIFF, 1. **2.** *Eccl.* A bishop; specif., the pope; = PONTIFF, 2.

pon′tiff (pŏn′tĭf), *n.* [F. *pontife*, fr. L. *pontifex, -ficis*, prob. orig. pathfinder, waymaker, fr. L. *pons, pontis*, bridge + *facere* to do.] **1.** *Rom. Relig.* A member of the council of priests forming the central body of the ***Pontifical College***, the highest priestly organization of Rome, presided over by the ***pontifex maximus.*** **2.** *Eccl.* A bishop; now usually, the pope.

pon·tif′i·cal (pŏn·tĭf′ĭ·kăl), *adj.* **1. a** Of or pertaining to a pontiff, bishop, or prelate; episcopal; specif., papal. **b** Having the dignity, dogmatism, etc., of a pontiff. **c** Celebrated by a bishop; as, *pontifical* Mass. — *n.* **1.** Now always *pl.* The vestments and insignia worn by a prelate in pontifical Mass. **2.** A book containing the offices, or forms for rites, etc., performed by a pontiff, or bishop.

pon·tif′i·cate (-ĭ·kāt), *n.* State, office, dignity, or term of office of a pontiff.

pon·tif′i·cate (-kāt), *v. i.* **a** To officiate as a pontiff. **b** To speak in the manner of, or as if with the authority of, a pontiff.

pon′til (pŏn′tĭl), *n.* = PUNTY.

Pon′tius (pŏn′shŭs; -tĭ·ŭs), *n.* [L.] The gens name of the Roman procurator, **Pon′tius Pi′late** (pī′lăt), under whom Jesus was crucified.

pon′ton (pŏn′tŭn; *by some* pŏn·tōōn′), *n.* [F.] *U. S. Army.* A pontoon.

pon′to·nier′ (pŏn′tō·nēr′), *n.* [F. *pontonnier.*] *Mil.* An individual engaged in constructing a pontoon bridge.

pon·toon′ (pŏn·tōōn′; 2), *n.* [F. *ponton*, fr. L. *ponto, -onis*, fr. *pons, pontis*, bridge.] **1.** A flat-bottomed lighter or other boat; esp., *Mil.*, a flat-bottomed boat or other portable float, such as a metallic cylinder, or a boatlike frame covered with waterproof material, used in building a floating **pontoon bridge**, for the passage of troops or vehicles. **2.** A float of an aircraft.

pon·toon′, *n.* *Brit.* Corruption of VINGT-ET-UN.

po′ny (pō′nĭ), *n.; pl.* PONIES (-nĭz). [From earlier *pawny*, prob. fr. OF. *poulenet*, dim. of *poulain* colt, fr. LL. *pullanus*, fr. L. *pullus* a young animal.] **1.** A small horse; esp. a horse of any of certain very small but stocky breeds, usually not over 14 hands (polo 14½ hands) in height. The broncos, mustangs, and cayuses of the western United States are sometimes called ponies regardless of size. **2.** *Slang, Eng.* Sum of £25. **3.** *U. S.* A translation used to avoid study in getting lessons; a crib. **4.** Something very small of its kind; as, *Colloq.*, a small liqueur glass or the liquor it will hold. — *v. t. & i.* *Slang, U. S.* To pay (money), esp. to settle an account; — with *up.*

pony express. The first rapid-transit postal and express system across western United States (1860–61), extending from St. Joseph, Mo., to Sacramento, Calif. Relays of ponies carried mails 1960 miles in 10 days.

pooch (pōōch), *n.* *Slang.* A dog.

pood (pōōd), *n.* [Russ. *pud*, ult. fr. L. See POUND the weight.] A Russian weight, equivalent to 36.113 lb.

poo′dle (pōō′d′l), *n.* [G. *pudel.*] A pet or gun dog of a basic breed of very high intelligence, having a coat of either wiry, curled hair, or long silky hair of any solid color.

pooh′-pooh′ (pōō′pōō′), *v. t. & i.* To make light (of).

pool (pōōl), *n.* [AS. *pōl.*] **1.** A small and rather deep body of (usually) fresh water, as one in a stream. **2.** A small body of standing water or other liquid; a puddle. **3.** A continuous area of porous sedimentary rock which yields petroleum.

pool, *n.* [F. *poule*, prop., a hen. See PULLET.] **1.** The aggregate stake played for in certain card games. **2. a** *Eng.* A game at billiards, in which each of the players stakes a certain sum and the winner takes all. **b** *U. S.* Any of various games of billiards played on a table having six pockets, with, usually, fifteen object balls and a cue ball. **3.** In a joint gambling venture, the total amount contributed to be staked, the resulting gains or losses to be divided proportionately; also, the combination of persons. **4.** Any aggregation of the interests or property of different persons made to further a joint undertaking by subjecting them to the same control and a common liability; also, the persons combining. Specif.: **a** *Com.* A common fund or combination of interests, esp. for speculating in, or manipulating the market price of, securities, grain, etc. **b** A combination between competing business houses or corporations for the control of traffic by removing competition. **5.** *Fencing.* A contest in which each member of a team successively engages each member of another team. **6.** *Med.* An accumulation of blood in any part of the body, as in the capillaries and veins of the peritoneal cavity, resulting from stagnating circulation. — **Syn.** See MONOPOLY. — *v. t.* To contribute to a common fund, on the basis of a mutual division of profits or losses; to make a common interest of. — *v. i.* To combine with others in a pool.

pool′room′ (pōōl′rōōm′), *n.* *U. S.* **1.** A room in which gambling on distant horse races, prize fights, etc., is carried on. **2.** A public room in which pool is played.

poon (pōōn), *n.*, *or* **poon tree.** [Singhalese *puna.*] Any of several East Indian trees (genus *Calophyllum*, family Clusiaceae), or their hard, light wood, used for masts, etc.

poop (pōōp), *n.* [F. *poupe*, fr. It. *poppa*, fr. L. *puppis.*] **1.** *Now Rare.* The after section of a vessel. **2.** *Naut.* A deck (**poop deck**) above the upper deck abaft the mizzen, sometimes forming the roof of a cabin (**poop cabin**). — *v. t.* **1. a** To break over the poop of. **b** To ship (a sea or wave) over the stern. **2.** *Slang.* To put out of breath or wind; also, to wear out or exhaust; — used esp. in past participial form.

poor (pōōr; 84), *adj.* [ME. *pore, poure*, fr. OF. *povre* (F. *pauvre*), fr. L. *pauper.*] **1.** Wanting in material riches or goods; needy; indigent; impoverished. **2.** Destitute of some normal or desirable quality; as: **a** Scanty; inadequate; as, a *poor* crop. **b** Not good, as in quality or workmanship; inferior. **c** Feeble; dejected; as, *poor* health; also, mean-spirited. **d** Lean; emaciated; as, a *poor* horse. **e** Barren; sterile; — of land. **f** Unfavorable; uncomfortable; as, the sick man had a *poor* night. **g** Wanting in elegance or marks of wealth or refinement; as, *poor* attire. **h** Inefficient; not satisfactory; as, a *poor* orator. **3.** *Colloq.* Worthy of pity or sympathy; as, *poor* vain fool. — **poor′ly,** *adv.* — **poor′ness,** *n.*

poor farm. *U. S.* A farm maintained at public expense for the support and employment of paupers.

poor′house′ (pōōr′hous′), *n.* A dwelling house for paupers maintained at public expense; almshouse.

poor law. A law providing for or regulating the public relief or support of the poor.

poor′-spir′it·ed (*see Pron.*, § 2), *adj.* Of a mean spirit; cowardly; base.

poor′tith (pōōr′tĭth), *n.* [OF. *povretet.*] *Scot.* Poverty.

poor white. *Contemptuous.* **1.** In the southern United States, a white person of neither property nor social position; — often called collectively **poor white trash**. 2. In South Africa, a white person of a low social class marked by poverty, inferior mentality or capacity to labor, etc., descended from Boer farmers.

pop (pŏp), *n.* [Of imitative origin.] **1.** A small, sharp explosive report. **2.** A shot from a rifle, pistol, etc. **3.** A beverage which expels the cork with a pop from the bottle. — *v. i.*; POPPED (pŏpt); POP′PING. **1.** To make, or to burst with, a pop, or sharp report. **2.** To go, enter, or issue forth suddenly; to dart; leap; as, to *pop* under the clothes. **3.** To protrude from the sockets. **4.** To shoot with a firearm. — *v. t.* **1.** To thrust, push, or put suddenly. **2.** To cause to burst open; as, to *pop* corn. **3.** *Colloq.* To fire off (a firearm, blast, etc.); hence, to shoot. — ***pop the question.*** *Colloq.* To propose marriage. — *adv.* Like or with a pop; suddenly.

pop′corn′ (pŏp′kôrn′), *n.* A type (*Zea mays everta*) of Indian corn having kernels which on exposure to dry heat are burst open by the explosion of the contained moisture, forming a white starchy mass; also, the corn when popped.

pope (pōp), *n.* [AS. *pāpa*, fr. LL. *papa*, fr. Gr. *papas*, *pappas*, father.] **1.** In the Roman Catholic Church, the bishop of Rome, the head of the church. **2.** One likened to the pope in authority or claims.

pope, *n.* [Russ. *pop*, fr. LGr. *papas*.] *Orthodox Ch.* A parish priest.

pope′dom (pōp′dŭm), *n.* Office of the or a pope.

Pope Joan (jōn). A card game resembling newmarket.

pop′er·y (pōp′ẽr·ĭ), *n.* [*often cap.*] Roman Catholicism, esp. its government and forms of worship; — a designation of disparagement.

pop′gun′ (pŏp′gŭn′), *n.* A child's toy gun for shooting pellets, with a popping noise, by compression of air.

pop′in·jay (pŏp′ĭn·jā), *n.* [OF. *papegai*, *papingay*, fr. Sp. *papagayo*, fr. Ar.] **1.** *Obs.* A parrot. **2.** A person likened to a parrot, as a talkative coxcomb. **3.** A target in the form of a parrot on a pole.

pop′ish (pōp′ĭsh), *adj.* Roman Catholic; papistic; — used opprobriously. — **pop′ish·ly**, *adv.* — **pop′ish·ness**, *n.*

pop′lar (pŏp′lẽr), *n.* [OF. *poplier*, fr. L. *populus* poplar.] **1. a** Any of a genus (*Populus*) of slender quick-growing trees of the willow family, including the aspens *P. tremula*, *P. tremuloides*, and *P. grandidentata*; the ***balsam poplar*** (*P. tacamahaca*), also known as ***balm of Gilead*** and ***tacamahac***, a North American shade tree; the European ***black poplar*** (*P. nigra*), of which the ***Lombardy poplar*** (*P. nigra italica*) is a variety; the cottonwood *P. balsamifera* (see COTTONWOOD); and the Eurasian ***white poplar*** (*P. alba*), cultivated in the United States. **b** The wood of any of these trees. **2.** *U. S.* The tulip tree; also, its wood.

pop′lin (pŏp′lĭn), *n.* [F. *popeline*, *papeline*, fr. It. *papalino* papal; — because made at Avignon, a papal town.] A corded fabric, usually of silk or worsted, used esp. for women's dresses.

pop·lit′e·al (pŏp·lĭt′ē·ăl; pŏp′lĭ·tē′ăl), *adj.* [L. *poples*, *-itis*, the ham.] *Anat.* Of or pertaining to the ham, or back part of the leg behind the knee joint, as the **popliteal nerve**, either of the two branches of the sciatic nerve.

pop′o′ver (pŏp′ō′vẽr), *n.* A quick bread made from batter rich in egg and expanded by baking into a hollow shell.

pop′per (pŏp′ẽr), *n.* **1.** One who or that which pops. **2.** A utensil for popping corn.

pop′pet (pŏp′ĕt; -ĭt), *n.* [Earlier form of PUPPET.] **1.** *Now Dial.* A small person; *Obs.*, a doll; also, a puppet. **2.** *Mach.* **a** An upright support or guide fastened at the bottom only, as a lathe poppethead. **b** Also **poppet valve**. A valve that rises perpendicularly to or from its seat. **3.** Any of the small pieces of wood on a boat's gunwale supporting the rowlocks.

pop′pet·head′ (-hĕd′), *n.* A lathe tailstock or headstock.

pop′pied (pŏp′ĭd), *adj.* **1.** Growing with poppies. **2.** Drugging or sleep-inducing; also, drugged; drowsy.

pop′ping crease. *Cricket.* See CREASE, *n.*, 2.

pop′ple (pŏp′'l), *v. i.* [ME. *poplen*.] To toss about, as water in a choppy sea. — *n.* A heaving of water, as by boiling.

pop′py (pŏp′ĭ), *n.*; *pl.* -PIES (-ĭz). [AS. *popig*, *popæg*, ult. fr. L. *papaver*.] **1.** Any of a genus (*Papaver*) of bristly-hairy herbs typifying a family (Papaveraceae, the poppy family) characterized by milky juice, showy regular flowers, and capsular fruit. Annual garden poppies are descended chiefly from the Eurasian white-flowered to purple-flowered ***opium poppy*** (*P. somniferum*) long cultivated as the source of opium, and from the red-flowered ***corn poppy*** or ***coquelicot*** (*P. rhoeas*) common in European cornfields. Perennial garden poppies are descended chiefly from the scarlet-flowered ***Oriental poppy*** (*P. orientale*) and the yellow-flowered or red-flowered ***Iceland poppy*** (*P. nudicaule*) of alpine or arctic America. See CALIFORNIA POPPY, PRICKLY POPPY. **2.** The extract from the plant used in medicines. **3.** The color poppy red.

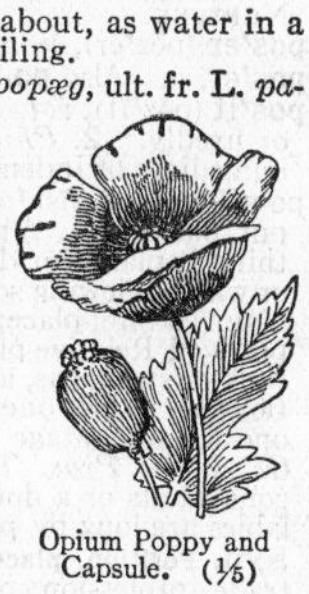

Opium Poppy and Capsule. (1/6)

pop′py·cock′ (pŏp′ĭ·kŏk′), *n.* *Colloq.* Empty talk; bosh; nonsense.

pop′py·head′ (-hĕd′), *n.* *Arch., Furniture, etc.* A raised ornament often in the form of a finial, as on the tops of the upright ends of seats in Gothic churches.

poppy red. A color, yellowish-red in hue, of very high saturation and medium brilliance. See COLOR.

pop′u·lace (pŏp′ū·lĭs; -lȧs), *n.* [F., fr. It., fr. *popolo* people, fr. L. *populus*.] The common people; the masses.

pop′u·lar (-lẽr), *adj.* [L. *popularis*, fr. *populus* people.] **1.** Of or pertaining to the common people, or the whole body of the people; carried on by the people; as, a *popular* election. **2.** Suitable to the public in general; as: **a** Easy to understand; plain. **b** Adapted to the means of the generality of people; hence, cheap. **3.** Having general currency; prevalent; as, a *popular* fallacy. **4.** Beloved or approved by the people. — **Syn.** See COMMON. — **pop′u·lar·ly**, *adv.*

popular front. [F. *Front Populaire*, Sp. *Frente Popular*.] A coalition of leftist, labor, and center parties in a common front against fascism and dictatorship.

pop′u·lar′i·ty (pŏp′ū·lăr′ĭ·tĭ), *n.* Quality or state of being popular; manifest approval of the people in general.

pop′u·lar·ize (pŏp′ū·lẽr·īz), *v. t.* To make popular. — **pop′u·lar·i·za′tion** (-ĭ·zā′shŭn; -ī·zā′-), *n.* — **pop′u·lar·iz′er** (-īz′ẽr), *n.*

pop′u·late (pŏp′ū·lāt), *v. t.* [ML. *populatus*, past part. of *populare*.] To furnish with inhabitants; to people.

pop′u·la′tion (-lā′shŭn), *n.* **1.** The whole number of people or inhabitants in a country, section, or area. **2.** Act or process of populating. **3.** The body of inhabitants of a given locality. **4.** *Biol.* The organisms, collectively, inhabiting an area or region. **5.** *Statistics.* A group of individuals or items; specif., in biometry, the entire group of organisms from which samples are taken for measurement.

Pop′u·list (pŏp′ū·lĭst), *n.* [L. *populus* people + *-ist*.] *U. S. Politics.* A member of the People's party or an advocate of its political doctrines, or **Pop′u·lism** (-lĭz′m). — **Pop′u·lis′tic** (-lĭs′tĭk), *adj.*

pop′u·lous (-lŭs), *adj.* [L. *populosus*.] Abounding in people; thickly inhabited. — **pop′u·lous·ly**, *adv.* — **pop′u·lous·ness**, *n.*

por′bea′gle (pôr′bē′g'l), *n.* A small viviparous shark (*Lamna nasus*) of northern seas, noted for its voracity.

por′ce·lain (pōr′sĕ·lĭn; pōrs′lĭn), *n.* [F. *porcelaine*, fr. It. *porcellana*, orig., the cowrie.] A fine translucent ware of superior whiteness, hardness, and sonority; china. — **por′ce·la′ne·ous, por′cel·la′ne·ous** (pōr′sĕ·lā′nē·ŭs; 58), *adj.*

porch (pōrch; 70), *n.* [OF. *porche*, fr. L. *porticus*.] **1.** *Arch.* A covered entrance to a building, commonly enclosed in part, projecting out from the main wall and having a separate roof. **2.** *Obs.* A portico; covered walk. **3.** *Chiefly U. S.* A veranda. See LOGGIA. — ***the Porch.*** A portico in Athens, where Zeno, the philosopher, taught his disciples.

por′cine (pôr′sīn; -sĭn), *adj.* [F., fr. L. *porcinus*, fr. *porcus* a swine.] Of, pertaining to, characteristic of, or like swine.

por′cu·pine (pôr′kū·pīn), *n.*; see PLURAL, *Note*, 3. [OF. & Pr. *porc espin*, fr. L. *porcus* swine + a deriv. of *spina* thorn, spine.] Any of certain rodents (as the genus *Hystrix* of Europe and Africa, *Erethizon* of North America) having sharp erectile, readily detachable spines mingled with their hair.

porcupine anteater. An echidna.

pore (pōr; 70), *v. i.* [ME. *pouren*, *puren*.] **1.** To gaze intently or searchingly. **2.** To read with profound attention; to study; as, to *pore* over books. **3.** To reflect deeply and continuously; as, to *pore* on the mysteries of nature.

pore, *n.* [F. *pore*, OF. *porre*, fr. L. *porus*, fr. Gr. *poros* passage, pore.] **1.** A minute opening or foramen, esp. in an animal or vegetable membrane, for transpiration, absorption, etc.; as, the *pores* of the sweat glands. **2.** In stone, etc., a small interstice admitting absorption or passage of liquid.

por′gy (pôr′gĭ), *n.*; *pl.* -GIES (-gĭz). See PLURAL, *Note*, 3. **a** A sparoid food fish (*Pagrus pagrus*), called ***red porgy***, of the Mediterranean and the Atlantic. It is crimson with blue spots. **b** Any of various related fishes, as the scup.

po·rif′er·an (pō·rĭf′ẽr·ăn), *n.* [L. *porus* pore + *ferre* to bear.] *Zool.* A member of a phylum (Porifera) constituted by the sponges. — **po·rif′er·ous** (-ŭs), *adj.*

po′rism (pō′rĭz'm; 70), *n.* [NL. *porisma*, fr. Gr. *porisma* a thing procured, a deduction from a demonstration, fr. *porizein* to bring, provide.] *Geom.* A proposition affirming the possibility of finding such conditions as will render a certain problem capable of innumerable solutions.

pork (pōrk; 70), *n.* [OF. *porc*, fr. L. *porcus* hog, pig.] **1.** The flesh of swine, fresh or salted, used for food. Cf. HAM, 3. **2.** *Slang, U. S.* Money, position, or favors obtained from the government, as a result of political patronage.

pork barrel. *Slang, U. S.* Appropriations from the Federal treasury, as for improving rivers and harbors, regarded as appropriated more for local political patronage than for really necessary improvements.

pork′er (pōr′kẽr; 70), *n.* A hog fattened for food.

pork′pie′ (pōrk′pī′), *n.*, *or* **pork pie.** A felt sports hat with the crown narrower at the top than at the bottom and flat on top and an upturned or partly upturned brim, suggestive of a dish used by the English for pork pie.

por·nog′ra·phy (pôr·nŏg′rȧ·fĭ), *n.* [Gr. *pornē* harlot + *-graphy*.] Obscene or licentious writing or painting. — **por′no·graph′ic** (pôr′nō·grăf′ĭk), *adj.*

po·ros′i·ty (pō·rŏs′ĭ·tĭ), *n.*; *pl.* -TIES (-tĭz). **1.** State of being porous; specif., the ratio of the volume of interstices of the material to the volume of its mass. **2.** A bore.

po′rous (pō′rŭs; 70), *adj.* Full of pores; permeable by liquids. — **po′rous·ness**, *n.*

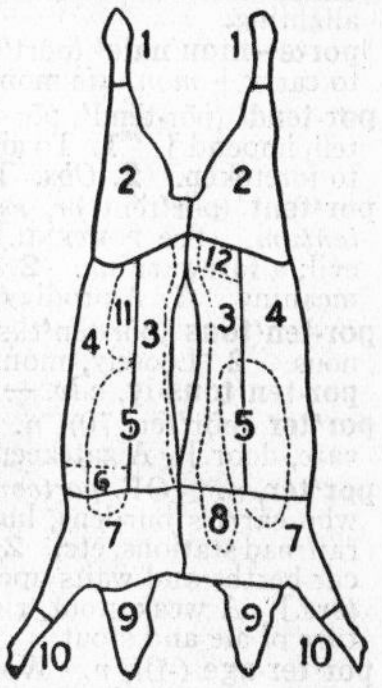

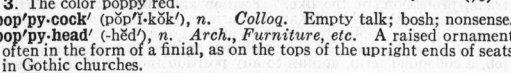

Cuts of Pork. 1, 1 Hind Feet; 2, 2 Hams; 3, 3 Pork Loins; 4, 4 Clear Bellies; 5, 5 Spareribs; 6 Brisket; 7, 7 Picnics; 8 Shoulder, New York style; 9, 9 Jowl Butts; 10, 10 Forefeet; 11 Leaf Fat; 12 Loin Butt.

por′phy·rin (pôr′fĭ·rĭn; *by some* pôr·fīr′ĭn), *Biochem.* Any of a group of iron-free or magnesium-free derivatives of pyrrole that form the basis of chlorophyll and hemin.

por′phy·rit′ic (pôr′fĭ·rĭt′ĭk), *adj.* **1.** Of or pert. to porphyry. **2.** *Petrog.* Characterized by distinct crystals, as of feldspar, quartz, or augite, in a fine-grained base.

por′phy·roid (pôr′fĭ·roid), *n.* *Petrog.* A more or less schistose, metamorphic rock with porphyritic texture.

por′phy·ry (-rĭ), *n.*; *pl.* -RIES (-rĭz). [OF. *porfire*, through It. & ML., fr. Gr. *porphyreos*, adj., *porphyra*, n., purple.] Orig., a rock consisting of feldspar crystals embedded in a compact dark-red or purple groundmass. Now, any igneous rock of porphyritic texture.

por′poise (pôr′pŭs), *n.*; *pl.* -POISES (-ĕz; -ĭz). See PLURAL, *Note*, 3. [OF. *porpeis*, *porpois*, lit., hog fish, fr. L. *porcus* swine + *piscis* fish.] **1.** Any of several small gregarious cetaceans (genus *Phocaena*); esp., the common porpoise (*P. phocaena*) of the North Atlantic and Pacific, five to eight feet long, having a blunt snout. **2.** Popularly, the common dolphin or the bottle-nosed dolphin. See DOLPHIN, *Illust.*

por′ridge (pŏr′ĭj), *n.* [From *pottage*; prob. influenced by ME. *porree* a kind of pottage.] A food made by boiling some vegetable or grain substance in water or milk, making a broth or thin pudding; as, pease *porridge*; oatmeal *porridge*.

por′rin·ger (pŏr′ĭn·jẽr), *n.* [Earlier *pottanger*, with intrusive *n*, for *pottager*, fr. F. *potager* a soup basin.] A dish, bowl, or cup for porridge.

port (pōrt; 70), *n.* [From *Oporto*, now *Porto*, Portugal.] A fortified wine of rich taste and aroma, usually dark red.

port, *n.* [From AS. *port*, and fr. OF. *port*, both fr. L. *portus*.] **1. A**

harbor; haven. **2.** *Com.* A place to which vessels may resort to discharge or receive their cargoes. **3.** *Revenue Law.* Short for **port of entry**, a designated locality, whether a nautical port or not, where foreign goods may be cleared through the customhouse.

port (pōrt; 70), *n.* [OF. *porte*, fr. L. *porta.*] **1.** *Scot.* A gate; portal. **2.** *Mach.* An opening for inlet or outlet of air, gas, steam, water, or other fluid, esp. in a valve seat or valve face; specif., the area of opening, in a cylinder face, of a passageway for the working fluid in an engine; also, any such passageway. **3.** *Naut.* An opening in a ship's side, as to admit light and air, load cargo, etc.; specif., an embrasure through which cannon may be discharged; also, the cover for a porthole.

port, *v. t.* [OF. *porter*, fr. L. *portare* to carry.] *Mil.* To carry in a position sloping across the body from right to left, as a rifle. — *n.* **1.** Carriage; bearing; demeanor. **2.** *Mil.* The position in which a weapon is carried when ported.

port (pōrt; 70), *n.* *Naut.* The left side of a ship (looking from stern toward bow); larboard. — *adj.* Larboard. — *v. t.* *Naut.* To turn or put to the port side of a ship.

port'a·ble (pōr'tȧ·b'l), *adj.* [F., fr. LL. *portabilis*, fr. *portare* to carry.] **1.** Capable of being borne; easily transported. **2.** Tolerable. — **port'a·bil'i·ty** (-bĭl'ĭ·tĭ), *n.*

por'tage (pōr'tĭj; 70), *n.* [F. See PORT to carry.] **1.** Act of carrying, or cost of carrying. **2.** A carrying of boats, goods, etc., overland between navigable waters; also, the route over which they are so carried; as, a rough *portage.*

por'tal (pōr'tăl; -t'l), *n.* [OF., fr. ML. *portale*, prop., neut. adj., fr. L. *porta* gate.] **1.** A door, gate, or entrance, esp. one that is grand and imposing. **2.** In Spanish American architecture, any porch or large roofed opening.

por'tal, *adj.* *Anat.* **a** Designating the transverse fissure on the under side of the liver where most of the vessels enter. **b** Hence, designating, or pertaining to, a large vein (**portal vein**) carrying the blood from the digestive organs and spleen to the liver, in the tissues of which it breaks up into capillaries.

por'ta·men'to (pōr'tȧ·mĕn'tō), *n.; pl.* -TI (-tē). [It., fr. *portare* to carry.] *Music.* Passage from one tone to another in a continuous glide through the intervening tones.

port'ance (pōr'tăns; 70), *n.* [OF.] *Archaic.* Port; carriage.

por'ta·tive (pōr'tȧ·tĭv), *adj.* [OF. *portatif.*] Capable of holding or carrying; as, the *portative* force of a magnet.

port·cul'lis (pōrt·kŭl'ĭs), *n.* [OF. *porte coleïce* a sliding door, fr. L. *colare, colatum*, to filter.] A grating of iron, hung in or over the gateway of a fortress or castle, to be let down to prevent entrance.

Porte (pōrt; 70), *n.* [F. *porte* gate. See PORT gate.] The government of the Turkish empire, officially called the ***Sublime Porte***, from the gate (*port*) of the sultan's palace at which justice was administered.

porte'-co·chere' (pōrt'kō·shâr'; *F.* pôrt'kô'shâr'; 70), *n.* [F. *porte-cochère.* See PORT gate; COACH.] **1.** *Arch.* A large gateway allowing vehicles to drive into a courtyard. **2.** *U. S.* Erroneously, a porch under which a vehicle may be driven to protect its occupants when alighting.

‖**porte'-mon'naie'** (pôrt'mô'nĕ'; *Angl.* pōrt'mŭn'ĭ), *n.* [F., fr. *porter* to carry + *monnaie* money.] A small purse.

por·tend' (pōr·tĕnd'; pôr-; 70), *v. t.* [L. *portendere, -tentum*, to foretell, impend.] **1.** To give an anticipatory sign, warning, or threat of; to foretoken. **2.** *Obs.* To signify. — **Syn.** See FORETELL.

por'tent (pōr'tĕnt *or, esp. Brit.,* pōr'tĕnt, pôr'-; 70), *n.* [L. *portentum.* See PORTEND.] **1.** An event or situation which presages evil; a forewarning. **2.** Prophetic character or significance; ominous meaning. **3.** A prodigy; a marvel.

por·ten'tous (pōr·tĕn'tŭs), *adj.* **1.** Of the nature of a portent; ominous. **2.** Loosely, monstrous; prodigious. — **Syn.** See OMINOUS. — **por·ten'tous·ly**, *adv.* — **por·ten'tous·ness**, *n.*

por'ter (pōr'tẽr; 70), *n.* [OF. *portier*, fr. LL. *portarius*, fr. *porta* gate, door.] A gatekeeper or doorkeeper.

por'ter, *n.* [OF. *porteour*, fr. LL., fr. L. *portare* to carry.] **1.** One who carries burdens, luggage, etc., for hire or for patrons at hotels, railroad stations, etc. **2.** *U. S.* An attendant who makes up Pullman-car berths and waits upon passengers. **3.** [That is, a liquor for *porters.*] A weak stout, rich in saccharine matter; — originally a mixture of ale and stout.

por'ter·age (-ĭj), *n.* Work of a porter or the charge made.

por'ter·house' (-hous'), *n.* **1.** A house having malt liquors, as porter, for sale. **2.** *Colloq.* Short for **porterhouse steak**, a choice steak with a large tenderloin, cut from the thick end of a beef. See BEEF.

port·fo'li·o (pōrt·fō'lĭ·ō; -fōl'yō; 70), *n.; pl.* -FOLIOS (-ōz; -yōz). [It. *portafoglio, portafogli*, fr. *portare* to carry + *foglio*, pl. *fogli*, leaf, sheet.] **1.** A portable case for keeping, usually without folding, loose papers, prints, etc. **2.** Such a case for documents of state; hence, the office and functions of a minister of state or cabinet member. **3.** A list of the commercial paper and securities owned, esp. by a bank or an investment trust.

port'hole' (pōrt'hōl'), *n.* **1.** *Naut.* An opening in a ship's side; a port. **2.** An opening, as in a wall, a military bunker, a tank, etc., esp. one through which to shoot.

Por'ti·a (pōr'shĭ·ȧ; -shȧ), *n.* The heroine of Shakespeare's *Merchant of Venice.*

por'ti·co (pōr'tĭ·kō), *n.; pl.* -COES or -COS (-kōz). [It., fr. L. *porticus.*] *Arch.* A colonnade or covered ambulatory. — ***the Portico.*** = THE PORCH (see under PORCH).

por·tiere' (pōr·tyâr'; -tĭ·âr'; *F.* pôr'tyâr'), *n.* [F. *portière*, fr. *porte* gate.] A curtain hanging across a doorway.

por'tion (pōr'shŭn; 70), *n.* [OF., fr. L. *portio.*] **1.** An allotted part; specif.: **a** A share received by gift or inheritance; a patrimony. **b** A dowry. **c** A share of food; a piece or amount served or regarded as sufficient for one person; a helping. **2.** One's lot or destiny. **3.** A part of a whole; as: **a** A constituent part. **b** A part abstracted from a whole; a limited quantity. — **Syn.** See PART; FATE. — *v. t.* [OF. *portionner.*] **1.** To divide into portions; to distribute in shares. **2.** To allot as a portion; specif., to dower. — **por'tion·less**, *adj.*

port'land ce·ment' (pōrt'lănd; 70). [From Isle of *Portland*, Eng.] A hydraulic cement made by burning and grinding a mixture of calcareous and argillaceous materials such as limestone and clay, limestone and shale, limestone and marl, chalk and clay, or limestone and iron blast-furnace slag.

port'ly (pōrt'lĭ), *adj.;* PORT'LI·ER (-lĭ·ẽr); PORT'LI·EST. [From PORT demeanor.] Dignified in appearance; stately; imposing, now esp. on account of bulk; corpulent. — **port'li·ness**, *n.*

port·man'teau (pōrt·măn'tō), *n.; pl.* -TEAUS (-tōz), -TEAUX (*E.* -tōz). [F. *porte-manteau*, fr. *porter* to carry + *manteau* mantle.] *Chiefly Brit.* A traveling bag or case, orig. one adapted for use on horseback; now, esp., a large suitcase.

portmanteau word. A word formed by arbitrary combination of two words (*slithy*, from *slimy* and *lithe*); — usually called *blend.*

port of entry. See 2d PORT, 3.

por'trait (pōr'trāt; -trĭt; 70), *n.* [F., orig. past part. of *portraire* to portray.] **1.** A pictorial representation of a person, esp. of the face, painted, drawn, engraved, photographed, or the like; a likeness, esp. one painted from life. **2.** Lifelike or realistic delineation, description, etc.

por'trait·ist (pōr'trāt·ĭst), *n.* One who makes, esp. paints, portraits.

por'trai·ture (-trȧ·tūr), *n.* [OF.] **1.** Act, practice, or art of making portraits; portrayal. **2.** A portrait.

por·tray' (pōr·trā'; 70), *v. t.* [OF. *portraire*, fr. L. *protrahere, -tractum*, to draw forth.] **1.** To represent by drawing, painting, engraving, etc.; to make a picture or image of; delineate; depict. **2.** To describe or depict in words; to describe vividly; also, to represent dramatically; act. — **por·tray'a·ble**, *adj.* — **por·tray'er**, *n.*

por·tray'al (-ăl), *n.* Act, process, or result of portraying; delineation; a portrait.

por'tress (pōr'trĕs; -trĭs), **por'ter·ess** (pōr'tẽr·ĕs; -ĭs), *n., fem.* of PORTER.

Por'tu·guese (pōr'tū·gēz; -gēs), *adj.* from PORTUGAL, *Gaz.* — *n.* **1.** *sing. & pl.* One of the people of Portugal, usually considered as typical representatives of the Iberian branch of the Mediterranean race. **2.** The Romance language of Portugal and Brazil, and the dialect (*Galician*) of the Spanish provinces of Galicia. See INDO-EUROPEAN LANGUAGES, *Table.*

Portuguese man-of-war. Any of several large siphonophores (genus *Physalia*) having a large, bladderlike sac or cyst, with a saillike crest on the upper side, by means of which they float at the surface.

por'tu·lac'a (pōr'tū·lăk'ȧ; 70), *n.* [L., purslane.] Any of a genus (**Por'tu·la'ca**, *pron.* -lā'kȧ; -lăk'ȧ) of mainly tropical succulent herbs of the purslane family, including the common purslane (*P. oleracea*) and the ***garden portulaca*** (*P. grandiflora*).

por'tu·la·ca'ceous (-lȧ·kā'shŭs), *adj.* Belonging to the purslane family (Portulacaceae). See PURSLANE.

‖**po·sa'da** (pō·sä'thä), *n.* [Sp.] A hotel; inn.

pose (pōz), *v. t.* [From *appose*, for *oppose.*] **1.** *Obs.* To question. **2.** To puzzle by or as by questioning; to nonplus.

pose, *v. t.* [OF. *poser* to place, put, fr. L. *pausare* to pause, in LL. also, to place, fr. L. *pausa* a pause; confused in LL., F., and E. with L. *ponere, posui, positum*, to put, place.] **1.** To claim to identify; as, to *pose* a poem as Shelley's. **2.** To propose or propound, as a question. **3.** To place in a studied attitude, with attention to posture and arrangement of draperies; as, to *pose* a model. — *v. i.* To assume a pose, or studied attitude, for a picture or as an affectation; to attitudinize. — *n.* **1.** A fixed or sustained posture, as for artistic effect or in affectation. **2.** A deliberately assumed mood; as, his cheerfulness is not a *pose.* **3.** Posing; attitudinizing.

Syn. **Pose, air** (*or* **airs**), **affectation, mannerism** mean an adopted way of speaking or behaving. **Pose** implies an attitude deliberately assumed in order to impress others; **air** may suggest acquirement through environment, but **airs** always implies artificiality and pretentiousness; **affectation** implies a trick of speech or behavior which strikes the observer as insincere; **mannerism** implies an acquired eccentricity that has become a habit.

Po·sei'don (pō·sī'dŏn), *n.* [L., fr. Gr. *Poseidōn.*] *Gr. Relig.* The god of the sea and of the watery element generally, son of Cronus and Rhea and husband of Amphitrite, worshiped as god of horses. His attributes include the dolphin, the horse, and the trident. See NEPTUNE.

pos'er (pōz'ẽr), *n.* A baffling question; a puzzle.

pos'er, *n.* Also **po·seur'** (pō·zûr'). One who poses.

pos'it (pŏz'ĭt), *v. t.* [L. *ponere, positum*, to place.] **1.** To set firmly or fixedly. **2.** *Philos.* To postulate or assert as fact (that which is immediate or indemonstrable); — contrasted with *infer.*

po·si'tion (pō·zĭsh'ŭn), *n.* [F., fr. L. *positio*, fr. *ponere, positum*, to put, place.] **1.** A positing, or placing. **2.** The manner in which anything is placed or disposed; hence: **a** Posture or attitude. **b** Manner or way of viewing something; mental attitude; as, to define one's *position.* **c** Site; place; station; hence, proper place; as, the *position* of a post. **d** Relative place, situation, or standing; specif., social or official rank or status; as, a person of *position.* **e** Office; employment; situation; as, to lose one's *position.* **f** Spot, place, or condition that gives one the advantage over another; as, to maneuver for *position.* **3.** *Gr. & Lat. Pros.* The state of having a short vowel followed by two consonants or a double consonant (as *x* or *z*); as, in *vŏlvŭnt* the syllables are long by *position.* — **po·si'tion·al** (-ăl; -'l), *adj.*

Syn. **Position, place, situation, office, post, job** mean an opening in a trade, profession, or the like. **Position** and **place** carry no further meaning; **situation** adds only an emphasis on its occupancy or need of an occupant; **office** applies to a position of trust or authority; **post** applies to a position attended by responsibility or involving onerous duties; **job**, a colloquial term, applies to any position thought of in terms of the work involved.

— *v. t.* To put in a or the proper position; also, to locate.

pos'i·tive (pŏz'ĭ·tĭv), *adj.* [OF. *positif*, fr. L. *positivus.*] **1.** Definitely or formally laid down or imposed; as, a *positive* order; hence, explicitly expressed; admitting of no doubt, qualification, or discretion; peremptory; explicit; definite; decisive; as, a *positive* statement; also, *Colloq.*, downright; absolute; as, a *positive* promise. **2.** Concerned with matters of practical experience; not speculative or theoretical. **3.** Independent of changing circumstances or relations; — opposed to *relative* and *comparative;* as, the idea of beauty is not *positive.* **4.** **a** Confident; certain; sometimes, overconfident; dogmatic. **b** Characterized by acceptance or approval; affirmative; as, a *positive* reply. **5.** Having a real existence, energy, character, or the like; actual; concrete; as, *positive* good. **6.** **a** *Bacteriol.* Affirming the presence of the organism or condition in question; as, a *positive* diphtheria culture. **b** *Biol.* Directed or moving toward a source of stimulation; as, a *positive* taxis. **7.** *Elec.* **a** Designating or pertaining to a kind of electricity. See ELECTRICITY, 2. **b** Specif.: (1) Charged with positive electricity. (2) Tending to lose electrons, and thus become positive [in sense (1)]. **8.** *Gram.* Of an adjective or adverb or its degree, having its simple form denoting no relation to increase or diminution. See COMPARISON, 2. **9.** *Mach.* Designating, or pertaining to, a motion or device which is definite, unyielding, constant, or certain in its action, as determined by unyielding parts or exactly controlled movements. **10.** *Math., Physics, etc.* **a** Numerically greater than zero; plus. **b** Reckoned or proceeding in a direction arbitrarily or conventionally taken as that of increase, onward motion, or the like. **11.** *Philos.* **a** Affirmative and constructive; — disting. from *skeptical.* **b** Empirical; subject to scientific verification; — disting. from *speculative.* **12.** *Photog.* Reproducing light and shade as in the original subject. — **Syn.** See SURE. — *n.* That which is positive; as: **a** *Gram.* The positive degree, or a form denoting it. **b** *Photog.* A print from a negative. — **pos'i·tive·ly,** *adv.* — **pos'i·tive·ness,** *n.*

pos'i·tiv·ism (pŏz'ĭ·tĭv·ĭz'm), *n.* **1.** Quality or state of being positive; certainty. **2.** [F. *positivisme.*] [*usually cap.*] A system of philosophy originated by Auguste Comte which excludes everything but the natural phenomena or properties of knowable things, together with their relations of coexistence and succession. — **pos'i·tiv·ist** (-ĭst), *adj. & n.* — **pos'i·tiv·is'tic** (-ĭs'tĭk), *adj.*

pos'i·tron (pŏz'ĭ·trŏn), *n.* [*positive* + *electron.*] *Physics & Chem.* A positively charged particle having the same mass and magnitude of charge as the electron, first detected in cosmic rays.

pos'se (pŏs'ē), *n.* [ML.; in L., infin., to be able.] **1.** *Law.* Short for POSSE COMITATUS. **2.** A force with legal authority; an armed band.

‖**pos'se co'mi·ta'tus** (kŏm'ĭ·tā'tŭs). [L. *posse* to be able, to have power, in ML., power + ML. *comitatus* a county.] **1.** *Law.* The entire body of inhabitants liable to be summoned by the sheriff to assist in preserving the public peace; also, the body of persons so summoned. **2.** = POSSE, 2.

pos·sess' (pŏ·zĕs'), *v. t.* [See POSSESSION.] **1.** To cause to own, hold, or control; to make the owner or holder, as of property, power, knowledge, etc. **2. a** To have and hold as property; to be master of; to own. **b** To have as a property, adjunct, attribute, or the like; as, to *possess* information. **3.** *Archaic.* **a** To gain; seize. **b** To bring under the control or influence (of some passion, idea, or the like); as, to *possess* one with indignation. **c** To inform; acquaint. **4.** To enter into and influence powerfully; to dominate; as, he was *possessed* with rage. **5.** To maintain in a condition of control or tranquillity; as, to *possess* one's soul in patience. — **Syn.** See HAVE.

pos·sessed' (pŏ·zĕst'), *adj.* **1.** Having as a possession or attribute; as, *possessed* of lands or wit. **2.** Influenced or controlled as by evil spirits, one's passions, a fixed idea; hence, mad; crazed. **3.** Self-possessed.

pos·ses'sion (pŏ·zĕsh'ŭn), *n.* [OF. *possession*, fr. L. *possessio*, fr. *possidere, possessum*, to possess.] **1.** Act or state of possessing; ownership; control; also, the state of being possessed. **2.** The thing possessed; in *pl.*, property in the aggregate; wealth; territory governed or controlled; as, foreign *possessions.* **3.** Fact or state of being dominated by an extraneous personality, a demon, passion, idea, or the like. **4.** Fact or state of being under one's own control; self-possession.

pos·ses'sive (-zĕs'ĭv), *adj.* **1.** Of or tending to possession; manifesting the desire to possess. **2.** *Gram.* Designating or pertaining to the case in English denoting ownership or some relation felt as analogous (*Dick's* hat; out of *harm's* way); also, designating a pronoun or construction, as with *of*, expressive of the same relation. Abbr. *poss.* Cf. GENITIVE. — *n. Gram.* **a** The possessive case or a word in that case; also, an equivalent case phrase (a story *of Lincoln's*), often called a ***double possessive.*** **b** A possessive pronoun.

☞ Present treatment of the apostrophe in forming possessives: (1) Nouns not ending in a sibilant sound, whether singular or plural, add *'s* (*dog's; men's*). (2) Singular nouns ending in an *s-* or *z-* sound, when of one syllable, add *'s* (*James's*); when of two or more syllables taking accent on the last, add *'s* (*Hortense's*); when of two or more syllables taking no accent on the last, add *'s* if the last syllable is not preceded by an *s-* or *z-* sound (*Thomas's*); but when the last syllable is preceded by an *s-* or *z-* sound, they add simply the apostrophe (*Moses'; for conscience'* sake; *Xerxes'*); proper nouns ending in *-es* [*pron.* -ēz], add only the apostrophe if the accent is on the penult (*Achil'les'*); but add *'s* otherwise (*Hercules's*). (3) Plural nouns ending in *s* or *es* add an apostrophe after the *s* (*boys'; fishes'*). Cf. *Punctuation* § 11. — **pos·ses'sive·ly,** *adv.* — **pos·ses'sive·ness,** *n.*

possessive adjective. An adjective formed from a personal pronoun, expressing possession (*my* hat).

pos·ses'sor (pŏ·zĕs'ẽr), *n.* One who possesses. — **pos·ses'sor·ship,** *n.*

pos·ses'so·ry (-ŏ·rĭ), *adj.* Of the nature of or arising from possession; having possession; being a possessor; possessive.

pos'set (pŏs'ĕt; -ĭt), *n.* [ME. *possot, poshote*, of uncert. origin.] A beverage of hot milk curdled, as by ale, wine, etc., and spiced.

pos'si·bil'i·ty (pŏs'ĭ·bĭl'ĭ·tĭ), *n.; pl.* -TIES (-tĭz). **1.** The state or fact of being possible. **2.** That which is possible.

pos'si·ble (pŏs'ĭ·b'l), *adj.* [OF., fr. L. *possibilis*, fr. *posse* to be able, fr. *potis* able, capable + *esse* to be.] **1.** Within the powers of performance, attainment, conception, etc., of an agent or activity expressed or implied; as, knowledge *possible* only to God; loosely, permissible; attainable; as, not *possible* to see the patient today. **2.** That may or may not occur; dependent on contingency; as, put by for *possible* emergencies. **3.** Potential, as by nature or circumstances; able or fitted to become, be used, or the like; as, a *possible* site for a capitol.

Syn. (1) **Possible, practicable, feasible** mean capable of being realized. **Possible** implies that a thing may exist or occur, given the proper conditions; **practicable**, that a plan, project, or the like, may be easily or readily effected by means at hand or under current conditions; **feasible**, that something proposed may be worked out or used so as to attain the ends desired.
(2) See PROBABLE.

pos'si·bly (-blĭ), *adv.* By possible means; perhaps

pos'sum (pŏs'ŭm), *n.* Short for OPOSSUM. — ***to play possum.*** To feign illness, ignorance, etc.; — from the opossum's habit of feigning death.

post (pōst), *n.* [From OF. *post*, and fr. AS. *post*, both fr. L. *postis.*] **1.** A piece of timber, metal, or the like, firmly fixed upright, esp. as a support; a pillar; prop. **2.** *Stock Exch.* Any of the places on an exchange floor at which trading in specified securities is carried on. — *v. t.* **1.** To affix to a post, wall, or other usual place for public notices; to placard. **2.** To publish, announce, or advertise as by the use of a placard; as, to *post* one for cowardice. **3. a** To affix public notices to. **b** To forbid to trespassers under penalty of legal prosecution, by notices along the boundaries; as, to *post* a brook. **4.** To enter (a name) on a postal list, as at clubs of a member behind in his dues.

post, *n.* [F. *poste*, fr. It. *posto*, fr. LL. *postum*, for *positum*, fr. *ponere, positum*, to place.] **1.** *Mil.* **a** The place at which a soldier is stationed. **b** The place at which a body of troops is stationed, or the troops there. **c** *U. S.* A local subdivision of certain veterans' organizations. **d** In the British Army, one of the two bugle calls (***first post*** and ***last post***) sounded at tattoo. **2.** A station or position, esp. one assigned; as, the *post* of duty. **3.** A position, situation, or office to which one is appointed; as, a *post* in the public service. **4.** A trading post or settlement. — **Syn.** See POSITION. — *v. t.* To station in a given place; to assign to a post, as a sentinel.

post, *n.* [F. *poste*, fr. It. *posta*, orig., a station, fr. LL. *posta*, for *posita*, fr. *ponere, positum*, to place.] **1.** Formerly, one who travels express with messages, letters, etc., as a courier or runner. **2.** Formerly, one of a series of stations for keeping horses for relays; also, a stage; hence, ***post horse.*** **3.** *Chiefly Brit.* **a** A single dispatch of postal matter; also, a mail or the mail. **b** A building for postal business; also, a letter box. **4.** A size of paper, 16″ × 20″; — from the watermark, a postman's horn. — *v. i.* To travel with post horses; hence, to ride or travel with haste. — *v. t.* **1.** To dispatch by the post or mail; to mail. **2.** *Colloq.* To inform; as, he is well *posted.* **3.** *Bookkeeping.* **a** To transfer or carry (an entry or item), esp. from the journal or daybook to the ledger; as, to *post* the cashbook; also, to enter (an item) properly in a book. **b** To complete (the ledger or other book) by the transfer to it and proper entry of all items in antecedent books; to make the proper entries in (all the books) to complete the record. — *adv.* With post horses; hence, at full speed; express.

post- (pōst-). [L., fr. *post*, adv. & prep., behind, after.] A prefix meaning: **1.** *After, subsequent, later*, as in *post*date, *post*script. **2.** *Behind* or *after* (in position), as in *post*fix; specif., *Anat. & Zool., behind* or *posterior to* (a specified part), as in:

postbrachial	**posthepatic**	**postthoracic**
postcerebellar	**postrenal**	**postuterine**

3. *Subsequent to*, as in *post*exilic; also as in:

post-Aztec	**postdiastolic**	**postnuptial**
postbaptismal	**postelection**	**post-Renaissance**
post-Biblical	**postembryonic**	**post-Revolutionary**
postcanonical	**posthypnotic**	**postseason**
postclassical	**postmarital**	**postsystolic**
post-Darwinian	**postnatal**	**postwar**

4. *Med. Occurring after and as a result of*, as in:

postanesthetic	**postparturient**	**postspasmodic**
postoperative	**postpuerperal**	**posttyphoid**

post'age (pōs'tĭj), *n.* The charge for the conveyance of a letter or other mailable matter by public post.

postage stamp. A government stamp required to be put on articles sent by mail in payment of the postage.

post'al (pōs'tăl; -t'l), *adj.* Of or pert. to the post office or mail service. — *n. Colloq., U. S.* Short for POSTAL CARD.

postal card. *U. S.* **1.** A card with a printed postage stamp sold by the government for transmission through the mails. **2.** Officially **post card.** Any private or unofficial card admitted to the mail on the affixing of a postage stamp.

post·ax'i·al (pōst·ăk'sĭ·ăl), *adj.* *Anat. & Zool.* Behind the axis of the body; esp., of or pertaining to the posterior side of the axis of a limb.

post bel'lum (pōst bĕl'ŭm). [L.] After the war; esp., *U. S.*, after the Civil War (1861–1865). — **post–bel'lum,** *adj.*

post'boy' (pōst'boi'), *n.* A boy who rides post; a carrier of dispatches or letters; a courier; also, a postilion.

post card, *or* **post'card'** (pōst'kärd'), *n.* **1.** *U. S.* See POSTAL CARD, 2. **2.** *Brit.* = POSTAL CARD, 1 & 2.

post chaise. *Hist.* A carriage for traveling post, having a closed body on four wheels and seating two to four.

post'date' (pōst'dāt'), *v. t.* To date after actual time of writing, issuing, etc.; as, to *postdate* a check or one's day of birth.

post'di·lu'vi·an (-dĭ·lū'vĭ·ăn; -dī-), *adj.* Existing or happening after the Flood. — *n.* One who lived or lives after the Flood.

post'er (pōs'tẽr), *n.* **1.** One who posts bills. **2.** A bill or placard, usually decorative or pictorial, for posting in a public place.

post'er, *n.* A fast traveler; also, a post horse.

poste res·tante' (pōst' rĕs·tänt'; *F.* pôst' rĕs'täɴt'). [F.] To be held at the post office until called for; — used in addressing letters; also, a post-office department having charge of letters so addressed. In the United States usually called *general delivery.*

pos·te'ri·or (pŏs·tēr'ĭ·ẽr), *adj.* [L., compar. of *posterus* coming after, fr. *post* after.] **1.** Later in time. **2.** Later in the order of proceeding, or moving. **3.** Situated behind; hinder; specif., *Anat.*, at or toward the hinder end of the body; caudal; hence, in human anatomy, dorsal. **4.** *Bot.* On the side next the axis of inflorescence; superior; — of an axillary flower. — **pos·te'ri·or·ly,** *adv.*

pos·te'ri·or'i·ty (-ŏr'ĭ·tĭ), *n.* State of being subsequent; — opposed to *priority.*

pos·te'ri·ors (pŏs·tēr'ĭ·ẽrz), *n. pl.* The buttocks.

pos·ter'i·ty (pŏs·tĕr'ĭ·tĭ), *n.* [F. *postérité*, fr. L. *posteritas.*] **1.** Offspring to the furthest generation; descendants; — contrasted with *ancestry.* **2.** All succeeding generations, collectively; future time.

pos'tern (pōs'tẽrn), *n.* [OF. *posterne, posterle*, fr. LL. *posterula*, fr. *posterus* coming after.] *Now Rare.* A back door or gate; a private or side way. — *adj.* Situated at the back, rear, or side.

post exchange. *Mil., U. S.* A store that sells articles and services to members of the armed forces and certain other authorized persons.

post'ex·il'ic (pōst'ĕg·zĭl'ĭk; -ĕks·ĭl'ĭk), **post'ex·il'i·an** (-ĭ·ăn), *adj.* After the exile; specif., *Jewish Hist.*, after the Babylonian captivity (after 597 B.C. or about 586).

post'fix (pōst'fĭks), *n.* [*post-* + *-fix* as in pre*fix.*] *Gram.* A letter, syllable, or word, added to the end of another word; a suffix. — (pōst-fĭks'), *v. t.* To annex; *Gram.*, to add to the end of another word; to suffix.

post'–free' (pōst'frē'; 2), *adj.* **1.** Free from charge for postage, as official governmental letters. **2.** *Chiefly Brit.* Postpaid.

post·gla'cial (pōst·glā'shăl), *adj.* *Geol.* Subsequent to the Pleistocene, or Glacial period; recent. See RECENT, 3.

post·grad'u·ate (-grăd'ū·āt), *adj.* Pert. to or designating graduates, or studies pursued after graduation. — *n.* A student pursuing such studies.

post'haste' (pōst'hāst'), *n.* Speed in traveling, as of a post or courier. — (*see Pron.*, § 2), *adv.* With great speed; by fastest means.

‖**post hoc, er'go prop'ter hoc** (pōst hŏk, ûr'gō prŏp'tẽr hŏk). [L.] *Logic.* After this, therefore on account of it; — a fallacy in arguing.

post'hu·mous (pŏs'tū·mŭs), *adj.* [LL. *posthumus*, fr. L. *postumus*, prop., last, hence, late born.] **1.** Born after the death of the father; as, a *posthumous* son. **2.** Published after the death of its author.

3. Following or occurring after one's death; as, *posthumous* fame. — **post′hu·mous·ly**, *adv.*

‖**pos′tiche′** (pôs′tēsh′), *adj.* [F.] Counterfeit; artificial. — *n.* **a** A substituted imitation; superadded ornament. **b** Counterfeiting; pretense.

pos·ti′cous (pŏs·tī′kŭs), *adj.* [L. *posticus.*] *Bot.* **a** Posterior. **b** Situated on the outer side of a filament.

pos·til′ion, pos·til′lion (pōs·tĭl′yŭn; pŏs-), *n.* [F. *postillon.*] One who rides as a guide the near horse of one of the pairs attached to a coach or post chaise.

post′im·pres′sion·ism (pōst′ĭm·prĕsh′ŭn·ĭz′m), *n. Art.* The theory or practice of certain artists in reaction against the scientific and naturalistic character of impressionism and neoimpressionism, characterized esp. by emphasis on the visual impression. Since postimpressionism stresses self-expression, it is a form of expressionism. Cézanne, Matisse, and Derain are among its chief exponents. See CUBISM. — **post′im·pres′sion·ist** (-ĭst), *n.* & *adj.* — **post′im·pres′sion·is′tic** (-ĭs′tĭk), *adj.*

post′li·min′i·um (-lĭ·mĭn′ĭ·ŭm), *n.* Also **post·lim′i·ny** (-lĭm′ĭ·nĭ). [L. *postliminium*, fr. *post* after + *limen, liminis*, a threshold.] *Internat. Law.* The right or rule of law (in full ‖**jus post′li·mi′ni·i** [jŭs pōst′lĭ·mĭn′ĭ·ī]) which, when persons or things taken by an enemy in war come again under the control of the state to which they belonged, revives their former rights.

post′lude (pōst′lūd), *n.* [*post* + *prelude.*] *Music.* A closing piece, esp. an organ voluntary at the end of a service.

post′man (-măn), *n.; pl.* -MEN (-mĕn). One who carries letters, etc.; formerly, a post or courier; now, a letter carrier.

post′mark′ (pōst′märk′), *n.* Any mark officially put on mail; strictly, the cancellation mark of a post office. Abbr. *pmk.* — *v. t.* To put a postmark on.

post′mas′ter (-mås′tẽr), *n.* **1.** One who has charge of a post office. Abbr. *P. M.* **2.** One who has charge of a station for travelers; one who supplies post horses.

postmaster general; *pl.* POSTMASTERS GENERAL. The chief officer of the post-office department of a government.

post′me·rid′i·an (pōst′mē·rĭd′ĭ·ăn), *adj.* [L. *postmeridianus.* See MERIDIAN.] Coming after the sun has passed the meridian; belonging to the afternoon.

post me·rid′i·em (mē·rĭd′ĭ·ĕm). [L.] After noon. Abbr. P.M.

post′mil·len′ni·al (pōst′mĭ·lĕn′ĭ·ăl), *adj.* Coming, or belonging to the period, after the millennium. Cf. PREMILLENNIAL. — **post′mil·len′ni·al·ism** (-ĭz′m), *n.* — **post′mil·len′ni·al·ist** (-ĭst), *n.*

post′mis′tress (pōst′mĭs′trĕs; -trĭs), *n.* A woman in charge of a post office.

post′–mor′tem (-môr′tĕm; 2), *adj.* [L., after death.] **1.** Occurring, made, or done after death. **2.** Pertaining to or used in a post-mortem examination. — *n.* A post-mortem examination.

post–mortem examination. *Med.* An autopsy.

post′–o′bit (pōst′ō′bĭt; -ŏb′ĭt), *adj.* Effective, or to take effect, after death. — *n.* Short for **post–obit bond**, a bond payable after the death of some person; esp., one made to secure payment of a loan with a bonus and interest.

‖**post ob′i·tum** (ŏb′ĭ·tŭm). [L.] After death.

post office. The governmental department for forwarding mail matter; an office under governmental superintendence where mail is distributed. Abbr. *P.O.* — **post′–of′fice**, *adj.*

post·or′bit·al (pōst·ôr′bĭ·tăl; -t'l), *adj. Anat.* & *Zool.* Situated behind the orbit, or eye socket.

post′paid′ (pōst′pād′; 2), *adj.* With postage prepaid.

post·pon′a·ble (pōst·pōn′ȧ·b'l), *adj.* That can be postponed.

post·pone′ (-pōn′), *v. t.* [L. *postponere, -positum*, fr. *post* after + *ponere* to place, put.] **1.** To defer; to put off; delay. **2.** To subordinate. — *v. i.* To delay; *Med.*, to delay in coming on. — **Syn.** See DEFER. — **post·pone′ment**, *n.* — **post·pon′er** (-pōn′ẽr), *n.*

post′po·si′tion (pōst′pō·zĭsh′ŭn), *n.* [See POSTPONE.] A placing after; state of being placed after.

post·pos′i·tive (pōst·pŏz′ĭ·tĭv), *adj.* Placed after or at the end of another word, often as enclitic or suffix. — *n.* A postpositive particle or word. — **post·pos′i·tive·ly**, *adv.*

post·pran′di·al (-prăn′dĭ·ăl), *adj.* Following a banquet; after-dinner; as, *postprandial* speeches.

post road. A road over which the mail is or was formerly carried.

pos·trorse′ (pŏs·trôrs′), *adj. Biol.* Retrorse; — opposed to *antrorse.*

post′script (pōst′skrĭpt; pōs′skrĭpt), *n.* [L. *postscriptum*, neut. past part. of *postscribere* to write after, fr. *post* after + *scribere* to write.] A note or series of notes appended to a completed letter, book, or the like, usually giving an afterthought. Abbr. *P.S.*, *p.s.* A second postscript is introduced by *P.P.S.* or *p.p.s.* (for *post postscriptum*).

pos′tu·lant (pŏs′tū·lănt), *n.* [F., fr. L. *postulans*, pres. part. of *postulare.* See POSTULATE.] A candidate for admission to a religious order in the stage preliminary to the novitiate.

pos′tu·late (-lāt), *n.* [L. *postulatum* request, prop., past part. of *postulare* to demand.] **1.** A proposition which is taken for granted or put forth as axiomatic; an underlying hypothesis. **2.** An essential prerequisite. — (-lāt), *v. t.* **1.** To demand; require; claim. **2.** To assume or claim as true, real, existent, or necessary; as, psychology that *postulates* a soul; to depend upon or start from the postulate of; as, his argument *postulates* the validity of reason. — **pos′tu·la′tion** (-lā′shŭn), *n.* — **pos′tu·la′tor** (-lā′tẽr), *n.*

pos′ture (pŏs′tūr), *n.* [F., fr. L. *positura*, fr. *ponere, positum*, to place.] **1.** Relative arrangement of the different parts, esp. of the body; characteristic or assumed bearing; specif., pose of a model or figure. **2.** Condition with reference to attitude of persons concerned, or disposition of things involved; as, a *posture* of defense. **3.** State of mind; attitude. — *v. i.* & *t.* To assume, or cause to assume, a posture; to pose. — **pos′tur·al** (-tūr·ăl), *adj.* — **pos′tur·er** (-ẽr), *n.*

pos′tur·ize (-tūr·īz), *v. t.* & *i.* To posture; pose.

post′vo·cal′ic (pōst′vō·kăl′ĭk), *adj.* Occurring immediately after a vowel sound.

po′sy (pō′zĭ), *n.; pl.* POSIES (-zĭz). [Contr. fr. POESY.] **1.** A brief sentiment or motto, as one inscribed on a ring. **2.** [Prob. from the use of flowers as of enigmatical significance.] A flower; nosegay.

pot (pŏt), *n. Scot.* & *N. of Eng.* A deep hole or pit.

pot, *n.* [Late AS. *pott.*] **1.** A metallic or earthen vessel of rounded form, variously used. **2.** Such a vessel with its contents; by ellipsis, a pot of drink; hence, drink; liquor; potation. **3.** = CHIMNEY POT. **4.** *Colloq.* **a** Of money, a large sum. **b** = POT SHOT. **c** The total of the bets at stake at one time. **d** = CHAMBER POT. **5.** A wicker vessel for catching fish, eels, lobsters, etc. — *v. t.;* POT′TED; POT′TING. **1.** To place in or as in a pot or pots; to preserve in pots; as, to *pot* ham. **2.** To shoot for the pot, that is, for cooking; to secure or hit by or as by a pot shot. **3.** *Colloq.* To secure; win; bag. — *v. i. Colloq.* To take a pot shot or shots.

po′ta·ble (pō′tȧ·b'l), *adj.* [F., fr. LL. *potabilis*, fr. *potare* to drink.] Drinkable. — *n.* In *pl.*, beverages.

‖**po′tage′** (pô′tȧzh′), *n.* A thick soup. — **Syn.** See SOUP.

pot′ash′ (pŏt′ăsh′), *n.* [After D. *potasch*, whence F. *potasse.*] **1.** Potassium carbonate, esp. from wood ashes. Purified potash is called *pearlash.* **2.** Caustic potash.

po·tass′ (pō·tăs′; pŏt′ăs), *n.* [F. *potasse.*] **1.** Also **po·tas′sa** (pō·tăs′ȧ). Potash. **2.** Potassium.

po·tas′si·um (pō·tăs′ĭ·ŭm; 58), *n.* [NL. See POTASH.] *Chem.* A soft white metal of the alkali group, occurring combined, as in sylvite, saltpeter, etc. Symbol, *K* (for NL. *kalium*); at. no., 19; at. wt., 39.100. Sp. gr., 0.86. — **po·tas′sic** (-ĭk), *adj.*

potassium bromide. See BROMIDE.

potassium carbonate. *Chem.* A white salt, K_2CO_3, forming a strongly alkaline solution, made from wood ashes, etc., used in making glass, soap, etc.

potassium chlorate. *Chem.* A colorless or white crystalline salt, $KClO_3$, a strong oxidizer used in explosives and matches.

potassium chloride. *Chem.* A colorless or white crystalline compound, KCl, found as sylvite, in plant and animal fluids, etc., and used as a fertilizer, etc.

potassium cyanide. *Chem.* A very poisonous crystalline salt, KCN, used in electroplating, etc.

potassium dichromate. *Chem.* A soluble salt, $K_2Cr_2O_7$, forming large orange-red crystals, used in dyeing, in photography, and as an oxidizing agent, etc.

potassium hydroxide. *Chem.* A white deliquescent solid, KOH, dissolving in water with much heat, to form a strongly alkaline and caustic liquid, used chiefly in making soap and as a reagent.

potassium nitrate. *Chem.* A crystalline salt, KNO_3, occurring as a product of nitrification in arable soils. It is a strong oxidizer and is used in making gunpowder, in preserving meat, in medicine, etc.

potassium permanganate. *Chem.* A dark-purple salt, $KMnO_4$, used as an oxidizer and disinfectant.

potassium sulfate. *Chem.* A white crystalline compound, K_2SO_4, used as a fertilizer, as a mild cathartic, etc.

po·ta′tion (pō·tā′shŭn), *n.* [OF. *potacion*, fr. L. *potatio*, fr. *potare.*] **1.** A drinking; a draft. **2.** A drink; beverage; alcoholic liquor.

po·ta′to (pō·tā′tō), *n.; pl.* -TOES (-tōz). [Sp. *patata* potato, orig., sweet potato, var. of *batata* sweet potato, fr. Taino *batata.*] **1.** The sweet potato. **2.** The edible starchy tuber of an American plant (*Solanum tuberosum*) of the nightshade family; also, the plant; — called also ***Irish potato*** *or* ***white potato.***

potato beetle *or* **bug**. A black-and-yellow striped beetle (*Leptinotarsa decemlineata*) that feeds on the leaves of the potato; — called also ***Colorado potato beetle.***

potato chips. Thin slices of potato (def. 2) fried crisp in deep fat.

potato worm. The large green white-striped larva of a hawk moth (*Sphinx quinquemaculata*).

‖**pot–au–feu** (pô′-tō′fû′), *n.* [F., lit., pot on the fire.] A dish of broth, meat, and vegetables boiled in a pot.

pot′bel′ly (pŏt′bĕl′ĭ), *n.* A protuberant belly. — **pot′bel′lied** (-ĭd), *adj.*

pot′boil′er (-boil′ẽr), *n.* A book, painting, etc., executed solely, and often hastily, for its monetary return.

pot′boy′ (-boi′), *n.* A boy who carries pots of ale, beer, etc.; a menial in a public house.

po·teen′ (pō·tēn′), **po·theen′** (-thēn′), *n.* [Ir. *poitīn* a small pot.] *Chiefly Ir.* Illicitly distilled whisky.

po′ten·cy (pō′tĕn·sĭ), *n.; pl.* -CIES (-sĭz). Also **po′tence** (-tĕns). [L. *potentia*, fr. *potens, -entis*, potent.] **1.** Quality or state of being potent; esp., ability to effect a certain result. **2.** Capability of developing in accordance with its nature; potentiality.

po′tent (pō′tĕnt), *adj.* [L. *potens, -entis*, pres. part. of *posse* to be able, have power, fr. *potis* able + *esse* to be.] **1.** Having or wielding authority, control, or dominion; puissant; mighty. **2.** Highly influential, effective, or cogent; as, a *potent* argument. **3.** Highly efficacious chemically or medicinally; as, a *potent* drug. **4.** Having the power of procreation. — **po′tent·ly**, *adv.* — **po′tent·ness**, *n.*

po′tent, *adj. Her.* Terminating in crutchlike figures; — said of a cross. See CROSS, *Illust.* (20).

po′ten·tate (pō′tĕn·tāt), *n.* [L. *potentatus* power, rule, ruler.] A sovereign or monarch wielding great power.

po·ten′tial (pō·tĕn′shăl), *adj.* **1.** *Now Rare.* Potent; influential; efficacious. **2.** Existing in possibility, not in actuality; possible or in the making, as opposed to actual or realized; latent; as, a *potential* hero or market. **3.** *Gram.* Designating or pertaining to that mood (**potential mood**) which expresses possibility, liberty, power, by the use of *may, can, might, could, would,* or *should.* — **Syn.** See LATENT. — *n.* **1.** That which is possible; potentiality. **2.** *Gram.* The potential mood; a verb form of that mood. Abbr. *pot.* **3.** *Math.* & *Physics.* Any of certain functions from which the intensity (or, in some cases, the velocity) at any point in a field may be readily calculated; specif., *Elec.*, the degree of electrification as referred to some standard, as that of the earth. — **po·ten′tial·ly**, *adv.*

potential energy. *Physics.* The energy which a piece of matter has because of its position, as a weight raised to a height, or because of the arrangement of parts, as a coiled spring, or the like.

po·ten′ti·al′i·ty (pō·tĕn′shĭ·ăl′ĭ·tĭ), *n.; pl.* -TIES (-tĭz). **1.** Potential character or condition; state of being possible, not actual. **2.** A possibility; a thing that may exist, occur, etc.; also, a person who may be chosen.

po′ten·til′la (pō′tĕn·tĭl′ȧ), *n.* [NL. dim. See POTENT.] Any of a large genus (*Potentilla*) of herbs of the rose family, the cinquefoils, or five-fingers, abundant in temperate regions.

po·ten′ti·om′e·ter (pō·tĕn′shĭ·ŏm′ē·tẽr), *n.* [*potential* + *-meter.*] **a** *Elec.* An instrument for measuring or comparing electromotive forces. **b** *Radio.* = VOLTAGE DIVIDER. — **po·ten′ti·o·met′ric** (-ō·mĕt′rĭk), *adj.*

poth′e·car′y (pŏth′ē·kĕr′ĭ; -kẽr·ĭ; 3), *n.; pl.* -IES (-ĭz). *Dial.* An apothecary.

po·theen′ (pō·thēn′). Var. of POTEEN.

poth′er (pŏth′ẽr; *now rarely* pŭth′ẽr), *n.* **1.** A choking cloud of dust, smoke, or steam. **2.** Bustle; fuss. — **Syn.** See STIR. — *v. t. & i.* To harass and perplex; worry; fuss.

pot′herb′ (pŏt′ûrb′; -hûrb′), *n.* Any herb boiled for food, esp. greens, or used to season food, as mint.

pot′hole′ (-hōl′), *n.* Any pit or hole; specif., a circular hole formed in the rocky beds of rivers by the grinding action of stones or gravel whirled round by the water.

pot′hook′ (-ho͝ok′), *n.* **1.** An S-shaped hook for hanging pots and kettles over an open fire. **2.** A hooked iron rod used to lift pots or lids. **3.** A written character resembling a pothook, as one used in teaching writing.

pot′house′ (-hous′), *n.* An alehouse; a low tavern.

pot′hunt′er (-hŭn′tẽr), *n.* **1.** A hunter who pots; esp., one who fills his bag in defiance of the rules or spirit of sport. **2.** A person who contests merely to win prizes. — **pot′hunt′ing,** *n. & adj.*

‖**po′tiche′** (pô′tēsh′), *n.; pl.* -TICHES (-tēsh′). [F., fr. *pot* a pot.] A vase with a separate cover, the body usually rounded or polygonal with nearly vertical sides.

po′tion (pō′shŭn), *n.* [OF., fr. L. *potio,* fr. *potare* to drink.] A draft; a dose; esp., a dose of a liquid medicine or of a poison.

pot′latch′ (pŏt′lăch′), *n.* [Chinook *patshatl* giving, a gift.] **1.** Among American Indians of the northwestern coast: **a** [*cap.*] The winter festival. **b** The ceremonial distribution of gifts during the festival. **2.** *Colloq.* **a** A large feast, often with gift giving. **b** A gift.

pot lead (lĕd). [D. *potlood.*] Graphite, or black lead, often used on the bottoms of racing vessels. — **pot′-lead′,** *v. t.*

pot′lick′er, pot′lik′ker (pŏt′lĭk′ẽr). Vars. of POT LIQUOR.

pot liquor. The liquid, esp. that suitable for soup, left in the pot after cooking meat, vegetables, etc.

pot′luck′ (pŏt′lŭk′), *n.* Whatever may be provided for a meal; hence, an ordinary, informal meal; such meals collectively.

pot′man (-măn), *n.; pl.* -MEN (-mĕn). A serving man in a public house.

pot marigold. A calendula, esp. *C. officinalis.*

pot′pie′ (pŏt′pī′), *n.* A meat pie cooked in a pot; esp., a fricassee with dumplings.

pot′pour′ri′ (pō′po͞o′rē′; pŏt′po͝or′ĭ), *n.* [F., fr. *pot* pot + *pourri,* past part. of *pourrir* to rot, fr. L. *putrere.*] A medley or mixture; specif.: **1.** A mixture, as of spiced flower petals in a jar, used to scent a room. **2.** A medley; sometimes, an anthology.

pot roast. A piece of meat, usually beef, cooked, by braising, usually on top of the stove.

pot′sherd′ (pŏt′shûrd′), *n.* [*pot* + *sherd* or *shard.*] *Now Archaeol.* A piece or fragment of a broken earthen pot.

pot shot. A pothunter's shot; hence, a shot, or any attack, that is unsportsmanlike or requires neither skill nor effort.

pot′stone′ (pŏt′stōn′), *n.* *Petrol.* An impure steatite, used in manufacturing culinary vessels, esp. in prehistoric times.

pot′tage (pŏt′ĭj), *n.* [OF. *potage,* fr. *pot* pot.] *Archaic.* A dish of vegetables, or vegetables and meat; a thick soup; potage. — **Syn.** See SOUP.

pot′ter (pŏt′ẽr), *n.* [From 2d POT.] One who makes earthenware vessels.

pot′ter (pŏt′ẽr), *v. i. & t.* Also, and in U. S. usually, **put′ter** (pŭt′ẽr). [Freq. of *pote* to poke, fr. AS. *potian.*] To busy oneself with trifles or futilely; trifle or dawdle (away). — *n.* Act or habit of pottering. — **pot′ter·er,** *n.* — **pot′ter·ing·ly,** *adv.*

pot′ter's field (pŏt′ẽrz). An old burial place for strangers at Jerusalem (*Matt.* xxvii. 7); hence, a burial place, esp. in a city, for paupers, unknown persons, and criminals.

potter's wheel. *Ceramics.* A horizontal disk, revolving on a vertical spindle, and carrying the clay in throwing.

pot′ter·y (pŏt′ẽr·ĭ), *n.; pl.* POTTERIES (-ĭz). [F. *poterie,* fr. *potier* potter, fr. *pot.*] **1.** A shop or factory where earthen vessels are made. **2.** Art of the potter; ceramics. **3. a** Ware made from clay, shaped and hardened by heat. **b** In a narrower sense, the coarser vessels so made. Cf. PORCELAIN.

pot′tle (pŏt′'l), *n.* [OF. *potel,* dim. of *pot* pot.] **1.** An old measure equal to a half gallon. **2.** A tankard of this capacity; by ellipsis, a pottle of wine, etc.; hence, liquor.

Pott's disease (pŏts). [After Percivall *Pott* (1714–1788), Eng. surgeon.] *Med.* Caries of the vertebrae, esp. tuberculous caries, often resulting in curvature of the spine.

pot′ty (pŏt′ĭ), *adj.* *Colloq.* **a** Trifling. **b** Slightly crazy.

pot′-val′iant (pŏt′văl′yănt; pŏt′văl′yănt), *adj.* Courageous when drunk.

pot′-wal′lop·er (pŏt′wŏl′ŭp·ẽr; pŏt′wŏl′-), *n.* *Eng. Hist.* A voter whose qualification for suffrage as a householder was being a boiler (walloper) of his own pot.

pouch (pouch), *n.* [OF. *pouche, poche.*] **1.** A small or moderate-sized bag, sack, or receptacle. **2.** Specif.: **a** *Archaic.* A money purse. **b** *Chiefly Scot.* A pocket in a garment. **c** A leather bag for ammunition; also, a wooden cartridge box. **d** A mailbag. **3.** That which is shaped like a pouch, as a cyst or sac; specif., *Zool.,* a sac or bag, esp. one for carrying the young, as on the abdomen of most marsupials, or for carrying food, as in the cheek of certain rodents. — *v. t.* To put in or as in a pouch; pocket. — *v. i.* **1.** To swallow; gorge. **2.** To form a pouch or baglike cavity.

pouched (poucht), *adj.* Having a pouch or pouches; as, a **pouched rat,** a gopher (sense 1).

pouf (po͞of), *n.* [F., a puff.] **1.** A puff, as of hair. **2.** A piece of furniture like an ottoman, usually circular with cushion seats on all sides.

pou·lard′ (po͞o·lärd′), *n.* [F. *poularde* pullet, fr. *poule* hen. See PULLET.] A pullet which has been sterilized for fattening; hence, a fat pullet. Cf. CAPON, 1.

poult (pōlt), *n.* [ME. *pulte,* contr. fr. *polet, poullet,* fr. OF. *poulet.* See PULLET.] A young turkey, or less commonly, a young chicken, pheasant, or the like.

poul′ter·er (pōl′tẽr·ẽr), *n.* *Archaic* **poul′ter** (-tẽr). [OF. *pouletier.*] One who deals in poultry.

poul′tice (pōl′tĭs), *n.* [Earlier *pultes,* fr. ML. *pultes* pap, pl. of L. *puls, pultis.*] A soft composition, usually heated and spread on a cloth, applied to a sore or inflamed part of the body, etc. — *v. t.;* -TICED (-tĭst); -TIC·ING (-tĭs·ĭng). To apply a poultice to.

poul′try (pōl′trĭ), *n.* [OF. *pouleterie.* See POULT.] Domesticated birds which serve as a source of food, either eggs or meat. They include chickens, turkeys, ducks, guinea fowl, pigeons, and pheasants.

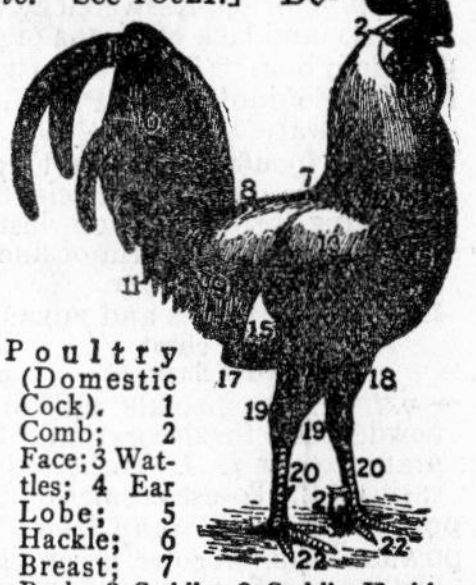

Poultry (Domestic Cock). 1 Comb; 2 Face; 3 Wattles; 4 Ear Lobe; 5 Hackle; 6 Breast; 7 Back; 8 Saddle; 9 Saddle Hackles; 10 Sickle Feathers; 11 Tail Coverts; 12 Tail Feathers; 13 Wing Bow; 14 Wing Coverts; 15 Secondaries; 17 Primaries; 18 Thighs; 19 Hocks; 20 Shanks or Legs; 21 Spur; 22 Toes.

pounce (pouns; 106), *n.* [F. *ponce* pumice, pounce, fr. L. *pumex, -icis,* pumice.] **1.** A powder, as of cuttlefish bone, formerly used to prevent ink from spreading. **2.** Powder, as charcoal dust, for making stenciled patterns. — *v. t.;* POUNCED (pounst); POUNC′ING (poun′sĭng). To dust, rub, finish, or stencil with pounce. — **pounc′er** (poun′sẽr), *n.*

pounce, *n.* The claw or talon of a bird of prey. — *v. i.* **1.** To swoop down, spring or leap, and seize with or as with the pounces, or talons; — with *on, upon,* or *at.* **2.** To spring or enter abruptly; as, to *pounce* into a room.

pounce, *n.* Act of pouncing; a sudden swoop or spring.

pounce, *v. t.* **1.** To emboss, as silver or gold, by hammering on the reverse side. **2.** To ornament by punching, cutting holes in, etc.; to cut the edge of in scallops; to pink.

poun′cet box (poun′sĕt; -sĭt). Also **poun′cet,** *n.* *Archaic.* A pomander.

pound (pound), *n.* [AS. *pund* (in comp.).] **1.** An enclosure, maintained by public authority, for confining animals taken in trespassing, or when at large; a pinfold. **2.** An enclosure for sheltering or trapping animals. **3.** A place of confinement, as for criminals. **4.** An area or space within which fish are kept, stowed, or caught. — *v. t.* To impound; pen up.

pound, *n.; pl.* POUNDS (poundz; 25), *collectively* POUND. [AS. *pund,* fr. L. *pondo.*] **1.** A unit of weight and of mass (see WEIGHT, *Tables* 1, 2, 3, & 4). Abbr. *lb.* (for L. *libra* pound); pl. *lb.* or *lbs.* **2. a** The monetary unit in several countries, as Great Britain (where it is called specifically the **pound sterling**), Australia, Egypt, Israel, Lebanon, Syria, and Turkey. See MONEY, *Tables.* **b** More fully **pound Scots.** A former Scotch money of account. It was originally equal to the English pound, but it gradually became debased until by 1603 when the Scotch and English Crowns were united it was equal to only 20 pence English.

pound, *v. t.* [AS. *punian* to bruise.] **1.** To reduce to a powder or pulp by beating. **2.** To strike heavily or repeatedly, as with the fist; pommel. — *v. i.* **1.** To strike or deliver heavy blows; beat. **2.** To move or come down heavily and with sounds as of pounding, as a person dancing, a horse running, or a ship meeting heavy seas. — *n.* A pounding; a heavy blow; thud. — **pound′er,** *n.*

pound′age (poun′dĭj), *n.* A sum or rate per pound; esp., a payment, tax, or the like of so much per pound sterling.

pound′age, *n.* **a** An impounding, as of cattle in a pound. **b** A fee for release of impounded animals.

pound′al (poun′dăl; -d'l), *n.* [From POUND a weight.] *Physics.* A unit of force which will impart to a mass of one pound an acceleration equal to one foot per second per second.

pound′cake′ (pound′kāk′), *n.* A kind of rich cake, the chief ingredients of which are measured in pounds.

pound′er (poun′dẽr), *n.* **1.** A thing weighing a pound. **2.** A thing weighing or having to do with something weighing a (specified) number of pounds; — used in combination; thus, a twelve-*pounder* may be a twelve-pound shell or a cannon firing such a shell.

pound′-fool′ish (*see Pron.,* § 2), *adj.* Incapable of dealing wisely with large sums or matters. See PENNY-WISE.

pound net. A fish trap consisting of a net or nets supported to form an enclosure with a narrow entrance.

pour (pōr; 70), *v. t. & i.* [ME. *pouren.*] **1.** To cause to flow or to flow in a stream or flood. **2.** To issue as if in a stream; to give or come forth freely, abundantly, or continuously. — *n.* A pouring, or the quantity poured; a flood; downpour. — **pour′er,** *n.* — **pour′ing·ly,** *adv.*

‖**pour′boire′** (po͞or′bwȧr′), *n.* [F.] Literally, (money) for drinking; hence, a gratuity; tip.

‖**pour le mé′rite′** (po͞or′ lẽ mā′rēt′). [F.] For merit; specif., **Pour le mérite,** the Prussian Order of Merit.

‖**pour′par′ler′** (po͞or′pȧr′lā′), *n.* [F.] An informal discussion.

pour′point (po͞or′point), *n.* [F.] *Hist.* A quilted doublet.

pour test (pōr). *Chem. & Mach.* A test to determine the lowest temperature (**pour point**) at which an oil, as a lubricating oil from petroleum, flows under given conditions.

pousse′-ca′fé′ (po͞os′kȧ′fā′), *n.; pl.* -FÉS (-fāz′). [F., fr. *pousser* to push + *café* coffee.] A drink served with after-dinner coffee; esp., *U. S.,* one made of various liqueurs of different specific gravities, poured so as to remain in separate layers.

pous·sette′ (po͞o·sĕt′), *n.* [F.] A dance figure in which one or more couples dance round and round with hands joined. — *v. i.* To perform a poussette.

pous′sie (po͞os′ĭ). Scot. var. of PUSSY, a hare.

‖**pou sto** (po͞o stō; pou stō). [Gr. *pou stō* where I may stand.] A place to stand upon; a basis for operations.

pout (pout), *n.;* see PLURAL, *Note,* 6. [AS. *pūte,* in *ǣlepūte* eelpout.] **a** Any of several fresh-water catfishes; esp., a horned pout (see HORNED POUT). **b** An eelpout.

pout, *v. i.* [ME. *pouten.*] To thrust out the lips, as in displeasure; hence, to look sullen. — *v. t.* To protrude or swell out (the lips); also, to say with a pout. — *n.* A pouting; *pl.,* a fit of pouting.

pout′er (pout′ẽr), *n.* **1.** One who pouts. **2.** A pigeon of a domestic breed with a distensible and often dilated crop.

pov′er·ty (pŏv′ẽr·tĭ), *n.* [OF. *poverté, povreté,* fr. L. *paupertas,* fr. *pauper* poor.] **1.** Quality or state of being poor or indigent; need; destitution. **2.** In monastic vows, renunciation as an individual of the right to own property. **3.** Inadequacy; scarcity. — **pov′er·ty-strick′en,** *adj.*

Syn. Poverty, indigence, penury, want, destitution mean the state of one in great need. Poverty implies an owning nothing or almost nothing; indigence, seriously straitened circumstances; penury, a cramping or oppressive lack of money; want and destitution, extreme poverty and lack of means of subsistence.

pow (pō; pou). Dial. var. of POLL, head.

POW (pē'ō'dŭb''l·ū) *or* **P.O.W.**; *pl.* POWs (-ūz) or P.O.W.'s. A prisoner of war.

pow'der (pou'dẽr), *n.* [OF. *poudre*, fr. *poldre*, fr. L. *pulvis, pulveris*.] **1.** The fine particles to which any dry substance is reduced by pounding, grinding, etc.; dust. **2.** A medicinal, cosmetic, or other preparation in the form of fine particles. **3.** Any of various solid explosives, as gunpowder.

☞ COMBINATIONS and PHRASES (in sense 3) are:

powder chest	powder horn	powder mill
powder flask	powder keg	powder room

— *v. t.* **1.** To sprinkle with or as with powder. **2.** To sprinkle like powder, esp. for decoration. **3.** To reduce to powder; pulverize, triturate. — *v. i.* **1.** To be reduced to powder; as, some salts *powder* easily. **2.** To use cosmetic powder. — **pow'der·er** (-ẽr), *n.*

pow'der, *v. i.* *Chiefly Dial.* To rush; ride very fast.

powder blue. A color, green-blue in hue, of low saturation and medium brilliance. See COLOR. — **pow'der-blue'** (*see Pron.*, § 2), *adj.*

powder metallurgy. The production of metallic objects by compressing powdered metal or alloy, with or without other material, and heating without thoroughly melting to solidify and strengthen.

powder monkey, powder boy. Formerly, a boy employed on war vessels to carry powder to the guns.

pow'der·y (pou'dẽr·ĭ), *adj.* **1.** Of the nature of, resembling, or of powder. **2.** Friable. **3.** Sprinkled with powder; dusty.

pow'er (pou'ẽr), *n.* [ME. *pouer, poer*, fr. OF. *poeir, pooir*, prop. infin., fr. VL. *potere*, for L. *posse, potesse*, to be able.] **1.** Ability to act; capacity for action or being acted upon; capability of producing or undergoing an effect; as, to have the *power*, but not the will, to work. **2.** A faculty, as of thinking or willing, of hearing, etc.; a mental or physical function; as, to use all his *powers* in an effort to succeed; the *power* of procreation. **3.** The possession of sway or controlling influence over others; also, a person, government, etc., invested with authority or influence or exercising control; as, the men in *power;* the great *powers* among nations. **4. a** *Archaic.* A military or naval force. **b** A superhuman agent; a spirit; as, the *powers* of darkness. **c** [*cap.*] *pl.* One of the orders of angels. **d** *Dial.* A host; multitude. **5.** Exerted energy; force; might; as, rent by lightning's *power*. **6.** Force or energy applied or applicable to work; specif., *Mech.*, mechanical or electrical force or energy.

☞ COMBINATIONS and PHRASES in this sense are:

power amplifier	power-driven, *adj.*	power-operated, *adj.*
powerboat	powerhouse	power plant
power cable	power line	power press
power drill	power loom	power station

7. *Law.* In general, authority, capacity, or right; as, *power* to contract; esp., authority or right to do or forbear derived by one person from another; as, a **power of attorney**, which is an instrument authorizing one to act as the attorney or agent of the person granting it; specif., an authority (a **power of appointment**) vested in one person (called *donee* or *appointor*) to dispose of, or create rights in, the property of another. **8.** *Math.* The product arising from the continued multiplication of a number into itself; as, 9 is the second *power* of 3. **9.** *Optics.* The degree to which an optical instrument magnifies. **10.** *Physics, etc.* The rate of transfer of energy, as in work done by an engine, or in absorption of energy in an electric system.

Syn. (1) Power, force, energy, strength, might mean the ability to exert effort. Power may imply latent or exerted, inherent or acquired, physical, mental, or spiritual ability to act or be acted upon; force implies the actual exhibition or exercise of active power; energy, power thought of as expended or ready to be expended; strength, power that resides in a person or thing that enables him or it to exert force or to resist pressure, attack, etc.; might, operative or effective power or force. (2) Power, authority, jurisdiction, control, command, sway, dominion mean the right to govern or determine. Power implies ability inherent or acquired; authority, power resident in or exercised by another; jurisdiction, the prescribed limits in which one exercises power; control, possession of authority to restrain or curb or of power to keep responsive to one's will; command, such power or authority that obedience ensues or is inexorably forced; sway, power marked by extent or scope of its influence; dominion, sovereign power or supreme authority.

power dive. A dive of an airplane accelerated by the power of the engine. — **pow'er-dive'**, *v. i. & t.*

pow'er·ful (pou'ẽr·fo͝ol; -f'l), *adj.* Full of, or having, power; potent; influential; cogent. — **pow'er·ful·ly**, *adv.*

pow'er·less, *adj.* **1.** Destitute of power, force, or energy; unable to produce any effect. **2.** Lacking requisite authority or sanction; not empowered. — **pow'er·less·ly**, *adv.* — **pow'er·less·ness**, *n.*

power pack. *Radio.* A unit consisting typically of transformer, rectifier, and filter for converting the voltage of power line or battery to that required for plate, screen, and filament circuits.

power politics. International politics by which each nation advances its interests through coercion on the basis of relative armed strength and by making capital of other nations' involvements.

pow'wow' (pou'wou'), *n.* [Of Algonquian origin.] **1.** Among North American Indians: **a** A priest, conjurer, or medicine man. **b** A ceremony, esp. of conjuration, marked by noise and feasting, and performed for cure of diseases, success in war, etc. **c** A conference of or with Indians. **2.** *U.S.* A conference or assembly resembling or likened to an Indian powwow. — (pou'wou'; pou'wou'), *v. i.* To hold a powwow.

pox (pŏks), *n.* [For *pocks*, ME. *pokkes*. See POCK. It is plural in form, but is used as a singular.] **a** Any of various diseases characterized by pustules or eruptions; as, chicken *pox*. **b** Without a qualifier, usually, syphilis.

poz'zuo·la'na (pŏt'swô·lä'nä), **poz'zo·la'na** (pŏt'sō-), *n.* [It.] *Petrog.* A siliceous rock of volcanic origin, first found near Puteoli (mod. Pozzuoli), Italy, used in preparing a hydraulic cement.

P.P. fac'tor (pē'pē'). Niacin or niacin amide. See VITAMIN.

PPI (pē'pē'ī'). [From *p*lan *p*osition *i*ndicator.] A radarscope on which spots of light representing reflections of radar waves indicate the range and bearing of objects, as airplanes, ships, buildings, cliffs.

prac'tic (prăk'tĭk), *n.* *Archaic.* Practice. — *adj.* *Obs.* Practical.

prac'ti·ca·ble (prăk'tĭ·kȧ·b'l), *adj.* [F. *praticable*, fr. *pratiquer* to practice. See PRACTICE.] **1.** Capable of being put into practice or accomplished; feasible; as, a *practicable* method. **2.** Capable of being used; usable; as, a *practicable* weapon. — **prac'ti·ca·bil'i·ty** (-bĭl'ĭ·tĭ), **prac'ti·ca·ble·ness**, *n.* — **prac'ti·ca·bly**, *adv.*

Syn. (1) See POSSIBLE.
(2) Practicable, practical are often confused. *Practicable* applies to that which has not yet been worked out or fully tested, but seems feasible; practical applies not only to things but to persons, and implies success in meeting the demands made by actual living, use, etc.; as, a *practicable* invention or scheme; a *practical* vehicle or person.

prac'ti·cal (prăk'tĭ·kăl), *adj.* [From *practic*, through obs. F. & LL., fr. Gr. *praktikos* fit for doing, practical, fr. *prassein* to do.] **1.** Of, pertaining to, or manifested in practice or action; — opposed to *theoretical, ideal,* or *speculative;* as, for *practical* purposes; *practical* politics. **2.** Capable of being turned to use or account; useful; as *practical* suggestion. **3.** Given or disposed to action as opposed to speculation, etc.; skillful or experienced from practice; capable of applying knowledge to some useful end; as, a *practical* mind; a *practical* electrician. **4.** That is such in practice, effect, or essential; virtual; as, the *practical* equivalence of terms. — **Syn.** See PRACTICABLE. — **prac'ti·cal'i·ty** (-kăl'ĭ·tĭ), *n.* — **prac'ti·cal·ly**, *adv.*

practical joke. A joke consisting in something done rather than said; esp., a trick played on a person.

prac'tice, prac'tise (prăk'tĭs), *v. t.*; -TICED or -TISED (-tĭst); -TIC·ING or -TIS·ING (-tĭs·ĭng). [OF. *practiser, pratiser*, for older *pratiquer*, fr. ML. *practicare*.] **1.** To do, perform, carry on, or exercise, esp. often or habitually. **2.** To perform or work at repeatedly; to acquire proficiency; as, to *practice* music. **3.** To follow or work at, as a profession; as, to *practice* law. **4.** To teach or accustom by practice; train; drill. — *v. i.* **1.** To act; operate; proceed. **2.** To perform certain acts often for proficiency. **3.** To pursue an employment or profession actively, esp. medicine or law. **4.** *Now Rare.* To scheme; plot; intrigue. **5.** To put something into practice; as, to *practice* rather than to preach. — **prac'tic·er, prac'tis·er** (-tĭs·ẽr), *n.*

Syn. Practice, exercise, drill mean to perform or make perform repeatedly. Practice further implies an accustoming and acquirement of proficiency; exercise, a strengthening or developing by keeping busy or at work; drill, a formation of correct habits by mechanical repetition.

prac'tice, *n.* [Earlier *practise*, fr. the v.] **1.** Actual performance or application of knowledge; — distinguished from *theory, profession*, etc.; as, engineering *practice*. **2.** Repeated or customary action; usage; habit; as, the *practice* of rising early. **3.** Usual mode or method of doing something; as, the *practice* is to use a local anesthetic; in *pl.* usually derogatory; as, the *practices* of tricksters. **4.** Stratagem; a scheme; plot. **5.** Systematic exercise for instruction or discipline; as, *practice* makes perfect; also, practical acquaintance, proficiency, etc., so acquired; as, to be out of *practice*. **6. a** The exercise of any profession or occupation; as, the *practice* of law. **b** Professional business or work, esp. as in incorporeal property; as, he sold his *practice*. **7.** *Arith.* A compendious method of performing multiplication by means of aliquot parts. **8.** *Law.* Established mode of conducting suits and prosecutions. — **Syn.** See HABIT.

prac'ticed, prac'tised (prăk'tĭst), *adj.* **1.** Experienced; skilled. **2.** Learned by practice; as, a *practiced* art.

prac·ti'tion·er (prăk·tĭsh'ŭn·ẽr), *n.* **1.** One who practices; esp., one who practices a profession. **2.** *Christian Science.* An authorized healer.

prae- (prē-). [L. *prae* before.] An equivalent or variant of PRE-, as in:

praecocial	praefect	praelector
praecox	praelection	praepositor

prae'di·al, pre'di·al (prē'dĭ·ăl), *adj.* [ML. *praedialis*, fr. L. *praedium* farm, land.] Of the nature of, or pertaining to, land or immovable property.

prae'mu·ni're (prē'mū·nī'rē), *n.* [Short for *praemunire facias*, where *praemunire* is a ML. corruption of L. *praemonere* to forewarn, cite.] *Eng. Law.* A form of writ for prosecuting certain offenses punishable by forfeiture and imprisonment; also, the offense or penalty.

prae·no'men (prē·nō'mĕn), *n.; pl.* -NOMINA (-nŏm'ĭ·nȧ). [L., fr. *prae* before + *nomen* name.] In ancient Roman names, the first of the usual three names (*praenomen, nomen, cognomen*), by which a person was distinguished from others of his family. — **prae·nom'i·nal** (-nŏm'ĭ·năl; -n'l), *adj.*

prae·pos'tor, pre·pos'tor (prē·pŏs'tẽr), *n.* A prepositor.

prae'ter- (prē'tẽr-). Var. of PRETER-.

prae·tex'ta (prē·tĕks'tȧ), *n.; pl.* -TEXTAE (-tē). [L. (sc. *toga*), fr. *praetextus*, past part. of *praetexere* to weave before, to fringe.] *Rom. Antiq.* A white robe with a purple border worn by a Roman boy before he assumed the toga virilis, and by girls until their marriage.

prae'tor, pre'tor (prē'tŏr), *n.* [L. *praetor*, for *praeitor*, fr. *praeire* to go before.] *Rom. Hist.* A magistrate next to the consul in rank, with, chiefly, judicial duties. — **prae·to'ri·al, pre·to'ri·al** (prē·tō'rĭ·ăl; 70), *adj.*

prae·to'ri·an, pre·to'ri·an (prē·tō'rĭ·ăn), *adj.* **1.** Praetorial. **2.** [*usually cap.*] Of, pertaining to, or designating the bodyguard (**Praetorian Guard**) of a Roman emperor. — *n.* **1.** A praetor or ex-praetor. **2.** [*cap.*] A soldier of the Praetorian Guard.

prag·mat'ic (prăg·măt'ĭk), *adj.* [L. *pragmaticus* busy, active, skilled in law and state affairs, systematic, fr. Gr. *pragmatikos*, fr. *pragma* a thing done, business, fr. *prassein* to do.] **1.** Of or pertaining to the affairs of a community or state; — chiefly in **pragmatic sanction** [*usually caps.*], one of certain royal decrees having the force of a fundamental law. **2.** Dealing with events so as to show their interconnection. **3.** Pragmatical; officious; opinionated. **4.** Practical; matter-of-fact. **5.** Of or pertaining to pragmatism. — *n.* **1.** A pragmatic sanction. **2.** A pragmatical person; a busybody; also, an opinionated person.

prag·mat'i·cal (-ĭ·kăl), *adj.* **1.** Practical; matter-of-fact. **2.** Objectionably busy; officious; fussy; also, conceited; dogmatic.

prag·mat'i·cal·ly, *adv.* of PRAGMATIC, PRAGMATICAL.

prag'ma·tism (prăg'mȧ·tĭz'm), *n.* **1.** Pragmatic quality or state or an instance of it. **2.** An American philosophical movement founded by C. S. Peirce and William James, and having as its characteristic doctrines that the meaning of conceptions is to be sought in their practical bearings, that the function of thought is as a guide to action, and that the truth is pre-eminently to be tested by the practical consequences of belief. — **prag'ma·tist** (-tĭst), *n. & adj.*

pra'hu (prä'ho͞o; prä'o͞o). Var. of PROA.

‖Prai'rial' (prē'ryȧl'), *n.* [F., fr. *prairie* meadow.] See REVOLUTIONARY CALENDAR.

prai′rie (prâr′ĭ; 6), *n.* [F., an extensive meadow, fr. OF. *praerie*, fr. L. *pratum* meadow.] A tract of grassland; specif., an extensive tract of level or rolling land in the Mississippi Valley, covered by coarse grass without trees.

prairie chicken. A grouse (*Tympanuchus cupido americanus*) of the Mississippi Valley.

prairie dog. An American burrowing rodent (genus *Cynomys*, esp. *C. ludovicianus* of the prairies), allied to the marmots. Prairie dogs live together in large colonies.

prairie schooner. *U.S.* A long canvas-covered wagon used esp. by emigrants crossing the prairies.

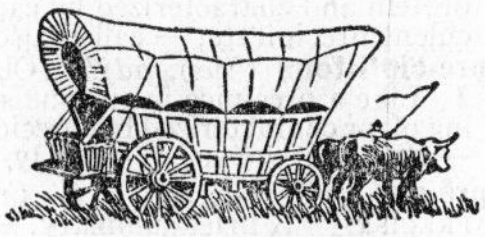
Prairie Schooner.

prairie wolf. A coyote.

praise (prāz), *v. t. & i.* [OF. *preisier*, fr. LL. *pretiare* to prize, fr. *pretium* price.] **1.** To express approbation (of); extol; commend. **2.** To glorify, esp. God, by homage; to magnify, esp. in song. — **Syn.** Eulogize, extol, acclaim, laud. — **Ant.** Blame. — *n.* **1.** Act of praising, or state of being praised; expressed approval; honor rendered. **2.** *Archaic.* The subject or reason of praise. — **prais′er** (prāz′ẽr), *n.*

praise′wor′thy (-wûr′thĭ), *adj.* Laudable. — **praise′wor′thi·ly,** *adv.* — **praise′wor′thi·ness,** *n.*

Pra′krit (prä′krĭt), *n.* [Skr. *prakṛtā* original, natural, usual, common.] The Aryan vernacular dialects of India, esp. the medieval vernaculars, as distinguished from Sanskrit; also, any one of these dialects. See INDO-EUROPEAN LANGUAGES, *Table.* — **Pra′krit,** *adj.*

pra′line (prä′lēn; prō′-; prā′-), *n.* [F.] A confection of nut kernels roasted in boiling sugar until brown and crisp.

prall′tril′ler (präl′trĭl′ẽr), *n.* [G.] *Music.* A melodic embellishment consisting of a principal tone, a tone one degree higher, and the principal tone again, all played as quickly as possible; — called also *inverted mordent.* Cf. MORDENT, *Illust.*

pram (prăm), *n.* Short for PERAMBULATOR, baby carriage.

prance (pråns; 9), *v. i.;* PRANCED (prånst); PRANC′ING (prån′sĭng). [ME. *prauncen.*] **1.** To spring from the hind legs, or move by so doing, as a horse in high mettle. **2.** To ride on a prancing horse; ride gaily or proudly. **3.** To swagger; also, to caper. — *v. t.* To cause (a horse) to prance. — *n.* A prancing; a prancing movement. — **pranc′er** (prån′sẽr), *n.* — **pranc′ing·ly,** *adv.*

pran′di·al (prăn′dĭ·ăl), *adj.* [L. *prandium* a repast.] *Now Humorous.* Of or pertaining to a repast, esp. dinner.

prang (prăng), *n. British Aviation Slang.* A crash. — *v. t. & i.* To crash (one's plane); to smash or destroy (a target or enemy plane).

prank (prăngk), *n.* A sportive or mischievous act; frolic; trick. — *v. i.* To play pranks.

prank, *v. t.* To dress gaily or showily; deck; also, dress up. — *v. i.* To make ostentatious show.

prank′ish, *adj.* Full of pranks; frolicsome; of the nature of a prank. — **prank′ish·ly,** *adv.* — **prank′ish·ness,** *n.*

prao (prou). Var. of PROA.

prase (prāz), *n.* [F., fr. L. *prasius*, fr. Gr. *prasios* of a leek-green, fr. Gr. *prason* a leek.] *Mineral.* A variety of indistinctly crystalline, translucent green quartz.

pra′se·o·dym′i·um (prā′zē·ō·dĭm′ĭ·ŭm; prā′sē·ō-), *n.* [NL., fr. Gr. *prasios* green + *didymium.*] *Chem.* A silvery white rare metallic element (see RARE-EARTH ELEMENT), a constituent of didymium. Its salts are green. Symbol, *Pr;* at. no., 59; at. wt., 140.92.

prate (prāt), *v. i. & t.* [MD. & MLG. *praten.*] To talk, esp. much and to little purpose; to chatter; babble; prattle. — *n.* Act of prating; idle talk. — **prat′er** (prāt′ẽr), *n.* — **prat′ing·ly,** *adv.*

prat′in·cole (prăt′ĭng·kōl; prā′tĭn-), *n.* [L. *pratum* meadow + *incola* inhabitant.] Any of a genus (*Glareola*) of limicoline birds.

pra·tique′ (prȧ·tēk′; prăt′ĭk; *F.* prȧ′tēk′), *n.* [F., prop., practice.] *Marine.* Permission to hold intercourse with a port given to a ship that has satisfied health regulations.

prat′tle (prăt′'l), *v. i. & t.;* -TLED (-'ld); -TLING (-lĭng). [MLG. *prätelen.* See PRATE.] To prate; esp., to talk or say lightly and artlessly; babble. — *n.* Trifling or childish talk or chatter; also, figuratively, a sound like prattling; as, the *prattle* of a brook. — **prat′tler** (-lẽr), *n.* — **prat′tling·ly,** *adv.*

pra′u (prä′o͞o; prou). Var. of PROA.

prawn (prôn), *n.* [ME. *prane.*] Any of numerous edible, shrimplike decapod crustaceans (genera *Pandalus, Peneus,* etc.) of tropical and temperate regions. — *v. i.* To fish for prawns. — **prawn′er** (-ẽr), *n.*

prax′is (prăk′sĭs), *n.* [NL., fr. Gr. *praxis*, fr. *prassein* to do.] Practice, esp. of an art, science, or technical occupation; — opp. to *theory.*

pray (prā), *v. t.;* PRAYED (prād); PRAY′ING. [OF. *preier*, fr. L. *precari*, fr. *prex, precis,* a prayer.] **1.** To entreat; implore. **2.** To supplicate or beg for; crave. **3.** To effect, bring, put, etc., by praying; — usually with an adverb as *out, into, down,* etc. — *v. i.* To make entreaty or supplication; to say prayers, esp. to God. — **pray′er** (-ẽr), *n.*

prayer (prâr), *n.* [OF. *preiere*, fr. L. *precarius* got by prayer, fr. *precari* to pray.] **1.** Act, practice, or an instance of praying; entreaty; earnest request. **2.** The offering of adoration, confession, supplication, thanksgiving, etc., to God or a god. **3.** The form of words used in praying; a formula of supplication, esp. one addressed to God. **4.** Often in *pl.* A form of religious service for public or common use, consisting largely of prayers; as, the ***Morning Prayer*** or the ***Evening Prayer*** of Anglican churches. **5.** That prayed for; specif., that part of a petition as to a legislature, or of a bill in equity, which specifies the thing desired or the relief sought. — **prayer′ful,** *adj.*

prayer book. A book containing prayers used at divine service; specif. [*caps.*], the Book of Common Prayer.

prayer meeting. A meeting or gathering for prayer to God, esp. one in which several or all offer prayer.

Prayer of Ma·nas′ses (mȧ·năs′ēz). A book of the Apocrypha. See BIBLE.

prayer wheel. *Lamaism.* A wheel or drum containing prayers which are deemed efficacious when the wheel turns.

pray′ing man′tis. See MANTIS.

pre- (prē-; prĕ-). [F. or L.; F. *pré-*, fr. L. *prae-* (ML. also *pre-*), pref., *prae,* adv. & prep., before.] A prefix denoting *priority;* specif.: **a** *Before in time; previously* or *previous;* as, **pre′ar·range′**, to arrange beforehand; **pre′al·lot′ment**, an advance allotment; — chiefly with verbs and their derivative nouns, as in:

preacceptance	precompose	preincarnation
preaccuse	preconceal	preincline
preaccustom	preconclude	preindicate
preacknowledge	precondemn	preinform
preacquaintance	precontract	preinstruct
preacquire	precook	prelimit
preactivity	precool	premove
preadjustment	predecay	prenotify
preadmission	predeclaration	preobject
preagreement	predeliberation	preobserve
preappoint	pre-engage	preorder
prearrangement	pre-establish	preprint
preascertain	pre-exact	prerelease
preassemble	pre-examine	preremit
prebake	pre-exhibition	presentence
prebid	pre-explode	preset
precast	pre-exposure	preshow
precelebration	preform	presurvey
precognition	preformulation	pretoken
precommunion	preheat	preview

b *Before in place; front; anterior;* as, **pre′ab·do′men**, the front part of the abdomen; **pre·cer′e·bral**, of or pertaining to the anterior brain; — chiefly with adjectives and nouns in scientific terminology. **c** *Prior in rank* or *degree; surpassingly* or *surpassing;* as in *pre*-eminent; — rarely an English formative. **d** *Prior to* (in time or place); *in advance* or *in front of; ahead of;* as, **pre′–Ar′mi·stice**, of the time prior to the Armistice (Nov. 11, 1918); **pre′ad·o·les′cent**, of the period preceding adolescence; **pre·al′tar**, placed before the altar; — chiefly with nouns used attributively, or with adjectives designating an event, period, school (literary, artistic, etc.), object, etc.; as in:

pre-Aaronic	preconvention	premodern
preadult	pre-election	premundane
pre-American	pre-Elizabethan	prenuptial
preanesthetic	prefeudal	preparental
pre-Aryan	pre-Gothic	preprandial
pre-Augustan	prehuman	pre-Revolution
prebaptismal	pre-Incan	presenile
precampaign	pre-Levitical	pre-Shakespearean
pre-Christian	premarital	pre-Victorian
preclassic	prematernity	prevocalic
preconsonantal	premedieval	prewar

e *Educ. Preparatory to; prerequisite to* (a type of training indicated by the second element); as, **pre·col′lege**, preparatory to college, *pre*medical, *pre*school, *pre*vocational.

preach (prēch), *v. i.* [OF. *preechier, prechier*, fr. L. *praedicare* to proclaim, fr. *prae-* + *dicare* to make known.] **1.** To proclaim tidings; specif., to proclaim the gospel; deliver a sermon. **2.** To exhort; sermonize. — *v. t.* **1.** To proclaim or utter in a sermon. **2.** To inculcate in discourse; as, to *preach* patience. **3.** To deliver (a sermon). — **preach′er,** *n.* — **preach′ing·ly,** *adv.*

preach′i·fy (-ĭ·fī), *v. i.* [*preach* + *-fy.*] *Colloq.* To preach ineptly or tediously.

preach′ing, *n.* Act or art of a preacher or an instance thereof; a sermon; a public religious service.

preach′ment (prēch′mĕnt), *n.* A preaching; a sermon; esp., a tedious exhortation; a religious harangue.

preach′y (prēch′ĭ), *adj.;* PREACH′I·ER (-ĭ·ẽr); PREACH′I·EST. *Colloq.* Given to preaching; having the style of preaching.

pre′am′ble (prē′ăm′b'l; prē·ăm′b'l), *n.* [OF. *preambule*, fr. ML., fr. LL. *praeambulus* walking before. See PRE-; AMBLE.] **1.** An introductory portion; a preface; specif., the introductory part of a statute, which states the reasons and intent of the law. **2.** An introductory fact or circumstance, esp. one that indicates what is to follow.

pre·ax′i·al (prē·ăk′sĭ·ăl), *adj.* *Anat.* In front of the axis of the body; in the arm, designating the radial side; in the leg, designating the tibial side.

preb′end (prĕb′ĕnd), *n.* [OF. *prebende*, fr. LL. *praebenda*, prop., things to be furnished, deriv. of *prae-* + *habere* to have.] The stipend or maintenance granted out of the estate of a cathedral or collegiate church to a canon or member of the chapter; also, the land or tithe from which the stipend comes, or the holding of it as a benefice. — **pre·ben′dal** (prē·bĕn′dăl; -d'l), *adj.*

preb′en·dar′y (prĕb′ĕn·dĕr′ĭ *or, esp. Brit.,* -dẽr·ĭ), *n.; pl.* -DARIES (-ĭz). One who receives a prebend; now, *Ch. of Eng.,* an honorary canon with the title but not the emoluments of a prebend.

Pre′–Cam′bri·an (prē′kăm′brĭ·ăn), *adj.* Of, pert. to, or designating the earliest division of geological history (equivalent to the Archeozoic and Proterozoic divisions) or the rocks formed during this time. — **Pre′–Cam′bri·an,** *n.*

pre·can′cel (prē·kăn′sĕl; -s'l), *v. t.;* -CAN′CELED (-sĕld; -s'ld) or -CAN′CELLED; -CAN′CEL·ING or -CAN′CEL·LING. [*pre-* + *cancel.*] To cancel (postage stamps) in advance of use; — chiefly in past participle (abbr. *precanc.*).

pre·car′i·ous (prē·kâr′ĭ·ŭs), *adj.* [L. *precarius* obtained by begging or prayer, fr. *prex, precis,* prayer.] **1.** Depending on the will or pleasure of another; held on sufferance; uncertain; as, *precarious* privileges. **2.** Taken for granted; unfounded; unwarranted; as, a *precarious* conclusion. **3.** Dependent on contingencies; exposed to hazards; insecure; as, to be in a *precarious* situation. — **Syn.** See DANGEROUS. — **pre·car′i·ous·ly,** *adv.* — **pre·car′i·ous·ness,** *n.*

prec′a·to′ry (prĕk′ȧ·tō′rĭ *or, esp. Brit.,* -tẽr·ĭ), *adj.* Also **prec′a·tive** (-tĭv). [LL. *precatorius, precativus.*] Of, pert. to, or of the nature of, or expressive of entreaty; supplicatory.

pre·cau′tion (prē·kô′shŭn), *n.* [F. *précaution*, fr. LL. *praecautio*, fr. L. *praecavere, -cautum,* to guard against beforehand, fr. *prae-* + *cavere* to be on one's guard.] **1.** Previous caution or care. **2.** A measure taken beforehand to ward off evil or secure good or success; as, to take *precautions* against accident. — **pre·cau′tion·al** (-ăl; -'l), *adj.*

pre·cau′tion·ar′y (-ẽr′ĭ *or, esp. Brit.,* -ẽr·ĭ), *adj.* Of, pertaining to, or of the nature of a precaution; advising or using caution beforehand.

pre·cau′tious (prē·kô′shŭs), *adj.* Using precaution; precautionary.

pre·cede′ (prē·sēd′; 2), *v. t. & i.* [F. *précéder*, fr. L. *praecedere, -cessum,* fr. *prae-* + *cedere* to go.] **1.** To go before as in rank or dignity; take precedence of. **2.** To be, go, or come before or in front of. **3.** To go before in order of time; to be earlier than.

pre·ced′ence (prē·sēd′ĕns; prĕs′ē·dĕns; prĕ′sē-), *n.* Also **pre·ced′en·cy** (-(d)ĕn·sĭ). A preceding; priority in time, importance, or esp., rank; specif., ceremonial priority or order; the order observed by persons of different rank on ceremonial occasions.

pre·ced′ent (prē·sēd′ĕnt), *adj.* Preceding; going before in time, order, arrangement, etc.

prec′e·dent (prĕs′ē·dĕnt; prē′sē-), *n.* Something done or said that may serve as an example to authorize or justify a subsequent act of the same or an analogous kind; esp., *Law,* a judicial decision, proceeding, or course of action, serving as a rule for future determinations in similar cases.

prec′e·den′tial (-dĕn′shăl), *adj.* Of the nature of, or constituting, a precedent; as, *precedential* acts.

pre·ced′ing (prē·sēd′ĭng), *adj.* That precedes; going before in time, order, arrangement, etc.; precedent.

Syn. Preceding, antecedent, foregoing, previous, prior, former, anterior mean being before. Preceding implies beforeness in time or in place; antecedent implies beforeness in time, especially as a cause; foregoing implies reference to that which has preceded, esp. in a discourse; previous always, and prior sometimes, apply to something made or occurring earlier, but *prior* often adds the implication of greater importance; former definitely implies comparison with that which is *latter,* anterior with that which is *posterior,* in place, in order, or in time.

pre·cent′ (prē·sĕnt′), *v. i. & t.* To act as precentor.

pre·cen′tor (-sĕn′tẽr), *n.* [LL. *praecentor,* fr. *praecinere* to sing before, fr. *prae-* + *canere* to sing.] A leader of the singing of a choir or congregation. — **pre′cen·to′ri·al** (prē′sĕn·tō′rĭ·ăl; 70), *adj.* — **pre·cen′tor·ship,** *n.*

pre′cept (prē′sĕpt), *n.* [OF. or L.; OF., fr. L. *praeceptum,* fr. *praecipere* to take beforehand, instruct, teach, fr. *prae-* + *capere* take.] **1.** Any commandment, instruction, or order intended as a rule of action or conduct; esp., a practical rule guiding behavior, technique, etc. **2.** *Law.* An order, warrant, or writ issued pursuant to law, esp. to an administrative officer. — **Syn.** See LAW.

pre·cep′tive (prē·sĕp′tĭv), *adj.* Giving precepts; of the nature of a precept; instructive. — **pre·cep′tive·ly,** *adv.*

pre·cep′tor (-tẽr), *n.* [L. *praeceptor.*] **1.** A teacher; specif., the master or principal of a school. **2.** The head of a preceptory. — **pre·cep′to·ral** (-tō·răl), **pre′cep·to′ri·al** (prē′sĕp·tō′rĭ·ăl; 70), *adj.* — **pre·cep′tor·ate** (prē·sĕp′tẽr·ĭt), *n.*

pre·cep′to·ry (-tō·rĭ), *adj.* Preceptive. — *n.; pl.* -RIES (-rĭz). [ML. *praeceptoria* an estate assigned to a preceptor.] A religious house of the Knights Templars, subordinate to the temple of the order in London; hence, a commandery. See COMMANDERY **a.**

pre·cep′tress (-trĕs; -trĭs), *n.* A female preceptor (def. 1).

pre·ces′sion (prē·sĕsh′ŭn), *n.* [LL. *praecessio,* fr. *praecedere, -cessum,* to go before. See PRECEDE.] Act of preceding in time, rank, or order; precedence. — **pre·ces′sion·al** (-ăl; -'l), *adj.*

precession of the equinoxes. *Astron.* A slow westward motion of the equinoctial points along the ecliptic, caused by lunisolar action upon the protuberant matter about the earth's equator, and bringing either equinox to the meridian sooner each day than it would otherwise come; — called specif. ***lunisolar precession.*** This precession is modified by a comparatively small eastward motion of the equinoxes caused by planetary action altering the plane of the earth's orbit; — called specif. ***planetary precession.*** Hence, the combined effect of lunisolar and planetary precession; — called specif. ***general precession.*** A complete revolution is accomplished in a cycle of nearly 26,000 years, called the *Platonic year,* or *great year.*

pre′cinct (prē′sĭngkt), *n.* [ML. *praecinctum,* fr. L. *praecingere, -cinctum,* to gird about, encompass. See PRE-; CINCTURE.] **1.** The enclosed or otherwise limited grounds, as of a church; hence, *pl.,* immediate surroundings; environs. **2.** Bounds; limited area; a boundary. **3.** A district made for administrative or similar purposes; esp., a division of a city for police control, or of a ward or county for election purposes.

pre′ci·os′i·ty (prĕsh′ĭ·ŏs′ĭ·tĭ), *n.; pl.* -TIES (-tĭz). [OF. *preciosité.*] Fastidious refinement, esp. in language.

pre′cious (prĕsh′ŭs), *adj.* [OF. *precios,* fr. L. *pretiosus,* fr. *pretium* price, value.] **1.** Of great price or value; costly; as, a *precious* stone. **2.** Highly esteemed or loved; dear. **3.** Fastidious; overrefined; as, *precious* language. **4.** Egregious; arrant; as, a *precious* fool. — **Syn.** See COSTLY. — *adv. Colloq.* Very; — an intensive. — **pre′cious·ly,** *adv.* — **pre′cious·ness,** *n.*

prec′i·pice (prĕs′ĭ·pĭs), *n.* [F. *précipice,* fr. L. *praecipitium,* fr. *praeceps, -cipitis,* headlong, fr. *prae-* + *caput, -pitis,* head.] A very steep or overhanging place, as the face of a cliff; an abrupt declivity; a cliff.

pre·cip′i·tance (prē·sĭp′ĭ·tăns), *n.* Also **pre·cip′i·tan·cy** (-tăn·sĭ). Action, fact, or quality of being precipitant, or precipitate; excessive or rash haste.

pre·cip′i·tant (-tănt), *adj.* [F. or L.; F. *précipitant,* fr. L. *praecipitans, -antis,* pres. part. of *praecipitare* to precipitate.] **1.** Falling or rushing headlong; rushing swiftly, violently, or recklessly. **2.** Very sudden or unexpected; abrupt. **3.** *Chem.* Falling as a precipitate. — *n. Chem.* Anything which causes the formation of a precipitate. — **pre·cip′i·tant·ly,** *adv.*

pre·cip′i·tate (-tāt), *adj.* [L. *praecipitatus,* past part. of *praecipitare* to precipitate, fr. *praeceps* headlong.] **1.** Falling, flowing, or rushing, with steep descent; hurled headlong. **2.** Acting with unwise haste; rash; headstrong. **3.** Extremely sudden or abrupt; as, a *precipitate* illness. **4.** Done without, or exhibiting the lack of, due deliberation or care; overhasty.

Syn. Precipitate, headlong, abrupt, impetuous, sudden mean showing undue haste or unexpectedness. Precipitate and headlong imply lack of forethought, and rashness, but *precipitate* applies usually to decisions or actions, and *headlong* to the persons or qualities involved; abrupt implies unceremoniousness, curtness, or a complete lack of warning; impetuous implies a vehement impulsiveness or impatience; sudden implies great hastiness and impetuosity.

— (-tāt), *v. t. & i.* **1.** To throw or dash headlong; cast or hurl down, as from a precipice. **2.** To move very rapidly; to urge or press on with haste or violence; to cause to happen suddenly, unexpectedly, or too soon; as, to *precipitate* a conflict. **3.** *Physics & Meteorol.* To condense or become condensed, as vapor, and fall as rain, etc. **4.** *Chem.* To separate or become separated as a precipitate.

— (-tāt *or, esp. Brit.,* -tĭt), *n.* A substance in a concrete state separated from a solution in consequence of some chemical or physical change caused by a reagent, cold, etc.

— **pre·cip′i·tate·ly,** *adv.* — **pre·cip′i·tate·ness,** *n.* — **pre·cip′i·ta′tive** (-tā′tĭv), *adj.* — **pre·cip′i·ta′tor** (-tā′tẽr), *n.*

pre·cip′i·ta′tion (-tā′shŭn), *n.* **1.** Act or an instance of precipitating, or state of being precipitated; that which is precipitated; specif.: **a** A headlong rush. **b** Precipitance; impetuosity. **c** A hastening; acceleration. **2.** *Chem.* A precipitating from a solution; also, a precipitate. **3.** *Meteorol.* A deposit on the earth of hail, mist, rain, sleet, or snow; also, the quantity of water deposited. **4.** *Spiritualism.* Materialization.

pre·cip′i·tin (prē·sĭp′ĭ·tĭn), *n.* [See PRECIPITATE; -IN.] *Immunol.* A specific antibody developed in response to inoculations of a foreign protein and characterized by causing at first turbidity and later a flocculent precipitate; — called also *coagulin.*

pre·cip′i·tous (-tŭs), *adj.* [Obs. F. *precipiteux.* See PRECIPICE.] **1.** Like a precipice in steepness; of the nature of a precipice; consisting of, or characterized by, precipices. **2.** Precipitant. **3.** Precipitate. — **Syn.** See STEEP. — **-tous·ly,** *adv.* — **-tous·ness,** *n.*

pré·cis′ (prā·sē′ *or, esp. Brit.,* prā′sē, prĕs′ē), *n. sing. & pl.* [F. See PRECISE.] A brief summary. — **Syn.** See COMPENDIUM.

pre·cise′ (prē·sīs′), *adj.* [F. *précis,* fr. L. *praecisus* cut off, brief, concise, deriv. of *prae-* + *caedere* to cut.] **1.** Exactly or sharply defined or stated; not vague or equivocal; as, *precise* directions. **2.** Minutely exact; not varying in the slightest degree from truth, accuracy, standard, etc.; as, a *precise* balance. **3.** Strictly conforming to rule or usage; punctilious; scrupulous; sometimes, overnice; very strict. — **Syn.** See CORRECT. — **pre·cise′ly,** *adv.* — **pre·cise′ness,** *n.*

pre·ci′sian (prē·sĭzh′ăn), *n.* One rigidly or ceremoniously exact in observing forms; esp. in religious observance; — formerly applied to the English Puritans. — **pre·ci′sian,** *adj.* — **pre·ci′sian·ism** (-ĭz′m), *n.*

pre·ci′sion (prē·sĭzh′ŭn), *n.* Quality or state of being precise; accuracy; definiteness. — *adj.* **1.** Adapted for extremely accurate scientific measurement; as, *precision* gauges. **2.** *Mil.* Adapted for extremely accurate aiming of projectiles or bombs, as by means of a bombsight; as, *precision* bombing. — **pre·ci′sion·ist** (-ĭst), *n.*

pre·clin′i·cal (prē·klĭn′ĭ·kăl), *adj. Med.* Of or pertaining to the period preceding symptomatic manifestations.

pre·clude′ (prē·klōōd′; 114), *v. t.* [L. *praecludere, -clusum,* fr. *prae-* + *claudere* to shut.] **1.** To put a barrier before; to shut up or out; impede; as, his acts *preclude* him from recognition. **2.** To shut out or obviate by anticipation; to render ineffectual, impossible, etc.; as, to *preclude* escape. — **Syn.** See PREVENT. — **pre·clu′sion** (-klōō′zhŭn), *n.* — **pre·clu′sive** (-sĭv), *adj.* — **pre·clu′sive·ly,** *adv.*

pre·co′cial (prē·kō′shăl), *adj.* [See PRECOCIOUS.] *Zool.* Designating birds covered with down and able to run about when newly hatched.

pre·co′cious (-shŭs), *adj.* [L. *praecox, -ocis,* fr. *praecoquere* to cook or ripen beforehand, fr. *prae-* + *coquere* to cook.] **1.** Exceptionally early in development, esp. mentally; forward; — chiefly of children. **2.** Of, pert. to, or suggesting precocity. — **pre·co′cious·ly,** *adv.* — **pre·co′cious·ness, pre·coc′i·ty** (-kŏs′ĭ·tĭ), *n.*

pre′con·ceive′ (prē′kŏn·sēv′), *v. t.* To conceive, or form an opinion of, beforehand; to form a previous notion of.

pre′con·cep′tion (-sĕp′shŭn), *n.* A preconceived idea; hence, a prejudice; a prepossession.

pre′con·cert′ (-sûrt′), *v. t.* To settle by prior agreement.

pre′con·di′tion (prē′kŏn·dĭsh′ŭn), *v. t.* To put in proper or desired condition, frame of mind, or the like, in advance.

pre′co·nize (prē′kō·nīz), *v. t.* [ML. *praeconizare* to proclaim, fr. L. *praeco, -onis,* a crier, a herald.] To proclaim or commend publicly; specif., *R.C.Ch.,* of the pope in consistory, to nominate to an ecclesiastical dignity.

pre·crit′i·cal (prē·krĭt′ĭ·kăl), *adj. Med.* Preceding a crisis.

pre·cur′sive (prē·kûr′sĭv), *adj.* Precursory; also, prognosticative.

pre·cur′sor (-sẽr), *n.* [L. *praecursor,* fr. *praecurrere* to run before, fr. *prae-* + *currere* to run.] One that precedes, esp. as a sign, indication, etc.; a forerunner; a harbinger. — **Syn.** See FORERUNNER.

pre·cur′so·ry (-sō·rĭ), *adj.* Of the nature of a precursor; preliminary; also, premonitory.

pre·da′ceous (prē·dā′shŭs), *adj.* Also **pre·da′cious** (-shŭs), *adj.* [L. *praeda* prey.] Living by preying on other animals; predatory. — **pre·da′ceous·ness, pre·da′cious·ness,** *n.* — **pre·dac′i·ty** (-dăs′ĭ·tĭ), *n.*

pre·date′ (prē·dāt′), *v. t.* To antedate.

pre·da′tion (prē·dā′shŭn), *n.* [L. *praedatio,* fr. *praedare* to plunder.] **1.** *Rare.* Depredation. **2.** *Ecology.* Predatory behavior.

predation pressure. *Ecology.* The effects of predacity on a species or community, esp. with respect to the survival of species serving as prey.

pred′a·tor (prĕd′ȧ·tẽr), *n.* [L. *praedator.*] A predatory organism, esp. a predaceous bird or mammal.

pred′a·to′ry (prĕd′ȧ·tō′rĭ *or, esp. Brit.,* -tẽr·ĭ), *adj.* [L. *praedatorius,* fr. *praedari* to plunder, fr. *praeda* prey.] **1.** Of, pertaining to, or characterized by plundering; practicing rapine; pillaging. **2.** Living by preying on other animals; predaceous; also, destructive to crops, buildings, etc., by consuming; as, *predatory* birds or insects. — **pred′a·to′ri·ly,** *adv.* — **pred′a·to′ri·ness,** *n.*

pre′de·cease′ (prē′dē·sēs′), *v. t. & i.* To die before.

pred′e·ces′sor (prĕd′ē·sĕs′ẽr; prĕd′ē·sĕs′ẽr; *or, esp. Brit.,* prē′dē-), *n.* [OF. *predecesseur,* fr. LL. *praedecessor,* fr. *prae-* + *decessor* a retiring officer, fr. *decedere.* See DECEASE.] **1.** One who or that which precedes; esp., one who has preceded another in any position, office, etc. **2.** An ancestor; a forefather.

pre·des′ig·nate (prē·dĕz′ĭg·nāt; prē·dĕs′-), *v. t.* **1.** To name or designate beforehand. **2.** *Logic.* To indicate the quantity of (a term or proposition) by prefixing a sign of quantity (*all; some; no*). — **pre′des·ig·na′tion** (prē′dĕz·ĭg·nā′shŭn), *n.*

pre·des′ti·nar′i·an (prē·dĕs′tĭ·nâr′ĭ·ăn; 6), *adj.* Of or pertaining to predestination. — *n.* One who accepts the doctrine of predestination. — **pre·des′ti·nar′i·an·ism** (-ĭz′m), *n.*

pre·des′ti·nate (prē·dĕs′tĭ·nāt), *adj.* [L. *praedestinatus,* past part. of *praedestinare* to predestine.] Predestinated. — (-nāt), *v. t.* To predestine.

pre·des′ti·na′tion (prē·dĕs′tĭ·nā′shŭn; prē′dĕs-), *n.* **1.** Act of predestinating, or state of being predestinated. **2.** *Theol.* The purpose or decree of God from eternity respecting all events; esp., the preordination of men to everlasting happiness or misery; election.

pre·des′tine (prē·dĕs′tĭn), *v. t.* To destine beforehand; to foreordain; specif., *Theol.,* to foreordain by divine decree or eternal purpose.

pre′de·ter′mine (prē′dē·tûr′mĭn), *v. t.* **1.** To determine beforehand; settle in advance. **2.** To give a tendency (to) beforehand; hence, to bias; prejudice. — **pre′de·ter′mi·na′tion** (-mĭ·nā′shŭn), *n.* — **pre′de·ter′mi·na′tive** (-tûr′mĭ·nā′tĭv; -nȧ·tĭv), *adj.*

pre′di·al (prē′dĭ·ăl). Var. of PRAEDIAL.

pred′i·ca·ble (prĕd′ĭ·kȧ·b'l), *adj.* That may be predicated; affirmable.

— *n.* **1.** Anything which may be predicated of a thing; an attribute. **2.** *Logic.* One of the five most general relations of attributes involved in logical division and predication, namely: genus, species, difference, property, and accident. — **pred'i·ca·bil'i·ty** (-bĭl'ĭ·tĭ), **pred'i·ca·ble·ness,** *n.* — **pred'i·ca·bly,** *adv.*

pre·dic'a·ment (prē·dĭk'ȧ·mĕnt; *in sense* 1, *also* prĕd'ĭ·kȧ-), *n.* [LL. *praedicamentum* that which is predicated, a quality.] **1.** The character, status, or classification assigned by a predication; specif., = CATEGORY, 1. **2.** Condition; situation; esp., an unpleasant, unfortunate, or trying position or situation.

Syn. **Predicament, dilemma, quandary, plight, fix, jam, pickle** mean a situation from which one extricates oneself with difficulty. **Predicament** implies a deeply perplexing problem; **dilemma** implies a predicament from which one escapes only by a choice of equally unsatisfactory alternatives; **quandary** stresses great puzzlement; **plight** stresses an unfortunate or trying situation; **fix** and **jam** are colloquial equivalents of *plight;* **pickle** means a distressing or sorry plight.

pred'i·cant (prĕd'ĭ·kănt), *adj.* Preaching. — *n.* A preacher.

pred'i·cate (prĕd'ĭ·kāt), *v. t.* [L. *praedicatus,* past part. of *praedicare* to proclaim. See PREACH.] **1.** To proclaim; affirm; also, preach. **2.** Specif., to assert to be a quality, attribute, or property (of); to affirm (one thing of another); as, to *predicate* whiteness of snow. **3.** To found; to base (upon); — not in good use. **4.** To involve as predicable; imply; as, snow *predicates* whiteness. **5.** Erroneously, to foretell. — *v. i.* To predicate something of another thing.

— (-kĭt), *adj.* **1.** Predicated. **2.** *Gram.* Belonging to the predicate; predicated by a verb requiring an attributive word, or complement, to complete it; as, a **predicate adjective** (Tom is *brave* but he looked *anxious*); **predicate noun** *or* **nominative** (Tom became *captain*); **predicate objective** (they chose Tom *captain*). — *n.* **1.** *Logic.* That which is affirmed or denied of a subject. In "paper is white, ink is not white," *whiteness* is the *predicate* affirmed of paper and denied of ink. **2.** *Gram.* The word or words in a sentence or clause which express what is said of the subject. The predicate is formed either by a notional verb, with or without objects or adverbial adjuncts, by a verb of incomplete predication with a complement, or by a copula or link verb with a noun or adjective. Abbr. *pred.*

pred'i·ca'tion (-kā'shŭn), *n.* **1.** Act or instance of predicating; affirmation; assertion. **2.** *Gram.* The expression of action, state, or quality by an element as constituting a predicate term; also, that which is so expressed. **3.** *Logic.* The affirming something of; esp., assignment of something to a class. — **pred'i·ca'tive** (prĕd'ĭ·kā'tĭv *or, esp. Brit.,* prē·dĭk'ȧ·tĭv), *adj.* — **pred'i·ca'tive·ly,** *adv.*

pred'i·ca·to'ry (prĕd'ĭ·kȧ·tō'rĭ *or, esp. Brit.,* -tĕr·ĭ), *adj.* Preaching; also, preached or proclaimed.

pre·dict' (prē·dĭkt'), *v. t. & i.* [L. *praedictus,* past part. of *praedicere* to predict, fr. *prae-* + *dicere* to say, tell.] To tell or declare beforehand; foretell; prophesy. — **Syn.** See FORETELL. — **pre·dict'a·ble** (-dĭk'tȧ·b'l), *adj.*

pre·dic'tion (prē·dĭk'shŭn), *n.* A predicting; also, that which is foretold; a prophecy. — **pre·dic'tive** (-tĭv), *adj.* — **pre·dic'tive·ly,** *adv.*

pre·dic'tor (-tēr), *n.* One who or that which predicts; specif., a mechanism for controlling antiaircraft fire that includes devices for calculating (or predicting) the precise position of an aircraft on the arrival of a shell.

pre'di·gest' (prē'dĭ·jĕst'; prē'dī-), *v. t.* To digest beforehand; to subject to predigestion.

pre'di·ges'tion (-jĕs'chŭn), *n.* Artificial digestion of food (as by enzymatic action) for use in impaired digestion.

pre'di·lec'tion (prē'dĭ·lĕk'shŭn; prĕd'ĭ-), *n.* [F. *prédilection,* fr. ML. *praediligere* to prefer, fr. *prae-* + *diligere, dilectum,* to choose.] A prepossession in favor of something; predisposition to choose or like; partiality.

Syn. **Predilection, prepossession, prejudice, bias** mean a feeling or idea which inclines one to make choice or judgment without forethought. **Predilection** implies a strong liking that ensues from one's temperament, experience, etc.; **prepossession,** a fixed conception in the light of which anyone or anything is judged; **prejudice,** a usually but not always unfavorable prepossession; **bias,** a distortion of one's judgment owing to a prepossession of any sort.

pre'dis·pose' (prē'dĭs·pōz'), *v. t.* **1.** To dispose or incline beforehand; give a tendency to; as, debility *predisposes* the body to disease; esp., to give a favorable bias to; to incline favorably. **2.** To dispose of or bequeath beforehand. — **Syn.** See INCLINE.

pre'dis·po·si'tion (-pō·zĭsh'ŭn), *n.* Act of predisposing, or state of being predisposed; a propensity; predilection; susceptibility; as, a *predisposition* to disease.

pre·dom'i·nance (prē·dŏm'ĭ·năns), *n.* Also **pre·dom'i·nan·cy** (-năn·sĭ). Quality or state of being predominant; ascendancy; prevalence.

pre·dom'i·nant (-nănt), *adj.* Having the ascendancy over others, because of strength, authority, numbers, etc.; superior in position, influence, etc.; prevailing. — **Syn.** See DOMINANT. — **pre·dom'i·nant·ly,** *adv.*

pre·dom'i·nate (-nāt), *v. i.* [*pre-* + *dominate.*] **1.** To be predominant; to prevail; rule; to have the mastery. **2.** To exceed in number; preponderate. — **pre·dom'i·na'tion** (-nā'shŭn), *n.* — **pre·dom'i·na'tor** (-nā'tēr), *n.*

pree (prē), *n. & v.* [For *preve* to prove. *Oxf. E. D.* See PROVE.] *Scot.* Taste; try. — ***pree the mouth of.*** *Chiefly Scot.* To kiss.

pre–em'i·nence (prē·ĕm'ĭ·nĕns), *n.* Quality or state of being pre-eminent; superiority; distinction.

pre–em'i·nent (-nĕnt), *adj.* [L. *praeeminens, -entis,* pres. part. of *praeeminere* to be prominent, surpass.] Eminent above others; prominent; superior, esp. in excellence. — **pre–em'i·nent·ly,** *adv.*

pre–empt' (prē·ĕmpt'), *v. t. & i.* [*pre-* + L. *emptio* a buying.] **1.** To settle upon (public land) with a right of pre-emption; take by pre-emption. **2.** To appropriate; seize upon to the exclusion of others. **3.** *Whist, Bridge, etc.* To make a bid aimed at shutting out shifts by the partner or bids by the opponents. — **Syn.** See ARROGATE. — **pre–emp'tive** (-ĕmp'tĭv), *adj.* — **pre–emp'tor** (-tôr), *n.* — **pre–emp'to·ry** (-tō·rĭ), *adj.*

pre–emp'tion (-ĕmp'shŭn), *n.* Act or right of purchasing before others; specif., *U. S.,* such a right formerly given under federal public land laws to citizens claiming under certain conditions a portion not exceeding a quarter section (160 acres) of public land.

preen (prēn), *n.* [AS. *prēon* a clasp.] *Now Dial.* A pin; a brooch.

preen, *v. t. & i.* [Prob. same word as *prune* to preen.] **1.** To trim or dress with or as with the beak, as the feathers or fur; — said of birds and some animals. **2.** To trim, dress, or smooth (oneself) up; to prink; primp. — **preen'er,** *n.*

pre'–ex·il'i·an (prē'ĕg·zĭl'ĭ·ăn; -ĕks·ĭl'ĭ·ăn), **pre'–ex·il'ic** (-ĕg·zĭl'ĭk; -ĕks·ĭl'ĭk), *adj.* [*pre-* + L. *ex(s)ilium* exile or E. *exile.*] Previous to the exile; specif., *Jewish Hist.,* belonging to, or occurring in, the period before the Babylonish exile, that is, before about 600 B.C.

pre'–ex·ist' (prē'ĕg·zĭst'; -ĭg-), *v. i. & t.* To exist before.

pre'–ex·ist'ence (-zĭs'tĕns), *n.* Existence in a former state, or previous to something else; specif., existence of the soul before its union with the body, esp. in the doctrine of transmigration. — **pre'–ex·ist'ent** (-tĕnt), *adj.*

pre·fab'ri·cate (prē·făb'rĭ·kāt), *v. t.* To fabricate all the parts of (as a house) at the factory, so that construction consists merely of assembling and uniting standardized parts. — **pre'fab·ri·ca'tion** (prē'făb·rĭ·kā'shŭn), *n.*

pref'ace (prĕf'ĭs; -ȧs), *n.* [OF., fr. L. *praefatio,* fr. *praefari* to say beforehand, fr. *prae-* + *fari, fatus,* to speak.] **1.** [*usually cap.*] In liturgies, the first part of the Eucharistic prayer; specif., the prelude to the Canon of the Mass. **2.** Something spoken or written as introductory or preliminary to a discourse, book, etc.; an introduction; prologue; foreword. — *v. t.;* -ACED (-ĭst; -ȧst); -AC·ING (-ĭs·ĭng). **1.** To introduce by, or commence with, a preface; to furnish with a preface. **2.** To be preliminary to.

pref'a·to'ry (prĕf'ȧ·tō'rĭ *or, esp. Brit.,* -tĕr·ĭ), *adj.* Pertaining to, or of the nature of, a preface; introductory; preliminary; as, *prefatory* remarks. — **pref'a·to'ri·ly,** *adv.*

pre'fect, prae'fect (prē'fĕkt), *n.* [OF. *prefect* (F. *préfet*), fr. L. *praefectus,* fr. *praefectus,* past part. of *praeficere* to set over, fr. *prae-* + *facere* to make.] **1.** In ancient Rome, any of various high officials or magistrates placed at the head of a particular command, charge, department, etc. **2.** In modern use, a president, chief officer, chief magistrate, or the like, as the head of any of the congregations of cardinals; in France, the chief administrative officer of a department. **3.** In Jesuit schools, a dean. **4.** In certain schools, a student monitor. Cf. PREPOSITOR.

pre'fec·ture (prē'fĕk·tūr), *n.* [L. *praefectura.*] The office, jurisdiction, residence, etc., of a prefect; also, the district governed by a prefect. — **pre·fec'tur·al** (prē·fĕk'tūr·ăl), *adj.*

pre·fer' (prē·fûr'), *v. t.;* -FERRED' (-fûrd'); -FER'RING. [OF. *preferer,* fr. L. *praeferre,* fr. *prae-* + *ferre* to bear.] **1.** To put in a higher position, rank, or the like; to advance, exalt; promote. **2.** To set above or before something else in estimation, favor, or liking; hold in greater favor; like better. **3.** To bring, put, or set (something) forward, or before one; to present; as, to *prefer* a claim against a person. **4.** *Law.* To give a preference or priority to. — **Syn.** See CHOOSE. — **pre·fer'rer,** *n.*

pref'er·a·ble (prĕf'ēr·ȧ·b'l), *adj.* Worthy to be preferred; more desirable. — **pref'er·a·bil'i·ty** (-bĭl'ĭ·tĭ), **pref'er·a·ble·ness,** *n.* — **pref'er·a·bly,** *adv.*

pref'er·ence (prĕf'ēr·ĕns), *n.* **1.** Act of preferring, or state of being preferred; higher estimation; prior choice; also, the power or opportunity of choosing. **2.** One who or that which is preferred. **3.** The act, fact, or principle of giving advantages to some over others. **4.** *Law.* Priority in the right to demand and receive satisfaction of an obligation. — **Syn.** See CHOICE.

preference share *or* **stock.** *Brit.* A share giving its owner a preference either as to receipt of dividends, to repayment in case of winding up, or as to both. Cf. PREFERRED STOCK.

pref'er·en'tial (prĕf'ēr·ĕn'shăl), *adj.* **1.** Of or pertaining to preference. **2.** Showing preference; as, *preferential* treatment; creating or employing a preference; as, a *preferential* tariff. **3.** Indicating one's preference, or order of choice, as of candidates in an election; as, *preferential* voting; a *preferential* ballot. — **pref'er·en'tial·ism** (-ĭz'm), *n.* — **pref'er·en'tial·ist** (-ĭst), *n.* — **pref'er·en'tial·ly,** *adv.*

preferential shop. A shop in which according to contract the management gives preference to members of the union, chiefly in hiring, layoffs, and dismissals, often also in promotions, work shifts, etc., but is free to hire outside of union membership if the union is unable to supply the workers needed.

preferential voting. A system of voting in which the voters indicate their preference between two or more candidates for an office, so that if no candidate receives a majority of first choices the one receiving the greatest number of first and second choices together is nominated or elected.

pre·fer'ment (prē·fûr'mĕnt), *n.* **1.** Act of preferring, or advancing in dignity or office; advancement; promotion. **2.** A position, appointment, or office of honor or profit.

pre·ferred' stock (prē·fûrd'). *U. S.* Stock which takes a dividend before other capital stock and on a distribution of assets participates ahead of the common stock; — essentially equiv. to the British *preference stock.*

pre'fig·u·ra'tion (prē'fĭg·ū·rā'shŭn), *n.* A prefiguring; a prototype. — **pre·fig'ur·a·tive** (prē·fĭg'ūr·ȧ·tĭv), *adj.*

pre·fig'ure (prē·fĭg'ūr), *v. t.* [F. or L.; F. *préfigurer,* fr. LL. *praefigurare.* See PRE-; FIGURE.] **1.** To show, suggest, or announce, by antecedent types and similitudes; hence, loosely, to foretell; foreshadow. **2.** To imagine beforehand. — **pre·fig'ure·ment,** *n.*

pre·fix' (prē·fĭks'; *in sense* 1, prē'fĭks'), *v. t.;* -FIXED' (-fĭkst'); -FIX'ING. [OF. *prefixer,* fr. L. *praefixus,* fr. *prae-* + *figere* to fix.] **1.** *Now Rare.* To set or fix beforehand. **2.** To put or fix before, or at the beginning of; to make, or add, as a prefix. — **pre·fix'ion** (prē·fĭk'shŭn), *n.*

pre'fix (prē'fĭks), *n.* That which is prefixed; esp., one or more letters or syllables combined or united with the beginning of a word to modify its signification, as *pre-* in *prefix, con-* in *conjure.* See COMBINING FORM. — **pre'fix·al** (prē'fĭk·săl; prē·fĭk'săl), *adj.* — **pre'fix·al·ly,** *adv.*

pre'for·ma'tion (prē'fôr·mā'shŭn), *n.* **1.** Previous formation. **2.** *Biol.* In full, ***theory of preformation.*** An old theory that every germ cell contained the organism of its kind fully formed, and that development consisted merely in increase in size. Cf. EPIGENESIS.

preg'na·ble (prĕg'nȧ·b'l), *adj.* [F. *prenable,* fr. *prendre* to take.] Capable of being taken, or captured; assailable; vulnerable. — **preg'na·bil'i·ty** (-bĭl'ĭ·tĭ), *n.*

preg'nan·cy (prĕg'năn·sĭ), *n.* **1.** Condition of being pregnant; state of being with young. **2.** Figuratively, quality of being laden with important meaning, etc.

preg'nant (-nănt), *adj.* [L. *praegnans, -antis,* fr. *prae-* + the root of *nasci* to be born, but in sense 3 fr., or confused with, F. *preignant* pressing, cogent.] **1.** Being with young; teeming; gravid. **2.** Teeming with, or full of, ideas; fertile; inventive; as, a *pregnant* wit. **3.** Heavy with important contents, significance, or issue; weighty; suggestive; potential. — **preg'nant·ly,** *adv.*

pre·hen'sile (prē·hĕn'sĭl; *see* -ILE), *adj.* [F. *préhensile,* fr. L. *prehendere, -hensum,* to seize.] Adapted for seizing or grasping, esp. by wrapping around; as, the *prehensile* tail of a monkey. — **pre'hen·sil'i·ty** (prē'hĕn·sĭl'ĭ·tĭ), *n.*

pre·hen'sion (-shŭn), *n.* **1.** *Chiefly Zool.* Act of taking hold, seizing, or grasping, as with the hand or other member. **2.** Mental apprehension; understanding.

pre'his·tor'ic (prē'hĭs·tŏr'ĭk), *adj.* Of, pertaining to, or existing in the period before written history. — **pre'his·tor'i·cal** (-ĭ·kăl), *adj.*

pre·his'to·ry (prē·hĭs'tō·rĭ), *n.* A history of the antecedents of an event; specif., prehistoric archaeology and anthropology; knowledge of man and his works before the written recording of history.

pre'ig·ni'tion (prē'ĭg·nĭsh'ŭn), *n. Engin.* Ignition in an internal-combustion engine while the inlet valve is open or before compression is completed.

pre·judge' (prē·jŭj'), *v. t. & i.* [F. *préjuger,* fr. L. *praejudicare.*] To judge before full and sufficient examination; pass judgment on beforehand. — **pre·judg'er** (-jŭj'ẽr), *n.* — **pre·judg'ment, pre·judge'ment,** *n.*

prej'u·dice (prĕj'ŏŏ·dĭs; 118), *n.* [OF., fr. L. *praejudicium,* fr. *prae-* + *judicium* judgment.] **1.** Injury due to some judgment or action of another, as in disregard of a person's right; — now chiefly in phrases; as, *in,* or *to, the prejudice of; **without prejudice,*** specif., *Law,* without damage to, or detraction from, one's own rights or claims. **2.** Preconceived judgment or opinion; unreasonable predilection or objection; esp., an opinion or leaning adverse to anything without just grounds or before sufficient knowledge. — **Syn.** See PREDILECTION. — *v. t.;* -DICED (-dĭst); -DIC·ING (-dĭs·ĭng). **1.** *Chiefly Legal.* To injure or damage by some judgment or action; hurt; impair; as, to *prejudice* a good cause. **2.** To cause to have prejudice; bias the mind of; as, to *prejudice* the members of a jury.

prej'u·di'cial (prĕj'ŏŏ·dĭsh'ăl), *adj.* Tending to injure or impair; hurtful; damaging. — **prej'u·di'cial·ly,** *adv.*

prel'a·cy (prĕl'ȧ·sĭ), *n.; pl.* -CIES (-sĭz). **1.** Office or dignity of a prelate. **2.** Prelates collectively; the body of ecclesiastical dignitaries. **3.** Church government by prelates; — chiefly a hostile term for *episcopacy.*

prel'ate (-ĭt), *n.* [OF. *prelat,* fr. ML. *praelatus,* fr. L. *praelatus,* used as past part. of *praeferre* to prefer.] An ecclesiastic of superior rank and authority; a dignitary of the church. — **pre·lat'ic** (prē·lăt'ĭk), *adj.*

prel'a·tism (prĕl'ȧ·tĭz'm), *n.* Prelacy (esp. sense 3). — **prel'a·tist** (-tĭst), *n.*

prel'a·ture (-tūr), *n.* [F. *prélature,* fr. ML. *praelatura.*] Prelacy (esp. senses 1 & 2).

pre·lect' (prē·lĕkt'), *v. i.* To discourse publicly; lecture. — **pre·lec'tion** (-lĕk'shŭn), *n.* — **pre·lec'tor** (-tẽr), *n.*

pre'li·ba'tion (prē'lī·bā'shŭn), *n.* [LL. *praelibatio,* fr. *praelibare* to taste beforehand.] A foretaste.

pre·lim'i·nar'y (prē·lĭm'ĭ·nĕr'ĭ *or, esp. Brit.,* -nẽr·ĭ), *adj.* [*pre-* + L. *liminaris* of a threshold, fr. *limen, liminis,* threshold.] Introductory; preceding the main discourse or business; prefatory. — *n.; pl.* -IES (-ĭz). Something preliminary, introductory or preparatory; a preparatory step, measure, etc.; by ellipsis, a preliminary examination; — chiefly in *pl.* — **pre·lim'i·nar'i·ly,** *adv.*

prel'ude (prĕl'ūd; prē'lūd), *n.* [F. *prélude,* fr. ML. *praeludium.* See PRELUDE, *v.*] **1.** An introductory performance, action, event, etc., preparing for the principal or a more important matter. **2.** *Music.* **a** A strain, section, or movement introducing the theme or chief subject, as of a fugue or suite. **b** An opening voluntary in a service. — (prĕl'ūd; prē'lūd; *formerly, & still occas.,* prē·lūd'), *v. i. & t.* [L. *praeludere, -lusum,* fr. *prae-* + *ludere* to play.] To serve as a prelude (to); provide an introduction (to) or prelude (of); specif., *Music,* to play a prelude (to). — **pre·lud'er** (prē·lūd'ẽr; prĕl'ū·dẽr), *n.*

pre·lu'sion (prē·lū'zhŭn), *n.* A prelude; introduction.

pre·lu'sive (-sĭv), **pre·lu'so·ry** (-sō·rĭ), *adj.* Of the nature of a prelude; introductory. — **pre·lu'sive·ly, pre·lu'so·ri·ly,** *adv.*

pre'ma·ture' (prē'mȧ·tūr'; prē'mȧ·tūr; *or, esp. Brit.,* prĕm'ȧ·tūr; 2), *adj.* [L. *praematurus,* fr. *prae-* + *maturus* ripe.] Happening, arriving, existing, or performed before the proper or usual time; too early; untimely. — **pre'ma·ture'ly,** *adv.* — **pre'ma·ture'ness,** *n.* — **pre'ma·tu'ri·ty** (-tū'rĭ·tĭ), *n.*

pre'max·il'la (prē'măks·ĭl'ȧ), *n.; pl.* -LAE (-ē). [NL.] *Anat. & Zool.* One of a pair of bones of the upper jaw of vertebrates, between and in front of the maxillae. — **pre·max'il·lar'y** (prē·măk'sĭ·lĕr'ĭ *or, esp. Brit.,* -măks·ĭl'ȧ·rĭ), *adj. & n.*

pre·med'ic (prē·mĕd'ĭk), *n. Colloq.* A premedical student.

pre·med'i·cal (-mĕd'ĭ·kăl), *adj.* Preceding medicine; specif., preceding and preparing for the regular study of medicine; as, the *premedical* course in a university; a *premedical* student.

pre·med'i·tate (prē·mĕd'ĭ·tāt), *v. t. & i.* [L. *praemeditatus,* past part. of *praemeditari,* fr. *prae-* + *meditari* to meditate.] To consider or revolve in the mind beforehand; to contrive, design, or deliberate before acting, speaking, etc. — **pre·med'i·ta'tive** (-tā'tĭv), *adj.* — **pre·med'i·ta'tor** (-tā'tẽr), *n.*

pre'med·i·ta'tion (prē'mĕd·ĭ·tā'shŭn), *n.* A premeditating; specif., *Law,* planning of an act beforehand such as to show intent to commit that act.

pre'mi·er (prē'mĭ·ẽr; prĕm'yẽr), *adj.* [F., fr. L. *primarius* of the first rank. See PRIMARY.] First; specif.: **a** Chief; principal. **b** Earliest. — (prē'mĭ·ẽr; prē·mẽr'; prĕm'yẽr), *n.* The first minister of state; more generally, chief officer; esp., the prime minister, as of France.

‖**pre·mière'** (prē·myâr'), *adj. fem.* [F.] First; chief. — *n. fem.; pl.* -MIÈRES (*F.* prē·myâr'). **a** The leading lady, esp. in a theatrical cast. **b** (*pron. usually* prē·mẽr') A first performance, as of a play.

pre'mil·le·nar'i·an (prē'mĭl·ē·nâr'ĭ·ăn; 6), *n.* One who holds the doctrine of premillennialism. — **pre'mil·le·nar'i·an,** *adj.* — **pre'mil·le·nar'i·an·ism** (-ĭz'm), *n.*

pre'mil·len'ni·al (prē'mĭ·lĕn'ĭ·ăl), *adj.* Coming before the millennium; previous to the millennium; — said esp. of the Second Advent. Cf. POSTMILLENNIAL.

pre'mil·len'ni·al·ism (-ĭz'm), *n.* The doctrine that the second coming of Christ precedes the millennium. — **pre'mil·len'ni·al·ist** (-ĭst), *n.*

prem'ise, prem'iss (prĕm'ĭs), *n.* [OF. *premisse,* fr. fem. of L. *praemissus,* past part. of *praemittere* to send before, fr. *prae-* + *mittere* to send. See MISSION.] **1.** A proposition antecedently supposed or proved; specif., *Logic,* a proposition stated or assumed as leading to a conclusion; either of the first two propositions of a syllogism (see MAJOR, *n.,* 4; MINOR, *n.,* 3). **2.** *pl. Law.* **a** Matters previously stated or set forth; hence, the part of a deed that states the names of the parties and sets forth the facts necessary to explain the transaction. **b** The stating part of a bill in equity setting forth the causes of complaint, the parties against whom redress is sought, etc. **c** The property conveyed in a deed; hence, a piece of land or real estate; sometimes, esp. in fire insurance, a building; as, to lease *premises.*

pre·mise' (prē·mīz'), *v. t.* **1.** To set forth beforehand, as introductory or as postulated; offer as premises, esp. to an argument. **2.** To presuppose or imply (something) as pre-existent; to postulate. — *v. i.* To make a premise.

pre'mi·um (prē'mĭ·ŭm; 58), *n.; pl.* PREMIUMS (-ŭmz). [L. *praemium,* orig., what one has got before or better than others, fr. *prae-* + *emere* take, buy.] **1.** A reward or recompense; a prize in a competition; also, any extra reward or compensation to spur competitors or workers. **2.** Something offered or given for the loan of money; bonus. **3.** A sum above the nominal or par value of anything; as, to sell stock at a *premium.* **4.** The consideration paid for a contract of insurance. **5.** *Econ.* The excess in purchasing power, or exchange value, of one form of money over another of the same nominal value, as of gold dollars over paper dollars. — ***at a premium.*** Above par; hence, unusually valuable, as because of rareness.

pre·mo'lar (prē·mō'lẽr), *adj. Anat. & Zool.* In front of or preceding the molar teeth; specif., designating, or pert. to, certain teeth of mammals in front of the true molars, in man termed *bicuspids.* — *n.* A premolar tooth. See TOOTH, *Illust.*

pre·mon'ish (prē·mŏn'ĭsh), *v. t. & i.* [*pre-* + *monish.*] To forewarn; to admonish beforehand.

pre'mo·ni'tion (prē'mō·nĭsh'ŭn), *n.* [LL. *praemonitio.*] A forewarning; a premonitory sign; a foreboding.

pre·mon'i·to'ry (prē·mŏn'ĭ·tō'rĭ *or, esp. Brit.,* -tẽr·ĭ), *adj.* Giving previous warning; as, *premonitory* symptoms.

pre·morse' (prē·môrs'), *adj.* [L. *praemorsus,* past part. of *praemordere* to bite off, fr. *prae-* + *mordere* to bite.] Bitten off; hence, *Chiefly Bot.,* irregularly truncate; as, a *premorse* root.

pre·na'tal (prē·nā'tăl; -t'l), *adj.* Before birth. — **pre·na'tal·ly,** *adv.*

pre·nom'i·nate (prē·nŏm'ĭ·nāt), *adj.* [L. *praenominatus,* past part.] *Obs.* Previously named.

pre·no'tion (prē·nō'shŭn), *n.* [L. *praenotio.*] Preconception; a preconceived idea formed without actual experience.

pren'tice, 'pren'tice (prĕn'tĭs), *adj.* Characteristic of an apprentice. — *n.* Aphetic for APPRENTICE.

pre·oc'cu·pan·cy (prē·ŏk'ū·păn·sĭ), *n.; pl.* -CIES (-sĭz). Act or right of occupying before another or others; preoccupation.

pre·oc'cu·pa'tion (-pā'shŭn; 2), *n.* Act of preoccupying, or state of being preoccupied; of the mind, engrossment.

pre·oc'cu·pied (prē·ŏk'ū·pīd), *adj.* **1.** Engrossed; lost in thought. **2.** Already occupied. **3.** *Biol.* Previously applied to some group and not available for use in a new sense; — of generic and specific names.

pre·oc'cu·py (-pī), *v. t.;* -PIED (-pīd); -PY'ING. **1.** To prepossess; to engage, occupy, or engross the attention of, beforehand. **2.** To occupy, or take possession of, before another.

pre·o'ral (prē·ō'răl; 70), *adj. Zool.* Situated in front of, or anterior to, the mouth. — **pre·o'ral·ly,** *adv.*

pre'or·dain' (prē'ôr·dān'), *v. t.* To foreordain; to decree or order beforehand. — **pre'or·di·na'tion** (-dĭ·nā'shŭn), *n.*

prep (prĕp), *adj. U. S.* Short for PREPARATORY; as, *prep* schools.

prep'a·ra'tion (prĕp'ȧ·rā'shŭn), *n.* **1.** Act, process, or an instance of making ready for use, service, etc.; equipment, training, manufacture, or the like. **2.** State of being prepared; preparedness. **3.** A preparatory act or measure. **4.** That which is prepared; specif., a medicinal substance fitted for use.

pre·par'a·tive (prē·păr'ȧ·tĭv), *adj.* Tending or serving to prepare or make ready; preparatory. — *n.* That which is preparative or preparatory; also, a preparation.

pre·par'a·tor (-tẽr), *n.* [LL. *praeparator.*] A preparer of specimens for scientific uses.

pre·par'a·to'ry (-tō'rĭ *or, esp. Brit.,* -tẽr·ĭ, -trĭ), *adj.* **1.** Preparing, or serving to prepare, for something; introductory; as, a *preparatory* school. **2.** Being prepared, esp. for college; undergoing training or instruction for something to follow; as, a *preparatory* student.

pre·pare' (prē·pâr'), *v. t.* [F. *préparer,* fr. L. *praeparare,* fr. *prae-* + *parare* to make ready.] **1.** To fit, adapt, or qualify beforehand for a particular purpose, end, or condition; to make ready. **2.** To procure as suitable or necessary; provide. **3.** To make or form, esp. by some specified process, compound, as in cooking, etc.; as, to *prepare* a medicine or foods. — *v. i.* **1.** To make ready. **2.** To make oneself ready. — **pre·par'ed·ly** (-pâr'ĕd·lĭ; -ĭd·lĭ), *adv.* — **pre·par'er** (-ẽr), *n.*

pre·par'ed·ness (-pâr'ĕd·nĕs; -ĭd-; -pârd'-; -nĭs), *n.* State of being prepared; specif., a state of military and naval preparation for adequate defense.

pre·pay' (prē·pā'), *v. t.;* see PAY. To pay, or to pay the charge upon, in advance or beforehand. — **pre·pay'ment,** *n.*

pre·pense' (prē·pĕns'), *adj.* [After OF. *purpensé* meditated.] Premeditated; aforethought; as, malice *prepense.*

pre·pon'der·ance (prē·pŏn'dẽr·ăns), *n.* Also **pre·pon'der·an·cy** (-ăn·sĭ). State of being preponderant; superiority or excess of weight, influence, number, etc.; an outweighing.

pre·pon'der·ant (-ănt), *adj.* Preponderating; superior in weight, force, etc. — **Syn.** See DOMINANT. — **pre·pon'der·ant·ly,** *adv.*

pre·pon'der·ate (-āt), *v. i.* [L. *praeponderatus,* past part. of *praeponderare.* See PRE-; PONDER.] **1.** To exceed in weight; hence, to turn the scale; to incline or descend, as the scale of a balance. **2.** To prevail; predominate. — *v. t. Obs.* To outweigh; overbalance. — **pre·pon'der·at'ing** (-āt'ĭng), *adj.* — **pre·pon'der·at'ing·ly,** *adv.* — **pre·pon'der·a'tion** (-ā'shŭn), *n.*

prep'o·si'tion (prĕp'ō·zĭsh'ŭn), *n.* [F. and L.; F. *préposition,* fr. L. *praepositio,* fr. *praeponere* to place before.] *Gram.* A word generally with some meaning of position, direction, time, or other abstract relation, used to connect a noun or a pronoun, in an adjectival or adverbial sense, with some other word. Abbr. *prep.*

prep'o·si'tion·al (-ăl), *adj.* Of, pert. to, of the nature of, or formed with a preposition; as, a *prepositional* phrase. — **prep'o·si'tion·al·ly,** *adv.*

pre·pos′i·tive (prḗ-pŏz′ĭ-tĭv), *adj. Gram.* Put before; prefixed. — *n.* A prepositive word.

pre·pos′i·tor (-tẽr), *n.* [Alteration of L. *praepositus.* See PROVOST.] *Eng.* At some public schools, a student entrusted with discipline; a monitor. — **pre·pos′i·to′ri·al** (-tō′rĭ-ăl; 70), *adj.*

pre′pos·sess′ (prḗ′pŏ-zĕs′), *v. t.* **1.** To possess or occupy before another. **2.** To preoccupy (one), so as to preclude other ideas, beliefs, etc.; hence, to bias or prejudice.

pre′pos·sess′ing (-zĕs′ĭng), *adj.* Tending to invite favor; attractive. — **pre′pos·sess′ing·ly**, *adv.*

pre′pos·ses′sion (-zĕsh′ŭn), *n.* A prepossessing; esp., a preoccupation of the mind by a prejudice, bias, etc. — **Syn.** See PREDILECTION.

pre·pos′ter·ous (prḗ-pŏs′tẽr-ŭs), *adj.* [L. *praeposterus,* fr. *prae-* + *posterus* latter.] Contrary to nature, reason, or common sense; irrational; hence, absurd; nonsensical; grotesque. — **pre·pos′ter·ous·ly**, *adv.* — **pre·pos′ter·ous·ness**, *n.*

pre·pos′tor (prḗ-pŏs′tẽr), *n.* = PREPOSITOR.

pre·po′ten·cy (-pō′tĕn·sĭ), *n.; pl.* -CIES (-sĭz). Quality or condition of being prepotent; *Biol.,* a marked capacity on the part of an individual, strain, or the like, to transmit a character or characters to the offspring.

pre·po′tent (-tĕnt), *adj.* [L. *praepotens.* See PRE-; POTENT.] **1.** Very powerful; predominant. **2.** *Biol.* Characterized by prepotency. — **pre·po′tent·ly**, *adv.*

pre′puce (prḗ′pūs), *n.* [F. *prépuce,* fr. L. *praeputium.*] The fold of skin that covers the glans of the penis; foreskin. — **pre·pu′tial** (prḗ-pū′shǎl), *adj.*

Pre′–Raph′a·el·ite, *n.* **a** Strictly, a member of a society, chiefly of artists, formed in England in 1848 to encourage fidelity to nature, sincerity, and delicacy of finish. **b** Popularly: (1) Any modern painter whose work recalls early ideals or methods, esp. in its attention to minute detail. (2) Any Italian painter of the epoch before Raphael. — **Pre′–Raph′a·el·ite,** *adj.* — **Pre′–Raph′a·el·it·ism,** *n.*

pre·req′ui·site (prḗ-rĕk′wĭ-zĭt), *adj.* Required before; necessary as a preliminary to a proposed effect or end; essential as a condition precedent. — *n.* Something prerequisite; something necessary to an end or effect; a condition precedent.

pre·rog′a·tive (prḗ-rŏg′a·tĭv), *n.* [OF., fr. L. *praerogativa* precedence in voting, privilege, fr. *praerogare* to ask before another, fr. *prae-* + *rogare* to ask.] **1.** Precedence, esp. by virtue of holding an office. **2.** A right to exercise a power or privilege in priority to, or to the exclusion of, others; esp., a right attached to an office or rank; as, the royal *prerogative.* **3.** A distinctive worth or excellence; a superiority. — *adj.* Pertaining to or having a prerogative.

prerogative court. Formerly, one of certain archiepiscopal courts (as York in England) having jurisdiction similar to that of probate courts; now, the probate court of New Jersey.

‖**pre′sa** (prā′sä), *n.; pl.* PRESE (-sā). [It., prop., a taking.] *Music.* A mark (written S:, +, ⁑, etc.) indicating where the successive voice parts of a canon, etc., take up the theme.

pres′age (prĕs′ĭj; *form.* prḗ-sāj′), *n.* [F. *présage,* fr. L. *praesagium,* fr. *praesagire* to forebode, fr. *prae-* + *sagire* to perceive keenly.] **1.** Something which foreshows or portends a future event; a prognostic; omen; augury. **2.** A presentiment; a foreboding; also, foreknowledge. **3.** A prediction. **4.** Ominous character; portent; as, of evil *presage.*

pre·sage′ (prḗ-sāj′), *v. t.; -SAGED′* (-sājd′); *-SAG′ING* (-sāj′ĭng). **1.** To give a presage of; portend. **2.** To have a presentiment of. **3.** To foretell; predict. — *v. i.* To utter or make a prediction. — **Syn.** See FORETELL. — **pre·sag′er** (-sāj′ẽr), *n.*

pres′by·o′pi·a (prĕz′bĭ-ō′pĭ·a; prĕs′-), *n.* [NL., fr. Gr. *presbys* an old man + *-opia.*] *Med.* A defect of vision associated with old age, characterized by recession of the near point of vision so that objects very near the eyes cannot be seen distinctly without convex glasses. — **pres′by·op′ic** (-ŏp′ĭk), *adj.*

pres′by·ter (prĕz′bĭ-tẽr; prĕs′-), *n.* [LL., an elder, fr. Gr. *presbyteros.* See PRIEST.] **1.** An elder in the early Christian church. **2.** A priest. **3.** In Presbyterian churches, an elder, especially a teaching elder, or minister.

pres·byt′er·ate (prĕz-bĭt′ẽr-āt; prĕs-), *n.* Office or position of a presbyter, or elder; also, a presbytery.

pres·byt′er·i·al (prĕz′bĭ-tẽr′ĭ-ăl; prĕs′-), *adj.* Also **pres·byt′er·al** (prĕz-bĭt′ẽr-ăl; prĕs-). *Now Rare.* Of or pert. to presbyters or a presbytery; presbyterian.

Pres′by·te′ri·an (-ăn), *adj.* [LL. *presbyterium* presbytery.] **a** [*not cap.*] Of or pert. to a presbyter or presbyters, or ecclesiastical government by presbyters. **b** Designating, or pert. to, a church or churches which uphold church government by presbyters, or elders, or to the doctrine, discipline, and worship of such churches. — *n.* A supporter of Presbyterianism; a member of a Presbyterian church.

Pres′by·te′ri·an·ism (-ĭz'm), *n.* That form of church government which invests presbyters, or elders, with all spiritual power and admits no prelates over them; also, the faith (orig. Calvinism) and polity of the Presbyterian churches, taken collectively.

pres′by·ter·y (prĕz′bĭ-tẽr′ĭ; -tẽr-ĭ; prĕs′-), *n.; pl.* -TERIES (-ĭz). **1.** In Presbyterian churches, a court consisting of the ministers and representative elders from the congregations within a district; also, the jurisdiction of such a court. **2.** That part of a church reserved for the officiating priests. **3.** *Chiefly R.C.Ch.* A priest's residence; rectory.

pre·school′ (prḗ-skōōl′; 2), *adj.* Of, pertaining to, or designating the period in a child's life, from infancy to the age of five, ordinarily preceding attendance at school.

pre′school′ (prḗ′skōōl′), *n.* A kindergarten or nursery school where children of preschool age, sometimes in age groups, are entered for observation and social and educational training.

pre′sci·ence (prḗ′shĭ·ĕns; prĕsh′ĭ-), *n.* [OF., fr. LL. *praescientia,* fr. L. *praesciens, -entis,* pres. part. of *praescire* to foreknow.] Foreknowledge of events; foresight; specif., omniscience with regard to the future. — **pre′sci·ent** (-ĕnt), *adj.* — **pre′sci·ent·ly**, *adv.*

pre·scind′ (prḗ-sĭnd′), *v. t.* [L. *praescindere* to cut off in front, fr. *prae-* + *scindere* to cut asunder.] To detach for purposes of thought; to separate in consideration; — with *from.*

pre·scribe′ (prḗ-skrīb′), *v. t.* [L. *praescribere, -scriptum,* fr. *prae-* + *scribere* to write.] **1.** To lay down as a guide, direction, or rule of action; dictate; ordain. **2.** *Law.* To outlaw or invalidate by prescription. **3.** *Med.* To designate or order the use of, as a remedy. — *v. i.* **1.** To give directions; dictate. **2.** *Law.* **a** To claim a title to a thing by right of prescription. **b** To become by prescription invalid or unenforceable; as, certain rights *prescribe* in twenty years. **3.** *Med.* To write or give medical prescriptions. — **pre·scrib′er** (-skrīb′ẽr), *n.*

pre·script′ (prḗ-skrĭpt′; prḗ′skrĭpt), *adj.* [L. *praescriptus,* past part.] Ordained by authority; prescribed.

pre′script (prḗ′skrĭpt), *n.* Thing prescribed; rule.

pre·scrip′ti·ble (prḗ-skrĭp′tĭ-b'l), *adj.* Depending on, derived from, or subject to prescription.

pre·scrip′tion (-shŭn), *n.* **1.** A prescribing or dictating; also, something prescribed, or ordered; a prescript. **2.** *Med.* A written direction for the preparation and use of a medicine; also, the medicine. See RECIPE, 1. **3. a** *Civil Law.* The operation of the law whereby rights might be established by long exercise of their corresponding powers or extinguished by prolonged failure to exercise such powers. **b** *Common Law.* Establishment of a claim of title by use and enjoyment during a time fixed by law; the right or title so acquired.

pre·scrip′tive (-tĭv), *adj.* **1.** Prescribing. **2.** Arising from, based on, or determined by prescription. — **pre·scrip′tive·ly**, *adv.*

pres′ence (prĕz′ĕns; -'ns), *n.* [OF., fr. L. *praesentia.* See PRESENT.] **1.** Act, fact, or state of being present. **2.** The space within one's immediate vicinity; also, formerly (in full **presence chamber**), the room in which a sovereign or other personage receives visitors. **3.** *Archaic.* An assembly, esp. of persons of rank. **4.** The person or personality of an individual; esp., the person of a superior, as a sovereign. **5.** Port; bearing; mien; as, a man of fine *presence.* **6.** An apparition; specter.

presence of mind. Self-control in an emergency, such that one can say and do the right thing; unshaken calmness and readiness of thought.

pres′ent (prĕz′ĕnt; -'nt), *adj.* [OF., fr. L. *praesens, -entis,* that is before one, pres. part. of *praeesse* to be before, fr. *prae-* + *esse* to be.] **1.** Being before, in view, or at hand; being in a certain place and not elsewhere; — opposed to *absent.* **2.** Now existing, or in process; begun but not ended; not past or future; as, the *present* Congress. **3.** *Now Rare.* Self-possessed; ready. **4.** *Obs.* Immediately operative or effective; instant. **5.** *Gram.* Expressing action or being in the time that now is or the time of speaking, in **present tense** (*I see* you), also of habitual action or general truth (the sun *shines* every day), in **present infinitive** (*to be, to do*), and in **present participle** (*being, doing*; see PARTICIPLE). The present tense used in telling of past events is the **historical present.** — *n.* **1.** Present time; the time being or contemplated. **2.** Present occasion or affair. **3.** *Gram.* The present tense, or a verb in it. *Abbr.* pres. **4.** *pl. Law.* Present letters or instrument, as a deed of conveyance, a lease, power of attorney, or other writing, as in "Know all men by these *presents.*" — **at present.** At the present time; just now. — **for the present.** Temporarily.

pre·sent′ (prḗ-zĕnt′), *v. t.* [OF. *presenter,* fr. L. *praesentare,* fr. *praesens,* adj. See PRESENT, *adj.*] **1.** To bring or introduce into the presence of someone, esp. a superior; introduce formally, as at court, or for acquaintance. **2.** To make a gift to. **3.** To put before a person for acceptance; offer as a gift; bestow formally. **4.** To represent; act; personate; perform. **5.** To exhibit or offer to view or notice; as, to *present* a fine appearance; to submit for consideration or action. **6.** To aim, point, or direct, as a weapon. **7.** *Eccl.* To nominate to a benefice. **8.** *Law.* **a** To lay, as a charge, before a court as an object of inquiry; to find or represent judicially. **b** To bring a formal public charge against; accuse; specif., *U. S.,* to bring an indictment or presentment against. **9.** *Mil.* To bring (a firearm or other weapon) to a prescribed position in response to a command "present arms." — **Syn.** See GIVE.

pres′ent (prĕz′ĕnt; -'nt), *n.* Anything presented; a gift.

pre·sent′a·ble (prḗ-zĕn′ta-b'l), *adj.* **1.** Capable of or admitting of being presented. **2.** In condition to be seen or inspected, esp. by the critical; being, in appearance; as, a *presentable* young woman. — **pre·sent′a·bil′i·ty** (-bĭl′ĭ-tĭ), **pre·sent′a·ble·ness**, *n.*

pre·sent′ arms. *Mil.* The command in response to which the rifle or other weapon is brought perpendicularly in front of the center of the body, the exact position varying with the arm and service; also, the position.

pres′en·ta′tion (prĕz′ĕn·tā′shŭn; prḗ′zĕn-), *n.* **1.** Act of presenting, or state of being presented; as: **a** Formal introduction, as at court. **b** Bestowal; donation. **2.** A present; gift. **3.** *Com.* = PRESENTMENT (of a negotiable instrument). **4.** *Eccl.* Nomination to a benefice; esp., application by a patron to the bishop for the institution of one so nominated. **5.** *Med.* The particular manner in which the child rests, in labor. **6.** *Philos. & Psychol.* A datum or perception; sensory appearance, whether in actual sensation or in a memory image.

pres′en·ta′tion·al (-ăl; -'l), *adj.* **1.** Of or pert. to a presentation or presentations. **2.** *Gram.* = NOTIONAL, 4.

pres′en·ta′tion·ism (-ĭz'm), *n.* A theory of knowledge which holds that reality is immediately presented in perception. — **pres′en·ta′tion·ist** (-ĭst), *n. & adj.*

pre·sent′a·tive (prḗ-zĕn′ta-tĭv), *adj.* **1.** That presents or serves to present with vividness or clearness, as an image or abstraction. **2.** *Eccl.* Subject to, or carrying the right of, presentation; as, a *presentative* benefice. **3.** *Philos. & Psychol.* Known or capable of being known directly rather than through cogitation; also, intuitive; perceptive.

pres′en·tee′ (prĕz′ĕn-tē′), *n.* One who is presented or to whom something is presented.

pre·sent′er (prḗ-zĕn′tẽr), *n.* One who presents.

pre·sen′ti·ment (prḗ-zĕn′tĭ-mĕnt), *n.* [MF.] A feeling that something will happen; esp., a premonition. — **pre·sen′ti·men′tal** (-mĕn′tăl), *adj.*

pre·sen′tive (prḗ-zĕn′tĭv), *adj.* Bringing a conception or notion directly before the mind; as, a *presentive* word. — **pre·sen′tive·ly**, *adv.* — **pre·sen′tive·ness**, *n.*

pres′ent·ly (prĕz′ĕnt-lĭ; -'nt-lĭ), *adv.* **1.** *Now Dial.* At once; immediately. **2.** Soon; shortly; before long. **3.** At the present time; now.

pre·sent′ment (prḗ-zĕnt′mĕnt), *n.* [OF. *presentement.*] **1.** Presentation. **2.** A setting forth to view; that which is presented or exhibited. **3.** *Commerce.* The act of offering at the proper time and place, a note, bill of exchange, or the like for acceptance, payment, etc. **4.** *Law.* The notice taken, or statement made, by a grand jury of any offense within their own knowledge or without a bill of indictment. **5.** *Philos.* A presentation; also, the content of a perception or thought.

present perfect. *Gram.* Expressing the act or state as completed at the time of speaking (I *have written*); as, *present perfect* tense or verb form.

pre·serv′a·tive (prḗ-zûr′vȧ·tĭv), *adj.* Having the power of preserving; tending to preserve. — *n.* A preservative agent; esp., *Foods,* a substance as sodium benzoate, added to food products to preserve them from decay.

pre·serve′ (prḗ-zûrv′), *v. t.* [OF. *preserver,* fr. LL. *praeservare,* fr. L.

prae before + *servare* to save.] **1.** To keep from injury or destruction; defend from evil; protect; save. **2.** To keep intact; specif.: **a** To keep from decaying. **b** To can, pickle, or the like, for future use. **3.** To maintain; retain; as, to *preserve* silence. **4.** *Hunting & Fishing.* To keep up and reserve for personal or special use; as, to *preserve* game or fish; to *preserve* a stream for fishing. — *v. i.* To make preserves; also, to keep a game preserve. — *n.* **1.** That which is preserved; now: **a** A preserved fruit; — commonly in *pl.* **b** Fruit cooked with sugar so as to keep its shape. **2.** A place in which game, fish, etc., are preserved for purposes of sport, for food, etc. — **pre·serv′a·ble,** *adj.* — **pres′er·va′tion** (prĕz′ẽr·vā′shŭn), *n.* — **pre·serv′er,** *n.*

pre·side′ (prē·zīd′), *v. i.* [F. *présider,* fr. L. *praesidere,* fr. *prae-* + *sedere* to sit.] **1.** To occupy the place of authority, as of president; to direct proceedings as chief officer. **2.** To occupy the leading place, esp. as the directing or featured instrumental performer at a concert, etc.; as, to *preside* at the organ. — **pre·sid′er** (-zīd′ẽr), *n.*

pres′i·den·cy (prĕz′ĭ·dĕn·sĭ), *n.; pl.* -CIES (-sĭz). **1.** Function or action of one who presides. **2.** The office or term of president; specif. [*often cap.*], the office of president of the United States. **3.** [*often cap.*] One of three great divisions, Madras, Bombay, and Bengal, of British India. **4.** *Mormon Ch.* A council of three, a president and two counselors, having jurisdiction throughout the church (***First Presidency***) or within any unit of the church.

pres′i·dent (prĕz′ĭ·dĕnt), *n.* [OF., fr. L. *praesidens, -entis,* pres. part. of *praesidere.* See PRESIDE.] One who presides, esp. by election or appointment; specif.: **a** A presiding officer, as of a legislative assembly. **b** The chief officer of a corporation, society, or the like. **c** [*often cap.*] The chief executive officer of a modern republic. Abbr. *Pres.* **d** The head of the hierarchy of the Mormon Church. Cf. PRESIDENCY, 4. — **pres′i·den′tial** (-dĕn′shăl), *adj.* — **pres′i·dent·ship,** *n.*

pre·sid′i·al (prē·sĭd′ĭ·ăl), *adj.* [L. *praesidium* a presiding over, defense, guard. See PRESIDE.] **1.** Also **pre·sid′i·ar′y** (-ẽr′ĭ; -ẽr·ĭ; 3). Of, pertaining to, or having a garrison; as, a *presidial* castle. **2.** Of or pert. to a presidio.

pre·si′di·o (prē·sē′dĭ·ō; *Sp.* prā·sē′thyō), *n.; pl.* -DIOS (-ōz; *Sp.* -thyōs). [Sp.] A garrisoned place; a military post; also, a Spanish penal settlement.

pre·sid′i·um (prē·sĭd′ĭ·ŭm), *n.* [L., lit., a presiding over, hence, defense, aid.] *Russian.* Any permanent administrative committee, esp. of the government.

pre·sig′ni·fy (prē·sĭg′nĭ·fī), *v. t.* [L. *praesignificare,* fr. *prae-* + *significare* to signify.] To signify beforehand; presage.

press (prĕs), *n.* [See 2d PRESS.] Impressment into service; specif., *Hist.,* compulsory enlistment or service; also, an official order or commission for impressing recruits.

press, *v. t.;* PRESSED (prĕst) or, *Rare,* PREST; PRESS′ING. [For *prest,* prob. misunderstood as a past part. and confused also with *press* to squeeze.] **1.** To force into service, esp. military or naval service. **2.** To use against one's will or contrary to one's (or its) nature; as, an awl *pressed* to do duty as a screwdriver.

press, *v. t.* [OF. *presser,* fr. L. *pressare,* fr. *premere, pressum,* to press.] **1.** To act upon by steady pushing or thrusting while in contact; bear upon; squeeze. **2.** To influence powerfully or irresistibly; constrain; force; compel. **3. a** *Obs.* To oppress. **b** To assail or effect so as to harass; as, to be hard *pressed* by poverty. **4. a** To squeeze so as to extract the juice or contents of; also, express; as, to *press* juice from grapes. **b** To squeeze so as to make compact, dense, or smooth; compress; specif., to iron, as clothes. **5.** To try to force or persuade; entreat; importune. **6.** *Archaic.* To crowd; to throng. **7.** To drive or urge on; speed up; ply hard; as, to *press* a horse in a race. **8.** To lay stress or emphasis on; urge insistently; as, to *press* one's point. **9.** To clasp in an embrace. — *v. i.* **1.** To exert pressure; as: **a** To force or push one's way through or ahead; speed ahead; also, to crowd; throng. **b** To bear weight; weigh down; — with *on* or *upon.* **c** To use argument or similar pressure. **2.** To demand haste or speed in action; as, time *presses.*

— *n.* **1.** Act of pressing or state of being pressed; pressure; as, the *press* of business. **2.** A crowd; a throng. **3.** An apparatus or machine by which any substance is cut, shaped, packed, expressed, stamped, etc., by pressure. Specif.: **a** In full ***printing press.*** Any machine for making impressions, esp. on paper, from an inked surface as of types, woodcuts, or copper plates. In a ***flat-bed cylinder press*** a revolving cylinder presses against a flat bed containing the printing form which passes underneath; in a ***rotary press*** revolving cylinders are employed for both the printing form and the impressional surface. **b** The place or building containing a press or presses. **4.** An upright case or closet for the safe keeping of articles; as, a clothes*press.* **5.** A clamping device, as for rackets or skis, to prevent warping. **6. a** The art, business, or process of printing; as, to go to *press.* **b** A printing or publishing establishment; also, its personnel. **c** Newspapers and periodicals, collectively. **d** Editorial or critical comment, or publicity in the press; as, the play had a good *press.* — **Syn.** See CROWD.

☞ COMBINATIONS and PHRASES (in sense 6) are:

press agent	**press clipping**	**press gallery**
press bureau	**press correspondent**	**pressroom**

press′board′ (prĕs′bōrd′; 70), *n.* A type of highly sized rag paper or board, sometimes containing a small admixture of wood pulp, — used in presses for finishing knit underwear.

press′er (prĕs′ẽr), *n.* One that presses.

presser foot. = FOOT, *n.,* 7.

press gang, *or* **press′gang′** (prĕs′găng′), *n.* [For *prestgang.* See 2d PRESS.] *Hist.* A detachment of men empowered to force men into military, or esp. naval, service.

press′ing, *adj.* Urgent; importunate. — **press′ing·ly,** *adv.*

press′man (prĕs′măn), *n.; pl.* -MEN (-mĕn). One who manages or operates a press; specif., a printer trained for presswork.

press′mark′ (prĕs′märk′), *n. Libraries.* A mark indicating the case, shelf, etc., where a book is located.

press money. = PREST MONEY, under PREST.

press of sail *or* **canvas.** As much sail as the wind permits.

pres′sor (prĕs′ẽr), *adj. Physiol.* Causing increase of pressure; as, *pressor* nerve fibers, stimulation of which causes a stronger contraction of the arteries and an increase of the arterial blood pressure. Cf. DEPRESSOR.

pres′sure (prĕsh′ẽr; 118), *n.* [OF., fr. L. *pressura,* fr. *premere.* See PRESS to squeeze.] **1.** A pressing, or state of being pressed; specif.: **a** A compression; a squeezing. **b** Weight or burden, as of distress. **c** A constraining force, influence, or impulse of any kind; as, to use moral *pressure.* **d** Exigent demands; as, *pressure* of business. **2.** Impression; stamp. **3.** *Elec.* Electromotive force. **4.** *Mech.* The action of a force against some opposing force; a force in the nature of a thrust, distributed over a surface.

pressure cabin. A pressurized cabin.

pressure cooker. A utensil for cooking or preserving foods by means of superheated steam under pressure.

pressure gauge. **1.** A gauge for indicating fluid pressure, as of steam. **2.** A device to measure the pressure of an explosive, as in a gun barrel.

pressure group. A minority group or a bloc that brings pressure to bear upon legislators and upon public opinion, as through lobbying or propaganda, to force or defeat legislation or alter public policy.

pres′sur·ize (prĕsh′ẽr·īz), *v. t.* To maintain near-normal atmospheric pressure inside (a sealed cabin of an aircraft) during high-level flight (above about 12,000 feet elevation), by means of a compressor or a pump, in order to supply occupants with sufficient air.

press′work′ (prĕs′wûrk′), *n.* Work done on or by a press, esp. a printing press; specif., that branch of printing concerned with the production of impressions from type, plates, etc.

prest (prĕst), *n.* [OF., fr. past part. of L. *praestare* to become surety for, fr. *prae-* + *stare* to stand.] *Obs.* **a** A loan. **b** An advance on wages; specif. (in full **prest money**), money advanced to men on enlisting in the British service. — *adj. Obs.* Ready.

pres′ter (prĕs′tẽr), *n.* [OF. *prestre,* fr. L. *presbyter.* See PRIEST.] A priest or presbyter; — *Obs.,* exc. as in **Prester John,** a legendary medieval priest and king of fabulous wealth, power, etc.

pres′ti·dig′i·ta′tion (prĕs′tĭ·dĭj′ĭ·tā′shŭn), *n.* [F., after F. *preste* nimble and L. *digitus* finger.] Sleight of hand; legerdemain. — **pres′ti·dig′i·ta′tor** (-dĭj′ĭ·tā′tẽr), *n.*

pres·tige′ (prĕs·tēzh′; prĕs′tĭj), *n.* [F., fr. L. *praestigium* delusion, illusion.] **1.** Power to command admiration; hence, éclat; renown. **2.** Ascendancy derived from general admiration or esteem; commanding position in men's minds. — **Syn.** See INFLUENCE.

pres·tis′si·mo (prĕs·tĭs′sē·mō), *adv.* [It., superl. of *presto.*] *Music.* At a very rapid pace; — a musical direction.

pres′to (prĕs′tō), *adv.* [It., quick, quickly, fr. LL. *praestus,* fr. *praesto* at hand.] **1.** Quickly; immediately. **2.** *Music.* At a rapid pace; — a direction. — *adj.* Rapidly performed or passing. — *n. Music.* A presto passage or movement.

pre·sume′ (prē·zūm′; 114), *v. t.* [OF. *presumer,* fr. L. *praesumere, -sumptum,* fr. *prae-* + *sumere* to take.] **1.** To take upon oneself without leave or warrant; dare; venture. **2.** To expect or assume, esp. with confidence; to take for granted; regard as probably true or as entitled to belief; as, innocence is *presumed* until guilt is proved. **3.** To raise a presumption of or that; as, a receipt for rent *presumes* payment of prior rent. — *v. i.* **1.** To act or proceed presumptuously or on a presumption; as, ignorance *presumes* where knowledge is timid. **2.** To go beyond what is right or proper; make encroachment; — with *on* or *upon.* — **pre·sum′a·ble** (-zūm′ȧ·b'l), *adj.* — **pre·sum′a·bly** (-blĭ), **pre·sum′ed·ly** (-zūm′ĕd·lĭ; -ĭd·lĭ; 30), *adv.* — **pre·sum′er,** *n.*

pre·sump′tion (prē·zŭmp′shŭn), *n.* **1.** *Now Rare.* A presuming. **2.** Quality of being presumptuous; effrontery; overconfidence. **3.** Ground for presuming, or believing probable; probable, but not conclusive, evidence; also, a conclusion based on such evidence. **4.** *Law.* An inference as to the existence of one fact not certainly known, from the known existence of some other fact.

pre·sump′tive (-tĭv), *adj.* Giving grounds for a presumption, or well-founded opinion or belief; as, *presumptive* evidence; also, based upon a presumption, or probability, or presumptive evidence of ownership, inheritance, culpability, or the like; as, a *presumptive* title to an estate. — **pre·sump′tive·ly,** *adv.*

presumptive heir. = HEIR PRESUMPTIVE.

pre·sump′tu·ous (prē·zŭmp′tū·ŭs), *adj.* [LL. *praesumptuosus.*] **1.** Overweeningly proud, self-confident, or venturesome; taking undue liberties; overbold. **2.** *Obs.* = PRESUMPTIVE. — **pre·sump′tu·ous·ly,** *adv.* — **pre·sump′tu·ous·ness,** *n.*

pre′sup·pose′ (prē′sŭ·pōz′), *v. t.* **1.** To suppose beforehand; to take for granted. **2.** To require as an antecedent logical condition; postulate; as, true knowledge of the external world *presupposes* the validity of perception. — **pre′sup·po·si′tion** (-sŭp·ō·zĭsh′ŭn), *n.*

pre′sur·mise′ (prē′sûr·mīz′), *n.* A presentiment.

pre·tence′ (prē·tĕns′; prē′tĕns; 2). Var. of PRETENSE.

pre·tend′ (prē·tĕnd′), *v. t.* [L. *praetendere, -tentum,* to stretch forward, pretend, assert, fr. *prae-* + *tendere* to stretch.] **1.** *Rare.* To hold before, as a disguise. **2.** To hold out the appearance of being, doing, having, feeling, etc.; to make a show or profession of falsely or with intent to deceive; feign; sham; as, to *pretend* illness or friendship. **3.** *Now Rare.* To allege as a reason, or excuse. — *v. i.* **1.** To put in a claim; allege a title; — with *to.* **2.** To simulate or feign a person, state, etc., as in play; to make believe. — **Syn.** See ASSUME.

pre·tend′ed (-tĕn′dĕd; -dĭd), *adj.* Professed or avowed but not genuine. — **pre·tend′ed·ly,** *adv.*

pre·tend′er (-tĕn′dẽr), *n.* **1.** One who pretends. **2.** A claimant; specif., a claimant to a throne; — in English history applied esp. [*cap.*] to the son (***Old Pretender*** *or* ***the Pretender***) and the grandson (***Young Pretender***) of James II.

pre·tense′, pre·tence′ (prē·tĕns′; prē′tĕns; 2), *n.* [Through AF. & ML., fr. L. *praetentus,* past part. of *praetendere.* See PRETEND.] **1.** A claiming; an asserted or implied claim; pretension; as, she makes no *pretense* to style. **2.** Pretentiousness; mere ostentation; also, a pretentious act, speech, etc.; as, free from *pretense* or *pretenses.* **3.** An aim; an endeavor to arrive (at); as, an index with no *pretense* at completeness. **4.** Pretext; excuse. **5.** A pretending, or simulation; false show.

pre·ten′sion (prē·tĕn′shŭn), *n.* **1.** An allegation; a pretext. **2.** A claim; esp., a claim, asserted or tacit, true or false (to something admirable); hence, any quality or feature that invites or aims to invite admiration or attention; as, his *pretension* to taste. **3.** *Rare.* Aspiration. **4.** Pretentiousness; a pretense or pretenses collectively. — **Syn.** See AMBITION.

pre·ten′tious (-shŭs), *adj.* Having or exhibiting pretensions or claims to admiration; specif.: **a** Ostentatious; showy. **b** Ambitious in scope, subject, etc.; as, a *pretentious* program. — **Syn.** See SHOWY. — **pre·ten′tious·ly,** *adv.* — **pre·ten′tious·ness,** *n.*

pre′ter- (prē′tẽr-). [L. *praeter* past, beyond, orig., compar. of *prae* before.] A prefix meaning: **a** *Past, beyond,* as in **pre′ter·le′thal,** beyond death. **b** [LL. & ML.] *Beyond the range or compass of,* as in:

preterhuman	**preterlegal**	**preterrational**

pret′er·it, pret′er·ite (prĕt′ẽr·ĭt), *adj.* [OF. *preterit*, fr. L. *praeteritus*, past part. of *praeterire* to pass by.] **1.** *Now Rare.* Past; bygone. **2.** *Gram.* Past, without reference to duration, in **preterit tense** (on arriving, I *wrote* to him). See PAST. — *n.* The preterit tense, or a verb in it; — called also *past absolute* (see PAST, *adj.*, 3). Abbr. *pret.*

pret′er·i′tion (prĕt′ẽr·ĭsh′ŭn), *n.* [LL. *praeteritio.*] **1.** A passing by or over. **2.** *Law.* A testator's passing over in silence of one or more of his (then existing) heirs. **3.** *Theol.* The Calvinistic doctrine that God passes over those not elect, leaving them to eternal death.

pre·ter′i·tive (prē·tĕr′ĭ·tĭv), *adj.* *Gram.* Used only or esp. in preterit tenses, as certain verbs.

pre′ter·mit′ (prē′tẽr·mĭt′), *v. t.*; -MIT′TED; -MIT′TING. [L. *praetermittere, -missum*, fr. *praeter* beyond + *mittere* to send.] **1.** To let pass; pass by or over; omit; neglect. **2.** To interrupt or break off; to intermit; suspend. — **pre′ter·mis′sion** (-mĭsh′ŭn), *n.*

pre′ter·nat′u·ral (-năt′ū·răl), *adj.* Beyond normal; esp., not miraculous but strange and inexplicable. — **pre′ter·nat′u·ral·ism** (-ĭz′m), *n.* — **pre′ter·nat′u·ral·ly**, *adv.*

pre′text (prē′tĕkst; *formerly, and still by some*, prē·tĕkst′), *n.* [F. *prétexte*, fr. L. *praetextus*, fr. *praetexere* to weave before, allege as an excuse, fr. *prae-* + *texere* to weave.] That which is alleged or assumed, in order to cloak the real intention or condition; excuse. — **Syn.** See APOLOGY.

‖**pre′ti·um la·bo′rum non vi′le** (prē′shĭ·ŭm lȧ·bō′rŭm nŏn vī′lē). [L.] The value of labor is not trifling; — motto of the Order of the Golden Fleece.

pre′tor (prē′tŏr), **pre·to′ri·an**, etc. Vars. of PRAETOR, PRAETORIAN.

pret′ti·fy (prĭt′ĭ·fī), *v. t.*; -FIED (-fīd); -FY′ING. [*pretty* + *-fy.*] To make pretty, esp. in a petty or overnice way.

pret′ty (prĭt′ĭ; 4), *adj.*; PRET′TI·ER (-ĭ·ẽr); PRET′TI·EST. [AS. *prættig* crafty, sly, fr. *præt, prætt*, deceit, trickery.] **1.** Pleasing by delicacy or grace; neat or elegant without grandeur; engaging but not elevating. **2.** Good; fine; excellent; — often ironical; as, a *pretty* trick. **3.** *Archaic & Scot.* Strong and brave; stout. **4.** Affectedly nice; foppish. **5.** *Chiefly Dial.* Moderately large; considerable. — **Syn.** See BEAUTIFUL. — *adv.* Moderately; in or to some degree. — *n.*; *pl.* -TIES (-ĭz). A pretty or dainty thing; *U.S.*, a knickknack. — **pret′ti·ly** (-ĭ·lĭ), *adv.* — **pret′ti·ness** (-ĭ·nĕs; -nĭs), *n.* — **pret′ty·ish**, *adj.*

pre·typ′i·fy (prē·tĭp′ĭ·fī), *v. t.*; -FIED (-fīd); -FY′ING. To prefigure; to exhibit previously in a type.

pret′zel (prĕt′sĕl), *n.* [G. *prezel, brezel.*] A brittle biscuit in the form of a twisted ring, glazed and salted.

pre·vail′ (prē·vāl′), *v. i.* [F. *prévaloir*, fr. L. *praevalere*, fr. *prae-* + *valere* to be strong or able.] **1.** To gain ascendancy; win mastery; triumph; — often with *over* or *against*. **2.** To be or become effective or effectual; succeed; as, her prayers *prevailed*. **3.** To urge successfully; work (*on, upon*, etc.) by arguments or persuasions. **4.** To be or become common; to be prevalent; predominate; as, Dutch names *prevail* in this region; also, to be in vogue; to be current; as, the custom still *prevails*. — **Syn.** See INDUCE.

pre·vail′ing (prē·vāl′ĭng), *adj.* **1.** Efficacious. **2.** Very generally current; most frequent; predominant; as, the *prevailing* belief. — **pre·vail′ing·ly**, *adv.* — **pre·vail′ing·ness**, *n.*

Syn. **Prevailing, prevalent, rife, current** mean generally circulated, accepted, or used at a certain time or in a certain place. **Prevailing** implies predominance, as in favor; but **prevalent** implies frequency (as, the *prevailing* pronunciation; a *prevalent* pronunciation); **rife** implies prevalence and increasing commonness (as, stories were *rife* about his achievements); **current**, applicable to that which is subject to change, also usually suggests prevalence at the present time (as, a *current* tendency).

prev′a·lent (prĕv′ȧ·lĕnt), *adj.* [L. *praevalens, -entis*, pres. part.] **1.** *Now Rare.* Being in ascendancy; dominant. **2.** Generally or extensively existing; occurring often or over a wide area; rife; as, a *prevalent* practice, disease, or opinion. — **Syn.** See PREVAILING. — **prev′a·lence** (-lĕns), *n.* — **prev′a·lent·ly**, *adv.*

pre·var′i·cate (prē·văr′ĭ·kāt), *v. i.* [L. *praevaricatus*, past part. of *praevaricari* to walk crookedly, collude, fr. *prae-* + *varicare* to straddle, fr. *varicus* straddling, fr. *varus* bent.] To deviate from the truth; speak equivocally or evasively; loosely, to lie. — **Syn.** See LIE. — **pre·var′i·ca′tion** (-kā′shŭn), *n.* — **pre·var′i·ca′tor** (-kā′tẽr), *n.*

‖**pré′ve·nance′** (prāv′näns′), *n.* [F.] Attentiveness to, or anticipation of, others' needs; also, an instance of this.

pre·ven′ience (prē·vēn′yĕns), *n.* **1.** Prevenient character or action. **2.** = PRÉVENANCE.

pre·ven′ient (-yĕnt), *adj.* [L. *praeveniens*, pres. part.] **1.** Preceding; hence, preventive. **2.** Antecedent; anticipatory; esp. in **prevenient grace**, grace operating on one's will before one turns to God.

pre·vent′ (prē·vĕnt′), *v. t.* [L. *praevenire, -ventum*, fr. *prae-* + *venire* to come.] **1.** *Archaic.* **a** To anticipate, as an occasion by being ready, or a wish by satisfying it. **b** To precede; outrun. **2.** To forestall; frustrate; circumvent. **3.** To keep from happening, existing, etc.; to render impossible, esp. by advance provisions; as, rain *prevented* his coming; to *prevent* war. **4.** To hinder (a person); — usually with *from*. — **pre·vent′a·ble, pre·vent′i·ble**, *adj.* — **pre·vent′er**, *n.* — **pre·ven′tion** (-vĕn′shŭn), *n.*

Syn. (1) **Prevent, anticipate, forestall** mean to deal with beforehand. **Prevent** now seldom implies a going before except when it also implies a frustration or a setting up of obstacles (as, to *prevent* an epidemic); **anticipate** implies a getting ahead as in using, treating, or the like, sometimes, so as to balk, but often, so as to prepare for something that comes later (as, to *anticipate* the invention of the airplane; to *anticipate* a payment on a loan); **forestall** implies a getting ahead so as to intercept or stop in its course (as, anxious to *forestall* criticism).
(2) **Prevent, preclude, obviate, avert, ward off** mean to hinder or stop something from coming, occurring, etc. **Prevent** implies the existence of an insurmountable obstacle; **preclude**, a shutting out of every possibility that a thing may happen; **obviate**, a forestalling of disagreeable eventualities by clearing away difficulties; **avert** and **ward off**, immediate and effective measures in the face of that which threatens.

pre·vent′a·tive (prē·vĕn′tȧ·tĭv), *n.* Preventive; — an irregular formation. — **pre·vent′a·tive**, *adj.*

pre·ven′tive (prē·vĕn′tĭv), *adj.* That prevents or tends to prevent; now, usually, devoted to or concerned with prevention; precautionary; as, *preventive* measures or medicine. — *n.* A preventive measure, situation, etc.; specif., *Med.*, a prophylactic. — **pre·ven′tive·ly**, *adv.* — **pre·ven′tive·ness**, *n.*

pre′view′ (prē′vū′), *n.* **1.** A view of a performance, exhibition, motion picture, etc., before it is open or shown to the public. **2.** A showing of snatches from a motion picture advertised for appearance in the near future; — in this sense often written **pre′vue′** (prē′vū′). — *v. t.* To see or show beforehand, esp. before public presentation.

pre′vi·ous (prē′vĭ·ŭs; 58), *adj.* [L. *praevius* going before, fr. *prae-* + *via* the way.] **1.** Going before, in time or order; preceding; antecedent; prior. **2.** *Colloq.* Premature; esp., speaking, judging, etc., prematurely or too quickly. — **Syn.** See PRECEDING. — **pre′vi·ous·ly**, *adv.* — **pre′vi·ous·ness**, *n.*

previous question. *Parliamentary Practice.* The question whether the main issue shall be voted on or not, at once, without further debate. In America the object of the motion is to hasten action; in England, to get rid of the subject for the time being.

pre·vise′ (prē·vīz′), *v. t.* [L. *praevisus*, past part. See PREVISION.] *Now Rare.* **a** To foresee. **b** To forewarn.

pre·vi′sion (-vĭzh′ŭn), *n.* [F. or L.; F. *prévision*, fr. L. *praevidere* to foresee.] Foresight; prescience; also, a prognostication; a forecast.

pre′vo·cal′ic (prē′vō·kăl′ĭk), *adj.* Occurring immediately before a vowel sound.

pre′vo·ca′tion·al (prē′vō·kā′shŭn·ăl; -'l), *adj.* *Educ.* Pertaining to or consisting in instruction or work, esp. in manual training or practical arts, given or required before admission to a vocational school.

pre′vue′, *n.* See PREVIEW, 2.

prex′y (prĕk′sĭ), *n.* Also **prex** (prĕks). *Slang.* College president.

prey (prā), *n.* [OF. *preie*, fr. L. *praeda.*] **1.** *Archaic.* Spoil; booty; plunder. **2.** Any animal seized by another to be devoured; hence, a person given up or seized as a victim. **3.** Act of seizing upon as prey. — *v. i.* **1.** To make raids for the sake of booty; to commit depredations. **2.** To seize; to seek or take food or victims through predaceousness; as, sharpers that *prey* on the poor. **3.** To have a wearing or exhausting effect; as, fears *preyed* upon his mind. — **prey′er** (prā′ẽr), *n.*

Pri′am (prī′ăm), *n.* [L. *Priamus*, fr. Gr. *Priamos.*] *Gr. Myth.* The last king of Troy, father of Hector and Paris. He was slain in the sack of Troy.

Pri·a′pus (prī·ā′pŭs), *n.* [L., fr. Gr. *Priapos.*] **1.** *Gr. & Rom. Relig.* The male generative power personified as a god. **2.** [*not cap.*] A phallus. — **Pri′a·pe′an** (prī′ȧ·pē′ăn), *adj.*

price (prīs), *n.* [OF. *pris* (F. *prix*), fr. L. *pretium.*] **1.** Value; worth; as, a pearl of great *price*. **2.** The quantity of one thing, usually money, exchanged or demanded in barter or sale for another; specif., the amount at which transactions take place in the market; as, today's *price* of wool. **3.** The terms for the sake of which something is undertaken; specif.: **a** That by which a person is or may be bribed; as, there is no *price* for this man. **b** Reward, esp. for capture; as, a *price* on his head. **c** Cost of obtaining; as, the *price* of liberty is eternal vigilance. — **Syn.** Charge, cost, expense.
— *v. t.*; PRICED (prīst); PRIC′ING (prīs′ĭng). **1.** To set a price on; fix the price of. **2.** *Colloq.* To ask the price of.

price′less (prīs′lĕs; -lĭs), *adj.* **1.** Of inestimable worth; invaluable. **2.** *Colloq.* Surprisingly amusing or absurd. — **Syn.** See COSTLY.

prick (prĭk), *n.* [AS. *prica* a point, dot.] **1.** A mark made by a pointed instrument; a puncture; a point; dot. **2.** A pointed instrument or weapon; *Archaic*, a goad. **3.** A pricking, or sensation of being pricked; a sting, as of remorse. — *v. t.* **1.** To pierce slightly with something pointed; make a small puncture or punctures in. **2.** To pain or sting, as with remorse. **3.** *Archaic.* To spur; goad; incite. **4.** To mark or designate by a puncture; to trace or outline by punctures. **5.** To erect into a point; as, the dog *pricked* up his ears; — hence, to **prick up one's ears**, to listen eagerly. **6.** *Far.* **a** To drive a nail into (a horse's foot) so as to cause lameness. **b** To nick. **7.** To trace on a chart, as a ship's course; — often with *off*. — *v. i.* **1.** To give or feel a small puncture or punctures; also, to be prickly. **2.** *Archaic.* To ride fast by use of goad; gallop. **3.** To point upward; to be erect. **4.** *Hort.* To transplant seedlings from pans to flat boxes; — with *off* or *out*. — *adj.* That pricks up or stands erect; as, *prick* ears. — **prick′er**, *n.* — **prick′ing·ly**, *adv.*

prick′-eared′ (prĭk′ērd′), *adj.* Having erect, pointed ears; — applied esp. in the 17th century by the Cavaliers to the Roundheads, whose close-cut hair made their ears conspicuous.

prick′et (prĭk′ĕt; -ĭt), *n.* [*prick* + *-et.*] **1.** A spike on which a candle is stuck; hence, a candlestick with such a point. **2.** [ME. *priket.*] A buck in his second year.

prick′le (prĭk′'l), *n.* [AS. *pricel.*] **1.** A small, sharp point; a fine, sharp process or projection; a spine; specif., *Bot.*, a sharp, pointed process or emergence arising from the subepidermal tissue. Cf. SPINE, 1. **2.** A pricking sensation. — *v. t. & i.*; -LED (-'ld); -LING (-lĭng). To prick; to pierce, prod, etc.; to tingle.

prick′ly (-lĭ), *adj.*; -LI·ER (-lĭ·ẽr); -LI·EST. **1.** Full of prickles; covered with prickles. **2.** Prickling; stinging. — **prick′li·ness**, *n.*

prickly ash. A prickly shrub or small tree (*Zanthoxylum americanum*) of the rue family, with yellowish flowers.

prickly heat. *Med.* A noncontagious cutaneous eruption of red pimples, with intense itching and tingling, caused by inflammation around the sweat ducts.

prickly pear. Any flat-jointed cactus (genus *Opuntia*); opuntia; also, its pear-shaped edible fruit.

prickly poppy. Any of a genus (*Argemone*) of plants of the poppy family, with prickly leaves and white or yellow flowers, esp. the ***Mexican poppy*** (*A. mexicana*). See CHICALOTE.

prick song. **1.** *Obs.* Music written, or noted; — so called from the points or notes. **2.** Descant; counterpoint.

pride (prīd), *n.* [ME. *pride, prute*, fr. AS. *prȳte*, fr. *prūt* proud.] **1.** Quality or state of being proud; specif.: **a** Inordinate self-esteem; conceit. See DEADLY SINS. **b** Lofty self-respect; a reasonable delight in one's position, achievements, possessions, etc. **2.** Proud behavior or treatment; insolence; arrogance; disdain. **3.** Show; ostentation; display. **4.** *Archaic.* Highest pitch; prime; glory; as, in the *pride* of one's life. **5.** A person or thing of which one is proud; hence, the pick; the flower. **6.** *Obs.* Mettle; hence, sexual desire. — *v. t.* To indulge in pride; rate highly; pique; plume; — used reflexively; as, to *pride* oneself upon one's skill.

pride′ful (prīd′fo͝ol; -f'l), *adj.* Full of pride; haughty; also, elated. — **pride′ful·ly**, *adv.* — **pride′ful·ness**, *n.*

pride of China. Also **pride of India.** = CHINA TREE.

‖**prie-dieu** (prē′dyû′), *n.* [F., lit., pray God.] A kneeling stand for praying, consisting of a bench for the knees and a rest for the elbows.

pri′er (prī′ẽr), *n.* Also **pry′er.** [From PRY.] One who pries; one who inquires narrowly, or is inquisitive.

priest (prēst), *n.* [AS. *prēost*, ult. fr. LL. *presbyter*, fr. Gr. *presbyteros* elder, older, n., an elder, compar. of *presbys* an old man.] **1.** One authorized or ordained to perform sacerdotal functions, esp. in Jewish or Christian rites; specif., one who offers the Eucharistic sacrifice. **2.** One of the clergy as distinguished from the laity. **3.** One whose function, spirit, etc., resembles that of a priest.

priest′craft′ (-krȧft′; 9), *n.* Priestly knowledge, skill, policies, or methods; — chiefly derogatory.

priest′ess, *n.* A woman priest, esp. of pagan antiquity.

priest′hood (prēst′hŏŏd), *n.* [AS. *prēosthād.*] **1.** Office, dignity, character, etc., of a priest. **2.** Priests collectively.

priest′ly (-lĭ), *adj.;* PRIEST′LI·ER (-lĭ·ẽr); PRIEST′LI·EST. Of or pertaining to priests; befitting or becoming a priest. — **priest′li·ness**, *n.*

priest′–rid′den, *adj.* Dominated by a priest or priests.

prig (prĭg), *v. t. & i.;* PRIGGED (prĭgd); PRIG′GING. *Chiefly Scot.* **a** To haggle; bargain hard. **b** To entreat; beg.

prig, *n.* **1.** *Obs.* A person; — in humorous or contemptuous use. **2.** An irritatingly self-sufficient or punctilious person. — **prig′ger·y** (-ẽr·ĭ), *n.* — **prig′gish**, *adj.* — **prig′gish·ly**, *adv.* — **prig′gish·ness**, *n.*

prig′gism (-ĭz′m), *n.* Behavior of a prig; priggishness.

prim (prĭm), *adj.;* PRIM′MER (-ẽr); PRIM′MEST. [OF. *prim, prime*, first, principal, fine, fr. L. *primus* first.] Formally precise; stiffly decorous. — *v. t.;* PRIMMED (prĭmd); PRIM′MING. To make prim; set, as lips, primly; to dress primly. — **prim′ly**, *adv.* — **prim′ness**, *n.*

pri′ma·cy (prī′mȧ·sĭ), *n.; pl.* -CIES (-sĭz). [OF. *primacie*, fr. ML. *primatia*, fr. LL. *primas* one of the first.] **1.** State of being prime, or first, as in time, place, rank, etc. **2.** The office, rank, or dignity of a primate; specif., *R.C.Ch.*, the supreme episcopal jurisdiction of the pope.

pri′ma don′na (prē′mȧ dŏn′ȧ; *It.* prē′mä dôn′nä); *pl.* PRIMA DONNAS (-ȧz), PRIME DONNE (*It.* prē′mā dôn′nā). [It., lit., first lady.] The principal woman singer in an opera or concert organization.

pri′ma fa′ci·e (prī′mȧ fā′shĭ·ē; fā′shĭ). [L., abl.] Literally, on first appearance.

pri′ma–fa′ci·e ev′i·dence. *Law.* Evidence sufficient to raise a presumption of fact or establish the fact in question unless rebutted. Hence, **prima–facie case.**

pri′mage (prī′mĭj), *n.* [Cf. PRIME, *adj.*] *Marine.* Formerly, a small gratuity made by shippers to the captain; now, usually, a small addition or percentage added to the freight and belonging to the owner.

‖**pri′ma (pri′mus) in′ter pa′res** (prī′mȧ [-mŭs] ĭn′tẽr pā′rēz). [L.] First among her (his) peers.

pri′mal (prī′măl), *adj.* [ML. *primalis*, fr. L. *primus* first.] **1.** First; original. **2.** First in importance; chief.

pri′ma·ri·ly (prī′mẽr·ĭ·lĭ; -mȧ·rĭ·lĭ; *emphatic also* prī·mâr′ĭ·lĭ; 2), *adv.* In the first place; originally; fundamentally.

pri′ma·ry (prī′mẽr·ĭ; -mȧ·rĭ), *adj.* [L. *primarius*, fr. *primus* first.] **1.** First in order of time or development or in intention; primitive; original; as, the *primary* meaning of a word; also, fundamental; radical; as, the *primary* causes of a war. **2.** First in dignity or importance; chief; principal; as, *primary* planets. **3.** Of the first order in successive divisions, combinations, or ramifications; as, *primary* nerves, compounds. **4.** First in order as being preparatory to something higher; as, *primary* schools. **5.** *Chem.* **a** Characterized by, or resulting from, the substitution of only one atom or group. **b** Designating or characterized by a carbon atom united (by a single valence) to only one chain or ring member. **6.** *Elec.* In an induction coil or transformer, pertaining to or designating the inducing current or its circuit; as, the *primary* coil. **7.** *Geol.* Belonging to Paleozoic and older formations. **8.** *Gram.* See SECONDARY, *adj.* **9.** *Zool.* Designating, or pertaining to, the principal feathers or quills on the distal joint of a bird's wing.

— *n.; pl.* -RIES (-ĭz). **1.** Something primary; the first in order, rank, etc. **2. a** *U. S.* A meeting of voters of the same political party to take first steps towards the nomination of candidates, as by choosing delegates to nominating conventions. **b** In full **primary election.** A preliminary election in which voters directly nominate for office the candidates of their own party. **3.** One of the primary colors. See COLOR, *n.*, 2. **4.** *Astron.* A planet as distinguished from its satellites. **5.** *Elec.* A primary coil. See PRIMARY, *adj.*, 6. **6.** *Zool.* A primary feather or quill. See PRIMARY, *adj.*, 9; BIRD, *Illust.;* POULTRY, *Illust.* (17).

primary accent. The strongest stress in the pronunciation of a word of two or more syllables; the mark (usually ′), to indicate this; thus the *primary accent* is on the first syllable of *horse′shoe′*. Cf. SECONDARY ACCENT.

primary cell. *Elec.* A cell that converts chemical energy into electrical energy by irreversible chemical reactions. Cf. SECONDARY CELL.

primary colors. See COLOR, *n.*, 2.

pri′mate (prī′mĭt), *n.* [OF. *primat*, fr. LL. *primas, -atis*, principal, chief, in ML., primate, fr. L. *primus* first.] **1.** One who is first in rank, quality, authority, or the like. **2.** *Eccl.* A bishop, usually an archbishop, who has precedence in a province, group of provinces, or a nation. In the Church of England, he has precedence over other bishops in his province. The archbishop of Canterbury has the title of ***Primate of All England***, and the archbishop of York, that of ***Primate of England***. **3.** *Zool.* One of an order (**Pri·ma′tes** [prī·mā′tēz]) of mammals consisting of man and the apes, monkeys, marmosets, and lemurs. — **pri·ma′tal** (prī·mā′tăl; -t′l), *adj. & n.* — **pri′mate·ship**, *n.* — **pri·ma′tial** (prī·mā′shăl), *adj.*

prime (prīm), *n.* [See PRIME, *adj.*] **1.** [AS. *prīm*, fr. L. *prima* (sc. *hora*) the first hour.] The first hour of the day; specif. [*cap.*], the first of the daytime canonical offices, or hours. See CANONICAL HOUR **a.** **2.** The earliest stage; beginning; hence, the dawn; the spring. **3.** The spring of life; youth; now, usually, the period of greatest health, strength, or beauty. **4.** That which is first in quality; the best; the pick. **5. a** Any of the first set of equal parts (originally and generally 60, sometimes 10) into which a unit, esp., a degree, is divided; a minute. **b** The accent (′) used to denote such a fraction and now also for many other purposes, as in algebra, thus *a′* (to be read *a prime*). **6.** *Arith.* A prime number. See PRIME, *adj.*, 5. **7.** *Music.* **a** A tone of the same staff degree as a given tone. **b** The pitch relation between two such tones, or their simultaneous combination. The perfect prime, represented by the ratio 1:1, is called also the *unison.* **c** The tonic, or keynote.

— *adj.* [OF., fr. L. *primus* first.] **1.** First in order of time; original; primeval; primitive. **2.** First in rank, degree, dignity, or importance; chief. **3.** First in excellence; of highest quality; as, *prime* wheat. **4.** Primary as opposed to derivative; as, a *prime* cause. **5.** *Math.* **a** Divisible by no number except itself or unity; as, 7 is a *prime* number; — opposed to *composite.* **b** Having no common divisor but 1; — used with *to;* as, 12 is *prime* to 25.

— *v. t.* **1.** To prepare for firing, as a firearm, by supplying with priming or a primer. **2.** Hence: **a** To put into working condition, as a pump by pouring water into the barrel or bucket. **b** To lay the first color, coating, or preparation upon (a surface), as in painting. **c** To make ready; instruct beforehand; post; as, to *prime* a witness. — *v. i.* **1.** To prime a gun, a pump, etc. **2.** *Steam Boilers.* To work so that fine water particles become mixed up with, and carried over by, the steam. — **prime′ly**, *adv.* — **prime′ness**, *n.*

prime conductor. *Elec.* The large conductor of a frictional electrical machine, serving to collect, accumulate, or retain the positive electricity.

prime cost. *Accounting.* The combined cost of direct labor and material in the production of an article.

prime meridian. A meridian from the intersection of which with the equator longitude is counted, both east and west. That of Greenwich is almost universally used.

prime minister. The responsible head of a ministry or executive government; a premier. Hence, **prime ministry.**

prime mover. a A natural agency applied by man to the production of power, such as muscular force. **b** An engine or machine which receives and modifies force and motion as supplied by some natural source, thereby driving other machinery, as a water wheel, or a turbine. **c** Figuratively, the original or the most effective force in any undertaking. **d** *U. S. Army.* A powerful tractor or truck, usually with all-wheel drive, for hauling artillery, moving stalled vehicles, etc.

prim′er (prīm′ẽr), *n.* A person or a thing that primes; specif., a cap, tube, or wafer containing percussion powder or other compound, for igniting an explosive charge.

prim′er (prĭm′ẽr; *Brit. now generally* prī′mẽr), *n.* [ML. *primarius.*] **1.** A book, orig. a prayer book, used in teaching children to read or spell; hence, an elementary textbook. **2.** (*pron.* prĭm′ẽr) *Print.* Either of two sizes of type: ***long primer*** (10 points) or ***great primer*** (18 points). See TYPE.

pri·me′ro (prī·mâr′ō), *n.* [Sp. *primera*, fr. *primero* first.] An old gambling card game.

pri·me′val (prī·mē′văl), *adj.* [L. *primaevus*, fr. *primus* first + *aevum* age.] Belonging to the first ages; pristine; primitive. — **pri·me′val·ly**, *adv.*

pri′mi·ge′ni·al (prī′mĭ·jē′nĭ·ăl), *adj.* [L. *primigenus, primigenius.*] First formed or generated; original.

pri′mine (prī′mĭn), *n.* [L. *primus* first.] *Bot.* **a** The outermost of the two integuments of an ovule. **b** Less commonly, the inner and earlier-formed integument.

prim′ing (prīm′ĭng), *n.* **1.** Act of one who primes. **2. a** The powder or other material used to fire a charge in a firearm or in blasting. **b** *Paint.* The first coating of paint, size, etc., laid on a surface to be painted.

pri·mip′a·ra (prī·mĭp′ȧ·rȧ), *n.* [L., fr. *primus* first + *parere* to bring forth.] *Med.* A woman parturient for the first time or having borne one child and no more. Cf. NULLIPARA, MULTIPARA. — **pri′mi·par′i·ty** (prī′mĭ·păr′ĭ·tĭ), *n.* — **pri·mip′a·rous** (prī·mĭp′ȧ·rŭs), *adj.*

prim′i·tive (prĭm′ĭ·tĭv), *adj.* [F. *primitif*, fr. L. *primitivus*, fr. *primus* first.] **1.** Of or pertaining to the beginning or origin, or to the earliest ages or period; original. **2.** Primary; radical; not derived; as, a *primitive* verb in grammar. **3.** Characterized by a quality or qualities belonging or ascribed to the original state of man, an institution, etc.; as, to live in *primitive* fashion. **4.** *Biol.* **a** Primordial. **b** Persisting, little evolved in structure, from ancestral types in remote geological ages; — of species or groups; as, the tuatara is a *primitive* type of reptile. — *n.* **1.** A primitive ancestor, inhabitant, or member. **2.** An artist or a work of art of a primitive period; esp., in painting and sculpture, one of the Middle Ages; also, a modern imitator or follower of such an artist. **3.** *Gram.* A radical or root word, as distinguished from a *derivative.* **4.** *Math.* The algebraic or geometric form from which another is derived. — **prim′i·tive·ly**, *adv.* — **-ness**, *n.*

prim′i·tiv·ism (-tĭv·ĭz′m), *n.* Belief in the superiority of primitive life, Christianity, etc. — **prim′i·tiv·ist** (-ĭst), *n.*

‖**pri′mo** (prē′mō), *n.* The first or leading part, as in a duet or trio.

pri′mo·gen′i·tor (prī′mō·jĕn′ĭ·tẽr), *n.* [ML., fr. L. *primus* first + *genitor* a begetter.] An ancestor; a forefather.

pri′mo·gen′i·ture (-tůr), *n.* [ML. *primogenitura*, fr. L. *primus* first + *genitura* birth, generation.] **1.** State of being the first-born of children of the same parents. **2.** *Law.* An exclusive right of inheritance belonging to the first-born.

pri·mor′di·al (prī·môr′dĭ·ăl), *adj.* [LL. *primordialis*, fr. L. *primordium* beginning, fr. *primus* first + *ordiri* to begin a web, begin.] **1.** First created or existing; rudimentary; as, *primordial* matter. **2.** First in order; primary; fundamental; elemental; as, *primordial* rights. **3.** *Biol.* Originally or earliest formed in the growth of an individual or organ; — opposed to *definitive.* — **pri·mor′di·al·ly**, *adv.*

primp (prĭmp), *v. i. & t.* To dress up; prink; preen.

prim′rose′ (prĭm′rōz′), *n.* [ME. *prymerose*, fr. OF. *primerole*, deriv. of ML. *primula*, fr. L. *primus* first.] **1.** Any of a genus (*Primula*) of perennial herbs typifying a family (Primulaceae, the primrose family), with large tufted basal leaves and showy various-colored flowers, esp. *P. vulgaris;* also, the cowslip (see COWSLIP, 1), the auricula, and the ***Chinese primrose*** (*P. sinensis*, with varicolored flowers, or *P. obconica*, with lilac or pink flowers); also, the flower. **2.** The evening primrose. **3.** Also **primrose yellow.** A color, reddish-yellow in hue, of medium saturation and high brilliance. See COLOR.

prim′rose′ (prĭm′rōz′), *adj.* **1.** Pert. to or abounding in primroses; hence, flowery; gay. **2.** Of primrose color. **3.** Gay; hence, devoted to sensual pleasures; — esp. in **primrose path.**

prim′sie (prĭm′sĭ), *adj.* *Scot.* Prim; demure.

prim′u·la (prĭm′ů·lȧ), *n.* = PRIMROSE, 1.

prim′u·la′ceous (-lā′shŭs), *adj.* [ML. *primula* primrose.] *Bot.* Belonging to the primrose family (Primulaceae). See PRIMROSE.

‖**pri′mum mo′bi·le** (prī′mŭm mŏb′ĭ·lē). [L.] In ancient and medieval astronomy, the outermost concentric sphere, carrying the spheres of the fixed stars and the planets in its daily revolution.

‖**pri′mus in′ter pa′res** (prī′mŭs ĭn′tẽr pā′rēz). [L.] First among (his) peers.

prince (prĭns; 106), *n.* [OF., fr. L. *princeps, -cipis*, the first, chief, fr. *primus* first + *capere* to take.] **1.** The one of highest rank; a sovereign; — now rarely applied to a female. **2.** A title given to the son of a sovereign, or to other members of a royal family. **3.** A title of nobility, esp. one in certain European countries ranking above, or in some cases below, that of duke. **4.** One at the head of, or very eminent in, a class or profession. — **prince′dom** (prĭns′dŭm), *n.*

Prince Albert. A long double-breasted frock coat for men.

prince consort. The husband of a queen regnant.

prince′kin (prĭns′kĭn), **prince′let, prince′ling,** *n.* A small or petty prince.

prince′ly (-lĭ), *adj.;* PRINCE′LI·ER (-lĭ·ẽr); PRINCE′LI·EST. Of or relating to a prince; regal; befitting or characteristic of a prince; noble; also, munificent. — **prince′li·ness,** *n.* — **prince′ly,** *adv.*

Prince of Darkness. The Devil; Satan.

Prince of Peace. Jesus Christ; — alluding to Isaiah ix. 6.

Prince of Wales. A title borne by the eldest son or heir apparent of the British sovereign.

prince's′-feath′er (prĭn′sĕz-; -sĭz-), *n.* An annual plant (*Amaranthus hybridus hypochondriacus*) often cultivated for its dense usually red spikes.

prin′cess (prĭn′sĕs; -sĭs; *in Brit. use, when attrib., usually* prĭn′sĕs, -sĭs; *otherwise* prĭn·sĕs′ *or* prĭn′sĕs), *n.* [F. *princesse.*] **1.** *Archaic.* A woman having sovereign power. **2.** The daughter or granddaughter of a sovereign; also, a female member of a royal family. **3.** The consort of a prince; as, the *princess* of Wales.

prin·cesse′ (prĭn·sĕs′; prĭn′sĕs, -sĭs), *adj.* Also **prin′cess** (prĭn′sĕs, -sĭs). [F., a princess.] Designating a one-piece, close-fitting dress or slip.

princess royal. The eldest daughter of a sovereign.

prin′ci·pal (prĭn′sĭ·păl; -p'l), *adj.* [OF., fr. L. *principalis,* fr. *princeps.*] Highest in rank, authority, or importance; chief; main. — *n.* **1.** A leader, chief, or head. **2. a** A capital sum placed at interest, due as a debt, or used as a fund; — disting. from *interest* or *profit.* **b** The main body of a decedent's estate, portion of estate, devise, or bequest; — disting. from *income.* **3.** *Archaic.* A fundamental point; a principle. **4.** *Arch. & Engin.* The construction which gives shape and strength to a roof, generally one of several trusses of timber or iron. **5.** *Educ.* A presiding or chief executive officer of a college, or esp. *U. S.,* of a school or academy. **6.** *Law.* **a** One who employs another to act for him. **b** One primarily liable on an obligation, as disting. from an *endorser, surety,* etc. **c** The chief actor in a crime, or an abettor present at it; — distinguished from an *accessory.* **7.** *Music.* **a** In English organs, the chief open metallic stop, an octave above the open diapason. **b** [*cap.*] An octave or 4-foot organ stop; — used in compound names. **c** A fugue subject; — opposed to *answer.* — **prin′ci·pal·ly,** *adv.* — **prin′ci·pal·ship′,** *n.*

prin′ci·pal′i·ty (-păl′ĭ·tĭ), *n.; pl.* -TIES (-tĭz). **1.** *Now Rare.* State or quality of being principal, or a principal. **2.** Territory or jurisdiction of a prince, or the country which gives title to a prince. **3.** In medieval angelology, one of an order of angels.

principal parts. *Gram.* Those forms of a verb from which its other forms can be derived — in English including the infinitive, the past tense, and the past participle (*play, played, played; ring, rang, rung*).

‖**prin′ci·pe** (*It.* prēn′chē·pā; *Sp.* prēn′thē·pā; *Pg.* prēɴ′sē·pĕ), *n.* [It., *principe,* Sp. & Pg. *príncipe.*] A prince; specif., in Spanish and Portuguese use, a title applied to the eldest son of a king.

prin·cip′i·um (prĭn·sĭp′ĭ·ŭm), *n.; pl.* -IA (-ȧ). [L.] A principle; esp., *pl.,* first principles; elements.

prin′ci·ple (prĭn′sĭ·p'l), *n.* [OF. *principe,* fr. L. *principium* beginning, foundation, fr. *princeps, -cipis.* See PRINCE.] **1.** A source or origin; primordial substance; ultimate basis or cause. **2.** An original faculty or endowment. **3.** A fundamental truth; a primary or basic law, doctrine, or the like. **4.** A settled rule of action; a governing law of conduct; also, such principles or loyalty to them; as, a man of no *principle.* **5.** Essential or characteristic constituent; that which gives a substance its essential properties; as, the active *principle* of a drug. **6.** The natural or mechanical law applied, as in a mechanical contrivance, or at work, as in a natural phenomenon; as, all these devices are based on the same *principle.* **7.** [*cap.*] *Christian Science.* Specif., divine Principle; — a synonym for God. — *v. t.;* PRIN′CI·PLED (-p'ld); PRIN′CI·PLING (-plĭng). To ground in a principle or principles; chiefly in *past part.,* esp. in combinations; as, high-*principled.*

prin′cox (prĭn′kŏks), *n.* Also **prin′cock** (-kŏk). [Prob. fr. *prim* + *cock.*] *Archaic.* A coxcomb; a pert youth.

prink (prĭngk), *v. t. & i.* To dress for show; bedeck (oneself); preen; — often with *up.* — **prink′er** (-ẽr), *n.*

print (prĭnt), *n.* [ME. *printe, prente,* fr. OF. *priente, preinte,* fr. past part. of *preindre* to press, print, fr. L. *premere.*] **1.** A mark made by pressure; a line, figure, etc., impressed; an imprint. **2.** A stamp, die, or mold; as, a butter *print;* also, that which receives an impression from a stamp, mold, etc. **3.** Printed state or form; as, put into *print.* **4.** Printed matter; esp., a printed publication. **5.** Printed letters; impression from type; as, small *print;* clear *print.* **6.** An impression taken from anything; specif., a lithograph, etching, photograph, or the like. **7.** A fabric figured by stamping. — ***in print.*** **a** In a printed form; published. **b** *Now Dial.* To the letter; with accurateness. **c** Still on sale by the publisher. — ***out of print.*** Not procurable from the publisher, the edition being exhausted. — *v. t.* **1.** To fix or impress, as a stamp, mark, character, idea, etc., into or upon something. **2.** To stamp something in or upon; to make an imprint on. **3.** Specif., to strike off an impression or impressions of, from type, or from stereotype, electrotype, or engraved plates, or the like; hence: **a** To do the typesetting, presswork, etc., of; as, to *print* books. **b** To stamp or impress characters, designs, etc., on, from plates, types, etc.; as, to *print* cards. **c** To publish in print; as, to *print* the disclosures. **4.** To form or write in characters like those of type. **5.** *Photog.* To make (a positive picture) from a negative, a drawing on transparent paper, or the like, upon a sensitized surface; — sometimes with *out.* — *v. i.* **1. a** To use or practice the art of typography. **b** To produce printed matter. **2.** To publish a book, article, music, or the like. **3.** To write letters or words in typographical characters.
— **print′a·ble,** *adj.*

print′er (prĭn′tẽr), *n.* **1.** One who prints; specif., one whose business is printing books, newspapers, magazines, engravings, etc., or one who works at printing, as a compositor or a pressman. **2.** A device used for printing, as a machine for printing from photographic negatives.

print′er's dev′il (prĭn′tẽrz). An apprentice in a printing office.

print′er·y (prĭn′tẽr·ĭ), *n.; pl.* -ERIES (-ĭz). **a** A place where cloth is printed. **b** A printing office or shop.

print′ing, *n.* Act, art, or practice or business of a printer; esp., typography.

printing press. See PRESS, *n.,* 3 **a.**

print′less (prĭnt′lĕs; -lĭs), *adj.* *Chiefly Poetic.* Making, bearing, or taking no imprint.

pri′or (prī′ẽr), *n.* [From AS. *prior* (fr. L.), and fr. OF. *priour, prior,* fr. L. *prior* former, superior, in ML. a prior.] **a** The coadjutor of an abbot ranking next to him in the monastery (***claustral prior***). **b** The superior of a priory (***conventual prior***). **c** The head of one of the houses of certain religious orders, as the Dominican or Augustinian. — **pri′or·ate** (-ĭt), *n.* — **pri′or·ship,** *n.*

pri′or, *adj.* [L., former, superior.] **1.** Preceding in the order of time; previous. **2.** Taking precedence because earlier, more important, etc. — **Syn.** See PRECEDING.

pri′or·ess (-ĕs; -ĭs), *n.* A nun whose position in an order of women corresponds to that of prior in an order of men.

pri·or′i·ty (prī·ŏr′ĭ·tĭ), *n.; pl.* -TIES (-tĭz). **1.** Quality of being prior. **2.** Superiority in rank, position, or privilege. **3.** Order of preference based on urgency, importance, or merit: **a** *U. S.* A wartime preferential rating assigned by the government for the delivery of products according to the relative need of each for national defense and the proportionate allocation of scarce materials. **b** Any preferential rating assigning rights to scarce products or materials, limited services, transportation, surplus property, or prescribing the order in which assignments are to be attended to.

pri′o·ry (prī′ô·rĭ), *n.; pl.* -RIES (-rĭz). [AF. *priorie,* fr. ML. *prioria.*] A religious house ranking next below an abbey. — **Syn.** See CLOISTER.

prise (prīz), *n. & v.* Var. of PRIZE.

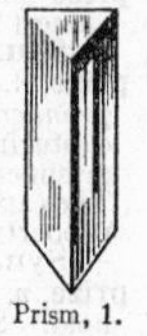

Prism, 1.

prism (prĭz'm; 65), *n.* [LL. *prisma,* fr. Gr. *prisma,* fr. *prizein, priein,* to saw.] **1.** *Geom.* A solid whose bases or ends are similar, equal, and parallel polygons, the faces being parallelograms. **2.** *Optics.* A transparent body bounded in part by two plane faces which are not parallel. **3.** *Cryst.* A form the faces of which are parallel to one axis; specif., one whose faces are parallel to the vertical axis, in distinction from *dome.* **4.** By extension, something which refracts light.

pris·mat′ic (prĭz·măt′ĭk), *adj.* Also **pris·mat′i·cal** (-ĭ·kăl). **1.** Of, pertaining to, or resembling a prism. **2.** Formed by a prism; resembling the colors formed by the refraction of light through a transparent prism. **3.** Hence, highly colored; brilliant. **4.** *Cryst.* Orthorhombic. — **pris·mat′i·cal·ly,** *adv.*

pris′moid (prĭz′moid), *n.* A solid like a prism but having unequal ends or bases so that the faces are trapezoids instead of parallelograms. — **pris·moi′dal** (prĭz·moi′dăl; -d'l), *adj.*

pris′on (prĭz′'n), *n.* [OF., fr. L. *prehensio, prensio,* a seizing, arresting.] **1.** A place or state of confinement or restraint, esp. of persons. **2.** A building or other place for the safe custody of criminals or others committed by lawful authority; specif., *U. S.,* a state prison.

pris′on·er (prĭz′'n·ẽr; prĭz′nẽr), *n.* A person under arrest, in custody, or in prison; hence, one who is involuntarily restrained.

pris′on·er's base (prĭz′'n·ẽrz; prĭz′nẽrz). An old game played by children; — called also **prisoner's bar** *or* **bars.**

pris′sy (prĭs′ĭ), *adj.;* PRIS′SI·ER (-ĭ·ẽr); PRIS′SI·EST. [A blend of *precise* and *sissy.*] *Colloq.* Prim and precise; finicky.

pris′tine (prĭs′tēn, -tĭn; *or, esp. Brit.,* -tīn), *adj.* [L. *pristinus.*] Belonging to the earliest period or state; primitive; hence, uncorrupted.

prith′ee (prĭth′ē; -ĭ), *interj.* [For earlier *preythe* (I) pray thee.] *Archaic.* I pray thee; — an exclamation expressing request.

pri′va·cy (prī′vȧ·sĭ; *Brit. also* prĭv′ȧ·sĭ), *n.; pl.* -CIES (-sĭz). **1.** State of being apart from company or observation; seclusion; also, secrecy. **2.** A place of seclusion.

‖**Pri·vat′do·cent′** (prē·vät′dô·tsĕnt′), *n.;* G. *pl.* -DOCENTEN (-tsĕn′tĕn). Also **Pri·vat′do·zent′.** [G. fr. *privat* private + *docent, dozent,* teacher.] An unsalaried university lecturer or teacher, esp. in Germany, remunerated by students' fees.

pri′vate (prī′vĭt), *adj.* [L. *privatus* apart from the state, private, prop. past part. of *privare* to bereave, deprive, fr. *privus* single, private.] **1.** Belonging to, or concerning, an individual; personal; one's own; not general or common; as, *private* property or opinions. **2.** Sequestered; secluded; as, to wish to be *private.* **3.** Not public in nature; not in public life or under public control; as, *private* schools or citizens. **4.** Not publicly known; secret; as, a *private* negotiation. — *n.* **1.** Someone or something that is private; also, privacy; as, to confer in *private.* **2.** *Mil.* A soldier below the grade of noncommissioned officer; as of 1948 in the U. S. Army, one grade above a recruit. Abbr. *pvt.* — **pri′vate·ly,** *adv.* — **pri′vate·ness,** *n.*

pri′va·teer′ (prī′vȧ·tēr′), *n.* **1.** An armed private vessel commissioned to cruise against the commerce or war vessels of the enemy. **2.** The commander, or one of the crew, of a privateer. — **pri′va·teers′man** (-tērz′măn), *n.*

private eye. *Slang.* A detective who is not a member of an official police force; a private detective.

private, first class. *Mil.* An enlisted man next below a corporal and above a private; as of 1948 in the U. S. Army, equal in grade to the former corporal but not a noncommissioned officer. Abbr. *Pfc.* or *Pfc*

pri·va′tion (prī·vā′shŭn), *n.* [OF., fr. L. *privatio.* See PRIVATE.] **1.** A depriving; deprivation, esp. of rank or office. **2.** State of being deprived of that which is needed; want of a necessity or necessities; as, to undergo severe *privations.* **3.** The absence of positive character or existence; also, the character or condition implicit in such absence.

priv′a·tive (prĭv′ȧ·tĭv), *adj.* [L. *privativus.*] **1.** Causing privation; depriving. **2.** Of, indicating, signifying, or predicating privation or negation; as, a *privative* prefix (*a-; un-, non-*); a *privative* term (*blind*); indifference is a *privative* state of mind. — *n.* Something characterized by privation; esp., a privative term, prefix, suffix, or conception. — **priv′a·tive·ly,** *adv.*

priv′et (prĭv′ĕt; -ĭt), *n.* **a** An ornamental shrub (*Ligustrum vulgare*) of the olive family, with half-evergreen leaves and small white flowers; also, any of various other species of the same genus. The privets (esp. the ***California privet,*** *L. ovalifolium*) are widely planted for hedges. **b** The shrub *Forestiera acuminata,* of the olive family.

priv′i·lege (prĭv′ĭ·lĭj), *n.* [OF., fr. L. *privilegium* a law for or against an individual, fr. *privus* private + *lex, legis,* law.] **1.** A right or immunity granted as a peculiar advantage or favor; a personal right, esp. in derogation of common right. **2.** A grant of a special right or immunity; a franchise or patent. **3.** A fundamental or sacred right; one of the rights guaranteed to all persons by modern constitutional governments. **4.** *Exchanges.* A call, put, spread, or straddle. — *v. t.;* -LEGED (-lĭjd); -LEG·ING (-lĭj·ĭng). To grant a privilege or privileges to; invest with a peculiar right, immunity, or prerogative; also, to exempt (from); — now often in *past part.;* as, the *privileged* classes; a *privileged* communication.

priv′i·ty (prĭv′ĭ·tĭ), *n.; pl.* -TIES (-tĭz). [OF. *priveté.*] **1.** *Obs.* Privacy; a private matter. **2.** Private knowledge; joint knowledge of a private matter. **3.** *Law.* A connection, or bond of union, between parties, as to some particular transaction; the relationship between privies (see PRIVY, *n.*, 1).

priv′y (prĭv′ĭ), *adj.* [OF. *privé*, fr. L. *privatus* private.] **1.** *Archaic.* **a** For private use or personal service; not public; — *Obs.*, except in *privy chamber, privy purse*, etc. **b** Hidden or clandestine; furtive. **2.** Secretly cognizant; privately aware as a party; — now with *to.* — *n.; pl.* PRIVIES (-ĭz). **1.** *Law.* Any of those persons having mutual or successive relationship to the same right of property. **2.** *Now Local.* A toilet, water closet, or the like. — **priv′i·ly**, *adv.*

privy council. A secret council; also, a private, or personal, council; esp.: [*caps.*] **a** *Eng. Hist.* The body of men appointed by the crown, without any patent or grant, to advise it in matters of state. **b** The similar body appointed to advise the governor or ruler, as in Canada, Japan, Jamaica, etc. Hence, **privy councilor** *or* **councillor.**

privy seal. In Great Britain, the seal which the king uses in grants, etc., which are to pass the great seal, or in lesser matters that do not require the great seal.

‖**prix fixe** (prē′ fēks′). [F., fixed price.] Table d'hôte (def. 2); also, the price charged for such a meal.

prize (prīz), *v. t.* [OF. *prisier*, fr. LL. *pretiare*, fr. *pretium* worth, value.] **1.** To appraise; price; rate. **2.** To value highly; to esteem. — **Syn.** See APPRECIATE.

prize, *n.* [OF. *prise* a seizing, hold, grasp, fr. *prendre* to take, fr. L. *prendere, prehendere*, past part. *prensus, prehensus.*] **1.** Act of capturing or taking; also, a thing or person seized by force, stratagem, or superior power. **2.** *Now Dial.* A lever; also, leverage. **3.** *Law.* The capture of anything by a belligerent using the rights of war, or the property captured; esp., the capture of a ship, or the ship captured. — **Syn.** See SPOIL. — *v. t.* To seize as a prize.

prize, *v. t.* [From *prize* a lever, fr. ME. *prise*, fr. OF. *prise* a taking hold. See 2d PRIZE.] To press, force, or move, esp. with a lever; to pry.

prize, *n.* [ME. *pris, prise.* See PRICE, PRIZE to value.] **1.** Something offered or striven for in competition or in contests of chance. **2.** Anything worth striving for; an advantage or privilege. **3.** *Hist.* A contest for a reward.

prize (prīz), *adj.* **1.** Having been awarded a prize; as, a *prize* essay; also, worthy of a prize; as, a *prize* effort. **2.** Awarded as a prize; as, a *prize* medal.

prize court. *Law.* A court having jurisdiction to adjudge upon captures at sea in time of war.

prize fight. An exhibition contest of pugilists for a stake or wager. Hence: **prize fighter; prize fighting.**

prize money. *Nav.* A portion of the proceeds of a captured vessel divided among the officers and men making the capture.

priz′er (prīz′ẽr), *n.* *Archaic.* One who contends for a prize.

prize ring. The ring for a prize fight; also, prize fighting.

‖**pro** (prō), *prep.* [L.] A Latin preposition signifying *for, before, forth.*

pro (prō), *adv.* For, on, or in behalf of, the affirmative side; — opposed to *con;* as, they debated it *pro* and con. — *n.* One who takes the affirmative side; an affirmative vote, argument, etc.

pro (prō), *n.; pl.* PROS (prōz). A professional; esp., a professional athlete. — **pro**, *adj.*

pro- (prō-; prŏ-). [L. *pro.* In F., L. *pro* often became *pour*, OF. also *por*, whence the E. *pur-*, as in *purchase, purvey.*] A prefix signifying in general *before, in front, forth, for, in behalf of, in place of, according to.* Special implications of sense are: **a** *Forth, forward, onward*, with the idea of *motion before* or *to the front*, as in proceed, to go before or forward, project, propel. **b** *In place of, for, instead of*, with the idea of *substitution*, as in pronoun, a word instead of a noun; also specif. in titles, *deputy*, as in proconsul, a person acting in place of a consul. **c** *For, in behalf of*, from the idea of *standing before* or *in front of for defense* or *protection*, as in procure, to gain, literally, to care for. **d** *For, in favor of, adherent to, partisan of*, as in proslavery, *pro*-Ally.

pro-. [Gr. *pro.*] A prefix meaning *before*, used to denote: **a** *Priority of place* with the sense of *position before, in front of*, as in proscenium. **b** *Priority of order* or *time*, in the sense of *occurring before, beforehand*, as in prologue, part spoken before (the main piece).

pro′a (prō′ȧ), *n.* [Malay *prao, prau*, boat.] A double-ended outrigger canoe of Malaysia, with large lateen sail.

pro′-Al·ly′ (prō′ă·lī′; -ăl′ī), *adj.* Favoring the Allies in World War I or World War II.

prob′a·bi·lism (prŏb′ȧ·bĭ·lĭz'm), *n.* **1.** The doctrine that certainty is impossible, but that probability suffices to govern belief and action. **2.** In casuistry, any of certain theories respecting moral obligation in cases where it is difficult to determine whether the law holds; specif., the theory that an opinion favoring liberty may be followed even though that for law is more probable, if that opinion commends itself to judicious minds or is supported by sound authority. — **prob′a·bi·list** (-lĭst), *n. & adj.*

prob′a·bil′i·ty (-bĭl′ĭ·tĭ), *n.; pl.* -TIES (-tĭz). **1.** Quality or state of being probable; likelihood; as, *probability* of guilt. **2.** That which is or appears probable. **3.** *Math.* The likelihood of the occurrence of any particular form of an event, estimated as the ratio of the number of ways in which that form might occur to the whole number of ways in which the event might occur in any form.

prob′a·ble (prŏb′ȧ·b'l), *adj.* [F., fr. L. *probabilis*, fr. *probare* to try, prove.] **1.** Supported by evidence strong enough to establish presumption, but not proof. **2.** *Now Rare.* Establishing a probability; as, *probable* evidence. **3.** Likely to be or become true or real; reasonably, but not certainly, to be believed or expected; as, *probable* events.

Syn. Probable, possible, likely mean such as may be or may become actual or true. **Probable** applies to that which is so reasonable or well evidenced that it almost induces belief; **possible**, to that which lies within the powers of performance, attainment, etc., of an agent or agency; **likely**, to that which is to all appearances as alleged, suggested, required, etc.

probable cause. *Law.* A reasonable ground of presumption that a charge is well founded.

prob′a·bly (prŏb′ȧ·blĭ), *adv.* In all probability; very likely; as, he is *probably* the best candidate.

pro′bang (prō′băng), *n.* A slender rod with a sponge on the end, for removing obstructions from the esophagus, etc.

pro′bate (prō′bāt *or, esp. Brit.*, prō′bĭt), *adj.* [L. *probatus*, past part. of *probare* to prove.] Of or belonging to a probate, or court of probate, or its jurisdiction. — *n.* *Law.* Official proof, esp. of an instrument offered as the last will and testament of a person deceased. — (prō′bāt), *v. t.* To make probate of, esp. of an instrument purporting to be the last will and testament of a person.

probate court. A court for the probate of wills, administration of estates, and related matters.

pro·ba′tion (prō·bā′shŭn), *n.* [F., fr. L. *probatio*, fr. *probare* to try, prove.] **1.** *Now Chiefly Scot.* Act of proving; proof. **2.** Any proceeding designed to ascertain truth, to determine character, qualification, etc.; trial or a period of trial; as, to engage a person on *probation.* **3.** In some universities, colleges, and schools, a status of trial for deficient or culpable students, usually marked by certain penalties. **4.** *Law.* The method of treating a convicted delinquent whereby he is released on a suspended sentence under supervision and upon specified conditions; also, the status of a convicted person so released; as, placed on *probation.* — **pro·ba′tion·al** (-ăl; -'l), **pro·ba′tion·ar′y** (-ĕr′ĭ *or, esp. Brit.*, -ẽr·ĭ), *adj.*

pro·ba′tion·er (-ẽr), *n.* **1.** One who is undergoing probation; one who is on trial, as a newly admitted student nurse. **2.** A convicted delinquent on probation.

probation officer. *Chiefly U. S.* In a municipal criminal court, an officer appointed by the magistrate to exercise supervision over, and receive regular reports from, an offender whose sentence is suspended.

pro′ba·tive (prō′bȧ·tĭv; prŏb′ȧ·tĭv), *adj.* **1.** Serving to test or try. **2.** Serving to prove.

pro′ba·to′ry (prō′bȧ·tō′rĭ *or, esp. Brit.*, -tẽr·ĭ), *adj.* Pertaining to, or serving for, proof; as, *probatory* evidence.

probe (prōb), *n.* [ML. *proba* examination, proof.] **1.** *Surg.* A slender instrument for examining a cavity, as a wound, ulcer, etc. **2.** An explorative examination or test; specif., *U. S.*, an inquiry directed to the discovery of evidence of wrongdoing; as, a legislative *probe.* — *v. t.* [From *probe*, n., and fr. L. *probare* to test.] **1.** To examine, as a wound, with a probe. **2.** To investigate thoroughly; as, to *probe* one's motive. **3.** To penetrate as with a probe; to pierce deeply. — **Syn.** See ENTER. — **prob′er** (prōb′ẽr), *n.*

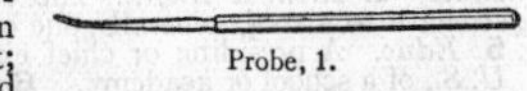
Probe, 1.

prob′i·ty (prŏb′ĭ·tĭ; prō′bĭ-), *n.* [F. *probité*, fr. L. *probitas*, fr. *probus* good, honest.] Tried virtue or integrity; uprightness. — **Syn.** See HONESTY.

prob′lem (prŏb′lĕm; -lĕm), *n.* [OF. *probleme*, fr. L. *problema*, fr. Gr. *problēma* anything thrown forward, deriv. of *pro-* + *ballein* to throw.] **1.** A question proposed for solution; hence, a perplexing question, situation, or person. **2.** *Math.* Anything that is required to be done. Cf. THEOREM, 2. — **Syn.** See MYSTERY. — *adj.* **1.** Dealing with a problem; of a play, novel, etc., having a plot presenting a problem of human conduct or relationship. **2.** Of a child, presenting a problem to those responsible for him because of misconduct or maladjustment.

prob′lem·at′i·cal (prŏb′lĕm·ăt′ĭ·kăl), *adj.* Also **prob′lem·at′ic** (-ĭk). Having the nature of a problem; difficult and uncertain; also, puzzling. — **Syn.** See DOUBTFUL. — **prob′lem·at′i·cal·ly**, *adv.*

‖**pro bo′no pu′bli·co** (prō bō′nō pŭb′lĭ·kō). [L.] For the public good.

pro′bos·cid′e·an (prō′bŏ·sĭd′ē·ăn), *adj.* Proboscidian.

pro′bos·cid′i·an (-ĭ·ăn), *adj.* [See PROBOSCIS.] *Zool.* Belonging to an order (Proboscidea) of ungulate mammals consisting of the elephants and their extinct allies. — **pro′bos·cid′i·an**, *n.*

pro·bos′cis (prō·bŏs′ĭs), *n.; pl.* PROBOSCISES (-ĕz; -ĭz), PROBOSCIDES (-ĭ·dēz). [L., fr. Gr. *proboskis*, fr. *pro-* + *boskein* to feed.] **1. a** The trunk of an elephant; also, any long flexible snout, as in the tapirs, shrews, etc. **b** Humorously, the human nose. **2.** *Zool.* Any of various tubular processes or prolongations of the head of animals, as in insects; a tubular sucking organ.

pro·caine′ (prō·kān′; prō′kān; *cf.* COCAINE), *n.* [*pro-* + *cocaine.*] *Pharm.* A local anesthetic ($C_{13}H_{20}O_2N_2HCl$) resembling cocaine, but less toxic.

pro·cam′bi·um (prō·kăm′bĭ·ŭm), *n.* [NL. See PRO-; CAMBIUM.] *Bot.* That meristematic tissue which forms the first units of vascular tissue. — **pro·cam′bi·al** (-ăl), *adj.*

pro′carp (prō′kärp), *n.* *Bot.* The female reproductive organ in certain red algae. Cf. CARPOGONIUM, SPOROCARP.

pro′ca·the′dral (prō′kȧ·thē′drăl), *n.* *Eccl.* A parish church used as a cathedral, as in a new diocese.

pro·ce′dur·al (prō·sē′dūr·ăl), *adj.* *Law.* Of or pertaining to procedure; as, a *procedural* contract, or one binding the maker to abide by the award of a court.

pro·ce′dure (-dūr; 118), *n.* [F. *procédure.*] **1.** Manner or method of proceeding in a process or course of action; also, a particular way of proceeding. **2.** The continuance of a process or operation; progress. **3.** Customary method of conducting business in a deliberative body; parliamentary order; as, rules of *procedure.*

pro·ceed′ (prō·sēd′), *v. i.* [OF. *proceder*, fr. L. *procedere, -cessum*, to go before, fr. *pro-* + *cedere* to move.] **1.** To move, pass, or go forward or onward; to advance. **2.** To issue or come forth as from a source or origin; to come (*from*). **3.** To go on in an orderly or regulated manner; to prosecute a design. **4.** *Law.* To begin and carry on a legal proceeding. — **Syn.** See SPRING.

pro′ceed (prō′sēd), *n.* Now only in *pl.* That which results, proceeds, or accrues from some possession or transaction; esp., the amount realized from a sale of property.

pro·ceed′ing (prō·sēd′ĭng), *n.* **a** = PROCEDURE, 1 & 2. **b** An act, measure or step in a course of business or conduct; a transaction; as, an illegal *proceeding.* **c** *pl.* Minutes of a society, board, etc.; as, to publish the commission's *proceedings.* **d** *Law.* (1) *pl.* The course of procedure in an action at law. (2) Any step or act taken in conducting litigation.

pro′ce·phal′ic (prō′sē·făl′ĭk), *adj.* *Zool.* Pertaining to, or forming, the front of the head.

proc′ess (prŏs′ĕs *or, esp. Brit.*, prō′sĕs), *n.; pl.* PROCESSES (-ĕz; -ĭz; *Anat. occas.* -ēz). [OF. *proces*, fr. L. *processus.* See PROCEED.] **1.** Act of proceeding; progress; advance. **2. a** Any phenomenon which shows a continuous change in time; as, the *process* of growth.

b A series of actions or operations definitely conducing to an end; continuous operation or treatment, esp. in manufacture; as, a *process* of making steel. **3.** *Biol.* Any marked prominence or projecting part; an outgrowth or extension. **4.** *Law.* The writ or mandate that serves as the means for bringing a defendant into court to answer in an action; in a broader sense, any writ, summons, or other writing by which a court exercises its jurisdiction; also, collectively, the whole of such mandates in an action or proceeding, or, in a still wider sense, the whole course of proceedings. **5.** *Print.* Photomechanical processes collectively, as distinguished from engraving by hand. — *v. t.* **1.** *Law.* To issue or take out process against, or to serve process upon. **2.** To subject to some special process or treatment, as in the course of manufacture. — *adj.* **1.** Processed; made according to a special process; as, *process* butter. **2.** Used in or using, or produced by, photomechanical processes; as, *process* plate.

proc′ess·ing tax. *U.S.* An agricultural adjustment tax levied on the first processing of specified basic agricultural commodities.

pro·ces′sion (prō·sĕsh′ŭn), *n.* [OF., fr. L. *processio.*] **1.** Progression as of a series; continuous course. **2.** A group, as of persons, carriages, etc., moving onward in an orderly manner; parade. — *v. i.* To go in procession.

pro·ces′sion·al (-ăl; -'l), *n. Eccl.* A hymn sung during a church procession, as of the choir and clergy into the church at the beginning of a service. — *adj.* Of, pertaining to, or moving in or as in a procession.

process printing. A method of printing, from half-tone plates, in three colors, yellow, red, and blue (and, usually, black), so that nearly any hue may be reproduced.

process server. A person who serves processes, such as summonses and subpoenas.

pro·cès′-ver·bal′ (prō·sā′vĕr·băl′; *F.* prô′sĕ′vĕr′bȧl′), *n.; pl.* PROCÈS-VERBAUX (-bō′). [F.] **1.** *Fr. Law.* An authenticated minute or statement of an official act for use as a basis of further action or for the acceptance of a superior. **2.** Any French official report.

pro·claim′ (prō·klām′), *v. t.* [L. *proclamare*, fr. *pro-* + *clamare* to call.] **1.** To make known by announcing in a public place; to publish abroad. **2.** Specif.: **a** To issue a proclamation outlawing (a person), prohibiting (a meeting), quarantining (a district), or the like. **b** To announce publicly the accession of (a sovereign). **3.** To manifest openly; to give outward evidence of. — **Syn.** See DECLARE. — **pro·claim′er** (-ẽr), *n.*

proc′la·ma′tion (prŏk′lȧ·mā′shŭn), *n.* **1.** Act of proclaiming; official publication. **2.** That which is proclaimed; specif., *Law*, a public notice by an official of some order, intended action, or state of facts.

pro·clit′ic (prō·klĭt′ĭk), *adj.* [NL. *procliticus*, fr. Gr. *proklinein* to lean forward.] *Gram.* Leaning forward (with reference to accent); — said of words which, having no accent of their own, are, in pronunciation, dependent on the following word. — *n.* A proclitic word.

pro·cliv′i·ty (prō·klĭv′ĭ·tĭ), *n.* [L. *proclivitas.*] Constitutional bent; disposition; inclination; propensity; as, a *proclivity* to study. — **Syn.** See LEANING.

Proc′ne (prŏk′nē), *n.* See PHILOMELA.

pro·con′sul (prō·kŏn′sŭl), *n.* [L., fr. *pro* for + *consul* consul.] **1.** *Rom. Hist.* An officer who discharged the duties of a consul without being himself consul, as in a province. **2.** *Chiefly Eng.* By extension, a governor in a modern colony, esp. one with wide powers. — **pro·con′su·lar** (-sū·lẽr), *adj.* — **pro·con′su·late** (-lāt), *n.* — **pro·con′sul·ship**, *n.*

pro·cras′ti·nate (prō·krăs′tĭ·nāt), *v. t. & i.* [L. *procrastinatus*, past part. of *procrastinare* to procrastinate, fr. *pro-* + *crastinus* of tomorrow, fr. *cras* tomorrow.] To put off from day to day; to defer; postpone. — **Syn.** See DELAY. — **pro·cras′ti·na′tion** (-nā′shŭn), *n.* — **pro·cras′ti·na′tor** (-nā′tẽr), *n.*

pro′cre·ant (prō′krē·ănt), *adj.* [L. *procreans*, pres. part.] Procreating; generating; producing; fruitful.

pro′cre·ate (-āt), *v. t.* [L. *procreatus*, past part. of *procreare*, fr. *pro-* + *creare* to create.] To generate and produce; to beget. — **pro′cre·a′tion** (-ā′shŭn), *n.* — **pro′cre·a′tive** (-ā′tĭv), *adj.* — **pro′cre·a′tor** (-ā′tẽr), *n.*

Pro·crus′te·an (prō·krŭs′tē·ăn), *adj.* [*often not cap.*] **1.** Of, pert. to, or like Procrustes. **2.** Harsh or inflexible in fitting (someone or something) to a preconceived idea, system, etc.; as, *Procrustean* discipline.

Pro·crus′tes (-tēz), *n.* [L., fr. Gr. *Prokroustēs*, fr. *prokrouein* to beat out, stretch.] *Gr. Antiq.* A legendary highwayman of Attica, who tied his victims upon an iron bed, and stretched or cut off their legs to adapt them to its length. He was slain by Theseus.

proc′to- (prŏk′tō-), **proct-**. [Gr. *prōktos* anus.] A combining form used to denote *rectum*, as in **proc·tec′to·my, proc′to·scope, proc·tos′to·my, proc·tot′o·my** (see -ECTOMY, etc.).

proc′to·dae′um (prŏk′tō·dē′ŭm), *n. Zool.* The posterior part of the alimentary canal. Cf. MESENTERON, STOMODAEUM.

proc·tol′o·gy (prŏk·tŏl′ō·jĭ), *n.* [*procto-* + *-logy.*] *Med.* The branch of medical science dealing with the anus and rectum. — **proc′to·log′ic** (prŏk′tō·lŏj′ĭk), **proc′to·log′i·cal** (-ĭ·kăl), *adj.* — **proc·tol′o·gist** (prŏk·tŏl′ō·jĭst), *n.*

proc′tor (prŏk′tẽr), *n.* [ME. *proketour, procutour*, contr. fr. *procuratour.* See PROCURATOR.] One employed to manage the affairs of another; a steward; a proxy. *Obs.* exc. in technical uses; as: **a** *Law.* A procurator in the civil and canon law. **b** An officer in a university or college who enforces order and obedience. **c** See KING'S PROCTOR. — **proc·to′ri·al** (prŏk·tō′rĭ·ăl), *adj.* — **proc′tor·ship**, *n.*

pro·cum′bent (prō·kŭm′bĕnt), *adj.* [L. *procumbens, -entis*, pres. part. of *procumbere* to fall or lean forward.] **1.** Lying with face down; prostrate. **2.** *Bot.* Trailing; prostrate; — said of stems.

pro·cur′a·ble (-kūr′ȧ·b'l), *adj.* Capable of being procured.

proc′u·ra·cy (prŏk′ū·rȧ·sĭ), *n.; pl.* -CIES (-sĭz). The office or act of a proctor or procurator; management for another.

pro·cur′ance (prō·kūr′ăns), *n.* Act of procuring; agency.

proc′u·ra′tion (prŏk′ū·rā′shŭn), *n.* **1.** Care; management; *Obs.* exc. meaning management of another's affairs; specif., *Civil Law*, in a broad sense, agency. **2.** A power of attorney; a proxy. **3.** Act of procuring; procurement. — **proc′u·ra·to′ry** (prŏk′ū·rȧ·tō′rĭ; prō·kū′rȧ·tō′rĭ; *or, esp. Brit.*, -tẽr·ĭ), *adj.*

proc′u·ra′tor (prŏk′ū·rā′tẽr), *n.* [OF. *procuratour*, fr. L. *procurator.*] **1.** *Rom. Antiq.* Under the empire, any of various imperial fiscal agents or administrators. **2.** *Law.* One who manages another's affairs; an agent; proctor. — **proc′u·ra·to′ri·al** (-rȧ·tō′rĭ·ăl; 70), *adj.*

pro·cure′ (prō·kūr′), *v. t.* [OF. *procurer*, fr. L. *procurare* to take care of, fr. *pro* for + *curare* to take care.] **1.** To obtain by any means; to acquire; gain; get. **2.** *Now Rare.* To contrive; effect; cause; as, to *procure* a favor to be granted. **3.** To obtain for illicit intercourse or prostitution. — *v. i.* To practice the trade of procurer. — **Syn.** See GET.

pro·cure′ment (-mĕnt), *n.* **1.** Act of procuring; acquisition. **2.** Accomplishment through the instrumentality of others; efficient management of an agent.

pro·cur′er (prō·kūr′ẽr), *n.* **1.** One who procures. **2.** A pander; pimp. — **pro·cur′ess**, *n.*

Pro′cy·on (prō′sĭ·ŏn), *n.* [L., a constellation which rises before the Dog Star, fr. Gr. *Prokyōn*, fr. *pro-* + *kyōn* dog.] A first-magnitude star in Canis Minor.

prod (prŏd), *v. t.;* PROD′DED; PROD′DING. To thrust a pointed instrument into; hence, to goad or incite, as to activity. — *n.* **1.** A prodding with or as with a pointed instrument; hence, a sharp reminder or reproof; a thrust; a dig. **2.** A pointed thing for prodding, as a goad, awl, or skewer. — **prod′der** (-ẽr), *n.*

prod′i·gal (prŏd′ĭ·găl; -g'l), *adj.* [Obs. F.] **1.** Given to reckless extravagance; as, *prodigal* spenders. **2.** Characterized by wasteful expenditure; lavish. **3.** Yielding abundantly; luxuriant. — **Syn.** See PROFUSE. — *n.* One who spends prodigally; a spendthrift. — **prod′i·gal·ly**, *adv.*

prod′i·gal′i·ty (-găl′ĭ·tĭ), *n.; pl.* -TIES (-tĭz). [OF. *prodigalité*, fr. LL. *prodigalitas*, fr. L. *prodigus* prodigal, fr. *prodigere* to squander, drive forth, fr. *pro-* (*prod-* only in comp.) forth + *agere* to drive.] Extravagance in expenditure; excessive liberality; waste.

pro·di′gious (prō·dĭj′ŭs), *adj.* [L. *prodigiosus*, fr. *prodigium* a prodigy.] **1.** *Obs.* Of the nature of a prodigy or omen; portentous. **2.** Out of the course of nature; marvelous; monstrous. **3.** Extraordinary in bulk, quantity, or degree; vast; huge. — **Syn.** See MONSTROUS. — **pro·di′gious·ly**, *adv.* — **pro·di′gious·ness**, *n.*

prod′i·gy (prŏd′ĭ·jĭ), *n.; pl.* -GIES (-jĭz). [L. *prodigium.*] **1.** *Archaic.* Something extraordinary, or out of the usual course of nature; hence, an omen; a sign. **2.** A wonder; a marvel. **3.** An abnormal occurrence, being, or the like. **4.** An extraordinary person, instance, deed, etc.; as, *prodigies* of valor; infant *prodigies.*

pro′drome (prō′drōm), *n.* [F., fr. L., fr. Gr. *prodromos* running before, fr. *pro-* + *dromos* a running.] *Med.* A premonitory symptom. — **prod′ro·mal** (prŏd′rō·măl), *adj.*

pro·duce′ (prō·dūs′; 114), *v. t.;* -DUCED′ (-dūst′); -DUC′ING (-dūs′ĭng). [L. *producere, -ductum*, to bring forward, produce, fr. *pro-* + *ducere* to lead.] **1.** To bring forward; to exhibit; show; as, to *produce* a witness in court. **2. a** To bring forth, as young, or as a natural product or growth; to bear; yield. **b** To cause to accrue; as, money at interest *produces* an income. **3.** To manufacture; as, he *produces* excellent pottery. **4.** To cause to be or to happen; to originate; to bring about. **5.** To bring out as a dramatic production; to introduce to the public, as a new star performer. **6.** *Obs.* To draw out; to lengthen. **7.** *Econ.* To make, or to create so as to be, available for satisfaction of human wants. **8.** *Geom.* To extend; prolong; as, to *produce* a side of a triangle. — *v. i.* To bring forth a product, products, or productions; to bear, yield, make, etc.

prod′uce (prŏd′ūs; prō′dūs; *orig.* prō·dūs′; 114), *n.* **1.** That which is produced, brought forth, or yielded; product; yield. **2.** The offspring (of an animal); get, as of a horse.

pro·duc′er (prō·dūs′ẽr), *n.* **1.** One who produces, brings forth, or generates. **2.** One who grows agricultural products, or manufactures crude materials into articles of use; — opposed to *consumer.* **3.** One who finances or is in general charge of the production of motion pictures, a play, opera, etc. **4.** A furnace or apparatus for producing combustible gas (**producer gas**) by circulating air or a mixture of air and steam through a layer of incandescent fuel, as coke. The gas consists chiefly of carbon monoxide, hydrogen, and nitrogen, and is used for fuel, for driving gas engines, etc.

pro·duc′ers' goods (-ẽrz). *Econ.* Goods that satisfy wants only indirectly as factors in the production of other goods, such as tools and raw material; — dist. from *consumers' goods.*

pro·duc′i·ble (-ĭ·b'l), *adj.* Capable of being produced.

prod′uct (prŏd′ŭkt; -ŭkt), *n.* [L. *productus*, past part. of *producere.* See PRODUCE.] **1.** Anything produced, as by generation, growth, labor, or thought. **2.** The amount, quantity, or total produced. **3.** *Chem.* A substance produced from one or more other substances as a result of chemical change; — distinguished from *educt.* **4.** *Math.* The number or quantity resulting from the multiplication together of two or more numbers or quantities; as, the *product* of 7 and 5 is 35. See MULTIPLICAND; MULTIPLIER, 2.

pro·duc′tion (prō·dŭk′shŭn), *n.* [F., fr. L. *productio* a lengthening.] **1.** Act or process of producing. **2.** That which is produced; product; specif., a literary or artistic work. **3.** *Econ.* The creation of economic value; the making of goods available for human wants.

pro·duc′tive (-tĭv), *adj.* **1.** Having the quality or power of producing, esp. in abundance; creative; fertile. **2.** Effective in bringing forth or forward; originative. **3.** Yielding or furnishing results, profits, or benefits; as, *productive* enterprises. **4.** *Econ.* Yielding, or devoted to the production of, a net return of wealth. — **pro·duc′tive·ly**, *adv.* — **pro·duc′tive·ness**, *n.*

pro′duc·tiv′i·ty (prō′dŭk·tĭv′ĭ·tĭ), *n.* Quality or state of being productive; productiveness.

pro′em (prō′ĕm), *n.* [OF. *proheme*, fr. L., fr. Gr. *prooimion*, fr. *pro-* + *oimē* song, poem.] Preface; prelude. — **pro·e′mi·al** (prō·ē′mĭ·ăl; 58), *adj.*

prof′a·na′tion (prŏf′ȧ·nā′shŭn), *n.* Act of profaning; specif., act of violating sacred things; desecration.

Syn. Profanation, desecration, sacrilege mean violation of that which is sacred. **Profanation** implies irreverence or contempt as shown in vulgar intrusion or vandalism; **desecration**, a loss of sacred character, as through pollution, defilement, or reduction to secular usage; **sacrilege**, a maltreatment of something sacred such as by unworthy reception of the sacraments.

pro·fan′a·to′ry (prō·făn′ȧ·tō′rĭ *or, esp. Brit.*, -tẽr·ĭ), *adj.* Profaning.

pro·fane′ (prō·fān′), *v. t.* [F. *profaner*, fr. L. *profanare.* See PROFANE, *adj.*] **1.** To violate or treat with irreverence, obloquy, or contempt (something regarded as sacred); to desecrate. **2.** To debase by a wrong, unworthy, or vulgar use. — *adj.* [F., fr. L. *profanus*, orig., before the temple, outside of it; hence, unholy, fr. *pro-* + *fanum* temple.] **1.** Not sacred or holy; not devoted to religion or religious ends; secular; — opposed to *sacred.* **2.** Not holy because unconsecrated, impure, or defiled; unsanctified. **3.** Not among the initiated; not possessing esoteric or expert knowledge. **4.** Serving to profane or defile that which is holy; blasphemous; irreverent. — **pro·fane′ly,** *adv.* — **pro·fane′ness, pro·fan′er** (prō·fān′ẽr), *n.*

pro·fan′i·ty (prō·făn′ĭ·tĭ), *n.; pl.* -TIES (-tĭz). **1.** Quality or state of being profane; irreverence; esp., blasphemy. **2.** Something profane; esp., profane language; blasphemy; cursing. — **Syn.** See BLASPHEMY.

pro′fert (prō′fẽrt), *n.* [L., he brings forward.] *Law.* An allegation in a pleading or on the record that the pleader produces an instrument in open court.

pro·fess′ (prō·fĕs′), *v. t.* [ME. *professed* bound by a vow, fr. OF. *profes,* masc., *professe,* fem., professed (monk or nun), fr. L. *professus,* past part. of *profiteri* to profess, fr. *pro-* + *fateri* to confess, own.] **1.** To declare or admit openly or freely; to avow; confess; as, to *profess* confidence in the president. **2.** To make profession of (a feeling, a quality, a belief, etc.); often narrowly, to pretend; as, to *profess* loyalty. **3.** To follow (a calling or profession) in which one is or claims to be an expert; as, to *profess* medicine. **4.** To confess one's faith in; to practice; observe; as, races which now *profess* Christianity. — *v. i.* To make a profession or one's profession.

pro·fessed′ (prō·fĕst′; *also, in poetry,* -fĕs′ĕd, -ĭd), *adj.* **1.** Openly declared or avowed. **2.** In religious use, having made one's profession (sense 6).

pro·fess′ed·ly (prō·fĕs′ĕd·lĭ; -ĭd·lĭ), *adv.* Avowedly or allegedly.

pro·fes′sion (prō·fĕsh′ŭn), *n.* **1.** A professing; open declaration; public avowal, as of religious faith and purpose. **2.** That which one professes; a declaration; avowal; specif., Christian or religious faith and purpose openly avowed. **3.** The faith in which one is professed; a religious system; also, a religious body. **4.** The occupation, if not commercial, mechanical, agricultural, or the like, to which one devotes oneself; a calling; as, the *profession* of arms, of teaching; the ***three professions,*** or the ***learned professions,*** of theology, law, and medicine. **5.** The body of persons engaged in a calling; as, the *profession* distrust him. **6.** *Eccl.* The taking of the vows that signify formal acceptance of the religious state, as by a monk.

pro·fes′sion·al (-ăl; -'l), *adj.* **1.** Of or pertaining to a profession; as, *professional* ethics. **2.** Characteristic of or conforming to the standards of a profession; as, distinctly *professional* work. **3. a** Engaging for livelihood or gain in an activity pursued, usually or often, for noncommercial satisfactions by amateurs; as, a *professional* golf player. **b** Engaged in by professional, as contrasted with amateur, performers; as, a *professional* race. **4.** Following a line of conduct as though it were a profession; hence, assumed; as, a *professional* patriot. — *n.* One who engages in anything professionally; a professional worker; — opposed to *amateur.* — **pro·fes′sion·al·ly,** *adv.*

pro·fes′sion·al·ism (-ĭz'm), *n.* **1.** Conduct, aims, qualities, etc., characteristic of a profession. **2.** The following of a profession, sport, etc., for livelihood or for gain; — opposed to *amateurism.*

pro·fes′sor (prō·fĕs′ẽr), *n.* [L., a teacher, a public teacher.] **1.** One who professes; esp., one who makes or has made a profession, as of faith or allegiance. **2.** *Educ.* One who publicly teaches, in the higher education or in the secondary-school grades, any branch of learning; specif., one on whom the title has been formally conferred by academic authority; as, a *professor* of mathematics. **3.** *Colloq.* Hence, one who teaches, or professes special knowledge in, any art, sport, or occupation requiring skill. **4.** *Angling.* An artificial fly with gray speckled wings, brown hackle, gold ribbing and tag, and scarlet tail. Cf. FLY, *Illust.* — **pro′fes·so′ri·al** (prō′fĕ·sō′rĭ·ăl; prŏf′ĕ-; 70), *adj.* — **pro′fes·so′ri·al·ly,** *adv.*

pro·fes′sor·ate (prō·fĕs′ẽr·ĭt), *n.* The office, or term of office, of a professor.

pro′fes·so′ri·ate (prō′fĕ·sō′rĭ·ĭt; prŏf′ĕ-), *n.* The professors of an academic institution; also, professorship.

pro·fes′sor·ship (prō·fĕs′ẽr·shĭp), *n.* The office, duties, or position of an academic professor.

prof′fer (prŏf′ẽr), *v. t.* [OF. *proffrir,* fr. *poroffrir,* fr. *por* for + *offrir* to offer.] To offer for acceptance; to make a tender of; to offer. — *n.* An offer; tender.

pro·fi′cien·cy (prō·fĭsh′ĕn·sĭ), *n.; pl.* -CIES (-sĭz). **1.** Progress, as in attaining skill. **2.** Quality or state of being proficient; expertness.

pro·fi′cient (-ĕnt), *n.* [L. *proficiens, -entis,* pres. part. of *proficere* to go forward, make progress.] One well advanced in any business, art, science, or branch of learning; an expert. — *adj.* Well advanced in any occupation, art, or branch of knowledge or skill; versed; adept. — **pro·fi′cient·ly,** *adv.* — **pro·fi′cient·ness,** *n.*

Syn. **Proficient, adept, skilled, skillful, expert** mean having great knowledge and experience in a trade or profession. **Proficient** implies competency above the average; **adept,** aptitude as well as proficiency; **skilled,** mastery of technique; **skillful,** adeptness and dexterity in execution or performance; **expert,** extraordinary proficiency or adeptness.

pro′file (prō′fīl *or, esp. Brit.,* -fēl), *n.* [It. *profilo,* fr. *profilare* to draw in profile, fr. *pro* (fr. L. *pro*) + *filo* stroke, line, fr. L. *filum* thread, outline.] **1.** A human head represented in a side view; hence, the outline of the face seen or represented sidewise. **2.** Contour; distinctive outline. **3.** A side or sectional elevation; as: **a** *Arch.* A section of any member at right angles with its main lines. **b** *Civil Engin.* A drawing showing a vertical section. **4.** A concise biographical sketch depicting a personality by vivid outlining and sharp contrast. — **Syn.** See OUTLINE. — *v. t.;* -FILED (-fīld; -fēld); -FIL·ING (-fīl·ĭng; -fēl·ĭng). To draw or write a profile of.

prof′it (prŏf′ĭt), *n.* [OF., fr. L. *profectus* advance, progress, profit.] **1.** Advantage. **2.** Accession of good; avail; gain; as, an office of *profit.* **3.** The excess of returns over expenditure in a given transaction or series of transactions; also, the excess of income over expenditure, as in a business, during a given period of time. Profit may be either: (1) the excess (called ***gross profit***) of gross receipts over the expenditures directly involved in production or purchase; or (2) the net proceeds (called ***net profit***) obtained by deducting from the gross proceeds all forms of expense or outlay. **4.** The ratio of profit (sense 3) for a given year to the amount of capital invested. **5.** Commonly in *pl.* The share of the employing classes in the distribution of the products of industry, as distinct from *wages* and *rent.* — *v. i.* **1.** *Obs.* To improve; to become proficient. **2.** To be of use or advantage; to avail. **3.** To derive benefit; gain; as, to *profit* by advice. — *v. t.* To benefit; advantage.

prof′it·a·ble (-ȧ·b'l), *adj.* Yielding or bringing profit or gain; lucrative; useful. — **Syn.** See BENEFICIAL. — **prof′it·a·ble·ness,** *n.* — **prof′it·a·bly,** *adv.*

profit and loss. *Accounting.* A summary account used at the end of an accounting period, to collect the balances of the nominal accounts, that the net profit or loss may be shown. Commonly referred to as *P. & L.* — **prof′it-and-loss′,** *adj.*

prof′it·eer′ (prŏf′ĭ·tēr′), *n.* [*profit* + *-eer.*] One who makes what is considered an unreasonable profit, as by taking advantage of a public need in time of war. — **prof′it·eer′,** *v. i.* — **prof′it·eer′ing,** *n.*

prof′it·less, *adj.* Without profit; unprofitable.

profit sharing. The system of paying workmen by giving them over and above their wages a percentage of the net profits of the business. — **prof′it-shar′ing,** *adj.*

prof′li·ga·cy (prŏf′lĭ·gȧ·sĭ), *n.* Quality or state of being profligate; dissolute character or conduct.

prof′li·gate (-găt), *adj.* [L. *profligatus,* past part. of *profligare* to dash to the ground, destroy.] **1.** Completely given up to dissipation; dissolute. **2.** Wasteful to the point of dissipation; prodigal. — *n.* A profligate person. — **prof′li·gate·ly,** *adv.* — **prof′li·gate·ness,** *n.*

prof′lu·ent (prŏf′lŏŏ·ĕnt), *adj.* [L. *profluens,* pres. part.] Flowing smoothly in or as in a stream.

‖**pro for′ma** (prō fôr′mȧ). [L.] For the sake of, or as a matter of, form.

pro·found′ (prō·found′), *adj.* [OF. *profond,* fr. L. *profundus,* fr. *pro-* + *fundus* bottom.] **1.** *Chiefly Poetic.* Of very great depth; unfathomable. **2.** Intellectually deep; thorough. **3.** Coming from, reaching to, or situated at a depth; deep-seated. **4.** Characterized by intensity, as of feeling or quality; as, *profound* respect, fear, etc. **5.** Of a bow, with body or head bent low in respect. — **Syn.** See DEEP. — **Ant.** Shallow. — *n. Poetic.* A deep; the deeps, as of the sea, of space, or of one's nature. — **pro·found′ly,** *adv.* — **pro·found′ness,** *n.*

pro·fun′di·ty (prō·fŭn′dĭ·tĭ), *n.; pl.* -TIES (-tĭz). [LL. *profunditas.*] **1.** Depth; profoundness. **2.** That which is profound; a deep; esp., an abstruse matter, theory, etc.

pro·fuse′ (prō·fūs′; 2), *adj.* [L. *profusus,* past part. of *profundere* to pour forth or out, fr. *pro-* + *fundere* to pour.] **1.** Pouring forth liberally; prodigal. **2.** Bountiful; lavish. — **pro·fuse′ly,** *adv.* — **pro·fuse′ness,** *n.*

Syn. **Profuse, lavish, prodigal, luxuriant, lush, exuberant** mean giving or given out abundantly. **Profuse** implies a pouring forth without restraint; **lavish,** the absence of all stint or measure; **prodigal,** lavishness that promises ultimate exhaustion of resources; **luxuriant,** a rich and splendid abundance; **lush,** a perfection in luxuriance; **exuberant,** vitality or vigor in that which produces abundantly.

pro·fu′sion (prō·fū′zhŭn), *n.* **1.** Profuse or lavish expenditure; prodigality. **2.** Abundance; lavish supply.

prog (prŏg), *v. i.;* PROGGED (prŏgd); PROG′GING. *Dial.* To poke, or search about, esp. in order to steal. — *n. Dial.* Food, esp. that got by begging or filching.

pro·gen′i·tor (prō·jĕn′ĭ·tẽr), *n.* [L., fr. *progignere, -genitum,* to bring forth, beget, fr. *pro-* + *gignere* to beget.] **1.** An ancestor in the direct line; a forefather. **2.** Precursor. — **pro·gen′i·tor·ship′,** *n.*

prog′e·ny (prŏj′ĕ·nĭ), *n.; pl.* PROGENIES (-nĭz). [OF. *progenie,* fr. L. *progenies,* fr. *progignere.* See PROGENITOR.] Offspring; issue.

pro·ges′ter·one (prō·jĕs′tẽr·ōn), *n.* [*pro-* + *ges*tation + *ster*ol + *-one.*] *Biochem.* A crystalline sex hormone, $C_{21}H_{30}O_2$, from corpus luteum, exhibiting progestin activity.

pro·ges′tin (prō·jĕs′tĭn), *n.* [*pro-* + *gest*ation + *-in.*] *Biochem.* Any substance that prepares the lining of the uterus for implantation of the fertilized ovum.

pro·glot′tid (prō·glŏt′ĭd), *n. Zool.* One of the segments of a tapeworm. They contain both male and female reproductive organs. — **pro·glot′tic** (-ĭk), *adj.*

pro·glot′tis (-ĭs), *n.; pl.* -TIDES (-ĭ·dēz). [NL., fr. Gr. *pro* forward + *glotta* the tongue.] *Zool.* A proglottid.

prog·nath′ic (prŏg·năth′ĭk), *adj.* Prognathous.

prog′na·thous (prŏg′nȧ·thŭs), *adj.* [*pro-* + Gr. *gnathos* jaw.] *Anat. & Zool.* Having the jaws projecting beyond the upper part of the face; — opposed to *opisthognathous.* See GNATHIC INDEX; FACIAL ANGLE, *Illust.* — **prog′na·thism** (-thĭz'm), **prog′na·thy** (-thĭ), *n.*

prog·no′sis (prŏg·nō′sĭs), *n.; pl.* -NOSES (-sēz). [LL., fr. Gr. *prognōsis* a knowing beforehand, deriv. of *pro-* + *gignōskein* to know.] **1.** Prognostication; a forecast. **2.** *Med.* Forecast of the course of a disease; also, the outlook afforded by this. Cf. DIAGNOSIS, 1.

prog·nos′tic (prŏg·nŏs′tĭk), *n.* [OF. *pronostique,* fr. L., fr. Gr. *prognōstikon.*] **1. a** A portent; sign; omen. **b** A prognostication; a forecast. **2.** *Med.* A symptom indicating the course of a disease. — *adj.* Of, pertaining to, or serving as ground for prognostication.

prog·nos′ti·cate (-tĭ·kāt), *v. t.* To foretell from signs or symptoms; to prophesy; predict; forecast. — **Syn.** See FORETELL. — **prog·nos′ti·ca′tive** (-kā′tĭv; -kȧ·tĭv), *adj.* — **prog·nos′ti·ca′tor** (-kā′tẽr), *n.*

prog·nos′ti·ca′tion (-kā′shŭn), *n.* **1.** Act of prognosticating; prediction; also, a forecast; a prophecy. **2.** That which foreshows; a foretoken. **3.** *Med.* Prognosis.

pro′gram (prō′grăm; -grăm), **pro′gramme** (prō′grăm), *n.* [L. and F.; F. *programme,* fr. LL. *programma* a public proclamation, manifesto, fr. Gr. *programma,* deriv. of *pro-* before + *graphein* to write.] **1.** *Hist.* A public notice. Specif.: **a** A proclamation. **b** A prospectus; syllabus. **2.** A brief outline of the order to be pursued, or the subjects embraced, in any public exercise, performance, etc.; as, a theater *program.* **3.** Hence, the performance or execution of selections (musical, dramatic, etc.) outlined on a program (sense 2). **4.** A plan of future procedure.

pro′gram (prō′grăm), *v. t.;* PRO′GRAMED (-grămd) or PRO′GRAMMED; PRO′GRAM·ING or PRO′GRAM·MING. Also **pro′gramme.** To arrange or furnish a program of or for; to enter in a program; to bill.

pro′gram·mat′ic (prō′grȧ·măt′ĭk), *adj.* Of, pertaining to, or of the nature of a program (esp. a plan or doctrine) or program music. — **pro′gram·mat′i·cal·ly** (-ĭ·kăl·ĭ), *adv.*

program music. Music that suggests things outside of itself, as distinguished from that which relies on tonal effect alone (see ABSOLUTE MUSIC); descriptive music.

program picture. A low-cost motion picture, acted by studio feature players, usually shown second on a double-feature program.

prog′ress (prŏg′rĕs *or, esp. Brit.,* prō′grĕs), *n.* [MF. *progresse* (fr. L. fem. n.), and *progres,* fr. L. *progressus,* fr. *progredi,* past part. *-gressus,* to go forward, fr. *pro-* + *gradi* to go.] **1.** Movement forward; onward course; progression. **2.** A journeying forward; expedition; tour. **3.** *Chiefly Hist.* An official journey or circuit, as of a judge. **4.** Advance to an objective; a going or getting ahead. **5.** Gradual betterment; as, assured of his *progress;* specif., progressive development or evolution of mankind as a process.

pro·gress′ (prō·grĕs′), *v. i.* **1.** To move forward; to proceed. **2.** To develop to a higher stage. — **Syn.** See ADVANCE. — **Ant.** Retrogress.

pro·gres′sion (prō̇·grĕsh′ŭn), *n.* **1.** Act of progressing, or moving forward. **2.** A continuous and connected series, as of acts, events, or steps; a sequence. **3.** *Astron.* The direct movement of the planets through the signs from west to east. **4.** *Math.* A discrete series that has a first but no last element, esp. one in which any intermediate element is related by a uniform law to the other elements. In an ***arithmetical progression*** *or* ***series*** the elements progress by a constant difference, as 1, 3, 5, 7, etc.; in a ***geometric progression*** *or* ***series*** the elements progress by a constant factor, as 2, 6, 18, 54, etc.; a ***harmonic progression*** is one in which the reciprocals of the terms are in arithmetical progression. **5.** *Music.* (1) Succession of tones or chords; the movement of the parts in harmony. (2) = SEQUENCE, 6. — **pro·gres′sion·al** (-ăl; -'l), *adj.*

pro·gres′sion·ist (-ĭst), *n.* One who believes in progress; esp., an evolutionist who emphasizes progress in the development of the species. — **pro·gres′sion·ism** (-ĭz'm), *n.*

prog′ress·ist (prŏg′rĕs·ĭst; prō′grĕs-), *n.* Progressionist.

pro·gres′sive (prō̇·grĕs′ĭv), *adj.* **1.** That progresses or moves forward or onward; advancing; — opposed to *retrograde.* **2.** Occurring or becoming effective by successive stages. **3.** Characterized by, evincing, or pertaining to progress; as, a *progressive* school system. **4.** Favoring or striving for progress, esp. in political and social methods. **5.** *Gram.* Designating a form (of verb or verbal) expressing the action or state as in progress or continuance. **6.** [*cap.*] *U.S. Politics.* Of or pert. to a Progressive party. — *n.* **1.** One who is progressive, esp. in political policy. **2.** [*cap.*] *U.S. Politics.* A member of a Progressive party. — **pro·gres′sive·ly,** *adv.* — **pro·gres′sive·ness,** *n.*

Progressive party. *U.S.* **a** The political party led by Theodore Roosevelt in 1912. **b** The political party led by Henry Wallace in 1948.

pro·gres′siv·ism (prō̇·grĕs′ĭv·ĭz'm), *n.* **1.** The principles or beliefs of progressionists or progressives. **2.** [*cap.*] *U.S. Politics.* The political doctrines advocated by a Progressive party.

pro·hib′it (prō̇·hĭb′ĭt), *v. t.* [L. *prohibitus,* past part. of *prohibere,* fr. *pro-* + *habere* to have, hold.] **1.** To forbid by authority; to interdict. **2.** To stop or prevent (a person); to hinder; debar. — **Syn.** See FORBID.

pro′hi·bi′tion (prō′ĭ·bĭsh′ŭn; prō′hĭ-), *n.* **1.** Act of prohibiting. **2.** A declaration or injunction forbidding some action. **3.** The forbidding by law of the sale and, sometimes, the manufacture and transportation, of alcoholic liquors as beverages.

pro′hi·bi′tion·ist (-ĭst), *n.* A person who favors the prohibition of the sale (or the manufacture and sale) of alcoholic liquors as beverages; specif., *U.S.* [*cap.*], a member of the **Prohibition party,** organized as a national political party 1869, having as its fundamental principle the prohibition by law of the manufacture, importation, transportation, and sale of alcoholic beverages.

pro·hib′i·tive (prō̇·hĭb′ĭ·tĭv), *adj.* Also **pro·hib′i·to′ry** (-tō′rĭ *or, esp. Brit.,* -tẽr·ĭ). That serves or tends to prohibit. — **pro·hib′i·tive·ly, pro·hib′i·to′ri·ly,** *adv.*

pro·ject′ (prō̇·jĕkt′; 2), *v. t.* [L. *projectus,* past part. of *proicere, projicere,* fr. *pro-* + *jacere* to throw.] **1.** To throw or cast forward. **2.** To cast about in the mind; to contrive; scheme. **3.** To cause to protrude, esp. as part of a structure. **4.** To cause (light or shadow) to fall into space, or (an image) upon a surface. **5.** To externalize and regard as objective or outside of oneself, as a sensation, image, or desire. **6.** *Geom., etc.* **a** To throw forward in a prescribed direction (as a point, line, area, etc.) so as to depict on a given surface. **b** More generally, to depict (one figure or extent) on another, according to any fixed correspondence. — *v. i.* To jut out; to protrude.

proj′ect (prŏj′ĕkt; -ĭkt), *n.* **1.** A plan or design; a scheme; proposal. **2.** A planned undertaking; specif., a definite piece of research. **3.** *Educ.* A task or problem, usually calling for constructive thought or action by the student, and involving the learning of a phase of schoolwork. — **Syn.** See PLAN.

pro·jec′tile (prō̇·jĕk′tĭl; 56), *adj.* **1.** Projecting or impelling forward; as, a *projectile* force. **2.** *Zool.* Capable of being thrust forward. — (prō̇·jĕk′tĭl; *Brit. also* prŏj′ĭk·tīl), *n.* A body projected by exterior force, and continuing in motion by its own inertia; specif., a missile for a firearm or cannon.

pro·jec′tion (prō̇·jĕk′shŭn), *n.* **1.** Act of projecting. **2.** A scheming or planning. **3.** A jutting out; also, a part that projects, or juts out; an extension beyond something else. **4.** Act of perceiving a mental object as spatially and sensibly objective; also, the object projected. **5.** *Geom., etc.* The operation of projecting lines and planes so that they intersect a given surface called the ***surface of projection;*** also, the picture so formed. **6.** *Map Making.* A method of representing upon a plane the surface of the earth or the celestial sphere. See AZIMUTHAL EQUIDISTANT PROJECTION, MERCATOR'S PROJECTION, ORTHOGRAPHIC PROJECTION, POLYCONIC PROJECTION. **7.** *Motion Pictures.* The display of motion pictures by throwing an image from them upon a screen. **8.** *Psychol.* The act of externalizing or objectifying what is primarily subjective; — opp. to *introjection.* — **pro·jec′tion·al** (-ăl; -'l), *adj.*

Syn. Projection, protrusion, protuberance, bulge mean an extension beyond the normal line or surface. **Projection** implies a jutting out, esp. at a sharp angle; **protrusion,** a thrusting out so as to seem a deformity; **protuberance,** a swelling out, esp. in rounded form; **bulge,** an expansion often caused by pressure.

pro·jec′tion·ist (-ĭst), *n.* An operator of a television equipment.

pro·jec′tive (prō̇·jĕk′tĭv), *adj.* **1.** That projects (in any sense); projecting. **2.** Pert. to, or produced by, projection.

projective geometry. That branch of geometry which deals with the properties of geometric configurations which remain invariant under projection.

pro·jec′tor (prō̇·jĕk′tẽr), *n.* **1.** One who forms projects; specif., a schemer; promoter. **2.** One that projects, as a device for projecting an object, ray, image, etc. **3.** *Motion Pictures.* = *motion-picture projector,* under MOTION PICTURE **b.** **4.** *Optics.* An optical instrument for projecting an image upon a screen, as a magic lantern.

‖**pro′jet′** (prō′zhĕ′), *n.* [F.] A plan; esp., a draft of a proposed measure or treaty.

pro·lac′tin (prō̇·lăk′tĭn), *n.* [*pro-* + *lact-* + *-in.*] *Biochem.* A hormone of the anterior lobe of the pituitary gland, inducing lactation in mammals and crop-gland secretion in birds.

pro·lam′in (prō̇·lăm′ĭn; prō′lȧ·mĭn), *n.* Also **pro·lam′ine** (-ĭn; -ēn). [*proline* + *ammonia* + *-ine.*] *Biochem.* Any of a class of simple proteins, insoluble in water and absolute alcohol, found esp. in seeds.

pro′lan (prō′lăn), *n.* [From L. *proles* offspring.] *Biochem.* A gonadotropic hormone found in urine in pregnancy and some other conditions.

pro·lapse′ (prō̇·lăps′), *n.* Also **pro·lap′sus** (-lăp′sŭs). [L. *prolapsus,* fr. *prolabi, prolapsus,* to fall forward, fr. *pro-* + *labi* to glide, fall.] *Med.* The falling down of an internal part, as of the uterus. — *v. i.* To fall or slip forward, down, or out, as in a prolapse.

pro′late (prō′lāt), *adj.* [L. *prolatus,* used as past part. of *proferre* to extend.] Stretched out; esp., elongated in the direction of a line joining the poles. Cf. OBLATE.

pro′leg′ (prō′lĕg′), *n.* [*pro-* for, in place of + *leg.*] *Zool.* One of the fleshy legs on the abdominal segments of the larvae of certain insects.

pro′le·gom′e·non (prō′lē·gŏm′ē·nŏn; -nŭn), *n.; pl.* -GOMENA (-nȧ). [Gr., neut. pass. pres. part. of *prolegein* to say beforehand.] A preliminary observation; a preface, as to a treatise; — used chiefly in *pl.*

pro′le·gom′e·nous (-nŭs), *adj.* Prefatory; also, given to needless or long prefatory remarks.

pro·lep′sis (prō̇·lĕp′sĭs *or, esp. Brit.,* -lēp′sĭs), *n.; pl.* -LEPSES (-sēz). [L., fr. Gr. *prolēpsis,* fr. *prolambanein* to take beforehand.] Anticipation; specif.: **a** *Rhet.* A figure by which objections are anticipated in order to weaken their force. **b** *Gram.* The applying of an adjective to a noun in anticipation, or to denote the result, of the action of the verb ("ere humane statute purged the *gentle* weal"). **c** *Chron.* An error in chronology, consisting in an event being dated before its actual time. — **pro·lep′tic** (-lĕp′tĭk), *adj.*

pro′le·tar′i·an (prō′lē·târ′ĭ·ăn), *adj.* [L. *proletarius,* fr. *proles* offspring.] Of or pert. to the proletarians; hence, *Obs.,* mean; vulgar. — *n.* **1.** Orig., one of the poorest and lowest class in a community or state. **2.** One of the wage-earning class; esp., a laborer for day wages not possessed of capital. — **pro′le·tar′i·an·ism** (-ĭz'm), *n.*

pro′le·tar′i·at (-ăt), *n.* [F. *prolétariat.*] Proletarians, collectively; the proletarian class.

pro·lif′er·ate (prō̇·lĭf′ẽr·āt), *v. i.* *Biol.* To grow by the rapid production of new parts, or new cells or buds. — **pro·lif′er·a′tion** (-ā′shŭn), *n.*

pro·lif′er·ous (-ŭs), *adj.* [L. *proles* offspring + *-ferous.*] **1.** *Bot.* **a** Reproducing freely by offsets, bulbils, gemmae, or other vegetative means. **b** Developing a leafy shoot from a normally terminal organ, as a flower or fruit. **2.** *Zool.* Proliferating; specif., of corals, producing a cluster of branchlets from a branch.

pro·lif′ic (prō̇·lĭf′ĭk), *adj.* [F. *prolifique,* fr. ML., fr. L. *proles* offspring.] **1.** Producing young or fruit; reproductive; now, usually, reproducing freely; fruitful; fecund. **2.** Highly inventive, propagative, etc.; as, a *prolific* brain. **3.** Causing, or characterized by, fruitfulness; as, a *prolific* season. — **Syn.** See FERTILE. — **Ant.** Barren. — **pro·lif′i·cal·ly** (-ĭ·kăl·ĭ), *adv.* — **pro·lif′ic·ness,** *n.*

pro′line (prō′lēn; -lĭn), *n.* Also **pro′lin.** [G. *prolin.*] *Biochem.* An amino acid, $C_5H_9NO_2$, formed by the decomposition of certain proteins.

pro·lix′ (prō̇·lĭks′; prō′lĭks; 2), *adj.* [F. *prolixe,* fr. L. *prolixus* extended.] **1.** Unduly prolonged, as by diffuseness; verbose. **2.** Indulging in verboseness; long-winded. — **Syn.** See WORDY. — **pro·lix′ly,** *adv.* — **pro·lix′ness,** *n.*

pro·lix′i·ty (prō̇·lĭk′sĭ·tĭ), *n.; pl.* -TIES (-tĭz). Quality or state of being prolix; long-windedness.

pro·loc′u·tor (prō̇·lŏk′ū·tẽr), *n.* [L., fr. *proloqui,* past part. *prolocutus,* to speak out.] One who speaks for another; a spokesman; a presiding officer; a chairman; specif., *Ch. of Eng.,* the presiding officer of the lower house of a convocation.

pro′log·ize (prō′lŏg·īz; -lō̇·jīz), *v. i.* To prologuize.

pro′logue (prō′lŏg; 74), *n.* [OF. *prologue,* fr. L. *prologus,* fr. Gr. *prologos,* fr. *pro-* + *logos* speech.] **1.** The preface or introduction to a discourse, poem, etc. **2.** One who delivers the prologue, as to a play. **3.** An introductory or prefatory act, event, etc.

pro′logu·ize (prō′lŏg·īz), *v. i.* To compose or deliver a prologue.

pro·long′ (prō̇·lŏng′; 74), *v. t.* [OF. *prolonguier, prolongier,* fr. LL. *prolongare,* fr. *pro-* + *longus* long.] **1.** To lengthen in time; to draw out; to continue. **2.** To lengthen in extent or range; as, to *prolong* a line. — **Syn.** See EXTEND. — **pro·long′er** (-lŏng′ẽr), *n.*

pro·lon′gate (-lŏng′gāt), *v. t.* To prolong; to extend in space or in time. — **pro′lon·ga′tion** (prō′lŏng·gā′shŭn), *n.*

pro·longe′ (prō̇·lŏnj′; *F.* prô′lôɴzh′), *n.* [F.] *Mil.* A rope with a hook and a toggle, sometimes used to drag a gun carriage.

prolonge knot. See KNOT, *Illust.* (10).

pro·lu′sion (prō̇·lū′zhŭn), *n.* [L. *prolusio,* fr. *proludere* to prelude, fr. *pro-* + *ludere* to play.] A trial performance, or introductory essay or exercise. — **pro·lu′so·ry** (-sō̇·rĭ), *adj.*

prom′e·nade′ (prŏm′ē·nȧd′; -nād′), *n.* [F., fr. *se promener* to walk, fr. MF. *pormener,* fr. LL. *prominare* to drive forward, fr. *pro-* + *minare* to drive (animals).] **1.** A walk, esp. in a public place, for pleasure, display, or exercise. **2.** A place for walking; a public walk. **3. a** A ceremonious opening of a formal ball, consisting of a march participated in by all the guests. **b** A ball or dance, esp. one given by a college or school class and then usually called **prom** (prŏm). — *v. i.* To take, or go on, a promenade. — **prom′e·nad′er** (-nȧd′ẽr; -nād′ẽr), *n.*

promenade deck. An upper deck of a passenger steamer, where passengers promenade. See DECK, *Illust.*

Pro·me′the·an (prō̇·mē′thē·ăn), *adj.* Of, pert. to, or like Prometheus; hence, life-giving; daringly original; creative.

Pro·me′theus (-thūs; -thē·ŭs), *n.* [L., fr. Gr. *Promētheus,* lit., Forethinker.] *Gr. Relig.* A Titan who stole fire from heaven and gave it to man. Zeus doomed him to be bound to Mt. Caucasus and to have a vulture daily consume his liver, and to continue this torment until some immortal should consent to die in Prometheus's stead. This Chiron did, and Hercules slew the vulture.

pro·me′thi·um (-thĭ·ŭm), *n.* Also **pro·me′the·um** (-thē·ŭm). [NL. See PROMETHEUS.] *Chem.* A rare-earth element discovered in 1947 as a fission product of uranium. Symbol, *Pm;* at. no., 61.

prom′i·nence (prŏm′ĭ·nĕns), *n.* **1.** Quality, state, or fact of being prominent, manifest, or conspicuous; distinction. **2.** Something prominent; a salient point, protuberance, projection, or the like.

prom′i·nent (-nĕnt), *adj.* [L. *prominens, -entis,* pres. part. of *prominere* to jut out, project.] **1.** Standing out, or projecting, beyond a surface or a line; jutting. **2.** Distinctly manifest; conspicuous. **3.** Of distinction; notable. — **Syn.** See NOTICEABLE. — **prom′i·nent·ly,** *adv.*

prom′is·cu′i·ty (prŏm′ĭs·kū′ĭ·tĭ; prō′mĭs-), *n.; pl.* -TIES (-tĭz). **1.** Indiscriminate mingling; promiscuousness; also, a heterogeneous mixture of persons, morals, etc. **2.** Promiscuous sexual union.

pro·mis′cu·ous (prō̇·mĭs′kū·ŭs), *adj.* [L. *promiscuus,* fr. *pro* before, in place of, for + *miscere* to mix.] **1.** Consisting of a heterogeneous mixture of persons or things. **2.** Indiscriminately distributed, applied, granted, etc.; as, *promiscuous* blame, intercourse. **3.** That is undiscriminating, irregular, casual, or the like; as, *promiscuous* standards. — **pro·mis'cu·ous·ly**, *adv.* — **pro·mis'cu·ous·ness**, *n.*

prom'ise (prŏm'ĭs), *n.* [From L. *promissum*, and fr. OF. *promesse*, fr. LL. *promissa*, fr. L. *promittere*, *-missum*, to put forth, promise, fr. *pro-* + *mittere* to send.] **1.** One's pledge to another to do or not do something specified; narrowly, a declaration which gives to the person to whom it is made a right to expect or to claim the performance or forbearance of a specified act. **2.** Ground for hope, expectation, or assurance, often specif., of eventual success. **3.** That which is promised. — *v. t.* **1.** To engage to do, give, make, obtain, etc.; to make (to another) a promise of; also, to give one's promise to. **2.** To assure; as, he will go, I *promise* you. **3.** To show or suggest beforehand; betoken; as, the clouds *promise* rain. — *v. i.* **1.** To make a promise. **2.** To give ground for expectations. — **Syn.** Engage, pledge, plight, covenant.

Prom'ised Land (prŏm'ĭst). = LAND OF PROMISE.

prom'is·ee' (prŏm'ĭs·ē'), *n.* *Law.* The person to whom a promise is made.

prom'is·er (prŏm'ĭ·sẽr), *n.* One who promises.

prom'is·ing, *adj.* Full of promise; likely; as, a *promising* young man. — **prom'is·ing·ly**, *adv.*

prom'i·sor (prŏm'ĭ·sôr *or, in contrast with* promisee, prŏm'ĭ·sôr'), *n.* *Law.* One who engages or undertakes.

prom'is·so'ry (prŏm'ĭ·sō'rĭ *or, esp. Brit.*, -sẽr·ĭ), *adj.* Containing a promise; as, a *promissory* note.

promissory note. *Law.* A written promise to pay on demand or at a fixed future time a certain sum of money to, or to the order of, a specified person or to bearer.

prom'on·to'ry (prŏm'ŭn·tō'rĭ *or, esp. Brit.*, -tẽr·ĭ, -trĭ), *n.*; *pl.* -RIES (-rĭz). [ML. *promontorium*, fr. L. *promunturium*.] **1.** A high point of land or rock projecting into the sea; a headland. Cf. 2d CAPE, 1. **2.** *Anat.* A prominence; protuberance.

pro·mote' (prō·mōt'), *v. t.* [L. *promotus*, past part. of *promovere* to move forward, promote, fr. *pro-* + *movere* to move.] **1.** To exalt in station, rank, or honor; to elevate; advance. **2.** To contribute to the growth or prosperity of (something in course); to further; as, to *promote* learning. **3.** *Educ.* To advance from a given grade or class as qualified for one higher. — **Syn.** See ADVANCE. — **Ant.** Impede.

pro·mot'er (-mōt'ẽr), *n.* **1.** One who or that which promotes. **2.** Specif., a person who alone or with others initiates, and takes the preliminary steps in, a scheme or undertaking for the organization of a company, the floating of bonds, stock, etc.

pro·mo'tion (prō·mō'shŭn), *n.* Act of promoting; as, engaged in the *promotion* of a corporate enterprise; advance in grade; as, a pupil meriting *promotion*.

pro·mo'tive (-tĭv), *adj.* Tending to promote.

prompt (prŏmpt; 89), *adj.* [F., fr. L. *promptus*, prop., brought forth, hence, visible, ready, quick, deriv. of *pro-* + *emere* to take.] **1.** Ready and quick to act as occasion demands; responding instantly. **2.** Done or rendered readily; given without delay or hesitation. **3.** Of or pertaining to prompting or a prompter, esp. of actors; as, a *prompt* table. — **Syn.** See QUICK. — *n.* **1.** *Com.* A limit of time given for payment of an account for produce purchased; also, the contract by which this time is fixed. **2.** A reminder. — *v. t.* **1.** To move (one) to action; to incite; as, poverty *prompted* them to riot. **2.** To remind (a person); specif., to remind (an actor, speaker, or the like) of words or topics forgotten; to give a cue to. **3.** To suggest (an act, thought, etc.); inspire. — **prompt'ly**, *adv.* — **prompt'ness**, *n.*

prompt'er (prŏmp'tẽr), *n.* One who prompts an actor, speaker, etc.

promp'ti·tude (prŏmp'tĭ·tūd), *n.* Quality or habit of being prompt; quickness in deciding, acting, etc.

pro·mul'gate (prō·mŭl'gāt *or, esp. Brit.*, prŏm'ŭl·gāt), *v. t.* [L. *promulgatus*, past part. of *promulgare*, fr. *provulgare*, fr. *pro-* + *vulgare* to publish.] **1.** *Chiefly Eccl.* To make known by open declaration, as a decree, or esp., a dogma. **2.** *Law.* **a** To make known or public the terms of (a proposed law). **b** To issue or give out (a law) by way of putting it into execution. — **Syn.** See DECLARE. — **pro'mul·ga'tion** (prō'mŭl·gā'shŭn; prŏm'ŭl-), *n.* — **pro·mul'ga·tor** (prō·mŭl'gā·tẽr; prŏm'ŭl·gā'tẽr; prŏm'ŭl-), *n.*

pro·mulge' (prō·mŭlj'), *v. t.*; -MULGED' (-mŭljd'); -MULG'ING (-mŭl'jĭng). To promulgate; publish; make known.

pro'nate (prō'nāt), *v. t.* & *i.* [LL. *pronatus*, past part. of *pronare* to bend forward.] To cause to assume, or to assume, a position of pronation.

pro·na'tor (prō·nā'tŏr), *n.* [ML.] *Anat.* A muscle which produces the motion of pronation.

pro·na'tion (prō·nā'shŭn), *n.* *Anat.* **a** Rotation of the forearm and hand or, loosely, of other joints, as the shoulder, hip, or knee, forward and toward the mid-line of the body. **b** The position resulting from such rotation, with the palm of the hand directed backward and the thumb next the body. Cf. SUPINATION.

prone (prōn), *adj.* [L. *pronus*.] **1.** Having a propensity or inclination; disposed; — with *to*; as, a mind *prone* to doubt. **2.** Inclined or willing to do something implied or specified. **3.** Downward: **a** Strictly, standing, lying, or placed so that the face and belly are in line with or upon the earth, floor, etc.; — opp. to *supine*; as, a *prone* position. **b** Loosely, prostrate; flat; — opp. to *erect*. **4.** *Poetic.* That descends, slopes, or moves downward. — **prone'ly**, *adv.* — **prone'ness**, *n.*

Syn. (1) See LIABLE.

(2) **Prone, supine, prostrate, recumbent** mean lying down. **Prone,** strictly, implies a posture with the front of the body turned toward the surface on which it lies (or, occasionally, stands); **supine,** a lying upon one's back; **prostrate,** the posture of one thrown in a prone (sometimes, supine) position; **recumbent,** the posture of one sleeping or resting.

pro·neph'ros (prō·nĕf'rŏs), *n.* [NL., fr. Gr. *pro* before + *nephros* a kidney.] *Embryol.* One of the anterior of the three pairs of embryonic renal organs of typical vertebrates.

prong (prŏng; 74), *n.* [ME. *prange*, *pronge*.] A tine of a fork; hence, a slender projecting part, as a point of an antler. — *v. t.* To stab, pierce, or break up (as soil) with a prong.

prong'horn' (-hôrn'), *n.*; see PLURAL, *Note*, 3. A peculiar antelopelike ruminant (*Antilocapra americana*) of the treeless parts of the western United States and Mexico.

pro·nom'i·nal (prō·nŏm'ĭ·năl; -n'l), *adj.* [LL. *pronominalis*.] *Gram.* Belonging to, or of the nature of, a pronoun; — in **pronominal adjective** (*these* books, *such* books, *his* books), **pronominal adverb** (*here, hence, thus, so*). — **pro·nom'i·nal·ly**, *adv.*

pro'noun (prō'noun), *n.* [F. *pronom*, fr. L. *pronomen*, fr. *pro* for + *nomen* name, noun.] *Gram.* A word used instead of a noun; one of a small group of words referring to persons or things either named, asked for, or understood in the context. Specifically called a ***personal pronoun*** when indicating the person or persons speaking or spoken to, or one or more persons or things or ideas spoken of (*I, me, he, she, it, we, they*, and all possessive pronouns, see below); a ***relative pronoun*** when referring back to a noun or pronoun and also linking a subordinate clause to a main clause (*who, whose, whom, which, that, as*); a ***demonstrative pronoun*** when pointing to an individual or idea already mentioned (*this, that, these, those*); an ***indefinite pronoun*** when giving an indefinite or general impression (*somebody, anybody, everything;* often also *somewhat, nothing, naught, aught,* usually classed as nouns); a ***possessive pronoun*** when indicating something as belonging to a person or thing (*mine, thine, his, hers, its, ours, yours, theirs*); a ***reflexive pronoun*** when referring to the person who does the action of the verb (compounds of personal pronouns plus *self* or *selves*); an ***intensive pronoun*** when emphasizing a preceding noun or pronoun (borrowing is *itself* a bad habit; he *himself*); an ***interrogative pronoun*** when asking the identity, nature, or possessor of whatever is in question (*who, what, which, whose, whom*); a ***reciprocal pronoun*** when indicating persons or things mutually affected (the phrases *each other, one another*). Abbr. *pron.*

pro·nounce' (prō·nouns'; 106), *v. t.*; -NOUNCED' (-nounst'); -NOUNC'ING (-noun'sĭng). [OF. *prononcier*, fr. L. *pronuntiare*, fr. *pro-* + *nunciare*, *nuntiare*, to announce.] **1.** To utter officially or ceremoniously; to deliver, as a decree. **2.** *Now Rare.* To declare publicly. **3.** To affirm or assert, as one's judgment; as, to *pronounce* one a brave man. **4.** To speak aloud, now esp. with reference to articulation or correct accent. **5.** To deliver, as a speech, effectively. — *v. i.* **1.** To make a pronouncement. **2.** To utter words or syllables. — **pro·nounce'a·ble**, *adj.* — **pro·nounc'er** (-noun'sẽr), *n.*

pro·nounced' (-nounst'), *adj.* Strongly marked; decided. — **pro·nounc'ed·ly** (-noun'sĕd·lĭ; -sĭd·lĭ), *adv.*

pro·nounce'ment (prō·nouns'mĕnt), *n.* A pronouncing; a declaration; a formal announcement.

pron'to (prŏn'tō), *adj.* & *adv.* [Sp.] *Colloq., U. S.* Quick; quickly; promptly.

pro·nu'cle·us (prō·nū'klē·ŭs), *n.*; *pl.* PRONUCLEI (-ī). [NL. See PRO-; NUCLEUS.] *Biol.* A gamete nucleus after the completion of maturation. In fertilization, two haploid gamete pronuclei fuse to form a diploid synkaryon or zygote nucleus.

pro·nun'ci·a·men'to (prō·nŭn'shĭ·ȧ·mĕn'tō; -sĭ·ȧ-), *n.*; *pl.* -TOS or -TOES (-tōz). [Sp. *pronunciamiento*.] A proclamation or pronouncement.

pro·nun'ci·a'tion (prō·nŭn'sĭ·ā'shŭn; -shĭ·ā'shŭn), *n.* Act or manner of pronouncing words; articulate utterance.

proof (prōōf; 85), *n.* [ME. *profe*, *prove* (after *prove*, v.), fr. *prefe*, *preve*, fr. OF. *preve*, *prueve*, fr. LL. *proba*. See PROVE.] **1.** That degree of cogency, arising from evidence, which convinces the mind of any truth or fact and produces belief; also, that which proves or tends to prove. Properly speaking, *proof* is the effect or result of evidence; evidence is the medium of proof. **2. a** Any effort, process, or operation designed to establish or discover a fact or truth; test; trial. **b** A test applied to substances to determine if they are of satisfactory quality, etc. **3.** Quality or state of having been proved or tried; as, armor of *proof*. **4.** Proof strength, that is, the minimum strength of proof spirit; sometimes, short for PROOF SPIRIT. Also, strength with reference to the standard for proof spirit. **5.** *Engraving & Etching.* A proof impression. **6.** *Law.* Evidence operating to determine the judgment of a tribunal. **7.** *Math.* An operation for testing the accuracy of a previous operation; a check. **8.** *Photog.* A test print made from a negative. **9.** *Print.* A trial impression, as from type, taken for correction or examination; — called also **proof sheet.**

— *adj.* [From *of proof*.] **1.** Firm or successful in resisting; as, *proof* against harm. **2.** Used in proving or testing, or serving as a proof. Specif., designating or pertaining to small samples of perfectly fine (i. e., pure) gold or silver prepared and kept in the United States mints and assay offices as standards. **3.** Of standard strength or quality, as spirits, vinegar, etc. Cf. PROOF SPIRIT.

-proof. A combining form of the adjective *proof*, denoting: **a** *Impervious to the penetration of*, as in water*proof*. **b** *Impervious to the adverse action of*, as in bomb*proof*. **c** *Able to withstand damage or destruction by*, as in tornado*proof*. **d** *As impervious as*, as in armor*proof*. **e** *Offering firm resistance to*, as in slander*proof*.

☞ Adjective compounds in *-proof* are formed freely, and their meanings can readily be understood from the above definitions. Most of these compounds are written as solid words; a few, esp. long ones, are hyphened. From such compounds, nouns may be formed by adding *-ness*. The compounds are also often used as verbs with the meaning of *to make proof against* (what is specified); as, to *waterproof* a surface.

proof'read' (prōōf'rēd'), *v. t.* & *i.*; see READ. To read and mark corrections in (printer's proof). — **proof'read'er**, *n.* — **proof'read'ing**, *n.*

proof spirit. A strong distilled alcoholic liquor, or mixture of alcohol and water, containing a standard amount of alcohol of a sp. gr. 0.7939 at 60° F. (in the United States one half of its volume).

prop (prŏp), *v. t.*; PROPPED (prŏpt), *Rare* PROPT; PROP'PING. [From PROP, *n.*] **1.** To support by placing something under or against or by being placed under or against; as, timbers that *prop* a falling roof. **2.** To sustain; strengthen. — *n.* [MD. *proppe* a prop, also (D. *prop*) stopple, stopper.] That which props or sustains; a support; a stay.

prop, *n.* *Theater.* Short for PROPERTY; — often used attributively.

prop, *n.* Short for PROPELLER.

pro'pae·deu'tic (prō'pē·dū'tĭk), **pro'pae·deu'ti·cal** (-tĭ·kăl), *adj.* [Gr. *propaideuein* to teach beforehand, fr. *pro-* + *paideuein* to bring up a child, fr. *pais*, *paidos*, a child.] Of, pert. to, or conveying preliminary instruction; introductory to any art or science.

pro'pae·deu'tic, *n.* **1.** A propaedeutic branch of knowledge. **2.** A preparatory or introductory course.

pro'pae·deu'tics (-tĭks), *n.*; see -ICS. The preliminary learning connected with any art or science.

prop'a·ga·ble (prŏp'ȧ·gȧ·b'l), *adj.* Capable of being propagated.

prop'a·gan'da (prŏp'ȧ·găn'dȧ; prō'pȧ-), *n.* [Abbr. fr. L. *de propaganda fide*. See PROPAGATE.] **1.** [*cap.*] *R.C.Ch.* **a** The Congregation of Propaganda. See CONGREGATION, 5 **b**. **b** More fully ***College of Propaganda***. A college instituted by Urban VIII (1623–44) to educate priests for missions. **2.** Any organized or concerted group, effort, or movement to spread particular doctrines, information, etc.

3. **a** A doctrine or ideas spread through propaganda (sense 2). **b** A plan for the propagation of a doctrine or system of principles.
prop′a·gan′dism (prŏp′ȧ·găn′dĭz′m; prō′pȧ-), *n.* The action, practice, or art of propagating doctrines, etc., or of using propaganda. — **prop′a·gan′dist** (-dĭst), *n. & adj.*
prop′a·gan′dize (-dīz), *v. t.* To subject to a propaganda.
prop′a·gate (prŏp′ȧ·gāt), *v. t.* [L. *propagatus*, past part. of *propagare* to propagate.] **1.** To cause to continue or multiply by generation. **2.** To cause to spread or extend. **3.** To transmit; to carry, as forward in space or time or through a medium; as, to *propagate* light. **4.** To spread from person to person; disseminate. **5.** *Obs.* To multiply; increase. — *v. i.* To have young or issue; to be produced by generation, or by seeds, cuttings, etc. — **prop′a·ga′tor** (-gā′tẽr), *n.*
prop′a·ga′tion (-gā′shŭn), *n.* Act of propagating; as: **a** Continuance by generation or successive production. **b** The spreading abroad of anything; diffusion; dissemination; as, the *propagation* of the gospel; the *propagation* of apple varieties. — **prop′a·ga′tive** (prŏp′ȧ·gā′tĭv), *adj.*
pro′pane (prō′pān), *n.* [*propyl* + *methane.*] *Chem.* A heavy gaseous hydrocarbon, $CH_3CH_2CH_3$, of the methane series, occurring naturally dissolved in crude petroleum.
pro′par·ox′y·tone (prō′păr·ŏk′sĭ·tōn), *n.* [Gr. *proparoxytonos*, adj. See PRO-; PAROXYTONE.] *Gram.* A word having the acute accent on the antepenult. — **pro′par·ox′y·tone, pro′par·ox′y·ton′ic** (-tŏn′ĭk), *adj.* — **pro′par·ox′y·tone,** *v. t.*
‖**pro pa′tri·a** (prō pā′trĭ·ȧ). [L.] For one's country.
pro·pel′ (prō·pĕl′), *v. t.;* PRO·PELLED′ (-pĕld′); PRO·PEL′LING. [L. *propellere, -pulsum*, fr. *pro-* + *pellere* to drive.] To impel forward or onward; to push ahead; to drive onward. — **Syn.** See PUSH.
pro·pel′lant (-pĕl′ănt), *n.* A propelling agent; specif.: **a** An explosive for propelling projectiles. **b** Fuel plus oxidizing agent used by a rocket engine.
pro·pel′lent (-ĕnt), *adj.* Driving forward; able or tending to propel. — *n.* Something that propels.
pro·pel′ler (-ẽr), *n.* One that propels; specif., a screw propeller. See SCREW PROPELLER; AIRPLANE, *Illust.*
pro·pend′ (prō·pĕnd′), *v. i.* [L. *propendere, -pensum*, fr. *pro-* + *pendere* to hang.] *Now Rare.* To be favorably inclined or disposed; to tend.
pro·pense′ (prō·pĕns′; 106), *adj.* [L. *propensus*, past part.] *Archaic.* Inclining toward; also, partial.
pro·pen′sion (-pĕn′shŭn), *n.* *Now Rare.* Propensity.
pro·pen′si·ty (-sĭ·tĭ), *n.; pl.* -TIES (-tĭz). **a** A natural inclination or bent. **b** A favorable disposition; a liking; bias. — **Syn.** See LEANING.
prop′er (prŏp′ẽr), *adj.* [OF. *propre*, fr. L. *proprius.*] **1.** *Archaic.* Belonging to one; one's own. **2.** Belonging to the natural or essential constitution; peculiar; distinctive; as, every animal has his *proper* instincts. **3.** Of or pertaining to the exact or specified part strictly so called; as, Greece *proper.* **4.** Befitting one's nature, qualities, etc.; right; fit. **5.** *Archaic.* Becoming in appearance; handsome. **6.** Fine; excellent. **7.** Strictly pertinent or applicable; correct; as, *proper* words in *proper* places. **8.** *Archaic.* Honest; chaste; respectable. **9.** Decorous; decent. **10.** *Eccl.* Special to, or appointed for, a particular day or festival. **11.** *Gram.* **a** Of a noun or name, naming a particular being or thing or, specifically, one that does not take a limiting modifier, regularly capitalized in English; — opp. to *common* (def. 8 **d**). See NOUN. **b** Of an adjective, naming a particular being or thing (*Mexican, Shakespearean*), regularly capitalized in English. **12.** *Her.* Represented in its natural color. — **Syn.** See FIT.
proper fraction. See FRACTION.
prop′er·ly (prŏp′ẽr·lĭ), *adv.* Suitably; fitly; rightly.
prop′er·tied (prŏp′ẽr·tĭd), *adj.* Possessing property.
prop′er·ty (prŏp′ẽr·tĭ), *n.; pl.* -TIES (-tĭz). [OF. *proprieté*, fr. L. *proprietas*, fr. *proprius* one's own, proper.] **1.** That which is proper to anything; a characteristic quality of a thing. **2.** An acquired or artificial quality; also, a peculiarity. **3.** Wealth; goods; specif., a piece of real estate. **4.** The exclusive right to possess, enjoy, and dispose of, a thing; ownership; in a broad sense, any valuable right or interest considered primarily as a source of wealth. **5.** That to which a person has a legal title; thing owned; an estate. **6.** *Logic.* An attribute common to all members of a class; thus, sweetness is a *property* of sugar. **7.** *Theater.* **a** *pl.* All the adjuncts of a play or motion picture except the painted scenery and the costumes of the actors; stage requisites. **b** *sing.* Any one of these articles. — **Syn.** See QUALITY.
pro′phase′ (prō′fāz′), *n.* *Biol.* An early stage in mitosis, preceding the metaphase, in which the spindle forms and the chromosomes split lengthwise.
proph′e·cy (prŏf′ē·sĭ), *n.; pl.* -CIES (-sĭz). [OF. *profecie*, fr. LL. *prophetia*, fr. Gr. *prophēteia*, fr. *prophētēs* prophet. See PROPHET.] **1.** The work or vocation of a prophet; utterance of a prophet. **2.** A declaration of something to come; prediction. **3.** *Bib.* A book of prophecies.
proph′e·si′er (-sī′ẽr), *n.* One who prophesies.
proph′e·sy (prŏf′ē·sī), *v. t.;* -SIED (-sīd); -SY′ING. **1.** To utter with or as with divine inspiration. **2.** To predict; foretell; as, to *prophesy* doom. **3.** *Rare.* To foreshow. — *v. i.* **a** To speak under the influence of religious experience, and hence as divinely inspired. *Ezek.* xxxvii. 7. **b** To give instruction in religious matters. **c** To utter predictions. — **Syn.** See FORETELL.
proph′et (prŏf′ĕt; -ĭt), *n.* [OF. *prophete*, fr. L. *propheta*, fr. Gr. *prophētēs* proclaimer of a revelation, fr. *pro* forth + *phanai* to speak.] **1.** One who speaks for another, esp. for God or a god. **2.** Hence: **a** *Chiefly Poetic.* A seer; specif., an inspired poet. **b** One who prophesies future events. **c** An effective spokesman for a group, a cause, or the like; as, *prophets* of socialism. **3.** *Jewish & Christian Theol.* One inspired by God to speak in his name, announcing future events. Cf. the PROPHETS. **4.** [*cap.*, with *the.*] **a** Among Moslems, Mohammed. **b** Among Mormons, Joseph Smith. **5.** *Christian Science.* A spiritual seer; disappearance of material sense before the conscious facts of spiritual Truth. *Mary Baker Eddy.* — **proph′et·ess,** *n.* — **proph′et·hood,** *n.*
pro·phet′ic (prō·fĕt′ĭk), *adj.* Also **pro·phet′i·cal** (-ĭ·kăl). Of or pertaining to a prophet or prophecy; interpretative; foretelling events. — **pro·phet′i·cal·ly,** *adv.*
Proph′ets, the. Certain books of the Old Testament, chiefly prophetic, constituting a division apart from the Law and the Hagiographa.
pro′phy·lac′tic (prō′fĭ·lăk′tĭk; prŏf′ĭ-), *adj.* [Gr. *prophylaktikos*, fr. *prophylassein* to guard against.] **1.** *Med.* Preventing, or guarding from, disease. **2.** That guards or preserves; protective. — *n.* *Med.* Anything that prevents disease, as fresh air, nutritious food, etc.; specif., a prophylactic medicine.
pro′phy·lax′is (-lăk′sĭs), *n.* [NL.] *Med.* Art of guarding against or preventing disease; preventive treatment.
pro·pine′ (prō·pēn′), *v. t.* [MF. *propiner*, fr. L. *propinare*, fr. Gr. *propinein*, fr. *pro-* + *pinein* to drink.] *Obs. exc. Scot.* To give, esp. as a token of friendship. — (-pēn′; -pīn′), *n.* *Scot.* A gift, esp. of money for drink.
pro·pin′qui·ty (prō·pĭng′kwĭ·tĭ), *n.* [OF. *propinquité*, fr. L. *propinquitas*, fr. *propinquus* near.] State of being near; specif.: **a** Nearness of blood; kinship. **b** Nearness in place or in time; proximity.
pro′pi·on′ic (prō′pĭ·ŏn′ĭk; -ō′nĭk), *adj.* [*proto-* + Gr. *piōn* fat.] *Chem.* Pertaining to or designating a fatty acid, $C_2H_5CO_2H$, a colorless, pungent liquid, produced in the distillation of wood, in the fermentation of glycerol, etc.
pro·pi′ti·ate (prō·pĭsh′ĭ·āt), *v.t.* [L. *propitiatus*, past part. of *propitiare* to propitiate, fr. *propitius* favorable.] To appease and render favorable; conciliate. — **Syn.** See PACIFY. — **pro·pi′ti·a·ble** (-ȧ·b'l), *adj.* — **pro·pi′ti·a′tive** (-ā′tĭv), *adj.*
pro·pi′ti·a′tion (-ā′shŭn), *n.* **1.** Act of propitiating. **2.** *Theol.* That which propitiates; atoning sacrifice; specif., the self-sacrifice and death of Jesus viewed as appeasing divine justice and effecting reconciliation between God and man.
pro·pi′ti·a′tor (prō·pĭsh′ĭ·ā′tẽr), *n.* One who propitiates.
pro·pi′ti·a·to′ry (prō·pĭsh′ĭ·ȧ·tō′rĭ *or, esp. Brit.*, -tẽr·ĭ), *adj.* Of or pertaining to propitiation; intended to propitiate; expiatory. — *n.* *Jewish Antiq.* The mercy seat.
pro·pi′tious (prō·pĭsh′ŭs), *adj.* [OF. *propicius*, fr. L. *propitius.*] **1.** Favorably disposed; graciously inclined; — said of a person or a divinity. **2.** That is of good omen; auspicious; as, a *propitious* sign. **3.** That favors or assists; helpful. — **Syn.** See FAVORABLE. — **pro·pi′tious·ly,** *adv.* — **pro·pi′tious·ness,** *n.*
prop′-jet′ en′gine. = TURBO-PROPELLER ENGINE.
prop′o·lis (prŏp′ō·lĭs), *n.* [L., fr. Gr. *propolis*, fr. *pro-* + *polis* city.] A brownish resinous material, of waxy consistency, collected by bees from the buds of trees and used as a cement.
pro·pone′ (prō·pōn′), *v. t.* [L. *proponere.*] *Now Scot.* **a** To propose; propound. **b** To put forward, as an excuse.
pro·po′nent (-pō′nĕnt), *n.* **1.** One who makes a proposal; one who lays down a proposition; hence, an advocate. **2.** *Law.* The propounder of a thing, as a will for probate.
pro·por′tion (prō·pōr′shŭn; 70), *n.* [OF. *proporcion, -tion*, fr. L. *proportio*, fr. the phrase *pro portione*, fr. *pro* before + *portio* part, share.] **1.** The relation of one portion to another, or to the whole, or of one thing to another, as respects magnitude, quantity, or degree; ratio; loosely, size; extent; degree; *pl.* dimensions. **2.** A share; quota. **3.** Symmetrical arrangement; symmetry; harmony; balance. **4.** *Math.* **a** The equality of ratios, or a relation among quantities such that the quotient of the first divided by the second equals that of the third divided by the fourth, — holding in a geometrical series and called also ***geometric proportion.*** Proportion is expressed by symbols preferably thus: $a/b = c/d$. The forms $a:b::c:d$ and $a:b = c:d$ were formerly much used. **b** = RULE OF THREE. — *v. t.* **1.** To adjust in a suitable proportion or relation; as, to *proportion* a penalty to an offense. **2.** To form or arrange symmetrically.
pro·por′tion·a·ble (-ȧ·b'l), *adj.* *Rare.* That is in proportion or is duly proportioned; proportional.
pro·por′tion·al (-ăl), *adj.* **1.** Determined with reference to proportions; as, *proportional* distribution of pupils. **2.** Proportionate; in proportion; — with *to;* as, his skill is *proportional* to his experience. **3.** *Math.* Having the same or a constant ratio; as, *proportional* quantities. — *n.* *Math.* Any number or quantity in a proportion. — **pro·por′tion·al′i·ty** (-ăl′ĭ·tĭ), *n.* — **pro·por′tion·al·ly,** *adv.*
Syn. **Proportional, proportionate, commensurate, commensurable** mean duly proportioned to something else. **Proportional** and **proportionate** are often interchangeable, the former being preferred when applied to several closely related things, and the latter when applied to one thing that bears a reciprocal relationship to another; **commensurate** and **commensurable** stress an equality between things dependent on, similar to, or otherwise related to one another.
proportional representation. A system of voting whereby the representative bodies elected are in proportion to the number of voters, thus making it possible for minorities to have representation in government. Abbr. *P. R.*
pro·por′tion·ate (-ĭt), *adj.* Being in proportion; proportionally adjusted; — now usually with *to;* as, representation *proportionate* to the population. — **Syn.** See PROPORTIONAL. — (-āt), *v. t.* To make proportionate; to proportion. — **pro·por′tion·ate·ly** (-ĭt·lĭ), *adv.*
pro·por′tion·ment (-mĕnt), *n.* A proportioning, or state of being proportioned.
pro·pos′al (prō·pōz′ăl; -'l), *n.* **1.** A proposing, or setting forth for consideration. **2.** Something proposed; an offer; a proposition; a scheme, a plan, a bid, or the like.
pro·pose′ (prō·pōz′), *v. t.* [F. *proposer*, fr. *pro-* (fr. L. *pro*) + *poser* to place.] **1.** To set before the mind; to state; propound; also, to picture in the mind. **2.** To offer for consideration or adoption; as, to *propose* terms of peace. **3.** To purpose; intend. **4.** To offer as a toast; to suggest drinking (as a toast). **5.** To nominate for membership. — *v. i.* **1.** To form or declare a plan or intention; as, man *proposes*, but God disposes. **2.** To make an offer of marriage. — **pro·pos′er** (-pōz′ẽr), *n.*
prop′o·si′tion (prŏp′ō·zĭsh′ŭn), *n.* [OF., fr. L. *propositio.*] **1.** *Archaic.* Act of setting or placing forth; act of offering. **2.** That which is proposed; proposal. **3.** *Colloq.* **a** A project or affair involving some action; as, in mining, an alluvial *proposition.* **b** A business undertaking; also, a commodity for marketing. **4.** *Logic.* An expression of anything which is capable of being believed, doubted, or denied; a verbal expression which is either true or false; statement. **5.** *Math.* A formal statement of a truth to be demonstrated, or of an operation to be performed, — in the first case called a *theorem;* in the second, a *problem.* **6.** *Rhet.* In argument, the point to be discussed or maintained, usually stated in sentence form near the outset. — **prop′o·si′tion·al** (-ăl; -'l), *adj.*
pro·pos′i·tus (prō·pŏz′ĭ·tŭs), *n.* [L.] *Law.* Literally, the person proposed; specif., the one whose relations are sought to be ascertained by a genealogical table. See CONSANGUINITY, *Illust.*
pro·pound′ (prō·pound′), *v. t.* [From earlier *propone*, fr. L. *proponere, -positum*, to set forth, propound, fr. *pro* for, before + *ponere* to put.] To offer for consideration; propose. — **pro·pound′er,** *n.*

pro·prae′tor, pro·pre′tor (prō·prē′tŏr), *n.* [L. *propraetor*, fr. *pro* for, before + *praetor* praetor.] *Rom. Hist.* A magistrate who, having served as praetor at Rome, was sent out to govern a province.

pro·pri′e·tar′y (prō·prī′ĕ·tĕr′ĭ *or, esp. Brit.,* -tĕr·ĭ), *n.; pl.* -IES (-ĭz). [ML. *proprietarius.*] **1.** A proprietor; owner; specif., *Amer. Hist.,* an owner or grantee of a proprietary colony. **2.** A body of property owners. **3.** *Pharm.* A nonpatented medicine the formula of which is kept secret except for the narcotic and poisonous ingredients. — *adj.* **1.** Of or pert. to a proprietary or proprietor; appertaining to, or holding, property; as, *proprietary* control. **2.** *U. S.* Made and marketed by a person having the exclusive right to manufacture and sell it; as, a *proprietary* medicine.

proprietary colony. *Amer. Hist.* A colony which had been granted to some individual or individuals with the fullest prerogatives of government.

pro·pri′e·tor (prō·prī′ĕ·tēr), *n.* [For older *proprietary.*] **1.** One who has the legal right or exclusive title to anything; an owner; also, in a wider sense, a person having an interest less than an absolute and exclusive right, as the usufruct, or present control and use, of property; as, the *proprietor* of the village inn. **2.** Specif., *Amer. Hist.,* a proprietary. — **pro·pri′e·tor·ship′**, *n.* — **pro·pri′e·tress**, *n.*

pro·pri′e·ty (-tĭ), *n.; pl.* -TIES (-tĭz). [OF. *proprieté.* See PROPERTY.] **1.** *Obs.* Private property. **2. a** *Obs.* Peculiarity. **b** *Obs.* Peculiar or true nature or condition. **3.** Quality of being proper or fitting; suitability; fitness; as, to question the *propriety* of the procedure. **4.** A rule or code or, sometimes, a sense of what is proper or fitting; also, the observance of such a standard, etc.; decorum; as, to observe *propriety* in all things; hence, ***the proprieties,*** the customs and manners of polite society. — **Syn.** See DECORUM.

pro′pri·o·cep′tive (prō′prĭ·ō·sĕp′tĭv), *adj.* [L. *proprius* one's own + *-ceptive* as in *receptive.*] *Physiol.* Activated by, pert. to, or designating stimuli produced within the organism by movement in its own tissues, as in muscle sense. Cf. INTEROCEPTIVE, EXTEROCEPTIVE.

pro′pri·o·cep′tor (-tēr), *n.* [NL.] *Physiol.* An internal receptor for stimuli originating in a somatic organ.

‖**pro′pri·o mo′tu** (prō′prĭ·ō mō′tū). [L.] = MOTU PROPRIO.

prop root. *Bot.* Any root which serves as a prop or support to the plant, as in maize or the mangrove.

prop·to′sis (prŏp·tō′sĭs), *n.* [NL., fr. Gr. *proptōsis* a fall forward.] *Med.* Protrusion, esp. of the eyeball.

pro·pul′sion (prō·pŭl′shŭn), *n.* [F. See PROPEL.] **1.** Act of driving forward or ahead; a propelling; as, steam *propulsion* of ships. **2.** Something that propels.

pro·pul′sive (-sĭv), *adj.* Tending, or having power, to propel; driving onward or forward; that impels.

pro′pyl (prō′pĭl), *n.* [*propionic* + *-yl.*] *Chem.* The univalent radical C_3H_7, of which propane is the hydride.

prop′y·lae′um (prŏp′ĭ·lē′ŭm), *n.; pl.* -LAEA (-ȧ). [L., fr. Gr. *propylaion,* fr. *pro-* + *pylē* gate.] *Classical Arch.* Any vestibule or entrance of architectural importance before a building or enclosure; — often in *pl.*

pro′pyl·ene gly′col (prō′pĭ·lēn glī′kōl; -kŏl). *Chem.* A sweet, colorless, viscous liquid, $C_3H_8O_2$, made from petroleum and otherwise, used as an antifreeze, germicide, solvent, etc.

prop′y·lite (prŏp′ĭ·līt), *n.* [Gr. *propylon* gateway + *-ite.*] *Petrog.* An altered form of andesite, important for its connection with certain ore deposits.

pro ra′ta (prō rā′tȧ; rä′tȧ). [L.] In proportion; proportionately; according to share or liability.

pro·rat′a·ble (prō·rāt′ȧ·b'l), *adj.* That can be prorated.

pro′rate′ (prō′rāt′; prō′rāt′), *v. t. & i.* [L. *pro rata* (sc. *parte*).] *Chiefly U. S.* To divide or distribute proportionally; to assess pro rata.

pro·ra′tion (prō·rā′shŭn), *n.* Act or instance of prorating; specif., limitation of the quantity of oil produced by each operator to some fractional part of his total productive capacity.

pro′ro·ga′tion (prō′rō·gā′shŭn), *n.* [F. or L.; F., fr. L. *prorogatio* prolongation, postponement.] A proroguing; specif., act of proroguing a deliberative body.

pro·rogue′ (prō·rōg′), *v. t.;* PRO·ROGUED′ (-rōgd′); PRO·RO′GUING (-rō′gĭng). [F. *proroger,* fr. L. *prorogare, -gatum,* to prolong, defer, fr. *pro-* + *rogare* to ask.] **1.** *Obs.* To postpone. **2.** *Parl. Practice.* To defer or end officially the meeting of (a legislative assembly); *Brit. Parl. Practice,* to end the session of (a parliament) by an order of the crown or of the representative of the crown. — **Syn.** See ADJOURN.

pro·sa′ic (prō·zā′ĭk), *adj.* [ML. *prosaicus,* fr. L. *prosa* prose. See PROSE.] **1.** Of or pertaining to prose; now, usually, characteristic of prose as distinguished from poetry. **2.** Dull; commonplace; humdrum. — **pro·sa′i·cal·ly** (-ĭ·kăl·ĭ), *adv.*

pro′sa·ism (prō′zā·ĭz'm), *n.* Quality of being prosaic; also, a prosaic phrase or expression.

pro·sce′ni·um (prō·sē′nĭ·ŭm), *n.* [L., fr. Gr. *proskēnion,* fr. *pro-* + *skēnē* tent, stage.] **1.** *Anc. Theater.* The stage. **2.** *Theater.* The part of the stage in front of the curtain; sometimes, the curtain and its framework.

pro·scribe′ (prō·skrīb′), *v. t.* [L. *proscribere, -scriptum,* to write before, publish, proscribe, fr. *pro-* + *scribere* to write.] **1.** *Rom. Antiq.* To publish or post the name of, as one whose property is forfeited or one condemned to death. **2.** To outlaw. **3.** To denounce and condemn; to interdict; as, to *proscribe* smoking. — **pro·scrib′er** (-skrīb′ēr), *n.*

pro·scrip′tion (-skrĭp′shŭn), *n.* **1.** *Chiefly Hist.* Act of proscribing. **2.** Interdiction; prohibition; hence, an imposed restriction. — **pro·scrip′tive** (-tĭv), *adj.* — **pro·scrip′tive·ly**, *adv.*

prose (prōz), *n.* [OF., fr. L. *prosa, prosa oratio,* fr. *prorsus, prosus,* straight on, fr. *proversus,* fr. *pro* forward + *versus,* past part. of *vertere* to turn.] **1.** The ordinary language in speaking or writing; — opposed to *verse* and to *poetry.* **2.** Unimpassioned or unimaginative discourse or expression. **3.** *R.C.Ch.* See SEQUENCE. — *adj.* **1.** Of or pert. to prose. **2.** Prosaic; ordinary; unembellished. — *v. t. & i.* To write, translate, or paraphrase in prose.

pro·sec′tor (prō·sĕk′tēr), *n.* [LL., an anatomist, fr. *prosecare* to cut up, fr. *pro-* + *secare* to cut.] One who makes dissections for anatomical demonstrations.

pros′e·cute (prŏs′ē·kūt), *v. t.* [L. *prosecutus,* past part. of *prosequi* to follow, pursue. See PURSUE.] **1.** To follow to the end; to pursue until finished; as, to *prosecute* the investigation. **2.** To engage in; to carry on; as, he will continue to *prosecute* his practice of the law. **3.** *Law.* **a** To seek to obtain, enforce, or the like, by legal process; as, to *prosecute* a claim. **b** To pursue (a person) by legal proceedings for redress or punishment, esp. because of some crime or breach of law. — *v. i. Law.* To institute and carry on a legal suit or prosecution; to sue.

pros′e·cut′ing at·tor′ney (-kūt′ĭng). *Law.* The attorney who conducts proceedings, esp. of a criminal nature, in a court on behalf of the government; a public prosecutor.

pros′e·cu′tion (prŏs′ē·kū′shŭn), *n.* **1.** Act or process of prosecuting; as, bent on the *prosecution* of his aims; during the *prosecution* of the inquiry. **2.** *Law.* **a** The institution and carrying on of a suit or proceeding in a court of law or equity, specif. of a criminal suit. **b** The party by whom criminal proceedings are instituted or conducted.

pros′e·cu′tor (prŏs′ē·kū′tēr), *n.* **1.** One who prosecutes. **2.** *Law.* **a** One who institutes an official prosecution before a court. **b** A public prosecuting attorney.

pros′e·lyte (prŏs′ē·līt), *n.* [OF. *proselite,* fr. LL. *proselytus,* fr. Gr. *prosēlytos,* orig., a newcomer, an alien.] A new convert, esp. to some religious sect, or to some opinion, system, or party. — **Syn.** See CONVERT. — *v. t. & i.* To convert; to make a proselyte of; to make proselytes.

pros′e·lyt·ism (-līt·ĭz'm; -lĭ·tĭz'm), *n.* **1.** Act or fact of becoming a proselyte. **2.** Act, practice, or result of proselyting, or making converts.

pros′e·lyt·ize (-līt·īz; -lĭ·tīz), *v. t. & i.* To proselyte.

pros′en·ceph′a·lon (prŏs′ĕn·sĕf′ȧ·lŏn), *n.* [NL., fr. Gr. *pros* toward, near to + E. *encephalon.*] See FOREBRAIN. — **pros′en·ce·phal′ic** (-sē·făl′ĭk), *adj.*

pros·en′chy·ma (prŏs·ĕng′kĭ·mȧ), *n.* [NL., fr. Gr. *pros* near + *parenchyma.*] *Bot.* One of two general types of tissue distinguishable in higher plants; — disting. from *parenchyma* in consisting of elongated cells, mostly with little living protoplasm. — **pros′en·chym′a·tous** (prŏs′ĕng·kĭm′ȧ·tŭs), *adj.*

pros′er (prōz′ēr), *n.* A writer of prose; also, one who talks or writes tediously.

Pro·ser′pi·na (prō·sûr′pĭ·nȧ), **Pros′er·pine** (prŏs′ēr·pīn *or, erroneously,* prō·sûr′pĭ·nē; *formerly also* prō·sûr′pĭn), *n.* Persephone.

‖**pro′sit** (prō′sĭt; *G.* -zĭt), *interj.* [L., 3d pers. sing. subj. present of *prodesse* to do good, fr. *pro* for + *esse* to be.] Literally, may it do (you) good; — a salutation in drinking healths.

pro·slav′er·y (prō·slāv′ēr·ĭ), *adj.* Favoring slavery; specif., *U. S. Hist.,* favoring noninterference with the institution of Negro slavery. — *n.* Advocacy of slavery.

pros′o·dist (prŏs′ō·dĭst), *n.* One versed in prosody.

pros′o·dy (-dĭ), *n.* [L. *prosodia,* fr. Gr. *prosōidia* a song with accompaniment, the tone or accent of a syllable, fr. *pros* to + *ōidē* song, ode.] The science or art of versification; specif.: **a** The systematic study of metrical structure, including varieties of poetic feet and meters, rhymes and rhyming patterns, types of stanzas and strophes, and fixed forms. **b** A particular system or theory of versification or of metrical composition; as, Horace's *prosody.*

☞ The principal symbols for representing features of prosody are: ′ ictus or accent; ˙ secondary accent; | a division between feet. Thus, My lóve|is líke|a réd,|red róse. In quantitative verse: ⏑ – is for an iamb; – ⏑ a trochee; – ⏑ ⏑ a dactyl; ⏑ ⏑ – an anapaest; – – a spondee; ⏑⏑ ⏑ or – ⏑⏑ a slightly shortened dactyl; ⏑ ⏑ – or ⏑⏑ – a slightly shortened anapaest.

— **pro·so′di·ac** (prō·sō′dĭ·ăk), **pros′o·di′a·cal** (prŏs′ō·dī′ȧ·kăl), *adj.* — **pro·sod′ic** (prō·sŏd′ĭk), **pro·sod′i·cal** (-ĭ·kăl), *adj.*

pro·so′po·poe′ia (prō·sō′pō·pē′yȧ), *n.* [L., fr. Gr. *prosōpopoiia,* fr. *prosōpon* a face, a person + *poiein* to make.] *Rhet.* Personification.

pros′pect (prŏs′pĕkt), *n.* [L. *prospectus,* fr. *prospicere, -spectum,* to look forward, fr. *pro-* + *specere* to look, see.] **1.** An extensive view, esp. of landscape. **2.** Relative aspect; outlook; exposure. **3.** An extended region which the eye overlooks at one time; scene. **4. a** Act of looking forward; anticipation. **b** That which is hoped for; expectation; probable result. **5.** A prospective customer, contestant, candidate, applicant, etc. **6.** *Mining.* **a** An unproved mineral occurrence; also, the property on which the mineral is found. **b** A partly developed mine. **c** The gold or other mineral secured in testing a sample of ore or gravel. — ***in prospect.*** That is expected or looked forward to; in view.

Syn. **Prospect, outlook, anticipation, foretaste** mean an advance realization of something to come. **Prospect** further implies expectation of an event, condition, or the like, of interest or of concern; **outlook,** a forecasting of the future; **anticipation,** a prospect or an outlook that involves advance suffering or enjoyment of that envisioned; **foretaste,** an advance experience, seldom in the imagination, which gives one a taste of what is or may be coming.

— *v. t. & i.* To explore or examine for something; as, to *prospect* a district for gold. — **pros′pec·tor** (prŏs′pĕk·tēr; prō·spĕk′tēr), *n.*

pro·spec′tive (prō·spĕk′tĭv), *adj.* That is in prospect; expected confidently. — **pro·spec′tive·ly**, *adv.*

pro·spec′tus (-tŭs), *n.* [L., a prospect, sight.] A preliminary statement of an enterprise, as a business undertaking, a literary work, a private school, etc., giving advance information calculated to arouse interest and win support.

pros′per (prŏs′pēr), *v. i.* [F. *prospérer,* fr. L. *prosperare,* fr. *prosper* or *prosperus.*] To succeed; thrive. — *v. t.* To render successful.

pros·per′i·ty (prŏs·pĕr′ĭ·tĭ), *n.; pl.* -TIES (-tĭz). Prosperous state or condition; successful progress; success.

Pros′per·o (prŏs′pēr·ō), *n.* In Shakespeare's *Tempest,* the Duke of Milan, who, being cast on an uninhabited island, by magic raises a tempest, in which his brother Antonio, who had deposed him, is shipwrecked upon the island. See ARIEL, CALIBAN.

pros′per·ous (prŏs′pēr·ŭs), *adj.* [AF., fr. OF. *prospere,* fr. L. *prosperus* or *prosper.*] **1.** That prospers; thriving; flourishing; successful. **2.** Favorable; auspicious. — **pros′per·ous·ly**, *adv.* — **pros′per·ous·ness**, *n.*

pros′tate (prŏs′tāt), *adj.* [Gr. *prostatēs* one who stands before, fr. *proïstanai* to set before, fr. *pro-* + *histanai* to set.] *Anat.* Designating a partly muscular, partly glandular body, the **prostate gland,** surrounding the commencement of the urethra of the male. — *n.* The prostate gland. — **pros·tat′ic** (prŏs·tăt′ĭk), *adj.*

pros′ta·to- (prŏs′tȧ·tō-), **prostat-.** *Med.* A combining form for *prostate,* as in **pros′ta·tec′to·my, pros′ta·tot′o·my.**

pros′the·sis (prŏs′thē·sĭs), *n.* [LL., fr. Gr. *prosthesis* an addition, fr. *pros* to + *tithenai* to put, place.] **1.** The addition to the human body of some artificial part, as a leg, eye, or tooth. **2.** *Gram.* The addition, esp. the prefixing, of a sound or syllable to a word (*be*loved; *y*-clad). — **pros·thet'ic** (prŏs·thĕt'ĭk), *adj.*

pros·thet'ics (prŏs·thĕt'ĭks), *n.*; see -ICS. The branch of surgery or dentistry that treats of prosthesis. — **pros'the·tist** (prŏs'thē·tĭst), *n.*

pros'tho·don'ti·a (prŏs'thō·dŏn'shĭ·ȧ), *n.* [NL.] Prosthetic dentistry. — **pros'tho·don'tist** (-tĭst), *n.*

Pro·stig'min (prō·stĭg'mĭn), *n.* A registered trade-mark applied to a synthetic drug, $C_{13}H_{22}N_2O_6S$ or $C_{12}H_{19}N_2O_2Br$, used for the relief or prevention of postoperative intestinal and bladder atony and for the control of severe myasthenia.

pros'ti·tute (prŏs'tĭ·tūt), *v. t.* [L. *prostitutus*, past part. of *prostituere* to prostitute, fr. *pro-* + *statuere* to place.] **1.** To submit to promiscuous lewdness, esp. for hire. **2.** To devote to base or unworthy purposes; as, to *prostitute* one's talents. — *adj.* [L. *prostitutus*, *-a*, past part.] Prostituted; now, chiefly, devoted to base purposes or ends; corrupt. — *n.* A woman given to indiscriminate lewdness for hire; a harlot. — **pros'ti·tu'tor** (-tū'tẽr), *n.*

pros'ti·tu'tion (-tū'shŭn), *n.* **1.** Act or practice of prostituting; as, the *prostitution* of one's abilities. **2.** Common and venal lewdness among a class of women.

pros'trate (prŏs'trāt), *adj.* [L. *prostratus*, past part. of *prosternere* to prostrate, fr. *pro-* + *sternere* to throw down.] **1.** Reclining with face on the ground in humble adoration; as, worshipers *prostrate* before an idol; hence, lying prone or supine. **2.** Thrown down; fallen prone; also, laid low; overthrown. **3.** *Bot.* Trailing on the ground; procumbent. — **Syn.** See PRONE. — (prŏs'trāt; *formerly, & still by some, esp. Brit.*, prŏs·trāt'), *v. t.* **1.** To throw prostrate; as, to *prostrate* oneself before an altar. **2.** To reduce to submission, exhaustion, or the like; as, business *prostrated* by a panic.

pros·tra'tion (prŏs·trā'shŭn), *n.* **1.** Act of prostrating, or state or fact of being prostrated. **2.** Complete exhaustion, impotence, or dejection.

pros'y (prōz'ĭ), *adj.*; PROS'I·ER (-ĭ·ẽr); -I·EST. **1.** Of or pert. to prose; prosaic. **2.** Dull and tedious. — **pros'i·ly**, *adv.* — **pros'i·ness**, *n.*

prot-. = PROTO-.

prot'ac·tin'i·um (prōt'ăk·tĭn'ĭ·ŭm), *n.* [NL.] See PROTOACTINIUM.

pro·tag'o·nist (prō·tăg'ō·nĭst), *n.* [Gr. *prōtagōnistēs*, fr. *prōtos* first + *agōnistēs* an actor, fr. *agōnizesthai* to struggle.] One who takes the leading part in a drama, novel, or story; hence, an active participant or leader.

pro'ta·mine (prō'tȧ·mēn; -mĭn), *n.* Also **pro'ta·min.** [See PROTO-; AMINE.] *Biochem.* Any of a class of proteins, strongly basic, noncoagulable by heat, and soluble in ammonia, yielding certain amino acids on hydrolysis.

prot'a·sis (prŏt'ȧ·sĭs), *n.* [L., fr. Gr. *protasis*, fr. *proteinein* to stretch before, forward, fr. *pro-* + *teinein* to stretch.] **1.** The introductory part of a play, preceding the epitasis. **2.** *Gram.* The subordinate clause expressing the condition in a conditional sentence; — distinguished from *apodosis.*

pro'te·an (prō'tē·ăn; prō·tē'ăn), *adj.* **1.** [*cap.*] Of or pertaining to, or characteristic of, Proteus. **2.** Exceedingly variable; readily assuming different shapes or forms.

pro'te·ase (prō'tē·ās), *n.* [*protein* + *-ase.*] *Biochem.* Any proteolytic enzyme.

pro·tect' (prō·tĕkt'), *v. t.* [L. *protectus*, past part. of *protegere*, lit., to cover in front, fr. *pro-* + *tegere* to cover.] **1.** To cover or shield from injury or destruction; to defend; guard. **2.** *Com. & Finance.* To see that (a note, draft, or other obligation) is paid or satisfied at maturity (114 *U. S.* 587); as, the consolidated company agreed to *protect* the bonds of the individual companies. **3.** *Econ.* To guard, shield, or foster by a protective tariff. — **Syn.** See DEFEND.

pro·tect'ed cruis'er (-tĕk'tĕd; -tĭd). A cruiser with no side or vertical armor, but with an armored deck.

pro·tect'ing, *adj.* Serving to protect or shield. — **pro·tect'ing·ly**, *adv.* — **pro·tect'ing·ness**, *n.*

pro·tec'tion (prō·tĕk'shŭn), *n.* **1.** Act of protecting; state or fact of being protected. **2.** A protecting person or thing. **3.** A safe-conduct; a passport. **4.** Government, oversight, or support of a protector or patron. **5.** *Econ.* The freeing of the producers of a country from foreign competition in their home market by the imposition of such duties on goods of foreign origin as will restrict or prevent their importation; also, the theory, policy, or system (called ***protective system***) favoring or practicing the imposition of such duties; — opposed to *free trade.*

pro·tec'tion·ism (prō·tĕk'shŭn·ĭz'm), *n.* *Econ.* The doctrine or policy of protection. — **pro·tec'tion·ist** (-ĭst), *n.*

pro·tec'tive (prō·tĕk'tĭv), *adj.* **1.** Protecting; affording protection; sometimes, self-protecting; as, *protective* coloring in birds. **2.** Based on or pertaining to the economic principles of protection. — **pro·tec'tive·ly**, *adv.*

protective tariff. *Econ.* A tariff protecting domestic producers, esp. one primarily designed to secure protection, as disting. from a tariff for revenue. See PROTECTION, 5.

pro·tec'tor (prō·tĕk'tẽr), *n.* **1.** One who protects; a defender; guardian; patron. **2.** Something serving to protect; a guard; as, a chest *protector.* **3.** *Eng. Hist.* **a** One having the care of the kingdom during the king's minority; a regent. **b** [*cap.*] Short for ***Lord Protector***, the title of Oliver Cromwell as head of the British Commonwealth (1653–1658), and of Richard Cromwell (1658–59). — **pro·tec'tor·ship**, *n.* — **pro·tec'tress**, *n.*

pro·tec'tor·ate (-ĭt), *n.* **1.** Government by a protector; also, the rank or office of a protector, or the period of his rule; esp. [*cap.*], the government of England (1653–59) under the Cromwells. **2.** A relation of authority assumed by one state over a dependent one, whereby the former protects the latter and shares in the management of its affairs; also, the authority so assumed, or the period of its exercise, or the country so protected.

pro·tec'to·ry (prō·tĕk'tō·rĭ), *n.* An institution for the protection of some class, as one for homeless children.

pro'té·gé (prō'tĕ·zhā; *F.* prō'tā'zhā'), *n. masc.*; *pl.* -GÉS (-zhāz; *F.* -zhā'); **pro'té·gée** (-zhā; *F.* -zhā'), *fem.*; *pl.* -GÉES (-zhāz; *F.* -zhā'). [F., past part.] One under the care and protection of another.

pro'te·ide (prō'tē·īd; -ĭd), **pro'te·id** (-ĭd), *n.* *Biochem.* Protein.

pro'te·in (prō'tē·ĭn; -tēn), *n.* [G. *protein*, fr. Gr. *prōteios* primary, holding first place.] **1.** *Biochem.* Any of a class of naturally occurring complex combinations of amino acids (containing carbon, hydrogen, nitrogen, oxygen, and usually sulfur), which are essential constituents of all living cells and also of the diet of the animal organism (see FOOD, *n.*, 1). They can be synthesized from nonamino nitrogenous material by plants, but apparently not by animals. **2.** The total nitrogenous material in vegetable or animal substance. — **pro'te·in**, *adj.*

pro'te·in·ase (prō'tē·ĭn·ās; -āz), *n.* *Biochem.* Any proteolytic enzyme.

pro tem'po·re (prō tĕm'pō·rē). [L.] For the time being; temporarily. Abbr. *pro tem.*

pro'te·ol'y·sis (prō'tē·ŏl'ĭ·sĭs), *n.* [NL., fr. *prote*id + *-lysis.*] *Biochem.* Splitting or hydrolysis of proteins with formation of simpler and soluble products, as in digestion. — **pro'te·o·lyt'ic** (-ō·lĭt'ĭk), *adj.*

pro'te·ose (prō'tē·ōs), *n.* [*prote*in + *-ose.*] *Biochem.* Any of a class of intermediate soluble protein derivatives formed by digestion with gastric and pancreatic juice, and also by the hydrolytic action of boiling dilute acids and alkalies, etc.; an albumose.

Prot'er·o·zo'ic (prŏt'ẽr·ō·zō'ĭk), *adj.* [Gr. *proteros* before, former + *zōē* life.] Of, pertaining to, or designating a division of geological history from the Archeozoic to the Paleozoic, or the rocks formed during this time. Fossils indicate the existence of annelid worms and of algae in this era. — **Prot'er·o·zo'ic**, *n.*

pro·test' (prō·tĕst'), *v. t.* [OF. *protester*, fr. L. *protestari*, fr. *pro-* + *testari* to be a witness, fr. *testis* witness.] **1.** To assert; affirm; aver. **2.** To make a protest against; as, to *protest* a witness. **3.** *Obs.* To call as a witness. **4.** To make a protest of (a bill of exchange or promissory note) with due service of notice of dishonor; — said of the notary or a party in interest. See PROTEST, *n.*, 3 **a**. — *v. i.* **1.** To make a protestation; to declare solemnly that one is telling truth. **2.** To enter a protest; object formally; dissent. — **Syn.** See ASSERT; OBJECT. — **pro·test'er**, *n.*

pro'test (prō'tĕst), *n.* **1.** A protestation; expostulation; complaint; also, an objection or remonstrance. **2.** A formal objection, as in writing, against some act, proceeding, condition, or the like; as, to pay a bill under *protest.* **3.** *Law.* **a** Strictly, a declaration in writing, made by a notary public on behalf of the holder of a bill or note, protesting against all parties liable for any loss or damage by the nonacceptance or nonpayment of the bill, or by the nonpayment of the note, as the case may be; popularly, the making of, or procuring to be made, such a declaration with due service of notice of dishonor. **b** A declaration made by the master of a vessel before a notary, consul, or other authorized officer, upon his arrival in port after a disaster, showing that any damage or loss sustained was not owing to the fault of the vessel, her officers, or crew. **c** A declaration made by a party, as before or while paying a tax, duty, or the like, which he deems illegal, to show that his action is not voluntary. **4.** *Sports.* An objection lodged with an official, as one against a player because of ineligibility.

prot'es·tant (prŏt'ĕs·tănt; prŏt'ĭs-; *in sense* 2 *also* prō·tĕs'tănt), *n.* [F., fr. L. *protestans*, *-antis*, pres. part. See PROTEST, *v.*] **1.** [*cap.*] **a** Originally, one of those German princes who submitted at the Diet of Spires (1529) a protest against an edict intended to crush the reform movement, and calling upon the emperor to summon a general council. **b** During the seventeenth century, an adherent of Lutheranism or Anglicanism; — not including, as later, Puritans, Presbyterians, and other dissenters. **c** Any Christian not of the Roman Catholic Church or the Eastern Church. The designation is rejected by many members of the churches of the Anglican Communion. **2.** One who makes or enters a protest. — (prŏt'ĕs·tănt; prŏt'ĭs-; *in sense* 1 *also* prō·tĕs'tănt), *adj.* **1.** Making a protest. **2.** [*cap.*] Of or pertaining to Protestants or their faith and practice.

Protestant Episcopal Church. The religious body which represents in the United States the Anglican Communion, organized as distinct from the Church of England in 1789.

prot'es·tant·ism (prŏt'ĕs·tănt·ĭz'm; prŏt'ĭs-), *n.* Quality or state of being protestant; specif. [*cap.*]: **a** State of being a Protestant; the principles or religion of the Protestants. **b** Protestants collectively.

prot'es·ta'tion (prŏt'ĕs·tā'shŭn), *n.* **1.** Act of protesting, or solemnly declaring true, existent, or the like; a public avowal; as, *protestations* of friendship. **2.** *Now Rare.* A protest; dissent.

Pro'teus (prō'tūs; -tē·ŭs), *n.* [L., fr. Gr. *Prōteus.*] *Gr. Myth.* A prophetic sea-god in the service of Poseidon. When seized, he would assume different shapes. Hence, one who easily changes his appearance or principles.

pro'tha·la'mi·on (prō'thȧ·lā'mĭ·ŏn), *n.*; *pl.* -MIA (-ȧ). Also **pro'tha·la'mi·um** (-ŭm); *pl.* -MIA. [NL., fr. Gr. *pro* before + *thalamos* (bridal) chamber.] A song in celebration of a marriage.

pro·thal'li·um (prō·thăl'ĭ·ŭm), *n.*; *pl.* -LIA (-ȧ). [NL.] *Bot.* The minute, reduced, thalloid gametophyte of the ferns and their allies (Pteridophyta). The prothallium bears sex organs (archegonia and antheridia). — **pro·thal'li·al** (-ăl), **pro·thal'line** (-thăl'ĭn; -īn), *adj.*

proth'e·sis (prŏth'ē·sĭs), *n.* [NL., fr. Gr. *prothesis* a placing in public, fr. *protithenai* to set before.] **1.** *Eastern Church.* **a** In full ***office of prothesis.*** The preparation and preliminary oblation of the bread and wine prior to the Liturgy proper. **b** The table or altar on which this is done. **c** The chapel (northern part of the bema) where this is done. **2.** = PROSTHESIS, 1 & 2. — **pro·thet'ic** (prō·thĕt'ĭk), *adj.* — **pro·thet'i·cal·ly** (-ĭ·kăl·ĭ), *adv.*

pro·thon'o·tar'y (prō·thŏn'ō·tĕr'ĭ; -tẽr·ĭ; prō'thō·nō'-), **pro·ton'o·tar'y** (prō·tŏn'ō-; prō'tō·nō'-), *n.*; *pl.* -IES (-ĭz). [LL. *protonotarius*, fr. Gr. *prōtos* first + L. *notarius* a scribe.] **1.** A chief notary or clerk. **2.** *R.C.Ch.* One of the seven members of the College of Prothonotaries Apostolic, who keep the records of consistories and canonizations and who sign the papal bulls; also, any of certain ecclesiastics holding this title as an honorary title. **3.** *Law.* A register or chief clerk of a court in certain states of the United States. — **pro·thon'o·tar'i·al** (prō·thŏn'ō·târ'ĭ·ăl; 6), *adj.*

pro·tho'rax (prō·thō'răks), *n.* [NL.] *Zool.* The anterior segment of the thorax of insects. See INSECT, *Illust.* — **pro'tho·rac'ic** (prō'thō·răs'ĭk), *adj.*

pro·throm'bin (prō·thrŏm'bĭn), *n.* = THROMBOGEN.

pro'tist (prō'tĭst), *n.* [Gr. *prōtistos* first.] *Biol.* Any one of the unicellular organisms collectively (Protista), including both protozoans and unicellular plants. — **pro·tis'tan** (prō·tĭs'tăn), *adj.* & *n.* — **pro·tis'tic** (-tĭk), *adj.*

pro'ti·um (prō'tĭ·ŭm; -shĭ·ŭm), *n.* [NL., fr. *prot-* + *-ium.*] *Chem.* The ordinary hydrogen isotope of mass number unity. Symbol, H^1

pro'to- (prō'tō-), **prot-.** [Gr. *prōtos.*] A combining form meaning *first*, used to denote: **1. a** *First in time*, as in *proto*col, *proto*type. **b** *First in status; chief in rank* or *importance; principal; chief; arch-*; as in *proto*notary. **2.** *Earliest among the forms that may be classed as* (specified); *original; primitive*; as in: **pro'to–Ar'yan, pro'to–Hel·len'ic.** **3.** *Astron. & Chem.* Short for PROTOMETALLIC. See PROTOMETALS. **4.** *Chem.* **a** The *first* or *lowest of a series*, or the one having (or supposed to have) the *smallest relative amount* of the element or radical indicated in the name to which it is prefixed, as in *protoxide*. **b** A substance that is held to be the *parent* of the substance to the name of which it is prefixed.

pro′to·ac·tin′i·um (prō′tō·ăk·tĭn′ĭ·ŭm), *n.* [NL.] *Chem.* A radioelement which by disintegration yields actinium. Symbol, *Pa*; at. no., 91; at. wt., 231. *Protactinium* is now the preferred spelling.

pro′to·col (prō′tō·kŏl), *n.* [F. *protocole*, fr. ML., fr. Gr. *prōtokollon* the first leaf glued to the rolls of papyrus and the notarial documents, fr. *prōtos* first + *kolla* glue.] **1.** An original copy, draft, minute, or record of a document or transaction. **2.** *Diplomacy.* A preliminary memorandum, as of resolutions arrived at in negotiation, often signed by the negotiators, as a basis for a final convention or treaty. **3.** The rules prescribing the etiquette in ceremonies of state; the code prescribing deference to rank and strict adherence to due order of preference and correct procedure, as in diplomatic exchange and ceremonies. — *v. i.* To make or write protocols.

pro′to·gine (-jĭn; -jēn), *n.* [F., fr. Gr. *prōtos* first + root of *gignesthai* to be born.] *Petrog.* An Alpine granite of gneissoid texture.

pro′to·lith′ic (prō′tō·lĭth′ĭk), *adj.* Designating, or pert. to, the earliest stone age; eolithic. See PALEOLITHIC.

pro′to·mar′tyr (-mär′tēr), *n.* [ML., fr. Gr. *prōtomartyr*.] The first martyr in any cause; — applied esp. to Stephen, the first Christian martyr.

pro′to·met′als (-mĕt′′lz), *n. pl.* *Physics & Chem.* Metals in a hypothetical form, indicated by certain spectral characteristics obtained at the highest available laboratory temperatures; as, ***pro′to·cal′ci·um, pro′to·mag·ne′si·um, pro′to·man′ga·nese.*** — **pro′to·me·tal′lic** (-mē·tăl′ĭk), *adj.*

pro′to·mor′phic (-môr′fĭk), *adj.* [*proto-* + *-morphic.*] *Biol.* Primitive. — **pro′to·morph** (prō′tō·môrf), *n.*

pro′ton (prō′tŏn), *n.* [NL., fr. Gr. *prōton*, neut. of *prōtos* first.] *Physics & Chem.* Nucleus of the atom of the light isotope of hydrogen, constituting the principal part of its mass and exhibiting a unit positive charge of electricity. It is believed to be a nuclear constituent of all atoms. Symbol, *p* or H^{1+} (no period) See ELECTRON.

pro′to·ne′ma (prō′tō·nē′mȧ), *n.*; *pl.* -MATA (-tȧ). [NL., fr. *proto-* + Gr. *nēma*, *nēmatos*, a thread.] *Bot.* The primary growth or thalloid stage of the gametophyte in mosses, corresponding somewhat to the prothallium in ferns.

pro·ton′o·tar′y. Var. of PROTHONOTARY.

pro′to·path′ic (prō′tō·păth′ĭk), *adj.* *Physiol. & Psychol.* Designating or pertaining to a primitive type of cutaneous reception or receptor, capable of only gross sensory discrimination. Cf. EPICRITIC.

pro′to·phlo′em (-flō′ĕm), *n.* *Bot.* The first-formed phloem developing from the procambium, consisting of narrow, thin-walled cells capable of a limited amount of stretching, and hence esp. suited to a region of rapid growth. Cf. PROTOXYLEM; see PHLOEM.

pro′to·plasm (prō′tō·plăz′m), *n.* [G. *protoplasma*, fr. Gr. *prōtos* first + *plasma* form, fr. *plassein* to mold.] *Biol.* **a** Orig., the formative material of animal embryos. **b** Later, cytoplasm. **c** Now, commonly, the essential substance both of the cell body and nucleus of cells of animals and plants, regarded as the only form of matter in which the phenomena of life are manifested. Protoplasm ordinarily is a viscous translucent material holding fine granules in suspension. — **pro′to·plas′mic** (-plăz′mĭk), *adj.*

pro′to·plast (-plăst), *n.* [Through F., fr. LL. *protoplastus* the first man, fr. Gr. *protoplastos* formed or created first, fr. *prōtos* first + *plastos* formed.] **1.** One that was first formed; specif., the hypothetical original ancestor or pair of ancestors of any species. **2.** *Biol.* **a** The protoplasmic cell contents, considered as a vital unit. **b** A plastid. — **pro′to·plas′tic** (-plăs′tĭk), *adj.*

pro′to·stele′ (-stēl′; -stē′lē), *n.* *Bot.* The solid stele characteristic of most roots and of the earliest portions of stems. See STELE. — **pro′to·ste′lic** (-stē′lĭk), *adj.*

pro′to·troph′ic (-trŏf′ĭk), *adj.* [*proto-* + *trophic.*] *Physiol.* Deriving nutriment from uncombined elements, as the nitrogen-fixing bacteria.

pro′to·type (prō′tō·tīp), *n.* [F., fr. NL., fr. Gr. *prōtotypon*, deriv. of *prōtos* first + *typos* type, model.] **1.** An original or model after which anything is copied; pattern; archetype. **2.** *Biol.* An ancestral form; an archetype. — **pro′to·typ′al** (-tīp′ăl), **pro′to·typ′ic** (-tĭp′ĭk), *adj.*

pro·tox′ide (prō·tŏk′sīd; -sĭd), *n.* Also **pro·tox′id.** [*prot-* + *oxide.*] *Chem.* That one of a series of oxides having the lowest proportion of oxygen (exclusive of suboxides).

pro′to·xy′lem (prō′tō·zī′lĕm), *n.* [*proto-* + *xylem.*] *Bot.* The first of the primary xylem (see XYLEM) to differentiate from the procambium. By some botanists, protoxylem is regarded as the primary xylem which differentiates from the procambium prior to any elongation of an organ.

pro′to·zo′a (prō′tō·zō′ȧ), *n.*, *pl.* of PROTOZOON.

pro′to·zo′an (prō′tō·zō′ăn), *n.*; *pl.* -ZOANS (-ănz). [*proto-* + Gr. *zōion* animal.] *Zool.* A member of a phylum (Protozoa) of animals whose chief characteristics are that the body consists of only a single cell and that they reproduce by fission. Most protozoans are too minute to be visible to the naked eye. They are mostly aquatic, abounding in the sea and in stagnant fresh water. Some are parasites. — **pro′to·zo′an** (-ăn), *adj.* — **pro′to·zo′ic** (-ĭk), *adj.*

pro′to·zo·ol′o·gy (-zō·ŏl′ō·jĭ), *n.* *Zool.* The study of the protozoa. — **pro′to·zo′o·log′i·cal** (-zō′ō·lŏj′ĭ·kăl), *adj.* — **pro′to·zo·ol′o·gist** (-zō·ŏl′ō·jĭst), *n.*

pro′to·zo′on (-zō′ŏn), *n.*; *pl.* PROTOZOA (-ȧ). [NL.] *Zool.* A protozoan.

pro·tract′ (prō·trăkt′), *v. t.* [L. *protractus*, past part. of *protrahere* to draw forth, fr. *pro-* + *trahere* to draw.] **1.** To draw out or lengthen in time or (rarely) in space; to prolong. **2.** *Surv.* To lay down the lines and angles of, with scale and protractor; to plot. **3.** *Zool.* To extend or protrude; — opp. to *retract.* — **Syn.** See EXTEND. **pro·trac′tive** (-trăk′tĭv), *adj.*

pro·trac′tile (-trăk′tĭl; 56), *adj.* Capable of being thrust out or protracted; protrusile.

pro·trac′tion (-shŭn), *n.* **1.** The act or an instance of protracting; extension; prolongation. **2.** *Surv.* A making of a plan drawn to scale. **3.** *Prosody.* The prolonging of a syllable beyond its usual value.

pro·trac′tor (-tēr), *n.* **1.** One who protracts, prolongs, or delays. **2.** An instrument for laying down and measuring angles on paper, used in drawing and plotting.

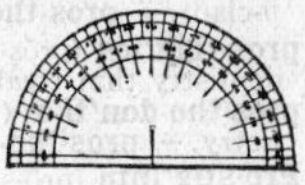
Protractor.

pro·trude′ (prō·trōōd′; 114), *v. t. & i.* [L. *protrudere*, *-trusum*, fr. *pro-* + *trudere* to thrust.] To thrust out; to project. — **pro·tru′si·ble** (-trōō′sĭ·b′l), *adj.*

pro·tru′sile (-trōō′sĭl; 56), *adj.* So made that it can be protruded or thrust out; as, a *protrusile* proboscis.

pro·tru′sion (prō·trōō′zhŭn; 114), *n.* A protruding; state of being protruded; that which protrudes or is protruded; as, the *protrusion* of its jaw. — **Syn.** See PROJECTION.

pro·tru′sive (-sĭv), *adj.* That protrudes or projects; protuberant; also, obtrusive in manner, speech, etc.; that forces attention. — **pro·tru′sive·ly**, *adv.*

pro·tu′ber·ance (prō·tū′bēr·ăns; 114), *n.* The quality, condition, or fact of being protuberant; also, that which is protuberant; a bulge. — **Syn.** See PROJECTION.

pro·tu′ber·an·cy (-ăn·sĭ), *n.* Protuberance.

pro·tu′ber·ant (-ănt), *adj.* [LL. *protuberans*, *-antis*, pres. part.] Bulging beyond the surrounding or adjacent surface; swelling. — **pro·tu′ber·ant·ly**, *adv.*

pro·tu′ber·ate (-āt), *v. i.* [LL. *protuberatus*, past part. of *protuberare* to bulge out, fr. L. *pro* forward + *tuber* a hump.] To bulge out.

pro′tyle (prō′tīl; -tĭl), *n.* Also **pro′tyl.** [*prot-* + Gr. *hylē* stuff, material.] *Chem. & Astron.* A hypothetical primordial substance supposedly differentiated into what are recognized as distinct chemical elements.

proud (proud), *adj.* [AS. *prūt*, *prūd*.] **1.** Feeling or manifesting pride; as: **a** Possessing or showing too great self-esteem; hence, arrogant; haughty. **b** Exulting (in); being highly pleased; — often with *of*; as, *proud* of one's country. **c** Having a feeling of proper self-respect or self-esteem. **2. a** *Obs.* Valiant. **b** Full of mettle; as, a *proud* steed. **3.** Giving reason or occasion for pride; admirable. **4.** Arising from, or produced by, pride; presumptuous. — **proud′ly**, *adv.*

Syn. (1) **Proud, arrogant, haughty, lordly, insolent, overbearing, supercilious, disdainful** mean exhibiting scorn for inferiors. **Proud**, not always derogatory, may imply imperiousness, conceit, or merely satisfaction; **arrogant** implies a disposition to claim more consideration than is due; **haughty**, consciousness of birth or station; **lordly**, pomposity or a display of power; **insolent**, haughtiness and contemptuousness; **overbearing**, intolerable insolence; **supercilious**, a manner that repels advances; **disdainful**, a more obvious and scornful superciliousness. (2) **Proud, vain, vainglorious** mean aware of one's excellence or superiority. **Proud** may imply justified or unjustified self-esteem; **vain**, an excessive desire to win the notice or praise of others; **vainglorious**, excessive vanity leading to boastfulness or an arrogant display of one's power, skill, influence, or the like.

proud flesh. *Med.* An abnormally abundant growth of granulation tissue in a wound or ulcer.

prov′a·ble (prōōv′ȧ·b′l), *adj.* That may be proved.

pro·vas′cu·lar tis′sue (prō·văs′kū·lēr). Procambium.

prove (prōōv), *v. t.*; PROVED (prōōvd); PROVED OR PROV′EN (prōōv′ĕn); PROV′ING. [OF. *prover*, fr. L. *probare* to try, approve, prove, fr. *probus* good, proper.] **1.** To try or to ascertain by an experiment or by a standard; to test; now, esp., to subject to a technical testing process; as, to *prove* cannon, gold, coal. **2.** *Archaic.* To know by trial; to experience. **3.** To establish or ascertain by argument or other evidence; to demonstrate; show. **4.** To ascertain or establish the genuineness or validity of; to verify; as, to *prove* a will. **5.** *Arith.* To test or verify, as the correctness of an operation or result. — *v. i.* **1.** *Obs.* To make trial; to essay. **2.** To be found by experience, trial, or result; to turn out to be; as, the report *proves* false.

prov′en (prōōv′ĕn), *adj.* Proved; esp., tried; tested; also, demonstrated.

prov′e·nance (prŏv′ē·năns), *n.* [F.] Origin; source.

Pro′ven·çal′ (prŏv′ĕn·säl′; prŏv′ĕn-; prō·vĕn′săl; *F.* prō′văN′sȧl′), *adj.* [F., fr. *Provence*, fr. L. *provincia* province.] Of or pertaining to Provence, its inhabitants, or their language. — *n.* **1.** A native or inhabitant of Provence. **2.** The Provençal language. From the 11th to the middle of the 14th century it was used in the lyric literature of the troubadours. See INDO-EUROPEAN LANGUAGES, *Table.*

prov′en·der (prŏv′ĕn·dēr; -ĭn·dēr), *n.* [OF. *provend(r)e*, fr. LL. *praebenda*. See PREBEND.] **1.** Dry food for domestic animals, as hay, oats, etc.; feed; specif., a mixture of ground oats and corn. **2.** *Now Humorous.* Food.

pro·ve′ni·ence (prō·vē′nĭ·ĕns; -vēn′yĕns; 58), *n.* [L. *proveniens*, *-entis*, pres. part. of *provenire* to come forth, fr. *pro* forth + *venire* to come.] Origin; source; provenance.

pro′ven·tric′u·lus (prō′vĕn·trĭk′ū·lŭs), *n.*; *pl.* -TRICULI (-lī). [NL.] *Zool.* In birds, the glandular or true stomach, situated between the crop and the gizzard.

prov′er (prōōv′ēr), *n.* One who proves; a tester.

prov′erb (prŏv′ûrb; -ērb), *n.* [OF. *proverbe*, fr. L. *proverbium*, fr. *pro-* + *verbum* word.] **1.** *Chiefly Bib.* A profound maxim; in Scriptural use, a parable; a truth couched obscurely. **2.** A brief epigrammatic saying that is a popular byword; a maxim; adage. **3.** A name, person, or thing that has become a byword. — *v. t.* **1.** To turn into a proverb; to make a byword of. **2.** To describe in or as in a proverb.

pro·ver′bi·al (prō·vûr′bĭ·ăl), *adj.* **1.** Of, pert. to, of the nature of, or characteristic of a proverb. **2.** That has become a proverb; commonly spoken of. — **pro·ver′bi·al·ly**, *adv.*

Prov′erbs (prŏv′ûrbz; -ērbz), *n. pl.*, *construed as sing.* A book of the Old Testament, containing wise maxims. See BIBLE.

pro·vide′ (prō·vīd′), *v. t.* [L. *providere*, *provisum*, fr. *pro-* + *videre* to see.] **1.** To look out for in advance; to procure beforehand. **2.** To supply for use; afford; yield. **3.** To furnish; stock. — *v. i.* **1.** To take precautionary measures in view of a possible need; — with *against* or *for*; as, to *provide* for his child's education. **2.** To make a proviso; to stipulate. **3.** To supply what is needed for sustenance; as, the Lord will *provide.*

pro·vid′ed (-vīd′ĕd; -ĭd), *conj.* It being provided; on condition; if; — often followed by *that.*

prov′i·dence (prŏv′ĭ·dĕns), *n.* **1.** *Obs. pron.* (prō·vīd′ĕns) The act of providing, exercising foresight, or preparing. **2.** Divine guidance or care; also, an act or instance of it. **3.** Prudence; economical character, policy, or habits; thrift. **4.** [*cap.*] God, conceived of as guiding men through his prescience, loving care, or intervention.

prov'i·dent (prŏv'ĭ·dĕnt), *adj.* [L. *providens, -entis,* pres. part. of *providere* to provide.] **1.** Making provision for the future. **2.** Prudent; frugal; saving. — **prov'i·dent·ly,** *adv.*

prov'i·den'tial (-dĕn'shăl), *adj.* **1.** Of, pert. to, or determined by Providence; as, *providential* guidance. **2.** That is or is like an intervention of Providence; lucky; highly opportune. — **Syn.** See LUCKY. — **prov'i·den'tial·ly,** *adv.*

pro·vid'er (prō·vīd'ẽr), *n.* One who provides.

pro·vid'ing (-ĭng), *conj.* In case that; provided.

prov'ince (prŏv'ĭns), *n.* [OF., fr. L. *provincia* duty, office, government of a province.] **1.** *Rom. Hist.* A region, remote from Rome, brought under Roman government. **2.** An administrative division of a country; as, the *provinces* of Prussia; specif.: **a** Any of those British colonies in America now united into the Dominion of Canada. **b** Before the Revolution, certain of the British colonies now a part of the United States. **3.** A region of country; a district. **4.** The proper business or duty of a person; jurisdiction; sphere. **5.** A department of knowledge or activity. **6.** *Usually pl.* A portion of a country, esp. one remote from the capital or largest city. In England, all of the country outside of London. **7.** *Biogeog.* Any division of less rank than a region. **8.** *Eccl.* A group of dioceses or, in England, a division of the country, over which an archbishop has jurisdiction. — **Syn.** See FUNCTION.

pro·vin'cial (prō·vĭn'shăl), *adj.* **1. a** Of, pert. to, or characteristic of a province. **b** Of or pert. to the provinces (esp. in British use), specif. the provinces of Canada. **2.** Exhibiting the ways or manners of a province; countrified; rude. **3.** Confined to a province; hence, narrow; limited; as, *provincial* interests. — *n.* A person belonging to a province; one who is provincial or who comes from the provinces. — **pro·vin'cial·ly,** *adv.*

pro·vin'cial·ism (-ĭz'm), *n.* **1.** Quality or state of being provincial. **2.** A characteristic, custom, etc., peculiar to a province or inhabitants of provinces. Specif., a word, or a manner of speaking, peculiar to a province.

pro·vin'ci·al'i·ty (prō·vĭn'shĭ·ăl'ĭ·tĭ), *n.* Provincialism.

prov'ing ground (proōv'ĭng). A place for scientific testing and experiment.

pro·vi'sion (prō·vĭzh'ŭn), *n.* [F., fr. L. *provisio.* See PROVIDE.] **1.** Act of providing, as the necessaries of life, or of preparing, as for a journey. **2.** That which is provided or prepared; preparation; provident care. **3.** Specif.: A store or stock of needed materials prepared beforehand; esp., a stock of food; hence, any kind of eatables collected or stored; food; — often in *pl.* **4.** That which is stipulated in advance; previous agreement; a proviso. — *v. t.* To supply with provisions esp. food.

pro·vi'sion·al (-ăl; -'l), *adj.* Of the nature of a temporary provision; adapted to present conditions, knowledge, etc., but subject to change; temporary; provisory; as, a *provisional* government. — *n. Philately.* A postage stamp issued for temporary use, as until a regular issue appears. — **pro·vi'sion·al·ly,** *adv.*

pro·vi'sion·ar'y (-ẽr'ĭ *or, esp. Brit.,* -ẽr·ĭ), *adj.* *Now Rare.* Provisional, or temporary.

pro·vi'sion·er (-ẽr), *n.* A furnisher of provisions.

pro·vi'so (prō·vī'zō), *n.; pl.* -SOS or -SOES (-zōz). [L., (it) being provided, abl. of *provisus,* past part. of *providere.* See PROVIDE.] An article or clause in any statute, contract, etc., by which a condition is introduced; a conditional stipulation.

pro·vi'so·ry (-zō·rĭ), *adj.* Provisional; conditional.

pro·vi'ta·min (prō·vī'tȧ·mĭn), *n.* [*pro-,* prefix meaning *undeveloped* (fr. L. *pro* before) + *vitamin.*] *Biochem.* A compound from which a vitamin is formed.

prov'o·ca'tion (prŏv'ō·kā'shŭn), *n.* [F., fr. L. *provocatio.*] The act or a cause of provoking; a challenge, cause of irritation, incitement, stimulus, etc.

pro·voc'a·tive (prō·vŏk'ȧ·tĭv), *adj.* Serving or tending to provoke, stimulate, or incense. — **pro·voc'a·tive,** *n.* — **pro·voc'a·tive·ly,** *adv.* — **pro·voc'a·tive·ness,** *n.*

pro·voke' (prō·vōk'), *v. t.* [F. *provoquer,* fr. L. *provocare* to call forth, fr. *pro-* + *vocare* to call.] **1.** *Obs.* To call forth; to summon. **2.** To excite (one), as to doing or feeling; to arouse. **3.** To incite to anger; to incense. **4.** To incite (emotion, action, activity, etc.); to stir up. — **pro·vok'er** (-vōk'ẽr), *n.* — **pro·vok'ing,** *adj.* — **pro·vok'ing·ly,** *adv.*

Syn. (1) **Provoke, excite, stimulate, pique, quicken** mean to arouse as if by pricking. **Provoke,** the least explicit term, suggests merely the result produced; **excite,** the rousing by stirring up or moving profoundly; **stimulate,** a rousing out of lethargy, indifference, or the like; **pique,** a stimulation by use of an irritant; **quicken,** a stimulation of vigor, energy, or the like, with beneficial result.
(2) See IRRITATE.

prov'ost (prŏv'ŭst; *mil.,* prō·vō'; *attrib.* prō'vō; 2), *n.* [From AS. *profost* (fr. LL.), and fr. OF. *provost,* fr. LL. *propositus,* for L. *praepositus* placed before, a chief. See PREPOSITION.] **1.** A superintendent; an official head. **2.** In Scottish burghs, the chief magistrate. **3.** *Obs.* The keeper of a prison. **4.** *Eccl.* The head of a cathedral or collegiate chapter. **5.** *Educ.* **a** The head of any of various English colleges. **b** In some American universities, a high administrative officer in charge of strictly educational activities. **6.** *Mil.* An officer of the military police. — **prov'ost·ship,** *n.*

pro'vost court (prō'vō; 2). *Mil.* A military court usually for the trial of minor offenses committed by either soldiers or civilians within an occupied hostile territory.

pro'vost guard (prō'vō; 2). *Mil.* A police detail of soldiers, under the authority of the provost marshal.

pro'vost mar'shal (prō'vō; 2). **a** *Mil.* An officer appointed as head of the military police. **b** *Nav.* An officer who has charge of prisoners on trial by court-martial, serves notices to witnesses, etc.

prow (prou), *n.* [F. *proue,* fr. L. *prora,* fr. Gr. *prōira.*] **1.** The bow of a vessel; stem; *Poetic,* the vessel. **2.** Something resembling the bow of a vessel, as the projecting fore part of an airship.

prow, *adj.* [OF. *prou, preu,* fr. L. *pro, prod,* in *prodesse* to be useful.] *Archaic.* Valiant; gallant.

prow'ess (prou'ĕs; -ĭs), *n.* **1.** Distinguished bravery; valor. **2.** A brave act. **3.** Superiority in ability, skill, technique, or the like. — **Syn.** See HEROISM.

prowl (proul), *v. i. & t.* [ME. *prollen* to search about.] To move about or wander stealthily. — *n.* Act of prowling, as for prey. — **prowl'er** (-ẽr), *n.*

prowl car. = SQUAD CAR.

prox'i·mal (prŏk'sĭ·măl), *adj.* **1.** Proximate; nearest, as to a point of attachment or origin, a body, or a center of motion. **2.** *Anat. & Biol.* Designating that end of a limb or other part which is nearest to the point of attachment; — opposed to *distal.*

prox'i·mate (-mĭt), *adj.* [L. *proximatus,* past part. of *proximare* to approach, fr. *proximus,* superl. of *propior* nearer, and *prope,* adv., near.] Very close, as in space, time, order, meaning, etc.; often, nearest; next preceding or following. — **prox'i·mate·ly,** *adv.*

prox·im'i·ty (prŏks·ĭm'ĭ·tĭ), *n.* [L. *proximitas.*] State of being next or very near; close propinquity.

proximity fuze. An electronic device that detonates a projectile within effective range of a target by means of the radio waves sent out from a tiny radio set in the nose of the projectile and reflected back to the set from the target; — called also *variable timing,* or *VT, fuze.*

prox'i·mo (prŏk'sĭ·mō), *adv.* [L., on the next, abl. of *proximus* next.] In or of the next month after the present; as, the 3d *proximo;* — abbr. *prox.*

prox'y (prŏk'sĭ), *n.; pl.* PROXIES (-sĭz). [ME. *prokecie,* contr. fr. *procuracie* procuracy.] **1.** The agency, function, sometimes office, of a procurator or deputy. **2.** Authority or power to act for another, as in voting; specif., a writing giving such authorization. **3.** A person authorized to act for another; substitute. — **Syn.** See AGENT.

prude (proōd), *n.* [F., prudish, orig., modest.] A person, commonly a woman, who is excessively or priggishly attentive to propriety; one who affects extreme modesty or reticence in speech, behavior, or dress.

pru'dence (proō'dĕns; 114), *n.* **1.** Ability to regulate and discipline oneself through the exercise of the reason; as, the cardinal virtue of *prudence.* **2.** Skill or sagacity in the management of practical, esp. business, affairs; provident use of resources.

pru'dent (proō'dĕnt), *adj.* [OF., fr. L. *prudens, -entis,* contr. fr. *providens.* See PROVIDENT.] Characterized by or manifesting prudence. Specif.: **a** Capable of directing or conducting oneself wisely and judiciously. **b** Cautious, circumspect, or discreet, as in conduct, choice of ends, or business management; not rash or ill-advised; highly sensible. — **Syn.** See WISE. — **pru'dent·ly,** *adv.*

pru·den'tial (proō·dĕn'shăl), *adj.* **1.** Proceeding from or characterized by prudence. **2.** Exercising prudence; discretionary; advisory. — **pru·den'tial·ly,** *adv.*

prud'er·y (proōd'ẽr·ĭ), *n.; pl.* -ERIES (-ĭz). Quality or state of being prudish; excessive or priggish modesty or decorousness; also, a prudish action or speech.

prud'ish (-ĭsh), *adj.* Like or of the nature of a prude. — **prud'ish·ly,** *adv.* — **prud'ish·ness,** *n.*

pru'i·nose (proō'ĭ·nōs), *adj.* [L. *pruinosus,* fr. *pruina* hoarfrost.] *Bot. & Zool.* Covered with whitish dust or bloom.

prune (proōn; 114), *n.* [OF., fr. LL. *pruna.* See PLUM.] **1.** Orig., a plum. **2.** Now, a plum of a type dried without the development of fermentation.

prune, *v. t. & i.* [ME. *prunen, proinen, pruinen,* fr. OF. *poroindre* to anoint.] To preen; trim; dress.

prune, *v. t. & i.* [Earlier *pruin, proin,* fr. OF. *proignier, prooignier.*] **1.** To lop or cut off the superfluous parts or branches (of); to trim. **2.** To cut off or cut out, as useless parts. — **prun'er** (proōn'ẽr), *n.*

pru·nel'la (proō·nĕl'ȧ), *n.* [F. *prunelle.*] A smooth woolen or mixed stuff, used for the uppers of shoes; more recently, a similar dress fabric usually in twill weave.

pru·nelle' (proō·nĕl'), *n.* [F., dim. of *prune.* See PRUNE, *n.*] A small yellow dried plum packed without the skin.

prun'ing hook (proōn'ĭng). A pole or rod with curved blade attached, used chiefly for removing spent or superfluous bramble canes.

pru'ri·ence (proōr'ĭ·ĕns), **pru'ri·en·cy** (-ĕn·sĭ), *n.* Fact or state of being prurient; lascivious desire or thought.

pru'ri·ent (-ĕnt), *adj.* [L. *pruriens, -entis,* pres. part. of *prurire* to itch.] Itching; longing; of persons, having lascivious longings; of desire, curiosity, or propensity, lewd. — **pru'ri·ent·ly,** *adv.*

pru·rig'i·nous (proōr·ĭj'ĭ·nŭs), *adj.* [F. *prurigineux,* fr. LL. *pruriginosus.*] *Med.* Tending to, caused by, or of the nature of prurigo.

pru·ri'go (proō·rī'gō), *n.* [L., itching, itch.] A chronic inflammatory skin disease marked by itching papules.

pru·ri'tus (proō·rī'tŭs; 114), *n.* [L.] *Med.* Itching. — **pru·rit'ic** (proōr·ĭt'ĭk), *adj.*

Prus'sian (prŭsh'ăn), *adj.* from PRUSSIA, *Gaz.* — *n.* **1.** One of the people of Prussia. **2.** The language of the Prussians. ***Old Prussian*** belonged to the Slavic languages of the Baltic region and became extinct in the 17th century. See INDO-EUROPEAN LANGUAGES, *Table.*

Prussian blue. Any of several complex cyanogen compounds of iron used in dyeing, etc., esp., ferric ferrocyanide, $Fe_4[Fe(CN)_6]_3$, the precipitation of which is used as a test for ferric iron.

Prus'sian·ism (prŭsh'ăn·ĭz'm), *n.* Policy, practice, or behavior of, or like that of, the Prussians; esp., Prussian militarism with its ideals of conquest and despotism.

prus'si·ate (prŭsh'ĭ·āt; prŭs'-), *n.* *Chem.* A salt of prussic acid; a cyanide. Also, a ferrocyanide or a ferricyanide.

prus'sic (prŭs'ĭk; proō'sĭk), *adj.* [F. *prussique.*] = HYDROCYANIC. Hence, **prussic acid** (= HYDROCYANIC ACID).

pry (prī), *n.; pl.* PRIES (prīz). [Corrupted fr. *prize* a lever, mistaken as a pl.] A lever or the like for prying; also, leverage. — *v. t.;* PRIED (prīd); PRY'ING. **1.** To raise or move, or pull (apart) with a pry; to prize. **2.** Hence, figuratively, to extract with difficulty.

pry, *v. i.* [ME. *prien.*] To look closely, scrutinizingly, or inquisitively; to peer curiously. — *n.* **1.** Curious inspection; impertinent peeping. **2.** A prying person. — **pry'er,** *n.*

pry'ing (prī'ĭng), *adj.* Peering; curious; inquisitive. — **Syn.** See CURIOUS. — **pry'ing·ly,** *adv.*

psalm (säm), *n.* [From AS. *psalm, sealm* (fr. LL.), and fr. OF. *salme, psaume,* fr. LL. *psalmus,* fr. Gr. *psalmos,* fr. *psallein* to pull, to play upon a stringed instrument.] A sacred song or poem. — *v. t.* To sing or extol in psalms.

psalm'ist (säm'ĭst), *n.* A writer or composer of sacred songs; — applied specif. [*usually cap.*] to David as the traditional author of many psalms.

psal'mo·dy (săl'mō·dĭ; säm'ō·dĭ), *n.* [LL. *psalmodia,* fr. Gr. *psalmōidia,* fr. *psalmos* psalm + *aeidein* to sing.] Act, practice, or art of singing psalms in worship; also, psalms collectively. — **psal'mo·dist** (-dĭst), *n.*

Psalms (sämz), *n. pl., construed as sing.* A book of the Old Testament. See BIBLE.

Psal'ter (sôl'tẽr), *n.* [AS. *psaltere*, fr. L.; ME. *sauter*, fr. OF. *sautier*, *saltier*, fr. L. *psalterium*. See PSALM.] The Book of Psalms; often, also, a book containing the Psalms, or a part of a book containing certain of the Psalms used in a religious service.

psal·te'ri·um (sôl·tē'rĭ·ŭm; săl-), *n.*; *pl.* -RIA (-ȧ). [L., a psaltery, psalter; — from the resemblance of the folds to the leaves of a book.] The third stomach of ruminants; the omasum; the manyplies. See RUMINANT, *Illust.*

psal'ter·y (sôl'tẽr·ĭ), *n.*; *pl.* -TERIES (-ĭz). [OF. *sautere*, *psalterie*, fr. L. *psalterium*. See PSALTER.] **1.** *Music.* An ancient stringed instrument of the zither type. **2.** [*cap.*] The Psalter.

psam'mite (săm'īt), *n.* [F., fr. Gr. *psammos* sand.] Any sandstone; — disting. from *psephite.*

pse'phite (sē'fīt; psē'-; 88), *n.* [Gr. *psēphos* pebble + *-ite.*] Any coarse fragmental rock composed of rounded pebbles, as conglomerate. Cf. PSAMMITE.

pseu·dax'is (sū·dăk'sĭs; psū-; 88), *n.* [NL.] *Bot.* A sympodium.

pseu'de·pig'ra·pha (sū'dē·pĭg'rȧ·fȧ; psū'-), *n. pl.* [NL.] Spurious works purporting to emanate from Biblical characters; apocrypha. — **pseu'dep·i·graph'ic** (-dĕp·ĭ·grăf'ĭk), **pseu'dep·i·graph'i·cal** (-ĭ·kăl), *adj.*

pseu'de·pig'ra·phous (-fŭs), *adj.* [Gr. *pseudepigraphos* falsely inscribed. See PSEUDO-; EPIGRAPH.] Inscribed with a false name.

pseu'do (sū'dō; psū'-; 88), *adj.* Sham; feigned; spurious.

pseu'do- (sū'dō-; psū'-), **pseud-**. [Gr., fr. stem of *pseudēs* false, *pseudein* to deceive.] **1.** A combining form meaning *fake, falsely*, used to denote: **a** *Sham; feigned.* **b** *Counterfeit; spurious.* **2.** In modern science: **a** *Deceptive resemblance to a* (specified) *thing.* **b** *Unreal; illusory.* **3.** *Chem. Resemblance to, isomerism with*, or *relation to*, the compound to the name of which it is prefixed.

pseu'do·a·quat'ic (-ȧ·kwăt'ĭk; -kwŏt'ĭk), *adj.* Growing in moist or wet places, but not truly aquatic.

pseu'do·carp (sū'dō·kärp; psū'-), *n.* *Bot.* A fruit which does not consist exclusively of the ripened ovary and its contents. The apple, fig, strawberry, etc., are examples. — **pseu'do·car'pous** (-kär'pŭs), *adj.*

pseu'do·clas'sic (-klăs'ĭk), *adj.* Pretending to be, or erroneously regarded as, classic. — **pseu'do·clas'sic**, *n.* — **pseu'do·clas'si·cism** (-ĭ·sĭz'm), *n.*

pseu'do·morph (sū'dō·môrf; psū'-), *n.* [Gr. *pseudomorphos*, fr. *pseudēs* false + *morphē* form.] **1.** An irregular or deceptive form. **2.** *Mineral.* A mineral having the characteristic outward form of another species; — used with *after*; as, limonite occurs as a *pseudomorph* after pyrite. — **pseu'do·mor'phic** (-môr'fĭk), *adj.* — **pseu'do·mor'phism** (-fĭz'm), *n.* — **pseu'do·mor'phous** (-fŭs), *adj.*

pseu'do·nym (sū'dō·nĭm; psū'-), *n.* [F. *pseudonyme*, fr. Gr.] A fictitious name; a pen name.

pseu·don'y·mous (sū·dŏn'ĭ·mŭs; psū-), *adj.* [Gr. *pseudōnymos*, fr. *pseudēs* false + *onyma*, *onoma*, a name.] Bearing or using a fictitious name, as a work or author. — **pseu'do·nym'i·ty** (sū'dō·nĭm'ĭ·tĭ; psū'-), *n.* — **pseu·don'y·mous·ly**, *adv.*

pseu'do·pod (sū'dō·pŏd; psū'-; 88), *n.* A pseudopodium.

pseu'do·po'di·um (-pō'dĭ·ŭm), *n.*; *pl.* -DIA (-ȧ). [NL.] *Zool.* A temporary protrusion or retractile process of the protoplasm of a cell, for moving about or taking up food.

psi (sī; psī; psē), *n.* [Gr.] The twenty-third letter (Ψ, ψ) of the Greek alphabet, equivalent to English *ps* as in hops.

psi·lan'thro·py (sī·lăn'thrō·pĭ; psī-), *n.* Also **psi·lan'thro·pism** (-pĭz'm). [Gr. *psilanthrōpos* merely human, fr. *psilos* bare, mere + *anthrōpos* a man.] The doctrine of the merely human existence of Christ.

psi·lom'e·lane (-lŏm'ē·lān), *n.* [Gr. *psilos* bare, mere + *melas*, *-anos*, black.] *Mineral.* A hydrous oxide of manganese occurring in smooth, botryoid iron-black or steel-gray forms, massive, or stalactitic.

psit'ta·co'sis (sĭt'ȧ·kō'sĭs; psĭt'-), *n.* [NL., fr. Gr. *psittakos* parrot + *-osis.*] *Med.* A contagious wasting disease of birds, esp. parrots. It is communicable to man, causing nausea and fever and, sometimes, bronchial pneumonia. Called also *parrot disease* or *fever.*

pso'as (sō'ăs; psō'-), *n.* [NL., fr. Gr. *psoa* a muscle of the loin.] *Anat.* Either of two muscles of the loin.

pso'ra (sō'rȧ; psō'-), *n.* [L., fr. Gr. *psōra.*] *Med.* Itching disease of the skin; specif.: **a** Scabies. **b** Psoriasis.

pso·ra'le·a (sō·rā'lē·ȧ; psō-), *n.* [NL., fr. Gr. *psōraleos* scabby.] *Bot.* Any of a genus (*Psoralea*) of herbs and shrubs of the pea family, esp. the breadroot.

pso·ri'a·sis (sō·rī'ȧ·sĭs; psō-), *n.* [NL., fr. Gr. *psōriasis*, fr. *psōra* psora.] *Med.* A chronic skin disease, characterized by red patches covered with white scales.

psych-. = PSYCHO-, as in **psy'cha·nal'y·sis.**

psy'chas·the'ni·a (sī'kăs·thē'nĭ·ȧ; psī'-; sī'kăs·thē·nī'ȧ; psī'-), *n.* [NL. See PSYCHO-; ASTHENIA.] *Psychopathol.* A neurotic condition characterized by obsessions, phobias, etc. — **psy'chas·then'ic** (sī'kăs·thĕn'ĭk; psī'-), *adj.* & *n.*

Psy'che (sī'kē; psī'-; 88), *n.* [L., fr. Gr. *Psychē* Psyche, fr. *psychē* the soul.] **1.** *Class. Myth.* A beautiful princess of whom Venus became jealous. Cupid, Venus's son, fell in love with Psyche, and Venus imposed many hardships on her; but Psyche was finally reunited with Cupid and made immortal. **2.** [*not cap.*] The human soul; also, the mind; the mental life.

Psyche knot. A style of wearing the hair in a projecting or conical coil at the back of the head.

psy·chi'a·try (sī·kī'ȧ·trĭ; psī-; sī'kĭ·ăt'rĭ; psī'-; 88), *n.* [NL. *psychiatria*, fr. Gr. *psychē* the mind + *iatreia* healing.] The medical specialty dealing with mental disorders, esp. with psychoses, but also with neuroses. — **psy'chi·at'ric** (sī'kĭ·ăt'rĭk; psī'-), **psy'chi·at'ri·cal** (-rĭ·kăl), *adj.* — **psy·chi'a·trist** (sī·kī'ȧ·trĭst; psī-; sī'kĭ·ăt'rĭst; psī'-), *n.*

psy'chic (sī'kĭk; psī'kĭk), *adj.* [Gr. *psychikos* of the soul or life, spiritual, fr. *psychē* breath, life, soul, fr. *psychein* to breathe, blow.] **1.** Of or pert. to the psyche, or soul or mind. **2.** Not physical; lying outside the realm of known physical processes; as, *psychic* forces. **3.** Sensitive to nonphysical forces; as, a *psychic* medium. — *n.* **1.** A person apparently sensitive to nonphysical forces; esp., *Spiritualism*, one capable of serving as a medium. **2.** The field of psychic phenomena.

psy'chi·cal (-kĭ·kăl), *adj.* **1.** Psychic. **2.** Of or pertaining to the mind; mental; — contrasted with *physical.* — **psy'chi·cal·ly**, *adv.*

psy'cho- (sī'kō-; psī'-; 88), **psych-.** [Gr. *psychē.*] A combining form meaning *life, soul*, denoting: **a** *Mind, mental processes and activities*, as in *psychology.* **b** *Psychological methods*, as in *psychoanalysis.* **c** *Psychic and*; — in adjectives, as in *psychophysical.*

psy'cho·a·nal'y·sis (-ȧ·năl'ĭ·sĭs), *n.* [NL., fr. *psycho-* + *analysis.*] A method of psychotherapeutic analysis resting on the theory that abnormal mental reactions are due to repression of desires consciously rejected but subconsciously persistent. — **psy'cho·an'a·lyt'ic** (-ăn'ȧ·lĭt'ĭk), **psy'cho·an'a·lyt'i·cal** (-ĭ·kăl), *adj.* — **psy'cho·an'a·lyt'i·cal·ly**, *adv.*

psy'cho·an'a·lyze (-ăn'ȧ·līz), *v. t.* To subject to psychoanalytical examination and treatment. — **psy'cho·an'a·lyst** (-lĭst), *n.*

psy'cho·bi·ol'o·gy (-bī·ŏl'ō·jĭ), *n.* The study of mental life and behavior in relation to other biological processes. — **psy'cho·bi'o·log'i·cal** (-bī'ō·lŏj'ĭ·kăl), **psy'cho·bi'o·log'ic** (-lŏj'ĭk), *adj.*

psy'cho·dra'ma (-drä'mȧ; -drăm'ȧ), *n.* A drama in which actors extemporize in meeting a given situation, thus exhibiting their natural psychological reactions, used esp. in treating the mentally ill. — **psy'cho·dra·mat'ic** (-drȧ·măt'ĭk), *adj.*

psy'cho·dy·nam'ic (-dī·năm'ĭk; -dĭ-), *adj.* Pertaining to or concerned with motives and other causative factors in mental life. — **psy'cho·dy·nam'ics** (-ĭks), *n.*; see -ICS.

psy'cho·gen'e·sis (-jĕn'ē·sĭs), *n.* [NL.] **1.** Genesis through an internal force, as opposed to *natural selection.* **2.** *Psychol.* The origin and development of the mind. — **psy'cho·ge·net'ic** (-jē·nĕt'ĭk), *adj.*

psy'cho·gen'ic (-jĕn'ĭk), *adj.* Originating in the mind; caused by mental influences; as, *psychogenic* nervous disorders.

psy·chog'no·sis (sī·kŏg'nō·sĭs; psī-; 88), *n.* [See -GNOSIS.] Any penetrating study of the psyche.

psy'cho·graph (sī'kō·grăf; psī'-; 9), *n.* A psychological biography or analysis of a person.

psy'cho·log'i·cal (sī'kō·lŏj'ĭ·kăl; psī'-), *adj.* Also **psy'cho·log'ic** (-ĭk). **1. a** Of, belonging to, concerning, or of the nature of psychology. **b** Loosely, mental. **2.** Intended to affect morale, as to weaken that of an enemy; as, *psychological* warfare. — **psy'cho·log'i·cal·ly**, *adv.*

psy·chol'o·gize (sī·kŏl'ō·jīz; psī-), *v. i.* To engage in psychological thought or investigation.

psy·chol'o·gy (sī·kŏl'ō·jĭ; psī-; 88), *n.* [NL. *psychologia.* See PSYCHO-; -LOGY.] **1.** The science which treats of the mind in any of its aspects; systematic knowledge and investigation of the phenomena of consciousness and behavior. **2.** The traits, feelings, actions, and attributes, collectively, of the mind; as, the *psychology* of a criminal. **3.** A treatise on the science of psychology. — **psy·chol'o·gist** (-jĭst), *n.*

psy·chom'e·try (-kŏm'ē·trĭ), *n.* **1.** *Occult.* Divination of facts about an object or its owner through contact with, or proximity to, the object. **2.** *Psychol.* Also **psy'cho·met'rics** (sī'kō·mĕt'rĭks; psī'-), see -ICS. Mental measurement, as of speed and precision of mental processes. — **psy·chom'e·tri'cian** (sī·kŏm'ē·trĭsh'ăn; psī-), **psy·chom'e·trist** (-kŏm'ē·trĭst), *n.* — **psy'cho·met'ric** (sī'kō·mĕt'rĭk; psī'-), *adj.*

psy'cho·mo'tor (sī'kō·mō'tẽr; psī'-), *adj.* Of or pertaining to muscular action ensuing directly from a mental process.

psy'cho·neu·ro'sis (-nū·rō'sĭs), *n.* [NL.] A neurosis based on conflict in which some impulse that has been blocked seeks expression in some disguised response or symptom; — distinguished from *traumatic neurosis.* — **psy'cho·neu·rot'ic** (-rŏt'ĭk), *adj.* & *n.*

psy'cho·path (sī'kō·păth; psī'-), *n.* One affected with psychopathy.

psy'cho·path'ic (-păth'ĭk), *adj.* **1.** Of, pertaining to, of the nature of, or characterized by psychopathy. **2.** Designating, or relating to, abnormal sensitiveness to spiritual phenomena; characterized by extreme susceptibility to religious emotion, conscientious doubts and fears, etc. **3.** Incorrectly, of or pertaining to psychotherapeutics. — **psy'cho·path'ic**, *n.*

psy·chop'a·thist (sī·kŏp'ȧ·thĭst; psī-), *n.* An alienist.

psy'cho·pa·thol'o·gy (sī'kō·pȧ·thŏl'ō·jĭ; psī'-; 88), *n.* The scientific study of mental disorders from the psychological point of view. — **psy'cho·pa·thol'o·gist** (-jĭst), *n.*

psy·chop'a·thy (sī·kŏp'ȧ·thĭ; psī-), *n.* [*psycho-* + *-pathy.*] **1.** Mental disorder in general. **2.** More commonly, mental disorder characterized by eccentricity, emotional instability, perversity of conduct, undue conceit and suspiciousness, or lack of common sense, social feeling, self-control, truthfulness, energy, or persistence. **3.** Incorrectly, psychotherapeutics.

psy'cho·phys'ics (sī'kō·fĭz'ĭks; psī'-), *n.*; see -ICS. The scientific study of the relations between mental and physical processes. — **psy'cho·phys'i·cal** (-ĭ·kăl), *adj.* — **psy'cho·phys'i·cist** (-ĭ·sĭst), *n.*

psy·cho'sis (sī·kō'sĭs; psī-), *n.*; *pl.* -SES (-sēz). [NL.] *Psychiatry.* Mental disease; any serious mental derangement; — a purely psychiatric term without the legal implications of the word *insanity.* — **Syn.** See INSANITY. — **psy·chot'ic** (-kŏt'ĭk), *adj.* & *n.*

psy'cho·so·mat'ic (sī'kō·sō·măt'ĭk; psī'-; 88), *adj.* Pertaining to the functional interrelationship between mind and body, as in **psychosomatic medicine**, which deals especially with bodily disorders induced by mental or emotional disturbances. — **psy'cho·so·mat'ics** (-ĭks), *n.*; see -ICS.

psy'cho·sur'ger·y (-sûr'jẽr·ĭ), *n.* Cerebral surgery employed in treating psychic symptoms; specif., leucotomy.

psy'cho·ther'a·peu'tics (-thĕr'ȧ·pū'tĭks), *n.*; see -ICS. Science and art of psychotherapy. — **psy'cho·ther'a·peu'tic** (-tĭk), *adj.* — **psy'cho·ther'a·peu'tist** (-tĭst), *n.*

psy'cho·ther'a·py (-thĕr'ȧ·pĭ), *n.* Mental treatment of illness, esp. of nervous diseases and maladjustments, as by suggestion, psychoanalysis, or re-education. — **psy'cho·ther'a·pist** (-pĭst), *n.*

psychro-. [Gr. *psychros.*] A combining form meaning *cold.*

psy·chrom'e·ter (sī·krŏm'ē·tẽr; psī-; 88), *n.* [*psychro-* + *-meter.*] A hygrometer, or instrument for measuring the aqueous vapor in the atmosphere, consisting essentially of two similar thermometers, the bulb of one being kept wet. Because of the cooling that results from evaporation (which is less on a moist day), the wet-bulb thermometer registers a lower temperature than the dry-bulb thermometer, the difference between the readings constituting a measure of the dryness of the atmosphere.

Ptah (p'tä; *Egypt.* p'tăĸ), *n.* [Egypt. *Ptaḥ.*] *Egypt. Relig.* The chief god of Memphis, worshiped as early as the 1st dynasty. He was regarded as shaper of the world and father of gods and men.

ptar'mi·gan (tär'mĭ·găn), *n.*; see PLURAL, *Note*, 3. [Gael. *tārmachan.*] Any of various species of grouse (genus *Lagopus*) of northern regions, having completely feathered feet.

PT boat (pē′tē′ bōt′). [For *patrol torpedo boat.*] *U.S. Navy.* A motor torpedo boat used for coastal patrol and convoy. See MOTOR TORPEDO BOAT.

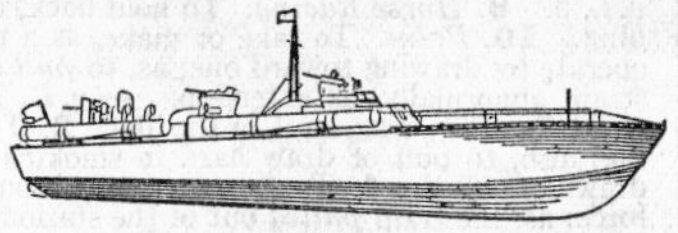

PT Boat.

pter′i·dol′o·gy (tĕr′ĭ-dŏl′ō-jĭ; p′tĕr′-; 88), *n.* [Gr. *pteris, pteridos,* fern + *-logy.*] The science or study of ferns. — **pter′i·do·log′i·cal** (-dō-lŏj′ĭ-kăl), *adj.* — **pter′i·dol′o·gist** (-dŏl′ō-jĭst), *n.*

pter′i·do·phyte′ (tĕr′ĭ-dō-fīt′; p′tĕr′-), *n.* [Gr. *pteris, -ridos,* fern + *-phyte.*] *Bot.* Any of a phylum (Pteridophyta) of plants, including the ferns and their allies. They represent the highest type of flowerless plants. — **pter′i·do·phyt′ic** (-fĭt′ĭk), **pter′i·doph′y·tous** (-dŏf′ĭ-tŭs), *adj.*

pter′o·dac′tyl (tĕr′ō-dăk′tĭl; p′tĕr′-; 88), *n.* [Gr. *pteron* feather, wing + *daktylos* finger, toe.] Any of an order (Pterosauria) of extinct flying reptiles, existing from the Lower Jurassic nearly to the close of the Mesozoic. They were destitute of feathers, and the supporting surface of the wings was a membrane which extended from the side of the body along the arm to the end of the enormously developed fourth digit.

pter′o·pod (tĕr′ō-pŏd; p′tĕr′-), *adj.* [Gr. *pteropous* wing-footed, fr. *pteron* feather, wing + *pous, podos,* foot.] *Zool.* Of or pertaining to a group (Pteropoda) of gastropod mollusks having the anterior lobes of the foot developed in the form of broad, thin, winglike organs, with which they swim at or near the surface of the sea. — **pter′o·pod,** *n.* — **pte·rop′o·dan** (tē-rŏp′ō-dăn; p′tē-), *adj. & n.*

pter′o·saur (-sôr), *n.* [Gr. *pteron* feather + *sauros* lizard.] A pterodactyl.

-pterous. [Gr. *pteron* wing.] *Bot. & Zool.* A combining form denoting *having* (so many or such) *wings,* as in brachy*pterous.*

pter′y·goid (tĕr′ĭ-goid; p′tĕr′-; 88), *adj.* [Gr. *pteryx, pterygos,* wing, fin + *-oid.*] *Anat.* Designating, pert. to, or in the region of the inferior portion of the sphenoid bone of the vertebrate skull. It comprises two **pterygoid processes,** each consisting of lateral and medial **pterygoid plates** fused in front but diverging posteriorly. — *n.* Any pterygoid element, as a muscle, nerve, or bone.

ptis′an (tĭz′ăn; tĭ-zăn′), *n.* [F. *ptisane, tisane,* fr. L. *ptisana* peeled barley, barley water, fr. Gr. *ptisanē,* fr. *ptissein* to peel, husk.] **1.** A decoction of barley with other ingredients. **2.** *Pharm.* A decoction, as of an herb, containing little if any medicinal agent. Cf. TISANE.

Ptol′e·ma′ic (tŏl′ē-mā′ĭk), *adj.* **1.** Of or pert. to Ptolemy the geographer and astronomer, who flourished at Alexandria about A.D. 130. **2.** Of or pert. to the Ptolemies, Greco-Egyptian rulers of Egypt from 323 B.C. to 30 B.C.

Ptolemaic system. *Astron.* The system maintained by Ptolemy, who supposed the earth to be the fixed center of the universe, about which the sun and stars revolve. The system was finally superseded by the Copernican system.

Ptol′e·ma′ist (-ĭst), *n.* A supporter of the Ptolemaic system.

pto′maine (tō′mān; tō-mān′; *now rarely* tō′mȧ-ēn; 2), *n.* Also **pto′main.** [It. *ptomaina,* fr. Gr. *ptōma* dead body.] *Biochem.* Any of a class of organic bases or alkaloids formed by the action of putrefactive bacteria on nitrogenous matter. Most are harmless; some may be poisonous.

ptomaine poisoning. Poisoning caused by ptomaines, or by substances once supposed to be ptomaines but now known to be specific bacterial poisons in spoiled food.

pto′sis (tō′sĭs; p′tō′-; 88), *n.* [NL., fr. Gr. *ptōsis* a falling.] *Med.* The falling down or prolapse of any part; specif., the drooping of the upper eyelid, as from paralysis of a muscle.

pty′a·lin (tī′ȧ-lĭn; p′tī′-), *n.* [Gr. *ptyalon* spittle.] *Biochem.* The amylase of saliva in man.

pty′a·lism (-lĭz′m), *n.* [Gr. *ptyalismos.*] Salivation, or excessive flow of saliva.

pub (pŭb), *n.* *Brit. Slang.* A public house; hotel or tavern.

pu′ber·ty (pū′bẽr-tĭ), *n.* [F. or L.; F. *puberté,* fr. L. *pubertas,* fr. *puber, pubes,* adult.] The state or quality of being first capable of begetting or bearing offspring; the period at which sexual maturity is reached. The age of puberty is commonly designated legally as fourteen for boys and twelve for girls.

pu·ber′u·lent (pū-bĕr′ū-lĕnt; -ōō-lĕnt), **pu·ber′u·lous** (-lŭs), *adj.* *Bot.* Minutely downy; covered with fine pubescence.

pu′bes (pū′bēz), *n.* [L., pubes (in sense 1 **a**), fr. *pubes* adult.] **1.** *Anat.* **a** The hair which appears upon the lower part of the hypogastric region at the age of puberty. **b** The pubic region. **2.** *Bot.* Pubescence.

pu·bes′cent (pū-bĕs′ĕnt; -′nt), *adj.* [F. or L.; F., fr. L. *pubescens, -entis,* pres. part. of *pubescere* to reach puberty, grow hairy.] **1.** Arriving at puberty; characteristic of or pertaining to this state. **2.** Downy or hairy; covered with soft fine hairs. — **pu·bes′cence** (-ĕns; -′ns), *n.*

pu′bic (pū′bĭk), *adj.* *Anat.* Pertaining to or designating the region of the pubes, or the pubis; as, the *pubic* symphysis.

pu′bis (pū′bĭs), *n.; pl.* PUBES (-bēz). [NL. See PUBES.] *Anat. & Zool.* The ventral and anterior of the three principal bones composing either half of the pelvis.

pub′lic (pŭb′lĭk), *adj.* [F., fr. L. *publicus* (after *pubes* adult), fr. *poplicus,* fr. *populus* people.] **1.** Of or pertaining to the people; relating to, belonging to, or affecting a nation, state, or community at large; — opposed to *private.* **2.** Open to common or general use, enjoyment, etc.; as, a *public* meeting. **3.** Open to the knowledge or view of all; generally seen, known, or heard. **4.** Engaged in activities, esp. unofficial activities, carried on for or before the public; as, men in *public* life. **5.** Having a civil, or official, status representing the public; as, a *public* prosecutor. — *n.* **1.** The general body of mankind, or of a nation, state, or community; the people, indefinitely; as, the American *public;* also, a particular body of people; as, the reading *public.* **2.** *Colloq., Brit.* A public house; an inn.

pub′lic–ad·dress′ sys′tem. An apparatus for broadcasting speech, music, or other sounds to a large audience, as in an auditorium or out of doors. It includes one or more microphones or other pickup devices, an audio-frequency amplifier, and one or more loud speakers. Called also *PA, P.A.,* or *p.a., system.*

pub′li·can (pŭb′lĭ-kăn), *n.* [OF. *publicain,* fr. L. *publicanus.*] **1.** *Rom. Antiq.* A farmer of the public revenues; hence, a collector of toll. **2.** *Brit.* Keeper of a public house.

pub′li·ca′tion (pŭb′lĭ-kā′shŭn), *n.* [F., fr. L. *publicatio.*] **1.** Act of publishing, or state of being published; public notification. **2.** The issuing to the public of copies of a book, engraving, or the like; hence, the business of printing, etc., such copies. **3.** That which is published; esp., any book, pamphlet, etc., offered for sale or to public notice.

public domain. The realm embracing property rights belonging to the community at large, subject to appropriation by anyone; specif., status unprotected by copyright or patent.

public house. In a general sense, any inn or hotel; esp., in British usage, any house where intoxicating liquors are sold by retail to be consumed on the premises.

pub′li·cist (pŭb′lĭ-sĭst), *n.* A writer on, or one versed in, international law, or law of nations; hence, loosely, any writer, as a journalist, on matters of public policy.

pub·lic′i·ty (pŭb-lĭs′ĭ-tĭ), *n.* **1.** Quality or state of being public. **2.** **a** Advertising of any kind. **b** Information designed to advance the interests of a place, person, cause, etc., usually appearing in public print. **c** Any matter which secures public attention; also, the attention so gained.

pub′li·cize (pŭb′lĭ-sīz), *v. t.* To give publicity to.

pub′lic·ly (pŭb′lĭk-lĭ), *adv.* **1.** In a public manner; openly. **2.** Through the agency or consent of the public; as, *publicly* managed utilities.

pub′lic·ness, *n.* Quality or state of being public.

public relations. **1.** The activities of a corporation, union, government, or other organization in building and maintaining sound and productive relations with special publics such as customers, employees, or stockholders, and with the public at large, so as to adapt itself to its environment and interpret itself to society. **2.** The state of such activities or the art of organizing them.

public school. **a** In Great Britain, any of various schools maintained by the community, wholly or partly under public control, or maintained largely by endowment and not carried on for profit; specif., and commonly, any of various select and usually expensive endowed schools which give a liberal education or prepare pupils for the universities. **b** In the United States, Scotland, and British colonies and dominions, an elementary or secondary school, now usually free, maintained by the local governmental authority. — **pub′lic–school′** (*see Pron.,* § 2), *adj.*

public servant. **1.** Any officer or employee of a governmental body. **2.** *U.S.* Any individual or corporation, as a public utility, rendering a public service.

public service. The business of supplying some commodity (as electricity, gas, water) or of providing some service (as transportation or communication) to any or all members of a community, where exercise of the calling involves some legal privilege or a natural or virtual monopoly.

pub′lic–serv′ice cor′po·ra′tion. A civil corporation organized to render a public service (which see).

public spirit. A spirit inspiring an interest in, and active efforts for, the public welfare.

public utility. Also **utility.** **1.** A business organization, such as a public-service corporation, performing some public service and subject to special governmental regulation. **2.** *Stock Exchange. Usually pl.* The shares of public-utility companies. — **pub′lic–u·til′i·ty** (*see Pron.,* § 2), *adj.*

Public Works Administration. *U.S.* A government agency (officially, the Federal Emergency Administration of Public Works) to provide employment through work on public projects, created by act of Congress, June 16, 1933, and administered by the secretary of the interior. Liquidated June 30, 1944.

pub′lish (pŭb′lĭsh), *v. t.* [OF. *publier,* fr. L. *publicare, publicatum.*] **1.** To make public; to divulge; to proclaim. **2.** To bring before the public, as for sale; esp.: **a** To print and issue from the press, as a book, newspaper, etc. **b** *U.S.* To put into circulation; as, to *publish* counterfeit paper. — **Syn.** See DECLARE. — **pub′lish·a·ble** (-ȧ-b′l), *adj.*

pub′lish·er (-ẽr), *n.* One who publishes; esp., one who issues from the press, and offers for sale, books, periodicals, music, maps, and the like.

puc·coon′ (pŭ-kōōn′), *n.* [See 1st POKE, *n.*] *Bot.* Any of several American plants yielding a red or yellow pigment; also, the pigment. Specif., the bloodroot.

puce (pūs), *n.* [F., fr. *puce* a flea, fr. L. *pulex, pulicis.*] A color, red in hue, of low saturation and low brilliance. See COLOR. — **puce,** *adj.*

puck (pŭk), *n.* [Also *pook,* fr. ME. *pouke,* fr. AS. *pūca.*] **1.** One of a class of evil spirits; a mischievous sprite; specif. [*cap.*], Robin Goodfellow. **2.** A disk of vulcanized rubber used in the game of ice hockey.

puck′a, puk′ka (pŭk′ȧ), *adj.* [Hind. *pakkā* cooked, ripe, solid.] *Colloq., Anglo-Indian.* Good of its kind; genuine.

puck′er (pŭk′ẽr), *v. i. & t.* [Freq. fr. POKE bag.] To contract or draw up into folds or wrinkles. — *n.* A bulge, fold, or wrinkle, made by puckering.

puck′er·y (-ĭ), *adj.* **1.** That puckers easily; also, puckered; as, *puckery* cloth. **2.** That causes puckering of the mouth.

puck′ish (pŭk′ĭsh), *adj.* [*also cap.*] Mischievous.

pud′ding (pōōd′ĭng), *n.* [ME. *pudding, poding.*] **1.** A piece of intestine stuffed with seasoned chopped meat, or the like, and boiled. **2.** A dessert having flour or some other cereal as a foundation, with added eggs, milk, fruit, sugar, spices, etc. Cf. YORKSHIRE PUDDING.

pudding stone. = CONGLOMERATE, *n.,* 2.

pud′dle (pŭd′′l), *n.* [ME. *puddel, podel,* dim. fr. AS. *pudd* ditch, furrow.] **1.** A very small pool of standing water. **2.** Clay, or a mixture of clay and sand, kneaded or worked, when wet, to render it impervious to water. — *v. t.;* -DLED (-′ld); -DLING (-lĭng). **1.** To make muddy; to muddle. **2.** **a** To make puddle (sense 2) of (clay or loam). **b** To make impervious to liquids by means of puddle. **3.** To subject (iron) to the process of puddling. **4.** *Agric.* To work while wet, as the soil in rice fields. — **pud′dler** (-lẽr), *n.*

pud′dling (pŭd′lĭng), *n.* **1.** *Hydraul. Engin.* **a** The process of working clay, loam, pulverized ore, etc., with water, to render it compact or impervious. **b** Puddle. See PUDDLE, *n.,* 2. **2.** *Metal.* The process of converting pig iron into wrought iron or, now rarely, steel, by subjecting it to heat and frequent stirring in a furnace (**puddling furnace**) in the presence of oxidizing substances.

pud′dock (pŭd′ŭk). Dial. var. of PADDOCK, toad.

pu′den·cy (pū′dĕn-sĭ), *n.* [LL. *pudentia,* fr. *pudens,* pres. part. of *pudere* to be ashamed.] Modesty; shamefacedness; extreme prudishness.

pu·den′dum (pū-dĕn′dŭm), *n.; pl.* PUDENDA (-dȧ). [NL., neut. of *pu-*

dendus that of which one ought to be ashamed, fr. *pudere* to be ashamed.] *Anat.* The external organs of generation, sometimes only of the female; the vulva.

pudg'y (pŭj'ĭ), *adj.* Short and thickset; dumpy. — **pudg'i·ly,** *adv.* — **pudg'i·ness,** *n.*

pueb'lo (pwĕb'lō), *n.; pl.* -LOS (-lōz). [Sp., a village, fr. L. *populus* people.] **1.** One of the Indian villages of Arizona, New Mexico, and adjacent regions, built of stone or adobe in the form of communal houses. **2.** [*cap.*] An Indian of one of the pueblos. The Pueblo Indians are industrious agriculturists, skilled in weaving, pottery, and basketry. **3.** Any Indian village of the southwestern U. S.

pu'er·ile (pū'ẽr·ĭl *or, esp. Brit.,* -īl; 56), *adj.* [F. or L.; F. *puéril,* fr. L. *puerilis,* fr. *puer* child, boy.] **1.** *Rare.* Juvenile. **2.** Childish; foolish; unthinking; as, a *puerile* remark. — **pu'er·ile·ly,** *adv.*

pu'er·il·ism (-ĭl·ĭz'm), *n.* Childish behavior, esp., *Psychiatry,* occurring as a symptom of mental disorder.

pu'er·il'i·ty (-ĭl'ĭ·tĭ), *n.; pl.* -TIES (-tĭz). **1.** The quality of being puerile; childishness. **2.** That which is puerile; a childish act, remark, etc.

pu·er'per·al (pū·ûr'pẽr·ăl), *adj.* [L. *puerpera* a lying-in woman, fr. *puer* child + *parere* to bear.] Of or pertaining to childbirth; as, a *puerperal* fever.

pu'er·pe'ri·um (pū'ẽr·pē'rĭ·ŭm), *n.* [L., childbirth.] *Med.* The state of a woman after childbirth.

puff (pŭf), *n.* [ME. *puf.*] **1.** A sudden and single emission of breath; hence, any sudden or short blast of wind; a slight gust; whiff. **2. a** A form of light pastry that has puffed in cooking. **b** A soft pad for applying powder to the skin or hair. **c** A soft, loose roll of hair. **d** A bed covering filled with cotton, wool, or down, and quilted or tufted. **3. a** A protuberance from swelling; as, a *puff* of flesh. **b** In clothing, a mass formed by a strip of material gathered at the edges and left loose in the center. **4.** An empty expression of praise, esp. one in a public journal. — *v. i.* **1.** To blow in puffs; to emit puffs of wind, smoke, steam, or breath. **2.** To become inflated; — usually with *up;* as, the sails *puffed* up. — *v. t.* **1.** To blow, emit, drive, or expel, with or as with a puff or puffs of wind, breath, etc. **2.** To swell or expand; to inflate. **3.** To praise exaggeratedly. **4.** *Toiletry.* To arrange in puffs, as the coiffure. — **puff'i·ness,** *n.* — **puff'y,** *adj.*

puff'ball' (-bôl'), *n.* Any of various fungi (family Lycoperdaceae) which are round in shape and discharge the ripe spores in a smokelike cloud when struck. Many of them are edible.

puff'er (pŭf'ẽr), *n.* **1.** One who or that which puffs. **2.** Any of numerous fishes (order Plectognathi) capable of inflating the body; — called also *globefish, swellfish,* or *blowfish.*

puff'er·y (-ĭ), *n.* Puffing publicity; fulsome praise.

puf'fin (pŭf'ĭn), *n.* [From PUFF.] Any of several sea birds (genera *Fratercula* and *Lunda*), esp. the ***Atlantic puffin*** (*F. arctica*) of the North Atlantic, about a foot long with short neck and a deep, grooved, parti-colored bill.

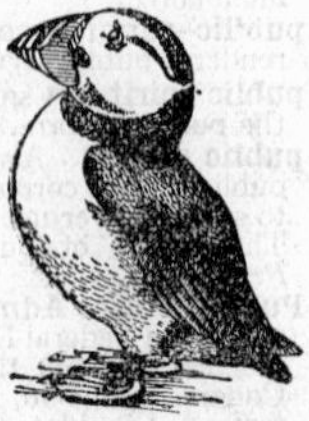
Puffin (*F. arctica*). (1/10)

puff paste. Dough used in making light, flaky pastries.

pug (pŭg), *n.* [Corrupted fr. PUCK.] **1.** A small usually close-haired dog of a breed believed to have originated in China probably from a common ancestor with the Pekingese. **2.** A pug nose.

pug, *v. t.;* PUGGED (pŭgd); PUG'GING. **1.** To mix and stir when wet, as clay for bricks, pottery, etc. **2.** To fill or stop with clay by tamping; to fill in with mortar for deadening sound. — *n.* Tempered or pugged clay.

pug, *n. Slang.* A pugilist.

pug, *n.* [Hind. *pag* foot.] *India.* Footprint; track. — *v. t. India.* To trace by pugs.

pug'gree (pŭg'rē), **pug'gry** (-rĭ), *n.* Also **pug'a·ree** (pŭg'ȧ·rē), **pug'ger·ee** (-ẽr·ē), **pug'ree** (pŭg'rē). [Hind. *pagrī* turban.] *India.* A light scarf wound around a hat or helmet to protect the head from the sun.

pu'gil·ism (pū'jĭ·lĭz'm), *n.* [L. *pugil* a pugilist, boxer.] The practice of boxing, or fighting with the fists. — **pu'gil·is'tic** (-lĭs'tĭk), *adj.*

pu'gil·ist (-lĭst), *n.* One who fights with his fists; esp., a professional prize fighter; a boxer.

pug·na'cious (pŭg·nā'shŭs), *adj.* [L. *pugnax, -acis,* fr. *pugnare* to fight, fr. *pugnus* fist.] Disposed to fight; combative. — **Syn.** See BELLIGERENT. — **pug·na'cious·ly,** *adv.* — **pug·na'cious·ness,** *n.* — **pug·nac'i·ty** (-năs'ĭ·tĭ), *n.*

pug'ree. Var. of PUGGREE.

pug nose. A nose turning upward at the tip and usually short and thick. — **pug'-nosed'** (*see Pron.,* § 2), *adj.*

puir (pür). Obs. exc. Scot. var. of POOR, PURE.

puis'ne (pū'nĭ), *adj.* [See PUNY.] *Law.* Younger or inferior in rank; junior. — *n.* A junior; esp., a puisne judge.

pu'is·sance (pū'ĭ·săns; pū·ĭs'-; -s'ns; pwĭs'ăns; -'ns), *n.* [F.] *Now Poetic.* Power; force.

pu'is·sant (-sănt; -s'nt), *adj.* [F., orig. a pres. part. fr. L. *posse* to be able.] Having power, authority, or mastery; potent; mighty; forcible. — **pu'is·sant·ly,** *adv.*

puke (pūk), *v. i. & t. & n.* Vomit.

puk'ka (pŭk'ȧ). Var. of PUCKA.

pul (pōōl), *n.* [Per. *pūl.*] A copper coin of Persia and Afghanistan, currently in Afghanistan equivalent to 1/100 of an afghani.

pul'chri·tude (pŭl'krĭ·tūd), *n.* [L. *pulchritudo,* fr. *pulcher* beautiful.] Beauty; loveliness.

pul'chri·tu'di·nous (-tū'dĭ·nŭs), *adj.* Endowed with physical beauty.

pule (pūl), *v. i.* To whimper, as a complaining child; to whine. — **pul'er** (pūl'ẽr), *n.*

pul'ing (pūl'ĭng), *adj.* Whining. — **pul'ing·ly,** *adv.*

pull (pōōl), *v. t.* [AS. *pullian.*] **1.** To exert force upon so as to cause, or tend to cause, motion toward the force; to draw. **2.** *Dial.* To pluck, as a fowl. **3.** To pluck; as, to *pull* flowers; hence, to extract; to draw out; as, to *pull* a tooth. **4.** To draw apart; to tear; rend. **5.** To stretch repeatedly, as a cooling candy. **6.** *Slang.* **a** To arrest; hence, to make a police raid upon. **b** To snatch in stealing. **c** *U. S.* To draw out; as, to *pull* a knife. **d** To put into daring execution; as, to *pull* stunts. **7.** *Slang.* To fail to give full force to; as, to *pull* one's punches in a boxing match. **8.** *Games.* To hit (a ball) in an oblique direction, as, *Golf,* in striking (the ball) so as to cause it to travel with a curve to the left of the intended line of play. Cf. SLICE, *v. t.,* 5. **9.** *Horse Racing.* To hold back, and so prevent from winning. **10.** *Print.* To take or make, as a proof. **11.** *Rowing.* To operate by drawing toward one; as, to *pull* an oar. **12.** *Sports.* To strain abnormally, as a tendon. — *v. i.* **1.** To use force or make efforts to draw, drag, haul, or the like. **2.** To take a draught in drinking; also, to puff or draw hard in smoking. **3.** To admit of being drawn or pulled. **4.** To get under way through the exercise of physical force; as, the train *pulled* out of the station.

Syn. Pull, draw, drag, haul, tug mean to move toward the exerting force. **Pull,** the general term, is usually followed by an adverb to indicate specific direction; **draw** implies a smoother or gentler motion than *pull;* **drag,** greater effort or more resistance; **haul,** a pulling or dragging with great exertion; **tug,** a strenuous pulling in an effort to move.

— *n.* **1.** Act of pulling (in various senses); also, the force exerted in pulling. **2.** Act of drinking; a drink. **3.** *Colloq.* A pulling with an oar or oars; a rowing. **4.** An ascent requiring effort; as, a long *pull* uphill. **5.** A knob, cord, wire, handle, or other device for pulling something; as, a bell *pull.* **6.** *Slang.* Influence; special favor. **7.** *Games.* Act or an instance of pulling the ball.

pul'let (pōōl'ĕt; -ĭt), *n.* [OF. *poulet,* dim. of *poule* a hen, fr. L. *pullus* young animal, young fowl.] A young hen, specif. one less than a year old.

pul'ley (pōōl'ĭ), *n.; pl.* -LEYS (-ĭz). [OF. *polie* (F. *poulie*).] **1.** A sheave or small wheel with a grooved rim, with or without the block in

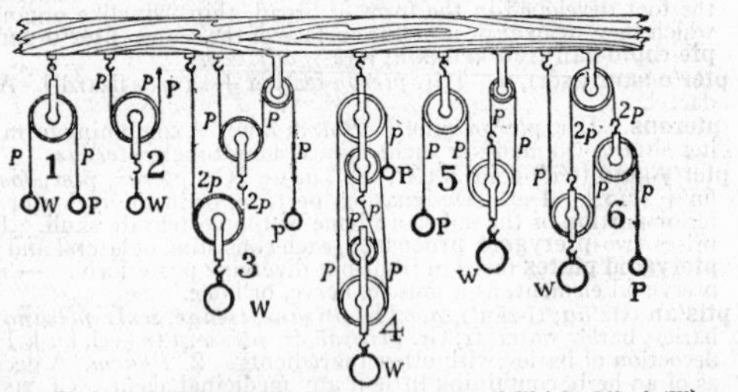

Pulley, 1. Various Tackles, showing theoretical ratios of Weight Lifted (*W*) to Applied Force (*P*). (1) *W* = *P;* (2) *W* = 2 *P;* (3, 4, 6) *W* = 4 *P;* (5) *W* = 3 *P.* The small *p*'s indicate tensions in the various cords.

which it runs, used singly with a rope or chain to change the direction and point of application of a pulling force, and in various combinations to increase the applied force, esp. for lifting weights. **2.** *Mech.* A pulley (as above) or pulleys with ropes to form a tackle, one of the simple machines. See SIMPLE MACHINE, *Illust.* **3.** *Mach.* Any wheel used to transmit power by means of a band, belt, or the like.

Pull'man car, *or* **Pull'man** (pōōl'măn), *n.* [After George M. *Pullman* (1831–97), who introduced them.] *U. S.* A railroad passenger car with specially comfortable furnishings, on which an extra fare is charged.

pul·lo'rum dis·ease' (pŭ·lō'rŭm). [L. *pullorum,* gen. pl. of *pullus* a young fowl.] *Veter.* A destructive, typically diarrheal, disease of chickens or, rarely, of related birds, caused by a toxin-producing bacterium (*Salmonella pullorum*) which may be transmitted in the egg or by contaminated food or water.

pull'-o'ver (pōōl'ō'vẽr), *adj.* That is put on by pulling over the head; as, a *pull-over* sweater, blouse, shirt. — **pull'-o'ver,** *n.*

pul'lu·late (pŭl'ū·lāt), *v. i.* [L. *pullulare* to sprout, fr. *pullulus* young animal, sprout, dim. of *pullus.* See PULLET.] To germinate; to produce abundantly; to teem; — now chiefly figurative. — **pul'lu·la'tion** (-lā'shŭn), *n.*

pul'mo·nar'y (pŭl'mō·nĕr'ĭ; pōōl'mō·nĕr'ĭ; -nẽr·ĭ), *adj.* [L. *pulmonarius,* fr. *pulmo, -onis,* lung.] Of, pertaining to, affecting, or resembling the lungs; having lungs; as, **pulmonary artery,** one conveying venous blood from the heart to the lungs; **pulmonary vein,** one returning arterial blood from the lungs to the heart. See HEART, *Illust.*

pul'mo·nate (-nāt), *adj. Zool.* **a** Having lungs or lunglike organs. **b** Belonging to a large order (Pulmonata) of gastropod mollusks having a lung or respiratory sac and comprising most land snails and slugs and many fresh-water snails. — *n.* A pulmonate gastropod.

pul·mon'ic (pŭl·mŏn'ĭk; pōōl-), *adj.* [L. *pulmo, -onis,* lung.] **1.** Pulmonary. **2.** Of or pert. to pneumonia; pneumonic.

Pul'mo'tor (pŭl'mō'tẽr; pōōl'-), *n.* A trade-mark for a respiratory apparatus for pumping oxygen or air into and out of the lungs, as of an asphyxiated person.

pulp (pŭlp), *n.* [F. *pulpe,* fr. L. *pulpa* flesh, pith.] **1.** A moist, slightly cohering mass, consisting of soft, undissolved animal or vegetable matter. **2.** The soft, succulent part of any fruit; also, the soft pith of certain stems. **3.** Any soft mass of vegetable matter, as of beets, from which most of the water has been extracted by pressure. **4.** *Anat.* The soft, highly vascular and sensitive tissue filling the central cavity of teeth. **5.** *Mining.* Pulverized ore mixed with water. **6.** *Paper Mfg.* The mixture of rag or wood fibers of which paper is made, when ground up and suspended in water. **7.** *Usually pl. Slang, U. S.* A magazine using rough-surfaced paper made of wood pulp; — often with derogatory implication of tawdry writing or sensational tone. Cf. SLICK, *n.,* 3. — *v. t.* **1.** To reduce to pulp. **2.** To deprive of the pulp, or integument. — *v. i.* To be or become pulpy. — **pulp,** *adj.*

pul'pit (pōōl'pĭt), *n.* [L. *pulpitum* scaffold, stage.] **1.** An elevated place or enclosed stage, in a church, in which the clergyman stands while preaching. **2.** Preachers as a class; also, preaching.

pul'pit·eer' (pōōl'pĭ·tēr'), *n.* A preacher; — contemptuous.

pulp'wood' (pŭlp'wōōd'), *n.* The soft wood of certain trees, mostly spruces and aspens, used in making paper.

pulp'y (pŭl'pĭ), *adj.;* PULP'I·ER (-pĭ·ẽr); PULP'I·EST. Like pulp; consisting of pulp; fleshy; succulent. — **pulp'i·ness,** *n.*

pul'que (pōōl'kā), *n.* [Sp., in Mexico.] A fermented drink made in Mexico from the juice of the maguey.

pul'sate (pŭl'sāt *or, esp. Brit.,* pŭl·sāt'), *v. i.* [L. *pulsatus,* past part. of *pulsare* to beat.] To beat; hence, to throb or move rhythmically; to vibrate with life.

pul'sa·tile (pŭl'sȧ·tĭl; 56), *adj.* Pulsating; throbbing, as a vascular tumor.
pul·sa'tion (pŭl·sā'shŭn), *n.* Rhythmical throbbing or vibrating, as of an artery; also, a beat or throb.
pul·sa'tor (pŭl·sā'tẽr), *n.* [L., a beater.] *Mach.* That which beats or throbs in working, as a pulsometer pump.
pul'sa·to'ry (pŭl'sȧ·tō'rĭ *or, esp. Brit.*, -tẽr·ĭ), *adj.* Capable of pulsating; throbbing.
pulse (pŭls), *n.* [OF. *pols, pouls*, fr. L. *puls, pultis*, a porridge made of meal, pulse, etc.] The edible seeds of various leguminous crops, as peas, beans, lentils, etc.; also, any plant yielding pulse.
pulse, *n.* [ME. *pous*, fr. OF. *pous* (fr. L.); ME. *puls*, fr. L. *pulsus* (sc. *venarum*) the beating of the pulse, the pulse, fr. *pellere, pulsum*, to beat.] **1.** A regular throbbing caused in the arteries by the contractions of the heart. **2.** Rhythmical beating, vibrating, or sounding; also, a pulsation or beat. **3.** Underlying sentiment, esp. as discoverable by skill in perception rather than by open inquiry. **4.** *Radio.* An electromagnetic wave or modulation thereof, of brief duration. — *v. i.* To exhibit a pulse or pulsation; throb. — *v. t. Radio.* To produce or modulate (electromagnetic waves) in the form of pulses.
pulse'-jet' en'gine. *Aeronautics.* A jet engine having in its forward end intermittent air-inlet valves, designed to produce a pulsating thrust by the intermittent flow of hot gases; — sometimes called also **pul'so·jet'** (pŭl'sō·jĕt').
pulse'-time' mod'u·la'tion. *Radio.* Modulation of the time intervals between successive pulses of constant duration and amplitude in accordance with a signal; specif., the system of multiplex high-frequency transmission using this method of modulation; — called also **pulse'-po·si'tion mod'u·la'tion.**
pul·sim'e·ter (pŭl·sĭm'ē·tẽr), *n.* [*pulse* + *-meter.*] An instrument for measuring the pulse, esp. its force and rate; a sphygmograph.
pul·som'e·ter (-sŏm'ē·tẽr), *n.* [*pulse* + *-meter.*] **1.** A type of displacement pump, with valves, for raising water by steam, without intervention of a piston or rotating parts. **2.** A sphygmograph, or pulsimeter.
pul'ver·ize (pŭl'vẽr·īz), *v. t. & i.* [F. or L.; F. *pulvériser*, fr. LL. *pulverizare*, fr. L. *pulvis* dust, powder.] **1.** To reduce, or be reduced, to a fine powder or dust, as by beating or grinding; triturate; comminute. **2.** To destroy as by smashing; to demolish, as an argument; to disintegrate. — **pul'ver·iz'a·ble** (-īz'ȧ·b'l), *adj.* — **pul'ver·i·za'tion** (-ĭ·zā'shŭn; -ī·zā'-), *n.* — **pul'ver·iz'er**, *n.*
pul·ver'u·lent (pŭl·vĕr'ū·lĕnt; -ŏŏ·lĕnt), *adj.* [L. *pulverulentus.*] **1.** Consisting of, or reducible to, fine powder; powdery; dusty. **2.** That crumbles easily; friable; — of rocks.
pul·vil'lus (pŭl·vĭl'ŭs), *n.; pl.* -LI (-ī). [L., a little cushion.] *Zool.* A pad or cushionlike organ on an insect's foot.
pul'vi·nate (pŭl'vĭ·nāt), **pul'vi·nat'ed** (-nāt'ĕd; -ĭd), *adj.* [L. *pulvinatus*, fr. *pulvinus* a cushion, an elevation.] **a** *Bot. & Zool.* Cushion-shaped. **b** *Bot.* Having a cushionlike enlargement (**pul·vi'nus** [pŭl·vī'nŭs]) of a petiole or of a secondary petiole at the point of insertion.
pu'ma (pū'mȧ), *n.; pl.* PUMAS (-mȧz). See PLURAL, *Note*, 3. [Sp., fr. Quechua *puma.*] The cougar; also, its fur.
pum'ice (pŭm'ĭs), *n., or* **pumice stone.** [OF. *pomis, pumis*, fr. L. *pumex, pumicis.*] A variety of volcanic glass, full of minute cavities and very light, — used, esp. powdered, for polishing. — *v. t.* To clean, smooth, etc., with pumice. — **pu·mi'ceous** (pū·mĭsh'ŭs), *adj.*
pum'mel (pŭm'ĕl; -'l). Var. of POMMEL.
pump (pŭmp), *n.* [Origin uncert.] A low shoe not fastened on, and gripping the foot only at the toe and heel.
pump, *n.* [MLG. *pumpe*, MD. *pompe* (D. *pomp*), prob. fr. Sp. *bomba.*] A device or machine that raises, transfers, or compresses fluids or that attenuates gases, esp. by suction or pressure, or both. See SUCTION PUMP, *Illust.* — *v. t.* **1.** To raise with a pump, as water. **2.** To propel, eject, emit, etc., in the manner of a pump or one using a pump; as, to *pump* bullets into a victim. **3.** To draw water, air, or the like, from. **4.** To subject to persistent searching, questioning, etc., in order to elicit something; also, to elicit by such efforts; as, unable to *pump* any news out of him. **5.** To operate by manipulating a lever, as if by a pump handle. **6.** To fill with air by means of a pump or bellows. — *v. i.* **1.** To work, or raise water, etc., with a pump. **2.** To move up and down like a pump handle. — **pump'er**, *n.*
pum'per·nick'el (pŭm'pẽr·nĭk''l; *G.* pŏŏm'pẽr-), *n.* [G.] A coarse, somewhat acid bread, made of unbolted rye.
pump'kin (pŭmp'kĭn; *colloq. and commonly* pŭng'kĭn), *n.* [From older *pompion, pompon*, fr. MF. *pompon*, fr. *popon, pepon*, fr. L. *pepo, peponis*, fr. Gr. *pepōn*, prop., ripe, mellow.] **1.** The round, deep-yellow, gourdlike fruit of a vine (*Cucurbita pepo*) of the gourd family, widely cultivated as food; also, the prickly-hairy vine. **2.** In England, any large variety of squash.
pump'kin·seed' (-sēd'), *n.* Any of various small fresh-water sunfishes, esp. the common sunfish. See SUNFISH.
pun (pŭn), *n.* A play on words of the same sound but different meanings or on different applications of a word, for the witty effect. — *v. i.;* PUNNED (pŭnd); PUN'NING. To make puns or a pun. — *v. t.* To persuade or affect by a pun.
‖**pu'na** (pōō'nä), *n.* [Sp., fr. Quechua *puna.*] A high bleak plateau region of the central Andes, esp. in Peru, Bolivia, and north Argentina, usually at an altitude of 7,000 to 13,000 feet.
punch (pŭnch), *n.* [Prob. fr. Hind. *pāc* five (ingredients), fr. Skr. *pañca.*] A beverage usually composed of wine or distilled liquor, water, milk, or tea, with sugar, lemon juice, and, often, spice or mint.
Punch, *n.* [Abbr. fr. PUNCHINELLO.] The principal character in a puppet show (**Punch'-and-Ju'dy show**) in which a little hook-nosed humpback, Punch, quarrels ludicrously with his wife, Judy.
punch, *v. t.* **1.** To prod with a stick; to poke; hence, to herd, as cattle. **2.** To strike, esp. with the fist. **3.** To perforate; to puncture; also, to make by perforating or puncturing; as, to *punch* holes in cloth. — **Syn.** See STRIKE. — *n.* **1.** A quick blow with the fist. **2.** *Colloq.* Effectively aimed force; as, a cartoon without *punch.* — **punch'er**, *n.*
punch, *n.* [Appar. fr. ME. *ponchon, ponson.* See PUNCHEON.] *Mach.* **a** A tool, usually a short rod of steel, variously shaped at one end, either solid or hollow and sharp-edged, for various uses, as perforating, marking, centering, embossing, starting a bolt out of a hole, etc.; specif., such a tapering tool for driving the heads of nails below the surface. **b** The tool used with a die; the upper die.
punch bowl. A large bowl for punch, lemonade, etc.
pun'cheon (pŭn'chŭn), *n.* [OF. *poinchon, poinçon*, fr. VL. *punctiare* to punch, prick, fr. L. *pungere, punctum.*] **1.** A figured die or punch, used by goldsmiths, cutlers, etc. **2.** *Carp.* A short, upright framing timber; also, a split log or heavy slab with the face smoothed, used esp. in early U. S. for flooring. **3.** [Perh. a different word.] A large cask of varying capacity; also, its volume as a measure. In England formerly the wine puncheon was 84 wine gallons (70 imperial gals.); the beer puncheon was equal to two barrels or 72 gallons.
pun'chi·nel'lo (pŭn'chĭ·nĕl'ō), *n.; pl.* -LOS, -LOES (-ōz). [From It. dial. for *pulcinella*, dim. of *pulcina* a chicken, fr. L. *pullus.*] **1.** A Punch; a buffoon. **2.** Any similarly squat grotesque person or animal.
punch'ing bag. A stuffed or inflated bag, usually suspended, to be punched for exercise or for training in boxing.
punch press. *Mach.* A press for working esp. on metal by the use of cutting, shaping, or combination dies.
punc'tate (pŭngk'tāt), **punc'tat·ed** (-tāt·ĕd; -ĭd), *adj.* [From L. *punctum* point.] Marked by dots; specif., *Bot. & Zool.*, dotted with minute spots. — **punc·ta'tion** (pŭngk·tā'shŭn), *n.*
‖**punc·ta'tim** (pŭngk·tā'tĭm), *adv.* [NL.] Point for point.
punc·til'i·o (pŭngk·tĭl'ĭ·ō; -yō), *n.; pl.* -IOS (-ĭ·ōz; -yōz). [From It. *puntiglio* and Sp. *puntillo*, dim. fr. *punto* point, fr. L. *punctum.*] **1.** A nice detail of conduct in a ceremony or in observance of a code. **2.** Exactness in observing details; punctiliousness; meticulosity.
punc·til'i·ous (-tĭl'ĭ·ŭs; -yŭs), *adj.* Attentive to punctilios; scrupulously exact in details or forms. — **Syn.** See CAREFUL. — **punc·til'i·ous·ly**, *adv.* — **punc·til'i·ous·ness**, *n.*
punc'tu·al (pŭngk'tū·ăl), *adj.* [ML. *punctualis*, fr. L. *punctus* point, fr. *pungere, punctum*, to prick.] **1.** Having the nature or a property of a point; specif., having fixity as a point in space; as, a *punctual* presence; also, having no extent or duration as a mathematical point; as, a *punctual* atom. **2.** Observant of nice points; punctilious. **3.** Attentive in regard to appointed or exact time; prompt. — **Syn.** See CAREFUL. — **punc'tu·al·ly**, *adv.* — **punc'tu·al·ness**, *n.*
punc'tu·al'i·ty (-ăl'ĭ·tĭ), *n.; pl.* -TIES (-tĭz). Quality or fact of being punctual; esp., characteristic promptness in keeping engagements.
punc'tu·ate (pŭngk'tū·āt), *v. t.;* -AT'ED (-āt'ĕd; -ĭd); -AT'ING. [ML. *punctuare*, fr. L. *punctus* point.] **1.** To separate (written matter) into sentences, clauses, etc., by points or stops. **2.** To break into or interrupt at intervals. **3.** To emphasize; as, jets *punctuating* the darkness. — *v. i.* To use punctuation marks.
punc'tu·a'tion (pŭngk'tū·ā'shŭn), *n.* Act or art of punctuating a writing, etc.; division of literary composition into sentences and members of a sentence by means of points indicating the structure of sentence parts for clearness. Chief points: the *period* [.], the *colon* [:], the *semicolon* [;], the *comma* [,]; also, the *interrogation point* [?], the *exclamation point* [!], *parentheses* [( )], the *dash* [—], *brackets* [[ ]], the *apostrophe* ['], the *hyphen* [-], *quotation marks* [" "] [' '], the *brace* [{ }], and the *ellipsis* [. . .] or [* * *]. Punctuation is *close* when the points, esp. commas, are used freely to mark the grouping and the separation of phrases, clauses, etc.; it is *open* when points are omitted wherever possible without ambiguity.
punc'tu·a'tor (pŭngk'tū·ā'tẽr), *n.* One who punctuates.
punc'ture (pŭngk'tūr), *n.* [L. *punctura*, fr. *pungere, punctum*, to prick.] Act of puncturing; also, a hole or slight wound resulting from puncturing. — *v. t.* **1.** To pierce with a pointed instrument. **2.** *Colloq.* To suffer a puncture of, as a tire. — *v. i.* To be susceptible of being punctured. — **punc'tur·a·ble** (-tūr·ȧ·b'l), *adj.*
pun'dit (pŭn'dĭt), *n.* [Hind. *paṇḍit*, fr. Skr. *paṇḍita* a learned man.] A learned teacher or critic; esp., *India*, a Brahman versed in Hindu science, laws, and religion.
pung (pŭng), *n.* [Earlier *tom pung*, a corrupt. of *toboggan* or its source.] *Local, U. S.* A type of sleigh with a boxlike body.
pun'gen·cy (pŭn'jĕn·sĭ), *n.* Quality or state of being pungent; keenness; sharpness; poignancy.
pun'gent (-jĕnt), *adj.* [L. *pungens, -entis*, pres. part. of *pungere, punctum*, to prick.] **1.** Causing a sharp sensation, as of the taste, smell, or feelings; pricking; acrid. **2.** Sharply painful; piercing; poignant. **3.** Of speech, etc., caustic; biting; also, stimulating. **4.** *Bot.* Prickly-pointed; hard and sharp. — **pun'gent·ly**, *adv.*
Syn. **Pungent, piquant, poignant, racy** mean sharp and stimulating in character. All are used figuratively as well as literally. **Pungent** implies power to sting or stimulate; **piquant,** to whet the appetite by tartness or pungency; **poignant,** to enter deeply as if by piercing; **racy,** to impress with its freshness, strength, and tang.
Pu'nic (pū'nĭk), *adj.* [L. *Punicus*, fr. *Poeni* the Carthaginians.] Pertaining to ancient Carthage or its inhabitants; hence, from the Roman view of their character, faithless; treacherous. — *n.* The language of ancient Carthage, a Phoenician dialect.
‖**Pu'ni·ca fi'des** (pū'nĭ·kȧ fī'dēz). [L.] Punic faith; hence, treachery.
pun'ish (pŭn'ĭsh), *v. t.* [OF. *punir*, fr. L. *punire, punitum*, for *poenire*, fr. *poena* punishment, penalty.] **1.** To afflict with pain, loss, or suffering for a crime or fault; to chasten. **2.** To inflict a penalty for (an offense) upon the offender; to visit (a fault, crime, etc.) with pain or loss; as, to *punish* treason with death. **3.** *Colloq.* To deal with harshly, roughly, or the like, so as to deplete in numbers, quantity, strength, etc.; as, a *punishing* assault. — *v. i.* To inflict punishment. — **pun'ish·er**, *n.*
Syn. **Punish, chastise, castigate, chasten, discipline, correct** mean to inflict pain, loss, etc., for a sin or fault. **Punish** implies subjection to a penalty for wrongdoing; **chastise,** corporal punishment; **castigate,** a lashing by tongue or pen; **chasten,** subjection to affliction or trial more as a test than a punishment; **discipline,** a punishing or chastening for the sake of bringing under control; **correct,** a punishing aimed at reforming an offender.
pun'ish·a·ble (-ȧ·b'l), *adj.* Deserving of, or liable to, punishment. — **pun'ish·a·bil'i·ty** (-bĭl'ĭ·tĭ), *n.*
pun'ish·ment (-mĕnt), *n.* **1.** Act of punishing. **2.** A penalty inflicted on an offender as a retribution, and incidentally for reformation and prevention. **3.** *Colloq.* Severe, rough, or disastrous treatment.
pu'ni·tive (pū'nĭ·tĭv), *adj.* Also **pu'ni·to'ry** (-tō'rĭ *or, esp. Brit.*, -tẽr·ĭ). That inflicts or is concerned with punishment or penalties; also, aiming at punishment; as, a *punitive* expedition.
Pun·ja'bi (pŭn·jä'bē), *n.* [Hind. *panjābī*, fr. *Panjāb* Punjab, fr. *panj* five + *āb* waters.] **1.** A native of the Punjab, India, peopled largely by Indo-Aryans. **2.** Panjabi.
punk (pŭngk), *n.* [Of Algonquian origin.] **1.** Wood so decayed as to be useful for tinder; touchwood. **2.** A spongy substance prepared from certain fungi (*Polyporus fomentarius* and related species), used as a styptic and as tinder; amadou.

punk (pŭngk), *n.* [Origin uncertain.] **1.** *Obs.* A prostitute. **2.** *Slang, U.S.* **a** A beginner; an inexperienced hand. **b** Something inferior or worthless. — *adj. Slang, U.S.* Very poor; bad; inferior; also, miserable; in poor health.

pun'kah (pŭng'kȧ), *n.* Also **pun'ka.** [Hind. *pankhā* a fan.] *India.* A large portable fan or a canvas-covered frame suspended from the ceiling for fanning a room.

punk'ie (pŭng'kĭ), *n.* Also **punk'y** (-kĭ). [D. *punki,* fr. Lenape (Delaware Indian dialect) *ponk,* lit., fine ashes, powder.] *U.S.* A biting midge (genus *Culicoides* or allied genera).

pun'ster (pŭn'stẽr), *n.* One who is addicted to punning.

punt (pŭnt), *n.* [AS., fr. L. *ponto* punt, pontoon.] **1.** *Chiefly Brit.* A narrow, flat-bottomed boat with square ends, usually propelled with a pole. **2.** *Football.* Act of punting the ball, or an instance of it. — *v. t.* **1.** To propel, as a punt, by pushing with a pole; also, to convey in a punt. **2.** *Football.* To kick (the ball) before it touches the ground, when let fall from the hands. — *v. i.* **1.** To boat or hunt in a punt. **2.** To punt a football.

punt, *v. i.* [F. *ponter,* fr. *ponte* a point, player against the bank, fr. Sp. *punto,* fr. L. *punctum* point.] To gamble; esp., to play against the banker, as at faro and baccarat. — *n.* A point in some games of chance; also, a punter.

punt'er (pŭnt'ẽr), *n.* One who punts or gambles.

pun'ty (pŭn'tĭ), *n.* [F. *pontil.*] *Glass Mfg.* An iron or steel rod used for fashioning hot glass; a pontil.

pu'ny (pū'nĭ), *adj.;* PU'NI·ER (-nĭ·ẽr); PU'NI·EST. [F. *puîné* younger, later born, fr. OF. *puisné,* fr. *puis* afterwards + *né* born.] **1.** *Obs.* Puisne. **2.** Slight or inferior in power, size, or importance; petty; weak; insignificant.

pup (pŭp), *n.* [From PUPPY.] A young dog; also, a young seal. — *v. i.;* PUPPED (pŭpt); PUP'PING. To bring forth whelps.

pu'pa (pū'pȧ), *n.; pl.* PUPAE (-pē), PUPAS (-pȧz). [NL., fr. L. *pupa* girl, doll, puppet.] *Zool.* An intermediate, usually quiescent, form assumed by metabolic insects after the larval stage, and maintained until the beginning of the adult, or imaginal, stage; a chrysalis. Cf. COCOON. — **pu'pal** (-păl), *adj.*

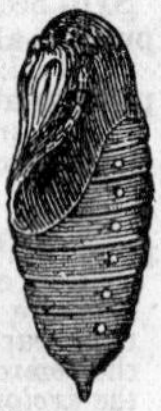

Pupa of a Moth (*Estigmene acraea*). Nat. size. Cf. WIGGLER, *Illust.*

pu'pate (pū'pāt), *v. i.* To become a pupa. — **pu·pa'tion** (pū·pā'shŭn), *n.*

pu'pil (pū'p'l; -pĭl), *n.* [F. *pupille,* n. fem., fr. L. *pupilla* the pupil of the eye, dim. of *pupa* girl.] The contractile aperture in the iris, round in most vertebrates, but in foxes and cats elliptical when contracted.

pu'pil, *n.* [F. *pupille,* n. masc. & fem., fr. L. *pupillus, pupilla,* dim. of *pupus* boy, *pupa* girl.] **1.** A youth of either sex under the care of an instructor or tutor. **2.** *Civil Law.* A boy or girl under the age of puberty and placed in charge of a guardian. — **Syn.** See SCHOLAR.

pu'pil·age (pū'pĭ·lĭj), *n.* Also **pu'pil·lage.** State or period of being a pupil.

pu'pil·lar'i·ty, pu'pi·lar'i·ty (pū'pĭ·lăr'ĭ·tĭ), *n. Chiefly Scots Law.* The period before puberty.

pu'pil·lar'y (pū'pĭ·lĕr'ĭ *or, esp. Brit.,* -lẽr·ĭ), *adj.* Of the pupil of the eye.

pu'pil·lar'y, *adj.* [L. *pupillaris.*] Of or pert. to a pupil or ward.

pu·pip'a·rous (pū·pĭp'ȧ·rŭs), *adj.* [*pupa* + *-parous.*] *Zool.* Of or pertaining to a division (Pupipara) of dipterous insects in which the young are born ready to become pupae, as in certain ticks.

pup'pet (pŭp'ĕt; -ĭt), *n.* [OF. *poupette,* dim. of (F. dial.) *poupe.*] **1.** A small image in human form; doll. **2.** A similar figure, often with jointed limbs, moved by hand or by strings or wires, as in a mock drama (**puppet show**); a marionette. **3.** One acting as another wills; a tool.

pup'pet·ry (-rĭ), *n.* **1.** Puppets, or puppetlike actions; mummery. **2.** The art of manipulating puppets.

pup'py (pŭp'ĭ), *n.; pl.* PUPPIES (-ĭz). [F. *poupée* doll, puppet.] **1.** The young of a canine animal; a whelp. **2.** A conceited, impertinent, or empty-headed youth; a silly fop.

puppy love. *Colloq.* = CALF LOVE.

pur (pûr). Var. of PURR.

pur'blind' (pûr'blīnd'), *adj.* [ME. *pur blind* totally blind.] **1.** Formerly, wholly blind or partly blind. **2.** That discerns imperfectly or obscurely; lacking in vision or understanding; obtuse. — **pur'blind'ness,** *n.*

pur'chas·a·ble (pûr'chĭs·ȧ·b'l), *adj.* Capable of being purchased; hence, venal; corrupt. — **pur'chas·a·bil'i·ty** (-bĭl'ĭ·tĭ), *n.*

pur'chase (pûr'chĭs), *v. t.* [OF. *porchacier, purchacier,* to pursue, to seek eagerly, fr. *por, pur,* for (fr. L. *pro*) + *chacier* to chase.] **1.** *Archaic.* To pursue and obtain; to acquire by seeking. **2.** To obtain by paying money or its equivalent; to buy for a price. **3.** To obtain by any outlay, as of labor, sacrifice, flattery, etc. **4.** To apply to (anything) a device for obtaining a mechanical advantage; to get a purchase upon; also, to move by a purchase (def. 4, below). **5.** *Law.* To acquire (real estate) by any means other than by descent or inheritance. — *n.* **1.** *Obs.* A seeking or procuring anything; also, acquisition. **2.** That which is obtained, in any manner; booty; now, specif., that obtained for a price in money. **3.** Acquisition for a price; buying. **4.** Any mechanical hold or advantage applied to the raising or moving of heavy bodies, as by a lever, tackle, or capstan; also, the apparatus. **5.** Income; yield; return; as, worth a year's *purchase.* **6.** *Law.* Acquisition of lands or tenements by any means other than descent or inheritance. — **pur'chas·er** (-chĭs·ẽr), *n.*

pur'dah (pûr'dȧ), *n.* [Hind. & Per. *pardah* veil.] A curtain or screen; esp., *India,* one used to seclude women.

pure (pūr; 114), *adj.* [OF. *pur,* fr. L. *purus.*] **1. a** Separate from all heterogeneous or extraneous matter; without alloy, stain, or taint; clear; unmixed; sheer. **b** Simple; mere. **c** Complete; absolute; as, *pure* nonsense. **2.** Free from what vitiates, weakens, or pollutes; faultless; as, he spoke *pure* French. **3.** Free from moral defilement or guilt; hence, innocent; guiltless. **4.** Chaste. **5.** Of unmixed blood or stock. **6.** Abstract; theoretic; as, *pure* science. **7.** *Bib.* Ritually clean. **8.** *Biol.* In genetics, homozygous; hence, breeding true with respect to a certain character or number of characters. **9.** *Kantianism.* Free from empirical elements; a priori. **10.** *Phonet.* Having an unvarying sound made with the oral speech organs in a fixed position; monophthongal. — **Syn.** See CHASTE.

Pure, Simon (pūr). A Pennsylvania Quaker in Mrs. Centlivre's comedy *A Bold Stroke for a Wife* (1718) who, impersonated in advance by Colonel Feignwell, is himself treated as an impostor; hence, **si'mon-pure',** *adj.,* genuine; authentic.

pure'bred' (pūr'brĕd'), *adj.* Of a recognized breed kept pure for many generations. — **pure'bred',** *n.*

pu·rée' (pū·rā'; pū'rā; *F.* pü'rā'), *n.* [F.] Food boiled to a pulp and rubbed through a sieve; also, a soup thickened with this. — **Syn.** See SOUP.

pure'ly (pūr'lĭ), *adv.* **a** Without admixture of anything injurious or foreign. **b** Merely; solely. **c** Chastely; innocently. **d** Completely.

pure'ness, *n.* State or quality of being pure; purity.

pur'fle (pûr'f'l), *v. t.;* -FLED (-f'ld); -FLING (-flĭng). [OF. *porfiler,* later *pourfiler,* fr. L. *pro* for + *filum* a thread.] **1.** To ornament the border of. **2.** To ornament or outline, as with metallic threads, jewels, or the like. — *n.* A hem, border, or trimming. — **pur'fling** (-flĭng), *n.*

pur·ga'tion (pûr·gā'shŭn), *n.* A purging; also, result of purging.

pur'ga·tive (pûr'gȧ·tĭv), *adj.* [F. *purgatif,* fr. L. *purgativus.*] Purging or tending to purge; cathartic. — *n. Med.* A purging medicine; a cathartic.

pur'ga·to'ri·al (-tō'rĭ·ăl; 70), *adj.* Also **pur'ga·to'ri·an** (-ăn). Expiatory; cleansing of sin; also, of or pert. to purgatory.

pur'ga·to'ry (pûr'gȧ·tō'rĭ *or, esp. Brit.,* -tẽr·ĭ), *n.* [OF. and ML.; OF. *purgatoire,* fr. ML. *purgatorium.* See PURGE.] **1.** *Theol.* An intermediate state after death for expiatory purification, esp. from venial sins. **2.** A place or state of temporary punishment. — *adj. Now Rare.* Purgative.

purge (pûrj), *v. t.;* PURGED (pûrjd); PURG'ING (pûr'jĭng). [OF. *purgier,* fr. L. *purgare,* earlier *purigare,* fr. *purus* pure.] **1.** To cleanse or purify by separating and carrying off whatever is impure, heterogeneous, or superfluous. **2.** To clear of guilt, or moral or ceremonial defilement. **3.** To remove in cleansing; to deterge. **4.** To clear of sediment, as a boiler, or of air, as a pipe. **5.** *Med.* To cause evacuations from, esp. the intestines. **6.** *Polit.* To rid or free (a state or party) by a purge; to get rid of (disloyal or suspect elements). — *v. i.* **1.** To become free of impurities, excess, etc., as by clearing. **2.** To have or produce frequent evacuations. — *n.* **1.** A purging; purgation. **2.** That which purges, esp. a cathartic. **3.** A ridding, as of a nation or party, of elements or members regarded as treacherous, disloyal, or suspect. — **purg'er** (pûr'jẽr), *n.*

pu'ri·fy (pū'rĭ·fī), *v. t. & i.;* -FIED (-fīd); -FY'ING. [OF. *purifier,* fr. L. *purificare,* fr. *purus* pure + *-ficare* (in comp.) to make.] To make or become pure; specif.: **a** To clear from material defilement; to free from impurities or noxious matter. **b** To free from guilt or moral blemish. **c** To free from that which is alien, extraneous, corrupting, etc., as a language of barbarisms. — **pu'ri·fi·ca'tion** (-fĭ·kā'shŭn), *n.* — **pu·rif'i·ca·to'ry** (pū·rĭf'ĭ·kȧ·tō'rĭ *or, esp. Brit.,* pū'rĭ·fĭ·kā'tẽr·ĭ), *adj.* — **pu'ri·fi'er** (pū'rĭ·fī'ẽr), *n.*

Pu'rim (pū'rĭm; pōō'rĭm; *Heb.* pōō·rēm'), *n.* [Heb. *pūr,* pl. *pūrīm,* a lot.] See JEWISH HOLIDAYS.

pu'rine (pū'rēn; -rĭn), *n.* Also **pu'rin** (-rĭn). [Abbr. fr. L. *purum* pure + NL. *uricum* uric acid + *-in.*] *Chem.* A colorless crystalline compound, $C_5H_4N_4$, the parent of compounds of the uric-acid group.

pur'ism (pūr'ĭz'm; 114), *n.* [F. *purisme.*] **1.** Rigid adherence to, or insistence upon, purity or nicety, esp. in use of words, etc.; also, an example of such adherence. **2.** The theory or practice of certain artists (about 1918) in reaction against cubism, characterized chiefly by the use of familiar recognizable objects in painting.

pur'ist (-ĭst), *n.* One solicitous, esp. oversolicitous, about purity or nicety, esp. in language. — **pu·ris'tic** (pū·rĭs'tĭk), *adj.*

Pu'ri·tan (pū'rĭ·tăn), *n.* [LL. *puritas* purity + *-an.*] **1.** *Eccl. Hist.* One who, in the time of Queen Elizabeth and the first two Stuarts, opposed traditional and formal usages, and advocated simpler forms of faith and worship than those established by law. **2.** [*often not cap.*] One who practices or preaches a more rigorous or professedly purer moral code than that which prevails. — **Pu'ri·tan, pu'ri·tan,** *adj.*

pu'ri·tan'i·cal (-tăn'ĭ·kăl), **pu'ri·tan'ic** (-ĭk), *adj.* **1.** [*cap.*] Of or pertaining to the Puritans or their doctrines and practice. **2.** Manifesting the influence of puritan beliefs or practices; morally rigorous; strict. — **pu'ri·tan'i·cal·ly,** *adv.* — **pu'ri·tan'i·cal·ness,** *n.*

Pu'ri·tan·ism (pū'rĭ·tăn·ĭz'm), *n.* [*often not cap.*] The doctrines, ideas, or practice of, or characteristic of, Puritans; austerity, esp. in matters of religion or conduct.

pu'ri·ty (pū'rĭ·tĭ), *n.* **1.** Quality or state of being pure; specif.: **a** Freedom from foreign admixture or deleterious matter. **b** Cleanness; freedom from foulness. **c** Freedom from guilt; innocence; chastity. **d** Freedom from sinister or improper motive. **e** Freedom from foreign words and idioms, or from barbarisms. **2.** Of color, saturation.

purl (pûrl), *v. t. & i.* [From PURL a border.] **1.** To purfle. **2.** Also **pearl** (pûrl). To finish lace with an edging of very small loops. **3.** Also **pearl.** To invert the stitches in knitting; to seam. — *n.* [From E. dial. *pirl* to twist, spin.] **1.** Gold or silver thread or twisted wire used in embroidering or in making edges, as on lace. **2.** Also **pearl.** A fine loop made in edging certain laces or lace braids. **3.** The plaited, fluted, or ruffled part of a ruff. **4.** Also **pearl.** [Perh. a diff. word.] *Knitting.* Inversion of stitches, producing a ribbed appearance.

purl (pûrl), *v. i.* **1.** To run swiftly round, as a small stream flowing among obstructions; to eddy; swirl; also, to make a murmuring sound. **2.** To move in circles, ripples, or undulations; to curl. — *n.* **1.** A purling or swirling stream or rill. **2.** A gentle murmur, as of purling water.

pur'lieu (pûr'lū), *n.* [Corrupted (by influence of *lieu* place) fr. OF. *puralée, poralée,* fr. *poraler* to go through.] **1.** *Eng. Hist.* Afforested land disafforested so as to remit to the former owners their rights. **2.** A place of resort; haunt; *pl.,* bounds. **3.** An outlying or adjacent district; *pl.,* environs; neighborhood.

pur'lin (pûr'lĭn), *n.* Also **pur'line.** *Arch.* In roofs, a horizontal member supporting the common rafters. See ROOF, *Illust.*

pur·loin' (pûr·loin'), *v. t. & i.* [OF. *purloignier* to retard, delay, fr. *pur, por,* for (fr. L. *pro*) + *loin* far, far off (fr. L. *longe*).] To steal; filch. — **Syn.** See STEAL. — **pur·loin'er** (-ẽr), *n.*

pur'ple (pûr'p'l), *n.* [From AS. *purpure* (fr. L.), and fr. OF. *purpre,* fr. L. *purpura* purple fish, purple dye, fr. Gr. *porphyra.*] **1.** A color of a hue between blue and red; one of the colors commonly called magenta, violet, lilac, mauve, etc.; in classical Hebrew and Greek literature, probably crimson. **2.** Cloth dyed purple, or a garment of such color; esp., a purple robe emblematic of rank or authority, specif. that worn by Roman emperors. **3.** Imperial or regal rank or power; also, *Colloq.,* exalted station. **4.** The cardinalate. — *adj.* **1.** Showing or having the color purple. **2.** Imperial; regal. **3.** Ornate; highly rhe-

torical. — *v. t.*; -PLED (-p'ld); -PLING (-plĭng). To make or dye purple. — *v. i.* To become or turn purple.
purple grackle. See GRACKLE.
Purple Heart, Order of the. *U. S.* A military order established by George Washington and re-established 1932 for granting decorations to soldiers wounded in service.
purple medic. Lucerne.
pur'plish (pûr'plĭsh), *adj.* Somewhat purple.
pur·port' (pûr·pōrt'; pûr'pōrt; 70), *v. t.* [OF. *purporter, porporter.* See PRO-; PORT to carry.] To convey or profess outwardly, as one's or its meaning or intention; to have the appearance, often specious, of being, intending, etc.; to profess; as, men *purporting* to be state police.
pur'port (pûr'pōrt; 70), *n.* Meaning; import; tenor; often, substance; gist; as, the *purport* of the conversation.
pur'pose (pûr'pŭs), *v. t. & i.* [OF. *purposer, pourposer,* fr. *pur, por,* for (fr. L. *pro*) + *poser* to place.] To propose as an aim to oneself; to intend; resolve. — *n.* **1. a** That which one sets before himself as an object to be attained; intention. **b** Resolution; determination. **2.** The object or result aimed at; as, energy applied to little *purpose.* **3.** The immediate subject or action; — in ***to the purpose,*** with relevancy. — **Syn.** See INTENTION. — **pur'pose·ful, pur'pose·less,** *adj.* — ***on purpose.*** Designedly; intentionally.
pur'pose·ly, *adv.* With a deliberate or express purpose.
pur'pos·ive (pûr'pŭs·ĭv), *adj.* **1.** Serving a useful function, though not as a result of design. **2.** Having or tending to fulfill a conscious purpose or design. — **pur'pos·ive·ly,** *adv.* — **pur'pos·ive·ness,** *n.*
pur'pu·ra (pûr'pū·rȧ), *n.* [L., purple, purple fish. See PURPLE.] *Med.* A disease marked by livid spots on the skin or mucous membranes, caused by extravasated blood. — **pur·pu'ric** (pûr·pū'rĭk), *adj.*
pur'pure (pûr'pûr), *n.* *Heraldry.* Purple.
purr, pur (pûr), *v. i.*; PURRED (pûrd); PURR'ING. [Imitative.] To utter a low, murmuring sound, as made by a cat when pleased. — *v. t.* To signify by purring. — *n.* The sound made by a purring cat, or a similar sound.
purse (pûrs), *n.* [AS. *purs,* fr. LL. *bursa,* fr. Gr. *byrsa* hide, skin, leather.] **1.** A small bag or pouch, esp. to carry money in; a pocketbook. **2.** A treasury; finances; as, the public *purse.* **3.** Any bag, pouch, or the like, like or likened to a money purse; as, the *purse* of some fishing nets. **4.** A sum of money offered as a prize, or a sum collected as a present. — *v. t.* **1.** To put into a purse. **2.** To pucker; knit.
purse crab. A large crab (*Birgus latro*) of tropical islands of the Indian and Pacific oceans, related to the hermit crab (which see) but having a broad symmetrical abdomen; — called also *palm crab* or *tree crab.* It lives in the ground, feeds on fruit, esp. coconuts, and weighs up to 20 pounds. Cf. CRAB, 1 **b**.
purse'-proud', *adj.* Proud because of one's wealth.
purs'er (pûr'sẽr), *n.* A clerk on a passenger vessel who keeps the accounts, as of freight, tickets, etc.
pur'si·ness (pûr'sĭ·nĕs; -nĭs), *n.* State of being pursy.
purs'lane (pûrs'lān; -lĭn), *n.* [OF. *porcelaine,* corrupt. fr. L. *porcilaca,* for *portulaca.*] Any plant of a family (Portulacaceae, the purslane family) of usually succulent herbs having perfect regular flowers with two sepals and 4–5 hypogynous petals. The common purslane (*Portulaca oleracea*), with succulent leaves, is used as a potherb, for salads, etc., and is common as a weed in gardens.
pur·su'ance (pẽr·sū'ăns), *n.* Act of pursuing; chiefly, a carrying out or into effect; prosecution; as, in *pursuance* of his researches.
pur·su'ant (pẽr·sū'ănt), *adj.* Acting or done in consequence or in prosecution; conformable; — with *to* or *of.*
pur·su'ant, pur·su'ant·ly, *adv.* Agreeably; conformably; as, *pursuant* to our contract.
pur·sue' (pẽr·sū'), *v. t.*; PUR·SUED' (-sūd'); PUR·SU'ING (-sū'ĭng). [OF. *porsivre, poursuir,* fr. L. *prosequi,* fr. *pro-* + *sequi* to follow.] **1.** To follow with a view to overtake; to chase. **2.** To seek; to use or adopt measures to obtain. **3.** To proceed along, with a view to some end, as to reach, accomplish, obtain, etc.; to follow, as a wise course. **4.** To prosecute or be engaged in, as one's studies. **5.** To continue to afflict, as illness or consequences. — *v. i.* To go in pursuit. — **Syn.** See FOLLOW. — **pur·su'er** (-sū'ẽr), *n.*
pur·suit' (pẽr·sūt'), *n.* [OF. *poursuite,* fr. the v. See PURSUE.] **1.** Act of pursuing. **2.** That which one pursues, or engages in, as a course of business or occupation; as, a literary *pursuit.* **3.** In full **pursuit plane.** A fighter; often specif., an offensive fighter of fair range for pursuit of enemy bombers. — **Syn.** See WORK.
pur'sui·vant (pûr'swĭ·vănt), *n.* [F. *poursuivant,* prop. pres. part. of *poursuivre.*] **1.** *Heralds' College.* A functionary ranking below a herald, but having similar duties. **2.** *Archaic.* A follower; attendant.
pur'sy (pûr'sĭ; *dial.* pŭs'ĭ), *adj.*; PUR'SI·ER (-sĭ·ẽr); PUR'SI·EST. [AF. *pursif,* fr. OF. *polsif* (F. *poussif*), ult. fr. L. *pulsare* to beat, throb.] **1.** Short-winded, esp. because of corpulence; fat. **2.** Swollen with pampering or luxurious living; characterized by or arising from arrogance of wealth, self-indulgence, etc.; as, *pursy* insolence.
pur'te·nance (pûr'tē·năns), *n.* [ME. *purtenaunce.*] *Archaic.* The pluck of an animal.
pu'ru·lence (pū'rōō·lĕns; pūr'ū-), *n.* Also **pu'ru·len·cy** (-lĕn·sĭ). Quality or state of being purulent; also, pus.
pu'ru·lent (-lĕnt), *adj.* [L. *purulentus,* fr. *pus, puris,* pus, matter.] *Med.* Of or consisting of pus; of the nature of pus; attended with suppuration. — **pu'ru·lent·ly,** *adv.*
pur·vey' (pûr·vā'), *v. t.* [OF. *porveeir, porveoir,* fr. L. *providere.*] To furnish or supply, as provisions.
pur·vey'ance (-ăns), *n.* **1.** Act of purveying or procuring, esp. provisions. **2.** *Eng. Law.* A providing of supplies or services for the crown by pre-emption or impressment.
pur·vey'or (-ẽr), *n.* **1.** A victualer; a caterer. **2.** *Eng.* An officer who formerly exacted provision, under the right of purveyance.
pur'view (pûr'vū), *n.* [OF. *porveü, pourveü,* provided, resolved. See PURVEY.] **1.** *Law.* The body of a statute, or its scope. **2.** The sphere or fixed limits of one's authority, competence, etc.; province; scope; field. **3.** Compass or reach of sight or understanding; as, a matter within the *purview* of ordinary men.
pus (pŭs), *n.* [L.] The yellowish-white opaque creamy matter produced by suppuration, chiefly exudate and disintegrating tissue with bacteria and leucocytes.
Pu'sey·ism (pū'zĭ·ĭz'm), *n.* Tractarianism (which see); — from E. B. Pusey (1800–82). — **Pu'sey·ite** (-īt), *n.*
push (pŏŏsh), *v. t.* [F. *pousser,* fr. L. *pulsare,* v. intens. fr. *pellere, pulsum,* to beat, push.] **1.** To press against with force in order to drive or impel; to move or endeavor to move away or ahead by steady pressure, without striking. **2.** To thrust forward, downward, or outward. **3.** To press or urge forward to completion with insistence; to prosecute with vigor or effectiveness, as a campaign. **4.** To bear hard upon so as to involve in difficulty, etc.; as, to be *pushed* for funds. — *v. i.* **1.** To press against something with steady force in order to impel. **2.** To press forward against opposition or with energy. **3.** To exert oneself continuously, vigorously, or obtrusively to gain an end, as success or social advancement.
Syn. **Push, shove, thrust, propel** mean to move ahead or aside by pressure or force. **Push** implies contact by the body exerting such force with the body to be moved; **shove,** the exercise of muscular strength or its like in forcing something along a surface; **thrust,** less steadiness but greater violence than *push;* **propel,** a driving forward or onward by a force imparting motion.
— *n.* **1.** Pressure or an exertion of pressure; as: **a** Extremity; emergency. **b** Any thrust, pressure, impulse, or force steadily applied without striking; a shove. **c** An advance overcoming obstacles. **2.** *Colloq.* Aggressive energy. **3.** *Slang.* **a** An influential or exclusive set. **b** *Australia.* A gang of larrikins. **4.** A part to be pushed, as the button of an electric bell.
push'ball' (pŏŏsh'bôl'), *n.* A game in which each of two sides tries to push an inflated, leather-covered ball, six feet in diameter, across the opponents' goal; also, the ball.
push button. A small knob which, when pushed, actuates a switch, bell, etc., by closing an electric circuit. — **push'-but'ton,** *adj.*
push'cart' (pŏŏsh'kärt'), *n.* A cart or barrow pushed by hand; — used chiefly by street venders.
push'er (-ẽr), *n.* One who or that which pushes.
push'ing, *part. adj.* Enterprising; energetic; also, forward. — **Syn.** See AGGRESSIVE.
push'o'ver (pŏŏsh'ō'vẽr), *n.* **1.** An opponent easy to defeat or capable of no effective resistance; as, backing political *pushovers;* wishful thinking that Japan would be a *pushover.* **2.** A victim either unwilling or too soft or gullible to resist the power of a particular attraction or appeal; a "sucker"; as, he is a *pushover* for that kind of advertising. **3.** An action or problem offering no difficulties; a "cinch"; as, the game was a *pushover* for the visiting team.
push'pin' (pŏŏsh'pĭn'), *n.* A steel point with projecting glass or metal head that may be pushed into a wall to support a picture, into a map as a marker, etc.
push'-pull' (pŏŏsh'pŏŏl'; 2), *adj.* *Radio.* Having or pertaining to a parallel arrangement of two circuit elements, as vacuum tubes, not in phase, such that their effects supplement each other; as, a *push-pull* amplifier, a *push-pull* circuit. — **push'-pull',** *n.*
Push'tu (pŭsh'tōō). Var. of PASHTO.
pu'sil·la·nim'i·ty (pū'sĭ·lȧ·nĭm'ĭ·tĭ), *n.* Quality or state of being pusillanimous; cowardliness.
pu'sil·lan'i·mous (-lăn'ĭ·mŭs), *adj.* [LL. *pusillanimis,* fr. *pusillus* very little + *animus* the mind.] **1.** Destitute of manly strength and firmness of mind; cowardly; of weak or mean spirit. **2.** Evincing or arising from weakness of spirit and want of courage; as, *pusillanimous* counsels. — **Syn.** See COWARDLY. — **pu'sil·lan'i·mous·ly,** *adv.*
puss (pŏŏs), *n.* **1.** A cat. **2.** A girl.
puss'ley (pŭs'lĭ), *n.* Also **puss'ly.** *U. S.* Purslane.
pus'sy (pŭs'ĭ), *adj.*; PUS'SI·ER (-ĭ·ẽr); PUS'SI·EST. *Med.* Full of or like pus.
puss'y (pŏŏs'ĭ), *n.*; *pl.* PUSSIES (-ĭz). [Dim. of *puss.*] **1.** A pet name for a cat. **2.** *Colloq.* A catkin of the pussy willow. **3.** *Scot. & Dial.* A hare.
puss'y·foot' (-fŏŏt'), *v. i.* *Both Slang.* **1.** To move warily or stealthily, as a cat does. **2.** To refrain from committing oneself, as in regard to a question at issue. — *n.* One who pussyfoots.
puss'y wil'low (pŏŏs'ĭ). Any willow (esp. the American *Salix discolor*) having large cylindrical silky aments.
pus'tu·lant (pŭs'tū·lănt), *adj.* [LL. *pustulans,* pres. part.] Producing pustules. — *n.* A pustulant medicine.
pus'tu·lar (-lẽr), *adj.* **1.** Of, pert. to, or of the nature of pustules. **2.** Covered with pustulelike prominences.
pus'tu·late (-lāt), *v. t. & i.* [LL. *pustulatus,* past part. of *pustulare* to blister, fr. *pustula.* See PUSTULE.] To form into pustules, or blisters. — (-lāt), *adj.* Covered with pustules.
pus'tu·la'tion (-lā'shŭn), *n.* Act of producing pustules; state of being pustulated; a pustule.
pus'tule (pŭs'tūl), *n.* [OF. or L.; OF., fr. L. *pustula.*] **1.** A small circumscribed elevation of the skin with an inflamed base, containing pus. **2.** Any small pimplelike or blisterlike elevation.
put (pŏŏt; *the pron.* pŭt *is common in dial., esp. in parts of Scotland; cf.* PUTT), *v. t.*; *past & past part.* PUT; *pres. part.* PUT'TING. [ME. *putten, puten,* fr. AS. *putian,* also *potian,* to push, thrust.] **1.** To thrust; push; impel. **2.** To throw or cast, esp., as in athletics, with a pushing motion "overhand"; as, to *put* the shot. **3.** To drive or force; hence, to incite; urge; constrain. **4.** To bring to a (stated or implied) position or place or relation; to place; lay; set; as, to *put* eggs in an incubator; to cause to be or exist in a specified relation, condition, or the like; as, to *put* things right; to *put* one to flight; to *put* into effect. **5.** To attach or attribute; as, to *put* a wrong construction on an act. **6.** To set before one for judgment, acceptance, or rejection; to offer; state; express. — *v. i.* To go or take one's course; betake oneself; — esp. hastily or in some manner or direction indicated by *for, about, back, in, out, to,* or the like.
put about. **1.** *Naut.* To change direction by tacking, wearing, or jibing, as a ship. **2.** To change or reverse one's course. — ***put across or over.*** *Slang, U. S.* To succeed in getting (something) done or accepted against opposition. — ***put by.*** **a** To reject. **b** To lay aside; to store up. — ***put forth.*** **a** To thrust out; to extrude. **b** To exert. **c** To leave a port or haven. — ***put in.*** *Naut.* To conduct into or enter a harbor. — ***put off.*** **a** To discard. **b** To divert; elude; frustrate; baffle. **c** To delay; defer; postpone. See DEFER, *Syn.* **d** *Colloq.* To disconcert. — ***put on.*** **a** To assume; feign. **b** To impose upon. — ***put out.*** **a** To eject or expel. **b** To shoot, as a sprout. **c** To provoke; vex; also, to inconvenience. **d** *Sports.* To cause to be "out." — ***put through.*** To carry, or to cause to go, through to completion, as a legislative measure. — ***put to it.*** To distress; to press hard; to perplex. — ***put up.*** **a** To offer; exhibit or expose. **b** To preserve, as jam or jelly. **c** To raise; erect. **d** To lodge or take lodgings. **e** To pay; as, to *put up* one's share; also, to provide

money. **f** To offer as a prize or stake. **g** *Slang.* To plan beforehand; prearrange. — ***put up with.*** To bear or suffer without recompense, punishment, or resentment; endure; tolerate.
— *n.* **1.** The act or an instance of putting, as the shot. **2.** *Exchanges.* A privilege which one buys of compelling the seller to accept a security or commodity at a stipulated price and time.
— *adj. Colloq.* Fixed; set; as, he stayed *put.*

pu·ta′men (pū·tā′mĕn), *n.* [L.] *Bot.* The stone of a drupaceous fruit, as of the peach.

pu′ta·tive (pū′tȧ·tĭv), *adj.* [LL. *putativus,* fr. *putare, putatum,* to reckon, think.] Commonly thought or deemed; supposed; reputed. — **pu′ta·tive·ly,** *adv.*

put′log′ (pŏŏt′lŏg′; pŭt′-; 74), *n. Arch.* One of the short timbers on which the flooring of a scaffold is laid.

put′–out′ (pŏŏt′out′), *n.; pl.* -OUTS. *Sports.* Act of putting a player out.

pu′tre·fac′tion (pū′trē·făk′shŭn), *n.* The decomposition of organic matter, esp. the typically anaerobic process of splitting of proteins, by bacteria and fungi, with formation of foul-smelling, incompletely oxidized products, as mercaptans and alkaloids. — **pu′tre·fac′tive** (-tĭv), *adj.*

pu′tre·fy (pū′trē·fī), *v. t. & i.;* PU′TRE·FIED (-fīd); PU′TRE·FY′ING. [F. *putréfier,* fr. L. *putrefacere* to make rotten, fr. *putrere* to be rotten + *facere* to make.] To render or become putrid; to decompose; to rot. — **Syn.** See DECAY. — **pu′tre·fi′er** (-fī′ẽr), *n.*

pu·tres′cent (pū·trĕs′ĕnt; -′nt), *adj.* [L. *putrescens,* pres. part. of *putrescere* to grow rotten.] **1.** Becoming putrid. **2.** Of putrefaction. — **pu·tres′cence** (-ĕns; -′ns), *n.*

pu·tres′ci·ble (-ĭ·b′l), *adj.* Liable to become putrid. — *n.* A putrescible substance.

pu′trid (pū′trĭd), *adj.* [L. *putridus,* fr. *putrere* to be rotten, fr. *puter, putris,* rotten.] **1.** Decomposed; esp., stinkingly rotten; also, tending to decomposition. **2.** Indicating, or proceeding from, decay. **3.** Figuratively, corrupt; foul; morally vicious. — **pu·trid′i·ty** (pū·trĭd′ĭ·tĭ), *n.* — **pu′trid·ness,** *n.* — **Syn.** See MALODOROUS.

‖**Putsch** (pŏŏch), *n.* [G., fr. Swiss dialect.] A petty rebellion or popular uprising.

putt (pŭt), *n.* [See PUT, *v.*] *Golf.* A stroke made on a putting green to play the ball into or near the hole. — **putt,** *v. t. & i.*

put′tee (pŭt′ĭ; pŭ·tē′), *n.; pl.* PUTTEES (-ĭz). Also **put′ty, put′tie** (pŭt′ĭ). [Hind. *paṭṭī* bandage, prop., piece, strip, fr. Skr.] A type of gaiter wrapped around the lower leg, either in the form of a leather legging or of a woolen or cotton strip wound spirally.

putt′er (pŭt′ẽr), *n. Golf.* **a** A club with a short shaft and almost perpendicular face, used in putting. See GOLF, *Illust.* **b** One who putts.

put′ter (pŏŏt′ẽr; *cf.* PUT, *v. t.*), *n.* One who puts something, as questions.

put′ter (pŭt′ẽr), **put′ter·er** (-ẽr). Vars. of POTTER, POTTERER.

put′ti·er (pŭt′ĭ·ẽr), *n.* One who putties, as a glazier.

putt′ing green (pŭt′ĭng). *Golf.* A space, prepared for accurate play, containing the hole into which the ball must be played.

put′ty (pŭt′ĭ), *n.; pl.* PUTTIES (-ĭz). [F. *potée* putty, potful, fr. *pot* pot.] **1.** A type of cement usually of whiting and boiled linseed oil, beaten or kneaded to the consistency of dough. **2.** Any of various other substances resembling putty (sense 1); as: **a** A mixture of ferric oxide and boiled linseed oil (***iron putty***), or of red and white lead and boiled linseed oil (***red-lead putty***), used by mechanics in making pipe joints, etc. **b** Short for **putty powder,** an oxide of tin, or of tin and lead, used in polishing glass, metal, etc. **3.** *Plastering.* A cement consisting of quicklime slaked with water to the consistency of cream, used, mixed with plaster of Paris or sand, for the third, or finishing, coat (**putty coat**). — *v. t.* To cement, or stop, with putty.

put′ty·root′ (-rōōt′; 85), *n.* An American orchid (*Aplectrum hyemale*) having a slender naked rootstock producing each spring a scape of brown flowers.

put′–up′ (pŏŏt′ŭp′), *adj. Colloq.* Planned or plotted ahead; prearranged; — usually in a bad sense; as, a *put-up* job.

puz′zle (pŭz′′l), *v. t.;* -ZLED (-′ld); -ZLING (-lĭng). [See PUZZLE, *n.*] **1.** To perplex; nonplus; to bewilder mentally. **2.** To solve or discover by labor or ingenuity; as, to *puzzle* out a mystery. — *v. i.* **1.** To be bewildered or perplexed. **2.** To search or try by experiment or guesswork, as over a problem.

Syn. **Puzzle, perplex, bewilder, distract, nonplus, confound, dumfound** mean to disturb and baffle. **Puzzle** stresses distressing difficulty in solving; **perplex,** worry and uncertainty as in making a decision or in trying to solve a problem; **bewilder,** a confusion of mind that prevents clear thinking; **distract,** agitation arising from conflicting interests; **nonplus,** an utter inability to say or do anything; **confound,** temporary mental paralysis; **dumfound,** a momentary confounding.

— *n.* [For *opposal,* in the sense of problem.] **1.** State of being puzzled; perplexity. **2.** Something which perplexes; a difficult problem; hence, a toy, device, or problem designed for testing ingenuity; as, a crossword *puzzle.* — **Syn.** See MYSTERY.

puz′zle·ment (-mĕnt), *n.* Puzzled state; perplexity.

puz′zler (pŭz′lẽr), *n.* One who or that which puzzles.

puz′zling (-lĭng), *adj.* That puzzles; perplexing.

PW (pē′dŭb′′l·ū) *or* **P.W.**; *pl.* PWs (-ūz) or P.W.'s. Prisoner of war.

PX (pē′ĕks′), *n.; pl.* PXs (pē′ĕk′sĕz; -sĭz). Post exchange (which see).

py- (pī-). = PYO-.

py·ae′mi·a, py·ae′mic. Vars. of PYEMIA, PYEMIC.

pyc·nid′i·um (pĭk·nĭd′ĭ·ŭm), *n.; pl.* -IA (-ȧ). [NL.] *Bot.* A flask-shaped spore fruit bearing conidiophores and conidia on the interior, occurring in certain imperfect fungi.

pyc·nom′e·ter (pĭk·nŏm′ē·tẽr), *n.* [Gr. *pyknos* thick, dense + *-meter.*] *Physics.* A standard vessel, often provided with a thermometer, for measuring and comparing the densities of liquids or solids.

pye (pī). Var. of 3d PIE.

py′e·li′tis (pī′ĕ·lī′tĭs), *n.* [NL., fr. Gr. *pyelos* basin + *-itis.*] Inflammation of the pelvis of the kidney.

py′e·lo·gram′ (pī′ĕ·lō·grăm′), *n.* Also **py′e·lo·graph′** (-gråf′). [Gr. *pyelos* basin + *-gram, -graph.*] An X-ray picture of the renal pelvis filled with an opaque solution through a ureteral catheter. — **py′e·lo·graph′ic** (-grăf′ĭk), *adj.* — **py′e·log′ra·phy** (-lŏg′rȧ·fĭ), *n.*

py·e′mi·a, py·ae′mi·a (pī·ē′mĭ·ȧ), *n.* [NL., fr. Gr. *pyon* pus + *-emia, -aemia.*] See BLOOD POISONING. — **py·e′mic, py·ae′mic** (-mĭk), *adj.*

py·gid′i·um (pī·jĭd′ĭ·ŭm), *n.; pl.* -IA (-ȧ). [NL., fr. Gr. *pygidion,* dim. of *pygē* rump.] *Zool.* A caudal structure, or the terminal body region, of various invertebrates. See ISOPOD, *Illust.*

pyg·mae′an, pyg·me′an (pĭg·mē′ăn), *adj.* Pygmy.

Pyg·ma′li·on (pĭg·mā′lĭ·ŏn; 58), *n.* See GALATEA.

Pyg′my (pĭg′mĭ), *n.; pl.* -MIES (-mĭz). Also **Pig′my.** [L. *pygmaeus,* fr. Gr. *pygmaios,* fr. *pygmē* fist, a measure of length.] **1.** One of a fabled race of dwarfs described by Greek authors. **2.** Specifically, one of a dwarf people in central Africa, averaging under five feet in stature. **3.** [*not cap.*] A short, insignificant person; a dwarf. — *adj.* [*not cap.*] Of or pertaining to the Pygmies; dwarfish.

py′ic (pī′ĭk), *adj. Med.* Purulent.

py′in (pī′ĭn), *n.* [*py-* + *-in.*] *Biochem.* A constituent of pus, apparently a protein precipitated by acetic acid.

py·ja′ma (pĭ·jä′mȧ; pī-; -jăm′ȧ), *n. Chiefly Brit.* Pajama.

pyk′nic (pĭk′nĭk), *adj.* [Gr. *pyknos* compact.] *Anthropol.* Characterized by a large abdomen, squatness, and general roundness of form; fat; stout. — *n.* A person of pyknic type.

py′lon (pī′lŏn), *n.* [Gr. *pylōn* gateway, fr. *pylē* gate.] **1. a** A gateway. **b** *Egypt. Arch.* A gateway of two truncated pyramids, with an entrance between. **c** Any monumental mass placed so as to flank an entrance, approach to a bridge, etc. **2.** A tower for supporting either end of a wire, as for a telegraph line, over a long span. **3.** *Aeronautics.* A post, tower, or the like, marking a prescribed course of flight.

py·lor′ic (pī·lŏr′ĭk; pĭ-), *adj. Anat. & Zool.* Of, pert. to, or in the region of the pylorus, or that part of the stomach from which the intestine leads.

py·lo′rus (pī·lō′rŭs; pĭ-; 70), *n.; pl.* -RI (-rī). [LL., fr. Gr. *pylōros* pylorus, gatekeeper, fr. *pylē* a gate + *ouros* guardian.] *Anat.* The opening from the stomach into the intestine.

py′o- (pī′ō-), **py-** (pī-). [Gr. *pyon* pus.] A combining form meaning: *Presence of pus in* or *with; due to pus; suppurative,* as in:

pyogenesis	**pyonephritis**	**pyopneumothorax**
pyogenic	**pyopericardium**	**pyothorax**
pyogenous	**pyophthalmia**	**pyoureter**

py′or·rhe′a, py′or·rhoe′a (pī′ō·rē′ȧ), *n.* [NL., fr. *pyo-* + *-rrhea.*] *Med.* A discharge of pus; specif.: ‖**py′or·rhe′a al·ve′o·la′ris** (ăl·vē′ō·lā′rĭs), purulent inflammation of the sockets of the teeth, leading usually to loosening of the teeth; Riggs' disease. — **py′or·rhe′al, -rhoe′al** (-ăl), *adj.*

py·o′sis (pī·ō′sĭs), *n.* [NL., fr. Gr. *pyōsis.*] *Med.* Suppuration.

pyr-. = PYRO-.

py·ral′i·did (pĭ·răl′ĭ·dĭd), *adj.* [L. *pyralis, -idis,* a kind of winged insect, fr. Gr. *pyralis.*] *Zool.* Belonging to a family (**Pyr·a·lid′i·dae** [pĭr′ȧ·lĭd′ĭ·dē]) of moths comprising, in most classifications, a vast and heterogeneous assemblage of small or medium-sized plainly colored, slender-bodied and long-legged species. — *n.* A pyralidid moth. — **py·ral′i·dan** (-dăn), *adj. & n.*

pyr′a·mid (pĭr′ȧ·mĭd), *n.* [L. *pyramis, -idis,* fr. Gr. *pyramis, -idos,* prob. fr. Egypt. *pi-mar* the pyramid.] **1.** A massive structure, typically of square ground plan, with four triangular faces meeting at a point, and used for tombs, as in ancient Egypt. **2.** Loosely, any conelike or triangular figure, object, or formation suggestive of a pyramid. **3.** *Cryst.* A form each face of which intersects the vertical axis and either two lateral axes, or, in the tetragonal system, one lateral axis. **4.** *Exchanges.* The series of operations involved in pyramiding. See PYRAMID, *v. i.* **5.** *Geom.* A figure having for its base a plane triangle, rectangle, or other polygon and for its sides several triangles with a common vertex and with their bases forming the sides of the base. **6.** *Hort.* A tree grown or pruned in pyramidal shape. **7.** *Psychol.* A tridimensional diagram to represent the relations of sensory qualities; as, a color *pyramid.* — ***the Pyramids.*** Three large pyramids at Giza, near Cairo, Egypt. See *Gaz.*

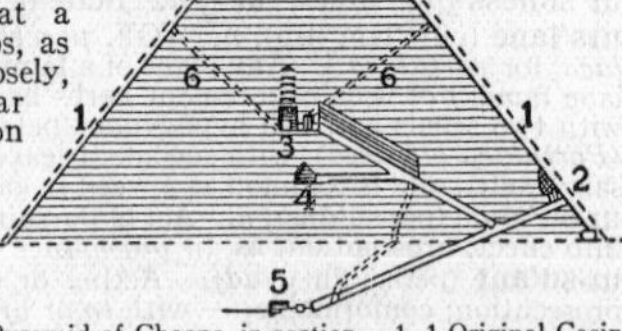

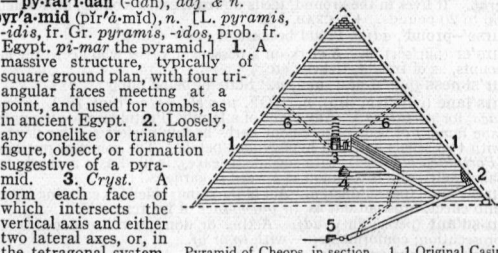

Pyramid of Cheops, in section. 1, 1 Original Casing of Limestone; 2 Entrance; 3 King's Chamber; 4 Queen's Chamber; 5 Underground Chamber; 6, 6 Air Passages.

— *v. i. Exchanges.* To enlarge one's holding or interest in a series of operations on a continued rise or decline by using the profits to buy or sell additional amounts on a margin. — *v. t.* **1.** To arrange or build up as if upon the base of a pyramid; to heap up. **2.** *Exchanges.* To use, or to deal in, in a pyramiding transaction.

py·ram′i·dal (pĭ·răm′ĭ·dăl; -d′l), *adj.* Of, pertaining to, or having the form of a pyramid. — **py·ram′i·dal·ly,** *adv.*

pyr′a·mid′i·cal (pĭr′ȧ·mĭd′ĭ·kăl), *adj.* Also **pyr′a·mid′ic** (-ĭk). [Gr. *pyramidikos.*] Pyramidal; pyramidlike.

Pyr′a·mus and This′be (pĭr′ȧ·mŭs, thĭz′bē). [L., fr. Gr. *Pyramos;* L., fr. Gr. *Thisbē.*] Legendary lovers of ancient Babylon who, according to Ovid, made love through a chink in a wall and planned a tryst. Thisbe, coming first, fled from a lioness, losing her garment, which Pyramus found smeared with blood; he killed himself, and Thisbe, returning, killed herself.

py′ran (pī′răn; pī·răn′), *n.* [From PYRONE.] *Chem.* A parent cyclic compound, C_5H_6O, whose ring consists of five carbon atoms and one oxygen atom.

py·rar′gy·rite (pī·rär′jĭ·rīt), *n.* [Gr. *pyr* fire + *argyros* silver.] *Mineral.* A silver antimony sulfide, Ag_3SbS_3, occurring in rhombohedral crystals or massive, and having a dark-red or black color with a metallic adamantine luster.

pyre (pīr), *n.* [L. *pyra,* fr. Gr. *pyra,* fr. *pyr* fire.] A combustible heap, usually of wood, for burning a dead body as a funeral rite; hence, any pile to be burnt.

py′rene (pī′rēn), *n.* [Gr. *pyrēn* stone of a fruit.] *Bot.* The stone or endocarp of a drupelet, as in the fruit of the huckleberry; hence, loosely, any small hard nutlet.

py·re′thrum (pī·rē′thrŭm; -rĕth′rŭm), *n.* [L., feverfew, fr. Gr. *pyrethron,* fr. *pyr* fire.] **1.** Any of several garden chrysanthemums with usually finely divided, often aromatic leaves, and showy white, lilac, or red (but not yellow) flowers. **2.** *Pharm.* A powder for exterminating insects.

py·ret′ic (pī·rĕt′ĭk), *adj.* [Gr. *pyretos* burning heat, fever, fr. *pyr* fire.] *Med.* Of or pert. to fever; febrile.

pyr′e·tol′o·gy (pĭr′ē·tŏl′ō·jĭ; pī′rē-), *n.* [Gr. *pyretos* fever + *-logy.*] That branch of medicine treating of fevers.

pyr′e·to·ther′a·py (pĭr′ē·tō·thĕr′ȧ·pĭ; pī′rē·tō-), *n.* [*pyreto-* (fr. Gr. *pyretos* fever) + *-therapy.*] *Med.* The treatment of disease by inducing fever.

Py′rex (pī′rĕks), *n.* A trade-mark applied to a variety of glasses and glassware usually resistant to heat, chemicals, or electricity.

py·rex′i·a (pī·rĕk′sĭ·ȧ), *n.* [NL., fr. Gr. *pyressein* to be feverish, fr. *pyretos* fever.] *Med.* The febrile condition; fever. — **py·rex′i·al** (-ăl), *adj.* — **py·rex′ic** (-sĭk), *adj.*

pyr·he′li·om′e·ter (pīr·hē′lĭ·ŏm′ē·tẽr; pĭr-), *n.* [*pyr-* + *helio-* + *-meter.*] *Astrophysics.* An instrument for measuring the sun's heat and energy.

pyr′i·dine (pĭr′ĭ·dēn; -dĭn), *n.* Also **pyr′i·din.** [*pyr*role + *-idine* as in tolu*idine.*] *Chem.* A colorless, liquid, nitrogenous base, C_5H_5N, of pungent odor, obtained in the distillation of bone oil, coal tar, etc., and by the decomposition of certain alkaloids. Parent of many organic compounds, as nicotine, it is used in denaturing alcohol, as a solvent, as a germicide, as a remedy for asthma, etc. — **py·rid′ic** (pī·rĭd′ĭk), *adj.*

pyr′i·dox′ine (pĭr′ĭ·dŏk′sēn; -sĭn), *n.* Also **pyr′i·dox′in** [*pyridine* with *ox(y)-* inserted.] Vitamin B_6 (see VITAMIN).

pyr′i·form (pĭr′ĭ·fôrm), *adj.* [ML. *pyrum,* for L. *pirum* a pear + *-form.*] Pear-shaped.

py′rite (pī′rīt), *n.* ; *pl.* PYRITES (-rīts). [L. *pyrites.*] A common mineral of a pale brass-yellow color and metallic luster, chemically iron disulfide, FeS_2, burned for making sulfuric acid; iron pyrites (see PYRITES).

py·ri′tes (pī·rī′tēz; pĭ-; pī′rīts), *n.* [L., fr. Gr. *pyritēs,* adj., *pyritēs lithos* a mineral which strikes fire, fr. *pyr* fire.] Any of a number of metallic-looking sulfides, as ***iron pyrites*** (= PYRITE), the commonest form, and ***copper pyrites*** (= CHALCOPYRITE) and ***tin pyrites*** (= STANNITE). See FOOL'S GOLD. — **py·rit′ic** (pī·rĭt′ĭk; pĭ-), **py·rit′i·cal** (-ĭ·kăl), *adj.*

py′ro- (pī′rō-; pĭr′ō-; *see note below*), **pyr-.** [Gr. *pyr, pyros,* fire.] A combining form meaning *fire,* used: **1.** To denote *fire* or *heat,* as in *pyr*heliometer. **2.** *Chem.* To imply an actual or theoretical *derivative by action of heat.* In inorganic chemistry *pyro-* is often used in naming an acid (**py′ro·ac′id**) derived from the ordinary form by the loss of one molecule of water from two of the acid. Thus $2H_3PO_4$ (ordinary phosphoric acid) — $H_2O = H_4P_2O_7$ (pyrophosphoric acid). **3.** *Geol.* To denote *due to the action of fire* or *heat.*

☞ The etymological pron. is pĭr′ō- (the *y* being short in Greek), but present usage decidedly prefers the long sound (ī) in most of these words.

py′ro·cat′e·chol (-kăt′ē·kōl; -chōl; -kŏl), *n.* Also **py′ro·cat′e·chin** (-chĭn; -kĭn). *Chem.* A white crystalline phenol, $C_6H_4(OH)_2(o)$, found in various plants, and variously formed, as by distillation of wood. It is used as a photographic developer.

py′ro·chem′i·cal (-kĕm′ĭ·kăl), *adj.* Pertaining to chemistry at high temperatures. — **py′ro·chem′i·cal·ly,** *adv.*

py′ro·clas′tic (-klăs′tĭk), *adj.* *Geol.* Formed by fragmentation as a result of volcanic or igneous action.

py′ro·con′duc·tiv′i·ty (-kŏn′dŭk·tĭv′ĭ·tĭ), *n.* *Elec.* Conductivity induced by application of heat.

py′ro·crys′tal·line (-krĭs′tăl·ĭn; -īn), *adj.* *Petrog.* Crystallized from a molten magma.

py′ro·e·lec′tric (-ē·lĕk′trĭk), *adj.* Of, pert. to, or exhibiting pyroelectricity. — *n.* A pyroelectric substance.

py′ro·e·lec′tric′i·ty (-ē·lĕk′trĭs′ĭ·tĭ), *n.* *Physics & Mineral.* Electric polarity produced on certain crystals by change of temperature.

py′ro·gal′late (-găl′āt), *n.* *Chem.* A salt or ether of pyrogallol.

py′ro·gal′lic (-găl′ĭk), *adj.* *Chem.* Pertaining to or designating an acid later called *pyrogallol.*

py′ro·gal′lol (-găl′ōl; -ŏl; -gă·lōl′), *n.* [*pyrogallic* + *-ol.*] *Chem.* A poisonous, bitter, white crystalline phenol, $C_6H_3(OH)_3$, obtained chiefly by the action of heat on gallic acid, and used as a photographic developer. It has weak acid properties, and hence is called also *pyrogallic acid.*

py′ro·gen ((pī′rō·jĕn; pĭr′ō-), *n.* *Med.* A fever-producing substance.

py′ro·gen′ic (-jĕn′ĭk), *adj.* [*pyro-* + *-genic.*] Also **py·rog′e·nous** (pī·rŏj′ē·nŭs). **1.** Producing or produced by heat, or, *Med.,* fever. **2.** *Geol.* Of igneous origin.

py′rog·nos′tics (pī′rŏg·nŏs′tĭks; pĭr′ŏg-), *n. pl.*; see -ICS. [*pyro-* + Gr. *gnōstikos* knowing.] *Mineral.* The characters of a mineral observed by the use of the blowpipe, as the degree of fusibility, flame coloration, etc.

py·rog′ra·phy (pī·rŏg′rȧ·fĭ), *n.* [*pyro-* + *-graphy.*] The art of producing designs or pictures, as on leather, by burning with hot instruments; also, a design or picture so made. — **py·rog′ra·pher** (-fẽr), *n.* — **py′ro·graph′ic** (pī′rō·grăf′ĭk; pĭr′ō-), *adj.*

py′ro·gra·vure′ (pī′rō·grȧ·vūr′; -grā′vūr; pĭr′ō-), *n.* [*pyro-* + F. *gravure* engraving.] Pyrography.

py′ro·lig′ne·ous (pī′rō·lĭg′nē·ŭs; pĭr′ō-), *adj.* [F. *pyroligneux,* fr. *pyro-* + L. *lignum* wood.] Obtained by destructive distillation of wood.

pyroligneous acid. An acid reddish-brown aqueous liquid, containing chiefly acetic acid and methanol.

pyroligneous alcohol *or* **spirit.** Methanol, esp. from wood.

py′ro·lig′nic (pī′rō·lĭg′nĭk; pĭr′ō-), *adj.* Pyroligneous.

py·rol′o·gy (pī·rŏl′ō·jĭ), *n.* [*pyro-* + *-logy.*] Mineralogy that treats of pyrognostics. — **py′ro·log′i·cal** (pī′rō·lŏj′ĭ·kăl; pĭr′ō-), *adj.*

py′ro·lu′site (pī′rō·lū′sīt; pī·rŏl′ū·sīt), *n.* [*pyro-* + Gr. *louein* to wash.] *Mineral.* Native manganese dioxide, MnO_2, a mineral of an iron-black or dark steel-gray color and metallic luster, usually soft, used in glassmaking, in making chlorine, oxygen, and spiegeleisen.

py·rol′y·sis (pī·rŏl′ĭ·sĭs), *n.* [NL., fr. *pyro-* + *-lysis.*] *Chem.* Chemical decomposition by the action of heat. — **py′ro·lyt′ic** (pī′rō·lĭt′ĭk; pĭr′ō-), *adj.*

py′ro·mag·net′ic (pī′rō·măg·nĕt′ĭk; pĭr′ō-), *adj.* *Physics.* Pertaining to, produced by, or acting by the combined agency of heat and magnetism.

py′ro·man′cy (pī′rō·măn′sĭ; pĭr′ō-), *n.* [OF. *piromance, pyromancie,* fr. ML., fr. Gr. *pyromanteia.* See PYRO-; -MANCY.] Divination by means of fire or flames.

py′ro·ma′ni·a (-mā′nĭ·ȧ), *n.* [NL., fr. *pyro-* + *-mania.*] *Psychiatry.* A persistent impulse to incendiarism. — **py′ro·ma′ni·ac** (-ăk), *n.* — **py′ro·ma·ni′a·cal** (-mȧ·nī′ȧ·kăl), *adj.*

py·rom′e·ter (pī·rŏm′ē·tẽr), *n.* [*pyro-* + *-meter.*] *Physics.* An instrument for measuring temperatures, esp. those beyond the range of mercurial thermometers, as by means of the change of electric resistance, the production of a thermoelectric current, the expansion of gases, the specific heat of solids, or the intensity of the heat or light radiated. — **py′ro·met′ric** (pī′rō·mĕt′rĭk; pĭr′ō-), **py′ro·met′ri·cal** (-rĭ·kăl), *adj.* — **py·rom′e·try** (pī·rŏm′ē·trĭ), *n.*

py′ro·mor′phite (pī′rō·môr′fīt; pĭr′ō-), *n.* [G. *pyromorphit,* fr. Gr. *pyr* fire + *morphē* form.] *Mineral.* A native lead chloride and phosphate, $(PbCl)Pb_4(PO_4)_3$, occurring in green, yellow, brown, gray, or white crystals or masses.

py′rone (pī′rōn; pī·rōn′), *n.* [G. *pyron.*] *Chem.* An unsaturated cyclic compound, $C_5H_4O_2$, one variety of which is the parent of several natural yellow dyes.

py′rope (pī′rōp), *n.* [OF. *pirope,* fr. L. *pyropus* a kind of red bronze, fr. Gr. *pyrōpos,* fr. *pyr* fire + *ōps* the eye, face.] *Mineral.* A variety of garnet, deep red in color, frequently used as a gem. Chemically it is $Mg_3Al_2(SiO_4)_3$.

py′ro·pho′bi·a (pī′rō·fō′bĭ·ȧ; pĭr′ō-), *n.* *Med.* Morbid dread of fire.

py′ro·phor′ic (-fŏr′ĭk), *adj.* [Gr. *pyrophoros* fire-bearing, fr. *pyr* fire + *pherein* to bear.] Light-producing; igniting spontaneously.

py′ro·phos·phor′ic ac′id (-fŏs·fŏr′ĭk; -fôr′ĭk). *Chem.* An acid, $H_4P_2O_7$, derived from orthophosphoric acid by the loss of water, either a sirupy liquid or a glasslike crystalline solid. See PHOSPHORIC ACID.

py′ro·pho·tom′e·ter (-fō·tŏm′ē·tẽr), *n.* *Physics.* An instrument for optical measurement of high temperatures.

py′ro·phyl′lite (-fĭl′īt), *n.* [*pyro-* + Gr. *phyllon* leaf.] *Mineral.* A hydrous aluminum silicate, $HAl(SiO_3)_2$, usually white or greenish and in its compact form used for making slate pencils.

py·ro′sis (pī·rō′sĭs), *n.* [NL., fr. Gr. *pyrōsis* a burning, an inflammation, fr. *pyroun* to burn.] *Med.* A disorder of the stomach characterized by a burning sensation with eructations of acid fluids; heartburn.

py′ro·stat (pī′rō·stăt; pĭr′ō-), *n.* [*pyro-* + *-stat* as in thermo*stat.*] An automatic device which, when exposed to accidental fire, actuates a mechanism for giving warning; also, *Physics,* a thermostat.

py′ro·sul′fate (-sŭl′fāt), *n.* *Chem.* A salt of pyrosulfuric acid.

py′ro·sul·fu′ric (-sŭl·fū′rĭk), *adj.* *Chem.* Designating an acid, $H_2S_2O_7$, crystalline when pure but commercially a thick, oily, fuming liquid.

py′ro·tech′nics (-tĕk′nĭks), *n.*; see -ICS. **1.** Also **py′ro·tech′ny** (pī′rō·tĕk′nĭ; pĭr′ō-). The art of making, or the manufacture and use of, fireworks. **2.** A spectacular display suggesting fireworks, as of oratory, emotion, wit, or virtuosity. — **py′ro·tech′nic** (-tĕk′nĭk), **py′ro·tech′ni·cal** (-nĭ·kăl), *adj.*

py′ro·tech′nist (-nĭst), *n.* One skilled in pyrotechnics.

py′ro·tox′in (pī′rō·tŏk′sĭn; pĭr′ō-), *n.* *Biochem.* A bacterial poison capable of inducing the symptoms of fever.

py′rox·ene (pī′rŏk·sēn), *n.* [F. *pyroxène,* fr. Gr. *pyr* fire + *xenos* a stranger; — so named by Haüy as not being native in igneous rocks.] *Mineral.* A common metasilicate, chiefly of calcium and magnesium, usually in short, thick, prismatic crystals or in massive forms, often laminated, next to feldspar the most frequent constituent of igneous rocks. H., 5–6. Sp. gr., 3.2–3.6. — **py′rox·en′ic** (pī′rŏks·ĕn′ĭk), *adj.*

py·rox′e·nite (pī·rŏk′sē·nīt), *n.* *Petrog.* An igneous rock, without olivine, composed essentially of pyroxene.

py·rox′y·lin (-sĭ·lĭn), *n.* Also **py·rox′y·line.** [*pyro-* + Gr. *xylon* wood.] A mixture of cellulose nitrates, esp. the lower nitrates, which is soluble in a mixture of ether and alcohol and in other organic solvents, less explosive than guncotton, and used in making celluloid, lacquers, etc.

Pyr′rha (pĭr′ȧ). See DEUCALION AND PYRRHA.

pyr′rhic (pĭr′ĭk), *n.* [Gr. *pyrrhichē.*] An ancient Greek martial dance accompanied by the flute. — **pyr′rhic,** *adj.*

pyr′rhic, *n.* [L. *pyrrhichius* (sc. *pes*), fr. Gr. *pyrrhichios* (sc. *pous*).] *Pros.* A foot consisting of two short syllables. — *adj.* Of, containing, or composed of pyrrhics.

Pyrrhic victory. A success gained at too great cost; — in allusion to remarks by Pyrrhus, King of Epirus, after his costly victory over the Romans at Asculum (279 B.C.).

Pyr′rho·nism (pĭr′ō·nĭz′m), *n.* **a** The doctrines of Pyrrho, founder of a school of skeptics in ancient Greece. **b** Hence, any extreme skepticism.

pyr′rho·tite (-tīt), *n.* Also **pyr′rho·tine** (-tĭn). [Gr. *pyrrhotēs* redness, fr. *pyrrhos* flame-colored, fr. *pyr* fire.] A bronze-colored mineral of metallic luster, an iron sulfide, usually massive, often containing nickel.

pyr′rhu·lox′i·a (pĭr′ōō·lŏk′sĭ·ȧ), *n.* [NL.] A large handsome finch (*Pyrrhuloxia sinuata*) of the southwestern United States and Mexico. The back is gray, the breast and crest rose-colored in the male, yellowish in the female.

pyr·role′ (pĭ·rōl′; pĭr′ōl), *n.* Also **pyr·rol′.** [G. *pyrrol,* fr Gr. *pyrrhos* fiery + L. *ol*eum oil.] *Chem.* A colorless, weakly basic liquid, C_4H_5N, smelling like chloroform, obtained by distillation of coal tar, bone oil, etc., and parent of many compounds and derivatives, as nicotine, chlorophyll, proteins, etc.

py·ru′vic (pī·rōō′vĭk; pĭ-), *adj.* [*pyr-* + L. *uva* grape.] *Chem.* Designating a colorless, liquid, ketonic acid, CH_3COCO_2H, having an odor like acetic acid, which is obtained by the dry distillation of racemic or tartaric acid.

Py·thag′o·re′an (pĭ·thăg′ō·rē′ăn; pī-), *adj.* Of or pertaining to Pythagoras (Greek philosopher of Samos), to whom is ascribed the doctrine of metempsychosis, or the school and system of his philosophy (**Py·thag′o·re′an·ism**). — **Py·thag′o·re′an,** *n.*

Pyth′i·a (pĭth′ĭ·ȧ), *n.* [Gr.] Apollo's priestess and prophetess at Delphi. See DELPHIAN. — **Pyth′ic** (-ĭk), *adj.*

Pyth′i·ad (-ăd), *n.* *Gr. Antiq.* The period, four years, between celebrations of the Pythian games.

Pyth′i·an (-ăn), *adj.* [L. *Pythius,* fr. Gr. *Pythios* belonging to Pytho, older name of Delphi.] *Gr. Antiq.* **a** Pertaining to Apollo, as patron or god of Delphi. **b** Designating, or pertaining to, the games (**Pythian games**) celebrated at Delphi every four years.

Pyth′i·as (-ăs), *n.* See DAMON.

py′tho·gen′ic (pī′thō·jĕn′ĭk; pĭth′ō-), *adj.* [Gr. *pythein* to rot + *-genic.*] Originating from decomposition or filth.

py′thon (pī′thŏn *or, esp. in sense* 2, -thŭn), *n.* [L. (in sense 1), fr. Gr. *Pythōn.*] **1.** [*cap.*] *Gr. Myth.* A monstrous serpent which arose from the mud left by the deluge which Deucalion survived and which dwelt in the caves of Mount Parnassus, where Apollo slew it. **2.** [LL. *Pytho,* Gr. *Pythōn.*] In the New Testament, a soothsaying spirit or daemon (*R. V. Acts* xvi. 16). **3.** Any of various large nonvenomous snakes (genus *Python* or family Pythonidae) closely related to the boas (see BOA, 1). **4.** Loosely, any large snake that crushes its prey. Cf. ANACONDA, 3; BOA, 2; BOA CONSTRICTOR, 2.

py'tho·ness (pī'thō·nĕs; -nĭs; pĭth'ō-), *n.* [OF. *phitonise* (F. *pythonisse*), fr. ML., fr. LL. *pythonissa.*] **1.** *Gr. Relig.* Apollo's Delphian priestess. **2.** Any woman supposed to have a spirit of divination.

py·thon'ic (pī·thŏn'ĭk; pĭ-), *adj.* [LL. *pythonicus*, fr. Gr. *pythōnikos.* See PYTHIAN.] **1.** Oracular; pretending to foretell events. **2.** Of, pert. to, or like a python (snake).

py·u'ri·a (pī·ū'rĭ·ȧ), *n.* [NL., fr. *py-* + *-uria.*] *Med.* A morbid condition in which pus is discharged in the urine.

pyx (pĭks), *n.* Also **pix.** [L. *pyxis* a box, fr. Gr. *pyxis* a box, esp. of boxwood, fr. *pyxos* the box tree or boxwood.] **1.** *Eccl.* **a** *Hist.* The vessel in which the Host is reserved; ciborium. **b** The little vessel, usually watch-shaped, in which the Eucharist is carried to the sick. **2.** More fully ***pyx chest.*** A box in the British mint as a place of deposit for certain sample coins reserved for a trial (***trial of the pyx***) of weight and fineness.

pyx·id'i·um (pĭks·ĭd'ĭ·ŭm), *n.; pl.* -IA (-ȧ). [NL., fr. Gr. *pyxidion*, dim. of *pyxis* a box. See PYX.] *Bot.* A capsule which dehisces into an upper and lower half, as in the plantain, purslane, etc.

pyx'ie (pĭk'sĭ), *n.* [From the botanical name, prob. confused with *pixy.*] A creeping evergreen shrub (*Pyxidanthera barbulata*) of the pine barrens of New Jersey and North Carolina, bearing mostly white early-blooming, star-shaped flowers.

pyx'is (pĭk'sĭs), *n.; pl.* PYXIDES (-sĭ·dēz). [L. See PYX.] **1.** *Gr. & Rom. Antiq.* A boxlike vase, generally cylindrical and furnished with a cover. **2.** A box; a jewel case. **3.** *Bot.* A pyxidium.

Q

Q, q (kū), *n.; pl.* Q's, q's, Qs, qs (kūz). **1.** The seventeenth letter of the English alphabet. Its history runs parallel with that of K. **2.** The sound of the letter Q. In English, this sign is normally used in combination with *u* to represent a voiceless labialized velar sound (*kw*), as in *qu*orum. See *Pron.*, § 91. **3.** As a *symbol*, the sixteenth or (see K, 3) the seventeenth in order or class.

Q fe'ver (kū' fē'vẽr). [From *Query fever*, by E. H. Derrick, Australian doctor who first recognized the disease in man.] A mild disease somewhat like typhus, characterized by high fever, chills, pains in the muscles, caused by a microorganism (*Rickettsia*) transmitted by ticks.

qua (kwā; kwä), *adv.* [L., abl. fem. of *qui* who.] In so far as; in the capacity or character of; as.

quack (kwăk), *v. i.* [Imitative.] To utter a sharp harsh cry; — said esp. of a duck. — **quack,** *n.*

quack, *n.* [From QUACKSALVER.] **1.** A boastful pretender to medical skill. **2.** Hence, a charlatan. — *adj.* Pert. to, or characterized by, boasting and unfounded pretension; pretending to cure diseases; as, a *quack* medicine. — *v. i.* To play the quack. — *v. t.* To treat as a quack would. — **quack'ish** (-ĭsh), *adj.*

quack'er·y (kwăk'ẽr·ĭ), *n.; pl.* -ERIES (-ĭz). Acts, arts, or pretensions of a quack; charlatanry.

quack grass. The couch grass *Agropyron repens.*

quack'sal·ver (kwăk'săl·vẽr), *n.* [D., now *kwakzalver.*] A quack; charlatan.

quad (kwŏd), *n.* [From QUADRAT.] *Print.* A quadrat.

quad, *n.* [From QUADRANGLE.] *Colloq.* Quadrangle.

quad. *Slang.* Var. of QUOD.

quad'ra·ge·nar'i·an (kwŏd'rȧ·jē·nâr'ĭ·ăn; 6), *adj.* [L. *quadragenarius*, fr. *quadrageni* forty each.] Forty years old. — *n.* A person forty years old; one in the forties.

Quad'ra·ges'i·ma (-jĕs'ĭ·mȧ), *n.* [LL., fr. L. *quadragesimus* the fortieth, fr. *quadraginta* forty.] *Eccl.* **a** *Obs.* The forty days of Lent. **b** More fully ***Quadragesima Sunday.*** The first Sunday in Lent.

quad'ra·ges'i·mal (-măl), *adj.* **1.** Consisting of forty; — said esp. of the Lenten fast. **2.** [*cap.*] Lenten.

quad'ran'gle (kwŏd'răng'g'l *or, esp. Brit.*, kwŏd·răng'g'l), *n.* [F., fr. LL. *quadrangulum.*] **1.** *Geom.* A plane figure having four angles and four sides; any figure having four angles. **2.** A quadrangular enclosure, esp. when surrounded by buildings; also, the buildings enclosing a quadrangle. **3.** The tract of country represented by one of the atlas sheets published by the U. S. Geological Survey. — **quad·ran'gu·lar** (kwŏd·răng'gū·lẽr), *adj.*

quad'rant (kwŏd'rănt), *n.* [L. *quadrans, -antis*, a fourth part.] **1.** The quarter of a circle, an arc of 90°; also, the area bounded by a quadrant and two radii. See MEASURE, *Table* 7. **2.** An instrument for measuring altitudes, consisting commonly of a graduated arc of 90°, with an index or vernier, and usually having a plumb line or spirit level for fixing the vertical or horizontal direction. **3.** *Anal. Geom.* Any of the four parts into which a plane is divided by rectangular co-ordinate axes lying in that plane. The upper right-hand part is the *first quadrant;* the others successively counterclockwise are the *second, third,* and *fourth.* **4.** *Mach.* Any piece shaped like, or suggestive of, the quadrant of a circle. — **quad·ran'tal** (kwŏd·răn'tăl; -t'l), *adj.*

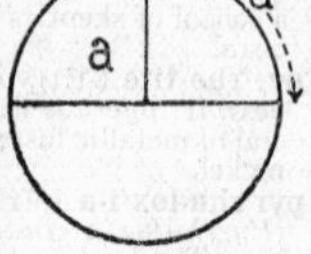

a, a Quadrants.

quad'rat (kwŏd'răt), *n.* [Var. of QUADRATE, *n.*] *Print.* A block of type metal lower than the letters, used in spacing and in blank lines.

quad'rate (-rāt), *adj.* [L. *quadratus* squared.] **1.** Square or approximately square. **2.** *Astrol.* Distant from each other 90°; — said of two heavenly bodies. **3.** *Her.* Expanded into a square at the junction of the arms; — said of a cross. See CROSS, *Illust.* (19). **4.** *Zool.* Designating or pertaining to a bony or cartilaginous element of each side of the skull, to which the lower jaw is articulated in most vertebrates below mammals. — *n.* **1.** A square; hence, anything resembling a square, as a rectangular space. **2.** An object square or cubical in form. **3.** *Zool.* The quadrate bone.
— (kwŏd'rāt; kwŏd·rāt'), *v. i.* To square; agree; correspond; — followed by *with.* — *v. t.* To make accordant with; conform to.

quad·rat'ic (kwŏd·răt'ĭk), *adj.* **1.** Square. **2.** *Math.* Marked by terms of second degrees as the highest; as, a **quadratic equation** is an equation in which the highest power of the unknown quantity is a square. — *n. Math.* A quadratic expression or equation.

quad·rat'ics (-ĭks), *n.;* see -ICS. *Math.* That branch of algebra treating of quadratic equations.

quad'ra·ture (kwŏd'rȧ·tūr), *n.* [L. *quadratura.*] **1.** Act or process of making square or of determining areas; specif., quadrature of the circle. **2.** *Obs.* Square shape; also, a square. **3.** *Astron.* **a** The relation of two celestial bodies when distant from each other 90°. **b** Either of two points on an orbit in a middle position between the syzygies; as, the *quadratures* of the moon (points where, the moon being in quadrature with the sun, one half of the lunar disk is illumined).

quadrature of the circle. *Math.* The problem of finding the side of a square exactly equal in area to a given circular area. Solution of this problem is not possible by geometric methods limited to the use of straight edge and compass alone.

quad·ren'ni·al (kwŏd·rĕn'ĭ·ăl; 58), *adj.* [L. *quadriennium* a space of four years, fr. *quadri-* + *annus* year.] **1.** Comprising, or lasting through, four years. **2.** Occurring once in four years. — **quad·ren'ni·al·ly,** *adv.*

quad·ren'ni·um (-ŭm), *n.; pl.* -NIA (-ȧ). [NL. See QUADRENNIAL.] A period of four years.

quad'ri- (kwŏd'rĭ-), **quadr-.** [L.; akin to L. *quattuor* four.] A combining form meaning *consisting of,* or *characterized by having, four.*

quad'ric (kwŏd'rĭk), *adj.* [L. *quadra* a square.] *Math.* Of or pertaining to the second degree; — used where there are more than two variables. — *n. Alg.* A quantic of the second degree. See QUANTIC.

quad'ri·cen·ten'ni·al (kwŏd'rĭ·sĕn·tĕn'ĭ·ăl; 58), *n.* The four-hundredth anniversary of any event; also, a celebration of it. — **quad'ri·cen·ten'ni·al,** *adj.*

quad'ri·ceps (kwŏd'rĭ·sĕps), *n.* [NL., fr. *quadri-* + L. *caput* head.] More fully ‖***quad'ri·ceps ex·ten'sor*** (ĕks·tĕn'sôr). *Anat.* The great extensor muscle of the front of the thigh. — **quad'ri·cip'i·tal** (-sĭp'ĭ·tăl), *adj.*

quad'ri·cy'cle (-sī'k'l), *n.* A four-wheeled cycle.

quad'ri·fid (-fĭd), *adj.* [L. *quadrifidus.* See -FID.] Divided, or deeply cleft, into four parts, as a petal.

quad'ri·fo'li·ate (-fō'lĭ·āt), *adj. Bot.* Having four leaves.

quad'ri·fo'li·o·late (-fō'lĭ·ō·lāt; -fō·lī'ō·lāt), *adj. Bot.* Having four leaflets.

quad·ri'ga (kwŏd·rī'gȧ), *n.; pl.* -GAE (-jē). [L.] *Rom. Antiq.* A chariot drawn by four horses abreast.

quad'ri·lat'er·al (kwŏd'rĭ·lăt'ẽr·ăl), *adj.* [L. *quadrilaterus.* See LATERAL.] Having four sides, and four angles; quadrangular. — *n.* **1.** *Geom.* A plane figure of four sides and four angles; a quadrangular figure. **2.** A quadrilateral area, as one defended by four fortresses supporting each other.

quad'ri·lin'gual (-lĭng'gwăl), *adj.* [*quadri-* + L. *lingua* tongue.] Using, or made up of, four languages.

qua·drille' (kwŏ·drĭl' *or, now esp. Brit.*, kȧ·drĭl'), *n.* [F., fr. Sp. *cuadrilla*, fr. *cuadro* battle square, fr. L. *quadrus* square.] A square dance of five figures, chiefly in $\frac{6}{8}$ and $\frac{2}{4}$ time, popular in the 19th century; also, music for this dance.

qua·drille', *n.* [F., fr. Sp. *cuartillo*, fr. *cuarto* fourth, quarter, fr. L. *quartus.*] An 18th-century game at cards.

quad·ril'lion (kwŏd·rĭl'yŭn), *n.* & *adj.* [F., formed like *million.*] See NUMERATION, *Table.* — **quad·ril'lionth** (-yŭnth), *n.* & *adj.*

quad'ri·no'mi·al (kwŏd'rĭ·nō'mĭ·ăl; 58), *n. Alg.* A polynomial of four terms. — **quad'ri·no'mi·al,** *adj.*

quad'ri·par'tite (-pär'tīt), *adj.* [L. *quadripartitus*, past part. of *quadripartire* to divide into four parts.] Consisting of, or divided into, four parts; of a contract, etc., drawn up in four corresponding parts; also, shared in by four persons, states, etc.; as, a *quadripartite* treaty.

quad'ri·syl'la·ble (kwŏd'rĭ·sĭl'ȧ·b'l), *n.* A word of four syllables. — **quad'ri·syl·lab'ic** (-sĭ·lăb'ĭk), *adj.*

quad'ri·va'lent (kwŏd'rĭ·vā'lĕnt; kwŏd·rĭv'ȧ·lĕnt), *adj.* [*quadri-* + L. *valens, -entis*, pres. part. See VALENCE.] *Chem.* Having a valence of four; tetravalent. — **quad'ri·va'lence** (-lĕns), **quad'ri·va'len·cy** (-lĕn·sĭ), *n.*

quad·riv'i·al (kwŏd·rĭv'ĭ·ăl), *adj.* [L. *quadrivium* a place where four ways meet, fr. *quadri-* + *via* way.] Having four ways or roads meeting in a point; also, of ways or roads, leading in four directions.

quad·riv'i·um (-ŭm), *n.* [L., lit., crossroads.] In medieval times, the four "liberal arts," arithmetic, music, geometry, and astronomy, forming the course for the three years of study between the B.A. and M.A. degrees. Cf. TRIVIUM.

quad·roon' (kwŏd·rōōn'), *n.* [Sp. *cuarterón*, fr. *cuarto* fourth.] The offspring of a mulatto and a white person; a person of quarter Negro blood.

quad·ru'ma·nous (kwŏd·rōō'mȧ·nŭs), *adj.* [L. *quadru-* in comp. (see QUADRI-) + *manus* hand.] *Zool.* **a** Having four hands. **b** Belonging to a group (Quadrumana) of mammals including all the primates except man. — **quad'ru·mane** (kwŏd'rōō·mān), *n.*

quad·rum'vi·rate (kwŏd·rŭm'vĭ·rāt), *n.* Also **quad·riv'i·rate** (-rĭv'ĭ·rāt). *Obs.* A group or association of four men.

quad'ru·ped (kwŏd'rōō·pĕd), *n.* [L. *quadrupes, -pedis*, fr. *quadru-* in comp. (see QUADRI-) + *pes, pedis*, a foot.] *Zool.* An animal having four feet. — *adj.* Having four feet. — **quad·ru'pe·dal** (kwŏd·rōō'pē·dăl; -d'l; kwŏd'rōō·pĕd'ăl; -'l), *adj.*

quad'ru·ple (kwŏd'rōō·p'l; kwŏd·rōō'p'l), *adj.* [F., fr. L. *quadruplus.*] **a** Consisting of four; fourfold; as, the *Quadruple* Alliance. **b** Taken in groups of four. — *adv.* Fourfold. — *n.* A sum or amount four times as great as another; a fourfold amount.

quad'ru·ple (kwŏd'rōō·p'l; kwŏd·rōō'-), *v. t.* & *i.;* -RU·PLED (-p'ld); -RU·PLING (-plĭng). **1.** To multiply by four; to increase fourfold. **2.** To total four times as many as.

quadruple measure *or* **time.** *Music.* A measure of four beats, the first and third being accented; also, the rhythm derived from use of this measure.

quad′ru·plet (kwŏd′rōō·plĕt; -plĭt; kwŏd·rōō′plĭt), *n.* **1.** A collection of four of a kind. **2.** One of four offspring born at one birth.

quad′ru·plex (kwŏd′rōō·plĕks), *adj.* [L.] **1.** Fourfold. **2.** *Teleg.* Pert. to a system by which four messages, two in each direction, may be sent simultaneously over one wire.

quad·ru′pli·cate (kwŏd·rōō′plĭ·kāt), *v. t.* [L. *quadruplicatus,* past part. of *quadruplicare,* fr. *quadruplex* fourfold.] To quadruple. — (-kāt), *adj.* Fourfold; specif., *Math.,* raised to the fourth power. — (-kāt), *n.* In *pl.:* Four things, as copies of a document, corresponding exactly in all ways. — **quad·ru′pli·ca′tion** (-kā′shŭn), *n.*

‖**quae′re** (kwē′rē), *v. imperative.* [L., imper. of *quaerere* to seek. See QUERY.] Inquire; question; see; — used to signify doubt or to suggest investigation. — *n.* A query.

quaes′tor (kwĕs′tŏr; kwēs′-), *n.* Also **ques′tor.** [L., fr. *quaerere, quaesitum,* to seek for, ask.] *Rom. Hist.* Any of a number of officials, originally judges at certain criminal trials, later treasurers of state. — **quaes·to′ri·al** (kwĕs·tō′rĭ·ăl; kwēs-; 70), *adj.* — **quaes′tor·ship,** *n.*

quaff (kwȧf; 9), *v. i. & t.* To drink deeply or repeatedly; to drink. — *n.* A drink. — **quaff′er** (-ẽr), *n.*

quag (kwăg; kwŏg), *n.* Quagmire.

quag′ga (kwăg′ȧ), *n.* [From Bantu dialects, of Hottentot origin.] **a** A South African wild ass (*Equus quagga*), now extinct, allied to the zebras. **b** Erroneously, a zebra.

quag′gy (kwăg′ĭ; kwŏg′ĭ), *adj.;* QUAG′GI·ER (-ĭ·ẽr); QUAG′GI·EST. **1.** Of the nature of a quagmire; boggy. **2.** By extension, flabby; yielding.

quag′mire′ (kwăg′mīr′; kwŏg′-), *n.* **1.** Soft, wet, miry land, which yields under the foot. **2.** A position or condition of difficulty, as of one caught in a quagmire.

qua′hog (kwô′hŏg; kwȧ·hŏg′), *n.* Also **qua′haug** (-hôg; -hŏg′). [Of Algonquian origin.] See CLAM, 1.

quaich, quaigh (kwāk), *n.* [Gael. *cuach,* fr. LL. *caucus.*] *Scot.* A shallow drinking vessel, with ears.

Quai d′Or′say′ (kā′ dôr′sā′). [F., lit., quay of Orsay, a French general.] A quay on the Seine in Paris, fronting on which are the offices of the French Ministry of Foreign Affairs; hence, the French Foreign Office.

quail (kwāl), *v. i.* To sink under trial or prospect of danger; to lose heart; hence, shrink; cower. — **Syn.** See RECOIL.

quail, *n.;* see PLURAL, *Note,* 3. [OF. *quaille,* of Teut. origin.] Any of various small gallinaceous game birds (family Phasianidae) related to the pheasants. All species are ground-nesting, partly insectivorous birds of open country, protectively colored in soft variegated shades. Specif., in the Old World, a migratory bird (*Coturnix coturnix*) and closely related species, in North America, the bobwhite and other nonmigratory forms, as the ***California quail*** (*Lophortyx californica*). See BOBWHITE, *Illust.*

quaint (kwānt), *adj.* [OF. *cointe,* fr. L. *cognitus* known, past part. of *cognoscere* to know.] **1.** *Obs.* Wise; expert; also, crafty. **2.** *Archaic.* Skillfully wrought; hence, graceful; nice; neat. **3. a** Strange; peculiar. **b** Strange but pleasing, esp. because of suggesting customs, dress, or the like, of former generations. — **Syn.** See STRANGE. — **quaint′ly,** *adv.* — **quaint′ness,** *n.*

quake (kwāk), *v. i.* [AS. *cwacian.*] **1.** To shake, vibrate, or quiver, either from not being solid, as soft, wet land, or from violent convulsion of any kind. **2.** To shudder; tremble. — *n.* A shaking or trembling; esp., an earthquake.

Quak′er (kwāk′ẽr), *n.* [From QUAKE, *v.*] One of a religious sect founded by George Fox, about 1650, the members of which call themselves *Friends.* The name *Quaker* was applied in derision in 1650 by a judge to Fox, who bade the justice tremble at the word of the Lord. — **Quak′er·ess** (-ĕs; -ĭs), *n.* — **Quak′er·ish** (-ĭsh), *adj.* — **Quak′er·ism** (-ĭz′m), *n.* — **Quak′er·ly** (-lĭ), *adj. & adv.*

Quaker gun. A dummy piece of artillery, usually of wood; — from the Quaker doctrine of nonresistance.

quak′er-la′dies, *n. pl.* Bluets.

Quaker meeting. A meeting of Quakers for worship, in which there often occur prolonged periods of silence; hence, *Colloq.,* any silent gathering of persons.

qual′i·fi·ca′tion (kwŏl′ĭ·fĭ·kā′shŭn), *n.* **1.** Act or an instance of qualifying, or state of being qualified. **2. a** Any endowment or acquirement which fits a person for a place, office, or employment; also, a requisite; an essential. **b** A condition that must be complied with for the attainment of a status, the perfection of a right, etc.; as, the *qualification* for citizenship. **3.** Modification; as, to promise without *qualification.*

qual′i·fied (kwŏl′ĭ·fīd), *adj.* **1. a** Competent; fit. **b** Having complied with conditions for an office, employment, etc. **2.** Limited or modified in some way, esp. as to the legal effect. — **Syn.** See ABLE. — **qual′i·fied·ly,** *adv.*

qual′i·fi′er (-fī′ẽr), *n.* **1.** One who or that which qualifies. **2.** *Gram.* A word, as an adjective or adverb, joined to another word to qualify or limit its meaning; a modifier.

qual′i·fy (-fī), *v. t.;* -FIED (-fīd); -FY′ING. [F. *qualifier,* fr. ML. *qualificare,* fr. L. *qualis* how constituted, as + *-ficare* (in comp.) to make.] **1. a** To reduce from a general to a particular or restricted form; to modify; limit; as, to *qualify* a statement. **b** To characterize by naming an attribute or attributes; to name descriptively. **2.** Hence, to soften; mitigate; abate; assuage. **3.** To fit, as for a place, office, character, or privilege; esp., to supply with legal authority. **4.** To modify the strength of, as liquors. **5.** *Gram.* To limit or modify the meaning of, as an adjective or adverb; to modify. — *v. i.* **1.** To be or become qualified; to be fit, as for an office. **2.** To obtain legal or competent power or capacity. **3.** In sports, to exhibit a required degree of ability in preliminary contests.

qual′i·ta′tive (kwŏl′ĭ·tā′tĭv), *adj.* Relating to or concerned with quality; as, *qualitative* analysis in chemistry; — contrasted with *quantitative.* — **qual′i·ta′tive·ly,** *adv.*

qual′i·ty (kwŏl′ĭ·tĭ), *n.; pl.* -TIES (-tĭz). [OF. *qualité,* fr. L. *qualitas,* fr. *qualis* how constituted, as.] **1.** *Now Rare.* Proper or essential being; nature. **2.** Hence, an attribute; characteristic. **3.** Class, kind, or grade; as, a fine *quality* of yarn. **4.** Distinctive trait, power, capacity, or virtue. **5.** Specif.: **a** Excellence of character; as, the thoroughbred shows *quality.* **b** An acquired trait; accomplishment. **c** *Now Rare.* Social status; as, persons of the best *quality;* hence, persons, collectively, of a high social status. **6.** *Acoustics.* That property of a tone which may distinguish it from another tone having the same pitch and loudness. **7.** *Logic.* The character, in a proposition, of being affirmative or negative. **8.** *Philos.* A property or attribute. **9.** *Phonet.* The identifying character of a vowel sound, determined chiefly by the resonance of the vocal chambers in uttering it; — contrasted with *quantity,* or duration.

Syn. **Quality, property, character, attribute** mean a characteristic mark or trait of a thing. **Quality,** the widest term, implies any characteristic, material or immaterial, individual or generic; **property** implies one that belongs by virtue of the thing's true or essential nature; **character,** a peculiar and distinctive quality of a thing, esp. of a class of things; **attribute,** a quality ascribed to a thing.

qualm (kwäm; kwôm), *n.* **1.** A sudden attack of illness, faintness, or pain, esp. nausea. **2.** Hence, a sudden misgiving or faintheartedness. **3.** A scruple; compunction.

Syn. **Qualm, scruple, compunction, demur** mean a misgiving about what one is doing or going to do. **Qualm** implies uneasiness lest one is not following his conscience or better judgment; **scruple,** doubt of the rightness, the justice, etc., of an act; **compunction,** a warning prick or sting of conscience; **demur,** hesitation caused by irresolution or objections to some act or suggestion.

qualm′ish, *adj.* **1.** Feeling qualms, esp. of nausea. **2.** Like, or of the nature of, a qualm; also, likely to produce qualms. — **qualm′ish·ly,** *adv.* — **qualm′ish·ness,** *n.*

quam′ash (kwŏm′ăsh; kwȧ·măsh′). Var. of CAMASS.

quan′da·ry (kwŏn′dȧ·rĭ *or, esp. Brit. and formerly,* kwŏn·dâr′ĭ), *n.; pl.* -RIES (-rĭz). A state of perplexity or doubt; a dilemma. — **Syn.** See PREDICAMENT.

‖**quand même** (käɴ′ mâm′). [F.] Even though; whatever may happen.

quan′dong′ (kwŏn′dŏng′), *n.* Also **quan′dang′** (-dŏng′), **quan′tong′** (-tŏng′), etc. [Native name.] An Australian tree (*Fusanus acuminatus,* family Santalaceae); also, its edible drupaceous fruit, or its edible nut (called also **quandong nut**).

quan′ta (kwŏn′tȧ), *n., pl.* of QUANTUM.

quan′tic (-tĭk), *n.* [L. *quantus* how much.] *Math.* A homogeneous algebraic function of two or more variables, in general containing only positive integral powers of the variables.

quan′ti·fy (kwŏn′tĭ·fī), *v. t.;* -FIED (-fīd); -FY′ING. [ML. *quantificare,* fr. L. *quantus* how much.] **1.** To modify or qualify with respect to quantity; also, to measure the quantity of. **2.** *Logic.* To render the logical quantity of a term explicit. — **quan′ti·fi·ca′tion** (-fĭ·kā′shŭn), *n.*

quan′ti·ta′tive (-tā′tĭv), *adj.* **1.** *Rare.* Having quantity, mass, or extent in space. **2.** That is, or that may be, estimated by quantity. **3.** Concerned with the measurement of phenomena, esp. with respect to its quantity; as, *quantitative* analysis; — contrasted with *qualitative.* **4.** Designating a type of verse having as its metrical unit a foot of determined time value and a rhythm dependent mainly on arrangement of long and short syllables. **5.** Of or pertaining to vowel quantity; as, a *quantitative* accent. — **quan′ti·ta′tive·ly,** *adv.*

quan′ti·ty (-tĭ), *n.; pl.* -TIES (-tĭz). [OF. *quantité,* fr. L. *quantitas,* fr. *quantus* how great, how much.] **1.** An amount or portion; either, a measurable or numerable amount; or, loosely, any amount capable of increase or decrease in kind. **2.** *Obs. exc. Math.* Spatial dimension, whether cubic, plane, or linear. **3.** Great amount; as, a medicine in *quantities,* that is, in large amounts. **4.** *Logic.* **a** With respect to terms taken generally, their extension or, less frequently, their intension. **b** With respect to propositions, their character as universal or particular (or, as some would add, singular). **5.** *Math.* Whatever may be operated upon according to fixed mutually consistent laws; — distinguished from a *magnitude.* **6.** *Music.* The relative duration of a tone. **7.** *Philos.* In general, that character of a thing by virtue of which measure or number is applicable to it, or it can be determined as more or less than some other. **8.** *Phonet.* The relative duration, or time length of a speech sound or sound-group. **9.** *Pros.* Length or brevity of vowel sounds or of syllables as measured by the time required to pronounce them. — **Syn.** See SUM.

quan′tum (kwŏn′tŭm), *n.; pl.* QUANTA (-tȧ). [L., neuter of *quantus* how much.] **1.** Quantity; amount. **2.** *Physics.* An elemental unit of energy according to the quantum theory (which see).

‖**quan′tum suf′fi·cit** (sŭf′ĭ·sĭt). [L.] As much as suffices.

quantum theory. *Physics.* A theory that in the emission or absorption of energy by atoms or molecules the process is not continuous but takes place by steps, each step being the emission or absorption of an amount of energy called the *quantum.*

quar′an·tine (kwŏr′ăn·tēn; 74), *n.* [It. *quarantina,* fr. *quaranta* forty, fr. L. *quadraginta.*] **1.** A period of forty days. **2.** The term, orig. of forty days, during which an arriving ship, suspected of infection, is restrained from intercourse with the shore; hence, such restraint, or the measures taken to enforce it; also, the place where prohibited vessels are stationed. Now, any forced stoppage of travel or intercourse, due to contagions or infections. **3.** A place, usually an isolation hospital, in which persons under quarantine are kept. **4.** A condition of isolation. — (kwŏr′ăn·tēn; kwŏr′ăn·tēn′), *v. t.* **1.** To place in quarantine. **2.** To isolate; to keep from normal relations or intercourse with, or effect upon, other persons, countries, etc.; as, to *quarantine* aggressor nations; to *quarantine* the war in Spain.

quar′rel (kwŏr′ĕl; 74), *n.* [OF., fr. dim. of L. *quadrum* a square.] **1.** *Now Hist.* A square-headed bolt or arrow, esp. for a crossbow. **2.** *Arch.* Any small quadrangular member, as a square of glass, esp. when set diagonally.

quar′rel, *n.* [OF. *querele, querelle,* fr. L. *querela, querella,* a complaint, fr. *queri* to complain.] **1.** *Now Rare.* Ground of complaint. **2.** A cause or case to be disputed or defended. **3.** A breach of concord, amity, or obligation; esp., angry dispute or strife.

Syn. **Quarrel, wrangle, altercation, squabble, spat, tiff** mean an angry, discordant dispute. **Quarrel** implies verbal strife followed by strained or severed relations; **wrangle,** a noisy, insistent dispute; **altercation,** a fight marked by quarreling and, often, blows; **squabble,** childish and unseemly wrangling; **spat** and **tiff,** a squabble over something insignificant.

— *v. i.;* -RELED (-ĕld) or -RELLED; -REL·ING or -REL·LING. **1.** To find fault; to cavil. **2.** To disagree; to be or become antagonistic. **3.** To dispute angrily or violently; to wrangle. — **quar′rel·er, quar′rel·ler** (-ẽr), *n.*

quar′rel·some (-sŭm), *adj.* Apt or disposed to quarrel; given to brawls or wrangling. — **Syn.** See BELLIGERENT. — **quar′rel·some·ly,** *adv.* — **quar′rel·some·ness,** *n.*

quar′ri·er (kwŏr′ĭ·ẽr), *n.* A worker in a stone quarry.

quar′ry (kwŏr′ĭ), *n.; pl.* -RIES (-ĭz). [From 1st QUARREL, *n.*] A square pane of glass, tile, or the like.

quar′ry, *n.; pl.* -RIES (-ĭz). [OF. *cuirée*, fr. *curée* (past part. of *curer* to clean) and fr. ML. *corata* entrails, with influence in OF. of *cuir* skin.] **1.** *Obs. Hunting.* A heap of the game killed. **2.** The object of the chase; game; esp., the game hunted with hawks. **3.** Hence, any prey.

quar′ry, *n.* [OF. *quarriere*, fr. *carre* squared stone, fr. L. *quadrum.* See QUADRATE.] An open excavation, usually for obtaining building stone, slate, or limestone. — *v. t.;* QUAR′RIED (-ĭd); QUAR′RY·ING. **1.** To dig or take from or as from a quarry. **2.** To make a quarry in; as, to *quarry* land.

quar′ry·ing, *n.* The business or occupation of extracting stone, marble, slate, etc., from quarries.

quart (kwôrt), *n.* [OF. *quarte*, n. fem., fr. *quart* fourth, fr. L. *quartus* fourth.] **1.** A measure of capacity. See MEASURE, *Tables* 10 & 11. **2.** A vessel or measure containing a quart.

quart (kärt), *n.* [F. *quarte.*] **1.** *Fencing.* = 1st CARTE. **2.** *Games.* In piquet and certain other card games, four cards of a suit in sequence, the highest four being the ***quart major.***

quar′tan (kwôr′tăn; -t'n), *adj.* [OF. *quartain*, in *fièvre quartaine*, L. *quartana*, fem. of *quartanus*, fr. *quartus* the fourth.] Of or pertaining to the fourth; specif., occurring every fourth day, reckoning inclusively. — *n. Med.* An intermittent fever which returns every fourth day, that is, with two days' intermission between paroxysms; esp., a quartan malaria. Cf. QUINTAN, TERTIAN.

‖**quarte** (kärt), *n.* [F.] *Fencing.* = 1st CARTE.

quar′ter (kwôr′tẽr), *n.* [OF. *quartier*, fr. L. *quartarius* a fourth part.] **1.** One of four equal parts into which anything is divided; a fourth part or portion. **2.** Specif.: **a** The fourth part of a hundredweight. **b** Eight bushels, formerly the fourth of a ton; — used esp. in measuring grain. **c** The fourth of a pound. **d** The fourth of a yard; a span; also, the fourth of a mile. **e** The fourth of a year. **f** A term of study in a college, etc.; — properly, a fourth of the school year. **g** The fourth of an hour; hence, the moment marking this. **h** *U. S. & Canada.* Twenty-five cents, a fourth of a dollar; also, a silver coin of this value. See MONEY, *Tables.* **i** *U. S.* Short for QUARTER SECTION. **3.** One limb of a quadruped with the adjacent parts. **4. a** The region under or considered as under any of the four conceived divisions of the horizon; hence, region; place; also, point; direction. **b** One of the four parts into which the horizon is regarded as divided; also, a cardinal point or division. **c** A point or direction of the compass. **d** A point, direction, person, place, etc., without definite localization; as, the news from that *quarter* was favorable. **5.** A division of a town, city, or county; a special district. **6.** Proper station; as: **a** Assigned position; post; as, a call to *quarters.* **b** Place of residence; shelter; — usually *pl.;* as, bachelor *quarters.* **c** *pl. Southern U. S.* A collection of cabins for Negroes on a plantation. **7.** Forbearance; clemency; as, no *quarter* from his creditors. **8.** *Astron.* A fourth part of the moon's period; also, quadrature. **9.** *Farriery.* The side of a horse's hoof between the toe and the heel. See HOOF, *Illust.* **10.** *Her.* **a** A bearing or charge occupying the first fourth part of the field. **b** Any of the four partitions into which the field is divided. See ESCUTCHEON, *Illust.* **11.** *Mil.* Clemency shown to a conquered enemy in not taking his life. **12.** *Naut.* **a** The after part of a vessel's side, generally corresponding in extent with the quarter-deck. **b** The part of the yardarm outside of the slings. **c** A station at which officers and men are posted in battle, drill, inspection, etc. **d** The fourth of a fathom. **e** The fourth of the distance from one point of the compass to another, being the fourth of 11° 15′, i. e., nearly 2° 49′; — called also ***quarter point.*** **13.** *Shoemaking.* That part of a boot or shoe which forms the side, from the heel to the vamp. **14.** *Sports.* **a** *Football.* Short for QUARTERBACK. **b** One of the four periods into which a game is divided. — ***at close quarters.*** In immediate contact; at close range.
— *v. t.* **1.** To divide into four equal parts. Hence, to divide or separate into parts, either more or less than four; as, to *quarter* an orange. Specif., to cleave asunder; to dismember. **2.** To shelter; to supply with lodging; esp., to assign to a certain place of shelter, as soldiers. **3.** To pass back and forth across an area in many directions; — said esp. of game dogs questing for game. **4.** *Her.* To arrange or bear, as different coats of arms, quarterly on one escutcheon; also, to add (a coat of arms) to another or others in this way. **5.** *Mach.* To adjust or locate at right angles, as cranks. — *v. i.* **1.** To lodge. **2.** To range over a region; specif., *Hunting,* to cover a field in sections, as a dog in search of game. **3.** *Naut.* To strike or blow on a ship's quarter, as the wind.
— *adj.* Consisting of, or equal to, a quarter.

quar′ter·age (kwôr′tẽr·ĭj), *n.* [OF.] **1.** A quarterly payment or allowance. **2.** Quarters or shelter, as for troops; also, the provision of, or the cost of providing, quarters.

quar′ter·back′ (-băk′), *n.* *Am. Football.* Formerly, a player who received the ball from the center and passed it to the runner; now, a back scarcely distinguishable in function from the other backs (*halfbacks, fullback*).

quarter crack. See SAND CRACK.

quarter day. A day regarded as beginning a quarter of the year, when quarterly payments, as rent, become due.

quar′ter–deck′, *n.* *Naut.* That part of the upper deck abaft the mainmast reserved as a promenade for the officers and, sometimes, cabin passengers.

quar′tered (kwôr′tẽrd), *adj.* **1.** Divided into quarters. **2.** Furnished with quarters; provided with shelter. **3.** Quartersawed; — said of lumber, commonly oak. See QUARTERSAW, *Illust.* **4.** *Her.* Divided into, or containing, quarters or quarterings.

quar′ter–fi′nal, *adj.* *Sports.* Designating or pert. to the round immediately preceding the semifinal round of a tournament. — **quar′ter–fi′nal,** *n.* — **quar′ter–fi′nal·ist,** *n.*

quar′ter·ing, *adj.* That quarters; specif.: **a** *Mach.* At right angles. **b** *Naut.* Coming from a point well abaft the beam, but not directly astern; — said of wind, waves, etc. — *n.* **1.** Division into quarters; hence, division in general. **2.** The act of driving or moving diagonally on a road. **3.** Assignment of quarters, as for soldiers. **4.** *Her.* **a** The division of an escutcheon containing different coats of arms into four or more compartments. **b** A quarter, or the coat of arms on it.

quar′ter·ly (kwôr′tẽr·lĭ), *adv.* **1.** By quarters; once in a quarter of a year. **2.** *Her.* In quarters, or quarterings; — said of a shield thus divided. — *adj.* **1.** Containing, or consisting of, a fourth part. **2.** Recurring during, or at the end of, each quarter. — *n.; pl.* -LIES (-lĭz). A periodical work published once a quarter.

quar′ter·mas′ter (-mȧs′tẽr; 9), *n.* **1.** *Mil.* A commissioned officer whose duty is to provide quarters, clothing, transportation, forage, subsistence, etc., for troops. **2.** *Naut.* A petty officer who attends to the helm, binnacle, signals, etc.

quar′tern (kwôr′tẽrn), *n.* [OF. *quarteron* fourth of a pound, or of a hundred.] **1.** A fourth part or quarter, as a fourth of a pint, or a gill. **2.** A loaf of bread weighing about four pounds.

quarter note. *Music.* See NOTE, *n.*

quar′ter–phase′, *adj.* *Elec.* Diphase.

quarter point. See QUARTER, *n.*, 12 e.

quar′ter·saw′ (kwôr′tẽr·sô′; 2), *v. t.;* see SAW. To saw (a log) into quarters and then into boards or veneer, to show the grain advantageously.

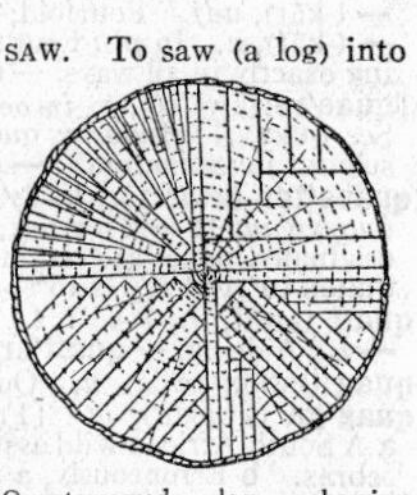
Quartersawed log, showing different ways of cutting the Quarters.

quarter section. **1.** A quarter. **2.** In the government system of land surveying of the United States and Canada, a tract of land half a mile square, containing 160 acres.

quarter sessions. **a** *Eng. Law.* A court of a limited original and appellate criminal jurisdiction, held quarterly by the justices of peace in counties and by the recorders in boroughs. **b** A similar court with criminal jurisdiction in some states of the United States.

quar′ter·staff′ (kwôr′tẽr·stȧf′; 9), *n.; pl.* -STAVES (-stāvz′; -stȧvz′). A staff, formerly common as a weapon, wielded with one hand in the middle and the other between middle and end.

quarter step. *Music.* A quarter tone.

quarter tone. *Music.* **a** An interval of one half a semitone or half step. **b** A tone at such an interval.

quar·tet′, quar·tette′ (kwôr·tĕt′), *n.* [F. *quartette*, fr. It. *quartetto*, dim. of *quarto* fourth, fr. L. *quartus* the fourth.] **1.** A group of four. **2.** *Music.* **a** A composition in four parts, each for a single performer. **b** The group of four performers of such music.

quar′tic (kwôr′tĭk), *adj.* [L. *quartus* fourth.] *Math.* Of the fourth degree. — *n. Alg.* A quantic of the fourth degree.

quar′tile (kwôr′tĭl; 56), *adj.* [ML. *quartilis*, fr. L. *quartus* the fourth.] **1.** *Statistics.* Designating a point so chosen that ¾ of the items of a frequency distribution are on one side of it and ¼ on the other. Cf. MEDIAN, *adj.*, 2. **2.** *Astrol.* Designating, or pertaining to, an aspect with a difference of 90° celestial longitude. — *n.* **1.** *Statistics.* A quartile point. **2.** *Astrol.* A quartile aspect.

quar′to (kwôr′tō), *adj.* [L. *in quarto* in fourth.] Having four leaves (eight pages) to the sheet; of the form or size of a quarto. — *n.; pl.* QUARTOS (-tōz). A size of a book, or of its pages, made by twice folding a sheet, making four leaves, measuring about 9½ × 12½ inches. Abbr. *4to* or *4°*.

quartz (kwôrts), *n.* [G. *quarz.*] *Mineral.* A form of silica (silicon dioxide, SiO_2) occurring in hexagonal crystals or in crystalline masses. It is the most common of all solid minerals and may be colorless and transparent, or colored.

quartz·if′er·ous (kwôrts·ĭf′ẽr·ŭs), *adj.* [*quartz* + *-ferous.*] Consisting of quartz; containing quartz.

quartz′ite (kwôrts′īt), *n.* A compact granular rock composed of quartz. It is a metamorphosed sandstone.

quartz lamp. A mercury-vapor lamp in a tube of quartz glass, which transmits most of the ultraviolet radiation.

quartz plate. *Elec.* A piece of quartz crystal cut in such a way as to be active piezoelectrically.

quash (kwŏsh; 74), *v. t.* [OF. *quasser*, in form fr. L. *quassare* to shake, break, but influenced by LL. *cassare* to annihilate.] *Law.* To abate, annul, or make void.

quash, *v. t.* [OF. *quasser* (F. *casser*), fr. L. *quassare* to shake, shatter.] To suppress; quell.

qua′si (kwā′sī; kwä′sĭ). [L.] As if; as though; as it were; in a manner; in a certain sense or degree; seeming; seemingly; — used as an adjective or an adverb, or as a prefix; as, a *quasi* argument, that which resembles, or is used as, an argument; **qua′si–his·tor′i·cal** (seemingly historical), **qua′si–hu′mor·ous, qua′si–se′ri·ous·ly.**

quasi contract. *Law.* An obligation similar to that upon contract and enforced by action as upon contract, imposed by law independently of the will of the person obliged.

qua′si–ju·di′cial (kwā′sī·jōō·dĭsh′ăl; kwä′sĭ-), *adj.* Having certain critical powers of inquiry like those of a judge or the judiciary.

quass (kvȧs). Var. of KVASS.

quas′si·a (kwŏsh′ĭ·ȧ; kwŏsh′ȧ), *n.* [NL., after Graman *Quassi*, a Surinam Negro who discovered its virtues about 1730.] *Pharm.* A drug extracted from the wood of certain tropical American trees (family Simaroubaceae, the ailanthus family, esp. *Quassia amara*). It is used in medicine as a bitter tonic and as a remedy for threadworms in children.

qua·ter′na·ry (kwȧ·tûr′nȧ·rĭ), *adj.* [L. *quaternarius* consisting of four each, containing four.] **1.** Consisting of four; by fours. **2.** [*cap.*] *Geol.* Of, pert. to, or designating the later principal division (cf. TERTIARY, 4) of the Cenozoic era, down to the present. It includes the Pleistocene or Glacial period and the Recent period. — *n.; pl.* -RIES (-rĭz). **1.** A group of four; also, the number four. **2.** [*cap.*] *Geol.* The Quaternary division or its system of rocks.

qua·ter′nate (kwȧ·tûr′nāt), *adj.* Composed of, or arranged in, sets of four; as, *quaternate* leaves.

qua·ter′ni·on (-nĭ·ŭn; 58), *n.* [LL. *quaternio*, fr. *quaterni* four each.] **1.** A set of four parts, things, or persons. **2.** *Math.* An operator, or factor, q, multiplication by which converts one vector, A, into another vector, B, by changing the direction and magnitude of vector A so that it agrees with that of vector B. **3.** *pl. Math.* The calculus of the quaternion.

qua·torze′ (kȧ·tôrz′), *n.* [F., fourteen, fr. L. *quattuordecim.*] The four aces, kings, queens, knaves, or tens, in piquet, counting as fourteen points.

quat′rain (kwŏt′rān), *n.* [F., fr. *quatre* four, fr. L. *quattuor, quatuor.*] *Pros.* A stanza of four lines.

qua′tre (kä′tẽr; *F.* kȧ′tr′), *n.* [F.] A card, die, or domino having four spots, or pips.

quat′re·foil′ (kăt′ẽr·foil′; kăt′rĕ-), *n.* [OF. *quatre* four + *foil, foille*, leaf.] A flower with four leaves, or a leaf with four leaflets; specif., *Arch.*, an ornamental foliation of four lobes or foils. See FOIL, *Illust.*

||**quat'tro·cen'to** (kwät'trō·chĕn'tō), *n. & adj.* [It., four hundred. Cf. CINQUECENTO.] The 15th century, when applied to Italian art or literature.

quat'tu·or·de·cil'lion (kwăt'ū·ôr·dē·sĭl'yŭn), *n.* See NUMERATION, *Table.*

qua'ver (kwā'vẽr), *v. i.* [Freq. fr. *quave*, ME. *cwavien.*] **1.** To tremble; shake. **2. a** To utter sound in tremulous tones. **b** *Music.* To trill with the voice or on an instrument. — *v. t.* To utter with quavers; esp., to sing with trills or quavers. — *n.* **1.** A tremulous tone. **2.** *Music.* See NOTE, *n.* — **qua'ver·y** (-ĭ), *adj.*

quay (kē; kwā), *n.* [OF. *kai, cay* (F. *quai*).] A stretch of paved bank or a solid artificial landing place beside navigable water, for convenience in loading and unloading ships.

quay'age (kē'ĭj; kwā'-), *n.* [F.] **1.** Charge for use of a quay. **2.** Room on or for quays; also, quays collectively.

quean (kwēn), *n.* [AS. *cwene.*] **1.** A jade; wench; slut. **2.** *Now Scot.* A woman, esp. an unmarried woman; a girl.

quea'sy (kwē'zĭ), *adj.;* QUEA'SI·ER (-zĭ·ẽr); QUEA'SI·EST. **1.** Presenting difficulties; hazardous. **2.** Nauseated; qualmish. **3.** Ill at ease; uncomfortable. **4.** Fastidious; squeamish. — **quea'si·ly,** *adv.* — **quea'si·ness,** *n.*

que·bra'cho (kā·brä'chō), *n.* [Sp., also *quiebrahacha*, lit., break-ax, from its hard wood.] **1.** Any of several tropical American trees or their very hard wood; specif.: **a** The ***white quebracho*** (*Aspidosperma quebracho*, family Apocynaceae, the dogbane family) of Chile and Argentina, whose bark, ***quebracho bark,*** is used as a tonic and antispasmodic. **b** A tree (*Quebrachia lorentzii*, family Anacardiaceae, the sumac family) of Argentina, known as ***red quebracho*** from its bright-red bark, which is rich in tannin and is used for dyeing. **2.** The wood or bark of any of these trees.

Quech'ua (kĕch'wä), *n.* [From native name.] **1.** Any Indian of the group of civilized tribes which constituted the dominant element in the Inca Empire. **2.** The language of the Quechuas, still spoken in many different dialects in Peru and Ecuador. See LANGUAGE, *Table.* — **Quech'uan** (-wăn), *adj.*

queen (kwēn), *n.* [AS. *cwēn* wife, queen, woman.] **1.** A wife of a king. **2.** A female monarch. **3.** A woman eminent in rank, power, or attractions. **4.** The fertile, or fully developed, female of social bees (**queen bee**), ants, and termites, whose function is to lay eggs; — disting. from the workers, soldiers, etc. See TERMITE, *Illust.* **5.** *Cards.* A playing card picturing a queen. **6.** *Chess.* The most powerful piece, moving as either a rook or a bishop in any given move. Abbr. *Q* (no period). — *v. t.* To make a queen of. — *v. i.* To act as, or wield the power of, a queen; — chiefly with *it.* — **queen'li·ness,** *n.* — **queen'ly,** *adj.*

Queen Anne's lace *or* **laces** (ănz). The wild carrot; — in allusion to the delicate white flowers in the flat-topped umbel.

Queen Anne style. a *Arch.* A style of English building of the early 18th century, characterized by modified classic ornament, and unpretentious design, by the use of red brickwork, in which even relief ornament is carved, and by general fitness for domestic architecture. **b** *Furniture.* A style prevalent in England under Dutch influence, about 1690–1750. It is marked by the increased use of upholstery and marquetry, the vogue of Oriental goods, and the greater attention to comfort.

queen dowager. The widow of a king.

Queen Mab (măb). A fairy queen, the midwife that delivers men of their dreams.

queen mother. A queen dowager who is mother of the reigning king or queen.

queen olive. A large, oblong olive with a small but long pit, grown in the region of Seville, Spain. Loosely, any olive of similar character.

queen post. One of two vertical tie posts in a roof truss, or similar framed truss. Cf. KING POST; ROOF, *Illust.*

queen regent. A reigning queen, either in behalf of another or (also **queen regnant**) in her own right.

Queen's Bench, queen's counsel, English, evidence, proctor, shilling. See KING'S BENCH, KING'S COUNSEL, etc.

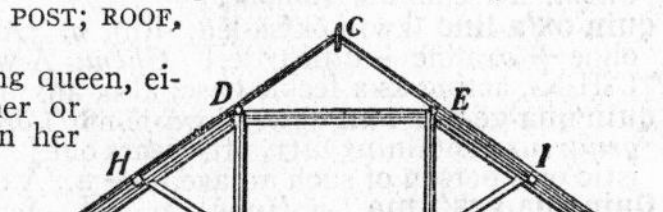

DG, EF Queen Posts; *AB* Tie Beam; *DE* Straining Piece; *AD, BE* Principal Rafters; *AC, BC* Rafters; *GH, FI* Struts.

queen truss. *Arch.* A truss framed with queen posts.

queer (kwẽr), *adj.* [Perh. fr. G. *quer* cross, oblique, athwart.] **1.** Differing in some odd way from what is ordinary; singular; peculiar. **2. a** *Slang.* Spurious; counterfeit. **b** *Colloq.* Suspicious; questionable. **c** *Colloq.* Eccentric. **3.** Not quite well; qualmish; faint. — **Syn.** See STRANGE. — *v. t.* To spoil the effect or success of as by ridicule; also, reflexively, to get (oneself) into a disadvantageous situation; as, he *queered* himself with the professor. — *n. Slang.* **1.** Counterfeit money. **2.** A homosexual. — **queer'ly,** *adv.* — **queer'ness,** *n.*

quell (kwĕl), *v. t.* [AS. *cwellan*, caus. to *cwelan* to die.] **1.** To overpower; subdue; suppress; destroy. **2.** To quiet; allay; pacify; as, to *quell* grief. — **quell'er** (-ẽr), *n.*

quench (kwĕnch), *v. t.* [AS. *cwencan* in *ācwencan*, causative to *cwincan* to decrease.] **1.** To extinguish; make an end of; as, to *quench* a fire. Hence, of emotions, sensations, etc., to subdue; suppress; as, to *quench* hate, love, etc. **2.** To extinguish by satisfying, as thirst; to slake. **3.** To cool suddenly, as heated steel, by immersion, usually in water or oil. — *v. i.* To become extinguished; to go out; — said of something burning; hence, of passions, etc., or of persons experiencing them, to subside; to become calm or cool. — **quench'a·ble,** *adj.* — **quench'er,** *n.* — **quench'less,** *adj.*

quer'ce·tin (kwûr'sē·tĭn), *n.* [See QUERCITRON.] *Chem.* A yellow crystalline dye, $C_{15}H_{10}O_7$, the dyestuff of quercitron. — **quer·cet'ic** (kwẽr·sĕt'ĭk; -sē'tĭk), *adj.*

quer'cine (-sĭn; -sīn), *adj.* [LL. *quercinus*, fr. *quercus* oak.] Pertaining to or designating the oak.

quer'cit·ron (kwûr'sĭt·rŭn), *n.* [For *querci-citron*, fr. L. *quercus* oak + F. *citron* (see CITRON).] **1.** The black oak (*Quercus velutina*); also, its bark, used in tanning and dyeing. **2.** A yellow dyestuff consisting of the ground or rasped inner bark of this tree.

que'rist (kwẽr'ĭst), *n.* [See QUERY.] An inquirer.

quern (kwûrn), *n.* [AS. *cweorn, cwyrn.*] **1.** A primitive hand mill for grinding grain. **2.** A small hand mill for grinding spices.

quer'u·lous (kwĕr'ū·lŭs; kwĕr'ōō-), *adj.* [L. *querulus*, LL. *querulosus*, fr. *queri* to complain.] **1.** Apt to find fault; habitually complaining. **2.** Expressing complaint; fretful; peevish. — **quer'u·lous·ly,** *adv.* — **quer'u·lous·ness,** *n.*

que'ry (kwẽr'ĭ), *n.; pl.* -RIES (-ĭz). [L. *quaere*, imper. sing. of *quaerere, quaesitum*, to seek or search for, ask.] **1.** A question; inquiry. **2.** A question in the mind; doubt. **3.** An interrogation point [?] as the sign of a question or of a doubt. — *v. t.;* -RIED (-ĭd); -RY·ING. **1.** To inquire into; ask. **2.** To address questions to. **3.** To question the truth or correctness of; specif., to mark with interrogation marks, as printer's proof, expressing doubt as to a detail. — *v. i.* To question or express doubt. — **Syn.** See ASK.

quest (kwĕst), *n.* [OF. *queste* (F. *quête*). See QUERY.] **1.** *Rare.* A jury of inquest. **2.** A seeking; adventure; esp., in medieval romance, a chivalrous enterprise, usually involving a journey. **3.** Those who make search collectively. — *v. i.* **1.** To search a trail, as of game; also, to bay; — said of a dog. **2.** To make a search; to go on a quest. — **quest'er,** *n.*

ques'tion (kwĕs'chŭn), *n.* [OF., fr. L. *quaestio*, fr. *quaerere* to ask.] **1. a** Act of asking; interrogation; inquiry. **b** That which is asked; query. **2.** Discussion; debate; hence, objection; doubt; as, true beyond *question.* **3.** Investigation; specif., a judicial or official investigation. **4.** A problem; matter to be inquired into. **5.** A subject or point of debate, or a proposition being or to be voted on, in a meeting, esp. in a legislative body; also, the putting such a subject or proposal to vote. — *v. i.* To ask questions; to inquire. — *v. t.* **1.** To inquire of by asking questions; to query; as, to *question* a witness. **2.** To doubt. **3.** To raise a question about; to dispute; as, to *question* a decision. — **Syn.** See ASK. — **ques'tion·ing·ly,** *adv.*

ques'tion·a·ble (-*ȧ*·b'l), *adj.* **1.** *Obs.* Admitting of being questioned; inviting inquiry. **2.** Open to doubt; not sure, exact, or decided. **3.** Dubious in nature or character; not of good repute; as, a *questionable* neighborhood. — **Syn.** See DOUBTFUL. — **ques'tion·a·ble·ness,** *n.* — **ques'tion·a·bly,** *adv.*

ques'tion·ar'y (-ẽr'ĭ *or, esp. Brit.,* -ẽr·ĭ), *n.* A questionnaire.

ques'tion·er (-ẽr), *n.* One who questions.

ques'tion·less, *adj.* Not to be questioned; indubitable; also, unquestioning. — *adv.* Unquestionably.

question mark. An interrogation point [?].

ques'tion·naire' (kwĕs'chŭn·âr'; *F.* kĕs'tyô'nâr'), *n.* [F.] A set of questions for submission to a number of persons to get data for an induction or calculation, as in a psychological investigation or an industrial report.

ques'tor (kwĕs'tẽr; kwēs'-), *n.* = QUAESTOR. — **ques'tor·ship,** *n.*

quet·zal' (kĕt·säl'), **que·zal'** (kĕ·säl'), *n.* [Sp. *quetzal, quetzale*, fr. Nahuatl *quetzalli* tail feather, esp. of the *quetzaltototl* quetzal.] **1.** A Central American trogon (*Pharomacrus mocinno*) having brilliant plumage, and, in the male, long upper tail coverts. It is the national emblem of Guatemala. **2.** *pl.* -ZALES (*pron.* -sä'lās). The gold currency unit of Guatemala. See MONEY, *Tables.*

queue (kū), *n.* [F.] **1.** A taillike plait of hair worn behind; a pigtail. **2.** A waiting line, as of persons before a ticket window. — *v. t. & i.* To arrange in or form a queue.

quey (kwā), *n.* [Dan. *qvie, kvie.*] *Scot.* A heifer.

quib'ble (kwĭb''l), *n.* **1.** *Rare.* A pun. **2.** An evasion of or a shift ing from the point at issue; an equivocation. — *v. i.* To indulge in a quibble or quibbles; to make use of equivocation. — **quib'bler** (-lẽr), *n.*

quick (kwĭk), *adj.* [AS. *cwic, cwicu, cwucu*, living.] **1.** *Archaic & Dial.* Living; animate. **2.** Manifesting a characteristic activity or quality suggestive of life; — of things; as: **a** Burning; — said of fire. Hence, fiery; intense. **b** Moving; shifting; — said of sand, earth, etc. **c** Fresh; bracing. **3.** Swift; rapid; speedy; as, a *quick* trot. **4.** Hence: **a** Prompt in action or thought; alert; ready; as, a *quick* wit. **b** Hasty; as, a *quick* temper. **c** Taking place rapidly; begun and terminated in an instant; as, a *quick* look. **5.** Sensitive; perceptive in a high degree; as, a *quick* ear. **6.** Productive; esp., pregnant; as, *quick* with child.

Syn. (1) See LIVING.
(2) See FAST.
(3) **Quick, prompt, ready, apt** mean able to respond without delay or hesitation. **Quick** implies native rather than acquired power; **prompt** implies, usually, the training or discipline that fits one for instant response; **ready,** more often applied to a person or his powers, implies facility, fluency, etc.; **apt** applies to the possession of such quickness or the like that makes for instant response.

— *adv.* In a quick manner; quickly.

— *n.* **1.** A living person or thing; — chiefly in ***the quick,*** the, or those, living. **2.** A live plant, or living plants collectively; esp., hawthorn; a quickset. **3.** Sensitive living flesh; as, to cut a fingernail to the *quick;* hence, a vital part.

— *v. t. Archaic.* To animate; stir up.

— **quick'ly,** *adv.* — **quick'ness,** *n.*

quick assets. *Accounting.* Cash on hand and all forms of merchandise which can be marketed at no great sacrifice.

quick bread. Any kind of bread, esp. biscuits, muffins, popovers, etc., whose leavening agent permits immediate baking of dough or batter mixture.

quick'en (kwĭk'ĕn), *v. t.* **1.** To make alive; to revive or resuscitate, as from death; hence, to excite; stimulate. **2.** To make lively, active, or sprightly; of medicine, liquor, or the like, to strengthen. **3.** To make quick or rapid; to accelerate; as, he *quickened* his pace. — *v. i.* **1.** To come to life; to become alive; to become vivified or enlivened. **2.** To reach the stage of pregnancy at which fetal movement is felt. **3.** To move faster; as, his pulse *quickened.* — **quick'en·er** (-ẽr), *n.*

Syn. (1) **Quicken, animate, enliven, vivify** mean to give life to. **Quicken** stresses renewal of life or activity, esp. in that which is inert; **animate,** the imparting of motion or activity, esp. to that which is mechanical or artificial; **enliven,** a stimulating influence that arouses from dullness, torpidity, etc.; **vivify,** a freshening influence that restores vitality.
(2) See PROVOKE.

quick fire. Firing of shots in rapid succession.

quick'-fire' (-fīr'; 2), *adj.* Also **quick'-fir'ing** (-fīr'ĭng). **a** Firing, or adapted for firing, in rapid succession. **b** *Ordn.* Shooting with short intervals between shots.

quick'-freeze' (kwĭk'frēz'), *v. t.* To freeze (food), for preservation, so rapidly that ice crystals formed are too small to rupture cell walls and consequently natural juices and flavor are not lost on thawing.

quick grass. See COUCH GRASS.

quick′ie (kwĭk′ĭ), *n.* Anything hastily produced or contrived, as by improvising, short cuts, or slapdash execution, for quick availability, as a movie or book, or to be begun and ended in less than the usual time, as a program, trip, strike, or drink. — **quick′ie,** *adj.*

quick′lime′ (kwĭk′līm′), *n.* Unslaked lime. See 1st LIME, 2.

quick′sand′ (-sănd′), *n.* Sand readily yielding to pressure; esp., a deep mass of loose sand mixed with water, into which a person or heavy object sinks.

quick′set′ (-sĕt′), *n.* **1.** A living plant or a live slip or cutting, esp. when set for a hedge; specif., the hawthorn. **2.** A hedge or thicket, esp. of hawthorn.

quick′sil′ver (-sĭl′vẽr), *n.* [*quick* living + *silver;* — from its fluidity.] The metal mercury. — **quick′sil′ver,** *v. t.*

quick′step′ (-stĕp′), *n.* *Music.* A spirited march, esp. in military quick time; also, a lively dance step.

quick time. *Mil.* A rate of marching in which 120 steps (of 30 inches each in the U. S. Army, and 33 inches each in the British Army) are taken in one minute. — **quick march.**

quick trick. At bridge, a card or combination that will win the first or second round of a suit, no matter who leads it, such as the ace, or both king and queen.

quick′-wit′ted (*see Pron.,* § 2), *adj.* Mentally alert. — **Syn.** See INTELLIGENT. — **quick′-wit′ted·ly,** *adv.* — **quick′-wit′ted·ness,** *n.*

quid (kwĭd), *n.* [Var. of CUD.] A portion suitable to be chewed; a cud; as, a *quid* of tobacco.

quid, *n.; pl.* QUID. *Brit. Slang.* A sovereign, or pound sterling.

quid′di·ty (kwĭd′ĭ·tĭ), *n.; pl.* -TIES (-tĭz). [ML. *quidditas,* fr. L. *quid* what, neut. of *quis* who.] **1.** The essence of a thing; that which answers the question, *Quid est?* or What is it? **2.** A subtle distinction; cavil; quibble.

quid′nunc′ (kwĭd′nŭngk′), *n.* [L. *quid nunc* what now?] One curious to know everything going on; a gossip.

‖**quid pro quo** (kwĭd prō kwō). [L., something for something.] One thing for, or in place of, another; tit for tat.

‖**¿quién sa′be?** (kyān sä′vā; 17). [Sp.] Who knows?

qui·es′cent (kwī·ĕs′ĕnt; -′nt), *adj.* [L. *quiescens, -entis,* pres. part. of *quiescere.*] At rest; motionless. — **Syn.** See LATENT. — **qui·es′cence** (-ĕns; -′ns); *also* **qui·es′cen·cy** (-ĕn·sĭ; -′n·sĭ), *n.* — **qui·es′cent·ly,** *adv.*

qui′et (kwī′ĕt), *adj.* [OF. *quiete,* fr. L. *quietus,* past part. of *quiescere* to rest, keep quiet.] **1.** In a state of rest or calm; without motion. **2.** Free from noise or disturbance; still; hushed. **3.** Not turbulent; gentle. **4.** Not excited, anxious, or wrought up; calm; peaceful. **5.** Not showy; modest; as, a *quiet* dress. **6.** Retired; secluded; as, a *quiet* nook. **7.** Enjoyed in peace and relaxation; as, a *quiet* cup of tea. **8.** *Com.* Displaying little business activity.
— *n.* [L. *quies, -etis.*] **1.** The state or condition of being quiet; silence, rest, repose, etc. **2.** The quality or character of being quiet, peaceful, calm, etc.
— *v. t.* To make quiet, as by pacifying, slowing up or stopping motion, etc.; to calm. — *v. i.* To become or grow quiet; — often with *down.*
— *adv.* In a quiet, peaceful, placid, or smooth manner. — **qui′et·er,** *n.* — **qui′et·ly,** *adv.* — **qui′et·ness,** *n.*

qui′et·en (kwī′ĕ·t'n), *v. t. & i.* *Chiefly Brit.* To make or become quiet.

qui′et·ism (kwī′ĕt·ĭz'm), *n.* [It. *quietismo.*] **1.** A system of religious mysticism, teaching that perfection and spiritual peace are attained by self-annihilation and passive absorption in contemplation of God and divine things. **2.** A quiet condition or habit, esp. of mind. — **qui′et·ist** (-ĭst), *n.*

qui′e·tude (kwī′ĕ·tūd), *n.* [F. *quiétude,* fr. LL. *quietudo.*] A state of being quiet; rest; repose; tranquillity.

qui·e′tus (kwī·ē′tŭs), *n.* [From ML. *quietus est* he is quiet.] Final acquittance, as from debt; hence, discharge from office or duty; discharge from life, i. e., death; also, that which quiets or extinguishes life or activity; as, to give a person his *quietus,* to kill him.

quill (kwĭl), *n.* [ME. *quil.*] **1. a** One of the large stiff feathers of a bird's wing or tail, esp. one of those of the wing; also, the hollow barrel or calamus of a feather. See FEATHER, *Illust.* **b** A spine of the hedgehog or porcupine. **2.** Something made from or like the quill of a feather, as a pen for writing. **3.** *Music.* **a** *Archaic.* A tube or pipe, as of cane or reed, of a musical instrument. **b** The plectrum made from a feather quill, with which the strings of certain instruments, as the lute, are plucked. **4.** *Pharm.* A roll of dried bark; as, a *quill* of cinnamon. **5.** *Weaving.* A spindle, or bobbin, as of reed, for the thread in a shuttle. — *v. t.* **1.** To plait in small cylindrical ridges, called **quill′ings,** as a ruffle. **2.** To wind on a quill, as thread.

quil·lai′ (kĭ·lī′), *n.* [Sp. *quillái, quillay,* fr. Araucan.] The soapbark tree (*Quillaja saponaria*) of Chile. Its bark, called **quillai bark,** *or* **quil·lai′a bark** (kĭ·lī′ȧ; kwĭ·lā′yȧ), is rich in saponin, and is commonly used as soap in Chile; in pharmacy it is used as a detergent.

quill driver. *Chiefly Contemptuous.* One who works with a pen; writer; clerk. — **quill driving.**

quil′let (kwĭl′ĕt; -ĭt), *n.* *Archaic.* A quibble.

quill′wort′ (kwĭl′wûrt′), *n.* Any of a genus (*Isoetes,* family Isoetaceae) of marsh plants with quill-shaped leaves.

quilt (kwĭlt), *n.* [OF. *cuilte, coilte,* fr. L. *culcita* bed, cushion, mattress.] **1.** Orig., a kind of mattress; now, a bed coverlet of two thicknesses with a filling of wool, cotton, down, etc. **2.** Anything quilted or like a quilt. — *v. t.* **1.** *Rare.* To fill, pad, or line like a quilt. **2.** To stitch or sew in layers, usually with some soft thick substance between, as in a bedquilt. **3.** To stitch or sew in lines or patterns, as in quilts. **4.** To fasten between pieces of material in the manner of a quilt; as, to *quilt* money in one's belt. — *v. i.* To make quilted work. — **quilt′er,** *n.*

quilt′ing, *n.* **1.** Act of one who quilts something. **2.** Material that is quilted or used for making quilts.

quin′a·crine (kwĭn′ȧ·krēn; -krĭn), *n.* [*quinine* + *acridine.*] A chemical compound derived from acridine. Its dihydrochloride, $C_{23}H_{30}ClN_3O.2HCl$, a yellow powder, is an antimalarial known also as *atebrin.*

qui′na·ry (kwī′nȧ·rĭ), *adj.* [L. *quinarius,* fr. *quini* five each.] Consisting of five; arranged by fives; quintuple.

qui′nate (kwī′nāt), *adj.* Composed of, or arranged in, sets of five; — said esp. of compound leaves with five leaflets.

quin·az′o·line (kwĭn·ăz′ō·lēn; -lĭn), *n.* Also **quin·az′o·lin.** [G. *chinazolin* (cf. CHINA BARK).] *Chem.* A colorless crystalline compound, $C_8H_6N_2$, regarded as derived from quinoline by substitution of a nitrogen atom for a certain CH group; also, any of various derivatives of this compound.

quince (kwĭns; 106), *n.* [Prop. a pl. fr. ME. *quyne, coyn,* fr. OF. *cooin,* fr. L. *cotoneum,* also *cydonium,* fr. Gr. *kydōnion* quince.] **1.** The applelike fruit of a central Asiatic tree (*Cydonia oblonga*). Its hard, acid flesh is used for marmalade, jelly, and preserves. **2.** The tree which bears this fruit.

quin·cun′cial (kwĭn·kŭn′shăl), *adj.* **1.** Of or arranged in a quincunx. **2.** *Bot.* **a** Having the leaves of a pentamerous calyx or corolla so imbricated that two are exterior, two are interior, and the other has one edge exterior and one interior; as, *quincuncial* estivation. **b** In phyllotaxy, 5-ranked.

quin′cunx (kwĭn′kŭngks), *n.; pl.* QUINCUNXES (-kŭngk·sĕz; -sĭz). [L., lit., five twelfths, fr. *quinque* five + *uncia* an ounce.] **1.** An arrangement of five things with one at each corner and one in the middle of a square. **2.** *Bot.* A quincuncial arrangement, as of the parts of a flower.

quin·dec′a·gon (kwĭn·dĕk′ȧ·gŏn), *n.* [L. *quindecim* fifteen + Gr. *gōnia* angle.] *Geom.* A figure, generally plane, with fifteen angles, and consequently fifteen sides.

quin′de·cen′ni·al (kwĭn′dē·sĕn′ĭ·ăl; 58), *adj.* [L. *quindecim* fifteen + *-ennial* as in bi*ennial.*] Of or pertaining to fifteen years or a fifteenth anniversary. — *n.* A quindecennial anniversary.

quin′de·cil′lion (-dē·sĭl′yŭn), *n.* See NUMERATION, *Table.*

quin′ic ac′id (kwĭn′ĭk). [See QUININE.] *Chem.* A white crystalline acid, $C_6H_7(OH)_4CO_2H$, obtained from cinchona bark, coffee beans, etc. It is a tetrahydroxy-cyclohexane-carboxylic acid.

quin′i·dine (kwĭn′ĭ·dēn; -dĭn), *n.* Also **quin′i·din.** *Chem.* An alkaloid isomeric with, and resembling, quinine, found in certain species of cinchona.

qui′nine (kwī′nīn; kwĭ·nēn′; kwĭn′ēn), *n.* Also **quin′in** (kwĭn′ĭn), **quin′i·a** (-ĭ·ȧ), **qui·ni′na** (kĭ·nē′nȧ), etc. [Sp. *quina,* fr. Quechua *quinquina* cinchona bark.] **a** *Chem.* An alkaloid, $C_{20}H_{24}N_2O_2$, extracted from cinchona bark as a bitter white crystalline substance. **b** *Pharm.* Any of the salts of this alkaloid, as the acetate, chloride, sulfate, etc., employed as a febrifuge, antiperiodic, and bitter tonic.

quin′nat salm′on (kwĭn′ăt). [Amer. Indian name.] A salmon (*Oncorhynchus tschawytscha*) of the Pacific coasts. Commercially it is the most important species.

quin′oid (kwĭn′oid), *n.* *Chem.* A quinonoid compound.

qui·noi′dine (kwĭ·noi′dēn; -dĭn), *n.* Also **qui·noi′din.** [*quinine* + *-oid.*] *Pharm.* A brownish resinous mixture of alkaloids obtained as a by-product in the extraction of cinchona bark for crystalline alkaloids, and sold as a substitute for quinine.

quin′o·line (kwĭn′ō·lēn; -lĭn), *n.* Also **quin′o·lin** [*quin*ine + *-ol,* 2 + *-ine.*] *Chem.* A nitrogenous base, C_9H_7N, obtained as a pungent colorless oil by the distillation of alkaloids, coal tar, bones, etc., and also by synthetic methods; by extension, any of various derivatives of it. Quinoline is the parent substance of a large number of compounds, including alkaloids, antiseptics, dyes, etc.

qui·none′ (kwĭ·nōn′; kwĭn′ōn), *n.* [*quinic* acid + *-one.*] *Chem.* **a** Either of two isomeric crystalline compounds, $C_6H_4O_2$. Specif., the yellow, pungent para compound obtained by the oxidation of quinic acid, hydroquinone, aniline, etc., used in tanning. **b** By extension, any of various compounds of which paraquinone is a type.

qui·non′i·mine (kwĭ·nŏn′ĭ·mēn; -mĭn), *n.* [*quinone* + *imine.*] *Chem.* A crystalline compound, $O:C_6H_4:NH$, regarded as derived from ordinary quinone by replacement of one oxygen atom by the imino group; also, a compound derived from any quinone by similar replacement.

quin′o·noid (kwĭn′ō·noid; kwĭ·nō′noid), *adj.* [*quinone* + *-oid.*] *Chem.* Resembling quinone.

quin·ox′a·line (kwĭn·ŏk′sȧ·lēn; -lĭn), *n.* Also **quin·ox′a·lin.** [*quin*oline + *ox*aline + *al*dehyde.] *Chem.* A white crystalline compound $C_8H_6N_2$, acting as a feeble base; also, any derivative of it.

quin′qua·ge·nar′i·an (kwĭn′kwȧ·jē·nâr′ĭ·ăn; 6), *adj.* [L. *quinquagenarius* containing fifty, fifty years old.] Fifty years old; characteristic of a person of such an age. — *n.* A quinquagenarian person.

Quin′qua·ges′i·ma (-jĕs′ĭ·mȧ), *n.* [L., fem. of *quinquagesimus* the fiftieth.] More fully **Quinquagesima Sunday.** The Sunday before Lent.

quin′que- (kwĭn′kwē-), **quinqu-.** [L. *quinque* five.] A combining form meaning *consisting of,* or *characterized by having, five,* as in **quin′que·loc′u·lar, quin′que·par′tite.**

quin′que·fo′li·ate (-fō′lĭ·āt), *adj.* *Bot.* Having five leaves.

quin′que·fo′li·o·late (-fō′lĭ·ō·lāt; -fō·lī′ō·lāt), *adj.* *Bot.* Having five leaflets. See LEAF, *Illust.* (26).

quin·quen′ni·ad (kwĭn·kwĕn′ĭ·ăd), *n.* A quinquennium.

quin·quen′ni·al (-ăl; 58), *adj.* [L. *quinquennis,* fr. *quinque* five + *annus* year.] Occurring once in five years, or at the end of every five years; also, lasting five years. — *n.* A quinquennial term or office. — **quin·quen′ni·al·ly,** *adv.*

quin·quen′ni·um (-ŭm), *n.; L. pl.* -NIA (-ȧ). [L.] A period of five years.

quin′que·va′lent (kwĭn′kwē·vā′lĕnt; kwĭn·kwĕv′ȧ·lĕnt), *adj.* *Chem.* Having a valence of five; pentavalent. — **quin′que·va′lence** (-lĕns), **quin′que·va′len·cy** (-lĕn·sĭ), *n.*

quin′sy (kwĭn′zĭ), *n.* [ML. *quinancia,* fr. Gr. *kynanchē* sore throat, dog's collar, fr. *kyōn* dog + *anchein* to choke.] *Med.* A severe inflammation of the throat, or parts adjacent, with swelling and fever; suppurative tonsillitis.

quint (kwĭnt; kĭnt; *formerly also as F.* kăNt), *n.* [F. *quinte,* fr. L. *quintus, quinta,* the fifth.] **1.** *Card Playing.* A sequence of five cards of the same suit in piquet. **2.** *Music.* **a** The interval of a fifth. **b** An organ stop giving tones a fifth higher than the normal pitch of the digitals.

quint (kwĭnt), *n.* *Colloq.* Short for QUINTUPLET.

quin′tain (kwĭn′tĭn), *n.* [OF. *quintaine,* ML. *quintana.*] *Obs. exc. Hist.* An object to be tilted at, as a post with a crosspiece supporting a target.

quin′tal (-tăl; -t'l), *n.* [F., fr. ML., fr. Ar. *qinṭār.*] **a** A hundredweight (see WEIGHT, *Table* 1). **b** One hundred kilograms (see METRIC SYSTEM, *Table* 5).

quin′tan (-tăn), *adj.* [L. *quintanus,* fr. *quintus* fifth.] Occurring as the fifth, after four others; also, occurring every fifth day, reckoning inclusively; as, a *quintan* fever. — *n.* *Med.* A quintan fever. Cf. QUARTAN, TERTIAN.

quinte (kăɴt), *n.* [F. See QUINT.] *Fencing.* A parry a little lower than carte, the fifth in the old order of teaching.

quint·es′sence (kwĭnt·ĕs′ĕns; -′ns; *formerly also* kwĭnt′-), *n.* [F., fr. ML. *quinta essentia* fifth essence.] **1.** The fifth or last and highest essence or power in a natural body. The ancient Greeks recognized four elements, fire, air, water, and earth. The Pythagoreans and Aristotle added a fifth, ether, of which the heavenly bodies were composed. **2.** The essence of a thing in its most concentrated form. **3.** The most typical example; the consummate instance of a quality, class, etc. — **quin′tes·sen′tial** (kwĭn′tĕ·sĕn′shăl), *adj.*

quin·tet′, quin·tette′ (kwĭn·tĕt′), *n.* [It. *quintetto*, dim. of *quinto* the fifth, a fifth part, fr. L. *quintus* the fifth.] **1.** *Music.* A composition for five voices or instruments; also, the group of five performers. **2.** Any set of five, or thing arranged for five.

quin′tile (kwĭn′tĭl; -tīl; 56), *n.* [L. *quintus* the fifth.] *Astrol.* The aspect of planets when separated the fifth part of the zodiac, or 72°.

quin·til′lion (kwĭn·tĭl′yŭn), *n.* & *adj.* [Formed like *million* fr. L. *quintus* the fifth.] See NUMERATION, *Table.* — **quin·til′lionth** (-yŭnth), *n.* & *adj.*

quin′tu·ple (kwĭn′tū·p′l; kwĭn·tū′p′l), *adj.* [F., fr. LL. *quintuplex*, fr. L. *quintus* fifth.] Multiplied by five; fivefold. — *v. t.* & *i.*; -TU·PLED (-p′ld); -TU·PLING (-plĭng). To make, or become, fivefold.

quin′tu·plet (kwĭn′tū·plĕt; -plĭt; kwĭn·tū′plĭt; kwĭn·tŭp′lĭt), *n.* [From QUINTUPLE.] **1.** A collection of five of a kind. **2.** One of five offspring born at one birth.

quin·tu′pli·cate (kwĭn·tū′plĭ·kāt), *v. t.* To quintuple. — (-kāt), *adj.* Fivefold. — (-kāt), *n.* A fifth exact copy of something.

quip (kwĭp), *n.* [From earlier *quippy*, fr. L. *quippe* forsooth, used ironically.] **1.** A smart, sarcastic turn or jest; also, a witty sally. **2.** A quibble. **3.** Something queer; an oddity. — **Syn.** See JEST. — **quip**, *v. t.* & *i.* — **quip′ster** (-stẽr), *n.*

qui′pu (kē′po͞o; kwĭp′o͞o), *n.* [Sp. *quipo*, fr. Quechua *quipu* knot.] A device used by the ancient Peruvians for counting and for recording important facts and events. It consisted of a main cord, from which hung smaller cords of various colors, each having a special meaning.

quire (kwīr), *n.* [OF. *quaier*, *caern*, a book of loose sheets, a quarter of a quire, fr. L. *quaterni* four each, by fours, fr. *quattuor* four.] A collection of 24 (sometimes 25) sheets of paper of the same size and quality, either not folded or having a single fold. Abbr. *qr.* Cf. REAM.

quire. Var. of CHOIR.

Quir′i·nal (kwĭr′ĭ·năl; kwĭ·rī′năl; -n′l), *n.* [L. *Quirinalis*, fr. *Quirinus*, ancient Roman god of war.] One of the seven hills of Rome, site of a palace used as a residence by the ruling house of Italy, later by the president of the republic; hence, the government in Italy, as disting. from the "Vatican," or papal government. — **Quir′i·nal**, *adj.*

quirk (kwûrk), *n.* **1.** A sudden turn, twist, or curve, as a flourish made by a pen in writing. **2.** A subterfuge; quibble; also, equivocation. **3.** A clever sally; a quip. **4.** An individual knack or peculiarity. **5.** *Arch.* A groove separating a bead or other molding from the adjoining members. — *v. t.* **1.** To give a quirk or quirks to; specif., to fashion, as molding, with quirks. **2.** To strike with a sudden jerk of a whip.

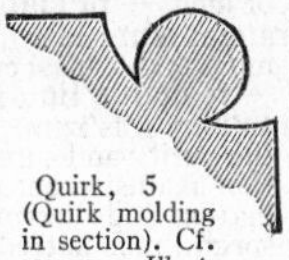

Quirk, 5 (Quirk molding in section). Cf. MOLDING, *Illust.*

quirt (kwûrt), *n.* [Mex. Sp. *cuarta* quirt, orig., a long whip.] A riding whip with a short handle and a lash of braided rawhide. — *v. t.* To strike with a quirt.

‖**quis cus·to′di·et ip′sos cus·to′des?** (kwĭs kŭs·tō′dĭ·ĕt ĭp′sōs kŭs·tō′dēz). [L.] Who shall keep the keepers themselves?

‖**qui s′ex′cuse′ s′ac′cuse′** (kē sĕks′küz′ sȧ′küz′). [F.] Who excuses himself accuses himself.

quis′ling (kwĭz′lĭng), *n.* Also **quis′ler** (kwĭz′lẽr). A traitor, esp. one who becomes the tool of the conqueror of his country; — after Major Vidkun Quisling, head of the Norwegian Nazi party, who on German invasion of Norway (April, 1940) accepted chief place in a Nazi-sponsored government.

‖**quis se′pa·ra′bit?** (kwĭs sĕp′ȧ·rā′bĭt). [L.] Who shall separate (us)? — motto of the Order of St. Patrick.

quit (kwĭt), *v. t.*; QUIT′TED or QUIT; QUIT′TING. [OF. *quitter*, *quiter*, fr. LL. *quietare* to set free, calm, fr. *quietus* quiet.] **1.** To set free; to clear; — now only reflexive. **2.** To discharge, as an obligation; to repay; pay up. **3.** *Archaic.* To conduct; acquit; — used reflexively. **4.** To have done with; hence: **a** To depart from; to leave. **b** To let go; surrender. **c** *Now U. S.* To discontinue; as, to *quit* work. — *v. i.* To go away; to leave; also, to stop doing a thing; specif., *Colloq.*, to leave one's employment. — **Syn.** See GO; STOP. — *adj.* [ME. *quit*, *quite*, fr. OF. *quitte*, *quite*.] Released from obligation, charge, penalty, etc.; absolved; acquitted; now usually, free; rid.

quitch (kwĭch), *n.*, *or* **quitch grass.** [AS. *cwice*; akin to *cwic* living.] See COUCH GRASS.

quit′claim′ (kwĭt′klām′), *n.* [See QUITCLAIM, *v.*] *Law.* A release of a claim; a deed of release; specif., an instrument by which some right, title, interest, or claim, which one person has in or to an estate held by himself or another, is released or relinquished to another, the grantor sometimes covenanting against persons who claim under himself, but not otherwise. In many states of the United States the *quitclaim* is more than a release, and is used as a simple conveyance for making a grant of lands. — *v. t.* [OF. *quite clamer* to call quit, declare quit.] *Law.* To release or relinquish a claim to.

quite (kwīt), *adv.* [ME., fr. the adj. *quite* discharged, free, clear, fr. OF. *quite*.] **1.** Completely; wholly. **2.** Positively; really; as, it is *quite* the rage. **3.** *Colloq.* To a great extent or degree; as, *quite* near.

‖**qui trans′tu·lit sus′ti·net** (kwī trăns′tū·lĭt sŭs′tĭ·nĕt). [L.] He who transplanted sustains; — motto of Connecticut.

quit′rent′ (kwĭt′rĕnt′), *n.* Often written **quit rent.** [*quit*, adj. + *rent*.] *Law.* A fixed rent, payable in commutation of certain feudal services; hence, any fixed rent due from a socage tenant.

quits (kwĭts), *adj.* [From QUIT, *adj.*] Even or equal (with another or each other) by the repayment of an obligation or the requital of a favor, injury, etc.

quit′tance (kwĭt′ăns), *n.* **1.** Discharge from a debt or an obligation; acquaintance. **2.** Recompense; requital.

quit′ter (-ẽr), *n.* One who quits or shirks; hence, a coward; a welsher.

quit′tor (-ẽr), *n.* [ME. *quiture*, *quetour*.] *Veter.* A disease of the feet of horses, asses, etc., affecting the cartilage of the foot (***cartilaginous quittor***), or the soft tissues just above the foot (***cutaneous quittor***).

qui va là? (kē vȧ lȧ′). [F.] Who goes there?

quiv′er (kwĭv′ẽr), *adj.* [AS. *cwifer*.] *Now Dial.* Nimble; lively.

quiv′er, *v. i.* [From QUAVER.] To shake or move with slight and tremulous motion; to tremble. — *n.* Act, fact, or state of quivering; a tremor.

quiv′er, *n.* [OF. *cuivre*, of Teut. origin.] A case or sheath for carrying arrows; also, the arrows in a quiver.

‖**qui vive** (kē vēv′). [F., lit., (long) live who?] The challenge of a French sentinel; — used like the English challenge: "Who goes there?" — ***on the qui vive.*** On the alert.

Quix′ote, Don. See DON QUIXOTE.

quix·ot′ic (kwĭks·ŏt′ĭk), **quix·ot′i·cal** (-ĭ·kăl), *adj.* [See DON QUIXOTE.] Like, or characteristic of, Don Quixote; idealistic but unpractical. — **Syn.** See IMAGINARY. — **quix·ot′i·cal·ly**, *adv.* — **quix′ot·ism** (kwĭk′sŏ·tĭz′m), *n.*

quiz (kwĭz), *n.*; *pl.* QUIZZES (-ĕz; -ĭz). [Origin uncert.] **1.** *Now Rare.* An eccentric person. **2. a** One who quizzes others. **b** A practical joke. **3.** *U. S.* Act or instance of quizzing; specif., an informal examination of a class by questions. — *v. t.*; QUIZZED (kwĭzd); QUIZ′ZING. **1.** To ridicule; chaff. **2.** *U. S.* To examine by close questioning. — **quiz′zer** (-ẽr), *n.*

quiz′zi·cal (kwĭz′ĭ·kăl), *adj.* **1.** Odd; eccentric; amusing. **2.** Showing mocking inquisitiveness; bantering; teasing. — **quiz′zi·cal·ly**, *adv.*

quo (kwō). Archaic & dial. var. of QUOTH.

‖**quo a′ni·mo** (kwō ăn′ĭ·mō). [L.] With what mind or intention.

quod (kwŏd), *n.* *Slang.* Prison.

‖**quod e′rat de′mon·stran′dum** (kwŏd ĕr′ăt dĕm′ŏn·străn′dŭm). [L.] Which was to be demonstrated. Abbr. *Q.E.D.*

‖**quod e′rat fa′ci·en′dum** (fā′shĭ·ĕn′dŭm). [L.] Which was to be done.

‖**quod vi′de** (vī′dē). [L.] Which see. Abbr., *q.v.*

quoin (koin; kwoin), *n.* [See COIN.] **1.** *Arch.* Orig., a solid exterior angle, as of a building; now, one of the selected pieces of material by which the corner is marked. **2.** A wedgelike piece of stone, wood, metal, etc., as one used as the keystone or a voussoir in an arch. **3.** *Print.* Any of various devices used in locking up a form within a chase, or type on a galley. — *v. t.* **1.** To wedge up with quoins, as a printer's form. **2.** To provide with quoins, as a wall corner.

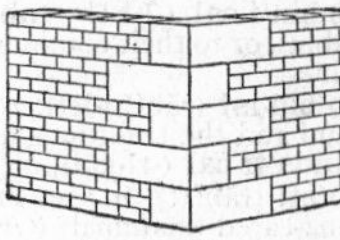

Quoins of Stone set in Brickwork.

quoit (kwoit; kwāt; *esp. Brit.*, koit), *n.* [ME. *coite*, prob. orig. a flat stone.] **1.** Orig., a discus; a flattened ring-shaped piece of iron, to be pitched at a fixed object in play. **2.** **quoits** (kwoits; kwāts; koits) (*pl.* in form but used with *sing.* verb). A game played with quoits. — *v. t.* To throw like a quoit.

quon′dam (kwŏn′dăm), *adj.* [L., formerly.] Having been formerly; former; sometime.

quo′rum (kwō′rŭm; 70), *n.* [L., of whom.] **1.** Orig., in England, the select number of justices of the peace some of whom, on account of their skill and discretion, were required to be present at the sessions of a court; later, all the justices of the peace collectively. **2.** A select body. **3.** Such a number of the officers or members of any body as is, when duly assembled, legally competent to transact business. The quorum of a body is an absolute majority of it, unless the authority by which the body was created fixes it at a different number.

quo′ta (kwō′tȧ), *n.*; *pl.* QUOTAS (-tȧz). [ML., fr. L. *quota* (sc. *pars*), fr. *quotus* of what number, how many, fr. *quot* how many.] **1.** A (certain) proportional part or share; the share assigned to each in a division or to each member of a body. **2.** The number of immigrants from any one country allowed by the immigration law to enter the United States during a year.

quo·ta′tion (kwō·tā′shŭn; *formerly also, and still by some*, kō-), *n.* **1.** Act of quoting or citing. **2.** That which is quoted or cited; a passage referred to, repeated, or adduced. **3.** *Com.* The naming or publishing of the current price of stocks, bonds, or any commodity; also, the price named.

quotation mark. One of the marks used in printing and writing to indicate the beginning and the end of matter quoted verbatim. In printing, quotation marks are two inverted commas ["] at the beginning and two apostrophes ["] at the end. A quotation within a quotation is generally set off by single marks; as, "The youth replies, 'I will!'" Commonly, however, in British practice and with increasing frequency in American practice single marks are used to set off the initial quotation and double marks a quotation within a quotation. At the end of a quotation the comma or period is regularly included within the quotation marks; the colon, semicolon, question mark, exclamation point, or dash is placed inside or outside according as it belongs to the quoted matter or to the whole sentence. In practice the colon and semicolon are regularly placed outside because quoted matter terminating at a colon or semicolon regularly drops the colon or semicolon in favor of the punctuation of the main clause. Thus: Do not say "I'm sorry"; say nothing. But, "The Lord is my shepherd" — he began — "I shall not want." See *Punctuation* § 10.

quote (kwōt; *formerly also, and still by some*, kōt), *v. t.* [ML. *quotare* to divide into chapters and verses, fr. L. *quotus*. See QUOTA.] **1. a** To cite a passage from; as, to *quote* Shakespeare. **b** To refer to or repeat (a passage), esp. as authority or illustration. **2.** To cite; adduce; as, to *quote* an instance. **3.** *Com.* To name (the current price of anything, as a commodity, stock, or bond). **4.** *Print. & Writing.* To set off by quotation marks. — *n.* *Colloq.* A quotation; also, a quotation mark. — **quot′a·ble** (kwōt′ȧ·b′l), *adj.*

quoth (kwōth; *formerly also* kwŭth; 4), *v. t.* [AS. *cwethan*, pret. *cwæth*, pl. *cwǣdon*.] *Archaic.* Said; — used in the first and third persons in the past tense, followed by its nominative, the word or words said being the object.

quoth′a (kwōth′ȧ), *interj.* [For *quoth'a* said he, *'a* being corrupted from *he*.] *Archaic.* Indeed! forsooth!

quo·tid′i·an (kwō·tĭd′ĭ·ăn; 58), *adj.* [OF. *cotidien*, *-ian*, fr. L. *quotidianus*, fr. *quotidie* daily, fr. *quotus* how many + *dies* day.] Daily; recurring daily; as, a *quotidian* fever. — **Syn.** See DAILY. — *n.* Any thing recurring daily, esp., *Med.*, an intermittent fever or ague.

quo′tient (kwō′shĕnt), *n.* [L. *quotiens*, *quoties*, how often, how many times, fr. *quot* how many.] *Arith.* The number or quantity resulting from the division of one number or quantity (the *dividend*) by another (the *divisor*). Cf. REMAINDER, 5.

quo war·ran′to (kwō wŏ·răn′tō); *pl.* QUO WARRANTOS (-tōz). [ML., by what warrant.] *Law.* **a** Orig., a writ of right by which one was required to show by what right he exercised any office, franchise, or liberty. **b** In modern practice, a proceeding for a like purpose begun by an information; also, the information, or the proceeding itself.

R

R, r (är), *n.; pl.* R's, R's, Rs, RS (ärz). **1.** The eighteenth letter of the English alphabet. It comes through the Latin from the Greek (*rhō*), which borrowed it from the Phoenician (Hebrew *rēsh*). **2.** The sound of the letter R. In English R in general denotes a voiced alveolar continuant or glide. See *Pron.*, § 92. **3.** As a *symbol*, used to denote or indicate the seventeenth or (see K, 3) eighteenth in order or class.

Ra (rä), *or* **Re** (rā), *n.* [Egypt. *Rē'*, *Rā*, the sun.] *Egypt. Relig.* The great god of the sun and the chief deity of historical Egypt, represented by the lion, cat, and falcon, and usually wearing the solar disk.

ra·ba'to (rȧ·bā'tō; -bä'tō), *n.* [F. *rabat*, fr. *rabattre* to beat down.] *Hist.* A rebato.

rab'bet (răb'ĕt; -ĭt), *n.* [OF. *rabat* a beating down, fr. *rabatre* to beat down.] A groove cut out of the edge or face of any body; esp., such a groove intended to receive another member, as a panel. — *v. t.*; -BET·ED; -BET·ING. **1.** To cut a rabbet in. **2.** To unite the edges of, as boards, in a rabbet joint. — *v. i.* To be joined by a rabbet.

rabbet joint. *Carp.* A joint formed by fitting together rabbeted boards or timbers. Cf. MATCHBOARD, *Illust.*

rab'bi (răb'ī; -ĭ), *n.; pl.* -BIS *or* -BIES (-īz; -ĭz). Also **rab'bin** (răb'ĭn). [LL., fr. Gr. *rhabbi*, fr. Heb. *rabbī* my great one.] Master; — used as a Jewish title; also, a Jewish teacher or doctor of the law.

Rab·bin'ic (ră·bĭn'ĭk), *n.* The language used by the Jewish theologians on Talmudic subjects and Biblical exegesis in early medieval times.

rab·bin'i·cal (-ĭ·kăl), **rab·bin'ic** (-ĭk), *adj.* Of or pertaining to the rabbis, or to their opinions, learning, or language, esp. in early medieval times.

rab'bin·ist (răb'ĭn·ĭst), *n.* One of the Jews who adhered to the Talmud and the traditions of the rabbis. — **rab'bin·is'tic** (-ĭs'tĭk), **rab'bin·is'ti·cal** (-tĭ·kăl), *adj.*

rab'bit (răb'ĭt), *n.;* see PLURAL, *Note*, 3. [ME. *rabet.*] **1.** A small long-eared mammal (*Oryctolagus cuniculus*) of the hare family (*Leporidae*), technically one of the lagomorphs, which differs from ordinary hares in producing naked young and in its burrowing habits; loosely, in America, any hare. See LEPORID. **2.** The pelt of any of these animals. **3.** Short for WELSH RABBIT. — *v. i.* To hunt rabbits.

rabbit fever. *Med.* Tularemia.

rabbit punch. *Boxing.* A short chopping blow delivered to the back of the neck or the base of the skull.

rab'bit·ry (răb'ĭt·rĭ), *n.; pl.* -RIES (-rĭz). A place where rabbits, esp. tame rabbits, are kept.

rab'ble (răb''l), *n.* [F. *râble*, fr. OF. *roable*, fr. L. *rutabulum.*] *Metal.* An iron bar with the end bent for use like a rake, used in puddling iron; any similar device used in a refining or roasting furnace. — *v. t.;* -BLED (-'ld); -BLING (-lĭng). To stir, skim, or gather with a rabble. — **rab'bler** (-lẽr), *n.*

rab'ble, *n.* [ME. *rabel* a pack (of hounds).] A tumultuous crowd; mob. — ***the rabble.*** *Contemptuous.* The populace. — *v. t.* To assault with a rabble; to mob.

rab'ble (răb''l), *v. t. & i.* *Obs.* To babble; gabble.

rab'ble·ment (răb''l·mĕnt), *n.* Disturbance; tumult.

Rab'e·lai'si·an (răb'ĕ·lā'zĭ·ăn), *adj.* Of or characteristic of Rabelais or his works; esp., marked by gross robust humor, extravagance of caricature or bold naturalism. — *n.* A student or imitator of Rabelais. — **Rab'e·lai'si·an·ism** (-ĭz'm), *n.*

Ra·bi'a (rȧ·bē'ȧ), *n.* [Ar. *Rabī'*, orig. spring.] See MOHAMMEDAN CALENDAR.

rab'id (răb'ĭd), *adj.* [L. *rabidus*, fr. *rabere* to rave.] **1.** Furious; raging. **2.** Going to extreme lengths in giving vent to a feeling or opinion; fanatical; as, a *rabid* socialist. **3.** Of, pertaining to, or affected with rabies. — **ra·bid'i·ty** (rȧ·bĭd'ĭ·tĭ) **rab'id·ness,** *n.* — **rab'id·ly,** *adv.*

ra'bies (rā'bēz; răb'ēz), *n.* [L.] *Med. & Vet.* An acute, often fatal, virus disease of the central nervous system, occurring chiefly among carnivorous animals, esp. the dog and wolf, but transmissible to man; canine madness; hydrophobia.

rac·coon', ra·coon' (ră·kōōn'), *n.;* see PLURAL, *Note*, 3. [Of Algonquian origin.] A small flesh-eating mammal (*Procyon lotor*) of North America, chiefly gray, with a bushy ringed tail, living largely in trees and active esp. at night; also, the fur of this animal.

race (rās), *n.* [OF. *raïz*, fr. L. *radix, -icis.*] A root (of ginger).

race, *n.* [ON. *rās.*] **1.** *Now Scot.* Act of rushing onward. **2.** **a** A strong or rapid current of water, or its channel. **b** A watercourse, esp. when used industrially, as for mining; also, the current flowing in such a course; as, a mill*race* for turning a water wheel. **3.** **a** Course, as of the sun; progress. **b** The onward course of life. **4.** **a** A contest of speed, as in running, riding, sailing; in *pl.*, usually, meeting for contests in the running of horses. **b** Any contest; as, the *race* for Congress. **5.** *Aeronautics.* = SLIP STREAM. **6.** *Mach.* A track or channel in which something rolls or slides, as a slide for a shuttle, a groove for the balls in a ball bearing. — *v. i.* **1.** To engage in a race; to compete in speed. **2.** To run swiftly; to move at top speed; to rush. **3.** *Mach.* To run too fast under a diminished load. — *v. t.* **1.** To run, sail, row, etc., a race with. **2.** To cause to contend in a race; to drive at high speed, as horses. **3.** To speed (an engine or motor) without a working load or in disengagement from the transmission. — **race,** *adj.*

race (rās), *n.* [F. *race*, fr. It. *razza.*] **1.** The descendants of a common ancestor; a family, tribe, people, or nation, believed to belong to the same stock; a lineage; a breed; also, a class or kind of individuals with common characteristics, habits, or the like; as, the *race* of doctors. **2.** Peculiar flavor, taste, or strength, as of wine; hence, *Now Rare*, piquancy, as of conversation. **3.** State of being one of a special ethnical stock, more narrowly, of a particular group or family; also, the qualities, features, etc., resulting from this; as, differences of *race*. **4.** *Obs.* A herd or stud; — of horses. *Shak.* **5.** *Biol.* **a** A group within a species, having similar characters which do not sufficiently distinguish from the specific type to form a separate species. **b** A geographical subspecies. **c** A group differing physiologically from the other members of a species; as, a disease-resistant *race* of wheat. **6.** *Ethnol.* A division of mankind possessing constant traits, transmissible by descent, sufficient to characterize it as a distinct human type.

race'course' (rās'kōrs'; 70), *n.* A course for racing horses, dogs, etc.

race horse. A horse bred or kept for racing.

ra·ceme' (rȧ·sēm'; rā-), *n.* [L. *racemus* a bunch of berries or grapes.] *Bot.* A type of simple inflorescence in which the elongated axis bears flowers on short stems in succession toward the apex, as in the lily of the valley, etc. See INFLORESCENCE, *Illust.* (1).

ra·ce'mic (rȧ·sē'mĭk; -sĕm'ĭk; rā-), *adj.* [See RACEME.] *Chem.* **a** Pert. to or designating an optically inactive variety of tartaric acid found with ordinary tartaric acid in the juice of grapes. **b** Pertaining to or designating compounds formed by the union of two optically different forms, especially the dextrorotatory and the levorotatory forms (in which case the compound is inactive). — **rac'e·mism** (răs'ē·mĭz'm; rȧ·sē'mĭz'm), *n.*

rac'e·mi·za'tion (răs'ē·mĭ·zā'shŭn; -mī·zā'shŭn), *n.* *Chem.* Act or process of changing from an optically active compound into a racemic compound or an inactive mixture of corresponding dextro and levo forms.

rac'e·mose (răs'ē·mōs), *adj.* [L. *racemosus* full of clusters.] Of the nature of or bearing a raceme; growing in the form of a raceme. See INFLORESCENCE, *Illust.*

racemose gland. *Anat.* A compound gland of freely branching ducts which end in acini so that the whole resembles somewhat a cluster of grapes. The pancreas is an example.

rac'er (rās'ẽr), *n.* **1.** One who races; anything with power to travel swiftly. **2.** An American black snake (*Coluber constrictor*). **3.** *Ordn.* A turntable to which the chassis is secured.

race riot. A riot animated by racial hatred; specif., *U.S.*, such a conflict between whites and Negroes.

race suicide. The gradual extinction of a race through the voluntary failure of its members to keep the birth rate as high as the death rate.

race track. A track over which races are run; a racecourse.

race'way' (rās'wā'), *n.* A canal for a current of water.

Ra'chel (rā'chĕl), *n.* *Bib.* The wife of Jacob.

ra'chis (rā'kĭs), *n.; pl.* RACHISES (-ĕz; -ĭz), RACHIDES (răk'ĭ·dēz; rā'kĭ-). [NL., fr. Gr. *rhachis, -ios.*] **1.** *Anat.* The spinal column. **2.** Any of various axial structures; as: **a** *Bot.* (1) The elongated axis of an inflorescence. (2) In compound leaves, the extension or prolongation of the petiole bearing the leaflets. **b** *Zool.* The distal part of the shaft of a feather which bears the web. See FEATHER, *Illust.*

ra·chi'tis (rȧ·kī'tĭs), *n.* [NL., fr. Gr. *rhachitis* (sc. *nosos*), fr. *rhachis, -ios*, spine.] Literally, inflammation of the spine; commonly, rickets. — **ra·chit'ic** (-kĭt'ĭk), *adj.*

ra'cial (rā'shăl), *adj.* Of, pert. to, or characteristic of a race or family of men. — **ra'cial·ly,** *adv.*

ra'cial·ism (-ĭz'm), *n.* Racial prejudice, expressing either favorable or unfavorable bias; esp., race hatred; also, racism. — **ra'cial·ist** (-ĭst), *n.* — **ra'cial·is'tic** (-ĭs'tĭk), *adj.*

rac'ism (rās'ĭz'm), *n.* Assumption of inherent racial superiority or the purity and superiority of certain races, and consequent discrimination against other races; also, any doctrine or program of racial domination and discrimination based on such an assumption. Also, less specif., race hatred and discrimination. — **rac'ist** (-ĭst), *n.*

rack (răk), *n.* [Var. of WRACK.] Destruction; — chiefly in ***rack and ruin.***

rack, *n.* **1.** Formerly, the neck and spine of a forequarter of veal, pork, or esp. mutton. **2.** Now: **a** The rib section of the fore part of a lamb or mutton carcass; — called specif. ***hotel rack.*** See LAMB, *Illust.* **b** *Meat Packing.* The fore part of a carcass.

rack, *v. i.* [Origin uncert.] To go with either gait called a rack. — *n.* A horse's gait, either pace or single-foot.

rack, *n.* [Prob. of Scand. origin.] A wind-driven mass of high, often broken, clouds. — *v. i.* To fly or scud, as vapor or broken clouds.

rack, *n.* [ME. *rake, rakke*, fr. ON. *rāk* stripe.] A path or course, esp. of storm clouds; also, a faint trace; a vestige.

rack, *v. t.* [Pr. *arraca.*] To draw off from the lees, as wine.

rack, *n.* [ME. *racke, rekke*, a framework, prob. fr. MD. & MLG. *rec* framework, *recken* to stretch.] **1.** A framework for holding fodder for cattle. **2.** An engine of torture consisting of a large frame having rollers at each end to which the limbs were fastened and between which the body was stretched. Hence, ***on the rack,*** in physical or mental anguish. **3.** A cause of anguish or the suffering produced. **4.** A straining or wrenching; as, the *rack* of storms. **5.** A framework, stand, or grating, on or in which articles are placed as for keeping or for display; as, a clothes *rack;* specif.: **a** A frame fitted to a wagon for carrying hay, straw, etc. **b** A box of pigeonholes into which items are sorted. **6.** *Mach.* A bar, straight or curved, with teeth on one face for gearing with those of a pinion, worm, etc.; also, a notched bar used as a ratchet to engage with a pawl, click, detent, or the like. See JACK, *Illust.* **7.** *Print.* A frame or receptacle for holding type cases. — *v. t.* **1.** To stretch or strain by force; to stretch on the rack or wheel. **2.** To torment; torture. **3.** To stretch up or raise beyond what is usual or fair; as, to *rack* one's brains over a problem; specif., of rents, to raise oppressively; to raise to a rack rent. **4.** To harass or oppress by exactions, as by rack rents. — **Syn.** See AFFLICT.

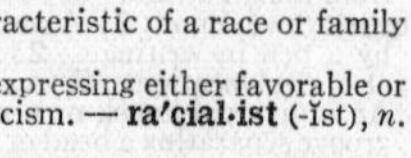

Rack (*R R*) and Pinion.

rack'et (răk'ĕt; -ĭt), *n.* [F. *raquette*, fr. Ar. *rāḥah* (pl. *rāḥāt*) the palm of the hand.] **1.** A form of light bat consisting of a netting stretched in an oval open frame with handle, used for striking the ball in tennis and similar games. **2.** *pl.* A game played with ball and rackets in a four-walled court. **3.** A snowshoe.

rack'et, *n.* [Prob. imitative.] **1.** Confused, clattering noise; noisy talk or sport. **2.** Social whirl or excitement; reveling. **3.** The strain of an ordeal; — with *the;* as, unable to stand the *racket.* **4.** *Slang.* **a** A fraudulent scheme. **b** Any method of exploitation for money, ranging from petty charlatanry, illicit business, and gambling schemes to an organized extortionary crime ring operating by use of violence, with hired legal protection and bribery of politicians. — *v. i.* **1.** To be given to gaiety. **2.** To make, or move with, a racket.

rack'et·eer' (răk'ĕ·tēr'; răk'ĭ-), *n.* [See 2d RACKET, 4; -EER.] *Law.* One who singly or in combination with others extorts money or advantages by threats of violence or of unlawful interference with business. — *v. i.* To practice as a racketeer. — **rack'et·eer'ing,** *n.*

rack'et·y (răk'ĕ·tĭ; -ĭ·tĭ), *adj.* **1.** Noisy; turbulent. **2.** Addicted to reveling; gay; dissipated.

rack'le (răk''l), *adj.* *Dial.* Headstrong; reckless.

rack railway *or* **railroad**. A railway having between its rails a rack (**rack rail**) that meshes with a gear wheel or pinion of the locomotive for traction on steep grades.

rack rent, *or* **rack'rent'** (răk'rĕnt'), *n.* [*rack* to stretch + *rent.*] An excessive or unreasonably high rent, esp. one at or near the full annual value of the tenement.

rack'–rent', *v. t.* To subject to rack rent.

rack'–rent'er, *n.* One who pays, or exacts, rack rent.

rack'work' (răk'wûrk'), *n.* Any mechanism having a rack.

ra'con (rā'kŏn), *n.* [*ra*dar bea*con.*] A radar beacon that sends out a coded signal in response to the proper radar signal received from a ship or aircraft, enabling the navigator to identify the beacon as well as to determine his own range and bearing from it.

rac'on·teur' (răk'ŏn·tûr'; *F.* rȧ'kôɴ'tûr'), *n.; pl.* -TEURS (-tûrz'; *F.* -tûr'). [F.] One who excels in storytelling.

ra·coon' (ră·kōōn'). Var. of RACCOON.

rac'quet (răk'ĕt; -ĭt). Var. of RACKET, a bat.

rac'y (rās'ĭ), *adj.;* RAC'I·ER (-ĭ·ẽr); RAC'I·EST. [From RACE tribe, family.] **1.** Having the distinctive quality of a thing in its native or genuine form; unspoiled, fresh, full-flavored, etc. **2.** Full of zest; spirited; often, piquant, pungent, brisk, etc. — **Syn.** See PUNGENT. — **rac'i·ly** (-ĭ·lĭ), *adv.* — **rac'i·ness** (-ĭ·nĕs; -nĭs), *n.*

rad (*Scot.* rȧd), *adj.* [ON. *hræddr.*] *Obs. exc. Scot.* Afraid.

ra'dar (rā'där), *n.* [*ra*dio *d*etecting *a*nd *r*anging.] A radio detecting device that emits and focuses a powerful scanning beam of ultra high-frequency waves and establishes through reception and timing of reflected waves the distance, altitude, and direction of motion of any object in the path of the beam, unhindered by darkness, storm, cloud, or fog. See RADIOLOCATOR. — **ra'dar·man** (-măn; -măn'), *n.*

ra'dar·scope (-skōp), *n.* [*radar* + oscillo*scope.*] See SCOPE, *n.*, 5.

rad'dle (răd''l), *v. t.* To interweave or twist together.

rad'dle, *n.* [Cf. RUDDLE.] Red ocher. — *v. t.* To paint with raddle.

rad'dle·man (-măn), *n.; pl.* -MEN (-mĕn). A dealer in raddle.

ra'di·al (rā'dĭ·ăl), *adj.* **1.** Arranged or having parts arranged like rays. **2.** Pertaining to or placed like a radius. **3.** Characterized by divergence as from a center; as, *radial* symmetry. **4.** *Anat.* Pertaining to, or in the region of, the radius (bone of the forearm). **5.** *Zool.* Pertaining to a ray or arm. — **ra'di·al·ly**, *adv.*

radial engine. *Mach.* An engine, usually an internal-combustion engine, having cylinders arranged radially like the spokes of a wheel. Cf. ROTARY ENGINE.

ra'di·an (rā'dĭ·ăn), *n.* [From RADIUS.] *Math.* The angle subtended by an arc of a circle equal in length to the radius of the circle.

ra'di·ance (-ăns), *n.* Also **ra'di·an·cy** (-ăn·sĭ). State or quality of being radiant; brilliancy; effulgence.

ra'di·ant (-ănt), *adj.* [L. *radians, -antis,* pres. part. of *radiare* to emit rays, fr. *radius* ray.] **1.** Radiating rays of light; emitting or reflecting beams of light; vividly shining; glowing; brilliant. **2.** Beaming with vivacity and happiness, joy, love, hope, etc. **3.** *Physics.* Emitted or transmitted by radiation; as, *radiant* energy. — **Syn.** See BRIGHT. — *n.* That which radiates; as: **a** *Astron.* The point in the heavens at which the visible paths of meteors appear to meet, when traced backward. **b** *Optics.* The point or object from which light emanates. — **ra'di·ant·ly**, *adv.*

radiant energy. *Physics.* Energy radiating, or traveling, as a wave motion; specif., the energy of electromagnetic waves, as radio waves, infrared rays, visible light, ultraviolet rays, X rays, and gamma rays.

radiant heating. = PANEL HEATING.

ra'di·ate (rā'dĭ·āt), *v. i.* [L. *radiatus,* past part. of *radiare* to irradiate, fr. *radius* ray.] **1.** To emit rays; to be radiant. **2.** To issue in rays, as light or heat. **3.** To proceed in a direct line or lines from; as, spokes *radiate* from a hub. — *v. t.* **1.** To emit in rays. **2.** To irradiate; to expose to radiation. **3.** To spread around as from a center; diffuse. — *adj.* Having rays or radial parts; radiated; radial; specif., *Zool.,* characterized by radial symmetry. — *n. Zool.* Any member of a group (Radiata) of invertebrates distinguished by having parts arranged radially around an axis, as in the coelenterates and echinoderms.

ra'di·a'tion (-ā'shŭn), *n.* **1.** Act or process of radiating; specif., the process by which energy is emitted from molecules and atoms owing to internal changes. **2.** That which is radiated, namely *radiant energy.* **3.** The combined processes of emission, transmission, and absorption of radiant energy. **4.** Radial arrangement. — **ra'di·a'tive** (rā'dĭ·ā'tĭv; -ȧ·tĭv), *adj.*

ra'di·a'tor (rā'dĭ·ā'tẽr), *n.* That which radiates something; specif., any of various devices for heating external objects or for cooling an internal substance by radiation, as a nest of pipes containing circulating steam, hot water, etc.

rad'i·cal (răd'ĭ·kăl), *adj.* [LL. *radicalis* having roots, fr. *radix, -icis,* a root.] **1.** Of, pert. to, or proceeding from the root. **2.** Original; fundamental; reaching to the center or ultimate source; affecting the vital principle or principles; hence, thoroughgoing; extreme. **3.** [*often cap.*] Of or pert. to radicals in politics. **4.** *Bot.* Proceeding from the root or from a rootlike stem; basal. **5.** *Math.* Of or pert. to a radix or root. — *n.* **1.** A root, or radical, part; hence, a fundamental. **2.** [*often cap.*] In politics, one who advocates radical and sweeping changes in laws and methods of government with the least delay. **3.** *Alg.* **a** A radical expression. **b** The radical sign. **4.** [F. *radical.*] *Chem.* **a** A fundamental constituent of a compound. **b** A group of atoms replaceable by a single atom or remaining unchanged during a series of reactions, and hence regarded as playing the part of a single atom. **5.** One of certain characters in Chinese writing, usually indicating part of its meaning. **6.** *Philol.* A root.

radical expression. *Alg.* An expression involving radical signs; specif., a surd.

rad'i·cal·ism (răd'ĭ·kăl·ĭz'm), *n.* State or quality of being radical; also, the doctrines or principles of political radicals.

rad'i·cal·ly (răd'ĭ·kăl·ĭ), *adv.* **1.** As regards root or source; in origin. **2.** In a radical or thoroughgoing manner.

radical sign. *Math.* The sign √ (originally the initial *r* of *radix*), placed before any expression, denoting that its root is to be extracted; thus, $\sqrt{a}$, $\sqrt[3]{(a+b)}$.

rad'i·cel (răd'ĭ·sĕl), *n.* [Dim. of *radix.*] *Bot.* A rootlet.

rad'i·cle (-k'l), *n.* [L. *radicula,* dim. of *radix, -icis,* root.] **1.** *Anat.* The rootlike beginning of a vessel or part, as of a nerve fibril. **2.** *Bot.* The lower portion of the axis of an embryo seedling; properly, the extremity or root portion; commonly, the hypocotyl, or both the hypocotyl and the root. See EMBRYO, *Illust.* **3.** *Chem.* = RADICAL, *n.*, 4.

ra'di·i (rā'dĭ·ī), *n., pl.* of RADIUS.

ra'di·o (rā'dĭ·ō), *n.; pl.* -DIOS (-ōz). [From *radiotelegraphy.*] **1.** **a** The transmission and reception of signals by means of electric waves without a connecting wire; the use of radiotelegraphy or radiotelephony. **b** A radio receiving set. **2.** *Colloq.* A radio message; a radiogram. — *adj.* **a** Of, employing, or operated by radiant energy, specifically that of electric waves; hence, pert. to or employed in radiotelegraphy, radiotelephony, etc. **b** Of or pert. to electric currents or phenomena of frequencies between about 15,000 and $(10)^{11}$ per second. Cf. AUDIO. **c** Pertaining to or used in radio or a radio set; specializing in radio; as, a *radio* engineer. — *v. t. & i.;* RA'DI·OED (-ōd); RA'DI·O·ING. To send, communicate, or inform by radiotelegraphy, radiotelephony, etc.

ra'di·o- (rā'dĭ·ō-). [From RADIUS.] A combining form denoting: **1.** *Radial, radially,* as in **ra'di·o·sym·met'ri·cal** (see SYMMETRICAL). **2.** *Anat. Radial and,* as in **ra'di·o–ul'nar**. **3.** [From *radio*meter.] *Chem. & Phys.* **a** *Radiant energy,* as in *radio*phone. **b** *Radioactive,* as in *radio*element. **c** *Radioactive isotopes,* esp. those produced artificially, as in **ra'di·o·so'di·um, ra'di·o·ti·ta'ni·um**. **4.** *Med.* **a** *From* or *by means of radiant energy,* esp. X rays, as in **ra'di·o·di'ag·no'sis**. **b** *By means of radium,* as in **ra'di·o·sur'ger·y**. **5.** *Radio,* as in **ra'di·o·a·cous'tics** (see -ICS), *radio*photography.

ra'di·o·ac·tiv'i·ty (-ăk·tĭv'ĭ·tĭ), *n.* *Physics & Chem.* The property or process whereby certain elements or isotopes (notably radium, uranium, thorium and their products), whether free or combined, spontaneously emit particles and/or rays by the disintegration of the nuclei of their atoms. Cf. ALPHA RAY, BETA RAY, GAMMA RAYS. *Artificial radioactivity* may be induced by bombarding nuclei with particles, as from a cyclotron. — **ra'di·o·ac'tive** (-ăk'tĭv), **ra'di·o–ac'tive**, *adj.* — **ra'di·o·ac'ti·vate** (-ăk'tĭ·vāt), *v. t.*

ra'di·o·au'to·graph (rā'dĭ·ō·ô'tō·grȧf; 9), *n.* [*radio-* + *autograph.*] A picture produced upon a sensitive surface, as of a photographic film, by the rays from a radioactive substance in the object.

radio beacon. A radio station which transmits special radio signals by which a receiver may determine his position. A radio beacon which transmits in such a way as to mark out a fixed straight line is a **radio range beacon.**

radio beam. See BEAM, 9.

ra'di·o·bi·ol'o·gy (rā'dĭ·ō·bī·ŏl'ō·jĭ), *n.* The branch of biology which deals with the effects produced by radiant energy on living organisms.

ra'di·o·broad'cast' (rā'dĭ·ō·brôd'kȧst'), *v. t.* To broadcast by radiotelegraph or radiotelephone. — **ra'di·o·broad'cast'er** (-kȧs'tẽr), *n.* — **ra'di·o·broad'cast'ing**, *n.*

ra'di·o·chem'is·try (-kĕm'ĭs·trĭ), *n.* The chemistry of radioactive phenomena. — **ra'di·o·chem'i·cal** (-ĭ·kăl), *adj.*

radio compass. A direction finder used for navigating a ship or aircraft.

ra'di·o·con·duc'tor (rā'dĭ·ō·kŏn·dŭk'tẽr), *n.* *Elec.* A substance or device that has its conductivity altered in some way by electric waves, as a coherer.

ra'di·o·el'e·ment (-ĕl'ē·mĕnt), *n.* A radioactive element.

ra'di·o–fre'quen·cy (-frē'kwĕn·sĭ), *adj.* Of or using a frequency or frequencies above 15,000 per second.

ra'di·o·gen'ic (-jĕn'ĭk), *adj.* [*radio-* + *-genic,* 2.] **1.** Produced by radioactivity; as, *radiogenic* lead. **2.** Eminently suitable for being broadcast by radio. Cf. TELEGENIC.

ra'di·o·gram' (rā'dĭ·ō·grăm'), *n.* **1.** A radiograph. **2.** A message transmitted by radiotelegraphy.

ra'di·o·graph' (-grȧf'; 9), *n.* [*radio-* + *-graph.*] A picture produced upon a sensitive surface, as of a photographic plate, by some form of radiation other than light; specif., an X-ray photograph. — *v. t.* To make a radiograph of. — **ra'di·og'ra·pher** (-ŏg'rȧ·fẽr), *n.* — **ra'di·o·graph'ic** (-ō·grăf'ĭk), *adj.* — **ra'di·o·graph'i·cal** (-ĭ·kăl), *adj.*

ra'di·og'ra·phy (rā'dĭ·ŏg'rȧ·fĭ), *n.* The art, practice, or act of making radiographs.

ra'di·o·i'so·tope (rā'dĭ·ō·ī'sō·tōp), *n.* [*radio-* + *isotope.*] *Physics & Chem.* A radioactive isotope.

ra'di·o·lar'i·an (rā'dĭ·ō·lâr'ĭ·ăn; 6), *n.* [From NL. dim. of L. *radius* radius.] *Zool.* Any of an extensive order (Radiolaria) of minute marine rhizopods having a siliceous skeleton of spicules and radiating threadlike pseudopodia.

ra'di·o·lo·ca'tion (rā'dĭ·ō·lō·kā'shŭn), *n.* A method of detecting the position and course of distant objects, esp. enemy aircraft and naval craft, by means of radiolocators, or radar.

ra'di·o·lo'ca·tor (-lō'kā·tẽr; -lō·kā'tẽr), *n.* A radio detector for locating, by means of reflected radio waves, objects beyond sight or hearing. The locator developed by the British is usually called *radiolocator,* the similar American device *radar* (which see).

ra'di·ol'o·gy (rā'dĭ·ŏl'ō·jĭ), *n.* The science of radioactive substances and X rays and its application, as in the diagnosis and cure of disease. — **ra'di·ol'o·gist** (-jĭst), *n.* — **ra'di·o·log'i·cal** (-ō·lŏj'ĭ·kăl), **ra'di·o·log'ic** (-ĭk), *adj.*

ra'di·o·me'te·or·o·graph' (rā'dĭ·ō·mē'tē·ŏr·ō·grȧf'; -mē'tē·ŏr'-; 9), *n.* = RADIOSONDE.

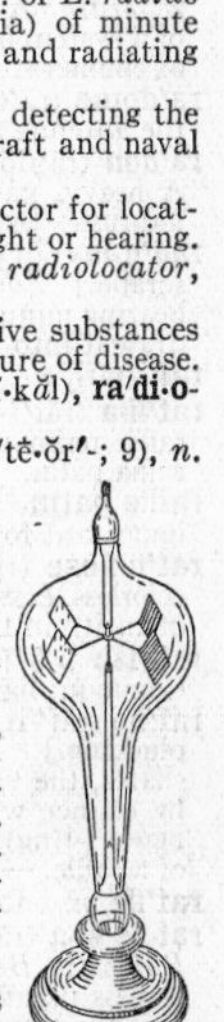

Radiometer.

ra'di·om'e·ter (-ŏm'ē·tẽr), *n.* [*radio-* + *-meter.*] *Physics.* An instrument designed to measure the intensity of radiant energy by the torsional twist of a suspended disk, blackened on one side, when exposed to sunlight or any source of radiant energy. — **ra'di·o·met'ric** (-ō·mĕt'rĭk), *adj.* — **ra'di·om'e·try** (-ŏm'ē·trĭ), *n.*

ra'di·on'ics (rā'dĭ·ŏn'ĭks), *n.;* see -ICS. [*radi-* (*radio-,* 1) + electr*onics.*] = ELECTRONICS.

ra'di·o·phone' (rā'dĭ·ō·fōn'), *n.* **1.** *Physics.* Any apparatus for the production of sound by radiant energy. **2.** A radiotelephone. — **ra'di·o·phon'ic** (-fŏn'ĭk), *adj.*

ra'di·o·pho·tog'ra·phy (-fō·tŏg'rȧ·fĭ), *n.* The transmission of photographs by means of radio. — **ra'di·o·pho'to·graph** (-fō'tō·grȧf; 9), *n.*

ra'di·os'co·py (rā'dĭ·ŏs'kō·pĭ), *n.* [*radio-* + *-scopy.*] Direct observation of objects opaque to light by means of some other form of radiant energy, as X rays. — **ra'di·o·scop'ic** (-ō·skŏp'ĭk), **ra'di·o·scop'i·cal** (-ĭ·kăl), *adj.*

ra'di·o·sen'si·tive (rā'dĭ·ō·sĕn'sĭ·tĭv), *adj.* *Med.* Sensitive to radiant energy; specif., capable of being injured or destroyed by it, as certain

tumors which can be destroyed by X rays. — **ra′di·o·sen′si·tiv′i·ty** (rā′dĭ·ō·sĕn′sĭ·tĭv′ĭ·tĭ), *n.*
ra′di·o·sonde′ (rā′dĭ·ō·sŏnd′), *n.* [F., fr. *radio* + *sonde* depth sounding.] *Meteorol.* A miniature radio transmitter with instruments attached which is carried by an unmanned balloon to an elevation of 15½ miles and dropped by parachute, for broadcasting by means of precise tone signals information on the humidity, temperature, and pressure.
radio spectrum. See SPECTRUM, 2.
ra′di·o·sym·met′ri·cal (rā′dĭ·ō·sĭ·mĕt′rĭ·kăl), *adj.* [*radio-* + *-symmetrical.*] Radially symmetrical; specif., *Bot.*, see SYMMETRICAL, 2 **a**.
ra′di·o·tel′e·gram (-tĕl′ē·grăm), *n.* A message transmitted by radiotelegraphy.
ra′di·o·te·leg′ra·phy (-tē·lĕg′rȧ·fĭ), *n.* [*radio-* + *telegraphy.*] Telegraphy carried on by the aid of radio waves, without connecting wires; wireless telegraphy. — **ra′di·o·tel′e·graph** (-tĕl′ē·grăf; 9), *n.* & *v. t.* — **ra′di·o·tel′e·graph′ic** (-tĕl′ē·grăf′ĭk), *adj.*
ra′di·o·te·leph′o·ny (-tē·lĕf′ō·nĭ), *n.* Telephony carried on by the aid of radio waves, without connecting wires. — **ra′di·o·tel′e·phone** (-tĕl′ē·fōn), *n.* — **ra′di·o·tel′e·phon′ic** (-tĕl′ē·fŏn′ĭk), *adj.*
ra′di·o·ther′a·py (-thĕr′ȧ·pĭ), *n.* *Med.* Treatment of disease by means of X rays or other forms of radioactivity.
ra′di·o·ther′my (rā′dĭ·ō·thûr′mĭ), *n.* [*radio* + Gr. *thermē* heat.] Diathermy by means of a short-wave radio machine.
ra′di·o·tho′ri·um (-thō′rĭ·ŭm), *n.* [NL.] *Chem.* A radioactive isotope of thorium, specif., one of mass number 228, formed from mesothorium 2.
radio tube. An electron tube.
ra′di·o·vi′sion (rā′dĭ·ō·vĭzh′ŭn), *n.* Television by radio.
rad′ish (răd′ĭsh), *n.* [F. and L.; F. *radis,* fr. It. *radice,* fr. L. *radix, -icis,* a root, esp. a radish.] The pungent fleshy root of a plant (*Raphanus sativus*) of the mustard family, eaten raw as a relish; also, the plant.
ra′di·um (rā′dĭ·ŭm), *n.* [NL., fr. L. *radius* ray.] *Chem.* An intensely radioactive metallic element found (combined) in minute quantities in pitchblende and other uranium minerals. Symbol, *Ra;* at. no., 88; at. wt., 226.05. By their rays (*alpha rays, beta rays,* and *gamma rays*), radium preparations ionize gases, affect photographic plates, cause sores on the skin, etc. The radioactivity of radium is a result of a disintegration of the atom. This breaking up occurs in several stages, the successive products being called *radon,* **radium A, radium B, radium C, C′,** *or* **C″, D, E, F, G.** Radium G is an isotope of lead. Radon is a heavy gas, the later products solids. Helium is formed by the accumulation of expelled alpha particles. Radium is believed to be formed indirectly by slow disintegration of uranium.
radium emanation. *Chem.* = RADON.
ra′di·um·ther′a·py (rā′dĭ·ŭm·thĕr′ȧ·pĭ), *n.* [*radium* + *-therapy.*] *Med.* Treatment of disease, esp. cancer, with radium, its emanations or active deposit.
ra′di·us (rā′dĭ·ŭs), *n.; pl.* RADII (-ī), RADIUSES (-ŭs·ĕz; -ĭz). [L., a staff, rod, radius, ray.] **1.** A radial part, as the movable limb of a sextant. **2.** A distance or circular limit defined by a radius of specified length; as, the four-mile cab *radius* in London; loosely, any area bounded by certain limits; as, the cruising *radius* of an aircraft. **3.** *Anat. & Zool.* The anterior (thicker and shorter) of the two bones of the forearm or forelimb. **4.** *Geom.* A right line extending from the center of a circle or sphere to the curve or surface. See CIRCLE, *Illust.* **5.** *Mech.* Distance from a center line or point to an axis of rotation; throw; eccentricity. **6.** *Zool.* In radially symmetrical animals, an imaginary radial plane dividing the body into similar parts.
ra′di·us vec′tor (vĕk′tŏr); *pl.* RADII VECTORES (rā′dĭ·ī vĕk·tō′rēz), RADIUS VECTORS. [NL. *vector* a bearer, carrier.] **1.** *Math.* A straight segment (or its length) from a fixed point (or pole, or center) to a variable point. **2.** *Astron.* A straight line joining the center of an attracting body with that of a body describing an orbit around it, as a line joining the sun and a planet or comet.
ra′dix (rā′dĭks), *n.; pl.* RADICES (răd′ĭ·sēz; rā′dĭ·sēz), RADIXES (rā′dĭk·sĕz; -sĭz). [L. *radix, -icis,* root.] **1.** *Bot.* The root of a plant. **2.** *Math.* A number that is arbitrarily made the fundamental number of a system of numbers. Thus, 10 is the *radix* of the decimal system of enumeration. **3.** *Philol.* A root; radical; etymon.
ra′dome (rā′dōm), *n.* [*radar* + *dome.*] A dome-shaped housing for the antenna assembly of a radar set, esp. on an aircraft.
ra′don (rā′dŏn), *n.* [*radium* + *-on* as in *argon, neon,* etc.] *Chem.* A heavy, gaseous element resembling argon, but radioactive. See RADIUM. Symbol, *Rn;* at. no., 86; at. wt., 222.
rad′u·la (răd′ū·lȧ), *n.; pl.* RADULAE (-lē). [L., a scraper, fr. *radere* to scrape.] *Zool.* In mollusks except bivalves, a horny band or ribbon, bearing minute teeth on its dorsal surface, serving to tear up food and draw it into the mouth. — **rad′u·lar** (-lẽr), *adj.*
raff (răf), *n.* The scum or dregs of society; riffraff.
raf′fi·a (răf′ĭ·ȧ; 58), *n.* [Malagasy *rafia, raofia.*] **a** Fiber from the raffia palm used for tying plants, basketmaking, hats, etc. **b** The raffia palm.
raffia palm. A pinnate-leaved palm (*Raphia ruffia*) of Madagascar, important for the fiber from its leafstalks.
raf′fi·nose (răf′ĭ·nōs), *n.* [F. *raffiner* to refine + *-ose.*] *Chem.* A colorless, crystalline, slightly sweet sugar, $C_{18}H_{32}O_{16}$, occurring in small quantity in the sugar beet, cottonseed, etc.
raff′ish (răf′ĭsh), *adj.* [*raff,* n. + *-ish.*] **1.** Disreputable; low. **2.** Common; flashy. — **raff′ish·ly,** *adv.* — **raff′ish·ness,** *n.*
raf′fle (răf′'l), *n.* [ME. *rafle* a dicing game, fr. OF. *rafle* a stripping, plucking.] A form of lottery, in which a number of persons pay, in shares, the value or assumed value of something, and then determine by chance which one shall have it. — *v. i.;* RAF′FLED (-'ld); RAF′FLING (-lĭng). To engage in a raffle. — *v. t.* To dispose of by means of a raffle. — **raf′fler** (-lẽr), *n.*
raf′fle, *n.* Refuse; *Naut. & Dial. Eng.,* a jumble or tangle.
raf·fle′si·a (ră·flē′zhĭ·ȧ; -zĭ·ȧ), *n.* [NL., after its discoverer, Sir T. S. *Raffles.*] *Bot.* Any of a genus (*Rafflesia*) of Malaysian stemless and leafless plants with huge flowers, usually exhaling a carrionlike odor. It is the type of a family (Rafflesiaceae, the rafflesia family) of chiefly Old World plants having imbricated scales in place of leaves, and apetalous flowers. — **raf·fle′si·a′ceous** (-ā′shŭs), *adj.*
raft (răft; 9), *n.* [For *raff* a heap.] *Colloq.* A large collection.
raft, *n.* [ME., fr. ON. *raptr* rafter.] A collection of logs, timber, etc., fastened together, for a support or for their conveyance. — *v. t.* To transport on or as a raft; also, to make into a raft. — *v. i.* To use a raft or to use something as a raft; to form a raft.
raft′er (răf′tẽr; 9), *n.* [AS. *ræfter.*] *Arch.* One of the sloping timbers of a roof. See ROOF, QUEEN POST, *Illusts.*
rafts′man (răfts′măn; 9), *n.* A man engaged in rafting.
rag (răg), *n.* [AS. *ragg* (in *raggig* shaggy), fr. ON. *rögg* a tuft, shagginess.] **1. a** A waste piece of cloth torn or cut off; a shred; tatter. **b** *pl.* Remnants of used clothing, utilized for paper, lint, shoddy, etc. **2.** *Usually pl.* Hence, mean or tattered attire. **3.** Something suggesting a rag or rags and considered of little worth or service; — used contemptuously, jocularly, or ironically. **4.** Shabby or low people. **5.** The stringy axis and the white fibrous membrane of citrus fruits.
rag, *n.* A large roofing slate, rough on one side.
rag, *v. t.;* RAGGED (răgd); RAG′GING. *Slang.* **a** To scold. **b** To banter; tease. — *n. Slang.* Boisterous merrymaking; — orig. of students at English universities.
rag′a·muf′fin (răg′ȧ·mŭf′ĭn), *n.* A disreputable tatterdemalion.
rage (rāj), *n.* [OF., for L. *rabies.*] **1.** *Obs.* Insanity. **2.** Anger accompanied with raving; overmastering wrath; a fit of fury. **3.** Violence or fury, as of a wind, sea, fire. **4.** Extreme vehemence of emotion or suffering, mastering the will; frenzy. **5.** Enthusiasm, excitement, or fervor, esp. at its height. **6.** The subject of eager desire; as, to be all the *rage.* — **Syn.** See ANGER; FASHION. — *v. i.;* RAGED (rājd); RAG′ING (rāj′ĭng). **1.** To be in a fury or frenzy; to rave fiercely; also, to be violent, as a storm. **2.** To prevail because beyond control, as a plague.
rag′ged (răg′ĕd; -ĭd), *adj.* **1.** Rough; shaggy. **2.** Having rough edges or surface; uneven; jagged. **3. a** Rent or worn into tatters, or till the texture is broken; as, a *ragged* coat. **b** Wearing ragged clothes; as, a *ragged* beggar. **4.** Wanting finish; irregular; defective; also, harsh; dissonant. — ***on the ragged edge.*** On the verge of losing or being without means, health, self-control, or the like. — **rag′ged·ly,** *adv.* — **rag′ged·ness,** *n.*
ragged robin. A perennial herb (*Lychnis floscuculi*) having pink flowers with narrow-lobed petals; — called also *cuckooflower.*
rag′gee (răg′ē), *n.* Also **rag′gi, rag′gy, ra′gi.** [Hind. *rāgī.*] An East Indian cereal grass (*Eleusine coracana*) yielding a staple food crop in the Orient.
rag′lan (răg′lăn), *n.* [After 1st Baron *Raglan* (d. 1855), Eng. general.] A loose overcoat with sleeves (**raglan sleeves**) that extend up to the neckline of the garment, giving a slanting seam line from under the arm to the neck.
rag′man′ (răg′măn′; -măn), *n.* [ME. *rag(g)eman.*] A man who collects, or deals in, rags.
Rag′na·rok′ (răg′nȧ·rŏk′), **Rag′na·rök′** (-nȧ·rûk′), *n.* [ON., fr. *regin, rögn,* gods + *rök* reason, origin, history.] *Norse Myth.* The "Twilight of the Gods," the final destruction of the world in the conflict between the Aesir (gods) and the powers of Hel led by Loki.
ra·gout′ (ră·gōō′), *n.* [F. *ragoût,* fr. *ragoûter* to restore one's appetite, fr. *re-* re- + *à* to + *goût* taste.] A dish made of pieces of meat stewed with vegetables and highly seasoned. — *v. t.;* RA·GOUTED′ (-gōōd′); -GOUT′ING (-gōō′ĭng). To make a ragout of.
rag′pick′er (răg′pĭk′ẽr), *n.* One who picks up rags and refuse as a means of livelihood.
rag′tag′ (-tăg′), *n., or* **rag, tag, and bobtail.** The rabble; the mob; riffraff.
rag′time′ (-tīm′), *n.* *Music.* **a** Rhythm characterized by more or less continuous syncopation in the melody. **b** *Colloq.* A type of music (**ragtime music**) characterized by a strongly syncopated melody superimposed upon a regularly accented accompaniment.
rag′weed′ (-wēd′), *n.* **a** *Eng.* The ragwort. **b** *U. S.* Any of several coarse herbs (genus *Ambrosia*) typifying a family (Ambrosiaceae, the ragweed family) having heads of flowers subtended by an involucre of bracts; esp. a very common weed (*A. elatior*) with deeply lobed or dissected leaves; and the ***great,*** *or* ***giant, ragweed*** (*A. trifida*), with trilobate leaves. The cockleburs (see COCKLEBUR) also belong to this family.
rag′wort′ (-wûrt′), *n.* Any of several plants (genus *Senecio*) of the aster family, as the ***golden ragwort*** (*S. aureus*) of the United States, having an open corymb of yellow-rayed flowers.
ra′ia, ra′yah (rä′yȧ), *n.* [F., fr. Turk. *ra'āya,* fr. Ar. *ra'āya,* coll. sing. *ra'īyah,* flock, herd.] A non-Moslem subject of the Ottoman Empire.
raid (rād), *n.* [Scot. form of *road.* See ROAD raid, way.] **1.** A hostile or predatory incursion; a foray; orig., an inroad or incursion of mounted men; hence, a sudden or rapid attack, as by an armed force of any kind, by a naval vessel or by a bomber. **2.** Sudden attack or invasion by officers of the law for the purpose of making arrests, seizing illicit stores, or the like. **3.** *Exchanges.* An attempt by professional operators to depress prices. — *v. t.* To make a raid upon or into. — *v. i.* To conduct or take part in a raid.
raid′er (rād′ẽr), *n.* **1.** One who raids; one who leads or participates in a raid. **2.** [*often cap.*] *U. S. Marines.* A member of a battalion specially trained for close-range fighting.
rail (rāl), *n.;* see PLURAL, *Note,* 3. [F. *râle,* fr. OF. *ralle, raale.*] Any of numerous small precocial wading birds (family Rallidae, subfamily Rallinae) structurally related to the cranes, and prized as game birds. They have short rounded wings, a short tail, and usually very long toes, which enable them to run on the soft mud of swamps. The family (Rallidae) includes also crakes, coots, gallinules, and allied forms. North American species include the ***king rail*** (*Rallus elegans*), ***clapper rail*** (*R. longirostris crepitans*), and the ***sora*** (which see); European species, the ***land rail,*** *or* ***corn crake*** (*Crex crex*), common in grainfields, and the ***water rail*** (*Rallus aquaticus*).
rail, *v. i.* [F. *railler.*] To revile or scold in harsh, insolent, or vituperative language; scoff; — with *at* or *against.* — **Syn.** See SCOLD. — *v. t.* To remove by railing. *Shak.* — **rail′er,** *n.*
rail, *n.* [OF. *reille,* fr. L. *regula* a straight piece of wood, rule.] **1.** A bar of timber or metal extending from one support to another, as a guard or barrier, as in fences, balustrades, etc., or as a support. **2.** A fence; railing. **3.** A bar, usually of rolled steel, forming a track for wheeled vehicles. **4.** Short for *railroad;* as, by *rail.* **5.** *Arch.* A horizontal piece in a frame or paneling. **6.** *Naut.* The plank that forms the top of the bulwarks. — *v. t.* To provide with rails or a railing; to fence.
rail′head′ (rāl′hĕd′), *n.* **1.** *Mil.* A point on a railroad at which supplies for troops are discharged for distribution or forwarding. **2.** In a railroad under construction, the farthest point to which the rails have been laid.

rail′ing, *n.* **1.** A barrier, as a fence or balustrade, consisting of rails and supports. **2.** Rails in general.

rail′ler·y (rāl′ẽr·ĭ; răl′-), *n.; pl.* -IES (-ĭz). [F. *raillerie*, fr. *railler* to scoff.] **1.** Jocose ridicule; pleasantry touched with satire; banter. **2.** A bantering act or speech. — **Syn.** See BADINAGE.

rail′road′ (rāl′rōd′), *n.* A permanent road or way having a line or lines of rails providing a track for freight and passenger cars and other rolling stock, usually designed to be drawn by locomotives and (as distinguished from *railway*) for heavy traffic; hence, such a road or line together with all the lands, buildings, rolling stock, franchises, and other assets pertaining thereto. Abbr. *R.R.* — *v. t. U. S.* **1.** To transport by railroad. **2.** *Colloq.* To send or put through in great haste or without due consideration; as, to *railroad* a bill through Congress. **3.** *Slang.* To get rid of by sending (to prison) on a fake charge.

rail′road′ing, *n.* Construction or operation of a railroad line; employment in the operation of a railroad; the business of managing a railroad, or of working as an employee of a railroad.

rail′way′ (-wā′), *n.* **1.** A railroad designed for light traffic; as, an electric street *railway;* also, esp. *Brit.*, a railroad. Abbr. *Ry.* **2.** Any track providing a runway for wheels; as, a parcel *railway* in a shop.

railway stitch. A stitch consisting of a loop of thread and a small finishing stitch, used for working small flowers and leaves. See STITCH, *Illust.*

rai′ment (rā′mĕnt), *n.* [Abbr. fr. *arraiment.* See ARRAY.] Clothing in general; vesture; garments.

rain (rān), *n.* [AS. *regn.*] **1.** Water falling in drops condensed from vapor in the atmosphere; also, the descent of such drops. **2.** A shower of rain; rainstorm; also, *pl.*, the rainy season. **3.** Rainy weather. **4.** A falling or driving of numerous particles; as, a *rain* of sparks. — *v. i.* **1.** To fall in drops from the clouds, as water. **2.** To send down rain. **3.** To fall like water from clouds. — *v. t.* To pour as from the clouds; to bestow profusely; shed copiously.

rain′band′ (rān′bănd′), *n.* *Physics & Meteorol.* A dark band in the solar spectrum caused by watery vapor in the atmosphere.

rain′bow′ (-bō′), *n.* [AS. *regnboga.*] *Meteorol.* A circular bow or arc exhibiting the several colors of the spectrum, and formed opposite the sun by the refraction and reflection of the sun's rays in drops of rain, or in spray, mist, etc.

rain check. A coupon guaranteeing a deferred admission that has been paid for, as to a baseball game in case of rain; also, an assurance of a deferred extension of hospitality or privilege; as, I'll take a *rain check* on that invitation; the parachute is a *rain check* on life.

rain′coat′ (rān′kōt′), *n.* A coat suited in make and material for wear in the rain.

rain′drop′ (-drŏp′), *n.* A drop of rain.

rain′fall′ (-fôl′), *n.* A fall of rain; the amount of water that falls in rain, snow, etc., in inches of depth.

rain gauge. An instrument for measuring the quantity of rain that falls at a given place and time; a pluviometer.

rain′proof′ (rān′prōōf′; 2), *adj.* See -PROOF. — (rān′prōōf′), *v. t.* To make rainproof.

rain′storm′ (-stôrm′), *n.* A storm of or with rain.

rain water. Water falling or fallen as rain, that has not collected soluble matter from the soil, and hence is soft.

rain′y (rān′ĭ), *adj.;* RAIN′I·ER (-ĭ·ẽr); RAIN′I·EST. Abounding with rain; wet; showery. — **rain′i·ness**, *n.*

raise (rāz), *v. t.* [ON. *reisa*, causative to *rīsa* to rise.] **1.** To cause to rise up; hence: **a** To awaken; arouse. **b** To stir up; incite. **c** *Chiefly Scot.* To madden. **d** To call up, as a spirit; to recall from death. **2.** To cause to arise, grow up, or come into being or to appear; to give rise to; hence: **a** To build up; erect. **b** To collect; levy; to gather or obtain for use or service, as money or troops. **c** To cause or procure to be bred or propagated, as hops or cattle. **d** To cause to arise, come forth, or appear; — with *up.* **e** To give rise to; occasion, as a smile or a racket. **f** To give vent to; utter. **g** To submit for consideration, as an objection. **3.** To elevate; heave; hence: **a** To elevate in rank, dignity, or the like; to exalt; advance; enhance. **b** To increase the strength or vehemence of; to intensify, invigorate, or heighten, as the voice or the spirits. **c** To elevate in degree according to some scale, as the pitch or the temperature. **d** To cause to increase in height, level, size, amount, etc., as the rent. **4.** To cause to rise, or become light, as by leaven. **5.** To end the operation of, as if by lifting away, as an injunction. **6.** *Cards.* To increase (the wager or bid); also, to wager more than (a previous better). **7.** *Com.* Of negotiable paper, to increase fraudulently the nominal value of. **8.** *Naut.* To cause (land or an object) to rise above the horizon and so appear to view, or to seem higher, by drawing nearer to it. — *v. i.* **1.** *Now Dial.* To rise; arise. **2.** *Cards.* To increase the wager or bid. — **Syn.** See LIFT.

— *n.* A raising in amount, as of stakes; specif., an increase in pay (cf. RISE, *n.*, 4).

raised (rāzd), *adj.* **1.** Done in relief; embossed; as, *raised* embroidery. **2.** *Cookery.* Made light with leaven; — used of bread, cake, etc., thus made light, as distinguished from such foods made light with cream of tartar, baking soda, etc.

rai′sin (rā′z′n), *n.* [OF. *raizin, reisin* (F. *raisin*), fr. L. *racemus* cluster of grapes or berries.] **1.** A grape of a special type dried in the sun or by artificial heat. **2.** A color, bluish-red in hue, of low saturation and very low brilliance. See COLOR.

‖**rai′son′ d′é′tat′** (rĕ′zôɴ′ dā′tȧ′). [F.] Reason, or interest, of state.

‖**rai′son′ d′ê′tre** (dâ′tr′). [F.] Reason or justification for existence.

‖**rai′son′né′** (rĕ′zō′nā′), *adj.* [F.] Arranged systematically; as, a catalogue *raisonné.*

raj (räj), *n.* [Hind. *rāj.*] *India.* Reign; rule.

ra′ja, ra′jah (rä′jȧ), *n.* [Hind. *rājā*, fr. Skr. *rājan.*] **1.** Title of an Indian king, prince, or chief, or of a Malay or Javanese ruler. **2.** One bearing this title.

Ra·jab′ (rȧ·jăb′), *n.* [Ar.] See MOHAMMEDAN CALENDAR.

Ra′jas·tha′ni (rä′jȧs·tä′nē), *n.* [Hind. *rājasthān* king's palace, part of Rajputana.] The Indo-Aryan language, a dialect of Western Hindi, spoken in Rajputana and neighboring regions. See INDO-EUROPEAN LANGUAGES, *Table.*

Raj′put (räj′pōōt), *n.* [Hind. *rājpūt*, fr. Skr. *rājaputra* king's son.] A member of a dominant and military caste, of Kshatriya rank, numerous in northern India.

rake (rāk), *v. i.* [AS. *racian.*] **1.** To pass with violence or rapidity. **2.** *Hunting.* **a** Of a hawk, to fly after game. **b** *Brit.* Of dogs, to run with the nose to the ground.

rake, *v. i.* [Origin uncert.] To incline from a perpendicular, as a mast or funnel. — *n.* **1.** Inclination from a perpendicular direction; slope. **2.** *Aeronautics.* The cutting away of the wing tip of an airplane at an angle so that the main supporting surfaces, seen from above, will appear of trapezoidal form. **3.** *Mach.* The angle between the top cutting surface of a tool and a plane perpendicular to the surface of the work.

rake, *n.* [AS. *raca, racu.*] An implement consisting of a bar with projecting pegs or prongs, set transversely, and used for gathering hay, stirring and spreading earth, etc.

rake (rāk), *v. t.* **1.** To scrape together, along, apart, etc., with or as with a rake; as, to *rake* a fire with a poker. **2.** To collect with laborious industry; to scrape together. **3.** To scrape or scratch with a rake to clear off something or to stir up the soil. **4.** To search through; to ransack. **5.** To sweep the length of (a ship, column, etc.) with gunfire; to enfilade. — **rak′er** (rāk′ẽr), *n.*

rake, *n.* [From *rakehell* a dissolute fellow.] A debauchee; a roué.

rake′hell′ (rāk′hĕl′), *n.* [*rake* to scrape + *hell.*] *Archaic.* A lewd, dissolute fellow; an utter profligate; a rake.

rake′hell′ (rāk′hĕl′), **rake′hell′y** (-ĭ), *adj.* Dissolute; debauched.

rake′-off′, *n.* *Slang, U. S.* A commission, profit, or rebate, often illegitimate, received by a party to a transaction.

ra′ki′, ra′kee′ (rȧ′kē′; răk′ē), *n.* [Turk. *rāqi*, fr. Ar. *'araq.*] A type of ardent spirits used in southern Europe and the East, distilled from grape juice, grain, etc.

rak′ish (rāk′ĭsh), *adj.* [See RAKE a debauchee.] Of or characteristic of a rake; lewd; as, *rakish* habits.

rak′ish, *adj.* [See RAKE inclination.] **1.** *Naut.* Having a smart appearance indicative of speed. **2.** Not straight or conventional in line, appearance, etc.; jauntily careless; sporty; as, a hat set at a *rakish* angle. — **rak′ish·ly**, *adv.* — **rak′ish·ness**, *n.*

‖**râle** (räl), *n.* [F.] *Med.* An abnormal sound, usually morbid, accompanying the normal sounds of breathing.

ral′len·tan′do (răl′ĕn·tăn′dō; *It.* räl′lăn·tän′dō), *adj.* [It.] *Music.* Gradually decreasing in tempo; — a direction. — *n.* *Music.* A passage or movement gradually decreasing in tempo.

ral′li·form (răl′ĭ·fôrm), *adj.* *Zool.* Like or related to the rails.

ral′line (răl′īn; -ĭn), *adj.* [NL. *rallus* rail (bird).] *Zool.* Like or pertaining to the rails.

ral′ly (răl′ĭ), *v. t.;* RAL′LIED (-ĭd); RAL′LY·ING. [F. *rallier*, fr. *re-* + *allier* to join. See ALLY, *v.*] **1.** To collect and reduce to order, as troops in confusion; also, to assemble for common action. **2.** To arouse to action; to revive. — *v. i.* **1.** To recover unity and strength by a reassembling of scattered forces. **2.** To collect one's vital powers or forces; to recuperate; revive. **3.** To join in active support. **4.** To recover strength after a decline in prices, as stocks. **5.** *Tennis, etc.* To engage in a rally. — *n.; pl.* -LIES (-ĭz). **1.** Act, process, or an instance of rallying; as, a stock market *rally.* **2.** *U. S.* A mass meeting intended to arouse group enthusiasm. **3.** In tennis, rackets, etc., a series of strokes interchanged between the players before a point is won.

ral′ly, *v. t. & i.* [F. *railler* to scoff.] To attack with, or indulge in, raillery; to banter. — **Syn.** See RIDICULE.

ram (răm), *n.* [AS. *ramm, ram.*] **1.** A male sheep. **2.** An engine of war used for butting, or battering. Specif.: **a** A battering-ram. **b** A beak projecting from the prow of a ship for piercing or cutting an enemy's vessel; also, a ship with such a beak. **3.** A hydraulic ram. **4.** [*cap.*] *Astron.* The constellation Aries. **5.** *Mach.* **a** The plunger of a hydrostatic press, force pump, etc. **b** The weight in a pile driver, or the like. — *v. t.;* RAMMED (rămd); RAM′MING. **1.** To make compact or to fill as by pounding or stamping; to cram; stuff. **2.** To force down by driving into the earth. **3.** To butt or strike against violently.

Ra′ma (rä′mȧ), *n.* [Skr. *Rāma.*] *Hindu Myth.* Either the sixth, seventh, or eighth incarnation of Vishnu. Of these the seventh, **Ra′ma·chan′dra** (-chŭn′drȧ) [Skr. *Rāmacandra*], is the most famous. See RAMAYANA.

Ram′a·dan′ (răm′ȧ·dän′), *n.* Also **Ram′a·zan′** (-zän′). [Ar. *Ramaḍān*, prop., the hot month.] In the Mohammedan year, the ninth month, when strict fasting is practiced; also, the fasting. See MOHAMMEDAN CALENDAR.

Ra·ma′ya·na (rä·mä′yȧ·nȧ), *n.* [Skr. *Rāmāyaṇa.*] A Sanskrit epic detailing the adventures of Ramachandra.

ram′ble (răm′b′l), *v. i.;* RAM′BLED (-b′ld); RAM′BLING (-blĭng). [Origin uncert.] **1.** To go from place to place, without an aim or goal; to roam. **2.** To talk or write in a desultory or pointless fashion. **3.** To extend or grow at random, as a vine. — *n.* A rambling; a walking trip.

ram′bler (-blẽr), *n.* One who or that which rambles; specif., *Hort.*, any clambering rose, esp. the ***crimson rambler*** (*Rosa barbierana*).

ram′bling (-blĭng), *adj.* Discursive; digressive; desultory.

Ram′bouil′let′ (räɴ′bōō′yĕ′; răm′bōō·lā), *n.* [From *Rambouillet*, France.] The French merino sheep, bred for both mutton and wool.

ram·bunc′tious (răm·bŭngk′shŭs), *adj.* *Colloq.* Wild or uncontrollable in conduct; unruly.

ram·bu′tan (răm·bōō′tăn), *n.* [Malay, fr. *rambut* hair.] A bright-red, spiny Malayan fruit closely related to the litchi nut; also, the tree (*Nephelium lappaceum*) of the soapberry family, bearing this fruit.

ram′e·kin, ram′e·quin (răm′ē·kĭn), *n.* [F. *ramequin.*] **1.** A preparation of cheese with bread crumbs or puff paste, eggs, etc., baked in a mold; — usually *pl.* **2.** A pottery dish for baking and serving any similar mixture; hence, food served in such a dish; as, chicken *ramekins.*

ram′ie (răm′ē), *n.* [Malay *rami* the plant.] An Asian perennial plant (*Boehmeria nivea*) of the nettle family; also, its strong, lustrous bast fiber capable of being spun and woven into various rather coarse lightweight fabrics resembling linen.

ram′i·fi·ca′tion (răm′ĭ·fĭ·kā′shŭn), *n.* **1.** Act or process of branching; specif., *Bot.*, arrangement of branches. **2.** A branch or offshoot; also, the resulting branched structure. **3.** A subdivision, an outgrowth, or a consequence; as, every *ramification* of his subject.

ram′i·form (răm′ĭ·fôrm), *adj.* [L. *ramus* branch + *-form.*] Branch-like; branched.

ram′i·fy (răm′ĭ·fī), *v. t. & i.;* -FIED (-fīd); -FY′ING. [F. *ramifier*, fr. ML. *ramificare*, fr. L. *ramus* branch + *-ficare* (in comp.) to make.] To divide or spread out into branches or ramifications; to branch out.

ram′-jet′ en′gine. *Aeronautics.* A jet engine having in its forward end a continuous inlet of air so that there is a compressing or "ramming" effect produced on the air taken in while the engine is in motion.

The compressed air that enters the combustion chamber and the constant burning of the fuel result in a continuous jet of hot gases.
ram'mer (răm'ẽr), *n.* A ramming instrument.
ram'mish (-ĭsh), *adj.* Like a ram; lustful; rank.
ra'mose (rā'mōs; rȧ·mōs'), *adj.* [L. *ramosus*, fr. *ramus* a branch.] Branched; consisting of or having branches.
ra'mous (rā'mŭs), *adj.* **a** Ramose. **b** Branchlike.
ramp (rămp), *v. i.* [OF. *ramper* to climb, creep.] **1. a** To be rampant, or in the posture of a beast rampant in heraldry. **b** To stand or advance with forelegs or with arms raised as if in menace; hence, to rage; storm; rampage. **2.** To rush about excitedly. — *n.* Act of ramping; a threatening or warlike advance or posture.
ramp, *n.* [F. *rampe*, fr. *ramper*.] **1.** A sloping roadway or passageway. **2.** *Arch.* A short bend, slope, or curve, usually in the vertical plane, where a handrail, coping, or the like changes its direction. **3.** *Fort.* An inclined plane serving as a way between different interior levels. See BASTION, *Illust.*
ram'page (răm'pāj *or*, *esp. Brit.*, răm·pāj'), *n.* [See RAMP, *v.*] Violent, riotous, reckless behavior.
ram·page' (răm·pāj'; răm'pāj), *v. i.* To go on a rampage; to storm or rush about wildly or excitedly. — **ram·pa'geous** (răm·pā'jŭs), *adj.* — **ram·pa'geous·ness**, *n.*
ramp'an·cy (răm'păn·sĭ), *n.* State of being rampant.
ramp'ant (-pănt), *adj.* [OF., pres. part.] **1.** Rearing upon the hind legs with forelegs extended. **2.** Threatening, extravagant, or unrestrained in bearing. **3.** Exuberant in growth or spread; as, superstition was *rampant*. **4.** *Arch.* Having one abutment higher than the other. **5.** *Her.* Standing and reared up, with head to the dexter side and one (usually dexter) foreleg raised above the other; — of lions, bears, etc. — **ramp'ant·ly**, *adv.*
ram'part (răm'pärt; -pẽrt), *n.* [F. *rempart*, fr. *remparer* to fortify, fr. *re-* re- + *emparer* to take possession of.] **1.** *Fort.* A broad embankment round a place, on which the parapet is raised. **2.** A bulwark; a protective barrier. — *v. t.* To surround or protect with a rampart.
ram'pi·on (răm'pĭ·ŭn), *n.* A European bellflower (*Campanula rapunculus*) having an edible tuberous root used with the leaves as a salad.
ram'rod' (răm'rŏd'), *n.* The rod used in ramming home the charge in a muzzle-loading firearm; now, a cleaning rod for small arms.
ram'shack'le (-shăk''l), *adj.* [From earlier *ranshackled*, fr. *ransackle*, freq. of RANSACK.] Loose-jointed; rickety; tumble-down.
ram'stam' (rȧm'stȧm'), *adj.* *Scot. & Dial.* Reckless; headstrong. — *adv.* Recklessly; headlong.
ram'til (răm'tĭl), *n.* [Hind. *rāmtil*.] A tropical herb (*Guizotia abyssinica*) of the aster family, cultivated in India for its seeds, which yield a valuable oil.
ram'u·lose (răm'ū·lōs), *adj.* [L. *ramulosus*, fr. *ramulus*, dim. of *ramus* a branch.] Having many small branches.
ra'mus (rā'mŭs), *n.; pl.* RAMI (-mī). [L.] *Biol.* A branch; a projecting part.
Ran (rän), *n.* [ON. *Rān*.] See AEGIR.
ran (răn), *past & improper past part.* of RUN.
rance (răns), *n.* [F.] A dull-red Belgian marble with blue-and-white markings.
ranch (rănch), *n.* Also, formerly, **ranche**. [See RANCHO.] **1.** *Western U. S. & Canada.* An establishment, with its estate, for the grazing and rearing of horses, cattle, or sheep; esp., the buildings occupied, barns, corrals, etc.; also, the persons on the estate. **2.** Loosely, a large farm; as, a fruit *ranch*. — *v. i.* To live or work on a ranch.
ranch'er (răn'chẽr), *n.* A ranchman.
ran·che'ro (răn·châr'ō), *n.; pl.* -ROS (-ōz). [Sp.] *Sp. Amer.* A herdsman employed on a ranch or rancho; also, sometimes, the owner.
ranch house. A one-story dwelling, typically having an informal interior plan and a low-pitched roof.
ranch'man (rănch'măn), *n.; pl.* -MEN (-mĕn). One who owns, occupies, or works on a ranch; a rancher.
ran'cho (răn'chō), *n.; pl.* -CHOS (-chōz). [Sp., prop., a mess, messroom.] *Sp. Amer.* **1.** A rude hut or collection of huts for herdsmen or farm laborers. **2.** A large grazing farm; — disting. from *hacienda*.
ran'cid (răn'sĭd), *adj.* [L. *rancidus*, fr. *rancere* to be rancid.] Having a rank smell or taste; hence, unpleasant; offensive. — **ran'cid·ness**, *n.*
ran·cid'i·ty (răn·sĭd'ĭ·tĭ), *n.* Quality or state of being rancid; a rancid odor or flavor, as of old oil.
ran'cor, ran'cour (răng'kẽr), *n.* [OF. *rancor*, *rancur*, fr. LL. *rancor* rancidity, rancor, fr. L. *rancere* to be rank or rancid.] Vehement ill will; intense malignity or spite; deep-seated enmity. — **Syn.** See ENMITY.
ran'cor·ous (răng'kẽr·ŭs), *adj.* Full of or evincing rancor. — **ran'cor·ous·ly**, *adv.* — **ran'cor·ous·ness**, *n.*
rand (rănd), *n.* [AS. *rand*, *rond*.] **1.** *Obs. exc. Dial.* A border or margin; a strip. **2.** *Shoe Mfg.* A leveling strip put on before the lifts of the heel.
ran'dom (răn'dŭm), *n.* [OF. *randon* violence, rapidity.] *Now Rare.* A haphazard course or progress. — ***at random.*** Without definite aim, direction, rule, or method; at haphazard. — *adj.* **1.** Coming, acting, made, occurring, etc., at random. **2.** *Biol.* Made as if at random but controlled so as to bring together certain individuals or classes, or to make representative; as, *random* breeding. — **ran'dom·ly**, *adv.*
Syn. **Random, haphazard, casual, desultory** mean showing the influence of accident rather than design. **Random** implies little or no guidance by a governing mind, eye, objective, or the like; **haphazard**, a being more or less at the mercy of chance or of natural or logical necessity; **casual**, a working, an acting, or the like, without deliberation, intention, or purpose; **desultory**, a jumping or skipping from one thing to another ungoverned by method or system.
rand'y (răn'dĭ; rȧn'dĭ), *adj.* *Scot.* Ill-mannered; coarse. — *n.* *Scot.* A sturdy beggar; also, a virago.
ra'nee. Var. of RANI.
rang (răng), *past* of RING, to sound.
range (rānj), *v. t.;* RANGED (rānjd); RANG'ING (rān'jĭng). [OF. *rangier*, var. of *rengier*, fr. *renc* row, rank, of Teut. origin.] **1.** To set in a row, or in rows; to dispose in the proper order. **2.** To place (a single individual, as oneself) among others in a line; hence, to espouse a cause, to join a party, etc. **3.** To dispose in a classified, or in systematic, order. **4.** To rove over or through. **5.** To lay off; to make even or straight. **6.** To train (a telescope). **7.** *Gun.* To determine the elevation necessary for a given distance; to give (a gun) such elevation. **8.** *Naut.* To arrange (an anchor cable) on deck. — *v. i.* **1.** To rove at large. **2.** To move over a surface so as to explore it, esp. as a hunting dog seeking game. **3.** To be ranked. **4.** To correspond in direction or line. **5. a** To have range; to be capable of projecting; as, the gun *ranges* three miles. **b** To change or differ within limits. **6.** *Bot. & Zool.* To be native to, or live in, a certain district or region. **7.** *Gun.* To obtain the range of an object by firing alternately over and short of it. — **Syn.** See LINE.
— *n.* **1.** A series of things in a line; a row; a rank. **2. a** A wandering or roving. **b** That which may be ranged over; esp., a sparsely populated and open region over which livestock may roam and feed. **3.** A series or chain of mountain peaks considered as forming one connected system; a ridge of mountains; as, the Appalachian *range*. **4.** A cookstove. **5.** An order; a class. **6.** *U. S.* In the public land system, a row or line of townships lying between two successive meridian lines six miles apart. **7.** Extent or space taken in or covered; compass; reach; scope; sphere. **8.** A line of direction; as, in *range* with a beacon. **9.** The limits of a series of actual or possible variations; as, a narrow *range* of choice. **10.** *Bot. & Zool.* The region throughout which a plant or animal naturally lives. **11.** *Gun.* **a** The horizontal distance to which a projectile is, or may be, propelled; also, the horizontal distance of the target from the gun. **b** A place where shooting is practiced. **12.** *Leather Mfg.* A part of a hide. See HIDE, *Illust.* **13.** *Statistics.* The difference between the least and greatest values of the variable of a frequency distribution.
— *adj.* Of or pert. to a range, or open region; as, *range* cattle.
range finder. **1.** *Gun.* An instrument, variously constructed, used to determine the distance of an object to be hit. **2.** *Photog.* A camera attachment for measuring the distance between the camera and an object.
rang'er (rān'jẽr), *n.* **1.** *Eng.* The keeper of a royal park or forest. **2.** A rover; wanderer. **3.** One of a body of mounted troops who range over a region. **4.** In America, a warden who patrols tracts of forests, esp. those owned by the nation. **5.** [*often cap.*] An expert in close-range fighting attached to a special American unit of assault troops corresponding to the British commando. — **rang'er·ship**, *n.*
rang'y (rān'jĭ), *adj.;* RANG'I·ER (-jĭ·ẽr); RANG'I·EST. Inclined or able to range far; hence, long-limbed and slender.
ra'ni, ra'nee (rä'nē), *n.* [Hind. *rānī*, fr. Skr. *rājñī*.] **1.** Title of a Hindu queen, a reigning princess, or a raja's wife. **2.** One bearing this title.
rank (răngk), *adj.* [AS. *ranc* strong, proud.] **1.** Luxuriant or vigorous in growth; grown to immoderate height; as, *rank* weeds. **2.** Producing luxuriantly; very (sometimes too) rich and fertile. **3.** Offensively gross or coarse; indecent. **4.** Strong-scented; rancid; offensive in smell or taste. **5.** Extreme; gross; utter; — only in reprobation; as, *rank* treason. **6.** *Obs. exc. Law.* Excessive. **7.** *Obs.* Lustful; ruttish. — **Syn.** See MALODOROUS: FLAGRANT. — **rank'ly**, *adv.* — **rank'ness**, *n.*
rank, *n.* [OF. *ranc*, var. of *renc* (F. *rang*), of Teut. origin.] **1.** A row; line; range; series; tier; as, mountains in *ranks*. **2.** Orderly arrangement; array; as, to form a crowd into *rank*. **3.** An aggregate of individuals classed together; a social class; as, *ranks* and orders of men. **4.** Grade of official standing; as, the *rank* of admiral. **5.** Degree of eminence or excellence; also, relative position; status; grade; as, a writer of the first *rank*. **6.** Elevated grade; high degree; also, high social position; distinction; eminence. **7.** *Chess.* A row of squares on the chessboard parallel to the sides next the players. **8.** *Mil.* **a** A line of soldiers ranged side by side in close order; — opposed to *file*. **b** *pl.* An army. **c** *pl.* The body of privates as distinguished from officers; as, he rose from the *ranks*. — *v. t.* **1.** To arrange in a line or lines; to draw up in a regular formation, as soldiers. **2.** To range in a class; to class; as, to *rank* Dante above Shakespeare. **3.** *Mil. & Nav.* To outrank; to take precedence of. — *v. i.* **1.** To be ranged in order, as of rank or merit; as, to *rank* below the average. **2.** To have the highest rank; to be senior; as, *ranking* colonel; to be supremely eminent.
rank and file. **a** *Mil.* The whole body of common soldiers. **b** Hence, those constituting the body of a party, nation, etc., as distinct from the heads or leaders.
rank'er (răngk'ẽr), *n.* [From RANK, *n.*] *Colloq., Mil.* One who serves or has served in the ranks; esp., a commissioned officer promoted from the ranks.
ran'kle (răng'k'l), *v. i.;* RAN'KLED (-k'ld); RAN'KLING (-klĭng). [OF. *rancler*, var. of *draoncler* to fester, deriv. of ML. *dracunculus* a sore, dim. of L. *draco* dragon.] To produce a festering or inflamed effect; to fester; as, the words *rankled* in his bosom.
ran'sack (răn'săk), *v. t.* [ON. *rannsaka* to explore, search a house, fr. *rann* house + *saka*; akin to ON. *sœkja* to seek.] **1.** To search every part of. **2.** To search through and carry away all valuables in; to pillage; as, to *ransack* the city. — **ran'sack·er** (-ẽr), *n.*
ran'som (răn'sŭm), *n.* [OF. *rançon*, *raençon*, fr. L. *redemptio*, fr. *redimere* to redeem. See REDEEM.] A redeeming of a captive by payment of a consideration; also, the consideration paid or demanded. — *v. t.* **1.** To redeem from captivity, slavery, or the like, by paying a price. **2.** To deliver, as from sin. — **Syn.** See RESCUE. — **ran'som·er** (-ẽr), *n.*
rant (rănt), *v. i.* [MD. *ranten*, *randen*, to dote, to be enraged.] **1.** To declaim, or talk noisily, excitedly, and extravagantly; to discourse in a bombastic, turgid fashion. **2.** To scold vehemently. **3.** *Now Dial.* To revel; carouse; to riot. — *n.* **1.** Ranting discourse or language. **2.** *Dial.* A noisy jollification. — **Syn.** See BOMBAST. — **rant'er**, *n.* — **rant'ing**, *adj.* — **rant'ing·ly**, *adv.*
ra·nun'cu·la'ceous (rȧ·nŭng'kū·lā'shŭs), *adj.* [See RANUNCULUS.] *Bot.* Belonging to the crowfoot family (Ranunculaceae). See CROWFOOT.
ra·nun'cu·lus (rȧ·nŭng'kū·lŭs), *n.; pl.* -LUSES (-lŭs·ĕz; -ĭz), -CULI (-lī). [L., a little frog, a medicinal plant, perh. crowfoot, dim. of *rana* a frog.] *Bot.* Any of a large genus (*Ranunculus*) of herbs, the crowfoots. See CROWFOOT.
rap (răp), *n.* [Origin uncert.] *Colloq.* Any coin of trifling value; hence, the least bit; as, I don't care a *rap*.
rap, *v. t.;* RAPPED (răpt), or, often, RAPT; RAP'PING. [From RAPT, *adj.*] **1.** To snatch away. **2.** To transport out of oneself; to enrapture; — in *past part.*
rap, *v. t. & i.;* RAPPED (răpt); RAP'PING. [See RAP a blow.] **1.** To strike with a quick, smart blow or blows. **2.** To utter suddenly and forcibly; to deliver with a bang. — *n.* [Of imitative origin.] **1.** A

quick, smart blow. **2.** A sound like that of knocking, ascribed to mediumistic agencies, as at spiritualistic séances.

ra·pa′cious (rȧ·pā′shŭs), *adj.* [L. *rapax, -acis,* fr. *rapere* to seize and carry off.] **1.** Excessively grasping or covetous; given to seizing or extorting what is coveted. **2.** Subsisting on prey; predaceous. **3.** Ravenous; voracious. — **ra·pa′cious·ly,** *adv.* — **ra·pa′cious·ness,** *n.*

ra·pac′i·ty (rȧ·păs′ĭ·tĭ), *n.* Quality of being rapacious.

rape (rāp), *n.* [L. *rapa, rapum.*] A European herb (*Brassica napus*) of the mustard family, grown as a forage crop for sheep and hogs. Its seeds yield rape oil and are a bird food.

rape, *n.* [F. *râpe,* ML. *raspa.*] The pomace of grapes, left after expression of the juice or must.

rape, *v. t.* [AS. & OF. *raper,* fr. L. *rapere, raptum.*] **1.** *Archaic.* To seize and take away by force; to plunder. **2.** To commit rape upon; to ravish. — *n.* **1.** A seizing by force; robbery. **2.** *Law.* The illicit carnal knowledge of a woman without her consent.

rape, *or* **rape′seed′, oil.** A fixed, nondrying or semidrying oil obtained from rapeseed, used as a lubricant, etc.; — called also *colza oil.*

rape′seed′ (rāp′sēd′), *n.* The seed of rape; also, the plant.

Raph′a·el (răf′ā·ĕl; -ĭ·ĕl; rā′fā·ĕl; -fĭ·ĕl), *n.* [LL., fr. Gr. *Rhaphaēl,* fr. Heb. *Rĕphā′ēl.*] An archangel mentioned in Hebrew literature. Milton represents him as sent by God to instruct Adam.

ra′phe (rā′fē), *n.* [NL., fr. Gr. *rhaphē* a seam or suture, fr. *rhaptein* to sew or stitch together.] **1.** *Anat.* The seamlike union of the two lateral halves of a part or organ, as of the tongue, having externally a ridge or furrow. **2.** *Bot.* **a** In anatropous ovules, that part of the cord or stalk united in growth to the outside covering, forming a ridge along the body of the ovule. See SEED, *Illust.* **b** In diatoms, the median line of a valve.

raph′i·des (răf′ĭ·dēz), *n. pl.* [NL., fr. Gr. *rhaphis, rhaphidos,* a needle.] *Bot.* Needle-shaped crystals, generally of calcium oxalate developed as metabolic by-products in plant cells.

rap′id (răp′ĭd), *adj.* [F. *rapide,* fr. L. *rapidus,* fr. *rapere* to seize and carry off, hurry away.] **1.** Very swift or quick in motion; fast-moving. **2.** Quick in action, thought, etc. **3.** Progressing or accomplished in much less than normal time; as, *rapid* growth. **4.** *Photog.* Adapted to short exposure. — **Syn.** See FAST. — **Ant.** Leisurely. — *n.* A part of a river where the current moves with great swiftness, the surface being usually broken by obstructions, but without actual waterfall; — usually in *pl.* — **rap′id·ly,** *adv.*

rap′id–fire′ (răp′ĭd-fīr′; 2), **rap′id–fir′ing,** *adj.* **1.** Firing, or adapted for firing, shots in rapid succession; — esp., *Ordnance,* of single-barreled guns of greater caliber than small arms. **2.** Proceeding with or characterized by rapidity or sharpness; as, a *rapid-fire* cross-examination.

ra·pid′i·ty (rȧ·pĭd′ĭ·tĭ), *n.* Quality or state of being rapid; swiftness; speed; fleetness; quickness.

ra′pi·er (rā′pĭ·ēr; 58), *n.* [F. *rapière.*] A straight two-edged sword, having a narrow, pointed blade.

rap′ine (răp′ĭn), *n.* [F. or L.; F., fr. L. *rapina,* fr. *rapere* to seize and carry off.] A plundering; spoliation; pillage; plunder.

rap′loch (răp′lŏk), *adj. Scot.* Coarse or rough and undyed. — *n. Scot.* A coarse, undyed, woolen cloth.

rap′pa·ree′ (răp′ȧ·rē′), *n.* [Ir. *rapaire, ropaire.*] *Hist.* An Irish freebooter; hence, a plunderer; vagabond.

rap·pee′ (ră·pē′), *n.* [F. *râpé,* prop., past part., grated.] A pungent snuff made from the ranker tobacco leaves.

rap′per (răp′ēr), *n.* [From RAP.] One who or that which raps; specif., a knocker of a door.

rap·port′ (ră·pōrt′; *F.* rȧ′pôr′; 70), *n.* [F., fr. *rapporter* to bring back, refer.] Relation of harmony, conformity, accord, or affinity; — esp. in ***in rapport*** *or* ‖***en rap′port′*** (äɴ rȧ′pôr′) [F.], in an intimate or harmonious relation.

‖**rap′proche′ment′** (rȧ′prôsh′mäɴ′), *n.* [F., fr. *rapprocher* to cause to approach again. See RE-; APPROACH.] A coming together; establishment or state of cordial relations.

rap·scal′lion (răp·skăl′yŭn), *n.* A rascal; a ne'er-do-well.

rapt (răpt), *part. adj.* [L. *raptus,* past part. of *rapere* to seize.] **1.** Lifted, as by supernatural force; transported, as in spirit or to another place. **2.** Transported with love, delight, etc.; enraptured. **3.** Wholly absorbed or engrossed, as in feeling or meditation. — **Syn.** See INTENT.

rap·to′ri·al (răp·tō′rĭ·ăl; 70), *adj.* [L. *raptor* a plunderer.] *Zool.* Living on prey; having feet modified with sharp curved claws, for seizing prey; — of a group of carnivorous birds consisting of the hawks, eagles, vultures, and owls.

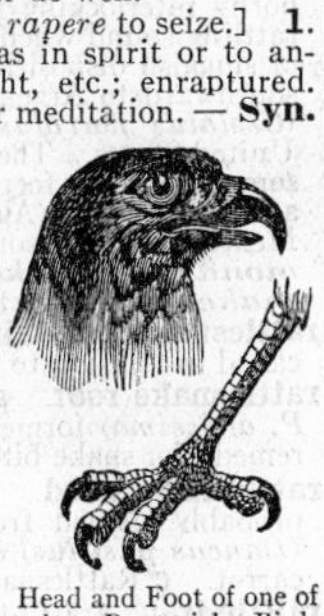

Head and Foot of one of the Raptorial Birds (*Ictinia plumbea*).

rap′ture (răp′tūr), *n.* [From RAPT, *adj.*] **1.** *Now Rare.* Act of transporting, or fact of being transported. **2.** State of being rapt, or carried out of oneself; spiritual or emotional ecstasy. **3.** An expression, or manifestation, of ecstasy; a rhapsody. — **Syn.** See ECSTASY. — *v. t. Poetic.* To transport; enrapture.

rap′tur·ous (-tūr·ŭs), *adj.* Feeling, expressing, or manifesting rapture; ecstatic. — **rap′tur·ous·ly,** *adv.* — **rap′tur·ous·ness,** *n.*

‖**ra′ra a′vis** (rā′rȧ ā′vĭs); *pl.* RARAE AVES (rā′rē ā′vēz). [L.] Literally, a rare bird; hence, a rarity; an extraordinary person or thing.

rare (râr), *adj.* [Also, dial., *rear,* fr. ME. *rere,* fr. AS. *hrēr.*] Not thoroughly cooked; underdone.

rare, *adj.* [F., fr. L. *rarus* thin, rare.] **1.** Not thick or dense; thin; as, *rare* atmosphere. **2.** *Obs.* Thinly scattered; not massed. **3.** Of an uncommon quality; unusually excellent; as, a person of *rare* charm. **4.** Seldom met with or occurring; very uncommon. **5.** Of a relatively small class; as, a *rare* gem. — **Syn.** See CHOICE; INFREQUENT.

rare′bit (râr′bĭt), *n. Cookery.* = WELSH RABBIT; — from false etymologizing of this jocose phrase as *rare bit.*

rare earth. *Chem.* Any of a series of very similar oxides (general formula, M_2O_3) of the rare-earth metals. They are obtained from widely distributed but relatively scarce minerals. — **rare′–earth′,** *adj.*

rare′–earth′ el′e·ment *or* **met′al.** *Chem.* Any of a group of very similar elements of successive atomic numbers, beginning with cerium 58 (sometimes with lanthanum 57) and extending through lutecium 71. See PERIODIC TABLE.

rar′ee show (râr′ē). [From Savoyard showmen's pron. of E. *rare show.*] A show carried in a box; hence, any cheap street show.

rar′e·fac′tion (râr′ē·făk′shŭn), *n.* Act or process of rarefying; state of being rarefied.

rar′e·fac′tive (-tĭv), *adj.* [L. *rarefacere, -factum,* to rarefy. See RAREFY.] Producing or marked by rarefaction.

rar′e·fy (râr′ē·fī), *v. t. & i.;* RAR′E·FIED (-fīd); RAR′E·FY′ING. [F. *raréfier,* fr. L. *rarus* rare + *-ficare* (in comp.) to make.] To make or become rare, thin, porous, or less dense; figuratively, to make more spiritual, refined, or the like.

rare′ly (râr′lĭ), *adv.* **1.** Seldom; not often. **2.** Finely; beautifully; excellently; with rare skill. **3.** In an exceptional degree; extremely; as, *rarely* beautiful.

rare′ness, *n.* State or quality of being rare; rarity.

rare′ripe′ (râr′rīp′), *adj.* [Dial. *rare,* var. of *rath* early, soon + *ripe.*] Early ripe. — *n.* An early ripening fruit or vegetable.

rar′i·ty (răr′ĭ·tĭ; râr′-), *n.; pl.* -TIES (-tĭz). **1.** Quality or state of being rare; as: **a** Thinness; as, the *rarity* (contrasted with the *density*) of gases. **b** Infrequency; scarcity. **c** Quality of being unusually excellent; as, *rarity* of phrasing. **2.** A thing valued for its scarcity.

ras′cal (răs′kăl *or, esp. Brit.,* räs′-), *n.* [OF. *rascaille,* fr. ONF. *rasque* filth, dirt.] **1.** *Now Rare.* One of the rabble. **2.** A mean, trickish fellow; a base, dishonest person; a rogue; knave; — also jocular; as, you young *rascal.* — *adj.* Of or pertaining to the rabble; low; mean; base.

ras·cal′i·ty (răs·kăl′ĭ·tĭ *or, esp. Brit.,* räs-), *n.; pl.* -TIES (-tĭz). The character or actions of a rascal; knavery; also, a rascally act.

ras′cal·ly (răs′kăl·ĭ *or, esp. Brit.,* räs′-), *adj.* Of, pertaining to, or characteristic of a rascal; meanly tricky; base; worthless· — often jocular. — *adv.* In a rascally fashion.

rase (rāz), *v. t.* [OF. *raser,* v. freq. fr. L. *radere, rasum,* to scrape.] *Now Rare.* **1.** To erase. **2.** To level to the ground; = RAZE, 3.

rash (răsh), *n.* [OF. *rasche, rache,* eruption, scurf.] A fine eruption or efflorescence on the body.

rash, *adj.* [ME. *rasch* quick.] **1.** Acting or given to acting without deliberation or caution; overhasty in decision, action, or speech; precipitate; reckless; imprudent. **2.** Characterized by or manifesting undue haste, too little reflection, or disregard for consequences. **3.** *Rare.* Quickly effective. *Shak.* — **Syn.** See ADVENTUROUS. — **rash′ly,** *adv.* — **rash′ness,** *n.*

rash (rȧsh). Scot. & N. of Eng. var. of RUSH, a plant.

rash′er (răsh′ēr), *n.* A thin slice, as of bacon or, more rarely, of ham, cut for broiling or frying.

ra·so′ri·al (rȧ·sō′rĭ·ăl; 70), *adj.* [L. *radere, rasum,* to scratch.] Habitually scratching the ground in search of food, as a fowl; gallinaceous.

rasp (rȧsp; 9), *v. t.* [OF. *rasper* to scrape, grate, rasp.] **1.** To rub or file with a rasp; to rub or grate with or as with a rough file. **2.** To grate harshly upon; to serve as an irritant to, as the nerves. **3.** To utter in an irritated or grating tone. — *v. i.* To grate or scrape. — *n.* **1.** A type of coarse file, with raised points forming the cutting prominences instead of lines as on the true file. **2.** Act or effect of rasping; rasping sound or sensation.

rasp′ber′ry (răz′bĕr′ĭ *or, esp. Brit.,* räz′bĕr·ĭ), *n.* [From earlier *rasp, raspis berry,* both fr. *raspis* raspberry.] **1.** The aggregate fruit of any of various brambles (genus *Rubus*) of the rose family, distinguished from the blackberry as being rounder and smaller and easily separated from the receptacle when ripe. The mass of drupelets composing the fruit are red, purple, black, or yellow. Also, the plant bearing this fruit. From the ***red raspberry*** of America (*R. strigosus*) and the ***black raspberry,*** *or* ***blackcap,*** of eastern America (*R. occidentalis*) are derived numerous garden varieties. See CLOUDBERRY, BRAMBLE. **2.** [Orig. E. slang.] A sound of contempt produced with vibration of the tongue between the lips.

raspberry sawfly. A yellow-and-black hymenopteron (*Blennocampa rubi*) of which the pale-green larvae are a serious pest of cane fruits, esp. on the Pacific coast. They feed on the leaves and may strip the plants.

rasped (rȧspt), *adj.* Of book edges, uncut but roughened with a coarse rasp to imitate a deckle edge.

rasp′er (rȧs′pēr; 9), *n.* One who or that which rasps.

rasp′ing, *adj.* Grating; scraping; raucous.

rasp′y (rȧs′pĭ; 9), *adj.;* RASP′I·ER (-pĭ·ēr); RASP′I·EST. **a** Like a rasp, or the sound made by a rasp; grating. **b** Irritable.

ras′ter (răs′tēr), *n.* [G., screen.] *Television.* The area upon which the image is reproduced in the cathode-ray tube of a receiving set.

ra′sure (rā′zhēr), *n.* [F. or L.; F., fr. L. *rasura,* fr. *radere, rasum,* to scrape.] Erasure; obliteration.

rat (răt), *n.* [AS. *ræt.*] **1.** Any of certain rodents (genus *Rattus,* and allied genera) distinguished from mice by their larger size and differences in the teeth. See RODENT, *Illust.* The best-known species are the ***brown,*** *or* ***Norway, rat*** (*R. norvegicus*), about ten inches long, excluding the tail; the ***black rat*** (*R. rattus*), a smaller species with a longer tail and larger ears; and the ***roof rat*** (*R. r. alexandrinus*), a variety of the black rat. Cf. MUSKRAT, WHITE RAT. **2.** [From the belief that rats desert a falling house or sinking ship.] *Slang.* A vile sneak or thieving fellow; a contemptible deserter or betrayer, as of fellow workmen. **3.** *Colloq., U. S.* A pad with tapering ends for the hair. — *v. i.;* RAT′TED (-ĕd; -ĭd); RAT′TING. **1.** To play the rat; specif., to forsake one's associates for one's own advantage. **2.** To catch or hunt rats, esp. with a dog.

rat′a·ble, rate′a·ble (rāt′ȧ·b'l), *adj.* **1.** Capable of being rated, appraised, or estimated. **2.** Proportional; as, a *ratable* distribution of an estate. **3.** *Eng.* Liable to taxation. — **rat′a·bil′i·ty, rate′a·bil′i·ty** (-bĭl′ĭ·tĭ), *n.* — **rat′a·bly, rate′a·bly,** *adv.*

rat′a·fi′a (răt′ȧ·fē′ȧ), *n.* Also **rat′a·fee′** (-fē′). [F. *ratafia.*] **1.** Any liqueur flavored with fruit kernels, esp. of a bitter almond flavor. **2.** A sweet almond-flavored biscuit.

rat′al (rāt′ăl), *n.* [*rate* + *-al.*] Amount at which a person is rated with reference to assessment. — **rat′al,** *adj.*

rat′a·plan′ (răt′ȧ·plăn′), *n.* [F.] The iterative sound or beating, as from a drum, or the hoofs of a galloping horse.

rat′bite′ fe′ver *or* **dis·ease′** (răt′bīt′). *Med.* An infectious disease, following the bite of a rat, with ulceration, relapsing fever, rash, etc. It is prevalent in Japan.

ratch (răch), *n.* [See RATCHET.] A notched bar with which a pawl or click works to prevent reversal of motion.

ratch′et (răch′ĕt; -ĭt), *n.* [F. *rochet* ratchet, bobbin.] **1.** A pawl, click, or detent, for holding or propelling a ratchet wheel, ratch, etc. **2.** A mechanism composed of a ratchet wheel and pawl.

ratchet jack. See JACK, *Illust.*

ratchet wheel. *Mach.* A circular wheel having teeth with which a reciprocating pawl engages.

rate (rāt), *v. t. & i.* [ME. *raten.*] To berate; chide; scold violently.

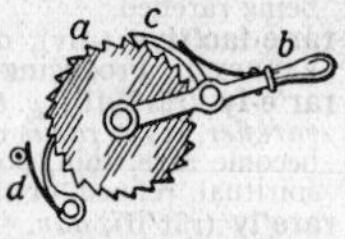

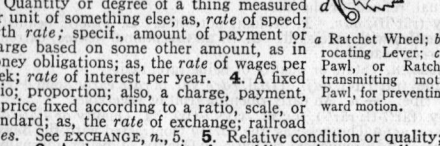

a Ratchet Wheel; *b* Reciprocating Lever; *c* Click, Pawl, or Ratchet for transmitting motion; *d* Pawl, for preventing backward motion.

rate, *n.* [OF., fr. L. *rata* (sc. *pars*), fr. *ratus*, past part. of *reri* to reckon.] **1.** *Obs.* Amount or quantity. **2.** Value; price. **3.** Quantity or degree of a thing measured per unit of something else; as, *rate* of speed; birth *rate;* specif., amount of payment or charge based on some other amount, as in money obligations; as, the *rate* of wages per week; *rate* of interest per year. **4.** A fixed ratio; proportion; also, a charge, payment, or price fixed according to a ratio, scale, or standard; as, the *rate* of exchange; railroad *rates.* See EXCHANGE, *n.*, 5. **5.** Relative condition or quality; rank; class. **6.** A charge per unit of a public-service commodity such as electricity, gas, water, or the like; as, an electric *rate* of 7 cents per kilowatt-hour. **7.** *Econ. Usually pl.* A unit charge or ratio used by the government for assessing taxes; esp., in England, a local tax; as, parish *rates.* **8.** *Insurance.* The amount of premium per unit of insurance, sometimes expressed as a percentage. — ***at any rate.*** **a** At the least; anyhow. **b** In any circumstances or event.
— *v. t.* **1.** *Now Rare.* To calculate the amount of. **2.** To consider; reckon. **3.** To appraise; value; specif., to assess the value of for a rate or tax. **4.** To settle the relative rank, class, or quality of; as, to *rate* a ship, a seaman. **5.** *U. S.* To arrange for the transportation of (goods, by rail, water, etc.) at a certain rate. — *v. i.* To be classed; to have rating or rank. — **Syn.** See ESTIMATE.

rate′a·bil′i·ty, rate′a·ble, rate′a·bly. Vars. of RATABILITY, RATABLE, etc.

ra′tel (rā′tĕl; rä′-), *n.* [S. Afr. D., for *rateldas*, fr. D. *raat* honeycomb + *das* badger.] A musteline, badgerlike mammal (genus *Mellivora*) of South Africa and India.

rate′pay′er (rāt′pā′ẽr), *n.* *Brit.* One who pays rates, or local taxes. — **rate′pay′ing,** *adj. & n.*

rat′er (rāt′ẽr), *n.* One who rates, or scolds.

rat′er (rāt′ẽr), *n.* One who rates, estimates, etc.

rathe (rāth), *adv.* Also **rath** (råth). [AS. *hrathe, hræthe.*] **1.** *Obs.* Quickly; soon. **2.** *Dial. & Poetic.* Early in the day, season, etc. — *adj.* [AS. *hræth* quick.] **1.** *Obs.* Quick; eager; speedy. **2.** *Dial. & Poetic.* Early in the day, season, etc. **3.** *Poetic.* Belonging to the early portion of the day, season, etc.

rath′er (råth′ẽr; 9), *adv.* [AS. *hrathor*, compar. of *hrathe, hræthe*, quickly, immediately.] **1.** *Obs. exc. Dial. Eng.* More quickly; earlier. **2.** More readily; preferably. **3.** On the other hand; to the contrary. **4.** Preferably from the point of view of wisdom, justice, etc. **5.** More properly; more correctly speaking. **6.** In some degree; somewhat.

raths′kel′ler (räts′kĕl′ẽr), *n.* [G., also *ratskeller*, prop., town-hall cellar.] A restaurant, usually below the street level, at which drinks are served, patterned after the German basement of a city hall where beer or wine is sold.

rat′i·cide (răt′ĭ·sīd), *n.* [See -CIDE, 1.] A substance used for killing rats. — **rat′i·cid′al** (-sīd′ăl; -′l; 2), *adj.*

rat′i·fi·ca′tion (răt′ĭ·fĭ·kā′shŭn), *n.* Act of ratifying; state of being ratified; confirmation; sanction.

rat′i·fy (răt′ĭ·fī), *v. t.*; -FIED (-fīd); -FY′ING. [OF. *ratifier*, fr. ML. *ratificare*, fr. L. *ratus* fixed by calculation, firm, valid + *-ficare* (in comp.) to make.] To approve and sanction, esp. formally; to confirm. — **rat′i·fi′er** (-fī′ẽr), *n.*

rat′i·né′ (răt′ĭ·nā′) *or* **ra·tine′** (ră·tēn′), *n.* [F. *ratiné* having had the nap frizzed or tufted.] A coarse loose-textured fabric, usually of cotton but also of silk, wool, worsted, rayon, or a mixture, woven with a rough surface full of nubs or knots, and used for dresses, suits, coats, etc.; — called also *sponge cloth.*

rat′ing (rāt′ĭng), *n.* Scolding; rebuke.

rat′ing, *n.* **1.** Classification according to grade; rank; class. **2.** Assessment of a tax. **3.** *Com.* An estimate as to the credit and responsibility of an individual or business concern. **4.** *Naut.* The relative standing or grade of a sailor in the ship's company; as, the *rating* of boatswain's mate. **5.** *Nav., Brit.* An enlisted man.

ra′tio (rā′shō; *as Latin*, rā′shĭ·ō), *n.* [L. See REASON.] **1.** Fixed or approximate relation, as between things or to another thing, in number, quantity, or degree; rate; proportion. **2.** *Now Rare.* A portion; a ration. **3.** *Finance.* The expression of the relative values of gold and silver as determined by the currency laws of a country. **4.** *Math.* The quotient of one magnitude divided by another of the same kind. *Ratio* was formerly regarded as different from *quotient* or a *fraction*, but no distinction is now ordinarily recognized.

ra′ti·oc′i·nate (răsh′ĭ·ŏs′ĭ·nāt), *v. i.* [L. *ratiocinatus*, past part. of *ratiocinari*, fr. *ratio* reason.] To reason. — **ra′ti·oc′i·na′tor** (-nā′tẽr), *n.*

ra′ti·oc′i·na′tion (-nā′shŭn), *n.* Reasoning or the process of exact thinking: also, a piece of reasoning. — **ra′ti·oc′i·na′tive** (-ŏs′ĭ·nā′tĭv), *adj.*

ra′tion (răsh′ŭn; rā′shŭn), *n.* [F., fr. L. *ratio* a reckoning, relation, in ML., ration.] **1.** An allowance; share. **2.** An allowance of provisions; an allotment or share as determined esp. by supply; as, the sugar *ration;* the gasoline *ration;* esp., *Mil. & Nav.*, a fixed daily allowance assigned to a soldier or a sailor for his subsistence. — *v. t.* **1.** To supply with rations. **2.** To allot in rations; as, to *ration* meats, sugar, oil.

ra′tion·al (răsh′ŭn·ăl; -′l), *adj.* [L. *rationalis.*] **1.** Having reason or understanding; reasoning. **2.** Of the nature of, based upon, derived from, concerned with, or characterized by reason. **3.** Agreeable to reason; intelligent; sensible. **4.** *Gr. & Lat. Pros.* Capable of being measured in terms of the mora or metrical unit; having the normal ratio between arsis and thesis. **5.** *Math.* Not involving a surd. — *n.* That which is rational. — **ra′tion·al·ly,** *adv.*

ra′tion·ale′ (răsh′ŭn·ăl′; -äl′; -ā′lē; -ä′lē), *n.* [L. *rationalis*, neut. *rationale.*] **1.** *Now Rare.* An explanation or exposition of the principles of some opinion, hypothesis, or the like. **2.** The underlying reason; rational foundation.

ra′tion·al·ism (răsh′ŭn·ăl·ĭz′m; -′l·ĭz′m), *n.* **1.** The practice of guiding one's opinions and actions solely by what is considered reasonable. **2.** *Philos.* The theory that reason is a source of knowledge in itself, superior to and independent of sense perceptions; — opposed to *sensationalism.* **3.** *Theol.* Explanation according to reason of what appears supernatural. — **ra′tion·al·ist** (-ĭst), *n.* — **ra′tion·al·is′tic** (-ĭs′tĭk), **ra′tion·al·is′ti·cal** (-tĭ·kăl), *adj.* — **ra′tion·al·is′ti·cal·ly,** *adv.*

ra′tion·al′i·ty (-ăl′ĭ·tĭ), *n.; pl.* -TIES (-tĭz). **1.** Quality or state of being rational, or having reasoning power. **2.** An opinion, practice, etc., that is rational. **3.** Rationalism.

ra′tion·al·ize (răsh′ŭn·ăl·īz; -′l·īz), *v. t.* **1.** To give a rational or rationalistic explanation of; as: **a** To make conformable to principles satisfactory to reason. **b** To explain or justify on rational or rationalistic grounds. **c** To free from elements not in harmony with rational or rationalistic principles; as, to *rationalize* the Greek myths. **2.** *Psychol.* To attribute (one's actions) to rational and creditable motives, without adequate analysis of the true motives. — **ra′tion·al·i·za′tion** (-ĭ·zā′shŭn; -ī·zā′-), *n.* — **ra′tion·al·iz′er** (-īz′ẽr), *n.*

rational number. An integer or ratio of two integers.

rat′ite (răt′īt), *adj.* [L. *ratis* a raft.] Having a flat breastbone; unkeeled. — *n.* Any of a division (Ratitae) of flightless birds with no keel to the breastbone, including the ostriches, emus, cassowaries, moas, etc.

rat′line, rat′lin (răt′lĭn), *n.* [Origin uncert.] *Naut.* **a** Small, usually three-stranded, tarred rope used for ratlines (sense **b**). **b** One of the small transverse ropes attached to the shrouds and forming a rope ladder.

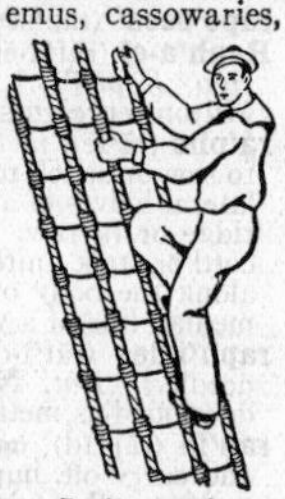
Ratlines and Shrouds.

ra·toon′ (ră·tōōn′), *n.* [Sp. *retoño.*] *Agric.* A shoot of a perennial plant, as of cotton or sugar cane; specif., one of the second year's growth from the root. — *v. i.* To sprout or spring up from the root, as sugar cane.

rats′bane′ (răts′bān′), *n.* [*rat* + *bane.*] Rat poison, esp. white arsenic (see ARSENIC).

rat·tan′ (ră·tăn′), *n.* [Malay *rotan.*] **1. a** Also **rattan palm.** Any climbing palm (genera *Calamus* and *Daemonorops*) remarkable for the great length of the stems. **b** A portion of one of these stems, used for walking sticks, wickerwork, etc. **2.** A cane or switch made from one of these stems.

rat·teen′ (ră·tēn′), *n.* [F. *ratine.*] In the 17th and 18th centuries, any of a variety of coarse woolen fabrics such as baize, drugget, and frieze.

rat′ten (răt′'n), *v. t. & i.* [E. dial. *ratten* a rat, hence, lit., to do mischief like a rat.] *Eng. Trade Union Cant.* To sabotage. — **rat′ten·er** (-ẽr), *n.*

rat′ter (răt′ẽr), *n.* One that rats; as: **a** One who deserts his party in adversity. **b** A person employed to catch rats; also, a rat-catching dog.

rat′tle (răt′'l), *v. t.*; RAT′TLED (-'ld); RAT′TLING (-lĭng). *Naut.* To furnish with ratlines; — often with *down.*

rat′tle, *v. i.* [ME. *ratelen.*] **1.** To make a rapid succession of short sharp noises, as of hard bodies striking against each other. **2.** *Colloq.* To chatter incessantly and aimlessly. **3.** To move or proceed with a clatter. — *v. t.* **1.** To cause to make a rattling sound. **2.** To say, perform, affect, etc., in a brisk, lively fashion, esp. with a rattle or clatter. **3.** To rouse; specif., to beat (a cover) for game; to chase hard (game, etc.). **4.** *Colloq.* To disconcert; confuse; agitate. — **Syn.** See EMBARRASS.
— *n.* **1.** A rapid succession of sharp, clattering sounds. **2.** An instrument with which a rattling sound is made. **3.** The sound-producing organ on a rattlesnake's tail. **4.** Noise; racket. **5.** The noise in the throat caused by air passing through mucus, chiefly observable at approach of death.

rat′tle·brained′ (răt′'l·brānd′), **rat′tle·head′ed** (-hĕd′ĕd; -ĭd; 2), **rat′tle·pat′ed** (-pāt′ĕd; -ĭd; 2), *adj.* Giddy; flighty; harebrained. — **rat′tle·brain′** (-brān′), **rat′tle·head′** (-hĕd′), **rat′tle·pate′** (-pāt′), *n.*

rat′tler (răt′lẽr), *n.* One that rattles; esp., a rattlesnake.

rat′tle·snake′ (răt′'l·snāk′), *n.* Any of certain American venomous snakes (family Crotalidae, genera *Sistrurus* and *Crotalus*) having horny interlocking joints at the end of the tail which make a sharp rattling sound when shaken; a rattler. They are thick-bodied snakes of sluggish disposition. They are distributed from southern Canada southward to Argentina. The ***banded,*** *or* ***timber, rattlesnake*** (*Crotalus horridus*) is the common species of the northeastern United States. The ***diamondback rattlesnake*** (*C. adamanteus*), sometimes eight feet long, is so named from the markings on the back, and occurs from Alabama and Georgia to Florida. In Texas, New Mexico, and Arizona the best-known species is the ***western diamond rattlesnake*** (*C. atrox*). Farther north the ***prairie rattlesnake*** (*C. confluentus*) is common. See FANG, *Illust.*

rattlesnake plantain. Any orchid of the genus *Peramium;* — so called in allusion to the checked or mottled leaves.

rattlesnake root. **a** Any of various plants (genus *Prenanthes*, esp. *P. altissima*) formerly of repute in the southern United States as a remedy for snake bites. **b** The senega root.

rattlesnake weed. **a** One of the hawkweeds (*Hieracium venosum*), probably named from its purple-veined leaves. **b** A weedy herb (*Daucus pusillus*) of the western United States, related to the wild carrot. **c** Rattlesnake plantain.

rat′tle·trap′ (răt′'l·trăp′), *n.* **1.** A rickety rattling vehicle. **2.** *Slang.* **a** A talkative person. **b** The mouth.

rat′tling (răt′lĭng), *adj.* That rattles; hence: **a** Lively; brisk. **b** *Colloq.* Remarkably fast, good, etc.

rat′tling (răt′lĭn). Var. of RATLINE.

rat′ton (răt′ŭn), *n.* *Dial.* A rat.

rat·toon′ (ră·tōōn′). Var. of RATOON.

rat′trap′ (răt′trăp′), *n.* A trap set for rats; hence, a situation in which one is hopelessly doomed.

rat′ty (răt′ĭ), *adj.* **1.** Characteristic of or abounding in rats. **2.** *Slang.* Shabby in appearance.

rau′cous (rô′kŭs), *adj.* [L. *raucus.*] Hoarse; disagreeably harsh; strident; as, a *raucous* voice. — **rau′ci·ty** (rô′sĭ·tĭ), *n.* — **rau′cous·ly,** *adv.* — **rau′cous·ness,** *n.*

raught (rôt; *Scot.* rôKT). Scot. & dial. past of REACH.

rav′age (răv′ĭj), *n.* [F., fr. *ravir* to ravish. See RAVISH.] **1.** Violently destructive action. **2.** Havoc or damage; ruin; devastation. — *v. t.*; RAV′AGED (-ĭjd); RAV′AG·ING (-ĭj·ĭng). To lay waste; plunder. — *v. i.* To commit ravages. — **rav′ag·er** (-ĭj·ẽr), *n.*

Syn. **Ravage, devastate, waste, sack, pillage, despoil** mean to lay waste by plundering or destroying. **Ravage** implies, usually, the cumulative effect of successive invasions, depredations, etc.; **devastate** and the less common **waste** imply the ruin and desolation which follow a ravaging; **sack** implies the capturing and stripping of valuable possessions by the victorious army; **pillage** implies a ruthless plundering by an invading or victorious army; **despoil**, much like *sack*, less often refers to towns or cities than to churches, palaces, etc.

rave (rāv), *v. i.* [OF. *raver, rever,* to rave, revel (F. *rêver* to dream, rave).] **1.** To talk irrationally, as in delirium; hence, to declaim passionately. **2.** To storm; rage. **3.** To talk with excessive enthusiasm; as, to *rave* about one's beauty. — *v. t.* To utter in madness or frenzy. — *n.* **1.** A raving. **2.** *Slang.* **a** An infatuation; crush. **b** An extravagant commendation. — *adj.* Extravagantly commendatory.

rav'el (răv'ĕl; -'l), *v. t.;* -ELED (-ĕld; -'ld) or -ELLED; -EL·ING or EL·LING. [MD. *ravelen,* D. *rafelen.*] **1.** *Dial & Poetic.* To let fall into a tangled mass; hence, to entangle; to make intricate. **2.** To unravel, untwist, unweave, or the like. **3.** To disentangle; to make plain. — *v. i.* **1.** *Obs.* To become entangled or confused. **2.** To become untwisted, unwoven, or unwound; to fray. — *n.* Act or result of raveling; as: **a** A tangled mass; a snarl. **b** Something raveled or torn; a raveling. — **rav'el·er, rav'el·ler,** *n.*

rave'lin (răv'lĭn), *n.* [F.] *Fort.* A detached work with two embankments which make a salient angle.

rav'el·ing, rav'el·ling (răv'ĕl·ĭng; -'l·ĭng), *n.* That which is raveled out; esp., a thread detached from a texture.

rav'el·ment (răv'ĕl·mĕnt; -'l·mĕnt), *n.* A ravel, or tangle.

rav'en (răv'ĕn), *v. t.* [OF. *raviner* to take by force, ravish.] **1.** *Obs.* To seize by violence. **2.** To devour eagerly. — *v. i.* To prey with rapacity; to feed greedily; to be or become ravenous. — *n.* Var. of RAVIN.

ra'ven (rā'vĕn), *n.* [AS. *hræfn.*] A glossy-black corvine bird (*Corvus corax*) of northern Europe, Asia, and America. See CROW. — *adj.* Of the glossy black color of the raven.

rav'en·ing (răv'ĕn·ĭng), *adj.* That ravens; devouring; rapacious; preying; voracious. — *n.* = RAVIN.

rav'en·ous (-ŭs), *adj.* [OF. *ravinos* rapacious, violent.] **1.** Rapacious; voracious. **2.** Eager for food, satisfaction, or gratification. — **rav'en·ous·ly,** *adv.* — **rav'en·ous·ness,** *n.*

rav'in (răv'ĭn), *n.* Rapine; rapacity; also, something seized as prey; prey. — *v. t. & i.* Var. of RAVEN.

ra·vine' (rȧ·vēn'), *n.* [F., fr. OF. *ravine* impetuosity, fr. L. *rapina* rapine.] A depression worn out by running water, larger than a gully and smaller than a valley.

rav'ing (rāv'ĭng), *n.* Irrational, wild, or extravagant utterance. — *adj.* Talking wildly or irrationally.

‖**ra·vi·o'li** (rä·vyô'lē; *Angl.* răv'ĭ·ō'lĭ), *n. pl.* [It., pl. of *ravi(u)olo.*] Little shells or cases of thin noodle dough, containing a savory forcemeat.

rav'ish (răv'ĭsh), *v. t.* [OF. *ravir,* fr. L. *rapere* to tear away, ravish.] **1.** To seize and carry away by violence. **2.** To transport with emotion, esp. with joy or delight. **3.** To abduct (a woman); hence, to rape. — **rav'ish·er,** *n.*

rav'ish·ing, *adj.* That ravishes; esp., that inspires joy or delight; as, *ravishing* beauty. — **rav'ish·ing·ly,** *adv.*

rav'ish·ment (-mĕnt), *n.* Act, means, or effect of ravishing; state of being ravished; esp., rapture; ecstasy.

raw (rô), *adj.* [AS. *hrēaw, hrēaw.*] **1.** Not cooked. **2.** In, or nearly in, the natural state; little changed by art; unwrought; specif.: **a** Not spun or twisted; as, *raw* silk. **b** Not mixed or diluted; as, *raw* spirits. **c** Not tanned; as, *raw* hides. **3. a** Not prepared for use or enjoyment; unfinished; untrained. **b** Not refined; rude; crude; also, indelicate; coarse. **4.** Deprived of skin; galled; as, a *raw* sore. **5.** Disagreeably damp or cold; bleak. — **Syn.** See RUDE. — *n.* A raw, sore, or galled place; a sensitive spot. — **raw'ly,** *adv.* — **raw'ness,** *n.*

raw'boned' (rô'bōnd'; 2), *adj.* Having little flesh; gaunt. — **Syn.** See LEAN.

raw'hide' (-hīd'), *n.* Untanned cattle skin; specif., a whip of untanned (or raw) hide twisted, braided, or rolled.

raw material. Material available or suitable for manufacture, development, training, etc., but still raw (sense 2).

raw silk. Reeled silk (before it is thrown).

rax (răks; *dial.* râks), *v. i. & t.* [AS. *raxan.*] *Scot.* To stretch; reach; strain.

ray (rā), *n.* [OF. *raie,* fr. L. *raia.*] *Zool.* Any of numerous elasmobranch fishes (order Batoidei) which have the body flattened dorsoventrally, with the eyes on the upper surface, and a much-reduced, often whiplike, caudal region. The chief rays include: the ***whip-tailed rays or whip rays,*** constituting a suborder (Masticura), including the ***sting ray or stingray or stingaree*** (family Dasyatidae) with one or more sharp, barbed dorsal spines, near the base of the whiplike tail, capable of inflicting severe wounds; the ***thick-tailed rays,*** constituting a suborder (Sarcura), including the ***electric ray,*** known also as ***crampfish, numbfish, or torpedo*** (family Torpedinidae) with the body disklike in front, a short tail, and a pair of electric organs between the head and the pectoral fins; numerous sharklike rays of a family (Rhinobatidae) found in all warm seas and variously called according to their shape ***fiddlerfish, guitarfish,*** etc.; and the ***skate*** (family Rajidae) and ***sawfish*** (see these terms). See DEVILFISH, *Illust.*

ray, *n.* [OF. *rai,* fr. L. *radius* a beam or ray.] **1.** One of the lines of light which appear to radiate from a bright object. Cf. BEAM, *n.,* 7. **2.** A glance; sight; perception; vision; — from an old theory of vision. **3. a** Light of a ray or rays; radiance. **b** Moral or intellectual light or a gleam of such light. **4.** A small amount; a particle; as, not a *ray* of courage. **5.** A thin line like a ray; esp., one of a number diverging from a center. **6.** *Bot.* **a** A ray flower. **b** A branch or flower stalk of an umbel. **c** A medullary ray. **7.** *Physics.* **a** A beam of light or, in general, of radiant energy. **b** The geometrical line, normal to the wavefront, in which light, heat, or the like, is propagated. **c** A stream of material particles traveling in the same line, as in radioactive phenomena. **8.** *Zool.* **a** One of the bony rods which extend and support the membrane in the fin of a fish. **b** One of the radiating divisions of the body of a radiate animal, as an arm of a starfish. — *v. i.* **1.** To shine; to emit rays; also, to issue as rays. **2.** To radiate. — *v. t.* **1.** To send forth or emit in rays. **2.** To expose to rays, as X rays, radiations from radium, or ultraviolet light.

ra'yah (rä'yȧ). Var. of RAIA.

ray flower. Also **ray floret.** *Bot.* One of the marginal flowers of the head in many plants of the aster family (Carduaceae), as the aster, goldenrod, daisy, and sunflower. See COMPOSITE, *Illust.*

ray'less (rā'lĕs; -lĭs), *adj.* Destitute of rays; hence: **a** Dark; blind. **b** Having no rays or raylike parts.

ray'on (rā'ŏn), *n.* [Arbitrarily formed in English (not fr. F. *rayon* ray), with suggestion of E. *ray* beam, light.] A synthetic fiber made by forcing a viscous solution of modified cellulose (usually viscose) through minute holes and drying the filaments; also, a yarn or fabric made from this material. — **ray'on,** *adj.*

raze (rāz), *v. t.* [F. *raser* to scrape, shave. See RASE.] **1.** To scrape; graze; wound slightly. **2.** To scrape, cut, or shave off; to erase. **3.** To lay level with the ground; demolish; hence, to overthrow; destroy; remove utterly.

ra·zee' (rā·zē'), *n.* [F. *vaisseau rasé,* fr. *raser* to raze, razee.] *Obs. Naut.* A ship having her upper deck cut away, and thus reduced to the next inferior class. — *v. t.;* RA·ZEED' (-zēd'); RA·ZEE'ING. To cut down to a less number of decks, as a ship.

ra'zor (rā'zẽr), *n.* [OF. *rasor,* fr. *raser.*] A keen-edged cutting instrument used in shaving.

ra'zor·back' (-băk'), *n.* **1.** A rorqual. **2.** A thin-bodied, long-legged, half-wild hog of the southeastern United States.

razz (răz), *n.* [From RASPBERRY, 2.] *Slang.* = RASPBERRY, *n.,* 2. — *v. t. & i. Slang, U.S.* To chaff; banter; tease.

r'–col'ored (är'kŭl'ẽrd), *adj.* Of vowels, pronounced with simultaneous *r* quality resulting from a following *r* sound formerly or still present. The retroflex vowels used for the *ur* and *er* in *further* in one type of American speech are *r-colored.*

re (rā; rē), *n.* [It., fr. L. *re*sonare to resound.] *Music.* A syllable applied in solmization to the second tone of the diatonic scale.

re (rē), *n.* [Abl. of L. *res* thing.] In or of the thing or matter; — commonly used prepositionally for *in re* in business correspondence; as, *re* your letter of the 3d instant.

re-. [F. or L.; F. *re-, ré-,* fr. L. *re-, red-.*] A prefix denoting: **1.** *Back,* esp. *back to an original* or *former state* or *position; backwards,* as in *re*trace, *re*cede; also, *back from advancing,* as in *re*frain. **2.** *Again;* — used chiefly to form words denoting *repetition* (of the action of the verb), as in *re*iterate or *re*invest, or *restoration* (to a previous state), as in *re*new.

Re (rā), *n. Egypt. Relig.* = RA.

re'ab·sorb' (rē'ăb·sôrb'), *v. t.* To absorb again. — **re'ab·sorp'tion** (-sôrp'shŭn), *n.*

reach (rēch), *v. t.* [AS. *rǣcan.*] **1.** To extend; to stretch out; to thrust out, as a limb. **2.** To strike, hit, or touch, with a missile. **3.** To hand over. **4.** To touch, strike, grasp, seize, or the like, by extending some part of the body, esp. the hand. **5.** To extend to; to stretch out as far as. **6.** To arrive at; to come to. **7.** To influence or impress. **8.** To communicate with; get in touch with.

Syn. **Reach, gain, compass, achieve, attain** mean to arrive at by effort. **Reach,** the broadest term, may be used in reference to anything arrived at by any degree of effort; **gain** implies a struggle to reach; **compass,** efforts to get around difficulties or to transcend limitations; **achieve,** skill or endurance as well as effort; **attain,** aspiration or ambition and an end beyond the scope or powers of most men.

— *v. i.* **1.** To stretch out the hand or arm. **2.** To extend in dimension, time, amount, action, influence, etc. **3.** To get or make its way (to a place, point, or the like); also, of a gun, the voice, the eye, or the like, to carry; as, as far as the eye can *reach.* **4.** To strain after something; to make efforts. **5.** *Naut.* To sail directly on one's course with the wind forward of the beam.

— *n.* **1.** Act of reaching, or stretching out. **2. a** An extent; stretch; expanse. **b** A level stretch, as between locks in a canal; an arm of the sea extending up into the land; a promontory or tongue of land. **3.** Power of seizing, obtaining, touching, or affecting something; esp., extent of such power. **4.** Extent or range of force, capacity, or the like. **5.** A coupling pole, esp. one joining the hind axle to the forward transverse bar of a wagon. **6.** *Naut.* A leg sailed by a vessel between tacks; also, a course of sailing with the wind forward of the beam but not enough so to compel tacking.

reach'er (rēch'ẽr), *n.* One who or that which reaches.

re·act' (rē·ăkt'), *v. i.* **1.** To act (*on* or *upon*) in turn or in return; to exert a return, reciprocal, or counteracting influence. **2.** To act in response, as to a stimulus, influence, or a reagent; to respond. **3.** To show a reaction, or reverse trend; to turn back to a prior condition, a lower price, or the like; as, stocks *reacted* markedly. **4.** Loosely, to act, behave, operate, function, etc., esp. under particular circumstances; as, how did he *react* when he heard the news?

re·act'ance (rē·ăk'tăns), *n.* [*react* + *-ance.*] *Elec.* That part of the impedance of an alternating-current circuit which is due to capacitance or inductance or both. It is expressed in ohms.

re·ac'tion (rē·ăk'shŭn), *n.* **1.** Reciprocal or return action or influence. **2.** A counter tendency; esp., in politics, a movement towards a former political or social policy. **3.** Retaliatory or responsive effect of stimulation; response; as, one's *reaction* to a piece of news. **4.** *Bacteriol. & Immunol.* The specific effect characteristically evoked in cells or tissues by a foreign substance, as in tests for infection. **5.** *Chem. & Physics.* **a** Chemical transformation or change; a chemical process or its manner or result. **b** A process involving change in atomic nuclei; — called specifically ***nuclear reaction.*** For example, the process by which uranium 239 disintegrates into neptunium and an electron is a nuclear reaction. **6.** *Mech.* The force which a body opposes to a force acting upon it. **7.** *Med.* **a** An action induced by vital resistance to some other action. **b** Depression or exhaustion of vital force consequent on overexertion or overstimulation. **c** Heightened activity succeeding depression or shock. **8.** *Physiol. & Psychol.* Activity aroused in an organism by a stimulus; a response.

re·ac'tion·ar'y (-ẽr'ĭ *or, esp. Brit.,* -ẽr·ĭ), *adj.* Of, pertaining to, characterized by, or favoring reaction, or a return to an older order. — *n.; pl.* -ARIES (-ĭz). One who favors reaction, esp. in politics or policies.

re·ac'tion·ist (-ĭst), *n.* A reactionary. — *adj.* Reactionary.

re·ac'tive (rē·ăk'tĭv), *adj.* That reacts, tends to react, or results from reaction.

re·ac'tor (-tẽr), *n.* **1.** One that reacts. **2.** A vat for an industrial chemical reaction. **3.** *Elec.* A device (as a coil, winding, or conductor of small resistance) used to introduce reactance into an alternating-current circuit. **4.** *Immunol.* An individual reacting positively to a foreign substance, esp. in test for disease. **5.** *Physics.* = PILE, *n.,* 5.

read (rēd), *v. t.;* READ (rĕd); READ'ING (rēd'ĭng). [AS. *rǣdan* to read, advise, counsel, guess.] **1.** To take in the sense of, as of language, by interpreting the characters with which it is expressed; to peruse. **2.** To utter aloud or render something written, esp. so as to give an interpretation of its significance. **3.** **a** To learn or be informed of by perusal. **b** To learn, or discover the nature of, by observing closely as if perusing a book. **4.** To interpret; hence, to foresee or foretell. **5.** To attribute (a meaning) to what is read; to infer as meant in something read. **6.** To make a special study of, as by perusing books on; as, to *read* law. **7.** To register; indicate; — of a meter, thermometer, etc. — *v. i.* **1.** To perform the act of reading the words of a book, letters, etc. **2.** To utter aloud what is written, either while perusing it or from memory. **3.** To inform oneself by reading; — usually with *of.* **4.** To have import, or be in effect, as to terms or the like, when read; as, this ticket *reads* to Boston. **5.** To be expressed by, or consist of, certain words; as, the passage *reads* thus in early manuscripts. **6.** To study, esp. by reading. — *n.* A period of reading.

read (rĕd), *adj.* Informed through reading; as, a well-*read* man.

read′a·ble (rēd′ȧ·b'l), *adj.* **a** Legible, as handwriting. **b** Easy to read, because interesting. — **read′a·bil′i·ty** (-bĭl′ĭ·tĭ), *n.* — **read′a·ble·ness,** *n.* — **read′a·bly,** *adv.*

read′er (rēd′ẽr), *n.* **1.** One who reads. **2.** Specif.: **a** A professional reciter; an elocutionist. **b** An employee who reads meters, indexes, etc. **c** A proofreader. **d** One who reads manuscripts offered for publication and advises regarding their merit. **3.** A book containing selections for reading. **4.** *Eccl.* One appointed or authorized to read the lessons or prayers, etc., in a place of worship. **5.** *Educ. & Law.* One who reads lectures or expounds subjects; a teacher; a lecturer.

read′er·ship (rēd′ẽr·shĭp), *n.* **1.** See -SHIP. **2.** The number of readers of a newspaper, periodical, a column, etc.; — distinguished from *circulation.*

read′i·ly (rĕd′ĭ·lĭ), *adv.* **1.** With cheerful readiness; without delay or objection. **2.** With promptness; quickly.

read′i·ness (rĕd′ĭ·nĕs; -nĭs), *n.* **1.** Quality of being ready; promptness; alacrity. **2.** State or fact of being ready.

read′ing (rēd′ĭng), *n.* **1.** Act of one who reads; as: **a** Perusal. **b** Recital of a bill in a legislature. **2.** That which is read; hence, a public recital or lecture. **3.** The form in which anything is written; a version. **4.** Study of books; literary scholarship. **5.** Written or printed matter intended to be read. **6.** Manner of rendering something written; as, an actor's *reading* of a part; also, interpretation; as, my *reading* of his character. **7.** That which is indicated so as to be read, as on the scale of a barometer. — *adj.* **1.** That reads or studies. **2.** Of or for reading; as, *reading* matter; a *reading* glass or lamp.

reading desk. A desk to support a book while reading, esp. in a church service; a lectern.

re′ad·just′ (rē′ȧ·jŭst′), *v. t.* To adjust anew; to rearrange. — **re′ad·just′er** (-jŭs′tẽr), *n.*

re′ad·just′ment (-mĕnt), *n.* Act or result of readjusting; specif., *Finance,* the reconstruction or rehabilitation of a corporation, effected usually by the voluntary action of the security holders. Cf. REORGANIZATION, 2.

re′ad·mis′sion (rē′ăd·mĭsh′ŭn), *n.* Act of readmitting.

re′ad·mit′ (rē′ăd·mĭt′), *v. t.* To admit again; to give entrance or access to again.

re′ad·mit′tance (-mĭt′ăns), *n.* Readmission.

read′y (rĕd′ĭ), *adj.*; READ′I·ER (-ĭ·ẽr); READ′I·EST. [AS. *rǣde, gerǣde.*] **1.** Prepared or supplied with what is needed for some act or event. **2.** Fitted or arranged for immediate use. **3.** Immediately liable; likely; — esp. with *to.* **4.** Willing; disposed. **5.** Dexterous; expert. **6.** Prompt; as, a *ready* answer. **7.** Offering itself at once; available; handy; as, *ready* assets; *ready* money. **8.** *Obs.* **a** Of payment, not deferred; promptly rendered. **b** Present; here; — used in answer to a roll call. — **Syn.** See QUICK.
— *v. t.*; READ′IED (-ĭd); READ′Y·ING. To make ready; to put in a state of order or preparation.
— *n.* **1.** *Colloq.* Ready money; cash; — often with *the.* **2.** *Mil.* A position of preparation in the manual of arms or in artillery drill, at which the piece is cocked or prepared for firing.

read′y-made′ (-mād′; 2), *adj.* Made beforehand, in anticipation of need; specif., made for general sale; as, *ready-made* clothing; hence, lacking originality or individuality; as, *ready-made* beliefs.

read′y-to-wear′, *adj.* Ready-made; — of clothing.

read′y-wit′ted (*see Pron.,* § 2), *adj.* Quick-witted.

re′af·firm′ (rē′ȧ·fûrm′), *v. t.* To affirm again in order to strengthen or confirm. — **re′af·firm′ance** (-fûr′măns), **re′af·fir·ma′tion** (rē′ăf·ẽr·mā′shŭn), *n.*

re·a′gent (rē·ā′jĕnt), *n.* *Chem., etc.* Any substance which, from its capacity for certain reactions, is used in detecting, examining, or measuring other substances, etc.

re′al (rē′ăl; *Sp.* rrē·äl′), *n.*; *pl.* REALS (rē′ălz), REALES (rrē·ä′lās). [Sp., fr. *real* royal, fr. L. *regalis.*] **a** The former silver coin unit of the Spanish monetary system, eight of which made the dollar. Cf. PIECE OF EIGHT. **b** (rē·äl′) Sing. of REIS.

re′al (rē′ăl; rē′ăl; 27), *adj.* [OF. (F. *réel*), fr. ML. *realis,* fr. L. *res, rei,* a thing.] **1.** Existent as a thing, state, or quality; having actuality; as, *real* events. **2.** Genuine; not artificial, counterfeit, or factitious; — often opposed to *ostensible;* as, the *real* reason. **3.** Relating to things or events, esp. to physical things, rather than to persons or opinions. **4.** Representing reality; corresponding to what is; true. **5.** *Law.* **a** Of or pertaining to things themselves; as, a *real* action; a *real* right; — opp. to *personal.* **b** Specif.: *Eng. & Amer. Law.* Pertaining to, or consisting of, things fixed, permanent, or immovable, as lands and tenements; as, *real* property, in distinction from personal property. **6.** *Math.* Having no imaginary part; as, a *real* number. **7.** *Philos.* **a** Actually existing; actual, as disting. from *fictitious* or *imaginary,* or the ideal. **b** Self-existent or pertaining to the self-existent; absolute, as opposed to *derivative* or *dependent;* fundamental and ultimate, as opposed to merely *apparent* or *phenomenal;* intrinsic and of the essence, as opp. to *nominal* or *relative.*
Syn. Real, actual, true mean correspondent to known or knowable facts. Real implies correspondence between what a thing seems to be and what it is; actual, occurrence or manifest existence; true, conformity to what is real or what is actual.
— *n.* Something which is real; also, with *the,* actual state of affairs; in a metaphysical sense, reality in general.

real estate *or* **property.** Lands, tenements, and hereditaments; freehold interests in landed property; property in houses and land. — **re′al-es·tate′,** *adj.*

re·al′gar (rē·ăl′gẽr), *n.* [ML. *realgar,* through Catalan & Sp., fr. Ar. *rahj al-ghār* powder of the mine.] *Mineral.* Arsenic monosulfide, AsS, an orange-red mineral of resinous luster, used in pyrotechny and formerly as a pigment.

re′al·ism (rē′ăl·ĭz'm; rē′ăl-), *n.* **1.** *Philos.* **a** The doctrine that universals exist outside the mind; — opposed to *nominalism.* Cf. CONCEPTUALISM. **b** The conception that objects of sense perception (and, sometimes, of cognition in general) are real in their own right, existing independently of their being known or related to mind; — opposed to *idealism.* **2.** Preoccupation with reality; scientific, as opposed to idealistic or speculative or sentimental, attitude, policy, etc.; now esp., the disposition to think and act in the light of things as they are and to repudiate visionary schemes. **3.** The theory that art or literature should conform to nature or to real life; also, practice of this theory; representation without idealization. See IMPRESSIONISM, 1; NATURALISM, 2; cf. SURREALISM.

re′al·ist (-ĭst), *n.* **1.** An adherent to or advocate of realism. **2.** An artist or writer who aims at realism in his work. — **re′al·ist,** *adj.*

re′al·is′tic (-ĭs′tĭk), *adj.* Of or pertaining to, or after the manner of, realism or realists. — **re′al·is′ti·cal·ly** (-tĭ·kăl·ĭ), *adv.*

re·al′i·ty (rē·ăl′ĭ·tĭ), *n.*; *pl.* -TIES (-tĭz). **1.** State, quality, or fact of being real; also, in art, etc., the character of being true to life or to fact. **2.** Someone real or something real; an actual person, event, situation, or the like. **3.** *Philos.* **a** That which has objective existence, and is not merely an idea. **b** That which is absolute or self-existent, as opposed to what is derivative or dependent; that which is ultimate.

re′al·i·za′tion (rē′ăl·ĭ·zā′shŭn; -ī·zā′shŭn; rē′-), *n.* **1.** A realizing, or state of being realized. **2.** An instance or product of realizing.

re′al·ize (rē′ăl·īz; rē′ăl-), *v. t.* **1.** To make real; to bring into concrete existence; to accomplish; as, to *realize* a project. **2.** To cause to seem real; as, to *realize* ancient history. **3.** To convert into actual money; as, to *realize* assets. **4.** To acquire as the result of plans and efforts; to gain; as, to *realize* large profits. Also, of property, to bring by sale or investment. **5.** To conceive vividly as real; as, he *realized* his danger. — *v. i.* To convert an intangible right or property into real (tangible) property; hence, to convert any kind of property into money. — **Syn.** See THINK. — **re′al·iz′a·ble** (-īz′ȧ·b'l), *adj.* — **re′al·iz′er,** *n.*

re′al·iz′ing (rē′ăl·īz′ĭng; rē′ăl-), *adj.* Characterized by vivid or clear realization; as, a *realizing* sense.

re·al′lo·cate (rē·ăl′ō·kāt), *v. t.* To allocate again. — **re′al·lo·ca′tion** (rē′ăl·ō·kā′shŭn), *n.*

re′al·ly (rē′ăl·ĭ; rē′-; 27), *adv.* In a real manner; actually.

realm (rĕlm), *n.* [OF. *reialme, reaume,* deriv. of L. *regalis* royal.] **1.** A kingdom. **2.** Hence, province; region; domain; as, the *realm* of fancy. **3.** *Biogeog.* A primary marine or terrestrial division of the earth's surface.

re′al Mc·Coy′, the. See McCOY.

re′al·ness (rē′ăl·nĕs; -nĭs; rē′ăl-), *n.* Quality or state of being real.

‖Re·al′po′li·tik′ (rā·äl′pō′lē·tēk′), *n.* [G.] Practical politics; often, cynically, reliance upon armed strength for gaining one's ends in national or international affairs.

re′al·tor (rē′ăl·tẽr; rē′ăl·tẽr; -tôr), *n.* [See REALTY.] *U. S.* A real-estate broker who is an active member of the National Association of Real Estate Boards.

re′al·ty (-tĭ), *n.* [*real* + *-ty.*] **1.** *Obs.* Loyalty; honesty. **2.** Real estate or property; a piece of real property.

real wages. Wages measured by their purchasing power, as distinct from *nominal wages,* measured in money.

ream (rēm; *dial. also* răm), *n.* *Dial.* Cream; also, froth. — *v. i.* To froth. — *v. t.* To skim the cream from.

ream (rēm), *n.* [OF. *rayme,* fr. Sp. *resma,* fr. Ar. *rizmah* bundle.] **1.** A quantity of paper, usually twenty quires, or 480 sheets, but sometimes 500 sheets, and in a printer's ***perfect ream*** 516 sheets. Abbr. *rm.* **2.** *pl. Colloq.* An enormous amount, as of something written, printed, or spoken; — often *reams and reams.*

ream, *v. t.* **1.** To widen the opening of (a hole); to bevel out. **2** To enlarge (a hole) with a reamer; to enlarge the bore of, as a gun, in this way; — often with *out.* **3.** To remove (a defective part, as in a bore) by reaming (sense 2, above); — with *out.*

ream′er (rēm′ẽr), *n.* One that reams; specif., *Mach.,* any of various rotating finishing tools with cutting edges for enlarging or shaping a hole.

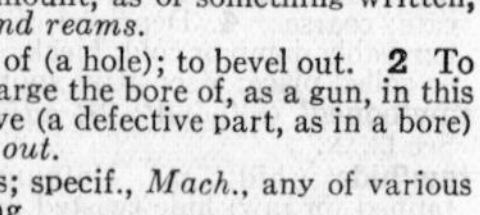
Reamers, Square and Fluted.

re·an′i·mate (rē·ăn′ĭ·māt), *v. t.* To animate anew; to revive. — **re′an·i·ma′tion** (rē′ăn·ĭ·mā′shŭn), *n.*

reap (rēp), *v. t.* [AS. *reopan, repan, ripan.*] **1.** To cut with a sickle, scythe, or machine, as grain; to gather, as a harvest, by cutting. **2.** To gather as the fruit of labor or of works; to harvest. **3.** To clear of a crop by reaping; as, to *reap* a field. — *v. i.* To reap something; to gather a harvest. — **reap′a·ble,** *adj.*

reap′er (-ẽr), *n.* One that reaps; specif., a **reap′ing ma·chine′,** any of various machines for reaping grain.

re′ap·pear′ (rē′ȧ·pēr′), *v. i.* To appear again.

re′ap·pear′ance (-ăns), *n.* A reappearing.

re′ap·point′ (rē′ȧ·point′), *v. t.* To appoint again. — **re′ap·point′ment,** *n.*

rear (rēr), *n.* [Shortened fr. ARREAR.] **1.** The unit of an army, fleet, or force which comes last; — opposite of *van.* **2.** The back of anything. **3.** The space or position behind, or at the back. — *adj.* Being at the back; hindmost.

rear, *v. t.* [AS. *rǣran* to raise, rear.] **1.** To raise upright; to set upright. **2.** To erect by building; to construct. **3.** To lift up; elevate; raise. **4.** To breed and raise. **5.** To foster; as, to *rear* offspring. — *v. i.* To rise up; esp., of a horse or other quadruped, to rise up on the hind legs. — **Syn.** See LIFT. — **rear′er,** *n.*

rear admiral. An officer in the navy, next in rank below a vice-admiral.

re·arm′ (rē·ärm′), *v. t.* To furnish with new or improved arms. — **re·ar′ma·ment** (-är′mȧ·mĕnt), *n.*

rear′most (rēr′mōst; -mŭst), *adj.* Farthest in the rear.

re′ar·range′ (rē′ȧ·rānj′), *v. t.* To arrange again or anew. — **re′ar·range′ment,** *n.*

rear′ward (rēr′wẽrd), *adj.* Rear; backward. — *adv.* At or toward the rear. — **rear′wards** (-wẽrdz), *adv.*

rear′ward′ (rēr′wôrd′), *n.* [AF. *rerewarde.* See WARD, *n.,* guard.] *Now Rare.* The rear; specif., the rear division of an army or fleet.

re′as·cend′ (rē′ȧ·sĕnd′), *v. t. & i.* To ascend again.

rea′son (rē′z'n), *n.* [OF. *raison,* fr. L. *ratio.*] **1.** **a** A statement offered as an explanation or justification of an act or procedure. **b** A consideration, motive, or judgment inducing or confirming a belief, influencing the will, or leading to an action. **2.** A ground or cause;

that in the reality which makes any fact intelligible. **3.** The power of comprehending and inferring; intellect. **4.** A sane or sound mind; sanity; sense; also, a sane or sound view or consideration. **5.** Due exercise of the reasoning faculty; right thinking. **6.** *Archaic.* **a** A formal reckoning. **b** Justice; propriety; specif., honorable treatment. — **Syn.** See CAUSE.

— ***by reason of.*** Because of. — ***in reason.*** **a** Justifiably. **b** That is reasonable, just, or possible.

— *v. i.* **1.** *Obs.* To hold argument; hence, to discourse. **2.** To talk persuasively; as, we *reasoned* with him for an hour. **3.** To use induction, deduction, or a combination of these in an effort to decide something. — **Syn.** See THINK. — *v. t.* **1.** To discuss or present the reasons for or against; to debate; argue. **2.** To seek a reason or reasons for; also, to infer or conclude. **3.** To explain, support, justify, etc., by adducing reasons. **4.** To persuade by reasoning. **5.** To think out systematically or logically. — **rea′son·er** (rē′z'n·ēr), *n.*

rea′son·a·ble (rē′z'n·ȧ·b'l), *adj.* **1.** Having the faculty of reason; rational. **2.** Just; fair-minded; of acts, thoughts, etc., agreeable to reason; not beyond the bounds of reason, logic, etc. **3.** Inexpensive; moderately priced. — **rea′son·a·bil′i·ty** (-bĭl′ĭ·tĭ), **rea′son·a·ble·ness,** *n.* — **rea′son·a·bly,** *adv.*

rea′son·ing (-ĭng), *n.* **1.** The drawing of inferences; thinking with a view to a conclusion believed to be valid. **2.** The proofs or arguments resulting from the use of reason.

rea′son·less, *adj.* Devoid of reason.

re′as·sem′ble (rē′ă·sĕm′b'l), *v. t. & i.* To assemble again. — **re′as·sem′bly** (-blĭ), *n.*

re′as·sert′ (rē′ă·sûrt′), *v. t.* To assert again.

re′as·sign′ (rē′ă·sīn′), *v. t.* To assign again. — **re′as·sign′ment,** *n.*

re′as·sume′ (rē′ă·sūm′), *v. t.* To assume again or anew.

re′as·sure′ (-shŏŏr′), *v. t.* To assure anew; specif.: **a** To restore confidence to. **b** *Insurance.* = REINSURE. — **re′as·sur′ance** (-shŏŏr′-ăns), *n.* — **re′as·sur′ing·ly,** *adv.*

Re′au·mur, Ré′au·mur (rā′ō·mūr; *F.* rā′ō′mür′), *adj.* Of or pert. to R. A. F. de Réaumur or the thermometric scale invented by him about 1730, in which 0° marks the freezing point and 80° the boiling point of water. Abbr. *R.* See THERMOMETER, *Illust.*

reave (rēv), *v. t.; past & past part.* REAVED (rēvd), REFT (rĕft); *pres. part.* REAV′ING. [AS. *rēafian.*] *Archaic.* To rob or plunder; despoil; seize. — **reav′er,** *n.*

reave, *v. t. & i. Archaic.* To burst; tear; split.

re′a·wak′en (rē′ă·wāk′ĕn), *v. t. & i.* To awaken again.

re′bap·tize′ (rē′băp·tīz′), *v. t.* To baptize again; also, to christen again. — **re·bap′tism** (rē·băp′tĭz'm), *n.*

re′bate (rē′bāt; *commonly* răb′ĕt; -ĭt), *n.* [See RABBET.] *Arch.* A rabbet. — *v. t.* To rabbet.

re′bate (rē′bāt; rē·bāt′), *n.* [MF. *rabat.* See REBATE, *v.*] Deduction; abatement; specif., payment back; as, a *rebate* of interest; a *rebate* to a shipper. — *v. t.* [OF. *rabattre,* fr. *re-* + *abattre* to beat down.] **1.** *Rare.* To diminish; reduce. **2.** *Archaic.* To blunt; to dull. **3.** To make a rebate of (an amount) or on (a bill); to give a rebate to (one). — **re′bat·er** (rē′bāt·ēr; rē·bāt′ēr), *n.*

re·ba′to (rē·bä′tō), *n.* [F. *rabat.*] *Hist.* A stiff flaring collar, as of lace.

re′bec, re′beck (rē′bĕk), *n.* [F. *rebec.*] *Music.* A stringed instrument believed to be the progenitor of the viol class.

Re·bec′ca, Re·bek′ah (rē·bĕk′ȧ), *n.* [Heb. *Ribhqāh.*] *Bib.* Wife of Isaac, mother of Esau and Jacob.

re·bel′ (rē·bĕl′), *v. i.;* -BELLED′ (-bĕld′); -BEL′LING. [OF. *rebeller,* fr. L. *rebellare* to make war again, fr. *re-* + *bellare* to make war, fr. *bellum* war.] **1.** To renounce, and resist by force, the authority of one's ruler or government. **2.** To oppose one in authority; to be insubordinate.

reb′el (rĕb′ĕl; -'l), *adj.* [OF. *rebelle,* fr. L. *rebellis.*] Of, pert. to, or characteristic of rebels or rebellion; rebellious.

reb′el, *n.* One who rebels or is in rebellion. — **reb′el·dom** (-dŭm), *n.*

re·bel′lion (rē·bĕl′yŭn), *n.* [OF., fr. L. *rebellio.*] **1.** Act of rebelling; revolt. **2.** Open resistance to, or defiance of, any authority.

Syn. **Rebellion, revolution, uprising, revolt, insurrection, mutiny** mean an outbreak against those in authority. **Rebellion** implies open, organized, and often armed, resistance; **revolution,** a successful rebellion involving a change, usually in government; **uprising,** an effort at rebellion; **revolt** and **insurrection,** an armed uprising that is quickly put down or is immediately effective; **mutiny,** an insurrection against those in authority, esp. on a ship at sea.

re·bel′lious (-yŭs), *adj.* **1.** That rebels; engaged in rebellion; also, of, pertaining to, or characteristic of a rebel, rebels, or rebellion. **2.** Resisting treatment or operation; refractory. — **re·bel′lious·ly,** *adv.* — **re·bel′lious·ness,** *n.*

re·bind′ (rē·bīnd′), *v. t.* To bind anew or again.

re·birth′ (rē·bûrth′; rē′bûrth′), *n.* **1.** A new or second birth. **2.** A renaissance; a revival.

reb′o·ant (rĕb′ō·ănt), *adj.* [L. *reboans,* pres. part. of *reboare,* fr. *re-* + *boare* to cry aloud.] Resounding loudly.

re′bop (rē′bŏp′), *n.* = BEBOP.

re·born′ (rē·bôrn′), *adj.* Born again; experiencing rebirth.

re·bound′ (rē·bound′), *v. i.* [OF. *rebondir* to spring back, re-echo.] **1.** To spring back on impact with another body. **2.** To resound; re-echo. **3.** *Archaic.* To leap or spring; as, to *rebound* with hope. — *v. t. Rare.* **1.** To send back as if by a rebound. **2.** To re-echo.

re·bound′ (rē·bound′; rē′bound′), *n.* **1.** Act of rebounding. **2.** Something reverberated or returned, as an echo. **3.** A mental or emotional recoil following disappointment; as, to marry on the *rebound.*

re·buff′ (rē·bŭf′), *n.* [MF. *rebuffe,* fr. It. *ribuffo, rabbuffo,* deriv. of *baruffare* to scuffle.] **1.** A curt refusal to meet an advance or offer; a snub. **2.** Any sharp check; a repulse. — *v. t.* **1.** To administer a rebuff to; to snub. **2.** To drive, beat, or blow back.

re·build′ (rē·bĭld′), *v. t.* To build again or anew. — **Syn.** See MEND.

re·buke′ (rē·būk′), *v. t.* [AF. *rebuker,* OF. *rebuchier* to repel.] **1.** *Now Rare.* To check; repress. **2.** To reprehend sharply; to reprimand. — **Syn.** See REPROVE. — *n.* A sharp reproof; reprimand. — **re·buk′er** (-bŭk′ēr), *n.*

re′bus (rē′bŭs), *n.* [L. *rebus* by things, abl. pl. of *res* a thing. See REAL actual.] A mode of expressing words and phrases by pictures of objects whose names resemble those words, or the syllables of which they are composed; hence, a form of riddle made up of such representations.

re·but′ (rē·bŭt′), *v. t.;* RE·BUT′TED; RE·BUT′TING. [OF. *rebouter* to repulse, drive back, fr. *re-* + *bouter* to push.] **1.** *Obs.* To drive back; repulse. **2.** To contradict; to refute, esp. formally, as by evidence and arguments. — **Syn.** See DISPROVE.

re·but′tal (-bŭt′ăl; -'l), *n.* Act of rebutting; specif., *Law,* the giving of evidence in a suit to destroy the effect of evidence introduced by the other side in the same suit.

re·but′ter (-ēr), *n.* [Prop. fr. OF. *rebouter,* inf. as n. See REBUT, *v.*] *Law.* The answer of a defendant in matters of fact to a plaintiff's surrejoinder.

re·but′ter, *n.* That which rebuts, or refutes.

re·cal′ci·trant (rē·kăl′sĭ·trănt), *adj.* [L. *recalcitrans,* pres. part. of *recalcitrare* to kick back, fr. *re-* + *calcitrare* to kick, fr. *calx* heel.] Stubbornly rebellious, obstinate in defying constituted authority; refractory. — **Syn.** See UNRULY. — *n.* One who is recalcitrant. — **re·cal′ci·trance** (-trăns), **re·cal′ci·tran·cy** (-trăn·sĭ), *n.*

re·cal′ci·trate (-trāt), *v. i. & t.* To kick backwards; now, to protest vigorously; to manifest stubborn opposition. — **re·cal′ci·tra′tion** (-trā′shŭn), *n.*

re′ca·les′cence (rē′kȧ·lĕs′ĕns; -'ns), *n.* *Metal.* The sudden liberation of heat by a metal when cooling through a certain critical temperature, as iron at 690° C. — **re′ca·lesce′** (-lĕs′), *v. i.;* RE′CA·LESCED′ (-lĕst′); RE′CA·LESC′ING (-lĕs′ĭng).

re·call′ (rē·kôl′), *v. t.* **1.** To call back; to summon to return. **2.** To call back to mind; to recollect. **3.** *Poetic.* To renew; revive. **4.** To revoke; annul; to take back; withdraw. — **Syn.** See REMEMBER. — **re·call′a·ble,** *adj.*

re·call′ (rē·kôl′; rē′kôl′), *n.* **1.** A calling back; a summons to return. **2.** Act of revoking, annulling, or the like. **3.** **a** *Mil.* A call on the trumpet, bugle, or drum, which calls soldiers back to the ranks, camp, etc. **b** *Nav.* A signal calling a boat or vessel back to a ship or squadron. **4.** *Polit. Science.* The right or procedure by which a public official may be removed from office by a vote of the people.

re·cant′ (rē·kănt′), *v. t.* [L. *recantare, -tatum,* to recant, fr. *re-* + *cantare* to sing, sound.] **1.** To withdraw or repudiate formally (opinions formerly expressed); to take back openly. **2.** To retract; revoke. — *v. i.* To retract a declaration, etc., esp. publicly. — **Syn.** See ABJURE. — **re′can·ta′tion** (rē′kăn·tā′shŭn), *n.* — **re·cant′er,** *n.*

re·cap′ (rē·kăp′), *v. t.;* RE·CAPPED′ (-kăpt′); RE·CAP′PING (-kăp′ĭng). To cement, mold, and vulcanize a strip of camelback upon the buffed and roughened surface of the tread of (a worn pneumatic tire); — distinguished from *retread.* — (rē′kăp′), *n.* A recapped tire. — **re·cap′pa·ble** (rē·kăp′ȧ·b'l), *adj.*

re′cap (rē′kăp), *n. Colloq.* Short for RECAPITULATION.

re′cap (rē′kăp), *v. t.;* RE′CAPPED (-kăpt); RE′CAP·PING. *Colloq.* Short for RECAPITULATE.

re·cap′i·tal·ize (rē·kăp′ĭ·tăl·īz), *v. t.* To capitalize again; to change the capitalization of. — **re·cap′i·tal·i·za′tion** (-ĭ·zā′shŭn; -ī·zā′-), *n.*

re′ca·pit′u·late (rē′kȧ·pĭt′ū·lāt), *v. t. & i.* [LL. *recapitulare, -latum,* fr. *re-* + *capitulum* a small head chapter, section.] To repeat or restate briefly, as the principal points in a discourse; to summarize.

re′ca·pit′u·la′tion (-lā′shŭn), *n.* **1.** A recapitulating; a concise summary. **2.** *Biol.* Repetition, in an individual, of phylogenetic development. **3.** *Music.* The third part of a sonata form. — **re′ca·pit′u·la′tive** (-pĭt′ū·lā′tĭv), **re′ca·pit′u·la·to′ry** (-lȧ·tō′rĭ; -tēr·ĭ), *adj.*

re·cap′ture (rē·kăp′tūr), *n.* **1.** Act of retaking by capture; specif.: *Internat. Law,* the retaking of a prize or goods. **2.** That which is recaptured. **3.** *Law, U. S.* In public utility law, a taking by the public of earnings or profits beyond some fixed amount. — (rē-), *v. t.* **1.** To capture again, as a prize. **2.** To bring to memory; recall.

re·cast′ (rē·kăst′; 9), *v. t.* To cast or found anew; to remold or remodel; as, to *recast* a cannon; to *recast* a poem. — **re·cast′** (-kăst′; rē′kăst′), *n.*

re·cede′ (rē·sēd′), *v. i.* [L. *recedere, recessum,* fr. *re-* + *cedere* to go.] **1.** To move back or away; to retreat; retire. **2.** To shrink in size, bulk, compass, frequency, intensity, or the like; as, the gums *recede;* the colleges would *recede* in importance. **3.** To withdraw, as a party to an agreement, a sponsor, etc.; — usually with *from;* as, he *receded* from his position. **4.** *U. S. Congress.* To withdraw its opposition to an amendment of the other house.

Syn. **Recede, retreat, retrograde, retract, back** mean to move backward. **Recede** may or may not imply actual movement for it stresses increasing distance from a fixed point in space or time, a fixed point of view, a fixed attitude, or the like; **retreat** implies withdrawal from a point or position reached; **retrograde,** a movement contrary to that which is normally progressive; **retract,** chiefly used in biology, a drawing back; **back,** often followed by an adverb such as *up, out,* or *down,* may be used interchangeably with any of the others.

re·cede′ (rē·sēd′), *v. t.* [*re-* + *cede.*] To cede back.

re·ceipt′ (rē·sēt′), *n.* [OF. *recete, recepte,* fr. L. *recepta,* fr. past part. of *recipere, receptum,* to receive.] **1.** A formula according to which things are to be taken or combined, or some effect is to be produced; a recipe. See RECIPE, 2. **2.** Act or fact of receiving or being received. **3.** That which is received in distinction from what is expended; — usually in *pl.;* as, the gross *receipts.* **4.** A writing acknowledging the taking or receiving of goods or money. — *v. t.* **a** *Rare. U. S.* To give a receipt for. **b** To put a receipt on; to mark paid; as, to *receipt* a bill. — *v. i. Rare. U. S.* To give a receipt.

re·ceipt′or (-ēr), *n.* One who receipts; *Law,* one who receipts as bailee for property taken by the sheriff.

re·ceiv′a·ble (rē·sēv′ȧ·b'l), *adj.* **1.** Capable of being received; specif., acceptable as legal; as, *receivable* certificates. **2.** Such that payment is due or callable; as, bills *receivable.*

re·ceiv′a·bles (-b'lz), *n. pl.* Accounts, accepted bills, or notes created in the course of business, due from others, or becoming due at an assignable date.

re·ceive′ (rē·sēv′), *v. t.* [OF. *receivre,* fr. L. *recipere,* fr. *re-* + *capere* to take, seize.] **1.** To take, as something that is offered, sent, paid, or the like; to accept. **2.** To admit; hence, to have capacity for; to hold; contain. **3.** To permit to enter, as into one's house; greet; as, to *receive* an actor with applause. **4.** To get, acquire, or the like, from an outside source; hence, to experience; to undergo. **5.** To gain the knowledge of from some communication; as, to *receive* a warning; also, *Now Rare,* to accept as true, valid, or the like; hence, to comprehend. **6.** To support, catch, bear, or the like; to take, as a blow on one's shield. — *v. i.* **1.** To be a recipient; to get. **2.** To receive visitors; as, she *receives* on Tuesdays. **3.** *Radio & Television.* To change incoming radio waves into perceptible signals.

Syn. **Receive, accept, admit, take** mean to let someone or something come to one. **Receive** ordinarily implies passiveness in the one receiving; **accept**, a measure of mental consent, or even of approval, but rarely, clear activity; **admit**, the act of receiving, often by allowing, permitting, or the like; **take**, a receiving by letting into one's hands, one's mind, one's possession, or the like.

re·ceiv'er (rē·sēv'ẽr), *n.* **1.** One who receives in any manner; hence, variously, a catcher, porter, etc. **2.** One appointed to receive money due; a treasurer. **3.** One who buys stolen goods from a thief, knowing them to be stolen. **4.** That which receives; a receptacle. **5.** *Chem.* **a** See RETORT, *Illust.* **b** A vessel to receive and contain gases. **6.** *Elec.* That portion of a telegraphic or telephonic apparatus by which the electric currents or waves are converted into visible or audible signals. See TELEPHONE, *Illust.* **7.** *Law.* **a** A person appointed to receive, and hold in trust, property under litigation. **b** *U.S.* A person appointed under a statute by some administrative officer to wind up some business of public interest, such as a bank. **8.** *Radio & Television.* A receiving set.

re·ceiv'er·ship (-shĭp), *n.* *Law.* **1.** The office or function of a receiver (sense 7). **2.** The state or condition of being in the hands of a receiver.

re·ceiv'ing set. An apparatus for receiving radio or television signals.

re'cen·cy (rē'sĕn·sĭ; -s'n·sĭ), *n.* State or quality of being recent.

re·cen'sion (rē·sĕn'shŭn), *n.* [F. or L.; F., fr. L. *recensio.*] **1.** A revising of a text (as of an ancient author) by an editor; esp., critical revision with intent to establish a definitive text. **2.** A text so established.

re'cent (rē'sĕnt; -s'nt), *adj.* [F. *récent*, fr. L. *recens, -entis.*] **1.** Lately formed, created, developed, used, etc. **2.** Of or pert. to a time relatively near. **3.** [*cap.*] *Geol.* Pert. to or designating the later period (cf. PLEISTOCENE) of the Quaternary division of the Cenozoic era, or the system of rocks formed during this period. — **re'cent·ly,** *adv.* — **re'cent·ness,** *n.*

re'cept (rē'sĕpt), *n.* [L. *receptum*, neut. past part. of *recipere.* See RECEIVE.] *Psychol.* A mental image or idea formed by successive percepts of the same or like objects, accentuating their common characters.

re·cep'ta·cle (rē·sĕp'tȧ·k'l; -tĭ·k'l), *n.* [L. *receptaculum*, fr. *receptare*, v. intens. fr. *recipere* to receive.] **1.** That which serves for receiving and containing something; a container. **2.** *Bot.* = TORUS, 3.

re·cep'tion (rē·sĕp'shŭn), *n.* [OF., fr. L. *receptio.* See RECEIVE.] **1.** Act of receiving; receipt; admission. **2.** Act of receiving visitors; ceremony of receiving guests. **3.** Manner of receiving; as, a cold *reception.* **4.** *Radio & Television.* Act or process of receiving.

re·cep'tion·ist (-ĭst), *n.* *Colloq., U.S.* An office employee, usually a woman, who greets callers.

re·cep'tive (-tĭv), *adj.* **1.** Able or inclined to take in, absorb, hold, or contain. **2.** *Physiol. & Psychol.* Pert. to receptors or to the reception of stimuli. — **re·cep'tive·ly,** *adv.* — **re·cep'tive·ness,** *n.* — **re'cep·tiv'i·ty** (rē'sĕp·tĭv'ĭ·tĭ; rĕs'ĕp-), *n.*

re·cep'tor (rē·sĕp'tẽr), *n.* [OF. *receptour*, fr. L. *receptor.*] **1.** A receiver. **2.** *Physiol.* A cell or group of cells which receives stimuli; a sense organ. **3.** *Telephony.* A receiver. **4.** *Wireless Teleg.* The entire receiving apparatus.

re·cess' (rē·sĕs'; rē'sĕs; *the 2d pron. is now usual in the U.S. for a period of intermission*), *n.* [L. *recessus*, fr. *recedere, -cessum.* See RECEDE.] **1.** An indentation, cleft, or the like, in a line or surface; in a room, an alcove, niche, or the like. **2.** A place of retirement, retreat, secrecy, or seclusion. **3.** Suspension of business or procedure for a short time; a short intermission, as of a legislative body, court, or school.

re·cess' (rē·sĕs'), *v. t.* **1.** To put into a recess; to set back; to seclude. **2.** To make a recess in; as, to *recess* a wall. — *v. i. Colloq., U.S.* To take a recess.

re·ces'sion (rē·sĕsh'ŭn), *n.* [L. *recessio.*] **1.** Act or fact of receding or retiring; withdrawal. **2.** The return procession, as of clergy and choir after a service. **3.** A slowing down of commercial and industrial activity marked by decrease in employment, profits, production, prices, and sales but less severe than a depression; also, a period of such slackening, usually a setback interrupting a recovery.

re·ces'sion, *n.* [*re-* + *cession.*] Act of ceding back.

re·ces'sion·al (-ăl; -'l), *adj.* Of or pertaining to recession. — *n.* **1.** A recessional hymn. **2.** A piece of music played at the end, as of a church service.

recessional hymn. A hymn sung during the recession of the clergy and choir from the chancel to the robing room.

re·ces'sive (rē·sĕs'ĭv), *adj.* **1.** Tending to go back; receding. **2.** *Biol.* Designating that member of a pair of allelomorphs which, when both contrasting factors are present, is subordinate to the other in its manifestation. — *n. Biol.* **a** A recessive character or factor. **b** An organism possessing recessive characters.

re·charge' (rē·chärj'), *v. t. & i.* [*re-* + *charge.*] To charge again, anew, or in return.

re·char'ter (rē·chär'tẽr), *v. t.* To charter again or anew.

‖ré'chauf'fé' (rā'shō'fā'), *n.; pl.* RÉCHAUFFÉS (-fā'). [F., lit., warmed over.] A dish of food warmed again; a rehash.

re·cher'ché' (rē·shẽr'shā'; rē·shär'shā), *adj.* [F.] *Often Jocose.* Sought out with care; choice; of rare quality or elegance.

re·cid'i·vism (rē·sĭd'ĭ·vĭz'm), *n.* State or quality of being recidivous; relapse; specif., *Criminol.*, a falling back into prior criminal habits, esp. after punishment. — **re·cid'i·vist** (-vĭst), *n.* — **re·cid'i·vis'tic** (-vĭs'tĭk), *adj.*

re·cid'i·vous (-vŭs), *adj.* [L. *recidivus*, fr. *recidere* to fall back.] Relapsing; tending to or marked by a falling back into prior habits, esp. criminal habits.

rec'i·pe (rĕs'ĭ·pē), *n.* [L., imper. of *recipere.* See RECEIVE.] **1.** A formula for compounding a medicine; also, the preparation compounded; — now usually *prescription.* Symbol ℞. **2.** A formula for making a dish in cookery; a receipt; — often preferred to *receipt.* **3.** A means prescribed for producing a desired result.

re·cip'i·ence (rē·sĭp'ĭ·ĕns), *n.* Also **re·cip'i·en·cy** (-ĕn·sĭ). Act of receiving or state of being recipient; receptiveness.

re·cip'i·ent (-ĕnt), *n.* [L. *recipiens, -entis*, receiving, pres. part.] One who or that which receives; a receiver. — *adj.* Receiving; receptive.

re·cip'ro·cal (rē·sĭp'rō·kăl), *adj.* [L. *reciprocus.*] **1.** Mutual; shared, felt, shown, or the like, by both sides; as, united in *reciprocal* affection. **2.** Corresponding to each other as by being equivalent or complementary; as, the *reciprocal* obligations of capital and labor. **3.** Interchangeable; convertible; also, inversely related. **4.** *Gram.* Expressive of mutual relation; — applied esp. to pronouns. See PRONOUN. **5.** *Math.* Used to denote different kinds of mutual relation; — often with reference to the substitution of reciprocals for given quantities.

Syn. **Reciprocal, mutual, common** mean shared, experienced, or the like, by each. **Reciprocal** implies a return in due measure by each of two sides, as of reproaches, courtesies, duties, etc.; **mutual**, though often used interchangeably with *reciprocal*, stresses a sharing equally and jointly rather than a return, and is often applicable to two or more persons who share certain feelings; **common** carries no implication of reciprocity, but merely a being shared with others; as, *reciprocal* obligations; our obligations are *mutual*, we are *mutual* friends; we have *common* friends.

— *n.* **1.** That which reciprocates or bears a reciprocal relation to another thing. **2.** *Math.* The quotient of unity divided by any quantity. The *reciprocal* of a fraction is the fraction inverted.

— **re·cip'ro·cal'i·ty** (-kăl'ĭ·tĭ), *n.* — **re·cip'ro·cal·ly,** *adv.*

re·cip'ro·cate (-kāt), *v. i.* [L. *reciprocatus*, past part. of *reciprocare* to move back and forth, reciprocate.] **1.** *Obs. exc. Mech.* To move forward and backward alternately; to act interchangeably. **2.** To make a return for something done or given; also, *Colloq.*, to return a compliment, good wishes, or the like. — *v. t.* **1.** To cause to move in alternate directions. **2.** To give and take reciprocally; to exchange mutually. **3.** To return in kind or degree; to repay. — **re·cip'ro·ca'tor** (-kā'tẽr), *n.*

re·cip'ro·cat'ing en'gine (-kāt'ĭng). An engine in which the piston moves to and fro; — disting. from *rotary engine* (sense 1).

re·cip'ro·ca'tion (rē·sĭp'rō·kā'shŭn), *n.* Act or fact of reciprocating. **a** Reciprocal motion, succession, action, or relationship. **b** Mutual exchange; as, *reciprocation* of courtesies. **c** A return in kind or of like value; as, *reciprocation* of his affection. **d** Correspondence or equivalence. — **re·cip'ro·ca'tive** (rē·sĭp'rō·kā'tĭv), *adj.*

rec'i·proc'i·ty (rĕs'ĭ·prŏs'ĭ·tĭ), *n.* **1.** State of being reciprocal; mutual dependence, co-operation, etc.; also, a reciprocation; an interchange, return in kind, etc. **2.** *Internat. Trade.* That relation or policy as to trade or other interests between countries under which special advantages are granted by one side in consideration of special advantages granted by the other.

re·ci'sion (rē·sĭzh'ŭn), *n.* [L. *recisio*, fr. *recidere, recisum*, to cut off, fr. *re-* + *caedere* to cut.] Act of rescinding or canceling.

re·cit'al (rē·sīt'ăl; -'l), *n.* **1.** Act of reciting. Specif.: **a** A rehearsing in detail; a particularized account. **b** Repetition of the words of another, as by reading; as, the *recital* of Hamlet. **2.** A story; narrative. **3.** *Music.* A program of music, vocal or instrumental; often, such a program presented by one person; — disting. from *concert.*

rec'i·ta'tion (rĕs'ĭ·tā'shŭn), *n.* [F. *récitation*, fr. L. *recitatio.*] **1.** Act of reciting. **2.** The delivery before an audience of something memorized; also, that which is so delivered. **3.** *Educ.* A class exercise in which students reply orally to questions for which preparation is expected; hence, loosely, any class exercise.

rec'i·ta·tive' (rĕs'ĭ·tȧ·tēv'), *n.* [It. *recitativo.*] *Music.* A species of musical recitation in which the words are delivered in a manner resembling declamation; also, a piece or passage of music intended for such recitation or rendered in this manner.

rec'i·ta'tive, *adj.* **1.** (rĕs'ĭ·tā'tĭv; rē·sīt'ȧ·tĭv) That recites; narrative. **2.** (rĕs'ĭ·tȧ·tēv') Of, pert. to, or having the style of recitative.

re·cite' (rē·sīt'), *v. t. & i.* [F. *réciter*, fr. L. *recitare, recitatum*, fr. *re-* + *citare* to call, cite.] **1.** To repeat, as something prepared or committed to memory. **2.** To tell over; to go over in particulars; to relate. **3.** To rehearse or repeat, as a lesson to an instructor. — **re·cit'er** (-sīt'ẽr), *n.*

reck (rĕk), *v. i.* [AS. *reccan, rēcan.*] *Archaic.* **1.** To take heed, care, or thought; to care; mind. **2.** To be of account or interest; to matter. — *v. t. Archaic.* **1.** To care for; to heed; regard. **2.** To concern.

reck'less (rĕk'lĕs; -lĭs), *adj.* [AS. *recceléas, rēceléas.*] **1.** Neglectful; indifferent; as, utterly *reckless* of danger. **2.** Characterized by lack of due caution; rash. — **Syn.** See ADVENTUROUS. — **Ant.** Calculating. — **reck'less·ly,** *adv.* — **reck'less·ness,** *n.*

reck'on (rĕk'ŭn), *v. t.* [AS. *gerecenian* to explain.] **1.** To count; compute; calculate. **2.** To consider; regard; as, to *reckon* him prosperous. **3.** To conclude, as after an enumerating of chances; hence, *Colloq.*, to think, suppose. **4.** *Obs.* To attribute (a quality, a relationship, etc.); to impute. — *v. i.* **1.** To make an enumeration or computation. **2.** To make up accounts; to settle. **3.** To rely; count; — followed by *on*; as, to *reckon* on one's coming. **4.** *Dial.* To think, suppose; guess. — **Syn.** See CALCULATE: RELY. — ***reckon without one's host.*** Orig., to reckon one's score without consulting one's landlord; hence, to ignore in a calculation or arrangement some essential consideration.

reck'on·er (-ẽr), *n.* **a** One who or that which reckons. **b** An aid to reckoning, esp. a book of tables, etc.; — often called ***ready reckoner.***

reck'on·ing, *n.* **1.** Act of one who reckons, or result of reckoning; calculation. Specif.: **a** The act or fact of accounting, as to God, for one's conduct. **b** *Archaic.* One's score, as at an inn. **2.** *Navig.* The calculation of a ship's position.

re·claim' (rē·klām'), *v. t.* [OF. *reclamer* (3d sing. pres. *reclaime*) to call back, fr. L. *reclamare, -matum*, to cry out against.] **1.** To call back from flight or disorderly action. **2.** To reduce from a wild to a tamed state, as an eagle; to tame and train; — said esp. of hawks. **3.** To call back to rectitude from moral transgression; to reform. **4.** To reduce to a desired state by discipline, labor, cultivation, etc.; to rescue from being wild, waste, or the like; as, to *reclaim* savages; to *reclaim* overflowed land, etc. **5.** To obtain, as rubber, from a waste product or by-product; to recover. — *v. i. Now Rare.* To cry out, esp. in protest; to object. — **Syn.** See RESCUE. — **re·claim'a·ble,** *adj.*

re–claim' (rē·klām'), *v. t.* To claim back; to demand the return of as a right; to attempt to recover possession of.

re'claim' (rē'klām'), *n.* A fresh claim; a renewed claim.

re·claim'ant (rē·klām'ănt), *n.* One who reclaims or, esp., protests or appeals.

re·claim'er (-ẽr), *n.* One who or that which reclaims; as, oil *reclaimers* are used to clarify used lubricants.

rec'la·ma'tion (rĕk'lȧ·mā'shŭn), *n.* [F. *réclamation*, fr. L. *reclamatio.* See RECLAIM.] Act or process of reclaiming; also, the industry of reclaiming waste; as, *reclamation* of swamp land; a *reclamation* plant.

‖ré·clame' (rā'klȧm'), *n.* [F., fr. *réclamer.* See RECLAIM.] Publicity; also, publicity seeking.

re·cline′ (rē·klīn′), *v. t. & i.* [OF. *recliner*, fr. L. *reclinare*, fr. *re-* + *clinare* to lean, incline.] To cause or permit to incline backwards or in a recumbent position; loosely, to lean; incline; rest. — **re·clin′er** (-klīn′ẽr), *n.*

re·cluse′ (rē·klōōs′; 114), *adj.* [OF. *reclus*, fem. *recluse*, fr. L. *reclusus*, fr. *recludere*, *-clusum*, to unclose, open, later, to shut up.] Shut up; sequestered; retired from the world or from public notice; solitary. — (rē·klōōs′; rĕk′lūs), *n.* A person who lives in seclusion, as a hermit.

re·clu′sion (rē·klōō′zhŭn; 114), *n.* Act of becoming, or state of being, a recluse; seclusion; specif., imprisonment, esp. solitary. — **re·clu′sive** (-sĭv), *adj.*

rec′og·ni′tion (rĕk′ŏg·nĭsh′ŭn), *n.* [F. *récognition*, fr. L. *recognitio*.] **1.** Act of recognizing; as: **a** Formal acknowledgment, as of a fact or a claim. **b** Acceptance as entitled to attention; as, *recognition* by the chair of one rising to speak in a meeting. **2.** Perception of identity as already known in fact or by description; as, *recognition* of a person or a portrait. **3.** *Internat. Law.* Acknowledgment of the independence of an insurgent or rebelling community or province. — **re·cog′ni·to′ry** (rē·kŏg′nĭ·tō′rĭ *or, esp. Brit.*, -tẽr·ĭ), *adj.*

re·cog′ni·zance (rē·kŏg′nĭ·zăns *or, esp. Law*, rē·kŏn′ĭ-), *n.* [OF. *reconoissance*, later *recognoissance*, deriv. of L. *recognoscere*, fr. *re-* + *cognoscere* to know.] **1.** *Law.* **a** An obligation of record entered into before some court or magistrate, making the performance of some act the condition of nonforfeiture. **b** The sum liable to forfeiture upon such an obligation. **2.** *Archaic.* A token; symbol; pledge; badge.

rec′og·nize (rĕk′ŏg·nīz), *v. t.* [See RECOGNIZANCE.] **1.** To know again; to perceive to be a person or thing previously known. **2.** To avow knowledge of; to admit with a formal acknowledgment. **3.** To acknowledge formally, as by special attention; to take notice of; specif.: **a** To acknowledge with a show of approval; as, to *recognize* services. **b** To acknowledge acquaintance with, as by salutation. **c** To acknowledge by admitting to a privileged status. **d** To acknowledge as the one entitled to be heard at the time, as one who offers to speak in a meeting. **4.** *Law.* **a** *Eng.* To make formal acknowledgment of as one's lord, ruler, or sovereign. **b** To acknowledge the independence of (a body which has thrown off the sovereignty of a state to which it was subject), thus entitling it to be treated as an independent state by the recognizing power. — **rec′og·niz′a·ble** (-nīz′ȧ·b'l), *adj.* — **rec′og·niz′a·bly**, *adv.*

rec′og·niz′er (-nīz′ẽr), *n.* One who recognizes.

re·coil′ (rē·koil′), *v. i.* [OF. *reculer*.] **1.** To retreat, draw back, or fall back. **2.** To spring back, as a released spring or a firearm in the act of discharging. **3.** To return to or as to the starting point.

Syn. **Recoil, shrink, flinch, wince, blench, quail** mean to draw back as through fear. **Recoil** implies a start, a movement away, or the like; **shrink**, a mental or physical drawing back from something painful or horrible; **flinch**, a desire to avoid or evade; **wince**, a physical movement showing recoil; **blench** and **quail**, a shrinking through faintheartedness or terror.

— *n.* **1.** Act of recoiling; now, esp., a rebound; a drawing or shrinking back. **2.** The state or condition of having recoiled; reaction. **3.** Specif.: The recoiling of a gun, spring, etc.; also, the distance through which a gun, spring, etc., recoils.

re·coin′ (rē·koin′), *v. t.* To coin anew or again.

re·coin′age (-ĭj), *n.* A coining, or a thing coined, anew.

re′-col·lect′ (rē′kŏ·lĕkt′), *v. t.* [L. *recollectus*, past part. of *recolligere* to collect; in some senses prob. fr. *re-* + *collect*.] To collect again, as something that has been scattered; also, to gather; rally; recover.

rec′ol·lect′ (rĕk′ŏ·lĕkt′), *v. t.* [L. *recollectus*, past part. of *recolligere* to collect.] **1.** To recall the knowledge of; to remember. **2.** To compose (oneself); to recover control over (oneself). **3.** To recall something forgotten to (oneself); as, he *recollected* himself in time. — *v. i.* To have a recollection; to call something to mind. — **Syn.** See REMEMBER.

rec′ol·lect′ed (-lĕk′tĕd; -tĭd), *adj.* **1.** Composed; calm; collected; as, cool and *recollected* at all times. **2.** Recalled to memory. — **rec′ol·lect′ed·ness**, *n.*

rec′ol·lec′tion (-lĕk′shŭn), *n.* **1.** Act of recollecting, or recalling to the memory; remembrance. **2.** The power of recalling ideas to the mind; memory; as, a weakened *recollection*. **3.** That which is recollected; reminiscence. — **Syn.** See MEMORY. — **rec′ol·lec′tive** (-tĭv), *adj.*

re′com·bine′ (rē′kŏm·bīn′), *v. t. & i.* To combine again.

re·com′fort (rē·kŭm′fẽrt), *v. t.* [OF. *reconforter*.] *Archaic.* To comfort; console; refresh.

re′com·mence′ (rē′kŏ·mĕns′), *v. t. & i.* [F. *recommencer*.] To commence again. — **re′com·mence′ment**, *n.*

rec′om·mend′ (rĕk′ŏ·mĕnd′), *v. t.* [ML. *recommendare*.] **1.** To commit; to consign; entrust; — now usually *commend*. **2.** To praise; now specif., to make a commendatory statement concerning (a person or thing). **3.** To commend; to offer or suggest with favoring representations. **4.** To make acceptable; to attract favor to; as, his manners *recommended* him. **5.** To advise; counsel.

rec′om·men·da′tion (-mĕn·dā′shŭn), *n.* **1.** Act of recommending. **2.** Something which recommends or commends; specif., a statement declaring what one recommends or expressing commendation.

rec′om·mend′a·to′ry (-mĕn′dȧ·tō′rĭ *or, esp. Brit.*, -tẽr·ĭ), *adj.* **1.** Serving to recommend, commend, or attract favorable attention. **2.** Offered as a recommendation; advisory.

rec′om·mend′er (-mĕn′dẽr), *n.* One who recommends.

re′com·mit′ (rē′kŏ·mĭt′), *v. t.* To commit again; as, to *recommit* a criminal to prison; specif., to refer again, as a bill, to a committee. — **re′com·mit′ment** (-mĕnt), **re′com·mit′tal** (-ăl; -'l), *n.*

rec′om·pense (rĕk′ŏm·pĕns), *v. t.* [OF. *recompenser*, fr. LL., fr. L. *re-* + *compensare* to compensate.] **1.** To give compensation to; to requite; compensate. **2.** To give an equivalent for; to pay for. — **Syn.** See PAY. — *n.* Compensation; an equivalent or a return for something done, suffered, or given.

re′com·pose′ (rē′kŏm·pōz′), *v. t.* **1.** To compose again; to recombine; also, to rearrange. **2.** To restore to composure. — **re′com·po·si′tion** (-kŏm·pō·zĭsh′ŭn), *n.*

re·con′cen·trate (rē·kŏn′sĕn·trāt), *v. t. & i.* To concentrate again; to concentrate thoroughly.

re′con·cen·tra′tion (rē′kŏn·sĕn·trā′shŭn), *n.* Act of reconcentrating; esp., concentration of the rural population in towns for convenience in administration, as in Cuba during the revolution of 1895–98.

rec′on·cil′a·ble (rĕk′ŏn·sīl′ȧ·b'l), *adj.* Capable of being reconciled. — **rec′on·cil′a·bil′i·ty** (-bĭl′ĭ·tĭ), **rec′on·cil′a·ble·ness**, *n.* — **rec′on·cil′a·bly**, *adv.*

rec′on·cile (rĕk′ŏn·sīl), *v. t.* [OF. or L.; OF. *reconcilier*, fr. L. *reconciliare*, fr. *re-* + *conciliare* to unite.] **1.** To cause to be friendly again; to bring back to harmony. **2.** To adjust; settle; as, to *reconcile* differences. **3.** To make consistent or congruous. **4.** To bring to acquiescence or quiet submission; as, to *reconcile* oneself to afflictions. — **Syn.** See ADAPT. — **rec′on·cile′ment**, *n.*

rec′on·cil′i·a′tion (-sĭl′ĭ·ā′shŭn), *n.* **1.** Act of reconciling, or state of being reconciled. **2.** Reduction to congruence; removal or explanation of inconsistency; harmony; as, a *reconciliation* of the Gospels.

rec′on·cil′i·a·to′ry (-sĭl′ĭ·ȧ·tō′rĭ *or, esp. Brit.*, -tẽr·ĭ), *adj.* Serving or tending to reconcile.

rec′on·dite (rĕk′ŭn·dīt; rē·kŏn′dīt), *adj.* [L. *reconditus*, past part. of *recondere* to put up again, conceal, fr. *re-* + *condere* to bring together.] **1.** Hidden from sight; concealed. **2.** Difficult to comprehend; abstruse. **3.** Dealing with what is abstruse; characterized by profound scholarship. — **rec′on·dite·ly**, *adv.* — **rec′on·dite·ness**, *n.*

re′con·di′tion (rē′kŏn·dĭsh′ŭn), *v. t.* **1.** To restore (something worn) to sound condition by readjustments and replacement of parts; as, a *reconditioned* typewriter. **2.** To re-educate (individuals); to change (emotional attitudes, habits, etc.).

re·con′nais·sance (rē·kŏn′ĭ·săns), *n.* Also **re·con′nois·sance** (-ĭ·săns). [F.] A survey; specif.: **a** *Engin.* An examination of a region preparatory to triangulation, etc. **b** *Geol.* A preliminary examination or survey. **c** *Mil.* An examination of a territory to gain information of enemy troops, of the terrain, or of resources.

rec′on·noi′ter, rec′on·noi′tre (rĕk′ŏ·noi′tẽr; rē′kŏ-), *v. t.* [F. *reconnoître* (now *reconnaître*). See RECOGNIZANCE.] To examine with the eye; to make a preliminary examination or survey of, esp. for military or engineering operations. — *v. i.* To make a reconnaissance. — **rec′on·noi′ter·er** (-ẽr), **rec′on·noi′trer** (-trẽr), *n.*

re·con′quer (rē·kŏng′kẽr), *v. t.* To conquer again.

re′con·sid′er (rē′kŏn·sĭd′ẽr), *v. t.* **1.** To consider again; to consider with a view to changing, as a plan. **2.** *Parliamentary Practice.* To take up for renewed consideration, as a motion or a vote previously acted on. — **re′con·sid′er·a′tion** (-ā′shŭn), *n.*

re′con·sign′ment (rē′kŏn·sīn′mĕnt), *n.* Consignment again or anew. — **re′con·sign′**, *v. t.*

re·con′sti·tute (rē·kŏn′stĭ·tūt), *v. t.* To constitute again. — **re·con′sti·tu′tion** (-tū′shŭn), *n.*

re′con·struct′ (rē′kŏn·strŭkt′), *v. t.* To construct again.

re′con·struct′ed (-strŭk′tĕd; -tĭd), *adj.* Made again or anew; rebuilt; also, of gems, artificially made.

re′con·struc′tion (-strŭk′shŭn), *n.* **1.** Act of reconstructing; also, something reconstructed. **2.** [*sometimes cap.*] *U.S. Hist.* The process of reorganizing the governments of the states which had passed ordinances of secession, and of re-establishing their constitutional relations to the national government, after the Civil War.

re′con·struc′tive (-tĭv), *adj.* Reconstructing; tending to reconstruct.

re′con·vene′ (rē′kŏn·vēn′), *v. i. & t.* To convene again.

re′con·vert′ (-vûrt′), *v. t. & i.* To convert back or again; specif.: **a** To convert (esp. an industry or plant) after termination of government contracts for production of war materials back to production of civilian goods. **b** To restore (a unit that has been refitted and adapted for using a different fuel) to use with the former type of fuel. — **re′con·ver′sion** (-vûr′shŭn; -zhŭn), *n.*

re′con·vey′ (-vā′), *v. t.* To convey back or to the former place or owner. — **re′con·vey′ance** (-ăns), *n.*

re·cord′ (rē·kôrd′), *v. t.* [OF. *recorder*, fr. L. *recordari* to remember, fr. *re-* + *cor*, *cordis*, the heart or mind.] To commit to writing, to printing, or the like; to write or enter in a book for the purpose of preserving authentic evidence of, or on a wax cylinder, rubber disk, etc., for reproduction, as by a phonograph; to register.

rec′ord (rĕk′ẽrd *or, esp. Brit.*, -ôrd), *n.* **1.** A recording or being recorded; reduction to writing as evidence; also, the writing so made; a register. **2.** That which is written to perpetuate a knowledge of events; also, that on which such record is made, as a monument. **3.** Specif.: **a** An official writing by which the acts of some public body or officer are recorded. **b** An authentic official copy of a document deposited in the keeping of some officer designated by law. **c** An official memorandum stating the proceedings of a court of justice. **d** The official copy of the various legal papers used in a case, together with memoranda of the proceedings of the court. **4.** The known facts in the course of anything, as in a public man's career. **5.** That which has been publicly achieved in any kind of competitive sport as recorded in some authoritative manner; also, the best of such achievements; as, to beat the *record*. **6.** Something made by perforating, indenting, grooving, or otherwise transforming an original blank, so that when operated upon by a special instrument or machine it will at any time perform a definite act of reproduction, esp. of sound; as, a phonograph *record*. **7.** *Obs.* Testimony; evidence. — ***off the record.*** Not to be quoted by the public press; not for publication.

— *adj.* Denoting a performance, occurrence, or condition which goes beyond others of its kind; as, *record* prices.

re·cord′er (rē·kôr′dẽr), *n.* **1.** One who records. **2.** A mechanical or electronic recording instrument, esp. when autographic, for registering pressure, speed, electric impulses, radiation, etc.; as, a facsimile *recorder*. **3.** A device that records sounds, for example, a phonograph or its pickup or a wire or tape recorder. **4.** A magistrate or judge with criminal jurisdiction in a city or borough. **5.** An old type of flute with a fipple, having eight holes and blown at the end. Recorder making and playing have been revived in the twentieth century.

record player. An electrical instrument for playing phonograph records either through the loud-speaker of a nearby radio set, to which it broadcasts signals, or through its own loud-speaker.

re·count′ (rē·kount′), *v. t.* [OF. *reconter* to relate, fr. *re-* again + *conter* to relate.] To relate in detail.

re–count′ (rē·kount′), *v. t.* To count again. — **re·count′** (rē·kount′; rē′kount′), *n.*

re·count′al (rē·koun′tăl; -t'l), *n.* A recounting; recital.

re·coup′ (rē·kōōp′), *v. t.* [F. *recouper*, fr. *re-* + *couper* to cut.] **1.** *Law.* To keep back rightfully (a part), so as to diminish a sum due; to take off (a part) from damages; to deduct. **2.** To get an equivalent or compensation for; as, to *recoup* one's losses. **3.** To compensate (oneself) for loss, damage, etc.; reimburse. — *n. Law.* Act of recouping. — **re·coup′a·ble**, *adj.* — **re·coup′ment**, *n.*

re·course′ (rē·kōrs′; rē′kōrs; 70), *n.* [OF. *recours*, fr. L. *recursus* a running back, fr. *recurrere, recursum*. See RECUR.] **1.** Resort or application for assistance; specif.: **a** Resort for the meeting of an obligation; — chiefly in ***without recourse***, words which when added to the endorsement of a negotiable instrument protect the endorser from liability to subsequent holders. **b** *Obs.* Access; admittance. **2.** Person or thing resorted to; source of aid.

re–cov′er (rē·kŭv′ẽr), *v. t.* To cover again or anew.

re·cov′er (rē·kŭv′ẽr), *v. t.* [OF. *recovrer*, fr. L. *recuperare*. See RECUPERATE.] **1.** To get again; win back; regain, as lost property or health. **2.** To overcome; get the better of, as a state of mind. **3.** To bring (oneself) back to normal health, poise, or status. **4.** To make up for; retrieve; as, to *recover* losses. **5.** *Archaic.* To gain; reach. **6.** To restore, as to consciousness. **7.** To rescue; deliver. **8.** To reclaim, as land from the sea, gold from ore, etc.; as, to *recover* sulfur in making soda. **9.** *Law.* **a** To gain as a compensation or return; as, to *recover* damages. **b** To obtain title to by final decree or judgment; as, to *recover* lands in ejectment or real action. **c** To gain by legal process; as, to *recover* judgment against a defendant. — *v. i.* To recover something; esp.: **a** To regain health or consciousness. **b** *Law.* To obtain a judgment in one's favor. **c** *Sports.* To make a recovery. — *n. Chiefly Sports.* Recovery. — **re·cov′er·a·ble**, *adj.* — **re·cov′er·er**, *n.*

re·cov′er·y (-ĭ), *n.; pl.* -ERIES (-ĭz). **1.** A recovering; restoration; repossession; reclamation; also, time taken or amount gained in recovering. **2.** Specif., restoration from sickness, weakness, or the like. **3.** *Fencing, Sparring, etc.* Act of regaining the position of guard after making an attack. **4.** *Rowing.* The movement of the body and oar or oars, after completion of a stroke, into position for the next stroke.

rec′re·ant (rĕk′rē·ănt), *adj.* [OF., pres. part. of *recreire* to surrender allegiance, ML. *recredere* to give up, fr. L. *re-* again, back + *credere* to entrust, believe.] **1.** Crying for mercy; cowardly; craven. **2.** Apostate; unfaithful to duty or allegiance. — **Syn.** See COWARDLY. — *n.* A coward; also, an apostate. — **rec′re·an·cy** (-ăn·sĭ), *n.* — **rec′re·ant·ly**, *adv.*

rec′re·ate (-āt), *v. t.* [L. *recreatus*, past part. of *recreare* to create anew, refresh, fr. *re-* + *creare* to create.] To give fresh life to; reanimate; esp., to refresh after toil or anxiety. — **Syn.** See AMUSE. — *v. i.* To take recreation. — **rec′re·a′tive** (-ā′tĭv), *adj.*

re′–cre·ate′ (rē′krē·āt′), *v. t.* To create anew. — **re′–cre·a′tion** (-ā′shŭn), *n.*

rec′re·a′tion (rĕk′rē·ā′shŭn), *n.* A recreating; refreshment of strength and spirits after toil; diversion or a mode of diversion; play. — **rec′re·a′tion·al** (-ăl; -'l), *adj.*

rec′re·ment (rĕk′rē·mĕnt), *n.* [F. or L.; F. *récrément*, fr. L. *recrementum*, fr. *re-* + *cernere, cretum*, to separate, sift.] **1.** Superfluous matter separated from that which is useful; dross; scoria. **2.** *Med.* A substance secreted from a part of the body, as a gland, and then absorbed by the body. — **rec′re·men′tal** (-mĕn′tăl; -t'l), *adj.* — **rec′re·men·ti′tious** (-mĕn·tĭsh′ŭs), *adj.*

re·crim′i·nate (rē·krĭm′ĭ·nāt), *v. i.* [ML. *recriminare*. See CRIMINATE.] To make a countercharge or accusation; to charge back fault or crime upon an accuser. — **re·crim′i·na′tion** (-nā′shŭn), *n.* — **re·crim′i·na′tive** (-nā′tĭv; -nȧ·tĭv), *adj.*

re·crim′i·na·to′ry (-nȧ·tō′rĭ; 3), *adj.* Having the character or nature of recrimination; recriminating.

re·cross′ (rē·krŏs′; 74), *v. t. & i.* To cross again.

re′cru·desce′ (rē′kroo͞·dĕs′), *v. i.;* -DESCED′ (-dĕst′); -DESC′ING (-dĕs′ĭng). [See RECRUDESCENT.] To break out again; renew activity. — **Syn.** See RETURN.

re′cru·des′cent (-dĕs′ĕnt; -'nt), *adj.* [L. *recrudescens, -entis*, pres. part., deriv. of *re-* + *crudescere* to become hard or raw.] That breaks out again; renewing morbid or dangerous activity after abatement; as, *recrudescent* discontent. — **re′cru·des′cence** (-ĕns; -'ns), **re′cru·des′cen·cy** (-ĕn·sĭ; -'n·sĭ), *n.*

re·cruit′ (rē·kroo͞t′; 114), *v. t.* [F. *recruter*, fr. *recrue, recrute*, recruiting, recruit, prop., a new growth, deriv. of *re-* + *croître* to grow, fr. L. *crescere*.] **1.** To strengthen or supply with new men or troops; to fill up by enlistment; also, to muster; raise. **2.** To provide with what is needed to correct or prevent exhaustion, etc.; replenish. **3.** To restore the vigor or health of. — *v. i.* **1.** To gain new supplies of men for service. **2.** To recover what has been lost or spent, esp. health; recuperate. — *n.* **1.** A newly enlisted soldier, sailor, or marine, — from 1948 the lowest U. S. Army grade. Abbr. *rct.* **2.** *Now Rare.* That which replenishes or repairs a loss. — **re·cruit′er**, *n.* — **re·cruit′ment**, *n.*

re·crys′tal·lize (rē·krĭs′tăl·īz), *v. t. & i.* To crystallize again or repeatedly. — **re′crys·tal·li·za′tion** (rē′krĭs·tăl·ĭ·zā′shŭn; -ī·zā′-), *n.*

rect-. **a** = RECTO-. **b** = RECTI-.

rec′tal (rĕk′tăl; -t'l), *adj.* Of, pertaining to, or in the region of the rectum.

rec′tan′gle (rĕk′tăng′g'l), *n.* [F., fr. LL. *rect(i)angulum*, fr. L. *rectus* right + *angulus* angle.] *Geom.* A right-angled parallelogram. The area of a rectangle is found by multiplying together two adjacent sides.

rec·tan′gu·lar (rĕk·tăng′gū·lẽr), *adj.* **1.** Having one or more right angles; having the shape of, or each of its surfaces shaped like, a rectangle. **2.** That meet, cross, lie, or the like, at a right angle. — **rec·tan′gu·lar′i·ty** (-lăr′ĭ·tĭ), *n.* — **rec·tan′gu·lar·ly**, *adv.*

rec′ti- (rĕk′tĭ-), **rect-.** [LL. *recti-*, fr. L. *rectus*.] A combining form meaning *straight*, as in **rec′ti·lin′e·al, rec′ti·nerved′, rec′ti·ros′tral.**

rec′ti·fi′er (rĕk′tĭ·fī′ẽr), *n.* One who or that which rectifies; specif., *Elec.*, a device for rectifying, as the ***half-wave rectifier*** which utilizes only half of each cycle of the alternating current or the ***full-wave rectifier*** which utilizes both halves of each cycle.

rec′ti·fy (rĕk′tĭ·fī), *v. t.;* -FIED (-fīd); -FY′ING. [F. *rectifier*, fr. LL. *rectificare*, fr. *rectus* right + *ficare* (in comp.) to make.] **1.** To make or set right; amend. **2.** To set right by adjustment or calculation; — esp. in ***to rectify a globe***, to adjust a globe in preparation for solving a problem. **3.** *Chem.* To refine or purify, esp. by repeated distillation; as, to *rectify* spirit. **4.** *Elec.* To make (an alternating or oscillating current) unidirectional, varying periodically between zero and a maximum. **5.** *Math.* To determine the length of (an arc of a curve). — **Syn.** See CORRECT. — **rec′ti·fi′a·ble** (-fī′ȧ·b'l), *adj.* — **rec′ti·fi·ca′tion** (-fĭ·kā′shŭn), *n.*

rec′ti·lin′e·ar (rĕk′tĭ·lĭn′ē·ẽr), *adj.* [*recti-* + *linear*.] **1.** Moving in or forming a straight line. **2.** Formed or bounded by straight lines; also, characterized by straight lines. — **rec′ti·lin′e·ar·ly**, *adv.*

rec′ti·tude (rĕk′tĭ·tūd), *n.* [F., fr. LL. *rectitudo*, fr. *rectus* right, straight.] **1.** *Now Rare.* Straightness. **2.** Undeviating adherence to moral standards; uprightness. **3.** Correctness of judgment or procedure.

rec′to (rĕk′tō), *n.; pl.* RECTOS (-tōz). [L., abl. of *rectus* right.] *Print.* The right-hand page; — opposed to *verso*.

rec′to- (rĕk′tō-), **rect-.** [From RECTUM.] *Anat. & Med.* A combining form used to denote: **a** *The rectum*, as in **rec·tec′to·my** (see -ECTOMY), **rec′to·cele**, hernia of the rectum. **b** *Rectal and*, as in **rec′to·ab·dom′i·nal.**

rec′tor (rĕk′tẽr), *n.* [L., fr. *regere, rectum*, to lead straight, rule.] **1.** A director; the chief. **2.** *Eccl.* The clergyman in charge of a church or parish; specif., *Ch. of Eng.*, such a clergyman who has the tithes, rights, and glebes of the parish. Cf. VICAR. **3.** The head of a university or school.

rec′tor·ate (-ĭt), *n.* [ML. *rectoratus*.] The office, rank, or term of a rector.

rec·to′ri·al (rĕk·tō′rĭ·ăl; 70), *adj.* Of or pertaining to a rector, a rectory, or a rectorate.

rec′to·ry (rĕk′tō·rĭ), *n.; pl.* -RIES (-rĭz). **1.** *Eng.* A benefice held by a rector. **2.** A parsonage.

rec′trix (rĕk′trĭks), *n.; pl.* RECTRICES (rĕk·trī′sēz). *Zool.* One of the quill feathers of the tail of a bird; — so called from their importance in controlling the direction of flight. — **rec·tri′cial** (rĕk·trĭsh′ăl), *adj.*

rec′tum (rĕk′tŭm), *n.; pl.* -TA (-tȧ). [NL. (sc. *intestinum*), fr. L. *rectus* straight.] *Anat. & Zool.* The terminal part of the intestine, from the sigmoid flexure to the anus.

rec′tus (-tŭs), *n.; pl.* RECTI (-tī). [NL. (sc. *musculus*), fr. L. *rectus* straight.] *Anat.* Any of several straight muscles, as of the abdomen, thigh, head, and eye.

re·cum′ben·cy (rē·kŭm′bĕn·sĭ), *n.* Recumbent position.

re·cum′bent (-bĕnt), *adj.* [L. *recumbens*, pres. part. of *recumbere* to lie down.] **1.** Leaning; reclining; lying; specif., *Biol.*, of a structure, tending to rest upon the surface from which it extends. **2.** Resting; reposing; inactive. — **Syn.** See PRONE. — **re·cum′bent·ly**, *adv.*

re·cu′per·ate (rē·kū′pẽr·āt), *v. t.* [L. *recuperatus*, past part. of *recuperare*.] To recover; regain; also, to restore to health. — *v. i.* To recover health, strength, or from losses; esp., to convalesce. — **re·cu′per·a′tion** (-ā′shŭn), *n.* — **re·cu′per·a′tor** (-ā′tẽr), *n.* — **re·cu′per·a·to′ry** (-ȧ·tō′rĭ *or, esp. Brit.*, -tẽr·ĭ), *adj.*

re·cu′per·a′tive (-ā′tĭv; -ȧ·tĭv), *adj.* Able or likely to recover or restore; tending to recovery; restorative.

re·cur′ (rē·kûr′), *v. i.;* -CURRED′ (-kûrd′); RE·CUR′RING. [L. *recurrere*, fr. *re-* + *currere* to run.] **1.** *Now Rare.* To resort; have recourse. **2.** To go or come back in thought or discourse; as, to *recur* to our former subject. **3.** To come again to mind. **4.** To come up again for consideration; as, the question often *recurs*. **5.** To occur, or appear, again, esp. after an interval; as, a *recurring* fever. — **Syn.** See RETURN.

re·cur′rent (rē·kûr′ĕnt), *adj.* [L. *recurrens, -entis*, pres. part.] **1.** Returning from time to time; recurring; also, reappearing. **2.** *Anat.* Running or turning back in direction, as a nerve, a vein, etc. — **Syn.** See INTERMITTENT. — **re·cur′rence** (-ĕns), *n.* — **re·cur′rent·ly**, *adv.*

re·cur′ring dec′i·mal. A circulating decimal.

re·cur′vate (rē·kûr′vāt), *adj.* [L. *recurvatus*, past part.] Recurved.

re·curve′ (rē·kûrv′), *v. t. & i.* To curve in an opposite or unusual direction; to bend back.

rec′u·san·cy (rĕk′ū·zăn·sĭ; rē·kū′-), *n.* [From L. *recusans*, pres. part. of *recusare* to refuse, object to, fr. *re-* + *causa* a cause, pretext.] State or offense of one who refuses to comply with or conform to some regulation or practice, esp. in religion; nonconformity; esp., *Eng. Hist.*, refusal to attend the services of the Established Church. — **rec′u·sant** (-zănt; -z'nt), *adj. & n.*

re·cuse′ (rē·kūz′), *v. t.* [OF. *recuser*, fr. L. *recusare*. See RECUSANCY.] *Chiefly Canon Law.* To reject; esp., to except to (a judge), as interested or incompetent.

red (rĕd), *adj.;* RED′DER (-ẽr); RED′DEST. [ME. *red, reed, read*, fr. AS. *rēad*.] **1.** Of the color or hue red. **2.** Suffused with redness; as: **a** Glowing from heat. **b** Flushed, as with shame or anger. **c** Bloodstained. **3.** [*often cap.*] **a** Revolutionary or anarchistic; esp., practicing or favoring revolutionary socialism. **b** Of or pertaining to any Communist party or a Communist-controlled country or its citizens. — *n.* **1.** Any of several colors whose hue ranges from that of blood to that of the ruby or of many roses; any of the colors of that portion of the physical spectrum lying between orange (red-yellow) and violet (reddish blue). See COLOR. **2.** Any pigment or dye that colors red. **3.** A thing or animal that is red; a redskin. **4.** [*often cap.*] **a** A revolutionary. **b** A member of a Communist party or citizen of a Communist-controlled country. — ***in the red.*** Showing a net loss.

red, *v. t. Dial.* Var. of REDD.

re·dact′ (rē·dăkt′), *v. t.* [L. *redactus*, past part. of *redigere*, fr. *red-, re-*, again, back + *agere* to drive.] **1.** To put in writing; specif., to frame; draft; as, to *redact* a proclamation. **2.** To reduce to good or suitable form; put in shape, as for publication; edit; revise. — **re·dac′tion** (-dăk′shŭn), *n.* — **re·dac′tor** (-tẽr), *n.*

red algae; *sing.* RED ALGA. *Bot.* See ALGA.

re·dan′ (rē·dăn′), *n.* [F., also *redent*, a double notching, fr. *re-* + *dens, dentis*, tooth.] *Fort.* A work having two parapets forming a salient angle. Redans joined by curtains are a form of fieldworks.

red′bird′ (rĕd′bûrd′), *n.* **a** The cardinal bird. **b** The scarlet tanager. **c** The summer tanager (see TANAGER).

red′–blood′ed (rĕd′blŭd′ĕd; -ĭd; 2), *adj.* Characterized by great vitality and courage.

red′breast′ (-brĕst′), *n.* **a** The robin. **b** The knot (a sandpiper). **c** In full, **red′–breast′ed bream.** A reddish-bellied sunfish (*Lepomis auritus*) of the eastern U. S.

red′bud′ (-bŭd′), *n.* Any American tree of the genus *Cercis* of the senna family; esp., one species (*C. canadensis*), with heart-shaped leaves and small pink flowers.

red′cap′ (-kăp′), *n.* **1.** A person wearing a red cap; specif.: **a** *U. S.* A railroad station porter. **b** *Brit. Slang.* One of the military police. **2.** The European goldfinch.

red′coat′ (-kōt′), *n.* One who wears a red coat; specif., a British soldier, as formerly the typical uniform was red.

red cross. A red-colored cross; hence: **a** St. George's cross, the national emblem of England. **b** = GENEVA CROSS. **c** [*cap.*] A hospital or ambulance service, usually a national society, for alleviating sufferings in war or calamity.

redd (rĕd), *v. t.* [Prob. the same word as ME. *reden*, fr. AS. *rǣdan* to arrange, put in order.] *Dial.* To clear or clean; make tidy.

red deer. **a** The common deer of temperate Europe and Asia (*Cervus* *elaphus*), a large species related to but smaller than the elk. The male is called in his first year a *calf* or *fawn*, in second year *brocket*, in third year *spay*, in fourth year *staggard*, in fifth year and older *stag* or *hart;* the adult female is called *hind*. See ANTLER, *Illust.* **b** The Virginia deer in its summer coat. Cf. DEER.

red'den (rĕd''n), *v. t. & i.* [From RED, *adj.*] To make or become red or reddish; flush; blush.

red'dish (rĕd'ĭsh), *adj.* Somewhat red; tinged with red.

red'dle (rĕd''l). Var. of RADDLE. — **red'dle·man** (-măn), *n.*

red drum, red drumfish. See DRUMFISH.

rede (rēd), *v. t.* [See READ, *v.*] *Archaic & Dial.* To advise or counsel. — *n. Archaic & Dial.* **1.** Counsel; advice. **2. a** A story; a tale. **b** Interpretation.

re·deem' (rē·dēm'), *v. t.* [F. or L.; F. *rédimer*, fr. L. *redimere, redemptum*, fr. *red-, re-*, re- + *emere* to buy.] **1.** To regain possession of by repurchase, or esp., payment of amount due as on a pledge or mortgage. **2.** To rescue or deliver, as from bondage, by paying a ransom. **3.** To buy off or take up, as by payment; as, to *redeem* bank notes with coin. **4.** To make amends for; atone for. **5.** To fulfill, as a promise. **6.** *Theol.* To rescue and deliver from the bondage of sin and the penalties of God's violated law. — **Syn.** See RESCUE. — **re·deem'a·ble**, *adj.*

re·deem'er (-ẽr), *n.* One who redeems; specif. [*cap.*], the Saviour of the world, Jesus Christ.

re'de·liv'er (rē'dē·lĭv'ẽr), *v. t.* To deliver back or again.

re'de·mand' (-dē·månd'), *v. t.* To demand back or again. — *n. Rare.* A redemanding. — **re'de·mand'a·ble**, *adj.*

re·demp'tion (rē·dĕmp'shŭn; 89), *n.* [OF., fr. L. *redemptio.*] **1.** Act of redeeming, or state of being redeemed; ransom; deliverance; reclamation. **2.** In religions generally, salvation; deliverance from what is regarded as evil; in Christianity, deliverance from the bondage and consequences of sin, as through Christ's atonement.

re·demp'tion·er (-ẽr), *n.* Formerly, one who, wishing to emigrate from Europe to America, secured passage on credit, binding himself to be sold into service by the master or the owner of the ship for a stipulated time.

re·demp'tive (rē·dĕmp'tĭv), *adj.* Serving or tending to redeem.

re·demp'to·ry (-tō·rĭ), *adj.* Of or pertaining to redemption; paid for ransom; serving to redeem.

re'de·pos'it (rē'dē·pŏz'ĭt), *v. t.* To deposit again. — **re'de·pos'it,** *n.*

re'de·ter'mine (-dē·tûr'mĭn), *v. t.* To determine anew.

re'de·vel'op (-dē·vĕl'ŭp), *v. t. & i.* To develop again; specif., *Photog.*, to tone (a developed image) by subjecting it to a suitable bleach. — **re'de·vel'op·er** (-ẽr), *n.* — **re'de·vel'op·ment** (-mĕnt), *n.*

red'fin' (rĕd'fĭn'), *n.* Any of certain cyprinoid fishes or suckers, as a small shiner (*Luxilus cornutus*) of North America.

red fir. a Any of several western American firs, as *Abies nobilis, A. magnifica* (the ***California red fir***), and *A. amabilis;* also, their reddish wood. **b** The Douglas fir.

red fire. A composition, usually containing a strontium salt, that burns with a red light, used in pyrotechny, etc.

red fox. See FOX.

red gum. See GUM, 5 **a**.

red'-hand'ed, *adj.* Also **red'-hand'** (*see Pron.*, § 2). Having hands red with blood; in the very act, as if with bloody hands; — of a person taken in the act of homicide; hence, fresh from the commission of crime. — **red'-hand'ed·ly**, *adv.* — **red'-hand'ed·ness**, *n.*

red'head' (rĕd'hĕd'), *n.* **1.** A person who has red hair, and esp. one with a quick temper. **2.** An American duck (*Nyroca americana*), allied to the canvasback.

red heat. State of being red-hot; the temperature at which a substance is red-hot.

red herring. 1. A herring cured with saltpeter and slowly dried so as to be red. **2.** A subject intended to divert attention from the main question; — often in *to draw a red herring across the track* (*path*, etc.).

red'-hot' (rĕd'hŏt'; 2), *adj.* Red from a high degree of heat; as, *red-hot* metal; hence: **a** Excited; furious; as, a *red-hot* debate. **b** Very fresh or new; as, *red-hot* news.

red Indian, *or* **Red Indian.** An American Indian; usually, one of the copper-colored Indians of North America.

red'in·gote (rĕd'ĭng·gōt), *n.* [F., fr. E. *riding coat.*] A long plain outside coat, now one worn by women.

red·in'te·grate (rĕd·ĭn'tē·grāt), *v. t.* To make whole again; renew; restore to integrity or soundness. — **red·in'te·gra'tion** (-grā'shŭn), *n.* — **red·in'te·gra'tive** (-grā'tĭv), *adj.*

re'di·rect' (rē'dĭ·rĕkt'; -dī-), *adj. Law. U. S.* Designating or pertaining to the examination of a witness by the party calling him, after the cross-examination.

re'di·rect', *v. t.* To direct again. — **re'di·rec'tion** (-rĕk'shŭn), *n.*

re·dis'count (rē·dĭs'kount), *v. t.* To discount again, as commercial paper. — *n.* Act of rediscounting; also, *Colloq.*, rediscounted commercial paper.

re'dis·cov'er (rē'dĭs·kŭv'ẽr), *v. t.* To discover again. — **re'dis·cov'er·y** (-ĭ), *n.*

re·dis'trict (rē·dĭs'trĭkt), *v. t.* To district anew; to revise the legislative, esp. Congressional, districts of.

red'i·vi'vus (rĕd'ĭ·vī'vŭs), *adj.* [L., fr. *red-, re-*, re- + *vivus* alive.] Living again; revived.

red lattice. Red latticework, — formerly common in the windows of alehouses; hence, an alehouse or tavern.

red lead (lĕd). Minium, Pb_3O_4, prepared as a bright-red powder by oxidizing massicot, used in glassmaking, etc.

red lead ore. *Mineral.* Crocoite.

red'-let'ter (*see Pron.*, § 2), *adj.* Specially happy; memorable; — from the use on calendars of red letters for church feasts.

red light. A red-colored light, esp. one used as a sign of danger or a signal to stop. — **red'-light'** (*see Pron.*, § 2), *adj.*

red'-light' dis'trict. A district in which disorderly houses, often indicated by a red light, are numerous.

red man. A redskin.

red'ness (rĕd'nĕs; -nĭs), *n.* Red coloring; state of being red.

red oak. Any of certain oaks (as *Quercus borealis, Q. velutina, Q. texana*) with hard, cross-grained wood; also, the wood. See OAK, *Illust.*

red ocher. *Mineral.* A red, earthy hematite, used as a pigment.

red'o·lent (rĕd'ō·lĕnt), *adj.* [OF., fr. L. *redolens, -entis*, pres. part. of *redolere* to diffuse an odor.] Odorous; fragrant; hence: **a** Suggestive (*of*), as in odor, atmosphere, etc. **b** Imbued (*with*); as, a tone *redolent* with contempt. — **red'o·lence** (-lĕns), *n.* — **Syn.** See FRAGRANCE. — **red'o·lent·ly**, *adv.*

red osier. a The willow *Salix purpurea*, with reddish twigs used for basketry; also, any of several related willows. **b** Also **red osier dogwood**. See DOGWOOD.

re·dou'ble (rē·dŭb''l; rē-), *v. t. & i.* [F. *redoubler.*] **1.** To double or become doubled, as in size, amount, or degree. **2.** To repeat; re-echo. **3.** *Bridge.* To double an opponent's double. — **re·dou'ble**, *n.*

re·dou'ble (rē·dŭb''l; 2), *v. t. & i.* To double again or back; as, a fox *redoubling* on his tracks.

re·doubt' (rē·dout'), *n.* [F. *redoute*, fr. It. *ridotto*, fr. ML. *reductus*, lit., a retreat, fr. L. *reducere*. See REDUCE.] *Fort.* **a** In permanent works, a work within an outwork. **b** A small, enclosed work, commonly temporary and used in fortifying tops of hills and passes, etc.

re·doubt'a·ble (-ȧ·b'l), *adj.* [OF. *redo(u)table.*] Formidable; dread; also, worthy of respect or reverence. — **re·doubt'a·ble·ness**, *n.* — **re·doubt'a·bly**, *adv.*

re·doubt'ed (-ĕd; -ĭd), *adj.* Redoubtable; renowned.

re·dound' (rē·dound'), *v. i.* [OF. *redonder* to overflow, fr. L. *redundare*, fr. *red-, re-*, re- + *undare* to rise in waves, fr. *unda* a wave.] **1.** *Obs.* **a** To rise or surge, as water; overflow. **b** To rebound. **c** To resound. **2.** To flow back as a consequence; come as a result; accrue. — **Syn.** See CONDUCE. — *n.* A redounding; return.

red'o·wa (rĕd'ō·wȧ; -vȧ), *n.* [F. & G., fr. Czech *rejdovák*, fr. *rejdovati* to steer around, drive.] Either of two popular ballroom dances of the 19th century, one in triple time, like a waltz, the other in ¾ time, like a polka.

red pepper. See PEPPER, 3.

red'poll' (rĕd'pōl'), *n.* Any of several small finches (genus *Acanthis*) the males of which have, usually, a red crown.

Red Polled (pōld). One of an English breed of hornless dairy cattle of a uniform reddish color, raised also for beef.

re·draft' (rē·dråft'; rē'dråft'; 2; 9), *n.* **1.** A draft on the maker or endorsers of a bill of exchange dishonored by the drawee, for the amount of the bill and charges. **2.** A second draft or copy.

re·draw' (rē·drô'), *v. t. & i.* To draw again; make a redraft. — **re·draw'**, *n.* — **re·draw'er** (-ẽr), *n.*

re·dress' (rē·drĕs'), *v. t.* [F. *redresser* to straighten. See RE-; DRESS.] **1.** To set right; make amends for; as, to *redress* wrongs. **2.** To correct or amend, as a fault or abuse. **3.** To make amends to; relieve. **4.** To adjust again (usually, the balances). **5.** To restore, as an airplane, to normal condition, position, etc. — **Syn.** See CORRECT. — (rē·drĕs'; rē'drĕs), *n.* **1.** Reparation of wrong; amends. **2.** A redressing; correction; reformation; — often with *of;* as, the *redress* of grievances. — **re·dress'er, re·dres'sor**, *n.*

red'root' (rĕd'ro͞ot'; 85), *n.* **a** An herb (*Lachnanthes tinctoria*, of the bloodwort family) of the eastern U. S., with sword-shaped leaves, woolly flowers, and a red root. **b** Any of several other plants, as the bloodroot and the alkanet *Alkanna tinctoria.*

red'skin' (-skĭn'), *n. & adj.* North American Indian.

red squirrel. See SQUIRREL.

red'start' (-stärt'), *n.* [*red* + *start* tail.] **1.** A small European singing bird (*Phoenicurus phoenicurus*) allied to the redbreast. **2.** A flycatching warbler (*Setophaga ruticilla*) of eastern North America.

red tape. Official routine; hence, necessary official delay; — from the tape used in tying up official documents. — **red'-tape'**, *adj.* — **red'-tap'ism** (rĕd'tāp'ĭz'm), *n.*

red'top' (rĕd'tŏp'), *n.* A pasture and forage grass (*Agrostis stolonifera major*) of eastern North America. See 3d BENT, *n.*, 2.

re·duce' (rē·dūs'), *v. t.;* -DUCED' (-dūst'); -DUC'ING (-dūs'ĭng). [L. *reducere, -ductum*, fr. *red-, re-* + *ducere* to lead.] **1.** *Obs.* **a** To recall to mind. **b** To lead back from error in conduct or religion. **2.** To draw together; now, to diminish, esp. in bulk, amount, or extent. **3.** To bring down; lower; degrade; as, to *reduce* a sergeant to the ranks. **4.** To bring to terms; humble; conquer; subdue; as, to *reduce* a fort or a person to submission. **5.** To bring into a certain order, arrangement, classification, etc.; as, to *reduce* language to rules. **6.** To bring from one form to another; as, statements *reduced* to writing. **7.** To bring to a certain state or condition by grinding, pounding, etc.; as, to *reduce* wood to pulp. **8.** To dilute, as a paint. **9.** *Arith.* To change the denominations of (a quantity) or the form of (an expression) without changing the value; as, to *reduce* fractions to their lowest terms. **10.** *Biol.* To subject to reduction (sense 2). **11.** *Chem.* **a** Also *Metal.* To bring to the metallic state by removal of nonmetallic elements; as, metals are *reduced* from their ores. **b** To deoxidize; to change from a higher to a lower positive valence. **c** To combine with, or subject to the action of, hydrogen. **12.** *Photog.* To render less dense, as a negative. **13.** *Surg.* To correct, as a fracture, by restoring displaced parts. — *v. i.* To become reduced in any way. — **Syn.** See DECREASE; CONQUER. — **re·duc'er** (-dūs'ẽr), *n.* — **re·duc'i·bil'i·ty** (-ĭ·bĭl'ĭ·tĭ), *n.* — **re·duc'i·ble** (-b'l), *adj.* — **re·duc'i·bly**, *adv.*

re·duc'tase (rē·dŭk'tās; -tāz), *n.* [*reduct*ion + diast*ase.*] Any enzyme that accelerates the process of reduction.

‖**re·duc'ti·o ad ab·sur'dum** (rē·dŭk'shĭ·ō ăd ăb·sûr'dŭm). [L.] Literally, reduction to absurdity; hence, disproof of a proposition, etc., by showing the absurdity to which it leads when carried to its logical conclusion.

re·duc'tion (rē·dŭk'shŭn), *n.* [F. or L.; F. *réduction*, fr. L. *reductio*. See REDUCE.] **1.** A reducing, or state of being reduced; also, a thing made by reducing, as a copy on a smaller scale, a reduced price, etc. **2.** *Biol.* **a** = MEIOSIS. **b** In a narrower sense, = HAPLOSIS. — **re·duc'tion·al** (-ăl; -'l), *adj.* — **re·duc'tive** (-dŭk'tĭv), *adj. & n.*

re·dun'dance (rē·dŭn'dăns), *n.* Redundancy.

re·dun'dan·cy (-dăn·sĭ), *n.* **1.** Quality, instance, or state of being redundant; superfluity; excess; specif., use of more words than needed to convey the thought. Cf. PLEONASM, TAUTOLOGY. **2.** That which is redundant; a superfluity.

re·dun'dant (-dănt), *adj.* [L. *redundans, -antis*, pres. part. of *redundare*. See REDOUND.] **1.** Exceeding what is natural, usual, or necessary; superfluous; as, a *redundant* foot in a verse; *redundant* words in a statement. **2.** Containing something excessive or superfluous; as, a *redundant* chord; specif., using more words than necessary; as, *redundant* style or language. **3.** Profuse; superabundant. — **Syn.** See WORDY. — **re·dun'dant·ly**, *adv.*

redundant verb. *Gram.* A verb that has alternative forms, as for the past tense (*hanged, hung*).

re·du′pli·cate (rē·dū′plĭ·kāt; 114), *adj.* [LL. *reduplicatus*, past part. See RE-; DUPLICATE.] Double; doubled. — (-kāt), *v. t. & i.* **1.** To redouble; repeat. **2.** *Philol.* To repeat all or part of (a radical element); to form by reduplication.

re·du′pli·ca′tion (-kā′shŭn), *n.* **1.** Act of redoubling, or state of being redoubled; also, a part folded back on itself. **2.** *Philol.* Repetition, commonly at the beginning of a word, of a radical element or a part of it, often accompanied by change of the radical vowel; as in Fr. *bonbon*, L. *murmur*, Eng. *knickknack*. — **re·du′pli·ca′tive** (-dū′plĭ·kā′tĭv), *adj.*

red′ware′ (rĕd′wâr′), *n.* [*red* + *ware* seaweed.] A large brown edible seaweed (*Laminaria digitata*) common off the New England coast.

red′–wat′ (-wŏt′), *adj.* *Scot.* Wet with blood.

red′wing′ (-wĭng′), *n.* **a** A European thrush (*Turdus musicus*) having the under wing coverts red. **b** The red-winged blackbird. See BLACKBIRD.

red′wood′ (-wo͝od′), *n.* **1.** Any wood yielding a red dye, or the tree furnishing the wood. **2.** Any of various trees having reddish wood. **3. a** An important coniferous timber tree (*Sequoia sempervirens*) of California, often attaining a height of 300 feet. **b** The handsome brownish-red light wood of this tree.

red′wood′ (rĕd′wo͝od′; -wōd′; -wo͝od′), *adj.* [*red* + *wood* mad.] *Scot.* Mad; furious.

red′–yel′low, *n.* The hue of the color cycle equally like and equally unlike the primary hues red and yellow. See COLOR. — **red′–yel′low** (*see Pron.*, § 2), *adj.*

re–ech′o (rē·ĕk′ō), *v. i. & t.* To echo back; reverberate. — *n.; pl.* -ECHOES (-ōz). The echo of an echo.

reed (rēd), *n.* [AS. *hrēod.*] **1.** Also **reed grass.** Any of various tall bamboolike grasses, esp. one species (*Phragmites communis*), or their slender, often jointed, stems. Cf. CANE, 3 **b**. **2.** A growth or mass of reeds. **3.** An arrow, as of a reed. **4.** A musical instrument or pipe made of the hollow joint of reed, cane, or the like. **5.** *Arch.* A type of molding. See MOLDING, *Illust.* **6.** *Bib.* An ancient Jewish measure of six cubits. **7.** *Music.* A thin, elastic tongue of cane, wood, or metal, fastened at one end to the mouthpiece of the clarinet, organ reed pipe, etc., or to a reed block or other fixture over an air opening, as in the reed organ or accordion, and set in vibration by the breath or other air current. Cf. DOUBLE-REED. **8.** *Weaving.* In a loom, a contrivance through which yarns are drawn. It consists of flat parallel slips. — *v. t.* **1.** To thatch with reeds. **2.** To decorate with reeds.

R Reed, 7 (Mouthpiece of a Clarinet).

reed′bird′ (-bûrd′), *n.* *Southern U. S.* See BOBOLINK.

reed′buck′ (-bŭk′), *n.; see* PLURAL, *Note*, 6. [Trans. of D. *rietbok.*] Any of a genus (*Redunca*) of African antelope of a fawn color. The females are hornless.

re–ed′i·fy (rē·ĕd′ĭ·fī), *v. t.* To rebuild.

reed′ing, *n.* [From REED, the plant.] *Arch. & Furniture.* **a** A small convex molding; a reed; — the reverse of *fluting*. See MOLDING, *Illust.* **b** Decoration by reeds, as on chair or table legs.

reed′ling (rēd′lĭng), *n.* [*reed* + 1st *-ling.*] A small, long-tailed European bird (*Panurus biarmicus*) which frequents reedy places. The male has a tuft of black feathers on each side of the face.

reed mace. *Eng.* The cattail.

reed organ. An organ in which the wind acts upon a set of free metal reeds.

reed pipe. *Music.* See PIPE, *n.*, 1.

reed stop. *Music.* A set of reed pipes, in an organ, controlled by a single stop knob.

re–ed′u·cate (rē·ĕd′ū·kāt), *v. t.* To educate again; esp., to rehabilitate through education. — **re′–ed·u·ca′tion** (rē′ĕd·ū·kā′shŭn), *n.*

reed′y (rēd′ĭ), *adj.;* REED′I·ER (-ĭ·ẽr); REED′I·EST. **1.** Abounding in or made of reeds. **2.** Like a reed; esp., long and slender. **3.** Having the quality of a reed instrument in tone. — **reed′i·ness**, *n.*

reef (rēf), *n.* [ON. *rif*, prob. same as ON. *rif* rib. See REEF of a sail.] **1.** A chain of rocks or ridge of sand lying at or near the surface of the water. **2.** *Mining.* A vein or lode.

reef, *n.* [ON. *rif* reef, prob. same as ON. *rif* rib. Cf. 1st REEF.] *Naut.* **a** That part of a sail taken in or let out in regulating size. **b** The reduction in sail area by reefing. — *v. t. & i.;* REEFED (rēft); REEF′ING. **a** To reduce (a sail) by rolling or folding up a part of it. **b** To lower or bring inboard wholly or partially (a spar), as a topmast or bowsprit; house.

reef′er (-ẽr), *n.* **1.** *Naut.* One who reefs. **2.** A close-fitting, usually double-breasted, jacket of thick cloth. **3.** *Slang.* A cigarette containing the narcotic marijuana.

reef knot. *Naut.* A kind of knot. See KNOT, *Illust.* (28).

reek (rēk), *n.* [AS. *rēc.*] **1.** *Now Dial.* Smoke. **2.** Vapor; fetid air; a fume. — *v. i.* **1.** To emit reek, or fumes; fume. **2.** To be permeated with or as with a reek; as, the room *reeked* of tobacco smoke. — *v. t.* **1.** To subject to the action of smoke, vapor, etc.; — chiefly technical. **2.** To emit as or as if a reek; to exude; as, his manner *reeks* prosperity. — **reek′er** (-ẽr), *n.* — **reek′y** (-ĭ), *adj.*

reel (rēl), *n.* **1.** A lively dance of the Scottish Highlanders, or its music. **2.** = VIRGINIA REEL.

reel, *n.* [AS. *hrēol.*] **1.** A revolvable device on which yarn, thread, etc., is wound. **2.** Specif.: **a** A form of small windlass for the butt end of a fishing rod. **b** A spool or bobbin to hold sewing silk, etc. **c** A flanged spool on which a photographic film is wound; hence, a strip of motion-picture film, usually 1000 or 2000 feet in length, wound on a spool. **3.** A quantity of thread, wire, etc., wound on a spool. — *v. t.* **1.** To wind upon a reel. **2.** To draw by reeling a line; as, to *reel* a fish in. — **reel′a·ble**, *adj.*

— ***reel off.*** **a** To take off by reeling, as silk from the cocoon. **b** To tell fluently, as a story.

reel, *v. i.* [From REEL, device.] **1.** To turn or move round and round; to whirl; specif.: **a** Of the eyes, to roll with dizziness, etc. **b** Of the mind, head, or the like, to be giddy; to be in a whirl. **2.** To give way; waver, as a line in battle. **3.** To walk or move unsteadily; sway; stagger. — *v. t.* To cause to reel, esp. to whirl. — *n.* A reeling.

re′–e·lect′ (rē′ē·lĕkt′), *v. t.* To elect again to an office. — **re′–e·lec′tion** (-lĕk′shŭn), *n.*

reel′er (rēl′ẽr), *n.* One who reels.

re′–e·merge′ (rē′ē·mûrj′), *v. i.* To emerge after being concealed, suppressed, etc. — **re′–e·mer′gence** (-mûr′jĕns), *n.*

re–em′pha·size (rē·ĕm′fȧ·sīz), *v. t.* To emphasize again.

re′–em·ploy′ (rē′ĕm·ploi′), *v. t.* To employ again. — **re′–em·ploy′ment**, *n.*

re′–en·act′ (rē′ĕn·ăkt′), *v. t.* To enact anew. — **re′–en·act′ment**, *n.*

re′–en·force′, etc. Vars. of REINFORCE, etc.

re′–en·gage′ (rē′ĕn·gāj′), *v. t.* To engage again.

re′–en·grave′ (-grāv′), *v. t.* To engrave again.

re′–en·list′ (rē′ĕn·lĭst′), *v. t.* To enlist again, as at the end of one's period of service. — **re′–en·list′ment**, *n.*

re–en′ter (rē·ĕn′tẽr), *v. t. & i.* To enter again.

re–en′ter·ing pol′y·gon. A polygon having one or more angles pointing inward (**re–entering angles**).

re–en′trance (rē·ĕn′trăns), *n.* A re-entering.

re–en′trant (rē·ĕn′trănt), *adj.* Re-entering; directed inwards. — *n.* A re-entrant angle, as in a fortification.

re–en′try (-trĭ), *n.* **1.** A second or new entry. **2.** In full **re–entry card.** *Whist & Bridge.* A card that by winning a trick will enable one to regain the lead. **3.** *Law.* A retaking possession; repossession.

reest (rēst), *v. i.* *Scot. & Dial.* To balk.

reest, *v. t. & i.* *Scot.* To cure or be cured by smoking.

re′–es·tab′lish (rē′ĕs·tăb′lĭsh), *v. t.* To establish again or anew. — **re′–es·tab′lish·ment**, *n.*

reeve (rēv), *n.* The female of the ruff (sandpiper).

reeve, *v. t.;* ROVE (rōv), or REEVED (rēvd); REEV′ING. [Origin uncert.] *Naut.* **a** To pass, as the end of a rope, through a hole in a block, cleat, or the like. **b** To fasten by passing through or around something. **c** To pass a rope through; as, to *reeve* a block.

reeve, *n.* [ME. *reve*, fr. AS. *gerēfa.*] *O. Eng. Hist.* An administrative official who was in part a steward, bailiff, or overseer.

re′–ex·am′i·na′tion (rē′ĕg·zăm′ĭ·nā′shŭn; -ĭg-), *n.* **1.** A second examination. **2.** *Law.* An examination made by a party calling a witness, after, and upon matters arising out of, the cross-examination.

re′–ex·am′ine (-zăm′ĭn), *v. t.* To subject to re-examination. — **re′–ex·am′in·er** (-ĭn·ẽr), *n.*

re′–ex·port′ (rē′ĕks·pōrt′; 70; *see* EXPORT), *v. t.* To export again; also, usually, to export (something imported). — **re–ex′port** (rē·ĕks′pōrt), *n.* — **re′–ex·por·ta′tion** (rē′ĕks·pōr·tā′shŭn), *n.*

re·face′ (rē·fās′), *v. t.* To supply with a new face, or front.

re·fash′ion (-făsh′ŭn), *v. t.* To fashion again.

re·fas′ten (-fás′'n; 9), *v. t.* To fasten again.

re·fect′ (rē·fĕkt′), *v. t.* [L. *refectus*, past part. of *reficere*, fr. *re-* + *facere* to make.] *Archaic.* To refresh, as with food or drink.

re·fec′tion (rē·fĕk′shŭn), *n.* [OF., fr. L. *refectio.* See REFECT.] **1.** Refreshment; esp., refreshment after hunger or fatigue. **2.** A repast; a lunch.

re·fec′to·ry (-tō·rĭ), *n.; pl.* -RIES (-rĭz). [ML. *refectorium.*] A dining hall, esp. in a monastery or convent.

refectory table. A long, narrow dining table; specif., an early, heavy standing table, or a trestle and board.

re·fer′ (rē·fûr′), *v. t.;* -FERRED′ (-fûrd′); -FER′RING. [OF. or L.; OF. *referer*, fr. L. *referre*, fr. *re-* + *ferre* to bear.] **1.** To regard, identify, or the like, as belonging or related (to); to assign as to a class, or cause. **2.** To send or direct (to some person or place), as for treatment, aid, decision, etc.; specif., to send for information regarding ability, character, etc. — *v. i.* **1.** To have relation or reference; relate; point. **2.** To direct attention; make reference. **3.** To have recourse; go (*to*) for information, support, etc.; as, to *refer* to the dictionary. — **ref′er·a·ble** (rĕf′ẽr·ȧ·b'l; rē·fûr′ȧ·b'l), **re·fer′ri·ble** (rē·fûr′ĭ·b'l), *adj.* — **re·fer′rer** (-ẽr), *n.*

Syn. (1) See ASCRIBE.
(2) **Refer, allude** mean to call attention to something by mentioning it. **Refer** suggests, usually, intentional introduction and distinct mention; **allude**, indirect mention as by a hint or a roundabout expression.

ref′er·ee′ (rĕf′ẽr·ē′), *n.* One to whom a thing is referred; as: **a** *Law.* An arbitrator; specif., *U. S.*, an attorney appointed to act as an officer of the court in determining, or reporting on, an issue referred to him in a pending proceeding or suit. **b** An umpire, as in certain games or sports; sometimes, specif., a judge of certain points of play, as, in American football, an official who is esp. the judge of matters connected with the progress of the ball, as distinguished from the *umpire*, who is, in general, judge of the acts of the players. — *v. t. & i.;* REF′ER·EED′ (-ēd′); REF′ER·EE′ING. To act as referee (for).

ref′er·ence (rĕf′ẽr·ĕns), *n.* **1.** Act of referring, or state of being referred. **2.** Relation; respect. **3.** A statement or remark referring (to something); an allusion. **4.** A sign or direction referring a reader to another passage or book. **5.** Direction to, or consultation of, books, periodicals, etc., for information; — chiefly attributive; as, *reference* books. **6.** Any person or thing referred to for information, recommendation, etc. **7.** A written statement of the qualifications of a person seeking employment, a position, etc.

ref′er·en′dum (-ĕn′dŭm), *n.; pl.* -DUMS (-dŭmz), -DA (-dȧ). [Neut. gerundive of L. *referre*. See REFER.] **1.** The principle or practice of referring measures passed upon or proposed by the legislative body to the electorate for approval or rejection; also, the right so to pass on laws, or the vote by which this is done. **2.** Hence, any similar method for ascertaining the will of a group of persons, as a labor union.

ref′er·ent (rĕf′ẽr·ĕnt), *n.* [L. *referens, -entis*, pres. part.] Someone or something that refers to another or, esp., that is referred to. — **ref′er·ent**, *adj.*

re·fer′ral (rē·fûr′ăl), *n.* Act of referring.

re′fill (rē′fĭl), *n.* A commercial product designed to fill again a special container originally sold with its contents.

re·fill′ (rē·fĭl′), *v. t.* To fill again. — **re·fill′a·ble**, *adj.*

re·fine′ (rē·fīn′), *v. t.* [*re-* + *fine* to make fine.] **1.** To reduce to a fine, unmixed, or pure state; to free from dross or alloy, as metals; to purify, as sugar, wine, etc. **2.** To free from dullness, earthiness, etc.; to elevate; as, to *refine* one's mind or thoughts. **3.** To improve or perfect as by pruning or polishing; as, to *refine* one's style. **4.** To free from what is coarse, vulgar, inelegant, or the like; as, an education that *refined* his taste. — *v. i.* **1.** To become pure or purer, elegant or more elegant. **2.** To make use of refinements, esp. in thought or language. **3.** To improve by introducing refinements; — with *on* or *upon;* as, to *refine* upon another's invention. — **re·fin′er** (-fīn′ẽr), *n.*

re·fined′ (-fīnd′), *adj.* That is purified, freed from dross, etc.; hence: **a** Highbred; fastidious; cultivated. **b** Marked by refinement of methods or execution; subtle, exact, etc.; as, the *refined* cruelty of a tyrant.

re·fine′ment (rē·fīn′mĕnt), *n.* **1.** A refining; state or quality of being refined. **2.** A product or outcome of a refining process; specif.: **a** A subtlety in reasoning; as, the *refinements* of logic. **b** An improvement; a contrivance, etc., that perfects.

re·fin′er·y (rē·fīn′ẽr·ĭ), *n.; pl.* -ERIES (-ĭz). A building and apparatus for refining, or purifying, esp. metals, oil, and sugar.

re·fit′ (rē·fĭt′), *v. t.;* RE·FIT′TED (-ĕd; -ĭd); RE·FIT′TING. To prepare for use again; fit out or supply again; repair; renovate. — *v. i.* To obtain repairs or fresh supplies or equipment. — *n.* A refitting; a repairing of damages or replacing of what is worn or useless.

re·flate′ (rē·flāt′), *v. i. & t.* To inflate again; to reinflate. — **re·fla′tion** (-flā′shŭn), *n.*

re·flect′ (rē·flĕkt′), *v. t.* [OF. *reflecter*, fr. L. *reflectere, reflexum*, fr. *re-* + *flectere* to bend.] **1.** To turn or direct; deflect; divert; as, to *reflect* the eye to a thing. **2.** To bend back; throw or cast back, esp. on being struck; as, this wall *reflects* heat waves. **3.** To give back an image or likeness of; mirror. **4.** To bring or cast as a result; as, to *reflect* credit on one. — *v. i.* **1.** *Obs.* To be reflected. **2.** To reflect light, heat, etc. **3.** To throw or turn back the thoughts (upon anything); meditate; contemplate. **4.** To cast or bring reproach, discredit, or the like. — **Syn.** See THINK. — **re·flect′er** (rē·flĕk′tẽr), *n.*

re·flect′ance (rē·flĕk′tăns), *n.* [*reflect* + *-ance.*] *Physics.* A measure of the ability of a surface to reflect radiant energy, ordinarily expressed as the ratio of the intensity of the reflected radiation to that of the incident radiation at normal incidence; — called also *coefficient of reflection.*

re·flec′tion (-flĕk′shŭn), *n.* **1.** A reflecting; esp., the return of light or sound waves from surfaces. **2.** That which is produced by such reflection; as: **a** Reflected light or heat. **b** A reflected image. **3.** Reproach cast; blame; a statement, etc., that casts reproach or discredit; an imputation. **4.** Mental consideration; contemplation; also, a conclusion reached after much thought. **5.** *Anat. & Zool.* The bending back of a part upon itself; also, the part so bent back. — **Syn.** See ANIMADVERSION. — **re·flec′tion·al** (-ăl; -′l), *adj.*

re·flec′tive (rē·flĕk′tĭv), *adj.* **1.** That reflects; specif., given to reflection; deliberative; thoughtful. **2.** Of, pertaining to, or caused by reflection; reflected. — **re·flec′tive·ly,** *adv.* — **re·flec′tive·ness,** *n.* — **re′flec·tiv′i·ty** (rē′flĕk·tĭv′ĭ·tĭ), *n.*

re·flec′tor (-tẽr), *n.* One that reflects; specif., a polished surface, as in a headlight, for reflecting rays of light.

‖**re·flet′** (rē·flĕ′), *n.* [F., reflection. See REFLEX.] Luster; special brilliancy of surface; — of pottery.

re′flex (rē′flĕks; 2), *adj.* [L. *reflexus*, past part. See REFLECT.] **1.** Bent, turned, or directed back; reversed in direction; specif.: **a** Of light, reflected. **b** *Now Rare.* Of thought or thinking, introspective. **2.** Produced in reaction, in resistance, or in return; as, a *reflex* consequence. **3.** *Physiol.* Pertaining to, or produced by, reflex action (see REFLEX, *n.*, 3). **4.** *Radio.* Of or pertaining to a type of receiving set with an amplifier tube or tubes functioning simultaneously as both a radio-frequency and an audio-frequency amplifier. **5.** Of more than 180° and less than 360°; — of an angle. — (rē′flĕks), *n.* **1.** *Now Rare.* Reflected heat, light, color, or the like; also, a reflex effect, operation, etc. **2.** A mirrored image; hence, a likeness, or copy; often, a concrete representation or expression. **3.** *Physiol.* An act, as a movement, performed involuntarily in consequence of a nervous impulse transmitted inward from a receptor, or sense organ, to a nerve center and outward to an effector, as a muscle or gland; also, the whole process (***reflex action***), culminating in such an act.

re·flex′ (rē·flĕks′), *v. t.* To bend, turn, or fold, back; reflect; — chiefly in *past part.*

re′flex cam′er·a. A camera in which the image formed by the lens is, for focusing purposes, viewed in a mirror.

re·flex′ion, re·flex′ion·al. Vars. of REFLECTION, etc.

re·flex′ive (rē·flĕk′sĭv), *adj.* **1.** Reflex. **2.** Reflective. **3.** *Gram.* **a** Denoting an action that is directed back upon the agent or subject, as in ***reflexive verb*** (the witness *perjured* himself). **b** See *reflexive pronoun*, under PRONOUN. — *n.* A reflexive pronoun or verb. — **re·flex′ive·ly,** *adv.* — **re·flex′ive·ness, re′flex·iv′i·ty** (rē′flĕk·sĭv′ĭ·tĭ), *n.*

re′flo·res′cence (rē′flō·rĕs′ĕns; -′ns), *n.* A blossoming anew.

re·flow′ (rē·flō′), *v. i.* To flow back; ebb.

ref′lu·ent (rĕf′lū·ĕnt; 114), *adj.* [L. *refluens*, pres. part.] Flowing back; ebbing. — **ref′lu·ence** (-ĕns), *n.*

re′flux (rē′flŭks), *n.* [*re-* + *flux.*] A flowing back; ebb; refluence; as, the flux and *reflux* of the tides.

re·for′est (rē·fŏr′ĕst; -ĭst), *v. t. & i.* To renew forest cover on (land) by seeding or planting. — **re′for·est·a′tion** (rē′fŏr·ĕs·tā′shŭn; -ĭs-), *n.*

re·forge′ (rē·fôrj′; -fōrj′), *v. t.* To forge again or anew; make over. — **re·forg′er** (-fôr′jẽr; -fōr′jẽr), *n.*

re·form′ (rē·fôrm′), *v. t.* [OF. *reformer*, fr. L. *reformare*, fr. *re-* + *formare* to form, fr. *forma* form.] To change into a new and improved form or condition; to improve by change of form, removal of faults or abuses, etc.; to restore to a former good state, or bring from bad to good; amend. — **Syn.** See CORRECT. — *n.* Amendment of what is vicious or depraved, or a case of it; correction of an abuse, a wrong, or errors. — **re·form′a·ble,** *adj.* — **re·form′a·tive,** *adj.* — **re·form′er, re·form′ist,** *n.*

re–form′ (rē·fôrm′), *v. t. & i.* To shape again or anew. — **re′–for·ma′tion** (rē′fôr·mā′shŭn), *n.*

ref′or·ma′tion (rĕf′ŏr·mā′shŭn), *n.* **1.** Act of reforming, or state of being reformed. **2.** [*cap.*] The important religious movement in western Christendom beginning early in the 16th century, which resulted in the formation of the various Protestant churches. — **ref′or·ma′tion·al** (-ăl; -′l), *adj.*

re·form′a·to′ry (rē·fôr′mȧ·tō′rĭ *or, esp. Brit.,* -tẽr·ĭ), *adj.* That tend to or aim at reformation; intended for reformation; as, *reformatory* measures or schools. — *n.; pl.* -RIES (-rĭz). A penal institution to which young offenders are committed for training and reformation.

re·formed′ (rē·fôrmd′), *adj.* **1.** Corrected; amended; esp., improved in character or life. **2.** [*cap.*] Pertaining to, or designating the body of Protestant churches originating in the Reformation or, in a more restricted sense, of those churches formed in various European countries by Zwingli, Calvin, and others who separated from Luther on the doctrine of the Lord's Supper, etc.

reform school. A reformatory for boys or girls.

re·fract′ (rē·frăkt′), *v. t.* [L. *refractus*, past part. of *refringere*, fr. *re-* + *frangere* to break.] **1.** *Med. & Optics.* To measure the refraction of (an eye, a lens). **2.** *Physics.* To subject (rays of light, etc.) to refraction. — **re·frac′tor** (-frăk′tẽr), *n.*

re·frac′tion (-frăk′shŭn), *n.* *Physics.* The deflection from a straight path suffered by a ray of light, heat, sound, or the like, in passing obliquely from one medium into another in which its velocity is different, as from air into water or from a denser to a rarer layer of air. — **re·frac′tion·al** (-ăl; -′l), *adj.*

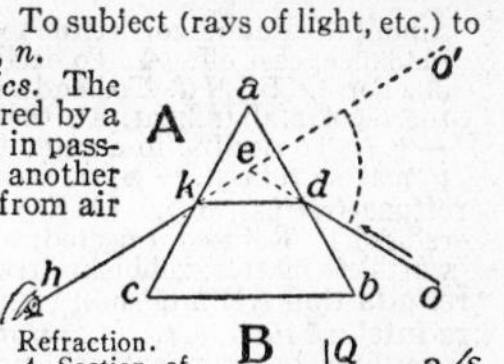

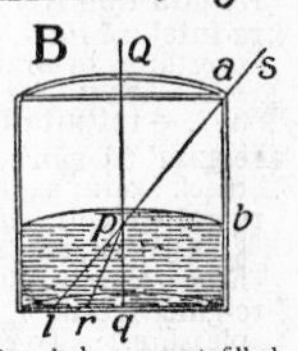

Refraction.
A Section of Prism, showing Refraction. The Incident Ray *od* is refracted at *d* and again at *k*, the Eye (*k*) seeing a virtual image of *o* at o′; *oeo′* Angle of Deviation.
B Section of Vessel, lower part filled with Water; *sl* Ray of Light in straight line; *spr* Ray of Light refracted; *Qq* Perpendicular; *spQ* Angle of Incidence; *rpq* Angle of Refraction. See also FOCUS, *Illust.*

re·frac′tive (-tĭv), *adj.* Serving, or having power, to refract, or deflect; of, pertaining to, or due to refraction. — **re·frac′tive·ly,** *adv.* — **re·frac′tive·ness, re′frac·tiv′i·ty** (rē′frăk·tĭv′ĭ·tĭ), *n.*

re′frac·tom′e·ter (rē′frăk·tŏm′ē·tẽr), *n.* [*refraction* + *-meter.*] *Physics.* Any of various instruments used for measuring refraction. — **re′frac·tom′e·try** (-trĭ), *n.*

re·frac′to·ri·ness (rē·frăk′tō·rĭ·nĕs; -nĭs), *n.* State, condition, or quality of being refractory; esp., the capacity of a material to resist a high temperature.

re·frac′to·ry (-tō·rĭ), *adj.* **1.** Obstinate; intractable; unmanageable. **2.** Resisting ordinary treatment; difficult to fuse, reduce, or the like; as, a *refractory* ore. — **Syn.** See UNRULY. — *n.* A refractory person or thing; esp., a refractory material. — **re·frac′to·ri·ly,** *adv.* — **re·frac′to·ri·ness,** *n.*

ref′ra·ga·ble (rĕf′rȧ·gȧ·b′l), *adj.* [ML. *refragabilis*, fr. L. *refragari* to oppose.] *Rare.* That may be controverted.

re·frain′ (rē·frān′), *v. t.* [OF. *refrener*, fr. L. *refrenare* (fr. *re-* back + *frenum* bridle), influenced prob. by OF. *refraindre* to restrain, moderate.] *Archaic.* To restrain; check; to curb. — *v. i.* To keep oneself from doing something implied or understood; forbear; abstain. — **re·frain′er,** *n.*

Syn. **Refrain, abstain, forbear** mean to keep oneself from doing or indulging in something. **Refrain** suggests, usually, the checking of an impulse; **abstain,** deliberate renunciation or self-denial; **forbear,** self-restraint and the exercise of patience or charity.

re·frain′, *n.* [OF., fr. *refraindre* to restrain, deriv. of L. *refringere*, lit., to break off.] The burden of a song; a phrase or verse which recurs regularly, esp. at the end of each stanza or division of a poem or song; also, the musical setting of such a phrase or verse.

re·fran′gi·ble (rē·frăn′jĭ·b′l), *adj.* [*re-* + L. *frangere* to break.] Capable of being refracted, as rays of light. — **re·fran′gi·bil′i·ty** (-bĭl′ĭ·tĭ), **re·fran′gi·ble·ness,** *n.*

re·fresh′ (rē·frĕsh′), *v. t.* [OF. *refreschier*, fr. *re-* + *fres* fresh.] **1.** To make fresh or fresher, as by cooling; to restore strength, spirit, etc., to. **2.** To revive, strengthen, or the like, by or as by renewing supplies; replenish; as, to *refresh* one's memory. **3.** To freshen up, as by cleaning; renovate. — *v. i.* **1.** To become fresh again; revive. **2.** To give, supply, or take refreshment. — **Syn.** See RENEW. — **re·fresh′ing·ly,** *adv.*

re·fresh′er (-ẽr), *n.* **1.** One that refreshes; specif.: **a** *Colloq.* A drink. **b** A reminder. **c** A refresher course. **2.** *Law.* An extra fee paid to counsel in a case adjourned from one term to another or unusually protracted. — *adj.* That is designed to refresh one's mind on subjects previously studied and partly forgotten or to inform one of new developments in some field; as, a *refresher* course; *refresher* training.

re·fresh′ment (-mĕnt), *n.* **1.** Act of refreshing, or state of being refreshed. **2.** That which refreshes; specif., food or drink; in *pl.*, a light meal; a lunch.

re·frig′er·ant (rē·frĭj′ẽr·ănt), *adj.* Cooling; refreshing. — *n.* A refrigerant agent or agency; specif.: **a** A medicine for allaying fever. **b** Any substance, as ice, liquid air, ammonia, or carbon dioxide, used in refrigeration.

re·frig′er·ate (-āt), *v. t.* [L. *refrigeratus*, past part. of *refrigerare*, fr. *re-* + *frigerare* to make cool, fr. *frigus, frigoris*, coolness.] To make or keep cold or cool; specif., to freeze or chill (food) for preservation. — **re·frig′er·a′tion** (-ā′shŭn), *n.* — **re·frig′er·a′tive** (-ā′tĭv; -ȧ·tĭv), *adj. & n.* — **re·frig′er·a·to′ry** (-ȧ·tō′rĭ *or, esp. Brit.,* -tẽr·ĭ), *adj.*

re·frig′er·a′tor (-ā′tẽr), *n.* That which refrigerates; specif., a box or room for keeping food or other articles cool; also, an apparatus for rapidly cooling heated liquids or vapors.

re·frin′gent (rē·frĭn′jĕnt), *adj.* [L. *refringens*, pres. part. of *refringere.* See REFRACT.] Refractive; refracting.

reft (rĕft), *past tense & past part.* of 1st REAVE.

ref′uge (rĕf′ūj), *n.* [OF., fr. L. *refugium*, fr. *re-* + *fugere* to flee.] **1.** Shelter or protection from danger, distress, etc. **2.** An asylum, or place where one is safe or protected; a shelter; a sanctuary; retreat. **3.** A means of resort; resource; a recourse. — *v. t. & i.* *Now Rare.* To give or take refuge.

ref′u·gee′ (rĕf′ū·jē′), *n.* [F. *réfugié.*] One who flees for safety; specif., a person who has fled or been ejected from his country of nationality or of habitual residence for reasons of race, religion, nationality, or political opinion or as a victim of one of the nazi, fascist, or quisling regimes; also, a German or Austrian resident of Jewish or foreign origin detained under nazi persecution, or returned thither after flight through the vicissitudes of war, and not yet resettled.

re·ful′gence (rē·fŭl′jĕns), *n.* Also **re·ful′gen·cy** (-jĕn·sĭ). [From L. *refulgens*, pres. part. of *refulgere* to flash back.] Quality or state of being radiant or resplendent; splendor; radiance. — **re·ful′gent,** *adj.* — **re·ful′gent·ly,** *adv.*

re·fund′ (rē·fŭnd′), *v. t.* [*re-* + *fund.*] To fund again or anew; specif., *Finance*, to borrow, as by the sale of bonds, in order to pay off an existing loan with the proceeds.

re·fund′ (rē·fŭnd′), *v. t.* [OF. or L.; OF. *refunder*, fr. L. *refundere*, fr. *re-* + *fundere* to pour.] **1.** *Now Rare.* To pour back. **2.** To return (money) in restitution, repayment, etc. — (rē·fŭnd′; rē′fŭnd), *n.* A refunding; amount refunded. — **re·fund′er,** *n.* — **re·fund′ment,** *n.*

re·fur′bish (rē·fûr′bĭsh), *v. t.* To brighten or freshen up.

re·fus′al (rē·fūz′ăl; -′l), *n.* **1.** A refusing; rejection; denial. **2.** The right to refuse or take before others; option.

re·fuse′ (rē·fūz′), *v. t.* [OF. *refuser*, fr. freq. of L. *refundere.* See REFUND to repay.] **1.** To decline to accept; reject. **2.** To decline to submit to or undergo; decline to do or give; deny; decline. **3.** *Obs.* To renounce; cast off. **4.** To decline to jump or leap over, as a fence; — of a horse. **5.** *Mil.* To bend or keep back (as a wing or a flank), out of the regular alignment; as, the right was *refused* along a crossroad. — *v. i.* To decline to accept; to withhold compliance or permission; to make a refusal. — **Syn.** See DECLINE. — **re·fus′er** (rē-fūz′ẽr), *n.*

ref′use (rĕf′ūs), *adj.* [ME. *refus*, prob. fr. OF. *refuse*, past part., refused.] Refused; rejected; worthless. — *n.* Rejected, useless, or worthless matter; rubbish; dregs, leavings, etc.

ref′u·ta′tion (rĕf′ū-tā′shŭn), *n.* A refuting; disproof.

re·fute′ (rē-fūt′), *v. t.* [L. *refutare* to repel, refute.] To disprove and overthrow by argument, evidence, or proof; prove to be false or erroneous. — **Syn.** See DISPROVE. — **ref′u·ta·ble** (rĕf′ū-tȧ-b'l; rē-fūt′ȧ-b'l), *adj.* — **ref′u·ta·bly** (-blĭ), *adv.* — **re·fut′er** (rē-fūt′ẽr), *n.*

re·gain′ (rē-gān′), *v. t.* **1.** To gain anew; recover. **2.** To get back to; reach again; as, to *regain* the shore.

re′gal (rē′găl), *adj.* [OF. or L.; OF., fr. L. *regalis*, fr. *rex, regis*, a king.] Of, pertaining to, suitable to, characteristic of, or like a king; hence, stately, splendid, etc. — **re′gal·ly**, *adv.*

re·gale′ (rē-gāl′), *v. t. & i.* [F. *régaler*, fr. *régal, régale*, fr. OF. *gale* pleasure.] To entertain or feast sumptuously or delightfully. — *n. Rare.* **a** A feast. **b** A delicacy. **c** Refreshment. — **re·gale′ment**, *n.*

re·ga′li·a (rē-gā′lĭ-ȧ; -gāl′yȧ), *n. pl.* [L., neut. pl. of *regalis* regal.] **1.** The emblems, symbols, etc., of royalty, such as the crown and scepter. **2.** Hence: **a** Decorations or insignia of an office or order. **b** Finery; special dress.

re·gal′i·ty (rē-găl′ĭ-tĭ), *n.; pl.* -TIES (-tĭz). **1.** Royalty; sovereignty; also, *Hist.*, sovereign power given by grant from the crown. **2.** A country or territory subject to the crown or to one granted sovereign power.

Re′gan (rē′găn), *n.* See KING LEAR.

re·gard′ (rē-gärd′), *v. t.* [F. *regarder*, fr. *re-* + *garder* to guard, heed, keep.] **1.** To keep in view; look at, esp. closely or attentively. **2.** To hold (one) in high esteem. **3.** To show respect or consideration for; heed. **4.** To take into consideration; take account of. **5.** To look upon so as to accept, treat, etc.; as, to *regard* one as a friend or with dislike. **6.** To have relation or respect to; concern; as, I agree with you as *regards* this. **7.** *Obs.* To look after; care for. — *v. i.* To look attentively; gaze; also, heed.

Syn. **Regard, respect, esteem, admire** mean to recognize a person's or thing's worth. **Regard**, the least explicit of these words, usually requires qualification to complete its meaning; **respect** implies a judgment of high valuation; **esteem** adds to *respect* the implication of warmth of feeling or close attachment; **admire** connotes enthusiastic appreciation and, sometimes, genuine affection.

— *n.* **1.** *Archaic.* Aspect; look; air. **2.** A look; glance; gaze. **3.** Attention; consideration; heed; care; concern. **4.** A consideration or motive. **5.** A respect, relation, or particular; as, in *regard* to your purchase. **6.** Respect; esteem; affection; — often in *pl.*, in expressions of esteem, etc.; as, my best *regards* to your brother. — ***in regard to, with regard to.*** With respect or relation to.

re·gard′ant (rē-gär′dănt), *adj.* [F.] *Her.* Depicted with the face in profile and looking backward.

re·gard′ful (rē-gärd′fo͝ol; -f'l), *adj.* **1.** Heedful; observant. **2.** Respectful. — **re·gard′ful·ly**, *adv.* — **re·gard′ful·ness**, *n.*

re·gard′ing, *prep.* Concerning; respecting.

re·gard′less, *adj.* Having or taking no regard; heedless; careless. — **re·gard′less·ly**, *adv.* — **re·gard′less·ness**, *n.*

re·gat′ta (rē-găt′ȧ), *n.; pl.* -TAS (-ȧz). [It.] Orig., a gondola race in Venice; now, a rowing or sailing race, or, usually, an organized series of such races.

re′ge·late (rē′jē-lāt; rē′jē-lāt′), *v. i.* *Physics.* To freeze together again; to undergo regelation, as ice.

re′ge·la′tion (-lā′shŭn), *n.* [*re-* + L. *gelatio* a freezing.] The refreezing of water that has resulted from the melting of ice under pressure.

re′gen·cy (rē′jĕn-sĭ), *n.; pl.* -CIES (-sĭz). **1.** The office of ruler; dominion; government. **2.** Esp., the office, jurisdiction, or dominion of a regent, or of a body of regents; deputed or vicarious government. **3.** A body of regents. **4.** The period during which a regent governs.

re·gen′er·a·cy (rē-jĕn′ẽr-ȧ-sĭ), *n.* State of being regenerated.

re·gen′er·ate (-ĭt), *adj.* [L. *regeneratus*, past part. of *regenerare*.] Regenerated; esp., *Theol.*, spiritually reborn.

re·gen′er·ate (-āt), *v. t.* **1.** *Theol.* To cause to be reborn spiritually. **2.** To reform completely. **3.** To generate anew; reproduce; re-create; revive. **4.** *Rare.* To re-establish on a better basis. **5.** To restore (a material) to its original strength or properties. **6.** *Elec.* To increase the amplification of by causing a part of the power in the output circuit to act upon the input circuit. **7.** *Mach.* To make use, by means of special devices, of heat, or the like, that would otherwise be lost. See REGENERATOR, 2. — *v. i.* **1.** To form again. **2.** To become regenerate; reform. — **re·gen′er·a′tion** (rē-jĕn′ẽr-ā′shŭn; rē′jĕn-), *n.* — **re·gen′er·a′tive** (rē-jĕn′ẽr-ā′tĭv; -ȧ-tĭv), *adj.* — **reg·en′er·a′tive·ly**, *adv.*

re·gen′er·a′tor (-ā′tẽr), *n.* **1.** One who or that which regenerates. **2.** *Mach.* A device used with hot-air engines, gas-burning furnaces, etc., in which the incoming air or gas is heated by contact with masses of iron, brick, etc., previously heated by the outgoing hot air or gas.

re′gent (rē′jĕnt), *adj.* [F. or L.; F. *régent*, fr. L. *regens, -entis*, pres. part. of *regere* to rule.] **1.** Exercising vicarious authority; acting as a regent. **2.** *Now Rare.* Ruling; regnant. — *n.* **1.** *Now Rare.* A governing authority or principle; also, a governor; ruler. **2.** One invested with vicarious authority; one who governs a kingdom in the minority, absence, or disability of the sovereign. **3.** *U.S.* One of a governing board, as of a university. — **re′gent·ship**, *n.*

reg′i·cide (rĕj′ĭ-sīd), *n.* [L. *rex, regis*, a king + *-cide*.] **1.** One who kills a king, esp. his own king; specif. [*often cap.*], *Eng. Hist.*, one of the judges who condemned Charles I to death. **2.** The killing or murder of a king. — **reg′i·cid′al** (-sīd′ăl; 2), *adj.*

re·gime′ (rā-zhēm′), *n.* Also **ré·gime′**. [F. *régime*.] Mode of rule or management; the prevailing governmental or social system.

reg′i·men (rĕj′ĭ-mĕn), *n.* [L. *regimen, -inis*, fr. *regere* to guide, rule.] **1.** A governing; administration; system. **2.** *Med.* A systematic course of diet, etc. **3.** *Gram.* A syntactical relation between words, as when one depends on another and is regulated by it in respect to case or mood; government.

reg′i·ment (rĕj′ĭ-mĕnt; *Brit. often* rĕj′mĕnt), *n.* [F. *régiment* a regiment of men, OF. also government, fr. LL. *regimentum* government, fr. *regere* to rule.] **1.** *Rare.* Governmental rule. **2.** *Mil.* A body of soldiers commanded by a colonel, and consisting of a number of companies, troops, or batteries. Cf. BRIGADE, 1. — (-mĕnt), *v. t.* **1.** *Mil.* To form into a regiment or into regiments. **2.** To assign to a regiment. **3.** To organize into groups, or units, esp. for central control; hence, to reduce to strict order or uniformity; as, an education that *regiments* children. — **reg′i·men′tal** (-mĕn′tăl; -t'l), *adj.*

reg′i·men′tals (rĕj′ĭ-mĕn′tălz; -t'lz), *n. pl.* The uniform worn by the officers and soldiers of a regiment; military dress; — not now in technical use.

reg′i·men·ta′tion (-mĕn-tā′shŭn), *n.* Act or process of regimenting; organization into groups.

‖**re·gi′na** (rē-jī′nȧ), *n.* [L.] Queen.

re′gion (rē′jŭn), *n.* [OF. *regium* (F. *région*), fr. L. *regio* a direction, boundary line, region, fr. *regere* to direct.] **1.** A large tract of land; an indefinite area; a country; province; district; specif., an administrative area or province, as in Soviet Russia. **2.** A part or division of the body or one of its parts. **3.** One of the portions into which the atmosphere is conceived of as divided according to height, or the sea according to depth; as, the middle *region* of the air. **4.** *Biogeog.* A faunal division of the world.

re′gion·al (-ăl; -'l), *adj.* **1.** Of or pertaining to a region, or territory; — often opposed to *local*. **2.** Of or pertaining to a region or division; sectional; local; as, *regional* symptoms. — **re′gion·al·ly**, *adv.*

reg′is·ter (rĕj′ĭs-tẽr), *n.* One who registers; a registrar; as, a *register* of deeds.

reg′is·ter, *n.* [OF. *registre*, fr. ML., fr. LL. *regesta*, pl., fr. *regerere*, *regestum*, to carry back, register, fr. *re-* + *gerere* to carry.] **1.** A written or printed record containing regular entries of items or details; a book for such a record; as, a municipal *register* (as of births, marriages, and deaths). **2.** An entry in a register, as of a parish. **3.** Registration; registry; as, a port of *register*. **4.** A device, as in a furnace, for regulating the admission of air; esp., one in a floor, wall, or the like, for heated or fresh air. **5.** Something which registers or records; esp., an automatic machine registering number of fares taken, amount of gas consumed, etc. **6.** *Music.* **a** The compass or range of a voice or instrument. **b** The series of tones produced by a particular adjustment of the vocal cords. In singing up the scale the register changes at the point where the vocal cords readjust themselves to reach the higher tones, all tones below this point being considered to be the ***chest,*** *or* ***thick, register***, all above, the ***head,*** *or* ***thin, register***. **7.** *Photog.* Correspondence in position between the focusing screen and the surface of the replacing sensitive film or plate. **8.** *Print.* Exact correspondence as in position of pages, columns, or lines on the opposite or reverse sides of the sheet, or of the several impressions in a design printed in parts; as, the blue parts of the advertisement are out of *register*.

— *v. t.* **1.** To enter in a register, official record, list, or roll; enroll. **2.** To record automatically; indicate; as, the thermometer *registered* zero. **3.** To make correspond exactly; to adjust and print (pages, etc.) in register. **4.** To secure special protection for (a letter, mail, etc.) by prepayment of a fee. **5.** To show, as an emotion, by facial expression, bodily movement, etc. — *v. i.* **1.** To enroll one's name, as in a hotel register, or in a list of voters. **2.** To correspond exactly; to be in register, or correct alignment. — **reg′is·ter·er** (-ẽr), *n.*

reg′is·tered (rĕj′ĭs-tẽrd), *adj.* Recorded; as: **a** Of bonds, shares, etc., having the owner's name entered in a register. **b** Designating purebred livestock, whose pedigree, etc., has been recorded by a recognized breed association. **c** Certificated; legally authenticated; as, a *registered* nurse or ship.

reg′is·tra·ble (-trȧ-b'l), *adj.* That may be registered.

reg′is·trant (-trănt), *n.* [From ML. *registrans*, pres. part.] One who registers his name.

reg′is·trar (rĕj′ĭs-trär; -trär′), *n.* [For older *registrer*.] One who keeps a register, or record, as of names; as, a *registrar* of voters; a college *registrar*.

reg′is·trate (rĕj′ĭs-trāt), *v. i.* [ML. *registratus*, past part. of *registrare*.] *Music.* To select and adjust organ stops.

reg′is·tra′tion (-trā′shŭn), *n.* **1.** A registering. **2.** An entry in a register. **3.** The body or number of persons registered. **4.** *Music.* The art or act of registrating; also, the combination of organ stops selected for the performance of a composition.

reg′is·try (rĕj′ĭs-trĭ), *n.; pl.* -TRIES (-trĭz). **1.** A registering; enrollment; registration. **2.** The state or fact of being entered in a register; as, a certificate of *registry*; specif., of a ship, (particular) nationality as evidenced by such an entry; as, ships of British or of Greek *registry*. **3.** The place where a register is kept; a place of registration. **4.** A register; an official record book or an entry in one.

‖**re′gi·us** (rē′jĭ-ŭs), *adj.* [L. *regius*, fr. *rex, regis*, a king.] Royal.

regius professor. An incumbent of a professorship founded by royal bounty, as at Oxford and Cambridge.

reg′let (rĕg′lĕt; -lĭt), *n.* [F. *réglet*, dim. of *règle* a rule, fr. L. *regula*. See RULE.] **1.** *Arch.* A flat, narrow molding. **2.** *Print.* **a** A low strip of wood, used like leads between lines, as in posters. **b** Reglets collectively, or material for them.

reg′ma (rĕg′mȧ), *n.* [NL., fr. Gr. *rhēgma, -atos*, fracture, fr. *rhēgnynai* to break.] *Bot.* A schizocarp consisting of three or more carpels, which burst elastically.

reg′nal (-năl; -n'l), *adj.* [ML. *regnalis*, fr. *regnum* reign.] Of or pertaining to a reign, kingdom, or king.

reg′nant (rĕg′nănt), *adj.* [L. *regnans, -antis*, pres. part. of *regnare* to reign.] **1.** Reigning; as, a queen *regnant*. **2.** Dominant; also, prevalent. — **reg′nan·cy** (-năn-sĭ), *n.*

‖**reg′nat po′pu·lus** (rĕg′năt pŏp′ū-lŭs). [L.] The people rule; — motto of Arkansas.

reg′o·lith (rĕg′ō-lĭth), *n.* [Gr. *rhegos* blanket + *-lith*.] *Geol.* The mantle of loose material consisting of soils, sediments, broken rock, etc., overlying the solid rock of the earth.

re·gorge′ (rē-gôrj′), *v. t.* [F. *regorger*, fr. *re-* + *gorger* to gorge.] To vomit up; disgorge; throw back. — *v. i.* To gush again; be thrown back.

re·grant′ (rē-grȧnt′; 9), *v. t.* To grant again; renew the grant of. — **re·grant′**, *n.*

re·greet′ (rē-grēt′), *v. t. & i.* To greet again or in return; to greet. — *n. Obs.* A regreeting; *pl.*, greetings.

re′gress (rē′grĕs), *n.* [L. *regressus*, fr. *regredi, regressus*, to go back, fr. *re-* + *gradi* to go.] **1.** Act or privilege of going or coming back; withdrawal; egress. **2.** Retrogression; retrogradation.

re·gress′ (rē-grĕs′), *v. i.* To make or undergo regress; retrograde. —

re·gres′sive (rē·grĕs′ĭv), *adj* — **re·gres′sive·ly**, *adv.* — **re·gres′sor** (-ẽr), *n.*

re·gres′sion (rē·grĕsh′ŭn), *n.* **1.** A regressing. **2.** *Psychoanalysis.* Return of the libido to earlier stages of development or to infantile objects of attachment.

re·gret′ (rē·grĕt′), *v. t.;* -GRET′TED; -GRET′TING. [OF. *regreter, regrater* (F. *regretter*).] **1.** To mourn the loss or death of; to miss poignantly. **2.** To have distress of mind or misgivings concerning; to be sorry for; as, to *regret* one's past mistakes. — *n.* **1.** A regretting; sorrow for what is lost or irreparable; remorse. **2.** An expression of sorrow, disappointment, etc.; specif., often *pl.*, a note politely declining an invitation; as, to send *regrets.* — **Syn.** See SORROW. — **re·gret′ta·ble**, *adj.* — **re·gret′ta·bly**, *adv.* — **re·gret′ter**, *n.*

re·gret′ful (-fo͝ol; -f'l), *adj.* Full of regret; indulging in regrets; repining. — **re·gret′ful·ly**, *adv.* — **re·gret′ful·ness**, *n.*

reg′u·lar (rĕg′ū·lẽr), *adj.* [OF. *reguler*, fr. L. *regularis*, fr. *regula* a rule, fr. *regere* to guide.] **1.** *Eccl.* Belonging to a religious order or community; under, or pertaining to, a religious rule; — opposed to *secular;* as, *regular* clergy. **2.** Formed, built, arranged, etc., according to rule, law, principle, or type; symmetrical; as, *regular* verse; *regular* features. **3.** Steady or uniform in course, practice, etc.; not characterized by variation from the normal or usual; as, a *regular* pulse; *regular* habits. **4.** Constituted, selected, conducted, etc., in conformity with established usage, rules, or discipline; duly authorized or qualified; as, the nomination was *regular.* **5** Undeviating in conformance to a standard as set by convention, a party, etc. **6.** *Colloq.* Thorough; unmitigated. **7.** *Bot.* Having the members of each whorl symmetrical in form; — of flowers. **8.** *Crystallog.* = ISOMETRIC, 2. **9.** *Gram.* Of a word or inflection, conforming to the normal or usual manner of inflection. Abbr. *reg.* **10.** *Internat. Law.* Designating soldiers properly recognized as legitimate combatants in war. **11.** *Math.* Of a polygon, both equilateral and equiangular; of a polyhedron, having equal faces. **12.** *Mil.* Of or belonging to the **regular army** the permanently organized body constituting the army of the state.

Syn. (1) **Regular, normal, typical, natural** mean of the usual or average sort or kind. **Regular** implies conformity to a rule, standard, or pattern; **normal**, lack of deviation from that discovered or established as the norm, or what is to be expected; **typical**, exhibition of the characters or characteristics common to the type or class; **natural**, action, behavior, or the like in accordance with a thing's nature, function, or the like.
(2) Methodical, systematic, orderly.

— *n.* **1.** A habitual or steady attendant, customer, or the like. **2.** *Eccl.* One of the regular clergy. **3.** A regular soldier.
— **reg′u·lar′i·ty** (-lăr′ĭ·tĭ), *n.* — **reg′u·lar·ly**, *adv.*

reg′u·lar·ize (-īz), *v. t.* To make regular, or conformable to law, rules, or the like; to make uniform.

regular year. See JEWISH CALENDAR.

reg′u·late (rĕg′ū·lāt), *v. t.* [L. *regulatus*, past part. of *regulare.*] **1.** To govern or direct according to rule; as, laws which *regulate* the succession of seasons. **2.** To bring under the control of constituted authority; to make regulations concerning; as, to *regulate* industries. **3.** To make regular, uniform, methodical, etc.; as, to *regulate* one's habits. **4.** To fix the amount, degree, or rate of, by adjusting, rectifying, etc.; as, to *regulate* speed. **5.** To adjust so as to work accurately or regularly; as, to *regulate* a clock. — **reg′u·la′tive** (-lā′tĭv), *adj. & n.* — **reg′u·la·to′ry** (-lȧ·tō′rĭ *or, esp. Brit.*, -lā·tẽr·ĭ; 3), *adj.*

reg′u·la′tion (-lā′shŭn), *n.* **1.** Act of regulating, or state of being regulated. **2.** A regulating principle or law; rule. — **Syn.** See LAW.

reg′u·la′tor (rĕg′ū·lā′tẽr), *n.* One who or that which regulates; as: **a** *Elec.* An automatic device for maintaining or adjusting the current, speed, etc., of a machine, transformer, or the like. **b** *Horol.* (1) A lever or index in a watch for making it go faster or slower. (2) A standard clock used for timing clocks. **c** *Mach.* A governor. **d** *Steam Engin.* (1) A balance valve for controlling the admission of steam to the steam chest in a locomotive. (2) A reducing valve or steam-pressure regulating device.

reg′u·lus (rĕg′ū·lŭs), *n.; pl.* -LUSES (-lŭs·ĕz; -ĭz); -LI (-lī). [L., a petty king, dim. of *rex, regis*, a king.] **1.** [*cap.*] *Astron.* A first-magnitude star in the constellation Leo. **2.** [ML.] *Chem. & Metal.* The impure mass of metal formed beneath the slag in smelting and reducing ores.

re·gur′gi·tate (rē·gûr′jĭ·tāt), *v. t. & i.* [ML. *regurgitare, regurgitatum*, fr. *re-* + LL. *gurgitare.*] To pour, gush, rush, or surge back; often, to vomit.

re·gur′gi·ta′tion (-tā′shŭn), *n.* A regurgitating; specif., *Biol. & Med.*, the casting up of incompletely digested food (as by certain birds feeding their young) or the backward flow of blood to the heart.

re′ha·bil′i·tate (rē′hȧ·bĭl′ĭ·tāt), *v. t.* [ML. *rehabilitare.*] **1.** To restore to a former capacity; reinstate. **2.** To restore to good repute; vindicate. **3.** To restore to solvency, efficiency, etc. **4.** To fit to make one's livelihood again; as, to *rehabilitate* disabled soldiers. — **re′ha·bil′i·ta′tion** (-tā′shŭn), *n.* — **re′ha·bil′i·ta′tive** (-tā′tĭv), *adj.*

re·hash′ (rē·hăsh′), *v. t.* To hash over again; to present or use again in another form; to restate, as old arguments.

re′hash (rē′hăsh), *n.* The action or product of rehashing; something rehashed and given a new name.

re·hears′al (rē·hûr′săl; -s'l), *n.* A rehearsing; recital.

re·hearse′ (rē·hûrs′), *v. t.* [OF. *rehercier* to harrow over again, repeat. See HEARSE.] **1.** To repeat; recite aloud formally; to say over. **2.** To recount or mention one by one; enumerate. **3.** *Now Rare.* To recount; relate; tell. **4. a** To go through, in private, in preparation for a more formal and public representation; as, to *rehearse* a play. **b** To train or instruct by rehearsal. — *v. i.* To recite esp. for practice; to engage in a rehearsal. — **re·hears′er** (-hûr′sẽr), *n.*

rei (rā), *n.* Incorrect Eng. sing. for Pg. *real* (coin), *pl.* REIS. See REIS.

‖**Reich** (rīĸ), *n.* [G.] Literally, "empire"; — used specifically in: ***First Reich,*** the Holy Roman Empire, from the crowning of Otto I in Rome, 962–1806; ***Second Reich*** (officially ***Deutsches Reich***), the German Empire, 1871–1918, established by Bismarck; ***Third Reich,*** the German totalitarian state, 1933–1945, under the dictatorship of the chancellor (known also as the *Führer*) with a consultative cabinet and a single political party (see NAZI). From 1919 to 1933 Germany was a republic. See WEIMAR REPUBLIC.

Reichs′bank′ (rīĸs′băngk′; *G.* -bängk′), *n.* [G.] The state bank of Germany in the Third Reich.

‖**Reichs′füh′rer** (-fü′rẽr), *n.* [G., lit., leader of the Reich.] Head of the Schutzstaffel; — title held by Heinrich Himmler.

reichs′mark′ (-märk′), *n.; pl.* -MARKS, -MARK. [G.] The monetary unit of Germany (Deutsches *Reich*), equal at par to 23.8 cents, as established by law in 1924; later, its gold content value was determined at 40.3 cents. In Western Germany it was replaced by the Deutsche mark June, 1948.

reichs′pfen′nig (-pfĕn′ĭg), *n.; pl.* -NIGS (-ĭgz), -NIGE (-ĭ·gĕ). [G.] Formerly, a minor bronze coin of Germany worth 1/100 reichsmark.

‖**Reichs′tag′** (-täĸ′), *n.* [G.] Formerly, the legislative assembly of Germany.

reif (rēf), *n.* [AS. *rēaf.*] *Chiefly Scot.* Robbery; plunder.

re′i·fy (rē′ĭ·fī), *v. t.;* -FIED (-fīd); -FY′ING. [L. *res* thing + E. *-fy.*] To convert (an abstraction or mental construction) into a supposed real thing; to attribute substantiality to; to hypostatize. — **re′i·fi·ca′tion** (rē′ĭ·fĭ·kā′shŭn), *n.*

reign (rān), *n.* [OF. *reigne, regne*, fr. L. *regnum*, fr. *regere* to guide, rule.] Royal authority; dominion; sway; also, time during which a sovereign rules. — *v. i.* **1.** To exercise sovereign power or authority; to govern as king or emperor. **2.** To be predominant; to prevail.

Reign of Terror. *Fr. Hist.* A period (1793–94) in the French Revolution, during which the country was terrorized by the ferocious measures of its temporary rulers.

re′im·burse′ (rē′ĭm·bûrs′), *v. t.* [*re-* + *imburse*, after F. *rembourser.*] **1.** To pay back; repay. **2.** To make restoration of an equivalent to (a person); indemnify. — **Syn.** See PAY. — **re′im·burse′ment**, *n.*

re′im·port′ (rē′ĭm·pōrt′; 70), *v. t.* To import again; to import (something previously exported, esp. in a raw state). — **re′im·port′**, *n.* — **re′im·por·ta′tion** (-pōr·tā′shŭn), *n.*

re′im·pose′ (-pōz′), *v. t.* To impose again. — **re′im·po·si′tion** (-pō·zĭsh′ŭn), *n.*

re′im·pres′sion (rē′ĭm·prĕsh′ŭn), *n.* A second impression, as of a book without change, or a reprint.

rein (rān), *n.* [OF. *rene, resne*, (F. *rêne*), deriv. of L. *retinere* to hold back.] **1.** The strap of a bridle, fastened to the curb or snaffle on each side, by which the rider or driver governs a horse or other animal; — usually in the *pl.* See BIT, HARNESS, *Illusts.* **2.** Often *pl.* **a** A curbing; check; hindrance. **b** Position of command; as, to take the *reins* of government. — *v. t.* **1.** To provide with reins. **2.** To check, stop, or direct, by or as by a pull at the reins; guide; control. — *v. i.* **1.** *Rare.* To submit to reins. **2.** To stop or slow up by or as by pulling the reins; — with *back, in,* or *up.* — ***to give rein to.*** To give free play to; as, *to give rein to* his imagination.

re′in·car′nate (rē′ĭn·kär′nāt), *v. t.* To incarnate again; to subject to reincarnation.

re′in·car·na′tion (-kär·nā′shŭn), *n.* The belief that the souls of the dead successively return to earth in new forms or bodies; hence, a rebirth of a soul in a new, esp. a human, body. Cf. METEMPSYCHOSIS. — **re′in·car·na′tion·ist**, *n.*

rein′deer′ (rān′dēr′), *n. sing. & pl.* [ON. *hreindȳri*, fr. *hreinn* reindeer + *dȳr* deer.] Any of several species of deer of the genus *Rangifer* inhabiting northern Europe, Asia, and America. American species are called *caribou.*

reindeer moss. A gray, erect, tufted and much-branched lichen (*Cladonia rangiferina*) which forms extensive patches on the ground in arctic and even in north-temperate regions. It forms a large part of the food of reindeer in the far north, and is sometimes eaten by man.

re′in·flate′ (rē′ĭn·flāt′), *v. t. & i.* To inflate again. — **re′in·fla′tion** (-flā′shŭn), *n.*

re′in·force′ (-fōrs′; 70), *v. t.* [*re-* + *enforce.*] To strengthen by the addition of something new, as new material; specif., to strengthen with additional troops or ships. — *n.* Something which reinforces, as a metal band over the rear part of guns. — **re′in·forc′er** (-fōr′sẽr), *n.*

re′in·forced′ con′crete (-fōrst′). Concrete in which metal, usually steel, is embedded in such a manner that the two materials act together in resisting forces.

re′in·force′ment (rē′ĭn·fōrs′mĕnt), *n.* **1.** Act of reinforcing, or state of being reinforced. **2.** That which reinforces; esp., *pl.* additional troops or ships to augment the strength of a military or naval force.

reins (rānz), *n. pl.* [OF., fr. L. *ren*, pl. *renes.*] *Archaic.* **1.** Kidneys, or the region of the kidneys; hence, loins. **2.** The seat of the feelings or passions, formerly localized in the loins.

re′in·sert′ (rē′ĭn·sûrt′), *v. t.* To insert again. — **re′in·ser′tion** (-sûr′shŭn), *n.*

re′in·stall′ (-stôl′), *v. t.* To install again. — **re′in·stall′ment, re′in·stal′ment**, *n.*

re′in·state′ (-stāt′), *v. t.* To instate again; to place again in possession, or in a former position. — **re′in·state′ment**, *n.*

re′in·sure′ (-sho͝or′), *v. t.* To insure again; specif.: **a** Of one insurance company, to transfer to another in whole or in part the liability assumed on a risk. **b** Of the second insurance company, to assume such liability in a transfer. — **re′in·sur′ance** (-sho͝or′ăns), *n.* — **re′in·sur′er** (-ẽr), *n.*

re·in′te·grate (rē·ĭn′tē·grāt), *v. t.* To integrate again; to restore to unity after disintegration. — **re·in′te·gra′tion** (-grā′shŭn), *n.*

re′in·ter′ (rē′ĭn·tûr′), *v. t.* To inter again or in another grave. — **re′in·ter′ment**, *n.*

re′in·tro·duce′ (-ĭn·trō·dūs′), *v. t.* To introduce again or anew. — **re′in·tro·duc′tion** (-dŭk′shŭn), *n.*

re′in·vest′ (rē′ĭn·vĕst′), *v. t. & i.* To invest again or anew; specif., to make new investments with money earned on old investments. — **re′in·vest′ment**, *n.*

re′in·vig′or·ate (-ĭn·vĭg′ẽr·āt), *v. t.* To invigorate again; make more vigorous. — **re′in·vig′or·a′tion** (-ā′shŭn), *n.*

reis (rās), *n. pl.; sing.* REAL (rē·äl′). [Pg., pl. of *real.*] A former Portuguese and Brazilian money of account; one thousandth of a milreis. Abbr. *Rs.*

re·is′sue (rē·ĭsh′ū; -o͞o), *n.* **1.** A second or repeated issue, as of a publication. **2.** *Philately.* A new issue of stamps for use as postage printed from the plates. Cf. REPRINT. — **re·is′sue**, *v. t.*

re·it′er·ate (rē·ĭt′ẽr·āt), *v. t.* [L. *reiteratus*, past part. of *reiterare.*] To repeat; to say or do over again or repeatedly. — **Syn.** See REPEAT. — **re·it′er·a′tion** (-ā′shŭn), *n.* — **re·it′er·a′tive** (-ā′tĭv), *adj.*

re·ject′ (rē·jĕkt′), *v. t.* [L. *rejectus*, past part. of *reicere, rejicere*, fr. *re-* + *jacere* to throw.] **1.** To refuse to acknowledge, believe, receive, etc.; decline to accept; refuse. **2.** To cast or throw away as useless, unsatisfactory, etc.; discard; relegate. **3.** To refuse to hear, receive, etc. (a person); repel. **4.** To refuse to grant, consider, or accede to. **5.** To spew out. **6.** *Obs.* To forsake. — **Syn.** See DECLINE. — **re·ject′er**, *n.* — **re·jec′tion** (-jĕk′shŭn), *n.*

re'ject (rē'jĕkt), *n.* A rejected person or thing.
re·jec'ta·men'ta (rē·jĕk'tȧ·mĕn'tȧ), *n. pl.* [NL.] Rejects; rubbish; specif., excrement.
re·jec'tion (rē·jĕk'shŭn), *n.* Act of rejecting, or state of being rejected; also, that which is rejected.
re·joice' (rē·jois'), *v. t.;* -JOICED' (-joist'); -JOIC'ING (-jois'ĭng). [OF. *resjoïr* (3d pl. pres. *resjoïssent*), fr. *re-* + OF. *esjoïr* to rejoice, fr. *es-* (L. *ex-*) + OF. *joïr*, fr. L. *gaudere* to rejoice.] To give joy to; to gladden. — *v. i.* To feel joy or great delight. — **re·joic'er** (-jois'ẽr), *n.*
re·joic'ing (-jois'ĭng), *n.* Act of one who rejoices; joy; also, an occasion or expression of joy.
re·join' (rē·join'), *v. i.* [F. *rejoindre*, fr. *re-* + *joindre* to join.] **1.** *Law.* To answer, as the defendant to the plaintiff's replication. **2.** (rē-) To join or come together again; to reunite. — *v. t.* **1.** (rē-) To join again. **2.** To say by way of answer or rejoinder. — **Syn.** See ANSWER.
re·join'der (-join'dẽr), *n.* [F. *rejoindre*, inf. as n.] **1.** *Law.* The defendant's answer to the replication. **2.** An answer; reply.
re·ju've·nate (rē·jo͞o'vē·nāt; 114), *v. t.* [*re-* + L. *juvenis* young.] **1.** To render youthful again; reinvigorate. **2.** *Phys. Geog.* **a** To stimulate, as by uplift, to renewed erosive activity; — said of streams. **b** To develop youthful features of topography in. — **Syn.** See RENEW. — **re·ju've·na'tion** (-nā'shŭn), *n.* — **re·ju've·na'tor** (-nā'tẽr), *n.*
re·ju've·nes'cence (-nĕs'ĕns; -'ns), *n.* **1.** A renewing of youth; a rejuvenation. **2.** *Biol.* A method of cell formation in which the entire protoplasm of an old cell escapes by rupture of the cell wall, and develops a new cell wall. — **re·ju've·nes'cent** (-ĕnt; -'nt), *adj.*
re·ju've·nize (rē·jo͞o'vē·nīz), *v. t.* To rejuvenate.
re·kin'dle (rē·kĭn'd'l), *v. t. & i.;* RE·KIN'DLED (-d'ld); RE·KIN'DLING (-dlĭng). To kindle again.
re·lapse' (rē·lăps'), *v. i.* [L. *relapsus*, past part. of *relabi*, fr. *re-* + *labi* to fall, slip, slide.] **1.** To slip back into a former condition after a change for the better; specif., to become ill again after convalescing, or to revert to evil habits after amendment, etc. **2.** To sink; lapse; as, to *relapse* into a stupor. — *n.* The act or fact of relapsing; esp., a recurrence, as of an illness, after improvement.
re·laps'ing fe'ver. *Med.* Any of several forms of acute infectious disease marked by recurring high fever lasting from five to seven days, and transmitted by a tick (*Ornithodoros moubata*) and various lice.
re·late' (rē·lāt'), *v. t.* [In part fr. earlier *relation, relative;* in part fr. F. *relater* to recount.] **1.** To recount; narrate. **2.** To connect or bring into relation; to establish relationship between. — *v. i.* To stand in some relation; to pertain; — with *to.* — **Syn.** See JOIN. — **re·lat'er** (-lāt'ẽr), *n.*
re·lat'ed (rē·lāt'ĕd; -ĭd), *adj.* **1.** Narrated; recounted. **2.** Connected by reason of an established or discoverable relation. **3.** *Music.* Having a close melodic or harmonic connection; — of tones, chords, or tonalities.
re·la'tion (rē·lā'shŭn), *n.* [OF. *relation*, or fr. L. *relatio*, fr. *relatus*, used as past part. of *referre.* See REFER.] **1.** Act of relating, or telling; also, that which is related; recital; account. **2. a** A person connected by blood or marriage; a relative. **b** Connection by blood or marriage; kinship. **3. a** Any aspect or quality which can be predicated only of two or more things taken together, as direction, resemblance, or of one thing considered as a factor of itself, as self-identity. **b** Connection; as, the *relation* of master to servant. **4.** Reference; respect; — esp. in phrase, *in relation to.* **5.** The mode in which one thing stands to another, or the mode in which two or more things stand to one another; as, the *relation* of father to son. **6.** State of being mutually or reciprocally interested, as in social or business matters; *pl.*, dealings; affairs; as, the foreign *relations* of a country. **7.** *Law.* **a** The referring of an act to a prior date as the time of its taking effect. **b** The act of a relator at whose instance a suit is begun.
re·la'tion·al (-ăl; -'l), *adj.* **1.** Of or pertaining to kinship. **2.** Of, pertaining to, or specifying a relation in general. See WORD, *n.* **3.** *Gram.* Pertaining to or designating a word, as *is, shall, who,* in which the meaning consists chiefly in indicating a relation of syntax; — distinguished from *notional.*
re·la'tion·ship, *n.* **1.** The state of being related. **2.** Kinship; consanguinity or affinity.
rel'a·tive (rĕl'ȧ·tĭv), *adj.* [F. or L.; F. *relatif*, fr. L. *relativus.*] **1.** Having relationship one to another; mutually related. **2.** Having relation, reference, or application; referring; pertaining; pertinent. **3.** Arising from relation; comparative; not absolute or independent. **4.** *Gram.* Referring to an antecedent; introducing a subordinate clause qualifying an expressed or implied antecedent; as, *relative* pronoun (see PRONOUN), adjective, or adverb. **5.** Involving or implying relationship; — said of names, terms, etc. **6.** *Music.* Having the same key signature; — said of major and minor keys and scales. — *n.* **1.** A being or object posited by virtue of its relationships. **2.** A person connected with another by blood or marriage; a kinsman or kinswoman. **3.** *Gram.* A relative pronoun or other word. Abbr. *rel.* — **rel'a·tive·ly,** *adv.* — **rel'a·tive·ness,** *n.*
relative clause. *Gram.* A clause adjunct introduced by a relative pronoun.
relative humidity. See HUMIDITY.
rel'a·tiv'i·ty (rĕl'ȧ·tĭv'ĭ·tĭ), *n.* **1.** State of being relative. **2.** *Philos.* The state of being dependent for existence or determined in nature, value, or some other quality by relation to something else. **3.** *Physics.* As formulated by Einstein, a mathematical development of the two postulates: (a) If two systems are in relative motion with a uniform linear velocity, it is impossible for observers in either system by observation and measurement of phenomena in the other to learn anything more about the motion than the fact that there is this relative motion; (b) measurements of the velocity of light in either system, regardless of the position of the source of light, always give the same numerical value. This development forms the *special*, or *restricted, theory of relativity.* By extension and deduction, Einstein developed a *general theory of relativity*, including formulas for the motions of the planets, etc.
relativity of knowledge. The doctrine that knowledge is relative to the limited nature of the mind and the conditions of knowing and hence not true to the nature of independent reality.
re·la'tor (rē·lā'tẽr), *n.* [L.] **1.** One who relates; a narrator. **2.** *Law.* A private person at whose relation, or in whose behalf, the attorney general allows an information in the nature of a quo warranto to be filed.
re·lax' (rē·lăks'), *v. t.* [L. *relaxare*, fr. *re-* + *laxare* to loose.] **1.** To make less firm, rigid, or tense; to slacken. **2.** To make less severe or strict; to mollify; as, to *relax* discipline. — *v. i.* **1.** To become lax, weak, or loose; to abate in tenseness. **2.** To abate in severity; to become less rigorous. **3.** To remit attention or effort; to seek recreation or rest. — **re·lax'er,** *n.*
re'lax·a'tion (rē'lăk·sā'shŭn; rĕl'ăk-), *n.* **1.** A relaxing, or state of being relaxed. **2.** Abatement or remission, as of a penalty, duty, etc. **3.** Diversion; recreation.
re·lay' (rē·lā'; rē'lā), *n.* [OF. *relai*, fr. *relaier* to leave, let.] **1.** A supply arranged beforehand for successive relief. Specif.: **a** A supply of horses, dogs, etc., kept in readiness to relieve others in the hunt, on a journey, etc. **b** A number of men who relieve others in carrying on some work. **2.** *Athletics.* Short for RELAY RACE; also, one of the legs, or divisions, of a relay race. **3.** *Elec.* An electromagnetic device operated by a variation in conditions of an electric circuit, and which, when so operated, operates, in turn, other devices, as a switch, in the same or a different circuit. Thus, in a telegraph system, a current too weak to operate a sounder may, by means of a delicate relay, communicate the signals to a local current of any desired strength. **4.** *Mach.* A relay apparatus; a servomotor. — *v. t.;* RE·LAYED' (-lād'; -lād); RE·LAY'ING. **1.** To pass on as if by relays; as, to *relay* news. **2.** *Elec.* To control or operate (the current or the like) by a relay. — (rē·lā'; rē'lā; 2), *adj.* *Mach.* Relating to, or having the characteristics of, an auxiliary apparatus put into action by a feeble force but itself capable of exerting greater force, used to control a powerful appliance.
re–lay' (rē·lā'), *v. t.;* RE·LAID' (-lād'); RE·LAY'ING. To lay again.
relay race. A race between groups of competitors each one of whom covers a specified portion of the entire course.
re–lease' (rē·lēs'), *v. t.* To lease again.
re·lease' (rē·lēs'), *v. t.* [OF. *relaissier* to let free, fr. L. *relaxare.* See RELAX.] **1.** To let loose again; to set free; to let go. **2.** To relieve, as from pain, trouble, penalty. **3.** To permit, at a specified date, but not before, the public performance, exhibition, publication, or sale of. **4.** *Obs.* To remit, as a payment, tax, etc.; to give remission for, as for sins. **5.** *Law.* To let go or give up, as a legal claim. — **Syn.** See FREE.
— *n.* **1.** Deliverance or relief from care, pain, trouble, etc. **2.** Discharge from obligation, as from a debt or claim; a relinquishment, as of a right or claim. **3.** Liberation or discharge from restraint, or an instrument granting this. **4.** A releasing for publication, circulation, or performance. See RELEASE, *v. t.*, 3. **5.** *Engin.* The act of permitting the working fluid, as steam, to escape from the cylinder at the end of the working stroke; also, the point in the cycle of operations at which this act occurs. **6.** *Law.* Any instrument by which a legal right is discharged; specif., a conveyance of a man's right in lands or tenements to another having an estate in possession; a quitclaim. **7.** *Mach.* A device adapted to hold or release a device or mechanism as required.
re·leas'er (rē·lēs'ẽr), *n.* One who or that which releases.
rel'e·gate (rĕl'ē·gāt), *v. t.* [L. *relegatus*, past part. of *relegare*, fr. *re-* + *legare* to send with a commission.] **1.** To exile (one); to banish; hence, to remove or dismiss (a person or thing) thereby putting (such) out of sight or mind; as, to *relegate* these comments to footnotes; to *relegate* religion out of one's life. **2.** To assign, as to a class or sphere; to consign by classifying or appraising. **3.** To submit for decision; to delegate; refer. — **Syn.** See COMMIT. — **rel'e·ga'tion** (-gā'shŭn), *n.*
re·lent' (rē·lĕnt'), *v. i.* [*re-* + L. *lentus* pliant, slow.] **1.** *Obs.* To melt; liquefy; soften. **2.** To become less severe, harsh, cruel, or the like; to soften in temper. — **Syn.** See YIELD. — *v. t. Obs.* **1.** To soften; hence, to mollify. **2.** To slacken; also, to give up; abandon.
re·lent'less, *adj.* Mercilessly harsh; stern. — **re·lent'less·ly,** *adv.* — **re·lent'less·ness,** *n.*
rel'e·vant (rĕl'ē·vănt), *adj.* [ML. *relevans*, pres. part., in L., raising, lifting up. See RELIEVE.] Bearing upon, or applying to, the case in hand; pertinent. — **rel'e·vance** (-văns), **rel'e·van·cy** (-văn·sĭ), *n.* — **rel'e·vant·ly,** *adv.*
Syn. Relevant, germane, material, pertinent, apposite, applicable, apropos mean related to or bearing upon the matter in hand. **Relevant** implies a traceable and significant connection; **germane,** a fitness for or appropriateness to the situation or occasion; **material,** so close an association with the matter in hand that it cannot be dispensed with; **pertinent,** so clear or decisive a relevance that it contributes to the understanding of the matter in hand; **apposite,** a felicitous pertinence; **applicable,** a bearing upon with especial fitness; **apropos,** appropriateness and opportuneness.
re·li'a·ble (rē·lī'ȧ·b'l), *adj.* Suitable or fit to be relied on; trustworthy. — **re·li'a·bil'i·ty** (-bĭl'ĭ·tĭ), *n.* — **re·li'a·ble·ness,** *n.* — **-a·bly,** *adv.*
re·li'ance (-ăns), *n.* **1.** Act of relying. **2.** State of one who relies; dependence; confidence; trust. **3.** Someone or something relied upon.
re·li'ant (-ănt), *adj.* That places reliance on something or in someone; confiding; trusting.
rel'ic (rĕl'ĭk), *n.* [OF. *relique*, fr. L. *reliquiae*, pl.] **1.** *Usually pl. Now Poetic.* A corpse. **2.** An object venerated by the faithful because of its association with a saint or other sacred person. **3.** *pl.* Ruins; residue. **4.** A survival; a vestige. **5.** A souvenir; memento; often, a monument of the past.
rel'ict (rĕl'ĭkt), *n.* [L. *relictus*, fem. *relicta*, past part. of *relinquere* to leave behind.] **1.** A widow. **2.** *Ecol.* A species or other group within a community representative of an earlier stage of development or of a different set of environmental conditions.
re·lief' (rē·lēf'), *n.* [OF. *relief*, prop., a lifting up. See RELIEVE.] **1.** Act of relieving or state of being relieved; succor; comfort; ease. **2.** Specif.: **a** Aid in the form of money or necessities for indigent persons. **b** Aid in time of danger or difficulty, esp. in war. **3.** Release from a post, or from the performance of duty; as, a *relief* of a sentry. **4.** That which removes or lessens evil, pain, etc.; that which gives succor, aid, or comfort. **5.** The person who relieves from performance of duty by taking the place of another; a relay. **6.** [Cf. It. *relievo.*] In sculpture, the projection of figures, ornament, etc., from a background; hence, a work of art so produced. The kinds of relief are named according to the degree of projection. In ***high relief*** (*alto-rilievo*) this is half or more than half the natural circumference. In ***low relief*** (*basso-rilievo, bas-relief*) it is slight, no part being entirely detached. Intermediate degrees of projection are sometimes called ***half relief*** (*mezzo-rilievo*). Very low relief, as on modern coins, is termed *stiacciato.* **7.** In drawing, painting, etc., the suggestion of spatial relations by the arrangement of lines, shadings, colors, etc. Hence, in general, vividness of outline due to contrast. **8.** *Cartography.* The parts of a map, collectively, which represent the configuration of the ground. **9.** *Feudal Law.* A fine or money composition which the

heir of a deceased tenant paid to his lord for the privilege of taking up the landed estate. Also, sometimes, an acknowledgment made by the heir of his vassal tenure of the lord. **10.** *Phys. Geog.* The elevations or inequalities, collectively, of a land surface.

relief map. A model of an area in which its inequalities of surface are shown in relief; also, a representation in perspective of such a model.

re·li'er (rē·lī'ēr), *n.* One who or that which relies.

re·lieve' (rē·lēv'), *v. t.* [OF. *relever* (3d sing. pres. *relieve*), fr. L. *relevare* to lift up, relieve, fr. *re-* + *levare* to raise.] **1.** To free, wholly or partly, from any burden, trial, evil, etc. **2.** To raise or remove, as anything which depresses or crushes; to alleviate; mitigate. **3.** To release from a post, station, or duty; as, to *relieve* a sentry. **4.** To ease of any burden, wrong, or oppression by judicial or legislative action, by indemnification, etc.; to right. **5.** To remove the monotony of, as by contrast and variety. **6.** To put in relief; to give prominence to; to set off by contrast. — **re·liev'a·ble**, *adj.* — **re·liev'er**, *n.*

Syn. **Relieve, alleviate, lighten, assuage, mitigate, allay** mean to make something less grievous. **Relieve** implies a lifting of enough of a burden to make it tolerable or capable of being forgotten for a time; **alleviate**, the temporary or partial nature of the relief; **lighten**, a reduction in weight of that which is burdensome or depressing; **assuage**, a softening, sweetening, or mollifying of something harsh or disagreeable; **mitigate**, a moderation of that which is violent or intense; **allay**, an effective calming or quieting.

re·lie'vo (rē·lē'vō), *n.; pl.* -vos (-vōz). [It. *rilievo.*] Relief (sense 6).

re·light' (rē·līt'), *v. t.* To light again.

‖**re·li'gieux'** (rē·lē'zhyû'), *n. masc., sing. & pl.;* ‖**re·li'gieuse'** (-zhyûz'), *pl.* -GIEUSES (-zhyûz'), *fem.* [F.] A religious; (*masc.*) a monk, or (*fem.*) a nun.

‖**re·li'gi·o la'i·ci** (rē·lĭj'ĭ·ō lā'ĭ·sī). [LL.] A layman's religion.

re·li'gion (rē·lĭj'ŭn), *n.* [OF., fr. L. *religio*, prop., taboo, restraint.] **1.** The service and adoration of God or a god as expressed in forms of worship. **2.** One of the systems of faith and worship. **3.** The profession or practice of religious beliefs; religious observances collectively; *pl.*, rites. **4.** Devotion or fidelity; conscientiousness. **5.** An awareness or conviction of the existence of a supreme being, arousing reverence, love, gratitude, the will to obey and serve, and the like; as, man only is capable of *religion.*

re·li'gion·ism (-ĭz'm), *n.* Strict practice of, or devotion to, religion; also, pretense of religion. — **re·li'gion·ist** (-ĭst), *n.*

re·lig'i·os'i·ty (rē·lĭj'ĭ·ŏs'ĭ·tĭ), *n.* Religiousness, esp. when intense, excessive, or affected.

re·li'gious (rē·lĭj'ŭs), *adj.* [OF. *religius, religious*, fr. L. *religiosus.*] **1.** Manifesting devotion to, or the influence of, religion; godly. **2.** Belonging to, or followed by, an order of religious; as, the *religious* life. **3.** Of or pert. to religion or religions; concerned with religion; teaching, or setting forth, religion. **4.** Scrupulously faithful or exact; conscientious. — **Syn.** See DEVOUT. — *n., sing. & pl.* Those or one devoted to a life of piety and religion; a monk or friar; a nun. — **re·li'gious·ly**, *adv.* — **re·li'gious·ness**, *n.*

Syn. **Religious, monk, friar, nun** mean a member of a religious order bound by the vows of poverty, chastity, and obedience. **Religious**, the comprehensive term, is applicable to either a man or a woman; **monk**, in strict use, to any male religious living in a cloister and devoting themselves to contemplation, prayer, and some chosen form of work; **friar**, strictly, to any male religious of a mendicant order whose members originally lived by alms and went about preaching the Gospel; **nun**, to any female religious, esp. one of the severer orders.

re·lin'quish (rē·lĭng'kwĭsh), *v. t.* [OF. *relinquir, relenquir*, fr. L. *relinquere* to leave behind, fr. *re-* + *linquere* to leave.] **1.** To withdraw from; to desist from; to abandon; quit. **2.** To give up; to renounce a claim to. — **re·lin'quish·er**, *n.* — **re·lin'quish·ment**, *n.*

Syn. **Relinquish, yield, resign, surrender, abandon, waive** mean to give up completely. **Relinquish** carries no added implication but often acquires color from its contextual associations; **yield** adds the ideas of concession or compliance; **resign**, of voluntary or deliberate relinquishment or sacrifice; **surrender**, of relinquishment after a struggle to retain; **abandon**, of completeness or finality in relinquishment; **waive**, of concession with no (or very little) compulsion.

rel'i·quar'y (rĕl'ĭ·kwĕr'ĭ *or, esp. Brit.,* -kwĕr·ĭ), *n.; pl.* -IES (-ĭz). [F. *reliquaire.* See RELIC.] A small box, casket, shrine, etc., for keeping or exhibiting a relic.

rel'ique (rĕl'ĭk; rē·lēk'). Var. of RELIC.

re·liq'ui·ae (rē·lĭk'wĭ·ē), *n. pl.* [L.] Remains; relics.

rel'ish (rĕl'ĭsh), *n.* [OF. *reles, relais*, what is left, remainder. See RELEASE.] **1.** A taste; characteristic flavor; now esp., a pleasing flavor. **2.** A quantity just sufficient to flavor; a dash. **3.** Taste, or power to discern and appreciate; often, personal taste; liking. **4.** Appetite; inclination. **5.** Something taken with food to render it more palatable or to stimulate appetite; a condiment. — **Syn.** See TASTE. — *v. t.* **1.** To add a relish, flavor, or zest to. **2.** To be pleased or gratified by; to enjoy. **3.** To eat or drink with pleasure; to like the taste of. — *v. i.* To have a characteristic, pleasing, or appetizing taste; to have a flavor; hence, to be pleasurable or acceptable. — **rel'ish·a·ble**, *adj.*

re·live' (rē·lĭv'), *v. t. & i.* To live again.

re·load' (rē·lōd'), *v. t. & i.* To load again.

re·lo'cate (rē·lō'kāt), *v. t.* To locate or allocate again. — **re'lo·ca'tion** (rē'lō·kā'shŭn), *n.*

re·lu'cent (rē·lū'sĕnt; -s'nt), *adj.* [L. *relucens*, pres. part. of *relucere.* See LUCENT.] Reflecting light; refulgent.

re·luct' (rē·lŭkt'), *v. i.* [L. *reluctari*, fr. *re-* + *luctari* to struggle.] To feel or show dislike or reluctance; to revolt.

re·luc'tance (rē·lŭk'tăns), *n.* **1.** State or quality of being reluctant; repugnance; unwillingness. **2.** *Elec.* The opposition offered by a magnetic substance to magnetic flux; ratio of the magnetomotive force acting on a magnetic circuit to the magnetic flux it produces.

re·luc'tan·cy (-tăn·sĭ), *n.* Reluctance.

re·luc'tant (-tănt), *adj.* [L. *reluctans, -antis*, pres. part. See RELUCT.] **1.** Struggling against; resisting. **2.** Characterized by reluctance; averse; unwilling; disinclined. — **Syn.** See DISINCLINED. — **re·luc'tant·ly**, *adv.*

rel'uc·tiv'i·ty (rĕl'ŭk·tĭv'ĭ·tĭ), *n.* *Elec.* Specific reluctance; the reluctance of a mass of the material one centimeter long and one square centimeter in cross section.

re·lume' (rē·lūm'), *v. t.* To rekindle; to light again.

re·lu'mine (rē·lū'mĭn), *v. t.* [LL. *reluminare.*] To relume.

re·ly' (rē·lī'), *v. i.;* -LIED' (-līd'); -LY'ING. [OF. *relier* to bind, bind together or again, fr. L. *religare*, fr. *re-* + *ligare* to bind.] To have confidence; trust; depend; — with *on.*

Syn. **Rely, trust, depend, count, reckon** mean to place full confidence. **Rely** *on* or *upon* implies a judgment based upon experience or association; **trust** *in* or *to*, complete assurance that another will not fail one; **depend** *on* or *upon*, a resting confidently for support or assistance; **count** *on* or **reckon** *on*, a taking into one's calculations as certain or assured.

re·main' (rē·mān'), *v. i.* [OF. *remaindre, remanoir* (3d sing. pres. *remaint*), fr. L. *remanere*, fr. *re-* + *manere* to stay, remain.] **1.** To be left after others have been removed or destroyed; to be left after a number or quantity has been subtracted or cut off. **2.** To be left as not included or comprised. **3.** To stay behind while others withdraw. **4.** To continue unchanged or undiminished; to abide; endure. — **Syn.** See STAY. — *n.* **1.** *Obs.* Stay. **2.** The portion surviving after a part has been destroyed or removed; remnant; remaining part; remainder; chiefly in *pl.* **3.** *pl.* **a** Posthumous works, esp. literary works. **b** A corpse.

re·main'der (-dēr), *n.* [OF. *remaindre*, inf. as n.] **1.** Residue; residuum; remnant. **2.** The person or persons of a company, family, etc., remaining after the departure or removal of a portion. **3.** Copies of a book remaining in the publisher's stock when sales have ceased or become unprofitable. **4.** *Law.* An estate in expectancy, which becomes an estate in possession upon the determination of a particular prior estate, created at the same time, and by the same instrument; — disting. from a *reversion*, in which the residual interest is reserved by the grantor. **5.** *Math.* That which is left after subtraction or any deduction; the undivided part, less than the divisor, left after division (cf. QUOTIENT). **6.** *pl. Philately.* Supplies of stamps left on hand after demonetization. — *adj.* Remaining; left over.

re·make' (rē·māk'), *v. t.* To make anew.

re·man' (rē·măn'), *v. t.* **1.** To man again or anew. **2.** To reimbue with courage or manliness.

re·mand' (rē·mȧnd'; 9), *v. t.* [F. *remander* to send word again, fr. LL. *remandare*, fr. *re-* re- + *mandare* to commit.] **1.** To recommit; to send back; specif., to recommit (a prisoner) temporarily. **2.** To commit or consign; to remit. — *n.* Act of remanding, or state of being remanded; also, a remanded prisoner.

rem'a·nent (rĕm'ȧ·nĕnt), *adj.* [L. *remanens*, pres. part. of *remanere.* See REMAIN.] Remaining; residual.

re·mark' (rē·märk'), *v. t.* [F. *remarquer*, fr. *re-* + *marquer* to mark.] **1.** *Obs.* To mark in a notable manner; to distinguish clearly. **2.** To take notice of, or to observe; perceive. **3.** To state; say. — *v. i.* To make a remark or remarks; to comment; — with *on.* — *n.* **1.** Act of remarking; notice or observation. **2.** The mention of that which deserves attention; comment; hence, also, a casual statement. **3.** *Engraving & Etching.* A remarque.

re·mark'a·ble (rē·mär'kȧ·b'l), *adj.* Worthy of being remarked or noticed; conspicuous; hence, uncommon; extraordinary. — **Syn.** See NOTICEABLE. — **re·mark'a·ble·ness**, *n.* — **re·mark'a·bly**, *adv.*

re·marque' (rē·märk'), *n.* [F.] *Engraving.* **a** A small design etched on the margin of a plate and supposed to be removed after the earliest proofs have been taken; also, any feature distinguishing a particular stage of the plate. **b** A print or proof so distinguished.

re·mar'ry (rē·măr'ĭ), *v. t. & i.;* RE·MAR'RIED (-măr'ĭd); RE·MAR'RY·ING. To marry again. — **re·mar'riage** (-ĭj), *n.*

re·me'di·a·ble (rē·mē'dĭ·ȧ·b'l; 58), *adj.* Capable of being remedied. — **re·me'di·a·bly**, *adv.*

re·me'di·al (-ăl), *adj.* [L. *remedialis.*] Affording a remedy; intended for a remedy; as, *remedial* treatment.

rem'e·di·less (rĕm'ē·dĭ·lĕs *or, esp. formerly,* rē·mĕd'ĭ·lĕs; -lĭs), *adj.* Not admitting of remedy; irreparable; irremediable.

rem'e·dy (rĕm'ē·dĭ), *n.; pl.* -DIES (-dĭz). [AF. (F. *remède*), fr. L. *remedium.*] **1.** Any medicine or application which puts an end to disease and restores health; also, one that relieves, but does not necessarily end, a morbid condition. **2.** That which corrects or counteracts an evil; a corrective; cure. **3.** *Coinage.* = TOLERANCE, 4. **4.** *Law.* The legal means to recover a right, or to prevent, or obtain redress for, a wrong. — *v. t.;* REM'E·DIED (-dĭd); REM'E·DY·ING. To provide or serve as a remedy for; to cure; relieve; correct; repair. — **Syn.** See CURE: CORRECT.

re·mem'ber (rē·mĕm'bēr), *v. t.* [OF. *remembrer*, fr. LL. *rememorari*, fr. *re-* + *memorare* to bring to remembrance, fr. *memor* mindful.] **1.** To have (a notion or idea) come into the mind again; to think of again; to recollect. **2.** To put in mind; to remind; — also used impersonally. **3.** **a** To be continually thoughtful or regardful of; as, to *remember* one's friends at Christmas. **b** To keep in mind as deserving a reward; hence, to reward. **4.** To retain in the memory. **5.** To recall to the mind of another; as, *remember* me to him. — *v. i.* **1.** To exercise or have the power of memory. **2.** To have a recollection or remembrance; — with *of;* — now regarded as incorrect. — **re·mem'ber·er**, *n.*

Syn. **Remember, recollect, recall, remind, reminisce** mean to put one in mind of something. **Remember** usually implies a keeping in memory; **recollect**, a bringing back to memory; **recall**, an effort to bring back to memory or, transitively, an impulsion that brings back to mind; **remind**, now usually transitive, a jogging of the memory; **reminisce**, a recollection of that past and gone.

re·mem'brance (rē·mĕm'brăns), *n.* **1.** Act of remembering; a recollecting. **2.** State of being remembered, or held in mind; memory; recollection. **3.** (One's) memory or ability to remember; hence, the period over which one's memory extends. **4.** A reminder; memento; souvenir. **5.** *pl.* Greetings recalling or betokening friendship. — **Syn.** See MEMORY.

Remembrance Day. *Canada.* See HOLIDAY, 3.

re·mem'branc·er (rē·mĕm'brăn·sēr), *n.* **1.** [*usually cap.*] Any of several officials of the Court of Exchequer in England. The only one now surviving is the ***king's (or queen's) remembrancer***, now an officer of the Supreme Court, responsible for the collection of debts due to the sovereign. **2.** A person who brings things to the mind of another; esp., formerly, one appointed to do so. **3.** A reminder; memento.

re'mex (rē'mĕks), *n.; pl.* REMIGES (rĕm'ĭ·jēz). [L. *remex, -igis*, an oarsman.] *Zool.* One of the quill or flight feathers of the wing of a bird. These are divided into primaries and secondaries. — **re·mig'i·al** (rē·mĭj'ĭ·ăl), *adj.*

rem'i·grant (rĕm'ĭ·grănt; -grănt), *n.* A migrant who returns.

re·mi'grate (rē·mī'grāt), *v. i.* To migrate again or back. — **re'mi·gra'tion** (rē'mī·grā'shŭn), *n.*

re·mil′i·ta·rize (rē·mĭl′ĭ·tȧ·rīz), *v. t.* To prepare or equip again with military forces, defenses, etc. — **re′mil·i·ta·ri·za′tion** (rē′mĭl·ĭ·tȧ·rĭ·zā′shŭn; -rī·zā′-), *n.*

re·mind′ (rē·mīnd′), *v. t. & i.* To put (one) in mind (of something); to cause to remember. — **Syn.** See REMEMBER. — **re·mind′er** (-mīn′dẽr), *n.*

re·mind′ful (-fo͝ol; -f'l), *adj.* Of persons, mindful; regardful; of things, awakening memories; — with *of.*

rem′i·nisce′ (rĕm′ĭ·nĭs′), *v. t. & i.* To indulge in or give oneself up to reminiscences. — **Syn.** See REMEMBER.

rem′i·nis′cence (-nĭs′ĕns; -'ns), *n.* [F. *réminiscence.*] **1.** Act, power, or fact of recalling past experience; recollection. **2.** *pl.* An account of one's memorable experiences; as, to publish G—'s *reminiscences.* **3.** A phrase, custom, feature, etc., so suggestive of another as to be regarded as an unconscious imitation, survival, or the like. **4.** *Philos.* In Platonism, the apprehension of perfect forms (ideas). — **Syn.** See MEMORY.

rem′i·nis′cent (-ĕnt; -'nt), *adj.* [L. *reminiscens, -entis,* pres. part. of *reminisci* to recollect.] **1.** Of the nature of, pertaining to, or marked by reminiscence. **2.** Given to or indulging in reminiscences. **3.** That reminds one, as of something previously known; as, a scene *reminiscent* of Pickwick's London.

re·mise′ (rē·mīz′), *v. t.* [From F. *remise* restoration, or fr. F. *remis,* past part. of *remettre.*] *Law.* To give, grant, or release a claim to; to deed.

re·miss′ (rē·mĭs′), *adj.* [L. *remissus,* past part. of *remittere.* See REMIT.] **1.** Negligent; careless. **2.** Showing neglect or inattention; negligently performed; lax. — **Syn.** See NEGLIGENT.

re·mis′si·ble (rē·mĭs′ĭ·b'l), *adj.* That may be remitted or forgiven. — **re·mis′si·bil′i·ty** (-bĭl′ĭ·tĭ), *n.*

re·mis′sion (rē·mĭsh′ŭn), *n.* **1.** Act of remitting; pardon; esp., remission of sin (which see). **2.** Cancellation or relinquishment of a claim, right, tax, debt, etc. **3.** Diminution of intensity, as of cold or heat. **4.** *Obs.* Slackening of strain; relaxation. **5.** Act of sending in payment, as money; remittance.

remission of sin *or* **sins.** Forgiveness of sin or sins; specif., *R.C.Ch.,* the remitting, through the sacrament of penance, of due or merited punishment for one's sins.

re·miss′ness, *n.* Quality or state of being remiss.

re·mit′ (rē·mĭt′), *v. t.;* -MIT′TED; -MIT′TING. [L. *remittere, remissum,* to send back, relax, fr. *re-* + *mittere* to send.] **1.** To forgive; pardon. **2.** To let slacken; mitigate; abate. **3.** To submit or refer (something) for consideration, judgment, decision, action, etc., now esp. to one in authority. **4.** *Now Rare.* To send back, esp. to custody; recommit. **5.** To refrain from exacting, inflicting, or enforcing; as, to *remit* a penalty. **6.** To restore, as to a former title or status. **7.** To put off; defer. **8.** *Obs.* **a** To surrender or resign. **b** To set free; release, as a prisoner. **9.** *Com.* To transmit or send, esp. to a distance, as money in payment of a demand, account, etc. **10.** *Law.* To send back (a proceeding) to an inferior court for further action. — *v. i.* **1.** To abate in force or in intensity. **2.** To send money, as in payment. — *n.* Act of remitting; esp., a transfer, as of a legal cause by one authority to another. — **re·mit′ta·ble,** *adj.* — **re·mit′ter,** *n.*

re·mit′tal (rē·mĭt′ăl; -'l), *n.* Remission, as of a penalty.

re·mit′tance (-ăns), *n.* Transmittal of money, bills, etc., esp. to a distance; also, the thing, esp. money, remitted.

re·mit′tent (-ĕnt), *adj.* Remitting; esp., temporarily abating. — *n.* A remittent fever. — **re·mit′tence** (-ĕns), **re·mit′ten·cy** (-ĕn·sĭ), *n.* — **re·mit′tent·ly,** *adv.*

remittent fever. *Med.* A fever in which the symptoms temporarily abate at regular intervals.

re·mit′tor (rē·mĭt′ẽr), *n.* One who makes a remittance.

rem′nant (rĕm′nănt), *n.* [See REMNANT, *adj.*] **1.** Residue; remainder. **2. a** A small fragment. **b** An unsold end of piece goods, as of cloth. **3.** A surviving trace, as of a custom, state, etc. — *adj.* [OF. *remenant, remanant,* pres. part. of *remanoir, remaindre.* See REMAIN.] Remaining; yet left.

re·mod′el (rē·mŏd′'l), *v. t.* To model anew; to reconstruct. — **Syn.** See MEND.

re·mold′, re·mould′ (rē·mōld′), *v. t.* To mold again or anew.

re·mon′e·tize (-mŏn′ē·tīz; -mŭn′-), *v. t.* To restore to use as legal tender; as, to *remonetize* silver. — **re·mon′e·ti·za′tion** (-tĭ·zā′shŭn; -tī·zā′-), *n.*

re·mon′strance (rē·mŏn′străns), *n.* [OF.] Act or instance of remonstrating; expostulation; protest.

re·mon′strant (-strănt), *adj.* Remonstrating; vigorously objecting or opposing. — *n.* One who remonstrates; specif. [*cap.*], *Eccl. Hist.,* one of the Arminians who in 1610 addressed, to the states of Holland, a remonstrance showing their differences from the strict Calvinists.

re·mon′strate (rē·mŏn′strāt), *v. t.* [ML. *remonstratus,* past part. of *remonstrare* to demonstrate, fr. L. *re-* + *monstrare* to show.] **1.** *Obs.* To point out; to demonstrate. **2.** To say or plead in protest, reproof, etc. — *v. i.* To present and urge reasons in opposition, as to an act, measure, or any proceedings. — **Syn.** See OBJECT. — **re′mon·stra′tion** (rē′mŏn·strā′shŭn; rĕm′ŏn-), *n.* — **re·mon′stra·tive** (rē·mŏn′strȧ·tĭv), *adj.* — **re·mon′stra·tor** (-strā·tẽr), *n.*

re·mon′tant (rē·mŏn′tănt), *adj.* [F., pres. part.] *Hort.* Flowering again; — applied to roses which bloom more than once in a season. — *n.* A remontant rose.

rem′on·toir′ (rĕm′ŏn·twär′; rē·môɴ′twȧr′), *n.* [F.] *Horol.* A device to give a uniform impulse to a pendulum.

rem′o·ra (rĕm′ō·rȧ), *n.* [L., hindrance.] **1.** Any of several fishes (genera *Echeneis, Remora,* family Echeneididae), with a suctorial disk on the head by which they cling to other fishes or to ships. **2.** A clog; drag; hindrance.

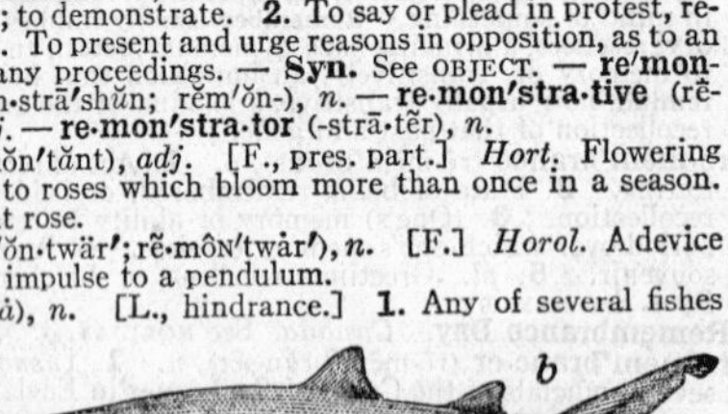

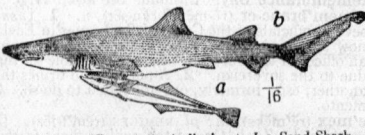

a Remora (*E. naucrates*) clinging to *b* a Sand Shark (*Odontaspis littoralis*).

re·morse′ (rē·môrs′), *n.* [OF. *remors,* fr. LL., fr. L. *remordere, remorsum,* to bite again; torment, fr. *re-* + *mordere* to bite.] **1.** Distress, like gnawing pain, excited by a sense of guilt; repentant regret. **2.** *Now Rare.* Pity; compassion. — **Syn.** See PENITENCE.

re·morse′ful (-fo͝ol; -f'l), *adj.* Full of remorse; springing from, or characterized by, remorse. — **re·morse′ful·ly,** *adv.* — **re·morse′ful·ness,** *n.*

re·morse′less, *adj.* Being without remorse or pity; merciless. — **re·morse′less·ly,** *adv.* — **re·morse′less·ness,** *n.*

re·mote′ (rē·mōt′), *adj.* [L. *remotus,* past part. See REMOVE.] **1.** Removed to, or situated at, a distance; distant; also, out of the way; secluded. **2. a** Foreign; alien; markedly divergent. **b** Not closely related or connected. **c** Separate; abstracted; hence, aloof; inaccessible. **d** Not proximate or acting directly; not primary. **e** Not obvious or striking; slight; as, a *remote* resemblance. — **Syn.** See DISTANT. — **re·mote′ly,** *adv.* — **re·mote′ness,** *n.*

re·mo′tion (rē·mō′shŭn), *n.* **1.** Act of removing; removal. **2.** *Obs.* Departure.

re·mould′ (rē·mōld′). Var. of REMOLD.

re·mount′ (rē·mount′), *v. t. & i.* To mount again. — (rē·mount′; rē′mount′), *n.* A fresh horse to take the place of one lost or disabled. — **re·mount′,** *adj.*

re·mov′a·ble (rē·mo͞ov′ȧ·b'l), *adj.* Admitting of being removed. — **re·mov′a·bil′i·ty** (-bĭl′ĭ·tĭ), **re·mov′a·ble·ness,** *n.* — **re·mov′a·bly,** *adv.*

re·mov′al (rē·mo͞ov′ăl), *n.* Act of removing; fact of being removed; dismissal; transference; change of residence.

re·move′ (rē·mo͞ov′), *v. t.* [OF. *removoir,* fr. L. *removere, remotum,* fr. *re-* + *movere* to move.] **1.** To change the location of; to transfer, esp. in order to re-establish. **2.** To move by lifting, pushing aside, or the like. **3. a** To dismiss from office; as, to *remove* a postmaster. **b** To assassinate. **c** To take away by death. **4.** To eradicate; to eliminate; as, to *remove* the causes of poverty. — *v. i.* **1.** To change one's location, station, or, esp., residence. **2.** To depart; to go away. — *n.* **1.** *Now Rare.* Act of removing. **2.** The transfer of one's business, or of one's domestic belongings, from one location to another; — in the United States usually called a *move.* **3.** The distance, space, or interval through which anything is removed; hence, a step or degree in any scale of gradation. **4.** *Rare.* Absence. **5.** *Eng.* A dish or course at a meal.

re·moved′ (rē·mo͞ovd′), *adj.* **1.** Distant in relationship; as, a first cousin twice *removed* (a first cousin's grandchild). **2.** Remote; far away. — **Syn.** See DISTANT.

re·mov′er (rē·mo͞ov′ẽr), *n.* One who or that which removes something, as a solvent for removing paint.

‖**re·mu′da** (rrā·mo͞o′thä; *Angl.* rē·mū′dȧ), *n.* [Sp.] The saddle horses collectively from which are chosen those to be used for the day.

re·mu′ner·ate (rē·mū′nẽr·āt), *v. t. & i.* [L. *remuneratus,* past part. of *remunerare, remunerari,* fr. *re-* + *munerare, -ari,* to give, present.] To pay an equivalent for (any service, loss, etc.), or to pay an equivalent to (one) for such service, etc.; to recompense; pay. — **Syn.** See PAY.

re·mu′ner·a′tion (-ā′shŭn), *n.* Act or fact of remunerating; also, that which remunerates; recompense; pay.

re·mu′ner·a′tive (rē·mū′nẽr·ā′tĭv; -ȧ·tĭv), *adj.* **1.** Serving to remunerate. **2.** Affording remuneration; profitable; gainful. — **re·mu′ner·a′tive·ly,** *adv.*

Re′mus (rē′mŭs), *n.* [L.] See ROMULUS.

ren′ais·sance′ (rĕn′ĕ·zäns′; -säns′; rē·nā′săns), *n.* [F., fr. *renaître* to be born again.] **1.** A new birth or revival. Specif. [*cap.*]: **a** The transitional movement in Europe between the medieval and the modern, marked esp. by revival of classical influence; also, the period (14th–16th centuries) during which this occurred. **b** The neoclassic style of art which prevailed at this epoch. **2.** Any period similarly characterized by vigorous activity along literary, artistic, or other lines.

Renaissance architecture. The style of building and decoration that arose in the early 15th century in Italy, based on the Roman classic orders and design.

re′nal (rē′năl; -n'l), *adj.* [F. or L.; F. *rénal,* fr. L. *renalis,* fr. *renes* kidneys, reins.] *Anat.* Of or pertaining to the kidneys; in the region of the kidneys.

re·name′ (rē·nām′), *v. t.* To name again or anew.

Ren′ard (rĕn′ẽrd). Var. of REYNARD.

re·nas′cence (rē·năs′ĕns; -'ns), *n.* **1.** Rebirth; revival. **2.** [*cap.*] The Renaissance.

re·nas′cent (-ĕnt; -'nt), *adj.* [L. *renascens,* pres. part. of *renasci* to be born again, fr. *re-* + *nasci* to be born.] Springing again into being or vigor; being born again, or reproduced.

ren·con′tre (rĕn·kŏn′tẽr; *F.* räɴ′kôɴ′tr'), *n.* [F.] Rencounter.

ren·coun′ter (rĕn·koun′tẽr), *v. t. & i.* [F. *rencontrer,* fr. *re-* + OF. *encontrer* to encounter.] *Now Rare.* To meet, esp. casually, as a friend. — *n.* [F. *rencontre,* fr. *rencontrer* to meet.] **1.** *Archaic.* A hostile meeting; a combat or duel. **2.** A personal contest of any sort, esp. in debate. **3.** A casual meeting with a person.

rend (rĕnd), *v. t.;* RENT (rĕnt); REND′ING. [AS. *rendan.*] **1.** To take from its place by a violent effort; to wrest. **2.** To tear violently asunder; to split. **3.** *Poetic.* To tear (clothes) from one's body in a frenzy. — *v. i.* To split asunder; burst. — **Syn.** See TEAR. — **rend′er,** *n.*

ren′der (rĕn′dẽr), *v. t.* [OF. *rendre* to give up, translate, cause to become, deriv. of L. *reddere, redditum,* fr. *red-, re-* + *dare* to give.] **1.** To give; deliver; transmit; as, to *render* a message. **2.** To melt down, extract, or clarify by melting; as, to *render* lard. **3.** To give up; yield; surrender; as, to *render* a city. **4.** To give or inflict in return or requital; as, to *render* thanks for blessings. **5.** To furnish for consideration; to deliver; as, to *render* an account. **6.** To pay back; restore; as, to *render* anything loaned. **7.** To pay as due, esp. as rent, tribute, or the like; as, to *render* homage. **8.** To cause to be or become; as, to *render* a fortress secure. **9.** To furnish; contribute; as, to *render* assistance. **10.** To represent or depict, as by painting, music, or the like; as, to *render* the role of Hamlet. **11.** To translate; as, to *render* Latin into English. **12.** *Plastering.* To apply a first coat to (a wall, etc.). — *v. i.* To give recompense. — *n.* A return in kind, services, or money, esp. in kind or service, as by a tenant to his superior. — **ren′der·a·ble** (-ȧ·b'l), *adj.* — **ren′der·er** (-ẽr), *n.*

ren′dez·vous (rän′dĕ·vo͞o; rĕn′-), *n.; pl.* -VOUS (-vo͞oz), formerly also -VOUSES (-vo͞o′zĕz). [F. *rendez-vous,* prop., render yourselves, repair to a place.] **1.** A place appointed for a meeting. **2.** A meeting by appointment. **3.** *Obs.* **a** A retreat; refuge. **b** A gathering of persons or things. — *v. i. & t.;* -VOUSED (-vo͞od); -VOUS′ING (-vo͞o′ĭng). To assemble; meet, esp. by appointment.

ren·di′tion (rĕn·dĭsh′ŭn), *n.* [MF.] Act or result of rendering; as:

a Surrender, as of a fort. b Translation, as of a foreign language. c Performance, as of a play, a musical selection, etc.

ren′e·gade (rĕn′ē·gād), *n.* [Sp. *renegado*, fr. ML. *renegatus*, fr. *renegare* to deny, fr. L. *re-* + *negare* to deny.] An apostate from one's faith, party, or the like, esp. one who deserts to a hostile faith, party, etc.; a traitor; turncoat. — *adj.* Traitorous; apostate. — *v. i.* To become a renegade.

ren′e·ga′do (rĕn′ē·gā′dō), *n., adj., & v.* [Sp.] = RENEGADE.

re·nege′ (rē·nēg′; rē·nĕg′; *popularly* rē·nĭg′), *v. t.;* RE·NEGED′ (-nēgd′; -nĕgd′; -nĭgd′); RE·NEG′ING (-nēg′ĭng; -nĕg′ĭng; -nĭg′ĭng). [ML. *renegare.*] To deny; renounce; as, to *renege* one's country. — *v. i.* 1. *Card Playing.* To fail to follow suit when able to do so, in violation of the rules of the game; to revoke. 2. *Colloq.* To go back upon a promise. — *n.* Act or fact of reneging. — **re·neg′er** (-nēg′ẽr; -nĕg′ẽr; -nĭg′ẽr), *n.*

re′ne·go′ti·ate (rē′nē·gō′shĭ·āt), *v. t. & i.* 1. To negotiate again. 2. To readjust (a government war contract or subcontract or the price stipulated) by negotiation with a price-adjustment board charged (under section 403 of Public Law 528, 77th Congress) with elimination of any excessive profits made out of the war. — **re′ne·go′ti·a·ble** (-ȧ·b'l), *adj.* — **re′ne·go′ti·a′tion** (-ā′shŭn), *n.*

re·new′ (rē·nū′), *v. t.* 1. To make new again; to restore to freshness or vigor; also, to gain again as new; as, to *renew* one's strength. 2. To make new spiritually; to regenerate. 3. To re-establish; rebuild; revive. 4. To repeat; go over again. 5. To recommence; resume; as, to *renew* an attack. 6. To replace; also, to restore to fullness; as, to *renew* water in a tank. 7. To grant or obtain an extension of; as, to *renew* a note. — *v. i.* 1. To become new, or as new. 2. To begin again; resume. 3. To make a renewal, as of a lease. — **re·new′a·ble,** *adj.*

Syn. **Renew, restore, refresh, renovate, rejuvenate** mean to make new or like new. **Renew** implies usually a replacing of that which is decayed, disintegrated, or the like; **restore,** a return to an original state after depletion, illness, etc.; **refresh,** a supplying of something that restores lost strength, animation, etc.; **renovate,** a renewal or refreshing of, usually, a material thing; **rejuvenate,** a restoration of youthful vigor, appearance, powers, etc.

re·new′al (rē·nū′ăl), *n.* A renewing, or state of being renewed.

ren′i- (rĕn′ĭ-; rē′nĭ-). Also **ren′o-.** [L. *ren, renis.*] A combining form denoting *kidney,* as in **ren′i·form** (see LEAF, *Illust.*), **ren′i·punc′ture.**

re′nin (rē′nĭn), *n.* [*reni* + *-in.*] *Biochem.* A protein found in the kidney, that increases blood pressure.

re·ni′tent (rē·nī′tĕnt; rĕn′ĭ·tĕnt), *adj.* [F. or L.; F. *rénitant*, fr. L. *renitens, -entis,* pres. part. of *reniti* to strive against.] 1. Resisting pressure. 2. Persistently opposed; recalcitrant. — **re·ni′ten·cy** (-tĕn-sĭ), *n.*

ren′net (rĕn′ĕt; -ĭt), *n.* [ME., fr. *rennen* to run.] 1. The contents of the stomach of an unweaned calf or other animal, or the lining membrane of the stomach, used for curdling milk; hence, also, any preparation of the stomach of animals which is used for that purpose. 2. Anything used to curdle milk. 3. *Biochem.* Rennin.

ren′nin (rĕn′ĭn), *n.* *Biochem.* An enzyme that coagulates milk. It is found in gastric juice, and also in various lower animals and plants.

ren′o- (rĕn′ō-; rē′nō-). = RENI-.

re·nom′i·nate (rē·nŏm′ĭ·nāt), *v. t.* To nominate again or anew, esp. for a term of office in immediate succession. — **re·nom′i·na′tion** (-nā′shŭn), *n.*

re·nounce′ (rē·nouns′), *v. t.;* -NOUNCED′ (-nounst′); -NOUNC′ING (-noun′sĭng). [OF. *renoncier*, fr. L. *renuntiare* to bring back word, announce, renounce, fr. *re-* + *nuntiare* to announce, fr. *nuntius* messenger.] 1. To give up, abandon, or resign; as, to *renounce* a title; to *renounce* faith. 2. To disclaim; to repudiate; cast off; as, to *renounce* one's son. 3. *Card Playing.* To disclaim having a card of (the suit led) by playing a card of another suit. — See ABDICATE (**Ant.** arrogate); ABJURE. — *v. i.* *Card Playing.* Not to follow suit, because holding no cards of the suit led. — **re·nounce′ment,** *n.*

ren′o·vate (rĕn′ō·vāt), *v. t.* [L. *renovatus*, past part. of *renovare*, fr. *re-* + *novare* to make new, fr. *novus* new.] 1. To restore to life, vigor, activity, etc. 2. To renew, make over, or repair. — **Syn.** See RENEW. — *adj.* Renovated. — **ren′o·va′tion** (-vā′shŭn), *n.* — **ren′o·va′tor** (-vā′tẽr), *n.*

re·nown′ (rē·noun′), *n.* [OF. *renon*, fr. *renomer* to make famous.] 1. Illustrious reputation; exalted fame; celebrity. 2. *Obs.* Report; rumor.

re·nowned′ (-nound′), *adj.* Having renown; celebrated. — **Syn.** See FAMOUS.

rens′se·laer·ite (rĕn′sĕ·lẽr·īt; rĕn′sĕ·lâr′īt), *n.* [After Stephen Van *Rensselaer*, Am. statesman.] *Mineral.* A soft, compact variety of talc, often worked into inkstands, etc.

rent (rĕnt), *past & past part.* of REND.

rent, *n.* [From E. dial. *rent* to rend.] 1. An opening made by rending or tearing; specif., a tear in cloth, a cleft in the earth, etc. 2. A schism; split in a party or organized group.

rent, *n.* [OF. *rente*, ult. fr. L. *reddere.* See RENDER.] 1. *Obs.* Revenue; income. 2. *Obs. exc. Colloq., U. S.* A piece of real property that is rented. 3. *Com. & Law.* a The return made by the tenant or occupant of land or corporeal hereditaments to the owner for the use thereof; commonly, a certain sum agreed upon between a tenant and his landlord, and paid at fixed intervals by the tenant to the landlord, for the use of land or its appendages. b The return made by a hirer of personal property to the owner for its use. 4. *Econ.* A return from a differential advantage for production, as in case of earnings due to natural resources, fertility, etc.; — as distinct from *profit* and *wages.* — *v. t.* 1. To take and hold under an agreement to pay rent. 2. To grant possession and enjoyment of for rent; to lease. — *v. i.* To be leased or let for rent. — **Syn.** See HIRE. — **rent′a·ble,** *adj.*

rent′al (rĕn′tăl; -t'l), *n.* [AF. (Anglo-Lat. *rentale*).] 1. A schedule of rents, with the names of the tenants, etc. 2. The amount of a rent or rents. — *adj.* Of or pertaining to rent; as, *rental* value, the amount for which a property will rent, generally stated on an annual basis.

‖**rente** (räNt), *n.* [F. See 3d RENT.] In France, annual income; specif., *pl.* (**rentes sur l'é′tat′** [räNt′ sür lā′tȧ′]), interests payable by the government on the consolidated debt; also, the bonds, stocks, etc., which represent this indebtedness.

rent′er (rĕn′tẽr), *n.* One who rents lands, tenements, or other property; — usually said of a lessee or tenant.

‖**ren′tier′** (räN′tyā′), *n.* [F. See 3d RENT.] One who owns rentes; hence, one who receives a fixed income from any source, as from land, stocks, bonds, etc.

re·num′ber (rē·nŭm′bẽr), *v. t.* To number again or anew.

re·nun′ci·a′tion (rē·nŭn′sĭ·ā′shŭn; -shĭ·ā′shŭn), *n.* Act or an instance of renouncing, or sacrificing, repudiating, etc.; renouncement. — **re·nun′ci·a′tive** (-nŭn′shĭ·ā′tĭv; -sĭ·ā′tĭv; -ȧ·tĭv), *adj.* — **re·nun′ci·a·to′ry** (-ȧ·tō′rĭ *or, esp. Brit.,* -tẽr·ĭ), *adj.*

re·oc′cu·py (rē·ŏk′ū·pī), *v. t.* To occupy again. — **re′oc·cu·pa′tion** (rē′ŏk·ū·pā′shŭn), *n.*

re·o′pen (rē·ō′pĕn), *v. t. & i.* 1. To open again. 2. To resume; recommence; as, to *reopen* an assault, a discussion.

re·or′der (rē·ôr′dẽr), *n.* *Com.* A subsequent order for goods given to the same person or dealer, esp. within a short time. — *v. t. & i.* To order again.

re′or·gan·i·za′tion (rē′ôr·găn·ĭ·zā′shŭn; -ī·zā′shŭn), *n.* 1. Act of reorganizing, or state of being reorganized. 2. *Finance.* The reconstruction of a business concern, usually rendered necessary by an actual or anticipated receivership. Cf. READJUSTMENT.

re·or′gan·ize (rē·ôr′găn·īz), *v. t. & i.* To organize again or anew; to effect a reorganization of. — **re·or′gan·iz′er** (-īz′ẽr), *n.*

re·o′ri·ent (rē·ō′rĭ·ĕnt), *adj.* *Rare.* Rising again.

rep, repp (rĕp), *n.* [Also *reps*, fr. F. *reps*, fr. E. *ribs*, pl. of *rib.*] A fabric of silk or wool, or both, having a corded or ribbed surface.

re·paint′ (rē·pānt′), *v. t. & i.* To paint again. — *n.* Anything, esp. a portion of a picture, which has been repainted.

re·pair′ (rē·pâr′), *v. i.* [OF. *repairer*, fr. LL. *repatriare* to return to one's country, fr. *re-* + *patria* native land.] 1. To go; betake oneself. 2. To return. — *n.* 1. A place of resort; haunt. 2. *Scot.* A concourse; a flocking, as of numbers of people to one place.

re·pair′, *v. t.* [OF. *reparer*, fr. L. *reparare*, fr. *re-* + *parare* to prepare.] 1. To restore to a sound or good state after decay, injury, etc. 2. To remedy, heal, or mend; as, to *repair* a break, a wound, etc. 3. *Now Rare.* To make amends for (an injury, injustice, etc.). — **Syn.** See MEND. — *n.* 1. Act or process of repairing; restoration to a sound state after decay, injury, etc.; also, an instance or a result of repairing. 2. The state of being repaired; also, condition with respect to soundness or need of repairing; as, in excellent *repair.* — **re·pair′a·ble,** *adj.* — **re·pair′er,** *n.*

re·pand′ (rē·pănd′), *adj.* [L. *repandus* bent backward.] *Bot.* Having a slightly undulating margin; — said of leaves.

rep′a·ra·ble (rĕp′ȧ·rȧ·b'l), *adj.* [L. *reparabilis.*] Capable of being repaired, mended, remedied, or made good. — **rep′a·ra·bly,** *adv.*

rep′a·ra′tion (-rā′shŭn), *n.* [OF. *reparacion*, fr. LL. *reparatio.* See REPAIR to mend.] 1. A repairing or keeping in repair; as, the *reparation* of wasted tissue; a church in need of constant *reparation.* 2. Act of making amends for a wrong, injury, etc.; also, the amends; compensation. 3. Specif. (usually in the *pl.*), compensation either in money or in materials, commodities, capital equipment, merchant vessels, and the like, payable by a defeated nation as war indemnity for direct damages and for loss from war expenditures, occupation costs, etc., sustained as a result of aggression by the defeated nation.

re·par′a·tive (rē·păr′ȧ·tĭv), *adj.* 1. Repairing, or tending to repair. 2. Tending or pertaining to reparation.

rep′ar·tee′ (rĕp′ẽr·tē′), *n.* [F. *repartie*, fr. *repartir* to reply, depart again.] A clever and witty retort; also, skill in making such replies; clever retorts collectively. — **Syn.** See WIT.

re′par·ti′tion (rē′pär·tĭsh′ŭn; rĕ′pẽr-), *n.* 1. Act, fact, or result of partitioning; distribution. 2. A second or an additional partition or distribution.

re·pass′ (rē·pȧs′; 9), *v. t. & i.* To pass through, over, or by way of, again, esp. in returning; to cross or pass again. — **re·pas′sage** (-păs′ĭj), *n.*

re·past′ (rē·pȧst′; 9), *n.* [OF., fr. *past* food, meal, fr. L. *pastus*, fr. *pascere, pastum,* to feed, with *re-* after OF. *repaistre* to feed.] 1. Food, now only that composing a meal; hence, a meal; feast. 2. Act of taking food; also, mealtime. — *v. t. & i. Rare.* To supply food to.

re·pa′tri·ate (rē·pā′trĭ·āt; *esp. Brit.,* rē·păt′rĭ-), *v. t. & i.* [LL. *repatriare.* See 1st REPAIR.] To restore or return to one's own country, allegiance, or citizenship; as, to *repatriate* prisoners of war. — **re·pa′tri·a′tion** (-ā′shŭn), *n.* — **re·pa′tri·a·ble** (-ȧ·b'l), *adj.*

re·pave′ (rē·pāv′), *v. t.* To pave again.

re·pay′ (rē·pā′), *v. t.* [OF. *repaier.*] 1. To pay back; refund; also, to make requital for; to recompense; return; as, to *repay* a loan, a kindness. 2. To pay back what is owed or due to (one). — *v. i.* To make payment, return, or requital. — **Syn.** See PAY. — **re·pay′a·ble,** *adj.* — **re·pay′ment,** *n.*

re·peal′ (rē·pēl′), *v. t.* [OF. *rapeler* to call back, fr. *re-* + *apeler* to call. See APPEAL.] 1. To recall, as a deed, grant, will, law, etc.; to revoke; rescind. 2. *Obs.* To recall; to summon to return, as from exile. 3. *Now Rare.* To renounce; to retract. — *n.* Revocation; rescission; abrogation; as, *repeal* of a law. — **re·peal′a·ble,** *adj.* — **re·peal′er,** *n.*

re·peat′ (rē·pēt′), *v. t.* [OF. *repeter*, fr. L. *repetere*, fr. *re-* + *petere* to attack, seek.] 1. To say or utter again; reiterate. 2. To make, do, or perform, again; to present, cover, etc., again. 3. To say over from memory; to recite; also, to say or utter after another; as, to *repeat* a poem or a teacher's words. — *v. i.* To say, utter, or do again what has been said, uttered, or done; specif., *U. S.,* to vote more than once at an election, in violation of law.

Syn. **Repeat, iterate, reiterate** mean to say or do again. **Repeat,** the usual term, may imply once or many times and the same agent or not; **iterate,** indefinite repetition, and **reiterate,** manifold repetition, esp. of something said.

— *n.* 1. Act of repeating; repetition. 2. A repetition or that which is repeated, as a reorder of merchandise, a repeated telegraph message, etc. 3. *Music.* a A passage to be repeated in performance. b A sign consisting of a vertical series of dots, placed before and after, or often only at the end of, a passage to be repeated.

re·peat′ed (rē·pēt′ĕd; -ĭd), *adj.* That is repeated; happening again and again. — **re·peat′ed·ly,** *adv.*

re·peat′er (-ẽr), *n.* 1. One who or that which repeats; specif., *U. S.,* one who repeats at an election. 2. *Educ.* A student enrolled in a grade, class, or course for the second (or a subsequent) time. 3. *Firearms.* A rapid-firing small arm, as a rifle, with a reservoir of cartridges. 4. *Horol.* A watch with a striking apparatus which, upon pressure of a spring, will indicate the time.

re·peat′ing dec′i·mal. *Math.* A decimal fraction in which only a single figure recurs or is repeated ad infinitum, as .133333 +; also, sometimes, a circulating decimal.

repeating firearm. A firearm that may be discharged many times in quick succession.

re·pel′ (rē·pĕl′), *v. t.;* -PELLED′ (-pĕld′); -PEL′LING. [L. *repellere, repulsum,* fr. *re-* + *pellere* to drive.] **1.** To drive back; repulse; as, to *repel* an enemy. **2.** To resist or oppose effectually; as, to *repel* an assault. **3.** To turn away; to reject; as, to *repel* a suit or suitor. **4.** To be incapable of adhering to, mixing with, or the like, as mercury to glass or oil with water. **5.** To cause aversion in; as, the prospect *repelled* him. **6.** *Physics.* To force or drive away or apart, or tend to do so, by mutual action at a distance; as, two like electric charges *repel* one another; — opposed to *attract.* — *v. i.* To exercise repulsion; to cause aversion.

re·pel′lent (rē·pĕl′ĕnt), *adj.* **1.** That repels or tends to repel. **2.** Arousing aversion or repugnance. — **Syn.** See REPUGNANT. — *n.* That which repels; specif.: **a** *Med.* A medicine which causes the disappearance of a tumor, eruption, etc. **b** A type of waterproof cloth.

re·pel′ler (-ẽr), *n.* One who or that which repels.

re′pent (rē′pĕnt), *adj.* [L. *repens, -entis,* creeping.] *Bot. & Zool.* Creeping; prostrate; reptant.

re·pent′ (rē·pĕnt′), *v. i. & t.* [OF. *repentir,* fr. L. *re-* + *poenitere* to make repent.] **1.** *Theol.* To amend or resolve to amend one's life as a result of contrition for one's sins. **2.** To change one's mind with regard to past or intended action, conduct, etc., on account of regret or dissatisfaction. **3.** To feel regret, contrition, or compunction for what one has done or omitted to do.

re·pent′ance (rē·pĕn′tăns), *n.* Act of repenting, or state of being penitent; specif., contrition for sins, with amendment of life. — **Syn.** See PENITENCE.

re·pent′ant (-tănt), *adj.* [OF., pres. part.] **1.** That repents, esp. for one's sins; penitent. **2.** Expressing or showing repentance. — **re·pent′ant·ly,** *adv.*

re·pent′er (-tẽr), *n.* One who repents.

re·peo′ple (rē·pē′p'l), *v. t.* [F. *repeupler.*] To people anew; also, to restock, as with animals.

re′per·cus′sion (rē′pẽr·kŭsh′ŭn), *n.* [F. or L.; F. *répercussion,* fr. L. *repercussio,* fr. L. *repercussus,* past part. of *repercutere* to drive back.] **1.** A driving back or being driven back; repulse; also, reflection; reverberation; as, *repercussion* of sound. **2.** A reciprocal action or effect; as, *repercussions* of the Treaty of Versailles. **3.** *Med.* The action of a repellent in reducing a swelling, etc. **4.** *Music.* **a** The reiteration of a tone or chord. **b** The re-entrance of a fugue subject and answer after the development of an episode. **5.** *Obstetrics.* Ballottement.

re′per·cus′sive (-kŭs′ĭv), *adj.* **1.** That causes or can cause repercussion; reverberating. **2.** Resounding; reverberated.

rep′er·toire (rĕp′ẽr·twär; -twôr), *or* ‖**ré′per′toire′** (*F.* rā′pĕr′twȧr′), *n.* [F. *répertoire.*] A list of dramas, operas, parts, etc., which a company or a person has rehearsed and is prepared to perform.

rep′er·to′ry (rĕp′ẽr·tō′rĭ *or, esp. Brit.,* -tẽr·ĭ), *n.; pl.* -RIES (-rĭz). [LL. *repertorium,* fr. *reperire* to find, acquire.] **1.** A treasury; storehouse; collection. **2.** = REPERTOIRE.

rep′e·tend (rĕp′ē·tĕnd; rĕp′ē·tĕnd′), *n.* [L. *repetendus* to be repeated, fr. *repetere* to repeat.] **1.** *Math.* A group of digits (including 0), which repeated indefinitely always in the same order constitutes a repeating or circulating decimal. **2.** A refrain; a recurrent tone, sound, or phrase.

rep′e·ti′tion (rĕp′ē·tĭsh′ŭn), *n.* [L. *repetitio.*] **1.** Act of repeating; reiteration. **2.** Act of reciting, as something learned; also, recital.

rep′e·ti′tious (-ŭs), *adj.* That repeats; containing repetition; esp., tediously repeating. — **rep′e·ti′tious·ly,** *adv.* — **rep′e·ti′tious·ness,** *n.*

re·pet′i·tive (rē·pĕt′ĭ·tĭv), *adj.* Repetitious.

re·phrase′ (rē·frāz′), *v. t.* To phrase anew.

re·pine′ (rē·pīn′), *v. i.* [*re-* + *pine* to languish.] To feel or express dejection or discontent; to complain; grumble.

re·place′ (rē·plās′), *v. t.* **1.** To place again; to restore to a former place, condition, etc. **2.** To take the place of; supplant; as, paper money *replaced* specie. **3.** To supply an equivalent for; as, to *replace* a lost book. **4.** To restore; pay back; as, to *replace* stolen money. — **re·place′a·ble,** *adj.* — **re·plac′er** (-plās′ẽr), *n.*

Syn. **Replace, displace, supplant, supersede** mean to put out of place or into the place of another. **Replace** implies, usually, a filling of a place once occupied by something lost, destroyed, dismissed, or the like; **displace,** an ousting, dislodging, etc., and filling the place of that which has been ousted, one idea, however, being stressed more than the other; **supplant,** strictly, a taking the place of one dispossessed by craft, fraud, or the like; **supersede,** replacing a person or thing that has become superannuated, obsolete, or otherwise inferior.

re·place′ment (-mĕnt), *n.* **1.** Act of replacing, or state of being replaced. **2.** *Cryst.* The removal of an edge or an angle by one or more faces. **3.** Something which replaces that which is worn out, discarded, etc. **4.** *Mil.* A trained individual available for assignment to a unit to replace a loss or complete a quota.

re·plant′ (rē·plȧnt′; 9), *v. t.* To plant again or anew.

re·play′ (rē·plā′), *v. t.* To play again. — **re·play′,** *n.*

re·plead′er (rē·plēd′ẽr), *n.* [*re-* + obs. *pleader,* fr. F. *plaider,* inf. as n.] *Law.* A second pleading; also, the right of pleading again.

re·plen′ish (rē·plĕn′ĭsh), *v. t.* [OF. *replenir,* fr. L. *re-* + *plenus* full.] **1.** To stock with persons, animals, or both. **2.** To supply fully. **3.** To fill again, esp. after having been emptied; to stock anew. — **re·plen′ish·er,** *n.* — **re·plen′ish·ment,** *n.*

re·plete′ (rē·plēt′), *adj.* [OF. *replet,* fr. L. *repletus,* past part. of *replere* to fill again, fill up, fr. *re-* + *plere* to fill.] **1.** Filled; filled to capacity; of persons, gorged with food or drink; surfeited. **2.** Provided abundantly; copiously supplied. — **Syn.** See FULL.

re·ple′tion (-plē′shŭn), *n.* Act of making, or state of being, replete; surfeit.

re·plev′i·a·ble (rē·plĕv′ĭ·ȧ·b'l), *adj.* Also **re·plev′i·sa·ble** (-ĭ·sȧ·b'l). Capable of being replevied.

re·plev′in (rē·plĕv′ĭn), *n.* [AF. *replevine,* fr. OF. *replevir* to protect, give security for, fr. *re-* + *plevir* to pledge.] *Law.* **a** The return to, or recovery by, a person of goods or chattels wrongfully taken or detained upon giving security to try the matter in court and return the goods if defeated in the action. **b** The writ by, or the action in, which goods and chattels are replevied. — *v. t. Law.* To replevy.

re·plev′y (-ĭ), *v. t.;* -PLEV′IED (-ĭd); -PLEV′Y·ING. [OF. *replevir.* See REPLEVIN.] *Law.* **a** To take or get back by a writ for replevin. **b** To seize under a writ of replevin; — said of a sheriff or bailiff. — *n. Law.* Replevin.

rep′li·ca (rĕp′lĭ·kȧ), *n.* [It., fr. *replicare* to repeat, reply.] **1.** *Fine Arts.* A reproduction or copy, as of a picture or statue, esp. by the maker of the original. **2.** A facsimile or very close copy. — **Syn.** See REPRODUCTION.

rep′li·cate (-kĭt), *adj.* Also **rep′li·cat′ed** (-kāt′ĕd; -ĭd). [L. *replicatus,* past part. of *replicare.* See REPLY.] Folded over or backward; folded back upon itself.

rep′li·ca′tion (-kā′shŭn), *n.* **1.** Reply; answer; specif., rejoinder. **2.** Return or repercussion, as of sound; echo. **3.** Act or result of reproducing; reproduction; copy.

re·pli′er (rē·plī′ẽr), *n.* One who replies.

re·ply′ (rē·plī′), *v. i.;* -PLIED′ (-plīd′); -PLY′ING. [OF. *repliier* to bend back, fr. L. *replicare* to fold back, make a reply, fr. *re-* + *plicare* to fold.] **1.** To make answer in words or writing; to respond; hence, to echo. **2.** To do something as response to something done; as, to *reply* to a signal. — *v. t.* To return as an answer; — usually with object clause. — **Syn.** See ANSWER. — *n.; pl.* REPLIES (-plīz′). That which is said, written, or done in answer to what is said, written, or done by another; answer; response.

‖**ré·pon′dez′ s'il vous plaît** (rā′pôɴ′dā′ sēl vōō plĕ′). [F.] Answer, if you please. Abbr. *R.S.V.P.*

re·port′ (rē·pōrt′; 70), *v. t.* [OF. *reporter* to carry back, carry, fr. L. *reportare* to bear or bring back.] **1.** To give an account of; to relate; tell. **2.** To repeat, as something heard, said, or received as a message; hence, to make minutes of, as a speech or debate; also, to prepare an account of; as, to *report* a trial. **3.** To give a formal or official account of; as, a treasurer *reports* the receipts. **4.** To prefer a charge of misconduct against (one) to a superior; as, to *report* a servant to his employer. **5.** *Parl. Practice.* To return or present (a matter officially referred) with the conclusions reached. — *v. i.* **1.** To give an account of oneself; as, promising to *report* weekly by letter. **2.** To make, issue, or submit, a report, esp. a formal report. **3.** To act as a reporter. **4.** To make one's presence, arrival, etc., known by presenting oneself; as, to *report* for duty. — *n.* **1.** Common talk; rumor; hence, fame; repute. **2.** **a** An account or relation, esp. of some matter specially investigated; as, the *report* of an expert. **b** An account, as of a speech, debate, etc. **c** An official statement of facts. **d** A statement of misconduct; as, the *reports* against three boys. **3.** An explosive noise; as, the *report* of a gun. **4.** *Law.* An account or statement of a judicial opinion or decision; also, *pl.,* the volumes containing such reports; as, Coke's *Reports.* — **re·port′a·ble,** *adj.*

re·port′er (rē·pōr′tẽr; 70), *n.* One who or that which reports. Specif.: **a** A person who makes authorized statements of law proceedings, or of legislative debates. **b** One who reports speeches, news, etc., for a newspaper or other periodical; also, one who gathers news.

rep′or·to′ri·al (rĕp′ŏr·tō′rĭ·ăl; rē′pŏr-), *adj.* Of, pertaining to, or characteristic of a reporter or reporters.

re·pos′al (rē·pōz′ăl; -'l), *n. Obs.* **a** Act of reposing, or of placing, as of trust. **b** Act or state of reposing, or resting.

re·pose′ (rē·pōz′), *v. t.* [From L. *repositus,* past part. of *reponere,* after verbs in *-pose.*] **1.** *Now Rare.* To deposit. **2.** To place or set (trust, hope, etc.); — with *in.*

re·pose′, *v. t.* [F. *reposer,* fr. LL. *repausare,* fr. L. *re-* + *pausare* to pause.] To lay at rest; to rest; as, to *repose* oneself on a couch. — *v. i.* **1.** To lie or be at rest; to take rest; also, to lie buried. **2.** To confide; rely. **3.** To lie; to be supported; as, his head *reposing* on a cushion. — *n.* **1.** State of reposing; rest; esp., sleep. **2.** Peace; calm. **3.** Composure of manner; quiet ease and dignity of bearing. **4.** *Fine Arts.* Harmony in the disposition of parts, colors, etc., such as gives rest to the eye or ear.

re·pose′ful (-fōōl; -f'l), *adj.* Full of repose; quiet. — **Syn.** See COMFORTABLE.

re·pos′it (rē·pŏz′ĭt), *v. t.* [L. *repositus,* past part. of *reponere* to put back, fr. *re-* + *ponere* to put.] To lay away; to deposit, as for safety.

re′po·si′tion (rē′pō·zĭsh′ŭn; rĕp′ō-), *n. Archaic, Scot.* Restoration to a position, possession, or office; reinstatement.

re·pos′i·to′ry (rē·pŏz′ĭ·tō′rĭ *or, esp. Brit.,* -tẽr·ĭ), *n.; pl.* -RIES (-rĭz). [L. *repositorium.*] A depository.

re′pos·sess′ (rē′pŏ·zĕs′), *v. t.* **1.** To possess again; to regain possession of. **2.** To restore to possession; also, *Scot.,* to reinstate. — **re′pos·ses′sion** (-zĕsh′ŭn), *n.*

‖**re·pous′sé′** (rē·pōō′sā′), *adj.* [F., past part., thrust back.] Formed in relief, as a pattern on thin metal beaten up from the reverse side; also, shaped or ornamented with patterns so made.

repp (rĕp). Var. of REP.

rep′re·hend′ (rĕp′rē·hĕnd′), *v. t.* [L. *reprehendere, -hensum,* to check, blame, fr. *re-* + *prehendere* to lay hold of.] To reprimand; reprove; blame; censure. — **Syn.** See CRITICIZE.

rep′re·hen′si·ble (-hĕn′sĭ·b'l), *adj.* Worthy of reprehension; culpable. — **rep′re·hen′si·bil′i·ty** (-bĭl′ĭ·tĭ), **rep′re·hen′si·ble·ness,** *n.* — **rep′re·hen′si·bly,** *adv.*

rep′re·hen′sion (-hĕn′shŭn), *n.* Act or an instance of reprehending; reproof; blame; censure. — **rep′re·hen′sive** (-sĭv), *adj.* — **rep′re·hen′sive·ly,** *adv.*

rep′re·sent′ (rĕp′rē·zĕnt′), *v. t.* [OF. *representer,* fr. L. *repraesentare, -tatum,* fr. *re-* + *praesentare* to place before, present.] **1.** To bring clearly before the mind; to present. **2.** To present by means of something standing in the place of; to typify; also, to serve as a sign or symbol of; as, words *represent* ideas. **3.** To portray or depict; as, to *represent* a landscape in a painting. **4.** To exhibit dramatically; to act the part or role of; as, to *represent* Hamlet. **5.** To give one's own impressions and judgment of; to state with the design of affecting action or judgment; as, he *represented* himself to be starving. **6.** To be the equivalent of; as, let x *represent* the momentum. **7.** To supply the place of; as, an attorney *represents* his client. **8.** To serve with delegated or deputed authority, as in a legislative body; as, the state was *represented* by six Republicans. **9.** To serve as a specimen, example, or instance of; as, a dozen nationalities were *represented* in the steerage. — **rep′re·sent′a·ble,** *adj.*

rep′re·sen·ta′tion (rĕp′rē·zĕn·tā′shŭn), *n.* **1.** Act or instance of representing. **2.** A likeness, picture, model, image, or other reproduction. **3.** A dramatic production or performance. **4.** Act of setting forth by a statement, account, or the like, esp. with a view to affecting action; also, such a statement or account so made; sometimes, specif., a protest. **5.** **a** The representing of a certain number, class, or interest in a legislative body; also, the system of choosing delegates to represent constituents, as in a legislature. **b** Delegates representing a constituency, collectively. 6. *Law.* A statement of fact incidental or collateral to a contract, made orally or in writing or by implication, on the faith of which the contract is entered into.

rep′re·sent′a·tive (-zĕn′tȧ·tĭv), *adj.* 1. Representing, portraying, or the like. 2. Being, or acting as, the agent for another, esp. by authority. 3. Pert. to, or founded on, representation of the many by delegates; as, a *representative* government. 4. Typical; as, a *representative* modern play. — *n.* One who or that which represents; specif.: **a** A person or thing that represents, or stands for, a number or class of persons or things; a type. **b** One who represents others or another in a special capacity; an agent or deputy; specif., one who represents a people or community in its legislative or governing capacity; esp., *U. S.*, a member of the lower house in the national Congress or in a state legislature. — **rep′re·sent′a·tive·ly,** *adv.* — **rep′re·sent′a·tive·ness,** *n.*

re·press′ (rē·prĕs′), *v. t.* [L. *repressus*, past part. of *reprimere.* See REPRIMAND.] 1. To check by or as by pressure; to restrain; curb. 2. *Now Rare.* To suppress by exercising force; to quell; also, to subdue. 3. To prevent the natural or normal expression, activity, or development of. — **re·press′er** (-ẽr), *n.* — **re·press′i·ble** (-ĭ·b'l), *adj.*

re·pressed′ (rē·prĕst′), *adj.* Suppressed; specif., *Psychoanalysis,* affected by psychoanalytic repression.

re·pres′sion (-prĕsh′ŭn), *n.* 1. Act or an instance of repressing; state of being repressed. 2. *Psychoanalysis.* The process by which unacceptable desires or impulses are excluded from consciousness and thus being denied direct satisfaction are left to operate in the unconscious.

re·pres′sive (-prĕs′ĭv), *adj.* Having power or tending to repress. — **re·pres′sive·ly,** *adv.* — **re·pres′sive·ness,** *n.*

re·prieve′ (rē·prēv′), *v. t.* [From earlier *repry*, fr. F. *repris*, past part. of *reprendre* (see REPRISE).] 1. To delay; postpone, esp. something evil. 2. To delay the punishment of; to suspend the execution of sentence on; to respite, as a condemned prisoner. 3. To give relief to for a time. — *n.* 1. Act of reprieving, or state of being reprieved. 2. A respite or temporary escape, as from death.

rep′ri·mand (rĕp′rĭ·mȧnd; 9), *n.* [F. *réprimande*, fr. L. *reprimendus*, fem. *reprimenda*, that is to be checked, fr. *reprimere* to check, fr. *re-* + *premere* to press.] A severe or formal reproof. — (rĕp′rĭ·mȧnd; rĕp′rĭ·mȧnd′), *v. t.* To reprove severely; to censure formally, esp. with authority. — **Syn.** See REPROVE.

re·print′ (rē·prĭnt′), *v. t.* To print again; to print a second or a new edition of. — **re·print′er,** *n.*

re′print′ (rē′prĭnt′; rē·prĭnt′), *n.* 1. A second or a new impression of a printed work; specif.: **a** A facsimile copy. **b** An offprint. 2. *Philately.* A stamp printed from an old plate, usually with different paper, ink, etc., and not intended for postal use. Cf. REISSUE.

re·pris′al (rē·prīz′ăl; -'l), *n.* [OF. *reprisaille.* See REPRISE.] 1. *Internat. Law.* The act or practice of resorting to force, short of war, to procure redress of grievances, orig. by seizing property or persons; also, an act or instance of this. 2. A prize. *Shak.* 3. Any act of retaliation; esp., in war, an act of retaliation against the enemy. 4. That paid as compensation or in restitution.

re·prise′ (rē·prīz′), *n.* [OF. *reprise*, fr. *reprendre, repris*, to take back, fr. L. *reprehendere.* See REPREHEND.] 1. *Obs.* Reprisal. 2. *Law.* A deduction or charge to be made yearly out of a manor or estate, such as rent charge, pensions, etc.; — usually in *pl.* 3. (*pron.* rē·prēz′; rē·prĕz′) *Music.* A repetition.

re·proach′ (rē·prōch′), *v. t.* [F. *reprocher.*] 1. To rebuke; censure; upbraid. 2. To cast reproach upon (one, one's life, character, repute, etc.); to bring into discredit. — **Syn.** See REPROVE. — *n.* 1. A cause or occasion of blame, censure, disgrace, or discredit; hence, disgrace, discredit, or the like, incurred. 2. Censure or blame; rebuke; a reproof. 3. One subjected to censure or scorn. — **re·proach′a·ble,** *adj.* — **re·proach′a·ble·ness,** *n.* — **re·proach′a·bly,** *adv.* — **re·proach′er,** *n.* — **re·proach′less,** *adj.*

re·proach′ful (-fŏŏl; -f'l), *adj.* 1. *Obs.* Involving or incurring reproach; shameful. 2. Expressing censure or rebuke; as, a *reproachful* word, glance. — **re·proach′ful·ly,** *adv.* — **re·proach′ful·ness,** *n.*

rep′ro·bate (rĕp′rō·bāt *or, esp. Brit.,* -bĭt), *adj.* [LL. *reprobatus*, past part. of *reprobare.* See REPROVE.] 1. *Archaic.* Rejected as not of standard purity or fineness; condemned. 2. Of, pertaining to, or characteristic of a scoundrel; vicious; corrupt. 3. *Theol.* Condemned or rejected by God's decree. Hence, morally abandoned; depraved; — said of persons. — *n.* A depraved, vicious, or unprincipled person; a scoundrel. — (-bāt), *v. t.* 1. To disapprove of; to condemn as unworthy. 2. To reject; to refuse to accept. 3. *Theol.* Of God, to reject, or foreordain to damnation. — **Syn.** See CRITICIZE.

rep′ro·ba′tion (rĕp′rō·bā′shŭn), *n.* 1. Act of reprobating; now usually, severe disapproval; censure. 2. *Theol.* Rejection by God's decree. Cf. PRETERITION, 3.

rep′ro·ba′tive (rĕp′rō·bā′tĭv), *adj.* Pertaining to or expressing reprobation. — **rep′ro·ba′tive·ly,** *adv.*

re′pro·duce′ (rē′prō·dūs′), *v. t.* To produce again; specif.: **a** To produce again by generation or the like. **b** To cause to exist again or anew. **c** To repeat. **d** To make an image, a copy, etc., of; to portray. **e** To present or exhibit again; as, to *reproduce* a play. **f** To revive mentally; to remember; recite. — *v. i.* To reproduce its kind; to produce offspring. — **re′pro·duc′er** (-dūs′ẽr), *n.* — **re′pro·duc′i·ble** (-ĭ·b'l), *adj.*

re′pro·duc′tion (-dŭk′shŭn), *n.* 1. Act or process of reproducing. 2. A copy, likeness, or reconstruction; as, to make a *reproduction* of the Elizabethan theater. 3. *Biol.* The process by which plants and animals give rise to offspring. In multicellular animals and plants, ordinary sexual reproduction involves the fusion or union of two *sex* or *germ cells*, one, the *egg*, derived from the female parent, and the other, the *sperm* or *spermatozoon*, from the male parent. From the cell thus produced (the ***fertilized egg***) the offspring develops.

Syn. Reproduction, duplicate, copy, facsimile, replica mean one thing made closely resembling another. **Reproduction** implies an exact or very close imitation of an existing thing; **duplicate**, a double or counterpart of a thing, exactly corresponding to it; **copy**, a more general term, anything reproduced by printing or striking off at the same time or by making separately; **facsimile**, a close reproduction in identical materials, but often differing in scale; **replica**, an exact reproduction of a statue, a painting, etc., made by the same artist and not clearly distinguishable from the original.

re′pro·duc′tive (rē′prō·dŭk′tĭv), *adj.* That reproduces or tends to reproduce; tending toward, or employed in, reproduction. — **re′pro·duc′tive·ly,** *adv.* — **re′pro·duc′tive·ness,** *n.*

re·proof′ (rē·prōōf′), *n.* [OF. *reprueve.* See PROOF, REPROVE.] 1. *Obs.* Reproach; disgrace. 2. Censure for a fault; reprimand; rebuke.

re·prov′al (rē·prōōv′ăl), *n.* Reproof.

re·prove′ (rē·prōōv′), *v. t.* [OF. *reprover* (3d sing. pres. *reprueve*), fr. LL. *reprobare* to disapprove, fr. *re-* + *probare* to test, prove.] 1. To chide as blameworthy; to rebuke. 2. To express disapprobation of; to censure. 3. *Obs.* To convince; convict. 4. *Obs.* To refute. — **re·prov′a·ble** (-prōōv′ȧ·b'l), *adj.* — **re·prov′er** (-prōōv′ẽr), *n.* — **re·prov′ing·ly,** *adv.*

Syn. Reprove, rebuke, reprimand, admonish, reproach, chide mean to criticize or censure adversely. **Reprove** implies an intent, often kindly, to correct a fault; **rebuke**, a sharp or stern reproof; **reprimand**, a rebuke that is formal and, often, public or official; **admonish**, warning or counsel; **reproach** and **chide**, dissatisfaction or displeasure, with a mild reproof or slight scolding.

rep′tant (rĕp′tănt), *adj.* [L. *reptans, -antis*, pres. part. of *reptare*, v. intens. fr. *repere.*] Creeping; repent.

rep′tile (rĕp′tĭl; -tīl), *n.* [LL., prop. neut. of *reptilis* reptant, fr. L. *repere, reptum*, to creep.] 1. An animal that crawls, or moves on its belly, as snakes, or on small, short legs, as lizards. 2. *Zool.* **a** Any of a class (Reptilia) of air-breathing vertebrates including the alligators and crocodiles, lizards, snakes, turtles, and their extinct allies; the reptiles. They have a completely ossified skeleton, a single occipital condyle, a distinct quadrate bone usually immovably articulated with the skull, and ribs attached to the sternum. In existing reptiles the body is usually covered with scales or bony plates. **b** In popular use, an amphibian. 3. A groveling or despicable person. — *adj.* 1. Creeping; reptant. 2. Groveling; low; despicable. 3. Of the nature of, or pertaining to, a reptile or reptiles.

rep·til′i·an (rĕp·tĭl′ĭ·ăn), *adj.* Of, pertaining to, like, or characteristic of a reptile or reptiles. — *n.* A reptile.

re·pub′lic (rē·pŭb′lĭk), *n.* [F. *république*, fr. L. *respublica* commonwealth, fr. *res* thing, affair + *publicus, publica*, public.] A state in which the sovereign power resides in a certain body of the people (the *electorate*), and is exercised by representatives elected by, and responsible to, them; also, the form of government of such a state.

re·pub′li·can (-lĭ·kăn), *adj.* 1. Of or pert. to, or having the characteristics of a republic. 2. Consonant with, or favoring, the principles of a republic. 3. Of, pert. to, designating, or connected with a political party called *republican*, specif., *U. S.* [*cap.*], the Republican party (which see). — *n.* 1. One who favors a republican government. 2. A member of a party called *republican*, specif., *U. S.* [*cap.*], of the Republican party.

re·pub′li·can·ism (-ĭz'm), *n.* 1. A republican form or system of government; the principles or theory of republican government. 2. Attachment to, or political sympathy for, a republican form of government. 3. [*cap.*] *U. S.* The principles and policy of the Republican party.

re·pub′li·can·ize (-īz), *v. t. & i.* To make republican in character, form, or principle. — **re·pub′li·can·i·za′tion** (-ĭ·zā′shŭn; -ī·zā′-), *n.*

Republican party. *U. S. Politics.* One of the two great parties. It was organized in 1854–56 for opposing the extension of slavery.

re′pub·li·ca′tion (rē′pŭb·lĭ·kā′shŭn), *n.* Act of republishing; also, something republished.

republic of letters. The collective body of literary or learned men; also, the field of literature.

re·pub′lish (rē·pŭb′lĭsh), *v. t.* To publish anew.

re·pu′di·ate (rē·pū′dĭ·āt), *v. t.* [L. *repudiatus*, past part. of *repudiare* to repudiate, reject, fr. *repudium* separation, divorce.] 1. *Hist.* To divorce or discard, as a wife. 2. To cast off, disown, or renounce, as a son. 3. To refuse to accept as true, just, or of rightful authority or obligation, as a pretender's claims. 4. To refuse to acknowledge or to pay; to disclaim, as debts. — **Syn.** See DECLINE. — **re·pu′di·a′tor** (-ā′tẽr), *n.*

re·pu′di·a′tion (-ā′shŭn), *n.* Act of repudiating, or fact of being repudiated; esp., the disowning of a debt.

re·pugn′ (rē·pūn′), *v. t.* [OF. *repugner*, fr. L. *repugnare, -natum*, fr. *re-* + *pugnare* to fight.] *Now Rare.* To oppose; resist; repel. — *v. i.* To strive in opposition.

re·pug′nance (rē·pŭg′năns), *n.* Also **re·pug′nan·cy** (-năn·sĭ). 1. Inconsistency, incompatibility, incongruity, or an instance of it; as, *repugnance* between the Gospel narratives. 2. Deep-rooted antagonism; aversion; antipathy.

re·pug′nant (-nănt), *adj.* [OF., fr. L. *repugnans, -antis*, pres. part.] 1. Opposed or reciprocally opposed; contradictory; irreconcilable; as, a principle *repugnant* to constitutional law. 2. That offers resistance; hostile; refractory. 3. Distasteful; repellent. — **re·pug′nant·ly,** *adv.*

Syn. Repugnant, repellent, abhorrent, distasteful, obnoxious, invidious mean so unlikable as to arouse antagonism or aversion. **Repugnant** implies a nature alien to one's ideas, principles, or tastes, and a stirring up of resistance or loathing; **repellent**, a forbidding or unlovely quality that causes one to back away; **abhorrent**, a repugnance that stimulates antagonism; **distasteful**, a contrariness to one's tastes or inclinations that causes shrinking; **obnoxious**, an objectionableness so great that one cannot tolerate it; **invidious**, a character such that it cannot be used, undertaken, etc., without creating ill will, odium, or the like.

re·pulse′ (rē·pŭls′), *v. t.* [L. *repulsus*, past part. of *repellere.* See REPEL.] 1. To repel, as an assault or an enemy; to beat back. 2. To repel by discourtesy, coldness, or denial, as a suitor; to rebuff; reject. — *n.* 1. Act of repelling, or fact of being repelled, in hostile encounter. 2. Denial; rejection; rebuff. — **re·puls′er,** *n.*

re·pul′sion (-pŭl′shŭn), *n.* 1. A repulsing, or fact of being repulsed. 2. A feeling of aversion; repugnance. 3. *Physics.* Act of repelling, or the force with which bodies, particles, or like forces, repel one another.

re·pul′sive (rē·pŭl′sĭv), *adj.* 1. Serving, or able, to repulse or repel; as, a *repulsive* force. 2. Repelling advances; forbidding. 3. Arousing aversion or disgust; offensive. — **re·pul′sive·ly,** *adv.* — **re·pul′sive·ness,** *n.*

re·pur′chase (rē·pûr′chĭs), *v. t.* To buy back. — *n.* A repurchasing. — **re·pur′chas·er** (-chĭs·ẽr), *n.*

rep′u·ta·ble (rĕp′ū·tȧ·b'l), *adj.* 1. Enjoying good repute; held in esteem; as, a *reputable* citizen, firm. 2. Employed widely or sanctioned by good writers; — of words. — **rep′u·ta·bil′i·ty** (-bĭl′ĭ·tĭ), *n.* — **rep′u·ta·bly,** *adv.*

rep′u·ta′tion (-tā′shŭn), *n.* 1. The character commonly imputed to a person or thing; one's reputed as distinct from one's inherent or real character; as, honorable in spite of his *reputation.* 2. Repute, or public esteem; fame; celebrity; distinction. 3. Good name; place in public esteem; as, to lose one's *reputation.* 4. A particular character ascribed to one in popular belief; as, to have the *reputation* of slighting one's work.

re·pute′ (rē·pūt′), *v. t.* [OF. or L.; OF. *reputer,* fr. L. *reputare* to count over, think over, impute, repute, fr. *re-* + *putare* to count, think.] To hold in thought; to account; esteem; — now usually in passive. — *n.* **1.** Reputation, or the character or status commonly ascribed to one; as, a man of ill *repute.* **2.** Fame; note; also, favor or degree of favor generally accorded; public esteem. **3.** Popular ascription; common talk or report; as, a fine fellow, by *repute.*

re·put′ed (-pūt′ĕd; -ĭd), *adj.* That has the reputation of being; popularly supposed. — **re·put′ed·ly,** *adv.*

re·quest′ (rē·kwĕst′), *n.* [OF. *requeste,* fr. past part. of L. *requirere.* See REQUIRE.] **1.** Act or an instance of asking for something or some action desired; entreaty; petition. **2.** That which is asked for; as, to grant a *request.* **3.** The condition or the fact of being requested; as: ***at or by request,*** in compliance with or response to a requesting; also, demand; as, his services are in *request.* — *v. t.* **1.** To ask for (something); to solicit. **2.** To make a request to or of (one); — followed by an infinitive; as, to *request* him to sign. — **Syn.** See ASK.

re′qui·em (rē′kwĭ·ĕm; rĕk′wĭ·ĕm), *n.* [Acc. of L. *requies* rest, the first word of the Mass.] **1.** [*usually cap.*] *R.C.Ch.* A Mass for the repose of a departed soul or souls. **2.** [*usually cap.*] *Music.* A setting of the Mass for the dead; also, a piece of like character on other words; hence, any grand musical service or hymn in honor of the dead. **3.** A song or chant inviting rest or repose.

‖**re′qui·es′cat** (rĕk′wĭ·ĕs′kăt), *n.* [L., fr. the phrase *requiescat in pace* may he (or she) rest in peace.] A prayer for the repose of a dead person.

re·quire′ (rē·kwīr′), *v. t.* [OF. *requerre* (3d sing. pres. *requiert*), deriv. of L. *re-* + *quaerere* to ask.] **1.** To demand; to claim as by right and authority; to exact; as, to *require* the surrender of property. **2.** To demand or exact as necessary or appropriate; to need; call for; as, the matter *requires* haste. **3.** *Archaic.* To request. **4.** To impose a compulsion upon; compel. — **Syn.** See DEMAND: LACK. — *v. i.* **1.** *Now Rare.* To ask. **2.** *Now Rare.* To be requisite. **3.** To need; to be under a necessity; as, man *requires* to be fed.

re·quire′ment (-mĕnt), *n.* **1.** A requiring. **2.** That which is required; specif., a requisite condition; a required quality, course, etc.; as, *requirements* for college entrance; also, a necessity; a need.

req′ui·site (rĕk′wĭ·zĭt), *adj.* [L. *requisitus,* past part. of *requirere,* fr. *re-* + *quaerere* to ask.] Required by the nature of things, by circumstances, or by the end in view; necessary. — *n.* That which is required, indispensable, or essential. — **req′ui·site·ly,** *adv.* — **req′ui·site·ness,** *n.*

req′ui·si′tion (-zĭsh′ŭn), *n.* **1.** Act of requiring as of right; formal application made by one officer or department to another for things needed in the service or business. **2.** State of being demanded or put into service; as, to put an orator in *requisition.* **3.** A requirement; as, the *requisitions* for a degree. — *v. t.* To make a requisition for or on; hence, to demand; press into service; as, to *requisition* horses for troops.

re·quit′al (rē·kwīt′ăl; -'l), *n.* [From REQUITE.] **1.** Act of requiting or fact of being requited; as, no hope of *requital.* **2.** Something given in return, compensation, or retaliation; recompense; as, a poor *requital* for his self-sacrifice.

re·quite′ (rē·kwīt′), *v. t.* [*re-* + *quit.*] **1.** To repay (as a benefit or injury); to make return for; as, to *requite* evil with good. **2.** To repay (a person) for a benefit or injury; to recompense; reward; as, to *requite* one for his services. **3.** To compensate for; as, the charms of travel *requite* its inconveniences. — **Syn.** See PAY. — **re·quit′er** (-kwīt′ēr), *n.*

re′ra·di·a′tion (rē′rā·dĭ·ā′shŭn), *n. Physics.* Radiation emitted by a body or system as a result of its absorbing radiation incident on it.

re·read′ (rē·rēd′), *v. t.* To read again.

rere·dos (rēr′dŏs; râr′ĕ-; rēr′ĕ-), *n.* [AF. *rere-* rear + *dos* back.] *Arch.* **a** A screen or partition wall, usually ornamental, behind an altar. **b** *Archaic.* The back of a fireplace.

rere′mouse′ (rēr′mous′), *n.; pl.* -MICE (-mīs′). [AS. *hreremūs.*] *Now Dial.* A bat.

re·roll′ (rē·rōl′), *v. t.* To roll again; to rewind.

re·run′ (rē·rŭn′; rē′rŭn′), *n.* A rerunning; specif., the presentation of a motion picture after its first run. — (rē·rŭn′), *v. t.;* see RUN. To run again.

‖**res** (rēz), *n.; pl.* RES (rēz). [L.] A thing; the particular thing or matter; — used esp. in phrases, chiefly legal.

‖**res ad·ju′di·ca′ta** (ă·jōō′dĭ·kā′tȧ). [L.] A matter finally decided on its merits by a court of competent jurisdiction. Such a matter cannot be litigated again between the same parties.

re·sail′ (rē·sāl′), *v. t. & i.* To sail again or back.

re·sal′a·ble (rē·sāl′ȧ·b'l), *adj.* That may be sold again.

re·sale′ (rē·sāl′; rē′sāl′; 2), *n.* A selling at second hand or at retail.

re·scind′ (rē·sĭnd′), *v. t.* [L. *rescindere, -scissum,* fr. *re-* + *scindere* to cut, split.] **1.** To abrogate; annul; cancel. **2.** To vacate or make void, as an act, by the enacting authority or by superior authority. — **re·scind′er,** *n.*

re·scis′sion (rē·sĭzh′ŭn), *n.* Act of rescinding.

re·scis′so·ry (rē·sĭs′ō·rĭ; rē·sĭz′-), *adj.* [LL. *rescissorius.*] Rescinding; revoking.

re′script (rē′skrĭpt), *n.* [L. *rescriptum,* past part. neut. of *rescribere,* fr. *re-* + *scribere* to write.] **1.** The written answer of a Roman emperor, or of the pope, to an inquiry upon some matter of law or state. **2.** An official or authoritative order or decree. **3.** A rewriting.

res′cue (rĕs′kū), *v. t.;* RES′CUED (-kūd); RES′CU·ING (-kū·ĭng). [OF. *rescourre,* fr. *re-* + *escorre* to move, shake, fr. L. *excutere* to shake out.] **1.** To free from any confinement, violence, danger, or evil. **2.** *Law.* To take forcibly from the custody of the law. **3.** To regain, or recover, by force. — *n.* A rescuing; deliverance from restraint, violence, or danger; also, *Law,* forcible removal of a person or goods from the custody of the law. — **res′cu·er** (rĕs′kū·ēr), *n.*

Syn. **Rescue, deliver, redeem, ransom, reclaim, save** mean to free from danger of death, destruction, or evil. **Rescue** implies release from imminent danger by prompt or vigorous action; **deliver,** release of a person (usually) from confinement, temptation, slavery, etc.; **redeem,** release from bondage or from penalties by giving what is demanded; **ransom,** a release of one enslaved or kidnaped by paying the amount demanded by his captor or owner; **reclaim,** a bringing back to a former state or condition of someone or something abandoned or debased; **save,** a rescue, deliverance, etc., and a continuance in existence or in usefulness.

re·seal′ (rē·sēl′), *v. t.* To seal again or anew.

re·search′ (rē·sûrch′; rē′sûrch; 2), *n.* [MF. *recerche* (F. *recherche*).] **1.** Careful search; a close searching. **2.** Studious inquiry; usually, critical and exhaustive investigation or experimentation having for its aim the revision of accepted conclusions, in the light of newly discovered facts. — *v. i.* To make researches. — **re·search′er,** *n.*

re·seat′ (rē·sēt′), *v. t.* To seat or set again.

‖**ré′seau′** (rā′zō′), *n.* [F.] A network; specif.: **a** *Astron.* A system of lines forming small squares of standard size, which is photographed, by a separate exposure, on the same plate with star images to facilitate measurements. **b** *Lacemaking.* In lace, a net ground or foundation.

re·sect′ (rē·sĕkt′), *v. t.* [L. *resectus,* past part. of *resecare* to cut off, fr. *re-* + *secare* to cut.] *Surg.* To cut or pare away; — distinguished from *excise.*

re·sec′tion (-sĕk′shŭn), *n.* [L. *resectio.*] The surgical removal of part of an organ or structure.

re·se′da (rē·sē′dȧ), *n.* [L., a kind of plant.] **1.** An herb (genus *Reseda*) typifying a family (Resedaceae, the mignonette family), having racemose flowers with cleft petals and many stamens. See MIGNONETTE. **2.** Also **ré′sé′da′** (rā′zā′dȧ′). The color of the mignonette flower, greenish-yellow in hue.

res′e·da′ceous (rĕs′ē·dā′shŭs), *adj.* [See RESEDA.] Belonging to the mignonette family (Resedaceae). See MIGNONETTE.

re·sell′ (rē·sĕl′), *v. t.* To sell again. — **re·sell′er,** *n.*

re·sem′blance (rē·zĕm′blăns), *n.* [AF.] **1.** Quality or state of resembling; similarity; also, a point of likeness. **2.** *Rare.* A copied likeness. **3.** *Rare.* Characteristic appearance. *Shak.* **4.** *Rare.* Probability. *Shak.* — **Syn.** See LIKENESS.

re·sem′ble (rē·zĕm′b'l), *v. t.;* -SEM′BLED (-b'ld); -SEM′BLING (-blĭng). [OF. *resembler,* fr. *re-* + *sembler* to seem, fr. L. *similare, simulare,* to imitate.] **1.** To be like or similar to. **2.** *Archaic.* To liken; to compare.

re·send′ (rē·sĕnd′), *v. t.* To send again; also, to send back.

re·sent′ (rē·zĕnt′), *v. t.* [F. *se ressentir de* to feel the effects of, fr. L. *re-* + *sentire* to feel.] To feel or express indignant displeasure at; as, to *resent* undue familiarity.

re·sent′ful (-fŏŏl; -f'l), *adj.* Full of resentment or inclined to resent. — **re·sent′ful·ly,** *adv.* — **re·sent′ful·ness,** *n.*

re·sent′ment (-mĕnt), *n.* A feeling of indignant displeasure because of something regarded as a wrong or insult; umbrage. — **Syn.** See OFFENSE.

res′er·va′tion (rĕz′ēr·vā′shŭn), *n.* **1.** Act of reserving, esp. for oneself; as, the *reservation* of a hotel room; the *reservation* of rights by the states; also, something reserved for a special use; as, to telegraph a hotel for a *reservation.* **2.** A promise or record of such engagement. **3.** A limiting condition; limitation; as, to yield without *reservation;* specif., ***mental reservation,*** the withholding of something that affects a statement, promise, etc., and which, if disclosed, would materially alter its import. **4.** *U.S.* A tract of the public land reserved for some special use, as for forests, for Indians, etc.

re·serve′ (rē·zûrv′), *v. t.* [OF. *reserver,* fr. L. *reservare, -vatum,* fr. *re-* + *servare* to keep.] **1.** To keep in store for future or special use. **2.** To retain or hold over to a future time; not to deliver or disclose at once. **3.** To set apart; to keep; — usually with *for* or *to.* **4.** To secure by stipulation; as, *reserved* seats. **5.** *Eccl.* To set aside at the time of a celebration of the Eucharist (a portion) for communion of the sick. — **Syn.** See KEEP.

— *n.* **1.** That which is reserved; a store; stock; extra supply. **2.** Something reserved for a particular purpose; specif., a tract of (esp. public) land reserved for a particular purpose; a reservation; as, forest *reserves.* **3.** Reservation; exception; qualification; as, a mental *reserve.* **4.** Self-restraint, closeness, or caution, in one's words and bearing toward others; lack of effusiveness or, sometimes, of cordiality. **5.** Forbearance from making a full explanation, complete disclosure, or free expression of one's mind; reticence. **6.** *Finance.* **a** That part of the assets of a bank specially kept in cash or in a more or less liquid form as a reasonable provision for meeting all demands which may be made upon it. **b** That portion of the earnings of a corporation set aside to meet future losses or contingent liabilities. **7.** *Mil.* **a** A force withheld temporarily from action so that it may be available to the commander when needed. **b** The military or naval forces of a country not serving with the colors during time of peace, but liable to call.

— *adj.* Constituting, or of the nature of, a reserve; as, a *reserve* supply; *reserve* troops.

reserve bank. A Federal Reserve Bank.

re·served′ (rē·zûrvd′), *adj.* **1.** Kept or set apart or aside for future or special use. **2.** Restrained in words or actions; cautious in communicating one's thoughts and feelings. — **Syn.** See SILENT. — **re·serv′ed·ly** (-zûr′vĕd·lĭ; -vĭd·lĭ), *adv.* — **re·serv′ed·ness,** *n.*

re·serv′ist (rē·zûr′vĭst), *n.* A member of the reserves of a military or naval organization.

res′er·voir (rĕz′ēr·vwôr; -vwär), *n.* [F. *réservoir,* fr. *réserver.* See RESERVE.] **1.** A place where anything is kept in store; specif.: **a** A place where water is collected and kept for use when wanted, chiefly in large quantity, as to supply a city. **b** A part of an apparatus in which a liquid is held; as, the *reservoir* of an oil lamp. **2.** A reserve; a store; an extra supply.

re·set′ (rē·sĕt′), *v. t.;* see SET. To set again, as type or a diamond.

re·set′tle (rē·sĕt′'l), *v. t. & i.* To settle again. — **re·set′tle·ment,** *n.*

‖**res ges′tae** (rēz jĕs′tē). [L.] Things done; deeds; exploits.

re·shape′ (rē·shāp′), *v. t.* To shape anew.

re·ship′ (rē·shĭp′), *v. t.;* RE·SHIPPED′ (-shĭpt′); RE·SHIP′PING. To ship again; specif., to put on board of a vessel a second time; to transfer to another ship. — *v. i.* To embark again or sign anew for service on a ship. — **re·ship′ment,** *n.*

re·side′ (rē·zīd′), *v. i.* [F. *résider,* fr. L. *residēre,* fr. *re-* + *sedere* to sit.] **1.** To dwell permanently or continuously; to have one's residence or domicile. **2.** To be present as an element; to inhere as a quality; to be vested as a right; as, the power *resides* in the electorate.

res′i·dence (rĕz′ĭ·dĕns), *n.* **1.** Act or fact of dwelling in a place for some time. **2.** Act or fact of living in some place, in the discharge of a duty or as a qualification for some benefit; as, the canon in *residence.* **3.** The place where one actually has his home. **4.** The seat of a power, prerogative, etc. **5.** The duration of one's abode in a place.

res′i·den·cy (-dĕn·sĭ), *n.; pl.* -CIES (-sĭz). The official residence of, or the territory subject to, a resident diplomatic agent or governor; specif., any of certain administrative divisions in the East Indies, India, etc.

res′i·dent (-dĕnt), *adj.* [OF., fr. L. *residens, -entis,* pres. part.] **1.**

Dwelling for a continued length of time; residing. **2.** Present; inherent. **3.** Of birds, not migratory. — *n.* **1.** One who resides in a place. **2.** A diplomatic agent residing at a foreign court or seat of government; specif., such an agent in a residency.

res′i·den′tial (rĕz′ĭ·dĕn′shăl), *adj.* **1.** Used as a residence or by residents. **2.** Adapted to, or occupied by, residences. **3.** Of, or connected with, residence or residences.

res′i·den′ti·ar′y (-dĕn′shĭ·ĕr′ĭ; -shȧ·rĭ), *adj.* Having residence; residing; resident. — *n.; pl.* -IES (-ĭz). **1.** An ecclesiastic who is or must be in residence, as for a certain time. **2.** One who is resident.

re·sid′u·al (rē·zĭd′ū·ăl), *adj.* Of, or of the nature of, a residue; left as a residuum. — *n.* A remainder; a residuum; specif.: **a** A residual product or substance. **b** *Math.* (1) The difference of the results obtained by observation, and by computation from a formula. (2) The difference between the mean of several observations and any one of them. **c** *Psychol.* Any internal aftereffect of experience or activity, which influences later behavior.

re·sid′u·ar′y (-ĕr′ĭ *or, esp. Brit.,* -ĕr·ĭ), *adj.* [See RESIDUE.] Residual; as, the *residuary* clause of a will, in which the residue of an estate is disposed of; a *residuary* legatee.

res′i·due (rĕz′ĭ·dū), *n.* [OF. *residu*, fr. L. *residuum*, neut. of *residuus* remaining, fr. *residēre*. See RESIDE.] **1.** That which remains after a part is taken, separated, or designated; remnant; remainder; rest. **2.** *Law.* The part of a testator's estate remaining after the satisfaction of all debts and previous devises and bequests.

re·sid′u·um (rē·zĭd′ū·ŭm), *n.; pl.* RESIDUA (-ȧ). [L.] **1.** That which remains after certain deductions are made; a residue; often, that left over; the leavings. **2.** A residual product, as that left after distillation of crude petroleum. **3.** *Law.* = RESIDUE, 2.

re·sign′ (rē·zīn′), *v. t.* [OF. *resigner*, fr. L. *resignare* to unseal, annul, resign, fr. *re-* + *signare* to seal, stamp.] **1.** To give up, as one's office; to surrender by a formal act; to yield; relinquish; as, to *resign* control of an estate. **2.** To commit as by yielding or abandoning; to give (oneself, etc.) over or up; to consign; as, to *resign* one to his fate. — *v. i.* To give up one's office or position; *U. S.*, to withdraw (*from*) formally; as, the governor has *resigned.* — **Syn.** See RELINQUISH: ABDICATE.

res′ig·na′tion (rĕz′ĭg·nā′shŭn; rĕs′ĭg-), *n.* **1.** Act or fact of resigning; surrender. **2.** State of being resigned or submissive; acquiescence; esp., quiet or patient submission.

re·signed′ (rē·zīnd′), *adj.* Submissive; acquiescent; uncomplaining. — **re·sign′ed·ly** (-zīn′ĕd·lĭ; -ĭd·lĭ; -zīnd′lĭ), *adv.* — **re·sign′ed·ness,** *n.*

re·sile′ (rē·zīl′), *v. i.* [From MF., fr. L. *resilire* to leap or spring back, withdraw, fr. *re-* + *salire* to spring.] To rebound; to return to its original position, as an elastic body.

re·sil′i·ence (rē·zĭl′ĭ·ĕns; 58), **re·sil′i·en·cy** (-ĕn·sĭ), *n.* Elasticity; hence, capability of a strained body to recover its size and shape after deformation, esp. when the strain is caused by compressive stresses.

re·sil′i·ent (-ĕnt), *adj.* [L. *resiliens*, pres. part. See RESILE.] **1.** Returning to, or resuming, the original position or shape; possessing resilience; specif., *Mech.*, capable of withstanding shock without permanent deformation or rupture. **2.** Elastic; buoyant. — **Syn.** See ELASTIC.

res′in (rĕz′ĭn; -′n), *n.* [F. *résine*, fr. L. *resina*, fr. Gr. *rhētinē*.] **1. a** Any of various amorphous, solid or semisolid natural organic substances, chiefly of plant origin, usually yellowish to dark brown, transparent to translucent, nonconductors of electricity, and soluble in organic solvents but not in water. **b** Specif., rosin. **2.** Any artificial product having most of the properties of the natural resins. — *v. t.* To treat, as by rubbing, with resin.

res′in·ate (rĕz′ĭ·nāt), *v. t.* To impregnate or flavor with resin.

res′in·if′er·ous (rĕz′ĭ·nĭf′ĕr·ŭs), *adj.* Yielding resin.

res′in·oid (rĕz′ĭ·noid), *adj.* More or less resinous. — *n.* **1.** A resinoid substance; specif., a synthetic resin. **2.** = GUM RESIN.

res′in·ous (-nŭs), *adj.* [L. *resinosus.*] **1.** Of, characteristic of, of the nature of, or obtained from resin. **2.** Electronegative.

re·sist′ (rē·zĭst′), *v. t.* [OF. *resister*, fr. L. *resistere*, fr. *re-* + *sistere*, v. causative of *stare* to stand.] **1.** To withstand; to be proof against; to be able to repel, as disease. **2.** To strive against; to exert oneself to counteract, defeat, or frustrate. **3.** To withstand the action of, as the metal *resists* acid. — *v. i.* To exert force in opposition; to offer resistance. — **Syn.** See OPPOSE. — *n.* Something that resists or prevents a certain action, as a protective coating that renders a fabric color-proof or a surface nonconducting or acidproof. — **re·sist′er,** *n.*

re·sist′ance (rē·zĭs′tăns), *n.* **1.** Act or capacity of resisting. **2.** Any opposing or retarding force. **3.** *Elec.* The opposition offered by a substance or body to the passage through it of an electric current; — the reciprocal of *conductance.*

resistance thermometer. See THERMOMETER.

re·sist′ant (rē·zĭs′tănt), *adj.* Making resistance; resisting. — *n.* One who or that which resists.

re·sist′i·ble (rē·zĭs′tĭ·b'l), *adj.* Capable of being resisted. — **re·sist′i·bil′i·ty** (-bĭl′ĭ·tĭ), *n.*

re·sis′tive (rē·zĭs′tĭv), *adj.* Tending to resist.

re′sis·tiv′i·ty (rē′zĭs·tĭv′ĭ·tĭ), *n.* Capacity for resisting; specif., *Elec.*, the electrical resistance of a cubic centimeter of any material; — the reciprocal of *conductivity.*

re·sist′less, *adj.* **1.** Incapable of being resisted; irresistible. **2.** Having no power to resist; offering no opposition. — **re·sist′less·ly,** *adv.* — **re·sist′less·ness,** *n.*

re·sis′tor (rē·zĭs′tẽr), *n.* *Elec.* A device offering electrical resistance used in an electric circuit for protection or control.

res ju′di·ca′ta (rēz jōō′dĭ·kā′tȧ). [L.] = RES ADJUDICATA.

res′na·tron (rĕz′nȧ·trŏn), *n.* [*resonator* + *-tron* as in *electron.*] A high-power, wide-frequency electron tube, used esp. in World War II to jam enemy radar.

res′o·jet′ en′gine (rĕz′ō·jĕt′). [*resonance* + *jet.*] *Aeronautics.* **a** A jet engine having in its forward end a continuously open air inlet and containing a diffuser, a combustion chamber, and an exhaust nozzle, dependent for operation upon resonance (a phenomenon illustrated by the vibrating column of air in a sounding open organ pipe), and designed to produce a pulsating thrust by the intermittent flow of hot gases. Fuel is supplied continuously to the combustion chamber, where it is mixed with air and ignited, and resonance occurs when the free vibrational period of the column of gases within the jet engine is the same as the period of the ignition cycle. **b** A pulse-jet engine whose operation depends upon resonance.

re·sole′ (rē·sōl′), *v. t.* To sole anew, as shoes.

re·sol′u·ble (rē·zŏl′ū·b'l; rĕz′ō·lū·b'l), *adj.* [LL. *resolubilis.*] Admitting of being resolved; soluble. — **re·sol′u·bil′i·ty** (-bĭl′ĭ·tĭ), *n.* — **re·sol′u·ble·ness,** *n.*

res′o·lute (rĕz′ō·lūt; 114), *adj.* [L. *resolutus*, past part. See RESOLVE.] Having, or characterized by, a decided purpose; determined; resolved; hence, bold; firm; steady. — **Syn.** See FAITHFUL. — *n.* One who is resolute, or daring. — **res′o·lute·ly,** *adv.* — **res′o·lute·ness,** *n.*

res′o·lu′tion (-lū′shŭn), *n.* **1.** Act or process of resolving, or reducing to simpler form; also, its result; answer; solution. **2.** Act of, or quality of mind admitting or productive of, resolving or determining; resoluteness; firmness; also, that which is resolved upon or decided upon; settled determination. **3.** A formal expression of the opinion or will of an assembly, adopted by vote. **4.** *Med.* A breaking up, disappearance, or termination, as of a fever. **5.** *Music.* The progression of a dissonant tone of a chord to a tone of another pitch so as to produce a consonant chord; also, the consonant tone or consonance so produced. — **Syn.** See COURAGE.

res′o·lu′tion·er (-ẽr), **res′o·lu′tion·ist** (-ĭst), *n.* One who makes or joins with others in a resolution.

re·solv′a·ble (rē·zŏl′vȧ·b'l), *adj.* Admitting of being resolved. — **re·solv′a·bil′i·ty** (-bĭl′ĭ·tĭ), **re·solv′a·ble·ness,** *n.*

re·solve′ (rē·zŏlv′), *v. t.* [L. *resolvere, -solutum*, to loosen, relax, fr. *re-* + *solvere* to loosen, dissolve.] **1.** *Archaic.* To dissolve. *Shak.* **2.** To separate or break up (into constituent parts or elements); to change or convert by disintegration (into); to transform, reduce, as by analysis, or convert (into, to); to analyze. **3.** To determine or decide; to settle, or settle on. **4.** To answer or solve, as a problem; to disentangle; unravel; explain; solve; hence, to clear up; as, to *resolve* a riddle. **5.** To convince; assure; — only reflexively. **6.** To express by resolution and vote; to declare or decide by a formal vote; as, the house *resolved* to appropriate no money. **7.** To change or convert by resolution or formal vote; as, the house *resolved* itself into a committee. **8.** *Chem.* To separate (a racemic compound) into its two components. **9.** *Music.* To make (one or more tones of chord) progress from a dissonance to a consonance. **10.** *Optics.* To distinguish between or render visible the separate parts of; as, to *resolve* lines in a spectrum. — *v. i.* **1.** To undergo resolution; to be reduced as by dissolving or analysis. **2.** To form a purpose or resolution; esp., to determine after reflection; as, to *resolve* on a better course of life. **3.** *Music.* To progress from a dissonance to a consonance. — **Syn.** See ANALYZE: DECIDE. — *n.* **1.** That which has been resolved; a determination; a resolution. **2.** Resolute quality; determination. — **re·solv′er,** *n.*

re·solved′ (rē·zŏlvd′), *part. adj.* Having a fixed purpose; determined. — **re·solv′ed·ly** (-zŏl′vĕd·lĭ; -vĭd·lĭ), *adv.*

re·sol′vent (-zŏl′vĕnt), *adj.* [L. *resolvens*, pres. part. of *resolvere.* See RESOLVE.] *Chiefly Med.* Having power to resolve; solvent. — *n.* **1.** *Med.* That which has power to disperse inflammatory or other lesions. **2.** A solvent.

re·solv′ing pow′er (rē·zŏl′vĭng). **1.** *Optics.* The ability of an optical instrument to form distinguishable images of objects separated by small angular distances. **2.** *Photog.* The ability of a film or plate to reproduce the fine detail of the optical image.

res′o·nance (rĕz′ō·năns), *n.* **1.** Act of resounding; quality or state of being resonant. **2.** *Chem.* The phenomenon shown by a molecule to which two or more structures, differing only in the disposition of electrons, can be assigned. Its effect is to increase stability. **3.** *Elec.* The state of adjustment of a circuit permitting a maximum flow of current when an electromotive force of a particular frequency is impressed. **4.** *Med.* The sound elicited on percussion, esp. of the lungs. **5.** *Music.* The intensification and enriching of a musical tone by supplementary vibration. **6.** *Physics.* The phenomenon shown by a vibrating system which responds with maximum amplitude under the action of a harmonic force; this occurs when the frequency of the applied force is the same as a natural frequency of the vibrating body.

res′o·nant (-nănt), *adj.* [L. *resonans*, pres. part. of *resonare* to resound. See RESOUND.] **1.** Resounding; ringing; re-echoing. **2.** Intensified and enriched by or as if by resonance; as, the *resonant* quality of Caruso's voice. **3.** *Physics.* Pertaining to, or exhibiting, resonance. — **res′o·nant·ly,** *adv.*

res′o·nate (-nāt), *v. i.* [L. *resonare, resonatum*, to resound.] *Physics & Chem.* To exhibit resonance; to vibrate sympathetically with some source of sound or electric oscillations.

res′o·na′tor (-nā′tẽr), *n.* [NL.] Anything that resounds or resonates; any device for giving resonance to sounds; *Radio*, the antenna system and other high-frequency circuits of a receiving apparatus.

re·sorb′ (rē·sôrb′), *v. t.* [L. *resorbere.*] To swallow or suck in again; reabsorb. — **re·sorp′tion** (-sôrp′shŭn), *n.*

res·or′cin·ol (rĕz·ôr′sĭ·nōl; -nŏl), **res·or′cin** (-ôr′sĭn), *n.* [*resin* + *orcinol.*] *Chem.* A colorless, crystalline phenol, $C_6H_4(OH)_2(m)$, obtained from certain resins, also artificially. It is used in making dyes and as an antiseptic.

re·sort′ (rē·zôrt′), *v. i.* [OF. *resortir*, fr. *re-* + *sortir* to go out.] **1.** To go, repair, or betake oneself, esp. frequently, customarily, or usually. **2.** To have recourse; to betake oneself for help, relief, or advantage.
— *n.* **1.** That to which, or one to whom, one resorts or looks for help; resource; refuge. **2.** Recourse; as, to have *resort* to force. **3.** Frequent, habitual, or general visiting; as, a place of popular *resort.* **4.** A place of frequent assembly; a haunt. **5.** A popular place of entertainment. — **Syn.** See RESOURCE.

re–sound′ (rē·sound′), *v. t. & i.* To sound again or anew.

re·sound′ (rē·zound′), *v. i.* [OF. *resoner*, fr. L. *resonare*, fr. *re-* + *sonare* to sound.] **1.** To be filled with sound; reverberate; as, the earth *resounded* with his praise. **2.** To echo; to produce an echo, as a horn. **3.** *Poetic.* To be proclaimed often, as one's name; to be renowned. — *v. t.* **1.** *Poetic.* To proclaim (one's praises, virtues, etc.); to extol loudly. **2.** To sound or utter in full, resonant tones. **3.** To reverberate; re-echo. — **re·sound′ing·ly,** *adv.*

re·source′ (rē·sōrs′; rē′sōrs; 70), *n.* [F. *ressource*, fr. OF. *resourdre* to spring forth or up again, fr. L. *resurgere*, fr. *re-* re- + *surgere* to rise.] **1.** A new or a reserve source of supply or support. **2.** *pl.* Available means; computable wealth in money, property, products, etc.; immediate and possible sources of revenue. **3.** Means of resort in exigency; expedient, stratagem, etc.; as, her usual *resource* was a smile. **4.** Possibility of relief or recovery; — in ***without resource.*** **5.** Skill in meeting a situation, rising to an occasion, etc.; resourcefulness.

Syn. Resource, resort, expedient, shift, makeshift, stopgap mean something to which one turns in absence of the usual means or source of supply. **Resource** or **resort** applies to anything upon which one falls back; **expedient**, to any device or contrivance when the usual one is not possible or at hand; **shift**, to a tentative or temporary expedient; **make-shift**, to an inferior thing used as a shift; **stopgap**, to any person or thing that for the moment supplies a need or fills a gap.

re·source′ful (rē·sōrs′fo͝ol; -f'l), *adj.* Characterized by resource; having great resources. — **re·source′ful·ness**, *n.*

re·spect′ (rē·spĕkt′), *v. t.* [L. *respectus*, past part. of *respicere* to look back, respect, fr. *re-* + *specere* to look, view.] **1.** To consider worthy of esteem; hence, to refrain from obtruding upon, as a person's privacy. **2.** To have reference to; to be concerned with. **3.** *Obs.* To consider; deem. *Shak.* — **Syn.** See REGARD. — *n.* **1.** Relation; relationship; reference; regard; as, with *respect* to. **2.** Act of noticing with attention; regard; consideration. **3.** Favor; esp., undue favor or bias; partiality; as, to show *respect* of persons. **4.** A point regarded; a particular; a point of view; as, in all *respects*. **5.** Esteem; deferential regard; also, honor. **6.** *pl.* Expressions of respect or deference; regards; as, to send one's *respects* to another. **7.** *Obs.* A consideration; motive.

re·spect′a·bil′i·ty (rē·spĕk′tȧ·bĭl′ĭ·tĭ), *n.; pl.* -TIES (-tĭz). **1.** State or quality of being respectable. **2.** Respectable persons collectively. **3.** A respectable convention; as, to observe the *respectabilities*.

re·spect′a·ble (rē·spĕk′tȧ·b'l), *adj.* **1.** Worthy of note; of consequence or repute. **2.** Worthy of respect, esteem, or deference; estimable; respected. **3.** Decent in behavior or character; now often, that respects the decencies or proprieties; conventionally correct in conduct. **4.** Rather large or numerous; fair in size, quantity, or quality; tolerable. — **re·spect′a·bly**, *adv.*

re·spect′er (-tẽr), *n.* One who respects; as, ***respecter of persons***, one whose decisions are influenced by bias toward persons. "God is no *respecter of persons*." *Acts* x. 34.

re·spect′ful (rē·spĕkt′fo͝ol; -f'l), *adj.* Marked by respect; showing deference. — **re·spect′ful·ly**, *adv.* — **re·spect′ful·ness**, *n.*

re·spect′ing, *prep.* In view of; with regard to.

re·spec′tive (rē·spĕk′tĭv), *adj.* **1.** *Now Rare.* Attentive; heedful. **2.** Relating to particular persons or things, each to each; several; as, their *respective* homes. **3.** *Obs.* Partial; discriminative. *Shak.* — **Syn.** See SPECIAL.

re·spec′tive·ly, *adv.* As relating to each; in particular; each to each; each in the order given.

re·spell′ (rē·spĕl′), *v. t.* To spell again.

‖**re′spi·ce fi′nem** (rĕs′pĭ·sē fī′nĕm). [L.] Look at the end.

re·spir′a·ble (rē·spīr′ȧ·b'l; rĕs′pĭ·rȧ·b'l), *adj.* Suitable for being breathed; also, capable of respiration.

res′pi·ra′tion (rĕs′pĭ·rā′shŭn), *n.* **1.** Act or process of breathing; inspiration and expiration. **2.** *Physiol.* The osmotic and chemical process or processes by which a plant or animal absorbs oxygen and gives off the products (esp. the carbon dioxide) formed by the oxidation in the tissues; — to be disting. from *photosynthesis*.

res′pi·ra′tor (rĕs′pĭ·rā′tẽr), *n.* **a** A device covering the mouth or nose, to prevent the inhalation of noxious substances or to allow the inhalation of medicated vapors or of gases. **b** A device for artificial respiration.

re·spir′a·to′ry (rē·spīr′ȧ·tō′rĭ; rĕs′pĭ·rȧ-), *adj.* *Physiol.* Of or pertaining to respiration; serving for respiration.

re·spire′ (rē·spīr′), *v. i.* [OF. *respirer*, fr. L. *respirare, respiratum*, fr. *re-* + *spirare* to breathe.] **1.** To breathe; to inhale and exhale air successively, to maintain the vitality of the blood. **2.** To have a breathing space; to recover hope or courage. — *v. t.* To breathe.

res′pite (rĕs′pĭt), *n.* [OF. *respit*, fr. L. *respectus* respect, delay. See RESPECT, *v.*] **1.** A putting off; postponement; delay. **2.** Temporary intermission of labor, or of any process or operation. **3.** *Law.* Temporary suspension of the execution of a capital offender; reprieve. — *v. t.* **1.** To grant a respite to. **2.** To delay or postpone.

re·splend′ence (rē·splĕn′dĕns), **re·splend′en·cy** (-dĕn·sĭ), *n.* State of being resplendent; splendor; luster.

re·splend′ent (-dĕnt), *adj.* [L. *resplendens, -entis*, pres. part. of *resplendere* to shine brightly, fr. *re-* + *splendere* to shine.] Shining brilliantly; lustrous; splendid. — **Syn.** See SPLENDID. — **re·splend′ent·ly**, *adv.*

re·spond′ (rē·spŏnd′), *v. i.* [OF. *respondre*, fr. L. *respondere, -sponsum*, fr. *re-* + *spondere* to promise.] **1.** To answer; to reply. **2.** To act, behave, etc., in response. **3.** *U. S.* To be answerable; as, the defendant is held to *respond* in damages. — **Syn.** See ANSWER. — *n.* *Arch.* An engaged pillar supporting an arch.

re·spond′ence (-spŏn′dĕns), *n.* Also **re·spond′en·cy** (-dĕn·sĭ). Act of responding; response; also, correspondence; agreement.

re·spond′ent (-dĕnt), *adj.* [L. *respondens, -entis*, pres. part.] **1.** *Obs.* Corresponding. **2.** Making response; answering. — *n.* One who responds; *Law*, one who answers in certain suits or proceedings, esp. in equity and admiralty; defendant.

re·sponse′ (rē·spŏns′), *n.* [OF. and L.; OF. *respons, response*, fr. L. *responsum*, fr. *respondere*. See RESPOND.] **1.** Act of responding; an answer. **2.** *Biol. & Psychol.* Any activity of an organism or of an effector organ or part, or the inhibition of previous activity, resulting from stimulation; a reaction. **3.** *Eccl.* **a** A verse, phrase, or word sung or said by the people or choir after or in reply to the priest or clergyman. **b** A responsory.

re·spon′si·bil′i·ty (rē·spŏn′sĭ·bĭl′ĭ·tĭ), *n.; pl.* -TIES (-tĭz). **1.** State or quality of being responsible; specif.: **a** Accountability; also, moral accountability; as, the *responsibilities* of parenthood. **b** Reliability; sometimes, ability to pay. **2.** A charge for which one is responsible or accountable; as, to seek relief from his *responsibilities*.

re·spon′si·ble (rē·spŏn′sĭ·b'l), *adj.* **1.** Liable to respond; accountable; answerable. **2.** Able to respond or answer for one's conduct and obligations; trustworthy. **3.** Involving responsibility or accountability. **4.** *Chiefly U. S.* Answerable as the primary cause, motive, or agent; — with *for*. **5.** *Ethics.* Having the character of a free moral agent. — **re·spon′si·ble·ness**, *n.* — **re·spon′si·bly**, *adv.*

Syn. **Responsible, answerable, accountable, amenable, liable** mean subject to an authority which may exact redress in case of default. **Responsible** implies such a relation between one who performs a task or duty, executes a trust, or the like, and the person or body imposing that task, duty, etc.; **answerable**, between one having a moral or legal obligation and a court, tribunal, etc., charged with oversight of its observance; **accountable**, between someone entrusted with something valuable and the person or being to whom he must account for its use; **amenable** and **liable**, between one subject to the control or censure of a higher authority and that authority itself.

re·spon′sions (rē·spŏn′shŭnz), *n. pl.* *Univ. of Oxford.* The first university examination for the B.A. degree.

re·spon′sive (-sĭv), *adj.* **1.** Answering. **2.** *Obs.* Correspondent. **3.** Ready or inclined to respond, or react in sympathy; as, to stir a *responsive* chord. **4.** Characterized by responses. — **re·spon′sive·ly**, *adv.*

re·spon′sive·ness, *n.* Quality of being responsive; *Mech.*, the rapidity with which a member, as an instrument pointer, comes to rest after a change of any kind.

re·spon′so·ry (rē·spŏn′sō·rĭ), *n.; pl.* -RIES (-rĭz). *Eccl.* A response; esp., an anthem sung or said after or during a lection.

‖**res·pu′bli·ca** (rēz·pŭb′lĭ·kȧ), *n.* [L.] Commonweal; commonwealth; state; republic.

rest (rĕst), *n.* [ME., fr. OF. *arest*. See ARREST.] *Medieval Armor.* A projection or attachment on the side of the breastplate to support the butt of the lance.

rest, *n.* [AS. *rest, ræst*, rest, bed, grave.] **1.** A place where one may rest; abode; stopping place; a place of shelter and lodging; as, travelers' *rests*. **2.** Repose; sleep; slumber. **3.** Freedom from activity; quiet; tranquillity. **4.** Hence: **a** Peace of mind or spirit. **b** *Rare.* Renewed vigor. *Shak.* **5.** The repose of death. **6.** Absence or cessation of motion, as a physical phenomenon; continuance in the same place; — opposed to *motion*. **7.** That on which anything rests or leans for support; a support. **8.** *Billiards & Pool.* A support for a cue; a bridge. **9.** *Music.* A rhythmic silence in music; also, a char-

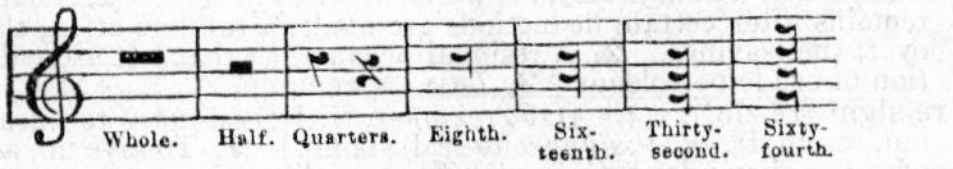
Whole.
Half.
Quarters.
Eighth.
Sixteenth.
Thirty-second.
Sixty-fourth.

Rests, 9.

acter that stands for such silence. **10.** *Pros.* A short pause in reading; a caesura.
— *v. i.* **1.** To get repose by lying down; esp., to sleep; also, to be dead. **2.** To cease from action or motion; to desist from exertion; to be still. **3.** To lie; to be fixed or supported; as, a column *rests* on its pedestal. **4.** To repose without anxiety; to trust, rely, depend; also, to be based or founded; as, the case *rests* on slender evidence. **5.** To remain or lie for action or accomplishment; as, the maintenance of peace *rests* with him alone. **6.** *Agric.* Of land, to remain idle or uncropped. **7.** *Law.* In practice, to bring to an end voluntarily the introduction of evidence. — *v. t.* **1.** To refresh by repose; to lay at rest. **2.** To place or lay, as on a support; to lean. **3.** To base or ground, as one's hopes. **4.** *Law.* In practice, to desist voluntarily from introducing evidence on.

rest (rĕst), *n.* [F. *reste*, fr. *rester* to remain, fr. L. *restare* to stay back, remain, fr. *re-* + *stare* to stand.] With *the*, that which is left after removal of a part; the remainder.

re·start′ (rē·stärt′), *v. t. & i.* To start again or afresh. — **re·start′**, *n.*

re·state′ (rē·stāt′), *v. t.* To state again or in a new form. — **re·state′ment**, *n.*

res′tau·rant (rĕs′tō·rănt; *Brit. also* rĕs′tō·räɴ), *n.* [F., fr. *restaurer*, fr. L. *restaurare*. See RESTORE.] A public eating house.

res′tau·ra·teur′ (rĕs′tō·rä·tûr′), *n.* [F.] A restaurant keeper.

rest cure. *Med.* Treatment of disease, as neurasthenia or tuberculosis, by rest and isolation in a good hygienic environment.

rest′ful (rĕst′fo͝ol; -f'l), *adj.* **1.** Giving, characterized by, or of the nature of rest; freeing from toil, trouble, etc. **2.** Being at rest; quiet. — **Syn.** See COMFORTABLE. — **rest′ful·ly**, *adv.* — **rest′ful·ness**, *n.*

rest′har′row (rĕst′hăr′ō), *n.* [See 1st REST; HARROW.] A European woody herb (*Ononis repens*) of the pea family, with pink flowers and long tough roots.

res′ti·form (rĕs′tĭ·fôrm), *adj.* [L. *restis* a rope + *-form*.] *Anat.* Designating a pair of cordlike masses (the **restiform bodies**) of nerve fibers on the dorsal surface of the medulla oblongata, connecting it with the cerebellum.

rest′ing, *adj.* *Biol. & Hort.* Dormant; quiescent; as, a *resting* spore, commonly invested with thickened cell wall to withstand cold, heat, dryness, etc.; also, of or pertaining to dormancy; as, a *resting* stage.

res′ti·tu′tion (rĕs′tĭ·tū′shŭn), *n.* [OF., fr. L. *restitutio*, fr. *restituere* to restore, fr. *re-* + *statuere* to put. See STATUTE.] **1.** Act of restoring; specif., restoration of anything to its rightful owner; act of giving an equivalent for loss, damage, etc. **2.** *Physics.* Return to, or recovery of, a former state, as of an elastic body.

res′tive (rĕs′tĭv), *adj.* [OF. *restif*, fr. L. *restare* to stay back, resist.] **1.** Stubbornly resisting control or guidance; of a horse, balky; hence, unmanageable. **2.** Uneasy; fidgeting about; as, the crowd grew *restive*. — **Syn.** See CONTRARY. — **res′tive·ly**, *adv.* — **res′tive·ness**, *n.*

rest′less, *adj.* **1.** Deprived of rest; uneasy. **2.** Not affording rest; unrestful; as, a *restless* night. **3.** *Poetic.* Never resting; unquiet; unceasing. **4.** Lacking in repose; averse to inaction; hence, unsettled, discontented. — **rest′less·ly**, *adv.* — **rest′less·ness**, *n.*

re·stock′ (rē·stŏk′), *v. t. & i.* To stock again; to provide new stock for, as a stream depleted of fish, etc.

res′to·ra′tion (rĕs′tō·rā′shŭn), *n.* **1.** Act of restoring, or state or fact of being restored; as: **a** Reinstatement; re-establishment. **b** Restitution. **c** Putting back into an unimpaired or much improved condition. **d** Putting back into nearly or quite the original form. **2.** A representation of the original form, as of a fossil animal or of a building. — ***the Restoration.*** *Eng. Hist.* The re-establishment of monarchy under King Charles II (1660–85).

re·stor′a·tive (rē·stōr′ȧ·tĭv; 70), *adj.* Of or pertaining to restoration; having power to restore. — *n.* Something that serves to restore, esp. a person to consciousness.

re·store′ (rē·stōr′; 70), *v. t.* [OF. *restorer*, fr. L. *restaurare*, fr. *re-* + *staurare* (in comp.) to place, fix.] **1.** To give back; to return. **2.** To re-establish; to put back into existence or use, as harmony among foes. **3.** To bring or put back; to put (a person) again in possession; as, to *restore* a king to the throne. **4.** To bring back to, or put back into, the former or original state; to repair; renew; specif.: **a** To reconstruct. **b** To reinstate in a former favor, position, office, etc. **c** To bring back to a healthy state. **d** To renovate, as a painting. **e** *Arch.* To repair and alter (a building) into nearly or quite the original form. — **Syn.** See RENEW. — **re·stor′er** (-stōr′ẽr), *n.*

re·strain′ (rē·strān′), *v. t.* [OF. *restraindre, restreindre*, fr. L. *restringere, restrictum*. See RE-; STRAIN, *v.*] **1.** To draw back again; to check; to repress or suppress; to curb. **2.** To limit or restrict, as power, trade, or a title. **3.** To deprive of liberty, as the insane. — **re·strain′a·ble**, *adj.* — **re·strain′ed·ly**, *adv.* — **re·strain′er**, *n.*

Syn. **Restrain, curb, check, bridle** mean to hold back from something, or in doing something. **Restrain**, the most comprehensive term, implies an intent to prevent or to keep within bounds; **curb**, a sharp drastic method that produces its effect immediately or prevents its free or efficient operation; **check**, something that impedes motion or progress; **bridle**, a keeping under control by subduing or holding in.

re·straint′ (rē·strānt′), *n.* [OF. *restrainte.*] **1.** Act, process, or means of restraining; restraining force or influence; a case of restraining or being restrained. **2.** State of being restrained; esp., confinement. **3.** Control over one's thoughts, feelings, etc., or their expression; reserve; reticence; constraint.

restraint of trade. Any attempt or intent to eliminate or stifle competition, to effect a monopoly, to maintain prices artificially, or otherwise to hamper or obstruct the course of trade and commerce as it would be if left to the control of natural and economic forces.

re·strict′ (rē·strĭkt′), *v. t.* [L. *restrictus*, past part. See RESTRAIN.] To restrain within bounds; to limit; confine. — **Syn.** See LIMIT. — **re·strict′ed**, *adj.* — **re·strict′ed·ly**, *adv.*

re·stric′tion (rē·strĭk′shŭn), *n.* **1.** That which restricts; a limitation; a regulation which restricts or restrains. **2.** Act of restricting, or state of being restricted; as, *restriction* of children within limits. — **re·stric′tion·ist**, *n.*

re·stric′tive (-tĭv), *adj.* **1.** Serving or tending to restrict; conveying restrictions. **2.** *Gram.* **a** Of an adjunct, expressing a limitation of reference; as, a *restrictive* adjective (*this* house). **b** Specif., of an adjective clause, essential to the definiteness of the meaning of the antecedent (the boys *who work* eat first); — opp. to *descriptive* (or *nonrestrictive*). — **re·stric′tive·ly**, *adv.*

re·string′ (rē·strĭng′), *v. t.* To string again or anew.

re·sult′ (rē·zŭlt′), *v. i.* [From ML., fr. L. *resultare* to spring back, fr. *re-* + *saltare* to leap, v. intens. fr. *salire.*] To proceed, spring, or arise, as a consequence, effect, or conclusion; to terminate; to end; — with *from* or *in.* — *n.* **1.** That which results, as a consequence, issue, or conclusion; sometimes, beneficial effect; fruit. **2.** Something obtained by calculation or investigation. — **Syn.** See EFFECT.

re·sult′ant (-zŭl′tănt), *adj.* Resulting or issuing; having the character of a result; equal in effect to two or more components, as forces. — *n.* That which results; a resultant force (see COMPOSITION OF FORCES).

re·sume′ (rē·zūm′; 114), *v. t.* [F. *résumer*, fr. L. *resumere, -sumptum*, fr. *re-* + *sumere* to take.] **1.** To assume or take again; to put on anew; to reoccupy. **2.** To enter upon or begin again; to recommence, as something interrupted. **3.** To take back to oneself. **4.** To take or pick up again; to go back to using. — *v. i.* To recommence.

ré′su·mé′ (rā′zū·mā′; *F.* rā′zü′mā′), *n.* [F., past part.] A summing up; an abridgment or summary.

re·sum′mon (rē·sŭm′ŭn), *v. t.* To summon again or anew.

re·sump′tion (rē·zŭmp′shŭn), *n.* Act or fact of resuming.

re·su′pi·nate (rē·sū′pĭ·nāt), *adj.* [L. *resupinatus*, past part. of *resupinare* to bend back. See RESUPINE.] *Bot.* Inverted in position, as the flowers of many orchids.

re·su′pi·na′tion (-nā′shŭn), *n.* A turning or twisting to an inverted position; a resupinate condition.

re′su·pine′ (rē′sū·pīn′), *adj.* [L. *resupinus*, fr. *re-* + *supinus* bent backward, supine.] Lying on the back; supine.

re·sur′face (rē·sûr′fĭs; -fȧs), *v. t.* To surface anew.

‖**re·sur′gam** (rē·sûr′găm). [L.] I shall rise again.

re·surge′ (rē·sûrj′), *v. i.;* -SURGED′ (-sûrjd′); -SURG′ING (-sûr′jĭng). [L. *resurgere.* See RESURRECTION.] To rise again; to be resurrected.

re·sur′gence (rē·sûr′jĕns), *n.* A rising again into life.

re·sur′gent (-jĕnt), *adj.* That rises again from death, torpor, decadence, etc.

res′ur·rect′ (rĕz′ŭ·rĕkt′), *v. t.* [From RESURRECTION.] To restore to life; to reanimate; to bring to view again (that which was forgotten or lost); also, to exhume.

res′ur·rec′tion (-rĕk′shŭn), *n.* [OF., fr. LL. *resurrectio*, fr. *resurgere, resurrectum*, to rise again, fr. *re-* + *surgere* to rise.] **1.** With *the.* **a** [*cap.*] The rising of Christ from the dead. **b** The rising again of all the human dead before the final judgment. **2.** A resumption of vigor; restoration; revival. **3.** *Christian Science.* Spiritualization of thought; a new and higher idea of immortality, or spiritual existence; material belief yielding to spiritual understanding. *Mary Baker Eddy.* — **res′ur·rec′tion·al** (-ăl; -′l), *adj.*

res′ur·rec′tion·ar′y (rĕz′ŭ·rĕk′shŭn·ĕr′ĭ *or, esp. Brit.*, -ẽr·ĭ), *adj.* Of the nature of resurrection; also, of or pert. to resurrectionism.

res′ur·rec′tion·ist (-ĭst), *n.* **1.** One who steals bodies from graves to sell to anatomists; a body snatcher; hence **res′ur·rec′tion·ism** (-ĭz′m). **2.** One who resurrects, revives, etc. **3.** A believer in the resurrection of the body.

re′sur·vey′ (rē′sẽr·vā′), *v. t.* To survey again or anew.

re·sur′vey (rē·sûr′vā), *n.* A second or new survey.

re·sus′ci·tate (rē·sŭs′ĭ·tāt), *v. t.* [L. *resuscitatus*, past part. of *resuscitare.*] To revivify; restore, esp. from apparent death or unconsciousness. — *v. i.* To revive. — **re·sus′ci·ta·ble** (-tȧ·b′l), *adj.* — **re·sus′ci·ta′tive** (-tā′tĭv), *adj.* — **re·sus′ci·ta′tor** (-tā′tẽr), *n.*

re·sus′ci·ta′tion (-tā′shŭn), *n.* Act of resuscitating, or state of being resuscitated; restoration; revival.

ret (rĕt), *v. t.;* RET′TED; RET′TING. [ME. *reten* to soak.] To soak or expose to moisture, as flax, hemp, or timber.

re·ta′ble (rē·tā′b′l), *n.* [F., fr. *rere-table; rere* is AF. for *rear.*] *Eccl.* A raised shelf or ledge above the table of an altar, on which are placed altar lights, flowers, etc.

re′tail (rē′tāl; 2), *n.* [AF., fr. OF. *retail* a cutting, fr. *retaillier* to cut off, diminish, divide into pieces.] The sale of commodities in small quantities or parcels; — opposed to *wholesale.* — (rē′tāl), *adj.* Of, engaged in, or connected with retailing commodities. — (rē′tāl *or, esp. in sense* 2 *& in Brit. use*, rē·tāl′), *v. t.* **1.** To sell in small quantities, as by the single yard, pound, gallon, etc.; to sell directly to the consumer. **2.** To relate in detail or to one person after another. — *v. i.* To sell at retail. — **re′tail·er** (rē′tāl·ẽr; rē·tāl′ẽr), *n.*

re·tain′ (rē·tān′), *v. t.* [OF. *retenir*, fr. L. *retinere*, fr. *re-* + *tenere* to hold, keep.] **1.** To keep in a fixed place or condition; as, lead *retains* heat. **2.** To hold or continue to hold in possession or use. **3.** To employ (a lawyer) by paying a retainer. **4.** To keep in mind or memory. — **Syn.** See KEEP. — **re·tain′a·ble**, *adj.* — **re·tain′ment**, *n.*

re·tained′ ob′ject (rē·tānd′). See OBJECT, *n.*, 4.

re·tain′er (rē·tān′ẽr), *n.* [OF. *retenir*, inf. used as n.] *Law.* **a** The act of a client by which he engages the services of a lawyer or counselor to maintain a cause, or of a professional adviser to obtain advice from him or to secure a prior claim on his services in case of need. **b** The fee paid.

re·tain′er, *n.* **1.** One who retains, maintains, or preserves. **2.** *Hist.* An adherent who gives occasional service and wears his master's livery.

re·tain′ing wall. A wall for sustaining a bank of earth liable to a landslide; also, a revetment.

re·take′ (rē·tāk′), *v. t.* **1.** To take or receive back. **2.** To recapture. **3.** *Motion Pictures.* To photograph again. — (rē′tāk′), *n. Colloq. Motion Pictures.* A second photographing or photograph of a scene. — **re·tak′er** (rē·tāk′ẽr), *n.*

re·tal′i·ate (rē·tăl′ĭ·āt), *v. i.* [L. *retaliatus*, past part. of *retaliare* to retaliate.] To return like for like; to make requital; esp., to return evil for evil. — **re·tal′i·a′tive** (-ā′tĭv; -ȧ·tĭv), *adj.*

re·tal′i·a′tion (-ā′shŭn), *n.* Act of retaliating; requital.

re·tal′i·a·to′ry (rē·tăl′ĭ·ȧ·tō′rĭ *or, esp. Brit.*, -tẽr·ĭ), *adj.* Tending to, involving, or of the nature of retaliation.

re·tard′ (rē·tärd′), *v. t.* [F. or L.; F. *retarder*, fr. L. *retardare, -datum*, fr. *re-* + *tardare* to make slow, fr. *tardus* slow.] To make slow or slower; to delay or impede the progress, course, or event of. — *v. i.* To be delayed. — **Syn.** See DELAY. — **Ant.** Accelerate. — *n.* Delay; retardation. — **re·tard′er**, *n.*

re′tar·da′tion (rē′tär·dā′shŭn), *n.* **1.** The action or an instance of retarding. **2.** The extent to which anything is retarded. **3.** Slowness of development or progress. **4.** *Music.* A suspension which resolves upwards. — **re·tard′a·to′ry** (rē·tär′dȧ·tō′rĭ *or, esp. Brit.*, -tẽr·ĭ), *adj.*

re·tard′ment (rē·tärd′mĕnt), *n.* Retardation.

retch (rĕch *or, esp. Brit.*, rēch), *v. i.* [AS. *hrǣcan* to clear the throat.] To make an effort to vomit; to strain, as in vomiting.

‖**re′te** (rē′tē), *n.; pl.* RETIA (-shĭ·ȧ; -tĭ·ȧ). [L., a net.] *Anat.* A net or network; a plexus.

re·tell′ (rē·tĕl′), *v. t.* To tell again; also, to count again.

re′tem (rē′tĕm), *n.* [Ar. *ratam*, pl.] A juniperlike desert shrub (*Retama raetam*) of Syria and Arabia, with tiny white flowers. It is the juniper of the Old Testament.

re′tene (rē′tēn; rĕt′ēn), *n.* [Gr. *rhētinē* pine resin.] *Chem.* A white crystalline hydrocarbon, $C_{18}H_{18}$, obtained from pine tar, certain fossil resins, etc.

re·ten′tion (rē·tĕn′shŭn), *n.* [OF., fr. L. *retentio.*] **1.** Act of retaining, or state of being retained. **2.** Retaining, or the ability to retain, things in mind; memory.

re·ten′tive (-tĭv), *adj.* Having the power, property, or capacity of retaining; specif., having a good memory; tenacious. — **re·ten′tive·ness**, *n.*

re′ten·tiv′i·ty (rē′tĕn·tĭv′ĭ·tĭ), *n.* The power of retaining; retentive force; specif., *Magnetism*, the capacity for retaining magnetism after the action of the magnetizing force has ceased.

‖**re·te·nue′** (rĕt·nü′), *n.* [F.] Self-restraint; self-control; discretion.

re′te·pore (rē′tē·pōr; 70), *n.* [L. *rete* net + *porus* pore.] *Zool.* Any of a genus (*Retepora*) of bryozoans which form delicate, corallike colonies.

re′ti·a′ri·us (rē′shĭ·ā′rĭ·ŭs; 6), *n.; pl.* -RII (-rĭ·ī). [L., fr. *rete* a net.] *Rom. Antiq.* A gladiator armed with a net and a trident.

re′ti·ar′y (rē′shĭ·ĕr′ĭ *or, esp. Brit.*, -ẽr·ĭ), *adj.* **1.** Of or pertaining to nets or the making of nets; netlike. **2.** Constructing a web to catch prey; — of a spider. **3.** Armed with a net; hence, skillful to entangle.

ret′i·cence (rĕt′ĭ·sĕns; -s′ns), *n.* Also **ret′i·cen·cy** (-sĕn·sĭ). Quality, state, or an instance of being reticent.

ret′i·cent (-sĕnt; -s′nt), *adj.* [L. *reticens*, pres. part. of *reticere* to keep silence, fr. *re-* + *tacere* to be silent.] Inclined to keep silent or uncommunicative. — **Syn.** See SILENT. — **Ant.** Frank. — **ret′i·cent·ly**, *adv.*

ret′i·cle (rĕt′ĭ·k'l), *n.* [See RETICULE.] A system of lines or wires in the focus of the eyepiece of an optical instrument.

re·tic′u·lar (rē·tĭk′ū·lẽr), *adj.* [NL. *reticularis.*] **1.** Reticulated; reticulate. **2.** Like a net in operation or effect; intricate.

re·tic′u·late (-lāt), *adj.* [L. *reticulatus.*] Resembling network; netted; having veins or fibers crossing like a network. — (-lāt), *v. t. & i.* To divide or mark so as to resemble or form network.

re·tic′u·la′tion (-lā′shŭn), *n.* Reticulated, or weblike, formation or appearance; network.

ret′i·cule (rĕt′ĭ·kūl), *n.* [F. *réticule*, fr. L. *reticulum*, dim. of *rete* a net.] **1.** *Optics.* = RETICLE. **2.** A small bag, originally of network, carried by women as a workbag or pocket.

re·tic′u·lum (rē·tĭk′ū·lŭm), *n.; pl.* RETICULA (-lȧ). [L., dim. of *rete* a net.] **1.** *Zool.* The second stomach of ruminants, in which folds of the mucous membrane form hexagonal cells. See RUMINANT, *Illust.* **2.** A netlike structure; a network; specif., *Biol.*, the meshwork of dense protoplasm detectable in most cells. See HYALOPLASM.

re′ti·form (rē′tĭ·fôrm; rĕt′ĭ-), *adj.* [NL. *retiformis.* See RETE; -FORM.] Composed of crossing lines and interstices; reticular; netlike.

ret′i·na (rĕt′ĭ·nȧ), *n.; pl.* RETINAS (-nȧz), RETINAE (-nē). [ML., fr. L. *rete* a net.] *Anat. & Zool.* The sensitive membrane of the eye, which receives the image formed by the lens and is connected with the brain by the optic nerve. See EYE, *Illust.* — **ret′i·nal** (-năl; -n′l), *adj.*

ret′i·nite (-nīt), *n.* [Gr. *rhētinē* resin + *-ite.*] *Mineral.* A form of fossil resin.

ret′i·ni′tis (-nī′tĭs), *n.* [NL., fr. *retina* + *-itis.*] *Med.* Inflammation of the retina.

ret′i·nol (rĕt′ĭ·nōl; -nŏl), *n.* [Gr. *rhētinē* resin + *-ol*, 2.] A yellowish oil obtained by the distillation of resin, used as a lubricant, as an antiseptic, etc.

ret′i·nos′co·py (-nŏs′kō·pĭ; rĕt′ĭ·nō·skō′pĭ), *n.* [*retina* + *-scopy.*] *Physiol.* Observation of the retina of the eye, as to determine the state of refraction. — **ret′i·no·scop′ic** (-nō·skŏp′ĭk), *adj.*

ret′i·nue (rĕt′ĭ·nū), *n.* [OF. *retenue*, fr. *retenu*, fem. *retenue*, past part. of *retenir* to retain, engage.] The body of retainers who follow a prince or other distinguished person; a train of attendants; suite.

re·tire′ (rē·tīr′), *v. i.* [F. *retirer*, fr. *re-* + *tirer* to draw.] **1.** To withdraw from action or danger; to retreat. **2.** To withdraw for the sake of privacy, seclusion, protection, or the like. **3.** To recede, or appear to do so; as, the shore *retires* in bays. **4.** To withdraw from office, a public station, business, or the like. **5.** To go to bed. — **Syn.** See GO. — *v. t.* **1.** To withdraw (a military force), esp. from before the enemy. **2.** To withdraw from circulation, or from the market; to take up or pay, as bonds. **3.** To designate as no longer qualified for active service, as a naval officer. **4.** *Baseball, Cricket, etc.* To put out (a batsman, side).

re·tired′ (rē·tīrd′), *adj.* **a** Secluded; solitary; sequestered. **b** Withdrawn from active duty or business. **c** Received by, or due to, a person who has retired.

re·tire′ment (rē·tīr′mĕnt), *n.* **1.** A retiring, or state of being retired: **a** Retreat, as of an army. **b** A withdrawing into seclusion. **c** A withdrawing from office, active service, etc. **d** Secluded condition; privacy. **e** Withdrawal from circulation; — said of currency. **2.** A place of seclusion.

re·tir′ing (rē·tīr′ĭng), *adj.* Reserved; shy; not forward.

re·tor′sion (rē·tôr′shŭn). Var. of RETORTION.

re·tort′ (rē·tôrt′), *v. t.* [L. *retortus*, past part. of *retorquere*, fr. *re-* + *torquere* to turn, twist.] **1.** To pay, cast, or hurl back, as an accusation. **2.** To make a like reply to, as to answer in kind. **3.** To answer, as an argument, by a counter argument of a like kind. — *v. i.* To make retort; to return an argument or charge. — *n.* A quick, sharp, witty, cutting, or severe reply, esp. one which turns the first speaker's statement against him. — **Syn.** See ANSWER.

re·tort′, *n.* [F. *retorte*, fr. ML. *retorta*, fem., fr. L. *retortus*, past part. of *retorquere*. So named from its bent shape. See RETORT, *v.*] A vessel in which substances are distilled or decomposed by heat.

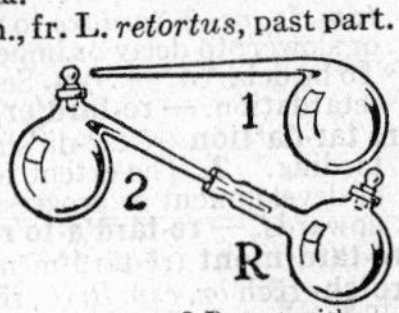

1 Retort; 2 Retort with Receiver (*R*).

re·tor′tion (rē·tôr′shŭn), *n.* **1.** Act of retorting. **2.** *Law.* Retaliation; — used chiefly in international law of treatment by one state of subjects of another state in the same way that state has treated the first state's subjects.

re·touch′ (rē·tŭch′), *v. t.* **1.** To touch again, or rework, in order to improve, as a picture or essay. **2.** *Photog.* To change, as a negative, by handwork, to remove unnatural effects of detail. — *n.* A retouching; a retouched detail. — **re·touch′er** (-ẽr), *n.*

re–trace′, re·trace′ (rē·trās′), *v. t.* [*re-* + *trace.*] To trace over again, as a drawing.

re·trace′ (rē·trās′), *v. t.* [F. *retracer.*] To trace the origin or early history of, by tracking its previous steps; to go over again with the eyes, or in memory; to go back upon (one's steps, etc.); to go over again in a reverse direction; as, to *retrace* one's way. — **re·trace′a·ble**, *adj.*

re·tract′ (rē·trăkt′), *v. t. & i.* [F. *rétracter*, fr. L. *retractare, -tatum*, to handle again, fr. *retrahere*. See RETREAT.] **1.** To draw back or in, as claws. **2.** To withdraw (an accusation or promise); to recall; recant; disavow. — **Syn.** See RECEDE: ABJURE. — **re·tract′a·ble**, *adj.* — **re′trac·ta′tion** (rē′trăk·tā′shŭn), *n.*

re·trac′tile (rē·trăk′tĭl; 56), *adj.* Capable of being drawn back or in. — **re′trac·til′i·ty** (rē′trăk·tĭl′ĭ·tĭ), *n.*

re·trac′tion (-shŭn), *n.* **1.** Act of withdrawing a declaration, accusation, promise, etc.; recantation; revocation. **2.** Act of retracting, or drawing back or in; state of being retracted.

re·trac′tive (-tĭv), *adj.* Serving to retract; that retracts.

re·trac′tor (-tẽr), *n.* [NL.] One who or that which retracts; specif., *Surg.*, an instrument to hold apart the edges of a wound during an operation.

re′tral (rē′trăl), *adj.* [L. *retro* backward + *-al.*] Situated at or toward the back; posterior.

re′trans·fer′ (rē′trăns·fûr′; rē·trăns′fûr), *v. t.* To transfer again.

re–tread′ (rē·trĕd′), *v. t. & i.* To tread again or back.

re·tread′ (rē·trĕd′), *v. t.;* RE·TREAD′ED; RE·TREAD′ING. To cement, mold, and vulcanize an entire new tread of camelback upon the bare cord fabric of (a worn pneumatic tire) after the buffing off of the remains of the old tread; — disting. from *recap.* — (rē′trĕd′), *n.* A retreaded tire.

re·treat′ (rē·trēt′), *n.* [OF. *retret, retrait, retraite*, fr. *retraire* to withdraw, fr. L. *retrahere*, fr. *re-* + *trahere* to draw.] **1.** Act of retiring, or withdrawing, as from what is difficult, dangerous, or disagreeable. **2.** A place of seclusion, privacy, safety, or resort; a refuge; asylum; hiding place; den. **3.** An asylum for insane persons, inebriates, etc. **4.** *Aeronautics.* The extent to which a plane, wing tip, or the like retreats. **5.** *Mil.* **a** The withdrawal, esp. when forced, of troops from the presence of an enemy, or from an advanced position; also, a signal for retreating. **b** A signal given in the army, by drum, trumpet, or the like, following evening roll call or parade and immediately followed by the sunset gun. — *v. i.* **1.** To make a retreat; to withdraw. **2.** *Aeronautics.* To slope backward; — of a plane, wing tip, etc. — **Syn.** See RECEDE. — *v. t.* To draw or lead back; *Chess*, to move (a piece) back.

re·trench′ (rē·trĕnch′), *v. t.* [MF. *retrencher*. See RE-; TRENCH, *v.*] **1.** To cut down; to lessen; reduce; curtail, as expenses. **2.** To cut off; to pare away; to remove. — *v. i.* To make retrenchments; specif., to economize. — **Syn.** See SHORTEN.

re·trench′ment (-mĕnt), *n.* **1.** Act or process of retrenching; curtailment; excision; specif., cutting down of expenses. **2.** *Fort.* A defensive work within another, usually a simple traverse or parapet and ditch.

re·tri′al (rē·trī′ăl), *n.* A second trial or test.

ret′ri·bu′tion (rĕt′rĭ·bū′shŭn), *n.* [OF., fr. L. *retributio.*] **1.** *Now Rare.* Recompense; return. **2.** That given or exacted in recompense; specif., punishment; esp., condign punishment in the hereafter.

re·trib′u·tive (rē·trĭb′ū·tĭv), **re·trib′u·to′ry** (-tō′rĭ *or, esp. Brit.*, -tẽr·ĭ), *adj.* Of, of the nature of, or involving retribution.

re·triev′al (rē·trēv′ăl; -′l), *n.* Act of retrieving; also, possibility of being retrieved or of recovering.

re·trieve′ (rē·trēv′), *v. t.* [For older *retreve*, fr. OF. *retrover* to find again, recover (3d sing. pres. *il retrueve*), fr. *re-* + *trover* to find.] **1.** *Hunting.* To discover and bring in (killed or wounded game). **2.** To recover, as by study or an effort of memory. **3.** To recover or regain; as, to *retrieve* freedom. **4.** To restore or revive, as one's character. **5.** To remedy the evil consequences of; repair, as a loss. — *v. i. Hunting.* To retrieve game. — *n.* **1.** Retrieval; possibility of recovery. **2.** Act of retrieving. — **re·triev′a·ble**, *adj.*

re·triev′er (-trēv′ẽr), *n.* **1.** Any dog used for retrieving; specif., one of a breed having a shapely head, straight forelegs, and strong hind quarters. **2.** One who retrieves.

ret′ro- (rĕt′rō- *or, esp. in physiological terms*, rē′trō-). [L., fr. *retro*, adv., backward, back, orig. compar. fr. *re-.*] A prefix signifying: **a** *Backward, back*, as in **ret′ro·act′**, to act backward, in return, or in opposition. **b** *Situated behind*, as in:

retrobuccal **retrofrontal** **retrorenal**

ret′ro·ac′tion (rĕt′rō·ăk′shŭn; rē′trō-), *n.* **1.** Retroactive operation, as of a law. **2.** A return, or reciprocal, action.

ret′ro·ac′tive (-ăk′tĭv), *adj.* Having relation to, or efficacy in, a prior time; specif., extending in effect to acts done prior to enactment, promulgation, or imposition; as, a *retroactive* law, tax. — **ret′ro·ac′tive·ly**, *adv.* — **ret′ro·ac·tiv′i·ty** (-ăk·tĭv′ĭ·tĭ), *n.*

ret′ro·cede′ (rĕt′rō·sēd′; rē′trō-), *v. i.* [L. *retrocedere*, fr. *retro* back + *cedere* to go.] To go back; to recede. — **ret′ro·ces′sion** (-sĕsh′ŭn), *n.*

re′tro·cede′ (rē′trō·sēd′; rĕt′rō-), *v. t.* [F. *rétrocéder.*] To cede or grant back. — **ret′ro·ces′sion** (rĕt′rō·sĕsh′ŭn; rē′trō-), *n.*

re′tro·choir (rē′trō·kwīr; rĕt′rō-), *n.* [*retro-* + *choir.*] *Arch.* The space left in a church behind the high altar or choir enclosure, sometimes used as a chapel.

ret′ro·flex (rĕt′rō·flĕks; rē′trō-), *v. t. & i.* [*retro-* + L. *flexus*, past part. of *flectere* to bend, turn.] To bend or turn abruptly backward; specif.: *Phonet.* **a** To raise and bend back the tip of (the tongue). **b** To produce (a sound) with the tongue in this position; as, a *retroflexed* r. — *adj.* Retroflexed.

ret′ro·flex′ion (rĕt′rō·flĕk′shŭn), *n.* Also **ret′ro·flec′tion.** **1.** Act of retroflexing, or state of being retroflexed. **2.** *Med.* The bending back of an organ upon itself, as of the uterus.

ret′ro·gra·da′tion (rĕt′rō·grā·dā′shŭn; rē′trō-), *n.* Act of retrograding, or state of being retrograde.

ret′ro·grade (rĕt′rō·grād; rē′trō-), *adj.* [L. *retrogradus*, fr. *retrogradi, -gressus*, to retrograde, fr. *retro-* + *gradi* to step.] **1.** *Astron.* Having a direction contrary to that of the general planetary course; directed from east to west; — of apparent or real motion of a celestial body; also, exhibiting such motion. **2.** Going, or inclined to go, from a better to a worse state; declining. **3.** Directed backward, or having a backward direction, motion, or tendency; as, a *retrograde* motion. **4.** Inverse; inverted. **5.** *Obs.* Opposed; contrary. *Shak.* **6.** *Biol.* Characterized by retrogression. — *v. i.* **1.** To go, move, or appear to move, backward; to recede. **2.** To decline from a better to a worse condition; to degenerate. — **Syn.** See RECEDE. — *v. t. Now Rare.* To turn back; to reverse.

ret′ro·gress (rĕt′rō·grĕs; rē′trō-; 2), *v. i.* [See RETROGRADE.] To move backwards; to revert to an earlier state or condition. — **Ant.** Progress.

ret′ro·gres′sion (-grĕsh′ŭn), *n.* Act or process of retrograding; specif.: **a** *Astron.* Retrogradation. **b** *Biol.* A passing from a higher to a lower state or type of organization or structure, in the course of the development of an animal.

ret′ro·gres′sive (rĕt′rō·grĕs′ĭv; rē′trō-), *adj.* Retrograding or tending to retrograde; moving or directed backward; going from a better to a worse state; specif., *Biol.*, exhibiting retrogression. — **ret′ro·gres′sive·ly**, *adv.*

re·trorse′ (rē·trôrs′), *adj.* [L. *retrorsus, retroversus*, fr. *retro* back + *vertere, versum*, to turn.] *Biol.* Bent backward or downward; postrorse; — opposed to *antrorse.* — **re·trorse′ly**, *adv.*

ret′ro·spect (rĕt′rō·spĕkt; rē′trō-), *v. i.* [L. *retrospicere*, fr. *retro* back + *specere, spectum*, to look.] **1.** To practice retrospection. **2.** *Now Rare.* To look or refer back. — *v. t.* To go back over in thought. — *n.* A looking back on things past; a review of the past.

ret′ro·spec′tion (-spĕk′shŭn), *n.* **1.** *Now Rare.* A looking back; reference to the past. **2.** Act, power, or mood of recollecting the past; also, a review of past events.

ret′ro·spec′tive (-tĭv), *adj.* **1.** Directed to the past; contemplative of or relative to things past. **2.** Retroactive. **3.** Characterized by or given to retrospection. — **ret′ro·spec′tive·ly**, *adv.*

ret′rous·sé′ (rĕt′rōō·sā′; *Brit. usually* rē·trōō′sā; *F.* rē·trōō′sā′), *adj.* [F., past part. of *retrousser* to turn up.] Turned up; — of the nose. Cf. PUG NOSE.

ret′ro·ver′sion (rĕt′rō·vûr′shŭn; rē′trō-), *n.* [*retro-* + L. *vertere, versum*, to turn.] **1.** A turning, bending, or looking back. **2.** State of being turned backward; displacement backwards; as, *retroversion* of the uterus.

re·try′ (rē·trī′), *v. t.* To try again.

re·turn′ (rē·tûrn′), *v. i.* [OF. *retourner*. See RE-; TURN.] **1.** To go or come back again to a place, person, or condition. **2.** To revert in thought, narration, argument, or practice. **3.** To speak in answer; to reply. — *v. t.* **1.** To render (usually an official account) to a superior; to report officially by a list or statement, as a list of killed or wounded; hence, to elect to an administrative body. **2.** To bring back to a tribunal or office, with a certificate of what has been done; to make return of, as a writ. **3.** To bring, carry, put, or send, back, as a borrowed book. **4.** To give in requital or recompense; to repay; reciprocate. **5.** To produce in return; to yield. **6.** To give back; to send or say in reply or response, as an answer, thanks. **7.** To cause to continue at an angle, chiefly at a right angle, as a wall. **8.** *Card Playing.* To lead in response to the lead of one's partner; as, in ***return a lead***, to lead a suit already led by another player. **9.** *Games.* To play back (the ball) to the one who delivered it. **10.** *Mil.* To replace (a weapon) in its receptacle.

Syn. **Return, revert, recur, recrudesce** mean to go or come back. **Return** may imply a going back to the starting point or a coming back from the place or condition where it belongs, esp. in turn; **revert**, a going back to a former state, to an original owner, to a previous decision, or the like; **recur**, a return of something that has previously happened, been experienced, or the like; **recrudesce**, a return to life or activity, as of something suppressed, kept under control, or the like.

— *n.* **1.** Act of returning to or from a place or condition; as, the *return* of one long absent; the *return* of health. **2.** Act of returning something or sending or bringing it back to the same place or condition; also, that which is so returned; specif., restitution; repayment; requital; a retort. **3.** The value of, or profit from, goods which come back in exchange for goods sent out as a mercantile venture; hence, the profit on, or advantage from, labor, an investment, etc.; often, in *pl.*, proceeds. **4.** Recurrence, as of an illness or anniversary. **5.** A bend or turn, as in a rod, stream, or gallery; a portion between two bends. **6.** An account, or formal report, of an action performed, and the like; as, election *returns.* **7.** A person or thing sent back; — usually *pl.* **8.** *Arch.* The continuation, most often at a right angle, of the face of a building, or any member, as a colonnade, molding, or mold. **9.** *Art.* The carrying of a molding or group of moldings at an angle, usually a right angle, as in a picture frame. **10.** *Card Playing.* A lead answering to a previous lead of one's partner. **11.** *Cricket, Tennis, etc.* Act of returning the ball; also, a ball returned. **12.** *Econ.* Specif., the rate of yield of product in any given process of production per unit of cost, esp. in an industrial process. **13.** *Law.* **a** The rendering back or delivery of a writ, precept, or execution, to the proper officer or court. **b** The certificate of an officer, precept, etc., endorsed on the document. **c** The sending back of a commission with the certificate of the commissioners.

— *adj.* **1.** Having or formed by a return, or change of direction; also, doubled upon itself. **2.** Returning or returned; recurring. **3.** Played, delivered, or given, in return. **4.** Used or taken in returning; as, a *return* cargo, journey; also, round-trip. **5.** That returns or permits return; as, a *return* current.

re·turn'a·ble (rḗ-tûr'nȧ-b'l), *adj.* **1.** Legally required to be returned, delivered, or rendered; as, a writ *returnable* at a certain date. **2.** That must be or may be returned; to be returned.

return ticket. A ticket good for a return journey; also, a round-trip ticket.

re·tuse' (rḗ-tūs'), *adj.* [L. *retusus*, past part. of *retundere* to beat back, blunt.] *Bot.* Having the apex rounded or obtuse, with a slight notch, as a leaf.

re·type' (rḗ-tīp'), *v. t.* To type over again.

Reu'ben (rōō'bĕn), *n.* [Heb. *Rĕ'ūben.*] *Bib.* See JACOB.

re·un'ion (rḗ-ūn'yŭn), *n.* **1.** Act of reuniting, or state of being reunited. **2.** A reuniting of persons after separation.

re·un'ion·ist (-ĭst), *n.* An advocate of reunion. — **re·un'ion·ism** (-ĭz'm), *n.* — **re·un'ion·is'tic** (-ĭs'tĭk), *adj.*

re'u·nite' (rḗ'ū-nīt'), *v. t. & i.* [ML. *reunire.*] To unite again; to join after separation.

rev (rĕv), *n.* *Colloq.* Short for REVOLUTION (of a motor).

rev, *v. t. & i.;* REVVED (rĕvd); REV'VING (rĕv'ĭng). *Aviation Slang.* To step (*up* or *down*) the number of revolutions per minute of (a motor).

re·val'u·ate (rḗ-văl'ū-āt), *v. t.* To valuate again; to set a different valuation upon. — **re·val·u·a'tion** (rḗ'văl-ū-ā'shŭn), *n.*

re·val'ue (rḗ-văl'ū), *v. t.; see* VALUE. To value again or anew.

re·vamp' (rḗ-vămp'), *v. t.* To vamp again or anew; also, *Colloq.*, to give a new form to while using the old materials.

re·veal' (rḗ-vēl'), *v. t.* [OF. *reveler*, fr. L. *revelare, -latum*, to unveil, reveal, fr. *re-* + *velare* to veil, fr. *velum* a veil.] **1.** To communicate or impart by supernatural means or agency. **2.** To divulge (something secret or hidden); to disclose. **3.** To open up to view; as, a painting *reveals* the painter. — **re·veal'a·ble,** *adj.* — **re·veal'er,** *n.*

Syn. Reveal, discover, disclose, divulge, tell, betray mean to make known that which has been or should be concealed. Reveal implies an unveiling, as of something not clear to human vision or beyond one's knowledge; discover, somewhat archaic, an uncovering of something concealed from view; disclose, sometimes a discovering, but more often the making known, of what has been kept secret; divulge, a disclosure that is not quite proper; tell, an imparting of that which is unknown or should be kept secret; betray, a divulging that represents a breach of faith or an unconscious disclosure.

— *n. Arch.* The side of an opening for a window, doorway, or the like, between the frame and the outer surface of the wall; also, the jamb.

re·veal'ment (-mĕnt), *n.* Act of revealing; disclosure.

rev·eil'le (rĕv'ĕ·lĭ; *now rare,* rḗ·văl'yĭ; *Brit.* rḗ·vĕl'ĭ, -văl'ĭ), *n.* [F. *réveillez*-vous, imper. of *se réveiller* to get awake, fr. *réveiller* to awaken, arouse.] *Mil. & Nav.* A signal, usually sounded by bugle, fife, or drum, at about sunrise, summoning soldiers or sailors to the day's duties.

rev'el (rĕv'ĕl; -'l), *v. i.;* REV'ELED (-ĕld; -'ld) *or* REV'ELLED; REV'EL·ING *or* REV'EL·LING. [OF. *reveler* to revolt, rebel, make merry, fr. L. *rebellare.* See REBEL.] **1.** To be festive in a riotous or noisy manner. **2.** To take great or intense delight or satisfaction (*in*). — *n.* **1.** Merrymaking; carousing; conviviality. **2.** A merry or noisy celebration of a feast, wedding, etc.

rev'e·la'tion (rĕv'ḗ·lā'shŭn), *n.* **1.** Act of revealing; the disclosing to others of what was before unknown to them; also, that which is revealed; often, a striking disclosure. **2.** *Theol.* A God's disclosure or manifestation of himself or of his will to man, as through some act, oracular words, signs, laws, etc. **b** That which is revealed by God to man. **3.** [*cap.*] In full **The Revelation of Saint John the Divine.** The last of the canonical books of the Bible; the Apocalypse. See BIBLE.

rev·e·la'tion·ist (-ĭst), *n.* **1.** The author of Revelation. **2.** One who accepts the scriptural account of the Creation.

rev'e·la'tor (rĕv'ḗ·lā'tẽr), *n.* A revealer.

rev'el·er, rev'el·ler (rĕv'ĕl·ẽr; rĕv''l-), *n.* One who revels.

rev'el·ry (rĕv'ĕl·rĭ; rĕv''l-), *n.* Reveling; merrymaking.

rev'e·nant (rĕv'ḗ·nănt), *n.* [F., pres. part. of *revenir* to return.] One returned from death or long absence; a ghost.

re·venge' (rḗ-vĕnj'), *v. t.;* RE·VENGED' (-vĕnjd'); RE·VENG'ING (-vĕn'-jĭng). [OF. *revengier, -chier,* fr. *re-* + *vengier, venchier,* to avenge, revenge, fr. L. *vindicare.* See VINDICATE.] **1.** To inflict harm or injury in return for; to exact satisfaction for; to vindicate by avenging. **2.** *Now Rare.* To avenge or seek vengeance for a wrong done (oneself or another). — *v. i. Archaic.* To take vengeance. — **Syn.** See AVENGE. — *n.* **1.** Act or instance of revenging; vindictive retaliation. **2.** The disposition or desire to seek vengeance. **3.** An opportunity of getting satisfaction, as a return match. — **re·veng'er** (-vĕn'-jẽr), *n.*

re·venge'ful (-fōol; -f'l), *adj.* Full of, or prone to, revenge; vindictive. — **re·venge'ful·ly,** *adv.* — **re·venge'ful·ness,** *n.*

rev'e·nue (rĕv'ḗ·nū), *n.* [OF. & F. *revenu,* prop. past part. of *revenir* to return, fr. L. *revenire,* fr. *re-* + *venire* to come.] **1.** Return from investment; income. **2.** An item of income; a source of income. **3.** The annual or periodical yield of taxes, excise, customs, duties, rents, etc., which a nation, state, or municipality collects for public use. **4.** The government department concerned with the collection of the national revenue.

revenue stamp. A stamp provided for raising money, as in prepayment of a tax on documents, proprietary articles, leases, mortgages, etc., and not valid for postage. — called also a *fiscal.*

re·verb' (rḗ·vûrb'), *v. t. & i.* [See REVERBERATE.] To reverberate.

re·ver'ber·ant (rḗ·vûr'bẽr·ănt), *adj.* Reverberating; resonant.

re·ver'ber·ate (-āt), *v. t.* [L. *reverberare* to strike back, repel, fr. *re-* + *verberare* to lash, beat, fr. *verber* a lash, whip.] **1.** To force or drive back; to repel; to echo, as sound; to reflect, as light or heat. **2.**

To subject to the action of a reverberatory furnace. — *v. i.* **1.** To rebound; to recoil; to be reflected or repelled. **2.** To resound; to continue, like a series of echoes. **3.** To be forced to strike (*upon*) or go (*over*), as flames in a furnace.

re·ver'ber·a'tion (rḗ·vûr'bẽr·ā'shŭn), *n.* **1.** Act of reverberating; reflection of light or heat rays, echo of sound, etc.; also, state of being reflected or re-echoed. **2.** That which is reverberated, as the re-echo of a sound, etc.

re·ver'ber·a'tive (-vûr'bẽr·ā'tĭv; -ȧ·tĭv), *adj.* Of the nature of reverberation; tending to reverberate.

re·ver'ber·a'tor (rḗ·vûr'bẽr·ā'tẽr), *n.* Something that produces reverberation; specif., a reflector of sound, heat, light, etc.

re·ver'ber·a·to·ry (-ȧ·tō'rĭ *or, esp. Brit.,* -tẽr·ĭ), *adj.* **1.** Acting by reverberation; forced back or diverted, as flame or heat on the material to be subjected to it. **2.** Designating a furnace (**reverberatory furnace**), kiln, etc., in which the heat is reflected from the roof on the material treated. Cf. BLAST FURNACE, OPEN-HEARTH. — *n.* A reverberatory furnace, kiln, or the like.

re·vere' (rḗ·vēr'), *n.* A revers.

re·vere' *v. t.* [F. or L.; F. *révérer,* fr. L. *revereri,* fr. *re-* + *vereri* to fear.] To regard with reverence; to venerate.

Syn. Revere, reverence, venerate, worship, adore mean to regard with profound respect or honor. Revere further implies tenderness of feeling and deference; reverence, an intrinsic and inviolate claim to respect; venerate, a regarding as holy, sacred, or sacrosanct; worship, homage by word or ceremonial, esp. to a divine being; adore, restricted to deity except in loose use, a personal approach and the performance of individual acts of worship.

rev'er·ence (rĕv'ẽr·ĕns), *n.* [OF. or L.; OF., fr. L. *reverentia.*] **1.** Honor or respect felt or manifested; deference. **2.** Profound respect mingled with love and awe. **3.** A gesture of respect, as an obeisance or curtsy. **4.** The state of being revered; dignity; exalted position. **5.** One called Reverend or entitled to reverence; — chiefly in phrases; as, *your Reverence,* a form of address to a clergyman (*Chiefly Dial. Irish*). — **Syn.** See HONOR. — *v. t.* To regard or treat with reverence. — **Syn.** See REVERE.

rev'er·end (-ĕnd), *adj.* [L. *reverendus,* gerundive of *revereri.*] **1.** Worthy of reverence; revered; — used esp. as a title of respect given to ecclesiastics. **2.** Of, pertaining to, or characteristic of the clergy. — *n. Colloq.* A clergyman.

rev'er·ent (-ĕnt), *adj.* [L. *reverens, -entis,* pres. part. of *revereri.* See REVERE.] Expressing, or characterized by, reverence or veneration; reverential; profoundly respectful. — **rev'er·ent·ly,** *adv.*

rev'er·en'tial (-ĕn'shăl), *adj.* Proceeding from, or expressing, reverence; reverent. — **rev'er·en'tial·ly,** *adv.*

rev'er·ie (rĕv'ẽr·ĭ), **rev'er·y** (-ĭ), *n.; pl.* REVERIES (-ĭz). [F. *rêverie,* fr. *rêver* to dream, rave.] **1.** State of being lost in thought; also, a musing. **2.** A fanciful product of the mind; a theory or notion, usually strange or impractical.

re·vers' (rḗ·vẽr'; rḗ·vâr'), *n. sing. & pl.* [F. See REVERSE.] *Dressmaking, Tailoring, etc.* A part turned or folded back so as to show the inside, or a piece put on in imitation of such a part, as the lapel of a coat.

re·ver'sal (rḗ·vûr'săl; -s'l), *n.* Act or process of reversing. Specif.: **a** *Law.* A change or overthrowing; as, the *reversal* of a judgment. **b** The causing to move or face in an opposite direction, or to appear in an inverted position; as, the *reversal* of objects by a lens.

re·verse' (rḗ·vûrs'), *adj.* [OF. *revers,* fr. L. *reversus,* past part. of *revertere.* See REVERT.] **1.** Turned back; opposite or contrary; as, the *reverse* order; specif., having the back presented to the observer or opponent. **2.** Acting or operating in a manner opposite to contrary. **3.** Effecting reverse movement; as, a *reverse* gear. — *n.* **1.** That which is directly contrary to something else; the opposite. **2.** Act of reversing; complete change; specif., a change from better to worse; misfortune; a check or defeat; as, the enemy met with a *reverse.* **3.** The back; — opposed to *obverse*; as, the *reverse* of a coin, medal, book leaf. **4.** *Mech.* A reversing gear, movement, etc. — *v. t.* **1.** To turn upside down; to invert. **2.** To turn completely about in position or direction. **3.** To revoke; annul; specif., *Law,* to overthrow by a contrary decision; as, to *reverse* a judgment. **4.** To change to the contrary in character or trend; as, to *reverse* a policy. **5.** To cause to go or move in the opposite direction; as, to *reverse* an electric current; specif., *Mach.,* to cause (an engine, machine, etc.) to perform its action in the opposite direction. — *v. i.* **1.** To turn or move in the opposite direction, as in waltzing. **2.** To put an engine, machine, etc., in reverse.

Syn. Reverse, transpose, invert mean to change to the opposite position. Reverse implies a change in side, order, direction, sequence, or the like; transpose, a reversed or exchanged position; invert, a turning upside down or inside out.

re·verse'ly (-lĭ), *adv.* In a reverse manner.

re·vers'er (rḗ·vûr'sẽr), *n.* One who or that which reverses.

re·vers'i·ble (-sĭ·b'l), *adj.* **1.** Capable of being reversed or of reversing; as, a chair with a *reversible* back. **2.** Capable of going through a series of movements, changes, etc., either backward or forward; as, in chemistry, a *reversible* reaction. **3.** Finished on both sides, so that either may be used; — said of fabrics. — **re·vers'i·bil'i·ty** (-bĭl'ĭ·tĭ), *n.* — **re·vers'i·bly,** *adv.*

re·ver'sion (rḗ·vûr'shŭn; -zhŭn), *n.* [OF., fr. L. *reversio* a turning back. See REVERT.] **1.** *Law.* The returning of an estate to the grantor or his heirs, by operation of law, after the grant has terminated. **2.** Right of succession or future possession or enjoyment. **3.** Act or instance of coming back, or returning, as to a former condition or faith. **4.** Act of reversing, or turning the opposite way, or state of being so turned. **5.** *Obs.* That which remains; residue. **6.** *Biol.* A return toward some ancestral type or condition; atavism; also, an organism or individual possessing such a character; a throwback.

re·ver'sion·al (-ăl; -'l), *adj.* Reversionary.

re·ver'sion·ar'y (rḗ·vûr'shŭn·ĕr'ĭ; rḗ·vûr'zhŭn-; *or, esp. Brit.,* -ẽr·ĭ), *adj.* Of, pertaining to, or of the nature of a reversion.

re·ver'sion·er (-ẽr), *n.* *Law.* One who has a reversion; loosely, any one having a vested right to a future estate.

re·vert' (rḗ·vûrt'), *v. i.* [OF. *revertir,* fr. L. *revertere, reversum,* fr. *re-* + *vertere* to turn.] **1.** To come or go back, as to a place, person, condition, or topic. **2.** *Biol.* To undergo reversion. **3.** *Law.* To return to the proprietor or his heirs at the end of a reversion. — **Syn.** See RETURN. — *n.* One who or that which reverts; specif., one who returns to a former faith. — **re·vert'i·ble** (-vûr'tĭ·b'l), *adj.*

rev'er·y (rĕv'ẽr·ĭ). Var. of REVERIE.

re·vest′ (rē·vĕst′), *v. t.* [OF. *revestir* (F. *revêtir*), fr. L. *revestire*, fr. *re-* + *vestire* to clothe, fr. *vestis* a garment.] **1.** To put on (clothing); to clothe (oneself) again. **2.** To vest again; to reinstate; reinvest; as, to *revest* a king in his kingdom. — *v. i.* To take effect or vest again, as a title; to revert to a former owner.

re·vet′ (rē·vĕt′), *v. t.*; -VET′TED; -VET′TING. [F. *revêtir*, prop., to clothe. See REVEST.] *Mil. & Civil Engin.* To face, as an embankment, with a revetment.

re·vet′ment (-mĕnt), *n.* [F. *revêtement.*] *Fort. & Engin.* A facing of stone, concrete, etc., to sustain an embankment; also, a retaining wall.

re·vict′ual (rē·vĭt′'l), *v. t. & i.* To victual again. — **re·vict′ual·ment**, *n.*

re·view′ (rē·vū′; *in senses* 1 & 2, rē-), *v. t.* [*re-* + *view.* See REVIEW, *n.*] **1.** *Obs.* To view or see again. **2.** To examine again; as, the officers viewed and *reviewed* the plans. **3.** To look back on; to take a retrospective view of. **4.** [From REVIEW, *n.*] To go over or examine deliberately; specif., to write a critical examination of; as, to *review* a new novel. **5.** *Law.* To re-examine judicially; as, a higher court may *review* the judgments of a lower one. **6.** *Mil.* To make a formal or official examination of the state of, as troops or the like. — *v. i.* To write reviews; to be a reviewer. — **re·view′a·ble** (-ȧ·b'l), *adj.*
— (rē·vū′), *n.* [MF. *reveue* (F. *revue*), fr. *revoir* to see again, fr. L. *revidere*, fr. *re-* + *videre* to see.] **1.** A general survey. **2.** A reexamination. **3.** A retrospective view, as of one's life. **4.** A critical account of a publication, dramatic production, exhibition, or the like, usually in a periodical; a critique. **5.** A periodical containing critical articles primarily. **6.** *Drama.* A revue. **7.** *Educ.* A repetition of a lesson some time after its first assignment. **8.** *Law.* Judicial re-examination, as of the proceedings of a lower tribunal of any kind by a higher. **9.** *Mil. & Nav.* An inspection, as of troops under arms, by a high officer to ascertain the state of discipline, equipment, etc.

re·view′al (rē·vū′ăl), *n.* Act of reviewing; a review.

re·view′er (-ẽr), *n.* One who reviews or re-examines; specif., a professional critic of books.

re·vile′ (rē·vīl′), *v. t. & i.* [OF. *reviler* to despise, regard as vile.] To subject to abuse, now only in speech; to rail or rail at. — **Syn.** See SCOLD. — **re·vile′ment**, *n.* — **re·vil′er** (-vīl′ẽr), *n.* — **re·vil′ing·ly**, *adv.*

re·vis′al (rē·vīz′ăl; -'l), *n.* Act of revising; revision.

re·vise′ (rē·vīz′), *v. t.* [F. *reviser*, fr. L. *revisere* to look back, revisit.] **1.** To look at or over again in order to correct or improve; as, to *revise* a printer's proof. **2.** To make a new, improved, or up-to-date version of; as, to *revise* the game laws. — **Syn.** See CORRECT. — *n.* **1.** Act of revising; revision. **2.** *Print.* A proof taken after corrections have been made. — **re·vis′er** (-vīz′ẽr), **re·vi′sor** (-vī′zẽr), *n.*

Re·vised′ Stand′ard Ver′sion (rē·vīzd′). See BIBLE.

Revised Version. See BIBLE.

re·vi′sion (rē·vĭzh′ŭn), *n.* **1.** Act of revising. **2.** That made by revising; a revised form or version. — **re·vi′sion·al** (-ăl; -'l), **re·vi′sion·ar′y** (-ĕr′ĭ *or, esp. Brit.*, -ẽr·ĭ), *adj.*

re·vis′it (rē·vĭz′ĭt), *v. t. & i.* To visit again. — *n.* A repeated visit. — **re′vis·it·a′tion** (rē′vĭz·ĭ·tā′shŭn), *n.*

re·vi′so·ry (rē·vī′zō·rĭ), *adj.* Having the power or purpose to revise; making revision; as, *revisory* body, power.

re·vi′tal·ize (rē·vī′tăl·īz), *v. t.* To give new life to. — **re′vi·tal·i·za′tion** (rē′vī·tăl·ĭ·zā′shŭn; -ī·zā′-), *n.*

re·viv′al (rē·vīv′ăl; -'l), *n.* **1.** Act or instance of reviving, or state of being revived; restoration. Specif.: **a** Renewed attention to something, as to literature. **b** Of a play, book, etc., a new presentation or publication. **c** In full, **revival of religion.** Renewed interest in religion, after indifference and decline; a period of religious awakening. **d** Reanimation from languor or depression; — applied to the health, spirits, etc. **e** Renewed flourishing state of something, as of commerce, arts, etc. **2.** An evangelistic meeting or series of meetings. **3.** *Law.* Restoration of force, validity, or effect; as, the *revival* of a debt barred by limitation.

re·viv′al·ism (-ĭz'm), *n.* **1.** The spirit or kind of religion or methods characteristic of religious revivals. **2.** Tendency or desire to revive or restore.

re·viv′al·ist (-ĭst), *n.* One who promotes religious revivals; specif., an evangelist.

Revival of Learning, Letters, *or* **Literature.** The Renaissance in its literary aspect.

re·vive′ (rē·vīv′), *v. i. & t.* [F. *revivre*, fr. L. *revivere*, fr. *re-* + *vivere* to live.] **1.** To restore or return to consciousness or life; to reanimate. **2.** To raise from languor, depression, or discouragement; to render or become active, operative, or flourishing again. **3.** To recover from a state of neglect or disuse; to restore; re-establish. **4.** To renew in the mind or memory; to reawaken; refresh. — **re·viv′er** (-vīv′ẽr), *n.*

re·viv′i·fy (rē·vĭv′ĭ·fī), *v. t. & i.* To cause to revive; to revive. — **re·viv′i·fi·ca′tion** (-fĭ·kā′shŭn), *n.*

rev′i·vis′cence (rĕv′ĭ·vĭs′ĕns; -'ns), **rev′i·vis′cen·cy** (-ĕn·sĭ; -'n·sĭ), *n.* Act of reviving, or state of being revived; restoration to life, vigor, etc. — **rev′i·vis′cent** (-ĕnt; -'nt), *adj.*

rev′o·ca·ble (rĕv′ō·kȧ·b'l), *adj.* [F. *révocable*, fr. L. *revocabilis.* See REVOKE.] Capable of being revoked. — **rev′o·ca·bil′i·ty** (-bĭl′ĭ·tĭ), *n.* — **rev′o·ca·bly**, *adv.*

rev′o·ca′tion (-kā′shŭn), *n.* **1.** *Obs.* Recall. **2.** Act of revoking; annulment; repeal; reversal; as, the *revocation* of an edict or a license. — **rev′o·ca·to′ry** (rĕv′ō·kȧ·tō′rĭ *or, esp. Brit.*, -tẽr·ĭ), *adj.*

re·vok′a·ble (rē·vōk′ȧ·b'l), *adj.* Revocable.

re·voke′ (rē·vōk′), *v. t.* [OF. *revoquer*, fr. L. *revocare*, fr. *re-* + *vocare* to call.] **1.** *Now Rare.* To bring back; to recall. **2.** To annul by recalling or taking back; to repeal; rescind. — *v. i.* *Card Playing.* To renege. — *n.* **a** An annulling. **b** *Card Playing.* A renege. — **re·vok′er** (-vōk′ẽr), *n.*

re·volt′ (rē·vōlt′; -vŏlt′), *n.* [F. *révolte*, fr. *révolter* to revolt, fr. It. *rivoltare*, fr. L. *revolvere.* See REVOLVE.] **1.** A casting off of allegiance; rebellion; insurrection. **2.** A movement or expression of vigorous dissent or refusal to accept. — **Syn.** See REBELLION. — *v. i.* **1.** To renounce allegiance; to rebel. **2.** To be disgusted or grossly offended; — with *at* or *against*; as, his nature *revolts* against such treatment. — *v. t.* To affect with disgust or loathing. — **re·volt′er**, *n.*

re·volt′ing (rē·vōl′tĭng; rē·vŏl′-), *adj.* Disgusting; shocking; offensive; nauseating. — **re·volt′ing·ly**, *adv.*

rev′o·lute (rĕv′ō·lūt), *adj.* [L. *revolutus*, past part. of *revolvere.* See REVOLVE.] Rolled backward or downward, as the margins or tips of some leaves.

rev′o·lu′tion (-lū′shŭn; 114), *n.* **1. a** Strictly, a progressive motion of a body round a center or axis, such that any line of the body remains throughout parallel to its initial position, to which it returns on completing the circuit. **b** Motion of any figure about a center or axis; — more accurately called *rotation.* **2.** Specif.: **a** Of a celestial body, act of going round in an orbit, or the time taken in going round in an orbit; also, apparent movement round the earth. **b** The rotation of a celestial body on its axis. **3.** Completion of a course, as of years, or of any recurring series of events. **4.** A total or radical change; as, a *revolution* in thoughts; specif., the ***industrial revolution***, the change following and resulting from the introduction of power-driven machinery to replace hand labor, occurring in England after 1760. **5.** *Polit. Sci.* A fundamental change in political organization, or in a government or constitution; the overthrow or renunciation of one government or ruler, and the substitution of another, by the governed; as, the ***American Revolution*** *or* ***Revolutionary War*** (1775–83), between the English colonies in America and England; the ***French Revolution*** (1789–99), between the French people on the one hand and the French king and nobles on the other; the ***English Revolution*** (1688), between the English people and King James II; the ***Russian Revolution*** (1917), by Russian soldiers and workers against the tsar and his ministers. — **Syn.** See REBELLION.

rev′o·lu′tion·ar′y (-ĕr′ĭ *or, esp. Brit.*, -ẽr·ĭ), *adj.* Of, pertaining to, characterized by, or of the nature of a revolution, esp. in government. — *n.*; *pl.* -IES (-ĭz). A revolutionist.

Revolutionary calendar. The calendar of the first French republic. It was substituted for the ordinary calendar by the National Convention in 1793, and began with the 22d of September, 1792, the day from which the existence of the republic was reckoned. The year was divided into twelve months of thirty days, with five additional days (*sans-culottides*) for festivals, and six in every fourth year. The names of the months with their English significance, and the approximate dates when they began, are:

Vendémiaire	Vintage	Sept. 22	**Floréal**	Blossom	Apr. 20
Brumaire	Fog	Oct. 22	**Prairial**	Pasture	May 20
Frimaire	Sleet	Nov. 21	**Messidor**	Harvest	June 19
Nivôse	Snow	Dec. 21	**Thermidor,** *or* **Fervidor**	Heat	July 19
Pluviôse	Rain	Jan. 20	**Fructidor**	Fruit	Aug. 18
Ventôse	Wind	Feb. 19			
Germinal	Seed	Mar. 21			

Revolutionary War. See REVOLUTION, 5.

rev′o·lu′tion·ist (rĕv′ō·lū′shŭn·ĭst), *n.* One engaged in a revolution; one who advocates revolutionary doctrines; a revolutionary.

rev′o·lu′tion·ize (rĕv′ō·lū′shŭn·īz), *v. t.* **1.** To overthrow the established government of. **2.** To imbue with revolutionary doctrines. **3.** To change completely.

re·volve′ (rē·vŏlv′), *v. t.* [OF. *revolver*, fr. L. *revolvere*, *-lutum*, fr. *re-* + *volvere* to roll, turn round.] **1.** To turn over and over (in the mind); to reflect upon; to ponder. **2.** To cause to go round in an orbit; also, to rotate. — **Syn.** See CONSIDER. — *v. i.* **1.** To move in a curved path round a center or axis; as, the planets *revolve* round the sun. **2.** To rotate; to perform a revolution. **3. a** To recur; as, the centuries *revolve.* **b** To circulate; as, an idea *revolving* in one's mind. — **re·volv′a·ble**, *adj.*

re·volv′er (rē·vŏl′vẽr), *n.* One that revolves; specif., a firearm (commonly a pistol) with a cylinder of several chambers so arranged as to revolve on an axis, and be discharged in succession by the same lock.

re·volv′ing (rē·vŏl′vĭng), *adj.* That revolves or recurs.

revolving fund. A fund set up for the purpose of carrying on specific activities or attaining certain objectives which, in turn, yield repayments in restoration of the fund, constituting a cycle.

re·vue′ (rē·vū′; *F.* rē·vü′), *n.* [F.] A form of burlesque in which recent events, esp. plays of the past year, are reviewed by imitations of their salient features and chief actors; also, loosely, a medley of songs, dances, etc.

re·vul′sion (rē·vŭl′shŭn), *n.* [F. or L.; F. *révulsion*, fr. L. *revulsio*, fr. *revellere*, *-vulsum*, to pluck away, fr. *re-* + *vellere* to pull.] **1.** *Med.* The diverting of any disease, or blood from a diseased region, from one part of the body to another. **2.** A strong pulling or drawing back or away; withdrawal. **3.** A sudden or strong reaction, reversion, or change. — **re·vul′sive** (-sĭv), *adj.*

re·ward′ (rē·wôrd′), *v. t.* [ONF. *rewarder* (OF. *reguarder*, *regarder*), of Teut. origin.] To make a return, or give a reward, to (a person) or for (a service, etc.); to requite; recompense; repay. — *n.* **1.** That which is given in return for good or evil done or received, as a prize for excellence in studies, money for the return of something lost, etc. **2.** *Law.* Compensation for services; esp., a special sum for extraordinary services. — **re·ward′er**, *n.*

re·wind′ (rē·wīnd′), *v. t. & i.*; RE·WOUND′ (-wound′); RE·WIND′ING. To wind again.

re·wire′ (rē·wīr′), *v. t. & i.* To wire (a house, a cable, an electric machine, or the like) anew.

re·word′ (rē·wûrd′), *v. t.* **1.** To repeat in the same words. **2.** To alter the wording of; to restate in other words.

re·work′ (-wûrk′), *v. t. & i.*; RE·WORKED′ (-wûrkt′); RE·WORK′ING. To work, or work over, again.

re·write′ (rē·rīt′), *v. t. & i.*; see WRITE. **1.** To write again. **2.** *U.S. Journalism.* To put into form for publication (the material supplied by a reporter). The resulting article is called a **re′write′** (rē′rīt′).

rex (rĕks), *n.* [L.] King.

Reyn′ard (rĕn′ẽrd; rā′närd), *n.* [OF. *Renard*, fr. OHG. The spelling *Reynard* is fr. a MD. form.] Proper name of the fox in the medieval beast epic *Reynard the Fox*; also [*not cap.*], a fox.

rhab′do·man′cy (răb′dō·măn′sĭ), *n.* [Gr. *rhabdos* rod, stick + *-mancy.*] Divination by rods or wands. — **rhab′do·man′tist** (-tĭst), *n.*

rha′chis (rā′kĭs). Var. of RACHIS.

Rhad′a·man′thus (răd′ȧ·măn′thŭs), **Rhad′a·man′thys** (-thĭs), *n.* [L. *Rhadamanthus*, fr. Gr. *Rhadamanthos, Rhadamanthys.*] *Gr. Myth.* A son of Zeus and Europa, made, after death, one of the judges in the lower world. — **Rhad′a·man′thine** (-thĭn), *adj.*

Rhae′tic (rē′tĭk), *adj.* *Geol.* Pertaining to or designating the uppermost division of the European Triassic; — in allusion to certain strata of the Rhaetian Alps (see *Gaz.*).

Rhae′to-Ro·man′ic (rē′tō·rō·măn′ĭk), *n.* The Romance dialects spoken in southeastern Switzerland, along the northern limits of Italy, and in Friuli. *Ladin* and *Romansh* have been used for some or all of them. See INDO-EUROPEAN LANGUAGES, *Table.*

-rha′gi·a (-rā′jĭ·*à*), **-rhage** (-rāj). Vars. of -RRHAGIA, -RRHAGE.

rham·na′ceous (răm·nā′shŭs), *adj.* [Gr. *rhamnos* a kind of prickly shrub.] *Bot.* Belonging to or designating the buckthorn family (Rhamnaceae). See BUCKTHORN.

rhap·sod′i·cal (răp·sŏd′ĭ·kăl), *adj.* Also **rhap·sod′ic** (-ĭk). Characteristic of, or of the nature of, a rhapsody; ecstatical. — **rhap·sod′i·cal·ly,** *adv.*

rhap′so·dist (răp′sō·dĭst), *n.* **1.** *Gr. Antiq.* One who recited a rhapsody; esp., a professional reciter of epic poems. **2.** One who writes or speaks rhapsodically.

rhap′so·dize (-dīz), *v. t. & i.* To utter or recite as, or in the manner of, a rhapsody.

rhap′so·dy (-dĭ), *n.; pl.* -DIES (-dĭz). [F. *r(h)apsodie,* fr. L. *rhapsodia,* fr. Gr. *rhapsōidia,* deriv. of *rhaptein* to sew together, unite + *ōidē* song.] **1.** *Gr. Antiq.* A portion of an epic poem, as of the *Iliad,* adapted for recitation; hence, a similar modern literary piece. **2.** A miscellaneous collection, as a literary miscellany. **3.** An ecstatic or highly emotional utterance or literary work. **4.** *Music.* An instrumental composition irregular in form, like an improvisation. — **Syn.** See BOMBAST.

rhat′a·ny (răt′*à*·nĭ), *n.* [Sp. *ratania, rataña,* fr. Quechua *rataña.*] **a** The dried root of either of two American shrubs, ***Peruvian,*** *or* ***knotty, rhatany*** (*Krameria triandra*) and ***Pará,*** *or* ***Brazilian, rhatany*** (*K. argentea*), used as an astringent. **b** Either plant.

Rhe′a (rē′*à*), *n.* [L., fr. Gr. *Rhea.*] **1.** *Gr. Relig.* Daughter of Uranus and Gaea, wife of Cronus, and mother of Zeus, Hades, Poseidon, Hera, Hestia, and Demeter, — hence called "Mother of the Gods." Rhea was identified by the Greeks with Cybele. **2.** [*not cap.*] *Zool.* A bird of a genus (*Rhea*) comprising the American ostriches. They are smaller than the African ostriches, and have three toes instead of two, and the head and neck feathered.

-rhe′a (-rē′*à*). Var. of -RRHEA.

Rhein′gold′ (rīn′gōld′; *G.* -gōlt′), *n.* Also Anglicized **Rhine′gold′** (rīn′gōld′). The title of the first part of Wagner's tetralogy of music dramas, *Der Ring des Nibelungen* (The Ring of the Nibelung). It is a piece of consecrated gold stolen from the Rhine and made into a ring by Alberich. When it is stolen from him, he lays a curse on it, so that it brings disaster to its possessors.

Rhen′ish (rĕn′ĭsh), *adj.* [L. *Rhenus* Rhine.] Of or pert. to the river Rhine or the region near it. — *n.* Rhine wine.

rhe′ni·um (rē′nĭ·ŭm), *n.* [L. *Rhenus* the Rhine + *-ium* as in *sodium.*] *Chem.* A rare metallic element resembling manganese. Symbol, *Re*; at. no., 75; at. wt., 186.31.

rhe′o- (rē′ō-). [Gr. *rheos.*] A combining form meaning *current;* — used chiefly in *Elec.,* as in *rheostat.*

rhe·ol′o·gy (rē·ŏl′ō·jĭ), *n.* [*rheo-* + *-logy.*] The science treating of the deformation and flow of matter. — **rhe·ol′o·gist** (-jĭst), *n.* — **rhe′o·log′ic** (rē′ō·lŏj′ĭk), **rhe′o·log′i·cal** (-ĭ·kăl), *adj.*

rhe·om′e·ter (rē·ŏm′ē·tẽr), *n.* [*rheo-* + *-meter.*] An instrument for measuring or regulating currents, esp. electrical currents or blood currents.

rhe′o·scope (rē′ō·skōp), *n.* [*rheo-* + *-scope.*] *Physics.* A galvanoscope. — **rhe′o·scop′ic** (-skŏp′ĭk), *adj.*

rhe′o·stat (-stăt), *n.* [*rheo-* + *-stat.*] *Elec.* A resistor for regulating a current by means of variable resistances. — **rhe′o·stat′ic** (-stăt′ĭk), *adj.*

rhe′o·tax′is (-tăk′sĭs), *n.* [NL., fr. *rheo-* + Gr. *taxis* an arranging.] *Biol.* A taxis in which mechanical stimulation by a stream of fluid, esp. water, is the directive factor.

rhe′o·trope (rē′ō·trōp), *n.* [*rheo-* + *-trope.*] *Elec.* A commutator for reversing a current.

rhe·ot′ro·pism (rē·ŏt′rō·pĭz′m), *n.* *Biol.* A tropism in which mechanical stimulation by a stream of fluid, esp. water, is the orienting factor.

rhe′sus (rē′sŭs), *n.* [NL., a name given (1797) by Jean B. Audebert (1759–1800), French naturalist, who says that it has no meaning.] An Indian short-tailed monkey (*Macaca mulatta*).

Rhe′sus (rē′sŭs), *n.* [L., fr. Gr. *Rhēsos.*] *Gr. Myth.* A Thracian ally of the Trojans. An oracle declared that Troy would not be taken should the horses of Rhesus drink from the Xanthus. See DIOMEDES.

Rhesus factor. See RH FACTOR.

rhe′tor (rē′tŏr), *n.* [L., fr. Gr. *rhētōr.*] **1.** *Hist.* A master or teacher of rhetoric. **2.** An orator.

rhet′o·ric (rĕt′ō·rĭk), *n.* [OF. *rhetorique,* fr. L. *rhetorica,* fr. Gr. *rhētorikē* (sc. *technē*), deriv. of *rhētōr* orator.] **1.** The art of expressive speech or of discourse, orig. of oratory, now esp. of literary composition; esp., the art of writing well in prose, as disting. from versification and elocution. Abbr. *rhet.* **2.** Hence: **a** Skillful or artistic use of speech. **b** Artificial elegance of language.

rhe·tor′i·cal (rē·tŏr′ĭ·kăl), *adj.* **1.** Of, pert. to, or proceeding from rhetoric; according to rhetoric. **2.** Emphasizing style, often at the expense of thought. — **rhe·tor′i·cal·ly,** *adv.*

rhetorical question. A question not intended to elicit an answer, but inserted for rhetorical effect.

rhet′o·ri′cian (rĕt′ō·rĭsh′ăn), *n.* **1.** A teacher or master of rhetoric. **2.** An eloquent writer or speaker.

rheum (ro͞om; 114), *n.* [OF. *reume* rheum, a cold, fr. L. *rheuma* rheum, fr. Gr. *rheuma.*] *Med.* A watery discharge from the mucous membranes, esp. from the eyes or nose; hence, a cold; catarrh; *Poetic,* tears.

rheu·mat′ic (ro͞o·măt′ĭk), *adj.* [OF. *reumatique,* fr. L., fr. Gr. *rheumatikos* subject to a flux. See RHEUM.] *Med.* Of, pert. to, affected with, or causing rheumatism. — *n.* **1.** One affected with rheumatism. **2.** *pl. Dial.* Rheumatism.

rheumatic fever. *Med.* An acute disease, chiefly in children and young adults and characterized by fever, inflammation and pain in and around the joints, inflammatory involvement of the pericardium and heart valves, etc.

rheu′ma·tism (ro͞o′m*à*·tĭz′m), *n.* [L. *rheumatismus* rheum, fr. Gr. *rheumatismos.* See RHEUM.] *Med.* Any of numerous morbid states characterized by stiffness of the joints or muscles, pain on motion, etc.; also, specif., rheumatic fever or rheumatoid arthritis.

rheu′ma·toid (-toid), *adj.* Also **rheu′ma·toi′dal** (-toi′dăl; -d′l). *Med.* **a** Resembling, or characteristic of, rheumatism. **b** Afflicted with rheumatism.

rheumatoid arthritis. *Med.* A disease or group of diseases characterized by inflammation of the joints and more or less persisting stiffness and deformity.

rheum′y (ro͞om′ĭ), *adj.;* RHEUM′I·ER (-ĭ·ẽr); RHEUM′I·EST. Of or pertaining to rheum; abounding in or causing rheum; affected with rheum.

Rh (är′āch′), *or* **Rhe′sus** (rē′sŭs), **fac′tor.** A substance present in the red blood cells of most persons and certain animals, as the *rhesus* monkey, in which it was first detected (whence the name). Serious effects may be suffered by an infant of an **Rh-pos′i·tive** father (one in whom this substance is present) and an **Rh-neg′a·tive** mother (one in whom this substance is absent), or by an *Rh-negative* person who receives repeated blood transfusions from an *Rh-positive* donor.

rhig′o·lene (rĭg′ō·lēn), *n.* [Gr. *rhigos* cold + L. *oleum* oil.] A very volatile petroleum product intermediate between cymogene and gasoline, used as a local anesthetic.

rhi′nal (rī′năl; -n′l), *adj.* [Gr. *rhis, rhinos,* the nose.] *Anat.* Of or pertaining to the nose; nasal; narial.

Rhine′gold′ (rīn′gōld′). Anglicized form of RHEINGOLD.

rhi′nen·ceph′a·lon (rī′nĕn·sĕf′*à*·lŏn), *n.; pl.* -LA (-l*à*). [NL., fr. Gr. *rhis, rhinos,* nose + *enkephalos* brain.] *Anat. & Zool.* The olfactory part of the brain. — **rhi′nen·ce·phal′ic** (-sē·făl′ĭk), *adj.*

rhine′stone′ (rīn′stōn′), *n.* [Trans. of F. *caillou du Rhin.*] A colorless imitation stone of high luster, made of glass or paste.

Rhine wine (rīn). Wine produced in the valley of the Rhine; also, wine of the same type produced elsewhere. Rhine wines are light, dry, white, and distinguished by their fine bouquet and their acidity.

rhi·ni′tis (rī·nī′tĭs), *n.* [NL., fr. *rhin-* + *-itis.*] *Med.* Inflammation of the nose, esp. of the mucous membrane.

rhi′no (rī′nō), *n.* [Origin obscure.] *Slang.* Money; cash.

rhi′no (rī′nō), *n.; pl.* RHINOS (-nōz). Short for RHINOCEROS.

rhi′no- (rī′nō-), **rhin-.** [Gr. *rhis, rhinos.*] A combining form meaning *nose,* as in *rhinitis.*

rhi·noc′er·os (rī·nŏs′ẽr·ŏs), *n.;* see PLURAL, *Note,* 3. [L., fr. Gr. *rhinokerōs, -ōtos,* fr. *rhis, rhinos,* the nose + *keras* horn.] Any of certain large, powerful, herbivorous, thick-skinned, three-toed mammals (family Rhinocerotidae) having one or two heavy upright horns on the snout.

rhi·nol′o·gy (rī·nŏl′ō·jĭ), *n.* [*rhino-* + *-logy.*] Medical science treating of the nose and its diseases. — **rhi·nol′o·gist** (-jĭst), *n.*

rhi′no·plas′ty (rī′nō·plăs′tĭ), *n.* Plastic surgery of the nose. — **rhi′no·plas′tic** (-plăs′tĭk), *adj.*

rhi′no·scope (rī′nō·skōp), *n.* [*rhino-* + *-scope.*] An instrument for examining the nose, its cavities, passages, etc.

rhi·nos′co·py (rī·nŏs′kō·pĭ), *n.* *Med.* Examination of the nasal cavity, etc., as by means of a speculum.

-rhi′za, -rrhi′za (-rī′z*à*). [NL.] *Bot. & Zool.* A combining form, from Greek *rhiza,* root, used to denote *a rootlike part.*

rhi′zo- (rī′zō-), **rhiz-.** [Gr. *rhiza.*] A combining form meaning *root,* as in **rhi·zoph′a·gous,** root-eating.

rhi·zo′bi·um (rī·zō′bĭ·ŭm), *n.; pl.* -BIA (-*à*). [NL., fr. *rhizo-* + Gr. *bios* life.] *Bacteriol.* Any of a genus (*Rhizobium*) of rod-shaped bacteria living symbiotically in nodules produced upon the roots of leguminous plants, where they fix atmospheric nitrogen.

rhi′zo·car′pous (rī′zō·kär′pŭs), *adj.* [*rhizo-* + *-carpous.*] *Bot.* Having perennial underground parts, but annual stems and foliage; — said of all perennial herbs.

rhi′zo·ceph′a·lous (-sĕf′*à*·lŭs), *adj.* [*rhizo-* + Gr. *kephalē* head.] *Zool.* Belonging to or designating an order (Rhizocephala) of extremely degenerate cirripeds which live as parasites on ordinary crabs and hermit crabs.

rhi′zo·gen′ic (-jĕn′ĭk), **rhi·zog′e·nous** (rī·zŏj′ē·nŭs), *adj.* *Bot.* Producing roots; as, *rhizogenic* tissue.

rhi′zoid (rī′zoid), *n.* [*rhiz-* + *-oid.*] *Bot.* In ferns, mosses, and liverworts, one of the rootlike filaments that attach the gametophyte to the substratum. — **rhi·zoi′dal** (rī·zoi′dăl; -d′l), *adj.*

rhi′zome (rī′zōm), *n.* [NL. *rhizoma,* fr. Gr. *rhizōma* mass of roots (of a tree), stem, race.] *Bot.* Any underground rootlike stem, sending up leafy shoots from the upper surface and emitting roots from the lower side. — **rhi·zom′a·tous** (rī·zŏm′*à*·tŭs; -zō′m*à*·tŭs), *adj.*

Rhizome of Solomon's-seal. *a* Stem of current year; *b, b* Scars from previous years; *c* Bud of following year.

rhi′zo·mor′phous (rī′zō·môr′fŭs), *adj.* [*rhizo-* + *-morphous.*] *Bot.* Having the form of a root; rootlike.

rhi′zo·pod (rī′zō·pŏd), *n.* [*rhizo-* + *-pod.*] *Zool.* Any of a division (Rhizopoda) of protozoans characterized by rootlike pseudopodia. — **rhi·zop′o·dan** (rī·zŏp′ō·dăn), *adj. & n.* — **rhi·zop′o·dous** (-dŭs), *adj.*

rhi′zo·pus (rī′zō·pŭs), *n.* [NL., fr. *rhizo-* + Gr. *pous* foot.] *Bot.* Any of a genus (*Rhizopus*) of fungi, including those of bread mold, those causing certain potato rots, etc.

rhi·zot′o·my (rī·zŏt′ō·mĭ), *n.* [*rhizo-* + *-tomy.*] *Surg.* The operation of cutting the afferent spinal nerve roots, as to relieve pain or spastic paralysis.

Rh-neg′a·tive, *adj.* See RH FACTOR.

rho (rō), *n.* [Gr. *rhō.*] The seventeenth letter (Ρ, ρ) of the Greek alphabet, equivalent to English *r.* See R.

rho′da·mine (rō′d*à*·mēn; -mĭn), *n.* Also **rho′da·min.** [Gr. *rhodon* rose + *amine.*] *Chem.* Any of a group of synthetic red or pink dyes. **rhodamine B** is prepared by fusing an amino derivative of phenol with phthalic anhydride.

Rhode Is′land Red (rōd ī′lănd). One of an American breed of domestic fowls having a long heavy body, smooth yellow or reddish legs, and rich brownish-red plumage.

Rhodes schol′ar·ship (rōdz). Any of a number of scholarships, each tenable for three years, at Oxford University, England, provided by the will of Cecil J. Rhodes, about 100 being open to candidates from certain British dominions and colonies and 96 to candidates from the United States. Hence, **Rhodes scholar.**

rho′dic (rō′dĭk), *adj.* *Chem.* Of, pertaining to, or containing rhodium, esp. in its higher valences.

rho′di·um (rō′dĭ·ŭm), *n.* [NL., fr. Gr. *rhodon* rose; — from the rose-red color of certain of its salts.] *Chem.* A rare element found esp. in platinum ores and separated as a hard grayish-white metal insoluble in acids and very difficult to fuse. Symbol, *Rh*; at. no., 45; at. wt., 102.91.

rho′do·chro′site (rō′dō·krō′sīt), *n.* [Gr. *rhodon* rose + *chrōsis* a coloring.] *Mineral.* A rose-red mineral consisting essentially of manganese carbonate, $MnCO_3$.

rho′do·den′dron (rō′dō·dĕn′drŏn), *n.* [L., fr. Gr. *rhododendron,* fr. *rhodon* rose + *dendron* tree.] *Bot.* Any of a large genus (*Rhododendron*) of mostly evergreen shrubs and trees of the heath family, natives of mountainous regions in the Northern Hemisphere. They have handsome white, pink, or rose-purple flowers. The ***great rhododendron*** (*R. maximum*) of eastern U. S. is the State flower of West Virginia; — called also ***great laurel*** (cf. LAUREL, 2). The ***pink rhododendron*** (*R. macrophyllum*) of the Pacific coast region is the State flower of Washington; — called also *California rosebay.*

rho′do·lite (rō′dō·līt), *n.* [Gr. *rhodon* rose + *-lite.*] *Mineral.* A pink or purple variety of garnet used as a gem.

rho′do·nite (-nīt), *n.* [Gr. *rhodon* the rose.] A pale-red triclinic mineral consisting essentially of a manganese silicate, $MnSiO_3$; manganese spar. It is often used as an ornamental stone, esp. in Russia.

rho·do′ra (rō·dō′rȧ; 70), *n.* [L., a kind of plant.] *Bot.* Any of a genus (*Rhodora*) of shrubs related to the rhododendron and found throughout Canada and New England. It has delicate pink flowers produced before or with the leaves in spring.

rhomb (rŏmb; rŏm), *n.* [F. *rhombe,* fr. L. *rhombus,* fr. Gr. *rhombos* rhomb, spinning top.] **1.** *Geom.* = RHOMBUS. **2.** *Cryst.* A rhombohedron.

rhom′ben·ceph′a·lon (rŏm′bĕn·sĕf′ȧ·lŏn), *n.* [NL.] See HINDBRAIN.

rhom′bic (rŏm′bĭk), **rhom′bi·cal** (-bĭ·kăl), *adj.* **1.** Having the form of a rhombus. **2.** *Cryst.* = ORTHORHOMBIC.

rhom′bo·he′dral (rŏm′bō·hē′drăl), *adj. Geom. & Cryst.* Related to, or presenting the form of, a rhombohedron.

rhom′bo·he′dron (-drŭn), *n.; pl.* -HEDRA (-drȧ). [Gr. *rhombos* rhomb + *hedra* base.] A six-sided prism whose faces are parallelograms.

rhom′boid (rŏm′boid), *n.* [F. *rhomboïde,* fr. L. *rhomboides,* fr. Gr. *rhomboeidēs* rhomboidal.] *Geom.* A parallelogram in which the angles are oblique and the adjacent sides are unequal. — *adj.* Also **rhom·boi′dal** (rŏm·boi′dăl; -d'l). Shaped more or less like a rhombus, or rhomb, or like a rhomboid.

rhom′bus (-bŭs), *n.; pl.* RHOMBUSES (-bŭs·ĕz; -ĭz), RHOMBI (-bī). [L.] *Geom.* **a** An equilateral parallelogram having its angles oblique. **b** A rhombohedron.

rhon′chus (rŏng′kŭs), *n.; pl.* -CHI (-kī). [L., a snoring, a croaking.] *Med.* A whistling or snoring heard on auscultation of the chest when the air channels are partly obstructed. Cf. RÂLE. — **rhon′chi·al** (-kĭ·ăl), **rhon′chal** (-kăl), *adj.*

Rh–pos′i·tive, *adj.* See RH FACTOR.

rhu′barb (ro͞o′bärb; 114), *n.* [OF. *reubarbe,* fr. ML. *rheubarbarum,* lit., barbarian rhubarb, fr. LL., fr. Gr. *rha, rhēon,* fr. *Rha* the Volga River.] **1.** Any of a genus (*Rheum*) of plants of the buckwheat family, including the common garden rhubarb (*R. rhaponticum*) and other species (esp. *R. officinale* and *R. palmatum*) yielding the commercial product. They are tall, coarse herbs with very large leaves and thick, succulent petioles. **2.** *Pharm.* The dried rhizome and roots of any of several herbs of this genus used as a purgative and stomachic bitter. **3.** The acid leafstalks of the common garden species, boiled with sugar and eaten as a sauce, or made into pies. **4.** *Slang.* A heated dispute or controversy; specif., a dispute on the field during a baseball game.

rhumb (rŭm; rŭmb), *n.* [F. *rumb,* Sp. & Pg. *rumbo.*] Any of the points of the mariner's compass.

rhum′ba (rŭm′bȧ). Var. of RUMBA.

rhum′ba·tron (rŭm′bȧ·trŏn), *n.* A pair of copper tanks in the klystron that convert the electron stream into the ultra-high-frequency current; also, the klystron.

rhumb line. A line on the surface of a sphere, which makes equal oblique angles with all meridians; a loxodromic curve. It is the path of a ship sailing always oblique to the meridian in the direction of one and the same point of the compass.

rhyme, rime (rīm), *n.* [ME. *rime, ryme,* verse, poetry, end rhyme, fr. OF. *rime,* perh. fr. L. *rhythmus* rhythm, or perh. of Teut. origin.] **1.** A composition in verse having correspondence of terminal sounds. Hence, rhyming verse or (chiefly *pl.*) poetry. **2.** *Pros.* **a** The correspondence, in two or more words or verses, of terminal sounds. See MASCULINE RHYME, FEMININE RHYME, EYE RHYME. **b** One of two or more words thus corresponding in sound. **c** A rhyming arrangement. — *v. i.* **1.** To make rhymes or verses. **2.** To accord in rhyme; to form a rhyme. — *v. t. Pros.* **a** To put into rhyme. **b** To compose (rhymed verse). **c** To make (words) rhyme; to use as rhyme. — **rhym′er, rim′er** (rīm′ẽr), *n.*

rhyme royal. *Pros.* A stanza of seven verses in iambic pentameter rhyming *a b a b b c c.* It was introduced into English by Chaucer.

rhyme′ster, rime′ster (rīm′stẽr), *n.* A mere rhymer; a maker of poor verse.

rhyn′cho·ce·pha′li·an (rĭng′kō·sē·fā′lĭ·ăn), *adj.* [Gr. *rhynchos* snout + *kephalē* head.] *Zool.* Belonging to or designating an order (Rhynchocephalia) of lizardlike reptiles. — *n.* One of this order of reptiles.

rhy′o·lite (rī′ō·līt), *n.* [Gr. *rhein* to flow + *-lite.*] *Petrog.* A very acid volcanic rock, the lava form of granite.

rhythm (rĭth'm; rĭth'm), *n.* [F. and L.; F. *rhythme,* fr. L. *rhythmus,* fr. Gr. *rhythmos* measured motion, measure, proportion; akin to Gr. *rhein* to flow.] **1.** The flow of cadences in written or spoken language; specif., *Pros.:* **a** The regular rise and fall of sounds (whether in pitch, stress, or speed) in verse when read with attention to quantities of syllables, accents, and pauses. **b** A particular metrical or rhythmical effect as produced by the prevailing kind of foot used; as, dactylic *rhythm.* **c** Rhythmical or metrical form. **2.** *Music.* **a** Regularity or flow of movement which groups by recurrent heavy and light accent. **b** A symmetrical and regularly recurrent grouping of tones according to accent and time value; as, a fandango *rhythm.* **c** A particular typical accent pattern that groups the beats of a composition or movement into measures; as, three-four *rhythm.* **3.** Movement marked by regular recurrence of, or regular alternation in, features, elements, phenomena, etc.; hence, periodicity.

rhyth′mic (rĭth′mĭk; rĭth′-), *adj.* Rhythmical. — *n.* Also **rhyth′mics** (-mĭks); see -ICS. The science or theory of rhythms; rhythmical system.

rhyth′mi·cal (-mĭ·kăl), *adj.* Marked by, or manifesting, rhythm; involving rhythm; as, *rhythmical* prose. — **-mi·cal·ly,** *adv.*

rhyth′mist (-mĭst), *n.* One who is versed in, or has a feeling for, rhythm.

ri′al (rī′ăl), *n.* [OF. *rial, real,* prop., royal.] The monetary unit and a silver coin of Iran, equal to 1⁄100 pahlavi. See MONEY, *Tables.*

Ri·al′to (rĭ·ăl′tō *or, esp. in sense* 1, rē·äl′tō), *n.* **1.** An island and district in Venice, a center of commercial activity; also, a famous marble bridge built about 1590 over the Grand Canal at Venice, connecting this island with the island San Marco. **2.** [*not cap.*] Hence, an exchange or market. **3.** In New York, a district on Broadway frequented by players and playgoers; hence, the theater district of any city.

ri′ant (rī′ănt), *adj.* [F. *riant,* pres. part. of *rire* to laugh, fr. L. *ridere.*] Laughing; gay. — **ri′ant·ly,** *adv.*

ri·a′ta (rē·ä′tȧ), *n.* [Sp. *reata.*] A lariat.

rib (rĭb), *n.* [AS. *rib, ribb.*] **1.** *Anat. & Zool.* One of the series of paired curved bony or partly cartilaginous rods which stiffen the lateral walls of the body of most vertebrates and protect the viscera. See THORAX, *Illust.* In man there are normally twelve pairs, classified into *true* and *false ribs* (which see). Cf. FLOATING RIBS. **2.** *Cookery.* A cut of meat including a rib or ribs. See BEEF, *Illust.* **3.** A wife; — alluding to Eve, as made from Adam's rib (*Genesis* ii. 21 ff.). **4.** Something likened to a rib; as: **a** A bar, rod, or the like, used to support or shape something; as, a *rib* of an umbrella. **b** An arched longitudinal frame of timber in an arch. **c** In Romanesque and Gothic vaulting, one of the arches, meeting and crossing one another, dividing the whole vaulted space into triangles. See GOTHIC, *Illust.* **5.** *Bot.* One of the primary veins, or nerves, of a leaf. **6.** *Shipbuilding.* A transverse member of the frame of a vessel, running from keel to deck. **7.** *Textiles.* One of the ridges marking certain weaves in a fabric. — *v. t.;* RIBBED (rĭbd); RIB′BING. **1.** To furnish, strengthen, or enclose, with ribs; to mark with ridges. **2.** [From colloq. *to poke in the ribs,* with similar meaning.] *Slang.* To make fun of; to tease; "kid."

rib′ald (rĭb′ăld; -'ld), *n.* [OF. *ribaut, ribault* (F. *ribaud*), of Teut. origin.] One who is ribald in speech or writing. — *adj.* Low, coarse, or scurrilous; esp., coarsely offensive in language; as, a *ribald* jest. — **Syn.** See COARSE.

rib′ald·ry (-rĭ), *n.* Ribald language.

rib′and (rĭb′ănd; *formerly* rĭb′ăn), *n.* A ribbon, esp. one used as a decoration.

rib′band′ (rĭb′bănd′; rĭb′ănd; rĭb′ăn), *n.* Also **rib′–band′, rib′and′.** [*rib* + *band.*] *Shipbuilding.* A long, narrow strip of timber or bar, esp. one bent and bolted longitudinally to the frames of a vessel, to hold them in position while the vessel is being built.

rib′bing (rĭb′ĭng), *n.* An arrangement of ribs, as in timberwork, veins in leaves, ridges in cloth, etc.

rib′ble–rab′ble (rĭb′'l·răb′'l), *n.* A rabble; also, loose, ribald, or incoherent chatter.

rib′bon (rĭb′ŭn), *n.* [OF. *riban, ruban.*] **1.** A fillet or narrow woven fabric of varying widths, commonly of silk or velvet, used for trimming, for badges, etc. **2.** A narrow strip or shred; *pl.,* tatters; as, sails torn to *ribbons.* **3.** An inked strip of cloth used in typewriters and stamping presses. **4.** Any of various things suggestive of a ribbon; as: **a** A long, thin, flat strip of metal, as of steel for a spring, a measuring tape, or the like. **b** *pl. Colloq.* Driving reins. **5.** *Mil.* A fillet or bar worn in lieu of a decoration, medal, or badge. **6.** *Shipbuilding.* = RIBBAND. — *v. t.* To adorn with or as with ribbons.

ribbon building. *Brit.* The building of houses and stores along main highways, esp. along roads leading from towns into country districts; hence, **ribbon development.**

rib′bon·fish′ (-fĭsh′), *n.;* see FISH. Any of certain elongate, greatly compressed marine fishes so called from their shape, as the dealfish, oarfish, etc.

ri′bo·fla′vin (rī′bō·flā′vĭn; 2), *n.* [*ribose* + *flavin.*] Vitamin B_2 (see VITAMIN).

ri′bose (rī′bōs), *n.* [From *ribonic,* fr. a G. transposition of *arabinose,* a sugar of the pentose class, + *-ose.*] *Chem.* A pentose, $C_5H_{10}O_5$, the D-variety of which is obtained especially from plant nucleic acids.

rib′wort′ (rĭb′wûrt′), *n., or* **ribwort plantain.** A species of plantain (*Plantago lanceolata*) with long, narrow, ribbed leaves, widely naturalized as a weed.

rice (rīs), *n.* [OF. *ris* (F. *riz*), fr. It. *riso,* through MGr., fr. Gr. *oryzon, oryza,* ult. fr. Skr.] **1.** An annual cereal grass (*Oryza sativa*) widely cultivated in warm climates for its seed, used for human food. **2.** Collectively, the grain or seeds of rice.

rice′bird′ (-bûrd′), *n.* **a** The Java sparrow (see SPARROW, 3 **b**). **b** *Southern U. S.* See BOBOLINK.

rice paper. **1.** A thin paper made from rice straw. **2.** By confusion, a kind of thin, delicate paper, brought from China, — used esp. for painting upon. It is made by cutting the pith of the **rice′–pa′per tree** (*Tetrapanax papyriferum*) into one sheet, which is pressed flat.

ric′er (rīs′ẽr), *n.* A kitchen utensil designed for pressing potatoes and similar cooked vegetables through a perforated container, the resulting product emerging as strings about the diameter of a grain of rice.

rich (rĭch), *adj.* [AS. *rīce* powerful, rich.] **1.** **a** Well supplied with land, goods, or money; wealthy. **b** Abundantly furnished; as, *rich* in paintings. **2.** Sumptuous; costly; valuable; as, *rich* presents. **3.** Abounding in superior, pleasing, or effective qualities; — esp. of articles of food or drink; as, *rich* cream; *rich* foods. **4.** Hence: **a** Of colors, vivid but pleasing. **b** Full and mellow in tone; as, a *rich* voice. **c** High in the combustible component; — said of a mixture of air and gas or vapor. Opposed to LEAN. **d** Pregnant with meaning; as, *rich* allusions or words. **5.** Abundant; bountiful; as, a *rich* crop. **6.** Producing abundantly; fruitful; as, *rich* soil or a *rich* mine. **7.** Abounding in humor; entertaining; hence, laughable; absurd; as, that is a *rich* idea. — **rich′ly,** *adv.* — **rich′ness,** *n.*

Syn. **Rich, wealthy, affluent, opulent** mean having possessions or the like in abundance. **Rich** implies more than enough to gratify normal desires or needs; **wealthy,** the possession of abundant money, income-producing property, or intrinsically valuable things; **affluent,** prosperity and the continuing increase of material possessions; **opulent,** ostentatious wealth, esp. as shown in lavish expenditure. — **Ant.** Poor.

rich′es (rĭch′ĕz; -ĭz), *n. pl.* Orig. a *sing.* [OF. *richece* (F. *richesse*).] That which makes one rich; wealth.

ri′cin (rī′sĭn; rĭs′ĭn), *n.* [L. *ricinus* the castor-oil plant.] *Chem.* A white poisonous protein in the castor bean.

ric′in·o·le′ic (rĭs′ĭ·nō·lē′ĭk; -nō′lē·ĭk), *adj.* [L. *ricinus* the castor-oil plant + *oleum* oil.] *Chem.* Pert. to or designating an oily unsaturated hydroxy acid, $C_{18}H_{34}O_3$.

ric′in·o′le·in (rĭs′ĭ·nō′lē·ĭn), *n.* *Chem.* The glycerol ester of ricinoleic acid forming the chief constituent of castor oil.

rick (rĭk), *n.* [AS. *hrēac.*] A stack or pile, as of grain, straw, or hay, in the open air, often thatched for protection. — *v. t.* To heap up in ricks, as hay, etc.

rick′ets (rĭk′ĕts; -ĭts), *n.* *Med.* A disease of early childhood, characterized by alterations in the bones due to defective deposit of calcium salts at their growing ends. The head becomes square and bulky and often the spinal column and long bones are bent. Rickets responds to treatment with sunlight or vitamin D. Called also *rachitis.*

rick·ett′si·a (rĭk·ĕt′sĭ·ȧ), *n.* [NL., after H. T. *Ricketts* (1871–1910), Am. pathologist.] *Bacteriol.* Any microorganism of a genus (*Rickettsia*) of bacteriumlike organisms, believed by some to be of protozoan nature, found in man in certain diseases, as trench fever and typhus. The organism is held to be transmitted by lice or ticks. — **rick·ett′si·al** (-ăl), *adj.*

rick′et·y (rĭk′ĕ·tĭ; -ĭ·tĭ), *adj.* **1.** Affected with rickets. **2.** Feeble in the joints; tottering; shaky; weak.

rick′ey (rĭk′ĭ), *n.* [Said to be after a Col. *Rickey.*] A drink made by squeezing the juice of a fresh lime into spirituous liquor and carbonated water; — usually preceded by the name of the liquor; as, a gin *rickey;* also, a similar nonalcoholic carbonated drink.

rick′le (rĭk′'l), *n.* *Scot. & Ir.* A small rick; a loose heap.

rick′rack′ (rĭk′răk′), *n.* [Redupl. of *rack* to stretch.] A form of openwork edging or insertion of serpentine braid.

rick′sha, rick′shaw (rĭk′shä; -shô), *n.* *Colloq.* Short for *jinrikisha;* — used by foreigners only.

ric′o·chet′ (rĭk′ō·shā′ *or, esp. Brit.,* -shĕt′), *n.* [F.] A glancing rebound or skipping, as of a projectile along the ground. — *v. i.;* -CHETED′ (-shād′) or -CHET′TED (-shĕt′ĕd; -ĭd); -CHET′ING (-shā′ĭng) or -CHET′TING (-shĕt′ĭng). To skip with glancing rebounds, as a projectile.

ric′rac′ (rĭk′răk′). Var. of RICKRACK.

ric′tus (rĭk′tŭs), *n.* [L., the aperture of the mouth.] **1.** The gape (of the mouth) of a bird. **2.** The mouth opening. — **ric′tal** (-tăl), *adj.*

rid (rĭd), *v. t.;* RID, RID′DED; RID′DING. [ME. *ruden, rydden,* fr. ON. *rythja* to clear (land), empty.] **1.** To free; disencumber; — followed by *of;* as, to *rid* one of his fears. **2.** *Now Rare.* To remove, as from peril; to rescue. **3.** *Now Rare.* To drive away; to make away with.

rid, *archaic past & past part.* of RIDE, *v. i.*

rid′a·ble (rīd′ȧ·b'l), *adj.* Possible or fit to be ridden (as a horse), or ridden over (as a road).

rid′dance (rĭd′ăns), *n.* **1.** Act of ridding or freeing. **2.** Deliverance; escape; as, *riddance* from adversity.

rid′den (rĭd′'n), *past part.* of RIDE.

rid′dle (rĭd′'l), *n.* [AS. *hriddel,* fr. *hrider.*] A sieve with coarse meshes. — *v. t.;* RID′DLED (-'ld); RID′DLING (-lĭng). **1.** To separate, as grain from chaff, with a riddle; to sift. **2.** To perforate so as to make like a riddle; as, a ship *riddled* with shot.

rid′dle, *n.* [For *riddels, s* being misunderstood as the plural ending; ME. *rydel, redels,* fr. AS. *rǣdels, rǣdelse.*] An enigma propounded for solution by guessing, esp. as a form of play; a conundrum. — **Syn.** See MYSTERY. — *v. t.* To explain; solve; unriddle. — *v. i.* To speak in or to propound riddles.

ride (rīd), *v. i.; past* RODE (rōd), *Archaic* RID (rĭd); *past part.* RID′DEN (rĭd′'n), *Archaic* RID, RODE; *pres. part.* RID′ING (rīd′ĭng). [AS. *rīdan.*] **1.** To be carried on the back of an animal, esp. on a horse which one manages; also, to be borne in or on a vehicle. **2.** To be borne as if on a horse or in a vehicle; as: **a** To be borne on or in a fluid; to float. **b** To overlap, as two leads or rules in printed matter, or two colors that should just border on each other. **3.** To be supported in motion; to be borne along; as, he *rode* on the wave of popularity. **4.** To support and carry one; as, a carriage *rides* easy or hard. **5.** *Slang, U. S.* To take its course without interference; as, let it *ride.* — *v. t.* **1.** To sit on and control so as to be carried; hence, to be carried along by, as if controlling. **2.** To perform or proceed over, while or by being mounted on a horse. **3.** To endure or survive, as a storm, a trial, etc.; — often with *out.* **4.** To domineer over; — often used in the past participle in composition. **5.** To mount oneself upon (a person or thing) as on a horse. **6.** *Colloq.* To carry in a position resembling that of one riding a horse. **7.** *Colloq.* To harass by criticism, ridicule, etc.; hence, tyrannize over. — ***ride herd.*** To act as a mounted cattle herdsman skilled in confining a drove to a particular place, and keeping off wild animals. — ***ride the beam.*** See BEAM.

Syn. **Ride, drive** mean to be carried along speedily by something. **Ride** stresses a being borne along in or upon something such as a horse's back, a motorcycle, or the like, and may or may not imply management of the rafters of that which bears one; **drive** stresses propulsion in a given direction and usually implies the action of an agent that controls the movements of a horse or the operation of the mechanism which supplies power.

— *n.* **1.** Act or fact of riding; esp., a journey on the back of an animal, or in or on any vehicle or conveyance. **2.** A road for riding; esp., a forest road.

ri′dent (rī′dĕnt), *adj.* [L. *ridens,* pres. part. of *ridere* to laugh.] *Rare.* Laughing or broadly smiling; riant.

rid′er (rīd′ẽr), *n.* **1.** One who rides; esp., one who rides on horseback. **2.** An addition or amendment to a document, often attached on a separate piece of paper; in legislative practice, an additional clause annexed to a bill while in course of passage. **3.** Something used to overlie or cover another, or to move along on some other piece, as a small adjusting weight on the beam of a balance. — **rid′er·less,** *adj.*

ridge (rĭj), *n.* [ME. *rigge,* fr. AS. *hrycg.*] **1.** The back, now the top of the back, of an animal. **2.** A range of hills or mountains. **3.** A raised line or strip, as of ground thrown up by a plow, or as on the surface of metal, cloth, or bone, etc. **4.** *Arch.* The intersection of two surfaces forming a salient angle. — *v. t. & i.;* RIDGED (rĭjd); RIDG′ING. To form into a ridge or ridges; to furnish or mark with ridges.

ridge′pole′ (-pōl′), *n.* Also **ridge′piece′** (-pēs′), **ridge′plate′** (-plāt′). *Arch.* The highest horizontal timber in a roof, receiving the upper ends of the rafters. See ROOF, *Illust.*

ridg′y (rĭj′ĭ), *adj.* Having ridges; rising in a ridge.

rid′i·cule (rĭd′ĭ·kūl), *n.* [F., adj. & n., fr. L. *ridiculus* ridiculous, neut. *ridiculum* a jest, fr. *ridere* to laugh.] **1.** The act or practice of exciting laughter at a person or thing by means of jesting words, caricature, mocking, etc.; slightly contemptuous banter. **2.** A laughing matter; of persons, a laughingstock; a butt. **3.** *Now Rare.* Quality of being ridiculous; ridiculousness. — *v. t.* To treat with ridicule; to laugh at mockingly or disparagingly. — **rid′i·cul′er** (-kūl′ẽr), *n.*

Syn. **Ridicule, deride, mock, taunt, twit, rally** mean to make an object of laughter. **Ridicule** implies belittling, sometimes maliciously; **deride,** contemptuous and, often, bitter ridicule; **mock,** scornful derision; **taunt,** mockery and reproach; **twit,** a taunting and casting up something to someone; **rally,** a mild taunting as if in fun.

ri·dic′u·lous (rĭ·dĭk′ū·lŭs), *adj.* Fitted to excite ridicule; unworthy of serious consideration; absurd. — **Syn.** See LAUGHABLE. — **ri·dic′u·lous·ly,** *adv.* — **ri·dic′u·lous·ness,** *n.*

rid′ing (rīd′ĭng), *n.* [For *thriding,* the initial *th* having been lost because of preceding *North.* See THIRD.] One of the three administrative jurisdictions (North Riding, West Riding, East Riding) of the county of York, in England. Hence, any similar division of any other county of the United Kingdom or other English-speaking country.

rid′ing, *n.* Act or state of one who rides. — *adj.* **1.** Employed to travel; traveling. **2. a** Used for riding on; as, a *riding* horse. **b** Used for riding or when riding; as, a *riding* whip.

ri·dot′to (rĭ·dŏt′ō), *n.; pl.* -DOTTOS (-ōz). [It., festival, resort, redoubt. See REDOUBT, *n.*] A public entertainment, consisting of music and dancing, often in masquerade, popular in England in the 18th century.

‖**ri·fa′ci·men′to** (rē·fä′chē·mĕn′tō), *n.; pl.* -TI (-tē). [It.] A remaking or recasting; an adaptation, as of a book.

rife (rīf), *adj.* [AS. *rīfe.*] **1.** Prevalent; current. **2.** Abounding; replete; — usually with *with;* as, the air is *rife* with rumors. — **Syn.** See PREVAILING.

Riff (rĭf), *n.* A Berber of Er Rif, hilly coastal region of Morocco. — **Riff′i·an** (rĭf′ĭ·ăn; 58), *n. & adj.*

rif′fle (rĭf′'l), *n.* **1.** *U. S.* A shallow, extending across the bed of a river; also, a rapid. **2.** A mode of shuffling cards. — *v. t. & i.* **1.** To form or flow over a riffle. **2.** To shuffle, as pages of a book or newspaper. **3.** To shuffle (cards) by slightly elevating the corners to let each part of the pack fall card by card into the other part, and then pushing them all together.

rif′fle, *n.* *Gold Mining.* **a** Any of various contrivances (as blocks, bars, etc.) laid on the bottom of a sluice or launder to make a series of grooves or interstices to catch and retain a mineral, as gold; also, sometimes, a groove or interstice so formed. **b** A bar or cleat in a riffle (as above), or in a cradle or similar gold-washing apparatus.

riff′raff′ (rĭf′răf′), *n.* [ME. *rif and raf* every scrap, fr. OF. *rif et raf.*] **a** Refuse; rubbish. **b** The rabble.

ri′fle (rī′f'l), *v. t.;* -FLED (-f'ld); -FLING (-flĭng). [OF. *rifler* to rifle, plunder, of Teut. origin.] **1.** To ransack; pillage. **2.** To steal and carry away, esp. by force.

ri′fle (rī′f'l), *v. t.* [F. *rifler* to file, scrape.] To groove internally with spiral channels; as, to *rifle* a gun barrel. — *n.* [For *rifled gun.*] **1.** A firearm having upon the surface of its bore spiral grooves to impart rotary motion to the projectile, insuring greater accuracy of fire. Cf. GUNLOCK, *Illust.* Specif.: **a** In popular use, such a firearm fired from the shoulder, in distinction from artillery and from pistols. **b** In military use, such a firearm fired from the shoulder and distinguished from a *carbine* by greater length and weight and by provision for a bayonet. **2.** *pl. Mil.* A body of soldiers armed with rifles. **3.** [Norm. F.] A strip of wood covered with emery, used for sharpening scythes.

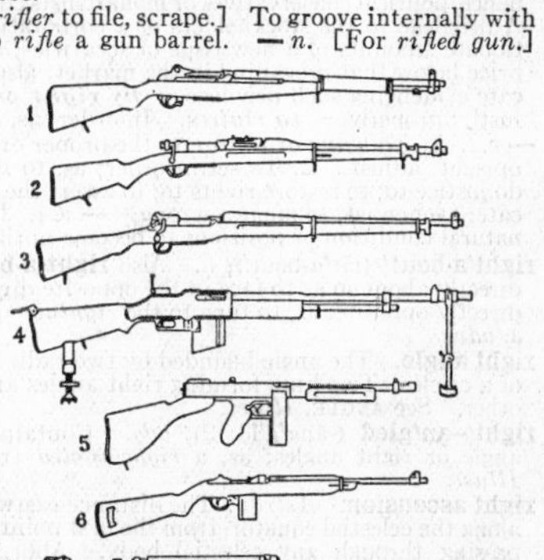

Rifles and Machine Guns. 1 Garand Semiautomatic Rifle; 2 Springfield Rifle; 3 Enfield Rifle; 4 Browning Automatic Rifle (BAR); 5 Thompson Submachine Gun; 6 Carbine; 7 Aircraft Gun.

ri′fle·man (rī′f'l·măn), *n.* **a** *Mil.* A soldier armed with a rifle. **b** One skilled in shooting with a rifle.

rifle pit. *Mil.* A short trench or excavation, with a parapet of earth in front, to shelter one or more skirmishers.

ri′fler (rī′flẽr), *n.* One who rifles; a robber.

ri′fling (rī′flĭng), *n.* **a** Act or process of making grooves in a gun barrel. **b** A system of spiral grooves cut in the surface of the bore of a gun, leaving intervening lands that cut into the projectile when fired or into a metal band secured to it and rotating it about its longer axis.

rift (rĭft), *n.* [Of Scand. origin.] A cleft; fissure. — *v. t. & i.* To cleave; rive; to split.

rift saw. A saw for rifting timber into boards, laths, etc.

rift′-sawed′, *adj.* Quartersawed. See QUARTERSAW, *Illust.*

rig (rĭg), *v. t.;* RIGGED (rĭgd); RIG′GING. [Of Scand. origin.] **1.** To fit the shrouds, stays, braces, etc., of (a vessel) to their respective masts, spars, etc.; to fit shrouds, stays, etc., to (a mast, spar, or the like); by extension, to assemble and adjust the parts of (an aircraft). **2.** To furnish with apparatus or gear; to equip. **3.** To dress; to clothe, esp. oddly. **4.** To arrange or manipulate, esp. fraudulently; as, to *rig* the market. — *n.* **1.** *Naut.* The distinctive shape, number, and arrangement, of sails and masts, which differentiate types of vessels, without reference to the hull; as, schooner *rig.* **2.** *Colloq.* Dress; esp., odd or fanciful clothing. **3.** Anything rigged up or fitted out; an outfit. Specif.: **a** A carriage with its horse or horses. **b** Tackle, apparatus, or machinery.

rig, *n.* [Northern form of RIDGE.] *Chiefly Scot.* A space between furrows in a plowed field.

rig′a·doon′ (rĭg′ȧ·do͞on′), *n.* [F. *rigodon, rigaudon.*] **1.** *Obs.* A lively dance with a jumping step for one couple. **2.** Music for this dance, usually in spirited duple measure.

Ri′gel (rī′jĕl; rī′gĕl), *n.* [Ar. *rijl* foot.] A first-magnitude star in the left foot of the constellation Orion.

rig′ger (rĭg′ẽr), *n.* **1.** One who rigs; also, one who erects scaffolding. **2.** Specif.: **a** One whose occupation is fitting the rigging of ships. **b** *Aeronautics.* One employed in assembling and aligning aircraft. **3.** In building operations, a scaffold to protect passers-by from falling objects.

rig′ging (-ĭng), *n.* **1.** The ropes, chains, etc., that support or raise and lower the masts and spars of a vessel, or serve to set and trim the sails, etc. **2.** Tackle; gear.

rig′ging, *n.* *Scot.* A ridge or roof of a house.

Riggs′′ dis·ease′ (rĭgz). [After J. M. *Riggs* (1810–85), Am. dentist.] *Med.* Pyorrhea alveolaris.

right (rīt), *adj.* [AS. *riht.*] **1.** Straight; not crooked; as, a *right* line. **2.** Upright; erect from a base; having its axis perpendicular to the base; not oblique; as, a *right* pyramid. **3.** Conformed to justice; according with duty; upright; — now commonly of acts or things only. **4.** Fit; suitable; also, most convenient. **5.** *Archaic.* Real; not spurious. **6.** Not mistaken or wrong; correct; as, a *right* solution. **7.** Well in body, mind, spirits, or the like; in good condition; also, normal mentally; sane. **8.** Designed to be placed or worn outward; hence, usually, most ornamental; as, the *right* side of a rug. **9.** Designating, or of or pert. to, that side of the body in man on which the muscular action is usually more skilled than on the other side; — opposed to *left;* hence, naming a side which corresponds to the right side of the body. **10. a** Designating an angle bounded by two lines perpendicular to each other; as, a *right* angle. See ANGLE, *Illust.* **b** Designating a triangle one of whose angles is a right angle; as, a *right* triangle. See TRIANGLE, *Illust.* — **Syn.** See CORRECT. — **Ant.** Wrong.

— *adv.* [AS. *rihte.*] **1.** In a right, or straight, line; directly; hence, immediately; next; as, *right* before me. **2.** According to right; righteously; as, to act *right.* **3.** In a suitable, desired, or fortunate manner; well. **4.** According to fact or truth; correctly. **5.** *Colloq.* Exactly; precisely; as, *right* here and now. **6.** In a great degree; very; extremely. **7.** Toward the right hand; as, some turned *right,* some left.

— *n.* **1.** That which is right or correct. Specif.: **a** Adherence to duty; obedience to lawful authority; freedom from guilt; specif., *Ethics,* that which is warranted by moral approval, the ideal of moral propriety. **b** Just or righteous action or decision; justice; as, to petition as a matter of *right.* **2.** That to which one has a just claim; any power or privilege vested in a person by the law, custom, etc. **3. a** The side, part, or the like, that is on or toward the right side (see RIGHT, *adj.,* 9). **b** The outward, or most finished, surface, as of a fabric. **4.** *Politics.* In some legislative bodies of Europe (as in France), those members collectively who have seats to the right of the presiding officer; also, the conservative or monarchical groups occupying these seats; hence, political conservatives or monarchists collectively. **5.** *Finance.* A privilege to the stockholders of a corporation to purchase proportionate amounts of a new issue of securities, generally at par or at a price below that prevailing in the market; also, the negotiable certificate evidencing such privilege. — ***by right or by rights.*** Rightly; justly; properly. — ***to rights.*** In order; as, to put a room *to rights.*

— *v. t.* **1.** To bring or restore to the proper or natural position; to set upright; adjust. **2.** To set in order; as, to *right* the room. **3.** To do justice to; to restore rights to; to assert the rights of; also, to vindicate; avenge; as, to *right* a wrong. **—** *v. i.* To recover the proper or natural condition or position; to become upright.

right′a·bout′ (rīt′ȧ·bout′), *n.* Also **right′a·bout′–face′.** A turning directly about so as to face in the opposite direction; also, the quarter directly opposite; as, to turn to the *rightabout.* — **right′a·bout′,** *adj. & adv.*

right angle. The angle bounded by two radii that intercept a quarter of a circle. Two lines forming right angles are perpendicular to each other. See ANGLE, *Illust.*

right′–an′gled (-ăng′g'ld; 2), *adj.* Containing or forming a right angle or right angles; as, a *right-angled* triangle. See TRIANGLE, *Illust.*

right ascension. *Astron.* The distance eastward or counterclockwise along the celestial equator, from the first point of Aries to the meridian passing through any celestial body. Abbr. *R.A.* and *Æ.*, also *α* (alpha).

right′eous (rī′chŭs), *adj.* [AS. *rihtwīs,* fr. *riht* right + *wīs* wise, prudent.] Doing, or according with, that which is right; upright; equitable; esp., free from wrong or sin; virtuous. — **Syn.** See MORAL. — **Ant.** Iniquitous. — **right′eous·ly,** *adv.*

right′eous·ness, *n.* **1.** The quality or state of being righteous. **2.** A righteous act or quality. **3.** The state or quality of being rightful or just.

right′er (rīt′ẽr), *n.* One who sets right or redresses wrong.

right′ful (-fo͝ol; -f'l), *adj.* **1.** *Rare.* Righteous. **2.** Equitable; just. **3.** Having a right or just claim according to laws. **4.** Belonging, held, or possessed, by right or by just claim. — **right′ful·ly,** *adv.* — **right′ful·ness,** *n.*

right hand. **1.** The hand on one's right; hence, right side. **2.** A reliable or indispensable person. **3.** The hand of greeting; hence, welcome; friendship.

right′–hand′, *adj.* **1.** Situated on the right. **2** Right-handed. **3.** Chiefly relied on; as, his *right-hand* man.

right′–hand′ed (*see Pron.,* § 2), *adj.* **1.** Using the right hand habitually or more easily than the left. **2.** Of, pert. to, adapted to, or done with the right hand. **3. a** Having the same direction or course as the movement of the hands of a watch viewed from in front; clockwise; — said of a twist, rotary motion, or spiral curve as viewed from a given direction with respect to the axis of rotation. **b** Having a structure involving a clockwise direction; as, a *right-handed* screw.

right–hand rope. Rope laid up and twisted in the same direction as plain-laid rope.

right′ist (rīt′ĭst), *n.* *Politics.* **a** A member of the right. See RIGHT, *n.,* 4. **b** A conservative, royalist, or the like, in politics. — **right′ist,** *adj.*

right line. A straight line.

right′ly, *adv.* [AS. *rihtlīce.*] **1.** Justly; uprightly. **2.** Properly; fitly. **3.** Correctly; exactly.

right′ness, *n.* Quality or state of being right; specif.: **a** Straightness. **b** Rectitude; uprightness. **c** Correctness; accuracy. **d** Suitability; appropriateness.

right of search. *Mar. Law.* The right of a belligerent to stop any merchant vessel of a neutral state on the high seas and make search to determine whether she has become liable to capture by violation of the laws of war, as by carrying contraband; — usually called in British works ***right of visit,*** or more properly, ***right of visit*** (or ***visitation***) ***and search.***

right of way, *or* **right′–of–way′,** *n.; pl.* RIGHTS OF WAY or RIGHTS-OF-WAY. **a** *Law.* A right of passage over another person's ground. **b** The land occupied by a railroad for its tracks, esp. for its main line; also, the strip of land over which a public road is built, or the strip over which an electric power transmission line passes. **c** A precedence in passing accorded to one wagon, car, train, boat, etc., over another, either by custom or by statute.

right triangle. A right-angled triangle. See TRIANGLE, *Illust.*

right whale. Any whalebone whale of the family Balaenidae; — said by whalers to be so called because regarded by whalers as the right kind to pursue, but probably named as the true, or typical, whale. Two chief species can be distinguished: (1) the ***bowhead*** (*Balaena mysticetus*) confined to arctic seas; (2) the ***southern right whale*** (*Eubalaena glacialis*) of temperate seas.

rig′id (rĭj′ĭd), *adj.* [L. *rigidus,* fr. *rigere* to be stiff.] **1.** Not pliant; stiff; unyielding; firm. **2.** Inflexibly fixed or set in opinion, conduct, etc.; not lax or indulgent; strict. **3.** Precise and accurate; as, *rigid* reasoning. **4.** *Aeronautics.* Of an airship, having the gas containers enclosed within compartments of a rigid hull which carries the cabins, gondolas, motors, etc. See AIRSHIP. — **ri·gid′i·ty** (rĭ·jĭd′ĭ·tĭ), *n.* — **rig′id·ly,** *adv.* — **rig′id·ness,** *n.*

Syn. (1) See STIFF.

(2) **Rigid, rigorous, strict, stringent** mean extremely severe or stern. **Rigid** implies uncompromising inflexibility; **rigorous,** imposition of severities or hardships and, usually, their acceptance; **strict,** undeviating conformity to rules, standards, requirements, etc.; **stringent,** impositions which limit, curb, or coerce.

rig′ma·role (rĭg′mȧ·rōl), *n.* [For *ragman roll,* fr. ME. *rageman* document + *roll.*] A succession of confused or foolish statements; rambling talk.

rig′ol (rĭg′ŏl), *n.* [F. *rigole* groove.] A ring; circle. *Shak.*

rig′or, rig′our (rĭg′ẽr), *n.* [OF. *rigour,* fr. L. *rigor,* fr. *rigere* to be stiff.] **1.** Rigidity; stiffness. **2.** Strictness; severity; harshness. **3.** An act or instance of severity, oppression, or cruelty. **4.** (rĭg′ẽr; rī′gẽr, -gôr) [L.] *Med.* A convulsive tremor, as in the chill preceding a fever. **5.** *Physiol.* A state of rigidity in organs, tissues, or cells, during which they are incapable of responding to stimuli. — **Syn.** See DIFFICULTY.

rig′or·ism, rig′our·ism (rĭg′ẽr·ĭz'm), *n.* Rigidity in principle or practice; strictness; austerity, as of life. — **rig′or·ist, rig′our·ist** (-ĭst), *n. & adj.* — **rig′or·is′tic, rig′our·is′tic** (-ĭs′tĭk), *adj.*

‖ri′gor mor′tis (rĭg′ẽr môr′tĭs; rī′gẽr, -gôr). [L., rigor of death.] The rigidity of the muscles that occurs at death.

rig′or·ous (rĭg′ẽr·ŭs), *adj.* **1.** Manifesting, exercising, or favoring, rigor; strict. **2.** Harsh; severe; as, *rigorous* winter. — **Syn.** See RIGID. — **rig′or·ous·ly,** *adv.* — **rig′or·ous·ness,** *n.*

Rigs′dag′ (rĭgz′däg′), *n.* The legislature of Denmark.

rigs′da′ler (rĭgz′dä′lẽr), *n.* [Dan.] = RIX-DOLLAR.

Rig–Ve′da (rĭg·vā′dȧ), *n.* [Skr. *Rgveda.*] See VEDA.

rig·wid′die (rĭg·wĭd′ĭ; rĭg′wĭd′ĭ), **rig·wood′ie** (rĭg·wo͝od′ĭ; rĭg′-wo͝od′ĭ), *adj.* *Scot.* Ropelike; scrawny.

rijks′daal′der (rīks′däl′dẽr; *colloq.* -däl′ẽr), *n.* [D.] = RIX-DOLLAR.

Riks′dag′ (rĭks′däg′), *n.* [Sw.] The Swedish legislature, or parliament.

rile (rīl), *v. t.* [See ROIL.] *Colloq., Chiefly U. S.* To roil; specif.: **a** To make turbid or muddy. **b** To irritate; vex.

ril′ey (rīl′ĭ), *adj.* *Colloq., U. S.* Roiled; specif.: **a** Turbid; muddy. **b** Irritated; also, irritable.

‖ri·lie′vo (rē·lyâ′vō), *n.* [It.] = RELIEF, *n.,* 6.

rill (rĭl), *n.* [LG. *rille,* D. *ril.*] A very small brook.

rill, rille (rĭl), *n.* [G. *rille* a furrow.] *Astron.* One of certain long narrow valleys on the moon.

rill′et (rĭl′ĕt; -ĭt), *n.* A little rill.

rim (rĭm), *n.* [AS. *rima.*] **1.** The border, edge, or margin of a thing, usually of something circular or curving. **2.** The outer part of a wheel, joined to the hub by the spokes; specif., a removable outer band on an automobile wheel, to which the tire is attached. — **Syn.** See BORDER. **—** *v. t.;* RIMMED (rĭmd); RIM′MING. **1.** To furnish with a rim; to border. **2.** To run around the rim of; as, in golf, a putt that *rimmed* the cup.

rime (rīm), *n.* [AS. *hrīm.*] White frost; hoarfrost. **—** *v. t.* To cover with rime.

rime, rim′er, rime′ster. Vars. of RHYME, etc.

ri′mose (rī′mōs; rī·mōs′), *adj.* Also **rim′ous** (rīm′ŭs). [L. *rimosus,* fr. *rima* chink.] Full of fissures or chinks.

rim′y (rīm′ĭ), *adj.* Abounding with rime; frosty.

rin (rĭn), *n. sing. & pl.* [Jap.] A Japanese money of account, equivalent to 1⁄10 of a sen.

rind (rīnd), *n.* [AS., bark, crust of bread.] The bark of a tree, the peel of a fruit, the crust of bread, or the outer layer of anything, as of a side of bacon.

rin′der·pest (rĭn′dẽr·pĕst), *n.* [G., fr. *rind,* pl. *rinder,* cattle + *pest* pest.] *Veter.* An infectious disease of cattle, less often of sheep and goats, marked by diphtheritic inflammation of the mucous membranes, esp. of the intestines.

ring (rĭng), *n.* [AS. *hring.*] **1.** A circlet of metal; now, a small circlet of precious metal to be worn on a finger. **2.** Any circular band of metal, wood, etc., used for holding, hanging, etc.; as, curtain *rings;* a key *ring.* **3.** The rim or border of a disk or wheel. **4.** A cut made into or around the trunk or a limb of a tree. **5.** Any circular line, figure, or object; a circular arrangement of things or persons. **6.** An exclusive combination of persons for a selfish, and often corrupt, purpose, as to control the market. **7.** A racecourse, usually circular; hence, an arena for competition or display. Specif.: **a** The arena of a circus, horse show, etc. **b** An enclosed space in which pugilists contest; hence, prize fighting. **8.** An enclosure devoted to betting at a horse race; hence, those who bet there, esp. the bookmakers. **9.** The field of a contest, esp. a political contest; as, he is in the *ring* for the governorship. **10.** *Bot.* Any one of the rings (***annual rings***) seen in cross sections of the stems of most trees, marking the annual growth of spring and summer wood. **11.** *Chem.* An arrangement of atoms represented in formulas or models as a ring; a closed chain. Cf. BEN-

ZENE RING, OPEN CHAIN. **12.** *Geom.* The plane figure between two concentric circles.
— v. t.; RINGED (rĭngd); RING′ING. **1.** To surround with a ring, or as with a ring; to encircle. **2.** To provide with a ring or with rings. **3.** *Hort. & Forestry.* To girdle; as, to *ring* trees. **4.** In games where rings are tossed at a mark, to throw a ring over (the mark). — *v. i.* **1.** To move in a ring, or rings; specif., *Falconry,* to rise in the air spirally. **2.** To form or take the shape of a ring or rings.

ring (rĭng), *v. i.;* RANG (răng) or RUNG (rŭng); RUNG; RING′ING. [AS. *hringan.*] **1.** To sound resonantly, as a bell. **2.** To be filled with a reverberating sound; also, to have the sensation of being filled with such a sound; as, his ears *ring.* **3.** To ring a bell, as in giving a summons. **4.** To be filled with report or talk; as, the whole town *rings* with his fame. **5.** To have a sound expressive of some quality; as, his words *rang* true. — *v. t.* **1.** To sound, esp. by striking, as a bell. **2.** To make (a sound), as by ringing a bell. **3.** To announce by or as if by ringing; as, to *ring* an alarm. **4.** To repeat often, loudly, or earnestly; as, to *ring* the praises of a deed. — ***ring the changes on.*** To present (the same facts or arguments) in a variety of ways.
— n. 1. A clear resonant sound made by, or as by, vibrating metals. **2.** Any loud sound, esp. one continued or reverberated. **3.** A set of bells. See CHANGE RINGING. **4.** A particular sound or character of utterance in speech or writing expressive of some quality; as, a *ring* of defiance, etc. **5.** The act or an instance of sounding a bell, as of a telephone, etc.; specif., a call on the telephone.

ring′bolt′ (rĭng′bōlt′), *n.* A bolt with a ring through one end.

ring′bone′ (-bōn′), *n. Veter.* Any bony outgrowth on the phalangeal bones of the horse, usually producing lameness.

ring′dove′ (-dŭv′), *n.* **a** A European pigeon (*Columba palumbus*), having on each side of the neck a whitish patch. **b** A dove (*Streptopelia risoria*) of southeastern Europe and much of Asia, allied to the turtledove.

ringed (rĭngd; *poet.* rĭng′ĕd; -ĭd), *adj.* **1.** Encircled with or as with a ring; forming or shaped like a ring; composed of rings. **2.** Wearing a wedding ring; hence, wedded.

rin′gent (rĭn′jĕnt), *adj.* [L. *ringens, -entis,* pres. part. of *ringi* to gape.] Gaping; esp., *Bot.,* having the lips separated like an open mouth; as, a *ringent* corolla.

ring′er (rĭng′ẽr), *n.* **1.** One who or that which rings, as a quoit that lodges so as to surround the peg. **2.** Any person of highest excellence in some particular activity.

ring′er, *n.* **1.** One who or that which rings, as a bell. **2.** *Slang.* **a** One that enters any competition under false representations as to his identity, past performances, etc. **b** Hence, one who strongly resembles another; as, that man is a *ringer* for so-and-so.

ring′lead′er (rĭng′lēd′ẽr; 2), *n.* [From RING a group.] A leader of any body of men or animals, specif. of a body of persons engaged in violation of law, as rioters.

ring′let (rĭng′lĕt; -lĭt), *n.* **1.** A small ring; a small circle. **2.** A curl; esp., a long curl of hair.

ring′mas′ter (-mȧs′tẽr; 9), *n.* One in charge of the performances within the ring, as in a circus.

Ring of the Ni′be·lung (nē′bĕ·lo͝ong). The ring made by the dwarf Alberich from the Rheingold. Its story is the theme of a tetralogy of music dramas (**Ring cycle**) by Richard Wagner, which collectively bear this name.

ring ouzel. A thrush (*Turdus torquatus*) allied to the European blackbird and the American robin. It is black, with a white bar across the breast.

ring′side′ (rĭng′sīd′), *n.* A place just outside a ring, esp. a ring where a contest occurs; hence, a place from which one may have a close view.

ring′ster (rĭng′stẽr), *n. Colloq.* A member of a ring, or clique, esp. of a political ring.

ring′-streaked′ (-strēkt′), *adj. Archaic,* **ring′-straked′** (-strākt′). Marked with circular bands or streaks, as of color.

ring′worm′ (rĭng′wûrm′), *n. Med. & Veter.* Any of several contagious diseases of the skin of man and domestic animals, caused by fungi, and characterized by ring-shaped discolored patches covered with vesicles and scales, and by disorders of the hair.

rink (rĭngk), *n.* [Scot., earlier *renk,* a course, a race, fr. OF. *renc.*] **1.** A smooth extent of ice marked off for curling. **2.** A division of a bowling green large enough for a match. **3.** In curling, quoits, or bowls, the players composing one side. **4.** An enclosed sheet of ice, usually artificial, for skating; a building containing such a rink; hence, also, a covered enclosure for roller skating.

rinse (rĭns), *v. t.* [OF. *rincer,* fr. *reïncier,* deriv. of L. *recens* fresh.] **1.** To wash lightly with water. **2.** To cleanse from the soap used in washing, by agitating in clear water. **3.** To remove (dirt, etc.) by washing lightly or in water only. — *n.* **1.** A wash. **2.** The water used to wash out remaining impurities, soap, etc. **3.** A cosmetic preparation for coloring the hair. — **rins′er** (rĭn′sẽr), *n.*

rins′ing (rĭn′sĭng), *n.* The water that has been used to rinse a vessel; hence, the last dregs; — usually in *pl.*

ri′ot (rī′ŭt), *n.* [OF. *riote* quarrel, dispute, ult. fr. L. *rugire* to roar.] **1.** Wild and loose festivity; revelry. **2.** Disorderly behavior; tumult. **3.** A vivid and confused view, noise, etc.; as, a *riot* of sound or color. **4.** *Law.* The tumultuous disturbance of the public peace by an unlawful assembly of three or more persons in the execution of some private object. — *v. i.* **1.** To indulge in excess of luxury, feasting, or the like; to revel. **2.** To create or engage in a disturbance or tumult. — *v. t.* To spend or pass in riot. — **ri′ot·er** (-ẽr), *n.*

Riot Act. 1. *Eng.* An act (1 Geo. I, st. 2, c. 5, 1715) providing that if any twelve persons are unlawfully assembled to the disturbance of the peace, they may be commanded by proclamation to disperse, and if they disregard such order they shall be guilty of felony. **2.** [*not cap.*] A strong, vigorous reproof or warning; as, he read the *riot act* to his son.

ri′ot·ous (rī′ŭt·ŭs), *adj.* Involving, or engaging in, riot; specif.: **a** Wanton; profligate. **b** Of the nature of a riot (sense 4); tumultuous.

rip (rĭp), *v. t.;* RIPPED (rĭpt); RIP′PING. [Appar. of Scand. or LG. origin.] **1.** To divide or separate the parts of by cutting or tearing. **2.** To take out or away by or as by cutting or tearing. **3.** To saw or split (wood) lengthwise of the grain or fiber. — *v. i.* **1.** To become torn apart or split asunder, esp., in a garment, by cutting or breaking stitches. **2.** *Colloq.* To go ahead or proceed headlong. **3.** *Colloq.* To break forth into vehement, often profane, utterance; — often with *out;* as, he *ripped* out with an oath. — **Syn.** See TEAR. — *n.* A rent made by ripping, esp. by a seam giving way; a tear.

rip, *n. Colloq.* A mean, vicious, or worthless thing or person.

rip, *n.* [Cf. RIPPLE a little wave.] A body of water made rough by the meeting of opposing tides or currents. Hence, **rip current, rip tide.**

rip (rĭp), *n.* [Northern form of *reap* handful of grain.] A small bunch of hay or of grain in the stalk.

ri·par′i·an (rĭ·pâr′ĭ·ăn; rī-), *adj.* [L. *riparius,* fr. *ripa* bank.] Of, pertaining to, or living on the bank of a river, of a lake, or of a tidewater; as, **riparian rights,** the rights of a person owning land containing or bordering on a watercourse or other body of water in or to its banks, bed, or waters.

rip′cord′ (rĭp′kôrd′), *n. Aeronautics.* **a** A cord by which the gasbag of a balloon may be ripped open for a limited distance to release the gas quickly and so cause immediate descent. **b** A cord the pulling of which permits a parachute to open.

ripe (rīp), *adj.* [AS. *rīpe.*] **1.** Ready for reaping or gathering; mature. **2.** Like ripened fruit in ruddiness and plumpness. **3.** Advanced by keeping to the state best for use; mellow; as, *ripe* cheese. **4.** Mature; perfected; consummate. **5.** Maturated; ready to discharge; — said of abscesses, etc. **6.** Ready for action or effect; prepared. **7.** *Slang.* Intoxicated. — **ripe′ly,** *adv.* — **ripe′ness,** *n.*

ripe, *v. t. & i.* [AS. *rȳpan.*] *Scot.* To search; ransack.

rip′en (rīp′ĕn), *v. i. & t.* **1.** To grow or make ripe; to become mature, as grain or fruit. **2.** To come or bring to completeness or to fitness for use, etc. — **rip′en·er** (-ẽr), *n.*

ri·poste′, ri·post′ (rē·pōst′), *n.* [F. *riposte.*] **1.** In fencing, a quick return thrust after a parry. **2.** A quick retort; a repartee. — *v. i.* To make a riposte, either verbally or in fencing; to retort quickly.

rip′per (rĭp′ẽr), *n.* **1.** One who or that which rips. **2.** *Slang.* Any person or thing very remarkable of its kind. **3.** = DOUBLE-RIPPER.

rip′ple (rĭp′'l), *n.* A toothed implement for removing seeds from flax, broomcorn, etc. — **rip′ple,** *v. t.*

rip′ple, *v. i.;* RIP′PLED (rĭp′'ld); RIP′PLING (-lĭng). **1.** To become fretted or ruffled on the surface, as water when agitated or running over rough shallows; as, a field of grain *ripples* in the wind. **2.** To flow in small ripples. **3.** To make a sound as of water running gently over rough shallows; as, her laughter *rippled.* — *v. t.* To fret or ruffle, as the surface of water. — *n.* **1.** The fretting or ruffling of the surface of water; hence, a little curling wave or an undulation. **2.** A sound such as is made by rippling water. — **rip′pler** (rĭp′lẽr), *n.*

rip′plet (rĭp′lĕt; -lĭt), *n.* A small ripple.

rip′pling (rĭp′lĭng), *adj.* That ripples. — **rip′pling·ly,** *adv.*

rip′rap′ (rĭp′răp′), *n. Masonry, U.S.* A foundation or sustaining wall of stones thrown together without order, as in deep water or on a soft bottom; also, stones so used. — *v. t.;* -RAPPED′ (-răpt′); -RAP′PING. *Masonry, U.S.* To form a riprap in or upon; to strengthen with a riprap.

rip′-roar′ing (-rōr′ĭng; 2), *adj.* Also **rip′-roar′i·ous** (-ĭ·ŭs). *Slang.* Noisily exciting; hilarious; as, a *rip-roaring* farce.

rip′saw′ (rĭp′sô′), *n.* [See RIP, *v. t.,* 3.] A saw with coarse teeth, used for cutting wood in the direction of the grain. See SAW, *Illust.*

rip′snort′er (rĭp′snôr′tẽr), *n.* See SNORTER, 2.

Rip′u·ar′i·an (rĭp′ū·âr′ĭ·ăn), *adj.* [ML. *ripuarius.*] Designating a group of Franks who established themselves in the 4th century on the Rhine near Cologne. — *n.* A Ripuarian Frank.

Rip′ van Win′kle (rĭp′ văn wĭng′k'l). The title and hero of a story in Irving's *Sketch Book.* He is a bibulous Dutch settler, put under a spell in the Catskill Mountains. He slept for twenty years, and then returned home to find that his wife was dead and he himself forgotten.

rise (rīz), *v. i.;* ROSE (rōz); RIS′EN (rĭz′'n); RIS′ING (rīz′ĭng). [AS. *rīsan.*] **1.** To move upward, as by walking, climbing, flying, etc. **2.** To emerge above the horizon; as, the sun *rose.* **3.** To ascend from the grave; to come to life. **4.** To reach or attain; to extend upward; as, the Alps *rise* far above the sea. **5.** To reach a higher level; as, the tide was *rising.* **6.** To attain to a better social, official, or financial position; to succeed; also, to do one's best to overcome a difficulty. **7.** To change from a lying, kneeling, or sitting to a higher position, esp. to a standing position. **8.** To get up from bed after sleep; as, he *rose* at six thirty. **9.** To end an official sitting; adjourn; as, the committee *rose.* **10.** To rebel; to take up arms. **11.** To increase, as in volume, price, degree, intensity, violence, loudness, or the like. **12.** To swell or puff up; to become light, as dough. **13. a** To come into being; to originate. **b** To emerge into sight; as, the land *rose* to view. **c** To become perceptible to other senses than sight; as, odor *rises* from the flower. **d** To come to mind; to be suggested; as, to make a picture *rise* in the imagination of an audience. — **Syn.** See SPRING.
— n. 1. Act of rising, or state of being risen; a moving upward. Specif.: **a** Emergence above the horizon. **b** An ascent from the grave. **c** An upward slope. **d** The upward spring of a fish to seize food or bait. **e** Elevation of the voice; upward change of key. **f** The amount or distance of an increase in size, distance upward, etc. **2.** Act of attaining a higher position or rank. **3.** *Slang.* Response to a provocation; a retort. **4.** Increase; advance, as of price, value, fame, and the like; specif., *Brit.,* an increase in wages or salary. **5.** Source; origin; as, the *rise* of a stream.

ris′er (rīz′ẽr), *n.* **1.** One who or that which rises, as in getting up in the morning. **2.** *Arch.* The upright piece of a step, from tread to tread. See STAIR, *Illust.*

ris′i·bil′i·ty (rĭz′ĭ·bĭl′ĭ·tĭ), *n.; pl.* -TIES (-tĭz). **1.** The quality of being able or inclined to laugh. **2.** *pl.* A person's sensibilities to what seems laughable.

ris′i·ble (rĭz′ĭ·b'l), *adj.* [F., fr. LL. *risibilis,* fr. *ridere, risum,* to laugh.] **1.** Disposed to laugh. **2.** Exciting laughter. **3.** Used in, or expressing, laughter; of or pertaining to laughter. — **Syn.** See LAUGHABLE.

ris′ing (rīz′ĭng), *adj.* **1.** Ascending; sloping upward; elevated; advancing. **2.** Increasing in wealth, power, distinction, intensity, etc. **3.** Growing; advancing to adult years; as, the *rising* generation. — *n.* **1.** Act of one who or that which rises (in any sense). **2.** That which rises; specif., a tumor; boil. *Lev.* xiii. 10. — *prep. Dial.* Approaching; nearing; as, he was *rising* sixteen years.

risk (rĭsk), *n.* [F. *risque,* fr. It. *risco, risico.*] **1.** Hazard; peril; exposure to loss or injury. **2.** *Insurance.* **a** The chance of loss or the perils to the subject matter of insurance covered by the contract; also, the degree of probability of such loss. **b** Short for *amount at risk,* that is, the amount which the company may lose. **c** Loosely, a person or thing considered with reference to the risk involved in placing insurance upon him or it. **d** The character of hazard involved in insurance; — usually with a qualifying word; as, war *risk,* fire *risk,* catastrophe *risk.* — *v. t.* **1.** To expose to risk, hazard, or peril; venture. **2.** To incur the risk or danger of.

risk capital. = VENTURE CAPITAL.

risk'y (rĭs'kĭ), *adj.;* RISK'I·ER (-kĭ·ẽr); RISK'I·EST. Attended with risk or danger. — **Syn.** See DANGEROUS.

‖**ri·sor·gi·men'to** (rē·sôr·jē·mān'tō), *n.* [It.] Literally, a revival; specif.: **a** The revival of learning in Italy in the 14th and 15th centuries, as distinguished from the Renaissance in France and northern Europe. **b** The movement for political unity in Italy in the 19th century.

‖**ri·sot'to** (rē·sôt'tō), *n.* [It.] Rice, cooked with meat gravy, and, often, with cheese.

ris·qué' (rĭs·kā'; 2), *adj. masc.;* **ris·quée'** (-kā'), *fem.* [F., past part. of *risquer* to risk.] Hazardous; esp., figuratively, verging upon impropriety or indecency; as, a *risqué* story.

‖**ris'so'lé'** (rē'sô'lā'), *adj.* [F.] Browned by frying in deep fat.

‖**ris'sole'** (rē'sôl'; rĭs'ōl), *n.* [F.] *Cookery.* A roll of rich minced meat or fish, covered with pastry and fried.

ri'tar·dan'do (rē'tär·dăn'dō; *It.* rē·tär·dän'dō), *adj.* [It.] *Music.* Retarding; rallentando; — used as a direction. — *n. Music.* A movement or passage in gradually slackening tempo.

rite (rīt), *n.* [L. *ritus.*] **1. a** A prescribed form of conducting a ceremony, esp. a religious ceremony; a ritual for a religious service, sacrament, or the like. **b** [*often cap.*] Liturgy; esp., one of the historical forms of the Eucharistic service. The rite now used for the Mass in Roman Catholic churches is in Latin and is called ***Roman rite** or **Roman liturgy.*** In the Orthodox Church and in some Uniat churches, the Eucharistic rite is in Greek and is called the ***Greek,** or **Byzantine, rite.*** **2.** A ceremonial act; esp., a religious ceremony; as, to perform the last *rites* of the Church. **3.** *Obs.* Established custom or usage. **4.** [*sometimes cap.*] *Eastern & Western Churches.* A division of the Church as determined by liturgy; specif., a patriarchate; as, Catholics of the Latin *Rite;* a Uniat of the Byzantine *Rite.*

‖**Rit'ter** (rĭt'ẽr), *n. sing. & pl.* [G.] A knight; specif., a member of one of the lowest orders of the nobility in Germany and Austria.

rit'u·al (rĭt'ū·ăl), *adj.* [L. *ritualis,* fr. *ritus* a rite.] Of or pert. to rites or a ritual. — *n.* [From RITUAL, *adj.*] **1.** The form of conducting worship; religious ceremonial. **2.** A code of ceremonies observed; as, the *ritual* of the Freemasons. **3.** A book containing ceremonial forms. — **rit'u·al·ly,** *adv.*

rit'u·al·ism (-ĭz'm), *n.* A conducting of religious worship according to a ritual; use or observance of a ritual; in a derogatory sense, excessive devotion to prescribed ritual forms in worship. — **rit'u·al·is'tic** (-ĭs'tĭk), *adj.* — **rit'u·al·is'ti·cal·ly** (-tĭ·kăl·ĭ), *adv.*

rit'u·al·ist (-ĭst), *n.* One skilled in, or attached to, a ritual; one who advocates or practices ritualism.

riv'age (rĭv'ĭj), *n.* [OF., fr. *rive* bank, fr. L. *ripa.*] *Archaic.* A bank, shore, or coast.

ri'val (rī'văl), *n.* [F. or L.; F., fr. L. *rivalis.*] **1.** An associate or companion. *Shak.* **2.** One of two or more striving to reach or obtain that which one only can possess; a competitor. **3.** One that equals another in the possession of desired qualities; as, fir is a *rival* of pine. — *adj.* Having the same pretensions or claims; competing. — *v. t.;* RI'VALED (-văld) or RI'VALLED; RI'VAL·ING or RI'VAL·LING. **1.** To be in competition with. **2.** To strive to equal or excel; to emulate. **3.** To possess qualities that equal those of another; as, water *rivals* steam as a source of power. — *v. i. Archaic.* To be in rivalry.

ri'val·ry (-rĭ), *n.; pl.* -RIES (-rĭz). Act of rivaling, or state of being a rival; a competition.

rive (rīv), *v. t. & i.;* RIVED (rīvd); RIVED or RIV'EN (rĭv'ĕn); RIV'ING (rīv'ĭng). [ME. *riven,* fr. ON. *rīfa.*] **1.** To tear apart. **2.** To rend asunder; to split; cleave. — **Syn.** See TEAR.

riv'er (rĭv'ẽr), *n.* [OF. *rivere, riviere,* river, fr. L. *riparius* belonging to a bank or shore, fr. *ripa* a bank.] **1.** A natural stream of water larger than a brook or a creek. **2.** Figuratively: A large stream; copious flow; as, *rivers* of oil.

river horse. A hippopotamus.

riv'er·ine (rĭv'ẽr·īn; -ĭn), *adj.* Of, pertaining to, formed by, or resembling a river or rivers; as, *riverine* traffic.

river novel. = ROMAN-FLEUVE.

riv'er·side' (rĭv'ẽr·sīd'), *n.* The side or bank of a river.

riv'et (rĭv'ĕt; -ĭt), *n.* [OF., fr. *river* to rivet.] A headed pin or bolt of metal used for uniting two or more pieces by passing the shank

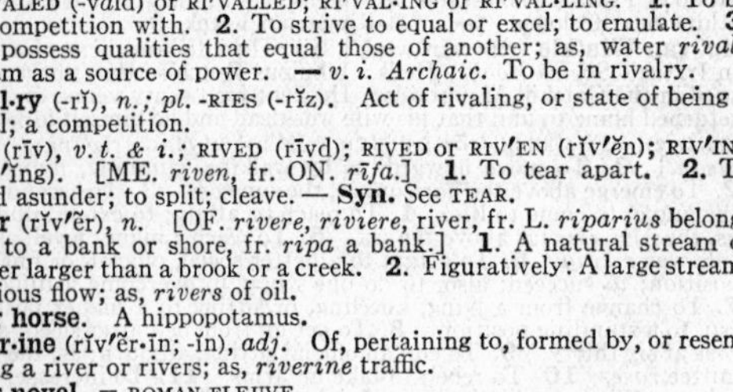

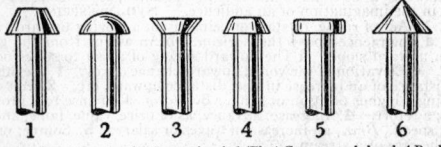

Rivetheads. 1 Conehead; 2 Buttonhead; 3 (Flat) Countersunk-head; 4 Panhead; 5 Flathead; 6 Steeple-head.

through a hole in each piece and then beating or pressing down the plain end so as to make a second head. — *v. t.* **1.** To fasten with a rivet, or with rivets. **2.** To upset the end or point of, as a metallic pin, rod, or bolt, by beating or pressing so as to form a head. **3.** To fasten firmly. **4.** To attract and hold (the attention). — **riv'et·er,** *n.*

‖**ri'vière'** (rē'vyâr'), *n.* [F., prop., stream.] A necklace of diamonds or other gems, esp. one of several strings.

riv'u·let (rĭv'ū·lĕt; -lĭt), *n.* [It. *rivoletto,* dim. fr. *rivolo,* fr. L. *rivulus,* dim. of *rivus* a brook.] A small stream.

rix'–dol'lar (rĭks'dŏl'ẽr), *n.* [Obs. D. *rijcksdaler* (D. *rijksdaalder*), lit., dollar of the realm.] Any of various nearly obsolete German, Dutch (2½ gulden), and Scandinavian silver coins, worth generally about $1.00.

Ri·zal' Day (rē·zäl'; -säl'). The thirtieth day of December, a legal holiday in the Philippine Islands, commemorating the death of the Filipino patriot José Rizal, who was shot without trial in 1896 by Spanish soldiers.

riz'zar (rĭz'ẽr), *v. t.* [MF. *ressoré,* past part.] *Scot.* To dry or cure (haddock) in the sun.

roach (rōch), *n.* [From COCKROACH.] A cockroach.

roach, *n.;* see PLURAL, *Note,* 6. [OF. *roche.*] **a** A European freshwater fish (*Rutilus rutilus*) of the carp family (Cyprinidae). It is silver white with a greenish back. **b** Any of various allied or similar fishes of the carp family.

roach, *n.* [Origin uncert.] **1.** *Naut.* A cutting away in a curve of the edge of a sail to prevent chafing or to secure a better fit. **2.** A sheet of water thrown upwards behind the float of a seaplane.

road (rōd), *n.* [Orig., a riding, fr. AS. *rād,* fr. *rīdan* to ride.] **1.** A place where one may ride; a highway. Abbr. *rd.* Cf. STREET, 1 **b.** **2.** Figuratively, way; path; as, the *road* to ruin. **3.** A place, less enclosed than a *harbor,* where ships may ride at anchor; a roadstead; — often in *pl.* **4.** Railroad; railway. — **road'side'** (-sīd'), *n. & adj.*

road agent. *Colloq., Chiefly Western U.S.* A highwayman, esp. on stage routes in unsettled districts.

road'bed' (rōd'bĕd'), *n.* **a** In railroads, the bed on which the superstructure (ties, rails, etc.) rests; also, the ballast on which the ties rest. **b** In common roads, the whole material laid in place and ready for travel.

road'block' (-blŏk'), *n.* **1.** *Mil.* A barricade built of concrete, logs, boards, sandbags, barbed wire, etc., often with traps or mines, for holding up the enemy's advance at a point on the road covered by heavy fire from shelter. **2.** Any similar road barricade, esp. one set up by law-enforcement officers.

road'house' (-hous'), *n.* An inn or similar place catering esp. to travelers by the road, as automobilists, etc.

road metal. Broken stone, cinders, etc., used in making and repairing roads, ballasting railroads, etc.

road roller. One that rolls roadways; specif., a machine with wide smooth rollers for packing down roads and pavements.

road runner. A bird (*Geococcyx californianus*) of the cuckoo family, of largely terrestrial habits, noted for running with great speed. It ranges from California to Mexico and Texas. It is called also *chaparral cock* (or, fem., *hen*).

road'stead (rōd'stĕd), *n.* [*road* + *stead* a place.] A protected place where ships may ride at anchor; = ROAD, 3.

road'ster (-stẽr), *n.* **1.** A horse used for driving, or for light work, on ordinary roads. **2. a** Formerly, a bicycle or tricycle adapted for ordinary use on common roads. **b** Now, an automobile with an open body having one cross seat and a luggage compartment in the rear, often containing a rumble seat. **3.** One who travels much on roads.

road'way' (-wā'), *n.* A road, esp. the traveled part of it.

roam (rōm), *v. i.* [ME. *romen.*] To go from place to place without any certain purpose or direction; to rove; wander. — *v. t.* To range or wander over. — *n.* Act of roaming; a wandering; ramble. — **roam'er** (-ẽr), *n.*

roan (rōn), *adj.* [MF. (F. *rouan*), fr. Sp. *roano.*] **1.** Bay, chestnut, red, or brown, with gray or white thickly interspersed; — said of a horse. **2.** Made of the leather called roan. — *n.* **1.** Roan color. **2.** A roan horse. **3.** A variety of low-grade sheepskin tanned with sumac and colored to imitate ungrained morocco.

roar (rōr; 70), *v. i. & t.* [AS. *rārian.*] **1.** To cry with a full, loud, continued sound; to bellow, as a bull. **2.** To make a loud, confused sound, as winds, waves, etc. **3.** To be boisterous or disorderly. **4.** To laugh out loudly. **5.** To make a loud noise in breathing, as horses having a certain disease. See ROARING, *n.,* 2. **6.** To go with a roar, as an engine. — *n.* The sound of roaring; a loud deep cry, a loud confused noise, outcry, etc. — **roar'er** (-ẽr), *n.*

roar'ing (rōr'ĭng; 70), *adj.* **1.** Making or characterized by a noise like a roar; as, *roaring* applause. **2.** *Colloq.* So busy, brisk, successful, or the like, as to suggest the roar of traffic, applause, or the like; as, we did a *roaring* business. — *n.* **1.** A loud, deep, prolonged sound, as of certain beasts or of winds or waves. **2.** *Veter.* An unsoundness of horses causing noisy respiration during exercise.

roast (rōst), *v. t.* [OF. *rostir,* of Teut. origin.] **1.** Orig., to cook by exposure before a fire; as, to *roast* meat on a spit; now, usually, to cook in an oven. **2.** To cook by surrounding with hot embers, ashes, etc. **3.** To dry and parch by exposure to heat; as, to *roast* coffee. **4.** *Colloq.* To banter, ridicule, or criticize severely. **5.** *Metal.* To heat with access of air, but without fusing, as to expel volatile matter or effect oxidation, and esp. to remove sulfur from sulfide ores. — *v. i.* **1.** To roast meat, fish, etc. **2.** To undergo the process of being roasted. — *n.* **1.** That which is roasted; a piece of meat, esp. of beef, roasted, or suitable for being roasted. See BEEF, *Illust.* **2.** Act or process of roasting. **3.** *Colloq.* A social gathering at which food is roasted before an open fire; as, a steak *roast;* a corn *roast.* — *adj.* [For *roasted.*] Roasted; as, *roast* beef.

roast'er (rōs'tẽr), *n.* **1.** One who roasts. **2.** A machine or contrivance for roasting. **3.** That which is adapted to roasting, esp. whole; specif.: **a** A sucking pig. **b** A young chicken.

rob (rŏb), *v. t.;* ROBBED (rŏbd); ROB'BING. [OF. *rober,* of Teut. origin.] **1.** To take something away from by force; to steal from. **2.** To deprive of, or withhold from, unjustly or injuriously; to defraud. **3.** *Law.* To take personal property in the possession of another from his person or his presence, feloniously and against his will, by violence or by putting him in fear. — *v. i.* To commit robbery.

rob'a·lo (rŏb'ȧ·lō; rō'bä-), *n.;* see PLURAL, *Note,* 3. [Sp. *róbalo.*] Any of a family (Centropomidae) of pikelike marine fishes of tropical America; esp., the largest species (*Centropomus undecimalis*), a valuable food fish.

rob'and (rŏb'ănd), *n.* Also **rob'bin** (rŏb'ĭn), etc. [Prob. fr. D. *raband,* prop., a yard band.] *Naut.* A piece of spun yarn or marline used to fasten the head of a sail to a spar.

rob'ber (rŏb'ẽr), *n.* One who robs.

robber fly. Any of numerous predaceous flies (family Asilidae), many of them of large size.

rob'ber·y (rŏb'ẽr·ĭ), *n.; pl.* -BERIES (-ĭz). [OF. *roberie.*] Act or practice of robbing; specif., *Law,* larceny of property from the person or immediate presence of another in possession thereof accomplished by violence or putting him in fear.

robe (rōb), *n.* [OF., orig., booty, plunder, of Teut. origin.] **1.** A long loose outer garment, esp. one of a flowing and elegant style or make; hence, a dress of state, rank, office, etc. **2.** *pl.* Dress; costume. **3.** A covering; mantle. **4.** *U.S.* A skin of an animal, or some other warm covering, to throw over or wrap around the legs, as when driving. — *v. t. & i.* To invest or clothe with a robe or robes; to dress; array.

‖**robe–de–cham'bre** (rôb'dē·shäN'br'), *n.* [F.] A dressing gown, esp. for a woman.

rob'in (rŏb'ĭn), *n.* [F., prop. dim. of *Robert.*] **1.** A small, warblerlike European bird (*Erithacus rubecula*) of the thrush family, having the back brownish olive and the throat and breast yellowish red. **2.**

In North America, a large thrush (*Turdus migratorius*), having the upper parts olivaceous gray, the head and tail blackish, and the breast and under parts chiefly dull reddish.

Rob′in Good′fel′low (rŏb′ĭn gŏŏd′fĕl′ō). A tricksy house sprite in the popular fairy mythology of England; Puck.

Robin Hood (hŏŏd). A legendary English outlaw, usually described as a yeoman, with his chief resort in the forest of Sherwood, in Nottinghamshire. The popular legends extol his courage, courtesy, and skill in archery, and his habit of robbing the rich for the benefit of the poor.

robin redbreast. The European or the American robin.

Rob′in·son Cru′soe (rŏb′ĭn·s'n krōō′sō). The usual title and hero of a romance (1719) by Defoe. He is a sailor, shipwrecked on an uninhabited island and living there for many years.

ro′ble (rō′blā), *n.* [Sp., oak, fr. L. *robur*.] Any of several oaks; esp., the white oak (*Quercus lobata*) of California.

rob′o·rant (rŏb′ō·rănt), *adj.* [L. *roborans*, pres. part. of *roborare* to strengthen, fr. *robur*, *roboris*, strength.] Strengthening. — *n.* A roborant drug.

ro′bot (rō′bŏt; rŏb′ŏt), *n.* [Czech *robota* compulsory service, work.] **1.** In Karel Čapek's play *R. U. R.* (Rossum's Universal Robots), one of a large number of artificially manufactured persons, mechanically efficient but devoid of sensibility; hence, a brutal, efficient, insensitive person; an automaton. **2.** Any automatic device that performs functions ordinarily ascribed to human beings, or operates with seemingly human intelligence. — **ro′bot·ism** (-ĭz'm), *n.* — **ro′bot·is′tic** (-ĭs′tĭk), *adj.* — **ro′bot·ize** (-īz), *v.* — **ro′bot·ry** (-rĭ), *n.*

robot bomb. A small pilotless jet-propelled airplane steered by a gyroscopic device and heavily loaded with explosives, which descends as an aerial bomb. Called also *flying bomb, buzz bomb, V-1*, etc.

ro′bur·ite (rō′bẽr·īt), *n.* [L. *robur* strength.] A mining explosive containing, according to one formula, chlorinated dinitrobenzene and ammonium nitrate.

ro·bust′ (rō·bŭst′; 2), *adj.* [L. *robustus* oaken, hard, strong, fr. *robur* strength, oak, heart of oak.] **1.** Having or evincing strength or vigorous health; strong; vigorous; sound. **2.** Rough; rude. **3.** Requiring strength or vigor. — **Syn.** See HEALTHY. — **ro·bust′ly**, *adv.* — **ro·bust′ness**, *n.*

ro·bus′tious (rō·bŭs′chŭs), *adj.* *Chiefly Humorous.* Robust; esp., rudely vigorous. — **ro·bus′tious·ly**, *adv.*

roc (rŏk), *n.* [Ar. *rukhkh*, fr. Per. *rukh*.] A fabulous bird of Arabia so huge that it bore off elephants to feed its young.

roc′am·bole (rŏk′ăm·bōl), *n.* [F., fr. G. *rockenbolle*, fr. *rocken*, *roggen*, rye + *bolle* bulb.] A European leek (*Allium scorodoprasum*) used for flavoring.

Roch′dale prin′ci·ples (rŏch′dāl). In co-operative marketing, the system whereby no credit is given, and all profits are distributed among customers; — from Rochdale, England.

Ro·chelle′ pow′der (rō·shĕl′). = SEIDLITZ POWDER.

Rochelle salt. [From *Rochelle*, France.] Potassium sodium tartrate, $KNaC_4H_4O_6.4H_2O$, a colorless crystalline salt, used as a mild purgative.

‖**roche mou′ton′née′** (rôsh′ mōō′tô′nā′). [F., sheep-shaped rock.] *Phys. Geog.* A rock worn round by glaciers.

roch′et (rŏch′ĕt; -ĭt), *n.* [OF., fr. *roc.* of Teut. origin.] *Eccl.* A close-fitting linen vestment resembling a surplice, worn esp. by bishops and privileged prelates in certain ceremonies.

rock (rŏk), *n.* [ONF. *roque* (OF. & F. *roche*).] **1.** A cliff of rock (see sense 3, below); as, the *rock* of Gibraltar. **2.** A large concreted mass of stony material; also, broken pieces of such masses. **3.** *Geol.* Any solid mineral matter occurring naturally in large quantities; also, a particular mass of it. **4.** That which resembles a rock (sense 3) in firmness; a defense; refuge. **5.** Anything which causes a disaster suggestive of the wreck of a vessel upon a rock; as, a business going on the *rocks*. **6.** *Colloq.* **a** A type of hard stick candy. **b** = ROCK CANDY. **c** A diamond. — **rock**, *adj.*

rock (rŏk), *v. t. & i.* [AS. *roccian*.] **1.** To move as in a cradle; to lull; quiet. **2.** To sway backward and forward, as a body resting on a support beneath; to vibrate. **3.** To affect in a specified manner by rocking; as, to *rock* one asleep. **4.** In mezzotint engraving, to prepare the surface of (a plate) by the use of the rocker. **5.** *Mining.* To wash (placer gravel) in a cradle or rocker. — **Syn.** See SHAKE. — *n.* Act or process of rocking; a rocking movement.

rock, *n.* [ME. (perh. fr. MD.) *roc*, *rokke*.] *Hist.* A distaff.

rock′a·way (rŏk′ȧ·wā), *n.* [From *Rockaway*, N. J., where they were made.] A light, low four-wheeled carriage with standing top, open at the sides.

rock bottom. The very bottom or foundation.

rock′-bot′tom (*see Pron.*, § 2), *adj.* The very lowest; as, *rock-bottom* prices.

rock′-bound′, *adj.* Encircled or girt with rocks.

rock brake. Any fern of the genus *Pellaea*.

rock candy. Sugar obtained in large crystals or crystalline masses by slow evaporation.

rock cress. See CRESS.

rock crystal. Transparent quartz.

rock′er (rŏk′ẽr), *n.* **1.** One who rocks a cradle. **2.** Either of the curving pieces of wood or metal on which a cradle, chair, etc., rocks; also, a rocking chair or rocking horse. **3.** Any of various devices that work with a rocking or to-and-fro motion; as: **a** *Engraving.* A tool for preparing the ground in mezzotint engraving. **b** *Mining.* = CRADLE, *n.*, 5. **4.** A skate with a curved blade.

rocker arm. *Mach.* An arm borne by a rockshaft.

rock′et (rŏk′ĕt; -ĭt), *n.* [F. *roquette*, fr. Pr. *rouqeto*, dim. fr. *eruca*, fr. L. *eruca* a sort of colewort.] **a** Orig., the **rocket salad** (*Eruca sativa*), an herb with pinnately lobed leaves and whitish-yellow flowers. **b** Any plant of the genus *Hesperis*, of the mustard family, esp. the ***garden rocket*** (*H. matronalis*).

rock′et, *n.* [It. *rocchetta*, prop. a bobbin, spool, dim. of *rocca* distaff; — from its resemblance in shape.] **1.** A firework consisting of a case filled with a combustible composition and fastened to a guiding stick. It is projected through the air by the reaction resulting from the rearward discharge of the gases liberated by combustion. **2.** A jet engine operating on the same principle as the firework; — called also **rocket engine, rocket motor**. It consists essentially of a combustion chamber and an exhaust nozzle, and is supplied with either liquid or solid propellants which provide the fuel and the oxygen needed for combustion, thus making this engine independent of the oxygen of the air. Rockets are used for the propulsion of bombs, shells, airplanes, automobiles, etc. Hence, **rock′et-pro·pelled′**, *adj.*, **rocket propulsion.** Cf. *jet engine*, under JET PROPULSION.

☞ The term *rocket* is commonly used attributively to designate: **a** *Rocket-propelled*, as in *rocket* bomb; *rocket* plane. **b** *Armed with rocket launchers*, as in *rocket* ship; *rocket* plane.

— *v. i.* **1.** To rise or dash swiftly and with force like a rocket. **2.** To rise straight up and swiftly when flushed; — said chiefly of pheasants.

rocket bomb. *Mil.* **a** An aerial bomb designed for release at low altitude and equipped with a rocket apparatus for giving it added momentum. **b** Any rocket-propelled bomb launched from the ground, for example, the V-2.

rocket launcher. *Mil.* A launcher consisting of a tube or cluster of tubes for firing rocket shells, for example, a three-tube launcher placed on the underside of an airplane wing or a one-tube ground launcher, the bazooka.

rock′et·ry (rŏk′ĕt·rĭ; rŏk′ĭt-), *n.* The study of, use of, or experimentation with rockets. — **rock′et·eer′** (rŏk′ĕ·tēr′; rŏk′ĭ-), **rock′et·er** (rŏk′ĕ·tẽr; rŏk′ĭ-), *n.*

Rock fever. [From the *Rock* (of Gibraltar).] = UNDULANT FEVER.

rock′fish′ (rŏk′fĭsh′), *n.*; see FISH. Any of various fishes that live among rocks or on rocky bottoms; as: **a** Any of various food fishes (genera *Sebastodes*, *Sebastichthys*, etc.) of northern Pacific coasts. **b** The striped bass. See BASS **b**. **c** Any of several groupers of Bermuda and Florida.

rock garden. *Hort.* A garden laid out in a rocky situation or built to reproduce the conditions of such a place, adapted to the growth of certain sorts of plants, as those requiring a cool, moist location.

rock′ing chair. A chair mounted on rockers.

rocking horse. A toy horse mounted on rockers.

rock oil. Petroleum.

rock rabbit. A pika.

rock′-ribbed′ (*see Pron.*, § 2), *adj.* **1.** Having ribs of, or like, rock. **2.** Strong; solidly established; also, inflexible.

rock′rose′ (rŏk′rōz′), *n.* Any plant of the genus *Cistus*, typifying a family (Cistaceae, the rockrose family) of shrubs and somewhat woody herbs; also, any plant of the genera *Helianthemum* and, in the U. S., *Crocanthemum*.

rock salt. Common salt (sodium chloride) occurring in solid form as a mineral; esp., salt in rocklike masses.

rock′shaft′ (rŏk′shȧft′; 9), *n.* *Mach.* A shaft that oscillates on its journals, instead of revolving.

rock′weed′ (-wēd′), *n.* Any coarse seaweed (family Fucaceae) growing attached to rocks, esp. species of *Fucus* and *Ascophyllum*.

rock wool. A fibrous woollike material made by blowing a jet of steam through molten rock, esp. limestone or siliceous rock, or through slag. It is used for heat insulation and for the absorption of sound.

rock′y (rŏk′ĭ), *adj.*; ROCK′I·ER (-ĭ·ẽr); -I·EST. **1.** Full of, or abounding in, rocks; consisting of rocks. **2.** Like a rock. **3.** Figuratively, hard; unfeeling; obdurate. — **rock′i·ness**, *n.*

rock′y, *adj.* *Slang.* Disposed to rock or totter, as after dissipation; hence, shaky; weak.

Rocky Mountain sheep. See MOUNTAIN SHEEP.

Rocky Mountain spotted fever. *Med.* An infection occurring in the Rocky Mountain region, marked by livid spots, chills, fever, etc., and transmitted to man by the bite of certain ticks.

ro·co′co (rō·kō′kō; rō′kō·kō′), *n.* [F., fr. *rocaille*.] A florid style of ornamentation characterized by curved lines and decoration of pierced shellwork, popular in Europe in the 18th century. — **ro·co′co**, *adj.*

rod (rŏd), *n.* [AS. *rodd*.] **1.** A straight and slender stick, as one cut fresh from a tree; hence, stock; race; tribe; as, of the *rod* of Jesse. **2.** Any slender bar. Specif.: **a** An instrument of punishment; figuratively, chastisement. **b** A scepter; hence, authority; tyranny; oppression. **c** A wand or similar badge of office, as carried by marshals, ushers, etc. **d** A fishing pole. **e** A bar or staff for measuring. **f** *Slang, U.S.* A pistol. **3.** A measure of length. See MEASURE, *Tables* 1 & 3. **4.** *Anat.* One of the long rod-shaped sensory bodies in the retina, responsive to faint light. **5.** *Bacteriol.* A bacterium shaped like a rod.

rode (rōd). See RIDE, *v.*

ro′dent (rō′dĕnt), *adj.* [L. *rodens*, *-entis*, pres. part. of *rodere* to gnaw.] **1.** Gnawing; biting. **2.** *Zool.* Pertaining to an order (Rodentia) of gnawing mammals having one pair of upper incisors, as rats, squirrels, beavers, and porcupines. — *n.* A rodent animal.

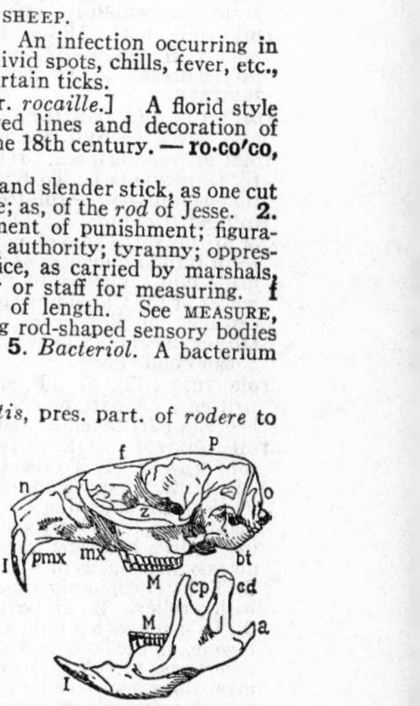

Skull of Rodent (Muskrat). *I, I* Incisors; *M, M* Molars; *n* Nasal; *f* Frontal; *p* Parietal; *o* Occipital; *z* Zygomatic Arch; *bt* Bulla Tympani; *mx* Maxillary; *pmx* Premaxillary; *cp* Coronoid Process; *cd* Condyle; *a* Angle of Mandible.

ro·den′ti·cide (rō·dĕn′tĭ·sīd), *n.* [*rodent* + *-cide*, 1.] A substance that kills rodents.

ro′de·o (rō′dē·ō; rō·dā′ō), *n.* [Sp., a going round.] **a** *Western U.S.* A roundup of cattle. **b** Figuratively, any spectacle likened to a roundup; specif., a public performance presenting the chief features of a roundup, as lariat throwing, horse breaking, etc.

rod′man (rŏd′măn), *n.* One whose work is done with a rod; specif., *Surveying*, the man who holds the leveling rod.

rod′o·mon·tade′ (rŏd′ō·mŏn·tād′; -täd′), *n.* [F., fr. It. *rodomontata*, fr. *Rodomonte*, the boastful king of Algiers in Italian romances of Orlando.] Vain boasting; bluster; rant. — *adj.* Boastful. — *v. i.* To boast; brag.

roe (rō), *n.*; see PLURAL, *Note*, 6. [AS. *rā*, *rāha*.] **a** The roe deer. **b** A hind or doe.

roe, *n.* [For *roan*, fr. ME. *rowne*, fr. ON. *hrogn*.] **a** The eggs of fishes, esp. when still enclosed in the ovarian membranes. **b** The eggs or ovaries of certain crustaceans, as the coral of the lobster.

roe′buck′ (rō′bŭk′), *n.* The male roe deer.

roe deer. [AS. *rāhdēor*.] A small, nimble, graceful European and Asiatic deer (*Capreolus capreolus*), with erect antlers, forked at the summit. Cf. DEER.

roent′gen, rönt′gen (rûnt′gĕn; rĕnt′-; rŭnt′-; -yĕn), *n.* [After Wilhelm Konrad *Röntgen*, Ger. physicist.] *Physics.* The international unit of quantity of roentgen, or X, rays.

roent'gen, rönt'gen (rûnt'gĕn; rĕnt'-; rŭnt'-; -yĕn), *adj.* [*also cap.*] Of or pertaining to X rays; as, *roentgen*, or *Roentgen*, apparatus.

roent'gen·ize, rönt'gen·ize (-īz), *v. t. Med.* To subject to the action of X rays.

roentgeno-, röntgeno-. A combining form meaning *roentgen*, or *X*, *rays*, as in **roent'gen·o·gram', rönt'gen·o·gram'** (rûnt'gĕn·ō·grăm'; rĕnt'-; rŭnt'-; -yĕn-), a roentgenograph.

roent'gen·o·graph', rönt'gen·o·graph' (rûnt'gĕn·ō·grȧf'; rĕnt'-; rŭnt'-; -yĕn-), *n.* A photograph made with X rays. — **roent'gen·o·graph'ic, rönt'gen·o·graph'ic** (-grăf'ĭk), *adj.* — **roent'gen·og'ra·phy, rönt'gen·og'ra·phy** (-ŏg'rȧ·fĭ), *n.*

roent'gen·ol'o·gy, rönt'gen·ol'o·gy (-ŏl'ō·jĭ), *n.* The branch of science dealing with X rays, esp. their use for diagnosis or treatment in medicine and dentistry. — **roent'gen·o·log'ic, rönt'gen·o·log'ic** (-ō·lŏj'ĭk), **roent'gen·o·log'i·cal, rönt'gen·o·log'i·cal** (-ĭ·kăl), *adj.* — **roent'gen·ol'o·gist, rönt'gen·ol'o·gist** (-ŏl'ō·jĭst), *n.*

roent'gen·o·scope, rönt'gen·o·scope (rûnt'gĕn·ō·skōp; rĕnt'-; rŭnt'-; -yĕn-), *n. Med.* A fluoroscope.

roent'gen·o·ther'a·py, rönt'gen·o·ther'a·py (-thĕr'ȧ·pĭ), *n. Med.* Treatment, as of a patient or a lesion of disease, by X rays.

roentgen, *or* **röntgen, ray.** [*also cap.*] X ray.

ro·ga'tion (rō·gā'shŭn), *n.* [OF. or L.; OF., fr. L. *rogatio*, fr. *rogare, rogatum*, to ask, beg.] **1.** *Eccl.* Litany; supplication; also (usually *pl.*), the ceremonies of Rogation days. **2.** *Rom. Antiq.* The proposal of a law by the consuls or the tribunes for passage by the people; also, the law or decree proposed.

Rogation days. *Eccl.* The three days before Ascension Day, observed as days of special supplication.

rog'a·to'ry (rŏg'ȧ·tō'rĭ *or, esp. Brit.*, -tĕr·ĭ), *adj.* [See ROGATION.] Seeking information; authorized to examine witnesses or ascertain facts; as, a *rogatory* commission.

Rog'er (rŏj'ẽr), *n.* [F.] **1.** Masc. proper name. **2.** [*also not cap.*] A black flag with white skull and crossbones, formerly used by pirates; — called also *Jolly Roger*.

Rog'er (rŏj'ẽr), *interj.* [Arbitrary identification of *R* for (message) received (and understood).] *Radio & Signaling.* All right; I understand; O.K.

rogue (rōg), *n.* [Origin unknown.] **1.** A vagrant; an idle, sturdy beggar; a tramp. **2.** A knave; cheat. **3.** Scamp; rascal. **4.** A rogue elephant. **5.** *Biol.* A chance variation; — usually applied to inferior or nontypical plants.

rogue elephant. A vicious elephant which separates from the herd and roams alone.

ro'guer·y (rō'gẽr·ĭ), *n.; pl.* -IES (-ĭz). **1.** Practices of a rogue; knavish tricks; cheating; fraud. **2.** Sportive tricks; mischievousness.

rogues' gallery (rōgz). A collection of portraits of persons arrested as criminals, for the use of the police.

rogue's march. Derisive music for a person driven away under popular indignation or official sentence, as when a soldier is drummed out of a regiment.

ro'guish (rō'gĭsh), *adj.* **1.** Knavish. **2.** Pleasantly mischievous; arch. — **ro'guish·ly,** *adv.* — **ro'guish·ness,** *n.*

roil (roil), *v. t.* [From F. *rouiller* to rust, earlier also, to make muddy, fr. OF. *rouil* mud, rust.] **1.** To render turbid by stirring up the dregs. **2.** To disturb (the temper); to ruffle; vex. — **Syn.** See IRRITATE.

roil'y (-ĭ), *adj.;* ROIL'I·ER (-ĭ·ẽr); ROIL'I·EST. Turbid; as, *roily* water; also, vexed. — **Syn.** See TURBID.

roist'er (rois'tẽr), *v. i.* [OF. *ruistre, ruiste*, prop. *adj.*, rude, violent, fr. L. *rusticus.*] To bluster or swagger; brag; also, to indulge in riotous festivity. — **roist'er·er** (-ẽr), *n.*

Ro'land (rō'lănd), *n.* [F., of G. origin.] A warden of the marches of Brittany, the hero of many romantic tales of the Charlemagne cycle; — in Italian romances of Charlemagne he is called *Orlando*. Legend made him a nephew of the emperor, and the most redoubtable defender of the Christians against the Saracens. He was killed at Roncesvalles, or Roncevaux, in 778. The phrase ***a Roland for an Oliver***, meaning a blow for a blow, alludes to a drawn combat between Roland and Oliver.

role, rôle (rōl), *n.* [F. *rôle*, the roll on which an actor's part was written.] A part, or character, performed by an actor in a drama; hence, a part taken or assumed by anyone.

roll (rōl), *v. t.* [OF. *roller, roler*, fr. L. *rotulus, rotula*, dim. of L. *rota* wheel.] **1.** To revolve by turning over and over; as, to *roll* a wheel. **2.** To move on rollers or small wheels. **3.** To wrap round on itself or on something else, or to form into a cylindrical body in that manner; as, to *roll* up a sheet of paper. **4.** To bind or involve by winding, as in a bandage; to enwrap. **5.** To drive or impel forward with an easy motion, as of rolling; as, a river *rolls* its waters to the ocean. **6.** To utter copiously, esp. with sounding words. **7.** To press or level with a roller. **8.** To beat with rapid, continuous strokes, as a drum. **9.** To utter with a trill; as, to *roll* one's r's. **10.** To sway from side to side, as the body in walking. **11.** *Print.* To ink with a roller or rollers; as, to *roll* a form. — *v. i.* **1.** To move, as a curved object may, along a surface by rotation without sliding. **2.** To move or be moved on wheels, as a carriage. **3.** To have an undulating form, as land. **4.** To turn or move circularly as on an axis; to incline first to one side, then to the other; as, the ship *rolled* heavily. Hence, to walk with a swinging gait; to swagger; sometimes, to stagger. **5.** To move, as waves, with alternate swell and depression. **6.** To be wound or formed into a ball. **7.** To make a loud or heavy rising and falling or rumbling noise, as thunder. **8.** To spread under a roller; as, the ink *rolls* well. **9.** To perform a periodical revolution; as, the *rolling* year. **10.** To trill; — said of certain birds. **11.** *Colloq.* To wallow; as, to *roll* in money. **12.** To be in a (specified) condition after being rolled; as, the metal *rolled* out in flat bars. — ***roll back.*** To reduce (a commodity price) to or toward a previous level on a national scale by government control devices.

— *n.* **1.** Act of rolling, or state of being rolled; also, a rolling movement; as, a *roll* in a walk. **2.** That which rolls; a roller. **3.** That which is rolled up. Specif.: **a** A document which may be rolled up; a scroll. **b** Hence, a register; record; also, a catalogue; list; specif., a muster roll. **c** A certain quantity, as of fabric or paper, rolled up to form a single package. **d** *Cookery.* Any of various food preparations rolled up for cooking or serving. **e** *Slang, U.S.* Paper money rolled into a wad; hence, money in general. **4.** A heavy, reverberatory sound, as of cannon, thunder, a drum. **5.** A swell or undulation on a surface, as of the ground; a low rounded ridge. **6.** A resounding, often rhythmical, flow of speech; as, the fine *roll* of the best verse. **7.** *Aeronautics.* A maneuver in which a complete revolution about the longitudinal axis is made, the horizontal direction of flight being approximately maintained.

roll'back' (rōl'băk'), *n.* Act or instance of rolling back.

roll call. **1.** Act or time of calling over a list of names, as among soldiers. **2.** A signal, as on a bugle, for such a call.

roll'er (rōl'ẽr), *n.* **1.** One that rolls, as a small wheel of a caster, the wheel of a roller skate, a stick on which to roll up a curtain, etc.; esp., a cylindrical body rolled along something, or between two bodies, for pressing or smoothing by pressure, for spreading a viscous liquid on a surface, for crushing, etc. **2.** A bandage; fillet. **3.** A pigeon proficient in aerial tumbling or rolling; also, any of certain Old World birds (family Coraciidae) which turn over in flight like tumbler pigeons. **4.** A canary having a song with a long recurrent trill. **5.** *Naut.* One of a series of long, heavy waves which roll in upon a coast, as after a storm.

roller bearing. *Mach.* A bearing in which the journal rotates in contact with a number of rollers usually contained in a cage. Cf. BALL BEARING.

roller coaster. A coasting apparatus consisting of a circular inclined railway with cars rolling upon it.

roller skate. A skate with wheels instead of a runner. — **roll'er-skate'** (*see Pron.*, § 2), *v. i.* — **roller skating.**

roller towel. An endless towel hung from a roller.

rol'lick (rŏl'ĭk), *v. i.* To move or play in a careless, swaggering manner; to frolic; sport.

rol'lick·ing, rol'lick·some (-sŭm), *adj.* Boisterously jovial.

roll'ing (rōl'ĭng), *n.* Act of one who or that which rolls, in various senses. — *adj.* **1.** Rotating on or as if on an axis. **2.** Moving on or as if on wheels or rollers. **3.** *U.S.* Having gradual, rounded undulations of surface; as, a *rolling* country. **4. a** Of sounds, rising and falling or rumbling, as thunder; trilled, as the song of a bird. **b** Of water, mist, smoke, etc., surging on or upward in billows. **5.** Having a turn over upon or toward itself; as, a *rolling* collar. **6.** Recurring; as, the *rolling* years. **7.** Lurching; swaying; as, a *rolling* gait.

rolling hitch. *Naut.* See KNOT, *Illust.* (21).

rolling mill. An establishment where metal, esp. iron and steel, is rolled into plates and bars.

rolling pin. A cylindrical piece of wood or other material for rolling out paste, dough, or, formerly, leather.

rolling stock. *Railroads.* The wheeled vehicles running or capable of running on the tracks or rails.

roll'-top' desk. A writing desk having a sliding cover made of parallel slats fastened to a flexible backing.

roll'way' (rōl'wā'), *n.* A way or road on which objects, as logs, are rolled or moved on rollers.

ro'ly-po'ly (rō'lĭ-pō'lĭ), *n.* [Redupl. based on ROLL, *v.*] **1.** A pudding of paste spread with fruit, rolled into a cylindrical form, and boiled, baked, or steamed. **2.** A roly-poly person or thing. — *adj.* Short and pudgy.

Ro·ma'ic (rō·mā'ĭk), *adj.* [ML. *Romaicus*, fr. Gr. *Rhōmaïkos* Roman.] Of or pert. to modern Greece or, esp., its language. — *n.* The modern Greek vernacular. See GREEK, *n.*, 4.

ro·maine' (rō·mān'), *n.* Also **romaine lettuce.** [F. *romaine*, fem. adj., Roman.] A variety (*Lactuca sativa longifolia*) of lettuce, with long spoon-shaped leaves and columnar heads.

Ro'man (rō'măn), *adj.* [OF. and L.; OF. *romain*, fr. L. *Romanus*, fr. *Roma* Rome.] **1.** Of, pert. to, or characteristic of Rome or the Roman people; as, the *Roman*, or Latin, language. **2.** Of or pert. to the Roman Catholic Church, or, more accurately, the Latin Rite; as, the *Roman* liturgy. **3.** [*now usually not cap.*] Designating a style of light-faced, upright type, having shaded strokes and characterized by serifs. See TYPE, *n.* — *n.* **1.** A native, inhabitant, or citizen of Rome, esp. of ancient Rome. **2.** Latin. **3.** [*now usually not cap.*] Roman type, letters, or print. **4.** Loosely, a Roman Catholic.

‖ro'man' (rô'mäɴ'), *n.* [F.] The generic name of a type of metrical tale, esp. in old French literature, an outgrowth from the chanson de geste.

‖ro'man' à clef (rô'mäɴ'-nȧ klā'). [F.] A novel with a key; that is, one in which real persons or actual events figure, under disguise.

Roman arch. The semicircular arch.

Roman calendar. The calendar (of twelve months) of the ancient Romans, from which our modern calendars are derived. In designating days of the month, the Romans reckoned backwards from three fixed points, the *calends*, the *nones*, and the *ides*. The calends were always the first day of the month. The ides fell on the 15th in March, May, July, and October, and on the 13th in other months. The nones came on the 8th day before the ides.

Roman candle. A straight cylindrical firework which discharges intermittent balls or stars of fire.

Roman Catholic. Of, pertaining to, or designating the Roman Catholic Church. Also, a member of that church.

Roman Catholic Church. That body of Christians of which the pope is the head; — called **Catholic Church** by its members.

Roman Catholicism. The faith, practice, polity, etc., of the Roman Catholic Church.

ro·mance' (rō·măns'), *n.* [F., fr. Sp. *romance*, fr. OF. *romanz.* See 2d ROMANCE.] *Music.* A short lyric tale set to music.

ro·mance' (rō·măns'; rō'măns), *n.* [OF. *romanz, romans*, something written in the vulgar tongue, in French, fr. L. *Romanice*, adv., in Roman fashion, fr. *Romanicus* Roman, fr. *Romanus.*] **1.** A species of tale, orig. in meter in the Romance dialects, afterward diffused in verse or prose, such as the tales of the court of Arthur; hence, any fictitious and wonderful tale; now, esp., a sort of novel, whose interest lies esp. in adventure, surprising incident, etc.; also, the class of literature including fiction of this type. **2.** Picturesque characteristic or nature; as, the *romance* of history. **3.** A romantically adventurous act or experience. **4.** A dreamy, imaginative habit of mind tending to dwell on the picturesquely unusual; as, a girl full of *romance.* **5.** A fictitious tale; a falsehood. **6.** [*cap.*] *Philol.* The Romance (or Romanic) languages. — (rō·măns'), *v. i.;* -MANCED' (-mănst'); -MANC'ING (-măn'sĭng). To write or tell romances; also, to indulge in romantic fancies. — **ro·manc'er** (rō·măn'sẽr), *n.*

Ro·mance' (rō·măns'; rō'măns; 2), *adj.* [F. *romance* in *langue romance* (now *romane*) Romance language, fr. OF. *romanz*, n. See 2d

ROMANCE.] Designating, or pertaining to, a language or languages developed from Vulgar Latin, including Italian, Spanish, Portuguese, French, Provençal, Romanian, etc. As a group these languages are called **Romance languages**. See INDO-EUROPEAN LANGUAGES, *Table.*

Roman Curia. = CURIA, 3.

Roman Empire. The empire of ancient Rome, which began under Augustus in 27 B.C. and lasted until A.D. 395, when it was divided into the ***Western Roman Empire*** and the ***Eastern Roman Empire***. Cf. HOLY ROMAN EMPIRE.

Ro′man·esque′ (rō′măn·ĕsk′), *adj.* [F.] **1.** *Art, esp. Arch.* Of, pertaining to, or designating a style somewhat resembling the Roman. **2.** Romance; esp., Provençal. — *n.* **a** Romanesque style. **b** A Romance language.

Romanesque architecture *or* **style.** The architecture or style which developed in Italy and western Europe between the Roman and the Gothic styles and characterized in its later development (after 1000) by the use of the round arch and vault, substitution for columns of piers, decorative use of arcades, and profuse ornament.

‖**ro′man′-fleuve′** (rô′mäɴ′flûv′), *n.* [F. *roman* novel + *fleuve* stream.] A type of novel, distinctively French but found also in English (sometimes called *saga novel*), which takes the form of a long and usually easygoing chronicle of persons comprising a family (with its generations), community, or other social group.

Ro·ma′nian (rō·mān′yăn; -mā′nĭ·ăn), *adj.* Also **Ru·ma′nian** (rōō-), **Rou·ma′nian** (rōō-). Of or pertaining to Romania. — *n.* **a** An inhabitant of Romania or one whose native speech is Romanian. **b** The language of Romania, a Romance language containing many words from other tongues, as the Slavic, Turkish, and Greek. See INDO-EUROPEAN LANGUAGES, *Table.*

Ro·man′ic (rō·măn′ĭk), *adj.* [L. *Romanicus.*] **1.** Related to the Roman people by descent; — of races and nations speaking any Romanic tongue. **2.** *Philol.* = ROMANCE, *adj.*

Ro′man·ism (rō′măn·ĭz′m), *n.* The tenets, customs, etc., of the Church of Rome; the Roman Catholic religion; — chiefly in disparagement. — **Ro′man·ist** (-ĭst), *n. & adj.*

Ro′man·ize (-īz), *v. t.* To make Roman; specif.: **a** To Latinize. **b** To convert to the Roman Catholic religion, etc. — *v. i.* To conform to, or lean toward, Roman Catholic beliefs, etc. — **Ro′man·i·za′tion** (-ĭ·zā′shŭn; -ī·zā′-), *n.*

Roman nose. A nose somewhat aquiline.

Roman numeral. See NUMBER, *Table.*

Ro·ma′nov (rŭ·mä′nŭf; *Angl.* rō′mȧ·nŏf), *n.* The Russian dynasty (1613–1917) founded by Mikhail Feodorovich Romanov.

Roman punch. A water ice made with lemon juice, sugar, beaten whites of eggs, and rum.

Ro′mans (rō′mănz), *n. pl., construed as sing.* The Epistle to the Romans, in the New Testament. See BIBLE.

Ro·mansh′, Ro·mansch′ (rō·mănsh′; -mänsh′), *n.* [Grisons *rumansch, rumonsch, romonsch.* See 2d ROMANCE.] The Rhaeto-Romanic dialects spoken in the Grisons, Switzerland. See INDO-EUROPEAN LANGUAGES, *Table.* — **Ro·mansh′, Ro·mansch′,** *adj.*

ro·man′tic (rō·măn′tĭk), *adj.* [F. *romantique,* fr. MF. *romant.*] **1.** Of or pert. to romance; involving or resembling romance; hence, fanciful; unreal; as, a *romantic* tale. **2.** Entertaining ideas suited to a romance; as, a *romantic* person. **3.** Of or pert. to the style of the Christian and popular literature and art of the Middle Ages, as opposed to the classical antique; characterized by freedom of fancy in conception and treatment. **4.** Characterized by picturesque strangeness or variety; suited to romance; also, fabulous; imaginary; not actual or real. — *n.* **1.** A romanticist. **2.** A romantic person, trait, etc. — **ro·man′ti·cal·ly** (-tĭ·kăl·ĭ), *adv.*

ro·man′ti·cism (-tĭ·sĭz′m), *n.* Romantic principles or characteristics generally; conformity to, or practice of, the romantic style. As a critical term *romanticism* generally denotes the principles, characteristics, or spirit of the movement, the ***romantic movement***, primarily in literature, for reasserting imagination and sentiment and emphasizing individualism in thought and expression as against the restrictive, formality of classicism (which see). — **ro·man′ti·cist** (-sĭst), *n.*

ro·man′ti·cize (-sīz), *v. t.* To consider in a romantic light; to attach romantic meaning or character to.

Rom′a·ny (rŏm′ȧ·nĭ), *n.* Also **Rom′ma·ny.** [Romany *romano, romani,* adj., gypsy.] A gypsy; also, the language of the gypsies, an Indic tongue spoken in many dialects, greatly corrupted and intermixed with words from European languages. See INDO-EUROPEAN LANGUAGES, *Table.* — **Rom′a·ny, Rom′ma·ny,** *adj.*

Rom′a·ny rye′ (rī′). One who sympathizes and associates with the gypsies, masters their language, etc.

ro·maunt′ (rō·mänt′; -mônt′), *n.* [MF. *romant.* See 2d ROMANCE.] A romance, esp. one in verse.

Ro′me·o (rō′mē·ō), *n.* **1.** In Shakespeare's *Romeo and Juliet,* the son of Montague, in love with Juliet, daughter of Capulet. A feud had long existed between the two houses. **2.** Hence, a lover.

Rom′ish (rōm′ĭsh), *adj.* Belonging or relating to Rome, or, esp., to the Roman Catholic Church; — chiefly used disparagingly. — **Rom′ish·ly,** *adv.* — **Rom′ish·ness,** *n.*

Rom′ney, *n., or* **Rom′ney Marsh** (rŏm′nĭ; rŭm′nĭ). [From *Romney,* or *Romney Marsh,* Kent, Eng.] A breed of sheep adapted to lowlying lands.

romp (rŏmp), *n.* [From earlier *ramp* a bold woman.] **1.** A person, esp. a girl, who romps. **2.** [From ROMP, *v.*] Boisterous play. **3.** *Horse Racing.* A fast but unforced pace; as, to win in a *romp.* — *v. i.* **1.** To play boisterously. **2.** *Slang. Horse Racing.* To run easily before the field.

romp′er (rŏmp′ẽr), *n.* **1.** One who romps. **2.** *pl.* A type of child's dress, with the lower part shaped like bloomers.

romp′ish, *adj.* Inclined to romp. — **romp′ish·ness,** *n.*

Rom′u·lus (rŏm′ū·lŭs), *n.* [L.] Legendary founder and first king of Rome. With his twin brother, Remus, he was thrown in infancy into the Tiber, but saved and suckled by a she-wolf. He slew Remus for leaping scornfully over the wall of his new city, Rome. He was carried to heaven by his father, Mars, and was deified by the Romans.

ron′deau (rŏn′dō; rŏn·dō′), *n.* [F. See ROUNDEL.] *Pros.* A fixed lyrical form of French origin running on two rhymes and consisting usually of thirteen lines and an unrhymed refrain taken from the beginning of the first line; a poem in this form. The rhymes and refrain are generally arranged; *aabba, aab* refrain, *aabba* refrain.

ron′del (rŏn′dĕl; -d'l), *n.* [See ROUNDEL.] *Pros.* A lyric form of French origin running on two rhymes and having commonly fourteen lines, of which the first two are repeated as a refrain at the seventh and eighth, and again at the thirteenth and fourteenth; a poem in this form.

ron·di′no (rŏn·dē′nō), **ron′do·let′to** (rŏn′dō·lĕt′ō), *n.* [Dim. of *rondo.*] *Music.* A short rondo.

ron′do (rŏn′dō; rŏn·dō′), *n.; pl.* RONDOS (-dōz). [It. *rondò,* fr. F. *rondeau.*] **1.** *Music.* A composition or movement in which the principal theme or first subject occurs at least three times in the same key, with contrasting themes in between. It is often the last movement of a sonata. **2.** = RONDEAU.

ron′dure (rŏn′dūr), *n.* [F. *rondeur* roundness.] A round; a circle.

ron′geur′ (rôɴ′zhûr′), *n.* [F., fr. *ronger* to gnaw.] *Surg.* An instrument for removing small pieces of bone.

rönt′gen, etc. See ROENTGEN, etc.

ron′yon (rŭn′yŭn), *n.* Also **ron′ion.** *Obs.* A mangy or scabby creature.

rood (rōōd), *n.* [AS. *rōd* a cross, measure of land, rod, pole.] **1.** *Eccl.* A cross or crucifix; esp., in medieval churches, a large crucifix at the entrance of the chancel (called also ***holy rood***), often supported on a beam (**rood beam**), or screen (**rood screen**). **2. a** A square measure equal usually to one fourth of an acre, or 40 square rods. **b** A linear measure varying locally, usually 7 or 8 yards, but sometimes a rod.

roof (rōōf; 85), *n.* [AS. *hrōf* top, roof.] **1.** *Arch.* The cover of any building. **2. a** A house; dwelling. **b** The top or summit. **3.** That which resembles, or corresponds to, the top of a house. — *v. t.* To cover with or as with a roof.

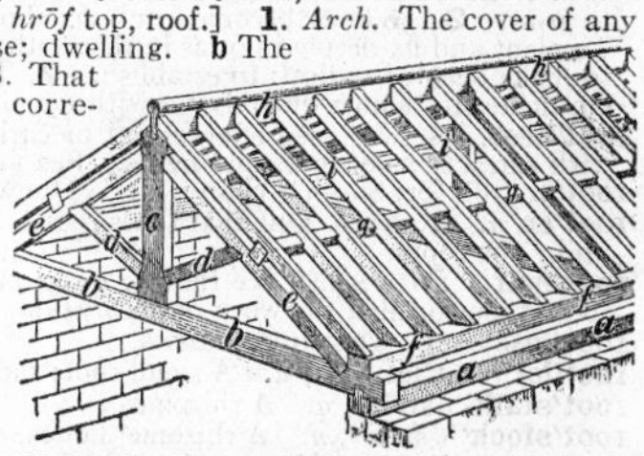

Timbers in a Common Gable Roof. *a a* Wall Plate; *b b* Tie Beam; *c* King Post; *d d* Struts; *e e* Principal Rafters; *f f* Pole Plate; *g g* Purlin; *h h* Ridgepole, or Ridgepiece; *i i* Common Rafters. Cf. QUEEN POST, *Illust.*

roof′er (rōōf′ẽr; 85), *n.* One who puts on or mends roofs.

roof garden. A garden on the flat roof of a building; esp., a garden where refreshments are served, on the roof of a high building, often with a stage for entertainments.

roof′ing, *n.* **a** Act of covering with a roof. **b** Materials for a roof, or materials forming a roof. — *adj.* Used, or fit or prepared for use, in building or covering roofs; as, *roofing* felt, slate, tile, tongs, etc.

roof′less, *adj.* **1.** Having no roof. **2.** Having no house or home; homeless.

roof′tree′ (rōōf′trē′), *n.* The ridgepole; hence, the roof itself; also, figuratively, the home; dwelling place.

rook (rŏŏk), *n.* [OF. *roc,* fr. Per. *rukh.*] *Chess.* A piece moving parallel to the sides of the board across any number of unoccupied squares. Abbr. *R* (no period).

rook, *n.* [AS. *hrōc.*] **1.** An abundant European corvine bird (*Corvus frugilegus*) about the size and color of the American crow. **2.** A cheat; sharper. — *v. t. & i.* To cheat.

rook′er·y (rŏŏk′ẽr·ĭ), *n.; pl.* -ERIES (-ĭz). **1.** The breeding place of a colony of rooks; also, the rooks. Also, a breeding place of other gregarious birds, as herons. **2.** The breeding ground of seals, esp. of fur seals. **3.** A dilapidated building with many rooms and occupants; also, a cluster of dilapidated buildings housing many occupants, as in a city slum.

rook′ie, rook′y (rŏŏk′ĭ), *n.* [From RECRUIT.] *Slang.* A raw recruit; hence, a novice; beginner.

rook′y (rŏŏk′ĭ), *adj.;* ROOK′I·ER (-ĭ·ẽr); ROOK′I·EST. *Rare.* Full of, or abounding in, rooks.

room (rōōm; 85), *n.* [AS. *rūm.*] **1.** Extent of space, great or small; compass; esp., unobstructed space. **2.** Space enclosed or set apart by a partition; an apartment or chamber; also, the people, collectively, in the apartment. **3.** *Obs.* Place or position; rank; station. **4.** Possibility of admission; opportunity; fit occasion; as, little *room* for disagreement. — *v. i. Chiefly U. S.* To occupy a room or rooms; lodge. — *v. t.* To accommodate with lodgings.

room′er (rōōm′ẽr), *n. Chiefly U. S.* A lodger.

room·ette′ (rōōm·ĕt′), *n.* A small private single bedroom with folding bed, toilet facilities, and sliding door opening on the center aisle of a certain type of Pullman car.

room′ful (rōōm′fŏŏl), *n.* As much or many as a room will hold; also, the persons or objects in a room.

room′ing house. A house in which furnished rooms, or apartments, are let to lodgers; a lodginghouse.

room′mate′ (rōōm′māt′), *n.* One of two or more occupying the same room or rooms.

room′y (rōōm′ĭ), *adj.;* -I·ER (-ĭ·ẽr); -I·EST. Having ample room; spacious. — **room′i·ly,** *adv.* — **room′i·ness,** *n.*

roor′back (rōōr′băk), *n.* Also, formerly, **roor′bach.** *U. S.* A defamatory falsehood published for political effect.

☞ The word originated in 1844, when there was published, to the detriment of James K. Polk, then a candidate for president, an extract purporting to be from *Roorback's Tour through the Western and Southern States in 1836.*

roose (rōōz; *Scot. also* rūz), *n. & v.* [ON. *hrōs.*] *Obs. exc. Dial.* Boast; vaunt; praise.

roost (rōōst), *n.* [AS. *hrōst* roost, perch.] **1.** A perch, as for fowls at night. **2.** Hence, a resting place; lodging. — *v. i.* To sit or rest, as fowls on a perch.

roost′er (rōōs′tẽr), *n.* **1.** *U. S.* The male of the domestic fowl; a cock. See POULTRY, *Illust.* **2.** *Slang.* A cocky, strutting, active person.

root (rōōt; 85), *v. i. & t.* [AS. *wrōtan.*] **1.** To turn up the earth with the snout, as swine. **2.** To poke around; to dig down into some mass in order to find something.

root, *v. i.* [Prob. fr. *rout* to shout, roar.] *Slang, U. S.* To shout for, or otherwise noisily applaud or encourage, a contestant, as in sports.

root (rōōt; 85), *n.* [AS. *rōt*, fr. ON. *rōt*.] **1.** *Bot.* In higher plants (ferns and seed plants), a portion of the plant body bearing neither leaves nor reproductive organs, but provided with a growing point and functioning as an organ of absorption, an aerating organ, a food reservoir, or a means of support. **2.** Popularly, any subterranean part of a plant. Cf. BULB, CORM, RHIZOME, TUBER. **3.** That which resembles a root in position or function. Specif.: **a** An ancestor; hence, an early race; stem. **b** The part of an organ by which it is attached, as that part of a tooth in the socket. See TOOTH, *Illust.* **c** The cause; source. **d** The lowest place, position, or part; hence, the essential point or part. **4.** *Math.* A quantity which, taken as a factor a number of times (indicated by the index), produces another quantity; thus, either + 3 or − 3 is a second *root* of 9, because either taken twice as a factor produces 9. **5.** *Music.* The tone from whose harmonics, or overtones, a chord is composed, often simply the lowest tone of a chord in its normal position. **6.** *Philol.* An uncompounded word or element, without prefix, infix, suffix, or inflectional ending. — **Syn.** See ORIGIN. — *v. i.* **1.** To fix the root; to take root and begin to grow. **2.** To be or become firmly fixed or established. — *v. t.* **1.** To plant and fix deeply in or as in the earth; to implant firmly; hence, to make deep or radical; to establish. **2.** To tear up by the root; to eradicate; to remove entirely; — with *up*, *out*, or *away*. — **root**, *adj.*

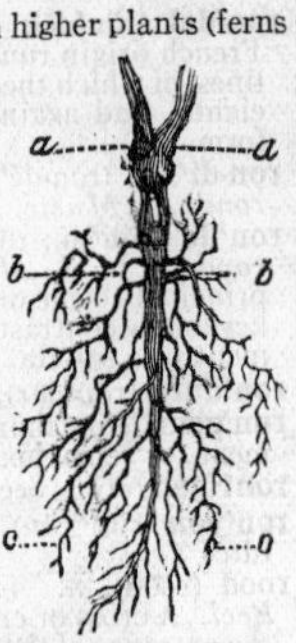

Root. *a, a* Crown; *b, b* Main Root; *c, c* Rootlets.

root beer. A sweetened effervescent or carbonated beverage flavored with extractions of roots and herbs. See BEER, 3.

root′er (rōōt′ẽr; 85), *n.* *Slang, U. S.* One who roots, or applauds.

root′er, *n.* **1.** *Rare.* One that takes root. **2.** One that roots or tears up by the roots.

root hair. *Bot.* A hairlike tubular outgrowth from near the tip of a rootlet, performing the work of absorption.

root′less, *adj.* Destitute of roots.

root′let (rōōt′lĕt; -lĭt), *n.* A small root; radicel. See ROOT, *Illust.*

root′stalk′ (-stôk′), *n.* A rhizome.

root′stock′ (-stŏk′), *n.* A rhizome; hence, a source.

root′y (rōōt′ĭ; 85), *adj.*; ROOT′I·ER (-ĭ·ẽr); ROOT′I·EST. Full of roots; like, or of the quality of, a root or roots. — **root′i·ness** (-ĭ·nĕs; -nĭs), *n.*

rope (rōp), *n.* [AS. *rāp*.] **1.** A large, stout cord made of strands of fiber or wire twisted or braided together. **2.** A hangman's noose; hence, punishment or death by hanging. **3.** A row or string of things united, as by braiding, twining, etc.; as, a *rope* of pearls. **4.** A viscous or glutinous formation in a ropy liquid. — *v. t.* **1.** To bind or tie with a rope. **2.** To connect or fasten together with a rope. **3.** To partition, separate, or divide, by means of a rope. **4.** *Western U. S.* To lasso (a steer, horse, etc.). **5.** *Slang, U. S.* To draw as if with a rope; to inveigle; lure; — with *in*. — *v. i.* To be formed into or to twist in the shape of rope. — *adj.* Of or pert. to rope or ropes. — **rop′er** (rōp′ẽr), *n.*

rope′danc′er (rōp′dȧn′sẽr), *n.* One who dances, walks, or performs acrobatic feats, on a rope extended through the air at some height. — **rope′danc′ing**, *n.*

rop′er·y (rōp′ẽr·ĭ), *n.* **1.** A place where ropes are made; ropewalk. **2.** *Obs.* Roguery; roguish tricks.

rope′walk′ (rōp′wôk′), *n.* A long covered walk, building, or room where ropes are manufactured.

rope′walk′er (-ẽr), *n.* An acrobat who walks a rope.

rop′y (rōp′ĭ), *adj.*; ROP′I·ER (-ĭ·ẽr); ROP′I·EST. **1.** Viscous; glutinous; as, *ropy* sirup. **2.** Resembling rope; stringy. — **rop′i·ly** (-ĭ·lĭ), *adv.* — **rop′i·ness** (-ĭ·nĕs; -nĭs), *n.*

roque (rōk), *n.* [Abbr. fr. *croquet*.] A form of croquet.

Roque′fort cheese, *or* **Roque′fort** (rōk′fẽrt; rôk′fôr′), *n.* A cheese, originally made at Roquefort, France, having a flavor caused by a blue mold (*Penicillium roquefortii*).

roq′ue·laure (rŏk′ĕ·lōr; rôk′lōr′), *n.* [F., after Duc de *Roquelaure*.] A knee-length cloak buttoned in front, worn after 1700.

ro·quet′ (rō·kā′; *Brit.* rō′kā, -kĭ), *v. t. & i.* *Croquet.* To hit (another's ball); — said of a ball or of the player who strikes it. — *n.* Act of roqueting.

ror′qual (rôr′kwăl), *n.* [F. (& G.), fr. Nor. *rörhval*, *röyrkval*, lit., red whale.] Any of a genus (*Balaenoptera*) comprising some of the largest whales; a finback.

Ror′schach test (rōr′shäk; *Angl.* rôr′shäk). [After Hermann *Rorschach* (1884–1922), Swiss psychiatrist.] A psychological test in which a subject is called upon to interpret what he sees in different inkblot designs, for analyzing intellectual and emotional processes, personality, response to environment, etc.

ro·sa′ceous (rō·zā′shŭs), *adj.* [L. *rosaceus*, fr. *rosa* rose.] *Bot.* **1.** Belonging to or designating the rose family. See ROSE, 1. **2.** Having a regular flower with five petals, as the rose.

ros·an′i·line (rōz·ăn′ĭ·lĭn; -līn; -lēn), *n.* Also **ros·an′i·lin.** [*rose* + *aniline*.] *Chem.* A white crystalline base, $NH_2(CH_3)C_6H_3C(OH)(C_6H_4NH_2)_2$, obtained in red-colored salts by oxidation of a mixture of aniline and orthotoluidine and paratoluidine. It is the parent of many aniline dyes.

ro′sa·ry (rō′zȧ·rĭ), *n.*; *pl.* -RIES (-rĭz). [ML. *rosarium* string of beads, series of prayers, garland of roses, in L., a rose garden, fr. *rosarius* of roses, fr. *rosa* a rose.] **1.** A bed or bush of roses, or place where roses grow. **2.** A string of beads used in counting prayers; esp., the prayers of the Rosary (sense 3). **3.** *Eccl.* [*cap.*] A form of devotion to the Virgin Mary consisting of fifteen decades of Ave Marias, each of which is preceded by a Pater Noster and ended with a Gloria Patri.

rose (rōz), *n.* [AS., fr. L. *rosa*, fr. Gr. *rhodon*, of Oriental origin.] **1.** Any of a genus (*Rosa*) of erect, climbing, or creeping shrubs with mostly prickly stems, pinnate leaves, and showy flowers, having five petals in the wild state, but double or semidouble in cultivation. The genus is the type of a family (Rosaceae, the rose family) of nearly cosmopolitan trees, shrubs, and herbs (order Rosales), including, besides the rose, blackberries, raspberries, strawberries, spiraeas, cinquefoils, the goatsbeard, etc. Also, a flower of this shrub. The rose is the floral emblem of England; the ***wild rose*** has been made the State flower of New York, North Dakota, and Iowa. See AMERICAN BEAUTY, CHEROKEE ROSE. **2.** A rosette, esp. one on a shoe. **3.** A perforated nozzle for delivering water in fine jets. **4.** = ROSE COLOR. **5.** *Jewelry.* A form in which diamonds and other gems are cut; also, a gem, esp. a diamond, so cut. **6.** *Naut.* **a** = COMPASS CARD. **b** A circular card with radiating lines, used in other instruments. — ***under the rose.*** A translation of L. *sub rosa*, in secret; under circumstances forbidding disclosure; — the rose being anciently a symbol of secrecy. — *v. t.* To render rose-colored; flush. — **rose′bud′** (-bŭd′), *n.* — **rose′bush′** (-bŏŏsh′), *n.*

rose (rōz), *past of* RISE.

ro′se·ate (rō′zē·āt; -ĭt), *adj.* **1.** Full of, consisting of, or made from roses. **2.** Resembling a rose; esp., tinged with the color rose; hence, figuratively, optimistic; as, *roseate* hopes. — **ro′se·ate·ly**, *adv.*

rose′bay′ (rōz′bā′), *n.* **a** The oleander. **b** Any species of rhododendron, esp. the great rhododendron or the pink rhododendron. See RHODODENDRON.

rose beetle *or* **bug.** A yellowish scarabaeid beetle (*Macrodactylus subspinosus*) often injuring rosebushes, etc.

rose campion. **a** See CAMPION. **b** The corn cockle.

rose cold. *Med.* A variety of hay fever occurring in the spring or early summer, attributed to rose pollen.

rose color. The color of a rose, deep pink or pale cardinal.

rose′–col′ored, *adj.* Of the color rose; hence, pleasing; alluring; also, optimistic.

rose fever. Rose cold.

rose geranium. *Hort.* Any of several South African herbs (genus *Pelargonium*, esp. *P. graveolens*), grown for their fragrant 3–5 lobed leaves and small pink flowers.

rose mallow. **a** Any of several plants (genus *Hibiscus*) of the mallow family, with large rose-colored flowers. **b** The hollyhock.

rose′mar′y (rōz′mâr′ĭ *or, esp. Brit.*, -mẽr·ĭ), *n.*; *pl.* -IES (-ĭz). [L. *rosmarinus*, fr. *ros* dew + *marinus* marine. In Eng. the word has been changed as if it meant the *rose of Mary*.] A fragrant shrub (*Rosmarinus officinalis*) of the mint family, of southern Europe and Asia Minor, used in cookery, perfumery, etc. It is an emblem of fidelity or constancy.

rose moss. The garden portulaca. See PORTULACA.

rose of Jer′i·cho (jĕr′ĭ·kō). A Syrian plant (*Anastatica hierochuntica*) of the mustard family, which rolls up when dry, and expands again when moistened.

rose of Shar′on (shâr′ŭn). **a** A Eurasian St.-John's wort (*Hypericum calycinum*) often cultivated for its large yellow flowers. **b** The althea.

ro·se′o·la (rō·zē′ō·lȧ), *n.* [NL., dim. fr. L. *roseus* rosy.] *Med.* Any rose-colored rash; specif., rubella.

ros′et (rŏz′ĭt), *n.* *Chiefly Scot.* Resin.

Ro·set′ta stone (rō·zĕt′ȧ). A piece of black basalt found in 1799 near the Rosetta mouth of the Nile, bearing a bilingual inscription (in hieroglyphics, demotic characters, and Greek), and famous as having given M. Champollion the first clue toward deciphering the Egyptian hieroglyphics.

ro·sette′ (rō·zĕt′), *n.* [F., dim. of *rose* a rose.] **1.** An imitation of a rose made of gathered or pleated material, of thread (as in lace), etc. **2.** Something resembling a rose, as in shape or color. **3.** *Arch.* An ornament somewhat like a roundel, and filled with leafage. **4.** *Bot.* A short internode bearing a cluster of leaves. See INVOLUCRE, *Illust.*

rose water. A watery solution of the odoriferous constituents of the rose, used as a perfume.

rose′–wa′ter, *adj.* Having the odor of rose water; hence, affectedly nice or delicate.

rose window. *Arch.* A circular window filled with tracery.

rose′wood′ (rōz′wŏŏd′), *n.* Any of several valuable cabinet woods of a dark-red or purplish color, streaked with black, obtained from various tropical trees, esp. of Brazil and Honduras; also, the trees yielding these woods.

Rosh Ha·sha′na (rōsh hä·shä′nä). Also **Rosh Ha·sho′noh** (hä·shô′nō). [Heb. *rōsh* head of + *hash-shānāh* the year.] See JEWISH HOLIDAYS.

Ro′si·cru′cian (rō′zĭ·krōō′shăn; rŏz′ĭ-), *n.* [After Christian *Rosenkreuz* (Lat. *Rosae Crucis*), described (1614) by J. V. Andreä as founder of a secret society in Germany in the 15th century.] An alleged member, in the 17th century and the early 18th century, of an esoteric order of philosophers deeply versed in the secrets of nature and mysticism. The society was revived in England in 1866 with the title *Societas Rosicruciana in Anglia* and on the continent in 1890. In America there are several fraternities named *Rosicrucian* that use the emblems of the rose and the cross and claim to share the esoteric teachings. — **Ro′si·cru′cian**, *adj.* — **Ro′si·cru′cian·ism** (-ĭz′m), *n.*

ros′i·ly (rōz′ĭ·lĭ), *adv.* of ROSY.

ros′in (rŏz′ĭn; -′n), *n.* [From RESIN.] The hard resin, amber-colored to almost black, left after distilling off the volatile oil of turpentine and used in varnishes and soaps, on violin bows, in driers for oils, etc. — *v. t.* To rub with rosin.

Ros′i·nan′te (rŏz′ĭ·năn′tē), *n.* [Sp. *Rocinante*, fr. *rocín* a jaded horse, a hack + *ante* before.] Don Quixote's steed, lean, bony, and unsound, but regarded by the knight as incomparable; hence, any worn-out nag; a jade.

ros′i·ness (rōz′ĭ·nĕs; -nĭs), *n.* Quality or state of being rosy.

ros′in·weed′ (rŏz′ĭn·wēd′), *n.* Any of various American plants having resinous foliage or odor; specif., the compass plant *Silphium laciniatum.*

ro·so′lio (rō·zôl′yō), *n.* [It., fr. ML. *ros solis* sundew, from which it was originally extracted.] A sweet cordial of the Mediterranean region, made of brandy, sugar, raisins, etc.

ros′tel·late (rŏs′tĕ·lāt), *adj.* [NL. *rostellatus*.] Having a small beak.

ros′ter (rŏs′tẽr; rōs′tẽr), *n.* [D. *rooster* a list.] **1.** *Mil. & Nav.* A roll or list of officers or enlisted men, subject to certain assignments for duty. **2.** Hence, any roll or list.

ros′tra (rŏs′trȧ), *n., pl.* of ROSTRUM.

ros′tral (-trăl), *adj.* [LL. *rostralis*.] Pert. to a rostrum.

ros′trate (-trāt), *adj.* Having a rostrum or beak.

ros′trum (rŏs′trŭm), *n.*; *pl.* -TRA (-trȧ), -TRUMS (-trŭmz). [L., beak, ship's beak, fr. *rodere*, *rosum*, to gnaw.] **1.** *Obs. exc. Hist. Rom. Antiq.* The curved end of a ship's prow, esp. the beak of a war galley. **2.** *pl.* ROSTRA. *Rom. Antiq.* The platform in the Forum where orations, pleadings, etc., were delivered. **3.** Hence, a stage for public speaking; the pulpit or platform. **4.** *Anat. & Zool.* A part suggesting a bird's beak.

ros′y (rōz′ĭ), *adj.*; ROS′I·ER (-ĭ·ẽr); ROS′I·EST. **1.** Resembling a rose.

specif., blooming; blushing; also, made of roses. **2.** Figuratively, promising success; as, *rosy* prospects; also, optimistic.

rot (rŏt), *v. i.;* ROT′TED; ROT′TING. [AS. *rotian.*] **1.** To decompose; decay. **2.** To become morally corrupt; to degenerate. — *v. t.* **1.** To cause to rot. **2.** To ret (flax, etc.) in order to separate the fiber. — **Syn.** See DECAY. — *n.* **1.** Process of rotting, or state of being rotten; decay; also, that which is rotting. **2.** *Slang.* Offensive nonsense. **3.** *Veter.* Any of a number of parasitic diseases, chiefly of sheep, characterized by rotting, emaciation, etc. — *interj.* An exclamation expressing irritation, disgust, etc.

ro′ta (rō′tȧ), *n.* [L., wheel.] **1.** A roll; roster. **2.** *R.C.Ch.* A court, called also ***Sacra Romana Rota*** (Sacred Roman Rota), of the Roman Curia, with jurisdiction, ordinarily appellate, in civil and ecclesiastical cases.

Ro·tar′i·an (rō·târ′ĭ·ăn), *n.* A member of any of a large number of clubs (**Ro′ta·ry Clubs**) having the same constitution and affiliated under an International Association of Rotary Clubs (***Rotary International***) and having as their motto "Service." — **Ro·tar′i·an·ism** (-ĭz′m), *n.*

ro′ta·ry (rō′tȧ·rĭ), *adj.* [LL. *rotarius*, fr. L. *rota* a wheel.] Turning, as a wheel on its axis; having parts that rotate; rotatory. — *n.* **1.** A rotary machine, as a rotary engine or a rotary press. **2.** A road junction formed around a central circular plot about which traffic moves in a counterclockwise direction only; — called also *traffic circle.*

rotary engine. **1.** Any of various engines in which power is applied by revolving wheels, as in a turbine, or by vanes, or the like, constrained to move in a circular path. Cf. RECIPROCATING ENGINE. **2.** A radial engine in which the cylinders revolve about a fixed crankshaft.

rotary press. See PRESS, *n.*, 3 **a**.

ro′tate (rō′tāt *or, esp. Brit.*, rō·tāt′), *v. i.* [L. *rotatus*, past part. of *rotare*, fr. *rota* wheel.] **1.** To turn, as a wheel, round an axis; to revolve. **2.** To perform any act, function, or operation in turn; to pass or alternate in a series. — *v. t.* **1.** To cause to rotate, or turn, as a wheel, around an axle; to revolve. **2.** To cause to succeed, pass, or act, in turn in a series; as, to *rotate* men in office. **3.** *Agric.* To cause to grow in rotation; as, to *rotate* crops. — **ro′tat·a·ble** (rō′tāt·ȧ·b′l; rō·tāt′-), *adj.*

ro′tate (rō′tāt), *adj.* Having the parts flat and spreading or radiating like those of a wheel; wheel-shaped.

ro·ta′tion (rō·tā′shŭn), *n.* **1.** Act of rotating, or turning on or as on an axis. See REVOLUTION, 1 **b**. **2.** Any return or succession in a series; as, *rotation* in office. — **ro·ta′tion·al** (-ăl; -′l), *adj.*

ro′ta·tive (rō′tȧ·tĭv), *adj.* **1.** Turning, as a wheel; rotary. **2.** Causing rotation; also, occurring in regular series.

ro′ta·tor (rō′tā·tẽr; rō·tā′tẽr), *n.* [L.] Anything that rotates; specif.: *Anat.* [*pl.* ROTATORES (rō′tȧ·tō′rēz; 70).] A muscle which partially rotates a part on its axis.

ro′ta·to′ry (rō′tȧ·tō′rĭ; *Brit. also* rō·tā′tō·rĭ), *adj.* **1.** Of, pert. to, or producing rotation; having parts that rotate; rotary. **2.** Going or following in rotation or succession.

rotche, rotch (rŏch), *n.* = DOVEKIE **b**.

rote (rōt), *n.* The noise produced by the surf on the shore.

rote, *n.* A fixed course or routine; hence, repetition of forms or phrases, often without attention to meaning.

rote, *n. Music.* = 1st CROWD.

ro′te·none (rō′t′n·ōn), *n. Chem.* A poisonous crystalline ketone, $C_{23}H_{22}O_6$, found in certain fish poisons and used as an insecticide.

ro′ti·fer (rō′tĭ·fẽr), *n.* [NL., fr. L. *rota* a wheel + *ferre* to bear.] One of a class (Rotifera) of minute, many-celled aquatic animals having the anterior end modified into a retractile disc (*corona*) bearing circles of strong cilia, which, when in motion, look like rapidly revolving wheels. They are most abundant in stagnant fresh water. — **ro·tif′er·al** (rō·tĭf′ẽr·ăl), *adj.* — **ro·tif′er·ous** (-ŭs), *adj.*

ro′tis′se·rie′ (rō′tēs′rē′), *n.* [F., fr. *rôtir* to roast.] **1.** A shop where roast meats are prepared and sold. **2.** *U.S.* A restaurant where patrons may select their meat and have it roasted in their view.

rot′l (rŏt′′l), *n.; pl.* ARTAL (är′täl). [Ar. *raṭl.*] A weight of North Africa, and of parts of Europe and Asia, corresponding to the pound, but varying greatly with the locality; also, a varying dry measure.

ro′to·graph (rō′tō·grȧf; 9), *n.* [L. *rota* wheel + *-graph.*] A photograph printed by a process in which a strip of sensitized paper is automatically fed under the negative so that a series of prints is made.

ro′to·gra·vure′ (-grȧ·vūr′; -grā′vūr), *n.* [L. *rota* wheel + *gravure.*] **1.** A process of photogravure in which the impression is produced by etched cylindrical plates affixed to the rollers of a rotary printing press; hence, an illustration so printed. **2.** Also **roto section.** A section of a newspaper devoted to rotogravure pictures.

ro′tor (rō′tẽr), *n.* [Short for *rotator.*] **1.** *Aeronautics.* A complete system of rotating blades or airfoils that supplies all or a major portion of the lift supporting an aircraft, as in a helicopter. Hence, **ro′tor·craft′** (rō′tẽr·krȧft′), **rotor plane, ro′ta·ry–wing′ air′craft′, ro′tat·ing–wing′ air′craft′.** **2.** *Mach.* A part that revolves in a stationary part; esp., the rotating member of an electrical machine.

rotor ship. *Naut.* A ship propelled by the wind acting on one or more revolving vertical cylinders (**rotors,** *or* **rotor masts**).

ro′to sec′tion (rō′tō). See ROTOGRAVURE, 2.

rot′ten (rŏt′′n), *adj.* [ON. *rotinn.*] **1.** Having rotted; putrid; hence, fetid. **2.** Unsound, as if rotted; not firm. **3.** Corrupt; esp., open to bribery. — **rot′ten·ly,** *adv.* — **rot′ten·ness,** *n.*

rotten borough. **1.** *Eng. Hist.* Any of the boroughs which, at the time of the Reform Act of 1832, contained but few voters, yet retained the privilege of sending a member to Parliament. **2.** Any political unit in a republican form of government that has much less than its due proportion of inhabitants.

rot′ten·stone′ (-stōn′), *n.* A decomposed siliceous limestone, used for polishing.

rot′ter (rŏt′ẽr), *n.* [From ROT, *v.*] *Slang.* A blackguard; more vaguely, a thoroughly objectionable person.

ro·tund′ (rō·tŭnd′), *adj.* [L. *rotundus.*] **1.** Round or rounded out; spherical. **2.** Rounded; full and flowing, as speech. — **ro·tun′di·ty** (-tŭn′dĭ·tĭ), *n.* — **ro·tund′ly,** *adv.* — **ro·tund′ness,** *n.*

ro·tun′da (rō·tŭn′dȧ), *n.* [It. *rotonda*, fr. L. *rotundus* round, fem. *rotunda.*] **1.** *Arch.* A round building, esp. one covered by a dome or cupola. **2.** A large round room; as, the *rotunda* of the Capitol.

‖**ro′tu′rier′** (rō′tü′ryā′), *n.; pl.* -RIERS (*F.* -ryā′). [F.] A person not of noble birth.

rou′ble (rōō′b′l), **rouche** (rōōsh). Vars. of RUBLE, RUCHE.

rou·é′ (rōō·ā′), *n.* [F.] A debauchee; rake.

rouge (rōōzh), *n.* [F.] **1.** A red powder consisting of ferric oxide used in polishing, as a pigment, etc. **2.** Any of various cosmetics used for giving a red color to the cheeks or lips. — *v. i. & t.;* ROUGED (rōōzhd); ROUG′ING (rōōzh′ĭng). To tint with rouge, as the cheeks.

rouge′ et noir′ (rōō′-zhā nwär′). [F., red and black.] Trente et quarante; — so called from the colors bet on.

rough (rŭf), *adj.* [AS. *rūh.*] **1.** Having inequalities, ridges, or projections on the surface; not smooth. Specif.: **a** Hairy; shaggy. **b** Not level; uneven; — of a piece of land, or of a road. **c** Tossed in waves; not calm; — of water. **2.** Coarse or rugged in character or appearance; unrefined. Specif.: **a** Harsh to the eye; as, a *rough* landscape. **b** Not cultivated; rude; as, *rough* peasants. **c** Harsh to the ear; discordant; as, a *rough* voice. **d** Harsh to the taste; as, *rough* whisky. **3.** Not tranquil; boisterous; tempestuous. **4.** Not gentle; harsh; surly; uncivil. **5.** In a crude or unfinished state; as, the *rough* lumber for a house; hence, hastily done or made and therefore confessedly imperfect; as, a *rough* estimate. **6.** Of fish, not game; not sought in sport. **7.** *Phonet.* Pronounced with a breathing or aspirate; aspirated; as, a *rough* vowel.

Syn. (1) **Rough, harsh, uneven, rugged, scabrous** mean not smooth or even. **Rough** implies points, bristles, ridges, or projections on the surface or exterior; **harsh,** a surface or texture distinctly unpleasant to the tactile sense or, by extension, to any sense or to one's nerves; **uneven,** a lack of uniformity in height, breadth, quality, etc.; **rugged,** a roughness, esp. of surface; **scabrous,** a scaliness, thorniness, prickliness, etc., as of surface.
(2) See RUDE.

— *n.* **1.** [Perh. orig. short for RUFFIAN.] A rowdy; ruffian. **2.** That which is rough; crude material. **3.** Ground uneven and covered with brush, stones, etc. **4.** *Golf.* Any portion of the course on which grass, weeds, etc., are allowed to grow freely; — opp. to *fairway.*

— *v. t.* **1.** To roughen. **2.** To shape, make, or dress, roughly. **3.** *Football, etc.* To subject (an opponent) to unnecessary and intentional violence.

rough it. **a** To endure hard or rude conditions of living. **b** To indulge in rough conduct or contention. — ***rough out.*** To draw, block out, etc., a piece of work hastily and rudely, with the intention of polishing it later.

— *adv.* In a rough manner; roughly.

rough′age (rŭf′ĭj), *n.* [From ROUGH, *adj.*] **a** Any rough or coarse substance. **b** *U.S.* Specif., coarse food or fodder, as food high in indigestible material, esp. cellulose, whose bulk stimulates peristalsis.

rough′–and–read′y, *adj.* Rude in nature, method, or manner, but effective in action or use.

rough′–and–tum′ble (*see Pron.*, § 2), *adj.* Characterized by violence not restrained by rule; as, a *rough-and-tumble* fight.

rough breathing. [Trans. of L. *spiritus asper.*] In Greek grammar, a mark of aspiration [ʽ] placed over initial vowels or over ρ (rho), thus ὡς is pronounced *hōs;* also, the sound thus indicated.

rough′cast′ (rŭf′kȧst′; 9), *n.* **1.** A rude model. **2.** A type of plastering made of lime, with a mixture of shells or pebbles, used for covering buildings. — *v. t.* **1.** To shape or form roughly; to block out. **2.** To plaster with roughcast. — **rough′cast′er,** *n.*

rough′dry′ (rŭf′drī′), *v. t.;* see DRY. In laundry work, to dry without smoothing or ironing. — **rough′dry′,** *adj.*

rough′en (rŭf′ĕn; -′n), *v. t. & i.* To make or become rough.

rough′er (-ẽr), *n.* One who roughs or roughs out anything.

rough′hew′ (rŭf′hū′; 2), *v. t.;* see HEW. **1.** To hew coarsely, without smoothing; as, to *roughhew* timber. **2.** To form crudely; roughcast.

rough′house′ (rŭf′hous′), *n.* An outbreak of violence or noisy sport, esp. among occupants of a house or room. — *v. t.* To handle roughly, but in a spirit of fun. — *v. i.* To start, or take part in, a roughhouse. *All Slang.*

rough′ly, *adv.* In a rough manner.

rough′neck′ (rŭf′nĕk′), *n. Slang.* One who is rough or uncouth, esp. in manners; a boor; also, a rowdy; tough.

rough′ness, *n.* Quality or state of being rough.

rough′rid′er (rŭf′rīd′ẽr; rŭf′rīd′ẽr; 2), *n.* One who breaks horses to the saddle or is accustomed to riding little-trained horses; *Colloq.*, an irregular cavalryman; hence [*cap.*], a member of the 1st U. S. Volunteer Cavalry, a regiment raised for the Spanish War of 1898, largely organized, and later commanded, by Theodore Roosevelt.

rough′shod′ (rŭf′shŏd′; 2), *adj.* Shod with calked shoes. — ***to ride roughshod.*** To ride or travel without regard to difficulties; hence, to tyrannize over.

rou·lade′ (rōō·läd′), *n.* [F., fr. *rouler* to roll.] *Music.* In vocal music, an ornament consisting of a quick run, arpeggio, or other figure, sung to one syllable; a vocal flourish.

rou·leau′ (rōō·lō′), *n.; pl.* ROULEAUX (-lōz′), ROULEAUS (-lōz′). [F., fr. *rôle.*] Literally, a little roll; specif., a roll of coins put up in paper.

rou·lette′ (rōō·lĕt′), *n.* [F., fr. OF. *roelete*, dim. of *roele.* See ROWEL.] **1.** A gambling game, in which a marble is spun around the inside of a bowl the inner portion of which, called a **roulette wheel,** is revolved in the opposite direction, and has around the bottom numbered red and black compartments, the compartment in which the ball finally comes to rest deciding the results of the wagers. **2.** Any of various toothed wheels or disks, as for producing rows of dots on engraved plates, or for making short consecutive incisions in paper to facilitate subsequent division. Hence, specif.: *Philately.* Separating incisions so made in sheets of stamps without removing any of the paper. Abbr. *roul.* — *v. t.;* ROU·LET′TED (-lĕt′ĕd; -ĭd); ROU·LET′TING. To make incisions in with a roulette.

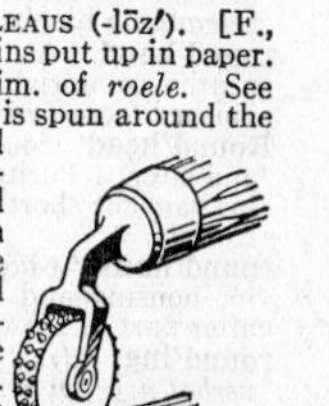

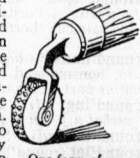

One form of Roulette, 2.

Rou·ma′nian (rōō·mān′yăn; -mā′nĭ·ăn). Var. of ROMANIAN.

round (round), *v. t. & i.* [From obs. or dial. *roun* to whisper, fr. AS. *rūnian.*] *Archaic.* To whisper; to utter in a whisper; to talk or say privately or secretly.

round, *adj.* [OF. *roont, reont,* fem. *roonde, reonde* (F. *rond*), fr. L. *rotundus.*] **1.** Spherical, circular, or globular. **2.** Circular in cross section; esp., cylindrical, as a rifle barrel. **3.** Having a curved outline or form, esp. one like the arc of a circle; rotund. **4.** Characterized by formation or movement in a circle; as, a *round* dance. **5.** Full; complete; not fractional; — said of numbers. **6.** Large; liberal in size or amount; as, a *round* sum. **7.** Not cramped or limited; specif.: **a** Free and vigorous in motion; as, a *round* pace. **b** Uttered or emitted with a full tone; as, a *round* voice. **c** Outspoken; plain and direct; as, a *round* oath. **8.** *Now Rare.* Polished; rounded; — said of language or style. **9.** Complete; esp., accomplished by a progression through a series of places, conditions, etc., with a final return to the starting point; as, a *round* trip. **10.** *Phonet.* Rounded; labialized; labial. See ROUND, *v. t.*, 6.

— *n.* **1.** Anything round, as a circle, globe, ring. **2.** A group; as, a *round* of politicians. **3.** A circular dance; round dance. **4.** A course ending where it began; a circuit; — often in *pl.;* as, to go the *rounds.* **5.** A series of changes, events, acts, or the like, ending where it began; as, the *round* of the seasons; hence, a complete circuit or range; as, the whole *round* of knowledge. **6.** A course of action, conduct, etc., performed by a number of persons in turn, or, loosely, simultaneously; as, a *round* of applause; also, a bout or turn of action participated in by two or more persons in competition; as, a *round* at cards. **7.** A rounded or curved part of anything. **8.** The round step of a ladder; a rung. **9.** = ROUND OF BEEF. **10.** State of being round or circular; roundness. **11.** *Archery.* A certain number of shots at given distances, recognized and named by rule or custom. **12.** *Boxing.* One of the periods into which a boxing contest is divided. **13.** *Mil.* **a** One shot discharged by each soldier, gun, or cannon of a command. **b** A unit of ammunition for one shot. **14.** *Music.* A polyphonic vocal composition in which three or four voices follow each other around in a species of canon in the unison. **15.** *Sports.* A period of play in a contest or match. — ***in the round.*** Of figures, giving the full form in projection on all sides; — distinguished from *relief.*

— *v. t.* **1.** To make round; also, to turn in, or as if in, a circle; to rotate. **2.** To surround; encircle. **3.** To complete; hence, to finish. **4.** To fill out to roundness or fullness of form. **5.** To go round wholly or in part; as, to *round* Cape Horn. **6.** *Phonet.* **a** To draw (the lips) together in a round opening, as in the pronunciation of *oo.* **b** To pronounce (a vowel or consonant) with rounding of the lips; to labialize. — ***round up.*** **a** To collect (cattle) by riding around them and driving them in. See ROUNDUP. **b** *Colloq.* To gather in, as scattered persons. — *v. i.* **1.** To grow round, rotund, or full; hence, to attain to fullness or perfection; also, with *into,* to develop. **2.** *Rare.* To go round; to make a circuit. **3.** To turn round; to wheel about.

— *prep.* **1. a** In a way to enclose on all sides; as, a rope *round* his neck. **b** In a way to pass close by all sides of successively. **2.** On all sides of or from all sides toward, so as to surround. **3.** In all directions from; here and there about; as, we looked *round* us.

— *adv.* **1. a** Circularly; around. **b** So as to reach all of an assemblage, or a number of places, in succession; as, to hand *round* cigars. **c** So as to pass around a thing; in circumference; as, a ball 10 inches *round.* **d** So as to present an opposite side; through a half circle, with one part not changing position; as, to face the clock *round;* hence, from one side, party, attitude of mind, or the like, to another. **2. a** Out in all directions from a point; as, to scatter handbills *round.* **b** In the vicinity; as, to spread among the farmers *round.* **c** *Chiefly U.S.* Hither and thither; as, to sit or dance *round.* **3.** On all sides of or from all sides toward a person or thing so as to confine, surround, or envelop.

round'a·bout' (round'*á*·bout'), *n.* **1.** Merry-go-round. **2.** A short, close jacket worn by boys, sailors, etc. — *adj.* **1.** Circuitous; indirect; as, *roundabout* methods. **2.** Encircling; comprehensive.

round angle. *Math.* The plane angle described by a half line in turning positively in a plane about its extremity as a center until it returns to its original position. It is equal to 360°.

round arch. An arch semicircular in its intrados curve. See ARCH, *Illust.*

round clam. The quahog. See CLAM.

round dance. **a** A country-dance in which participants form a ring, sometimes separating into couples. **b** A ballroom dance in which couples revolve counterclockwise.

round'ed (roun'dĕd; -dĭd), *adj.* **1.** Made round or spherical; also, polished; finished; of speech, deep and sonorous. **2.** *Phonet.* Formed by rounding the lips; labialized.

roun'del (roun'dĕl), *n.* [OF. *rondel* a roundelay (F. *rondel, rondeau*), orig., a dim. fr. *rond.* See ROUND, *adj.*] **1.** [OF. *rondele* (F. *rondelle*).] Anything having a round form; a round figure. **2.** *Arch.* A circular panel, window, or niche. **3.** *Poetry.* **a** Var. of RONDEL. **b** An English modified rondeau.

roun'de·lay (roun'dĕ·lā), *n.* [OF. *rondelet,* dim. of *rondel.* See ROUNDEL.] **1. a** A song in which a simple strain is often repeated. **b** A round dance. **2.** *Archaic Poetry.* A kind of poem or song with a refrain recurring frequently or at fixed intervals as in a rondel.

round'er (roun'dẽr), *n.* **1.** One who makes rounds; specif.: **a** [*cap.*] A Methodist preacher who goes around a circuit. **b** *Slang.* One who makes the rounds of disreputable resorts; a dissolute spendthrift. **2.** One or that which makes something round; specif., a tool for making an edge or surface round. **3.** *pl.* A game, chiefly English, somewhat resembling baseball.

round hand. A style of penmanship in which the letters are formed in nearly an upright position, and each separately distinct; — distinguished from *running hand.*

Round'head' (round'hĕd'), *n.* *Eng. Hist.* In the reign of Charles I and later, a Puritan or member of the Parliamentary party who wore his hair cut short; — so called in derision by the Cavaliers, who wore ringlets.

round'house' (-hous'), *n.* **1.** *Obs.* A lockup. **2.** A circular building for housing and repairing locomotives. **3.** *Naut.* A cabin on the after part of the quarter-deck.

round'ing, *adj.* **1.** Round or nearly round. **2.** [From ROUNDING, *verbal n.*] Of or pertaining to, or used for or in, rounding something.

round'ish, *adj.* Somewhat round. — **round'ish·ness,** *n.*

round'let (round'lĕt; -lĭt), *n.* [OF. *rondelet.*] A little circle or round object; a disk.

round'ly (-lĭ), *adv.* In a round form or manner.

round'ness, *n.* Quality or state of being round.

round of beef. The part of the thigh below the aitchbone, or between the rump and the leg. The inside muscles are often called *top* (round) and those outside *bottom* (round). See BEEF, *Illust.*

round robin. **1.** A written petition, protest, etc., with signatures in a circle so as not to indicate who signed first. **2.** A letter sent from person to person in a group, to which each recipient in turn contributes an additional message. **3.** A tournament, as in chess or tennis, in which each contestant is matched against every other player.

round'-shoul'dered (round'shōl'dẽrd; 2), *adj.* Having the shoulders stooping, rounded, or projecting.

rounds'man (roundz'măn), *n.; pl.* -MEN (-mĕn). **a** *U.S.* A police officer ranking next below a sergeant; — so called because he makes rounds of inspection. **b** *Eng.* A retail deliveryman who sells bread, milk, etc.

round steak. A beefsteak cut from the round.

Round Table. **1. a** A huge circular marble table, at which King Arthur and his knights were accustomed to sit. **b** The knights of King Arthur collectively. **2.** [*not caps.*] Hence, any meeting place of a group for conference, discussion, etc.; also, the group meeting for such a purpose. — **round'-ta'ble,** *adj.*

round trip. A trip to a place and back. — **round'-trip',** *adj.*

round turn and half hitch. See KNOT, *Illust.* (22).

round'up' (round'ŭp'), *n.* **1.** *Western U.S.* Act of gathering together cattle on the range by riding around them and driving them in, as for branding. Also, the men and horses engaged in a roundup, collectively. **2.** *Colloq., U.S.* Hence, a gathering in of scattered persons or things; as, a *roundup* of criminals.

round'worm' (-wûrm'), *n.* A nematode worm, as distinguished from a flatworm.

roup (roup; rōōp), *n.* [From MD. *roepen* to shout.] *Obs. exc. Scot. & Dial.* Auction.

roup (rōōp), *n.* [Prob. of imitative origin.] **1.** Hoarseness; a cold. **2.** *Veter.* A disease of poultry, characterized by hoarseness, discharge from the nostrils and eyes, etc.

roup'et (roup'ĭt; rōōp'-), *adj.* *Scot.* Roupy.

roup'y (rōōp'ĭ), *adj.* **1.** *Scot.* Hoarse. **2.** *Veter.* Affected with roup; pertaining to the roup of poultry.

rouse (rouz), *n.* [From CAROUSE.] **1.** *Obs.* A bumper of liquor, esp. a toast. **2.** A carousal; drinking frolic.

rouse, *v. i. & t.* *Naut.* To haul strongly and all together.

rouse, *v. t. & i.* [Origin uncert. Cf. AROUSE.] **1.** To start from a covert or lurking place. **2.** To wake from sleep or repose. **3.** To excite to activity; to stir up. — *n.* Act of rousing; a sudden start, as from inaction; also, a signal for action. — **rous'er** (rouz'ẽr), *n.*

rous'ing (rouz'ĭng), *adj.* **1.** Having power to awaken or excite; as, a *rousing* appeal. **2.** *Colloq.* That rouses astonishment; remarkable; as, a *rousing* lie.

roust'a·bout' (roust'*á*·bout'), *n.* **1.** *U.S.* **a** A wharf laborer or deck hand, esp. on a river steamboat; in mines, oil fields, etc., a general laborer. **b** A shiftless vagrant who lives by chance jobs. **2.** On ranches in the western United States, a handy man.

rout (rout), *v. i.* [AS. *hrūtan.*] *Dial.* To snore loudly.

rout (rout; rōōt), *v. i.* [ON. *rauta.*] *Obs. exc. Dial.* To roar; bellow; bray. — (rout), *n.* *Archaic.* A bellowing; uproar.

rout (rout), *v. i.* [Var. of 1st ROOT.] To root, search, or rummage, as a swine. — *v. t.* **1.** To root up. **2.** To scoop out, as with a gouge; specif., *Print., Engraving, etc.,* to cut away (blank parts of an engraving, electrotype, etc.) with a tool (router).

rout, *n.* [OF. *route* a throng, defeat, fr. VL. *rupta,* fr. L. *rumpere, ruptum,* to break.] **1.** *Obs.* A throng. **2.** A tumultuous mob; hence, the rabble. **3.** A band of retainers; a retinue. **4.** State of being disorganized and thrown into confused flight. **5.** *Archaic.* A fashionable assembly; esp., a large evening party. **6.** *Law.* A disturbance of the peace by persons assembled with intent to do a thing, which, if executed, would make them rioters. — **Syn.** See CROWD. — *v. t.* To put to rout; defeat utterly. — **Syn.** See CONQUER.

route (rōōt; rout), *n.* [OF. (& F.) *route,* fr. L. *rupta* (sc. *via*), fr. *ruptus,* past part. of *rumpere* to break; hence, lit., a broken or beaten way.] **1.** The course or way which is or is to be traveled. **2.** *Mil.* An order for troops to march from one place to another, esp. that part of the order which indicates the location of headquarters for each evening. **3.** *Med.* The path in, or part of, the body through which a remedy is administered; as, the alimentary *route.* — *v. t.;* ROUT'ED; ROUT'ING. **1.** To send, forward, or transport, by a certain route. **2.** To prearrange and direct the order and course of procedure of, as a series of operations; also, to send through such procedure; as, to *route* copy in an editorial office. — **rout'er** (rōōt'ẽr), *n.*

rout'er (rout'ẽr), *n.* One that routs, or scoops out; a device for routing; as: **a** A routing plane. See PLANE, *Illust.* **b** *Mach.* A machine with a revolving vertical spindle and cutter for milling out the surface of wood or metal, as for blanks on an electrotype. — **rout'er,** *v. t.*

routh (rōōth; routh), *n.* *Chiefly Scot.* Abundance.

rou·tine' (rōō·tēn'; 2), *n.* [F., fr. *route* way. See ROUTE.] **1.** A round daily or frequently pursued; esp., the regular course of business or official duties. **2.** Any regular procedure adhered to by habit. — **rou·tine',** *adj.*

rout'ing plane (rout'ĭng). See PLANE, *Illust.* (3).

rou·tin'ism (rōō·tēn'ĭz'm), *n.* Adherence to routine; mechanical regularity in work, etc. — **rou·tin'ist** (-ĭst), *n.*

‖**roux** (rōō), *n.* [F. *beurre roux* brown butter.] A cooked mixture of flour and butter used to thicken soup and sauces.

rove (rōv), *v. t.* **1.** To draw through an eye or similar aperture. **2.** *Textiles.* **a** To draw out into flakes; card, as wool. **b** To draw out and twist slightly, as slivers of wool or cotton, before spinning. — *n.* A roll or sliver of wool, cotton, silk, etc., drawn out and slightly twisted; — also collective.

rove, *n.* A copper washer upon which the end of a nail is clinched in boat building.

rove, *v. i.* [Prob. fr. MF. *rouer* to roam, ramble.] To wander; to ramble. — *v. t.* To wander over or through. — *n.* A roving; a ramble.

rove, *past & past part.* of REEVE.

rove beetle. Any of a numerous family (Staphylinidae) of long-bodied beetles which are often found on decaying animal and vegetable matter, and can run swiftly.

rove'-o'ver (rōv'ō'vẽr), *adj.* *Pros.* Designating a type of verse in sprung rhythm in which the end of one line and the beginning of the next form one foot.

rov'er (rōv'ẽr), *n.* One who runs a roving machine; also, the machine.

rov'er, *n.* [MD. *rōver* robber, fr. *rōven* (D. *rooven*) to rob.] **1.** A pirate; also, a pirate ship. **2.** A wanderer; vagrant. **3.** *Archery.* **a** A casual mark. **b** One of a series of fixed marks at long range. **4.** *Croquet.* **a** Also **rover ball.** A ball which has passed through all the arches but has not yet hit the stake. **b** Its player.

rov'ing (rōv'ĭng), *n.* The operation of forming a rove, or twisted sliver of wool, cotton, etc.; also, a rove.

row (rou), *n.* [Prob. fr. *rouse,* n., taken as a pl.] *Colloq.* A noisy or turbulent quarrel; a brawl; fuss. — *v. t.* To pick or have a row with. — *v. i.* To engage in a row.

row (rō), *v. t.* [AS. *rōwan.*] **1.** To propel with oars along the surface of water. **2.** To convey in a boat propelled with oars. **3.** To be equipped with (a stated number of oars). **4.** In contests: **a** To ply (a given oar or oars). **b** To match rowing strength and skill against. — *v. i.* **1.** To use an oar or oars in propelling a boat. **2.** To be moved by oars. — *n.* A rowing; an excursion in a rowboat. — **row'er,** *n.*

row (rō), *n.* [AS. *rāw, rǣw.*] **1.** A series of persons or things in a continued line; rank; file. **2.** A line of houses, close together, constituting an architectural whole, or a division of a street, or a short street; as, Rochester *Row,* in London. — *v. t.* To arrange in a row.

row. Scot. & N. of Eng. var. of ROLL.

row'an (rō'ăn; rou'ăn), *n.* **a** In full **rowan tree.** A Eurasian tree (*Sorbus aucuparia*) of the apple family, with flat corymbs of white flowers followed by red berrylike pomes. **b** Either of two related American trees (*S. americana* and *S. decora*), usually called *mountain ash.* **c** In full **row'an·ber'ry.** The fruit of the rowan tree.

row'boat' (rō'bōt'), *n.* A boat designed to be rowed.

row'dy (rou'dĭ), *n.; pl.* -DIES (-dĭz). One who engages in rows, or in rough behavior; a rough. — *adj.;* ROW'DI·ER (-dĭ·ēr); ROW'DI·EST. Characteristic of, or of the nature of, a rowdy. — **row'di·ly,** *adv.* — **row'di·ness,** *n.*

row'dy·ish (-ĭsh), *adj.* Rowdylike; noisy and rough. — **row'dy·ish·ly,** *adv.* — **row'dy·ish·ness,** *n.* — **row'dy·ism** (-ĭz'm), *n.*

row'el (rou'ĕl), *n.* [OF. *roele, rouele,* prop., a little wheel, fr. ML. *rotella* little wheel, dim. fr. L. *rota* wheel.] A little wheel on some spurs, having a number of radiating sharp points. — *v. t.;* ROW'ELED (-ĕld) or ROW'ELLED; ROW'EL·ING or ROW'EL·LING. To spur, esp. with a rowel.

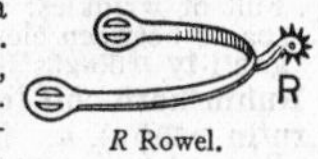

R Rowel.

row'en (rou'ĕn), *n.* A second-growth crop; aftermath.

row'lock (rō'lŏk; rŭl'ŭk), *n.* [For earlier *oarlock.*] A device serving as a support for an oar in rowing.

rowte (rout). Scot. var. of ROUT, roar, noise.

roy'al (roi'ăl), *adj.* [OF. *roial, reial* (F. *royal*), fr. L. *regalis,* fr. *rex, regis,* king.] **1.** Kingly; regal; of or pertaining to the crown or the king or sovereign; also, of or pertaining to the government of a kingdom; as, the *royal* army and navy. **2.** Under the patronage of royalty; holding a charter granted by the sovereign. **3.** Characteristic of or befitting a king; magnificent; majestic. **4.** Very large, excellent, or the like, of its kind. — *n.* **1.** Any of certain sizes of paper (as 19 × 24 or 20 × 25 inches), originally bearing as watermark the royal crest, a fleur-de-lis, of France. **2.** *Naut.* A small sail on the royal mast immediately above the topgallant sail. See SAIL, *Illust.* — **roy'al·ly,** *adv.*

royal antler. See ANTLER, *Illust.*

royal blue. A color, reddish-blue in hue, of very high saturation and low brilliance. See COLOR. — **roy'al–blue'** (-blōō'; 2), *adj.*

royal coachman. *Angling.* An artificial fly with white wings, peacock-herl body with red band, brown hackle, and gold tag. Cf. FLY, *Illust.*

royal fern. A fern (*Osmunda regalis*) with large bipinnate fronds bearing panicled sporophylls at their summit.

roy'al·ism (roi'ăl·ĭz'm), *n.* The principles of monarchical government; adherence to a king or a royal government.

roy'al·ist (-ĭst), *n.* An adherent of royalism; specif. [*cap.*]: **a** A supporter of Charles I of England; a Cavalier. **b** An adherent of George III or the British government in the American Revolution. **c** An adherent of the Bourbon dynasty in France. — **roy'al·ist, roy'al·is'tic** (-ĭs'tĭk), *adj.*

royal mast. The mast next above the topgallant mast.

royal palm. A tall, graceful, pinnate-leaved palm (*Roystonea regia*) of southern Florida and Cuba, widely planted for ornament throughout the tropics.

royal purple. A color, bluish blue-red in hue, of high saturation and low brilliance. See COLOR. — **roy'al–pur'ple** (roi'ăl·pûr'p'l; 2), *adj.*

roy'al·ty (roi'ăl·tĭ), *n.; pl.* -TIES (-tĭz). [OF. *roialté, royaulté.*] **1.** Royal station, birth, etc.; kingship. **2.** The person of a king; collectively, royal persons. **3.** Kingliness; regal quality or nature; magnificence; pomp. **4.** A royal domain. **5.** A right or perquisite of a sovereign, as a seigniorage on gold and silver coined at the mint, or a percentage paid to the crown of gold or silver taken from mines. **6.** Hence: **a** A share of the product or profit (as of a mine, forest, etc.) reserved by the owner for permitting another to use the property. **b** A compensation paid to the owner of a patent or a copyright for the use of it or the right to act under it.

-rrha'gi·a (-rā'jĭ·ȧ), **-rrhage** (-rāj). [NL. *-rrhagia,* fr. Gr. *-rrhagia,* fr. *rhēgnynai* to burst.] *Med.* A combining form meaning *a bursting forth, abnormal* or *excessive discharge* or *flow,* as in *bronchorrhagia.* Derivative adjectives are formed in **-rrhag'ic** (-răj'ĭk).

-rrhagy. = -RRHAGIA.

-rrhe'a, -rrhoe'a (-rē'ȧ). [NL., fr. Gr. *-rrhoia,* fr. *rhein* to flow.] *Med.* A combining form denoting *flow, discharge,* as in *diarrhea.*

-rrhi'za (-rī'zȧ). Var. of -RHIZA.

rub (rŭb), *v. t.;* RUBBED (rŭbd); RUB'BING. [ME. *rubben.*] **1.** To subject (a body) to the action of something moving over its surface with pressure and friction. **2.** To scour, polish, erase, apply, smear, etc., by or as by rubbing. **3.** To cause to move with pressure and friction along a surface; as, to *rub* the hands together. — *v. i.* **1.** To graze, grate, or similarly come in contact. **2.** To fret or chafe with friction. **3.** To move or pass with friction or difficulty; as, to *rub* through the world. **4.** To admit of being rubbed. — *n.* **1.** A rubbing; friction. **2.** That which rubs; hindrance; obstruction. **3.** Something grating to the feelings, as sarcasm or harsh criticism. **4.** An unevenness of surface or of character; a roughness; a fault.

rub'–a–dub' (rŭb'ȧ·dŭb'), *n.* [Imitative.] A repeated clamor, as of drumbeats; a clatter.

Ru·bái'yát' (rōō·bī'yăt'; rōō·bī'yăt; rōō'bī·yăt), *n. pl.* [Ar. *rubāʽīyāt,* pl. of *rubāʽīyah* quatrain, fem. of *rubāʽī* composed of four.] Stanzas consisting of four hemistichs or four lines; — the title of a poem in quatrains by Omar Khayyám, or its translation by Edward FitzGerald.

ru·basse' (rōō·bȧs'), *n.* [F. *rubace.*] A variety of quartz stained a ruby red.

ru·ba'to (rōō·bä'tō), *adj.* [It.] Literally, robbed; specif., *Music,* fluctuating; — applied to tempo. — *n.* A tempo in which some notes are shortened that others may be lengthened.

rub'ber (rŭb'ēr), *n.* **1.** One who rubs, as a polisher, masseur, etc. **2.** An instrument or thing used in rubbing, as an eraser, whetstone, etc. **3.** [From its earliest European use, the making of erasers.] **a** A substance obtained from the milky juice (**rubber latex:** cf. LATEX) of many tropical plants, and usually characterized by elasticity; — called also *caoutchouc* and *India rubber.* Perfectly pure rubber is a white unsaturated hydrocarbon having the composition $(C_5H_8)_x$ or $(C_{10}H_{16})_x$. To increase its useful properties, crude rubber is worked on rolls to make it more plastic, then compounded with other materials, molded and vulcanized. **b** Any of certain synthetic products resembling natural rubber in its properties. **4.** Something made of rubber, as an overshoe. — **rub'ber·y,** *adj.*

rub'ber, *n.* In some games, as whist, the odd game when there is a tie between the players; also, a contest determined by the winning of two out of three games.

rub'ber·ize (rŭb'ēr·īz), *v. t.* To coat or impregnate with rubber or a rubber solution or preparation, as silk.

rub'ber·neck' (rŭb'ēr·nĕk'), *n. Slang, U. S.* One who cranes his neck or gapes in curiosity. — **rub'ber·neck',** *v. i. & t.*

rubber plant. Any of several plants which yield rubber (see RUBBER, 3); specif., a commonly cultivated East Indian tree (*Ficus elastica*) of the mulberry family.

rub'ber–stamp', *v. t.* To stamp, endorse, or the like, with an imprint made by a rubber stamping device (**rubber stamp**); hence, *Colloq.,* to endorse or approve as a mere matter of routine.

rub'bish (rŭb'ĭsh), *n.* [ME. *robys, rubus, robous.*] Waste or rejected matter; trash; debris. — **rub'bish·y** (-ĭ), *adj.*

rub'ble (rŭb''l), *n.* [ME. *robyl, robel;* akin to RUBBISH.] **1.** Waterworn or rough broken stones, broken bricks, etc., used in coarse masonry, or in filling courses of walls; also, rubblework. **2.** Rough stone as it comes from the quarry. **3.** Any mass made up of rough irregular pieces; a collection of loose broken pieces. — **rub'ble,** *adj.* — **rub'bly** (-lĭ), *adj.*

rub'ble·work' (-wûrk'), *n.* Masonry of unsquared or rudely squared stones, irregular in size and shape.

rub'down' (rŭb'doun'), *n.* Act of rubbing or chafing; esp. the rubbing of the body, as after a bath.

rube (rōōb; 114), *n. Slang.* An awkward, unsophisticated person; a rustic.

ru'be·fa'cient (rōō'bē·fā'shĕnt), *adj.* [L. *rubefaciens,* pres. part. of *rubefacere* to make red.] Causing redness, as of the skin. — *n. Med.* An external application producing redness of the skin. — **ru'be·fac'tion** (-făk'shŭn), *n.*

ru·bel'la (rōō·bĕl'ȧ), *n.* [NL., fr. L. *rubellus* reddish.] *Med.* An acute specific disease milder than measles but with a similar eruption; — called also *German measles.*

ru·bel'lite (-bĕl'īt), *n.* [L. *rubellus* reddish, dim. of *ruber* red.] *Mineral.* A red tourmaline used as a gem.

Ru'ben (rōō'bĕn), *n. Douay Bib.* Reuben. See JACOB.

ru·be'o·la (rōō·bē'ō·lȧ), *n.* [NL., fr. L. *rubeus* reddish.] **a** The measles. **b** Rubella. — **ru·be'o·lar** (-lēr), *adj.*

ru·bes'cent (rōō·bĕs'ĕnt; -'nt), *adj.* [L. *rubescens, -entis,* pres. part. of *rubescere* to grow red.] Growing or becoming red; reddening; flushing. — **ru·bes'cence** (-ĕns; -'ns), *n.*

ru'bi·a'ceous (rōō'bĭ·ā'shŭs), *adj.* [L. *rubia* madder.] Belonging to the madder family (Rubiaceae). See MADDER.

ru'bi·celle (rōō'bĭ·sĕl), *n.* See SPINEL.

Ru'bi·con (rōō'bĭ·kŏn), *n.* [L. *Rubico.*] *Anc. Geog.* A small river between Italy and cisalpine Gaul. By leading an army across this river, contrary to government orders, Caesar precipitated the civil war which made him supreme; hence, ***to pass, or cross, the Rubicon*** is to take the irrevocable decisive step.

ru'bi·cund (-kŭnd), *adj.* [L. *rubicundus,* fr. *rubere* to be red.] Inclining to redness; ruddy. — **ru'bi·cun'di·ty** (-kŭn'dĭ·tĭ), *n.*

ru·bid'i·um (rōō·bĭd'ĭ·ŭm), *n.* [NL., fr. L. *rubidus* red.] *Chem.* A soft, silvery metal which decomposes water with violence and inflames spontaneously in air. Symbol, *Rb;* at. no., 37; at. wt., 85.48.

ru·big'i·nous (rōō·bĭj'ĭ·nŭs), *adj.* Also **ru·big'i·nose** (-nōs). Rust-colored; also, affected with rust.

ru'bi·ous (rōō'bĭ·ŭs), *adj.* [See RUBY.] *Rare.* Red; ruby.

ru'ble (rōō'b'l), *n.* Also **rou'ble.** [Russ. *rubl'.*] The monetary unit of the U.S.S.R., divided into 100 kopecks; also, a silver coin of this value. See MONEY, *Tables.*

ru'bric (rōō'brĭk), *n.* [OF. *rubrique, rubriche,* fr. L. *rubrica* red earth for coloring, fr. *ruber* red.] **1.** *Archaic.* Red ocher. **2.** In early manuscripts or print, any part in red, esp. a title page or part of it, or an initial letter or letters. **3.** Hence, because anciently printed in red: **a** The title of a statute or law. **b** A rule for the conduct of a liturgical service; as, the *rubrics* of the Mass. **c** A section heading of a discourse or writing; a head. **4.** Red. **5.** A prescribed or established form, method, etc.

ru'bri·cal (-brĭ·kăl), *adj.* Of, pert. to, or according to the rubrics, esp. liturgical rubrics. — **ru'bri·cal·ly,** *adv.*

ru'bri·cate (rōō'brĭ·kāt), *v. t.* [L. *rubricatus,* past part. of *rubricare* to color red.] To mark or distinguish with red, as titles in a book; also, to provide with rubrics. — **ru'bri·ca'tion** (-kā'shŭn), *n.* — **ru'bri·ca'tor** (-kā'tēr), *n.*

ru·bri'cian (rōō·brĭsh'ăn), *n.* One versed in rubrics.

ru'by (rōō'bĭ; 114), *n.; pl.* RUBIES (-bĭz). [OF. *rubi* (F. *rubis*), fr. L. *rubeus* red.] **1.** A precious stone, a red crystallized variety of corundum; — called also ***true, or Oriental, ruby.*** See CORUNDUM; SAPPHIRE, 1 **b.** **2.** A thing made of the ruby; esp., *Horol.,* a bearing, roller, or other part, made of ruby or a substitute material. **3.** The color of the ruby, red in hue, of high saturation and low brilliance. See COLOR. **4.** Something like or likened to a ruby, esp. in color, as red wine or a carbuncle. **5.** *Eng.* A size of type (5½ point); — called *agate* in U. S. See TYPE.

ruby spinel. See SPINEL.

ruche (rōōsh), *n.* [F. *ruche* ruche, beehive, fr. OF. *rusche* beehive, fr. ML. *rusca* bark.] A plaited, quilled, or goffered strip of lace, net, or the like, used as an edging for collars, cuffs, etc. — **ruch'ing** (rōōsh'ĭng), *n.*

ruck (rŭk; *dial.* rŏŏk), *n.* [Of Scand. origin.] The undistinguished multitude; the crowd of ordinary persons or things.

ruck, *n. & v. t. & i.* [ON. *hrukka.*] Wrinkle; pucker.

ruck'sack' (rŭk'săk'; *G.* rŏŏk'zäk'), *n.* [G.] A loose flat bag supported on the back by straps over the shoulders.

‖**Rück'um'laut** (rük'ŏŏm'lout), *n.* [G., fr. *rück* back + *umlaut* mutation.] In the Germanic languages, absence of umlaut of the stem vowel because of the loss of an *i* in the following syllable before the umlaut period.

ruc'tion (rŭk'shŭn), *n.* [From the Irish *insurrection* of 1798.] *Dial.* An uproar; rough-and-tumble fight.
rud·beck'i·a (rŭd·bĕk'ĭ·ȧ), *n.* [NL., after Olaus *Rudbeck* (1630–1702), Sw. botanist.] Any of a genus (*Rudbeckia*) of North American herbs of the aster family, the coneflowers, having showy, mostly yellow, rayed flowers, and a conical chaffy receptacle. See BLACK-EYED SUSAN, GOLDEN GLOW.
rudd (rŭd), *n.* [From *rud* redness, AS. *rudu.*] A fresh-water European fish (*Scardinius erythrophthalmus*) of the carp family.
rud'der (rŭd'ẽr), *n.* [AS. *rōther* a paddle.] **1.** A flat piece or structure of wood or metal, hinged vertically at a vessel's stern so that when it is turned the vessel turns also in the same direction. **2.** In an aircraft, a hinged or pivoted surface, usually attached at the rear end, serving to control its direction of flight by impressing yawing moments on the craft. See AIRPLANE, *Illust.* **3.** That which guides or governs the course (of a person or thing). — **rud'der·less,** *adj.*
rud'der·post' (-pōst'), *n.* *Naut.* **a** = RUDDERSTOCK. **b** An additional sternpost, in single-screw vessels, to which the rudder is attached.
rud'der·stock' (-stŏk'), *n.* *Naut.* That part of a rudder by which it is pivoted to the sternpost or rudderpost.
rud'dle (rŭd''l), *n.* [From *rud* redness, ruddle, AS. *rudu.*] Red ocher; raddle. — *v. t.*; RUD'DLED (-'ld); RUD'DLING (-lĭng). To color with ruddle; redden.
rud'dle·man (rŭd''l·măn; rŏŏd''l-), *n.* A raddleman.
rud'dock (rŭd'ŭk), *n.* [AS. *rudduc.*] The European robin.
rud'dy (rŭd'ĭ), *adj.*; RUD'DI·ER (-ĭ·ẽr); RUD'DI·EST. [AS. *rudig.*] **1.** Reddish. **2.** Having a healthy reddish color.
ruddy duck. An American duck (*Erismatura jamaicensis rubida*) having a broad bill and a wedge-shaped tail. The adult male has the upper parts largely rich brownish red.
rude (rōōd; 114), *adj.* [OF., fr. L. *rudis.*] **1.** Characterized by roughness; crude; also, of weather, storms, etc., harsh; severe; violent. **2.** Lacking delicacy or refinement; boorish; unpolished; uncouth; hence, of low rank. **3.** Savage; now usually, uncivil; impolite; impudent. **4.** Not carefully made or worked out; rough; makeshift; as, a *rude* estimate. **5.** Unskillful; inexpert. **6.** Rugged; sturdy; vigorous; as, *rude* health. — **rude'ly,** *adv.* — **rude'ness,** *n.*
Syn. **Rude, rough, crude, raw, callow, green** mean lacking in qualities that make for finish or refinement. **Rude** implies indifference to or ignorance of form in any sense, esp. good form; **rough** implies more harshness or violence than *rude* and more culpable ignorance or inexperience; **crude**, applied literally to that unprocessed, unrefined, untreated, etc., suggests remoteness from that which is highly developed, civilized, etc.; **raw**, literally uncooked, suggests being untested, inexperienced, or unfinished; **callow**, applied mostly to youths, suggests showing signs of immaturity, even when reaching manhood; **green** suggests an unripeness or unfitness showing itself in inexperience, unreadiness for work or use, or the like.
rudes'by (rōōdz'bĭ), *n.* *Archaic.* A rude fellow.
ru'di·ment (rōō'dĭ·mĕnt), *n.* [L. *rudimentum*, fr. *rudis* unwrought, ignorant, rude.] **1.** That which is undeveloped; an unfinished beginning. **2.** A first principle of any art or science; a first step. **3.** *Biol.* **a** An organ or part just beginning to develop or, esp., one arrested in its development at an early stage. **b** The remains of a part functional only in an earlier stage of the same individual or in his ancestors. — **ru'di·men'tal** (-mĕn'tăl; -t'l), *adj.*
ru'di·men'ta·ry (-mĕn'tȧ·rĭ), *adj.* **1.** Of or pert. to rudiments; elementary. **2.** *Biol.* Having the character of a rudiment; imperfectly developed; also, vestigial. — **ru'di·men'ta·ri·ly,** *adv.* — **ru'di·men'ta·ri·ness,** *n.*
rue (rōō; 114), *n.* [OF. *rue*, fr. L. *ruta*, fr. Gr. *rhytē.*] A strong-scented, perennial woody herb (*Ruta graveolens*) whose bitter leaves are used in medicine. It is the type of a family (Rutaceae, the rue family) of herbs, shrubs, and trees, often glandular and strong-scented, and including also the citrus fruits, the fraxinella, etc.
rue (rōō), *v. t.*; RUED (rōōd); RU'ING (rōō'ĭng). [AS. *hrēowan* to grieve, make sorry.] To suffer remorse for; to repent of; hence, to regret having entered into, as a bargain; to wish undone, nullified, nonexistent, etc. — *v. i.* To feel regret; repent. — *n.* Disappointment; regret; *Scot.*, compassion; repentance. — **ru'er** (rōō'ẽr), *n.*
rue anemone. A delicate vernal herb (*Anemonella thalictroides*) of the crowfoot family, with white flowers resembling those of the wood anemone.
rue'ful (rōō'fŏŏl; -f'l), *adj.* **1.** Lamentable; pitiable. **2.** Mournful; sorrowful; regretful. **3.** Merciful; pitiful. — **rue'ful·ly,** *adv.* — **rue'ful·ness,** *n.*
ru·fes'cent (rōō·fĕs'ĕnt; -'nt), *adj.* [L. *rufescens*, pres. part. of *rufescere* to become reddish, fr. *rufus* red.] Reddish. — **ru·fes'cence** (-ĕns; -'ns), *n.*
ruff (rŭf), *n.* [OF. *roffle, ronfle*, fr. *triomphe.*] **a** *Obs.* A game similar to whist. **b** Act of trumping. — *v. i. & t.* To play a trump card on a lead of another suit; trump; *Bridge*, to lead a suit that one's partner can trump.
ruff, ruffe (rŭf), *n.* [ME. *rowe, ruffe*, prob. fr. ROUGH, *adj.*] A small fresh-water European perch (*Acerina cernua*).
ruff (rŭf), *n.* **1.** A type of stiffly-starched, wheel-shaped collar worn by both men and women in the late 16th and 17th centuries. **2.** Something suggestive of such a collar, as, *Zool.*, a fringe of hair or feathers on the neck. **3.** *fem.* REEVE. A sandpiper of Europe and Asia (*Philomachus pugnax*). The males during the breeding season have a fringe of erectile feathers on the neck. — **ruffed** (rŭft), *adj.*
ruffed grouse (rŭft). A North American grouse (*Bonasa umbellus*) valued as a game bird in the eastern U. S. and Canada; — called *partridge* in the North and *pheasant* in the South.
ruf'fi·an (rŭf'ĭ·ăn; rŭf'yăn), *n.* [F. *rufian*, fr. It. *ruffiano.*] A cruel, brutal fellow. — *adj.* Brutal; cruel. — **ruf'fi·an·ism** (-ĭz'm), *n.* — **ruf'fi·an·ly,** *adj.*
ruf'fle (rŭf''l), *v. t.*; -FLED (-'ld); -FLING (-lĭng). [ME. *ruffeln.*] **1.** To make into a ruff or ruffle; draw into puckers, plaits, or folds. **2.** To furnish with ruffles. **3.** To erect in or like a ruff, as feathers. **4.** To discompose; disturb; specif.: **a** To roughen the surface of, as water. **b** To irritate; vex. **5.** To disarrange; rumple. **6.** To riffle (leaves of a book); to shuffle (cards). — *n.* **1.** That which is ruffled; specif., a plaited or gathered strip of lace, cambric, etc.; frill. **2.** State or an instance of being ruffled; as: **a** Irritation. **b** A commotion; brawl. **c** A ripple. — **ruf'fly** (-lĭ), *adj.*
ruf'fle, *v. i.* [ME. *ruffelen* to struggle, swagger.] **1.** To grow rough, boisterous, or turbulent; also, to fight. **2.** To put on airs; swagger. — **ruf'fler** (-lẽr), *n.*
ruf'fle, *n.* *Mil.* A low, vibrating beat of a drum, not so loud as a roll.
ru'fous (rōō'fŭs), *adj.* [L. *rufus.*] Of any of several colors, averaging reddish red-yellow in hue, of high saturation and high brilliance. See COLOR.
rug (rŭg), *n.* [Of Scand. origin.] A piece of thick, heavy, napped or piled fabric, used for floor covering, a lap robe, etc.; also, a fur mat, etc. Cf. CARPET, *n.*, 1; ORIENTAL RUG.
rug (*dial.* rŭg, rōōg), *v. t. & i. & n.* [ME. *ruggen*, of Scand. origin.] *Dial.* Pull; wrench; tear; haul.
ru'ga (rōō'gȧ), *n.*; *pl.* RUGAE (-jē). [L.] *Nat. Hist.* A wrinkle; fold; — chiefly in *pl.* — **ru'gate** (-gāt), *adj.*
Rug'by (rŭg'bĭ), *n.* Also **Rugby football.** [Because orig. played at *Rugby* school, Eng.] A variety of football game. See FOOTBALL, *n.*, 2.
rug'ged (rŭg'ĕd; -ĭd), *adj.* **1.** Having a rough, uneven surface; not smooth; irregular; rough. **2.** Specif.: **a** Not kept even; unkempt. **b** Rough with bristles or hair; shaggy. **c** Full of furrows and ridges; seamed; wrinkled. **3.** Harsh; hard; austere; sometimes, sour; surly; crabbed. **4.** Rude, as in manners; uncivil; ungracious. **5.** Turbulent; stormy. **6.** Rough to the ear; harsh. **7.** Robust; sturdy; hardy. — **Syn.** See ROUGH. — **rug'ged·ly,** *adv.* — **rug'ged·ness,** *n.*
Rug'ger (rŭg'ẽr), *n.* *Colloq., Brit.* = RUGBY.
ru'gose (rōō'gōs; rōō·gōs'), *adj.* [L. *rugosus*, fr. *ruga* a wrinkle.] Full of wrinkles; specif., *Bot.*, having the veinlets sunken and the spaces between elevated, as certain leaves. — **ru'gose·ly,** *adv.* — **ru·gos'i·ty** (rōō·gŏs'ĭ·tĭ), *n.*
Ruhm'korff coil (rōōm'kôrf). = INDUCTION COIL.
ru'in (rōō'ĭn), *n.* [OF. *ruine*, fr. L. *ruina*, a falling, ruin.] **1.** *Now Rare.* A falling or tumbling down. **2.** Such change in anything as to destroy it or impair its effectiveness; destruction. **3.** The cause or the causing of such destruction or impairment; as, drink will be the *ruin* of him. **4.** That which is fallen down and become worthless from injury or decay; as, his mind is a *ruin*; esp., *pl.*, the remains of a dilapidated house, city, or the like. **5.** State of being decayed, destroyed, wrecked, etc.; as, to go to *ruin.* — *v. t. & i.* To bring, fall, go, or come, to ruin; specif.: **a** To bankrupt. **b** To deprive (a woman) of chastity. — **ru'in·a·ble,** *adj.* — **ru'in·er,** *n.*
ru'in·ate (rōō'ĭ·nāt), *v. t.* To ruin. — *adj.* Ruined. — **ru'in·a'tion** (-nā'shŭn), *n.*
ru'ined (rōō'ĭnd), *adj.* In ruins; gone to ruin.
ru'in·ous (rōō'ĭ·nŭs; 114), *adj.* **1.** Causing, or tending to cause, ruin; destructive. **2.** Ruined; dilapidated; as, a wall in a *ruinous* state. **3.** Composed of, or consisting of, ruins. — **ru'in·ous·ly,** *adv.* — **ru'in·ous·ness,** *n.*
rule (rōōl; 114), *n.* [OF. *riule, reule*, fr. L. *regula* a ruler, rule, model, fr. *regere, rectum*, to lead straight, direct.] **1.** A prescribed guide for conduct, action, usage (as of words), etc.; a regulation; precept. **2.** Uniform or established course; systematic method or practice; as, my *rule* is to rise at six o'clock. **3.** The regular course of things; as, we have cold winters as a *rule.* **4.** *Obs.* Behavior. **5.** Act or time of ruling; government; reign; as, during the *rule* of Elizabeth. **6.** A ruler (sense 3); also, a straight line as drawn by a ruler. **7.** *Eccl.* The laws or regulations prescribed by the founder of a religious order for observance by its members; as, the *rule* of St. Dominic. **8.** *Law.* An order or direction made by a court, usually in writing, regulating court practice (***general rule***) or regulating the action of parties in special cases (***special rule***). **9.** *Math.* A determinate method prescribed for performing any operation. **10.** *Print.* A thin plate of metal (usually brass), the height of ordinary type, with a line or lines as its face. — **Syn.** See LAW.
— *v. t.* **1.** To control; govern; manage. **2.** To direct by influence or counsel; guide; as, to be *ruled* by those one loves. **3.** To be the dominant note, character, etc., of; as, quiet humor *rules* the essay. **4.** To decide; specif., *Law*, to give as a direction, order, or determination of the court. **5.** To moderate or restrain; as, to *rule* one's passions. **6.** To mark with straight parallel lines, esp. with the aid of a ruler. — *v. i.* **1.** To exercise supreme authority; — often with *over.* **2.** To be in general, or as a rule; as, prices *rule* lower today. **3.** *Law.* To lay down a rule or order of court; to decide an incidental point. — **Syn.** See GOVERN; DECIDE.
rule of three. *Math.* The rule for finding the fourth term of a proportion where three are given. The rule states that the product of the means equals the product of the extremes.
rule of thumb. **a** Any rude measurement, calculation, etc.; — from using the thumb as a rule. **b** Judgment based on practical experience rather than on scientific knowledge.
rul'er (rōōl'ẽr; 114), *n.* **1.** One who rules; specif., a sovereign. **2.** A worker or a machine that rules paper. **3.** A smooth-edged strip of wood, metal, etc., used for guiding a pen or pencil in drawing lines, for measuring, etc.; a straightedge. — **rul'er·ship,** *n.*
rul'ing (-ĭng), *n.* **1.** Act of one who rules; government. **2.** Act of drawing ruled lines; also, a ruled line. **3.** *Law.* A decision or rule of a judge or a court, esp. on a point of law. — *adj.* Predominant; also, prevailing.
rum (rŭm), *n.* **1.** An alcoholic liquor distilled from fermented molasses or other cane product. **2.** *U. S.* Any intoxicating liquor; intoxicants.
rum, *adj.* [From obs. *rum, rome*, a slang word for good.] *Slang.* **a** Queer; odd. **b** Dangerous; "tough."
Ru·ma'nian (rōō·mān'yăn; -mā'nĭ·ăn; 58). Var. of ROMANIAN.
‖rum'ba (rōōm'bä; *U. S.* rŭm'bȧ), *n.* [Sp., prob. of Afr. origin.] A Cuban Negro dance or, *U. S.*, an imitation of it.
rum'ble (rŭm'b'l), *v. i.*; -BLED (-b'ld); -BLING (-blĭng). [ME. *romblen.*] **1.** To make a low, heavy, rolling sound. **2.** To speak in a low, rolling tone; also, to move or stir about heavily and noisily. — *v. t.* **1.** To utter in a low, rolling voice. **2.** To polish or otherwise treat in a rumble (sense 2). — *n.* **1.** A low, heavy, continuous sound like that made by heavy wagons or thunder. **2.** A tumbling barrel; — called also **rum'bler** (rŭm'blẽr). See TUMBLING BARREL. **3. a** A seat for servants, behind the body of a carriage. **b** In full **rumble seat.** A folding seat in the back of the covered part of an automobile. Cf. DICKEY, 3. — **rum'bler** (-blẽr), *n.* — **rum'bling·ly,** *adv.*
ru'men (rōō'mĕn), *n.*; *pl.* -MINA (-mĭ·nȧ). [L. *rumen* gullet.] **1.** The first stomach of ruminants. See RUMINANT, *Illust.* **2.** The cud of a ruminant.
ru'mi·nant (rōō'mĭ·nănt), *adj.* [L. *ruminans, -antis*, pres. part.] **1.** Chewing the cud; of or pertaining to ruminants. **2.** Given to, or

engaged in, ruminating, or pondering. — *n.* Any of a division (**Ru′mi·nan′ti·a** [ro͞o′mĭ·năn′shĭ·*ȧ*]) of even-toed hoofed mammals including those that chew the cud, as the oxen, sheep, goats, antelopes, giraffes, deer, and camels. The herbaceous food, swallowed partly chewed, passes into the first chamber of the complex stomach, the rumen or the reticulum, whence it is regurgitated in masses and thoroughly masticated and mixed with saliva while the animal is at rest. It is then swallowed and passes through the reticulum and omasum into the abomasum, where it is acted on by gastric juice.

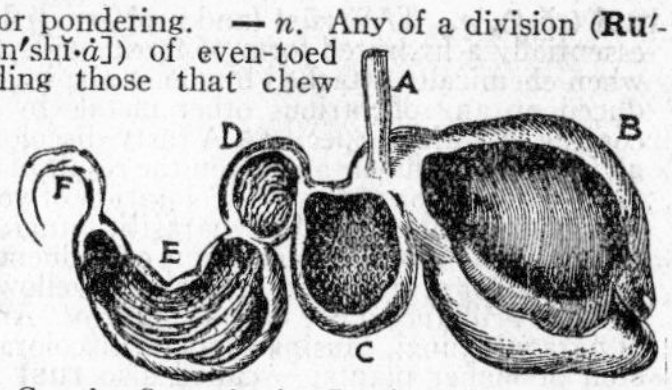

Complex Stomach of a Ruminant, cut away. *A* Esophagus; *B* Rumen; *C* Reticulum; *D* Omasum, Psalterium, or Manyplies; *E* Abomasum; *F* Intestine.

ru′mi·nate (ro͞o′mĭ·nāt), *v. i. & t.* [L. *ruminatus*, past part. of *ruminari, -nare*, fr. *rumen, -inis*, throat.] **1.** To chew the cud; to chew again what has been chewed slightly and swallowed. **2.** To bring to mind and consider again and again; muse; ponder. — **Syn.** PONDER. — **ru′mi·nat′ing·ly** (-nāt′ĭng·lĭ), *adv.* — **ru′mi·na′tion** (-nā′shŭn), *n.* — **ru′mi·na′tive** (-nā′tĭv), *adj.* — **ru′mi·na′tor** (-nā′tẽr), *n.*

rum′mage (rŭm′ĭj), *n.* [MF. *arrumage*, fr. *arrumer* to stow goods in the hold of a ship.] **1.** *Obs.* The stowage of, or a place for stowing, cargo in a ship. **2.** A careful searching with turning over of things; hence, an upheaval; confusion. **3.** In full **rummage sale.** A sale of accumulated odds and ends, as discarded or unsalable articles; esp., such a sale for charity. — *v. t. & i.*; -MAGED (-ĭjd); -MAG·ING (-ĭj·ĭng). **1.** To search by looking into every corner, and turning over all the contents (of); ransack. **2.** To bring to light by or as by a thorough search; to collect as by searching. — **rum′mag·er** (-ĭj·ẽr), *n.*

rum′mer (rŭm′ẽr), *n.* [D. *roemer, romer.*] A large tall glass or drinking cup.

rum′my (rŭm′ĭ), *adj.*; -MI·ER (-ĭ·ẽr); -MI·EST. *Slang.* Rum; queer; odd.

rum′my (rŭm′ĭ), *n.* A card game in which the object is to be the first to match all of one's cards into sets or sequences of three or more by drawing from and discarding on the stock.

rum′my, *n. Slang, U. S.* A drunkard.

ru′mor, ru′mour (ro͞o′mẽr; 114), *n.* [OF. *rumor, rumour*, fr. L. *rumor.*] **1.** *Obs.* A prolonged, indistinct noise. **2.** A popular report; common talk; hence, notoriety; reputation. **3.** A story current but not authenticated. — *v. t.* To noise abroad; spread by rumor.

rump (rŭmp), *n.* [ME. *rumpe*, of Scand. origin.] **1.** The posterior end of an animal, generally including the buttocks. See DOG, *Illust.* **2.** Among butchers, the piece of beef behind the upper part of the sirloin. See BEEF, *Illust.* **3.** The hind end; fag end; a remnant.

rum′ple (rŭm′p'l), *v. t. & i.*; RUM′PLED (-p'ld); RUM′PLING (-plĭng). [MD. *rumpelen, rompelen.*] To make uneven; crumple; tousle; muss. — *n.* A crease; wrinkle.

rum′pus (rŭm′pŭs), *n. Colloq.* A disturbance; fracas.

rumpus room. A room set apart in a home, usually in the basement, and suitably furnished for games, parties, and recreation by the family and guests, both children and adults.

rum′run′ner (rŭm′rŭn′ẽr), *n.* One engaged in bringing prohibited alcoholic liquor ashore or across a border; one illegally transporting alcoholic liquor. — **rum′run′ning,** *n.*

run (rŭn), *v. i.*; RAN (răn) or, *Dial.*, RUN; RUN; RUN′NING. [ME. *rinnen, rennen*, fr. ON. and fr. AS. *rinnan* (pret. *ran*, past part. *gerunnen*), and *iernan, irnan*, to run (pret. *orn, arn, earn*, past part. *urnen*).] **1.** To move swiftly, smoothly, or with quick action, as a stream, wagon, person, etc.; go rapidly; hasten. **2.** Specif.: To move rapidly by springing steps so that there is an instant in each step when neither foot touches the ground. **3.** To move, go, pass, or proceed; specif.: **a** To go back and forth; ply; as, the boat *runs* between Albany and New York. **b** To steal off; flee. **4.** To contend in a race, an election, etc.; also, to win a (specified) place in a contest; as, his horse *ran* third. **5.** To turn, as a wheel; rotate; hence, to turn, as on a hinge; hinge. **6.** To migrate or move in schools; — said of fish; esp., to ascend a river to spawn. **7.** To extend; reach; as, his memory *runs* not so far back. **8.** To pass from one condition to another; as, to *run* in debt. **9.** To flow; course; as, her blood *ran* cold. **10.** To become fluid or flowing, as sap, melting iron, etc. **11.** To grow or develop, or tend to do so. **12.** To spread or dissolve, as a dyed color in washing. **13.** To discharge pus, etc. **14.** To have a course or direction; as, the line *runs* east. **15.** To accrue or become payable in due course, as interest. **16.** To be written, inscribed, worded, or the like; as, the song *runs* as follows. **17.** To creep, climb, or extend up or along; spread. **18.** To be continuously and on the average (as specified); as, the fish *run* large at this season. **19.** To keep continuously in motion, action, etc.; as, his tongue *runs* on. **20.** To make numerous drafts or demands for payment, as upon a bank; — with *on.* **21.** To keep recurring, as ideas, tunes, etc., in the mind. **22.** To pass as current; circulate. **23.** *Law.* To continue in or have force, effect, or operation; also, to accompany as a valid obligation or right.

— *v. t.* **1.** To cause to run, as a horse, an engine, a metal, a plant, etc. **2.** To bring to a specified condition by, or as if by, running; as, he *ran* the firm into debt. **3.** To pursue; hunt. **4.** To pass over or cover by, or as if by, running; as, to *run* the streets. **5.** To go through or perform by, or as by, running; as, to *run* a race. **6.** To follow (a specified way); to pursue (a course). **7.** To pursue in thought; trace; as, to *run* the rumor back to its source. **8.** To cause to enter or go in; thrust; as, to *run* a nail in the foot; to cause to move, flow, slide, etc., as in some specified direction, into a certain position, etc.; as, to *run* cards in a file. **9.** To mold or cast, as bullets. **10.** To mark out, as a boundary line. **11.** To smuggle (contraband or dutiable goods). **12.** To encounter or incur, as a danger or risk. **13.** To vie with, as in a race. **14.** *U. S.* To manage (a hotel). **15.** To sew with stitches that form a continuous line. **16.** In certain games, to make (a number of successful shots, strokes, or the like) in succession. — ***run a blockade.*** To get to, or away from, a blockaded port in safety. — ***run in or on.*** *Print.* To make (matter) continuous without a paragraph or break. — ***run the gantlet.*** To suffer the punishment of the gantlet; hence, to go through the ordeal of severe criticism or ill treatment at many hands.

— *n.* **1.** Act of running; specif.: **a** Act of migrating, or ascending a river to spawn; — said of fish; also, a school of migrating fish. **b** A quickened gallop. **c** A continuing in a certain course or series; as, a *run* of good luck. **d** A continuing urgent demand, esp. one on a bank or treasury for payment of its obligations. **2.** A series; sequence; esp., an unbroken succession, as of performances, of successful shots or strokes, of melodic tones, etc. **3.** A swift watercourse; brook. **4.** That which runs, or flows, during a certain time. **5.** The usual or normal kind, character, type, or group; as, the common *run* of people. **6.** The distance covered, or amount of work turned out, during a special course, time, or operation. **7.** A range of ground for feeding or exercising stock; as, a sheep *run;* a poultry *run;* hence, *Colloq.*, freedom to range at will. **8.** Course; passage, as in time, events, etc.; as, in the long *run;* specif.: **a** A trip; a journey. **b** Route. **c** A coasting course. **9.** A lengthwise ravel in a knitted fabric, as in silk hose. **10.** A contest, esp. a hard-fought contest. **11.** See BOWERBIRD. **12.** In certain games, a score unit, made by completing a prescribed course. **13.** *Colloq.* Freedom to go about at will. **14.** *Naut.* The after part of the underwater body from where it begins to curve or slope upward and inward, to the stern.

— *adj.* **1.** Melted or made from molten material; cast. **2.** *Colloq.* Smuggled.

run′a·bout′ (rŭn′*ȧ*·bout′), *n.* **1.** A gadder; vagabond. **2.** **a** A type of light uncovered wagon. **b** *Automobiles.* A light roadster. **c** A light motorboat.

run′a·gate (rŭn′*ȧ*·gāt), *n.* [ME. *renegat*, fr. ML. *renegatus*, confused with E. *run*, and dial. *agate*, adv., on the way. See RENEGADE.] A fugitive; runaway; also, a vagabond.

run′a·way′ (rŭn′*ȧ*·wā′), *n.* **1.** A fugitive. **2.** A running away, esp. of a horse or team; also, a horse that is running away. — *adj.* **1.** Fleeing; fugitive. **2.** Accomplished by elopement, or during flight; as, a *runaway* marriage. **3.** Orig., *Racing*, won by a long lead; hence, decisive; as, a *runaway* victory. **4.** *Com.* Subject, as prices, to rapid changes, usually toward higher levels; as, a *runaway* market.

run′ci·ble spoon (rŭn′sĭ·b'l). A fork with three broad prongs, one sharp-edged and curved like a spoon.

run′ci·nate (rŭn′sĭ·nāt), *adj.* [L. *runcinatus*, past part. of *runcinare* to plane off, fr. *runcina* a plane.] *Bot.* Pinnately cut with lobes pointing downwards. See LEAF, *Illust.* (17).

run′dle (rŭn′d'l), *n.* [Var. of *roundel.*] **1.** A round; a step of a ladder; a rung. **2.** Something which rotates about an axis, as a wheel.

rund′let (rŭnd′lĕt; -lĭt), *n.* Also **run′let.** [OF. *rondelet*, dim. of *rondelle* a little tun, fr. *rond* round.] A small barrel of varying capacity; hence, an old liquid measure about 18 wine (or U. S.) gallons (68 liters).

run′-down′ (rŭn′doun′; 2), *adj.* **a** Dilapidated. **b** Exhausted; worn out. **c** Of a watch or clock, stopped for want of winding.

rune (ro͞on; 114), *n.* [AS., Dan., and ON.; AS. *rūn* a rune, a secret, a mystery.] **1.** Any of the characters of the alphabet formerly in general use by the Teutonic, or Germanic, peoples from about the 3d century A.D. **2.** *pl.* Old Finnish poetry expressed in runes; sometimes, old Norse poetry. **3.** Mystery; magic. — **ru′nic** (ro͞o′nĭk), *adj.*

rung (rŭng), *n.* [AS. *hrung* a staff, rod, pole.] **1.** *Scot. & N. of Eng.* A stout staff or cudgel. **2.** One of the rounds of a chair or of a ladder, the spoke of a wheel, etc.

rung, *past & past part.* of RING.

run′-in′ (rŭn′ĭn′), *n.* **1.** Something inserted, as a paragraph in printed matter or one term within the definition of another in a dictionary. **2.** *Slang, U. S.* An altercation; quarrel. — **run′-in′,** *adj.*

run′kle (rŭng′k'l; ro͝ong′-), *n. & v. Obs. exc. Scot.* Wrinkle.

run′let (rŭn′lĕt; -lĭt), *n.* [*run* + *-let.*] A runnel.

run′let. Var. of RUNDLET.

run′nel (rŭn′ĕl; -'l), *n.* [From ME. *rinel*, influenced by *run.*] A rivulet; a brook; streamlet.

run′ner (rŭn′ẽr), *n.* **1.** One that runs, as a racer, an engine driver, a horse, etc.; as: **a** One who runs errands, makes reports, etc., as for a bank. **b** *Colloq.* A smuggler. **c** *U. S.* One employed to solicit patronage, as for a hotel, etc. **d** A manager or director; an operator. **e** A messenger. **2.** **a** Either of the longitudinal pieces on which a sled or sleigh slides; also, the blade of a skate. **b** A part, as a groove, on or in which something slides. **3.** A long, narrow strip of material, as of roofing; specif.: **a** A long narrow rug for a corridor. **b** A long table or dresser scarf. **4.** A ravel in a stocking. **5.** *Bot.* **a** A slender prostrate branch which roots at the joints or end, forming new plants. **b** A plant which spreads by this method. **6.** *Hort.* Any of several varieties of twining beans, esp. the scarlet runner. **7.** *Zool.* A jurel (*Paratractus*, or *Caranx, crysos*) common from Cape Cod southward.

run′ner-up′, *n.* One who runs up; specif., the competitor in a contest who finishes next to the winner.

run′ning (rŭn′ĭng), *n.* **1.** Act of one that runs, in various senses; as: **a** Management. **b** Racing. **2.** Strength or ability to run. **3.** *Colloq.* A trip or journey. — *adj.* **1.** Moving or advancing by or as if by running; specif.: **a** Of a horse, moving or racing at a run; also, trained to run. **b** Of water, flowing. **2.** Continuous; as, a *running* fire of musketry. **3.** Successive; as, two days *running.* **4.** Measured in a straight line; linear; as, per *running* foot. **5.** Flowing; easy; cursive; as, a *running* hand in writing. **6.** Discharging pus; as, a *running* sore. **7.** Of or pert. to a run, as of a train, a candidate, etc.

running board. *U. S.* A footboard, as on the side of an automobile.

running gear. The wheels and axles of a vehicle, and their attachments, in distinction from the body; all the working parts of a locomotive or other machine.

running hand. A form of rapid writing in which the letters are usually slanted and the words formed without lifting the pen; — distinguished from *round hand.*

running head, running headline. *Print.* A headline repeated on consecutive pages in a book or the like.

running knot. See KNOT, *Illust.* (13). Hence, **running noose.**

running mate. **1.** A horse entered in a race to set the pace for part of the distance for another horse of the same owner or stable. **2.** A candidate running for a subordinate place on a ticket for political or other office, esp. a vice-presidential candidate. **3.** *Colloq.* A person frequently seen in close association with another.

running title. The title of a volume as printed at the top of the left-hand pages or, sometimes, all pages.

run′off′ (rŭn′ŏf′), *n.* **1.** The water which is removed from the soil over the surface or through drains beneath the surface. **2.** A final race, contest, or the like, to decide an earlier one that has ended without a decision in favor of any one competitor.

run′-on′ (rŭn′ŏn′), *adj.* That is run on or appended, as in printed matter; as, a *run-on* entry. — **run′-on′,** *n.*

runt (rŭnt), *n.* [Scot., an old cow, an old, withered woman.] **1.** Any animal unusually small of its kind. **2.** A dwarf; a person of small or stunted growth. **3.** *Obs. exc. Dial.* The dead stump of a tree; also, the stem of a plant. — **runt′ish**, *adj.* — **runt′y**, *adj.* — **runt′i·ness**, *n.*

run′way′ (rŭn′wā′), *n.* **1.** The channel of a stream. **2.** A beaten path made by animals; also, a poultry run. **3.** A way or track for wheeled vehicles, for planes in landing or taking off, etc. **4.** *Bowling.* A track over which balls are returned to the players.

ru·pee′ (ro͞o·pē′; ro͞o′pē), *n.* [Hind. *rūpiyah*, fr. Skr. *rūpya* silver.] **a** The monetary unit in several countries, as India, Pakistan, Burma, and Ceylon. See MONEY, *Tables.* **b** A silver coin of India; also, a nickel coin of Pakistan. **c** A paper currency note of the value of a rupee.

rup′ture (rŭp′tŭr), *n.* [F. or L.; F. *rupture*, fr. L. *ruptura*, fr. *rumpere, ruptum*, to break.] **1.** A breaking apart, or state of being broken apart. **2.** Breach of peace or concord; specif., open hostility or war between nations. **3.** *Med.* Hernia. — **Syn.** See FRACTURE. — *v. t. & i.* To break; burst; cause a rupture of or in. — **rup′tur·a·ble** (rŭp′tŭr·ȧ·b'l), *adj.*

rup′tured duck (rŭp′tŭrd). *Colloq.* The symbol of an eagle with outspread wings depicted in the discharge emblem for personnel of the U. S. armed forces.

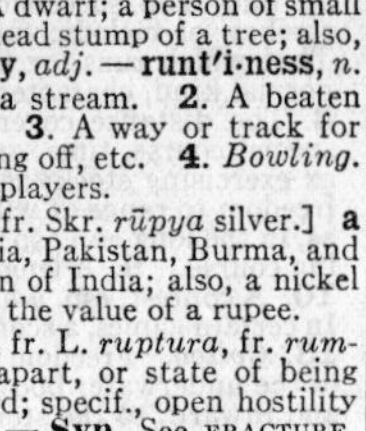

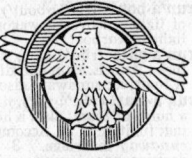

Ruptured Duck.

ru′ral (ro͝or′ăl; 114), *adj.* [F., fr. LL. *ruralis*, fr. *rus, ruris*, the country.] Of or pert. to the country, as disting. from a city or town; designating or pertaining to country people, or country occupations, esp. agriculture; rustic. — **ru′ral·ism** (-ĭz'm), **ru·ral′i·ty** (ro͞o·răl′ĭ·tĭ), *n.* — **ru′ral·ist** (ro͝or′ăl·ĭst), *n.* — **ru′ral·ly**, *adv.*

Syn. **Rural, rustic, pastoral, bucolic** mean characteristic of country life. **Rural** esp. suggests agricultural pursuits or simple community life; **rustic** more clearly suggests a contrast to city life, often connoting rudeness or lack of polish; **pastoral** suggests a more idyllic life than *rural* and, often, apartness from the world; **bucolic**, in current use, carries a strong implication of loutishness.

rural dean. See ARCHPRIEST **a.**

rural free delivery. Free delivery of mail on routes in country districts. Abbr. *R. F. D.*

ru′ral·ize (ro͝or′ăl·īz), *v. t. & i.* To make or become rural; to rusticate. — **ru′ral·i·za′tion** (-ĭ·zā′shŭn; -ī·zā′-), *n.*

ruse (ro͞oz; 114), *n.* [F., a trick, detour, fr. *ruser* to dodge.] An artifice; trick. — **Syn.** See TRICK.

rush (rŭsh), *n.* [AS. *rysc, risc.*] **1.** Any of a genus (*Juncus*), typifying a family (Juncaceae, the rush family) of plants with cylindrical, often hollow, stems; also, less correctly, any of several species of *Scirpus.* Rushes are used in plaiting mats, etc. **2.** The merest trifle; a straw. — **rush′y** (rŭsh′ĭ), *adj.*

rush, *v. i. & t.* [ME. *russhen*, fr. AF. *russher, russer*, OF. *ruser, reüser.*] **1.** To move, push, or urge forward with impetuosity, violence, or haste. **2.** To act or do with undue haste, or without due deliberation or preparation. **3.** To make an onset on; charge; carry by assault. **4.** *Football.* To advance the ball or carry (the ball) forward by a rush or rushes. — *n.* **1.** A rushing; a violent motion or course. **2.** A thronging of many people to some new place, as in search of newly discovered gold; also, Australia, a new gold field. **3.** An onset; attack; combat; specif., *U. S.*, a trial of strength between two classes, as in college, for temporary possession of a walk, fence, cane, etc. **4.** *Colloq.* That which by its accumulation or pressure causes unusual activity; as, a *rush* of business. **5.** *Amer. Football.* **a** One of certain players in the **rush line**, the forward line of attack or defense. **b** Act of carrying the ball. **6.** *Motion Pictures.* A first print from scenes exposed on the previous day, projected for inspection. — *adj.* Requiring a rush in performing, preparing, etc.; as, a *rush* order. — **rush′er**, *n.* — **rush′ing·ly**, *adv.*

rush candle. A candle made of the pith of certain rushes dipped in grease. Hence, **rush light.**

ru′sine ant′ler (ro͞o′sĭn; -sīn). An antler with a simple brow tine and a simple fork at the tip of the beam.

‖**rus in ur′be** (rŭs ĭn ûr′bē). [L.] The country in the city.

rusk (rŭsk), *n.* [Sp. *rosca* a roll, twist (of bread).] **1.** A light, soft, crusty bread made with yeast and eggs; also, a form of sweet biscuit. **2.** Bread or cake browned or crisped in an oven; often, also, such bread pulverized.

Russ (rŭs), *n.; pl.* RUSS, RUSSES (rŭs′ĕz; -ĭz). [F. *Russe.*] **1.** A Russian, or the Russians. **2.** The Russian language. — **Russ**, *adj.*

Rus′sell·ite (rŭs′'l·īt), *n.* See JEHOVAH'S WITNESSES.

rus′set (rŭs′ĕt; -ĭt), *n.* [OF. *rousset, rosset*, dim. of *rous, ros*, red, fr. L. *russus;* akin to E. RED.] **1.** Orig., homespun cloth or clothing, often russet in color; hence, country dress. **2.** Any of a group of browns varying in hue from reddish red-yellow to red-yellow. See COLOR. **3.** Any apple of a group of winter apples having rough skins of a russet color. — **rus′set**, *adj.*

Rus′sia leath′er (rŭsh′ȧ). Leather made from various skins by tanning with barks of the willow, birch, or oak, and then rubbing the flesh side with birch oil, which imparts a peculiar odor and protects from insects; — used in fine bookbinding, for purses, etc.

Rus′sian (rŭsh′ăn), *adj.* Of or pertaining to Russia, its inhabitants, or their language. — *n.* **1.** One of the people of Russia; esp., a member of the dominant Slavic-speaking race, or races, of Russia. The Russian-speaking peoples are subdivided into the ***Great Russians***, of the central and northeastern areas; the ***Little Russians***, of Little Russia (see in *Gaz.*); and the ***White Russians, or Byelorussians***, in White Russia. **2.** The chief Slavic language of Russia. It includes: ***Great Russian***, the standard literary language; ***Little Russian, or Ukrainian***, spoken in Ukraine and southern Poland; and ***White Russian, or Byelorussian***, spoken in western Soviet Russia and northeastern Poland. See INDO-EUROPEAN LANGUAGES, *Table.*

Russian Church. Before 1917, the established Orthodox church of the Russian Empire.

Russian dressing. Mayonnaise dressing with pungent additions, as chili sauce, or chopped pickles, pimientos, etc.

Rus′sian·ize (rŭsh′ăn·īz), *v. t.* To make Russian.

Russian Revolution. See REVOLUTION, 5.

Rus′so- (rŭs′ō-). A combining form denoting: **a** *Russia, Russians*, as in **Rus′so·phile, Rus′so·pho′bi·a.** **b** *Russian and;* — in adjectives, as in **Rus′so-Chi′nese′, Rus′so-Ger′man, Rus′so-Greek′, Rus′so-Jap′a·nese′, Rus′so-Pol′ish, Rus′so-Turk′ish.**

rust (rŭst), *n.* [AS. *rūst* (and prob. *rust*).] **1.** The reddish coating, essentially a hydrated form of ferric oxide (Fe_2O_3), formed on iron as when chemically attacked by moist air; by extension, the coating produced on any of various other metals by corrosion. **2.** A rustlike coating or stain. Specif.: **a** A rusty discoloration found on cured fish, giving it a bad flavor and often the result of bacterial colonies. **b** Any morbid brown or reddish discoloration of vegetation or fruit; esp., one in higher plants caused by parasitic fungi. See sense 6, below. **3.** Corrosive or injurious accretion or influence. **4.** Inaction; idleness. **5.** The color of iron rust, reddish red-yellow in hue, of high saturation and low brilliance. See COLOR. **6.** *Bot.* Any of an order (Uredinales) of parasitic fungi, causing spots or discolorations on the leaves, stems, etc., of higher plants; — called also **rust fungus.** They are often heteroecious, as the ***wheat rust*** *Puccinia graminis*, whose alternate host is the common barberry. — *v. i. & t.* **1.** To contract or cause to contract rust. **2.** To affect or be affected with rust. **3.** To turn to or become rust in color. **4.** To impair or corrupt by or as by time or indolence. — **rust′a·ble**, *adj.*

rus′tic (rŭs′tĭk), *adj.* [L. *rusticus*, fr. *rus, ruris*, the country.] **1.** Of or pertaining to the country; rural. **2.** Awkward; unpolished; boorish. **3.** Befitting the country; plain; simple; specif., designating a type of rough furniture made of rough limbs often with the bark left on. **4.** *Masonry.* Rusticated; as, a *rustic* joint. — **Syn.** See RURAL. — *n.* **1.** An inhabitant of the country, esp. one rude, coarse, or dull. **2.** A rural person naturally simple in character or manners. — **rus′ti·cal** (-tĭ·kăl), *adj. & n.* — **rus′ti·cal·ly**, *adv.*

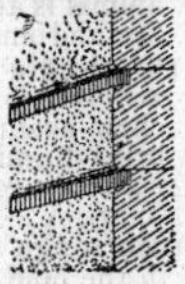

Rustic Joints.

rus′ti·cate (rŭs′tĭ·kāt), *v. i. & t.* [L. *rusticatus*, past part. of *rusticari* to rusticate. See RUSTIC.] **1.** To go into, or reside in, the country or to force to do so; banish or be banished to the country; specif., to suspend, esp. from college. **2.** To cause to become rustic. **3.** *Masonry.* To bevel or rabbet, as blocks on the edges so as to make the joints conspicuous. — **rus′ti·ca′tion** (-kā′shŭn), *n.* — **rus′ti·ca′tor** (-kā′tẽr), *n.*

rus·tic′i·ty (rŭs·tĭs′ĭ·tĭ), *n.; pl.* -TIES (-tĭz). Quality or state of being rustic; rustic crudeness, simplicity, etc.

rus′tle (rŭs′'l), *v. i. & t.;* -TLED (-'ld); -TLING (-lĭng). [ME. *rustle, rustel*, of imitative origin.] To make or cause to make a rustle. — *n.* A succession or confusion of small sounds, like those made by shaking leaves or straw, by the swish of silk, etc. — **rus′tler** (-lẽr), *n.*

rus′tle, *v. i. & t.* [A modern blend of *rush* and *hustle.*] **1.** *Slang, U. S.* To act with or get by a display of energy and rushing. **2.** *Orig. Western U. S.* To steal, as cattle.

rus′tler (rŭs′lẽr), *n.* **1.** One who or that which rustles; a hustler. **2.** *Orig. Western U. S.* A cattle thief.

rust′y (rŭs′tĭ), *adj.;* RUST′I·ER (-tĭ·ẽr); RUST′I·EST. **1.** Covered or affected with rust; stiff in action, as if clogged with rust. **2.** Impaired by disuse or neglect. **3.** Of the color rust. — **rust′i·ly**, *adv.* — **rust′i·ness**, *n.*

rust′y, *adj.* [From *resty*, var. of RESTIVE.] Stubborn; obstinate; rebellious; — esp. in the phrase *to ride*, or *turn, rusty*, to become stubborn or rebellious.

rut (rŭt), *n.* [F., fr. OF. *ruit*, fr. L. *rugitus* roaring, fr. *rugire* to roar.] Sexual desire or oestrus of deer, cattle, and other mammals; heat; also, the period during which it exists. — *v. i.;* RUT′TED; RUT′TING. To have rut. — *v. t.* To cover in copulation.

rut (rŭt), *n.* [OF. *rote, route*, way. See ROUTE.] **1.** A track worn by a wheel or by habitual passage of anything; a groove in which anything runs. **2.** A routine method of action or procedure from which one is not easily stirred. — *v. t.;* RUT′TED; RUT′TING. To make a rut or ruts in.

ru′ta·ba′ga (ro͞o′tȧ·bā′gȧ), *n.* [Sw. dial. *rotabagge.*] A variety of turnip (*Brassica napobrassica*) commonly with a very large elongated yellowish root. See TURNIP, 1.

ru·ta′ceous (ro͞o·tā′shŭs), *adj.* [L. *rutaceus*, fr. *ruta* rue.] Belonging to the rue family (Rutaceae). See RUE.

ruth (ro͞oth; 114), *n.* [ME. *reuthe, reowthe*, fr. AS. *hrēow(e)* sad.] **1.** Compassion for misery of another; pity. **2.** Sorrow; esp., repentance; regret; remorse. — **Syn.** See PITY.

Ruth (ro͞oth), *n.* [LL., fr. Heb. *Rūth.*] **a** An Old Testament heroine. **b** A book of the Old Testament. See BIBLE.

Ru·the′ni·an (ro͞o·thē′nĭ·ăn; -thēn′yăn; 58), *n.* One of a branch of the Little Russians, formerly of Galicia in Austria, now chiefly of Ruthenia (see RUTHENIA, in *Gaz.*); also, their Slavic language, the Little Russian (see RUSSIAN, *n.*, 2). — **Ru·the′ni·an**, *adj.*

ru·then′ic (ro͞o·thĕn′ĭk; -thē′nĭk), *adj.* *Chem.* Of or pertaining to ruthenium; — used specif. of compounds in which ruthenium has a relatively high valence.

ru·the′ni·ous (ro͞o·thē′nĭ·ŭs), *adj.* *Chem.* Of or pertaining to ruthenium; — used specif. of compounds in which ruthenium has a relatively low valence.

ru·the′ni·um (-ŭm), *n.* [NL., fr. ML. *Ruthenia* Russia, the metal having been found in the Ural Mountains.] *Chem.* A rare metal of the platinum group, associated with platinum ores. Symbol, *Ru;* at. no., 44; at. wt., 101.7; sp. gr. (crystalline form), 12.2.

ruth′ful (ro͞oth′fo͝ol; -f'l), *adj.* Full of ruth; pitiful; causing sorrow.

ruth′less, *adj.* Having no ruth; cruel; pitiless. — **ruth′less·ly**, *adv.* — **ruth′less·ness**, *n.*

ru′ti·lant (ro͞o′tĭ·lănt), *adj.* [L. *rutilans*, pres. part. See RUTILE.] Having a reddish glow; shining.

ru′tile (ro͞o′tēl; -tīl), *n.* [F. *rutile*, G. *rutil*, fr. L. *rutilus* red, golden red.] *Mineral.* A mineral consisting of titanium dioxide, TiO_2, usually of a reddish-brown color and brilliant metallic luster. It usually contains a little iron. H., 6–6.5. Sp. gr., about 4.2.

rut′tish (rŭt′ĭsh), *adj.* Inclined to rut; lustful; salacious.

rut′ty (rŭt′ĭ), *adj.;* RUT′TI·ER (-ĭ·ẽr); RUT′TI·EST. Full of ruts, as a road. — **rut′ti·ness** (-ĭ·nĕs; -nĭs), *n.*

-ry (-rĭ). A reduced form of the suffix -ERY; as in jewel*ry*.

rye (rī), *n.* [Romany *rei, rai*, lord.] *Gypsy.* A gentleman.

rye, *n.* [AS. *ryge.*] **1.** A hardy annual cereal grass (*Secale cereale*) widely cultivated as a food grain. **2.** The seeds or grain of this plant. **3.** Whisky distilled from rye.

ryke (rīk; rēk), *v. i.* *Scot.* To reach.

rynd, rind (rīnd; rĭnd), *n.* [ME. *rynd.*] A piece of iron crossing the hole in the upper millstone by which the stone is borne on the spindle.

ry′ot (rī′ŏt), *n.* [Hind. *raiyat, ra'iyat*, fr. Ar. *ra'iyah.*] *India.* A peasant or cultivator of the soil.

S

S, s (ĕs), *n.; pl.* S's, s's, Ss, ss (ĕs′ĕz; -ĭz). **1.** The nineteenth letter of the English alphabet. It comes through the Latin from the Greek (*sigma*), which borrowed the character from the Phoenician (Hebrew *sin, shin*). **2.** The sound or any sound of the letter S. See *Pron.* § 96. **3.** Anything having the shape of the letter S. **4.** As a *symbol*, eighteenth or (see K, 3) nineteenth in order or class.

-s. **1.** [ME. *-s, -es,* fr. AS. *-as,* masc. ending.] The suffix used to form the common case plural of most nouns, abbreviations, figures, and symbols (for plurals in *-es,* see PLURAL, 2; see also *Orthography* §§ 12, 13, 14). In specific use: Adverbial plural suffix added to nouns that denote time or occasion to indicate the predicated action or state as repeated or usual at, on, or during such times (he goes, or is at, home Sunday*s*, holiday*s*, mealtime*s*, noon hour*s*, weekend*s*; winter*s* our birds migrate southward). The function of the adverbial plural suffix was in older English served by the adverbial genitive. See 2d -s. **2.** [ME. *-s, -es,* a Northern form replacing Midland *-eth* (AS. bind*eth* he binds).] The suffix used to form the third person singular indicative of English verbs (fall*s*).

-s. An adverbial suffix, as in toward*s*, need*s*; — orig. the genitive ending, as in Sunday*s*, of a Sunday.

-'s. [ME. *-s, -es,* fr. AS. *-es,* gen. sing., masc. and neut. ending.] The suffix used to form the possessive of nouns, as in boy*'s*, man*'s*, women*'s*.

's. Colloquial contraction of *is, has,* and (in let*'s*) *us.*

S′-1′, S′-2′, S′-3′, S′-4′ (ĕs′wŭn′, etc.). *U. S. Army.* The four sections of the staff, of a regiment or smaller unit, in charge respectively of personnel and administration, intelligence, operations and training, and supply. S-1 is the adjutant of a unit. Cf. G-1, G-2, etc.

sab′a·dil′la (săb′ȧ·dĭl′ȧ), *n.* [Sp. *cebadilla,* dim. of *cebada* barley.] A Mexican plant (*Schoenocaulon officinalis*) of the bunchflower family; also, its seeds, used as a source of veratrine and in the preparation of an insecticide.

Sa′ba·ism (sā′bȧ·ĭz′m), *n.* [Heb. *ṣābhā* host (of heaven), army + *-ism.*] Star worship. — **Sa′ba·ist** (-ĭst), *n.*

Sab′a·oth (săb′ā·ŏth; sȧ·bā′ŏth), *n. pl.* [LL., fr. LGr. *Sabaōth,* fr. Heb. *ṣĕbhā′ōth* armies.] *Bib.* Armies; hosts; — used twice in the English Bible, in *the Lord of Sabaoth.*

Sab′ba·tar′i·an (săb′ȧ·târ′ĭ·ăn; 6), *n.* [L. *Sabbatarius.*] **1.** One who keeps the seventh day of the week as holy, in conformity with the letter of the fourth commandment. **2.** One who favors strict observance of the Sabbath. — **Sab′ba·tar′i·an,** *adj.* — **Sab′ba·tar′i·an·ism** (-ĭz′m), *n.*

Sab′bath (săb′ăth), *n.* [From AS. *sabat* (fr. L.) and fr. OF. *sabat* (F. *sabbat*), fr. L. *sabbatum,* fr. Gr., fr. Heb. *shabbāth* day of rest, fr. *shābath* to rest.] **1.** The seventh day of the week in the Jewish calendar, the period from Friday evening to Saturday evening, kept as a day of rest and worship by the Jews and some Christians. **2.** Sunday, among Christians a day of rest and worship. **3.** [*not cap.*] A time of rest or repose. — **Syn.** See SUNDAY.

Sabbath school. = SUNDAY SCHOOL.

Sab·bat′i·cal (sȧ·băt′ĭ·kăl), *adj.* Also **Sab·bat′ic** (-ĭk). [Gr. *sabbatikos,* fr. *sabbaton.*] **1.** Of or suited to the Sabbath. **2.** [*Usually not cap.*] Of the nature of the Sabbath or a similarly recurring period of rest; as, *sabbatical* leave. Cf. SABBATICAL YEAR **b.** — **Sab·bat′i·cal·ly,** *adv.*

sab·bat′i·cal, Sab·bat′i·cal, *n.* **1.** A sabbatical year or leave of absence. **2.** *pl.* Sabbatical, or Sunday, clothes.

sabbatical year. **a** *Jewish Antiq.* Every seventh year, in which the Israelites were commanded to suffer their fields to lie without tillage. **b** A leave of absence granted every seventh year, as to a college professor, for rest, travel, or research.

Sa·bel′li·an (sȧ·bĕl′ĭ·ăn), *n.* One of a group of early Italian peoples comprising Sabines, Samnites, and others; also, a minor group of pre-Latin dialects, comprising a little-known branch of the Italic languages, related to Oscan. See INDO-EUROPEAN LANGUAGES, *Table.*

sa′ber, sa′bre (sā′bẽr), *n.* [F. *sabre,* fr. G. *sabel* (now *säbel*), of Slav. origin.] A cavalry sword with a somewhat curved blade for cutting and thrusting. — *v. t.;* SA′BERED or SA′BRED (-bẽrd); SA′BER·ING (-bẽr·ĭng) or SA′BRING (-brĭng). To strike or cut with a saber.

sa′ber-toothed′, sa′bre-toothed′, *adj.* Having long sharp canine teeth.

saber-toothed tiger. Any of various extinct catlike mammals of a subfamily (Machairodontinae) of the cat family, found from the Oligocene to the Pleistocene and characterized by the lengthening of the upper canines.

Sa′bine (sā′bīn *or, esp. Brit.,* săb′īn), *adj.* [L. *Sabinus.*] Of the ancient Sabines, whose chief seat was the Apennines northeast of Latium. — *n.* One of the Sabine people; also, their language, a dialect of the Sabellian branch of Italic. See INDO-EUROPEAN LANGUAGES, *Table.*

sa′ble (sā′b'l), *n.;* see PLURAL, *Note,* 3. [OF., fr. ML. *sabelum,* of Slav. origin.] **1.** A carnivorous mammal (*Martes zibellina*) allied to the martens, found in northern Europe and parts of northern Asia; also, a North American animal related to it. **2.** The fur or pelt of this animal. **3.** The color of the fur of this animal; black. **4.** A mourning garment; — usually *pl.* **5.** *Her.* Black. **6.** *Painting.* A brush made from hair of the sable. — *adj. Poetic.* Black in color; dark.

sable antelope. A large handsome African antelope (*Egoceros niger*) having large curved ringed horns.

sa′bot′ (sȧ′bō′; săb′ō), *n.* [F. (OF. *çabot*), after *bot, botte,* boot, fr. *savate* old shoe.] **1.** A type of wooden shoe worn by the peasantry in various European countries. **2.** *Mil.* A piece of soft metal formerly attached to a projectile, to take the grooves of the rifling.

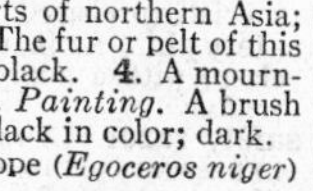

Sabot, 1.

sab′o·tage′ (săb′ō·täzh′; săb′ō·tĭj; *F.* sȧ′bô′tȧzh′), *n.* [F., fr. *saboter* to practice sabotage, to work carelessly, orig., to tread with wooden shoes, fr. *sabot.*] **1.** Malicious waste or destruction of an employer's property by workmen, as during labor troubles. **2.** Commission by a civilian or enemy agent within a country of any destructive act designed to impede the armed forces, or any act or neglect that retards essential industry, public services, etc. — (săb′ō·täzh′), *v. t. & i.;* -TAGED′ (-täzhd′); -TAG′ING (-täzh′ĭng). To practice sabotage (on); to destroy.

sab′o·teur′ (săb′ō·tûr′), *n.* [F.] One who resorts to sabotage.

sa′bre (sā′bẽr). Var. of SABER.

sa′bre·tache′ (sā′bẽr·tăsh′; săb′ẽr-), *n.* [F., fr. G. *säbeltasche,* fr. *säbel* saber + *tasche* a pocket.] *Mil.* A leather case or pocket sometimes worn, suspended on the left from the saber belt, by cavalry.

sab′u·lous (săb′ū·lŭs), *adj.* [L. *sabulosus,* fr. *sabulum* sand.] Sandy; gritty. — **sab′u·los′i·ty** (-lŏs′ĭ·tĭ), *n.*

sac (săk), *n.* [F., fr. L. *saccus* a sack.] A baglike part of an animal or plant, often containing some special fluid. See FANG, *Illust.*

Sac (săk; sôk), *n.* One of a tribe of Algonquian Indians formerly dwelling along the upper Mississippi.

sac′a·ton′ (săk′ȧ·tōn′), *n.* [Sp. *zacatón,* aug. of *zacate, sacate,* grass, fr. Nahuatl.] Zacatón, esp. a coarse perennial grass (*Sporobolus wrightii*), useful for hay in alkaline regions.

sac′cate (săk′āt), *adj.* [L. *saccus* a sack, bag.] *Biol.* Having the form of a sac or pouch.

sac′cha·rate (săk′ȧ·rāt), *n.* *Chem.* **a** A salt or ester of saccharic acid. **b** A compound of a sugar with the oxide of calcium, barium, or the like.

sac·char′ic (sȧ·kăr′ĭk), *adj.* **1.** Of or obtained from saccharine substances. **2.** *Chem.* Pertaining to or designating a diacid, $(CHOH)_4(CO_2H)_2$, occurring in three optically different modifications, D-, L-, and DL-.

sac′cha·ride (săk′ȧ·rīd; -rĭd), *n.* *Chem.* **a** A compound with sugar; a saccharate. **b** A carbohydrate; specif., a monosaccharide. **c** An ester of sucrose.

sac·char′i·fy (sȧ·kăr′ĭ·fī; săk′ȧ·rĭ·fī), *v. t.;* -FIED (-fīd); -FY′ING. [ML. *saccharum* sugar + *-fy.*] To convert into, or to impregnate with, sugar. — **sac·char′i·fi·ca′tion** (sȧ·kăr′ĭ·fĭ·kā′shŭn; săk′ȧ·rĭf′ĭ-), *n.*

sac′cha·rim′e·ter (săk′ȧ·rĭm′ē·tẽr), *n.* [Gr. *sakchari* sugar + *metron* measure.] Any device for measuring the amount of sugar in a solution, esp. a form of polarimeter. Cf. SACCHAROMETER.

sac′cha·rin (săk′ȧ·rĭn), *n.* Also **sac′cha·rine** (-rĭn; -rēn). [ML. *saccharum* sugar, fr. L., fr. Gr. *sakcharon,* through Pali, fr. Skr. *śarkarā* gravel, grit, sugar.] A coal-tar crystalline product, $C_7H_5NO_3S$, several hundred times sweeter than cane sugar, used as a sugar substitute. Cf. CRYSTALLOSE.

sac′cha·rine (-rĭn; -rīn), *adj.* **1.** Of or of the nature of sugar; sweet; yielding sugar. **2.** Ingratiatingly or sickishly sweet. — **sac′cha·rin′i·ty** (-rĭn′ĭ·tĭ), *n.*

sac′cha·ro- (săk′ȧ·rō-), **sacchar-.** [Gr. *sakcharon* sugar.] A combining form meaning: **a** *Sugar,* as in **sac′cha·rif′er·ous.** **b** *Saccharine and,* as in **sac′cha·ro·far′i·na′ceous.**

sac′cha·roid (săk′ȧ·roid), **sac′cha·roi′dal** (-roi′dăl; -d'l), *adj.* [*sacchar-* + *-oid.*] Resembling loaf sugar; crystalline and granular; — chiefly of stone.

sac′cha·rom′e·ter (-rŏm′ē·tẽr), *n.* Any device for measuring the amount of sugar in a solution, esp. a hydrometer with a special scale. Cf. SACCHARIMETER.

sac′cha·rose (săk′ȧ·rōs), *n.* Sucrose. See SUGAR.

sac′cu·lat′ed (săk′ū·lāt′ĕd; -ĭd), *adj.* Also **sac′cu·late** (-lāt). Formed of or having a series of saclike expansions.

sac′cule (săk′ūl), *n.* [L. *sacculus,* dim. fr. *saccus* sack.] A little sac.

sac′cu·lus (săk′ū·lŭs), *n.; pl.* SACCULI (-lī). [L., little sack.] A little sac; esp., *Anat.,* the saccule of the ear.

sac′er·do′tal (săs′ẽr·dō′tăl; -t'l), *adj.* [F., fr. L. *sacerdotalis,* fr. *sacerdos, -otis,* a priest.] **1.** Of priests; relating to the priestly office or function. **2.** Characterized by a belief in a divinely authorized priesthood. — **sac′er·do′tal·ly,** *adv.*

sac′er·do′tal·ism (-ĭz′m), *n.* **1.** The priesthood, its character, office, or function. **2.** The doctrine that ordination confers special powers and rights necessary for the exercise of the ministry.

sa′chem (sā′chĕm), *n.* [Of Algonquian origin.] **1.** A North American Indian chief, orig. chief of a confederation. **2.** Any one of the twelve governors of the Tammany Society.

sa·chet′ (sȧ·shā′ *or, esp. Brit.,* săsh′ā), *n.* [F., dim. of *sac.*] A scent bag, or perfumed pad, packed with perfumed powder (**sachet powder**).

sack (săk), *n.* [Formerly *seck,* for *wyne seck* dry wine, fr. F. *vin sec,* fr. L. *siccus* dry, harsh.] Formerly, any of various strong white wines from southern Europe.

sack, *n.* [F. *sac,* fr. It. *sacco,* fr. VL. (ML.) *saccare* to sack, take by force.] The plundering of a captured town. — *v. t.* To plunder or pillage after capture; to loot. — **Syn.** See RAVAGE. — **sack′er** (-ẽr), *n.*

sack, *n.* [AS. *sacc,* fr. L. *saccus,* fr. Gr. *sakkos,* of Sem. origin.] **1.** A bag, typically large, oblong, and of coarse material. **2.** A varying measure of capacity, being the quantity contained in a sack. In the United States a sack averages 3 bu.; a sack of salt, 215 lb.; cotton, 140 lb.; flour for export, 140 lb.; flour or meal, usually 100 lb. **3.** *Slang.* Discharge; dismissal. **4.** Also **sacque** (săk). A short loose-fitting coat, worn by women or children. — *v. t.* **1.** To put or pack in a sack or sacks. **2.** *Slang.* To discharge; dismiss. **3.** To defeat decisively in a contest.

sack′but (săk′bŭt), *n.* [F. *saquebute,* deriv. of MF. *saquer* to pull + *bouter* to thrust.] **1.** *Music.* An early form of the slide trombone. **2.** [Mistranslation of Aram. *sabbĕkhā,* Dan. iii.] Probably a form of harp.

sack′cloth′ (-klŏth′; 74), *n.* Coarse cloth; sacking; also, garb of penitence, in the Bible probably of goats' or camels' hair.

sack coat. A man's short, loose-fitting, single-breasted or double-breasted coat for informal wear.

sack′ful (săk′fo͝ol), *n.* The quantity that fills a sack.

sack′ing, *n.* Stout coarse cloth of which sacks are made.

sack′less, *adj.* [AS. *saclēas.* See 1st SAKE; -LESS.] **1.** *Archaic.* Guiltless. **2.** *Scot.* **a** Dispirited. **b** Harmless.

sack race. A race in which each contestant has his legs in a sack.

sacque (săk). Var. of SACK, a coat.

sa′cral (sā′krăl), *adj.* [L. *sacer,* neut. *sacrum,* sacred.] **1.** Of or for religious rites. **2.** [NL. *sacralis.*] *Anat.* Pertaining to or in the region of the sacrum.

sac′ra·ment (săk′rȧ·mĕnt), *n.* [OF. *sacrement,* fr. L. *sacramentum,* fr. *sacrare.* See SACRED.] **1.** *Eccl.* One of certain religious ceremonies distinguished in Christian rites as instituted or recognized by Christ. The Roman Catholic and the Eastern churches recognize seven sacraments, viz., baptism, confirmation, the Eucharist, penance, extreme unction, holy orders, and matrimony; Protestants, only baptism and the Lord's Supper. **2.** With *the* and often *cap.*, the Eucharist; also, *R.C.Ch.*, usually with *blessed* or *holy*, the consecrated Host. **3. a** A token or symbol. **b** An oath, as in compurgation. **4.** A spiritual covenant, as between God and man.

sac′ra·men′tal (săk′rȧ·mĕn′tăl; -t'l), *adj.* Of or pertaining to the Christian sacraments; of the nature of a sacrament. — *n.* *R.C.Ch.* A rite or a sacred object like a sacrament but instituted by the church.

sac′ra·men·tar′i·an (-mĕn·târ′ĭ·ăn; 6), *adj.* *Eccl.* Of or pertaining to sacraments or [*cap.*] the Sacramentarians. — *n.* [*cap.*] One who holds the sacraments to be simply visible symbols; — applied to Zwinglians and Calvinists.

sa·crar′i·um (sȧ·krâr′ĭ·ŭm), *n.; pl.* -IA (-ȧ). [L., fr. *sacer* sacred.] **1.** *Rom. Antiq.* A shrine or sanctuary. **2.** *Eccl.* **a** Anciently, the sanctuary. **b** *R.C.Ch.* = PISCINA.

sa′cred (sā′krĕd; -krĭd), *adj.* [Orig. past part. of ME. *sacren* to consecrate, fr. OF., fr. L. *sacrare*, fr. *sacer* sacred, holy.] **1.** Dedicated; set apart in honor of, or as dear to, one, as a god; hence, devoted exclusively to a certain person or end. **2.** Holy; hallowed by association with the divine or the consecrated; hence, entitled to reverence and respect; as, a *sacred* memory. **3.** Of or pertaining to religion, its doctrines, rites, history, etc.; religious; as, *sacred* vestments. Cf. 2d TEMPORAL, 2. **4.** Inviolable or inviolate; not to be profaned. **5.** Accursed; baleful. — **sa′cred·ly**, *adv.* — **sa′cred·ness**, *n.*

sacred baboon. A baboon (*Papio hamadryas*) venerated by the ancient Egyptians.

sac′ri·fice (săk′rĭ·fīs; -fīs; -fīz), *n.* [OF., fr. L. *sacrificium*, fr. *sacer* sacred + *-ficare* to make.] **1.** An offering to a deity of animal or vegetable life or of food, drink, incense, or the like. **2.** Anything consecrated and offered to God or to a divinity. **3.** Destruction or surrender of some desirable thing in behalf of a higher object, or devotion of it to a claim deemed more pressing; also, the thing so devoted or given up. **4.** A loss of profit or grievous loss incurred in selling under unfavorable conditions. **5.** *Baseball.* Short for SACRIFICE HIT. — (săk′rĭ·fīs; -fīz), *v. t.;* -FICED (-fīst; -fīzd); -FIC′ING (-fīs′ĭng; -fīz′ĭng). **1.** To offer as a sacrifice; to immolate. **2.** To suffer loss of, give up, renounce, or destroy, for an end regarded as superior. **3.** *Colloq.* To sell at a sacrifice. **4.** *Baseball.* To advance (a base runner) by a sacrifice hit. — *v. i.* To offer up or perform rites of a sacrifice. — **sac′ri·fic′er** (-fīs′ẽr; -fīz′ẽr), *n.*

sacrifice hit. *Baseball.* A bunt or a fly ball (called then specif. **sacrifice fly**) that allows a runner to advance a base while the batter is put out.

sac′ri·fi′cial (săk′rĭ·fĭsh′ăl), *adj.* Of, pert. to, of the nature of, or involving sacrifice. — **sac′ri·fi′cial·ly**, *adv.*

sac′ri·lege (săk′rĭ·lĕj; -lĭj), *n.* [OF., fr. L. *sacrilegium*, fr. *sacrilegus* one who steals sacred things, fr. *sacer* sacred + *legere* to gather, pick up.] The crime of stealing or desecrating that which is sacred. — **Syn.** See PROFANATION.

sac′ri·le′gious (-lē′jŭs; -lĭj′ŭs), *adj.* Committing or involving sacrilege. — **sac′ri·le′gious·ly**, *adv.* — **sac′ri·le′gious·ness**, *n.*

sa′cring (sā′krĭng), *n.* Consecration, esp. of the sacramental elements.

sacring bell. **a** A small hand bell rung at the Elevation in the Mass. **b** The tolling of the church bell to announce the Elevation.

sac′ris·tan (săk′rĭs·tăn), *n.* [ML. *sacristanus*, fr. *sacrista*, fr. L. *sacer* sacred.] An officer in charge of the sacristy; also, a sexton.

sac′ris·ty (-tĭ), *n.; pl.* -TIES (-tĭz). [ML. *sacristia*.] A room in a church where the sacred utensils, vestments, etc., are kept; a vestry.

sa′cro- (sā′krō-; săk′rō-). [From SACRUM.] *Anat.* A combining form denoting: **a** *The sacrum*, as in **sa·crot′o·my** (sā·krŏt′ō·mĭ). **b** *Sacral and*, as in **sa′cro·sci·at′ic**.

sa′cro- (sā′krō-). A combining form for *sacred*.

sa′cro·il′i·ac (sā′krō·ĭl′ĭ·ăk; săk′rō-), *adj.* [1st *sacro-* + *iliac*.] Of, pert. to, or involving the sacrum and ilium or the joint between these parts; as, *sacroiliac* strain. — *n.* The joint between sacrum and ilium.

sac′ro·sanct (săk′rō·săngkt), *adj.* [L. *sacrosanctus*.] Most sacred; inviolable; — often ironical. — **sac′ro·sanc′ti·ty** (-săngk′tĭ·tĭ), *n.*

sa′crum (sā′krŭm), *n.; pl.* -CRA (-krȧ). [NL., fr. L. *os sacrum* the lowest bone of the spine, lit., sacred bone.] *Anat. & Zool.* That part of the vertebral column directly connected with, or forming a part of, the pelvis, in man consisting of five united vertebrae.

sad (săd), *adj.;* SAD′DER (-ẽr); SAD′DEST. [AS. *sæd* satisfied, sated.] **1.** *Archaic.* Firmly established. **2.** Affected with or expressive of grief; downcast; gloomy. **3.** Characterized by or associated with sorrow; melancholy. **4.** Afflictive; grievous. **5.** Dull; somber; — of colors. **6. a** Shocking; wicked; — often playfully. **b** *Slang.* Inferior.

sad′den (săd′'n), *v. t. & i.* To make or become sad.

sad′dle (săd′'l), *n.* [AS. *sadol*.] **1.** A leather-covered seat for a rider on horseback or on a bicycle, motorcycle, etc. (see BICYCLE, *Illust.*); also, the position of a person riding on such a seat; as, ***in the saddle***, in a position to dictate or command. **2.** Something suggestive of or analogous to a saddle; also, any of various devices suggestive of a saddle; as: **a** A saddlelike ridge or marking. **b** The bearing of an axle box. **c** In bookbinding, the central or middle part of the back of the binding. **d** A strip of leather arching over the instep and containing the lacing eyelets, esp. of an Oxford-style shoe, extending from the shank on one side to the shank on the other side, often of a contrasting color with the rest of the shoe, as brown on white. Hence, **saddle shoe**. **3.** *Cookery.* The whole upper back portion of a carcass, including both loins; as, a *saddle* of mutton; also, such a piece cooked for food. **4.** *Harness.* A padded part worn on a horse's back, being fastened with a girth. See HARNESS, *Illust.* **5.** *Ordn.* In some types of carriage, the part which supports the trunnions. **6.** *Phys. Geog. & Meteorol.* A ridge connecting two higher elevations. **7.** *Poultry.* The rear part of the back of a male fowl, extending to the tail. See POULTRY, *Illust.* (8). — *v. t.;* SAD′DLED (-'ld); SAD′DLING (-lĭng). **1.** To put a saddle upon. **2.** To fix as a charge or burden upon; to load; encumber. **3.** To place the burden of or responsibility for; — with *upon*. — **sad′dle**, *adj.*

sad′dle·bag′ (-băg′), *n.* A large bag or pouch, usually one of a pair, carried hanging from one side of a saddle.

sad′dle·bow′ (-bō′), *n.* The bow or arch in the front, or the pieces forming the front, of a saddle.

sad′dle·cloth′ (-klōth′; 74), *n.* A cloth used under a saddle.

saddle horse. A horse of any of various mixed breeds, esp. suited for riding because of its strong back.

sad′dler (săd′lẽr), *n.* A maker, repairer, or seller of saddles and other equipment for horses.

saddle roof. A roof having two gables and one ridge.

sad′dler·y (săd′lẽr·ĭ), *n.; pl.* SADDLERIES (-ĭz). The trade, articles of trade, or shop, of a saddler.

saddle soap. A mild soap made with some added unsaponified oil, in the form of a paste or bar for cleansing and conditioning leather.

sad′dle-tree′ (săd′'l·trē′), *n.* **1.** The frame of a saddle. **2.** *U.S.* The tulip tree *Liriodendron tulipifera*.

Sad′du·cee (săd′ū·sē), *n.* [LL. *Sadducaei*, pl., fr. Gr. *Saddoukaioi*, fr. Heb. *Tsaddūqīm*.] One of a sect among the ancient Jews that denied the resurrection, personal immortality, future retribution, fate, the existence of angels, and postulated the freedom of the will. — **Sad′du·ce′an** (-sē′ăn), *adj. & n.* — **Sad′du·cee·ism** (săd′ū·sē·ĭz'm), *n.*

sad′i′ron (săd′ī′ẽrn), *n.* [*sad* (obs.) heavy.] A flatiron.

sad′ism (săd′ĭz'm; sā′dĭz'm; säd′ĭz'm), *n.* [F. *sadisme;* — after Count de *Sade* (1740–1814), who depicted the perversion.] **a** A sexual perversion in which gratification is got by torturing the loved person. Cf. MASOCHISM. **b** Love of cruelty, conceived as manifesting sexual desire. **c** Loosely and popularly, abnormal delight in cruelty. — **sad′ist** (-ĭst), *n. & adj.* — **sa·dis′tic** (sȧ·dĭs′tĭk; sā-), *adj.* — **sa·dis′ti·cal·ly** (-tĭ·kăl·ĭ), *adv.*

sad′ly (săd′lĭ), *adv.* In a sad manner or way.

sad′ness (-nĕs; -nĭs), *n.* State, quality, or fact of being sad.

Syn. **Sadness, depression, melancholy, melancholia, dejection, gloom** mean an attack of low spirits. **Sadness**, the general term, apart from the context carries no suggestion of the cause or extent of low spirits; **depression** suggests a mood or state of mind when one feels let down, discouraged, or the like; **melancholy** sometimes suggests a settled state of depression (now more often called **melancholia**) but usually implies a not unpleasant mood characterized by pensive sadness or deep seriousness; **dejection** implies a mood of one who is downcast or dispirited by a passing event; **gloom** implies the effect produced by any one of these moods or states of mind on the person afflicted or on others.

Sa·far′ (sȧ·fär′), *n.* [Ar. *Ṣafar*.] See MOHAMMEDAN CALENDAR.

sa·fa′ri (sȧ·fä′rĭ), *n.* [Ar., referring to a journey, traveling.] *E. Africa.* A journey or expedition, esp., a hunting expedition; also, its caravan, with camels, etc.

safe (sāf), *adj.;* SAF′ER (sāf′ẽr); SAF′EST. [OF. *sauf*, fr. L. *salvus* safe, well.] **1.** Freed from injury or risk; unhurt; as, to arrive *safe;* secure from threat of danger, harm, or loss. **2.** Affording safety; as, a *safe* harbor. **3.** Without risk of mishap or failure; as, a *safe* policy. **4.** Trustworthy; as, a *safe* guide. **5.** Made incapable of doing harm; in secure custody. — **safe′ly**, *adv.* — **safe′ness**, *n.*

Syn. **Safe, secure** mean free from danger. **Safe** may or may not imply previous danger but it always suggests freedom from it at the time suggested; **secure** implies freedom from apprehension of danger or risk.

— *n.* A place or receptacle specially designed for keeping articles safe; specif., a steel box or chest, often built into a wall or vault, for valuables.

safe′blow′ing (-blō′ĭng), *n.* Use of explosives to open a safe to be burglarized. — **safe′blow′er**, *n.*

safe′break′er (-brāk′ẽr), *n.* One who breaks open safes to steal. — **safe′break′ing**, *n.*

safe′-con′duct, *n.* That which assures a safe passage, esp. in an enemy's country; as: **a** Protection by a convoy or guard. **b** A writing, pass, or warrant of security, enabling one to travel with safety.

safe deposit. A place, as a vault that is proof against fire, flood, and theft, to store valuables safely. — **safe′-de·pos′it**, *adj.* — **safe′-de·pos′it box, vault**, etc.

safe′guard′ (sāf′gärd′), *n.* [OF. *sauvegarde*, prop., a safekeeping.] A means of protection; specif.: **a** A convoy or escort. **b** A pass; safe-conduct. **c** A precautionary measure or stipulation. **d** A technical contrivance to prevent accident. — *v. t.* To provide a safeguard for. — **Syn.** See DEFEND.

safe hit. *Baseball.* A hit enabling the batter to reach first base without the aid of an error.

safe′keep′ing (sāf′kēp′ĭng), *n.* A preserving in safety.

safe′ty (sāf′tĭ), *n.* **1.** Condition of being safe; freedom from danger or hazard. **2.** Quality of being devoid of whatever exposes one to danger or harm; safeness. **3.** *Rare.* Close custody. **4.** A keeping of oneself or others safe, esp. from danger of accident or disease. **5.** A protective device, as on a firearm, to prevent accidental discharge. **6.** *Amer. Football.* Any act resulting in the ball's being declared dead on, above, or behind the goal line, in the possession of a player guarding his own goal, provided the impetus which sent the ball to or across the line was given by the side defending the goal; also, a score (2 points) so made. **7.** *Baseball.* A safe hit. — *adj.* **1.** Made or planned so as to ensure the safety of the user, operator, etc., as in **safety glass**. **2.** Of or pertaining to the safeguarding of the public, or of a group of employees, or the like, from accident; as, *safety* measures, rules; *safety* engineers.

safety belt. **1.** = LIFE BELT. **2.** A belt or strap for fastening a person to some object, esp. to prevent his falling.

safety lamp. A miner's lamp constructed to avoid explosion of gas. In the original ***Davy lamp***, invented by Sir Humphry Davy, the flame is enclosed by fine wire gauze.

safety match. A match which can be ignited only on a surface specially prepared.

safety pin. A pin, used esp for fastening clothes, made in the form of a clasp, with a guard covering its point so that it will not prick the wearer.

safety razor. A razor provided with a guard or guards for the blade to prevent cutting the skin.

safety valve. **1.** An automatic escape or relief valve for a steam boiler, hydraulic system, or the like. **2.** An outlet or vent for pent-up energy, emotion, etc.

safety zone. A space in a street or road reserved for the use of pedestrians and marked in some way, as by painted lines.

saf′flow′er (săf′lou′ẽr), *n.* [Earlier also *safflore, saflor*, fr. OF. *saflor, saffleur*, fr. OIt. *saffiore, zaffrole*. All forms influenced by words for flower.] **1.** An Old World thistlelike herb (*Carthamus tinctorius*) of the aster family, having large orange-colored flower heads. **2.** A red dyestuff, also a drug, prepared from these flower heads.

saf′fron (săf′rŭn), *n.* [OF. *safran*, fr. ML. *safranum*, ult. fr. Ar. *za'farān*.] **1.** A species of crocus (*Crocus sativus*) with purple flowers. **2.** The orange-colored aromatic, pungent dried stigmas of this plant, used to color and flavor foods, and formerly as a dyestuff, etc. **3.** The color saffron yellow. — *adj.* Of the color saffron yellow.

saffron yellow. A color, yellowish red-yellow in hue, of high saturation and high brilliance; — called also *saffron* and *crocus*. See COLOR.

saf′ra·nine (săf′rȧ·nēn; -nĭn), *n.* Also **saf′ra·nin.** [See SAFFRON.] **1.** *Chem.* Any of a class of synthetic dyes, usually red, amino derivatives of certain bases. **2.** Any of various mixtures of safranine salts used in dyeing and as a microscopic stain.

saf′role (săf′rōl), *n.* Also **saf′rol** (-rōl; -rŏl). [F. *safran* saffron + *-ol*, 2.] *Chem.* A poisonous oil, $C_{10}H_{10}O_2$, chief constituent of oil of sassafras, used for perfuming, etc.

sag (săg), *n.* **1.** Fact, state, instance, or degree of sagging. **2.** A part or place that is sunken, as in a roadbed. **3.** Drift, as of a vessel to leeward. — *v. i.;* SAGGED (săgd); SAG′GING. **1.** To droop, sink, or settle, as through being pressed down or losing tautness, esp. at the middle, as a cable. **2.** To lose firmness, resiliency or vigor; to yield under pressure, as the spirits; to fall gradually, as prices. **3.** *Naut.* To drift.

sa′ga (sä′gȧ), *n.* [ON.] **1.** A medieval story, historical or legendary or both, of an Icelandic hero or family. **2.** A modern epiclike narrative like an Icelandic saga.

sa·ga′cious (sȧ·gā′shŭs), *adj.* [L. *sagax, sagacis.*] **1.** Keen in sense perception, esp. in scenting. **2.** Of keen penetration and judgment; discerning and farsighted in judging men, motives, and means; shrewd. — **Syn.** See SHREWD. — **sa·ga′cious·ly,** *adv.* — **sa·ga′cious·ness,** *n.*

sa·gac′i·ty (sȧ·găs′ĭ·tĭ), *n.; pl.* -TIES (-tĭz). Quality of being sagacious; keenness of discernment or judgment.

sag′a·more (săg′ȧ·mōr; 70), *n.* A lesser chief or tribal chief among certain North American Indians; a sachem.

saga novel. See ROMAN-FLEUVE.

sage (sāj), *n.* [OF. *sauge,* fr. L. *salvia,* fr. *salvus* well, in allusion to its reputed healing virtues.] **a** A half-shrubby mint (*Salvia officinalis*) with grayish-green leaves, used in flavoring meats, etc.; also, any other species of this genus; as, the ***scarlet sage*** (*S. splendens*) and the ***clary sage*** (*S. sclarea* and *S. horminum*). **b** The sagebrush.

sage (sāj), *adj.;* SAG′ER (sāj′ẽr); SAG′EST. [OF., fr. L. *sapiens* and (or) *sapidus,* fr. *sapere* to be wise.] **1.** Eminent in wisdom, esp. wisdom gained through experience and reflection. **2.** Proceeding from, or characterized by, wisdom, prudence, and good judgment; as, *sage* counsel. **3.** *Now Rare.* Grave; solemn. — **Syn.** See WISE. — *n.* [OF.] A profound philosopher or wise counselor; also, a venerable man sound in judgment. — **sage′ly,** *adv.* — **sage′ness,** *n.*

sage′brush′ (-brŭsh′), *n.* Any of several hoary undershrubs (genus *Artemisia,* esp. *A. tridentata*) of the aster family, with a bitter juice and sagelike odor, of the western alkaline plains of the U. S., adopted as the State flower of Nevada.

sage grouse. A large grouse (*Centrocercus urophasianus*) native of the sagebrush plains of western North America. The male and female are often called specif. **sage cock** and **sage hen.**

sage sparrow. See SPARROW.

sag′ger (săg′ẽr), *n.* [E. *dial. saggard* a sagger, contr. fr. *safeguard.*] *Ceramics.* A box made of fire clay, in which delicate pieces are fired either for biscuit or for glaze; also, the clay of which saggers are made.

sag′it·tal (săj′ĭ·tăl; -t′l), *adj.* [NL. *sagittalis,* fr. L. *sagitta* arrow.] **1.** Of, pertaining to, or like an arrow or arrowhead. **2.** *Anat. & Zool.* **a** Designating the suture between the parietal bones of the skull. **b** Designating, situated in, or pertaining to, the median vertical longitudinal plane, dividing an animal into right and left halves; or any plane parallel thereto.

Sag′it·ta′ri·us (săj′ĭ·tâ′rĭ·ŭs), *n.; gen.* -TARII (-ī). [L., lit., an archer.] **a** A southern constellation pictured as a centaur shooting an arrow. **b** The ninth sign [♐] of the zodiac, which the sun enters about Nov. 22. See ZODIAC.

sag′it·tate (săj′ĭ·tāt), *adj.* [NL. *sagittatus,* fr. L. *segitta* arrow.] Shaped like an arrowhead. See LEAF, *Illust.* (21).

sa·git′ti·form (sȧ·jĭt′ĭ·fôrm; săj′ĭ·tĭ-), *adj.* Sagittate.

sa′go (sā′gō), *n.* [Malay *sagu.*] A starch prepared from the pith of an East Indian and Malaysian palm (**sago palm,** genus *Metroxylon*), used in puddings and for stiffening textiles.

sa·gua′ro (sȧ·gwä′rō; sȧ·wä′rō), *n.; pl.* -ROS (-rōz). [Sp., of Piman origin.] An arborescent cactus (*Carnegiea gigantea*) of the southwestern U. S. and Mexico, attaining a height of 60 feet. The blossom is the State flower of Arizona.

sa′hib (sä′ĭb), *n.* [Hind. *sāhib,* fr. Ar. *ṣāhib* master, lord.] *India.* **a** [*usually cap.*] The title used by natives when addressing, or speaking of, a European gentleman. **b** Master; — specif. used among Hindus and Mohammedans in titles of men of rank; as, Raja *Sahib.*

saice (sīs). Var. of SYCE.

said (sĕd; 4), *past tense & past part.* of SAY. Hence: *adj.* Before-mentioned; — in legal style.

sail (sāl), *n.* [AS. *segel, segl.*] **1.** An extent of canvas or other fabric by means of which the wind is used to propel vessels through the water, — of two main types, *fore-and-aft* (as on a schooner: see 1st *Illust.,* below) and *square* (as on a full-rigged ship: see 2d *Illust.*). See also illustrations at BRIG, HERMAPHRODITE BRIG, KETCH, LATEEN SAIL, LUGSAIL, SHARPIE, and SLOOP. **2. a** Sails collectively; as, under full *sail.* **b** A sailing vessel; also, sailing vessels collectively. **3.** Anything suggestive of a sail; as: **a** *Poetic.* A wing. **b** The extended surface of the arm of a windmill. **4.** [From the verb.] A passage by a sailing vessel; a voyage. — *v. i.* **1. a** To be conveyed in a vessel on water, orig. only in a craft propelled by the wind. **b** To take trips in a sailboat for pleasure. **2.** To be impelled by the action of wind upon sails; hence, to move on water by any motive power. **3.** To glide through the air without apparent exertion, as a bird; hence, to move in a stately manner or arrogantly. **4.** To begin a water voyage. — *v. t.* **1.** To move or journey upon, as in a ship by means of sails or other motive power. **2.** To manage the motion of (a vessel).

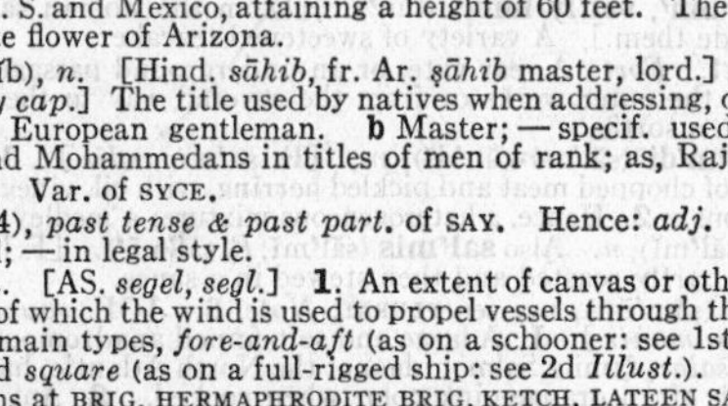

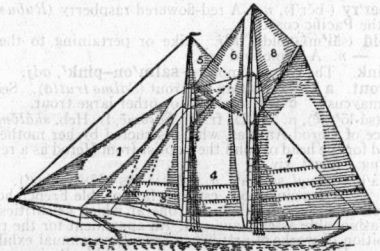

Schooner's Sails. (An inner and outer jib are sometimes fitted instead of one jib.) 1 Flying Jib; 2 Jib; 3 Forestaysail; 4 Foresail; 5 Fore Gaff-topsail; 6 Maintopmast Staysail; 7 Mainsail; 8 Main Gaff-topsail.

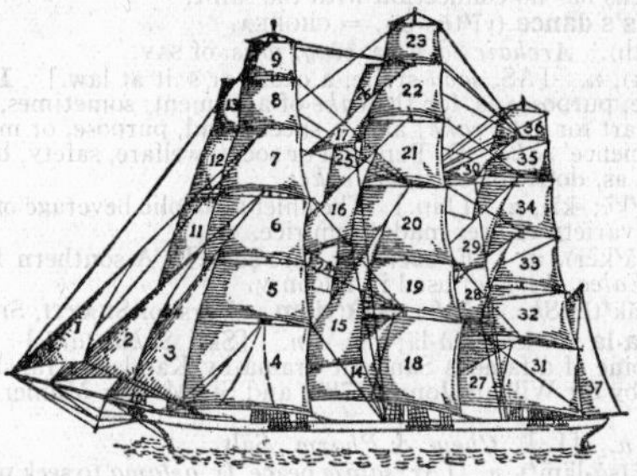

Full-rigged Ship under All Plain Sail. 1 Flying Jib; 2 Jib; 3 Fore-topmast Staysail; 4 Foresail; 5 Lower Fore-topsail; 6 Upper Fore-topsail; 7 Fore-topgallant Sail. 8 Foreroyal; 9 Fore-skysail; 10 Lower Studding Sail (never on the main); 11 Fore-topmast Studding Sail; 12 Fore-topgallant Studding Sail; 13 Foreroyal Studding Sail; 14 Main Staysail; 15 Main-topmast Staysail; 16 Main-topgallant Staysail; 17 Main-royal Staysail; 18 Mainsail; 19 Lower Main Topsail; 20 Upper Main Topsail; 21 Main-topgallant Sail; 22 Main Royal; 23 Main Skysail; 24 Main-topmast Studding Sail; 25 Main-topgallant Studding Sail; 26 Main-royal Studding Sail; 27 Mizzen Staysail; 28 Mizzen-topmast Staysail; 29 Mizzen-topgallant Staysail; 30 Mizzen-royal Staysail; 31 Mizzen Sail; 32 Lower Mizzen Topsail; 33 Upper Mizzen Topsail; 34 Mizzen-topgallant Sail; 35 Mizzen Royal; 36 Mizzen Skysail; 37 Spanker.

sail′boat′ (sāl′bōt′), *n.* A boat propelled by a sail or sails; — seldom applied to larger vessels.

sail′cloth′ (-klŏth′; 74), *n.* **a** A very heavy canvas or duck used for sails, tents, etc. **b** A piece of such material used as a sail, a covering, etc.

sail′er (sāl′ẽr), *n.* A vessel considered with regard to the way it navigates a body of water; as, a heavy *sailer.*

sail′fish′ (sāl′fĭsh′), *n.; see* FISH. **a** Any of a genus (*Istiophorus*) of large pelagic fishes related to the swordfish, but having teeth, scales, and a very large dorsal fin. **b** The basking shark (see SHARK).

sail′ing, *n. Naut.* The art of managing a vessel; navigation; also, the art or method of determining the course to be followed to reach a given point. In ***plane sailing*** the earth's curvature is disregarded, the course being plotted as if sailed on a plane surface; in ***spherical,*** *or* ***circular, sailing*** allowance is made for the curvature of the earth's surface, as in ***parallel sailing*** in which the course is along a parallel; in ***great-circle sailing*** the course is along a great circle (see CIRCLE, *n.,* 9) of the globe, the shortest distance between two points.

sail′or (sāl′ẽr), *n.* **1.** One who sails; a mariner; technically, a common seaman. **2.** One who travels by water, considered with reference to his susceptibility to seasickness; as, a good or bad *sailor.* **3.** A type of straw hat with a flat rounded top and brim. — **sail′or·ly,** *adj.*

sail′or's-choice′ (sāl′ẽrz-), *n. sing. & pl.* **a** A small porgy (*Lagodon rhomboides*). **b** The pigfish *Orthopristis chrysopterus.*

sail′plane′ (sāl′plān′), *n. Aeronautics.* A glider with a wing load small enough to enable it to rise in an upward air current. — **sail′plane′,** *v. i.*

sain (sān), *v. t.* [AS. *segnian,* fr. L. *signare* to mark.] *Archaic & Dial.* To cross (oneself).

sain′foin (sān′foin), *n.* [F., fr. *saint* sacred (fr. L. *sanctus*) + *foin* hay (fr. L. *fenum*), confused with *sain* wholesome (fr. L. *sanus*).] A Eurasian pink-flowered perennial forage herb (*Onobrychis viciaefolia*) of the pea family.

saint (sānt; *unaccented, as in Saint Agnes,* sănt; 4), *n.* [OF. *saint, seint* (F. *saint*), fr. L. *sanctus* holy, fr. past part. of *sancire* to render sacred.] **1.** A holy or godly person; esp., one regenerated and sanctified or undergoing sanctification. **2.** One of the beatified souls. **3.** *Eccl.* One recognized or acknowledged as having achieved sanctification; esp., such a one who is canonized by the church. Abbr. *St.;* pl. *SS.* **4.** [*cap.*] A member of one of certain religious bodies designated *Saints.* **5.** One extraordinarily charitable, patient, self-denying, etc.; as, enough to provoke a *saint.* — (sānt), *v. t.* To call saint; to canonize.

Saint Ag′nes's Eve. The night of January 20, when a maiden may have a revelation as to her future husband.

St. An′drew's cross. See CROSS, *Illust.* (9).

Saint An′tho·ny's cross. A tau cross. See CROSS, *Illust.* (10).

Saint Anthony's fire. Erysipelas or ergotism.

Saint Ber·nard′ (bẽr·närd′). A giant dog of a breed taking its name from the hospice of Saint Bernard in the Swiss Alps, where it has been bred for nearly 1000 years.

saint′ed (sān′tĕd; -tĭd), *adj.* **1.** Of, befitting, or resembling a saint or saints. **2.** Saintly; virtuous; pious. **3.** *Rare.* Entered into heaven; dead.

St. El′mo's fire *or* **light** (ĕl′mōz). [From the patron saint of sailors.] A flamelike appearance sometimes seen in stormy weather at prominent points on a ship; a corposant.

St. George's cross. *Her.* A Greek cross gules. See CROSS, *Illust.*

saint′hood, *n.* Saintly state; also, saints collectively.

St. James's Palace. The London residence of the British sovereigns from William III to the accession of Victoria in 1837. The ***Court of St. James's*** is still the official designation of the British court.

St.-John's′-wort′, *n.* Any of a genus (*Hypericum*) of herbs and shrubs having pentamerous and showy yellow flowers. The genus is typical of a family (Hypericaceae, the St.-John's-wort family).

St. Law′rence skiff. [From the *St. Lawrence* River.] See SKIFF.

saint′ly (sānt′lĭ), *adj.;* -LI·ER (-lĭ·ẽr); -LI·EST. Like or befitting a saint; holy; pious. — **saint′li·ness,** *n.*

Saint Nich′o·las (nĭk′ō·lȧs). A bishop of Myra, Asia Minor (d. ?345).

He is the patron saint of Russia, and of mariners, merchants, and children. As the bearer of presents to children on Christmas Eve, his name has been corrupted to *Santa Claus.*

Saint Pat′rick's Day (păt′rĭks). March 17, commemorating St. Patrick, patron saint of Ireland.

saint′ship (sānt′shĭp), *n.* Character or qualities of a saint.

Saint Val′en·tine's Day (văl′ĕn·tīnz). Feb. 14, observed in honor of Saint Valentine, a Christian martyr of the 3d century. The sending of love tokens has no connection with the saint.

St. Vi′tus's dance (vī′tŭs·ĭz). = CHOREA.

saith (sĕth). *Archaic 3d pers. sing. pres.* of SAY.

sake (sāk), *n.* [AS. *sacu* strife, a cause or suit at law.] **1.** End or objective; purpose; as, for the *sake* of argument; sometimes, ultimate end; as, art for art's *sake;* also, a special end, purpose, or motive; as, for conscience' *sake.* **2.** Personal or social welfare, safety, benefit, or the like; as, do it for both our *sakes.*

sa′ke (sä′kĕ; -kĭ), *n.* [Jap.] The chief alcoholic beverage of the Japanese, a variety of beer made from rice.

sa′ker (sā′kẽr), *n.* [F. *sacre,* fr. Ar. *ṣaqr.*] A southern European falcon (*Falco cherrug*) used in falconry.

Sak′ti (săk′tē; *Skr.* shŭk′-), **Sak′tism.** Vars. of SHAKTI, SHAKTISM.

Sa·kun′ta·la (sȧ·kōōn′tȧ·lä; shȧ-), *n.* [Skr. *Sakuntalā.*] The title and heroine of a famous Sanskrit drama by Kalidasa, translated into English by Sir William Jones (1789) and Sir Monier Monier-Williams (1853).

sal (săl), *n.* [L.] *Chem. & Pharm.* Salt.

sa·laam′ (sȧ·läm′), *n.* [Ar. *salām* peace, fr. *aslama* to seek peace, surrender.] A salutation or compliment of ceremony in the East by word or act; an obeisance, performed by bowing very low and placing the right palm on the forehead. — **sa·laam′**, *v. i. & t.*

sal′a·ble (sāl′ȧ·b'l), *adj.* Capable of being sold; marketable. — **sal′a·bil′i·ty** (-bĭl′ĭ·tĭ), *n.* — **sal′a·bly,** *adv.*

sa·la′cious (sȧ·lā′shŭs), *adj.* [L. *salax, -acis,* fond of leaping, lustful.] Having a propensity to venery; lustful; lecherous. — **sa·la′cious·ly,** *adv.* — **sa·la′cious·ness,** *n.*

sal′ad (săl′ăd), *n.* [OF. *salade,* fr. Pr. *salada,* fr. L. *sal* salt.] **1. a** A cold dish of green vegetables such as lettuce, cress, or endive, usually dressed with oil, vinegar, and seasonings. **b** Any cold dish of meat, shellfish, fruit or vegetables, served singly or in combinations, with mayonnaise or other dressing. **2.** Any green herb grown for salad; specif., *U. S.,* lettuce.

salad days. Days of youthful inexperience.

salad dressing. A savory sauce for a salad, as mayonnaise.

sal′a·man′der (săl′ȧ·măn′dẽr), *n.* [OF. *salamandre,* fr. L., fr. Gr. *salamandra.*] **1.** A mythical animal having the power to endure fire without harm. **2.** In the theory of Paracelsus, a being inhabiting the element fire. **3.** Any of numerous amphibians (order Caudata, in U. S. esp. genus *Ambystoma*), superficially resembling lizards, but scaleless and covered with a soft, moist skin, and breathing by gills in the larval stage. Cf. NEWT. **4.** Any of various articles used in connection with the fire, as a culinary utensil for browning pastry, a portable stove or incinerator, etc. — **sal′a·man′drine** (-măn′drĭn), *adj.*

sa·la′mi (sä·lä′mē), *n.* [It.] Highly seasoned sausage made of pork and beef, either dried and of good keeping qualities or fresh and requiring refrigeration.

sal ammoniac, *or* **sal′-am·mo′ni·ac,** *n.* Ammonium chloride, NH_4Cl, a white salt.

sal′a·ried (săl′ȧ·rĭd), *adj.* Receiving or yielding a salary.

sal′a·ry (săl′ȧ·rĭ), *n.; pl.* -RIES (-rĭz). [AF. *salarie,* OF. *salaire,* fr. L. *salarium* pension, stipend, orig., salt money, fr. *sal* salt.] Fixed compensation regularly paid, or stipulated to be paid, for services, as by the year, quarter, month, or week; stipend. — **Syn.** See WAGE.

‖**sal At′ti·cus** *or* **At′ti·cum** (săl ăt′ĭ·kŭs, -kŭm). [L.] Attic salt; wit.

sale (sāl), *n.* [Late AS. *sala,* fr. ON. *sala.*] **1.** *Law.* Act of selling; a contract whereby the ownership of property is transferred from one person to another for a sum of money or, loosely, for any consideration. **2.** Opportunity of selling or being sold; demand; market. **3.** Exhibition for selling; status of being purchasable; — as in ***on sale, for sale.*** **4.** Public disposal to the highest bidder; auction. **5.** A selling off of surplus, shopworn, or other marked-down goods, at bargain prices.

sale′a·ble, sale′a·bil′i·ty. Vars. of SALABLE, etc.

sal′ep (săl′ĕp), *n.* [F. & Sp., fr. Ar. *saḥlab,* corrupt. of *khuṣa al-tha'lab* the fox's testicles.] The dried tubers of any of various orchids, used for food like tapioca.

sal′e·ra′tus (săl′ĕ·rā′tŭs), *n.* [NL. *sal aeratus;* — because "fixed air" (carbon dioxide) is evolved on treatment with acids.] Literally, aerated salt, potassium or sodium bicarbonate, commonly the latter; baking soda.

sales′clerk′ (sālz′klûrk′), *n.* A salesman at a counter.

sales′man (-măn), *n.; pl.* -MEN (-mĕn). [*sale's* + *man.*] One whose occupation is to sell, as merchandise, land, securities, etc., either in a store or within a given territory. — **sales′wom′an** (-wōōm′ăn), *n.; pl.* -WOMEN (-wĭm′ĕn; -ĭn). — **sales′man·ship,** *n.*

sales tax. A tax assessed upon receipts from sales of goods.

sale′work′ (sāl′wûrk′), *n.* Work done for sale, esp. carelessly or slightingly.

Sa′li·an (sā′lĭ·ăn; 58), *adj.* Denoting a tribe of Franks established in the 4th century on the river Sala (now IJssel). — *n.* A Salian Frank.

Sal′ic (săl′ĭk; sā′lĭk), *adj.* [F. *salique,* fr. the Salian Franks, LL. *Salii.*] Of or pertaining to the Salian Franks, or the Salic law.

sal′i·ca′ceous (săl′ĭ·kā′shŭs), *adj.* [L. *salix, salicis,* willow.] Belonging to the willow family (Salicaceae). See WILLOW.

sal′i·cin (săl′ĭ·sĭn), *n.* Also **sal′i·cine** (-sĭn; -sēn). [F. *salicine,* fr. L. *salix, -icis,* willow.] *Chem.* A bitter white crystalline glucoside, $C_{13}H_{18}O_7$, found in the bark and leaves of several species of willow (*Salix*) and poplar, used in medicine as an antipyretic, tonic, etc.

Salic law. a A fifth-century compilation of the laws of Germanic tribes. **b** The provision of this law excluding women from inheriting land; hence, the rule excluding women from dynastic succession in France and Spain.

sal′i·cyl′ate (săl′ĭ·sĭl′āt; sȧ·lĭs′ĭ·lāt; săl′ĭ·sĭl′ăt), *n. Chem.* A salt or ester of salicylic acid.

sal′i·cyl′ic (săl′ĭ·sĭl′ĭk), *adj.* [*salicin* + *-yl* + *-ic.*] *Chem.* Pertaining to or designating a colorless crystalline acid, $C_6H_4(OH)CO_2H$, used as an antiseptic and (in its salts) in treating rheumatism.

sa′li·ence (sā′lĭ·ĕns; 58), **sa′li·en·cy** (-ĕn·sĭ), *n.* **1.** The quality of being salient; prominence; emphasis. **2.** A salient feature, detail, or the like.

sa′li·ent (-ĕnt), *adj.* [L. *saliens, -entis,* pres. part. of *salire* to leap.] **1.** Leaping; bounding; jumping. **2.** Projecting outwardly; as, a *salient* angle. See BASTION, *Illust.* **3.** Prominent; conspicuous; noticeable; as, one's *salient* traits. — **Syn.** See NOTICEABLE. — *n.* **1.** *Fort.* A salient angle or part. **2.** *Mil.* An outwardly projecting part of a trench system or line of defense. — **sa′li·ent·ly,** *adv.*

sa′li·en′ti·an (sā′lĭ·ĕn′shĭ·ăn; -shăn), *adj.* [See SALIENT.] *Zool.* Belonging to an order (Salientia) of Amphibia, whose members are tailless in the adult state and have long hind legs usually adapted for leaping, including the frogs, toads, and tree toads. — *n.* A salientian amphibian.

sa·lif′er·ous (sȧ·lĭf′ẽr·ŭs), *adj.* [L. *sal* salt + *-ferous.*] Producing, or impregnated with, salt.

sal′i·fy (săl′ĭ·fī), *v. t.;* -FIED (-fīd); -FY′ING. [F. *salifier.*] *Chem.* **a** To combine or impregnate with a salt. **b** To form a salt with; to convert into a salt.

sal·im′e·ter (săl·ĭm′ē·tẽr), *n.* = SALINOMETER.

sa·li′na (sȧ·lī′nȧ), *n.* [Sp., fr. L. *salinae,* pl., saltworks, fr. *sal* salt. See SALT.] **1.** A salt marsh, pond, or lake, enclosed from the sea. **2.** A place where salt is made; a saltern; saltworks.

sa′line (sā′līn), *adj.* [F. *salin.* See SALINA.] **1.** Consisting of or containing salt. **2.** Of or characteristic of salt or salts; salty. **3.** *Pharm. & Med.* Consisting of or pert. to the salts of the alkali metals or of magnesium; as, a *saline* cathartic.

— (sā′līn *or, esp. Brit.,* sȧ·līn′), *n.* **1.** A natural deposit of any soluble salt; a salina. **2.** A metallic salt; esp., a salt of potassium, sodium, or magnesium with a cathartic action. **3.** *Physiol.* A saline solution, esp. one isotonic with the body fluids.

sa·lin′i·ty (sȧ·lĭn′ĭ·tĭ), *n.* Saline quality or degree; saltness.

sal′i·nom′e·ter (săl′ĭ·nŏm′ē·tẽr), *n.* [L. *sal* salt + *-meter.*] An instrument, as a specially graduated hydrometer, for measuring the amount of salt in a solution.

Sa·lique′ (sȧ·lēk′; săl′ĭk). Var. of SALIC. *Shak.*

Salis′bur′y steak (sôlz′bĕr′ĭ; -bẽr·ĭ; -brĭ). = HAMBURG STEAK.

Sa′lish (sā′lĭsh), *n.* A Salishan Indian; esp., a Flathead.

Sa′lish·an (sā′lĭsh·ăn; săl′ĭsh-), *adj.* Pert. to an American Indian linguistic family, formerly of southern British Columbia and areas in Washington, Oregon, Idaho, and Montana.

sa·li′va (sȧ·lī′vȧ), *n.* [L.] The weakly alkaline fluid secreted by the glands discharging into the mouth; spittle.

sal′i·var′y (săl′ĭ·vẽr′ĭ *or, esp. Brit.,* -vẽr·ĭ), *adj. Physiol.* Of or pertaining to saliva or the glands (**salivary glands**) which secrete it.

sal′i·vate (săl′ĭ·vāt), *v. t.* [L. *salivatus,* past part. of *salivare* to salivate.] To produce an abnormal flow of saliva in, as by use of mercury. — *v. i.* To secrete saliva.

sal′i·va′tion (-vā′shŭn), *n.* Act or process of salivating; an excessive secretion of saliva; ptyalism.

‖**salle à man′ger′** (sȧl′ ȧ män′zhā′). [F.] Dining room.

sal′len·ders (săl′ĕn·dẽrz), *n. pl.* [F. *solandres, solandre.*] *Veter.* An eczematous eruption on the hind leg of a horse.

sal′let (săl′ĕt; -ĭt), *n.* [F. *salade,* fr. It. *celata,* fr. L. (cassis) *caelata,* fr. *caelare, caelatum,* to engrave in relief.] A light 15th-century helmet with a projection over the neck. See HELMET, *Illust.* (7, 8).

sal′low (săl′ō), *n.* [ME. *sallow, salwe,* fr. AS. *sealh.*] Any European broad-leaved willow, esp. a species (*Salix caprea*) called the ***great sallow.***

sal′low, *adj.* [AS. *salu.*] Of a pale reddish-yellow color, suggesting sickliness; — of the skin, complexion, etc. — *v. t.* To make sallow. — **sal′low·ish,** *adj.* — **sal′low·ness,** *n.*

sal′low·y (săl′ō·ĭ), *adj.* Abounding in sallows, or willows.

sal′ly (săl′ĭ), *n.; pl.* -LIES (-ĭz). [F. *saillie,* fr. *saillir* to gush out, project, in OF. also to leap, dance, fr. L. *salire* to leap, spring.] **1.** A rushing or bursting forth; specif., a sortie of the besieged upon the besiegers. **2.** An excursion, esp. one away from the usual track; a trip or jaunt. **3.** A flight of fancy, liveliness, wit, or the like; a clever or witty remark or passage. — *v. i.* To leap or burst forth, as troops to attack besiegers.

Sal′ly Lunn′, sal′ly lunn′ (lŭn′). [From the woman said to have first made them.] A variety of sweetened teacake.

sally port. *Fort.* A rear gate, or an underground passage, from the inner to the outer works or from the covered way to the glacis, for troops in a sortie.

sal′ma·gun′di (săl′mȧ·gŭn′dĭ), *n.* [F. *salmigondis.*] **1.** A mixed dish, as of chopped meat and pickled herring, with oil, vinegar, pepper, and onions. **2.** Hence, a heterogeneous mixture; a medley; potpourri.

sal′mi (săl′mĭ), *n.* Also **sal′mis** (săl′mĭ; *F.* sȧl′mē′). [F.] A ragout of game partly roasted and then stewed in a sauce.

salm′on (săm′ŭn), *n.;* see PLURAL, *Note,* 6. [OF. *saumon,* fr. L. *salmo, salmonis.*] **1.** A large and soft-finned anadromous game fish (*Salmo salar,* family Salmonidae) of the North Atlantic, having excellent flesh of an orange-pink color when cooked. **2.** Any of certain fishes closely allied to the above; esp., those of a genus (*Oncorhynchus*) of the northern North Pacific; also, the ceratodus. See QUINNAT SALMON, BLUEBACK SALMON. **3.** The color of the salmon's flesh, reddish red-yellow in hue, of medium saturation and high brilliance. See COLOR. — *adj.* Of the color salmon.

salm′on·ber′ry (-bĕr′ĭ), *n.* A red-flowered raspberry (*Rubus spectabilis*) of the Pacific coast.

sal′mo·noid (săl′mō·noid), *adj.* Like or pertaining to the typical salmons. — *n.* A salmonoid fish.

salmon pink. The color salmon. — **salm′on-pink′,** *adj.*

salmon trout. a The European sea trout (*Salmo trutta*). See TROUT. **b** The namaycush. **c** The steelhead or other large trout.

Sa·lo′me (sȧ·lō′mē), *n.* [LL., fr. Gr. *Salōmē,* fr. Heb. *shālōm* peace.] *Bib.* Niece of Herod Antipas, who, instructed by her mother, Herodias, asked for the head of John the Baptist from Herod as a reward for her dancing. *Matt.* xiv. 8.

‖**sa′lon′** (sȧ′lôN′; *Angl.* sȧ·lŏn′), *n.; pl.* SALONS (-lôN′; -lŏnz′). [F. See SALOON.] **1.** A drawing room, esp. in a fashionable French home. **2.** A reception in a French salon, esp. one at which celebrities gather; hence, a fashionable assemblage. **3.** An apartment for the reception and exhibition of works of art; hence [*cap.*], an annual exhibition of paintings, sculptures, etc., by living artists, held in Paris.

sa·loon′ (sȧ·lōōn′), *n.* [F. *salon,* fr. It. *salone,* augm. of *sala* hall, room, of G. origin.] **1.** A spacious apartment for reception of guests or for works of art; a large drawing room. **2.** A hall, usually decorated, serving as a drawing room, ballroom, or for some other (specified) purpose; as, the dining *saloon* of a ship. **3.** A large cabin on shipboard, esp. for first-class passengers. **4.** *Brit.* **a** Also **saloon carriage.** A first-class railway coach without compartments. **b** Also **saloon car.** A type of automobile resembling a sedan. **5.** *U.S.* A shop where intoxicating liquors are sold and drunk.

sa·loop′ (sȧ·lo͞op′), *n.* [From *salop, salup,* vars. of SALEP.] **1.** = SALEP. **2.** A hot drink made from an infusion of salep, or of sassafras.

sal′pa (săl′pȧ), *n.* [NL., fr. L. *salpa* kind of stockfish, fr. Gr. *salpē.*] *Zool.* Any of a genus (*Salpa*) of transparent barrel-shaped or fusiform free-swimming oceanic tunicates common in warm latitudes. — **sal′pi·form** (-pĭ·fôrm), *adj.*

sal′pi·glos′sis (săl′pĭ·glŏs′ĭs), *n.* [NL., fr. Gr. *salpinx* trumpet + *glōssa* tongue; — in allusion to the tonguelike stigma.] Any of a small genus (*Salpiglossis*) of Chilean plants of the nightshade family with large funnel-shaped varicolored flowers often beautifully marked.

sal·pin′go- (săl·pĭng′gō-), **salping-.** [Gr. *salpinx, salpingos,* trumpet.] A combining form denoting: **a** *A Eustachian tube.* **b** *A Fallopian tube,* as in **sal′pin·gi′tis.**

sal′pinx (săl′pĭngks), *n.; pl.* SALPINGES (săl·pĭn′jēz). [NL., fr. Gr. *salpinx, -ingos,* a trumpet.] *Anat.* **a** A Eustachian tube. **b** A Fallopian tube.

sal′si·fy (săl′sĭ·fĭ), *n.* [F. *salsifis,* fr. It. *sassefrica.*] A European biennial herb (*Tragopogon porrifolius*) of the chicory family, with a long spindle-shaped edible root.

sal soda, *or* **sal′so′da** (săl′sō′dȧ), *n.* See SODIUM CARBONATE.

salt (sôlt; 10), *n.* [AS. *sealt.*] **1.** Sodium chloride (NaCl) used to season food, as a preservative, etc.; — called also ***common salt.*** **2.** = SALTCELLAR. **3.** That which preserves or purifies; a corrective; as, the *salt* of skepticism; allowance; modification; as in ***with a grain of salt,*** with reserve or corrective allowance. **4.** That which gives piquant or pungent flavor; hence: **a** Savor; smack; seasoning. **b** Piquancy; wit; pungency; as, Attic *salt.* **5.** *Colloq.* A sailor. **6.** *Chem.* Any of a class of compounds formed when the acid hydrogen of an acid is partly or wholly replaced by a metal or a metallike radical. The names of salts of *-ous* acids end in *-ite;* salts of *ic* acids end in *-ate;* with a few exceptions. **7.** *Med. pl.* **a** Any mineral salt or saline mixture used as an aperient or cathartic. **b** Smelling salts. — *adj.* **1.** Abounding in or cured with salt; smelling or tasting of salt. **2.** Overflowed with salt water. — *v. t.* **1.** To add salt to; to preserve with salt or in brine. **2.** To season as if with salt. **3.** To supply with salt, as cattle. **4.** To enrich artificially, usually with fraudulent intent, as a mine, by secretly placing valuable mineral in some of the working places. — ***salt away, salt down.*** To prepare with, or pack in, salt for preserving, as meat; *Colloq.,* to save or invest safely, as money. — ***salt out.*** To precipitate (a dissolved substance) from a solution by the addition of some salt.

salt, *adj. Obs.* Salacious; lustful. *Shak.*

sal′tant (săl′tănt), *adj.* [L. *saltans,* pres. part of *saltare* to dance.] Leaping; jumping; dancing.

sal′ta·rel′lo (săl′tȧ·rĕl′ō), *n.* [It., fr. L. *saltare* to jump.] **a** An Italian dance, running with a hop step beginning each measure. **b** Music for this dance.

sal·ta′tion (săl·tā′shŭn), *n.* **1.** A jumping; a leap. **2.** A sudden or abrupt change; an advance by a leap. **3.** *Evolution.* Mutation.

sal′ta·to′ri·al (săl′tȧ·tō′rĭ·ăl), *adj.* Of the nature of, marked by, or adapted for leaping; saltatory.

sal′ta·to′ry (săl′tȧ·tō′rĭ *or, esp. Brit.,* -tẽr·ĭ), *adj.* **1.** Of or pertaining to dancing. **2.** Making or adapted to making leaps and bounds.

salt′cel′lar (sôlt′sĕl′ẽr), *n.* [ME. *salte seler* saltcellar, fr. OF. *saliere* saltcellar, ult. fr. L. *sal* salt.] A small vessel for holding salt at table.

salt′ed (sôl′tĕd; -tĭd), *adj.* **1.** Treated, seasoned, or filled with salt. **2.** Seasoned; hardened; experienced. **3.** *Colloq. Veter.* Immune against a contagious disease, because of having recovered from it.

salt′er (-tẽr), *n.* **1.** One who manufactures, or deals in, salt. **2.** One who salts (esp. meat, fish, or hides).

salt′ern (sôl′tẽrn), *n.* [AS. *sealtern, -ærn,* fr. *sealt* salt + *ærn, ern,* place, house.] A place where salt is made by boiling or by evaporation.

sal′tier, sal′tire (săl′tẽr), *n.* [OF. *sautoir,* fr. ML. *saltatorium* a sort of stirrup, fr. L. *saltatorius* saltatory.] *Her.* A charge consisting of a cross formed by a bend dexter and a bend sinister crossing in the center.

sal′ti·grade (săl′tĭ·grād), *adj.* [L. *saltus* a leap + *-grade.*] *Zool.* Having feet or legs formed for leaping.

salt′i·ness (sôl′tĭ·nĕs; -nĭs), *n.* Salty quality.

salt′ish, *adj.* Somewhat salt.

salt lick. = LICK, *n.,* 4.

salt marsh. Flat land subject to overflow by salt water.

salt′ness, *n.* Quality, state, or condition of being salt.

salt′pe′ter, salt′pe′tre (sôlt′pē′tẽr), *n.* [OF. *salpetre,* fr. ML. *sal petrae,* lit., rock salt; — so called because it exudes from rocks.] **1.** Potassium nitrate; niter. **2.** = SODIUM NITRATE; — called also ***Chile saltpeter.***

salt rheum. *Med.* Eczema.

salt′works′ (sôlt′wûrks′), *n. sing. & pl.* A saltern.

salt′wort′ (-wûrt′), *n.* **a** Any of a genus (*Salsola*) of plants of the goosefoot family, as a thistlelike pest (*S. pestifer*), or species (*S. kali* and *S. soda*) used in making soda ash. **b** The glasswort (*Salicornia*).

salt′y (sôl′tĭ), *adj.;* -I·ER (-tĭ·ẽr); -I·EST. **1.** Of, seasoned with, or containing salt. **2.** Having a quality suggestive of salt; agreeably provocative; as, *salty* humor, remarks.

sa·lu′bri·ous (sȧ·lū′brĭ·ŭs; 114), *adj.* [L. *salubris,* fr. *salus* health, safety.] Conducive to well-being, esp. physical well-being; beneficial; healthful. — **sa·lu′bri·ous·ly,** *adv.* — **sa·lu′bri·ous·ness,** *n.* — **sa·lu′bri·ty** (-brĭ·tĭ), *n.*

sa·lu′ki (sȧ·lo͞o′kĭ), *n.* [Ar. *salūqī* from or pert. to *Salūq,* ancient city in South Arabia.] A swift, keen-sighted, graceful hunting dog of a breed bred in Persia, Arabia, and Egypt for hundreds of years. It has a long narrow head, silky ears, and silky coat ranging in color from white or cream to black or black and tan.

‖**sa′lus po′pu·li su·pre′ma lex es′to** (sā′lŭs pŏp′ū·lī sū·prē′mȧ lĕks ĕs′tō). [L.] Let the welfare of the people be the supreme law; — motto of Missouri.

sal′u·tar′y (săl′ū·tĕr′ĭ *or, esp. Brit.,* -tẽr·ĭ), *adj.* [F. or L.; F. *salutaire,* fr. L. *salutaris,* fr. *salus, -utis,* health, safety.] **1.** Promoting health; curative; as, *salutary* exercise. **2.** Conducive to a beneficial outcome; bringing ultimate compensations; as, *salutary* suffering. — **sal′u·tar′i·ly,** *adv.* — **sal′u·tar′i·ness,** *n.*

sal′u·ta′tion (-tā′shŭn), *n.* Act of saluting, as an expression of courtesy; also, a phrase or gesture of greeting; specif., the introductory words of a letter, as "Dear Sir."

sa·lu′ta·to′ri·an (sȧ·lū′tȧ·tō′rĭ·ăn; 70), *n.* *U.S.* The graduating student (commonly second highest in rank) in a school or college who pronounces the salutatory oration. Cf. VALEDICTORIAN.

sa·lu′ta·to′ry (sȧ·lū′tȧ·tō′rĭ *or, esp. Brit.,* -tẽr·ĭ), *adj.* *U.S.* Expressing salutations; speaking a welcome; — esp. of the oration introducing commencement exercises in a school or college. — *n.; pl.* -RIES (-rĭz). An address of greeting; specif., *U.S.,* such an address delivered at a school or college commencement.

sa·lute′ (sȧ·lūt′; 114), *v. t.* [L. *salutare, -tatum,* fr. *salus, -utis,* health, safety.] **1.** To address with expressions of kind wishes and courtesy; to greet. **2.** Hence, to compliment by an act of ceremony, as by a bow. **3.** *Mil. & Nav.* **a** To honor, as some person, by a discharge of cannon, by dipping colors, etc. **b** To exhibit a mark of deference to a superior by assuming a prescribed position with the hand, rifle, sword, etc. — *v. i.* To make a salute. — *n.* **1.** A gesture expressing welcome, recognition, or courtesy. **2.** *Mil. & Nav.* The position of the hand, rifle, sword, etc., or the attitude of a person saluting a superior. — **sa·lut′er** (-lūt′ẽr), *n.*

sal′u·tif′er·ous (săl′ū·tĭf′ẽr·ŭs), *adj.* [L. *salutifer.*] *Now Rare.* Salutary.

sal′va·ble (săl′vȧ·b′l), *adj.* [LL. *salvare* to save, fr. *salvus* safe.] Capable of being saved or salvaged.

sal′vage (săl′vĭj), *n.* [F., fr. LL. *salvare.*] **1.** The compensation paid for saving a ship or its cargo from the perils of the sea, or for the lives, property, etc., rescued in a wreck; also, the act of saving a ship or its cargo; also, that which is saved from destruction in a wreck, fire, etc. **2.** *Fire Insurance.* Insured goods rescued from fire, or their value as allowed, or their proceeds on being sold. — *v. t.;* -VAGED (-vĭjd); -VAG·ING (-vĭj·ĭng). To rescue or save from wreckage, ruin, or the like. — **sal′vag·er** (-vĭj·ẽr), *n.*

Sal′var·san (săl′vẽr·săn), *n.* A trade-mark applied to arsphenamine.

sal·va′tion (săl·vā′shŭn), *n.* [OF., fr. LL. *salvatio,* fr. *salvare* to save.] **1.** The saving of man from the spiritual consequences of sin; esp., deliverance from sin and eternal damnation through the atonement of Christ; redemption. **2.** Preservation from destruction, failure, or other evil. **3.** The source, cause, or means, of preservation from danger or difficulty. **4.** *Christian Science.* Life, Truth, and Love understood and demonstrated as supreme over all; sin, sickness, and death destroyed. *Mary Baker Eddy.*

Salvation Army. A religious and charitable organization on military lines, founded in 1865 by William Booth for evangelization and social betterment of the poor and degraded. — **Sal·va′tion·ism** (săl·vā′shŭn·ĭz′m), *n.* — **Sal·va′tion·ist** (-ĭst), *n. & adj.*

salve (säv; săv), *n.* [AS. *sealf.*] **1.** A healing ointment. **2.** A remedial or soothing influence or agency. **3.** Something laid on like a salve, as flattery. — *v. t.* **1.** *Archaic.* To apply salve to. **2.** To quiet, allay, or assuage, as something irritated; as, to *salve* one's wounded vanity.

salve (sălv), *v. t.* [From SALVAGE.] To salvage.

sal′ve (săl′vē), *interj.* [L. See SALVO a volley.] Hail!

sal′ver (săl′vẽr), *n.* [F. *salve,* fr. Sp. *salva* foretasting, fr. *salvar* to save, taste, fr. LL. *salvare* to save.] A tray, as for visiting cards.

sal′ver·form (săl′vẽr·fôrm), **sal′ver–shaped′** (-shāpt′), *adj.* *Bot.* Tubular, with a spreading limb; — said of a gamopetalous corolla.

sal′vi·a (săl′vĭ·ȧ), *n.* [L. See SAGE a plant.] *Bot.* Any of a genus (*Salvia*) of herbs or shrubs of the mint family, the sages, having a 2-lipped open calyx and two anthers; commonly, the scarlet sage (see SAGE). Cf. CLARY.

sal′vo (săl′vō), *n.; pl.* -VOS (-vōz). [ML. *salvo jure,* lit., right being reserved.] *Rare.* **1.** A proviso; a quibbling excuse. **2.** A means of saving one's name, feelings, etc.

sal′vo (săl′vō), *n.; pl.* -VOS, -VOES (-vōz). [It. *salva* volley, salute, fr. L. *salve* hail!, voc. of *salvus* well, taken as imper. of *salvere* to be well.] **1.** *Mil.* A series of shots by a battery, each gun firing one round in turn after a prescribed interval. **2.** A simultaneous discharge of shots or bombs: **a** *Nav.* A discharge of two or more guns of the same battery at the same time at the same target. **b** A release of a rack of bombs all at the same time from an aircraft, or the bombs so released. **3.** A burst of shouts or cheers from a crowd; as, a *salvo* of applause.

‖**sal vo·la′ti·le** (săl vō·lăt′ĭ·lē). [NL.] A variable mixture of ammonium bicarbonate, NH_4HCO_3, and ammonium carbonate, $NH_2CO_2NH_4$, the base of common smelling salts.

sal′vor (săl′vẽr), *n.* A salvager.

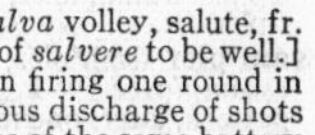

Samaras. 1 Ash; 2 Elm; 3 Maple.

sam′a·ra (săm′ȧ·rȧ; sȧ·mā′rȧ), *n.* [L. *samara, samera,* an elm seed.] *Bot.* A dry, indehiscent, winged fruit, usually one-seeded as in the ash or elm, but sometimes two-seeded (***double samara***) as in the maple; — called also *key* or *key fruit.*

Sa·mar′i·tan (sȧ·măr′ĭ·tăn), *n.* **1.** A native or inhabitant of Samaria, an ancient city and region of Palestine. **2.** One ready and generous in helping fellow beings in distress. *Luke* x. 30–37. — **Sa·mar′i·tan,** *adj.*

sa·ma′ri·um (sȧ·mā′rĭ·ŭm; 6), *n.* [NL., fr. E. *samarskite.*] *Chem.* A rare, metallic element discovered spectroscopically in samarskite in 1879. Symbol *Sm* or *Sa;* at. no., 62; at. wt., 150.43.

sa·mar′skite (sȧ·mär′skīt), *n.* [After Col. *Samarski,* Russ. mine official.] *Mineral.* A velvet-black orthorhombic mineral containing iron, calcium, uranium, cerium, etc. It is a source of the thorium oxide in incandescent gas mantles.

sam′ba (săm′bȧ), *n.* [Pg., of African origin.] A Brazilian dance of African origin characterized by a dip and upspring, with a bending of the knee at each beat of the music. — **sam′ba,** *v. i.*

sam′bar (săm′bẽr; säm′-), *n.* See PLURAL, *Note,* 3. Also **sam′bur.** [Hind. *sābar, sābar,* fr. Skr. *śambara.*] Any of several large Asiatic deer having a maned neck; esp., the Indian species (*Cervus,* or *Rusa, aristotelis*).

sam′bo (săm′bō), *n.* [Sp. *zambo* Negro, mulatto, monkey.] An Indian or mulatto and Negro half-breed.

Sam Browne belt (broun). *Mil.* A leather waist belt supported by a light strap passing over the right shoulder.

sam′bur. Var. of SAMBAR.

same (sām), *adj.* [ON. *same, samr* (Dan. & Sw. *samme*).] With the definite article or a demonstrative pronoun: **1.** Being one without addition, change, or discontinuance; identical; as, to hold the *same* views with another. **2.** Of two or more: Agreeing or corresponding exactly or so closely as to be undistinguishable from each other; as, on the *same* day every year; of one uniform type or style. **3.** Unchanged in nature or behavior; equally desirable. — *adv.* In the same way; with equal readiness; equally. — *pron.* The same person, thing, act, etc.

Syn. **Same, selfsame, very, identical, equivalent, equal** mean not different or not differing from one another. **Same** may imply, as **selfsame** does invariably, that the things under consideration are one thing and not two or more things, or it may imply numerical difference between them with no difference in kind, appearance, or the like; **very,** like *selfsame,* implies no difference in number but suggests agreement between a desire or an intent and its fulfillment; **identical** may imply selfsameness or sameness, but also suggests absolute likeness; **equivalent** implies an amounting to the same thing, esp. when set against each other; **equal** implies no difference in amount, number, value, etc.

same′ness, *n.* **1.** State of being the same; identity. **2.** Hence, want of variety; tedious monotony.

sam′iel (săm′yĕl), *n.* [Turk. *sam* poison + *yel* wind.] The simoom.

sam′i·sen (săm′ĭ·sĕn), *n.* [Jap., fr. Chin. (Pek.) *san*[1] *hsien*[4], lit., three strings.] *Music.* A Japanese banjolike instrument having only three strings.

sam′ite (săm′īt; sā′mīt), *n.* [OF. *samit,* through ML. fr. MGr. *hexamiton,* fr. *hexamitos* woven with six threads, fr. Gr. *hex* six + *mitos* a thread.] *Hist.* A heavy silk fabric, interwoven with gold or silver.

sam′let (săm′lĕt; -lĭt), *n.* [Contr. fr. *salmon* + *-let.*] A young or small salmon; a parr.

Sam′nite (săm′nīt), *n.* One of an ancient people, an offshoot of the Sabines, in Italy. — **Sam′nite,** *adj.*

Sa·mo′an (sȧ·mō′ăn), *adj.* Of or pertaining to Samoa or its inhabitants. — *n.* One of the natives of Samoa, among the purest in type of the Polynesians; also, their language.

Sam′o·thra′cian (săm′ō·thrā′shăn), *adj.* [Gr. *Samothrakios.*] Of Samothrace, or designating mysteries for which it was famous. — *n.* An inhabitant of Samothrace.

sam′o·var (săm′ō·vär; săm′ō·vär′), *n.* [Russ., lit., self-boiler.] A Russian urn for making tea.

Sam′o·yed′, Sam′o·yede′ (săm′ō·yĕd′), *n.* [Russ. *Samoyed.*] **1.** One of a Siberian Mongolian people, hunters and fishers, related to the Finns. **2.** An arctic dog of a breed originating in western Siberia, having powerful loins and head and a white or cream coat.

Sam′o·yed′, Sam′o·yede′, *adj.* Also **Sam′o·yed′ic** (-yĕd′ĭk). Of or pertaining to the Samoyeds or their language. — *n.* The language of the Samoyeds.

samp (sămp), *n.* [Of Algonquian origin.] *U.S.* Coarse hominy.

sam′pan (săm′păn), *n.* [(After Chin. *san*[1]-*pan*[3], fr. Pg.) fr. earlier *champan, champana,* fr. Pg. *champão, champana.*] A skiff, used in the river and harbor traffic of China and Japan, propelled usually with a scull.

Sampan.

sam′phire (săm′fīr), *n.* [F. *l'herbe de Saint Pierre* herb of Saint Peter.] **a** A fleshy European plant (*Crithmum maritimum*) of the carrot family, sometimes pickled. **b** A common glasswort (*Salicornia europaea*).

sam′ple (sȧm′p'l; 9), *n.* [OF. *essample, example,* fr. L. *exemplum.* See EXAMPLE.] A part of anything presented for inspection, or shown as evidence of the quality of the whole; a specimen. — **Syn.** See INSTANCE. — *v. t.;* -PLED (-p'ld); -PLING (-plĭng). To test a sample of; to judge as to quality from samples. — **sam′pler** (-plēr), *n.*

sam′pler (sȧm′plēr; 9), *n.* [ME. *samplere* original, model, fr. OF. *essamplaire.*] **1.** A piece of needlework, made orig. to preserve a pattern, later, one made as a sample of skill, showing embroidered letters or verses. **2.** Any of various devices for extracting samples, as from a bag of grain.

sam′pling (-plĭng), *n.* A small part of anything selected as a sample for inspection or analysis; also, the act, process, or technique of selecting a suitable sample.

sam′shu (săm′shōō), *n.* [Chinese.] An alcoholic liquor distilled in China from rice or large millet; also, in general, a spirituous drink.

Sam′son (săm′s'n), *n.* [LL., fr. Gr. *Sampsōn,* fr. Heb. *shimshōn,* lit., sun's man.] An Israelite judge (*Judges* xiii. ff.), of great physical strength.

Sam′u·el (săm′ū·ĕl), *n.* [LL., fr. Gr. *Samouēl,* fr. Heb. *Shĕmūēl,* lit., his name is *El* (God).] **a** A famous Hebrew judge and prophet. **b** Either of the books of Samuel in the Old Testament. See BIBLE.

sam′u·rai (săm′ōō·rī), *n. pl. & sing.* [Jap.] In the former feudal system of Japan, the class, or a member of the class, of military retainers of the daimios, constituting the gentry or lesser nobility.

san′a·tive (săn′ȧ·tĭv), *adj.* Curative; healing.

san′a·to′ri·um (-tō′rĭ·ŭm; 70), *n.; pl.* L. -RIA (-ȧ), E. -RIUMS (-ŭmz). [NL. See SANATORY.] **1.** A health resort; specif., a high-altitude summer station in the tropics. **2.** An establishment for the treatment of the sick, esp. one using natural therapeutic agents; a sanitarium; as, a tuberculosis *sanatorium.*

san′a·to′ry (săn′ȧ·tō′rĭ *or, esp. Brit.,* -tēr·ĭ), *adj.* [LL. *sanatorius,* fr. L. *sanare* to heal.] Conducive to health; curative; also, of or pertaining to healing.

san′be·ni′to (săn′bĕ·nē′tō), *n.* [Sp. *sambenito,* fr. *San Benito* Saint Benedict.] **1.** Originally, a sackcloth coat worn by penitents on being reconciled to the church. **2.** A yellow garment resembling a scapular, worn by penitents at the auto-da-fé; also, a similar garment in black, painted with flames, figures of devils, etc., worn by those brought forth for punishment at the auto-da-fé.

San′cho Pan′za (săn′chō păn′zȧ; *Sp.* sän′chō pän′thä). The squire of Don Quixote. He is a short, potbellied peasant, ignorant and credulous, but shrewd and with a store of proverbial wisdom.

sanc′ti·fied (săngk′tĭ·fīd), *adj.* Free of sin; set apart to sacred duty or use; consecrated; also, sanctimonious.

sanc′ti·fy (-fī), *v. t.* [OF. and L.; OF. *saintifier, sanctifier,* fr. LL. *sanctificare,* fr. *sanctus* holy + *-ficare* (in comp.) to make.] **1.** To make sacred or holy; specif., to set apart to a sacred office or to religious use or observance; to hallow. **2.** To make free from sin; to purify, as the affections of men. **3.** To impart or impute sacredness or inviolability to; to give sanction to; as, the intention *sanctifies* the deed. **4.** To render productive of holiness or piety. — **sanc′ti·fi·ca′tion** (-fĭ-kā′shŭn), *n.* — **sanc′ti·fi′er** (-fī′ēr), *n.*

sanc′ti·mo′ni·ous (săngk′tĭ·mō′nĭ·ŭs; 58), *adj.* **1.** *Obs.* Holy; saintly. **2.** Making a show of sanctity; hypocritically pious. — **Syn.** See DEVOUT. — **sanc′ti·mo′ni·ous·ly,** *adv.* — **sanc′ti·mo′ni·ous·ness,** *n.*

sanc′ti·mo′ny (săngk′tĭ·mō′nĭ *or, esp. Brit.,* -mŭn·ĭ), *n.* [OF. *sanctimonie,* fr. L. *sanctimonia,* fr. *sanctus* holy.] **1.** *Obs.* Holiness. **2.** Outward or artificial saintliness; hypocritical devoutness.

sanc′tion (săngk′shŭn), *n.* [F. or L.; F., fr. L. *sanctio, -onis,* fr. *sancire* to render sacred or inviolable.] **1.** Formerly, a decree (cf. *pragmatic sanction,* under PRAGMATIC, *adj.*); now, solemn or ceremonious ratification; confirmation; approbation. **2.** That which induces observance of law or custom; specif.: **a** *Ethics.* Any consideration, principle, or influence, which impels to moral action or determines the moral judgment as valid. **b** *Law.* The detriment, loss of reward, or other coercive intervention, annexed to a violation of a law as a means of enforcing the law. **3.** A coercive measure adopted, usually by several nations in concert, for forcing a nation violating international law to desist or yield to adjudication, as by withholding loans or limiting trade relations or by military force or blockade. — *v. t.* To give sanction to; to ratify. — **Syn.** See APPROVE. — **sanc′tion·ist** (-ĭst), *n. & adj.*

sanc′ti·ty (săngk′tĭ·tĭ), *n.; pl.* -TIES (-tĭz). [From L. *sanctitas,* and fr. OF. *saincteté, saintité* (fr. L.) See SAINT.] **1.** Holiness of life and character; saintliness. **2.** Sacredness; inviolability; religious binding force; as, the *sanctity* of an oath; *pl.,* sacred obligations, rites, etc.

sanc′tu·ar′y (săngk′tū̇·ĕr′ĭ *or, esp. Brit.,* -ēr·ĭ), *n.; pl.* -IES (-ĭz). [From L. *sanctuarium,* and fr. OF. *saintuaire, sainctuarie* (fr. L.). See SAINT.] **1.** A consecrated place; specif.: **a** The temple at Jerusalem, or the most retired part of it, the ***holy of holies,*** housing the ark of the covenant. **b** The most sacred part of any religious building, esp. the vicinity of the altar. **c** A church or temple. **d** *Gr. & Rom. Antiq.* A place consecrated to some god or gods, as a grove, or an enclosure containing a temple. **2.** **a** A sacred and inviolable asylum; a place of refuge. **b** Immunity from law by entering such a place.

sanc′tum (săngk′tŭm), *n.; pl.* SANCTUMS (-tŭmz), sometimes SANCTA (-tȧ). [L., neut. of *sanctus* holy.] A sacred place; hence, a place of retreat, where one is free from intrusion.

sanc′tum sanc·to′rum (săngk·tō′rŭm; 70). [L.] **a** The holy of holies; the most holy place. **b** One's strictly private retreat; — often jocose.

Sanc′tus (săngk′tŭs), *n.* [L., holy. See SAINT.] The last part of the Preface of the Mass, beginning Sanctus, Sanctus, Sanctus; also, a corresponding English prayer.

Sanctus bell. A bell rung by the server at the Sanctus.

sand (sănd), *n.* [AS.] **1.** A loose granular material resulting from the disintegration of rocks. **2.** *Usually pl.* A tract, region, or deposit of sand; beach. **3.** The sand in the hourglass or a grain of it; hence, the moments of one's life. **4.** *Slang.* Courage; grit. **5.** A color, reddish-yellow in hue, of low saturation and medium brilliance. See COLOR. — **Syn.** See FORTITUDE. — *v. t.* **1.** To sprinkle, powder, or mix with sand. **2.** To fill, as harbors, with sand, as by action of currents. **3.** To smooth by rubbing with sand or sandpaper.

san′dal (săn′dăl; -d'l), *n.* Sandalwood.

san′dal, *n.* [L. *sandalium,* fr. Gr. *sandalion,* dim. of *sandalon.*] **1.** A form of shoe consisting of a sole strapped to the foot; a protection for the foot, covering its lower surface only. Sandals are much worn among Orientals, and are a part of the official dress of Roman Catholic bishops and abbots. **2.** A strap to hold on a slipper or low shoe; sometimes, a fancy slipper, with openwork in vamp and quarter. **3.** A rubber overshoe cut low. — **san′daled, san′dalled** (-dăld; -d'ld), *adj.*

san′dal·wood′ (-wŏŏd′), *n.* [OF. *sandal, santal,* through ML. fr. LGr. *santalon, sandanon,* ult. fr. Skr.] **1.** The compact, close-grained, fragrant, yellowish heartwood of an Indo-Malayan parasitic tree (*Santalum album*), type of a family (Santalaceae, the sandalwood family) of herbs, shrubs, or rarely trees, having clustered apetalous flowers and a nut or drupe for a fruit. The wood is much used in ornamental carving and cabinetwork. Also, the tree that yields this wood. **2.** Any of various other trees or their fragrant wood, as the ***red sandalwood,*** an East Indian tree (*Lingoum santalinum*) of the pea family, or its heavy red dyewood.

san′da·rac (săn′dȧ·răk), *n.* [L. *sandaraca,* fr. Gr. *sandarakē.*] **1.** Realgar. **2.** A brittle, faintly aromatic translucent resin obtained from the sandarac tree, used in making varnish and as incense.

sandarac tree. A large tree (*Tetraclinis articulata*) of the pine family, of Morocco, with fragrant wood used in building and as the source of the resin sandarac.

sand′bag′ (sănd′băg′), *n.* A bag filled with sand, used as in fortifications, as ballast, as a weapon. — *v. t.;* see BAG. **1.** To bank or stop up with sandbags. **2.** To hit or stun with a sandbag. — **sand′bag′ger,** *n.*

sand bar. A ridge of sand built up by currents, as in a river.

sand′blast′ (sănd′blȧst′; 9), *n.* A stream of sand projected by air or steam for engraving or cutting glass, stone, etc., for cleaning files, removing scale from metals, etc.; also, the apparatus used to apply it. — **sand′blast′,** *v. t.*

sand′-blind′, *adj.* [ME., fr. (assumed) *samblind,* fr. AS. *sam-* half (akin to L. *semi-*) + *blind.*] Purblind; weak-sighted.

sand′box′ tree, *or* **sand′box′** (sănd′bŏks′), *n.* A tropical American tree (*Hura crepitans*) with a woody capsule which, when dry, bursts and scatters the seeds.

sand′bur′, sand′burr′ (-bûr′), *n.* Any of several weeds of waste places, having burlike fruit; as: **a** A North American nightshade (*Solanum rostratum*) with prickly foliage and racemose yellow flowers. **b** An annual bristly herb (*Franseria acanthicarpa*), allied to the cocklebur.

sand′-cast′, *v. t.* *Metal.* To make (a casting) by pouring metal in sand. — **sand casting.**

sand crack. *Veter.* A fissure or lesion in the horn of the hoof wall, often causing lameness. When in the front wall, it is known as *toe crack,* and is most common in the hind feet; when in the lateral parts of the wall, as *quarter crack,* and is nearly always in the fore feet.

sand′cul′ture (sănd′kŭl′tū̇r), *n.* A form of hydroponics in which the roots of plants are established in sand.

sand dollar. Any of several flat circular sea urchins (esp. *Echinarachnius parma*) which live on sandy bottoms.

Sand Dollar (*E. parma*). (½)

sand eel. The sand launce.
sand′er (săn′dẽr), *n.* One who or that which sands; as: **a** A device for sanding surfaces. **b** A sandpapering machine.
sand′er·ling (-lĭng), *n.* [See 1st -LING.] A small sandpiper (*Crocethia alba*) with largely gray-and-white plumage.
sand flea. **a** Any flea found in sandy places. **b** The chigoe. **c** A beach flea.
sand fly. Any of certain small dipterous biting flies, esp. of *Phlebotomus* and related genera.
sand′glass′ (sănd′glȧs′; 9), *n.* An instrument for measuring time by the running of sand. See HOURGLASS.
sand grouse. Any of numerous birds (family Pteroclidae) inhabiting arid parts of southern Europe, Asia, and Africa, closely allied to the pigeons in structure.
san′dhi (săn′dĭ), *n.* [Skr. *saṁdhi* a placing together.] *Phonet.* Assimilation resulting when words are pronounced without pause between them, as when *horseshoe* is pronounced *hôrsh′shōō′*, or *don't you* is pronounced *dōn′chōō.*
sand hog. *Slang.* A workman who works under compressed air as in driving tunnels by the pneumatic-caisson method.
sand′i·ness, *n.* Quality or state of being sandy.
sand launce. Any of several small, elongate, marine teleost fishes (*Ammodytes* or allied genera) which remain buried in sandy beaches at ebb tide.
sand lily. A low acaulescent herb (*Leucocrinum montanum*) of the lily family, common in the western United States.
sand′-lot′, *adj.* Of or pertaining to a lot or piece of sandy ground, esp. as the scene of unorganized sports of boys from city streets; as, *sand-lot* baseball. — **sand lotter.**
sand′man′ (sănd′măn′), *n.* The genie of folklore who makes children sleepy; — in allusion to the rubbing of their eyes as if there were sand in them.
sand martin. See SWALLOW, *n.*, 1.
sand′pa′per (sănd′pā′pẽr), *n.* Paper covered on one side with sand glued fast, used for smoothing and polishing. — *v. t.* To rub with sandpaper.
sand′pip′er (-pīp′ẽr), *n.; see* PLURAL, *Note*, 3. Any of numerous small shore birds distinguished from the plovers chiefly by the longer and soft-tipped bill. The common sandpiper of Europe (*Actitis hypoleuca*) frequents inland streams and ponds, as does the allied ***spotted sandpiper*** (*A. macularia*) common throughout North America. Cf. DUNLIN, 1st KNOT, SANDERLING.
sand′stone′ (-stōn′), *n.* A sedimentary rock consisting of sand, usually quartz, united by some cement, as silica, iron oxide, etc.
sand′storm′ (-stôrm′), *n.* A storm of wind that drives clouds of sand along a desert.
sand table. A table with boxlike top, holding sand for children to mold, or bearing a relief model of a section of terrain built to scale of hardened sand, for study or demonstration of military tactics.
sand verbena. Any of several western American herbs (genus *Abronia*) of the four-o'clock family, having flowers like the verbena, esp. two species (*A. latifolia* and *A. umbellata*) of the Pacific coast.
sand′wich (sănd′wĭch; *Brit. usually* săn′wĭj *or* -wĭch), *n.* [After John Montagu, 4th Earl of *Sandwich* (1718–92).] **1.** Two or more slices of bread with other food, as meat, cheese, or savory mixture, spread between them. **2.** Something resembling a sandwich in arrangement. — *v. t.* To make into a sandwich; also, to insert between two other persons or things of different character.
sandwich man. A man with two advertising boards suspended one before and one behind him.
sand′wort′ (sănd′wûrt′), *n.* Any of a genus (*Arenaria*) of low tufted herbs of the pink family, found in dry, sandy regions.
sand′y (săn′dĭ), *adj.;* SAND′I·ER (-dĭ·ẽr); SAND′I·EST. **1.** Consisting of or containing sand; full of sand; covered or sprinkled with sand. **2.** Resembling sand; specif.: **a** Unstable. **b** Of the color sand.
sane (sān), *adj.* [L. *sanus* sane, healthy.] **1.** Mentally sound; possessing a rational mind. **2.** Of the mind, sound; not deranged; acting rationally. **3.** Proceeding from a sound mind; as, a *sane* proposal. — **Syn.** See WISE. — **sane′ly**, *adv.* — **sane′ness**, *n.*
San′for·ized (săn′fẽr·īzd), *n.* A trade-mark applied to cotton or linen woven fabrics and products made therefrom which, before tailoring or manufacture, have been mechanically treated under the control and periodic testing of the trade-mark proprietor so as to substantially eliminate subsequent shrinkage.
sang (săng), *past of* SING.
san′ga·ree′ (săng′gȧ·rē′), *n.* [Sp. *sangría*, lit., bleeding, fr. *sangre* blood, fr. L. *sanguis.*] A tropical drink, of wine, water, and sometimes brandy, sweetened and spiced.
‖**sang-froid** (säɴ′frwä′), *n.* [F., cold blood.] Freedom from agitation; coolness in trying circumstances. — **Syn.** See EQUANIMITY.
San′graal′ (săng′grāl′), **San′gre·al** (săng′grē·ăl), *n.* [See SAINT; GRAIL.] The Holy Grail. See GRAIL.
sangui-. [L. *sanguis.*] A combining form meaning *blood*, as in: **san·guic′o·lous** (săng·gwĭk′ō·lŭs), **san·guif′er·ous**, **san·guiv′o·rous.**
san′gui·na′ri·a (săng′gwĭ·nā′rĭ·ȧ; 6), *n.* [NL., fr. L. (herba) *sanguinaria* an herb that stanches blood.] **a** The bloodroot. **b** *Pharm.* Its rhizome and roots used as an expectorant and emetic.
san′gui·nar′y (săng′gwĭ·nĕr′ĭ *or, esp. Brit.*, -nẽr·ĭ), *adj.* [L. *sanguinarius*, fr. *sanguis* blood.] **1.** Attended with or concerning much bloodshed; bloody; specif., harsh in inflicting the death penalty. **2.** Bloodthirsty; eager to shed blood. **3.** Consisting of or indicating blood. — **san′gui·nar′i·ly**, *adv.* — **san′gui·nar′i·ness**, *n.*
san′guine (săng′gwĭn) *adj.* [OF. *sanguin*, fr. L. *sanguineus*, fr. *sanguis* blood.] **1.** Red, like blood. **2.** In early physiology, having blood as the dominant humor; now, characterized by abundant and active circulation of blood; as, a *sanguine* bodily temperament, one marked by a ruddy complexion, and by cheerful and hopeful spirits. **3.** Hence, warm; ardent; also, disposed to be hopeful; anticipating the best. **4.** Sanguinary; bloodthirsty. — **san′guine·ly**, *adv.* — **san′guine·ness**, *n.*
san·guin′e·ous (săng·gwĭn′ē·ŭs), *adj.* **1.** Of the color of blood; crimson. **2.** Of, pertaining to, or containing blood. **3.** Abounding with blood; sanguine; hence, having a sanguine temperament; hopeful.
san·guin′o·lent (-ō·lĕnt), *adj.* [F., fr. L. *sanguinolentus*, fr. *sanguis* blood.] Of, containing, or tinged with blood.
San′he·drin (săn′[h]ē·drĭn; săn·hē′drĭn; săn·hĕd′rĭn), *n.* Also **San′he·drim** (-drĭm). [LHeb. *sanhedrīn*, fr. Gr. *synedrion*, fr. *syn* with + *hedra* seat.] *Jewish Antiq.* Assembly; esp. ***Great Sanhedrin***, the supreme council and tribunal of the Jews, consisting of 71 members having religious, civil, and criminal jurisdiction.
san′i·cle (săn′ĭ·k'l), *n.* [OF., fr. ML. *sanicula*, fr. L. *sanus* healthy.] Any of a genus (*Sanicula*) of umbelliferous American herbs of the carrot family, formerly reputed to have healing powers.
sa′ni·es (sā′nĭ·ēz), *n.* [L.] *Med.* A thin, blood-tinged fluid discharged from ulcers or infected wounds.
sa′ni·ous (-ŭs), *adj.* [L. *saniosus*, fr. *sanies.*] **1.** *Med.* Pert. to or like sanies; thin and serous with a bloody tinge. **2.** *Med.* Discharging sanies.
san′i·tar′i·an (săn′ĭ·târ′ĭ·ăn; 6), *adj.* Of or pertaining to health or the laws of health; sanitary. — *n.* One especially interested or versed in sanitary measures.
san′i·tar′i·ly (săn′ĭ·tĕr′ĭ·lĭ; -tẽr·ĭ·lĭ), *adv.* of SANITARY.
san′i·tar′i·um (săn′ĭ·târ′ĭ·ŭm), *n.; pl.* -IUMS (-ŭmz), -IA (-ȧ). [NL.] A health retreat; an institution for the recuperation and treatment of victims of physical or mental disorders; a sanatorium.
san′i·tar′y (săn′ĭ·tĕr′ĭ *or, esp. Brit.*, -tẽr·ĭ), *adj.* [F. *sanitaire*, fr. L. *sanitas* health.] Of or pert. to health, or to the preservation or restoration of health; hygienic; as, *sanitary* regulations; free from agencies injurious to health; as, *sanitary* markets. — *n.; pl.* -IES (-ĭz). A water closet, urinal, etc., fitted with sanitary plumbing.
san′i·ta′tion (-tā′shŭn), *n.* A rendering sanitary; use of sanitary measures; also, science of sanitary conditions.
san′i·ty (săn′ĭ·tĭ), *n.* [F. *sanité*, fr. L. *sanitas*, fr. *sanus* sound, healthy.] Soundness or health of mind.
san′jak′ (sȧn′jăk′), *n.* [Turk. *sanjāq*, *sānjāq*, lit., flag.] Formerly, in Turkey, a district or subdivision of a vilayet.
San Jo·se′ scale (săn′ [h]ō·zā′). A scale insect (*Aspidiotus perniciosus*) very destructive to fruit trees; — first introduced into the United States at San Jose, California.
sank (săngk), *past of* SINK.
San′khya (säng′kyȧ), *n.* [Skr. *sāṁkhya.*] One of the six orthodox systems of Hindu philosophy, dualistic in nature.
san′nup (săn′ŭp), *n.* [Of Algonquian origin.] **1.** A married male Indian. **2.** An ordinary warrior as distinguished from a chief.
sans (sănz; *F.* säɴ), *prep.* [F., fr. L. *absentia*, abl., in the absence of, with loss of initial syllable after L. *sine* without.] *Archaic.* Without; deprived or destitute of.
San′scrit (săn′skrĭt). Var. of SANSKRIT.
sans′-cu·lotte′ (sănz′kū·lŏt′; *F.* säɴ′kü′lȯt′), *n.* [F., without breeches.] **1.** *Fr. Hist.* Literally, a fellow without breeches; — applied by the aristocrats at the time of the Revolution to the republicans, who rejected short breeches for pantaloons. Cf. CARMAGNOLE, 2. **2.** A radical republican; violent revolutionist. — **sans′-cu·lot′tic** (sănz′kū·lŏt′ĭk), **sans′-cu·lot′tish** (-ĭsh), *adj.* — **sans′-cu·lot′tism** (-ĭz′m), *n.*
sans′-cu′lot′tide′ (säɴ′kü′lȯ′tēd′; sănz′kū·lŏt′ĭd), *n.* Also **sans′-cu·lot′tid.** See REVOLUTIONARY CALENDAR.
‖**sans doute** (säɴ dōōt′). [F.] Without doubt; certainly.
san′sei′ (sän′sā′), *n.; pl.* SANSEI, SANSEIS (-sāz′). [Jap. *san* third + *sei* generation.] An American citizen born of nisei parents in the U. S.
san′se·vie′ri·a (săn′sĕ·vẹr′ĭ·ȧ), *n.* [NL.] Any of a genus (*Sansevieria*) of tropical plants of the lily family, some of which are grown for their decorative sword-shaped leaves. Most species yield a fiber used in making bowstrings, cordage, and cloth, both plant and fiber being called also *bowstring hemp.*
‖**sans gêne** (säɴ zhâɴ′). [F.] Without constraint or embarrassment; easy.
San′skrit (săn′skrĭt), *n.* Also **San′scrit.** [Skr. *saṁskṛta*, lit., prepared, cultivated, fr. *sam* together + *kṛ* to do, make.] **a** The ancient Aryan (*Indo-Iranian*) language of the Hindus of India, including the language of the Vedas, often termed ***Vedic Sanskrit*** (see VEDA), as well as the later ***classical Sanskrit***, which is essentially a literary language, preserved in a great and varied literature, as the Mahabharata, Ramayana, Sakuntala, etc. **b** Specif., the classical language as distinguished both from Vedic and from the vernacular Prakrit (which see). It possesses special interest to philology because it retains many of the supposed characteristics of the parent Indo-European language. See INDO-EUROPEAN LANGUAGES. — *adj.* Of, pert. to, or written in Sanskrit. — **San·skrit′ic** (săn·skrĭt′ĭk), *adj.* — **San′skrit·ist**, *n.*
‖**sans peur et sans re·proche′** (säɴ pûr′ ā säɴ rē·prôsh′). [F.] Without fear and without reproach; — said esp. of the Chevalier de Bayard.
sans′-ser′if (sănz′sĕr′ĭf), *n.* [F. *sans* without + E. *serif.*] Printing type with no serifs. See TYPE.
‖**sans sou′ci′** (säɴ sōō′sē′). [F.] Without worry; carefree.
San′ta Claus *or* **Klaus** (săn′tȧ klôz; săn′tĭ). [U. S. colonial corrupt. of D. *Sant Nikolaas.*] See SAINT NICHOLAS.
san′ta·la′ceous (săn′tȧ·lā′shŭs), *adj.* [ML. *santalum* sandalwood.] Belonging to the sandalwood family (Santalaceae). See SANDALWOOD.
san·ton′i·ca (săn·tŏn′ĭ·kȧ), *n.* [NL., fr. L. *herba santonica*, fr. *Santoni* a people of Aquitania.] **a** The European wormwood *Artemisia pauciflora.* **b** An anthelmintic drug consisting of its dried flower heads.
san′to·nin (săn′tō·nĭn), *n.* Also **-nine.** *Chem. & Pharm.* A colorless, crystalline, slightly bitter compound, $C_{15}H_{18}O_3$, occurring in santonica and used as an anthelmintic.
‖**Saor′stat′** (sâr′stôt′), *n.* [Ir. *saor* free + *stāt* state.] Free state; specif., ***Saor′stat′ Eir′eann*** (âr′ĭn), the Irish Free State.
sap (săp), *n.* [AS. *sæp.*] **1.** The juices of a plant, esp. the watery solution which circulates through the vascular tissue in woody plants. **2.** Sapwood, or alburnum. **3.** Any liquid or humor essential to life, health, or vigor, as blood; vital juice; vitality. **4.** *Slang.* A saphead. — *v. t.* To drain (sap) as by sucking; to drain of sap.
sap, *n.* [F. *sappe*, *sap.* See SAP, *v.*] *Mil.* An extension of a trench dug from within the trench itself; esp., one dug from the attacker's lines to a point beneath the enemy's works. — *v. t.;* SAPPED (săpt); SAP′PING. [F. *sapper*, *saper*, fr. *sappe*, *sape*, mattock, fr. LL. *sappa.*] **1.** To subvert by digging or wearing away the foundation; un-

dermine. **2.** To unsettle or weaken; to exhaust gradually. **3.** *Mil.* To operate against, or pierce, by saps. — **Syn.** See WEAKEN. — *v. i. Mil.* To proceed by, or to execute, saps.

sap'a·jou (săp'ȧ·jo͞o; *F.* sȧ'pȧ'zho͞o'), *n.* [F., of Tupian origin.] A capuchin monkey.

sa·pan'wood' (sȧ·păn'wo͝od'), *n.* [D. *sapanhout*, fr. Malay *sapañ.*] A red dyewood obtained from an East Indian tree (*Caesalpinia sappan*) of the senna family; also, the tree itself.

sap'head' (săp'hĕd'), *n. Colloq.* A weak-minded, stupid fellow; a dupe. — **sap'head'ed** (-ĕd; -ĭd; 2), *adj.*

sa·phe'nous (sȧ·fē'nŭs), *adj.* [ML. *saphena* a vein in the leg, fr. Ar. *ṣāfin.*] *Anat.* Designating, pertaining to, or in the region of, the two principal superficial veins of the leg, the long one passing up the medial side of the leg, the short one passing behind the outer malleolus and up the back of the leg.

sap'id (săp'ĭd), *adj.* [L. *sapidus.* See SAGE, *adj.*] Having savor or flavor; sensible to organs of taste; also, palatable. — **sa·pid'i·ty** (sȧ·pĭd'ĭ·tĭ), *n.* — **Syn.** See TASTE.

sa'pi·ent (sā'pĭ·ĕnt), *adj.* [OF., fr. L. *sapiens, -entis*, pres. part. of *sapere* to taste, have sense, know.] Wise; sage; discerning; — often ironical. — **Syn.** See WISE. — **sa'pi·ence** (-ĕns), **sa'pi·en·cy** (-ĕn·sĭ), *n.* — **sa'pi·ent·ly**, *adv.*

sap'in·da'ceous (săp'ĭn·dā'shŭs), *adj.* [From *Sapindus*, type genus, fr. L. *sapo* soap + *Indicus* Indian.] Belonging to the soapberry family (Sapindaceae). See SOAPBERRY.

sap'less (săp'lĕs; -lĭs), *adj.* Destitute of sap.

sap'ling (-lĭng), *n.* **1.** A young tree. **2.** A youth.

sap'o·dil'la (săp'ō·dĭl'ȧ), *n.* [Sp. *sapotillo, zapotillo*, dim. of *sapote, zapote.* See SAPOTA.] **a** A tropical evergreen tree (*Achras zapota*) with hard reddish wood. Its latex yields chicle. It typifies a family (Sapotaceae, the sapodilla family) of tropical trees or shrubs with milky juice and fleshy, often edible, fruits. Many genera (esp. *Palaquium* and *Payena*) yield gutta-percha, gums, etc. **b** Also **sapodilla plum.** The rough-skinned brownish fruit of this tree.

sap'o·na'ceous (-nā'shŭs), *adj.* [ML. *saponaceus*, fr. L. *sapo, -onis*, soap.] Resembling soap; soapy; slippery.

sa·pon'i·fi·ca'tion (sȧ·pŏn'ĭ·fĭ·kā'shŭn), *n.* [F.] **1.** Act, process, or result of conversion into soap. **2.** *Chem.* The hydrolysis of any ester into the corresponding alcohol and acid; hence, any hydrolysis.

sa·pon'i·fy (sȧ·pŏn'ĭ·fī), *v. t. & i.*; -FIED (-fīd); -FY'ING. [F. *saponifier*, fr. L. *sapo, -onis*, soap. See -FY.] To convert into soap; to subject to, or to undergo, saponification. — **sa·pon'i·fi'a·ble** (-fī'ȧ·b'l), *adj.* — **sa·pon'i·fi'er** (-fī'ẽr), *n.*

sap'o·nin (săp'ō·nĭn), *n.* Also **sap'o·nine** (-nĭn; -nēn). [F. *saponine*, fr. L. *sapo, -onis*, soap.] *Chem.* Any of a group of glucosides occurring in many plants, as in soapwort, soapbark, etc., and characterized by their property of producing a soapy lather. Commercial saponin, a mixture of saponins, is used as a foam producer in beverages and fire extinguishers, as a detergent, etc.

sap'o·nite (săp'ō·nīt), *n.* [Sw. *saponit*, fr. L. *sapo, -onis*, soap.] *Mineral.* A hydrous magnesium aluminum silicate, occurring in soft, soapy, amorphous masses, filling veins and cavities in serpentine, diabase, etc. Sp. gr., 2.24–2.30.

sa'por, sa'pour (sā'pôr; -pẽr), *n.* [L.] That property of a thing affecting the sense of taste; savor; flavor. — **sap'o·rif'ic** (săp'ō·rĭf'ĭk), *adj.* — **sap'o·rous** (săp'ō·rŭs), *adj.*

sa·po'ta (sȧ·pō'tȧ), *n.* [NL., fr. Sp. *sapote, zapote*, fr. Nahuatl *tzapotl.*] The sapodilla.

sap'o·ta'ceous (săp'ō·tā'shŭs), *adj.* Belonging to the sapodilla family (Sapotaceae). See SAPODILLA.

sap·pan'wood' (sȧ·păn'wo͝od'), *n.* = SAPANWOOD.

sap'per (săp'ẽr), *n.* One who saps; *Mil.*, a member of an engineer unit trained to execute sapping. See 2d SAP, *v. t.*, 3.

Sap'phic (săf'ĭk), *adj.* **1.** Of or pert. to Sappho, a Lesbian poetess (c. 600 B.C.) famous for love lyrics. **2.** [*often not cap.*] Erotic. Cf. LESBIAN. **3.** Designating, or pert. to, any of certain verse forms used by Sappho. — *n.* A Sapphic verse.

Sap·phi'ra (să·fī'rȧ), *n.* See ANANIAS.

sap'phire (săf'īr), *n.* [OF. *safir* (F. *saphir*), fr. L. *sapphirus*, fr. Gr. *sappheiros*, ult. fr. Skr.] **1. a** A precious stone of transparent rich-blue corundum. **b** More widely, a pure variety of corundum in transparent or translucent crystals used as a gem; also, such a gem. Such varieties are distinguished according to color as: WHITE SAPPHIRE (clear or colorless), PURPLE SAPPHIRE or ORIENTAL AMETHYST, GREEN SAPPHIRE or ORIENTAL EMERALD, YELLOW SAPPHIRE or ORIENTAL TOPAZ. The ruby (red corundum) is almost never called *sapphire.* **2.** In full ***sapphire blue.*** A color, greenish-blue in hue, of medium saturation and low brilliance. See COLOR. — **sap'phire**, *adj.*

sap'phir·ine (săf'ẽr·ĭn; -īn), *adj.* Of sapphire; like sapphires, as in color or hardness. — *n. Mineral.* **a** A pale-blue or green magnesium aluminum silicate, usually granular. **b** A blue variety of spinel.

sap'py (săp'ĭ), *adj.*; SAP'PI·ER (-ĭ·ẽr); SAP'PI·EST. **1.** Abounding with sap. **2. a** Vital. **b** Having substance; pithy. **3.** *Slang.* Foolish; silly.

sa·pre'mi·a, sa·prae'mi·a (sȧ·prē'mĭ·ȧ), *n.* [NL., fr. *sapr-* + *-emia.*] *Med.* A morbid condition in which the products of putrefactive bacteria are present in the blood.

sap'ro- (săp'rō-), **sapr-.** [Gr. *sapros.*] A combining form meaning *rotten*, as in **sap'ro·lite**, disintegrated rock; specif.: **a** *Dead* or *decaying organic matter*, as in **sa·proph'a·gous.** **b** *Saprophytic*, as in *sapremia.*

sap'ro·gen'ic (-jĕn'ĭk), *adj.* [*sapro-* + *-genic.*] Of, pertaining to, capable of, or resulting from the production of putrefaction. — **sa·prog'e·nous** (sȧ·prŏj'ē·nŭs), *adj.*

sap'ro·phyte (săp'rō·fīt), *n.* [*sapro-* + *-phyte.*] *Biol.* Any organism living on dead or decaying organic matter. Cf. AUTOPHYTE. — **sap'ro·phyt'ic** (-fĭt'ĭk), *adj. & n.*

sap'sa·go (săp'sȧ·gō), *n.* [Corrupt. fr. G. *schabzieger*, fr. *schaben* to shave, scrape + *zieger* whey, whey cheese.] A hard green Swiss cheese, mixed with blue melilot.

sap'suck'er (săp'sŭk'ẽr), *n.* Any of several small American woodpeckers (genus *Sphyrapicus*) which feed partly on sap; esp., the ***yellow-bellied sapsucker*** (*S. varius*).

sap'wood' (-wo͝od'), *n.* Alburnum; the usually lighter, more porous, and younger wood, beneath the bark and extending to the heartwood of the tree.

sar'a·band (săr'ȧ·bănd), *n.* [F. *sarabande*, fr. Sp. *zarabanda.*] **a** A rude, lively Spanish dance, performed with castanets; also, the music for it. **b** A stately court dance evolved from this dance and fashionable in the 17th and 18th centuries.

Sar'a·cen (săr'ȧ·sĕn), *n.* [LL. *Saracenus.*] Orig. a nomad of the deserts between Syria and Arabia; later, an Arab; hence, a Moslem, esp. as hostile to the Crusaders. — **Sar'a·cen**, *adj.* — **Sar'a·cen'ic** (-sĕn'ĭk), **Sar'a·cen'i·cal** (-ĭ·kăl), *adj.*

Sar'ah (sâr'ȧ; sā'rȧ; 6), *n. Bib.* Also **Sa'rai** (sā'rī; sâr'ā·ī). The wife of Abraham and the mother of Isaac.

Sa·ran' (sȧ·răn'), *n.* A trade-mark applied to a group of tough, flexible thermoplastics that can be formed into waterproof and chemically resistant filaments, fabrics, pipe, film, molded parts, and protective coatings.

Sar'a·to'ga trunk (săr'ȧ·tō'gȧ). [From *Saratoga*, N. Y.] A very large traveling trunk.

sarc-. = SARCO-.

sar'casm (sär'kăz'm), *n.* [F. or L.; F. *sarcasme*, fr. L. *sarcasmos*, fr. Gr. *sarkasmos*, fr. *sarkazein* to tear flesh like dogs, bite the lips in rage, speak bitterly, fr. *sarx, sarkos*, flesh.] **1.** A keen or bitter taunt; a cutting gibe or rebuke. **2.** The use of bitter, caustic, or stinging remarks expressing contempt, often by ironical statement; also, the language of such remarks. — **Syn.** See WIT.

sar·cas'tic (sär·kăs'tĭk), *adj.* Expressing, or expressed by, sarcasm; characterized by, or of the nature of, sarcasm; given to the use of sarcasms. — **sar·cas'ti·cal·ly** (-tĭ·kăl·ĭ), *adv.*

sarce'net, sarse'net (särs'nĕt; -nĭt), *n.* [AF. *sarzinett*, dim. fr. ME. *sarzin* Saracen.] A soft silk fabric, in plain or twill weave, much used for linings.

sar'co- (sär'kō-), **sarc-.** [Gr. *sarx, sarkos.*] A combining form meaning: **a** *Flesh*, as in:

sarcogenic	sarcolysis	sarcophilous
sarcogenous	sarcolytic	sarcosepsis

b *Combined with sarcoma*, as in **sar'co·ad'e·no'ma, sar'co·car'ci·no'ma, sar'co·en'chon·dro'ma.**

sar'co·carp (sär'kō·kärp), *n.* [*sarco-* + *-carp.*] *Bot.* **a** A mesocarp, esp. when fleshy, as in the peach. See ENDOCARP, *Illust.* **b** Improperly, any fleshy fruit.

sar·co'ma (sär·kō'mȧ), *n.*; *pl.* SARCOMATA (-mȧ·tȧ), SARCOMAS (-mȧz). [NL., fr. Gr. *sarkōma, -atos*, fr. *sarx, sarkos*, flesh.] *Med.* Any malignant growth derived from nonepithelial tissue of mesodermal embryonic origin, as connective tissue, lymphoid tissue, cartilage, bone, etc. Cf. CANCER, CARCINOMA. — **sar·co'ma·toid** (-toid), *adj.* — **sar·co'ma·tous** (-kō'mȧ·tŭs; -kŏm'ȧ·tŭs), *adj.*

sar·co'ma·to'sis (-tō'sĭs), *n.* [NL]. *Med.* A morbid condition characterized by a sarcoma.

sar·coph'a·gus (sär·kŏf'ȧ·gŭs), *n.*; *pl.* -GI (-jī), -GUSES (-gŭs·ĕz; -ĭz). [L., fr. Gr. *sarkophagos*, prop., eating flesh, fr. *sarx, sarkos*, flesh + *phagein* to eat.] **1.** A limestone used among the Greeks for coffins, because it disintegrated within a few weeks the flesh of bodies deposited in it. **2.** A coffin or chest-shaped tomb of such stone; hence: **a** A stone coffin. **b** A large coffin exposed to view in the open air or in a tomb.

sar'cous (sär'kŭs), *adj.* [Gr. *sarx, sarkos*, flesh.] *Anat.* Pertaining to flesh or muscle.

sard (särd), *n.* Also **sar'dine** (sär'dĭn; -dīn). [L. *sarda*, fr. Gr. *sardion*, or *sardios* (sc. *lithos*), i. e., Sardian stone, fr. *Sardeis* Sardis, capital of Lydia.] A deep orange-red variety of chalcedony, classed by some as a variety of carnelian.

sar·dine' (sär·dēn'; sär'dēn), *n.*; see PLURAL, *Note*, 3. [F., fr. L. *sardina, sarda*, fr. Gr. *sardēnē, sarda.*] **1.** The young of the pilchard (*Sardinia pilchardus*) when of a size suitable for preserving for food. **2.** Any of various small fishes resembling the true sardines or similarly preserved for food.

sar'di·us (sär'dĭ·ŭs), *n.* [LL. *sardius, lapis sardius.* See SARD.] **1.** A sard. **2.** *Bib.* A gem in the Hebrew high priest's breastplate, possibly a ruby or a sard.

sar·don'ic (sär·dŏn'ĭk), *adj.* [F. *sardonique*, fr. L. *sardonius*, fr. Gr. *sardonios, sardanios.*] Bitterly scornful; disdainfully or sneeringly derisive. — **sar·don'i·cal·ly** (-ĭ·kăl·ĭ), *adv.*

sar'do·nyx (sär'dō·nĭks), *n.* [L., fr. Gr. *sardonyx.* See SARD; ONYX.] A variety of onyx having layers of sard.

sar·gas'so (sär·găs'ō), *n.* [Pg. *sargasso, sargaço*, fr. *sarga, sargo*, a kind of grape.] Also **sargasso weed.** A seaweed of the genus *Sargassum*; a gulfweed.

sar·gas'sum (-ŭm), *n.* [NL., fr. Pg. *sargasso.*] Any of a genus (*Sargassum*) of fucoid seaweeds, the gulfweeds, of the warmer parts of the Atlantic.

sa'ri (sä'rē), *n.* [Hind. *sāṛhī, sāṛī.*] The chief garment of a Hindu woman, a long cloth wrapped round the waist to cover the legs, draped full in front, and then wound over the bosom, the left shoulder, and sometimes the head.

sark (särk), *n.* [AS. *serc, serce.*] *Archaic.* A shirt.

sar·men'tose (sär·mĕn'tōs), *adj.* [L. *sarmentum* twig.] *Bot.* Producing slender prostrate branches or runners.

sa·rong' (sȧ·rŏng'), *n.* [Malay *saroṅ.*] **a** The skirtlike garment made of a long strip of cloth, worn by both sexes in the Malay Archipelago, Ceylon, and some parts of India. **b** Cloth for such garments.

Sar·pe'don (sär·pē'dŏn), *n.* [L., fr. Gr. *Sarpēdōn.*] *Gr. Myth.* A son of Zeus and Europa. He became king of Lycia and Zeus gave him the privilege of living three generations.

sar'ra·ce'ni·a (săr'ȧ·sē'nĭ·ȧ), *n.* [NL., after D. *Sarrazin* of Quebec.] Any of a genus (*Sarracenia*) of insectivorous bog herbs, the American pitcher plants, typifying a family (Sarraceniaceae, the American pitcher-plant family), and having pitcher-shaped or tubular leaves with an arched or hooded flap at the apex. — **sar'ra·ce'ni·a'ceous** (-ā'shŭs), *adj.*

sar'sa·pa·ril'la (säs'[ȧ·]pȧ·rĭl'ȧ; särs'[ȧ·]pȧ-), *n.* [Sp. *zarzaparrilla.*] **1.** Any of various tropical American species of *Smilax.* **2.** The dried cordlike roots of any of these, used as a mild tonic and alterative. **3.** A carbonated beverage of sarsaparilla flavor.

sarse'net (särs'nĕt; -nĭt). Var. of SARCENET.

sar'tor (sär'tẽr; -tôr), *n.* [LL.] *Chiefly Humorous.* A tailor.

sar·to'ri·al (sär·tō'rĭ·ăl; 70), *adj.* **1.** Of or pertaining to a tailor or tailored garments. **2.** *Anat.* Of or pertaining to the sartorius. — **sar·to'ri·al·ly**, *adv.*

sar·to'ri·us (-ŭs), *n.* [NL., fr. LL. *sartor* a patcher, tailor, fr. *sarcire, sartum*, to patch, mend.] *Anat.* A muscle, the longest in man, crossing the front of the thigh obliquely. It assists in rotating the leg to the position assumed in sitting like a tailor, that is, cross-legged.

sar′tor re·sar′tus (sär′tẽr[-tôr] rē·sär′tŭs). [LL.] The tailor re-tailored; [*caps.*] title of a book by Thomas Carlyle.

Sar′um use (sâr′ŭm). The liturgical use, or the order of divine service, of Sarum (Salisbury) in the late medieval period. Hence, **Sarum office, Sarum rubric.**

sash (săsh), *n.; pl.* SASHES (-ĕz; -ĭz), or, collectively, SASH. [Appar. fr pl. *sashes, shashes, shasses,* fr. F. sing. *châssis* a frame, sash.] The framing in which panes of glass are set in a glazed window or door; hence, loosely, the movable part of a window.

sash, *n.; pl.* SASHES. [Ar. *shāsh.*] A long band of silk or other material, worn originally wound around the head as a turban, but now around the waist as a girdle or over the shoulder as part of a uniform.

sa·shay′ (să·shā′), *v. i.* [Corrupt. of *chassé.*] To perform a chassé, or glide; hence, *U. S. Slang.*, to step mincingly; to skip.

sa′sin (sā′sĭn), *n.* The black buck.

sas′ka·toon′ (săs′kȧ·tōōn′), *n.* [Cree *misâskwatomin.*] A shadbush (*Amelanchier alnifolia*), with purple fruit.

sass (săs; sȧs). Dial. var. of SAUCE.

sas′sa·by (săs′ȧ·bĭ), *n.; pl.* -BIES (-bĭz). A large South African antelope (*Damaliscus lunatus*).

sas′sa·fras (săs′ȧ·frăs), *n.* [Sp. *sasafrás,* appar. from confusion with Sp. *saxafrax, saxifraga,* saxifrage.] **1.** Any American tree of a genus (*Sassafras*) of aromatic trees of the laurel family, with soft yellow wood. **2.** *Pharm.* The dried bark of the root of *S. variifolium,* used as a diaphoretic, a flavoring agent, and aromatic bitters. It yields an aromatic, volatile oil used in perfumes.

Sas·sa′ni·an (să·sā′nĭ·ăn; 58), *n. & adj.* Sassanid.

Sas·san′i·dae (să·săn′ĭ·dē), *n. pl.* [From *Sassan,* whose grandson Ardashir became king.] A dynasty of Persian kings, from A.D. 226 to 641. — **Sas′sa·nid, Sas′sa·nide** (săs′ȧ·nĭd), *n. & adj.*

Sas′se·nach (săs′ĕ·năk), *n.* [Ir. *sasanach.*] *Scot. & Ir.* A Saxon; an Englishman; a Lowlander.

sas′sy (săs′ĭ), **sas′sy·wood′** (-wŏŏd′), *n.* [W. Afr. *sassy.*] A West African tree (*Erythrophloeum guineënse*) of the senna family, with poisonous wood and bark (**sassy bark**) used as an ordeal poison.

sass′y (săs′ĭ; sȧs′-). *U. S.* Dial. var. of SAUCY.

sat (săt), *past & past part.* of SIT.

Sa′tan (sā′tăn; -t'n), *n.* [Heb. *ṣāṭān* adversary.] **1.** In Christian theology, the great adversary of man; the Devil. According to the Talmud, he was an archangel, cast out of heaven for disobedience and pride. Milton follows this in *Paradise Lost.* **2.** [*often not cap.*] A fiend; a devil.

sa·tang′ (sȧ·tăng′), *n. sing. & pl.* [Siamese *satăn.*] *Thailand.* A bronze coin and money of account, equal to 1/100 baht.

sa·tan′ic (să·tăn′ĭk), *adj.* Also **sa·tan′i·cal** (-ĭ·kăl). Of, pertaining to, or like Satan; devilish; infernal. — **sa·tan′i·cal·ly,** *adv.*

Sa′tan·ism (sā′tăn·ĭz′m), *n.* Worship of Satan; specif., a cult, real or fictitious, which travesties Christian rites. — **Sa′tan·ist** (-ĭst), *n.*

satch′el (săch′ĕl), *n.* [OF. *sachel,* fr. L. *saccellus,* dim. of *saccus.* See SACK bag.] A small bag, carried either by hand or slung from the shoulder; a valise.

sate (sāt), *v. t.* [Prob. shortened fr. *satiate.*] **1.** To satisfy or gratify to the full, as a desire. **2.** To gratify to the point of weariness or loathing; satiate. — **Syn.** See SATIATE.

sate (săt; sāt). *Archaic past & past part.* of SIT.

sa·teen′ (să·tēn′), *n.* [From SATIN.] A cotton fabric with a glossy surface resembling satin.

sat′el·lite (săt′ĕ·līt), *n.* [F., fr. L. *satelles, -itis,* an attendant.] **1.** An attendant attached to a prince or other powerful person; hence, an obsequious dependent or follower, or a subordinate associate. **2.** *Astron.* An attendant body, revolving about a larger one, its primary; esp., in the solar system, a secondary planet. **3.** Something attendant, accompanying, or closely related but subordinate or secondary, as: **a** A state politically and economically dominated by a powerful neighboring state. **b** A subordinate population center, usually an independent city or town, whose economic life is controlled by the activities of a nearby metropolis. **c** One of a number of subsidiary airfields of limited facilities surrounding a main air base. — **Syn.** See FOLLOWER. — **sat′el·lite,** *adj.*

sa′tem lan′guages (sä′tĕm; sā′-). See INDO-EUROPEAN LANGUAGES.

sa′ti·a·ble (sā′shĭ·ȧ·b'l; sā′shȧ·b'l), *adj.* That may be sated or satiated. — **sa′ti·a·bil′i·ty** (-bĭl′ĭ·tĭ), **sa′ti·a·ble·ness,** *n.* — **sa′ti·a·bly,** *adv.*

sa′ti·ate (sā′shĭ·āt), *adj.* [L. *satiatus,* past part. of *satiare* to satisfy, fr. *satis* enough.] Filled to satiety; sated. — (-āt), *v. t.* **1.** *Now Rare.* To sate; satisfy fully. **2.** To gratify to repletion or loathing; to surfeit; glut. — **sa′ti·a′tion** (-ā′shŭn), *n.*

Syn. **Satiate, sate, surfeit, cloy, pall, glut, gorge** mean to fill or be filled to repletion. **Satiate** and **sate** once implied, and still sometimes imply, complete satisfaction, but both (esp. *satiate*) now more often suggest repletion that has destroyed interest or desire; **surfeit** implies a nauseating repletion; **cloy,** the resulting disgust or boredom of such surfeiting; **pall,** the loss of power in that which surfeits to stimulate one's interest or appetite; **glut,** excess in feeding or supplying; **gorge,** a glutting almost to the point of bursting or choking.

sa·ti′e·ty (sȧ·tī′ĕ·tĭ), *n.* [F. *satiété,* fr. L. *satietas,* fr. *satis* enough.] State of being satiated; an excess of gratification of any desire or need, finally resulting in wearisomeness or loathing.

sat′in (săt′ĭn; -'n), *n.* [OF., prob. fr. Ar. *zaytūnī,* fr. *Zaytūn* (Marco Polo's *Zaitun*), fr. Chin. *Tzŭ-t'ing,* formerly a great seaport in Fukien Province, China.] A fabric woven in satin weave (see under WEAVE, *n.*) having close texture, lustrous face, and dull back, orig. of silk only, commonly of rayon or nylon. — *adj.* Pert. to or made of satin.

sat′i·net′ (săt′ĭ·nĕt′), *n.* Also **sat′i·nette′.** [F., fr. *satin.*] **a** An imitation satin. **b** *U. S.* A fabric of cotton warp and woolen filling, used for outer garments.

sat′in·flow′er (săt′ĭn·flou′ẽr), **sat′in·pod′** (-pŏd′), *n.* = HONESTY, 2.

satin stitch. *Embroidery.* A stitch worked in close parallel lines over a design, producing a satiny surface, nearly alike on both sides.

sat′in·wood′ (săt′ĭn·wŏŏd′), *n.* **1.** An East Indian tree (*Chloroxylon swietenia*) of the mahogany family; also, its yellowish-brown wood. **2.** The tree *Zanthoxylum flavum* of the rue family, of Florida and the West Indies, with orange-colored wood used for furniture and implements.

sat′in·y (-ĭ), *adj.* Of or like satin; lustrous.

sat′ire (săt′īr), *n.* [F., fr. L. *satira, satura,* a poetic medley, fr. *satura* (sc. *lanx*) a dish filled with various fruits, a medley, fr. *satur* full of food, sated.] **1.** A poem or prose work holding up human vices, follies, etc., to ridicule or scorn. **2.** Trenchant wit, irony, or sarcasm, used for the purpose of exposing and discrediting vice or folly. — **Syn.** See WIT.

sa·tir′ic (să·tĭr′ĭk), **sa·tir′i·cal** (-ĭ·kăl), *adj.* **1.** Of, pertaining to, or of the nature of satire; as, *satiric* verse. **2.** Usually *satirical.* Given to, or skilled in, the use of satire; specif., ironically censorious; severe in ridiculing men, manners, or things. — **sa·tir′i·cal·ly,** *adv.* — **sa·tir′i·cal·ness,** *n.*

sat′i·rist (săt′ĭ·rĭst), *n.* One who satirizes; esp., one who writes satire.

sat′i·rize (-rīz), *v. t. & i.* To denounce satirically, in or as in a satire. — **sat′i·riz′er** (-rīz′ẽr), *n.*

sat′is·fac′tion (săt′ĭs·făk′shŭn), *n.* **1.** The act of satisfying; the state of being satisfied. **2.** That which satisfies; esp.: **a** *Theol.* Atonement that meets the demands of divine justice or righteousness. **b** Reparation for an insult, as by duel or apology. **c** Satisfactory answer or information. **d** Settlement of a claim or demand; payment.

sat′is·fac′to·ry (-făk′tō·rĭ), *adj.* Giving or producing satisfaction; of a kind to meet requirements or expectations. — **sat′is·fac′to·ri·ly** (-rĭ·lĭ), *adv.* — **sat′is·fac′to·ri·ness** (-rĭ·nĕs; -nĭs), *n.*

sat′is·fy (săt′ĭs·fī), *v. t.;* -FIED (-fīd); -FY′ING. [OF. *satisfier,* fr. L. *satisfacere,* fr. *satis* enough + *facere* to make.] **1.** In general, to fill up the measure of a want of (a person or a thing); hence, to gratify fully the desire of; to make content. **2. a** To give what is due to; as, to *satisfy* a creditor. **b** To answer or discharge, as a claim, debt, legal demand, or the like; pay off; requite. **3.** *Obs.* To expiate. **4. a** To set at rest the mind of; convince; free from uncertainty; as, I am *satisfied* that he is guilty. **b** To answer convincingly; solve; as, to *satisfy* a doubt. **5.** To be so constituted as to fulfill the requirements of; as, to *satisfy* a condition. — *v. i.* To give satisfaction or gratification; to leave nothing to be desired. — **sat′is·fi′er** (-fī′ẽr), *n.* — **sat′is·fy′ing·ly,** *adv.*

Syn. (1) **Satisfy, content** mean to appease one's desires or longings. **Satisfy** implies full appeasement, esp. of one's needs, requirements, etc.; **content,** appeasement to the point where one is not disturbed or disquieted.
(2) See PAY.

sa′trap (sā′trăp *or, esp. Brit.,* săt′răp), *n.* [L. *satrapes,* fr. Gr. *satrapēs,* fr. OPer. *shathrapāvan* satrap.] **1.** The governor of a province in ancient Persia. **2.** A petty prince; a despotic subordinate official.

sa′trap·y (sā′tră·pĭ; săt′ră-), *n.; pl.* -TRAPIES (-pĭz). The government, jurisdiction, or rank, of a satrap.

sat′u·ra·ble (săt′ū·rȧ·b'l), *adj.* Capable of being saturated. — **sat′u·ra·bil′i·ty** (-bĭl′ĭ·tĭ), *n.*

sat′u·rant (-rănt), *n. & adj.* (One) that saturates.

sat′u·rate (-rāt), *v. t.* [L. *saturatus,* past part. of *saturare* to saturate, fr. *satur* full of food, sated.] **1.** To cause to become completely penetrated, impregnated, or soaked. **2.** To treat, furnish, charge, etc., (with something) to the point (**saturation point**) where no more can be absorbed, dissolved, retained, sold at the current price, etc.; as, water *saturated* with salt; the market is *saturated* with goods. **3.** *Chem.* To cause to combine till there is no further tendency to combine; to neutralize. **4.** *Mil.* To blanket completely (a target area, as a factory district) with aerial bombs dropped nearly simultaneously by a concentration of bombers in close formation. — **Syn.** See SOAK. — (-rāt), *adj.* **1.** *Chiefly Poetic.* Saturated. **2. a** Very deep or intense; — of colors. **b** = SATURATED, 3 **a.** — **sat′u·rat′er** (-rāt′ẽr), **sat′u·ra′tor** (-rā′tẽr), *n.*

sat′u·rat′ed (-rāt′ĕd; -ĭd), *adj.* **1.** Filled to repletion; holding by absorption, solution, combination, or the like, all that is possible; as, a *saturated* atmosphere. **2.** Thoroughly soaked with moisture; wet. **3. a** *Color.* Having very high saturation, as some of the spectrum colors. See COLOR. **b** *Optics.* Not diluted with white; — said of pure colors like those of the spectrum. **4.** *Chem.* **a** Denoting the most concentrated solution that can remain in the presence of an excess of the dissolved substance. **b** Denoting a compound that does not tend to unite directly with another compound; — applied esp. in *Org. Chem.* to compounds containing no double or triple bonds. **5.** *Petrog.* Of minerals and rocks, containing the greatest possible amount of combined silica.

sat′u·ra′tion (-rā′shŭn), *n.* **1.** Act or process of saturating, or state of being saturated. **2.** Of chromatic colors: **a** Freedom or degree of freedom from admixture with white. **b** (As used in definitions in this book) That attribute which determines their degree of difference from a gray of the same brilliance. See COLOR, *n.*, 2, and *Illust.* **3.** *Magnetism.* State of maximum magnetization; the point where further increase in intensity produces only an equal increase in density.

saturation bombing. Bombing in which the target area is saturated. See SATURATE, *v. t.*, 4.

Sat′ur·day (săt′ẽr·dĭ; -dā; 13), *n.* [AS. *Sæterdæg, Sæterndæg,* lit., Saturn's day.] The seventh and last day of the week; the Jewish Sabbath. Abbr. *Sat.*

Sat′urn (săt′ẽrn), *n.* [L. *Saturnus,* prob. fr. the root of *serere, satum,* to sow.] **1.** *Rom. Relig.* An ancient god of the seed sowing, later identified with the Greek Cronus and, like him, fabled to have been king during an ancient golden age. **2.** *Astron.* The planet next in magnitude to Jupiter, and next more remote from the sun. It is remarkable for its engirdling rings which are composed of a dense swarm of small solid bodies. It revolves about the sun at a mean distance of 886,000,000 miles. Symbol, ♄. See PLANET, *Table.* **3.** *Alchem. & Old Chem.* The metal lead.

Sat′ur·na′li·a (săt′ẽr·nā′lĭ·ȧ; 58), *n. pl.; rarely, n. sing.,* **Sat′ur·na′le** (-lē). [L.] **1.** *Rom. Relig.* The festival of Saturn, beginning Dec. 17. **2.** [*not cap.*] A period or occasion of general license, as in excesses of vice; — sometimes construed as *sing.* — **Sat′ur·na′li·an** (-ăn), *adj.*

Sa·tur′ni·an (să·tûr′nĭ·ăn), *adj.* **1.** Of or pertaining to the god Saturn, whose age or reign is called the golden age; hence, of an age, reign, etc., marked by peace, happiness, and contentment. **2.** Of, pertaining to, or influenced by the planet Saturn.

sa·tur′ni·id (-nĭ·ĭd), *n. & adj.* [From *Saturnia,* type genus, fr. L. *Saturnius* Saturnian.] (One) of a widely distributed family (Saturniidae) of moths with a stout hairy body and strong wide wings. American species include the Io moth, Polyphemus moth, Luna moth, and Cecropia moth.

sat′ur·nine (săt′ẽr·nīn), *adj.* [F. *saturnin.*] **1.** [*cap.*] Saturnian (sense 2); born under Saturn. **2.** Heavy; grave; gloomy; dull; — the opposite of *mercurial;* as, a *saturnine* person or temper. **3.** Of, pertaining to, or resembling lead; also, affected by lead poisoning. — **Syn.** See SULLEN. — **sat'ur·nine·ly,** *adv.*

‖Sat'ya·gra'ha (sŭt'yȧ·grŭ'hȧ), *n.* [Lit., truth-grasping, fr. Skr. *satya* + *graha.*] *India.* A politico-religious movement initiated in 1919, favoring passive resistance and non-co-operation as means of opposing abuses.

sat'yr (săt'ẽr; sā'tẽr), *n.* [L. *satyrus,* fr. Gr. *satyros.*] **1.** [*often cap.*] *Gr. Myth.* A sylvan deity or demigod, often depicted with the tail and ears of a horse, given to riotous merriment and lasciviousness. **2. a** A lecherous man. **b** A man having satyriasis. **3.** Any of many brown and gray butterflies (family Agapetidae) often with ocelli on the wings. — **sa·tyr'ic** (sȧ·tĭr'ĭk), **sa·tyr'i·cal** (-ĭ·kăl), *adj.*

sat'y·ri'a·sis (săt'ĭ·rī'ȧ·sĭs), *n.* [NL., fr. Gr. *satyriasis.* See SATYR.] *Med.* Insatiable venereal appetite in the male.

sauce (sôs), *n.* [OF. *sauce, sause,* fr. L. *salsa,* fem. of *salsus* salted, past part. of *salire* to salt, fr. *sal* salt.] **1.** A condiment or composition of condiments eaten with food as a relish; esp., a fluid dressing for meat, fish, puddings, etc. **2.** A thing which adds piquancy or zest. **3.** *Colloq.* Sauciness. **4.** *Dial.* (*dial.* sôs, säs, săs). Any garden vegetable eaten with meat; — called also ***garden sauce.*** **5.** *U. S.* Stewed or preserved fruit; as, apple *sauce.* — *v. t.;* SAUCED (sôst); SAUC'ING (sôs'ĭng). **1.** To dress (food) with a sauce; also, to season, flavor, etc. **2.** To temper, as with a condiment, the severity or harshness of. **3.** To make poignant, pungent, or sharp; give zest. **4.** *Colloq.* To be saucy to.

sauce'box' (-bŏks'), *n.* *Colloq.* A saucy person; a pert child.

sauce'pan' (-păn'), *n.* A small metal vessel with a handle, used for stewing, etc., orig. for cooking sauce.

sau'cer (sô'sẽr), *n.* [OF. *saussier, saussiere,* fr. *sausse.* See SAUCE.] **1.** A small shallow dish in which a cup is set at table. **2.** A saucerlike or saucer-shaped thing.

sau'cy (sô'sĭ), *adj.;* SAU'CI·ER (-sĭ·ẽr); SAU'CI·EST. [From SAUCE.] Showing impertinent boldness or forwardness; impudent; pert. — **sau'ci·ly,** *adv.* — **sau'ci·ness,** *n.*

sauer'kraut' (sour'krout'), *n.* [G., fr. *sauer* sour + *kraut* cabbage.] Cabbage cut fine and allowed to ferment in a brine made of its own juice with salt.

sau'ger (sô'gẽr), *n.* A pike perch (*Cynoperca canadensis*) similar to the walleye, but smaller.

saugh (souк; sôк; säк), *n.* *Chiefly Scot.* The sallow.

Saul (sôl), *n.* [LL. *Saul, Saulus,* fr. Gr. *Saulos,* fr. Heb. *Shā'ūl.*] *Bib.* **a** The first king of Israel. **b** The original name of the apostle Paul; — often **Saul of Tar'sus** (tär'sŭs).

sau'na (sou'nȧ), *n.* [Finnish.] The Finnish bath in steam from water thrown on heated stones, accompanied by stroking with cedar or birch boughs; also, the bathhouse.

saun'ter (sôn'tẽr; sän'-), *v. i.* To walk about idly; stroll slowly or aimlessly. — **saun'ter·er** (-ẽr), *n.*

sau'rel (sô'rĕl), *n.* [F.] Any of a genus (*Trachurus*) of carangoid fishes (esp. *T. trachurus* and *T. symmetricus*) of Europe and America.

sau'ri·an (sô'rĭ·ăn), *n.* [Gr. *saura, sauros,* a lizard.] One of a group (Sauria) of reptiles, including the lizards, and in older classifications the crocodiles and various extinct groups of more or less lizardlike form, as the dinosaurs and ichthyosaurs. — *adj.* Belonging to the Sauria; lizardlike.

sau'ro- (sô'rō-), **saur-.** [Gr. *sauros.*] A combining form meaning *lizard.*

sau'ro·pod (-pŏd), *n. & adj.* [*sauro-* + *-pod.*] (One) belonging to a group (Sauropoda) of dinosaurs, consisting of herbivorous forms with a long neck and tail, small head, and more or less plantigrade five-toed limbs. — **sau·rop'o·dous** (sô·rŏp'ō·dŭs), *adj.*

-sau'rus (-sô'rŭs). [NL., fr. Gr. *sauros.*] *Zool. & Paleontol.* A suffix meaning *lizard,* used in names of genera. Corresponding names of families, classes, etc., are formed in **-sau'ri·dae, -sau'ri·a,** and of individuals in **-sau'rid, -saur.** Derivative adjectives are formed in **-sau'ri·an.**

sau'ry (sô'rĭ), *n.; pl.* -RIES (-rĭz). [NL. *saurus.* See -SAURUS.] A slender long-beaked fish (*Scombresox saurus*) related to the flying fishes, and found in the temperate parts of the Atlantic.

sau'sage (sô'sĭj), *n.* [ONF. *saussiche* (OF. & F. *saucisse*), fr. VL. *salsicia,* fr. L. *salsus* salted.] **1.** Meat (esp. pork) minced and highly seasoned, and commonly enclosed in a prepared intestine of some animal. **2.** Also **sausage balloon.** *Army Slang.* An elongated captive observation balloon.

sau·té' (sō·tā'), *adj.* [F., past part. of *sauter,* prop., to jump.] *Cookery.* Fried lightly and quickly in a little hot fat while being frequently turned over. Hence: **sau·té',** *v. t.;* SAU·TÉED' (-tād'); SAU·TÉ'ING. — *n.* A sautéed dish.

sau·terne' (sō·tûrn'; *as if F.,* sō'tẽrn'), *n.* Also **sau·ternes'** (sō·tûrn'; *F.* sō'tẽrn'). [From *Sauternes,* Gironde, France.] A variety of sweet white wine. See BORDEAUX, YQUEM.

‖sauve qui peut (sōv' kē pû'). [F.] Save himself who can; hence, a complete rout.

sav'age (săv'ĭj), *adj.* [OF. *sauvage,* fr. L. *silvaticus* belonging to a wood, wild, fr. *silva* a wood.] **1.** Of or pertaining to the forest; in a state of nature; wild. **2.** Untamed; not domesticated; as, *savage* beasts. **3.** *Archaic.* Uncultivated; growing wild. **4.** Uncivilized; barbarous; also, unpolished; rude. **5.** Cruel; fierce; ferocious. — **Syn.** See FIERCE; BARBARIAN. — *n.* **1.** A human being living in a state little removed from that of animals; one completely uncivilized. **2.** A savage, or brutal, person; also, one lacking in civility or manners. — *v. t.* To attack savagely; to treat with savagery. — **sav'age·ly,** *adv.* — **sav'age·ness,** *n.*

sav'age·ry (săv'ĭj·rĭ), *n.; pl.* -RIES (-rĭz). **1.** Savage disposition, action, or act. **2.** State of being savage, or uncivilized. Cf. BARBARISM, CIVILIZATION. **3.** Savages or savage beasts collectively.

sav'ag·ism (săv'ĭj·ĭz'm), *n.* Savagery.

sa·van'na, sa·van'nah (sȧ·văn'ȧ), *n.* [Sp. *zavana* (now *sabana*), fr. Taino *zabana.*] **1.** A treeless plain; an open, level region, esp. in Florida. **2.** *Biogeog.* A tropical or subtropical grassland containing scattered trees and drought-resistant undergrowth.

sa·vant' (să·vän'; să·vänt'), *n.; pl.* SAVANTS (să·vänz'; să·vänts'). [F., fr. *savoir* to know, fr. L. *sapere.*] A man of learning; one versed in literature or science; a scholar.

save (sāv), *v. t.* [OF. *salver, sauver,* fr. LL. *salvare,* fr. *salvus* saved, safe.] **1.** To make safe; to rescue or deliver from danger. **2.** To preserve; safeguard; — often with *from* and in phrases such as ***save appearances, save face,*** etc. **3.** To avoid losing by being in time; catch; as, to *save* the mail. **4.** To rescue from evil life; reclaim; also, to redeem; as, to *save* sinners. **5.** To lay by; hoard; as, to *save* money. **6.** To keep from being spent, wasted, or lost; as, to *save* one's time or strength. **7.** To reserve (for a special purpose, use, etc.); to preserve by careful or sparing use. **8.** To avoid or enable (one) to avoid; as, to *save* one labor. — **Syn.** See RESCUE. — *v. i.* **1.** To preserve something from danger, destruction, loss, waste, etc. **2.** To lay by money or goods. **3.** To keep; last; as, food that will *save.* — ***save, or saving, your reverence.*** An apology for an unseemly expression made in the presence of a priest or clergyman. — **sav'a·ble** (sāv'ȧ·b'l), **save'a·ble,** *adj.* — **sav'er** (sāv'ẽr), *n.*

save, *prep.* [F. *sauf,* prop. adj., safe.] *Archaic.* **1.** With the exception of; not including. **2.** Except; but; as, no duties *save* to eat and sleep. — *conj.* **1.** Were it not that; also, unless; — now usually with *that.* **2.** But; except; — followed by a pronoun in the nominative.

save'-all', *n.* Any of various devices for saving waste, loss, or injury; as: **a** Overalls. **b** A child's bank. **c** A receptacle for leakage, waste products, etc.

sav'e·loy (săv'ĕ·loi), *n.* [F. *cervelas,* fr. It. *cervellata,* fr. *cervello* brain, fr. L. *cerebellum,* dim. of *cerebrum* brain.] A form of ready-cooked, highly seasoned pork sausage.

sav'in, sav'ine (săv'ĭn), *n.* [From late AS. *safine, savine* and OF. *savine,* fr. L. *sabina* savin.] **a** A Eurasian juniper (*Juniperus sabina*) with dark foliage and small yellowish-green berries. **b** Either of two North American junipers, *J. virginiana* and *J. horizontalis.*

sav'ing (sāv'ĭng), *adj.* That saves; as: **a** Preserving; rescuing; esp., *Theol.,* leading to salvation; as, *saving* grace. **b** Economizing; frugal; economical. **c** Offsetting or compensating; as, one *saving* quality, its humor. **d** Making reservation or exception; as, a *saving* clause. — *n.* **1.** Act of saving. **2.** Economy in outlay or cost; as, a *saving* of ten per cent. **3.** That which is saved; specif., *pl.,* sums saved from time to time, and kept unexpended. **4.** *Chiefly Law.* Exception; reservation. — **sav'ing·ly,** *adv.*

sav'ing, *prep. & conj.* Save; except.

sav'ings bank (sāv'ĭngz). A bank the business of which is to receive and invest small deposits, and pay compound interest thereon.

sav'ior, sav'iour (sāv'yẽr), *n.* [OF. *sauveour, salveor,* fr. LL. *salvator,* fr. *salvare* to save.] **1.** One who saves or delivers. **2.** [*cap.*] In this sense **Saviour.** Jesus Christ, the Redeemer.

‖sa'voir'-faire' (sȧ'vwȧr'fâr'), *n.* [F.] Literally, knowing how to do; readiness in doing, saying, etc., the proper or graceful thing. — **Syn.** See TACT.

‖sa'voir'-vi'vre (-vē'vr'), *n.* [F.] Literally, knowing how to live; good breeding; social ease and grace.

sa'vor, sa'vour (sā'vẽr), *n.* [OF. *savor, savour,* fr. L. *sapor.* See SAGE, *adj.*] **1. a** That property of a thing which affects the organs of taste or (less often) smell; taste and odors; flavor; relish. **b** A distinguishing taste or smell. **2.** Distinctive quality; characteristic property. **3.** Power to arouse interest or zest; as, a book without *savor.* **4.** *Archaic.* Repute. Cf. ODOR. — **Syn.** See TASTE. — *v. i.* **1.** To have the distinctive taste, smell or quality of; smack; — with *of.* — *v. t.* **1.** To impart flavor, scent, tone, or the like, to. **2.** To have the flavor or quality of; to indicate presence of. **3.** To taste or smell with pleasure; delight in; hence, to appreciate discriminatingly. — **sa'vor·er, sa'vour·er,** *n.* — **sa'vor·less, sa'vour·less,** *adj.* — **sa'vor·ous,** *adj.*

sa'vor·y, sa'vour·y (sā'vẽr·ĭ), *adj.;* -I·ER (-ĭ·ẽr); -I·EST. **1.** Having a grateful savor; appetizing. **2.** Hence, agreeable; piquant. — **sa'vor·i·ness, sa'vour·i·ness,** *n.*

sa'vor·y, *n.* Also **sa'vour·y.** [Appar. through OF., fr. L. *satureia;* influenced by *savory,* adj.] **1.** An aromatic European mint (*Satureia hortensis*), much used in cooking; — called also ***summer savory.*** **2.** [From SAVORY, *adj.*] *Brit.* A small highly seasoned dish served as a course at the end of a dinner, in contrast to the sweet.

sa·voy' (sȧ·voi'), *n.* [F. *chou de Savoie* cabbage of Savoy.] *Hort.* A cabbage of a race having compact heads and wrinkled and curled leaves.

Sa·voy'ard (sȧ·voi'ẽrd; *F.* sȧ'vwȧ'yȧr'), *n.* **1.** A native or inhabitant of Savoy. In Europe, Savoyards are well known as itinerants with hurdy-gurdy and monkey. **2.** An ardent admirer, actor, producer, etc., of Gilbert and Sullivan operas, most of which were first produced at the Savoy Theatre, London. — **Sa·voy'ard,** *adj.*

saw (sô), *n.* [AS. *sagu.*] A saying; proverb; maxim.

saw, *n.* [AS. *sagu, sage.*] **1.** A cutting tool or instrument, with a thin flat blade having a continuous series of teeth on the edge. **2.** Any of various analogous tools or devices without teeth, which cut by wearing out a kerf. **3.** A tool or machine having a saw (senses 1 and 2) for cutting. — *v. t.;* SAWED (sôd); SAWED or SAWN (sôn); SAW'ING. **1.** To cut or separate with a saw. **2.** To form by cutting with a saw. **3.** To rend or slice (as the air with one's arms) with motions suggestive of those made in sawing; also, to produce by similar movements of a bow; as, to *saw* out a tune on a violin. — *v. i.* **1.** To use a saw. **2.** To cut, as a saw. **3.** To be cut with a saw. — **saw'er** (sô'ẽr), *n.*

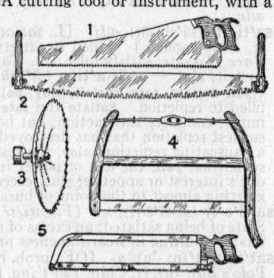

Saws. 1 Ripsaw; 2 Two-man Saw; 3 Concave Circular, or Buzz, Saw; 4 Bucksaw; 5 Butcher's Saw.

saw, *past tense* of SEE.

saw'buck' (sô'bŭk'), *n.* [D. *zaagbok.*] *U. S.* **a** A sawhorse. **b** *Slang.* A ten-dollar bill.

saw'dust' (-dŭst'), *n.* Dust or small fragments of wood, stone, etc., made by the cutting of a saw.

saw'fish' (-fĭsh'), *n.;* see FISH. Any of several sharklike viviparous rays (genus *Pristis*) having a flattened elongate snout with a row of toothlike structures along each edge. They live principally in tropical America and Africa. They reach a length of from ten to twenty feet. See 1st RAY.

saw'fly' (-flī'), *n.* Any of numerous hymenoptera chiefly of the family Tenthredinidae or the superfamily Tenthredinoidea, the female of which usually has an ovipositor with a pair of sawlike organs.

saw grass. Any of certain sedges (esp., any species of *Cladium*) having the leaf edges set with sharp teeth.

saw'horse' (sô'hôrs'), *n.* A form of rack on which wood is laid for sawing by hand, orig. one with X-shaped ends.

saw log. A log of suitable size for sawing into lumber.

saw'mill' (sô'mĭl'), *n.* A mill or machine for sawing logs.

sawn (sôn), *past part. & part. adj.* of SAW.

saw palmetto. **a** A stemless palm (*Serenoa serrulata*) of the southern U. S. **b** A similar palm (*Paurotis wrightii*) of the West Indies and Florida.

saw pit. See SAWYER, 1.

saw set. An instrument used to give set to saw teeth.

saw'-toothed' (sô'tōōtht'), *adj.* Having a tooth or teeth like those of a saw; serrate.

saw'yer (sô'yẽr), *n.* [*saw* + *-yer* as in *lawyer*.] **1.** One whose occupation is to saw; specif., either of the two men who saw timber over a pit (***saw pit***), one (***top sawyer***) standing above the timber, the other (***bottom, or pit, sawyer***) below it. **2.** Any of several large longicorn beetles whose larvae bore large holes in timber or dead trees.

sax'a·tile (săk'sȧ·tĭl; 56), *adj.* [L. *saxatilis*, fr. *saxum* a rock.] Pertaining to rocks; saxicoline.

Saxe'-Co'burg and Go'tha, House of (săks'kō'bûrg, gō'tȧ). The royal family of Great Britain 1901 to 1917, during the reign of Edward VII and part of the reign of George V. See WINDSOR, HOUSE OF.

sax'horn' (săks'hôrn'), *n.* [After Antoine *Sax* of Belgium and Paris, who invented it (c. 1840).] *Music.* One of a family of brass-wind instruments with valves, characterized by fullness and evenness of tone, large compass, and simple manipulation. The alto saxhorn is the *althorn* (which see).

sax·ic'o·line (săks·ĭk'ō·lĭn; -līn), *adj.* Also **sax·ic'o·lous** (-lŭs). [L. *saxum* rock + *colere* to inhabit.] *Bot. & Zool.* Inhabiting or growing among rocks.

sax'i·frage (săk'sĭ·frĭj), *n.* [OF., fr. L. *saxifraga*, fr. *saxifragus* rock-breaking, fr. *saxum* rock + *frangere* to break.] Any of a genus (*Saxifraga*) or of its related genus (*Micranthes*) of plants with showy pentamerous flowers and often with basal, tufted leaves. The genus *Saxifraga* typifies a family (Saxifragaceae, the saxifrage family) of widely distributed herbs of arctic and temperate regions. — **sax'i·fra·ga'ceous** (-frȧ·gā'shŭs), *adj.*

Sax'on (săk's'n), *n.* [OF., fr. LL. *Saxo*, pl. *Saxones*, of Teut. origin.] **1. a** One of a Germanic people who dwelt in what is now Holstein. They, with the Angles and Jutes, conquered and colonized most of England. **b** One of the Saxon or Anglian conquerors of England; an Anglo-Saxon. **c** One of the people of modern Saxony. **2.** The language of the Saxons. ***Old Saxon***, or the language of the original Saxon tribes, and ***Anglo-Saxon***, the language of the Saxons of England, are Low German tongues. The language of modern Saxony is High German. See INDO-EUROPEAN LANGUAGES, *Table.* — *adj.* **a** Of or pertaining to the Saxons, their country, or their language. **b** Anglo-Saxon. — **Sax'on·ism** (-ĭz'm), *n.*

Sax'o·ny (săk'sō·nĭ), *n.* **1.** A glossy woolen fabric. **2.** A fine, closely twisted knitting yarn.

sax'o·phone (săk'sō·fōn), *n.* [Antoine *Sax*, the inventor (see SAXHORN) + Gr. *phōnē* tone.] *Music.* A wind instrument combining the reed mouthpiece of a clarinet with a bent conical tube of metal, equipped with finger keys. — **sax'o·phon'ist** (-fōn'ĭst; *esp. Brit.*, săk·sŏf'ō·nĭst), *n.*

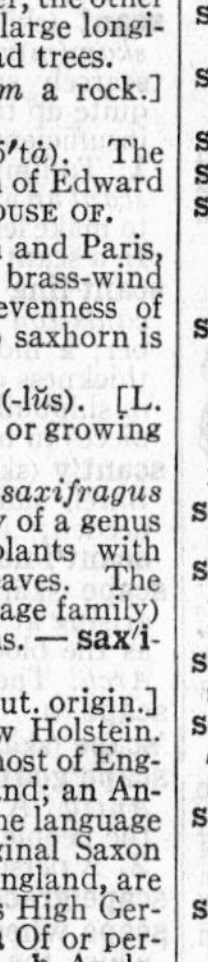

Alto Saxophone.

sax'tu'ba (săks'tū'bȧ), *n.* [See SAXHORN; TUBA.] A saxhorn, esp. one of the larger sizes.

say (sā), *n. & v. t.* [For *assay*.] *Obs.* = ASSAY.

say, *v. t.*; SAID (sĕd), from AS. *sægde*; SAY'ING. [AS. *secgan*.] **1.** To utter or give utterance to; as, to *say* yes. **2.** To express in words; tell; speak; declare. **3.** To state, or be able to state, positively; to declare with assurance; as, no one can *say* where he is. **4.** To repeat; recite; as, to *say* one's prayers. **5.** To suggest as an estimate; — in the imperative, let us assume; as, he has, *say* fifty thousand dollars. **6.** To state as common opinion or belief; as, it is *said* to be so. — *v. i.* To speak; declare; make a statement. — *n.* **1.** That which is said or to be said; esp., the opportunity to express an opinion; as, to have one's *say*. **2. a** One's turn to say or do something; a voice; as, to have a *say* in an affair. **b** *U. S.* With *the*. The power of final decision; as, who has the *say* in this matter? — **say'er** (sā'ẽr), *n.*

sa'yid (sī'ĭd; sä'yĭd), *n.* Also **say'yid** (sī'yĭd). [Ar. *sayyid*.] Lord; prince; — a Moslem title applied esp. to a descendant of Mohammed through his daughter Fatima and cousin Ali.

say'ing (sā'ĭng), *n.* That which is said; a statement, esp. a proverbial one; aphorism.

says (sĕz; 4), *pres. indic. 3d pers. sing.* of SAY, to utter.

say'-so' (sā'sō'), *n.* *Colloq.* **a** One's unsupported assertion. **b** Right of final decision; say. **c** An authoritative direction; a dictum.

'sblood (z'blŭd), *interj.* *Archaic.* An abbreviation of *God's blood*; — used as an oath.

scab (skăb), *n.* [ME. *scab*, *scabbe*, of Scand. origin.] **1.** A crust over a sore, wound, etc. **2.** *Slang.* A dirty, paltry fellow; a scoundrel. **3.** *Trade-Unionism.* A workman who works for lower wages than, or under conditions contrary to, those prescribed by the trade-union; also, one who takes the place of a striker. **4.** *Plant Pathol.* **a** Any of various bacterial or fungous diseases frequently characterized by crustlike spots. **b** One of the crustlike spots in any of these diseases. **5.** *Veter.* The mange. — *v. i.*; SCABBED (skăbd); SCAB'BING. **1.** To become covered with a scab. **2.** To work as a scab.

scab'bard (skăb'ẽrd), *n.* [AF. *escaubers*, *escauberz*, pl., *escalberc*, sing., through OF. fr. OHG.] A sheath for a sword, dagger, etc. — *v. t.* To put in a scabbard.

scab'ble (skăb''l), *v. t.* To dress roughly, as stone.

scab'by (skăb'ĭ), *adj.*; SCAB'BI·ER (-ĭ·ẽr); SCAB'BI·EST. **1.** Covered with, full of, or consisting of scabs. **2.** Diseased with the scab. **3.** *Colloq.* Mean; shabby; contemptible; stingy. — **scab'bi·ly**, *adv.* — **scab'bi·ness**, *n.*

sca'bi·es (skā'bĭ·ēz), *n.* [L.] The itch; mange. — **sca'bi·et'ic** (-ĕt'ĭk), *adj.*

sca'bi·o'sa (skā'bĭ·ō'sȧ; skăb'ĭ-), *n.* [NL. See SCABIOUS, *n.*] Any of a genus (**Sca'bi·o'sa**) of herbs of the teasel family (Dipsacaceae) having terminal flower heads subtended by a leafy involucre. See SCABIOUS, *n.*

sca'bi·ous (skā'bĭ·ŭs), *adj.* [F. or L.; F. *scabieux*, fr. L. *scabiosus*, fr. *scabies* itch.] **1.** Scabby. **2.** Pertaining to, or like, scabies; as, *scabious* eruptions.

sca'bi·ous, *n.* [ML. *scabiosa* (sc. *herba*); — because supposed to be a remedy for scabies.] Any scabiosa, esp. the ***sweet scabious*** (*S. atropurpurea*), and the ***field scabious*** (*S. arvensis*).

sca'brous (skā'brŭs), *adj.* [LL. *scabrosus*, fr. L. *scaber* rough.] **1.** Rough to the touch, like a file; scurfy; scaly. **2. a** Beset with difficulties; knotty. **b** Risqué; salacious. — **Syn.** See ROUGH. — **sca'brous·ly**, *adv.* — **sca'brous·ness**, *n.*

scads (skădz), *n. pl.* *Slang, U. S.* **a** Money. **b** An exceedingly large quantity or number.

scaf'fold (skăf'ŭld; -ōld), *n.* [OF. *escafaut*.] **1.** An elevated and, usually, temporary platform; specif.: **a** One to support workmen, tools, etc., as in building. **b** One on which a criminal is executed. **c** *Hist.* An out-of-door stage. **2.** *U. S.* A loft for grain. **3.** Scaffolding.

scaf'fold·ing, *n.* A scaffold or system of scaffolds; also, materials for scaffolds.

scagl·io'la (skăl·yō'lȧ), *n.* [It. *scagliuola*.] A gypsum and glue imitation of ornamental stone.

scal'a·ble (skāl'ȧ·b'l), *adj.* Capable of being scaled.

sca·lade' (skȧ·lād'), *n.* *Obs.* = ESCALADE.

scal'age (skāl'ĭj), *n.* **1.** An allowance or percentage by which anything is scaled down, as listed weights, to compensate for shrinkage. **2.** Act of scaling in weight, quantity, or dimensions. **3.** The amount that logs or timber scale or measure.

sca'lar (skā'lẽr), *adj.* [L. *scalaris*. See SCALE ladder.] **1.** Describable by a number; that can be represented by a point on a scale; as, a *scalar* quantity. **2.** *Math.* Of or relating to a scalar, a process using scalars, or the product of a process using scalars. — *n.* *Math.* In vector analysis and quaternions, an undirected quantity; a quantity fully described by a number; — disting. from a *vector*.

sca·la're (skȧ·lâr'ē; -lä'rā), *n.* [NL., fr. L. *scalaris* like a ladder.] See ANGELFISH **c**.

sca·lar'i·form (skȧ·lăr'ĭ·fôrm), *adj.* [L. *scalaris* like a ladder + *-form*.] Resembling a ladder; having bars or markings like the rounds of a ladder; as, *scalariform* cells in plants.

sca·la'tion (skā·lā'shŭn), *n.* *Zool.* Structure and arrangement of scales.

scal'a·wag, scal'la·wag (skăl'ȧ·wăg), *n.* **1.** *Colloq.* A scamp. **2.** *Slang, U. S.* A white Southerner who acted as a Republican during the reconstruction period after the Civil War.

scald, skald (skôld; skäld), *n.* [ON. *skāld*.] One of the ancient Scandinavian poets and historiographers; a Norse reciter of heroic poems, eulogies, etc.

scald (skôld), *v. t.* [ONF. *escalder* (OF. *eschalder*), fr. LL. *excaldare*, fr. *ex* + *calidus* warm, hot.] **1.** To burn with, or as if with, hot liquid or steam. **2.** To bring to a temperature just below the boiling point. **3.** To subject to the action of boiling water. — *v. i.* To scald something; to pain, as if scalded. — *n.* **1.** A scalding; a burn or injury caused by scalding. **2.** *Plant Pathol.* **a** Any of several parasitic diseases; as, cranberry *scald*. **b** A burning and browning of plant tissues as a result of intense heat, and sometimes also of intense light.

scald, scalled (skôld), *adj.* [From *scall*.] Scabby; scurvy.

scald (skôld), *n.* *Obs.* Scurf; morbid scab.

scale (skāl), *n.* [ON. *skāl* bowl, balance.] **1.** Either dish of a balance; hence, usually *pl.*, the balance itself; a weighing machine. **2.** That which evaluates or determines alternatives; as, the *scales* of Justice. **3.** [*cap.*] *pl. Astron.* The sign or constellation Libra. — *v. t. & i.* **1.** To weigh or be weighed in scales. **2.** To have a weight (of); weigh.

scale, *n.* [ME. *scale*, *skale*, fr. OF. *escale* cup, husk (F. *écale* husk, chip), fr. the Teutonic stems of SHALE and 1st SCALE.] **1. a** A small, flattened, rigid plate forming part of the external body covering, esp. of fishes and reptiles. **b** Such scales collectively. **2.** Any small, thin, dry lamina shed from the skin, as in many skin diseases. **3.** Any lamina, layer, or leaf suggestive of a fish scale. **4.** A thin coating, covering, film, or incrustation. **5.** Short for SCALE INSECT. **6.** *Bot.* **a** Also **scale leaf**. One of the scalelike leaves serving in most seed plants to protect a bud before expansion. **b** Any thin, membranous, chaffy, or woody bract. **7.** *Metal.* Formerly *pl.* The black scaly coating of oxide (esp. magnetic oxide, Fe_3O_4) on the surface of heated iron; also, a similar coating upon other metals. — *v. t.* **1.** To strip or clear of scales or scale. **2.** To take off in thin layers or scales; to pare off. **3.** To form into scales or to form scale on; cover with scales. **4.** To throw, as a thin, flat stone, so that the edge cuts the air or so that it skips on a water surface. **5.** *Chiefly Scot.* To disperse. — *v. i.* **1.** To separate and come off in scales. **2.** To shed scales. **3.** To become incrusted with a hard deposit, as a boiler.

scale, *n.* [It. or L.; It. *scala*, fr. L. *scala*, usually *pl.* *scalae*, staircase, ladder.] **1.** A ladder; a rung; a series of steps; — now, figuratively, a means of ascent. **2.** Anything graduated, esp. when used as a measure or rule (see VERNIER, *Illust.*) specif.: **a** A series of spaces marked by lines, representing proportionately larger distances, or registering something, as the height of mercury (see THERMOMETER, *Illust.*); esp., a divided line on a map, chart, indicating the scale (sense 4) by which distances can be measured. **b** A mathematical instrument, consisting of a slip of wood, ivory, or metal, with one or more sets of spaces graduated and numbered on its surface, for measuring or laying off distances, dimensions, etc. **c** A basis for a numeral system; as, the decimal *scale*. **3.** A progressive graduated series; a graded system from the lowest to the highest; as, a *scale* of wages; buying stocks on a *scale*; also, a degree, point, or grade on such a scale; as, a low *scale* of existence. **4.** Relative dimensions, without difference in proportion of parts; esp., proportion in dimensions between a drawing, map, etc., and that represented; as, drawn to a *scale* of one inch to a mile. **5.** Scalage. **6.** *Educ. & Psychol.* A graded series of tests or of performances used in rating individual intelligence or achievement. **7.** *Music.* A graduated series of tones, ascending or descending in order of pitch according to a specified scheme of their intervals. — *v. t.* **1.** To climb by, or as if by, a ladder; ascend by climbing. **2.** To grade; graduate; hence, to judge proportionately. **3.** To reduce according to a fixed ratio or scale; — sometimes with *down*; as, to *scale* down debts, etc. **4.** To measure or estimate the board feet of (logs, timber). — *v. i.* **1.** To afford an ascent; to climb. **2.** To rise in a graduated series. — **Syn.** See ASCEND.

scale'board' (skāl'bōrd'; *colloq.* skăb'ẽrd), *n.* [*scale* plate, layer + *board*.] A very thin board; specif.: **a** *Print.* A very thin slip of wood or cardboard formerly used in justifying. **b** A thin leaf of wood used for veneering, for splints, etc.

scale insect. Any of numerous small but very prolific homopterous insects (family Coccidae), the young of which suck the juices of plants. Certain of these insects produce lac; others yield dyes, as cochineal; and many are garden pests. See LOUSE, 2; LAC· COCHINEAL.

scale leaf. See 2d SCALE, *n.*, 6 **a**.

scale moss. Any foliose hepatic or liverwort; — from the imbricated scalelike leaves.

sca·lene′ (skā·lēn′), *adj.* [LL. *scalenus*, fr. Gr. *skalēnos*.] **1.** *Geom.* **a** Having the sides and angles unequal; — of a triangle. See TRIANGLE, *Illust.* **b** Having the axis inclined to the base; as, a *scalene* cone. **2.** *Anat.* Designating or pertaining to a muscle (**scalene muscle**, *or* **sca·le′nus** [skā·lē′nŭs]), one of certain deeply situated muscles, each of which extends from cervical vertebrae to the first or second rib.

scal′er (skāl′ẽr), *n.* **1.** One who or that which scales. **2.** *Physics.* An electronic device that operates a recorder after a specified number of impulses appearing too rapidly for individual recording.

scall (skôl), *n.* [ON. *skalli* a bald head.] A scurf.

scal′la·wag (skăl′ȧ·wăg). Var. of SCALAWAG.

scalled (skôld), *adj.* = 3d SCALD.

scal′lion (skăl′yŭn), *n.* [ONF. *escalogne*, fr. L. *Ascalonia* (sc. *caepa* onion), fr. *Ascalo, -onis*, Ascalon (Ashkelon), seaport in Palestine.] **a** The shallot. **b** The leek. **c** Any onion forming a thick basal portion without a bulb.

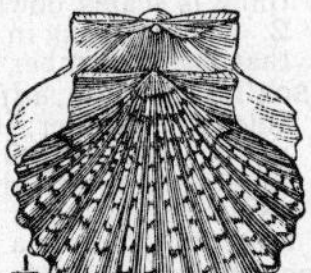

¼

Scallop (*Vola jacobaea*).

scal′lop (skŏl′ŭp; skăl′-), *n.* [OF. *escalope* shell, of Teut. origin.] **1.** **a** Any of numerous marine bivalve mollusks (family Pectinidae) having the shell radially ribbed and the edge undulated. Scallops swim by opening and closing the valves. They have a single large adductor muscle. **b** *Usually pl.* The adductor muscle of any of the edible scallops used as food. **2.** One of the valves of a scallop shell or a similarly shaped dish, used for baking. **3.** One of a continuous series of circle segments, angular projections, or the like, forming a border, as on lace or embroidery. — *v. t.* **1.** To edge with scallops. **2.** *Cookery.* To bake in a scallop (sense 2), casserole, etc., as oysters or tomatoes prepared with bread crumbs and other ingredients; also, to bake in a sauce, as potatoes or fish. — **scal′lop·er**, *n.*

scal′ly·wag (skăl′ĭ·wăg). Var. of SCALAWAG.

scalp (skălp), *n.* [ME., of Scand. origin.] **1.** **a** That part of the integument of the human head usually covered with hair. **b** The corresponding part of many animals, esp. wolves, foxes, etc. **c** A part of the human scalp which North American Indians cut or tore from an enemy as a token of victory. **d** Hence, a trophy of victory. **2.** **a** *Dial.* A projecting mass as of rock or mud. **b** *Poetic.* A mountain cap. **3.** *Finance.* A small profit from scalping. — *v. t.* **1.** To deprive of the scalp. **2.** To buy and sell so as to make small, quick profits; specif., to buy (tickets, etc.), and peddle them at other than official or stated prices. — *v. i.* To make a small, quick profit by slight fluctuations of the market. — **scalp′er**, *n.*

scal′pel (skăl′pĕl), *n.* [L. *scalpellum*, dim. of *scalprum* scalper, knife.] *Surg.* A small, straight knife with a thin blade.

scalp lock. A long tuft of hair left on the crown of the head by the warriors of some tribes of American Indians.

scal′y (skāl′ĭ), *adj.*; SCAL′I·ER (-ĭ·ẽr); SCAL′I·EST. **1.** Covered or abounding with scales, or scale. **2.** That scales, or flakes. **3.** Having, or composed of, scalelike laminae or plates. **4.** Infested with scale insects. **5.** *Slang.* Mean; despicable. — **scal′i·ness** (-ĭ·nĕs; -nĭs), *n.*

scaly anteater. A pangolin (genus *Smutsia*).

scam′mo·ny (skăm′ō·nĭ), *n.* [L. *scammonia, scammonea*, fr. Gr. *skammōnia*.] **1.** A twining species of convolvulus (*Convolvulus scammonia*) of Asia Minor. **2.** A cathartic resin from its root.

scamp (skămp), *n.* A rascal; a worthless fellow. — *v. t.* To perform hastily and imperfectly; to skimp; scant. — **scamp′er**, *n.*

scam′per (skăm′pẽr), *v. i.* [D. or F.; obs. D. *schampen*, fr. OF. *escamper, eschamper*.] To run or move in a quick, hurried manner. — *n.* A scampering; a hasty flight.

scan (skăn), *v. t.*; SCANNED (skănd); SCAN′NING. [L. *scandere, scansum*, to climb, scan.] **1.** *Pros.* To go through (verse) foot by foot distinguishing the metrical structure; recite metrically. **2.** To examine point by point; scrutinize; also, *Colloq.*, to look over hastily; as, to *scan* a newspaper. **3.** *Elec.* In reproducing a television image, to cause (a surface) to be traversed by a rapid succession of narrow lines (**scanning lines**), varying in brightness, into which an image has been resolved by a device for **scanning** (successive exposure of small portions of it), at the transmitting end. In ***mechanical scanning*** the scanning lines are produced by a beam of light directed by a mechanical part, as a rotating perforated disk (**scanning disk**). In ***electrical***, *or* ***electronic, scanning*** the lines are produced by a beam of electrons sweeping over the surface. **4.** *Radar.* To cause (a prescribed region) to be traversed by a directive beam. Cf. SCANNER **b**. — **Syn.** See SCRUTINIZE. — *v. i.* **1.** **a** To scan verse. **b** *Pros.* To conform to or reveal a definite metrical pattern; as, the line will not *scan*. **2.** *Elec.* To scan a surface in reproducing a television image. — *n.* A scanning; also, range of vision. — **scan′na·ble** (skăn′ȧ·b′l), *adj.*

scan′dal (skăn′dăl; -d′l), *n.* [From F. *scandale* and ME. *scandle*, fr. OF. *escandle*; F. & OF. separately fr. LL. *scandalum* stumbling block, temptation, fr. Gr. *skandalon* a trap.] **1.** The distressing effect on others of unseemly or unrighteous conduct; esp., an occasion of another's lapse in faith or morals; as, to give *scandal* to one's children. **2.** Opprobrium, ignominy, or disgrace; as, to the *scandal* of the service. **3.** That which offends established moral conceptions or disgraces all who are associated or involved; as, the mayor's administration is a gross *scandal*. **4.** Defamatory talk; malicious gossip; backbiting; as, untouched by the breath of *scandal*. — **Syn.** See OFFENSE: DISGRACE. — *v. t.*; -DALED (-dăld; -d′ld) or -DALLED; -DAL·ING or -DAL·LING. **1.** *Now Dial.* To defame. **2.** *Obs.* **a** To bring reproach upon. **b** To scandalize. — **scan′dal·mon′ger** (-mŭng′gẽr), *n.*

scan′dal·ize (-īz), *v. t.* To horrify or shock the moral sense of. — **scan′dal·i·za′tion** (-ĭ·zā′shŭn; -ī·zā′-) *n.* — **scan′dal·iz′er** (-īz′ẽr), *n.*

scan′dal·ous (-ŭs), *adj.* **1.** Giving scandal; scandalizing; also, bringing shame or infamy; as, *scandalous* actions. **2.** Defamatory; libelous; as, a *scandalous* story. — **scan′dal·ous·ly**, *adv.*

scan′dent (skăn′dĕnt), *adj.* [L. *scandens, -entis*, pres. part. of *scandere* to climb.] Climbing; as, a *scandent* plant.

scan′di·a (-dĭ·ȧ), *n.* [NL. See SCANDIUM.] *Chem.* Scandium oxide, Sc_2O_3, obtained as a white infusible powder.

scan′dic (skăn′dĭk), *adj.* *Chem.* Of or pert. to scandium.

Scan′di·na′vi·an (skăn′dĭ·nā′vĭ·ăn; -nāv′yăn; 58), *adj.* Of or pertaining to Scandinavia, its peoples, or languages. — *n.* **1.** A native or inhabitant of Scandinavia. **2.** The Scandinavian languages, or any of them; Old Norse. See INDO-EUROPEAN LANGUAGES, *Table*.

scan′di·um (skăn′dĭ·ŭm), *n.* [NL., fr. L. *Scandia* Scandinavia + *-ium* as in sod*ium*.] *Chem.* A rare trivalent metallic element. Symbol, *Sc*; at. no., 21; at. wt., 44.96.

scan′ner (-ẽr), *n.* One that scans; specif.: **a** *Elec.* A scanning disk (see SCAN, *v. t.*, 3). **b** *Radar.* An antenna assembly for emitting signals and intercepting those reflected back as it turns through a prescribed angle.

scan′sion (skăn′shŭn), *n.* *Pros.* Act of scanning.

☞ For scansion signs see PROSODY.

scan·so′ri·al (skăn·sō′rĭ·ăl; 70), *adj.* *Zool.* Pertaining to, capable of, or adapted for, climbing.

scant (skănt; 9), *adj.* [ME. *skant*, fr. ON. *skam(m)t*, neut. of *skam(m)r* short, brief.] **1.** Not full, large, or plentiful; barely or scarcely sufficient; meager. **2.** Wanting a trifle of, or not coming quite up to, the full measure; as, *scant* weight. **3.** Having a small or insufficient supply; — used with *of*. — **Syn.** See MEAGER. — *v. t.* **1.** To limit in number, amount, etc.; to provide scantily; stint; as, to *scant* an allowance of food. **2.** To fail to give in full or in full measure; to make less than is just, exact, etc. — (skănt; *dial.* skänt), *adv. Dial.* In a scant manner; scarcely. — **scant′ly**, *adv.*

scant′ling (skănt′lĭng), *n.* [From earlier *scantillon*, fr. ONF. *escantillon* a sample, pattern.] **1.** A small quantity, amount, or number; a modicum. **2.** Measure or dimensions, esp. of breadth and thickness of timber, stone, etc., in building, or the sizes of frames, etc., in shipbuilding. **3.** A small piece of lumber, esp. one of the upright pieces in house framing; stud.

scant′y (skăn′tĭ), *adj.*; -I·ER (-tĭ·ẽr); -I·EST. [From SCANT, *adj.*] **1.** Barely sufficient; meager; as, a *scanty* diet. **2.** Somewhat less than is needed; insufficient. — **Syn.** See MEAGER. — **scant′i·ly**, *adv.* — **scant′i·ness**, *n.*

scape (skāp), *n.* [L. *scapus* shaft, stem, stalk.] **1.** *Bot.* A peduncle arising at or beneath the surface of the ground in acaulescent plants, as the bloodroot, tulip, etc. **2.** *Zool.* A shaft as of a feather. **3.** *Arch.* The shaft of a column.

scape, *n.* **1.** *Dial.* An escape. **2.** *Obs.* A slip; fault; escapade.

'scape (skāp), *v. t. & i.* To escape; — formerly written *scape*.

scape′goat′ (skāp′gōt′), *n.* [See 'SCAPE to escape.] **1.** *Jewish Antiq.* A goat upon whose head were symbolically placed the sins of the people, after which he was suffered to escape into the wilderness. **2.** A person or thing bearing blame for others.

scape′grace′ (-grās′), *n.* An incorrigible rascal.

scape wheel. *Horol.* The wheel in an escapement into the teeth of which the pallets play.

scaph′oid (skăf′oid), *adj.* [Gr. *skaphē* boat + *-oid*.] Boat-shaped. — *n.* *Anat.* The navicular of the carpus or tarsus.

scapi-. [L. *scapus*.] A combining form meaning *stalk, shaft*, as in **sca′pi·form, sca·pig′er·ous.** See -FORM; -GEROUS.

scap′o·lite (skăp′ō·līt), *n.* [Gr. *skapos* staff, shaft + *-lite*.] *Mineral.* Any of a group (**scapolite group**) of minerals consisting essentially of aluminum, calcium, and sodium; specif., a species containing 46 to 54 per cent of silica; — called also *wernerite*.

sca′pose (skā′pōs), *adj.* [1st *scape* + *-ose*.] *Bot.* Scape-bearing; resembling, or consisting of, a scape.

scapul-. = SCAPULO- (which see), as in **scap′u·lal′gi·a.**

scap′u·la (skăp′ū·lȧ), *n.*; *pl.* SCAPULAE (-lē), SCAPULAS (-lȧz). [L.] *Anat. & Zool.* The shoulder blade; in most mammals the principal, or sometimes the only, bone of the pectoral arch. See THORAX, *Illust.*

scap′u·lar (-lẽr), *adj.* Of or pertaining to the shoulder, the scapula, or scapulars. — *n.* [F. and ML.; F. *scapulaire*, fr. ML. *scapularium, scapulare*, fr. L. *scapula* shoulder blade.] **1.** *Eccl.* **a** In a monk's habit, a sleeveless outer garment which falls from the shoulders. **b** A badge of membership in an order, usually worn over the shoulders. **2.** *Surg.* A bandage passing over the shoulder to support it, or to retain another bandage in place. **3.** **a** *Anat. & Zool.* A scapula. **b** *Zool.* A scapular feather. See BIRD, *Illust.* (14).

scap′u·lar′y (-lẽr′ĭ *or, esp. Brit.*, -lẽr·ĭ), *adj. & n.* Scapular.

scap′u·lo- (skăp′ū·lō-). [From SCAPULA.] A combining form denoting: **a** *Scapula*, as in **scap′u·lo·pex′y.** See -PEXY. **b** *Scapular and*, as in **scap′u·lo·cla·vic′u·lar, scap′u·lo·hu′mer·al, scap′u·lo·spi′nal, scap′u·lo·tho·rac′ic, scap′u·lo·ul′nar, scap′u·lo·ver′te·bral**, etc.

scar (skär), *n.* [ON. *sker* a skerry, cliff.] **a** An isolated or protruding rock. **b** A steep, rocky eminence.

scar, *n.* [OF. *escare* eschar, fr. L. *eschara*, fr. Gr. *eschara* hearth, fireplace, scab. The meaning has been influenced in E. by obs. *scar* crack.] **1.** A mark left by the healing of an injury, burn, ulcer, etc. **2.** A mark or indentation left on a stem or branch by the fall of a leaf; also, *Zool.*, a cicatrix. **3.** A lasting effect of an injury to one's feelings, reputation, etc. — *v. t. & i.*; SCARRED (skärd); SCAR′RING. To mark or become marked with a scar; leave a scar (upon).

scar′ab (skăr′ăb), *n.* [F. *scarabée*, fr. L. *scarabaeus*.] A scarabaeus (beetle or symbol); also, any dung beetle.

scar′a·bae′id (skăr′ȧ·bē′ĭd), *n. & adj.* [L. *scarabaeus* beetle + 2d *-id*.] (One) belonging to a large family (Scarabaeidae) of stout-bodied beetles with lamellate antennae, including the dung beetles, chafers, etc. — **scar′a·bae′an** (-ăn), *adj. & n.* — **scar′a·bae′oid** (-oid), *adj.*

scar′a·bae′us (-ŭs), *n.*; *pl.* -BAEUSES (-ĕz; -ĭz), -BAEI (-bē′ī). [L.] **1.** A large black, or nearly black, dung beetle (*Scarabaeus sacer*) regarded by the ancient Egyptians as symbolic of resurrection and immortality. **2.** *Egyptol.* A conventionalized representation of a scarabaeid; also, a gem cut in this image.

Scarabaeus, 1. (¼)

scar′ab·oid (skăr′ăb·oid), *adj.* **a** *Zool.* Scarabaeoid. **b** Of the nature of, or resembling, a scarabaeus (image).

Scar′a·mouch′ (skăr′ȧ·mouch′; -mōōsh′), *n.* [F. *Scaramouche*, fr. It. *Scaramuccia*, lit., skirmish.] A boastful poltroon, a stock character in old Italian comedy; hence [*sometimes not cap.*], a cowardly buffoon.

scarce (skârs), *adj.* [ONF. *escars*, deriv. of L. *excerptus*, past part. of *excerpere* to pick out, and hence to contract, shorten.] **1.** Deficient in quantity or number compared with the demand; not abundant. **2.** Hard to find; uncommon; rare. — **Syn.** See INFREQUENT. — **Ant.** Abundant. — *adv.* Scarcely (see FLAT, *adj.*, 13). — **scarce′ness**, *n.*

scarce′ly (skârs′lĭ), *adv.* **1.** By a narrow margin; barely; hardly. **2.** Certainly not or, sometimes, probably not; as, you will *scarcely* believe that.

scarce′ment (-mĕnt), *n.* *Engin.* An offset, or retreat, in the thickness of a wall, bank of earth, etc.

scar′ci·ty (skâr′sĭ·tĭ), *n.* Condition of being scarce; scarceness; specif., want of provisions for the support of life; as, a beleaguered city suffers *scarcity.*

scare (skâr), *v. t.* [ON. *skirren,* fr. *skjarr* shy, afraid.] To frighten or strike with sudden fear; alarm. — *v. i.* To be scared; to take alarm. — *n.* Fright; esp., a sudden fright occasioned by a trifle, a misjudgment, etc. — **scar′er** (skâr′ẽr), *n.* — **scar′ing·ly,** *adv.*

scare′crow′ (-krō′), *n.* **1.** An object, usually suggesting a human figure, set up to frighten crows, etc., away from crops; hence, anything terrifying without danger. **2.** A person clad in rags and tatters.

scare′head′ (-hĕd′), *n.* *U.S.* A headline in enormous print.

scare′mon′ger (-mŭng′gẽr), *n.* An alarmist.

scarf (skärf), *n.; pl.* SCARVES (skärvz), SCARFS (skärfs). [ONF. *escarpe,* orig., pilgrim's scrip, of Teut. origin.] **1.** A broad band of fabric worn loosely over the shoulders, about the neck, over the head, or around the waist. **2.** Specif.: **a** A military or official sash, usually indicative of rank. **b** A muffler or tippet. **c** A cravat with broad falling ends. **3.** A runner, as for a dresser. — *v. t.* **1.** To wrap, cover, or adorn, with or as with a scarf. **2.** To wrap or throw on (a scarf or mantle) loosely.

scarf (skärf), *v. t.* [From *scarf* scarf joint, of Scand. origin.] **1.** To unite, as pieces of timber or metal, by a scarf joint. **2.** To form a scarf on the end or edge of, as for a joint. **3.** *Whaling.* To cut scarfs in, and flense. — *n.; pl.* SCARFS. **1.** Either of the chamfered or cut-away ends that fit together to form a scarf joint. **2.** In full **scarf joint.** A joint made by chamfering, halving, notching, or otherwise cutting away, two pieces to correspond to each other and securing them together after overlapping by bolting, riveting, or the like. **3.** *Whaling.* A groove or channel along a whale's body. — **scarf′er,** *n.*

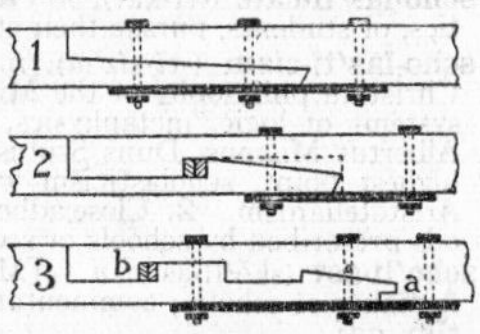

1–3 Forms of Scarf Joints; *a* Cog; *b* Key.

scarf′skin′ (skärf′skĭn′), *n.* *Anat.* The epidermis.

scar′i·fi·ca′tion (skăr′ĭ·fĭ·kā′shŭn), *n.* A scarifying; also, scratches or incisions made by scarifying.

scar′i·fi·ca′tor (skăr′ĭ·fĭ·kā′tẽr), *n.* [NL.] *Med.* An instrument for making slight cuts in the skin.

scar′i·fy (skăr′ĭ·fī), *v. t.* [F. *scarifier,* fr. L. *scarificare, scarifare,* fr. Gr. *skariphasthai* to scratch.] **1.** To scratch or cut the skin of; esp., *Med.,* to make small incisions in, for drawing blood without opening a large vein. **2.** To lacerate, as the feelings. **3.** *Agric.* **a** To stir or pulverize (the surface soil). **b** To scratch (hard-coated seeds) to aid germination. **c** To make cuts in the bark of (a tree). — **scar′i·fi′er** (-fī′ẽr), *n.*

scar′i·ous (skâr′ĭ·ŭs), *adj.* [F. *scarieux,* fr. NL. *scariosus.*] *Bot.* Thin and membranous in texture, as a bract.

scar′la·ti′na (skär′lȧ·tē′nȧ), *n.* [NL.] *Med.* Scarlet fever. — **scar′la·ti′noid** (-tē′noid; skär·lăt′ĭ·noid), *adj.*

scar′let (skär′lĕt; -lĭt), *n.* [ME. *scarlat, scarlet,* prop., a stuff, later, a color, fr. OF. *escarlate,* fr. ML., fr. Ar. *siquillāt.*] **1.** A color, yellowish-red in hue, of very high saturation and medium brilliance. See COLOR. **2.** Scarlet cloth or clothes. — *adj.* **1.** Of the color scarlet. **2.** Whorish; — in reference to *Rev.* xvii.

scarlet fever. *Med.* An acute contagious febrile disease caused by a type of streptococcus (*Streptococcus scarlatinae*) and characterized by inflammation of the fauces and a scarlet rash.

scarlet letter. A scarlet A, once used as a mark of adultery.

scarlet runner. Also **scarlet runner bean.** A tropical American high-climbing bean (*Phaseolus coccineus*) with large bright-red flowers and red-and-black seeds.

scarlet tanager. See TANAGER.

Scarlet Woman. The Roman Catholic Church; — an opprobrious epithet in allusion to *Rev.* xvii. 1–6.

scarp (skärp), *n.* [Aphetic for ESCARP.] **1.** *Fort.* The side of a ditch next the parapet. **2.** A steep descent or declivity. — *v. t.* To cut down vertically or to a steep slope.

scart (skärt), *v. t. & i. & n.* *Scot. & Ir.* Scratch; scrape.

scarves (skärvz), *n., pl.* of 1st SCARF.

scar′y (skâr′ĭ), *adj.;* SCAR′I·ER (-ĭ·ẽr); SCAR′I·EST. *Colloq.* Easily scared; timid; also, causing fright; alarming.

scat, scatt (skăt), *n.* [ON. *skattr.*] A tax; tribute.

scath (skăth), etc. Dial. vars. of SCATHE, etc.

scathe (skāṯẖ), *n.* [ON. *skathi* (Dan. *skade,* Sw. *skada*).] *Archaic & Dial.* Harm; damage; injury; hurt; misfortune. — *v. t.* **1.** *Archaic & Dial.* To do harm to; to injure. **2.** To injure by fire; scorch; hence, to assail with withering denunciation. — **scathe′less,** *adj.*

scath′ing (skāṯẖ′ĭng), *adj.* Injuring, as by blasting or burning; as, a *scathing* rebuke. — **scath′ing·ly,** *adv.*

scat′o- (skăt′ō-). [Gr. *skōr, skatos.*] A combining form, meaning *ordure,* as in **sca·toph′a·gous, sca·tos′co·py.**

sca·tol′o·gy (skȧ·tŏl′ō·jĭ), *n.* [*scato-* + *-logy.*] Study of excrement; hence, study of the obscene, esp. in literature. — **scat′o·log′ic** (skăt′ō·lŏj′ĭk), **scat′o·log′i·cal** (-ĭ·kăl), *adj.*

scat′ter (skăt′ẽr), *v. t. & i.* [ME. *scateren, schateren.* See SHATTER.] **1.** To separate and go or send in different directions; disperse. **2.** To dissipate or become dissipated. **3.** To strew or be strewn widely; distribute. **4.** *Obs.* To squander. **5.** *Physics.* **a** To reflect irregularly and diffusely. **b** To diffuse and spread out (radiation).

Syn. Scatter, disperse, dissipate, dispel mean to cause to separate or break up. Scatter may imply a casting at will but more often it suggests the use or operation of force; disperse implies a wider separation of units and a quick breaking up of a mass or assemblage; dissipate implies complete disintegration or dissolution and final disappearance; dispel implies a driving away as if by scattering.

— *n.* A scattering; the extent of dispersion; also, that which is scattered.

— *adj.* Adapted to being scattered or strewn; as, *scatter* rugs.

— **scat′ter·er,** *n.* — **scat′ter·ing·ly,** *adv.*

scat′ter·brain′ (-brān′), **scat′ter·brains′** (-brānz′), *n.* *Colloq.* A person incapable of concentration or attention. — **scat′ter·brained′** (-brānd′), *adj.*

scat′ter·good′ (-gŏŏd′), *n.* One who wastes; a spendthrift.

scat′ter·ing, *adj.* **1.** Found or placed far apart or at irregular intervals. **2.** Divided among several or many, as votes among candidates.

scaup duck (skôp). [From *scaup,* obs. var. of *scalp.*] Any of certain ducks (genus *Nyroca* and subgenus *Marila*); esp., one (*N. marila*) of northern regions, related to the canvasback and the redhead.

scaur (skär; skôr). Scot. & Ir. var. of SCARE; SCAR.

scav′enge (skăv′ĕnj; -ĭnj), *v. t. & i.;* -ENGED (-ĕnjd; -ĭnjd); -ENG·ING (-ĕn·jĭng; -ĭn·jĭng). [From SCAVENGER.] **1.** To cleanse, as streets, yards, etc., from filth; to clean up filth, esp. street refuse. **2.** *Internal-Combustion Engines.* To remove burned gases from the cylinder after a working stroke. **3.** *Metal.* To clean and purify (molten metal) by taking up foreign elements in chemical union.

scav′en·ger (skăv′ĕn·jẽr; -ĭn·jẽr), *n.* [With intrusive *n* fr. ME. *scavager* an officer with various duties.] A person, animal, or thing that scavenges.

sce·nar′i·o (sē·nâr′ĭ·ō; sē·nä′rĭ·ō; shȧ·nä′-), *n.; pl.* -NARIOS (-ōz). [It.] **1.** (Pl. also SCENARI [shȧ·nä′rē]) An outline or synopsis of a play, the book of an opera, etc., showing the scenes and the entrances and exits of the actors. **2.** *Motion Pictures & Television.* The plot of a play prepared for production of a film or live show, showing its development scene by scene and giving essential details for acting. Cf. SCREENPLAY.

sce·nar′ist (sē·nâr′ĭst; -nä′rĭst), *n.* A writer of scenarios.

scend (sĕnd), *v. i.* [Var. of *send,* taken as aphetic for *ascend.*] *Naut.* To lift or heave upward, esp. in a seaway. Cf. PITCH, *v. i.,* 5. — *n.* The upward movement of a pitching vessel.

scene (sēn), *n.* [F. *scène,* fr. L. *scena, scaena,* fr. Gr. *skēnē* a covered place, tent, stage.] **1.** One of the divisions of a drama; esp.: **a** A division of an act during which there is no change of place or lapse in continuity of time. **b** A part of a drama or narrative presenting a single situation, dialogue, or the like; an episode. **2.** The place in which the action of a play, story, etc., is laid; hence, place of occurrence or action; setting. **3.** Something viewed as a whole or as a detached unit; as, a sylvan *scene;* the American *scene.* **4.** Stage setting or scenery; — often *pl.;* as, behind the *scenes.* **5.** One of a series of actions and events, esp. as represented in literature or art. **6.** An exhibition of strong feeling; sometimes, an affected demonstration. **7.** *Hist.* The stage on which a play is exhibited.

scen′er·y (sēn′ẽr·ĭ), *n.* **1.** The painted scenes or hangings of a stage, with their accessories. **2.** The general aspect of a landscape; the array of impressive natural prospects and imposing features of a particular place.

sce′nic (sē′nĭk; sĕn′ĭk), *adj.* **1.** Of or pertaining to the stage, a stage setting, or stage representation; as, *scenic* effects. **2.** Of or pertaining to natural scenery; picturesque; as, *scenic* marvels. **3.** Representing graphically an action, event, or episode; as, a *scenic* bas-relief.

sce′ni·cal (sē′nĭ·kăl; sĕn′ĭ-), *adj.* Scenic.

sce·nog′ra·phy (sē·nŏg′rȧ·fĭ), *n.* [From L., fr. Gr. *skēnographia,* fr. *skēnē* scene, stage + *graphein* to write.] **1.** Art or act of representing in perspective. **2.** Such art applied to the painting of stage scenery, as by the Greeks. — **sce′no·graph′ic** (sē′nō·grăf′ĭk; sĕn′ō-), *adj.*

scent (sĕnt), *v. t.* [ME. *sent,* fr. OF. *sentir* to feel, smell.] **1.** To perceive by the olfactory organs; smell; as, to *scent* game; hence, to get or have an inkling of; as, to *scent* a plot. **2.** To imbue or fill with odor. — *v. i.* To hunt animals by means of the sense of smell. — *n.* **1.** The effluvia from a substance which affect the sense of smell; odor; specif.: **a** The odor left by one (esp. an animal) along one's track; as, the dogs found the *scent;* hence, track leading to discovery; as, to throw one off the *scent.* **b** A characteristic odor. **2.** Power of scenting; sense of smell. **3.** A class, or one of a class, of perfumes. **4.** Bits of paper dropped in the game of hare and hounds. — **Syn.** See SMELL: FRAGRANCE. — **scent′less,** *adj.*

scep′ter, scep′tre (sĕp′tẽr), *n.* [OF. *ceptre, sceptre,* fr. L. *sceptrum,* fr. Gr. *skēptron* staff, scepter.] A baton or staff borne by a sovereign as an emblem of authority; also, royal or imperial authority; sovereignty. — *v. t.;* -TERED or -TRED (-tẽrd); -TER·ING (-tẽr·ĭng) or -TRING (-trĭng). To endow with the scepter; invest with royal authority.

scep′tic (skĕp′tĭk), **scep′ti·cal,** etc. Vars. of SKEPTIC, etc.

schat′chen (shät′ḵĕn), *n.* [Yiddish, fr. NHeb. *shadhkhān.*] A marriage broker, esp. among certain Jews.

sched′ule (skĕd′ūl; *Brit.* shĕd′ūl), *n.* [After ML. *schedula,* fr. ME. & OF. *cedule,* fr. LL. *scedula,* dim. of L. *scheda, scida,* a leaf of paper or papyrus, fr. Gr. *schidē* a split piece of wood, fr. *schizein* to split.] **1.** *Obs.* A document. **2.** A formal list; often, a list, catalogue, or inventory, annexed to a larger document, as to a will. **3.** An appended statement of supplementary details, as accompanying a legal or legislative document; as, *Schedule* D of the tariff bill. **4.** A tabular statement of times of projected operations, recurring events, arriving and departing trains, etc.; a timetable. — *v. t.;* -ULED (-ūld); -UL·ING (-ūl·ĭng). **1.** To form into, or place in, a schedule; as, to *schedule* a new train; to add in a schedule or appendix, as to an act. **2.** *Colloq.* To appoint, assign, or designate to do or receive something at a fixed time in the future. — **sched′u·lar** (skĕd′ū·lẽr; shĕd′-), *adj.*

schee′lite (shā′līt; shē′-), *n.* [After K. W. *Scheele,* Sw. chemist.] *Mineral.* Native calcium tungstate, $CaWO_4$, a source of tungsten and its compounds.

schef′fer·ite (shĕf′ẽr·īt), *n.* [After H. T. *Scheffer* (1710–59), Sw. chemist.] *Mineral.* A brown to black variety of pyroxene, containing manganese and frequently much iron.

Sche·her′a·zade′, Queen (shĕ·hĕr′ȧ·zäd′; -hẽr′ȧ-; -zä′dĕ). The fictitious relator of the stories of the *Arabian Nights.*

sche′ma (skē′mȧ), *n.; pl.* SCHEMATA (-mȧ·tȧ). [L. See SCHEME.] Scheme, plan, outline, or diagram; specif., *Logic,* a syllogistic figure.

sche·mat′ic (skē·măt′ĭk), *adj.* Of or pertaining to a scheme (systematic plan) or a schema; diagrammatic; revealing schematism. — **sche·mat′i·cal·ly** (-ĭ·kăl·ĭ), *adv.*

sche′ma·tism (skē′mȧ·tĭz′m), *n.* [NL. *schematismus.*] The disposition of constituents in a pattern or according to a scheme; a systematic disposition of parts; design.

sche′ma·tize (-tīz), *v. i. & t.* [Gr. *schēmatizein.*] To form, or to form into, a scheme or schemes; to arrange schematically. — **sche′ma·ti·za′tion** (-tĭ·zā′shŭn; -tī·zā′-), *n.*

scheme (skēm), *n.* [L. *schema* a rhetorical figure, shape, figure, fr. Gr. *schēma, schēmatos,* shape, outline, plan.] **1.** *Archaic.* A diagram, design, or outline. **2.** A plan or program of something to be done;

specif.: **a** An enterprise; a project; as, an irrigation *scheme.* **b** A crafty, unethical project. **c** A visionary project. **3.** A systematic plan; a system; also, a complexity revealing design or system; as, the metrical *scheme* of a sonnet. **4.** A plan in tabulated form. **5.** *Astrol.* A representation of the aspects of the planets at a given time; a figure. — **Syn.** See PLAN. — *v. t.* To devise or contrive a scheme for; design; project; plot. — *v. i.* To form plans or designs; to devise intrigue. — **schem′er** (skēm′ẽr), *n.*

schem′ing (skēm′ĭng), *adj.* Given to forming schemes; artful.

scher·zan′do (skĕr·tsän′dō; -tsăn′dō), *adj.* [It., pres. part.] *Music.* Jesting; in a sportive manner; — a direction.

scher′zo (skĕr′tsō), *n.; pl.* SCHERZOS (-tsōz), SCHERZI (-tsē). [It.] *Music.* A sprightly, humorous, instrumental composition or movement, commonly in quick triple measure.

Schick test (shĭk). [After Dr. Bela *Schick,* of Vienna.] A test in which cutaneous injection of a diluted diphtheria toxin causes, in a subject susceptible to diphtheria, an area of reddening and induration.

schil′ler (shĭl′ẽr), *n.* [G., play of colors.] *Mineral.* A bronzelike iridescent luster, as in hypersthene.

schil′ler·ize (-īz), *v. t. Mineral.* To impart a schiller to. — **schil′ler·i·za′tion** (-ĭ·zā′shŭn;-ī·zā′-), *n.*

schil′ling (shĭl′ĭng), *n.* [G.] **a** A former minor coin denomination of Germany. **b** Since 1925 the gold monetary unit of Austria (see MONEY, *Tables*); also, a coin of copper and nickel.

schip′per·ke (skĭp′ẽr·kĭ), *n.* [Dial. D., prop., little boatman, dim. of D. *schipper;* because used as a watchdog on boats.] A small dog of a breed originating in Belgium. It has a foxlike head, erect ears, a broad chest, thickset body, and black coat.

schism (sĭz′m), *n.* [OF. *cisme, scisme,* fr. LL. *schisma,* fr. Gr. *schisma,* fr. *schizein* to split.] **1.** Division or separation. **2.** Specif., *Eccl.,* formal division or separation in the Christian church; also, the offense of seeking to produce division in a church. **3.** A schismatic body or faction.

schis·mat′ic (sĭz·măt′ĭk), *adj.* Of, pertaining to, or characteristic of schism; of the nature of, or tending to, schism; guilty of schism. — *n.* One who creates or takes part in schism. — **schis·mat′i·cal** (-ĭ·kăl), *adj.* — **schis·mat′i·cal·ly,** *adv.*

schist (shĭst), *n.* [F. *schiste,* fr. L. *schistos* that cleaves easily (of stone), fr. Gr. *schistos* divided, divisible.] *Petrog.* Any metamorphic crystalline rock having a foliated structure and readily split into slabs or sheets.

schist′ose (shĭs′tōs), **schist′ous** (-tŭs), *adj.* Of or pertaining to schist; having the nature or structure of schist.

schis′to·so·mi′a·sis (shĭs′tō·sō·mī′ȧ·sĭs), *n.* [NL., fr. *schistosome* (fr. Gr. *schistos* cleft + *-some*) + *-iasis.*] *Med. & Veter.* A disease caused by infestation of the blood with **schis′to·somes** (shĭs′tō·sōmz), trematodes of the genus *Schistosoma* (syn. *Bilharzia*), affecting the intestines, urinary bladder, liver, spleen, etc. Certain snails, in which part of the life cycle of the schistosome takes place, act as intermediate hosts in the transmission of the disease. Called also *bilharziasis.*

schiz′o- (skĭz′ō-), **schiz-.** [Gr. *schizein* to cleave, split.] A combining form denoting *division* or *cleavage.*

schiz′o·carp (-kärp), *n.* [*schizo-* + *-carp.*] *Bot.* A dry compound fruit which splits at maturity into several indehiscent one-seeded carpels. — **schiz′o·car′pous** (-kär′pŭs), *adj.*

schiz′o·gen′e·sis (-jĕn′ē·sĭs), *n.* [NL., fr. *schizo-* + *-genesis.*] *Biol.* Reproduction by fission.

schiz′oid (skĭz′oid), *adj.* [*schiz-* + *-oid.*] Resembling schizophrenia or a schizophrenic. — **schiz′oid,** *n.*

schiz′o·my·cete′ (skĭz′ō·mī·sēt′), *n.; pl.* -MYCETES (-mī·sēts′). [*schizo-* + Gr. *mykēs, mykētos,* fungus.] *Bot.* A plant of the class (Schizomycetes) consisting of the bacteria.

schiz′o·my·co′sis (-mī·kō′sĭs), *n.* [NL.] *Med.* Any disease caused by the presence of schizomycetes.

schiz′o·phre′ni·a (-frē′nĭ·ȧ), *n.* [NL., fr. *schizo-* + Gr. *phrēn* mind, heart.] A type of psychosis characterized by loss of contact with environment and by disintegration of personality. — **schiz′o·phrene** (skĭz′ō·frēn), *n.* — **schiz′o·phren′ic** (-frĕn′ĭk), *adj. & n.*

schiz′o·phyte (skĭz′ō·fīt), *n.* [*schizo-* + *-phyte.*] *Bot.* One of a division or phylum (Schizophyta) of plants comprising the so-called fission plants. They are either unicellular or filamentous, consisting of a chain of cells, or occasionally united into cell colonies. They multiply only by fission or by asexual spores. — **schiz′o·phyt′ic** (-fĭt′ĭk), *adj.*

schiz′o·pod (-pŏd), *n.* Any of a formerly recognized order (Schizopoda) of shrimplike crustaceans with a soft carapace. — **schiz′o·pod,** *adj.* — **schi·zop′o·dous** (skĭ·zŏp′ō·dŭs; skĭ-), *adj.*

schiz′o·thy′mi·a (skĭz′ō·thī′mĭ·ȧ), *n.* [NL., fr. *schizo-* + Gr. *thymos* spirit.] *Psychiatry.* A schizoid condition or temperament remaining within the bounds of normality; — opposed to *cyclothymia.* — **schiz′o·thy′mic** (-mĭk), *adj.*

schle·miel′, schle·mihl′ (shlĕ·mēl′), *n.* [Yiddish, fr. Heb. *Shĕlūmī-ēl* (Numbers i. 6), lit., God is welfare.] *Slang.* An ill-starred or ineffectual fellow; a chump, saphead, or oaf.

schlie′ren (shlē′rĕn), *n. pl.* [G.] **1.** *Petrog.* Small masses or streaks in igneous rocks which differ from the main body. **2.** *Physics.* Regions of varying refraction in a medium caused by differences in pressure, detectable by photographing a beam of light. Hence, **schlieren effect, schlieren photography.** — **schlie′ric** (-rĭk), *adj.*

schmaltz (shmôlts), *n.* [Through Yiddish, fr. G. *schmalz* lard, melted fat, butter. See 2d SMELT.] *Slang.* Sentimental, esp. fulsomely sentimental, music or sentimentalism in art expression.

schna′bel (shnä′bĕl), *n.* [G.] See WHITEFISH.

schnap′per (shnăp′ẽr; snăp′ẽr), *n.* [E. *snapper* a kind of fish, altered to accord with G. *schnapper.*] A snapper (*Pagrosomus auratus*) of Australia and New Zealand.

schnapps (shnăps; shnäps), *n.* [G., a dram of spirits.] Strong Holland gin.

schnau′zer (shnou′zẽr), *n.* [G., prop., snarler.] A terrier of a breed originating in Germany at least 500 years ago. It has a long head, with small ears and heavy eyebrows, mustache, and beard, and a wiry coat.

schnit′zel (shnĭt′sĕl), *n.* [G.] A veal cutlet variously seasoned and garnished, often with lemon, sardines, and capers.

schnor′chel, schnor′kel (shnôr′kĕl), *n.* See SNORKEL.

schnor′rer (shnōr′ẽr), *n.* [Yiddish, fr. G. *schnurrer,* fr. *schnurren* to hum, whir, hence, from the musical instrument used by strolling beggars, to beg.] Among the Jews, a beggar.

schol′ar (skŏl′ẽr), *n.* [OF. *escoler, escolier,* LL. *scholaris* belonging to a school, fr. L. *schola* school.] **1.** One who attends a school; a student. **2.** A student who holds an academic scholarship. **3.** One who has engaged in advanced study and acquired knowledge in some special field. **4.** A literate person; specif., one who can read and write.

Syn. Scholar, pupil, student, disciple mean one who studies under a teacher. Scholar, as here compared, stresses enrollment in a school and the fact of being instructed; pupil stresses a teacher's personal care and oversight; student, generally applicable to one who studies or loves to study, is often specifically applied to one who attends a higher institution of learning; disciple, now archaic in this sense, approaches *pupil* but stresses devoted adherence to the teachings of the master.

schol′arch (skŏl′ärk), *n.* [Gr. *scholarchēs,* fr. *scholē* school + *archein* to rule.] The head of a school, esp. of an Athenian school of philosophy.

schol′ar·ly (skŏl′ẽr·lĭ), *adj.* Like, characteristic of, or suitable to a scholar, or learned person; learned. — *adv.* Like or as befits a scholar.

schol′ar·ship, *n.* **1.** Character or qualities of a scholar; learning. **2.** A foundation for the support of a scholar or student, as in a college.

scho·las′tic (skō·lăs′tĭk), *adj.* [L. *scholasticus,* fr. Gr. *scholastikos,* fr. *scholazein* to have leisure, keep a school, fr. *scholē.* See 2d SCHOOL.] **1.** [*often cap.*] Of or pert. to the Schoolmen and divines of the Middle Ages; as, *scholastic* philosophy. **2.** Characterized by, or suggestive of, the logic or methods of the medieval Schoolmen; hence, pedantic; formal. **3.** Pert. to or suiting a scholar or schools; academic; as, *scholastic* rank; often, specif., of or pert. to secondary schools; as, *scholastic* competitions. — *n.* **1.** [*usually cap.*] A Christian philosopher of the Middle Ages; a Schoolman. **2.** One who deals with philosophical or theological problems in the spirit of Scholasticism; depreciatively, a pedant; a formalist. — **scho·las′ti·cal** (-tĭ·kăl), *adj. & n.*

scho·las′ti·cate (-tĭ·kāt), *n. R.C.Ch.* A place where Jesuit scholastics, or students, pursue their studies.

scho·las′ti·cism (-tĭ·sĭz′m), *n.* **1.** [*usually cap.*] The dominant Christian philosophy of the Middle Ages and early Renaissance; the systems of logic, metaphysics, theology, etc., expounded chiefly by Albertus Magnus, Duns Scotus, and esp., Thomas Aquinas. At its highest point, scholasticism was intellectualistic and grounded on Aristotelianism. **2.** Close adherence to traditional teachings or methods prescribed by schools or sects.

scho′li·ast (skō′lĭ·ăst), *n.* [ML. *scholiasta,* fr. LGr. *scholiastēs.*] A maker of scholia; commentator; annotator. — **scho′li·as′tic** (-ăs′tĭk), *adj.*

scho′li·um (-ŭm), *n.; pl.* SCHOLIA (-ȧ), SCHOLIUMS (-ŭmz). [ML., fr. Gr. *scholion,* fr. *scholē.* See 2d SCHOOL.] **1.** A marginal annotation, esp. one by an early grammarian on a classic text. **2.** A remark or observation subjoined, but not essential, to a demonstration or reasoning.

school (skōōl), *n.* [D. See 1st SHOAL.] A large number of one kind of fish or aquatic animals swimming together; a shoal. — *v. i.* To swim together in schools, or shoals.

school, *n.* [From AS. *scōl* (fr. L.) and fr. OF. *escole* (F. *école*), fr. L. *schola,* fr. Gr. *scholē* leisure, that in which leisure is employed, lecture, a school.] **1.** An institution for teaching children. See GRAMMAR SCHOOL, SECONDARY SCHOOL, HIGH SCHOOL. Hence: **a** The body of pupils attending a school. **b** A session of an institution of instruction. **c** A schoolhouse. **2.** Any place or means of learning or discipline. **3.** A place for lectures, esp., in the Middle Ages, for lectures in logic, metaphysics, and theology. **4.** The process of being educated in institutions for teaching the young, usually not including colleges; also, attendance at a school. **5.** A place for instruction in any branch of knowledge; also, the institution or the collective body of teachers and learners in such a place. **6.** A faculty for specialized higher education, usually within a university; as, a medical or law *school.* **7.** The disciples or followers of a teacher; a sect in philosophy, theology, science, etc.; as, the Socratic *school;* the homeopathic *school.* **8.** *Fine Arts.* **a** A group, as of painters or musicians, under a common local or personal influence producing a general similarity in their work. **b** The artists or art of a country or region. **9.** *Mil. & Nav.* The regulations, collectively, governing the drill of individuals or of a unit; also, the exercises carried out in accordance with such regulations; as, the *school* of the soldier.

☞ COMBINATIONS are:

schoolbag	schoolgirl	schoolroom
schoolbook	schoolhouse	schoolteacher
schoolboy	schoolmaid	schoolwork
schoolfellow	schoolmate	schoolyard

— *v. t.* **1.** To educate in an institution of learning. **2.** To teach or train. — **Syn.** See TEACH.

— *adj.* **1.** Pertaining to a school or schools. **2.** Of or pertaining to the Schoolmen.

school board. A board in charge of local public schools.

school′ing, *n.* **1.** Instruction in school; also, the act or means of teaching. **2.** *Archaic.* Chastisement for correction; reproof. **3.** Cost of instruction and maintenance in school. **4.** The teaching and training of horses and riders, esp. in a school of horsemanship.

school′man (skōōl′măn), *n.* One versed in the niceties of academical disputation; esp. [*usually cap.*], a philosopher or divine of the schools of the Middle Ages; a Scholastic.

school′mas′ter (-màs′tẽr; 9), *n.* **1.** A man who teaches a school; one of the masters of a school. **2.** One who or that which disciplines and directs. **3.** A snapper (*Lutianus apodus*) of the West Indies and southern United States. — **school′mis′tress** (-mĭs′trĕs; -trĭs), *n.*

schoon′er (skōōn′ẽr), *n.* [From dial. *scoon* to skim, slip.] *Naut.* A fore-and-aft-rigged vessel, typically having two masts, with the smaller sail on the foremast and the mainmast stepped nearly amidships. See SAIL, 1st *Illust.*

schoon′er, *n. U. S.* A large tall drinking glass for beer or ale.

schooner rig. A fore-and-aft rig. See SAIL, 1st *Illust.* — **schoon′er-rigged′** (-rĭgd′), *adj.*

Scho′pen·hau′er·ism (shō′pĕn·hou′ẽr·ĭz′m), *n.* The philosophy of the German pessimistic philosopher Arthur Schopenhauer, who taught that life is an evil to be cured only by overcoming the will to live.

schorl (shôrl), *n.* [G. *schörl.*] *Mineral.* Tourmaline, esp. the black variety. — **schor·la′ceous** (shôr·lā′shŭs), *adj.*

schot′tische, schot′tish (shŏt′ĭsh; shŏ·tēsh′), *n.* [G. *schottisch* Scottish.] A 19th-century round dance in $\frac{2}{4}$ time, similar to the polka, but slower; also, its music.

‖**Schreck′lich·keit** (shrĕk′lĭk·kīt), *n.* [G.] Frightfulness; atrociousness. See FRIGHTFULNESS, 2.

‖**schrik** (skrĭk), *n.* [D.] *S. Africa.* A sudden fright; panic.

schuit, schuyt (skoit), *n.* [D. *schuit.*] A Dutch vessel with bluff bows and usually rounded stern.

schuss (sho͝os), *n.* [G., a scooting, shooting. See 1st SHOT.] *Skiing.* A straight high-speed run; also, a straightaway course. — **schuss,** *v. i.;* SCHUSSED (sho͝ost); SCHUSS′ING.

‖**Schutz′staf′fel** (sho͝ots′shtä′fĕl), *n.* [G. protective force (lit., grade, rank).] A unit of fanatical Nazis wearing black uniforms with brown shirts, created in 1923 by Himmler as bodyguard to "der Führer," later organized into divisions for service with the regular army; — often called *Blackshirts,* after the Italian Fascisti. Abbr. *SS* or *S.S.*

schwa (shwä; shvä), *n.* [G., fr. Heb. *shewa.*] In phonetics, an unaccented, obscure vowel sound, that of *a* in idea, *e* in quiet, *o* in atom, *u* in circus, etc., represented in the alphabet of the International Phonetic Association by the symbol ə (inverted *e*); also, the symbol itself.

schwei′zer·kä′se (shvīt′sẽr·kâ′zĕ), **schwei′zer,** *n* [G. *schweizerkäse.*] Swiss cheese.

‖**Schwer′punkt′** (shvār′po͝ongkt′), *n.* [G., lit., center of gravity.] *Mil.* An offensive tactic used by the Germans in World War II in which an armored striking force is thrust against a narrow sector of the enemy front for the execution of a breakthrough; also, the sector singled out for the thrust.

sci·ae′noid (sī·ē′noid), *adj.* [L. *sciaena* a kind of fish, fr. Gr. *skiaina.*] Of or pert. to an order (Percomorphi) of carnivorous spiny-finned fishes comprising the kingfishes, drumfishes, etc., most of which have a large air bladder by which they produce a peculiar sound. — *n.* A sciaenoid fish.

sci′a·gram (sī′ȧ·grăm), **sci′a·graph,** etc. Vars of SKIAGRAM, etc.

sci·am′a·chy (sī·ăm′ȧ·kĭ), *n.* [Gr. *skiamachia, skiomachia,* fr. *skia* a shadow + *machē* battle.] A fighting with a shadow; futile combat, as with an imaginary foe.

sci·at′ic (sī·ăt′ĭk), *adj.* [F. *sciatique,* through ML. & L., fr. Gr. *ischiadikos,* fr. *ischion* hip joint, ischium.] **1.** Of or pertaining to the hip; in the region of, or affecting, the hip; ischial. **2.** Of, pertaining to, afflicted with, or caused by sciatica.

sci·at′i·ca (-ĭ·kȧ), *n.* [NL.] *Med.* Neuritis or neuralgia of the **sciatic nerve,** a nerve running down the back of the thigh. Popularly, any painful affection of the hip and adjoining parts.

sci′ence (sī′ĕns), *n.* [OF., fr. L. *scientia,* fr. *sciens, -entis,* pres. part of *scire* to know.] **1.** Knowledge obtained by study and practice. **2.** Any department of systematized knowledge. **3.** Art or skill; — chiefly humorous or sporting; as, the *science* of boxing. **4.** A branch of study concerned with observation and classification of facts, esp. with the establishment of verifiable general laws, chiefly by induction and hypotheses; as, mathematical *science.* **5.** Specif., accumulated knowledge systematized and formulated with reference to the discovery of general truths or the operation of general laws. **6.** Esp., such knowledge when it relates to the physical world; — called also *natural science.* **7.** [*cap.*] *Christian Science.* Christian Science.

sci·en′tial (sī·ĕn′shăl), *adj.* **1.** Pertaining to, or producing knowledge. **2.** Having efficient knowledge; capable.

sci′en·tif′ic (sī′ĕn·tĭf′ĭk), *adj.* [LL. *scientificus.*] **1.** Concerned with, or treating of, science or sciences; as, *scientific* training. **2.** Of, pertaining to, or used in science, esp. natural science, or a branch of science; as, *scientific* apparatus. **3.** Agreeing with, or conducted or prepared strictly according to, the principles and practice of exact science; as, *scientific* research. **4.** Conducted or systematized after the manner of science; applying expert knowledge or technical skill, as in sports, warfare, business; as, *scientific* management. — **sci′en·tif′i·cal·ly** (-ĭ·kăl·ĭ), *adv.*

sci′en·tist (sī′ĕn·tĭst), *n.* **1.** One learned in science, esp. natural science; a scientific investigator. **2.** [*cap.*] *Christian Science.* A Christian Scientist.

scil′i·cet (sĭl′ĭ·sĕt), *adv.* [L., fr. *scire* to know + *licet* it is permitted.] To wit; namely; videlicet; also, (to be) understood or supplied; — preceding the word that is to be supplied. Abbr. *scil.* or *sc.*

scim′i·tar, scim′i·ter (sĭm′ĭ·tẽr), *n.* [F. *cimeterre,* or It. *scimitarra.*] A saber having a curved blade with the edge on the convex side, used chiefly by Moslems, esp. Arabs and Persians.

Scimitar.

scin′coid (sĭng′koid), *adj.* Also **scin·coi′di·an** (sĭng·koi′dĭ·ăn). [L. *scincus* + *-oid.*] See SKINK, *n.*] Like or pertaining to the skinks. — **scin′coid, scin·coi′di·an,** *n.*

scin·til′la (sĭn·tĭl′ȧ), *n.* [L.] A spark or barely perceptible manifestation; the slightest trace.

scin′til·lant (sĭn′tĭ·lănt), *adj.* [L. *scintillans,* pres. part. of *scintillare* to sparkle.] Emitting sparks.

scin′til·late (-lāt), *v. i. & t.* [L. *scintillare, -latum,* fr. *scintilla* a spark.] **1.** To emit sparks; to spark. **2.** To gleam or emit quick flashes as if throwing off sparks; as, wit that *scintillates;* also, to sparkle or twinkle, as the fixed stars. — **Syn.** See FLASH.

scin′til·lat′ing (-lāt′ĭng), *adj.* That scintillates; sparkling; as, *scintillating* wit. — **scin′til·lat′ing·ly,** *adv.*

scin′til·la′tion (-lā′shŭn), *n.* **1.** Act of scintillating. **2.** A spark or flash emitted in scintillating. **3.** *Astron.* The twinkling of stars or of the planet Mercury.

sci′o·graph (sī′ō·grȧf), **sci′o·graph′ic,** etc. Vars. of SKIAGRAPH, etc.

sci′o·lism (sī′ō·lĭz′m), *n.* [LL. *sciolus,* dim. of *scius* knowing, fr. *scire* to know.] Superficial knowledge. — **sci′o·list** (-lĭst), *n.* — **sci′o·lis′tic** (-lĭs′tĭk), *adj.*

sci·om′a·chy (sī·ŏm′ȧ·kĭ), *n.* Sciamachy.

sci′o·man′cy (sī′ō·măn′sĭ), *n.* [Gr. *skia* a shadow + *-mancy.*] Divination by consulting the shades of the dead.

sci′on (sī′ŭn), *n.* [OF. *cion* (F. *scion*).] **1.** Also **ci′on.** *Hort.* A detached shoot, or other portion of a plant consisting of more than one bud, capable of propagation; specif., such a part removed and prepared for grafting. See GRAFTAGE, *Illust.*

☞ The older spelling *cion* is now adopted by most American nurserymen and horticulturists.

2. Hence, a descendant; as, a *scion* of a royal stock.

‖**sci′re fa′ci·as** (sī′rē fā′shĭ·ăs) [L., do you cause to know.] *Law* A judicial writ founded upon some matter of record and requiring the party proceeded against to show cause why the record should not be enforced, annulled, or vacated; also, the proceeding so instituted.

scir′rhus (skĭr′ŭs), *n.; pl.* -RHI (-ī), -RHUSES (-ŭs·ĕz; -ĭz). [NL., fr. L *scirros,* fr. Gr. *skirrhos, skiros,* hard.] *Med.* A hard cancerous tumor. — **scir′rhoid** (-oid), *adj.* — **scir·rhos′i·ty** (skĭ·rŏs′ĭ·tĭ), *n.* — **scir′rhous** (skĭr′ŭs), *adj.*

scis′sile (sĭs′ĭl; 56), *adj.* [F., fr. L. *scissilis,* fr. *scindere, scissum,* to cut, split.] Capable of being cut smoothly or split easily.

scis′sion (sĭzh′ŭn; sĭsh′ŭn), *n.* [F., fr. LL. *scissio,* fr. *scindere, scissum,* to cut, split.] Act of cutting, dividing, or splitting, or state of being cut, divided, or split; fission.

scis′sor (sĭz′ẽr), *v. t.* To cut or cut off with scissors.

scis′sors (sĭz′ẽrz), *n. pl.* [OF. *cisoires,* fr. LL. *cisorium* a cutting instrument, pl. *cisoria,* fr. L. *caedere* to cut. The modern spelling is due to a mistaken derivation from ML. *scissor* one who cleaves or divides, a tailor, fr. L. *scindere, scissum,* to cut, split.] **1.** A cutting instrument working like shears but smaller; — often called *pair of scissors.* **2.** *Gymnastics.* Any of several feats in which, while vaulting, the legs are moved in a manner suggesting the opening and closing of scissors; — construed as *singular.* **3.** *Wrestling.* A hold in which one contestant clasps the other's head or body with his legs; — construed as *singular.*

scissors, *or* **scissor, kick.** *Swimming.* A form of kick in which the legs are moved in a fashion resembling the opening and closing of scissors.

scis′sor·tail′ (sĭz′ẽr·tāl′), *n.* Also **scis′sor–tailed′ fly′catch′er.** A flycatcher (*Muscivora forficata*) of the southern U. S. and Mexico, having a forked tail.

sci′u·rine (sī′ū·rīn; -rĭn), *adj.* [L. *sciurus* squirrel.] *Zool.* Belonging to or designating a family (Sciuridae) of rodents consisting of the true squirrels, ground squirrels, marmots, and their allies. — **sci′u·rine,** *n.*

sci·u′roid (sī·ū′roid), *adj.* [L. *sciurus* + *-oid.*] Squirrellike; *Bot.,* resembling the tail of a squirrel, as the spikes of barley and certain other grasses.

sclaff (sklȧf), *n.* [Imitative.] **1.** *Scot.* A slight blow; also, the accompanying noise. **2.** *Golf.* The stroke made by one who sclaffs. — *v. i. Golf.* To strike the ground behind the ball before hitting the ball. — *v. t. Golf.* To scrape (the club) on the ground, in a stroke, before hitting the ball; to make (a stroke) in that way. — **sclaff′er** (-ẽr), *n.*

scle′ra (sklē′rȧ), *n.* [NL., fr. Gr. *sklēros* hard. See SKELETON.] *Anat.* The sclerotic coat of the eyeball. See SCLEROTIC, *adj.,* 1.

scle·ren′chy·ma (sklē·rĕng′kĭ·mȧ), *n.* [NL., fr. Gr. *sklēros* hard + *-enchyma* as in par*enchyma.*] *Bot.* In higher plants, a tissue composed of cells which have the cell walls thickened and lignified, and which are usually without living protoplasm and incapable of further growth when mature. Cf. COLLENCHYMA. — **scle′ren·chym′a·tous** (sklē′rĕng·kĭm′ȧ·tŭs), *adj.*

scle·ri′a·sis (sklē·rī′ȧ·sĭs), *n.* [NL., fr. Gr. *sklēriasis,* fr. *sklēros* hard.] *Med.* Induration of any part.

scle′rite (sklēr′īt), *n.* [Gr. *sklēros* hard.] *Zool.* A hard chitinous or calcareous plate, piece, or spicule. — **scle·rit′ic** (sklē·rĭt′ĭk), *adj.*

scle·ri′tis (sklē·rī′tĭs), *n.* [NL.] Sclerotitis.

scle′ro- (sklēr′ō-; sklĕr′ō-), **scler-.** [Gr. *sklēros* hard.] A combining form used to denote: **a** *Fibrous; hard;* as in *sclero*derma. **b** *Med. Pertaining to the sclera and,* as in **scle′ro·i·ri′tis.**

scle′ro·der′ma (-dûr′mȧ), *n.* [NL., fr. *sclero-* + *derma.*] A disease characterized by diffuse or circumscribed rigidity and hardness of the skin.

scle′ro·der′ma·tous (-dûr′mȧ·tŭs), *adj.* Having a hard external covering, as of bony plates or horny scales.

scle′roid (sklēr′oid), *adj. Bot. & Zool.* Hard; indurated.

scle·ro′ma (sklē·rō′mȧ), *n.; pl.* -MATA (-mȧ·tȧ). [NL., fr. Gr. *sklērōma,* fr. *sklēros* hard.] *Med.* Induration, or an induration, of tissues.

scle·rom′e·ter (-rŏm′ē·tẽr), *n. Mineral.* An instrument for determining the relative hardnesses of materials.

scle·ro′sal (sklē·rō′săl; -s'l), *adj.* Pert. to, or producing, sclerosis.

scle·rosed′ (sklē·rōst′; sklēr′ōzd), *adj.* Affected with sclerosis; indurated.

scle·ro′sis (sklē·rō′sĭs), *n.; pl.* -ROSES (-sēz). [NL., fr. Gr. *sklērōsis.*] **1.** *Med.* Induration by increase of interstitial connective tissue; also, degenerative replacement of tissue of the spinal cord or brain by neuroglia. **2.** *Bot.* Hardening by lignification.

scle·rot′ic (-rŏt′ĭk), *adj.* [NL. *scleroticus,* fr. Gr. *sklēros* hard.] **1.** *Anat. & Zool.* Designating, or pertaining to, the dense, fibrous, opaque white outer coat of the eyeball. See EYE, *Illust.* **2.** *Bot., Med., etc.* Affected with sclerosis. **3.** Pertaining to sclerosis. — *n.* The sclerotic coat of the eyeball; = SCLERA.

scle′ro·ti′tis (sklē′rō·tī′tĭs; sklĕr′ō-), *n.* [NL. See SCLEROTIC; -ITIS.] *Med.* Inflammation of the sclera. — **scle′ro·tit′ic** (-tĭt′ĭk), *adj.*

scle·ro′ti·um (sklē·rō′shĭ·ŭm), *n.; pl.* -TIA (-ȧ). [NL., fr. Gr. *sklēros* hard.] *Bot.* In certain higher fungi, a compact mass of hardened mycelium stored with reserve food material. — **scle·ro′tial** (-shăl), *adj.*

scle·rot′o·my (-rŏt′ō·mĭ), *n.* [*sclero-* + *-tomy.*] *Surg.* The cutting of the sclera, as in operating for glaucoma.

scle′rous (sklēr′ŭs), *adj.* [Gr. *sklēros.*] Hard; indurated.

scoff (skŏf; 74), *n.* [ME. *scof.*] **1.** A derisive or mocking expression of scorn, derision, or contempt. **2.** An object of scorn, mockery, or derision. — *v. i.* To manifest contempt by derisive acts or language. — *v. t.* To deride; to mock at. — **scoff′er,** *n.* — **scoff′ing·ly,** *adv.*

Syn. **Scoff, jeer, gibe, fleer, gird, sneer, flout** mean to show one's scorn in derision or mockery. **Scoff** stresses insolence, irreverence, incredulity, etc., as its motives; **jeer,** a coarser, more vulgar, and less keenly critical attitude than *scoff;* **gibe,** a taunting either good-naturedly or in sarcastic derision; **fleer,** a grinning or laughing derisively; **gird,** an attacking by scoffing or jeering; **sneer,** an insulting through contemptuous facial expression, manner of phrasing, or tone of voice; **flout,** refusal to heed by disdaining or scorning.

scold (skōld), *n.* [ME. *scold(e), scald.*] One addicted to abusive, orig. ribald, speech. — *v. i. & t.* **1.** *Obs.* To brawl; rail. **2.** To utter harsh rebuke; chide severely. — **scold′er,** *n.* — **scold′ing,** *adj. & n.* — **scold′ing·ly,** *adv.*

Syn. **Scold, upbraid, berate, rail, revile, vituperate** mean to reproach angrily and, often, abusively. **Scold** implies a rebuking in irritation or ill temper justly or unjustly; **upbraid,** a censuring on definite and, often, justifiable grounds; **berate,** a prolonged and, often, abusive scolding; **rail,** followed usually by *at* or *against,* an abusive or scoffing berating; **revile,** a scurrilous, abusive attack; **vituperate,** a violent reviling.

scold′ing, *or* **scold's, bri′dle.** = BRANK, 2.

scol′e·cite (skŏl′ē·sīt; skō′lē-), *n.* [G. *scolezit,* fr. Gr. *skōlēx* worm.] *Mineral.* A zeolite, of the natrolite group, a hydrous silicate of calcium and aluminum, $CaAl_2Si_3O_{10}3H_2O$.

sco'lex (skō'lĕks), *n.; pl.* SCOLECES (skō·lē'sēz), often also SCOLICES (skŏl'ĭ·sēz; skō'lĭ-). [NL., fr. Gr. *skōlēx* worm, grub.] *Zool.* The head of a tapeworm either in the larva (bladder worm) or adult stage.

sco'li·o'sis (skō'lĭ·ō'sĭs; skŏl'ĭ-), *n.* [NL., fr. Gr. *skoliōsis* crookedness, fr. *skolios* crooked.] *Med.* A lateral curvature of the spine.

scol'lop (skŏl'ŭp), **scol'lop·er.** Vars. of SCALLOP, etc.

scol'o·pen'drid (skŏl'ō·pĕn'drĭd), *n.* [L. *scolopendra* a kind of multiped, fr. Gr. *skolopendra.*] *Zool.* One of a family (Scolopendridae) of centipedes. — **scol'o·pen'drid,** *adj.* — **scol'o·pen'drine** (-drīn; -drĭn), *adj.*

scom'broid (skŏm'broid), *adj.* [L. *scomber* mackerel + *-oid.*] *Zool.* Like, or pertaining to, the mackerel family (Scombridae) or their allies (group Scombroidea). — *n.* A scombroid fish.

sconce (skŏns), *n.* [OF. *esconse* lantern, hiding place, fr. ML. *sconsa,* fr. *absconsa,* fr. L. *abscondere, absconsum,* to hide.] A bracket candlestick or group of candlesticks secured to a wall.

sconce, *n.* [D. *schans* sconce, bulwark, wall, orig., of, or with, wickerwork.] **1.** A protection, cover, shelter, etc. **2.** *Colloq.* The head; skull; also, brains; sense. **3.** *Fort.* A detached defensive work. **4.** A fine; penalty. — *v. t.;* SCONCED (skŏnst); SCONC'ING (skŏn'sĭng). To provide with a sconce, or fortified defense; entrench; screen.

sconce, *v. t.* To mulct; fine.

sconce, *v. t.* Clipped form of ENSCONCE.

scone (skōn; skŏn; skŭn), *n. Orig. Scot.* A flat, round or triangular teacake, usually unsweetened, cooked quickly on a griddle.

scoop (skōōp), *n.* [ME. *scope.*] **1.** A large ladle. **2.** A deep shovel, or similar implement for digging, dipping, or shoveling. **3.** Act of scooping, or taking with a scoop or ladle; a motion like that made with a scoop. **4.** A basinlike cavity; a hollow. **5.** *Newspaper Slang.* = BEAT, *n.*, 10. **6.** *Colloq.* An amount of something obtained in large quantity, as if with a scoop, as large profits in speculation. **7.** *Surg.* A spoon-shaped instrument, used in extracting certain substances or foreign bodies. — *v. t.* **1.** To take out or up with or as with a scoop. **2. a** To empty by lading; as, to *scoop* a boat dry. **b** To make hollow, as a scoop or dish; to dig out. **3.** To fashion by or as by scooping; — often with *out.* **4.** *Colloq.* To gather in, as if with a scoop; as, to *scoop* in a good profit. **5.** *Newspaper Slang.* To get a scoop, or a beat, on (a rival). See BEAT, *n.*, 10. — **scoop'er,** *n.* — **scoop'ful,** *n.*

scoot (skōōt), *n.* *Colloq.* A sudden scooting, or darting. — *v. i.* *Colloq.* To go suddenly and swiftly; to dart; scud. — *interj. Colloq.* Begone quickly.

scoot'er (-ẽr), *n.* **1.** *Local, U. S.* A strongly built sailboat having a flat bottom shod with steel runners, and a sharply rising stem, for sailing through water or over ice as either is met with. **2.** A child's vehicle consisting of a narrow board mounted on two wheels tandem, and guided by a handle attached to the front wheel. The child stands with one foot on the board and pushes with the other foot.

scoot'er. Var. of SCOTER.

scop (skŏp; skōp), *n.* [AS. *scop, sceop.*] *Hist.* A bard; poet.

scope (skōp), *n.* [It. *scopo,* fr. L. *scopus, scopos,* fr. Gr. *skopos* a watcher, mark, aim.] **1.** *Archaic.* Ultimate intention. **2.** Room for free outlook, aim, or action; liberty. **3. a** Distance within which a missile carries. **b** Length; extent; as, *scope* of cable. **4. a** Range of view, intent, or mental activity. **b** The range within which an activity displays itself; as, the *scope* of Napoleon's genius. **5.** Short for *oscilloscope;* specif., one in the form of a cathode-ray tube with a fluorescent screen, constituting the visual indicator in a radar set and sometimes called a *radarscope.*

-scope (-skōp). [Gr. *skopein* to view. See SCOPE.] A combining form denoting a *means,* usually *an instrument, for viewing* or *observing,* as in micro*scope.*

sco·pol'a·mine (skō·pŏl'ȧ·mēn, -mĭn; skō'pō·lȧ·mēn'; -lăm'ĭn), *n.* Also **-min.** [G. *scopolamin,* fr. NL. *Scopolia* a genus of plants (after G. A. *Scopoli* (1723–88), of Pavia, Italy) + *amine.*] *Chem.* An alkaloid, $C_{17}H_{21}NO_4$, occurring in the roots of certain plants (esp. genus *Scopolia*) of the nightshade family. It is used with morphine to produce twilight sleep.

-scopy. [Gr. *skopein* to view.] A combining form denoting *viewing, scrutiny, observation,* as in micro*scopy.*

scor·bu'tic (skôr·bū'tĭk), *adj.* Also **scor·bu'ti·cal** (-tĭ·kăl). [F. *scorbutique,* fr. ML. *scorbutus* scurvy.] *Med.* Of, pertaining to, or like scurvy; diseased with scurvy.

scorch (skôrch), *v. t.* **1.** To parch the surface of by heat; to heat so as to change color and texture without consuming. **2.** To affect painfully with burning criticism, sarcasm, etc. **3.** *Archaic.* To burn; to destroy by or as by fire. **4.** *Mil.* To devastate completely before abandoning to the enemy. — *v. i.* **1.** To become scorched. **2.** *Colloq.* To ride or drive at great, usually excessive, speed.

scorch, *v. t.* [Cf. SCOTCH to score.] *Obs. exc. Dial. Eng.* Cut; slash.

scorched earth (skôrcht). A policy adopted by retreating armies of demolishing cities, utility plants, railways, food stores, crops, fuel, and other property of use to the enemy.

scorch'er (skôr'chẽr), *n.* One that scorches; specif.: *Chiefly Slang.* **a** Anything very hot, as a day; hence, anything withering or caustic, as a rebuke. **b** One who rides or drives at an excessive speed.

scorch'ing, *adj.* Parching or shriveling with heat; hence, withering; stinging; as, a *scorching* criticism. — **scorch'ing·ly,** *adv.*

score (skōr; 70), *n.* [ME. *scor,* fr. ON. *skor* notch, tally.] **1.** A notch or incision, esp. one made as a tally mark or for keeping account. **2.** A line or long mark, as a scratch; esp., a mark as a starting point or a goal; a taw. **3.** An account or reckoning kept by making marks on a tally; hence, any account; also, amount due. **4.** An obligation or injury kept in mind for requital; as, to settle old *scores.* **5.** Account; reason; motive; as, excused on the *score* of illness. **6.** *Colloq.* A successful move, stroke, etc. **7.** A group of twenty, as being the number represented by a notch on a tally; hence, in *pl.*, a large number; as, the disease killed *scores.* **8.** The number of points gained by contestants in a contest; hence, an account of points made. **9.** Degree of success in a test; hence, rating as of an individual or a school. **10.** *Music.* The original draft, or its transcript, of a composition, with the parts for instruments or voices written on staffs. **11.** *Psychol. & Educ.* A number expressing the degree of success in a test, in terms of the amount performed, time required, or difficulty surmounted, or of the excellence of the performance. **12.** The stark, inescapable facts, and often the unglossed prospects, of a situation; as, those bomber crews knew the *score;* the home folks have no idea what the *score* is; to find out the *score* in the fight against fascism.
— *v. t.* **1.** To mark with lines, scratches, or notches; to notch. **2.** To record by cuts or notches. **3.** To mark with lines or notches, as in keeping account. **4.** To keep record or account of by or as by notches on a tally; to record; charge. **5. a** To list; reckon; — often with *up.* **b** To enter a record of the indebtedness of; — often with *up.* **6.** In games, sports, etc.: **a** To enter the score of. **b** To gain for addition to the score, as points, runs, etc. **c** To count or have as value; as, a touchdown *scores* six. **d** To place to one's score. **7.** To rate by quality, as livestock, fruit, etc.; to grade, as a test. **8.** To berate; scold. **9.** To achieve as a gain; as, to *score* a success. **10.** *Cookery.* To gash in lines, as liver. **11.** *Music.* To orchestrate or arrange. — *v. i.* **1.** To run up a score, or account of indebtedness. **2.** *Rare.* To mark lines, as by incision. **3. a** To keep the score in a game. **b** To make or count a point or points, as in a game; to tally. — **scor'er** (skōr'ẽr), *n.*

sco'ri·a (skō'rĭ·ȧ; 70), *n.; pl.* SCORIAE (-ē). [L., fr. Gr. *skōria,* fr. *skōr* dung, ordure.] Refuse from melting of metals, reduction of ores, etc.; dross; slag; also, slaggy lava. — **sco'ri·a'ceous** (-ā'shŭs), *adj.*

sco'ri·fy (skō'rĭ·fī; 70), *v. t.;* -FIED (-fīd); -FY'ING. [*scoria* + *-fy.*] To reduce to scoria, or slag. — **sco'ri·fi·ca'tion** (-fĭ·kā'shŭn), *n.*

scorn (skôrn), *n.* [ME. *scorn, scarn,* fr. OF. *escarn,* of Teut. origin.] **1.** Disdain; an emotion involving both anger and disgust; also, derision. **2.** An expression of extreme contempt; gibe; flout; taunt. **3.** An object of extreme disdain, contempt, or derision. — *v. t.* **1.** *Archaic.* To treat with extreme contempt; to mock; deride. **2.** To hold in, or reject with, extreme contempt; to contemn; disdain. — *v. i.* *Archaic.* To scoff; to mock. — **Syn.** See DESPISE. — **scorn'er,** *n.*

scorn'ful (-fŏŏl; -f'l), *adj.* Full of scorn or contempt; disdainful; contemptuous. — **scorn'ful·ly,** *adv.* — **scorn'ful·ness,** *n.*

scor·pae'noid (skôr·pē'noid), *adj.* [L. *scorpaena* a kind of fish, fr. Gr. *skorpaina.*] *Zool.* Belonging to or designating a family (*Scorpaenidae*) of marine spiny-finned fishes. — **scor·pae'nid** (-nĭd), **scor·pae'noid** (-noid), *n.*

Scor'pi·o (skôr'pĭ·ō), *n.* [L., a scorpion.] **a** [*gen. Rare,* SCORPIONIS (-ō'nĭs).] A southern constellation partly in the Milky Way, and adjoining Libra. **b** The eighth sign of the zodiac, marked ♏ in almanacs. See ZODIAC.

scor'pi·oid (-oid), *adj.* [Gr. *skorpioeidēs,* fr. *skorpios* a scorpion + *eidos* form.] **1.** *Zool.* Like a scorpion; pertaining to the order (Scorpionida) constituted by the true scorpions. **2.** *Chiefly Bot.* Curved at the end, like a scorpion's tail; circinate; — chiefly of inflorescence.

scor'pi·on (skôr'pĭ·ŭn; 58), *n.* [OF., fr. L. *scorpio, scorpius,* fr. Gr. *skorpios.*] **1.** Any of an order (Scorpionida) of arachnids having an elongated body and a narrow segmented tail bearing a venomous sting at the tip. **2.** *Bib.* A kind of scourge, prob. one armed with metal points. 1 *Kings* xii. 11. **3.** Something which incites to action like the sting of an insect. **4.** [*cap.*] *Astron.* = SCORPIO.

Scorpion (*Androctonus occitanus*). (⅖)

scot (skŏt), *n.* [From ON. *skot,* and fr. OF. *escot,* of Teut. origin.] Money assessed or paid; a tax.

Scot, *n.* [LL. *Scoti, Scotti,* pl.] **1.** One of a Gaelic people of northern Ireland who settled in Scotland about the 5th century and gave it their name. **2.** A native or inhabitant of Scotland; a Scotchman.

scot and lot. **a** A parish assessment formerly laid on subjects in Great Britain according to their ability to pay. **b** Figuratively, obligations of every kind regarded collectively.

scotch (skŏch), *v. t.* [AF. *escocher* to make an incision, cut, fr. OF. *coche* nock, notch, nick.] **1.** To cut superficially; to score; also, to gash; to wound. **2.** Hence, to crush; stamp out. **3.** To block with a wedge, chock, etc., as a wheel, to prevent slipping. — *n.* **1.** A slight cut or notch; a score. **2.** A wedge to prevent slipping or rolling; a chock.

Scotch (skŏch), *adj.* Of, pert. to, or characteristic of Scotland, its language, or its inhabitants; Scottish; hence, *Humorous,* parsimonious.

Syn. **Scotch, Scottish, Scots** mean of or belonging to Scotland. **Scotch,** the most recent of these terms, is now found in careful use only in idiomatic phrases or where the other terms would be thought affected (as, *Scotch* whisky; a *Scotch* nurse); **Scottish** is now generally used in Scotland and in precise literary use in England and America (as, *Scottish* literature or character); **Scots,** the oldest term in Scotland, is now again acquiring favor there but is used elsewhere only in certain phrases (as, *Scots* law; a pound *Scots*).

— *n.* **1.** Collectively, the people of Scotland; the Scots. **2.** The dialect or dialects spoken by the people of Scotland. **3.** Short for SCOTCH WHISKY.

Scotch'man (skŏch'măn), *n.; pl.* -MEN (-mĕn). A Scot.

Scotch terrier. = SCOTTISH TERRIER.

Scotch whisky. Whisky distilled in Scotland, esp. from malted barley.

Scotch woodcock. Eggs cooked in any form and served on toast or crackers with anchovy paste.

sco'ter (skō'tẽr), *n.;* see PLURAL, *Note,* 3. Any of several sea ducks (genera *Oidemia* and *Melanitta*) inhabiting the northern coasts of the Old and New World, usually called *coots* in America, but not to be confounded with the true coots (genus *Fulica*). Common American species include the ***white-winged scoter*** (*M. deglandi*) and ***surf scoter*** (*M. perspicillata*). The common scoter of the British coasts is the ***black scoter*** (*O. nigra*). Cf. SURF DUCK.

scot'-free' (skŏt'frē'; 2), *adj.* Without payment of scot; untaxed; hence, without penalty, injury, or the like; clear; unhurt.

sco'ti·a (skō'shĭ·ȧ; -shȧ), *n.* [L., fr. Gr. *skotia* darkness, a sunken molding in the base of a pillar, so called from the dark shadow it casts, fr. *skotos* darkness.] *Arch.* A type of molding. See MOLDING, *Illust.* (9); BASE, *Illust.*

Sco'tia (skō'shȧ), *n.* [LL.] *Poetic.* Scotland.

Sco'tism (skō'tĭz'm), *n.* The system and school of John Duns Scotus (see *Biog.*).

Scot'land Yard' (skŏt'lănd). A short street off Whitehall in London, until 1890 the headquarters of the Metropolitan Police; hence, the detective department of the Metropolitan Police force.

scot'o- (skŏt'ō-; skō'tō-). [Gr. *skotos.*] A combining form meaning *darkness.*

Scot'o- (skŏt'ō-; skō'tō-). A combining form from Late Latin *Scotus,* Scot, meaning *Scottish (and),* as in **Scot'o-I'rish.**

sco·to'ma (skō·tō'mȧ), *n.; pl.* -MATA (-mȧ·tȧ). [LL., fr. Gr. *skotōma.*] *Med.* A blind or dark spot in the visual field.

Scots (skŏts), *adj.* [For older *Scottis* Scottish.] Of or pertaining to the Scottish; as, *Scots* law; a pound *Scots* (1s. 8d.). — **Syn.** See SCOTCH. — *n.* The Scottish language or dialect.

Scots'man (skŏts'măn), *n.* A Scot.

☞ *Scotsman* is the form now commonly used by Scots.

Scot'ti·cism (skŏt'ĭ-sĭz'm), *n.* An idiom, or mode of expression, peculiar to Scottish people.

Scot'tish (skŏt'ĭsh), *adj.* Of or pertaining to the inhabitants of Scotland, their country, language, or literature; Scots. — **Syn.** See SCOTCH. — *n.* **a** The Scottish language; Scots. See INDO-EUROPEAN LANGUAGES, *Table.* **b** Collectively, the Scots.

Scottish rite. *Freemasonry.* The ceremonial observed by one of the Masonic systems (the Ancient and Accepted Scottish rite); also, the system itself, which confers thirty-three degrees. Cf. YORK RITE.

Scottish terrier. A dog of a breed originating in Scotland. It has short legs, a large head with small prick ears and a powerful muzzle, a broad, deep chest, and a tail about seven inches long.

Scot'ty (skŏt'ĭ), *n.* *Colloq.* **a** A Scot; — a nickname. **b** A Scottish terrier.

scoun'drel (skoun'drĕl), *n.* A mean, worthless fellow; a villain. — *adj.* Base; mean. — **scoun'drel·ly** (-ĭ), *adj.*

scour (skour), *v. i.* [Prob. OF. *escorre, escourre,* to run out or forth, fr. L. *excurrere* to run forth.] To run swiftly, or move sweepingly, esp. in pursuit or search of something. — *v. t.* To pass over, or traverse, swiftly (a region, etc.) as if in search of something; as, to *scour* a book for quotations.

scour, *v. t.* [Prob. fr. MD. *schuren,* fr. OF. *escurer* to cleanse.] **1.** To rub hard for the purpose of cleansing; to make clean and bright by friction. **2.** To remove as if by rubbing or cleaning; esp., to sweep away; as, to *scour* the invaders from the land. **3.** To purge; as, to *scour* a horse. **4.** To cleanse from grease, dirt, etc.; as, to *scour* wool. **5.** To flush with a current of water; as, to *scour* a ditch. — *v. i.* **1.** To scour things by rubbing, washing, etc. **2.** To cleanse anything, esp. in a liquid. **3.** To become clean and bright by rubbing. — *n.* **1.** Act of scouring. **2.** A place scoured, esp. by running water. **3.** The cleansing agent used in scouring wool, etc. **4.** *usually pl.* Diarrhea or dysentery, as in cattle.

scour'er (-ẽr), *n.* **a** One whose work is at scouring. **b** A thing used for scouring; specif., a cathartic.

scour'er, *n.* [See SCOUR to run.] One who scours the streets, esp. by night; a roisterer or night thief.

scourge (skûrj), *v. t. & i.;* SCOURGED (skûrjd); SCOURG'ING (skûr'jĭng). [OF. *escorgier,* fr. L. *corrigia* strap, whip.] **1.** To whip; lash; flog. **2.** To punish with severity; chastise; afflict, esp. for sins or faults. — *n.* **1.** A lash, switch, or whip. **2.** A means of inflicting punishment, vengeance, or suffering, esp. as divine castigation; hence, a punishment; also, an infliction or affliction. — **scourg'er** (skûr'jẽr), *n.*

scour'ing rush (skour'ĭng). = HORSETAIL, 2 **a**; specif., the common horsetail (*Equisetum hyemale*) used, esp. in Europe, as a scouring material.

scour'ings (-ĭngz), *n.* Refuse removed in scouring; specif., refuse removed in scouring grain.

scouse (skous), *n.* *Naut.* A sailor's baked dish. Bread scouse contains no meat. See LOBSCOUSE.

scout (skout), *v. i.* [ME. *scouten.* See SCOUT, *n.*] To look or search; specif., *Mil.,* to reconnoiter; *Rare,* to keep watch. — *v. t.* To observe, watch, look for, or follow, as a scout; also, to reconnoiter. — *n.* [OF. *escoute* scout, spy, fr. *escouter, escolter,* to listen, hear, ult. fr. L. *auscultare* to listen to.] **1.** Act of scouting or reconnoitering. **2.** A person sent out to gain tidings, or to keep watch. **3.** = BOY SCOUT; GIRL SCOUT. **4.** *Colloq.* Fellow; chap. **5.** A college servant; — so called at Oxford University. **6.** *Aeronautics.* An airplane used for scouting purposes. **7.** *Mil. & Nav.* A soldier or a vessel sent out in war to reconnoiter. **8.** *Sports.* A person sent out to secure first-hand information as to the style of play, tactics, players, etc., of rival teams or clubs.

scout, *v. t. & i.* [Of Scand. origin.] To reject with contempt, as something absurd; to flout; scoff; as, to *scout* a suggestion. — **Syn.** See DESPISE.

scout car. A fast, armored, military reconnaissance vehicle with four-wheel drive and open top.

scout'er (skout'ẽr), *n.* **1.** One who scouts. **2.** Any adult active member (over 18 years) of the boy scouts' organization.

scouth (skōōth), *n.* *Scot.* Room; scope; also, plenty.

scout'ing, *n.* **1.** Act of one who scouts. **2.** The activities collectively of boy and girl scouts.

scout'mas'ter (skout'mȧs'tẽr), *n.* Leader of a band of scouts; specif., a leader of a troop of boy scouts.

scow (skou), *n.* [D. *schouw.*] A large flat-bottomed boat, with broad, square ends, — used as a lighter.

scowl (skoul), *v. i.* [ME. *scoulen.*] **1.** To draw down or wrinkle the brows, as in frowning; to look sullen, severe, or angry. **2.** To look gloomy or threatening. — *v. t.* To affect, influence, etc., by or as if by scowling. — **Syn.** See FROWN. — *n.* **1.** A wrinkling of the brows, as in ill humor. **2.** Hence, a gloomy or threatening aspect. — **scowl'er,** *n.* — **scowl'ing·ly,** *adv.*

scrab'ble (skrăb''l), *v. i. & t.;* -BLED (-'ld); -BLING (-lĭng). [D. *schrabbelen,* freq. of *schrabben.*] **1. a** To scrape, paw, or scratch with the hands or feet. **b** To struggle by or as by scraping with the hands. **2.** To clamber or scramble. **3.** To scribble; scrawl. — *n.* A scrabbling; as: **a** A scramble. **b** A scribble; scrawl.

scrag (skrăg), *n.* Any of various persons, animals, or objects that are lean and tough; specif.: **a** A scrawny person or animal. **b** The nape of the neck, esp. in a sheep (see SHEEP, *Illust.*) — *v. t.;* SCRAGGED (skrăgd); SCRAG'GING. *Colloq.* To seize, pull, or twist the neck of; to hang by the neck; to garrote.

scrag'gly (skrăg'lĭ), *adj.* Irregular; jagged; unkempt.

scrag'gy (-ĭ), *adj.;* SCRAG'GI·ER (-ĭ-ẽr); SCRAG'GI·EST. **1.** Rough; rugged. **2.** Lean and bony; scrawny. — **scrag'gi·ness,** *n.*

scraich, scraigh (skrāk). Scot. vars. of SCREECH.

scram (skrăm), *v. i.* [From SCRAMBLE.] *Slang.* To get out; go away; chiefly imperative.

scram'ble (skrăm'b'l), *v. i.;* -BLED (-b'ld); -BLING (-blĭng). [Nasalized form of *scrabble.*] **1.** To move or clamber with or on hands and feet or knees; to progress clumsily, as if on all fours. **2.** To struggle with others for something on the ground; hence, to struggle unceremoniously for something. **3.** To spread irregularly; as, a *scrambling* village. — *v. t.* **1.** To collect by scrambling; as, to *scramble* up wealth. **2.** To toss or mix together confusedly, as cards. **3.** To cook (eggs) by frying the mixed yolks and whites in milk or butter; as, *scrambled* eggs. — *n.* A scrambling; a jostling and pushing to get something one wants. — **scram'bler** (-blẽr), *n.*

scran'nel (skrăn''l), *adj.* **1.** *Archaic exc. Dial. Eng.* Slight; thin; lean. **2.** Hence, harsh; unmelodious; as, a *scrannel* voice; *scrannel* music.

scrap (skrăp), *n.* [ON. *skrap.*] **1.** *pl.* Fragments of food. **2. a** A small detached piece; a bit; as, a *scrap* of paper. **b** Specif., a fragment of something written or printed; an extract; as, to read *scraps* of a letter. **3.** *pl.* The crisp substance that remains after trying out animal fat; as, pork *scraps.* **4.** Fragments of material discarded as waste in manufacturing operations, or machines, tools, equipment, or parts of these, no longer in serviceable condition, which are valuable only as raw material for reprocessing; as, classes of *scrap* include metal, rubber, textiles, rope, paper, leather, lumber, plastics, and equipment made of these. — *v. t.;* SCRAPPED (skrăpt); SCRAP'PING. To make into scrap or scraps; to discard as refuse; as, to *scrap* machinery, methods. — **Syn.** See DISCARD. — *adj.* **1.** In the form of scraps or fragments. **2.** Used and discarded, or in such condition as to be unfit for further use; as, *scrap* iron. **3.** Made up of odds and ends; as, a *scrap* dinner.

scrap, *n. & v. i.* *Slang.* Fight; quarrel.

scrap'book' (skrăp'bo͝ok'), *n.* A blankbook in which printed items, pictures cut from papers, etc., may be pasted.

scrape (skrāp), *v. t.* [AS. *scrapian,* or (prob.), fr. ON. *skrapa.*] **1.** To rub over the surface of with a sharp or rough instrument; to make smooth or clean by or as by rasping; also, to grate harshly over; specif., in highway maintenance, to draw a road grader over. **2.** To remove by scraping (as above). **3.** To collect by or as by a process of scraping. **4.** To draw roughly over; to rub so as to make a grating sound. — *v. i.* **1.** To scrape anything, esp. with a grating sound. **2.** To gather and hoard goods, esp. money, little by little. **3.** To play (a violin, etc.) with a rough, unmusical tone. **4.** To draw back the foot along the ground or floor when making a bow; as, bowing and *scraping.* **5.** To manage to make one's way with difficulty; as, to *scrape* along. — *n.* **1. a** Act of scraping. **b** The effect of scraping, as a scratching sound. **2.** A bow made by drawing back the foot. **3.** A disagreeable predicament.

scrap'er (skrāp'ẽr), *n.* **1.** One who scrapes. Specif.: **a** One who acquires avariciously and saves penuriously. **b** A fiddler; also, a barber; — usually contemptuous. **2.** A tool or apparatus that scrapes; an instrument or implement with which something is scraped.

scrap'per (skrăp'ẽr), *n.* One who or that which scraps.

scrap'ple (skrăp''l), *n.* [Dim. of SCRAP.] An article of food made by boiling together scraps of meat, usually pork, with chopped herbs and flour or Indian meal.

scrap'py (skrăp'ĭ), *adj.;* SCRAP'PI·ER (-ĭ-ẽr); SCRAP'PI·EST. Consisting of scraps; fragmentary.

scrap'py, *adj.* *Colloq.* Combative; determinedly aggressive. — **scrap'pi·ly,** *adv.*

scratch (skrăch), *v. t.* [ME. *cracchen,* blended with ME. *scratten* to scratch.] **1.** To scrape with the claws or nails. **2.** To rub and tear or mark the surface of with something sharp or ragged. **3.** To scrape or rub to allay irritation, cause a pleasant sensation, or the like; as, to *scratch* a dog's neck. **4.** *Colloq.* To write or draw hastily or roughly; scribble. **5.** To scrape along a rough surface; as, to *scratch* a match. **6.** To withdraw (an entry from competition); as, his horse was *scratched* in the third race. **7.** To cancel or expunge as by drawing a line through; as, to *scratch* an item from an account. **8.** *U. S. Politics.* To mark (a ballot) so as to vote for most of the candidates of one party, but for some of another party. — *v. i.* **1.** To use the claws or nails in tearing, wounding, digging, etc. **2.** To rub one's head, back, etc., with something rough. **3.** To gather money by hard work and hoarding. **4.** To scrape lightly with a slight grating sound; as, a pen *scratching.* **5.** *Billiards & Pool.* To make a scratch.

— *n.* **1.** A mark or injury produced by scratching. **2.** *Colloq.* A written scrawl; scribble. **3.** An act, instance, or sound of scratching. **4.** The line from which contestants start in a race; hence, figuratively, nothing; as, circulation rose from *scratch* to 50,000. **5.** A line formerly drawn across a prize ring, up to which boxers were brought to join fight; hence, trial or proof of courage; as, to come up to the *scratch.* **6.** In a contest where handicaps are allowed, the starting time, station, etc., of a competitor who neither is allowed odds nor receives a penalty. **7.** *Billiards.* A shot which scores by chance; hence, in general, a fluke. **8.** *Billiards & Pool.* A shot which involves a penalty; hence, esp., a miss. **9.** *pl. Veter.* Scratches (which see).

— *adj.* **1.** Made as, or used for, a tentative effort; as, *scratch* paper. **2.** Made or done by chance and not in the way intended; as, a *scratch* hit. **3.** Arranged or put together with little selection of material; haphazard; as, a *scratch* dinner. **4.** In sports, without handicap or allowance.

scratch'er (skrăch'ẽr), *n.* One who or that which scratches.

scratch'es (-ĕz; -ĭz), *n. pl., usually construed as a sing. Veter.* An affection of the skin of the hollow of the fetlock of horses, accompanied with swelling, heat, tenderness, and sometimes suppuration.

scratch hit. *Baseball.* A hit credited as such to a batter when ordinarily he would have been out, as when a fly ball drops untouched between two fielders each of whom hesitates in the attempt to catch it.

scratch test. *Med.* A test for determining a person's susceptibility, made by rubbing an extract of the allergy-producing substance in question into small breaks or scratches in the skin.

scratch'y (skrăch'ĭ), *adj.;* SCRATCH'I·ER (-ĭ-ẽr); -I·EST. **1. a** Making a scratching noise. **b** Having the appearance of scratches. **2.** Uneven; straggling.

scrawl (skrôl), *v. t. & i.* To draw or mark awkwardly and irregularly; to write hastily and carelessly; to scribble. — *n.* Scrawled writing; a bit of careless or inelegant writing. — **scrawl'er** (-ẽr), *n.* — **scrawl'y** (-ĭ), *adj.*

scraw'ny (skrô'nĭ), *adj.* *U. S.* Thin; rawboned. — **Syn.** See LEAN.

screak (skrēk), *v. i.* To screech or creak, as a hinge. — *n.* A screech; creaking.

scream (skrēm), *v. i.* [ME. *scremen,* perh. fr. ON. *skræma* to scare, terrify.] **1.** To cry out with a shrill voice; to utter a sharp outcry. **2.** *Colloq.* To speak or write with intense, hysterical expressions; as, he wrote in *screaming* headlines; also, to have a vivid, startling effect; as, *screaming* colors. — *v. t.* To utter with or as with a scream; as, to *scream* an alarm. — *n.* A sharp, shrill cry.

scream'er (-ẽr), *n.* **1.** A person who screams. **2.** *Slang.* Anything of remarkable excellence, as a good shot at golf. **3.** *Slang.* A writing or person that makes one scream from thrills or mirth. **4. a** *Printers' Slang.* An exclamation mark. **b** *Cant, U.S. Journalism.* A sensationally startling headline. **5.** *Zool.* Any of a small group of South American birds (family Anhimidae) comprising the ***crested screamers*** (genus *Chauna*) and the ***horned screamer*** (*Anhima cornuta*).

scream'ing, *adj.* **1.** Uttering screams. **2.** Having the nature of a scream; like a scream. **3.** Evoking screams, as of mirth; as, a *screaming* farce. — **scream'ing·ly**, *adv.*

scree (skrē), *n.* [From the pl. *screes*, fr. ON. *skrītha* a landslip on a hillside.] *Brit.* A pebble; a stone; also, a heap of stones or debris.

screech (skrēch), *v. i.* [Also, formerly, *scritch*, ME. *skrichen*, of imitative origin.] To utter a harsh, shrill scream; to shriek; also, to make a sound resembling a scream or shriek. — *v. t.* To utter as or with a screech. — *n.* A harsh, shrill scream, or a sound resembling this. — **screech'er** (-ẽr), *n.*

screed (skrēd), *n.* [AS. *screāde.*] **1.** *Dial.* A fragment; shred; also, a strip or band. **2.** *Scot.* **a** A tearing; rent. **b** A drink or drinking bout. **3.** A long list or discourse; sometimes, a tirade; diatribe. **4.** Also **floating screed.** A strip, as of plaster of the thickness planned for the coat, laid on as a guide. — *v. t. & i. Scot.* To rend; tear.

screen (skrēn), *n.* [OF. *escren, escran.*] **1.** A partition or curtain that cuts off inconvenience, injury, or danger; a protective barrier; as, a fire *screen;* a window *screen.* **2.** A perforated plate or meshed fabric, usually mounted on a frame, used to separate coarser from finer parts, as of sand; a coarse sieve. **3.** *Arch.* A wall or partition, often ornamental, carried up to a certain height for separation and protection. **4.** *Mil.* A body of troops thrown out toward the enemy to protect a command or an area. **5.** *Motion Pictures.* A surface upon which a picture or series of pictures is projected; hence, the motion pictures, collectively. **6.** *Nav.* A formation of light vessels about a formation of heavier vessels for protection, as from submarines or destroyers. **7.** *Photoengraving.* Two pieces of optical glass, ruled in opposite directions, used in half-tone reproduction. **8.** *Physics.* A piece of apparatus designed to prevent agencies in one part affecting other parts; as, optical and magnetic *screens.* **9.** *Television.* The part of a television set on which the picture appears.
— *v. t.* **1.** To cut off from inconvenience, injury, or danger. **2.** To shelter or conceal with or as with a screen. **3.** To pass, as coal, gravel, ashes, etc., through a screen; to sift. **4.** To post as a notice upon a screen. **5.** To project (as a picture) upon a screen; also, to adapt (a story, drama, etc.) to motion-picture reproduction. **6.** *Chiefly Mil.* To pass through a standardized test (**screen'ing test**) for sorting out candidates of superior capacity, aptitude, and personality, as for advanced training, special assignment, etc., or for eliminating those patently unfit for induction. — *v. i.* To be screenable; esp., *Motion Pictures,* to undergo, or be suitable for, projection on a screen. — **Syn.** See HIDE. — **screen'a·ble**, *adj.* — **screen'er**, *n.*

screen'ings (-ĭngz), *n. pl.* **a** Material which has been screened. **b** Refuse after screening, as in cleaning wheat, rice, barley, etc.

screen'play' (skrēn'plā'), *n.* The written form of a story prepared for motion-picture production, including description of characters, scenes and settings, dialogue, and stage directions. See SCRIPT.

screw (skrōō; 114), *n.* [Formerly *scrue*, fr. OF. *escroue* female screw, ult. fr. L. *scrofa* sow.] **1.** A common mechanical device consisting in its simplest form of a continuous helical rib, or thread, with the cylindrical shank from which it projects (see SIMPLE MACHINE, *Illust.*); — called specif. *external*, or *male, screw.* Also, the corresponding part into which an external, or male, screw advances and fits when turned; — called specif. *internal*, or *female, screw.* **2. a** A screwlike form; a spiral. **b** A turn of a screw; also, any twist like the turn of a screw. **c** A screwlike device, as a tool with a worm for pulling corks; a corkscrew. **3.** *Colloq.* [Cf. Dan. *skrog* a carcass.] A worn-out horse. **4.** *Brit.* A small packet of tobacco, pepper, etc.; — so called because often wrapped in a bit of twisted paper. **5.** A sharp bargainer; skinflint. **6.** *Slang.* **a** A prison guard; turnkey. **b** *Chiefly Brit.* Salary; pay. **7.** A screw propeller. **8.** = THUMBSCREW, 2.

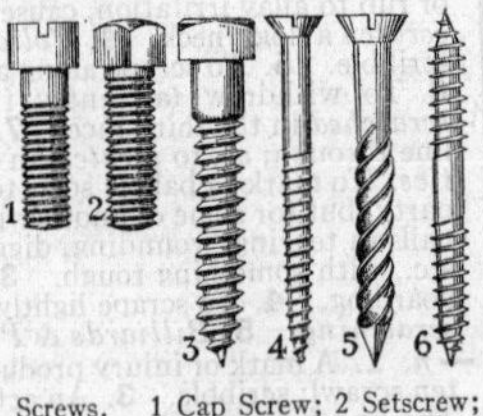

Screws. 1 Cap Screw; 2 Setscrew; 3 Lag Screw, or Coach Screw; 4 Flathead Screw; 5 Drive Screw; 6 Dowel Screw.

— *v. t.* **1.** To turn, as a screw; to apply a screw to; to press, insert, move, or the like, by a screw or screws. **2. a** To twist; contort; as, to *screw* the eyes. **b** To twist or strain, esp. to suit one's purposes. **3.** To fasten with or as with a screw. **4.** To tighten (a musical string) by turning the screws or keys; figuratively, to make tense; as, *screwing* up courage. **5.** To force as if by the pressure of screws. **6.** Hence, to practice extortion upon. — *v. i.* **1.** To turn as or like a screw. **2.** To turn with a twisting motion. **3.** To practice extortion or exactions.
— *adj.* **1.** Of, pertaining to, or operated by, a screw or screw propeller. **2.** Having a screw (sense 1) or screw thread, so as to be capable of being screwed in or on; as, **screw auger** (see AUGER, *Illust.*), **screw cap, screw collar, screw hook, screw nut, screw plug, screw post.**

screw'ball' (skrōō'bôl'), *n.* **1.** Anything crazily eccentric, as: **a** *Baseball.* A pitched ball with a crazy break opposite to a curve. **b** Fervid swing music. **2.** *Slang.* One conspicuous for dizzily fantastic ideas or wildly irrational behavior. — *adj.* Crazily eccentric; zany.

screw bean. a The twisted sweet pod of a shrub or small tree (*Prosopis pubescens*) of the southwestern United States. **b** The tree itself, commonly called *tornillo.*

screw driver, *or* **screw'driv'er** (skrōō'drīv'ẽr), *n.* A tool for turning screws.

screwed (skrōōd), *adj.* **1.** Having threads like those of a screw. **2.** Twisted; contorted. **3.** *Slang.* Intoxicated.

screw'er (skrōō'ẽr), *n.* One who or that which screws.

screw eye. A screw with a head in the form of a loop or eye.

screw jack. A jackscrew.

screw pine. Any plant of the genus *Pandanus*, typifying a family (Pandanaceae, the screw-pine family) characterized by slender palmlike stems, often with huge prop roots, and by terminal crowns of swordlike leaves; esp. *P. tectorius* of Polynesia.

screw propeller. A device consisting of a central hub with radiating blades placed and twisted so that each forms part of a helical surface, used to propel ships, aircraft, etc.

screw thread. *Mach.* The projecting helical rib of a screw; also, one complete turn of it.

screw'y (skrōō'ĭ), *adj. Slang, U.S.* Crackbrained; fantastically or ridiculously absurd; freakish; preposterous.

scrib'ble (skrĭb''l), *v. t.;* -BLED (-'ld); -BLING (-lĭng). [ML. *scribillare*, fr. L. *scribere.*] **1.** To write hastily or carelessly; to scrawl. **2.** To fill or cover with careless or worthless writing. — *v. i.* To scrawl; to make meaningless marks. — *n.* Hasty or careless writing; scrawl.

scrib'bler (-lẽr), *n.* One who scribbles; a writer of worthless or inferior matter; an author of small reputation.

scribe (skrīb), *n.* [L. *scriba*, fr. *scribere* to write.] **1.** An official or public writer acting usually as a clerk. **2.** A copier of manuscripts. **3.** Penman; author; writer; journalist; — used humorously. **4.** *Jewish Religion & Hist.* A doctor or teacher of the law. **5.** Any of various pointed instruments for marking wood, metal, bricks, etc.; a scriber. — *v. i. & t.* **1.** To work as a scribe; to write. **2.** To mark (wood, metal, brick, etc.) by scratching lines with a pointed instrument, as a pair of compasses, to indicate how the piece is to be cut or shaped. — **scrib'al** (skrīb'ăl; -'l), *adj.*

scrib'er (skrīb'ẽr), *n.* One that scribes; specif., a pointed tool for marking off wood, metal, etc., to be cut.

scrieve (skrēv), *v. i.* To glide along. — *v. t.* To reel off (a story or song). *Both Scot.*

scrim (skrĭm), *n.* A light, coarse, cotton or linen fabric, used in embroidery, for window curtains, etc.

scrim'mage (skrĭm'ĭj), *n.* [An alteration of SKIRMISH.] **1.** Formerly, a skirmish; now, a confused struggle. **2. a** *Rugby Football.* A loose scrummage. **b** *Amer. Football.* The play following the putting in play of the ball by the center lineman of the team in possession of the ball. It does not end until the ball is dead. — *v. i. & t.* **1.** To search busily. **2.** *Football.* To take part in, or to throw into, a scrimmage. — **scrim'mag·er** (-ĭj·ẽr), *n.*

scrimp (skrĭmp), *v. t.* **1.** To be niggardly in providing for; as, to *scrimp* a son for money. **2.** To make too small, short, scanty, etc.; to skimp. — *v. i.* To be niggardly. — **scrimp'i·ly**, *adv.* — **scrimp'i·ness**, *n.* — **scrimp'y**, *adj.;* SCRIMP'I·ER (-ĭ·ẽr); SCRIMP'I·EST.

scrim'shaw' (skrĭm'shô'), *v. i. & t. Naut.* To do any neat small mechanical job; specif., to ornament, as shells, ivory, etc., by engraving. — *n. Naut.* A neat piece of mechanical work; anything that is scrimshawed.

scrip (skrĭp), *n.* [ME. *scrippe*, fr. ML. *scrippum.*] *Archaic.* A small bag or wallet.

scrip, *n.* [From SCRIPT.] **1.** A writing, as a certificate, schedule, or list. **2.** A small piece or scrap, esp. of paper. **3.** Any of various documents used as evidence that the holder or bearer is entitled to receive something, as stock or a fractional share of stock, an allotment of land, etc. Cf. SCRIP DIVIDEND. **4.** *Colloq., U.S.* A piece of the fractional paper currency formerly issued in the United States; a "shinplaster"; also, such currency collectively.

scrip dividend. *Finance.* A dividend in scrip instead of cash, usually convertible into stock.

script (skrĭpt), *n.* [OF. and L.; OF. *escript, escrit*, fr. L. *scriptum* something written, fr. *scribere, scriptum,* to write.] **1.** *Rare.* A writing. **2.** *Law.* An original or principal instrument or document. **3.** Written characters; a system of writing. **4.** *Print.* Type made in imitation of handwriting. See TYPE. **5.** *Theater.* Short for MANUSCRIPT. **6.** A typescript; specif., *Motion Pictures & Television*, the typescript or mimeographed or published form of a screenplay for use during the shooting of a picture. **7.** *Radio.* The typed text or dialogue, often with suggestions to director and cast, from which the spoken part of a program is presented for broadcasting. — **script'-writ'er**, *n.*

scrip·to'ri·um (skrĭp·tō'rĭ·ŭm; 70), *n.; pl.* SCRIPTORIA (-ȧ). [ML., fr. L. *scribere, scriptum,* to write.] The room in a monastery set apart for the scribes or copyists.

scrip'tur·al (skrĭp'tůr·ăl), *adj.* **1.** Written or pert. to writing. **2.** Of, pert. to, contained in, or according to, the Scriptures; Biblical. — **scrip'tur·al·ly**, *adv.*

scrip'ture (-tůr), *n.* [L. *scriptura.* See SCRIPT.] **1.** *Archaic.* Anything written; document; inscription. **2.** [*cap.*] The books of the Old and the New Testament, or of either of them; the Bible; — used chiefly in *pl.*, with *the* (and often *Holy*); as, the Holy *Scriptures.* **3.** *Rare.* [*cap.*] A passage from the Bible; a text. **4.** Any sacred writing; as, Buddhist *scripture.*

scrive'ner (skrĭv'nẽr; skrĭv'ĕn·ẽr), *n.* [From older *scrivein*, fr. OF. *escrivain*, fr. L. *scribere* to write.] **1.** A professional or public writer; scribe; amanuensis. **2.** A notary.

scrod (skrŏd), *n. U.S.* A young cod (esp. *Gadus morrhua*) prepared in strips cut across the grain, as for broiling.

scrof'u·la (skrŏf'ů·lȧ), *n.* [ML., fr. LL. *scrofulae*, pl., dim. fr. *scrofa* a breeding sow.] *Med.* A tuberculous condition, with enlargement and cheesy degeneration of the lymphatic glands, particularly of the neck; king's evil.

scrof'u·lous (-lŭs), *adj.* **1.** Pertaining to or affected with scrofula. **2.** Resembling scrofula; hence, morally contaminated. — **scrof'u·lous·ly**, *adv.* — **scrof'u·lous·ness**, *n.*

scrog (skrŏg), *n.* [ME. *skrogg.*] *Scot. & Dial.* A stunted shrub, bush, or branch; scrub. — **scrog'gy** (-ĭ), *adj.*

scroll (skrōl), *n.* [Earlier *scrowle* (after *rowle* roll), fr. ME. *scrowe*, fr. OF. *escroe, escroue*, of Teut. origin.] **1.** A roll of paper or parchment; hence, a writing; schedule; list; also, a draft; outline. **2.** Something, usually an ornament, in form resembling a roll of paper, esp. one loosely or only partly rolled, as any of various spiral forms in ornamental design. **3.** The curved head of viol instruments. See VIOLIN, *Illust.*

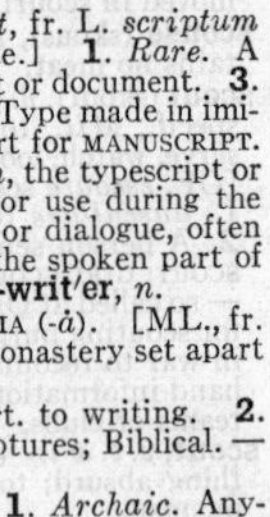
Scroll.

scroll saw. A ribbonlike saw stretched in a frame, adapted for sawing curved outlines; also, a machine in which such a saw is worked by foot or power.

scroll'work' (skrōl'wûrk'), *n.* Ornamental work having a scroll or scrolls as the essential feature; also, thin woodwork cut into designs with a scroll saw.

Scrooge, Eb'en·e'zer (ĕb'ĕn·ē'zẽr skrōōj'). In Dickens's *Christmas Carol*, a hard, avaricious man visited by spirits on Christmas Eve and made kindly by what they show him of human life.

scroop (skrōōp), *v. i.* [Imitative.] *Dial.* To creak; squeak; grate. — **scroop**, *n.*

scroph'u·lar'i·a'ceous (skrŏf'ū·lâr'ĭ·ā'shŭs), *adj.* [From *Scrophularia*, type genus.] *Bot.* Belonging to the figwort family (Scrophulariaceae). See FIGWORT.

scro'tum (skrō'tŭm), *n.*; *pl.* -TA (-tȧ), -TUMS (-tŭmz). [L.] The external bag or pouch containing the testicles, found in most mammals. — **scro'tal** (-tăl; -t'l), *adj.*

scrouge (skrouj; skrōōj), *v. & n.* *Colloq.* Crowd; press.

scrounge (skrounj; skrōōnj), *v. t. & i.* [Prob. fr. E. dial. *scr(o)unge* to squeeze.] *Slang.* To steal slyly; pilfer; also, to cadge; sponge. — **scroung'er** (skroun'jẽr; skrōōn'-), *n.*

scrub (skrŭb), *n.* [Dan. *skrub.*] **1.** Vegetation consisting chiefly of dwarf or stunted trees and shrubs; also, a tract covered with such vegetation, esp. a palmetto barren of the southern United States, or the "bush" of Australia. **2.** An undersized or inferior person; also, one who works hard and lives meanly; a drudge. **3.** *Forestry.* A low, straggling tree of inferior quality. **4.** *Sports.* A player not belonging to the regular team, crew, etc. **5.** *Stock Breeding.* A domestic animal of mixed or unknown parentage, usually without definite type; a mongrel. — *adj.* **1.** Undersized; inferior; paltry. **2.** *Sports.* Of a crew, nine, eleven, or other team, composed of "scrubs"; hence, hastily got together without careful selection; as, a *scrub* team; also, of a game or other contest, participated in by scrub teams.

scrub, *v. t.*; SCRUBBED (skrŭbd); SCRUB'BING. [Of LG. or Scand. origin.] **1.** To rub hard in washing; to wash with rubbing; as, to *scrub* a floor. **2.** To wash (a gas). — *v. i.* To rub something hard, or to cleanse by rubbing, as with a wet brush. — *n.* Act or process of scrubbing.

scrub'bed (skrŭb'ĕd; -ĭd), *adj.* *Archaic.* Scrubby.

scrub'ber (skrŭb'ẽr), *n.* One who scrubs, or that which scrubs or is used for scrubbing, as a brush; specif., *Gas Mfg.*, any of various apparatus for washing (scrubbing) coal gas or other gases.

scrub'by (skrŭb'ĭ), *adj.*; SCRUB'BI·ER (-ĭ·ẽr); -BI·EST. **1.** Of the nature of scrub; stunted. **2.** Having much scrub, or underbrush. **3.** *Colloq.* Insignificant; paltry.

scrub typhus. = TSUTSUGAMUSHI DISEASE.

scruff (skrŭf), *n.* The nape of the neck.

scrum (skrŭm). Short for SCRUMMAGE.

scrum'mage (skrŭm'ĭj; *dial. also* skrōōm'-), *n.* **1.** Scot. & dial. Eng. var. of SCRIMMAGE. **2.** Specif., *Rugby Football*, a certain play or formation (in which players of each side close round the ball) used to restart the play as after certain minor infractions. — *v. t. & i.*; -MAGED (-ĭjd); -MAG·ING (-ĭj·ĭng). *Rugby Football.* To play or place (the ball) in, or form, a scrummage. — **scrum'mag·er** (-ĭj·ẽr), *n.*

scrump'tious (skrŭmp'shŭs), *adj.* *Slang.* **a** Nice; particular; fastidious. **b** Very fine; capital; "dandy."

scrunch (skrŭnch), *v. t. & i.* *Colloq.* To crunch; also, to crush; squeeze. — **scrunch,** *n.*

scru'ple (skrōō'p'l), *n.* [F. and L.; F. *scrupule*, fr. L. *scrupulus* a small sharp stone.] **1.** A minute portion; a small part; specif.: *Rom. Antiq.* **a** The smallest unit of weight, 1/288 of an as or 1/24 of an ounce. **b** A coin, worth during the Republic about $0.75. **2.** An apothecaries' weight. See WEIGHT, *Table* 3. **3.** Hesitation as to action or decision from the difficulty of determining what is right or fitting. — **Syn.** See QUALM. — *v. i. & t.*; SCRU'PLED (-p'ld); SCRU'PLING (-plĭng). To have scruples, esp. conscientious ones.

scru'pu·lous (skrōō'pū·lŭs), *adj.* Full of or having scruples; inclined to scruple; careful; exact; punctilious. — **Syn.** See CAREFUL; UPRIGHT. — **scru'pu·los'i·ty** (-lŏs'ĭ·tĭ), *n.* — **scru'pu·lous·ly,** *adv.* — **scru'pu·lous·ness,** *n.*

scru·ta'tor (skrōō·tā'tẽr), *n.* [L.] One who investigates or scrutinizes; a scrutineer.

scru'ti·neer' (skrōō'tĭ·nēr'), *n.* A scrutinizer or examiner, esp. of votes at an election.

scru'ti·nize (skrōō'tĭ·nīz; 114), *v. t. & i.* To examine closely; to make a scrutiny. — **scru'ti·niz'er** (-nīz'ẽr), *n.* — **scru'ti·niz'ing·ly,** *adv.*

Syn. **Scrutinize, scan, inspect, examine** mean to look at critically or searchingly. **Scrutinize** stresses close attention to minute detail; **scan,** close analytic observation, now esp. in reference to the metrical structure of verse; **inspect,** a careful observation or, esp. in military or industrial use, a searching scrutiny for defects, errors, or the like; **examine,** a close scrutiny in order to determine nature, condition, or the like.

scru'ti·ny (-nĭ), *n.*; *pl.* -NIES (-nĭz). [L. *scrutinium*, fr. *scrutari* to search, examine.] **1.** Close examination; minute inspection; critical observation. **2.** *Parliamentary Practice.* An official examination, as by a committee, of the votes given at an election.

scud (skŭd), *v. i.*; SCUD'DED; SCUD'DING. **1.** To move or run swiftly. **2.** *Naut.* To be driven swiftly, or to run, before a gale. — *n.* **1.** Act of scudding; a driving along. **2.** Loose, vapory clouds driven swiftly by the wind; also, *Scot. & Dial. Eng.*, a gust of wind, or a driving mist. **3.** *Scot. & Ir.* A slap; spank.

scu'do (skōō'dō), *n.*; *pl.* SCUDI (-dē). [It., a crown, a dollar, a shield, fr. L. *scutum* a shield.] A silver coin, and money of account, used (from the 17th to the 19th century) in Italy and Sicily, usually approximating 97 cents; also, a gold coin of the same value.

scuff (skŭf), *v. t. & i.* To walk without lifting the feet; to shuffle. — *n.* **1.** A noise of or as of scuffing. **2.** A variety of slipper without quarter or counter.

scuf'fle (skŭf''l), *v. i.*; SCUF'FLED (-'ld); SCUF'FLING (-lĭng). **1.** To struggle at close quarters with disorder and confusion. **2.** To scuff; shuffle. — *n.* A rough haphazard struggle with scrambling and confusion.

scul·dud'der·y (skŭl·dŭd'ẽr·ĭ), *n.* *Scot. & U. S.* Grossness; obscenity. Cf. SKULDUGGERY.

sculk (skŭlk), **sculk'er.** Vars. of SKULK, etc.

scull (skŭl), *n.* [ME., of unknown origin.] *Naut.* **a** An oar used at the stern to propel a boat by sculling. **b** One of a pair of short oars, usually less than ten feet in length, for one person. **c** *Obs.* A small rowboat. — *v. t. & i.* *Naut.* To propel (a boat) with a scull or sculls. — **scull'er** (-ẽr), *n.*

scull, *n.* [Gael. or ON.] *Scot.* A large shallow wicker basket, esp. for carrying produce.

scul'ler·y (skŭl'ẽr·ĭ), *n.*; *pl.* -IES (-ĭz). [OF. *escuelerie* the office of keeping dishes, fr. *escuele* a dish, fr. L. *scutella* a salver.] A place where culinary utensils are cleaned and kept; also, a room near the kitchen, for the coarse work. — **scul'ler·y,** *adj.*

scul'lion (skŭl'yŭn), *n.* [OF. *escouillon, escouvillon*, a swab.] *Archaic.* A kitchen menial; also, in contempt, fellow; wretch.

scul'pin (skŭl'pĭn), *n.*; see PLURAL, *Note*, 3. **a** Any of numerous spiny, large-headed, broad-mouthed, usually scaleless, fishes constituting a family (Cottidae), esp. one of a genus (*Acanthocottus*) abundant in the North Atlantic. **b** A fish (*Scorpaena guttata*) of the southern California coast.

‖**sculp'sit** (skŭlp'sĭt). [L.] He (or she) carved or engraved (it).

sculp'tor (skŭlp'tẽr), *n.* [L., fr. *sculpere, sculptum*, to carve, fr. *scalpere* to cut, scratch.] **1.** One who sculptures. **2.** Hence, an artist who designs works of sculpture, his model being usually in a plastic material, from which model the marble is cut or the bronze is cast. — **sculp'tress** (-três; -trĭs), *n.*

sculp'ture (skŭlp'tūr), *n.* [L. *sculptura.*] **1.** Act or art of carving, cutting, or hewing wood, stone, metal, etc., into statues, ornaments, etc.; hence, the act or art of producing figures and groups, now esp. in marble or bronze. **2.** Carved work in stone, wood, metal, etc. — *v. t.* **1.** To form with the chisel or other tool on, in, or from wood, stone, metal, etc.; to carve; engrave. **2.** *Phys. Geog.* To change in form by erosion. — **sculp'tur·al** (-tūr·ăl), *adj.*

sculp'tur·esque' (skŭlp'tūr·ĕsk'), *adj.* In the manner of, or resembling, sculpture; statuelike; majestic. — **sculp'tur·esque'ly,** *adv.* — **sculp'tur·esque'ness,** *n.*

scum (skŭm), *n.* [ME. *scume*, fr. MD. *schūm* (D. *schuim*).] **1. a** Extraneous matter risen to the surface of liquids; any foul, filmy covering floating on a liquid, as on a stagnant pool. **b** The scoria of metals in a molten state; dross. **2.** Refuse; offscourings; hence, a rabble of low people. — *v. t.*; SCUMMED (skŭmd); SCUM'MING. To take the scum from; to skim. — *v. i.* **1.** *Obs.* To rise as scum. **2.** To form a scum; to become covered with scum.

scum'ble (skŭm'b'l), *v. t.*; SCUM'BLED (-b'ld); SCUM'BLING (-blĭng). [Freq. of SCUM.] *Painting & Drawing.* **a** To render softer by covering with a thin coat of opaque color; also, to apply (a color) in this manner. **b** To soften the lines or colors of (a drawing) by rubbing lightly with a stump, the finger, etc. **c** To paint, draw, or produce by either of these processes. — *n.* A softened effect produced by scumbling; also, material put on in scumbling; the quantity, as of paint, used for scumbling.

scum'my (skŭm'ĭ), *adj.*; SCUM'MI·ER (-ĭ·ẽr); SCUM'MI·EST. **1.** Covered with scum. **2.** Of the nature of or like scum; hence, contemptible; mean; scurvy.

scun'ner (skŭn'ẽr), *n.* *Dial.* Dislike; prejudice. — (skŭn'ẽr; skōōn'-), *v. t. & i.* *Scot. & Dial.* To loathe; to sicken with disgust.

scup (skŭp), *n.*; see PLURAL, *Note*, 6. [North Amer. Indian *mishcŭppaŭog*, pl.] A marine food fish (*Stenotomus versicolor*) of the sea-bream family (Sparidae), common on the Atlantic coast of the United States; — called also *porgy*. See SPAROID.

scup'per (skŭp'ẽr), *n.* *Naut.* An opening cut through the waterway and bulwarks of a ship, so that water falling on deck may flow overboard. — *v. t.* *Slang, Brit.* To put or leave in difficulty; to massacre in a surprise attack.

scup'per·nong (-nŏng), *n.* [From *Scuppernong* river and lake in N. Carolina.] **1.** An American grape, a form of the muscadine (*Muscadinia rotundifolia*) of the southern Atlantic States. It is large, yellowish-green, and of plumlike flavor. **2.** An aromatic wine made from this grape.

scurf (skûrf), *n.* [AS. *scurf, sceorf.*] **1.** Branlike material which becomes detached from the epidermis in thin dry scales, esp. in an abnormal skin condition. **2. a** Anything like flakes or scales adhering to a surface. **b** Hence, the foul remains of anything adherent. — **scurf'y,** *adj.*

scur'rile (skûr'ĭl; 56), *adj.* Also **scur'ril.** [L. *scurrilis*, fr. *scurra* buffoon, jester.] Scurrilous.

scur·ril'i·ty (skŭ·rĭl'ĭ·tĭ), *n.*; *pl.* -TIES (-tĭz). Quality or state of being scurrilous; also, a scurrilous remark or act. — **Syn.** See ABUSE.

scur'ril·ous (skûr'ĭ·lŭs; 117), *adj.* **1.** Using, or given to using, the language of low buffoonery. **2.** Containing low indecency or abuse; coarsely opprobrious; obscenely jocular. — **scur'ril·ous·ly,** *adv.* — **scur'ril·ous·ness,** *n.*

scur'ry (skûr'ĭ), *v. i.*; SCUR'RIED (-ĭd); SCUR'RY·ING. [Appar. a blend of *scatter* and *hurry.*] To hasten briskly; to scamper. — *n.* **1.** Act of scurrying. **2.** A short run or race, esp. on horseback.

scur'vy (skûr'vĭ), *adj.*; SCUR'VI·ER (-vĭ·ẽr); SCUR'VI·EST. [From SCURF.] **1.** *Obs.* Covered or affected with scurf or scabs; scurfy. **2.** Mean; contemptible; as, a *scurvy* trick. — **Syn.** See CONTEMPTIBLE. — **scur'vi·ly,** *adv.* — **scur'vi·ness,** *n.*

scur'vy, *n.* [From SCURVY, *adj.*] *Med.* A disease characterized by hemorrhage, esp. into the skin and mucous membranes, by spongy gums, debility, etc. It results from a lack of vitamin C.

scurvy grass. Any of several cresses, esp. one (*Cochlearia officinalis*) of arctic regions, a remedy for scurvy.

scut (skŭt), *n.* **1.** The short erect tail of an animal, esp. of a hare or rabbit. **2.** *Slang.* A contemptible fellow.

scu'tage (skū'tĭj), *n.* [ML. *scutagium*, fr. L. *scutum* shield.] *Feud. Law.* A tax levied upon a tenant of a knight's fee in commutation for military service.

scu'tate (-tāt), *adj.* [L. *scutatus* armed with a shield.] **1.** *Bot.* Peltate (see LEAF, *Illust.*). **2.** *Zool.* Covered by bony or horny plates, or large scales.

scutch (skŭch), *v. t.* **1.** To separate the woody fiber from (flax, hemp, etc.) by beating; to swingle. **2.** To dress the fiber of (cotton or silk) by beating. — *n.* A scutcher.

scutch'eon (skŭch'ŭn), *n.* **a** Contr. of ESCUTCHEON. **b** Anything shaped like an escutcheon; specif., *Zool.*, a scute.

scutch'er (skŭch'ẽr), *n.* An implement or machine for scutching hemp, flax, etc.; a scutch.

scute (skūt), *n.* [L. *scutum* a shield, buckler.] *Zool.* Any external bony or horny plate, as on a reptile, a fish, etc.

scu'tel·late (skū'tĕ·lāt), *adj.* [L. *scutella* a platter.] *Bot. & Zool.* Platterlike in form.

scu·tel'late (skū·tĕl'āt; skū'tĕ·lāt), *adj.* [NL. *scutellatus*, fr. *scutellum*, dim. of L. *scutum* shield.] *Zool.* Covered with scales or small plates.

scu'tel·la'tion (skū'tĕ·lā'shŭn), *n.* The entire covering, or arrangement, of scales, as on the legs of a bird.

scu·tel'lum (skū·tĕl'ŭm), *n.*; *pl.* -LA (-ȧ). [NL., neut. dim. of L. *scutum* a shield.] **1.** *Bot.* Any of several small shield-shaped parts or organs. **2.** *Zool.* A plate or scale, as one of the transverse scales on the tarsi and toes of birds.

scu'ti·form (skū'tĭ·fôrm), *adj.* [L. *scutum* shield + *-form.*] Shield-shaped; scutate.

‖**scu'to bo'nae vo'lun·ta'tis tu'ae co'ro·nas'ti nos** (skū'tō bō'nē vŏl'ŭn·tā'tĭs tū'ē kŏr'ō·năs'tī nōs). [L.] Thou hast crowned us with a shield of thy good will; — motto of Maryland.

scut'ter (skŭt'ẽr; skoot'ẽr), *v. i. & t.* To scuttle; scurry. — *n. Scot. & Dial.* A rapid scurry.

scut'tle (skŭt''l), *n.* [AS. *scutel.*] **1.** A shallow, open basket for carrying grain, etc. **2.** A utensil for carrying coal; coal scuttle.

scut'tle, *v. i.;* -TLED (-'ld); -TLING (-lĭng). To run swiftly; scurry. — *n.* A quick pace; a short swift run.

scut'tle, *n.* [MF. *escoutille,* fr. Sp. *escotilla.*] **1.** A small opening, as in a wall or roof, furnished with a lid. **2.** *Naut.* A small opening or hatchway in the deck of a ship, large enough to admit a man, and with a lid for covering it; also, a like hole in the side or bottom of a ship. — *v. t.* To cut a hole through the bottom, deck, or sides of (a vessel); specif., to sink, or attempt to sink (a vessel) by cutting holes through the bottom of.

scuttle butt *or* **cask.** Formerly, on shipboard, a butt or cask containing water for the day's use; now, a drinking fountain on a ship. Hence, **scut'tle·butt'** (skŭt''l·bŭt'), *n. U. S. Navy Slang.* Rumor; gossip.

scu'tum (skū'tŭm), *n.; pl.* -TA (-tȧ). [L.] **1.** *Rom. Antiq.* An oblong leather-covered shield, esp. for heavy-armed infantry. **2.** *Zool.* A bony or horny plate; a scute.

Scyl'la (sĭl'ȧ), *n.* [L., fr. Gr. *Skylla.*] A rock on the Italian coast opposite the whirlpool Charybdis off the Sicilian coast. The ancients personified both as female monsters. — ***between Scylla and Charybdis.*** Between two dangers, either of which is difficult to avoid without encountering the other.

scyphi-. *Bot.* A combining form for *scyphus,* as in **scy·phif'er·ous, scy'phi·form, scy·phiph'o·rous.**

scy'pho·zo'an (sī'fō·zō'ăn), *n.* [Gr. *skyphos* cup + *zōion* animal.] *Zool.* Any of a class (Scyphozoa) of coelenterates including certain jellyfishes. — **scy'pho·zo'an,** *adj.*

scy'phus (sī'fŭs), *n.; pl.* -PHI (-fī). [L., a cup, fr. Gr. *skyphos.*] **1.** *Gr. Antiq.* A deep cup or bowl. **2.** *Bot.* A cup-shaped part, as the corona of some flowers.

scythe (sīth), *n.* [AS. *sīthe, sigthe.*] An instrument for mowing grass, grain, etc., by hand, composed of a long, curving blade, with a sharp edge, made fast at one end to a long, bent handle (the *snath*). — *v. t.* To cut with or as with a scythe; mow.

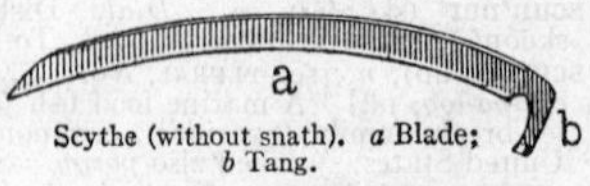

Scythe (without snath). *a* Blade; *b* Tang.

Scyth'i·an (sĭth'ĭ·ăn; sĭth'-ĭ-), *adj.* Of or pert. to the region anciently inhabited by the Scythians, or its inhabitants or their language. — *n.* **1.** One of an ancient people of nomadic habits and famed for savagery, who dwelt north of the Black Sea and east of Lake Aral. **2.** The language of the Scythians, of Iranian origin. See INDO-EUROPEAN LANGUAGES, *Table.*

'sdeath (zdĕth), *interj. Archaic.* Corrupted form of *God's death,* used as an expletive.

sea (sē), *n.* [AS. *sǣ.*] **1.** One of the larger bodies of salt water, less than an ocean. **2.** An inland body of water, esp. if large or if salt or brackish; as, the Caspian *Sea;* sometimes, a small fresh-water lake; as, the *Sea* of Galilee. **3.** The ocean. **4. a** *Naut.* The disturbance of the ocean due to the wind blowing; as, there was a high *sea.* **b** Surface motion on a large body of water, or its direction; a heavy swell or wave. **5.** Something suggesting a sea; as, a *sea* of faces; a *sea* of troubles. **6.** The expanse of the high seas as a field of life; as, to follow the *sea.* — ***at sea.*** **a** On the sea; on a sea voyage. **b** Figuratively: Lost; bewildered. — **sea,** *adj.*

sea anchor. a *Naut.* A drag, typically an open canvas cone, thrown overboard to retard the drifting of a vessel and to keep her head to the wind. Cf. DRAG SAIL. **b** *Aeronautics.* A similar device to restrain a seaplane resting on the water.

sea anemone. Any of numerous anthozoans (order Actiniaria) whose form, bright colors, and tentacles about the mouth often give them a superficial resemblance to a flower. See ACTINIA, *Illust.*

sea bass (băs). Any of numerous marine fishes of a widely distributed family (Serranidae); — often used as a general name for fishes of that family but applied specif. along the Atlantic coast of the United States to a valuable food and game fish (*Centropristes striatus*). See BASS.

Sea'bee' (sē'bē'), *n.* [construction *b*attalion.] A member of one of the construction battalions organized as a volunteer branch of the Civil Engineer Corps of the U. S. Navy, for building aviation and ship facilities, artillery emplacements, and other naval installations, and defending them.

sea'board' (sē'bōrd'; 70), *n.* [*sea* + *board,* F. *bord* side.] The seacoast; country bordering a seacoast. — **sea'board',** *adj.*

sea bread. Ship biscuit.

sea calf. = SEA DOG, 1 **b.**

sea'coast' (sē'kōst'), *n.* The shore or border of the land adjacent to the sea or ocean.

sea cow. 1. Any sirenian, as a manatee or dugong. **2. a** A walrus. **b** *Rare.* A hippopotamus.

sea crayfish. See LOBSTER, 1.

sea cucumber. A holothurian (esp. of the genus *Cucumaria*), as the common American and European species (*C. frondosa*).

sea devil. a = DEVILFISH. **b** = ANGELFISH **a.**

sea dog. 1. a A dogfish. **b** The seal *Phoca vitulina;* — also known as *harbor seal* and *sea calf.* **2.** An experienced sailor. **3.** Formerly, a pirate or a privateer.

sea'dog' (sē'dŏg'; 74), *n.* = FOGDOG.

sea'drome' (-drōm'), *n. Aeronautics.* A floating airdrome serving as an intermediate landing place.

sea duck. See DUCK.

sea eagle. a See EAGLE, 1. **b** *Local, U. S.* The osprey.

sea'-ear', *n.* An abalone.

sea fan. Any of an order (Gorgonacea) of anthozoans which branch in a fanlike form, esp. *Gorgonia flabellum* of Florida and the West Indies.

sea'far'er (sē'fâr'ẽr), *n.* A mariner.

sea'far'ing (-ĭng), *n.* Traveling over the sea or seas as a pursuit or recreation; esp., the mariner's calling. — *adj.* Of, given to, or engaged in seafaring.

sea fight. An engagement between vessels at sea.

sea'flow'er (sē'flou'ẽr), *n.* A sea anemone or related actinozoan.

sea foam. a Foam of sea water. **b** Meerschaum.

sea food. Edible salt-water shellfish or fish.

sea'fowl' (sē'foul'), *n.* Any bird which frequents the sea, as an auk, gannet, gull, tern, or petrel.

sea front. The water front of a seaside place.

sea gate. A gate, beach, channel, or the like, which gives access to the sea or a sea.

sea'girt' (sē'gûrt'), *adj.* Surrounded by the sea.

sea'go'ing (sē'gō'ĭng), *adj.* **a** Adapted for, or for use in, sailing the open sea. **b** Seafaring. — **sea'go'ing,** *n.*

sea green. A color, yellowish yellow-green in hue, of medium saturation and high brilliance. See COLOR. — **sea'-green'** (-grēn'; 2), *adj.*

sea gull. Any gull frequenting the sea.

sea hog. A porpoise.

sea holly. A European herb (*Eryngium maritimum*) of the carrot family.

sea horse. 1. *Gr. & Rom. Myth.* A fabulous creature, half horse and half fish, driven by sea-gods or ridden by the Nereids. **2.** A walrus. **3.** Any of a number of small lophobranch fishes mostly of one genus (*Hippocampus*), related to the pipefishes, and found in most warm seas. **4.** A large whitecap.

Sea Horse, 3 (*H. hudsonius*). (¼)

sea'-is'land, *adj.* Of certain islands along the coast of South Carolina and Georgia; as, *sea-island* cotton (see COTTON).

sea kale. A European fleshy plant (*Crambe maritima*) of the mustard family, used as a potherb.

sea king. [After ON. *sækoningr,* AS. *sæcyning.*] A Norse pirate-chief of royal blood. Cf. VIKING.

seal (sēl), *n.; see* PLURAL, *Note,* 3. [AS. *seolh.*] **1.** A marine aquatic carnivorous mammal (group Pinnipedia, family Phocidae or Otariidae) found mostly in cold regions, and hunted for its fur, hide, and oil; specif., the ***fur seal,*** any of certain eared seals having a dense, soft, highly valued underfur; esp., one of the species (*Callorhinus alascanus*) which breeds on the Pribilof Islands. **2.** = SEALSKIN. **3.** A leather made from the skin of a seal. ***pin seal*** is leather from a very young seal. **4.** Also **seal brown.** A brown, yellowish red-yellow in hue, of low saturation and low brilliance. See COLOR. — *v. i.* To hunt seals.

seal, *n.* [OF. *seel,* fr. L. *sigillum* a little image, seal, dim. of *signum* a mark, sign.] **1. a** Any device bearing a design so made that it can impart an impression in relief upon a soft tenacious substance, as clay or wax. **b** An impression thus made. **c** The wafer, or the like, bearing the impression. **2.** That which seals or secures, as a wax wafer on an envelope or a fastening on a door; hence, a guaranty; an assurance; a pledge. **3.** *Eng. Chiefly pl.* The indication or mark of office; as, to resign the *seals* of the secretary of state. **4.** Any device to prevent the passage or return of gas or air into a pipe or container, as by keeping filled with liquid a deep bend in a pipe. **5.** A stamp affixed to something; esp., an ornamental stamp, as one used on Christmas letters and packages. **6.** *Law.* Any impression, device, sign, or mark given the effect of a seal (sense 1) either by statute law or by American local custom recognized by judicial decision. — *v. t.* **1.** To set or affix a seal to; hence, to authenticate; ratify; as, to *seal* a deed. **2.** To fasten with a seal or with something that closes securely; hence, to enclose; make fast; as, vessels *sealed* in ice. **3. a** To test or compare and mark with a stamp, esp. as an evidence of standard exactness, legal size, or merchantable quality. **b** To give under, or as under, seal; to grant authentically. **4.** To determine irrevocably or indisputably; as, this *sealed* his fate. **5.** *Elec.* To complete the movement of, after the contacting parts touch each other. **6.** *Mormon Ch.* To solemnize for eternity, as a marriage or an adoption of a child. — **seal'a·ble,** *adj.*

seal. Var. of SEEL.

sea lavender. Any marine herb of the genus *Linonium.*

sea lawyer. *Naut.* An argumentative, captious sailor.

sea legs. *Sailors' Slang.* Ability to walk steadily on a ship at sea; hence, freedom from seasickness; as, to get one's *sea legs,* to get accustomed to the rolling and pitching of a vessel.

seal'er (sēl'ẽr), *n.* Someone or something that seals; specif., an officer who tests and certifies, as weights.

seal'er, *n.* A mariner or a vessel engaged in hunting seals.

seal'er·y (-ĭ), *n.; pl.* -ERIES (-ĭz). The occupation of hunting seals; also, a place where seals are hunted.

sea lettuce. Any seaweed of a genus (*Ulva,* family Ulvaceae), the green fronds of which are sometimes eaten.

sea level. The level of the surface of the sea, esp. at its mean position, midway between mean high and low water.

sea lily. A crinoid, esp. one of the stalked forms.

seal'ing wax. A resinous composition, plastic when warm, used to seal letters and documents, dry cells, etc.

sea lion. Any of several large, eared seals of the Pacific. The largest (*Eumetopias jubata,* syn. *E. stelleri*) reaches a length of about 12 feet.

seal ring. A ring engraved with a seal; a signet ring.

seal'skin' (sēl'skĭn'), *n.* The fur or pelt of a fur seal; also, a coat or other garment of this material. — **seal'skin',** *adj.*

sea lungwort. A fleshy herb (*Mertensia maritima*) of the borage family, of northern coasts, with long-stalked flowers.

Sea'ly·ham ter'ri·er (sē'lĭ·hăm; -ăm). Also **Sea'ly·ham,** *n.* A short-legged, strong-jawed terrier of a breed developed at Sealyham, a Welsh estate, about 1860.

seam (sēm), *n.* [AS. *sēam.*] **1.** The fold or line formed by sewing together two pieces of cloth, leather, etc. **2.** A line of junction; a line, groove, ridge, or interstice, formed by or between abutting edges. **3.** *Chiefly Scot.* Needlework, or the material for it. **4.** A line left by a cut or wound; a scar; also, a wrinkle. **5.** *Geol. & Mining.* A thin stratum; of coal or other valuable mineral, a bed, whether thin or not. — *v. t.* **1.** To join by a seam; make the seams of. **2.** To line, scar, wrinkle, furrow, etc. **3.** *Knitting.* To make an apparent seam in, as a stocking, by a line of purled stitches; hence, to purl. — *v. i.* **1.** *Dial.* To sew. **2.** To become fissured or ridgy; crack open. **3.** *Knitting.* To do seaming. — **seam'er** (-ẽr), *n.*

sea'-maid', *n.* Also **sea'-maid'en.** *Poetic.* A mermaid; also, a sea-goddess or sea nymph.

sea'man (sē'măn), *n.; pl.* -MEN (-mĕn). **1.** One skilled in seamanship. **2.** One whose occupation is to assist in the handling of ships at sea; a sailor; mariner. The term is often restricted to deck hands. A skilled and experienced seaman is called an ***able-bodied seaman,*** *or* ***able seaman*** (abbr. *A.B.*); one of some experience but less fully skilled is usually called an ***ordinary seaman*** (abbr. *O.D.* or *O.S.*). **3.** *U. S. Navy.* A nonrated enlisted man, below a petty officer.

sea′man·like′ (sē′măn·līk′), *adj.* & *adv.* Indicating seamanship; characteristic of a good seaman.

sea′man·ship, *n.* The skill of a good seaman; the art, or skill in the art, of navigating a vessel.

sea′mark′ (sē′märk′), *n.* **1.** A line on a coast marking the tidal limit. **2.** An elevated object serving to guide mariners; a beacon; a landmark.

sea mew. A sea gull; esp., the European *Larus canus.*

sea mile. See MEASURE, *Table* 9.

seam′less (sēm′lĕs; -lĭs), *adj.* Having no seam.

sea mouse. A large, broad, marine polychaetous annelid (*Aphrodite* or allied genus) covered with hairlike setae.

seam′stress (sēm′strĕs; -strĭs; sĕm′-), *n.* Also **semp′stress** (sĕmp′-strĕs; sĕm′-; -strĭs). [From older *seamster*, prop. fem., fr. AS. *sēamestre.* See SEAM.] Any woman who does sewing; esp., a woman whose occupation is plain sewing rather than dressmaking.

seam′y (sēm′ĭ), *adj.*; SEAM′I·ER (-ĭ·ẽr); SEAM′I·EST. **1.** Having, marked by, or like a seam or seams; seamed. **2.** Showing rough seams, as the underside of a garment; hence: **a** Worse; less pleasant or presentable; as, the *seamy* side of city life. **b** Disreputable; degraded.

Sean′ad Eir′eann (săn′ăd âr′ĭn). [Ir. *seanad* senate + *Eireann* of Ireland.] The upper house, or Senate, of the legislature (Oireachtas) of the Republic of Ireland. See DAIL EIREANN.

sé′ance′ (sā′äns′; sā′äns), *n.* [F., fr. *seoir* to sit, fr. L. *sedere.*] **1.** A sitting; a session. **2.** A meeting of spiritualists to receive spirit communications.

sea onion. a The official squill (*Urginea scilla*). **b** The squill *Scilla verna.*

sea otter. An otter (*Enhydra lutris*) of the North Pacific coasts, whose pelt furnishes a very valuable fur.

sea pen. Any of numerous polyps (*Pennatula* and allied genera) whose colonies have a featherlike form.

sea′plane′ (sē′plān′), *n.* An airplane designed to rise from and alight on the water.

sea′port′ (-pōrt′; 70), *n.* A port, harbor, or town, on the seashore and accessible to seagoing vessels.

sea power. a Naval strength. **b** A nation having naval strength, esp. formidable naval strength. Cf. LAND POWER.

sea purse. Horny egg case of skates and of certain sharks.

sea′quake′ (sē′kwāk′), *n.* A submarine earthquake.

sear (sēr), *n.* [F. *serre* a grasp, fr. LL. *serare* to bolt, bar, and LL. *serrare* to saw.] The catch in a gunlock holding the hammer at cock or half cock.

sear, sere (sēr), *adj.* [AS. *sēar.*] **1.** Dried up; withered. **2.** Worn with age or use; hence, exhausted of vigor; effete.

sear (sēr), *v. t.* [AS. *sēarian.*] **1.** To wither; dry up. **2.** To burn, scorch, or brown, esp. the surface of, as in cauterizing or in cooking meat; also, to brand with a heated iron (**sear′ing i′ron**). **3. a** To harden; to make callous. **b** To brand; to mark as with a stigma. — *v. i.* To be or become sear. — *n.* The mark, scar, or brand left by searing.

sea raven. A sculpin (*Hemitripterus americanus*) of the northern Atlantic coast of America.

search (sûrch), *v. t.* [OF. *cerchier*, fr. LL. *circare* to go about, fr. L. *circum, circa,* around.] **1.** To look over and through for the purpose of finding something; explore; examine; rummage. **2.** To seek by looking, inquiry, investigation, etc.; make search for; — often with *out.* **3.** To probe; tent; hence, to pierce or penetrate. **4.** To subject to a thorough inspection, as for concealed weapons. **5.** *Law. Colloq.* To examine (a public record), as for information pertinent to the title to land. — *v. i.* To seek; make a search. — *n.* **1.** Act or action of searching; an endeavor to find, ascertain, recover, or the like. **2.** Specif.: **a** Examination; critical scrutiny; survey. **b** Research; investigation. **3.** *Rare.* A person or party that searches. **4.** Power or range of searching, esp. of penetrating. **5.** *Mar. Law.* Act of boarding and inspecting a vessel, on the high seas, in exercise of right of search (which see). — **search′a·ble,** *adj.* — **search′er,** *n.*

search′ing, *adj.* Exploring thoroughly; scrutinizing; as, a *searching* examination; penetrating; as, *searching* cold. — **search′ing·ly,** *adv.*

search′light′ (sûrch′līt′), *n.* An apparatus for projecting a powerful beam of light of approximately parallel rays, usually devised so that it can be swiveled about; also, the beam of light projected by it.

search warrant. *Law.* A warrant legally issued, authorizing a search, as for stolen or smuggled goods.

sea robin. Any of several gurnards, esp. American species of a genus (*Prionotus*) having red or brown on the body and fins.

sea room. *Naut.* Space at sea to maneuver safely.

sea rover. One who roves the sea; hence, a pirate.

sea′scape (sē′skāp), *n.* **1.** A view of or over the sea. **2.** A picture representing a scene at sea.

sea′scout′ing (sē′skout′ĭng), *n.*, *or* **sea scouting.** That branch of the boy-scout program which provides training for older boys in seamanship and water activities. — **sea′scout′,** *n.*, *or* **sea scout.**

sea serpent. A large marine animal resembling a serpent, often reported to have been seen, but never proved to exist.

sea′shore′ (sē′shōr′; 2; 70), *n.* The seacoast; specif., *Law,* all the ground between the ordinary high-water and low-water marks. — **sea′shore′,** *adj.*

sea′sick′ness (-sĭk′nĕs; -nĭs), *n.* Nausea, prostration, etc., caused by the motion of a ship. — **sea′sick′,** *adj.*

sea′side′ (-sīd′), *n.* The land bordering the sea; seacoast.

sea snake. 1. Any of numerous venomous snakes (family Hydrophidae), that, with one known exception, live in the sea, esp. in the warmer parts of the Indian and Pacific oceans. **2.** A sea serpent.

sea′son (sē′z'n), *n.* [OF. *seson, seison* (F. *saison*), prop., the sowing time, fr. L. *satio* a sowing.] **1.** A period in which a special type of agricultural work is normal and a particular type of weather prevails. **2.** The suitable, fitting, natural, or opportune time or occasion; as, the *season* for rest; in good *season.* **3.** A relatively short period of time; a while. **4.** One of the divisions of the year, as spring, summer, autumn, and winter. **5. a** Time of flourishing, development, activity, marketing, etc.; as, the social *season.* **b** The complementary period of inactivity; — used ironically with such adjectives as *dead, dull, off.* **6.** [From SEASON, *v.*] *Obs.* That which seasons; seasoning. **7.** *Eccl.* Any of certain periods in the Christian year; as, the *season* of Christmas; the Lenten *season.* — *v. t.* **1.** To render palatable by adding salt, pepper, spice, or the like; hence, to make pungent, piquant, etc. **2.** To treat by some process that will put it in condition for use; as, to *season* lumber or tobacco. **3.** To habituate; acclimatize; inure. **4.** *Archaic.* To qualify by admixture; temper; as, mercy *seasons* justice. — *v. i.* To become seasoned, inured, hardened, dried (as lumber), or the like. — **sea′son·er,** *n.*

sea′son·a·ble (-ȧ·b'l), *adj.* Occurring in good or proper time; opportune; in keeping with the season; timely. — **sea′son·a·ble·ness,** *n.* — **sea′son·a·bly,** *adv.*

Syn. Seasonable, timely, opportune, pat mean occurring or coming appropriately. **Seasonable** implies appropriateness to the time or moment; **timely,** such appropriateness to the moment as to be of genuine service or value; **opportune,** such concurrence of circumstances as to make the moment advantageous; **pat,** a perfect adaptability to a situation and coming, usually, just when needed.

sea′son·al (-ăl; -'l), *adj.* Of, pertaining to, occurring at, or affected by the season or seasons; as, *seasonal* storms; *seasonal* industries. — **sea′son·al·ly,** *adv.*

sea′son·ing, *n.* That which seasons; esp., a condiment.

season ticket. A ticket giving its holder a privilege for a specified season, as daily transportation between two places, or entrance to all games at a certain field. Cf. COMMUTATION TICKET.

sea squirt. A simple ascidian.

seat (sēt), *n.* [ME. *sete, sete,* fr. ON. *sæti.*] **1.** Posture or way of sitting, as on horseback. **2. a** The place at, or the thing on, which one sits. **b** A right to sit; a sitting; a membership; as, to win a *seat* in Congress. **c** Space to sit in; as, to buy two *seats.* **3.** A place of abode, residence, etc.; site; location. **4.** Specif.: **a** A capital or other center of government; as, a county *seat.* **b** A locality in which a (specified) thing or condition is prevalent; as, a *seat* of learning. **5.** A chair, stool, bench, pew, etc., or the part of it on which one sits. **6.** The buttocks. **7.** A part or surface on which another part or surface rests. — *v. t.* **1.** To place in or on a seat; cause to sit down, settle, etc.; install; fix in place, etc. **2.** To provide seats or sittings for; furnish with seats. **3.** To put a seat in; to repair the seat of.

sea tangle. Any of various seaweeds or kelps, esp. of the genus *Laminaria;* tangle.

seat′ing, *n.* **1.** Act of providing with a seat or seats; also, the making of seats. **2. a** Material for covering or upholstering seats. **b** *Mach.* A seat (sense 7); also, a part or surface that beds on a seat.

sea′train′ (sē′trān′), *n.* A form of ocean-going steamship for carrying freight cars.

sea urchin. Any of a class (Echinoidea) of echinoderms, esp. one of somewhat flattened globular form having a thin brittle shell covered with movable spines.

Sea Urchin (*Strongylocentrotus drobachiensis*). (⅕) See also OVUM, *Illust.*

sea wall. A wall to resist encroachments of the sea.

sea′wan (sē′wȧn), **sea′want** (-wȧnt). Vars. of SEWAN.

sea′ward (sē′wẽrd), *n.* The direction or side away from land to the open sea. — *adj.* Directed or situated toward the sea. — *adv.* Also **sea′wards** (-wẽrdz). Toward the sea or ocean.

sea′ware′ (-wâr′), *n.* Sea wrack used esp. as manure.

sea′way′ (-wā′), *n.* *Naut.* **a** A moderate or rough sea; — chiefly in *in a seaway.* **b** A vessel's headway. **c** The sea as a route for travel; also, one of the ocean traffic lanes. **d** A deep inland waterway that admits ocean shipping.

sea′weed′ (-wēd′), *n.* Any plant growing in the sea; specif., any marine alga, as kelp, dulse, sea lettuce, etc.

sea′wor′thy (-wûr′thĭ), *adj.* Fit for a sea voyage; able to stand stormy weather. — **sea′wor′thi·ness,** *n.*

sea wrack. Seaweed, esp. of the large species, as rockweeds and kelps.

se·ba′ceous (sē·bā′shŭs), *adj.* [L. *sebaceus,* fr. L. *sebum* tallow, grease.] *Physiol.* Of, pert. to, or like fatty matter, or sebum; esp., secreting sebum, as certain glands (**sebaceous glands**) in the deeper layer of the skin.

se·bac′ic (sē·băs′ĭk; -bā′sĭk), *adj.* [L. *sebum* tallow.] *Chem.* Pert. to or designating a crystalline acid, $C_8H_{16}(CO_2H)_2$, variously obtained, as by dry distillation of oleic acid.

sebi-. [L. *sebum.*] A combining form meaning *tallow, suet,* as in **se·bif′er·ous, se·bip′a·rous.** See -FEROUS; -PAROUS.

seb′or·rhe′a, seb′or·rhoe′a (sĕb′ŏ·rē′ȧ), *n.* [NL., fr. L. *sebum* tallow + *-rrhea.*] *Med.* A morbidly increased discharge of sebaceous matter on the skin; stearrhea.

se′bum (sē′bŭm), *n.* [L., tallow, grease.] *Anat.* The fatty matter secreted by the sebaceous glands.

‖sec (sĕk), *adj.* [F.] Dry; — of wine. Cf. BRUT; SWEET, *adj.*, 9.

se′cant (sē′kănt), *adj.* [L. *secans, -antis,* pres. part. of *secare* to cut.] Cutting; as, a *secant* line. — *n.* **1.** *Geom.* A line that cuts another; esp., a straight line cutting a curve in two or more points. See CIRCLE, *Illust.* **2.** *Trig.* A right line drawn from the center of a circle through one end of a circular arc to a tangent drawn from the other end; the ratio of this line to the radius of the circle. Abbr. *sec.*

‖sec′co (săk′kō; *Angl.* sĕk′ō), *adj.* [It.] Dry. — *n.* Also **secco painting.** Painting on dry plaster.

se·cede′ (sē·sēd′), *v. i.* [L. *secedere, secessum,* fr. *se-* aside + *cedere* to go, move.] To withdraw from an organization, communion, or federation; esp., to withdraw formally from a political or religious body. — **se·ced′er** (-sēd′ẽr), *n.*

se·cern′ (sē·sûrn′), *v. t.* & *i.* [L. *secernere.* See SECRETE.] **1.** To separate; discriminate. **2.** *Physiol.* To secrete. — **se·cern′ent,** *adj.* — **se·cern′ment,** *n.*

se·ces′sion (sē·sĕsh′ŭn), *n.* **1.** Act of, or condition following, seceding; withdrawal. **2.** [*often cap.*] *U. S.* The withdrawal of a state from the national Union, as that of eleven states in 1860–61. — **se·ces′sion·al** (-ăl; -'l), *adj.*

se·ces′sion·ist (-ĭst), *n.* One who upholds secession; specif. [*often cap.*], *U. S. Hist.*, one who held that a state has the right to separate from the Union at its will; esp., one who participated in, or sympathized with, the Secession in 1860–61. — **se·ces′sion·ism** (-ĭz'm), *n.*

Seck′el (sĕk′'l; sĭk′'l), *n.* [After the owner of the farm near Philadelphia where it originated.] A small, reddish-brown sweet and juicy pear of an American variety.

se·clude′ (sē·klo͞od′; 114), *v. t.* [L. *secludere, seclusum,* fr. *se-* aside + *claudere* to shut.] **1.** To shut up apart; withdraw into, or place in, solitude; isolate. **2.** *Now Rare.* To deny admission to; debar; expel; exclude. **3.** To screen; protect by shutting off or being shut off; — chiefly in *past part.*; as, a *secluded* spot. — **se·clud′ed·ly,** *adv.* — **se·clud′ed·ness,** *n.*

se·clu′sion (-klo͞o′zhŭn), *n.* **1.** A secluding; state or fact of being secluded; isolation. **2.** A secluded place; a place of retirement. — **Syn.** See SOLITUDE. — **se·clu′sive** (-sĭv), *adj.* — **se·clu′sive·ly,** *adv.* — **se·clu′sive·ness,** *n.*

sec′ond (sĕk′ŭnd; -ŭnt), *n.* [F. *seconde.* See SECOND, *adj.*] **1.** The sixtieth part of a minute of time or of a degree. Abbr. *sec.* or *s.*; as, 4 m. 10 *sec.* See MEASURE, *Tables* 6, 7, & 8. **2.** *Colloq.* A moment; an instant.

sec′ond, *adj.* [OF., fr. L. *secundus* second, prop., following, fr. root of *sequi* to follow.] **1.** Immediately following the first; — the ordinal of *two.* See NUMBER, *Table.* **2.** Next to the first in order of place or time; hence, occurring again; another; other. **3.** Of the same kind as another; as, a *second* Cato. **4.** Next to the first in value, power, excellence, dignity, rank, or degree; hence, secondary; subordinate; inferior. **5.** *Music.* Lower in pitch; rendering a part of lower pitch. — *adv.* In second place, rank, etc.
— *n.* **1.** One who or that which is second, as in place, time, rank, merit, etc. **2.** The next in order or series after the first. **3.** One who attends another for his support and aid; a backer; an assistant; specif., one who acts as another's aid in a duel or prize fight. **4.** An article of merchandise of a grade inferior to the best or below the standard; specif., *pl.*, a coarse or inferior kind of flour or bread made from it. **5.** One twelfth of an inch; a line. **6.** *Music.* **a** The interval embracing two diatonic degrees. **b** A tone at this interval. **c** The harmonic combination of two tones a second apart. **d** The second part in a concerted piece; popularly, the alto.
— (sĕk′ŭnd), *v. t. & i.* **1.** To act as a second (of); assist; support. **2.** To encourage or reinforce; further; forward. **3.** *Parl. Practice.* To support, as a motion, by adding one's voice to that of the mover or proposer, esp. as a preliminary to further debate or a vote.
— **sec′ond·er,** *n.* — **sec′ond·ly,** *adv.*

Second Advent. *Theol.* The second coming of Christ, expected by many Christians, to judge both the living and the resurrected dead.

Second Adventist. = ADVENTIST.

sec′ond·ar′y (sĕk′ŭn·dĕr′ĭ *or, esp. Brit.,* -dĕr·ĭ), *adj.* **1.** Next below the first in importance; of second place or class. **2.** Immediately derived from or dependent on that which is original or primary; as, a *secondary* cause or authority. **3.** That is used to second or is resorted to in the second place; auxiliary; as, *secondary* bases. **4.** Of or pertaining to the second order of a series; belonging to a second stage in process of growth, manufacture, etc.; subsequent in origin or development; as, *secondary* tissue. **5.** *Chem.* Characterized by or resulting from the substitution of two atoms or groups; specif., designating or characterized by a carbon atom which is united by two valences to chain or ring members. **6.** *Educ.* Intermediate between elementary and collegiate. **7.** *Elec.* In an induction coil or transformer, pert. to or designating the induced current or its circuit; as, the *secondary* coil; *secondary* winding. **8.** *Geol.* [*cap.*] Mesozoic. **9.** *Gram.* Expressive of past fact; — of tenses (Latin imperfect, historical perfect, and pluperfect, and Greek aorist), as distinguished from *primary* tenses (present, perfect, future, future perfect). **10.** *Zool.* Designating, or pert. to, the second (that is, lower) joint of the wing of a bird, or its quills. — *n.* **1.** Anyone or anything that is secondary; esp., one not a principal; a subordinate. **2.** *Elec.* A secondary circuit or coil. **3.** *Zool.* A secondary feather or quill. See BIRD, POULTRY, *Illusts.* — **sec′ond·ar′i·ly,** *adv.*

secondary accent. *Phonet.* A stress next weaker than the strongest in the same word; the mark (′ in this Dictionary) to indicate this; as in *horse′shoe′, reg′ulat′ed.* Cf. PRIMARY ACCENT.

secondary cell. *Elec.* A cell that converts chemical energy into electrical energy by reversible chemical reactions. It may be recharged by passing a current through it in the opposite direction to that of its discharge. Called also *storage cell.* Cf. PRIMARY CELL.

secondary school. A school providing secondary education, as an American high school or an English public school.

second childhood. State or time of dotage.

sec′ond–class′ (*see Pron.,* § 2), *adj.* **1.** Of or pertaining to a class next below the first, as in a school, a ship, the postal service, etc. **2.** Second-rate; mediocre.

Second Coming. *Theol.* = SECOND ADVENT.

se·conde′ (sē·kŏnd′; *F.* sẽ·gôɴd′), *n.* [F., fr. *second* second.] *Fencing.* A position in parrying.

second fiddle. A subordinate part or role; also, a second choice; — chiefly in the phrase *to play,* or *be, second fiddle.*

sec′ond·hand′ (sĕk′ŭnd·hănd′; 2), *adj.* **1.** Not original or primary; derived. **2.** Used previously; not new. **3.** Pert. to, or dealing in, secondhand clothes, etc.

second hand. **a** An intermediate person or thing; — now only in ***at second hand,*** indirectly; through an intermediary. **b** The hand marking seconds on a timepiece.

second mortgage. A mortgage the lien of which is subordinate to that of a prior mortgage.

second nature. Acquired, rather than innate, character or disposition; also, fixed, ingrained habit or habits.

‖**se·con′do** (sā·kŏn′dō), *n.*; *pl.* -DI (-dē). [It.] *Music.* The second part in a concerted piece, esp. the lower part in a pianoforte duet, or its performer.

sec′ond–rate′ (*see Pron.,* § 2), *adj.* Of second, or inferior, quality, value, etc.; mediocre; lacking excellence. — **sec′ond–rat′er** (-rāt′ẽr), *n.*

second sight. The power of seeing beyond the visible; intuitive, visionary, or prophetic power.

sec′par′ (sĕk′pär′), *n.* = PARSEC.

se′cre·cy (sē′krĕ·sĭ), *n.* [From SECRET.] **1.** Quality or state of being secret; concealment. **2.** The practice or quality of being secretive; reticence.

se′cret (sē′krĕt; -krĭt), *adj.* [OF., fr. L. *secretus,* past part. of *secernere* to put apart, separate, fr. *se-* aside + *cernere.*] **1.** Hidden from others; revealed to none or to few; as, keep this matter *secret.* **2.** Faithful to a secret; secretive; close. **3.** Withdrawn from intercourse or notice; secluded; retired. **4.** Beyond ordinary comprehension; inscrutable; also, esoteric. **5.** Constructed so as to escape observation; as, a *secret* drawer. **6.** Not declared or avowed as such; as, a *secret* agent.
Syn. **Secret, covert, stealthy, furtive, clandestine, surreptitious, underhand, underhanded** mean done, managed, etc., without attracting observation. **Secret** implies concealment on any grounds or for any motive; **covert,** a not being open or avowed; **stealthy,** an attempt to gain one's end through quietness and, often, deceit; **furtive,** a sly or cautious stealthiness; **clandestine,** secrecy and, usually, an evil or illicit end; **surreptitious,** a stealthiness, furtiveness, etc., in violation of a right, a law, a code, or the like; **underhand, underhanded,** secrecy with fraud.
— *n.* **1.** Something kept secret, undisclosed, or unrevealed. **2.** A thing not discovered, or not explained; a mystery; in art or industry, a device or fact concealed from general knowledge; as, a trade *secret.* **3.** Secrecy; as, to meet in *secret.* *Rare* exc. in phrase ***in secret.*** **4.** The key to the solution of something; hidden cause or explanation; as, the *secret* of his success. **5.** *Liturgics.* [*cap.*] Prayers said in a low voice by the celebrant just before the Preface in the Mass. — **se′cret·ly,** *adv.*

sec′re·tar′i·at (sĕk′rē·târ′ĭ·ăt; -ăt), *n.* Also **sec′re·tar′i·ate** (-ĭt). [F. *secrétariat.*] **1.** The office, offices, or the like, of a department headed by a secretary. **2.** The entire body of secretaries in an office. **3.** The department headed by a governmental secretary.

sec′re·tar′y (sĕk′rē·tĕr′ĭ *or, esp. Brit.,* -tẽr·ĭ), *n.*; *pl.* -TARIES (-ĭz). [ML. *secretarius,* orig., a confidant, fr. L. *secretum* a secret.] **1.** *Obs.* **a** A confidant. **b** An amanuensis. **2.** **a** A confidential clerk, esp. one who attends to correspondence, records, etc., of a private or confidential character. **b** In a corporation, society, etc., one having oversight of, or responsibility for, the correspondence, records, etc., of the organization. **c** An officer of state whose business is to superintend and manage the affairs of a particular department of government. Abbr. *sec.* or *secy.* **3.** A writing desk; specif., such a desk with a top section for books (called also **secretary bookcase**). — **sec′re·tar′i·al** (-târ′ĭ·ăl), *adj.* — **sec′re·tar′y·ship,** *n.*

secretary bird. [From its crest, which suggests a bunch of pens stuck behind the ear.] A large long-legged African bird of prey (*Sagittarius serpentarius*) which feeds largely upon reptiles.

sec′re·tar′y–gen′er·al, *n.*; *pl.* SECRETARIES-GENERAL. A chief or superior secretary.

se·crete′ (sē·krēt′), *v. t.* [L. *secretus* separated, secret, hidden, past part. of *secernere.* See SECRET.] **1.** To keep secret or hidden; esp., to deposit in a place of hiding; conceal. **2.** *Physiol. & Biol.* To separate, elaborate, and emit as a secretion. — **Syn.** See HIDE. — **se·cre′tor** (-krē′tẽr), *n.*

se·cre′tin (sē·krē′tĭn), *n.* *Biochem.* An intestinal hormone capable of stimulating the pancreas to secrete.

se·cre′tion (-shŭn), *n.* **1.** A secreting or concealing. **2.** *Physiol. & Biol.* **a** Act or process of secreting. **b** That which is secreted; material separated (usually from the blood in animals, and the protoplasts in plants), elaborated, and discharged by a cell or cells, esp. (in animals) by the epithelial cells of glands, as saliva from the salivary glands. Cf. EXCRETION. — **se·cre′tion·ar′y** (-ẽr′ĭ *or, esp. Brit.,* -ẽr·ĭ), *adj.*

se·cre′tive (sē·krē′tĭv; *in sense* 1, *also* sē′krē·tĭv), *adj.* **1.** Disposed to keep or to make secrets, esp. of one's own concerns; not frank; reticent. **2.** *Physiol. & Biol.* Secretory. — **Syn.** See SILENT. — **se·cre′tive·ly,** *adv.* — **se·cre′tive·ness,** *n.*

se·cre′to·ry (sē·krē′tō·rĭ), *adj.* *Physiol.* Secreting; connected with, or promoting, secretion. — *n.* A secretory organ or gland.

secret service. The detective service of a government. In the U. S. it is a division under the Treasury Department, chiefly charged with the suppression of counterfeiting, the protection of the President, investigations of tax-law and loan-law violations. It also aids other government departments in personnel and espionage investigations, etc.

secret society. A society having a secret ritual, oath, sign of recognition, or the like.

sect (sĕkt), *n.* [F. *secte,* fr. L. *secta,* fr. *sequi* to follow; often confused with L. *secare, sectum,* to cut.] **1.** *Obs.* A class, order, or kind of men. **2.** A group having in common a leader or a distinctive doctrine; a following; a school, as of philosophy. **3.** A group holding similar views; a party. **4.** In religion: **a** A party dissenting from an established or parent church; a body of sectaries. **b** One of the organized bodies of Christians; a denomination.

sect, *n.* [L. *secare, sectum,* to cut.] A section; a part.

-sect (-sĕkt), **-sect′ed** (-sĕk′tĕd; -tĭd). [L. *secare, sectum,* to cut.] Suffixes meaning *cut, divided,* as in bi*sected,* vivi*sect.*

sec·tar′i·an (sĕk·târ′ĭ·ăn; 6), *adj.* Of, pert. to, or characteristic of sectaries or sects. — *n.* **1.** *Hist.* [*often cap.*] A sectary; a dissenter. **2.** One of a sect, esp. of a religious sect. **3.** A narrow or bigoted denominationalist.

sec·tar′i·an·ism (-ĭz′m), *n.* Sectarian spirit or beliefs; exclusive or narrow-minded attachment to a sect.

sec·tar′i·an·ize (-īz), *v. t.* To imbue with sectarian principles or feelings; subject to a sect.

sec′ta·ry (sĕk′tȧ·rĭ), *n.* [F. *sectaire,* or ML. *sectarius.*] **1.** An adherent, esp. a zealous adherent, of a sect. **2.** [*often cap.*] A dissenter from the established church; specif., a Protestant nonconformist, esp. an Independent.

sec′tile (sĕk′tĭl; 56), *adj.* [F., fr. L. *sectilis,* fr. *secare, sectum,* to cut.] Capable of being severed smoothly by the knife. — **sec·til′i·ty** (sĕk·tĭl′ĭ·tĭ), *n.*

sec′tion (sĕk′shŭn), *n.* [F. or L.; F., fr. L. *sectio,* fr. *secare, sectum,* to cut.] **1.** Act or instance of cutting; separation by cutting; also, a part separated; a division; portion; slice. **2.** A distinct part of a writing; usually, a subdivision of a chapter; also, a division of a law. Symbol §. **3.** The description or representation of anything as it would appear if cut through by a plane. In mechanical drawing, as in these illustrations of a cannon, a ***longitudinal section*** (*a*) usually represents the object cut through its center lengthwise and vertically; a ***cross,* or *transverse, section*** (*b*), as cut crosswise and vertically; and a ***horizontal section*** (*c*), as cut through its center horizontally. ***oblique sections*** are made at various angles. **4.** A distinct part of a country or people, community, class, or the like. **5.** One of the portions, of one square mile each (640 acres), into which the public lands of the United States are divided. See MEASURE, *Table* 4. **6.** One of component parts that may be assembled or reassembled, as of a bookcase. **7.** *Biol.* A natural subdivision of a classificatory group, esp. of a genus, but often of a family or other group. **8.** *Bookbinding.* A signature (sense 4 **c**). **9.** *Micros.* A very thin slice. Cf. MICROTOME. **10.** *Mil. & Nav.* A subdivision of a tactical

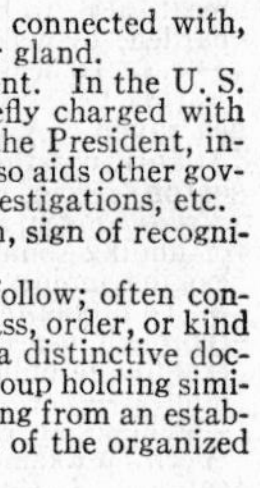

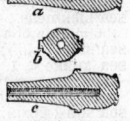

Section, 3.

unit or part of a unit. **11.** *Railroads.* **a** In a sleeping car, a division including an upper and a lower berth. **b** A portion of the permanent way under the care of a particular set of men. Hence: **section boss, crew, gang, hand, man.** **c** One of two or more trains running on the same schedule. — **Syn.** See PART.
— *v. t.* **1.** To cut or separate into sections; make a section of. **2.** To shade, as a drawing, so as to indicate a section; represent in sections.

sec′tion·al (sĕk′shŭn·ăl; -′l), *adj.* **1.** Of, pertaining to, or characteristic of a section. **2.** Consisting of, or divided into, sections; as, a *sectional* bookcase. — **sec′tion·al·ly,** *adv.*

sec′tion·al·ism (-ĭz′m), *n.* *Chiefly U.S.* Undue devotion to the interests peculiar to a section of the country; sectional feeling, spirit, prejudice, etc.

sec′tion·al·ize (-īz), *v. t.* **1.** To make sectional. **2.** *Chiefly U.S.* To divide according to geographical sections or local interests. — **sec′tion·al·i·za′tion** (-ĭ·zā′shŭn; -ī·zā′-), *n.*

sec′tor (sĕk′tẽr), *n.* [LL., prop., a cutter.] **1.** *Geom.* The figure bounded by two radii and the included arc of a circle, ellipse, or other central curve. See CIRCLE, *Illust.* **2.** A mathematical instrument, consisting of two rulers connected at one end by a joint, and marked with several scales. **3.** *Mil.* A subdivision of a defensive system or position assigned to a commander as an area of responsibility. — *v. t.* To divide into, or furnish with, sectors.

sec·to′ri·al (sĕk·tō′rĭ·ăl; 70), *adj.* Of, relating to, or shaped like a sector or the sectors of a circle.

sec′u·lar (sĕk′ū·lẽr), *adj.* [OF. and L.; OF. *seculer,* fr. L. *saecularis,* fr. *saeculum* a race, age, the world.] **1.** Of or pert. to the worldly or temporal as distinguished from the spiritual or eternal; specif.: **a** Not under church control; nonecclesiastical; civil; as, *secular* courts or education. **b** Not sacred; profane; as, *secular* music. **2.** *Eccl.* Not bound by monastic vows or rules; not belonging to a religious order; as, the *secular* clergy; — opp. to *regular.* **3.** Coming or observed once in an age or a century; as, *secular* phenomena. **4.** Existing or continuing through ages or centuries; centuries-old. **5.** Of, pertaining to, or advocating secularism; as, a *secular* review. — *n.* *Eccl.* **a** A secular ecclesiastic, as a parish priest. **b** A layman. — **sec′u·lar·ly,** *adv.*

sec′u·lar·ist (-ĭst), *n.* One who rejects every form of religious faith and worship, and undertakes to live accordingly; also, one who believes that education and other civil matters should be without religious element. — **sec′u·lar·ism** (-ĭz′m), *n.* — **sec′u·lar·is′tic** (-ĭs′tĭk), *adj.*

sec′u·lar′i·ty (-lăr′ĭ·tĭ), *n.; pl.* -TIES (-tĭz). **1.** State or quality of being secular. **2.** The character of being nonreligious or divorced from religion; secularism. **3.** A secular concern, affair, etc.

sec′u·lar·ize (sĕk′ū·lẽr·īz), *v. t.* To render secular; specif.: **a** To authorize (a monk or nun) to live outside the monastery or convent. **b** To transfer from ecclesiastical to civil or lay use, possession, or control; as, to *secularize* a hospital. **c** To deprive of a religious character, observance, etc.; as, to *secularize* Sunday. **d** To convert to, or imbue with, secularism. — **sec′u·lar·i·za′tion** (-ĭ·zā′shŭn; -ī·zā′-), *n.* — **sec′u·lar·iz′er** (-īz′ẽr), *n.*

se′cund (sē′kŭnd; sĕk′ŭnd), *adj.* [L. *secundus* following. See SECOND, *adj.*] *Bot.* Arranged on one side only; unilateral, as flowers in some racemes, spikes, etc.

sec′un·dine (sĕk′ŭn·dīn; -dĭn), *n.* **1.** Afterbirth; — chiefly in *pl.* **2.** *Bot.* Second coat, or integument, of an ovule.

‖**se·cun′dum** (sē·kŭn′dŭm), *prep.* [L.] According to.

se·cure′ (sē·kūr′), *adj.* [L. *securus,* fr. *se-* without + *cura* care.] **1.** *Archaic.* **a** Free from fear, care, or anxiety; easy in mind. **b** Confident; not feeling doubt. **2.** Safe; as: **a** Not exposed to danger. **b** In safe possession or keeping. **c** Affording safety; as, a *secure* retreat. **d** So strong, stable, or firm as to ensure safety; as, a *secure* foundation. **3.** Assured; sure; certain. — **Syn.** See SAFE. — *v. t.* **1.** To make secure; shield; guard; — with *from* or *against;* as, to *secure* troops from a surprise attack. **2.** To ensure the payment of or to, as by a pledge, etc.; as, to *secure* a loan or a creditor. **3.** To make fast; as, to *secure* a door. **4.** To get possession of, esp. something eagerly sought or competed for; acquire; obtain; also, engage. — *v. i.* To be or become secure; to have or provide security; — with *against.* — **Syn.** See ENSURE: GET. — **se·cure′ly,** *adv.* — **se·cure′ness,** *n.* — **se·cur′er** (-kūr′ẽr), *n.*

Se·cu′ri·ties and Ex·change′ Com·mis′sion (sē·kū′rĭ·tĭz). *U.S.* A government commission of five members, organized, July 6, 1934, to supervise, under the Securities Exchange Act of 1934 and the Securities Act of 1933, registration of security issues and transactions in outstanding securities, and under the Public Utility Act of 1935 to regulate the public utility holding companies. Abbr. *SEC*

se·cu′ri·ty (sē·kū′rĭ·tĭ), *n.* **1.** The quality or condition of being secure; specif.: **a** Freedom from exposure to danger; protection; safety or a place of safety. **b** Feeling of or assurance of safety or certainty; freedom from anxiety or doubt. **2.** That which secures; a means of protection, defense, etc. **3.** *Law.* **a** Something given, deposited, or pledged, to make secure the fulfillment of an obligation, the payment of a debt, etc.; surety. **b** One who becomes surety for another, or engages himself for the performance of another's obligation. **4.** *Chiefly pl.* An evidence of debt or of property, as a bond, stock certificate, or other instrument, etc.

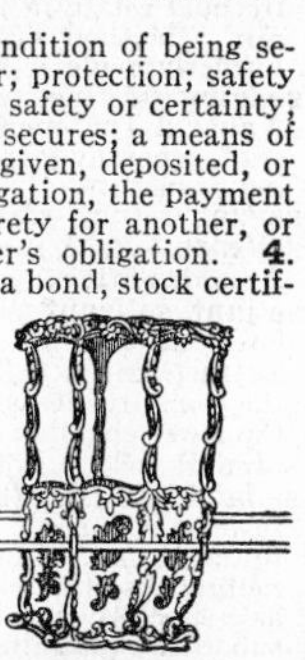
Sedan Chair.

se·dan′ (sē·dăn′), *n.* [Appar., via Sicily, fr. Sp. *sillón,* fr. *silla,* fr. L. *sella* chair, saddle, sedan.] **1.** Also **sedan chair.** A portable chair or covered vehicle for carrying one person, usually borne on poles by two men. **2.** A type of enclosed automobile having one compartment for from four to seven persons.

se·date′ (sē·dāt′), *adj.* [L. *sedatus,* past part. of *sedare, sedatum,* to allay, calm.] **1.** Uninfluenced by that which disturbs; quiet; calm; — now chiefly of mental habits, processes, etc.; as, a *sedate* judgment. **2.** Of a staid or grave nature or constitution; not inclined to levity. — **Syn.** See SERIOUS. — **se·date′ly,** *adv.* — **se·date′ness,** *n.*

se·da′tion (sē·dā′shŭn), *n.* *Med.* The act of making calm or allaying nervous excitement or the state of being calmed, specif. by the use of sedatives.

sed′a·tive (sĕd′ȧ·tĭv), *adj.* Tending to calm, moderate, or tranquilize; specif., *Med.*, allaying irritability and irritation; assuaging pain. — *n.* A sedative agent or remedy.

‖**se de·fen·den′do** (sē dĕf′ĕn·dĕn′dō). [L.] Defending himself.

sed′en·tar′y (sĕd′ĕn·tĕr′ĭ *or, esp. Brit.,* -tẽr·ĭ), *adj.* [F. *sédentaire,* fr. L. *sedentarius,* fr. *sedere* to sit.] **1.** Characterized by, or requiring, sitting; as, a *sedentary* employment. **2.** Stationary; settled; not migratory; as, *sedentary* birds. **3.** Accustomed to sit much or long; as, a *sedentary* man. **4.** *Zool.* Permanently attached, as an oyster or barnacle. — **sed′en·tar′i·ly,** *adv.*

sedge (sĕj), *n.* [AS. *secg.*] **a** Any of a genus (*Carex*) of grasslike plants, often growing in dense tufts in marshy places. The genus is typical of a family (Cyperaceae, the sedge family) distinguished from the grasses chiefly by having achenes and solid stems. **b** Hence, any plant of this family.

se·dil′i·a (sē·dĭl′ĭ·ȧ), *n. pl.; sing.* SEDILE (-dī′lē). [L., pl. of *sedile* seat.] *Eccl.* Seats, usually three, in the chancel for the officiating clergy during intervals of service.

sed′i·ment (sĕd′ĭ·mĕnt), *n.* [F. *sédiment,* fr. L. *sedimentum* a settling, fr. *sedere* to sit.] **1.** The matter which settles to the bottom from a liquid; lees; dregs. **2.** *Geol.* Material, or a mass of it, deposited, as by water.

sed′i·men′ta·ry (-mĕn′tȧ·rĭ), *adj.* Also **sed′i·men′tal** (-tăl; -t′l). **1.** Of, pertaining to, or containing sediment; as, *sedimentary* deposits. **2.** Formed by or from deposits of sediment, esp.: (1) of fragments of other rock transported from their sources and deposited in water, as sandstone and shale; (2) by precipitation from solution, as rock salt and gypsum; (3) from calcareous remains of organisms, as limestone. — **sed′i·men′ta·ri·ly,** *adv.*

sed′i·men·ta′tion (-mĕn·tā′shŭn), *n.* The act or process of depositing sediment.

se·di′tion (sē·dĭsh′ŭn), *n.* [OF., fr. L. *seditio,* orig. a going aside.] Excitement of discontent against the government, or of resistance to lawful authority.

Syn. Sedition, treason mean a serious offense in defiance of allegiance. **Sedition** implies conduct leading to commotion or resistance to authority but without overt acts; **treason,** conduct marked by overt act or acts aiming at overthrow of government, betrayal to the enemy, or the like.

se·di′tion·ar′y (-ĕr′ĭ *or, esp. Brit.,* -ẽr·ĭ), *adj.* Seditious. — *n.* An inciter or promoter of sedition.

se·di′tious (sē·dĭsh′ŭs), *adj.* **1.** Of, pertaining to, of the nature of, or tending to excite sedition. **2.** Disposed to arouse, or take part in, sedition. — **se·di′tious·ly,** *adv.* — **se·di′tious·ness,** *n.*

se·duce′ (sē·dūs′), *v. t.;* SE·DUCED′ (-dūst′); SE·DUC′ING (-dūs′ĭng). [L. *seducere, seductum,* fr. *se-* aside + *ducere* to lead.] **1.** To persuade (one), as into disobedience or disloyalty. **2.** To lead or draw (one) astray, as into an evil, foolish, or disastrous course; to tempt or entice. **3.** To induce to evil; to corrupt; specif., to induce to surrender chastity. — **Syn.** See LURE. — **se·duce′ment,** *n.* — **se·duc′er** (-dūs′ẽr), *n.* — **se·duc′i·ble** (-ĭ·b′l), *adj.*

se·duc′tion (sē·dŭk′shŭn), *n.* **1.** Act of seducing; enticement, esp. to wrongdoing. **2.** That which seduces.

se·duc′tive (-tĭv), *adj.* Tending to seduce; alluring; tempting. — **se·duc′tive·ly,** *adv.* — **se·duc′tive·ness,** *n.*

se·duc′tress (-trĕs; -trĭs), *n.* A woman who seduces.

se·du′li·ty (sē·dū′lĭ·tĭ), *n.* Sedulous activity.

sed′u·lous (sĕd′ū·lŭs), *adj.* [L. *sedulus,* fr. *sedulo* busily, zealously, prop., in good earnest.] Diligent in application or pursuit; steadily industrious. — **Syn.** See BUSY. — **sed′u·lous·ly,** *adv.* — **sed′u·lous·ness,** *n.*

se′dum (sē′dŭm), *n.* [L., houseleek.] *Bot.* Any of a genus (*Sedum*) of fleshy, widely distributed herbs of the orpine family; the stonecrop. *S. acre* is the common stonecrop.

see (sē), *n.* [OF. *sie, sied,* fr. L. *sedes* seat.] **1.** *Obs.* A seat; esp., a throne. **2.** *Eccl.* The seat of the power or authority of a bishop; the diocesan center; hence, the rank, office, power, etc., of a bishop. The ***Apostolic, or Holy, See*** is the see of the pope as bishop of Rome.

see (sē; 4), *v. t.;* SAW (sô); SEEN (sēn); SEE′ING. [AS. *sēon.*] **1.** To perceive by the eye; to behold; descry. **2.** To undergo; experience; as, to *see* service. **3.** To witness as present or contemporary; as, that year *saw* many changes. **4.** To look at, examine, or scrutinize. **5.** To take care or heed; — followed by a noun clause; as, *see* that you do what is necessary. **6.** To accompany in person; to escort. **7.** To meet and converse with, as in an interview. **8.** To discern; understand. **9.** In poker and similar games at cards, to meet (a bet) or to equal the bet of (a player). — *v. i.* **1.** To have the power of sight. **2.** To look. *Obs.,* exc. imper. or interj.: Look! behold! lo! **3.** To comprehend; discern. **4. a** To make investigation; as, run and *see.* **b** To have knowledge by experience; as, we shall *see.*

Syn. See, look, watch mean to perceive something by use of the eyes. **See** stresses the reception of visual impressions; **look,** the directing of the eyes to in order to see; **watch,** a following with the eyes.

see′catch′ (sē′kăch′), **see′catch′ie** (sē′kăch′ĭ), *n.* [Russ. *sekach.*] *Alaska.* A grown male fur seal.

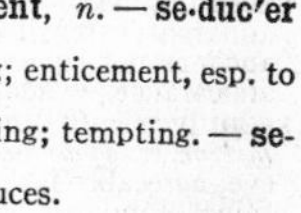

Seed. *A* Seed of Violet, enlarged. *B* Same in Vertical Section; *c* Cotyledons; *ca* Hypocotyl; *e* Endosperm; *h* Hilum; *r* Raphe.

seed (sēd), *n.; pl.* SEED or SEEDS (sēdz). [AS. *sǣd;* akin to AS. *sāwan* to sow.] **1.** The grains or ovules of plants used for sowing; also, one of these grains. **2.** Progeny; descendants; as, the *seed* of David. **3.** That from which anything springs; as: **a** First principle; source. **b** Stock; ancestry. **4.** The stage or condition of bearing seed; hence, overripeness; decay; as, gone to *seed.* **5.** Young oysters suitable for transplanting. **6.** *Agric.* Any propagative portion of a plant. **7.** *Biol. & Physiol.* Semen; milt. **8.** *Bot.* The small body produced by flowering plants which contains an embryo capable of developing by germination; a fertilized and ripened ovule. Cf. PLUMULE, *Illust.*
— *v. t.* **1.** To sprinkle with or as with seed; to sow. **2.** To extract the seeds from (stone fruit, as raisins). **3.** *Sports.* In arranging a tournament, to modify (the draw for positions) by so distributing the names of superior contestants that any possibility of their meeting in the early rounds is eliminated. — *v. i.* **1.** To sow seed; plant. **2.** To bear or shed seed. **3.** To go to seed. — **seed,** *adj.* — **seed′less,** *adj.*

seed′cake′ (-kāk′), *n.* A cake or cooky containing aromatic seeds, such as caraway.

seed′case′ (-kās′), *n.* A seed vessel.

seed coat. *Bot.* The integument of a seed. See TESTA.

seed coral. Small bits of coral used in ornaments.

seed′er (sēd′ẽr), *n.* **1.** An implement used for planting or sowing seeds. **2.** An apparatus for seeding fruit.

seed leaf. An original leaf of a seed embryo.

seed′ling (sēd′lĭng), *n.* **1.** *Hort.* A plant grown from seed. See PLUMULE, *Illust.* **2.** *Forestry.* Any young tree under three feet in height.
seed oyster. A young oyster, esp. of a size suitable for transplantation.
seed pearl. A very small and, often, irregular pearl.
seed plant. = SPERMATOPHYTE.
seeds′man (sēdz′măn), *n.; pl.* -MEN (-mĕn). Also **seed′man** (sēd′-măn). **1.** A sower. **2.** A person who deals in seeds.
seed′time′ (sēd′tīm′), *n.* The season of sowing seeds.
seed vessel. Any dry hollow fruit which contains seeds.
seed weevil. Any of numerous small weevils, esp. of the genus *Apion*, which live in seeds.
seed′y (sēd′ĭ), *adj.;* SEED′I·ER (-ĭ·ẽr); SEED′I·EST. **1.** Abounding with seeds; bearing seeds; having run to seeds; also, containing seeds. **2.** *Colloq.* Worn out; shabby; also, spiritless; feeling or looking wretched. — **seed′i·ly**, *adv.* — **seed′i·ness**, *n.*
see′ing (sē′ĭng), *n.* Sight; vision or power of vision. — *adj.* Having the power of sight or discernment.
see′ing, *conj.* In view of the fact that; inasmuch as.
See′ing Eye (sē′ĭng ī′). An institution near Morristown, N. J., in which dogs are bred and trained as lifetime companions and guides of blind persons.
seek (sēk), *v. t.;* SOUGHT (sôt); SEEK′ING. [AS. *sēcan.*] **1.** To go in search of; to look for. **2.** To try to reach or come to; to resort to. **3.** To inquire for; to beseech; entreat. **4.** To try to acquire. **5.** To try; attempt; — followed by an infinitive. **6.** To search; look through; explore. — *v. i.* **1.** To make search or inquiry. **2.** *Archaic.* To go or resort; have recourse; apply. — **seek′er**, *n.*
seel (sēl), *v. t.* [OF. *siller, ciller*, fr. *cil* eyelash, fr. L. *cilium.*] **1.** *Falconry.* To close the eyes of, as a hawk, by drawing threads through the lids. **2.** To shut or close, as the eyes; to blind.
see′ly (sē′lĭ), *adj.* [AS. *sǣlig.*] *Archaic & Dial.* Weak; feeble; poor; wretched; frail.
seem (sēm), *v. i.* [ME. *semen* to seem, become, befit, of Scand. origin.] **1.** To be in appearance; to look to be; to appear. **2.** To offer itself to view or notice as existing. **3.** To appear to one's own mind or opinion; as, I *seem* to feel no pain. **4.** In a negative expression, to find out how (to do something); as, I cannot *seem* to unlock the door. **5.** With the expletive *it:* **a** To be apparently so; as, it *seems* to me that this is drudgery. **b** To have the appearance of being; as, it *seemed* best to compromise. **c** To present such outward signs; as, it *seemed* as if the hour would never come. **d** To come to be known; as, he was, it *seems*, a spy. — **seem′er**, *n.*
seem′ing, *adj.* Having a semblance, usually as differing from reality; apparent; ostensible. — **Syn.** See APPARENT. — *n.* External appearance, as not corresponding to inner nature or as deceptive; specious appearance. — **seem′ing·ly**, *adv.*
seem′ly (sēm′lĭ), *adj.;* SEEM′LI·ER (-lĭ·ẽr); SEEM′LI·EST. [ON. *sœmiligr*, fr. *sœmr* becoming, fit.] **1.** Having properties pleasing to the eye; agreeably fashioned. **2.** Fitting or proper in respect to conventional standards of good form or taste; decorous. **3.** *Obs.* Suited to the occasion, purpose, or one's character or position; fit. — *adv.* Becomingly; appropriately; decently. — **seem′li·ness**, *n.*
seen (sēn), *past part.* of SEE.
seep (sēp), *v. i.* *Both Scot. & U. S.* To run or leak through fine pores and interstices; to ooze; to percolate slowly. — *n.* A spot where water or petroleum oozes out slowly and gathers in a pool.
seep (sēp), *n.* [*sea* + *peep.*] An amphibious jeep.
seep′age (sēp′ĭj), *n.* *Scot. & U. S.* Act or process of seeping; fluid that has seeped through porous material.
se′er, *n.* **1.** (*pron.* sē′ẽr) One who sees. **2.** (*pron.* sēr) One who foresees events; a prophet.
seer (sēr; sär). Variant of SER.
seer′ess (sēr′ĕs; -ĭs), *n.* Female seer; prophetess.
seer′suck′er (sēr′sŭk′ẽr), *n.* [Hind. *śīrśakar*, fr. Per. *shīrushakar* kind of cloth, lit., milk and sugar.] A light linen fabric, usually striped and of slightly puckered weave; also, a similar cotton fabric.
see′saw′ (sē′sô′), *n.* [Redupl. fr. SAW to cut with a saw.] **1.** A children's pastime of riding on the ends of a plank balanced in the middle, one end going up as the other goes down; also, a plank or board so used. **2.** Any action likened to the motion of a seesaw, as a race in which two contestants frequently alternate in the lead. **3.** *Whist.* A crossruff. — *adj.* Moving up and down or to and fro. — *v. i. & t.* To play at seesaw; hence, to move back and forth or up and down; also, to alternate in the lead.
seethe (sēth), *v. t. & i.;* SEETHED (sēthd); SEETH′ING (sēth′ĭng); *Obs. forms: past* SOD (sŏd); *past part.* SOD′DEN (sŏd′'n). [AS. *sēothan.*] **1.** *Archaic.* To boil or stew. **2.** To soak or saturate in a liquid. **3.** To move or issue in a state of ebullition or violent agitation; as, the rapids *seethed*. **4.** To suffer violent internal excitement. — *n.* Act of seething or state of being seethed.
se·gar′ (sē·gär′). Var. of CIGAR.
seg′gar (sĕg′ẽr). Var. of SAGGER.
seg′ment (sĕg′mĕnt), *n.* [L. *segmentum*, fr. *secare* to cut off.] **1.** Any of the parts into which a body naturally separates or is divided; a section. **2.** *Geom.* **a** A part cut off from a figure by a line or plane; esp., that part of a circular area bounded by a chord and an arc of that circle, or so much of the area as is cut off by the chord. See CIRCLE, *Illust.* **b** The part of a sphere cut off by a plane, or included between two parallel planes. **c** Any of the finite parts of a divided line. — **Syn.** See PART. — *v. t. & i.* To separate into segments; to divide by, or undergo, segmentation. — **seg·men′tal** (sĕg·mĕn′tăl; sĕg′mĕn·tăl; -t'l), *adj.* — **seg·men′tal·ly**, *adv.* — **seg′men·tar′y** (sĕg′mĕn·tĕr′ĭ *or, esp. Brit.,* -tẽr·ĭ), *adj.*
seg′men·ta′tion (sĕg′mĕn·tā′shŭn), *n.* Act or process of dividing into segments, or state of being so divided; esp., *Biol. & Embryol.*, the formation of many cells from a single cell; cleavage, as in a developing egg.
segmentation cavity. *Embryol.* A blastocoele.
‖**se′gno** (sā′nyō), *n.* [It.] *Music.* A sign; specif., the sign marking the beginning or end of a repeat, 𝄋 or :𝄋:.
se′go (sē′gō), *n.* Also **sego lily.** [Of Shoshonean origin.] A perennial herb (*Calochortus nuttallii*) of western North America; also, its edible bulb. The blossom is the State flower of Utah.
seg′re·gate (sĕg′rē·gāt), *adj.* [L. *segregatus*, past part. of *segregare* to separate, fr. *se-* aside + *grex, gregis*, a flock, herd.] Set apart; separate; select. — (-gāt), *v. t.* To separate or cut off from others or from the general mass; to isolate; seclude. — *v. i.* **1.** To separate from the general mass, and collect together, as in crystallization. **2.** *Biol.* To undergo segregation.
seg′re·ga′tion (-gā′shŭn), *n.* **1.** Act of segregating, or state of being segregated; separation from a general mass or main body; specif., isolation or seclusion of a particular group of persons. **2.** A segregated portion. **3.** *Biol.* The separation of allelomorphic genes or characters, typically during meiosis. See MENDEL'S LAW. — **seg′re·ga′tive** (sĕg′rē·gā′tĭv), *adj.*
‖**se′gui·dil′la** (sā′gē·thē′lyä), *n.* [Sp.] **1.** A Spanish stanza of four or seven short verses partly assonant. **2.** *pl.* An air to which a group of such stanzas is sung, and its accompanying dance.
‖**sei·cen′to** (sā·chĕn′tō), *n.* [It., six hundred. Cf. CINQUECENTO.] The 17th century, as a period of Italian art or literature.
seiche (sāsh), *n.* [Swiss F.] An oscillation of the surface of a lake or landlocked sea, varying in period from a few minutes to several hours.
Seid′litz pow′der *or* **pow′ders** (sĕd′lĭts). [From resemblance to the natural water of the village of *Sedlitz*, Bohemia.] Effervescing salts consisting of two separate powders, one of sodium bicarbonate and Rochelle salt and the other of tartaric acid. They are mixed in water, and drunk as a mild cathartic. Called also *Rochelle powder*.
sei·gneur′ (sēn·yûr′; *F.* sĕ′nyûr′). [F.] A lord; seignior.
seign′ior (sēn′yẽr), *n.* [OF. *seignor*, fr. acc. of L. *senior* elder.] **1.** A lord; esp., the lord of a manor. **2.** A title of honor or of address, corresponding to *Sir.* — **seign′ior·al** (-ăl), **sei·gno′ri·al** (sēn·yō′rĭ·ăl), *adj.*
seign′ior·age (-ĭj), *n.* **1.** Something claimed or taken by virtue of sovereign prerogative. **2.** Specif., the difference between the circulating value of a coin and the cost of the bullion and the minting.
seign′ior·y (-ĭ), *n.; pl.* -IES (-ĭz). **1.** *Hist.* Lordship; dominion. **2.** The territory over which a lord holds jurisdiction. **3.** A right appertaining to feudal superiority.
seine (sān; sĕn), *n.* [AS. *segne*, fr. L. *sagena*, fr. Gr. *sagēnē.*] *Fishing.* A large net, one edge having sinkers, and the other, floats. — *v. t. & i.* To fish with a seine.
seise (sēz), *v. t.* [Var. of SEIZE.] To put in possession; to take possession of. *Archaic*, except in legal use.
sei′sin (sē′zĭn). Var. of SEIZIN.
seism (sīz'm; sīs'm), *n.* [See SEISMIC.] An earthquake.
seis′mic (sīz′mĭk; sīs′-), **seis′mi·cal** (-mĭ·kăl), *adj.* Also **seis′mal** (-măl). [Gr. *seismos* earthquake, fr. *seiein* to shake.] Of, pertaining to, of the nature of, subject to, or caused by an earthquake.
seis′mism (-mĭz'm), *n.* [Gr. *seismos* earthquake.] Earthquake phenomena, collectively.
seis′mo- (sīz′mō-; sīs′mō-). [Gr. *seismos.*] A combining form meaning *earthquake*, as in *seismology*.
seis′mo·gram (-grăm), *n.* *Physics.* The record of an earth tremor.
seis′mo·graph (sīz′mō·gráf; sīs′-; 9), *n.* [*seismo-* + *graph.*] *Physics.* An apparatus to register the shocks and motions of earthquakes. — **seis·mog′ra·pher** (sīz·mŏg′rȧ·fẽr; sīs-), *n.* — **seis′mo·graph′ic** (sīz′mō·grăf′ĭk; sīs′-), *adj.* — **seis·mog′ra·phy** (sīz·mŏg′rȧ·fĭ; sīs-), *n.*
seis·mol′o·gy (sīz·mŏl′ō·jĭ; sīs-), *n.* The science of earthquakes and attendant phenomena. — **seis′mo·log′ic** (sīz′mō·lŏj′ĭk; sīs′mō-), **seis′mo·log′i·cal** (-ĭ·kăl), *adj.* — **seis′mo·log′i·cal·ly**, *adv.* — **seis·mol′o·gist** (sīz·mŏl′ō·jĭst; sīs-), *n.*
seis·mom′e·ter (-mŏm′ē·tẽr), *n.* [*seismo-* + *-meter.*] An accurate form of seismograph indicating the actual movements of the ground. — **seis′mo·met′ric** (sīz′mō·mĕt′rĭk; sīs′-), **seis′mo·met′ri·cal** (-rĭ·kăl), *adj.*
seis′mo·scope (sīz′mō·skōp; sīs′-), *n.* An instrument for recording only the time or occurrence of earthquakes. — **seis′mo·scop′ic** (-skŏp′ĭk), *adj.*
seize (sēz), *v. t.* [OF. *seisir, saisir*, fr. LL. *sacire* to effect legal possession.] **1.** Orig., to put in possession of a feudal holding. **2.** **a** To confiscate; annex; as, to *seize* a fief. **b** To take possession of by force. **3.** To lay hold of suddenly or forcibly; to clutch. **4.** To take prisoner; arrest. **5.** To affect so as to oppress or overwhelm; as, *seized* with dizziness. **6.** To grasp with the mind; comprehend. **7.** *Naut.* To bind or fasten together with a lashing of small stuff, as yarn or marline; as, to *seize* ropes. — *v. i.* To take or lay hold suddenly or forcibly; to grasp. — **Syn.** See TAKE. — **seiz′a·ble** (sēz′ȧ·b'l), *adj.* — **seiz′er** (-ẽr), *n.*
sei′zin, *or, commonly,* **sei′sin** (sē′zĭn), *n.* [OF. *saisine.*] *Law.* Orig., possession, whether of land or chattels; later, possession of a freehold estate in land by one having title thereto. — ***livery of seizin.*** Method by which the ceremonial conveyance of land was formerly made.
seiz′ing (sēz′ĭng), *n.* **1.** Act of grasping suddenly or forcibly. **2.** *Naut.* **a** The operation of fastening together or lashing with small stuff, generally tarred; also, the cord or lashing so used. **b** The fastening so made.
sei′zor (sē′zẽr; -zôr), *n.* *Law.* One who seizes.
sei′zure (sē′zhẽr), *n.* **1.** Act of seizing, or state of being seized. **2.** A sudden attack, as of a disease; a fit.
se′jant, se′jeant (sē′jănt), *adj.* [F. *séant*, pres. part. of *seoir* to sit, fr. L. *sedere.*] *Her.* Sitting, as a lion or other beast.
Sejm (sām), *n.* [Pol. *sejm* assembly.] Assembly, or Diet; specif., the Constituent Assembly of the Polish Republic (1918–22), and later the lower chamber of the Polish Parliament.
sel, sell (sĕl). Scot. & dial. vars. of SELF.
se·la′chi·an (sē·lā′kĭ·ăn), *adj.* [Gr. *selachos* a fish having cartilages instead of bones.] *Zool.* Pertaining to a group (Selachii) of elasmobranch fishes. In the broadest senses it comprises either all the elasmobranchs or all except the chimaeras. In restricted senses, it ranks as a subclass or order comprising the existing sharks and rays, or as a suborder containing the existing sharks as disting. from the rays. — **se·la′chi·an**, *n.*
sel′a·gi·nel′la (sĕl′ȧ·jĭ·nĕl′ȧ), *n.* [NL., dim. fr. L. *selago, -ginis*, name of a plant.] *Bot.* Any of a genus (*Selaginella*) of mosslike fern allies constituting a family (Selaginellaceae).
se′lah (sē′lȧ), *n.* [Heb. *selāh.*] *Bib.* Probably, a musical or liturgical sign of some kind, occurring often in the Psalms and three times in Habakkuk iii. Hence, a pause.
se·lam′lik (sē·läm′lĭk), *n.* [Turk. *selāmliq*, fr. Ar. *salām* + Turk. suff. *-liq.*] In a Turkish house, the men's quarters, where guests are received.
sel′dom (sĕl′dŭm), *adv.* [AS. *seldan, seldon, seldum.*] Rarely; not often. — *adj. Archaic.* Rare; infrequent.

se·lect′ (sē·lĕkt′), *adj.* [L. *selectus*, pres. part. of *seligere* to select, fr. *se-* aside + *legere* to gather.] **1.** Taken from a number of the same or an analogous kind by preference; picked. **2.** Of special excellence; choice. **3.** Fastidious in selecting; nice in choosing. — *v. t. & i.* To take by preference from among others; to pick out. — **Syn.** See CHOOSE. — **se·lect′ness**, *n.*

se·lect′ee′ (sē·lĕk′tē′), *n. U. S.* One inducted into military service under the Selective Service System.

se·lec′tion (sē·lĕk′shŭn), *n.* **1.** A selecting or state of being selected. **2.** One that is selected; a collection of things chosen. **3.** *Biol.* Specif., any process, natural (see NATURAL SELECTION) or artificial, which results or tends to result in preventing certain individuals or groups of organisms from surviving and propagating, and in allowing others to do so. — **Syn.** See CHOICE.

se·lec′tive (-tĭv), *adj.* **1.** Of, pert. to, or characterized by selection; selecting or tending to select. **2.** *Radio.* Pert. to or designating the degree of ability of a circuit or apparatus to respond to a desired frequency and not to others. — **se·lec′tiv′i·ty** (-tĭv′ĭ·tĭ), *n.*

Selective Service System. *U. S.* A government agency set up by the Selective Training and Service Act of Sept. 16, 1940 for the mobilization of the nation's manpower. Re-established by the Selective Service Act of 1948, for supplying manpower to the armed services. Abbr. *SSS*

se·lect′man (sē·lĕkt′măn), *n.; pl.* -MEN (-mĕn). One of a board of officers chosen annually in towns in the New England States, except Rhode Island, to transact public business.

se·lec′tor (sē·lĕk′tẽr), *n.* One that selects.

Se·le′ne (sē·lē′nē), *n.* [Gr. *Selēnē*, fr. *selēnē* moon.] *Gr. Relig.* The goddess of the moon, merged in Artemis and Hecate. See ENDYMION.

se·le′nic (sē·lē′nĭk; -lĕn′ĭk), *adj. Chem.* Of, pertaining to, or containing selenium, in a relatively high valence.

selenic acid. An acid, H_2SeO_4, whose aqueous solution dissolves gold, copper, iron, etc.

se·le′ni·ous (sē·lē′nĭ·ŭs), *adj. Chem.* Of, pertaining to, or containing selenium, esp. in a relatively low valence.

sel′e·nite (sĕl′ē·nīt; sē·lē′nīt), *n.* [L. *selenites*, fr. Gr. *selēnitēs* (sc. *lithos*), fr. *selēnē* the moon; — so called because supposed to wax and wane with the moon.] *Mineral.* A variety of gypsum in crystals or crystalline masses.

se·le′ni·um (sē·lē′nĭ·ŭm), *n.* [NL., fr. Gr. *selēnē* the moon; — from its resemblance to *tellurium* (fr. L. *tellus* the earth).] *Chem.* A nonmetallic element, resembling sulfur and tellurium chemically and obtained chiefly as a by-product in copper refining. The electrical conductivity of the gray metal-like form of selenium varies with the intensity of its illumination. Symbol, *Se;* at. no., 34; at. wt., 78.96. Selenium is used in various photoelectric devices, as talking films.

selenium cell. *Elec.* A piece of metallic selenium in circuit with a battery and a galvanometer, used in certain optical experiments because, under the action of light, the electrical resistance of selenium changes.

sel′e·nog′ra·phy (sĕl′ē·nŏg′rȧ·fĭ), *n.* [Gr. *selēnē* the moon + *-graphy.*] The science of the physical features of the moon. — **sel′e·nog′ra·pher** (-fẽr), **sel′e·nog′ra·phist** (-fĭst), *n.* — **se·le′no·graph′ic** (sē·lē′nō·grăf′ĭk), *adj.*

sel′e·nol′o·gy (-nŏl′ō·jĭ), *n.* [Gr. *selēnē* the moon + *-logy.*] That branch of astronomy which treats of the moon; loosely, selenography. — **sel′e·nol′o·gist** (-jĭst), *n.*

Se·leu′cid (sē·lū′sĭd), *n.* One of the **Se·leu′ci·dae** (-sĭ·dē), a dynasty (312–64 B.C.) which, at the height of its power, ruled over Bactria, Persia, Babylonia, Syria, and part of Asia Minor. It was founded by Seleucus Nicator, a general of Alexander the Great. — **Se·leu′cid, Se·leu′ci·dan** (-sĭ·dăn), *adj.*

self (sĕlf), *adj.* [AS. *self, seolf, sylf.*] **1.** *Obs.* Same; identical. **2.** **a** Having its own or a single nature or character, as in color, composition, etc.; as, *self*-colored. **b** Of the same material, color, etc., as that which it accompanies; as, a *self* trimming. — *n.; pl.* SELVES (sĕlvz). **1.** The identity of anything considered abstractly. **2.** An individual considered as an identical person; a being regarded as having personality; a being in its relations to its own identity. **3.** Personal interest or advantage; selfishness.

self-. The noun *self* used as a prefix in many compounds, and denoting: **a** The *person* or *thing affected*, as in *self*-conscious. **b** The *agent* that of itself acts in a manner implied by the word with which it is joined; the *subject* of the action; as in *self*-pollinated. **c** With adverbial force: (1) *To, with, for,* or *toward oneself*, as in *self*-centered. (2) *Of* or *in oneself inherently*, as in *self*-evident. **d** With adjectival force: (1) *Obs. Personal; individual.* (2) *Independent*, as in *self*-government. **e** *Automatic;* — in nouns denoting, or adjectives describing, apparatus, as in *self*-loading.

self′-a·base′ment, *n.* Abasement of oneself.

self′-a·buse′, *n.* **1.** Abuse of oneself, one's powers, one's faculties. **2.** Masturbation; self-pollution.

self′-act′ing, *adj.* Acting of or by itself; automatic.

self′-ad·dressed′, *adj.* Addressed for return to the sender and enclosed or to be enclosed in a communication for the convenience of one making reply; — applied to an envelope or card.

self′-as·ser′tion, *n.* Act of asserting oneself, or one's own rights or claims. — **self′-as·ser′tive**, *adj.* — **Syn.** See AGGRESSIVE.

self′-as·sured′, *adj.* Self-reliant; complacent. — **self′-as·sur′ance**, *n.*

self′-cen′tered, self′-cen′tred (*see Pron.*, § 2), *adj.* Centered in itself, or in oneself; independent; absorbed in self.

self′-col′ored, self′-col′oured, *adj.* Of a single color.

self′-com·mand′, *n.* Command of oneself; self-control.

self′-com·pla′cent, *adj.* Satisfied with one's own character and acts; self-satisfied. — **self′-com·pla′cence, self′-com·pla′cen·cy**, *n.* — **self′-com·pla′cent·ly**, *adv.*

self′-com·posed′, *adj.* Calm; collected.

self′-con·ceit′, *n.* An overweening opinion of one's own powers; vanity. — **self′-con·ceit′ed**, *adj.*

self′-con′fi·dence, *n.* Quality or state of being self-confident; self-reliance; often, overconfidence.

self′-con′fi·dent, *adj.* Confident of one's own strength or powers; self-reliant. — **self′-con′fi·dent·ly**, *adv.*

self′-con′scious, *adj.* **1.** Conscious of one's acts or states as belonging to, or originating in, oneself. **2.** Embarrassed by consciousness of oneself, one's awkwardness, failure, etc., in social relations. — **self′-con′scious·ly**, *adv.* — **self′-con′scious·ness**, *n.*

self′-con·tained′, *adj.* Sufficient in itself; independent. Hence: **a** Reserved; uncommunicative. **b** Showing self-control. **c** *Mach.* Having all essential working parts so contained in a case or framework that they do not depend on appliances or fastenings outside of the machine.

self′-con·tent′, *n.* Self-satisfaction; self-complacency.

self′-con·tent′ment, *n.* Self-satisfaction.

self′-con′tra·dic′tion, *n.* Contradiction of oneself or itself. — **self′-con′tra·dic′to·ry**, *adj.*

self′-con·trol′, *n.* Control of oneself.

self′-de·ceit′, *n.* Act of deceiving oneself, or state of being deceived by oneself; self-deception.

self′-de·cep′tion, *n.* Self-deceit.

self′-de·fense′, self′-de·fence′, *n.* Act of defending one's own person, property, or reputation. — **self′-de·fen′sive**, *adj.*

self′-de·lu′sion, *n.* Self-deception.

self′-de·ni′al, *n.* Denial of oneself; forbearance from gratifying one's own desires.

self′-de·ny′ing, *adj.* Forbearing to gratify oneself; showing self-denial. — **self′-de·ny′ing·ly**, *adv.*

self′-de·struc′tion, *n.* Destruction of oneself; specif., suicide.

self′-de·ter′mi·na′tion, *n.* **1.** Determination of one's acts by oneself without external compulsion. **2.** *International Law.* Decision by the population of a territorial unit as to its future political status. — **self′-de·ter′min·ing**, *adj. & n.*

self′-de·ter′mined, *adj.* Determined by itself.

self′-de·vo′tion, *n.* Devotion of oneself, esp. in service or sacrifice. — **self′-de·vo′tion·al**, *adj.*

self′-dis′ci·pline, *n.* Correction or government of oneself for the sake of improvement.

self′-dis·trust′, *n.* Lack of confidence in oneself.

self′-driv′en, *adj.* Driven by itself; automotive.

self′-ed′u·cat′ed, *adj.* Educated by one's own efforts, without formal instruction, or without pecuniary assistance. — **self′-ed′u·ca′tion**, *n.*

self′-es·teem′, *n.* Self-respect; also, self-conceit.

self′-ev′i·dent, *adj.* Evident without proof or reasoning.

self′-ex·am′i·na′tion, *n.* Examination into one's own state, conduct, and motives; introspection.

self′-ex′e·cut′ing, *adj.* Providing for its own execution; containing clauses giving effect to its provisions by operation of law upon the happening of a contemplated event; — said of laws, treaties, etc.

self′-ex·ist′ent, *adj.* Existing, as God, of or by himself, independent of any other being or cause. — **self′-ex·ist′ence**, *n.*

self′-ex·plain′ing, *adj.* Self-explanatory.

self′-ex·plan′a·to′ry, *adj.* Explaining itself; capable of being understood without explanation.

self′-ex·pres′sion, *n.* Expression of one's own personality, as through art, music, etc.

self′-for·get′ful, *adj.* Forgetful of self; unselfish.

self′-ful·fill′ment, self′-ful·fil′ment, *n.* Fulfillment of one's hopes or ambitions by one's own powers or efforts.

self′-gov′erned, *adj.* Having self-government; independent. — **self′-gov′ern·ing**, *adj.*

self′-gov′ern·ment, *n.* **1.** Self-control; self-command. **2.** Hence, government by the joint action of the mass of people constituting a civil body; also, the state of being so governed; specif., democratic government.

self′-hard′en·ing, *adj. Metal.* Designating, or pertaining to, any of various steels that harden when heated to above a red heat and cooled in air without quenching. — **self′-hard′ened**, *adj.*

self′heal′ (sĕlf′hēl′), *n.* **a** A blue-flowered Eurasian mint (*Prunella vulgaris*) naturalized throughout North America. It was supposed to possess healing properties. **b** Any of several plants with like reputation, as the sanicle, etc.

self′-help′, *n.* Act of aiding or providing for oneself, without depending on the aid of others.

self′hood (sĕlf′ho͝od), *n.* **1.** That by which one is oneself; individuality; also, one's personality. **2.** Selfishness.

self′-i·den′ti·ty, *n.* The identity of a thing with itself; identity of subject and object in life and consciousness.

self′-im·por′tance, *n.* An exaggerated estimate of one's own importance or merit, esp. as manifested; self-conceit. — **self′-im·por′tant**, *adj.* — **self′-im·por′tant·ly**, *adv.*

self′-im·prove′ment, *n.* Improvement of oneself by one's own action.

self′-in·clu′sive, *adj.* Including within itself.

self′-in·duced′, *adj.* Produced by self-induction.

self′-in·duc′tion, *n. Elec. & Magnetism.* The inducing of an electromotive force in a circuit by a varying current in the same circuit.

self′-in·dul′gence, *n.* Indulgence of one's appetites, desires, etc. — **self′-in·dul′gent**, *adj.* — **self′-in·dul′gent·ly**, *adv.*

self′-in·i′ti·at′ed, *adj.* Initiated by oneself.

self′-in·sur′ance, *n.* Insurance of oneself or one's own interests, as by laying aside a fund for the purpose.

self′-in′ter·est, *n.* The interest or advantage of oneself; esp., disposition to pursue personal advantage.

self′ish (sĕl′fĭsh), *adj.* Caring unduly or supremely for oneself; regarding one's own comfort, advantage, etc., in disregard, or at the expense, of that of others. — **self′ish·ly**, *adv.* — **self′ish·ness**, *n.*

self′-knowl′edge, *n.* Knowledge of oneself.

self′less, *adj.* Having no regard to self; unselfish.

self′-liq′ui·dat′ing, *adj. Colloq., U. S. Com.* Designating a commercial transaction in which the normal course of business leads to the conversion of goods into cash in a short time, as the sale of goods in great current demand.

self′-load′ing, *adj.* That loads itself by its own action.

self′-love′, *n.* Love of oneself; amour-propre; regard for one's own happiness, benefit, etc. — **self′-lov′ing**, *adj.*

self′-made′ (*see Pron.*, § 2), *adj.* **1.** Made by oneself or itself. **2.** Having risen from poverty or obscurity unaided, esp. without pecuniary aid; as, a *self-made* man.

self′-mas′ter·y, *n.* Self-command; self-control.

self′-mor′ti·fi·ca′tion, *n.* Mortification of one's own body.

self′-o·pin′ion, *n.* Opinion, esp. high opinion, of oneself.

self′-o·pin′ion·at′ed, *adj.* **a** Conceited. **b** Stubborn.

self′-o·pin′ioned, *adj.* Self-opinionated.

self′-pit′y, *n.* Pity felt for oneself.
self′-pol′li·nat′ed, *adj.* *Bot.* Pollinated by the anthers of the same flower. Cf. CROSS-POLLINATION. — **self′-pol′li·nate**, *v. t.* — **self′-pol′li·na′tion**, *n.*
self′-pol·lu′tion, *n.* Masturbation. — **self′-pol·lut′er**, *n.*
self′-por′trait, *n.* A portrait of oneself made by oneself.
self′-pos·sessed′, *adj.* Having or exhibiting self-possession; composed in mind, manner, etc.; calm.
self′-pos·ses′sion, *n.* Control or command over one's powers; self-command; presence of mind; composure. — **Syn.** See CONFIDENCE.
self′-pres′er·va′tion, *n.* Preservation of oneself from destruction, injury, loss, etc.; also, the tendency to this regarded as an instinct or natural law.
self′-pride′, *n.* Pride in oneself or that which pertains to oneself.
self′-pro·duced′, *adj.* Produced by powers within oneself or itself.
self′-pro·pel′ling, *adj.* Containing within itself the means for its own propulsion. — **self′-pro·pelled′**, *adj.*
self′-pro·tec′tion, *n.* Protection of oneself from injury, loss, etc.
self′-re′al·i·za′tion, *n.* Fulfillment by oneself of the possibilities of one's character or personality.
self′-re·cord′ing, *adj.* Autographic.
self′-re·gard′, *n.* Regard for, or consideration of, one's own self or interests; also, self-respect.
self′-reg′is·ter·ing, *adj.* Registering automatically.
self′-re·la′tion, *n.* Self-identity.
self′-re·li′ance, *n.* Reliance upon one's own efforts, powers, etc.; confidence in oneself.
self′-re·li′ant, *adj.* Reliant upon oneself.
self′-re·nun′ci·a′tion, *n.* Act of renouncing one's own wishes, etc.; self-sacrifice. — **self′-re·nun′ci·a·to′ry**, *adj.*
self′-re·proach′, *n.* Act of reproaching oneself.
self′-re·proach′ful, *adj.* Reproachful of oneself.
self′-re·proof′, *n.* Act of reproving oneself; censure of one's own conduct by one's own judgment.
self′-re·spect′, *n.* Respect for oneself; laudable self-esteem. — **self′-re·spect′ing**, *adj.*
self′-re·straint′, *n.* Restraint over self; self-control.
self′-right′eous, *adj.* Righteous in one's own esteem; pharisaical. — **self′-right′eous·ly**, *adv.*
self′-ris′ing, *adj.* That rises of itself, specif. without the addition of leaven, as certain flour.
self′-sac′ri·fice, *n.* Sacrifice of oneself, or one's interest, for others or from conscience. — **self′-sac′ri·fic′ing**, *adj.*
self′same′ (sĕlf′sām′; 2), *adj.* [*self*, adj. + *same*.] Precisely the same; identical. Cf. SELF, *adj.*, 1. — **Syn.** See SAME. — **self′same′ness**, *n.*
self′-sat′is·fac′tion, *n.* Satisfaction with oneself, one's position, powers, or person; self-complacency.
self′-sat′is·fied, *adj.* Satisfied with oneself or one's actions, etc.; self-complacent.
self′-seek′er, *n.* One who seeks only or unduly his own interest, advantage, or pleasure.
self′-seek′ing, *n.* Act or habit of seeking primarily one's own interest or happiness; selfishness. — **self′-seek′ing**, *adj.*
self′-serv′ice, *adj.* Designating a type of restaurant or café, or a store, where the patrons help themselves, wholly or in part, to food or goods to be paid for upon leaving. — **self′-serv′ice**, *n.*
self′-sown′ (*see Pron.*, § 2), *adj.* Sown or disseminated autonomically, or by inanimate agencies, as by wind, water currents, etc.
self′-start′er, *n.* *Internal-Combustion Engines.* Any of various more or less automatic attachments for starting an engine, other than the simple starting crank or an auxiliary turning engine.

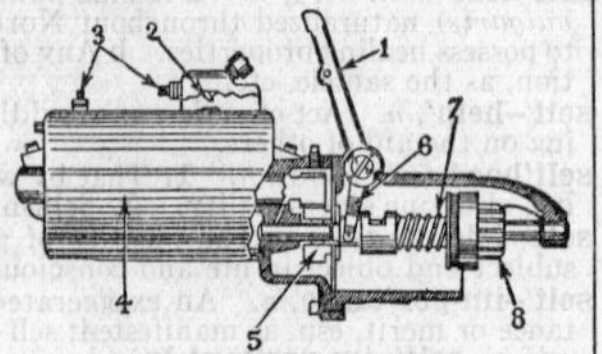

Self-starter (automobile). 1 Contact Arm; 2 Switch and Plunger; 3 Terminal Posts; 4 Motor; 5 Reduction Gear; 6 Shift Yoke; 7 Shift Spring; 8 Pinion.

self′-styled′, *adj.* Styled or called by oneself; soi-disant.
self′-suf·fi′cient, *adj.* **1.** Able to accomplish one's own aims without external aid or co-operation. **2.** Having an overweening confidence in one's own abilities; hence, haughty; overbearing. — **self′-suf·fi′cien·cy**, *n.*
self′-suf·fic′ing, *adj.* Self-sufficient.
self′-sup·port′, *n.* Independent support of oneself or itself.
self′-sup·port′ed, *adj.* Supported by oneself or itself. — **self′-sup·port′ing**, *adj.*
self′-sur·ren′der, *n.* Surrender of self; the yielding up of oneself, one's will, etc., to some influence or person.
self′-sus·tain′ing, *adj.* Maintaining, or capable of maintaining, oneself by one's independent efforts.
self′-taught′ (sĕlf′tôt′; 2), *adj.* Taught by oneself; having little or no formal instruction.
self′-will′, *n.* One's own will, esp. when opposed to that of others; obstinacy.
self′-willed′, *adj.* Governed by one's own will; not yielding to the wishes of others; obstinate.
self′-wind′ing (-wīn′dĭng), *adj.* *Horol.* Of a clock, etc., wound automatically, as at intervals by an electric motor.
self′-wrong′, *n.* Wrong done to oneself.
Sel·juk′ (sĕl·jōōk′; sĕl′jōōk), *n.* [Turk. *Seljūq*, the eponymous ancestor.] A member of any of several Turkish dynasties which ruled over a great part of western Asia in the 11th, 12th and 13th centuries. — **Sel·juk′, Sel·juk′i·an** (-ĭ·ăn), *adj.*
sell (sĕl), *v. t.*; SOLD (sōld); SELL′ING. [AS. *sellan, syllan*, to give, deliver, sell.] **1.** To deliver or hand over in breach of duty, trust, etc.; to betray. **2.** To deliver into bondage, esp. for money. **3.** To dispose of or manage for profit instead of in accord with conscience, justice, etc.; as, to *sell* one's vote. **4.** *Slang.* To impose upon; trick. **5.** To transfer (property) for a consideration; to give up for a consideration; to convey; — opposed to *buy*. **6.** To deal in as an article of sale; as, to *sell* groceries. — *v. i.* **1.** To dispose of commodities or property; to make sales. **2.** To be sold; to find buyers. — ***sell out.*** **1.** To dispose of completely by sale. **2.** *Slang.* To betray one's cause or associates for a compensation. **3.** *Exchanges.* To sell in open market (stocks or commodities carried on margin when this margin is not maintained); also, to sell the stocks or commodities of (a person) in this way and for this reason. — *n. Colloq.* A hoax.
sell. Var. of SELF (see SEL).
sell′er (sĕl′ẽr), *n.* One who sells; a dealer; vendor.
sell′ing, *adj.* **1.** That sells readily; salable. **2.** Engaged in selling; making a business of selling.
sell′ing-plat′er (sĕl′ĭng·plăt′ẽr), *n.* A horse that runs in selling races.
selling race. *Horse Racing.* A race in which horses are entered to be sold at a certain price, the weights imposed varying as these prices.
sell′out′ (sĕl′out′), *n.* **1.** *Slang.* Act or instance of selling out; specif., the exhaustion of the supply of an article of merchandise due to an unusual demand. **2.** *Theat. Slang.* A show for which all the seats have been sold.
Selt′zer (sĕlt′sẽr), *n.*, *or* **Seltzer water.** A mineral water from Nieder Selters, in Wiesbaden, Germany; also, an artificially prepared water of similar composition.
sel′vage, sel′vedge (sĕl′vĭj), *n.* [*self* + *edge*, i. e., its own proper edge.] **1.** The edge or an edge of a woven fabric, so formed as to prevent raveling. **2.** The edge plate of a lock through which the bolt is projected.
selves (sĕlvz), *n., pl.* of SELF.
se·man′teme (sē·măn′tēm), *n.* [F. *sémantème*. See SEMANTICS.] *Linguistics.* An element of language that expresses a definite image or idea; a base. It may be a word (*tree, play*) or part of a word (*tree*-s, *play*-ing). Cf. MORPHEME **a**.
se·man′tic (sē·măn′tĭk), *adj.* [Gr. *sēmantikos*. See SEMANTICS.] **1.** Pertaining to meaning in language; as, pitch may have *semantic* value. **2.** Of or pertaining to semantics.
se·man′tics (sē·măn′tĭks), *n.*; see -ICS. [After F. *sémantique*, fr. Gr. *sēmantikos* significant meaning, fr. *sēmainein* to signify, fr. *sēma* a sign.] **1.** *Philol.* The science of meanings, as contrasted with *phonetics*, the science of sounds; the historical and psychological study and the classification of changes in the signification of words or forms, viewed as normal and vital factors in linguistic development. **2.** That science dealing with the relations between symbols ("signs") and what they refer to and with human behavior in reaction to symbols, including unconscious attitudes, influences of social institutions, and epistemological and linguistic assumptions, and having as an objective the systematization of the language of science and the unification of knowledge. Called also *significs*. — **se·man′ti·cal** (-tĭ·kăl), *adj.* — **sem′an·ti′cian** (sĕm′ăn·tĭsh′ăn; sē′măn-), **se·man′ti·cist** (sē·măn′tĭ·sĭst), *n.*
sem′a·phore (sĕm′ȧ·fōr; 70), *n.* [Gr. *sēma* a sign + *-phore*.] **1.** A signal telegraph, as an apparatus used esp. on railroads for giving signals by the disposition of lanterns, flags, oscillating arms, etc. **2.** A form of visual signaling in which the operator uses a flag in each hand. — *v. t. & i.* To signal by semaphore.
se·ma′si·ol′o·gy (sē·mā′sĭ·ŏl′ō·jĭ), *n.* [Gr. *sēmasia* signification + *-logy*.] *Philol.* Semantics. — **se·ma′si·o·log′i·cal** (-ō·lŏj′ĭ·kăl), *adj.* — **se·ma′si·ol′o·gist** (-ŏl′ō·jĭst), *n.*
se·mat′ic (sē·măt′ĭk), *adj.* [Gr. *sēma, sēmatos*, sign, token.] *Biol.* Serving as a warning, as the conspicuous colors of certain noxious or poisonous animals.

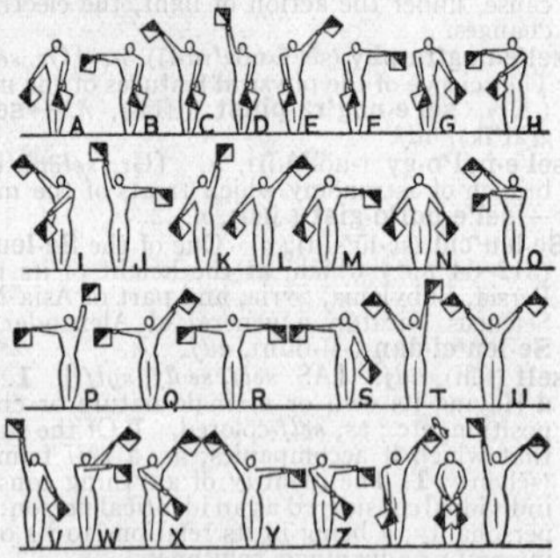

Semaphore Alphabet. Letters *A* through *J* may be read for the numerals 1, 2, 3, 4, 5, 6, 7, 8, 9, 0, but numbers in a message should be spelled out. Several letters have special meanings, as *C* for Answering Sign and *J* for Attention Sign (also indicated by rapid alternation of *U* and *R*). The three positions following *Z* are: Error (successive *E's* broken by rotating raised arm); Front, or Break; and Numerals Follow. In the overhead groups (*DJV* and *KPT*) the arm in some codes may be bent at right angles at the elbow.

sem′bla·ble (sĕm′blȧ·b'l), *adj.* [OF., fr. *sembler* to seem, resemble, fr. L. *similare, simulare*.] *Archaic.* **a** Like; alike; similar. **b** Suitable. **c** Apparent; ostensible; seeming. — *n. Archaic.* Resemblance. — **sem′bla·bly** (-blĭ), *adv.*
sem′blance (sĕm′blăns), *n.* [OF.] **1.** One's outward appearance; form. **2.** Countenance; aspect. **3.** An image; likeness. **4.** Resemblance, actual or apparent; similarity. **5.** Seeming; esp., specious appearance or seeming; also, mere show.
se·mé′ (sē·mā′), *adj.* [F., sown.] *Her.* Covered with small figures, as of flowers or stars.
se′mei·ol′o·gy (sē′mī·ŏl′ō·jĭ), *n.* [Gr. *sēmeion* sign + *-logy*.] Science or art of signs. Specif.: **a** *Med.* Symptomatology. **b** Art of using signs in signaling or in expressing thought.
se′mei·ot′ic (-ŏt′ĭk), *adj.* Also **se′mei·ot′i·cal** (-ĭ·kăl). [Gr. *sēmeiōtikos*, fr. *sēmeion* a mark, sign.] **1.** Relating to signs or to the language of signs. **2.** *Med.* Of or pertaining to signs or symptoms of diseases.
se′men (sē′mĕn), *n.*; *pl.* SEMINA (sĕm′ĭ·nȧ). [L., fr. the root of *serere, satum*, to sow.] *Physiol.* The viscid whitish fluid produced in the male reproductive organs, which contains the spermatozoa and hence serves to fertilize the eggs.
se·mes′ter (sē·mĕs′tẽr), *n.* [Gr., fr. L. *semestris* half-yearly, fr. *sex* six + *mensis* month.] **1.** Orig. a period of six months. **2.** Hence, either of the two periods of instruction, commonly about eighteen weeks in length, into which the academic year is often divided. — **se·mes′tral** (-trăl), **se·mes′tri·al** (-trĭ·ăl), *adj.*
sem′i- (sĕm′ĭ-). [L.] A prefix denoting *half*; specif.: **a** *Approximately half; partly;* as in *semi*permeable. **b** *Precisely half; halved* or *bisected;* as in *semi*breve, *semi*dome. **c** *Occurring* or *coming twice*, as in *semi*monthly. Cf. BI-, 2. **d** *In one half*, esp. for half the length or on one of two sides, as in *semi*round; also, *in some particular*, as in *semi*vowel. **e** *No more than half; in low degree; only partly; incompletely;* as in *semi*civilized, *semi*final, *semi-*

official, *semi*oviparous, *semi*precious. **f** *Little more than; little better than,* as in *semi*mute.

☞ For words below see *semi-* and the combining words.

semiadherent
semiallegiance
semiannual
semiannually
semiaquatic
semiarc
semiarid
semiattached
semiautonomous
semibarbaric
semibarbarism
semibarbarous
semibay
semiblind
semicentenarian
semi-Christian
semicircumference
semicivilized
semicoagulated
semicollapsible
semicoma
semicomatose
semiconic
semiconical
semiconscious
semiconversion
semicrystalline
semicylindrical
semidaily
semidarkness
semidelirious
semidesert
semidetached
semideveloped
semidiameter
semidivine
semidomesticated
semidry
semidrying
semieducated
semiellipse
semielliptical
semienclosed
semifeudal
semifitting
semiflexion
semifloating
semiformal
semigelatinous
semiglobe
semiglobular
semi-Gothic
semihexagonal
semihumorous
semi-idleness
semi-independence
semi-independent
semi-intoxicated
semi-intoxication
semi-invalid
semiliquid
semiliterate
semiloyalty
semimajor
semimilitary
semimonopoly
semimute
seminarcosis
semiobscurity
semiopaque
semiorganized
semiovoid
semiparalysis
semiperishable
semiphilosophical
semipinnate
semiplastic
semipolitical
semiporous
semiprofessional
semipublic
semiradial
semireligious
semi-Romanized
semi-Russian
semiscientific
semiserious
semisixth
semiskilled
semi-Slavic
semismile
semisoft
semisolid
semistarvation
semisuspension
semisymmetric
semitechnical
semi-Tory
semitranslucent
semitransparency
semitransparent
semitropical
semitubular
semiurban
semiviscid
semivitreous
semivitrified
semiyearly

sem′i·au′to·mat′ic (sĕm′ĭ·ô′tō·măt′ĭk), *adj.* **1.** Not wholly automatic. **2.** *Firearms.* That employs gas pressure or force of recoil and mechanical spring action in ejecting the empty cartridge case after the first shot and loading the next cartridge from the magazine, but that requires release and another pressure of the trigger for firing each successive shot. See AUTOMATIC, *adj.*, 3.

sem′i·breve′ (sĕm′ĭ·brēv′), *n.* *Music.* A note having half the time value of the breve. See NOTE, *n.*

sem′i·cen·ten′ni·al (-sĕn·tĕn′ĭ·ăl; 58), *adj.* Of or pertaining to, or occurring at the completion of, half of a century. — *n.* A fiftieth anniversary or its celebration.

sem′i·cir′cle (sĕm′ĭ·sûr′k'l), *n.* **1.** The half of a circle. **2.** A body or arrangement of objects in the form of half of a circle. — **sem′i·cir′cu·lar** (-sûr′kū·lẽr), *adj.*

sem′i·cir′cu·lar ca·nal′. Any of the loop-shaped tubular parts of the labyrinth of the ear of vertebrates. See EAR, *Illust.*

sem′i·co′lon (sĕm′ĭ·kō′lŏn), *n.* *Punctuation.* A point [;] used in printing and writing chiefly in a co-ordinating function between major sentence elements, separating them with more distinctness than comma or dash. Cf. COLON.

sem′i·di·ur′nal (-dī·ûr′năl; -n'l), *adj.* **1.** Pert. to, or accomplished in, half a day; also, occurring twice a day. **2. a** Pert. to the arc (or traversed in the time) between the meridian and a celestial body's rising or setting. **b** Occurring approximately every half day; as, the *semidiurnal* tides.

sem′i·dome′ (sĕm′ĭ·dōm′), *n.* *Arch.* A roof or ceiling covering a semicircular, or nearly semicircular, room or recess.

sem′i·fi′nal (-fī′năl; -n'l), *adj.* *Sports.* Half final; — used in tournaments and similar contests of the round, or matches, or heats in it, before the final or last round. — *n.* A semifinal match or heat; also, *pl.*, a semifinal round.

sem′i·fi′nal·ist (-fī′năl·ĭst), *n.* *Sports.* Any of the contestants that meet in the semifinal round or heat.

sem′i·flu′id (sĕm′ĭ·flōō′ĭd; 114), *adj.* Imperfectly fluid; very viscous but not solid. — *n.* A semifluid substance.

sem′i·lu′nar (-lū′nẽr), *adj.* Shaped like a half-moon.

semilunar valve. *Anat.* Any of the crescent-shaped flaps (three between the heart and the aorta, and three between the heart and the pulmonary artery) which are forced apart by pressure in the ventricles during systole and pushed together by pressure in the arteries during diastole, thus preventing regurgitation of blood into the ventricles. Cf. HEART, *Illust.*

sem′i·month′ly (sĕm′ĭ·mŭnth′lĭ), *adj.* Coming or made twice in a month. — *n.* Something done or made every half month, esp. such a periodical. — **sem′i·month′ly,** *adv.*

sem′i·nal (sĕm′ĭ·năl; -n'l), *adj.* [OF., fr. L. *seminalis,* fr. *semen, seminis,* seed.] **1.** Pertaining to, containing, or consisting of seed or semen. **2.** Holding the relation of source, or first principle; germinal; originative; as, *seminal* virtue. — **sem′i·nal·ly,** *adv.*

sem′i·nar′ (sĕm′ĭ·när′), *n.* [G. (fr. L.). See SEMINARY.] A group of (usually graduate) students engaged, under a professor, in original research; also, the course of study, or the room of meeting.

sem′i·nar′y (sĕm′ĭ·nĕr′ĭ *or, esp. Brit.,* -nẽr·ĭ), *n.; pl.* -IES (-ĭz). [L. *seminarium,* fr. *seminarius* pert. to seed.] **1.** An academy; now, often, a private secondary school. **2.** An institution for the training of candidates for the priesthood or ministry; hence **sem′i·nar′i·an** (-nâr′ĭ·ăn), one of the students in a seminary. **3.** The place, condition, or original stock whence anything is brought or produced.

sem′i·nif′er·ous (sĕm′ĭ·nĭf′ẽr·ŭs), *adj.* [L. *semen, seminis,* seed + *-ferous.*] **a** *Bot.* Producing seed; seed-bearing. **b** *Zool. & Anat.* Producing semen.

sem′i·niv′o·rous (-nĭv′ō·rŭs), *adj.* [See SEMEN; -VOROUS.] Feeding on seeds.

Sem′i·nole (sĕm′ĭ·nōl), *n. sing. & pl.; pl.* also SEMINOLES (-nōlz). One of a tribe of Muskhogean Indians, orig. settled in Florida, removed in 1843 for the most part to the Indian Territory. — **Sem′i·nole,** *adj.*

sem′i·of·fi′cial (sĕm′ĭ·ŏ·fĭsh′ăl), *adj.* Half official; having some official authority. — **sem′i·of·fi′cial·ly,** *adv.*

se′mi·ol′o·gy (sē′mĭ·ŏl′ō·jĭ), **se′mi·ot′ic,** etc. Vars. of SEMEIOLOGY, etc.

sem′i·o·vip′a·rous (sĕm′ĭ·ō·vĭp′ȧ·rŭs), *adj.* Bearing imperfectly developed young, as a marsupial.

sem′i·pal′mate (-păl′măt), *adj.* Also **sem′i·pal′mat·ed** (-māt·ĕd; -ĭd). *Zool.* Having the anterior toes joined only part way down with a web.

sem′i·par′a·sit′ic (-păr′ȧ·sĭt′ĭk), *adj.* **1.** *Biol.* Usually parasitic but capable of leading a saprophytic life. **2.** *Bot.* Containing chlorophyll and therefore capable of performing photosynthesis, as mistletoe.

sem′i·per′me·a·ble (-pûr′mē·ȧ·b'l), *adj.* Permeable to certain (smaller) fluid particles, as of water, but not to other (larger) particles, as of a dissolved substance; — said of membranes. See OSMOSIS.

sem′i·por′ce·lain (-pōr′sĕ·lĭn; -pōrs′lĭn; 70), *n.* A porcelain like earthenware in its lack of translucency or inferior finish.

sem′i·post′al (-pōs′tăl; -t'l), *adj. & n.* (A postage stamp) sold at a premium over its postal value, as for various humanitarian purposes.

sem′i·pre′cious (-prĕsh′ŭs), *adj.* Of less value than those called precious, as amethyst, garnet, etc.

sem′i·qua′ver (sĕm′ĭ·kwā′vẽr), *n.* *Music.* See NOTE, *n.*

Se·mir′a·mis (sē·mĭr′ȧ·mĭs), *n.* A legendary Assyrian queen, noted for beauty, wisdom, and voluptuousness.

sem′i·rig′id (sĕm′ĭ·rĭj′ĭd), *adj.* Of an airship, having a flexible gas container with an attached stiffening keel that carries the load. See AIRSHIP.

sem′i·round′ (sĕm′ĭ·round′; 2), *adj.* Round on one side and flat on the other. — *n.* A semiround object.

Sem′ite (sĕm′īt; sē′mīt), *n.* **1.** A descendant of Shem. **2.** A member of a Caucasian race now chiefly represented by the Jews and Arabs, but in ancient times including the Babylonians, Assyrians, Aramaeans, Phoenicians, etc.

Se·mit′ic (sē·mĭt′ĭk), *adj.* **1.** Of or pert. to the Semites or, sometimes, the Jews. **2.** Designating or pert. to a family of inflectional languages possessing records of great antiquity, including Phoenician, Hebrew, Aramaic, Arabic, and Ethiopic. See LANGUAGE, *Table.*

Se·mit′ics (-ĭks), *n.;* see -ICS. The language, literature, and history of Semitic peoples studied scientifically.

Sem′i·tism (sĕm′ĭ·tĭz'm; sē′mĭ-), *n.* **1.** Semitic character or qualities; also, a Semitic idiom or expression. **2.** Policy, esp. political policy, favorable to Jews; a predisposition in favor of Jews.

Sem′i·tist (-tĭst), *n.* **1.** A specialist in Semitics; a Semitic scholar. **2.** A person favoring, or disposed to favor, the Jews.

sem′i·tone′ (sĕm′ĭ·tōn′), *n.* *Music.* Literally, half a tone; the tone at a half step; less properly, the half step itself. — **sem′i·ton′ic** (-tŏn′ĭk), *adj.*

sem′i·trail′er (-trāl′ẽr), *n.* A nonautomotive trucking vehicle the forward part of which is supported by the truck tractor that hauls the vehicle.

sem′i·vow′el (sĕm′ĭ·vou′ĕl), *n.* *Phonet.* A sound partaking of the nature of a vowel and a consonant (English *w* or *y;* also, according to some, *l, m, n, ng, r, s, sh, x*).

sem′i·week′ly (-wēk′lĭ), *adj.* Coming, made, or done once every half week. — *n.* That which comes or happens once every half week, esp. a periodical published every half week. — **sem′i·week′ly,** *adv.*

sem′o·li′na (sĕm′ō·lē′nȧ), *n.* [It. *semolino,* dim. of *semola* bran, fr. L. *simila* the finest wheat flour.] The purified middlings of durum or other hard wheat, used for macaroni and similar edible pastes.

‖**sem′per e′a·dem** (sĕm′pẽr ē′ȧ·dĕm). [L.] Always the same; — motto of Queen Elizabeth I of England.

‖**sem′per fi·de′lis** (fĭ·dē′lĭs). [L.] Always faithful; — motto of the U. S. Marine Corps.

‖**sem′per i′dem** (ī′dĕm). [L.] Always the same.

‖**sem′per pa·ra′tus** (pȧ·rā′tŭs). [L.] Always ready; — motto of the U. S. Coast Guard.

sem′pi·ter′nal (sĕm′pĭ·tûr′năl; -n'l), *adj.* [ML. *sempiternalis,* fr. L. *sempiternus,* fr. *semper* always.] Everlasting; eternal. — **sem′pi·ter′ni·ty** (-nĭ·tĭ), *n.*

‖**sem′pli·ce** (sĕm′plē·chā), *adj.* [It.] *Music.* Simple; plain; unaffected; — used as a direction.

‖**sem′pre** (sĕm′prā), *adv.* [It., fr. L. *semper.*] *Music.* Always; throughout; as, *sempre* piano.

semp′stress (sĕmp′strĕs; sĕm′-; -strĭs). Var. of SEAMSTRESS.

sen (sĕn), *n. sing. & pl.* [Jap., fr. Chin. *ch'ien*².] A Japanese copper coin, 1/100 of a yen.

sen′a·ry (sĕn′ȧ·rĭ), *adj.* [L. *senarius,* fr. *seni* six each.] Of or pert. to six; sextuple; *Math.*, using six as a radix, or base.

sen′ate (sĕn′ĭt; -ȧt), *n.* [OF. *senat,* fr. L. *senatus,* fr. *senex,* gen. *senis,* old, an old man.] **1.** Literally, an assembly of old men; hence, an assembly with the highest deliberative and legislative functions; specif.: **a** *Ancient Rome.* The supreme council of the state, originally only advisory and wholly patrician, but early including plebeians. **b** The upper and less numerous branch of various legislatures, as of France, the United States, etc. **c** In general, a legislative body; a state council. **2.** The governing body of certain universities.

sen′a·tor (sĕn′ȧ·tẽr), *n.* [OF. *senatour,* fr. L. *senator.*] A member of a senate. — **sen′a·tor·ship′,** *n.*

sen′a·to′ri·al (-tō′rĭ·ăl; 70), *adj.* **1.** Of, pertaining to, or befitting a senator or a senate. **2.** *U.S.* Entitled to elect a (state) senator; as, *senatorial* districts.

‖**se·na′tus con·sul′tum** (sē·nā′tŭs kŏn·sŭl′tŭm); *pl.* SENATUS CONSULTA (-tȧ). [L.] Also **se·na′tus·con·sult′** (-kŏn·sŭlt′; -kŏn′sŭlt), *n.* A decree of the ancient Roman senate.

send (sĕnd), *v. t.;* SENT (sĕnt); SEND′ING. [AS. *sendan.*] **1.** To transmit or cause to be transmitted; specif.: **a** To cause to be conveyed by an agent to a destination; to dispatch, as by post or telegraph; also, to commission to go; to direct by reference, as to an encyclopedia. **b** To cause to come, happen, be, etc.; to bestow; as, a child *sent* to bless a marriage bed. **c** To dispatch for a course or term, as a son to college. **2.** To cause to issue; specif., to discharge, as smoke; to cause to issue in sound, or to resound, as music or a cry; to emit, as light or heat. **3.** To force to go; specif.: **a** To propel or discharge with an aim, as a bullet. **b** To force to depart; drive; as, to *send* the rebels flying. **c** To use force or influence so as to impel; as, to *send* up a rocket. **d** To transmit by pulsation, as a current; *Radio,* to transmit. — *v. i.* **1.** To dispatch an agent to convey a message or to do an errand; to dispatch a missive. **2.** *Naut.* **a** To be carried forward by the impulse of a wave; as, the ship *sends* violently. **b** = SCEND, *v. i.* **3.** *Swing Music Cant.* To play or sing with, or to inspire to, the spontaneous improvisations of swing music. — ***send for.*** To request by message to come or be brought. — *n.* **1.** *Naut.* **a** The impulse of a wave by which a vessel is carried bodily. **b** = SCEND, *n.* **2.** *Swing Music Cant.* An instance of swinging a piece of music; as, a *send* of jive.

sen′dal (sĕn′dăl; -d'l), *n.* [OF. *cendal*, ult. fr. Gr. *sindōn* a fine Indian cloth.] A thin silk fabric used in the Middle Ages, possibly of Chinese origin.

send′er (sĕn′dẽr), *n.* One who sends; transmitter.

send′-off′, *n.* *Colloq.* A demonstration of good will to one starting on a journey, in a new business, etc.

Sen′e·ca (sĕn′ē·kȧ), *n.* One of a tribe of Iroquoian Indians of western New York, the most warlike of the Five Nations.

sen′e·ga (sĕn′ē·gȧ), *n.* The dried root of a North American milkwort, the **senega root** *or* **senega snakeroot** (*Polygala senega*) containing an irritating saponin and used as an expectorant; also, the plant.

se·nes′cent (sē·nĕs′ĕnt; -'nt), *adj.* [L. *senescens*, pres. part. of *senescere* to grow old.] Growing old; aging. — **se·nes′cence** (-ĕns; -'ns), *n.*

sen′es·chal (sĕn′ĕ·shăl; sĕn′ĭ-), *n.* [OF., fr. ML. *seniscalcus*, fr. OHG. *siniscalh*, prop., senior servant.] The bailiff, steward, or major-domo representing his medieval lord in the feudal courts and in the management of his estate.

se′nile (sē′nīl; -nĭl), *adj.* [L. *senilis*, fr. *senex*, gen. *senis*, old, an old man.] **1.** Of, pertaining to, exhibiting, or characteristic of old age. **2.** *Phys. Geol.* Approaching the end of a cycle of erosion.

se·nil′i·ty (sē·nĭl′ĭ·tĭ), *n.* Quality or state of being senile; old age or its physical and mental infirmity.

sen′ior (sēn′yẽr), *adj.* [L., compar. of *senex*, *senis*, old.] **1.** Elder; — indicating (abbr. *Sr.*; in England *Sen.*) the older of two in the family, school, etc., bearing the name. **2.** More advanced in dignity, rank, or office; as, *senior* member. **3.** Belonging to the final year of the course in American colleges, universities, high schools, etc.; as, *senior* class. — *n.* **1.** A person older than another. **2.** One older in office, or whose entrance upon office was anterior to that of another. **3.** An undergraduate in his final year at an American college, etc. **4.** *Eng. Universities.* A senior fellow.

sen·ior′i·ty (sēn·yŏr′ĭ·tĭ), *n.*; *pl.* -TIES (-tĭz). **1.** Quality or state of being senior; priority of birth, office, or service. **2.** The status secured by length of service for a company, to which certain rights, as promotion, attach. **3.** *Eng. Universities.* The body of senior fellows of a college.

sen′na (sĕn′ȧ), *n.* [ML. *senna*, *sena*, fr. Ar. *sana*.] **1.** Any of a genus (*Cassia*) of herbs, shrubs, and trees, natives of warm regions, esp. of certain species whose leaves yield a drug (see def. 2; see also CASSIA). They belong to a family (Caesalpiniaceae, the senna family) typified by a large genus (*Caesalpinia*) of tropical trees, including the brazilwood and divi-divi, with showy flowers, fruit borne in pods, bipinnate leaves, and, often, spiny branches. The ***American, or wild, senna*** is *Cassia marilandica*. **2.** *Pharm.* The dried leaflets of certain species of cassia (esp. *Cassia acutifolia*, *C. angustifolia*), used as a purgative.

sen′net (sĕn′ĕt; -ĭt), *n.* *Obs. exc. Hist.* A signal call on a trumpet or cornet for entrance or exit on the stage.

sen′night (sĕn′īt; -ĭt), *n.* Also **se′n′night.** [For *seven-night.*] *Archaic.* A week.

sen′nit (sĕn′ĭt), *n.* [Prob. fr. *seven* + *knit*.] *Naut.* A braided cord or fabric of plaited rope yarns or other small stuff.

‖**se·ñor′** (sā·nyôr′), *n.*; *pl.* -ÑORES (-nyō′rās) (abbr. *Sr.*); ‖**se·ño′ra** (sā·nyō′rä), *n.* (abbr. *Sra.*); ‖**se′ño·ri′ta** (sā′nyō·rē′tä), *n.* (abbr. *Srta.*). [Sp.] Spanish titles of courtesy corresponding respectively to the English *Mr.* or *Sir*, *Mrs.* or *Madam*, and *Miss*; also, a gentleman, lady, or young lady.

sen·sa′tion (sĕn·sā′shŭn), *n.* [ML. *sensatio*, fr. LL. *sensatus* gifted with sense, fr. *sensus* sense.] **1. a** That mode of mental functioning referred to immediate stimulation of the bodily organism, including seeing, hearing, smelling, etc.; specif., the direct result of the present stimulation of the sense organs, as disting. from *perception*, which involves the combination of different sensations and the utilization of past experience in recognizing the objects and facts from which the present stimulation arises. **b** The power of responding to stimulation. **c** A sense datum. **2.** A somewhat indefinite bodily feeling; as, a *sensation* of buoyancy. **3.** A state of excited interest or feeling, or its cause; as, the murder caused a *sensation*.

sen·sa′tion·al (-ăl; -'l), *adj.* **1.** Of or pertaining to sensation or the senses, or sensationalism. **2.** Suited or intended to excite temporarily great interest or emotion; melodramatic; emotional. — **sen·sa′tion·al·ly**, *adv.*

sen·sa′tion·al·ism (-ĭz'm), *n.* **1.** The use or effect of subject matter and literary treatment calculated to arouse excited interest and emotional response. **2.** *Ethics.* The doctrine that feeling is the sole criterion of good; sensualism. **3.** *Philos.* The doctrine that all our knowledge originates in sensation or sense perceptions, or, in a narrower meaning, that all knowledge is made up of sense elements. **4.** *Psychol.* = SENSATIONISM. — **sen·sa′tion·al·ist** (-ĭst), *n.* — **sen·sa′tion·al·is′tic** (-ĭs′tĭk), *adj.*

sen·sa′tion·ism (sĕn·sā′shŭn·ĭz'm), *n.* *Psychol.* A system of psychology based upon sensations as the constituent elements of all conscious experience. — **sen·sa′tion·ist** (-ĭst), *n.*

sense (sĕns; 106), *n.* [F. or L.; F. *sens*, fr. L. *sensus*, fr. *sentire*, *sensum*, to perceive, feel.] **1.** Sensuous perception, now esp. when aesthetic or emotional; also, chiefly *pl.*, one of its avenues of perception. **2.** Sentience; intelligence. **3.** Sense perception; sensation; sensibility. **4.** Sound perception and reasoning; correct judgment; also, that which is sound, or reasonable; as, no *sense* in waiting. **5.** A sensation, as of thirst. **6.** A perception, realization, or discernment, as of the value of money. **7.** Hence, moral perception or appreciation, as of friendly offices; a perceptive notion, as of coming danger; a self-conscious motivating awareness, as of shame. **8.** Formerly, the faculty of receiving mental impressions through certain bodily organs or of perceiving bodily changes; also, any special faculty of sensation; as, the ***five senses*** of sight, hearing, smell, taste, and touch. **9.** (1) A specialized mechanism or function by which an animal is receptive and responsive to a certain class of stimuli, typically external, as in the senses of sight, hearing, touch, pain, etc., but also internal, as in the case of the kinesthetic and organic senses. (2) The total function comprising the several senses, in distinction from the functions of movement, thought, etc. **10.** Power of perception; also, an ability to perceive; as, a *sense* of direction. **11.** Faculty of intellectual and aesthetic understanding and appreciation; as, a *sense* of beauty or humor. **12.** An instinctive comprehension of the fine points, and acuteness in mastering a game or the like; as, a musical *sense*. **13.** One of the differing meanings which a word may bear, often as segregated in a dictionary entry; also, meaning; signification. **14.** That which is felt or is held as a sentiment, view, or opinion; judgment; as, the *sense* of the meeting. **15.** [F. *sens*.] Direction; trend; course.

Syn. (1) **Sense, common sense, gumption, judgment** (*or* **judgement**), **wisdom** mean ability to reach intelligent conclusions. **Sense** or, more often, **common sense** implies a capacity for making practical, or prudent and reasonable, decisions; **gumption**, a colloquial term, a capacity for estimating the better possibility, such as success or failure; **judgment**, an ability to comprehend the significance of facts or conditions; **wisdom**, a common sense and judgment far above the average.

(2) See MEANING.

— *v. t.* **1.** To become aware of, as danger or dislike. **2.** *Chiefly Colloq., U.S.* To grasp; comprehend; understand.

sense datum. Any component of experience directly due to the stimulation of a sense organ.

sense′less, *adj.* Destitute of, deficient in, or contrary to sense; specif.: **a** Insensible; unconscious. **b** Deficient in knowledge, appreciation, or reasoning power; stupid. **c** Lacking good sense; nonsensical. **d** Purposeless; meaningless; as, a *senseless* custom. — **sense′less·ly**, *adv.* — **sense′less·ness**, *n.*

sense organ. *Physiol.* An organ specialized to receive certain stimuli, which it transforms into sensations; a receptor.

sense perception. Perception by the senses, as distinguished from intellectual perception.

sense stress. *Phonet.* = SENTENCE STRESS.

sen′si·bil′i·ty (sĕn′sĭ·bĭl′ĭ·tĭ), *n.*; *pl.* -TIES (-tĭz). **1.** Ability to perceive or to receive sensation; as, tactile *sensibility*. **2.** Peculiar susceptibility to impression, pleasurable or painful; acuteness of feeling; — often *pl.* **3.** Mental receptivity; ready discernment, as of truth. **4.** Delicacy or sensitiveness of an instrument. **5.** *Lit. & Art.* Refined sensitiveness in emotion and taste with especial responsiveness to the pathetic.

sen′si·ble (sĕn′sĭ·b'l), *adj.* [OF., fr. L. *sensibilis*.] **1.** Capable of being perceived by the senses; hence, also, perceptible to the mind. **2.** Perceptibly large; appreciable. **3.** Capable of receiving impressions from external objects; as, *sensible* to sound. **4.** Cognizant; aware; also, perceiving so clearly as to be convinced; as, *sensible* of having made a mistake. **5.** *Archaic.* Having or exhibiting nice perception or acute feeling; sensitive; as, *sensible* in grief. **6.** Characterized by good or common sense; intelligent; reasonable. — **Syn.** See MATERIAL: PERCEPTIBLE: AWARE: WISE. — **sen′si·ble·ness**, *n.* — **sen′si·bly**, *adv.*

sen′si·tive (sĕn′sĭ·tĭv), *adj.* [F. *sensitif*, fr. ML. *sensitivus*. See SENSE.] **1.** That conveys or receives sense impressions; as, *sensitive* nerves. **2.** Of or pertaining to the senses or sensation; sensory; as, *sensitive* muscular motions excited by irritation. **3.** Having the capacity of receiving impressions from external objects; as, *sensitive* creatures. **4.** Having quick and acute sensibility, either to action of objects or to impressions; highly susceptible. **5.** Susceptible; — with *of* or *to*; specif., fluctuating or liable to fluctuation; as, a *sensitive* market. **6.** *Biol.* Capable of being stimulated or excited by certain external agents, as light, gravity, contact, etc. **7.** *Bot.* Responding by movement to stimuli, as the sensitive plant. **8.** *Chem. & Photog.* Readily affected or changed by certain agents. **9.** *Mech.* Capable of indicating minute differences; delicate; as, *sensitive* scales. **10.** *Med.* Abnormally susceptible; sensitized. **11.** *Radio.* High in sensitivity. — **Syn.** See LIABLE. — **sen′si·tive·ly**, *adv.* — **sen′si·tive·ness**, *n.*

sensitive plant. A tropical American herb (*Mimosa pudica*; see MIMOSA), also cultivated in greenhouses, whose leaflets close tight and whose leafstalk droops when touched.

sen′si·tiv′i·ty (sĕn′sĭ·tĭv′ĭ·tĭ), *n.*; *pl.* -TIES (-tĭz). **1.** Quality or state of being sensitive. **2.** *Psychol.* The capacity of an organism or of a sense organ to respond to stimulation; irritability; also, the degree of such responsiveness. **3.** *Radio.* The degree to which a receiving set responds to incoming waves.

sen′si·tize (sĕn′sĭ·tīz), *v. t.* **1.** *Chem. & Photog.* To render sensitive. **2.** *Immunol.* To render sensitive to, or unusually susceptible to the action of, a serum by repeated injection. — **sen′si·ti·za′tion** (-tĭ·zā′shŭn; -tī·zā′-), *n.* — **sen′si·tiz′er** (-tīz′ẽr), *n.*

sen′si·tom′e·ter (-tŏm′ē·tẽr), *n.* *Optics.* An instrument for measuring sensitivity, as of the eye.

sen·so′ri·al (sĕn·sō′rĭ·ăl; 70), *adj.* Pertaining to the sensorium or to sensation; sensory.

sen·so′ri·um (-ŭm), *n.*; *pl.* -RIUMS (-ŭmz), -RIA (-ȧ). [LL., fr. *sentire*, *sensum*, to feel.] *Physiol. & Psychol.* **a** The brain regarded as the center for all the senses and for sensation. **b** The entire sensory apparatus.

sen′so·ry (sĕn′sō·rĭ), *adj.* **a** Pertaining to sensation or to the senses. **b** Conveying nerve impulses from the sense organs to the nerve centers; as, the *sensory* nerves.

sen′su·al (sĕn′shōō·ăl; *by some* sĕns′ū·ăl; 118), *adj.* [F. or L.; F. *sensuel*, fr. L. *sensualis*, fr. *sensus* sense.] **1.** *Now Rare.* Sensory; also, sensuous. **2.** Pert. to, or consisting in, the gratification of the senses, or the indulgence of appetite; fleshly. **3.** Devoted to the pleasures of sense and appetite; voluptuous; sometimes, lewd. **4.** Indicating sensuality, or voluptuousness; as, a *sensual* mouth. **5.** Pert. to the doctrine of sensationalism. — **Syn.** See CARNAL: SENSUOUS. — **Ant.** Ascetic, spiritual. — **sen′su·al·ly**, *adv.*

sen′su·al·ism (-ĭz'm), *n.* **1.** Subjection to sensual appetite; pursuit of sensual pleasures. **2.** *Aesthetics.* Stress on the sensuous qualities of an object or on the sensuous as the chief element of beauty. **3.** *Ethics.* The view that gratification of the senses is the highest good. **4.** *Philos.* Sensationalism.

sen′su·al·ist (-ĭst), *n.* **1.** One who is sensual. **2.** One who holds to a doctrine of sensualism. — **sen′su·al·is′tic** (-ĭs′tĭk), *adj.*

sen′su·al′i·ty (-ăl′ĭ·tĭ), *n.*; *pl.* -TIES (-tĭz). Quality or state of being sensual; voluptuousness.

sen′su·al·ize (sĕn′shōō·ăl·īz; sĕns′ū-), *v. t.* To make sensual; debase by carnal gratifications. — **sen′su·al·i·za′tion** (-ĭ·zā′shŭn; -ī·zā′-), *n.*

sen′su·ous (sĕn′shōō·ŭs; sĕns′ū-; 118), *adj.* **1.** Of or pertaining to the senses or sensible objects; addressing the senses. **2.** Characterized by sense impressions or imagery addressing the senses; as, *sensuous* description. **3.** Highly susceptible to influence through the senses. — **sen′su·ous·ly**, *adv.* — **sen′su·ous·ness**, *n.*

Syn. **Sensuous, sensual, luxurious, voluptuous, epicurean** mean giving pleasure by gratifying the senses. **Sensuous** implies delight in beauty of color, sound, form, etc.; **sensual**, gratification of appetites impelled by gluttony or lust; **luxurious**, inducing a pleasant languor, delightful ease, etc.; **voluptuous**, abandonment to sensuous or, esp., sensual enjoyments; **epicurean**, sensuous or, less often, sensual delight in eating, drinking, and the like.

sent (sĕnt), *past & past part.* of SEND.
sent, *n.* A minor coin of Estonia, 1/100 of a kroon.
sen′tence (sĕn′tĕns), *n.* [OF., fr. L. *sententia*, for *sentientia*, fr. *sentire* to feel, think.] **1.** A stated opinion, esp. one given after deliberation; a decision; determination. **2.** *Archaic.* A maxim; axiom. **3.** *Gram.* A unit of speech consisting of a meaningful arrangement of words, or merely a word, that expresses an assertion, a question, a command, a wish, or an exclamation, and typically containing a subject and a predicate (*He played ball;* It. *parto*, I depart) or only a predicate (*Go home*). Such sentences are sometimes called ***full sentences***, as distinguished from ***minor sentences***, which generally consist of a completive word or phrase (Where is John? —*At home*), an interjection (*Ouch!*), or an exclamation (*Heavens above!*). Classified according to meaning, sentences expressive of assertion are *declarative*, of questioning *interrogative*, of command or request *imperative*, of emotion *exclamatory*. In speech, declarative, imperative, and exclamatory sentences regularly close with a falling intonation, interrogative sentences with a rising intonation when *yes* or *no* is expected in the answer, otherwise with a falling intonation. In writing, declarative and imperative sentences are usually closed with periods, interrogative sentences with question marks, and exclamatory sentences with exclamation marks. *Simple* sentences consist of one independent clause, *compound* sentences of more than one independent clause, *complex* sentences of one independent clause and one or more dependent clauses, *compound-complex* sentences of two or more independent clauses and one or more dependent clauses. **4.** *Law.* A judicial determination; a decree; in criminal courts, commonly, the order by which the court imposes penalty upon a person found guilty, or the punishment or penalty so imposed. **5.** *Music.* A complete musical idea; a period. — *v. t.;* -TENCED (-tĕnst); -TENC·ING (-tĕn·sĭng). To pronounce sentence on; to prescribe the punishment of. — **sen′tenc·er** (-tĕn·sẽr), *n.*
sentence stress. Also **sentence accent.** *Phonet.* The normal variation in the degrees of prominence given to the successive words of a sense group, which is essential to the meaning of the group.
sen·ten′tious (sĕn·tĕn′shŭs), *adj.* [L. *sententiosus.*] **a** Terse and energetic in expression; pithy. **b** Abounding in axioms or maxims. **c** Marked by pompous formality. **d** Given to making aphorisms. — **sen·ten′tious·ly**, *adv.* — **sen·ten′tious·ness**, *n.*
sen′ti·ence (sĕn′shĭ·ĕns; -shĕns; 58), *n.* Also **sen′ti·en·cy** (-shĭ·ĕn·sĭ; -shĕn·sĭ). **1.** Sentient being or state; consciousness. **2.** Inchoate consciousness; sensation, as disting. from perception and thought.
sen′tient (sĕn′shĕnt; -shĭ·ĕnt), *adj.* [L. *sentiens, -entis*, pres. part.] **1.** Capable of sensation and consciousness. **2.** Experiencing sensation and feeling. — *n.* A sentient being; also, the mind. — **sen′tient·ly**, *adv.*
sen′ti·ment (sĕn′tĭ·mĕnt), *n.* [OF. *sentement* (F. *sentiment*), fr. ML. *sentimentum*, fr. L. *sentire* to feel, think.] **1.** Feeling; sensibility; also, tender susceptibility; as, less *sentiment* and more sense. **2.** A mental attitude, thought, or judgment permeated or prompted by feeling; as, religious *sentiment;* in general, an emotional disposition, sometimes excessively emotional, with reference to some object or class of objects. **3. a** A complex organization of ideas and instincts, built up in the course of the individual's experience. **b** A particular view, opinion, or judgment, esp. one colored by feeling. **4. a** The significance of an expression as distinguished from the verbal form. **b** A maxim, saying, or toast as colored by feeling. **5.** Refined feeling; delicate sensibility; as, an artistic style characterized by *sentiment.* — **Syn.** See FEELING; OPINION.
sen′ti·men′tal (-mĕn′tăl; -t'l), *adj.* **1.** Of the nature of, or characterized or dominated by, sentiment; as, *sentimental* motives. **2.** Having an excess of sentiment or sensibility; affectedly tender; mawkishly emotional. **3.** Characterized by the expression of sentiment or sentiments; as, *sentimental* music. — **sen′ti·men′tal·ly**, *adv.*
sen′ti·men′tal·ism (-ĭz'm), *n.* Quality or state of being sentimental; disposition to favor or indulge in sentiment.
sen′ti·men′tal·ist (-ĭst), *n.* One disposed to indulge in sensibility or sentimentalities.
sen′ti·men·tal′i·ty (sĕn′tĭ·mĕn·tăl′ĭ·tĭ), *n.; pl.* -TIES (-tĭz). Quality or state of being sentimental, esp. to excess.
sen′ti·men′tal·ize (-mĕn′tăl·īz; -t'l·īz), *v. t.* To imbue with sentiment. — *v. i.* To think or act sentimentally.
sen′ti·nel (sĕn′tĭ·nĕl; -n'l), *n.* [F. *sentinelle*, fr. It. *sentinella.*] One who watches or guards; *Mil.*, a soldier set to guard an army, camp, etc., from surprise; a sentry. — *v. t.;* -NELED (-nĕld; -n'ld) or -NELLED; -NEL·ING or -NEL·LING. **1.** To watch over as a sentinel. **2.** To furnish with a sentinel. **3.** To post as sentinel.
sen′try (sĕn′trĭ), *n.; pl.* -TRIES (-trĭz). **1.** One, esp. a soldier, placed on guard. **2.** Guard; watch.
sentry box. A hut or box to shelter a sentinel at his post.
Se·nu′si (sĕ·nōō′sē), *n.* Also **Se·nus′si.** One of a North African Moslem sect, famous for its fanaticism and belligerent attitude. — **Se·nu′si·an** (-sĭ·ăn), *adj.*
se′pal (sē′păl; sĕp′ăl), *n.* [F. *sépale*, NL. *sepalum*, proposed by Necker.] *Bot.* A leaf or division of the calyx. See CALYX: CARPEL, *Illust.* — **se′paled, se′palled** (sē′păld; sĕp′ăld), *adj.*
-sep′al·ous (-sĕp′ăl·ŭs). [*sepal* + *-ous.*] A combining form denoting *having* (so many or such) *sepals.*
sep′a·ra·ble (sĕp′ȧ·rȧ·b'l), *adj.* Capable of being separated or distinguished. — **sep′a·ra·bil′i·ty** (-bĭl′ĭ·tĭ), **sep′a·ra·ble·ness**, *n.* — **sep′a·ra·bly**, *adv.*
sep′a·rate (-rāt), *v. t.* [L. *separatus*, past part. of *separare* to separate, fr. *se-* aside + *parare* to prepare.] **1.** To disunite, disconnect, or sever, as friends. **2.** To part by a legal separation, as man and wife. **3.** To form or keep apart by something intervening; to keep apart by occupying the space between; to intervene. **4.** To set apart from others for a special use. **5.** To isolate from a combination or mixture, as gold from an alloy. — *v. i.* **1.** To withdraw, as in quitting association; also, to part company; as, the family *separated.* **2.** To come apart; become detached. **3.** To cease to live as man and wife. **4.** To become disengaged as a separate body; as, crystals may *separate* from a solution.
Syn. **Separate, part, divide, sever, sunder, divorce** mean to cause to break into parts or to keep apart. **Separate** may imply any of several causes, such as dispersion, removal of one from the others, or the presence of an intervening thing; **part,** the separation of persons or things that have been in close union or association; **divide,** commonly, a separation into pieces or sections by cutting, breaking, or the like; **sever,** violence, esp. in the removal of a part or member; **sunder,** a violent rending or wrenching apart; **divorce,** a separation usually of two persons or things, so that each goes its own way.
— (-rĭt), *adj.* **1. a** Unconnected; not united or associated; distinct. **b** Divided from another or others; disjoined; disconnected. **2.** Being apart from others; withdrawn from social intercourse; solitary; secluded; as, *separate* confinement. **3.** Disunited from the body; disembodied. **4.** Pertaining to one only; not shared; as, *separate* rooms. **5.** Particular; as, every *separate* item. — **Syn.** See SINGLE. — **sep′a·rate·ly**, *adv.* — **sep′a·rate·ness**, *n.*
sep′a·ra′tion (sĕp′ȧ·rā′shŭn), *n.* **1.** Act of separating, or state of being separated or separate. **2.** Point or line of division. **3.** *Law.* **a** Divorce. **b** A cessation of cohabitation between husband and wife by agreement.
separation center. A demobilizing station or camp of one of the armed services for separation or discharge of personnel from military service.
sep′a·ra′tist (sĕp′ȧ·rā′tĭst; -rĭt·ĭst), *n.* **1.** An advocate of separation. **2.** One who withdraws from a church; a seceder; dissenter; nonconformist; schismatic; sectary. **3.** [*usually cap.*] A secessionist. — **sep′a·ra·tism** (-rĭt·ĭz'm), *n.*
sep′a·ra′tive (-rā′tĭv; -rĭ·tĭv), *adv.* Tending to cause separation.
sep′a·ra′tor (-rā′tẽr), *n.* [LL.] Any of various apparatus for separating a mixture into its constituent parts; specif.: **a** A machine for separating cream from milk; a creamer. **b** An apparatus for dressing ore, removing slate from coal, etc.
Se·phar′dim (sē·fär′dĭm), *n. pl.* [Heb. *Sĕphārādhīm.*] Jews who are descendants of the former Jews of Spain and Portugal, as a rule darker than the northern Jews (Ashkenazim). — **Se·phar′dic** (-dĭk), *adj.*
se′pi·a (sē′pĭ·ȧ), *n.; pl.* SEPIAS (-ȧz), SEPIAE (-ē). [L., fr. Gr. *sēpia.*] **1.** Any of several cuttlefishes (*Sepia* or an allied genus) having an internal calcareous shell. **2.** A pigment of rich brown color prepared from the ink, or black secretion, of various cuttlefishes, and used esp. in water-color painting. **3.** The color of sepia, a brown, yellowish red-yellow in hue, of low saturation and low brilliance. See COLOR. **4.** *Photog.* A print the image of which resembles sepia. — *adj.* Of sepia or the color of sepia.
se′pi·o·lite (sē′pĭ·ō·līt), *n.* = MEERSCHAUM, 1.
se′poy (sē′poi), *n.* [Pg. *sipae, sipaio*, fr. Hind. & Per. *sipāhī*, fr. *sipāh* army.] A native of India employed as a soldier by a European power, esp. by Great Britain.
sep′pu′ku (sĕp′pōō′kōō), *n.* [Jap.] See HARA-KIRI.
sep′sis (sĕp′sĭs), *n.* [NL., fr. Gr. *sēpsis* putrefaction.] *Med.* A poisoned state caused by absorption of pathogenic bacteria from a region of infection into the blood stream.
sept (sĕpt), *n.* [Var. of SECT.] **1.** In ancient Ireland, a clan. **2.** *Anthropol.* A social group in which all are believed to have descended from a single ancestor.
sep′ta (sĕp′tȧ), *n., pl. of* SEPTUM.
sep′tal (sĕp′tăl; -t'l), *adj.* Of a septum or septa.
sep·tar′i·um (sĕp·târ′ĭ·ŭm), *n.; pl.* -IA (-ȧ). [NL., fr. L. *septum, saeptum*, enclosure, partition. See SEPTUM.] *Geol.* A concretionary nodule, usually of limestone or clay ironstone, intersected within by cracks filled with calcite, barite, etc. — **sep·tar′i·an** (-ăn), *adj.*
sep′tate (sĕp′tāt), *adj.* [NL. *septatus.* See SEPTUM.] Divided by, or having, a septum or septa.
sep·tec′to·my (sĕp·tĕk′tō·mĭ), *n.* [*septum* + *-ectomy.*] Surgical removal of part of the nasal septum.
sep′tem- (sĕp′tĕm-), **sept-.** [L. *septem.*] A combining form meaning *seven, seventh*, as in **sep′tem·par′tite**, divided into seven parts.
Sep·tem′ber (sĕp·tĕm′bẽr), *n.* [L., fr. *septem* seven, as being the seventh month of the old Roman year.] The ninth month of the year, containing 30 days. Abbr. *Sept., Sep.*
Sep·tem′brist (-brĭst), *n.* A participant in the massacres (***September Massacres***) of Royalists in Paris, September 2–6, 1792.
sep′te·nar′y (sĕp′tē·nĕr′ĭ *or, esp. Brit.*, -nẽr·ĭ; sĕp·tē′nȧ·rĭ), *adj.* [L. *septenarius*, fr. *septeni* seven each, fr. *septem* seven.] **1.** Septuple. **2.** Hebdomadal. — *n.; pl.* -IES (-ĭz). **1.** The number seven; also, a group of seven, specif. of seven years. **2.** *Pros.* A verse of seven feet or stresses.
sep′ten·de·cil′lion (sĕp′tĕn·dē·sĭl′yŭn), *n.* See NUMERATION, *Table.*
sep·ten′ni·al (sĕp·tĕn′ĭ·ăl; 58), *adj.* [L. *septennium* a period of seven years, fr. *septennis* of seven years.] Lasting seven years; also, happening or returning once in every seven years. — **sep·ten′ni·al·ly**, *adv.*
sep·ten′tri·o·nal (sĕp·tĕn′trĭ·ō·năl; -n'l), *adj.* [OF., fr. L. *septentrio* the northern regions.] Of or pertaining to the north; boreal.
sep·tet′, sep·tette′ (sĕp·tĕt′), *n.* [From L. *septem* seven, after *duet.*] **a** A set of seven persons or objects. **b** *Music.* A composition for seven instruments or voices.
sep′tic (sĕp′tĭk), *adj.* [L. *septicus*, fr. Gr. *sēptikos*, fr. *sēpein* to make putrid.] **a** Putrefactive. **b** Produced by putrefaction or morbid germs; as, *septic* poisoning. — *n.* A substance that promotes putrefaction.
sep′ti·ce′mi·a, sep′ti·cae′mi·a (sĕp′tĭ·sē′mĭ·ȧ), *n.* [NL., fr. Gr. *sēptikos* putrefactive + *-emia.*] See BLOOD POISONING. — **sep′ti·ce′mic, sep′ti·cae′mic** (-mĭk), *adj.*
sep′ti·cid′al (sĕp′tĭ·sīd′ăl; -'l; 2), *adj.* [*septum* + L. *caedere* to cut.] *Bot.* Dehiscing at the lines of union of the carpels. Cf. LOCULICIDAL.
septic sore throat. *Med.* A severe sore throat caused by certain streptococci and marked by fever, prostration, inflammation of the tonsils, and other evidences of toxemia.
septic tank. A tank in which the solid matter of continuously flowing sewage is disintegrated by bacteria.
sep·tif′ra·gal (sĕp·tĭf′rȧ·găl), *adj.* [*septum* + L. *frangere, fractum*, to break.] *Bot.* Dehiscing by sundering of the valves of a capsule from the dissepiments.
sep·til′lion (sĕp·tĭl′yŭn), *n. & adj.* [F., fr. L. *septem* seven, after *million.*] See NUMERATION, *Table.* — **sep·til′lionth** (-yŭnth), *n.*
sep′tu·a·ge·nar′i·an (sĕp′tū·ȧ·jē·nâr′ĭ·ăn), *adj.* Septuagenary. — *n.* A person in his seventies; a person of an age between seventy and seventy-nine years, inclusive.
sep′tu·ag′e·nar′y (-ăj′ē·nĕr′ĭ; *Brit.* -ȧ·jē′nȧ·rĭ), *adj.* [L. *septuagenarius*, fr. *septuageni* seventy each.] Consisting of seventy; also, seventy years old; pertaining to one seventy years old. — *n.; pl.* -IES (-ĭz). A septuagenarian.
Sep′tu·a·ges′i·ma (sĕp′tū·ȧ·jĕs′ĭ·mȧ), *n.* [L., fem. of *septuagesimus*

seventieth, fr. *septuaginta* seventy.] More fully **Septuagesima Sunday**. The third Sunday before Lent.

Sep'tu·a·gint (sĕp'tū̇·ȧ·jĭnt), *n.* [L. *septuaginta* seventy.] The pre-Christian Greek version of the Old Testament still in use in the Eastern Church; — so called from the legend that the translation was made by seventy emissaries from Jerusalem for Ptolemy II (about 270 B.C.). See BIBLE.

sep'tum (sĕp'tŭm), *n.; pl.* -TA (-tȧ). [L. *septum, saeptum,* an enclosure, hedge, fence, fr. *sepire, saepire,* to hedge in, enclose.] Any dividing wall, partition, or the like; specif.: **a** *Biol.* A wall separating two cavities or masses of softer tissue in an organism. **b** *Physics.* The membrane separating two liquids in osmosis.

sep'tu·or (sĕp'tū̇·ôr), *n.* [F.] *Music.* A septet.

sep'tu·ple (sĕp'tū̇·p'l; sĕp·tū'p'l), *adj.* [LL. *septuplus.*] **1.** Consisting of seven; sevenfold; by sevens. **2.** *Music.* Having seven beats to the measure. — *v. t.;* -PLED (-p'ld); -PLING (-plĭng). To multiply by seven.

sep'tu·plet (sĕp'tū̇·plĕt; -plĭt; sĕp·tū'plĭt), *n.* One of seven offspring born at one birth.

sep'ul·cher, sep'ul·chre (sĕp'ŭl·kẽr), *n.* [OF. *sepulchre,* fr. L. *sepulcrum, -chrum,* fr. root of *sepelire, sepultum,* to bury.] **1.** A tomb; burial vault. **2.** *Eccl.* A repository for relics, as in an altar. — *v. t.* To bury; inter; entomb.

se·pul'chral (sē·pŭl'krăl), *adj.* **1.** Of or pert. to burial, the grave, or monuments to the dead. **2.** Suggestive of, or befitting, a sepulcher: **a** Gloomy; funereal. **b** Unnaturally low and grave; — of sound. — **se·pul'chral·ly,** *adv.*

sep'ul·ture (sĕp'ŭl·tū̇r), *n.* [OF., fr. L. *sepultura,* fr. *sepelire, sepultum,* to bury.] **1.** Act of burying; burial; interment. **2.** A sepulcher.

se·qua'cious (sē·kwā'shŭs), *adj.* [L. *sequax, -acis,* fr. *sequi* to follow.] **1.** Inclined to follow a leader. **2.** Slavishly compliant, esp. in opinion; as, *sequacious* zeal. **3.** Having or observing logical sequence. — **se·qua'cious·ly,** *adv.* — **se·quac'i·ty** (-kwăs'ĭ·tĭ), *n.*

se'quel (sē'kwĕl), *n.* [F. *séquelle,* fr. L. *sequela,* fr. *sequi* to follow.] **1.** That which follows; specif., logical consequence; inference. **2.** A result which ensues; consequence; effect. **3.** The events which ensue; also, outcome; upshot. **4.** A literary work continuing the course of a narrative begun in one preceding.

se·que'la (sē·kwē'lȧ), *n.; pl.* SEQUELAE (-lē). [L.] **a** A consequence; necessary concomitant. **b** *Med.* A morbid condition left as the result of a disease.

se'quence (sē'kwĕns), *n.* [OF. See SEQUENT.] **1.** State or fact of being sequent; succession; consecutiveness. **2.** A series having continuity and connection, and often uniformity, as of reflections or of poems, usually sonnets, united by a single theme. **3.** That which follows later or as a consequence; result. **4.** The order of events in time; simple succession. **5.** *Card Playing.* Three or more cards of the same suit in immediately consecutive order of value. **6.** *Music.* A succession of repeated harmonic or melodic phrases rising or falling usually by the regular diatonic degrees in the same scale. **7.** *Motion Pictures.* A section of a film story showing an uninterrupted episode without time lapses, titles, or breaks in the action. **8.** *R.C.Ch.* A hymn or rhythm introduced in the Mass on some occasions, and sung after the epistle and gradual; — called also a *prose.*

se'quent (-kwĕnt), *adj.* [L. *sequens, -entis,* pres. part. of *sequi* to follow.] Following; specif.: **a** Succeeding in time. **b** Following as an effect. — *n.* That which follows, esp. as a result; a sequence or sequel.

se·quen'tial (sē·kwĕn'shăl), *adj.* Succeeding or following in order or as a result. — **se·quen'tial·ly,** *adv.*

se·ques'ter (sē·kwĕs'tẽr), *v. t.* [OF. *sequestrer,* fr. LL. *sequestrare* to give up for safekeeping, fr. L. *sequester* a trustee.] **1.** To set apart; to separate; segregate. **2.** *Archaic.* To seclude; withdraw; — often reflexively. **3.** *Law.* **a** To take possession of, as property from the owner, until a demand is satisfied, a decree performed, etc. **b** *Internat. Law.* To confiscate or seize and appropriate under the right of pre-emption. — **se·ques'tra·ble** (-trȧ·b'l), *adj.*

se·ques'tered (sē·kwĕs'tẽrd), *adj.* Retired; secluded.

se·ques'trate (sē·kwĕs'trāt), *v. t.* **1.** *Archaic.* To sequester. **2.** To confiscate. — **se'ques·tra'tor** (sē'kwĕs·trā'tẽr; sĕk'wĕs-; sē·kwĕs'trā·tẽr), *n.*

se'ques·tra'tion (sē'kwĕs·trā'shŭn; sĕk'wĕs-), *n.* **1.** Act of sequestering or state of being sequestered; separation; seclusion, as from society. **2.** *Law.* The sequestering of property; removal of property from the person in possession of it, esp. pending some further proceeding affecting it.

se·ques'trum (sē·kwĕs'trŭm), *n.; pl.* -TRA (-trȧ). [NL. See SEQUESTER.] *Med.* A portion of dead tissue, esp. bone, which becomes separated from the sound portion.

se'quin (sē'kwĭn; sĕk'ĭn), *n.* [F. *sequin,* fr. It. *zecchino,* fr. *zecca* mint, fr. Ar. *sikkah* a die, stamp.] **1.** An obsolete gold coin of Italy and Turkey worth about $2.25. **2.** A metal disk or spangle used for ornamentation in costume, etc.

se·quoi'a (sē·kwoi'ȧ), *n.* [NL., after *Sequoya* (Cherokee *Sikwâyĭ*), inventor of the Cherokee syllabary.] *Bot.* Either of two species of huge, coniferous, Californian trees of the pine family which reach a height of over 300 feet; the big tree, or ***giant sequoia*** (*Sequoiadendron giganteum,* syn. *Sequoia gigantea*), or the redwood *Sequoia sempervirens* (see REDWOOD, 3 **a**). See CONE, *Illust.*

ser (sēr), *n.* Also **seer.** [Hind. *ser,* Per. *sīr.*] A varying weight of India, usually 1/40 of a maund. The government ser contains 80 tolas = 2.057 lb., or 0.933 kg.

se'ra (sēr'ȧ), *n., pl.* of SERUM.

‖**sé'rac'** (sā'răk'), *n.* [Swiss F., orig., a kind of solid cheese.] A pinnacle of ice among the crevasses of a glacier.

se·ragl'io (sē·răl'yō; sē·räl'yō), *n.; pl.* SERAGLI (-yē), SERAGLIOS (-yōz). [It. *serraglio,* orig., an enclosure of palisades (confused with Turk. *serāi* palace), fr. LL. *serrare* to close, lock up.] **1.** A harem; a place for keeping wives or concubines. **2.** Formerly, any palace of the sultan.

se·ra'i (sĕ·rä'ē; -rī'), *n.* [Turk. *serāi* palace, house, inn, fr. Per. *sarāi.*] In the East, a caravansary. Hence, a seraglio.

se·rail' (sĕ·rāl'), *n.* [F. *sérail.*] Seraglio.

se·ra'pe (sĕ·rä'pā), *n.* [Sp. *serape, sarape.*] A blanket worn as an outer garment by Spanish Americans.

ser'aph (sĕr'ăf), *n.; pl.* SERAPHIM (-ȧ·fĭm), SERAPHS (-ăfs). [Heb. *sĕrāphīm,* pl.] One of an order of celestial beings, conceived as fiery and purifying ministers of Jehovah. The seraphim are usually ranked as the highest order of angels, immediately above the cherubim.

se·raph'ic (sē·răf'ĭk), *adj.* Also **se·raph'i·cal** (-ĭ·kăl). Of, pertaining to, resembling, or befitting a seraph; angelic. — **se·raph'i·cal·ly,** *adv.*

ser'a·phim (sĕr'ȧ·fĭm), *n.* The Hebrew plural of SERAPH; — erroneously used as a sing., with pl. *seraphims,* in the King James Bible (*Is.* vi. 2, 6).

Se·ra'pis (sē·rā'pĭs), *n.* [L., fr. Gr. *Sarapis, Serapis.*] *Egypt., Gr., & Rom. Relig.* A god in whom were united the attributes of Osiris and Apis.

Serb (sûrb), *n.* [Serb. *Srb, Srbn.*] **a** A member of a Slavic tribe settled in the Roman province of Moesia, later forming the kingdom of Serbia. **b** A Serbian or his language. — *adj.* Serbian.

Ser'bi·an (sûr'bĭ·ăn; 58), *adj.* Of or pertaining to Serbia. — *n.* One of the people of Serbia, or of the race dominant in Serbia; also, their language. See SERBO-CROATIAN.

Ser'bo–Cro·a'tian (sûr'bō·krō·ā'shăn), *n.* The Slavic language dominant in Yugoslavia. The Roman alphabet is widely used, but the Cyrillic prevails in Serbia and Montenegro. See INDO-EUROPEAN LANGUAGES, *Table.* — **Ser'bo–Cro·a'tian,** *adj.*

Ser·bo'ni·an (sẽr·bō'nĭ·ăn; 58), *adj.* [Gr. *Serbōnis.*] Of or pertaining to Lake Serbonis (now dry) in Egypt in which Herodotus relates that whole armies were engulfed.

sere (sēr), *adj.* [Var. of SEAR.] Dried up; withered.

sere, *n.* [From L. *serere* to join, connect, with suggestion of L. *series* series.] *Ecol.* The complete cycle of changes in an area, from the initial condition to the climax condition.

ser'e·nade' (sĕr'ĕ·nād'), *n.* [F. *sérénade,* fr. It. *serenata.*] *Music.* Music as sung or played in the open air at night, esp. for gallantry, under the windows of ladies. — *v. t. & i.* To entertain with or perform a serenade. — **ser'e·nad'er** (-nād'ẽr), *n.*

ser'e·na'ta (sĕr'ĕ·nä'tȧ), *n.; pl.* -TAS (-tȧz), -TE (-tā). [It.] **a** A cantata of a pastoral or dramatic character; — so called by Handel. **b** An orchestral composition, midway between the earlier suite and the modern symphony; — so called by Mozart.

se·rene' (sē·rēn'), *adj.* [L. *serenus.*] **1.** Bright, clear, and calm; shining with clear, steady light. **2.** Placid; unruffled. **3.** Tranquil. **4.** Used as a title of princes; as, His *Serene* Highness. — **Syn.** See CALM. — *n.* A serene expanse of sky, sea, etc. — **se·rene'ly,** *adv.*

se·ren'i·ty (sē·rĕn'ĭ·tĭ), *n.; pl.* -TIES (-tĭz). **1.** Quality or state of being serene; composure; repose. **2.** Used as a title for the Roman emperor, the pope, bishops, etc.; as, Your *Serenity.*

serf (sûrf), *n.* [F., fr. L. *servus* servant, slave.] Orig., a slave; now usually, a person bound to the soil and more or less subject to the will of the owner. — **serf'age** (sûr'fĭj), **serf'dom** (sûrf'dŭm), **serf'hood** (-hŏŏd), *n.*

serge (sûrj), *n.* [OF. *sarge* (F. *serge*), fr. L. *serica* silk fabric.] **a** A twilled worsted fabric, used for suits, coats, and dresses. **b** A similarly twilled fabric, as of silk, used for lining.

ser'gean·cy (sär'jĕn·sĭ), *n.; pl.* -CIES (-sĭz). Office or function of a sergeant.

ser'geant, ser'jeant (sär'jĕnt), *n.* In England *serjeant* is preferred as naming a lawyer, otherwise *sergeant.* [OF. *sergent, sarjant,* fr. L. *serviens, -entis,* pres. part. of *servire* to serve.] **1.** *O. Eng. Feudal Law.* A personal attendant upon a soldier in war. **2.** Also **ser'jeant–at–law'.** *Eng.* One of a former ranking order of barristers acting for the king in the deciding of cases in his courts. **3.** = SERGEANT AT ARMS. **4.** Abbr. *sgt.,* or *sergt.* **a** An officer in a police force, in the United States ranking next below captain (sometimes lieutenant). **b** *Mil.* The highest noncommissioned officer. In the U. S. Army, formerly in four grades: ***master sergeant*** or ***first sergeant, technical sergeant, staff sergeant,*** and ***sergeant*** (4th grade); as of 1948, in three grades: ***master sergeant, sergeant, first class,*** and ***sergeant.*** See CORPORAL, 1. — **ser'geant·ship, ser'jeant·ship,** *n.*

sergeant at arms. An officer of any legislative or judicial body appointed to preserve order, arrest offenders, etc.

sergeant fish. **a** A striped, pelagic, somewhat mackerellike fish (*Rachycentron canadus*). **b** A robalo (*Centropomus undecimalis*).

sergeant major; *pl.* SERGEANTS MAJOR. In the U. S. Army a position held by either a master sergeant or a technical sergeant at a headquarters, to assist the adjutant and to supervise the enlisted men on duty at the headquarters.

se'ri·al (sēr'ĭ·ăl), *adj.* Of, consisting of, or arranged in a series, rank, or row; as, *serial* pictures; appearing in successive parts or numbers; as, a *serial* story. — *n.* **1.** A serial publication. **2.** A writing published in successive numbers of a periodical. — **se'ri·al·ly,** *adv.*

se'ri·al·ize (sēr'ĭ·ăl·īz), *v. t.* To arrange or publish in serial form. — **se'ri·al·i·za'tion** (-ĭ·zā'shŭn; -ī·zā'-), *n.*

se'ri·ate (sēr'ĭ·āt), *adj.* Arranged in a series or succession. — **se'ri·ate·ly,** *adv.*

se'ri·a'tim (sēr'ĭ·ā'tĭm; sĕr'ĭ-), *adv.* [ML.] In a series; one after another; serially.

se·ri'ceous (sē·rĭsh'ŭs), *adj.* [LL. *sericeus,* fr. *sericus* silken.] **1.** Of, pert. to, or consisting of silk; silky. **2.** *Bot.* Covered with very soft silky hairs.

ser'i·cul'ture (sĕr'ĭ·kŭl'tū̇r), *n.* [See SERICEOUS; CULTURE.] The production of raw silk by raising silkworms. — **ser'i·cul'tur·al** (-kŭl'tū̇r·ăl), *adj.* — **ser'i·cul'tur·ist** (-ĭst), *n.*

ser'i·e'ma (sĕr'ĭ·ē'mȧ; -ā'mȧ), *n.* [NL., fr. Tupi *seriema,* lit., crested.] **a** A large, long-legged crested bird (*Cariama cristata*) of southern Brazil. **b** A similar smaller bird (*Chunga burmeisteri*) of northern Argentina.

se'ries (sēr'ēz; -ĭz), *n. sing. & pl.* [L.; akin to L. *serere, sertum,* to join or bind together.] **1.** A number of things or events standing or succeeding in order, and connected by a like relation; a spatial or temporal succession of persons or things, as calamities, payments, etc. **2.** A set of volumes or numbers issued successively and having some connection, whether of subject, form, authorship, or publication; as, the Belles-Lettres *Series.* **3.** *Elec.* The arrangement of connecting the separate parts of a circuit successively end to end to form a single path for the current, parts so arranged being ***in series;*** — opp. to *parallel.* **4.** *Geol.* A division of rocks, smaller than a system, comprising those formed in an epoch. Cf. EPOCH, 4; SYSTEM, 7. **5.** *Math.* A succession of terms each derived from one or more of the preceding by a fixed law. See PROGRESSION, *n.,* 4. **6.** *Rhet.* A group of successive co-ordinate sentence elements joined together; as, an a, b, and c *series.*

series winding. *Elec.* A winding in which the armature and the field magnet are in series with the external circuit; — opposed to *shunt winding.* — **se'ries–wound'** (-wound'), *adj.*

ser′if (sĕr′ĭf), *n.* One of the fine lines of a letter, esp. a fine cross stroke at the top or bottom. See TYPE, *Illust.*

ser′i·graph (sĕr′ĭ·gràf), *n. Graphic Arts.* A color print, strictly an artist-made color print, produced by serigraphy.

se·rig′ra·phy (sè·rĭg′rà·fĭ), *n.* [See SERICEOUS; -GRAPHY.] *Graphic Arts.* A printing process of Chinese and Japanese origin in which semi-liquid pigment is pressed with a squeegee through a fine-mesh silk screen or bolting cloth to form the given design upon any desired surface by means of a stencil (one stencil for each color), which may be painted on the screen with shellac or tusche and glue or cut out of an impervious material like paper or metal and cemented to the screen or photographically reproduced on the screen impregnated with a light-sensitive emulsion; — restricted by artists to the making of original prints by an artist after his own design in distinction from *silk-screen printing*, which is applied to the process used commercially or for reproduction. — **se·rig′ra·pher** (-fẽr), *n.*

ser′in (sĕr′ĭn), *n.* [F.] A small European finch (*Serinus canarius*), related to the canary.

ser′ine (sĕr′ēn, -ĭn; sĕr′ēn, -ĭn), **ser′in**, *n.* [L. *sericus* silken.] *Chem.* A crystalline compound, $CH_2OHCH(NH_2)CO_2H$, obtained as a product of protein splitting.

se·rin′ga (sè·rĭng′gà), *n.* [F. & Pg. See SYRINGA.] Any of several Brazilian trees (genus *Hevea*) of the spurge family, yielding rubber.

se′ri·o·com′ic (sḗr′ĭ·ô·kŏm′ĭk), *adj.* Also **se′ri·o·com′i·cal** (-ĭ·kăl). Having a mixture of seriousness and sport.

se′ri·ous (sḗr′ĭ·ŭs), *adj.* [F. *sérieux*, fr. ML. *seriosus*, fr. L. *serius*.] **1.** Grave in disposition or manner; earnest; thoughtful; solemn. **2.** Being in earnest; not jesting. **3.** Demanding earnestness of thought or endeavor. **4.** Important; weighty. **5.** Addressed to grave moods. **6.** Giving rise to apprehension; attended with danger; as, a *serious* injury. — **se′ri·ous·ly**, *adv.* — **se′ri·ous·ness**, *n.*

Syn. Serious, grave, solemn, sedate, staid, sober, earnest mean showing signs of deep thought, absorption in important affairs, or the like. **Serious** implies a concern for what really matters; **grave**, somberness of expression or attitude; **solemn**, gravity that is highly impressive; **sedate**, a composed and decorous seriousness; **staid**, a settled sedateness, often a prim self-restraint; **sober**, seriousness of purpose; **earnest**, soberness with sincerity and, often, zealousness.

ser′jeant (sär′jĕnt), **ser′jeant·ship**, etc. Vars. of SERGEANT, etc.

ser′mon (sûr′mŭn), *n.* [OF., fr. L. *sermo*, -*onis*, a speaking, discourse.] **1.** A discourse delivered in public, usually by a clergyman, for the purpose of religious instruction, and grounded on a passage of Scripture. **2.** A lecture on one's conduct or duty; a homily; hence, an annoying harangue.

ser′mon·ize (sûr′mŭn·īz), *v. i. & t.* To compose or deliver a sermon (to); to preach; esp., to discourse didactically or dogmatically; also, to lecture; admonish. — **ser′mon·iz′er** (-īz′ẽr), *n.*

Sermon on the Mount. The discourse of Christ recorded in Matthew v, vi, and vii, and in Luke vi. 20–49.

se′ro- (sḗr′ô-). [From SERUM.] A combining form indicating: **a** *Connection with*, or *relation to*, *serum*, as in **se·rol′o·gy**, the science treating of the reactions, preparation, use, etc., of serums. **b** *Serous and*, as in **se′ro·mu′cous**.

se·ros′i·ty (sè·rŏs′ĭ·tĭ), *n.; pl.* -TIES (-tĭz). **1.** Quality or state of being serous; thin or watery consistency. **2.** A thin watery animal fluid, as synovial fluid.

ser′o·tine (sĕr′ô·tĭn; -tīn), **se·rot′i·nous** (sè·rŏt′ĭ·nŭs), *adj.* [L. *serotinus*, fr. *serus* late.] Late, esp. in developing or flowering.

se′rous (sḗr′ŭs), *adj.* [F. *séreux.* See SERUM.] *Physiol.* **a** Thin; watery; like serum; as, a *serous* fluid. **b** Of or pertaining to serum.

serous fluid. Any of various thin watery fluids in cavities of the body, esp. those lined by serous membranes.

serous membrane. *Anat.* Any of certain thin, reflected, lining membranes, as the peritoneum, pericardium, etc.

ser′ow (sĕr′ō), *n.* [Native dialect *să-ro* the long-haired goat of Tibet.] Any of several goat antelopes (genus *Capricornis*) of eastern Asia. They are usually rather dark, heavily built animals, the larger forms having distinct manes.

ser′pent (sûr′pĕnt), *n.* [OF., fr. L. *serpens*, -*entis*, fr. *serpens*, pres. part. of *serpere* to creep.] **1. a** *Archaic.* Any noxious creature that creeps, hisses, or stings. **b** A snake; esp., a large snake. **2.** A subtle, treacherous, malicious person. **3.** A variety of firework having a serpentine motion. **4.** An obsolete bass wind instrument of the trumpet type.

ser′pen·tine (sûr′pĕn·tēn; -tīn), *adj.* [F. *serpentin*, fr. LL. *serpentinus.*] **1.** Of or like a serpent. **2.** Like the serpent; subtly wily or tempting; diabolic. **3.** Winding or turning one way and the other; sinuous.

ser′pen·tine (-tēn), *n.* [OF.] A mineral or rock, essentially a hydrous magnesium silicate, $H_4Mg_3Si_2O_9$, usually dull-green, often with a mottled appearance.

ser·pi′go (sẽr·pī′gō), *n.* [ML., fr. L. *serpere* to creep.] Any creeping or spreading skin disease, esp. ringworm. — **ser·pig′i·nous** (-pĭj′ĭ·nŭs), *adj.*

ser′ra·noid (sĕr′à·noid), *adj.* [L. *serra* a saw + -*oid.*] Of or pertaining to a family (Serranidae) of carnivorous perchlike fishes comprising the black sea bass and allies and including, sometimes, the true groupers, jewfish, etc. — *n.* A serranoid fish.

ser′rate (sĕr′āt), *adj.* Also **ser′rat·ed** (-āt·ĕd; -ĭd). [L. *serratus*, fr. *serra* a saw.] Notched or toothed on the edge, like a saw; specif., *Bot.*, having marginal teeth pointing forward or toward the apex; as, a *serrate* leaf. Cf. DENTATE.

ser·ra′tion (sĕ·rā′shŭn), *n.* **a** Condition of being serrate. **b** A formation resembling the toothed edge of a saw. **c** One of the teeth in a serrate margin.

ser′ra·ture (sĕr′à·tụr), *n.* Serration.

ser′ried. See SERRY.

ser′ru·late (sĕr′ụ̇·lāt; sĕr′ŏŏ-), *adj.* Also **ser′ru·lat·ed** (-lāt′ĕd; -ĭd). [L. *serrula* a little saw, dim. of *serra* a saw.] Finely serrate.

ser′ru·la′tion (-lā′shŭn), *n.* **1.** State of being serrulate. **2.** One of the teeth in a serrulate margin.

ser′ry (sĕr′ĭ), *v. i. & t.* [F. *serré*, past part. of *serrer* to press.] To press together, esp. in ranks; — chiefly in form **ser′ried** (-ĭd), *part. adj.*

ser′tu·lar′i·an (sûr′tụ̇·lâr′ĭ·ăn; 6), *adj. Zool.* Any of a genus (*Sertularia*) of delicate branching hydroids. — *n.* A sertularian hydroid.

se′rum (sḗr′ŭm), *n.; pl.* SERUMS (-ŭmz), SERA (-à). [L.] **1.** The watery portion of an animal fluid remaining after coagulation; esp.: **a** Blood serum; often, specif., immune blood serum, which contains specific immune bodies, as antitoxins or agglutinins; as, antitoxic *serum.* **b** The whey of milk. **2.** Any serous fluid, normal or pathological. **3.** The watery part of a vegetable fluid.

ser′val (sûr′văl), *n.* [F., fr. Pg. *lobo cerval* lynx, fr. L. *lupus* wolf + *cervus* stag.] A long-legged African wildcat (*Felis capensis*) having large untufted ears.

serv′ant (sûr′vănt), *n.* [OF. *servant*, pres. part. of *servir* to serve, fr. L. *servire.*] **1.** A person employed by another for menial offices, or for other labor; as, a domestic *servant*; one who exerts himself for the benefit of another, his master; specif., an official of a government; as, a public *servant.* **2.** A slave.

serve (sûrv), *v. i.* [Late AS. *servian*, fr. OF. *servir*, fr. L. *servire* to serve, to be a servant or slave.] **1.** To labor as a servant. **2.** To discharge the requirements of an office or public duty, as on a jury. **3.** To do military, naval, or similar service. **4.** To discharge the obligations of a term of forced or voluntary service, as an indenture. **5.** To help persons to food at table. **6.** To answer a purpose. **7.** To be usable as a substitute. **8.** To be favorable, as occasion. **9.** *Tennis.* To deliver the service. — *v. t.* **1.** To exert oneself continuously or statedly for; specif., in a religious sense, to obey and worship. **2.** To comply with the commands or demands of, as one's appetite. **3.** To perform the official duties belonging to, or required in or for, as a church. **4.** To render military or naval service to; to fight for. **5.** To go through (a period of service) by indenture, enlistment, or sentence. **6.** To render services so as to benefit, help, or promote; as, to *serve* mankind. **7. a** To wait upon at table. **b** To deliver in readiness to be partaken of, esp. at table. **8.** To treat; to behave oneself to; to requite; as, he *served* me very ill. **9.** To furnish or supply, as with light and heat. **10.** To copulate with; to cover; — of male animals. **11.** To answer the needs of; as, an excuse that *served* my purpose. **12.** To be sufficient for, as a period of time. **13.** To contribute or conduce to; to promote. **14.** To answer the needs of (one) in place of something; — with *for*; as, a sofa *serves* one for a seat and a couch. **15.** *Games.* In tennis, rackets, etc., to put (the ball) in play by delivering it by a stroke to one's opponent. **16.** *Law.* **a** To bring to notice, deliver, or execute, actually or constructively, as a process. **b** To make legal service upon (a person). **17.** *Mil. & Naval.* To operate (guns) in action. **18.** *Naut.* To wind spun yarn, canvas, wire, etc., tightly around (a rope or stay, etc.) to protect it, as from chafing. — *n. Tennis, etc.* Act or turn of serving; the ball as served.

serv′er (sûr′vẽr), *n.* **1.** One who serves; specif.: **a** *Eccl.* The celebrant's assistant at Low Mass. **b** *Games.* The player who serves the ball. **2.** That which serves, as a tray for dishes; a salver.

serv′ice (sûr′vĭs), *n.*, or **service tree.** [From ME. *serves*, pl. of obs. *serve*, fr. AS. *syrfe* service tree.] A European tree (*Sorbus domestica*) resembling the mountain ash but with larger and edible fruit. The related *S. torminalis* is often distinguished as **wild service tree.** See CHECKER, *n.*, 3. **b** *U. S.* Any shadbush.

serv′ice, *n.* [OF. *servise*, *service* (F. *service*), fr. L. *servitium.* See SERVE.] **1.** The occupation or status of a servant; as, placed out at *service.* **2.** Performance of labor for the benefit of another, or at another's command. **3.** Duty done or required; office. **4.** *Hist.* The attentions and devotion of a gallant to his mistress. **5.** Profession of respect; — used in complimentary salutations. **6.** Spiritual serving as shown by obedience, good works, and love; as, dedicated to the *service* of God. **7. a** An official religious duty performed; appropriate religious rites; as, a burial *service.* **b** A particular celebration of public worship. **8.** Performance of official duties for a sovereign or state; as, public *service*; also, a particular duty of such work; as, jury *service.* **9.** A branch of public employment; also, those collectively in it; as, the civil *service.* **10. a** Military duty; also, its performance. **b** Military organization, esp. (*pl.*) combined; as, the armed *services.* **11.** A set of articles for a particular use; as, a dinner *service.* **12.** Conduct contributing to the advantage of another or others; as, a *service* to the cause of freedom; also, useful office; benefit. **13.** Act or means of supplying some general demand, esp. of conducting some public utility; as, gas or water *service.* **14.** A set of musical settings of portions of the liturgy, esp. of the choral canticles, chants, etc. **15.** *Usually pl.* Any result of useful labor which does not produce a tangible commodity; as, railroads perform *services.* **16.** *Animal Breeding.* Act of covering. **17.** *Com.* Accommodations to a dealer or consumer to promote the sale and use of a product. **18.** *Games.* **a** Act or turn at serving the ball. **b** The ball served. **19.** *Law.* Act of bringing to notice; the execution of any writ or process. **20.** *Naut.* The materials used for serving a rope, etc., as spun yarn, lines, etc.

— *adj.* **1.** In active service. **2.** Facilitating service; used by servants. **3.** For ordinary use; as, *service* uniform; — contrasted with *dress* or *full-dress* (uniform). **4.** Pert. to business; as, the *service* entrance.

— *v. t.; var.* SERV′ICED (-vĭst) SERV′IC·ING (-vĭs·ĭng). To perform services of maintenance, supply, repair, installation, etc., for or upon.

serv′ice·a·ble (-à·b'l), *adj.* **1.** *Archaic.* Willing to be of service; obliging. **2. a** Capable of, or fit for, the performance of duty. **b** Doing service; fit for use or service; beneficial; advantageous. **3.** Lasting or wearing well in use; as, *serviceable* shoes. — **serv′ice·a·bil′i·ty** (-bĭl′ĭ·tĭ), *n.* — **serv′ice·a·ble·ness**, *n.*

serv′ice-ber′ry (sûr′vĭs·bĕr′ĭ), *n.* **a** The fruit of any service tree. **b** The shad bush.

service clasp. See CLASP.

service club. An organization for the promotion of the common interests of its members and to help the community welfare, as a Rotary, Kiwanis, or Lions club.

serv′ice-man′ (sûr′vĭs·măn′; -măn), *n.; pl.* -MEN (-mĕn′; -mĕn). **a** One who performs or has performed military service. **b** One whose work is servicing.

service medal. *Mil.* A medal awarded for service during a specified time or in a specified campaign or expedition. Cf. DECORATION, 3.

service station. An establishment where service may be obtained for automobiles, as the furnishing of gasoline, oil, water, air, greasing, and general repairing.

service stripe. A stripe, or one of several stripes, worn usually on the sleeve of a uniform, to indicate length of service or, *U. S. Army*, number of enlistments.

service tree. See 1st SERVICE.

ser′vi·ette′ (sûr′vĭ·ĕt′), *n.* [F.] A table napkin.

ser′vile (sûr′vĭl *or*, esp. Brit., -vīl), *adj.* [L. *servilis*, fr. *servus* a servant or slave.] **1.** Of or pertaining to a slave or slaves; consisting of slaves; as, a *servile* revolt. **2.** *Archaic.* Held in subjection; enslaved. **3. a** Befitting a slave or servant. **b** Characteristic of a slave; slavish;

as, *servile* flattery. **c** Behaving like a slave; meanly submissive; cringing; fawning. — **Syn.** See SUBSERVIENT. — **ser′vile·ly**, *adv.* — **ser′vile·ness**, *n.* — **ser·vil′i·ty** (sẽr·vĭl′ĭ·tĭ), *n.*

ser′vi·tor (sûr′vĭ·tẽr), *n.* One who serves; an attendant; one who acts under another; a follower or adherent.

ser′vi·tude (sûr′vĭ·tūd), *n.* [F., fr. L. *servitudo.*] **1.** Condition of a slave; slavery; serfdom; bondage. **2.** Service required as a punishment for crime. **3.** *Law.* A right in virtue of which the object (as land) is subject to a certain use or enjoyment by another person or for the benefit of another thing.

Syn. **Servitude, slavery, bondage** mean the state of being subject to a master. **Servitude**, a more or less rhetorical term, implies in general lack of liberty to do as one pleases, but specifically, lack of freedom to determine one's acts, laws, conditions of living, etc.; **slavery**, subjection to a master who owns one's person and may treat one as property; **bondage**, the state of being bound, formerly as a serf but now, more often, like a prisoner by chains, to a state of complete subjection to the will of another.

ser′vo (sûr′vō), *n.* Short for SERVOMOTOR, SERVOMECHANISM; hence, **ser′vo**, *adj.*

ser′vo con·trol′ (sûr′vō). *Aeronautics.* An auxiliary device to reinforce by an aerodynamic or mechanical relay the pilot's effort in operating a control. A small hinged auxiliary airfoil at the trailing edge of an aileron, elevator, or rudder is frequently used for the purpose.

Ser′vo–Cro·a′tian (sûr′vō-). Var. of SERBO-CROATIAN.

ser′vo·mo′tor (sûr′vō·mō′tẽr), *n.* [F. *servo-moteur* (fr. L. *servus* slave + L. *movere, motum,* to move).] **1.** A relay apparatus. **2.** Any power-driven mechanism, commonly an electric motor, which supplements a primary control operated by a comparatively feeble force. In one type the primary control is a simple lever; in another the primary control is an automatic device such as a photoelectric cell or a meter for measuring position, speed, voltage, etc., to whose variations the motor responds, so that it is used as a correctional or compensating device, as in a gyropilot or in a gun-aiming apparatus. An apparatus that includes a servomotor is often called a **ser′vo·mech′a·nism** (-mĕk′ȧ·nĭz′m).

ses′a·me (sĕs′ȧ·mē), *n.* [F. and L.; F. *sésame,* fr. L., fr. Gr. *sēsamon, sēsamē.*] **1.** An East Indian hairy herb (*Sesamum indicum*); also, its small flattish seed (**sesame seed**), yielding an oil (**sesame oil**) and used as food and in making soap. **2.** [*cap.*] = OPEN SESAME.

ses′a·moid (sĕs′ȧ·moid), *adj.* [Gr. *sēsamoeidēs* like sesame.] Of, pert. to, or designating a nodular mass of bone or cartilage in a tendon, esp. at a joint or bony prominence. — *n.* A sesamoid bone or cartilage.

ses′qui- (sĕs′kwĭ-). [L., one half more, one and a half.] A combining form denoting: **1.** *One and a half times,* as in *sesqui*centennial. **2.** That *three* atoms or equivalents of the (specified) element or radical are combined with *two* of another, as in iron **ses′qui·ox′ide**, Fe_2O_3.

ses′qui·cen·ten′ni·al (-sĕn·tĕn′ĭ·ăl; 58), *adj.* [*sesqui-* + *centennial.*] Of or pertaining to a century and a half. — *n.* The one hundred and fiftieth anniversary, or its celebration.

ses′qui·pe·da′li·an (-pē·dā′lĭ·ăn), *adj.* Also **ses·quip′e·dal** (sĕs-kwĭp′ē·dăl; sĕs′kwĭ·pē′dăl; -d'l). [L. *sesquipedalis.* See SESQUI-; PEDAL.] **a** Measuring or containing a foot and a half; — sometimes humorously applied to long words. **b** Given to using long words. — *n.* A very long word.

ses′sile (sĕs′ĭl; 56), *adj.* [L. *sessilis* low, dwarf, fr. *sedere, sessum,* to sit.] **1.** *Bot.* Attached directly by the base; not raised upon a stalk or peduncle. **2.** *Zool.* Permanently attached; not free to move about.

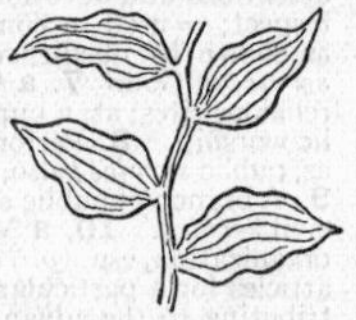

Sessile Leaves.

ses′sion (sĕsh′ŭn), *n.* [F., fr. L. *sessio,* fr. *sedere, sessum,* to sit.] **1.** *Archaic.* A sitting or being seated. **2.** The actual or constructive sitting of a court, council, legislature, etc.; as, a *session* of Congress; also, a single sitting or the period of sitting. **3.** *Educ.* A period of conducting classes or giving instruction; as, a morning *session;* the winter *session.* **4.** *pl.* **a** *Eng. Law.* The sittings or a sitting of justices of peace, as in ***petty sessions,*** when held without a jury, for trial of minor offenses. **b** *U. S.* The sittings or a sitting of a justice's court, as to grant innkeepers' licenses, to lay out highways, etc. — **ses′sion·al** (-ăl; -'l), *adj.*

ses′terce (sĕs′tûrs), *n.* [L. *sestertius* (sc. *nummus*), fr. *sestertius* two and a half.] *Rom. Antiq.* A coin orig. of silver, later of brass, equal to ¼ denarius.

ses·ter′ti·um (sĕs·tûr′shĭ·ŭm; -shŭm), *n.; pl.* -TIA (-ȧ). [L. See SESTERCE.] *Rom. Antiq.* A money of account equal to one thousand sesterces.

ses·tet′ (sĕs·tĕt′; sĕs′tĕt), *n.* [It. *sestetto,* fr. *sesto* sixth, fr. L. *sextus,* fr. *sex* six.] **1.** *Music.* A sextet. **2.** *Pros.* The last six lines of a sonnet of the Italian type.

ses·ti′na (sĕs·tē′nȧ), *n.; pl.* -TINE (-nā), -TINAS (-nȧz). [It.] A lyrical fixed form distinguished by its six six-line stanzas, its six end words repeated in a different order in each stanza, and a three-line envoy in which are distributed these six words.

Set (sĕt), *n.* [Gr. *Sēth,* fr. Egypt. *Setesh,* the god of evil.] *Egypt. Relig.* An evil divinity, brother and enemy of Osiris, having a beast's head with pointed snout.

set (sĕt), *v. t.;* SET; SET′TING. [AS. *settan.*] **1.** To seat or cause to sit, as on a throne; specif., to put (a fowl) on eggs to hatch them, or to put (eggs) into a nest for a fowl to sit on, or into an incubator; also [cf. SET, *v. i.,* 2], *Scot.,* to suit; become. **2.** To fix in a situation or direction; specif.: **a** To put to stay in a place. **b** To fix in position to snare or seize, as a net or trap. **c** To direct with fixed attention and preoccupation; as, to *set* one's heart on or one's trust in. **d** To appoint to a position; post; station; as, a supervisor *set* over us. **3.** To establish; specif.: **a** To ordain or fix as a time, limit, or regulation; prescribe. **b** To furnish as a pattern or an example. **c** To allot or appoint as a task; to propound for solution or prescribe for study; assign. **4.** To move with fixed direction; specif.: **a** To cause to be, become, do, etc.; to dispose; start; as, to *set* houses afire; to *set* one at ease. **b** To incite to hostility, as brother against brother. **c** To put and fix in a direction; direct; as, to *set* one's face toward home. **d** To adjust in conformity with some standard, as a clock. **5.** To put in readiness; specif.: **a** To put into a desired position, adjustment, or condition; to regulate; as, wheels *set* close together. **b** To put in order for immediate use, as a table or a lathe. **c** Hence, to put a smooth edge on (a razor or tool), to adjust the teeth of (a saw), etc. **d** To adjust (a measuring instrument) to a desired position. **6.** To beset; specif.: **a** To adorn with something infixed or affixed; to stud; dot. **b** To fix, as a precious stone, in a border of metal; to place in or amid something which serves as a setting, as glass in a sash. **7.** To place in estimation; specif.: **a** To fix at or adjust to a certain amount, as a price, fine, or ransom. **b** To value; to rate; to estimate; — with *at.* **8.** To put in a fixed state; specif.: **a** To fix firmly; to make fast, rigid, or immobile, as one's jaw. **b** To make unyielding or obstinate, as one's mind. **c** To render stiff or solid; esp., to convert into curd, as milk for cheese. **d** To wager. **9.** Technically: **a** *Baking.* To lay aside (dough, batter, etc., in which yeast has been added) to rise. **b** *Hunting.* To point out the seat or position of, as game. **c** *Music.* To adapt, as words to music, or music to words. **d** *Naut.* To spread or have spread to the wind, as the sails. **e** *Print.* To compose; to arrange in words, lines, etc., as type. **f** *Surg.* To restore to normal position or connection when dislocated or fractured. — *v. i.* **1.** To brood; — of hens. **2.** To fit or suit; as, the coat *sets* well. **3.** To pass below the horizon; — of a heavenly body; hence, to wane; pass away. **4.** To move with fixed direction; specif.: **a** To begin to move; to start; — now, exc. in *dial.,* with *out, on, forth,* or *forward.* **b** To have a certain direction in motion, inclination, or tendency; as, the current *sets* to the north. **5.** To take on a fixed condition; specif.: **a** To become rigid or permanent; to become hardened, as by chemical action or cooling. **b** To become fast or permanent; — of a color. **6.** *Hort.* To adhere to the parent plant and initiate growth or normal development, as a result of some stimulus, esp. pollination; — of a blossom, fruit, or seed. **7.** *Hunting.* To indicate the position of game.

set about. To begin to do. — ***set aside.*** **a** To discard; dismiss. **b** To reserve for a purpose. **c** To annul. — ***set back.*** To hinder; check; reverse the progress of. — ***set down.*** To enter in writing; to consider; to attribute. — ***set forth.*** To publish; promulgate; expound. — ***set in.*** To begin; to become prevalent. — ***set off.*** **a** To embellish; to intensify by or serve as a contrast. **b** To start (one), as to laughing. **c** To explode. — ***set on.*** **a** To assail; attack. **b** To incite; instigate. — ***set sail.*** To spread the sails; to begin a voyage. — ***set to.*** To begin actively or earnestly, as to fight or argue. — ***set up.*** **a** To raise, as a cry; also, to elevate. **b** To begin; establish; organize. **c** To rouse to anger or hostility. — ***set upon.*** To assail, esp. violently.

— *adj.* **1.** Fixed by authority or appointment; prescribed. **2.** Deliberately conceived or expressed; as, in *set* terms. **3.** *Now Dial.* Obstinate. **4. a** Immovable; rigid. **b** Persistent; settled; as, *set* rains. **c** Settled in build; as, a figure heavily *set.* **d** Built in; as, a *set* tub.

— *n.* [Senses 5 to 8 orig. fr. OF. *sette,* fr. L. *secta.*] **1.** The hardening of a plastic or liquid substance, as by chemical action or by cooling or drying. **2.** Form; build; also, carriage; as, the *set* of one's shoulders. **3.** Direction or course, as of the wind. **4.** *Chiefly Colloq.* Manner of fitting; fit; as, the *set* of a coat. **5.** A number of things of the same kind that belong or are used together. **6.** A series associated by common authorship or publication. **7.** A number of persons associated by custom, opinion, or the like; a clique. **8.** A clutch (of eggs). **9.** In dancing, the number necessary to execute a square dance; also, the figures executed. **10.** *Hort.* **a** A young plant or rooted cutting ready for setting out. **b** A small tuber, bulb, corm, or the like; as, an onion *set.* **11.** *Mech.* **a** Permanent change of form due to repeated or excessive stress, as from compression, tension, bending, twisting, etc. **b** Sidewise deflection of a saw-toothed point. **12.** *Motion Pictures.* Any artificial and formal setting for a scene of a photoplay. **13.** *Philately.* A series of stamps or a part of a series. **14.** *Radio.* A receiving set. **15.** [Orig. fr. OF. *sette* sequence.] *Tennis.* A group of games in which one side wins six to the opponent's four or less.

se′ta (sē′tȧ), *n.; pl.* SETAE (-tē). [L. *seta, saeta,* a bristle.] *Bot. & Zool.* Any slender, bristlelike organ or part.

se·ta′ceous (sē·tā′shŭs), *adj.* [NL. *setaceus,* fr. L. *seta* a bristle.] **a** Set with, or consisting of, bristles. **b** Bristlelike in form or texture.

set′back′ (sĕt′băk′), *n.* **1.** An unexpected check or reverse. **2.** *U. S.* An eddy or countercurrent. **3.** *Arch.* A withdrawal of the face of a building to a line to the rear of the building line, or to the rear of the wall below, required by many building codes to assure adequate sunlight reaching the streets and the lower floors of adjacent buildings.

set chisel. A chisel or punch with broad flat end, for stripping off rivet heads and the like.

Seth (sĕth), *n.* [Heb. *Shēth.*] *Bib.* A son of Adam.

seti-. [L. *seta.*] A combining form meaning *bristle,* as in: **se·tif′er·ous, se′ti·form, se·tig′er·ous, se·tip′a·rous.**

set′off′ (sĕt′ŏf′; 74), *n.* **1.** That which is set off against another thing. **2.** *Law.* The discharge of a debt by setting against it a distinct claim in favor of the debtor; also, the claim itself.

se′ton (sē′t'n), *n.* [ML. *seto, setonis,* fr. L. *seta* bristle.] *Med. & Veter.* A few threads, horsehairs, or the like, introduced beneath the skin to form an issue; also, the issue.

se′tose (sē′tōs; sē·tōs′), *adj.* [L. *setosus.*] Setaceous.

set′screw′ (sĕt′skrōō′), *n.* A machine screw screwed through one part tightly upon or slightly into another part, to prevent relative movement. See CHUCK, SCREW, *Illusts.*

‖**set′te·cen′to** (sĕt′tā·chĕn′tō), *n.* [It., seven hundred. Cf. CINQUECENTO.] The 18th century, esp. in Italian art and literature.

set·tee′ (sĕ·tē′), *n.* [From SET.] A long seat with a back, for several persons; also, a medium-sized sofa.

set′ter (sĕt′ẽr), *n.* **1.** One who sets; as, a *setter* of bounds; a type*setter;* a *setter-on* (or inciter). **2.** A gun dog of a type formerly trained to set, or crouch, on finding game but now to stand rigid and point. The three chief breeds are *English, Gordon,* and *Irish setters.*

set′ting (sĕt′ĭng), *n.* **1.** Act of one that sets. **2.** That in which something, as a gem, is set. **3.** The temporal and spatial environment of the action of a narrative. **4.** The music composed for a poem, psalm, etc. **5.** The eggs incubated by a fowl at one time. **6.** The scenic environment of a play, including the physical surroundings, properties, buildings, etc., within which the action takes place.

set′tle (sĕt′'l), *n.* [AS. *setl.*] A long wooden bench with arms, a high solid back, and an enclosed foundation often serving as a chest.

set′tle, *v. t.;* SET′TLED (-'ld); SET′TLING (-lĭng). [AS. *setlan,* fr. *setl.*] **1.** To place in a position to remain; as, to *settle* troops in barracks; to plant with inhabitants; to colonize; people. **2.** To cause to sink; to render close or compact, as the contents of a barrel by shaking; also, to restore to a smooth or passable condition, as the ground, or a road. **3.** *Colloq.* To reduce to order or good behavior; to put in one's place. **4.** To place in a fixed or permanent condition, as peace or order; to make firm, steady, or stable; to establish, as one's mind; to establish in business, in a home, or the like. **5.** To settle by agreement, as a price. **6.** To secure to one by legal form, as a right or an estate. **7.** To clear of dregs and impurities by causing them to sink. **8.** To render quiet; to calm; compose. **9.** To put in order or adjustment, as one's room or an estate for disposal at death. **10.** To determine, as something ex-

posed to doubt or question; to free from uncertainty or wavering; also, to appoint definitely, as a date. **11.** To close by payment, as accounts; to liquidate. **12.** To adjust, as something in discussion; to compose; pacify. **13.** *Law.* To conclude (a lawsuit) by agreement between the parties. — **Syn.** See DECIDE.
— *v. i.* **1.** To alight, as creatures flying; to descend and stay, as night. **2.** To sink; specif.: **a** To sink gradually to a lower level; to subside. **b** To fall to the bottom, as dregs. **c** To become firm, dry, and hard, as the ground after frost. **3.** To become established in a fixed location or direction, as dust or the wind; set. **4.** To fix one's residence; to establish abode. **5.** To decide; determine; resolve. **6.** To leave an irregular, and take up a methodical, way of life; esp., to assume the duties of a householder. **7.** To clarify by depositing sediment, as wine. **8.** To adjust differences or accounts; to come to an agreement.

set'tle·ment (sĕt''l·mĕnt), *n.* **1.** Act of settling, or state of being settled; establishment in business, office, condition, etc.; also, bestowal under legal sanction; formal presentation; specif.: **a** Payment or adjustment of an account; composure of doubts or differences; adjustment; also, condition of affairs thus adjusted. **b** Colonization. **2.** That which settles or is settled, established, or fixed; a place or region newly settled; also, a small village. **3.** An institution, maintained amidst a congested city population, to render educational, recreational, and other services to the community. **4.** A community formed by a religious body; as, a Shaker *settlement.* **5.** *Arch.* The gradual sinking of a structure; *pl.*, fractures or dislocations caused by settlement. **6.** *Law.* **a** A settled place of abode; residence. **b** A disposition of property for the benefit of someone, usually through the medium of trustees.

set'tler (sĕt'lẽr), *n.* One who settles something; one who settles in a new region; a colonist.

set'tling (sĕt'lĭng), *n.* **1.** Act of one who settles. **2. a** Subsidence. **b** *pl.* Lees; dregs.

set'tlor (sĕt'lẽr), *n.* *Law.* One who makes a settlement or creates a trust of property.

set'-to' (sĕt'tōō'), *n.; pl.* SET-TOS (-tōōz'). *Colloq.* A contest, as in boxing, usually vigorous and brief; a bout.

set'up' (sĕt'ŭp'), *n.* **1.** The manner in which something is set up; organization; make-up; specif.: **a** *U. S.* Carriage of the body. **b** An arrangement, as of scientific apparatus. **2.** *Slang.* **a** A task or contest purposely made easy. **b** A match arranged with an opponent who can easily be defeated.

sev'en (sĕv'ĕn), *n. & adj.* [AS. *seofon.*] See NUMBER, *Table.*

Seven against Thebes, the. In Greek legend, the expedition of seven heroes against Thebes, undertaken to aid Polynices to recover a share in the kingship, which his brother Eteocles had usurped. An oracle promised success to whichever brother their father Oedipus should favor, but he cursed both, and the brothers slew each other.

seven deadly sins. See DEADLY SINS.

sev'en·fold' (sĕv'ĕn·fōld'; 2), *adj. & adv.* See -FOLD.

Seven Hills. The seven hills upon and about which was built the city of Rome. According to tradition, Romulus built upon the *Palatine* hill (later the site of the palaces of the Caesars), though later he united with his settlement those upon the *Capitoline* and *Quirinal.* The *Caelian*, the *Aventine*, the *Esquiline* and *Viminal*, were added later.

seven seas *or* **Seven Seas.** All the waters or oceans of the world.

sev'en·teen' (sĕv'ĕn·tēn'; 2), *n. & adj.* [AS. *seofontiene, -tȳne, -tēne.*] See NUMBER, *Table.* — **sev'en·teenth'** (-tēnth'; 2), *n. & adj.*

sev'en·teen'-year' lo'cust. A cicada (*Cicada septendecim*), of the United States, which has in the North a life of seventeen years, in the South of thirteen years, mostly spent underground in the nymphal condition, from which it emerges as an adult, living only a few weeks. See CICADA.

sev'enth (sĕv'ĕnth), *n.* **1.** See NUMBER, *Table.* **2.** *Music.* **a** An interval embracing seven diatonic degrees. **b** A tone at this interval. **c** The harmonic combination of two tones a seventh apart. **d** The seventh tone of a scale, reckoning up from the tonic. — **sev'enth**, *adj.* — **sev'enth·ly**, *adv.*

seventh chord. *Music.* A chord comprising a fundamental tone with its third, fifth, and seventh.

sev'enth-day' (sĕv'ĕnth·dā'; 2), *adj.* Pertaining to or observing the seventh day; esp., advocating observance of Saturday as the Sabbath.

seventh heaven. **1.** *Mohammedanism.* The last and highest of the abodes of bliss. **2.** A state of extreme joy or rapture.

sev'en·ty (sĕv'ĕn·tĭ), *n. & adj.* [AS. hund-*seofontig, seofontig.*] See NUMBER, *Table.* — ***the Seventy.*** **a** *Jewish Antiq.* The Great Sanhedrin (see SANHEDRIN). **b** The seventy disciples sent out two and two by Jesus to preach and heal. — **sev'en·ti·eth** (-tĭ·ĕth; -ĭth), *n. & adj.*

sev'en·ty-five', *n.* *Mil.* A 75 mm. gun, esp. the fieldpiece of that caliber used by the armies of France.

sev'en·ty·fold' (-fōld'; 2), *adj. & adv.* See -FOLD.

sev'en-up', *n.* *Cards.* A game for two, three, or four players in which seven points constitute a game.

Seven Wonders of the World. Seven remarkable objects of the ancient world, usually enumerated as: 1. The pyramids of Egypt. 2. The Pharos of Alexandria. 3. The walls and hanging gardens of Babylon. 4. The temple of Artemis (Diana) at Ephesus. 5. The statue of the Olympian Zeus (Jupiter) by Phidias. 6. The mausoleum erected by Queen Artemisia at Halicarnassus. 7. The Colossus of Rhodes.

sev'er (sĕv'ẽr), *v. t. & i.* [OF. *sevrer* to separate, fr. L. *separare.*] **1.** To separate, as one from another, physically or mentally; divide; part; sunder; disunite; dissociate; specif., to part by violence, as by cutting, rending, etc. **2.** To cut or break open or apart; disjoin; as, to *sever* an arm. — **Syn.** See SEPARATE.

sev'er·a·ble (-ȧ·b'l), *adj.* Capable of being severed; specif., *Law*, capable of being divided into legally independent rights or obligations; esp. of a contract of which the part one party is to perform consists of distinct items.

sev'er·al (sĕv'ẽr·ăl), *adj.* [AF., fr. ML. *separalis*, fr. L. *separ* separate, different, fr. *separare.*] **1.** Individual; single; distinct. **2.** Respective; peculiar; as, their *several* roads. **3.** Diverse; different; as, two *several* items. **4.** Consisting of an indefinite number more than two, but not very many; divers; sundry. — **sev'er·al·ly**, *adv.*

sev'er·al·ty (-tĭ), *n.* **1.** A holding by individual right. **2.** Separate character or state. — ***in severalty.*** *Law.* In or of one's own right; without a joint interest in any other person; as, an estate held *in severalty.*

sev'er·ance (sĕv'ẽr·ăns), *n.* [AF., fr. OF. *sevrance.*] Act of severing, or state of being severed; partition.

se·vere' (sē·vẽr'), *adj.* [F. *sévère*, fr. L. *severus.*] **1.** Serious in feeling or manner; sedate; grave; austere. **2. a** Very strict in discipline; harsh; rigorous. **b** Unsparing in exaction, punishment, or censure; as, a *severe* judge or reprimand. **3. a** Rigidly methodical or adherent to rule or principle; accurate; exact; as, *severe* reasoning. **b** Of style, not employing unnecessary ornament, etc.; austerely plain. **4.** Inflicting discomfort or pain hard to endure; sharp; afflictive; violent; extreme; as, *severe* cold. **5.** Difficult to be sustained; taxing; arduous; rigorous; as, a *severe* test. — **se·vere'ly**, *adv.* — **se·vere'ness**, *n.*

Syn. **Severe, stern, austere, ascetic** mean given to or showing discipline or restraint. **Severe** refers not only to persons but to things for which persons are responsible, or by which they are afflicted, and suggests no laxity or indulgence but an uncompromising quality; **stern** stresses inflexibility and inexorability of temper or character; **austere** stresses absence of warmth, color, animation, etc., and a dispassionate or starkly simple quality; **ascetic** stresses self-denial, abstention from that which is merely pleasurable, and, in modern use, the courting of that which is painful or disagreeable.

se·ver'i·ty (sē·vĕr'ĭ·tĭ), *n.; pl.* -TIES (-tĭz). Quality or state of being severe; specif.: **a** Gravity or austerity; seriousness. **b** Extreme strictness; harshness. **c** Quality or power of distressing or paining. **d** Cruel treatment; sharpness of punishment. **e** Exactness. **f** Plainness or chasteness of style, as in art.

Sè'vres ware, *or* **Sè'vres** (sâ'vr'), *n.* A costly porcelain manufactured at Sèvres, France.

sew (sō), *v. t.;* SEWED (sōd); SEWED, SEWN (sōn); SEW'ING. [AS. *siwan, seowian.*] **1.** To unite or fasten by stitches made with thread and needle. **2.** To affect or bring by sewing; — often with *up;* specif., to close or enclose by sewing. — *v. i.* To practice sewing, esp. as an occupation. — **sew'a·ble**, *adj.*

sew'age (sū'ĭj), *n.* The contents of a sewer or drain; refuse liquids or matter carried off by sewers.

se'wan (sē'wȧn), *n.* [D. *sewan, zeawant*, of Algonquian origin.] Unstrung shell beads used as money among the Algonquian Indians of New England. Cf. WAMPUM.

sew'er (sō'ẽr), *n.* One who or that which sews, or stitches.

sew'er (sū'ẽr), *n.* [AF. *asseour*, fr. OF. *asseoir* to seat, set.] In medieval Europe, a household officer of rank, in charge of serving the dishes at table.

sew'er (sū'ẽr), *n.* [OF. *sewiere, seuwiere*, a sluice or channel for draining a pond, ult. fr. L. *ex* out + a derivative of *aqua* water.] An artificial, usually subterranean, conduit to carry off water and certain waste matter.

sew'er·age (sū'ẽr·ĭj), *n.* **1.** Removal of sewage and surface water by sewers. **2.** The system of sewers in a city, town, etc. **3.** = SEWAGE.

sew'ing (sō'ĭng), *n.* **1.** Act or occupation of one who sews. **2.** Material that has been, or is to be, sewed.

sewing machine. A machine for sewing or stitching.

sewing silk. Hard twisted silk thread used in sewing.

sewn (sōn), *past part.* of SEW.

sex (sĕks), *n.* [F. *sexe*, fr. L. *sexus.*] **1.** One of the two divisions of organisms formed on the distinction of male and female; males or females collectively. **2.** The character of being male or female, or of pertaining to the distinctive function of the male or female in reproduction.

sex- (sĕks-). [L. *sex.*] A combining form meaning *six.*

sex'a·ge·nar'i·an (sĕk'sȧ·jē·nâr'ĭ·ăn; 6), *adj.* Sixty years of age; of or pertaining to a sexagenarian. — *n.* A person of from sixty to sixty-nine years old.

sex·ag'e·nar'y (sĕks·ăj'ē·nĕr'ĭ *or, esp. Brit.*, -nẽr·ĭ), *adj.* [L. *sexagenarius*, fr. *sexageni* sixty each.] **1.** Pertaining to or designating the number sixty; proceeding by sixties. **2.** Sexagenarian. — *n.; pl.* -IES (-ĭz). A sexagenarian.

sexagenary cycle. A period of 60 years (embracing the smaller cycles of 60 days) employed by the Chinese in reckoning time. See CHINESE CALENDAR.

Sex'a·ges'i·ma (sĕk'sȧ·jĕs'ĭ·mȧ), *n.* More fully, **Sexagesima Sunday.** [L.] *Eccl.* The second Sunday before Lent.

sex'a·ges'i·mal (-măl), *adj.* [L. *sexagesimus* sixtieth.] Pertaining to, or founded on, the number sixty.

sex appeal. Quality, esp. personal charm, which serves to draw together individuals of opposite sexes.

sex·cen'te·nar'y (sĕks·sĕn'tē·nĕr'ĭ; -sĕn·tĕn'ȧ·rĭ; *see* CENTENARY), *adj.* Of or pert. to six hundred, esp. six hundred years. — *n.* A sexcentenary division, period, etc.

sex chromosome. *Biol.* A chromosome in certain plants and animals supposed to determine sex. The presence of two ***X chromosomes***, one each from the male and female in the fertilized egg, causes a female to be developed; the presence of a ***Y chromosome*** (both an X chromosome and a Y chromosome are produced by the male) causes a male to be developed.

sex'de·cil'lion (sĕks'dē·sĭl'yŭn), *n.* See NUMERATION, *Table.*

sex·en'ni·al (sĕks·ĕn'ĭ·ăl), *adj.* [L. *sexennium* a period of six years, *sexennis* of six years, fr. *sex* six + *annus* a year.] Lasting six years, or happening once in six years. — *n.* A sexennial event. — **sex·en'ni·al·ly**, *adv.*

sex hormone. *Biochem.* Any hormone having an effect, usually stimulatory, on the growth or function of the reproductive organs or on the development of secondary sex characters; esp., one produced in the ovaries or testes.

sex hygiene. That division of hygiene which deals with sex and sexual conduct as bearing on the health of the individual and the community.

sex'i- (sĕk'sĭ-). = SEX-, as in **sex'i·va'lent.**

sex'less, *adj.* Without sex; neuter. — **sex'less·ness**, *n.*

sex'-linked' (sĕks'lĭngkt'), *adj.* *Biol.* Pertaining to or designating any factor located in the sex chromosomes of either sex, or any character dependent on them.

sex·ol'o·gy (sĕks·ŏl'ō·jĭ), *n.* The branch of science which deals with matters pertaining to sex. — **sex·ol'o·gist** (-jĭst), *n.*

sex·par'tite (sĕks·pär'tīt), *adj.* [*sex-* + *partite.*] Divided into six parts; made up of six parts.

sext (sĕkst), *n.* [L. *sexta*, fem. of *sextus* sixth, ordinal of *sex* six.] [*often cap.*] *Eccl.* One of the canonical hours, being the sixth hour or 12 M.; hence, an office recited at this time, or now often somewhat earlier. See CANONICAL HOUR.

Sex'tans (sĕks'tănz), *n.; gen.* SEXTANTIS (sĕks·tăn'tĭs). [L.] *Astron.* A constellation on the equator south of Leo.

sex′tant (sĕks′tănt), *n.* [L. *sextans, -antis,* sixth part, fr. *sextus* sixth.] An instrument for measuring angular distances, used, esp. at sea, to observe altitudes so as to ascertain latitude and longitude.

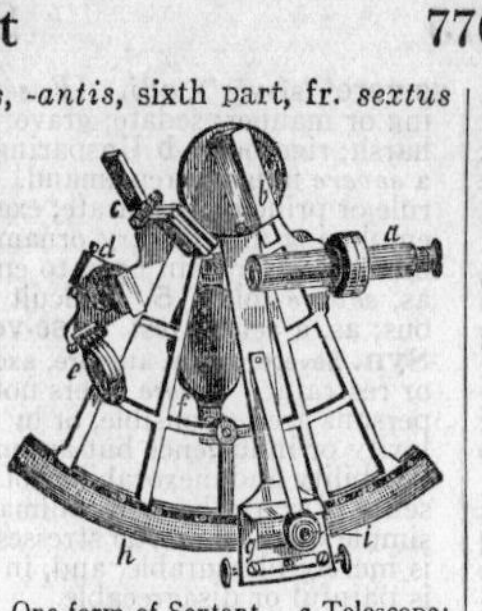

One form of Sextant. *a* Telescope; *b* Index Mirror on upper end of Alidade; *c* Back Shades or Screens of colored glass; *d* Horizon Glass; *e* Fore Shades or Screens of colored glass; *f* Handle; *g* Lower part of Alidade with Vernier; *h* Graduated Arc or Limb; *i* Microscope.

sex·tet′, sex·tette′ (sĕks·tĕt′), *n.* [L. *sextus* sixth + E. *-et.*] **1.** *Music.* A composition in six voice parts, or for six instruments; also, the six performers of such a piece. **2.** Any group or set of six persons or things.

sex′tile (sĕks′tĭl; 56), *adj.* [L. *sextilis* sixth (month), of a sixth (part).] *Astrol.* Measured by sixty degrees; fixed or indicated by a distance of sixty degrees. — *n. Astrol.* The aspect or position of two heavenly bodies when distant from each other sixty degrees.

sex·til′lion (sĕks·tĭl′yŭn), *n.* [F., fr. L. *sextus* sixth, after *million.*] See NUMERATION, *Table.* — **sex·til′lion,** *adj.* — **sex·til′lionth** (-yŭnth), *n.* & *adj.*

sex′to·dec′i·mo (sĕks′tō·dĕs′ĭ·mō), *adj.* [L., abl. of *sextusdecimus* the sixteenth.] Having sixteen leaves to a sheet, as a book. — *n.; pl.* -MOS (-mōz). A size of a book, or of its pages, measuring about $4\frac{1}{2} \times 6\frac{3}{4}$ inches, as a maximum; — usually written 16mo, or 16°, and called also *sixteenmo.*

sex′ton (sĕks′tŭn), *n.* [OF. *secrestein,* fr. ML. *sacristanus.* See SACRISTAN.] An underofficer in a church, now, usually, one who takes care of the church property, rings the bell for services, and in some cases digs graves.

sex′tu·ple (sĕks′tū·p'l; sĕks·tū′p'l), *adj.* [From L. *sex* six, after *quadruple.*] **1.** Consisting of six; sixfold. **2.** *Music.* Having six beats to the measure; as, *sextuple* time, rhythm, measure. — *v. t.* & *i.; -*PLED (-p'ld); -PLING (-plĭng). To multiply sixfold.

sex′tu·plet (sĕks′tū·plĕt; -plĭt; sĕks·tū′plĭt), *n.* [From *sextuple,* after *triplet.*] **1.** A group or set of six of a kind. **2.** One of six offspring produced at one birth.

sex′u·al (sĕk′shŏŏ·ăl; *the more formal* sĕks′ū·ăl *is preferred by many*), *adj.* [LL. *sexualis,* fr. *sexus* sex.] **1.** Pert. to or associated with sex or the sexes. **2.** *Biol.* Having sex; — opposed to *asexual.* — **sex′u·al·ly,** *adv.*

sexual generation. See ALTERNATION OF GENERATIONS.

sex′u·al′i·ty (-ăl′ĭ·tĭ), *n.* **1.** Quality or state of being sexual; possession or exercise of sexual functions, appetites, etc. **2.** Undue preoccupation with what is sexual. **3.** The constitution and life of the individual as related to sex.

sfer′ics (sfĕr′ĭks), *n. sing.* & *pl.* [From var. spelling atmo*sferics.*] *U.S.Army.* An electronic detector of storms using a directional antenna and cathode-ray tube for plotting electrical discharges from distances up to 3000 miles.

‖**sfor·zan′do** (sfôr·tsän′dō), ‖**sfor·za′to** (-tsä′tō), *adj.* [It. *sforzando,* pres. part., and *sforzato,* past part., of *sforzare* to force.] Accented; — a musical direction. Abbr. *sf, sfz* Symbol, >

Sha·ban′ (shȧ·bän′), *n.* [Ar. *sha'bān.*] See MOHAMMEDAN CALENDAR.

shab′by (shăb′ĭ), *adj.;* SHAB′BI·ER (-ĭ·ẽr); SHAB′BI·EST. [From AS. *scæb, sceabb,* scab.] **1.** Threadbare and faded from wear; appearing worn out. **2.** Clothed with worn or seedy garments. **3.** Mean; despicable; as, *shabby* treatment. — **shab′bi·ly,** *adv.* — **shab′bi·ness,** *n.*

shab′by-gen·teel′, *adj.* Maintaining a genteel though shabby appearance. — **shab′by-gen·til′i·ty,** *n.*

Sha·bu′oth (shä·vōō′ōth; shȧ·vōō′ōs), *n. pl.* See JEWISH HOLIDAYS.

shack (shăk), *n.* *Colloq., U. S.* & *Canada.* A hut; shanty.

shack, *v. t.* *Colloq., U. S.* To chase; to retrieve, as a ball.

shack′le (shăk′'l), *n.* *Usually pl.* [AS. *scacul, sceacul.*] **1.** Something that confines the legs or arms; a manacle; fetter. **2.** That which prevents free action, as if by fetters. **3.** Any of various devices for making something fast, as a U-shaped piece with a pin through the ends; a clevis. — *v. t.;* SHACK′LED (-'ld); SHACK′LING (-lĭng). **1.** To confine the limbs of, so as to prevent free motion; to fetter; chain. **2.** To hinder; impede; cumber. **3.** To secure with a shackle. — **Syn.** See HAMPER. — **shack′ler** (-lẽr), *n.*

shad (shăd), *n.;* see PLURAL, *Note,* 6. [AS. *sceadd.*] Any of several herringlike fishes (genus *Alosa*) differing from the typical herrings in having the body relatively deep. The common shad (*A. sapidissima*) occurs along the Atlantic coast of North America and ascends rivers in early spring to spawn. It is a valuable American food fish.

shad′ber′ry (-bĕr′ĭ; -bẽr·ĭ), *n.* The fruit of the shadbush; also, the plant.

shad′-blow′ (-blō′), *n.* The shadbush.

shad′bush′ (-bŏŏsh′), *n.* Any of a genus (*Amelanchier*) of American white-flowered shrubs or small trees, with small edible berrylike pomes ripening in June or July.

shad′dock (shăd′ŭk), *n.* [After a Captain *Shaddock,* who brought the seed from the East Indies to Barbados in 1696.] **a** A pear-shaped citrus fruit (*Citrus maxima*) resembling the grapefruit but having coarse dry flesh of poor quality. **b** The tree which bears this fruit.

shade (shād), *n.* [AS. *sceadu, scead.*] **1.** Comparative obscurity owing to interception of the rays of light; darkness. **2.** A spot not exposed to sunlight; hence, a secluded retreat. **3.** Relative obscurity or retirement. **4. a** A color which, with respect to brilliance only, resembles black more closely than median gray resembles black; — contrasted with *tint.* **b** Degree of brilliance or luminosity of a color or colors; as, differing in *shade.* **5.** A minute variation, as of thought, belief, expression, etc.; nuance; as, *shades* of meaning in synonyms. **6. a** *Archaic.* A shadow. **b** *pl.* The shadows which gather as darkness comes on. **7. a** *pl.* Phantoms. *Shak.* **b** Spirit; ghost. **8.** That which intercepts, or shelters from, light or the rays of the sun; screen, as for a window. **9.** *Painting, Drawing, etc.* Representation of a shaded surface by darker pigment, closely repeated lines, or the like. — **Syn.** See COLOR. — ***the shades.*** The nether world; Hades, abode of disembodied spirits. — *v. t.* **1.** To screen by intercepting radiated light or heat. **2.** To hide partly by or as by a shadow. **3.** To darken; obscure; dim. **4.** To mark with gradations of light or color. **5.** To change by gradual transition or qualification. **6.** *Com.* To lessen slightly, as the price of anything. **7.** *Painting, etc.* **a** To represent the effect of shade or shadow on (an object). **b** To add shading to (a drawing or painting). — *v. i.* To undergo or exhibit minute difference or variation, as of color, value, meaning, etc. — **shade′less,** *adj.*

shad′ing (shād′ĭng), *n.* The color, lines, etc., by which darkness or shadow is represented in a drawing or painting.

sha·doof′ (shä·dōōf′), *n.* [Ar. *shādūf.*] A counterpoised sweep used in Egypt for raising water.

shad′ow (shăd′ō), *n.* [ME. *shadowe, schadewe,* fr. an inflexional form of AS. *sceadu* shade.] **1.** Shade within defined limits; obscurity within a space from which rays from a source of light are cut off by an interposed body. Also, the image made by such an obscured space on a surface that cuts across it; as, the *shadow* of a man. **2.** Protecting cover; shelter. **3.** *Obs.* A shaded place; seclusion. **4.** A small degree or portion; a trace. **5.** *pl.* Darkness; as, night's *shadows;* figuratively, an influence casting gloom, etc.; as, hate is a *shadow.* **6.** A reflected image, as in a mirror. **7.** An imaginary vision. **8.** A spiritual apparition; specter. **9.** An indistinct image of some person or thing; hence, a type or symbol. **10.** Vestige; remnant. **11.** An inseparable companion. **12.** One who shadows as a spy or detective. **13.** *Painting, etc.* A shaded or darker portion of a picture. — *adj.* Having form without substance; specif., *Brit.,* formulated or constructed in outline, so as to be capable of quick completion when needed; as, a *shadow* war cabinet; a *shadow* factory. — *v. t.* **1.** To throw a shadow upon. **2.** *Archaic.* **a** To shelter from the sun. **b** To protect; shelter. **3.** To cloud; darken. **4.** To represent faintly, mystically, etc. **5.** To attend or follow and watch closely, esp. secretly. **6.** *Painting, Drawing, etc.* To shade. — **shad′ow·er** (-ō·ẽr), *n.* — **shad′ow·less,** *adj.*

shad′ow·box′ (shăd′ō·bŏks′), *v. t.* To box with an imaginary opponent, esp. as a form of training. — **shad′ow·box′ing,** *n.*

shad′ow·graph (shăd′ō·gråf; 9), *n.* **1.** Also **shadow play.** A drama exhibited by throwing the shadows of invisible puppets, sometimes of living actors, on a screen. **2.** An image or picture made on a surface by the shadow of some object; specif., a skiagraph.

shad′ow·y (shăd′ō·ĭ), *adj.* **1.** Of the nature of a shadow, esp. as being impalpable or transitory; unsubstantial; unreal. **2.** Full of, or causing, shade or shadow. **3.** *Obs.* Faintly representative; hence, dimly embodying; symbolic. **4.** Dim as a shadow; vague; as, the *shadowy* past.

shad′y (shād′ĭ), *adj.;* SHAD′I·ER (-ĭ·ẽr); SHAD′I·EST. **1.** Abounding in or causing shade. **2.** Sheltered from the sun's rays. **3.** *Colloq.* Of or pertaining to shade or darkness; hence, better kept in darkness; disreputable; as, a *shady* business. — **shad′i·ly,** *adv.* — **shad′i·ness,** *n.*

shaft (shåft; 9), *n.* [AS. *sceaft.*] **1.** The long handle of a spear or the like; hence, a spear; lance. **2.** The stele of an arrow; an arrow, esp. for the longbow. See ARROW, *Illust.* **3.** A pole; specif.: **a** A flagstaff. **b** The pole, or tongue, of a vehicle; also, a thill. **4.** Anything regarded as a shaft to be thrown or darted; a missile; as, *shafts* of light, of ridicule. **5.** A long slender part, esp. when cylindrical; as: **a** The stem of a tree. **b** The part of a candlestick supporting its branches. *Ex.* xxv. 31. **c** The handle or helve of certain tools, etc., as of a hammer, whip, golf club, etc. **d** A column, obelisk, or the like. **6.** *Arch.* **a** The cylindrical pillar of a column, between the capital and the base. See BASE, IONIC, ORDER, *Illusts.* **b** A vertical opening through the floors of a building; as, an elevator *shaft.* **7.** *Mach.* A bar, now usually of steel, used to support rotating pieces or to transmit power; as, a propeller *shaft.* **8.** *Mining.* A vertical or inclined opening made for finding or mining ore, raising water, etc. **9.** *Zool.* The stem of a feather. See FEATHER, *Illust.*

shaft′ing (shåf′tĭng), *n.* Shafts or material for shafts.

shag (shăg), *n.* [AS. *sceacga* a bush of hair.] **1.** Coarse, matted wool, hair, etc. **2.** Formerly, a worsted or silk cloth with a velvet nap. **3.** Long, coarse nap of cloth; also, pile. **4.** A tangled mass. **5.** A strong, coarse tobacco cut into fine shreds. — *v. t.;* SHAGGED (shăgd); SHAG′GING. To make hairy or shaggy; hence, to make rough.

shag, *v. t.* *Colloq., U. S.* To chase; to retrieve, as a ball. — *v. i.* To dance the shag. — *n.* A dance step consisting of a hopping movement on one foot then on the other followed by a quick descent on each in turn.

shag′bark′ (-bärk′), *n.* A hickory (*Carya ovata*), the outer shaggy bark of which peels off in long strips; also, its wood. It yields the best of the commercial hickory nuts.

shag′gy (shăg′ĭ), *adj.;* SHAG′GI·ER (-ĭ·ẽr); SHAG′GI·EST. **1.** Rough with or as if with long hair or wool. **2. a** Unkempt; — of persons. **b** Unpolished; — of manners. **3.** Having a rough nap or surface. — **shag′gi·ness,** *n.*

shag′gy-mane′, *n., or* **shaggy-mane mushroom.** A common edible mushroom (*Coprinus comatus*) with elongated shaggy white pileus and white spores; — called also **shaggy cap.** See FUNGUS, *Illust.*

sha·green′ (shȧ·grēn′), *n.* [F. *chagrin,* fr. Turk. *ṣāghrī.*] **1.** A variety of untanned leather prepared in Russia and the East, covered with small round granulations. **2.** The rough skin of certain sharks and rays when covered with small close-set tubercles, suggesting shagreen leather.

shah (shä), *n.* [Per. *shāh.*] The title of the ruler in certain Eastern countries, esp. Persia.

Sha·hap′ti·an (shä·hăp′tĭ·ăn), *adj.* Pertaining to or designating an American Indian linguistic family formerly occupying the upper valley of the Columbia River. See NEZ PERCÉ. — **Sha·hap′ti·an,** *n.*

shai·tan′, shei·tan′ (shī·tän′), *n.* [Ar. *shaiṭān* (fr. Heb.). See SATAN.] After Mohammedan usage: **a** [*also cap.*] An evil spirit; the Devil. **b** *Colloq.* A fiend.

shak′a·ble (shāk′ȧ·b'l), **shake′a·ble,** *adj.* That may be shaken.

shake (shāk), *v. i.;* SHOOK (shŏŏk); SHAK′EN (shāk′ĕn); SHAK′ING. *Dial. past. part.* SHAKED (shākt); *past part.* SHAKED *or* SHOOK. [AS. *scacan, sceacan.*] **1. a** To be agitated with irregular vibratory motion; to tremble; quiver. **b** To totter; become unsteady. **2.** To quake under physical or mental disturbance, as cold, palsy, fear. **3.** *Music.* To make a trill or shake. — *v. t.* **1.** To cause to go, move, or the like, by or as by agitating; specif.: **a** To throw off by a jolting or vibrating motion. *Shak.* **b** To dislodge; eject; as, to *shake* fruit from a tree. **2. a** To cause to move with quick or violent vibrations; to make to tremble. **b** To set vibrating or quaking. **3.** To brandish, wave, or flourish. **4.** To cause to waver or to be infirm; as, nerves *shaken* by fear. **5.** To put in a location or condition by repeated shakes, as in mixing, etc.; as, to *shake* down hay. **6.** To clasp (a person's hand) as in greeting. **7.** *Dicing.* To rattle (the dice) before casting. **8.** *Music.* To give a tremulous tone to; to trill.

Syn. **Shake, agitate, rock, convulse** mean to move up and down or to and fro with more or less violence. **Shake**, the general word, always carries this basic implication but usually also implies a particular intent or purpose; **agitate** suggests usually a violent and somewhat prolonged tossing or stirring; **rock** suggests a swinging or swaying motion, often suggesting an upheaving; **convulse** suggests a violent pulling to or fro or a wrenching, as or as if of the body in a paroxysm.

— *n.* **1.** A shaking; hence, specif.: **a** Tremor. **b** *Slang.* A shaking off or dismissal. **c** *Slang.* A moment; as, in two *shakes.* **d** *Colloq.* An earthquake shock. **2.** Result of shaking; a quivering motion as in trembling, quaking, shivering, jerking, etc. **3.** A thing produced by shaking; as: **a** A fissure in strata or in rock. **b** In timber, a fissure or crack, usually caused by frost or wind during growth; also, fissured or cracked places or parts, collectively. Cf. WIND SHAKE. **4.** *Music.* A rapid alternation of a principal tone with another represented on the next degree of the staff above it; a trill. — ***the shakes.*** **a** Any disease accompanied by marked trembling. **b** Nervous agitation, esp. from fear.

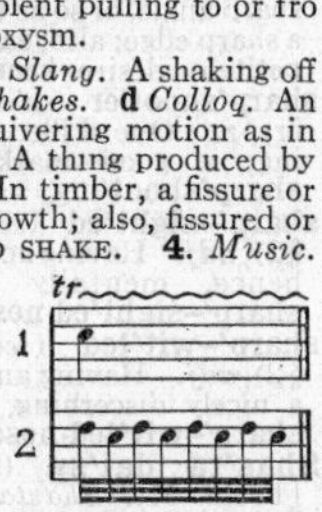

Shake, 4. 1 As written; 2 As performed.

shake′down′ (shāk′doun′), *n.* **1.** An improvised bed, as one made on the floor by spreading bedclothes over straw. **2.** *Slang.* = BREAKDOWN, 3. **3.** *Slang.* An instance or means of getting money from a person by persuasion or compulsion.

shakedown cruise. *Nav.* A cruise made by a newly commissioned ship to habituate the crew to the ship.

shak′er (shāk′ẽr), *n.* **1.** One who or that which shakes; esp., a machine or device used in shaking; as, a cocktail *shaker.* **2.** [*cap.*] One of a dwindling religious celibate sect, the ***Millennial Church;*** — popularly named from movements in dancing, originally a part of their worship. — **Shak′er·ess** (-ĕs; -ĭs), *n.* — **Shak′er·ism** (-ĭz′m), *n.*

Shake·spear′e·an (shāk·spēr′ē·ăn), *adj.* Also **Shak·sper′i·an** (-ĭ·ăn). Of, pert. to, or in the style of Shakespeare or his works. — *n.* A scholar specializing in Shakespeare or his writings.

Shake′speare–Ba′con Con′tro·ver′sy (shāk′spēr·bā′kŭn). A discussion arising from the attempt of Miss Delia Bacon (1811–59) to show that Sir Francis Bacon wrote the dramas attributed to Shakespeare.

shake′–up′, *n.* **1.** Act or process of shaking, agitating, or jarring as by physical shock. **2.** A reorganization resulting in change of personnel.

shak′ing (shāk′ĭng), *n.* **1.** Act of one that shakes. **2.** The ague; as, **shaking palsy,** a chronic progressive nervous disease, marked by muscular tremor, weakness, and a peculiar gait.

shak′o (shăk′ō), *n.; pl.* SHAKOS (-ōz). [F., fr. Hung. *csákó,* prop., peaked (cap).] A stiff military cap with high crown and plume.

Shak′ti (shŭk′tĭ), *n.* [Skr. *śakti.*] *Hinduism.* **a** [*not cap.*] Power; force. **b** The female energy or principle. **c** = DEVI.

Shak′tism (-tĭz′m), *n.* The worship of Shakti.

shak′y (shāk′ĭ), *adj.;* SHAK′I·ER (-ĭ·ẽr); SHAK′I·EST. **1.** Easily shaken; tottering; unsound. **2.** Trembling; tremulous. **3. a** Lacking stability of mind or character; unsettled. **b** *Colloq.* Questionable; unreliable. — **shak′i·ly,** *adv.* — **shak′i·ness,** *n.*

shale (shāl), *n.* [G. *schale,* husk, shell.] *Petrog.* A fissile rock formed by the consolidation of clay, mud, or silt, having a finely stratified or laminated structure and composed of minerals essentially unaltered since deposited. Bituminous shale upon distillation yields **shale oil.**

shall (shăl; *unstressed* shăl; 4), *v.; pres. sing.,* 1st & 3d persons SHALL, 2d SHALT, *pl.* SHALL; *past* SHOULD. Infinitive and participles lacking. [AS. *scal, sceal,* I am obliged (orig. a pret. indic.), pret. *scolde, sceolde,* inf. *sculan.*] As an auxiliary verb, followed by the infinitive without *to:* Am (is, are, etc.) obliged; must. Hence, am (is, are, etc.) to; — forming future-tense phrases. See also SHOULD. *Shall,* when used in the 2d or 3d person, is expressive of some authority or compulsion on the speaker's part, as in thou *shalt* not kill. Conventional rules call for *shall* in the 1st person to express mere futurity; for *will* in the 1st person with its primary force of volition or willingness, as in "Dead or alive I *will* go"; for *will* in the 2d and 3d persons to express mere futurity; for the form in the question that is expected in the answer. However, in colloquial English, frequently also in literary language, *will* is used in all persons to express mere futurity.

shal·loon′ (shă·lōōn′), *n.* [F. *chalon,* fr. *Châlons,* France, where first made.] A woolen fabric of twill weave.

shal′lop (shăl′ŭp), *n.* [F. *chaloupe.* See SLOOP.] A light open boat, used chiefly on rivers, propelled by oars or sails or by both.

shal·lot′ (shă·lŏt′), *n.* [MF. *eschalotte,* with change of suff., fr. OF. *eschaloigne.* See SCALLION.] **a** *Bot.* An onionlike plant (*Allium ascalonicum*) producing small clustered bulbs used like garlic for flavoring. **b** A small onion.

shal′low (shăl′ō), *adj.* [ME. *schalowe.*] **1.** Not deep; shoal. **2.** Not deep intellectually; superficial. — **Syn.** See SUPERFICIAL. — *n.* A shallow place in a body of water; a shoal. — *v. t. & i.* To make or become shallow. — **shal′low·ly,** *adv.* — **shal′low·ness,** *n.*

shalt (shălt), *2d pers. sing.* of SHALL.

sham (shăm), *n.* [Prob. fr. *sham,* dial. var. of SHAME.] **1.** Formerly, a trick; hoax. **2.** Anything that simulates an article of personal or household linen and is used in its place or as a decoration or covering; as, a pillow *sham.* **3.** A substitute, imitation, or counterfeit purporting to be the real thing. — **Syn.** See IMPOSTURE. — *adj.* **1.** False; feigned; as, a *sham* battle. **2.** That shams or is made or used as a sham; as, *sham* jewelry. — *v. t.;* SHAMMED (shămd); SHAM′MING. **1.** To deceive or delude with false pretenses; to trick. **2.** To assume the character or the effects of; counterfeit; feign. — *v. i.* To make false pretenses; to deceive. — **Syn.** See ASSUME.

sha′man (shä′măn; shăm′ăn), *n.* [Russ., fr. Tungusic *samān,* perh. ult. fr. Skr. *śramaṇa* beggar monk.] A priest or conjurer of shamanism; loosely, a medicine man. — *adj.* Of or pert. to a shaman or shamanism.

sha′man·ism (-ĭz′m), *n.* Primarily, the primitive religion of the Ural-Altaic peoples of northern Asia and Europe, in which the unseen world of gods, demons, and ancestral spirits is conceived to be responsive only to the shamans. Hence, any similar religion, esp. that of some American Indians. — **sha′man·ist** (-ĭst), *n. & adj.* — **sha′man·is′tic** (-ĭs′tĭk), *adj.*

Sha′mash (shä′măsh), *n.* [Assyr.-Bab.] *Semitic Relig.* The chief sun-god, a beneficent power which drives away winter and storms and brightens the earth with verdure.

sham′ble (shăm′b'l), *n.* [AS. *scamel, sceamol,* a bench, stool, fr. L. *scamellum,* dim. of *scamnum.*] **1.** A bench or stall for marketing merchandise, esp. meats. **2.** A slaughterhouse; abattoir; figuratively, a place or scene of slaughter or of destruction; — used in plural (*shambles*), but sometimes construed as singular; as, war turned the town into a *shambles.*

sham′ble (shăm′b'l), *v. i.;* -BLED (-b'ld); -BLING (-blĭng). To walk clumsily; to shuffle along. — **sham′ble,** *n.*

shame (shām), *n.* [AS. *scamu, sceamu.*] **1. a** Painful emotion excited by a consciousness of guilt, shortcoming, or impropriety. **b** Susceptibility to such feeling or emotion. **2.** Disgrace; dishonor. **3.** That which brings discredit or reproach; as, it's a *shame.* — **Syn.** See DISGRACE. — *v. t.* **1.** To make ashamed; to excite in (a person) a consciousness of guilt. **2.** To cover with reproach or ignominy; to put to shame; to disgrace. **3.** To bring or drive (a person) by shame.

shame′faced′ (-fāst′), *adj.* [For *shamefast,* fr. AS. *scamfæst.* See SHAME, *n.;* FAST firm.] **1.** Modest; also, bashful. **2.** Ashamed; abashed. — **shame·fac′ed·ly** (shām·fās′ĕd·lĭ; -ĭd·lĭ; shām′fāst′lĭ), *adv.* — **shame·fac′ed·ness,** *n.*

shame′ful (shām′fōōl; -f'l), *adj.* **1.** Bringing shame or disgrace; disgraceful. **2.** Exciting the feeling of shame; indecent; scandalous. — **shame′ful·ly,** *adv.* — **shame′ful·ness,** *n.*

shame′less, *adj.* **1.** Destitute of shame; wanting modesty; brazen. **2.** Indicating want of sensibility to shame or disgrace; impudent; brazen; barefaced. — **Ant.** Decent, chaste, virtuous. — **shame′less·ly,** *adv.* — **shame′less·ness,** *n.*

sham′mer (shăm′ẽr), *n.* One who shams; impostor.

sham′my (shăm′ĭ), *n.* [F. *chamois* a chamois, shammy leather.] **1.** *Zool.* The chamois. **2.** = CHAMOIS, *n.,* 2.

sham′ois, sha·moy′ (*pron., see* CHAMOIS). Vars. of CHAMOIS.

sham·poo′ (shăm·pōō′), *v. t.;* SHAM·POOED′ (-pōōd′); SHAM·POO′ING. [Hind. *cāpo,* imper. of *cāpnā* to shampoo.] **1.** To massage. **2.** To cleanse and treat (the hair and scalp), usually with soap and water; to give such a cleansing and treatment to (a person). — *n.* **1.** Act or process or fact of shampooing. **2.** A preparation to be used in shampooing. — **sham·poo′er** (-ẽr), *n.*

sham′rock (shăm′rŏk), *n.* [Ir. *seamrōg,* dim. of *seamar* trefoil, clover, honeysuckle.] A trifoliolate plant used as a floral emblem by the Irish. The original shamrock is variously considered to have been a hop clover (*Trifolium dubium*), regarded by many as the true shamrock, the wood sorrel *Oxalis acetosella,* the white clover, or the black medic. See CLOVER; 1st MEDIC; WOOD SORREL.

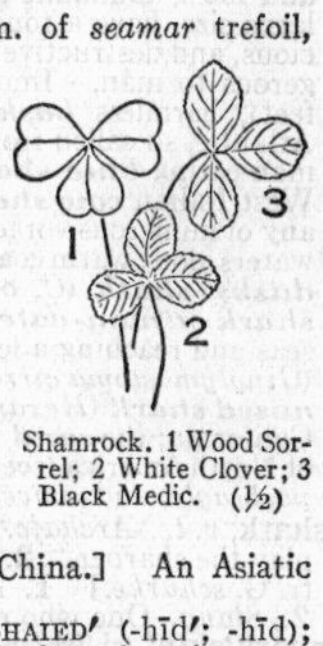

Shamrock. 1 Wood Sorrel; 2 White Clover; 3 Black Medic. (½)

Shan (shăn; shän), *n.* A member of a group of Mongoloid tribes of southeastern Asia; also, their language, a branch of the Thai of the Indo-Chinese family. See LANGUAGE, *Table.*

shan′dry·dan (shăn′drĭ·dăn), *n.* *Dial. & Slang.* An old-fashioned chaise or gig; a rickety vehicle.

shan′dy·gaff (shăn′dĭ·găf), *n.* A beverage made by mixing beer and ginger beer or ginger ale.

Shang′hai (shăng′hī), *n.* [From *Shanghai,* China.] An Asiatic breed of domestic fowls.

shang·hai′ (shăng·hī′; shăng′hī), *v. t.;* SHANG·HAIED′ (-hīd′; -hīd); SHANG·HAI′ING. [From *Shanghai,* China.] To drug, intoxicate, or render insensible and ship as a sailor; hence, to bring by deceit and coercion.

Shan′gri–La′ (shăng′grē·lä′), *n.* [Fanciful name using Tibetan *La* mountain pass.] A nonexistent idyllic land depicted as a utopia in James Hilton's novel *Lost Horizon* (1933).

shank (shăngk), *n.* [AS. *sceanca.*] **1. a** The lower part of the leg; in man, the part between the knee and the ankle; in various animals, the part apparently corresponding thereto. **b** Specif., in dressed beef, a cut from the upper part of the foreleg. See BEEF, *Illust.* Cf. SHIN. **2.** The entire leg; as, to rest one's weary *shanks.* **3.** Hence: **a** That part of an instrument, tool, or other thing, which connects the acting part with a handle or other part, as the straight part of a fishhook, the middle part of an anchor (see ANCHOR, *Illust.*), the loop forming an eye to a button, etc. **b** *Colloq.* The final part; as, the *shank* of the evening. **4.** *Shoe Mfg.* The narrow part of the sole beneath the instep; also, the metal or fiber piece that gives it form. See SHOE, *Illust.* **5.** *Type Founding.* The body of a type. See TYPE, *Illust.* — *v. i.* **1.** To decay or fall off, as a leaf, flower, or capsule, on account of disease affecting the supporting footstalk. **2.** *Chiefly Scot.* To travel on foot; — sometimes with *it.*

shan′ny (shăn′ĭ), *n.* A European blenny (*Blennius pholis*), olive green with irregular dark spots.

shan't (shänt; shȧnt; 9). Colloquial contraction of *shall not.*

shant′ey, shant′y (shăn′tĭ). Vars. of CHANTEY.

Shan·tung′ (shăn·tŭng′), *n.* [From *Shantung* prov., China.] A variety of pongee with a rough surface.

shan′ty (shăn′tĭ), *n.; pl.* -TIES (-tĭz). [Can. F. *chantier.*] A small, mean dwelling; a hut.

shape (shāp), *n.* [AS. *sceap* in *gesceap* creation, creature, fr. the root of *scieppan, sceppan,* to shape, effect.] **1.** Spatial form; as, the *shape* of a ball, jellyfish. **2.** A characteristic visible form; hence, assumed appearance; guise. **3.** Bodily contour, esp. of the trunk; specif., figure. **4.** A phantom; apparition. **5.** Form of embodiment, as in words; form, as of thought; esp., relatively definite form; as, beginning to take *shape.* **6.** Condition or state of being; as, he is in bad *shape.* **7.** A thing having a particular form; as, a hatter's *shape.* **8.** *Cookery.* A mold for shaping jelly, etc. — **Syn.** See FORM.

— *v. t.;* SHAPED (shāpt); SHAPED, *Archaic* SHAP′EN (shāp′ĕn); SHAP′ING. [ME. *shapen, schapen,* fr. the n. *schap* shape. See SHAPE, *n.*] **1.** To form or create; esp., to mold into a particular form; to fashion. **2.** *Obs.* To ordain; decree. **3.** To design; plan; arrange. **4.** To embody in definite form, as in words. **5.** To adapt, as to purpose; to adjust. **6.** To direct the course of, as conduct, life. — **Syn.** See MAKE. — *v. i.* **1.** To happen; befall. **2.** To suit; conform. **3.** *Colloq.* To develop to definite form in character, proficiency, etc., as an athletic team; show promise. — **shap′er** (shāp′ẽr), *n.*

shape′less, *adj.* **1.** Destitute of shape or regular form. **2.** Wanting symmetry; misshapen; — opposed to *shapely.* — **shape′less·ly,** *adv.* — **shape′less·ness,** *n.*

shape′ly (shāp′lĭ), *adj.;* -LI·ER (-lĭ·ẽr); -LI·EST. Well-formed; symmetrical. — **shape′li·ness,** *n.*

shard (shärd), *n.* [AS. *sceard,* orig. a past part. from the root of *sceran* to shear, cut.] **1.** A fragment of a brittle substance, as of an earthen vessel. Also, a shell, scale, or the like. **2.** Hence, a fragment.

shard (shärd), *n.* The hard wing cover, or elytrum, of a beetle.

share (shâr), *n.* [AS. *scear.*] *Agric. Mach.* A plowshare. See PLOW, *Illust.*

share, *n.* [AS. *scearu, scaru*, fr. *sceran* to shear, cut.] **1.** *Obs.* A portion; part. **2.** A portion pertaining to an individual; often, one's full or fair portion; as, his *share* of luck. **3.** Specif.: **a** The part allotted to one of a number owning together any property or interest. **b** Any of a certain number of equal portions into which any property is divided; as, a ship owned in 64 *shares.* Specif., any of the equal interests or rights into which the entire capital stock of a corporation is divided, the ownership of shares being regularly evidenced by certificates. Cf. STOCK, *n.*, 18 **c**.

☞ *Stock* is usually called *shares* in England.

— *v. t.* **1.** To divide and distribute in portions; to apportion; divide. **2.** To partake of, use, experience, or enjoy, with others. — *v. i.* To have a share; participate. — **shar′er** (shâr′ẽr), *n.*

Syn. **Share, participate, partake** mean to have, get, use, etc., in common with another or others. **Share** implies either the granting or receiving of the privilege to use, possess, enjoy, etc.; **participate**, a taking part, as in a discussion, an undertaking, or the like; **partake**, a taking one's part or share of a meal, a pleasure, a burden, or the like.

share′crop′per (shâr′krŏp′ẽr), *n.* *Southern U. S.* A tenant farmer who, provided with credit for seed, tools, living quarters, and for food at the landlord's commissary, works the land and receives a certain share of the value of the crop, minus charges, as for drainage, fencing, and credit advances. — **share′crop′**, *v. i.*

share′hold′er (shâr′hōl′dẽr), *n.* One who holds or owns a share or shares in a joint fund or property; esp., a holder of shares in a corporation.

shark (shärk), *n.* [Prob. named from its rapacity and fr. SHARK a crafty person.] Any of numerous elasmobranch fishes, mostly marine and most abundant in warm seas. They are usually of medium or large size, have a tough, usually dull-gray skin, are very active, voracious, and destructive of other fishes, and the larger ones are often dangerous to man. Important kinds include: the very large (up to 40 feet), harmless ***basking shark*** (*Cetorhinus maximus*) of North Atlantic, so called from its habit of basking at the surface; the pelagic man-eating ***blue shark*** (*Prionace glauca*); the large European and West Indian ***cow shark*** (*Hexanchus griseus*); the ***ground shark***, any of numerous voracious sharks (genus *Carcharias*) found in shallow waters along warm coasts, as the ***cub shark*** (*C. commersonii*) and the ***dusky shark*** (*C. obscurus*) of North Atlantic; the ***man-eating shark*** or ***man-eater*** (*Carcharodon carcharias*) found in all warm seas and reaching a length of over 30 feet; the ***nurse shark*** or ***gata*** (*Ginglymostoma cirratum*) of warmer parts of Atlantic; the ***shovel-nosed shark*** (*Hexanchus corinus* and *Notorhynchus maculatus*) of California; the ***sand shark*** (genus *Odontaspis*) of the Atlantic coast of North America (see REMORA, *Illust.*), and the *dogfish, hammerhead, porbeagle*, and *shovelhead* (see these terms).

shark, *v. t.* *Archaic.* To get rapaciously or by fraud. — *v. i.* **1.** To play the sharper. **2.** To live by shifts and stratagems. — *n.* [Prob. fr. G. *schurke.*] **1.** A rapacious, crafty person; as, a mortgage *shark.* **2.** *Slang.* One who excels greatly along some line.

shark′skin′ (shärk′skĭn′), *n.* **1.** The skin of a shark or leather made from it. **2. a** A worsted suiting in a twill-like weave with a hard sleek finish. **b** A fabric with a sleek chalky appearance, made chiefly of rayon, sometimes of cotton, usually in a basket weave.

sharp (shärp), *adj.* [AS. *scearp.*] **1.** Having a very thin edge or fine point; keen. **2.** Terminating in a point or edge; not obtuse or rounded; somewhat pointed. **3.** Composed of hard, angular grains; gritty, as sand. **4.** Steep; abrupt; as, a *sharp* curve. **5.** Well-defined; distinct. **6. a** To the taste or smell, pungent; acid; sour. **b** To the hearing, piercing; shrill. **c** To the eye, instantaneously brilliant. **d** Cold; nipping; — of air, etc. **7.** Painful; distressing; as, *sharp* pain. **8.** Cutting in language or import; as, a *sharp* answer. **9.** Severe; harsh; as, a *sharp* temper. **10.** Of keen perception; acute; penetrating; as, a *sharp* eye. **11. a** Eager; keen; — of the appetite. **b** Conducted with eagerness; impetuous. **12.** Brisk; active. **13.** Very attentive; as, a *sharp* watch. **14.** *Music.* Opposed to *flat.* **a** Raised a semitone in pitch; as, C-*sharp* (C ♯), which is a half step higher than C. **b** So high as to be out of tune, or above true pitch. **c** Of a key or tonality, having a signature in sharps. **15.** *Phonet.* Voiceless; surd. Cf. FLAT, *adj.*, 17 **b**.

Syn. **Sharp, keen, acute** mean markedly edged or pointed. **Sharp**, applicable to things with an edge or point, implies a cutting or piercing quality and, often, its disagreeableness, its distinctness, or the like; **keen**, applicable esp. to things with an edge, suggests a poignant, a zestful, or a bracing quality; **acute**, applicable to an angle or end formed by lines or edges converging in a sharp point, suggests a power to penetrate and is figuratively applied to tones, the hearing, thinkers, and the like.

— *v. t.* *Music.* To raise in pitch, as a musical tone; esp., to raise by a half step. — *v. i.* *Music.* To sing or play above the true pitch.

— *adv.* [See FLAT, *adj.*, 13.] In a sharp manner; esp.: **a** To a point or edge; piercingly. **b** *Colloq.* Precisely; exactly. **c** Briskly; quickly; abruptly.

— *n.* **1.** A sharp edge or point. **2.** *Slang.* **a** An expert. **b** A sharper. **3.** A sewing needle having a very slender point; — usually *pl.* **4.** *Music.* **a** A tone or note one half step higher than a tone or note named. **b** A character (♯) on a degree of the staff, indicating a pitch a half step higher than the degree would indicate without it. A ***double sharp*** (× or ✕) indicates that a note is to be a whole step higher in pitch than it would be without any sharp.

— **sharp′ly**, *adv.* — **sharp′ness**, *n.*

sharp′en (shär′pĕn), *v. t.* & *i.* To make or become sharp or sharper.

sharp′en·er (-ẽr), *n.* One who or that which sharpens, esp. tools, gears, or the like; specif., in full ***pencil sharpener***, a device for sharpening the point of a lead pencil or the like by pressure against a rotating blade or cutting edges.

sharp′er (shär′pẽr), *n.* A swindler; a cheating gamester.

sharp′-eyed′ (*see Pron.*, § 2), *adj.* Keen-sighted; hence, keen in observing or penetrating.

sharp′-fanged′ (*see Pron.*, § 2), *adj.* Having sharp fangs; hence, sarcastic.

sharp′-freeze′, *v. t.* To quick-freeze, often for 8 or 10 hours, at a temperature of −30° F. to −10° F. in preparation for storage in a locker. — **sharp′-freez′er**, *n.*

sharp′ie (shär′pĭ), *n.* *Local, U. S. Naut.* A long, sharp, flat-bottomed boat, with one or two masts each carrying a triangular sail.

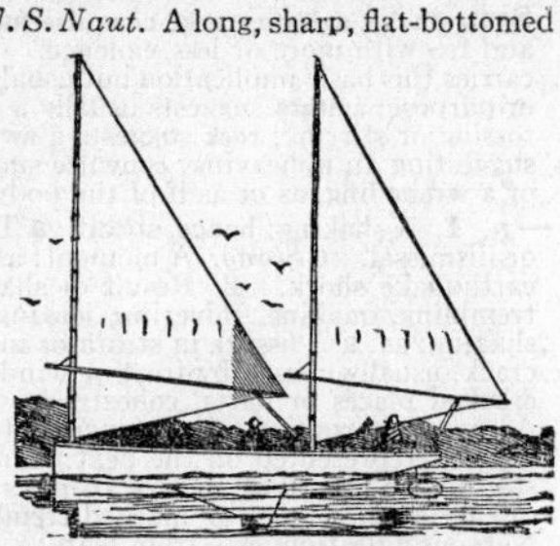

Sharpie with Centerboard down and Leg-of-Mutton Sails extended by Sprits.

sharp′-set′, *adj.* Set at a sharp angle, or so as to present a sharp edge; also, eager in appetite or desire; keen.

sharp′shoot′er (shärp′shōōt′ẽr), *n.* One skilled in shooting; a good marksman. — **sharp′shoot′ing**, *n.*

sharp′-sight′ed (*see Pron.*, § 2), *adj.* Having acute sight; hence, mentally keen. — **sharp′-sight′ed·ness**, *n.*

sharp′-wit′ted (*see Pron.*, § 2), *adj.* Having an acute, or a nicely discerning, mind. — **sharp′-wit′ted·ness**, *n.*

Shas′ta dai′sy (shăs′tȧ). [From Mt. *Shasta*, Calif.] A large-flowered garden variety of *Chrysanthemum maximum*, a perennial herb from the Pyrenees, resembling the common oxeye daisy.

Shas′tan (shăs′tăn), *adj.* & *n.* = COMANCHEAN.

shat′ter (shăt′ẽr), *v. t.* [ME. *schateren, scateren.*] **1.** *Obs.* To scatter; disperse. **2.** To break at once into pieces; to dash, burst, or part violently, into fragments. **3.** To render unsound; damage. — *v. i.* To burst or break into fragments. — *n.* A fragment of anything shattered; — used chiefly in *in, into*, or *to, shatters.*

shave (shāv), *v. t.*; SHAVED (shāvd); SHAVED or SHAV′EN (shāv′ĕn); SHAV′ING. [AS. *scafan, sceafan.*] **1.** To cut or pare off by the sliding or drawing movement of a razor; specif., to cut off or remove (hair, as the beard) close to the skin by a razor. **2.** To make bare or smooth by cutting off closely the surface or surface covering of; as, to *shave* the face. **3. a** To cut off closely. **b** To cut off thin slices from; to cut in thin slices. **4.** To skim along or near the surface of; to pass close to or touch lightly in passing. — *v. i.* To use a razor for removing the beard or hair; hence, to be hard and severe in a bargain.

— *n.* [Senses 2, 3, 4, fr. SHAVE, *v.*] **1.** [AS. *sceafa* a plane.] Any of various tools for shaving or cutting thin slices. **2.** A thin slice; a shaving. **3.** Act or operation of shaving, esp. the beard. **4.** *Colloq.* Act of passing very near to, so as almost to graze; as, a close *shave.*

shave′ling (shāv′lĭng), *n.* **1.** *Contemptuous.* A priest; — from his tonsure. **2.** Stripling; youth.

shav′er (shāv′ẽr), *n.* **1.** One who shaves. **2.** One who is sharp at bargains or shrewd in dealing, or who fleeces people. **3.** *Colloq.* & *Dial.* A chap; lad; youngster.

shave′tail′ (shāv′tāl′), *n.* **1.** An untrained mule. **2.** *Soldiers' Slang.* A recently appointed second lieutenant; — humorously so called with allusion to the young unbroken army mules.

Sha′vi·an (shā′vĭ·ăn; 58), *n.* An admirer or devotee of George Bernard Shaw, his writings, or his social theories. — **Sha′vi·an**, *adj.*

shav′ie (shāv′ĭ), *n.* *Scot.* A trick; prank; practical joke.

shav′ing (shāv′ĭng), *n.* **1.** Act of one who or that which shaves. **2.** That which is shaved off; a thin slice pared off with a knife, plane, etc.

shaw (shô), *n.* [ME. *schawe* thicket, grove, fr. AS. *scaga.*] **1.** *Archaic* & *Dial.* A thicket; small wood or grove. **2.** *Scot.* The tops of potatoes or turnips.

shawl (shôl), *n.* [Per. *shāl.*] A square or oblong outer garment made of textile or netted fabric, used, esp. by women, as a loose covering for the neck and shoulders.

shawm (shôm), *n.* [OF. *chalemie*, var. of *chalemel*, dim. fr. L. *calamus* reed, reed pipe.] *Music.* An obsolete wind instrument of the oboe class.

Shaw·nee′ (shô·nē′; 2), *n.*; *pl.* SHAWNEE, SHAWNEES (-nēz′). [Shawnee *Shawunogi* southerners, fr. *shawun* south.] An Indian of an Algonquian tribe formerly dwelling in Tennessee and South Carolina.

Shaw·wal′ (shô·wäl′), *n.* [Ar. *shawwāl.*] See MOHAMMEDAN CALENDAR.

shay (shā), *n.* [From CHAISE, mistaken as pl.] *Dial.* & *Colloq.* A chaise.

she (shē; 4), *pron.*; *nom.* SHE; *poss.* HER (hûr; 4) or HERS (hûrz); *obj.* HER; *pl. nom.* THEY (thā); *poss.* THEIR (thâr) or THEIRS (thârz); *obj.* THEM (thĕm; 4). [AS. *sēo, sīo*, fem. of the definite article, originally a demonstrative pronoun.] **1.** The woman or female being previously designated. **2.** That or any woman; as, *she* of the golden hair. — *n.* A woman or girl; a female person or animal.

she-. A combining form of *she*, denoting *a female of a* (specified) *class*, as in **she′-bear′**, **she′-mon′ster**; also, *womanly; of* or *for women.*

shea butter (shē). [Mandingo *si, se*, the shea tree, written *shea* by Mungo Park.] A solid white fat obtained from the seeds of the ***shea tree***, an African tree (*Butyrospermum parkii*). It is used as a food, illuminant, etc.

sheaf (shēf), *n.*; *pl.* SHEAVES (shēvz). [AS. *scēaf.*] **1.** A quantity of the stalks and ears of wheat, rye, or other grain, bound together; a bundle of grain or straw. **2.** Something likened to a sheaf of grain, as arrows filling a quiver. — *v. t.* To gather and bind into a sheaf.

shear (shēr), *v. t.*; SHEARED (shērd) or, *Archaic*, SHORE (shōr; 70); SHEARED or SHORN (shōrn); SHEAR′ING. [AS. *sceran, scieran, scyran.*] **1.** To cut off the hair from; to shave; as, with crown *shorn.* **2.** To cut, clip, or sever from something, esp. wool from sheep; also, to cut something from; as, to *shear* sheep. **3.** *Scot.* & *Dial.* To reap or cut with a sickle. **4.** To deprive by or as by cutting; as, *shorn* of power. **5.** To cut with shears or a similar instrument, as a bar of metal. — *v. i.* **1.** To cut through with, as with a sword; to cleave a way. **2.** To shear crops; to use a sickle in reaping. **3.** *Mech.* To become divided, as a body under the action of a shear. — *n.* **1. a** A pair of shears; — now in the plural or attributive. See SHEARS, 1. **b** One blade of a pair of shears. **2.** A shearing; — used esp. in designating the age of sheep; as, a two-*shear* ram. **3.** Act, means, or result of shearing. **4.** That which is shorn, as a shorn animal or a fleece. **5.** *Mach.* Any of various machines for shearing metal, esp. sheet metal. **6.** *Mech.* **a** Internal force tangential to the section on which it acts; shearing force. **b** An action or stress, resulting from applied forces, which causes or tends to cause two contiguous parts of a body to slide relatively to each other in a direction parallel to their plane of contact; — called also **shear′ing stress**. **c** See SHEARS, 3. — **shear′er** (-ẽr), *n.*

shears (shērz), n. pl. **1.** Any of various cutting instruments operating by the action of opposed cutting edges of metal; in effect, large powerful scissors. **2.** Something likened to a pair of shears; specif.: **a** Obs. A pair of wings. **b** A hoisting apparatus consisting of two (sometimes more) spars fastened together at their upper ends, resting on their spread heels, steadied by a guy or guys, and provided with tackle; — called also **shear** (or **sheer**) **legs. 3.** Mach. The bed piece of a machine tool on which a table or slide rest is secured; a way; as, the shears of a lathe or planer; — sometimes written **shear.**

shear′wa′ter (shēr′wô′tẽr; -wŏt′ẽr), n. [shear + water.] Any of numerous oceanic birds (chiefly of the genus Puffinus, order Procellariiformes), related to the petrels and albatrosses. In flight they usually skim close to the waves.

A form of Shears, 2 b.

sheat′fish′ (shēt′fĭsh′), n.; pl., see FISH. A large catfish (Silurus glanis) of central and eastern Europe.

sheath (shēth), n.; pl. SHEATHS (shēthz). [AS. scǣth, scēath.] **1.** A case for a sword, knife, etc.; a scabbard. **2.** Any covering resembling or likened to a sheath (sense 1), esp. one in animals and plants. **3.** Bot. The base of a leaf when sheathing a stem or branch, as in grasses; any sheathlike spathe; an ocrea, or sheathing stipule, etc. **4.** Zool. An elytrum of a beetle. — v. t. = SHEATHE.

sheath′bill′ (shēth′bĭl′), n. Any of several sea birds constituting a family (Chionididae), confined to the colder parts of the Southern Hemisphere; — so called from a horny sheath over the base of the upper mandible.

sheathe (shēth), v. t. **1.** To put into a sheath, case, or scabbard; to enclose or cover as with a sheath or case. **2.** To plunge or bury in flesh, as a sword or tusk; also, to retract or draw in (a claw). **3.** To fit or furnish with or as with a sheath. **4.** To case or cover with something which protects, as in boards, sheets of metal, etc.; as, to sheathe a ship with copper. — **sheath′er** (shēth′ẽr), n.

sheath′ing (shēth′ĭng), n. **1.** Act of one who sheathes. **2.** That which sheathes; specif., the covering of a ship's bottom and sides. **3.** Arch. The first covering of boards, or of waterproof material, on the outside wall of a frame house or on a timber roof; also, the material so used. — adj. Enclosing or investing with a sheath.

sheath knife (shēth). A knife carried in a sheath.

shea tree. See SHEA BUTTER.

sheave (shēv; shĭv), n. [Var. of shive, ME. schive.] **a** The grooved wheel or pulley of a pulley block. See BLOCK, Illust. **b** Any grooved wheel or pulley.

sheave (shēv), v. t. To gather and bind into a sheaf or sheaves.

sheaves (shēvz), n., pl. of SHEAF (shēvz; shĭvz), pl. of SHEAVE.

she-bang′ (shḗ-băng′), n. Slang. Establishment; contrivance; outfit; concern.

She-bat′ (shḗ-bät′), n. [Heb. Shĕbāt.] See JEWISH CALENDAR.

she-been′ (shḗ-bēn′), n. [Ir. sībīn, sēibīn, little mug, inferior ale.] A place where liquor is sold without a license. — v. i. To keep a shebeen. Both Chiefly Ir. & Scot.

shed (shĕd), n. [Var. of SHADE, n.] **1.** A slight structure built for shelter or storage, as a penthouse, lean-to, etc. **2.** A place of shelter, as a hut, cottage, lair, etc.

shed (shĕd), v. t.; SHED; SHED′DING. [AS. scādan, scēadan, to part, separate.] **1. a** To pour forth in drops; as, to shed tears. **b** To pour out; emit; as, to shed favors. **2.** To cause to flow or fall from a cut or wound; as, to shed the blood of a victim. **3.** To diffuse, esp. so as to impart, as light, heat, influence; as, the sun sheds light. **4.** To throw off by repelling, as rays and light; as, ducks shed water. **5.** To cast or throw off, as a natural covering of hair, feathers, shell. — v. i. **1.** To part with, or let fall, some covering, integument, growth, etc., as a skin, seeds, fruit, or leaves. — **Syn.** See DISCARD. — n. **1.** A shedding or spilling; — only in comb., as in blood shed. **2.** Colloq. That which is or has been shed, as a cocoon, the molted shell of a crab, etc.

shed′der (shĕd′ẽr), n. **1.** One who or that which sheds. **2.** A crab or lobster about to molt its shell; also, Local, U. S., a crab that has just shed its shell.

sheen (shēn), adj. [AS. scīene, scēne, scȳne.] Beautiful; bright. — v. i. To show a sheen, or luster. — n. **1.** Brightness; luster. **2.** Shining attire.

sheen′y (shēn′ĭ), adj. Lustrous with sheen; shining; radiant.

sheep (shēp), n. sing. & pl. [AS. scēp, scēap.] **1.** Any ruminant of a genus (Ovis) allied to the goats, esp. any of numerous domesticated

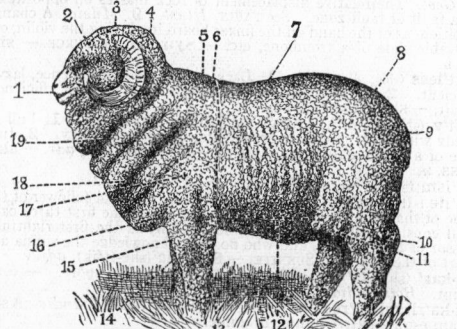

Sheep. 1 Muzzle; 2 Forehead; 3 Poll; 4 Scrag; 5 Withers; 6 Girth; 7 Loin; 8 Rump; 9 Tail; 10 Hock; 11 Stifle; 12 Underline; 13 Elbow; 14 Knee; 15 Arm; 16 Brisket; 17 Shoulder; 18 Apron; 19 Throat. Cf. LAMB, Illust.

varieties kept for their flesh (mutton), wool, and skin. Well-known breeds are the Cheviot, Corriedale, Cotswold, Dorset Horn, Hampshire Down, Leicester, Lincoln, Merino, Oxford Down, Romney, Shropshire, Southdown, and Suffolk. Cf. ARGALI, MOUFLON, MOUNTAIN

SHEEP. 2. A timid, defenseless creature; also, a bashful or silly fellow. **3.** Leather of sheepskin, as for bookbinding; sheepskin. —

sheep′herd′er (-hûr′dẽr), n.

sheep′ber′ry (-bĕr′ĭ; -bĕr·ĭ), n. A North American shrub or small tree (Viburnum lentago) having white flowers in flat cymes; also, its black edible berry.

sheep′cote′ (-kōt′; -kŏt′), n. Also **sheep′cot′** (-kŏt′), n. A sheepfold.

sheep′-dip′, n. Veter. A liquid preparation, as of tobacco, arsenic, creosote, etc., to dip sheep in to disinfect them.

sheep dog. A dog used to tend sheep; esp., a collie.

sheep′fold′ (shēp′fōld′), n. A fold or pen for sheep.

sheep′herd′er (-hûr′dẽr), n. Chiefly U. S. A herder on a sheep run. — **sheep′herd′ing,** n. & adj.

sheep′ish, adj. Like a sheep in meekness, stupidity, or timidity. — **sheep′ish·ly,** adv. — **sheep′ish·ness,** n.

sheep ked (kĕd). A degenerate blood-sucking dipterous insect (Melophagus ovinus) which conveys sheep trypanosomiasis (— loosely called sheep tick. See 1st TICK, n. 2.

sheep laurel. A North American dwarf shrub (Kalmia angustifolia), resembling the mountain laurel but with smaller red flowers. It is poisonous to young stock.

sheep′man (shēp′măn), n.; pl. -MEN (-mĕn). A man who breeds, tends, or raises sheep.

sheep's eye (shēps). A shy, longing, usually amorous, glance.

sheep′shank (shēp′shăngk′), n. **1.** Literally, the shank of a sheep; hence, something thin and slender, weak, or the like. **2.** See KNOT, Illust. (12).

sheeps′head′ (shēps′hĕd′), n. **1.** The head of a sheep, esp. as prepared for eating. **2.** A silly or stupid person; blockhead. **3.** See PLURAL, Note, 3. A sparoid food fish (Archosargus probatocephalus) of the Atlantic and Gulf coasts of the United States, having broad incisor teeth.

sheep′shear′ing (shēp′shēr′ĭng), n. **1.** Act of shearing sheep. **2.** The time, or a feast at the time, of shearing sheep. — **sheep′shear′er** (-ẽr), n.

sheep′skin′ (-skĭn′), n. **1.** The skin of a sheep, or leather prepared from it; also, parchment. **2.** Colloq. A diploma.

sheep sorrel. See 1st SORREL a.

sheep tick. = SHEEP KED.

sheep′walk′ (shēp′wôk′), n. A pasture for sheep.

sheer (shēr), adj. [ME. schere pure, bright, prob. fr. ON. skærr.] **1.** Obs. Bright; shining. **2.** Pure; undiluted; as, sheer ale. **3.** Being what it seems to be; unqualified; utter; as, sheer folly. **4.** Taken or acting in dissociation from all else; as, by sheer force. **5.** Perpendicular, or very steep, without break. **6.** Very thin or transparent; diaphanous. — **Syn.** See STEEP. — adv. **1.** Altogether; completely. **2.** Perpendicularly; steeply. — **sheer′ly,** adv. — **sheer′ness,** n.

sheer, v. i. [From SHEAR to divide.] **1.** To decline or deviate from a course. — v. t. To cause to sheer. — n. Naut. **a** The longitudinal upward curvature of the deck, gunwale, and lines of a vessel, when viewed from the side. **b** The position of a vessel riding to a single anchor and heading toward it. **c** A turn, deviation, or change in a course.

sheer legs. See SHEARS, 2 b.

sheet (shēt), n. [AS. scīete, scēte, scȳte, a sheet, piece of linen cloth.] **1.** A broad piece of cloth, usually linen or cotton; esp., one used as an article of bedding next to the body. **2.** A broad piece of paper; esp., a single piece of any of the sizes prepared for writing on or printing on; hence, a letter, a newspaper, etc.; also, in pl., the unbound pages of a book. **3.** A broad stretch or surface, as of water, ice, etc. **4.** In general, a piece of anything that is usually very thin in relation to its length and breadth; as, a sheet of glass, tin. **5.** A flat baking utensil of tinned metal, usually with a lip on the front edge for handling; as, a cooky sheet. **6.** Geol. Any body of rock, gravel, ice, etc., that is long and wide as compared with its thickness. **7.** Philately. A complete printing of stamps on a single piece of paper as it leaves the press and before it is cut into panes. — v. t. **1.** To wrap in, or cover with, a sheet; to shroud. **2.** To furnish with a sheet or sheets.

sheet, n. [AS. scēatlīne, scēata the lower corner of a sail.] **1.** Naut. Often in pl. A rope or chain which regulates the angle at which a sail is set in relation to the wind. **2.** Naut. pl. The spaces not occupied by thwarts at either end of an open boat; — called respectively **fore-sheets** (at the bow) and **stern sheets** (at the stern). — v. t. Naut. To haul upon by means of a sheet; — used only in **to sheet home,** to extend (a square sail) by hauling upon the sheets until it is set as flat as possible.

sheet anchor. [ME. scheten to shoot, AS. scēotan.] **1.** Naut. Formerly, the main anchor, carried in the waist of a ship. Cf. 5th BOWER. **2.** Anything regarded as a main support or dependence in danger.

sheet bend. Naut. A bend or hitch for temporarily fastening a rope to the bight of another rope or to an eye. See KNOT, Illust. (34).

sheet glass. Glass made in large sheets directly from the furnace or by making a cylinder and flattening it.

sheet′ing, n. Act or process of forming into, disposing in, or covering with, sheets; also, material, such as cotton or linen cloth, made into or suitable for sheets.

sheet lightning. Lightning in sheetlike form, due to reflection and diffusion by the clouds and sky.

sheet metal. Metal in the form of a sheet. Similarly, **sheet iron, sheet steel, sheet tin,** etc.

sheik, sheikh (shēk; shāk), n. [Ar. shaykh, lit., old man.] **1.** An Arab chief; — now also used as an Arabic title of respect. **2.** Slang. A man supposed to be endowed with an irresistible fascination in the eyes of romantic young women; — from The Sheik, a novel (1921) by Edith M. Hull.

sheik′dom, sheikh′dom (shēk′dŭm; shāk′-), n. [See -DOM.] The region under a sheik's rule.

shei·tan′ (shī·tän′). Var. of SHAITAN.

shek′el (shĕk′ĕl; -'l), n. [Heb. shegel, fr. shāqal to weigh.] An ancient weight and money unit of Babylonia, hence also of the Phoenicians, Hebrews, etc.; also, a coin having this weight. The ordinary Hebrew shekel for gold was probably 252⅔ grains (about $10.88); for silver, 224½ grains.

She·ki′nah (shḗ·kī′nà), n. [Heb. shĕkhīnāh the earthly presence (dwelling) of God, fr. shākhan to dwell.] Jewish Theol. The Divine Manifestation, through which God's presence is felt by man.

shel′drake′ (shĕl′drāk′), *n.*; see PLURAL, *Note*, 3. [E. dial. *sheld* variegated + *drake*.] **a** Any of various Old World ducks (genera *Tadorna* and *Casarca*), esp. the common European species (*T. tadorna*) slightly larger than the mallard. **b** Any merganser; also, locally, any of various other ducks.

shelf (shĕlf), *n.*; *pl.* SHELVES (shĕlvz). [AS. *scielfe, scylfe.*] **1. a** A thin, flat, usually long and narrow, piece fastened horizontally, as against a wall, to hold objects. **b** One of several similar pieces in a closet, bookcase, or the like. **c** The books or other contents of a shelf. **2.** Something resembling a shelf or ledge; as: **a** A sandbank or ledge of rocks; a reef or shoal. **b** A flat, projecting layer of rock. **c** *Mining & Geol.* A stratum with a shelflike surface. — ***on the shelf.*** Put aside as of no present use or value.

shelf ice. An extensive ice sheet which originates on land and continues out to sea beyond the depths at which it rests upon the sea bottom.

shell (shĕl), *n.* [AS. *scell, sciell, scyll.*] **1. a** A hard rigid covering of an animal, as a mollusk. See GASTROPOD, *Illust.* **b** The hard or tough outer covering of an egg, esp. a bird's egg. See EGG, *Illust.* **2. a** The outside part of a fruit or seed; a nutshell, pod, or husk. **b** *pl.* Cocoa shells. **3. a** Shell material or, collectively, shells, esp. of mollusks, turtles, or tortoises; tortoise shell. **b** *pl.* Unslaked limestone. **4.** Something resembling or likened to a shell (sense 1) in some way, as a frail framework; as, the *shell* of a house. **5. a** Outside covering; as, the *shell* of a ship; also, a casing without substance. **b** An impersonal attitude or manner which conceals feeling; as, to come out of one's *shell*. **6.** A shell-bearing mollusk. **7.** *Chem.* One of the concentric series of electrons in the atom, or the space occupied by such a series. **8.** *Cookery.* An edible case, as of pastry, made to receive a filling. **9.** *Firearms.* A metal or paper case which holds the charge of powder and shot or bullet used with breech-loading small arms. See CARTRIDGE, *Illust.* **10.** *Fireworks.* A spherical case containing explosive material which bursts after having been thrown high into the air. **11.** *Ordn.* A hollow projectile for cannon, containing an explosive bursting charge. **12.** *Rowing.* A light long racing boat, only wide enough to accommodate one oarsman on a seat, with a frame covered with very thin wood. — *v. t.* **1.** To take out of the shell, husk, pod, etc. **2. a** To strip or remove the shell of. **b** To separate the kernels of (an ear of Indian corn, wheat, oats, etc.) from the cob, ear, or husk. **3.** To throw shells or bombs at, upon, or into; to bombard. — *v. i.* **1.** To fall or scale off, as a shell, crust, etc. **2.** To cast the shell; to fall out of the pod or husk; as, nuts *shell* in falling. — **shell**, *adj.*

shel·lac′ (shĕ·lăk′; shĕl′ăk), *n.* Also **shel·lack′, shell′-lac′.** [*shell* + *lac*, trans. of F. *laque en écailles* lac in thin plates.] **1.** Purified lac resin, esp. in thin layers or flakes, used in insulating materials, in varnishes, sealing wax, etc. **2.** A preparation of lac dissolved in alcohol, used in filling wood, as a varnish, etc. — *v. t.*; -LACKED′ (shĕ·lăkt′; shĕl′ăkt); -LACK′ING. **1.** To coat or treat with shellac. **2.** *Slang, U.S.* To beat; hence, to defeat. — **shel·lack′er** (shĕ·lăk′ẽr; shĕl′ăk·ẽr), *n.*

shell′back′ (shĕl′băk′), *n.* *Slang.* An old sailor; an old salt.

shell′bark′ (shĕl′bärk′), *n.* The shagbark.

shell bean. Any variety of bean grown esp. for the seeds, which are used as a vegetable when mature but undried.

shell′fire′ (shĕl′fīr′), *n.* *Mil.* Firing or shooting of shells; as, the courage of troops under *shellfire*.

shell′fish′ (shĕl′fĭsh′), *n.*; *pl.*, see FISH. [AS. *scylfisc.*] Any aquatic invertebrate animal having a shell, esp. a mollusk or a crustacean.

shell game. A sleight-of-hand swindling game; hence, any game in which the victim has no chance to win. Cf. THIMBLERIG.

shell jacket. A semiformal tight-fitting jacket, short in the back, often used in tropical countries in place of the tuxedo.

shell′proof′ (shĕl′pro͞of′; 2), *adj.* Capable of resisting shells or bombs; bombproof.

shell shock. *Psychiatry.* Any of numerous psychoneurotic conditions, akin to hysteria, appearing in soldiers exposed to modern warfare. — **shell′-shock′**, *v. t.*

shell′y (shĕl′ĭ), *adj.*; SHELL′I·ER (-ĭ·ẽr); SHELL′I·EST. **1.** Abounding in, or covered with, shells; as, a *shelly* shore. **2.** Of, pertaining to, or like a shell.

shel′ter (shĕl′tẽr), *n.* [AS. *scildtruma* a troop of men with shields, fr. *scild* shield + *truma* a band of men.] **1.** That which covers or defends; a protection or place of protection; a refuge. **2.** State of being covered and protected; protection. — **Syn.** Asylum, sanctuary, refuge. — *v. t.* **1.** To be a shelter for; to provide with a shelter; to shield; protect. **2.** To screen or cover from injury, attack, notice, etc. **3.** To place under shelter or protection. — *v. i.* To take or provide shelter; remain sheltered. — **shel′ter·er**, *n.* — **shel′ter·less**, *adj.*

shelter tent. A small tent, usually consisting of two or more pieces of waterproof cotton duck fixed for buttoning or tying; — in soldiers' slang called also *dog tent*.

shel′ty, shel′tie (shĕl′tĭ), *n.*; *pl.* -TIES (-tĭz). A Shetland pony.

shelve (shĕlv), *v. i.* [Prob. fr. *shelf* a ledge.] To incline; to be sloping, esp. gradually. — *v. t.* **1.** To furnish with shelves. **2.** To place on a shelf or to store on shelves; hence, to lay on the shelf; to dismiss from service; as, to *shelve* an officer.

shelv′ing, *n.* **1.** Act of fitting up shelves. **2.** Act of laying on a shelf, or on the shelf; putting off or aside; as, the *shelving* of a claim. **3.** Material for shelves; shelves collectively.

Shem (shĕm), *n.* *Bib.* Eldest son of Noah.

Shem′ite (shĕm′īt), *n.* Semite. — **Shem·it′ic** (shĕm·ĭt′ĭk), *adj.*

she·nan′i·gan (shĕ·năn′ĭ·găn), *n.* *Colloq.* Trickery.

shend (shĕnd), *v. t.*; SHENT (shĕnt); SHEND′ING. [AS. *scendan.*] *Archaic & Dial.* To blame, reproach, or revile; to disgrace, or put to shame or confusion.

She′ol (shē′ōl), *n.* [Heb. *shĕʼōl.*] The underworld; the abode of the dead; hell; Hades.

shep′herd (shĕp′ẽrd), *n.* [AS. *scēaphyrde.*] **1.** A herder of sheep. **2.** *Bib. & Eccl.* A pastor. — *v. t.* To tend as a shepherd; to gather, guard, herd, lead, or drive, as a shepherd. — **shep′herd·ess**, *n.*

shepherd, *or* **shepherd's, dog.** A sheep dog; a collie.

shep′herd's pie (shĕp′ẽrdz). A meat pie with a mashed potato crust.

shep′herd's-purse′, *n.* An annual herb (*Capsella bursa-pastoris*) of the mustard family, bearing pouchlike pods.

sher′ard·ize (shĕr′ẽr·dīz), *v. t.*; -IZED (-dīzd); -IZ′ING (-dīz′ĭng). [After *Sherard* Cowper-Coles, inventor of the process.] To galvanize by treating with zinc and heating in a tightly closed retort.

Sher′a·ton (shĕr′ȧ·t′n; -tŭn), *adj.* Designating a light, elegant style in furniture, developed around 1800 by Thomas Sheraton, an English designer, and marked by straight lines and graceful proportions.

sher′bet (shûr′bĕt; -bĭt), *n.* [Turk. & Per. *sharbat*, fr. Ar. *sharbah* a drink.] **1.** A refreshing drink, made of diluted fruit juice. **2.** A water ice.

sherd (shûrd). Var. of SHARD.

she·rif′ (shĕ·rēf′), *n.* Also **she·reef′.** [Ar. *sharīf* noble.] **1.** An Arab prince or chief. **2.** A descendant of Mohammed through his daughter Fatima; — used as a title. Hence, a high dignitary among Mohammedans.

sher′iff (shĕr′ĭf), *n.* [AS. *scīr-gerēfa.* See SHIRE; 3d REEVE.] The chief executive officer of a shire or county, charged with the execution of the laws and the preservation of the peace. — **sher′iff·dom** (-dŭm), *n.*

sher′lock, Sher′lock (shûr′lŏk), *n.* *Colloq.* A detective; — from Sherlock Holmes, chief character in a series of stories by Sir Arthur Conan Doyle (1859–1930).

sher′ris (shĕr′ĭs), *n.* *Archaic.* Sherry.

sher′ry (shĕr′ĭ), *n.* [From *sherris*, taken as pl., fr. *Xeres* (now *Jerez*) de la Frontera, a Spanish town near Cádiz.] A still white wine made near Jerez; hence, a wine of this type made elsewhere.

sherry cobbler. A beverage prepared with sherry, water, lemon or orange, sugar, ice, etc.

Shet′land po′ny (shĕt′lănd). A small, stocky, hardy breed of ponies which originated in the Shetland Islands.

Shetland wool. A fine, thin, loosely twisted worsted, spun from wool of Shetland sheep.

sheugh, sheuch (shŭk), *n.* *Scot.* A ditch; trench.

shew (shō). Var. of SHOW, *n. & v.*

shew′bread′ (shō′brĕd′), **show′bread′**, *n.* *Jewish Antiq.* Bread of exhibition, unleavened bread which priests placed before Yahweh in the sanctuary (*Ex.* xxv. 30).

Shi′ah (shē′ȧ), *n.* = SHIITE.

shib′bo·leth (shĭb′ō·lĕth), *n.* [Heb. *shibbōleth* an ear of corn, stream.] **1.** *Bib.* The word by which the Gileadites distinguished the fugitive Ephraimites, who pronounced it *sibboleth. Judges* xii. **2.** Hence, criterion, test, or watchword; a party cry or pet phrase.

shied (shīd), *past & past part.* of SHY.

shiel (shēl), *n.* *Scot. & N. of Eng.* A shieling; hut.

shield (shēld), *n.* [AS. *scild, sceld, scyld.*] **1.** A broad piece of defensive armor, carried on the arm or in the hand, — formerly in general use. **2.** A person or thing that protects or defends; defense; shelter. **3.** An adjunct of dress, as a piece of rubberized silk, worn inside a part of the clothing liable to be soiled by perspiration, etc. **4.** A fixture over moving parts of machinery, or parts carrying electricity, etc., in order to protect persons from injury. **5.** *Her.* The escutcheon or field on which are placed the bearings in coats of arms. See ESCUTCHEON, *Illust.* **6.** *Ordn.* An armored screen, usually attached to the carriage, protecting an otherwise exposed gun. **7.** *Tunneling & Mining.* An iron or steel framework moved forward in excavating to support the ground ahead of the concrete, brickwork, or other lining. **8.** *Zool.* A protective structure likened to a shield, as a large scale, a carapace, etc. — *v. t. & i.* **1.** To cover with or as with a shield; to defend; protect. **2.** *Archaic.* To avert, as a misfortune; forbid. — **Syn.** See DEFEND. — **shield′-bear′er**, *n.* — **shield′er**, *n.* — **shield′-shaped′**, *adj.*

shiel′ing (shēl′ĭng; -ĭn), *n.* Also **sheal′ing.** [Of Scand. origin.] *Chiefly Scot.* A hut, as that of shepherds, sportsmen, etc.

shi′er (shī′ẽr), **shi′est**, *adj., compar. & superl.* of SHY.

shift (shĭft), *v. t.* [AS. *sciftan* to divide.] **1.** To exchange for or replace by another or others; to change; as, to *shift* the clothes. **2.** To move or remove, as from one place or person to another; to transfer; as, to *shift* the blame. **3.** *Philol.* To change phonetically, esp. by Grimm's law. — *v. i.* **1.** To change position, abode, form, etc.; hence, to change one's clothing. **2. a** To resort to shifts; esp., to live by one's wits. **b** To practice evasive methods. **c** To get along; as, left to *shift* for oneself. **3.** To shift gears, as in operating an automobile. **4.** *Philol.* To become changed phonetically, esp. by Grimm's law. — *n.* **1.** An effort; a means to accomplish an end; as, to ***make*** **(*a*)** ***shift*** to do something. **2.** An expedient or scheme tried in difficulty; often, a trick; dodge; fraud. **3. a** A change of clothes. **b** A woman's chemise. **4.** A change in direction; as, a *shift* of wind. **5.** The change of one set of workmen for another; hence, a spell of work; also, a set of workmen who work in turn with other sets; as, a night *shift*. **6.** Act of shifting; change of place, attitude, etc.; transfer, as of responsibility. **7.** *Amer. Football.* A lateral change of position, esp. from one side of the line to the other, made, just before the ball is put in play, by one or more players of the side in possession of the ball. **8.** *Geol.* The relative displacement of rock masses on opposite sides of a fault or fault zone. See FAULT, *Illust.* **9.** *Music.* A change in position, as of the hand on the finger board in playing the violin, or the movable slide of a trombone, etc. — **Syn.** See RESOURCE. — **shift′er**, *n.*

shift′less (-lĕs; -lĭs), *adj.* **1.** Lacking in expedients; hence, lazy; inefficient. **2.** Manifesting, or characteristic of, lack of efficiency or thrift. — **shift′less·ness**, *n.*

shift′y (shĭf′tĭ), *adj.*; SHIFT′I·ER (-tĭ·ẽr); SHIFT′I·EST. **1.** Full of or ready with shifts; fertile in expedients; sometimes, tricky. **2.** Indicative of a tricky nature; as, *shifty* eyes. — **shift′i·ly**, *adv.* — **shift′i·ness**, *n.*

Shi′ism (shē′ĭz'm), *n.* The tenets held by the Shiites.

Shi′ite (-īt), **Shi′ah** (-ȧ), *n.* [Ar. *shī'ī* a partisan or follower of (Ali).] One of that branch of the Moslems who reject the first three caliphs, and consider Ali, Mohammed's son-in-law, as the first rightful successor of Mohammed, and who do not acknowledge the sunna as any part of the law. Cf. SUNNITE. — **Shi·it′ic** (shē·ĭt′ĭk), *adj.*

shi·kar′ (shĭ·kär′), *n.* [Per. *shikār.*] Hunting; sport. — *v. t.* To hunt. *Both India.*

shi·ka′ri, shi·ka′ree (shĭ·kä′rē), *n.* [Per. *shikārī.*] *India.* A sportsman; esp., a native hunter or guide.

shill (shĭl), *adj.* [AS. *scyl* sonorous.] *Dial.* Shrill.

shil·le′lagh, shil·la′lah (shĭ·lā′lē), *n.* Also **shil·le′lah, shil·la′la.** *Irish.* A cudgel; — from Shillelagh, Ireland, famous for its oaks.

shil′ling (shĭl′ĭng), *n.* [AS. *scilling.*] **1.** A British silver coin and money of account, equal to twelve pence, or the twentieth part of a pound. Abbr. s. Symbol / (as: twelve shillings, 12/-). See MONEY, *Tables.* **2. a** A coin and money of account of Scotland in use previous to 1707, later worth only one English penny. **b** Any of several related moneys of the Continent, as the German schilling or the Danish skilling. **3.** *U. S. Hist.* In the thirteen colonies, a corresponding denomination of money differing in value in different colonies.

shil′ly-shal′ly (shĭl′ĭ-shăl′ĭ), *v. i.* [Redupl. of *shall I.*] To act irresolutely; hence, to occupy oneself with trifles. — *n.* Irresolution; also, occupation with trifles. — *adj.* Hesitating; irresolute.

shilp′it (shĭl′pĭt), *adj.* *Scot.* **a** Weak; feeble; sickly; puny. **b** Thin; flat; insipid, as drink.

shi′ly (shī′lĭ). Var. of SHYLY.

shim (shĭm), *n.* [Origin uncert.] A thin slip of wood, metal, stone, etc., often tapered, used to fill in, as in leveling a stone in building, or a railroad tie, etc. — *v. t.;* SHIMMED (shĭmd); SHIM′MING. To fill out, or level up, by the use of a shim or shims.

shim′mer (shĭm′ẽr), *v. i.* [AS. *scimrian.*] To shine with a tremulous or fitful light; glimmer. — **Syn.** See FLASH. — *n.* A fitful, tremulous light; a glimmer.

shim′my, shim′mey (shĭm′ĭ), *n.* [From *chemise,* taken as pl.] **1.** *Dial. & Colloq.* A chemise. **2.** A jazz dance characterized by shaking movements of the body. **3.** Abnormal vibration, as in the front wheels of an automobile. — *v. i.* **1.** To shake or tremble in, or as if in, dancing a shimmy. **2.** To vibrate abnormally, as the wheels of an automobile.

shin (shĭn), *n.* [AS. *scinu.*] **a** The front part of the leg below the knee. **b** Specif., in beef cattle, the lower part of the foreleg; — distinguished from *shank.* — *v. t. & i.;* SHINNED (shĭnd); SHIN′NING. To use the shins in climbing; to climb, esp. as a mast, tree, etc., by embracing it alternately with the arms or hands and legs; — often with *up;* as, to *shin* up a mast.

shin′bone′ (shĭn′bōn′), *n.* The tibia.

shin′dig (shĭn′dĭg), *n.* [Cf. SHINDY.] *Slang, U. S.* A festive occasion with dancing.

shin′dy (shĭn′dĭ), *n.; pl.* SHINDIES (-dĭz). [Origin uncert.; cf. Gael. *sinteag* a skip, jump.] **a** *Slang.* Uproar; fracas; row. **b** *Slang, U. S.* A dance; party; "shindig."

shine (shīn), *v. i.;* SHONE (shōn; shŏn; *in British use usually* shŏn), *Archaic* SHINED (shīnd); SHIN′ING (shīn′ĭng). [AS. *scīnan.*] **1.** To emit rays of light; to give light. **2.** To be bright by reflection of light; to gleam; also, to be conspicuously clear or evident. **3.** To be eminent; to exhibit brilliant intellectual powers. — *v. t.* **1.** To cause to shine. **2.** [In this sense the past *shined* is common.] *Colloq.* To make bright with polish; as, to *shine* shoes. — *n.* **1.** Radiance; illumination. **2.** Luster; gloss; sheen. **3.** Brilliance; splendor. **4.** Sunshine; fair weather; as, rain or *shine.* **5.** *Slang.* **a** *U. S.* A liking; fancy; as, to take a *shine* to a person. **b** A caper; prank; monkeyshine. **6.** *Colloq.* A polish given to shoes; also, a single polishing of a pair of shoes.

shin′er (shīn′ẽr), *n.* **1.** One that shines; esp., something bright or sparkling. **2.** *Slang.* A black eye, as from a blow. **3.** Any of numerous small silvery fresh-water American fishes (genus *Notropis* and allied genera) of the carp family.

shin′gle (shĭng′g'l), *n.* **1.** *Chiefly Brit.* Coarse, rounded detritus or alluvial material, as on the seashore, differing from ordinary gravel only in the larger size of the stones. **2.** A place, as a beach, strewn with shingle. — **shin′gly** (-glĭ), *adj.*

shin′gle, *n.* [ME., for *shindle,* fr. L. *scindula, scandula.*] **1.** A piece of wood sawed or rived thin and small, with one end thinner than the other, for covering roofs, etc. **2.** *Humorous, U. S.* A signboard, as of a lawyer's or doctor's office. **3.** A short haircut. — *v. t.;* -GLED (-g'ld); -GLING (-glĭng). **1.** To cover with shingles, as a roof. **2.** To cut or bob (the hair) closely. — **shin′gler** (-glẽr), *n.*

shin′gle, *v. t.* To subject, as iron, to the process of expelling cinder and impurities by hammering and squeezing.

shin′gles (shĭng′g'lz), *n.* [ML. *cingulus,* fr. L. *cingulum* girdle, fr. *cingere* to gird.] An acute inflammatory skin disease of nervous origin, marked by vesicles and neuralgic pains; — called also *herpes zoster.*

shin′ing (shīn′ĭng), *adj.* **a** Emitting or reflecting light, esp. steadily; radiant; resplendent. **b** Splendid; illustrious; brilliant. — **shin′ing·ly,** *adv.*

shin′leaf′ (shĭn′lēf′), *n.* Any herb of the genus *Pyrola,* esp. *P. elliptica* and *P. americana.* See WINTERGREEN, 1.

shin′ny, shin′ney (shĭn′ĭ), *n.* Hockey as informally played by schoolboys, etc.; also, the curved stick used in the game. — **shin′ny, shin′ney,** *v. i.*

shin′ny (shĭn′ĭ), *v. i.* *Colloq., U. S.* To climb by use of the shins; to shin; — chiefly with *up.*

shin′plas′ter (shĭn′plȧs′tẽr), *n.* **1.** A plaster applied to sore shins. **2.** Formerly, *Slang,* a piece of poorly secured paper money. Specif.: **a** Any one of the notes of small value issued by private bankers during the depression of 1837. **b** *U. S. & Canada.* See FRACTIONAL CURRENCY.

Shin′to′ (shĭn′tō′), *n.* [Jap. *Shintō,* lit., the way of the gods, fr. *shin* gods + *tō* way.] The ethnic cult and religion of the Japanese, consisting chiefly in the reverence shown to the spirits of imperial ancestors and historical personages, and to some deities of nature. — **Shin′to·ism** (-tō·ĭz'm), *n.* — **Shin′to·ist** (-ĭst), *n. & adj.*

shin′y (shīn′ĭ), *adj.;* SHIN′I·ER (-ĭ·ẽr); SHIN′I·EST. **1.** Bright; radiant; unclouded. **2.** Polished; glossy.

ship (shĭp), *n.* [AS. *scip.*] **1.** Any large seagoing vessel; also, a vessel's officers and crew, collectively. **2.** Specif., *Naut.,* a vessel with a bowsprit and three masts (foremast, mainmast, and mizzenmast), with, rarely, a fourth mast, each composed of a lower mast, a topmast, and a topgallant mast, and, sometimes, higher masts. See SAIL, *Illust.* **3.** In general, any vessel not of the kind propelled by oars, paddles, or the like. **4.** Symbolically, one's fortune or affairs; as, when one's *ship* comes home. **5.** An airship; also, an airplane.

☞ COMBINATIONS are:

shipbuilder	**shipload**	**shipwright**
shipbuilding	**shipowner**	**shipyard**

— *v. t.;* SHIPPED (shĭpt); SHIP′PING. **1. a** To put or receive on board of a ship, or other vessel, for transportation. **b** *U. S.* To transport, or commit for transportation. **2.** *Colloq.* Hence, to send away; to get rid of. **3.** To take into a boat; as, to *ship* a gangplank; specif., to draw in (an oar or scull) from its rowlock; also, to take in (water) over the side; as, to *ship* a sea or wave. **4.** To put in place for use; as, to *ship* the tiller. **5.** To engage for service on a ship, as seamen. — *v. i.* **1.** To embark on a ship. **2.** To engage to serve on shipboard.

-ship (-shĭp). [AS. *-scipe.*] A noun-forming suffix added chiefly to nouns denoting persons, but orig. to adjectives, as in hard*ship.* It denotes: (1) *State, condition,* or *quality,* as in son*ship,* friend*ship;* (2) *office, dignity,* or *profession,* as in clerk*ship,* author*ship;* (3) *art* or *skill,* as in horseman*ship;* (4) *something showing, exhibiting,* or *embodying a quality* or *state,* as in town*ship;* court*ship,* act of paying court, etc. (5) *One entitled to a* (specified) *rank, title,* or *appellation;* — used with possessive pronouns, as in Your Lord*ship.*

ship biscuit. Also **ship bread.** Hard biscuit prepared for use on shipboard; hardtack; pilot biscuit.

ship′board′ (shĭp′bōrd′; 70), *n.* A ship's side; by extension, a ship; — in adverbial phrases; as, on *shipboard.*

ship canal. A canal deep enough for seagoing vessels.

ship chandler. A dealer in supplies for ships. — **ship chandlery.**

ship′lap′ (shĭp′lăp′), *adj.* *Carp.* Cut away for a portion of the width on both edges, but on opposite sides, so as to make a flush joint with similar pieces.

ship′man (-măn), *n.* **1.** *Archaic.* A seaman; sailor. **2.** = SHIPMASTER.

ship′mas′ter (-mȧs′tẽr), *n.* The master or commander of a vessel other than a war vessel.

ship′mate′ (-māt′), *n.* One who serves on the same ship with another; a fellow sailor.

ship′ment (-mĕnt), *n.* Act or process of shipping; dispatch of goods for transportation; also, the goods shipped.

ship money. *Eng. Hist.* An impost levied at various times on ports, towns, etc., to provide ships for national defense.

ship of the line. *Nav.* Formerly, a ship of war large enough to have a place in the line of battle.

ship′pa·ble (shĭp′ȧ·b'l), *adj.* That can be shipped.

ship′pen (shĭp′ĕn). Var. of SHIPPON.

ship′per (shĭp′ẽr), *n.* One who ships goods; broadly, one who sends goods by any form of conveyance.

ship′ping, *n.* **1.** Act or business of one who ships goods. **2.** The collective body of ships in one place, or belonging to one port, country, etc.; vessels, generally; tonnage.

shipping clerk. **1.** *Brit.* In commercial offices, a clerk who arranges for the shipping of goods, esp. abroad. **2.** *U. S.* An employee in charge of the packing and delivery of goods.

shipping room. A room, as in a factory, from which goods are shipped.

ship′pon (shĭp′ŭn), *n.* [AS. *scypen.*] *Scot.* Cow barn.

ship′-rigged′ (shĭp′rĭgd′), *adj.* Rigged as a ship, that is, with three masts and square sails; also, square-rigged. See SAIL, *Illust.*

ship′shape′ (shĭp′shāp′), *adj.* Arranged in a manner befitting a ship; trim; tidy; orderly. — **ship′shape′,** *adv.*

ship's papers (shĭps). *Mar. Law.* The papers with which a vessel is required to be provided for due inspection.

ship′way′ (shĭp′wā′), *n.* **a** The ways on which a ship is built. **b** A ship canal.

ship′worm′ (-wûrm′), *n.* Any of certain peculiar marine clams (esp. *Teredo navalis*) which burrow in submerged wood and damage piles of wharves, wooden ships, etc.

ship′wreck′ (-rĕk′), *n.* **1.** A wrecked ship or its parts; wreckage. **2.** The destruction or loss of a vessel, as by sinking or grounding. **3.** Figuratively, ruin; irretrievable loss or failure. — *v. t.* To destroy, as a ship at sea, by grounding or foundering; to wreck.

shire (shīr; *as suffix* -shĭr *or* -shẽr), *n.* [AS. *scīr* a division, county.] **1.** In England, a territorial division, usually identical with a county, orig. under an earl and later under the sheriff, officer of the king. In England, in official use, *shire* is now replaced by *county.* **2.** [*cap.*] A breed of heavy draft horses (**shire horse**), chiefly from the central counties of England.

shirk (shûrk), *v. t.* [See SHIRK, *n.*] To avoid; evade; — implying meanness or fraud; as, to *shirk* duty, danger. — *v. i.* To evade an obligation. — *n.* [Prob. var. of SHARK crafty person.] One who evades duty, labor, or the like. — **shirk′er,** *n.*

shirr (shûr), *n.* *Sewing.* A series of close parallel runnings drawn up so as to make the material between them set full by gathers. — *v. t.* **1.** *Sewing.* To make a shirr or shirrs in. **2.** *Cookery.* To break (eggs) into a dish with cream or crumbs and bake in the oven or on the fire.

shirt (shûrt), *n.* [AS. *scyrte* a short garment, shirt, kirtle.] Any of certain garments for the upper part of the body; specif.: **a** A loose garment of men and boys worn under a coat or vest. **b** A close-fitting undergarment. — **shirt′less,** *adj.* — **shirt′mak′er,** *n.*

shirt′ing, *n.* Cloth suitable for making shirts.

shirt′waist′ (shûrt′wāst′; 2), *n.* A tailored blouse or shirt, usually with collar and cuffs, having ends that are tucked in under a skirt or trousers held in place by a belt.

shit′tah (shĭt′ȧ), *n., or* **shittah tree.** [Heb. *shiṭṭāh,* pl. *shiṭṭīm.*] A tree of the wood of which the ark, altars, etc., of the Jewish tabernacle were made. The tree was probably an acacia (*Acacia seyal*).

shit′tim (shĭt′ĭm), *n., or* **shittim wood.** The wood of the shittah tree.

Shi′va (shē′vȧ), **Shi′va·ism,** etc. Vars. of SIVA, SIVAISM, etc.

shiv′a·ree′ (shĭv′ȧ·rē′), *n. & v.* Corrupt. of CHARIVARI.

shiv′er (shĭv′ẽr), *n.* [ME. *schivere, scifre.*] One of the small pieces or splinters into which a brittle thing is broken by sudden violence; — generally in *pl.* — *v. t. & i.* To break into many small pieces or splinters; to shatter.

shiv′er, *v. i.* [ME. *chiveren, cheveren.*] To tremble; quiver; shake, as from cold or fear. — *v. t.* *Naut.* To cause (a sail) to shake by steering close to the wind. — *n.* Act of shivering; tremble; quiver.

shiv′er·y (shĭv′ẽr·ĭ), *adj.* Easily shivered; brittle.

shiv′er·y (shĭv′ẽr·ĭ), *adj.* Inclined to, characterized by, or causing shivering or trembling; tremulous; shivering.

shoal (shōl), *n.* [AS. *scolu, sceolu,* a company, crowd.] A crowd; throng; esp. of fish. — *v. i.* To throng; to school, as fish.

shoal, *adj.* [ME. *schold,* fr. AS. *sceald.*] Having little depth; shallow; as, *shoal* water. — *n.* **1.** A place where a sea, river, etc., is shallow; a shallow. **2.** A sand bank or bar which makes the water shoal; — applied only to elevations (not rocky) on which there is a depth of water of 6 fathoms or less. — *v. i.* To become shallow gradually; to shallow. — *v. t.* **a** To come to a shallow or less deep part of; as, a ship *shoals* her water by advancing into that which is less deep. **b** To cause to become shallow or less deep.

shoat (shōt), *n.* A shote; a young hog; a pig.

shock (shŏk), *n.* [ME. *schokke.*] A pile of sheaves of grain, as wheat, rye, etc., set up in the field. Cf. SHOOK c, STOOK. — *v. t. & i.* To collect or make up into a shock or shocks.

shock (shŏk), *n.* [F. *choc*, fr. *choquer* to shock.] **1.** The impact of individuals or groups in combat. **2.** A blow, impact, collision, or violent shake or jar; also, the effect of such violence; as, an earthquake *shock*. **3.** A sudden agitation of the mental or emotional sensibilities, or an event causing this. **4.** The sudden stimulation caused by the discharge, through the animal system, of electricity. **5.** *Med.* **a** A state of profound depression of the vital processes resulting from wounds, hemorrhage, crushing injuries, blows, etc. **b** A stroke of paralysis. — *v. t.* **1.** *Obs.* To cause to shake; to encounter with violence. **2.** To strike with surprise, horror, or disgust. **3.** To cause to undergo a physical, esp. a nervous, shock. **4.** To drive into or out of as if by a shock; as, to *shock* the truth out of a person. **5.** *Physiol.* To subject (a body) to the action of an electrical discharge. — *v. i.* To collide.

shock, *n.* **1.** Short for **shock dog**, a long-haired dog. **2.** A thick, bushy mass, as of hair. — *adj.* Bushy; shaggy.

shock absorber. *Mach.* Any of several types of devices for absorbing the energy of sudden impulses or shocks in machinery or structures, as springs of automobiles.

shock′er (shŏk′ẽr), *n.* One who or that which shocks grain.

shock′er, *n.* *Brit.* One that shocks, or startles; esp., a sensational tale; as, a shilling *shocker*. Cf. DREADFUL, *n.*; DIME NOVEL.

shock′head′ed (shŏk′hĕd′ĕd; -ĭd; 2), *adj.* Also **shock′-head′**. Having a thick and bushy head of hair.

shock′ing, *adj.* Causing to shake or to recoil with horror or disgust; offensive. — **Syn.** See FEARFUL. — **shock′ing·ly,** *adv.*

shock tactics. *Mil.* Tactics, esp. of cavalry, in which **shock action**, or an attack in massed formation, is employed.

shock therapy. The treatment of mental disorders by means of an artificially induced state of shock resulting from the administration of chemicals or of an electric current.

shock troops. *Mil.* Troops specially chosen for offensive work because of their high morale, training, and discipline. Hence, **shock battalion, shock corps, shock force,** etc.

shod (shŏd), *past & past part.* of SHOE.

shod′dy (shŏd′ĭ), *n.* **1.** A variety of reclaimed wool, obtained by pulling apart worsteds or woolens; — disting. from *mungo* by length of fiber and by the superior quality of fabrics manufactured from it. **2.** Any fabric manufactured from reclaimed wool. **3.** A cloth of inferior quality made of reclaimed wool. **4.** Refuse or inferior articles or matter of any kind. **5.** An inferior person or thing claiming superiority; also, pretentious vulgarity, as in society, art, etc. — *adj.*; SHOD′DI·ER (-ĭ·ẽr); SHOD′DI·EST. **1.** Made of shoddy; as, *shoddy* cloth. **2.** Not genuine; sham; as, *shoddy* aristocracy.

shoe (sho͞o), *n.*; *pl.* SHOES (sho͞oz), or, *Now Archaic & Dial.*, SHOON (sho͞on). [AS. *scōh, sceōh.*] **1.** A covering for the human foot, having a thick sole and heel and a lighter upper, usually of leather, but often of cloth. In England, and now to some extent in the United States, the word is used to designate a low shoe, as an Oxford, the high shoe being called a *boot*. **2.** Anything suggestive of, or likened to, a shoe; specif.: **a** A horseshoe. **b** A metal band on the runner of a sled, sleigh, etc. **c** A drag under a wheel of a vehicle to retard motion in going down hill. **d** The part of a brake which presses on a vehicle wheel to retard its motion. See HYDRAULIC, *Illust.* **e** A socket or ferrule, as of iron, to protect the point of a wooden pile, pole, cane, staff, or the like. **3.** *Automobiles.* The external rubber-and-fabric casing of a pneumatic tire, which protects the air-filled inner tube. See TIRE, *Illust.* **4.** *Elec.* The sliding contact member of a current collector; as, a third-rail *shoe* of a subway car. **5.** *Mach.* A plate interposed between a moving part and the stationary part on which it bears. — *v. t.*; SHOD (shŏd); SHOE′ING. **1.** To put a shoe or shoes on; to furnish with a shoe or shoes. **2.** To cover for protection, strength, or ornament.

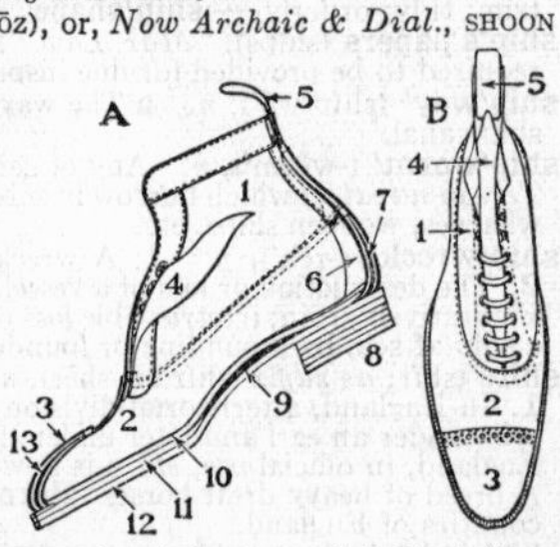

Shoe, 1. *A* Section, and *B* Front View. 1 Top; 2 Vamp; 3 Cap; 4 Tongue; 5 Pull Strap; 6 Backstay; 7 Counter; 8 Heel; 9 Shank; 10 Insole; 11 Slipsole; 12 Outsole; 13 Toe Box.

shoebrush	shoemaker	shoeshop
shoelace	shoemaking	shoestring

shoe′bill′ (sho͞o′bĭl′), *n.* A wading bird (*Balaeniceps rex*) allied to the storks and herons. It inhabits the valley of the White Nile.

shoe′black′ (sho͞o′blăk′), *n.* A bootblack.

shoe′horn′ (-hôrn′), *n.* A curved piece, as of horn, wood, or metal, to aid in slipping on a shoe.

sho′er (sho͞o′ẽr), *n.* One who shoes horses.

shoe tree. = BOOT TREE.

sho′far (shō′fär). Var. of SHOPHAR.

shog (shŏg), *n. & v. t. & i.* *Dial.* Shake; jog.

sho′gun′ (shō′go͝on′), *n.* [Jap. *shō-gun*, fr. Chin. (Pek.) *chiang*[4]*-chün*[1] leader of an army.] A title of military governors of Japan, who usurped power until by the revolution of 1867–68 the office was abolished and the power of the emperor restored. Cf. TYCOON, 1. — **sho′gun′ate** (-āt), *n.*

shone (shōn; shŏn; *Brit. usually* shŏn), *past* of SHINE.

shoo (sho͞o), *interj.* An exclamation used in frightening away animals, esp. fowls; hence, *jocular*, begone! — *v. t. & i.*; SHOOED (sho͞od); SHOO′ING. To drive away by crying "shoo!"

shook (sho͝ok), *n.* *Com.* **a** A set of staves and headings sufficient in number for one hogshead, cask, barrel, etc. **b** A set of parts of boxes, tops, bottoms, sides, and ends, ready to be put together. **c** A shock of sheaves.

shook. Past & archaic or dial. past part. of SHAKE.

shool (sho͞ol), *v. i. & t. & n.* *Dial.* Shovel.

shoon (sho͞on). Archaic & dial. pl. of SHOE.

shoot (sho͞ot), *v. t.*; SHOT (shŏt); SHOOT′ING. [AS. *scēotan.*] **1.** To let fly, or cause to be driven, with force, as an arrow, bullet, etc. **2.** To hit, or often, to kill or wound, with a missile discharged from a firearm. **3.** To discharge (a bow, gun, etc.). **4.** To push into or out of a fastening, as a bolt, key, or lock. **5.** To throw or cast suddenly, often with force. **6.** To emit; dart, as a ray of light. **7.** To discharge, dump, or the like, esp. into some desired place. **8.** To variegate as if by sprinkling color in streaks or patches; as, silk *shot* with silver. **9.** To thrust forward; protrude; as, a plant *shoots* out a bud. **10.** To pass rapidly along; as, to *shoot* a rapid. **11.** To take the altitude of; as, he used his transit to *shoot* a star. **12.** *Carp.* To plane straight or true; to fit by planing. **13.** *Gambling.* To throw or cast (the dice), as in craps. **14.** *Hunting.* To do shooting for game in or on; as, to *shoot* a park. **15.** *Mining.* To cause to explode, as a blast. **16.** *Photog. & Motion Pictures.* To photograph; film; as, to *shoot* a scene. **17.** *Sports.* To propel (a ball, puck, or the like) toward the goal; also, to score (a goal) by so doing. — *v. i.* **1.** To move, drive, or rush swiftly. **2.** To dart with a piercing sensation; as, *shooting* pains. **3.** To cause an engine or weapon to discharge a missile; hence, to hunt. **4.** To be discharged; go off; — of firearms; also, to project a missile; as, to *shoot* three miles. **5.** To protrude; jut. **6. a** To grow; sprout, as plants, hair, etc.; hence, to develop; mature. **b** To germinate; bud. **7.** *Photog. & Motion Pictures.* **a** To take a photograph. **b** To photograph a scene of a motion picture. **c** To start the cameras in photographing a scene. **8.** *Sports.* To play by propelling the ball, marble, or the like (in a certain way). — *n.* **1.** *Archaic.* Act of shooting. **2. a** A hunting trip or hunting party. **b** A shooting match. **3.** A sending out of new growth; also, the new growth; as: **a** A stem with its leaves. **b** A budding antler. **4.** = CHUTE, *n.*, 2. **5.** A twinge of pain. **6.** A movement of rapid thrusting; as, a *shoot* of the arms away from the body. **7.** *Rowing.* The pace between strokes.

Syn. **Shoot, branch, bough, limb** mean an outgrowth from a shrub or tree. **Shoot,** applicable also to any plant, stresses actual growing and therefore applies chiefly to any young undeveloped member; **branch** stresses division and applies to any more or less fully developed member whether it emanates from the trunk or from one of its subdivisions; **bough,** often used interchangeably with *branch*, carries however a weak implication of division and a strong one of being covered with foliage; **limb,** applicable chiefly to large trees, suggests usually one of the divisions made by forking of the trunk.

shoot′er (sho͞ot′ẽr), *n.* One who or that which shoots.

shoot′ing box. A cabin or small house in the country for use in the shooting season; — called also **shooting lodge.**

shooting gallery. A range, usually covered, with targets for practice with firearms.

shooting iron. *Slang, U. S.* A firearm.

shooting star. **1.** A meteor. **2.** A North American perennial herb (*Dodecatheon meadia*) with entire, oblong leaves and showy flowers; — called also *American cowslip.*

shop (shŏp), *n.* [AS. *sceoppa* treasury.] **1.** A store. **2.** A room or building devoted to a particular line in a factory; as, a machine *shop*. **3.** Subject matter, esp. details, pertaining to a person's occupation, business, profession, etc.; as, to talk *shop*. — *v. i.*; SHOPPED (shŏpt); SHOP′PING. To visit shops for purchasing or inspecting goods.

shopgirl	shopkeeping	shopwindow
shopkeeper	shopman	shopwoman

sho′phar (shō′fär), *n.* Also **sho′far.** [Heb. *shōphār.*] A horn, as of a ram, used as a trumpet by the ancient Hebrews as in battle or upon sacred festivals, or still used in synagogues, as on the Day of Atonement.

shop′lift′er (shŏp′lĭf′tẽr), *n.* [*shop* + *lift* to steal.] One who steals from a shop goods exposed for sale. — **shop′lift′ing,** *n.*

shop′per (shŏp′ẽr), *n.* **1.** One who shops. **2.** One who makes a business of buying goods at retail for others.

shop′walk′er (shŏp′wôk′ẽr), *n.* One who walks about in a shop to oversee employees and direct customers.

shop′worn′ (-wōrn′; 70), *adj.* Somewhat worn or marred by having been kept in a shop.

sho′ran (shō′răn; shô′răn), *n.* [*sho*rt *ra*nge *n*avigation.] A system of short-range navigation in which radar signals transmitted by an airplane are intercepted and rebroadcast by two ground stations of known position, and utilized to determine the range of the aircraft from each station. Cf. LORAN.

shore (shōr; 70), *n.* [ME. *schore.*] A prop or support placed against or beneath anything to prevent sinking or sagging. — *v. t.* To support by a shore or shores; prop.

shore, *n.* [ME. *schore*, fr. AS. (assumed) *score*, prob. fr. *scieran*, prop., that which is shorn off, edge.] The land bordering a body of water, esp. a large body; the coast. — **shore′less,** *adj.*

shore, *v. t.* *Scot.* **a** To offer. **b** To threaten; also, to scold.

shore. Archaic & dial. past tense & past part. of SHEAR; — form used among sheep raisers in Australia.

shore bird. A bird of a suborder (Charadrii), most of which frequent the seashore, as the plover, snipe, etc.

shore cod. See COD.

shore patrol. The military police of the U. S. Navy. *Abbr.* SP

shor′ing (shōr′ĭng; 70), *n.* Act of supporting with a prop or shore; also, a system of shores, or props.

shorn (shōrn; 70), *past part.* of SHEAR.

short (shôrt), *adj.* [AS. *scort, sceort.*] **1.** Not long from end to end; of brief length. **2.** Not tall. **3.** Of a compass or range having little extent. **4.** Not great in distance. **5.** Not extended in time; brief. **6.** Not retentive for more than a brief period; — of memory. **7.** Of a bill, commercial paper, etc., payable at an early date, as ten or thirty days or less. **8.** Concise; succinct; as, a *short* poem. **9.** Curt; abrupt; as, a *short* answer. **10.** Not coming up to a measure, standard, etc.; as, the money in the cashier's hands was *short*, that is, less than what the accounts called for. **11.** Not reaching to some mark, bound, etc.; as, his arrow fell *short*. **12.** With *of*: Less than; not equal or equivalent to; as, nothing *short* of war. **13.** Insufficiently provided or supplied; as, to be *short* of money. **14. a** Easily broken, friable, crisp, as pastry. **b** Of metals, brittle under certain conditions, as steel, brittle when hot (***hot-short***) because of an excess of sulfur or when cold (***cold-short***) because of an excess of phosphorus. **15.** *Finance & Com.* **a** Not having goods or property that one has sold; as, to be *short* of wheat. **b** Of the nature of or pert. to a sale of securities or commodities which the seller does not possess, or has not contracted for, at the time of the sale; as, a *short* sale. **16.** *Phonet.* Of speech sounds, having relatively small duration. **17.** *Pros.* Of a syllable or vowel, of relatively brief duration. — **Syn.** See BRIEF. — **Ant.** Long.

— *n.* **1.** *Dial.* A summing up. **2.** A thing or part that is short; specif.: **a** A fish, lobster, etc., short of the length required for legal keeping. **b** A motion picture shorter than the usual in duration. **3.** *pl.* **a** Short trousers; formerly, smallclothes. **b** Short loose-fitting pants reaching part way to the knee, esp. for wear in sports. **4.** *pl.* Things that fall short of expectation or correctness in value, quantity, and the like. **5.** *pl.* Refuse, clippings, or trimmings, thrown off in various manufacturing processes and used for inferior products. **6.** *Colloq. Baseball.* Shortstop. **7.** *Elec.* = SHORT CIRCUIT. **8.** *Exchanges.* One who has made a short sale. See SHORT SALE. **9.** *Mil.* A shot which falls short of the target. **10.** *Milling. pl.* A by-product of wheat milling which includes the germ, fine bran, and some flour. **11.** *Phonet. & Pros.* A short sound or its symbol; also, a short syllable. — ***in short.*** In few words; in brief; by way of summary. — *adv.* **1.** In a short manner; briefly; abruptly; curtly; harshly. **2.** So as not to attain the expected length, distance, point, or goal; as, to throw *short.* **3.** *Exchanges.* In the character or condition of one who is short; as, to sell stocks *short.*

short account. *Stock Exchange.* **a** The account of a short seller. **b** The aggregate of the open short sales in a given subject of trade, or in the market as a whole.

short′age (shôr′tĭj), *n.* Deficiency in the amount required; deficit.

short′-arm′, *adj.* *Boxing.* Having, or delivered with, the arm or reach shortened; as, a *short-arm* blow.

short′bread′ (shôrt′brĕd′), *n.* A crisp, sweet cake rich in butter, and sometimes containing chopped nuts or fruit.

short′cake′ (-kāk′), *n.* **a** A crisp, short, often unsweetened, biscuit, cookie, or teacake. **b** A dessert made usually of very short baking-powder-biscuit dough spread with sweetened fruit, as strawberries.

short′change′ (-chānj′), *v. t.;* -CHANGED′ (-chānjd′); -CHANG′ING (-chān′jĭng). *Colloq.* To give (one) less than the correct change, esp. after a sale; hence, to cheat. — **short′chang′er** (-chān′jẽr), *n.*

short circuit. *Elec.* A circuit through a small resistance, esp. one which acts as a shunt to a circuit of large resistance. — **short′-cir′cuit,** *v. t.*

short′com′ing (shôrt′kŭm′ĭng; shôrt′kŭm′ĭng; 2), *n.* A failing, or coming short; deficiency; defect.

short′-com′mons, *n. pl.* A scanty ration of food.

short covering. *Stock & Produce Exchanges.* Buying in securities or other property to close out a short sale.

short cut. **1.** A route more direct than that ordinarily taken. **2.** A way of accomplishing something more directly and quickly than by ordinary procedure.

short′-cut′, *v. i.* To take a short cut.

short′en (shôr′t′n), *v. t. & i.* To make or become short or shorter. — ***shorten sail.*** *Naut.* To reduce the amount of sail, as by reefing and/or furling. — **short′en·er** (-ẽr), *n.*

Syn. **Shorten, curtail, abbreviate, abridge, retrench** mean to reduce in extent. **Shorten** commonly implies reduction in length of dimension or duration; **curtail,** a docking or cutting that leaves a thing incomplete or inadequate; **abbreviate,** a shortening, usually of a word or phrase, by contraction or the like; **abridge,** a reduction in compass or scope with the retention of relative completeness; **retrench,** a reduction in something felt to be excessive.

short′en·ing (shôr′t′n·ĭng; shôrt′nĭng), *n.* **1.** Act of making or becoming short or shorter. **2.** That which shortens pastry, cake, etc.; any fat fit for such use.

Short′er Cat′e·chism. A catechism prepared by the Westminster Assembly and used by the Presbyterian Church.

short′hand′ (shôrt′hănd′), *n.* A rapid method of writing by substituting characters or symbols for letters, words, etc.; stenography. Cf. LONGHAND. — *adj.* **a** Using shorthand; as, a *shorthand* reporter. **b** Written in shorthand. — *v. t.* To write in shorthand.

short′hand′ed (-hăn′dĕd; -dĭd; 2), *adj.* Short of the regular number of servants, helpers, or "hands."

Short′horn′ (-hôrn′), *n.* An animal of a red, white, and roan breed of beef cattle, originating in northern England. These cattle are also valuable for dairy purposes, esp. a strain that has been developed into a breed called ***Milking Shorthorn.***

short′ish (shôr′tĭsh), *adj.* Somewhat short.

short′-lived′ (shôrt′līvd′ *or, esp. Brit.,* -lĭvd′; 2), *adj.* Not living or lasting long.

short′ly, *adv.* **1.** In a short time; soon. **2.** In few words; briefly. **3.** Abruptly; curtly.

short′ness, *n.* Quality or state of being short.

short sale. *Exchanges.* A contract of sale of securities or other property which one does not possess but hopes to obtain later on more advantageous terms. — **short seller.** — **short selling.**

short shrift. **a** Brief time to confess before dying. **b** A brief respite.

short′sight′ed (shôrt′sīt′ĕd; -ĭd), *adj.* **1.** Not able to see far; nearsighted; myopic. **2.** Lacking foresight; also, characterized by lack of foresight. — **short′sight′ed·ly,** *adv.* — **short′sight′ed·ness,** *n.*

short snort′er. [From (slang) *short snort* quick drink (bought by loser).] **1.** A member of an informal club to which a pilot, crew member, or passenger who has made a transoceanic flight is eligible and each member of which carries a dollar bill (or pound note), autographed by at least two members, which he must present on demand or forfeit a dollar bill (or pound note) to each member present. **2.** A dollar bill (or pound note) endorsed by short snorters as a membership certificate.

short′-spo′ken (shôrt′spō′kĕn; 2), *adj.* *Colloq.* Speaking in a quick or brief manner; hence, gruff; curt; also, laconic.

short′stop′ (-stŏp′), *n.* **1.** In baseball, a player stationed between second and third base. **2.** *Photog.* A bath or solution serving to stop the developing process.

short story, *or* **short′-sto′ry,** *n.* In narrative literature, a relatively brief prose story usually characterized by uniformity of tone and dramatic intensity, and having as a plot a single action represented at the crisis. — **short′-sto′ry** (2), *adj.*

short′-tem′pered (shôrt′tĕm′pẽrd; 2), *adj.* Having a quick temper.

short′-term′ (-tûrm′; 2), *adj.* Designating a financial obligation or a negotiable paper which matures within a relatively short term.

short ton. See TON, 1 **a.**

short wave. *Radio.* A hertzian wave of sixty-meter wave length or less. — **short′-wave′** (-wāv′; 2), *adj.*

short′-wind′ed (-wĭn′dĕd; -dĭd; 2), *adj.* Having a quick, difficult respiration, as in asthma or panting; easily put out of breath, as by exercise.

Sho·sho′ne·an (shō·shō′nē·ăn; shō′shō·nē′ăn), *adj.* Designating an important North American Indian linguistic stock extending from the Rocky Mountains to the Sierra Nevada.

Sho·sho′ni, Sho·sho′ne, Sho·sho′nee (shō·shō′nē), *n.* An Indian of an important Shoshonean tribe of western Wyoming and Colorado and parts of Idaho, Utah, and Nevada.

shot (shŏt), *n.; pl.* SHOTS (shŏts), SHOT. [AS. *scot* a shooting, *gesceot* a missile.] **1.** Act of shooting; a directed discharge from a firearm, as in warfare, hunting, etc. **2.** Orig., a missile, as an arrow; now, a projectile designed to be discharged from a firearm. **3.** Anything thrown, cast forth, or let fly, with force; also, a remark so directed as to have a telling effect. **4.** A guess; conjecture; also, an attempt. **5.** *Slang.* A dose shot into the body, as by injection; as, a *shot* of cocaine; also, a single drink of liquor. **6.** The flight of a missile, or the distance which it is, or can be, thrown; figuratively, reach; range; as, within ear*shot.* **7.** [AS. *scot, sceot.*] A reckoning to be paid, or one's share of it; scot. **8.** One who shoots, esp. with a firearm; a marksman; as, an excellent *shot.* **9.** *Athletics.* A spherical weight, usually, for men's events, weighing not less than 16 pounds, to be put (see PUT, *v. t.,* 2) in competition for distance. **10.** *Firearms.* A small globular mass, or pellet, of lead, for use esp. in shotguns. See CARTRIDGE, *Illust.* **11.** *Games.* A stroke, as in billiards, hockey, curling, etc. **12.** *Mining, Quarrying, etc.* A blast, as of dynamite. **13.** *Motion Pictures.* The film record of a scene or series of scenes of a motion picture. **14.** *Photog.* A snapshot or longer exposure.

shot (shŏt), *past & past part.* of SHOOT. Hence: *part. adj.* **1.** That has discharged or been discharged; also, that has sprouted. **2.** Woven, as silk, or dyed, as a mixed fabric, so as to be changeable in tint; variegated; of colors, changeable. **3.** *Slang.* Intoxicated; also, used up; worn out.

shote (shōt), *n.* A young hog; a shoat.

shot′gun′ (shŏt′gŭn′), *n.* A smooth bore gun designed for firing shot at short range.

shot′-put′ (shŏt′po͝ot′), *n.* *Athletics.* A field event consisting in putting the shot for distance. See SHOT, *n.,* 9. — **shot′-put′ter,** *n.*

shot′ten (shŏt′'n), *adj.* [Past part. of *shoot,* fr. AS. *scoten, sceoten,* past part. of *scēotan.*] Having ejected the spawn and so of inferior food value; as, *shotten* herring; hence, worthless.

should (sho͝od; 4), *past tense* of SHALL. [AS. *scolde, sceolde.* See SHALL.] As auxiliaries *should* and *would* are used: **1.** To form a tense expressive of action, etc., as impending in the past; as, I said that I *should* go. **2.** To form the conditional mood (as, I *should* go, I *should* have gone), used esp.: **a** In the conclusion in sentences of rejected condition; as, if I had tried, I *should* not have failed. **b** In conditional clauses expressive of uncertainty or reserve; as, *should* you come, I shall meet you. **c** In statements, requests, etc., which it softens; as, so it *should* seem. In these uses, according to conventional rules, the choice between *should* and *would* is based on the distinctions between *shall* and *will* (see under SHALL). However, except as in **b,** *would* is often used instead of *should* in colloquial English and frequently also in literary language. **3.** *Should,* esp. when stressed, is also used to express moral obligation; as, you *should* be sorry.

shoul′der (shōl′dẽr), *n.* [AS. *sculdor.*] **1. a** In man, the laterally projecting part of the body formed by the bones and muscles where the arm joins the trunk. **b** In animals, the corresponding region. **2.** *Chiefly in pl.* The upper part of the back, forming that part of the human frame on which it is easiest to carry a burden. **3.** That which supports or sustains; as, the blame rests on my *shoulders.* **4.** A projecting part like or likened to a shoulder (def. 1 **a**); also, the part of a garment at the wearer's shoulder. **5.** The upper joint of the foreleg and adjacent parts of an animal, dressed for market. See BEEF, *Illust.* **6.** *Fort.* The angle of a bastion between the face and flank. **7.** *Leather Mfg.* A part of a hide. See HIDE, *Illust.* **8.** *Print.* The part of the top of a type which projects beyond the base of the raised character. See TYPE, *Illust.* **9.** *Roads.* Either edge of a road. — *v. t. & i.* **1.** To push or thrust with or as with the shoulder; jostle. **2.** To take or bear upon the shoulder; hence, to assume the burden of; as, to *shoulder* a debt.

shoulder blade. = SCAPULA.

shoulder knot, mark, strap. A knot, mark, or strap worn on the shoulder, esp., *Mil. & Nav.,* to show rank.

should′na (sho͝od′nȧ). Scot. var. of *should not.*

should′n't (sho͝od′'nt). Colloq. contraction of *should not.*

shouldst (sho͝odst), *2d pers. sing.* of SHOULD.

shout (shout), *v. i.* [ME. *shouten,* of uncert. origin.] To utter a sudden loud cry. — *v. t.* To utter with a shout. — *n.* A loud burst of voices; a sudden outcry.

shout′er (shout′ẽr), *n.* One who shouts.

shove (shŭv), *v. t. & i.* [AS. *scūfan.*] **1.** To push along by the direct application of strength. **2.** To push aside, or away, carelessly or rudely. — **Syn.** See PUSH. — *n.* Act of shoving; a forcible push. — **shov′er** (shŭv′ẽr), *n.*

shov′el (shŭv′'l), *n.* [AS. *scofl.*] **1.** A long-handled scooplike implement used to lift and throw earth, coal, grain, etc.; also, the amount contained in such a scooplike implement; as, a *shovel* of coal. **2.** A shovel hat. — *v. t.;* -ELED or -ELLED (-'ld); -EL·ING or -EL·LING. **1.** To take up and throw with a shovel. **2.** To dig or clean out with a shovel. **3.** To throw or convey roughly or in the mass, as if with a shovel.

shov′el-bill′ (-bĭl′), *n.* A shoveler (duck).

shov′el·board′ (-bōrd′; 70), *n.* [Cf. SHUFFLE, SHOVE.] = SHUFFLEBOARD, 2.

shov′el·er, shov′el·ler (shŭv′'l·ẽr), *n.* **1.** A laborer who works with a shovel. **2.** Any of a genus (*Spatula*) of river ducks, so called from the large broad bill, esp. *S. clypeata,* which is widely distributed, esp. in the Northern Hemisphere.

shovel hat. A broad-brimmed hat, turned up at the sides like a shovel, worn by some clergy of the English Church.

shov′el·head′ (shŭv′'l·hĕd′), *n.* **a** A shark (*Reniceps tiburo*) allied to the hammerhead, but with head narrower and less hammer-shaped. **b** The shovel-nosed sturgeon.

shov′el·nose′ (-nōz′), *n.* A shovel-nosed animal.

shov′el-nosed′ (-nōzd′), *adj.* Having a broad, flat head, nose, or beak.

shovel-nosed sturgeon. A small sturgeon (*Scaphirhynchus platorhynchus*) of the Mississippi Valley, which has a broad, flattened snout.

show (shō), *v. t.;* SHOWED (shōd); SHOWN (shōn) or SHOWED; SHOW′ING. Also, *esp. Brit.,* **shew** (shō), SHEWED (shōd); SHEWN (shōn); SHEW′ING. [AS. *scēawian* to look, see, view.] **1.** To present to sight; exhibit; display. **2.** To bestow; confer; as, to *show* favor. **3.** To reveal the character of (oneself) as being or having (some quality); as, to *show* oneself cruel. **4.** To reveal; make known; as, to *show* one's designs. **5.** To explain something to; to teach; instruct. **6.** To allege; plead; — now esp. in *Law;* as, to *show* cause. **7.** To prove; demonstrate; as, to *show* the truth of a statement. **8.** To direct; guide; conduct. **9.** To give indication of by record; as, a clock *shows* the hour. — *v. i.* **1.** To manifest oneself or itself; to appear. **2.** To seem; appear. **3.** To make its appearance; to be present. **4.** To be noticeable; as, does the spot *show?* **5.** *Racing Slang.* To be third, or at least third, in a race. **6.** *Theater.* To give a performance. — ***show off.*** To make an ostentatious display (of).

Syn. (1) **Show, manifest, evidence, evince, demonstrate** mean to reveal or serve to reveal something not plain. **Show** implies inference from acts, looks, words, or the like; **manifest,** a fuller, plainer, more indubitable revelation; **evidence,** a serving as proof of the actuality or existence of something in question; **evince,** a showing by outward marks or tokens; **demonstrate,** an evincing through a display of feeling.

(2) **Show, exhibit, display, expose, parade, flaunt** mean to present so as to invite notice or attention. **Show** implies enabling another to see or look at; **exhibit,** a putting forward prominently or openly; **display,** a putting in position where one may see to advantage; **expose,** a bringing from concealment and a displaying; **parade,** an ostentatious or arrogant display; **flaunt,** a shameless, boastful, and often offensive parade.

— *n.* **1.** A bringing to view; exhibition. **2.** A demonstrative display; as, a *show* of force. **3.** False semblance; pretense. **4.** Sign; trace; as, some *show* of reason. **5.** External appearance. **6.** Ostentatious display; pomp. **7.** *Colloq.* Opportunity; chance; as, he hasn't a *show* of winning. **8.** An indication of metal in a mine, gas or oil in a well, etc.; as, a *show* of gold. **9.** A thing to behold; a sight. **10.** A spectacle; exhibition. **11.** *Colloq.* A theatrical performance. **12.** *Slang.* Third place in a race.

— *adj.* **1.** That makes a show; that is displayed or used for displaying something; as, a *show* animal; a *show* window. **2.** Of or pertaining to a show or to the theater; as, *show* folk.

show bill. A broad sheet containing an advertisement.

show′boat′ (shō′bōt′), *n.* A passenger steamship, as the old sidewheelers on the Mississippi, part of it converted into a theater and carrying a troupe of players.

show′bread′ (-brĕd′). Var. of SHEWBREAD.

show′case′ (-kās′), *n.* A glazed case, box, etc., to display and protect shopkeepers' wares, articles in museums, etc.

show′down′ (-doun′), *n.* A definite disclosure of facts, intentions, resources, etc.

show′er (shō′ẽr), *n.* One who shows or exhibits.

show′er (shou′ẽr), *n.* [AS. *scūr.*] **1.** A fall of rain, of short duration. **2.** An emission of drops, rays, etc., as of tears, blood, light. **3.** That which resembles a shower; as, a *shower* of sparks. **4.** A party given to a prospective bride, where gifts are presented; as, a linen *shower.* **5.** Short for SHOWER BATH. — *v. t.* **1.** To wet copiously with water or other liquid in the form of spray, fine streams, or drops. **2.** To bestow liberally; to scatter in abundance. — *v. i.* **1.** To rain or fall in or as in a shower. **2.** To bathe in a shower bath. — **show′er·y** (-ĭ), *adj.*

shower bath. A bath in which water is showered on the person; also, the apparatus for such a bath.

show′ing (shō′ĭng), *n.* A display or exhibition; as, a *showing* of millinery; also, a presentation of some fact, condition, or the like; as, a bad financial *showing.*

show′man (shō′măn), *n.* **1.** One who exhibits or helps to exhibit a show. **2.** One who is adept at exhibiting things to advantage. — **show′man·ship,** *n.*

shown (shōn), *past part.* of SHOW.

show′-off′ (shō′ôf′), *n.* **1.** Act of showing off; display, esp. when pretentious. **2.** *Colloq.* One who shows off.

show′room′ (-rōōm′), *n.* A room where merchandise is exposed for sale, or where samples are displayed.

show′y (shō′ĭ), *adj.;* SHOW′I·ER (-ĭ·ẽr); SHOW′I·EST. Making an attractive show; also, ostentatious. — **show′i·ly,** *adv.* — **show′i·ness,** *n.*

Syn. **Showy, pretentious, ostentatious, pompous** mean given to excessive outward display. **Showy** implies an attempt at an imposing or striking appearance but usually suggests cheapness or poor taste; **pretentious,** a showiness not justified by the thing's value or the person's standing; **ostentatious,** vainglorious display or parade; **pompous,** an ostentatiousness dictated by a love of ceremony or by an exaggerated sense of self-importance.

showy orchis. See ORCHIS.

shrank (shrăngk), *past* of SHRINK.

shrap′nel (shrăp′nĕl; -n′l), *n. sing. & pl.* [After Gen. Henry *Shrapnel* (1761–1842), of the Brit. Army.] *Mil.* A case or shell provided with a bursting charge, and filled with balls, exploded in flight by a time fuse.

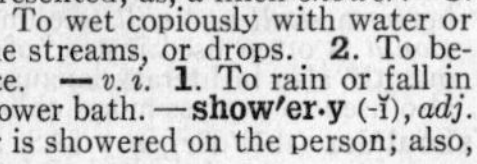

Shrapnel. 1 Combination Fuse, time and percussion; 2 Steel Case; 3 Shrapnel Balls; 4 Central Tube; 5 Guncotton; 6 Loose Powder.

shred (shrĕd), *n.* [AS. *scrēade.*] A long, narrow piece cut or torn off; a strip. In general, a fragment; particle. — *v. t.;* SHRED or SHRED′DED; SHRED′DING. [AS. *scrēadian.*] To cut or tear into shreds.

shred′der (shrĕd′ẽr), *n.* One that shreds.

shrew (shrōō), *n.* [ME., fr. AS. *scrēawa,* the animal, because supposed to be venomous.] **1.** A scolding or brawling woman; a termagant. **2.** [AS. *scrēawa.*] Any of numerous small mouselike mammals (family Soricidae), with a long pointed snout, very small eyes, and velvety fur.

shrewd (shrōōd), *adj.* [For *shrewed* (cf. DOGGED).] **1.** *Obs.* **a** Evil; bad. **b** Shrewish; as, a *shrewd* wench. **c** Dangerous. **2.** *Obs.* Mischievous. **3.** *Archaic.* Artful; cunning; as, *shrewd* tempers. **4.** Able in practical affairs; astute. **5.** Biting; piercing; sharp; as, a *shrewd* wind. — **shrewd′ly,** *adv.* — **shrewd′ness,** *n.*

Syn. **Shrewd, sagacious, perspicacious, astute** mean acute in perception and judgment. **Shrewd** implies acumen, hardheadedness, and an almost uncanny ability to see below the surface; **sagacious,** discernment, penetration, judiciousness, and often farsightedness; **perspicacious,** unusual power to see through and to understand that which is dark or hidden; **astute,** a combination of shrewdness, perspicacity, and ability to keep one's counsel.

shrew′ish (shrōō′ĭsh), *adj.* Having the qualities of a shrew; having a scolding disposition; peevish. — **shrew′ish·ly,** *adv.* — **shrew′ish·ness,** *n.*

shrew′mouse′ (shrōō′mous′), *n.* A shrew.

shriek (shrēk), *v. i.* [ME. *schriken,* fr. or akin to ON. *skrækja.*] To utter a sharp, shrill sound or cry, as do some birds and beasts; to scream, as in fright, horror, or wild laughter; also, to make a sound like a shriek; as, horns *shrieked.* — *v. t.* To utter sharply and shrilly. — *n.* A shrill, wild cry, as of terror, pain, or wild laughter. — **shriek′er,** *n.*

shriev′al (shrēv′ăl), *adj.* Of or pert. to a sheriff.

shriev′al·ty (-tĭ), *n.; pl.* -TIES (-tĭz). The office, term of office, or sphere of jurisdiction, of a sheriff.

shrieve (shrēv). Var. of SHERIFF.

shrieve (shrēv). Pseudoarchaic var. of SHRIVE.

shrift (shrĭft), *n.* [AS. *scrift* (akin to ON. *skript*), fr. root of AS. *scrīfan* to shrive.] **1.** *Archaic.* The act of shriving; a confessing of one's sins or a hearing of a penitent's confession in the sacrament of penance. **2.** Confession or disclosure to anyone. Cf. SHORT SHRIFT.

shrike (shrīk), *n.* [AS. *scrīc* thrush.] Any of numerous oscine birds of the family Laniidae. The typical genus (*Lanius*) is characterized by a strong notched bill hooked at the tip. Its members feed chiefly on insects, and often impale their prey on thorns. The term ***butcherbird*** is often applied to its larger species, including *L. excubitor* of Europe and *L. borealis* of northern North America, which sometimes kill small birds and mammals. The ***loggerhead shrike*** (*L. ludovicianus*) occurs in the southeastern United States.

shrill (shrĭl), *adj.* [ME. *shrille.*] **1.** Having or emitting a sharp, high-pitched tone or sound. **2. a** Accompanied by such sounds; as, *shrill* gaiety. **b** Sharp; keen; bright; clear. — *adv.* Shrilly. — *v. i. & t.* To utter or emit an acute, piercing sound; also, to sound with a sharp, shrill tone. — *n.* A shrill sound. — **shrill′ness,** *n.* — **shril′ly** (shrĭl′lĭ), *adv.*

shrimp (shrĭmp), *n.;* see PLURAL, *Note,* 3. **1.** Any of numerous small, mostly marine, macruran crustaceans (*Crago* and allied genera) having a slender body, long legs, and a depressed abdomen. Many are used as food. **2.** A little contemptible person or thing.

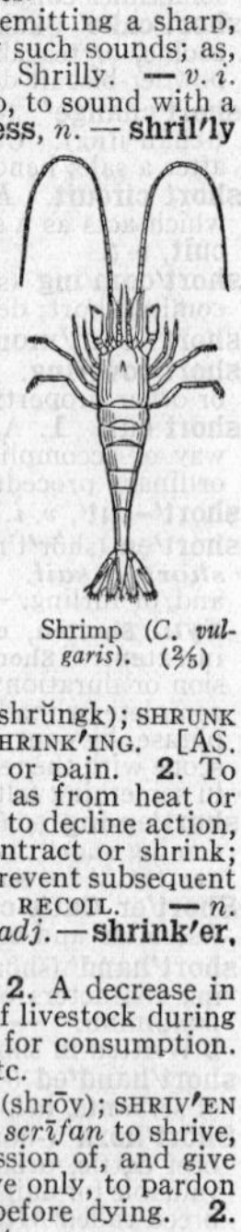
Shrimp (*C. vulgaris*). (2/5)

shrine (shrīn), *n.* [AS. *scrīn,* fr. L. *scrinium* a case, box.] **1.** A case, box, or receptacle, esp. for sacred relics. **2.** The tomb of a saint or other sacred person. **3.** A place or object hallowed from its associations. **4.** [*cap.*] Short for ***Ancient Arabic Order of Nobles of the Mystic Shrine,*** a secret order said to have been originated at Mecca about A.D. 646. In the modern order, only Knights Templar or thirty-second-degree Masons are eligible for admission, though the order is not Masonic. — *v. t.* To enshrine.

Shrin′er (shrīn′ẽr), *n.* A member of the Order of the Mystic Shrine. See SHRINE, *n.,* 4.

shrink (shrĭngk), *v. i.;* SHRANK (shrăngk) or SHRUNK (shrŭngk); SHRUNK or (chiefly as *part. adj.*) SHRUNK′EN (shrŭngk′ĕn); SHRINK′ING. [AS. *scrincan.*] **1.** To huddle; cower, as with horror or pain. **2.** To contract to a less compass; to become compacted, as from heat or wetting; hence, to lessen in value. **3.** To withdraw; to decline action, as from fear or distaste. — *v. t.* To cause to contract or shrink; specif., *Textiles,* to prepare (cloth) by shrinkage to prevent subsequent shrinking. — **Syn.** See CONTRACT (**Ant.** swell): RECOIL. — *n.* Shrinkage; contraction; also, recoil. — **shrink′a·ble,** *adj.* — **shrink′er,** *n.* — **shrink′ing·ly,** *adv.*

shrink′age (shrĭngk′ĭj), *n.* **1.** Act of shrinking. **2.** A decrease in value; depreciation. **3.** Specif., the loss in weight of livestock during shipment and in the process of preparing the meat for consumption. **4.** The amount of such contraction, depreciation, etc.

shrive (shrīv), *v. t. & i.;* SHRIVED (shrīvd) or SHROVE (shrōv); SHRIV′EN (shrĭv′ĕn) or SHRIVED; SHRIV′ING (shrīv′ĭng). [AS. *scrīfan* to shrive, impose penance.] **1.** *Archaic.* To hear the confession of, and give absolution to, in the sacrament of penance; in passive only, to pardon the sins of (one so confessing); as, to be *shriven* before dying. **2.** *Obs.* To confess the sins of (oneself), esp. to a priest.

shriv′el (shrĭv′'l), *v. i. & t.;* -ELED or -ELLED (-'ld); -EL·ING or -EL·LING. **1.** To draw, or be drawn, into wrinkles; to shrink and form corrugations. **2.** To become reduced to inanition, helplessness, or inefficiency; as, faculties that *shrivel.*

shroff (shrŏf), *n.* [Ar. *ṣarrāf.*] *East Indies, China, etc.* A banker, or changer of money; also, a bank expert who tests silver coins. — **shroff,** *v. t. & i.*

Shrop′shire (shrŏp′shĭr; -shẽr), *n.* [From *Shropshire,* county of England.] One of an English breed of black-faced hornless sheep, larger than a Southdown.

shroud (shroud), *n.* [AS. *scrūd* a garment, clothing.] **1.** That which covers or shelters like a garment. **2.** The dress for the dead; a winding sheet. **3.** *Naut.* One of the ropes leading, usually in pairs, from a vessel's mastheads to give lateral support to the masts. See RATLINE, *Illust.* — *v. t.* **1. a** *Archaic.* To protect; shelter. **b** *Obs.* To conceal; to veil. **2.** To veil by obscurity, or disguise; as, *shrouded* in mystery. **3.** To cover with a shroud, or winding sheet; to dress for the grave. — *v. i. Archaic.* To take or seek shelter. — **shroud′less,** *adj.*

shroud′-laid′, *adj.* Composed of four strands, and laid right-handed with a core; — of rope.

shrove (shrōv), *past* of SHRIVE.

Shrove′tide′ (shrōv′tīd′), *n.* [See SHRIVE; TIDE.] The days, usually three, before Ash Wednesday; — so called as being the time for confession preparatory to Lent. Hence, **Shrove Sunday, Monday, Tuesday.** Cf. CARNIVAL, 1.

shrub (shrŭb), *n.* [Ar. *shurb* drink, colloq. *sharāb.*] A liquor composed of fruit acid, esp. lemon juice and sugar, usually with spirit to preserve it.

shrub, *n.* [AS. *scrybb* shrubbery.] A low, usually several-stemmed, woody plant; a bush.

shrub′ber·y (shrŭb′ẽr·ĭ), *n.; pl.* -BERIES (-ĭz). A growth of shrubs; shrubs collectively.

shrub′by (shrŭb′ĭ), *adj.;* SHRUB′BI·ER (-ĭ·ẽr); SHRUB′BI·EST. **1.** Covered with shrubs. **2.** Shrublike in size, habit, or growth. — **shrub′bi·ness,** *n.*

shrug (shrŭg), *v. t. & i.;* SHRUGGED (shrŭgd); SHRUG′GING. To draw up or contract (the shoulders), esp. by way of expressing dislike, dread, doubt, or the like. — **shrug**, *n.*

shrunk (shrŭngk), *past & past part.* of SHRINK.

shrunk'en (shrŭngk'ĕn), *past part. & part. adj.* of SHRINK.

shuck (shŭk), *n.* **1.** A shell, husk, or pod; esp., the outer covering of a nut, or of Indian corn. **2.** *U.S.* The shell of an oyster or clam. **3.** *U.S.* Something of little or no value; — used in various colloquial phrases, as *not to care shucks, not worth shucks,* etc. — *v. t.* **1.** To strip of the shucks, or husks; as, to *shuck* nuts, corn, etc. **2.** To remove (oysters) from the shell. — **shuck'er**, *n.*

shud'der (shŭd'ẽr), *v. i.* [ME. *shoderen, schuderen.*] To tremble convulsively or shake with fear, horror, or aversion; quake. — **shud'der**, *n.* — **shud'der·ing·ly**, *adv.*

shud'na (shōōd'nȧ). Scot. var. of *should not.*

shuf'fle (shŭf''l), *v. t.;* SHUF'FLED (-'ld); SHUF'FLING (-lĭng). [Orig., a freq. fr. the root of *shove.* See SHOVE; cf. SCUFFLE.] **1.** To mix in a mass without order. **2.** At cards, to mix by successive, supposedly chance, changes of order of individual cards. **3.** To move or perform with a dragging gait; as, to *shuffle* the feet. **4.** To shift from place to place; also, to introduce or remove clumsily or trickily. — *v. i.* **1.** To introduce or extricate oneself shiftily; — with *in, into,* or *out of.* **2.** *Cards.* To mix a pack by repeatedly forming two sections and inserting the cards of one here and there between those of the other. **3.** To act shiftily; hence, to evade questions; to prevaricate. **4.** To make shift; to proceed awkwardly or with difficulty. **5. a** To move or walk in a slovenly, dragging manner. **b** To dance in a lazy, nonchalant manner with sliding and tapping motions of the feet. — *n.* **1.** Act of shuffling; specif., the mixing up of cards in a pack before dealing; also, the right of shuffling, or one's turn to shuffle, the cards. **2.** A trick; evasion; equivocation. **3.** A slovenly, dragging motion; specif., a sliding or scraping step in dancing; also, a dance characterized by such a step.

shuf'fle·board' (-bōrd'; 70), *n.* **1.** A board on which a game was formerly played by driving pieces of metal or money to reach certain marks; also, the game. **2.** A somewhat similar game played on the deck of a ship.

shuf'fler (shŭf'lẽr), *n.* **a** One given to shuffling; also, one who shuffles cards. **b** A scaup duck.

shun (shŭn), *v. t.;* SHUNNED (shŭnd); SHUN'NING. [AS. *scunian.*] To avoid deliberately, esp. as a practice; to keep clear of. — **Syn.** See ESCAPE. — **shun'ner** (shŭn'ẽr), *n.*

shunt (shŭnt), *v. t.* [E. dial., to move, push, stand aside, fr. ME. *shunten* to avoid.] **1.** To turn off to one side; to shift; as, to *shunt* cattle into a corral; *Railroads,* to switch, as a car or train, from one track to another. **2.** *Elec.* To provide with, or place upon, a shunt. — *v. i.* To move aside, esp. out of the way; also, to turn off; to shift. — *n.* A turning, or thrusting aside; specif.: **a** *Railroads.* A switch. **b** *Elec.* A conductor joining two points in a circuit so as to form a parallel or derived circuit through which a portion of the current may pass, in order to regulate the amount passing in the main circuit. Hence, **shunt circuit, shunt field, shunt lamp,** etc. — **shunt'er**, *n.*

shunt winding. *Elec.* A winding so arranged as to divide the armature current and lead a portion of it around the field magnet; — opposed to *series winding.* — **shunt'-wound'** (shŭnt'wound'), *adj.*

shure (shür). Scot. past of SHEAR, reap.

shut (shŭt), *v. t.;* SHUT; SHUT'TING. [AS. *scyttan* to shut or lock up.] **1.** To fasten with a bolt; now, to close so as to hinder ingress or egress. **2.** To forbid entrance into; to bar. **3.** To confine by enclosure; as, *shut* in prison. **4.** To fold together, as a knife; to close over, as the fingers. **5.** *Obs.* To exclude. — *v. i.* To close itself or become closed. — *adj.* **1.** Closed or fastened; as, a *shut* door. **2.** *Now Dial.* Rid; clear; free; — with *of.* **3.** *Phonet.* Formed with complete closure of the oral and nasal passages (the stops *p, b,* etc.); stopped. — *n.* **1.** Act or time of shutting; close; as, the *shut* of a door. **2.** The line of union of two pieces of welded metal.

shut'down' (-doun'), *n.* A shutting down; discontinuance, esp. of work in a factory or the like.

shut'-in', *adj.* **1.** Confined to one's home; — said of invalids. **2.** *Psychiatry.* Prone to seek isolation from other people; as, a *shut-in* personality. — *n.* An invalid confined to his home, a room, or his bed.

shut'off' (shŭt'ôf'; 74), *n.* That which shuts off.

shut'out' (-out'), *n.* Act of shutting out; specif.: **a** A lockout. **b** *Sports.* A preventing from scoring; hence, a game in which one side fails to score.

shut'ter (shŭt'ẽr), *n.* **1.** One who or that which shuts. **2.** A movable cover or screen for a window; a blind. **3.** *Photog.* A mechanical device of various forms, attached to a camera for opening and closing to expose the film or plate. — *v. t.* To cover or furnish with a shutter.

shut'tle (shŭt''l), *n.* [AS. *scytel* missile.] **1.** An instrument used in weaving for passing the woof thread between the warp threads. **2.** The sliding thread holder in a sewing machine; hence, any of various rotary, vibrating, or oscillating, devices used for the same purpose. **3.** *U.S.* A shuttle train. — *v. t. & i.;* -TLED (-'ld); -TLING (-lĭng). To move backward and forward, like a shuttle. — *adj.* That moves backward and forward like a shuttle.

shut'tle·cock' (shŭt''l·kŏk'), *n.* **1.** A cork stuck with feathers batted with a battledore in an old game (*battledore and shuttlecock*) or the similar object used in the game of badminton. **2.** The game of battledore and shuttlecock. — *v. t.* To send or toss to and fro; to bandy.

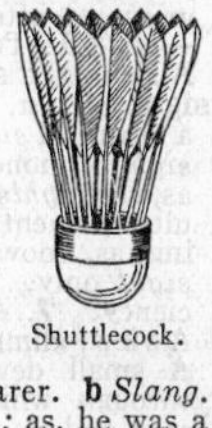

Shuttlecock.

shuttle train. A train running back and forth over a short route, as to an outlying town.

shy (shī), *adj.;* SHI'ER (shī'ẽr) or SHY'ER; SHI'EST or SHY'EST. [AS. *sceōh.*] **1.** Easily frightened; timid. **2.** Disposed to avoid a person or thing through caution or timidity; distrustful; wary. **3.** Reserved; bashful. **4. a** Scant; very light; as, that tree is a *shy* bearer. **b** *Slang.* Lacking; inadequately supplied; — sometimes with *on;* as, he was a bit *shy* on brains. **c** *Slang.* Short; not having paid; — used esp. in poker playing.

Syn. **Shy, bashful, diffident, modest, coy** mean disinclined to intrude or obtrude. **Shy** implies a shrinking from familiarity or contact with others; **bashful**, an instinctive shrinking from public notice that usually shows in awkward demeanor; **diffident**, a distrust of one's ability, one's opinion, or the like, that gives rise to hesitation; **modest**, an absence of undue confidence in oneself or one's powers; **coy**, an assumed or affected shyness.

— *v. i.;* SHIED (shīd); SHY'ING. **1.** To shrink; recoil. **2.** To start suddenly aside through fright or suspicion; — said esp. of horses. — *n.;* *pl.* SHIES (shīz). A sudden start aside.

shy, *v. t. & i.* To throw sidewise with a jerk; as, to *shy* a stone. — *n.* **1.** Act of shying; a throw. **2.** Hence, a verbal fling; a sneer. **3.** = COCKSHY. — **shy'er** (shī'ẽr), *n.*

Shy'lock (shī'lŏk), *n.* **1.** A revengeful Jewish moneylender in Shakespeare's *Merchant of Venice.* **2.** An extortionate creditor.

shy'ly (shī'lĭ), *adv.* In a shy manner.

shy'ness, *n.* Quality or state of being shy.

shy'ster (shī'stẽr), *n.* [Appar. after a New York attorney, Scheuster, frequently rebuked in court (1840 ff.) for pettifoggery.] *U.S.* One who is professionally unscrupulous, esp. in the practice of law or politics; a pettifogger.

si (sē), *n.* [It.] *Music.* See TI.

si'a·la·gog'ic (sī'ȧ·lȧ·gŏj'ĭk), **si'a·lo·gog'ic** (sī'ȧ·lō-), *adj.* *Med.* Promoting the flow of saliva. — *n.* A sialagogue.

si·al'a·gogue (sī·ăl'ȧ·gŏg; 74), **si·al'o·gogue** (sī·ăl'ō-), *n.* [Gr. *sialon* saliva + *-agogue.*] An agent promoting the flow of saliva.

si'a·lid (sī'ȧ·lĭd), **si·al'i·dan** (sī·ăl'ĭ·dăn), *adj.* [Gr. *sialis* a kind of bird.] Belonging to a family (Sialidae) of insects (order Megaloptera) including the hellgrammite and allies. — **si'a·lid, si·al'i·dan**, *n.*

si'a·loid (sī'ȧ·loid), *adj.* Resembling saliva.

si'a·mang (sē'ȧ·măng; syä'măng), *n.;* *pl.* SIAMANGS (-măngz). [Malay *siamañ.*] A black gibbon (*Symphalangus syndactylus*) of Sumatra, largest of the gibbons.

Si'a·mese' (sī'ȧ·mēz'; -mēs'; 2), *n.* **1.** *sing. & pl.* One of the people of Siam; specif., a member of the dominant race of Siam since the 13th century, the most progressive representative of the Thai stock. **2.** The language of the Siamese, a branch of the Thai of the Indo-Chinese family. See LANGUAGE, *Table.* — **Si'a·mese'**, *adj.*

Siamese cat. A slender cat of an oriental breed with sleek short fur light-colored on the body and distinctively dark on ears, paws, tail, and face.

Siamese twins. An instance of double monstrosity, Chang and Eng (1811–74), born in Siam of Chinese extraction. They were united, between the xiphoid cartilages, by a thick fleshy ligament. Hence, any similar or double monster.

sib (sĭb), *n.* [AS. *sibb, gesib.* See GOSSIP.] **1.** Kindred, collectively; relatives. **2.** A blood relation; a kinsman. **3.** In genetics, a brother or sister, considered irrespective of sex; *pl.,* offspring of the same parents. **4.** *Anthropol.* = CLAN, 3. — *adj.* Related by blood; akin.

sib'i·lant (sĭb'ĭ·lănt), *adj.* [L. *sibilans, -antis,* pres. part. of *sibilare* to hiss.] Making a hissing sound; esp., *Phonet.,* uttered with, or accompanied by, a hissing sound (*s, ch*). — *n.* A sibilant speech sound or its symbol. The sibilants in English are *s, z, sh, zh, ch, j.* — **sib'i·lance** (-lăns), **sib'i·lan·cy** (-lăn·sĭ), *n.* — **sib'i·lant·ly**, *adv.*

sib'i·late (-lāt), *v. t. & i.* [L. *sibilare* to hiss.] To pronounce with initial *s;* also, to hiss. — **sib'i·la'tion** (-lā'shŭn), *n.*

sib'ling (sĭb'lĭng), *n.* One of two or more children of the same parents but not necessarily of the same birth; — usually in *pl.*

sib'yl (sĭb'ĭl; -'l), *n.* [L. *sibylla,* fr. Gr. *sibylla.*] *Gr. & Rom. Myth.* Any of a number of prophetesses credited to parts of the ancient world; hence, a prophetess; fortune teller. — **si·byl'ic, si·byl'lic** (sĭ·bĭl'ĭk), **sib'yl·line** (sĭb'ĭ·līn; -lĭn), *adj.*

Sib'yl·line Books. *Rom. Relig.* A collection of oracles, in Greek, said to have been bought from the sibyl of Cumae by Tarquin the Proud.

‖**sic** (sĭk), *adv.* [L.] Thus; — sometimes inserted [*sic*] to note that an expression, spelling, or the like, exactly reproduces the original.

sic (sĭk). Dial. var. of SUCH.

sic'ca·tive (sĭk'ȧ·tĭv), *adj.* [LL. *siccativus.*] Drying; causing to dry. — *n.* That which promotes drying; a drier.

sice (sīs). Var. of SYCE.

Si·cil'ian Ves'pers (sĭ·sĭl'yăn; -ĭ·ăn; 58). The great massacre of the French in Sicily by the natives, in 1282, which began at Palermo on the Monday of Easter week, at the hour of vespers.

sick (sĭk), *v. t.* [Dial. var. of SEEK, *v.*] **1.** To seek; chase; attack; — used chiefly of or to a dog. **2.** To incite, as a dog; — chiefly with *on.*

sick, *adj.* [AS. *sēoc.*] **1.** Affected with disease; ill. **2. a** *Colloq.* Accompanying or suggestive of sickness; sickly; as, a *sick* smile. **b** Pertaining or relating to the sick; as, *sick* insurance. **c** Designed for, or put to, the use of a sick person; as, a *sick*bed. **3.** Affected with, or attended by, nausea; inclined to vomit. **4.** Unsound or unfit in condition. **5.** Pale; wan; — of light, color, etc. **6. a** *Obs.* Unsound in spiritual or moral state. **b** Mentally unsound. **7.** Permeated by an emotion, as of grief, desire, or disgust, that causes physical distress; also, disgusted; surfeited. **8.** Depressed and longing for something; languishing; — with *for;* as, to be *sick* for one's home. **9.** *Agric.* Of soils, incapable of producing profitable yields of certain crops; as, clover-*sick;* less commonly, infested with disease organisms. — *n.* A sick person; also, sick people, collectively.

Syn. **Sick, ill** mean not in good health. **Sick** is commoner in this sense in the United States than in England, where **ill** is preferred and *sick* is often restricted in meaning to "nauseated."

sick bay. *Naut.* A section in a vessel, esp. a war vessel or transport, used as a dispensary and hospital. Cf. 2d BAY, *n.,* 5.

sick'bed' (sĭk'bĕd'), *n.* The bed upon which one lies sick.

sick'en (sĭk'ĕn), *v. t. & i.* To make or become sick.

sick'en·er (-ẽr), *n.* Something that tends to sicken.

sick'en·ing (-ĭng), *adj.* Causing sickness; specif., causing disgust; nauseating. — **sick'en·ing·ly**, *adv.*

sick'er, sik'er (sĭk'ẽr), *adj.* [AS. *sicor,* fr. L. *securus* sure.] *Now Scot.* Sure; safe; dependable.

sick headache. *Med.* A variety of headache attended with, or due to, disorder of the stomach and nausea.

sick'ish, *adj.* **1.** *Archaic.* Somewhat sick. **2.** Somewhat nauseated or nauseating. — **sick'ish·ly**, *adv.* — **sick'ish·ness**, *n.*

sic'kle (sĭk''l), *n.* [AS. *sicol, sicel.*] **1.** An agricultural implement consisting of a curved metal blade with a handle fitted on a tang. **2.** [*cap.*] *Astron.* A group of six stars in the constellation Leo.

Sic'kle (sĭk''l). Var. of SECKEL.

sic'kle-bill' (-bĭl'), *n.* Any of various birds with a strongly curved bill, as a curlew.

sickle feather. See POULTRY, *Illust.* (10).

sick'ly (sĭk'lĭ), *adj.;* SICK'LI·ER (-lĭ·ẽr); SICK'LI·EST. **1.** Somewhat sick; ailing. **2.** Produced by, or associated with, sickness; as, a *sickly* complexion. **3.** Characterized by the presence of sickness; as, a *sickly* season; also, producing disease. **4. a** Appearing as if sick;

languid; pale. **b** Resembling in state a sickly person. **5. a** Tending to produce nausea; sickening. **b** Hence, mawkish; disgusting. — *adv.* In a sick manner or condition; ill. — *v. t.;* SICK'LIED (-lĭd); SICK'LY-ING. To make sick or sickly, esp. in hue. — **sick'li·ness,** *n.*

sick'ness (sĭk'nĕs; -nĭs), *n.* **1.** Diseased condition; illness. **2.** A malady; disease. **3.** Nausea; qualmishness.

‖**sic pas'sim** (sĭk păs'ĭm). [L.] So everywhere.

‖**sic sem'per ty·ran'nis** (sĕm'pĕr tĭ·răn'ĭs; tī-). [L.] Ever thus to tyrants; — motto of Virginia.

‖**sic tran'sit glo'ri·a mun'di** (trăn'sĭt glō'rĭ·ȧ mŭn'dī). [L.] So passes away the glory of the world.

‖**sic'ut pa'tri·bus, sit De'us no'bis** (sĭk'ŭt păt'rĭ·bŭs, sĭt dē'ŭs nō'bĭs). [L.] As with our fathers, may God be with us.

sid'dur (sĭd'o͝or), *n.* [Heb. *siddūr* order, arrangement.] *Jewish Relig.* The Jewish daily prayer book, containing both Hebrew and Aramaic prayers.

side (sīd), *adj.* [AS. *sīd.*] *Scot. & Dial.* Long and flowing; hanging low; — esp. of garments.

side, *n.* *Slang.* Swaggering manner; pretentiousness.

side, *n.* [AS. *sīde.*] **1.** A surface forming a border or face of an object. **2. a** Any outer portion of a thing considered as facing in a particular direction; as, the upper *side* of a sphere. **b** An aspect or part regarded as contrasted with some other; a phase; as, the bright *side* of poverty. **3.** A slope or declivity, as of a hill. **4. a** A bounding line of a geometrical figure; as, the *side* of a square. **b** One of the surfaces that define or limit a solid, esp. one of the longer surfaces. **5.** The right or left part of the trunk of the body; one of the halves of a human or animal body. **6.** The space beside one. **7.** A place, space, or direction with respect to a center or a line of division; as, altars on either *side.* **8.** The attitude or activity of one person or group with respect to another; part; as, one's *side* of an agreement. **9.** A body of partisans or contestants, as in games; as, victory for neither *side.* **10.** A line of descent traced through one parent; as, the grandfather on one's mother's *side.* Cf. CONSANGUINITY, *Illust.* **11.** *Billiards.* Sidewise spin imparted to a ball. **12.** *Naut.* The outer surface of a ship on either side above the water line. **13.** *Theater.* An actor's lines. — **Syn.** See PHASE. — ***off side.*** See in *Vocab.* — ***on side.*** Not off side.

— *adj.* **1.** Of or pertaining to a side, or the sides; being on the side, or toward the side; lateral. **2.** Hence, indirect; oblique; as, a *side* view or remark.

— *v. t.* **1.** To push or thrust aside; to put aside. **2.** To furnish with sides; as, to *side* a house, a book. — *v. i.* To embrace the opinions of one party, or engage in its interest, in opposition to another party; to take sides.

side arms. *Mil. & Nav.* Weapons worn at the side or in the belt, as sword, revolver, bayonet, etc.

side band. *Radio.* The band of frequencies on either side of the carrier frequency, produced by the process of modulation.

side'board' (sīd'bōrd'; 70), *n.* **1.** A piece of dining-room furniture for holding articles of table service. **2.** *Slang, pl.* Side whiskers.

side'burns' (-bûrnz'), *n. pl.* = BURNSIDES.

side'car' (-kär'), *n.* A car attached to a motorcycle for a passenger seated abreast of the cyclist.

side'check' (-chĕk'), *n.* A checkrein at the side of the horse's head.

sid'ed (sīd'ĕd; -ĭd), *adj.* Having sides, as in lop*sided,* four-*sided.*

side'–dress' (sīd'drĕs'), *v. t.* *Agric.* To nourish (growing plants) by working fertilizer (**side dressing**) into the soil along one side of each row, esp. by means of a cultivator.

side'head' (sīd'hĕd'), *n.* A subhead placed at or in the side of text matter, usually the left side of the first line of a paragraph.

side'hill' (sīd'hĭl'; 2), *n.* *Now U. S.* Hillside.

side issue. An issue apart from the main point.

side light. **1.** Light from the side; hence, information or an illustration coming incidentally. **2.** *Naut.* The red light on the port bow or the green light on the starboard bow carried by vessels under way at night.

side line. **1.** A line attached to the side of a thing. **2. a** A line of goods sold in addition to one's principal articles of trade. **b** A course of business pursued outside of one's regular occupation; a by-line. **3.** A transportation line running to one side of the main line. **4.** *Sports.* A line, usually at right angles to a goal line or end line, marking a side of a court, field of play, etc. **5.** Often **side lines.** **a** *Sports.* The space immediately outside the lines along either side of the field. **b** The standpoint of those not immediately participating.

side'ling (sīd'lĭng), *adv.* [*side* + 2d *-ling.*] Sidelong; also, obliquely. — *adj.* Inclining to or directed toward one side; also, sloping; figuratively, indirect.

side'long' (-lŏng'; 74), *adv.* [See SIDELING, *adv.*] **1.** Laterally; obliquely. **2.** On the side; as, to lay a thing *sidelong.* — *adj.* **1.** Slanting; oblique. **2.** Directed sideways; indirect, as a glance or smile.

side'piece' (-pēs'), *n.* A piece forming, or contained in, the side of something.

si·de're·al (sī·dēr'ē·ăl), *adj.* [L. *sidereus,* fr. *sidus, sideris,* constellation, star.] **1.** Of or relating to the stars or constellations; starry; astral. **2.** *Astron.* Measured by the apparent motion of fixed stars; as, *sidereal day,* the interval between two successive transits of the first point of Aries over the upper meridian of any place, equal to 23 h. 56 m. 4.09 s. of mean solar time. A sidereal day has 24 **sidereal hours,** each of 60 **sidereal minutes,** each minute of 60 **sidereal seconds.**

sid'er·ite (sĭd'ĕr·īt), *n.* [L. *sideritis* loadstone, fr. Gr. *sidēritēs, -ritis,* of iron, fr. *sidēros* iron.] *Mineral.* **a** Formerly, loadstone. **b** Native ferrous carbonate, $FeCO_3$, a valuable ore. **c** Meteoric iron. — **sid'er·it'ic** (-ĭt'ĭk), *adj.*

sid'er·o- (sĭd'ĕr·ō-), **sider-.** [Gr. *sidēros.*] A combining form meaning *iron,* as in **sid'er·o·lite',** a stony-iron meteorite, **sid'er·o'sis,** a lung disease caused by inhaling iron particles.

sid'er·o-. [L. *sidus, sideris.*] A combining form meaning *star,* as in **sid'er·o·stat',** a device to reflect a star's rays in a constant direction.

side'sad'dle (sīd'săd''l), *n.* A saddle for women, in which the rider sits with both feet on the same side of the horse.

side show. **a** A small show accompanying or a part of a main exhibition, as of a circus. **b** An incidental diversion.

side'slip' (sīd'slĭp'), *v. i.;* see SLIP. **1.** To skid, as an automobile. **2.** *Aeronautics.* To slide sideways in a downward direction along the lateral axis of an airplane, the axis being in an inclined position. If sideslipping occurs when turning, it is the opposite of skidding. **3.** *Skiing.* To slip sideways. — **side'slip',** *n.*

side'split'ting, *adj.* Affecting the sides convulsively, as laughter.

side step. A step aside, as in boxing, to avoid a blow.

side'–step', *v. i.;* see STEP. To take a side step; hence, to avoid meeting issues. — *v. t.* To avoid, as a blow; also, to evade, as a decision.

side stroke. A type of stroke made by a swimmer while lying on his side, in which the arms are moved alternately forward and backward while the legs execute a scissors kick.

side'swipe' (sīd'swīp'), *v. t. & i.* *Colloq.* To strike with a glancing blow along the side. — **side'swipe',** *n.*

side'track' (-trăk'), *v. t.* **1.** *Railroads.* To transfer to a siding. **2.** *Colloq.* Hence, to switch off, as from a purpose. — *n.* **1.** *Railroads.* A siding. **2.** A position in which one is sidetracked.

side'walk' (-wôk'), *n.* A walk for foot passengers at the side of a street or road; a foot pavement.

side'ward (-wẽrd), **side'wards** (-wẽrdz), *adj. & adv.* (Moving or tending) toward one side.

side'way' (-wā'), *adv. & adj.* = SIDEWAYS.

side'ways' (-wāz'), *adv.* **1.** From the side; as, viewed *sideways.* **2.** With one side advanced; as, to lie *sideways.* **3.** To, toward, or at one side; obliquely. — *adj.* Moving or tending toward one side.

side'–wheel', *adj.* Designating a form of steamer (**side'–wheel'er**) having a paddle wheel on each side.

side whisker. A whisker at the side of the face; — chiefly *pl.*

side'wind'er (sīd'wīn'dẽr), *n.* **1.** Any of several rattlesnakes. **2.** *Slang.* A heavy swinging blow from the side.

side'wise' (-wīz'), *adv. & adj.* Sideways.

sid'ing (sīd'ĭng), *n.* **1.** *U. S.* Boards forming the exposed surface of outside walls of frame buildings. **2.** *Railroads.* A short track connected with the main track; sidetrack.

si'dle (sī'd'l), *v. i.;* SI'DLED (-d'ld); SI'DLING (-dlĭng). [From SIDE.] To go or move with one side foremost; to move sidewise, esp. in a furtive advance. — **si'dle,** *n.*

‖**siè'cle** (syĕ'kl'), *n.* [F.] Century; age.

siege (sēj), *n.* [OF. *sege, siege* (F. *siège*) a seat, a siege, deriv. of L. *sedere* to sit.] **1.** *Archaic.* A seat; esp., a throne. **2. a** The besetting of a fortified place by an army to compel surrender; a besieging. **b** A continued attempt to gain possession. **c** *Colloq.* A long, wearying time. **3.** *Obs.* Place; seat; also, rank; station. — *v. t.;* SIEGED (sējd); SIEG'ING (sēj'ĭng). To besiege.

Siege Perilous. [See SIEGE, *n.,* 1.] The seat of danger at King Arthur's Round Table, reserved for the knight destined to achieve the quest of the Holy Grail and fatal to all others who should occupy it.

Sieg'fried (sēg'frēd; *G.* zēk'frēt), *n.* [G.] The hero of various German legends, esp. of the *Nibelungenlied.* He wins the hoard of the Nibelungs, a magic sword, and a cap (or cloak) rendering its wearer invisible. He slays a dragon and makes himself invulnerable by bathing in its blood. He aids Gunther to win Brunhild, and himself weds Kriemhild, Gunther's sister. Wagner makes Siegfried release from enchantment and wed the Valkyrie Brünnhilde before falling in love with Gutrune.

Siegfried line. [After the G. hero, *Siegfried.*] = LIMES, 2.

si·en'na (sĭ·ĕn'ȧ), *n.* [It. *terra di Siena,* fr. *Siena* in Italy.] An earthy substance, brownish-yellow when raw and orange-red or reddish-brown when burnt, used as a pigment. It owes its color to oxides of iron and, usually, of manganese.

si·er'ra (sĭ·ĕr'ȧ), *n.* [Sp., prop., a saw, fr. L. *serra.*] **1.** A ridge of mountains with a serrated or irregular outline. **2.** Any of certain mackerellike fishes, as the cero and pintado.

si·es'ta (sĭ·ĕs'tȧ), *n.* [Sp.] A short rest, esp. at midday.

‖**sieur** (syûr), *n.* [F., abbr. fr. *seigneur.*] Sir; — a title of respect used, esp. formerly, by the French.

sieve (sĭv), *n.* [AS. *sife.*] An apparatus with meshes through which the finer particles of a pulverized or granulated substance are passed to separate them from the coarser particles. — *v. t. & i.* To sift.

sieve tube. *Bot.* A tube, characteristic of phloem tissue, which consists of an end-to-end series of thin-walled living cells (**sieve cells**) having no nucleus when mature; also, a sieve cell.

sift (sĭft), *v. t.* [AS. *siftan.*] **1.** To pass through or as through a sieve. **2.** Hence: **a** To subject to close questioning. **b** To examine critically or minutely; as, to *sift* the evidence. **3.** To separate with or as with a sieve, as the fine part of a substance from the coarse; as, to *sift* flour. **4.** To scatter by or as by passing through a sieve; as, to *sift* sugar on a cake. — *v. i.* **1.** To sift something with, or as with, a sieve. **2.** To pass through, or as through, a sieve. — **sift'er,** *n.*

sig'a·to'ka (sĭg'ȧ·tō'kȧ), *n.* [From *Sigatoka,* a river on Viti Levu, Fiji Is.] *Plant Pathol.* A serious leaf spot disease of bananas, esp. in tropical America, caused by the mold *Cercospora musae,* the imperfect stage of *Mycosphaerella musicola.*

sigh (sī), *v. i.* [ME. *sihen, sighen,* fr. *sihte,* past tense of *sichen, siken,* to sigh, fr. AS. *sīcan.*] **1.** To make a deep single audible respiration, esp. as an expression of fatigue, grief, etc. **2.** To lament; grieve; — often with *for.* **3.** To make a sound like sighing, as a wind. — *v. t.* **1.** To express by sighs. **2.** To lament or mourn over. — *n.* A sighing; a sound of or as of sighing. — **sigh'er** (sī'ẽr), *n.*

sight (sīt), *n.* [AS. *gesiht, gesihth.*] **1.** A view; esp., a spectacle; as, a beautiful *sight.* **2.** *Colloq.* A great number, quantity, or sum; as, a *sight* of money. **3.** A thing regarded as worth seeing; — chiefly *pl.;* as, the *sights* of the city. **4. a** The power of seeing; vision. **b** Faculty of mental or spiritual perception. **5. a** Act of seeing or looking; as, known by *sight.* **b** Inspection; as, a letter intended for your *sight* only. **6. a** Mental view; judgment. **b** *Obs.* Insight; proficiency. **7.** An observation taken by means of a sighting device. **8.** A view; glimpse. **9.** The range of view; as, out of one's *sight.* **10.** A small device with an aperture through which objects are to be seen and by which their direction is ascertained; as, the *sight* of a quadrant, of a gun. — ***at sight.*** As soon as seen, or presented to sight; as, a draft payable *at sight,* that is, on demand or presentation. — *v. t.* **1.** To get sight of; to see; as, to *sight* land. **2. a** To look at through or as through a sight; as, to *sight* an object, as a star. **b** To give the proper elevation and direction to by a sight or sights; as, to *sight* a

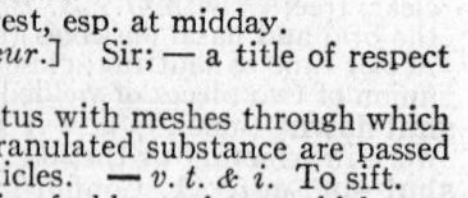

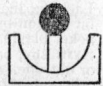

Sight, 10. Aiming Patterns for Peep Sight and Open Sight. Cf. TARGET, *Illust.*

rifle. **3.** To equip with sights; also, to adjust the sights of. See SIGHT, *n.*, 10. — *v. i.* **1.** To take aim by a sight. **2.** To look carefully in a given direction.

sight bill, draft (or the like). A bill, draft, etc., directing payment at sight, that is, on presentation.

sight′hole′ (sīt′hōl′), *n.* A peephole.

sight′less, *adj.* **1.** Wanting sight; blind. **2.** Invisible.

sight′ly (sīt′lĭ), *adj.*; -LI·ER (-lĭ·ẽr); -LI·EST. **1.** Pleasing to the sight; comely. **2.** *U. S.* Affording a fine view; as, a *sightly* eminence. — **sight′li·ness,** *n.*

sight rhyme. See EYE RHYME.

sight′-see′ing, *adj.* Engaged in, or devoted to, seeing sights; as, a *sight-seeing* tour. — *n.* Act of seeing sights. — **sight′-se′er** (-sē′ẽr), *n.*

sight unseen. = UNSIGHT, UNSEEN.

sig′il (sĭj′ĭl), *n.* [L. *sigillum* a seal.] **1.** A seal; signet. **2.** *Magic.* An astrological image having conjured into it the power of the stars. — **sig′il·lar′y** (sĭj′ĭ·lẽr′ĭ *or, esp. Brit.,* -lẽr·ĭ), *adj.*

sig′ma (sĭg′mȧ), *n.* [Gr.] The 18th letter (Σ, σ, ς) of the Greek alphabet, corresponding to Eng. *S, s.*

sig′mate (-māt), *adj.* [From SIGMA.] Having the shape or form of the Greek sigma or the letter S.

sig′moid (sĭg′moid), *adj.* [Gr. *sigmoeidēs.* See SIGMA; -OID.] **1.** Curved in two directions, like the letter S or the Greek ς. **2.** *Anat.* Pertaining to the sigmoid flexure of the intestine. — **sig·moi′dal** (sĭg·moi′dăl; -d'l), *adj.*

sigmoid flexure. a *Zool.* An S-shaped curve. **b** *Anat.* The contracted and crooked part of the intestine above the rectum. It is the lowest part of the colon.

sign (sīn), *n.* [OF. *signe,* fr. L. *signum.*] **1.** A conventional symbol representing an idea, as a word, letter, or mark. **2.** A motion, action, or gesture by which a thought is expressed, or a command or wish made known. **3.** A publicly displayed notice on a building, office, etc., to advertise the business there transacted, or the name of the person or firm conducting it. **4.** Something indicating the existence of a thing; a token. **5.** A prodigy; an omen. **6.** A trace; vestige; as, no *sign* of life. **7.** *Astron.* One of the twelve divisions of the ecliptic or zodiac. See ZODIAC. **8.** *Hunting, U. S.* A trace; a spoor; as, a bear sign. **9.** *Math.* A character indicating the relation of quantities, or an operation performed on them; as, the *signs* + (plus), − (minus), ÷ (of division), etc.; also, any abbreviation or conventional mark having a fixed meaning; as, the integral *sign* ∫, the radical sign √, etc. **10.** *Med.* An objective evidence of disease; that is, one appreciable by someone other than the patient. Cf. SYMPTOM, 1. **11.** *Music.* Any character used in notation, as a flat, sharp, etc.

Syn. **Sign, mark, token, note, symptom** mean a sensible indication of that not apparent to the senses. **Sign** is applicable to anything that gives such an indication whether a printed notice, a symbolic device, a manifestation as of a mood, or the like; **mark** suggests something impressed upon or inherently characteristic of a thing, esp. in contrast to an outward manifestation; **token** suggests something that serves as proof of that which has no physical existence; **note** suggests a distinguishing mark or characteristic; **symptom** suggests any outward indication of inward change as in the human body or the body politic.

— *v. t.* **1. a** To consecrate, bless, or mark with a sign, esp. with the sign of the cross. **b** To represent or indicate by a sign. **2. a** To affix a signature to. **b** To write (a signature); as, to *sign* one's name. **c** To assign or convey formally; as, to *sign* over property to a buyer. **3.** To signify by, or express in, a sign language. **4.** To hire by securing the signature of; as, the manager has *signed* a new player. — *v. i.* **1.** To write one's name, esp. as a token of assent or obligation. **2.** To make a sign or signal. — ***sign off.*** *Radio.* To announce the end (of a message, program, etc.) and discontinue transmitting. — ***sign on.*** To engage oneself for work by signature.

sig′nal (sĭg′năl; -n'l), *n.* [F., fr. LL. *signale,* neut. of *signalis,* adj., fr. L. *signum* sign.] **1.** A token; sign. **2. a** A sign, event, or watchword which has been agreed upon as the occasion of concerted action. **b** That which incites to action. **3.** A sign made to give notice of something, as of a command. **4.** At cards, a play indicating, to one's partner, desire for a certain lead. **5.** *Elec.* The intelligence, message, or effect conveyed in telegraphy or telephony. — *adj.* **1.** Noticeable; distinguished from what is ordinary; as, a *signal* exploit. **2.** Used in signaling; as, a *signal* beacon. — **Syn.** See NOTICEABLE. — *v. t. & i.*; -NALED (-năld; -n'ld) or -NALLED; -NAL·ING or -NAL·LING. **1.** To communicate by signals. **2.** To notify by a signal. — **sig′nal·er, sig′nal·ler,** *n.*

sig′nal·ize (sĭg′năl·īz), *v. t.* **a** To make signal; to distinguish. **b** To point out carefully or distinctly. **c** To signal.

sig′nal·ly, *adv.* Notably; as, *signally* wise.

sig′nal·man (sĭg′năl·măn; sĭg′n'l-), *n.* A man whose business is to manage or display signals.

sig′nal·ment (-mĕnt), *n.* [F. *signalement.*] Description by peculiar, appropriate, or characteristic marks; specif., the systematic description of a person for purposes of identification.

sig′na·to′ry (sĭg′nȧ·tō′rĭ *or, esp. Brit.,* -tẽr·ĭ), *adj.* Joining in a signature; bound by the terms of a signed agreement; as, *signatory* powers. — *n.*; *pl.* -RIES (-rĭz). A signer with another or others.

sig′na·ture (sĭg′nȧ·tūr; 118), *n.* [F. *signature,* or ML. *signatura,* fr. L. *signare, signatum,* to mark.] **1. a** The name of any person, written with his own hand. **b** Act of signing one's name. **2.** *Music.* Short for KEY SIGNATURE, TIME SIGNATURE. **3.** *Pharm.* That part of a prescription which contains the directions to the patient, usually prefaced by *S* or *Sig.* **4.** *Print.* **a** A letter or figure at the bottom of the first page of each sheet of a book or pamphlet, to direct the binder in arranging the sheets; — called also **signature mark. b** A printed sheet containing a number of pages, as 4, 8, 12, 16, etc., folded as one unit and forming a section of a book or pamphlet. **c** Hence, in bookbinding, such a printed sheet or set of sheets folded into four, or some multiple of four, pages. **5.** *Radio & Television.* A tune, musical number, or sound effect with which a particular program is regularly introduced or concluded, or both; — called also *theme.*

sign′board′ (sīn′bōrd′; 70), *n.* A board for or bearing a notice or sign, originally of a shop or inn.

sign′er (sīn′ẽr), *n.* One who signs.

sig′net (sĭg′nĕt; -nĭt), *n.* [OF.] **1.** A seal, esp. one used officially to give authority to a document. **2.** The impression made by or as by a seal or signet. — *v. t.* To mark or authenticate with a signet.

signet ring. A ring containing a signet, or seal.

sig·nif′i·cance (sĭg·nĭf′ĭ·kăns), *n.* Also **sig·nif′i·can·cy** (-kăn·sĭ). **1.** That which is signified; meaning; import. **2.** Importance; consequence. **3.** Suggestiveness; signification. — **Syn.** See MEANING; IMPORTANCE.

sig·nif′i·cant (-kănt), *adj.* [L. *significans, -antis,* pres. part.] **1.** Having a meaning; esp., full of import; expressive. **2.** Suggesting or containing some covert or special meaning. **3.** Important; momentous. — *n.* A thing which has significance.

sig·nif′i·cant·ly, *adv.* In a significant manner.

sig′ni·fi·ca′tion (sĭg′nĭ·fĭ·kā′shŭn), *n.* **1.** Act of signifying; a making known by signs or other means. **2.** That which is signified; meaning. — **Syn.** See MEANING.

sig·nif′i·ca′tive (sĭg·nĭf′ĭ·kā′tĭv; -kȧ·tĭv), *adj.* Significant.

sig·nif′ics (sĭg·nĭf′ĭks), *n.*; see -ICS. = SEMANTICS, 2.

sig′ni·fy (sĭg′nĭ·fī), *v. t.*; -FIED (-fīd); -FY′ING. [OF. *signifier,* fr. L. *significare,* fr. *signum* a sign + *-ficare* (in comp.) to make.] **1.** To show by a sign; to communicate by words, signals or the like; to make known. **2.** To mean; denote; import. — *v. i.* To have meaning; to matter; — often used impersonally. — **sig′ni·fi′er** (-fī′ẽr), *n.*

si′gnior (sēn′yôr), *n.* Sir; Mr.; — English form of the Italian *signor.*

sign language. 1. = DACTYLOLOGY. **2.** The gesture language of the Plains Indians inhabiting the Great Plains of western U. S. and Canada, used for communication between different tribes.

sign manual. A signature. Specif., the king's signature on a royal grant, placed at the top of the document.

‖**si′gnor** (sē′nyôr), *n.* [It.] **1.** [*cap.*] See SIGNORE. **2.** A lord or gentleman, esp. an Italian of distinction.

‖**si·gno′ra** (sē·nyō′rä), *n.*; *pl.* -RE (-rā). [It.] Madam; Mrs.; — a title of address or respect among Italians.

‖**si·gno′re** (sē·nyō′rā), *n.*; *pl.* -RI (-rē). [It.] Sir; Mr.; — a title of address or respect among Italians. When used before a person's name the form is **Si′gnor.**

‖**si·gno·ri′na** (sē·nyō·rē′nä), *n.*; *pl.* SIGNORINE (-nā). [It.] Miss; — a diminutive of *signora.*

‖**si·gno·ri′no** (-nō), *n.*; *pl.* SIGNORINI (-nē). [It.] Young gentleman; master; — a diminutive of *signore.*

si′gno·ry (sē′nyō·rĭ). Var. of SEIGNIORY.

sign′post′ (sīn′pōst′), *n.* A post bearing a sign; specif., a guidepost; hence, figuratively, a guide; beacon.

Si′gurd (zē′gōort), *n.* [ON. *Sigurthr.*] See BRYNHILD, FAFNIR.

‖**si jeu′nesse′ sa′vait′, si vieil′lesse′ pou′vait′!** (sē zhû′nĕs′ĕ sȧ′vĕ′, sē vyĕ′yĕs′ pōō′vĕ′). [F.] If youth knew, if age were able!

sike (sīk; sĭk), *n.* [AS. *sīc.*] *Chiefly Scot.* A small stream; a rill; also, a ditch; gully; ravine.

sik′er (sĭk′ẽr). Obs. exc. dial. Eng. var. of SICKER.

Sikh (sēk), *n.* [Hind., prop., a disciple.] An adherent of Sikhism. — **Sikh,** *adj.*

Sikh′ism (-ĭz'm), *n.* The tenets of a Hindu sect founded by Guru Nanak about A.D. 1500 in the Punjab. It involves belief in one god, prohibits idolatry, abolishes caste, and refuses to recognize Brahmanical supremacy.

si′lage (sī′lĭj), *n.* [From *ensilage,* after *silo.*] *Agric.* Fodder for winter use cut, compressed, and preserved by its own fermentation in an airtight chamber, as a silo.

si′le·na′ceous (sī′lē·nā′shŭs), *adj.* Syn. of CARYOPHYLLACEOUS.

si′lence (sī′lĕns), *n.* [OF., fr. L. *silentium.* See SILENT.] **1.** State of keeping or being silent; forbearance from speech or other noise; muteness. **2.** Absence of mention: **a** Oblivion; obscurity. **b** Secrecy; failure to make something known. **3.** Absence of sound or noise; stillness. — *v. t.*; -LENCED (-lĕnst); -LENC·ING (-lĕn·sĭng). **1.** To compel or reduce to silence; to still. **2.** To put to rest; to quiet. **3.** *Mil.* Specif., to cause to cease hostile firing, esp. by return fire. — *interj.* Be silent.

si′lenc·er (sī′lĕn·sẽr), *n.* One that silences; as: **a** The muffler of an exhaust. **b** A silencing device for firearms, etc.

si′lent (sī′lĕnt), *adj.* [L. *silens, -entis,* pres. part. of *silere* to be silent.] **1.** Making no utterance: **a** Speechless; mute. **b** Taciturn; not loquacious. **2.** Free from noise; still. **3.** Performed or borne without utterance; as, *silent* prayer, grief. **4.** Making no mention; as, history is *silent* as to this; also, unmentioned. **5.** Performed without sound; as, the *silent* drama. **6.** Maintaining a state of inactivity; as, a *silent* volcano. — **si′lent·ly,** *adv.* — **si′lent·ness,** *n.*

Syn. **Silent, taciturn, reticent, reserved, secretive** mean showing restraint in speaking to others. **Silent** implies a habit of saying no more than is absolutely necessary; **taciturn,** a temperamental disinclination to speech; **reticent,** a disposition to keep one's own counsel or to withhold much that could be said; **reserved,** a temperamental indisposition to the give and take of familiar intercourse; **secretive,** a displeasing reticence that gives the impression of concealing something. — **Ant.** Talkative.

silent butler. A receptacle with a hinged lid for the temporary holding of litter, as from ash trays.

‖**si′lent le′ges in′ter ar′ma** (sī′lĕnt lē′jēz ĭn′tẽr är′mȧ). [L.] The laws are silent in time of war.

silent partner. A partner who has no voice in the business (as between the partners).

silent service. *Colloq.* With *the.* The navy; often specif., esp. *U. S.,* the submarine service.

si·le′nus (sī·lē′nŭs), *n.*; *pl.* -NI (-nī). [L. *Silenus,* fr. Gr. *Seilēnos.*] *Gr. Myth.* One of a type of minor woodland deities, sometimes not distinguished from the satyrs.

si·le′sia (sī·lē′zhȧ; -zhĭ·ȧ; -shȧ; -shĭ·ȧ; sĭ-), *n.* **1.** A linen cloth, originally made in Silesia. **2.** A twilled cotton fabric.

Si·le′sian (-zhăn; -zhĭ·ăn; -shăn; -shĭ·ăn), *adj. & n.* from SILESIA, *Gaz.*

si′lex (sī′lĕks), *n.* [L., a flint, a pebble.] Silica, SiO_2, esp. in the form of quartz, etc.

sil′hou·ette′ (sĭl′ōō·ĕt′), *n.* [F., after Etienne de *Silhouette,* French politician.] A representation of the outlines of an object filled in with some uniform color; a profile of this kind, such as a shadow appears to be. — **Syn.** See OUTLINE. — *v. t.* To represent by a silhouette; to project upon a background, like a silhouette.

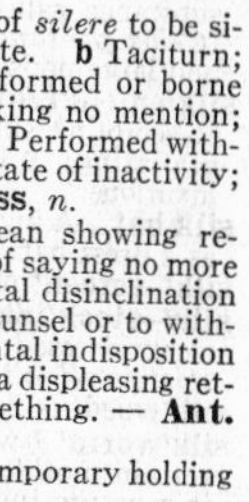

Silhouette.

silic-. = SILICO-.

sil′i·ca (sĭl′ĭ·kȧ), *n.* [NL., fr. L. *silex, silicis,* a flint.] *Chem.* Silicon dioxide, SiO_2, occurring as quartz, etc., and as opal.

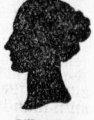

silica gel. *Chem.* A form of colloidal silica, like coarse sand in appearance, but possessing many fine pores and therefore extremely absorbent.

sil'i·cate (sĭl'ĭ·kāt), *n.* *Chem.* A compound regarded as a salt or ester of any of the silicic acids.

si·li'ceous (sĭ·lĭsh'ŭs), *adj.* [L. *siliceus.*] **1.** Of, pertaining to, containing, or like silica. **2.** Growing in a soil composed largely of silica.

si·lic'ic (sĭ·lĭs'ĭk), *adj.* *Chem.* Pertaining to, derived from, or containing silica or silicon.

silicic acid. Any of various weakly acid substances obtained as gelatinous masses by treating certain silicates with acids, dehydration, and otherwise.

sil'i·cide (sĭl'ĭ·sīd; -sĭd), *n.* *Chem.* A binary compound of silicon with an element or a radical.

sil'i·cif'er·ous (sĭl'ĭ·sĭf'ẽr·ŭs), *adj.* [L. *silex, silicis,* a flint + *-ferous.*] Producing, containing, or united with silica.

si·lic'i·fied wood (sĭ·lĭs'ĭ·fīd). Quartz formed by the replacement of wood by infiltration and crystallization of a silica solution.

si·lic'i·fy (-fī), *v. t.;* -FIED (-fīd); -FY'ING. [L. *silex, silicis,* a flint + *-fy.*] To convert into or to impregnate with silica. — **si·lic'i·fi·ca'tion** (-fĭ·kā'shŭn), *n.*

si·li'cious (sĭ·lĭsh'ŭs), *adj.* Siliceous.

si·li'ci·um (sĭ·lĭsh'ĭ·ŭm; sĭ·lĭs'-), *n.* [NL.] = SILICON.

sil'i·cle (sĭl'ĭ·k'l), *n.* [L. *silicula,* dim. of *siliqua* pod.] *Bot.* A silique broader than it is long.

sil'i·co- (sĭl'ĭ·kō-), **silic-.** [From SILICON.] *Chem.* A combining form denoting: **a** The *presence of silicon* or *its compounds.* **b** In adjectives, *silicic and,* as in **sil'i·co·al'ka·line.**

sil'i·con (sĭl'ĭ·kŏn), *n.* [See SILICA.] *Chem.* A nonmetallic element occurring abundantly (always combined) in nature, being, next to oxygen, the chief elementary constituent of the earth's crust. Symbol, *Si;* at. no., 14; at. wt., 28.09. Crystalline silicon is used in steelmaking as a deoxidizer and hardener. It melts at 1420° C. (2588° F.) and can be cast like iron.

sil'i·cone (sĭl'ĭ·kōn), *n.* [*silicon* + *-one.*] *Chem.* Any of a class of polymeric organic silicon compounds obtained as oils, greases, or plastics, and used especially for water- and heat-resistant lubricants, varnishes, binders, and electric insulators.

sil'i·co'sis (sĭl'ĭ·kō'sĭs), *n.* [NL., fr. *silic-* + *-osis.*] *Med.* A disease of the lungs caused by the inhalation of silicate or quartz dust.

si·lic'u·lose (sĭ·lĭk'ū·lōs), **si·lic'u·lous** (-lŭs), *adj.* *Bot.* **a** Bearing silicles. **b** Of the form or appearance of a silicle.

si·lique' (sĭ·lēk'; sĭl'ĭk), *n.* [F., fr. L. *siliqua* a pod or husk.] *Bot.* A narrow many-seeded capsular fruit with two parietal placentae, especially characteristic of the mustard family, consisting of two valves usually separated by a partition from which both valves lift away at dehiscence.

sil'i·quose (sĭl'ĭ·kwōs), **sil'i·quous** (-kwŭs), *adj.* *Bot.* Bearing or having the form of a silique.

silk (sĭlk), *n.* [AS. *seolc, seoloc.*] **1.** The fine, strong, lustrous fiber produced by various insect larvae, generally to form their nest or cocoon; esp., that produced by certain caterpillars (the silkworms) and used for weaving into fabrics. **2.** Thread, cloth, or a garment of the above material; specif., *Eng.,* a gown worn by the king's (or queen's) counsel, or barrister of high rank; hence, ***to take silk,*** to become a king's counsel. **3.** A filament resembling silk, as that produced by certain spiders. **4.** Something silklike, as the styles on an ear of Indian corn. — *adj.* **a** Pertaining to or made of silk; silken; as, a *silk* ribbon. **b** Resembling silk. — *v. i.* *U. S.* To blossom; — said of maize.

silk'a·line', silk'a·lene' (sĭl'kȧ·lēn'), *n.* A soft, thin cotton fabric, having a smooth finish resembling silk.

silk'-cotton tree. **a** Any of a family (Bombacaceae, the silk-cotton family) of tropical trees, including the balsa and baobab, having palmate leaves and large, dry or fleshy fruit containing usually woolly seeds. The seeds of certain species are enveloped by a cottony or silky substance called **silk cotton.** **b** Specif., a tropical American tree (*Ceiba pentandra*), called also *ceiba* or *kapok tree,* with large trunk and large pods yielding silk cotton. See KAPOK.

silk'en (sĭl'kĕn), *adj.* **1.** Of or pertaining to silk; made of silk. **2.** Resembling silk; as: **a** Soft and lustrous. **b** Agreeably smooth; ingratiating. **c** Delicate; as, a *silken* touch. **3.** Dressed in silk; hence, luxurious.

silk hat. A high cylindrical hat with a silk-plush finish, worn by men as a dress hat.

silk'-screen' print'ing. See SERIGRAPHY. — **silk'-screen' print.**

silk'-stock'ing (*see Pron.,* § 2), *adj.* Wearing silk stockings; hence, richly dressed; aristocratic. — *n.* A luxurious person; also, *U. S. Hist., Colloq.,* a Federalist or Whig.

silk'weed' (sĭlk'wēd'), *n.* = MILKWEED.

silk'worm' (-wûrm'), *n.* [AS. *seolcwyrm.*] The larva of any of certain moths, which spins a strong silk in constructing its cocoon. The common silkworm is the larva of a bombycid moth (*Bombyx mori*) which is yellow and measures about an inch and a half across the extended wings.

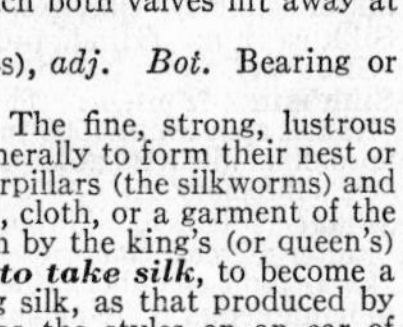

Silkworm (*B. mori*). (⅔) Adult Female and Larva.

silk'y (sĭl'kĭ), *adj.;* SILK'I·ER (-kĭ·ẽr); SILK'I·EST. **1.** Silken. **2.** *Bot.* Covered with soft hairs pressed close to the surface, as a leaf. — **silk'i·ly,** *adv.* — **silk'i·ness,** *n.*

sill (sĭl), *n.* [AS. *syl, syll.*] The basis of a thing; esp., a horizontal piece, as a timber, which forms the lowest member of a frame, or supports a structure; as, the *sill* or *sills* of a house, of a bridge, etc. Hence: **a** The timber or stone at the foot of a door; the threshold. **b** The timber or stone on which a window frame stands, or the lowest piece in a window frame.

sil'la·bub (sĭl'ȧ·bŭb), *n.* **1.** A dish made by mixing wine or cider with milk, forming a soft curd; also, sweetened cream, flavored with wine and beaten to a stiff froth. **2.** Anything frothy but unsubstantial; esp., florid language.

sil'ler (sĭl'ẽr). Scot. & N. of Eng. var. of SILVER, money.

sil'li·man·ite (sĭl'ĭ·măn·īt), *n.* [After *B. Silliman* (1779–1864), Am. chemist.] *Mineral.* A brown, grayish, or pale-green aluminum silicate, Al_2SiO_5, in orthorhombic crystals which often pass into fibrous or columnar forms.

sil'ly (sĭl'ĭ), *adj.;* SIL'LI·ER (-ĭ·ẽr); SIL'LI·EST. [AS. *sǣlig, gesǣlig,* happy, good, fr. *sǣl* good fortune, happiness.] **1. a** *Archaic.* Helpless; frail; — in compassion or endearment. **b** *Scot. & N. of Eng.* Weak; sickly. **2.** Rustic; plain; humble. **3. a** *Orig. Scot.* Weak in intellect; witless. **b** Lacking in sense; foolish; fatuous. **4.** Proceeding from or characterized by weakness of mind or by folly; absurd; stupid. — **Syn.** See SIMPLE. — *n.* *Colloq.* A silly person. — **sil'li·ly,** *adv.* — **sil'li·ness,** *n.*

si'lo (sī'lō), *n.; pl.* SILOS (-lōz). [Sp., fr. L. *sirus,* fr. Gr. *siros.*] Originally a pit or vat, now usually a circular structure of wood, concrete, etc., for packing away fodder to convert it into silage. — *v. t.* *Agric.* To place in a silo, as fodder; to ensile.

Si·lo'am (sĭ·lō'ăm; sī-), *n.* *Bib.* A spring and pool of water near Jerusalem. *John* ix. 7.

silt (sĭlt), *n.* [ME. *sylt,* prob. of Scand. origin.] **a** Loose sedimentary material (rock particles less than 1/16 millimeter in diameter) suspended in water. **b** A deposit of sediment, as by a river. — *v. t. & i.* To choke or obstruct with silt or mud. — **silt'y,** *adj.*

si·lun'dum (sĭ·lŭn'dŭm), *n.* [*silicon* + *carborundum.*] A very hard variety of silicon carbide, SiC, formed in the electric furnace and used for electric resistors, etc.

Sil'u·res (sĭl'ū·rēz), *n. pl.* [L.] A people of ancient Britain, described by Tacitus as occupying chiefly southern Wales, and probably of Iberian origin.

Si·lu'ri·an (sĭ·lū'rĭ·ăn; sī-), *adj.* **1.** Of or pert. to the Silures, or their place of habitation. **2.** *Geol.* Of, pert. to, or designating that period of the Paleozoic era between the Ordovician and Devonian, or the system of rocks formed during this period. It is marked by coral-reef building and the appearance of great crustaceans. The Silurian originally was divided into the ***Upper Silurian,*** now called simply *Silurian,* and ***Lower Silurian,*** now called *Ordovician.* — **Si·lu'ri·an,** *n.*

si·lu'rid (sĭ·lū'rĭd; sī-), *n.* [L. *silurus* a sort of river fish, fr. Gr. *silouros.*] Any of a family (Siluridae) of catfishes; — now usually restricted to several fresh-water genera of Europe and Asia. — **si·lu'rid,** *adj.* — **si·lu'roid** (-roid), *adj. & n.*

sil'va, syl'va (sĭl'vȧ), *n.; pl.* -VAS (-vȧz), -VAE (-vē). [L., a wood, forest.] **a** The forest trees of a region or country, considered collectively. **b** A description of, or treatise on, the trees of a given region.

sil'van (sĭl'văn). Var. of SYLVAN.

sil'ver (sĭl'vẽr), *n.* [AS. *seolfor, siolfur.*] **1.** A white metallic element, sonorous, ductile, very malleable, and capable of a high degree of polish. It also has the highest thermal and electric conductivity of any substance. Symbol, *Ag* (Latin *argentum*); at. no., 47; at. wt., 107.880. **2.** Silver as a commodity; as, *silver* has risen. **3.** Coin made of silver; silver money; money (in general). **4.** Silverware; an article, or articles collectively, of domestic use, as tableware, made of or plated with silver. **5. a** Anything having the luster or appearance of silver. **b** A neutral gray of medium brilliance. **6.** *U. S. Photog.* A salt of silver, esp. the nitrate.
— *adj.* **1.** Made of, or coated or plated with, silver. **2.** Resembling silver; silvery. **3.** Giving a clear, ringing sound; soft and clear. **4.** Eloquent; — of the tongue. **5.** Of or pertaining to silver; relating to silver; as, the *silver* legislation. **6.** Designating a twenty-fifth anniversary, as of a wedding. **7.** Advocating the adoption of silver as a standard of currency; as, the *silver* party.
— *v. t.* **1.** To cover with silver, as by electroplating. **2.** To coat with a substance, as a metal, resembling silver; as, to *silver* a glass with an amalgam. — **sil'ver·er,** *n.*

silver age. **a** In ancient literature, the period between A.D. 14 and 180, notable for the writings of Martial, Tacitus, Juvenal, etc. **b** *Class. Myth.* The second age of the world, when men lost the virtues of the golden age.

silver bell. Also **sil'ver-bell' tree.** A medium-sized tree (*Halesia carolina*) of the storax family, of the southeastern United States, cultivated for its bell-shaped white flowers.

sil'ver·ber'ry (sĭl'vẽr·bĕr'ĭ), *n.* A silvery North American shrub (*Elaeagnus argentea*) related to the buffalo berry.

silver bromide. See BROMIDE.

silver certificate. A certificate issued by a government that there has been deposited with it silver to a specified amount, payable to the bearer on demand. In the United States and its possessions, it is issued against the deposit of silver coin, and is legal tender for all debts, public and private, and for public charges, taxes, duties, and dues.

silver chloride. *Chem.* A compound, AgCl, sensitive to light, and used esp. for photographic, or light-sensitive, papers.

silver doctor. *Angling.* An artificial fly, usually tied with brown, green, blue, red, and yellow wings, silver-tinsel body, and yellow, red, blue, and green tail. Cf. FLY, *Illust.*

silver dollar. See DOLLAR, 1 **d.**

sil'ver·fish' (sĭl'vẽr·fĭsh'), *n.;* see FISH. **1.** Any of various silvery fishes; as: **a** The tarpon. **b** A silvery variety of the goldfish. **c** A silversides. **2.** A small wingless insect (genus *Lepisma,* esp. *L. saccharina*) found in houses and sometimes injurious to sized papers, starched clothes, etc.

silver fox. See FOX, 1 **a.**

sil'ver·ing (sĭl'vẽr·ĭng), *n.* Act or process of covering with silver; also, the silverlike film on a silvered object, or a silvery appearance.

sil'ver·ly (sĭl'vẽr·lĭ), *adv.* With silvery appearance or sound.

sil'vern (sĭl'vẽrn), *adj.* *Archaic.* Made of silver; resembling, or characteristic of, silver.

silver nitrate. *Chem.* A colorless crystalline salt, $AgNO_3$, obtained by dissolving silver in nitric acid, and evaporating. In contact with organic matter it turns black. It is used as a chemical reagent, in photography, and in medicine as an antiseptic, etc.

sil'ver·sides' (sĭl'vẽr·sīdz'), *n. sing. & pl.* Also **sil'ver·side'** (-sīd'). **a** Any of certain small fishes (family Atherinidae) related to the gray mullets, having a silvery stripe along each side of the body; also, any fish of that family. **b** Any of various fresh-water minnows of the carp family.

sil'ver·smith' (-smĭth'), *n.* One whose occupation is to manufacture utensils, ornaments, etc., of silver.

silver standard. A standard, esp. in a monetary system, by which silver is the measure of value.

Silver Star Medal. *Mil., U. S.* A medal, first issued 1932, consisting of a bronze star with an oak wreath and small silver star at its center, awarded for gallantry in action in any war.

sil'ver-tongued' (sĭl'vẽr·tŭngd'; 2), *adj.* Eloquent.

sil'ver·ware' (-wâr'), *n.* Collectively, dishes, vases, ornaments, etc., esp. tableware, made of silver.

sil′ver·weed′ (sĭl′vẽr·wēd′), *n.* **a** A perennial herb (*Argentina anserina*) of the rose family, with leaves silvery-white beneath. **b** A prostrate cinquefoil (*Potentilla argentea*) of the North Temperate Zone, densely white-tomentose beneath.

sil′ver·y (sĭl′vẽr·ĭ), *adj.* **1.** Resembling, or having the luster of, silver. **2.** Having the clear, musical tone of silver. **3.** Full of silver. — **sil′ver·i·ness**, *n.*

sil′vi·cul′ture (sĭl′vĭ·kŭl′tūr), *n.* [L. *silva* forest + E. *culture.*] The art of producing and caring for a forest. — **sil′vi·cul′tur·al** (-kŭl′tūr·ăl), *adj.* — **sil′vi·cul′tur·ist** (-ĭst), *n.*

‖**s'il vous plaît** (sēl′ vōō plĕ′). [F.] If you please.

si·mar′ (sĭ·mär′), *n.* [F. *simarre*, fr. It. *cimarra* long coat, fr. Ar. *sammūr* the weasel.] A loose robe for women.

sim′a·rou′ba (sĭm′ȧ·rōō′bȧ), *n.* [NL., fr. Carib (in Guiana) *simarouba.*] *Bot.* Any of a genus (*Simarouba*) of tropical American trees of the ailanthus family, with drupaceous fruit. The bark of most species is a bitter tonic.

sim′a·rou·ba′ceous (-rōō·bā′shŭs), *adj.* *Bot.* Belonging to the ailanthus family (Simaroubaceae). See AILANTHUS.

Sim′e·on (sĭm′ē·ŭn), *n.* *Bib.* **1.** See JACOB. **2.** A devout man of Jerusalem, who saw the infant Jesus in the temple and uttered the song known as the Nunc Dimittis. *Luke* ii. 25–35.

Sim·hath′ To·rah′ (sĭm·käth′ tō·rä′; sĭm′käs tō′rä). Also **Simchas′ To·rah′**. See JEWISH HOLIDAYS.

sim′i·an (sĭm′ĭ·ăn), *adj.* [L. *simia* an ape.] Resembling, characteristic of, or pertaining to the apes and monkeys; apelike. — *n.* Any monkey or ape, esp. an anthropoid ape.

sim′i·lar (sĭm′ĭ·lẽr), *adj.* [F. *similaire*, fr. L. *similis* like, similar.] **1.** Nearly corresponding; having a general likeness. **2.** *Geom.* Having the same shape, differing only in size and position; — of two figures. — **sim′i·lar·ly**, *adv.*

Syn. **Similar, alike, akin, analogous, parallel, homogeneous, uniform** mean closely resembling each other. **Similar** implies an impossibility of being mistaken for each other; **alike**, close likeness to superficial view though obviously distinct; **akin**, essential rather than superficial likenesses; **analogous**, though radically different as in categories, a possession of common likenesses; **parallel**, a marked likeness in their course or development; **homogeneous**, likeness in kind, sort, or class; **uniform**, lack of variance or variation in given instances.

sim′i·lar′i·ty (sĭm′ĭ·lăr′ĭ·tĭ), *n.; pl.* -TIES (-tĭz). **1.** Quality or state of being similar; likeness. **2.** A point in which things are similar. — **Syn.** See LIKENESS.

sim′i·lar·ly (sĭm′ĭ·lẽr·lĭ), *adv.* In like manner.

sim′i·le (sĭm′ĭ·lē; -lē), *n.; pl.* -LES (-lēz; -lēz). [L., neut. of *similis.*] *Rhet.* A figure of speech by which one thing, action, or relation is likened or explicitly compared, often with *as* or *like*, to something of different kind or quality.

‖**si·mi′li·a si·mi′li·bus cu·ran′tur** (sĭ·mĭl′ĭ·ȧ sĭ·mĭl′ĭ·bŭs kū·răn′tẽr). [L.] Likes are cured by likes; like cures like.

‖**si′mi·lis si′mi·li gau′det** (sĭm′ĭ·lĭs sĭm′ĭ·lī gô′dĕt). [L.] Like takes pleasure in like.

si·mil′i·tude (sĭ·mĭl′ĭ·tūd), *n.* [OF., fr. L. *similitudo.*] **1.** Similarity; resemblance. **2.** **a** A simile. **b** A parable. **c** An allegory. **3.** **a** One that is like or similar; a facsimile. **b** Semblance; form. — **Syn.** See LIKENESS.

sim′i·ous (sĭm′ĭ·ŭs), *adj.* [L. *simia* an ape.] Simian.

sim′mer (sĭm′ẽr), *v. i. & t.* [From earlier *simper*, of imitative origin.] **1.** To boil gently; to be on the point of boiling. **2.** To be in a state of incipient agitation.

sim′nel (sĭm′nĕl; -n'l), *n.* [OF. *simenel, siminel, seminel*, cake or bread of wheat flour, fr. L. *simila*, ult. fr. Bab. *samīdu* fine flour.] *Archaic.* A variety of bread made of fine flour; a kind of biscuit.

si·mo′le·on (sĭ·mō′lē·ŭn), *n.* *Slang, U. S.* A dollar.

Si′mon (sī′mŭn), *n.* [L., fr. Gr. *Simōn*, fr. Heb. *Shim'ōn.*] *Bib.* **a** Also **Si′mon Pe′ter**. The apostle surnamed Peter. **b** One of the disciples of Jesus. **c** A brother or relative of Jesus.

si·mo′ni·ac (sĭ·mō′nĭ·ăk), *n.* One who practices simony

sim′o·ni′a·cal (sĭm′ō·nī′ȧ·kăl), *adj.* Of, pert. to, guilty of, or tainted by simony. — **sim′o·ni′a·cal·ly**, *adv.*

Si′mon Le·gree′. See LEGREE.

Si′mon Ma′gus (sī′mŭn mā′gŭs). [L. *magus* magician.] *Bib.* A Samaritan sorcerer, converted by the apostle Philip (*Acts* viii. 9–24) and severely rebuked by Peter for offering money to purchase the power of giving the Holy Ghost.

si′mon-pure′ (*see Pron.*, § 2), *adj.* [See PURE, SIMON.] Genuine.

‖**si mo′nu·men′tum re·qui′ris, cir·cum′spi·ce** (sī mŏn′ū·mĕn′tŭm rē·kwī′rĭs, sẽr·kŭm′spĭ·sē). [L.] If you seek (his) monument, look around; — epitaph of Sir Christopher Wren in St. Paul's, London.

sim′o·ny (sĭm′ō·nĭ; sī′mō-), *n.* [OF. *simonie*, fr. ML. *simonia*, fr. *Simon.* See SIMON MAGUS.] Traffic in that which is sacred; specif., the crime of buying or selling ecclesiastical preferment. Cf. BARRATRY, 1. — **sim′o·nism** (-nĭz'm), *n.* — **sim′o·nist** (-nĭst), *n.*

si·moom′ (sĭ·mōōm′), *n.* Also **si·moon′**. [Ar. *samūm.*] A hot, dry, violent wind laden with dust, that blows occasionally in Arabia, Syria, etc.

simp (sĭmp), *n.* *Slang.* Short for SIMPLETON.

sim′per (sĭm′pẽr), *v. i.* To smile in a silly manner. — *n.* An affected, silly smile; a smirk. — **sim′per·er**, *n.* — **sim′per·ing·ly**, *adv.*

sim′ple (sĭm′p'l), *adj.;* SIM′PLER (-plẽr); SIM′PLEST. [OF., fr. L. *simplex*, fr. *sem-* one, one and the same (in L. *semel* once, *similis* like).] **1.** Single; uncompounded; uncombined; elementary. **2.** Mere; not other than; as, the *simple* truth. **3.** Free from complexity; not complicated; as, a *simple* sentence (see SENTENCE); not elaborate; uninvolved; as, a *simple* machine; hence, not hard to understand or solve; as, a *simple* problem. **4.** Absolute; having no limitation; as, in fee *simple*. **5.** **a** Not given to duplicity; undesigning; straightforward; as, *simple* dealing. **b** Devoid of ostentation; unaffected; natural. **6.** **a** Of humble birth or station. **b** Plain; unadorned; as, *simple* dress. **c** Not luxurious; plain; as, a *simple* diet. **d** Insignificant; trifling. **7.** **a** Ignorant; not wise. **b** Lacking sense; foolish. **8.** *Bot.* Without subdivision or branches, as a stem; having only one blade, or not compound, as a leaf; consisting of a single carpel, as an ovary. **9.** *Chem.* Elementary; also, unmixed. **10.** *Music.* **a** Not compound. See TIME, *n.*, 19. **b** Without overtones; as, a *simple* tone. **c** Free from elaboration or figuration. **Syn.** (1) See EASY. (2) **Simple, foolish, silly, fatuous, asinine** mean actually or apparently deficient in intelligence. **Simple** implies intelligence of a child or an incapacity for dealing with problems involving mental effort; **foolish** implies the character of being an imbecile or an idiot, or of appearing like one; **silly**, though not implying actual mental deficiency, suggests a failure to act as a rational being, esp. by ridiculous behavior; **fatuous** suggests foolishness, stupidity, and inanity and is often used in contempt; **asinine**, also a term of contempt, implies an intelligence equal to that of an ass, considered the most stupid of beasts of burden.
— *n.* **1.** **a** A person of humble condition. **b** An ignorant or simple-minded person. **2.** A medicinal plant; — each vegetable being supposed to constitute a simple remedy. **3.** Something not mixed or compounded; specif., *Pharm.*, a medicinal preparation composed of but one ingredient.
— **sim′ple·ness**, *n.*

simple fraction. See FRACTION.

simple fruit. A fruit that matures from a single ovary; — opposed to *collective*, or *compound, fruit* (see COMPOUND, *adj.*, 2).

simple honors. *Bridge.* Three honors held by the same side, in the trump suit.

simple interest. See INTEREST, 4.

simple machine. Any of six (or more) mechanisms formerly considered elements composing all machines: (1) *lever*, (2) *inclined plane*, (3) *wheel and axle*, (4) *screw*, (5) *pulley*, (6) *wedge*.

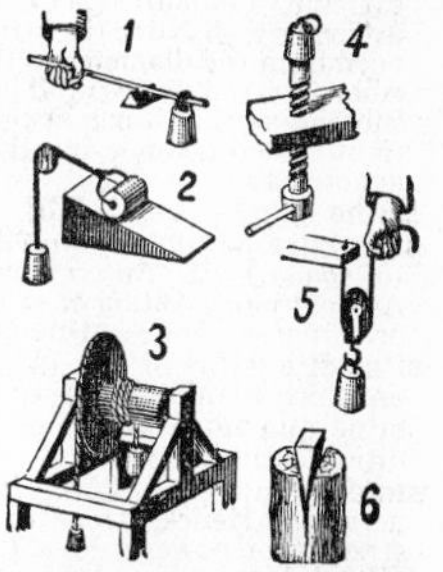

Simple Machines. 1 Lever; 2 Inclined Plane; 3 Wheel and Axle; 4 Screw; 5 Pulley; 6 Wedge.

sim′ple-mind′ed (*see Pron.*, § 2), *adj.* Devoid of subtlety; also, foolish; simple. — **sim′ple-mind′ed·ly**, *adv.* — **sim′ple-mind′ed·ness**, *n.*

sim′ple·ton (sĭm′p'l·tŭn), *n.* [Humorous formation on *simple*, as if a surname in *-ton.*] A person lacking in common sense; a silly person; fool. — **Syn.** See FOOL.

sim′plex (sĭm′plĕks), *adj.* [L. See SIMPLE.] **1.** Simple; uncompounded. **2.** *Teleg.* Pertaining to a system in which only one message is sent over a line at a time. Cf. MULTIPLEX, 2.

sim′pli·ci·den′tate (sĭm′plĭ·sĭ·dĕn′tāt), *adj.* [L. *simplex, -icis*, simple + *dens, dentis*, tooth.] *Zool.* Belonging to a former suborder (Simplicidentata) of rodents, containing all but the hares, rabbits, and pikas. It is characterized by a single pair of upper incisors.

sim·plic′i·ty (sĭm·plĭs′ĭ·tĭ), *n.; pl.* -TIES (-tĭz). **1.** Quality or state of being simple, or uncompounded. **2.** Quality or state of being not complex; clearness; plainness. **3.** **a** Artlessness of mind; lack of duplicity. **b** Plainness in manners or mode of life; also, rusticity. **4.** Silliness; folly.

sim′pli·fy (sĭm′plĭ·fī), *v. t.;* -FIED (-fīd); -FY′ING. [See SIMPLE; -FY.] To make simpler; to show an easier or shorter process for doing, etc. — **sim′pli·fi·ca′tion** (-fĭ·kā′shŭn), *n.* — **sim′pli·fi′er** (-fī′ẽr), *n.*

sim′ply (sĭm′plĭ), *adv.* **1.** In a simple manner; as: **a** Merely. **b** Without art or subtlety. **c** Stupidly. **2.** *Colloq.* Really; truly.

sim′u·la′cre (sĭm′ū·lā′kẽr), *n.* [OF.] Image; likeness.

sim′u·la′crum (sĭm′ū·lā′krŭm), *n.; pl.* -LACRA (-krȧ). [L. See SIMULATE.] **1.** An image. **2.** A vague, unreal semblance; a sham.

sim′u·lant (sĭm′ū·lănt), *adj.* [L. *simulans, -antis*, pres. part.] Simulating (something which it is not); — esp. in *Biol.;* as, a stamen *simulant* of a petal, etc.

sim′u·lar (-lẽr), *n.* = SIMULATOR. — *adj.* Simulated; also, simulative.

sim′u·late (-lāt), *adj.* [L. *simulatus*, past part. of *simulare* to simulate, fr. *similis* like.] Feigned. — (-lāt), *v. t.* To assume the appearance of, without the reality; to feign. — **Syn.** See ASSUME. — **sim′u·la′tor** (-lā′tẽr), *n.*

sim′u·la′tion (-lā′shŭn), *n.* Act of simulating; feigning.

sim′u·la′tive (sĭm′ū·lā′tĭv), *adj.* Characterized by or tending to simulation. — **sim′u·la′tive·ly**, *adv.*

si′mul·cast′ (sī′mŭl·kȧst′; sĭm′ŭl-; 9), *v.t. & i.* [*simul*taneous + broad*cast.*] To broadcast by radio and television simultaneously. — *n.* A broadcast of a program by radio and television simultaneously; also, a program thus broadcast.

si′mul·ta′ne·ous (sī′mŭl·tā′nē·ŭs; sĭm′ŭl-), *adj.* [From L. *simul* at the same time.] Taking place or operating at the same time. — **Syn.** See CONTEMPORARY. — **si′mul·ta′ne·ous·ly**, *adv.* — **si′mul·ta′ne·ous·ness, si′mul·ta·ne′i·ty** (-tȧ·nē′ĭ·tĭ), *n.*

simultaneous equations. *Alg.* Two or more equations satisfied by the same sets of values of the unknown quantities.

sin (sĭn), *adv., prep., & conj.* *Scot.* Since.

sin, *n.* [AS. *synn, syn.*] **1.** Transgression of the law of God. See DEADLY SINS. **2.** An offense, in general; misdemeanor. — **Syn.** See OFFENSE. — *v. i.;* SINNED (sĭnd); SIN′NING. **1.** To violate the divine law by actual transgression or by neglect. **2.** To violate human rights, law, or propriety; to transgress. — *v. t.* **1.** To do or commit wrongly, as a sin. **2.** To effect, bring about, etc., by a sin or sins.

sin·al′bin (sĭn·ăl′bĭn), *n.* [L. *sinapis* mustard + *alba*, fem. adj., white.] *Chem.* A crystalline glucoside, $C_{30}H_{42}N_2O_{15}S_2$, in white-mustard seeds.

sin′a·pine (sĭn′ȧ·pēn; -pĭn), *n.* Also **sin′a·pin**. [L. *sinapi(s)* mustard.] *Chem.* An alkaloid, $C_{16}H_{25}NO_6$, in the seeds of black mustard.

sin′a·pism (-pĭz'm), *n.* [L. *sinapismus*, fr. Gr. *sinapismos* the use of a mustard blister, deriv. of *sinapi* mustard.] *Med.* A plaster of powdered mustard seed, or containing its volatile oil. It is a powerful irritant.

since (sĭns; 106), *adv.* [For *sins*, contr. fr. ME. *sithens, sithenes*, (*-s* being an adv. ending; see 2d -s), deriv. of AS. *siththan, syththan, seoththan*, afterward, after.] **1.** **a** From a definite past time until now. **b** Subsequent to a certain past time and before the present; as, appointed last year, and *since* reappointed. **2.** In the time past, counting backward from the present. — *prep.* From the time of; subsequently to; after. — *conj.* **1.** At any time in the past after or later than. **2.** Elapsed from the time when. **3.** Seeing that; because.

sin·cere′ (sĭn·sēr′), *adj.;* -CER′ER (-sēr′ẽr); -CER′EST. [F. *sincère*, fr. L. *sincerus.*] **1.** *Archaic.* Pure; unadulterated. **2.** Honest; free from hypocrisy or dissimulation; as, a *sincere* friend. **3.** Being in reality what it appears to be; genuine; real. **4.** *Obs.* Whole; uninjured. — **sin·cere′ly**, *adv.* — **sin·cere′ness**, *n.*

Syn. **Sincere, wholehearted, heartfelt, hearty, unfeigned** mean genuine in feeling or expression. **Sincere** stresses a revelation of just what one feels, thinks, or sees, and no more, and an unwillingness to embellish or exaggerate; **wholehearted**, a sincerity and earnestness, as in devotion to a person, a cause, or the like; **heartfelt**, depth as well as genuineness of feeling outwardly expressed; **hearty**, honesty, warmth, and exuberance in display of feeling; **unfeigned**, spontaneousness and lack of simulation.

sin·cer′i·ty (sĭn·sĕr′ĭ·tĭ), *n.* Quality or state of being sincere; honesty of mind or intention; freedom from simulation.

sin′ci·put (sĭn′sĭ·pŭt; -pŭt), *n.* [L., half a head, fr. *semi-* half + *caput* the head.] *Anat.* **a** The forehead. **b** The upper half of the skull. — **sin·cip′i·tal** (sĭn·sĭp′ĭ·tăl; -t'l), *adj.*

Sind′bad the Sail′or (sĭnd′băd; sĭn′-). A character whose adventures are told in the *Arabian Nights.*

Sin′dhi (sĭn′dē), *n.* [Ar. *Sindi*, fr. *Sind* India, fr. Skr.] The Prakrit language spoken in Sind, having many loan words from Persian. See INDO-EUROPEAN LANGUAGES, *Table.*

sine (sīn), *n.* [L. *sinus* gulf, bosom, used as trans. of Ar. *jayb* bosom of a garment.] *Math.* **a** Formerly, the perpendicular drawn from one extremity of an arc of a circle to the diameter drawn through the other extremity. **b** Now, the ratio of the length of this perpendicular (reckoned from the diameter to the circle) to that of the radius of the circle. Abbr. *sin* (no period). The sine of a plane angle is the sine of the arc subtending that angle at the center of a circle of unit radius; or, in a right-angled triangle, it is that ratio of the side opposite the angle to the hypotenuse.

‖**si′ne** (sī′nē), *prep.* [L.] Without.

si′ne·cure (sī′nē·kūr; sĭn′ē·kūr), *n.* [ML. *sine* without + *cura* cure (of souls).] **1.** An ecclesiastical benefice without cure of souls. **2.** Any office or position of value which involves little or no responsibility or active service. — **si′ne·cur′ist** (-kūr′ĭst), *n.*

si′ne di′e (sī′nē dī′ē). [L.] Without day; without appointing a day on which to appear or assemble again.

‖**si′ne qua non** (kwā nŏn′). [L.] An indispensable thing or condition; a necessity.

sin′ew (sĭn′ū), *n.* [AS. *sinu, seonu.*] **1.** A tendon. **2. a** *Obs.* A nerve. **b** Hence, strength; nervous energy. **3.** That which supplies strength or power. — *v. t.* To knit or strengthen as with sinews. — **sin′ew·less,** *adj.*

sin′ew·y (sĭn′ū·ĭ), *adj.* **1.** Having sinews, esp. strong and well-developed sinews. **2.** Pertaining to, consisting of, or resembling a sinew or sinews. **3.** Nervous; vigorous; firm; tough.

sin′fo·ni′a (sĭn′fō·nē′ȧ; *It.* sēn·fō·nē′ä), *n.*; *pl.* SINFONIE (-nē′ā). [It.] *Music.* = SYMPHONY, 3.

sin′fo·niet′ta (sĭn′fŭn·yĕt′ȧ), *n.* [It., dim. of *sinfonia* symphony.] **a** A symphony of less than standard length, or requiring fewer instruments, or both. **b** A small symphony orchestra, esp. an orchestra of strings only.

sin′ful (sĭn′fŏŏl; -f'l), *adj.* Tainted with, or full of, sin; wicked. — **sin′ful·ly,** *adv.* — **sin′ful·ness,** *n.*

sing (sĭng), *v. i.*; SANG (săng) or SUNG (sŭng); SUNG; SING′ING. [AS. *singan.*] **1.** To produce musical tones by means of the voice, with musical inflections and modulations; specif., to deliver songs, arias, or the like, in the character of a professional singer. **2.** To produce harmonious sounds, as those made by birds, brooks, etc. **3.** To make a small, shrill sound; as, missiles *sing* through the air. **4.** To relate or celebrate something in poetry; also, to compose verses. **5.** To hum; to ring; — of the ears. — *v. t.* **1.** To utter with musical inflections. **2.** To celebrate in song or in verse. **3.** To chant; intone; as, to *sing* Mass. **4.** To express enthusiastically; as, to *sing* one's praises. **5. a** To bring to a (specified) state by singing; as, to *sing* a child to sleep. **b** To accompany, or attend on, with singing. — *n.* **1.** *Colloq.* A singing, esp. in company. **2.** A small shrill sound, as of a bullet in flight. — **sing′a·ble,** *adj.*

singe (sĭnj), *v. t.*; SINGED (sĭnjd); SINGE′ING (sĭn′jĭng). [AS. *sengan*; perh. orig., to cause to sing, from the *singing* sound often produced when a substance is singed.] **1.** To burn superficially; to scorch. **2. a** To remove the nap of (cloth) by exposing it to scorching heat. **b** To remove the hair or down from (a plucked fowl, etc.) by passing over a flame. — *n.* A burning of the surface; a slight burn.

sing′er (sĭng′ẽr), *n.* One who or that which sings.

Sin′gha·lese′ (sĭng′gȧ·lēz′; -lēs′; 2), *or* **Sin′ha·lese′** (sĭn′hȧ-), *adj.* [Skr. *Siṁhala* Ceylon.] Literally, of or pertaining to Ceylon; hence, designating, or pertaining to, the principal race of Ceylon, or their language. They are of mixed Aryan and Dravidian stock, and mostly Buddhists. — *n.* **1.** *sing. & pl.* A member of the Singhalese race. **2.** The language of the Singhalese, an Aryan tongue with many Dravidian words. See INDO-EUROPEAN LANGUAGES, *Table.*

sing′ing birds (sĭng′ĭng). See OSCINE, *n.*

sin′gle (sĭng′g'l), *adj.* [OF. *sengle, single*, fr. L. *singulus.*] **1.** One only, as disting. from more than one; individual. **2.** Alone; without company or aid. **3. a** Unmarried. **b** Pert. to, or characteristic of, celibacy; as, a *single* life. **4. a** Having but one feature or part; as, a *single* blow, line. **b** *Archaic.* Of low strength; — disting. from *double*; as, *single* ale. **5. a** Not deceitful; honest; sincere. **b** Free from defect; — of the eye or vision; as, an eye *single* to what is just. **6.** Peculiar to or involving one person only; as, his *single* strength. **7.** Performed by one person, or one on each side. **8.** Having one principal working part; as, a *single* plow, having one share. **9.** For the use of one person or family only; as, a *single* house. **10.** *Hort.* Having only the normal number of petals or rays; as, a *single* rose. **11.** *Teleg.* = SIMPLEX, *adj.*, 2.

Syn. **Single, sole, unique, solitary, separate, particular** mean one as distinguished from two or more or all others. **Single** implies unaccompaniment or lack of support by any other; **sole**, the only one that exists, acts, has power, or the like; **unique**, the only one of its kind or character in existence; **solitary**, a standing by itself as a sole instance or a unique thing; **separate**, singleness and disconnection from every other one; **particular**, numerical distinctness from every other instance, member, or example, as of the class under consideration.

— *v. t.*; SIN′GLED (-g'ld); SIN′GLING (-glĭng). To select, as one person or thing, from among a number; — usually with *out* or *from*; as, to *single* one out for mention. — *v. i.* **1.** To take the gait called single-foot; — said of horses. **2.** *Baseball.* To make a base hit. — *n.* **1.** A separate individual person or thing. **2.** *Baseball.* A base hit. **3.** *Cricket.* A hit for one run. **4.** *Sports.* **a** *Lawn Tennis.* A game with but one player on each side; — usually in *pl.* **b** *Golf.* A match between two players, as distinguished from a *foursome.*

single bowknot. See KNOT, *Illust.* (30).

sin′gle-breast′ed (*see Pron.*, § 2), *adj.* Designating a coat, waistcoat, or the like, which laps over the breast only enough for buttoning, and has buttons on one edge only.

single combat. Combat between two persons.

single entry. Something involving only one entry; specif., *Bookkeeping*, a method of bookkeeping in which debts owing to and by a concern are the only facts recorded. Cf. DOUBLE ENTRY. — **sin′gle-en′try,** *adj.*

single file. A line of men marching one behind another.

sin′gle-foot′, *n.* A gait of the horse in which each foot strikes singly, and there are alternately one and two feet on the ground. — *v. i.* To proceed by means of single-foot.

sin′gle·hand′ed (sĭng′g'l·hăn′dĕd; -dĭd; 2), *adj.* **1.** Managed or done by one person or with one hand. **2.** Working alone; unassisted. — **sin′gle·hand′ed·ly,** *adv.*

sin′gle·heart′ed (-här′tĕd; -tĭd; 2), *adj.* Having an honest heart. — **sin′gle·heart′ed·ly,** *adv.*

single knot. See KNOT, *Illust.* (16).

sin′gle-mind′ed (-mīn′dĕd; -dĭd; 2), *adj.* **1.** Guileless; singlehearted. **2.** Having a single purpose. — **sin′gle-mind′ed·ly,** *adv.* — **sin′gle-mind′ed·ness,** *n.*

sin′gle-name′ pa′per. *Banking.* A promissory note with no endorsement other than that of the maker.

sin′gle·ness, *n.* Quality or state of being single.

sin′gle-phase′ (sĭng′g'l·fāz′; 2), *adj.* Pertaining to a circuit energized by a single alternating electromotive force.

sin′gle·stick′ (-stĭk′), *n.* Formerly, a stout cudgel; now, a stick used for hitting and fencing; also, the game or sport of fencing with these sticks.

sin′gle·stick′er (-stĭk′ẽr), *n.* *Naut. Colloq.* A sloop.

sin′glet (sĭng′glĕt; -glĭt), *n.* An undershirt or jersey.

single tax. *Econ.* A tax to be levied on a single object, specif. land, as the sole source of public revenue, a policy proposed about 1750 by the physiocrats and later popularized by Henry George. — **sin′gle-tax′** (*see Pron.*, [§ 2), *adj.*

sin′gle·ton (sĭng′g'l·tŭn), *n.* [Humorous formation on *single*, after surname *Singleton.*] In certain card games, as whist, a card which is the only one of its suit held in a given hand at the deal.

sin′gle·tree′ (sĭng′g'l·trē′; -trĭ), *n.* [From SWINGLETREE.] The pivoted or swinging bar to which the traces of a harnessed horse are fixed; a whippletree. Cf. DOUBLETREE.

single wing back formation. See WING BACK FORMATION.

sin′gly (sĭng′glĭ), *adv.* **1.** Individually; severally. **2.** Singlehanded. **3.** As or by a single individual.

sing′song′ (sĭng′sŏng′; 74), *n.* **1.** Verse with marked and regular rhythm; a jingling song; hence, doggerel. **2.** A tone of voice with monotonous rise and fall of pitch. **3.** *Brit.* A social gathering for, or an entertainment of, singing. — *adj.* Having a monotonous cadence or rhythm.

sin′gu·lar (sĭng′gū·lẽr), *adj.* [OF. *singulier, singuler*, fr. L. *singularius, singularis*, fr. *singulus* single.] **1. a** *Philos.* Individual; separate. **b** Of or pertaining to a single unit or individual; hence, private; peculiar to oneself or itself. **2.** Distinguished; excelling others; exceptional; as, of *singular* attainments. **3.** Unusual; strange; as, a *singular* phenomenon; also, odd; whimsical. **4.** Unique; unparalleled. **5.** *Gram.* Designating, or pertaining to, a word form denoting one person, thing, or instance; — opposed to *dual* and *plural.* **6.** *Law.* Each; individual; as, to convey several parcels of land, all and *singular.* **7.** *Logic.* Of or pertaining to a single instance or to something considered by itself; as, a *singular* proposition. — **Syn.** See STRANGE. — *n.* **1.** *Gram.* The singular number, the inflectional form denoting it, or a word in that form. Abbr. *sing.* **2.** *Logic.* That which is considered by itself or as a single term. — **sin′gu·lar·ly,** *adv.* — **sin′gu·lar·ness,** *n.*

sin′gu·lar′i·ty (sĭng′gū·lăr′ĭ·tĭ), *n.*; *pl.* -TIES (-tĭz). **1.** Quality or state of being singular. **2.** That which is singular; a singular person, thing, act, etc.; esp., a distinctive character or quality; a peculiarity.

sin′gu·lar·ize (sĭng′gū·lẽr·īz), *v. t.* To make singular.

Sin′ha·lese′ (sĭn′hȧ·lēz′; -lēs′; 2). Var. of SINGHALESE.

Sin′i·cism (sĭn′ĭ·sĭz'm), *n.* [LL. *Sinae* the Chinese.] Anything, esp. a custom, peculiar to the Chinese.

Sin′i·fy (sĭn′ĭ·fī), *v. t.* To modify by Chinese influence.

sin′i·grin (sĭn′ĭ·grĭn), *n.* [From NL. *Sinapis nigra* a synonymic name.] *Chem.* A crystalline glucoside, $C_{10}H_{16}KNO_9S_2$, found esp. in the seeds of black mustard (*Brassica nigra*). On hydrolysis it yields dextrose, allyl mustard oil, and potassium hydrogen sulfate.

sin′is·ter (sĭn′ĭs·tẽr), *adj.* [L.] **1.** On or toward the left hand; left. **2.** Wrong; dishonest; corrupt. **3.** Inauspicious; disastrous; evil; adverse; as, *sinister* influences. **4.** Indicative of lurking evil or harm; as, a *sinister* glance. **5.** *Her.* See ESCUTCHEON, *Illust.* — **sin′is·ter·ly,** *adv.* — **sin′is·ter·ness,** *n.* — **sin′is·ter·wise′** (-wīz′), *adv.*

Syn. **Sinister, baleful, malign** mean seriously threatening evil or disaster. **Sinister** rarely applies to that which obviously threatens, but rather to that which is known by experience to be its signs or to act covertly, insidiously, or the like; **baleful** imputes perniciousness, destructiveness, and the like, both to that which works openly and that which works occultly or obliquely; **malign** imputes an inherent evil or harmfulness to the thing so described.

sin′is·tral (sĭn′ĭs·trăl; sĭ·nĭs′-), *adj.* **1.** Of or pertaining to the left; on or inclining to the left; — opposed to *dextral.* **2.** Left-handed. **3.** *Conchol.* Having the aperture to the left of the axis, when facing the observer, with the apex pointing upward; — said of the shells of certain gastropod mollusks of which the whorls form a clockwise spiral mounting from the aperture to the apex. **4.** Of some flatfishes, having the left side uppermost. — **sin′is·tral·ly,** *adv.*

sin′is·tro- (sĭn′ĭs·trō-; sĭ·nĭs′trō-), **sinistr-.** [L. *sinister.*] A combining form meaning *left-*; specif.: **a** *Of, in,* or *pertaining to the left,* as in **sin′is·tro·cer′e·bral.** **b** *Direction* or *displacement toward the left,* as in **sin′is·tro·gy·ra′tion.** **c** *Better developed in,* or *using preferentially, the left,* as in **sin′is·troc′u·lar, sin′is·tro·dex′tral.**

sin′is·trorse (sĭn′ĭs·trôrs; sĭn′ĭs·trôrs′), *adj.* [L. *sinistrorsus, sinistroversus,* turned toward the left side, fr. *sinister* left + *versum, vorsum,* turned.] **1.** *Bot.* Twining spirally upward around an axis from right to left; — applied as the opposite of *dextrorse* (which see). **2.** *Conchol.* Sinistral. — **sin′is·trorse·ly,** *adv.*

sin'is·trous (sĭn'ĭs·trŭs; sĭ·nĭs'-), *adj.* **1.** Unfortunate; ill-omened. **2.** Malign or baleful. **3.** Sinistral.

sink (sĭngk), *v. i.;* SANK (săngk) or SUNK (sŭngk); SUNK (*Obs.* SUNK'EN [-ĕn] — now used as *adj.*); SINK'ING. [AS. *sincan.*] **1.** To become submerged or swallowed up; as, the ship *sinks;* to go down so as to be partly covered; as, the feet *sink* in snow. **2.** To descend lower and lower; to subside; as, the sun *sinks* in the west. **3. a** To fall or drop slowly, as to the ground; hence, to give way; fall, as in ruin. **b** To fall to a lower level, as a river. **c** To diminish in volume or apparent height. **d** To become or appear hollow or depressed; as, with old age his cheeks *sink.* **e** To fall to a lower pitch or tone; as, his voice *sank* to a whisper. **f** To die down, as flame. **g** To slope; dip; — of land. **4. a** To penetrate; as, water *sinks* in the earth. **b** Hence, to enter so as to impress lastingly. **5.** To decline, fall, or pass into a state considered as lower; as, to *sink* in the social scale; specif., to degenerate. **6.** To diminish; decline; — of prices, etc. **7.** To fail in health or in strength. **8.** To lapse from mental activity; as, to *sink* to sleep. — *v. t.* **1.** To cause to sink or fall. Specif.: **a** To submerge. **b** To lower, as the voice. **c** To degrade; debase. **d** To ruin; destroy. **e** To diminish in price, etc. **2.** To make (a depression) by digging or cutting, etc.; as, to *sink* a well; also, to place or fix in a depression thus made; as, to *sink* a post. **3.** To ignore; set aside; suppress; as, they agreed to *sink* their differences. **4.** To invest (capital) in a more or less permanent holding; often, to invest to one's loss; as, sums *sunk* in speculations.

— *n.* **1.** A drain to carry off filthy water; a sewer. **2.** A place in which vice, corruption, etc., collect. **3.** A shallow vessel connected with a drain and usually with a water supply, as for kitchen drainage. **4.** *Geol.* A depression in the land surface, esp. one having a saline lake with no outlet. — **sink'a·ble,** *adj.*

sink'age (sĭngk'ĭj), *n.* **1.** Act, process, or degree of sinking. **2.** A panel or surface depressed or set back from the main surface. **3.** *Printing.* The dropping down from the top of the page, or the lowered position, of matter as at the beginning of a chapter; also, extent of such lowering.

sink'er (sĭngk'ẽr), *n.* **1.** Something that sinks, as a weight on a fishline to sink it. **2.** One whose work is to sink a (specified) thing; as, a shaft *sinker.* **3.** *Slang, U. S.* A doughnut.

sink'hole' (sĭngk'hōl'), *n.* A hollow place in which drainage collects, esp. one opening at the bottom into an underground channel.

sink'ing fund (sĭngk'ĭng). The aggregate of sums of money, set apart usually at fixed intervals, and deposited or invested to extinguish a debt, or for other purposes.

sin'less (sĭn'lĕs; -lĭs), *adj.* Without sin; free from sin. — **sin'less·ly,** *adv.* — **sin'less·ness,** *n.*

sin'ner (sĭn'ẽr), *n.* One who sins; esp., one who sins without repenting; hence, an incorrigible transgressor.

Sinn Fein (shĭn fān). [Ir. *sinn féin* we ourselves.] **1.** A policy or movement advocating the advancement of Ireland along national lines and its political separation from Great Britain. **2.** Also, the body of extreme Irish Nationalists who opposed the establishment of the Irish Free State. — **Sinn Fein'er.** — **Sinn Fein'ism.**

Sin'o- (sĭn'ō-; sī'nō-). [See SINOLOGUE.] A combining form used to denote: **a** *Chinese;* — in nouns, as in *Sinology.* **b** *Chinese and;* — in adjectives, as in **Sin'o–A·mer'i·can, Sin'o–Ger'man, Sin'o–Jap'a·nese', Sin'o–Rus'sian, Sin'o–So'vi·et, Sin'o–Ti·bet'an.**

Sin'o·logue (sĭn'ō·lŏg; sī'nō-; 74), *n.* [Gr. *Sinai* (whence LL. *Sinae*) an Oriental people mentioned by Ptolemy + Gr. *logos* discourse.] A student of, or one versed in, the Chinese language, literature, or history.

Si·nol'o·gy (sĭ·nŏl'ō·jĭ; sī-), *n.* That branch of systematized knowledge which treats of the Chinese, their culture, language, etc. — **Sin'o·log'i·cal** (sĭn'ō·lŏj'ĭ·kăl; sī'nō-), *adj.* — **Si·nol'o·gist** (sĭ·nŏl'ō·jĭst; sī-), *n.*

sin'syne (sĭn'sīn), *adv. Scot.* Since that time.

sin'ter (sĭn'tẽr), *n.* [G.] Literally, dross of iron; cinder; — applied in geology to certain evaporation deposits of spring or lake water.

sin'u·ate (sĭn'ū·āt), *adj.* [L. *sinuatus,* past part. of *sinuare* to wind, bend, fr. *sinus* a bend.] Sinuous; wavy; — said esp. of leaves. — **sin'u·at'ed** (-āt'ĕd; -ĭd), *adj.* — **sin'u·ate·ly,** *adv.* — **sin'u·a'tion** (-ā'shŭn), *n.*

sin'u·ous (sĭn'ū·ŭs), *adj.* [L. *sinuosus,* fr. *sinus* a bent surface, a curve.] **1.** Bending in and out; of a serpentine or wavy form; winding. **2.** *Bot.* Sinuate. — **sin'u·os'i·ty** (-ŏs'ĭ·tĭ), *n.* — **sin'u·ous·ly,** *adv.* — **sin'u·ous·ness,** *n.*

si'nus (sī'nŭs), *n.; pl.* SINUS, SINUSES (-ĕz; -ĭz). [L., a bent surface, curve.] **1. a** A bend. **b** An opening or hollow. **2.** *Anat. & Zool.* A cavity; a recess or depression; esp.: **a** A cavity in the substance of a bone of the skull which communicates with the nostrils and contains air; as, the frontal *sinus,* etc. **b** A channel for venous blood. **c** A dilatation in a canal or vessel. **3.** *Bot.* A depression between adjoining lobes, as of a leaf. **4.** *Med.* A long narrow cavity or tract through which pus discharges.

si'nus·i'tis (sī'nŭs·ī'tĭs; sĭn'ū·sī'-), *n.* [NL., fr. *sinus* + *-itis.*] *Med.* Inflammation of a sinus (sense 2 **a**).

si'nus·oid (sī'nŭs·oid), *n.* A curve of sines. — **si'nus·oi'dal** (-oi'dăl; -d'l), *adj.*

si'nus·oi'dal pro·jec'tion. In map making, an equal-area representation of the surface of the earth on a plane, with the equator and central meridian as straight lines and the parallels of latitude correct to scale. Other meridians are curved lines (sinusoids) and distances along them are not constant or correct. This projection is especially good for large areas in low latitudes, as continents of South America or Africa.

Si'on (sī'ŭn), *n.* = ZION.

-sion. See -TION.

Siou'an (sōō'ăn), *adj.* Pertaining to or designating one of the great linguistic families of North American Indians formerly inhabiting a large area between the Mississippi and the Rocky Mountains. See LANGUAGE, *Table.*

Sioux (sōō; *pl.* sōō *or* sōōz), *n. sing. & pl.* An Indian of an important group of Siouan tribes, calling themselves ***Dakota.*** The Sioux are warlike and of fine physique.

Sioux State. North Dakota; — a nickname.

sip (sĭp), *v. t.;* SIPPED (sĭpt), or, *Rare* or *Ref. Sp.,* SIPT; SIP'PING. [ME. *sippen.*] **1.** To drink in small quantities or little by little; as, to *sip* tea. **2.** To take sips from; to taste. — *v. i.* To take a sip or sips of something. — *n.* **1.** Act of sipping. **2.** A slight taste.

sipe (sīp), *v. i. Scot.* To seep; percolate.

si'phon (sī'fŏn; -fŭn), *n.* [F., fr. L. *sipho, -onis,* fr. Gr. *siphōn* a siphon, pipe.] **1.** A pipe or tube bent to form two legs of unequal length, by which a liquid can be transferred to a lower level, over an intermediate elevation, by atmospheric pressure forcing the liquid up the shorter branch of the pipe immersed in it, while the excess of weight of the liquid in the longer branch (when once filled) causes a flow. **2.** Short for SIPHON BOTTLE. **3.** *Zool.* Any of various tubular organs in animals, as in some mollusks, gastropods, etc., for drawing in or ejecting fluids. See CLAM, GASTROPOD, *Illusts.* — *v. t.* To convey, or draw off, by or as by a siphon. — *v. i.* To pass by means of a siphon.

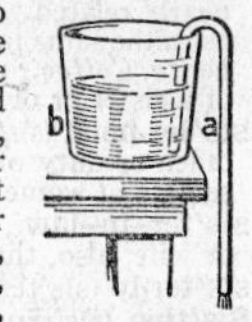

a Siphon, through which liquid flows from Vessel *b.*

siphon bottle. A bottle for holding aerated water. The water is driven out by the gas through a bent tube in the neck of the bottle.

si'pho·no·phore' (sī'fō·nō·fōr'; sī·fŏn'ō-; 70), *n.* [Gr. *siphōn* siphon, tube + *-phore.*] *Zool.* Any of an order (Siphonophora) of hydrozoans consisting of certain free-swimming or floating pelagic forms, mostly delicate, transparent, and colored.

si'pho·no·stele' (sī'fō·nō·stēl'; -stē'lē), *n.* [Gr. *siphōn* siphon, tube + *stele.*] *Bot.* A hollow cylindrical stele, with or without pith, as in the stems of ferns.

sip'pet (sĭp'ĕt; -ĭt), *n.* [See SIP, SOP.] **1.** A small piece, esp. of toast, soaked in milk, broth, etc.; a small piece of toasted or fried bread for garnishing. **2.** A fragment.

‖**si quae'ris pen·in'su·lam a·moe'nam, cir·cum'spi·ce** (sī kwē'rĭs pĕn·ĭn'sū·lăm ȧ·mē'năm, sẽr·kŭm'spĭ·sē). [L.] If thou seekest a beautiful peninsula, look around; — motto of Michigan.

sir (sûr; 4), *n.* [ME. *sir, ser,* fr. *sire.* See SIRE.] **1. a** *Obs.* A man of social authority or rank; a lord; master; — in this sense usually *sire.* **b** One suitably addressed by the title "Sir." **2.** A title prefixed [*cap.*] to the Christian name of a knight or a baronet; also, sometimes prefixed [*not cap.*] to his title of rank; as, *sir* knight. **3.** Hence: **a** Used as a fanciful or derisive title; as, *sir* oracle. **b** *Archaic.* Used as a title of respect for a priest; as, *sir* John. **4.** [*often cap.*] A respectful title used in addressing a man without using his name.

sir·dar' (sẽr·där'), *n.* [Hind. & Per. *sardār,* fr. Per. *sar* head, top + *dār* holding.] **1.** In India, etc., a native chief; also, a high military officer. **2.** In India, a head palanquin bearer or a body servant. **3.** In Turkey, Egypt, etc., a commander in chief, esp. the commander in chief of the Anglo-Egyptian army.

sire (sīr), *n.* [OF. *sire,* fr. L. *senior* older.] **1.** *Obs.* A person of authority; a lord; master. **2.** A title of respect, now used only in addressing a sovereign. **3.** A male progenitor; father; — now *Poetic* exc. in composition. **4.** The male parent of an animal, esp. of a horse. — *v. t.* To beget; procreate; — specif. of beasts, esp. stallions.

si'ren (sī'rĕn; -rĭn), *n.* [L., fr. Gr. *seirēn.*] **1.** [*also cap.*] *Gr. Relig.* One of a group of minor divinities or deities associated with death, and sometimes represented as carrying off souls, or as mourning for the dead. They are represented with the heads, and sometimes the busts and arms, of women, but otherwise with the forms of birds. **2.** Hence: Something insidious or deceptive; esp., an enticing, dangerous woman. **3.** A device for sounding signals of warning, as on an automobile. **4.** [F. *sirène,* properly, a siren in sense 1.] *Acoustics.* An apparatus producing musical tones by the rapid interruption of a current of air, steam, or other fluid by a perforated rotating disk or disks, used in acoustical investigations and, in a large form, as a fog signal. **5.** *Zool.* One of a genus (*Siren*) of eel-shaped amphibians having small forelimbs, but destitute of hind legs and pelvis, and having permanent external gills as well as lungs.

— *adj.* Of or pertaining to a siren; bewitching, like a siren.

si·re'ni·an (sī·rē'nĭ·ăn), *n.* [L. *siren.*] Any of an order (Sirenia) of aquatic herbivorous mammals, as the manatee, dugong, etc.

Sir'i·us (sĭr'ĭ·ŭs), *n.* [L., fr. Gr. *Seirios,* prop., scorching.] A star of the constellation Canis Major, the brightest star in the heavens; — called also the *Dog Star.*

sir'loin' (sûr'loin'), *n.* [OF. *surlonge,* fr. *sur* upon + *longe* loin.] A loin of beef, or a part of a loin; esp., in the United States, the part next behind the porterhouse. See BEEF, *Illust.*

si·roc'co (sĭ·rŏk'ō), *n.; pl.* -COS (-ōz). [It. *sirocco, scirocco,* fr. Ar. *sharq* the rising of the sun, the east.] **1. a** A hot, dust-laden wind from the Libyan deserts, experienced chiefly in Italy, Malta, and Sicily. **b** A warm, moist, oppressive southeast wind, in the same regions. **2.** In general, any hot or warm wind of cyclonic origin.

sir'rah (sĭr'ȧ), *n.* [From SIR.] *Archaic.* A term of address implying inferiority, used in anger, contempt, etc.

sir'–rev'er·ence, *n.* [L. *salva reverentia,* where *salva* is adj.] *Obs.* An equivalent of *save your reverence,* used apologetically before any unseemly expression.

sir'up, syr'up (sĭr'ŭp; sûr'-; 117), *n.* [OF. *sirop,* fr. Ar. *sharāb* a drink, sirup, fr. *shariba* to drink.] **1.** A thick, sticky liquid made from the juice of fruits, herbs, etc., boiled with sugar; as, pears preserved in their own *sirup.* **2.** Hence, any concentrated, more or less sticky, aqueous solution of sugar, either without admixture (as the ***simple sirup*** of pharmacy) or variously flavored or medicated, or obtained in an incompletely refined state as in the manufacture of cane sugar or of glucose. Cf. GLUCOSE, 2; MAPLE SIRUP; MOLASSES; SORGHUM, 2; SUGAR. — **sir'up·y, syr'up·y** (-ĭ), *adj.*

‖**sir'vente'** (sẽr'väNt'), *n.* [F.] A type of Provençal song satirizing the vices of society; — often used by the 12th- and 13th-century troubadours.

si'sal (sī'săl; sĭs'ăl; sē·säl'), *n.* Also **sisal hemp.** [From *Sisal,* Yucatan.] A strong durable white fiber, derived from the leaves of a West Indian agave (*Agave sisalina*) and used for hard fiber cordage. Also, the plant.

sis'kin (sĭs'kĭn), *n.* [G. dial. *sisschen.*] A small, sharp-billed, chiefly greenish and yellowish finch (*Spinus spinus*) of temperate Europe and Asia, allied to the goldfinch.

sis'mo·graph (sĭs'mō·grȧf), **sis'mo·graph'ic,** etc. Vars. of SEISMOGRAPH, etc.

sis'sy (sĭs'ĭ), *n.; pl.* SISSIES (-ĭz). *Colloq.* An effeminate boy or man. — **sis'sy,** *adj.* — **sis'sy·ish,** *adj.*

sis'ter (sĭs'tẽr), *n.* [ME. *sister, suster,* of Scand. origin.] **1.** A female person or, by extension, animal, considered in her relation to another person or animal, having the same parents (***whole sister***), or one parent in common (***half sister***). Cf. SIB, *n.,* 3. **2.** A member of a sisterhood; — used in the *pl.* as the title of many religious orders of women. **3.** One of the same kind or condition, regarded as nearly related. **4.** A woman closely associated with another person, as in the same faith, society, etc. **5.** A head nurse in a hospital ward; hence, *Colloq.*, nurse. — *adj.* Having or suggesting the relationship of a sister or of sisters; sisterly.

sis′ter·hood (sĭs′tẽr·ho͝od), *n.* **1.** State or relation of being a sister; the office or duty of a sister. **2.** Sisters, collectively; in religious use, a society of women united in one faith or order.

sis′ter–in–law′, *n.; pl.* SISTERS-IN-LAW. The sister of one's husband or wife; also, the wife of one's brother.

sis′ter·ly (sĭs′tẽr·lĭ), *adj.* Like or becoming a sister.

Sis′tine (sĭs′tēn; -tĭn; *or, esp. Brit.,* -tīn), **Six′tine** (sĭks′tĭn), *adj.* [It. *sistino*, NL. *Sixtinus.*] Of or pertaining to any of the popes named Sixtus.

Sistine Chapel. The pope's private chapel in the Vatican at Rome, built by Pope Sixtus IV, and decorated with frescoes by Michelangelo and others.

Sistine Madonna. A famous Madonna painted by Raphael for the Church of St. Sixtus (San Sisto) at Piacenza and now in the Dresden Gallery.

sis′trum (sĭs′trŭm), *n.* [L., fr. Gr. *seistron*, fr. *seiein* to shake.] A metallic instrument, a light frame with transverse metal rods, jingled in the ancient Egyptian ceremonies associated with the worship of Isis.

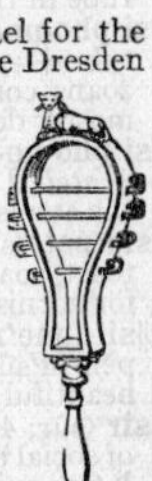

Sistrum.

Sis′y·phus (sĭs′ĭ·fŭs), *n.* [L., fr. Gr. *Sisyphos.*] *Gr. Myth.* A crafty and avaricious king of Corinth, condemned in Hades to roll up a hill a huge stone, which constantly rolled back. — **Sis′y·phe′an** (sĭs′ĭ·fē′ăn), *adj.*

sit (sĭt), *v. i.;* SAT (săt), *Archaic* SATE (săt, *rarely* sāt); SAT, *Obs.* SIT′TEN (sĭt′′n); SIT′TING. [AS. *sittan.*] **1.** To rest upon the haunches; to occupy a seat. **2.** To perch or roost with the body drawn up close, as birds. **3.** To occupy a place as a member of an official body; as, to *sit* in Congress. **4.** To hold a session; — said of assemblies, courts, etc. **5.** To cover and warm eggs for hatching; to brood; incubate; as, a *sitting* hen. **6. a** To take a position for a certain purpose, as for one's picture; as, to *sit* for a painter. **b** To pose as a model. **7.** To remain inactive or quiescent; to rest in any condition. **8. a** To be located. **b** To be supported; lie, rest, or bear; — with *on* or *upon*. **9.** To be adjusted; to fit; as, a coat *sits* well. **10.** To baby-sit. — *v. t.* **1.** To seat (oneself). **2.** To seat or place in position. **3.** To keep one's seat upon; as, to *sit* a horse.

sit′–down′, *n., or* **sit–down strike.** A cessation of work and refusal to be ejected from continuous occupation of shop, plant, or like place of employment, as a worker's protest and means toward forcing compliance with demands.

site (sīt), *n.* [L. *situs*, fr. *sinere, situm*, to let, past part, *situs* placed, lying, situate.] **1.** The local position of an edifice, town, monument, etc. **2.** The seat or scene of any (specified) thing.

sith (sĭth), *adv., conj., & prep.* [See SINCE.] *Archaic.* Since; afterwards; seeing that.

sit′–in′, *n.* = SIT-DOWN.

sito-. [Gr. *sitos.*] A combining form meaning: **a** *Grain, food,* as in **si·tol′o·gy**, a treatise on diet. **b** *Eating,* as in **si′to·ma′ni·a, si′to·pho′bi·a.**

si·tos′ter·ol (sī·tŏs′tẽr·ōl; -ŏl), *n.* Also **si·tos′ter·in** (-ĭn). [*sito-* + chole*sterol.*] *Chem.* A white crystalline alcohol, $C_{27}H_{46}O$, resembling cholesterol, found in wheat embryos, Calabar beans, and elsewhere.

sit′ter (sĭt′ẽr), *n.* One who sits; specif., = BABY SITTER.

sit′ting, *n.* **1.** Act or posture of one that sits, as for a portrait or bust; also, the period of time involved. **2.** A brooding over eggs for hatching, as by fowls; also, the number of eggs covered by a fowl in a single brooding. **3.** A session; as, a *sitting* of a court, legislature, etc.; also, the period of its duration. **4.** A seat in a church, theater, etc. — *adj.* **1.** That sits; specif.: **a** Being in the position of one who sits. **b** That is setting; as, a *sitting* hen. **c** That holds a seat; as, a *sitting* member. **2.** Pertaining to, or used in or for, sitting; as, a *sitting* room.

sitting room. A living room.

sit′u·ate (sĭt′ū·āt), *adj.* [ML. *situatus*, fr. *situare* to place, fr. *situs* situation, site.] *Chiefly Law.* Having its site; located. — (-āt), *v. t.* To place (one) in a situation; give a place to.

sit′u·at′ed (-āt′ĕd; -ĭd), *adj.* **1.** Having a site or location; located. **2.** Circumstanced; — of persons.

sit′u·a′tion (-ā′shŭn), *n.* **1.** Manner in which an object is placed; location; also, a locality. **2.** State of being located; position, as regards conditions and circumstances. **3.** Relative combination of circumstances at a moment; a critical or unusual state of affairs; specif., in narrative and drama, a particular complex of affairs at a given moment in the action. **4.** Position or place of employment. — **Syn.** See STATE: POSITION.

si′tus (sī′tŭs), *n.* [L.] Situation; position; esp., the natural position, as of a part of a plant, organ of a body, etc.

sitz bath (sĭts). [G. *sitzbad.*] A tub in which one bathes in a sitting posture; also, a bath so taken.

sitz′mark′ (sĭts′märk′; *G.* zĭts′märk′), *n.* [G., lit., seat mark.] *Skiing.* A depression left in the snow by a skier falling backward.

Si′va (sē′vȧ; shē′vȧ), **Shi′va** (shē′vȧ), *n.* [Skr. *Śiva*, prop., friendly, auspicious.] One of the supreme deities of Hinduism, when regarded as one member of the Hindu triad (see TRIMURTI), representing the principle of destruction, and also the reproductive or restoring power. — **Si′va·ism, Shi′va·ism** (-ĭz′m), *n.* — **Si′va·ist, Shi′va·ist** (-ĭst), *n.* — **Si′va·is′tic, Shi′va·is′tic** (-ĭs′tĭk), *adj.*

Si·van′ (sē·vän′), *n.* [Heb.] See JEWISH CALENDAR.

si′ver (sī′vẽr), *n. Scot.* An open drain.

six (sĭks), *n.* [AS. *six, seox, siex.*] **1.** See NUMBER, *Table.* **2.** Something having as an essential feature six units or members, as a playing card with six pips, a six-cylindered engine or automobile, etc. — **six**, *adj.*

six′fold′ (-fōld′; 2), *adj. & adv.* See -FOLD.

Six Nations. A confederation of North American Indians formed by the union of the Tuscaroras and the Five Nations. See IROQUOIS.

six′pence (sĭks′pĕns), *n.* The sum of six pence; also, an English silver coin of this value. See MONEY, *Tables.*

six′pen′ny (-pĕn′ĭ; -pĕn·ĭ), *adj.* **1.** Of the value of, or costing, sixpence; hence, of trifling worth; cheap; trashy. **2.** Designating a size of nails. See -PENNY.

six′score′ (-skōr′; 2; 70), *adj.* Six times twenty.

six′–shoot′er, *n. Colloq.* A firearm, esp. a revolver, which can be fired six times without reloading.

sixte (sĭkst), *n.* [F., fr. *six* six.] *Fencing.* The sixth parry, the same as *tierce* with the fingernails turned up.

six′teen′ (sĭks′tēn′; 2), *n. & adj.* [AS. *sixtēne, sixtȳne.*] See NUMBER, *Table.*

six′teen′mo (sĭks′tēn′mō), *n.; pl.* -MOS (-mōz). A book of sheets folded each into sixteen leaves; sextodecimo.

six′teenth′ (sĭks′tēnth′; 2), *n.* **1.** See NUMBER, *Table.* **2.** *Music.* A sixteenth note. — **six′teenth′**, *adj.*

sixteenth note. *Music.* See NOTE, *n.*

sixth (sĭksth), *n.* **1.** See NUMBER, *Table.* **2.** *Music.* **a** An interval embracing six diatonic degrees. **b** A tone at this interval. **c** The harmonic combination of two tones a sixth apart. **d** The sixth tone of a scale counting upwards. — **sixth**, *adj.* — **sixth′ly**, *adv.*

sixth chord. *Music.* A chord made up of a tone with its third and its sixth, usually regarded as the first inversion of a triad; — called also ***chord of the sixth.***

sixth column. a The aggregate of persons in a country at war who assist the subversive activities of the fifth column, esp. by defeatist talk, spreading rumors, and the like. **b** Any group organized to combat the fifth column.

sixth sense. A power of perception like but not one of the five senses; often, a keen intuitive power.

Six′tine (sĭks′tĭn). Var. of SISTINE.

six′ty (sĭks′tĭ), *n. & adj.* [AS. *siextig, sixtig.*] See NUMBER, *Table.* — **six′ti·eth** (-tĭ·ĕth; -ĭth), *n. & adj.*

six′ty·fold′ (-fōld′; 2), *adj. & adv.* See -FOLD.

six′ty–fourth′ note. *Music.* See NOTE, *n.*

siz′a·ble (sīz′ȧ·b′l), *adj.* Of suitable bulk; usually, large. — **siz′a·ble·ness**, *n.* — **siz′a·bly**, *adv.*

siz′ar (sīz′ẽr), *n.* Also **siz′er.** [From *size* a settled allowance.] A student in the universities of Cambridge (Eng.) and Dublin who receives from the university an allowance towards his college expenses. Formerly he had certain services to perform.

size (sīz), *n.* [Abbr. fr. *assize.*] **1.** Physical magnitude, extent, or bulk; dimensions. **2.** Character or status with reference to importance, correspondence to needs, etc.; as, the office demands a man of larger *size.* **3.** *Obs.* A settled allowance, as of food or drink. **4.** One of a set of the conventional specified measurements in which shoes, gloves, dresses, suits, etc., are made up for sale. **5.** *Colloq.* Actual state of affairs; true condition. **6.** Sizable amount, character, etc. — *v. t.* **1.** *Obs.* To fix the weight, measure, capacity, etc., of. **2.** To adjust, grade, or classify, according to size. **3.** *Colloq.* To form a judgment of.

size, *n.* [F. *assise* a setting, fixing, layer.] Any of various glutinous materials, as preparations of glue or flour, used for filling the pores in the surface of paper, fiber, plaster, etc., or, in bookbinding, for applying color, gold leaf, or the like to book covers. — *v. t.* To cover, stiffen, or glaze, with or as with size; to prepare with size.

size′a·ble (sīz′ȧ·b′l), etc. Var. of SIZABLE, etc.

-sized (-sīzd) *or* **-size** (-sīz). Having a specified size; — used in combinations mostly either *-sized* or *-size* at choice, as full-*sized* or full-*size*, life-*sized* or life-*size*, man-*sized* or man-*size;* in some compounds more commonly *-sized* in combination with adjectives and *-size* in combination with nouns, as good-*sized*, also good-*size;* medium-*sized*, also medium-*size;* family-*size*, also family-*sized;* pocket-*size*, also pocket-*sized*. Often compounds with *-sized* are preferred in formal writing, with *-size* in informal language.

siz′ing (sīz′ĭng), *n.* The process of applying size (see 2d SIZE, *n.*); also, size.

siz′zle (sĭz′′l), *v. i.;* SIZ′ZLED (-′ld); SIZ′ZLING (-lĭng). [Imitative.] To make a hissing sound; to fry, or to shrivel up, with a hissing sound. — *n.* A hissing sound, as of something frying over a fire.

siz′zling (-lĭng), *adj.* That sizzles; very hot; as, a ***sizzling*** spell of weather. — **siz′zling·ly**, *adv.*

skald (skôld; skäld). Var. of 1st SCALD.

skat (skät), *n.* [G., fr. It. *scartare* to discard.] A three-hand card game; also, one of the scoring combinations in this game.

skate (skāt), *n.; see* PLURAL, *Note,* 3. [ON. *skata.*] Any of numerous rays (genus *Raja* and allied genera of family Rajidae). Their pectoral fins are greatly developed and give the animal a rhomboidal shape. Among the best-known species are the common ***gray skate*** (*R. batis*) of Europe, the ***smooth,*** *or* ***barn-door, skate*** (*R. laevis*) of the American Atlantic coast, and a large species (*R. binoculata*) of the Pacific coast. See 1st RAY.

skate, *n.* [For *skates*, fr. D. *schaats* skate, stilt, fr. OF. *escace, escache*, stilt, of Teut. origin.] **1.** A metallic runner with a frame shaped to fit the sole of a shoe, to be fastened under the foot, and used for gliding on ice. **2.** A roller skate. — *v. i.* To glide along on skates, esp. as a form of exercise.

skate, *n. Slang, U. S.* An old decrepit horse.

skat′er (skāt′ẽr), *n.* **a** One that skates. **b** = WATER STRIDER.

skat′ole (skăt′ōl), *n.* Also **skat′ol** (-ōl; -ŏl). [Gr. *skōr, skatos*, dung + *-ol.*] *Chem.* A compound, C_9H_9N, formed by putrefaction of albuminous matter and found in the human intestine and in excrement.

skean (shkēn; skēn), *n.* [Ir. & Gael. *sgian.*] A dagger; dirk; — of weapons formerly used in Ireland and the Scottish Highlands.

ske·dad′dle (skē·dăd′′l), *v. i.;* -DLED (-′ld); -DLING (-lĭng). [E. dial. also to spill, scatter.] To flee; to run away. — *n.* Act of skedaddling. *Both Colloq.*

skee (skē), *n.* = SKI.

skeet (skēt), *n.* A form of trapshooting in which clay targets are thrown in such a way as to duplicate the angles of flight found in wing shooting.

skeg (skĕg), *n.* [D. *scheg(ge)*, fr. Dan. *skjeg.*] The afterpart of the keel of a vessel near the sternpost; now, esp., the part connecting the keel with the bottom of the rudderpost in a single-screw vessel.

skeigh (skēk), *adj. Scot.* Shy; mettlesome; proud.

skein (skān), *n.* [OF. *escaigne.*] **1.** A quantity of yarn, thread, silk, etc., put up after it is taken from the reel in a loose twisted loop. **2.** Something suggesting the twistings of a skein (def. 1), as in shape or arrangement.

skel′e·tal (skĕl′ē·tăl; -t′l), *adj.* Of or pertaining to, or of the nature of, a skeleton.

skel′e·ton (skĕl′ē·tŭn; -t′n), *n.* [NL., fr. Gr. *skeleton* (sc. *sōma*) a dried body, mummy, fr. *skeletos* dried up, parched, and akin to Gr. *skellein* to dry up, parch.] **1.** The bones, collectively, of a human being or other vertebrate; the bony or more or less cartilaginous framework supporting the soft tissues and protecting the internal organs. In *Biol.*, broadly, the whole of the more rigid parts, esp. the supporting and protective structures, of any animal. **2.** Something as meager, rigid, or devitalized, as a skeleton; specif., an emaciated person or animal. **3.** The framework of a thing, as of a building, literary work, etc. — *adj.* Consisting of or resembling a skeleton.

skel′e·ton·ize (skĕl′ē·tŭn·īz), *v. t.* To prepare a skeleton of; also, to reduce to a skeleton; specif., *Mil.*, to reduce (as a regiment) to a number of men and officers far below its complement.

skeleton key. *Locks.* A key with a large part of the bit filed away to enable it to open locks as a master key.

skel′lum (skĕl′ŭm), *n.* [D. *schelm.*] *Scot.* Rogue.

skelp (skĕlp), *n.* [Imitative.] *Scot., Ire., & Dial. Eng.* **1.** A smart blow; slap. **2.** A squall. — *v. t. Scot., Ire., & Dial. Eng.* To strike; slap; beat. — *v. i.* To step lively.

skene (shkēn; skēn). Var. of SKEAN.

skep (skĕp), *n.* [ON. *skeppa.*] **1.** A coarse round farm basket. **2.** A beehive, esp. one of twisted straw.

skep′tic (skĕp′tĭk), *adj.* Also **scep′tic** (skĕp′-). [F. *sceptique*, fr. L. *scepticus*, fr. Gr. *skeptikos* thoughtful, reflective.] Skeptical; esp., of, pert. to, or characteristic of philosophical skepticism. — *n.* **1.** One who believes in skepticism as a doctrine or employs skepticism as a method; specif. [*usually cap.*], a member of one of the ancient skeptical schools. **2.** One who carries a critical or incredulous attitude into his inquiries, or who is given to doubting. **3.** One who doubts, or disbelieves in, Christianity.

skep′ti·cal, scep′ti·cal (-tĭ·kăl), *adj.* **1.** Of, pertaining to, or characteristic of a skeptic or skepticism; characterized by skepticism. **2.** *Theol.* Doubting or denying the fundamentals of religion, freedom, immortality, God, providence, revelation. — **-ti·cal·ly**, *adv.* — **-ti·cal·ness**, *n.*

skep′ti·cism, scep′ti·cism (-tĭ·sĭz′m), *n.* **1.** *Philos.* The doctrine that all knowledge is uncertain; also, the method of suspended judgment, criticism, or doubt, characteristic of skeptics. *Skepticism* as a point of view is opposed to *dogmatism*, and appears as a reaction from it. **2.** A doubting state of mind. **3.** Doubt of, or unbelief in, theistic religion or Christianity. — **Syn.** See UNCERTAINTY.

sker′ry (skĕr′ĭ), *n.; pl.* -RIES (-ĭz). [ON. *sker.*] *Chiefly Scot.* A rocky isle; a reef.

sketch (skĕch), *n.* [D. *schets*, fr. It. *schizzo* a sketch, fr. L., fr. Gr. *schedion* an improvisation.] **1.** An outline or rough draft or plan of any design; esp., in the fine arts, such a representation of an object or scene as records its chief features; a preliminary draft. **2.** A short literary composition somewhat like the short story and the essay but intentionally slight in treatment, discursive in style, and familiar in tone. **3.** A short theatrical piece, esp. in vaudeville. — **Syn.** See COMPENDIUM. — *v. t.* To make a rough draft or sketch of. — *v. i.* To make, esp. to draw or paint, a sketch or sketches. — **sketch′er**, *n.*

sketch′book′ (-bŏŏk′), *n., or* **sketch book.** A book of or for sketches.

sketch′y (ĭ), *adj.*; SKETCH′I·ER (-ĭ·ẽr); SKETCH′I·EST. Of the nature of a sketch; roughly outlined; also, wanting in completeness, clearness, or the like; vague. — **sketch′i·ly**, *adv.* — **sketch′i·ness**, *n.*

skew (skū), *v. i.* [ONF. *eskiuer*, *escuer*, OF. *eschiuver* to shun, avoid.] **1.** *Colloq.* To take an oblique direction or course; to twist; swerve. **2.** *Dial.* To squint; to look askance. — *v. t.* **1.** To make, set, cut, etc., on the skew. **2.** To distort; pervert. — *adj.* **1.** Set, placed, or running, obliquely; slanting; — now chiefly technical. **2.** Not symmetrical; more developed on one side or in one direction than another. — *n.* A deviation from a straight line; a slant.

skew arch. An arch whose jambs are not at right angles with the face.

skew′back′ (skū′băk′), *n.* The course of masonry, the stone, or the iron plate, having an inclined face, against which the voussoirs of a segmental arch abut.

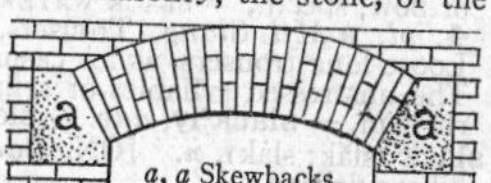

a, a Skewbacks.

skew′bald′ (-bôld′), *adj.* [ME. *skewed* piebald.] Of horses, etc., marked with patches of white and some other color.

skew′er (skū′ẽr), *n.* [Appar. fr. E. dial. *skiver* skewer.] **1.** A pin for fastening meat to a spit, or for keeping it in form while roasting. **2.** Any of various things used like such a pin. — *v. t.* To fasten as with skewers.

skew′ness, *n.* **1.** The fact or quality of being skew; distortion. **2.** *Statistics.* The state or quality of a frequency distribution of being bunched together on one side of the average and of tailing out on the other side.

ski (skē; *see note below*), *n.; pl.* SKI (skē) or SKIS (skēz). [Nor., fr. ON. *skīth.*] One of a pair of wooden, metal, or plastic strips bound one on each foot and used for gliding over snow. — *v. i.* To glide on skis in travel or as a pastime.

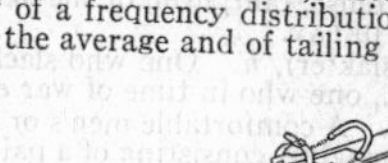
Ski and Binding.

☞ Norwegian *ski*, and *ski-* in Swedish *skida*, "ski," are pronounced shē, and shē is a frequent pronunciation in England.

ski′a·gram (skī′ȧ·grăm), *n.* A skiagraph.

ski′a·graph (-grȧf; 9), *n.* A shadowlike image or picture made on a sensitive surface, esp. by X rays. — *v. t.* To make a skiagraph of. — **ski·ag′ra·pher** (skī·ăg′rȧ·fẽr), *n.*

ski·ag′ra·phy (skī·ăg′rȧ·fĭ), *n.* [Gr. *skiagraphia*, fr. *skiagraphos* drawing in light and shade, fr. *skia* a shadow + *graphein* to delineate.] The art or science of making skiagraphs; — now used chiefly of X rays. — **ski′a·graph′ic** (skī′ȧ·grăf′ĭk), **ski′a·graph′i·cal** (-ĭ·kăl), *adj.*

ski′a·scope (skī′ȧ·skōp), *n.* [Gr. *skia* a shadow + *-scope.*] *Med.* A device for determining the refractive state of the eye by observing the retinal lights and shadows.

ski·as′co·py (skī·ăs′kō·pĭ), *n.* Examination of the eye by means of a skiascope.

skid (skĭd), *n.* [From Scand.] **1.** A timber, bar, rail, or the like, used in pairs or sets to form a slideway or rollway, as for an incline from a truck to the sidewalk. **2.** A shoe or clog placed under a wheel to prevent its turning when descending a hill; a drag. **3.** *Aeronautics.* A runner used as a member of the landing gear and designed to aid the aircraft in landing or taxiing. **4.** *Naut. Usually pl.* A wooden fender hung over a vessel's side to protect it in handling cargo, etc. **5.** Act of skidding; sideslip. — *v. t.*; SKID′DED; SKID′DING. **1.** To protect, support, check, etc., with or on a skid or skids. **2.** To haul along, slide downward, or hoist, on or as on skids. — *v. i.* **1.** To slide without rotating; — said of a wheel held from turning while the vehicle moves onward. **2.** To fail to grip the roadway; specif., to slip sideways; — said esp. of a cycle or automobile. **3.** *Aeronautics.* To slide sidewise away from the center of curvature when turning. See SIDESLIP.

skid, *v. i.* [Var. of SCUD.] To scud.

skid·doo′ (skĭ·dōō′), *v. i.* [From SKEDADDLE.] *Slang.* To get out; vamoose.

skid fin. *Aeronautics.* A fore-and-aft vertical surface, placed above the upper wing, giving lateral stability.

ski′er (skē′ẽr), *n.* One who skis.

skiff (skĭf), *n.* [F. *esquif*, fr. It. *schifo*, fr. OHG. *skif.*] **1.** A light rowboat. **2.** A boat with centerboard and spritsail, light enough to be rowed; — in full *St. Lawrence skiff.*

ski′ing (skē′ĭng), *n.* The sport of sliding on skis.

ski·jor′ing (skē·jŏr′ĭng; 70), *n.* [Nor. *skikjöring*, fr. *ski* ski + *kjöring* driving.] A winter sport in which a person wearing skis is drawn over snow or ice, usually by a horse.

ski jump. A jump made by a person wearing skis; also, a course or track especially prepared for such jumping.

skil′ful, skil′ful·ly, etc. Vars. of SKILLFUL, etc.

skill (skĭl), *n.* [ON. *skil* a distinction, discernment.] **1.** *Obs.* **a** Understanding; judgment. **b** Reason or ground for doing, saying, etc. **2.** The ability to use one's knowledge effectively; technical proficiency. **3.** A particular art or science; now, a developed or acquired ability. — **Syn.** See ART.

skill, *v. i.* [ON. *skilja* to separate, distinguish.] *Archaic.* To make a difference; also, to avail; — used impersonally; as, what *skills* it how we die?

skilled (skĭld), *adj.* **1.** Having skill; expert. **2. a** Of workmen or labor, having or requiring such training in one occupation as would involve industrial loss in a transference to other occupations; — opposed to *unskilled.* **b** Of or pertaining to workmen proficient in the handling of machinery; as, a *skilled* mechanic. **3.** Requiring skilled workmen; as, the *skilled* trades. — **Syn.** See PROFICIENT.

skil′let (skĭl′ĕt; -ĭt), *n.* A saucepan or, *U.S.*, a frying pan.

skill′ful, skil′ful (skĭl′fŏŏl; -f'l), *adj.* Possessed of, or displaying, skill; expert. — **Syn.** See PROFICIENT. — **skill′ful·ly, skil′ful·ly**, *adv.* — **skill′ful·ness, skil′ful·ness**, *n.*

skil′ling (skĭl′ĭng; *Swed. & Norw.* shĭl′-), *n.* A former money of account in Sweden, Norway, Denmark, etc., worth less than one cent; also, the coin.

skim (skĭm), *v. t.*; SKIMMED (skĭmd); SKIM′MING. [OF. *escumer*, fr. OHG. *scūm.* See SCUM.] **1.** To clear (a liquid) from scum or floating substance; to take off (a film, scum, etc.) from a liquid; as, to *skim* cream from milk; also, to remove scum, etc., from the contents of, as a pot. **2.** To read or examine superficially and rapidly; as, to *skim* a book. **3.** To pass swiftly or lightly over; as, gulls that *skim* the waves. **4.** To throw (a stone) so as to skip or ricochet along the water. **5.** *Chem.* = TOP, *v. t.*, 7. — *v. i.* **1.** To pass lightly or hastily; to glide or skip along the surface; esp., to give a cursory glance or consideration; — usually with *over.* **2.** To become coated with a film or scum. — *n.* **1.** *Rare.* Scum; film. **2.** Act of skimming. **3.** Something skimmed; specif., skim milk. — *adj. Rare.* Skimmed, as milk.

skim′ble–scam′ble (skĭm′b'l·skăm′b'l; skĭm″'l·skăm″'l), *adj.* Also **skim′ble–skam′ble.** Rambling; unconnected; senseless.

skim′mer (skĭm′ẽr), *n.* **1.** One who or that which skims. **2.** A utensil used for skimming. **3.** Any of several long-winged marine birds (genus *Rhynchops*) allied to the terns.

skim milk. Milk from which the cream has been taken.

skim′ming (skĭm′ĭng), *n.* That which is skimmed from a liquid; — chiefly in *pl.*

skimp (skĭmp), *v. t. & i.* To scrimp; also, to scamp. — *adj.* Scanty; meager. *Both Colloq.*

skimp′y (skĭmp′ĭ), *adj.*; SKIMP′I·ER (-ĭ·ẽr); SKIMP′I·EST. *Colloq.* **a** Scanty; skimp. **b** Stingy. — **skimp′i·ly**, *adv.* — **skimp′i·ness**, *n.*

skin (skĭn), *n.* [ON. *skinn.*] **1.** The integument of an animal, separated from the body; specif., *Com.*, that of a small animal, as a calf, sheep, or goat, as disting. from the *hide* of a large animal; the pelt of an animal made up into an article for use. **2.** A vessel of skin, used for liquids. **3.** The external integument of an animal. **4.** One's life; — in phrase *to save one's skin.* **5.** The outermost layer, or surface, of anything, likened to a skin; as, the *skin* of a casting; a rind, peel, etc., as of fruit. **6.** *Slang.* **a** A contemptible person; specif., a skinflint. **b** A cheat; a sharper. **7.** *Gems.* The outermost layer of nacreous matter composing a pearl. **8.** *Shipbuilding.* The shell of a vessel. — *v. t.*; SKINNED (skĭnd); SKIN′NING. **1.** To cover with or as with skin. **2.** To strip the skin from; to flay, peel, etc. **3.** *Slang.* To strip of money or property. — *v. i.* To become covered with or as with skin.

skin′bound′ (skĭn′bound′), *adj.* Having the skin adhering closely to the flesh; hidebound; affected with scleroderma.

skin′–deep′ (-dēp′; 2), *adj.* Only as deep as the skin; hence, superficial. — **skin′–deep′**, *adv.*

skin diving. The sport of submerging without a diving helmet or suit but with a breathing device. — **skin diver.**

skin effect. *Elec.* An effect characteristic of current distribution in a conductor at high frequencies, by virtue of which the current is greater at the surface (or "skin") of the conductor than in its interior.

skin′flint′ (skĭn′flĭnt′), *n.* One so miserly as to skin a flint in order to make a saving; a niggard.

skink (skĭngk), *n.* [L. *scincus*, fr. Gr. *skinkos.*] Any of a group of pleurodont lizards (family Scincidae) mostly small, with stout scales.

skink, *v. t.* [MD. *schinken*, *schenken.*] *Archaic & Dial.* To draw or pour out, as drink.

skink′ing, *adj. Scot.* Watery; thin.

skin′ner (skĭn′ẽr), *n.* **1.** One who deals in skins or hides; specif., one who removes, cures, or dresses skins. **2.** = SKIN, *n.*, 6 **b.** **3.** *Colloq.*, *U.S.* A mule or horse driver.

skin′ny (skĭn′ĭ), *adj.*; SKIN′NI·ER (-ĭ·ẽr); SKIN′NI·EST. **1.** Of the nature of, or like, skin. **2.** Thin; emaciated. — **Syn.** See LEAN. — **skin′ni·ness**, *n.*

skin′tight′ (skĭn′tīt′; 2), *adj.* Closely fitted to the figure.

ski′o·gram (skī′ō·grăm), **ski′o·graph** (-grăf; 9), *n.* A skiagraph.

skip (skĭp), *v. i.;* SKIPPED (skĭpt); SKIP′PING. [ME. *skippen.*] **1.** To move with leaps and bounds; to caper; also, to ricochet. **2.** To pass from point to point omitting or disregarding the intervals, as in reading, writing, etc. **3.** *Colloq.* To leave hurriedly; to escape; — often with *out.* **4.** *Educ. U. S.* To be promoted to a grade beyond the next higher. — *v. t.* **1.** To leap lightly over; as, to *skip* the gutter. **2.** *Colloq.* To cause to ricochet; as, to *skip* a stone. **3.** To pass over or by without notice, mention, or effect. — *n.* **1.** A light leap or bound; esp., a gait, often adopted by children, made up of alternating hops and steps. **2.** A passing over or omission due to calculation, neglect, chance, etc. **3.** *Music.* A melodic progression by more than a degree at once.

skip (skĭp), *n. Curling, Bowling, etc.* The captain of a side, who advises his men as to the play, controls the sweeping, etc. — *v. t.* To direct as skip.

skip bombing. Bombing technique according to which bombers swoop low like torpedo planes to release bombs close to shipmast level so that they explode underwater against the ship's side. — **skip′-bomb′**, *v. t.*

skip′jack′ (skĭp′jăk′), *n.;* see PLURAL, *Note,* 3. *Zool.* Any of various fishes that play at the surface of the water, as the bonito (*Sarda sarda*), saury, etc.

skip′per (skĭp′ẽr), *n.* **1.** One who or that which skips. **2.** Any of various skipping insects. **3.** The saury (*Scombresox saurus*) or other allied fish. **4.** Any of numerous small, stout-bodied lepidopterous insects (family Hesperiidae) commonly regarded as true butterflies, from which they differ in venation and form of the antennae.

skip′per, *n.* [MD. *schipper.*] In nautical use, the master of a fishing or small trading vessel; hence, loosely, the master of any vessel.

skirl (skĭrl; skûrl), *v. t. & i.* [Of Scand. origin.] *Scot. & Dial.* To scream; to sound shrilly, as a bagpipe. — *n. Scot. & N. of Eng.* A shrill sound, as that made by bagpipes.

skir′mish (skûr′mĭsh), *v. i.* [OF. *escremir, eskermir,* to fence, fight.] To fight as skirmishers; to engage in a skirmish. — *n.* A slight fight in war, usually incidental to larger movements. — **Syn.** See ENCOUNTER.

skir′mish·er (-ẽr), *n.* One who skirmishes. Specif., *Mil.,* one of the soldiers deployed, in extended order, as in a combat formation.

skirr (skûr), *v. i.* To move, fly, etc., hastily; to scurry, esp. with a whirring sound. — *v. t. Now Chiefly Dial.* **a** To scour, as for clearing of enemies. **b** To skim over; also, to cause to glide or skim. — *n.* A whirr, as of birds in flight.

skirt (skûrt), *n.* [ON. *skyrta* a shirt, a kind of kirtle, Sw. *skört* a skirt, *skjorta* a shirt.] **1.** The lower hanging part of a coat, dress, or like garment; specif., a separate outer garment for women or girls covering the body from the waistline down; also, a petticoat or underskirt. **2.** Something that hangs down in the manner of a skirt; specif., *pl.,* on a saddle, the flaps covering the sidepieces on which the stirrups are hung to the saddle. **3.** *pl.* The environs, as of a city. **4.** A rim, border, etc. **5.** *Slang.* A girl or woman. — *v. t.* **1.** To border; to run along the edge of. **2.** To envelop in the manner of a skirt; also, to give a border or edging to; — usually with *with.* **3.** To go or pass around or about, now esp., to avoid crossing or discovery; as, the army *skirted* the marsh. — *v. i.* To be or lie or move along the edge; as, to *skirt* along a coast.

skit (skĭt), *n.* **1.** A jeer or gibe. **2.** *Scot.* A jest or hoax. **3.** A satirical or humorous story, sketch, or the like, often outwardly serious. **4.** *Drama.* A brief burlesque or comic sketch included in a dramatic performance, as a revue.

skite (skīt), *n. Scot. & Dial.* **a** A sudden shower. **b** A glancing blow; a buffeting. **c** A squirting or squirt.

skit′ter (skĭt′ẽr), *v. i.* **1.** To glide lightly or hurriedly; esp., *U. S.,* to skip along a surface. **2.** *Angling.* To draw a hook through, or along the surface of, the water with a twitching or quivering motion. — *v. t.* To cause to skitter.

skit′tish (skĭt′ĭsh), *adj.* [E. dial. *skit* to caper as a restive horse, to skip.] **1.** Excessively lively or frivolous in nature, action, etc.; capricious. **2.** Easily frightened; restive; — chiefly of horses. **3.** Coy; shy. — **skit′tish·ly,** *adv.* — **skit′tish·ness,** *n.*

skit′tle (skĭt′'l), *n.* [Of Scand. origin.] **1.** In form **skit′tles** (-'lz), construed as *sing.,* except in attributive use, as **skittle alley.** The game of ninepins. **2.** One of the pins used in this game. **3.** *pl.* Play; enjoyment; — in phrase *not all beer and skittles.* See BEER AND SKITTLES.

skive (skīv), *v. t.* [ON. *skīfa.*] To cut off, as leather, rubber, etc., in thin layers or pieces; to shave or pare.

skiv′er (skīv′ẽr), *n.* **1.** A cheap, soft leather, made of the grain side of a split sheepskin, usually tanned in sumac, and dyed. **2.** The cutting tool used in splitting leather or skins. **3.** One who skives leather.

skiv′vies (skĭv′ĭz), *n. pl.* [E. dial. *skivie, skaivie* askew, silly, fr. Sc. Gael. *skaivie,* fr. ON. *skeifr* oblique, crooked.] *U. S. Navy.* Underwear.

sklent (sklĕnt), *v. i.* To slant; also, to fib. — *n.* A slant; also, an untruth. — *adj.* Slanting. *All Scot.*

skoal (skōl), *interj.* An exclamation pledging health in drinking. — **skoal,** *n. & v.*

skreegh, skreigh (skrēk; skrāk). Scot. vars. of SCREECH.

sku′a (skū′ȧ), *n.* Also **skua gull.** [Of Scand. origin.] Any jaeger (esp. of genera *Catharacta* and *Stercorarius*), as the ***great skua*** (*C. skua*) of the North Atlantic. See GULL.

skul·dug′ger·y (skŭl·dŭg′ẽr·ĭ), *n. Humorous.* Trickery.

skulk (skŭlk), *v. i.* [OF. Scand. origin.] **1.** To hide, or get out of the way, in a sneaking manner; to lurk. **2.** To shirk; malinger. — **Syn.** See LURK. — *n.* One who skulks. — **skulk′er,** *n.*

skull (skŭl), *n.* [ME. *skulle,* of Scand. origin.] **1.** The skeleton of the head of a vertebrate; the bony or cartilaginous framework which encloses and protects the brain and chief sense organs, and supports the jaws. See FACIAL ANGLE, *Illust.* **2.** The head, esp. as the seat of intelligence; the brain; mind.

skull and crossbones. A representation of the human skull over crossbones. It is a symbol of death.

skull′cap′ (skŭl′kăp′), *n.* **1.** A close-fitting cap; esp., a light brimless cap for indoor wear. **2.** Any of various plants (genus *Scutellaria*) of the mint family, the calyx of whose flower appears, when inverted, like a helmet.

skunk (skŭngk), *n.;* see PLURAL, *Note,* 3. [Of Algonquian origin.] **1.** A common mammal (genus *Mephitis*) of temperate North America, allied to the weasels and minks. It has the power of ejecting an offensive odorous secretion produced in two perineal glands. Also, the fur or pelt of this animal. **2.** *Vulgar.* A low, contemptible person. — *v. t. Slang, U. S.* To defeat, as in cards, so completely that one's opponent fails to score.

skunk cabbage. **a** A perennial herb (*Symplocarpus foetidus*) of the arum family, of eastern North America and Asia, which sends up in early spring a cowl-shaped brownish-purple spathe having an unpleasant odor. **b** In the Pacific coast states, a somewhat similar plant (*Lysichiton camstschatcense*) of the arum family.

sky (skī), *n.; pl.* SKIES (skīz). [ON. *sky̅* cloud, cloudy sky.] **1.** Orig., a cloud; now, the upper atmosphere usually with reference to cloudiness; — chiefly in *pl.* **2.** The apparent arch, or vault, of heaven; the firmament. **3.** Heaven; the celestial regions or powers. **4.** Weather; climate. — *v. t.;* SKIED (skīd) or SKYED; SKY′ING. **1.** *Colloq.* To lift, throw, bat, etc., towards the sky, as a ball. **2.** *Colloq.* To hang (a picture) in the top row in an exhibition, or very near the ceiling.

sky blue. The color of the sky, blue in hue, of medium saturation and medium brilliance. See COLOR. — **sky′-blue′** (*see Pron.,* § 2), *adj.*

Skye terrier (skī). [From Isle of *Skye,* Inner Hebrides, Scotland.] A terrier of a very old breed originating in Scotland, having a long head, a long and low body, and short and straight legs.

sky′ey (skī′ĭ), *adj. Poet.* Of or like the sky; ethereal.

sky′lark′ (skī′lärk′), *n.* The common Old World lark (*Alauda arvensis*), noted for its song, uttered as it rises in almost perpendicular flight.

sky′lark′, *v. i.* To frolic boisterously; to run or skip about in a sportive manner. — **sky′lark′er,** *n.*

sky′light′ (-līt′), *n.* A window in a roof, ceiling, etc.

sky line. **1.** The visible horizon. **2.** The outline or silhouette of an object or objects against the sky; as, the *sky line* formed by New York's skyscrapers.

sky pilot. *Slang.* **a** A chaplain or missionary; also, a clergyman. **b** *Aeronautics.* A licensed pilot.

sky′rock′et (skī′rŏk′ĕt; -ĭt), *n. Fireworks.* A rocket that ascends and explodes high in the air. — *v. i. Colloq.* To rise like a skyrocket; — often of prices, etc.

sky′sail′ (skī′sāl′; *naut.* skī′s'l), *n. Naut.* The sail above the royal.

sky′scrap′er (-skrāp′ẽr), *n.* A very tall building.

sky′ward (-wẽrd), **sky′wards** (-wẽrdz), *adv.* Toward the sky. — *adj.* Directed to the sky or to heaven.

sky wave. *Radio.* That portion of electric waves which is reflected from the upper ionized portion of the atmosphere. Cf. GROUND WAVE.

sky′writ′ing (skī′rīt′ĭng), *n.* The forming of written signals in the air by smoke emitted from an aircraft. — **sky′writ′er** (-ẽr), *n.* — **sky′write′** (-rīt′), *v.*

slab (slăb), *n.* [ME. *slab, slabbe, sclabbe.*] **1.** A thick plate or slice of anything. **2.** *Baseball Slang.* The pitcher's plate. **3.** *Logging.* The outside piece, with or without the bark, taken from a log in sawing it into boards. — *v. t.* **1.** To saw, cut, or form into slabs; also, to saw the outside slab or slabs from (a log). **2.** To cover with slabs, as in roofing or paving.

slab, *adj. Archaic.* Thick; viscous.

slab′ber (slăb′ẽr), *v. i., v. t., & n.* Slobber.

slab′-sid′ed (slăb′sīd′ĕd; -ĭd; 2), *adj. Colloq.* Having flat sides; hence, tall or long and lank.

slack (slăk), *adj.* [AS. *slæc.*] **1.** Not using due care; remiss. **2.** Slow, sluggish, or listless. **3.** Blowing or flowing at low speed; — of a wind, tide, etc. **4.** Relaxed; not tight; as, a *slack* rope; hence, lacking in firmness; weak; soft. **5.** Wanting in activity; not busy; as, a *slack* season. **6.** Inadequate; lacking in finish or perfection. — **Syn.** See NEGLIGENT. — *v. t. & i.* **1.** To make or become slack; to slacken; to moderate, loosen, relax, etc. **2.** To slake. — *n.* **1.** The part of anything that hangs loose without strain. **2.** Cessation in movement or flow; specif., = SLACK WATER. **3.** A lull in activity; a dull season. **4.** *pl.* **a** *Mil. Slang.* Trousers, esp. when worn without puttees. **b** Loose long trousers, as for casual wear by men or women. **5.** *Pros.* The unstressed syllables or syllable of a foot; — used esp. of sprung rhythm. — **slack′ly,** *adv.* — **slack′ness,** *n.*

slack (slăk; slȧk), *n.* [ON. *slakki.*] *Scot. & Dial.* A pass between hills; a dell.

slack (slăk), *n. Mining.* The finest screenings of coal produced at a mine, undesirable for fuel unless cleaned.

slack′-baked′ (-bākt′), *adj.* Underdone; also, figuratively, undeveloped physically or mentally; half-baked.

slack′en (slăk′ĕn), *v. i.* To become slack, slow, or negligent. — *v. t.* **1.** To retard; moderate; abate; as, to *slacken* one's pace. **2.** To make less tense, taut, firm, or the like; as, to *slacken* a sail, or rope. — **Syn.** See DELAY.

slack′er (slăk′ẽr), *n.* One who slacks or shirks (work or any obligation); esp., one who in time of war evades military service.

slack suit. A comfortable men's or women's suit for casual or sportswear or lounging, consisting of a pair of slacks and jacket top or sport shirt usually of the same material and color.

slack water. Of tidal waters, the period when there is no horizontal motion of water at the surface.

slag (slăg), *n.* [MLG. *slagge.*] **1.** The dross, or scoria, of a metal; cinder. **2.** The scoriaceous lava from a volcano.

slain (slān), *past part.* of SLAY.

slake (slāk; *see note below*), *v. t.* [AS. *slacian, sleacian,* to grow slack, fr. *slæc,* slack.] **1.** *Obs.* **a** To make slack or loose; to lessen the tension of. **b** To reduce; to make less. **2.** To slacken in speed, force, etc. **3.** *Archaic.* To relieve, as pain; to assuage. **4.** To allay; to satisfy; quench; as, to *slake* thirst. **5.** To cause (lime) to heat and crumble by treatment with water; to hydrate. — *v. i.* **1.** *Obs.* To slacken one's efforts, etc. **2.** To slake lime, one's thirst, etc.; also, of lime, to become slaked. **3.** To crumble or disintegrate; — said of lime, coal, etc.

☞ The pron. slăk is common in current use, esp. with reference to lime.

sla′lom (slä′lŭm; slā′-), *n.* [Nor.] Skiing, usually in a race against time, in a zigzag downhill course.

slam (slăm), *n.* **1.** An old card game identified with ruff. **2.** A winning of all the tricks of a deal (called, in bridge, ***grand slam,*** the winning of all but one of the thirteen tricks being called a ***little,*** *or* ***small, slam***).

slam, *v. t. & i.;* SLAMMED (slămd); SLAM′MING. **1.** To shut noisily; to bang. **2.** To put in place with undue noise or in a hurry; as, to *slam* a trunk down. **3.** *Colloq.* To criticize vigorously. — *n.* **1.** A heavy impact. **2.** A banging noise, as in shutting a door. **3.** *Colloq.* A violent criticism.

slan'der (slăn'dẽr *or, esp. Brit.,* slän'dẽr), *n.* [OF. *esclandre, esclande,* fr. LL. *scandalum* stumbling block. See SCANDAL.] Defamation, oral or written; specif., *Law,* a false report maliciously uttered and tending to injure the reputation of another. Cf. LIBEL. — *v. t.* To utter slander against; to defame. — **Syn.** See MALIGN. — **slan'der·er** (-ẽr), *n.* — **slan'der·ous** (-ŭs), *adj.* — **slan'der·ous·ly,** *adv.* — **slan'der·ous·ness,** *n.*

slang (slăng), *n.* **1.** Cant of thieves, beggars, gypsies, etc. **2.** The jargon of a particular calling or class of society. **3.** Language comprising certain widely current terms having a forced, fantastic, or grotesque meaning, or exhibiting eccentric humor or fancy. — **Syn.** See DIALECT. — *v. t.* To address with slang or ribaldry; to abuse. — *v. i.* To use slang or vulgar abuse. — **slang'i·ly,** *adv.* — **slang'i·ness,** *n.* — **slang'y,** *adj.*

slank (slăngk), *Archaic past* of SLINK.

slant (slánt; 9), *adj.* [Cf. Sw. dial. *slant* slippery. See SLANT, *v.*] Inclined from a direct line; sloping; oblique. — *n.* **1.** A slanting direction, line, or plane; slope; inclination. **2.** *Colloq.* **a** A peculiar or personal attitude or opinion; as, a new *slant* on the problem. **b** A slanting view; a glance; as, to take a *slant* at him. — *v. i. & t.* [ME. *slenten* to slope, slide, of Scand. origin; cf. Sw. *slinta* to slide.] To turn or incline from a right line or a level; to slope. — **slant'ing,** *adj.* — **slant'ing·ly,** *adv.* — **slant'ly,** *adv.* — **slant'ways'** (-wāz'), *adv.* — **slant'wise'** (-wīz'), *adv. & adj.*

slap (slăp; slȧp), *n.* [ME. *slop,* fr. MD. *slop.*] *Scot. & Ir.* A pass; breach; gate; notch.

slap (slăp), *n.* [LG. *slappe,* of imitative origin.] A blow, esp. one from or as from the open hand; also, a rebuff; insult. — *adv.* Suddenly; instantly. — *v. t.;* SLAPPED (slăpt); SLAP'PING. **1.** To strike with or as with the open hand. **2.** To put, place, or throw with careless haste or force. — **Syn.** See STRIKE.

slap'dash' (-dăsh'; 2), *adv.* Also **slap'-bang'** (-băng'; 2). With impetuous force and suddenness. — *adj.* Characterized by careless haste or force.

slap'jack' (-jăk'), *n.* **1.** *U. S.* A griddlecake; flapjack. **2.** A child's card game.

slap'stick' (slăp'stĭk'), *n.* **1.** A device made of two flat pieces of wood, sometimes used in farce by one actor in striking another in such a way as from the loud noise to make it appear that the blow was a severe one. **2.** Use of this device or of rapid, usually violent, physical activity, for comic effect. **3.** Comedy characterized by slapstick (def. 2). — *adj.* Using slapstick; as, *slapstick* comedy.

slash (slăsh), *v. t.* [ME. *slaschen.*] **1.** To cut by sweeping strokes, esp. when made at random; specif., to cut in long slits; gash. **2.** To lash; scourge. **3.** To cut slits in (a garment) so as to expose an underlying color. **4.** To reduce sharply; as, to *slash* appropriations. — *v. i.* To strike violently and at random with or as with an edged instrument, to cut or censure recklessly. — *n.* **1.** Act of slashing; also, a long cut made by or as by slashing; a gash. **2.** An ornamental slit in a garment. **3.** In a forest, an open tract strewn with debris, as from logging; also, such debris. — **slash'er,** *n.*

slash (slăsh), *n.* *Local, U. S.* Swampy low-lying land.

slash'ing, *n.* A slash (in any sense); a cutting, gashing, or lashing. — *adj.* **1.** Merciless in attack; as, a *slashing* editorial. **2.** Dashing; vigorous. **3.** *Slang.* Huge; immense; as, a *slashing* dinner. — **slash'ing·ly,** *adv.*

slash pine. **a** A pine (*Pinus caribaea*) of the coast region of the southern United States, — found in swampy low-lying lands (slashes) in Florida. Also, its hard wood. **b** The loblolly *P. taeda.*

slat (slăt), *v. t.;* SLAT'TED; SLAT'TING. *Dial.* **1.** To hurl or throw. **2.** To strike; pummel. — *v. i.* To flap, as a loose sail, or as halyards against a mast. — *n.* *Dial.* A resounding slap or blow.

slat, *n.* [ME. *sclat,* fr. OF. *esclat* fragment, splinter.] A thin, narrow bar, esp. of wood or metal; a lath; as, the *slats* of a Venetian blind, of a bedstead. — *v. t.* To make or equip with slats.

slate (slāt), *n.* [OF. *esclate,* fem. of *esclat.* See 2d SLAT.] **1.** A dense, fine-grained rock produced by the compression (metamorphism) of clays, shales, etc., so as to develop a characteristic cleavage. **2.** A prepared piece of slate used for various purposes; esp.: **a** A thin, flat piece for roofing; a tile. **b** A framed tablet of slate used for writing on. **3.** Something noted on or as on a slate. Specif.: **a** A record of one's misdeeds; — chiefly in phrase, a ***clean slate,*** an unspotted or cleared record. **b** *U. S.* A list of candidates prepared for nomination or for election. **4.** The average color of common slate, blue-red in hue, of very low saturation and low brilliance. See COLOR. — *v. t.* **1.** To cover with slate or a slatelike substance. **2.** To register (as on a slate and subject to revision) for an appointment, for consideration, etc.

slate, *v. t.* [AS. *slǣtan* to bait.] **1.** To thrash; punish. **2.** To reprimand; to criticize slashingly.

slat'er (slāt'ẽr), *n.* **1.** One who lays slates. **2.** Any of various isopod crustaceans; esp., a sow bug or wood louse.

slat'er, *n.* One who slates, or censures violently; a severe critic.

slath'er (slăth'ẽr; slā'thẽr), *v. t.* *Colloq.* To spread on thick; to use, spend, etc., in quantities. — **slath'er,** *n.*

slat'ing (slāt'ĭng), *n.* **a** The work of a slater. **b** Slates, collectively.

slat'ted (slăt'ĕd; -ĭd), *adj.* Having slats, or marks like slats; made of slats.

slat'tern (slăt'ẽrn), *n.* An untidy, slovenly woman; a slut. — **slat'tern·ly,** *adj. & adv.*

slat'y (slāt'ĭ), *adj.;* SLAT'I·ER (-ĭ·ẽr); SLAT'I·EST. Of the nature of, like, or containing slate; also, slate-colored.

slaugh'ter (slô'tẽr), *n.* [ON. *slātr* butchers' meat, but modified by ME. *slaught, slaht,* slaughter, fr. AS. *sleaht, sliht;* both from the root of E. *slay.*] Act of killing; as: **a** The butchering of cattle or other beasts for market. **b** Great destruction of lives, esp. human lives in battle; carnage. — **Syn.** Massacre, butchery. — *v. t.* **1.** To butcher; to kill for the market, as beasts. **2.** To kill, esp. violently and ruthlessly or in large numbers. — **slaugh'ter·er,** *n.*

slaugh'ter·house' (-hous'), *n.* A building where beasts are butchered for the market; an abattoir.

slaugh'ter·ous (-ŭs), *adj.* Destructive; murderous.

Slav (släv; slăv), *n.* [G. *Slave,* F. *slave,* ML. *Slavus.*] A person speaking a Slavic language as his native tongue; hence, a person of the prevailing type or race among the Slavic-speaking peoples. The northern Slavs are the Russians, Poles, Czechs, Sorbs, Slovaks, and others; the south, or southern, Slavs are the Bulgarians and Yugoslavs (Serbians, Croats, and Slovenes).

slave (slāv), *n.* [OF. *esclave,* fr. ML. *Sclavus, Slavus,* Slav, fr. LGr. *Sklabos.*] **1.** One whose person and services are under the control of another as owner or master. **2.** One who has lost control of himself, freedom of action, etc.; as, a *slave* to ambition or of drink. **3.** A drudge. — *v. i.* To labor as a slave; to drudge; toil. — *v. t.* *Rare.* To enslave. — **slave,** *adj.*

slave ant. Any ant made a slave of by ants of other species (called **slave'-mak'ing ants,** *or* **slave makers**).

slave driver. One who superintends slaves at work; hence, a cruel taskmaster. — **slave'-drive',** *v. t.*

slave'hold'er (slāv'hōl'dẽr), *n.* One who holds slaves. — **slave'hold'ing,** *adj. & n.*

slav'er (slăv'ẽr), *v. i.* To suffer spittle, etc., to run from the mouth; to drool. — *v. t.* To smear with saliva; to slobber. — *n.* **1.** Saliva driveling from the mouth. **2.** Drivel; an offensive outpouring (of words, etc.).

slav'er (slāv'ẽr), *n.* **1.** A person engaged in, or a ship used in, trade in slaves, esp. in buying them and transporting them from their homes for sale. **2.** = WHITE SLAVER.

slav'er·y (-ĭ), *n.* **1.** Continued and wearisome labor; drudgery. **2.** The condition of, or like that of, a slave; bondage. **3.** The institution of slaveholding. — **Syn.** See SERVITUDE.

slav'ey (slāv'ĭ; *Brit. also* slăv'ĭ), *n.; pl.* SLAVEYS (-ĭz). *Colloq.* A servant; now usually, a maid of all work.

Slav'ic (släv'ĭk; slăv'-), *adj.* Of or pert. to the Slavs or their languages; Slavonic. — *n.* The group of related languages spoken by the Slavs. See INDO-EUROPEAN LANGUAGES, *Table.*

Slav'i·cism (-ĭ·sĭz'm), **Slav'ism** (-ĭz'm), *n.* Slavic races, culture, character, institutions, or the like.

slav'ish (slāv'ĭsh), *adj.* **1.** Of, pert. to, or befitting a slave; servile. **2.** Belonging to or inducing slavery; tyrannical; as, *slavish* laws. **3.** Permitting or manifesting no freedom of choice or judgment; as, a *slavish* translation. — **Syn.** See SUBSERVIENT. — **slav'ish·ly,** *adv.* — **slav'ish·ness,** *n.*

Slav'o- (släv'ō-; slăv'ō-). A combining form for *Slav.*

slav·oc'ra·cy (slāv·ŏk'rȧ·sĭ), *n.* [*slave* + *-cracy.*] *U. S. Politics.* Formerly, the persons or interests representing slavery, or using influence to preserve or advance slavery.

Sla·vo'ni·an (slȧ·vō'nĭ·ăn; 58), *adj.* Of or pertaining to Slavonia, the Slavs, or the Slavic race or language. — *n.* **1.** An inhabitant of Slavonia. **2.** Slavonic.

Sla·von'ic (slȧ·vŏn'ĭk), *adj.* = SLAVONIAN. — *n.* The Slavic language.

Slav'o·phile (släv'ō·fīl; -fĭl; slăv'-), **Slav'o·phil** (-fĭl), *n.* [*Slavo-* + *-phile.*] One who greatly admires the Slavs, their institutions, art, etc. — **Sla·voph'i·lism** (slȧ·vŏf'ĭ·lĭz'm; släv'ō·fĭl·ĭz'm; slăv'-), *n.*

Sla·voph'o·bist (slȧ·vŏf'ō·bĭst), *n.* [*Slavo-* + Gr. *phobos* fear.] One who fears or dislikes the Slavs.

slaw (slô), *n.* [D. *sla,* contr. fr. *salade* salad, fr. F. *salade.*] Sliced cabbage served as a salad. Cf. COLESLAW.

slay (slā), *v. t.;* SLEW (slōō); SLAIN (slān); SLAY'ING. [AS. *slēan* to strike, slay.] **1.** *Obs.* To smite; knock. **2.** To put to death by violence; to kill; destroy. — **Syn.** See KILL. — **slay'er** (slā'ẽr), *n.*

sleave (slēv), *v. t.* [AS. *slǣfan.*] To separate and divide, as silk thread. — *n.* **1.** Also **sleave silk.** Sleaved silk; floss; untwisted silk that tangles easily. **2.** A tangle.

slea'zy (slā'zĭ; slē'zĭ), *adj.;* SLEA'ZI·ER (-zĭ·ẽr); SLEA'ZI·EST. [E. dial.; cf. dial. *sleeze, slease,* to part asunder, said of badly woven cloth.] Wanting firmness of texture or substance; flimsy. — **Syn.** See LIMP. — **slea'zi·ness,** *n.*

sled (slĕd), *n.* [MD. *sledde.*] **1.** A vehicle on runners used for conveying loads, esp. over snow or ice; a sledge. **2.** A small vehicle with runners for sliding on snow or ice. — *v. t.;* SLED'DED; SLED'DING. To transport on a sled. — *v. i.* To travel or be carried on a sled.

sled'der (slĕd'ẽr), *n.* **1.** One who drives a sled. **2.** A horse or other animal that draws a sled.

sled'ding (slĕd'ĭng), *n.* **1.** Use of a sled, as for transportation. **2.** State of the snow which admits of using sleds. **3.** State of one's affairs with reference to one's ability to get along; as, business was hard *sledding.*

sledge (slĕj), *n.* Also **sledge hammer.** [AS. *slecg.*] A large, heavy hammer, usually wielded with both hands.

sledge, *n.* [MD. *sleedse.*] **1.** *Eng.* A sleigh. **2.** A strong vehicle with low runners, or one made of plank slightly turned up at one end without runners, used for transporting loads, esp. upon snow or ice; a sled. — *v. i. & t.;* SLEDGED (slĕjd); SLEDG'ING (slĕj'ĭng). To travel or convey in a sledge.

sleek (slēk), *v. t.* [See SLEEK, *adj.*] To make smooth or glossy by polishing, brushing, etc.; hence, to tidy or freshen in appearance. — *adj.* [ME. *slike.* See SLICK, *adj.*] **1.** Sleeked, as by rubbing; smooth and glossy. **2.** Smooth in speech or manner; bland; often, hypocritically smooth and unctuous. — **sleek'ly,** *adv.* — **sleek'ness,** *n.*

sleek'en (-ĕn), *v. t.* To make smooth or gentle; to sleek.

sleek'er (-ẽr), *n.* One that sleeks, as a tool for smoothing leather.

sleek'it (-ĭt), *adj.* *Scot.* Sleek; crafty.

sleep (slēp), *n.* [AS. *slǣp.*] **1.** A natural, temporary, and periodical diminution of sensation, feeling, and thought, amounting in heavy slumber to an almost complete cessation of conscious life. **2.** A state resembling sleep; as: **a** A state of inactivity, torpor, or the like. **b** The repose of death; death. **c** The state of an animal during hibernation. **3.** *Plant Physiol.* Nyctitropism. — *v. i.;* SLEPT (slĕpt); SLEEP'ING. **1.** To take rest in a state of sleep; to slumber. **2.** To be or rest in a state like sleep, as that of death, inertness, torpidity, or quiescence. **3.** To spin so quickly and smoothly that its motion is imperceptible; — of a top. **4.** *Plant Physiol.* To assume a nyctitropic position. — *v. t.* **1.** To be slumbering in; — followed by a cognate object; as, to *sleep* a dreamless sleep. **2.** To spend, use up, or get rid of in or by sleep; — with *away, off;* as, to *sleep* away the hours. **3.** *Colloq.* To have or provide sleeping accommodations for.

sleep'er (slēp'ẽr), *n.* **1.** One who sleeps. **2.** A piece of timber, stone, or steel, on or near the ground to support some superstructure, to keep in place the rails of a railroad (= TIE, *n.,* 8), to receive floor joists, etc.; a stringpiece. **3.** Also **sleeping car.** A railroad car with compartments and berths for sleeping. **4.** Anything unpromising and unnoticed that attains a startling value or importance, as: **a** A race horse long ignored as a possible winner that unexpectedly wins. **b** In the book trade, a disregarded item that is found to demand a price well above that assigned. **c** A movie that brings returns out of proportion to its cost and far exceeding the expectations of the producers.

sleep′ing bag. A bag, usually waterproof and often warmly lined, in which one may sleep, esp. outdoors.

sleeping partner. One whose relation as a business partner is kept from the public.

sleeping sickness. **1.** *Med.* A serious disease, prevalent in parts of West and South Africa, marked by fever, protracted lethargy, weakness, tremors, and wasting, caused by certain trypanosomes transmitted by the bite of tsetse flies (genus *Glossina*). **2.** Any epidemic encephalitis producing somnolence. Cf. ENCEPHALOMYELITIS.

sleep′less (slēp′lĕs; -lĭs), *adj.* Having or taking no sleep or rest. — **sleep′less·ly,** *adv.* — **sleep′less·ness,** *n.*

sleep′walk′er (-wôk′ẽr), *n.* A somnambulist. — **sleep′walk′ing,** *n.*

sleep′y (slēp′ĭ), *adj.;* SLEEP′I·ER (-ĭ·ẽr); SLEEP′I·EST. **1.** Drowsy; inclined to sleep; hence, phlegmatic; sluggish. **2.** Of or manifesting drowsiness. **3.** Tending to induce sleep; soporiferous. — **sleep′i·ly,** *adv.* — **sleep′i·ness,** *n.*

sleepy sickness. = SLEEPING SICKNESS, 2.

sleet (slēt), *n.* [ME. *sleet, slete.*] **1.** Fine driving icy particles, often with rain; also, a mixture of rain and snow. **2.** Popularly, the icy glaze that forms when cold rain falls on terrestrial objects below the freezing point. — *v. i.* To shower sleet. — **sleet′y** (-ĭ), *adj.*

sleeve (slēv), *n.* [AS. *slīef, slēf, slȳf.*] **1.** The part of a garment covering an arm only. **2.** *Mach.* A tubular part designed to fit over another part. — **sleeve′less,** *adj.*

sleigh (slā), *n.* [D. *slee,* fr. *slede.*] A vehicle on runners, used for transporting persons or goods on snow or ice. — *v. i.* To drive or travel in a sleigh.

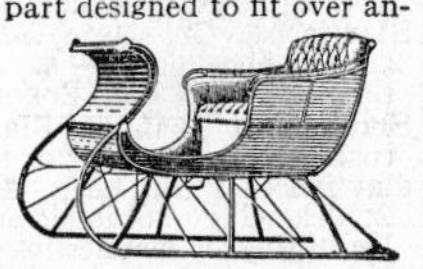

Sleigh.

sleight (slīt), *n.* [ON. *slǣgth,* fr. *slǣgr* sly, cunning.] **1.** *Now Rare.* Craft. **2.** A sly artifice; a stratagem; trick. **3.** Dexterity; skill; deftness.

sleight of hand. A trick or tricks requiring skillful manual manipulation; legerdemain; also, expertness in such tricks.

slen′der (slĕn′dẽr), *adj.* [ME. *slendre, sclendre.*] **1.** Small or narrow in circumference or width in proportion to the length or height; thin; slim. **2.** Weak; feeble; slight; as, *slender* hope. **3.** Limited in quality, size, etc.; meager; inadequate; as, *slender* means. **4.** Frugal; abstemious; as, a *slender* diet. **5.** *Phonetics.* Of a vowel, close. — **Syn.** See THIN. — **slen′der·ly,** *adv.* — **slen′der·ness,** *n.*

slen′der·ize (-īz), *v. t. & i.* To make or become slender; to reduce (one's) bodily weight.

slept (slĕpt), *past & past part.* of SLEEP.

sleuth (slōōth; 114), *n.* [ON. *slōth* track.] **1.** A sleuthhound. **2.** *Colloq.* A detective. — *v. i.* [From SLEUTHHOUND.] To play the detective.

sleuth′hound′ (-hound′), *n.* [See SLEUTH.] **1.** A hound that tracks animals by the scent; specif., a bloodhound. **2.** *U. S.* A sleuth, or detective.

slew (slōō; 114), *n.* [Var. of SLOUGH a wet place.] A wet or marshy place; a river inlet. See 1st SLOUGH, 2.

slew, *v. t. & i.* To slue; to twist. — *n.* A twist.

slew, slue (slōō; 114), *n.* [Ir. *sluagh.*] *Colloq.* A large number; as, a *slew* of people.

slew (slōō; 114), *past* of SLAY.

slice (slīs), *n.* [OF. *esclice, esclisse,* thin piece of wood, of Teut. origin.] **1.** A thin, flat piece cut off and across something. **2.** A spatula for spreading paint, ink, etc. **3.** A knife with wedge-shaped blade, for serving; as, a fish *slice;* also, one for turning meat, etc., when cooking in a pan. **4.** *Golf.* A sliced stroke. See SLICE, *v. t.,* 5. — *v. t.;* SLICED (slīst); SLIC′ING (slīs′ĭng). **1.** To cut into slices; to cut into or across with or as with a knife. **2.** To remove as a slice; — usually with *off.* **3.** To cut so as to divide into shares or parts, as an estate into farms. **4.** To use a slice (the implement) for removing, spreading, etc., as ink; to clear with a slice bar. **5.** *Golf.* To strike (the ball) so that the face of the club draws inward across the face of the ball, causing it to curve toward the right in flight (with a right-handed player). Cf. HOOK, *n.,* 7. — *v. i.* To slice something, as a ball in golf. — **slice′a·ble,** *adj.* — **slic′er** (slīs′ẽr), *n.*

slice bar. A form of fire iron with a broad, flat end, for stirring a fire of coals, clearing out ashes, etc.

slick (slĭk), *v. t.* [AS. *slician.* See SLICK, *adj.*] To make sleek or smooth; to polish; — often with *up.* — *adj.* [ME. *slike;* akin to AS. *slician* to make smooth, ON. *slīkr* smooth.] **1.** *Now Dial.* Sleek. **2.** Smart; clever; now often, adroit in trickery. **3.** Sleeked over with oil, or the like. — *n.* **1.** A device for slicking. **2.** A smooth surface of water, as caused by a film of oil or by the sweep of a ship's stern. **3.** Also **slick paper.** *Slang, U. S.* A magazine using calendered paper with a glossy finish; — often with implication of urbanity or smartness in content. Cf. PULP, *n.,* 7. — *adv.* In a slick manner.

slick′en·side′ (slĭk′ĕn·sīd′), *n.* [E. dial. *slicken* smooth + *side, n.*] *Geol.* A smooth, striated, polished surface produced on rock by friction; — usually in *pl.*

slick′er (slĭk′ẽr), *n.* **1.** *U. S.* A long, loose waterproof coat. **2.** *Colloq.* A clever trickster or cheat.

slide (slīd), *v. i.;* SLID (slĭd); SLID, SLID′DEN (slĭd″n); SLID′ING (slīd′ĭng). [AS. *slīdan.*] **1.** To move smoothly along a surface; to slide. **2.** Specif., to move over snow or ice with a smooth, uninterrupted motion, as on a sled, or esp., on the feet. **3.** To slip or fall by a loss of footing, balance, support, or the like; as, the packages *slid* from her arms. **4.** To move, esp. to crawl, flow, or speed, with marked smoothness or ease; as, a roadster *slid* up the hill. **5.** To pass quietly, secretly, stealthily, etc., so as not to observe or be observed; — often with *let,* to allow (a thing, or a thing's outcome) to become a matter of indifference. **6.** To pass by easy gradations, as from prose into poetry. — *v. t.* **1.** To cause to slide, esp. by a push along an incline or slippery surface. **2.** To pass with unobtrusive dexterity; to slip; as, to *slide* in a word.

— *n.* **1.** Act, motion, or an instance of sliding. **2.** The descent of a mass, as of earth, rock, or snow, down a hillside; as, a land*slide;* also: **a** The track of bare rock or earth left by a landslide. **b** The mass of earth or rock deposited by a landslide. **3.** That which operates, adjusts, etc., by sliding, as a cover for an aperture. **4.** That on which anything moves by sliding. **5. a** A plate of glass or other transparent material on which is a picture to be projected, as by a magic lantern. **b** A plate on which is an object to be examined with a microscope. **6.** *Music.* **a** A grace consisting of two or more small notes moving by adjacent degrees and leading to a principal note. **b** A portamento. **c** In the trumpet and trombone, a U-shaped section of tube, pushed out and in to produce the tones between the fundamental and its harmonics.

— **slid′er** (slīd′ẽr), *n.*

slide fastener. A fastener consisting of two rows of metal or plastic teeth on strips of tape for binding to the edges of an opening, as of a garment or a bag, and having a sliding piece which closes the opening by drawing the teeth into interlocking position.

slide knot. A form of slipknot. See KNOT, *Illust.* (11).

slide rule. An instrument consisting of a ruler with a medial slide, ruler and slide being graduated with similar logarithmic scales, labeled with the corresponding antilogarithms.

slide valve. *Engines.* Any valve which opens and closes a passageway by sliding over a port; specif., a particular valve often used in steam engines for alternately admitting steam to the piston and releasing it.

slide′way′ (slīd′wā′), *n.* A way along which something slides.

slid′ing scale (slīd′ĭng). **1.** A flexible scale of fees, prices, wages, etc., capable of being adjusted at need. **2. a** A scale for raising or lowering imposts in proportion to the fall or rise of prices. **b** *Econ.* A scale of workmen's wages under which the wages depend, more or less, upon the selling price of the product, the rate of pay rising and falling with the price.

sli′er (slī′ẽr), **sli′est,** *compar. & superl.* of SLY.

slight (slīt), *adj.* [ME. *slight, sleght,* orig., level, smooth, flat.] **1.** Slender; slim; frail; flimsy. **2.** Not strong in intellect or character; foolish; silly. **3.** Scanty; meager; as, the rewards were *slight.* **4.** Without weight, solidity, importance, etc.; insignificant; trivial; superficial; not severe or intense. — **Syn.** See THIN. — *v. t.* **1.** To treat as slight, or unimportant; to make light of. **2.** To treat with disdain or indifference; to ignore discourteously. **3.** To perform or attend to carelessly and inadequately; as, to *slight* one's work. — **Syn.** See NEGLECT. — *n.* Act of slighting; an instance of being slighted, or treated indifferently or superciliously; a humiliating discourtesy. — **slight′ly,** *adv.* — **slight′ness,** *n.*

slight′ing, *adj.* Offering a slight; as, a *slighting* remark. — **slight′ing·ly,** *adv.*

sli′ly (slī′lĭ). Var. of SLYLY.

slim (slĭm), *adj.;* SLIM′MER (-ẽr); SLIM′MEST. [Formerly, bad, slight, awry, fr. D. *slim.*] **1.** *Chiefly Dial.* **a** Mean; worthless. **b** Cunning; sly. **2.** Of small thickness in proportion to the height or length; slender. **3.** Slight in substance, structure, quality, amount, etc.; esp., scanty; spare; as, a *slim* chance. — **Syn.** See THIN. — *v. t. & i.;* SLIMMED (slĭmd); SLIM′MING. To make or become slender. — **slim′ly,** *adv.* — **slim′ness,** *n.*

slime (slīm), *n.* [AS. *slīm.*] **1.** Soft, moist earth or clay; viscous mud. **2.** Any viscous substance, esp. one that is dirty or offensive. **3.** The mucous secretion of the skin of slugs, land snails, catfishes, etc. — *v. t.;* SLIMED (slīmd); SLIM′ING (slīm′ĭng). **1.** To smear or cover with slime. **2.** To remove slime from, as from fish for canning.

slime mold *or* **fungus.** A myxomycetous organism. See MYXOMYCETOUS.

slim′sy (slĭm′zĭ; -sĭ), *adj.;* SLIM′SI·ER (-zĭ·ẽr; -sĭ·ẽr); SLIM′SI·EST. Also **slimp′sy** (slĭmp′sĭ). [Appar. fr. *slim,* after *flimsy.*] *Colloq., U. S.* Flimsy; frail.

slim′y (slīm′ĭ), *adj.;* SLIM′I·ER (-ĭ·ẽr); SLIM′I·EST. Of, resembling, or of the nature of slime; viscous; glutinous; also, covered with, or yielding, slime. — **slim′i·ly,** *adv.* — **slim′i·ness,** *n.*

sling (slĭng), *n.* [ME. See SLING, *v.*] **1.** An instrument, as a short strap with two strings fastened to its ends, for throwing stones by centrifugal force; also, *Colloq.,* a slingshot. **2.** A slinging of or as of a missile; a violent stroke. — *v. t.;* SLUNG (slŭng); SLING′ING. [AS. *slingan* to wind, twist.] **1.** To throw (stones, etc.) with a sling. **2.** To throw forcibly away from one; to fling. — **Syn.** See THROW. — **sling′er** (slĭng′ẽr), *n.*

sling, *n.* **1.** A strap, chain, rope, or the like, used to hold securely something to be hoisted, lowered, carried, or suspended; as, a strap attached to a firearm or pack, or a hanging bandage put around the neck to support the arm or hand. **2.** *Naut. Usually pl.* A chain or rope attached to and supporting a yard or hooked at the bow and stern of a boat for lowering and hoisting aboard. — *v. t.* **1.** To place in a sling or slings for hoisting or lowering; also, to move, hoist, or the like, by slings. **2.** To suspend by or as by a sling, as a rifle.

sling (slĭng), *n.* *Colloq., U. S.* A drink made of spirits, esp. gin, with water, sugar, and sometimes lemon, and served either hot or iced.

sling′er ring (slĭng′ẽr). A tubular ring fitted round the propeller hub of an airplane through which a spray of antifreeze solution is spread by centrifugal force over the propeller blades to prevent formation of ice.

sling′shot′ (slĭng′shŏt′), *n.* A forked stick with an elastic band attached for shooting small stones or the like; a catapult.

slink (slĭngk), *v. i.;* SLUNK (slŭngk); SLINK′ING. Archaic past SLANK. [AS. *slincan.*] To go or move stealthily or furtively, as in fear or shame. — *v. t.* To cast prematurely; as, a cow that *slinks* her calf. — **Syn.** See LURK. — *n.* The young of a beast (esp. a calf) brought forth prematurely. — *adj.* Produced prematurely. — **slink′ing·ly,** *adv.*

slip (slĭp), *v. i.;* SLIPPED (slĭpt); SLIP′PING. Archaic past SLIPT. [ME. *slippen,* fr. MD. or MLG. *slippen.*] **1.** To escape without being observed; to leave quietly, secretly, or without ceremony; as, they *slipped* out one by one. **2.** To pass one or from one unawares; to escape one's memory, notice, mouth, grasp, etc., esp. through one's negligence; as, to let an opportunity *slip.* **3.** To move as if sliding or gliding; as, the music *slipped* into a waltz. **4.** To slide on or down a slippery surface; as, to *slip* on a peel. **5.** To fall into error or fault; to err; as, even good men *slip.* **6.** To slide out of place, from off a support, out of one's hold, etc.; as, the tool *slipped* and cut me. **7.** *Colloq.* To fall off, or decline, slightly; to deteriorate; as, prices have *slipped.* — *v. t.* **1.** To allow to slip or let pass unnoticed or undone; to skip. **2.** To escape from one's (memory, tongue, etc.) by inadvertence, negligence, etc.; as, the data *slipped* my mind. **3.** To cause (something) to slip, esp. to slide easily, as into or out of its place; as, to *slip* a ring on one's finger; also, to effect the slipping off of, as a dog's collar. **4.** To let loose in pursuit of game, as a hound. **5.** To slink (young). **6.** To put, pass, insert, etc., quickly, quietly, or secretly, as a cartridge into a gun. **7.** *Colloq.* To put (*on*) or take (*off*) hurriedly.

— *n.* **1.** A form of sloping pier extending out into the water to serve as a landing place for vessels; in U. S., a ship's berth between two piers or

wharves. **2.** An evading or eluding. **3.** Act or an instance of slipping, or sliding down, out of place, etc.; hence, a sudden mishap. **4.** A blunder; esp., a trivial error. **5.** A transgression; a false step. **6.** A leash or string by which a dog is held. **7.** Any covering easily slipped on; specif.: **a** A one-piece garment worn under a thin dress. **b** A child's pinafore or frock. **c** A case for a pillow. **8.** A small whetstone having a cross section in general like that of a wedge, usually with one or both edges rounded. **9.** The difference between the operating or effective and the calculated or potential force, volume, speed, etc., as between the volume displaced and the volume of liquid delivered by a pump; leakage. **10.** *Cricket.* The position of a fielder, or the fielder himself, on the off side of the wicket, usually to the rear of the wicketkeeper. **11.** *Geol. & Mining.* Any movement dislocating the parts of a rock mass; also, the result of such a movement. **12.** *Naut.* The difference between a vessel's actual speed and the speed which she would have if the propelling instrument acted upon a solid. **13.** *Shipbuilding.* An inclined plane on which a vessel is built or repaired. — **Syn.** See ERROR.
— *adj.* That permits easy slipping on, off, along, through, etc.; as, a *slip* coat; a *slip* bolt; a *slip* noose.

slip (slĭp), *n.* [ME. *slyp* slime, curd, fr. AS. *slipa* viscous substance.] Potter's clay in a liquid state, used in the casting process and for decoration, or as a cement.

slip, *n.* [MD. or MLG. *slippe.* See SLIP to cut.] **1.** A cutting or cion, as for planting or grafting. **2.** A long narrow strip of material. **3.** A young and slender person; a stripling. **4.** A strip or piece of paper used for a memorandum, a record, note, etc.; as, deposit *slips.* **5.** *U. S.* A long seat or narrow pew. — *v. t.* [MD. or MLG. *slippen* to cut, slit.] **1.** To take cuttings from (a plant). **2.** To equip, mark, etc., with a slip or slips.

slip cover. **1.** A removable cover esp. for an overstuffed chair, couch, or the like. **2.** A paper or fabric cover readily slipped on or off a book; a jacket.

slipe (slīp), *v. t. Scot.* To strip. — *v. t. Scot.* To glide; slip.

slip′knot′ (slĭp′nŏt′), *n., or* **slip knot.** A knot which slips along the rope around which it is made. See KNOT, *Illust.* (13).

slip noose. A noose with a running knot, as on a lariat.

slip′-on′, *n.* A garment easily slipped on or off; specif., a garment, as a sweater, blouse, etc., that one gets into or out of by pulling over the head.

slip′o′ver (slĭp′ō′vẽr), *adj.* That slips over (a box, book, chair, etc.). — *n.* Something that slips over, as a frame, case, garment, etc.

slip′page (slĭp′ĭj), *n.* Act or amount of slipping; *Mach.,* loss in working, as in transmission of power; difference between theoretical and actual output.

slip′per (slĭp′ẽr), *adj.* [AS. *slipor.*] *Now Dial.* Slippery.

slip′per, *n.* **1.** A form of light shoe that may be slipped on with ease and worn in undress. **2.** One that slips.

slip′pered (-ẽrd), *adj.* Provided with or wearing slippers.

slip′per·y (slĭp′ẽr·ĭ), *adj.;* -I·ER (-ĭ·ẽr); -I·EST. [From 1st SLIPPER.] **1.** Allowing or causing anything to slip or move easily upon the surface. **2.** Liable or apt to slip away. **3.** *Now Rare.* Wanton. *Shak.* **4.** Unreliable; untrustworthy; tricky; shifty. — **slip′per·i·ness** *n.*

slippery elm. A North American elm (*Ulmus fulva*) with hard wood and fragrant, mucilaginous inner bark; also, the bark, used as a demulcent.

slip ring. *Elec.* In a dynamo or motor, one of two or more continuous conducting rings from which the brushes take, or to which they deliver, current. See MAGNETO, *Illust.* — **slip′-ring′,** *adj.*

slip′shod′ (slĭp′shŏd′), *adj.* **1.** Wearing shoes or slippers down at the heel. **2.** Exceedingly slovenly.

slip′slop′ (-slŏp′), *n.* [Redupl. of SLOP.] *Colloq.* **1.** Weak, poor, or flat liquor; slops. **2.** Twaddle; gabble.

slip′sole′ (slĭp′sōl′), *n.* A thin insole placed in a shoe for warmth or more accurate fit. See SHOE, *Illust.*

slip stream. The stream of air driven aft by the propeller of an aircraft, having a velocity relative to the engine greater than that of the surrounding body of still air.

slip′-up′, *n. Colloq.* A slight mistake; a slip (def. 4).

slit (slĭt), *v. t.;* SLIT; SLIT′TING. [AS. *slītan* to slit, tear.] **1.** To cut lengthwise; slash; cleave; also, to sever. **2.** To cut into long, narrow strips, as leather into straps. — *n.* A long incision; also, any long, very narrow opening. — **slit′ter,** *n.*

slith′er (slĭth′ẽr), *v. i.* [E. dial. *slidder,* fr. AS. *sliderian.*] **1.** To slide on, or as on, a loose, gravelly slope. **2.** To move, glide, or walk as if slipping or sliding, often in snakelike fashion. — *v. t.* To send sliding; to make slide; to slip.

slith′y (slĭth′ĭ), *adj.* See PORTMANTEAU WORD.

slit trench. *Mil.* A narrow trench, often V-shaped or cross-shaped, deeper than a foxhole, for protection against shellfire and aerial bombs.

sliv′er (slĭv′ẽr), *n.* [AS. *slīfan* to split.] **1.** A long slender piece cut or, esp., rent off; a sharp, slender fragment; a splinter. **2.** *Textile Mfg.* **a** A strand or slender roll of cotton or other fiber from a carding machine ready for roving or slubbing. **b** Wool, in a ribbonlike form, from the combing machine. — *v. t.* To cut or rend into slivers; to reduce to sliver or slivers; to slice or shred, as lettuce. — *v. i.* To split into, or become surfaced with, slivers.

slob (slŏb), *n.* [Ir. *slab.*] **1.** *Chiefly Ire.* Mud; ooze; a mud flat. **2.** *Newfoundland.* Soft or mushy ice or snow. **3.** *Contemptuous.* A clumsy or dull, slovenly person.

slob′ber (slŏb′ẽr), *v. i.* To let saliva fall or dribble from the mouth; to slaver; drool; also, to gush sentimentally. — *v. t.* To wet and smear with dribbling saliva. — (slŏb′ẽr), *n.* **1.** Dribbling saliva. **2.** Driveling speech, utterance, kissing, etc. — **slob′ber·er** (-ẽr), *n.*

sloe (slō), *n.* [AS. *slā.*] **a** Also **sloe plum.** The astringent fruit of the blackthorn *Prunus spinosa;* also, the tree itself. **b** Any of various American wild plums (as *P. americana, P. allegheniensis*).

sloe′-eyed′ (slō′īd′), *adj.* Having bluish or purplish-black eyes, like the color of sloes.

sloe gin. A spirit distilled from grain and rectified but flavored with fresh sloes instead of juniper berries.

slog (slŏg), *v. t.;* SLOGGED (slŏgd); SLOG′GING. [See SLUG a blow.] To strike with heavy and, sometimes, aimless blows, as in cricket or boxing. — *v. i.* To plod, as through mire; to plug doggedly. — *n.* A hard blow. — **slog′ger** (-ẽr), *n.*

slo′gan (slō′găn), *n.* [Gael. *sluagh-ghairm,* fr. *sluagh* army + *gairm* a call.] **1.** The war cry, or gathering word, of a Highland clan in Scotland. **2.** A word or phrase associated by usage with a particular party, group, etc.; a catchword. **3.** A brief, striking phrase adopted for use in advertising a product, industry, etc.

sloid, slojd (sloid). Vars. of SLOYD.

sloop (slōōp), *n.* [D. *sloep,* earlier *sloepe* (whence F. *chaloupe*).] A fore-and-aft-rigged vessel with one mast and a single headsail jib.

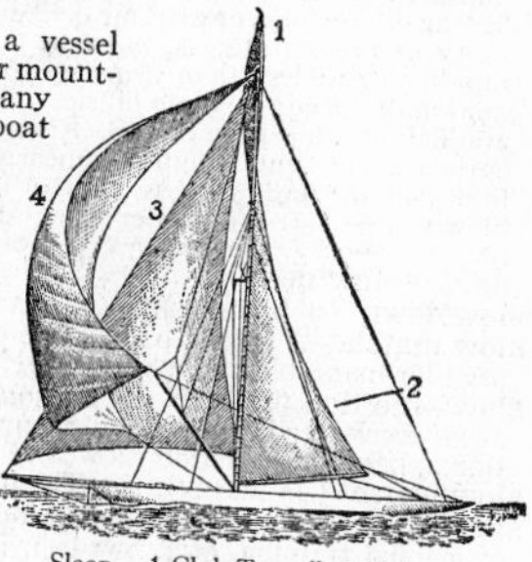

Sloop. 1 Club Topsail; 2 Mainsail; 3 Balloon Jib; 4 Spinnaker.

sloop of war. *Nav.* Orig., a vessel rigged as a ship, brig, or schooner mounting from 10 to 32 guns; later, any war vessel larger than a gunboat with guns on one deck only.

slop (slŏp), *n.* [MD. *slop;* akin to AS. *oferslop.*] **1.** Any outer or loose garment, as a smock. **2.** *pl. Hist.* Loose breeches. **3.** *pl.* Cheap ready-made clothes; *Naut.,* clothing and other articles sold to sailors; such clothes and also small stores; hence, **slop′shop′** (slŏp′shŏp′), *n.*

slop, *n.* [ME. *sloppe* a puddle, fr. AS. *sloppe* in *cūsloppe, cūslyppe,* the droppings of a cow.] **1.** Soft mud; slush. **2.** *Usually pl.* Thin, tasteless drink or liquid food. **3.** Water or other liquid spilled or thrown about; a spot soiled or wet with spilled liquid. **4.** *Often pl.* **a** Kitchen or similar waste with nutritive matter, fed to animals. **b** Dirty liquid refuse from toilet bowls or jars. **5.** *Often pl. Distilling.* Mash after removal of the alcohol. — *v. t. & i.;* SLOPPED (slŏpt); SLOP′PING. **1.** To spill or be spilled as a liquid, esp. by the motion of the vessel containing it. **2.** To slobber or spill liquid upon. **3.** *Colloq.* To gush; slobber; — with *over.*

slop basin, slop bowl. A basin or bowl for receiving the rinsings of tea or coffee cups at the table; also, a basin or bowl for slops, waste water from cleaning, etc.

slope (slōp), *v. i.* **1.** To take an oblique course. **2.** To have a slant, as in surface, position, direction, etc.; to incline. — *v. t.* To cause to incline or slant. — *n.* **1.** A natural or artificial incline, as a hillside or terrace. **2.** The degree of deviation from the horizontal or perpendicular. **3.** A sloping position, direction, line, surface, etc. **4.** The part of a continent draining to a particular ocean; as, the Pacific *slope.* — *adj. Poetic.* Sloping; slanting. — **slop′er** (slōp′ẽr), *n.*

slop′ing (slōp′ĭng), *adj.* Inclining or inclined; oblique. — **slop′ing·ly,** *adv.* — **slop′ing·ness,** *n.*

slop′py (slŏp′ĭ), *adj.;* SLOP′PI·ER (-ĭ·ẽr); SLOP′PI·EST. [From 2d SLOP.] **1.** Wet so as to spatter easily; slushy; wet as with something slopped over. **2.** *Colloq.* Slovenly; careless; messy. **3.** *Colloq.* Disagreeably effusive. — **slop′pi·ly,** *adv.* — **slop′pi·ness,** *n.*

slop′work′ (slŏp′wûrk′), *n.* **1.** Manufacture of cheap ready-made clothing. **2.** Hasty, slovenly work. — **slop′work′er,** *n.*

slosh (slŏsh), *v. i.* To wallow or flounder with splashing or dripping through water, mire, etc. — *v. t.* **1.** To move about vigorously in liquid. **2.** *Dial.* To hit. — *n.* Slush.

slot (slŏt), *n.* [OF. *esclot.*] **1.** An aperture, now esp. one long and narrow, as a seating for a key, or a narrow opening through which a coin can be pushed. **2.** *Aeronautics.* A nozzle-shaped opening through a wing, usually near the leading edge, to promote smooth flow and thus maintain lift and prevent or delay the stalling of the wing. — *v. t.;* SLOT′TED (-ĕd; -ĭd); SLOT′TING. To cut a slot in.

slot, *n.* [OF. *esclot,* fr. ON. *slōth* track.] The track of a deer; hence, any track or trail.

sloth (slŏth; slōth; 74), *n.* [From *slow.*] **1.** Disinclination to action or labor; laziness; indolence. **2.** Any of several slow-moving, arboreal, edentate mammals of the tropical forests of South and Central America, as the ***three-toed sloths*** (genus *Bradypus*), having three claws, and the ***two-toed sloths*** (genus *Choloepus*), two claws, on each front foot.

sloth bear. A bear (*Melursus labiatus*) of India and Ceylon with long snout and mobile tongue and lips.

sloth′ful (slŏth′fŏŏl; slŏth′-; -f'l), *adj.* Addicted to sloth; sluggish; indolent. — **Syn.** See LAZY. — **sloth′ful·ly,** *adv.* — **sloth′ful·ness,** *n.*

slot machine. A machine the operation of which is started by dropping a coin into a slot.

slouch (slouch), *n.* **1.** A lazy lubber; a person without energy or ambition. **2.** A gait or posture characterized by ungainly stooping of head and shoulders or undue relaxation of body muscles. **3.** Droop, as of a hat brim. — *v. i.* **1.** To move, walk, stand, sit, etc., with a slouch. **2.** To hang down flaccidly, as a hat brim. — *v. t.* To cause to droop.

slouch hat. A soft hat with a wide and flexible brim.

slouch′y (slouch′ĭ), *adj.;* SLOUCH′I·ER (-ĭ·ẽr); SLOUCH′I·EST. Slouching, esp. in gait or posture. — **slouch′i·ly,** *adv.* — **slouch′i·ness,** *n.*

slough (slou; *in sense* 2, slōō), *n.* [ME. *slogh, slough,* fr. AS. *slōh.*] **1.** A place of deep mud or mire. **2.** (*pron.* slōō) Also **slew, slue.** A swamp; also: **a** An inlet from a river. **b** *U. S.* A tide flat or bottom-land creek. **3.** A state of moral degradation or spiritual dejection.

slough (slŭf), *n.* [ME. *slughe, slouh.*] **1.** The skin, commonly the castoff skin, of a snake; cast (def. 11). **2.** *Med.* The dead mass separating from an ulcer or gangrenous tissues. — *v. i.* **1.** To be shed or cast off, as diseased tissue; also, to shed or cast off one's skin, an excrescence, a habit, etc.; — often with *away* or *off.* **2.** *Med.* To separate in the form of dead matter from the living tissues. — *v. t.* **1.** To cast off; to discard. **2.** At bridge, to get rid of (a card) to avoid losing a trick with it. — **Syn.** See DISCARD.

Slo′vak (slō′văk; slō·văk′), *n.* [Czechoslovak *slovák,* orig., a Slav.] **1.** One of a northern Slavic people of central Czechoslovakia. **2.** The language of the Slovaks, related to Czech. See INDO-EUROPEAN LANGUAGES, *Table.* — **Slo′vak,** *adj.* — **Slo·va′ki·an** (slō·vä′kĭ·ăn; -văk′ĭ·ăn), *adj. & n.*

slov′en (slŭv′ĕn), *n.* [MD. *slof* careless + ME. *-ein.*] One habitually negligent of neatness or cleanliness, esp. in dress or person.

Slo′vene (slō′vēn), *n.* [G. *Slowene.*] One of a southern Slavic group usually classed with the Serbs and Croats, now dwelling in Yugoslavia. — **Slo′vene,** *adj.*

Slo·ve′ni·an (slō·vē′nĭ·ăn; 58), *adj.* Slovene. — *n.* **a** A Slovene. **b** The language of the Slovenes, closely akin to Serbo-Croatian. See INDO-EUROPEAN LANGUAGES, *Table.*

slov'en·ly (slŭv'ĕn·lĭ), *adj.;* -LI·ER (-lĭ·ẽr); -LI·EST. **1.** Having the habits of a sloven; lazy and slipshod in any way. **2.** Characteristic of a sloven. — *adv.* In a slovenly manner. — **slov'en·li·ness**, *n.*

slow (slō), *adj.* [AS. *slāw.*] **1.** Mentally dull; stupid; also, inert; phlegmatic. **2.** Not ready or prompt in moving, working, etc.; manifesting dilatoriness or extreme deliberation; as, a *slow* worker. **3.** Not hasty or precipitate; as, *slow* to take offense. **4.** Moving without rapidity or at less than usual speed; also, characterized by retarded motion or speed; as, *slow* music. **5.** Not happening in a short time; gradual; as, *slow* growth. **6.** Registering behind or below that which is the correct time, weight, or measure. **7.** Such as to hinder or prohibit fast or rapid progress, play, or the like; as, a *slow* track. — *adv.* Slowly. — *v. t.* To render slow; also, to retard; delay. — **Syn.** See DELAY. — *v. i.* To go slower; — often with *up* or *down.* — **slow'ly**, *adv.* — **slow'ness**, *n.*

slow'down' (slō'doun'), *n.* *Colloq.* A slowing down.

slow match. A match, or fuse, made so as to burn slowly and evenly, used for firing blasting charges, etc.

slow'–mo'tion pic'ture. A motion picture recorded on film exposed at an accelerated rate, so that when projected at normal speed the action appears inordinately slow.

slow'worm' (slō'wûrm'), *n.* The blindworm.

sloyd (sloid), *n.* [Sw. *slöjd* skill, dexterity, skilled labor.] A system of manual training, orig. Swedish, using wood carving as a means of training in the use of tools.

slub (slŭb), *v. t.;* SLUBBED (slŭbd); SLUB'BING. To draw out and twist slightly, as slivers of wool. — *n.* A slubbed roll of wool, cotton, or silk; *pl.*, thick places in cotton rovings, slivers, and yarns.

slub'ber (slŭb'ẽr), *v. t.* *Now Dial.* **1.** To daub; stain. **2.** To do in a slovenly way; to botch; scamp.

sludge (slŭj), *n.* **1.** Mud; esp., a muddy deposit on tideland, a river bed, etc.; ooze. **2.** New sea ice; slob. **3.** A muddy or slushy mass, deposit, or the like; specif.: **a** The precipitated solid matter produced by water and sewage treatment processes. **b** Mud from a drill hole in boring. **c** Muddy sediment in a steam boiler.

slue (slo͞o; 114), *v. t. & i.;* SLUED (slo͞od); SLU'ING (slo͞o'ĭng). Also **slew.** To turn, twist, or swing about a fixed point, usually the axis, as a spar; *Colloq.*, to twist; veer. — *n.* Act or process of sluing a body; also, the position of a body when slued.

slue, *n.* A slough, or swamp. See 1st SLOUGH, 2.

slue. Var. of SLEW, a large number.

slug (slŭg), *n.* [ME. *slugge* sluggard, *sluggen* to be slothful.] **1.** Any of numerous terrestrial pulmonate gastropods (genus *Limax*) related to the ordinary land snails, but having the shell rudimentary and often buried in the mantle, or entirely lacking. **2.** Any smooth, soft larva of a sawfly or moth which creeps like a mollusk. **3.** A slow-moving animal.

slug, *n.* **1.** An unshaped or roughly shaped piece of metal such as one that can be inserted in the slot of various machines to operate them; specif. one used as a missile for a gun, as in old-time muskets; hence, a small bullet for air guns. **2.** The British engineering unit of mass, — equal in pounds to the number of feet per second per second of acceleration of a freely falling body at the location in question. **3.** A single drink, as of liquor. **4.** *Print.* **a** A strip of metal, usually six points (1/12 inch) thick, less than the height of type, used esp. to space between lines. **b** A strip the height of type, as one with a figure for temporary identifying use, or a line of type cast in one piece. — *v. i.* To become changed in shape, as bullets, by passing through the bore.

slug, *n.* [Also *slog*, of uncert. origin; cf. D. *slag* a blow, E. *slay.*] *Colloq.* A heavy blow, esp. with the fist. — *v. t.;* SLUGGED (slŭgd); SLUG'GING. To hit hard or heavily as with the fist, a bat, etc. — **slug'ger**, *n.*

slug'gard (slŭg'ẽrd), *n.* [*slug* + *-ard.*] A person habitually lazy; a drone. — *adj.* Sluggish; lazy.

slug'gish (slŭg'ĭsh), *adj.* **1.** Given to idling or procrastinating; slothful. **2.** Not easily aroused to activity; as, a *sluggish* liver. **3.** Markedly slow in movement, flow, etc. **4.** Of business, etc., dull; stagnant. — **slug'gish·ly**, *adv.* — **slug'gish·ness**, *n.*

sluice (slo͞os; 114), *n.* [OF. *escluse*, fr. LL. *exclusa* (also *clusa*), fr. L. *excludere, -clusum*, to shut out. See EXCLUDE.] **1. a** An artificial passage for water, fitted with a valve or gate, as in a millstream, for stopping or regulating the flow. **b** A body of water pent up behind a floodgate. **2.** A water gate or floodgate; a dock gate. **3.** A stream flowing through a floodgate; also, a channel serving to drain or carry off surplus water. **4.** A long, inclined trough, launder, or flume, for washing auriferous earth, floating down logs, etc.; specif., *Gold Mining*, such a contrivance paved with riffles, etc., to hold the quicksilver for catching the gold. — *v. t.;* SLUICED (slo͞ost); SLUIC'ING (slo͞os'ĭng). **1.** To draw off by or through a sluice. **2.** To wash with or in a stream of water running through or from a sluice. **3.** To transport in a sluice, as logs. — *v. i.* To pour, as from a sluice. — **sluice gate.** — **sluice'way'** (-wā'), *n.*

sluit (slo͞ot), *n.* [D. *sloot.*] *S. Africa.* A gully or gulch, made by heavy rains in sun-baked soil.

slum (slŭm), *n.* [Origin uncert.] **1.** A thickly populated street or alley marked by squalor or wretched living conditions. **2.** *Usually pl.* A city district comprising such streets. — *v. i.;* SLUMMED (slŭmd); SLUM'MING. To visit slums, as for study. — **slum'mer** (-ẽr), *n.*

slum'ber (slŭm'bẽr), *v. i.* [AS. *slūma* slumber.] **1.** To sleep; sometimes, to sleep lightly; to drowse. **2.** To be or remain in a state of negligence, sloth, unawareness, etc. — *n.* Sleep, esp. light sleep; doze. — **slum'ber·er** (-ẽr), *n.*

slum'ber·ous (-ŭs), *adj.* Also **slum'brous** (slŭm'brŭs). **1.** Slumbering; somnolent. **2.** Inviting slumber.

slum'ber·y (-ĭ), *adj.* Slumbering; slumberous.

slump (slŭmp), *v. i.* **1.** To fall or sink suddenly, as through thin ice or into a bog. **2.** To drop or slide down abruptly, as sails or debris; of persons, to collapse in a heap; also, to hold a drooping posture or gait. **3.** To decline or fall off abruptly, as stocks. — *n.* A marked decline or falling off, as in attention, interest, activity, prices, or in business.

slung (slŭng), **slunk** (slŭngk), *past & past part.* of SLING, SLINK.

slung shot. A small mass of metal or stone fixed on a flexible handle, strap, or the like, used as a weapon.

slur (slûr), *v. t.;* SLURRED (slûrd); SLUR'RING. **1.** *Dial.* To besmirch; sully. **2.** To cast aspersions upon; to calumniate; traduce. **3.** *Print.* To blur; mackle. — *n.* **1.** A stain or blot; hence, reproach; stigma. **2.** An aspersion; calumny. **3.** *Print.* A blurred spot; a mackle.

slur, *v. t.* **1.** To slide or slip over without due mention, consideration, or emphasis. **2.** *Music.* **a** To perform (two or more successive tones of different pitch) in a smooth or connected manner. **b** To mark (notes) with a slur. **3.** *Phonet.* To pass over in pronunciation so lightly as to obscure or quite suppress, as a sound or syllable. — *n.* **1.** *Music.* **a** A curved line [⌣ or ⌢] connecting notes that are to be sung to the same syllable, or performed without a break, as when made in one continued breath of a wind instrument, or with one stroke of a bow. **b** The combination of two or more slurred tones; a legato effect. **2.** *Phonet.* A slurred sound.

slur'ry (slûr'ĭ), *n.; pl.* -RIES (-ĭz). A thin, watery mixture, as liquid mud, cement, mortar, etc.

slush (slŭsh), *n.* **1.** Partly melted snow; watery snow. **2.** Soft mud or mire. **3.** A soft mixture of grease and other materials, used for protecting the surface of metal parts against corrosion; esp., a mixture of white lead and lime with which the bright parts of machines are painted to be preserved from oxidation. **4.** Gush; drivel. **5.** Refuse grease and fat from cooking, esp. on shipboard. **6.** Paper pulp in water suspension. — *v. t.* **1.** To wet, splash, or paint with slush. **2.** To fill in with mortar, cement, etc. — **slush'y** (-ĭ), *adj.*

slush fund. **1.** *Nav.* A fund derived from the sale of refuse and used for small luxuries. **2.** *Slang, U.S.* A fund for use in bribery, or for corruptive propaganda.

slut (slŭt), *n.* **1.** A slovenly woman; a slattern. **2.** A lewd woman; a harlot. **3.** A bitch. — **slut'tish** (-ĭsh), *adj.* — **slut'tish·ly**, *adv.* — **slut'tish·ness**, *n.*

sly (slī), *adj.;* SLI'ER (slī'ẽr) or SLY'ER; SLI'EST or SLY'EST. [ME. *sli, slegh, sleih*, fr. ON. *slægr.*] **1.** *Now Dial.* Wise in practical affairs; skillful; shrewd. **2.** Artfully or meanly cunning; crafty; wily; marked by duplicity. **3.** Secret or secretive; dissembling. **4.** Lightly mischievous; roguish; as, *sly* jests. — **sly'ly, sli'ly** (slī'lĭ), *adv.* — **sly'ness**, *n.* — ***on the sly.*** *Colloq.* Furtively.

Syn. **Sly, cunning, crafty, tricky, foxy, wily, artful** mean attaining one's ends by devious means. **Sly** implies lack of candor showing itself in underhandedness, furtiveness, or duplicity; **cunning,** the use of such intelligence as one has in overreaching or circumventing; **crafty,** clever cunning; **tricky,** unscrupulous cunning; **foxy,** shrewd craftiness or trickiness; **wily,** astuteness in tricking; **artful,** insinuating or ingratiating craftiness.

slype (slīp), *n.* [Origin uncert.] *Arch.* A narrow passageway, esp. one between the transept and chapter house or deanery in certain English cathedrals.

smack (smăk), *n.* [AS. *smæc* taste, savor.] **1.** Characteristic taste or flavor; also, a perceptible taste or tincture. **2.** A small quantity; a taste; a bit. — **Syn.** See TASTE. — *v. i.* **1.** To have a smack; as, tea that *smacks* of tannin. **2.** To have or show a trace or suggestion.

smack, *n.* [Cf. MD. *smack*, D. *smak.*] **1.** A quick, sharp noise made by rapidly compressing and opening the lips in gusto, kissing, etc. **2.** A loud kiss; a buss. **3.** A resounding slap or crack. — *v. t.* **1.** To close and open (lips) so as to produce a smack. **2.** To kiss or slap with a smack. — *v. i.* To make or give a smack or smacks. — *adv.* With the sudden violence of a smack; also, completely.

smack, *n.* [D. *smak*, MLG. *smacke.*] *Naut.* A sailing vessel, commonly a sloop or cutter, used chiefly in coasting and fishing; in the United States, often specif., a fore-and-aft rigged fishing boat with a well in which fish are kept alive.

smack'ing, *adj.* Brisk; spanking; as, a *smacking* breeze.

small (smôl), *adj.* [AS. *smæl.*] **1.** Relatively little in size; diminutive. **2.** Little in quantity, amount, value, duration, extent, etc.; consisting of members or units few in numbers, little in size, low in value; as, *small* change. **3.** Limited or slight in degree, intensity, scope, etc.; trifling. **4.** Minor in rank, ability, or degree; as, *small* poets; *small* offenders. **5.** Carrying on a small business; as, a *small* tradesman. **6.** Having only petty interests or narrow sympathies; petty; mean. **7.** Humiliated. **8.** Gentle; soft; — of the voice; also, diluted or weak; thin. **9.** Of little consequence; trivial. **10.** Humble; modest; as, a *small* beginning.

Syn. **Small, little, diminutive, petite, tiny, miniature, wee, minute** mean conspicuously below the average in size. **Small** and **little** are often used interchangeably, but *small* only is possible when size is determined by capacity, value, number, and the like, and *little* when there is the intent to hint at a thing's pettiness, insignificance, etc., or to suggest tenderness, pathos, or the like; **diminutive** implies extreme or abnormal smallness or littleness; **petite,** applied usually to girls or to women, smallness and trimness; **tiny,** extreme diminutiveness; **miniature,** representation on a very small or diminutive scale; **wee** is a more homely term than *diminutive;* **minute,** a more formal term than *tiny.* — **Ant.** Large.

— *adv.* In a small way; esp., faintly; timidly; as, to sing *small.*

— *n.* **1.** *pl.* **a** In any trade, small-sized articles such as notions, small breads, or rolls, etc. **b** Smallclothes. **2.** The small or slender part, as of the back. **3.** A small person. **4.** *pl. Eng.* = RESPONSIONS.

small arms. *Mil. & Nav.* Arms carried on the person and used in the hands; now, generally, only portable firearms. Cf. RIFLE, *Illust.*

small beer. **a** Weak, watery beer. **b** Something or someone of little importance. **c** Contemptuously; as, to think *small beer* of one.

small capital. See 1st CAPITAL, *n.*, 1; SMALL CAPITAL, p. 1158.

small change. Money consisting of small coins; hence, something as trifling, petty, or as quickly circulated as small change.

small'clothes' (smôl'klōthz'; *colloq.* -klōz'), *n. pl.* The close-fitting knee breeches worn in the 18th century.

small fry. **1.** The young of fishes (see 1st FRY). **2.** Little fellows of no consequence. **3.** Small children.

small hours. The early hours of the morning.

small'ish (smôl'ĭsh), *adj.* Below normal size.

small'–mind'ed (*see Pron.*, § 2), *adj.* Narrow; petty; ungenerous. — **small'–mind'ed·ness**, *n.*

small'ness (smôl'nĕs; -nĭs), *n.* Quality or state of being small.

small potatoes. Something or someone of trivial importance or worth; often, a meanly petty person or act.

small'pox' (smôl'pŏks'), *n.* [*small* + *pox, pocks.*] *Med.* A contagious, febrile disease characterized by a peculiar pustular eruption; variola.

small stores. *Nav.* Small articles like tobacco, soap, etc., issued monthly by the paymaster of a war vessel to members of the crew and charged to their accounts.

small stuff. *Naut.* Spun yarn, marline, and other small rope designated usually by the number of threads or yarns which it contains.

small'sword' (smôl'sōrd'), *n.* A light, tapering sword for thrusting, used chiefly in dueling and fencing.

small talk. Light or trifling conversation; chitchat.
smalt (smôlt), *n.* [F., fr. It. *smalto.*] A deep-blue pigment prepared by fusing together silica, potash, and oxide of cobalt, and grinding to powder the glass thus formed.
smalt'ite (smôl'tīt), **smalt'ine** (-tĭn; -tēn), *n.* *Mineral.* A tin-white or gray isometric mineral of metallic luster, essentially a compound of cobalt and arsenic, usually containing iron and nickel.
‖**smal'to** (zmäl'tō), *n.; pl.* SMALTI (-tē). [It.] Colored glass, or a piece of it, used in mosaic work.
smar'agd (smăr'ăgd), *n.* [OF. *smaragde,* fr. L. *smaragdus.* See EMERALD.] The emerald.
sma·rag'dine (smȧ·răg'dĭn), *adj.* Of or pertaining to emerald; of the color emerald. — *n.* Smaragd.
sma·rag'dite (-dīt), *n.* [From its emerald color.] *Mineral.* A green foliated amphibole.
smart (smärt), *v. i.* [AS. *smeortan.*] **1.** To cause, or be the cause or seat of, a sharp, poignant pain; also, to feel or have such a pain. **2.** To feel acutely remorseful. **3.** To endure sharp pain; esp., to pay a heavy or stinging penalty, as for an offense. — *adj.* **1.** Causing a smarting pain; stinging. **2.** That smarts; pricking; poignant; as, a *smart* sensation. **3.** Vigorously active; alert and dexterous. **4.** Brisk; spirited; lively; as, a *smart* pace. **5.** Quick in learning, contriving, scheming, etc.; shrewd; also, manifesting adroitness; sometimes, questionably sharp or shrewd. **6.** Keenly or alertly witty; pungent. **7.** Dashing in appearance; esp., stylishly dressed. **8.** Combining dash, style, and elegance; as, a *smart* hat. **9.** Of, characteristic of, or patronized by an exclusive and ultrafashionable social group called the **smart set**. — *n.* **1.** A smarting pain or pains; esp., a stinging local pain. **2.** Poignant grief or remorse. — **smart'ly**, *adv.* — **smart'ness**, *n.*
smart aleck. *Colloq., U. S.* A cheaply clever, bumptious person.
smart'en (smär't'n), *v. t.* To make smart or, esp., spruce.
smart money. **1.** *Brit.* Money allowed to soldiers or sailors for injuries received. **2.** A sum paid by an employer to an injured employee. **3.** = EXEMPLARY DAMAGES.
smart'weed' (smärt'wēd'), *n.* The water pepper *Persicaria hydropiper.*
smash (smăsh), *v. t.* [Prob. imitative, with influence of *mash.*] **1.** To break in pieces by violence; to shatter. **2.** To destroy utterly; to wreck; to cause to collapse. **3.** *Lawn Tennis, etc.* To hit (the ball) with a hard overhand stroke. — *v. i.* **1.** To go to pieces suddenly, by collision or pressure. **2.** To move or be propelled with great violence, as through a thicket. — *n.* **1.** A breaking or dashing to pieces, or the sound of breaking to pieces; also, *Colloq.,* a wreck due to collision. **2.** Utter collapse; ruin; specif., bankruptcy. **3.** A drink of spirits, with ice, water, sugar, and mint; also, a drink made with crushed or squeezed fruit. **4.** *Lawn Tennis, etc.* A hard overhand stroke. — **smash'er** (-ẽr), *n.*
smash'up' (-ŭp'), *n.* A disastrous collision; also, a collapse, as in health or finances.
smat'ter (smăt'ẽr), *v. t.* [ME. *smateren* to chatter, prate.] To speak so as to reveal a spotty or superficial knowledge; as, to *smatter* French; also, to dabble in; to study bits of. — *n.* A smattering. — **smat'ter·er** (-ẽr), *n.* — **smat'ter·ing·ly**, *adv.*
smat'ter·ing, *n.* Superficial, piecemeal knowledge.
smaze (smāz), *n.* [*smoke* + *haze.*] A combination of haze and smoke similar to smog in appearance but less damp in consistency.
smear (smēr), *n.* [AS. *smeoru, smeru,* fat, grease.] **1.** Originally, a fat, oily substance; ointment; now, a viscous or sticky substance. **2.** Hence, a spot made by or as by an unctuous or adhesive substance; a blotch; daub; smudge. **3.** A smearing; vilification. **4.** *Bacteriol., etc.* Material smeared on a surface, as of a microscopic slide or of a medium for cultivating bacteria. — *v. t.* **1.** To overspread with something unctuous, viscous, or adhesive; to daub; also, to spread all over or in patches. **2.** To besmirch, sully, defame; specif., to vilify by applying a debasing epithet (***smear word***) or by secretly and maliciously spreading gross charges or imputations. **3.** *Slang, U. S.* To rout, repulse, or frustrate completely; to smother.
smear'case' (smēr'kās'), *n.* *U. S.* Cottage cheese.
smed'dum (smĕd'ŭm), *n.* [AS. *smedema, smedma.*] *Scot.* **1.** The flour of ground malt; hence, powder. **2.** Spirit; vigor.
smeek (smēk), *n. & v.* [AS. *smēocan,* v.] *Scot.* Smoke.
smell (smĕl), *v. t.;* SMELLED (smĕld) or SMELT (smĕlt); SMELL'ING. [ME. *smellen, smillen, smullen.*] **1.** To perceive by the excitation of the olfactory nerves; to get the odor or scent of. **2.** To detect or become aware of, as if by the sense of smell; as, to *smell* a plot. **3.** To seek or find in the manner of a dog on the scent; as, to *smell* out a secret. — *v. i.* **1.** To exercise the sense of smell; — now, with *at,* or *Colloq., of.* **2.** To have an odor; to give forth an aroma. **3.** To have an offensive odor. — *n.* **1.** The process, function, or power of smelling; the special sense by which certain properties (called *odor*) of bodies are perceived through an end organ responsive to diffusing chemical substances; the olfactory sense. **2.** The property of a thing which affects the olfactory organs; an odor, fragrance, stench, etc. **3.** A quality that suggests an influence or connection; smack; as, a *smell* of anarchy. **4.** An act or instance of smelling; as, take a *smell.*
Syn. **Smell, scent, odor, aroma** mean that property which makes a thing perceptible to the olfactory sense. **Smell** implies merely the sensation and gives no hint of its quality or character; **scent**, a physical emanation or effluvium (often delicate) from that smelled; **odor** is preferable to *scent* when an abundance of effluvia is suggested, and is therefore used more often when a clearly perceptible smell is indicated; **aroma** suggests a penetrating, pungent (but usually pleasant) odor.
smell'ing salts. An aromatic preparation of carbonate of ammonium and some scent, used to relieve faintness or headache.
smell'y (smĕl'ĭ), *adj.;* SMELL'I·ER (-ĭ·ẽr); SMELL'I·EST. Having a smell; esp., ill-smelling.
smelt (smĕlt), *n.* See PLURAL, *Note,* 3. [AS.] Any of certain small food fishes (family Osmeridae, esp. genus *Osmerus*) which closely resemble the trout in general structure. They live along the coasts and ascend the rivers to spawn, or are landlocked in lakes.
smelt, *v. t.;* SMELT'ED (-ĕd; -ĭd); SMELT'ING. [MD. or MLG. *smelten.*] To melt or fuse, as ore, usually to separate the metal; hence, to reduce; to refine; to flux or scorify; as, to *smelt* tin. — *v. i.* To smelt a metal; to be smelted or fused.
smelt, *past & past part.* of SMELL.
smelt'er (smĕl'tẽr), *n.* **1.** A furnaceman who smelts ore. **2.** An owner of a smeltery. **3.** A smelting establishment, or **smelt'er·y** (-ĭ).
smew (smū), *n.* A merganser (*Mergus albellus*) of northern Europe and Asia, white-crested in the male.
smi'lax (smī'lăks), *n.* [L., bindweed, fr. Gr. *smilax.*] **1.** *Bot.* Any of a genus (*Smilax*) of plants, the greenbriers, typifying a family (Smilacaceae, the smilax family) of somewhat woody vines, having leaves with one to five prominent parallel veins, dioecious flowers, and globose berries. Several tropical species of smilax yield sarsaparilla. **2.** A delicate greenhouse twining plant (*Asparagus asparagoides*), with ovate, bright-green false leaves. — **smi'la·ca'ceous** (smī'lȧ·kā'shŭs), *adj.*
smile (smīl), *v. i.* [ME. *smilen.*] **1.** To have, produce, or exhibit a smile; to look with a smile. **2.** To look with amusement or ridicule. **3.** To be propitious; as, fortune *smiled* on him. — *v. t.* **1.** To express by a smile. **2.** To affect in a certain way with a smile or by smiling; as, to *smile* away her tears. — *n.* **1.** A change of facial expression involving a brightening of the eyes and an upward curving of the corners of the mouth, expressive of amusement, pleasure, affection, irony, derision, etc. **2.** *Poetic.* An appearance as bright as a smile; as, the *smiles* of fortune. — **smil'er** (smīl'ẽr), *n.* — **smil'ing·ly**, *adv.*
smirch (smûrch), *v. t.* [ME. *smorchen.*] **1.** To smear with that which stains, or makes dirty. **2.** To sully or blacken (one's honor, reputation, etc.); to tarnish. — *n.* A smutch; smear; blotch.
smirk (smûrk), *v. i.* [ME. *smirken,* fr. or akin to AS. *smercian, smearcian,* to smile.] To smile in an affected manner; to simper. — *n.* An affected smile; a simper.
smite (smīt), *v. t.;* SMOTE (smōt); SMIT'TEN (smĭt''n), SMIT (smĭt), or SMOTE; SMIT'ING (smīt'ĭng). [AS. *smītan* to smear.] **1.** To strike, esp. with the hand or something held in the hand. **2.** To destroy the life or vigor of, as by a stroke, a disease, etc. **3.** To punish as by a stroke; to chasten. **4.** To cause to strike; to hurl, drive, hammer, etc.; as, to *smite* one's hands together. **5.** To strike or impress forcibly; as, *smitten* with amazement. **6.** To bring distress to; trouble; as, his conscience *smote* him. — *v. i.* **1.** To deliver or deal a heavy blow or blows with or as with a weapon. **2.** To hit, pass, pierce, etc., with sudden force. — **Syn.** See STRIKE. — **smit'er** (smīt'ẽr), *n.*
smith (smĭth), *n.* [AS.] One who forges with the hammer; a worker in metals.
smith'er·eens' (smĭth'ẽr·ēnz'), **smith'ers** (smĭth'ẽrz), *n. pl.* [Ir. *smidirīn,* dim. of *smiodar* a piece, fragment.] Fragments; atoms; flinders.
smith'er·y (smĭth'ẽr·ĭ), *n.; pl.* -ERIES (-ĭz). **1.** The work, art, or trade of a smith. **2.** A smithy.
smith'son·ite (smĭth's'n·īt), *n.* [After J. L. M. *Smithson.*] *Mineral.* **a** Native zinc carbonate, $ZnCO_3$; — called also *calamine.* **b** = CALAMINE **a**.
smith'y (smĭth'ĭ *or, esp. Brit.,* smĭth'ĭ), *n.; pl.* SMITHIES (-ĭz). [Cf. AS. *smiththe,* ON. *smithja.*] The workshop of a smith, esp. a blacksmith; a smithery.
smit'ten (smĭt''n), *past part.* of SMITE; specif.: *adj.* **a** Grievously afflicted. **b** *Colloq.* Deeply enamored.
smock (smŏk), *n.* [AS. *smocc.*] **1.** A woman's chemise; shift. **2.** An overgarment like the smock frock in shape, used, esp. by women, to protect the clothes. — *v. t.* **1.** To clothe in a smock. **2.** To gather in lines joined at regular intervals, so as to produce a shirred effect. See SMOCKING.
smock frock. A coarse frock or long shirt, worn over the other dress, as by farm laborers, esp. in Europe.
smock'ing (smŏk'ĭng), *n.* Shirred work done in chain stitch, featherstitch, or the like.
smog (smŏg), *n.* [A blend of *smoke* and *fog.*] *U. S.* A fog made heavier and darker by the smoke of a city.
smok'a·bles (smōk'ȧ·b'lz), *n. pl.* Cigars, cigarettes, etc.
smoke (smōk), *n.* [AS. *smoca.*] **1.** The gaseous products of burning organic materials, as wood, coal, tobacco, rendered visible by the presence of small particles of carbon, which finally settle as soot. **2.** Act or fact of smoking; hence: **a** A mass or column of smoke (sense 1); also, a smudge. **b** A period given to smoking tobacco. **3.** Fume, vapor, dust, etc., resembling smoke. **4.** Something as unsubstantial, ephemeral, or beclouding as smoke; as, his plans ended in *smoke.* **5.** *Slang.* Something to smoke, as a cigar or cigarette. **6.** *Physical Chem.* A suspension, in a gas, of solid particles. — *v. i.* **1.** To emit or exhale smoke; to steam; reek. **2.** To emit smoke unduly or improperly, as a lamp. **3.** To move as smoke or so as to raise smoke, dust, etc.; to speed. **4.** To inhale and exhale the fumes of tobacco, or the like. — *v. t.* **1.** To subject to the action of smoke. Specif.: **a** To fumigate, as in disinfecting or exterminating vermin. **b** To stupefy, as bees, or to drive away, as mosquitoes, by a smoke. **c** To blacken or discolor with smoke, as a glass. **d** To cure (meat, fish, etc.) with smoke. **2.** To force one from concealment into the open; as, to *smoke* out an enemy. **3.** To inhale and puff out the smoke of, as tobacco; to use in smoking. **4.** To detect or suspect, as a plot or a trickster.
smoke'house' (smōk'hous'), *n.* A building where meat or fish is cured by subjecting it to a dense smoke.
smoke'jack' (-jăk'), *n.* *Hist.* A device for turning a spit by a wheel moved by ascending gases in a chimney.
smoke'less (-lĕs; -lĭs), *adj.* Making or having little or no smoke; as, **smokeless powder**, any of a class of powders (usually a nitrate of cellulose, alone or mixed) producing little or no smoke on explosion.
smok'er (smōk'ẽr), *n.* **1.** One who or that which smokes; specif., a person who smokes tobacco. **2.** *Colloq.* A smoking car or compartment. **3.** A gathering for smoking and social intercourse.
smoke screen. A curtain of heavy smoke, often produced by chemicals, used as a concealing screen, as for naval vessels.
smoke'stack' (smōk'stăk'), *n.* A pipe or tube serving as a chimney, as of a locomotive, factory, or steamship.
smoke tree. Either the European species (*Cotinus coggygria*) or the American species (*C. americanus*) of a shrub of the sumac family, bearing large panicles of minute flowers suggestive of smoke.
smok'y (smōk'ĭ), *adj.;* SMOK'I·ER (-ĭ·ẽr); SMOK'I·EST. **1.** Emitting smoke, esp. in large quantities. **2.** Like, or of the nature or color of, smoke. **3.** Filled with smoke; as, a *smoky* atmosphere. **4.** Tarnished with smoke. — **smok'i·ly** (-ĭ·lĭ), *adv.* — **smok'i·ness** (-ĭ·nĕs; -nĭs), *n.*
smoky quartz. Cairngorm.
smol'der, smoul'der (smōl'dẽr), *n.* Smoke; smother; smudge. — *v. i.* **1.** To burn and smoke without flame; to waste away by slow combustion. **2.** To exist in suppressed or smothered activity, as a feud. **3.** To manifest suppressed anger, jealousy, etc.; as, his eyes *smoldered* with hatred.
smolt (smōlt), *n.* A salmon about two years old, then silvery, as it first descends to the sea. Cf. GRILSE, PARR.

smooch (smōōch), *v. t. & n. U. S.* Smutch.
smooch, *v. i.* [Prob. imitative.] *Slang.* To kiss; embrace; make love.
smooth (smōōth), *adj.* [AS. *smōth.*] **1.** Having an even surface; devoid of surface roughness. **2.** Without hair, either naturally or as a result of shaving. **3.** Free from all that would obstruct or impede progress; as, a *smooth* trail. **4.** Even and uninterrupted in flow, flight, etc.; moving without breaks; not jerky, jarring, or jolting. **5.** Unruffled; serene; equable; as, a *smooth* disposition. **6.** Plausibly flattering; ingratiating. **7.** Agreeable to one's ear, palate, feelings, etc.; bland; mild; not pungent or acrid; as, a *smooth* wine. **8.** Evenly spread or arranged; as, *smooth* hair. **9.** Having its points, ridges, etc., leveled by wear or use; as, a *smooth* tire. **10.** *Mech. & Physics.* Causing no resistance to a body sliding along its surface; frictionless. — **Syn.** See LEVEL: EASY: SUAVE.
— *adv.* Smoothly (see FLAT, *adj.*, 13).
— *v. t.* **1.** To make smooth, level, or even on the surface. **2.** To free from that which is harsh, crude, or disagreeable; to refine, polish, etc., as one's verses. **3.** To free from obstruction, or difficulty; to make easy; as, to *smooth* one's way. **4.** To soothe, esp. with blandishments. **5.** To palliate; to gloze; to minimize, esp. in order to allay anger, ill will, etc.; — often with *over.* **6.** To level; — with *down* or *away.*
— *n.* **1.** The smooth part of anything. **2.** An act of smoothing.
— **smooth'er**, *n.* — **smooth'ly**, *adv.* — **smooth'ness**, *n.*
smooth'bore' (smōōth'bōr'; 70), *adj. Firearms.* Having a bore of smooth surface; — disting. from *rifled.*
smooth breathing. [Trans. of L. *spiritus lenis.*] In Greek grammar, a mark ['] indicating the absence of a preceding *h* sound from the initial vowel over which it is placed (*lēnai*, pronounced ē·ĕn'ī).
smooth'en (smōōth'ĕn), *v. t. & i.* To make or become smooth.
smor'gas·bord' (smôr'gȧs·bôrd'; *Swed.* smûr'gōs·bōōrd'), *n.* [Sw. *smörgåsbord*, lit., bread-and-butter table.] A Swedish type of luncheon or supper served buffet style and consisting of many hors d'oeuvres, hot and cold meats, smoked and pickled fish, sausages, cheeses, salads, relishes, desserts, often fifty different dishes.
smote (smōt), *past & past part.* of SMITE.
smoth'er (smŭth'ẽr), *n.* [ME. *smorther*, fr. AS. *smorian.*] **1.** Thick, stifling smoke held in suspension; a suffocating smudge. **2.** State of being stifled or suppressed. **3.** A dense suffocating fog, cloud of dust, mass of driving spray or snow, etc. **4.** A confused multitude of things; a welter. — *v. t.* **1.** To destroy the life of by suffocation. **2.** To cause to smolder or die down; to deaden, suppress, stifle, etc., by or as by covering up, as a fire, a yawn, one's griefs, a rebellion. **3.** *Cookery.* To cook in a covered dish, esp. with a thick covering of something. **4.** To cover up so as to conceal; to hush up. — *v. i.* **1.** To be suffocated or stifled. **2.** *Now Dial.* To smolder. **3.** To be suppressed or deprived of vent, as wrath. — **smoth'er·y** (-ĭ), *adj.*
smoul'der (smōl'dẽr). Var. of SMOLDER.
smudge (smŭj), *n.* [ME. *smogen* to smear.] **1.** Thick or suffocating smoke. **2.** A smoldering mass of combustibles placed to windward for driving off insects, protecting fruit from frost, etc. **3.** A stain or smutch; a smear. — *v. t.;* SMUDGED (smŭjd); SMUDG'ING (smŭj'ĭng). **1.** To smoke or to protect (as an orchard) by means of a smudge. **2.** To smutch; soil; begrime. — *v. i.* To make a smudge or become smudged. — **smudg'i·ly**, *adv.* — **smudg'i·ness**, *n.* — **smudg'y**, *adj.*
smug (smŭg), *adj.;* SMUG'GER (-ẽr); SMUG'GEST. [LG. *smuk.*] **1.** Trim or smart in dress; spruce. **2.** Scrupulously clean, neat, or correct; tidy. **3.** Highly self-satisfied; complacent. — **smug'ly**, *adv.* — **smug'ness**, *n.*
smug'gle (smŭg''l), *v. t. & i.;* -GLED (-'ld); -GLING (-lĭng). [LG. *smuggeln.*] **1.** To import or export secretly, contrary to the law, or without paying the duties imposed by law. **2.** To convey clandestinely. — **smug'gler** (-lẽr), *n.*
smut (smŭt), *n.* [LG. *smutt.*] **1.** Matter that smuts, or blackens, as soot or coal dust; also, a spot or soil made by such matter. **2.** Indecent or ribald language; obscenity. **3.** *Bot.* **a** Any of certain destructive diseases of plants, esp. cereals, producing black masses of spores (sori), which are covered in the ***kernel smuts***, open dusty masses in the ***naked smuts***, and found chiefly on the leaves in the ***flag smuts***. **b** The parasitic fungus (order Ustilaginales) causing such a disease. — *v. t.;* SMUT'TED; SMUT'TING. To stain or taint with smut. — *v. i.* **1.** To give off smut; to crock. **2.** To gather smut; to be affected by smut.
smutch (smŭch), *n.* A dark stain; a smudge. — *v. t.* To blacken, as with soot; to smudge. — **smutch'y** (-ĭ), *adj.*
smut'ty (smŭt'ĭ), *adj.;* -TI·ER (-ĭ·ẽr); -TI·EST. **1.** Soiled or tainted with smut; affected with smut fungus. **2.** Obscene; indecent. **3.** Like smut in color, etc.; sooty; dusky. — **smut'ti·ly**, *adv.* — **smut'ti·ness**, *n.*
smy'trie (smī'trĭ; smĭt'rĭ), *n. Scot.* A collection; litter.
snack (snăk), *n.* [Earlier, a snap, bite (as of a dog), fr. dial. *snack* to snap.] **1.** A share; — in ***to go snacks***, to share. **2.** A taste; a smack; a bit. **3.** A slight, hasty repast.
snaf'fle (snăf''l), *n.* [Cf. D. *snavel* a beak, snout, Fris. *snaffel* mouth.] Also **snaffle bit.** A plain slender jointed bridle bit without curb. — *v. t.;* -FLED (-'ld); -FLING (-lĭng). To restrain or check with a snaffle.
sna·fu' (snă·fōō'), *adj.* [*s*ituation *n*ormal: *a*ll *f*ouled *u*p.] *Navy & Army Slang.* Snarled or stalled in confusion; awry. — *n.* Confusion; a muddle. — *v. t.;* SNA·FUED' (-fōōd'); SNA·FU'ING. To snarl up.
snag (snăg), *n.* [Of Scand. origin.] **1.** A stump or base of a branch lopped off. **2.** A rough, sharp, or jagged projecting part; specif., a projecting tooth; also, a stump of a tooth. **3.** A tree or branch embedded in a river or lake bottom and not visible on the surface. **4.** A concealed or unexpected difficulty or obstacle. **5.** One of the secondary branches of an antler; a branch of a tine. — *v. t.;* SNAGGED (snăgd); SNAG'GING. **1.** To catch in or as in a snag so as to be pierced, rent, etc. **2.** *U. S.* To clear of snags. — **snag'ged** (snăg'ĕd; -ĭd), *adj.* — **snag'gy** (-ĭ), *adj.;* SNAG'GI·ER (-ĭ·ẽr); SNAG'GI·EST.
snag'gle·tooth' (snăg''l·tōōth'), *n.* An irregular, broken, or projecting tooth. — **snag'gle–toothed'** (-tōōtht'), *adj.*
snail (snāl), *n.* [AS. *snægel, snegel.*] **1.** Any of numerous gastropod mollusks; esp., one of terrestrial habits (chiefly family Helicidae) having a well-developed spiral shell into which the animal can withdraw for protection. Cf. GASTROPOD. **2.** A slow-moving person; a drone.
snail'–paced' (snāl'pāst'), *adj.* Moving very slowly.
snake (snāk), *n.* [AS. *snaca.*] **1.** Any of numerous limbless reptiles (group Ophidia, order Squamata) having a very elongate body, some of which have certain salivary glands modified into poison glands and certain upper teeth developed into grooved or tubular fangs. **2.** A worthless or treacherous fellow. — *v. t.* **1.** To wind (one's way) in the manner of a snake; to move sinuously. **2.** *Colloq., U. S.* To drag or draw forcibly or at full length, as a log; also, to skid (logs). — *v. i.* To crawl or move like a snake, sinuously.
snake'bird' (-bûrd'), *n.* [So named from its snakelike neck.] Any of several fish-eating birds (genus *Anhinga*, order Pelecaniformes), allied to the cormorants but having a very long slender neck and a sharp-pointed bill.
snake fence. *U. S.* A worm fence.
snake'head' (snāk'hĕd'), *n.* An American herb, the turtlehead *Chelone glabra.*
snake'mouth' (-mouth'), *n.* A bog orchid (*Pogonia ophioglossoides*) of eastern North America and Japan, with pink flowers.
snake'root' (-rōōt'; 85), *n.* Any of numerous plants, mostly reputed to cure snake bites; also, the roots of any of these; esp.: ***Virginia snakeroot*** (*Aristolochia serpentaria*); the bugbane (*Cimicifuga racemosa*); ***senega snakeroot*** (see SENEGA); ***white snakeroot*** (*Eupatorium urticaefolium*); ***button snakeroot*** (which see).
snake'weed' (-wēd'), *n.* **1.** Any of several weedy herbs associated with snakes because of a fancied structural similarity, use in snake-bite cures, or common habitat, esp. the snakeroot and plantain. **2.** Any of several American composites of the genus *Gutierrezia.*
snak'y (snāk'ĭ), *adj.;* SNAK'I·ER (-ĭ·ẽr); SNAK'I·EST. **1.** Of, formed of, or entwined with snakes or serpents; as, the *snaky* rod (see CADUCEUS). **2.** Snakelike; serpentine; sinuous; wriggly. **3.** Sly; treacherous; perfidious; venomous; spiteful. **4.** Abounding in snakes.
snap (snăp), *v. i.;* SNAPPED (snăpt); SNAP'PING. [MD. or MLG. *snappen.*] **1.** To dart forward to bite; to make a pounce or snatch; as, a fish *snaps* at the bait. **2.** To utter sharp, biting words; to bark out irritable retorts. **3.** To break short or in two, esp. with a sharp crackling sound; as, the mast *snapped* off; also, to give way to undue strain. **4.** To give forth a sharp, cracking noise or noises, as a fire; to emit a report or click, as a firearm. **5.** To close, fit something, etc., with a snap, or click, as a lock. **6.** To emit flashes of anger, wit, sarcasm, etc.; as, his eyes *snapped.* — *v. t.* **1.** To grasp or snatch suddenly with or as with the teeth; to bite off sharply. **2.** To gain by surprise seizure as a prize; to secure speedily or accept on the spot; — usually with *up.* **3.** To speak to curtly and irritably, esp. so as to hurt or confuse; — usually with *out;* as, to *snap* out his criticisms. **4.** To break sharply and suddenly; to break short or in two, as a knife blade. **5.** To cause (something) to crack, click, or make a report, as a whip; to close, open, or fit into with a snap, as a lock. **6.** To project with a snap; to fillip. **7.** *Amer. Football.* To put (the ball) in play by passing it back with a quick motion. **8.** *Photog.* To snapshot (a person or thing).
— *n.* **1.** A snapping; a biting, snatching, sudden breaking, etc. **2.** *Slang.* **a** An easy, remunerative position. **b** An easy task, course of study, etc.; a cinch. **3.** A bite; a bit; — now only in *not to care a snap.* **4.** A sharp report, caused by a snapping apart, off, etc.; as, to lock with a *snap.* **5.** A sudden interval or spell of (biting cold) weather. **6.** A hook, catch, or fastening which closes or locks with a click; as, the *snap* of a bracelet. **7.** *Colloq.* Snappiness; vigor; life; also, pungency; crispness, as of speech; also, a sharp retort. **8.** A thin brittle cookie or wafer; as, a ginger*snap.* **9.** A snapshot.
— *adj.* **1.** Secured, given, done, carried through, etc., suddenly or without due process or deliberation; as, a *snap* judgment. **2.** That snaps, or shuts, fastens, etc., with a click or by means of a device which snaps; as, a *snap* fastener or hook.
— *adv.* With a snap.
snap'back' (snăp'băk'), *n. Football.* **a** Act of snapping back the ball. **b** *Chiefly Can.* The center.
snap bean. = STRING BEAN.
snap'drag'on (snăp'drăg'ŭn), *n.* **1.** Any of several garden plants (genus *Antirrhinum*, esp. *A. majus*) of the figwort family, having showy white, crimson, or yellow bilabiate flowers fancifully likened to the face of a dragon. **2.** A game in which raisins are snatched from burning brandy, and eaten; also, that which is so eaten.
snap'per (snăp'ẽr), *n.* **1.** One who or that which snaps. **2. a** A snapping turtle (see TURTLE, 1). **b** A snapping beetle. See ELATER, 3 **a.** **3.** See PLURAL, *Note*, 3. **a** Any of numerous active carnivorous basslike marine fishes (family Lutianidae, esp. genus *Lutianus*) of warm seas, mostly edible. **b** Any of various other fishes, as the young of the bluefish.
snap'per–back' (-băk'), *n. Am. Football.* The center.
snap'ping bee'tle. = ELATER, 3 **a.**
snapping turtle. See TURTLE, 1.
snap'pish (snăp'ĭsh), *adj.* **1.** That snaps, or attempts to bite; also, given to angry, irritable speech; testy; irascible; as, a *snappish* old man. **2.** Tart; peevish; cross; petulant; as, a *snappish* reply. — **snap'pish·ly**, *adv.* — **snap'pish·ness**, *n.*
snap'py (snăp'ĭ), *adj.;* SNAP'PI·ER (-ĭ·ẽr); SNAP'PI·EST. **1.** Snappish. **2.** That snaps. **3.** *Colloq.* Full of snap, or life, briskness, pungency, smartness, etc.; as, *snappy* conversation. — **snap'pi·ly**, *adv.* — **snap'pi·ness**, *n.*
snap roll. *Aviation.* A maneuver in which an airplane is made by quick movement of the controls to complete a full revolution in the manner of a corkscrew, while maintaining its approximate horizontal direction. — **snap'–roll'**, *v. i.*
snap shot. A quick offhand shot, made without aiming.
snap'shot' (snăp'shŏt'), *n.* A photograph made automatically in a very short interval, such as 1/25 second, usually with a hand camera. — *v. t. & i.;* -SHOT'TED; -SHOT'TING. To photograph by a snapshot.
snare (snâr), *n.* [AS. *sneare*, fr. ON. *snara* snare, noose.] **1.** A contrivance, often consisting of a noose, for entangling birds or rabbits; a trap; gin. **2.** Anything by which one is entangled, involved in difficulties, impeded, or inveigled; a lure. **3.** One of the gut strings of a snare drum. **4.** *Surg.* A wire loop for removing tumors or the like by tightening and avulsion. — *v. t.* **1.** To catch with or as with a snare; to ensnare; entangle. **2.** To lure or entice; to capture by guile; to inveigle. — **Syn.** See CATCH. — **snar'er** (snâr'ẽr), *n.*
snare drum. The smaller common military double-headed drum, having (for greater resonance) a catgut string or strings stretched across its lower head. See DRUM, *Illust.*
snark (snärk), *n.* [A blend of *snake* and *shark.*] A nonsense creature invented by Lewis Carroll (Charles L. Dodgson), in his poem *The Hunting of the Snark* (1876).
snarl (snärl), *n.* [From SNARE.] A tangle, esp. of hairs or thread; a knot; also, a tangled situation; a complication. — *v. t.* **1.** To get into a tangle. **2.** To make excessively complicated. — *v. i.* To become tangled.

snarl (snärl), *v. i.* [From earlier *snar.*] **1.** To growl with a snapping or gnashing of the teeth, as an angry dog. **2.** To give vent to anger in surly language. — *v. t.* To utter or express with a snarl or by snarling. — *n.* A snarling; a surly, angry growl. — **snarl'er,** *n.* — **snarl'ing·ly,** *adv.*
snash (snăsh), *n. & v. Chiefly Scot.* Abuse.
snatch (snăch), *v. i.* [ME. *snacchen, snecchen.*] To attempt to seize something suddenly; as, to *snatch* at a rope. — *v. t.* **1.** To grasp abruptly or hastily; to seize before it passes; to seize or grab suddenly without permission, ceremony, or right. **2.** To remove with suddenness. **3.** *Slang, U. S.* To kidnap. — **Syn.** See TAKE. — *n.* **1.** A snatching at or of something. **2.** A snatched opportunity or period of time; as, to sleep in *snatches.* **3.** Something as brief, fragmentary, or hurried as if snatched or done in snatched time, as a short spell, or stint, an excerpt from a song, disconnected portion of talk or story, etc. **4.** *Slang, U. S.* Kidnaping, or a kidnaping. — **snatch'er,** *n.*
snatch block. A block which can be opened on one side to receive the bight of a rope.
snath (snăth), *n.* Also **snathe** (snāth). [AS. *snǣd.*] The handle of a scythe.
sneak (snēk), *v. i.* [Akin to ME. *sniken,* AS. *snīcan* to creep.] **1.** To move furtively or slinkingly; to creep or steal so as to be unobserved. **2.** To act the coward; to cringe. — *v. t.* To move, bring, or make off with, in a furtive manner. — **Syn.** See LURK. — *n.* **1.** A mean, sneaking person. **2.** A sneaking; a furtive move; an unobserved escape. **3.** *Slang. pl.* = SNEAKER, 2.
sneak'er (snēk'ẽr), *n.* **1.** One who or that which sneaks. **2.** *U. S. usually pl.* Soft, light shoes, usually of canvas with rubber soles, esp. for athletic wear.
sneak'ing, *adj.* **1.** Cowardly; furtive. **2.** Not openly avowed, as if something to be ashamed of; also, of an opinion, that is merely a suspicion. — **sneak'ing·ly,** *adv.*
sneak thief. A thief who steals whatever he can reach without using violence or breaking into buildings.
sneak'y (snēk'ĭ), *adj.;* SNEAK'I·ER (-ĭ·ẽr); SNEAK'I·EST. Like, or characteristic of, a sneak. — **sneak'i·ly,** *adv.* — **sneak'i·ness,** *n.*
sneck (snĕk), *v. & n. Scot. & Dial.* Latch.
sned (snĕd), *v. t.* [AS. *snǣdan.*] *Scot. & Ir.* To lop; prune.
sneer (snẽr), *v. i.* [ME. *sneren.*] To smile or laugh with facial expressions of scorn or contempt; hence, to speak or write in a scornfully jeering or derisive manner. — *v. t.* **1.** To utter with a sneer or sneeringly. **2.** To affect by sneering. — **Syn.** See SCOFF. — *n.* Act of sneering; a sneering expression. — **sneer'er** (-ẽr), *n.*
sneer'ing, *adj.* Marked by a sneer; derisive. — **sneer'ing·ly,** *adv.*
sneesh (snēsh), *n.* [From *sneezing powder.*] *Scot., Ir., & Dial.* Snuff.
sneeze (snēz), *v. i.* [ME. *snesen,* altered form of ME. *fnesen,* fr. AS. *fnēosan.*] To make a sudden, violent, spasmodic, and audible expiration of breath. — *n.* Act or fact of sneezing. — **sneez'er** (snēz'ẽr), *n.*
sneeze'weed' (-wēd'), *n.* A North American yellow-flowered perennial herb (*Helenium autumnale*) the odor of which is said to cause sneezing.
sneeze'wort' (snēz'wûrt'), *n.* A strong-scented Eurasian perennial herb (*Achillea ptarmica*) of the aster family.
snell (snĕl), *adj.* [AS.] **1.** *Dial.* Quick; swift; acute. **2.** Keen; piercing. **3.** Harsh; severe.
snell, *n.* A short line of horsehair, gut, etc., by which a fishhook is attached to a longer line.
snick (snĭk), *v. t.* [Prob. fr. SNICK AND SNEE.] **1.** To cut slightly; to nick. **2.** *Cricket.* To hit (a ball) a light glancing blow. — *n.* **1.** A small cut or snip; a nick. **2.** *Cricket.* A light glancing blow given to a bowled ball.
snick and snee. [D. *steken* to stab + D. *snijen, snijden,* to cut; with assimilation of *st* to *sn.*] To thrust and cut; hence, also **snick'-a-snee',** a combat with knives.
snick'er (snĭk'ẽr), *v. i.* [Imitative.] **1.** To laugh in a partly suppressed manner, with audible catches of voice; to giggle. **2.** To whinny; to nicker. — *v. t. Colloq.* To utter with a snicker. — *n.* A smothered giggle.
snick'er·snee' (-snē'), *n.* [Corrupt. of SNICK AND SNEE.] A knife, as a bowie knife.
snide (snīd), *adj.* Betraying subtly implied derision; slyly sarcastic. — *n.* A snide person or thing.
sniff (snĭf), *v. i.* [Imitative.] **1.** To draw air audibly up the nose. **2.** To snuff, as in suspicion, offense, or contempt. — *v. t.* **1.** To inhale audibly through the nose. **2.** To recognize, perceive, or detect, by or as by sniffing; to scent, as danger. — *n.* An act or the sound of sniffing; that which is sniffed.
snif'fle (snĭf''l), *v. i.;* -FLED (-'ld); -FLING (-lĭng). **1.** To snuffle, as a person with catarrh. **2.** To snivel; whimper. — *n.* A snuffle.
sniff'y (snĭf'ĭ), *adj.;* SNIFF'I·ER (-ĭ·ẽr); SNIFF'I·EST. *Colloq.* Disdainful; supercilious.
snig'ger (snĭg'ẽr), *v. i. & n.* Snicker. — **snig'ger·er** (-ẽr), *n.*
snig'gle (snĭg''l), *v. i.;* -GLED (-'ld) -GLING (-lĭng). [From E. dial. *snig* an eel.] To fish for eels by thrusting the baited hook into their dens. — *v. t.* To catch by sniggling.
snip (snĭp), *v. t.;* SNIPPED (snĭpt); SNIP'PING. [D. *snippen.*] **1.** To cut at one stroke or in a series of short quick strokes with shears or scissors; to clip suddenly or by bits. **2.** To remove by cutting. — *n.* **1.** A small piece that is snipped off; a shred; hence, a fragment or bit. **2.** *Usually pl.* Small hand shears for cutting sheet metal. **3.** A single stroke of shears, or the like; a clip.
snipe (snīp), *n.;* see PLURAL, *Note,* 6. [ME. *snype,* of Scand. origin.] **1.** Any of certain limicoline birds (genus *Capella*) related to the woodcocks and frequenting bogs and marshes, and highly valued as game. The ***common, or whole, snipe*** (*C. gallinago*) of Europe and the ***American, or Wilson's, snipe*** (*C. delicata*) are larger than the Old World ***jacksnipe, or half snipe*** (genus *Limnocryptes*). **2.** A sniping shot. See SNIPE, *v. i.,* 2. **3.** *Slang, U. S.* A butt of a smoked cigar or cigarette. — *v. i.* **1.** To shoot or hunt snipe. **2.** To shoot at detached men of an enemy's forces at long range, esp. when not in action. — **snip'er** (snīp'ẽr), *n.*
snip'pet (snĭp'ĕt; -ĭt), *n.* [Dim. of SNIP, *v.*] A small part, piece, or thing. — **snip'pet·y** (-ĕ·tĭ; -ĭ·tĭ), *adj.*
snip'py (snĭp'ĭ), *adj.;* SNIP'PI·ER (-ĭ·ẽr); SNIP'PI·EST. **1.** Fragmentary; unduly brief or curt. **2.** *Colloq.* **a** Snappish. **b** Putting on airs; supercilious. — **snip'pi·ness,** *n.*
snitch (snĭch), *v. t. Slang.* To snatch; pilfer. — *v. i. Slang.* To inform; betray. — *n. Slang.* One who snitches, or informs. — **snitch'er** (-ẽr), *n.*
sniv'el (snĭv''l), *v. i.;* -ELED (-'ld) or -ELLED; -EL·ING or -EL·LING. [ME. *snivelen, snevelen.*] **1.** To run at the nose. **2.** To snuff mucus up the nose audibly; to snuffle. **3.** To cry or whine with snuffling, as children. **4.** To affect emotion in a whining manner. — *n.* **1.** Mucus in or from the nose. **2.** A sniveling or snuffling or sniffling. **3.** Affected emotion; also, affected pathos. — **sniv'el·er,** *n.*
snob (snŏb), *n.* [Origin uncert.] **1.** One who blatantly imitates, fawningly admires, or vulgarly seeks association with those whom he regards as his superiors. **2.** One who by his conduct makes evident that he sets excessive store by rank, wealth, and social eminence, to the detriment of merit. **3.** One who repels the advances of those whom he regards as his inferiors; as, an intellectual *snob.*
snob'ber·y (snŏb'ẽr·ĭ), *n.* Snobbish conduct; snobbishness.
snob'bish (snŏb'ĭsh), *adj.* Of, characteristic of, or befitting a snob. **snob'bish·ly,** *adv.* — **snob'bish·ness,** *n.*
snod (snŏd), *adj. Chiefly Scot.* Trimmed; smooth.
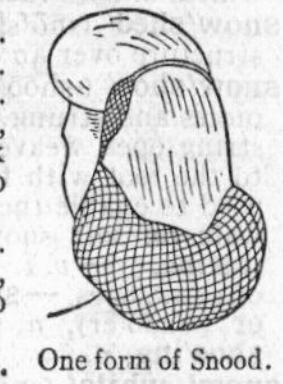
One form of Snood.
snood (snōōd), *n.* [AS. *snōd.*] **1.** *Chiefly Scot.* A band or ribbon for encircling a woman's hair. **2.** A coarse hair net or fabric bag worn by women, sometimes attached to a hat, for holding the back hair loosely folded against the nape. — *v. t.* To secure with a snood.
snook (snōōk), **snowk** (snouk; snōk; snōōk), *v. i.* [E. dial. *snook* to search out, to follow by the scent, fr. ME. *snoken* to sniff, smell.] *Scot. & Dial.* To sniff; to pry about.
snool (snōōl), *v. t. Scot.* To cow; snub. — *v. i. Scot.* To cringe.
snoop (snōōp), *v. i.* [D. *snoepen.*] *U. S.* To look or pry about in a sneaking or meddlesome manner, as for law violations. — *n.* One who snoops. — **snoop'er** (-ẽr), *n.*
snoop'y (-ĭ), *adj.;* SNOOP'I·ER (-ĭ·ẽr); SNOOP'I·EST. *Colloq., U. S.* Given to snooping.
snoot (snōōt), *n. Colloq.* **1.** Var. of SNOUT; hence, vulgarly, the nose. **2.** The face; a grimace, esp. one expressing contempt.
snoot'y (-ĭ), *adj.;* SNOOT'I·ER (-ĭ·ẽr); SNOOT'I·EST. *Colloq., U. S.* Haughtily contemptuous.
snooze (snōōz), *n.* [Origin uncert.] *Colloq.* A short sleep; a nap. — *v. i. Colloq.* To doze; to drowse.
snore (snōr; 70), *v. i.* [ME. *snoren.*] To breathe during sleep with a rough noise due to vibration of the soft palate. — *v. t.* To spend in snoring. — *n.* Act or noise of snoring. — **snor'er** (snōr'ẽr), *n.*
snor'kel (snôr'kĕl), **schnor'kel** (shnôr'-), *n.* Also **schnor'chel** (shnôr'kĕl); in British use, **snort** (snôrt). [From G. *schnorchel.*] A twin air-intake and exhaust tube for submarines, protrusible above the surface to allow operation by diesels at cruising speed while submerged to periscope depth.
snort (snôrt), *v. i.* [ME. *snorten;* akin to E. SNORE.] **1.** To force the air with violence through the nose, so as to make a noise, as do high-spirited horses. **2.** To laugh loudly, usually with a contemptuous or angry snort. — *v. t.* **1.** To utter with, or express by, a snort. **2.** To expel or emit with or as with a snort. — *n.* **1.** Act of snorting, or the sound produced; a noisy expulsion of air through the nose. **2.** A single drink of liquor, usually straight, taken in one draft.
snort'er (snôr'tẽr), *n.* **1.** One that snorts. **2.** Anything strikingly noisy, violent, intense, extraordinary, etc.; — often in the intensive form *ripsnorter.* **3.** = SNORT, *n.,* 2.
snout (snout), *n.* [ME. *snoute, snute.*] **1.** The long, projecting nose of a beast, as of swine; also, the anterior prolongation of the head of various animals, as of a weevil; a rostrum. **2.** *Colloq.* The nose. **3.** Something resembling a nose, as the nozzle of a pipe, hose, kettle, etc.
snout beetle. Any of a group (Rhynchophora) of beetles consisting of the curculios, or true weevils; — so called because the head is usually produced into a snout or beak.
snow (snō), *n.* [AS. *snāw.*] **1.** Small tabular and columnar crystals of frozen water formed directly from the water vapor of the air when its temperature at the time of condensation is lower than 0°C. (32°F.). **2.** The descent or a shower of such crystals; also, a mass, usually more or less consolidated, of such crystals after falling. **3.** *Poetic.* **a** White hair. **b** A mass of white petals, spray, etc. **4.** *Slang.* Cocaine. **5.** *Chem.* Any of various congealed substances of snowlike appearance; as, ***carbon-dioxide snow,*** solidified carbon dioxide, which vaporizes without melting and is used as a refrigerant. **6.** Small, transient, light or dark spots on a television screen resulting from the same causes as those that produce static in radio.
☞ COMBINATIONS are:

snowbank	snow-clad	snowscape
snowbound	snow-crested	snowslide
snow-capped	snowdrift	snowstorm

— *v. i.* To fall in or as snow; as, it had been *snowing.*
— *v. t.* **1.** To scatter or shower down like snow. **2.** To cover, shut in, or imprison, with or as with snow; as, the train was *snowed* under.
snow apple. = FAMEUSE.
snow'ball' (snō'bôl'), *n.* **1.** A round mass of snow pressed or rolled together. **2.** Any of certain cultivated white-flowered viburnums, as the guelder-rose (which see). — *v. i.* **1.** To form a snowball, esp. by rolling; hence, to accumulate in the manner of a rolled snowball. **2.** To throw snowballs. — *v. t.* To pelt with snowballs.
snow'ber'ry (-bĕr'ĭ; -bẽr·ĭ), *n.* A North American shrub (*Symphoricarpos racemosus*) of the honeysuckle family, with white berries; also, any of several related species.
snow'bird' (-bûrd'), *n.* **a** The snow bunting. **b** See JUNCO.
snow'bird', *n.* [See SNOW, 4; BIRD, 5.] *Slang.* A cocaine addict.
snow'-blind' (-blīnd'), *adj.* Affected with **snow blindness,** temporary blindness caused by the glare of the sun upon snow.
snow'-broth', *n.* Snow just melted; hence, very cold liquor.
snow bunting. A finch (*Plectrophenax nivalis*) of northern regions, allied to the longspurs.
snow'bush' (snō'bŏŏsh'), *n.* Any of several white-flowered shrubs, esp. one (*Ceanothus velutinus*) of California.
snow'drop' (-drŏp'), *n.* **1. a** A bulbous European herb (*Galanthus nivalis*) of the amaryllis family, bearing nodding white flowers that often appear while the snow is on the ground. **b** A flower or bulb of this plant. **2.** The common anemone (*Anemone quinquefolia*).
snow'fall' (-fôl'), *n.* A fall of snow; specif., the snow that falls in a single storm or in a given period.

snow'flake' (snō'flāk'), *n.* **1.** A flake or crystal of snow. **2.** The snow bunting. **3.** Any of a genus (*Leucojum*) of bulbous plants of the amaryllis family, esp. one (*L. vernum*) resembling the snowdrop.

snow'i·ly (snō'ĭ·lĭ), *adv.* In a snowy manner.

snow'i·ness (-ĭ·nĕs; -nĭs), *n.* State or quality of being snowy.

snow lily. A handsome Rocky Mountain dogtooth violet (*Erythronium grandiflorum*) with showy white flowers.

snow line *or* **limit.** The lowest limit of perpetual snow.

snow plant. A fleshy, bright-red saprophytic herb (*Sarcodes sanguinea*) growing in coniferous woods at high altitudes on the sierras of California, often appearing in early spring while snow is on the ground.

snow'plow' (snō'plou'), *n.* **1.** A plow, or any device functioning in the manner of a plow, used for clearing away snow. **2.** *Skiing.* The double stem used for slowing down or stopping. — **snow'plow'**, *v. i.*

snow pudding. A cold light pudding, made usually by folding whipped whites of eggs into a lemon jelly.

snow'shed' (snō'shĕd'), *n.* A shelter to protect from snow, as a long structure over an exposed part of a railroad.

snow'shoe' (-shōō'), *n.* A light oval frame of wood having two crosspieces and strung with a six-string open weave, attached to the foot with thongs and used to enable the wearer to walk on soft snow without sinking. — *v. i.* To travel on snowshoes. — **snow'sho'er** (-shōō'ĕr), *n.* — **snow'shoe'ing**, *n.*

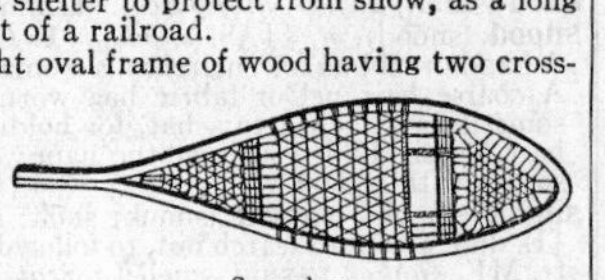

Snowshoe.

snow'-white' (snō'hwīt'; 2), *adj.* White as snow.

snow'y (snō'ĭ), *adj.;* SNOW'I·ER (-ĭ·ĕr); SNOW'I·EST. **1.** Marked by, abounding in, or covered with snow. **2.** White, like snow; as, *snowy* hair. **3.** Pure; spotless.

snub (snŭb), *v. t.;* SNUBBED (snŭbd); SNUB'BING. [ON. *snubba* to snub, chide.] **1.** To check or stop with a cutting retort. **2.** To check suddenly while running out (a rope, chain, etc.); hence, to check the motion of, as a boat, a log, or a baited fish, by snubbing a rope, chain, or line. **3.** To treat with contempt or neglect; to slight designedly; also, to affect in a specified way by such treatment; as, *snubbed* into silence. — *n.* **1.** A rebuke or slight; now, usually, an intentional discourtesy; a rebuff. **2.** Act or result of snubbing (a vessel). — *adj.* Slightly turned up and enlarged or flattened at the end; — of the nose.

snub'ber (snŭb'ĕr), *n.* **1.** One that snubs; esp., a device for snubbing. **2.** *Automobiles.* A shock absorber.

snub'-nosed' (-nōzd'; 2), *adj.* Having a snub nose.

snuff (snŭf), *n.* **1.** The charred part of a candlewick. **2.** A disagreeable or worthless remainder. — *v. t.* **1.** To crop the snuff of (a candle) by pinching, the use of snuffers, etc. **2.** To extinguish by or as by the use of snuffers.

snuff, *v. t.* [MD. *snuffen.*] **1.** To draw in, or to inhale, forcibly through the nose; to sniff. **2.** To detect by smelling; to scent; smell. **3.** To sniff in order to examine; — said of dogs, horses, etc. — *v. i.* **1.** To inhale through the nose noisily; to sniff or smell inquiringly, as a horse, dog, etc. **2.** *Obs.* To sniff loudly in or as in disgust. **3.** To inhale snuff; to take snuff. — *n.* **1.** Act of snuffing; sniff. **2.** A preparation of pulverized tobacco to be snuffed up the nostrils; also, the amount taken at once; a pinch.

snuff'box' (snŭf'bŏks'), *n.* A small box for holding snuff.

snuff'er (snŭf'ĕr), *n.* **1.** A device for cropping and holding the snuff of a candle. **2.** One who snuffs a light.

snuff'er, *n.* One who snuffs, or sniffs.

snuf'fle (snŭf''l), *v. i.;* SNUF'FLED (-'ld); SNUF'FLING (-lĭng). [Freq. of *snuff.*] **1.** To snuff, or sniff, audibly and repeatedly, as a dog in smelling. **2.** To breathe through the nose when it is obstructed, making a sniffing sound. **3.** To speak through or as through the nose; — often used of hypocritical persons. — *n.* **1.** Act or fact of snuffling; the sound made in snuffling. **2.** A nasal twang; also, canting, sanctimonious speech. **3.** *pl. Med.* A condition of obstructed respiration caused by a catarrhal nasal discharge. — **snuf'fler** (-lĕr), *n.*

snuff'y (snŭf'ĭ), *adj.;* SNUFF'I·ER (-ĭ·ĕr); SNUFF'I·EST. **1.** Like snuff, as in color, nature, etc. **2.** Addicted to the use of snuff. **3.** Disagreeable; horrid. **4.** Soiled with snuff. — **snuff'i·ness**, *n.*

snug (snŭg), *adj.;* SNUG'GER (-ĕr); SNUG'GEST. [Prob. of LG. origin.] **1.** Of a ship or its parts, manifesting seaworthiness in design, arrangements, etc. **2.** Serenely comfortable; peacefully secure; as, longing to be *snug* at home. **3.** Compact; neat; trim; often, small but comfortable; tidy; modest; sometimes, sizable; as, a *snug* income. **4.** Secreted; close; concealed. **5.** Tight; not loose; as, a *snug* fit. — **Syn.** See COMFORTABLE. — *v. i.;* SNUGGED (snŭgd); SNUG'GING. *Dial.* To lie close; to snuggle. — *v. t.* **1.** To make snug, or comfortable, trim, etc. **2.** *Naut.* To make ready for a gale by reducing sail, lowering topmast, lashing movables, etc. — *adv.* Snugly; neatly. — **snug'ly**, *adv.* — **snug'ness**, *n.*

snug'ger·y (snŭg'ĕr·ĭ), *n.; pl.* -IES (-ĭz). A snug, cozy place, esp. a small room or den.

snug'gle (snŭg''l), *v. i.;* -GLED (-'ld); -GLING (-lĭng). [Freq. of *snug.*] To cuddle; also, curl up comfortably. — *v. t.* To draw, as one's head, or another, close, as for comfort; to cuddle. — **snug'gle**, *n.*

so (sō; 4), *adv.* [ME. *so, sa, swa,* fr. AS. *swā.*] **1.** In that or like manner; specif.: **a** Just as has been done, said, thought, proposed, etc.; as, if he *so* chooses. **b** As described, professed, or named in a preceding word or phrase; as, he was always called *so.* **2.** In that degree; specif.: **a** To that degree described in the preceding context; as, he was *so* discouraged. **b** In or to a high degree; exceedingly; as, his style is *so* dull. **c** To a certain unspecified extent or degree; as, he dared come only *so* near. **3.** In such manner or such a manner; to such degree or extent; also, with the end in view. **4.** Denoting sequence or consequence; specif.: **a** For this or that reason; therefore. **b** By reason of that; on that account. **c** In the way of final outcome or conclusion. **5.** In the following manner; thus.

— *conj.* **1.** Provided that; if only; — often with *that.* **2.** *Colloq.* With the result that; as, he was sick, *so* they were quiet; also, in order that; as, be quiet *so* he can sleep.

— *pron.* **1.** Approximately that; as, I have read a page or *so.* **2.** Such as has been specified; the same; as, in America the foreigner who remains *so* is called a greenhorn.

— *interj.* An exclamation expressing: **a** Approval; let it be so; that will do. **b** Surprised dissent.

so (sō), *n.* *Music.* Sol.

soak (sōk), *v. i.* [AS. *socian.*] **1.** To become saturated or softened, etc., by saturation. **2.** To enter by pores or interstices; to percolate; also, to penetrate one's mind. **3.** To drink intemperately. — *v. t.* **1.** To saturate with a liquid; to drench. **2.** To subject to immersion, so as to soften, macerate, etc. **3.** To draw in, as by suction or absorption; as, a sponge *soaks* up water. **4.** To drink (liquor) to excess. **5.** *Slang.* **a** To sock; punch. **b** To extract money from, esp. by charging exorbitantly. **c** To pawn.

Syn. **Soak, saturate, drench, steep, impregnate** mean to subject to a liquid or the like until thorough permeation is attained. **Soak** implies immersion and resulting absorption and, often, an end to be gained; **saturate** an effect (rather than the process of soaking, diluting, etc.) where no more liquid can be absorbed or, figuratively, where an infusion is complete; **drench**, a thorough wetting or the like by something poured; **steep**, an extraction of the essence of one thing so as to make it part and parcel of the other, as tea leaves in boiling water; **impregnate**, an interpenetration of one thing with another (not invariably a liquid) until thoroughly imbued with it.

— *n.* **1.** Act or process of soaking; also, state of being soaked. **2.** *Slang.* **a** A hard blow; punch. **b** A sot; drunkard. **c** Pawn; as, to put in *soak.* **3.** The liquid in which anything is soaked. — **soak'er**, *n.*

soak'age (sōk'ĭj), *n.* **1.** Act or process of soaking, or state of being soaked. **2.** Liquid gained by absorption or lost by seepage.

so'-and-so', *n.* An unnamed or unspecified person or thing.

soap (sōp), *n.* [AS. *sāpe.*] **1.** A cleansing agent, made usually by action of alkali on fat or fatty acids (in the form of their glyceryl esters), and consisting essentially of sodium or potassium salts of such acids. **2.** *Chem.* By extension, any salt of one of the fat acids. **3.** *Slang.* Money; esp., *U. S.,* money used for bribery. — *v. t.* To rub soap over.

soap'bark' (-bärk'), *n.* **a** Also **soapbark tree.** A Chilean tree (*Quillaja saponaria*) of the rose family, with shining leaves and terminal white flowers. **b** The bark of this tree, which yields a soapy lather, and is used in cleaning, in emulsifying oils, etc. See QUILLAI. **c** Also **soapbark tree.** Any of several tropical American shrubs (genus *Pithecolobium,* as *P. bigeminum*) of the mimosa family, having saponaceous bark.

soap'ber'ry (-bĕr'ĭ; -bĕr·ĭ), *n.* Also **soapberry tree.** Any of a genus (*Sapindus*) typifying a family (Sapindaceae, the soapberry family) of chiefly tropical trees, shrubs or vines, with exstipulate leaves and baccate or capsular, often edible, fruit; esp., *S. saponaria,* called also *chinaberry;* also, its fruit, used in tropical America for cleaning clothes.

soap'box' (sōp'bŏks'), *n.* Also **soap box.** **a** A box for holding soap, esp. a packing box. **b** By extension, a hastily improvised platform such as a packing box from which a street orator speaks. — **soap'box'**, *adj.*

soap'less soap. See DETERGENT, *n.*

soap opera. *Slang.* A radio serial drama offered on a daytime commercial program chiefly for housewives.

soap'stone' (sōp'stōn'), *n.* *Petrog.* Steatite, a soft stone with a soapy feel. See TALC.

soap'suds' (-sŭdz'), *n. pl.* Suds made with soap.

soap'wort' (-wûrt'), *n.* A European perennial herb (*Saponaria officinalis*), of the pink family, widely naturalized in the United States. It has coarse pink or white flowers. The bruised leaves are detergent.

soap'y (sōp'ĭ), *adj.;* SOAP'I·ER (-ĭ·ĕr); SOAP'I·EST. **1.** Smeared with soap. **2.** Containing soap; saponaceous. — **soap'i·ly**, *adv.* — **soap'i·ness**, *n.*

soar (sōr; 70), *v. i.* [OF. *essorer,* F. *s'essorer* to soar, *essorer* to expose to the air (for drying), deriv. of L. *ex* out + *aura* air.] **1.** To fly aloft, as a bird; to sail upward; to hover in the upper air. **2.** To lift one's thoughts, spirits, etc., far above the earth or earthly things. **3.** To rise high above the ordinary level in any scale; as, prices *soared.* **4.** *Aeronautics.* To fly without engine power and without loss of altitude. — **Syn.** Ascend, mount, rise. — *n.* **1.** Soaring range, distance, or height; as, beyond the *soar* of fancy. **2.** Act of soaring; upward flight. — **soar'er**, *n.*

sob (sŏb), *v. i.;* SOBBED (sŏbd); SOB'BING. [ME. *sobben.*] **1.** To weep with convulsive heavings of the breast, or contractions of the throat. **2.** To make a sound suggestive of a sob or sigh. — *v. t.* **1.** To bring to a certain state by sobbing; as, to *sob* oneself to sleep. **2.** To utter with sobs. — *n.* A sigh, cry, or wail, accompanied by a convulsive catching of the breath. — **sob'bing·ly**, *adv.*

so·be'it (sō·bē'ĭt), *conj.* Provided; if it be so that.

so'ber (sō'bĕr), *adj.* [OF. *sobre,* fr. L. *sobrius.*] **1.** Habitually temperate in the use of liquor. **2.** Not drunk. **3.** Serious or subdued in mood, expression, appearance, color, etc.; solemn; grave; sedate. **4.** *Scot.* **a** Poor; feeble; ailing. **b** Humble; simple. **5.** Not affected by passion, excitement, or prejudice; well-balanced; as, a *sober* head in a panic. — **Syn.** See SERIOUS. — *v. t. & i.* To make or become sober. — **so'ber·ly**, *adv.* — **so'ber-mind'ed** (*see Pron.,* § 2), *adj.* — **so'ber·ness**, *n.*

So·bran'je (sō·brän'yĕ), *n.* Also **So·bran'ye.** [Bulg.] The former unicameral national assembly of Bulgaria.

so·bri'e·ty (sō·brī'ĕ·tĭ), *n.* [F. *sobriété,* fr. L. *sobrietas.*] The state or quality of being sober; specif.: **a** Habitual temperance. **b** Habitual moderation. **c** Sedateness; gravity.

so'bri·quet (sō'brĭ·kā; *F.* sô'brē'kĕ'), *n.* [F.] A fanciful epithet or appellation; a nickname.

sob sister. *Slang, U. S.* A woman journalist who writes sentimental news articles; also, *Rare,* a mawkishly sentimental person.

soc'age (sŏk'ĭj), *n.* [AF., fr. *soc.* See SOKE.] *Law.* Orig., in medieval England, the status, tenure, or holding of a sokeman; later, any tenure having the incidents of such tenure, which were fealty, relief, suit of court, and escheat, with freedom from scutage, wardship, and marriage. — **soc'ag·er** (-ĭj·ĕr), *n.*

so'-called' (sō'kôld'; 2), *adj.* Commonly named; thus termed; — implying doubt as to the correctness or propriety of so designating the person or thing; as, this *so-called* American; *so-called* education.

soc'cer (sŏk'ĕr), *n.* [Corrupt. fr. *association.*] Association football. See FOOTBALL, *n.,* 2.

so'cia·bil'i·ty (sō'shȧ·bĭl'ĭ·tĭ), *n.; pl.* -TIES (-tĭz). Sociable character, disposition, atmosphere, etc.

so'cia·ble (sō'shȧ·b'l), *adj.* [F. or L.; F., fr. L. *sociabilis,* fr. *sociare* to associate, fr. *socius* a companion.] **1.** Inclined by nature to companionship with others of the same species; — now usually *social.* **2.** Friendly, affable, or companionable; also, characterized by pleasant social relations. — **Syn.** See GRACIOUS. — *n.* *U. S.* An informal party designed to promote friendly relations in a group, esp. of church members; a social. — **so'cia·ble·ness**, *n.* — **so'cia·bly** (-blĭ), *adv.*

so'cial (sō'shăl), *adj.* [F. or L.; F., fr. L. *socialis*, fr. *socius* an associate, ally.] **1.** *Hist.* Of, pertaining to, or between, allies or confederates; as, the *Social* War. **2.** That is spent, taken, enjoyed, etc., in the company of one's friends or equals; as, agreeable *social* relations. **3.** *Rare.* Sociable by nature or inclination, or in character. **4.** Consisting of, pertaining to, or characteristic of society, or the pleasure-seeking world. **5.** Gregarious by nature and habit; as, man is by nature a *social* creature. **6.** Of or pertaining to society as an organism or as a group of interrelated, interdependent persons; as, the *social* order; *social* ethics. **7.** Of or pertaining to the welfare of human society, esp. welfare work for the benefit of the poor; as, a *social* center or settlement. **8.** Of or pertaining to human beings in their physical contacts or to evils resulting from such contacts, as overcrowding; as, *social* hygiene; specif., pertaining to venereal contagion; as, *social* diseases. **9.** Socialistic or communistic; as, *social* theories; — often used in names of political parties; as, *Social* Democratic party. **10.** *Bot.* Naturally growing in groups or masses. **11.** *Zool.* Living together and breeding in more or less organized communities; as, *social* ants, bees, etc. — *n.* A social gathering; a sociable.

Social Credit. The doctrine advanced by Major C. H. Douglas (Eng. engineer and economist, born 1879) that the returns of industry are largely unearned increment and, along with all interest, belong to the community and should be returnable to consumers in dividends.

social evil. Prostitution.

so'cial·ism (sō'shăl·ĭz'm), *n.* A political and economic theory of social organization based on collective or governmental ownership and democratic management of the essential means for the production and distribution of goods; also, a policy or practice based on this theory. Cf. COLLECTIVISM, FABIANISM, MARXISM, BOLSHEVISM, COMMUNISM.

so'cial·ist (-ĭst), *n.* One who advocates or practices the doctrines of socialism. — *adj.* Socialistic.

so'cial·is'tic (-ĭs'tĭk), *adj.* Of, pert. to, or based on socialism; favoring socialism.

so'cial·ite (sō'shăl·īt), *n.* [Colloq. *social light*, in this sense, taken humorously as *social* + *-ite*.] *U.S.* A person socially prominent.

so'ci·al'i·ty (sō'shĭ·ăl'ĭ·tĭ), *n.; pl.* -TIES (-tĭz). **1.** Sociability. **2.** The tendency, esp. in human beings, to form social groups.

so'cial·ize (sō'shăl·īz), *v. t.* **1.** To render social; esp., to train for social environment. **2.** To adapt to social needs or uses. **3.** To render socialistic; to regulate by the theories or practices of socialism; as, to *socialize* industries. **4.** *Educ.* To bring about the active participation of pupil and teachers in. — **-i·za'tion** (-ĭ·zā'shŭn; -ī·zā'-), *n.*

so'cial·ized med'i·cine (-īzd). Administration by an organized group, a state, or a nation of medical and hospital services to suit the needs of all members of a class or classes or all members of the population, deriving funds from assessments, philanthropy, taxation, or other sources. Often identified with one particular form, *state medicine.*

so'cial·ly (sō'shăl·ĭ), *adv.* In a social manner.

social register. A register, or directory, of persons socially prominent.

social science. **a** The science that deals with human society or its elements, as family, state, or race, and with the relations and institutions involved in man's existence and well-being as a member of an organized community; — sometimes synonymous with *sociology.* **b** One of a group of sciences dealing with special phases of human society, as economics, sociology, ethics, etc.

social security. **1.** Public provision of the means necessary to enable individual citizens of a country to lead a personally satisfying and socially useful life, including adequate housing, education, recreation, health safeguards, and full employment, as well as adequate income. **2.** [*often caps.*] *U.S.* A government program, established in 1935, designed to inaugurate social security, and gradually extended in the meantime, that includes provisions for contributory old-age and survivors' insurance and unemployment insurance, also approval of, and contributions to, State plans for assistance to the aged, permanently disabled and blind persons, child welfare, and maternal and child health services.

social service. Any activity designed to promote social welfare.

social settlement. = SETTLEMENT, 3.

so·ci'e·tal (sō·sī'ĕ·tăl; -t'l), *adj.* Of society, esp. organized society.

so·ci'e·ty (sō·sī'ĕ·tĭ), *n.; pl.* -TIES (-tĭz). [F. *société*, fr. L. *societas*, fr. *socius* an associate.] **1.** Companionship or association with one's fellows; usually, friendly or intimate intercourse. **2.** The social order, esp. as a state or system restricting the individual; community life. **3.** Hence: **a** Any portion of a community regarded as a unit distinguishable by particular aims or standards of living or conduct; as, to move in polite *society.* **b** That part of the community which marks itself apart as a leisured class, with much time given to formal social affairs, fashionable sports, etc. **4.** A voluntary association of individuals for common ends; as, a *society* of lawyers. **5.** *Ecology.* A unit assemblage of plants within an association; — often called *plant society.* **6.** *Eccl.* In Congregational churches in the United States, a corporation connected with a local church, having control of the ownership of the church buildings and the determination and payment of the minister's salary; — called also *parish.* Cf. CONGREGATION, 4. **7.** *Sociol.* An enduring, co-operating social group so functioning as to maintain itself and perpetuate the species.

Society of Friends. The sect of Friends, or Quakers. See FRIEND, *n.*, 5.

Society of Jesus. See JESUIT, *n.*, 1. Abbr. *S. J.*

society verse. [F. *vers de société.*] A light, finished kind of lyrical poetry, suited to amuse polite society.

So·cin'i·an (sō·sĭn'ĭ·ăn), *adj.* Of or pert. to Socinus, or Socinianism. — **So·cin'i·an,** *n.*

So·cin'i·an·ism (-ĭz'm), *n. Eccl. Hist.* The tenets of Faustus Socinus (Sozzini), an Italian theologian (1539–1604), who denied leading Catholic and Protestant doctrines, as the Trinity and the divinity of Christ, and offered rationalistic explanations of sin, salvation, and the like.

socio-. [F. *socio-*, fr. L. *socius* companion.] A combining form denoting: **a** *Society, social.* **b** *Social and.* **c** *Sociological and.*

so'ci·ol'o·gy (sō'sĭ·ŏl'ō·jĭ; sō'shĭ-), *n.* [*socio-* + *-logy.*] The science of the origin and evolution of society, or of the forms, institutions, and functions of human groups. Cf. SOCIAL SCIENCE. — **so'ci·o·log'ic** (-ō·lŏj'ĭk), **so'ci·o·log'i·cal** (-ĭ·kăl), *adj.* — **so'ci·o·log'i·cal·ly,** *adv.* — **so'ci·ol'o·gist** (-ŏl'ō·jĭst), *n.*

sock (sŏk), *n.* [AS. *socc* a sock, kind of shoe, fr. L. *soccus* a kind of low-heeled light shoe.] **1.** A shoe worn by actors of comedy in ancient Greece and Rome; hence, comedy as a form of art. Cf. BUSKIN. **2.** A stocking with a short leg.

sock, *v. t.* [Origin uncert.] *Slang.* To hurl, drive, or strike violently; also, to beat. — **sock,** *n.*

sock·dol'a·ger (sŏk·dŏl'ȧ·jẽr), *n.* [Corrupt. of *doxology.*] *Slang, U.S.* **a** That which settles a matter, as a decisive blow. **b** Something unusually large.

sock'et (sŏk'ĕt; -ĭt), *v. t.* To provide with, or support in or by, a socket. — *n.* [AF. *soket*, dim. of OF. *soc* plowshare.] An opening or hollow that forms a holder for something; as, a *socket* for a candle or an electric bulb; a *socket* for the shaft of a golf club, etc.

sock'eye' salm'on (sŏk'ī'). = BLUEBACK SALMON.

so'cle (sŏk''l; sō'k'l), *n.* [F., fr. It. *zoccolo*, also, wooden shoe.] *Arch.* A projecting member, usually molded, at the foot of a wall or pier, or beneath the base of a column, pedestal, or the like.

So·crat'ic (sō·krăt'ĭk), *adj.* Of or pertaining to Socrates, the Grecian sage and teacher (469–399 B.C.), or his philosophy or methods. — *n.* A follower of Socrates; esp., any of the Greek philosophers directly influenced by him. — **So·crat'i·cal·ly** (-ĭ·kăl·ĭ), *adv.*

Socratic irony. Pretended ignorance or willingness to learn from others assumed for the sake of making their errors conspicuous by means of adroit questioning.

Socratic method. The method of instruction used by Socrates, consisting of questionings the object of which is to elicit a consistent expression of something supposed to be implicitly known by all rational beings.

sod (sŏd). Obs. past of SEETHE.

sod, *n.* [MD. & MLG. *sode.*] **1.** That stratum of the soil filled with the roots of grass, herbs, etc.; turf; sward; also, a piece of such surface; a turf. **2.** The grass-covered earth; the soil. — *v. t.;* SOD'DED; SOD'DING. To cover with sod.

so'da (sō'dȧ), *n.* [It. & ML., fr. ML. *sodanum*, prop., headache remedy, fr. *soda* headache, fr. Ar. *ṣudā'* splitting headache.] **1.** Sodium carbonate (which see). **2.** Sodium bicarbonate (which see). **3.** Sodium hydroxide (which see). **4.** Sodium oxide, Na_2O. **5.** In *soda alum, soda salts*, etc., sodium. **6.** Short for SODA WATER. Also, a drink containing soda water. **7.** *Faro.* The card that shows face up in the dealing box before play begins.

soda ash. Commercial anhydrous sodium carbonate.

soda biscuit. **a** A biscuit leavened with sodium bicarbonate and sour milk or buttermilk. **b** A soda cracker.

soda cracker. A lightly baked crisp cracker made from yeast dough neutralized with soda.

soda fountain. An apparatus with delivery tube, faucets, etc., for drawing soda water; also, a counter where soda water is served.

soda jerk *or* **jerker.** A counterman who dispenses carbonated drinks and ice cream at a soda fountain.

soda lime. A mixture of caustic soda (sodium hydroxide) and slaked lime, used to absorb moisture, gases, etc.

so'da·lite (sō'dȧ·līt), *n.* [*soda* + *-lite.*] *Mineral.* A transparent to translucent mineral of vitreous or greasy luster, found in certain igneous rocks. It is a silicate of sodium and aluminum with some chlorine $Na_4(AlCl)Al_2(SiO_4)_3$.

so·dal'i·ty (sō·dăl'ĭ·tĭ), *n.; pl.* -TIES (-tĭz). [L. *sodalitas*, fr. *sodalis* a comrade.] **1.** Fellowship. **2.** A fellowship (of men or women); specif., *R.C.Ch.*, a devotional and charitable lay association.

soda water. **1.** A beverage consisting of a weak solution of sodium bicarbonate, with some acid to cause effervescence. **2.** A beverage consisting of water charged with carbon dioxide and flavored.

sod'den (sŏd''n). Obs. past part. of SEETHE. — *adj.* **1.** *Rare.* Boiled; steeped. **2.** As flaccid or as spent as if unduly stewed; dulled, esp. by dissipation; as, *sodden* features. **3.** Heavy or soggy because of imperfect baking or boiling; as, *sodden* biscuits. **4.** Soaked; heavy with moisture; saturated. — *v. t. & i.* To make or become sodden. — **sod'den·ly,** *adv.* — **sod'den·ness,** *n.*

so'di·um (sō'dĭ·ŭm; 58), *n.* [NL., fr. SODA.] *Chem.* A soft, waxy, silver-white metallic element of the alkali group, occurring abundantly (always combined), as in common salt, Chile saltpeter, borax, etc. Symbol, *Na* (*natrium*); at. no., 11; at. wt., 22.997. Melting point, 97.5° C. Sodium is chemically very active.

sodium benzoate. A colorless or white salt, $NaC_7H_5O_2$, used as a food preservative, and in medicine.

sodium bicarbonate. A white crystalline salt, $NaHCO_3$, having a slight alkaline taste, and used in cookery, in baking powders, in medicine, etc.; — called also *baking soda, saleratus*, etc.

sodium carbonate. Any carbonate of sodium; soda; specif., a salt, Na_2CO_3, of strong alkaline taste. A hydrated form, $Na_2CO_3.10H_2O$ (*sal soda* or *washing soda*), has transparent crystals. Sodium carbonate is used in making soap, chemical reagents, etc., in softening water, in scouring and bleaching, in medicine, photography, etc.

sodium chlorate. *Chem.* A colorless crystalline salt, $NaClO_3$, used as an oxidizing agent.

sodium chloride. Common salt. See SALT, *n.*, 1.

sodium cyanide. *Chem.* A white, deliquescent, poisonous salt, NaCN, used in electroplating, fumigating, etc.

sodium dichromate. A red crystalline salt, $Na_2Cr_2O_7$.

sodium hydroxide. A white, brittle solid, NaOH, used in making soap, rayon, and paper, and in bleaching.

sodium hyposulfite. **a** See SODIUM THIOSULFATE. **b** A crystalline water-soluble salt, $Na_2S_2O_4$, used esp. in dyeing and bleaching.

sodium, *or* **so'di·um-va'por, lamp.** *Elec.* An electric lamp containing sodium vapor and electrodes between which a luminous discharge takes place, used esp. for lighting highways.

sodium nitrate. *Chem.* A colorless deliquescent salt, $NaNO_3$, used as a fertilizer. It occurs in natural beds in Chile and is exported as *Chile saltpeter.*

sodium thiosulfate. A colorless or white salt, $Na_2S_2O_3$; — less correctly *sodium hyposulfite.* It is the "hypo" of the photographer, and used as a fixing agent.

Sod'om (sŏd'ŭm), *n.* **1.** *Bib.* A city or country the wickedness and destruction of which, with the neighboring ***Gomorrah***, are described in Genesis xviii and xix. **2.** A city or country notorious for vice and corruption.

Sod'om·ite (-īt), *n.* **a** An inhabitant of Sodom. **b** [*not cap.*] One guilty of sodomy.

sod'om·y (sŏd'ŭm·ĭ), *n.* [OF. *sodomy*, fr. *Sodome* Sodom.] Carnal copulation in any of certain unnatural ways.

so·ev'er (sō·ĕv'ẽr), *adv.* [*so* + *ever.*] **a** Following an adjective preceded by *how* or in the superlative with *the*, to any possible or known extent; as, how fair *soever* she may be. **b** Following a noun modified by *all, any, no, what,* etc., at all; of any or every kind that may be specified; as, he gives no information *soever.*

-so·ev'er (-sō·ĕv'ẽr). An intensive suffix added to *who, what, where, when, how,* etc., and indicating any out of all conceivable persons, things, places, times, ways, etc.

so'fa (sō'fȧ), *n.* [Ar. *ṣuffah.*] A type of lounge usually upholstered and with back and arms. Cf. CHESTERFIELD, DAVENPORT.

sofa bed. An upholstered sofa that can be made to serve as a double bed by lowering its hinged upholstered back to horizontal position; — distinguished from *studio couch.*

so'far (sō'fär), *n.* [*so*und *f*ixing *a*nd *r*anging.] A system for determining the location of a deep (around 4000 feet) underwater explosion at sea by means of triangulation based on the reception of the sound by three widely separated shore stations. It can be used to locate survivors who drop a special bomb into the sea, as from a lifeboat.

so'-fa' syl'la·bles. See SOL-FA SYLLABLES.

sof'fit (sŏf'ĭt), *n.* [F. and L.; F. *soffite* fr. It. *soffito, soffita,* fr. L. *suffixus,* past part., fastened beneath.] *Arch.* The underside of a subordinate part or member of a building, such as a staircase, archway, cornice, etc. See EXTRADOS, *Illust.*

soft (sŏft; 74), *adj.* [AS. *sōfte,* adj. & adv., orig. adv., the adj. being *sēfte.*] **1.** That has a soothing or quietly agreeable quality; affecting the senses in a gentle and pleasant way; lacking in acidity, harshness, stiffness, coarseness, or like quality offensive to the sense of taste, sight, hearing, or touch. **2.** Of a person or his looks, words, etc.: **a** Mild; conciliatory. **b** Emotionally susceptible; effeminate. **3.** Easily yielding to physical pressure; unresistant to molding, cutting, wear, etc. **4.** Relaxed by ease; untrained for hardship. **5.** Characterized by freedom from substances, as calcium and magnesium salts, which prevent formation of lather with soap; — said of water. **6.** Gently curved; not sharply defined; having blurred or vague outlines; as, a *soft* focus or contour. **7.** *Colloq., U.S.* Of beverages, not spirituous or alcoholic. **8.** Having starchy kernels low in gluten which yield a weak flour; — of wheats. **9.** *Phonet.* Of *c* and *g,* pronounced as in *city, gem,* etc. **10.** *Photog.* Having relatively little contrast. **11.** *Physics.* Designating or pertaining to rays, esp. X rays, of low penetrating power.

Syn. **Soft, bland, mild, gentle, lenient** mean devoid of all roughness, harshness, or intensity. **Soft** implies a subdual of all that is vivid, intense, forceful, and the like, until it is pleasantly agreeable; **bland** implies the absence of anything that might disturb, excite, stimulate, etc.; **mild** and **gentle** imply moderation of something that is often harsh, rough, violent, etc., so that it becomes soothing or agreeable; **lenient** implies a relaxing or assuasive quality.

— *adv.* Softly; gently; quietly; lightly.

— *n.* **1.** That which is soft; softness; a soft object or material. **2.** *Colloq.* A soft person; softy; a softhead.

— *interj. Archaic.* An exclamation urging silence or less haste; be quiet! not so fast!

— **soft'ly,** *adv.* — **soft'ness,** *n.*

soft'ball' (sŏft'bôl'), *n.* A modified form of baseball played out of doors with a soft ball larger than a baseball; also, the ball used in this game.

soft chancre. *Med.* = CHANCROID.

soft coal. Bituminous coal.

sof'ten (sŏf'ĕn; -'n; 74; *cf.* OFTEN), *v. t. & i.* **1.** To make or become soft or softer. **2.** *Mil.* To weaken in power to resist and in morale by means of preliminary aerial bombardment and other harassment in preparation for invasion; — often with *up.* — **sof'ten·er** (-ẽr), *n.*

sof'ten·ing of the brain. **a** *Med.* A localized softening of the brain substance. **b** Popularly, dementia.

soft'-finned' (sŏft'fĭnd'; 2), *adj. Zool.* Having fins in which the membrane is supported entirely or almost entirely by soft or articulated rays; — opp. to *spiny-finned.*

soft'head' (-hĕd'), *n.* A simpleton; simple person.

soft'heart'ed (-här'tĕd; -tĭd; 2), *adj.* Tenderhearted.

soft'-ped'al, *v. t. & i.;* see PEDAL. To play with the soft pedal; hence, *Slang.,* to soften; subdue; tone down.

soft pedal. **1.** *Music.* A foot lever on a piano used to produce a soft tone. **2.** *Slang.* Figuratively, a restraint or curb; esp., a ban upon talk.

soft'-shell' (sŏft'shĕl'), **soft'-shelled'** (-shĕld'), *adj.* Having a soft shell; as, a *soft-shelled* clam (see CLAM); *soft-shelled,* or *soft-shell,* crab (see CRAB); *soft-shelled* turtle (see TURTLE).

soft soap. **a** A semifluid soap. **b** *Colloq.* Flattery.

soft'-soap', *v. t. & i.* **a** To smear or treat with soft soap. **b** To flatter, wheedle, or gush over. — **soft'-soap'er,** *n.*

soft'-spo'ken (sŏft'spō'kĕn; 2), *adj.* Speaking softly; having a mild or gentle voice; hence, mild; suave.

soft'wood' (-wŏŏd'), *n.* **1.** **a** Any wood light in texture, nonresistant, and easily worked. **b** *Forestry.* The wood of a coniferous tree. **2.** Any tree having soft wood. — **soft'wood',** *adj.*

soft wood. = SOFTWOOD, 1 **a** & **b**.

soft'y (sŏf'tĭ), *n.; pl.* SOFTIES (-tĭz). *Colloq.* **a** A silly or sentimental person. **b** A weakling.

Sog'di·an (sŏg'dĭ·ăn), *n.* **1.** One of an ancient Iranian people dwelling in Sogdiana, the region of modern Bokhara. **2.** The Iranian language of ancient Sogdiana.

sog'gy (sŏg'ĭ), *adj.;* SOG'GI·ER (-ĭ·ẽr); SOG'GI·EST. [From E. dial. *sog* to soak.] Saturated with moisture; soaked; sodden. — **sog'gi·ly,** *adv.* — **sog'gi·ness,** *n.*

So·ho' (sō·hō'; sō'hō; 2), *n.* A district in London south of Oxford Street, since 1685 chiefly a foreign quarter. It is famous for its restaurants.

‖**soi'-di'sant'** (swȧ'dē'zäɴ'), *adj.* [F., fr. *soi* oneself + *disant,* pres. part. of *dire* to say.] Self-styled; — used disparagingly; hence, pretended; would-be.

‖**soi'gné'** (swȧ'nyā'), *adj. masc.,* ‖**soi'gnée'** (-nyā'), *fem.* [F.] Painstakingly attended to; often, well-groomed.

soil (soil), *v. t.* [OF. *soillier,* fr. *soil* miry place, fr. L. *suile* pigsty, fr. *sus* a swine.] **1.** To stain or defile morally; to corrupt. **2.** To make unclean, esp. superficially; to dirty. **3.** To smirch, as one's honor; to disgrace. — *v. i.* To become soiled or dirty. — *n.* **1.** A marsh or tract of water, in which hunted game takes refuge; — esp. in phrases; as, to run (or go) to *soil.* **2.** [From the v.] The act or fact of soiling; a stain, smudge, spot, etc. **3.** That which soils; filth. **4.** Hence, manure; fertilizing dung.

soil, *n.* [AF., fr. OF. *sueil, suel,* fr. L. *solum* floor, ground.] **1.** Firm land; earth. **2.** The upper layer of earth which may be dug, plowed, etc.; specif., the loose surface material of the earth in which plants grow. **3.** A country or land; a region. **4.** Any substance, medium, etc., in which something may take root and grow; as, social discontent is the *soil* in which anarchy thrives.

soil, *v. t.* [OF. *saoler, saouler,* to satiate, fr. L. *satullare,* fr. *satullus,* dim. of *satur* sated.] To feed, as stock, in the barn or an enclosure, with fresh grass or green food; also, to purge by feeding on green food.

soil'age (soil'ĭj), *n. Agric.* Green crops grown for feeding confined animals.

soil pipe. A pipe for carrying off liquid wastes from toilets.

soil'ure (soil'ūr), *n.* Act of soiling; also, a stain; smirch.

soi·ree', ‖**soi'rée'** (swä·rā'; *F.* swȧ'rā'), *n.* [F. *soirée.*] An evening party.

so'ja (sō'jȧ; sō'yȧ), *n.* Also **soja bean.** [NL., Sp., & D. *soja.* See SOY.] The soybean.

so·journ' (sō·jûrn'; sō'jûrn; *Brit. usually* sŏj'ûrn, -ẽrn; sŭj'-), *v. i.* [OF. *sojorner, sejorner,* deriv. of L. *sub* under, about + *diurnus* of the day.] To dwell in a place as a temporary resident or as a stranger. — (sō'jûrn; sō·jûrn'; *Brit. usually* sŏj'ûrn, -ẽrn; sŭj'-), *n.* A temporary stay. — **so·journ'er,** *n.*

soke (sōk), *n.* [ML. *soca,* fr. AS. *sōcn* attack, prosecution.] *Early Eng. Law.* **a** The right to hold court and do justice, with the franchise to receive certain fees or fines arising from it; jurisdiction over certain territory or certain men. **b** The district over which such jurisdiction or franchise extended.

soke'man (sōk'măn), *n.; pl.* -MEN (-mĕn). *Early Eng. Law.* A man who is under the soke of another.

Sol (sŏl), *n.* [L.] **1.** The sun. **2.** *Alchem.* Gold. **3.** *Rom. Relig.* The sun-god.

sol (sōl; sŏl), *n.* [It.] *Music.* A syllable applied in solmization of the fifth tone of any diatonic scale.

sol (sŏl), *n.* [OF.] *Hist.* Formerly, a French money of account; also, a coin, at first of silver and later of copper.

sol (sōl), *n.; pl.* SOLS (sōlz), SOLES (sō'lās). [Sp.] A silver coin and money of account of Peru, equal to 100 centavos. See MONEY, *Tables;* LIBRA, 2.

sol (sŏl; sōl), *n.* [From *sol*ution.] *Chem.* A fluid colloidal solution or system. Cf. HYDROSOL.

‖**so'la** (sō'lȧ), *adj.* See SOLUS.

sol'ace (sŏl'ĭs; -ȧs), *n.* [OF. *solaz, soulas,* fr. L. *solacium, solatium,* fr. *solari* to console.] Alleviation of grief or anxiety; also, a source of relief, consolation, etc. — *v. t.;* -ACED (-ĭst; -ȧst); -AC·ING (-ĭs·ĭng). **1.** To give comfort to in grief or misfortune; to console. **2.** To make cheerful; esp., to amuse. **3.** To allay; assuage; soothe. — **Syn.** See COMFORT. — **sol'ace·ment,** *n.* — **sol'ac·er** (sŏl'ĭs·ẽr), *n.*

sol'a·na'ceous (sŏl'ȧ·nā'shŭs), *adj.* [L. *solanum* nightshade + *-aceous.*] *Bot.* Belonging to the nightshade family (Solanaceae). See NIGHTSHADE.

so'lan goose (sō'lăn). The common gannet.

‖**so·la'no** (sō·lä'nō), *n.* [Sp.] A hot, oppressive east wind of the Mediterranean, esp. on the eastern coast of Spain; also a cloudy, rain-bringing wind of the same locality and direction.

so·la'num (sō·lā'nŭm), *n.* [L., nightshade.] *Bot.* Any of a genus (*Solanum*) of herbs, shrubs, or trees of the nightshade family.

so'lar (sō'lẽr), *adj.* [L. *solaris,* fr. *sol* the sun.] **1.** Of, from, or pertaining to, the sun, esp. as affecting the earth; as, *solar* heat; measured by the earth's course in relation to the sun; as, *solar* time; *solar* month, year (see MONTH, YEAR); hence, pert. to or reckoned by solar time; as, *solar* calendar. **2.** Produced, or operated, by the action of the sun's light or heat; as, a *solar* engine.

solar constant. The number expressing the quantity of radiant solar heat received at the outer layers of the earth's atmosphere on a unit of surface in a unit of time, which is 1.94 calories per square centimeter of surface in a minute.

so·lar'i·um (sō·lâr'ĭ·ŭm), *n.; pl.* -LARIA (-ȧ). [L.] An apartment exposed to the sun, as for the treatment of illness by the administration of sun baths.

so'lar·ize (sō'lẽr·īz), *v. t.* **1.** To expose to sunlight; to affect in some way by the action of the sun's rays. **2.** *Photog.* To injure by overexposure of the sensitive surface. — **so'lar·i·za'tion** (-ĭ·zā'shŭn; -ī·zā'-), *n.*

solar plexus. *Anat.* **1.** A nervous plexus situated in the abdomen behind the stomach and in front of the aorta and the crura of the diaphragm. It contains several ganglia, and distributes filaments to the abdominal viscera. **2.** *Colloq.* The pit of the stomach.

solar system. The sun, with the group of celestial bodies which, held by its attraction, revolve round it.

so·la'ti·um (sō·lā'shĭ·ŭm), *n.; pl.* SOLATIA (-ȧ). [L. See SOLACE, *n.*] A compensation, as for injured feelings.

sold (sōld), *past & past part.* of SELL.

sol'dan (sŏl'dăn), *n.* [OF. *soldan, soudan,* sultan.] *Hist.* In the Middle Ages, the ruler of a Mohammedan country; sultan; esp., the sultan of Egypt.

sol'der (sŏd'ẽr), *n.* [Formerly *soldure, souder,* fr. OF. *soudure* solder, fr. *souder, soulder,* to solder, fr. L. *solidare* to make solid.] **1.** A metal or metallic alloy used when melted to join metallic surfaces. Solders which melt readily are ***soft solders;*** others fusing at a red heat are ***hard solders.*** **2.** Hence, anything which unites or cements. — *v. t.* **1.** To join by solder. **2.** To unite securely; to cement. **3.** Hence, to mend; patch; — often with *up.* — *v. i.* To be or become united by or as by a solder. — **sol'der·er,** *n.*

sol'dier (sōl'jẽr), *n.* [OF. *soldier, soudier,* fr. *soulde, soude,* pay, wages, fr. L. *solidus* a piece of money (hence, soldier's pay).] **1.** One engaged in military service. **2.** An enlisted man in military service, as distinguished from a commissioned officer. **3.** A skilled warrior. **4.** A militant leader or worker in any cause. **5.** **a** In most termites or white ants, one of a caste of wingless individuals differing more or less from the workers in their larger size, very large head, and long jaws. See TERMITE, *Illust.* **b** In certain true ants, one of a type of workers distinguished by the large head and jaws. — *v. i.* **1.** To serve as a soldier. **2.** To make a pretense of working, while doing only enough to escape punishment; to malinger. — **sol'dier·ship,** *n.*

sol'dier·ly, *adj.* Like or befitting a soldier; brave; martial.

soldier of fortune. One who follows a military career wherever there is promise of profit, adventure, or pleasure.

sol'dier's med'al (sōl'jẽrz). A decoration awarded, since July 2, 1926, to members of the U. S. Army or its reserve units, or to personnel temporarily on duty with the army, for heroism not involving actual conflict with an enemy.

sol'dier·y (sōl'jẽr·ĭ), *n.; pl.* -IES (-ĭz). A body of soldiers; soldiers, collectively; the military.

sol'do (sŏl'dō; *It.* sôl'dō), *n.; pl.* -DI (-dē). [It. See SOU.] A small Italian coin and money of account, worth generally 1/20 of the lira.

sole (sōl), *n.* [From AS. and (or) F. *sole*, both fr. L. *solea*.] **1.** The undersurface of the foot. **2.** The part of a shoe, boot, etc., on which the sole of the foot rests. See SHOE, *Illust.* **3.** The bottom or lower part of anything, or that on which anything rests. **4.** *Golf.* The bottom of the club head. — *v. t.* **1.** To furnish with a sole. **2.** *Golf.* To place (the club) on its sole, as in addressing the ball.

sole, *n.* [OF., fr. Pr. *sola*, fr. L. *solea*, lit., sole of a shoe.] **1.** Any of certain flatfishes distinguished by the small mouth, small gill openings, and small eyes placed close together. The common sole of Europe (*Solea solea*) is one of the finest food fishes. **2.** Any of certain other flatfishes (as *Eopsetta jordani* and *Psettichthys melanostictus* of the Pacific coast of the United States), excellent food fishes.

sole, *adj.* [OF. and L.; OF. *soul, sol*, fr. L. *solus*.] **1.** *Law.* Single; unmarried; as, a feme *sole*. **2.** *Archaic.* Alone; solitary; isolated. **3.** That is the only one; one and no more; one and only; as, the *sole* heir. **4.** Acting, working, moving, etc., without assistance or interference. **5.** Belonging, granted, or attributed, to the one person or group specified. — **Syn.** See SINGLE.

sol'e·cism (sŏl'ē·sĭz'm), *n.* [F. *solécisme*, fr. L., fr. Gr. *soloikismos*, deriv. of *soloikos* speaking incorrectly, from the corruption of the Attic dialect among the Athenian colonists of Soli (Gr. Soloi) in Cilicia.] **1.** An ungrammatical combination of words in a sentence, loosely, any minor blunder in speech. Cf. BARBARISM, 1; IMPROPRIETY, 3. **2.** A breach of etiquette or decorum.

sol'e·cis'tic (sŏl'ē·sĭs'tĭk), *adj.* Pertaining to, of the nature of, or involving a solecism; incorrect or unseemly.

sole'ly (sōl'lĭ), *adv.* **1.** Without another; singly; alone. **2.** Exclusively; entirely; as, done *solely* for money.

sole Mar'gué·ry' (sōl' mär'gĕ·rē'). [*Marguéry*, a Paris café that featured the dish.] A dish of sole cooked in white wine and served in a rich sauce.

sol'emn (sŏl'ĕm), *adj.* [OF. *solemne, solempne*, fr. L. *solemnis, sollemnis*, fr. *sollus* all, entire + *annus* a year.] **1.** Observed with all the ceremony established by liturgy or tradition; as, Easter is a *solemn* feast. **2.** *Obs.* **a** Very important. **b** Sumptuous; splendid. **3.** Stately; formal; as, *solemn* state dinners. **4.** Performed, uttered, etc., under circumstances that indicate a religious sanction of all implied by one's act or words; as, to take a *solemn* oath on the Bible. **5.** Awe-inspiring; sublime. **6.** Highly serious; grave; deeply earnest. **7.** Somber; gloomy; as, a suit of *solemn* black. **8.** *Law.* Made in form; conforming with all legal requirements. — **Syn.** See SERIOUS. — **sol'emn·ly,** *adv.* — **sol'emn·ness,** *n.*

so·lem'ni·ty (sō·lĕm'nĭ·tĭ), *n.; pl.* -TIES (-tĭz). **1.** Ceremonious observance of an occasion or event; formality. **2.** A solemn rite, utterance, ceremony, etc. **3.** Seriousness, dignity, gravity, or the like. **4.** *Eccl.* Solemn, or full, liturgical celebration of a service, feast day, or the like.

sol'em·nize (sŏl'ĕm·nīz), *v. t.* **1.** To commemorate or observe with solemnity or in due fashion. **2.** To perform with pomp or ceremony; specif., to unite a couple in (marriage), with religious ceremony. **3.** To make solemn, serious, or exalted. — **sol'em·ni·za'tion** (-nĭ·zā'shŭn; -nī·zā'-), *n.* — **sol'em·niz'er** (-nīz'ẽr), *n.*

so'le·noid (sō'lē·noid; sō·lē'noid), *n.* [Gr. *sōlēn* channel, pipe + *-oid*.] *Elec.* A tubular coil for the production of a magnetic field. When traversed by a current the solenoid, or helix, acts in general like a magnet, with the south pole at the end at which the current flows clockwise to an observer facing it. — **so'le·noi'dal** (sō'lē·noi'dăl; -d'l), *adj.* — **so'le·noi'dal·ly,** *adv.*

sole trader. A feme-sole trader.

sol'–fa' (sōl'fä'; sŏl'-), *v. i.;* SOL'-FAED' (-fäd'); SOL'-FA'ING. [It. *solfa* the gamut, from the syllables *fa, sol.*] To sing the notes of the gamut; also, to sing in sol-fa syllables. — *v. t.* To sing to solmization syllables. — *n. Music.* **a** The syllables used in sol-faing. See SOL-FA SYLLABLES. **b** The gamut. **c** Solmization. **d** See TONIC SOL-FA. — **sol'–fa'ist** (-fä'ĭst), *n.*

sol–fa syllables. *Music.* Syllables applied to reading music; — now often called *so-fa syllables.* For the major scale the spellings most common in the United States are: *do, re, mi, fa, sol* (*so*), *la, ti, do.*

‖**sol·fa·ta'ra** (sōl·fä·tä'rä), *n.* [It., fr. *solfo* brimstone, sulfur, fr. L. *sulfur.*] *Geol.* A volcanic area or vent which yields only hot vapors and gases, in part sulfurous.

sol·feg'gio (sŏl·fĕj'ō), *n.; pl.* -GI (-ē) -GIOS (-ōz). [It., fr. *solfa* the gamut.] *Music.* **a** The application of the sol-fa syllables to the tones of the scale or to melodies or other voice parts. **b** An exercise in scales, using sol-fa syllables.

so·lic'it (sō·lĭs'ĭt), *v. t.* [F. *solliciter*, fr. L. *sollicitare, solicitare, -atum*, fr. *sollicitus* wholly (i. e., violently) moved, fr. *sollus* whole + *citus*, past part. of *ciere* to move.] **1.** To entreat; importune; now, often, to approach with a request or plea, as in selling, begging, etc. **2.** To try to obtain by asking for; as, to *solicit* an office, a favor, a contribution. **3.** To tempt (a person); to lure; specif., of a woman, to accost (a man) for immoral purposes. — *v. i.* To make solicitation; to importune; petition. — **Syn.** See ASK: INVITE.

so·lic'i·ta'tion (-ĭ·tā'shŭn), *n.* **1.** The practice, act, or an instance, of soliciting; often, specif., an entreaty; importunity. **2.** Incitement; allurement.

so·lic'i·tor (sō·lĭs'ĭ·tẽr), *n.* **1.** One who solicits; specif., one whose occupation it is to solicit contributions for a fund, etc.; as, no *solicitors* allowed in this building. **2.** *Law:* **a** *Eng.* Any person admitted to practice law and conduct litigation in any court. The solicitor is distinguished from the barrister in not having the right of audience (the right to plead in open court), except in a few minor courts. **b** The law officer of a city, town, department, or government; as, the city *solicitor.* — **Syn.** See LAWYER.

solicitor general; *pl.* SOLICITORS GENERAL. The second law officer in the government of Great Britain; also, a similar officer under the United States government; also, the chief law officer in some states of the United States.

so·lic'it·ous (sō·lĭs'ĭ·tŭs), *adj.* [L. *sollicitus, solicitus.* See SOLICIT, *v.*] **1.** Full of concern or fears; apprehensive. **2.** Full of desire; eager; anxiously willing. **3.** *Rare.* Meticulously careful. — **so·lic'it·ous·ly,** *adv.* — **so·lic'it·ous·ness,** *n.*

so·lic'i·tude (-ĭ·tūd), *n.* [F. *sollicitude*, fr. L. *sollicitudo.*] **1.** State of being solicitous; anxiety; also, excessive care or attention. **2.** *pl.* Causes of care or concern. — **Syn.** See CARE.

sol'id (sŏl'ĭd), *adj.* [F. *solide*, fr. L. *solidus.*] **1.** Not hollow; having its interior filled with matter. **2.** Cubic; three-dimensional; as, a *solid* foot (of 1728 *solid* inches); *solid* geometry. **3.** Compact; not disintegrated, loose, or spongy. **4.** Capable of resisting, up to a certain limit, forces tending to deform; rigid; not soft or fluid. **5.** Not weak, light, flimsy, etc.; sound; strong; also, stable, genuine, vigorous, etc. **6.** Of persons: **a** Having sound judgment. **b** Serious-minded; often, well-established financially. **c** Serious in purpose or character; not trivial. **7. a** Even or unbroken in surface; as, a *solid* panel. **b** Entirely of one metal or containing the minimum of alloy necessary to impart hardness; as, *solid* gold. **c** Designating a color, background, etc., all of one tone. **d** Unbroken; joined without a hyphen; — said of a compound word. **8. a** *Colloq.* Of time, without a break; as, to stand for three *solid* hours. **b** Of a group or group opinion, feeling, or vote, unanimous; as, a *solid* delegation. **9.** *Print.* Not having the lines separated by leads; not open. — **Syn.** See FIRM. — *n.* **1.** A magnitude that has three dimensions (length, breadth, and thickness); a part of space bounded on all sides, as a cube, a sphere. **2.** A solid substance or body. All substances which do not perceptibly flow are called *solids.* — **sol'id·ly,** *adv.* — **sol'id·ness,** *n.*

sol'i·da'go (sŏl'ĭ·dā'gō), *n.* [NL., fr. L. *solidare* to strengthen, unite; in allusion to its reputed healing qualities.] *Bot.* Any of a genus (*Solidago*) of chiefly North American herbs of the aster family, the goldenrods, adopted as State flowers by Alabama, Kentucky, and Nebraska.

solid angle. *Math.* The angle formed by three or more planes meeting at a point, as at the vertex of a cone.

sol'i·dar'i·ty (sŏl'ĭ·dăr'ĭ·tĭ), *n.; pl.* -TIES (-tĭz). [F. *solidarité.*] An entire union of interests and responsibilities in a group; community of interests, objectives, standards, etc. — **Syn.** See UNITY.

solid geometry. That branch of geometry which deals with the figure of three-dimensional space whose plane sections are the figure studied in plane geometry.

so·lid'i·fy (sō·lĭd'ĭ·fī), *v. t. & i.;* -FIED (-fīd); -FY'ING. [*solid* + *-fy.*] To make or become solid, or compact, or hard; to reduce (a fluid) to a solid state; often, to crystallize. — **so·lid'i·fi·ca'tion** (-fĭ·kā'shŭn), *n.*

so·lid'i·ty (-ĭ·tĭ), *n.; pl.* -TIES (-tĭz). **1.** The state, quality, or property of being solid. **2.** Moral, mental, or financial soundness. **3.** *Geom.* Volume; space within a closed surface.

sol'i·dus (sŏl'ĭ·dŭs), *n.; pl.* SOLIDI (-dī). [L.] **1. a** *Rom. Antiq.* A gold coin having an intrinsic value of about $3.02, issued at Byzantium (hence later called *bezant*) and circulated in Europe (6th–15th century). **b** [ML.] A medieval money of account equal to twelve denarii. **2.** The oblique stroke /, orig. a long *ſ* (s), abbrev. for *shilling;* — sometimes used instead of a horizontal line (—) in fractions, as 5/8 for $\frac{5}{8}$, in separating denominations in expressing a sum of money, as £3/12/6 (= £3 12s. 6d.), etc.

sol'i·fid'i·an (sŏl'ĭ·fĭd'ĭ·ăn), *n.* [L. *solus* alone + *fides* faith.] *Eccl.* One who holds that faith alone, without achievement or personal merit, is sufficient to insure salvation. — **sol'i·fid'i·an,** *adj.*

so·lil'o·quize (sō·lĭl'ō·kwīz), *v. i.* To utter a soliloquy; to talk to oneself. — **so·lil'o·quist** (-kwĭst), **so·lil'o·quiz'er** (-kwīz'ẽr), *n.* — **so·lil'o·quiz'ing·ly,** *adv.*

so·lil'o·quy (-kwĭ), *n.; pl.* -QUIES (-kwĭz). [LL. *soliloquium*, fr. *solus* alone + *loqui* to speak.] Act of talking to oneself; a discourse made by one in solitude to oneself; a monologue.

sol'ip·sism (sŏl'ĭp·sĭz'm), *n.* [L. *solus* alone + *ipse* self.] *Philos.* The theory or belief: **a** That the self knows and can know nothing but its own modifications and states. **b** That the self is the only existent thing. — **sol'ip·sist** (-sĭst), *n.*

sol'i·taire (sŏl'ĭ·târ; sŏl'ĭ·târ'), *n.* [F., fr. L. *solitarius.*] **1.** = SOLITARY, *n.* **2.** A single diamond, or other gem, set alone. **3.** A game which one person can play alone; — applied to many card games.

sol'i·tar'y (sŏl'ĭ·tĕr'ĭ *or, esp. Brit.,* -tẽr·ĭ, -trĭ), *adj.* [L. *solitarius*, fr. *solitas* solitude, fr. *solus* alone.] **1.** Being, living, or going alone or without companions; also, lonely. **2.** Taken, passed, performed, endured, etc., alone. **3.** Of places, unfrequented, desolate, or the like. **4.** Single; sole. **5.** *Bot.* Not associated with other individuals or organs of the same kind; as, a *solitary* pine or flower. **6.** *Zool.* Living habitually alone; not living in communities or colonies; as, *solitary* bees. — **Syn.** See ALONE: SINGLE. — *n.; pl.* -TARIES (-ĭz). One who lives or seeks to live a solitary life; a recluse; specif., a hermit. — **sol'i·tar'i·ly,** *adv.* — **sol'i·tar'i·ness,** *n.*

sol'i·tude (sŏl'ĭ·tūd), *n.* [OF., fr. L. *solitudo*, fr. *solus* alone.] **1.** State of being alone, or remote from society; loneliness; seclusion. **2.** A lonely place, as a desert.

Syn. **Solitude, isolation, seclusion** mean the state of one who is alone. **Solitude** may imply a condition of being apart from all human beings or of being cut off by wish or compulsion from one's neighbors, friends, or housemates; **isolation** stresses detachment from others, often, but not necessarily, because of circumstances beyond one's control; **seclusion**, a shutting away or keeping apart of oneself or another, often connoting confinement, withdrawal from the world, or retirement to a quiet life.

sol'ler·et (sŏl'ẽr·ĕt; sŏl'ẽr·ĕt'), *n.* [OF. *soleret*, dim. of *soler* shoe.] A flexible steel shoe. See ARMOR, *Illust.*

sol'mi·za'tion (sŏl'mĭ·zā'shŭn), *n.* [F. *solmisation*, fr. *solmiser* to sol-fa; — from the notes *sol, mi.*] *Music.* Act, practice, or system of using a set of syllables to denote the tones of a scale; sol-fa notation. See SOL-FA SYLLABLES.

so'lo (sō'lō), *n.; pl.* SOLOS (-lōz), SOLI (-lē). [It., lit., alone, fr. L *solus* alone.] **1.** An air, strain, or a whole piece, played or sung by a single person with or without accompaniment. **2.** Any performance in which the performer has no partner or associate, as a dance, flight in an airplane, etc. **3.** *Card Playing.* Any of a number of games in which one plays alone against the others or without a partner. — *adj.* Performing a solo; performed as a solo; alone. Specif.: *Music.* **a** Not arranged for several voices or instruments; as, a *solo* composition. **b** Performed by one voice or instrument; as, *solo* part or parts. — *adv.* Alone; as, to fly *solo.*

so'lo·ist (sō'lō·ĭst), *n.* One who performs a solo.

Sol'o·mon (sŏl'ō·mŭn), *n.* [From LL., fr. Gr. *Solomōn, Salōmōn*, fr. Heb. *Shĕlōmōh*, fr. *shālōm* peace.] *Bib.* Son of David and king of Israel and Judah in the 10th century B.C., noted for his wisdom, and reputed author of Proverbs, Canticles, Ecclesiastes, and Wisdom of Solomon; hence, a very wise man.

Sol'o·mon's seal (sŏl'ō·mŭnz). An emblem consisting of two triangles forming a six-pointed star, formerly used as an amulet, esp. to guard against fever.

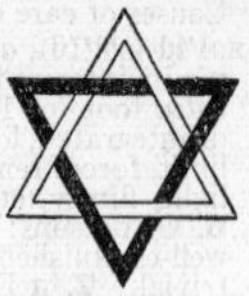

Solomon's Seal.

Sol'o·mon's-seal', *n.* Any of a genus (*Polygonatum*) of plants, of the lily-of-the-valley family, so called from the scars on the thick rootstock. See RHIZOME, *Illust.*

So'lon, so'lon (sō'lŏn; -lŭn), *n.* [From *Solon*, the Athenian lawgiver.] A legislator; wise man.

sol'stice (sŏl'stĭs), *n.* [OF., fr. L. *solstitium*, fr. *sol* sun + *sistere, statum*, to stand still, cause to stand.] **1.** *Astron.* **a** The point in the ecliptic at which the sun is farthest from the equator, north or south, namely: the first point of the sign Cancer and the first point of the sign Capricorn, the former being the ***summer solstice***, the latter the ***winter solstice***, in northern latitudes; — so called because the sun then apparently stands still in its northward or southward motion. **b** The time of the sun's passing the solstices, namely, about June 22 and December 22. **2.** Hence, furthest or highest point; limit.

sol·sti'tial (sŏl·stĭsh'ăl), *adj.* Of, or characteristic of, a solstice, esp. the summer solstice; happening, appearing, etc., at a solstice.

sol'u·bil'i·ty (sŏl'ū·bĭl'ĭ·tĭ), *n.; pl.* -TIES (-tĭz). **1.** Quality or state of being soluble. **2.** The amount of a substance which will dissolve in a given amount of another substance.

sol'u·ble (sŏl'ū·b'l), *adj.* [OF., fr. LL. *solubilis*, fr. *solvere, solutum*, to loosen, dissolve.] **1.** Susceptible of being dissolved; capable of passing into solution. **2.** That can be solved, as a problem; susceptible of being explained. — **sol'u·ble·ness**, *n.* — **sol'u·bly**, *adv.*

soluble glass. = WATER GLASS.

‖so'lus (sō'lŭs), *masc. adj.*, **so'la** (sō'lȧ), *fem.* [L.] Alone; — chiefly used in stage directions, etc.

sol'ute (sŏl'ūt; sō'lūt), *n.* A dissolved substance.

so·lu'tion (sō·lū'shŭn), *n.* [OF. *solucion*, fr. L. *solutio*, fr. *solvere, solutum*, to loosen, dissolve.] **1.** Act or process of solving a problem, etc., or the fact or state of its being solved; also, explanation; clearing up. **2.** A breaking; disruption; breach; — in phrases ***solution of continuity, connection***, or the like. **3.** The condition of being dissolved, or reduced to a liquid or held suspended in a solvent; also, a liquid containing a dissolved substance. **4.** *Math.* The process or result of solving, or finding the answer to, a problem; also, the answer. **5.** *Med.* **a** The termination of a disease; resolution. **b** A crisis. **c** A liquid medicine. **6.** *Physical Chem.* **a** The act or process by which a substance (solid, liquid, or gas) is homogeneously mixed with a liquid (or, by extension, a solid or gas) called the *solvent;* also, the state of being so mixed. **b** A homogeneous mixture (typically liquid) formed by the above process. In true solutions the molecules of the dissolved substance (called the *solute*) are dispersed among those of the solvent.

solv'a·ble (sŏl'vȧ·b'l), *adj.* Susceptible of solution, explanation, etc. — **solv'a·bil'i·ty** (-bĭl'ĭ·tĭ), *n.*

Sol'vay proc'ess (sŏl'vā). [After Ernest *Solvay* of Couillet, near Charleroi, Belgium, the inventor.] A process for making soda from common salt by passing carbon dioxide into ammoniacal brine. Sodium bicarbonate is precipitated, then converted into carbonate by calcining.

solve (sŏlv), *v. t.* [L. *solvere, solutum.*] **1.** To clear up (what is obscure or difficult); to explain; resolve; to find the solution of; as, to *solve* a mystery or problem. **2.** To pay (as a debt). — **solv'er**, *n.*

sol'ven·cy (sŏl'vĕn·sĭ), *n.; pl.* -CIES (-sĭz). Quality or state of being solvent.

sol'vent (sŏl'vĕnt), *adj.* [L. *solvens, -entis*, pres. part.] **1.** Able or sufficient to pay all legal debts. **2.** That dissolves or can dissolve; as, *solvent* fluids; the *solvent* action of water. — *n.* **1.** A substance (usually liquid) capable of, or used in, dissolving something. Cf. ALKAHEST. **2.** Something which solves; a solution.

so'ma (sō'mȧ), *n.* [NL., fr. Gr. *sōma* body.] *Anat. & Zool.* All of any organism except the germ cells.

-so'ma. [See SOMA.] A combining form meaning *body.*

So·ma'li (sō·mä'lē), *n.* **1.** One of a Hamitic race of Somaliland, many tribes of which are intermixed with Negro and Arab blood. **2.** The language of the Somalis.

so·mat'ic (sō·măt'ĭk), *adj.* [Gr. *sōmatikos*, fr. *sōma* the body.] **1.** Of, pert. to, or affecting the body; corporeal; physical. **2.** *Anat.* Of or pert. to the wall of the body, esp. as distinguished from the viscera; parietal. **3.** *Psychol.* Of or pertaining to the body, as distinguished from the mind, the brain, or the central nervous system. — **Syn.** See BODILY.

somatic cell. One of the cells of the body which become differentiated and compose the tissues, organs, and parts of that individual; — opp. to *germ cell.*

so·mat'ics (sō·măt'ĭks), *n.; see* -ICS. = SOMATOLOGY.

so'ma·to- (sō'mȧ·tō-), **somat-**. [Gr. *sōma, sōmatos.*] A combining form meaning *body*, as in *somatology.*

so'ma·tol'o·gy (-tŏl'ō·jĭ), *n.* [*somato-* + *-logy.*] **1.** The science of general properties of material substances. **2.** *Anthropol.* The comparative study of the structure, functions, and development of the human body. — **so'ma·to·log'ic** (-tō·lŏj'ĭk), **so'ma·to·log'i·cal** (-ĭ·kăl), *adj.* — **so'ma·tol'o·gist** (-tŏl'ō·jĭst), *n.*

so'ma·to·pleure' (sō'mȧ·tō·plo͝or'; 114), *n.* [*somato-* + Gr. *pleura* side.] *Embryol.* In the embryos of craniate vertebrates, the outer, or parietal, of the two layers into which the lateral part of the mesoblast splits. The somatopleure forms the body wall.

som'ber, som'bre (sŏm'bẽr), *adj.* [F. *sombre.*] **1.** So shaded as to be dark and gloomy; as, a *somber* forest, sky. **2.** Melancholy; grave; depressing. — **som'ber·ly, som'bre·ly**, *adv.* — **som'ber·ness, som'bre·ness**, *n.*

som·bre'ro (sŏm·brâr'ō), *n.; pl.* -ROS (-ōz). [Sp., fr. *sombra* shade.] A form of broad-brimmed hat, usually of felt, orig. worn in Spain and in Spanish America.

som'brous (sŏm'brŭs), *adj.* Somber.

some (sŭm; 4), *adj.* [AS. *sum.*] **1.** A certain; one; now, always, a certain unknown or unspecified; as, *some* person knocked. **2.** That is of an unspecified but appreciable or not inconsiderable quantity, amount, extent, degree, etc. **3.** Being one, a part, or an unspecified number of the class, group, etc., named or implied; as, *some* gems are hard. **4.** About; more or less; as, *some* two or three persons. **5.** *Slang, U.S.* That is important, striking, etc.; as, that was *some* party. — *pron.* **1.** Some one; a certain person or thing among a number. **2.** A certain (indefinite) quantity, portion, or number, as distinguished from the rest.

-some (-sŭm). **a** [AS. *-sum.*] An adjective suffix having primarily the sense of *like* or *same*, and indicating a considerable degree of the thing or quality denoted in the first part of the compound. **b** [AS. *sum.* See SOME.] A noun suffix used with numerals and denoting *together, in all*, as in four*some.*

-some (-sōm). [Gr. *sōma.*] Combining form meaning *body*, as in **cen'tro·some, chro'mo·some.**

some'bod'y (sŭm'bŏd'ĭ; -bŭd·ĭ), *pron.* One or some person of no certain or known identity; as, *somebody* else's (formerly *somebody's* else) business.

some'bod'y, *n.; pl.* -BODIES (-ĭz). A person of position or importance; as, to think oneself a *somebody.*

some'deal' (-dēl'), *adv. Archaic.* In some measure; somewhat.

some'how (-hou), *adv.* In one way or another; in some way not yet known or designated; by some means.

some'one' (sŭm'wŭn'), *pron.* Some person; somebody. — *n.* A somebody.

som'er·sault (sŭm'ẽr·sôlt), *n.* [OF. *sombresault*, through Pr. fr. L. *supra* above + *saltus* a leap.] A leap or jump in which a person turns his heels over his head. — *v. i.* To turn a somersault.

som'er·set (-sĕt), *n. & v. i. & t.* Somersault.

some'thing (sŭm'thĭng), *n.* **1.** Some thing undetermined, or not definitely understood or remembered. **2.** Some thing definite but not specified; — opposed to *nothing;* as, *something* to live for. **3.** A person of consequence; a somebody. — *adv. Colloq.* In some degree; somewhat.

some'time' (-tīm'), *adv.* **1.** *Archaic.* At some past time; once; formerly. **2.** *Rare.* Sometimes; occasionally. **3.** At one time or other in the future. **4.** At some not specified or definitely known time. — *adj.* Having been formerly; former; as, a *sometime* professor of English.

some'times' (-tīmz'; 2), *adv.* **1.** At times; now and then; occasionally. **2.** *Obs.* = SOMETIME, *adv.*, 1.

some'way' (sŭm'wā'), *adv.* Also **some way, some'ways'** (-wāz'). *Colloq.* In some way; somehow.

some'what' (sŭm'hwŏt'), *n.* **1.** An indefinite or unspecified amount or degree; a part, more or less. **2.** Some unspecified or indeterminate thing; something. **3.** An important or noteworthy person or thing. — *adv.* In some degree or measure; a little; as, he is *somewhat* changed.

some'when' (-hwĕn'), *adv.* Sometime.

some'where' (-hwâr'), *adv.* In or to some place unknown or not specified; in one place or another. — *n.* An undetermined or unnamed place.

some'whith'er (-hwĭth'ẽr), *adv.* To some place; in some direction or other.

some'why' (-hwī'), *adv.* For some reason or another.

some'wise' (-wīz'), *adv.* Someway. *Obs.*, except in the phrase *in somewise.*

so'mite (sō'mīt), *n.* [Gr. *sōma* body.] *Anat. & Zool.* One of the longitudinal series of segments into which the body of many animals is divided. — **so·mit'ic** (sō·mĭt'ĭk), *adj.*

som·nam'bu·late (sŏm·năm'bū·lāt), *v. i. & t.* [L. *somnus* sleep + *ambulare, ambulatum*, to walk.] To walk when asleep. — **som·nam'bu·lant** (-lănt), *adj.* — **som·nam'bu·la'tion** (-lā'shŭn), *n.* — **som·nam'bu·la'tor** (-lā'tẽr), *n.*

som·nam'bu·lism (-lĭz'm), *n.* A sleep or sleeplike state in which walking and other acts are performed; also, the actions characteristic of this state. — **som·nam'bu·list** (-lĭst), *n.* — **som·nam'bu·lis'tic** (-lĭs'tĭk), *adj.*

som'ni·fa'cient (sŏm'nĭ·fā'shĕnt), *adj.* [L. *somnus* sleep + *faciens, -entis*, pres. part. of *facere* to make.] Sleep-producing. — *n.* A sleep-producing drug; a hypnotic or soporific.

som·nif'er·ous (sŏm·nĭf'ẽr·ŭs), *adj.* [L. *somnifer*, fr. *somnus* sleep + *ferre* to bring.] Sleep-inducing; soporific.

som·nif'ic (sŏm·nĭf'ĭk), *adj.* [L. *somnificus.*] Somniferous.

som'no·lence (sŏm'nō·lĕns), *n.* Also **som'no·len·cy** (-lĕn·sĭ). Sleepiness; drowsiness.

som'no·lent (-lĕnt), *adj.* [F., fr. L. *somnolentus*, fr. *somnus* sleep.] Sleepy; drowsy; inclined to sleep. — **som'no·lent·ly**, *adv.*

son (sŭn), *n.* [AS. *sunu.*] **1.** A human male considered with reference to his parents or either of them. **2.** **a** A male descendant; in *pl.*, descendants in general. **b** A son-in-law. **c** An adopted male child; a foster son. **3.** [*cap.*] Jesus Christ, esp. as the second person of the Trinity; as, Father, *Son*, and Holy Ghost. **4.** Any male person considered with reference to his source, origin, native country, etc.

so'nance (sō'năns), *n.* **1.** A sound; a tune. **2.** Quality or state of being sonant.

so'nant (-nănt), *adj.* [L. *sonans, -antis*, pres. part. of *sonare.*] **1.** Of or pertaining to sound; sounding. **2.** *Phonet.* Of speech sounds, voiced; intonated; tonic; vocal; — opposed to *surd, voiceless, breathed, atonic.* — *n. Phonet.* A sonant sound or its symbol.

so'nar (sō'när), *n.* [*sound navigation ranging.*] An apparatus that detects the presence and location of submarines, underwater mines, or the like, by means of inaudible high-frequency vibrations which are reflected back to it from the objects; — called *asdic* by the British.

so·na'ta (sō·nä'tȧ), *n.* [It., fr. It. & L. *sonare* to sound.] *Music.* A composition for one or two instruments, usually in three or four movements contrasted in rhythm and mood but related in tonality and having unity of sentiment and style.

sonata form. The form of a sonata, specif., of the first movement consisting of: (1) the ***exposition***, in which the principal and secondary subjects are presented; (2) the ***development***, in which one or both subjects are worked out or developed; (3) the ***recapitulation***, in which both subjects are repeated followed by a coda.

son'a·ti'na (sŏn'ȧ·tē'nȧ; *It.* sō·nä·tē'nä), *n.; pl.* -NAS (-nȧz), *It.* -NE (-nā). [It.] *Music.* A short or simplified sonata.

son'der·class' (zŏn'dẽr·klȧs'; 9), *n.* [G. *sonderklasse* special class.] *Yachting.* A class of yachts (**sonder**, *or* **sonder yacht**), small in size, the total of water-line length, width of beam, and draft not being over thirty-two feet.

song (sŏng; 74), *n.* [AS. *song, sang.*] **1.** The act, practice, or art of singing; also, that which is sung. **2.** Poetical composition; poetry;

verse. **3.** Specif., a lyrical poem or ballad, esp. one adapted to being set to music. **4.** A trifle; a pittance; as, to buy a rug for a *song*. **5.** *Music.* A melody or musical setting for a lyric poem or ballad.
song′bird′ (sŏng′bûrd′), *n.* A bird that utters a succession of musical notes; also, a person, esp. a woman, who sings like a songbird.
song′ful (-fo͝ol; -f'l), *adj.* Disposed to sing; melodious.
Song of Solomon, The. Also **Song of Songs.** *Bib.* A Hebrew poem, partly dramatic, partly lyrical, traditionally ascribed to Solomon. It is also known as the ***Canticles*** or, in Douay Bible, the ***Canticle of Canticles.*** See BIBLE.
Song of the Three Children. A part of the Old Testament Apocrypha. See BIBLE.
song sparrow. See SPARROW, 2.
song′ster (sŏng′stẽr; 74), *n.* [AS. *sangestre*, fem.] **1.** One who sings or is skilled in singing. **2.** A songbird. — **song′stress** (-strĕs; -strĭs), *n.*
son′ic (sŏn′ĭk), *adj.* [L. *sonus* sound + *-ic.*] **1.** Of, pertaining to, or utilizing sound waves; as, a *sonic* altimeter. **2.** Of, pertaining to, or designating the speed of sound in air, that is, about 1087 feet per second (or about 738 miles per hour).
sonic barrier. The sudden large increase in aerodynamic drag that occurs as the speed of an aircraft approaches the speed of sound.
sonic depth finder. An instrument for determining the depth of water, as of the ocean, by means of sound waves produced by the instrument and reflected from the bottom back to the instrument.
son′-in-law′, *n.; pl.* SONS-IN-LAW. The husband of one's daughter; a man in his relationship to his wife's parents.
son′net (sŏn′ĕt; -ĭt), *n.* [F., fr. It. *sonetto*, fr. OF. & Pr. *sonet* a little song, dim. of *son* song, music.] A fixed verse form of Italian origin, consisting of fourteen lines, typically five-foot iambics, and treating, usually, a single emotion, sentiment, or reflection. Two standard types of sonnets, varying in verse groupings and rhyming schemes, are recognized: **a** The ***Italian sonnet***, also called the ***Petrarchan, or regular, sonnet***, in which the lines are grouped into an octave of two quatrains running on two rhymes (thus, *abba, abba*) and a sestet of two tercets on two or three rhymes, having more freedom of arrangement, but commonly running *cdc, dcd*, or *cde, cde*. **b** The ***English, Elizabethan, or Shakespearean, sonnet***, in which the lines are grouped into three quatrains and a couplet, with rhyme scheme *abab, cdcd, efef, gg*. The ***Spenserian sonnet*** unites the quatrains by interlacing the rhymes: *abab, bcbc, cdcd, ee*. — *v. i. & t.* To compose sonnets; to celebrate in sonnets.
son′net·eer′ (sŏn′ĕ·tēr′; -ĭ·tēr′), *n.* A composer of sonnets. — *v. t. & i.* To sonnet.
son′ny (sŭn′ĭ), *n.* Diminutive of SON; — used familiarly as in addressing a boy.
so·nom′e·ter (sō·nŏm′ē·tẽr), *n.* [L. *sonus* a sound + *-meter.*] = AUDIOMETER.
so·nor′i·ty (sō·nŏr′ĭ·tĭ), *n.; pl.* -TIES (-tĭz). Quality or state of being sonorous; sonorousness; resonance.
so·no′rous (sō·nō′rŭs; *Brit. also* sŏn′ō·rŭs), *adj.* [L. *sonorus*, fr. *sonor, -oris*, a sound.] **1.** Giving sound, as when struck; resonant. **2.** Loud or full in sound; richly resonant. **3.** High-sounding; impressive. — **so·no′rous·ly**, *adv.* — **so·no′rous·ness**, *n.*
-sonous. [L. *sonus* a sound.] A combining form denoting *sounding*, as in multi*sonous*.
son′ship (sŭn′shĭp), *n.* State or relation of being a son.
son′sy, son′sie (sŏn′sĭ), *adj.* [From Gael. & Ir. *sonas* prosperity, health.] *Scot., Ir., & Dial. Eng.* **a** Lucky. **b** Buxom; comely. **c** Good-natured. **d** Comfortable; also, plentiful.
soom (so͞om). *Scot. & N. of Eng.* var. of SWIM.
soon (so͞on; 85), *adv.* [AS. *sōna.*] **1.** At once; without delay. **2.** With reference to an implied time or the present, shortly after; also, shortly; in a short time. **3.** Promptly; speedily; quickly. **4.** Before the usual time; early. **5.** Readily, willingly.
soon′er (-ẽr), *n.* **1.** *Slang, U. S.* In the western U. S., one who settles on government land before it is legally open to settlement in order to gain the prior claim that the law gives to the first settler when the land is opened to settlement; hence, one who does a thing prematurely, in order to get an unfair advantage. **2.** [*cap.*] *U. S.* A native or inhabitant of Oklahoma, the **Sooner State**; — a nickname.
soot (so͝ot; so͞ot), *n.* [AS. *sōt.*] A black substance formed by combustion, or disengaged from fuel in combustion, adhering to the sides of the chimney or pipe conveying the smoke; strictly, the fine powder, chiefly of carbon, which colors smoke. — *v. t.* To coat or cover with soot.
sooth (so͞oth), *adj.* [AS. *sōth.*] **1.** *Archaic.* True; real. **2.** *Poetic.* Soothing; sweet; soft. — *n. Archaic.* Truth; reality. — **-ly**, *adv.*
soothe (so͞oth), *v. t.* [AS. *sōthian.*] **1.** *Obs.* To humor by complying. **2.** To please (one) as by approval, flattery, etc.; gratify by humoring, cajoling, etc. **3.** To still; assuage; mitigate. — *v. i.* To exert a pacifying or tranquilizing influence. — **sooth′er** (so͞oth′ẽr), *n.*
sooth′fast′ (so͞oth′făst′), *adj.* [AS. *sōthfæst*, prop., fast or firm with respect to truth.] *Archaic.* True; genuine; also, truthful; honest; faithful. — **sooth′fast′ly**, *adv.* — **sooth′fast′ness**, *n.*
sooth′ing (so͞oth′ĭng), *adj.* Calming; also, having a sedative effect, as, *soothing* sirup. — **sooth′ing·ly**, *adv.*
sooth′say′ (so͞oth′sā′), *v. i.* To foretell.
sooth′say′er (-sā′ẽr), *n. Hist.* One who foretells events.
sooth′say′ing, *n.* **1.** Art or practice of making predictions. **2.** *Hist.* A prediction; prophecy.
soot′y (so͝ot′ĭ; so͞ot′ĭ), *adj.;* SOOT′I·ER (-ĭ·ẽr); SOOT′I·EST. **1.** Of, pert. to, or providing soot; soiled with soot; blackened. **2.** Soot-colored; brownish-black. — **soot′i·ness**, *n.*
sop (sŏp), *v. t.;* SOPPED (sŏpt); SOP′PING. [AS. *soppian.*] **1.** To steep or dip in, or as if in, a liquid. **2.** To soak; wet; also, to mop (*up*), as water. — *v. i.* To ooze through or percolate; to soak in. — *n.* [AS. *sopp;* akin to E. SUP to sip.] **1.** *Now Dial.* Any food steeped or dipped in liquid; esp., a piece of bread, toast, etc., dipped in water, milk, gravy, or the like. **2.** A conciliatory bribe, gift, etc.
soph (sŏf), *n.* A sophomore.
soph′ism (sŏf′ĭz'm), *n.* [OF. *soffime, sophisme*, fr. L., fr. Gr. *sophisma*, deriv. of *sophos* wise.] **1.** An argument, esp. a formal one, intended to deceive; also, an argument embodying a subtle fallacy, but not intended as a deception. **2.** Specious reasoning; sophistry.
Soph′ist (-ĭst), *n.* **1.** One of a class of teachers of rhetoric, philosophy, and the art of successful living, in ancient Greece, who became prominent about the middle of the 5th century B.C. They were often adroit and specious in their reasoning. **2.** [*not cap.*] A thinker; philosopher; now, usually, a captious or fallacious reasoner. — **Soph′ist, soph′ist**, *adj.*
soph′ist·er (-ĭs·tẽr), *n.* **1.** A Sophist or sophist. **2.** At Oxford and Cambridge Universities, a student in his second (***junior sophister***) or third (***senior sophister***) year of residence.
so·phis′tic (sō·fĭs′tĭk), **so·phis′ti·cal** (-tĭ·kăl), *adj.* Of or pertaining to sophists, a Sophist, or sophistry; also, of the nature of a sophism. — **so·phis′ti·cal·ly**, *adv.* — **so·phis′ti·cal·ness**, *n.*
so·phis′ti·cate (-tĭ·kāt), *v. t.* [ML. *sophisticatus*, past part. of *sophisticare* to sophisticate.] To deprive of genuineness, naturalness, or simplicity; to disillusion; to make worldly-wise. — *n.* A sophisticated person.
so·phis′ti·cat′ed (sō·fĭs′tĭ·kāt′ĕd; -ĭd), *adj.* Also **so·phis′ti·cate** (-kāt). Deprived of original simplicity; made artificial, or, more narrowly, highly complicated, refined, subtilized, etc.; of persons, made wise, esp. worldly-wise, through experience, disillusionment, or the like; hence, of such a character as to appeal to worldly-wise persons; as, *sophisticated* novels.
so·phis′ti·ca′tion (-kā′shŭn), *n.* **1.** Sophistry; sophistical reasoning. **2.** Act or process of sophisticating, or state of being sophisticated; specif., quality or character of being intellectually sophisticated, as through experience.
soph′ist·ry (sŏf′ĭs·trĭ), *n.; pl.* -RIES (-trĭz). **1.** Sophistical or deceptively subtle reasoning or argumentation. **2.** A sophistical argument; a sophism.
soph′o·more (sŏf′ō·mōr; 70), *n.* [(After Gr. *sophos* wise, and *mōros* fool, foolish), fr. earlier *sophomer, sophumer*, a second-year student, fr. *sophom, sophum*, obs. vars. of SOPHISM.] **1.** A student in the second year of a four-year college course; one next above a freshman. **2.** *Local, U. S.* A second-year student in a high school.
soph′o·mor′ic (-mŏr′ĭk), *adj.* Of, pertaining to, resembling, or characteristic of a sophomore; hence, immature; shallow; bombastic; superficial.
Soph′o·ni′as (sŏf′ō·nī′ăs), *n. Douay Bib.* Zephaniah. See BIBLE.
So′phy (sō′fĭ; sŏf′ĭ), *n.* Also **So′phi.** [Per. (fr. Ar.) *Safawi*, a Persian dynasty.] *Archaic.* A former title of kings of Persia.
-sophy. [Gr. *sophia* skill, knowledge.] A combining form denoting *knowledge pertaining to a* (specified) *field.*
so′por (sō′pẽr; -pôr), *n.* [L.] Profound sleep; stupor.
so′po·rif′er·ous (sō′pō·rĭf′ẽr·ŭs; sŏp′ō-), *adj.* [L. *soporifer*, fr. *sopor* a heavy sleep + *ferre* to bring.] Soporific.
so′po·rif′ic (-rĭf′ĭk), *adj.* [L. *sopor* a heavy sleep + *facere* to make.] **1.** Causing, or tending to cause, sleep. **2.** Of or characterized by sleepiness or lethargy; as, *soporific* symptoms. — *n.* A sleep-inducing drug.
sop′ping (sŏp′ĭng), *adj.* Wet through; soaking.
sop′py (sŏp′ĭ), *adj.;* SOP′PI·ER (-ĭ·ẽr); SOP′PI·EST. **1.** Soaked or saturated; very wet or sloppy. **2.** *Slang, Brit.* Foolishly or extravagantly sentimental.
so·pran′o (sō·prăn′ō; -prä′nō), *n.; pl.* -OS (-ōz), -I (-ē). [It., fr. *soprano* superior, highest, fr. *sopra* above, fr. L. *supra.*] *Music.* **a** The treble; the highest quality of voice, typically covering two octaves or more up from middle C. **b** A part for such a voice. **c** A singer, esp. a woman, with a treble voice. Cf. COLORATURA SOPRANO, MEZZO-SOPRANO. — *adj.* Of or pert. to the soprano (voice or part); having a high or treble range.
so′ra (sō′rȧ; 70), *n., or* **sora rail.** A small short-billed North American rail (*Porzana carolina*).
sorb (sôrb), *n.* [F. *sorbe*, the fruit, fr. L. *sorbum*, the fruit, *sorbus*, the tree.] **a** Any of various European trees of the apple family, as the service tree. **b** The fruit of any tree so called. Cf. SORB APPLE.
Sorb, *n.* [G. *Sorbe*, of Slav. origin.] One of a Slavic people whose present representatives are the Wends living in Saxony and Brandenburg.
sorb apple. The fruit of the service tree.
Sor′bi·an (sôr′bĭ·ăn), *adj.* Of or pertaining to the Sorbs or their language. — *n.* **a** A Sorb. **b** The Slavic language of the Sorbs; Wendish. See INDO-EUROPEAN LANGUAGES, *Table.*
Sor′bon·ist (sôr′bŏn·ĭst), *n.* [F. *sorboniste.*] A doctor of, or student at, the Sorbonne.
Sor·bonne′ (sôr·bŏn′), *n.* [F.] **a** Orig., a house founded at Paris in 1257 by Robert de Sorbon, chaplain of Louis IX, for the society of poor theological students established by him. **b** Later, the faculty of theology, suppressed in 1792. **c** Now, the seat of the courses of the faculties of science and letters of the University of Paris.
sor′cer·er (sôr′sẽr·ẽr), *n.* One who practices sorcery; a wizard. — **sor′cer·ess** (-ĕs; -ĭs), *n.*
sor′cer·y (-ĭ), *n.; pl.* -CERIES (-ĭz). [OF. *sorcerie*, fr. *sorcier* a sorcerer, fr. L. *sors, sortis*, a lot, fate, destiny.] The use of power gained from the assistance or control of evil spirits, esp. for divining; necromancy; witchcraft. — **sor′cer·ous** (-ŭs), *adj.*
sor′did (sôr′dĭd), *adj.* [F. *sordide*, fr. L. *sordidus;* akin to L. *sordere* to be dirty.] **1.** Filthy; dirty. **2.** Vile; base; gross; despicable. **3.** Meanly avaricious; covetous; niggardly. **4.** *Bot. & Zool.* Of a dirty or muddy color. — **Syn.** See MEAN. — **sor′did·ly**, *adv.* — **sor′did·ness**, *n.*
sor·di′no (sôr·dē′nō), *n.; pl.* -NI (-nē). [It.] *Music.* = MUTE, *n.*, 2.
sore (sōr; 70), *adj.* [AS. *sār.*] **1.** Distressing; painful; grievous; extremely unpleasant. **2.** Sensitive to pain from pressure; tender; inflamed or ulcerated. **3.** Temperamentally sensitive; easily grieved or irritated. **4.** *Colloq.* Offended; disgruntled. — *n.* **1.** A place where the skin and flesh are ruptured or bruised, so as to be tender or painful; an ulcer or a boil. **2.** A source of pain or vexation; an affliction. — *adv. Archaic.* Sorely. — **sore′ly**, *adv.* — **sore′ness**, *n.*
sore′head′ (sōr′hĕd′), *n. Colloq., U. S.* A disgruntled person; sometimes, specif., a politician disgruntled because of failure of election or appointment. — **sore′head′**, *adj.*
sor′ghum (sôr′gŭm), *n.* [NL., also *sorgum*, fr. It. *sorgo.*] **1.** Any of a genus (*Sorghum*) of tropical cereal grasses, one species of which (*S. vulgare*) is especially cultivated for fodder, grain, or for sirup. Certain varieties grown for forage or for their sweet juices are known as **sor′go** (sôr′gō), and also as ***sweet, saccharine, or sugar sorghum.*** **2.** Sirup from the juice of any sorgo, resembling cane sirup but containing much invert sugar.
so′ri (sō′rī), *n., pl.* of SORUS.
sor′i·cine (sŏr′ĭ·sīn; -sĭn; sō′rĭ-; 70), *adj.* [L. *soricinus*, fr. *sorex, soricis*, a shrew.] Belonging to a subfamily (Soricinae) typical of a family (Soricidae) of mouselike mammals, the shrews; hence, shrewlike.

so·ri'tes (sṓ-rī'tēz), n. [L., fr. Gr. *sōreítēs* (sc. *syllogismos*), prop., heaped up (hence, a heap of syllogisms), fr. *sōros* a heap.] *Logic*. An abridged series of syllogisms in a series of propositions so arranged that the predicate of the first is the subject of the second, and so on, the conclusion uniting the subject of the first proposition with the predicate of the last. — **so·rit'i·cal** (sṓ-rĭt'ĭ-kăl), *adj*.

sorn (sôrn), *v. i. Scot*. To impose (on another) for bed and board; beg.

so·rop'ti·mist (sṓ-rŏp'tĭ-mĭst), n. [See SORORITY; OPTIMIST.] A member of a **Soroptimist Club**, one of an international Association of Soroptimist Clubs, composed of professional and executive business-women associated primarily for service.

so'ror·ate (sō'rŏr-āt), n. [L. *soror* sister.] The marriage of one man with two or more sisters, usually successively, after the first wife has been found to be barren or after her death. Cf. LEVIRATE.

so·ror'i·cide (sṓ-rŏr'ĭ-sīd), n. [LL. *sororicidium*; L. *sororicida*. See SISTER; -CIDE.] Act of one who kills his own sister; one who commits such an act. Cf. FRATRICIDE.

so·ror'i·ty (-ĭ-tĭ), n.; pl. -TIES (-tĭz). [L. *soror* sister.] A club of girls or women, as in a college.

so·ro'sis (sṓ-rō'sĭs), n. 1. [NL., fr. Gr. *sōros* a heap.] *Bot*. A collective fruit formed by the union of many flowers into a fleshy or pulpy mass, as in the mulberry and pineapple. 2. [Irreg. fr. L. *soror* sister.] *U. S.* A women's club.

'sorp'tion (sôrp'shŭn), n. *Physical Chem*. Process of taking up and holding either by adsorption or absorption.

sor'rel, n. [OF. *surele*, fr. *sur* sour.] *Bot*. Any of various plants having sour juice; as: **a** A plant of the genus *Rumex*, esp. the common sorrel (*R. acetosa*), and the *sheep sorrel* (*R. acetosella*) of dry places, with pleasant acid-tasting leaves. **b** = WOOD SORREL a.

sor'rel, n. [OF. *sorel*, dim. of *sor* sorrel.] 1. A brown, red-yellow in hue, of medium saturation and medium brilliance. See COLOR. 2. An animal of a sorrel color, as a horse; specif., a male fallow deer in its third year. See FALLOW DEER. — **sor'rel**, *adj*.

sorrel tree. A small tree (*Oxydendrum arboreum*) of the heath family, with white flowers and sour evergreen leaves.

sor'row (sŏr'ō; 74), n. [AS. *sorg, sorh*. Not akin to SORRY.] 1. Suffering or sadness arising from loss, disappointment, etc. 2. Contrition; penitence. 3. A cause of grief or sadness; a trouble; affliction. **Syn.** Sorrow, grief, anguish, woe, regret mean distress of mind. Sorrow implies a sense of one's own or another's loss or a sense of guilt; grief, a poignant sorrow for some definite cause; anguish, excruciating or torturing grief or dread; woe, deep or inconsolable grief or misery; regret, a pain of mind caused by deep disappointment, fruitless longing, or the like.

— *v. i.* To feel sorrow; to grieve. — **sor'row·er**, n.

sor'row·ful (-fŏŏl; -f'l), *adj*. Full of, expressive of, characterized by, or inducing sorrow. — **sor'row·ful·ly**, *adv*. — **sor'row·ful·ness**, n.

sor'ry (sŏr'ĭ; 74), *adj.*; sor'ri·er (-ĭ-ẽr); sor'ri·est. [AS. *sārig* sad, fr. *sār*, n., sore, grief, pain. Not akin to SORROW.] 1. Causing sorrow; grievous. 2. Grieved for a loss, a mistake, a sin, etc.; feeling sorrow, regret, or penitence. 3. Melancholy; dismal; gloomy; mournful. 4. Poor; mean; pitiful; contemptible. — **Syn.** See CONTEMPTIBLE. — **sor'ri·ly**, *adv*. — **sor'ri·ness**, n.

sort (sôrt), n. [OF., fr. L. *sors, sortis*.] *Obs*. A lot; hence, fate; destiny; also, divination by lot.

sort, n. [OF. *sorte*, fr. L. *sors, sortis*, a lot, part.] 1. A group having the same or similar characteristics; a kind, class, order, or species. 2. Way; fashion; manner. 3. Character; quality; nature; as, people of evil *sort*. 4. *Print*. Any character or type considered as a separate element in a font; — usually in *pl*. — **Syn**. See TYPE. — *of a sort*, *of sorts*. Of a different kind, or kinds; now, usually disparagingly, of a rather poor kind, or kinds. — *out of sorts*. **a** *Print*. With some sorts of type deficient or exhausted. **b** *Colloq*. Out of order; ill; disturbed. — *v. t.* 1. To put in a certain place or rank according to kind, class, sort, etc.; to classify. 2. *Obs. exc. Dial*. To put to rights; adjust. 3. *Scot*. To punish; as by scolding or beating. — **Syn**. See ASSORT. — *v. i.* 1. To consort. 2. To suit; harmonize. — **sort'a·ble**, *adj*. — **sort'er**, n.

sor'tie (sôr'tē), n. [F., fr. *sortir* to go out.] 1. A sally of troops from a besieged place against the besiegers. 2. *Mil. Aviation*. One mission or attack by a single plane.

sor'ti·lege (sôr'tĭ-lĕj; -lĭj), n. [OF., fr. ML. *sortilegium*, fr. L. *sortilegus* foretelling, as n., a soothsayer, fr. L. *sors, sortis*, a lot + *legere* to gather.] Divination by lots; hence, sorcery; witchery; enchantment.

so'rus (sō'rŭs), n.; pl. SORI (-rī). [NL., fr. Gr. *sōros* a heap.] *Bot*. A cluster of spores, sporangia, or analogous reproductive bodies, as the so-called *fruit dots* on fern fronds, the spots or pustules of fungus spores on a host, or a cluster of reproductive gemmae on a lichen thallus.

SOS (ĕs'ō'ĕs'). The letters of the distress signal (- - - - - - - - -) prescribed by the International Radiotelegraphic Convention of 1912 for use by ships, airships, etc.

☞ *SOS* is a code signal only, and not an abbreviation.

so'so' (sō'sō'), *adj*. Also **so'-so'**, **so so**. *Colloq*. Neither very good nor very bad; middling; passable.

so'-so', *adv*. Also so so. Tolerably; passably.

so·ste·nu'to (sŏs-tā·nōō'tō; *Angl.* sŏs'tĕ·nōō'tō), *adj*. [It.] *Music*. Sustained; — applied esp. to a movement or passage the tones of which are to be sustained to their full nominal value, or to a passage the tones of which are to be somewhat prolonged. — n. A sostenuto movement or passage.

sot (sŏt), n. [OF., fool, fr. ML. *sottus*.] A person besotted by excessive drinking; a habitual drunkard.

so·te·ri·ol'o·gy (sṓ-tē·rĭ-ŏl'ō-jĭ), n. [Gr. *sōtēria* safety + -*logy*.] Theology dealing with salvation as effected by Jesus Christ. — **so·te'ri·o·log'ic** (-ō-lŏj'ĭk), **so·te'ri·o·log'i·cal** (-ĭ-kăl), *adj*.

So'thic (sō'thĭk; sŏth'ĭk), *adj*. Also **So'thi·ac** (sō'thĭ-ăk). [Gr. *Sōthiakos*, fr. *Sōthis* the Dog Star, fr. Egypt. *Septit*.] Of, pertaining to, or named from **So'this** (sō'thĭs), or Sirius, the Dog Star.

Sothic cycle or period. *Astron*. A cycle of 1460 Sothic years in the Egyptian calendar. The **Sothic year** had 365 days and 6 hours.

so'tol (sō'tŏl; sō-tōl'), n. [Sp. *sotol, zotol*, fr. Nahuatl *tzotolli*.] Any yuccalike plant (genus *Dasylirion*, esp. *D. texanum*, *D. wheeleri*, etc.) of the southwestern United States.

sot'ted (sŏt'ĕd; -ĭd), *adj*. Besotted.

sot'tish (sŏt'ĭsh), *adj*. Like a sot; doltish; also, drunken. — **sot'tish·ly**, *adv*. — **sot'tish·ness**, n.

‖sot'to vo'ce (sŏt'ō vō'chā; sôt'ō vō'chā). [It.] Under the breath; in an undertone; hence, privately; as an objection uttered *sotto voce*.

sou (sōō), n.; pl. SOUS (sōōz; F. sōō). [F., fr. L. *solidus* a gold coin.] 1. = 3d SOL. 2. *France*. Popularly, the prewar bronze 5-centime piece, equivalent to ½₀ franc.

sou·a'ri nut (sōō-ä'rē). [F. *saouari, sawarri*.] The edible nutlike seed of a South American tree (genus *Caryocar*, typical of the family Caryocaraceae, the souari-nut family), esp. of *C. nuciferum*.

sou'bise' (sōō-bēz'), n. [F.] A white or brown sauce containing onions; — called also **soubise sauce**.

sou·brette' (sōō-brĕt'), n. [F., fr. Pr. *soubreto*, fem. of *soubret* affected, coy.] *Theater*. Originally, in comedies, an intriguing lady's maid; hence, a coquettish maidservant or frivolous young woman, or the actress playing such a part. — **sou·bret'tish** (-brĕt'ĭsh), *adj*.

sou'bri·quet (sōō'brĭ-kā). Var. of SOBRIQUET.

sou·car', sow·car' (sou-kär'), n. [Hind. *sāhūkār*, fr. Skr. *sādhu* straight.] *Anglo-Ind*. A native banker.

Sou'chong' (sōō'shŏng'; *Chin.* -chŏng'), n. [Chin. (Pek.) *hsiao²-chung²* small or fine sort.] [*sometimes not cap*.] A black tea (see TEA, 1 b) from China.

‖souf·flé' (sōō'flā'; sōō'flā), *adj*. [F., lit., puffed.] Puffed by or in cooking, as omelet, crackers, or sliced potato; — also Anglicized as **souf·fléed'** (-flād'; -flād). — *n*. A delicate spongy hot dish, made from a sweet or savory mixture, lightened by stiffly beaten whites of eggs.

souf'fle (sōō'f'l), n. [F.] *Med*. A murmuring or blowing sound heard on auscultation.

sough (sŭf; sou), n. [AS. *swōgan* to sound.] 1. A hollow moaning; a murmuring, sighing sound, as of the wind. 2. *Scot. & Ir.* **a** A vague or flying rumor. **b** A whiz or whistle, as of a missile. 3. *Scot.* A singsong tone. — *v. i.* 1. To make a sough; sigh; as, the wind *soughing* through the trees. 2. *Scot.* To preach or pray in a singsong tone.

sought (sôt), *past & past part.* of SEEK.

soul (sōl), n. [AS. *sāwel, sāwl*.] 1. An entity conceived as the essence, substance, animating principle, or actuating cause of life, or of the individual life, esp. of individual life manifested in thinking, willing, and knowing. In many religions it is regarded as immortal and separable from the body at death. 2. The physical or spiritual principle in general, esp. as informing the universe. 3. Man's moral and emotional nature, esp. as manifested in or communicated by what he writes, composes, etc. 4. The seat of real life, vitality, or action. 5. The leader; moving spirit; also, the embodiment. 6. Courage; spirit; fervor; spiritual force. 7. A person; as, a kind *soul*. 8. A disembodied spirit. 9. [*cap*.] *Christian Science*. A synonym for God. **Syn.** Soul, spirit, as here compared, mean an immaterial entity distinguishable from and superior to the body. **Soul** is the preferred term when the connection with the body is in mind, or its functions, responsibilities, or special qualities are suggested; **spirit**, when an opposition to that which is material, corporeal, etc., is in mind, and its movement, activity, or the like, is suggested; as, to save one's *soul*; to lift up one's *spirit* in prayer.

soul'ful (-fŏŏl; -f'l), *adj*. Full of, or expressing, deep feeling. — **soul'ful·ly**, *adv*.

soul'less (-lĕs; -lĭs), *adj*. Having no soul, or no greatness or nobleness of mind or feeling. — **soul'less·ly**, *adv*.

sou mar·qué' (sōō' mär'kā'). [F.] **a** An 18th-century minor coin of base metal, orig. issued for use in France but later restruck for the colonies. **b** *U. S.* (*pron.* mär'kē'; -kā') Little or nothing; a trifle.

sound (sound), *adj*. [ME. *sound, sund*, fr. AS. *gesund*.] 1. Free from flaw, defect, or decay; undamaged or unimpaired. 2. Healthy; not weak or diseased; robust; — of body or mind. 3. Firm; strong; safe; also, figuratively, secure; trustworthy. 4. Solid in structure; also, firm in texture; stable. 5. Founded in truth or right; not fallacious or faulty. 6. Showing good judgment or good sense; as, *sound* advice. 7. Orthodox, as in religion, politics, theories, etc. 8. Thorough. 9. Undisturbed; profound; — of sleep. 10. Legal; valid. — **Syn**. See HEALTHY; VALID. — **sound'ly**, *adv*. — **sound'ness**, n.

sound, n. [AS. & ON. *sund*.] 1. A long passage of water (wider and more extensive than a strait) connecting two larger bodies, as a sea and the ocean, or forming a channel between the mainland and an island. 2. The air bladder of a fish.

sound (sound), *v. t*. [OF. *sonder*.] 1. To measure the depth of, esp. by a line and plummet; fathom. 2. To find, or try to find, the thoughts, motives, or the like, of; probe; — often with *out*. 3. *Med*. To explore, as the bladder, with a sound. 4. To remove the sound, and other organs, from (fish). — *v. i.* 1. To ascertain the depth of water as with a sounding line. 2. To dive down suddenly, as a fish when hooked. — n. 1. A sounding. 2. *Med*. Any long probe, for exploring cavities of the body. — **sound'a·ble**, *adj*.

sound, n. [OF. *son*, fr. L. *sonus*.] 1. The sensation of hearing; that which is heard; specif.: **a** *Psychophysics*. Sensation due to stimulation of the auditory nerves and auditory centers of the brain, usually by vibrations transmitted in a material medium, commonly air, affecting the organ of hearing. **b** *Physics*. Vibrational energy which occasions such a sensation. Sound is propagated by progressive longitudinal vibratory disturbances (**sound waves**). Cf. PITCH, *Illust*. 2. A tone or noise of a special quality or character; as, a *sound* of rejoicing. 3. Import or implications of something heard, read, etc.; as, I don't like the *sound* of this letter. 4. *Archaic*. Rumor; fame. 5. Noise without meaning; mere noise. 6. Hearing distance; earshot.

— *v. i.* 1. To make a noise or sound. 2. To be conveyed in sound; to be communicated by speech. 3. To convey a certain impression or sound; hence, to seem; appear; as, the story *sounds* false. 4. *Obs. exc. Law*. To have, or tend in, its significance, import, nature, effect, or the like; — with *in*, and formerly *into, to, against*; as, *to sound in tort*, to have the nature or effect of tort. — *v. t.* 1. To cause to sound; to produce the sound of. 2. *Now Rare*. To utter; express audibly. 3. To order, indicate, or proclaim, by a sound or sounds; as, the clock *sounds* noon. 4. To celebrate by or as by sounds. 5. To examine by causing to emit sounds; as, to *sound* the chest.

sound barrier. = SONIC BARRIER.

sound'board' (sound'bōrd'; 70), n. 1. A thin resonant board, as the belly of a violin, so placed in an instrument as to reinforce its tones by sympathetic vibration. 2. = SOUNDING BOARD, 2.

sound bow (bō). The thick part of a bell against which the clapper strikes. See BELL, *Illust*.

sound box. 1. That part of a phonograph which contains the mechanism reproducing the sounds. 2. A chamber in a musical instrument for increasing its sonority, as a violin body.

sound'er (soun'dẽr), *n.* One that sounds; specif., an electromagnetic instrument used in telegraphy for recording sounds. See TELEGRAPH.
sound'ing, *adj.* Making or emitting sound; hence, resonant; sonorous; high-sounding. — **sound'ing·ly,** *adv.*
sound'ing, *n.* [From SOUND to fathom.] **1.** Act of one that sounds (in any sense). **2.** *Naut.* **a** Measurement of depth as by line or plummet; also, the depth so ascertained. **b** *pl.* Any part of the ocean, or other water, where a hand sounding line will reach bottom.
sounding board. **1.** *Music.* = SOUNDBOARD, 1. **2.** A structure over a pulpit or rostrum to give distinctness to a speaker's voice.
sounding line. *Naut.* A line, wire, or cord, weighted at one end with a plummet (**sounding lead**) used in sounding.
sound'less, *adj.* Not sounding. — **sound'less·ly,** *adv.*
sound motion picture. A motion picture with synchronized sound effects, as speech, music, etc.
sound'proof' (sound'proof'; 2), *adj.* Impervious to sound. — *v. t.* To make soundproof; to insulate so as to obstruct the passage of sound, as floors and partitions. — **sound'proof'ing,** *n.*
sound track. The area on a motion-picture film that carries the sound record.

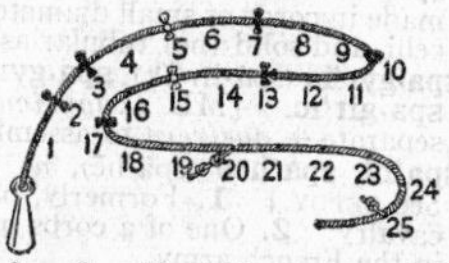

Sounding Line with Lead, marked off in fathoms. At Mark 2, two leather strips; Mark 3 and Mark 13, three leather strips; Mark 5 and Mark 15, white cloth; Mark 7 and Mark 17, red cloth; Mark 10, leather strip with hole; Mark 20, two knots; Mark 25, one knot. Other numbers are Deeps.

soup (sōōp), *n.* [F. *soupe,* of Teut. origin.] **1.** A liquid food, consisting of the broth of meat or vegetables or both, or of milk or thin cream sauce mixed with a purée of vegetables, shellfish, or the like. **2.** Something having or suggesting the consistency of soup, as a heavy fog.
Syn. **Soup, broth, stock, bouillon, consommé, pottage, potage, purée, bisque, chowder** mean a fluid food made by boiling and seasoning meat, fish, or vegetables, or a combination of these. **Soup** designates any dish of this sort; **broth,** the liquid (often concentrated) in which any meat or vegetable has been boiled; **stock,** usually, broth used as a basis for a more elaborate soup; **bouillon** and **consommé,** concentrated and clarified broths, the former of beef and the latter, usually, of veal or chicken; **pottage,** or its more modern French equivalent, **potage,** a thick soup made usually of meat and vegetables thoroughly cooked; **purée,** properly fish, meat, or vegetables boiled to a pulp and rubbed through a sieve, but now a soup made by the addition of this to stock or a creamed sauce; **bisque,** a particularly rich purée, often made of shellfish; **chowder,** a soup made typically of clams or fish with salt pork, onion, potatoes and, usually, crackers and milk.
soup (sōōp), *n.* [Corruption of *supe,* for *supercharge.*] *Slang.* Horsepower. — ***soup up.*** *Slang.* **a** To step up the horsepower of (an engine) as by supercharging and increasing the compression. **b** To step up the propulsive power and speed of (as an old plane, jalopy, or rocket); to boost the performance of (a device). **c** To impart zip to (as a play).
soup'çon' (sōōp'sôN'), *n.* [F.] A suspicion; a suggestion; hence, a very small portion; a taste.
sour (sour), *adj.* [AS. *sūr.*] **1.** Having an acid or tart taste, like vinegar and the juices of most unripe fruits. **2.** Changed, as by fermentation, so as to be acid, rancid, or musty; also, of or pertaining to fermentation. **3.** Having a vapor, emanation, or odor suggesting something acid or rancid. **4.** Distasteful; bitter; unpleasant; of persons, their words, etc., cross; crabbed; morose. **5.** Cold and wet; as, a *sour* day. **6.** Acid in reaction; — said of soils. **7.** Of gasoline, etc., containing sulfur compounds.
Syn. **Sour, acid, acidulous, tart** mean devoid of sweetness. **Sour** usually applies to that which through fermentation or decay has lost its sweetness or freshness; **acid,** to that which has such a taste naturally or normally; **acidulous** and **tart,** to that which is acid, *acidulous* implying a less-than-average acidity, and *tart* a sharp but agreeable acidity.
— *n.* **1.** A sour or acid substance; figuratively, that which is disagreeable or distasteful. **2.** Specif., a mildly acid solution used to neutralize alkali, in the process of bleaching; also, a treatment with such a sour. **3.** An acid beverage.
— *v. i. & t.* To become or to make sour.
— **sour'ish,** *adj.* — **sour'ly,** *adv.* — **sour'ness,** *n.*
source (sōrs; 70), *n.* [OF. *sourse,* deriv. of L. *surgere* to lift, to spring up. See SURGE.] **1.** The beginning of a stream of water or the like; a spring; a fountain. **2.** The origin; the first or ultimate cause. **3.** A person, book, document, etc., that supplies information. **4.** The individual, company, or corporation initiating a payment, as of dividends, interest, etc.; as, a tax paid at the *source.* — **Syn.** See ORIGIN.
sour cherry. See CHERRY, 1.
sour·dine' (sōōr·dēn'), *n.* [F., fr. It. *sordina.*] **1.** *Hist.* One of several low-toned or soft-toned musical instruments. **2.** A mute; specif., a trumpet mute.
sour'dough' (sour'dō'), *n.* A Canadian or Alaskan prospector; — so called from the habit of carrying **sour dough,** a fermented dough used as a leaven in making bread.
sour grapes. Things which persons affect to despise because they cannot possess them.
sour gum. See GUM, 5 **a.**
sour'sop' (sour'sŏp'), *n.* A small tropical American tree (*Annona muricata*), of the custard-apple family; also, its large edible fruit, with soft spines on its skin and a slightly acid, fibrous pulp.
sou'sa·phone (sōō'zȧ·fōn), *n.* [After J. P. *Sousa,* Am. bandmaster, its originator + *-phone.*] *Music.* A large circular tuba with a flaring bell facing toward the front.
souse (sous), *n.* [OF. *sous, solz,* of G. origin.] **1.** Something steeped in pickle, as pigs' feet. **2.** Brine. **3.** [From the v.] A sousing. **4.** *Slang, U.S.* A habitual drunkard. — *v. t. & i.* **1.** To pickle. **2.** To plunge in a liquid. **3.** To drench or become drenched. **4.** *Slang, U.S.* To make or become drunk.
souse (sous), *n.* [ME. *sours.*] *Falconry.* **a** A rising in flight, as a bird; — esp. in the phrase *at (the) souse.* **b** A swooping; a swoop, as of a hawk on its quarry. — *v. i. & t.* To swoop or pounce (down on), esp. in attacking prey. — *adv.* With a swoop; suddenly.
‖**sou'tache'** (sōō'tȧsh'), *n.* [F.] A trimming or embroidery braid, made of silk, wool, cotton, or tinsel.
sou·tane' (sōō·tän'), *n.* [F., fr. It. *sottana,* fr. *sotto* under, fr. L. *subtus* below, beneath, fr. *sub* under.] The cassock worn by Roman Catholic priests.
sou'ter (sōō'tẽr), *n.* [AS. *sūtere,* fr. L. *sutor,* fr. *suere* to sew.] *Chiefly Scot.* A shoemaker; cobbler.
south (south; *see note below*), *n.* [AS. *sūth,* for *sunth.*] **1.** The cardinal point directly opposite the north. See COMPASS CARD, *Illust.* **2.** A country, region, or section, farther to the south than another. **3.** [*cap.*] That part of the United States south of Mason and Dixon's line, the Ohio River, and the southern boundaries of Missouri and Kansas. — *adj.* Situated at the south, or in a southern direction; proceeding toward the south or coming from the south; southern; also, of, pert. to, or indigenous in the south. — *adv.* To, toward, in, or (*Rare*) from, the south.
☞ The pron. sou, chiefly nautical, is a recognized colloquialism in compounds, as *southeast, southwest,* etc.
south (south; *cf.* MOUTH, *v.*), *v. i.* To turn toward the south.
South African, *adj.* Of or pert. to South Africa, esp. to the Union of South Africa. — *n.* A native or inhabitant of South Africa; esp., an Afrikaner.
South African Dutch. = AFRIKAANS.
south by east. *Navig. & Surv.* One point, or 11° 15', east of due south; S. 11° 15' E. See COMPASS CARD, *Illust.*
south by west. *Navig. & Surv.* One point, or 11° 15', west of due south; S. 11° 15' W. See COMPASS CARD, *Illust.*
South'down' (south'doun'), *n.* A small short-wooled hornless sheep of an English breed producing superior mutton.
south'east' (south'ēst'; *see* SOUTH, *n.*), *n.* The point of the horizon between, and equally distant from, the south and the east; also, a part or region relatively southeast. See COMPASS CARD, *Illust.* — (-ēst'; 2), *adj.* Of, pert. to, situated or proceeding toward, or coming from the southeast. — *adv.* Toward, or from, the southeast. — **south'east'ern,** *adj.* — **south'east'ern·most,** *adj.* — **south'east'ern,** *adv., adj., & n.* — **south'east'ward·ly,** *adj. & adv.* — **south'east'wards,** *adv.*
southeast by east. *Navig. & Surv.* One point, or 11° 15', east of due southeast; S. 56° 15' E. See COMPASS CARD, *Illust.*
southeast by south. *Navig. & Surv.* One point, or 11° 15', south of due southeast; S. 33° 45' E. See COMPASS CARD, *Illust.*
south'east'er (south'ēs'tẽr; *see* SOUTH, *n.*), *n.* A storm, strong wind, or gale coming from the southeast.
south'east'er·ly, *adj.* Proceeding toward, or coming from, the southeast. — **south'east'er·ly,** *adv.*
south'er (south'ẽr), *n.* A wind or storm from the south.
sou'ther (sô'thẽr), **sow'ther,** *n.* Dial. vars. of SOLDER.
south'er·ly (sŭth'ẽr·lĭ; *formerly also* south'-), *adj.* Southern. — **south'er·ly,** *adv.* — **south'er·li·ness,** *n.*
south'ern (-ẽrn), *adj.* [AS. *sūtherne.*] **1.** Of or pertaining to, or situated in or toward, the south; proceeding from or toward the south; facing southward. **2.** *U. S.* [*cap.*] Of or pert. to the South. — *n.* A native of the south, esp. [*cap.*] *U. S.,* of the South. — **south'ern·most,** *adj.*
Southern Cross. Four bright stars in the Southern Hemisphere, situated as if at the extremities of a Latin cross; also, the constellation of which the four stars above are the brightest.
Southern Crown. = CORONA AUSTRALIS.
south'ern·er (sŭth'ẽr·nẽr), *n.* A native or inhabitant of the south; esp. [*cap.*] *U. S.,* of the South.
southern lights. = AURORA AUSTRALIS.
south'ern·ly (sŭth'ẽrn·lĭ), *adj. & adv.* Southerly.
south'ern·most (-mōst), *adj.* Farthest south.
south'ern·wood' (sŭth'ẽrn·wood'), *n.* A shrubby European wormwood (*Artemisia abrotanum*), used in beer.
south'ing (south'ĭng), *n.* **1.** Tendency or progress southward. **2.** *Astron.* **a** The passage of a celestial body across the meridian of a place in the Northern Hemisphere. **b** South declination. **3.** *Surv. & Navig.* Difference of latitude to the south from the last point of reckoning.
south'paw' (south'pô'), *adj.* *Sports.* Using the left hand in pitching, throwing, or the like. — **south'paw',** *n.*
South Pole. The southernmost point of the earth; the southern extremity of the earth's axis. Its zenith is the **south pole of the heavens.** See also in *Gaz.*
south'ron (sŭth'rŭn; south'-), *n.; pl.* SOUTHRON or SOUTHRONS (-rŭnz). [From SOUTHERN, after *Briton, Saxon.*] A southerner; specif. [*usually cap.*]: *Scot.* **a** An Englishman. **b** Englishmen. — **south'ron,** *adj.*
south'-south'east', south'-south'west', *adj.* Lying or situated in or leading to, a direction or point halfway between south and southeast (southwest); blowing or coming from that direction. — *adv.* Toward or from a point in that direction. — *n.* A direction or point halfway between south and southeast (southwest); two points, or 22° 30', east (west) of due south; S. 22° 30' E. (W.). See COMPASS CARD, *Illust.*
south'ward (south'wẽrd; *naut.* sŭth'ẽrd), **south'wards** (-wẽrdz; -ẽrdz), *adv.* Toward the south.
south'ward, *adj.* Lying or moving toward the south. — **south'ward,** *n.* — **south'ward·ly,** *adv.*
south'west' (south'wĕst'; *see* SOUTH, *n.*), *n.* The point of the horizon or direction between, and equally distant from, the south and west; a part or region relatively southwest. See COMPASS CARD, *Illust.* — *adj.* Of, pert. to, or situated in or toward, the southwest; proceeding toward the southwest; of the wind, blowing from the southwest. — *adv.* Toward, in, or from, the southwest. — **south'west'ern,** *adj.* — **south'west'ern·most,** *adj.* — **south'west'ward,** *adj., adv., & n.* — **south'west'ward·ly,** *adj. & adv.* — **south'west'wards,** *adv.*
southwest by south. *Navig. & Surv.* One point, or 11° 15', south of due southwest; S. 33° 45' W. See COMPASS CARD, *Illust.*
southwest by west. *Navig. & Surv.* One point, or 11° 15', west of due southwest; S. 56° 15' W. See COMPASS CARD, *Illust.*
south'west'er (south'wĕs'tẽr; *see* SOUTH, *n.*), *n.* **1.** A storm, gale, or strong wind from the southwest. **2.** *Rare.* A sou'wester.
south'west'er·ly, *adj.* Toward or from the southwest; as, a *southwesterly* course; a *southwesterly* wind.
sou've·nir' (sōō'vē·nēr'; sōō'vē·nēr), *n.* [F., prop., inf., to remember, fr. L. *subvenire* to come up, come to mind. See SUBVENE.] That which serves as a reminder; memento.
sou''west'er (sou'wĕs'tẽr), *n.* **1.** A southwester. **2.** A hat of painted canvas, oiled cloth, or the like, with a flap at the back, worn, esp. at sea, in stormy weather.

sov'er·eign (sŏv'ĕr·ĭn; sŏv'rĭn; sŭv'-), *adj.* [OF. *soverain, sovrain,* deriv. of L. *super* above. Modern spelling is due to a supposed connection with *reign.*] **1.** Chief or highest; supreme. **2.** Supreme in power; superior in position to all others; specif., princely; royal. **3.** Independent of, and unlimited by, any other; possessing, or entitled to, original and independent authority or jurisdiction; as, a *sovereign* state. **4.** Efficacious; effectual, as a remedy. — **Syn.** See DOMINANT: FREE. — *n.* **1.** A person, body of men, or state, vested with sovereign authority. **2.** A British gold coin worth one pound sterling; — from the effigy of the monarch on the obverse. See MONEY, *Tables.* — **sov'er·eign·ly,** *adv.*

sov'er·eign·ty (sŏv'ĕr·ĭn·tĭ; sŏv'rĭn·tĭ; sŭv'-), *n.; pl.* -TIES (-tĭz). **1.** Quality or state of being sovereign or a sovereign. **2.** Specif.: **a** The status, dominion, or rule of a sovereign. **b** Supreme political power or authority.

so'vi·et (sō'vĭ·ĕt; sō'vĭ·ĕt'; sō·vyĕt'; sŏv'ĭ·ĕt), *n.* [Russ. *sovet.*] **1.** A council; specif.: **a** [*often cap.*] Either one of two governing bodies (***village soviets, town soviets***) consisting of representatives of workmen, soldiers, and peasants, in the Union of Soviet Socialist Republics. A soviet is the supreme local authority and it sends deputies to each of the higher bodies (soviet congresses) having authority over larger units. The highest governmental body of all is the ***Supreme Soviet*** or ***Council.*** **b** Any of various similar socialistic bodies elsewhere. **2.** [*cap.*] **a** With *the.* The Union of Soviet Socialist Republics. **b** *pl.* The people, leaders, or armed forces of the U.S.S.R. — **so'vi·et,** *adj.* — **so'vi·et·dom** (-dŭm), *n.*

so'vi·et·ism (sō'vĭ·ĕt·ĭz'm; sō'vĭ·ĕt'-; sō·vyĕt'-; sŏv'ĭ·ĕt-), *n.* The form of government carried on through soviets; communism; Bolshevism. — **so'vi·et·ist** (-ĭst), *n.* — **so'vi·et·i·za'tion** (sō'vĭ·ĕt·ĭ·zā'shŭn; -ī·zā'-; sō'vĭ·ĕt'-; sō·vyĕt'-; sŏv'ĭ·ĕt-, -ĕt'-), *n.* — **so'vi·et·ize** (-īz), *v. t.*

sov'ran (sŏv'răn), **sov'ran·ty.** Vars. of SOVEREIGN, etc.

sow (sou), *n.* [AS. *sugu.*] **1.** The adult female of swine. See SWINE, 1. **2.** *Metal.* **a** A channel leading to molds in the pig bed. **b** A mass of metal solidified in such a channel or mold.

sow (sō), *v. t.;* SOWED (sōd); SOWN (sōn) or SOWED; SOW'ING. [AS. *sāwan.*] **1.** To scatter, as seed, upon the earth for growth; to plant by strewing. **2.** To scatter seed upon, in, or over, as a field. **3.** To spread abroad; disperse; disseminate; also, to implant. — *v. i.* To scatter seed for growth. — **sow'er,** *n.*

so·war' (sō·wär'; -wôr'), *n.* [Per. *sawār* horseman.] In India, a native cavalryman; also, a mounted orderly.

sow'bel'ly (sou'bĕl'ĭ), *n.* *Colloq., U.S.* Fat salt pork or bacon.

sow bug (sou). [From SOW, *n.*] A wood louse (genus *Oniscus,* and allies) that cannot roll up like the pill bugs. See WOOD LOUSE.

sow·car' (sou·kär'). Var. of SOUCAR.

sow'ens (sō'ĕnz; sōō'ĕnz), *n. pl.* [Gael. *sūghan* the liquid of which sowens are made, fr. *sūgh* juice.] *Dial.* Porridge from oat husks.

sowth (sōōth). Scot. var. of SOUGH.

sow thistle (sou). Any weed of a genus (*Sonchus,* esp. *S. oleraceus*) of weeds said to be eaten by swine.

sox (sŏks). Var. of *socks, pl.* of SOCK.

soy (soi), *n.* [Jap. *shōyū,* fr. Chin. (Pek.) *chiang*[4]*-yu*[2].] **1.** A Chinese and Japanese sauce for fish, etc., made by subjecting beans (esp. soybeans) to long fermentation and then to long digestion in brine. **2.** In full, **soy'bean'** (soi'bēn'). Also **so'ya** (sō'yȧ). An Asiatic legume (*Glycine soja,* syn. *G. max*), or its seed, which yields oil, flour, and meal. The legume is widely grown in China, Japan, and the United States.

so'zin (sō'zĭn), *n.* [Gr. *sōzein* to save.] *Biochem.* Any defensive protein normally in the animal body.

spa (spä; spô), *n.* [From *Spa,* Belgium.] A mineral spring; hence, a resort with mineral springs.

space (spās), *n.* [OF. *espace,* fr. L. *spatium* space.] **1.** That which is characterized by extension in all directions, boundlessness, and indefinite divisibility; the subject of determinations of position and direction. **2.** *Math.* The aggregate of points, or ordered sets of *n* numbers ($x_1, \dots x_n$). **3.** A limited extension in one, two, or three dimensions: a part marked off in some way. **4.** Specif., reservation; accommodations, as on a train. **5.** An interval between two points of time; duration. **6.** Opportunity; chance. **7.** *Archaic.* A while. **8.** *Advertising.* The page or part of a page of a periodical used for advertising, or the number of agate lines so used in a newspaper. *Trade Slang, U. S.* **9.** *Music.* A degree, or open place, of the staff. **10.** *Print.* A small piece cast lower than the face of the type used to separate words. **11.** *Teleg.* The interval during which the key is open, or not in contact, in operation. **12.** Popularly, the region beyond the earth's atmosphere, esp. that between and beyond the planets and stars. — *v. t.;* SPACED (spāst); SPAC'ING (spās'ĭng). To place at intervals; to arrange with spaces between. — **spac'er** (spās'ĕr), *n.*

space charge. *Elec.* The electrons in the space between the filament and the plate in an electron tube.

space'-lat'tice, *n.* *Physical Chem.* The geometrical arrangement of the atoms in a crystal, as determined by X-ray analysis.

space'ship' (spās'shĭp'), *n.* An imaginary aircraft of the future for interplanetary travel outside the earth's atmosphere.

space time. The four-dimensional order within which every physical existent may be "located" by specifying its four co-ordinates, three spatial and one temporal; the whole of physical reality, or any circumscribed portion, conceived as a four-dimensional array of long-lasting, extended things. — **space'-time',** *adj.*

space'-time' con·tin'u·um. See FOURTH DIMENSION.

spa'cial (spā'shăl). Var. of SPATIAL.

spa'cious (spā'shŭs), *adj.* [OF. *spacieux,* fr. L. *spatiosus.*] **1.** Vast in extent; roomy. **2.** Large or magnificent in scale; expansive. — **spa'cious·ly,** *adv.* — **spa'cious·ness,** *n.*

spade (spād), *n.* [AS. *spædu, spada.*] **1.** A digging implement heavier than a shovel and adapted for being pushed into the ground with the foot. **2.** A spade-shaped instrument; as: **a** A cutting instrument used in flensing. **b** *Ordn.* A prong on the underside of the trail of a gun carriage to check recoil. — ***to call a spade a spade.*** To call a thing by its right name, however coarse; to tell plain facts in plain words. — *v. t. & i.* To dig, or to pare off, with a spade. — **spade'ful,** *n.* — **spad'er** (spād'ĕr), *n.*

spade, *n.* [Sp. *espada,* lit., a sword (Spanish cards bearing the figure of a sword), fr. L. *spatha,* fr. Gr. *spathē.*] **a** A black, somewhat spadelike figure on playing cards of one suit. **b** A card of this suit, or, usually *pl.,* the suit.

spade'fish' (-fĭsh'), *n.;* see FISH. **a** A deep-bodied spiny-finned food fish (*Chaetodipterus faber*) found on the coasts from Cape Cod to Cuba. **b** The paddlefish.

spa·di'ceous (spā·dĭsh'ŭs), *adj.* [L. *spadix, -icis,* a date-brown or nut-brown color. See SPADIX.] **1.** Of a bright, clear, brown or chestnut color. **2.** *Bot.* Bearing flowers on, or of the nature of, a spadix.

spa'dix (spā'dĭks), *n.; pl.* SPADICES (spā·dī'sēz). [L., a palm branch broken off, with its fruit, fr. Gr. *spadix.*] *Bot.* A spike with a fleshy or succulent axis, usually enclosed in a spathe.

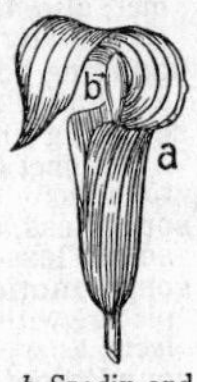

b Spadix and *a* Spathe of Jack-in-the-Pulpit.

spae (spā), *v. i.* [ON. *spā.*] *Chiefly Scot.* To foretell.

spa·ghet'ti (spȧ·gĕt'ĭ), *n.* [It., pl. of *spaghetto,* dim. of *spago* cord.] A food paste resembling macaroni, but made in cords of small diameter, but larger than vermicelli, and solid (not tubular as in macaroni).

spa·gyr'ic (spȧ·jĭr'ĭk), **spa·gyr'i·cal** (-ĭ·kăl), *adj.* Also **spa·gir'ic.** [ML. *spagyricus,* fr. Gr. *span* to draw, separate + *ageirein* to assemble.] *Hist.* Alchemical.

spa'hi, spa'hee (spä'hē), *n.* [Turk. & Per. *sipāhī.* See SEPOY.] **1.** Formerly, one of a corps of Turkish cavalry. **2.** One of a corps of Algerian native cavalry in the French army.

spake (spāk). Archaic past tense of SPEAK.

spale, spail (spāl), *n.* *Dial.* A lath; splinter.

spall (spôl), *n.* [ME. *spalle.*] A chip or fragment, esp. of stone. — *v. t.* *Mining.* To break up or reduce by chipping with a hammer. See HAMMER, *Illust.* (8). — *v. i.* To give off spalls; to chip or crumble.

spal·peen' (spăl·pēn'; spăl'pēn), *n.* [Ir. *spailpīn.*] *Anglo-Ir.* A scamp; rascal; — often used playfully.

span (spăn), *n.* [AS. *spann.*] **1.** The space from the end of the thumb to the end of the little finger when extended; in English measure, 9 inches (22.86 cm.). **2.** Any extent, stretch, reach, or spread, between two limits; specif.: **a** A limited space of time. **b** Spread or extent between abutments or supports; also, the portion thus extended. See BRIDGE, *Illust.* **c** *Aeronautics.* The maximum distance, laterally from tip to tip of an airplane. **3.** [D.; cf. G. *gespann.*] A pair of horses, mules, or other animals, driven together. — *v. t.;* SPANNED (spănd); SPAN'NING. [Partly fr. SPAN, *n.,* and partly fr. AS. *spannan.*] **1.** To measure by the hand with fingers and thumb extended, or by encompassing with the fingers; hence, to measure. **2.** To extend over, reach across, or (*Obs.*), encompass; to reach from one side or limit to the other of so as to cover or connect.

span (spăn). Archaic past of SPIN.

span'drel (spăn'drĕl; -drĭl), *n.* [Origin uncert.] *Arch.* The space between the exterior curve of an arch and the enclosing right angle; or the space between such curves of contiguous arches and a horizontal line above them, or another arch above and enclosing them.

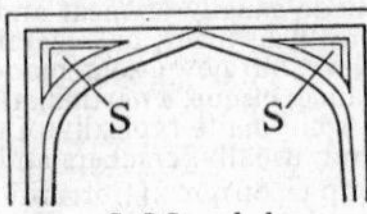

S, S Spandrels.

spa·ne'mi·a, spa·nae'mi·a (spȧ·nē'mĭ·ȧ), *n.* Also **span'e·my** (spăn'ē·mĭ). [NL., fr. Gr. *spanos* scarce + *-emia.*] *Med.* Anemia. — **spa·ne'mic, spa·nae'mic** (-nē'mĭk; -nĕm'ĭk), *adj.*

spang (spăng), *adv.* *Colloq.* Straight; directly; as, he ran *spang* into me.

span'gle (spăng'g'l), *n.* [Dim. of AS. *spange* clasp.] A small plate or boss of shining metal; esp., one of such plates stitched on a dress; a sparkling bit. — *v. t.;* -GLED (-g'ld); -GLING (-glĭng). To set or sprinkle with or as with spangles. — *v. i.* To gleam with or as with spangles; glitter.

Span'iard (spăn'yĕrd), *n.* A native or citizen of Spain.

span'iel (spăn'yĕl; *colloq. or dial.* spăn''l), *n.* [OF. *espagnol, espagneul,* orig. the same word as *espagnol* Spanish, fr. L. *Hispania* Spain.] **1.** Any of numerous breeds of small or medium-sized dogs, usually with long hair and large drooping ears. Spaniels are divided into three main classes: (1) ***field spaniels,*** adapted for hunting small game, including the ***springer spaniel*** and the smaller ***cocker spaniel*** and ***clumber spaniel;*** (2) ***water spaniels,*** which are larger and have curly hair; (3) ***English toy spaniels,*** as the black-and-tan ***King Charles spaniel*** and the typically chestnut-and-white ***Blenheim spaniel.*** **2.** A cringing, servile, fawning person.

Span'ish (spăn'ĭsh), *adj.* Of or pertaining to Spain, the Spaniards, or their language. — *n.* **1.** The chief language of Spain and of countries colonized by Spaniards, esp. the Spanish American countries. Cf. CASTILIAN; see INDO-EUROPEAN LANGUAGES, *Table.* **2.** The people of Spain, collectively; the Spaniards.

Spanish American, *adj.* **a** Designating, or pert. to, those countries of America in which Spanish is the national language. See SPANISH AMERICA, in *Gaz.* **b** In this use **Span'ish-A·mer'i·can,** *adj.* Designating, or pertaining to, the war between Spain and the United States in 1898. — *n.* A native or citizen of a Spanish American country, esp. one of Spanish descent.

Spanish bayonet. Any of several yuccas, esp. one species (*Yucca aloifolia*) with rigid spine-tipped leaves.

Spanish fly. See BLISTER BEETLE.

Spanish influenza. The influenza.

Spanish Main. The mainland of Spanish America, esp. the northern coast of South America; improperly, the southern portion, or the whole, of the Caribbean Sea.

Spanish moss. The long moss.

Spanish needles. The barbed achenes of a common beggar-ticks (*Bidens bipinnata*); also, the plant itself.

Spanish onion. Any of several varieties of large-bulbed, mild-flavored onions; — in the United States originally applied only to imported stock but now used more broadly.

Spanish paprika. A mild bright-red pepper (*Capsicum tetragonum*) of Spanish origin; also, the plant.

spank (spăngk), *v. i.* [From SPANKING, *adj.*] To move quickly, dashingly, or spiritedly.

spank, *v. t.* [Imitative.] To strike, or to strike the buttocks of, as with the open hand. — *n.* A spanking; a slap, esp. on the buttocks.

spank'er (spăngk'ĕr), *n.* **1.** One who or that which spanks. **2.** *Naut.* **a** The fore-and-aft sail on the aftermast of a square-rigged vessel. See SAIL, *Illust.* **b** The aftermast and the sail thereon in a schooner of four or more masts.

spank'ing, *adj.* [Prob. of Scand. origin.] **1.** That spanks, or moves briskly; lively; esp., of a wind, fresh; strong. **2.** *Slang.* Remarkable of its kind.

span′ner (spăn′ẽr), *n.* **1.** One who or that which spans. **2.** A tool, having a jaw or socket at either or both ends to turn a bolt, nut, pipe, etc.; a wrench.

span′–new′ (spăn′nū′; 2), *adj.* [ON. *spān-nȳr*, fr. *spānn* chip + *nȳr* new.] Quite new; brand-new.

span′worm′ (spăn′wûrm′), *n.* The larva of any geometrid moth.

spar (spär), *n.* [MLG.] Among miners, any of various nonmetallic minerals, usually cleavable and lustrous.

spar, *n.* [ME. *sparre.*] **1.** A mast, yard, boom, gaff, etc. **2.** One of the main lateral members of the wing of an airplane, usually of wood or tubular steel. — *v. t.;* SPARRED (spärd); SPAR′RING. To equip with spars.

spar, *v. i.* [F. *esparer* (now *éparer*) to kick, fr. It. *sparare* to kick, fling, fr. *parare* to parry.] **1.** To fight or strike with the feet or spurs, as cocks do. **2.** To box with the fists, esp. scientifically. — *n.* An offensive or defensive movement in sparring; a boxing match.

SPAR, Spar (spär), *n.; pl.* -s. A member of the Women's Reserve of the U. S. Coast Guard Reserve, known as **SPARS** (spärz), from the Coast Guard motto, "Semper Paratus — Always Ready."

spar′a·ble (spăr′ȧ·b'l), *n.* [Corrupt. fr. *sparrow bill.*] A variety of small nail used by shoemakers.

spar buoy. See BUOY, 1.

spare (spâr), *v. t.* [AS. *sparian*, fr. *spær* sparing, saving.] **1.** To refrain from using, indulging in, exercising, etc.; to employ frugally or rarely; stint; as, to *spare* no expense; to *spare* the rod. **2.** To free, relieve, or exempt (one) from (something); as, to *spare* one pain or trouble. **3.** To deprive oneself of; to do without; dispense with; as, I cannot *spare* another dollar. **4.** To forbear to destroy, punish, or accuse; show mercy to; as, the victors *spared* the vanquished. — *v. i.* **1.** To be frugal or parsimonious. **2.** To refrain from doing harm; show mercy. — *adj.* **1.** Not being used; held in reserve, as for emergency; as, a *spare* room. **2.** Surplus; superfluous; as, *spare* time. **3.** Parsimonious; chary; not liberal or profuse. **4.** Wanting flesh or fat; lean; gaunt. **5.** Scanty; frugal; as, a *spare* diet. — **Syn.** See LEAN: MEAGER. — *n.* **1.** That which has not been used or expended. **2.** A spare, or duplicate, part. **3.** *Bowling.* Act of knocking down all the pins in the first two bowls of a frame; also, the score thus made. — **spare′ly,** *adv.* — **spare′ness,** *n.* — **spar′er** (spâr′ẽr), *n.*

spare′rib′ (-rĭb′), *n.* [Also *ribspare;* appar. fr. MLG.] A cut of meat, esp. of pork, consisting of the thin ends of the ribs. See PORK, *Illust.*

sparge (spärj), *v. t. & i.;* SPARGED (spärjd); SPARG′ING (spär′jĭng). [OF. *espargier*, fr. L. *spargere.*] To sprinkle; spatter. — **sparge,** *n.* — **sparg′er** (spär′jẽr), *n.*

spar′ing (spâr′ĭng), *adj.* That spares; hence, careful; provident. — **spar′ing·ly,** *adv.*

Syn. **Sparing, frugal, thrifty, economical** mean careful in the use of one's money or resources. **Sparing** stresses abstention or restraint; **frugal,** simplicity in food, dress, and ways of living; **thrifty,** good management and industry; **economical,** prudence, lack of wastefulness, and use to the best advantage.

spark (spärk), *n.* [AS. *spærca, spearca.*] **1.** A small particle of fire or ignited substance emitted by a body, esp. by one in combustion. **2.** Anything sparklike; as: **a** A sparkle; a flash. **b** A particle capable of being kindled or developed; a germ; as, not a *spark* of life. **3.** *Elec.* **a** The light accompanying a sudden disruptive discharge between two conductors separated by air or some similar medium. **b** The discharge in a spark plug or the mechanism controlling it. **c** Short for SPARK TRANSMITTER, SPARK TRANSMISSION; — chiefly in attributive use; as, a *spark* station. — *v. i. Elec.* To produce sparks; specif., to have the electric ignition working, as in internal-combustion engine or the igniter. — *v. t.* To stir into activity, esp. into intense, sustained, and integrated activity, often with an implication of firing with zeal, spurring, or inspiriting.

spark, *n.* [ON. *sparkr* lively, sprightly.] **1.** A showy, gay man; gallant. **2.** A lover; beau. — *v. i. & t. Colloq.* To play the spark (to); court. — **spark′ish,** *adj.*

spark arrester. **1.** *U. S.* Any of various contrivances to prevent the escape of sparks, as from a smokestack. **2.** *Elec.* A device to minimize or prevent sparking at a place where a circuit is made and broken.

spark coil. *Elec.* An induction coil, esp. of an internal-combustion engine, wireless telegraph apparatus, etc.

spark′er (spär′kẽr), *n.* **1.** One who or that which sparks, as a spark plug. **2.** *Elec.* A spark arrester.

spark gap. *Elec.* The space between high potential terminals through which the discharge passes.

spark generator. A generator of alternating current which utilizes the discharge of a condenser through a spark gap as the source of its alternating-current power.

spark′ing plug. = SPARK PLUG, 1.

spar′kle (spär′k'l), *n.* [Dim. of *spark*, or fr. *sparkle*, v.] **1.** A little spark; a scintillation; also, quality of sparkling. **2.** Animation; liveliness. — *v. i. & t.;* SPAR′KLED (-k'ld); SPAR′KLING (-klĭng). **1.** To emit sparks (of); to emit, or reveal by, gleams of light; scintillate; flash. **2.** To effervesce. — **Syn.** See FLASH.

spar′kler (-klẽr), *n.* One that sparkles; specif.: **a** A firework consisting usually of a heavy wire partly coated with a composition which on burning emits brilliant sparks. **b** A gem that sparkles, as a diamond or ruby.

spar′kling (-klĭng), *adj.* **1.** Emitting sparks; flashing. **2.** Animated; lively. **3.** Effervescing or effervescent; of beverages, containing carbon dioxide under pressure. — **spar′kling·ly,** *adv.*

spark plug. **1.** In an internal-combustion engine, a part fitting into the cylinder head, carrying two electrodes separated by an air gap across which the current from the ignition system discharges, forming the spark for combustion. **2.** *Colloq., U. S.* One who, as a member of a group or team, imparts fire, energy, and spirit to his fellows. — **spark′–plug′,** *v. t.*

spark transmitter. *Radio.* A transmission set that utilizes the discharge of a condenser through a spark gap as a source of its alternating-current power. — **spark transmission.**

spar′ling (spär′lĭng), *n.* [ME. *sperling*, fr. OF. *esperlinge, esperlenc.*] The European smelt (*Osmerus eperlanus*).

spar′oid (spâr′oid; spăr′-), *adj.* [L. *sparus* gilthead + *-oid.*] Of or pertaining to the family (Sparidae) of deep-bodied, spiny-finned marine fishes, the sea breams, related to the grunts and snappers and including the porgies, scup, and sheepshead, and the common European species *Pagellus centrodontus.* — *n.* A sparoid fish.

spar′row (spăr′ō), *n.* [AS. *spearwa.*] **1.** Any finch of the genus *Passer*, esp. the Eurasian ***house sparrow*** (*P. domesticus*) naturalized in America as the ***English sparrow,*** and the smaller ***tree sparrow*** (*P. montanus*) of Europe. **2.** By extension, any of numerous finches (esp. of the genera *Spizella, Melospiza, Amphispiza*) resembling the house sparrow in size and color; as: the ***chipping sparrow*** (*Spizella passerina*) which often nests near or on buildings, the ***field sparrow*** (*S. pusilla*), and a ***tree sparrow*** (*S. arborea*) breeding in northern North America and wintering in U. S.; the American ***song sparrow*** (*Melospiza melodia*) noted for its sweet cheerful song, and the ***swamp sparrow*** (*M. georgiana*) of eastern North America; the ***sage sparrow*** (*Amphispiza belli* and *A. nevadensis*) inhabiting sagebrush regions in western North America. **3.** Any of certain other birds (not finches); as: **a** A common European warbler (*Prunella modularis*), called ***hedge sparrow.*** **b** A weaverbird (*Munia oryzivora*), called ***Java sparrow,*** native to Java but a common cage bird.

spar′row·grass′ (spăr′ō·grȧs′; 9), *n. Colloq.* Corrupt. of ASPARAGUS.

sparrow hawk. **1.** Any Old World hawk of certain small species of *Accipiter*, esp. *A. nisus.* See HAWK. **2.** A small North American falcon (*Falco sparverius*) closely allied to the European kestrel.

sparse (spärs), *adj.* [L. *sparsus*, past part. of *spargere* to strew, scatter.] Having few or widely scattered component units or elements; not thickly grown, settled, etc.; thinly scattered. — **Syn.** See MEAGER. — **sparse′ly,** *adv.* — **sparse′ness, spar′si·ty** (spär′sĭ·tĭ), *n.*

Spar′ta·cist (spär′tȧ·sĭst), *n.* A member of the **Spar′ta·cus par′ty** (-kŭs), a party organized in Germany in 1918 along extreme socialistic lines.

Spar′tan (spär′t'n), *adj.* Of or pertaining to Sparta, esp. ancient Sparta, in Laconia, ruled by a Dorian people noted for their military organization, rigorous discipline, and valor; hence, hardy; undaunted. — *n.* A citizen of Sparta; a person of great fortitude. — **Spar′tan·ism** (-ĭz'm), *n.*

spar′te·ine (-tē·ēn; -ĭn), *n.* Also **spar′te·in.** [Gr. *spartos* the broom + *-ine.*] *Chem.* A liquid alkaloid, $C_{15}H_{26}N_2$, extracted from the common broom.

spasm (spăz'm), *n.* [OF. *spasme*, fr. L. *spasmus*, fr. Gr. *spasmos*, fr. *spaein, span*, to draw, cause convulsion.] **1.** *Med.* An involuntary and unnatural muscular contraction. In ***clonic spasms*** contractions and relaxations alternate. In ***tonic spasms*** the contraction is steady and prolonged, as in tetanus. **2.** A sudden, violent, and temporary effort, emotion, etc.

spas·mod′ic (spăz·mŏd′ĭk), *adj.* [ML. *spasmodicus*, fr. Gr. *spasmōdēs*, fr. *spasmos* a convulsion + *eidos* likeness.] **1.** *Med.* Of, pertaining to, affected or characterized by a spasm or spasms. **2.** Characterized by fitfulness; lacking continuity; intermittent; as, *spasmodic* zeal. **3.** Subject to outbursts of emotional excitement; excitable. — **Syn.** See FITFUL. — **spas·mod′i·cal** (-ĭ·kăl), *adj.* — **spas·mod′i·cal·ly,** *adv.*

spas′tic (spăs′tĭk), *adj.* [L. *spasticus*, fr. Gr. *spastikos.*] *Med.* Of or pertaining to spasm; spasmodic; esp., pertaining to tonic spasm; tetanic. In **spastic paralysis** there is a steady and prolonged contraction of the muscles affected. — **spas′ti·cal·ly** (-tĭ·kăl·ĭ), *adv.*

spat (spăt), *n.* A young oyster or other bivalve mollusk; — chiefly collectively. — *v. i.* To emit spawn.

spat, *n.* [Short for SPATTERDASH.] A form of short cloth or leather gaiter.

spat, *v. i.;* SPAT′TED; SPAT′TING. *Colloq.* To slap, as with the hand; also, to dispute; quarrel. — *n. Colloq.* A slap; hence, a petty quarrel. — **Syn.** See QUARREL.

spat. Past & occasional past part. of SPIT, to eject.

spate (spāt), *n.* **1.** *Brit.* A freshet; a heavy rainstorm. **2.** An excessive quantity; a rush, as of words.

spa·tha′ceous (spȧ·thā′shŭs), *adj.* Also **spa′thal** (spā′thăl). *Bot.* Having a spathe; of the nature of a spathe.

spathe (spāth), *n.* [F., fr. L. *spatha*, fr. Gr. *spathē.*] *Bot.* The large sheathing bract or pair of bracts enclosing an inflorescence, esp. a spadix, on the same axis, as in the calla. See SPADIX, *Illust.* — **spa′those** (spā′thōs; spăth′ōs), *adj.*

spath′ic (spăth′ĭk), *adj.* Also **spath′ose** (spăth′ōs). Like spar; foliated or lamellar.

spath′u·late (spăth′ū·lāt). *Chiefly Bot.* Var. of SPATULATE.

spa′tial (spā′shăl), *adj.* Of or pertaining to space. — **spa′ti·al′i·ty** (spā′shĭ·ăl′ĭ·tĭ), *n.* — **spa′tial·ly,** *adv.*

spa′ti·o·tem′po·ral (spā′shĭ·ō·tĕm′pō·răl), *adj.* Of or pertaining to space time; having extent and duration.

spat′ter (spăt′ẽr), *v. t.* **1.** To splash with a liquid; spot or soil by splashing. **2.** To scatter by splashing; sprinkle around. **3.** To injure by aspersion; defame. — *v. i.* To spurt forth in drops. — *n.* **1.** Act or noise of spattering, or state of being spattered; a splashing. **2.** A drop or splash spattered on something; a spot or stain due to spattering. — **spat′ter·ing·ly,** *adv.*

spat′ter·dash′ (-dăsh′), *n.* [*spatter* + *dash.*] An old form of puttee; a legging; — chiefly in *pl.*

spat′ter·dock′ (-dŏk′), *n.* The common yellow water lily (*Nuphar advenum*); also, any plant of the same genus or of the related genus *Nymphaea.*

spat′u·la (spăt′ū·lȧ), *n.* [L. *spatula, spathula*, dim. of *spatha* a spatula.] A flexible knifelike implement, as one for spreading paints, drugs in compounding prescriptions, certain foods in cooking processes, etc. — **spat′u·lar** (-lẽr), *adj.*

spat′u·late (-lāt), *adj.* Shaped like a spatula; spoon-shaped. See LEAF, *Illust.* (10).

spa′viet (spā′vĭt; spȧv′ĕt), *adj. Scot. & Ir.* Spavined.

spav′in (spăv′ĭn), *n.* [OF. *esparvain, esparvin.*] *Veter.* A disease of the hock of horses, marked by a small bony enlargement inside of the leg, due to a sprain or a violent effort. — **spav′ined** (-ĭnd), *adj.*

spawn (spôn), *v. t. & i.* [OF. *espandre*, prop., to shed, spread, fr. L. *expandere* to spread out.] **1.** To produce or deposit (spawn). **2.** To bring forth; generate, esp. in vast quantities; — used in contempt. **3.** *Hort.* To plant with spawn (sense 3). — *n.* **1.** The eggs of fishes, oysters, and other aquatic animals. **2.** *Contemptuous.* Any product or offspring; also, numerous issue. **3.** The mycelium of fungi, esp. that of cultivated mushrooms, prepared for propagating purposes. — **spawn′er,** *n.*

spay (spā), *v. t.* [AF. *espeier*, OF. *espeer* to cut with sword.] To remove the ovaries of (a female animal).

spay, *n.* See RED DEER.

speak (spēk), *v. i.;* SPOKE (spōk); SPO′KEN (spō′kĕn); SPEAK′ING.

Archaic past SPAKE, *past part.* SPOKE. [AS. *specan, spreccan.*] **1.** To utter words or articulate sounds with the ordinary voice. **2.** To express opinions; talk; as, *speak* for yourself. **3.** To utter a speech, discourse, or the like; to address a public assembly formally. **4.** To make mention. **5.** To convey sentiments, ideas, etc., as if by utterance; as, features that *speak* of self-will. **6.** To sound, as does a bugle. **7.** To ask; make application or demand; as, to *speak* for tickets. — *v. t.* **1.** To utter by speaking; express orally; as, to *speak* words of wisdom. **2.** To declare orally; express in words; as, to *speak* the truth. **3.** To express or declare in any way; as, fame *speaks* him honest. **4.** To sound the praises of; extol. **5.** To use, or be able to use, in talk or conversation; as, to *speak* Latin. **6.** To address; esp., *Naut.*, to hail, as a vessel. — ***speak by the book.*** To speak with minute exactness. — **speak′a·ble**, *adj.*

Syn. **Speak, talk, converse** mean to express one's thoughts orally. **Speak**, the most general term, implies any utterance ranging from the most to the least coherent; **talk** implies an auditor or auditors and connected discourse or colloquy; **converse** implies interchange in talk of thoughts, opinions, etc.

speak′-eas′y *or* **speak′eas′y** (spēk′ēz′ĭ), *n. Slang, U. S.* An illicit drinking place.

speak′er (spēk′ẽr), *n.* **1.** One who speaks; specif.: **a** One who makes a public address. **b** One who is the mouthpiece of others; esp., one who presides over a deliberative assembly. **2.** A book of selections for declamation. **3.** *Radio.* = LOUD-SPEAKER. — **speak′er·ship**, *n.*

speak′ing, *adj.* **1.** Uttering speech; used for conveying speech. **2.** Lifelike; expressive; animated. — *n.* Act of uttering words; also, utterances of one who speaks; hence, oratory; as, a course in public *speaking.*

speaking tube. **a** A pipe through which conversation may be conducted, as between parties located in different rooms. **b** Also **speaking trumpet.** A trumpet-shaped instrument for intensifying the sound of the human voice.

spean (spēn), *v. t. Scot. & Ir.* To wean.

spear (spēr), *n.* [AS. *spere.*] **1.** A weapon with long shaft and sharp head or blade for thrusting or throwing; also, its sharp head.

☞ *Spear* is used attributively with the force of *paternal;* as, the *spear* side, that is, the male line of a family, as opposed to the *spindle* side. Cf. DISTAFF, 2.

2. A sharp-pointed instrument with barbs, for stabbing fish and other animals. **3.** A spearman. **4.** [Var. of SPIRE, influenced by *spear* weapon.] A shoot, as of grass; a spire; a reed; also, any young shoot or sprout. — *v. t.* To pierce or strike with, or as with, a spear. — *v. i.* To pierce like a spear; also, to shoot into a long stem, as a plant. — **spear′er** (-ẽr), *n.*

spear′fish′ (-fĭsh′), *n.;* see FISH. Any of several large, powerful, pelagic fishes (genus *Tetrapturus*) allied to the marlins and sailfishes.

spear′head′ (spēr′hĕd′), *n.* **1.** The head or point of a spear. **2.** The foremost point, person, or body in an attack, drive, enterprise, or the like.

spear′man (-măn), *n.* One armed with a spear.

spear′mint′ (-mĭnt′), *n.* [From its spire-shaped inflorescence.] The common garden mint (*Mentha spicata*), yielding an aromatic oil.

spear′wort′ (-wûrt′), *n.* Any of several species of crowfoot (*Ranunculus*) having spear-shaped leaves, esp. the **spear crowfoot** (*R. flammula*).

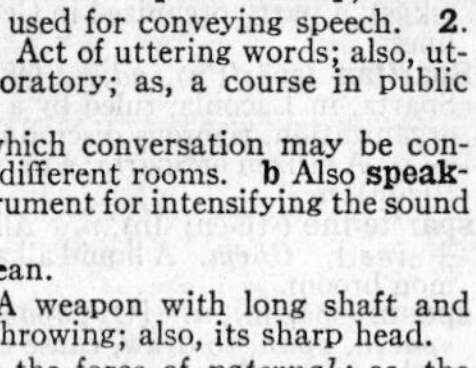
Spearheads.

spe′cial (spĕsh′ăl), *adj.* [OF. or L.; OF. *especial*, fr. L. *specialis.* See ESPECIAL.] **1.** Distinguished by some unusual quality; uncommon; noteworthy. **2.** Having an individual character or trait; peculiar; unique; as, this case is *special.* **3.** Of or pertaining to a species; specific. **4.** Particularly favored or loved; intimate; as, a *special* friend. **5.** Additional to the regular; extra; as, a *special* edition or dividend. **6.** Designed or selected for a particular purpose, occasion, or the like; as, a *special* diet. **7.** Confined to a definite field of action; specialized; limited; as, a *special* act of Congress.

Syn. **Special, especial, specific, particular, individual, respective, concrete** mean of or belonging to one only. **Special** stresses a quality, character, identity, or use of its own; **especial**, a pre-eminence among others of the same kind; **specific**, a quality or character distinguishing a species or an individual; **particular**, a distinguishing mark of an individual; **individual**, unequivocal reference to one of a class or group; **respective**, reference to each one of several, esp. in the order named; **concrete**, individuality and actuality of existence or experience.

— *n.* A special person or thing; variously, a special correspondent, edition, order, train, etc.

— **spe′cial·ly**, *adv.*

special delivery. Delivery, for an additional fee, of mail matter by special postal messenger ahead of the regular delivery.

special handling. *U. S. Post Office.* Handling, for an additional fee, of parcels (fourth-class matter) as first-class matter (letters), except that they do not receive immediate delivery at the office of destination.

spe′cial·ism (spĕsh′ăl·ĭz′m), *n.* Practice or policy of specializing; devotion to a specialty; as, medical *specialism;* also, an instance of specializing.

spe′cial·ist (-ĭst), *n.* One who devotes himself to some special branch of activity in his business, profession, studies, etc.; a specializing physician, scholar, broker, etc. — **spe′cial·ist, spe′cial·is′tic** (-ĭs′tĭk), *adj.*

spe′ci·al′i·ty (spĕsh′ĭ·ăl′ĭ·tĭ), *n.; pl.* -TIES (-tĭz). [F. *spécialité.*] **1.** A special or distinguishing mark or characteristic; in *pl.*, details; particulars. **2.** A specialty (senses 3, 4, 5).

spe′cial·ize (spĕsh′ăl·īz), *v. t.* **1.** To particularize; specif., to endorse (a check, draft, etc.) so as to designate a particular payee. **2.** To apply or restrict to a particular use or end; as, to *specialize* one's efforts. **3.** *Biol.* To develop (an organism or one of its parts) so as to become structurally adapted to the performance of a particular function, or to environment. — *v. i.* **1.** To concentrate one's efforts on a particular subject, line of research, etc.; to restrict oneself to a special branch or field of activity within one's profession or business. **2.** *Biol.* To become specialized. — **spe′cial·i·za′tion** (-ĭ·zā′shŭn; -ī·zā′-), *n.*

special pleading. **a** *Law.* The allegation of special or new matter to avoid the effect of matter pleaded by the opposite side and admitted. **b** Popularly, argument that presents one phase as if it covered the entire question at issue.

spe′cial·ty (spĕsh′ăl·tĭ), *n.; pl.* -TIES (-tĭz). [OF. *especialté.*] **1.** State of being special. **2.** A speciality (sense 1). **3.** In merchandising, an article or class of articles having special features, uses, or the like, or receiving special attention; as, a dealer in *specialties.* **4.** That in which one specializes or has special knowledge; a branch of knowledge, art, science, or business, to which one especially devotes himself; as, brain surgery is his *specialty.* **5.** A contract or obligation under seal; a contract by deed.

spe′ci·a′tion (spē′shĭ·ā′shŭn), *n. Biol.* The evolutionary process by which species are formed; the process by which variations become fixed.

‖**spe′ci·e** (spē′shĭ·ē; -shē), *abl.* of L. *species* sort, kind. Used in *in specie:* In kind; in (its own or a specified) form.

spe′cie (spē′shĭ), *n.* Coin, usually of gold or silver.

spe′cies (spē′shĭz *or, esp. in the pl.*, spē′shēz; *L.* spē′shĭ·ēz), *n. sing. & pl.* [L., a sight, outward appearance, shape, form, sort, kind.] **1.** A mental image or sensuous presentation; an object of thought considered as the similitude of an object in nature. **2.** *R.C.Ch.* The appearance of bread or of wine which the respective transubstantiated Eucharistic elements have; hence, the consecrated elements. **3.** A sort; kind; variety. **4.** *Obs.* Specie. **5.** *Biol.* A category of classification lower than a genus or subgenus and above a subspecies or variety; a group of animals or plants which possess in common one or more distinctive characters, and do or may interbreed and reproduce their characters in their offspring; a distinct kind or sort of animal or plant. See VARIETY, 5, *Note.* **6.** *Logic.* A class of individuals having common attributes and designated by a common name; specif., a logical division of a genus or more comprehensive class.

spec′i·fi′a·ble (spĕs′ĭ·fī′ȧ·b'l), *adj.* Capable of being specified.

spe·cif′ic (spē·sĭf′ĭk), *adj.* [ML. *specificus*, fr. L. *species* a particular sort or kind. See -FIC.] **1.** Of, pertaining to, characterizing, or constituting a species; as, the *specific* differences between the dog and the wolf. **2.** Precisely formulated or restricted; specifying; explicit; as, a *specific* statement. **3.** *Med.* **a** Exerting a peculiar influence over any part; preventing or curing disease by a peculiar adaptation; — of a remedy. **b** Due to a particular microorganism or virus; — of a disease. **4.** *Physics.* **a** Designating any of various arbitrary physical constants, as the ratio in quantity of one substance to a standard substance of the same volume; as, **specific gravity**, the ratio of the weight of any volume of a substance to the weight of an equal volume of some substance taken as a standard or unit as, usually, water for solids and liquids and air or hydrogen for gases. (Abbr. *sp. gr.*) **b** Designating a quantity per unit area; as, **specific luminous intensity** (luminous intensity per unit area of source). — **Syn.** See SPECIAL; EXPLICIT. — *n.* **1.** Anything peculiarly adapted to its purpose. **2.** *Med.* A specific remedy. — **spe·cif′i·cal** (-ĭ·kăl), *adj.* — **spe·cif′i·cal·ly**, *adv.* — **spec′i·fic′i·ty** (spĕs′ĭ·fĭs′ĭ·tĭ), *n.*

spec′i·fi·ca′tion (spĕs′ĭ·fĭ·kā′shŭn), *n.* **1.** *Now Rare.* Determination of a thing in its specific (sense 1) or particular character. **2.** A specifying, or designation of particulars. **3.** A statement containing a minute description or enumeration of particulars, as of the terms of a contract, details of construction not shown in an architect's drawings, etc.; also, any item of such a statement.

specific heat. *Physics.* The ratio of the quantity of heat required to raise the temperature of a body one degree to that required to raise an equal mass of water one degree.

spec′i·fy (spĕs′ĭ·fī), *v. t.;* SPEC′I·FIED (-fīd); SPEC′I·FY′ING. [OF. *specifier*, fr. ML. *specificare.* See SPECIES; -FY.] **1.** To name or state explicitly or in detail. **2.** To include as an item in a specification; as, to *specify* portland cement.

spec′i·men (spĕs′ĭ·mĕn), *n.* [L., fr. *specere* to look, behold.] **1.** A part, or one of a number, intended to show the kind and quality of the whole; a sample. **2.** *Colloq.* An individual; person; as, a tough *specimen.* — **Syn.** See INSTANCE.

spe′cious (spē′shŭs), *adj.* [L. *speciosus* good-looking, specious.] **1.** *Obs.* Outwardly pleasing; showy. **2.** Apparently but deceptively fair, just, or correct; appearing well at first view; plausible; as, *specious* reasoning. — **Syn.** See PLAUSIBLE. — **spe′cious·ly**, *adv.* — **spe′cious·ness, spe′ci·os′i·ty** (spē′shĭ·ŏs′ĭ·tĭ), *n.*

speck (spĕk), *n.* [AS. *specca.*] **1.** A small discoloration; a small spot, esp. from stain or decay. **2.** A bit; a particle. — *v. t.* To produce specks on or in.

speck′le (spĕk′'l), *n. & v. t.* Speck; spot.

specs (spĕks). *Colloq.* Short for *spectacles.*

spec′ta·cle (spĕk′tȧ·k'l; -tĭ·k'l), *n.* [OF., fr. L. *spectaculum*, fr. *spectare* to look at, behold.] **1.** Something exhibited, esp. as unusual and notable; a noteworthy sight. **2.** Specif., a public display appealing to the eye by its mass, proportions, color, etc. **3.** *pl.* A device to aid vision or protect the eyes, consisting usually of two lenses in a metal frame with a bridge, or nosepiece, and bows. **4.** *pl.* Any aid to vision, esp. mental vision of a specified or implied character; also, sometimes, a bias; a view colored by prejudice; as, to see events through rosy *spectacles.* **5.** *sing.* or *pl.* Anything suggesting a pair of spectacles, as a frame containing the red and green glasses in a semaphore.

spec′ta·cled (-k'ld), *adj.* Having, wearing, or, *Zool.*, having spots or patches suggesting, spectacles.

spec·tac′u·lar (spĕk·tăk′ū·lẽr), *adj.* Of, pertaining to, or of the nature of a spectacle; exciting wonder and admiration by unusual display. — *n.* Spectacular sights, action, or display. — **spec·tac′u·lar·ly**, *adv.*

spec·ta′tor (spĕk·tā′tẽr; spĕk′tā·tẽr), *n.* [L.] One who looks on or beholds; a beholder; onlooker; looker-on. — **spec·ta′tress** (spĕk·tā′trĕs; -trĭs), **spec·ta′trix** (-trĭks), *n. fem.*

spec′ter, spec′tre (spĕk′tẽr), *n.* [F. *spectre*, fr. L. *spectrum* image, specter, fr. *specere* to look.] A visible disembodied spirit; apparition.

spec′tra (-trȧ), *n., pl.* of SPECTRUM.

spec′tral (spĕk′trăl), *adj.* **1.** Of, like, or pertaining to a specter; ghostly. **2.** Of, pertaining to, or made by the (or a) spectrum. — **spec·tral′i·ty** (spĕk·trăl′ĭ·tĭ), *n.* — **spec′tral·ly**, *adv.*

spec′tro- (spĕk′trō-). [From SPECTRUM.] A combining form denoting: **a** *Pertaining to radiant energy* or *the analysis of radiation in a spectrum*, as in **spec′tro·chem′i·cal, spec′tro·chem′is·try, spec′tro·col′or·im′e·try, spec′tro·gram, spec′tro·graph, spec·trol′o·gy, spec′tro·pho·tog′ra·phy, spec′tro·tel′e·scope.** **b** *Spectroscope* or *spectroscopic and*, as in:

spectrobolometer	spectromicroscope	spectropolariscope
spectroelectric	spectropolarimeter	spectroradiometer

spec′tro·he′li·o·gram′ (-hē′lĭ·ō·grăm′), *n.* [*spectro-* + *helio-* +

-gram.] *Astrophysics.* A photograph of the sun made by monochromatic light, and showing the sun's faculae and prominences.
spec'tro·he'li·o·graph' (spĕk'trō·hē'lĭ·ō·grȧf'; 9), *n.* *Astrophysics.* An apparatus for making spectroheliograms.
spec'tro·he'li·o·scope' (-skōp'), *n.* [*spectro-* + *helio-* + *-scope.*] *Astrophysics.* Usually, the spectroheliograph; more properly, a similar instrument used for visual, as distinguished from photographic, observations.
spec·trom'e·ter (spĕk·trŏm'ē·tẽr), *n.* *Physics.* **a** An instrument for determining the index of refraction. **b** A spectroscope fitted for measurements of the spectra observed with it.
spec'tro·pho·tom'e·ter (spĕk'trō·fō·tŏm'ē·tẽr), *n.* *Optics.* An instrument for comparing the intensities of the corresponding colors of two spectra. — **spec'tro·pho·tom'e·try** (-trĭ), *n.*
spec'tro·scope (spĕk'trō·skōp), *n.* *Physics.* An optical instrument for forming spectra. — **spec'tro·scop'ic** (-skŏp'ĭk), **spec'tro·scop'i·cal** (-ĭ·kăl), *adj.* — **spec'tro·scop'i·cal·ly**, *adv.* — **spec·tros'co·pist** (spĕk·trŏs'kō·pĭst; spĕk'trō·skō'pĭst), *n.* — **spec·tros'co·py** (-pĭ), *n.*
spec'trum (spĕk'trŭm), *n.; pl.* -TRA (-trȧ), -TRUMS (-trŭmz). [L. See SPECTER.] **1.** *Physics.* The series of images formed when a beam of radiant energy is subjected to dispersion and then brought to focus, so that the component waves are arranged in the order of their wave lengths; hence, any series of radiant energies arranged in order of wave length. The ***visible spectrum*** has wave lengths between 3,800 and 8,000 angstrom units and when of sufficient intensity evokes in the eye a series of colors ranging from red (evoked by waves 760 millimicrons in length) to violet (385 millimicrons). **2.** *Radio.* The range of wave lengths of radio waves (from about 30,000 meters to 3 centimeters, or, in terms of frequencies, from 10 to 10,000,000 kilocycles); — called also *radio spectrum.*
spectrum analysis. The investigation of substances or bodies by means of their spectra.
spec'u·la (spĕk'ū·lȧ), *n., pl.* of SPECULUM.
spec'u·lar (spĕk'ū·lẽr), *adj.* [L. *specularis.* See SPECULUM.] Of, pertaining to, or having the qualities of a speculum (in any sense); specif., *Med.*, conducted with the aid of a speculum.
spec'u·late (-lāt), *v. i.* [L. *speculatus*, past part. of *speculari* to spy out, observe.] **1.** *Now Rare.* To contemplate; see mentally. **2.** To ponder a subject in its different aspects and relations; meditate; esp., to theorize from conjectures without sufficient evidence. **3.** *Com.* To enter into a transaction or venture the profits of which are conjectural or subject to chance; specif., to buy or sell with the expectation of profiting by fluctuations in price. — **Syn.** See THINK. — **spec'u·la'tion** (-lā'shŭn), *n.*
spec'u·la'tive (spĕk'ū·lā'tĭv; -lȧ·tĭv), *adj.* Of, pert. to, or of the nature of speculation; given to speculating; of ideas, theoretical; of a business venture, a security, etc., involving risks. Cf. PRACTICAL, 1. — **spec'u·la'tive·ly**, *adv.* — **spec'u·la'tive·ness**, *n.*
spec'u·la'tor (-lā'tẽr), *n.* [L., a spy, explorer.] One who speculates; specif., one who speculates in stocks, bonds, etc. — **spec'u·la·to'ry** (-lȧ·tō'rĭ *or, esp. Brit.*, -tẽr·ĭ), *adj.*
spec'u·lum (spĕk'ū·lŭm), *n.; pl.* SPECULA (-lȧ), SPECULUMS (-lŭmz). [L., fr. *specere* to look, behold.] **1.** A mirror, esp. of metal. **2.** A reflector in an optical instrument. **3.** *Med. & Surg.* An instrument for dilating certain passages of the body for viewing. **4.** *Zool.* A patch of color on the secondaries of most ducks and some other birds, as domestic fowls.
sped (spĕd), *past & past part.* of SPEED.
speech (spēch), *n.* [AS. *spǣc, spēc, sprǣc, sprēc;* akin to AS. *specan, sprecan*, to speak.] **1.** The faculty of uttering articulate sounds or words to express thoughts; the power of speaking. **2.** Act or manner of speaking; communication or expression of thoughts in spoken words. **3.** That which is spoken; uttered words expressive of thought; also, talk; conversation. **4.** A formal public discourse; oration; address. **5.** A particular language; a tongue; a dialect. **6.** *Archaic.* Common saying; report.
speech area. *Ling.* An area where a certain language (as French), a dialect (as Scottish), or a linguistic feature (as German *t-* instead of *z-*) prevails.
speech community. *Ling.* A group of people speaking a mutually intelligible language or dialect, whether living in the same area, contiguous areas, or noncontiguous areas.
speech form. See LINGUISTIC FORM.
speech'i·fy (spēch'ĭ·fī), *v. i.;* -FIED (-fīd); -FY'ING. [*speech* + *-fy.*] *Derisive.* To make a speech; harangue.
speech island. [Transl. of G. *sprachinsel.*] A speech area within a speech area; as, Gottschee (Kočevje) is a German *speech island* in Yugoslavia.
speech'less, *adj.* **1.** Destitute or deprived of speech. **2.** Not speaking for a time; dumb; silent. **3.** Not expressed in, or conveyed by, words; as, *speechless* grief. — **speech'less·ly**, *adv.* — **speech'less·ness**, *n.*
speech reading. = LIP READING.
speed (spēd), *n.* [AS. *spēd* success, swiftness.] **1.** *Archaic.* Prosperity in an undertaking; success; as, to wish one good *speed.* **2.** Act or state of moving swiftly; swiftness; rapidity; dispatch. **3.** Rate of motion; also, rate of performance as indicated by ratio of the amount of work accomplished to time taken. **4.** In automotive vehicles, a transmission gear. — **Syn.** See HASTE. — *v. i.;* SPED (spĕd), SPEED'ED; SPEED'ING. **1.** *Obs.* To go; to fare. **2.** *Archaic.* **a** To experience any fortune, good or ill; fare. **b** To succeed; prosper. **3.** To make haste; to go, drive, etc., fast, esp. too fast. — *v. t.* **1.** To promote; further; aid; favor. **2.** To wish Godspeed to. **3.** To cause to make haste; dispatch with celerity; force to increase speed; accelerate. **4.** *Mach., etc.* To set, adjust, or design, to or for a definite speed or speeds. — *adj.* Of or pertaining to speed; denoting something which regulates, indicates, or attains speed; as in:

speedboat	speed counter	speed limit
speed clock	speed gear	speed reducer
speed controller	speed indicator	speed trap

— **speed'er** (-ẽr), *n.* — **speed'ster** (-stẽr), *n.*
speed·om'e·ter (spēd·ŏm'ē·tẽr), *n.* [*speed* + *-meter.*] **a** An instrument for indicating speed or velocity; a tachometer. **b** A device which measures distance as well as speed; an odometer.
speed'way' (spēd'wā'), *n.* A road on which speeding is allowed.
speed'well (-wĕl), *n.* Any of a genus (*Veronica*) of herbs of the figwort family, with small colored flowers; esp., the common speedwell (*V. officinalis*) and the ***germander speedwell*** (*V. chamaedrys*).
speed'y (spēd'ĭ), *adj.;* -I·ER (-ĭ·ẽr); -I·EST. Marked by speed. — **Syn.** See FAST. — **Ant.** Dilatory. — **speed'i·ly**, *adv.* — **speed'i·ness**, *n.*
speel (spēl), *v. t. & i.* *Scot.* To climb.
speer, speir (spēr), *v. i.* [AS. *spyrian* to inquire, prop., to follow the track.] *Chiefly Scot.* To ask; inquire. — *v. t.* *Chiefly Scot.* **1.** To inquire concerning; to ask for. **2.** To find by searching or asking.
speiss (spīs), *n.* [G. *speise*, lit., food.] *Metal.* A mixture of impure metallic arsenides produced as a regulus in smelting certain ores.
spe'le·ol'o·gy (spē'lē·ŏl'ō·jĭ), *n.* [Gr. *spēlaion* cave + *-logy.*] The scientific study of caves. Cf. SPELUNKER. — **spe'le·o·log'i·cal** (-ō·lŏj'ĭ·kăl), *adj.* — **spe'le·ol'o·gist** (-ŏl'ō·jĭst), *n.*
spell (spĕl), *v. t.* [AS. *spelian.*] **1.** *Now Cant.* To supply the place of for a time; relieve. **2.** To allow an interval of rest to; as, he *spelled* his horse. — *v. i.* *Colloq.* To rest from work for a time. — *n.* **1.** The relief of one person by another in any work or duty. **2.** One's turn at work, or the like. **3.** A period of rest from work; a recess or vacation. **4.** Any relatively short period; hence, *Colloq.:* **a** Any relatively short distance. **b** A fit, as of illness or depression.
spell, *n.* [AS., a saying, tale, speech.] **1.** A spoken word or form of words supposed to have magic power; an incantation. **2.** A charm; spellbinding influence; fascination. — *v. t.* To put under, or as under, a spell; bewitch; charm.
spell (spĕl), *v. t.;* SPELLED (spĕld) or SPELT (spĕlt); SPELL'ING. [OF. *espeller* (F. *épeler*), of Teut. origin.] **1.** To name, write, or print in order the letters of (a word), esp. the proper letters. **2.** To constitute the letters of; hence: **a** To make up; compose. **b** To signify; import; as, such an act *spells* ruin. **3.** To read slowly and with difficulty; as, to *spell* out a letter. **4.** To trace by or as if by characters, marks, or qualities; find out, as by study. — *v. i.* To spell a word or words.
spell'bind' (-bīnd'), *v. t.;* see BIND. [From SPELLBOUND.] To bind or hold by or as if by a spell or charm; fascinate; charm. — **spell'bind'er** (-bīn'dẽr), *n.*
spell'bound' (-bound'), *adj.* [*spell* charm + *bound*, past part.] Entranced; fascinated.
spell'er (spĕl'ẽr), *n.* One who spells words; also, *U. S.*, a **spell'ing book**, a book with exercises for teaching how to spell.
spell'ing, *n.* Act of one who spells; formation of words by letters; orthography. Abbr. *sp.*
spelt (spĕlt), *n.* [AS., fr. LL. *spelta.*] The wheat *Triticum spelta* or any of its varieties. See WHEAT.
spelt, *past & past part.* of SPELL.
spel'ter (spĕl'tẽr), *n.* Zinc; — so called esp. in commerce.
spe·lunk'er (spē·lŭngk'ẽr), *n.* [L. *spelunca* cave.] One who makes a hobby of exploring caves and studying phenomena observable in them. Cf. SPELEOLOGIST. — **spe·lunk'** (spē·lŭngk'), *v. i.*
spence, spense (spĕns), *n.* [OF. *despense*, deriv. of L. *dispendere, -pensum.* See DISPENSE.] *Chiefly Scot.* A pantry; buttery.
spen'cer (spĕn'sẽr), *n.* A trysail abaft the foremast or mainmast.
spen'cer, *n.* [After the 2d Earl *Spencer* (1758–1834).] A short jacket reaching to the waist.
Spen·ce'ri·an (spĕn·sēr'ĭ·ăn), *adj.* Of or pertaining to Herbert Spencer or Spencerianism. — **Spen·ce'ri·an**, *n.*
Spen·ce'ri·an, *adj.* Of, pert. to, or characteristic of a form of slanting handwriting introduced by P. R. Spencer, Am. teacher (1800–64).
Spen·ce'ri·an·ism (-ĭz'm), *n.* The synthetic philosophy of Herbert Spencer, the central idea of which is the mechanistic evolution of the cosmos from relative simplicity to relative complexity.
spend (spĕnd), *v. t.;* SPENT (spĕnt); SPEND'ING. [From OF. *despendre* (fr. L. *dispendere*), and fr. AS. *spendan*, fr. L. *expendere* to weigh out, expend.] **1.** To consume by using; to lay out, exhaust, or distribute, in payment, giving, use, or the like; to expend. **2.** To bestow; confer; also, to give at a sacrifice. **3.** To consume wastefully; squander; exhaust; wear out. **4.** To pass the time of. — *v. i.* **1.** To expend, consume, or waste, anything. **2.** To be or become wasted or consumed.
spend'er (spĕn'dẽr), *n.* One who spends; esp., one who spends lavishly; a prodigal; a spendthrift.
spend'ing mon'ey. Money set apart for extra (not necessary) personal expenses; pocket money.
spend'thrift' (spĕnd'thrĭft'), *n.* One who spends profusely or improvidently; a prodigal. — **spend'thrift'**, *adj.*
Spen·se'ri·an stan'za (spĕn·sēr'ĭ·ăn). The stanza used by Edmund Spenser (see *Biog.*) in *The Faerie Queene*, consisting of eight decasyllabic lines and an alexandrine, and rhyming *ababbcbcc.*
spent (spĕnt), *adj.* Exhausted, esp. of effective quality.
sperm (spûrm), *n.* [OF. *esperme*, fr. LL., fr. Gr. *sperma, -atos*, fr. root of *speirein* to sow.] **1.** *Biol.* **a** The male fecundating fluid; semen. **b** A spermatozoon or spermatozoid. **2.** **a** Short for SPERMACETI. **b** Sperm oil.
-sperm (-spûrm). A combining form denoting *seed.*
sperm-. = SPERMO-.
sper'ma·ce'ti (spûr'mȧ·sē'tĭ; -sĕt'ĭ), *n.* [ML., fr. LL. *sperma* sperm + *ceti*, gen. of *cetus* a whale.] A waxy solid separating from the oil of the sperm whale, dolphin, etc., used esp. in making candles.
-sper'mal (-spûr'măl). = -SPERMOUS.
sper'ma·ry (spûr'mȧ·rĭ), *n.; pl.* -RIES (-rĭz). *Zool.* An organ in which spermatozoa are developed; sperm gland; testis.
sper·mat'ic (spẽr·măt'ĭk), *adj.* Pertaining to sperm or a testis; carrying or abounding in sperm; seminal; testicular.
spermatic cord. *Anat.* The cord which suspends the testicle within the scrotum and contains the vas deferens and vessels and nerves of the testicle.
sper'ma·tid (spûr'mȧ·tĭd), *n.* [Gr. *sperma, -atos*, seed.] *Biol.* One of the cells which arise by division of the secondary spermatocytes and become spermatozoa.
sper·ma'ti·um (spẽr·mā'shĭ·ŭm), *n.; pl.* -TIA (-ȧ). [NL.] *Bot.* **a** In red algae, a nonmotile male gamete. **b** In certain fungi and lichens, any of certain similar cells apparently functioning as male gametes.
sper'ma·to- (spûr'mȧ·tō-), **spermat-.** [Gr. *sperma, spermatos.*] A combining form meaning *sperm, seed, germ*, equivalent to *spermo-*, as in **sper'ma·tog'e·nous, sper'ma·toid.**
sper'ma·to·cyte' (-sīt'), *n.* [*spermato-* + *-cyte.*] *Biol.* A cell giving rise to sperm cells or spermatozoa; in recent usage, a cell of the last generation (***secondary spermatocyte***) or next to the last generation (***primary spermatocyte***) preceding the spermatozoon.
sper'ma·to·gen'e·sis (-jĕn'ē·sĭs), *n.* [NL., fr. *spermato-* + *-genesis.*]

Biol. The formation of spermatozoa. — **sper′ma·to·ge·net′ic** (spûr′mȧ·tō·jē·nĕt′ĭk), *adj.*

sper′ma·to·go′ni·um (spûr′mȧ·tō·gō′nĭ·ŭm), *n.; pl.* -GONIA (-ȧ). [NL., fr. *spermato-* + Gr. *gonē* offspring.] *Biol.* **a** *Zool.* One of the primitive male germ cells. **b** *Bot.* A spermogonium. — **sper′ma·to·go′ni·al** (-ăl), *adj.*

sper′ma·to·phore′ (spûr′mȧ·tō·fōr′; 70), *n.* *Zool.* A special capsule, packet, or mass, enclosing a number of spermatozoa, extruded by the male of various animals, as annelids, mollusks, and some vertebrates. — **sper′ma·toph′o·ral** (-tŏf′ō·răl), *adj.*

sper′ma·to·phyte′ (-fīt′), *n.* Any plant of a phylum (Spermatophyta) embracing the highest plants, or those that produce seeds; a seed, or flowering, plant; a phanerogam; — opposed to *cryptogam.* — **sper′ma·to·phyt′ic** (-fĭt′ĭk), *adj.*

sper′ma·tor·rhe′a, sper′ma·tor·rhoe′a (spûr′mȧ·tō·rē′ȧ), *n.* [NL., fr. *spermato-* + *-rrhea.*] *Med.* Abnormally frequent involuntary emission of semen without orgasm.

sper′ma·to·zo′id (-tō·zō′ĭd), *n.* Also **sper′ma·to·zo′oid** (-oid). [*spermatozoon* + Gr. *eidos* form.] *Bot.* A motile male gamete or male sexual cell, usually developed within an antheridium, and liberated in the presence of water.

sper′ma·to·zo′on (-ŏn), *n.; pl.* -ZOA (-ȧ). [NL., fr. *spermato-* + Gr. *zōion* an animal.] *Zool.* A male sexual cell or sperm cell of an animal, whose function is the fertilization of the egg. Spermatozoa are capable of active spontaneous movement. — **sper′ma·to·zo′al** (-ăl), **sper′ma·to·zo′an** (-ăn), **sper′ma·to·zo′ic** (-ĭk), *adj.*

sper′mic (spûr′mĭk), *adj.* Pertaining to sperm.

-sper′mic (-spûr′mĭk). = -SPERMOUS.

sperm′ine (spûr′mēn; -mĭn), *n.* Also **sperm′in.** [See SPERM.] *Biochem.* A crystalline aliphatic base, $C_{10}H_{26}N_4$, found in semen, in various body tissues, and in yeast.

sper′mo- (spûr′mō-), **sperm-.** A combining form meaning *seed, germ,* as in **sper′mo·phyte.**

sper′mo·go′ni·um (-gō′nĭ·ŭm), *n.; pl.* -NIA (-ȧ). [NL., fr. *spermo-* + Gr. *gonē* offspring.] *Bot.* A flask-shaped or depressed receptacle in which spermatia are produced in certain fungi and lichens.

sperm oil. See SPERM WHALE.

sper′mo·phile (spûr′mō·fīl; -fĭl), *n.* [Gr. *sperma* a seed + *-phile.*] Any of numerous burrowing rodents (genus *Citellus* and allied genera) of northern Europe, Asia, and North America, called also *gopher* and *ground squirrel* (see SQUIRREL, 1). They live in colonies, chiefly in open areas, and do great damage to crops. The best-known Old World species is the *suslik* (which see). A common species of the Great Plains of the United States is the ***striped spermophile*** *or* ***striped gopher*** (*C. tridecemlineatus*).

sper′mous (spûr′mŭs), *adj.* Resembling sperm.

-sper′mous (-spûr′mŭs). Also **-sper′mal** (-măl), **-sper′mic** (-mĭk). [See SPERM.] Combining forms signifying *having* (such or so many) *seeds* or *germs; seeded;* as in multi*spermous.*

sperm whale. A large whale (*Physeter catodon*) of the warmer parts of all oceans; — called also *cachalot.* Its head has a large closed cavity containing a fluid mixture of spermaceti and a valuable pale-yellow lubricant oil (**sperm oil**).

sper′ry·lite (spĕr′ĭ·līt), *n.* [After F. L. *Sperry,* Sudbury, Ontario.] *Mineral.* An arsenide of platinum, $PtAs_2$, occurring in grains and minute isometric crystals of a tin-white color. It is found near Sudbury, Ontario, Canada and is the only compound of platinum known to occur in nature.

spes′sart·ite (spĕs′ẽr·tīt), *n.* [From *Spessart,* Germany.] A red or yellow variety of garnet, chemically $Mn_3Al_2(SiO_4)_3$.

spew (spū), *v. t. & i.* [AS. *spiwian, spīwan.*] To eject from or as from the stomach; vomit; pour forth. — *n.* That which is spewed; vomit. — **spew′er** (spū′ẽr), *n.*

sphac′e·late (sfăs′ē·lāt), *v. i.* [NL. *sphacelare, -latum,* to mortify, fr. Gr. *sphakelos* gangrene.] *Med.* To become gangrenous; mortify. — **sphac′e·la′tion** (-lā′shŭn), *n.*

sphae′ro- (sfē′rō-; sfĕr′ō-), **sphaer-.** [Gr. *sphaira* ball, sphere.] A combining form denoting *sphere, spherical.*

sphag′nous (sfăg′nŭs), *adj.* Pertaining to or abounding in sphagnum.

sphag′num (-nŭm), *n.* [NL., fr. Gr. *sphagnos* a kind of moss.] **1.** Any of a genus (*Sphagnum*) of mosses, sole type of a family (Sphagnaceae); the peat mosses. **2.** A mass of these plants used by florists in packing, potting, etc., or in making surgical dressings and similar pads.

sphal′er·ite (sfăl′ẽr·īt; sfā′lẽr-), *n.* [Gr. *sphaleros* treacherous, uncertain.] *Mineral.* A widely distributed ore of zinc, essentially of zinc sulfide, ZnS. H., 3.5–4. Sp. gr., 3.9–4.1. Called also *blende* or *zinc blende.*

sphene (sfēn), *n.* [F. *sphène,* fr. Gr. *sphēn* wedge; from a form of its crystals.] *Mineral.* Titanite, esp. when light-colored.

sphe′no- (sfē′nō-), **sphen-.** [Gr. *sphēn.*] A combining form meaning *wedge, wedge-shaped;* specif., *Anat.,* denoting *connection with,* or *relation to, the sphenoid bone.*

sphe′noid (sfē′noid), *adj.* [Gr. *sphēnoeidēs,* fr. *sphēn* a wedge + *eidos* form.] **1.** Wedge-shaped. **2.** *Anat.* Designating or pertaining to a winged compound bone of the base of the cranium. — **sphe·noi′dal** (sfē·noi′dăl; -d'l), *adj.*

spher′al (sfēr′ăl), *adj.* Of, pertaining to, or like a sphere; hence, symmetrical; harmonious.

sphere (sfēr), *n.* [OF. *espere* (F. *sphère*), fr. L. *sphaera,* fr. Gr. *sphaira* sphere, ball.] **1.** *Geom.* A body of space bounded by one surface all points of which are equally distant from a point within called its *center.* **2.** Any globe or globular body, esp. a celestial one. **3.** *Astron.* **a** The apparent surface of the heavens (half of which forms the dome of the visible sky). **b** In ancient astronomy, one of the revolving spherical transparent shells in which stars, sun, planets, and moon were supposed to be set. **4.** Circuit or range of action, knowledge, or influence; compass; province; place or scene of action or existence. **5.** Rank; order of society; social position or class. **6.** *Obs.* An orbit. **7.** The atmosphere; the heavens. — *v. t.* **1.** To place in or as in a sphere or among the spheres; ensphere. **2.** To form into a sphere.

-sphere (-sfēr). [Gr. *sphaira* sphere.] A combining form meaning: **a** *A representation of spherical lines or bodies,* as in plani*sphere.* **b** *A spherical enveloping layer,* as in atmo*sphere.* **c** *A spherical mass forming a body,* as in oö*sphere.*

spher′ic (sfĕr′ĭk), *adj.* = SPHERICAL, 1 & 2.

spher′i·cal (-ĭ·kăl), *adj.* **1.** Sphere-shaped; globular. **2.** Of, pert. to, or dealing with a sphere or spheres; having to do with a sphere or with the properties of a sphere; as, *spherical* angle; ***spherical geometry*** (which treats of spherical magnitudes); ***spherical trigonometry*** (trigonometry applied to spherical triangles and polygons). Cf. SOLID, *adj.,* 2. **3.** Of or pert. to the celestial spheres. — **spher′i·cal·ly,** *adv.*

spherical angle. *Math.* The angle between two intersecting arcs of great circles of a sphere, measured by the plane angle formed by the tangents to the arcs at the point of intersection.

spherical polygon. *Geom.* A figure analogous to a plane polygon, formed on a sphere by arcs of great circles.

spherical sailing. See SAILING.

spherical triangle. *Math.* A figure on a sphere formed by the arcs of three great circles that intersect each other.

sphe·ric′i·ty (sfē·rĭs′ĭ·tĭ), *n.; pl.* -TIES (-tĭz). Quality or state of being spherical; roundness.

spher′ics (sfĕr′ĭks), *n.* Mathematics dealing with circles, figures, and other magnitudes of a sphere produced by planes intersecting it; spherical geometry and spherical trigonometry.

sphe′roid (sfēr′oid), *n.* A figure almost a sphere, but not spherical. — **sphe′roid, sphe·roi′dal** (sfē·roi′dăl; -d'l), *adj.* — **-roi′dal·ly,** *adv.*

sphe′roi·dic′i·ty (sfēr′oi·dĭs′ĭ·tĭ), *n.* Also **sphe·roi′di·ty** (sfē·roi′dĭ·tĭ). Quality or state of being spheroidal.

sphe·rom′e·ter (sfē·rŏm′ē·tẽr), *n.* [F. *sphéromètre.*] An instrument for measuring the curvature of surfaces.

spher′ule (sfĕr′ōōl), *n.* [LL. *sphaerula.*] A little sphere or spherical body.

spher′u·lite (sfĕr′ōō·līt), *n.* *Petrog.* A spherical crystalline body of radiating fibers, in some vitreous volcanic rocks, as obsidian. — **spher′u·lit′ic** (-lĭt′ĭk), *adj.*

spher′y (sfēr′ĭ), *adj.* *Poetic.* **1.** Spherical; starlike. *Shak.* **2.** Of the spheres.

sphinc′ter (sfĭngk′tẽr), *n.* [LL., fr. Gr. *sphinktēr;* akin to Gr. *sphingein* to bind tight.] *Anat. & Zool.* A ringlike muscle surrounding, and able to contract or close, a natural opening. — **sphinc′ter·al** (-ăl), *adj.*

sphinx (sfĭngks), *n.; pl.* SPHINXES (sfĭngk′sĕz; -sĭz), SPHINGES (sfĭn′jēz). [L., fr. Gr. *sphinx.*] **1.** *Gr. Myth.* A monster having typically a lion's body, wings, and the head and bust of a woman; specif., ***the Sphinx,*** of Thebes, who proposed a riddle to all passers and upon their failure to guess it destroyed them. Oedipus guessed the riddle, the Sphinx slew herself, and he became king of Thebes. The riddle: What creature walks in the morning upon four feet, at noon upon two, at evening upon three? The answer: Man, as a baby on hands and knees, later on his feet, and in old age with a staff. **2.** A person of inscrutable character and purposes; any person or monster thought of as like the sphinx. **3.** *Egypt. Archaeol.* An image of a recumbent lion having the head of a man (an *androsphinx,* as ***the Sphinx*** at Giza representing Harmachis, the morning sun), a ram (*criosphinx*), or a hawk (*hieracosphinx*). **4.** *Zool.* A hawk moth.

sphra·gis′tic (sfrȧ·jĭs′tĭk), *adj.* [Gr. *sphragistikos* of or for sealing, fr. *sphragis* a seal.] Of or like engraved seals.

sphra·gis′tics (-tĭks), *n.;* see -ICS. The science of seals.

sphyg′mic (sfĭg′mĭk), *adj.* [Gr. *sphygmos* the pulse.] *Physiol.* Of or pertaining to the pulse.

sphyg′mo- (sfĭg′mō-). [Gr. *sphygmos.*] *Med.* A combining form meaning *pulse,* as in **sphyg′mo·gram,** a tracing of curves corresponding with the beats of the heart.

sphyg′mo·graph (-grȧf; 9), *n.* [*sphygmo-* + *-graph.*] *Physiol.* An instrument which records graphically the movements of the pulse; a pulsimeter. — **sphyg′mo·graph′ic** (-grăf′ĭk), *adj.*

sphyg′moid (sfĭg′moid), *adj.* *Physiol. & Med.* Resembling the pulse; pulselike.

sphyg′mo·ma·nom′e·ter (sfĭg′mō·mȧ·nŏm′ē·tẽr), *n.* [*sphygmo-* + *manometer.*] An instrument for measuring blood pressure, esp. arterial blood pressure.

sphyg·mom′e·ter (sfĭg·mŏm′ē·tẽr), *n.* *Physiol.* An instrument for measuring the strength of the pulse beat.

sphyg′mus (sfĭg′mŭs), *n.* [NL., fr. Gr. *sphygmos.*] *Physiol.* The pulse.

spi′ca (spī′kȧ), *n.; pl.* SPICAE (-sē). [L., an ear, as of grain.] **1.** *Archaeol.* An ear of wheat. **2.** [*cap.*] *Astron.* A star of the first magnitude in the constellation Virgo.

spi′cate (spī′kāt), *adj.* [L. *spicatus,* past part. of *spicare* to furnish with spikes, or ears.] *Bot. & Zool.* Having the form of a spike; arranged in a spike or spikes.

spic·ca′to (spēk·kä′tō), *adj.* [It., past part. of *spiccare* to detach.] *Music.* Detached; performed with springing bow; — a direction for stringed instruments.

spice (spīs), *n.* [OF. *espice,* fr. L. *species* sort, kind.] **1.** A specimen; a small portion or admixture; modicum; touch. **2.** Any of various aromatic vegetable productions, as pepper, nutmeg, cloves, etc., used in cookery to season food and to flavor sauces, pickles, etc. **3.** A pungent or fragrant odor. **4.** That which gives zest or pungency; a piquant flavoring; as, variety is the *spice* of life. — *v. t.;* SPICED (spīst); SPIC′ING (spīs′ĭng). To season with or as with spices.

spice′ber′ry (spīs′bĕr′ĭ; -bẽr·ĭ), *n.; pl.* -RIES (-ĭz). **a** Wintergreen, or checkerberry. **b** A tree (*Eugenia rhombea*) of the myrtle family, of Florida, with orange or blackish fruit.

spice′bush′ (-bŏŏsh′), **spice′wood′** (-wŏŏd′), *n.* = BENZOIN, 2.

spic′er·y (spīs′ẽr·ĭ), *n.; pl.* -IES (-ĭz). [OF. *espicerie.*] **1.** Spices. **2.** A repository of spices. **3.** A spicy quality.

spic′i·ly (spīs′ĭ·lĭ), *adv.* In a spicy manner; pungently.

spic′i·ness (-ĭ·nĕs; -nĭs), *n.* Quality of being spicy.

spick′-and-span′, *or, more fully,* **spick′-and-span′-new′,** *adj.* [Var. of SPIKE a nail.] Quite new; brand-new; also, neat and trim.

spic′u·la (spĭk′ū·lȧ), *n.; pl.* -LAE (-lē). [NL., dim. of L. *spica.*] A spicule; prickle. — **spic′u·lar** (-lẽr), *adj.*

spic′u·late (-lāt), *adj.* [L. *spiculatus,* past part. of *spiculare* to sharpen, point.] Covered with spicules.

spic′ule (spĭk′ūl), *n.* [F., fr. L. *spiculum* a little point, a dart.] **1.** A minute, slender pointed body; a needlelike body, esp. of bony material. **2.** *Zool.* One of the minute calcareous or siliceous bodies which support the tissues of various invertebrates, as sponges, radiolarians, holothurians, etc.

spic′u·lum (-ū·lŭm), *n.; pl.* SPICULA (-lȧ). [L., a little point.] *Zool.* **a** Any of various small spicular organs, as the spines of an echinoderm. **b** A spicule.

spic'y (spīs'ĭ), *adj.;* SPIC'I·ER (-ĭ·ẽr); SPIC'I·EST. **1.** Flavored with, containing, or characteristic of, spice or spices; aromatic. **2.** Abounding with spices. **3.** Piquant; pungent; sometimes, savoring of the scandalous.

spi'der (spī'dẽr), *n.* [ME. *spithre,* fr. AS. *spinnan* to spin; — so named from spinning its web.] **1.** Any of various arachnids comprising an order (Araneida) and having a body with but two main divisions: a cephalothorax bearing four pairs of walking legs, and an unsegmented abdomen bearing two or more pairs of spinnerets for spinning threads of silk used in making cocoons for their eggs, nests for themselves, or webs for entangling their prey. **2.** A person conceived of as like a spider, as in craft. **3.** A metal pan with a handle, used in frying food. Originally it had long legs, for use over coals. **4.** A trivet or tripod to support pans or pots over a fire. **5.** A cultivator attachment for pulverizing the ground.

spider monkey. Any of a genus (*Ateles*) of American monkeys ranging from southern Mexico to Paraguay. They have long slender limbs, the thumb being absent or rudimentary and the tail very long and prehensile.

spider phaeton. A very high, light carriage, having a covered seat in front and a footman's seat behind.

spi'der·wort' (spī'dẽr·wûrt'), *n.* Any of a genus (*Tradescantia*) of plants having ephemeral blue or violet flowers with slender hairy stamens.

spi'der·y (spī'dẽr·ĭ), *adj.* Resembling a spider.

spie'gel·ei'sen (spē'gĕl·ī'zĕn), *n.* Also **spie'gel, spiegel iron.** [G., fr. *spiegel* mirror + *eisen* iron.] A variety of pig iron containing manganese up to 15–20 per cent.

spiel (spēl), *n.* [G. *spiel* play, *spielen* to play.] *Slang, U.S.* A speech or talk. — *v. i. Slang, U.S.* To talk.

spiel'er (spēl'ẽr), *n.* **1.** *Colloq., U.S. & Austral.* A professional sharper. **2.** *Slang, U.S.* A speaker, esp. one stationed outside a store or place of amusement to act as a crier.

spier (spēr). Var. of SPEER, ask.

spi'er (spī'ẽr), *n.* One who spies; a spy.

spiff'y (spĭf'ĭ), *adj.;* SPIFF'I·ER (-ĭ·ẽr); SPIFF'I·EST. *Slang.* Neat; fine-looking; smart.

spig'ot (spĭg'ŭt), *n.* A peg used to stop the vent in a cask; the plug of a cock; *U.S.*, a faucet or cock.

spike (spīk), *n.* [L. *spica* ear of grain, tuft of a plant.] **1.** An ear of corn or grain. **2.** *Bot.* A racemose inflorescence in which the flowers are sessile along the axis, as in the common plantain. A spike that is branched and resembles a panicle is termed *compound.* See INFLORESCENCE, *Illust.* (6 & 7).

spike, *n.* [ME.] **1.** Any of various pointed objects or projections, usually slender; as: a pointed iron set with point upward, as on a wall to prevent passage; pointed projections on the sole of a shoe to prevent slipping; a spine, as on some fishes. **2.** A form of very large nail. **3.** Anything shaped like such a projection or nail; as: **a** A young mackerel not over six inches long. **b** An unbranched antler of a young deer. **4.** *pl. Baseball.* Three projections formed by turning up the edges of the metal plate fastened to the sole or heel of a player's shoe to prevent slipping. — *v. t.* **1.** To fasten or furnish with spikes. **2.** To pierce, cut, impale, or the like, with or on a spike. **3.** To put an end to or block, as a proposed plan. **4.** *Mil.* To disable (a cannon) temporarily by driving a spike into the vent.

spike lavender. A European mint (*Lavandula spica*).

spike'let (spīk'lĕt; -lĭt), *n. Bot.* A small spike; specif., one of the small, few-flowered bracted spikes that make up the compound inflorescence of grasses and sedges.

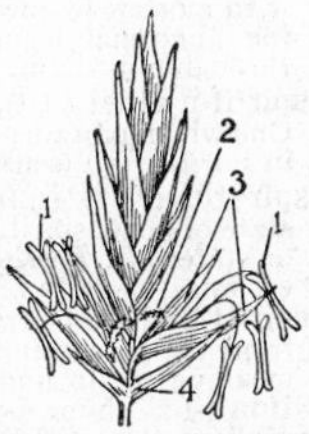

Spikelet of Meadow Fescue (*Festuca elatior*). 1, 1 Anthers; 2 Pistil; 3, 3 Paleae; 4 Glume.

spike'nard (spīk'nẽrd; -närd), *n.* [ML. *spica nardi.* See 1st SPIKE; NARD.] **1. a** A fragrant ointment of the ancients. **b** An East Indian aromatic plant (*Nardostachys jatamansi*) of the valerian family, from which the above is believed to have been derived. **2.** An American herb (*Aralia racemosa*) of the ginseng family, with aromatic root and panicled umbels.

spile (spīl), *n.* [MLG., a splinter, wooden peg.] **1.** A small plug, used to stop a vent. **2.** *U.S.* A spout inserted in a tree for conducting sap. **3.** A large stake driven into the ground as a support for some superstructure; a pile. — *v. t.* To supply with a spile or spiles; to pile; also, to draw off through a spile.

spil'i·kin, spil'li·kin (spĭl'ĭ·kĭn), *n.* [From 1st SPILL.] **1.** One of a number of small pieces or pegs, of bone, for playing certain games, as jackstraws, or for counting in cribbage. **2.** *pl.* A game played with these.

spil'ing (spīl'ĭng), *n.* Piling; piles collectively.

spill (spĭl), *n.* [Partly fr. E. dial. *spell* splinter; partly fr. MD. *spille,* D. *spil.*] **1.** A splinter. **2.** A slender piece; as: **a** A peg for plugging a hole; a spile. **b** A metallic rod or pin. **c** A roll of paper, or slip of wood, used for lighting lamps, pipes, etc.

spill (spĭl), *v. t.;* SPILLED (spĭld) or SPILT (spĭlt); SPILL'ING. [AS. *spillan* to destroy.] **1.** To cause accidentally, or allow unintentionally, to fall, flow, or run out, usually with the result of losing or wasting; hence, to lose, or suffer to be scattered; as, to *spill* water; to *spill* sand. **2.** To shed, as blood. **3.** To let become known, as news; to allow to leak out, as secrets. **4.** *Colloq.* To throw out or off accidentally. **5.** *Naut.* To relieve (a sail) from the pressure of the wind. — *v. i.* To fall or run out or over and thus usually be lost or wasted. — *n.* A spilling; that which is spilled; as: **a** *Colloq.* A throwing out or off accidentally, as from a motorcycle. **b** *Colloq.* A downpour. **c** A spillway.

spill'age (-ĭj), *n.* That which spills or is spilled over.

spill'way' (-wā'), *n. Hydraul. Engin.* A passage for superfluous water in a reservoir or river; a paved apron or a dam or part of a dam, etc., over which water flows.

spi'lo·site (spī'lō·sīt), *n.* [Gr. *spilos* a spot + *-ite.*] *Petrog.* A spotted schistose rock produced by contact metamorphism of clay slate, usually by diabase.

spilth (spĭlth), *n.* Spilling; something spilt; also, waste or refuse, as of the street.

spin (spĭn), *v. t.;* SPUN (spŭn), *Archaic* SPAN (spăn); SPUN; SPIN'NING. [AS. *spinnan.*] **1.** To draw out and twist into threads, by hand or machinery; to produce by drawing out and twisting a fibrous material. **2.** To form (a thread of silk, or a web, cocoon, etc.) by the extrusion of a viscous, rapidly hardening fluid; — of spiders, silkworms. **3.** To form or produce by a slow process, or by degrees; to prolong; protract; — usually with *out.* **4.** To shape in manufacture into threadlike form; — usually in past participle; as, *spun* glass. **5.** To twirl, as a top. — *v. i.* **1.** To make yarn or thread from fiber by drawing and twisting, as a jenny. **2.** To form a thread or threads, as a spider. **3.** To whirl; to revolve, as a top; to feel as if revolving, as one's head. **4.** *Colloq.* To move swiftly, as on a bicycle. **5.** To fish with spinning bait, as spoon bait; to troll.

— *n.* **1.** Act of spinning; the movement imparted by spinning; specif.: **a** A whirl or twirl, as of a baseball pitched with a curve. **b** Act of moving swiftly for a period, as in riding or sailing; as, to take a *spin* round the track. **2.** *Aviation.* An aerial maneuver consisting of a combination of roll and yaw, with the longitudinal axis of the airplane inclined steeply downward.

spin'ach (spĭn'ĭch; -ĭj; 21), *n.* [OF. *espinache, espinage,* through ML. & Sp., fr. Ar. *isbānakh, isfānākh.*] A potherb (*Spinacia oleracea*) of the goosefoot family, cultivated for its edible leaves.

spi'nal (spī'năl; -n'l), *adj.* [LL. *spinalis.*] **1.** *Anat.* **a** Of, pert. to, or near the backbone. **b** Pert. to spines or a spine (pointed process). **2.** *Physiol.* Of, dependent upon, or affecting the spinal cord, as in **spinal anesthesia, spinal anesthetic.** — *n.* A spinal anesthetic.

spinal canal. The canal (containing the spinal cord) formed by the arches on the dorsal side of the vertebrae.

spinal column. *Anat. & Zool.* The articulated series of small bones or vertebrae forming the backbone; the spine. See VERTEBRA, *Illust.*

spinal cord. *Anat.* The longitudinal cord of nervous tissue extending from the brain along the back in the spinal canal.

spin'dle (spĭn'd'l), *n.* [AS. *spinel;* akin to AS. *spinnan* to spin.] **1. a** In hand spinning, a round stick tapering toward each end, with a notch or catch at one end to hold the yarn. **b** The long, round, slender rod or pin in spinning wheels by which the thread is twisted, and on which, when twisted, it is wound. **2.** A spindle-shaped piece or figure; specif.: **a** The fusee of a watch. **b** *Biol.* The spindle-shaped figure of fibers of achromatic substance formed during mitosis. **3.** Any slender pin or rod suggestive of a spinning-machine spindle, esp. one which turns, or on which something turns; specif.: **a** In a lock, the bar or shaft that actuates the latch or bolt. **b** A short decorative turned piece, as in a baluster. **c** *Mach.* An arbor, mandrel, axle, or shaft; esp., a revolving piece less in size than a shaft; as, the live *spindle* of a lathe, that imparts motion to the work. **4.** A hydrometer. **5.** A yarn measure containing, in cotton yarn, 15,120 yards; in linen yarn, 14,400 yards. **6.** A round pile or pipe placed on a rock or shoal as an aid to navigation. — *adj.* **1.** Of or pertaining to spindles; like a spindle, esp. in shape; fusiform. **2.** Pertaining to the mother or the mother's side in descent; as, *spindle* kin. — *v. i.;* SPIN'DLED (-d'ld); SPIN'DLING (-dlĭng). **1.** To shoot or grow into a long slender stalk. **2.** To grow to stalk or stem rather than flower or fruit. — *v. t.* To shape like a spindle.

spin'dle–leg'ged (-lĕg'ĕd; -ĭd; -lĕgd'), **spin'dle–shanked'** (-shăngkt'), *adj.* Having long slender legs.

spin'dle·legs' (-lĕgz'), **spin'dle·shanks'** (-shăngks'), *n. pl., construed as sing. Colloq.* A person with slender legs, or shanks.

spindle tree. Any of a genus (*Evonymus,* family Celastraceae) of shrubs or trees with hard wood used for spindles.

spin'dling (spĭn'dlĭng), *adj.* Long and slender, or disproportionately tall and slender; as, a *spindling* tree or boy. — *n.* A spindling person, plant, or object.

spin'dly (spĭn'dlĭ), *adj.* Spindling.

spin'drift' (spĭn'drĭft'), *n.* Sea spray; spoondrift.

spine (spīn), *n.* [OF. and L.; OF. *espine,* fr. L. *spina* thorn, spine.] **1.** *Bot.* Any stiff, sharp-pointed process, as of the thistle, distinguished from a *thorn* by the absence of vascular tissue, and from *prickle,* which is of subepidermal origin. **2.** *Anat. & Zool.* A stiff sharp process, as of the porcupine or sea urchin; specif.: **a** A spicule. **b** A stiff unsegmented fin ray of a fish. **3.** The backbone, or spinal column. **4.** Backbone; spirit. **5.** *Bookbinding.* The back of a book.

spi·nel' (spĭ·nĕl'; spĭn'ĕl), *n.* Also **spi·nelle'.** [F. *spinelle,* fr. It., fr. L. *spina* thorn, prickle; from its pointed crystals.] *Mineral.* A hard (H., 8) mineral consisting essentially of magnesium and aluminum, and of various colors. ***Ruby spinel,*** a variety of spinel used as a gem, is called ***spinel ruby*** when deep red, ***balas, or balas ruby,*** when rose-red, ***rubicelle*** when yellow or orange-red, ***almandine*** when violet.

spine'less (spīn'lĕs; -lĭs), *adj.* **1.** Having no spine; invertebrate; also, having a flexible spinal column; figuratively, without backbone, or courage. **2.** Having no spines, thorns, or prickles. — **spine'less·ly,** *adv.* — **spine'less·ness,** *n.*

spi·nes'cent (spī·nĕs'ĕnt; -'nt), *adj.* [LL. *spinescens, -entis,* pres. part. of *spinescere* to grow thorny, fr. *spina* a thorn.] Spiny; spinose; tending toward spininess.

spin'et (spĭn'ĕt; -ĭt; spĭ·nĕt'), *n.* [F. *espinette,* fr. It. *spinetta,* prob. after Giovanni *Spinetti* (fl. 1500), of Venice.] **a** An obsolete small form of harpsichord. **b** A type of compactly built upright piano.

spi·nif'er·ous (spī·nĭf'ẽr·ŭs), **spi·nig'er·ous** (-nĭj'ẽr·ŭs), *adj.* Bearing a spine or spines.

spin'i·fex (spĭn'ĭ·fĕks), *n.* [NL., fr. L. *spina* spine + *facere* to make.] *Bot.* Any of a genus (*Spinifex*) of Australian grasses, the seeds of which bear an elastic spine.

spin'na·ker (spĭn'ȧ·kẽr), *n.* [Said to be fr. *Sphinx,* name of a yacht (1866).] *Naut.* A large triangular sail set upon a long light pole (**spinnaker boom**), used when running before the wind. See SLOOP, *Illust.*

spin'ner (spĭn'ẽr), *n.* **1.** One who or that which spins. **2.** *Aeronautics.* A fairing, usually conical and made of sheet metal, which is attached to the propeller boss and revolves with it. See AIRPLANE, *Illust.* **3.** *Angling.* A spoon, blade, or wings which revolve when drawn through the water. See LURE, *Illust.* **4.** *Football.* A play in which the ball carrier spins around in the attempt to deceive the opponents as to where he plans to strike the line.

spin'ner·et (spĭn'ẽr·ĕt), *n.* [Dim. of *spinner.*] **1.** *Zool.* An organ for producing a thread of silk from the secretion of the silk glands, as in spiders and certain caterpillars. **2.** Also **spin'ner·ette'** (spĭn'ẽr·ĕt'). *Rayon Mfg.* A small plate with fine holes through which the cellulose solution passes into the solidifying medium, thus spinning filaments.

spin′ney (spĭn′ĭ), *n.* Also **spin′ny.** [OF. *espinei*, fr. L. *spinetum*, fr. *spina* thorn.] *Eng.* A copse; a thicket.

spin′ning, *n.* The operation or business of making fibrous materials into yarn or thread. — **spin′ning,** *adj.*

spinning frame. *Spinning.* A machine that finally draws, twists, and spools the yarn.

spinning jenny. *Mach.* An engine or machine for spinning wool or cotton by means of many spindles.

spinning wheel. A hand- or foot-driven machine for spinning yarn or thread, in which a wheel drives a single spindle.

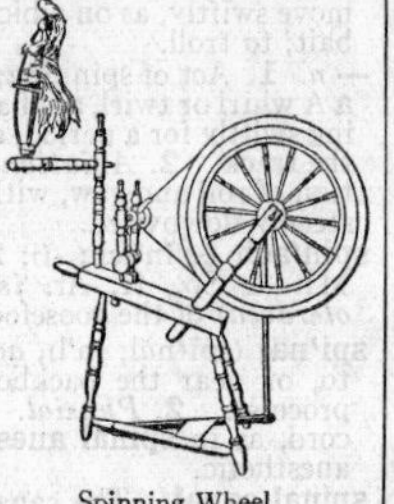
Spinning Wheel.

spi′nose (spī′nōs; spī·nōs′), *adj.* [L. *spinosus*, fr. *spina* thorn.] Full of or armed with spines. — **spi′nose·ly,** *adv.*

spi·nos′i·ty (spī·nŏs′ĭ·tĭ), *n.* Spinose or spinous quality or state; figuratively, a pointed or cutting remark; also, a thorny part or thing.

spi′nous (spī′nŭs), *adj.* Having the form of a spine or thorn; spinelike; also, spinose; spiny.

spinous process. *Anat. & Zool.* The median spinelike or platelike dorsal process of the neural arch of a vertebra. See VERTEBRA, *Illust.*

Spi·no′zism (spĭ·nō′zĭz′m), *n.* The philosophy of Benedictus (or Baruch) de Spinoza, who taught that all reality is One Substance, God, of which thought and extension (or mind and physical reality) are two aspects or attributes. — **Spi·no′zist** (-zĭst), *n.*

spin′ster (spĭn′stẽr), *n.* [ME., fr. *spin* + *-ster.*] **1.** A woman who spins. **2.** Formerly, a title given to unmarried women of the gentle classes from a viscount's daughter down; now, an unmarried woman. **3.** Popularly, an old maid. — **spin′ster·hood,** *n.* — **spin′ster·ish,** *adj.*

spin·thar′i·scope (spĭn·thăr′ĭ·skōp), *n.* [Gr. *spintharis* spark + *-scope.*] A small instrument containing a minute particle of a radium compound mounted in front of a fluorescent screen and viewed with magnifying lenses.

spi′nule (spī′nūl; spĭn′ūl), *n.* [L. *spinula*, dim. of *spina* a spine.] A minute spine. — **spin′u·lose** (spĭn′ū·lōs; spī′nū-), *adj.*

spin′y (spīn′ĭ), *adj.* **1.** Covered with spines; thorny; prickly. **2.** Abounding with difficulties. — **spin′i·ness,** *n.*

spiny anteater. An echidna.

spin′y–finned′ (-fĭnd′; 2), *adj.* Having fins with one or more stiff, unbranched rays, without transverse segmentation; — of acanthopterygian fishes. Cf. SOFT-FINNED.

spiny lobster. See LOBSTER.

spi′ra·cle (spī′rȧ·k'l; spĭr′ȧ-), *n.* [L. *spiraculum*, fr. *spirare* to breathe.] **1.** A breathing hole; blowhole; vent. **2.** *Zool.* In most terrestrial arthropods, one of the stigmata or external apertures of the tracheae, placed along the sides of the thorax and abdomen.

spi·rae′a (spī·rē′ȧ), *n.* Also **spi·re′a.** [L., fr. Gr., fr. *speira* a coil.] *Bot.* Any of a genus (*Spiraea*) of shrubs of the rose family, with small perfect white or pink flowers in dense racemes, corymbs, cymes, or panicles. See MEADOWSWEET, BRIDAL WREATH, HARDHACK.

spi′ral (spī′răl), *adj.* [See 1st SPIRE.] **1.** Winding, coiling, or circling round a center or pole and gradually receding from (or approaching) it; as, the *spiral* curve of a watch spring. **2.** Helical, like the thread of a screw. **3.** *Geom.* Of or like a spiral. — *n.* **1.** *Geom.* **a** The path (generally plane) of a point moving spirally. **b** A helix. **2.** Anything that has a spiral form; also, a single turn or coil in a spiral object. **3.** *Football.* A kick or pass in which the ball rotates on its long axis. **4.** *Aviation.* A flight in a spiral path. **5.** *Econ.* A continuously spreading and accelerating increase or decrease, as in cost, prices, or wages; hence, ***inflationary spiral***, a general accelerating inflation developing through a vicious circle of cause and effect: higher prices of commodities, higher wages, larger flow of money, greater demand for commodities, still higher prices, and so on; conversely, ***deflationary spiral***, a cumulative deflation following a reverse cycle: excess of prices over demand, slackening sales, reduced production, lower wages, reduced employment, shrinking demand, and so on to-ward depression. — *v. i.*; SPI′RALED (-răld) or -RALLED; -RAL·ING or -RAL·LING. To move in a spiral course; *Aviation*, to cause an airplane to follow a spiral path, esp. in descending. — *v. t.* To form into a spiral; twist spirally. — **spi′ral·ly,** *adv.*

spiral nebula. *Astron.* One of a large class of celestial structures exhibiting spiral form in their whorls and general configuration, now regarded as other milky ways.

spiral spring. See SPRING, *Illust.*

spi′rant (spī′rănt), *n.* [L. *spirans, -antis*, pres. part. of *spirare* to breathe.] *Phonet.* A consonant uttered with decided friction of the breath against some part of the oral passage; a fricative, as *f, s, sh.* — **spi′rant,** *adj.*

spire (spīr), *n.* [F., fr. L. *spira* a coil, twist, fr. Gr. *speira.*] **1.** A spiral; a coil, as of a serpent. **2.** *Zool.* The upper part of a spiral shell.

spire, *n.* [AS. *spīr* shoot, stalk.] **1.** A slender tapering blade or stalk, as of grass. **2.** The top of anything, as a deer's horn, that tapers to a point; the sharp tip. **3.** A tapering roof or analogous pyramidal construction surmounting a tower; loosely, a steeple. — *v. i.* To shoot up taperingly like a spire.

spi·re′a (spī·rē′ȧ), *n.* Var. of SPIRAEA.

spired (spīrd), *adj.* Spiral, or having a spire.

spi′reme (spī′rēm), *n.* [Gr. *speirēma, speirama*, a coil.] *Biol.* The chromatin of a cell nucleus, when in the form of a thread. See MITOSIS.

spi·rif′er·ous (spī·rĭf′ẽr·ŭs), *adj.* *Zool.* **a** Having a spiral part or organ. **b** Spired.

spi·ril′lum (spī·rĭl′ŭm), *n.*; *pl.* -LA (-ȧ). [NL., dim. fr. L. *spira* a coil.] *Bacteriol.* Any of a genus (*Spirillum*) of long, curved, flagellate bacteria; by extension, any spiral thread-shaped microorganism. See BACTERIA; cf. SPIROCHETE.

spir′it (spĭr′ĭt), *n.* [OF. or L.; OF. *espirit, esperit*, fr. L. *spiritus;* akin to L. *spirare* to breathe, blow.] **1.** The breath of life; life, or the life principle, conceived as a kind of vapor animating the body, or, in man, mediating between body and soul. **2.** The life principle viewed as the "breath" or gift of deity; hence, the agent of vital and conscious functions in man; the soul. **3.** [*often cap.*] In the abstract, life or consciousness viewed as an independent type of existence. **4.** [*cap.*, often with *the.*] One manifestation of the divine nature; the Holy Spirit. **5.** Any supernatural being, esp. one able to possess a person; an apparition; a specter; also, sometimes, a sprite; elf. **6.** An individual; a person; — esp. with reference to characteristics of mind or temper; as, a bold *spirit.* **7.** *Often pl.* Temper or disposition of mind; mood; as, to be in good *spirits.* **8.** Stimulated or high spirits; vivacity, ardor, quick resentment, courage, etc.; as, to reply with *spirit.* **9.** Enthusiastic loyalty; as, college *spirit.* **10.** Intent; real meaning; — opposed to *letter* (def. 4); also, characteristic quality; as, the *spirit* of an enterprise. **11. a** *Alchemy.* Any of four substances, sulfur, sal ammoniac, mercury, and orpiment. **b** *Old Chem.* Any liquid produced by distillation. **c** The liquid, containing ordinary alcohol and water, distilled from any alcoholic liquid or mash; — often *pl.* **d** Any of certain volatile liquids obtained by distillation of petroleum, shale, wood, etc. **12.** [*cap.*] *Christian Science.* A synonym for God. **13.** *Dyeing.* Any of various solutions, esp. of tin salts, used as mordants; as, aniline *spirit.* **14.** *Pharm.* An alcoholic solution of a volatile substance; — popularly called also *essence.* — **Syn.** See SOUL: COURAGE. — *v. t.* **1.** To inspirit; hence, to animate with vigor; to hearten; encourage. **2.** To convey rapidly and secretly, as if by the agency of a spirit; — often with *away* or *off.* — *adj.* **1.** Of spirits or spiritualism. **2.** That operates by means of or by combustion of alcoholic spirits; as, a *spirit* lamp.

spir′it·ed (spĭr′ĭ·tĕd; -tĭd), *adj.* **1.** *Obs.* Having spirit; also, animated by a spirit. **2.** Animated; full of spirit or fire. — **spir′it·ed·ly,** *adv.* — **spir′it·ed·ness,** *n.*

spir′it·ing, *n.* Action, work, or service of a spirit. *Shak.*

spir′it·ism (spĭr′ĭt·ĭz′m), *n.* = SPIRITUALISM, 3. — **spir′it·ist** (-ĭst), *n.* — **spir′it·is′tic** (-ĭs′tĭk), *adj.*

spir′it·less, *adj.* Destitute of spirit. — **spir′it·less·ly,** *adv.*

spirit level. A level in which the adjustment to the horizon is shown by the position of a bubble in alcohol.

spirit, *or* **spirits, of hartshorn.** See AMMONIA.

‖**spi·ri·to′so** (spē·rē·tō′sō), *adj.* [It.] *Music.* Animated; spirited; — used as a direction.

spir′it·ous (spĭr′ĭ·tŭs), *adj.* *Rare.* Refined; pure. *Milton.*

spirit rapping. An alleged form of communication with the spirits of the dead by rapping, as on a table.

spir′its, *or* **spir′it, of tur′pen·tine** (spĭr′ĭts). Oil of turpentine. See TURPENTINE.

spirits, *or* **spirit, of wine.** Alcohol; rectified spirit.

spir′it·u·al (spĭr′ĭt·ū·ăl), *adj.* **1.** Of or consisting of, spirit; incorporeal. **2.** Of the intellectual and higher endowments of the mind; intellectual. **3.** Of the moral feelings or states of the soul. **4.** Of the soul or its affections as influenced by the divine Spirit; pure; holy; — opposed to *carnal.* **5.** Of sacred things or the church; sacred; as, *spiritual* songs; not lay or temporal; ecclesiastical; as, lords *spiritual* and temporal. — *n.* **1.** *pl.* Sacred matters; esp., church affairs. **2.** A type of religious song peculiar to Negroes of the southern United States, with strongly marked rhythm, and the graphic narrative method of the folk ballad. — **spir′it·u·al·ly,** *adv.* — **spir′it·u·al·ness,** *n.*

spiritual incest. *Eccl. Law.* Cohabitation between persons spiritually allied by baptism or confirmation.

spir′it·u·al·ism (spĭr′ĭt·ū·ăl·ĭz′m), *n.* **1.** Spirituality. **2.** The doctrine that all that exists is spirit; idealism, esp. metaphysical idealism. See IDEALISM, 1 **a.** **3.** A belief that departed spirits hold intercourse with mortals by means of physical phenomena, as by rapping, or during abnormal mental states, as in trances, commonly manifested through a medium; the practices of spiritualists.

spir′it·u·al·ist (-ĭst), *n.* **1.** A spiritually minded person. **2.** *Philos.* One who maintains the doctrine of spiritualism. **3.** One who believes in spiritualism (sense 3); a spiritist. — **spir′it·u·al·is′tic** (-ĭs′tĭk), *adj.*

spir′it·u·al′i·ty (spĭr′ĭt·ū·ăl′ĭ·tĭ), *n.*; *pl.* -TIES (-tĭz). **1.** Quality or state of being spiritual; spiritual-mindedness. **2.** Incorporeal quality or state. **3.** *Eccl. Law.* That which belongs to the church, or to an ecclesiastic, or to religion.

spir′it·u·al·ize (spĭr′ĭt·ū·ăl·īz), *v. t.* **1.** To render spiritual; to purify from the corrupting influences of the world. **2.** To give a spiritual meaning to; to understand in a spiritual sense. — **spir′it·u·al·i·za′tion** (-ĭ·zā′shŭn; -ī·zā′-), *n.*

spir′it·u·al·ty (-ăl·tĭ), *n.* The clergy.

‖**spi′ri′tu′el′** (spē′rē′tü′ĕl′), *adj. masc.*, **spi′ri′tu′elle′** (-ĕl′), *fem.* [F.] Refined; ethereal; also, sprightly.

spir′it·u·ous (spĭr′ĭt·ū·ŭs), *adj.* Containing, or of the nature of, spirit (alcohol); ardent; as, *spirituous* liquors.

spir′i·tus as′per (spĭr′ĭ·tŭs ăs′pẽr). [L.] *Gr. Gram.* A rough breathing (which see).

spir′i·tus fru·men′ti (frōō·mĕn′tī). [L. *frumenti* of grain.] Whisky.

spir′i·tus le′nis (lē′nĭs). [L.] *Gr. Gram.* A smooth breathing (which see).

spirit writing. *Spiritualism.* Automatic writing under the control of abnormal influences.

spiro-. [L. *spirare* to breathe.] *Med.* A combining form meaning *respiration*, as in **spi·rom′e·ter** (spī·rŏm′ē·tẽr), an instrument for measuring the breathing capacity of the lungs; hence, **spi·rom′e·try,** *n.*

spi′ro·chete, spi′ro·chaete (spī′rō·kēt), *n.* [Gr. *speira* coil + *chaitē* hair.] *Bacteriol.* Any of the spirally undulating microorganisms of an order (Spirochaetales) of slender bacteria, including those causing syphilis and relapsing fever. Cf. SPIRILLUM.

spi′ro·che·to′sis, spi′ro·chae·to′sis (-kē·tō′sĭs), *n.* A disease caused by spirochetes, as ***avian spirochetosis***, a destructive febrile disease of domestic fowls and other birds, caused by a spirochete (*Borrelia anserina*).

spi′ro·graph (spī′rō·grȧf; 9), *n.* [*spiro-* + *-graph.*] *Physiol.* An instrument recording respiratory movements.

spi′ro·gy′ra (-jī′rȧ), *n.* [NL., fr. Gr. *speira* coil + *gyros* a ring.] *Bot.* Any of a genus (*Spirogyra*) of green fresh-water algae with spiral chlorophyll bands.

spi′roid (spī′roid), *adj.* [See SPIRE a spiral; -OID.] Like a screw or spiral.

spirt (spûrt), *v.* & *n.* Spurt; gush; squirt; jet; flare.

spir′u·la (spĭr′ū·lȧ; -ŏŏ·lȧ), *n.* [NL., dim. fr. L. *spira* a coil.] *Zool.* Any of a genus (*Spirula*) of small dibranchiate cephalopods having a many-chambered shell in a flat spiral.

spir′y (spīr′ĭ), *adj.* Of a spiral form; curled; serpentine.

spir'y (spīr'ĭ), *adj.* Of or like a spire; tall, slender, and tapering; also, abounding in spires.

spit (spĭt), *n.* [AS. *spitu.*] **1.** A slender, pointed iron rod for holding meat over a fire. **2.** A small point of land or narrow shoal running into a body of water from the shore. — *v. t.*; SPIT'TED; SPIT'TING. To thrust a spit through; to fix upon a spit; to impale.

spit, *v. t.*; SPAT (spăt), often SPIT; SPIT'TING. [AS. *spittan.*] **1.** To eject from the mouth; to expectorate. **2.** To eject; to give or send out as if by spitting, as snow or fire. **3.** To light (a fuse). — *v. i.* **1.** To eject saliva; — often with *on, upon,* or *at,* as showing contempt. **2.** To rain or snow slightly. **3.** To make a noise like that of expectoration, as a cat. — *n.* **1.** Spittle; saliva; also, the act of spitting. **2.** A frothy secretion resembling saliva, exuded by spittle insects; also, a spittle insect. **3.** A sprinkle of rain or flurry of snow. **4.** *Dial.* Perfect likeness; counterpart; as, he is the *spit* (or *spit and image,* etc.) of his father.

spit'al (spĭt'ăl; -'l), *n.* [ME. *spitel.* See HOSPITAL.] *Archaic.* A lazaretto; hence, refuge.

spit'ball' (spĭt'bôl'), *n.* **1.** Paper chewed and rolled into a ball, to be thrown as a missile. **2.** *Baseball.* A variety of pitched ball, now illegal, produced by moistening one side of the ball with saliva.

spitch'cock' (spĭch'kŏk'), *n.* [Lit., split-cook.] An eel split or cut up and cooked. — *v. t.* To prepare for eating as a spitchcock.

spite (spīt), *n.* [Shortened fr. ME. *despit* despite.] **1.** Ill will with the disposition to irritate, annoy, or thwart; petty malice; grudge; rancor. **2.** *Rare.* Vexation; mortification. *Shak.* — **Syn.** See MALICE. — ***in spite of.*** In defiance or contempt of; notwithstanding. — *v. t.* **1.** To treat maliciously; to thwart; shame; mortify. **2.** *Obs. exc. Scot.* To fill with spite; to vex.

spite'ful (-fo͝ol; -f'l), *adj.* Filled with, or showing, spite; malicious. — **spite'ful·ly,** *adv.* — **spite'ful·ness,** *n.*

spit'fire' (spĭt'fīr'), *n.* A violent, irascible, or passionate person.

spit'ter (spĭt'ẽr), *n.* **1.** One who puts meat on a spit. **2.** A young deer whose antlers begin to shoot.

spit'ter, *n.* One who ejects saliva from the mouth.

spit'tle (spĭt''l), *n.* [From SPIT to eject.] **1.** Saliva; spit. **2.** The frothy secretion of a spittle insect.

spittle insect. Any of numerous leaping homopterous insects (family Cercopidae) whose larvae secrete froth. See CUCKOO SPIT.

spit·toon' (spĭ·to͞on'), *n.* A receptacle for spit; a cuspidor.

spitz dog (spĭts). [G. *spitz, spitzhund,* fr. *spitz* pointed.] = POMERANIAN, *n.,* 2.

Spit'zen·burg (spĭt'sĕn·bûrg), *n.* Any of several varieties of pointed red-and-yellow winter apples.

spiv (spĭv), *n.* [Proposed origins: from police abbr. of "*s*uspected *p*ersons and *i*tinerant *v*agrants"; from the reverse of VIPS, very important persons; var. of 19th-cent. slang *spiff* a spiffy or flashy dresser.] *Brit. Slang.* One who lives by his wits, without working; hence, a slacker.

splanch'nic (splăngk'nĭk), *adj.* [Gr. *splanchnon* an entrail.] *Anat.* Of or pert. to the viscera; visceral.

splanch'no- (splăngk'nō-). [Gr. *splanchnon* an entrail.] A combining form meaning *the viscera,* as in **splanch·nol'o·gy, splanch·not'o·my** (see -LOGY, -TOMY).

splash (splăsh), *v. t.* [From PLASH to splash.] **1.** To strike and dash about (water, mud, etc.). **2.** To scatter water, mud, etc., upon in quantities; to bespatter. **3.** To make (one's or its way) with splashing. **4.** To cause to appear splashed or bespattered; as, fields *splashed* with poppies. **5.** *Logging.* To drive (logs) by releasing a head of water confined by a dam (**splash dam**) made for the purpose. — *v. i.* **1.** To strike and dash about water, mud, etc. **2.** To fall or strike with a splashing noise. **3.** To scatter about; to spatter. — *n.* **1.** Liquid splashed; a spot or daub from it; also, the sound of liquid being splashed. **2.** Act of striking the water. **3.** A blotch. **4. a** *Logging.* Act of splashing logs. **b** The water impounded and then released suddenly to splash logs.

splash'board' (-bōrd'; 70), *n.* **1.** A dashboard. **2.** A plank used to close a sluice or spillway of a dam.

splash'er (splăsh'ẽr), *n.* One that splashes; also, a guard to keep off splashes, as over a wheel.

splat (splăt), *n.* The single, flat, thin member of a chair back rising from seat rail to top rail.

splat'ter (splăt'ẽr), *v. i. & t. & n.* Spatter.

splay (splā), *v. t.* [From DISPLAY.] **1.** To spread out; expand. **2.** To dislocate, as a shoulder bone. **3.** To slope or slant, as the side of a door or window. — *v. i.* To spread out; also, to slope or slant. — *n.* **1.** Spread; expansion. **2.** *Arch.* A slope or bevel, esp. of the sides of a door or window. See MOLDING, *Illust.* (14). — *adj.* Spread out; turned outward; awkward; ungainly. — **splay'-kneed',** *adj.* — **splay'-leg'ged,** *adj.* — **splay'-toed',** *adj.*

splay'foot' (-fo͝ot'), *n.* A foot abnormally flattened and spread out; specif., *Med.,* a flat foot, or the deformity flatfoot. — **splay'foot', splay'foot'ed,** *adj.*

spleen (splēn), *n.* [OF. or L.; OF. *esplen,* fr. L. *splen,* fr. Gr. *splēn.*] **1.** *Anat. & Zool.* A highly vascular glandlike ductless organ near the stomach or intestine of most vertebrates, concerned with final destruction of blood cells, storage of blood, and production of lymphocytes; the milt. It was formerly believed to be the seat of emotions or passions. **2.** *Archaic.* Melancholy; low spirits. **3.** Anger; latent spite; malice. **4.** *Obs.* A sudden impulse or whim; caprice. — **Syn.** See MALICE.

spleen'ful (-fo͝ol; -f'l), *adj.* Full of or affected with spleen; ill-humored; melancholy; fiery. — **spleen'ful·ly,** *adv.*

spleen'wort' (-wûrt'), *n.* Any of a genus (*Asplenium*) of ferns having linear or oblong sori borne obliquely on the upper side of a veinlet.

splen'dent (splĕn'dĕnt), *adj.* [L. *splendens, -entis,* pres. part.] **1.** Shining; glossy. **2.** Illustrious; brilliant.

splen'did (splĕn'dĭd), *adj.*; -DID·ER (-ẽr); -DID·EST. [L. *splendidus,* fr. *splendere* to shine.] **1.** Possessing or displaying splendor; specif.: **a** Shining; brilliant. **b** Showy; magnificent; gorgeous. **2.** Illustrious; grand; glorious. **3.** Excellent; very good or fine. — **splen'did·ly,** *adv.* — **splen'did·ness,** *n.*

Syn. **Splendid, resplendent, gorgeous, glorious, sublime, superb** mean transcendently impressive. **Splendid** implies an outshining the usual or customary; **resplendent,** a glowing or blazing splendor; **gorgeous,** a sumptuous splendor particularly in its display of color; **glorious,** a radiance that heightens beauty or distinction; **sublime,** an elevation or exaltation almost beyond human comprehension; **superb,** a grandeur, magnificence, or the like, that reaches the highest point conceivable.

splen·dif'er·ous (splĕn·dĭf'ẽr·ŭs), *adj.* [*splendor* + *-ferous.*] *Humorous.* Splendid; gorgeous.

splen'dor, splen'dour (splĕn'dẽr), *n.* [OF. or L.; OF. *esplendor, -dour,* fr. L. *splendor,* fr. *splendere* to shine.] **1.** Great brightness; brilliant luster; brilliancy. **2.** Magnificence; pomp; glory. — **splen'dor·ous** (-dẽr·ŭs), **splen'drous** (-drŭs), *adj.*

sple·net'ic (splē·nĕt'ĭk), *adj.* [LL. *spleneticus.*] **1.** Splenic. **2.** Affected with spleen; hence, melancholy; also, malicious; peevish; fretful. — **Syn.** See IRASCIBLE. — *n.* One with a splenetic disposition. — **sple·net'i·cal** (-ĭ·kăl), *adj.* — **sple·net'i·cal·ly,** *adv.*

splen'ic (splĕn'ĭk; splē'nĭk), *adj.* [L. *splenicus,* fr. Gr. *splēnikos.*] Of, pertaining to, or located in the spleen.

sple'ni·us (splē'nĭ·ŭs), *n.* [NL.] *Anat.* A flat muscle of each side of the back of the neck. — **sple'ni·al** (-ăl), *adj.*

sple'no- (splē'nō-; splĕn'ō-), **splen-.** [Gr. *splēn, splēnos.*] A combining form denoting *the spleen,* as in **sple·nec'to·my, sple·ni'tis, sple·not'o·my.** (See -ECTOMY, etc.)

spleu'chan (splo͞o'kăn), *n.* [Gael. *spliūchan.*] *Scot. & Ir.* A pouch, as for holding tobacco or money.

splice (splīs), *v. t.*; SPLICED (splīst); SPLIC'ING (splīs'ĭng). [D. *splissen, splitsen.*] **1.** To unite, as two ropes or parts of a rope, by interweaving the strands. **2.** To unite, as spars, timbers, rails, etc., by lapping the two ends together, or by applying a piece which laps upon the two ends, and then making fast. **3.** *Slang.* To unite in marriage; to marry. — *n.* **1.** A joining or junction made by splicing. **2.** *Slang.* Marriage; a wedding.

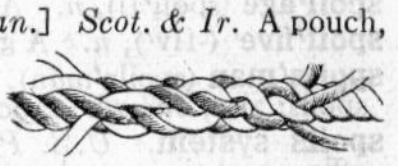

Splice, 1.

splic'er (splīs'ẽr), *n.* One who or that which splices; *Naut.,* a fid used in splicing. Cf. MARLINESPIKE, *Illust.*

spline (splīn), *n.* A thin wood strip, used in building construction.

splint (splĭnt), *n.* [MD. or MLG. *splinte.*] **1.** A piece split off; a splinter. **2.** A thin strip of wood interwoven with others to make a chair seat, basket, etc. **3.** *Medieval Armor.* One of the thin plates or strips of metal usually overlapping in armor, allowing free movement. **4.** *Surg.* An appliance, as of wood, metal, or plaster of Paris, used to keep in place, or protect, an injured part. **5.** *Veter.* An exostosis, or bony enlargement, caused by periostitis, on the upper part of the cannon bone of the horse, ordinarily on the inside of the leg. — *v. t.* To fasten or confine with splints, as a broken limb; to support or brace as with splints.

splint bone. *Veter.* One of the rudimentary, splintlike metacarpal or metatarsal bones on either side of the cannon bone in the limbs of the horse and allied animals.

splin'ter (splĭn'tẽr), *n.* [MD.] A thin piece split or rent off lengthwise; a sliver. — *v. t.* **1.** To split or rend into long, thin pieces; to shiver. **2.** To splint, as a limb. — *v. i.* To become split into long pieces; to shiver. — **splin'ter·y** (-ĭ), *adj.*

splinter bar. **1.** A crossbar in a coach or other vehicle to support the springs. **2.** A whippletree

split (splĭt), *v. t.*; SPLIT; SPLIT'TING. [MD. *splitten.*] **1.** To divide lengthwise or in the direction of the grain or layers; to rive; cleave. **2.** To burst; rend; tear asunder; figuratively, to ruin. **3.** To divide into parts or shares, as booty or commissions; to separate into divisions, factions, etc., as a political party. **4.** *Chem.* To divide or separate into components; also, to remove by such division; as, to *split* off carbon dioxide. — *v. i.* **1.** To divide lengthwise or in the direction of the grain or layers. **2.** To part asunder; to be rent. **3.** *Colloq.* To separate into factions. **4.** *Slang.* To betray confidence; to peach. — **Syn.** See TEAR. — ***split hairs.*** To make overnice or oversubtle distinctions. — ***split one's vote or ticket.*** To vote for candidates of different parties at the same election. — ***split the difference.*** To reach agreement by compromise involving equal concessions by each disputant. — *n.* **1.** A splitting; also, a crack, rent, or fissure. **2.** A breach or separation, as in a political party. **3.** A splinter; a fragment. **4.** *Slang.* **a** Share of booty. **b** A half pint, half glass, half portion. **5.** A mixed sweet composed of sliced fruit (esp. banana), ice cream, nuts, and sirups. **6.** *Basketwork.* Any of the three or four strips into which osiers are cleft for certain work. **7.** *Bowling.* A position of pins left standing, such that a spare is almost impossible. **8.** *Gymnastics.* The feat of going down to the floor so that the legs extend in a straight line. **9.** *Leather Mfg.* One of two or more thicknesses into which a skin is divided. — *adj.* **1.** Divided; fractured. **2.** Cleft for use either singly or in combination; as, *split* bamboo. **3.** *Stock Exchanges.* Of quotations, given in sixteenths, quotations in eighths being regular; as, 10$\frac{3}{16}$ is a *split* quotation. — **split'ter,** *n.*

split infinitive. *Gram.* The infinitive with *to,* taking a modifier between the *to* and the verbal (*to* really *learn*). The splitting has been widely objected to, but it sometimes is desirable or necessary, esp. to avert ambiguity.

split'-lev'el, *adj.* Divided vertically so that the floor level of rooms in one part is approximately midway between the levels of two successive stories in an adjoining part; — of a dwelling.

split'ting, *adj.* *Colloq.* Rending; piercing; very severe; as, a *splitting* headache.

splore (splōr), *n.* *Scot.* A frolic; carousal; broil.

splotch (splŏch), *n. & v.* Spot; blotch.

splurge (splûrj), *n.* [Imitative.] *Colloq.* An ostentatious demonstration or effort. — *v. i.*; SPLURGED (splûrjd); SPLURG'ING (splûr'jĭng). *Colloq.* To make a splurge.

splut'ter (splŭt'ẽr), *v. i. & t.* [Imitative.] **1.** To make a noise as of spitting. **2.** To speak or utter hastily and confusedly; to sputter. — *n.* A confused noise, as of hasty speaking. — **splut'ter·er,** *n.*

spode (spōd), *n.* A fine pottery or porcelain made at the works of Josiah Spode (1754–1827) at Stoke, Staffordshire, Eng.

spod'u·mene (spŏd'ū·mēn), *n.* [Gr. *spodoumenos,* pres. part. pass. fr. *spodoun* to burn to ashes, fr. *spodos* ashes.] *Mineral.* A monoclinic mineral occurring in prismatic crystals, often of great size. It is a silicate of lithium and aluminum.

spoil (spoil), *v. t.*; SPOILED (spoild) or SPOILT (spoilt); SPOIL'ING. [OF. *espoillier,* fr. L. *spoliare,* fr. *spolium* hide, arms or armor stripped from an enemy, spoil.] **1.** To strip or deprive by violence; to rob; despoil; as, to *spoil* one of his goods. **2.** *Archaic.* To take by force; plunder. **3.** To impair seriously; vitiate; mar; ruin. **4.** To impair the disposition of, as by overindulgence; as, to *spoil* a child. — **Syn.** See INDULGE. — *v. i.* **1.** To plunder; rob. **2.** To become corrupted or tainted; to decay, as fruit. — **Syn.** See DECAY. — ***be spoiling for.*** *Colloq.* To have an eager desire for. — *n.* **1.** The plunder taken from the enemy in war; pillage; booty; loot. **2.** Public offices and their emoluments regarded as the peculiar property of a successful party to be bestowed for its own advantage; — commonly *pl.* **3.** That which is gained by special effort; as, literary *spoils* from Europe. **4.** *Now Rare.* Spoliation. **5.** *Obs.* Impairment; corruption. **6.** An object for plundering; a prey. **7.** Refuse earth, rock, etc., excavated, as in dredging. — **spoil'er,** *n.*

Syn. Spoil (*or* **spoils**), **pillage, plunder, booty, prize, loot** mean that which is taken from another by force or craft. **Spoil,** or now more commonly **spoils,** refers to that which belongs by right or custom to the victor, originally in battle, but now often in a political contest; **pillage** implies more open violence or lawlessness; **plunder,** a more general term, applies to that taken not only in war, but in banditry, robbery, etc.; **booty** implies plunder to be shared or divided; **prize** implies spoils captured on the high seas or territorial waters of the enemy; **loot,** a very derogatory term for *plunder,* now applies esp. to that taken from the victims of a catastrophe.

spoil'age (spoil'ĭj), *n.* Act of spoiling; also, something spoiled.

spoil'five' (-fīv'), *n.* A game at cards.

spoils'man (spoilz'măn), *n.* One who serves a party for a share of the spoils; also, one who sanctions such practice.

spoils system. *U.S. Politics.* The practice of regarding public offices and their emoluments as plunder to be distributed to members of the victorious party. Cf. MERIT SYSTEM.

spoke (spōk), *n.* [AS. *spāca.*] **1.** The radius or ray of a wagon wheel; any of the small bars which are inserted in the hub, or nave, and which serve to support the rim or fellies. See WHEEL, *Illust.* **2.** Any of the radiating bars on any wheel; esp., *Naut.,* any of the projecting handles of a steering wheel. **3.** A rung, or round, of a ladder. — *v. t.* To furnish with spokes.

spoke, *past and archaic past part.* of SPEAK.

spo'ken (spō'kĕn), *past part.* of SPEAK; specif.: *part. adj.* **a** Uttered; delivered by word of mouth; oral; — opposed to *written;* as, the *spoken* word. **b** Speaking; as, well-*spoken.*

spoke'shave' (spōk'shāv'), *n.* A drawing knife or small transverse plane with end handles, for rounding small pieces.

spokes'man (spōks'măn), *n.* One who speaks as the representative of another or others. — **spokes'wom'an** (-wo͝om'ăn), *n.*

‖**spo'li·a o·pi'ma** (spō'lĭ·ȧ ō·pī'mȧ). [L.] The richest spoils; the arms taken on the field by the victorious from the vanquished general.

spo'li·a'tion (spō'lĭ·ā'shŭn), *n.* [L. *spoliatio,* fr. *spoliare* to spoil.] **1.** Act of plundering; despoliation; specif., robbery in war; esp., the authorized plundering of neutrals at sea. **2.** *Admiralty & Internat. Law.* The destruction of a ship's papers when she is suspected of smuggling, carrying contraband, etc. **3.** *Law.* Injury done to, or change made in, a document by a stranger to the document. — **spo'li·a'tor** (spō'lĭ·ā'tẽr), *n.*

spon·da'ic (spŏn·dā'ĭk), *adj.* [F. or L.; F. *spondaïque,* fr. L. *spondaicus,* better *spondiacus,* fr. Gr. *spondeiakos.*] Of or constituting a spondee; characterized by spondees; as, a *spondaic* hexameter, one having a spondee in the fifth foot.

spon'dee (spŏn'dē), *n.* [F. or L.; F. *spondée,* fr. L. *spondeus,* fr. Gr. *spondeios* (sc. *pous*), fr. *spondē* a drink offering, libation. At libations slow, solemn melodies were used, chiefly in this meter.] *Pros.* A foot of two long syllables, as in *lēgēs.* In English accentual verse so-called spondees are usually trochees.

spon'dy·lo- (spŏn'dĭ·lō-), **spondyl-.** [Gr. *spondylos.*] A combining form denoting *vertebra,* as in **spon'dy·li'tis,** inflammation of the vertebrae.

sponge (spŭnj), *n.* [OF. *esponge,* fr. L. *spongia,* fr. Gr. *spongia, spongos.*] **1.** The elastic porous mass of interlacing horny fibers which forms the internal skeleton of certain marine animals (phylum Porifera) which are, except in the larval stage, permanently attached, growing in a plantlike fashion and remarkable for their power of absorbing water, becoming soft when wet without losing their toughness; also, one of these animals or a colony of them. **2.** A piece of the above substance; also, act of bathing or wiping with a sponge. **3.** *Now Colloq.* One who lives upon others; a parasite. **4.** One that absorbs or takes in anything freely, as a sponge does water. **5.** Any spongelike substance; as: **a** Raised dough. **b** A porous pudding of gelatin, beaten egg whites, etc. **c** Any of various metals as platinum, obtained in spongelike form, usually by reduction without fusion. **6.** An absorbent pad of cotton used in surgical operations. — ***to chuck, throw, or toss up*** (*or* ***in***) ***the sponge.*** *Colloq.* To abandon the struggle; acknowledge defeat; submit; — from the practice of boxers' seconds throwing a sponge into the ring as a concession of defeat. — *v. t.;* SPONGED (spŭnjd); SPONG'ING (spŭn'jĭng). **1.** To cleanse, wipe, or wet with a sponge. **2.** To wipe out with a sponge; to efface. **3.** To absorb. **4.** *Now Colloq.* To get without cost in a mean, cringing, or underhand way; to cadge. — *v. i.* **1.** To absorb, as a sponge. **2.** *Colloq.* To get a living, a meal, etc., meanly at the expense of another or by imposition. **3.** To fish for sponges. — **spong'er** (spŭn'jẽr), *n.*

sponge'cake' (-kāk'), *n.* A cake without butter in which eggs are the chief leavening agent.

sponge cloth. = RATINÉ.

spong'ing house (spŭn'jĭng). *Eng. Law.* A house in which debtors were formerly kept for a day to give them a chance to compromise with their creditors.

spon'gy (spŭn'jĭ), *adj.;* SPON'GI·ER (-jĭ·ẽr); SPON'GI·EST. **1.** Of the nature of, or like, a sponge; elastic and porous; absorbent; of an open, loose, pliable texture. **2.** *Obs.* Rainy. *Shak.* — **spon'gi·ness** (-jĭ-nĕs; -nĭs), *n.*

spon'sion (spŏn'shŭn), *n.* [L. *sponsio,* fr. *spondere, sponsum,* to promise solemnly.] **1.** Act of becoming surety; a formal pledge, esp. one made on behalf of another person. **2.** *Internat. Law.* An act or engagement on behalf of a state by an agent not specially authorized for the purpose.

spon'son (-sŭn; -s'n), *n.* **1.** A projection from a ship's side, as a bracket; specif., a projecting gun platform, or an air chamber along the rail of a canoe for stability. **2.** A light, air-filled structure protruding from the hull of a seaplane to give it steadiness as it rests on water.

spon'sor (spŏn'sẽr), *n.* [L., fr. *spondere, sponsum,* to engage oneself, promise.] **1.** One who binds himself to answer for another's default; a surety. **2.** Hence, one who assumes, or one to whom is delegated, responsibility for some other person or thing. **3.** *Eccl.* One who at the baptism of an infant professes the Christian faith in its name, and guarantees its religious education; a godfather or godmother. **4.** A business firm that pays the broadcaster and performers for a radio program that introduces advertising of its product. — *v. t.* To be or stand sponsor for; to accept responsibility for. — **spon·so'ri·al** (spŏn·sō'rĭ·ăl; 70), *adj.* — **spon'sor·ship,** *n.*

spon'ta·ne'i·ty (spŏn'tȧ·nē'ĭ·tĭ), *n.; pl.* -TIES (-tĭz). **1.** Quality or state of being spontaneous; spontaneous action or movement. **2.** That quality, innate power, or influence which determines the character.

spon·ta'ne·ous (spŏn·tā'nē·ŭs), *adj.* [LL. *spontaneus,* fr. L. *sponte* of free will, voluntarily.] **1.** Proceeding from natural feeling, temperament, or disposition, or from a native internal tendency, without constraint. **2.** Proceeding from, or acting by, internal impulse, energy, or natural law, without external force; self-acting. **3.** Produced without being planted, or without human labor; indigenous. — *adv.* Spontaneously. — **spon·ta'ne·ous·ly,** *adv.* — **spon·ta'ne·ous·ness,** *n.*

Syn. Spontaneous, impulsive, instinctive, automatic, mechanical mean, as here compared, acting or activated without deliberation. **Spontaneous** also implies lack of prompting, and naturalness; **impulsive,** the acting under stress of emotion or spirit of the moment; **instinctive,** acting unconsciously as or as if by instinct; **automatic** and **mechanical,** engaging neither the mind nor the emotions and suggesting a machine in quick or perfunctory response.

spontaneous combustion. Self-ignition in a substance through chemical action of its constituents, as in the oxidation of oily rags.

spontaneous generation. *Biol.* The generation of living from nonliving matter; abiogenesis; autogenesis; — from a belief, now abandoned, that organisms found in putrid organic matter arose spontaneously from it.

spon·toon' (spŏn·to͞on'), *n.* [F. *sponton, esponton,* fr. It. *spontone, spuntone,* fr. *punto* point, fr. L. *punctum.*] A type of short pike formerly borne by subordinate officers of infantry.

spoof (spo͞of), *n.* [Orig., a game, invented, with the name, by Arthur Roberts (b. 1852), Eng. comedian.] *Slang.* Deception; hoax. — *v. t. & i. Slang.* To deceive; hoax.

spook (spo͝ok), *n.* [D.] *Now Humorous.* A spirit; ghost. — **spook'ish** (-ĭsh), *adj.* — **spook'y** (-ĭ), *adj.;* SPOOK'I·ER (-ĭ·ẽr); SPOOK'I·EST.

spool (spo͞ol), *n.* [MD. *spoele* (D. *spoel*).] **1.** A cylinder, with a rim or ridge at each end and an axial hole for a pin or spindle, used to wind thread or yarn on; a reel. **2.** Something like, or likened to, a spool. — *v. t.* To wind on a spool.

spoon (spo͞on), *n.* [ME. *spon* spoon, chip, fr. AS. *spōn* a chip.] **1.** An implement consisting of a small bowl (usually a shallow oval) with a handle, used esp. in cooking or eating. **2.** Anything which resembles a spoon; as: **a** *Angling.* A slightly curved piece of metal, or the like, used as bait; — called also **spoon bait.** Cf. SPOON HOOK; LURE, *Illust.* **b** *Nav. Ordn.* An extension outboard of the top of a torpedo tube for keeping a torpedo horizontal when launched. **3.** *Golf.* A wooden club with more loft than a driver or brassie, having also a slightly shorter and stiffer shaft. See GOLF, *Illust.* — *v. t.* **1.** To take up in or as in a spoon; also, to shape or hollow out like the bowl of a spoon. **2.** *Croquet, Golf, etc.* To push or shove (a ball) with a lifting motion. — *v. i.* **1.** To fish with a spoon bait. **2.** *Slang.* To act with silly and demonstrative fondness. **3.** *Croquet, Golf, etc.* To spoon a ball.

spoon'bill' (-bĭl'), *n.* Any of several wading birds (genera *Platalea* and *Ajaia*) closely allied to the ibises, having the bill greatly expanded and flattened at the tip. See BILL, *Illust.*

spoon bread. Bread made of corn meal or rice with milk, eggs, shortening, and leavening and so soft that it must be served with a spoon.

spoon'drift' (-drĭft'), *n.* [*spoom* (= *spume*) + *drift.*] Spray blown from waves during a gale at sea; spindrift.

spoon'er·ism (spo͞on'ẽr·ĭz'm), *n.* [After Rev. Wm. A. *Spooner* (1844–1930), of Oxford, Eng.] An accidental transposition of sounds, usually the initial sounds, of two or more words (a *bl*ushing *cr*ow, for a *cr*ushing *bl*ow).

spoon'-fed', *adj.* Fed with a spoon; hence: **a** Pampered. **b** Given no opportunity for initiative.

spoon'ful (spo͞on'fo͝ol), *n.; pl.* -FULS (-fo͝olz). As much as a spoon contains or can contain; specif., a teaspoonful.

spoon hook. A form of lure for fishing, consisting of a spoon on a swivel attached to the line, in connection with a hook or hooks. Cf. LURE, *Illust.*

spoor (spo͝or; 84), *n.* [D.] A track or trail of a wild animal. — *v. i. & t.* To track by a spoor or trail.

spo·rad'ic (spō·răd'ĭk), *adj.* [ML. *sporadicus,* fr. Gr. *sporadikos* scattered.] Occurring occasionally, singly, or apart from others of the same kind, or in scattered instances; separate; single. — **Syn.** See INFREQUENT. — **spo·rad'i·cal·ly** (-ĭ·kăl·ĭ), *adv.*

spo'ra·do·sid'er·ite (spō'rȧ·dō·sĭd'ẽr·īt), *n.* [Gr. *sporas, -ados,* scattered + *siderite.*] The commonest form of meteorite, mostly crystalline with grains of iron disseminated through it.

spo·ran'gi·um (spō·răn'jĭ·ŭm), *n.; pl.* -GIA (-ȧ). [NL., fr. Gr. *sporos* a sowing, seed + *angeion* receptacle.] *Bot.* A spore case; specif., the sac or receptacle within which asexual spores are produced. In bacteria and certain algae and fungi the sporangium is often a single cell (mother cell) giving rise endogenously to one or a few spores. — **spo·ran'gi·al** (-ăl), *adj.*

spore (spōr; 70), *n.* [NL. *spora,* fr. Gr. *spora* a sowing, seed; akin to Gr. *speirein* to sow.] *Biol.* Any of various primitive reproductive bodies (or resistant resting cells), typically unicellular, produced by plants and some protozoans. — *v. i. Bot.* To form or develop spores, as a plant.

spore case. *Bot.* A case containing spores; sporangium.

spore fruit. *Bot.* Any specialized structure which produces spores, as an ascocarp.

spo'ro- (spō'rō-), **spor-.** [Gr. *spora* a seed.] A combining form meaning *spore,* as in **spo·rif'er·ous.**

spo'ro·carp (-kärp), *n.* [*sporo-* + *-carp.*] *Bot.* **a** In the red algae (Rhodophyceae) and ascomycetous fungi, the multicellular body which develops from a fertilized archicarp or procarp; a cystocarp. It produces asexual spores called *carpospores.* **b** In mosses, the sporogonium.

spo'ro·cyst (-sĭst), *n.* [*sporo-* + *-cyst.*] **1.** *Zool.* **a** (1) The cast or cyst secreted by certain protozoans preliminary to sporulation. (2) A protozoan in such an encysted condition. **b** In certain trematode worms, a saclike stage which buds off cells from the membrane lining its internal cavity. **2.** *Bot.* A unicellular resting cell which may give rise to asexual spores.

spo′ro·gen′e·sis (spō′rō·jĕn′ē·sĭs), *n.* [NL.] *Biol.* **a** Reproduction by spores. **b** Spore formation. — **spo·rog′e·nous** (spō·rŏj′ē·nŭs), *adj.*

spo′ro·go′ni·um (-gō′nĭ·ŭm), *n.; pl.* -NIA (-ȧ). [NL. See SPORO-; -GONY.] *Bot.* The sporophyte in mosses and liverworts, typically consisting of a stalk (*seta*) bearing a capsule (*theca*) in which spores are produced.

spo·rog′o·ny (spō·rŏg′ō·nĭ), *n.* *Zool.* In sporozoans, the process of formation of sporozoites from a zygote or **spo′ront** (spō′rŏnt; 70).

spo′ro·phore (spō′rō·fōr; 70), *n.* *Bot.* A spore-bearing branch or organ.

spo′ro·phyll (-fĭl), *n.* Also **spo′ro·phyl.** *Bot.* A spore-bearing leaf; a leaf more or less modified in form and structure which develops sporangia.

spo′ro·phyte (-fīt), *n.* *Bot.* In plants exhibiting alternation of generations, the individual or generation which bears asexual spores; — distinguished from *gametophyte*.

-sporous. A combining form used to signify *having* (such or so many) *spores*.

spo′ro·zo′an (spō′rō·zō′ăn), *n.* [NL., fr. *sporo-* + *-zoa*.] *Zool.* Any member of a class (Sporozoa) of protozoans consisting of parasitic forms, which pass through a life history comprising both asexual and sexual generations, in the course of which reproduction by sporulation takes place. The group includes various pathogenic members, as the malaria parasite. — **spo′ro·zo′an,** *adj.*

spo′ro·zo′ite (-īt), *n.* *Zool.* In sporozoans, one of a group of spindle-shaped infective forms produced by repeated divisions of a zygote.

spor′ran (spŏr′ăn), *n.* [Gael. *sporan*, fr. LL. *bursa* purse.] A pouch of skin with the hair or fur on, worn in front of the kilt by Highlanders in full dress.

sport (spōrt; 70), *n.* [Abbr. fr. ME. *desport, disport.* See DISPORT.] **1.** That which diverts, and makes mirth; pastime; diversion. **2.** A diversion of the field, as hunting, fishing, racing, games, esp. athletic games, etc.; also, any of various similar games usually played under cover, as bowling, rackets, basketball, etc. **3. a** Pleasantry; raillery; as, he questioned them in *sport*. **b** Mock; mockery; derision. **4. a** A plaything. **b** A butt for mirth or derision; a laughingstock. **5.** Amorous play. *Shak.* **6.** One who has a sporting instinct; as, *Colloq.:* **a** A gambler. **b** One devoted to the gayer pleasures and pastimes. **7.** *Biol.* **a** A sudden spontaneous deviation or variation from type; a mutation. **b** *Bot.* A bud variation. — **Syn.** See FUN. — *v. t.* **1.** *Obs.* To amuse (oneself). **2.** *Colloq.:* To wear or use in public, esp. with ostentation. — *v. i.* **1.** To play; frolic; also, to wanton. **2.** To engage in sports. **3.** To speak or act in jest; to trifle. **4.** *Biol.* **a** To vary abruptly from type; to mutate. **b** *Bot.* To exhibit bud variation. — *adj.* Adapted to use in connection with outdoor sports; as, *sport* clothes.

sport′ful (-fo͝ol; -f'l), *adj.* Full of sport; diverting; merry; frolicsome. — **sport′ful·ly,** *adv.* — **sport′ful·ness,** *n.*

sport′ing, *adj.* **a** Of or engaging in sport or sports; sportsmanlike; calling for sportsmanship. **b** Such as might be tried, done, said, etc., by a contender in sports; — used esp. in such phrases as *a sporting chance, a sporting thing to do.*

spor′tive (spōr′tĭv; 70), *adj.* **1.** Tending to or engaged in sport; gay; frolicsome; not serious. **2.** Relating to sports, esp. field sports. **3.** *Obs.* Wanton. *Shak.* — **spor′tive·ly,** *adv.* — **spor′tive·ness,** *n.*

sports (spōrts), *adj.* Pertaining to, or suitable for, outdoor games; as, *sports* clothes.

sport, *or* **sports, shirt.** Any shirt styled for sportswear as distinguished from business or dress wear; specif., a loose, buttoned or pull-over casual shirt, typically with open neck, deep-folding collar, short or long sleeves, and square bottom to be worn inside or out.

sports′man (spōrts′măn), *n.; pl.* -MEN (-mĕn). **1.** One who pursues sports, esp. of the field. **2.** One who in sports is fair and generous; a good loser and a graceful winner. — **sports′man·like′** (-līk′), *adj.* — **sports′man·ly,** *adj.* — **sports′wom′an** (-wo͝om′ăn), *n.; pl.* -WOMEN (-wĭm′ĕn; -ĭn).

sports′man·ship, *n.* Skill in or devotion to sports; esp., conduct becoming to a sportsman, involving honest rivalry and graceful acceptance of results.

sports′wear′ (spōrts′wâr′), *n.* Clothing suitable for wearing while engaged in various sports; also, an occasion on which such clothing may be worn.

sport′y (spōr′tĭ; 70), *adj.;* SPORT′I·ER (-tĭ·ẽr); SPORT′I·EST. *Colloq.* Characteristic of a sport or a sporting man; also, given to gay dissipation. — **sport′i·ness,** *n.*

spor′u·la′tion (spŏr′ū·lā′shŭn), *n.* *Biol.* Formation of spores; esp., division into many small spores (esp. after encystment). — **spor′u·late** (spŏr′ū·lāt), *v. i.*

spor′ule (spŏr′ūl), *n.* *Biol.* A small spore.

spot (spŏt), *n.* [ME.] **1.** A mark on a substance made by foreign matter; a blot. **2.** A stain on character or reputation; reproach; fault; blemish. **3.** A small part differing, as in color, finish, or material, from the main part, or from the ground upon which it is; as, the *spots* of a leopard. **4.** A small extent of space; any particular place or area. **5.** A small sciaenoid food fish (*Leiostomus xanthurus*) of the Atlantic coast, with a black spot behind the shoulders. **6.** One of a variety of domestic pigeons, white with a dark tail and a dark patch on the forehead. — ***on, or upon, the spot.*** **a** Immediately; without further consideration. **b** *Slang.* In peril; in danger of the death penalty, as for betrayal of secrets; — often in *put on the spot,* to murder. — *v. t.;* SPOT′TED; SPOT′TING. **1.** To mark in or with spots; to stain. **2.** To blemish; taint; disgrace. **3.** *Colloq.* To mark or note so as to insure recognition; hence, to recognize; to detect; loosely, to espy. **4.** To place on an appointed or desired spot. **5.** *Mil.* To locate accurately on the ground or on a map. — *adj.* **1. a** On hand for immediate delivery after sale; as, *spot* wheat. **b** Paid or ready for payment at once upon delivery; — of cash. **2.** *Com.* Involving immediate cash payment; as, a *spot* transaction; engaged in, or making a specialty of, cash transactions; as, a *spot* firm; the *spot* market. **3.** *Radio.* **a** Originating in and broadcast from a local station; as, *spot* broadcasting. **b** Designating an announcement made between programs on a network or a local station. — **spot′ta·ble,** *adj.*

spot′less, *adj.* Without a spot; esp., free from reproach or impurity. — **spot′less·ly,** *adv.* — **spot′less·ness,** *n.*

spot′light′ (spŏt′līt′), *n.* **1. a** A projected spot or circle of light, used to illuminate brilliantly a single person or object or group on the stage. **b** Hence, conspicuous public notice. Cf. LIMELIGHT, 2 **b**. **2.** An accessory automobile light with an adjustable focusing device.

spot′ted (spŏt′ĕd; -ĭd), *adj.* **1.** Marked with spots. **2.** Sullied; tarnished.

spotted crake. A small European rail (*Porzana porzana*) similar to the American sora.

spotted crane's-bill. The wild geranium (*Geranium maculatum*). See GERANIUM.

spotted fever. *Med.* **a** = TYPHUS. **b** = CEREBROSPINAL MENINGITIS. **c** = ROCKY MOUNTAIN SPOTTED FEVER.

spotted hemlock. See COWBANE.

spot′ter (spŏt′ẽr), *n.* One that spots; as: **a** *U.S.* A detective; esp., a person employed to detect dishonesty and irregularities. **b** *Mil.* One who locates the position of an enemy target for a gun crew. **c** *Railroads, U.S.* A device on a car for marking irregularities in the track.

spot′ty (spŏt′ĭ), *adj.;* -TI·ER (-ĭ·ẽr); -TI·EST. **1.** Full of, or marked with, spots. **2.** Irregular; lacking uniformity; as, a *spotty* market. — **spot′ti·ness,** *n.*

spous′al (spouz′ăl; -'l), *n.* *Usually pl.* Nuptials. — *adj.* Of or celebrating marriage.

spouse (spous; spouz), *n.* [OF. *espous, espos,* fem. *espouse,* fr. L. *sponsus, sponsa,* prop. past part. See SPONSOR.] A husband or wife. — (spouz), *v. t. Archaic.* To wed; espouse.

spout (spout), *v. t.* [ME. *spouten* to spout, vomit.] **1.** To throw out forcibly and abundantly, as liquids; to eject in a jet. **2.** To recite in an oratorical or pompous manner. **3.** *Slang.* To pawn. — *v. i.* **1.** To issue with violence, or in a jet, as a liquid through a narrow orifice, or from a spout. **2.** To eject liquid or material in a jet. **3.** To declaim. — *n.* **1.** That through which anything spouts; a discharging lip, pipe, or orifice. **2.** A discharge or jet of water or other liquid from or as if from a pipe, esp. when rising in a column; specif., a waterspout. **3.** A shoot or lift formerly used in a pawnbroker's shop; *Slang,* a pawnshop. — **spout′er,** *n.*

sprag (sprăg), *n.* A billet of wood or a rod used as a prop or for checking a vehicle from running backward. — *v. t.* To prop, support, or check the motion of (a vehicle) by means of a sprag.

sprag, *n.* *New England.* A young codfish.

sprain (sprān), *v. t.* [OF. *espreindre* to press, force out, fr. L. *exprimere.* See EXPRESS, *adj.*] To weaken, as a joint or muscle, by sudden and excessive exertion. — *n.* **1.** Act of spraining; sudden or violent overstrain or wrenching. **2.** The condition caused by such overstrain.

sprang (sprăng), *past* of SPRING.

sprat (sprăt), *n.* [AS. *sprott.*] A small European herring (*Clupea sprattus*) closely allied to the common herring; also, any of several other species of small herring.

sprat′tle (sprăt′'l), *n. & v.* *Scot.* Scramble; struggle.

sprau′chle (spräk′'l), *v. t.* *Scot. & Ir.* To clamber.

sprawl (sprôl), *v. i.* [AS. *sprēawlian.*] **1.** To move, when lying down, with awkward extension and motions of the limbs. **2.** To spread the limbs carelessly in a recumbent position. **3.** To spread irregularly, as vines; to spread ungracefully, as handwriting. — *v. t.* To cause to spread out ungracefully or irregularly. — *n.* Act or posture of sprawling. — **sprawl′er,** *n.*

spray (sprā), *n.* [ME.] A collective mass of small branches and foliage, esp. when horizontal, as those of hemlock; also, something resembling this, as a decorative design or ornament, as of brilliants.

spray, *n.* [From earlier *spray* to sprinkle, fr. MD. *sprayen.*] **1.** Water flying in small drops or particles, as blown from waves. **2.** A jet of fine medicated vapor or a liquid dispersed by a sprayer, as for applying a medicine, insecticide, etc.; also, an instrument for such application, as an atomizer; also, the material so applied. — *v. t. & i.* **1.** To scatter or let fall in spray. **2.** To throw or discharge spray upon. — **spray′er,** *n.*

spread (sprĕd), *v. t.;* SPREAD; SPREAD′ING. [AS. *sprǣdan.*] **1.** To scatter, strew, or disperse; to distribute over a surface. **2.** To extend in length and breadth, or in breadth only; to stretch or flatten out; open; unfurl, as a sail. **3.** To extend or distribute over a period of time; to prolong or protract. **4.** To stretch forth or extend, as the legs or wings. **5. a** To divulge, as news; to disseminate. **b** To propagate, as a disease. **c** To diffuse, as effluvia; to emit. **6. a** To cover or overlay with something, as a floor with rugs. **b** To prepare; to set and furnish, as with provisions. **7.** To recount; to record, or enter, as resolutions upon the minutes. **8.** To push apart; as, the locomotive has *spread* the rails. — *v. i.* **1.** To become dispersed, distributed, or scattered; as, this paint *spreads* well. **2.** To extend in length and breadth in all directions, or in breadth only; to be extended. **3. a** To be made known more extensively, as news. **b** To be disseminated from one to another, as disease. **c** To diffuse, as an odor. **4.** To be forced, or to become, apart or farther apart; to separate. — *n.* **1. a** Act of spreading; extension; as, the *spread* of learning. **b** Extent of being spread out; capability of expansion; as, the *spread* of a bird's wing. **c** Dispersion or diffusion; as, the *spread* of disease. **2.** Extent; compass; expanse; also, intervening space. **3.** A cloth used to cover a table or a bed. **4.** *Colloq.* A meal; a feast; a banquet, usually informal. **5.** Anything, as jam, used to spread on bread. **6.** The distance from tip to tip of an airplane, inclusive of ailerons. **7.** *Advertising.* Matter set across a page instead of in a column. **8.** *Newspapers.* Two pages facing each other. **9.** *Exchanges, U.S.* An option in the nature of a put and call in which the put price is different from the call price.

spread eagle. The figure of an eagle with wings raised and legs extended; hence, anything resembling such a figure, as a figure in fancy skating, etc.

spread′-ea′gle, *adj.* *Colloq., U.S.* Pretentious or exaggerated in style; bombastic; esp., exaggeratedly patriotic. — *v. t.* To fix in the position of a spread eagle; specif., *Naut.,* to lash (a man) to the shrouds with arms and legs extended. — *v. i.* To execute a spread eagle, as in skating, diving, etc.

spread′er (sprĕd′ẽr), *n.* One who or that which spreads; as: **a** A device for scattering something. **b** A small knife for spreading butter at table. **c** A bar for holding apart two stays, bars, wires, etc.

spree (sprē), *n.* **1.** A frolic. **2.** A drunken carousal.

spri′er (sprī′ẽr), **spri′est,** *compar. & superl.* of SPRY.

sprig (sprĭg), *n.* [ME. *sprigge.*] **1.** A small shoot or twig; also, an ornament in the form of a twig or a stemmed flower. **2.** *Humorous.* A scion; a youth. **3.** A brad with no head; also, one of the small triangular pieces of tin plate or zinc to hold a pane of glass in the sash. — *v. t.;* SPRIGGED (sprĭgd); SPRIG′GING. **1.** To mark or adorn with sprigs, as muslin. **2.** To deprive or strip (a shrub, a tobacco plant, etc.) of a sprig or sprigs; also, to pluck (a sprig or sprigs). **3.** To drive sprigs, or brads, into.

sprigged (sprĭgd), *adj.* Adorned with sprigs; as, *sprigged* muslin.

spright′ly (sprīt′lĭ), *adj.;* -LI·ER (-lĭ·ẽr); -LI·EST. Having animation; lively; brisk; gay. — **Syn.** See LIVELY. — *adv.* Spiritedly. — **spright′li·ness,** *n.*

sprig′tail′ (sprĭg′tāl′), *n. Local, U.S.* The pintail duck. See PINTAIL **a.**

spring (sprĭng), *v. i.;* SPRANG (sprăng) or SPRUNG (sprŭng); SPRUNG; SPRING′ING. [AS. *springan.*] **1.** To leap; bound. **2. a** To start or rise suddenly, as from a covert. **b** To spurt; dart; shoot. **c** To bound to one's feet. **3.** To be resilient; to be elastic. **4.** To become warped, as a piece of timber. **5. a** To shoot up, out, or forth; to issue as a plant from seed, a stream from its source, etc. **b** *Archaic & Poetic.* Specif., of the day, to dawn. **c** To result, as from a cause, reason, or principle. **6.** To tower; to be higher; as, the spire *springs* far above the roof. **7.** To explode; — said of a mine. **8.** *Arch.* To start from the impost, rounding upward and outward; — said of a vault or arch.

Syn. Spring, arise, rise, originate, derive, flow, issue, emanate, proceed, stem mean to come up or out of something into existence. **Spring** specifically implies emergence; **arise** and **rise,** a coming into existence or notice, but *rise* usually stresses an ascent; **originate,** a definite source or starting point; **derive,** a prior existence in another form which serves as its source; **flow,** an origin as in a spring or reservoir; **issue,** emergence as if from a womb; **emanate,** the coming of something immaterial as from a source; **proceed,** the place of origin, derivation, or the like; **stem,** an outgrowth, as from a root or a branch.

— *v. t.* **1.** To cause to spring, leap up, dart forth, issue, etc. **2.** To disclose suddenly; also, to announce; reveal. **3. a** To crack or split. **b** To bend or strain so as to weaken; as, to *spring* a mast. **c** To cause to open, as a leak through the seams of a ship. **4.** To cause to explode; as, to *spring* a mine. **5.** To cause to close suddenly, as parts of a trap. **6.** To bend by force, as something stiff or strong; as, to *spring* the watchcase open; to force or put by bending, as a beam into its sockets; as, to *spring* in a bar. **7.** To pass over by leaping; as, to *spring* a fence. **8.** *Slang.* To release from jail or custody.

— *n.* [AS., a source of water, a springing.] **1.** Any source of supply, esp. that of a stream; an issue of water from the earth. **2.** Act of springing; as: **a** A leap; bound; also, the distance covered by a jump. **b** A flying back; resilience. **3.** Hence: **a** The first stage; time of growth and progress. **b** Season of the year when plants begin to vegetate and grow; the vernal season, usually including March, April, and May in the middle latitudes north of the equator. Spring of the astronomical year begins with the vernal equinox and ends with the summer solstice. **4.** An elastic body or device that recovers its original shape when released after being distorted. **5.** Capacity for springing; elasticity; hence, vigor; energy. **6.** That by which action, or motion, is produced or propagated; cause; origin; motive. **7.** *Scot.* A lively tune or dance. **8.** *Arch.* The line or plane at which an arch or vault curve springs from its impost. **9.** *Naut.* A crack, fissure, or permanent deformation in a mast or yard. — **Syn.** See MOTIVE.

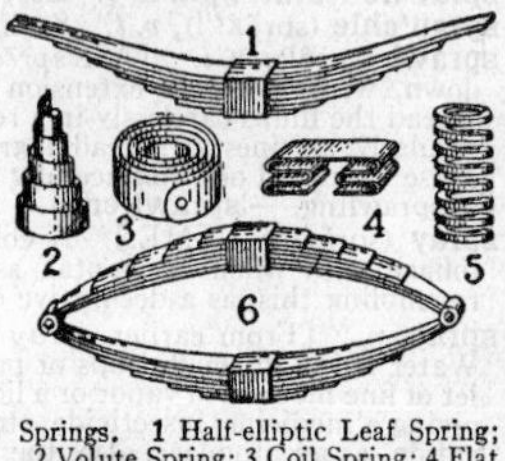

Springs. 1 Half-elliptic Leaf Spring; 2 Volute Spring; 3 Coil Spring; 4 Flat Spring; 5 Spiral Spring; 6 Elliptic Leaf Spring.

— *adj.* **1.** Of or pert. to spring; planted or occurring in the spring. **2.** Pert. to, fitted with, or acting like, a spring; resilient. **3.** Suspended on or having springs.

spring′al (sprĭng′ăl), **spring′ald** (-ăld), *n.* [Scot. *springald, springel,* fr. Scot. & E. *spring.*] *Archaic.* An active young man; a stripling.

spring beauty. Any of a genus (*Claytonia*) of plants, esp. one (*C. virginica*) which sends up in early spring a 2-leaved stem bearing delicate pink flowers.

spring′board′ (sprĭng′bōrd′; 70), *n.* **a** An elastic board, secured at the ends, or at one end, used in performing feats of agility or in exercising. **b** A stiff but springy board, projecting over water, from which bathers may dive.

spring′bok′ (-bŏk′), *n.;* see PLURAL, *Note,* 6. [D. *springbok,* lit., springbuck.] A South African gazelle (*Antidorcas euchore*) noted for its grace and for its habit of springing suddenly into the air.

spring′buck′ (-bŭk′), *n.* The springbok.

springe (sprĭnj), *n.* [ME. *sprenge.*] A noose fastened to a spring to catch small game; a snare; trap.

spring′er (sprĭng′ẽr), *n.* **1.** One who or that which springs. **2.** A springer spaniel. See SPANIEL. **3. a** A grampus. **b** The springbok. **4.** *Arch.* The stone or other solid which forms the impost. The skewback is one form of springer. See ARCH, *Illust.* **5.** A young chicken, larger than a broiler and smaller than a roaster; a fryer.

spring fever. *Humorous.* The lazy listless feeling that comes to persons with the first warm days of spring.

Spring′field ri′fle (sprĭng′fēld). [From *Springfield,* Mass., where a United States armory is located.] The breech-loading magazine .30 caliber rifle of the bolt type adopted in 1903 for use by the U. S. Army; — officially designated *United States rifle, Model of 1903.* See RIFLE, *Illust.*

spring′halt′ (sprĭng′hôlt′), *n.* Stringhalt. — **spring′halt′,** *adj.*

spring′head′ (-hĕd′), *n.* A fountain or source.

spring′ing line, *or* **spring′ing** (sprĭng′ĭng), *n. Arch.* The line, usually horizontal, from which an arch springs.

spring′i·za′tion (sprĭng′ĭ·zā′shŭn; -ī·zā′-), *n.* [*spring* + *-ization.*] = VERNALIZATION.

spring′tail′ (sprĭng′tāl′), *n.* Any of numerous small thysanuran insects (suborder Collembola). They have two elastic caudal stylets which can be bent and then suddenly extended like a spring, thus enabling them to leap.

spring tide. See TIDE, *n.,* 3.

spring′time′ (-tīm′), *n.* Also **spring′tide′** (-tīd′). The season of spring; the time or period of spring.

spring′y (sprĭng′ĭ), *adj.;* -I·ER (-ĭ·ẽr); -I·EST. **1.** Resembling a spring; elastic; resilient. **2.** Abounding with springs; wet; spongy. — **Syn.** See ELASTIC. — **spring′i·ly,** *adv.* — **spring′i·ness,** *n.*

sprin′kle (sprĭng′k'l), *v. t.;* -KLED (-k'ld); -KLING (-klĭng). [ME. *sprenkelen.*] **1.** To scatter in drops or particles. **2.** To scatter on; to spot, as with color. — *v. i.* **1.** To scatter a liquid, or any fine substance, so that it may fall in particles. **2.** To rain lightly in scattered drops. — *n.* A sprinkling; esp., a slight rain. — **sprin′kler** (-klẽr), *n.*

sprin′kler sys′tem (-klẽr). A system for protection against fire, in which pipes are distributed for conveying water or other extinguishing fluid to outlets for fire extinguishment.

sprin′kling (-klĭng), *n.* Act of one that sprinkles or a quantity sprinkled: as **a** A small quantity falling in scattered drops. **b** A small number scattered, or as if scattered, here and there; as, a *sprinkling* of people.

sprint (sprĭnt), *v. i.* [ME. *sprenten* to leap, run.] To run at top speed. — *n.* **1.** Act of sprinting; hence, a short period of intense work. **2.** *Sports.* A short-distance race, requiring contestants to go at top speed. — **sprint′er,** *n.*

sprit (sprĭt), *n.* [AS. *sprēot.*] *Naut.* A pole or spar which crosses a fore-and-aft sail diagonally. See SHARPIE, *Illust.*

sprite (sprīt), *n.* [OF. & F. *esprit,* fr. L. *spiritus.*] **1.** A shade; ghost; also, an apparition. **2.** An elf; fairy; goblin. **3.** The white crab (see CRAB, 1 **a**).

sprit′sail′ (sprĭt′sāl′; *naut.* -s'l), *n. Naut.* A sail extended by a sprit.

sprock′et (sprŏk′ĕt; -ĭt), *n. Mach.* **a** A tooth or projection, as on a wheel, shaped so as to engage with a chain. **b** A sprocket wheel.

sprocket wheel. A wheel with cogs or sprockets to engage with the links of a chain. See BICYCLE, *Illust.*

sprout (sprout), *v. i.* [AS. *sprūtan.*] To germinate, as a seed; to push out new shoots; hence, of the earth, to bring forth young shoots. — *v. t.* To cause to sprout; as, rain *sprouts* seed. — *n.* **1.** The shoot of a plant. **2.** Something resembling a sprout; offshoot; scion. **3.** *pl.* = BRUSSELS SPROUTS.

spruce (sprōōs; 114), *n.* [ME. *Spruce* Prussia, fr. *Pruce,* fr. ML. *Prussia;* — because first known as a native of Prussia.] **1. a** Any evergreen tree of the genus *Picea.* Spruces are handsome trees with dense foliage forming a conical head. Varieties include: ***black spruce*** (*P. mariana*) of northeastern North America, with inferior wood; ***blue spruce or Colorado spruce*** (*P. pungens*), a tall wide-spreading tree often planted for ornament; the ***Colorado blue spruce*** (*P. pungens kosteriana*), derived from the Colorado spruce; ***red spruce*** (*P. rubens*) of eastern North America, important as chief source of pulp wood; ***white spruce*** (*P. glauca*) of North America, with short blue-green leaves and slender cones. See CONE, *Illust.* **b** The wood of any of these trees. **2.** Any of several other coniferous trees, as the Douglas fir (often called ***Douglas spruce***), and the ***balsam spruce*** (*Abies lasiocarpa*), a tall tree of western North America, with silvery bark and bluish-green foliage.

spruce, *adj.* **1.** Neat and dapper; smart; trim. **2.** Overnice; fussy. — *v. t. & i.;* SPRUCED (sprōōst); SPRUC′ING (sprōōs′ĭng). *Now Colloq.* To dress smartly; — often with *up.* — **spruce′ly,** *adv.* — **spruce′ness,** *n.*

spruce beer. A beverage flavored with spruce, esp. one made from its twigs and leaves boiled with molasses or sugar and fermented with yeast.

sprue (sprōō), *n. Founding.* **a** The hole through which metal is poured into the gate and thence into the mold. **b** The waste piece cast in this hole.

sprue, *n. Med.* A tropical disease with chronic diarrhea and other digestive disturbance.

sprung (sprŭng), *past & past part.* of SPRING.

sprung rhythm. *Pros.* A type of rhythm in which the stress is always on the first syllable of the foot and the feet are mixed in types but equal in length and strength. The feet in sprung rhythm may consist of one, two (trochee), three (dactyl), four (paeon) or even more syllables.

spry (sprī), *adj.;* SPRI′ER or SPRY′ER (-ẽr); SPRI′EST or SPRY′EST. Nimble; active; brisk. — **Syn.** See AGILE. — **spry′ly,** *adv.* — **spry′ness,** *n.*

spud (spŭd), *n.* [ME.] **1.** A sharp, narrow spade, used esp. for digging up large-rooted weeds. **2.** *Dial. & Colloq.* A potato. — *v. t.;* SPUD′DED; SPUD′DING. To dig with a spud.

spud′der (spŭd′ẽr), *n.* A tool that removes bark from timber; a barker.

spue (spū). Obs. exc. dial. var. of SPEW.

spume (spūm), *n.* [OF. or L.; OF. (*e*)*spume,* fr. L. *spuma.*] Frothy matter on liquids; foam; scum. — *v. i.* [L. *spumare.*] To froth; foam. — **spu′mous** (spū′mŭs), *adj.* — **spum′y** (spūm′ĭ), *adj.;* SPUM′I·ER (-ĭ·ẽr); SPUM′I·EST.

‖**spu·mo′ne** (spōō·mō′nā), *n.* [It.] Italian ice cream, a frozen dessert resembling mousse, and usually containing chopped nuts, fruit, etc.

spun (spŭn), *past & past part.* of SPIN.

spun glass. Glass drawn into a thread while liquid.

spunk (spŭngk), *n.* [Gael. *spong* tinder, sponge, Ir. *sponnc,* fr. L. *spongia* sponge.] **1.** Wood that readily takes fire; touchwood; also, tinder made from a fungus; punk. **2.** A spark; a little fire; also, a sulfur match. **3.** *Colloq.* Spirit; mettle; also, anger; passion. — *v. i.* To kindle.

spunk′ie (spŭngk′ĭ), *n. Scot. & Dial.* **a** The ignis fatuus. **b** Liquor; spirits.

spunk′y (spŭngk′ĭ), *adj.;* -I·ER (-ĭ·ẽr); -I·EST. Full of spunk; spirited; plucky. — **spunk′i·ly,** *adv.* — **spunk′i·ness,** *n.*

spun rayon. **a** Yarn made from cut rayon filaments drawn out and twisted into threads as in the spinning of silk, cotton, etc. **b** A fabric woven from this yarn to simulate any of the classical fabrics such as cotton, wool, linen, and silk, with added original texture and surface effects, as the silklike luster of sharkskin.

spun yarn. *Naut.* Small rope, or stuff, formed of two or more rope yarns loosely twisted, used for seizings, etc.

spur (spûr), *n.* [AS. *spura, spora.*] **1.** A pointed implement secured to a rider's heel, to urge the horse by its pressure. See ROWEL, *Illust.* **2.** A goad to action; stimulus. **3.** Something projecting like, or suggesting, a spur; as: **a** A projecting root or branch of a tree. **b** Ergot of rye. **c** A gaff for a gamecock. **d** A climbing iron. **4.** Any stiff, sharp spine, as on the wings and legs of certain birds; esp., the spine on a cock's leg. See POULTRY, *Illust.* (21). **5.** A ridge or lesser elevation that extends laterally from a mountain, or range of mountains. **6.** *Arch.* **a** A short wooden brace of a post. **b** A griffe. **7.** *Bot.* Any hollow projecting spurlike appendage of a corolla or calyx, as in the flowers of larkspur, columbine, etc. **8.** *Carp.* A brace strengthening a post and some connected part, as a crossbeam; a strut. **9.** *Fort.* In fortifications, a reinforcing buttress of masonry. **10.** *Railroading.* Short for SPUR TRACK. — **Syn.** See MOTIVE. — ***on the spur of the moment.*** On hasty impulse; prompted by the occasion.

— v. t.; SPURRED (spûrd); SPUR′RING. **1.** To prick with spurs; hence, to incite; stimulate; instigate; drive. **2.** To put spurs on; as, a *spurred* boot; also, to strike or gash with, or as with, a spur. **— v. i.** To spur on one's horse; to hasten.

spurge (spûrj), *n.* [OF. *espurge*, fr. *espurgier* to purge, fr. L. *expurgare*. See EXPURGATE.] Any of certain plants (genus *Euphorbia* and related genera, family Euphorbiaceae, the spurge family), mostly shrubby and yielding a bitter milky juice.

spur gear. *Mach.* The simplest form of toothed wheel, with radial teeth parallel to the axis; also, gearing consisting of such wheels. See IDLE WHEEL, *Illust.* **— spur gearing.**

spurge laurel. A low Eurasian shrub (*Daphne laureola*) with oblong evergreen leaves and yellow flowers.

spu′ri·ous (spū′rĭ·ŭs), *adj.* [L. *spurius.*] **1.** Illegitimate; bastard. **2.** Not proceeding from the true source; not genuine; counterfeit; false. **3.** *Bot.* False; superficially like but morphologically unlike; as, a *spurious* fruit. **— spu′ri·ous·ly,** *adv.* **— spu′ri·ous·ness,** *n.*

spurn (spûrn), *v. t.* [AS. *spurnan* to kick, offend.] **1.** To drive back or away as with the foot; to kick. **2.** To reject with disdain. **— Syn.** See DECLINE. **— v. i. 1.** *Obs.* To kick. **2.** To manifest disdain in rejecting anything. **— n. 1.** A kick. **2.** Disdainful rejection; contemptuous treatment. **— spurn′er,** *n.*

spurred (spûrd), *adj.* Wearing or provided with spurs; also, having spurlike shoots or spines.

spur′ri·er (spûr′ĭ·ẽr), *n.* One who makes spurs.

spur′ry (spûr′ĭ; 117), *n.* Also **spur′rey.** [D. *spurrie.*] **a** A small white-flowered European weed (*Spergula arvensis*) with whorled filiform leaves. **b** Any of several other small herbs of the chickweed family.

spurt (spûrt), *v. i. & t.* [Also *spirt*; orig. same word as *sprit*, fr. AS. *spryttan.*] To gush out; to issue, expel, or force out, as a liquid, in a stream or jet; to squirt. **— n.** A sudden gushing forth; a jet.

spurt, *n.* A sudden manifestation of energy; increased exertion for a short time; also, a sudden rise in prices, activity, etc. **— v. i.** To make a spurt.

spur′tle (spûr′t'l), *n.* *Scot.* A stick for stirring porridge.

spur track. A track, diverging from a main or branch line, over which no regular train service is maintained.

spur wheel. *Mach.* A spur gear (which see).

sput′ter (spŭt′ẽr), *v. i.* [Imitative.] **1.** To emit saliva from the mouth in small particles, as in rapid speaking; to splutter. **2.** To utter words hastily and indistinctly. **3.** To throw out anything, as jets of steam, with a noise like that made by one sputtering. **— v. t. 1.** To eject rapidly and in small particles, with a spluttering sound. **2.** To utter spasmodically and confusedly. **— n. 1.** Act or sound of sputtering. **2.** Moist matter thrown out in small detached particles. **3.** Confused and excited speech; hence, fuss; ado. **— sput′ter·er,** *n.*

spu′tum (spū′tŭm), *n.; pl.* SPUTA (-tȧ). [L., fr. *spuere, sputum*, to spit.] That which is expectorated; spittle.

spy (spī), *v. t.*; SPIED (spīd); SPY′ING. [OF. *espier*, of Teut. origin.] **1.** To watch secretly; to play the spy upon. **2.** To gain sight of; to espy; see. **3.** To discover by close examination. **— v. i. 1.** To search narrowly; to scrutinize. **2.** To watch secretly; to play the spy. **— n.; pl.** SPIES (spīz). **1.** One who watches, esp. secretly or furtively, the conduct of others. **2.** One who, acting clandestinely or on false pretenses, obtains or seeks to obtain information in the zone of operations of a belligerent, with the intention of communicating it to the hostile party. **3.** Act of spying.

spy′glass′ (spī′glȧs′; 9), *n.* A small telescope.

squab (skwŏb; 73), *n.* [Of Scand. origin.] **1.** A nestling of a pigeon or similar bird. **2.** A short fat person. **3.** A cushion; also, a sofa. **— adj. 1.** Fat; short and thick. **2.** Unfledged; recently hatched; as, a *squab* pigeon.

squab′ble (skwŏb′'l), *v. i.*; -BLED (-'ld); -BLING (-blĭng). To quarrel noisily; to wrangle. **— v. t.** *Print.* To disarrange so that the letters or lines need readjustment; — said of type that has been set up. **— n.** A noisy dispute; a wrangle. **— Syn.** See QUARREL. **— squab′bler** (-lẽr), *n.*

squad (skwŏd; 73), *n.* [F. *esquade* (now *escouade*), fr. Sp. *escuadra* or It. *squadra*, prop., a square.] **1.** *Mil.* A small party of men grouped for drill, inspection, or other purposes. **2.** Hence, any small group engaged in some common enterprise or effort; as, a football *squad.* **— v. t.**; SQUAD′DED; SQUAD′DING. To arrange in squads.

squad car. A police automobile especially equipped with short-wave radio telephone connection with headquarters; — called also *cruiser* and *prowl car.*

squad′ron (skwŏd′rŭn; 73), *n.* [It. *squadrone*, fr. *squadra.* See SQUAD.] **1.** Loosely, any body of men in regular formation; an organized mass. **2.** In the U. S. Army, a unit composed of a headquarters troop and two or more troops of cavalry. **3.** *Mil. Aviation.* A flight formation made up of 2, 3, or 4 flights directed as a unit. **4.** *Nav.* A unit of a fleet. In the U. S. Navy a squadron consists of one or more divisions of battleships, destroyers, or aircraft. **— v. t.** To form into, or arrange in, squadrons.

squal′id (skwŏl′ĭd), *adj.* [L. *squalidus.* See SQUALOR.] Dirty through neglect; filthy; hence, mean; poor. **— Syn.** See DIRTY. **— squal′id·ly,** *adv.* **— squal′id·ness,** *n.*

squall (skwôl), *n.* **1.** A gust of wind, often with rain or snow. **2.** *Colloq.* A disturbance. **— v. i.** To blow a squall.

squall, *v. i. & t.* To cry out or scream violently. **— n.** A harsh, piercing cry; a squawk. **— squall′er,** *n.*

squall′y (skwôl′ĭ), *adj.*; SQUALL′I·ER (-ĭ·ẽr); SQUALL′I·EST. Abounding with, or threatening, squalls; gusty.

squal′or (skwŏl′ẽr; *now rarely* skwā′lẽr), *n.* [L., roughness, filth, dirt; akin to L. *squalere* to be foul, *squalidus* filthy.] Squalidness; miserable and unkempt condition.

squa′lus (skwā′lŭs), *n.* [L.] One of a genus (*Squalus*) of dogfish, or small sharks.

squa′ma (skwā′mȧ), *n.; pl.* SQUAMAE (-mē). [L., a scale.] *Biol.* A scale or scalelike structure.

squa′mate (skwā′māt), *adj.* [LL. *squamatus.*] Scaly.

squa·ma′tion (skwȧ·mā′shŭn), *n.* **a** State of being squamate. **b** The arrangement of scales on an animal.

squa′mo- (skwā′mō-). *Anat.* A combining form for *squama*, denoting: **a** *Squamosely*, as in **squa′mo·cel′lu·lar, squa′mo·ep′i·the′li·al.** **b** *Squamous and*, as in **squa′mo·pa·ri′e·tal, squa′mo·sphe′noid, squa′mo·tem′po·ral,** etc.

squa·mo′sal (skwȧ·mō′săl), *adj.* Scalelike; specif.: **a** *Anat.* Squamous. **b** *Zool.* Designating, or pertaining to, a membrane bone of the skull of many vertebrates corresponding to the squamous portion of the temporal bone of man. **— n.** The squamosal bone.

squa′mose (skwā′mōs; skwȧ·mōs′), *adj.* Squamous. **— squa′mose·ly,** *adv.* **— squa′mose·ness,** *n.*

squa′mous (skwā′mŭs), *adj.* [L. *squamosus*, fr. *squama* a scale.] Covered with, or consisting of, scales; resembling a scale; scaly; specif., *Anat.*, designating, or pert. to, the anterior upper portion of the temporal bone of man and various mammals. **— squa′mous·ly,** *adv.* **— squa′mous·ness,** *n.*

squam′u·lose (skwăm′ū·lōs; skwā′mū-), *adj.* Minutely squamous.

squan′der (skwŏn′dẽr), *v. t. & i.* **1.** *Archaic.* To scatter; disperse. **2.** To spend lavishly or wastefully; to dissipate. **— n.** Act or instance of squandering. **— squan′der·er,** *n.*

square (skwâr), *n.* [OF. *esquarre, esquerre*, deriv. of L. *ex* out + *quadra* a square.] **1.** *Geom.* A parallelogram having four equal sides and four right angles. Abbr. *sq.* **2.** Hence, anything of, or approximating to, this form. **3.** An instrument having at least one right angle and two or more straight edges, used to lay out or test square work. **4.** A quadrilateral area bounded by streets; also, the distance along one side of such an area. **5.** An open place or area, as one formed at the meeting of two or more streets. **6.** *Obs.* A rule, principle, or standard. **7.** *Agric.* The three bracts subtending the flower of the cotton plant. **8.** *Arith. & Alg.* The product of a number or quantity multiplied by itself; thus, 81 is the *square* of 9. **9.** *Mil.* A body of troops formed in a square.

— *on the square.* **a** At right angles; not obliquely. **b** *Colloq.* In an open, fair manner; honestly; honorably. **— *out of square.*** **a** Not at right angles; obliquely. **b** Not regular or in order; also, incorrectly.

— v. t. 1. To form with four equal sides and four right angles. **2.** To form with right angles and straight lines, or flat surfaces; as, to *square* mason's work; also, to measure in order to find the deviation from a right angle, straight line, or plane surface. **3.** To bring approximately to a right angle; as, to *square* one's shoulders. **4.** To compare with, or reduce to, any given standard; to adjust; regulate. **5.** To make even, so as to leave no remainder or difference; to balance; settle. **6.** *Slang.* To induce to favorable action or attitude by a gift, esp. a corrupt one; to bribe. **7.** To place accurately in position, as in bearings. **8.** To mark the surface of (paper, etc.) into squares. **9.** *Math.* **a** To multiply (a number or a quantity) by itself. **b** To find the number of areal units, as square feet, in (a given area); also, to find a square equal in area to; as, to try to *square* the circle. **10.** *Sports.* To cause the score of (a match) to become equal. **— v. i. 1.** To agree; suit; fit. **2.** To take an attitude of offense or defense; esp., to take an attitude ready for boxing. **3.** *Colloq.* To settle things; esp., to pay the reckoning. **4.** *Golf.* To make the scores equal. **— Syn.** See AGREE.

— adj. 1. *Geom.* Having four equal sides and four right angles. **2.** Forming a right angle; turning at a right angle; hence, figuratively, diverging or divergent. **3.** Squared; converted from a linear unit into a square unit of area having the same length of side; as, a *square* foot (the area of a square the side of which is one foot). See MEASURE, *Tables* 3 & 4. **4.** Having a shape broad for the height; as, a man of a *square* frame; hence, brawny; sturdy. **5.** Exactly adjusted; well-made. **6.** Honest; just; fair. **7.** Even; leaving no balance; as, to make accounts *square.* **8.** *Colloq.* Of one eating or drinking, hearty; vigorous; of a meal, or the like, substantial; satisfying. **9.** Straightforward; unequivocal; as, a *square* denial. **10.** *Naut.* At right angles with the mast and keel; — said of the yards of a square-rigged vessel. **— adv. 1.** Honestly. **2.** So as to face, or be face to face. **3.** Directly; with nothing intervening. **4.** Firmly; solidly. **5.** In a square shape.

— square′ly, *adv.* **— square′ness,** *n.*

square bracket. *Print.* = BRACKET, *n.*, 4 **a.**

square dance. Any dance, as a quadrille, in which the dancers are arranged to form a square.

squared circle *or* ring (skwârd). *Colloq.* The prize ring.

square deal. *Colloq.* **a** An honest dealing of playing cards. **b** Fair or honest treatment; an honest transaction.

square′head′ (skwâr′hĕd′), *n.* **a** *Colloq.* A Scandinavian. **b** *Slang, U.S.* Since World War I, a German.

square knot. A knot in which the terminal and standing parts are together and parallel each to the other; a reef knot. See KNOT, *Illust.* (28).

square measure. The measure of areas in square units, as square feet; also, a system of such units. See MEASURE, *Tables* 3 & 4; METRIC SYSTEM, *Tables* 2 & 3.

squar′er (skwâr′ẽr), *n.* One who or that which squares; a workman who squares timber, stone, etc.

square′-rigged′ (skwâr′rĭgd′; 2), *adj.* *Naut.* Having the principal sails extended on yards suspended horizontally at the middle; — opposed to *fore-and-aft-rigged.* See BARK, SAIL, *Illusts.* **— square′-rig′ger,** *n.*

square root. *Math.* A second root. See ROOT, *n.*, 4.

square sail. *Naut.* A four-sided sail extended on a yard suspended at the middle from a mast.

square shooter. *Colloq.* An honest person; one who plays fairly and justly. **— square shooting.**

square′-toed′ (skwâr′tōd′; 2), *adj.* **1.** Having the toe square. **2.** Old-fashioned; conservative; precise; prim.

square′-toes′ (-tōz′), *n.* *Humorous or Contemptuous.* An old-fashioned precise person.

squar′ing the cir′cle (skwâr′ĭng). = QUADRATURE OF THE CIRCLE.

squar′rose (skwăr′ōs; skwŏ·rōs′), *adj.* Also **squar′rous** (skwăr′ŭs). [L. *squarrosus* scurfy, scabby.] **a** *Bot. & Zool.* Rough with divergent scales or processes. **b** *Bot.* Thickly crowded and rigid; as, *squarrose* leaves.

squash (skwŏsh), *n.* [Of Algonquian origin; cf. Massachuset Indian *askoot-asquash* squash, lit., eaten green.] The fruit of a plant or vine (genus *Cucurbita*) of the gourd family; also, the vine or plant which bears it. Cultivated squashes are varieties of three species: the true winter varieties, as the ***Hubbard squash*** and ***turban squash***, are varieties of *C. maxima*; the *cushaw* (which see), ***Canada crookneck***, and ***winter crookneck***, are varieties of *C. moschata*; the ***summer squashes***, of both scallop-shaped and crookneck types, belong to the same species as the pumpkin (*C. pepo*).

squash, *v. t.* [OF. *esquasser.* See EX-; QUASH to crush.] **1.** To beat or press into pulp or a flat mass; to crush. **2.** To suppress; put down;

quash; as, to *squash* a revolt. — *v. i.* **1.** To fall heavily and helplessly; esp., to flatten out at impact. **2.** To squeeze; press; as, four *squashed* into one seat. **3.** *Colloq.* To squelch; ooze. — *n.* **1.** Something soft and easily crushed. **2.** A sudden fall of a heavy, soft body; also, the sound produced by such a fall. **3.** A crushed mass. **4.** The squelching sound made by walking on damp, soft ground. **5.** **a** Also **squash tennis.** A game much like rackets, played in a walled court with a rubber ball and a bat like a tennis racket. **b** Short for SQUASH RACKETS. **6.** A drink, one ingredient of which is some fruit juice; esp., short for LEMON SQUASH. — *adv.* With a squash, or a squashing sound. — **squash'er,** *n.*

squash bug. A large black American insect (*Anasa tristis,* family Coreidae) injurious to squash vines.

squash rackets. A game similar to rackets but played on a small court with a rubber ball, and a racket like that used in the game of rackets except for a shorter handle.

squash'y (skwŏsh'ĭ), *adj.;* SQUASH'I·ER (-ĭ·ẽr); SQUASH'I·EST. Easily squashed; soft; esp., boggy or muddy. — **squash'i·ly,** *adv.* — **squash'i·ness,** *n.*

squat (skwŏt), *v. t.;* SQUAT'TED or SQUAT; SQUAT'TING. [OF. *esquater, -tir.*] To cause to crouch or squat; — chiefly reflexive. — *v. i.* **1.** To sit down upon the hams or heels. **2.** To sit or keep close to the ground to escape observation, as a partridge or rabbit. **3.** To settle on land, esp. new or unoccupied land, without right or title; also, to settle on public land under government regulation with a view to acquiring title. — *adj.* **1.** Seated on the hams or heels; crouching. **2.** Short and thick, like the figure of an animal squatting. — **squat'ness,** *n.* — *n.* **1.** The act of squatting; also, the posture of one that squats. **2.** The place where one squats; esp., the hole or lair of an animal, as a hare.

squat'ter (skwŏt'ẽr), *n.* One who or that which squats, as on new land or on government land.

squatter sovereignty. *U. S. Hist.* The doctrine that the squatters, or actual residents, of a territory had the right to make their own laws.

squat'ty (skwŏt'ĭ), *adj.;* SQUAT'TI·ER (-ĭ·ẽr); SQUAT'TI·EST. Squat; dumpy; thickset.

squaw (skwô), *n.* [Of Algonquian origin.] An American Indian woman; among Indians, any woman; a female.

squaw'fish' (-fĭsh'), *n.;* see FISH. A large fish (*Ptychocheilus oregonensis*) of the carp family, found in the Pacific-coast rivers from central California northward.

squawk (skwôk), *v. i.* [Imitative.] To utter a harsh, abrupt scream, as a fowl; hence, *Colloq.,* to complain in a loud raucous voice; protest. — *v. t.* To utter with a harsh loud scream. — *n.* **1.** Act or noise of squawking. **2.** *Colloq.* A noisy, raucous complaint. **3.** The black-crowned night heron. See NIGHT HERON. — **squawk'er,** *n.*

squaw man. A white man married to an Indian woman and, usually, living as one of her tribe.

squaw'root' (skwô'rōōt'; 85), *n.* A North American scaly herb (*Conopholis americana,* family Orobanchaceae, the broomrape family) parasitic on oak and hemlock roots.

squeak (skwēk), *v. i.* [Prob. of imitative origin.] **1.** To utter or make a squeak. **2.** *Slang.* To break silence, or secrecy, as from fear of pain or punishment; to confess; betray. — *v. t.* To utter or speak in a shrill piping tone. — *n.* A sharp, shrill, usually short cry or sound. — ***a narrow, close, or near squeak.*** *Colloq.* A close escape. — **squeak'i·ly,** *adv.* — **squeak'i·ness,** *n.* — **squeak'y,** *adj.*

squeak'er (-ẽr), *n.* One who or that which squeaks.

squeal (skwēl), *v. i.* **1.** To utter a squeal. **2.** *Colloq.* **a** To complain; protest. **b** To turn informer; to betray a secret. — *v. t.* To utter with, or as if with, a squeal. — *n.* **1.** A shrill, sharp, somewhat prolonged cry. **2.** Act or instance of squealing. — **squeal'er,** *n.*

squeam'ish (skwēm'ĭsh), *adj.* [ME. *squaymous, sweymous,* prob. fr. ME. *sweem, swem,* dizziness.] **1.** Having a stomach easily nauseated; queasy; qualmish. **2.** Fastidious; easily disgusted or offended. — **Syn.** See NICE. — **squeam'ish·ly,** *adv.* — **squeam'ish·ness,** *n.*

squee'gee (skwē'jē; skwē·jē'), *n.* A device with a handle and a transverse piece at one end of it set with a strip of leather or rubber, used for drying decks, pavements, windows, etc., by squeezing off the superfluous water; hence, a smaller similar device used by photographers, lithographers, and others. — *v. t.* To smooth, press, or treat with a squeegee.

squeeze (skwēz), *v. t.* [AS. *cwēsan, cwӯsan.*] **1.** To exert pressure on opposite sides or parts of; to compress. **2.** To gain or procure by or as if by pressure; as, to *squeeze* juice from a lemon. **3.** To force, thrust, or cause to pass, by pressure; as, to *squeeze* water through felt. **4.** To oppress, as with burdens, taxes, etc. **5.** *Colloq.* To bring influence to bear upon (a person, group, etc.) to do something or to extort money or benefit; also, to extract or extort (money, advantage) by influence or pressure. **6.** *Cant.* To make a squeeze of. See SQUEEZE, *n.,* 4. **7.** *Bridge.* To constrain (an adversary) to unguard a suit by discarding. — *v. i.* **1.** To give way before pressure; as, oranges that *squeeze* well. **2.** To exert pressure, as with the hand. **3.** To urge one's way, or to pass, by pressing; to crowd. — ***squeeze the shorts.*** *Exchanges.* To force parties who have sold (stocks, produce, or the like) short to pay high prices for covering their deliveries. See SHORT, *adv.,* 3. — *n.* **1.** Act or instance of squeezing; pressure, as in a crowd. **2.** A firm pressing of another's hand; a hug. **3.** A quantity squeezed or pressed out from something, as juice from an orange. **4.** A facsimile impression of an object made in a plastic substance by forcing it into the depressions of the object. **5.** *Colloq.* Influence used to extort favors, money, etc. **6.** An actual or threatened elimination of operating margin, as of a retailer, because of low ceiling prices and rising replacement cost. **7.** *Bridge.* A play or a situation in which one is squeezed. **8.** *Exchanges.* Act or instance of squeezing the shorts.

squeeze play. **a** *Baseball.* A form of hit-and-run play in which, when there is a runner on third base and not more than one out, the batter bunts a pitched ball previously designated by signal, and the runner starts for the home plate as soon as the pitcher makes a motion to pitch that ball. **b** *Bridge.* A play in which an opponent is forced by his discard to give up command of one suit or to unguard his possible taking card in another suit.

squeez'er (skwēz'ẽr), *n.* One who or that which squeezes.

squelch (skwĕlch), *n.* [Imitative.] *Colloq.* **1.** A sound as of one walking in mud or slush. **2.** A squelcher (retort). — *v. t.* To fall or stamp on so as to crush; to quell or crush; hence, to discomfit or disconcert; suppress. — *v. i.* To make a sound like that made by one walking in mud or slush.

squelch'er (skwĕl'chẽr), *n.* *Colloq.* One who or that which squelches; esp., an effective retort.

sque·teague' (skwē·tēg'), *n. sing. & pl.* Also **sque·tee'** (-tē'). [From a Narraganset Indian name.] A common marine food fish (*Cynoscion regalis*) of the eastern coast of North America and, by extension, any of several closely related fishes. Cf. WEAKFISH.

squib (skwĭb), *n.* **1.** A pipe, tube, or ball of paper filled with powder to be fired so as to burn and often to explode with a crack. **2.** A broken firecracker, the powder in which burns with a fizz. **3.** A brief witty or sarcastic writing or speech; a lampoon. — *v. i.;* SQUIBBED (skwĭbd); SQUIB'BING. **1.** To speak, write, or publish squibs. **2.** To fire a squib. **3.** To move about restlessly. **4.** To explode with a slight sharp crack, as of a rifle. — *v. t.* **1.** To throw, use, or explode, like a squib. **2.** To make squibs or lampoons against.

squid (skwĭd), *n.;* see PLURAL, *Note,* 3. [From *squit,* dial. var. of SQUIRT.] Any of numerous ten-armed cephalopods (esp., any species of *Loligo, Ommastrephes*) having a long, tapered body and a caudal fin on each side. Cf. CUTTLEFISH.

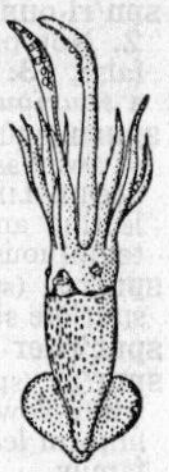
Squid (*O. sagittatus*). (1/6)

squiffed (skwĭft), *adj.* Also **squif'fy** (skwĭf'ĭ). *Slang.* Intoxicated.

squil'gee (skwĭl'jē; skwē'jē), *n.* Also **squill'gee, squil'la·gee** (skwĭl'ȧ·jē). **1.** A squeegee. **2.** *Naut.* A strap, or becket, and a toggle, used to confine a studding sail while being set. — *v. t.* To squeegee.

squill (skwĭl), *n.* [L. *squilla, scilla,* sea onion, fr. Gr. *skilla.*] **a** A bulbous herb (*Urginea maritima,* of the lily family) of southern Europe and northern Africa; *pl.,* its bulbs or roots, dried, sliced, and used as an expectorant, cardiac stimulant, and diuretic. **b** Any of a genus (*Scilla*) of plants of the lily family.

squil'la (skwĭl'ȧ), *n.; pl.* -LAS (-ȧz), -LAE (-ē). [L., sea onion, also, prawn, shrimp. See SQUILL.] Any of a genus (*Squilla*) of stomatopod crustaceans, which burrow in the mud or beneath stones in shallow water along the seashore.

squinch (skwĭnch), *n.* [From earlier *sconcheon, scuncheon,* fr. OF. *escoinson.*] *Arch.* An arch, lintel, corbeling, or the like, carried across the corner of a room to support a superimposed mass.

squin'ny (skwĭn'ĭ), *n. & v.* *Obs.* Squint; peep.

squint (skwĭnt), *adj.* [Aphetic for *asquint.*] **1.** Looking obliquely; looking askance or with envy, disdain, or distrust. **2.** *Med.* Not having the optic axes coincident; — said of the eyes; cross-eyed. — *v. i.* **1.** To see or look obliquely or askance, or with a furtive glance; also, to peer with eyes partly closed. **2.** To deviate from a true line; hence, to have an indirect bearing or implication. **3.** *Med.* To be cross-eyed, or strabismic. — *v. t.* **1.** To cause to squint, or look obliquely or askance. **2.** *Colloq.* To close (the eyes) partly, as in excess of light. — *n.* **1.** Act, fact, or habit of squinting. **2.** Deviation from the ordinary; trend; bent. **3.** *Arch.* A hagioscope. **4.** *Med.* Strabismus. A ***convergent squint*** is one in which the eye turns inward (toward the nose); a ***divergent squint,*** one in which the eye turns outward. — **squint'er,** *n.*

squint'-eyed' (-īd'), *adj.* Having eyes that squint; specif., cross-eyed; hence, looking askance; prejudiced; malignant.

squin'y (skwĭn'ĭ; skwĭ'nĭ). Var. of SQUINNY.

squire (skwīr), *n.* [Aphetic for *esquire.* See ESQUIRE.] **1.** A shield-bearer or armor-bearer of a knight. **2.** In England, a title of dignity next in degree below *knight,* and above *gentleman,* applied esp. to a rural landed proprietor; hence, also, in both England and America, a title of office and courtesy, perhaps most usually given to justices of the peace. **3.** A male attendant on a great personage; also, *Colloq.,* a gallant devoted to a lady; a lover. — *v. t. & i.* To attend or act as a squire; to escort; accompany.

squire'arch·y, squir'arch·y (skwīr'är·kĭ), *n.* [*squire* + *-archy.*] **1.** The gentry collectively; the landed proprietor class. **2.** Government by the English landed gentry; — in allusion to the influence of the English landed gentry in the House of Commons, esp. before the Reform Bill of 1832.

squirm (skwûrm), *v. i.* To twist about with contortions like an eel or a worm; to wriggle; writhe. — *n.* Act or fact of squirming; a wriggling. — **squirm'y** (skwûr'mĭ), *adj.*

squir'rel (skwûr'ĕl *or, esp. Brit.,* skwĭr'-; 117), *n.* [OF. *esquireul, escuriuel,* fr. dim. fr. VL. *scurius,* for L. *sciurus,* fr. Gr. *skiouros,* fr. *skia* shade + *oura* tail.] **1.** Any of various small or medium-sized rodents of the family Sciuridae; specif.: **a** Any of numerous arboreal forms having a long bushy tail and strong hind legs, including the common Old World species (*Sciurus vulgaris*) and North American species, as the ***red squirrel or chickaree*** (*S. hudsonicus*), ***gray squirrel*** (*S. carolinensis*) of the east and midwest, ***fox squirrel*** (*S. niger niger*) of the pinelands of the south. Varieties of the gray and fox squirrels are known as ***black squirrel.*** **b** Any of numerous burrowing forms, called specif. ***ground squirrel,*** including the chipmunks and spermophiles (see these terms). **2.** The fur of any of these animals. **3.** Any of various rodents of allied families; as: **a** Any of the ***flying squirrels*** (family Petauristidae) which have parachutelike folds of skin connecting the fore and hind legs enabling them to make long leaps. **b** *Australia.* Any of certain flying phalangers (see PHALANGER).

squirrel corn. A North American herb (*Dicentra canadensis,* family Fumariaceae) with much-divided leaves and a scapose raceme of cream-colored flowers.

squirt (skwûrt), *v. i. & t.* To eject liquid in a thin spurt; to spurt. — *n.* **1.** An instrument, as a syringe, for squirting a liquid. **2.** A jet; figuratively, a quantity ejected forcibly and suddenly as from a small orifice. **3.** Act of squirting. **4.** *Colloq.* An impudent youth; whippersnapper. — **squirt'er,** *n.*

squirt'ing cu'cum·ber. A Mediterranean plant (*Ecballium elaterium*) with oblong fruit which bursts from the peduncle when ripe, forcibly ejecting the seeds.

squish (skwĭsh), *v. t. & i.* *Dial.* To squash. — **squish,** *n.*

stab (stăb), *v. t.;* STABBED (stăbd); STAB'BING. [Var. of *stob,* fr. *stob* a stake, stick.] To pierce with or as with a pointed weapon; also, to thrust or drive, as a pointed implement. — *v. i.* To thrust or give a wound with or as if with a pointed weapon; pierce. — *n.* A thrust of, or a wound given by or as if by, a pointed weapon. — **stab'ber** (-ẽr), *n.*

Sta'bat Ma'ter (stä'bät mä'tẽr; stā'băt mā'tẽr). [L., the mother was standing; — so called from its first two words.] A Latin hymn commemorating the sorrows of Mary, mother of Jesus, as she followed him to his crucifixion; also, a musical setting of this hymn.

sta'bile (stā'bĭl; stăb'ĭl), *adj.* [L. *stabilis.* See STABLE, *adj.*] Stationary; not moving; — specif., in electrotherapeutics, opposed to *labile;* as, *stabile* electrodes.

sta·bil'i·ty (stȧ·bĭl'ĭ·tĭ), *n.* **1.** State or quality of being stable, or firm. **2.** Steadiness or firmness of character, resolution, or purpose; constancy. **3.** *Obs.* Fixedness; — as opposed to *fluidity.* **4.** *Mech. & Aeronautics.* That property of a body which causes it, when disturbed from a condition of equilibrium or steady motion, to develop forces or moments which tend to restore the body to its original condition. **5.** *R.C.Ch.* A vow binding a monk for life to one monastery.

sta'bi·li·za'tor (stā'bĭ·lĭ·zā'tẽr; stăb'ĭ-), *n.* A stabilizer.

sta'bi·lize (stā'bĭ·līz; stăb'ĭ-), *v. t.* **1.** To make stable, steadfast, or firm. **2.** To hold steady; to prevent fluctuations; as, to *stabilize* prices. **3.** *Aeronautics.* To maintain, or to make it possible to maintain, the equilibrium of (an aircraft) by means of fixed surfaces or gyroscopic or other devices not manipulated by the pilot. — **sta'bi·li·za'tion** (-lĭ·zā'shŭn; -lī·zā'-), *n.*

sta'bi·liz'er (-līz'ẽr), *n.* One that renders stable; specif.: **1.** A substance added to an explosive to render it less liable to spontaneous decomposition. **2.** *Aeronautics.* **a** A mechanical device, as a gyroscope, to stabilize the motion of an aircraft. **b** A fixed surface acting to stabilize the motion of an aircraft, esp. a horizontal tail surface to stabilize the pitching motion. See AIRPLANE, *Illust.*

sta'ble (stā'b'l), *adj.* [OF. *estable* (F. *stable*), fr. L. *stabilis;* akin to L. *stare* to stand.] **1.** Firmly established; fixed; steadfast. **2.** Steady in purpose; constant. **3.** Durable; enduring. **4.** So placed as to resist forces tending to cause motion or distortion. **5.** *Chem.* Not decomposing readily. — **Syn.** See LASTING. — **sta'ble·ness,** *n.* — **sta'bly** (stā'blĭ), *adv.*

sta'ble, *n.* [OF. *estable* (F. *étable*), fr. L. *stabulum;* akin to L. *stare* to stand.] **1.** A building for beasts to lodge and feed in; esp., a building having stalls, as for horses. **2.** *Racing Slang.* The horses of a certain racing stable collectively; also, all the persons concerned with the management of a certain stable collectively. — *v. t. & i.;* STA'BLED (stā'b'ld); STA'BLING (-blĭng). To put, keep, or lodge in or as in a stable. — **sta'ble·man,** *n.*

sta'bling (stā'blĭng), *n.* Accommodation (for horses) in a building; also, the building.

stab'lish (stăb'lĭsh). Archaic aphetic form of ESTABLISH.

stac·ca'to (stȧ·kä'tō; *It.* stäk·kä'tō), *adj.* [It., past part., detached.] *Music.* Disconnected; cut short in performing; hence, marked by short, clear-cut playing or singing of tones or chords; — indicated by a vertical stroke or by a dot (**staccato mark**) placed over or under a note. Opposed to *legato.*

stack (stăk), *n.* [ON. *stakkr.*] **1.** A large pile of hay, grain in the sheath, straw, or the like. **2.** A more or less orderly pile or heap; in the game of poker, a pile of chips sold to or won by a player. **3.** An English unit of measure for coal and wood as fuel, equal to 108 cu. ft. (4 cu. yd.). **4.** *Colloq.* A large quantity or number, as of money. **5.** A vertical pipe; as, a smoke*stack.* **6.** *Arch.* **a** A number of flues embodied in one structure rising above a roof. **b** Any chimney or conduit for smoke. **7.** *Libraries.* **a** A structure of bookshelves for compact storage of books. **b** Any collection of bookcases compactly arranged. **c** A building housing such a structure. **8.** *Mil.* A pyramidal self-supporting pile of arms, esp. of three rifles or carbines interlocked. — *v. t.* To pile up. — **stack'er,** *n.* — ***stack cards.*** *Card Playing.* To arrange cards secretly for cheating; hence, *Slang,* to have the odds fixed in advance.

stack'er (stăk'ẽr), *n. & v.* Also **stach'er** (stäk'ẽr). *Scot. & Dial. Eng.* Stagger.

stac'te (stăk'tē), *n.* [L., myrrh, fr. Gr. *staktē,* prop., fem. of *staktos* oozing out in drops.] A spice used by the ancient Jews to prepare incense. *Ex.* xxx. 34.

stad'dle (stăd''l), *n.* Also **stad'le.** [AS. *stathol, stathul,* a foundation, firm seat.] The lower part of a stack, as of hay; also, its supporting frame or base; hence, any supporting framework.

stad'hold'er (stăd'hōl'dẽr), **stadt'hold'er** (stăt'-), *n.* [D. *stadhouder,* fr. *stad* place, city + *houder* holder.] **a** Orig., a viceroy in a province of the Netherlands. **b** Later, the chief executive officer of the United Provinces of the Netherlands. — **stad'hold'er·ate** (- āt), **stad'hold'er·ship,** *n.*

sta'di·a (stā'dĭ·ȧ), *n.* [It. See STADIUM.] **1.** *Surv.* **a** A temporary station. **b** *Chiefly Eng.* A **stadia rod,** a graduated rod used in connection with a surveying instrument to measure distances. **2.** *Mil.* A form of range finder consisting of a graduated stick held at arm's length.

sta'di·om'e·ter (stā'dĭ·ŏm'ē·tẽr), *n.* [*stadium* + *-meter.*] **1.** A toothed wheel with an index for measuring plotted curves, broken lines, etc., by running over the line. **2.** A form of theodolite for plotting bearings directly.

sta'di·um (stā'dĭ·ŭm), *n.; pl.* STADIA (-ȧ). [L., a stadium (in sense 1), fr. Gr. *stadion.*] **1.** A Greek measure of length. The Attic stadium was 607 English feet (185.2 m.); the Olympic, 630.8 ft. (192.3 m.); the Asiatic, 1/30 parasang (492 to 738 ft.). **2.** *Gr. Antiq.* A course for foot races, with tiers of seats for spectators. **3.** *pl.* STADIUMS (-ŭmz). A similar modern structure, with its enclosure used for athletic games, etc. **4.** = STAGE, *n.,* 4.

staff (stȧf), *n.* [G. *staffieren* to fill out, adorn, fr. D., fr. OF. *estoffe* stuff.] A building material made of a composition of plaster of Paris and hemp fiber, cast in molds and wired or nailed in place.

staff (stȧf; 9), *n.; pl.,* in senses 1 & 2, either STAVES (stāvz; stȧvz) or STAFFS (stȧfs); in senses 3–7, STAFFS. [AS. *stæf* staff.] **1.** A pole, stick, or bar, used for various purposes. **2.** **a** A long stick carried in the hand for support; hence, a support. **b** A cudgel or club. **c** A pole, stick, or wand, as an ensign of authority. **d** A pole on which a flag is displayed. **e** The long handle of certain weapons, as a lance or poleax. **f** Any of various graduated sticks or rules, as used in building, surveying, etc. **3.** A body of assistants to a superintendent or manager; as, a hospital *staff;* also, the body of officers of administration and instruction of an educational institution. **4.** The group of officers and aides-de-camp appointed to attend upon, and serve as escort to, a civil executive, esp. a president or governor. **5.** *Eccl.* A rod with a cross, forming part of a bishop's insignia. See VESTMENT, *Illust.* **6.** *Mil.* An establishment of officers, not having command, but having administrative and executive duties. **7.** *Music.* The horizontal lines, with their spaces, on which music is written; — called also *stave.* See PITCH, *Illust.* **8.** *Nav.* **a** The officers not in line to succeed to command, as the officers of the supply, medical, chaplains', etc., corps. **b** Officers detailed to serve on the staff of the commander of a fleet or lesser unit. — *adj.* Of or pertaining to a military or similar staff; as, a *staff* officer. — *v. t.;* STAFFED (stȧft); STAFF'ING. To supply (an organization, or the like) with a staff, as of officers or teachers.

staff officer. An officer serving on a staff.

staff of life. Bread or its equivalent.

stag (stăg), *n.;* see PLURAL, *Note,* 3. [ME., fr. AS. *stagga,* prop., an adult male, of birds or animals, and so in E. dial.] **1.** **a** The adult male of the red deer (which see); a hart. **b** Any male deer of this genus (*Cervus*), as the caribou. **2.** *Scot.* Often **staig.** A colt. **3.** A male animal castrated after maturity. **4.** A man at a social gathering unaccompanied by a woman; also, a social gathering of men only. — *adj.* Of or for stags (sense 4); as, a *stag* dinner.

stag, *v. t.;* STAGGED (stăgd); STAG'GING. *Slang.* To spy upon; to trail or "tail."

stag beetle. Any of numerous, mostly large, lamellicorn beetles (family Lucanidae) the males of which have mandibles suggesting the antlers of a stag.

stage (stāj), *n.* [OF. *estage* dwelling, story (of a building), situation, stage, fr. L. *stare* to stand.] **1.** A platform; specif.: **a** A scaffold; staging. **b** An elevated platform, esp. one on which an orator may speak, an exhibition be presented, or the like. **2.** The scene of any noted action, event, or career. **3.** A place of rest on a traveled road; a station; a place for a relay of horses. Hence: **a** The distance between two places of rest on a road. **b** A degree of progression in any pursuit, process, or the like; as, a *stage* of one's life. **c** A stagecoach; as, a parcel sent by *stage.* **4.** *Biol.* One of several periods in the development and growth of many animals and plants; as, the pupa *stage.* **5.** *Econ. & Sociol.* One of the steps into which the material development of man or a race is divided; as, the pastoral *stage.* **6.** *Geol.* A minor subdivision of a stratigraphic series. **7.** *Microscopy.* The small platform of the stand of a microscope on which the object for examination is placed. See MICROSCOPE, *Illust.* **8.** *Radio.* An element or part in a complex contrivance, as, in a multitube amplifier, one tube with its associated apparatus. **9.** *Theater.* **a** The raised flooring in a theater where plays are enacted. **b** The whole space at the back of the proscenium, including wings, flies, greenroom, etc. **c** Hence, the theater; the drama; also, theatrical profession. — *v. t.;* STAGED (stājd); STAG'ING (stāj'ĭng). To exhibit on or as on a stage; specif., to put (a play) on the stage.

stage'coach' (-kōch'), *n.* A coach that runs regularly between stations, for the conveyance of passengers.

stage'craft' (-krȧft'; 9), *n.* Skill in dramatic composition or production.

stage director. *Theater.* One who prepares a play for production, arranging stage effects, instructing actors in the interpretation of their parts, etc.

stage fright. Nervousness felt at appearing before an audience.

stage'hand' (stāj'hănd'), *n.* *Theater.* One of the handlers of scenery, lights, etc., who assist the director and stage manager.

stage'–man'age, *v. t.* To arrange or exhibit with an eye to striking effect; as, to *stage-manage* a wedding.

stage manager. *Theater.* One in control of the stage during the production of a play. The same person is sometimes also the stage director.

stag'er (stāj'ẽr), *n.* **1.** One who has long acted on the stage of life; a person of long experience; — usually with *old.* **2.** *Archaic.* A player; actor.

stage'–struck', *adj.* Fascinated by the stage; esp., seized by a passionate desire to become an actor.

stage whisper. A loud whisper by an actor, audible to the spectators but supposed not to be heard by one or more of the actors; any similar whisper.

stag'gard (stăg'ẽrd), **stag'gart** (-ẽrt), *n.* See RED DEER.

stag'ger (stăg'ẽr), *v. i.* [ON. *stakra* to push, stagger, fr. *staka* to punt, push.] To reel to one side and the other; to sway; totter; also, to tremble; to waver in purpose or action; to hesitate. — *v. t.* **1.** To cause to reel, sway, tremble, waver, etc. **2.** To arrange (working hours) so that some businesses open and close at different times from others; also, to arrange (work, jobs, etc.) so that groups of employees may be employed at alternating intervals. **3.** *Aeronautics.* To adjust (as the wings of a biplane) so that the leading edge of one wing projects beyond the leading edge of another wing. — *n.* **1.** A reeling or tottering movement of the body in trying to walk or stand. **2.** *Aeronautics.* The amount of advance of the leading edge of an upper wing of an airplane with two or more supporting planes, over that of a lower, expressed as percentage of gap. **3.** *In pl. form* **stag'gers** (-ẽrz), *construed as sing.* *Veter.* A diseased condition of horses and other animals which causes reeling, sudden falling, and other signs of nervous disorder; — often called ***blind staggers.*** — **stag'ger·er,** *n.* — **stag'ger·ing·ly,** *adv.*

stag'ger·bush' (-bo͝osh'), *n.* A shrub (*Neopieris mariana*) of the eastern United States, poisonous to stock.

stag'gie (stăg'ĭ), *n.* *Scot.* A young horse.

stag'hound' (stăg'hound'), *n.* A breed of hounds formerly used in hunting the stag, the wolf, etc.

stag'ing (stāj'ĭng), *n.* **1.** = SCAFFOLD, 1 **a;** a scaffolding. **2.** *Theater.* The act or art of putting a play on the stage.

Stag'i·rite (stăj'ĭ·rīt), *n.* A native of Stagira, in ancient Macedonia; esp., Aristotle.

stag'nant (stăg'nănt), *adj.* [L. *stagnans, -antis,* pres. part.] **1.** Not flowing; hence, foul from want of motion; as, a *stagnant* pond. **2.** Not active; dull; as, business is *stagnant.* — **stag'nan·cy** (-năn-sĭ), *n.* — **stag'nant·ly,** *adv.*

stag'nate (-nāt), *v. i.* [L. *stagnatus,* past part. of *stagnare* to stagnate, fr. *stagnum* a piece of standing water.] To be or become stagnant. — **stag·na'tion** (stăg·nā'shŭn), *n.*

stag'y, stage'y (stāj'ĭ), *adj.;* STAG'I·ER (stāj'ĭ·ẽr); STAG'I·EST. Having characteristics of the stage; theatrical. — **stag'i·ly,** *adv.* — **stag'i·ness,** *n.*

Stahl'helm' (shtäl'hĕlm'), *n.* [G., steel helmet.] A military organization of German ex-soldiers of monarchist sympathies, formed after World War I.

staid (stād), *archaic past & past part.* of STAY. Hence, *adj.,* fixed; also, sober; grave; sedate. — **Syn.** See SERIOUS. — **staid'ly,** *adv.* — **staid'ness,** *n.*

stain (stān), *v. t.* [Abbr. fr. DISTAIN.] **1.** To discolor with foreign matter; to foul. **2.** To impart color to or suffuse with color. **3.** To taint or corrupt; as, *stained* with vice. **4.** To spot with guilt or infamy. **5.** To color, as wood, glass, paper, cloth, or the like, by processes affecting, chemically or otherwise, the material **itself**; as, to *stain* glass. — *v. i.* To give or receive a stain. — *n.* **1.** Act of staining or state of being stained. **2. a** A discoloration by foreign matter; a spot. **b** Taint of guilt; stigma. **c** A natural spot of a color different from the ground. **3.** A dye, pigment, or the like, used in staining. **4.** A dye used in microscopy to render visible minute and transparent structures, to differentiate tissue elements, or to produce specific microchemical reactions. — **Syn.** Blot, stigma, brand. — **stain'a·ble,** *adj.* — **stain'less,** *adj.* — **stain'less·ly,** *adv.*

stained glass (stānd). Glass colored or stained. As used in windows, etc., it may be glass colored throughout by metallic oxides fused into it, or white glass cased with colored glass or into whose surface the pigments have been burned.

stain'er (stān'ẽr), *n.* One that stains; as: **a** A workman who stains (wood, furniture, etc.). **b** A pigment used to give color to paint. **c** Any of several insects that stain the material on which they feed.

stain'less steel (stān'lĕs; -lĭs). An alloy steel practically immune to rusting and ordinary corrosion, having chromium as its essential alloying constituent.

stair (stâr), *n.* [AS. *stǣger;* akin to AS. *stīgan* to ascend, rise.] **1.** *Archaic exc. Scot.* A staircase. **2.** Any one step of a series for ascending or descending, as in a building. **3.** A step by which one progresses, or may progress, from one stage or elevation to another, as in rank, power, etc. **4.** *pl.* A flight of steps; a staircase.

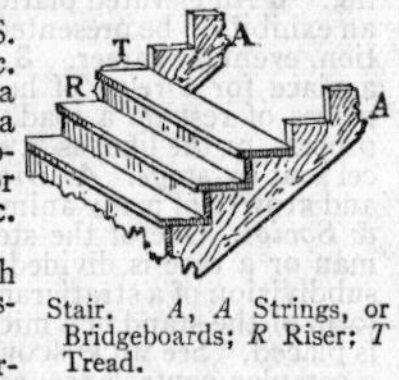

Stair. *A, A* Strings, or Bridgeboards; *R* Riser; *T* Tread.

stair'case' (-kās'), *n.* A flight of stairs with their supporting framework, casing, balusters, etc.

stair'head' (-hĕd'), *n.* The head of a staircase.

stair'way' (-wā'), *n.* The way up or down a staircase.

stair well. A compartment, extending vertically through a building, in which stairs are placed.

staith (stāth), *n.* [From AS. *stæth* bank, shore, and ON. *stöth* landing place.] *Chiefly N. of Eng.* A stage or wharf for transshipment, esp. of coal, as from railway cars into vessels; also, an embankment.

stake (stāk), *n.* [AS. *staca.*] **1.** A pointed piece, as of wood, driven, or to be driven, into the ground as a mark, support, etc. **2.** The post to which a person is bound to be burned; hence, death by such burning. **3.** A stick inserted upright in a loop, eye, or mortise, at the side or end of a cart, flatcar, etc., to retain the load. **4.** That which is staked, or hazarded, for gain or loss; esp., a gambler's capital. **5.** Short for GRUBSTAKE. **6.** The prize set in any contest; — often in *pl.* — ***at stake.*** Involved; implicated; hence, in jeopardy. — *v. t.* **1.** To mark the limits of by stakes. **2.** To fasten up or support with stakes, as plants; also, to tether to a stake. **3.** To hazard; wager. **4. a** Short for GRUBSTAKE. **b** *Slang.* To back financially.

stake'hold'er (-hōl'dẽr), *n.* The holder of a wager.

Sta·kha'no·vism (stȧ·kä'nō·vĭz'm), *n.* *Russia.* A voluntary efficiency system according to which Russian workers on a piecework basis step up their production by teamwork and sharp division of labor within working units, by improving technique, and by competition among units, with rewards of bonuses and special privileges; — so called after its initiator, Aleksei Grigorievich Stakhanov, a coal miner.

sta·lac'tite (stȧ·lăk'tīt; stăl'ăk·tīt), *n.; pl.* -TITES (-tīts). [Gr. *stalaktos* oozing out in drops, dropping.] **1.** *Geol.* A deposit of calcium carbonate resembling an icicle, hanging from the roof or sides of a cavern. Cf. STALAGMITE. **2.** A similar formation of other material, as of lava. — **stal'ac·tit'ic** (stăl'ăk·tĭt'ĭk), **stal'ac·tit'i·cal** (-ĭ·kăl), *adj.*

sta'lag' (stä'läg'; *G.* shtä'läκ'), *n.* [G. *stammlager* base camp.] A German prison camp for noncommissioned officers and privates.

sta·lag'mite (stȧ·lăg'mīt; stăl'ăg·mīt), *n.* [Gr. *stalagmos* a dropping, dripping.] **1.** *Geol.* A deposit of calcium carbonate like an inverted stalactite, formed on the floor of a cave by the drip of calcareous water. Cf. STALACTITE. **2.** A similar formation of other material. — **stal'ag·mit'ic** (stăl'ăg·mĭt'ĭk), **stal'ag·mit'i·cal** (-ĭ·kăl), *adj.*

stale (stāl), *adj.* [ME.] **1. a** Vapid or tasteless from age; as, *stale* beer. **b** Not freshly made; as, *stale* bread. **2.** Worn out by use or familiarity; trite; commonplace. **3.** Impaired in vigor or energy by prolonged activity; — orig. used of overtrained athletes. **4.** *Law.* Impaired in legal force or effect, as a lien, by reason of laches or being allowed to rest without use, action, or demand. — *v. t.* **1.** To make stale, or vapid, as beer or ale; in general, to destroy the charm or freshness of. **2.** To render common; to cheapen. — *v. i* To grow or become stale, as ale or beer; in general, to grow uninteresting, esp. by repetition. — **stale'ly,** *adv.* — **stale'ness,** *n.*

stale, *v. i.* [ME. *stalen.*] Of horses and cattle, to urinate. — *n.* Urine of horses or cattle.

stale'mate' (-māt'), *n.* [ME. *stale* stalemate, fr. AF. *estale,* prop., a fixed position.] **1.** *Chess.* The position of the king when, although not in check, he cannot move without being placed in check and there is no other piece which can be moved. A game so ending is a draw. **2.** Hence, a drawn contest; a deadlock. — *v. t.* **a** *Chess.* To subject to a stalemate. **b** Hence, to bring to a standstill.

Sta'lin·ism (stä'lĭn·ĭz'm; stăl'ĭn-), *n.* Leninism as transformed by J. Stalin (see *Biog.*) in consolidating his regime in the U.S.S.R.

Sta'lin·ist (-ĭst), *n.* An adherent of Stalinism.

stalk (stôk), *n.* [ME. *stalke.*] **1.** The stem or main axis of a plant; as, a *stalk* of wheat. **2.** That which is like, or likened to the stem of a plant, as the stem of a quill; *Zool.,* a long narrow stem or peduncle supporting some part, etc. Cf. EYESTALK. **3.** *Bot.* Any supporting organ, as a petiole, stipe, peduncle, pedicel, etc. — **stalked** (stôkt), *adj.* — **stalk'less,** *adj.*

stalk, *v. i.* [AS. be*stealcian* to walk stealthily.] **1.** *Obs.* To walk or steal along furtively. **2.** To approach one's quarry stealthily. Cf. STILL-HUNT. **3.** To walk with haughty bearing; figuratively, of famine, pestilence, etc., to be prevalent; to spread. — *v. t.* To approach, as game, under cover or by stealth. — *n.* **1.** Act or process of stalking game or other quarry. **2.** A stately or haughty step. — **stalk'er,** *n.*

stalk'ing-horse', *n.* **1.** A horse, or a figure like a horse, behind which a hunter stalks game; a mask or pretense. **2.** *Politics.* A candidate put up to divide the opposition or to hide someone's real candidacy.

stall (stôl), *n.* [AS. *steall, stall,* a place, seat, or station, a stable.] **1.** A place where horses or cattle are kept; a stable; esp., the compartment for one horse, ox, or the like. **2.** A small booth in which business is conducted; also, a bench, table, or the like, on which articles are exposed for sale; as, a butcher's *stall.* **3.** A seat, esp. one with arms; specif.: **a** A seat in the choir of a church having its back and sides wholly or partly enclosed; — called specif. ***choir stall.*** **b** A church pew. **4.** A sheath for a finger or thumb; a cot. **5.** A space marked off for the parking of a motor vehicle. **6.** *Aeronautics.* The condition resulting from stalling. See STALL, *v. i.,* 4. **7.** *Theater, Chiefly Eng.* One of the seats in the front part of the orchestra; hence, *pl.* (with *the*), the front part of the orchestra or that part of the audience seated there. — *v. t.* **1. a** To put into or keep in a stall or stable. **b** *Archaic.* To fatten by stall feeding; as, a *stalled* ox. See STALL-FEED. **2.** To check or stop by causing to become fast in mud, snow, or the like; to mire; hence, to stop or check undesiredly; as, to *stall* an engine by too great a load. **3.** *Obs.* To install in office. — *v. i.* **1. a** To live in, or be lodged in, a stall. **b** To kennel, as dogs. **2.** To stick fast, as a team in mire; hence, to stop undesiredly, as an engine from an overload. **3.** In contests, to do less than one's best, so as to deceive for any purpose. **4.** *Aeronautics.* To lose, from any cause, the relative air speed necessary for control; to lose velocity below the minimum at which an airplane can sustain itself.

stall (stôl), *n.* [From earlier *stale* a decoy, fr. AF. *estale.*] *Slang.* A story, excuse, etc., used to delay or impede action.

stall, *v. t. Colloq.* To stave off; keep at a distance, as by some trick; — usually with *off;* as, to *stall* off an enemy, a request. — *v. i. Slang.* To keep a given situation going by some trick until relief or change can be effected.

stall'-feed', *v. t.;* -FED'; -FEED'ING. To feed and fatten in a stall or on dry fodder; as, to *stall-feed* an ox.

stal'lion (stăl'yŭn), *n.* [OF. *estalion, estalon,* fr. OHG. *stal* a stable.] A male horse not castrated.

stal'wart (stôl'wẽrt; stŏl'-), *adj.* [AS. *stǣlwyrthe, -wierthe,* serviceable.] Stout; strong; sturdy; also, brave; resolute. — **Syn.** See STRONG. — *n.* **1.** A stalwart person. **2.** An unwavering partisan, esp. in politics. — **stal'wart·ly,** *adv.* — **stal'wart·ness,** *n.*

stal'worth (stôl'wûrth; stŏl'-), *adj. Archaic.* Stalwart.

sta'men (stā'mĕn), *n.; pl.* STAMENS (-mĕnz), *or, Now Rare,* STAMINA (stăm'ĭ·nȧ). [L., the warp, a thread, fiber.] *Bot.* The microsporophyll in seed plants; that organ of the flower giving rise to the male fertilizing cell. It consists of the *anther* and the *filament.* See CARPEL, FILAMENT, *Illusts.*

stam'i·na (stăm'ĭ·nȧ), *n.* [L., pl. of STAMEN the warp.] *Orig. as pl., now as sing.* Vigor; capacity for enduring.

stam'i·nal (-năl), *adj.* **1.** Of, pertaining to, constituting, or exhibiting stamina. **2.** Also **sta·min'e·al** (stȧ·mĭn'ē·ăl). Of, pertaining to, or consisting of a stamen or stamens.

stam'i·nate (-nāt), *adj. Bot.* Having or producing stamens; specif., of diclinous flowers, having stamens but no pistils. Cf. PISTILLATE; see AMENT, *Illust.*

stam'i·ni- (stăm'ĭ·nĭ-), **stamin-.** [L. *stamen, -minis.*] *Bot.* A combining form meaning *stamen,* as in **stam'i·nif'er·ous, stam'i·nig'er·ous.** See -FEROUS, -GEROUS.

stam'i·no'di·um (-nō'dĭ·ŭm), *n.; pl.* -DIA (-ȧ). Also **stam'i·node** (stăm'ĭ·nōd). [NL. See STAMEN; -OID.] *Bot.* An abortive or sterile stamen.

stam'i·no'dy (stăm'ĭ·nō'dĭ), *n. Bot.* Metamorphosis of a flower organ into a stamen.

stam'mel (stăm'ĕl; -'l), *n.* [F. *estamel.*] **a** A coarse woolen fabric usually dyed red. **b** The shade of red of this cloth.

stam'mer (stăm'ẽr), *v. i. & t.* [AS. *stamerian;* akin to AS. *stamur, stamer,* stammering.] To speak with involuntary stops in uttering syllables and words.

Syn. **Stammer, stutter** mean to speak stumblingly. **Stammer** usually implies fear, embarrassment, or a sudden shock as its cause; **stutter,** a constitutional defect, either of speech organs or of nerves.

— *n.* Act or instance of stammering; stutter.

— **stam'mer·er** (-ẽr), *n.* — **stam'mer·ing·ly,** *adv.*

stamp (stămp), *v. t.* [ME. *stampen;* akin to AS. *stempan.*] **1.** *Dial.* To crush; bray. **2. a** To strike or beat forcibly with the bottom of the foot. **b** To bring down (the foot) forcibly and noisily. **3.** To impress or imprint with some mark; hence, to fix deeply or indelibly, as by impressing. **4.** To cut out, bend, or indent, by a stamp, die, etc. **5.** To indicate as by a mark or stamp; to mark; distinguish. **6.** To impress with an official stamp; as, to *stamp* a bill "Paid"; also, to put a stamp on; as, to *stamp* a letter. — *v. i.* **1.** *Obs.* To strike; crush. **2.** To strike the foot forcibly and noisily downward, as in anger. — *n.* **1.** Act of stamping. **2.** That which stamps: **a** Any instrument for making impressions, as a die. **b** A heavy pestle, raised by water or steam power, for crushing ores. **3.** The mark, impression, design, etc., made by stamping. **4.** Specif., an official mark set on things chargeable with a government duty or tax, or on papers legally requiring execution under certain conditions, to signify that the duty or tax has been paid, or the conditions fulfilled. Also, a paper adhesive label affixed for a similar purpose. **5.** A stamped or printed device or slip of paper, issued by the government at a fixed price, and required by law to be affixed to, or stamped on, certain papers or things, as evidence that the government dues are paid. **6.** A trading stamp. **7.** A character or reputation, good or bad, fixed as if by imprinting; distinctive mark. **8.** Make; cast; form; character; as, a man of the same *stamp.* **9.** Value or authority, as if given by an official stamp. — **stamp'less,** *adj.*

Stamp Act. An act of the British Parliament (1765, repealed 1766) imposing a duty on all paper, vellum, and parchment used in the American colonies, and declaring all writings on unstamped materials null and void.

stam·pede' (stăm·pēd'), *n.* [Sp. *estampida* (in America) a stampede, *estampido* a crackling.] **1.** A wild, headlong scamper, or running away, of a number of animals; hence, any sudden flight or dispersion. **2.** Any sudden unconcerted moving or acting together of a number of persons, as from some common impulse. — *v. i.* **1.** To run away in a panic. **2.** Hence, to move or act together suddenly and unconcertedly; also, to act in a hasty or frightened manner. — *v. t.* To cause to stampede. — **stam·ped'er** (-pēd'ẽr), *n.*

stamp'er (stămp'ẽr), *n.* **1.** One who stamps, specif., in an industrial operation; as, card *stamper;* metal *stamper.* **2.** An implement for pounding or stamping. **3.** Any of various stamping machines, as for powdering calcined flints, cleansing fabrics in a revolving vessel, etc.

stamp'ing ground. A favorite or habitual resort.

stamp mill *or* **stamp'ing mill.** A mill in which ore is crushed with stamps.

stance (stăns), *n.* [OF. *estance* a standing, position.] **1.** *Scot.* Station; position, as for a building; site. **2.** Mode of standing or being placed; posture. **3.** *Golf.* A player's position after he places his feet preparatory to making a stroke.

stanch (stänch; stȧnch; 9), **staunch** (stônch; stänch), *v. t.* [OF. *estanchier.*] **1.** To stop or check the flowing of, as blood; to stop the flowing of blood from; as, to *stanch* a cut. **2.** *Archaic & Dial.* To quench; quell. — *v. i.* To cease flowing or bleeding. — *adj.* [OF. *estanc*, fem. *estanche.*] **1.** Watertight; sound; as, a *stanch* ship; hence, firm; strong. **2.** Loyal; steady; true; steadfast. — **Syn.** See FAITHFUL. — **stanch′er**, *n.* — **stanch′ly, staunch′ly**, *adv.* — **stanch′ness, staunch′ness**, *n.*

stan′chion (stăn′shŭn *or, esp. Brit.*, stän′-), *n.* [OF. *estanchon, estançon*, deriv. of L. *stans, stantis*, standing.] **1.** An upright bar, brace, or support, as for a roof, a ship's deck, etc. **2.** A pair of uprights made to form a yoke for securing cattle in a barn. — *v. t.* **1.** To provide with stanchions. **2.** To secure, as cattle, by stanchions.

stand (stănd), *v. i.*; STOOD (stŏŏd); STAND′ING. [AS. *standan.*] **1.** To take, or be at rest in, an upright or firm position; as: **a** To support oneself on the feet in an erect position; — opposed to *lie, sit, kneel*, etc. **b** To be, grow, or become, upright in its proper place, as a tree, a pillar, etc. **c** To take or occupy a (certain) standing position; as, to *stand* aloof. **d** To attain a (specified) height when erect; as, he *stands* six feet tall. **2.** To occupy or hold a place; to be located. **3.** To pause; stop. **4.** To remain unchanged or unimpaired; to abide; last. **5.** To hold one's ground; to maintain one's position. **6.** To be fixed or steadfast, as in defense or antagonism; as, to *stand* for temperance. **7.** To act in resistance, as to an enemy. **8.** To have or maintain a relative position or rank; as, he *stands* first in line of promotion. **9.** To hesitate; scruple; as, he will not *stand* at murder. **10.** To be in some particular state; as, he *stands* accused; to *stand* on guard. **11.** To agree; accord. **12.** To be a candidate; to run; as, he will *stand* for re-election. **13.** To collect and remain; as, tears *stand* in her eyes; also, to be stagnant; as, *standing* water. **14.** *Naut.* To hold a course at sea; as, to *stand* for the harbor. — *v. t.* **1.** To set upright; to cause to stand. **2.** To endure; sustain; tolerate. **3.** To resist; withstand; face with courage and steadfastness. **4.** To submit to; as, to *stand* trial. **5.** *Colloq.* To pay for (drinks). — **Syn.** See BEAR.

stand a chance, a show, etc. To have a chance. — ***stand by.*** **a** To be near; to be present. **b** To be set aside with disregard. **c** To defend; support; as, to *stand by* one's party. **d** *Naut.* To be or get ready; to be ready to act in relation to; as, *stand by* the main sheet. **e** *Radio.* (1) Of a transmitting station, to be ready to send out signals, etc., but not actually doing so. (2) Of a receiving station, to remain tuned in for a transmitting station until it starts transmitting. — ***stand down.*** To leave the witness box, as after giving evidence. — ***stand for.*** To represent; to be a symbol for; as, the judicial ermine *stands for* justice. — ***stand in.*** **a** To cost. **b** *Colloq.* To keep on good terms, as with the hope of favors. — ***stand off.*** **a** To keep oneself at a distance. **b** Not to comply. **c** To hold at bay, as an assailant; to put off, as a dun. **d** *Naut.* To steer away from the shore. — ***stand on.*** *Naut.* To continue on the same tack or course. — ***stand on** or **upon.*** **a** To depend upon. **b** To insist on; as, to *stand on* one's rights. — ***stand one in stead.*** To be of use or advantage. — ***stand one's ground.*** To stand firm. — ***stand out.*** **a** To be prominent. **b** To persist in resistance; not to yield. **c** To steer away from shore. **d** To endure; last. — ***stand over.*** To postpone, or be postponed. — ***stand pat.*** **a** *Poker.* To choose to play one's hand as dealt, without resorting to the draw. **b** Hence, *Colloq.*, to oppose change of any kind. — ***stand to.*** **a** To ply; as, to *stand to* one's oars. **b** To hold oneself in readiness for action, as in response to an alarm. **c** To support, as a policy. — ***stand up for.*** To defend; justify; support. — ***stand up to.*** To meet fairly and fully, as a danger, a foe.

— *n.* **1.** Act of standing. **2.** Specif., a halt or stop, esp. for defense or resistance. **3.** A station, as of a soldier, watchman, etc. **4.** Specif.: **a** The place where a witness stands to testify in court. **b** A raised platform whence a race or other spectacle may be viewed; grandstand. **5.** A stall or booth for business; any location for business. **6.** A small table; also, something on or in which anything may be placed for support; as, an umbrella or music *stand.* **7.** *Obs. exc. Dial.* A suit, set, or the like; of soldiers, a troop; as, a *stand* of armor; a *stand*, or hive, of bees. **8.** A growth of plants or trees, esp. with regard to the number or distribution upon a given area. **9.** *Theater.* On a tour, any of the stops made to give a performance; also, a town where such a stop is made; as, a one-night *stand.*

stand′ard (stăn′dẽrd), *n.* [OF. *estandart*, prob. of Teut. origin. In some senses fr. E. *stand*, influenced in form by the word fr. F. meaning banner.] **1. a** A figure adopted as an emblem by a people; as, the eagle was the *standard* of the Roman legion; specif., *Her.*, a long, narrow, tapering flag used by a noble or leader on special occasions; — disting. from a *banner.* **b** The personal flag of the ruler of a state; loosely, a banner. **2.** That which is set up and established by authority as a rule for the measure of quantity, weight, extent, value, or quality. **3.** That which is established by authority, custom, or general consent, as a model or example; criterion; test. **4.** A structure built for, or serving as, a base or support for something; as, the *standard* for a vase. **5.** *Chiefly Technical.* An upright support, as either of the end supports of a lathe, a stand for a lamp, an upright rod for carrying overhead electric wires, etc. **6.** *Bot.* A vexillum. **7.** *Coinage.* **a** The fineness and legal weight of the metal used in coins. **b** The standard of value for a monetary system, being in modern systems gold (the ***gold standard***) or silver (the ***silver standard***). **8.** *Educ., Chiefly Brit.* A grade or class (in a school). **9.** *Hort.* A tree, shrub, or herb, grown with an erect treelike stem, and not dwarfed by grafting or trained upon a wall or trellis.

Syn. **Standard, criterion, gauge, yardstick, touchstone** denote the means of determining what a thing should be. **Standard** applies to any definite rule, principle, or measure established by authority; **criterion** implies a measure or test of a thing's quality, such as goodness, beauty, etc.; **gauge**, in literal use, a standard of measurement but, in figurative use, a criterion; **yardstick** and **touchstone** are figuratively used in place of *criterion.*

— *adj.* **1.** Being, affording, or according with, a standard for comparison and judgment. **2.** Having a recognized and permanent value. **3.** *Printing.* Of type, normal in height, width, or weight of face. See TYPE, *n.*

stand′ard-bear′er, *n.* An officer or soldier of an army, company, battery or troop, who bears a standard; hence, the leader of any organization or movement.

stand′ard·bred′ (stăn′dẽrd·brĕd′), *adj.* Bred to conform to standards; as, the American *Standardbred* horse, a light-harness type bred for speed.

standard candle. See CANDLE, 3.

standard dollar. *U. S.* The monetary unit; before 1934 a dollar of 25.8 grains of gold, .900 fine; since Jan. 31, 1934, a dollar of 15.238 grains of gold, .900 fine.

stand′ard·ize (stăn′dẽr·dīz), *v. t.* To reduce to, or compare with, a standard; to render standard. — **stand′ard·i·za′tion** (-dĭ·zā′shŭn; -dī·zā′-), *n.* — **stand′ard·iz′er** (-dīz′ẽr), *n.*

standard time. The civil time established by law or by general usage over a region or country; for each zone of 15° of longitude around the world the time varies by 1 hour; however, where a country overlaps a zone or more, in order to have a uniform national time, its legal time may differ by ½ hour or less from the neighboring zone. In England, the standard time is the time when the sun crosses the meridian that passes through Greenwich (the mean solar time of Greenwich, or ***Greenwich time***). In the U. S., there are four official standards of time, ***Eastern, Central, Mountain,*** and ***Pacific***, corresponding to the mean local times of the 75th, 90th, 105th, and 120th meridians west, or 5, 6, 7, and 8 hours respectively slower than Greenwich. In addition to these standards Canada has ***Atlantic*** time, 4 hours slower than Greenwich, ***Newfoundland*** time, 3½ hours slower than Greenwich, and ***Yukon*** time, 9 hours slower than Greenwich.

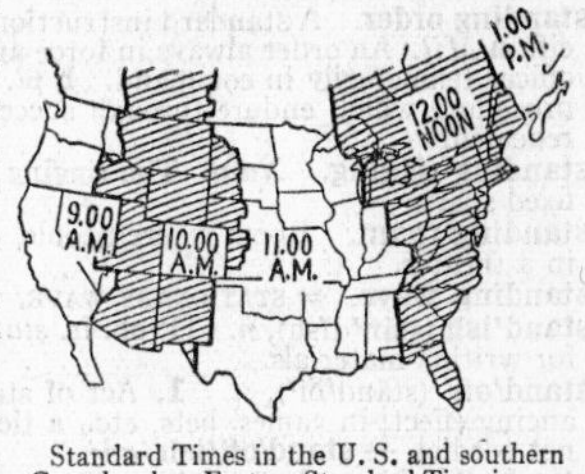

Standard Times in the U. S. and southern Canada when Eastern Standard Time is noon.

STANDARD TIME AROUND THE WORLD

TIME COMPARED WITH GREENWICH TIME AND WASHINGTON, D. C., NOON

NOTE. A day, Sunday, Sept. 6, begins at the *date line* (which see) in the Pacific and moves west. Wellington, N. Z., long. 174° 50′ E, is 12 hours ahead of Greenwich. When it is 12 o'clock noon at Greenwich it is 12 o'clock midnight that evening (Sunday) at Wellington and 7 o'clock that morning at Washington. When it is 12 o'clock noon at Washington it is 5 o'clock the next morning (Monday, Sept. 7) at Wellington and 5 o'clock (17 o'clock) that afternoon (Sunday) at Greenwich.

	Difference in time from Greenwich			Local time when it is noon at Washington
——180°——INTERNATIONAL DATE LINE——180°——				
	hr.	*min.*		
Wellington, N. Z.; Wake Island, 166° 35′ E	12		fast	5 A.M.*
New Caledonia	11		"	4 A.M.*
Sydney, N. S. W.; Port Moresby, Papua	10		"	3 A.M.*
Tokyo, Japan	9		"	2 A.M.*
Manila, P. I.; Shanghai, China	8		"	1 A.M.*
Djakarta, Java; Singapore, British Malaya	7	30	"	12 30 A.M.*
Calcutta, India; Bombay, "	5	30	"	10 30 P.M.
Baghdad, Iraq; Moscow, U. S. S. R.	3		"	8 P.M.
Cairo, Egypt; Cape Town, South Africa	2		"	7 P.M.
Rome, Italy; Berlin, Germany; Paris, France	1		"	6 P.M.
London, England	0		"	5 P.M.
Freetown, Sierra Leone	1		slow	4 P.M.
Rio de Janeiro, Brazil; Buenos Aires, Argentina	3		"	2 P.M.
Halifax, N. S. (Atlantic)	4		"	1 P.M.
Caracas, Venezuela	4	30	"	12 30 P.M.
New York, N. Y. (Eastern); Ottawa, Can.; Lima, Peru	5		"	12 noon (Sunday)
Chicago, Ill. (Central); St. Louis, Mo. "; Mexico City, Mexico	6		"	11 A.M.
Denver, Colo. (Mountain); Edmonton, Alberta	7		"	10 A.M.
San Francisco, Calif. (Pacific); Portland, Ore. "; Juneau, Alaska	8		"	9 A.M.
Honolulu, Hawaii; Tahiti, Society Islands	10		"	7 A.M.
Aleutian Is., Alaska	11		"	6 A.M.
Midway Island (transpacific airport), long. 177° 20′ W†	12		"	5 A.M.
——180°——INTERNATIONAL DATE LINE——180°——				

* The morning of the next day, Monday, Sept. 7.
† Actually uses the same time as Honolulu.

stand′-by′, *n.* One that can be relied upon either for regular use or for an emergency.

stand·ee′ (stăn·dē′), *n.* *Colloq.* One who stands, as at a theatrical performance.

stand′er (stăn′dẽr), *n.* One who or that which stands.

stand′fast′ (stănd′făst′; 9), *n.* A firm, fixed, or settled position. — **stand′fast′**, *adj.*

stand′-in′, *n.* **1.** A preferred or favorable position. **2.** *Motion Pictures.* Someone employed to stand in the place of an actor or actress until lights and cameras are ready.

stand′ing, *adj.* **1.** Upright or erect; as, *standing* grain. **2.** At rest; esp., not being operated, as a factory, tool; specif., of water, not flowing; stagnant. **3.** Remaining at the same level, degree, amount, etc., for an indeterminate period; as, a *standing* offer. **4.** Established by law, custom, or the like; permanent; as, a *standing* army. **5.** Not movable; as, a *standing* bed. Cf. TRUCKLE BED. **6.** Done from a standing position; as, a *standing* jump. — *n.* **1.** Act of one who stands or comes to a stand; stand or stance. **2.** Place to stand in; station; location. **3.** Length of service, esp. as determining rank, pay, etc.; hence, position or condition in society; reputation; as, a man of high *standing.* **4.** Maintenance of position or condition; duration; as, a custom of long *standing.*

standing army. A permanent army of paid soldiers.

standing order. A standard instruction, or series of instructions; specif.: **a** *Mil.* An order always in force and not subject to change by an officer temporarily in command. **b** *pl. Parl. Practice.* The rules for procedure which endure through successive sessions until vacated or repealed.

standing rigging. *Naut.* The rigging which sustains the masts and fixed spars.

standing room. Room where people, esp. spectators, may stand, as in a theater.

standing wave. = STATIONARY WAVE.

stand'ish (stăn'dĭsh), *n.* [Prob. fr. *stand* + *dish.*] A stand, or case, for writing materials.

stand'off' (stănd'ôf'), *n.* **1.** Act of standing off. **2.** A counterbalancing effect; in games, bets, etc., a tie; a draw. — *adj.* Reserved; not cordial. — **stand'off'ish,** *adj.*

stand oil. Linseed oil thickened by heating to about 600° F. for several hours, used in paints, varnishes, etc.

stand'out' (stănd'out'), *n.* **a** Something outstanding, as for excellence, taste, etc. **b** *Colloq.* One who refuses to join or co-operate with a group.

stand'pat' (-păt'), *adj.* *Colloq.* Of or pert. to or characterized by the policy of standing pat. — **stand'pat'ter** (-păt'ẽr), *n.*

stand'pipe' (-pīp'), *n.* A high vertical pipe or reservoir for water, used to secure a uniform pressure.

stand'point' (-point'), *n.* A fixed point or station; a position from which objects or principles are viewed and judged.

stand'still' (-stĭl'), *n.* A stop; a state of rest. — *adj.* That stands still; that maintains things in a fixed or static condition; as, a *standstill* agreement.

stand'-up', *adj.* **1.** Erect; upright; specif., of a collar, stiff and high with no fold. **2.** *Colloq.* Done, taken, etc., while standing; as, a *stand-up* lunch.

stang (stăng; stȧng), *v. t. & i. & n.* [ON. *stanga* to prick.] *Chiefly Scot.* Sting; throb; ache.

stan'hope (stăn'hōp; stăn'ŭp), *n.* [After Fitzroy *Stanhope* (1787–1864), Brit. clergyman.] A style of buggy typically with high seat and closed back and a heavy erect piece at each side.

stank (stăngk; stȧngk), *n.* [OF. *estanc.*] *Chiefly Scot. & Dial.* **a** Pond; pool; ditch. **b** Reservoir. **c** Dam; weir.

stank (stăngk), *past* of STINK.

stan'na·ry (stăn'ȧ·rĭ), *n.; pl.* -NARIES (-rĭz). [ML. *stannaria,* fr. L. *stannum* tin.] *Eng.* A tin mine; tinworks.

stan'nic (stăn'ĭk), *adj.* [L. *stannum* tin.] *Chem.* Of, pertaining to, or containing tin, specif. in its valence of four. Cf. STANNOUS.

stan'nite (-īt), *n.* *Mineral.* A steel-gray mineral of a metallic luster; tin pyrites. It is a compound of tin, copper, iron, and sulfur, and sometimes zinc.

stan'nous (-ŭs), *adj.* *Chem.* Pert. to, or containing, tin, specif. in its valence of two. Cf. STANNIC.

stan'num (-ŭm), *n.* [L., also *stagnum,* alloy of silver and lead (LL., tin).] Tin. Chemical symbol, *Sn* (no period).

stan'za (stăn'zȧ), *n.; pl.* -ZAS (-zȧz). [It., a room, a stanza, fr. L. *stans,* pres. part. of *stare* to stand.] *Pros.* **a** A recurring unit of a poem consisting of a group of verses, or lines, which are combined normally according to a typical scheme; as, the *stanzas* of Gray's Elegy. **b** Any group of verses comprising a division of a poem. — **Syn.** See VERSE. — **stan·za'ic** (stăn·zā'ĭk), *adj.*

sta·pe'li·a (stȧ·pē'lĭ·ȧ), *n.* [NL., after J. B. van *Stapel* (d. 1636), botanist of Leiden.] *Bot.* Any of a genus (*Stapelia*) of African evil-smelling plants of the milkweed family with succulent, leafless, toothed stems like the joints of a cactus.

sta'pes (stā'pēz), *n.* [LL. *stapes, stapedis,* a stirrup.] *Anat. & Zool.* The innermost ossicle of the ear of mammals. See EAR, 1 & *Illust.* — **sta·pe'di·al** (stȧ·pē'dĭ·ăl), *adj.*

staph'y·lo- (stăf'ĭ·lō-), **staphyl-.** [Gr. *staphylē.*] A combining form meaning *bunch of grapes,* used to denote: **a** *Uvula,* as in **staph'y·lo·plas'ty.** **b** *Staphylococcic.*

staph'y·lo·coc'cus (-kŏk'ŭs), *n.; pl.* -CI (-sī). [NL., fr. *staphylo-* + *-coccus.*] *Bacteriol.* Any of a genus (*Staphylococcus*) of Gram-positive bacteria (family Coccaceae) which often form grapelike clusters and are parasites on the skin and mucous membranes. — **staph'y·lo·coc'cal** (-kŏk'ăl), **staph'y·lo·coc'cic** (-kŏk'sĭk), *adj.*

staph'y·lor'rha·phy, staph'y·lor'a·phy (-lŏr'ȧ·fĭ), *n.* [*staphylo-* + Gr. *rhaptein* to sew.] *Surg.* The plastic operation of uniting a cleft palate.

sta'ple (stā'p'l), *n.* [AS. *stapol* post, pillar.] A loop of metal bent and formed with two points to be driven into wood, etc., to hold a hook, pin, or the like; also, a similarly shaped piece of thin wire, driven through papers, etc., and clinched to bind them. — *v. t.* To secure by a staple or staples.

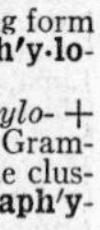

Staple.

sta'ple, *n.* [OF. *estaple,* fr. MD. *stapel* a support, stake, mart.] **1.** *Hist.* A settled mart; emporium. **2.** Hence, place of supply; source; also, storehouse. **3.** The principal commodity of traffic in a market. **4.** The principal constituent in anything; chief item; as, gossip was the chief *staple* of conversation. **5.** Unmanufactured material; raw material. **6.** A fiber of raw wool, cotton, flax, etc., in its natural state, or when carded or combed; the length, fineness, condition, of any kind, lot, or esp. grade, of such fibers. — *adj.* **1.** Established in commerce; occupying the markets; as, a *staple* trade. **2.** Regularly produced in large quantities; hence, principal; chief; as, wool was the *staple* commodity of England at that period. — *v. t.;* STA'PLED (-p'ld); STA'PLING (-plĭng). To sort according to its staple; as, to *staple* cotton.

sta'pler (stā'plẽr), *n.* **1.** A dealer in staple goods. **2.** One employed to assort wool according to its staple. **3.** A machine that binds papers with wire staples.

star (stär), *n.* [AS. *steorra.*] **1.** Any of the luminous bodies seen in the heavens; specif., *Astron.,* any self-luminous celestial body, exclusive of comets, meteors, and nebulae; — as distinguished from the much smaller bodies, known as planets, that shine by reflected light. Astronomically, the sun is a star of average brightness, size, and probable age. Cf. GIANT, *n.,* 3. **2.** A conventional figure having five or more points, taken as representing a star; any formation suggesting or likened to such a figure. **3.** An asterisk [thus, *]; — used as a reference to a note, etc. **4.** A person of brilliant qualities, who stands out pre-eminently among his fellows. **5. a** *Astrol. Usually pl.* A planet or a configuration of the planets regarded as influencing one's destiny. **b** Hence, destiny; fortune. **6.** *Mil., U.S.* A star-shaped emblem; specif.: **a** In full, ***battle star.*** An addition in the form of a bronze star authorized to be worn on a service ribbon to correspond to a battle clasp (see CLASP, *n.,* 3) on a service medal. Five bronze stars may be replaced by a single silver star. **b** A gold star awarded to U. S. naval personnel in lieu of a second award of the same decoration. **7.** *Theater & Motion Pictures.* An actor or actress who plays a principal role or roles. **8.** [*cap.*] *Yachting.* A boat of the Star Class (which see).
— *v. t.;* STARRED (stärd); STAR'RING. **1.** To set or adorn with stars; to bespangle; as, a robe *starred* with gems. **2.** To mark with a star, as being superior; also, to mark with or as with an asterisk. **3.** *Theater & Motion Pictures.* To present in the principal, or star, role. — *v. i.* **1.** To have the appearance of, or to suggest, a star; esp., to shine as a star; hence, to be brilliant or prominent. **2.** *Theater & Motion Pictures.* To play as a recognized star. — *adj.* **1.** Of or pertaining to a star or stars. **2.** Of outstanding excellence; pre-eminent.

star apple. A tropical American tree (*Chrysophyllum cainito*); also, its apple-shaped, edible fruit. The carpels present a starlike figure when cut across.

star'board (stär'bōrd; -bẽrd), *n.* [AS. *stēorbord,* i. e., steer side.] *Naut.* That side of a vessel on the right hand of a person who stands on board facing the bow; — opposed to *port* (formerly *larboard*). — *adj.* *Naut.* Pert. to the starboard. — *adv.* Toward the starboard side. — *v. t. & i.* *Naut.* To put or move to the right, or starboard, side.

Star Boat. *Yachting.* A boat of the Star Class (which see).

starch (stärch), *n.* [ME. *starche, sterche,* fr. *sterchen* to starch, fr. AS. *stercan* to stiffen, fr. *stearc* stiff.] **1.** A white, odorless, tasteless, granular or powdery complex carbohydrate, $(C_6H_{10}O_5)_x$, widely disseminated among plants, esp. in seeds, bulbs, and tubers. It is an important constituent of food, and is used in making commercial glucose, for stiffening linen, etc. **2.** A stiff, formal manner; stiffness. **3.** *Slang, U.S.* Energy; vim. — *v. t.* To stiffen with or as if with starch. — **starch'i·ness,** *n.* — **starch'y,** *adj.*

Star Chamber. [Appar. from the *stars* on the ceiling of the room where it sat.] **a** *Eng. Hist.* An ancient high court exercising wide civil and criminal jurisdiction. It could proceed on mere rumor or examine witnesses; it could apply torture. **b** Hence [*not cap.*], any secret or irresponsible tribunal. — **star'-cham'ber** (*see Pron.,* § 2), *adj.*

starch sirup. See GLUCOSE, 2.

Star Class. [Arbitrary designation: five-pointed red star.] *Yachting.* A large international one-design class of racing sloops (22 ft. 7½ in. over all), with a fin keel of cast iron (885 lb.), a Marconi mainsail (about 215 sq. ft.), and a jib (50 sq. ft.).

stare (stâr), *v. i.* [AS. *starian.*] **1.** To gaze or look fixedly, as through fear, wonder, etc. **2.** To be very conspicuous because of size, brilliancy, or the like; as, *staring* colors. **3.** Of hair, to stand on end; bristle. — *v. t.* To look earnestly at; commonly, to affect in a specified way by a fixed gaze; as, to *stare* one out of countenance. — **Syn.** See GAZE. — *n.* Act or fact of staring; a fixed look. — **star'er** (stâr'ẽr), *n.*

star facet. One of the eight small triangular facets which abut on the table in the bezel or crown of a brilliant. See BRILLIANT, *Illust.*

star'fish' (stär'fĭsh'), *n.; pl.,* see FISH. Any of a class (Asteroidea) of echinoderms having a body of radially disposed arms (usually five); an asteroid. Starfishes feed largely on mollusks, and some are very destructive to oysters.

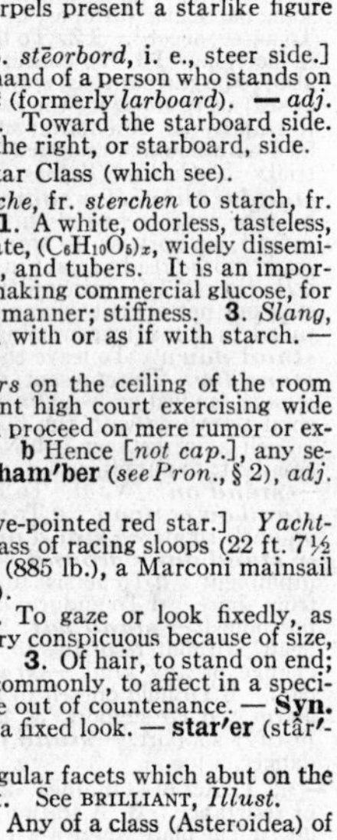

Starfish (*Asterias vulgaris*). (¼)

star'flow'er (-flou'ẽr), *n.* Any of several plants having star-shaped pentamerous flowers; as: **a** The star-of-Bethlehem. **b** Any of a genus (*Trientalis,* esp. *T. americana*) of plants of the primrose family.

star'gaze' (-gāz'), *v. i.* To gaze at, or as if at, stars.

star'gaz'er (-gāz'ẽr), *n.* **1.** One who gazes at the stars; an astrologer; sometimes, jocosely, an astronomer. **2.** Any of several spiny-finned marine fishes (family Uranoscopidae) whose eyes are on top of the head.

star'gaz'ing (-gāz'ĭng), *n.* **1.** Act or practice of a stargazer. **2.** Hence, absent-mindedness; abstraction.

star grass. Any of a genus (*Hypoxis*) of herbs of the amaryllis family, with small star-shaped flowers.

stark (stärk), *adj.* [AS. *stearc.*] **1.** Stiff; rigid; as, *stark* in death. **2.** *Obs. exc. Dial.* Intractable; obdurate. **3.** Harsh; of weather, violent; of persons, severe; stern; of scenery, barren; desolate. **4.** Unadorned; bare; as, the *stark* narrative. **5.** *Archaic.* Strong; firm. **6.** Sheer; utter; as, *stark* folly. — **Syn.** See STIFF. — *adv.* In a stark manner; severely; also, entirely; absolutely; as, *stark* mad. — **stark'ly,** *adv.*

star'less (stär'lĕs; -lĭs), *adj.* Without stars.

star'let (-lĕt; -lĭt), *n.* **1.** A little star. **2.** A young movie actress who has shown promise in supporting roles and is being coached and publicized for starring roles.

star'light' (-līt'), *n.* The light given by the stars. — *adj.* Also, *Rare,* **star'light'ed.** Lighted by the stars.

star'like' (-līk'), *adj.* Resembling a star.

star'ling (stär'lĭng), *n.* [AS. *stærlinc,* fr. *stær* starling.] **1.** Any passerine bird of a genus (*Sturnus*) or of a family (Sturnidae) native to Europe. The European starling is dark brown (in summer glossy greenish black) and spotted with yellowish white. It has been introduced in the U. S., Australia, and New Zealand. **2.** A structure of piles driven round the piers of a bridge for protection and support.

star'lit' (stär'lĭt'), *adj.* Lighted by the stars.

star'-nosed' (-nōzd'), *adj.* Designating a common American mole, the

star-nosed mole, *or* **star′nose′** (stär′nōz′) (*Condylura cristata*), of somewhat aquatic habits, having small radiating fleshy processes surrounding the nostrils.

star of Bethlehem. The star which guided the Magi to Bethlehem, to the infant Jesus. *Matt.* ii. 9.

star′-of-Beth′le·hem, *n.* Any of a genus (*Ornithogalum,* esp. *O. umbellatum*) of plants of the lily family, with greenish flowers, naturalized in the eastern United States.

starred (stärd), *adj.* **1.** Adorned with or as with stars. **2.** *Theater.* Presented as a star.

star′ry (stär′ĭ), *adj.;* STAR′RI·ER (-ĭ·ẽr); STAR′RI·EST. **1.** Of or pert. to the stars; studded with stars. **2.** Consisting of, or proceeding from, the stars; stellar. **3.** Shining like stars; sparkling. **4.** Arranged in rays like those of a star; stellate. **5.** Aspiring to starlike heights.

Stars and Bars. The first flag of the "Confederate States of America," having three bars, of red, white, and red respectively, and a blue union with white stars, in a circle, to the number of the seceded states.

Stars and Stripes. The flag of the United States, of thirteen horizontal stripes, alternately red (7) and white (6), and a union having, in a blue field, white stars to represent the states, one for each; — popularly so called.

star sapphire. A sapphire which, when cut with a convex surface (cabochon) and polished, exhibits asterism.

star shell. *Mil.* A shell which on bursting releases a shower of brilliant stars, — for signaling, illuminating, etc.

star shower. A meteoric shower.

star′-span′gled (stär′spăng′g'ld), *adj.* Spangled with stars.

Star-Spangled Banner, The. **a** The Stars and Stripes. **b** A poem by Francis Scott Key, written during the bombardment of Fort McHenry, near Baltimore, 1814. It was adopted as the national anthem of the United States in 1931.

start (stärt), *n.* [AS. *steort.*] A tail. *Obs., exc.* in composition; as, red*start.*

start, *v. i.* [ME. *sterten.*] **1.** To move suddenly and quickly, as with a spring, from one's position; to dart; jump. **2.** To protrude, or seem to protrude; as, in horror, his eyes *started* from their sockets. **3.** To give an involuntary convulsive twitch or spring, as in surprise, pain, etc. **4.** To set out; commence; begin. **5.** To become somewhat displaced or loosened; as, a seam has *started.* — *v. t.* **1.** To cause to start; to rouse; as, to *start* a hare. **2.** *Scot.* To startle; alarm. **3.** To set going, running, flowing, or the like; as, to *start* a train, rumor. **4.** To open up (a topic, subject); to broach. **5.** To cause to be displaced or loosened; as, to *start* a tooth, a bolt. **6.** To enter in a contest, as a horse race. **7.** *Naut.* To tap and begin drawing from; as, to *start* a water cask. — **Syn.** See BEGIN.

— *n.* **1.** Act of starting; sudden involuntary motion, as due to surprise, fear, etc. **2.** A spasmodic and brief effort. **3.** A sudden, capricious impulse; a sally; also, movement under a sudden, capricious impulse. **4.** A part that has started or become loosened or displaced. **5.** The beginning, as of a journey or a course of action. **6.** The place of beginning. **7.** A lead or handicap at the beginning of a competition; an advantage; as, to have a *start* of ten yards in a race.

start′er (stär′tẽr), *n.* **1.** One who or that which starts; as: **a** The first in a series. **b** An official of a bus line, or the like, who sees that cars leave at scheduled times. **c** = SELF-STARTER. **2.** *Sports.* **a** One who starts as a competitor in a race. **b** An official who has charge of competitors at the start of a race, and who gives the starting signal.

star thistle. A spiny European knapweed (*Centaurea calcitrapa*) with purple flowers; also, a related species (*C. solstitialis*) with yellow flowers; — called also *caltrop.*

star′tle (stär′t'l), *v. i.;* -TLED (-t'ld); -TLING (-tlĭng). [AS. *steartlian* to stumble.] To start or move suddenly as in surprise, fear, etc. — *v. t.* To frighten suddenly and, usually, not seriously; to cause to start. — *n.* A start or shock, as in alarm. — **star′tler** (-tlẽr), *n.*

star′tling (-tlĭng), *adj.* Causing sudden fear, surprise, anxiety, or the like. — **star′tling·ly,** *adv.*

star·va′tion (stär·vā′shŭn), *n.* Act of starving, or state of being starved.

starve (stärv), *v. i.* [ME. *sterven* to die, fr. AS. *steorfan.*] **1.** To perish with hunger; also, to suffer extreme hunger. **2.** *Now Dial.* To perish or suffer with cold. **3.** Hence, to suffer from any want; to be in need. — *v. t.* **1.** To kill with hunger; also, to distress or subdue by famine. **2.** *Now Dial.* To freeze to death. **3.** To destroy or disable by want of any kind. — **starv′er** (stär′vẽr), *n.*

starve′ling (-lĭng), *n.* One that pines or is thin from lack of food or nutriment. — *adj.* Hungry; lean; pining with want.

stash (stăsh), *v. t.* [Appar. a blend of *store* and *cache.*] *Slang, U.S.* To hide or store in a secret place for future use; also, to quit or stop. — *v. i.* To stop or stall. — *n.* Something stashed away or the place where it is stashed.

sta′sis (stā′sĭs; stăs′ĭs), *n.; pl.* STASES (stā′sēz). [NL., fr. Gr. *stasis* a standing still.] *Physiol.* A stoppage of the normal flow of fluids in any organs or vessels of the body. Specif.: **a** A slackening of the blood current, as in passive congestion. **b** Impaired motion of the intestines with retention of the feces.

-stat (-stăt). A combining form, Greek *-statēs,* as in *hydrostatēs* hydrostatic balance, used to denote *apparatus to render* (something) *stationary,* as in gyro*stat,* thermo*stat.*

state (stāt), *n.* [ME. *stat,* fr. OF. and L.; OF. *estat* (F. *état*), fr. L. *status* a standing, position, fr. *stare, statum,* to stand.] **1.** Mode or condition of being; nature; condition. **2.** Condition of mind; esp., an abnormal mental condition, as caused by fear, anger, etc.; as, to work oneself into a *state.* **3.** Condition with reference to wealth, social position, etc.; standing; esp., high rank; eminence. **4.** Condition of living; specif., elaborate condition befitting a person of rank and wealth; hence, formal dignity, pomp, or the like. **5.** *Archaic.* A person of high rank, as a noble. **6.** *Obs.* An estate; special class of persons. **7.** *pl.* The bodies that constitute the legislature of a country; estates. **8.** A political body, or body politic; any body of people occupying a definite territory and politically organized under one government, esp. one that is not subject to external control. **9.** [*often cap.*] Any of a number of commonwealths, or bodies politic, constituting a sovereign state (in sense 8) by their union, as in the United States. **10.** Territory or government of a state (sense 8 or 9). **11.** The entity collectively constituted by the body politic, territory, and government of a state; as, the Department of *State.*

Syn. State, condition, situation, status mean the way in which a person or thing manifests its existence or quality. State may imply a form of existence without relation to space, time, etc., but usually implies the sum of the qualities or characters involved in a thing's existence at a given time or place (as, Hell is not a place but a *state;* the present *state* of industry); condition equals *state* only in concrete use (as, the present *condition* of industry); situation implies a juncture of circumstances (as, industry is in a hopeful *situation*); status, one's state as determined by certain factors, such as age, sex, and the like (as, her *status* as a widow entitles her to a third of her husband's estate).

— *adj.* **1.** Suitable, or used, for ceremonial occasions. **2.** Of or pertaining to the body politic, or government; as, *state* papers.

— *v. t.* **1.** To set; settle; fix; as, to *state* the time for the meeting. **2.** To set forth in detail or in gross; to narrate; as, to *state* the proposition. — **state′hood** (stāt′ho͝od), *n.*

state′craft′ (stāt′krȧft′), *n.* The art of conducting state affairs; state management; statesmanship.

stat′ed (stāt′ĕd; -ĭd), *adj.* **a** Settled; regular. **b** Declared; avowed. **c** Formulated; recorded. — **stat′ed·ly,** *adv.*

State flower. In the United States, the floral emblem of a state, selected by the legislature, the school children, or otherwise.

state′house′ (stāt′hous′), *n.* Also **state house.** *U.S.* The building in which a state legislature sits; a state capitol.

state′less (-lĕs; -lĭs), *adj.* Being without a state or without nationality; as, looking forward to a *stateless* society; *stateless* persons.

state′ly (stāt′lĭ), *adj.;* STATE′LI·ER (-lĭ·ẽr); STATE′LI·EST. Evincing state, or lofty dignity. — **Syn.** See GRAND. — *adv.* In a stately manner. — **state′li·ness,** *n.*

state medicine. Administration and control by the national government of medical and hospital services for the whole population, medical and hospital personnel being employed by the government and funds raised by taxation.

state′ment (stāt′mĕnt), *n.* **1.** Act of stating or presenting, orally or on paper. **2.** That which is stated; recital; account; relation. **3.** *Com.* An abstract of an account showing the balance due.

state prison. *U.S.* Any prison maintained in a state under state laws.

sta′ter (stā′tẽr), *n.* [LL., fr. Gr. *statēr.*] The local coin unit, of gold or silver, in the Greek city-states, varying in value. The gold stater of Macedon weighed 135 grains and was worth $9.84 intrinsically.

state, *or* **states′, rights.** *U.S.* Constitutionally, all rights not vested by the Constitution of the United States in the federal government, nor forbidden by it to the separate states. Politically, such rights as claimed formerly with respect to the Southern States (see SOUTH, *n.,* 3), including esp. the right of a state to secede from the Union peaceably and at will.

state′room′ (stāt′ro͞om′), *n.* **1.** A cabin on shipboard. **2.** *Railroads.* An individual apartment on a railroad car.

state's attorney (stāts). *U.S.* A legal officer appointed to represent the state in the courts.

state's evidence. *Law, U.S.* Evidence for the government or the people; — chiefly in *to turn state's evidence.* See KING'S EVIDENCE.

States′-Gen′er·al, *n.* **1.** In France before the Revolution, the assembly of the three orders (the clergy, the nobility, and the third estate). **2.** The legislature of the Netherlands.

state′side′ (stāt′sīd′), *adj.* Of or pertaining to, done or occurring in, or received from, the continental United States. — *adv.* In or to the United States.

states′man (stāts′măn), *n.* [*state's,* possessive of *state* + *man.*] A man versed in the principles and art of government; esp., one who shows wisdom in treating or directing public matters; also, a man occupied with the affairs of government and influential in shaping its policy. — **states′man·like′,** *adj.* — **states′man·ly,** *adj.* — **states′-man·ship,** *n.*

state socialism. A form of socialism which advocates utilizing the power of the state to equalize income and opportunity. — **state socialist.**

state university. *U.S.* A university operated under the general control, and forming part of the system of public education, of a state.

stat′ic (stăt′ĭk), *adj.* Also **stat′i·cal** (-ĭ·kăl). [Gr. *statikos* causing to stand, skilled in weighing, fr. *histanai* to cause to stand, to weigh.] **1.** Acting by mere weight without motion; as, *static* pressure. **2.** Pertaining to bodies or forces at rest or in equilibrium; — opp. to *dynamic.* **3.** Pert. to passive, as distinguished from active, elements. **4.** Figuratively, resting; quiescent; not active. **5.** *Econ.* **a** Dealing with absolute quantities of goods or money, such as capital, rather than with rates of movement from hand to hand, such as income. **b** Less correctly, but oftener, dealing with problems as they present themselves in a stable state of society. **6.** *Elec.* Of, pert. to, or designating stationary charges of electricity; also, producing such charges, as by rubbing unlike bodies together; as, a *static* machine. **7.** *Radio.* Of, pert. to, or caused by static or atmospherics. — **stat′i·cal·ly,** *adv.*

stat′ic (stăt′ĭk), *n.* *Radio.* Disturbing effects produced in radio receiving apparatus by atmospheric electric phenomena, as by an electrical storm; atmospherics.

stat′ics (stăt′ĭks), *n.;* see -ICS. [See STATIC.] That branch of mechanics which treats of the equilibrium of forces, or relates to bodies as held in equilibrium by the forces acting on them; — disting. from *dynamics.*

static tube. A tube used to measure static pressure of the air, as distinct from the pressure resulting from the impact of air.

sta′tion (stā′shŭn), *n.* [OF. *stacion, estacion,* fr. L. *statio,* fr. *stare, statum,* to stand.] **1.** *Rare.* Posture. **2.** The place where anything stands, esp. where a person or thing habitually stands or is appointed to remain for a time. **3.** Specif.: **a** A regular stopping place in a stage, omnibus, or railroad route; also, the building or buildings connected with it; a depot. **b** In Australasia, a sheep run or cattle run, with its buildings. **c** A place or region to which a government ship or fleet is assigned for duty. **d** In India, the place of residence of British military or civil officers in a district. **4.** Post assigned; sphere of duty or occupation. **5.** Situation; position; location. **6.** Social standing or condition of life; state; rank; as, a man of lowly *station.* **7.** *Biol.* The most characteristic portion of the range of a plant or animal. Cf. HABITAT. **8.** *Radio.* The place in which a transmitting or receiving station is located; also, the assemblage of apparatus for transmitting or receiving. — *v. t.* To appoint or assign to a post, place, etc.

sta′tion·ar′y (-ĕr′ĭ *or, esp. Brit.,* -ẽr·ĭ), *adj.* **1.** Fixed in a certain station, place, course, or the like; not moving or appearing to move; stable; fixed. **2.** Not changing condition; neither improving nor getting worse.

stationary engine. A steam engine permanently placed.

stationary wave. *Physics.* A type of wave in which there are nodes, or points of no motion, between which the medium vibrates. Stationary waves result when two similar waves travel simultaneously and in opposite directions through a medium, as in a vibrating violin string.

sta′tion·er (stā′shŭn·ẽr), *n.* [ML. *stationarius.*] **1.** *Obs.* A bookseller or publisher. **2.** One who sells paper, pens, inkstands, pencils, blankbooks, etc.

sta′tion·er′y (-ẽr′ĭ *or, esp. Brit.,* -ẽr·ĭ), *n.* The articles usually sold by stationers, as paper, pens, ink, pencils, blankbooks, etc. — **sta′tion·er′y,** *adj.*

station house. A house at a post or station; specif., a police station.

sta′tion·mas′ter (stā′shŭn·màs′tẽr), *n.* An employee responsible for the operation of a railroad station.

sta′tions of the cross. [*often cap.*] *Eccl.* A series, usually fourteen, of representations (images or pictures) in a church or, sometimes, on roads leading to some church or shrine, of the stages of Christ's passion.

station wagon. Also **beach wagon.** A passenger automobile like a sedan except that the body, orig. of paneled wood, has a surface resembling wood, removable rear seats, and a hinged tail gate to admit baggage.

stat′ism (stāt′ĭz'm), *n.* Concentration of economic controls and planning in the hands of a highly centralized state government.

stat′ist, *n.* **1.** (stăt′ĭst) Statistician. **2.** (stāt′-) Advocate of statism.

stat′ist (stāt′ĭst), *adj.* Of, pert. to, or advocating statism.

sta·tis′tic (stȧ·tĭs′tĭk), *adj.* Statistical. — *n.* **1.** = STATISTICS. **2.** Any statistical element.

sta·tis′ti·cal (-tĭ·kăl), *adj.* Of or pert. to statistics; dealing with statistics. — **sta·tis′ti·cal·ly,** *adv.*

stat′is·ti′cian (stăt′ĭs·tĭsh′ăn), *n.* One versed in, or engaged in compiling, statistics.

sta·tis′tics (stȧ·tĭs′tĭks), *n.;* see -ICS. [From *statistic.*] **1.** (*Construed as sing.*) The science of the collection and classification of facts on the basis of relative number or occurrence as a ground for induction; systematic compilation of instances for the inference of general truths. **2.** (*Construed as pl.*) Classified facts respecting any particular class or interest; esp., those facts which can be stated in numbers.

stat′o·cyst (stăt′ō·sĭst), *n.* *Zool.* An organ of equilibrium or balancing organ common among invertebrate animals. Typically it consists of a fluid-filled vesicle in which are suspended calcareous particles, **stat′o·liths** (-lĭths). Cf. OTOCYST.

sta′tor (stā′tẽr), *n.* [NL., fr. L. *stare* to stand.] *Mach.* A stationary part in or about which another part (the rotor) revolves, esp. when both are large, as the stationary member of an electrical machine.

stat′o·scope (stăt′ō·skōp), *n.* [Gr. *statos* standing, fixed + *-scope.*] **1.** *Physics.* A sensitive form of aneroid barometer for recording small changes in atmospheric pressure. **2.** An instrument for registering the rise and fall of an aircraft.

stat′u·ar′y (stăt′ū·ẽr′ĭ *or, esp. Brit.,* -ẽr·ĭ), *n.; pl.* -ARIES (-ĭz). **1.** One who makes statues. **2.** The branch of sculpture treating of figures in the round. **3.** A collection of statues. — **stat′u·ar′y,** *adj.*

stat′ue (stăt′ū), *n.* [OF., fr. L. *statua.*] The likeness of a living being sculptured in some solid substance, as marble, bronze, or wax.

Statue of Liberty. A colossal copper statue on Bedloe's Island in New York harbor designed by the French sculptor F. A. Bartholdi to commemorate the 100th anniversary of American independence. It is the figure of a woman bearing a torch aloft in her right hand, "Liberty Enlightening the World."

stat′u·esque′ (stăt′ū·ĕsk′), *adj.* Resembling a statue; having the massive dignity of a statue. — **stat′u·esque′ly,** *adv.* — **stat′u·esque′ness,** *n.*

stat′u·ette′ (-ĕt′), *n.* [F., dim.] A small statue.

stat′ure (stăt′ūr), *n.* [OF., fr. L. *statura,* orig., an upright posture.] **1.** Natural height; — usually of persons. **2.** Development; growth. — **Syn.** See HEIGHT.

sta′tus (stā′tŭs; stăt′ŭs), *n.* [L.] **a** State or condition of a person. **b** Position of affairs. — **Syn.** See STATE.

‖**sta′tus in quo** (ĭn kwō), ‖**sta′tus quo.** [L., state in which.] The state in which anything is; the state existing. Cf. IN STATU QUO.

‖**sta′tus quo an′te bel′lum** (ăn′tē bĕl′ŭm). State existing before the war.

stat′u·ta·ble (stăt′ū·tȧ·b'l), *adj.* Made or imposed by statute; statutory; also, made in conformity to statute.

stat′ute (stăt′ūt), *n.* [OF. (*e*)*statut* (F. *statut*), fr. LL., fr. L. *statutus,* past part. of *statuere* to set, ordain.] Something declared as fixed or established; hence: **a** A law enacted by the legislative branch of a government. **b** An act of a corporation or of its founder intended as a permanent rule; as, the *statutes* of a university. — **Syn.** See LAW.

statute law. The law as stated in statutes.

statute mile. See MEASURE, *Table* 1.

statute of limitations. *Law.* A statute assigning a certain time after which rights cannot be enforced by action.

stat′u·to′ry (stăt′ū·tō′rĭ *or, esp. Brit.,* -tẽr·ĭ), *adj.* Enacted, acquired, or imposed by statute.

staum′rel (stôm′rĕl), *adj.* *Scot.* Half-witted.

staunch (stônch; stänch), **staunch′ly,** etc. Vars. of STANCH, etc.

stau′ro·lite (stô′rō·līt), *n.* [Gr. *stauros* a cross + *-lite.*] *Mineral.* A native silicate of iron and aluminum, $HFeAl_5Si_2O_{13}$, in prismatic crystals, often twinned so as to resemble a cross. — **stau′ro·lit′ic** (-lĭt′ĭk), *adj.*

stau′ro·scope (-skōp), *n.* [Gr. *stauros* a cross + *-scope.*] *Cryst.* A modified polariscope used to find the position of planes of light vibration in crystals.

stave (stāv), *n.* [From *staves,* pl. of STAFF.] **1.** A stick; cudgel; staff. **2.** Any of a number of narrow strips placed edge to edge to form the sides, covering, or lining of a vessel or structure, as of a cask, a pail, etc. **3.** Any of the bars of a rack, ladder, etc. **4.** A set of verses, as a stanza. **5.** *Music.* = 2d STAFF, 7.

stave, *v. t.;* STAVED (stāvd) or STOVE (stōv); STAV′ING (stāv′ĭng). [From STAVE, *n.*] **1.** To break in a stave or the staves of; to break a hole in; — often with *in;* as, to *stave* in a boat. **2.** To furnish with staves. **3.** To keep at a distance, as by force or craft; to ward off; — usually with *off;* as, to *stave* off trouble. — *v. i.* **1.** To break; to be stove, as a ship. **2.** *Colloq. & Dial.* To walk or move rapidly; rush.

staves (stāvz), *n., pl.* of STAFF, STAVE.

staves′a·cre (stāvz′ā·kẽr), *n.* [OF. *stafisagre,* fr. ML. *staphis agria,* fr. Gr. *staphis* raisin + *agrios* wild.] A Eurasian larkspur (*Delphinium staphisagria*); also, its seeds, violently emetic and cathartic.

staw (stô). Scot. past of STEAL.

stay (stā), *n.* [AS. *stæg.*] **1.** *Naut.* A large, strong rope, now usually of wire, used to support a mast. **2.** Hence, a guy rope or the like. — ***in stays.*** *Naut.* In the act of going about from one tack to another. — *v. t.* **1.** To fasten with stays, as a smokestack. **2.** *Naut.* To incline (a mast) forward or aft, or to one side, by the stays. — *v. i.* *Naut.* To tack; to go about, as a ship.

stay, *v. t.;* STAYED (stād) or, *Archaic,* STAID (stād); STAY′ING. [OF. *estayer,* fr. *estaie* a prop, strut.] **1.** To stop from falling; to prop; hold up. **2.** To use as a basis; also, to serve as a basis for; to found. **3.** To satisfy for a time, as the stomach by food; to sustain. **4.** To endure; to resist successfully. **5.** *Sporting Slang.* To hold out through; as, to *stay* the distance. — *n.* **1.** That which serves as a prop; a support. **2.** *pl.* A corset stiffened with whalebone or other material.

stay, *v. i.* [OF. *ester* to stand, fr. L. *stare.*] **1.** *Now Rare.* To rest; rely. **2.** To cease from motion or action; specif.: **a** To delay; wait. **b** To remain; dwell. **c** To stand still; not to retreat. **3.** *Rare.* To attend as a servant; — with *on.* **4.** *Colloq.* To have powers of endurance; as, a horse *stays* well. **5.** At poker, to remain in a hand by seeing an ante, bet, or raise. — *v. t.* **1.** To hold from proceeding; to stop; check; also, to hinder; delay. Specif., to stop or suspend the progress of by judicial proceedings or executive mandate. **2.** To wait for; to await. **3.** To pacify; allay; as, to *stay* the broil.

Syn. (1) **Stay, remain, wait, abide, tarry, linger** mean to continue in a place. **Stay** often specifically connotes the status of a visitor or guest; **remain,** a continuance after others have left or departed; **wait,** a staying in expectation or readiness; **abide,** stable residence or a patient waiting for an outcome; **tarry,** a not proceeding when it is time to do so; **linger,** a tarrying, often because of disinclination to depart. (2) See DEFER.

— *n.* [From STAY to stop.] **1.** That which stays, stops, or checks; a hindrance; check. **2.** *Obs.* Restraint; moderation. **3.** A halt; stand; stop; specif., a stopping, or a suspension, of procedure or execution by judicial proceedings or executive mandate. **4.** Continuance in a place; sojourn. **5.** *Colloq.* Quality of, or capacity for, endurance.

stay′er (stā′ẽr), *n.* One who or that which stays.

stay′-in′ strike, *or* **stay′-in′,** *n.* *Brit.* An organized slowing down by workers without deserting their posts to press for adjustment of a grievance. Cf. SIT-DOWN.

stay′sail′ (stā′sāl′; *naut.* stā′s'l), *n.* *Naut.* Any sail on a stay. See SAIL, *Illusts.*

stead (stĕd), *n.* [AS. *stede.*] **1.** Place, or spot, in general. *Now Dial.,* except in composition. **2.** Place or room which another had, has, or might have; as, another was chosen in his *stead.* **3.** Advantage; service; avail; — esp. in the phrase *to stand in stead,* to be of service or advantage. — *v. t.* To be of avail to; to help; benefit.

stead′fast, sted′fast (stĕd′fàst; -fȧst), *adj.* [AS. *stedefæst,* that is, fast in place.] **1.** Firmly established or fixed; firm. **2.** Unchanging; not fickle or wavering. — **Syn.** See FAITHFUL. — **stead′fast·ly, sted′fast·ly,** *adv.* — **stead′fast·ness, sted′fast·ness,** *n.*

stead′ing (stĕd′ĭng; -ĭn), *n.* *Scot.* A farmhouse and offices.

stead′y (stĕd′ĭ), *adj.;* -I·ER (-ĭ·ẽr); -I·EST. [From STEAD, *n.;* prob. under the influence of *steadfast.*] **1.** Firm in position; fixed; stable. **2.** Assured or direct, as in movement; unfaltering; hence, not easily upset; not nervous. **3.** Constant; not fickle or wavering; resolute. **4.** Regular; uninterrupted; as, *steady* work. **5. a** Grave; staid. **b** Not given to dissipation. **6.** *Naut.* Of a vessel, keeping nearly upright in a seaway.

Syn. Steady, uniform, even, equable mean much the same throughout its course or extent. **Steady** implies regularity and lack of deviation as in movement or character; **uniform,** a sameness of all the elements, units, instances, etc.; **even,** a lack of variation in quality, character, etc.; **equable,** an inherent quality that makes for lack of variability.

— *v. t. & i.;* STEAD′IED (-ĭd); STEAD′Y·ING. To make or become steady. — *interj.* **1.** An exclamation enjoining calmness and self-control. **2.** *Naut.* An order to the steersman to keep the vessel's head pointing as it is.

— *n.* *Slang.* One's steady companion or sweetheart

— **stead′i·er,** *n.* — **stead′i·ly,** *adv.* — **stead′i·ness,** *n.*

steak (stāk), *n.* [ON. *steik.*] **1.** A slice of meat cut from a fleshy part of a carcass; hence, such a slice broiled or ready for broiling, and cut from beef unless otherwise qualified (see BEEF, *Illust.*); also, a cross-section slice of a large fish; as, a cod *steak.* **2.** Meat, esp. beef meat, minced for cooking in the manner of a steak; as, hamburg *steak.*

steal (stēl), *v. t.;* STOLE (stōl); STO′LEN (stō′lĕn); STEAL′ING. [AS. *stelan.*] **1.** To take and carry away feloniously. **2.** To appropriate to oneself furtively or secretly; as, to *steal* a kiss. **3.** To move, convey, or introduce by stealth; to smuggle; as, to *steal* her eggs into another bird's nest. **4.** *Baseball.* To gain (a base) without the aid of a hit or of an error; — said of a base runner. — *v. i.* **1.** To practice, or be guilty of, theft. **2.** To move furtively or clandestinely.

Syn. Steal, pilfer, filch, purloin mean to take from another in a manner that eludes observation. **Steal** may refer to any surreptitious taking not only of money or valuables but of anything comparable in any way; **pilfer** now usually implies stealing in small amounts; **filch** adds an implication of snatching surreptitiously; **purloin,** a removing or a carrying off for one's own use or purposes.

— *n.* **a** An act of stealing. **b** Anything stolen.

steal′age (-ĭj), *n.* Act of stealing; larceny; theft; also, the proceeds of a theft.

steal′er (-ẽr), *n.* One who steals; a thief.

steal′ing, *n.* **1.** Act of one who steals; theft. **2.** Stolen goods; — chiefly in *pl.* — *adj.* Thieving.

stealth (stĕlth), *n.* [ME. *stelthe, stalthe;* akin to STEAL.] **1.** *Archaic.* Theft. **2.** *Obs.* The thing stolen. **3.** *Obs.* Act of going furtively. **4.** Secret procedure or action.

stealth′y (stĕl′thĭ), *adj.* Accomplished secretly or furtively; also, acting clandestinely; furtive; sly. — **Syn.** See SECRET. — **stealth′i·ly** (stĕl′thĭ·lĭ), *adv.* — **stealth′i·ness,** *n.*

steam (stēm), *n.* [AS. *stēam* vapor, smoke, odor.] **1.** The invisible gas or vapor into which water is converted when heated to the boiling point; water in the state of vapor. Cf. WATER VAPOR. **2.** Specif.: **a** Water vapor under pressure to supply energy for heating, cooking or mechanical work; also, the power so generated. **b** Power; force; energy. **3.** The mist formed by the condensation, on cooling, of water vapor; visible vapor; — popularly so called. **4.** Hence, any exhalation; as, a *steam* of incense. **5. a** Steam vessel; as, to travel by *steam.*

b Travel by, or a trip or ride in, a steam vessel. — *adj.* Using steam as in providing heat or driving power; operated or driven by steam; as, a *steam* engine; also, subjected to, or treated or processed by, steam; conveying steam. — *v. i.* **1.** To emit steam or vapor. **2.** To rise or pass off as vapor. **3.** To move or travel by the agency of steam. — *v. t.* To expose to the action of steam, as for softening or cooking.
☞ COMBINATIONS and PHRASES are:
steamcar steampipe steam shovel

steam'boat' (stēm'bōt'), *n.* A boat propelled by steam.
steam boiler. A boiler for producing steam.
steam chest. Also **steam box.** The chamber from which steam is distributed to a steam-engine cylinder.
steam engine. An engine driven or worked by steam. — **steam'-en'gine,** *adj.*
steam'er (stēm'ẽr), *n.* **1.** Something that generates or emits steam. **2.** Something, as an engine or vehicle, driven by steam. **3.** Specif., a vessel propelled by steam; a steamship. Abbr. *str.* **4.** A vessel in which articles are subjected to steam, as in washing, cookery, etc.
steam fitter. A workman who installs or repairs steampipes, their fittings, etc. — **steam fitting.**
steam roller *or* **steam'roll'er** (stēm'rōl'ẽr), *n.* A steam-driven road roller; figuratively, *Colloq.*, a power or force that ruthlessly or arbitrarily overcomes opposition.
steam'-roll'er *or* **steam'roll'er,** *v. t.* Also **steam'-roll'** *or* **steam'-roll'.** **1.** To crush or flatten with or as if with a steam roller. **2.** To overwhelm or coerce by ruthlessly overriding with massed forces; as, the majority *steam-rollered* the conference; also, to make (as a path) or to push (as legislation, either to passage or defeat) by thus overwhelming, overriding, or crushing opposition. — *v. i.* To roll resistlessly with crushing power.
steam'ship' (stēm'shĭp'), *n.* A ship or seagoing vessel propelled by the power of steam; a steamer. Abbr. *SS* or *S.S.*
steam table. A steam-heated table, as for keeping food warm.
steam'y (stēm'ĭ), *adj.*; STEAM'I·ER (-ĭ·ẽr); STEAM'I·EST. Consisting of, or resembling, steam; vaporous. — **steam'i·ly** (-ĭ·lĭ), *adv.* — **steam'i·ness** (-ĭ·nĕs; -nĭs), *n.*
ste·ap'sin (stē·ăp'sĭn), *n.* [G., fr. *stearin* + *pepsin.*] = LIPASE.
ste'a·rate (stē'ȧ·rāt), *n.* *Chem.* A salt or ester of stearic acid.
ste·ar'ic (stē·ăr'ĭk; stēr'ĭk), *adj.* *Chem.* Pertaining to, obtained from, or like stearin or tallow.
stearic acid. *Chem.* A white crystalline fatty acid, $CH_3(CH_2)_{16}CO_2H$, obtained by saponifying tallow or other hard fats containing stearin. Commercial stearic acid (stearine) is commonly a mixture of stearic and palmitic acids.
ste'a·rin (stē'ȧ·rĭn; stēr'ĭn), *n.* Also, in senses 2 & 3, **ste'a·rine** (-rĭn; -rēn). [F. *stéarine*, fr. Gr. *stear* tallow, suet.] **1.** *Chem.* A white crystalline solid, $C_3H_5(C_{18}H_{35}O_2)_3$, an ester of glycerol and stearic acid, found in many animal and vegetable fats. **2.** The solid portion of any fat; — disting. from *olein.* **3.** *Com.* Stearic acid.
ste'a·rop'tene (stē'ȧ·rŏp'tēn), *n.* [*stearic* + *elaeoptene.*] *Chem.* The part of an essential oil separated as a solid on cooling or long standing; — distinguished from *elaeoptene.*
ste'ar·rhe'a, ste'ar·rhoe'a (stē'ă·rē'ȧ), *n.* [NL., fr. Gr. *stear* tallow, suet + *-rhea.*] *Med.* Seborrhea.
ste'a·tite (stē'ȧ·tīt), *n.* [L. *steatitis*, fr. Gr. *stear, steatos*, fat, tallow.] *Mineral.* A massive variety of talc, used for utensils, etc.; soapstone. — **ste'a·tit'ic** (-tĭt'ĭk), *adj.*
ste'a·to·py'gi·a (stē'ȧ·tō·pī'jĭ·ȧ; -pĭj'ĭ·ȧ), *n.* Also **ste'a·top'y·gy** (-tŏp'ĭ·jĭ). [NL., fr. Gr. *stear, steatos*, fat + *pygē* rump.] An excessive development of fat on the buttocks, esp. of females. Among living races it is most common among the Hottentots and some Negro peoples. — **ste'a·to·pyg'ic** (-pĭj'ĭk), **ste'a·to·py'gous** (-pī'gŭs), *adj.*
stech (stĕk), *v. t. & i.* *Scot.* **a** To cram; gorge. **b** To pant.
sted'fast, sted'fast·ly, etc. Vars. of STEADFAST, etc.
steed (stēd), *n.* [AS. *stēda* studhorse, war horse.] *Literary.* A horse, esp. a spirited horse.
steek (stēk; stāk), *v. i. & t.* [ME. *steken.*] *Chiefly Scot.* **1.** To sew. **2.** To shut; close. — *n.* *Scot.* A stitch.
steel (stēl), *n.* [AS. *stēl, stēli, stȳle.*] **1.** A commercial form of iron containing carbon in any amount up to about 1.7 per cent as an essential alloying constituent, and malleable when under suitable conditions; — distinguished from *cast iron* by its malleability and lower carbon content. Steel is now almost entirely produced by refining molten pig iron. For commercial purposes steel is often classified in three grades of hardness: low-carbon (roughly less than 0.25 per cent carbon), called ***mild or soft steel;*** medium-carbon (roughly 0.25 to 0.60 per cent), called ***medium steel;*** and high-carbon (roughly more than 0.60 per cent), called ***hard steel.*** Cf. CAST IRON, INGOT IRON, WROUGHT IRON, CRUCIBLE STEEL, CHROME STEEL, MANGANESE STEEL, VANADIUM STEEL. **2.** An instrument or implement of steel; as: **a** A sword or dagger. **b** An instrument, usually a fluted round rod with a handle, for sharpening knives. **c** A piece of steel for striking sparks from flint. **d** A strip of steel used for stiffening. **3.** Steellike quality; hardness; coldness. **4.** *Colloq.* Market quotation for shares in a steel company; *pl.*, the quotations for companies in the steel manufacturing business. **5.** = STEEL GRAY. — *adj.* Of or made of steel; also, resembling steel. — *v. t.* **1.** To overlay, point, or edge with steel. **2.** To make hard or strong; hence, to make resolute.
☞ COMBINATIONS are:
steelmaker steelmaking steelworker

steel blue. Any of the blue colors assumed by steel at certain temperatures in tempering. — **steel'-blue',** *adj.*
steel engraving. Process of engraving on steel; also, an impression from an engraved steel plate.
steel gray. A nearly neutral gray of medium brilliance, slightly bluish. Cf. COLOR. — **steel'-gray',** *adj.*
steel'head' (stēl'hĕd'), *n.*; see PLURAL, *Note*, 6. **a** A North American trout (*Salmo gairdneri*) found from California to Alaska. **b** The rainbow trout *S. irideus* (see TROUT, 1).
Steel Helmet. A member of the Stahlhelm (which see).
steel wool. Fine steel shavings, used for cleaning, polishing, etc.
steel'work' (stēl'wûrk'), *n.* **1.** Any work in steel; articles, or a part, parts, or the whole of any construction, of steel. **2.** *pl.* **A** shop or establishment where steel is made.
steel'y (stēl'ĭ), *adj.*; STEEL'I·ER (-ĭ·ẽr); STEEL'I·EST. **1.** Made of steel. **2.** Resembling steel, as in hardness, color, etc. — **steel'i·ness** (-ĭ·nĕs; -nĭs), *n.*

steel'yard (stēl'yärd; *colloq.* stĭl'yẽrd), *n.* [See STEEL; 1st YARD.] A form of balance in which the object is suspended from the shorter arm of a lever, and its weight found by moving a counterpoise along the longer arm to produce equilibrium.

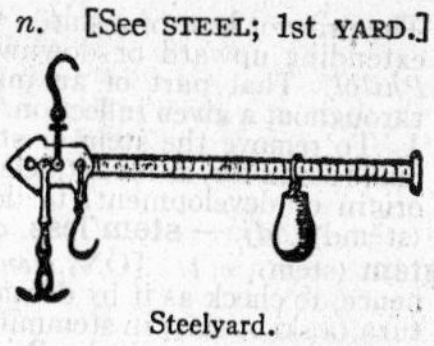

Steelyard.

steen'bok' (stēn'bŏk'; stān'-). Var. of STEINBOK.
steep (stēp), *adj.* [AS. *stēap.*] **1.** Lofty; high. **2.** Making a large angle with the plane of the horizon; precipitous; as, a *steep* hill. **3.** Mounting or falling precipitously; as, *steep* ruin. **4.** *Colloq.* Extreme; also, too great, high, heavy, etc. — *n.* A precipitous place. — **steep'ly,** *adv.* — **steep'ness,** *n.*
Syn. Steep, abrupt, precipitous, sheer mean having an incline approaching the perpendicular. Steep implies such sharpness of pitch that ascent or descent is extremely difficult; abrupt, a sharper pitch and a sudden break in the level; precipitous, a headlong descent like that of a precipice; sheer, perpendicularity that shows practically no break in its line.
steep, *v. t.* [ME. *stepen.*] **a** To soak in or as in a liquid; to extract the essence of by soaking. **b** Figuratively, to saturate; imbue with. — *v. i.* *Colloq.* To undergo the process of soaking in a liquid; as, the tea is *steeping.* — **Syn.** See SOAK. — *n.* State or process of steeping; also, something steeped, or a vessel or bath used in steeping. — **steep'er,** *n.*
steep'en (stēp'ĕn), *v. t. & i.* To make or become steeper.
stee'ple (stē'p'l), *n.* [AS. *stēpel, stȳpel*, tower.] *Arch.* The tall structure, usually topped with a spire, surmounting a church tower; also, a church tower.
stee'ple·bush' (-bo͝osh'), *n.* = HARDHACK.
stee'ple·chase' (-chās'), *n.* A race across country by horsemen; hence, a race over a course obstructed by such obstacles as hedges, walls, etc. — **stee'ple·chas'er** (-chās'ẽr), *n.*
steeple jack. *Colloq.* A man who makes a business of climbing steeples, etc., as for making repairs.
steer (stēr), *n.* [AS. *stēor.*] **a** A male bovine animal castrated before sexual maturity; an ox. **b** *U.S. & Brit. Colonies.* Any male cattle raised for beef.
steer, *v. t.* [AS. *stīeran, stȳran, stēoran.*] **1.** Orig., to direct the course of (a vessel) by means of a rudder; hence, to direct the course of by mechanical means; as, to *steer* an automobile. **2.** Hence, to guide; control; direct. **3.** To set and pursue (a course). — *v. i.* **1.** To direct the course of a vessel, a vehicle, etc. **2.** To take a direction, or course; to obey the helm; as, the boat *steers* easily. **3.** To pursue a course of action. — **Syn.** See GUIDE. — *n.* *Slang, U.S.* Advice as to procedure; a tip. — **steer'a·ble,** *adj.* — **steer'er,** *n.*
steer, *v. t.* [Var. of STIR.] *Scot.* To disturb; injure. — *v. i.* To hasten. — *n.* A poke; disturbance.
steer'age (stēr'ĭj), *n.* **1.** Act or practice of steering. **2.** Direction; guidance; management. **3.** *Naut.* **a** The effect of the helm on a ship. **b** In a passenger vessel, a section for passengers paying the smallest fares and receiving inferior accommodations. See THIRD CLASS.
steer'age·way' (-wā'), *n.* *Naut.* A rate of motion sufficient to make a vessel answer the helm.
steer'ing com·mit'tee. In a legislative body, a committee which determines the order in which business shall be taken up; hence, any group with similar powers.
steering wheel. A wheel with which one steers, as one that controls the movements of a ship's rudder or the front wheels of an automobile.
steers'man (stērz'măn), *n.* One who steers; helmsman.
steeve (stēv), *v. t.* [F. *estiver*, fr. L. *stipare* to compress.] To stow, as in a vessel's hold, by means of a steeve or jackscrew; to stuff; store. — *n.* A spar, with a block at one end, used in stowing cotton bales, etc.
steeve, *v. i. & t.* *Shipbuilding.* To turn upward at an angle with the horizon or the line of the keel; — of the bowsprit. — *n.* Also **steev'ing.** The angle which a bowsprit makes with the horizon, or with the keel.
steg'o·my'ia (stĕg'ō·mī'yȧ), *n.* [NL., fr. Gr. *stegos* a roof + *myia* fly.] *Zool.* Any of a former genus (*Stegomyia*) of mosquitoes; specif., the yellow-fever mosquito (*Aëdes aegypti*).
steg'o·sau'rus (-sô'rŭs), *n.* [NL., fr. Gr. *stegos* a roof + *-saurus.*] *Paleontol.* Any of a genus (*Stegosaurus*) of large armored dinosaurs of the Upper Jurassic rocks of Colorado and Wyoming.
stein (stīn), *n.* [G.] An earthenware mug, esp. for beer, commonly holding about a pint; also, the quantity of beer which it holds.
stein'bok' (-bŏk'), *n.* [D. *steenbok*, fr. *steen* stone + *bok* buck.] Any small antelope (genus *Raphicerus*, esp. *R. campestris*) of South Africa and East Africa.
stele (stēl), *n.* [AS. *stela, steola* stalk, stem.] A handle; shaft; specif., *Archery*, the long slender body of an arrow.
ste'le (stē'lē), *n.* [L. and Gr.; L. *stela*, fr. Gr. *stēlē* a post, an upright stone.] **1.** *Gr. & Rom. Antiq.* A slab or pillar of stone used as a gravestone; also, a pillar bearing an inscription. **2.** (*pron.* stēl; stē'lē) *Bot.* The central cylinder in the stems and roots of vascular plants.
stel'lar (stĕl'ẽr), *adj.* [LL. *stellaris*, fr. *stella* star.] **1.** Of or pert. to stars; astral; like a star. **2.** Chief; leading; principal; star. **3.** Of a theatrical or film star.
stel'late (-āt), *adj.* Also **stel'lat·ed** (-āt·ĕd; -ĭd). [L. *stellatus* set with stars, starry.] Resembling a star, as in shape; radiated. — **stel'late·ly,** *adv.*
stel·lif'er·ous (stĕ·lĭf'ẽr·ŭs), *adj.* [L. *stellifer*, fr. *stella* star + *ferre* to bear.] Abounding with stars.
stel'li·form (stĕl'ĭ·fôrm), *adj.* [L. *stella* a star.] Star-shaped.
stel'lu·lar (-ū·lẽr), *adj.* [LL. *stellula* little star.] **1.** Starlike; radiated. **2.** Marked with starlike spots of color.
stem (stĕm), *n.* [AS. *stemm, stefn, stæfn*, tree stem, stem or stern of a vessel.] **1.** The main trunk of a tree or other plant; specif., *Bot.*, any axis which develops buds and shoots instead of roots. **2.** Hence: **a** Any part which supports leaves or flowers; a stalk or stock. **b** A peduncle, petiole, or pedicel; as, the *stem* of an apple. **c** A bunch of bananas. **3.** The stock, or a branch, of a family; as, a noble *stem.* **4.** Anything resembling or likened to the stem of a plant; as, the *stem* of a pipe; specif.: **a** Of a watch, a shaft which projects from the case. **b** In some locks, the round portion about which the ordinary key turns. **c** A main or heavy stroke of a letter. See TYPE, *Illust.* **5.**

The prow or bow of a ship. 6. *Music.* The short perpendicular line extending upward or downward from the oval part of a note. 7. *Philol.* That part of an inflected word which remains unchanged throughout a given inflection. — *v. t.;* STEMMED (stĕmd); STEM′MING. 1. To remove the stem or stems from; as, to *stem* cherries. 2. To make stems for, as for artificial flowers. — *v. i.* To have or trace one's origin or development; to derive. — **Syn.** See SPRING. — **stemmed** (stĕmd), *adj.* — **stem′less**, *adj.* — **stem′mer**, *n.*

stem (stĕm), *v. t.* [ON. *stemma.*] 1. To stop or dam up, as a river; hence, to check as if by damming; specif., to stanch. 2. *Skiing.* To turn (a ski or skis) in stemming. — *v. i.* 1. To check oneself; also, to be checked or stanched. 2. *Skiing.* To retard oneself by forcing the heel of one ski (***single stemming***) or of both skis (***double stemming***) outward from the line of progress. — *n. Skiing.* Act or instance of stemming.

stem, *v. t.* [From the STEM of a ship.] Of a vessel, to make headway against (an adverse current, or the like); hence, to progress against (anything regarded as adverse); as, to *stem* the tide of public opinion.

stem′son (stĕm′s'n), *n.* [See STEM, *n.*, KEELSON.] *Shipbuilding.* A piece of curved timber bolted to the stem and keelson in a ship's frame near the bow.

stem turn. *Skiing.* A turn executed by unweighting and stemming the intended outside ski, so that the ski points converge, and then weighting the outside ski.

stem′-wind′er (stĕm′wīn′dẽr), *n.* 1. *Colloq.* A stem-winding watch. 2. *Slang.* Someone or something first-rate.

stem′-wind′ing (-wīn′dĭng; 2), *adj.* Wound by an inside mechanism turned by the knurled knob at the outside end of the stem. — **stem′-wind′**, *v. t.*

sten (stĕn), **stend** (stĕnd), *n. & v. Scot.* Leap; bound.

stench (stĕnch), *n.* [AS. *stenc.*] A stink.

sten′cil (stĕn′sĭl; -s'l), *n.* [OF. *estencele* spangle, spark, fr. L. *scintilla* spark.] 1. A piece of thin sheet metal, parchment, paper, or the like, so perforated that when it is laid on a surface and color or ink is applied, a desired figure is produced. 2. A pattern or design produced by stenciling. — *v. t.;* -CILED (-sĭld; -s'ld) or -CILLED; -CIL·ING or -CIL·LING. To mark or paint with a stencil. — **sten′cil·er**, **sten′cil·ler**, *n.*

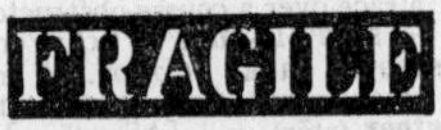

Stencil.

Sten gun (stĕn). [After *S*heppard and *T*urpin (its designers) + *En*gland.] A British machine carbine having only 45 parts and weighing from 6 lbs. 6 oz. to 8 lbs., that uses any rimless 9 mm. ammunition, and fires 550 rounds per minute.

sten′o- (stĕn′ō-). [Gr. *stenos.*] A combining form meaning *narrow, little, close,* as in **sten′o·pet′al·ous**, having narrow petals; **sten′o·phyl′lous**, having narrow leaves.

sten′o·graph (stĕn′ō·grăf; 9), *v. t.* To write in stenographic characters. — *n.* A production of stenography.

ste·nog′ra·pher (stē·nŏg′rȧ·fẽr), *n.* One skilled in, or employed to do, stenography.

ste·nog′ra·phy (-fĭ), *n.* [*steno-* + *-graphy.*] The art of writing in shorthand; shorthand; also, loosely, the making of shorthand notes and subsequent transcription of them, esp. in typewriting. — **sten′o·graph′ic** (stĕn′ō·grăf′ĭk), **sten′o·graph′i·cal** (-ĭ·kăl), *adj.* — **sten′o·graph′i·cal·ly**, *adv.*

ste·no′sis (stē·nō′sĭs), *n.* [NL., fr. Gr. *stenōsis*, fr. *stenos* narrow.] *Med.* A narrowing of the opening or cavity of any passage, tube, or orifice.

sten′o·type (stĕn′ō·tīp), *n.* [*steno-* + *-type.*] A letter or combination representing a phonogram in stenotypy.

sten′o·typ′y (stĕn′ō·tīp′ĭ; stē·nŏt′ĭ·pĭ), *n.* A type of phonogrammic writing using ordinary script.

Sten′tor (stĕn′tôr), *n.* [L., fr. Gr. *Stentōr.*] A herald, in the *Iliad*, with a very loud voice; hence [*usually not cap.*], any person having a loud voice.

sten·to′ri·an (stĕn·tō′rĭ·ăn; 70), *adj.* Extremely loud.

step (stĕp), *n.* [AS. *stæpe, stepe.*] 1. An advance or movement made by one removal of the foot; a pace; hence, in *pl.*, progress. 2. A rest for the foot in ascending or descending, as a round of a ladder, a stair, etc. 3. A degree, rank, or plane in a series of progress. 4. The space passed over by one movement of the foot in walking or running; as, a *step* of three feet. 5. A small space or distance. 6. A footstep; footprint. 7. Gait; manner of walking; also, the sound of a step; footfall. 8. Proceeding; measure; esp., any of successive progressive measures towards a result. 9. *Dancing.* Any combination of foot movements and body movements constituting a simple unit or a pattern that is repeated; as, the waltz *step.* 10. *Mach.* One of a series of offsets, or parts, resembling the steps of stairs. 11. *Music.* **a** A scale or staff degree. **b** The interval between two contiguous degrees of the staff or scale. See HALF STEP, WHOLE STEP. **c** = WHOLE STEP. 12. *Naut.* In general, a frame intended to receive an upright shaft; specif., such a framing supporting the heel of a mast. 13. *Radio.* = STAGE, 8.

— *v. i.;* STEPPED (stĕpt) or, *Poetic,* STEPT (stĕpt); STEP′PING. 1. To advance or recede by raising and moving one foot to another resting place, or by moving each foot in succession. 2. To go on foot; to walk; esp., to go a short distance. 3. To move with slow, graceful, grave, or resolute steps. 4. *Colloq.* To move smartly or briskly. 5. To come, as into a position or condition, at a single stroke; as, to *step* into a job. 6. To press down with the foot; as, to *step* on a self-starter. — *v. t.* 1. To set or place, as the foot. 2. To step through (the movements of a dance) in a stately manner; as, to *step* a minuet. 3. To measure by stepping; hence, to divide, as a space, or to form, as a series of marks, by successive measurements, as with dividers; as, to *step* a distance. 4. **a** To provide with steps, as by cutting; as, to *step* a hillside. **b** To alter, as in position, rate, etc., by or as if by a series of regulated steps; — usually with adverbs (as *back, down, up*) indicating direction of change. 5. *Naut.* **a** To fix the foot of in its step and so to erect (a mast). **b** To place (a deck) in position.

step- (stĕp-). [AS. *stēop-.*] A combining form denoting relative by virtue of a remarriage, esp. the remarriage of a parent, as in **step′fa′ther**, the husband of one's mother by a subsequent marriage, **step′moth′er**, **step′par′ent**; **step′child′**, the child of one's wife or husband by a former marriage, **step′daugh′ter**, **step′son′**; **step′broth′er**, a son of one's stepparent by a former marriage, **step′sis′ter**; **step′aunt′**, **step′grand′par′ent**, **step′un′cle**, etc.

step′dame′ (stĕp′dām′), *n. Archaic.* A stepmother.

step′-down′, *adj.* That steps down, or decreases gradually; as, a *step-down* transformer or gear. Cf. STEP-UP.

step′-in′, *adj.* Put on by being stepped into, as certain types of women's undergarments, pumplike shoes, etc. — **step′-in′**, *n.*

step′lad′der (stĕp′lăd′ẽr), *n.* A portable set of steps, esp. one with flat broad steps in place of rungs.

steppe (stĕp), *n.* [Russ. *step′*; cf. F. & G. *steppe.*] One of the vast tracts in southeastern Europe and in west central Asia, generally level and without forests.

step′per (stĕp′ẽr), *n.* One who or that which steps, as a fast horse, a dancer, etc.

step′ping-stone′ (stĕp′ĭng·stōn′), *n.* 1. A stone projecting above the surface of water or mud, on which to step in walking. 2. Hence, a means of progress or advancement.

step turn. *Skiing.* A turn executed in a downhill traverse by lifting the upper ski from the ground, placing it several inches higher up the hill and slightly forward, then weighing it and bringing the lower ski parallel.

step′-up′, *adj.* That steps up, or increases in steps; as, a *step-up* transformer or gear. Cf. STEP-DOWN.

-ster (-stẽr). [AS. *-estre, -istre.*] A suffix denoting orig. *the female agent*, esp. *one who does something with skill* or *as an occupation*, as in song*ster*, spin*ster* (orig., a woman who spins). Such formations came later to be regarded as masculine, some of them giving rise to new feminines in *-stress*, as in seam*stress* (from older seam*ster*), song*stress*. In the modern period the suffix is joined to nouns (road*ster*, gang*ster*) and, more rarely, to adjectives (old*ster*, young*ster*), the notion of agency tending to be lost, and the suffix often having a depreciatory sense (as in dab*ster*, rhyme*ster*).

ster′co·ra′ceous (stûr′kō·rā′shŭs), *adj.* [L. *stercus, -oris,* dung.] Of, pert. to, or of the nature of dung.

ster′co·ric′o·lous (-rĭk′ō·lŭs), *adj.* [L. *stercus, -oris,* dung + *-colous.*] Living in dung.

ster′co·rous (stûr′kō·rŭs), *adj.* Stercoraceous.

ster·cu′li·a′ceous (stẽr·kū′lĭ·ā′shŭs), *adj.* [From L. *Sterculius*, the deity that presided over manuring, fr. *stercus* dung; — in allusion to the fetid odor.] *Bot.* Belonging to the chocolate family (Sterculiaceae). See CHOCOLATE TREE.

stere (stẹr; *F.* stâr), *n.* [F. *stère*, fr. Gr. *stereos* solid.] A cubic meter. See METRIC SYSTEM, *Table* 6.

ster′e·o- (stĕr′ē·ō-; stẹr′ē·ō-), **ster′e-.** [Gr. *stereos* solid.] A combining form meaning *solid, a solid body,* as in *stereo*taxis; specif.: **a** Stereoscopic. **b** *Chem.* In three dimensions in space.

ster′e·o·bate (-bāt), *n.* [L. *stereobata*, fr. Gr. *stereos* solid + *bates* that treads or covers.] *Arch.* A substructure of masonry as visible above the ground level.

ster′e·o·chem′is·try (-kĕm′ĭs·trĭ), *n.* Chemistry dealing with the arrangement of atoms and molecules in space.

ster′e·o·chro′my (stĕr′ē·ō·krō′mĭ; stẹr′ē-), *n.* [*stereo-* + Gr. *chrōma* color.] A process of mural painting in which the pigment is fixed by reactions between the lime, water glass, etc. — **ster′e·o·chro′mic** (-krō′mĭk), *adj.*

ster′e·o·gram′ (-grăm′), *n.* [*stereo-* + *-gram.*] A diagram or picture representing objects with an impression of solidity or relief; also, a stereograph.

ster′e·o·graph′ (-grȧf′; 9), *n.* Any picture prepared for the stereoscope. — **ster′e·o·graph′**, *v. t. & i.*

ster′e·og′ra·phy (stĕr′ē·ŏg′rȧ·fĭ; stẹr′ē-), *n.* [*stereo-* + *-graphy.*] Art of delineating the forms of solid bodies on a plane; a branch of solid geometry, showing the construction of all solids that are regularly defined. — **ster′e·o·graph′ic** (-ō·grăf′ĭk), **ster′e·o·graph′i·cal** (-ĭ·kăl), *adj.* — **ster′e·o·graph′i·cal·ly**, *adv.*

ster′e·o·i·som′er·ism (-ō·ī·sŏm′ẽr·ĭz′m), *n. Chem.* Isomerism depending on arrangement of atoms in space. — **ster′e·o·i′so·mer** (-ī′sō·mẽr), *n.* — **ster′e·o·i′so·mer′ic** (-ī′sō·mĕr′ĭk), *adj.*

ster′e·om′e·try (stĕr′ē·ŏm′ē·trĭ; stẹr′ē-), *n.* Art of determining the volumes and other metrical elements of solid figures. Cf. PLANIMETER. — **ster′e·o·met′ric** (-ō·mĕt′rĭk), **ster′e·o·met′ri·cal** (-rĭ·kăl), *adj.* — **ster′e·o·met′ri·cal·ly**, *adv.*

ster′e·o·phon′ic (-ō·fŏn′ĭk), *adj.* Giving the effect of coming from two or more directions; — of sound reproduced.

ster′e·op′sis (-ŏp′sĭs), *n.* [NL., fr. *stere-* + *-opsis.*] Stereoscopic vision.

ster′e·op′ti·con (-ŏp′tĭ·kŏn), *n.* [NL. See STEREO-; OPTIC.] A form of the magic lantern, using chiefly photographic pictures and an intense light, and often made double so as to produce dissolving views.

ster′e·o·scope′ (stĕr′ē·ō·skōp′; stẹr′ē-), *n.* An optical instrument with two eyeglasses, for assisting the observer to combine the images of two pictures taken from points of view a little way apart, and thus to get the effect of solidity or depth.

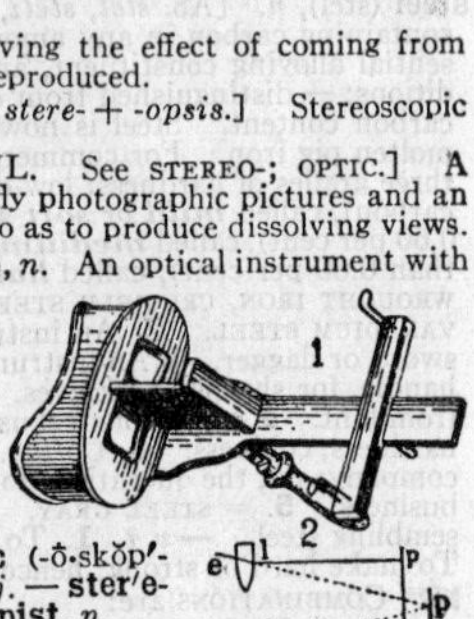

1 Stereoscope. 2 Diagram. Rays from *p* and *p′* by lenses *l, l′* are so refracted to the eyes at *e, e′* as to appear to come from one point *P.*

ster′e·os′co·py (-ŏs′kō·pĭ; -ō·skō′pĭ), *n.* 1. The science which deals with stereoscopic effects and methods. 2. The seeing of objects as in three dimensions. — **ster′e·o·scop′ic** (-ō·skŏp′ĭk), **ster′e·o·scop′i·cal** (-ĭ·kăl), *adj.* — **ster′e·o·scop′i·cal·ly**, *adv.* — **ster′e·os′co·pist**, *n.*

ster′e·o·tax′is (stĕr′ē·ō·tăk′sĭs; stẹr′ē-), *n. Biol.* A taxis in which contact with a solid body is the directive factor.

ster′e·ot′ro·pism (-ŏt′rō·pĭz′m), *n. Biol.* A tropism in which contact with a solid or a rigid surface is the directive factor.

ster′e·o·type′ (stĕr′ē·ō·tīp′; stẹr′ē-), *n.* 1. *Print.* **a** A plate made by taking a mold or matrix of a printing surface and making from this a cast in type metal. **b** Stereotypy. 2. Hence, anything undistinguished by individual marks, as if produced from a stereotype. — *v. t.* 1. To prepare for printing in stereotype; to make stereotype plates of, as a book. 2. Hence, to repeat without variation; to hackney. — **ster′e·o·typ′er** (-tīp′ẽr), *n.*

ster′e·o·typed′ (-tīpt′), *adj.* Produced as if from a stereotype; lacking originality or individuality. — **Syn.** See TRITE.

ster′e·o·typ′y (stĕr′ē·ō·tīp′ĭ; stẹr′ē-; -ŏt′ĭ·pĭ), *n.* 1. The art or process of making or of printing from stereotype plates. 2. Frequent, almost mechanical, repetition of the same posture or form of speech, as in the mannerisms of dementia praecox. — **ster′e·o·typ′ic** (stĕr′ē-ō·tĭp′ĭk; stēr′ē-), *adj.*

ster′ic (stĕr′ĭk; stēr′ĭk), **ster′i·cal** (-ĭ·kăl), *adj.* [*stereo-* + *-ic* (cf. def. of STEREOCHEMISTRY).] *Chem.* Relating to the arrangement of atoms in space; spatial.

ster′ile (stĕr′ĭl *or, esp. Brit.*, stĕr′īl), *adj.* [L. *sterilis.*] **1.** Barren; not fertile. **2.** Incapable of, or unfitted for, reproduction. **3.** Ineffective; useless; as, *sterile* gold. **4.** *Bacteriol.* Free from living microorganisms, as bacteria or their viable spores; as, a *sterile* fluid. **5.** *Bot.* **a** Incapable of bearing, or characterized by lack of, fruit or spores; as, a *sterile* plant; unable to germinate; as, a *sterile* seed. **b** Bearing only stamens, or entirely neutral; as, a *sterile* flower. — **ste·ril′i·ty** (stē·rĭl′ĭ·tĭ), *n.*

Syn. **Sterile, barren, impotent, unfruitful, infertile** mean lacking the power to produce offspring or bear fruit. **Sterile** implies inability to reproduce its kind because of an organic defect or the like; **barren**, a lack of issue or return; **impotent**, a lack of the power of procreation; **unfruitful** is close to *barren*, but is more often applied to land, vegetation, or efforts of any sort which bring forth nothing worth while; **infertile** implies sterility both literally and figuratively. — **Ant.** Fertile.

ster′i·li·za′tion (stĕr′ĭ·lĭ·zā′shŭn; -lī·zā′shŭn), *n.* Act or process of sterilizing; also, state of being sterile or sterilized; specif., the act or process of killing all living cells, esp. microorganisms. Cf. PASTEURIZATION.

ster′i·lize (stĕr′ĭ·līz), *v. t.* Also **ster′i·lise.** To make sterile; specif.: **a** To exhaust of fertility, as land. **b** To deprive of the power of reproducing, specif. by surgical removal or inhibition of function of the reproductive organs. **c** To render powerless or useless, as by inhibiting normal productive functions; as, to *sterilize* gold. **d** *Bacteriol.* To free from living microorganisms, as by physical or chemical agents. Cf. PASTEURIZE. — **ster′i·liz′er** (-līz′ẽr), *n.*

ster′let (stûr′lĕt; -lĭt), *n.* [Russ. *sterlyad′*; cf. F. & G. *sterlet.*] A small sturgeon (*Acipenser ruthenus*) found in the Caspian Sea and its rivers, esteemed for its flavor. The finest caviar is made from its roe.

ster′ling (stûr′lĭng), *n.* [ME., prob. fr. AS. *steorra* star.] **1.** The standard of fineness of lawful British coin; for silver (**sterling silver**) formerly 0.925, since 1920, 0.500; for gold, formerly 0.995, now 0.9166 or 11/12. **2.** Sterling silver .925 fine, standard for manufactured articles, as tableware. — *adj.* **1.** Of or concerned with sterling (sense 1); payable in sterling; as, *sterling* exchange. **2.** Manufactured of sterling silver (see sense 2, above). **3.** Of full value; genuine; as, *sterling* merit.

stern (stûrn), *adj.* [AS. *styrne, stierne.*] **1.** Having a certain hardness or severity as of nature or manner; austere. **2.** Hard or severe in aspect; forbidding. **3.** Stout; sturdy; as, a *stern* resolve. — **Syn.** See SEVERE. — **stern′ly,** *adv.* — **stern′ness,** *n.*

stern, *n.* **1.** The rear end of a vessel or boat. **2.** The hinder part of anything. — **stern,** *adj.*

ster′nal (stûr′năl), *adj.* Pertaining to the sternum.

stern chase. *Nav.* A chase in which the pursuing vessel follows in the path of the vessel pursued.

stern chaser. *Nav.* A gun so placed as to be able to fire astern at a vessel that may be in chase.

stern′fore′most (stûrn′fōr′mōst; -mŭst), *adv.* With the stern in advance; hence, backwards; also, awkwardly.

stern′most (stûrn′mōst; -mŭst), *adj.* Farthest astern.

ster′no- (stûr′nō-). [From *sternum.*] A combining form denoting *sternal and*; as in **ster′no·cla·vic′u·lar, ster′no·cos′tal, ster′no·mas′toid.** See CLAVICULAR, etc.

stern′post′ (stûrn′pōst′), *n.* *Shipbuilding.* The principal member at the stern of a vessel, extending from keel to deck.

stern′son (stûrn′s′n), *n.* Also **stern knee, sternson knee.** [See STERN, *n.*; cf. STEMSON.] *Shipbuilding.* The end of a keelson, to which the sternpost is bolted.

ster′num (stûr′nŭm), *n.*; *pl.* -NA (-nȧ), -NUMS (-nŭmz). [NL., fr. Gr. *sternon* the breast, chest.] *Anat. & Zool.* The compound bone or cartilage connecting the ribs (in man, the upper seven pairs) in front in most vertebrates above fishes; the breastbone. See THORAX, *Illust.*; cf. EPISTERNUM, MANUBRIUM, GLADIOLUS, XIPHISTERNUM.

ster′nu·ta′tion (stûr′nū·tā′shŭn), *n.* [L. *sternutatio*, fr. *sternutare* to sneeze.] The act, fact, or noise of sneezing. — **ster·nu′ta·tive** (stẽr·nū′tȧ·tĭv), **ster·nu′ta·to′ry** (-tō′rĭ *or, esp. Brit.*, -tẽr·ĭ), *adj.*

stern′way′ (stûrn′wā′), *n.* *Naut.* Movement of a ship backward, or with her stern foremost.

stern′-wheel′er, *n.* *Colloq., U. S.* A paddle steamer having a stern wheel instead of side wheels.

ster′oid (stĕr′oid), *n.* [*sterol* + *-oid.*] *Chem.* Any of a class of compounds containing the carbon ring system of the sterols and including the sterols, certain hormones and glycosides, etc.

ster′ol (stĕr′ōl; -ŏl), *n.* [From chole*sterol.*] Any of a class of solid alcohols, as cholesterol, widely distributed in plants and animals.

ster′tor (stûr′tẽr), *n.* [NL., fr. L. *stertere* to snore.] *Med.* Act or fact of producing a snoring sound; snoring.

ster′to·rous (stûr′tō·rŭs), *adj.* [L. *stertere* to snore.] Characterized by a deep snoring, as in apoplexy; hence, hoarsely breathing. — **ster′to·rous·ly,** *adv.* — **ster′to·rous·ness,** *n.*

stet (stĕt). [L., subj. 3d pers. sing. of *stare* to stand, remain.] *Print.* Let it stand; — used to signify that something once marked for omission is to remain. — *v. t.*; STET′TED; STET′TING. *Print.* To direct to remain after having been marked for omission; to mark with the word *stet.*

steth′o- (stĕth′ō-), **steth-.** [Gr. *stēthos.*] A combining form meaning *breast, chest*, as in **ste·thom′e·ter,** a device for measuring expansion of the chest during respiration.

steth′o·scope (-skōp), *n.* *Med.* An instrument used in auscultation, as of the chest, to convey to the ear the sounds produced in the body. — **steth′o·scop′ic** (-skŏp′ĭk), **steth′o·scop′i·cal** (-ĭ·kăl), *adj.* — **steth′o·scop′i·cal·ly,** *adv.* — **ste·thos′co·pist** (stē·thŏs′kō·pĭst; stĕth′ō·skō′pĭst), *n.* — **ste·thos′co·py,** *n.*

ste′ve·dore′ (stē′vĕ·dōr′; 70), *n.* [Sp. *estivador* packer, deriv. of L. *stipare* to press.] One who works at, or is responsible for, the unloading and loading of a vessel in port. — **ste′ve·dore′,** *v. t. & i.*

ste′ve·dore′s′ knot (-dōrz′). See KNOT, *Illust.* (3)

stew (stū), *v. t. & i.* [ME. *stuwen* to bathe, fr. OF. *estuver.*] **1.** To boil slowly, or with a simmering heat; to seethe. **2.** *Colloq.* To worry. — *n.* **1.** A brothel; — used chiefly in *pl.* **2.** [From STEW, *v.*] A dish prepared by stewing; esp., such a dish of meat and vegetables (cf. IRISH STEW); also, *Obs.*, a stewpan. **3.** *Colloq.* A state of agitating worry.

stew′ard (stū′ẽrd), *n.* [AS. *stīweard, stigweard*, fr. *stī, stig*, house, hall, sty + *weard* warden.] **1.** An officer or employee in a large family, or on a large estate, to manage the domestic concerns, supervise servants, collect rents or income, keep accounts, etc. **2.** An administrator, or supervisor; a manager. **3.** A person employed on board ship to do the catering, superintend culinary affairs, etc.; also, on passenger ships, an employee who attends to the passengers' comfort or, on airplanes and buses, a similar attendant. — **stew′ard·ess,** *n.* — **stew′ard·ship,** *n.*

Stew′art (stū′ẽrt), *n.* See STUART.

stew′pan′ (stū′păn′), *n.* A pan used for stewing.

stey (stā), *adj.* *Scot. & Dial. Eng.* Steep.

sthe·ni′a (sthē·nī′ȧ; sthē′nĭ·ȧ), *n.* [NL., fr. Gr. *sthenos.*] *Med.* Strength; vigor; — opposed to *asthenia.*

sthen′ic (sthĕn′ĭk), *adj.* [Gr. *sthenos* strength.] **a** *Med.* Strong; active; — said esp. of morbid states that are attended with excessive action of the vital processes. **b** *Psychol.* Indicative of vigor; as, the *sthenic* emotions.

‖**stiac·cia′to** (styät·chä′tō), *adj. & n.* [It., crushed, flattened.] See RELIEF, *n.*, 6.

stib′ine (stĭb′ēn; -ĭn), *n.* Also **stib′in.** [See STIBIUM.] *Chem.* A colorless poisonous gas, SbH_3, produced by the action of hydrogen on antimony or one of its compounds.

stib′i·um (stĭb′ĭ·ŭm), *n.* [L. *stibium, stibi*, fr. Gr. *stibi, stimmi.*] Antimony. Chem. symbol, *Sb* (no period). — **stib′i·al** (-ăl), *adj.*

stib′nite (stĭb′nīt), *n.* *Mineral.* Native antimony trisulfide, Sb_2S_3, occurring in orthorhombic, lead-gray, lustrous crystals and also massive.

stich (stĭk), *n.* [Gr. *stichos* a row, line.] *Pros.* A verse or line. — **stich′ic** (stĭk′ĭk), *adj.*

sti·chom′e·try (stĭ·kŏm′ē·trĭ), *n.* [Gr. *stichos* row, line + *-metry.*] Division of the text of a book into lines, esp. into lines fitted to the sense, a method used before punctuation was adopted. — **stich′o·met′ric** (stĭk′ō·mĕt′rĭk), **stich′o·met′ri·cal** (-rĭ·kăl), *adj.*

-stichous. [Gr. *stichos* row, line.] *Bot. & Zool.* A combining form denoting *having* (such or so many) *rows.*

stich′wort′ (stĭch′wûrt′). Var. of STITCHWORT.

stick (stĭk), *n.* [AS. *sticca.*] **1.** A woody piece or part of a tree or shrub; as: **a** A shoot or slender branch cut or broken off, esp. when dry and dead. **b** A stem or branch, of any size, cut or gathered, esp. for fuel or timber. **2.** A stalk, as of celery. **3.** Any long slender piece of wood; a rod; wand; staff. Specif.: **a** Short for WALKING STICK. **b** A staff, club, etc., used as a weapon. **4.** Anything resembling a stick in shape or use; as, a *stick* of candy, dynamite. **5.** *Brit.* A number of bombs arranged for release from a bombing plane in a series across a target. **6.** *Colloq.* A person who is dull, inert, or lifeless. **7.** A portion of liquor, as brandy, put into water, tea, etc. **8.** A thrust with a pointed instrument; a stab. **9.** Quality or fact of sticking or adhering. **10.** An impediment; also, stoppage; delay; demur. **11.** *Aeronautics.* The vertical lever by which certain of the principal controls of an airplane are operated. **12.** *Naut. Colloq.* A mast. **13.** *Print.* **a** A composing stick. **b** A stickful. **14.** *Sports.* **a** A hockey stick; a lacrosse player's crosse. **b** A racing hurdle.

— *v. t.*; STUCK (stŭk); STICK′ING. **1.** To pierce with something pointed; to stab; hence, to kill by piercing. **2.** To push, thrust, or drive, so as to pierce. **3.** Loosely, to shove; poke; as, to *stick* out one's arm; to *stick* one's chin out. **4.** To fasten by thrusting in; as, to *stick* a flower in one's buttonhole; hence, also, to adorn with things fastened on as by piercing; as, a coat *stuck* with badges. **5.** To set with something pointed; as, a cushion *stuck* with pins. **6.** To impale; transfix; hence, to affix or mount by transfixing; as, to *stick* insect specimens. **7.** To attach by, or as by, causing to adhere to the surface; as, to *stick* a stamp on an envelope. **8.** *Colloq.* To smear with viscous or glutinous matter. **9.** *Colloq.* To pose; puzzle; as, to *stick* one with a problem. **10.** *Slang.* **a** To compel to pay, as by beating in a gamble; hence, loosely, to charge. **b** To get the better of, esp. fraudulently; to cheat. — *v. i.* **1.** To become infixed by means of a pointed end. **2.** To become affixed by adhesion; to adhere. **3.** To remain where placed; to stay. **4.** To keep close, as in pursuit or competition; as, to *stick* to one's heels. **5.** To hold fast or adhere resolutely; to cling; as, to *stick* to a friend; also, to put up with conditions; to endure; as, ready to *stick* through thick and thin. **6.** To apply oneself industriously; as, to *stick* to business. **7.** To protrude; as, his hair *sticks* up. **8.** To become blocked, wedged, or jammed; as, to *stick* in the mud. **9.** To be puzzled; to hesitate; balk; scruple; as, a man who will *stick* at nothing.

Syn. **Stick, adhere, cohere, cling, cleave** mean to become closely attached. **Stick** implies attachment by affixing or as by gluing together; **adhere**, by deliberate acceptance or by growing together; **cohere**, a sticking together of parts so that they form a mass or unified whole; **cling**, attachment by hanging on, as by the arms, the tendrils, etc.; **cleave**, close and strong attachment, as in marriage.

stick, *v. t.*; STICKED (stĭkt); STICK′ING. [From STICK, *n.*] **1.** To supply sticks or brush as a prop for, as for a vine. **2.** [From STICK, *n.*, 13.] *Print.* To compose; to set, or arrange, in a composing stick.

stick′er (stĭk′ẽr), *n.* **1.** One who or that which sticks, as a pointed weapon or implement. **2.** One who or that which adheres or causes adhesion, as a gummed label to be affixed by moistening; specif., *U. S.* = PASTER, 2. **3.** *Slang.* Something puzzling; a poser. **4.** *Philately.* A hinge.

stick′ful (-fo͝ol), *n.*; *pl.* -FULS (-fo͝olz). *Print.* As much set type as fills a composing stick. See COMPOSING STICK.

stick′ing plas′ter. Adhesive plaster for closing wounds, etc.; court plaster.

stick insect. Any of various orthopterous insects (family Phasmatidae) usually wingless, with a long round body, sticklike in form and color.

stick′it (stĭk′ĭt; stĕk′ĭt), *adj.* *Scot.* Stuck; hence, having failed; — applied specif. to a person who has failed in, or given up, a calling; as, a *stickit* doctor or minister.

stick′le (stĭk′'l), *v. i.*; STICK′LED (-'ld); STICK′LING (-lĭng). [Prob. fr. ME. *stightlen* to arrange, govern, freq. of *stihten*, fr. AS. *stihtan, stihtian.*] **1.** To contend, esp. stubbornly and, usually, on insufficient grounds. **2.** To feel scruples; to scruple; demur. — **stick′ler** (-lẽr), *n.*

stick′le·back′ (stĭk′'l·băk′), *n.* [Dial. *stickle* stubble, bristle + *back.*] Any of numerous small scaleless fishes (family Gasterosteidae) having two or more free spines in front of the dorsal fin.
stick′pin′ (stĭk′pĭn′), *n.* An ornamental pin for a cravat.
sticks (stĭks), *n.* *Colloq.* With *the.* Timberlands; hence, sections of a country remote from centers of civilization.
stick′seed′ (stĭk′sēd′), *n.* Any plant of the genus *Lappula;* — in allusion to the bristly, adhesive fruit. The common stickseed (*L. echinata*), called also ***burseed***, is adventive as a weed in the United States.
stick′tight′ (-tīt′), *n.* The bur marigold.
stick′–to′–it·ive (stĭk′tōō′ĭt·ĭv), *adj.* That sticks resolutely or unswervingly, as to a task, purpose, etc.; dogged. — **stick′–to′–it·ive·ly**, *adv.* — **stick′–to′–it·ive·ness**, *n.*
stick′–up′, *n.* *Slang.* A holdup.
stick′weed′ (stĭk′wēd′), *n.* The common ragweed.
stick′y (-ĭ), *adj.;* STICK′I·ER (-ĭ·ẽr); STICK′I·EST. **1.** Having the quality of adhering; viscous; gluey. **2.** *Colloq.* Humid and hot. — **stick′i·ly**, *adv.* — **stick′i·ness**, *n.*
stiff (stĭf), *adj.* [AS. *stīf.*] **1.** Not easily bent; not flexible or pliant. **2.** Not moving with ease; not limber. **3.** Tense; taut; as, a *stiff* rein. **4.** Not liquid or fluid; thick and tenacious. **5.** Dense; tightly packed, as soil. **6.** Not natural and easy; lacking grace; awkward. **7.** Of a breeze, current, or the like, having force not easily opposed; strong. **8.** *Scot.* Sturdy; robust. **9.** Not easily subdued; unyielding; stubborn. **10.** Strong; — of an intoxicant or a medicine; as, a *stiff* dose. **11.** Harsh; severe; as, a *stiff* sentence. **12.** Difficult; as, a *stiff* ascent. **13.** *Colloq.* **a** Of prices, high; steep. **b** Unyielding; firm in prices; as, a *stiff* market. **14.** *Naut.* Bearing a press of canvas without much inclination; as, a *stiff* vessel.
Syn. **Stiff, rigid, inflexible, tense, stark** mean impossible to bend or make yield. **Stiff** implies merely the condition, except when used figuratively; **rigid** implies stiffness so great that it cannot be bent without breaking; **inflexible** stresses simply an incapacity for being bent; **tense,** a stretching or straining to a point where there is actual or seeming loss of elasticity; **stark,** now chiefly dialectal, a stiffness associated with loss of life, vitality, or fluidity.
— *n.* *Slang.* **a** A corpse. **b** An awkward, clumsy fellow. — **stiff′ly**, *adv.* — **stiff′ness**, *n.*
stiff′en (stĭf′ĕn), *v. t. & i.* To make or become stiff or stiffer. — **stiff′en·er** (-ẽr), *n.*
stiff′–necked′ (stĭf′nĕkt′; 2), *adj.* Stubborn; obstinate.
sti′fle (stī′f'l), *v. t.;* STI′FLED (-f'ld); STI′FLING (-flĭng). [ME. *stuf(f)len,* appar. fr. OF. *estouffer, estofer.*] **1.** To stop the breath of; to choke; to suffocate; also, to cause the death of by such means. **2.** To extinguish; quench; as, to *stifle* a fire. **3.** To smother; to keep or choke back; as, to *stifle* one's sobs. — *v. i.* **1.** To die by reason of obstruction of the breath. **2.** To suffer difficulty in breathing, as by reason of air charged with smoke. — **sti′fler** (-flẽr), *n.* — **sti′fling**, *adj.* — **sti′fling·ly**, *adv.*
sti′fle, *n.* Also **stifle joint.** [Origin uncert.] *Veter.* The joint next above the hock in the hind leg of certain quadrupeds, esp. horses and dogs, corresponding to the knee in man. See DOG, HORSE, *Illusts.*
stig′ma (stĭg′mȧ), *n.; pl.* STIGMATA (-mȧ·tȧ) or, esp. in senses 1, 2, 6, STIGMAS (-mȧz). [L., a mark, a brand, fr. Gr. *stigma, -atos,* the prick or mark of a pointed instrument, a spot, mark.] **1.** A brand, as upon a slave or criminal. **2.** Any mark of infamy or disgrace. **3.** A sign of blemish, taint, etc.; specif., any mark, label, or the like, designed to indicate deviation from some norm or standard; as, the label *Slang* is a *stigma* attached to many definitions. **4.** *pl.* Marks resembling the wounds on the crucified body of Christ, believed to have been supernaturally impressed upon the bodies of certain persons, as St. Francis of Assisi. **5.** *Anat. & Zool.* A small spot, mark, scar, or a minute hole. **6.** *Bot.* The part of the pistil of a flower which receives the pollen grains, and on which they germinate. **7.** *Med.* **a** A red speck upon the skin, esp. one due to extravasation of blood produced by nervous influence or by capillary congestion. **b** One of the signs or marks characterizing a disease.
stig·mas′ter·ol (stĭg·măs′tẽr·ōl; -ŏl), *n.* [Physo*stigma,* the genus including the Calabar bean + *sterol.*] *Chem.* A crystalline sterol, $C_{29}H_{47}OH$, obtained from the oils of Calabar beans and soybeans.
stig·mat′ic (stĭg·măt′ĭk), *adj.* Also **stig·mat′i·cal** (-ĭ·kăl). **1.** Of the nature of, or marked with, a stigma, or stigmas or stigmata. **2.** *Optics.* Anastigmatic; — said esp. of a bundle of rays which intersect at a single point. — *n.* One marked with stigmata.
stig′ma·tism (stĭg′mȧ·tĭz'm), *n.* **1.** Condition characterized by the presence of stigmata. **2.** Condition of a lens or of the refractive media of the eye, in which rays of light from one point are brought to a single focal point. Cf. ASTIGMATISM.
stig′ma·tize (-tīz), *v. t.* Also **stig′ma·tise.** **1.** To mark with a stigma; esp., to brand. **2.** To set a mark of disgrace on. **3.** To produce stigmata upon. See STIGMA, 4, 7. — **stig′ma·ti·za′tion** (-tĭ·zā′shŭn; -tī·zā′-), *n.* — **stig′ma·tiz′er** (-tīz′ẽr), *n.*
stil′bene (stĭl′bēn), *n.* [See STILBITE.] *Chem.* A hydrocarbon, $C_6H_5CH{:}CHC_6H_5$, used in making dyes.
stil·bes′trol, stil·boes′trol (stĭl·bĕs′trōl; -trŏl), *n.* [*stil*bene + *oestrus* + *-ol,* 1.] *Biochem.* **a** Properly, a crystalline synthetic compound, $C_{14}H_{12}O_2$, having little estrogenic activity. **b** Diethylstilbestrol.
stil′bite (stĭl′bīt), *n.* [F. *stilbite,* fr. Gr. *stilbein* to glitter, shine.] *Mineral.* Native hydrous silicate of aluminum, calcium, and sodium, often occurring in sheaflike aggregations of crystals.
stile (stīl), *n.* [AS. *stigel* a step, ladder.] A step, or set of steps, for ascending and descending, in passing a fence or wall; also, a turnstile.
stile, *n.* [Origin uncert.; cf. D. *stijl.*] One of the upright pieces in framing or paneling, into which the secondary members are tenoned.
sti·let′to (stĭ·lĕt′ō), *n.; pl.* -TOS, -TOES (-ōz). [It., dim. of *stilo* a dagger, fr. L. *stilus* a pointed instrument.] **1.** A type of dagger with a slender, pointed blade. **2.** A pointed instrument for making eyelet holes, etc. — *v. t.* To stab with a stiletto.
still (stĭl), *adj.* [AS. *stille.*] **1.** Motionless; quiet; also, inactive. **2.** Not disturbed by agitation or noise; calm; tranquil. **3.** Uttering no sound; silent; hushed. **4.** Comparatively quiet or silent; soft; low; subdued. **5.** Not sparkling or effervescent, owing to absence of carbon dioxide; — said esp. of wines. **6.** Of a photograph, not exhibiting motion.
— *n.* **1.** *Poetic.* Absence of noise; silence. **2.** *Colloq.* **a** A still alarm. **b** A still-life picture. **3.** *Photog.* A still photograph; specif., *Motion Pictures,* an individual photograph, as of some part of a motion picture, used for advertising purposes.
— *v. t.* **1.** To stop, as physical movement or agitation; to quiet. **2.** To calm; allay. **3.** To silence. — *v. i.* To become still, quiet, etc.
still, *adv.* **1.** *Poetic.* Always; ever; continually. **2.** **a** To this or that time; at present; yet; as, words *still* used. **b** In the future as now and before. **c** After that; after what is stated; as, he *still* feared. **3.** Even more; even yet; as, *still* better. — *conj.* Nevertheless; yet.
still, *v. t. & i.* [L. *stillare* to drop, drip.] *Now Rare.* To drop, or cause to fall by drops; to drip.
still, *v. t. & i.* [Shortened fr. *distill.*] *Obs.* = DISTILL.
still, *n.* [From STILL to distill.] **1.** A vessel used in distilling liquids, esp. alcoholic liquors; a retort. Sometimes, the whole apparatus used in vaporization and condensation. **2.** A distillery.
still alarm. An alarm of fire without sounding the signal apparatus, as by a call by telephone.
still′birth′ (stĭl′bûrth′), *n.* The birth of a dead fetus.
still′born′ (-bôrn′), *adj.* Dead at birth; figuratively, lifeless when produced; falling flat.
still hunt. *U.S.* **a** A hunting for game in a quiet manner, or under cover; stalking. **b** Hence, *Colloq.,* the quiet, cautious pursuit of any object. — **still′–hunt′**, *v. t. & i.*

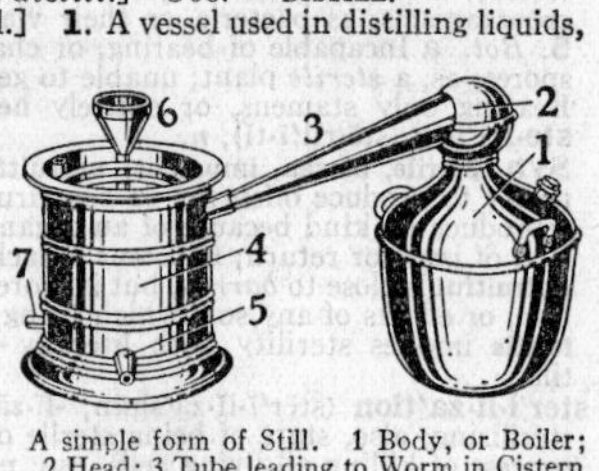

A simple form of Still. 1 Body, or Boiler; 2 Head; 3 Tube leading to Worm in Cistern of cold water (4); 5 Outlet from Worm; 6 Inlet to Cistern; 7 Outlet for overflow.

still life. *Fine Arts.* That kind of subject in a picture consisting of inanimate objects, as fruit, etc.; also, a picture having this kind of subject. — **still′–life′** (-līf′; 2), *adj.*
still′ness (stĭl′nĕs; -nĭs), *n.* Quiet; silence; calm.
Still′son wrench (stĭl′s'n). A wrench, bearing the trade-mark Stillson, having an adjustable L-shaped jaw sliding in a sleeve pivoted to, and loosely embracing, the handle. Pressure on the handle increases the grip. See WRENCH, *Illust.*
still′y (stĭl′ĭ), *adj.;* STILL′I·ER (-ĭ·ẽr); STILL′I·EST. Still; quiet; calm.
stil′ly (stĭl′lĭ), *adv.* Quietly; noiselessly.
stilt (stĭlt), *n.* [ME. *stilte.*] **1.** One of two poles constructed with a step or loop to raise the foot above the ground in walking. **2.** A tall pile or post forming one of the supports of a primitive building, a rude pier, or the like. **3.** See PLURAL, *Note,* 3. Any of certain very long-legged three-toed limicoline birds (genera *Himantopus* and *Cladorhynchus*) allied to the avocets. They chiefly inhabit inland ponds and marshes, nesting in small colonies. — *v. t.* To raise on stilts.
stilt′ed (stĭl′tĕd; -tĭd), *adj.* Elevated; hence: **a** Pompous or formal. **b** Of an arch, raised above the impost on courses of masonry.
Stil′ton (stĭl′t'n; -tŭn), *n., or* **Stilton cheese.** One of the principal English cheeses, sold orig. at Stilton, Huntingdonshire. It is rich, unpressed, of waxy texture, and permeated with a blue-green mold.
stime (stīm), *n.* *Scot. & Dial.* Glimpse.
stim′u·lant (stĭm′ū·lănt), *adj.* [L. *stimulans,* pres. part. See STIMULATE.] *Rare.* That stimulates. — *n.* **1.** That which stimulates. **2.** An alcoholic beverage; — popularly so called because of the apparent stimulation experienced by one who drinks an alcoholic beverage, resulting from the depression of certain nervous centers. **3.** *Physiol.* An agent that produces a temporary increase of vital activity.
stim′u·late (-lāt), *v. t.* [L. *stimulatus,* past part. of *stimulare* to goad on, incite, fr. *stimulus* a goad.] **1.** To excite, rouse, or spur on as if with a goad. **2.** To arouse by an intoxicating beverage; — popularly so used. See STIMULANT, *n.,* 2. **3.** *Physiol.* To excite the activity of (a nerve or an irritable muscle), as by electricity. — *v. i.* To act as a stimulant. — **Syn.** See PROVOKE. — **stim′u·lat′ing** (-lāt′ĭng), *adj.* — **stim′u·la′tor** (-lā′tẽr), **stim′u·lat′er** (-lāt′ẽr), *n.*
stim′u·la′tion (-lā′shŭn), *n.* **1.** Act of stimulating, or state of being stimulated; quickened activity. **2.** *Physiol.* The irritating action of various stimuli on muscles, nerves, etc., by which activity is caused.
stim′u·la′tive (stĭm′ū·lā′tĭv; -lȧ·tĭv), *adj.* Having power, or tending, to stimulate. — **stim′u·la′tive**, *n.*
stim′u·lus (stĭm′ū·lŭs), *n.; pl.* -LI (-lī). [L.] **1.** Something that rouses the mind or spirits, or incites to activity; an incentive. **2.** *Physiol. & Psychol.* Any agent or environmental change capable of influencing the activity of living protoplasm, as exciting the activity of a muscle or organ, of initiating an impulse in a nerve, or of exciting a specific end organ of sensation.
sti′my (stī′mĭ). Var. of STYMIE.
sting (stĭng), *v. t.;* STUNG (stŭng), *Archaic* STANG (stăng); STING′ING (stĭng′ĭng). [AS. *stingan.*] **1.** To prick painfully; as: **a** To pierce or wound with a poisonous or irritating sting. **b** To affect with sharp quick pain or smart; as, hail *stung* their faces. **2.** To cause to suffer acutely; as, *stung* with remorse. **3.** *Slang.* To pain by robbing, charging exorbitantly, etc. **4.** To stimulate; incite. — *v. i.* **1.** To use a sting; to give pain, as by a sting. **2.** To give a keen burning pain or smart. — *n.* **1.** The act of stinging; specif., the thrust of a sting (def. 6) into the flesh; also, a wound or pain caused by stinging. **2.** A goad; stimulus. *Shak.* **3.** The point of an epigram or sarcasm. **4.** Stinging force, quality, or capacity. **5.** *Bot.* = STINGING HAIR. **6.** *Zool.* Any of various sharp organs of offense and defense, esp. when connected with a poison gland or otherwise adapted to wound by piercing and inoculating a poisonous secretion. — **sting′ing·ly**, *adv.*
sting′a·ree (stĭng′ȧ·rē; stĭng′ȧ·rē′), *n.* [Corrupt. fr. STING RAY.] A sting ray (see 1st RAY).
sting′er (stĭng′ẽr), *n.* One that stings; specif.: **a** An animal or plant that stings. **b** The sting of an insect, etc. **c** *Colloq.* A stinging blow, remark, etc. **d** *Slang, Brit.* A whisky and soda.
sting′ing hair (stĭng′ĭng). *Bot.* A glandular hair whose swollen base secretes a stinging fluid, as in nettles.
stin′go (stĭng′gō), *n.* [From STING.] *Slang.* **a** Sharp or strong liquor, esp. ale or beer. **b** Zest; zip.
sting ray, *or* **sting′ray′** (stĭng′rā′), *n.* See 1st RAY.
sting′y (stĭng′ĭ), *adj.;* STING′I·ER (-ĭ·ẽr); STING′I·EST. Stinging; able to sting.
stin′gy (stĭn′jĭ), *adj.;* STIN′GI·ER (-jĭ·ẽr); STIN′GI·EST. [From dial. *stinge* a sting.] **1.** Very close; miserly. **2.** Scanty; as, a *stingy* crop. — **stin′gi·ly**, *adv.* — **stin′gi·ness**, *n.*

Syn. **Stingy, close, niggardly, parsimonious, penurious, miserly** mean unwilling to share one's possessions with others. **Stingy** implies a lack of generosity; **close**, a tight grip on one's possessions; **niggardly**, such stinginess and closeness that one gives the smallest amount possible; **parsimonious**, a frugality that leads to niggardliness; **penurious**, a niggardliness so great as to give the appearance of poverty; **miserly**, a sordid avariciousness that motivates penuriousness.

stink (stĭngk), *v. i.;* STANK (stăngk) or STUNK (stŭngk); STUNK; STINK'ING. [AS. *stincan* to have a smell (good or bad).] To emit a smell or odor, now only an offensive smell; hence, to be in bad repute. — *v. t.* To cause to stink; to affect by a stink; — often with *up.* — *n.* A disgusting odor; stench.

stink'ard (stĭngk'ẽrd), *n.* [*stink* + *-ard.*] *Now Dial. & Slang.* One who stinks; specif., a paltry fellow.

stink'bug' (stĭngk'bŭg'), *n.* Any of various bugs (order Hemiptera) which emit a disagreeable odor.

stink'er (stĭngk'ẽr), *n.* **1.** One that stinks; as: **a** A stinkpot. **b** *Slang.* A stinkard. **2.** Any of several large petrels of an offensive odor.

stink'horn' (stĭngk'hôrn'), *n.* Any of an order (Phallales, esp. *Ithyphallus impudicus*) of ill-smelling fungi.

stink'ing, *adj.* That stinks; rank. — **Syn.** See MALODOROUS. — **stink'ing·ly,** *adv.*

stinking smut. = 2d BUNT.

stink'pot' (stĭngk'pŏt'), *n.* A vessel of stinking materials; specif., *Mil. & Nav.*, a jar charged with materials of an offensive and suffocating smell, formerly sometimes thrown upon an enemy's deck.

stink'stone' (-stōn'), *n.* Any stone which emits a fetid smell on being struck or rubbed, owing to the decomposition of organic matter.

stink'weed' (-wēd'), *n.* Any of various strong-scented or ill-smelling plants, as the Jimson weed, ailanthus, etc.

stink'wood' (-wŏŏd'), *n.* Any of several trees with a wood of unpleasant odor; also, the wood.

stint (stĭnt), *v. t.* [ME. *stinten, stenten, stunten,* to cause to cease, to cease, fr. AS. *styntan* to blunt, dull.] **1.** *Archaic.* To put an end to; to stop. **2.** To restrain within certain limits; to confine; to restrict, esp. with respect to a share or allowance. — *v. i.* **1.** *Archaic & Dial.* To stop; desist. **2.** To be sparing or frugal. — *n.* Also **stent** (stĕnt). [See STINT, *v.*] **1.** *Obs.* Cessation. **2.** Restraint; limitation; also, limit; bound. **3.** Quantity or task assigned. — **Syn.** See TASK. — **stint'er,** *n.*

stint, *n.;* see PLURAL, *Note,* 3. Any of several small sandpipers, esp. the dunlin.

stipe (stīp), *n.* [F., fr. L. *stipes* a stock, branch.] *Bot.* A short stalk; as: **a** In mycology, the stem supporting the cap or pileus. See FUNGUS, *Illust.* **b** In ferns, the petiole of the frond. **c** In seed plants, a stalklike prolongation of the torus beneath the ovary.

sti'pel (stī'pĕl), *n.* [See STIPULE.] *Bot.* Stipule. — **sti·pel'late** (stī·pĕl'āt; stī'pĕl·āt), *adj.*

sti'pend (stī'pĕnd), *n.* [OF. *stipende, -die,* fr. L. *stipendium,* fr. *stips,* gen. *stipis,* a gift, donation, given in small coin + *pendere* to weigh or pay out.] Settled pay or compensation for services. — **Syn.** See WAGE.

sti·pen'di·ar'y (stī·pĕn'dĭ·ĕr'ĭ *or, esp. Brit.,* -ẽr·ĭ), *adj.* **1.** Receiving wages or salary; performing services for a stated compensation. **2.** Rendering tribute or taxes, as in money or services. — *n.; pl.* -IES (-ĭz). **1.** One who receives a stipend. **2.** A tribute-paying estate or tenant.

sti'pes (stī'pēz), *n.; pl.* STIPITES (stĭp'ĭ·tēz). [L., a stock.] **1.** *Zool.* A stalk, stem, or peduncle. **2.** *Zool.* The second basal segment of a maxilla of an insect or crustacean. — **sti'pi·form** (stī'pĭ·fôrm), **stip'i·ti·form'** (stĭp'ĭ·tĭ·fôrm'), *adj.*

stip'i·tate (stĭp'ĭ·tāt), *adj.* [NL. *stipitatus,* fr. L. *stipes.* See STIPE.] *Bot.* Having, or borne on, a stipe.

stip'ple (stĭp''l), *v. t.;* -PLED (-'ld); -PLING (-lĭng). [D. *stippelen* to make points, to spot, dot.] **1.** To engrave by means of dots, in distinction from engraving in lines. **2.** To render in paint, ink, etc., by small, short touches which together produce an even or softly graded shadow. Hence, to apply (paint, etc.) by repeated small touches. — *n.* Also **stip'pling** (-lĭng). **1.** In the graphic arts, any mode of execution by which gradation of light and shade is produced by separate touches; also, the effect so produced. **2.** Any effect, esp. in nature, resembling a stipple. — **stip'pler** (-lẽr), *n.*

stip'u·late (stĭp'ū·lāt), *v. i.* [L. *stipulatus,* past part. of *stipulari* to stipulate.] To agree to do or forbear anything; to bargain; contract. — *v. t.* To arrange definitely, as a covenant; to specify (something) as being a condition of agreement. — **stip'u·la'tor** (-lā'tẽr), *n.*

stip'u·late (-lāt), *adj.* Also **stip'u·lat'ed** (-lāt'ĕd; -ĭd). *Bot.* Furnished with stipules.

stip'u·la'tion (-lā'shŭn), *n.* Act of stipulating; a contracting or agreeing, or that which is agreed upon; also, any condition in an agreement. — **stip'u·la·to'ry** (stĭp'ū·lȧ·tō'rĭ *or, esp. Brit.,* -tẽr·ĭ), *adj.*

stip'ule (stĭp'ūl), *n.* [F., fr. L. *stipula* a stalk, stem.] *Bot.* One of the pair of appendages borne at the base of the leaf in many plants. — **stip'u·lar** (-ū·lẽr), *adj.*

stir (stûr), *v. t.;* STIRRED (stûrd); STIR'RING. [AS. *styrian.*] **1.** To change the position of in any manner; to move, esp. slightly. **2.** To impart movement to: **a** To disturb the relative position of the particles or parts of, as of a fluid, by passing something through it; hence, more broadly, to agitate; disturb. **b** To move briskly; to bestir; — usually reflexive. **3.** To rouse; specif.: **a** To excite; inflame; stimulate. **b** To awaken or start up; hence, to bring into notice or debate; to moot. — *v. i.* **1.** To move; esp., to move slightly; to change one's position. **2.** To be in motion; specif.: **a** To be active or busy. **b** *Archaic.* To be roused or excited. **3.** To become the object of notice; to be current. **4.** To be stirred; as, the starch paste *stirs* easily. — *n.* **1.** Act or result of stirring; agitation; activity; movement. **2. a** Public disturbance; disorder. **b** *Colloq.* A pother; to-do. **3.** A jog; poke.

Syn. **Stir, bustle, flurry, pother, fuss, ado** mean excitement or hurry accompanying an action or event. **Stir** suggests brisk and restless movement of a crowd; **bustle**, a noisy, obtrusive, or self-important display of energy; **flurry**, nervous agitation and undue haste; **pother** and **fuss**, flurry and fidgety activity; **ado**, fussiness and waste of energy.

stir, *n.* [Prob. fr. AS. *stēor, stȳr,* discipline, punishment.] *Slang.* A prison; jail.

stir'a·bout' (stûr'ȧ·bout'), *n.* A porridge of oatmeal or corn meal boiled in water or milk and stirred.

stirk (stûrk), *n.* [AS. *styric, stirc,* a young bull or heifer.] A bullock or heifer in the second year.

stir'pi·cul'ture (stûr'pĭ·kŭl'tūr), *n.* [L. *stirps, stirpis,* stem, stock + *cultura* culture.] The breeding of special stocks or races. — **stir'pi·cul'tur·al** (-kŭl'tūr·ăl), *adj.*

stirps (stûrps), *n.; pl.* STIRPES (stûr'pēz). [L., stem, stock.] **1.** Stock; race; family. Hence, *Law,* the person from whom a family is descended. **2.** *Biol.* The total of the organic units which are found in, and determine the development of, a fertilized egg.

stir'rer (stûr'ẽr), *n.* One who or that which stirs.

stir'ring (stûr'ĭng), *adj.* **a** Active; bustling. **b** Rousing; inspiring. — **stir'ring·ly,** *adv.*

stir'rup (stĭr'ŭp; stûr'ŭp; 117), *n.* [AS. *stigrāp.*] **1.** A form of ring, horizontal in one part for receiving the foot of the rider, attached by a strap to the saddle, used to aid in mounting and as a support while riding. **2.** Any piece resembling or likened to a stirrup (sense 1), as such a piece used as a support, clamp, etc., in carpentry and machinery. **3.** *Naut.* A rope secured to a yard, with a thimble in its lower end for supporting a footrope.

stirrup bone. *Anat.* The stapes.

stirrup cup. A cup of wine or the like taken by a rider about to depart; hence, a farewell cup; a parting glass.

stirrup leather *or* **strap.** The strap suspending a stirrup.

stirrup pump. A portable hand pump for throwing a jet or spray of a liquid, which is set in a container or a brook and held firm by one's foot on a bracket or stirrup.

stitch (stĭch), *n.* [AS. *stycce* a piece.] *Dial.* Any space passed over; distance; also, a space of time.

stitch, *n.* [AS. *stice* a pricking.] **1.** A local sharp and sudden pain, esp. in the side or back. **2.** In sewing, a single pass of a needle, or the loop or turn of the thread, twine, or the like thus made and left in the fabric, or, in surgical sewing, in the skin or flesh. **3.** A single turn of the thread round the needle in knitting, crocheting, netting, etc.; a link; or loop, of yarn. **4.** In crocheting, sewing, etc., an arrangement of stitches, or method of stitching in some particular style. **5.** *Colloq.* Any least part of a fabric or dress; as, to wet every *stitch* of one's clothes. — *v. t.* **1.** To form stitches in; esp., to sew in such a manner as to show a line of stitches. **2.** To sew together by stitches. **3.** To unite by means of staples; as, to *stitch* the flaps of a fiber box. — *v. i.* To practice stitching, or needlework.

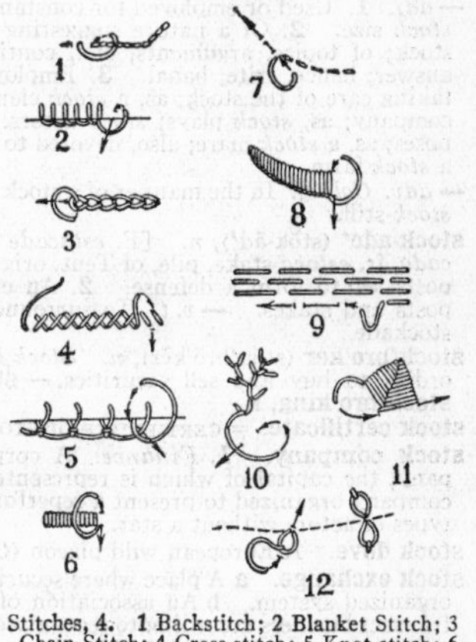

Stitches, 4. 1 Backstitch; 2 Blanket Stitch; 3 Chain Stitch; 4 Cross-stitch; 5 Knot stitch; 6 Overcast Stitch; 7 Running Stitch; 8 Buttonhole Stitch; 9 Darning Stitch; 10 Featherstitch; 11 Fishbone Stitch; 12 Railway, or Daisy, or Loop, or Picot, Stitch. See also HEMSTITCH, *Illust.*

stitch'er (stĭch'ẽr), *n.* One who or a machine that stitches.

stitch'wort' (stĭch'wûrt'), *n.* [AS. *sticwyrt.*] Any of a genus (*Alsine*) of chickweeds.

stith'y (stĭth'ĭ; stĭth'ĭ), *n.; pl.* STITHIES (-ĭz). [ON. *stethi* an anvil.] **1.** An anvil. **2.** A smithy; forge. — *v. t.;* STITH'IED (-ĭd); STITH'Y·ING. To forge on an anvil. *Shak.*

sti'ver (stī'vẽr), *n.* [D. *stuiver.*] **1.** A Dutch coin and money of account, worth about two cents. **2.** A thing of little worth.

sto'a (stō'ȧ), *n.; pl.* STOAE (-ē) or STOAS (-ȧz). [Gr. See STOIC.] *Gr. Arch.* A portico, walled at the back, and with a front colonnade to afford a sheltered promenade.

stoat (stōt), *n.* See PLURAL, *Note,* 3. [ME. *stot.*] The common European ermine, esp. in the brown summer coat; broadly, any ermine or weasel having a black tail tip.

stob (stŏb), *n.* [See STAB.] *Now Dial.* A stake or post.

stoc·ca'do (stŏ·kä'dō; -kā'dō), **stoc·ca'ta** (-tȧ), *n.* [F. and It.; F. *estocade,* fr. It. *stoccata,* fr. *stocco* rapier, fr. F. *estoc* a thrusting sword.] *Archaic.* A stab; thrust.

stock (stŏk), *n.* [AS. *stocc* a stock, trunk, stick.] **1. a** A stump; a wooden post. **b** A block of wood. **c** Hence, something without consciousness or life. **2.** A person who is dull, stupid, or lifeless like a block. **3.** That which serves for firm support, as a pillar or post; the part in which others are inserted, or to which they are attached; specif.: **a** The handle by which bits are held in boring; a bitstock; brace. See BRACE, *Illust.* **b** The butt, or handle, as of a whip, fishing rod, etc. **4. a** The main stem of a plant; the trunk. **b** A rhizome. **5. a** The original progenitor; the original, as a man, a race, or a language, from which others have descended or been derived. **b** The race or line of a family; lineage. Cf. CONSANGUINITY, *Illust.* **c** A strain, race, or group of genetically closely related individuals in a breed or species. **6.** *pl.* A frame of timber, with holes for the feet and hands, to confine offenders by way of punishment. **7.** *pl.* The frame or timbers on which a ship rests while building; hence, ***on the stocks,*** under construction. **8.** *pl.* A frame in which an animal, as a horse or cow, may be secured, as for shoeing. **9. a** The fund or capital which an individual or a firm employs in the conduct of business, trading, investing, etc. **b** A merchant's or manufacturer's store of goods; hence, store; supply on hand. **c** *Slang.* A part interest in something; loosely, the value of such interest; as, she set a great *stock* by him. **10.** Raw material; as, paper *stock;* soap *stock.* **11.** A rich extract of the soluble parts of meat, fish, poultry, etc., used as a basis for soups, gravies, etc. **12.** Livestock. **13.** *Obs.* A covering for the leg, or leg and foot. **14.** A close-fitting wide cravat for the neck. **15. a** Cabbage or colewort. **b** Any of a genus (*Matthiola*) of plants, as the gillyflower, or ***common stock*** (*Matthiola incana*); ***ten-weeks stock*** (*M. incana annua*). **16.** *Agric. Mach.* The frame of a plow, to which the handles, share, colter, etc., are secured. See PLOW, *Illust.* **17.** *Cards & Dominoes.* That portion of a pack of cards or set of dominoes not distributed to the players at the beginning of certain games. **18.** *Finance.* **a** The part of a tally formerly given to the creditor in a transaction. **b** The debt or fund represented by such a stock or a series of them; hence, a debt or fund due to individuals for money loaned at interest, or the securities representing such debt or fund. **c** *Chiefly U. S.* Shares or holdings, collectively, in a corporate business enterprise, attested by certificates of ownership. The aggregate par value of all shares outstanding constitutes the capital stock of the company. Certificates bearing no face value are called ***no-par stock***. *Stock* in the U. S. corresponds to *share* in English usage. See CAPITAL STOCK, COMMON STOCK, PREFERRED STOCK. **19.** *Firearms.* **a** In portable firearms, the wooden part to which the barrel and other parts are secured. **b** In rapid-fire guns, the connecting arm between the slide and the shoulder piece. **c** In field-gun carriages, the long beam which forms the basis of the carriage body. In modern field-gun carriages it is called the *trail*. See TRAIL, *n.*, 4 **b**. **20.** *Hort.* The stem or plant in which a graft is inserted; also, any plant from which slips or cuttings are taken. See GRAFTAGE, *Illust.* **21.** *Joinery.* The block of wood or metal frame which constitutes the body of a plane, and in which the plane iron is fitted. See PLANE, *Illust.* **22.** *Mach.* A holder for a threading die for cutting screw threads on bolts, etc. See DIE, *Illust.* **23.** *Naut.* The crosspiece of an anchor. See ANCHOR, *Illust.* **24.** *Theater.* A stock company; also, the plays collectively presented by one. **25.** *Zool.* A compound organism; an aggregate or colony of connected zooids. — **Syn.** See SOUP.

— *v. t.* **1.** *Obs. exc. Hist.* To put in the stocks, as a culprit. **2.** To provide with a stock, as a rifle; to secure by or to a stock; as, two plows *stocked* to one frame. **3.** To provide with stock; as, to *stock* a farm. **4.** To keep on hand, as for sale. — *v. i.* **1.** To send out new shoots, as from the crown of a plant. **2.** To put in stock, or supplies.

— *adj.* **1.** Used or employed for constant service; kept in stock; as, a *stock* size. **2.** Of a nature suggesting something regularly kept in stock; of topics, arguments, etc., continually repeated; as, a *stock* answer; hence, trite; banal. **3.** Employed in handling, checking, or taking care of the stock; as, a *stock* clerk. **4.** Of or pert. to a stock company; as, *stock* plays; *stock* actors. **5.** Kept for breeding purposes; as, a *stock* mare; also, devoted to the breeding of livestock; as, a *stock* farm.

— *adv. Colloq.* In the manner of a stock or wooden block; as, he stood *stock*-still.

stock·ade′ (stŏk·ād′), *n.* [F. *estacade* stockade, boom, fr. Pr. *estacado*, fr. *estaca* stake, pile, of Teut. origin.] **1.** *Mil.* A line of stout posts set to form a defense. **2.** An enclosure, or pen, made with posts and stakes. — *v. t.* To surround, fortify, or protect, with a stockade.

stock′bro′ker (stŏk′brō′kẽr), *n.* *Stock Exchange.* One who executes orders to buy and sell securities. — **stock′bro′ker·age** (-ĭj), *n.* — **stock′bro′king,** *n.*

stock certificate. = CERTIFICATE OF STOCK.

stock company. **1.** *Finance.* A corporation or joint-stock company, the capital of which is represented by stock. **2.** *Theater.* A company organized to present a repertory and composed of the stock types of actors without a star.

stock dove. A European wild pigeon (*Columba oenas*).

stock exchange. **a** A place where security trading is conducted on an organized system. **b** An association of stockbrokers who meet and transact business according to recognized forms and regulations.

stock farm. A farm chiefly devoted to the rearing of livestock, esp. beef cattle, horses, sheep, and hogs. — **stock farmer.** — **stock farming.**

stock′fish′ (stŏk′fĭsh′), *n.* Fish dried hard in the open air, without salt, esp. cod, haddock, hake, etc.

stock′hold′er (-hōl′dẽr), *n.* One who is a holder or proprietor of stock or stocks.

stock′i·net′ (stŏk′ĭ·nĕt′), *n.* An elastic knitted textile fabric used for stockings, undergarments, etc.

stock′ing (stŏk′ĭng), *n.* [From STOCK, *n.*, 13.] **1.** A close-fitting covering for the foot and leg, usually knit or woven. Cf. SOCK, 2. **2.** Any of various things resembling such covering. — **stock′ing·less,** *adj.*

stocking cap. A long, knitted, cone-shaped cap with a tassel or pompon at the apex, worn chiefly for sports or by children.

stock in trade. **a** The goods kept for sale by a shopkeeper. **b** The aggregate of things necessary to carry on a business.

stock′ish (stŏk′ĭsh), *adj.* Like a stock; stupid.

stock′job′ber (stŏk′jŏb′ẽr), *n.* *Stock Exchange.* One who deals in stocks: **a** *London Stock Exchange.* A member of the exchange who deals with other brokers, but not with the public. **b** *U. S.* A stockbroker; — often derogatory. — **stock′job′ber·y** (-ĭ), *n.* — **stock′job′bing,** *n.*

stock′man (-măn), *n.; pl.* -MEN (-mĕn). **1.** One who keeps records of, or works on, stock. **2.** *Australia & U. S.* One owning, or in charge of, livestock; a ranchman, herder, etc.

stock market. **a** A stock exchange. **b** The business of buying and selling which goes on in such a place. **c** The course of prices on the stock exchange.

stock′pile′ (stŏk′pīl′), *n.* A storage pile; specif., a reserve supply of an essential raw material, processed food, or the like, accumulated within a country for use during a war-induced shortage. — *v. t. & i.;* STOCK′PILED′ (-pīld′); STOCK′PIL′ING (-pīl′ĭng). To accumulate a stockpile (of).

stock′pot′ (stŏk′pŏt′), *n.* A pot in which soup (stock) is prepared; hence, a receptacle containing a mixture of materials.

stock raising. The rearing of livestock, esp. beef cattle, horses, sheep, and hogs. — **stock raiser.**

stock room. A storage place for supplies or goods used in a business.

stock′–still′ (stŏk′stĭl′; 2), *adj.* Still as a stock, or fixed post.

stock′y (stŏk′ĭ), *adj.;* STOCK′I·ER (-ĭ·ẽr); STOCK′I·EST. Short and thick; thickset; sturdy. — **stock′i·ly,** *adv.* — **stock′i·ness,** *n.*

stock′yard′ (stŏk′yärd′), *n.* A yard for stock; specif., one where cattle, sheep, swine, and horses are kept temporarily for slaughter, market, or shipping.

stodge (stŏj), *v. t. & i.* To stuff full, as with food; surfeit.

stodg′y (stŏj′ĭ), *adj.;* STODG′I·ER (-ĭ·ẽr); STODG′I·EST. **1.** Satiating; said of food. **2.** Stuffed; crammed; hence: **a** Short and thickset. **b** Lumpish; dull; lacking lightness and vivacity; uninspired. — **stodg′i·ly,** *adv.* — **stodg′i·ness,** *n.*

stoe′chi·ol′o·gy (stē′kĭ·ŏl′ō·jĭ), **stoe′chi·om′e·try.** Vars. of STOICHIOLOGY, STOICHIOMETRY.

sto′gie, sto′gy (stō′gĭ), *n.* [From Cones*toga* wagon, whose drivers wore heavy boots and were fond of coarse cigars.] **1.** A stout coarse boot or shoe; a brogan. **2.** A type of inexpensive, though not necessarily inferior, coarse slender cylindrical cigar.

Sto′ic (stō′ĭk), *n.* [L. *stoicus*, fr. Gr. *stōikos*, fr. *stōikos*, adj., lit., of or pert. to a colonnade, fr. *stoa* a roofed colonnade, a porch, esp., a porch in Athens where the Stoics taught.] **1.** A member of the school of philosophy founded by Zeno about 308 B.C. The Stoics taught that the wise man should be free from passion, unsubdued by joy or grief, willingly submissive to natural law. **2.** [*not cap.*] One apparently or professedly indifferent to pleasure or pain.

sto′ic (stō′ĭk), *adj.* Also **sto′i·cal** (-ĭ·kăl). **1.** [*cap.*] Of, pert. to, or resembling the Stoics or their doctrines. **2.** Not affected by passion or feeling; esp., manifesting indifference to pleasure or pain. — **Syn.** See IMPASSIVE. — **sto′i·cal·ly,** *adv.* — **sto′i·cal·ness,** *n.*

stoi′chi·ol′o·gy (stoi′kĭ·ŏl′ō·jĭ), *n.* Also **stoi′chei·ol′o·gy** (stoi′kī-), **stoe′chi·ol′o·gy** (stē′kĭ-). [Gr. *stoicheion* a first element + *-logy*.] Physiology which treats of the elements composing animal tissues.

stoi′chi·om′e·try (-ŏm′ē·trĭ), *n.* Also **stoi′chei·om′e·try, stoe′chi·om′e·try.** [Gr. *stoicheion* a first principle, or element + *-metry*.] *Chem.* **a** Calculation of the combining weights, etc., of the elements. **b** The branch treating of the laws of chemical combination and of the relations between the properties of substances and their composition. — **stoi′chi·o·met′ric** (-ō·mĕt′rĭk), **stoi′chi·o·met′ri·cal** (-rĭ·kăl), *adj.*

Sto′i·cism (stō′ĭ·sĭz′m), *n.* **1.** The opinions, maxims, or philosophical system, of the Stoics. **2.** [*not cap.*] The principle or practice of showing indifference to pleasure or pain; impassiveness.

stoit (stōt; stoit), **stoit′er** (-ẽr), *n. & v. i.* *Scot.* Stagger; lurch.

stoke (stōk), *v. t.* [OF. *estoquier* to thrust, stab, of Teut. origin.] To poke or stir up, as a fire; hence, to tend, as a furnace, boiler, etc.; to supply with fuel. — *v. i.* To stir up a fire; hence, to tend the fires of furnaces.

stoke′hold′ (-hōld′), *n.* *Naut.* The space in front of the boilers of a ship, from which the furnaces are fed; also, a room containing a ship's boilers.

stoke′hole′ (-hōl′), *n.* A stokehold; also, the opening into a furnace.

stok′er (stōk′ẽr), *n.* [D. See STOKE, *v.*] One employed to tend a furnace, esp. of a marine steam boiler; also, a machine for feeding a fire.

sto·ke′si·a (stō·kē′zhĭ·ȧ; -sĭ·ȧ), *n.* [NL., after Jonathan *Stokes*, Eng. botanist.] Any of a genus (*Stokesia*) of perennial herbs of the aster family (Carduaceae) of the southern United States. The only known species (*S. laevis*), known as **Stokes's as′ter** (stōk′sĭz), has large asterlike heads of blue flowers.

stole (stōl), *n.* [AS. *stole*, fr. L. *stola*, fr. Gr. *stolē* a garment.] **1.** A long loose garment reaching to the feet. **2.** *Eccl.* A vestment, consisting of a long narrow band worn around the neck and falling from the shoulders, of bishops and priests. See VESTMENT, *Illust.* **3.** A woman's long fur or cloth garment for the neck and shoulders.

stole. Past & archaic & dial. past part. of STEAL.

sto′len (stō′lĕn), *past part.* of STEAL.

stol′id (stŏl′ĭd), *adj.* [L. *stolidus*.] Dull; not easily excited; impassive. — **Syn.** See IMPASSIVE. — **sto·lid′i·ty** (stō·lĭd′ĭ·tĭ), *n.* — **stol′id·ly,** *adv.* — **stol′id·ness,** *n.*

sto′lon (stō′lŏn), *n.* [L. *stolo, -onis*.] **1.** *Bot.* **a** A slender branch or shoot developing a bud and root at the tip or at both node and tip. **b** A runner or rootstock used to propagate certain grasses; — usually *pl.* **2.** *Zool.* An extension of the body wall, from which buds are developed, giving rise to new zooids which usually remain united.

sto′lo·nif′er·ous (stō′lō·nĭf′ẽr·ŭs; stŏl′ō-), *adj.* *Bot. & Zool.* Bearing or developing stolons.

sto′ma (stō′mȧ), *n.; pl.* STOMATA (stō′mȧ·tȧ; stŏm′ȧ-). [NL., fr. Gr. *stoma, -atos*, a mouth.] *Biol.* Any of various small mouthlike openings, esp. in the lower animals or in the epidermis of plants.

stom′ach (stŭm′ăk), *n.* [OF. *estomac*, fr. L. *stomachus* gullet, liking, vexation, fr. Gr. *stomachos* stomach, throat, gullet, fr. *stoma* mouth.] **1. a** In man and most vertebrates, the saclike dilation of the alimentary canal beyond the esophagus, or gullet, in which the earlier stages of digestion take place. **b** In invertebrates, any digestive cavity. **2.** Hence, appetite in general; inclination; desire; as, he had no *stomach* for further fighting. **3.** Particular disposition or mental attitude; as: **a** Temper; spirit. **b** *Obs.* Pride; arrogance. *Shak.* **c** *Obs.* Anger; resentment. **4.** The belly; abdomen; — a common but erroneous use. — *v. t.;* STOM′ACHED (stŭm′ăkt); STOM′ACH·ING. **1.** To resent; to take offense at. **2.** To bear without overt resentment; to brook; to put up with; as, he could not *stomach* criticism.

stom′ach–ache′ (-āk′), *n.* Pain in the stomach.

stom′ach·er (stŭm′ăk·ẽr), *n.* An ornamental covering for the front of the upper body, formerly worn by both men and women.

sto·mach′ic (stō·măk′ĭk), *adj.* Also **sto·mach′i·cal** (-ĭ·kăl). **1.** Of or pertaining to the stomach. **2.** Strengthening to the stomach. — *n. Med.* A stomachic tonic. Cf. CARDIAC, *n.*

stomach tooth. A lower canine, esp. of the first dentition. Its appearance is often attended with gastric disturbance.

stom′ach·y (stŭm′ăk·ĭ), *adj.* *Dial. Eng.* **a** Spirited; obstinate. **b** Irritable. **c** Having a paunch.

sto′ma·ta (stō′mȧ·tȧ; stŏm′ȧ-), *n., pl.* of STOMA.

stom′a·tal (stŏm′ȧ·tăl; stō′mȧ-), *adj.* *Bot. & Zool.* Pertaining to, or of the nature of, a stoma.

sto·mat′ic (stō·măt′ĭk), *adj.* **1.** Of or pert. to the mouth. **2.** *Bot.* Pert. to, or of the nature of, a stoma.

sto′ma·ti′tis (stō′mȧ·tī′tĭs; stŏm′ȧ-), *n.* [NL., fr. *stomat-* + *-itis*.] *Med.* Inflammation of the mouth, as thrush.

stom′a·to- (stŏm′ȧ·tō-; stō′mȧ·tō-), **stomat-.** [Gr. *stoma, stomatos*.] A combining form meaning *mouth*, as in *stomat*itis, and the following: **sto·mat′o·my, stom′a·to·plas′ty, stom′a·to·sep′sis** (see -TOMY, etc.).

sto′ma·tol′o·gy (stō′mȧ·tŏl′ō·jĭ; stŏm′ȧ-), *n.* [*stomato-* + *-logy*.] *Med.* Science of the mouth and its diseases.

stom′a·to·pod′ (stŏm′ȧ·tō·pŏd′; stō′mȧ-), *n.* *Zool.* Any of an order (Stomatopoda) of malacostracan, marine crustaceans including the squillas, having the gills on the appendages of the abdomen. They live in holes in shallow water.

stom′a·tous (stŏm′ȧ·tŭs; stō′mȧ-), *adj.* Having stomata or a stoma.

-stom′a·tous (-stŏm′ȧ·tŭs; -stō′mȧ-). = -STOMOUS.

-stome (-stōm). [Gr. *stoma*.] A combining form signifying *mouth*, *mouthlike aperture*.

sto′mo·dae′um, sto′mo·de′um (stō′mō·dē′ŭm; stŏm′ō-), *n.; pl.*

-DAEA (-*à*). [NL., fr. Gr. *stoma, -atos,* mouth + *hodaios* on the way.] *Embryol. & Zool.* The anterior or oral part of the alimentary canal or tract. Cf. MESENTERON, PROCTODAEUM. — **sto′mo·dae′al, sto′mo·de′al** (stō′mō·dē′ăl; stŏm′ō-), *adj.*

-stomous. [Gr. *stoma* mouth.] A combining form meaning *-mouthed,* denoting *having a* (specified) *type of mouth.*

stomp (stŏmp). Dial. var. of STAMP, STUMP.

-stomy. [Gr. *stoma* mouth.] A combining form (*Surg.*) denoting *an operation establishing an artificial opening, usually permanent* (into some part or parts), as in gastro*stomy*, ileo*stomy*.

stone (stōn), *n.* [ME. *ston, stan,* fr. AS. *stān.*] **1.** Concreted earthy or mineral matter: **a** A small piece of rock. **b** Rock or rocklike matter as a material, esp. for building. **2.** A specific piece of rock; as: **a** A block of stone set up, as for a boundary mark, etc.; esp., a gravestone. **b** A grindstone; also, a whetstone. **3.** Something resembling a small stone; as: **a** A hailstone. **b** A testicle. **4.** A precious stone; a gem. **5.** *pl.* STONE. A varying unit of weight, now legally 14 lb. in Great Britain. See WEIGHT, *Table* 1. **6.** *Bot.* The hard endocarp of a drupaceous fruit, as of a peach; hence, popularly, any hard, stonelike seed. See ENDOCARP, *Illust.* **7.** *Lithography.* The surface upon which the drawing or design to be printed is drawn; specif., a fine-grained yellowish or grayish limestone so used. **8.** *Med.* A concretion (def. 2 **a**) or calculus, esp. one in the kidney, bladder, or gall bladder. **9.** *Print.* A stand or table with a smooth, flat top, originally of stone, on which to impose type; — called also *imposing stone.* — *v. t.* **1. a** To pelt with stones. **b** To pelt to death with stones. **2.** *Obs.* To make like stone; to harden. **3.** To remove the stones or seeds of. **4.** To wall, face, line, or fortify with stones. — *adj.* Pertaining to, or consisting or made of stone or stoneware.

Stone Age. The first known period of human culture characterized by the use of stone tools and preceding the Age of Bronze; — now generally divided into the paleolithic, the eolithic, and the neolithic periods. See AGE, *n.*, 6.

stone′-blind′ (*see Pron.*, § 2), *adj.* As blind as a stone; totally blind.

stone′-broke′, *adj. Slang.* Utterly broke; penniless.

stone bruise. A sore spot on the bottom of the foot without laceration, caused by a bruise from a stone or rounded object.

stone′chat′ (stōn′chăt′), *n.* A common European singing bird (*Saxicola torquata*). See CHAT, *n.*, 3.

stone′crop′ (-krŏp′), *n.* [AS. *stāncropp.*] Any of a genus (*Sedum,* esp. *S. acre,* the common stonecrop) of mosslike plants with pungent fleshy leaves and yellow flowers; also, any of various other plants of the orpine family.

stone′cut′ter (-kŭt′ẽr), *n.* **a** One who cuts or dresses stone. **b** A machine for dressing stone. — **stone′cut′ting,** *n.*

stone′-deaf′, *adj.* As deaf as a stone; totally deaf.

stone fly. Any insect of the order Plecoptera. The larvae are aquatic, furnished with tracheal gills, and are carnivorous. The adults are used by anglers for bait.

stone fruit. Any fruit with a stony endocarp; a drupe.

stone lily. A fossil crinoid.

stone′ma′son (stōn′mā′s'n), *n., or* **stone mason.** A mason who works or builds in stone. — **stone′ma′son·ry** (-rĭ), *n.*

stone parsley. A slender herb (*Sison amomum*) of the carrot family, having aromatic seeds used as a condiment.

ston′er (stōn′ẽr), *n.* One who or that which stones.

stone roller. a An American fresh-water fish (*Hypentelium nigricans*) of the sucker family. **b** A common American fish (*Campostoma anomalum*) of the carp family.

stone′wall′ (stōn′wôl′), *v. i.* **1.** *Cricket.* To play entirely on the defensive; — said of a batsman. **2.** *Polit. Cant, Australia.* To engage in obstructive tactics. — **stone′wall′er** (-ẽr), *n.*

stone′ware′ (-wâr′), *n.* Low-grade rough-textured ceramic ware made impermeable to liquids by a high degree of vitrification and usually glazed with salt or other vitreous materials.

stone′work′ (-wûrk′), *n.* **1.** Any work concerned with the shaping, setting, etc., of stone, as in masonry, jewelry, etc.; also, the resulting work. **2.** *pl.* An establishment where stones are cut, esp. for masonry; also, one where stoneware is made. — **stone′work′er** (-wûr′kẽr), *n.*

stone′wort′ (-wûrt′), *n.* Any of a family (Characeae) of chlorophyll-bearing submersed thallophytes having jointed stems with whorls of leaves at the nodes.

ston′ish (stŏn′ĭsh), **ston′ish·ment** (-mĕnt), etc. *Now Dial.* Aphetic for ASTONISH, etc.

ston′y (stōn′ĭ), *adj.;* STON′I·ER (-ĭ·ẽr); STON′I·EST. **1.** Abounding in stone or stones. **2.** *Archaic & Poetic.* Consisting or made of stone. **3.** Pert. to, like, or characteristic of stone. Hence, inflexible; pitiless; also, appearing as if petrified; still, cold, and rigid. **4.** Petrifying; stupefying. **5.** *Slang.* Stone-broke; without money. — **ston′i·ly,** *adv.* — **ston′i·ness,** *n.*

ston′y-broke′, *adj. Slang.* Stone-broke; penniless.

stony coral. Any coral with hard calcareous skeleton.

ston′y·heart′ed (stōn′ĭ·här′tĕd; -tĭd; 2), *adj.* Unfeeling; cruel; pitiless; merciless.

stood (stŏŏd), *past & past part.* of STAND.

stooge (stōōj), *n. Slang.* **a** Orig., in vaudeville, an actor who from a seat in the audience heckled or baited the chief comedian on the stage; hence, any actor whose main function is to feed lines to the chief comedian. **b** Any person who plays a subordinate role to some principal. — *v. i.* To act as a stooge.

stook (stŏŏk), *n. Brit.* A shock of corn.

stool (stōōl), *n.* [AS. *stōl* a seat.] **1.** A single seat without a back. **2.** A bench for the feet or the knees; a footstool; as, a kneeling *stool.* **3.** A seat used in evacuating the bowels; hence, a discharge from the bowels; also, fecal matter. **4.** [Dial. *stool* a stump, esp. one from which young shoots spring.] **a** A tree stump, or group of stumps, esp. one giving rise to shoots; hence, a base or stock from which shoots, layers, stalks, leaves, etc., are thrown out. **b** A stand, or growth, of plants with developing stems or shoots. **5. a** A pole or the like to which a bird, as a pigeon, is fastened as a decoy. **b** *U. S.* The bird thus fastened; a stool pigeon; also, a decoy. — *v. i.* **1.** To form a stool; to throw out shoots after the manner of a stool. **2.** To evacuate the bowels.

stool pigeon. a A pigeon used as a decoy to draw others within a net. **b** Hence, a person used as a decoy; esp., a spy used by the police; an informer.

stoop (stōōp), *n.* [ON. *stolpi.*] *Dial.* Post or pillar.

stoop, *v. i.* [AS. *stūpian.*] **1. a** To bend forward and downward. **b** Specif., to assume habitually a bent position, as a forward inclination of head and shoulders. **2.** To lower oneself, as in dignity or conduct; to condescend; as, to *stoop* to flattery. **3.** To yield; submit; to assume a position of humility or subjection. **4. a** To sink down; alight. **b** To pounce; swoop.

Syn. Stoop, condescend, deign mean to descend below one's level in order to do something. **Stoop** implies a descent not only in rank or dignity but often from a relatively high moral plane to a much lower one; **condescend,** a stooping, by one actually exalted, to accommodate himself to intercourse with his inferiors; **deign,** a reluctant or unwilling condescension, esp. when in a haughty frame of mind.

— *v. t.* **1.** To bend forward and downward. **2.** *Rare.* To prostrate; to subject.

— *n.* **1. a** Act of stooping. **b** A habitual forward bend of the back and shoulders. **2.** Descent, as from dignity or superiority; condescension; an act or position of submission, concession, etc. **3.** The descent of a bird on its prey; swoop.

stoop, *n.* [D. *stoep.*] *U. S.* Orig., a covered porch with seats, at a house door; hence, any porch; veranda.

stoop. Var. of STOUP; obs. var. of STUPE.

stop (stŏp; 73), *v. t.;* STOPPED (stŏpt) or, *Chiefly Poetic,* STOPT; STOP′PING. [AS. *stoppian* (in comp.).] **1.** To close, as an aperture, by filling or obstructing; hence: **a** To stanch, as a wound. **b** To obstruct; to render impassable. **c** To fill up, as a crack in a wall. **2.** To cause to cease; to suppress; check; hold back. **3.** To arrest the progress or action of; intercept; as, to *stop* a train; also, to withhold; as, the firm *stopped* his pay. **4.** Specif.: **a** To check by deadly means, as rifle fire, etc.; hence, kill. **b** To parry, as a blow. **c** To instruct one's banker not to honor or pay; as, to *stop* a check. **5.** *Bridge.* To hold an honor card and enough protecting cards in (a suit) to block the suit before an opponent can run off too many tricks in it. **6.** *Exchanges.* To place a stop order on; as, he *stopped* the stock a point below the previous close. See STOP ORDER. **7.** *Music.* To regulate the pitch of, as a violin string, by pressing it with the finger, or a wind instrument tube, by closing one or more finger holes. **8.** *Rhet.* To punctuate. — *v. i.* **1.** To cease to go on; to halt. **2.** To cease activity or operation. **3.** *Colloq.* To stay; tarry. **4.** To become choked; to clog, as a pipe.

Syn. Stop, cease, quit, discontinue, desist mean to suspend or cause to suspend activity. **Stop** applies primarily to action or progress or to that which is thought of as moving or progressing; **cease** applies to that which is thought of as being, or as having existence (as, one *stops* a car, but *ceases* driving a car); **quit** is an Americanism for *stop* or *cease;* **discontinue** applies to any activity, such as an occupation or employment (as, to *discontinue* the practice of law); **desist** implies forbearance or restraint as the motive for stopping (as, he *desisted* from further questioning).

— *n.* **1.** Act of stopping, or state of being stopped; check; obstruction. **2.** An end; finish. **3.** A stay; sojourn. **4.** Hence, a stopping place; also, an inn. **5.** An obstacle; obstruction; specif., a plug; stopper. **6.** An order stopping payment of a check, or the like. **7.** In telegrams, cables, etc., a word used to indicate a punctuation point, esp. a period. **8.** *Exchanges.* A stop order. See STOP ORDER. **9.** *Mach.* A device for arresting or limiting motion. **10.** *Music.* **a** The closing of an aperture in the air passage, or pressure of the finger upon a string, of an instrument, so as to alter the pitch of its tone; hence, any contrivance by which the pitch of an instrument is so regulated. **b** A graduated set of organ pipes of like kind and tone quality. A ***complete stop*** has one pipe at least for each digital; a ***partial stop*** has pipes for only part of its keyboard compass; a ***mixture stop*** has more than one pipe to each digital. An 8-*foot stop* (so called from the approximate length of an open pipe sounding the lowest C on the manuals) sounds pitches corresponding with the notation; a 16-*foot stop* and a 32-*foot stop* sound pitches an octave and two octaves lower, respectively; a 4-*foot stop* and a 2-*foot stop,* an octave and two octaves higher. **c** A corresponding set of reeds of a reed organ. **d** In full, **stop knob.** In an organ, one of the handles by which the player draws or shuts off a particular stop, or controls a coupler, etc. **11.** *Naut.* A piece of small line, or the like, used to bind or secure something; as, to secure a furled sail with *stops.* **12.** *Phonet.* Complete stoppage of the breath passage by the raised velum and the lips or the tongue, or by the closed glottis; a consonant so formed (*p, b, t, d, k, g*), or the glottal stop. By some are also included the nasals, *m, n, ng,* formed by oral, without nasal, closure. Opposed to *continuant.* **13.** *Photog.* The aperture of a lens, usually adjustable by a diaphragm. **14.** *Punctuation.* One of the marks of punctuation indicating a break, pause, or transition in the sentence; esp., a period.

stop′cock′ (stŏp′kŏk′), *n.* A cock or valve for stopping or regulating the flow through a pipe, etc.

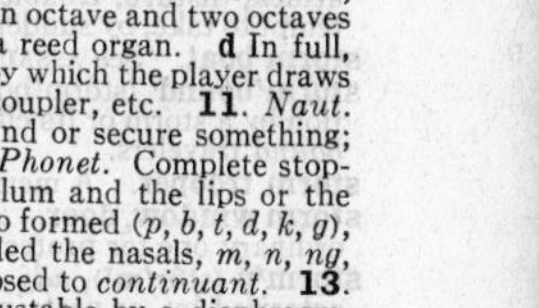
Stopcocks.

stope (stōp), *n. Mining.* An excavation underground for the removal of ore, formed by mining the ore from a block of ground. — *v. t. & i. Mining.* To extract (ore) from a stope.

stop′gap′ (stŏp′găp′), *n.* That which closes or fills up an opening or gap; hence, a temporary expedient. — **Syn.** See RESOURCE.

stop light. 1. A traffic light, usually red, giving a signal to stop. **2.** A light on the rear of a motor vehicle illuminated when the vehicle's foot brake pedal is depressed.

stop′-loss′, *adj.* Designed to prevent further loss.

stop order. Also **stop-loss order.** *Exchanges.* A limited order which becomes an order to sell or buy at the market whenever a designated quotation is reached.

stop′o′ver (stŏp′ō′vẽr), *n.* A stop at an intermediate point in one's journey; also, a place so stopped at.

stop′page (stŏp′ĭj), *n.* Act of stopping, or arresting motion, progress, or action; also, state of being stopped; a halt; obstruction.

stop payment. *Banking.* A depositor's order to a bank to refuse to honor a specified check drawn by him.

stopped (stŏpt), *adj.* **1.** Closed; obstructed. **2.** Checked; barred. **3.** Spoken or written with a stop. **4.** *Music.* **a** Of an organ pipe, closed at the top and producing thereby a pitch approximately an octave lower than that of an open pipe of the same length. **b** Obtained by stopping a string, pipe, finger hole, etc., of an instrument.

stop′per (stŏp′ẽr), *n.* One that stops or closes, as a cork, plug, etc. — *v. t.* To close or secure with a stopper.

stop'ple (stŏp''l), *n.* [ME. *stoppel.*] A stopper. — *v. t.; -*PLED (-'ld); -PLING (-lĭng). To stopper.

stop watch. A watch having a hand or hands that can be started or stopped at will, for exact timing, as of a race.

stor'age (stōr'ĭj; 70), *n.* **1.** Act of storing, or state of being stored; specif., the safekeeping of goods in a warehouse or other depository. **2.** Space, or a place, for the safekeeping of goods. **3.** The price charged for keeping goods in a storehouse. **4.** *Elec.* The production, by means of electric energy, of certain chemical reactions which, when allowed to reverse themselves, generate electricity again without serious loss.

storage battery. *Elec.* A connected group of electrochemical cells for the generation of electrical energy in which the cells after being discharged may be restored to a charged condition by passing a current through them in a direction opposite to the flow of current on discharge.

storage cell. *Elec.* A secondary cell.

sto'rax (stō'răks; 70), *n.* [L. *storax, styrax*, fr. Gr. *styrax.*] **1.** Any tree of the genus *Styrax*, typical of a family (Styracaceae, the storax family) of shrubs and trees bearing flowers with a 5-lobed corolla and ten stamens, and a dry or drupaceous fruit. **2.** A resin derived from various trees of the storax family (esp. *Styrax officinalis*). **3.** A fragrant balsam obtained from the bark of an Asiatic tree (*Liquidambar orientalis*) used as an expectorant and in perfumery.

store (stōr; 70), *v. t.* [OF. *estorer* to construct, restore, store, fr. L. *instaurare* to renew, restore.] **1.** To furnish; provide, esp. for a future time or need. **2.** To accumulate; to lay away. **3.** To deposit in a store, warehouse, etc., for preservation. — *n.* **1.** Orig., that which is stored for future use; now, *pl.*, articles, esp. of food, accumulated for some specific object; supplies, as of provisions, arms, etc. **2.** That which is accumulated; a source from which supplies may be drawn; a reserve fund. **3.** An abundance; a great quantity. **4.** A storehouse; warehouse. **5.** *U. S., Can., etc.* Any place where goods are kept for sale; a shop. — ***in store.*** In the position of being accumulated; in readiness for use; as, I have a surprise *in store* for you.

store'house' (-hous'), *n.* A building for storing goods, esp. provisions; magazine; warehouse; store.

store'keep'er (-kēp'ẽr), *n.* **1.** One in charge of stores, esp. military stores. **2.** One who keeps a store, or shop.

store'room' (-rōōm'), *n.* A room for storing supplies.

sto'rey (stō'rĭ). Var. of STORY (of a building).

sto'ried (stō'rĭd; 70), *adj.* **1.** Adorned with designs representing scenes from story or history. **2.** Having a history; celebrated in story or history.

sto'ried, *adj.* Having stories; — often in combination; as, a three-*storied* house.

sto'ri·ette' (stō'rĭ·ĕt'; 70), *n.* [*story* + *-ette.*] A brief story or tale.

stork (stôrk), *n.* [AS. *storc.*] Any of various large, mostly Old World, wading birds (family Ciconiidae) having a long, stout bill, allied to the ibises and herons. The common European ***white stork*** (*Ciconia ciconia*) is white with black wing quills and greater coverts.

stork's'-bill' (stôrks'bĭl'), *n.* See GERANIUM, 2.

storm (stôrm), *n.* [AS.] **1.** A disturbance of the atmosphere, attended by wind, rain, snow, hail, sleet, or thunder and lightning; hence, often, a heavy fall of rain, snow, or hail. **2.** A shower or furious flight of objects, esp. of missiles violently thrown; as, a *storm* of arrows. **3.** A civil, political, economic, social, or domestic commotion or tumult; violence. **4.** A vehement outburst, as of passion, excitement, etc. **5.** *Mil.* A determined assault on a fortified place. **6.** *Naut.* On one (Beaufort's) wind scale, a wind of velocity between 64 and 75 miles per hour. — *v. i.* **1.** To blow with violence; also, to rain, hail, snow, etc. **2.** To rage; to be angry. **3.** To rush about or move impetuously, violently, etc.; as, the mob *stormed* through the streets. — *v. t.* To attack, disturb, trouble, as with a tempest; *Mil.*, to attack, and attempt to take, by sudden assault. — **Syn.** See ATTACK. — **storm'er,** *n.*

storm boat. See ASSAULT BOAT.

storm'bound' (stôrm'bound'), *adj.* Cut off from outside communication by a storm or its effects; stopped or delayed by storms; as, *stormbound* travelers.

storm trooper. A member of the Sturmabteilung.

storm window, door. An additional window (door) placed outside the ordinary one for protection against severe weather.

storm'y (stôr'mĭ), *adj.; STORM'I·ER* (-mĭ·ẽr); STORM'I·EST. **1.** Characterized by, or pertaining to, a storm; tempestuous. **2.** Turbulent; violent. — **storm'i·ly,** *adv.* — **storm'i·ness,** *n.*

stormy petrel. **a** Any of certain small petrels (esp. ***Hydrobates pelagicus***, a small sooty-black bird marked with white on wing coverts and tail coverts) which frequent the north Atlantic and Mediterranean. **b** A harbinger of trouble; — from the belief that the petrel is active before a storm.

Stor'ting', Stor'thing' (stōr'tĭng'; 70), *n.* [Nor. *storting*, fr. *stor* great + *ting* assembly, court.] The Parliament of Norway.

sto'ry (stō'rĭ), *n.; pl.* -RIES (-rĭz). [Appar. same as 2d STORY; perh. orig. applied to a tier of pointed windows or of sculptures.] A set of rooms on the same floor or level; a floor, or the habitable space between two floors. Also, a horizontal division of a building's exterior, considered architecturally and not necessarily corresponding exactly with the stories within. See FLOOR.

sto'ry, *n.* [OF. *estoire*, fr. L. *historia*. See HISTORY.] **1.** *Archaic.* **a** A connected narration of past events. **b** A history. **2. a** An account of some incident. **b** A report; statement. **c** An anecdote, esp. an amusing one. **3.** In literature: **a** A narrative in either prose or verse; a tale; esp., a fictitious narrative less elaborate than a novel. **b** The plot of a narrative. **4.** *Colloq.* A fib; a lie. **5.** *U. S. Journalism.* Any news article. — *v. t.;* -RIED (-rĭd); -RY·ING. **1.** *Archaic.* To narrate or describe in story. **2.** To adorn with a story, or scene from history, etc.

sto'ry·tell'er (-tĕl'ẽr), *n.* A teller of story or stories. — **sto'ry·tell'ing,** *adj. & n.*

stoss (stōs; *G.* shtōs), *adj.* [G., a thrust.] *Geol.* Facing toward the direction from which an overriding glacier impinged; — said of the side of a hill or a rock.

sto·tin'ka (stō·tĭng'kȧ), *n.; pl.* -KI (-kĭ). [Bulg.] A minor coin denomination of Bulgaria, equal to $\frac{1}{100}$ lev.

stound (stound; stōōn(d)), *n.* [AS. *stund.*] **1.** *Archaic & Dial.* A time, esp. a short time; instant. **2.** *Obs. exc. Dial.* A heavy blow; a twinge; pang; thrill. — *v. i. Scot. & Dial. Eng.* To be in pain; throb; ache.

stoup (stōōp), *n.* [From Scand. and LG.; cf. ON. *staup.*] **1.** A vessel for liquids; specif.: **a** *Scot.* A bucket, pail, or small cask. **b** A drinking vessel. **2.** *Eccl.* A basin at the entrance of Roman Catholic churches for holy water.

stour (stōōr), *n.* [OF. *estour, estor*, tumult, combat.] *Archaic & Dial.* **a** Conflict. **b** Tumult. **c** A storm; a stiff breeze. **d** Dust, esp. in the air; chaff; also, spray; fog.

stout (stout), *adj.* [OF. *estout* bold, strong, proud, foolish, of Teut. origin.] **1.** Strong of character; specif.: **a** Brave; bold. **b** Firm; determined; sometimes, obstinate; uncompromising. **2.** Physically or materially strong; specif.: **a** Sturdy; vigorous. **b** Firm; stanch; enduring. **c** Solid; substantial. **3.** Forceful; as, a *stout* attack; sometimes, violent; as, a *stout* wind. **4.** Having a bulky body; thickset. — **Syn.** See STRONG. — *n.* **1.** A stout person; also, in garment trade, a dress or suit designed for a stout figure. **2.** A malt liquor brewed with malt and roasted malt.

stout'heart'ed (-här'tĕd; -tĭd; 2), *adj.* Having a stout heart or spirit; brave. — **stout'heart'ed·ly,** *adv.*

stout'ly (stout'lĭ), *adv.* In a stout manner.

stout'ness (-nĕs; -nĭs), *n.* Quality or state of being stout.

stove (stōv), *n.* [MD. or MLG.; akin to AS. *stofa* a room for a warm bath.] **1.** An apparatus, often including a metal enclosure, for generating or retaining heat for warming a room, for culinary purposes, for heating tools, etc. **2. a** A kiln, as for firing pottery. **b** A drying room or box used in various manufactures. — **stove'mak'er** (-māk'ẽr), *n.*

stove (stōv), *past & past part.* of STAVE.

stove'pipe' (-pīp'), *n.* **1.** Pipe, or a pipe, of sheet steel, used as a stove chimney or to connect a stove with a flue. **2.** *Colloq., U. S.* Short for **stovepipe hat,** the common tall silk hat.

sto'ver (stō'vẽr), *n.* [ME. See ESTOVERS.] **a** *Now Dial. Eng.* Fodder, esp. for winter, as straw or stubble. **b** The mature cured stalks of grain, from which the ears have been removed, used as feed for livestock.

stow (stō), *v. t.* [ME. *stowen*, fr. *stowe* a place, fr. AS. *stōw.*] **1.** To place or arrange in a compact mass; pack; as, to *stow* freight. **2.** To hide; lodge. **3.** To arrange anything compactly in; as, to *stow* a box. **4.** To hold; to furnish room for. **5.** *Slang.* To put aside; cease; as, *stow* that sort of talk.

stow, *v. t. Scot. & Dial. Eng.* To cut; crop; trim.

stow'age (stō'ĭj), *n.* **1.** Act or method of stowing; also, place in which things may be stowed; capacity for holding goods. **2.** State of being stowed. **3.** That which is stowed. **4.** Money paid for stowing goods.

stow'a·way' (stō'ȧ·wā'), *n.* One who conceals himself on a vessel, train, airship, etc., to obtain a passage.

stown'lins (stoun'lĭnz), *adv. Scot.* By stealth.

stowp (stōp). Scot. & dial. var. of STOUP, a beaker.

stra·bis'mus (strȧ·bĭz'mŭs), *n.* [NL., fr. Gr. *strabismos*, fr. *strabizein* to squint.] *Med.* A visual disorder marked by inability to direct both eyes to the same object, due to in-co-ordination of the muscles of the eyeballs; squint. When the lines of vision converge the condition is known as *cross-eye;* when they diverge, as *walleye.* — **stra·bis'mic** (-mĭk), **stra·bis'mi·cal** (-mĭ·kăl), *adj.*

stra·bot'o·my (-bŏt'ō·mĭ), *n.* *Surg.* The operation of cutting one or more eyeball muscles to cure strabismus.

strad'dle (străd''l), *v. i.;* -DLED (-'ld); -DLING (-lĭng). [Freq., akin to STRIDE.] **1.** To stand, sit, or walk, with the legs wide apart; esp., to sit astride. **2.** Hence, loosely, to sprawl. **3.** *Colloq.* To be noncommittal, or to favor or seem to favor two apparently opposite sides. **4.** *Exchanges.* To buy in one market and sell short in another. — *v. t.* **1.** To stand, sit, or be, astride of. **2.** *Colloq.* To be noncommittal in regard to, or to favor, or seem to favor, both sides of; as, to *straddle* an issue. — *n.* **1.** Act or position of one who straddles. **2.** The distance between the feet or legs of one straddling. **3.** *Colloq.* A noncommittal or equivocal position. **4.** *Exchanges.* **a** An option giving the holder the double privilege of a put and a call. **b** *Produce Exchanges.* The state of being long in one market, and short in another. — **strad'dler** (-lẽr), *n.*

Strad'i·var'i·us (străd'ĭ·vâr'ĭ·ŭs), *n.* A violin made by Antonio Stradivari (1644–1737) of Cremona, Italy.

strafe (strāf; sträf), *v. t.* [From G. phrase *Gott strafe England*, God punish England (1914).] To punish; to shell or bombard fiercely; to subject (a target) to rapid fire, esp. from machine guns in low-flying airplanes. — **strafe,** *n.* — **straf'er** (strāf'ẽr; sträf'-), *n.*

strag'gle (străg''l), *v. i.;* -GLED (-'ld); -GLING (-lĭng). **1.** To wander from the direct course; rove; stray. **2.** To wander off from others of its kind. — **strag'gler** (-lẽr), *n.*

strag'gly (-lĭ), *adj.* Straggling; spread out irregularly.

straight (strāt), *adj.* [ME. *streight, streght*, prop. past part. of *strecchen* to stretch, AS. *streht*, past part. of *streccan* to stretch, extend.] **1.** Having an invariable direction (*Newcomb*); lying evenly throughout its extent (*Euclid*); — said of a line. **2.** Having the general characteristics of a straight line; — opposed to *curved, crooked, curly*, etc. **3.** Direct; uninterrupted; unbroken; specif.: **a** *Slang.* Reliable; as, a *straight* tip. **b** Keeping true to a correct course or method; as, *straight* thinking. **c** *Colloq.* Candid; frank. **4.** Conforming to justice and rectitude; upright. **5.** Properly ordered or arranged; correct. **6.** Unmixed; undiluted; unmodified; as, whisky *straight.* **7.** *Polit. Cant, U. S.* Making no exceptions in one's support of a principle, party, etc.; as, a *straight* Republican; to vote a *straight* ticket. **8.** *Slang, U. S.* Having a fixed price for each regardless of the number sold; as, cigars ten cents *straight.* **9.** *Card Playing.* Composed of cards in a regular sequence, as the ace, king, queen, jack, and ten; as, a *straight* flush (cf. 4th FLUSH). **10.** *Mech.* Having the cylinders arranged in a single straight line; — of a type of internal-combustion engine. — *adv.* In a straight manner, course, line, etc. — *n.* **1.** Something straight; specif.: **a** A straight line. **b** *Slang.* A true statement. **2.** In various games or other contests, a sequence of shots, strokes, etc., resulting in a perfect score. **3.** *Poker, etc.* A straight hand of five cards. **4.** *Racing.* **a** With *the*, the section of a track between the last turn and the winning post; homestretch. **b** In horse racing, first place at the finish; — opposed to *place* and *show.* — *v. t. Chiefly Scot.* To straighten. — **straight'ly,** *adv.* — **straight'ness,** *n.*

straight angle. An angle whose sides lie in the same straight line but extend in opposite directions from the vertex.

straight'-arm', *v. t.* *Amer. Football.* To ward off (an opponent) with the arm held straight.

straight′a·way′ (strāt′ȧ·wā′), *adj.* Straightforward; continuous in direction; proceeding in a straight line. — *n.* A straight course, or a straight part of a course.
straight′edge′ (strāt′ĕj′), *n.* A bar or slip, as of wood or metal, with a straight edge for testing straight lines and surfaces, drawing straight lines, etc.
straight′en (strāt′'n), *v. t. & i.* To make or become straight. — **straight′en·er** (-ẽr), *n.*
straight face. A face giving no evidence of emotion, esp. of amusement. — **straight′–faced′** (-fāst′; 2), *adj.*
straight′–flute′, *adj.* Having straight flutes. See DRILL, *Illust.*
straight′for′ward (strāt′fôr′wẽrd), *adv.* Also **straight′for′wards** (-wẽrdz). In a straightforward manner.
straight′for′ward (-fôr′wẽrd; 2), *adj.* Proceeding in a straight course or manner; hence, honest; frank. — **straight′for′ward·ly,** *adv.* — **straight′for′ward·ness,** *n.*
straight′–line′, *adj.* **1.** *Mech.* Designating a linkage or equivalent device (called ***straight-line motion***) designed to produce or copy motion in a straight line. **2.** *Mach.* Having the principal parts arranged in a straight line, as the steam and air cylinders of a compressor.
straight′–out′ (strāt′out′; 2), *adj.* *Colloq., U.S.* Acting without concealment; hence, thoroughgoing.
straight′way′ (-wā′; 2), *adv.* Immediately; forthwith.
strain (strān), *n.* [AS. *strēon, strion,* gain, acquisition, begetting.] **1.** Orig., begetting; hence, race; stock; family. **2.** **a** Hereditary character or disposition. **b** A trace; streak; as, a *strain* of fanaticism. **3.** *Now Rare.* Sort; kind. **4.** In domestic animals, those which have a common lineage but not distinguishing characters sufficient to constitute a breed. See BREED, *n.*, 1 **b**. **5.** A sustained note or movement; a passage or flight, as of song or of the imagination. **6.** **a** The tenor, burden, tone, manner, style, of a song, poem, speech, book, etc., or of a course of action or conduct; as, he spoke in a noble *strain.* **b** Mood; temper; as, he was in a philosophizing *strain.* **7.** *Hort.* A group of plants differing little if any in morphology, yet physiologically distinct, with some additional quality, esp. a desirable one, as greater yield or vigor. **8.** *Music.* A tune or air.
strain, *v. t.* [OF. *estraindre, estreindre,* fr. L. *stringere* to draw tight.] **1.** To draw tight; to stretch. **2.** To exert to the utmost; as, to *strain* every nerve in running. **3.** To press closely; to hug; — now in phrase *to strain to one's breast.* **4.** **a** To filter. **b** To remove by filtration or the like. **5.** To stretch beyond its proper limit; as, to *strain* the law. **6.** To injure by overexertion; to sprain; as, to *strain* the wrist. **7.** To injure by drawing, stretching, or the exertion of force; as, the gale *strained* the timbers of the ship; also, to overtax (one's strength, emotions, etc.). **8.** *Obs.* To force; constrain. **9.** *Mech.* To cause a change of form or size by the application of external force. — *v. i.* **1.** To make violent efforts; to strive. **2.** To sustain a strain, wrench, or distortion. **3.** To be filtered; to percolate. **4.** To make great difficulty; to balk; as, to *strain* at a gnat.
— *n.* **1.** Act of straining, or state of being strained; specif.: **a** Excessive tension. **b** Excessive exertion. **c** A sprain; wrench. **2.** *Mech.* **a** Deformation or distortion due to stress or force. **b** Sometimes, stress, thrust, or force, generally.
strain′er (strān′ẽr), *n.* One who or that which strains; as: **a** A screen, sieve, filter, etc. **b** Any of various devices for stretching or tightening something.
strain′ing piece *or* **beam.** A short piece of timber in a truss, used to hold in place the ends of struts or rafters. See QUEEN POST, *Illust.*
strait (strāt), *adj.* [OF. *estreit,* fr. L. *strictus* drawn together, close, tight.] **1.** *Archaic.* **a** Narrow. **b** Restricted. **c** Tight; close; constricted. **2.** *Archaic.* Strict; scrupulous; rigid. **3.** **a** Distressful. **b** Straitened; limited as to resources. — *n.* **1.** *Archaic.* A narrow passage. **2.** A (comparatively) narrow passageway connecting two large bodies of water; — often in *pl.* with sing. sense. **3.** *Rare.* A neck of land; isthmus. **4.** A situation of perplexity or distress; — often in *pl.;* as, reduced to great *straits.* — **Syn.** See JUNCTURE. — **strait′ly,** *adv.* — **strait′ness,** *n.*
strait′en (strāt′'n), *v. t.* **1.** To make strait, or narrow; hence, to contract; confine. **2.** **a** *Rare.* To restrict; hamper. **b** To distress or embarrass in means or in condition of life; — chiefly in the *past part.;* as, a man *straitened* in his circumstances; *straitened* circumstances.
strait jacket. A strong tight coat for restraining the violently insane or delirious criminals, etc.
strait′–laced′ (strāt′lāst′; 2), *adj.* **1.** **a** Laced tightly, as stays. **b** Wearing, or bound with, tight stays. **2.** Excessively strict in manners, morals, or opinion.
Straits dollar (strāts). See DOLLAR, 1 **a**.
strake (strāk), *n.* *Shipbuilding.* One breadth of planks or plates along the bottom or sides of a vessel, reaching from the stem to the stern.
stra·mash′ (strȧ·măsh′; străm′ăsh), *n.* *Scot.* Disturbance.
stra·min′e·ous (strȧ·mĭn′ē·ŭs), *adj.* [L. *stramineus,* fr. *stramen* straw.] Of or like straw; also, straw-colored.
stra·mo′ni·um (strȧ·mō′nĭ·ŭm), *n.* Also **stram′o·ny** (străm′ō·nĭ). [NL.] **1.** The thorn apple (*Datura*); esp., the Jimson weed. **2.** *Pharm.* The dried leaves of the Jimson weed, used in medicine, esp. in asthma.
strand (strănd), *n.* [AS.] A shore, esp. of the ocean, a sea, or an arm of the ocean. — *v. t. & i.* **1.** To run, drift, or drive (a ship) on a strand, or aground. **2.** To place in a position, esp. an unfavorable position, which one cannot leave; also, in passive, to be left alone and destitute.
strand, *n.* [OF. *estran,* of Teut. origin.] **1.** Any of the fibers, as of yarn, twisted into a ropelike mass; also, the rope, cable, etc., thus made. **2.** **a** Any of two or more wires twisted together into a single ropelike cable. **b** Hence, any twisted or plaited ropelike structure; as, a *strand* of pearls. — *v. t.* To break a strand of (a rope).
strange (strānj; 46), *adj.;* STRANG′ER (strān′jẽr); STRANG′EST. [OF. *estrange,* fr. L. *extraneus* external, foreign, fr. *extra* on the outside.] **1.** *Archaic.* Of another country; foreign; alien. **2.** Of or pert. to some other kind, character, or place. **3.** Extraordinary, as in size, quantity, etc.; hence, unnatural; queer. **4.** Not before known, heard, or seen; new; unfamiliar. **5.** Reserved; shy. **6.** Unaccustomed; inexperienced. — *adv.* Strangely. — **strange′ly,** *adv.* — **strange′ness,** *n.*
Syn. **Strange, singular, unique, peculiar, eccentric, erratic, odd, queer, quaint, outlandish** mean varying from the usual or ordinary. **Strange** suggests unfamiliarity and may be applied to that which is foreign, unnatural, inexplicable, etc.; **singular** suggests individuality or a puzzling strangeness; **unique,** in loose use, implies singularity and the fact of being without a known parallel; **peculiar,** a marked distinctiveness; **eccentric,** a wide divergence from the beaten track; **erratic,** a capricious eccentricity; **odd,** a departure from the normal or regular; **queer,** a dubious or questionable oddness; **quaint,** an old-fashioned but pleasant oddness; **outlandish,** an uncouth or bizarre oddness.
stran′ger (strān′jẽr), *n.* **1.** One who is strange; specif.: **a** A foreigner. **b** A guest, visitor, or intruder. **c** A person with whom one is unacquainted. **d** One ignorant of, or unfamiliar with, a specified object. **2.** *Law.* One not privy or party to an act, contract, or title; a mere intruder or intermeddler.
stran′gle (străng′g'l), *v. t. & i.;* -GLED (-g'ld); -GLING (-glĭng). [OF. *estrangler,* fr. L. *strangulare,* fr. Gr. *strangalan,* fr. *strangalē* a halter.] **1.** To choke to death by compressing the throat, as with the hand or a rope; to throttle. **2.** To stifle, choke, or suffocate in any manner. **3.** To suppress; repress. — **stran′gler** (-glẽr), *n.*
strangle hold. **a** In wrestling, a hold by which one's opponent is choked. **b** Any force or influence that chokes or suppresses freedom of movement or expression.
stran′gles (străng′g'lz), *n. pl., construed as sing.* An infectious febrile disease of horses, marked by congestion of mucous membranes, etc.
stran′gu·late (străng′gū·lāt), *v. t.* [L. *strangulare, -latum,* to choke.] To compress, choke, or strangle, specif., *Med.,* so as to stop circulation, or prevent the passage of fluid; as, a *strangulated* hernia.
stran′gu·la′tion (-lā′shŭn), *n.* **1.** Act of strangling, or state of being strangled; any abnormal constriction. **2.** *Med.* Inordinate compression or constriction, as of the throat, esp. such as causes a suspension of breathing.
stran′gu·ry (străng′gū·rĭ), *n.* [L. *stranguria,* fr. Gr. *strangouria,* fr. *stranx, strangos,* a drop + *ouron* urine.] *Med.* A painful discharge of urine, drop by drop.
strap (străp), *n.* [Dial. var. of *strop,* fr. ME. *strope, stroppe,* fr. OF. *estrop,* and fr. AS. *stropp,* fr. L. *stroppus, struppus,* fr. Gr. *strophos* band, cord.] **1.** A narrow strip or thong of some flexible material used for securing, wrapping, or holding together things or parts of things. **2.** Something consisting of, serving as, or resembling, a strap (sense 1), as a loop on a boot (a boot strap) a strip of leather for sharpening a razor (a strop), a shoulder strap, etc. — *v. t.;* STRAPPED (străpt); STRAP′PING. **1.** To secure with a strap. **2.** To beat with a strap. **3.** To sharpen (a razor) by rubbing on a strap; to strop. — **strap′per,** *n.*
strap′hang′er (străp′hăng′ẽr), *n.* *Colloq.* A passenger in a streetcar, bus, or train, who clings for support while standing to one of the short straps or similar devices running along the aisle. — **strap′hang′** (-hăng′), *v. i.*
strap·pa′do (stră·pā′dō; -pä′dō), *n.;* *pl.* -DOES (-dōz). [It. *strappata.*] A former torture, consisting in hoisting the subject by a rope and letting him fall to the length of the rope; also, the machine used in the infliction of this torture.
strap′ping (străp′ĭng), *adj.* *Colloq.* Monstrous; whopping.
strass (străs), *n.* [G., after Joseph *Strasser* (18th cent.), Ger. jeweler.] A brilliant lead glass used in the manufacture of artificial gems; paste.
strass, *n.* [F. *strasse,* fr. It. *straccio.*] Silk refuse in skein making.
stra′ta (strā′tȧ; străt′ȧ), *n., pl.* of STRATUM.
strat′a·gem (străt′ȧ·jĕm), *n.* [F. *stratagème,* through It. & L. fr. Gr. *stratēgema,* fr. *stratēgein* to be leader of an army, fr. *stratēgos* a general, fr. *stratos* army + *agein* to lead.] A trick in war for deceiving the enemy; hence, in general, deception; ruse. — **Syn.** See TRICK.
stra·te′gic (stră·tē′jĭk; -tĕj′ĭk), *adj.* Also **stra·te′gi·cal** (-tē′jĭ·kăl; -tĕj′ĭ·kăl). **1.** Of or pertaining to strategy; marked by strategy; important in strategy. **2.** Required for the conduct of war but obtainable at least in part only from outside the country; — chiefly of raw material. Cf. CRITICAL. **3.** *Mil.* Designed or trained specially for devastating bases and industrial centers and wrecking communications to the rear of enemy lines; — of bombing or air forces. Cf. TACTICAL. — **stra·te′gi·cal·ly,** *adv.*
stra·te′gics (stră·tē′jĭks), *n.;* see -ICS. Strategy.
strat′e·gist (străt′ē·jĭst), *n.* One skilled in strategy.
strat′e·gy (-jĭ), *n.* **1.** The science and art of employing the armed strength of a belligerent to secure the objects of a war, esp. the large-scale planning and directing of operations in adjustment to combat area, possible enemy action, political alignments, etc.; also, an instance of it. **2.** Use of stratagem or artifice; intrigue.
strath (străth; *Scot.* strȧth), *n.* [Gael. *srath.*] A flat, wide river valley or its bottom land.
strath′spey′ (străth′spā′; străth′spā′), *n.* A lively Scottish dance, resembling the reel, but slower; also, the music for this dance.
stra·tic′u·late (strȧ·tĭk′ū·lāt), *adj.* [Dim. fr. *stratum.*] *Geol. & Min.* Characterized by thin parallel strata.
strat′i·form (străt′ĭ·fôrm), *adj.* *Anat.* Having the form of stratum; designating a cartilage embedded in a groove in a bone to form a smooth surface over which a tendon passes.
strat′i·fy (străt′ĭ·fī), *v. t.;* -FIED (-fīd); -FY′ING. [F. *stratifier,* fr. ML. *stratificare.*] **1.** To form, deposit, or arrange, in strata, or layers. **2.** *Hort.* To preserve (tree seeds) by spreading in layers alternating with sand or earth. — **strat′i·fi·ca′tion** (-fĭ·kā′shŭn), *n.*
stra·tig′ra·phy (strȧ·tĭg′rȧ·fĭ), *n.* [*stratum* + *-graphy.*] **a** The arrangement of strata. **b** Geology which treats of the arrangement of strata. — **strat′i·graph′ic** (străt′ĭ·grăf′ĭk), **strat′i·graph′i·cal** (-ĭ·kăl), *adj.* — **strat′i·graph′i·cal·ly,** *adv.*
stra′to- (strā′tō-). [From STRATUS.] A combining form denoting *stratus and,* as in **stra′to–cu′mu·lus** (-kū′mū·lŭs), stratified cumulus, consisting of large balls or rolls of dark cloud which often cover the whole sky, esp. in winter. See CLOUD, *Illust.*
stra·toc′ra·cy (strȧ·tŏk′rȧ·sĭ), *n.;* *pl.* -CIES (-sĭz). [Gr. *stratos* army + *-cracy.*] Government based on an army; a military government. — **strat′o·crat′ic** (străt′ō·krăt′ĭk), *adj.*
strat′o·sphere (străt′ō·sfēr; strā′tō-), *n.* [See STRATUM; -SPHERE.] *Meteorol.* The upper portion of the atmosphere, above seven miles, more or less (depending on latitude, season, and weather) in which temperature changes but little with altitude and clouds of water never form. — **strat′o·spher′ic** (-sfĕr′ĭk), **strat′o·spher′i·cal** (-ĭ·kăl), *adj.*
stra′tum (strā′tŭm; străt′ŭm), *n.;* *pl.* -TA (-tȧ; -ȧ), -TUMS (-tŭmz;

-ŭmz). [L., a covering, fr. *sternere, stratum,* to spread.] **1.** A bed or layer artificially made; as, a *stratum* of turf. **2.** A region of the sea or atmosphere conceived of as analogous to a stratum of the earth. **3.** A part of a historical or sociological series representing a stage of development; also, a contemporary group representative of such a stage, esp. in education. **4.** *Biol.* A layer of tissue. **5.** *Geol.* A sheetlike mass of sedimentary rock or earth of one kind, usually in layers between beds of other kinds. See FAULT, *Illust.*

stra'tus (strā'tŭs), *n.; pl.* STRATI (-tī). [L. *stratus* a spreading out, scattering.] *Meteorol.* A cloud form of great width and low altitude (2000 to 7000 feet). See CLOUD, *Illust.*

straucht, straught (străkt; strôkt). Scot. vars. of STRAIGHT.

stra·vage' (strȧ·vāg'), **stra·vaig'** (-vāg'), *n. & v.* [OF. *estravaguer.*] *Scot. & Dial.* Saunter; stroll.

straw (strô), *n.* [AS. *strēaw.*] **1.** Collectively, stalks of grain after threshing. **2.** A stalk or stem of grain, as of wheat, rye, oats, etc. **3.** A thing of smallest worth; a trifle. — *adj.* **1.** Of or like straw; of the color of straw. **2.** Of the worth of a straw; hence, of little or no value. **3.** Made as if with straw or straws; as, a *straw* man for the enemy's shots; of voting, etc., not official; as, a *straw* vote taken by letters of inquiry to ascertain the relative strength of opposing candidates.

straw'ber'ry (-bĕr'ĭ; -bẽr·ĭ), *n.* The juicy, edible, usually red fruit of a genus (*Fragaria*) of plants of the rose family; also, the plant (called a **strawberry vine**) which bears this fruit.

strawberry bass. The calico bass (see BASS **b**).

strawberry bush. A North American shrub (*Evonymus americanus*) having crimson pods, and seeds with a scarlet aril; also, the wahoo (*E. atropurpureus*).

strawberry shrub. Any of a genus (*Calycanthus*) of shrubs so called from the fragrance of the dark-red flowers. The genus is typical of a family (Calycanthaceae, the strawberry-shrub family).

strawberry tomato. Any of several annual and perennial herbs (genus *Physalis*) of warm or temperate countries, commonly planted for their small yellow or greenish tomatolike fruit or as ornamentals for their showy, bladderlike calyces; — called also *husk tomato, ground cherry.*

strawberry tree. A European evergreen tree (*Arbutus unedo*) with racemose white flowers, and strawberrylike fruit.

straw'board' (strô'bōrd'; 70), *n.* Common paper board made of straw pulp, used for packing, making boxes, etc.

straw boss. **1.** A subforeman who becomes acting foreman in the absence of the foreman, as in a camp or mill or on a ranch. **2.** In industry, a leader of a small gang of workers who carries his share of the work and serves as supervisor and expediter.

straw color. A light-yellow color, like that of dry straw. — **straw'-col'ored, straw'-col'oured,** *adj.*

straw'flow'er (strô'flou'ẽr), *n.* Any of several everlasting flowers. See EVERLASTING, *n.*, 3.

straw man. A man of straw; hence, variously, a nonentity; a puppet; a perjured witness.

straw wine. Wine from grapes dried in the sun, as on straw. The wine is sweet and liqueurlike.

straw'worm' (strô'wûrm'), *n.* **a** A caddis worm. **b** Any of several small hymenopterous insects (family Chalcididae) whose larvae injure the straw of wheat, etc.

stray (strā), *v. i.* [OF. *estraier,* prop. adj., stray, astray.] **1.** To wander, as from a direct course; to deviate. **2.** To wander from company, from confinement, or from the proper limits; to rove; roam. — *n.* **1.** Any domestic animal wandering at large or lost. **2.** A person or thing that strays; a straggler; waif. **3.** *pl. Radio.* Electrical effects that disturb reception. — *adj.* **1.** Having gone astray; wandering. **2.** Incidental; unrelated; isolated; as, a *stray* remark. — **stray'er** (strā'ẽr), *n.*

streak (strēk), *n.* [ME. *streke,* var. of *strike* streak, stroke, line, fr. AS. *strica.*] **1.** A line or mark of a different color or texture from the ground; a stripe. **2.** A vein of any mineral. **3.** A vein of character or temperament; a trait; also, a trace; strain. **4.** *Colloq., U.S.* A layer; as, bacon with a *streak* of lean; a *streak* of luck. **5.** *Bacteriol.* Inoculum implanted in a line or stripe. **6.** *Mineral.* The color of the fine powder of a mineral, as obtained by scratching or by rubbing against a hard white surface. It is often an important distinguishing character. — *v. t.* To form streaks or stripes in or on; to stripe.

streak'y (-ĭ), *adj.;* STREAK'I·ER (-ĭ·ẽr); STREAK'I·EST. Streaked; marked with streaks; of persons, their moods, etc., uneven; variable. — **streak'i·ly,** *adv.* — **streak'i·ness,** *n.*

stream (strēm), *n.* [AS. *strēam.*] **1.** A current or course of water or other fluid, flowing on the earth, as a river, brook, etc.; specif., any course of running liquid. **2.** A steady flow, as of water, air, gas, etc.; speed, force, amount, or direction of flow; specif., of light, a ray. **3.** Anything issuing or moving with continued succession of parts; as, a *stream* of words. **4.** A continued course; as, the *stream* of history. — *v. i.* **1.** To issue or flow in a stream. **2.** To pour out, or emit, a stream or streams; as, *streaming* eyes. **3.** To issue, shoot, or pass swiftly, as light, a comet, etc. **4.** To extend or stretch out at length, or in a line, often wavy; as, a flag *streams* out. **5.** To move forward in a body with a continuous motion; as, the crowd *streamed* into the hall. — *v. t.* **1.** To cause to flow; to pour; as, his eyes *streamed* tears. **2.** To cause to stream in the air; as, to *stream* a banner.

stream'er (strēm'ẽr), *n.* **1.** A flag which floats in the wind; specif., a long, narrow, ribbonlike flag. **2.** Hence, any long, narrow, wavy strip like or suggesting a banner floating in the wind. **3.** A stream or column of light shooting upward from the horizon, as in the aurora borealis. **4.** A newspaper headline that runs the full width of a page.

streamer fly. *Angling.* Any large wet fly with long feathers streaming out behind the hook and from the head. Cf. FLY, *Illust.*

stream'ing, *n.* *Biol.* The slow steady flowing motion of living protoplasm in a cell.

stream'let (strēm'lĕt; -lĭt), *n.* A small stream.

stream'line' (-līn'), *n.* **1.** The path of a small portion of a fluid relative to a solid body with respect to which the fluid is moving. **2.** A contour designed to decrease air resistance. — (2), *adj.* Of or pert. to a streamline; designating a motion or flow that is free from turbulence, like that of a free particle moving in a streamline; hence, *Mech.,* designating a surface, body, etc., designed to afford an unbroken flow of a fluid about it; as, a *streamline* body for an automobile or airplane. — *v. t.* To design or construct with a streamline form.

stream'lined' (strēm'līnd'; 2), *adj.* **1.** Expertly fashioned or refashioned so as to offer a minimum of resistance to swift, smooth progress, operation, or presentation, esp. in highly condensed form to suit up-to-date needs and tastes. **2.** Stripped of encumbrances; brought up to date; modernized.

streamline flow. Fluid flow in which the velocity at a given point is constant in magnitude and direction.

stream'lin'er (strēm'līn'ẽr), *n.* A streamlined train; also, a streamlined bus or airplane.

stream of consciousness. *Psychol.* Individual conscious experience considered as a series of processes continuously moving forward in time.

stream'-of-con'scious·ness nov'el. A novel telling its story by recording the current of thought of one or more of its characters.

streek (strēk), *v. t.* [ME. *streken,* var. of *strechen,* fr. AS. *streccan.* See STRETCH.] *Scot.* **1.** To stretch; extend. **2.** To lay out, as a corpse. — *n. Scot.* Stretch; extent.

street (strēt), *n.* [AS. *strǣt,* fr. LL. *strata* (sc. *via*) a paved way, prop. fem. past part. of *sternere, stratum,* to spread.] **1. a** *Obs.* Orig., a paved road. **b** Now, commonly, a thoroughfare, esp. in a city, town, or village; — disting. from an *alley* or *lane,* or from a county or state road (*highway*). *Street* usually includes the sidewalks or footpaths on either side, and often the bordering houses, lots, etc. Abbr. *St.* **2.** Hence, the occupants of the buildings on a street, collectively; as, the *street* was agog with curiosity. — ***the street.*** The street or vicinity in a city where its main financial business is carried on.

street Arab. A homeless vagabond in the streets of a city, particularly an outcast boy or girl; a gamin.

street'car' (strēt'kär'), *n.* A car, usually a passenger car, running on the public streets, usually on rails, often as a trackless trolley; a tram.

street certificate. *Stock Exchanges.* A certificate of stock, endorsed in blank by the registered owner and guaranteed by a broker, which circulates freely from seller to buyer in the market without requiring a transfer on the books of the corporation.

street railway. A line operating streetcars and/or buses.

street'walk'er (strēt'wôk'ẽr), *n.* A common prostitute who seeks trade in the streets. — **street'walk'ing,** *n. & adj.*

strength (strĕngth; strĕngkth; 68), *n.* [AS. *strengthu;* akin to E. STRONG.] **1.** The quality or state of being strong; capacity for exertion or endurance; force; power. **2.** Power to resist force; solidity or toughness. **3.** Power of resisting attacks; impregnability. **4.** Legal or moral force; as, the *strength* of law or public opinion. **5.** Intensity; vehemence; specif.: **a** Intensity or degree, esp. of potency of effect; — of liquors, solutions, etc. **b** Intensity; — said of light, color, sound, or odor. **c** Vigor of expression. **6.** Force as measured in numbers; amount, numbers, or power of any body, as of an army. **7.** One regarded as embodying or affording force or firmness; support. **8.** *Exchanges, Markets, etc.* Maintenance of, or a rising tendency in, a price level; firmness of prices. — **Syn.** See POWER.

strength'en (strĕng'thĕn), *v. t. & i.* To make, grow, or become stronger. — **strength'en·er** (-ẽr), *n.*

stren'u·ous (strĕn'ū·ŭs), *adj.* [L. *strenuus.*] **1.** Eagerly pressing or urgent; zealous; ardent. **2.** Marked by or requiring zealous energy. — **Syn.** See VIGOROUS. — **stren'u·ous·ly,** *adv.* — **stren'u·ous·ness, stren'u·os'i·ty** (-ŏs'ĭ·tĭ), *n.*

strep'i·tous (strĕp'ĭ·tŭs), *adj.* Also **strep'i·tant** (-tănt). [L. *strepitus* noise, din.] Clamorous; noisy; boisterous.

strep'to·coc'cus (strĕp'tō·kŏk'ŭs), *n.; pl.* STREPTOCOCCI (-kŏk'sī). [NL., fr. Gr. *streptos* curved + *-coccus.*] *Bacteriol.* Any microorganism of a genus (*Streptococcus*) of nonmotile, Gram-positive bacteria, occurring in pairs or chains and dividing in one plane only. Several species are virulently pathogenic and cause various acute diseases affecting the sinuses, lungs, spinal cord, joints, blood, etc. Cf. DIPLOCOCCUS. — **strep'to·coc'cal** (-kŏk'ăl), **-coc'cic** (-sĭk), *adj.*

strep'to·my'cin (strĕp'tō·mī'sĭn), *n.* [From *Streptomyces;* see -IN.] An antibacterial substance produced by a soil microorganism (*Streptomyces griseus*), effective in animal experiments against the bacteria of certain diseases, as tularemia, typhoid fever, and tuberculosis.

strep'to·thri'cin (-thrī'sĭn; -thrĭs'ĭn), *n.* [From NL. *Streptothrix* (fr. Gr. *streptos* curved + Gr. *thrix* hair) + *-in.*] *Biochem.* An antibacterial substance similar to streptomycin in origin and action.

stress (strĕs), *v. t.* [Abbr. fr. *distress,* and fr. OF. *estrecier,* fr. L. *strictus,* past part. of *stringere* to bind tight.] **1.** To subject to the action of external forces; esp., to overstrain. **2.** To subject to phonetic stress; to accent. **3.** To emphasize. — *n.* **1.** Pressure; strain; esp., intense strain; as, under the *stress* of circumstances; hence, urgency; significance; as, to lay *stress* on one argument. **2.** Intense effort; strained exertion. **3.** *Mech.* Mutual force or action between contiguous surfaces of bodies caused by external force, as tension, shear, etc.; the cohesive force or molecular resistance in a body opposing such action. Specif., intensity of this force, commonly expressed in pounds per square inch. **4.** *Music.* Accent. **5.** *Phonet.* Force of utterance given to a speech sound, syllable, or word, increasing its relative loudness; accent. **6.** *Pros.* **a** Emphasis or weight given syllables that carry the ictus; also, emphasis given syllables that are accented in speech as distinguished from those accented because of a metrical scheme. **b** Any syllable which carries the ictus.

-stress. [*-ster* + *-ess.*] A suffix denoting a *feminine agent,* now esp. *one who does something with skill* or *as an occupation,* as in seam*stress,* song*stress.*

stretch (strĕch), *v. t.* [AS. *streccan.*] **1.** To reach out; extend; esp., to extend (oneself, one's limbs or body); as, he *stretched* himself out on the bed. **2.** To draw out or extend in length or breadth; to expand. **3.** To make tense; to strain; as, to *stretch* a muscle. **4.** To cause to reach or continue; to extend; as, to *stretch* a wire between two posts. **5.** To extend too far; hence, to do violence to; to exaggerate; as, to *stretch* the truth. **6. a** *Slang.* To fell as with a blow. **b** *Chiefly Dial.* To lay out for burial. **7.** *Obs.* To execute by hanging. — *v. i.* **1.** To be extended in length or in breadth, or both; to spread. **2.** To extend or spread oneself, or one's limbs; as, he yawned and *stretched.* **3.** To be extended without breaking; as, rubber *stretches* easily. **4.** *Colloq.* To strain the truth; to exaggerate. **5.** *Colloq.* To be hanged; to hang. — **stretch'a·ble** (-ȧ·b'l), *adj.*
— *n.* **1.** Act of stretching, or state of being stretched; tension; strain; effort. **2.** A length or distance; as, grassy *stretches* of land; also, a continuous space of time. **3.** The extent to which anything may be stretched; extreme reach. **4.** *Colloq.* A sentence or term of imprisonment; as, he did a *stretch* in Sing Sing. **5.** Course; direction. **6.** A walk to relieve fatigue; as, to take a *stretch* over the countryside. **7.** Either of the straight sides of a racecourse with curving ends; specif., the homestretch.

stretch'er (-ẽr), *n.* **1.** One who or that which stretches; specif., any of various devices or machines for stretching or expanding something. **2.** In framed work, a timber or rod used as a tie, esp. when horizontal. **3.** A litter, usually of canvas stretched on a frame, for carrying disabled or dead persons. **4.** *Masonry.* A brick or stone laid with its length parallel to the face of the wall.

stretch'er–bear'er, *n.* Also **stretch'er·man** (strĕch'ẽr·măn). A man who carries one end of a stretcher (sense 3).

stretch'–out', *n.* *Colloq., U.S.* A system of mill operation in which operatives are required to do extra work, esp. to operate more machines than formerly, either with slight or with no additional pay. — **stretch'–out',** *adj.*

stret'to (strĕt'tō), *n. masc.; pl.* -TI (-tē), -TOS (-tōz). Also **stret'ta** (-tä), *fem.; pl.* -TE (-tā), -TAS (-täz). [It., close or contracted, pressed, fr. L. *strictus,* past part. See STRICT.] *Music.* **a** In a fugue, the crowding of answer upon subject; the division of a fugue, properly following the development of the theme. **b** A concluding passage performed in a quicker tempo; — usually *stretta* in this sense.

strew (strōō; *also, archaic,* strō), *v. t.;* STREWED (strōōd; strōd); STREWED or STREWN (strōōn; strōn); STREW'ING. [AS. *strewian, streowian.*] **1.** To spread by scattering. **2.** To cover by or as if by scattering something over or on; also, to be dispersed over. **3.** To disseminate; to spread abroad.

stri'a (strī'ȧ), *n.; pl.* STRIAE (-ē). [L., a furrow, channel.] A minute groove, or channel; a threadlike line or narrow band, esp. when one of a series of parallel lines.

stri'ate (strī'āt), *v. t.* To mark with striae. — (-āt), *adj.* Striated.

stri'at·ed (-āt·ĕd; -ĭd), *adj.* [L. *striatus,* past part. of *striare* to furnish with channels.] Marked with striae.

stri·a'tion (strī·ā'shŭn), *n.* **1.** Fact or state of being striated; also, arrangement of striae. **2.** A stria.

strick (strĭk), *n.* [ME. *stric, strik.*] **a** A bunch of hackled flax, jute, etc., prepared for drawing into slivers. **b** Any of the pieces into which a layer of floss silk is cut after the first carding or combing.

strick'en (strĭk'ĕn), *past part.* of STRIKE. Hence: *adj.* **1.** Smitten; wounded; as, the *stricken* deer. **2.** Worn out; hence, incapacitated in any way. **3.** Leveled off even with the top of the container; as, a *stricken* measure of grain.

strick'le (strĭk''l), *n.* [AS. *stricel.*] **1.** An instrument to strike grain. See STRIKE, *v. t.,* 16 **a**. **2.** An instrument for whetting scythes; a rifle. **3.** *Founding.* A template consisting of a board or plate with a beveled edge used to sweep or strike up a mold, core, etc., in sand or loam. — *v. t.* To smooth or form with a strickle.

strict (strĭkt), *adj.* [L. *strictus,* past part. of *stringere* to draw or bind tight.] **1.** *Archaic.* Drawn close; tight; also, tense. **2.** Governed or governing by exact rules; rigorous. **3.** Exact; precise; as, *strict* construction of a law. **4.** *Bot.* Erect, as a plant or stem; straight, and not drooping, as a flower. — **Syn.** See RIGID. — **strict'ly,** *adv.* — **strict'ness,** *n.*

stric'tion (strĭk'shŭn), *n.* [L. *strictio.*] A constriction.

stric'ture (strĭk'tūr), *n.* [L. *strictura* a contraction.] **1.** *Obs.* Strictness. *Shak.* **2.** A binding or contraction; specif., *Med.,* a morbid contraction of any passage of the body; also, the contracted part. **3.** An adverse criticism; censure. — **Syn.** See ANIMADVERSION.

stride (strīd), *v. i.;* STRODE (strōd), *Obs.* STRID (strĭd); STRID'DEN (strĭd''n), *Obs.* STRID; STRID'ING (strīd'ĭng). [AS. *strīdan* to stride, straddle.] **1.** To walk with long steps, esp. in a pompous manner; also, to walk or run with long and measured steps. **2.** *Rare.* To straddle. — *v. t.* **1.** To pass over at a step; to step over. **2.** To straddle; bestride. — *n.* **1.** Act of striding; also, a long step. **2.** A cycle of movements in locomotion, as of a horse, completed when the animal's feet regain the initial relative positions on the ground; also, the distance traversed in such a movement. **3.** Figuratively, a stage of progress; advance; as, great *strides* in education. — **strid'er** (strīd'ẽr), *n.*

stri'dent (strī'dĕnt), *adj.* [L. *stridens, -entis,* pres. part. of *stridere* to make a grating or creaking noise.] Harsh-sounding; grating; shrill. — **Syn.** See VOCIFEROUS. — **stri'dence** (-dĕns), **stri'den·cy** (-dĕn·sĭ), *n.* — **stri'dent·ly,** *adv.*

stri'dor (strī'dẽr), *n.* [L.] A harsh, shrill, or creaking noise; specif., *Med.,* a harsh whistling sound during respiration in cases of obstruction of the air passages.

strid'u·late (strĭd'ū·lāt), *v. i.* [See STRIDULOUS.] To make a shrill, creaking noise, such as is made by the males of many insects, as katydids, crickets, and grasshoppers. — **strid'u·la'tion** (-lā'shŭn), *n.* — **strid'u·la·to'ry** (strĭd'ū·lȧ·tō'rĭ *or, esp. Brit.,* -tẽr·ĭ), *adj.*

strid'u·lous (-lŭs), *adj.* [L. *stridulus.* See STRIDENT.] Making a shrill, creaking sound. — **strid'u·lous·ly,** *adv.* — **strid'u·lous·ness,** *n.*

strife (strīf), *n.* [OF. *estrif.* See STRIVE.] **1.** *Archaic.* Earnest endeavor. **2.** Exertion or contention for superiority; emulation. **3.** Altercation; conflict; fight. — **Syn.** See DISCORD.

strig'il (strĭj'ĭl), *n.* [L. *strigilis;* akin to L. *stringere* to graze, scrape.] **1.** *Gr. & Rom. Antiq.* An instrument for scraping the skin, as after the bath. **2.** *Zool.* In many insects, a comblike structure at the apex of the front tibia, used to clean the antennae and other parts of the body.

stri'gose (strī'gōs; strĭ·gōs'), *adj.* [NL. *strigosus,* fr. L. *striga* a furrow.] **1.** *Bot.* Set with stiff bristles, as a leaf; hispid. **2.** *Zool.* Marked with fine, closely set grooves.

strike (strīk), *v. t.;* STRUCK (strŭk); STRUCK or STRICK'EN (strĭk'ĕn), *Obs.* STROOK (strŏŏk), STRUCK'EN (strŭk'ĕn; strŏŏk'ĕn); STRIK'ING (strīk'ĭng). [ME. *striken* to strike, stroke, proceed, fr. AS. *strīcan* to go, proceed.] **1.** To touch or hit with force; to smite. **2.** To come in collision with; to attack as a hawk, blast as a thunderbolt, etc. **3.** To inflict, as a blow. **4.** To dash; cast; as, to *strike* one's head on a stone; to separate or hurl with a sharp blow; as, the shackles were *struck* from him; also, to smear; daub. **5.** *Obs.* To stroke; as, to *strike* one's hair. **6. a** To afflict; punish, as if with blows. **b** Of a snake, to sink fangs into. **7.** To produce by a stroke or blow; as, to *strike* a light; hence, to produce suddenly; as, to *strike* terror to one's heart. **8.** To cause to ignite by hitting, rubbing, etc.; as, to *strike* a match; specif., *Elec.,* to cause (an arc) to form, as between electrodes of an arc lamp. **9.** To impress with a die or dies, punch, or the like, as a coin or medal. **10.** To cause to enter or penetrate; as, a tree *strikes* its roots deep. **11.** To affect sensibly with some strong emotion; as, to *strike* the mind with surprise; of a thought, idea, etc., to occur to; as, it never *struck* me before. **12.** To affect by or as if by a blow; as, to *strike* one blind. **13.** To cause to sound; as, to *strike* up a march. **14.** *Colloq.* To come or light upon, esp. suddenly; as, my eye *struck* a strange word. **15.** *Obs.* To fight or wage (battle). **16. a** To level, as a measure of grain, by scraping off with a straight instrument what is above the level of the top. **b** To strickle, as a mold in founding. **17.** To catch and hold the admiration or love of; to attract. **18.** To arrive at by computation; as, to *strike* a balance. **19.** To make and ratify; as, to *strike* a bargain. **20.** To lower; haul down; as, to *strike* a flag. **21.** To remove, cancel, or the like, with or as with a stroke of the pen. **22.** To assume (a posture). **23.** *Slang.* To make an urgent request of; as, he *struck* a friend for a job. **24.** *Angling.* To hook (a fish), esp. by a sharp pull on the line. **25.** *Whaling.* To harpoon or shoot (a whale) with a bomb. — *v. i.* **1.** To advance; proceed; as, to *strike* into the fields. **2.** To pass quickly; to dart. **3.** *Colloq.* To come upon something suddenly. **4.** To deliver a blow or attack; hence, to deal blows; to fight; also, to aim a blow; as, he *struck* at me, but missed; of a snake, to attempt to sink the fangs into its prey. **5.** To hit; collide; dash; clash. **6.** To sound, as a clock, by percussion, or as if with blows. **7.** To lower a flag, or colors, in token of respect, or to signify surrender. **8.** To quit work in order to obtain, or resist, a change in conditions of employment. **9.** To pierce; penetrate; as, a chill that *strikes* to our very bones. **10.** *Angling.* To seize the bait; — said of a fish. **11.** *Hort.* To take root; — said esp. of cuttings of plants.

Syn. (1) **Strike, hit, smite, slap, swat, punch** mean to deal or deliver a blow to or upon. **Strike** usually suggests aiming and dealing a blow and the production of the intended effect; **hit** more often stresses the impact of the blow or the reaching of the mark aimed at; **smite** is more emphatic than *strike;* **slap** implies a striking with an open hand; **swat** implies a hitting with a crushing blow; **punch** implies a hitting with a closed fist.
(2) See AFFECT.

strike a balance. To find the difference between the debit and credit sides, as of an account. — ***strike camp.*** To take down the tents or huts of a camp. — ***strike dead or dumb.*** To confound; to astonish. — ***strike hands.*** To clasp hands; hence, to make a compact. — ***strike home.*** To give a blow which reaches its object. — ***strike it rich.*** To find a rich vein or deposit of ore; hence, to meet with financial good fortune. — ***strike off.*** **a** To erase from a list or the like; to deduct, as from an account. **b** *Print.* To print. — ***strike oil.*** To find petroleum when boring for it; hence, *Slang, U. S.,* to make a lucky hit financially. — ***strike out.*** **a** To produce by collision; to force out; as, to *strike out* sparks with steel. **b** To blot out; to efface; to erase. **c** To devise; invent; contrive. **d** To start suddenly; as, to *strike out* at a sharp pace. **e** *Baseball.* To be put out for not hitting the ball fairly in three opportunities during one's turn at the bat; to cause to strike out. — ***strike up.*** **a** To begin to sing, sound, or play. **b** To raise or emboss (metal, etc.) as by blows or pressure in a die. **c** *Colloq.* To form, or enter upon, suddenly, as a friendship or acquaintance.

— *n.* **1.** Act of striking. **2.** A strickle for leveling, as a measure of grain, etc., or for striking up a mold in founding. **3.** Act of quitting work; specif., such an act done by mutual understanding by a body of workmen as a means of enforcing compliance with demands made on their employer. **4.** A sudden finding of rich ore in mining, of oil, or the like; hence, any sudden success or good fortune. **5.** *Angling.* Act of striking the bait. **6.** *Baseball.* Any actual or constructive striking at the pitched ball, three of which, if the ball is not hit fairly, cause the batter to be put out. **7.** *Bowling.* Act of leveling all the pins with the first bowl; also, the score thus made. **8.** *Brewing.* The unit quantity of malt used in making ale or beer; also, excellence of quality. **9.** *Coining.* The quantity or number of coins, or the like, struck at one time. **10.** *Geol. & Mining.* The direction of a line formed by the intersection of a stratum with a horizontal plane.

strike'break'er (strīk'brāk'ẽr), *n.* Any person hired to do the work of one who is on strike.

strike'break'ing (-brāk'ĭng), *n.* Coercive measures designed to break up a strike or strikes.

strik'er (strīk'ẽr), *n.* One who or that which strikes, in any sense; specif.: **a** A blacksmith's helper. **b** The hammer of the striking mechanism in a clock. **c** A harpooner; rarely, a harpoon. **d** A workman on strike. **e** *U. S. Army.* A soldier employed in his spare time by an officer to do odd jobs. Cf. BATMAN. **f** *U. S. Navy.* A nonrated enlisted man who is working for a petty officer's rating.

strik'ing (strīk'ĭng), *adj.* Remarkable; surprising. — **Syn.** See NOTICEABLE. — **strik'ing·ly,** *adv.*

string (strĭng), *n.* [AS. *streng.*] **1.** A small cord or slender strip of leather, or the like, used esp. for binding or tying things. **2.** A thread or cord strung with a number of objects; hence, a line or series of things arranged on or as if on a thread; a series; as, a *string* of beads; a *string* of arguments. **3.** Hence, a group of contestants ranked according to rated skill; as, players on the third *string.* **4. a** The cord of a musical instrument, commonly of gut or wire, as of a piano, harp, or violin. **b** *pl.* Stringed instruments, esp. of an orchestra; also, the players on such instruments. Cf. WIND, *n.,* 9. **5.** A fiber, as of a plant. **6.** *Obs.* A nerve or tendon of an animal body. **7.** *Colloq. pl.* Conditions attached to an offer, deal, etc. **8. a** *Arch.* Short for STRINGCOURSE, STRINGPIECE. **b** A notched board supporting the treads and risers of wooden stairs; a bridgeboard. See STAIR, *Illust.* **9.** *Billiards & Pool.* **a** The line from behind and over which the cue ball must be played after being out of play, as by being pocketed; — called also *string line.* **b** Act of stringing for the right to make the opening shot in a game. See STRING, *v. i.,* 3. **10.** *Horse Racing.* The horses collectively which belong to one stable or owner. — *v. t.;* STRUNG (strŭng); STRUNG, or, *Rare,* STRINGED (strĭngd); STRING'ING (strĭng'ĭng). **1.** To furnish with strings; hence, to strengthen; brace. **2.** To adjust or tune the string or strings of, as of a stringed instrument; hence, to make tense. **3.** To thread on or as on a string; as, to *string* beads. **4.** To deprive of strings; as, to *string* beans. **5.** To tie, hang, fasten, etc., with a string or strings; as, to *string* one's shoes. **6.** To extend or stretch like a string; as, to *string* cables. **7.** *Slang.* To hoax; josh. — *v. i.* **1.** To form into a string or strings, as on being stretched. **2.** To move or progress in a string, or series. **3.** *Billiards & Pool.* To make the cue ball rebound from the foot cushion so as to stop as near as possible to the head cushion or to the string line, as for determining the order of play.

string bass. The contrabass, largest of the viols.

string bean. *Often pl.* STRING BEANS. Any of certain varieties of beans (esp. genus *Phaseolus,* as *P. vulgaris*) grown for the pods, edible when young; — so called from the strings on the pods. One variety with tender golden yellow pods is called ***wax bean or butter bean.***

string'board' (strĭng'bōrd'; 70), *n.* *Arch.* A board or built-up facing used in building stairs to cover the ends of the steps, as to hide the true string. Cf. STAIR, *Illust.*

string′course′ (strĭng′kōrs′; 70), *n.* *Arch.* A horizontal band in a building, forming a part of the design.

stringed (strĭngd), *adj.* **1.** Having strings, as certain musical instruments (**stringed instruments**); also, produced by strings. **2.** Tied with a string.

strin′gen·cy (strĭn′jĕn·sĭ), *n.* Quality or state of being stringent; specif.: **a** Strictness; severity; rigor. **b** Tightness; lack of ease or plenty, as in financial circles. **c** Cogency, as of an argument.

‖**strin·gen′do** (strēn·jĕn′dō), *adj.* [It.] *Music.* Urging or hastening the tempo, as to a climax; — a direction.

strin′gent (strĭn′jĕnt), *adj.* [L. *stringens, -entis,* pres. part. See STRAIN, *v.*] **1.** Strict in requirements; rigid. **2.** Tight; characterized by scarcity of money to be loaned or invested; as, a *stringent* stock market. **3.** Convincing; cogent. — **Syn.** See RIGID. — **strin′gent·ly**, *adv.*

string′er (strĭng′ẽr), *n.* **1.** One who or that which strings. **2.** *Mach.* **a** A long horizontal timber to connect uprights in a frame, or to support a floor or the like. **b** A stringpiece. **c** A tie in a truss, etc. **3.** *Railroads.* A longitudinal member extending the distance between adjacent joints on the chord of a truss of a bridge and carrying the track.

string′halt′ (strĭng′hôlt′), *n.* [Cf. SPRINGHALT.] A lameness in the horse, due to muscular spasms in the hind legs.

string line. *Billiards & Pool.* See STRING, *n.*, 9 a.

string′piece′ (strĭng′pēs′), *n.* *Arch.* The heavy squared timber lying along the top of the piles forming a dock front or timber pier.

string tie. A narrow necktie.

string′y (strĭng′ĭ), *adj.*; STRING′I·ER (-ĭ·ẽr); STRING′I·EST. **1.** Consisting of strings, or small threads; fibrous. **2.** Ropy; viscid; gluey. **3.** Like or suggestive of a string or strings; thin and long; sometimes, wiry; sinewy; as, a *stringy* cowboy. — **string′i·ness**, *n.*

strip (strĭp), *v. t.*; STRIPPED (strĭpt) or, *Rare,* STRIPT; STRIP′PING. [AS. *strȳpan* in *bestrȳpan* to plunder.] **1.** To deprive; divest; plunder; esp., to deprive or divest of a covering, clothing, or the like; to skin; peel. **2.** To pull or tear off, as a covering; to remove; as, to *strip* the skin from a beast. **3.** To make bare or clear, as by cutting, grazing, removing objects from, etc. **4.** To milk dry, esp. with a peculiar movement of the hand at the last of a milking; as, to *strip* a cow. **5.** *Mach.* To tear off or break the thread from (a bolt or nut). **6.** *Mil. & Naut.* To dismantle; as, to *strip* a machine gun, a ship. **7.** *Tobacco Culture.* **a** To pick the cured leaves from the stalks of (tobacco). **b** To remove the midrib from (tobacco leaves). — *v. i.* To take off, or become divested of, clothes or covering; to undress. — *n.* [Prob. due to confusion of *stripe,* n., and *strip,* v.] **1.** A narrow or relatively long piece; as, a *strip* of cloth; a *strip* of land. **2.** Act of stripping or despoiling; destruction. **3.** *Philately.* Three or more stamps attached in a row, either horizontally or vertically. **4.** Also **air′strip′** (âr′strĭp′), **landing strip.** A long narrow hard-surfaced area or runway suitable for the take-off and landing of aircraft, usually laid out in the direction of the prevailing wind; also, a portable runway in sections of thin perforated steel sheets laid flat and hooked together. Specif., ***flight strip,*** strip constituting an auxiliary landing field alongside a highway as a dispersal area for military aircraft or for emergency landings, etc.

strip cropping *or* **planting.** Planting of crops in alternating strips of fibrous-rooted and loose-rooted growth, practiced on hill slopes to minimize erosion.

stripe (strīp), *n.* [MD. *stripe, strijp.*] **1.** A line, or long narrow division of anything of a different color or structure from the ground. **2.** A strip attached to something of a different color or material. **3.** A weal or welt; hence, a stroke such as might raise a welt on the skin; a damaging blow. **4.** Color indicating, or symbolic of, something; hence, character; type; sort; as, men of the same political *stripe.* **5.** *Mil.* **a** A piece of braid, as on the sleeve of an officer's coat, to indicate rank or length of service. **b** *pl. Now Soldiers' Slang.* A chevron. **6.** *Weaving.* A pattern or cloth with lines or narrow bands, differently colored, or raised or depressed, from the ground. — *v. t.* To make stripes upon; to variegate with stripes.

striped (strīpt; strīp′ĕd; -ĭd), *adj.* Having stripes of different colors; as, **striped squirrel**, a chipmunk.

strip′er (strīp′ẽr), *n.* *Slang.* One who wears stripes on his sleeve, to indicate rank or length of service; — used in the U. S. Navy, generally in combination; as: ***one-striper,*** an ensign; ***four-striper,*** a captain; etc.

strip′ling (strĭp′lĭng), *n.* [*strip* + 1st *-ling;* as if a small strip from the main stock or stem.] A lad.

strip′per (strĭp′ẽr), *n.* One who or that which strips.

strip tease. *Theat.* In burlesque, an act in which an actress, usually at the end or as a part of a song number, removes her clothing before the audience, piece by piece. — **strip′–tease′**, *adj.* — **strip′–teas′er**, *n.*

strive (strīv), *v. i.*; STROVE (strōv), sometimes STRIVED (strīvd); STRIV′EN (strĭv′ĕn), often STRIVED, rarely STROVE; STRIV′ING (strīv′ĭng). [OF. *estriver,* of Teut. origin.] **1.** To make efforts; to labor hard; — followed by an infinitive. **2.** To struggle in opposition; to contend; contest; battle. **3.** *Obs.* To vie; compete. — **Syn.** See ATTEMPT. — **striv′er** (strīv′ẽr), *n.*

stro·bi′la (strō·bī′lȧ), *n.*; *pl.* -LAE (-lē). [NL., fr. Gr. *strobilē* a plug of lint shaped like a pine cone, fr. *strobilos* anything twisted, a pine cone.] *Zool.* A linear series of similar structures, as the segmented body of a tapeworm or a chain of larval scyphozoan jellyfishes. — **strob′i·late** (strŏb′ĭ·lāt), *adj.*

strob′i·la′ceous (strŏb′ĭ·lā′shŭs), *adj.* [See STROBILE.] *Bot.* Pert. to or like a strobile; also, bearing strobiles.

strob′ile (strŏb′ĭl; 56), *n.* Also **strob′il** *or* **strob′i·lus** (-ĭ·lŭs). [F. or LL.; F. *strobile,* fr. LL. *strobilus* a pine cone, fr. Gr. *strobilos.*] *Bot.* A conelike aggregation of sporophylls bearing sporangia, as in the club mosses, horsetails, etc.; specif.: **a** In gymnospermous plants, a cone. **b** In seed plants, the spikelike pistillate inflorescence of the hop. See HOP, *Illust.*

strob′o·scope (strŏb′ō·skōp), *n.* [Gr. *strobos* a whirling + *-scope.*] An instrument for studying the successive phases of a periodic or varying motion by means of light periodically interrupted. — **strob′o·scop′ic** (-skŏp′ĭk), **strob′o·scop′i·cal** (-ĭ·kăl), *adj.*

strob′o·tron (strŏb′ō·trŏn), *n.* [*strobo*scope + elec*tron* tube.] A gas-filled electron tube with a cold cathode, used esp. as a source of stroboscopic light.

strode (strōd), *past* of STRIDE.

stroke (strōk), *n.* [ME. *strok, strook, strak,* fr. *striken.* See STRIKE, *v.*] **1.** Act or fact of striking; an impact; blow; knock. **2.** The effect of a striking; injury. **3.** A sudden action resulting in impact or in a quick, sharp result, suggesting a blow; as, a *stroke* of lightning; a *stroke* of fortune; hence, the result of such action; esp., any sudden attack of disease; as, a *stroke* of apoplexy; sometimes, specif., an attack of paralysis; a shock. **4.** An effort by which something is done, produced, or accomplished; also, something done or accomplished by such an effort. **5.** The sound of striking, esp. of the striking of a clock. **6.** A throb or beat, as of the heart. **7.** One of a series of beats or movements against a resisting medium; as, the *stroke* of an oar in rowing, of a swimmer, etc.; also, the type or character or rate of such a movement; as, a fast *stroke;* to keep the *stroke* at 38 beats a minute. **8.** A movement, usually with a tool, implement, or the like; as, a *stroke* of a pen; figuratively, a delicate or clever touch in a narrative, description, or the like. **9.** A mark or dash made, or appearing as if made, by a stroke of a pen, engraving tool, etc.; as, a blurred *stroke.* **10.** In certain games, as lawn tennis, a striking of the ball in a particular manner; as, a chop *stroke.* **11.** *Mach.* The movement, or the distance of the movement, in either direction, of the piston plunger, piston rod, crosshead, etc., as of an engine or a pump. **12.** *Rowing.* A rower who pulls the oar (**stroke oar**) nearest the stern and sets the rate of rowing for all the oarsmen.

stroke (strōk), *v. t.* [ME. *stroken, straken,* fr. AS. *strācian.*] **1.** To rub gently in one direction; hence, to soothe. **2.** To sound, as a gong or a clock, with a stroke. **3.** *Rowing.* To set the stroke for (the crew of a rowing boat) or for the crew of (a rowing boat); to row as stroke of.

stroll (strōl), *v. i.* To wander on foot; to rove; specif.: **a** To ramble idly or leisurely. **b** To go from one place to another in search of occupation, profit, or the like; as, a *strolling* musician. — *v. t.* To walk leisurely along; as, to *stroll* the streets. — *n.* A strolling; a leisurely walk.

stroll′er (-ẽr), *n.* **1.** One who strolls or saunters. **2.** A vagrant; tramp. **3.** A strolling player; an itinerant actor. **4.** Any of various types of baby carriage.

stro′ma (strō′mȧ), *n.*; *pl.* STROMATA (-tȧ). [L., a bed covering, fr. Gr. *strōma* couch, bed.] *Anat.* **a** The connective tissue or framework of an organ. **b** The colorless framework of a red blood corpuscle, nerve cell, etc. — **stro·mat′ic** (strō·măt′ĭk), *adj.*

stro′mey′er·ite (strō′mī′ẽr·īt), *n.* [After Friedrich *Stromeyer* (d. 1835), Ger. chemist.] *Mineral.* A steel-gray sulfide of silver and copper $(Ag,Cu)_2S$, of metallic luster.

strone (strōn), *n. & v.* *Scot. & Ir.* Spout; stream.

strong (strông; 74), *adj.* [AS. *strang, strong.*] **1.** Having great physical power to act; vigorous; robust. **2.** Having moral or intellectual power. **3.** Having great resources, as of wealth, numbers, etc.; as, a *strong* bank, army, party. **4.** Reaching a certain degree or limit in respect to strength or numbers; as, an army ten thousand *strong.* **5.** Effective or efficient, esp. in a specified direction; as, a *strong* voice. **6.** Forceful; cogent. **7.** Intense in degree or quality; not mild, weak, or the like. **8.** *Obs.* Flagrant; outrageous. **9.** Moving with rapidity or force; violent; as, a *strong* tide; specif., of the wind, of a velocity of 25 to 38 miles per hour. Cf. BEAUFORT'S SCALE. **10.** Ardent; zealous; as, a *strong* Whig. **11.** Full of spirit; as, *strong* liquors. **12.** Solid; not easily injured; not easily subdued or taken; as, a *strong* beam; a *strong* fortress. **13.** Well-established; firm; as, a *strong* custom. **14.** *Colloq.* Having an offensive or too intense odor or flavor; rank. **15.** *Com.* Tending to steady or higher prices; firm; as, a *strong* market. **16.** *Gram.* Pert. to or designating a verb, or its conjugation, which forms its past tense by a variation in the root vowel, and its past participle (usually) by the addition of *-en* (*strive, strove, striven; break, broke, broken; drink, drank, drunk*); — called also *irregular,* and opposed to *weak,* or *regular.*

Syn. **Strong, stout, sturdy, stalwart, tough, tenacious** mean showing great power as in acting or resisting. **Strong** usually suggests power that resists destructive forces or is potent in a high degree; **stout,** an ability to endure hard use, severe pain, or any stress or strain, without giving way; **sturdy,** strength derived from vigorous growth, a determined spirit, solid construction, etc.; **stalwart,** an unassailability, impregnability, and complete dependability; **tough,** strength arising from a texture or spirit that is firm and unyielding; **tenacious,** strength shown in retaining that which has been gained or in adhering to a support, position, idea, etc. — **Ant.** Weak.

— *adv.* Strongly; — in combinations, as *strong*-beating, *strong*-knit.

strong′–arm′ (-ärm′; 2), *adj.* *Colloq.* Having or using force, esp. undue force; as, *strong-arm* methods.

strong′–arm′, *v. t.* *Colloq.* To use force upon; assault; beat up; rob by violence.

strong′bark′ (-bärk′), *n.* A small tree (*Bourreria ovata,* family Ehretiaceae) of southern Florida and the West Indies. It has strong, hard, brown wood and edible berries.

strong′box′ (-bŏks′), *n.* A strongly made chest or case for money or valuables.

strong drink. Intoxicating liquor.

strong′hold′ (strông′hōld′), *n.* A fortified place; fastness.

strong′ly, *adv.* In a strong manner; vehemently; emphatically.

strong′–mind′ed (-mīn′dĕd; -dĭd; 2), *adj.* Having a vigorous mind; esp., of women, having or affecting masculine qualities of mind. — **strong′–mind′ed·ly**, *adv.* — **strong′–mind′ed·ness**, *n.*

strong room. A room for money or valuables, usually specially constructed to be fireproof and burglarproof.

strong′–willed′ (strông′wĭld′; 2), *adj.* Having a strong will; determined; sometimes, obstinate.

stron′gyle (strŏn′jĭl), *n.* Also **stron′gyl.** [Gr. *strongylos* round.] *Veter.* Any of certain roundworms constituting a family (Strongylidae), related to the hookworms; esp., any of those species (*Strongylus* and closely allied genera) that are parasitic in the alimentary tract and tissues of the horse.

stron′gy·lo′sis (strŏn′jĭ·lō′sĭs), *n.* [NL.] *Veter.* Infestation by roundworms of the genus *Strongylus.*

stron′ti·a (strŏn′shĭ·ȧ), *n.* [NL.] *Chem.* **a** Strontium monoxide, SrO, a white solid, resembling lime and baryta. **b** Loosely, strontium hydroxide, $Sr(OH)_2$.

stron′ti·an (-shĭ·ăn; -shăn), *n.* Strontium, esp. in the form of some compound, as strontia or strontianite.

stron′ti·an·ite (strŏn′shĭ·ăn·īt), *n.* [From *Strontian,* in Argyll Co.,

Scotland.] *Mineral.* Native strontium carbonate, $SrCO_3$, in various forms and colors.
stron'ti·um (strŏn'shĭ·ŭm; -tĭ·ŭm), *n.* [NL. See STRONTIANITE.] *Chem.* A bivalent element, an alkaline-earth metal, occurring naturally only in combination. Symbol, *Sr;* at. no., 38; at. wt., 87.63. Strontium compounds color a flame crimson, and some are used in fireworks. — **stron'tic** (-tĭk), *adj.*
strook (strŏŏk). Obs. past part. of STRIKE.
strop (strŏp), *n.* [See STRAP.] A strap; specif., a strap for sharpening a razor. — *v. t.;* STROPPED (strŏpt); STROP'PING. To sharpen, as a razor, on a strop.
stro·phan'thin (strō·făn'thĭn), *n.* [*Strophanthus,* type genus (Gr. *strophē* a turning + *anthos* flower).] A bitter, poisonous glucoside extracted from certain tropical plants of the apocynaceous genus *Strophanthus,* used as a cardiac stimulant.
stro'phe (strō'fē), *n.* [Gr. *strophē,* lit., a turning; akin to Gr. *strephein* to twist, turn.] **1.** In the Greek choral dance, the movement of the chorus while turning from one side to the other of the orchestra. **2.** *Pros.* **a** The strain, or part of the choral ode, sung during the strophe (sense 1). **b** A stanza. — **stroph'ic** (strŏf'ĭk; strō'fĭk), **stroph'i·cal** (strŏf'ĭ·kăl; strō'fĭ-), *adj.*
stroph'u·lus (strŏf'ū·lŭs), *n.* [NL., dim. fr. Gr. *strophos* a twisted band or cord.] *Med.* A form of miliaria, of several varieties, occurring esp. in infants.
stroud (stroud), *n.* [Appar. fr. *Stroud,* Eng.] A coarse blanket or garment formerly used in trading with some North American Indians.
strove (strōv), *past & rare past part.* of STRIVE.
strow (strō), *v. t.;* STROWED (strōd); STROWN (strōn) or STROWED; STROW'ING. *Archaic.* To strew.
stroy (stroi), *v. t. & i. Archaic.* To destroy.
struck (strŭk), *past & past part.* of STRIKE.
struck, *adj.* Closed or affected by a labor strike.
struck'en (strŭk'ĕn; strŏŏk'ĕn). Obs. past part. of STRIKE.
struck jury. *Law.* A special jury of 12 members selected from 48, these being reduced to 24 by the attorney for each side striking out the names of twelve. The jury is then chosen by the ordinary methods.
struck measure. A measure, as of grain, leveled off.
struc'tur·al (strŭk'tūr·ăl), *adj.* **1.** Of or pertaining to structure or a structure. **2.** Involved in, or caused by, structure, esp. the economic structure; as, modern *structural* unemployment. **3.** *Biol.* Of or pertaining to organic structure; as, a *structural* element. **4.** *Geol.* Of, pertaining to, or resulting from the effects of folding or faulting of the earth's crust; tectonic. — **struc'tur·al·ly,** *adv.*
structural formula. See FORMULA, 4.
structural iron, steel. *Engin. & Arch.* Iron or steel made in shapes best adapted for structural uses, such as I-shaped and T-shaped beams.
struc'ture (strŭk'tūr), *n.* [L. *structura,* fr. *struere, structum,* to arrange, construct.] **1.** Manner of building; form; construction. **2.** Something constructed or built, as a building, a dam, a bridge. **3.** Arrangement of parts, of organs, or of constituent tissues or particles, in a substance or body. **4.** Figuratively, the interrelation of parts as dominated by the general character of the whole; as, the *structure* of society.
stru'del (shtrōō'dĕl; strōō'-), *n.* [G.] A dessert of pastry made by rolling and baking a paper-thin sheet of dough spread with a filling, usually of fruit.
strug'gle (strŭg''l), *v. i.;* -GLED (-'ld); -GLING (-lĭng). [ME. *strogelen, struglen.*] To put forth great efforts; to labor hard; to strive; contend. — *v. t.* **1.** To effect, accomplish or dispose of, in some specified way, by struggling. **2.** *Rare.* To struggle over. — **Syn.** See ATTEMPT. — *n.* **1.** A violent effort or exertion. **2.** Contest; strife. — **strug'gler** (-lẽr), *n.* — **strug'gling·ly,** *adv.*
strum (strŭm), *v. t. & i.;* STRUMMED (strŭmd); STRUM'MING. [Imitative.] To play on, or as on, a stringed musical instrument unskillfully, idly, or noisily; thrum. — *n.* Act or sound of strumming. — **strum'mer,** *n.*
stru'ma (strōō'mȧ), *n.; pl.* -MAE (-mē). [L., a scrofulous tumor.] **1.** *Med.* **a** Scrofula. **b** Goiter. **2.** *Bot.* A cushionlike swelling, as at the base of the capsule in many mosses. — **stru·mat'ic** (strōō·măt'ĭk), **stru'mose** (strōō'mōs; strōō·mōs'), **stru'mous** (strōō'mŭs), *adj.*
strum'pet (strŭm'pĕt; -pĭt), *n.* A prostitute; harlot.
strung (strŭng), *past & past part.* of STRING.
strunt (strŭnt; strōōnt), *n. & v. Scot.* Pique.
strut (strŭt), *v. i.;* STRUT'TED (-ĕd; -ĭd); STRUT'TING. [ME. *struten, strouten,* to swell, fr. AS. *strūtian.*] To walk with a lofty, proud gait; to swagger. — *n.* **1.** The act of strutting; a pompous step or walk. **2.** *Engin., Arch., etc.* Any bar or piece designed to resist pressure, or compressive stress, in the direction of its length. See QUEEN POST, ROOF, *Illusts.*
strut, *v. t.* To provide, stiffen, support, or hold apart with or as with a strut or struts.
stru'thi·ous (strōō'thĭ·ŭs), *adj.* [L. *struthio* ostrich, fr. Gr. *strouthiōn.*] Of or belonging to an order (Struthiones) of flightless ratite birds, including chiefly ostriches, emus, and cassowaries; narrowly, of the genus (*Struthio*) including the African ostriches.
strut'ter (strŭt'ẽr), *n.* One who struts.
strut'ting, *adj.* That struts. — **strut'ting·ly,** *adv.*
strych'ni·a (strĭk'nĭ·ȧ), *n.* [NL.] *Obs.* Strychnine.
strych'nic (-nĭk), *adj.* Of, pertaining to, or produced by strychnine; as, *strychnic* poisoning.
strych'nine (strĭk'nĭn; -nēn; -nīn), **strych'nin,** *n.* [F. *strychnine,* fr. L. *strychnos* a kind of nightshade, fr. Gr. *strychnos.*] *Chem.* A poisonous alkaloid, $C_{21}H_{22}N_2O_2$, obtained from various plants of the genus *Strychnos* (see STRYCHNOS), as nux vomica. It is used as a tonic and stimulant for the central nervous system.
strych'nin·ism (-nĭn·ĭz'm), *n. Med.* Morbid condition produced by the excessive use of strychnine.
strych'nos (strĭk'nŏs), *n.* [NL. See STRYCHNINE.] Any of a genus (*Strychnos*) of tropical trees and woody vines (family Loganiaceae). Many species yield valuable drugs. See BRUCINE, CURARE, STRYCHNINE.
Stu'art (stū'ẽrt), *n.* Also **Stew'art.** A member of a royal family in Scotland and England. Robert II was the first king of Scotland of this family (1370). In 1603 James VI of Scotland became James I of England, and Charles I, Charles II, and James II were other reigning members of this house in Great Britain.
stub (stŭb), *n.* [AS. *stubb, stybb.*] **1.** The stump of a tree. **2.** The short blunt part of anything after the larger part has been broken off or used up; as, the *stub* of a pencil. **3.** In a checkbook, etc., a small part of each leaf attached to the back for memoranda of the contents of the part torn away; also, any similar counterfoil, as the coupon of a theater ticket. **4.** Something short, blunt, etc.; specif.: **a** A pen with a short, blunt nib. **b** A stub nail. — *v. t.;* STUBBED (stŭbd); STUB'BING. **1.** To grub up by the roots, as weeds. **2.** To remove stubs from; as, to *stub* land. **3.** To strike, as one's foot, against a stub, a stone, or other object.
stub, *adj.* Stocky; thickset; squat.
stub'bed (stŭb'ĕd; -ĭd; stŭbd), *adj.* **1.** Reduced to, or resembling, a stub; short and blunt. **2.** Abounding in stubs. **3.** Hardy; rugged. — **stub'bed·ness,** *n.*
stub'ble (stŭb''l), *n.* [OF. *estouble, estuble,* fr. LL., for L. *stipula* stubble, stalk.] **1.** The stumps of wheat, corn, or other grain left in the ground, as after reaping. **2.** A rough surface or growth resembling stubble. — **stub'bled** (-'ld), *adj.* — **stub'bly** (-lĭ), *adj.*
stub'born (stŭb'ẽrn), *adj.* [ME. *stoburn, stiborn,* prob. fr. AS. *stubb, stybb,* a stub.] **1.** *Obs.* Sturdy. **2.** Fixed, resolute, or unyielding; esp., obstinate. **3.** Performed or carried on in an unyielding, obstinate, or persistent manner; as, *stubborn* strife. **4.** Difficult to handle, manage, or treat; refractory; as, a *stubborn* ore. — **Syn.** See OBSTINATE. — **stub'born·ly,** *adv.* — **stub'born·ness,** *n.*
stub'by (stŭb'ĭ), *adj.;* STUB'BI·ER (-ĭ·ẽr); STUB'BI·EST. **1.** Abounding with stubs. **2.** Short, thick, and stiff, as bristles. **3.** Stocky; thickset.
stub nail. An old horseshoe nail; a nail broken off; also, a short thick nail.
stuc'co (stŭk'ō), *n.; pl.* -COES, -COS (-ōz). [It., of Teut. origin.] A plastic material used to form a hard covering for exterior walls; esp., a fine plaster used for internal decorations and fine work; hence, stuccowork. In modern building, *stucco* is generally ***cement stucco,*** made of portland cement, sand, and, commonly, a small percentage of lime. — *v. t.* To decorate with stucco; to coat with stucco. — **stuc'co·er** (-ō·ẽr), *n.*
stuc'co·work' (-wûrk'), *n.* Work done in stucco.
stuck (stŭk), *past & past part.* of STICK.
stuck'-up' (-ŭp'), *adj. Colloq.* Self-important and supercilious; conceited; snobbishly aloof. — **stuck'-up'ness,** *n.*
stud (stŭd), *n.* [AS. *stōd.*] **1.** A collection of horses, kept primarily for breeding. **2.** The place where such a collection of horses is kept. **3.** A studhorse; also, any male animal kept for breeding. — ***at stud.*** Available for breeding; — of a male animal.
— *adj.* **a** Kept for breeding; as, a *stud* mare. **b** Of, pert. to, or connected with a stud.
stud, *n.* [AS. *studu* a post.] **1.** A kind of nail with a large head, used chiefly for ornament; an ornamental knob; boss. **2.** A detachable buttonlike device to be inserted through buttonholes or eyelets and serve as a fastener, for ornament, etc. **3.** An iron brace across the link of a chain cable. **4.** *Building.* A scantling; esp., one of the uprights in lath-and-plaster partitions and in furring, upon which the laths are nailed or to which boards are nailed in frame buildings. **5.** *Cards.* Short for *stud poker* (see POKER). **6.** *Mach.* A short rod or pin, projecting from something, and sometimes forming a journal. — *v. t.;* STUD'DED; STUD'DING. **1.** To supply with studs, or props, as supports; as, a low-*studded* room. **2.** To adorn with or as with a stud, studs, or knobs. **3.** To set with detached ornaments or prominent objects; as, a plain *studded* with farms.
stud'book' (-bŏŏk'), *n.* Also **stud book.** A registry of the pedigrees and performances of horses.
stud'die (stŭd'ĭ; stĭd'ĭ). Scot. & dial. var. of STITHY.
stud'ding (stŭd'ĭng), *n.* Material for studs or joists; studs or joists, collectively; scantling.
stud'ding sail (stŭn's'l *or, esp. as a literary term,* stŭd'ĭng sāl). *Naut.* A light sail set at the side of a principal square sail of a vessel in free winds. See SAIL, *Illust.*
stu'dent (stū'dĕnt; 114), *n.* [L. *studens, -entis,* pres. part. of *studere* to study.] **1.** A learner; scholar; esp., one who attends a school. **2.** One who studies; an attentive and systematic observer; as, a *student* of life. — **Syn.** See SCHOLAR.
student lamp. An adjustable reading lamp.
stu'dent·ship, *n.* **1.** State of being a student. **2.** *Chiefly Brit.* A scholarship or fellowship.
stud'horse' (stŭd'hôrs'), *n.* A stallion, esp. one kept for breeding.
stud'ied (stŭd'ĭd), *adj.* **1.** Made the subject of study. **2.** *Rare.* Qualified by study; learned. **3.** Premeditated; planned; designed; as, a *studied* insult. — **stud'ied·ly,** *adv.* — **stud'ied·ness,** *n.*
stu'di·o (stū'dĭ·ō), *n.; pl.* -DIOS (-ōz). [It., prop., study.] **1.** The working room of a painter, sculptor, etc. **2.** A place where motion pictures are made. **3.** *Radio & Television.* A room or series of rooms maintained by a transmitting station and equipped for the transmission of programs. — **stu'di·o,** *adj.*
studio couch. An upholstered backless couch that can be made to serve as a double bed by sliding from underneath it the frame of a single cot; — distinguished from *sofa bed.*
stu'di·ous (stū'dĭ·ŭs), *adj.* **1.** Given to or pursuing study. **2.** Diligent in attention; carefully earnest. **3.** *Rare.* Planned; deliberate; studied. **4.** *Poetic.* Favorable to study. — **stu'di·ous·ly,** *adv.* — **stu'di·ous·ness,** *n.*
stud poker. See POKER.
stud'work' (stŭd'wûrk'), *n.* Work supported, strengthened, held together, or ornamented by studs.
stud'y (stŭd'ĭ), *n.; pl.* STUDIES (-ĭz). [OF. *estudie,* fr. L. *studium.*] **1.** Application of the mind to books, arts, or any subject, for acquiring knowledge. **2.** Act or process of acquiring by one's own efforts knowledge of a subject. **3.** Any branch of learning that is studied; any object of attentive consideration. **4.** Earnest and reasoned effort, desire, or thought; as, his *study* is to do right. **5.** Mental absorption; profound thought or meditation; as, he was in a brown *study.* **6.** A building or room devoted to study or literary work; hence, any private room reserved for the use of the master of the house. **7.** In the fine arts and in literature, a rendering of any object or scene, primarily intended only for the information, instruction, or assistance of the maker; as, a *study* of heads for a figure picture. Also, a rendering of anything made as a result of careful investigation; as, a *study* in New England types. **8.** *Music.* A piece for special practice; an étude. — **Syn.** See ATTENTION. — *v. i.;* STUD'IED (-ĭd); STUD'Y·ING. **1.** To apply the mind to books or learning. **2.** To fix the mind closely upon a subject; also, to ponder; meditate. **3.** To endeavor

with thought and planning; to be intelligently zealous. 1 *Thess.* iv. 11.
— v. t. 1. To consider attentively; to make a study of; as, to *study* nature, mankind. **2.** To devise with deliberation; as, to *study* variety in composition. **3.** To read and examine so as to learn and understand; as, to *study* a lesson. **4.** To concentrate upon (a subject) as a part of one's education; as, to *study* geology. — **Syn.** See CONSIDER.

study hall. In some schools, a room set aside for study.

stuff (stŭf), *n.* [OF. *estoffe.*] **1.** Material to be worked up in manufacture or out of which anything is to be or may be formed; raw material; hence, any material regarded indefinitely; as, lava is curious *stuff.* **2.** The elemental part; essence; as, he was of good *stuff.* **3.** Loosely, any kind of matter, whether solid, liquid, or gaseous; matter. **4.** Goods; personal property. **5.** Fabric of any kind; sometimes, specif., woolen or worsted fabric. **6.** A medicine; a potion. **7.** Refuse; hence, nonsense; trash; — often as an interjection; as, *stuff* and nonsense!
— v. t.; STUFFED (stŭft); STUFF′ING. **1.** To fill by crowding something into; to cram. **2.** To fill the cavity of with a particular material to secure some end; as: **a** To fill with soft packing; as, to *stuff* a sofa cushion. **b** To fill the skin of, usually when mounting as a specimen in lifelike form. **c** To fill to repletion; as, she *stuffed* herself on candy. **d** To put filling in, as in the cavity of a tooth. **3.** To crowd or fill with information, ideas, emotions, etc.; as, to *stuff* a pupil with historical dates. **4.** *U. S.* To put fraudulent votes into (a ballot box). **5.** To stop up; to plug, as a hole, by packing material into it. **6.** To crowd in; to pack. **7.** To choke up, as with a cold. **8.** *Cookery.* To fill with a seasoning composition of bread, meat, condiments, etc.; as, to *stuff* a turkey. **9.** *Leather Mfg.* To impregnate (leather) with a fat, as a mixture of oil and tallow, to soften and preserve it. **— v. i.** To feed gluttonously; to cram.

stuffed shirt (stŭft). *Slang, U. S.* A person of pompous or imposing appearance and actual insignificance.

stuff′ing, *n.* **1.** Act or process of, or that which is used for, filling anything; as, the *stuffing* of a saddle or a cushion. **2.** *Cookery.* Any seasoning preparation used to stuff poultry or roasts; dressing.

stuffing box. *Mach.* A device to prevent leakage along a piston rod or other moving part in a cylinder containing steam, water, etc. It consists of a box or chamber made by enlarging the hole, and a gland or follower to compress the contained packing. See VALVE, *Illust.*

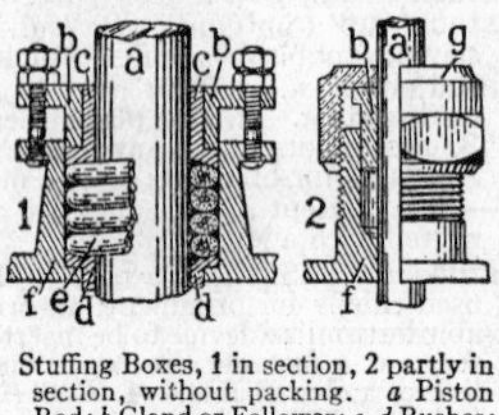

Stuffing Boxes, 1 in section, 2 partly in section, without packing. *a* Piston Rod; *b* Gland or Follower; *c, d* Bushes; *e* Packing, partly broken away; *f* Cylinder; *g* Stuffing Nut.

stuffing nut. See STUFFING BOX, VALVE, *Illusts.*

stuff′y (stŭf′ĭ), *adj.;* STUFF′I·ER (-ĭ·ẽr); STUFF′I·EST. **1.** *Colloq.* Angry and obstinate; sulky. **2.** Ill-ventilated; close, as a room; also, of persons, feeling choked up, as from a cold in the head. **3.** *Colloq.* **a** Stodgy; old-fogyish. **b** Prim; strait-laced. — **stuff′i·ly,** *adv.* — **stuff′i·ness,** *n.*

Stu′ka (stōō′kȧ; stŏŏk′ȧ; *G.* shtōō′kä), *n.* [G., fr. *Sturzkampfflugzeug* dive fighter.] A German dive bomber with backswept wings.

stull (stŭl), *n.* *Mining.* A round timber used to support the sides or back of a mine working, or one of a series of supports wedged between the walls of a stope to hold up a platform.

stul′ti·fy (stŭl′tĭ·fī), *v. t.;* -FIED (-fīd); -FY′ING. [L. *stultus* foolish + *-fy.*] **1.** To make or cause to appear stupid or foolish; to make a fool of. **2.** To frustrate, invalidate, or reduce to futility, esp. through debasing or repressive influences; as, the veto provision *stultifies* the reconstruction program; impatient of *stultifying* routine. **3.** *Law.* To allege to be of unsound mind and not responsible. — **stul′ti·fi·ca′tion** (-fĭ·kā′shŭn), *n.* — **stul′ti·fi′er** (-fī′ẽr), *n.*

stum (stŭm), *n.* [D. *stom* must.] Grape juice unfermented or arrested in fermentation, often added to revive fermentation in wine. **— v. t.;** STUMMED (stŭmd); STUM′MING. To revive (wine) by adding stum to it.

stum′ble (stŭm′b'l), *v. i.;* STUM′BLED (-b'ld); STUM′BLING (-blĭng). [ME. *stumblen, stomblen.*] **1.** To trip in walking, running, etc.; stagger because of a false step. **2.** To walk unsteadily or clumsily; hence, to speak, act, or perform anything, blunderingly. **3.** To trip morally; sin. **4.** To come or happen by chance; — with *on, upon,* or *against.* **— v. t. 1.** To cause to stumble or trip. **2.** To perplex; confound. **— n.** A stumbling; a trip; a false step. — **stum′bler** (-blẽr), *n.* — **stum′bling·ly,** *adv.*

stum′bling block. Any cause of stumbling, perplexity, or error; any obstacle or impediment to steady progress.

stump (stŭmp), *n.* [ME. *stumpe, stompe.*] **1.** The part of a tree or plant remaining in the earth after the stem or trunk is cut off. **2.** The basal portion of a limb, tooth, etc., left after the rest is removed. **3.** A stumplike remnant; a butt; a stub. **4.** A short stocky person or animal. **5. a** A heavy tramping sound; a clump. **b** *pl. Slang.* The legs. **6.** [Cf. F. *estompe.*] A short, thick, pointed roll, usually of leather or paper, used for shading crayon or pencil drawings by rubbing. **7.** A platform for political speaking, often in early days a tree stump. **8.** *Colloq.* A dare, or challenge. **9.** *Cricket.* Any of the three pointed rods stuck in the ground to form with the bails a wicket.
— v. t. 1. To reduce to a stump; lop. **2.** To clear of stumps, as land. **3.** *Colloq.* **a** To walk over or strike with a stump (sense 5 **a**); to stub, as the toes. **b** *U. S.* To nonplus; foil; as, the question *stumped* him; hence, to dare; challenge; as, he *stumped* me to jump the fence. **c** *U. S.* To travel over, in electioneering; as, to *stump* a state. **4.** To tone or treat with a stump (sense 6). **5.** *Cricket.* Of the wicket-keeper, to put out (a batsman out of his ground) by displacing a bail with the bowled ball. **— v. i. 1.** To walk clumsily or with thumps, as if on wooden legs; hobble. **2.** To make speeches on the stump.

stump′age (stŭmp′ĭj), *n.* The value of standing timber; also, the timber itself, or the right to cut it.

stump′y (stŭmp′ĭ), *adj.;* STUMP′I·ER (-ĭ·ẽr); STUMP′I·EST. **1.** Full of stumps. **2.** *Colloq.* Short and thick; stubby.

stun (stŭn), *v. t.;* STUNNED (stŭnd); STUN′NING. [OF. *estoner* to stun, resound.] **1.** To make senseless or dizzy by a blow or other violence. **2.** To overpower or confound with noise, sudden emotion, or the like; to daze; stupefy. **— n.** The condition of being stunned; also, that which stuns.

stung (stŭng), *past & past part.* of STING.

stunk (stŭngk), *past & past part.* of STINK.

stun′ner (stŭn′ẽr), *n.* One who or that which stuns; hence, *Slang,* one that is extraordinarily beautiful, excellent, etc.

stun′ning (stŭn′ĭng), *adj.* That stuns; as, *stunning* blows, news; hence, *Slang,* strikingly beautiful, excellent, etc. — **stun′ning·ly,** *adv.*

stun′sail, stun′s'le (stŭn′s'l). Contr. of STUDDING SAIL.

stunt (stŭnt), *n.* [Prob. var. of STINT a task.] *Colloq.* A feat of skill, strength, or the like, esp. one done to attract attention. **— v. i.** To perform stunts.

stunt, *v. t.* [From E. dial. *stunt* stunted, fr. AS. *stunt* dull, stupid. See STINT.] To hinder from normal growth; dwarf; check. **— n.** A stunting; a stunted thing.

stu′pa (stōō′pȧ), *n.* [Skr. *stūpa.*] A hemispherical or cylindrical mound or tower, esp. one serving as a Buddhist shrine.

stupe (stūp; 114), *n.* [L. *stupa, stuppa,* tow, fr. Gr. *stypē.*] *Med.* Cloth or tow dipped in water or medicaments and used as a dressing.

stu′pe·fa′cient (stū′pē·fā′shĕnt; 114), *adj.* [L. *stupefaciens, -entis,* pres. part. of *stupefacere* to stupefy.] Stupefying; inducing stupefaction. **— n.** *Med.* Anything stupefacient; a narcotic.

stu′pe·fac′tion (-făk′shŭn), *n.* Act of stupefying, or state of being stupefied; insensibility of mind or feeling; also, extreme astonishment or bewilderment.

stu′pe·fac′tive (stū′pē·făk′tĭv; stū′pē·făk′tĭv), *adj.* Stupefacient.

stu′pe·fy (stū′pē·fī), *v. t.;* -FIED (-fīd); -FY′ING. [F. *stupéfier,* fr. L. *stupefacere,* fr. *stupere* to be stupefied. See STUPID; -FY.] To make stupid or dull; or deprive of sensibility; make torpid. — **stu′pe·fi′er** (-fī′ẽr), *n.*

stu·pen′dous (stū·pĕn′dŭs), *adj.* [L. *stupendus* astonishing, fut. pass. part. of *stupere* to be astonished at.] Wonderful; amazing; esp., astonishing in magnitude or elevation. — **Syn.** See MONSTROUS. — **stu·pen′dous·ly,** *adv.* — **stu·pen′dous·ness,** *n.*

stu′pid (stū′pĭd; 114), *adj.* [L. *stupidus,* fr. *stupere* to be stupefied.] **1.** Lacking in understanding; in a state of stupor; stupefied. **2.** Sluggish in understanding; slow-witted; crassly foolish. **3.** Resulting from, or showing, mental dullness; foolish; witless; as, a *stupid* book. **— n.** A stupid person. — **stu′pid·ly,** *adv.* — **stu′pid·ness,** *n.*

Syn. **Stupid, dull, dense, crass, dumb** mean conspicuously lacking in power to absorb ideas or impressions. **Stupid** implies a benumbed or dazed state of mind that may be congenital or temporary; **dull,** a slow or sluggish mind, sometimes resulting from disease, or the like; **dense,** a thickheadedness, a stockishness, or the like; **crass,** a grossness that makes the mind incapable of analysis, evaluation, etc.; **dumb,** obtuseness and inarticulateness.

stu·pid′i·ty (stū·pĭd′ĭ·tĭ), *n.; pl.* -TIES (-tĭz). Stupidness; dullness of understanding; a stupid act, remark, etc.

stu′por (stū′pẽr), *n.* [L.] **1.** Condition in which sense or feeling is suspended or greatly diminished; insensibility; lethargy. **2.** Marked unresponsiveness to stimuli; esp., extreme mental or moral insensitiveness. — **Syn.** See LETHARGY. — **stu′por·ous,** *adj.*

stur′died (stûr′dĭd), *adj.* *Veter.* Affected with the sturdy.

stur′dy (-dĭ), *adj.;* STUR′DI·ER (-dĭ·ẽr); STUR′DI·EST. [OF. *estourdi* stunned, giddy, thoughtless, rash.] **1.** Resolute; firm; unyielding; as, *sturdy* patriotism. **2.** Strong and vigorous; lusty; robust; as, a *sturdy* boy; also, hardy; stout; as, a *sturdy* oak. — **Syn.** See STRONG. — **stur′di·ly,** *adv.* — **stur′di·ness,** *n.*

stur′dy, *n.* [OF. *estourdi* giddiness.] *Veter.* Gid.

stur′geon (stûr′jŭn), *n.* See PLURAL, *Note,* 3. [OF. *esturgeon,* of Teut. origin.] Any of certain edible ganoid fishes, mostly of large size, constituting a family (Acipenseridae) widely distributed in the North Temperate Zone. The roe is made into caviar, and the air bladder into isinglass.

‖**Sturm′ab′tei′lung** (shtŏŏrm′äp′tī′lŏŏng), *n.* [G., lit., storm section.] A private army of bullies, known as *storm troopers* or *Brownshirts,* assembled by Adolf Hitler about 1923, which after 1934 was covertly reorganized as a national militia. Abbr. *SA* or *S.A.*

‖**Sturm′ und Drang′** (shtŏŏrm′ ŏŏnt dräng′). [G.] Storm and stress; in Germany, a late 18th-century movement to free literature from domination by French neoclassicism.

sturt (stûrt), *n.* [Var. of STRUT.] *Scot.* Disturbance.

sturt′in (stûr′tĭn), *adj.* *Scot.* Frightened; staggered.

stut′ter (stŭt′ẽr), *v. i. & t.* [Freq. of E. dial. *stut.*] To hesitate or stumble in uttering words; to utter with spasmodic repetitions or pauses. — **Syn.** See STAMMER. **— n.** Act of stuttering; a stammer. — **stut′ter·er,** *n.* — **stut′ter·ing·ly,** *adv.*

sty (stī), *n.; pl.* STIES (stīz). [AS. *stī, stig.*] **1.** A pen for swine. **2.** A filthy, low, or vicious place. **— v. t. & i.;** STIED (stīd); STY′ING. To lodge or pen in or as in a sty.

sty, *n.* Also **stye.** [From older *styanye* (understood as *sty on eye*), fr. *styan,* AS. *stīgend,* fr. *stīgan* to rise.] *Med.* An inflamed swelling of a sebaceous gland at the margin of an eyelid.

Styg′i·an (stĭj′ĭ·ăn), *adj.* [L. *Stygius.*] Of or pertaining to the river Styx; hence: **a** Infernal; gloomy. **b** Inviolable, as an oath sworn by the Styx.

styl-. = STYLO-.

sty′lar (stī′lẽr), *adj.* Of, pertaining to, or resembling a style; styliform.

style (stīl), *n.* [OF. *style, stile,* fr. L. *stilus,* (incorrect) *stylus,* a style, or writing instrument, manner of writing. In senses 2 **e** and 8, influenced in form and meaning by Gr. *stylos* a pillar.] **1.** An instrument used by the ancients in writing on waxed tablets. **2.** Anything resembling the ancient style in shape or use; as: **a** A pen. **b** A graver. **c** An etching needle. **d** A phonograph needle. **e** The pin, or gnomon, of a dial. **f** *Surg.* A stylet; probe. **3.** Mode of expressing thought in language; esp., such use of language as exhibits the spirit and personality of an artist; characteristic mode of expression; as, a terse *style.* **4.** Distinctive or characteristic mode of presentation, construction, or execution in any art, employment, or product, esp. in any fine art; also, distinctive manner or mode of singing, playing, behaving, etc. **5.** The quality which gives distinctive character and excellence to artistic expression; as, his writing lacks *style.* **6.** Status or character of being in vogue or in accord with the accepted standard of elegance; fashionable mode; as, to dine in *style;* a woman of *style.* **7.** Mode of address or designation; a title. **8.** *Bot.* A filiform prolongation of the ovary, commonly bearing the stigma at its apex. **9.** *Chron.* A mode of reckoning time; a calendar; — in the phrases *Old Style* and *New Style.* See NEW STYLE, OLD STYLE. **10.** *Print.* Manner or plan followed in dealing with certain details of typography, forms of expression, etc., as spelling, capitalization, word division, and punctuation, often embodied in a book called a **style′book′**. **11.** *Zool.* A slender bristlelike process. — **Syn.** See FASHION. — *v. t.* **1.** To entitle; to name or call. **2.** To fashion in, or bring into accord with, the accepted style. — **styl′er** (stīl′ẽr), *n.*

-style (-stīl). [Gr. *stylos* a pillar.] A combining form denoting *(one) having* (so many) *pillars.*

sty′let (stī′lĕt; -lĭt), *n.* [F., fr. It. *stiletto.*] **1.** A stiletto. **2.** *Surg.* A probe for examining wounds, fistulas, etc. **3.** *Zool.* A bristlelike organ or appendage.

sty′li·form (stī′lĭ·fôrm), *adj.* Resembling a style.

styl′ish (stīl′ĭsh), *adj.* Having style; conforming to fashion; modish. — **styl′ish·ly**, *adv.* — **styl′ish·ness**, *n.*

styl′ist (-ĭst), *n.* **1.** One emphasizing style; esp., an author whose work is distinguished for style (sense 5). **2.** One who advises concerning style in clothes, furnishings, etc. — **sty·lis′tic** (stī·lĭs′tĭk), **sty·lis′ti·cal** (-tĭ·kăl), *adj.* — **sty·lis′ti·cal·ly**, *adv.*

sty′lite (stī′līt), *n.* [LGr. *stylitēs*, fr. *stylos* a pillar.] *Eccl. Hist.* One of a class of ascetics who lived on tops of pillars. Simeon Stylites of Antioch (d. 459) was the most famous. — **sty·lit′ic** (stī·lĭt′ĭk), *adj.* — **sty′lit·ism** (stī′lĭt·ĭz′m), *n.*

styl′ize (stīl′īz), *v. t.* To conform to a style; conventionalize; specif., *Fine Arts,* to represent or design according to a style or stylistic pattern rather than according to nature. — **styl′i·za′tion** (-ĭ·zā′shŭn), *n.* — **styl′iz·er** (stīl′īz·ẽr), *n.*

sty′lo- (stī′lō-), **styl-**. [Gr. *stylos.*] A combining form meaning *pillar,* as in *stylo*bate, *styl*ite. Specif.: **a** *Bot. & Zool. Characterized by a style or stylar process.* **b** *Anat. Styloid and,* as in:

styloglossal · stylomandibular · stylomaxillary
stylohyoid · stylomastoid · stylopharyngeal

sty′lo·bate (stī′lō·bāt), *n.* [L. *stylobates, stylobata,* fr. Gr. *stylobatēs,* fr. *stylos* a pillar + *batēs* one that treads.] *Arch.* The continuous flat coping, or pavement, on which a row of columns is supported. See ORDER, *Illust.*

sty′lo·graph (-grăf), *n.* Also **sty′lo·graph′ic pen.** A type of fountain pen with a conical point; hence, loosely, any fountain pen.

sty·log′ra·phy (stī·lŏg′rȧ·fĭ), *n.* [*style* + *-graphy.*] A mode of writing or tracing lines by means of a style or similar instrument. — **sty′lo·graph′ic** (stī′lō·grăf′ĭk), **sty′lo·graph′i·cal** (-ĭ·kăl), *adj.*

sty′loid (stī′loid), *adj.* [Gr. *styloeidēs,* fr. *stylos* pillar.] Styliform; specif., *Anat.,* of or pertaining to any **styloid process**; such as: **a** A long, slender process from the lower side of the temporal bone of man. **b** A projection on the inner back part of the distal end of the ulna.

sty′lo·lite (stī′lō·līt), *n.* [*stylo-* + *-lite.*] *Geol.* A small, longitudinally grooved column, of the same material as the rock (usually limestone) in which it occurs.

sty′lo·po′di·um (stī′lō·pō′dĭ·ŭm), *n.; pl.* -DIA (-ȧ). [NL. See STYLE, sense 8; -PODIUM.] *Bot.* The conical swelling or expansion at the base of the style in plants of the carrot family.

sty′lus (stī′lŭs), *n.* [L. See STYLE.] **1.** A style, or writing instrument, esp. one for making carbon copies. **2.** In a phonograph: **a** In recording, a pointed piece moved by the vibrations given to the diaphragm by a sound, thereby producing an indented record. **b** In reproducing sound, the needle.

sty′mie (stī′mĭ), *n.* Also **sti′my** (stī′mĭ). *Golf.* A condition which exists on the putting green when the ball nearer the hole lies in the line of play of the other ball. — *v. t.* To impede by a stymie; hence, to block or check as if by a stymie; as, to *stymie* a plan.

styp′sis (stĭp′sĭs), *n.* [LL., fr. Gr. *stypsis* a steeping in an astringent. See STYPTIC.] Application or use of styptics.

styp′tic (stĭp′tĭk), *adj.* [L. *stypticus,* fr. Gr. *styptikos,* fr. *styphein* to contract.] Producing contraction, as of blood vessels; stopping bleeding; astringent. — *n.* A styptic medicine. — **styp′ti·cal** (-tĭ·kăl), *adj.* — **styp·tic′i·ty** (stĭp·tĭs′ĭ·tĭ), *n.*

sty′ra·ca′ceous (stī′rȧ·kā′shŭs), *adj.* [L. *styrax, storax,* storax.] Belonging to the storax family (Styracaceae). See STORAX.

sty′rene (stī′rēn; stĭr′ēn), *n.* Also **sty′ro·lene** (stī′rō·lēn). *Chem.* An unsaturated hydrocarbon, $C_6H_5CH{:}CH_2$, prepared from cinnamic acid, and otherwise, as a fragrant liquid. It is used especially for making plastics (see POLYSTYRENE).

stythe (stīth), *n.* [E. dial., also *stife.*] *Mining.* Chokedamp.

Styx (stĭks), *n.* [L., fr. Gr. *Styx, Stygos.*] *Gr. Myth.* The chief river of the lower world, which it encircled seven times.

su′a·ble (sū′ȧ·b′l), *adj.* *Law.* Capable of being sued in court. — **su′a·bil′i·ty** (-bĭl′ĭ·tĭ), *n.*

sua′sion (swā′zhŭn), *n.* [L. *suasio,* fr. *suadere, suasum,* to advise, persuade.] A convincing or persuading; persuasion; as, moral *suasion.* — **sua′sive** (-sĭv), *adj.*

suave (swäv; swāv), *adj.* [F., fr. L. *suavis* sweet, pleasant.] Blandly pleasing; smoothly polite; urbane; polished. — **suave′ly**, *adv.* — **suave′ness**, **suav′i·ty** (swăv′ĭ·tĭ; swä′vĭ·tĭ), *n.*

Syn. **Suave, urbane, diplomatic, bland, smooth, politic** mean ingratiatingly tactful and well-mannered. **Suave** specifically suggests the power to encourage easy and frictionless intercourse; **urbane,** a high degree of cultivation and poise and a wide social experience; **diplomatic,** urbanity and an ability to deal with ticklish situations tactfully; **bland,** the absence of irritating qualities and a mild or gentle manner; **smooth,** suavity, often assumed; **politic,** shrewdness plus tact and suavity. — **Ant.** Bluff.

‖**sua′vi·ter in mo′do, for′ti·ter in re** (swăv′ĭ·tẽr ĭn mō′dō, fôr′tĭ·tẽr ĭn rē′). [L.] Gently in manner, strongly in deed.

sub (sŭb), *n.* *Colloq.* Short for SUBMARINE, SUBORDINATE, SUBWAY, SUBALTERN, SUBSTITUTE, SUBLIEUTENANT, etc.

sub, *adj.* Auxiliary; subordinate; as, a *sub* post office.

sub, *v. i.;* SUBBED (sŭbd); SUB′BING. To act as a substitute.

sub, *n.* *Photog.* Short for SUBSTRATUM. — *v. t.* To apply a substratum to (a film or plate).

sub- (sŭb-; *many compounds of sub-, esp. nouns, have variable accent, dependent upon position and emphasis;* 2). [L. *sub* under, below; sometimes *sus-* before *c, p,* or *t* by dropping *b* of a collateral *subs-.*] A prefix signifying, in general, *under, below, beneath,* as in:

subbasement · subcellar · subfloor

Specif., esp. in English formations: **1.** **a** *In an inferior degree; somewhat, slightly, almost, nearly,* as in: **sub·ac′id,** slightly acid; **sub·au′di·ble,** almost audible; and in:

subangular · subfuscous · submetallic
subarid · subhuman · subrational
subastringent · subincandescent · subround
subcontiguous · sublethal · subtotal

b *Next lower than, subordinate to, inferior in rank,* etc., as in: **sub′-dean′**, an under dean; deputy or substitute of a dean; **sub′deb·u·tante′**, one just below a debutante in age; and in:

subagency · subdialect · sublieutenancy
subagent · subeditor · sublieutenant
subchairman · subfreshman · subofficer
subchief · subinspector · substation
subconstable · subleader · subtreasury

c *Forming, or so as to form, a further division, a repetition,* or *a continuation of,* as in: **sub′dis′trict,** a subdivision of a district; **sub-cul′ture,** to culture (bacteria) anew on a fresh medium; and in:

subclassify · subsale · substage
subderivative · subsection · subtenure
subprovince · subsegment · subzone

d In classifications, *below the category of, but above the category which follows,* as in: **sub·phy′lum,** a category below a phylum, but above a class; **sub′class′**, a category below a class, but above an order; **sub·or′der, sub·fam′i·ly, sub·ge′nus,** etc.; hence, **sub′ge·ner′ic, sub·or′di·nal, sub′spe·cif′ic,** etc. **2.** *Anat. Situated under* or *on the ventral side of,* as in: **sub′au·ric′u·lar,** located below the ear; also, *a part so situated,* as in: **sub·cor′tex,** the parts of the brain below the cerebral cortex. Also:

subarachnoid · sublabial · suborbital
subaxillary · sublingual · subpleural
subepidermal · subnasal · subserous
subgenital · suboccipital · subvaginal

3. *Chem.* **a** *Having less than the amount normal in* (the compound named), as in: **sub·car′bide,** a carbide with less than the ordinary amount of carbon. **b** *Basic;* — prefixed to the name of a salt, as in: **sub·ac′e·tate,** basic acetate; **sub·ni′trate, sub·sul′fate,** etc. **4.** *Geog. & Geol. Near the base of; bordering upon,* as in: **sub·al′pine,** of mountains below the timber line; **sub·arc′tic,** of the region bordering on the Arctic Circle; **sub′ant·arc′tic, sub′e·qua·to′ri·al,** etc. **5.** *Math. Inversely;* — prefixed to adjectives qualifying *ratio,* as in: **sub·trip′li·cate ra′tio,** the inverse ratio of the cubes, similarly, **sub·dou′ble, sub′du·ple, sub·du′pli·cate,** etc. **6.** *Med. (One) under the typical in degree,* as in: **sub′a·cute′**, not quite acute, yet not chronic; **sub′de·lir′i·um,** a mild delirium; **sub·fe′brile, sub′in·flam·ma′tion,** etc.

su′bah·dar′, su′ba·dar′ (sōō′bä·där′), *n.* [Per. & Hind. *ṣūbahdār,* fr. Ar. *ṣūbah* province + Per. *dār* holder, keeper.] *India.* **a** A governor of a province. **b** The chief native officer of a native company in the British Army.

sub·al′tern (sŭ·bôl′tẽrn; *U.S. also, Brit. usu.,* sŭb′′l·tẽrn), *adj.* [F. *subalterne,* fr. LL. *subalternus,* fr. L. *sub* under + *alternus* alternate.] **1.** Ranked below; subordinate. **2.** *Logic.* Particular, with reference to a related universal; as, a *subaltern* proposition. **3.** *Mil., chiefly Brit.* Ranking below a captain; — of a commissioned officer. — *n.* **1.** A subordinate. **2.** *Logic.* A subaltern proposition. **3.** *Mil., chiefly Brit.* A commissioned officer below the rank of captain.

sub·al′ter·nate (sŭb·ôl′tẽr·nĭt; -ăl′-), *adj.* *Bot.* Alternate, but with a tendency to become opposite.

sub·a′que·ous (sŭb·ā′kwē·ŭs), *adj.* **1.** Being under or beneath the surface of water; submarine. **2.** *Geol.* Formed or occurring in or under water.

sub·at′om (sŭb·ăt′ŭm; *see* SUB-), *n.* *Chem. & Physics.* A component part of an atom.

sub′a·tom′ic (sŭb′ȧ·tŏm′ĭk), *adj.* *Chem. & Physics.* Of, pertaining to, or designating: **a** The inside of the atom or phenomena occurring there. **b** Particles smaller than the atom or phenomena associated with them.

sub′au·di′tion (sŭb′ô·dĭsh′ŭn), *n.* [LL. *subauditio.*] Act of understanding, or supplying, something not expressed, as a word or meaning; also, that which is so understood or supplied.

sub′base′ (sŭb′bās′), *n.* *Arch.* The lowest member of a base when divided horizontally, or of a baseboard, etc.

sub′bass′ (sŭb′bās′), *n.* Also **sub′base′**. *Organ Building.* A 16-foot or 32-foot stop, with very deep low tones. See STOP, *n.,* 10 **b.**

sub′bing (sŭb′ĭng), *n.* *Photog.* **a** The application of a substratum to a film or plate. **b** A substratum.

sub·cal′i·ber, sub·cal′i·bre (sŭb·kăl′ĭ·bẽr), *adj.* **a** Smaller than the caliber of a gun; as, a *subcaliber* projectile fired through a tube of small caliber clamped to, or inserted in, a gun in target practice. **b** Of, pertaining to, used in, or effected by firing a subcaliber projectile.

sub′car·ti·lag′i·nous (sŭb′kär·tĭ·lăj′ĭ·nŭs), *adj.* *Anat. & Zool.* **a** Under a cartilage. **b** Partially cartilaginous.

sub′ce·les′tial (sŭb′sē·lĕs′chăl), *adj.* Beneath the heavens; hence, mundane; *Astron.,* exactly beneath the zenith. — *n.* One belonging to the subcelestial regions.

sub′chas′er (sŭb′chās′ẽr), *n.* *Nav.* = SUBMARINE CHASER.

sub·chlo′ride (sŭb·klō′rīd; -rĭd), *n.* Also **sub·chlo′rid.** *Chem.* A chloride containing a relatively small proportion of chlorine; as, *subchloride* of mercury, HgCl.

sub·cla′vi·an (-klā′vĭ·ăn), *adj.* [*sub-* + L. *clavis* a key. See CLAVICLE.] *Anat.* Under the clavicle; designating, or pertaining to, the subclavian artery, vein, or muscle. — *n.* A subclavian artery, groove, vein, etc.

subclavian artery. *Anat. & Zool.* The proximal part of the main artery of the arm or forelimb.

subclavian groove. *Anat.* Either of two grooves (for the subclavian artery and vein) on the first rib.

subclavian muscle. *Anat.* A small muscle extending from the first rib and its cartilage to the under surface of the clavicle.

subclavian vein. *Anat.* The proximal part of the main vein of the arm.

sub·clin′i·cal (sŭb·klĭn′ĭ·kăl), *adj.* *Med.* Slightly abnormal; not detectable by the usual clinical tests; — said of abnormal physical states.

sub′com·mit′tee (sŭb′kŏ·mĭt′ē; *see* SUB-; 2), *n.* An under committee; a part or division of a committee.

sub·con′scious (sŭb·kŏn′shŭs), *adj.* **1.** Of the nature of mental operation yet not present in consciousness; as, *subconscious* conflict of desires. **2.** Of the lowest degree of consciousness; belonging to the margin of consciousness. — *n.* Subconscious activity, sometimes conceived as an entity or agent. — **sub·con′scious·ly,** *adv.* — **sub·con′scious·ness,** *n.*

sub·con′tract (sŭb·kŏn′trăkt; *see* SUB-), *n.* A contract under, or subordinate to, a previous contract. — (sŭb′kŏn·trăkt′), *v. t. & i.* To contract under, or for the performance of part or all of, another contract. — **sub′con·trac′tor** (sŭb′kŏn·trăk′tẽr; sŭb·kŏn′trăk·tẽr), *n.*

sub′con·tra·oc′tave (sŭb′kŏn·trȧ·ŏk′tāv), *n.* *Music.* The octave below the contraoctave. See PITCH, *Illust.*

sub′cu·ta′ne·ous (sŭb′kū·tā′nē·ŭs), *adj.* Being, living, used, performed, etc., under the skin; as, a *subcutaneous* needle or parasite. — **sub′cu·ta′ne·ous·ly**, *adv.*

sub·dea′con (sŭb·dē′kŭn), *n.* *Eccl.* One in holy orders ranking below a deacon, whose duties include (in the Roman Catholic and Eastern Churches) the preparation of the holy vessels for the Mass or Eucharist. — **sub·dea′con·ate** (-āt), **sub′di·ac′o·nate** (sŭb′dī·ăk′ō·nāt), *n.*

sub·deb′ (sŭb·dĕb′), *n.* *Colloq., U.S.* A subdebutante (see SUB-, 1 **b**).

sub′di·vide′ (sŭb′dĭ·vīd′; 2), *v. t. & i.* To divide again; specif., *Real Estate,* to divide (a tract of land) into lots to sell before developing or improving them. — **sub′di·vi′sion** (-vĭzh′ŭn; *see* SUB-), *n.*

sub·dom′i·nant (sŭb·dŏm′ĭ·nănt), *n.* *Music.* The fourth tone above, or fifth below, the tonic. — **sub·dom′i·nant**, *adj.*

sub·duct′ (sŭb·dŭkt′), *v. t. & i.* To withdraw; subtract. — **sub·duc′tion** (-dŭk′shŭn), *n.*

sub·due′ (sŭb·dū′), *v. t.* [OF. *soduire* to seduce (fr. L. *subducere* to draw or lead away; see SUBDUCE), but prob. confused in AF. with L. *subdere,* past part. *subditus,* to subdue.] **1.** To conquer and bring into subjection; also, to vanquish; crush. **2.** To overcome, as by persuasion, kindness, self-control, etc.; as, to *subdue* the passions. **3.** To reduce in intensity, force, or degree; lower; as, to *subdue* a fever or one's voice. **4.** To bring into cultivation, as land. — **Syn.** See CONQUER. — **sub·du′a·ble** (-dū′ȧ·b'l), *adj.* — **sub·du′al** (-ăl), *n.* — **sub·du′er** (-ẽr), *n.*

su·ber′ic (sū·bĕr′ĭk; sū-), *adj.* [F. *subérique,* fr. L. *suber* the cork tree.] Of or pert. to cork; *Chem.,* designating a white crystalline diacid, $(CH_2)_6(CO_2H)_2$, obtained from cork and various fatty oils and acids.

su′ber·in (sū′bẽr·ĭn), *n.* Also **su′ber·ine** (-ĭn; -ēn). *Biochem.* A fatty or waxy substance, the basis of cork.

su′ber·i·za′tion (-ĭ·zā′shŭn; -ī·zā′shŭn), *n.* *Bot.* Conversion of the cell walls into cork tissue by development of suberin, as when a callus forms over a wound.

su′ber·ize (sū′bẽr·īz), *v. t.* [L. *suber* cork.] *Bot.* To effect suberization of.

su′ber·ose (-ōs), *adj.* Also **su′ber·ous** (-ŭs). *Bot.* Having a corky texture; suberized.

sub·gla′cial (sŭb·glā′shăl), *adj.* Of or pertaining to the bottom of a glacier. — **sub·gla′cial·ly**, *adv.*

sub′group′ (sŭb′grōōp′; *see* SUB-), *n.* **a** *Biol.* A subdivision of a group. **b** *Chem.* A subdivision of a group in the periodic table. See PERIODIC TABLE.

sub′head′ (sŭb′hĕd′), *n.* **1.** Also **sub·head′ing** (sŭb·hĕd′ĭng). A heading of a subdivision, as a chapter, etc. **2.** In a college, school, etc., an official next below the head.

sub·in′dex (sŭb·ĭn′dĕks), *n.; pl.* -DICES (-dĭ·sēz). *Math.* A character affixed below to a symbol, to distinguish it in its class; a subscript; thus, a_0, b_1, c_2, x_n have 0, 1, 2, *n* as *subindices.*

sub′in·feu′date (sŭb′ĭn·fū′dāt), *v. t. & i.* Also **sub′in·feud′** (-fūd′). To make subinfeudation (of).

sub′in·feu·da′tion (-fū·dā′shŭn), *n.* *Feudal Law.* The granting of lands by a vassal lord to another to hold as vassal of himself; also, the tenure of a vassal so holding land. — **sub′in·feu′da·to′ry** (-fū′dȧ·tō′rĭ *or, esp. Brit.,* -tẽr·ĭ), *n.*

sub·ir′ri·gate (sŭb·ĭr′ĭ·gāt), *v. t.* To irrigate below the surface, as by a system of underground porous pipes. — **sub′ir·ri·ga′tion** (sŭb′ĭr·ĭ·gā′shŭn), *n.*

‖**su′bi·to** (sōō′bē·tō), *adv.* [It. & L.] *Music.* At once; suddenly; — in directions; as, *piano subito,* soft at once.

sub·ja′cent (sŭb·jā′sĕnt; -s'nt), *adj.* [L. *subjacens,* pres. part. of *subjacere* to lie under.] Lying under; also, being lower, though not directly below. — **sub·ja′cen·cy** (-sĕn·sĭ; -s'n·sĭ), *n.*

sub′ject (sŭb′jĕkt; -jĭkt), *adj.* [OF. *suget, subject,* fr. L. *subjectus,* past part. of *subjicere, subicere,* to throw or place under, fr. *sub-* + *jacere* to throw.] **1.** Under the power or dominion of another; specif., *International Law,* owing allegiance to, or being a subject of, a particular sovereign or state. **2.** Exposed; liable; prone; disposed; as, *subject* to temptation. **3.** Dependent upon or exposed to (some contingent action); — with *to;* as, the treaty is *subject* to ratification.

Syn. See LIABLE.

— *n.* **1.** One who is placed under the authority, dominion, control, or influence of another or of something else. **2.** Specif., one subject to a monarch or ruler; in a wider sense, one who owes allegiance to a sovereign power or state. **3.** One who or that which is operated upon, experimented with, tested, studied, etc.; specif., *Anat.,* a dead body for dissection. **4.** That concerning which anything is said or done; the thing or person treated of, represented, etc.; matter; theme; topic. **5.** One of the branches of learning studied in an educational institution. **6.** *Gram.* The word or word group denoting that of which anything is affirmed or predicated. Abbr. *subj.* **7.** *Logic.* That term of a proposition which denotes what the proposition is about; also, the denotation of such a term; topic of an affirmation or denial. **8.** *Music.* The principal theme, or melodic phrase, on which a composition or a movement is based. **9.** *Philos.* **a** That of which a quality, attribute, or relation may be affirmed or in which it may inhere. **b** Hence, substance; substratum; esp., substantive reality; the real, conceived as material or essential being. **c** The thinking agent; the mind, ego, or reality of whatever sort, which supports, or assumes the form of, mental operations. — **Syn.** See CITIZEN.

sub·ject′ (sŭb·jĕkt′), *v. t.* **1.** *Obs.* To make subjacent. **2.** To bring under control or dominion; subjugate. **3.** To make liable; predispose; — with *to.* **4.** To make accountable; — with *to.* **5.** Of an experiment, test, etc., to submit or expose as a subject; — with *to;* as, to *subject* a substance to heat. — **sub·jec′tion** (-jĕk′shŭn), *n.*

sub·jec′tive (sŭb·jĕk′tĭv; sŭb-; 2), *adj.* **1.** Pertaining to, or having the character or quality of, a subject. **2.** Exhibiting or affected by personal bias, emotional background, etc.; as a *subjective* judgment; a *subjective* poem. **3.** *Gram.* Nominative; as, the *subjective* case. **4.** *Med.* Perceptible to the patient only; — of symptoms. **5.** *Philos.* **a** *Obs.* Pertaining to the subject, as the real or essential being of that which supports qualities, attributes, or relations. **b** Of, pertaining to, or determined by the mind, ego, or consciousness, as the subject of experience and knowledge; belonging to reality as perceived or known as opposed to reality as independent of mind; as, to hold that space is *subjective.* **c** Conditioned by personal characteristics of mind, or by particular states of mind; as, the *subjective* element in apprehension. **6.** *Psychol.* **a** Resulting from conditions within the brain and sense organs; as, *subjective* sensations. **b** Requiring or exhibiting introspection. — **sub·jec′tive·ly**, *adv.* — **sub·jec′tive·ness**, **sub′jec·tiv′i·ty** (sŭb′jĕk·tĭv′ĭ·tĭ), *n.*

sub·jec′tiv·ism (sŭb·jĕk′tĭv·ĭz'm), *n.* **1.** *Metaph.* **a** The theory which limits knowledge to conscious states and elements. Cf. IDEALISM **b**. **b** A theory which attaches great or supreme importance to the subjective elements in experience. See KANTIANISM. **2.** *Ethics.* **a** The doctrine that the supreme good is the realization of some type of subjective experience or feeling, as pleasure. **b** The doctrine that individual feeling or apprehension is the ultimate criterion of the good and the right. — **sub·jec′tiv·ist** (-ĭst), *n.* — **sub·jec′ti·vis′tic** (-tĭ·vĭs′tĭk), *adj.*

subject matter. Matter presented for consideration in statement or discussion; subject of thought or study.

sub·join′ (sŭb·join′), *v. t.* [MF. *subjoindre,* fr. L. *subjungere.*] To annex; append.

‖**sub ju′di·ce** (sŭb jōō′dĭ·sē). [L.] Before the judge, or court; under judicial consideration.

sub′ju·gate (sŭb′jŏŏ·gāt; 114), *v. t.* [L. *subjugatus,* past part. of *subjugare* to subjugate, fr. *sub-* + *jugum* a yoke.] **1.** To bring under the yoke of power or dominion; subdue. **2.** To make subservient; subject. — **Syn.** See CONQUER. — **sub′ju·ga′tion** (-gā′shŭn), *n.* — **sub′ju·ga′tor** (-gā′tẽr), *n.*

sub·junc′tion (sŭb·jŭngk′shŭn), *n.* **1.** Act of subjoining, or state of being subjoined. **2.** Something subjoined.

sub·junc′tive (-tĭv), *adj.* [LL. *subjunctivus,* fr. *subjungere, -junctum,* to subjoin.] *Gram.* Designating or pert. to that mood (**subjunctive mood**) of a verb representing the denoted action or state not as fact but as contingent, possible, doubtful, desirable, etc. — *n.* The subjunctive mood; also, a form denoting it. Abbr. *subj.*

sub·king′dom (sŭb·kĭng′dŭm; *see* SUB-), *n.* *Biol.* A primary division of a kingdom, now usually called a *phylum.*

sub′lap·sar′i·an (sŭb′lăp·sâr′ĭ·ăn), *n.* [See SUB-; LAPSE.] *Eccl. Hist.* One of that class of Calvinists who consider the election of grace as a remedy for an existing evil rather than as a part of God's original purpose in regard to men. Cf. SUPRALAPSARIAN. — **sub′lap·sar′i·an**, *adj.* — **sub′lap·sar′i·an·ism** (-ĭz'm), *n.*

sub′lease′ (sŭb′lēs′; *see* SUB-), *n.* A lease by a tenant or lessee to another person of part or all of the leased premises. — (sŭb·lēs′), *v. t. & i.* To make a sublease of. — **sub′les·see′** (sŭb′lĕs·ē′), *n.* — **sub·les′sor** (sŭb·lĕs′ôr; sŭb′lĕs·ôr′), *n.*

sub·let′ (sŭb·lĕt′), *v. t. & i.;* see LET. To sublease.

sub′li·mate (sŭb′lĭ·māt), *v. t.* [L. *sublimatus,* past part. of *sublimare* to raise, elevate (in ML. in sense 1), fr. *sublimis* high.] **1.** To cause to sublime; as, to *sublimate* sulfur. **2.** *Psychoanalysis.* To direct the energy of (an impulse) from its primitive aim to one that is culturally or ethically higher. — *adj.* **a** Sublimated. **b** Refined; elevated. — (-māt), *n.* *Chem.* A product obtained by the process of subliming. — **sub′li·ma′tion** (-mā′shŭn), *n.*

sub·lime′ (sŭb·līm′; 2), *adj.* [F. or L.; F., fr. L. *sublimis.*] **1.** *Archaic.* Upraised; lofty. **2.** Elevated or exalted; noble; as, *sublime* truths. **3.** [*cap.*] As a title, supreme; as, the *Sublime* Porte (see PORTE). **4.** Awakening an uplifting emotion; producing a sense of elevated beauty, grandeur, etc.; as, *sublime* scenery. **5.** *Poetic.* Elevated by joy; elated. — **Syn.** See SPLENDID. — *n.* That which is sublime; quality of sublimity. — *v. t.* To make or cause to be sublime; variously, to exalt; refine; purify. — *v. i.* To pass from the solid to the gaseous state, and again condense to solid form, without apparently liquefying; also, esp. *Physics,* to pass directly from the solid to the gaseous state. — **sub·lime′ly**, *adv.* — **sub·lime′ness**, *n.* — **sub·lim′er** (-līm′ẽr), *n.*

sub·lim′i·nal (sŭb·lĭm′ĭ·năl; -n'l; *often* -lī′mĭ-), *adj.* [*sub-* + L. *limen* threshold.] *Psychol.* Below the threshold of consciousness or beyond the reach of personal awareness; subconscious; also, too small or weak to be perceived, felt, etc.; as, a *subliminal* stimulus. — *n.* The subconscious. — **sub·lim′i·nal·ly**, *adv.*

sub·lim′i·ty (sŭb·lĭm′ĭ·tĭ), *n.; pl.* -TIES (-tĭz). Quality, state, or instance, of being sublime.

sub′lu·nar′y (sŭb′lū·nẽr′ĭ; -nẽr·ĭ; sŭb·lū′nẽr·ĭ), *adj.* Also **sub·lu′nar** (sŭb·lū′nẽr). [See LUNAR.] Situated beneath the moon; hence, terrestrial; mundane; earthly.

sub′ma·chine′ gun (sŭb′mȧ·shēn′). A lightweight, automatic or semiautomatic portable firearm employing ammunition of pistol caliber and designed usually for firing from the shoulder. See RIFLE, *Illust.*

sub·mar′gin·al (sŭb·mär′jĭ·năl; -n'l), *adj.* **1.** *Econ.* Under the minimum allowing economic return; as, *submarginal* land. See MARGIN, 5. **2.** *Biol.* Near the margin; next to a marginal part or structure. — **sub·mar′gin·al·ly**, *adv.*

sub′ma·rine′ (sŭb′mȧ·rēn′; 2), *adj.* Being, acting, growing, or used under water in the sea. — (sŭb′mȧ·rēn′), *n.* **1.** A submarine creature, mine, etc. **2.** A submarine torpedo boat. — (sŭb′mȧ·rēn′), *v. t.* *Colloq.* To make an attack upon or to sink by means of a submarine.

submarine chaser. *Nav.* Any vessel fitted to operate offensively against submarines.

sub′max·il′la (sŭb′măk·sĭl′ȧ), *n.; pl.* -LAE (-ē). [NL.] *Anat. & Zool.* The lower jaw or inferior maxillary bone; in man, the mandible.

sub·max′il·lar′y (sŭb·măk′sĭ·lẽr′ĭ; -măks·ĭl′ȧ·rĭ), *adj.* *Anat.* **a** Below the lower jaw. **b** Designating, or pertaining to, a salivary gland (**submaxillary gland**) inside of and near the lower edge of either side of the mandible. — *n.; pl.* SUBMAXILLARIES (-ĭz). A submaxillary artery, bone, etc.

sub·me′di·ant (sŭb·mē′dĭ·ănt), *n.* *Music.* The sixth tone above, or the third below, the tonic.

sub·merge′ (sŭb·mûrj′), *v. t. & i.* [L. *submergere, submersum,* fr. *sub-* + *mergere* to plunge.] **1.** To put under or plunge into water. **2.** To cover or become covered with or as with water; inundate. — **sub·mer′gence** (-mûr′jĕns), *n.* — **sub·mer′gi·bil′i·ty** (-jĭ·bĭl′ĭ·tĭ), *n.* — **sub·mer′gi·ble** (-mûr′jĭ·b'l), *adj. & n.*

sub·merse′ (sŭb·mûrs′), *v. t.* [L. *submersus,* past part. of *submergere.*] To submerge. — **sub·mer′sion** (-mûr′shŭn), *n.*

sub·mersed′ (-mûrst′), *adj.* Submerged; growing, adapted to grow, or operating under water.

sub·mers′i·ble (-mûr′sĭ·b'l), *n.* Loosely, a submarine. — *adj.* Capable of being submersed or of operating or functioning while submersed.

sub′mi·cro·scop′ic (sŭb′mī·krō·skŏp′ĭk), *adj.* Too small to be seen through the microscope.

sub·miss′ (sŭb·mĭs′), *adj.* [L. *submissus*, past part. of *submittere*. See SUBMIT.] *Archaic.* Submissive; obsequious.

sub·mis′sion (-mĭsh′ŭn), *n.* [OF., fr. L. *submissio* a letting down, lowering.] **1.** Act of submitting; esp., surrender of person and power to the control of another. **2.** Submissiveness; obedience; compliance. **3.** Act of submitting something for consideration, inspection, etc.; as, *submission* of a passport for inspection.

sub·mis′sive (-mĭs′ĭv), *adj.* Inclined or ready to submit; expressing submission; yielding; meek. — **sub·mis′sive·ly,** *adv.* — **sub·mis′sive·ness,** *n.*

sub·mit′ (sŭb·mĭt′), *v. t.;* SUB·MIT′TED (-ĕd; -ĭd); SUB·MIT′TING. [L. *submittere*, fr. *sub-* + *mittere* to send.] **1.** To leave or commit to the discretion or judgment of another or others; refer. **2.** To yield, resign, or surrender to power, will, or authority; — often with the reflexive pronoun. **3.** To offer or put forward as an opinion; venture to affirm; as, we *submit* that the charge is not proved. — *v. i.* **1.** To yield one's person to the power of another; surrender. **2.** To yield or defer to the opinion or authority of another. **3.** To be submissive; yield resignedly. — **Syn.** See YIELD. — **sub·mit′tal** (-ăl), *n.* — **sub·mit′ter** (-ẽr), *n.*

sub·mon′tane (sŭb·mŏn′tān), *adj.* [*sub-* + L. *mons, montis*, mountain.] Situated at the foot or near the base of a mountain or mountains. — **sub·mon′tane·ly,** *adv.*

sub·mul′ti·ple (-mŭl′tĭ·p'l), *n.* A number or quantity that divides another exactly; an aliquot part.

sub·nor′mal (-nôr′măl), *adj.* Below the normal; less than normal; specif., *Psychol.*, having less than normal intelligence. — *n.* A subnormal person. — **sub′nor·mal′i·ty** (sŭb′nôr·măl′ĭ·tĭ), *n.*

sub′o·ce·an′ic (sŭb′ō·shē·ăn′ĭk), *adj.* *Geol.* Situated, taking place, or formed, beneath the bottom of the ocean.

sub·or′di·nate (sŭ·bôr′dĭ·nĭt), *adj.* [ML. *subordinatus*, past part. of *subordinare*, fr. *sub-* + *ordinare* to arrange.] **1.** Placed in a lower class or rank; as, *subordinate* officers. **2.** Inferior in order, nature, importance, etc.; as, a *subordinate* position. **3.** Pert. to or involving dependence or subjection in order or rank: **a** Submissive to authority. **b** *Gram.* (1) Also **sub·or′di·nat′ing** (-nāt′ĭng). Joining word groups or words with dependent rank to others in the sentence; subordinative or subordinating; as, a *subordinate* conjunction. (2) Subordinated or dependent; as, a *subordinate* clause. — *n.* One who stands in order or rank below another; — disting. from a *principal.* — (-nāt), *v. t.* **1.** To place in a lower order or class; to make or consider as of less value or importance. **2.** To make subservient; as, to *subordinate* the passions to reason. — **sub·or′di·na′tion** (-nā′shŭn), *n.* — **sub·or′di·na′tive** (-nā′tĭv; -nȧ·tĭv), *adj.*

sub·or′di·na′tion·ism (-nā′shŭn·ĭz'm), *n.* The doctrine that the second and third persons of the Trinity are subordinate to the first person. — **sub·or′di·na′tion·ist** (-ĭst), *n.* & *adj.*

sub·orn′ (sŭb·ôrn′; sŭb-), *v. t.* [F. *suborner*, fr. L. *subornare*, fr. *sub* under, secretly + *ornare* to equip.] **1.** To procure privately or unlawfully, as a person by bribery to commit some crime; incite secretly; instigate. **2.** *Law.* To procure (another) to commit perjury; as, to *suborn* witnesses. — **sub·orn′er,** *n.*

sub′or·na′tion (sŭb′ôr·nā′shŭn), *n.* Act of suborning; specif., *Law*, the crime of procuring a person to commit perjury. — **sub·or′na·tive** (sŭb·ôr′nȧ·tĭv), *adj.*

sub·ox′ide (sŭb·ŏk′sīd; -sĭd), *n.* Also **sub·ox′id.** *Chem.* An oxide containing a relatively small proportion of oxygen.

sub′plot′ (sŭb′plŏt′), *n.* A subordinate plot, as in a play.

sub·poe′na (sŭb·pē′nȧ; sŭb-; sŭ·pē′-), *n.* Also **sub·pe′na.** [NL., fr. L. *sub* under + *poena* punishment.] *Law.* A writ commanding the person designated in it to attend court under a penalty for failure. — *v. t.;* -NAED (-nȧd); -NA·ING. To serve or summon with a subpoena.

sub·prin′ci·pal (sŭb·prĭn′sĭ·păl; -p'l), *n.* **a** An under principal. **b** *Carp.* A secondary rafter or the like. **c** *Music.* In an organ, an open diapason subbass.

sub′re′gion (sŭb′rē′jŭn; *see* SUB-), *n.* *Biogeog.* One of the primary divisions of a region. — **sub·re′gion·al** (sŭb·rē′jŭn·ăl; -'l), *adj.*

sub·rep′tion (sŭb·rĕp′shŭn), *n.* [L. *subreptio*, fr. *subripere, subreptum.* See SURREPTITIOUS.] **1.** A deliberate misrepresentation or an inference drawn from it. **2.** *Law.* The obtaining of a gift or other property, esp. ecclesiastical preferment, by concealing the truth. — **sub′rep·ti′tious** (sŭb′rĕp·tĭsh′ŭs), *adj.*

sub′ro·gate (sŭb′rō·gāt), *v. t.* [L. *subrogatus*, past part. of *subrogare.* See SURROGATE.] To put in the place of another; to substitute.

sub′ro·ga′tion (-gā′shŭn), *n.* A subrogating; specif., *Law*, the substitution of one for another as a creditor, the new creditor succeeding to the former's rights.

‖**sub ro′sa** (sŭb rō′zȧ). [L.] Under the rose (see under ROSE, *n.*); covertly; privately; confidentially.

sub·scap′u·lar (sŭb·skăp′ū·lẽr), *adj.* *Anat.* Beneath the scapula; on, or pertaining to, the under (in man the anterior) surface of the scapula.

sub·scribe′ (sŭb·skrīb′), *v. t.* [L. *subscribere, subscriptum*, fr. *sub-* + *scribere* to write.] **1.** To write underneath; to sign (one's name) to a document. **2.** To sign with one's own hand; to give consent to, as something written, by writing one's name beneath; as, to *subscribe* a bond. **3.** To attest by writing one's name beneath; as, clerks *subscribe* copies of records. **4.** To give assent or support to overtly; favor; sanction. **5.** To promise to give or contribute, esp. in writing. — *v. i.* **1.** To sign one's name to a document. **2.** To give one's consent in or as in writing; often, to express assent; — usually with *to;* as, I *subscribe* to that statement. **3.** To set down one's name as token of a promise to give something, as money; also, loosely, to give something in accordance with such a promise. **4.** To agree to take and pay for something, as stock, or a journal, esp. by signing a formal agreement. — **Syn.** See ASSENT. — **sub·scrib′er** (-skrīb′ẽr), *n.*

sub′script (sŭb′skrĭpt), *adj.* [L. *subscriptus*, past part.] Written below; as, iota *subscript;* — said specif., *Math.*, of a subindex. — *n.* A subscript sign, letter, etc. Cf. SUPERSCRIPT.

sub·scrip′tion (sŭb·skrĭp′shŭn), *n.* **1.** Act of subscribing, as to a journal, to charity. **2.** That which is subscribed; specif.: **a** A signed paper. **b** The signature attached to a paper. **c** Consent or attestation by underwriting the name. **d** Sum or amount of sums subscribed. **3.** *Eccl.* The acceptance of articles or other tests tending to promote uniformity; esp., *Ch. of Eng.*, formal assent to the Thirty-nine Articles of 1563 and the Book of Common Prayer. — **sub·scrip′tive** (-tĭv), *adj.* — **sub·scrip′tive·ly,** *adv.*

sub′se·quence (sŭb′sē·kwĕns), *n.* Also **sub′se·quen·cy** (-kwĕn·sĭ). Act or state of being subsequent; also, that which follows subsequently; a later or following event.

sub′se·quent (-kwĕnt; -kwĕnt), *adj.* [F. or L.; F. *subséquent*, fr. L. *subsequens, -entis*, pres. part. of *subsequi* to follow, succeed.] Following in time, order, or place; later; succeeding. — **sub′se·quent·ly,** *adv.* — **sub′se·quent·ness,** *n.*

sub·serve′ (sŭb·sûrv′), *v. t.* [L. *subservire*, fr. *sub-* + *servire* to serve.] To serve in a subordinate capacity or manner; to be subservient or instrumental to; promote.

sub·ser′vi·ence (-sûr′vĭ·ĕns), *n.* Also **sub·ser′vi·en·cy** (-ĕn·sĭ). **1.** State of being subservient. **2.** Willingness to serve another's purposes; servility; truckling.

sub·ser′vi·ent (-ĕnt), *adj.* **1.** Fitted or disposed to subserve; useful in an inferior capacity. **2.** Servile; truckling. — **sub·ser′vi·ent·ly,** *adv.*

Syn. **Subservient, servile, slavish, menial, obsequious** mean showing or requiring extreme compliance or abject obedience. **Subservient** implies subordination, as in position or state of mind, and often a cringing or truckling; **servile,** work or character typical of slaves or servants of low degree; **slavish,** abject, debased servility; **menial,** in current use, lowness or meanness in character or degree; **obsequious,** a revealing of one's sense of inferiority in the presence of one's superiors.

sub′shrub′ (sŭb′shrŭb′), *n.* An undershrub.

sub·side′ (sŭb·sīd′), *v. i.* [L. *subsidere*, fr. *sub-* + *sidere* to sit down, settle.] **1.** To sink or fall to the bottom; settle, as lees. **2.** To tend downward; descend. **3.** *Colloq.* To sink; fall; as, he *subsided* into a chair. **4.** To fall into a state of quiet; become tranquil; abate. — **Syn.** See ABATE. — **sub·sid′ence** (sŭb·sīd′ĕns *or, esp. Brit.*, sŭb′sĭ·dĕns), *n.*

sub·sid′i·ar′y (sŭb·sĭd′ĭ·ĕr′ĭ *or, esp. Brit.*, -ẽr·ĭ), *adj.* [L. *subsidiarius.* See SUBSIDY.] **1.** Furnishing aid; auxiliary; tributary; as, a *subsidiary* stream; esp., aiding in a subordinate or inferior status or capacity; secondary. **2.** Of, pertaining to, or constituting a subsidy; aiding by, or aided by, a subsidy; as, *subsidiary* payments to allies. — *n.; pl.* -IES (-ĭz). **1.** One who or that which contributes aid or supplies; an auxiliary. **2.** *Finance.* In full, **subsidiary company.** A company controlled by another company which owns at least a majority of its shares. **3.** *Music.* A subordinate theme or motive. — **sub·sid′i·ar′i·ly** (-ĭ·lĭ), *adv.*

sub′si·dize (sŭb′sĭ·dīz), *v. t.* [From SUBSIDY.] To furnish with a subsidy; as: **a** To purchase the assistance of by the payment of a subsidy. **b** To aid or promote, as a private enterprise, with public money; as, to *subsidize* a steamship line. — **sub′si·di·za′tion** (-dĭ·zā′shŭn; -dī·zā′-), *n.* — **sub′si·diz′er** (-dīz′ẽr), *n.*

sub′si·dy (sŭb′sĭ·dĭ), *n.; pl.* -DIES (-dĭz). [AF. *subsidie*, fr. L. *subsidium* the troops stationed in reserve in the third line of battle, reserve, support.] **1.** Any gift made by way of financial aid. **2.** Formerly, in England, money granted by parliament to the crown and raised by special taxation. **3. a** A sum of money granted by one state to another, as to aid in the prosecution of a war. **b** A government grant to assist a private enterprise deemed advantageous to the public; a subvention.

sub·sist′ (sŭb·sĭst′), *v. i.* [L. *subsistere* to stand still, stay, remain alive, fr. *sub-* + *sistere* to stand.] **1.** To have existence; to exist or continue to exist. **2.** To retain the present state; abide. **3.** To be maintained with food and clothing; live. **4.** *Philos.* **a** To hold true or good. **b** To have the character of being logically conceivable and being the subject of true statements. — *v. t.* To support with provisions; maintain.

sub·sist′ence (-sĭs′tĕns), *n.* **1.** Act or condition of subsisting; specif.: **a** Being; existence. **b** *Obs.* Persistence; continuance. **c** Inherency; as, the *subsistence* of qualities in bodies. **2.** Means of support; provisions; supplies; also, maintenance; livelihood. **3.** *Philos.* **a** The mode by which substance becomes individualized, or, as applied to human personality, a singular rational substance wholly self-contained and endowed with inalienable rights. **b** The status of that which subsists (sense 4 **b**).

sub·sist′ent (-tĕnt), *adj.* **1.** Having being; subsisting; existing. **2.** Having subsistence (esp. sense 3 **a**).

sub′soil′ (sŭb′soil′), *n.* The bed or stratum of weathered material which underlies the surface soil. — *v. t.* To turn or stir up the subsoil of. — **sub′soil′er** (-ẽr), *n.*

sub·so′lar (sŭb·sō′lẽr), *adj.* [See SOLAR.] Being under the sun; having the sun in the zenith; terrestrial; mundane; specif., situated between the tropics.

sub·son′ic (-sŏn′ĭk), *adj.* [*sub-* + *sonic.*] *Physics.* Of, pertaining to, or designating a speed less than that of sound in air, that is, less than about 1087 feet per second (or about 738 miles per hour); also, moving, capable of moving, or utilizing air currents moving, at such a speed. Cf. SUPERSONIC.

‖**sub spe′ci·e ae·ter′ni·ta′tis** (sŭb spē′shĭ·ē [-shē] ē·tûr′nĭ·tā′tĭs). [L.] Under the aspect of eternity; in its essential or universal form or nature.

sub·spe′cies (sŭb·spē′shĭz *or, esp. in the pl.*, -spē′shēz; *see* SPECIES; 2), *n.* [NL.] *Biol.* A division of a species; a variety or race; a category ranking next below a species.

sub′stance (sŭb′stăns), *n.* [OF., fr. L. *substantia*, fr. *substare* to be under or present, stand firm.] **1.** That which underlies all outward manifestations; real, unchanging essence or nature of a thing; that in which qualities inhere; that which constitutes anything what it is. **2.** Essential element or elements; characteristic components; as, the ideas are the same in *substance.* **3.** Essential import; gist; as, the *substance* of what he said. **4.** Material of which a thing is made; hence, solidity; body; as, to test the *substance* of concrete; also, a material object, as distinguished from something visionary or shadowy. **5.** Material possessions; estate; property; resources; as, to waste one's *substance.* **6.** *Chem.* Any particular kind of matter, whether element, compound, or mixture; any chemical material of which bodies (sense 6) are composed. **7.** *Christian Science.* Spirit.

sub·stand′ard (sŭb·stăn′dẽrd), *adj.* Below the or a standard; specif.: **a** *U. S. Statute Law.* Below the standard of the Federal Food and Drugs Act and not labeled as below the standard. **b** *Linguistics.* Conforming to a pattern of linguistic usage existing within a speech community, but not that of the prestige group in that community, in choice of word (*set*, for *sit*), form of word (*kilt*, for *killed*), pronunciation (*twicet*, for *twice*), grammatical construction (the beans *is* growing), or idiom (*all to once*, for *all at once*).

sub·stan′tial (sŭb·stăn′shăl), *adj.* [OF. *substantiel*, fr. LL. *substantialis.*] **1.** Of, pertaining to, or having substance. **2.** Not seeming or imaginary; not illusive; real; true. **3.** Having substance, or body; strong; stout; solid; firm. **4**. Possessed of goods; moderately wealthy; responsible; as, *substantial* men. **5**. That is such in substance or in the main; as, a *substantial* victory. **6**. Considerable; large; as, a *substantial* gain. **7**. Nourishing and plentiful; as, a *substantial* meal. — *n*. Something substantial. — **sub·stan′ti·al′i·ty** (-shĭ·ăl′ĭ·tĭ), *n*. — **sub·stan′tial·ly**, *adv*. — **sub·stan′tial·ness**, *n*.

sub·stan′tial·ism (sŭb·stăn′shăl·ĭz′m), *n*. *Philos*. **a** The doctrine that constant realities underlie phenomena. **b** The doctrine that matter is a real substance rather than an aggregation of centers of force. — **sub·stan′tial·ist** (-ĭst), *n*.

sub·stan′ti·ate (sŭb·stăn′shĭ·āt), *v. t*. **1**. To impart substance to. **2**. To establish the existence or truth of by proof or competent evidence; verify. **3**. To put into substance or concrete form. — **Syn**. See CONFIRM. — **sub·stan′ti·a′tion** (-ā′shŭn), *n*. — **sub·stan′ti·a′tive** (-ā′tĭv), *adj*.

sub′stan·tive (sŭb′stăn·tĭv), *adj*. [OF. *substantif*, fr. LL. *substantivus*.] **1**. Independent and self-subsistent; not derivative or dependent. **2**. Considerable; substantial. **3**. Having real and continued existence; not transitive; abiding. **4**. Of the substance, as distinguished from that which is accidental or qualifying; essential. **5**. *Dyeing*. Not needing a mordant. **6**. *Gram*. Betokening or expressing existence; as, the *substantive* verb *to be*. **7**. *Law*. Pertaining to or constituting the essential part or principles; as, the law *substantive*. — **sub′stan·ti′val** (sŭb′stăn·tī′văl; sŭb′stăn·tĭv·ăl), *adj*.

sub′stan·tive, *n*. **1**. A substantive or self-subsistent entity or thing. **2**. *Gram*. **a** A noun. **b** A pronoun, verbal noun, or any part of speech used as a noun equivalent. — **-tive·ly**, *adv*. — **-tive·ness**, *n*.

sub·stit′u·ent (sŭb·stĭt′ū·ĕnt), *n*. [L. *substituens*, pres. part. See SUBSTITUTE.] *Chem*. Any atom or group substituted for another, or entering a molecule in place of some other part. — **sub·stit′u·ent**, *adj*.

sub′sti·tute (sŭb′stĭ·tūt), *n*. [L. *substitutus*, past part. of *substituere* to put under, put in the place of, fr. *sub-* + *statuere* to put, place.] **1**. A person or thing put in place of another; one replacing another. **2**. *Ling*. A word which replaces another word, a phrase, or a clause, in a context. **3**. *Mil*. A person who enlists for military service in the place of a conscript or drafted man. — *v. t. & i*. **1**. To put or serve in the place of another person or thing; exchange. **2**. To replace; take the place of (something or someone). — **sub′sti·tu′tion** (-tū′shŭn), *n*. — **sub′sti·tu′tion·al** (-ăl), *adj*. — **sub′sti·tu′tion·al·ly**, *adv*. — **sub′sti·tu′tion·ar′y** (-ĕr′ĭ *or, esp. Brit*., -ĕr·ĭ), *adj*.

sub′sti·tu′tive (-tū′tĭv), *adj*. Tending to afford or furnish a substitute; making, or capable of, substitution.

sub′strate (sŭb′strāt), *n*. **a** A substratum. **b** *Biochem*. A substance acted upon, as by an enzyme.

sub·strat′o·sphere (sŭb·străt′ō·sfēr; -strā′tō-), *n*. *Aviation*. The region of the atmosphere below the stratosphere and above an elevation of about 3½ miles, suitable for flying aircraft but requiring protective devices such as oxygen masks, pressurized cabins, supercharged engines, etc.

sub·stra′tum (sŭb·strā′tŭm), *n*.; *pl*. -TA (-tȧ). [L., neut. of *substratus*, past part. of *substernere* to strew under, fr. *sub-* + *sternere* to strew.] **1**. That which is laid or spread under; foundation. **2**. *Agric*. The subsoil. **3**. *Biol*. The substance or base on which an organism grows. **4**. *Metaph*. Substance considered as supporting attributes or accidents; the permanent subject of qualities or cause of phenomena. **5**. *Photog*. A thin coating, usually of hardened gelatin, on cellulosic material, glass, or paper, to facilitate the adhesion of the sensitive emulsion. — **sub·stra′tal** (-tăl; -t′l), **sub·stra′tive** (-tĭv), *adj*.

sub·struc′tion (sŭb·strŭk′shŭn), *n*. [L. *substructio*, fr. *substruere*, *substructum*, to build beneath, fr. *sub-* + *struere* to build.] *Arch*. Underbuilding; substructure.

sub·struc′ture (-strŭk′tūr; 2), *n*. Groundwork; specif.: **a** *Arch*. Foundation, as of a building. **b** *Railroads*. The earth roadway supporting the ballast and track. — **sub·struc′tur·al** (-tūr·ăl), *adj*.

sub·sume′ (sŭb·sūm′), *v. t*. [*sub-* + *sumere* to take.] To include or classify within a category, as individual under species, or particular under universal, principle under major principle, etc.

sub·sump′tion (-sŭmp′shŭn), *n*. **1**. Act of subsuming, or state of being subsumed. **2**. *Logic*. **a** That which is subsumed. **b** The minor premise of a syllogism.

sub·tan′gent (sŭb·tăn′jĕnt), *n*. *Geom*. The intercept on the axis of abscissas between the ordinate and tangent drawn to the same point in a curve.

sub·tem′per·ate (-tĕm′pẽr·ĭt), *adj*. *Geog*. Slightly temperate; of or pert. to the colder parts of the Temperate Zones.

sub·ten′ant (-tĕn′ănt; *see* SUB-), *n*. One who rents from a tenant; a sublessee. — **sub·ten′an·cy** (-ăn·sĭ), *n*.

sub·tend′ (sŭb·tĕnd′), *v. t*. [L. *subtendere*, fr. *sub-* + *tendere*, *tentum* or *tensum*, to stretch, extend.] **1**. To extend under, or be opposite to; as, a chord *subtends* an arc. **2**. *Bot*. To enclose or embrace in its axil; as, a bract *subtending* a flower.

sub′ter- (sŭb′tẽr-). [L. *subter*, adv. & prep., orig. compar. of *sub* under.] A prefix, meaning *below, beneath, underneath, less than*; — opposed to *super-*, as in **sub′ter·con′scious**, **sub′ter·nat′u·ral**, **sub′ter·sur′face**.

sub′ter·fuge (sŭb′tẽr·fūj), *n*. [F., fr. LL. *subterfugium*, fr. L. *subterfugere* to flee secretly, escape, fr. *subter* under + *fugere* to flee.] A device, plan, or the like, for escaping censure, evading an issue, etc. — **Syn**. See DECEPTION.

sub′ter·rane (-tĕ·rān), *n*. A cave or underground room.

sub′ter·ra′ne·an (-rā′nē·ăn), *adj*. Also **sub′ter·ra′ne·ous** (-ŭs). [L. *subterraneus*, fr. *sub-* + *terra* earth.] Being or lying under the surface of the earth; hence, hidden; secret.

sub′tile (sŭb′tĭl; sŭt′′l), *adj*. [F. *subtil*, for OF. *soutil*, under L. influence. See SUBTLE.] **1**. Subtle; tenuous; elusive, as an odor. **2**. Wily; cunning; crafty. — **sub′tile·ly**, *adv*. — **sub′tile·ness**, **sub·til′i·ty** (sŭb·tĭl′ĭ·tĭ), *n*.

sub′til·ize (sŭb′tĭl·īz; sŭt′′l·īz), *v. t. & i*. To make subtile; to use subtlety; to introduce fine-drawn distinctions into the use, discussion, or interpretation of; as, to *subtilize* Shakespeare's sonnets. — **sub′til·i·za′tion** (-ĭ·zā′shŭn; -ī·zā′-), *n*.

sub′til·ty (-tĭ), *n*.; *pl*. -TIES (-tĭz). Subtlety.

sub′ti′tle (sŭb′tī′t′l; 2), *n*. **1**. A secondary title, esp. of a book or play; hence, a book title repeated in a subordinate position, as over the first page of text. **2**. *Motion Pictures*. A brief statement thrown on the screen, generally preceding a scene which it explains.

sub′tle (sŭt′′l), *adj*. [OF. *soutil* (F. *subtil*), fr. L. *subtilis*, orig., woven fine, fr. *sub* under + stem of *tela* a web, *texere* to weave.] **1**. Subtile, or rare; tenuous. **2**. Mentally acute; given to or characterized by refinements of thought, insight, perception, etc.; analytic. **3**. Cunningly made or contrived; ingenious. **4**. Subtile, or crafty; artful. **5**. Insidiously or quietly active; as, *subtle* poisons. — **sub′tle·ness**, *n*. — **sub′tly** (sŭt′lĭ), *adv*.

sub′tle·ty (-tĭ), *n*.; *pl*. -TIES (-tĭz). **1**. Quality or state of being subtle; esp., the power or practice of drawing delicate distinctions. **2**. Something subtle; esp., a delicate distinction.

sub·ton′ic (sŭb·tŏn′ĭk), *n*. See LEADING TONE.

sub·tor′rid (sŭb·tŏr′ĭd), *adj*. Subtropical.

sub·tract′ (sŭb·trăkt′), *v. t. & i*. [L. *subtractus*, past part. of *subtrahere* to draw from beneath, withdraw, fr. *sub-* + *trahere*.] To withdraw or take away, as a part from a whole or one number from another; deduct. — **sub·tract′er**, *n*.

sub·trac′tion (sŭb·trăk′shŭn), *n*. **1**. Act, operation, or an instance, of subtracting. **2**. *Math*. Act or process of subtracting one number or quantity from another. It is denoted by the **subtraction sign** or **mark** (−).

sub·trac′tive (-tĭv), *adj*. **1**. Tending to subtract; involving subtraction. **2**. *Math*. Having the negative or minus sign (−).

sub′tra·hend′ (sŭb′trȧ·hĕnd′), *n*. [L. *subtrahendus* that is to be subtracted.] *Math*. The number or quantity to be subtracted from another (called the *minuend*). See REMAINDER, 5.

sub·trop′i·cal (sŭb·trŏp′ĭ·kăl), *adj*. Also **sub·trop′ic** (-ĭk). Nearly tropical; of, pert. to, or designating regions bordering on the tropical zone. — **sub·trop′ics** (-ĭks), *n. pl*.

su′bu·late (sū′bū·lāt), *adj*. [NL. *subulatus*, fr. L. *subula* an awl.] Linear and tapering to a fine point; awl-shaped.

sub′urb (sŭb′ûrb), *n*. [OF. *suburbe*, fr. L. *suburbium*, fr. *sub* under, below, near + *urbs* a city.] **1**. An outlying part of a city; a smaller place adjacent to a city; in *pl*. with *the*, the residential districts on the outskirts of a city. **2**. *pl*. The confines; periphery; environs.

sub·ur′ban (sŭb·ûr′băn; sŭb-), *adj*. Of, pertaining to, or characteristic of the suburbs; specif., *U. S*., blending the urban and rural. — *n*. A suburbanite.

sub·ur′ban·ite (-īt), *n*. A dweller in the suburbs.

sub·ur′bi·a (sŭb·ûr′bĭ·ȧ), *n*. The suburbs of a city; also, suburbanites collectively.

sub·ur′bi·car′i·an (sŭb·ûr′bĭ·kâr′ĭ·ăn), *adj*. [LL. *suburbicarius*, equiv. to L. *suburbanus* suburban.] Being in the suburbs or near the city; of or pertaining to the suburbs; — applied to the six dioceses nearest Rome.

sub·vene′ (sŭb·vēn′), *v. i*. [L. *subvenire* to come to one's assistance, come up.] To come under, esp. as a support; to happen by way of relief or aid.

sub·ven′tion (-vĕn′shŭn), *n*. **1**. A subvening. **2**. A grant of money; esp., a subsidy from a government or foundation. — **sub·ven′tion·ar′y** (-ĕr′ĭ *or, esp. Brit*., -ĕr·ĭ), *adj*.

‖**sub ver′bo** (sŭb vûr′bō). Also ‖**sub vo′ce** (vō′sē). [L.] Under the word; — used in reference to any entry in a dictionary, index, etc. Abbr. *s.v.*

sub·ver′sal (sŭb·vûr′săl), *n*. Subversion.

sub·ver′sion (-vûr′shŭn; -zhŭn), *n*. [OF., fr. LL. *subversio*. See SUBVERT.] **1**. Act of subverting, or state of being subverted; overthrow; utter ruin; destruction. **2**. That which subverts. — **sub·ver′sive** (-sĭv), *adj*.

sub·vert′ (sŭb·vûrt′), *v. t*. [OF. or L.; OF. *subvertir*, fr. L. *subvertere*, *subversum*, fr. *sub-* + *vertere* to turn.] **1**. To overturn; overthrow; ruin utterly. **2**. To undermine the morals, allegiance, or faith of; corrupt. — **sub·vert′er**, *n*.

‖**sub vo′ce**. See SUB VERBO.

sub′way′ (sŭb′wā′), *n*. An underground way or passage; esp.: **a** A passage under a street, for pedestrians, or for the running of water or gas mains, telephone wires, etc. **b** *U. S*. An underground electric railway.

suc′ce·da′ne·um (sŭk′sē·dā′nē·ŭm), *n*.; *pl*. -NEA (-ȧ). [NL., fr. *succedaneus* substituted.] A substitute. — **suc′ce·da′ne·ous** (-ŭs), *adj*.

suc·ceed′ (sŭk·sēd′), *v. i*. [OF. or L.; OF. *succeder*, fr. L. *succedere*, *successum*, to go under, go up, follow, be successful, fr. *sub-* + *cedere* to go along.] **1**. To come next after another, as into an office, an inheritance, etc.; specif., to inherit the sovereignty. **2**. To follow another in order; to come after another in sequence; ensue. **3**. *Obs*. To descend, as an estate; devolve. **4**. To attain the desired object or end; to be successful. — *v. t*. **1**. To follow (one) next after as heir or successor; fill the vacancy left by. **2**. To follow; be consequent or subsequent to. — **Syn**. See FOLLOW. — **suc·ceed′er**, *n*.

suc·cen′tor (sŭk·sĕn′tẽr), *n*. [LL., an accompanier in singing, ult. fr. *sub* under, after + *canere* to sing.] *Eccl*. A precentor's assistant, esp. in some monasteries and cathedrals.

‖**suc′cès′ d'es′time′** (sük′sĕ′ dĕs′tēm′). [F.] The reception accorded a play which wins critical respect but is not a popular success.

suc·cess′ (sŭk·sĕs′), *n*. [L. *successus*. See SUCCEED.] **1**. *Obs*. That which ensues; outcome; issue. **2**. Degree or measure of succeeding, or attaining one's desired end. **3**. Favorable termination of a venture; often, specif., the attainment of wealth, fame, etc. **4** A successful person or thing; one achieving success (sense 3). **5**. *Obs*. A succession.

suc·cess′ful (-fōōl; -f′l), *adj*. Resulting or terminating favorably or as desired; also, achieving success, wealth, position, or the like. — **suc·cess′ful·ly**, *adv*.

suc·ces′sion (sŭk·sĕsh′ŭn), *n*. [OF. or L.; OF., fr. L. *successio*. See SUCCEED.] **1**. The order in which or the conditions under which one person after another succeeds to a property, a dignity, a title, or, esp., a throne; also, the right of a person or line to succeed to a throne, etc., or the line having such a right. **2**. A succeeding; sequence; as, disasters came in rapid *succession*. **3**. A number of persons or things that follow each other in sequence; a continuous series. **4**. *Law*. **a** The change in legal relations by which one person comes into the enjoyment of, or becomes responsible for, the rights or liabilities of another person, as of a son to the estate or rank of his father; also, the right or duty so to take another's place, or the rights and duties succeeded to. **b** The act or fact of becoming beneficially entitled to the estate of a deceased person. — **suc·ces′sion·al**, *adj*. — **suc·ces′sion·al·ly**, *adv*.

suc·ces′sive (sŭk·sĕs′ĭv), *adj*. **1**. Following in succession or serial order; following each other without interruption. **2**. Characterized by, or produced in, succession. — **Syn**. See CONSECUTIVE. — **suc·ces′sive·ly**, *adv*. — **suc·ces′sive·ness**, *n*.

suc·ces′sor (sŭk·sĕs′ẽr), *n.* [OF. *successur, successor,* fr. L. *successor.* See SUCCEED.] One who or that which follows; esp., one who succeeds to a throne, title, estate, or office; — a correlative of *predecessor.*

suc·cinct′ (sŭk·sĭngkt′), *adj.* [L. *succinctus,* past part. of *succingere* to gird below or from below, tuck up, fr. *sub-* + *cingere* to gird.] **1.** *Archaic.* Girded; close-fitting. **2.** Compressed into a narrow compass; concise; terse; short; brief; curt. — **Syn.** See CONCISE. — **Ant.** Discursive. — **suc·cinct′ly,** *adv.* — **suc·cinct′ness,** *n.*

suc·cin′ic (sŭk·sĭn′ĭk), *adj.* [F. *succinique,* fr. L. *succinum, sucinum,* amber.] *Chem.* Pertaining to or designating a colorless crystalline diacid, $(CH_2CO_2H)_2$, in amber and lignite, etc., and also produced artificially.

suc′cor, suc′cour (sŭk′ẽr), *n.* [OF. *sucurs, socors, secors,* fr. ML. *succursus,* fr. L. *succurrere.* The loss of final *s* is due to mistaking the older form as pl. See SUCCOR, *v.*] **1.** Aid; help; assistance; relief. **2.** The person or thing that brings relief. — *v. t.* [OF. *sucurre, soucourre,* fr. L. *succurrere, succursum,* to run under, run to the aid of, help, fr. *sub-* + *currere* to run.] To go to the aid of when in want or distress; relieve. — **suc′cor·a·ble, suc′cour·a·ble,** *adj.* — **suc′cor·er, suc′cour·er,** *n.*

suc′co·ry (sŭk′ō·rĭ), *n.* [From *cicoree, sycory,* early vars. of *chicory,* after MLG. *suckerīe,* MD. *sūkerīe.*] Chicory.

suc′co·tash (-tăsh), *n.* [Am. Indian *misickquatash* an ear of corn, lit., the grains are whole.] Beans and kernels of sweet corn, cooked together.

suc′cu·ba (sŭk′ū·bȧ), *n.; pl.* -BAE (-bē). [L., strumpet.] = SUCCUBUS.

suc′cu·bus (sŭk′ū·bŭs), *n.; pl.* -BI (-bī), -BUSES (-bŭs·ĕz; -ĭz). [ML., fr. L. *succubare* to lie under, fr. *sub-* + *cubare* to lie down.] A demon, esp. one assuming female form to have sexual intercourse with men in their sleep. Cf. INCUBUS.

suc′cu·lent (-lĕnt), *adj.* [L. *succulentus, suculentus,* fr. *succus, sucus,* juice.] **1.** Full of juice; juicy; specif., *Bot.,* having juicy tissues, as most cacti. **2.** Full of vitality, freshness, etc.; not arid, thin, lifeless, etc. — **suc′cu·lence** (-lĕns), **suc′cu·len·cy** (-lĕn·sĭ), *n.* — **suc′cu·lent·ly,** *adv.*

suc·cumb′ (sŭ·kŭm′), *v. i.* [L. *succumbere,* fr. *sub-* + *cumbere* (in comp.) to lie down.] To sink down; yield; give way; specif., to give up one's life; — often with *to;* as, to *succumb* to temptation or pneumonia. — **Syn.** See YIELD.

suc·cur′sal (sŭ·kûr′săl), *adj.* [F. *succursale.*] Subsidiary; auxiliary; of the nature of a branch or offshoot; as, a *succursal* church of a cathedral.

suc·cuss′ (sŭ·kŭs′), *v. t.* To shake violently; esp., *Med.,* to perform succussion upon (a patient).

suc′cus·sa′tion (sŭk′ŭ·sā′shŭn), *n.* [L. *succussare* to jolt, v. intens.] A shaking; succussion. — **suc·cus′sa·to′ry** (sŭ·kŭs′ȧ·tō′rĭ *or, esp. Brit.,* -tẽr·ĭ), *adj.*

suc·cus′sion (sŭ·kŭsh′ŭn), *n.* [L. *succussio,* fr. *succutere* to fling up, toss up, fr. *sub-* + *quatere* to shake.] A shaking, esp. with violence; specif., *Med.,* a shaking of the body to ascertain if fluid is present in a cavity, esp. the thorax. — **suc·cus′sive** (-kŭs′ĭv), *adj.*

such (sŭch; 4), *adj.* [AS. *swelc, swilc, swylc.*] **1.** Of this or that kind, character or degree; of the sort, quality, etc., specified or implied; as, *such* love as hers is rare; avoid *such* topics. **2.** Of the same class, type, or category; similar; as, poets, *such* as Spenser, Milton, and Blake. **3.** Before-mentioned; as, in default of *such* issue. **4.** *Colloq.* So extreme of its kind; — used intensively esp. in exclamations; as, *such* a boy!; *such* a day! — *pron.* **1.** Such a person or thing; often, such persons or things; as, "the father of *such* as dwell in tents" *Gen.* iv. 20. **2.** This or that, which has been or is being stated, exemplified, etc.; as, *such* was the result of his efforts.

such′like′ (sŭch′līk′), *adj.* Of like kind; similar.

suck (sŭk), *v. t.* [AS. *sūcan.*] **1.** To draw (a liquid, esp. mother's milk), with the mouth. **2.** To draw liquid from, by action of the mouth; as, to *suck* an orange; specif., to suck (sense 1) milk from (the mother's breast). **3.** To ply the tongue, lips, or the like, in or as if in sucking (something); often, to consume by licking or sipping; as, to *suck* a lollipop. **4.** To draw, draw in, take up, etc., by or as by suction, absorption, inhalation, or the like; as, plants *suck* water from the ground. — *v. i.* **1.** To suck something. **2.** To draw milk from the breast or udder. **3.** To draw air; — of a pump that fails to draw fluid because of low water or a defective valve. — *n.* **1.** Act of sucking; suction; a sucking movement. **2.** That which is drawn into the mouth by sucking; specif., mother's milk. **3.** *Colloq.* A small draft; a sip.

suck′er (sŭk′ẽr), *n.* **1.** One who or that which sucks; a suckling. **2.** *Colloq.* **a** *Now Rare.* A parasite. **b** One easily duped or gulled. **3. a** The piston or bucket of a pump. **b** The valve of a pump bucket. **4.** A pipe, etc., through which water, smoke, or the like, is drawn by suction. **5. a** In various animals, an organ for adhering or holding. **b** A mouth adapted for sucking or for adhering or both, as that of a leech. **6.** Any of numerous fresh-water fishes (family Catostomidae) closely related to the carps. **7.** *Colloq.* A lollipop. **8.** *Bot.* A haustorium. **9.** *Hort.* A shoot from the roots or lower part of the stem of a plant. — *v. t. & i.* To strip off, or to send out, suckers, or shoots.

suck′fish′ (sŭk′fĭsh′), *n.;* see FISH. **a** A remora. **b** A California fish (*Caularchus maeandricus*) having a sucker on the under side of the body.

suck′le (sŭk′'l), *v. t. & i.;* -LED (-'ld); -LING (-lĭng). [Freq. of SUCK.] To give suck (to); to nurse at the breast or udder; rear; foster. — **suck′ler** (-lẽr), *n.*

suck′ling (-lĭng), *n.* A child or animal before it is weaned.

su′cre (so͞o′krā), *n.* [Sp., after Antonio José de *Sucre,* S. Am. liberator.] The monetary unit of Ecuador, containing 100 centavos (see MONEY, *Tables*); also, a silver coin of this value.

su′crose (sū′krōs), *n.* [F. *sucre* sugar. See SUGAR.] *Chem.* Cane or beet sugar; saccharose. See SUGAR.

suc′tion (sŭk′shŭn), *n.* [L. *sugere, suctum,* to suck.] **1.** *Now Chiefly Technical.* Act or process of, or capacity for, sucking. **2.** Act or process of exerting a force upon a solid, liquid, or gaseous body by reason of a reduced air pressure over part of its surface; also, the force so exerted. **3.** *Mach.* A suction pipe or fitting; an inlet for a pump, air compressor, or the like. — *adj.* **1.** Producing or effecting suction, or operating by means of suction; as, a *suction* pump or stroke. **2.** Of or pert. to a machine or device that operates by suction; as, the *suction* pipe of a suction pump.

suction pump. The common type of pump, in which the fluid to be raised is pushed by atmospheric pressure into the partial vacuum under the retreating bucket on the upstroke, reflux being prevented by a nonreturn, or suction, valve in the pipe.

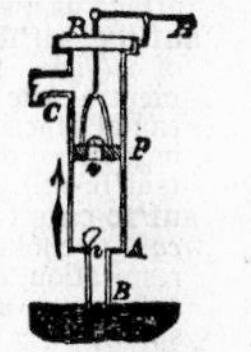

Suction Pump, in section. *AC* Cylinder, or Barrel; *AB* Pipe; *H* Handle; *P* Bucket, or Piston; *R* Rod; *v, v* Valves.

suction stop. *Phonet.* = CLICK, *n.,* 3.

suc·to′ri·al (sŭk·tō′rĭ·ăl; 70), *adj.* **a** Fitted for sucking; serving to adhere or draw up fluid by suction. **b** Provided with suctorial organs; living by sucking the blood or juices of animals or plants.

Su·dan′ic (so͞o·dăn′ĭk; -dän′ĭk), *adj.* Pertaining to a group of languages spoken across northern Africa from Senegal to Ethiopia, which includes many tongues of indeterminate relationship, such as Tshi, Mandingo, Yoruba. See LANGUAGE, *Table.*

su·dar′i·um (sū·dâr′ĭ·ŭm), *n.; pl.* -IA (-ȧ). Also **su′da·ry** (sū′dȧ·rĭ). [L. *sudarium,* fr. *sudare* to sweat.] A cloth for wiping sweat from the face; a handkerchief; specif., the sweat cloth of Veronica; also, a veronica. See VERONICA.

su′da·to′ri·um (sū′dȧ·tō′rĭ·ŭm; 70), *n.; pl.* -RIA (-ȧ). [L.] A sweating room in a bathing establishment.

su′da·to′ry (sū′dȧ·tō′rĭ *or, esp. Brit.,* -tẽr·ĭ), *adj.* [L. *sudatorius,* fr. *sudare* to sweat.] Of or pert. to a sudatorium. — *n.* A sudatorium.

sudd (sŭd), *n.* [Ar.] The floating vegetable matter which often makes the White Nile unnavigable.

sud′den (sŭd′'n; -ĭn), *adj.* [OF. *sodain, sudain,* fr. L. *subitaneus,* fr. *subitus* sudden.] **1.** Happening or coming unexpectedly; unforeseen; unprepared for. **2.** Characterized by or manifesting hastiness; precipitate; headlong. **3.** Come upon, or met with, unexpectedly; as, a *sudden* turn in the road. **4.** Hastily prepared, effected, etc.; as, a *sudden* cure. — **Syn.** See PRECIPITATE. — *adv.* Suddenly. — *n.* An unexpected occurrence; also, suddenness. *Obs.,* except in phrases ***all of a sudden, on a sudden.*** — **sud′den·ly,** *adv.* — **sud′den·ness,** *n.*

‖**su′dor** (sū′dôr), *n.* [L.] Sweat; perspiration; exudation. — **su′dor·al** (sū′dẽr·ăl), *adj.*

su′dor·if′er·ous (sū′dẽr·ĭf′ẽr·ŭs), *adj.* [NL. *sudoriferus.* See SUDOR; -FEROUS.] Producing or secreting sweat; as, *sudoriferous* glands. — **su′dor·if′er·ous·ness,** *n.*

su′dor·if′ic (-ĭf′ĭk), *adj.* [NL. *sudorificus.*] Causing or inducing sweat; diaphoretic; as, *sudorific* herbs. — *n.* A sudorific agent or medicine; a diaphoretic.

Su′dra (so͞o′drȧ), *n.* [Skr.] A Hindu of the lowest of the four great castes. Cf. BRAHMAN, KSHATRIYA, VAISYA.

suds (sŭdz), *n. pl.* Also **sud** (sŭd), *n. sing.* Soapy water, esp. when frothy; also, the lather or froth on soapy water.

suds′y (sŭd′zĭ), *adj.* Full of suds; frothy; foamy.

sue (sū; 114), *v. t.;* SUED (sūd); SU′ING (sū′ĭng). [OF. *sivre, sievre* (pres. ind. 3d sing. *il siut, suit,* he follows), fr. L. *sequi, secutus,* to follow.] **1.** To make petition to or for; solicit; urge. **2.** To pay court or suit to; woo. **3.** *Law.* **a** To go to (a court) in order to obtain legal redress therein. **b** To seek justice or right from (a person) by legal process; prosecute judicially. **c** To proceed with, as an action, and follow it up to its proper termination; gain by legal process. — *v. i.* **1.** To make a request or application; entreat; plead; — with *for* or *to.* **2.** To pay court; woo. **3.** *Law.* To take legal proceedings in court; to seek, as for damages, in law. — **su′er** (sū′ẽr), *n.*

suède (swād; *F.* swĕd), *n.* [F. *Suède* Sweden.] **1.** A tanned skin, with the flesh side rubbed into a nap. **2.** Also **suède cloth.** A napped fabric prepared so as to simulate the surface of such a tanned skin.

su′et (sū′ĕt; -ĭt), *n.* [Dim. fr. AF. *sue,* OF. *sieu, seu, siu,* fr. L. *sebum.*] The hard fat about the kidneys and loins in beef and mutton, which, when tried out, forms tallow.

suf-. An assimilated form of SUB- before *f.*

suf′fer (sŭf′ẽr), *v. t.* [OF. *sufrir, sofrir,* fr. L. *sufferre,* fr. *sub-* + *ferre* to bear.] **1.** To submit to or be forced to endure; bear as a victim or patient (sense 3). **2.** To undergo; experience; pass through; as, to *suffer* alteration. **3.** To have power to resist or sustain; — chiefly in negative statements; as, not able to *suffer* the cold. **4.** To allow; permit; tolerate; put up with; as, to *suffer* fools gladly. — *v. i.* **1.** To undergo pain of body or mind. **2.** *Archaic.* To endure or tolerate an evil, injury, etc. **3.** To sustain loss or damage. — **Syn.** See BEAR. — **suf′fer·er,** *n.*

suf′fer·a·ble (-ȧ·b'l), *adj.* That may be suffered, or tolerated; endurable. — **suf′fer·a·ble·ness,** *n.* — **suf′fer·a·bly,** *adv.*

suf′fer·ance (sŭf′ẽr·ăns), *n.* **1.** *Rare.* **a** Patient endurance; long-suffering. **b** Pain; misery; suffering. **2.** Consent or sanction implied by a lack of interference or the nonenforcement of a prohibition; passive or tacit permission; as, he remains here on *sufferance.* **3.** Power or ability to endure or withstand; as, it is beyond *sufferance.*

suf′fer·ing (sŭf′ẽr·ĭng; sŭf′rĭng), *n.* State or experience of one who suffers; also, pain; distress. — **Syn.** See DISTRESS. — *adj.* That suffers. — **suf′fer·ing·ly,** *adv.*

suf·fice′ (sŭ·fīs′; -fīz′), *v. i.;* -FICED′ (-fīst′; -fīzd′); -FIC′ING (-fīs′ĭng; -fīz′ĭng). [OF. *soufire,* F. *suffire* (cf. *suffisant,* pres. part., OF. *soufisant*), fr. L. *sufficere* to put under, substitute, avail for, suffice, fr. *sub-* + *facere* to make.] **1.** To meet or satisfy a need; to be sufficient. **2.** To be competent, capable, equal to a task, etc. — *v. t.* To be enough for; satisfy. — **suf·fic′er** (-fīs′ẽr; -fīz′ẽr), *n.*

suf·fi′cien·cy (sŭ·fĭsh′ĕn·sĭ), *n.; pl.* -CIES (-sĭz). **1.** Sufficient means to meet one's needs; competency; also, a modest but not parsimonious scale of living; as, an elegant *sufficiency.* **2.** Quality or state of being sufficient; adequacy; also, with *a,* enough. **3.** Self-sufficiency; self-confidence.

suf·fi′cient (-fĭsh′ĕnt), *adj.* [L. *sufficiens, -entis,* pres. part.] **1.** Equal to the end proposed; adequate; enough. **2.** *Archaic.* Adequately qualified; competent; fit. **3.** Having a sufficiency; responsible; good (sense 11). — **suf·fi′cient·ly,** *adv.*

Syn. **Sufficient, enough, adequate, competent** mean commensurate to a requirement. **Sufficient** or **enough** implies satisfying a need exactly, with nothing wanting or nothing in excess; **adequate,** measuring up to a just, fair, and sometimes inexacting standard of what is requisite; **competent,** answering all requirements or an adequate adaptation to the end in view.

suf·fix′ (sŭ·fĭks′), *v. t.* [See SUFFIX, *n.*] To add or annex to the end; attach as a suffix. — **suf·fix′ion** (sŭ·fĭk′shŭn), *n.*

suf′fix (sŭf′ĭks), *n.* [NL. *suffixum*, fr. L., neut. of *suffixus*, past part. of *suffigere* to affix, fr. *sub-* + *figere* to fix.] **1.** An abstract element at the end of a word serving a derivative, formative, or inflectional function, as *-ly* in man*ly*, *-ness* in sweet*ness*, *-ed* in hat*ed*, *-er* in soon*er*. See COMBINING FORM. **2.** *Math.* A subindex. — **suf′fix·al** (sŭf′ĭk·săl), *adj.*

suf′fo·cate (sŭf′ō·kāt), *v. t. & i.* [L. *suffocatus*, past part. of *suffocare* to choke, fr. *sub-* + *fauces* throat.] **1.** To kill or die by stopping respiration, as by strangling or asphyxiation. **2.** To stifle, choke, or smother. — **suf′fo·cat′ing·ly** (-kāt′ĭng·lĭ), *adv.* — **suf′fo·ca′tion** (-kā′shŭn), *n.* — **suf′fo·ca′tive** (-kā′tĭv), *adj.*

Suf′folk (sŭf′ŭk), *n.* [From *Suffolk*, England.] **a** A hornless sheep of an English breed producing excellent mutton. **b** A chestnut-colored heavy draft horse of an English breed.

suf′fra·gan (sŭf′rȧ·găn), *n.* [OF., fr. ML. *suffraganeus*, confused with L. *suffragans, -antis*, pres. part. of *suffragari* to support with one's vote. See SUFFRAGE.] In full, **suffragan bishop**. A bishop who serves as an assistant to the bishop of a diocese. — *adj.* **1.** Subject or subordinate to (a metropolitan or a metropolitan see); — of a diocesan bishop or his diocese. **2.** Assisting a diocesan bishop; — of a class of bishops.

suf′frage (sŭf′rĭj), *n.* [OF. and L.; OF., fr. L. *suffragium.*] **1.** An intercessory prayer; a supplication. **2.** A vote given in deciding a controverted question, or in the choice of a person for an office or trust; assent; vote. **3.** The right of voting in political matters, or the exercise of such right; the franchise.

suf′fra·gette′ (sŭf′rȧ·jĕt′), *n.* A woman advocate of suffrage for her sex. — **suf′fra·get′tism** (-jĕt′ĭz'm), *n.*

suf′fra·gist (sŭf′rȧ·jĭst), *n. & adj.* (One) advocating an extension of the suffrage, esp. to women.

suf′fru·tes′cent (sŭf′rōō·tĕs′ĕnt; -'nt), *adj.* *Bot.* Becoming partly woody and perennial at the base, as the stems of some plants.

suf·fru′ti·cose (sŭ·frōō′tĭ·kōs), *adj.* *Bot.* Woody and perennial at the base but remaining herbaceous above.

suf·fu′mi·gate (sŭ·fū′mĭ·gāt), *v. t. & i.* [L. *suffumigatus*, past part. of *suffumigare* to fumigate from below.] To fumigate from below, as in medication of parts of the body. — **suf·fu′mi·ga′tion** (-gā′shŭn), *n.*

suf·fuse′ (sŭ·fūz′), *v. t.* [L. *suffusus*, past part. of *suffundere* to overspread, fr. *sub-* + *fundere* to pour.] To overspread, as with a fluid, tinge, or tint. — **Syn.** See INFUSE. — **suf·fu′sion** (-zhŭn), *n.* — **suf·fu′sive** (-fū′sĭv), *adj.*

Su′fi (sōō′fē), *n.* [Ar. *ṣūfi*, lit., man of wool, ascetic.] An adherent of Sufism.

Su′fism (sōō′fĭz'm), *n.* A system of Mohammedan mysticism developed, esp. in Persia, into an elaborate symbolism much used by the poets. — **Su·fis′tic** (sōō·fĭs′tĭk), *adj.*

sug′ar (shŏŏg′ẽr), *n.* [OF. *sucre, sukere*, fr. ML. *succarum*, through Ar. & Per. fr. Skr. *ṣarkarā* gravel, grit, sugar.] **1.** A sweet carbohydrate, colorless or white when pure, chiefly derived from the sugar cane and the sugar beet; — called specif. *cane sugar*, *beet sugar* (when made from beets), *sucrose*, and *saccharose*. Crude cane sugar is often sold as *brown sugar*. Some sugar is also made from the sap of certain palm trees (*palm sugar*), maple trees (*maple sugar*), etc. ***granulated sugar***, a pure, white sugar prepared as crystalline granules, is commonly used in cooking and at table. ***powdered sugar*** is derived from granulated sugar by grinding, and includes ***confectioner's sugar*** which is highly refined and in the form of an extremely fine powder. Sugar forms fine monoclinic crystals melting at 186° C. (367° F.), which dissolve in about half their weight of water. Chemically, it is a disaccharide of the formula $C_{12}H_{22}O_{11}$, formed by union of one molecule of dextrose with one of levulose. **2.** By extension, any of a class of sweet, soluble compounds comprising the simpler carbohydrates. Among the important natural sugars are *sucrose* or *cane sugar* (see def. 1, above), *dextrose* or *grape sugar*, *levulose* or *fruit sugar*, *lactose* or *milk sugar*, and *maltose* or *malt sugar*. Cf. INVERT SUGAR, MOLASSES, SIRUP, SORGHUM. — *v. t.* **1.** To impregnate, season, or sprinkle with sugar; to mix sugar with. **2.** To sweeten, as something distasteful; to sugar-coat; — often with *over*. — *v. i.* To form sugar; to granulate; to become crystalline like sugar.

sugar apple. The sweetsop.

sugar beet. See BEET, 1.

sug′ar·ber′ry (shŏŏg′ẽr·bĕr′ĭ), *n.* The hackberry.

sug′ar·bush′ (-bŏŏsh′), *n.* *U. S.* = SUGAR ORCHARD.

sugar cane. A stout, tall perennial grass (*Saccharum officinarum*), with an ample terminal panicle, extensively cultivated in warm regions for its sugar.

sug′ar–coat′, *v. t.* To coat with sugar; hence, to make superficially attractive or palatable. — **sug′ar–coat′ing**, *n.*

sug′ared (shŏŏg′ẽrd), *adj.* Honeyed; sugar-coated.

sug′ar·house′ (shŏŏg′ẽr·hous′), *n.* A building where sugar is made or, *U. S.*, where maple sap is boiled and maple sugar and sirup made.

sug′ar·ing off (shŏŏg′ẽr·ĭng). The action or process of converting maple sap into sugar; also, a gathering of persons to assist in the process and to make merry afterwards.

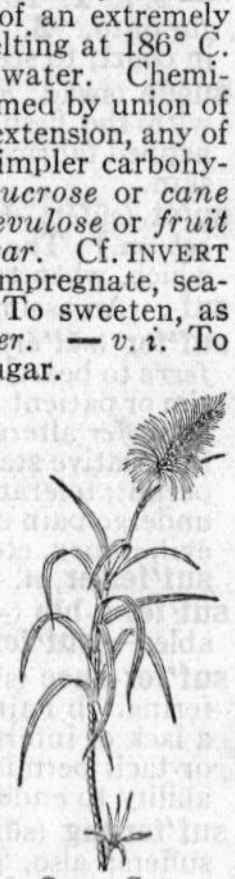

Sugar Cane. (1/100)

sugar loaf. A loaf or mass of refined sugar, usually conoidal. — **sug′ar–loaf′**, *adj.*

sugar of lead. = LEAD ACETATE.

sugar maple. See MAPLE.

sugar of milk. Lactose.

sugar orchard. A grove or collection of sugar maples (see MAPLE).

sugar pine. See PINE.

sug′ar·plum′ (shŏŏg′ẽr·plŭm′), *n.* A candy or sweetmeat made up in small balls or disks; a bonbon.

sug′ar·y (shŏŏg′ẽr·ĭ), *adj.* **1.** Like, containing, or consisting of sugar; tasting of sugar. **2.** Ostentatiously sweet; saccharine. — **sug′ar·i·ness**, *n.*

sug·gest′ (sŭg·jĕst′; sŭ·jĕst′), *v. t.* [L. *suggestus*, past part. of *suggerere* to put under, furnish, suggest, fr. *sub-* + *gerere* to carry.] **1.** To arouse, often by indirect means, the thought of, the desire for, the temptation to commit, or the like. **2.** Of things, to call to mind, as by association of ideas; specif. of a word, to call to mind (as an involved idea or ideas). **3.** To serve as a motive or inspiration for. **4.** To advance by way of suggestion. — **sug·gest′er**, *n.*

Syn. Suggest, imply, hint, intimate, insinuate mean to convey an idea or thought by indirect means. Suggest stresses a putting into the mind as a result of association of ideas, an awakening of a desire, etc.; imply, a suggesting of an idea involved (but not expressed) in a statement, a word, or the like; hint, the use of covert or remote suggestion; intimate, a more or less delicate suggestion; insinuate, an artful or unpleasant suggestion, conveyed by a tone, a manner of expression, etc.

sug·gest′i·ble (-jĕs′tĭ·b'l), *adj.* **1.** Easily influenced by suggestion or, specif., hypnotic suggestion. **2.** That may be suggested. — **sug·gest′i·bil′i·ty** (-bĭl′ĭ·tĭ), *n.*

sug·ges′tion (sŭg·jĕs′chŭn; sŭ·jĕs′-), *n.* **1.** The act or an instance of suggesting; also, that which is suggested. **2.** The mental process by which one thought leads to another, esp. through association of ideas. **3.** A trace; a slight touch; hint; as, a *suggestion* of fatigue. **4.** *Psychol.* The uncritical acceptance of an idea or proposal made by a person to whom the subject is docile and submissive; as, hypnotic *suggestion.*

sug·ges′tive (-tĭv), *adj.* **1.** Tending to suggest; full of suggestions; stimulative of thought. **2.** Tending to suggest what is improper, indecent, or the like. — **sug·ges′tive·ly**, *adv.* — **sug·ges′tive·ness**, *n.*

sugh (sōōk). Obs. ex. Scot. var. of SOUGH.

su′i·cid′al (sū′ĭ·sīd′ăl; -'l; 2), *adj.* Pertaining to, of the nature of, or suggestive of suicide. — **su′i·cid′al·ly**, *adv.*

su′i·cide (sū′ĭ·sīd), *n.* [L. *sui* of oneself + *-cide*, 2.] **1.** Act or an instance of taking one's own life voluntarily and intentionally; esp., *Law*, by a person past the age of discretion and of sound mind. **2.** Ruin of one's own interests. **3.** [L. *sui* of oneself + *-cide*, 1.] One who voluntarily and intentionally takes his own life. — *v. i.* *Colloq.* To commit suicide.

‖**su′i ge′ne·ris** (sū′ī jĕn′ĕ·rĭs). [L.] Of his, her, or its own kind; in a class by itself; unique; peculiar.

‖**su′i ju′ris** (jōō′rĭs). [L., in one's own right.] *Law.* Of full legal capacity, as distinguished from the limited capacity of those under some legal disability, as infancy.

su′int (sū′ĭnt; swĭnt), *n.* [F., fr. *suer* to sweat.] The dried perspiration of sheep, deposited in the wool, yielding potash.

suit (sūt; 114), *n.* [OF. *siute, sieute* (F. *suite*), fr. L. *sequi*. See SUE.] **1.** Orig., a livery, a uniform (as of a fraternity), a habit, or the like. **2.** A series or group of things forming a unit or constituting a complement; a set; — now usually *suite*, except in *suit* of armor, apparel, cards, clothes. **3.** Act or an instance of suing, or seeking by entreaty; solicitation; a plea; a petition; specif., wooing. **4.** *Cards.* One of the four sets of cards which constitute a pack. Cf. POKER, *Illust.* **5.** *Law.* Orig., the following or attending upon a court to obtain justice there; hence, an action or process in a court for the recovery of a right or claim; legal application to a court for justice. — *v. t.* **1.** To dress or attire. **2.** To answer the requirements of; to meet the desires or needs of; to please; satisfy. **3.** To fit or adapt (a thing) *to;* to accommodate. **4.** To be fitted or adjusted to; to accord with; befit; become. — *v. i.* To agree; to accord; to be fitting; to correspond.

suit′a·ble (sūt′ȧ·b'l), *adj.* That is suited to one, one's needs, wishes, or condition, the proprieties, etc.; appropriate; fitting. — **Syn.** See FIT. — **Ant.** Unsuitable. — **suit′a·bil′i·ty** (-bĭl′ĭ·tĭ), *n.* — **suit′a·ble·ness**, *n.* — **suit′a·bly**, *adv.*

suit′case′ (sūt′kās′), *n.* Also **suit case**. A flat rectangular valise or traveling bag large enough to contain a suit.

suite (sūt). Var. of SUIT (in various senses).

suite (swēt), *n.* [F.] **1.** A retinue; the personal staff accompanying a ruler, diplomat, or dignitary on official business. **2.** A number of things constituting a set, series, complement, sequence, or the like; as, a *suite* of rooms; specif., a set of matched furniture for a specified room; as, a bedroom *suite*. **3.** *Music.* **a** One of the old instrumental forms, consisting of a series of dances in the same or related keys. **b** A modern instrumental composition free as to the character and number of its movements.

suit′ing (sūt′ĭng), *n.* A fabric designed for suits.

suit′or (sūt′ẽr), *n.* **1.** One who sues, petitions, or entreats; a petitioner. **2.** A wooer. **3.** *Law.* A party to a suit.

su′ki·ya′ki (sōōk′ĭ·yä′kĭ; *Jap.* skē·yä′kē), *n.* [Jap.] A popular Japanese dish consisting of thin slices of meat fried with onions or other vegetables, with a little soya sauce, sake, and sugar.

Suk·koth′ (sōōk·ōth′), *n. pl.* Also **Suk′kos, Suc′cos** (sōōk′ŏs). [Heb. *sukkōth.*] See JEWISH HOLIDAYS.

sul′cate (sŭl′kāt), *adj.* Also **sul′cat·ed** (-kāt·ĕd; -ĭd). [L. *sulcatus*, past part. of *sulcare* to furrow.] Scored with furrows; grooved. — **sul·ca′tion** (sŭl·kā′shŭn), *n.*

sul′cus (sŭl′kŭs), *n.; pl.* SULCI (-sī). [L., a furrow.] A furrow; a groove; fissure; esp., *Anat.*, a shallow furrow on the surface of the brain separating convolutions.

sulf-, sulph-. *Chem.* A combining form denoting *presence of sulfur as an ingredient*, as in **sulf·am′mo·ni′um.**

☞ For words beginning *sulf-* or *sulph-*, the *f* spelling is preferred by American chemists and is common in American use generally, but *ph* is not infrequent, especially in nonscientific writing, and is the commoner British spelling.

sul′fa, sul′pha (sŭl′fȧ), *adj.* *Pharm. & Chem.* Designating or pertaining to a class of synthetic organic drugs related chemically to sulfanilamide. They act destructively on certain types of disease-producing bacteria. — *n.; pl.* SULFAS (-fȧz). A sulfa drug.

sul′fa·di′a·zine (sŭl′fȧ·dī′ȧ·zēn; -zĭn), **sul′fa·di′a·zin**, *n.* [*sulfa*nilamide + *di-* + azote nitrogen + *-ine.*] *Chem. & Pharm.* A sulfa drug, $C_{10}H_{10}N_4O_2S$, used in the treatment of pneumonia and other infections.

sul′fa·guan′i·dine (sŭl′fȧ·gwăn′ĭ·dēn; -gwä′nĭ·dēn; -dĭn), **sul′fa·guan′i·din**, *n.* [*sulfa*nilamide + *guanidine* (by oxidation from *guano*).] *Chem. & Pharm.* A sulfa drug, $C_7H_{10}N_4O_2S$ used esp. in treating intestinal infections; — called also **sul′fa·nil′yl·guan′i·dine** (sŭl′fȧ·nĭl′ĭl-).

sul′fa·mer′a·zine (sŭl′fȧ·mĕr′ȧ·zēn; -zĭn), **sul′fa·mer′a·zin**, *n.* [*sulfa* + Gr. *meros* part + *azine.*] *Chem. & Pharm.* A crystalline sulfa drug, $C_{11}H_{12}N_4O_2S$, a methyl derivative of sulfadiazine and similarly used.

sul′fa·nil′a·mide (sŭl′fȧ·nĭl′ȧ·mīd; -mĭd), *n.* [*sulfanil*ic acid + *amide.*] *Chem. & Pharm.* A white crystalline compound, *p*-$NH_2C_6H_4SO_2NH_2$, the amide of sulfanilic acid, used esp. in the treatment of certain infections, as gonorrhea, septicemia, sore throat, etc.

sul′fa·nil′ic ac′id (sŭl′fȧ·nĭl′ĭk). [From *sulf*uric + *anil*ine.] *Chem.*

A crystalline acid, $C_6H_4(NH_2)SO_3H$, obtained from aniline and used in making dyes, etc.

sul'fa·pyr'a·zine (sŭl'fȧ·pĭr'ȧ·zēn; -zĭn), **sul'fa·pyr'a·zin,** *n.* [*sulfa* + *pyrazine*.] *Chem. & Pharm.* A sulfa drug, $C_{10}H_{10}N_4O_2S$, used similarly to sulfadiazine.

sul'fa·pyr'i·dine (sŭl'fȧ·pĭr'ĭ·dēn; -dĭn), **sul'fa·pyr'i·din,** *n.* [*sulfanilamide* + *pyridine*.] *Chem. & Pharm.* A sulfa drug, $C_{11}H_{11}N_3O_2S$, used similarly to sulfanilamide.

sulf·ar'se·nide (sŭlf·är'sē·nīd; -nĭd), *n.* Also **sulf·ar'se·nid.** A compound which is both a sulfide and an arsenide.

Sul'fa·sux'i·dine (sŭl'fȧ·sŭk'sĭ·dēn; -dĭn), *n.* A trade-mark applied to a sulfa drug, $C_{13}H_{13}N_3O_5S_2$, a derivative of sulfathiazole and succinic acid, used esp. for the prophylaxis and treatment of dysentery caused by bacteria.

sul'fate (sŭl'fāt), *n.* [F., fr. NL. *sulphas, -atis*.] *Chem.* A salt or ester of sulfuric acid. — *v. t.* **1.** To treat or impregnate with sulfuric acid or a sulfate; to convert into sulfate. **2.** *Elec.* To form a deposit of a whitish scale (sulfate of lead) on (the plates of a storage battery). — *v. i.* To become sulfated.

sulfate process. A process for making wood pulp (**sulfate pulp**) by boiling wood chips under pressure with an alkaline solution of sodium sulfate. Hence, **sulfate paper.**

sul'fa·thi'a·zole (sŭl'fȧ·thī'ȧ·zōl), *n.* [*sulfanilamide* + *thiazole*.] *Chem. & Pharm.* A sulfa drug, $C_9H_9N_3O_2S_2$, used especially in the treatment of pneumococcus and staphylococcus infections.

sul'fat·ize (sŭl'fāt·īz), *v. t.* To convert into sulfate, as sulfide ores by roasting.

sul'fide (sŭl'fīd; -fĭd), *n.* Also **sul'fid.** *Chem.* A compound of sulfur with an element or radical; a salt or ester of hydrogen sulfide; — formerly called *sulphuret.*

sul'fi·nyl (sŭl'fĭ·nĭl), *n.* [*sulfine* (= *sulfonium*) + *-yl*.] *Org. Chem.* The bivalent radical >SO.

sul'fite (sŭl'fīt), *n.* [F.] *Chem.* A salt or ester of sulfurous acid. — **sul·fit'ic** (sŭl·fĭt'ĭk), *adj.*

sul'fo-, sul'pho- (sŭl'fō-). *Chem.* A combining form denoting *sulfur;* specif.: **a** Denoting *the presence of the sulfonic-acid group; sulfonic.* **b** Denoting *the presence of the sulfonyl group.* **c** Denoting *the presence of sulfuric acid.* — **sul'fo** (-fō), *adj.*

sul'fo·nal (sŭl'fō·năl; sŭl'fō·năl'), *n.* Sulfonmethane.

sul·fon'a·mide (sŭl·fŏn'ȧ·mīd; -mĭd), *n.* Also **sul·fon'a·mid.** [*sulfon-* (sulfonic acid) + *amide*.] *Chem.* The amide of a sulfonic acid; as, para-amino-benzene-*sulfonamide* (= sulfanilamide).

sul'fo·nate (sŭl'fō·nāt), *n.* *Chem.* A salt or ester of a sulfonic acid. — *v. t.* To introduce the sulfonic group into; to convert into a sulfonic acid.

sul'fone (sŭl'fōn), *n.* [G. *sulfon*.] *Chem.* Any of a class of compounds containing the sulfonyl group (SO_2) doubly united, by its sulfur, with carbon.

sul·fon'ic (sŭl·fŏn'ĭk), *adj.* *Chem.* Pertaining to or designating the equivalent acid group SO_3H.

sulfonic acid. Any of the acids containing the sulfonic group, and regarded as derived from sulfuric acid by replacement of hydroxyl.

sul·fo'ni·um (sŭl·fō'nĭ·ŭm), *n.* [NL., fr. *sulfur* + *ammonium*.] *Chem.* A univalent radical or cation, SH_3.

sul'fon·meth'ane (sŭl'fŏn·mĕth'ān; sŭl'fŏn-), *n.* *Pharm.* A crystalline compound, $(CH_3)_2C(SO_2C_2H_5)_2$, used as a hypnotic and sedative.

sul'fo·nyl (sŭl'fō·nĭl; -nēl), *n.* [*sulfone* + *-yl*.] *Org. Chem.* The bivalent radical >SO_2.

sul'fur, sul'phur (sŭl'fẽr), *n.* [L. *sulfur, sulphur, sulpur*.] **1.** *Chem.* A nonmetallic element occurring naturally, free or combined. It is a constituent of proteins. Symbol, *S;* at. no., 16; at. wt., 32.066. Native sulfur occurs in yellow orthorhombic crystals, in masses, crusts, and powder. H., 1.5–2.5. Sulfur burns in air with a blue flame and suffocating odor. It is used in making gunpowder, matches, etc., for vulcanizing rubber, in medicine as a laxative and diaphoretic, in ointments for the skin, etc. **2.** *Usually* **sul'phur.** Any of numerous yellow or orange pieridine butterflies, as the ***clouded sulphur*** (*Eurymus,* or *Colias, philodice*), the common yellow butterfly of the eastern U. S., and in the South the ***cloudless sulphur*** (*Callidryas eubule*).

sul'fu·rate (sŭl'fū·rāt), *adj.* Of or pert. to sulfur; sulfureous. — (-rāt), *v. t.* To sulfurize. — **sul'fu·ra'tion** (-rā'shŭn), *n.*

sulfur dioxide. A heavy, pungent gas, SO_2, easily condensed to a colorless liquid. It is used in making sulfuric acid, in bleaching, as a preservative, and in refrigerating machines, etc.

sul·fu're·ous, sul·phu're·ous (sŭl·fū'rē·ŭs), *adj.* Like sulfur; sulfurous. — **sul·fu're·ous·ly,** *adv.* — **-ous·ness,** *n.*

sul'fu·ret (sŭl'fū·rĕt), *n.* A sulfide. — *v. t.;* -RET'ED or -RET'TED; -RET'ING or -RET'TING. To combine or impregnate with sulfur.

sul·fu'ric (sŭl·fū'rĭk), *adj.* Of, pertaining to, or containing sulfur, esp. in a higher valence.

sulfuric acid. *Chem.* A heavy, corrosive, oily liquid, H_2SO_4, colorless when pure, early made by distilling green vitriol, whence the name *oil of vitriol.* See VITRIOL.

sul'fu·rize (sŭl'fū·rīz; sŭl'fẽr·īz), *v. t.;* -RIZED (-rīzd); -RIZ'ING (-rīz'ĭng). *Chem.* To combine or impregnate with sulfur or any of its compounds; specif., to fumigate or bleach with sulfur fumes. — **sul'fu·ri·za'tion** (-rĭ·zā'shŭn; -rī·zā'-), *n.*

sul'fu·rous, sul'phu·rous (sŭl'fū·rŭs; sŭl·fū'rŭs; *the 2d pron. is common in chemical terminology, as in* sul·fu'rous ac'id, *etc.*), *adj.* **1.** Of, pert. to, or containing, sulfur, esp. in a lower valence. **2. a** Of or pert. to brimstone or hell-fire; infernal. **b** Fiery; scorching; heated; as, *sulphurous* language. — **-rous·ly,** *adv.*

sulfurous acid. An acid, H_2SO_3, not known in the free state but forming a series of salts (the *sulfites*).

sul'fur·yl (sŭl'fẽr·ĭl; -ēl; sŭl'fū·rĭl), *n.* [*sulfur* + *-yl*.] *Inorg. Chem.* The bivalent radical >SO_2.

sulk (sŭlk), *v. i.* [See SULKY, *adj.*] To become sullen or morose in mood, esp. in resentment. — *n.* State of one sulking; a sulky mood, humor, etc. — often *pl.*

sulk'y (sŭl'kĭ), *adj.;* SULK'I·ER (-kĭ·ẽr); SULK'I·EST. [For *sulken,* fr. AS. *solcen* slothful, remiss, deriv. of *āseolcan* to be weak or slothful.] **1.** Sulking or inclined to sulk; given to fits of sulking. **2.** [From the noun.] Having wheels and a seat for the driver; as, a *sulky* plow. — **Syn.** See SULLEN. — **sulk'i·ly,** *adv.* — **sulk'i·ness,** *n.*

sulk'y, *n.; pl.* SULKIES (-kĭz). [From SULKY, *adj.;* because for only one person at a time.] A light two-wheeled carriage for a single person.

sul'lage (sŭl'ĭj), *n.* [F. *souiller* to soil.] **1.** Refuse; sewage. **2.** Filth; filthiness. **3.** Silt; mud deposited by water. **4.** Scoria on molten metal in the ladle.

sul'len (sŭl'ĕn; -ĭn), *adj.* [Through OF., fr. L. *solus* alone.] **1.** Ill-humoredly unsociable; hence, gloomily silent; morose; glum. **2.** Gloomy; dismal; sad. **3.** Dull or heavy, as in sound or color; somber; of mournful tone. **4.** Moving sluggishly; as, a *sullen* brook. **5.** Baleful; unpropitious. — **sul'len·ly,** *adv.* — **sul'len·ness,** *n.*

Syn. **Sullen, glum, morose, surly, sulky, crabbed, saturnine, gloomy** mean showing a disagreeable and forbidding mood or disposition. **Sullen** implies a silent ill humor and a refusal to be sociable; **glum,** a dismal silence because of low spirits or depressing circumstances; **morose,** a glumness characterized by bitterness; **surly,** gruffness and sullenness of speech or manner; **sulky,** a mood of peevish sullenness; **crabbed,** a forbidding, harsh, and ill-natured disposition; **saturnine,** a heavy, forbidding aspect and, often, taciturnity; **gloomy,** a depression in mood or disposition that makes one seem sullen or glum.

sul'ly (sŭl'ĭ), *v. t. & i.* [F. *souiller*. See SOIL to foul.] To make or become soiled or tarnished; defile. — **Syn.** Smirch, foul. — *n.; pl.* SULLIES (-ĭz). Soil; tarnish; stain.

sulph-, sul'pha, sul'phate, sul'phide, sul'phur, sul·phu'ric, sul'phu·rous, etc. Variants of SULF-, SULFA, SULFATE, SULFIDE, SULFUR, SULFURIC, SULFUROUS, etc.
☞ See *Note* at SULF-.

sul'phur–bot'tom, *n.* A whalebone whale (*Sibbaldus musculus*), the largest of living mammals, reaching an average length of 76 feet and found in the Atlantic, Pacific, and Antarctic oceans. The color is bluish gray with a few irregular white or yellowish-white spots on the under parts.

sulphur yellow. A color, yellow in hue, of medium saturation and very high brilliance. See COLOR.

sul'tan (sŭl'tăn; sōōl·tän'), *n.* [F., fr. Ar. *sulṭān* sultan, dominion.] **1.** A ruler, or sovereign; esp., a ruler of a Mohammedan state; — a title of any Mohammedan prince; specif., the ruler of the Turks; hence, **sul'tan·ship** (an office abolished in 1922). **2. a** [*cap.*] A breed of white domestic fowls having the legs and toes heavily feathered. **b** A sultana bird.

sul·tan'a (sŭl·tăn'ȧ; sŭl·tä'nȧ), *n.* [It.] **1.** The wife, or sometimes the mother, sister, or daughter, of a sultan. **2.** A mistress, esp. of a royal personage. **3.** Also **sultana bird.** A gallinule (genus *Porphyrio*) with handsome blue and greenish plumage. **4.** A pale-yellow seedless grape, grown as a source of raisins and of a delicate white wine.

sul'tan·ate (sŭl'tăn·āt), *n.* The rule, dominion, or office of a sultan.

sul'tan·ess (sŭl'tăn·ĕs; -ĭs; sŭl·tän'-), *n.* A sultana.

sul'try (sŭl'trĭ), *adj.;* SUL'TRI·ER (-trĭ·ẽr); SUL'TRI·EST. [From *sweltry,* adj., fr. SWELTER, *v.*] **1.** Very hot and moist, or close and oppressive; sweltering. **2.** Burning hot; as, a *sultry* sun. **3.** Hot, as with passion or anger. — **sul'tri·ly,** *adv.* — **sul'tri·ness,** *n.*

Su'lu (sōō'lōō), *n.* [Malay *Sulu'* (written *Suluk*).] A member of the most prominent tribe of Moros, of the Sulu Archipelago; also, their language. — **Su'lu·an** (-ăn), *adj. & n.*

sum (sŭm), *n.* [OF. *summe, somme,* fr. L. *summa,* fr. *summus* highest.] **1.** An amount; an indefinite (unless specified) amount of money. **2.** The whole amount; the aggregate; as, within the *sum* of human experience. **3.** A summary or epitome; also, the gist. **4.** *Archaic.* Utmost degree; height. **5.** The number or quantity resulting from the addition of two or more numbers or quantities (see ADDEND, AUGEND); an aggregate; a total; as, the *sum* of 5 and 7 is 12. **6.** The numbers to be added; also, *Colloq.,* any arithmetical problem.

Syn. **Sum, amount, aggregate, total, whole, number, quantity** mean a result gained by putting together all in a given group or mass. **Sum** implies a result of simple addition of figures or particulars; **amount,** a combination of all the sums, weights, or measures under consideration; **aggregate,** a result reached by counting individuals or items in a group or collection; **total** and **whole** stress the completeness or inclusiveness of the result; **number** is often used in place of *aggregate,* especially where *amount* may not be used (as, the *number* present; a small *number* of potatoes); **quantity,** in technical use, is referable to anything measurable in extent, duration, volume, etc., but in ordinary use, applies only to things measurable in bulk but still countable (as, a small *quantity* of apples).

— *v. t.;* SUMMED (sŭmd); SUM'MING. **1.** To calculate the amount or total of. **2.** To epitomize; summarize; to recapitulate, as evidence. — ***sum up.*** To recapitulate points, arguments, etc., as evidence.

su'mac, su'mach (shōō'măk; sū'măk), *n.* [OF. *sumac,* ML. *sumach,* fr. Ar. *summāq*.] **1.** Any of several trees, shrubs, or woody vines of two closely related genera (*Rhus* and *Toxicodendron*) with pyramidal panicles of small crimson one-seeded drupes, and in one genus (*Toxicodendron*) smooth fruits and foliage poisonous to the touch; also, the wood of any species. The sumac is typical of a family (Anacardiaceae, the sumac family) of trees and shrubs having small dioecious flowers and drupaceous fruits. The family includes the commercially important mango, pistachio, and varnish tree. See POISON SUMAC. **2.** A material used in tanning and dyeing, consisting of the dried and powdered leaves, panicles, etc., of various species of sumac (esp. *R. coriaria*).

Su·me'ri·an (sōō·mẽr'ĭ·ăn), *adj.* Also **Su·mi'ri·an** (sōō·mẽr'ĭ·ăn). Of Sumer (see *Gaz.*). — *n.* **1.** A native of Sumer. **2.** The agglutinative language of the Sumerians, the pre-Semitic population of the lower Euphrates valley.

‖**sum'ma cum lau'de.** See CUM LAUDE.

sum'ma·rize (sŭm'ȧ·rīz), *v. t. & i.* To tell in, reduce to, or make a summary; to present briefly. — **sum'ma·ri·za'tion** (-rĭ·zā'shŭn; -rī·zā'-), *n.* — **sum'ma·riz'er** (-rīz'ẽr), *n.*

sum'ma·ry (-rĭ), *adj.* [ML. *summarius*. See SUMMARY, *n.*] **1.** Comprehensive; esp., summarizing concisely. **2.** Done without delay or formality; as, *summary* vengeance; specif., *Law,* of, pert. to, or using a summary procedure; used in, or done by, summary proceeding. — **Syn.** See CONCISE. — **Ant.** Circumstantial. — **sum'ma·ri·ly** (sŭm'ȧ·rĭ·lĭ; *emphat. also* sŭm·âr'ĭ·lĭ), *adv.* — **sum'ma·ri·ness** (sŭm'ȧ·rĭ·nĕs; -nĭs), *n.*

sum'ma·ry, *n.; pl.* -RIES (-rĭz). [L. *summarium,* fr. *summa* sum. See SUM, *n.*] An abstract, abridgment, or compendium, esp. of a preceding discourse.

sum·ma'tion (sŭm·ā'shŭn), *n.* **1.** Act of summing, or of forming a sum, or total amount; addition. **2.** An aggregate, esp. one formed by accumulation or accretion.

sum'mer (sŭm'ẽr), *n.* [AS. *sumor, sumer*.] The season of the year in any region in which the sun shines most directly there; the warmest period of the year. — *v. i.* To pass the summer. — *v. t.* To keep or carry through the summer; as, to *summer* stock on upland pastures. — **sum′mer**, *adj.*

sum′mer (sŭm′ẽr), *n.* [F. *sommier* rafter, beast of burden.] A large horizontal beam or stone, used esp. in building; as: **a** The lintel of a door or window. **b** A stone forming the cap of a pier to support a lintel, arch, etc. **c** A principal floor timber.

sum′mer·house′ (-hous′), *n.* A rustic covered structure in a garden or park, to provide a shady retreat in summer.

sum′mer·sault, sum′mer·set. Vars. of SOMERSAULT, SOMERSET.

sum′mer·time′ (sŭm′ẽr·tīm′), *n.* The summer season; a summerlike period.

summer time. *Chiefly Brit.* Daylight-saving time.

sum′mer·y (sŭm′ẽr·ĭ), *adj.* Of, like, or fit for summer.

sum′mit (sŭm′ĭt), *n.* [OF. *sommette*, dim. of *som, sum*, fr. L. *summum*, fr. *summus* highest.] **1.** The apex; the top; the highest point. **2.** The utmost height; the highest degree; acme.

Syn. **Summit, peak, pinnacle, climax, apex, acme, culmination, meridian, zenith** mean the highest point attained or attainable. **Summit** implies the topmost level yet attained or attainable; **peak**, the highest point, esp. among other high points; **pinnacle**, a dizzy and, often, insecure height; **climax**, the highest point, as in force, interest, etc., in an ascending series; **apex**, the highest point where all ascending lines (efforts, ambitions, etc.) converge; **acme**, a point which exhibits the perfection of a thing; **culmination**, the outcome of a movement, a growth, or a development which represents its attained objective; **meridian**, the stage when a living and growing thing reaches its fullest development and vigor; **zenith** adds to *meridian* the implications of luster and distinction.

sum′mon (sŭm′ŭn), *v. t.* [OF. *sumundre, semondre*, fr. L. *summonēre* to remind privily, fr. *sub-* + *monēre* to admonish, warn.] **1.** To issue a call to convene; to convoke. **2.** To bid to come; to send for; also, to cite by authority; to call formally, as to appear in court. **3.** To call forth or evoke, esp. by an act of the will. **4.** *Mil.* To call upon to surrender. — **sum′mon·er**, *n.*

Syn. **Summon, call, cite, convoke, convene, muster** mean to demand the presence of. **Summon** specifically implies the exercise of authority or power; **call**, a more ordinary and colloquial term than *summon*, is often used in its place; **cite** implies a summons to court, often to answer a charge; **convoke**, a summons to assemble, esp. for legislative or deliberative purposes; **convene**, a call to assemble; **muster**, a summons to an army, ship's company, or the like, for action, inspection, parade, etc.

sum′mons (sŭm′ŭnz), *n.; pl.* SUMMONSES (-ŭn·zĕz; -zĭz). [OF. *sumunse, semonse*, participial n. fr. *sumundre, semondre*, to summon.] **1.** The act of summoning; a call by authority to appear at a place named, or to attend to some duty. **2.** A call, signal, knock, etc., that summons. **3.** *Law.* A warning or citation to appear in court; specif., a written notification, signed by the proper officer, to be served on a person, and warning him to appear in court at a day specified, to answer to the plaintiff upon pain of judgment against the defendant for default in so doing. — *v. t. Colloq.* To take out a summons against.

‖**sum′mum bo′num** (sŭm′ŭm bō′nŭm). [L.] The supreme or highest good, from which others are derived.

sump (sŭmp), *n.* [MLG., a marsh.] **1.** (*pron.* sŭmp, sŏŏmp) A pit or reservoir, serving as a drain or receptacle for fluids; specif.: **a** A cesspool. **b** A pit at the lowest point in a circulating or drainage system, as in the oil-circulating system of an internal-combustion engine; — called sometimes **sump pit**. **2.** [G. *sumpf*, lit., marsh.] *Mining.* **a** The lowest portion of a shaft, into which the water drains. **b** An excavation ahead of the regular work in driving a tunnel or sinking a shaft.

sumph (sŭmf; sŏŏmf), *n. Scot.* A stupid or sulky person.

sump′ter (sŭmp′tẽr), *n.* [OF. *sommetier* driver of a pack horse. See SUMMER a beam.] A pack horse or mule; a beast of burden. — **sump′ter**, *adj.*

sump′tu·ar′y (sŭmp′tū̍·ẽr′ĭ *or, esp. Brit.*, -ẽr·ĭ), *adj.* [L. *sumptuarius*, fr. *sumptus* expense, cost, fr. *sumere, sumptum*, to take, spend, fr. *sub-* + *emere* to take, buy.] Relating to or regulating expenditure, esp. on clothes, food, etc.; controlling extravagance; as *sumptuary* edicts.

sumptuary law. A law designed to regulate habits primarily on moral or religious grounds, justified under the police power of the state.

sump′tu·ous (sŭmp′tū̍·ŭs), *adj.* [F. *somptueux*, fr. L. *sumptuosus*, fr. *sumptus* expense, cost.] Involving large outlay or expense; costly; lavish; hence, luxurious; splendid. — **Syn.** See LUXURIOUS. — **sump′tu·ous·ly**, *adv.* — **sump′tu·ous·ness**, *n.*

sun (sŭn), *n.* [AS. *sunne.*] **1.** The luminous celestial body round which the earth and other planets revolve, and from which they receive light and heat. Symbol, ⊙. Its mean distance from the earth is 92,900,000 miles; its linear diameter, 864,000 miles; its mass, 332,000 times that of the earth; its mean density, about one fourth that of the earth. **2.** The heat or light radiated from the sun (def. 1); sunshine. **3.** Sunrise or sunset; — in phrases; as, *from sun to sun.* **4.** A celestial body like the sun; a luminary center of a system. **5.** A sunlike object, as a round firework. — *v. t.;* SUNNED (sŭnd); SUN′NING. To expose to the sun's rays; to warm, dry, air, bleach, etc., in or as if in the sun. — *v. i.* To sun oneself.

sun bath. Therapeutic exposure to the sun's rays.

sun′beam′ (sŭn′bēm′), *n.* A beam or ray of the sun.

sun′bird′ (-bûrd′), *n.* **a** Any of numerous small, brilliantly colored singing birds (family Nectariniidae), native to Africa and the East Indies, somewhat resembling hummingbirds. **b** The sun bittern.

sun bittern. Either of two peculiar Central and South American birds (*Eurypyga helias* and *E. major*) allied to the herons, rails, and cranes.

sun′bon′net (sŭn′bŏn′ĕt; -ĭt), *n.* A poke bonnet, with a cape at the back, worn to shield the head, face, and neck from the sun.

sun′bow′ (-bō′), *n. Poetic.* A rainbow; an iris.

sun′burn′ (-bûrn′), *n.* Superficial inflammation of the skin from exposure to the sun's rays; also, the red or brown color so caused. — *v. t. & i.* To burn by the sun.

sun′burst′ (-bûrst′), *n.* **1.** A burst of sunlight, esp. through a break in clouds. **2.** A jeweled brooch representing a sun surrounded by rays.

sun′dae (sŭn′dĭ), *n.* [Also *sunday*, obscurely fr. *Sunday*.] A portion of plain ice cream served with crushed fruit, sirups, nuts, etc.

sun dance. A ceremonial dance performed at the summer solstice among many Indians of the Great Plains.

Sun′day (sŭn′dĭ; 13), *n.* [AS. *sunnandæg.*] The first day of the week; the Christian Sabbath. Abbr. *Sun.*

Syn. **Sunday, Sabbath** are synonyms only in Christian use. Strictly **Sunday** names the first day of the week, and **Sabbath** the day devoted to rest and worship. Since the Jews have traditionally celebrated Saturday as the Sabbath and Christians, with some exceptions, Sunday, the term *Sabbath* is permissible in place of *Sunday* only when it clearly refers to the day of rest and worship.

Sun′day-go′-to-meet′ing, *adj. Humorous.* Pertaining to, or appropriate for, Sunday churchgoing.

Sunday, *or* **Sabbath, school.** A school held on Sunday for religious education; also, its teachers and pupils.

sun′der (sŭn′dẽr), *v. t.* [AS. *sundrian* (in comp.), or *syndrian;* akin to AS. *sundor* asunder, separately.] To force apart or separate by rending, cutting, breaking, etc.; to part or sever. — **Syn.** See SEPARATE. — ***in sunder.*** Into parts; apart; asunder.

sun′der·ance (-ăns), *n.* Act of dividing or separating; severance.

sun′dew′ (sŭn′dū′; 114), *n.* Any of a genus (*Drosera*) of bog-inhabiting insectivorous herbs having viscid glands on the leaves, and typical of a family (Droseraceae, the sundew family).

sun′di′al (-dī′ăl), *n.* An instrument to show the time of day by the shadow of a gnomon, or style.

sun disk. *Archaeol.* A disk with conventionalized wings, in Egypt the symbol of Ra the sun-god, and in the Near East, symbol of Ashur.

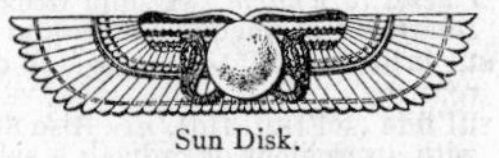

Sun Disk.

sun′dog′ (sŭn′dŏg′; 74), *n.* **1.** A parhelion. **2.** A small halo, nearly round, on the parhelic circle.

sun′down′ (-doun′), *n.* Sunset.

sun′down′er (-ẽr), *n. Colloq.* A tramp, orig. an Australian swagman, who comes to a station at sunset for food and shelter.

sun′-dried′ (-drīd′), *adj.* Dried by the sun, as raisins.

sun′dries (sŭn′drĭz), *n. pl.* Miscellaneous articles, details, or items of inconsiderable size or amount.

sun′drops′ (-drŏps′), *n. pl.* Any of several day-flowering herbs (genus *Kneiffia*) related to the evening primroses.

sun′dry (sŭn′drĭ), *adj.* [AS. *syndrig* separate, special, several.] Several; divers; various; miscellaneous.

sun′fast′ (-fȧst′; 9), *adj.* Not capable of being faded by sunlight.

sun′fish′ (-fĭsh′), *n.;* see FISH, *Note.* **1.** A large marine plectognath fish (*Mola mola*) with high dorsal and anal fins and a body nearly oval in outline due to a sharply truncated posterior extremity. It may attain a length of ten feet and a weight in excess of two tons. **2.** Any of numerous American perchlike fresh-water fishes (family Centrarchidae); esp., the common species, or pumpkinseed (*Eupomotis gibbosus*).

sun′flow′er (-flou′ẽr), *n.* Any of a genus (*Helianthus*) of plants of the aster family, having large yellow-rayed flower heads and bearing seeds which serve as stock food and which yield an edible oil. The common sunflower (*H. annuus*) is the State flower of Kansas.

Sunflower State. Kansas; — a nickname.

Sung (sŏŏng), *n.* [Chin. (Pek.) *Sung*⁴.] A dynasty in Chinese history, A.D. 960–1127, active in literature, philosophy, and art.

sung (sŭng), *past & past part.* of SING.

sun′glass′ (sŭn′glȧs′; 9), *n.* **1.** = BURNING GLASS. **2.** *Optics. pl.* Spectacles made of a glass or transparent plastic which protects the eyes from the glare of the sun.

sun′glow′ (-glō′), *n.* A brownish-yellow or rosy flush often seen in the sky before sunrise or after sunset, due to solar rays diffracted by particles in the air.

sun′-god′, *n. Myth.* A god representing the sun or one of its aspects, as Ra, Shamash, Helios, etc.

sunk (sŭngk), *past & past part.* of SINK.

sunk′en (sŭngk′ĕn), orig. *past part.* of SINK; hence: *adj.* **a** That has sunk down, in, below, etc.; also, situated in a depression; as, a **sunken garden.** **b** Lying on the bottom of a river or other water.

sun′ket (sŭng′kĭt; sŏŏng′-), *n.* [From Scot. form of *somewhat* something.] *Scot.* Food; esp., a dainty.

sunk fence. A ditch with a retaining wall, used to divide lands without defacing a landscape; a ha-ha.

sun lamp. An electric lamp designed to produce ultraviolet radiation including some of the same wave lengths as those in sunlight, used especially for therapeutic treatments.

sun′less (sŭn′lĕs; -lĭs), *adj.* Having no sun or sunlight.

sun′light′ (-līt′), *n.* The light of the sun.

sun′lit′ (-lĭt′), *adj.* Lighted by the sun.

sunn (sŭn), *n.*, *or* **sunn hemp.** [Hind. *san*, fr. Skr. *śaṇa.*] **a** An East Indian plant (*Crotalaria juncea*) of the pea family, with slender branches, simple leaves, and yellow flowers. **b** The valuable fiber of this plant, lighter and stronger than jute, and used for ropes, bags, etc.

Sun′na, Sun′nah (sŏŏn′ȧ), *n.* [Ar. *sunnah.*] *Moham. Relig.* The theory and practice of orthodox Islam.

Sun′nite (sŏŏn′īt), *n.* [From SUNNA.] One of a Moslem sect who acknowledge the first four caliphs to be the rightful successors of Mohammed. Cf. SHIITE.

sun′ny (sŭn′ĭ), *adj.;* -NI·ER (-ĭ·ẽr); -NI·EST. **1.** Of, from, or in the sun or sunshine; bright with sunshine. **2.** Exposed to, brightened by, etc., the sun's rays. **3.** Like the sun or sunshine; merry; gay. — **sun′ni·ness**, *n.*

sun parlor. Also **sun′room′** (sŭn′rōōm′), *n.* A glass-enclosed porch or living room with a sunny exposure.

sun′rise′ (sŭn′rīz′), *n.* **1.** The apparent rising of the sun above the horizon; also, the accompanying atmospheric effects. **2.** The time when the upper limb of the sun appears above the sensible horizon as a result of the diurnal rotation of the earth.

sun′set′ (-sĕt′), *n.* **1.** The apparent descent of the sun below the horizon; also, the accompanying atmospheric effects. **2.** The time when the upper limb of the sun disappears below the sensible horizon (see HORIZON, 3 **a**) as a result of the diurnal rotation of the earth.

sun′shade′ (-shād′), *n.* Anything used as a protection from the sun's rays; as: **a** A parasol. **b** An awning.

sun′shine′ (-shīn′), *n.* **1.** The sun's light; the sun's direct rays; hence: **a** The warmth and light given by the sun's rays. **b** A spot or surface on which the sun's light shines. **2.** Sunniness, happiness, graciousness, etc., or their source. — **sun′shin′y** (-shīn′ĭ), *adj.*

Sunshine State. Florida; sometimes, South Dakota and New Mexico; — a nickname.
sun′spot′ (sŭn′spŏt′), *n.* One of the dark spots that appear from time to time on the sun's surface, usually visible only with the telescope. Their appearance is frequently accompanied by magnetic storms on the earth.
sun′stroke′ (-strōk′), *n. Med.* An affection, often fatal, caused by exposure to the sun or excessive heat and marked by prostration and, usually, high fever.
sun′-struck′, *adj.* Affected with sunstroke.
sun′up′ (sŭn′ŭp′), *n.* Sunrise.
sun′ward (-wẽrd), **sun′wards** (-wẽrdz), *adv.* Toward the sun.
sun′ward (-wẽrd), *adj.* Facing the sun.
sun′wise′ (-wīz′), *adv.* Clockwise.
sun worship. Pagan or primitive worship of the sun as a deity or as a symbol of deity; heliolatry. — **sun worshiper.**
‖**su′o ju′re** (sū′ō jōō′rē). [L.] In one's own right.
‖**su′o lo′co** (lō′kō). [L.] In its proper place.
sup (sŭp), *v. t.;* SUPPED (sŭpt); SUP′PING. [(With influence of *supper*), fr. ME. *soupen*, fr. AS. *sūpan*, to drink.] *Archaic & Dial.* To take into the mouth in sips, as a liquid or liquid food. — *v. i.* To take liquid food into the mouth a little at a time; to sip. — *n.* A mouthful, as of liquor or broth.
sup, *v. i.* [OF. *super, soper*, combined with ME. *soupen* to drink.] **1.** To eat the evening meal. **2.** To make one's supper; — with *off.* — *v. t.* To provide with supper.
su′per (sū′pẽr), *n.* **1.** *Slang.* **a** Also **supe** (sūp; sōōp). Short for SUPERNUMERARY; esp., a supernumerary actor. **b** Short for SUPERINTENDENT. **c** In trade, a superfine or superior grade; an extra large size, or the like. **2.** Also **su′per·hive′** (-hīv′). A removable upper section of a beehive. See HIVE, *Illust.* **3.** *Bookbinding.* A thin, loosely woven, open-meshed starched cotton fabric, used esp. for reinforcing books. — *adj. Chiefly Slang.* **a** Superfine; excellent; first-rate. **b** *Ironical.* Excessively manifesting loyalty, etc.; as, a *super* American. — *v. t. Bookbinding.* To reinforce with super.
su′per- (sū′pẽr-; 114). [L. *super* over, above.] A prefix signifying *above, over;* specif.: **1. a** *Situated on* or *at the top of*, as in **su′per·gla′cial, su′per·soil′**. **b** *Over and above*, as in quantity, quality, or degree; *more than*, as in **su′per·stand′ard**. **c** *Now Rare. Superior in status*, as in **su′per·sov′er·eign**. **d** *That surpasses all* or *most others of its kind*, as in power or size, as in **su′per·state′**. **e** *Exceeding; in excess*, as in **su′per·re·fined′**. **f** *In addition; extra*, as in *super*tax. **g** *Secondarily*, as in **su′per·par′a·site**. **2. a** *Anat., Bot., & Zool. Situated over, at the upper part*, or *on the dorsal side of*, as in **su′per·glot′tal, su′per·or′bit·al**. **b** *Bot. & Zool. Constituting a more inclusive classification than* (that specified), as in *super*family. **c** *Anat. Superior*, as in **su′per·max·il′la**, the maxilla, or upper jaw. **3.** *Chem. Having the* (specified) *ingredient in a large*, or *unusually large, proportion*, as in *super*phosphate; — superseded by *per-, bi-, di-, acid*, etc. **4.** *Med. That exceeds the norm*, as in **su′per·pig′men·ta′tion.**
su′per·a·ble (sū′pẽr·ȧ·b'l), *adj.* [L. *superabilis*, fr. *superare* to surmount, fr. *super* above, over.] Capable of being overcome or conquered; surmountable.
su′per·a·bound′ (-ȧ·bound′), *v. i.* To be very, or too, abundant; to abound to excess or to an unusual extent.
su′per·a·bun′dant (-ȧ·bŭn′dănt), *adj.* Abounding to an abnormal degree or to excess. — **su′per·a·bun′dance** (-dăns), *n.* — **su′per·a·bun′dant·ly,** *adv.*
su′per·add′ (-ăd′), *v. t.* [L. *superaddere.*] To add over and above; to add, as something adventitious, out of the ordinary, etc. — **su′per·ad·di′tion** (-ă·dĭsh′ŭn), *n.*
su′per·an′nu·ate (-ăn′ū·āt), *v. t.* [*super-* + L. *annus* year.] To retire and pension because of old age or infirmity. — *v. i.* To become antiquated; — used in past part. — **su′per·an′nu·a′tion** (-ā′shŭn), *n.*
su·perb′ (sū·pûrb′), *adj.* [L. *superbus*, fr. *super* over + the root of *fui* I was, E. *be.*] **1.** Noble; majestic. **2.** Rich; sumptuous. **3.** Supremely good of its kind; as, a *superb* technique. — **Syn.** See SPLENDID. — **su·perb′ly,** *adv.* — **su·perb′ness,** *n.*
su′per·cal′en·der (sū′pẽr·kăl′ĕn·dẽr), *n.* A calender consisting of a stack of highly polished rolls, used to give an extra finish to paper, etc. — **su′per·cal′en·der,** *v. t.*
su′per·car′go (-kär′gō), *n.; pl.* -CARGOES, -CARGOS (-gōz). [From earlier *supracargo*, fr. Sp. *sobrecargo.*] An officer in a merchant ship in charge of the commercial concerns of the voyage.
su′per·charge′ (-chärj′), *v. t.* **1.** To charge over, beyond, to excess, or in addition. **2.** To supply a charge to the intake of an internal-combustion engine or other prime mover at a pressure higher than that of the surrounding atmosphere. **3.** = PRESSURIZE.
su′per·charg′er (sū′pẽr·chär′jẽr), *n.* A device, such as a blower or compressor, for pressurizing the cabin of an airplane or for increasing the volume air charge of an internal-combustion engine over that which would normally be drawn in through the pumping action of the pistons. Cf. TURBOSUPERCHARGER.

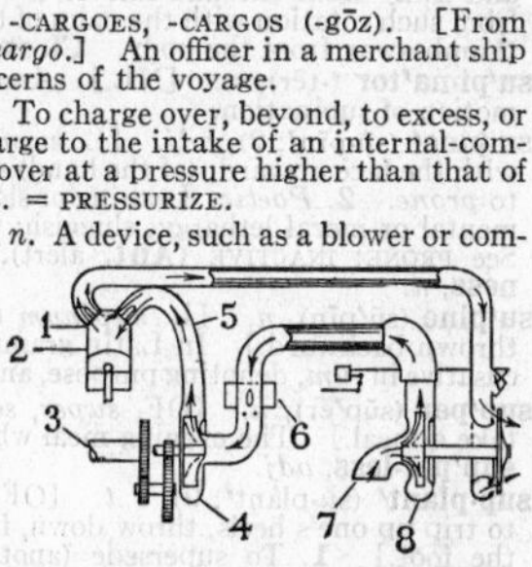

Supercharger (simplified combination of internal centrifugal and external exhaust-driven types). 1 Exhaust Valve; 2 Cylinder; 3 Crankshaft; 4 Internal Supercharger; 5 Intake Pipe; 6 Carburetor; 7 Air Intake; 8 Turbosupercharger.

su′per·cil′i·ar′y (sū′pẽr·sĭl′ĭ·ẽr′ĭ *or, esp. Brit.,* -ẽr·ĭ), *adj.* [L. *supercilium* eyebrow.] *Anat. & Zool.* Pertaining to the eyebrow; supraorbital.
su′per·cil′i·ous (-ĭ·ŭs), *adj.* [L. *superciliosus*, fr. *supercilium* an eyebrow, pride, fr. *super* over + *cilium* eyelid.] Lofty with pride; haughtily contemptuous. — **Syn.** See PROUD. — **-ly,** *adv.* — **-ness,** *n.*
su′per·class′ (sū′pẽr·klȧs′; 9), *n. Zool. & Bot.* A category equivalent to or below a subphylum, and above a class.
su′per·cool′ (-kōōl′), *v. t. & i. Physical Chem.* To cool below the freezing point without solidification.
su′per·dom′i·nant (-dŏm′ĭ·nănt), *n. Music.* = SUBMEDIANT.
su′per·dread′nought′ (-drĕd′nôt′), *n.* See DREADNOUGHT.
su′per·e′go (-ē′gō; -ĕg′ō), *n.* [*super-* + *ego.*] *Psychoanalysis.* The ego as developed along the lines of self-criticism and moral conscience.
su′per·em′i·nent (-ĕm′ĭ·nĕnt), *adj.* [L. *supereminens*, pres. part. of *supereminere.* See SUPER-; EMINENT.] Eminent in a superior degree; of surpassing quality, etc. — **su′per·em′i·nence** (-nĕns), *n.* — **su′per·em′i·nent·ly,** *adv.*
su′per·er′o·gate (-ĕr′ō·gāt), *v. i.* [LL. *supererogatus*, past part. of *supererogare* to spend over and above.] To do more than is required by duty or obligation.
su′per·er′o·ga′tion (-gā′shŭn), *n.* Act or fact of supererogating; also, supererogatory character or nature. In the Roman Catholic Church, ***works of supererogation*** are those good deeds believed to have been done by saints, or capable of being done by men, over and above what is needed for their own salvation.
su′per·e·rog′a·to′ry (-ē·rŏg′ȧ·tō′rĭ; -tẽr·ĭ; -ẽr′ō·gȧ·tẽr·ĭ), *adj.* **1.** Observed or performed to an extent not enjoined, or not required. **2.** Superfluous; nonessential.
Syn. Supererogatory, gratuitous, uncalled-for, wanton mean given or done without compulsion and, sometimes, without warrant. **Supererogatory** implies a giving above and beyond that which is required by the laws, rules, etc.; **gratuitous**, a voluntary giving without expectation of recompense or reward or, sometimes, without provocation; **uncalled-for** and, in loose use, *gratuitous*, a lack of need that suggests also impertinence or absurdity; **wanton**, not only a lack of provocation but a malicious or sportive motive.
su′per·fam′i·ly (-făm′ĭ·lĭ), *n. Zool. & Bot.* A category of classification ranking next above a family.
su′per·fe′cun·da′tion (-fē′kŭn·dā′shŭn; -fĕk′ŭn-), *n. Physiol.* Successive fertilization of two or more ova from the same ovulation.
su′per·fe′tate (-fē′tāt), *v. i.* [L. *superfetare*, fr. *super* above, over + *fetare* to bring forth.] *Physiol.* To conceive after a prior conception, but before the birth of the offspring.
su′per·fe·ta′tion (-fē·tā′shŭn), *n.* **1.** Conception during pregnancy. **2.** Fertilization of an ovule by two or more kinds of pollen. **3.** Uninterrupted cumulative development; overproduction; also, an instance of this.
su′per·fi′cial (-fĭsh′ăl), *adj.* [LL. *superficialis.*] **1.** Of or pert. to the superficies, or surface; lying on, not penetrating below, or affecting only, the surface; of measurements, square. **2.** Concerned only with the obvious or apparent; cursory; hasty; not profound; shallow. **3.** Not significant or genuine. **4.** That is seen at first view; external. — **su′per·fi′cial·ly,** *adv.* — **su′per·fi′cial·ness,** *n.*
Syn. Superficial, shallow, cursory mean lacking in depth or solidity. **Superficial** implies a concern with surface aspects or an avoidance of all but them; **shallow**, a more generally derogatory term, a lack of depth in knowledge, reasoning, emotions, or the like; **cursory**, a lack of thoroughness or care for details.
su′per·fi′ci·al′i·ty (-fĭsh′ĭ·ăl′ĭ·tĭ), *n.; pl.* -TIES (-tĭz). Quality of being superficial; that which is superficial.
su′per·fi′ci·es (-fĭsh′ĭ·ēz; -fĭsh′ēz), *n.* [L., fr. *super* above, over + *facies* make, figure, shape.] **1.** The surface; the exterior part or face, as of a sphere or a region. **2.** The purely external aspect.
su′per·fine′ (sū′pẽr·fīn′; 2), *adj.* **1.** Very refined or delicate; too nice. **2.** Extra fine; — of merchandise.
su′per·flu′i·ty (-flōō′ĭ·tĭ; 114), *n.; pl.* -ITIES (-tĭz). **1.** Superabundance, as of money, possessions, etc.; wealth. **2.** Excess supply, use, expenditure, etc.; more than is necessary or advantageous.
su·per′flu·ous (sū·pûr′flōō·ŭs; 114), *adj.* [L. *superfluus* overflowing, fr. *super* over, above + *fluere* to flow.] **1.** In excess of what is sufficient, necessary, normal, or desirable; superabundant; surplus. **2.** Extravagant; wasteful. — **su·per′flu·ous·ly,** *adv.* — **su·per′flu·ous·ness,** *n.*
su′per·fuse′ (sū′pẽr·fūz′), *v. t. & i.* [L. *superfusus*, past part. of *superfundere.*] **1.** To pour or be poured over or on something. **2.** *Physical Chem.* To supercool. — **su′per·fu′sion** (-fū′zhŭn), *n.*
su′per·heat′ (sū′pẽr·hēt′), *n.* The extra heat imparted to a vapor in superheating it from a dry and saturated condition; also, the range of temperature passed through. — (sū′pẽr·hēt′), *v. t.* **1.** To overheat. **2. a** To heat a liquid above its boiling point without converting it into vapor. **b** To heat (a vapor, esp. steam, not in contact with its own liquid) so that it possesses more than enough heat to remain a dry gas at the given pressure. — **su′per·heat′er** (-hēt′ẽr), *n.*
su′per·het′er·o·dyne′ (-hĕt′ẽr·ō·dīn′), *adj. Radio.* Pertaining to a form of heterodyne reception in which beats are produced of a frequency above audibility but below that of the received signals, the current of the beat frequency being then rectified, amplified, and rectified again to reproduce the music, etc. — *n.* A radio set for superheterodyne reception.
su′per·high′way′ (-hī′wā′), *n.* A highway consisting of four or more lanes and designed for fast-moving traffic, as by providing overpasses or underpasses for crossroads and making crossroads accessible by cloverleaf intersections.
su′per·hive′ (sū′pẽr·hīv′), *n.* See SUPER, *n.*, 2.
su′per·hu′man (-hū′măn), *adj.* **1.** Above the human; divine. **2.** Beyond human capacity or normal human power. — **su′per·hu·man′i·ty** (-hū·măn′ĭ·tĭ), *n.* — **su′per·hu′man·ly,** *adv.*
su′per·im·pose′ (-ĭm·pōz′), *v. t.* To lay or impose (one thing) over or above. — **su′per·im′po·si′tion** (-ĭm′pō·zĭsh′ŭn), *n.*
su′per·in·cum′bent (-ĭn·kŭm′bĕnt), *adj.* Lying or resting on something else. — **su′per·in·cum′bence** (-bĕns), *n.* — **su′per·in·cum′ben·cy** (-bĕn·sĭ), *n.*
su′per·in·duce′ (-ĭn·dūs′), *v. t.* [L. *superinducere.*] To introduce (something) by way of addition or superimposition; to bring in over or above that already existing. — **su′per·in·duc′tion** (-ĭn·dŭk′shŭn), *n.*
su′per·in·tend′ (sū′pẽr·ĭn·tĕnd′; -prĭn·tĕnd′), *v. t.* [LL. *superintendere.* See INTEND.] To have or exercise the charge and oversight of; to oversee with the power of direction; to supervise.
su′per·in·tend′ence (-tĕn′dĕns), *n.* The function of superintending; supervision.
su′per·in·tend′en·cy (-dĕn·sĭ), *n.* The office of a superintendent; superintendence.
su′per·in·tend′ent (sū′pẽr·ĭn·tĕn′dĕnt), *n.* One who has the oversight and charge of some place, institution, department, or the like. Abbr. *supt.* — *adj.* Superintending.
su·pe′ri·or (sū·pēr′ĭ·ẽr; sŭ-; 118), *adj.* [OF., fr. L. *superior*, compar. of *superus* being above, fr. *super* above, over.] **1.** More elevated in place or position; higher; upper. **2.** Higher in rank or office; more exalted in dignity. **3.** Extremely excellent of its kind; far above in comparison; as, of *superior* flavor; *superior* to his associates. **4.** Larger as in numbers or amount; of greater value, significance, validity, etc.; as, one's *superior* title to an estate. **5.** Courageously or

serenely indifferent, as to something painful or disheartening. **6.** Affecting or assuming superiority; supercilious, arrogant, domineering; as, a *superior* air. **7.** More comprehensive; as, a genus is *superior* to a species. **8.** *Astron.* **a** Farther from the sun than the earth; — said of the planets Mars, Jupiter, Saturn, Uranus, Neptune, and Pluto. **b** Farther from the earth than is the sun; as, a *superior* conjunction of Venus. **9.** *Bot.* Above and adnate to the ovary; of an ovary, free from the other floral organs. **10.** *Print.* Standing at the top of the line; as, in y^n, *n* is a *superior* letter. — *n.* **1.** One who surpasses another, as in rank, station, office, or merit. **2.** *Eccl.* The head of a monastery, convent, etc. A nun in this position is often called a ***mother superior.*** — **su·pe′ri·or·ly,** *adv.*

su·pe′ri·or′i·ty (sŭ·pēr′ĭ·ŏr′ĭ·tĭ; sŭ-), *n.* Quality or state of being superior; a superior characteristic.

superiority complex. See COMPLEX, *n.*, 2.

su′per·ja′cent (sū′pēr·jā′sĕnt; -s′nt), *adj.* [L. *superjacens,* pres. part. of *superjacere,* fr. *super* above + *jacere* to lie.] Overlying.

su·per′la·tive (sŭ·pûr′lȧ·tĭv), *adj.* [OF. *superlatif,* fr. LL. *superlativus,* fr. *superlatus* excessive.] **1.** *Gram.* Expressing the highest or utmost (or, with *least,* the lowest) degree or amount of the quantity, manner, etc., denoted. Abbr. *superl.* See COMPARISON, 2. **2.** Surpassing all other; supreme; as, *superlative* wisdom. **3.** Exaggerated; excessive. — *n.* **1.** *Gram.* The superlative degree; also, a form or word denoting it. **2.** The utmost degree of something; the peak or acme. — **su·per′la·tive·ly,** *adv.* — **su·per′la·tive·ness,** *n.*

su′per·lu′na·ry (sū′pēr·lū′nȧ·rĭ), *adj.* Also **su′per·lu′nar** (-lū′nẽr). Being above the moon; not belonging to this world.

su′per·man′ (sū′pēr·măn′), *n.* [Trans. of G. *übermensch.*] An ideal superior man of the future to be characterized by surpassing physique and capacity to dominate; popularly, a man of superhuman powers.

su′per·mar′ket (-mär′kĕt; -kĭt), *n.* A departmentalized, usually self-service, retail market of a chain-store system or an independent selling foods and other household merchandise.

su·per′nal (sŭ·pûr′năl), *adj.* [OF., fr. L. *supernus,* fr. *super* above.] **1.** Being in or coming from heaven or belonging to a realm above and beyond this world. **2.** Of or in the sky; celestial; hence, exalted. **3.** Excellent beyond earthly quality. — **su·per′nal·ly,** *adv.*

su′per·na′tant (sū′pēr·nā′tănt), *adj.* [L. *supernatans,* pres. part. of *supernatare* to swim above.] Floating on the surface.

su′per·nat′u·ral (-năt′ṳ·răl), *adj.* **1.** Of, or proceeding from, an order of existence beyond nature, or the visible and observable universe. **2.** Ascribed to agencies above or beyond nature; miraculous. — *n.* With *the,* the divine operation, intervention, etc.; hence, something miraculous or marvelous. — **su′per·nat′u·ral·ly,** *adv.* — **su′per·nat′u·ral·ness,** *n.*

su′per·nat′u·ral·ism (-ĭz′m), *n.* **1.** Quality or state of being supernatural. **2.** Belief in the supernatural order of existence; specif., any doctrine that asserts the control and guidance of nature and men by an invisible power or powers. — **su′per·nat′u·ral·ist** (-ĭst), *n.* — **su′per·nat′u·ral·ist, su′per·nat′u·ral·is′tic** (-ĭs′tĭk), *adj.*

su′per·nor′mal (-nôr′măl), *adj.* **1.** Superior to the norm or average; as, a *supernormal* pupil. **2.** Exceeding the natural powers of man; as, a *supernormal* experience or manifestation.

su′per·no′va (-nō′vȧ), *n.; pl.* -NOVAE (-vē), -NOVAS (-vȧz). [NL.] *Astron.* A nova hundreds of times as bright as common novae. The brightest known supernovae attain luminosities equivalent to hundreds of millions of suns. Two types of supernovae with distinct spectra and light curves occur in larger stellar systems about once every 400 years. In A.D. 1054 a supernova gave rise to the luminous Crab nebula in the constellation Taurus.

su′per·nu′mer·ar′y (sū′pēr·nū′mēr·ĕr′ĭ *or, esp. Brit.,* -ẽr·ĭ), *adj.* [LL. *supernumerarius.*] **1.** Exceeding the number stated or prescribed; extra. **2.** Exceeding a necessary, usual, or required number or quantity; superfluous. — *n.; pl.* -IES (-ĭz). **1.** A supernumerary person or thing. **2.** In theaters, a person not a regular actor, but employed to appear, as in a mob scene or a spectacle.

su′per·or′der (sū′pēr·ôr′dẽr), *n.* *Biol.* A category between an order and a class or a subclass.

su′per·or·gan′ic (-ôr·găn′ĭk), *adj.* Above or superior to the organic; hence, psychical.

su′per·phos′phate (-fŏs′fāt), *n.* **1.** An acid phosphate. **2.** A soluble mixture of phosphates used as a fertilizer, made from insoluble mineral phosphates by treatment with sulfuric acid.

su′per·phys′i·cal (-fĭz′ĭ·kăl), *adj.* Above or beyond physics; not explainable on physical principles.

su′per·pose′ (sū′pēr·pōz′), *v. t.* [F. *superposer.* See SUPER-; POSE.] **1.** To place or lay over or above; to superimpose with or often without contact. **2.** *Aeronautics.* To place (main supporting surfaces) one above another. **3.** *Geom.* To lay (a figure) upon another, making all the parts coincide with like parts. Cf. CONGRUENT, 2. — **su′per·pos′a·ble** (-pōz′ȧ·b'l), *adj.* — **su′per·po·si′tion** (-pō·zĭsh′ŭn), *n.*

su′per·posed′ (-pōzd′), *adj.* *Bot.* Growing or situated vertically over another part or organ.

su′per·pow′er (-pou′ẽr), *n.* **1.** A theoretical political entity conceived as having authority over other states, esp. over the most powerful states. **2.** Electric power developed by the utilization of all available water-power sites or existing steam-power plants in a large area, as connected parts of one system.

su′per·sat′u·rate (-săt′ṳ·rāt), *v. t.* To add to beyond saturation. — **su′per·sat′u·ra′tion** (-rā′shŭn), *n.*

su′per·scribe′ (-skrīb′), *v. t.* [L. *superscribere, -scriptum,* fr. *super* over + *scribere* to write.] To write or engrave (anything) on the top or outside; to write a name, address, etc., on the outside or cover of; to address.

su′per·script (sū′pēr·skrĭpt), *adj.* Written above; — opposed to *subscript.* — *n.* *Math.* Any index or mark written above, as in a^3, b'', c^n. Cf. SUBSCRIPT.

su′per·scrip′tion (-skrĭp′shŭn), *n.* **1.** Act of superscribing. **2.** That which is written or engraved on the surface, outside, or above something else; inscription; title; an address on a letter or envelope.

su′per·sede′ (-sēd′), *v. t.* [OF. *superseder, superceder,* fr. L. *supersedere, -sessum,* to sit above, be superior to, forbear, omit, fr. *super* above + *sedere* to sit.] **1.** To cause to be set aside; force out of use as inferior; as, new methods *supersede* old. **2.** To take the place, room, or position of; to replace. **3.** To displace, or pass over, so as to appoint a successor or make way for another; to supplant. — **Syn.** See REPLACE. — **su′per·sed′er** (-sēd′ẽr), *n.*

su′per·se′de·as (-sē′dē·ăs), *n.* [L., suspend, set aside.] *Law.* A writ or order commanding a stay of legal proceedings, as a writ to stay an officer from proceeding under another writ or an order staying proceedings of an inferior court.

su′per·se′dure (-sē′dṳr), *n.* A superseding, or setting aside.

su′per·sen′si·ble (-sĕn′sĭ·b'l), *adj.* Above that which is apparent to the senses; spiritual; psychical.

su′per·sen′so·ry (-sĕn′sō·rĭ), **su′per·sen′su·al** (-sĕn′shōō·ăl; *cf.* SENSUAL), *adj.* Supersensible; transcending sense.

su′per·serv′ice·a·ble (-sûr′vĭs·ȧ·b'l), *adj.* Too officious; obtrusively meddling.

su′per·ses′sion (-sĕsh′ŭn), *n.* Supersedure.

su′per·son′ic (-sŏn′ĭk), *adj.* [*super-* + *sonic.*] *Physics.* **a** Pertaining to vibrations and waves whose frequencies are greater than those which affect the human ear, that is, greater than about 20,000 per second. **b** Designating a speed exceeding that of sound in air, that is, greater than about 1087 feet per second (or about 738 miles per hour); also, moving, capable of moving, or utilizing air currents moving at a speed greater than that of sound; as, *supersonic* aircraft, a *supersonic* wind tunnel. Cf. SUBSONIC.

su′per·son′ic, *n.* A supersonic wave; hence, *pl.,* the branch of science which treats of supersonic phenomena.

su′per·sti′tion (sū′pēr·stĭsh′ŭn), *n.* [OF., fr. L. *superstitio,* orig., soothsaying, fr. *superstare* to stand over, fr. *super* over + *stare* to stand.] **1.** An irrational abject attitude of mind toward the supernatural, nature, or God, proceeding from ignorance, unreasoning fear of the unknown or mysterious, a belief in magic or chance, or the like. **2.** Any belief, conception, act or practice resulting from such a state of mind. **3.** Such conceptions, practices, etc., collectively.

su′per·sti′tious (sū′pēr·stĭsh′ŭs), *adj.* Of, proceeding from, characterized by, or manifesting superstition. — **su′per·sti′tious·ly,** *adv.* — **su′per·sti′tious·ness,** *n.*

su′per·stra′tum (sū′pēr·strā′tŭm), *n.* An overlying stratum.

su′per·struct′ (-strŭkt′), *v. t.* [L. *superstructus,* past part. of *superstruere* to build upon, fr. *super* over + *struere* to build.] To build over or on a structure; to erect on a foundation.

su′per·struc′ture (sū′pēr·strŭk′tṳr; 2), *n.* **1.** Any structure or edifice built as a vertical extension of something else. **2.** *Arch.* All that part of a building above the basement. **3.** *Naut.* The structural part of a vessel, esp. a war vessel, above the main deck. Cf. DECK, *Illust.* **4.** *Railroads.* The ties, rails, fastenings, etc., in distinction from the roadbed.

su′per·sub′tle (-sŭt′'l), *adj.* Too subtle. — **su′per·sub′tle·ty,** *n.*

su′per·tax′ (sū′pēr·tăks′), *n.* A tax in addition to the usual or normal tax; *U. S.,* a surtax.

su′per·ton′ic (-tŏn′ĭk), *n.* *Music.* The note next above the keynote; the second tone of the scale.

su′per·vene′ (-vēn′), *v. i.* [L. *supervenire, -ventum,* to come over or upon, fr. *super* over + *venire* to come.] To come or happen as something additional, unlooked for, or extraneous; to be added or to follow closely. — **Syn.** See FOLLOW. — **su′per·ven′tion** (-vĕn′shŭn), *n.*

su′per·ven′ient (-vēn′yĕnt), *adj.* Coming or occurring as something additional, extraneous, or unexpected. — **su′per·ven′ience** (-yĕns), *n.*

su′per·vise′ (sū′pēr·vīz′; sū′pēr·vīz), *v. t.* [ML. *supervisus,* past part. of *supervidere* to oversee, fr. L. *super* over + *videre* to see.] To oversee for direction; to superintend. — *v. i.* To exercise supervision.

su′per·vi′sion (sū′pēr·vĭzh′ŭn), *n.* **1.** Act of supervising. **2.** *Educ.* The direction and critical evaluation of instruction, esp. in public schools.

su′per·vi′sor (-vī′zẽr; sū′pēr·vī′zẽr), *n.* **1.** One who supervises; superintendent. **2.** *U. S.* An elected official standing at the head of the administration of a township or other county subdivision. **3.** *Educ.* An officer of a school system who has supervision over the courses and the teachers giving instruction in a special subject, as music. — **su′per·vi′sor·ship,** *n.*

su′per·vi′so·ry (sū′pēr·vī′zō·rĭ), *adj.* Of or pertaining to supervision; supervising; as, *supervisory* duties.

su′pi·nate (sū′pĭ·nāt), *v. t. & i.* [L. *supinare, supinatum,* to bend or lay backward, fr. *supinus* supine.] To cause to assume, or to assume, a position of supination.

su′pi·na′tion (-nā′shŭn), *n.* *Anat.* **a** Rotation of the forearm and hand or, loosely, of other joints, as the shoulder, hip, or knee, backward and away from the mid-line of the body. **b** The position resulting from such rotation with the palm of the hand directed forward and the thumb away from the body. Cf. PRONATION.

su′pi·na′tor (-tẽr), *n.* [NL.] *Anat.* A muscle which produces the motion of supination.

su·pine′ (sŭ·pīn′; 2), *adj.* [L. *supinus.*] **1.** Lying on the back, or with the face upward; (of the hand) marked by supination; — opposed to *prone.* **2.** *Poetic.* Leaning or sloping backward. **3.** Manifesting mental or moral lethargy; sluggish; without stamina; abject. — **Syn.** See PRONE: INACTIVE (**Ant.** alert). — **su·pine′ly,** *adv.* — **su·pine′ness,** *n.*

su′pine (sū′pīn), *n.* [L. *supinum* (sc. *verbum*), fr. *supinus* bent or thrown backward.] In Latin grammar, a verbal noun having an accusative in *-um,* denoting purpose, and an ablative of specification in *-u.*

sup′per (sŭp′ẽr), *n.* [OF. *super, soper,* prop., an infinitive, to sup, take a meal.] The evening meal when dinner is taken at midday. — **sup′per·less,** *adj.*

sup·plant′ (sŭ·plȧnt′; 9), *v. t.* [OF. *supplanter,* fr. L. *supplantare* to trip up one's heels, throw down, fr. *sub* under + *planta* the sole of the foot.] **1.** To supersede (another), esp. by force, trickery, or treachery. **2.** To uproot; to eradicate, often so as to replace; as, to *supplant* fear by curiosity. **3.** To take the place of; to supersede; as, free verse has not *supplanted* metrical verse. — **Syn.** See REPLACE. — **sup′plan·ta′tion** (sŭp′lăn·tā′shŭn), *n.* — **sup·plant′er,** *n.*

sup′ple (sŭp′'l), *adj.* [OF. *supple, souple,* fr. L. *supplex* suppliant.] **1.** Soft in texture; yielding; flexible when bent or twisted. **2.** Yielding; compliant; hence, unduly complaisant; obsequious. **3.** Of the mind, its acts, etc., bending easily to changing demands; adaptable; alertly responsive; resilient. — **Syn.** See ELASTIC. — *v. t. & i.; SUP′*-PLED (-'ld); SUP′PLING (-lĭng). To render or become supple; to mollify; alleviate. — **sup′ple·ly,** *adv.* — **sup′ple·ness,** *n.*

sup′ple·jack′ (-jăk′), *n.* Any of various woody climbers having tough, pliant stems (esp. *Berchemia scandens*).

sup′ple·ment (sŭp′lē·mĕnt), *n.* [L. *supplementum,* fr. *supplere* to fill up.] **1.** That which supplies a want or makes an addition to something already organized or set apart. **2.** A continuation of a book or paper, to make good its deficiencies, correct errors, or provide special features. **3.** *Trig.* The quantity by which an arc or an angle falls short of 180°, or an arc falls short of a semicircle. — (-mĕnt), *v. t.* To fill up or supply by additions; to fill the deficiencies of. — **sup′ple·men′tal** (sŭp′lē·mĕn′tăl; -t'l), *adj.*

sup′ple·men′ta·ry (sŭp′lē·mĕn′tȧ·rĭ), *adj.* Added as a supplement; additional; being, or serving as, a supplement; as, a *supplementary* volume, arc, angle.

sup′ple·to′ry (sŭp′lē·tō′rĭ *or, esp. Brit.,* -tẽr·ĭ), *adj.* [LL. *suppletorius.*] Supplying deficiencies; supplementary.

sup′pli·ance (sŭp′lĭ·ăns), *n.* *Now Rare.* Supplication.

sup′pli·ant (-ănt), *n.* [F. See SUPPLIANT, *adj.*] One who supplicates; petitioner. — *adj.* [F., pres. part. of *supplier* to entreat, fr. OF. *sopleier, souploier,* fr. L. *supplicare* to supplicate.] **1.** Supplicating; entreating; humbly imploring. **2.** Expressive of supplication. — **sup′pli·ant·ly,** *adv.*

sup′pli·cant (sŭp′lĭ·kănt), *adj.* [L. *supplicans,* pres. part.] Entreating; asking submissively. — *n.* One who supplicates; a suppliant.

sup′pli·cate (-kāt), *v. i.* [L. *supplicatus,* past part. of *supplicare* to supplicate, fr. *sub-* + root of *plicare* to fold, bend.] To make a humble entreaty; esp., to implore God. — *v. t.* **1.** To entreat for; to ask for earnestly and humbly. **2.** To entreat as a supplicant. — **Syn.** See BEG. — **sup′pli·cat′ing·ly** (-kāt′ĭng·lĭ), *adv.*

sup′pli·ca′tion (-kā′shŭn), *n.* Act of supplicating; a humble petition. — **Syn.** Entreaty, solicitation.

sup′pli·ca·to′ry (sŭp′lĭ·kȧ·tō′rĭ *or, esp. Brit.,* -tẽr·ĭ), *adj.* Expressing supplication; beseeching.

sup·ply′ (sŭ·plī′), *v. t.* [OF. *supplier, souploier,* fr. L. *supplere, -pletum,* fr. *sub-* + *plere* to fill.] **1.** To add (something essential or wanting); as, to *supply* missing words. **2.** To fill adequately; as, unable to *supply* the demand. **3.** To furnish or provide; specif.: **a** To give (something desired, needed, etc.); to afford; yield; as, this *supplies* proof. **b** To fill the needs of; to furnish with supplies, equipment, or the like; as, to *supply* roots with moisture. **4.** To fill or take temporarily (a place, office, etc.); to serve as substitute for another in; as, to *supply* a pulpit. — *v. i.* To serve as a substitute. — *n.; pl.* -PLIES (-plīz′). **1.** *Obs.* Assistance. **2.** Act of supplying, filling a want, providing something, etc. **3.** That which supplies or is supplied; specif.: **a** *Obs.* Reinforcements; — in *pl.* or *sing.* **b** A substitute clergyman or teacher. **c** The quantity (esp. of a commodity) at hand or needed; as, to send for a fresh *supply.* **d** *Chiefly pl.* Provisions, clothing, arms, raw materials, etc., set aside to be dispensed at need; stores. **e** *Chiefly pl.* An amount of money provided, as by parliament or congress, to meet the annual national expenditures. **4.** *Econ.* The quantity of any article offered at a given price. Cf. DEMAND, *n.,* 5. — *adj.* **1.** Serving to contain, deliver, or regulate a supply. **2.** Serving as a substitute; as, a *supply* teacher. — **sup·pli′er** (sŭ·plī′ẽr), *n.*

sup′ply (sŭp′lĭ). Var. of SUPPLELY.

sup·port′ (sŭ·pōrt′; 70), *v. t.* [OF. *supporter,* fr. L. *supportare* to convey, in ML., to support, sustain, fr. *sub-* + *portare* to carry.] **1.** To hold up or in position; to bear the weight or stress of; to keep from sinking or falling; also, to sustain (a load). **2.** To endure, esp. in silence; bear; tolerate; as, he could not *support* their taunts. **3.** To uphold (one) by aid or countenance; to take the side of, esp. in a dispute, an election, etc.; as, to *support* the defendant in an action; also, to uphold or defend as valid, right, just, etc., as a cause or a policy. **4.** To verify or substantiate, as a charge. **5.** To pay the costs of or maintain, as a project; also, to furnish with funds or means for maintenance; as, to *support* his brother's family. **6.** To maintain, as conversation, combustion, or the gold standard. **7.** To keep (a person) from fainting, sinking, yielding, or the like; to comfort or strengthen. **8.** *Theater.* **a** To assume and act, as a part. **b** To act with (a star); as, a fine company *supported* him.

Syn. **Support, uphold, advocate, back, champion** mean to favor actively one that meets opposition. **Support,** the least explicit term, implies only this and in itself gives no clue as to the assistance rendered; **uphold** implies more extended support to something attacked or challenged; **advocate** suggests urging or pleading; **back** suggests support from behind, as by lending assistance when falling or failing; **champion** suggests public defense in unjust attack or when too weak to advocate its own cause.

— *n.* **1.** Act or operation of supporting; the state of being supported. **2.** One who or that which supports; supporting means; a prop.

sup·port′a·ble (sŭ·pōr′tȧ·b'l), *adj.* That can or may be supported; endurable. — **sup·port′a·bil′i·ty** (-bĭl′ĭ·tĭ), **sup·port′a·ble·ness,** *n.* — **sup·port′a·bly,** *adv.*

sup·port′er (-pōr′tẽr), *n.* **1.** One who or that which supports; a support; specif., an adherent; an advocate. **2.** A band or elastic appliance for supporting any part of the body; also, a garter. **3.** *Her.* A figure of a man or animal, placed one on each side of an escutcheon, and exterior to it.

sup·port′ing, *adj.* That props up, confirms, etc.

sup·pos′a·ble (sŭ·pōz′ȧ·b'l), *adj.* That may or can be supposed; conceivable. — **sup·pos′a·bly** (-blĭ), *adv.*

sup·pos′al (sŭ·pōz′ăl; -'l), *n.* A supposing; supposition.

sup·pose′ (sŭ·pōz′), *v. t.* [OF. *supposer, suposer,* fr. L. *sub* under + OF. *poser* to place.] **1.** To lay down as a hypothesis or assumption; to accept tentatively as true, as for the sake of argument or exposition. **2.** To expect; — now only passive; as, I am *supposed* to attend. **3.** To incline to believe; to think probable or in keeping with the facts. **4.** To believe on slight grounds; presume. **5.** To presuppose. — *v. i.* To conjecture; to think; opine.

sup·posed′ (sŭ·pōzd′), *adj.* Accepted as such, often on slight grounds; erroneously imputed; sometimes, imagined. — **sup·pos′ed·ly** (-pōz′ĕd·lĭ; -ĭd·lĭ), *adv.*

sup′po·si′tion (sŭp′ō·zĭsh′ŭn), *n.* [OF., fr. L. *suppositio* a placing under, a substitution, fr. *supponere, suppositum,* to put under, substitute.] **1.** That which is supposed; a theory or surmise; as, mere *suppositions.* **2.** Act of supposing; assumption; as, given to *supposition.* — **sup′po·si′tion·al** (-ăl), *adj.* — **sup′po·si′tion·al·ly,** *adv.*

sup·pos′i·ti′tious (sŭ·pŏz′ĭ·tĭsh′ŭs), *adj.* **1.** Fraudulently substituted for something else; spurious; counterfeit. **2.** Of the nature of a supposition; hypothetical. — **sup·pos′i·ti′tious·ly,** *adv.* — **sup·pos′i·ti′tious·ness,** *n.*

sup·pos′i·tive (-pŏz′ĭ·tĭv), *adj.* Characterized by, involving, or implying supposition; supposed. — *n.* *Gram.* A word denoting or implying supposition (*if, granting, provided*). — **sup·pos′i·tive·ly,** *adv.*

sup·pos′i·to′ry (-tō′rĭ *or, esp. Brit.,* -tẽr·ĭ), *n.; pl.* -RIES (-rĭz). [LL. *suppositorium,* neut. of *suppositorius* that is placed underneath.] *Med.* An easily fusible preparation, usually in the form of a cone or cylinder, for introduction into the rectum, vagina, etc.

sup·press′ (sŭ·prĕs′), *v. t.* [L. *suppressus,* past part. of *supprimere* to suppress. See SUB-; PRESS to squeeze.] **1.** To put down by authority, force, or pressure, as a revolt; to quell; crush; subdue. **2.** To keep from public knowledge; as: **a** To refrain from divulging, as a scandal. **b** To prohibit or interdict the publication or revelation of, as a book. **3.** To keep from giving vent to; to repress, as anger; hence, to exclude from conscious and overt activity, as a desire. **4.** To check the flow or discharges of; as, to *suppress* a hemorrhage. — **sup·pres′sor** (-ẽr), *n.* — **sup·press′i·ble,** *adj.*

sup·pres′sion (-prĕsh′ŭn), *n.* **1.** Act or an instance of suppressing; state of being suppressed. **2.** *Psychoanalysis.* The forcible exclusion of an idea or desire from conscious and overt activity.

sup·pres′sive (-prĕs′ĭv), *adj.* Tending to suppress.

sup′pu·rate (sŭp′ū·rāt), *v. i.* [L. *suppuratus,* past part. of *suppurare,* fr. *sub* under + *pus, puris,* matter.] To generate pus; maturate.

sup′pu·ra′tion (-rā′shŭn), *n.* Act or process of suppurating; pus or a pus condition; maturation.

sup′pu·ra′tive (sŭp′ū·rā′tĭv; -rȧ·tĭv), *adj.* Tending to suppurate; attended with, or promoting, suppuration.

‖**su′pra** (sū′prȧ), *adv.* [L.] Above; previously (in a book).

su′pra- (sū′prȧ-; 114). [L. *supra,* adv., above. See SUPER-.] A prefix in general equivalent to *super-,* as in **su′pra·nat′u·ral, su′pra·ra′tion·al,** used esp. in forming scientific adjectives denoting *above in position; on the dorsal side of;* as in:

supra-abdominal	**suprailiac**	**supratemporal**
suprahepatic	**supranasal**	**supravaginal**

su′pra·lap·sar′i·an (-lăp·sâr′ĭ·ăn), *n.* [See SUPRA-; LAPSE.] *Eccl. Hist.* One of the Calvinists believing the fall and redemption to be instrumental to the carrying out of the decree of election. Cf. SUBLAPSARIAN. — **su′pra·lap·sar′i·an,** *adj.* — **su′pra·lap·sar′i·an·ism** (-ĭz′m), *n.*

su′pra·lim′i·nal (-lĭm′ĭ·năl; -n'l; *cf.* LIMINAL), *adj.* *Psychol.* Above the threshold of consciousness. Cf. SUBLIMINAL.

su′pra·mo·lec′u·lar (-mō·lĕk′ū·lẽr), *adj.* Above, or more complex than, a molecule; composed of many molecules.

su′pra·or′bit·al (-ôr′bĭ·tăl; -t'l), *adj.* *Anat.* Above the orbit of the eye.

su′pra·pro′test (-prō′tĕst), *n.* [After It. *sopra protesto* upon protest.] *Law.* An acceptance of a bill by a third person for the honor of the drawer after protest for nonacceptance or nonpayment by the drawee.

su′pra·re′nal (-rē′năl), *adj.* *Anat.* Situated above, or anterior to, the kidneys; designating, or pert. to, the suprarenal glands; adrenal. — *n.* A suprarenal gland.

suprarenal extract. *Biochem.* A solution of the active principle of the suprarenals. See ADRENALIN.

suprarenal gland, body, *or* **capsule.** *Anat.* A ductless gland, in most vertebrates near the anterior (in man the upper) end of each kidney; — called also *adrenal gland.* It produces secretions which diminish fatigue, increase the heartbeat, constrict the small arteries, etc.

su·prem′a·cy (sū·prĕm′ȧ·sĭ; sōō-), *n.* **1.** State of being supreme; also, supreme authority or power. **2.** The position of being established as superior to all others; as, the naval *supremacy.*

Syn. **Supremacy, ascendancy** mean the position of being first as in power or influence. **Supremacy** implies superiority over all others, as in numbers, quality, or prestige; **ascendancy** may or may not imply supremacy, but it always involves the idea of domination or of predominant power.

su·preme′ (sū·prēm′; sōō-; 2; 118), *adj.* [L. *supremus,* superl. of *superus* that is above, upper, fr. *super* above.] **1.** Highest in rank or authority; holding power which cannot be overruled; also, of or characteristic of one having such rank or power; as, *supreme* command. **2.** Highest in degree, quality, etc.; not exceeded by any other; utmost; as, *supreme* folly; also, characterized by highest excellence, achievement, etc.; as, *supreme* among poets. **3.** Ultimate; final; — as in **supreme sacrifice,** the sacrifice of one's life. — **su·preme′ly,** *adv.* — **su·preme′ness,** *n.*

Supreme Being. The eternal and infinite Spirit; God.

Supreme Court. *U. S.* The highest judicial body in the government; hence, a similar high tribunal in many of the states.

sur-. [F. *sur* over, above, OF. *sur, sour,* fr. L. *super.*] A prefix equivalent to *over-, super-,* as in *sur*charge.

su′ra (sōō′rȧ), *n.* [Ar. *sūrah,* a step, a degree.] One of the sections or chapters of the Koran.

su′rah (sōō′rȧ; sū′rȧ), *n.* [From *Surat,* India.] A soft twilled fabric of silk or silk and rayon.

su′ral (sū′răl), *adj.* [NL. *suralis,* fr. L. *sura* calf of the leg.] *Anat.* Of or pert. to the calf of the leg.

sur′base′ (sûr′bās′), *n.* *Arch.* A molding, or series of moldings, at the top of the base of a pedestal, podium, or wall. See DADO, *Illust.*

sur′based′ (-bāst′), *adj.* *Arch.* **a** Having a surbase. **b** [F. *surbaissé.*] Having the curve center below the springing line of imposts; — of an arch or vault.

sur·cease′ (sûr·sēs′), *v. t.* [F. *sursis,* past part. of *surseoir* to suspend, defer, in OF., to delay, forbear, fr. L. *supersedere.* *Surcease* is not related to E. *cease,* but has been influenced by it. See SUPERSEDE.] *Archaic.* To put an end to. — *n.* *Archaic.* Cessation; end.

sur·charge′ (-chärj′; 2), *v. t.;* -CHARGED′ (-chärjd′); -CHARG′ING (-chär′jĭng). [F. *surcharger.* See SUR-; CHARGE.] **1.** To overcharge. **2.** To overload; overburden. **3.** To fill to excess or repletion; to fill to overflowing. **4.** To print or write a surcharge on (postage stamps). **5.** *Equity.* To show an omission in (an account) for which credit ought to have been given.

sur′charge′ (sûr′chärj′; sûr·chärj′), *n.* **1.** A charge over the usual or normal rate. **2.** An excessive charge, load, or burden. **3.** An overprint on a postage stamp to give it a new postal value; loosely, an overprint or surprint. Abbr. *sur.* **4.** *Equity.* A surcharging. — **sur·charg′er** (sûr·chär′jẽr), *n.*

sur′cin′gle (sûr′sĭng′g'l), *n.* [OF. *surcengle,* fr. *sur-* + *cengle* girdle, fr. L. *cingula,* fr. *cingere* to gird.] **1.** A belt, band, or girth passing over a saddle, or over anything on a horse's back, to bind it fast. **2.** *Now Rare.* The girdle or cincture of a cassock.

sur′coat′ (sûr′kōt′), *n.* [OF. *surcote.* See SUR-; COAT.] *Hist.* An outer coat or cloak; specif., a tunic-like cloak worn over armor.

sur′cu·lose (sûr′kū·lōs), *adj.* *Bot.* Producing suckers.

surd (sûrd), *adj.* [L. *surdus* deaf, dim, dull.] **1.** *Math.* Involving irrational numbers; not expressible in rational numbers; radical; irrational. **2.** *Phonet.* Of speech sounds, voiceless; — opposed to *sonant, voiced.* — *n.* **1.** *Math.* An irrational number; thus, $\sqrt{3}$ and π are *surds.* **2.** *Phonet.* A surd speech sound.

sure (shŏŏr; 84), *adj.* [OF. *sur, seür* (F. *sûr*), fr. L. *securus.*] **1.** *Now Rare.* Secure, esp. from being harmed or doing harm. **2.** Firm or fast; not likely to be overthrown or displaced, or to yield; stable; as, a *sure* footing; also, unfailing; enduring; as, a *sure* faith. **3.** Assured in mind; having no doubt, fear, etc.; as, he is *sure* of his ground; also, certain; confident that one is right; as, *sure* of one's facts. **4.** Entirely trustworthy or dependable; reliable. **5.** Admitting of no doubt or qualification; indubitable; indisputable. **6.** Bound to come about or to happen; assured; of persons, bound; destined; as, he is *sure* to succeed. — **sure′ness,** *n.*

Syn. **Sure, certain, positive, cocksure** mean having or showing no doubt of one's opinion or conclusion. **Sure** usually stresses the subjective state of assurance; **certain,** the basing of the conclusion or conviction on definite grounds or on indubitable evidence; **positive,** conviction or full confidence in the rightness or correctness of one's opinion or conclusion; **cocksure,** presumptuous or overconfident positiveness. — **Ant.** Unsure.

— *adv.* **1.** Surely; infallibly; really. **2.** *Now Slang.* Undoubtedly; indeed; — used as an intensive esp. in replies and statements.

sure′-foot′ed (*see Pron.*, § 2), *adj.* Not liable to stumble or fall.

sure′ly (shŏŏr′lĭ), *adv.* **1.** In a sure manner; securely; infallibly. **2.** Assuredly; indeed; — used often as an interjection or an affirmative particle, or to qualify a statement.

sure′ty (shŏŏr′tĭ; -ĕ·tĭ), *n.; pl.* -TIES (-tĭz). **1.** State of being sure; certainty; security; sure knowledge. **2. a** That which confirms or makes sure; a guarantee; ground of confidence or security. **b** Security for payment or for the performance of some act. **3.** A sponsor or a bondsman. **4.** *Law.* One bound with and for another who is primarily liable (the *principal*); one legally liable for the debt, default, or failure of another. — **sure′ty·ship,** *n.*

surf (sûrf), *n.* [Formerly *suffe,* of unknown origin.] The swell of the sea which breaks upon the shore; also, the sound or foam caused by the breaking billows.

sur′face (sûr′fĭs; -fås), *n.* [F., after L. *superficies.* See SUR-; FACE.] **1.** The exterior of an object or body; the face or faces of a three-dimensioned thing. **2.** Superficial aspect. **3.** *Aeronautics.* An airfoil used for sustentation or control, or to increase stability. **4.** *Geom.* A two-dimensional locus of points; superficies; as, a spherical *surface.*

— *adj.* **1.** Pert. to or at a surface. **2.** Superficial.

— *v. t.;* -FACED (-fĭst; -fåst); -FAC·ING (-fĭs·ĭng). **1.** To give a surface to; to make smooth or to plane, as lumber; to finish, as by polishing or varnishing; to apply a surface layer to, as a road. **2.** To bring to the surface, as a submarine. — *v. i.* **1.** To work on or at the surface, as a miner. **2.** To come to the surface; as, the submarine *surfaced.* — **sur′fac·er** (sûr′fĭs·ẽr), *n.*

surface plate. *Mach.* A steel instrument of precision with dressed flat surface, used as a standard of flatness.

surface tension. *Physics.* That property, due to molecular forces, by which the surface film of all liquids tends to bring the contained volume into a form having the least superficial area.

surf′bird′ (sûrf′bûrd′), *n.* A shore bird (*Aphriza virgata*) of the Pacific coasts of America, allied to the turnstones. Its tail is blackish at the tip and white at the base.

surf′board′ (sûrf′bōrd′; 70), *n.* A long, narrow board used in the sport of riding the surf, as in Hawaii. Cf. AQUAPLANE.

surf′boat′ (-bōt′), *n.* A boat for use in heavy surf.

surf duck. A scoter, esp. the surf scoter (see SCOTER).

sur′feit (sûr′fĭt), *n.* [OF. *surfait, sorfait,* excess, crime, fr. *surfaire* to get the advantage, prop., to overdo, fr. *sur* over + *faire* to make, do.] **1.** Excess; superfluity; overabundant supply. **2.** Intemperate or immoderate indulgence, as in food or drink. **3.** Any morbid condition arising from excess in eating and drinking. **4.** Disgust caused by excess; satiety. — *v. t.* To feed, supply, give, etc., to surfeit; cloy. — *v. i.* To indulge to satiety. — **Syn.** See SATIATE. — **sur′feit·er,** *n.*

surf fish. Any of a family (Embiotocidae) of small or medium-sized viviparous fishes which live in shallow water along the Pacific coast of North America.

surge (sûrj), *n.* [From L. *surgere, surrectum,* to raise, rise, fr. *subs* (for *sub*) under + *regere* to direct, prob. through F.] **1.** A great, rolling swell of water; a billow; also, such swells collectively. **2.** A swelling or sweeping forward like that of an oncoming billow; a violent rising and falling; as, a *surge* of emotion. **3.** *Elec.* A transient and abnormal rush of current in a circuit. **4.** *Naut.* The tapered part of a windlass barrel or a capstan. — *v. i.;* SURGED (sûrjd); SURG′ING (sûr′jĭng). **1.** To rise in surges; to swell as though agitated; hence, to move, blow, etc., with a surge or in surges. **2.** *Elec.* To rise suddenly to an excessive or abnormal value, as current or potential. **3.** *Naut.* To slip, as around a windlass; — said of a rope. — *v. t. Naut.* To let go or slacken gradually, as a rope.

sur′geon (sûr′jŭn), *n.* [AF. *surgien,* contr. fr. OF. *serurgien, cirurgien* (F. *chirurgien*). See CHIRURGEON.] One who practices surgery. Cf. PHYSICIAN.

sur′geon·cy (-sĭ), *n.* The position of a surgeon.

sur′geon's knot (sûr′jŭnz). Any of several knots used in tying ligatures, stitches, etc. See KNOT, *Illust.* (32, 33).

sur′ger·y (sûr′jẽr·ĭ), *n.* [OF. *surgerie,* contr. fr. *serurgerie, cirurgerie.*] **1.** Medical science, art, and practice concerned with the correction of deformities and defects, the repair of injuries, etc., by manual and instrumental operations. **2.** A surgeon's operating room or laboratory. **3.** The work done by a surgeon. **4.** The treatment of other than human diseases by methods analogous to those of a surgeon; as, tree *surgery.*

sur′gi·cal (sûr′jĭ·kăl), *adj.* **1.** Of or pertaining to surgeons or surgery; done by or used in surgery. **2.** Subsequent to an operation by a surgeon, and often involving infection; as, *surgical* fever, *surgical* kidney. — **sur′gi·cal·ly,** *adv.*

su′ri·cate (sū′rĭ·kāt), *n.* [F. *surikate,* of uncert. origin.] A burrowing mammal (*Suricata tetradactyla*) of the civet family native to Cape Colony, allied to the mongooses, but having only four toes.

sur′ly (sûr′lĭ), *adj.;* -LI·ER (-lĭ·ẽr); -LI·EST. [From earlier *sirly,* fr. *sir.*] **1.** *Now Rare.* Arrogant. **2.** Ill-natured, abrupt, and rude; crabbed; churlishly cross. — **Syn.** See SULLEN. — **sur′li·ly,** *adv.* — **sur′li·ness,** *n.*

sur·mise′ (sûr·mīz′), *v. t.* [See SURMISE, *n.*] To imagine or infer on slight grounds; to guess. — **Syn.** See CONJECTURE.

sur·mise′ (sûr·mīz′; sûr′mīz), *n.* [OF. *surmise, sormise,* accusation, fr. *surmetre, sormetre,* to impose, accuse, fr. *sur, sor* (see SUR-) + *metre,* to put, set, fr. L. *mittere* to send.] A thought or idea based on scanty evidence; a guess; conjecture.

sur·mount′ (sûr·mount′), *v. t.* [OF. *surmonter, sormonter.* See SUR-; MOUNT, *v.*] **1.** *Now Rare.* To surpass; exceed; transcend. **2.** To conquer or overcome, as an obstacle. **3.** To get to the top of, or lie at the top of. — **Syn.** See CONQUER. — **sur·mount′a·ble,** *adj.*

sur·mul′let (sûr·mŭl′ĕt), *n.* See PLURAL, *Note,* 3. [F. *surmulet.*] See MULLET, 2.

sur′name′ (sûr′nām′), *n.* [*sur-* + *name,* after ME. *sournoun,* fr. OF. *so(u)rnon.*] **1.** *Archaic.* An agnomen (Richard *Cœur de Lion;* Lorenzo *the Magnificent*). **2.** The part of the name of individuals which is common to the family; family name; — distinguished from *Christian name* and *given name.* — (sûr′nām′; sûr·nām′), *v. t.* To give a surname, esp. an additional name, to.

sur·pass′ (sẽr·pås′; 9), *v. t.* [F. *surpasser,* fr. *sur* over + *passer* to pass.] **1.** To be superior to in quality, degree, performance, etc.; to exceed. **2.** To transcend the reach, capacity, or powers of. — **Syn.** See EXCEED. — **sur·pass′a·ble,** *adj.*

sur·pass′ing, *adj.* That surpasses; eminently excellent. — *adv.* Surpassingly. — **sur·pass′ing·ly,** *adv.* — **sur·pass′ing·ness,** *n.*

sur′plice (sûr′plĭs), *n.* [OF. *surpliz, sorpeliz,* deriv. of L. *super* over + LL. *pellicium, pelliceum,* a robe of fur, L. *pellicius* made of skins.] *Eccl.* An outer vestment of white linen worn usually over the cassock by the Roman Catholic and Anglican clergy in various offices and, in England, by choristers.

sur′plus (sûr′plŭs; -plŭs), *n.* [OF. See SUR-; PLUS.] **1.** That which remains when use or need is satisfied; excess; overplus. **2.** *Accounting.* **a** An excess of net income over fixed charges and dividends during a given period. **b** The aggregate excess of assets over liabilities accumulated by a business enterprise during its history, except so far as they have been made the basis for new issues of stock. — *adj.* Being or constituting a surplus.

sur′plus·age (sûr′plŭs·ĭj), *n.* **1.** Surplus; excess. **2.** Nonessential words. **3.** *Law.* In pleading, unnecessary or irrelevant matter.

sur′print′ (sûr′prĭnt′), *v. t.* [*sur-* + *print.*] To print (as a name) over (previously printed matter). — *n.* That which is surprinted.

sur·pris′al (sẽr·prīz′ăl), *n.* Act or fact of surprising, or state of being surprised; surprise.

sur·prise′ (-prīz′; 32), *v. t.* [OF. *surpris,* fem. *surprise,* past part. of *surprendre, sorprendre.* See SUR-; 2d PRIZE.] **1.** To seize by attacking unexpectedly. **2.** To come upon or attack unexpectedly. **3.** To take (one) unawares, as in an act; to come upon without warning. **4.** To strike with amazement because unexpected or different from that anticipated. **5.** To lead on or drive (one) by means of a surprise attack or request, as into unwonted generosity; also, to bring to light by such means; to detect or elicit; as, to *surprise* a secret.

Syn. **Surprise, astonish, astound, amaze, flabbergast** mean to impress one forcibly because unexpected. **Surprise** has another and older sense now slightly less common, implying a coming upon with startling effect, but this has given way in ordinary use to another which stresses the impression produced; **astonish** now implies a surprising so much as to seem almost incredible; **astound** stresses the shock more than *astonish;* **amaze** stresses bewilderment, perplexity, or wonder; **flabbergast** stresses an astounding and dumfounding.

— *n.* [OF., fr. fem. of past part. of *surprendre.* See SURPRISE, *v. t.*] **1.** Act of coming upon, or taking, unawares; surprisal. **2.** Something surprising; an occasion for, a cause of, or a quality arousing astonishment, etc. **3.** State of being surprised; emotion excited by what is sudden and unexpected; astonishment. — **sur·pris′er** (-prīz′ẽr), *n.*

sur·pris′ing (sẽr·prīz′ĭng), *adj.* Astonishing; amazing. — **sur·pris′ing·ly,** *adv.* — **sur·pris′ing·ness,** *n.*

sur′ra, sur′rah (sōōr′ȧ; sûr′ȧ), *n.* [Marathi *sūra* a wheezing sound.] *Veter.* A severe Old World febrile and hemorrhagic disease of domesticated animals caused by a protozoan (*Trypanosoma evansi*). It is commonly fatal in horses, mules, and camels, while cattle and dogs often recover.

sur·re′al·ism (sŭ·rē′ăl·ĭz′m; sûr·rē′-), *n.* [F. *surréalisme.*] *Art.* A modern French movement in art and literature, influenced by Freudianism, purporting to express the subconscious mental activities by presenting images without order or sequence, as in a dream. Cf. ABSTRACTION, 6; COLLAGE. — **sur·re′al·ist** (-ĭst), *n.* & *adj.* — **sur·re′al·is′tic** (-ĭs′tĭk), *adj.* — **sur·re′al·is′ti·cal·ly** (-tĭ·kăl·ĭ), *adv.*

sur′re·but′tal (sûr′rē·bŭt′ăl), *n.* *Law.* Act of supporting, or giving evidence to maintain, a surrebutter.

sur′re·but′ter (-bŭt′ẽr), *n.* *Law.* The reply of a plaintiff to a defendant's rebutter.

sur′re·join′der (sûr′rē·join′dẽr), *n.* *Law.* The answer of a plaintiff to a defendant's rejoinder.

sur·ren′der (sŭ·rĕn′dẽr), *v. t.* [OF. *surrendre,* fr. *sur-* + *rendre* to give up. See SUR-; RENDER.] **1.** To yield to the power of another; to give up possession of (anything) upon compulsion or demand. **2.** To give up completely; to relinquish. **3.** *Obs.* To render back; to give in return. — *v. i.* To give up oneself into the power of another; to yield. — **Syn.** See RELINQUISH. — *n.* [AF. (OF. *surrendre* to deliver up), inf. as n.] **1.** A yielding or resigning one's person, or the possession of something, into the power of another. **2.** *Insurance.* The voluntary cancellation of the legal liability of the company by the insured and beneficiary for a consideration (called the **surrender value**).

sur′rep·ti′tious (sûr′ĕp·tĭsh′ŭs; 117), *adj.* [L. *surrepticius, subrepticius,* fr. *surripere* to snatch away, withdraw privily, fr. *sub-* + *rapere* to snatch.] **1.** Done, made, acquired, etc., by stealth, or without proper authority; clandestine. **2.** Acting, or doing something, clandestinely; stealthy. — **Syn.** See SECRET. — **sur′rep·ti′tious·ly,** *adv.* — **sur′rep·ti′tious·ness,** *n.*

sur′rey (sûr′ĭ; 117), *n.* [From *Surrey,* Eng.] A four-wheeled, two-seated pleasure carriage.

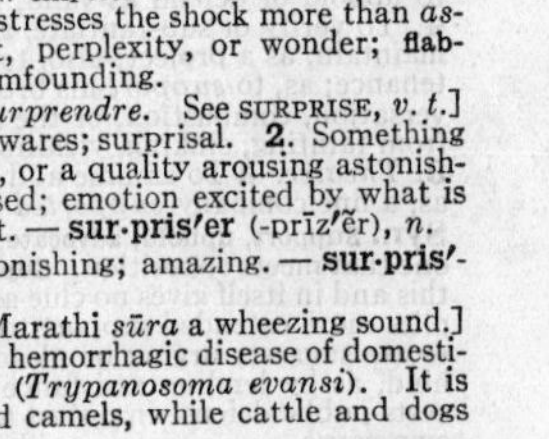
Surrey.

sur′ro·gate (sûr′ō·gāt; 117), *v. t.* [L. *surrogatus,* past part. of *surrogare, subrogare,* to substitute, fr. *sub-* + *rogare* to ask.] To put in the place of another, as successor, agent, or substitute; specif.: **a** *Law.* To subrogate. **b** *Civil Law.* To appoint (another) as successor to oneself. — (-gāt), *n.* **1.**

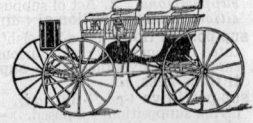

A deputy; substitute. **2.** *Ch. of Eng.* The deputy of an ecclesiastical judge, esp. of a bishop or his chancellor. **3.** *Law, U.S.* In some states, a judicial officer who has jurisdiction over the probate of wills, the settlement of estates, guardianships, etc.

sur·round′ (sŭ·round′), *v. t.* [OF. *suronder* to overflow, fr. LL. *superundare*, fr. L. *super* over + *undare* to rise in waves, overflow, fr. *unda* wave. The English sense and form are due to the influence of E. *round*.] **1.** To enclose on all sides; encompass. **2.** To encircle; as, a wall *surrounds* the city. **3.** *Mil.* To enclose, as a body of troops, so as to cut off communication or retreat; to invest, as a city.

sur·round′ing, *n.* **1.** The action of that which surrounds. **2.** *pl.* The circumstances, conditions, etc., by which one is surrounded; environment. — *adj.* Enveloping.

sur–roy′al (sûr·roi′ăl), *n.* See ANTLER, *Illust.*

‖**sur′sum cor′da** (sûr′sŭm kôr′dȧ). [L. *sursum* upward + *corda* hearts.] **1.** Literally, lift up your hearts; — first words of a versicle beginning the Preface of the Mass. **2.** A call to fervor, courage, etc.

sur′tax′ (sûr′tăks′), *n.* A special tax over and above the general charge upon a whole class; specif., *U. S.*, a graduated income tax, in addition to the normal income tax, imposed on the amount by which the net income of any individual exceeds a certain sum. — (sûr′tăks′; sûr·tăks′), *v. t.* To impose an additional tax, or surtax, on.

sur·tout′ (sûr·to͞ot′; -to͞o′; *F.* sür′to͞o′), *n.* [F., fr. *sur* over + *tout* all.] A man's long close-fitting overcoat.

sur·veil′lance (sûr·vāl′ăns; -vāl′yăns), *n.* [F., fr. *surveiller* to watch over, fr. *sur* over + *veiller* to watch, fr. L. *vigilare*.] Oversight; close supervision; now usually, constant guard; close watch.

sur·veil′lant (-vāl′ănt; -vāl′yănt), *n.* [F.] An overseer; supervisor; a guardian of law and order.

sur·vey′ (sẽr·vā′), *v. t.* [OF. *surveoir, sorveeir*, fr. *sur, sor*, over + *veoir, veeir*, to see, fr. L. *videre*.] **1.** To examine with reference to condition, situation, value, etc. **2.** To view with a scrutinizing eye; inspect. **3.** To determine and delineate the form, extent, position, etc., of, as a tract of land, by taking linear and angular measurements, and by applying the principles of geometry and trigonometry.

sur′vey (sûr′vā; sẽr·vā′), *n.* **1.** The act or an instance of surveying; also, something surveyed. **2.** A critical inspection, often official, to provide exact information; often, a study of an area with respect to a certain condition, or its prevalence; as, a *survey* of the schools. **3.** A comprehensive view; — often attributive; as, a *survey* course in history. **4.** The operation of finding and delineating the contour, dimensions, position, etc., as of any part of the earth's surface; also, a measured plan and description of any region. — **Syn.** See COMPENDIUM.

sur·vey′ing (sẽr·vā′ĭng), *n.* Act or occupation of one who makes surveys. Specif., that branch of applied mathematics which teaches the art of making surveys.

sur·vey′or (-ẽr), *n.* **1.** One who surveys; as, a *surveyor* of highways, ordnance, etc. **2.** One who practices the art of surveying. **3.** *Customs, U.S.* An officer whose duties include ascertaining the quantity, condition, and value of merchandise brought into a port. — **sur·vey′or·ship,** *n.*

sur·vey′or's chain (sẽr·vā′ẽrz). See CHAIN, *n.*, 4.

surveyor's level. A level consisting of a telescope, with a spirit level attached, mounted on a tripod and revolving on a vertical axis.

surveyor's measure. A system of measurement having the surveyor's chain as a unit, used in land surveying. See MEASURE, *Table* 4.

sur·viv′al (sẽr·vīv′ăl), *n.* **1.** A living or continuing longer than another person or thing. **2.** One that survives. **3.** *Anthropol.* Any usage or belief, remaining from ancient times, the origin of which is often unknown.

survival of the fittest. *Biol.* See NATURAL SELECTION.

survival value. *Biol.* Utility (of the characters of an organism) in the struggle for existence.

sur·viv′ance (sẽr·vīv′ăns), *n.* [F.] Survival.

sur·vive′ (sẽr·vīv′), *v. i.* [F. *survivre*, fr. L. *supervivere*, fr. *super* over + *vivere* to live.] To remain alive or existent. — *v. t.* To live beyond the life or existence of; outlive. — **Syn.** See OUTLIVE. — **sur·viv′ing** (-vīv′ĭng), *adj.* — **sur·vi′vor** (-vī′vẽr), **sur·viv′er** (-vīv′ẽr), *n.*

sur·vi′vor·ship, *n.* **1.** State of being a survivor. **2.** *Law.* The right of the survivor or survivors of two or more persons having joint interests in an estate or other property to take the interest of any of the number dying.

Su·san′na (sū·zăn′ȧ), *n.* A book of the Apocrypha. See BIBLE.

sus·cep′ti·bil′i·ty (sŭ·sĕp′tĭ·bĭl′ĭ·tĭ), *n.; pl.* -TIES (-tĭz). **1.** State or quality of being susceptible; capability of receiving impressions. **2.** A susceptible temperament; hence, *pl.*, feelings; sensibilities. **3.** *Magnetism.* A coefficient equal to the ratio of the magnetization to the magnetizing force. Symbol, *k* (no period).

sus·cep′ti·ble (sŭ·sĕp′tĭ·b'l), *adj.* [ML. *susceptibilis*, fr. L. *suscipere, -ceptum*, to take up, admit, fr. *sus-* for *subs-* (see SUB-) + *capere* to take.] **1.** Of such a nature as to admit or permit; — with *of;* as, a theory *susceptible* of proof. **2.** Such in constitution or temperament as to be unresistant; exposed or liable through weakness, sensitiveness, etc.; as, a person *susceptible* to infection. **3.** Easily affected or moved; responsive; as, *susceptible* children. — **Syn.** See LIABLE. — **sus·cep′ti·ble·ness,** *n.* — **sus·cep′ti·bly,** *adv.*

sus·cep′tive (sŭ·sĕp′tĭv), *adj.* Receptive; also, susceptible. — **sus′cep·tiv′i·ty** (sŭs′ĕp·tĭv′ĭ·tĭ), *n.*

sus′lik (sŭs′lĭk), *n.* [Russ.] A squirrellike burrowing rodent (*Citellus citillus*) of northeastern Europe and northwestern Asia; also, its mottled grayish-brown fur. See SPERMOPHILE.

sus·pect′ (sŭs·pĕkt′; sŭs′pĕkt; 2), *adj.* [OF. *suspect, souspect*, fr. L. *suspectus*, past part. of *suspicere*. See SUSPECT, *v.*] Regarded with suspicion; suspected.

sus′pect (sŭs′pĕkt; sŭs·pĕkt′), *n.* One who is suspected.

sus·pect′ (sŭs·pĕkt′), *v. t.* [F. *suspecter*, fr. L. *suspicere, -pectum*, to look up, admire, to look at secretly or askance, mistrust, fr. *sub-* + *specere* to look.] **1.** To have doubts of; distrust. **2.** To imagine (one) to be guilty, culpable, etc., on slight evidence, or without proof. **3.** To imagine (something) to be, or be true, likely, probable, etc.; to surmise. — *v. i.* To imagine something true or likely; to be suspicious.

sus·pend′ (sŭs·pĕnd′), *v. t.* [OF. *suspendre*, fr. L. *suspendĕre, -pensum*, fr. *sus-*, for *subs-* (see SUB-) + *pendĕre* to hang.] **1.** To debar temporarily from any privilege, office, function, etc.; as, to *suspend* a student. **2.** To cause to cease for a time, as an action, process, use, etc.; to stop temporarily; as, to *suspend* publication; to make temporarily inoperative; as, to *suspend* the rules. **3.** To withhold for a time on certain conditions; as, to *suspend* sentence on a convicted man. **4.** To hold in an undetermined state, awaiting fuller information; as, to *suspend* judgment. **5.** To hang, esp. so as to be free on all sides except at the point of support; as, to *suspend* a ball by a thread; also, to maintain from falling or sinking by some invisible support, or now, esp., by gravity, buoyancy, or the like; as, dust *suspended* in the air. **6.** To hold fixed in wonder, contemplation, etc. — **Syn.** See EXCLUDE: DEFER. — *v. i.* **1.** To cease temporarily from operation or activity. **2.** Specif., to stop payments, or fail to meet obligations or engagements; said of a commercial firm or a bank.

sus·pend′ed an′i·ma′tion. Temporary suspension of the vital functions, as in persons nearly drowned.

sus·pend′er (sŭs·pĕn′dẽr), *n.* **1.** One who or that which suspends. **2.** That by which something is, or may be, suspended; specif.: **a** *U. S.* One of the two straps arranged to pass over the shoulders and to be fastened to the trousers to hold them up; — commonly in *pl.*, or called a ***pair of suspenders.*** Cf. 2d BRACE, *n.*, 4. **b** *Brit.* A garter.

sus·pense′ (sŭs·pĕns′), *n.* [F. *suspens*, adj., *en suspens* in suspense, fr. L. *suspensus*, past part.] **1.** State of being suspended; temporary cessation; suspension. **2.** Mental uncertainty; anxiety. **3.** Indecisiveness; lack of certainty.

suspense account. *Bookkeeping.* An account for the temporary entry of charges or credits, pending determination of their ultimate disposition.

sus·pen′sion (sŭs·pĕn′shŭn), *n.* **1.** Act of suspending, or state or period of being suspended. **2.** A device by which something, as a magnetic needle, is suspended; specif., the system of springs, etc., supporting the upper part of a vehicle on the axles. **3.** *Commerce.* Stoppage of payment of obligations or engagements; failure; — said of commercial firms, banks, etc. **4.** *Eccl.* A penalty by which a cleric is forbidden to exercise the power of orders or office or to enjoy the fruits of his benefice. **5.** *Horol.* The act, process, or manner in which the pendulum or balance of a timepiece is suspended. **6.** *Music.* **a** The holding over of one or more tones of a chord into the following chord, thus producing a momentary discord, suspending the concord which the ear expects. **b** The tone or tones thus held over. **7.** *Physics.* The state of a solid when its particles are mixed with, but undissolved in, a fluid or another solid; also, any substance in this state. Cf. COLLOID. **8.** *Physical Chem.* A two-phase system consisting of a finely divided solid dispersed in a solid, liquid, or gas. **9.** *Rhet.* A holding in suspense, as through a series of clauses.

suspension bridge. A bridge which has its roadway suspended from two or more cables usually passing over towers and securely anchored at the ends. See BRIDGE, *Illust.*

suspension periods *or* **points.** *Punctuation.* Spaced periods in a row, usually three, terminally four, used to mark an interruption or attention-holding pause in a sentence. See *Punctuation* § 1.

sus·pen′sive (sŭs·pĕn′sĭv), *adj.* **1.** Suspending or, esp., stopping temporarily. **2.** Characterized by suspense, suspended judgment, indecisiveness, or the like. **3.** Characterized by or manifesting suspension; as, *suspensive* sentences. — **sus·pen′sive·ly,** *adv.*

sus·pen′soid (sŭs·pĕn′soid), *n.* *Physical Chem.* A colloidal solution the dispersed particles in which are solid. Cf. EMULSOID.

sus·pen′sor (-sẽr), *n.* [ML.] A suspensory.

sus·pen′so·ry (-sō·rĭ), *adj.* **1.** Suspended; also, fitted or serving to suspend; as, a *suspensory* muscle. **2.** Suspending; temporarily leaving undetermined. — *n.* That which suspends, or holds up; specif., *Med.*, a bandage or bag for supporting a part, esp. the scrotum.

suspensory ligament. *Anat.* In the eye, an annular fibrous membrane supporting the lens. See EYE, *Illust.*

sus. per coll. (sŭs′ pûr kŏl′). Abbreviation of Latin **sus·pen′sus per col′lum** (sŭs·pĕn′sŭs pûr kŏl′ŭm) hanged by the neck; — used chiefly in a record of ancestors, as a notation indicating one legally executed.

sus·pi′cion (sŭs·pĭsh′ŭn), *n.* [OF. *sospeçon*, fr. LL. *suspectio* a looking up to, an esteeming highly, later (after L. *suspicio*), suspicion, fr. *suspicere*. See SUSPECT.] **1.** Act, fact, or an instance of suspecting; imagination of something wrong, without proof, or on slight evidence; also, the mental uneasiness aroused in one who suspects; mistrust. **2.** An inkling; hint. — **Syn.** See UNCERTAINTY. — *v. t.* *Dial.* To suspect.

sus·pi′cious (-pĭsh′ŭs), *adj.* **1.** Such as to arouse suspicion; questionable. **2.** Inclined to suspect; prone to suspicion. **3.** Manifesting or indicative of suspicion; as, a *suspicious* glance. — **sus·pi′cious·ly,** *adv.* — **sus·pi′cious·ness,** *n.*

sus′pi·ra′tion (sŭs′pĭ·rā′shŭn), *n.* A long sigh.

sus·pire′ (sŭs·pīr′), *v. i.* [L. *suspirare* to breathe out, sigh, fr. *sub-* + *spirare* to breathe.] *Chiefly Poet.* To fetch a long breath; to sigh.

sus·tain′ (sŭs·tān′), *v. t.* [OF. *sustenir, sostenir*, fr. L. *sustinere*, fr. *sus-*, for *subs-* (see SUB-) + *tenere* to hold.] **1.** *Rare.* To give support, often military support, to. **2.** To provide for the support of; to supply with sustenance; as, provisions to *sustain* an army. **3.** To maintain, or cause to continue, in existence or a certain state, or in force or intensity; to keep up; prolong; as, to *sustain* conversation for hours. **4.** To bear up from or as from below; support the weight of; to hold up. **5.** To keep (one, one's mind or spirits, etc.) from sinking or giving way; to buoy up. **6. a** To endure without failing or yielding; to bear up under. **b** To suffer or undergo, as an injury. **7.** To support as true, legal, etc.; now, usually, to allow or admit as valid; as, the court *sustained* the suit. **8.** To support by adequate proof; to corroborate or confirm. — **sus·tain′a·ble,** *adj.* — **sus·tain′er,** *n.*

sus·tain′ing pro′gram. *Radio.* A program that is paid for by a station or network and has no commercial sponsor.

sus′te·nance (sŭs′tē·năns), *n.* **1.** Means of support; now, often, food; also, nourishment. **2.** Act or fact of sustaining, or state of being sustained; a supplying or being supplied with the necessaries of life. **3.** That which sustains or gives support, strength, etc. — **Syn.** See FOOD.

sus′ten·tac′u·lar (sŭs′tĕn·tăk′ū·lẽr), *adj.* [L. *sustentaculum* a support.] *Anat.* Supporting; as, *sustentacular* ligaments.

sus′ten·ta′tion (-tā′shŭn), *n.* [OF. *sustentacion*, fr. L. *sustentatio*, fr. *sustentare* to support.] **1.** A sustaining or being sustained; chiefly: **a** Maintenance; upkeep. **b** Preservation. **c** Maintenance of life, courage, etc. **d** Provision with support or nourishment. **e** Physical support; as, air so thin as to afford no *sustentation* for an airship. **2.** That which sustains or provides sustenance; a support.

sus′ten·ta′tive (sŭs′tĕn·tā′tĭv; sŭs·tĕn′tȧ·tĭv), **sus·ten′tive** (sŭs·tĕn′tĭv), *adj.* That sustains; pertaining to or giving sustentation.

sus·ten′tion (sŭs·tĕn′shŭn), *n.* Sustentation.

su·sur′rant (sū̇-sûr′ănt), *adj.* [L. *susurrans*, pres. part. of *susurrare* to whisper.] Whispering.

su·sur′rate (-āt), *v. i.* [L. *susurrare.*] To whisper; murmur. — **su′·sur·ra′tion** (sū′sŭ-rā′shŭn), *n.*

su·sur′rus (-ŭs), *n.* [L.] A whispering sound.

sut′ler (sŭt′lẽr), *n.* [Early D. *soeteler* (D. *zoetelaar*), fr. *soetelen* to undertake low offices.] One who follows an army and sells to the troops provisions, liquors, and the like. — **sut′ler·ship**, *n.*

su′tra (sōō′trȧ), *n.* [Skr. *sūtra* a thread, string of rules, aphorisms.] Also **sut′ta** (sŏŏt′ȧ). **1.** *Brahmanism.* **a** A precept; an aphorism. **b** A collection of aphorisms. **2.** *Buddhism.* The narrative parts of the Pali Buddhist scriptures, especially the dialogues of the Buddha.

sut·tee′ (sŭ-tē′), *n.* [Hind. *sattī, satī*, fr. Skr. *satī* a faithful wife, fem. of *sat, sant*, existing, real, true, good, pres. part. of *as* to be.] A Hindu widow who cremates herself, or is cremated, on the funeral pile of her husband; also, such cremation. The practice, forbidden by the British, is now uncommon. — **sut·tee′ism** (-ĭz′m), *n.*

su′ture (sū′tûr), *n.* [F., fr. L. *sutura*, fr. *suere, sutum*, to sew or stitch.] **1.** Act of sewing; also, the seam or seamlike line along which two things or parts are sewed or united. **2.** *Anat.* The line of union, or seam, in an immovable articulation, like those between the bones of the skull; also, such an articulation itself. **3.** *Bot.* **a** The line, or seam, formed by the union of two adjacent margins. **b** A line of dehiscence. **4.** *Surg.* **a** The act, process, or method of stitching skin or other structures, as to unite the edges of a wound or to fasten an organ in place. **b** The stitch so used. — *v. t.* To unite by sutures; to join by sewing or stitching. — **su′tur·al** (-tûr-ăl), *adj.* — **su′tur·al·ly**, *adv.*

‖**su′um cui′que** (sū′ŭm kī′kwē; kwī′kwē). [L.] To each his own.

su′ze·rain (sū′zĕ-rān; sōō′-), *n.* [F., fr. *sus* above, fr. L. *susum, sursum* (fr. *sub* under + *versum*, past part. of *vertere* to turn), after the analogy of *souverain*, E. *sovereign*.] **1.** A superior lord, to whom fealty is due; a feudal lord; overlord. **2.** *Internat. Law.* A state that exercises political control over another state, in relation to which it is sovereign. — *adj.* Sovereign; paramount.

su′ze·rain·ty (-tĭ), *n.* The dominion, authority, or relation of a suzerain in respect of the subject person or state.

svelte (svĕlt), *adj.* [F.] Slender; lithe; lissome.

swab (swŏb), *v. t.;* SWABBED (swŏbd); SWAB′BING. [From *swabber.*] To use a swab upon; to wipe or clean with or as if with a swab. — *n.* **1.** A form of mop for cleaning or wiping floors, decks, etc. **2.** A bit of cloth, cotton, or the like, for applying medicaments or for removing discharges from mucous membranes, etc.; also, a specimen taken with such a piece of fabric, cotton, etc. **3.** A sponge attached to a long handle, for cleaning the bore of a firearm. **4.** *Slang.* A lumpish, useless person; lout.

swab′ber (swŏb′ẽr), *n.* [D. *zwabber.*] **1.** One who uses a swab; hence, one fit only for menial work. **2.** A swab.

swad′dle (swŏd′'l), *v. t.;* -DLED (-'ld); -DLING (-lĭng). [See SWADDLE, *n.*] **1.** To bind (a newborn infant) with bands of cloth, or swaddling clothes; hence, to treat as an infant. **2.** To swathe; to wrap up, as with bandages. — *n.* [AS. *swathian* to swathe.] Anything used to swaddle with, as a cloth or band.

swad′dling clothes (-lĭng). Also **swaddling bands, clouts**, etc. Bands or clothes wrapped round an infant, esp. a newborn infant; hence, period of infancy or immaturity; also, the limitations of, or restrictions imposed upon, the very immature.

Swa·de′shi (swȧ-dā′shĭ), *n.* [Skr. *svadeśin* native, national, fr. *svadeśa* own country.] *India.* A phase of the struggle for swaraj, aiming at the production and use of home manufactures and the boycott of foreign goods.

swag (swăg), *n.* **1. a** *Australasia.* A tramping bushman's luggage, rolled up in a long bundle. **b** Any roll or bag of luggage. **2.** A swaying motion; lurch. **3.** *Slang.* Booty; plunder; also, spoils. — *v. i.;* SWAGGED (swăgd); SWAG′GING. **1.** To sway; lurch; also, to tip, cant, or list. **2.** To sag, as by its own weight. **3.** *Australasia.* To tramp carrying a swag.

swage (swāj), *n.* [OF. *souage* (F. *suage*).] A tool used by workers in metals for shaping their work, by holding the swage on the work, or the work on the swage, and striking with a hammer or sledge; also, a swage block. Cf. ANVIL, *Illust.* — *v. t.;* SWAGED (swājd); SWAG′ING (swāj′ĭng). To shape by means of a swage.

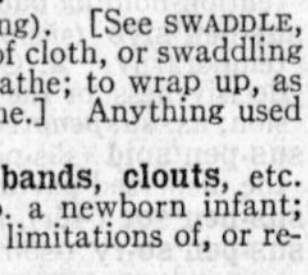

Blacksmith's Swages. 1 Bottom Swage; 2 Top Swage.

swage block. *Smithing, etc.* A perforated block of cast iron or steel, having grooved sides and adapted for use in heading bolts and swagging bars of various sizes.

swag′ger (swăg′ẽr), *v. i.* [Freq. of SWAG.] **1.** To walk with a conceited or lordly swing or strut. **2.** To boast or brag noisily. — *n.* The act of swaggering; the walk, manner, or attitude, etc., of one who swaggers. — **swag′ger·er**, *n.* — **swag′ger·ing·ly**, *adv.*

swagger stick. *Mil.* A short light canelike stick, for carrying in the hand.

swag′man (swăg′măn), *n.* *Chiefly Australasia.* One, esp. a bushman, traveling with a swag. Cf. SUNDOWNER.

Swa·hi′li (swä-hē′lē), *n. sing. & pl.* [Ar. *sawāhil* coasts + suff. *-i* belonging to.] A member of a Mohammedan Bantu people of Zanzibar and the neighboring coasts; also, their language. — **Swa·hi′li, Swa·hi′li·an** (-lē-ăn), *adj.*

swain (swān), *n.* [ON. *sveinn* a boy, servant.] A young peasant; a rustic; esp., in pastoral poetry, a country gallant. — **swain′ish**, *adj.* — **swain′ish·ness**, *n.*

swale (swāl), *n.* **1.** *Dial.* Shade. **2.** A piece of meadow, often one marshy and rank with vegetation.

swal′low (swŏl′ō), *n.* [AS. *swealwe, swalewe, swalwe.*] **1.** *Zool.* Any of a family (Hirundinidae) of small long-winged passerine birds noted for their graceful flight and regular migrations. Swallows occur in all parts of the world except New Zealand and polar regions. The common European swallow (*Hirundo rustica*) is called in England ***chimney swallow.*** Common North American swallows include the ***bank swallow, or sand martin*** (*Riparia riparia*), the ***barn swallow*** (*Hirundo erythrogaster*), and the ***cliff swallow*** (*Petrochelidon albifrons*). See MARTIN. **2.** Any of certain swifts, superficially like swallows, as the chimney swift (see SWIFT).

swal′low, *v. t.* [ME. *swolewen, swolwen, swelwen, swelghen*, fr. AS. *swelgan.*] **1.** To take through the gullet, or esophagus, into the stomach; to receive into the body through the mouth and throat. **2.** Hence, to take in or absorb in any manner; to seize and engulf, consume, or the like. **3.** *Colloq.* To accept, as statements, without investigation or question. **4.** To retract; recant; as, to *swallow* one's words. **5.** To put up with; as, forced to *swallow* his jibes. **6.** To refrain from giving vent to; as, to *swallow* one's resentment. — *v. i.* To swallow something; to perform the motions characteristic of swallowing, esp. in emotion. — *n.* **1.** The gullet; throat. **2.** The act of swallowing; hence, swallowing capacity; appetite; liking. **3.** As much as is swallowed at once. **4.** *Naut.* The aperture in a block between the sheave and frame through which the rope reeves. See BLOCK, 5, *Illust.* — **swal′low·er**, *n.*

swallow dive. *Chiefly Brit.* = SWAN DIVE.

swal′low·tail′ (swŏl′ō-tāl′), *n.* **1.** A swallow's tail, or a tail similarly forked and tapering. **2.** Any of numerous large butterflies (genus *Papilio* and allied genera) having the border of the hind wing produced into a taillike process. The ***tiger swallowtail*** (*P. glaucus*), the ***black swallowtail*** (*P. polyxenes*), and the ***zebra swallowtail*** (*Iphiclides marcellus*) are North American species. **3.** A swallow-tailed coat.

swal′low–tailed′ (-tāld′), *adj.* Having a deeply forked tail like that of a barn swallow.

swallow–tailed coat. A man's full-dress coat; a claw hammer; — from its two long tapering skirts at the back.

swal′low·wort′ (swŏl′ō-wûrt′), *n.* **a** = CELANDINE **a.** **b** A European twining vine (*Cynanchum vincetoxicum*), the root of which has been used as an emetic, cathartic, and diuretic. **c** Any of several other plants of the milkweed family.

swam (swăm), *past* of SWIM.

swa′mi, swa′my (swä′mĭ), *n.* [Hind. *svāmī*, fr. Skr. *svāmin* possessor, lord.] Master; lord; pundit. In American usage the term is often equivalent to *yogi, fakir*, etc.

swamp (swŏmp; 74), *n.* [Prob. of LG. origin.] Wet, spongy land, saturated, but not usually covered, with water; also, a tract of such land. — *adj.* Of or pertaining to a swamp; growing or dwelling in swamps. — *v. t.* **1.** To plunge or sink into, or as if into, a swamp. **2.** To submerge with or as if with a liquid; to deluge. **3.** *Naut.* To cause (a boat) to become filled with water; to sink by filling with water. — *v. i.* To sink or stick in or as in a swamp; to become entangled or submerged. — **swamp′ish**, *adj.* — **swamp′y**, *adj.*

swamp azalea, honeysuckle, *or* **pink.** See AZALEA.

swamp fever. Malaria.

swamp′land′ (swŏmp′lănd′), *n.* = SWAMP.

swamp sparrow. See SPARROW, 2.

swamp white oak. A large, flaky-barked oak (*Quercus bicolor*) of the eastern United States, resembling white oak but with smaller, less prominently lobed leaves.

swan (swŏn; 73), *n.;* see PLURAL, *Note*, 3. [AS.] **1.** Any of certain heavy-bodied, very long-necked, aquatic birds (subfamily Cygninae) of the duck family (Anatidae). With two exceptions all have pure-white plumage when adult. They are related to, but larger than, the geese, fly strongly when once started, and are very graceful when swimming. Cf. COB; CYGNET; 3d PEN. **2.** Something that suggests a swan because of its whiteness, grace, or (fabled) power of melody (see SWAN SONG); hence, specif., a poet. **3.** [*cap.*] *Astron.* The constellation Cygnus.

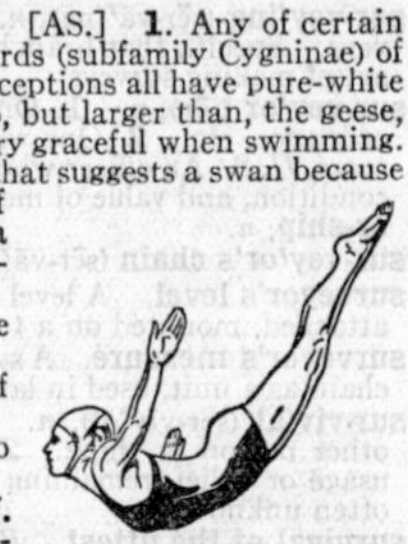

Swan Dive.

swan dive. A type of fancy dive. See *Illust.*

swang (swăng). Archaic & dial. past of SWING.

swan′herd′ (swŏn′hûrd′), *n.* One who tends swans.

swank (swăngk; swȧngk), **swank′y** (-ĭ), *adj.* **1.** *Scot.* Active; full of life. **2.** *Slang.* Ostentatiously smart and dashing. — **swank, swank′y**, *n.* — **swank′i·ly** (-ĭ-lĭ), *adv.* — **swank′i·ness** (-ĭ-nĕs; -nĭs), *n.*

swan maiden. *Teut. Myth.* An elf or fairy capable of becoming a maiden or swan at will by donning or doffing a magic garment, the **swan shift**, of swan's feathers.

swan′ner·y (swŏn′ẽr-ĭ), *n.; pl.* -NERIES (-ĭz). A place where swans are bred or kept.

swan's′–down′ (swŏnz′doun′), *n.* **1.** The down, or fine soft feathers, of the swan, used as trimming, for powder puffs, etc. **2.** *Textiles.* Commonly **swans′down′.** **a** A soft, thick cloth of wool mixed with silk, rayon, or cotton. **b** Canton flannel (see FLANNEL, 2).

swan′skin′ (swŏn′skĭn′), *n.* **1.** The skin of a swan with the down, or feathers. **2.** Any of various soft-napped or soft-surfaced cotton or woolen fabrics, as Canton flannel (see FLANNEL, 2). — **swan′skin′**, *adj.*

swan song. The song anciently fabled to be sung by a swan when dying; hence, a poetic, musical, or artistic work composed shortly before the artist's death.

swan′–up′ping (-ŭp′ĭng), *n.* [From *swan* + *up*, prep. & adv.] *Eng.* The practice or process of marking young swans or cygnets, for the owners; specif., an annual expedition for this purpose on the river Thames.

swap (swŏp), *v. t. & i.;* SWAPPED (swŏpt); SWAP′PING. Also **swop** (swŏp). [ME. *swappen* to strike, to move swiftly.] *Colloq.* To exchange; barter. — *n.* *Colloq.* An exchange; barter.

‖**swa·raj′** (swȧ-räj′), *n.* [Skr. *svarāj* self-ruling, *svārājya* independent rule.] *India.* **1.** Political independence; national self-government, or home rule. **2.** [*cap.*] The party of India advocating independence. — **swa·raj′ism** (-ĭz′m), *n.* — **swa·raj′ist** (-ĭst), *n. & adj.*

sward (swôrd), *n.* [AS. *sweard* skin, covering.] The grassy surface of land; turf. — *v. t. & i.* To produce sward (upon); to cover, or be covered, with sward.

sware (swâr). Archaic past of SWEAR.

swarm (swôrm), *n.* [AS. *swearm.*] **1.** A great number of honeybees emigrating from a hive in company with a queen to start a new colony elsewhere; also, loosely, a colony of honeybees settled in a hive. **2.** Any moving, esp. migratory, multitude; a dense crowd in motion; a throng. **3.** *Biol.* An aggregation of free-floating or free-swimming unicellular organisms; — applied usually to zoospores. — *v. i.* **1.** To collect and depart from a hive in a body to form a new colony; — said of bees. **2.** To migrate, move, or assemble in a crowd, like bees; to throng together. **3.** To contain a swarm, esp. a throng of beings in motion; to teem; — usually with *with;* as, the book *swarmed* with errors. **4.** *Biol.* To escape in a swarm, as zoospores from a sporangium. — *v. t.* To fill with a swarm; to throng.

swarm (swôrm), *v. i. & t.* [Origin uncert.] To climb; shin; mount; — commonly with *up;* as, to *swarm* up a pole.
swarm'er (swôr'mẽr), *n.* **1.** One who or that which swarms; one of a swarm. **2.** *Biol.* A swarm spore.
swarm spore. *Biol.* A zoospore, or a planogamete; any minute motile spore produced in large numbers.
swart (swôrt), *adj.* [AS. *sweart* black.] Swarthy.
swarth (swôrth), *n.* [AS. *swearth.*] *Dial.* = SWARD.
swarth, *adj.* Swart; swarthy.
swarth (swôrth). Var. of SWATH.
swarth'y (swôr'thĭ; -thĭ), *adj.;* -I·ER (-thĭ·ẽr; -thĭ·ẽr); -I·EST. Being of a dark color, complexion, etc.; dusky; swart. — **Syn.** See DUSKY. — **swarth'i·ly,** *adv.* — **swarth'i·ness,** *n.*
swart'ness (swôrt'nĕs; -nĭs), *n.* The quality or state of being swart.
swash (swŏsh), *v. i.* [Imitative.] **1.** To move, dash, strike, etc., with a splashing sound. **2.** To bluster; swagger. — *v. t.* To dash; esp., to cause to splash; as, to *swash* water in a pail. — *n.* **1.** Blustering noise; swagger. **2.** A body of dashing, splashing water; specif.: *U. S.* **a** A narrow sound or channel of water lying within a sandbank, or between a sandbank and the shore. **b** A bar over which the sea washes. **3.** A splashing of water against something; as, the *swash* of the waves against a pier.
swash'buck'ler (-bŭk'lẽr), *n.* [*swash* + *buckler* shield.] A boasting soldier; a swaggerer; a bravo. — **swash'buck'ler·ing, swash'buck'ling** (-lĭng), *n. & adj.*
swash'er (swŏsh'ẽr), *n.* A swashbuckler.
swash'ing, *adj.* That swashes; as: **a** Splashing. **b** Swashbuckling.
swash letters. A style of italic letters having flourishes at top and bottom; thus: *A R P N*
swas'ti·ka, swas'ti·ca (swŏs'tĭ·kȧ; swăs'-), *n.* [Skr. *svastika,* fr. *svasti* welfare, fr. *su* well + *asti* being, prop., is.] **1.** A symbol or ornament in the form of a Greek cross with the ends of the arms bent at right angles. **2.** A rectilinear swastika, with oblique arms, having the prolongations of the arms turning clockwise, adopted as the official emblem of the Nazis and the Third Reich; — called also *fylfot.* See GAMMADION, HAKENKREUZ. — **swas'ti·kaed** (-kȧd), *adj.*

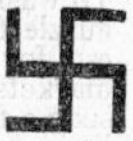
Swastika.

swat (swŏt), *v. t.* *Chiefly U. S.* To hit hard or crushingly. — **Syn.** See STRIKE. — **swat,** *n.* — **swat'ter,** *n.*
swat. Obs. exc. dial. past & past part. of SWEAT.
swat. Var. of SWOT, *n. & v.* — **swat'ter,** *n.*
swatch (swŏch), *n.* A sample of fabric, leather, etc.; a characteristic specimen.
swath (swôth; swŏth), **swathe** (swāth), *n.* [AS. *swæth, swathu,* a track, trace.] **1.** A row, strip, etc. **2.** The sweep of a scythe in mowing or cradling, or the path cut in one course. **3.** A windrow of cut grain or grass as left by the scythe or mowing machine. **4.** The sweep or reach of someone or something that cuts as a scythe; esp., in ***cut a swath,*** to cut a figure; to make a display.
swathe (swāth; swŏth), *v. t.* [AS. *swathian.*] **1.** To swaddle with a band, bandage, or the like; also, to wrap around in the manner of a bandage. **2.** To envelop in the manner of a swaddle or band; as, fog *swathed* the river. — *n.* A bandage; a band. — **swath'er** (swāth'ẽr; swŏth'-), *n.*
swats (swȧts), *n. pl.* *Scot.* Drink; new ale.
sway (swā), *v. i.* [ME. *sweyen,* prob. fr. ON. *sveigja* to bend, swing, sway.] **1.** To turn one's way; to bend one's course. **2.** To swing from side to side; to oscillate; fluctuate. **3.** To lean; incline; veer. **4.** To rule; govern. — *v. t.* **1.** To cause to swing, oscillate, or fluctuate. **2.** To cause to bend or swerve; to deflect; divert; also, to have a controlling influence over; as, motives that *swayed* the elections. **3.** To wield, as a scepter; also, to govern; control. **4.** *Naut.* To hoist or set up; — often with *up.* — **Syn.** See SWING: AFFECT. — *n.* **1.** The action or an instance of swaying or being swayed; oscillation, fluctuation, deflection, etc.; also, a ruling or governing. **2.** The sweep, force, or momentum of something swaying or swayed; now, usually, preponderating force or influence. **3.** Sovereign power; dominion. — **Syn.** See POWER.
sway'-back' (-băk'), *n.* An abnormally hollow condition, or sagging, of the back, found esp. among horses.
sway'-backed' (-băkt'), *adj.* Also **sway'-back', swayed** (swād). Having the back abnormally hollow or sagged; hence, characterized by weakness suggestive of a sway-back.
Swa'zi (swä'zē), *n.* A Bantu of an intelligent, industrious tribe of Zulu origin of Swaziland in South Africa.
sweal (swēl), *v. t. & i.* [AS. *swelan,* v. i.] *Now Dial.* To melt or waste away.
swear (swâr), *v. i.;* SWORE (swōr), formerly SWARE (swâr); SWORN (swōrn); SWEAR'ING. [AS. *swerian.*] **1.** To utter a solemn declaration, with an appeal to God for the truth of what is affirmed; to affirm solemnly by an object regarded as sacred, as the Bible, the Koran, etc. **2.** To make a solemn promise, threat, vow, etc.; to vow. **3.** To use profane or blasphemous language; to curse. **4.** *Law.* To take oath; to give evidence or state on oath. — *v. t.* **1.** To declare or assert as true; to promise or vow, or the like, with a solemn appeal to God, on oath, or on one's word of honor; to pledge sacredly; also, loosely, to assert or promise emphatically. **2.** To utter or take (an oath); as, to *swear* a false oath. **3.** To declare, charge, or confirm upon or under oath; as, he *swore* treason against his friend. **4.** *Law.* To put to an oath (which see); to administer an oath to. — **swear'er,** *n.* — ***swear by.*** **1.** To take an oath by. **2.** To have confidence in. — ***swear off.*** To vow to give up; to renounce.
swear'ing, *pres. part. & verbal n.* of SWEAR. — **Syn.** See BLASPHEMY.
sweat (swĕt), *v. i.;* SWEAT or SWEAT'ED, *Obs.* SWAT (swŏt); SWEAT'ING. [AS. *swǣtan,* fr. *swat,* n., sweat.] **1.** To excrete sensible moisture through the pores of the skin; to perspire. **2. a** To exude moisture, as green plants when closely packed, cheese in ripening, etc. **b** To ferment; — of tobacco, etc. **3.** To condense or gather surface moisture in beads; as, stones *sweat* at night. **4.** To be excreted, or exuded through pores or a porous surface; to ooze. **5.** *Colloq.* To labor in such manner as to cause perspiration; to drudge. — *v. t.* **1.** To emit or seem to emit from pores; to exude. **2.** To cause to exude or lose moisture; specif., to subject to fermentation, as the leaves of tobacco. **3.** To soak with perspiration; as, to *sweat* a collar. **4** To cause to perspire; as, his physicians *sweated* him. **5.** To get rid of or lose by or as if by sweating or being sweated; as, to *sweat* off one's surplus fat. **6. a** To heat so as to extract an easily fusible constituent; as, to *sweat* bismuth ore. **b** To heat, as solder, until it melts and runs, esp. between surfaces to unite them. **7.** To extract something valuable from (a person or thing) by unfair means; to fleece; specif., to remove particles of (a gold coin) by shaking it with others in a bag. **8.** To make to sweat, as by overwork; hence, to oppress (a worker) by exacting labor at low wages and under unfair or unhealthful conditions. **9.** *Slang.* To give (a prisoner) the third degree. — *n.* **1.** Perspiration. **2.** A sweating or being sweated; as, the doctor advised a *sweat.* **3.** Moisture gathering in drops on the surface of any substance; as, *sweat* on a pitcher. **4.** *Archaic.* Hard work; drudgery. **5.** *Obs.* The sweating sickness. **6.** *Manège.* An exercise given a horse before a race. — **sweat'i·ly,** *adv.* — **sweat'i·ness,** *n.* — **sweat'y,** *adj.*
sweat'band' (swĕt'bănd'), *n.* A band, as of leather, in a hat, to protect it from sweat.
sweat'box' (-bŏks'), *n.* Any device for sweating products, as hides in tanning, dried figs, raisins, etc.
sweat'ed (swĕt'ĕd; -ĭd), *adj.* That has been made to sweat; specif., subject or subjected to the sweating system; as, a *sweated* industry.
sweat'er (swĕt'ẽr), *n.* **1.** One who sweats. **2.** An employer of labor who makes use of the sweating system. **3.** Something that induces sweating; a sudorific. **4.** A knitted (or crocheted) jacket, jumper, or blouse.
sweat gland. *Anat.* A gland which secretes perspiration, occurring, in man, in great numbers in most of the skin, and consisting of a tube (*duct*) extending spirally from a minute orifice (*pore*) in the surface and ending in a convoluted spherical mass deep in the derma or in the subcutaneous tissue.
sweat'ing sick'ness. A febrile epidemic disease characterized by profuse sweating, sometimes fatal within two or three hours, that appeared in England in 1485, 1507, 1517, 1528, and 1551.
sweating system. A system of taking advantage of the necessities of employees to drive them to the limit of their powers of labor, usually for unduly low wages; often specif., the employment of employees in sweatshops.
sweat shirt. A type of pull-on sweater used by athletes before and after exercising.
sweat'shop' (swĕt'shŏp'), *n.* A shop in which workmen are employed for long hours and low wages, and under unhealthy conditions.
Swede (swēd), *n.* [MLG. & MD.] **1.** One of the people of Sweden. **2.** [*often not cap.*] A rutabaga.
Swe'den·bor'gi·an (swē'd'n·bôr'jĭ·ăn), *n.* One who holds the doctrines taught by Emanuel Swedenborg (1688–1772), a Swedish philosopher and religious writer. He taught that the Lord Jesus Christ is the one only God, and that there is a spiritual or symbolic sense to the Scriptures, which God revealed through him (Swedenborg). — **Swe'den·bor'gi·an,** *adj.* — **Swe'den·bor'gi·an·ism,** *n.* — **Swe'den·borg·ism** (swē'd'n·bôrg·ĭz'm), *n.*
Swed'ish (swēd'ĭsh), *adj.* Of or pert. to Sweden, its inhabitants, or their language. — *n.* **1.** The Swedish people collectively; — with *the.* **2.** The language of Sweden, which as a literary language began to develop in the 14th century. See INDO-EUROPEAN LANGUAGES, *Table.*
Swedish massage. *Med.* Massage together with **Swedish movements,** a system of exercise of different muscles and joints of the body.
Swedish turnip. A rutabaga; a swede.
swee'ny (swē'nĭ), *n.* In horses, an atrophy of the muscles, esp. of the shoulder.
sweep (swēp), *v. t.;* SWEPT (swĕpt); SWEEP'ING. [ME. *swepen;* akin to ME. *swopen.* See SWOOP, *v.*] **1.** To brush away or off by vigorous and repeated motions; hence, to destroy or efface by continuous onslaughts. **2.** To clean by brushings; hence, to strip or clear by repeated blows, strokes, gusts, or the like. **3.** To gather or collect in the manner of sweepings; to gather in, esp. at one stroke; as, to *sweep* the coins into one's pocket. **4.** To touch or come in contact with (a surface) in the manner of a brush; as, her fingers *swept* the strings. **5.** To range over; to traverse; also, to cover, as a wide field of vision; as, his eyes *swept* the horizon. — *v. i.* **1.** To clean a room, chimney, etc., with or as with a broom. **2.** To move over the surface of something with swiftness, force, etc. **3.** To trail one's skirts in moving; hence, to move with stateliness; as, she *swept* from the room. **4.** To have a wide compass; to extend in a curve or long stretch; as, the valley *sweeps* off to the right. — *n.* **1.** The action or an act of sweeping; esp., a clearing out or away. **2.** A sweeping movement or an effect of one; as, the downward *sweep* of an eagle; sometimes, a blow; stroke. **3.** The compass of a sweeping movement, survey, course, etc.; range of extent; scope; as, within the *sweep* of a telescope. **4.** A curving or flowing line or contour. **5.** *Usually pl.* That swept up; sweepings. **6.** One who sweeps; a sweeper; specif., a chimney sweeper. **7.** A hand water-raising device consisting of a long pole or timber pivoted to the top of a tall post and used to raise and lower a bucket. **8.** = SWEEPSTAKE, 1. **9.** *Card Playing.* In cassino, a pairing or combining of all the cards on the board, and so removing them all; in whist, the winning of all the tricks in a hand. **10.** *Naut.* A long oar used in boats or small vessels, either to propel or steer them. **11.** *Physics.* The process of settling or tendency (of a substance) to settle into thermal equilibrium. — **sweep'er,** *n.*
sweep'back' (swēp'băk'), *n.* The acute angle between the lateral axis of an airplane and the axis of a wing.
sweep'ing, *n.* **1.** The act, duty, etc., of one who or that which sweeps. **2.** *pl.* Things collected by sweeping; rubbish; refuse. — *adj.* **1.** That sweeps, in any sense. **2.** Covering the whole range; complete, or nearly so; as, a *sweeping* victory; often, general and indiscriminate; as, a *sweeping* accusation. — **Syn.** See INDISCRIMINATE. — **sweep'ing·ly,** *adv.* — **sweep'ing·ness,** *n.*
sweep'stake' (swēp'stāk'), *n.* Also **sweep'stakes'** (-stāks'), *sing. & pl.* **1.** The whole stake on an event, esp. on a horse race, a given amount being put up by each contestant and sometimes additional prizes added, and the stake awarded either all to the winner or in shares to several; also, a race or other contest for such a stake or stakes. **2.** Always spelled *sweepstakes.* A lottery offering to distribute sweepstakes as prizes.
sweep ticket. A ticket giving one a chance in a sweepstake.
sweep'y (swēp'ĭ), *adj.* *Chiefly Poet.* That sweeps; sweeping in motion, line, or force.
sweer (swẽr; swēr), *adj.* [AS. *swǣr.*] *Scot.* **a** Slow; indolent. **b** Reluctant; loath.
sweer. Scot. & dial. var. of SWEAR.
sweet (swēt), *adj.* [AS. *swēte.*] **1.** Pleasing to the taste; having an agreeable taste such as that of sugar; — opposed to *sour* or *bitter.* **2.** Hence, pleasing or agreeable in general. **3.** Dear; beloved; — formerly common in address; as, my *sweet* sir. **4.** Not salt or salted;

fresh; as, *sweet* water; *sweet* butter. **5.** Having a fresh taste; fresh; — opposed to *sour, rancid, stale, putrescent*, etc. **6.** Of land, suitable for crops; not dank or acid; — opposed to *sour*. **7.** *Colloq.* Easily managed; smooth-running; noiseless; as, a *sweet* motor. **8.** *Chem.* **a** Free from excess of acid, sulfur, or corrosive salts. **b** Of gasoline, etc., free from sulfur compounds. **9.** *Liquors.* Sweet to the taste; not brut, or dry (see DRY, *adj.*, 4); — said esp. of wines. **10.** *Swing Music.* = CORNY, 3. — *adv.* Sweetly. — *n.* **1.** That which is sweet to the taste, smell, etc. Specif.: **a** *Eng.* A sweet dish served for dessert. **b** *pl.* Confectionery, preserves, etc.; candy. **c** *Colloq., U. S.* A sweet potato. **2.** A sweet or enjoyable experience. **3.** A sweet or dear person; a beloved. **4.** Sweet quality, taste, smell, etc.; sweetness.

sweet alyssum. A perennial European herb (*Lobularia maritima*) having clusters of small fragrant white flowers.

sweet bay. **a** The true laurel (*Laurus nobilis*). **b** An American magnolia (*Magnolia virginiana*) abundant along the Atlantic coast and Gulf of Mexico from Massachusetts to Texas.

sweet′bread′ (swēt′brĕd′), *n.* The thymus or pancreas of an animal (esp. a calf) used for food, the thymus being the ***throat sweetbread*** or ***neck sweetbread***, the pancreas the ***stomach sweetbread***.

sweet′bri′er (-brī′ẽr), *n.* Also **sweet′bri′ar** (-ẽr). A European rose (*Rosa eglanteria*) with stout recurved prickles and single pink flowers.

sweet cherry. See CHERRY.

sweet corn. A type of Indian corn (*Zea mays saccharata*), with kernels containing a high percentage of sugar, and adapted for table use when in the milk stage.

sweet′en (swēt′'n), *v. t.* **1.** To make sweet, pleasant, or gratifying to a sense, the mind, or the feelings. **2.** To add sugar to; hence, *Slang:* **a** At poker, to add chips to (a jack pot). **b** *Finance.* To include high-class securities in the collateral for (a loan). **3.** To mollify; soften. — *v. i.* To become sweet. — **sweet′en·er** (-′n·ẽr), *n.*

sweet′en·ing (swēt′'n·ĭng; -nĭng), *n.* **1.** Act or process of making sweet. **2.** That which sweetens; specif., *Local, U. S.*, molasses (***long sweetening***) or sugar (***short sweetening***).

sweet fern. **a** Any of several ferns (genus *Dryopteris*). **b** A small North American shrub (*Comptonia asplenifolia*) having sweet-scented or aromatic fernlike leaves.

sweet flag *or* **calamus.** A perennial marsh herb (*Acorus calamus*) having long flaglike leaves and a pungent rootstock; — called also *calamus*.

sweet gum. See GUM, 5 **a**.

sweet′heart′ (swēt′härt′), *n.* One beloved; a lover.

sweet′ie (swēt′ĭ), *n.* *Colloq.* A sweetheart.

sweet′ing, *n.* **1.** A darling; sweetheart. **2.** A sweet apple.

sweet′ish (swēt′ĭsh), *adj.* Somewhat sweet; also, sickishly sweet. — **sweet′ish·ly,** *adv.* — **sweet′ish·ness,** *n.*

sweet′ly (swēt′lĭ), *adv.* In a sweet manner.

sweet marjoram. See MARJORAM.

sweet′meat′ (swēt′mēt′), *n.* *Usually pl.* Any food rich in sugar, as cake, candy, etc.; specif.: **a** A candied or crystallized fruit. **b** A confection; a candy.

sweet′ness, *n.* Quality or state of being sweet.

sweet oil. Any mild edible oil, as olive oil.

sweet pea. A garden plant (*Lathyrus odoratus*) having slender, climbing stems, and large fragrant flowers.

sweet pepper. See PEPPER, 3.

sweet potato. A tropical vine (*Ipomoea batatas*), related to the morning-glory, having variously shaped leaves and purplish flowers; also, its large, thick, sweet, and mealy tuberous root, which is cooked and eaten as a vegetable.

sweet scabious. See SCABIOUS.

sweet′-scent′ed (*see Pron.*, § 2), *adj.* Having a fragrant scent.

sweet′shop′ (swēt′shŏp′), *n.* A confectionery store.

sweet′sop′ (swēt′sŏp′), *n.* A tropical American tree (*Annona squamosa*); also, its edible sweet, pulpy fruit, which has a thick, green scaly rind and shining black seeds.

sweet William. Also **sweet william.** A Eurasian pink (*Dianthus barbatus*) having small flowers of many colors in dense umbellike clusters.

swell (swĕl), *v. i.;* SWELLED (swĕld); SWELLED or SWOL′LEN (swōl′ĕn); SWELL′ING. [AS. *swellan.*] **1.** To increase in volume; to grow larger; to dilate. **2.** To become puffed up with pride; to behave in an arrogant manner. **3.** To bulge; protrude, esp. in a curve. **4.** To become augmented in force, intensity, degree, etc. **5.** *Colloq.* To play the dandy or swell. — *v. t.* **1.** To increase the volume, size, value, or the like, of; to cause to rise, dilate, or increase. **2.** To puff up or inflate, as with pride. **3.** *Music.* To augment gradually in loudness, as a tone. — **Syn.** See EXPAND. — **Ant.** Shrink. — *n.* **1. a** A swelling, as in the body. **b** A bulge; protuberance. **c** A wave or an unbroken series of them. **d** A rounded elevation; also, a tract of rising ground. **e** A can, or tin, of fruit or vegetables bulged through fermentation of its contents. **2.** The act or process of swelling. **3.** *Colloq.* One conspicuous in the world, commonly in the world of fashion. **4.** *Music.* **a** A gradual increase and decrease of the loudness or volume of sound; the crescendo and diminuendo combined; also, the sign indicating this (<>). **b** A device in an organ for governing the loudness of the tones. — *adj.* **1.** *Colloq.* Stylish; smartly clothed; fashionable. **2.** *Slang.* Tiptop; first-rate.

swell box. *Music.* A box or chamber, in an organ, containing the reeds or a set of pipes, and having shutters that open or shut to regulate the volume of tone.

swell′fish′ (swĕl′fĭsh′), *n.; pl.*, see FISH. = PUFFER, 2.

swell′ing, *n.* **1.** Act of that which swells, or state of being swollen. **2.** A protuberance; esp., *Med. & Veter.*, a morbid protuberance or enlargement. — *adj.* That swells.

swel′ter (swĕl′tẽr), *v. i.* [Freq. of ME. *swelten* to die, swoon, fr. AS. *sweltan* to die.] To be faint from heat; to be oppressed by heat; to perspire profusely; to sweat. — *v. t.* **1.** To oppress with heat; to cause to sweat. **2.** *Archaic.* To exude; — chiefly in *past part.* — *n.* Sultry heat; also, profuse perspiration.

swel′ter·ing, *adj.* That swelters or causes sweltering; — of persons, heat, etc. — **swel′ter·ing·ly,** *adv.*

swept (swĕpt), *past & past part.* of SWEEP.

swerve (swûrv), *v. i. & t.* [AS. *sweorfan* to wipe off, file, polish.] To move or deviate from a straight line or course; to deflect; to turn aside.

Syn. **Swerve, veer, deviate, depart, digress, diverge** mean to turn aside or off. **Swerve** may be used literally and figuratively in reference to a person or thing; **veer**, used chiefly in wind and ships, implies a change in direction; **deviate**, a turning from a customary or prescribed course; **depart**, a deviation from a traditional, conventional, or long-accepted, etc., course or type; **digress**, a departing from the subject of one's discourse; **diverge**, often used as equal to *depart*, strictly implies a separation of a course or path into two or more branches.

— *n.* Act or instance of swerving; also, something that swerves.

swev′en (swĕv′ĕn), *n.* [AS. *swefen, swefn*, sleep, dream.] *Archaic.* Sleep; also, a dream.

swift (swĭft), *adj.* [AS.] **1.** Moving or capable of moving with great speed; rapidly running, flying, flowing, etc. **2.** Happening without warning or delay or in very short time. **3.** Quick to respond; ready; alert; prompt. — **Syn.** See FAST. — *adv. Poetic.* Swiftly. — *n.* **1.** Any of the large cylinders that carry forward the material in a carding machine; also, a similar cylinder in other machines. **2.** A reel, or turning instrument, for winding yarn, thread, silk, etc. **3.** Any of a family (Apodidae) of small, plainly colored birds allied to the hummingbirds and goatsuckers, but superficially resembling swallows (see SWALLOW, 2). The common American species (*Chaetura pelagica*) is called ***chimney swift*** from its habit of nesting and roosting in disused chimneys. **4.** Any of several lizards (esp. genus *Sceloporus*) which run swiftly. — **swift′ly,** *adv.* — **swift′ness,** *n.*

swift′er (swĭf′tẽr), *n.* *Naut.* **a** A rope used to retain the bars of the capstan in their sockets while men are turning it. **b** A rope used to encircle a boat longitudinally, to strengthen and protect her sides. **c** The forward shroud of a lower mast. — *v. t.* *Naut.* To tauten, as slack standing rigging, by bringing the shrouds nearer together.

swig (swĭg), *n.* *Colloq.* A long draft, or drink. — *v. t. & i.;* SWIGGED (swĭgd); SWIG′GING. *Colloq.* To drink in long drafts; to gulp. — **swig′ger,** *n.*

swill (swĭl), *v. t. & i.* [AS. *swilian, swillan*, to wash, gargle.] **1.** To wash; drench; as, to *swill* the decks. **2.** To swallow greedily; to guzzle (liquid or liquor). — *n.* **1. a** A semiliquid food for animals, esp. for swine, composed of the animal or vegetable refuse of kitchens, markets, or stores, mixed with water or skimmed or sour milk; also, such a food made of distillery waste. **b** Garbage. **2.** The swilling of liquor; swilled liquor; also, a swig.

swim (swĭm), *v. i.;* SWAM (swăm), *Dial. & Archaic* SWUM (swŭm); SWUM; SWIM′MING. [AS. *swimman.*] **1.** To move or propel oneself in water by natural means, as by hands and feet, by fins, etc. **2.** To move with a motion likened to that of swimming; to slip or glide smoothly and quietly. **3.** Not to sink; to float on a liquid; hence, not to be submerged by troubles, etc. **4.** To be immersed or covered, filled, etc., with or as with a liquid; as, the meat *swims* in gravy. — *v. t.* **1.** To move over or on, cover, cross, etc., by propelling oneself through water; as, to *swim* a stream. **2.** To cause or compel to swim or float; as, to *swim* a horse across a river. — *n.* **1.** Act of swimming; also, a gliding motion likened to or suggesting that of swimming. **2.** = SWIM BLADDER. **3.** The current of influence, fashion, popular favor, etc.; — in phrase *to be in the swim*. — **swim′mer,** *n.*

swim, *n.* [AS. *swīma.*] A temporary dizziness or unconsciousness; a swoon. — *v. i.* To be dizzy; also, to reel or appear to reel; as, the lights *swam* before him.

swim bladder. The air bladder of a fish.

swim′mer·et (swĭm′ẽr·ĕt), *n.* [Dim. of *swimmer.*] *Zool.* One of the series of small unspecialized appendages under the abdomen of many crustaceans and best developed in the macrurans. In some cases they are used for swimming, but usually their chief function is to carry the eggs.

swim′ming (swĭm′ĭng), *n.* **1.** The act, art, or sport, of swimming and diving. **2.** Vertigo; dizziness. — *adj.* **1.** That swims; capable of, or habituated to, swimming; adapted to, or used in or for, swimming. **2.** Filled or flooded with or as with water; as, *swimming* eyes. **3.** Being affected by dizziness; as, a *swimming* brain.

swimming bladder. The air bladder of a fish.

swim′ming·ly, *adv.* In the easy manner of one swimming; now usually, prosperously.

swin′dle (swĭn′d'l), *v. i. & t.;* -DLED (-d'ld); -DLING (-dlĭng). [G. *schwindeln* to be dizzy, cheat.] To obtain money or property from one by fraud or deceit; to cheat or defraud. — **Syn.** See CHEAT. — *n.* Act or process of swindling; a cheat. — **swin′dler** (-dlẽr), *n.*

swin′dling (-dlĭng), *n.* Act of one who swindles.

swine (swīn), *n. sing. & pl.* [AS. *swīn.*] **1.** An omnivorous hoofed mammal (family Suidae, type genus *Sus*) with stout body covered with bristles, short legs, and a long snout; a hog or pig; a boar (male) or a sow (female). The term *swine* is chiefly used collectively and applied esp. to the domestic varieties (cf. BOAR, 2). Chief domestic breeds include *Berkshire, Chester White, Duroc-Jersey*, and *Poland China*. **2.** A stupid, doltish, or sensual person.

swine′herd′ (-hûrd′), *n.* A keeper of swine.

swine pox. *Old Med.* A variety of the chicken pox, with acuminated vesicles containing a watery fluid.

swing (swĭng), *v. t.;* SWUNG (swŭng); SWING′ING (swĭng′ĭng); *Archaic & Dial. past* SWANG (swăng). [AS. *swingan* to scourge, fly, flutter.] **1.** To wield, as a weapon, with a flourish or sweep. **2.** To hang by hinges, end supports, etc., so as to permit oscillation or turning; as, to *swing* hammocks on the deck. **3.** To make oscillate; to move to and fro, as in a swing; also, to make rotate or pivot, as around an axis, on a hinge, etc.; as, to *swing* troops into line. **4.** *U. S.* To handle successfully; manage; as, to *swing* a bond issue. **5.** *Swing Music.* To play, or direct in playing, in the style of swing music.

— *v. i.* **1.** To hang; to be suspended; specif., to be executed by hanging. **2.** To oscillate; to sway to and fro. **3.** To turn as on a pivot or hinge; to wheel; as, the door *swung* open. **4.** To march or walk with free, swaying movements of the limbs; as, the troops *swung* along the road. **5.** To use a swing. See SWING, *n.*, 6. **6.** *Swing Music.* To play in the style of swing music.

Syn. (1) **Swing, wave, flourish, brandish, thrash** mean to wield or to move to and fro, up and down, or the like. **Swing** usually implies regularity in movements; **wave**, undulating or fluttering movements; **flourish**, ostentation, triumph, or bravado in swinging or waving something held by the hand; **brandish**, similar motions that, however, suggest a menacing or threatening; **thrash**, a noisy, vigorous swinging suggestive of movements of a flail threshing grain.

(2) **Swing, sway, oscillate, vibrate, fluctuate, waver, undulate** mean to move or cause to move from one direction to its opposite. **Swing** implies movement of that suspended, hinged, or the like, but carries no implication as to whether it is rhythmical, regular, intermittent, or not; **sway**, a swinging motion as of something flexible or unsteady or

not properly supported; **oscillate**, a swinging in the manner of a pendulum; **vibrate**, a stronger implication of shaking than of swinging though the latter is usually suggested; **fluctuate**, irregular alternations suggestive of waves driven by a high wind; **waver**, movements suggestive of reeling and tottering; **undulate**, a wavelike motion associated with a fairly calm sea.

— *n.* [AS. *geswing.*] **1.** A swinging stroke or blow. **2.** Indulgence of one's natural bent; hence, free scope; as, to be given full *swing* in the business. **3.** Act or process of swinging or causing to swing; as, the *swing* of a pendulum; also, the arc or range through which an object swings; a swinging movement or such movements collectively; as, the *swing* with which men march together. **4.** Course or period of existence, influence, etc.; turn; also, natural, normal, or requisite measure of energy or activity; as, a *swing* of fortune. **5.** The driving power of something swung, hurled, flung, etc.; impetus. **6.** That which swings or is swung, as a pendulum. Specif., an apparatus for recreation, commonly consisting of a rope, the two ends of which are fastened overhead and in the loop of which is placed a board or seat on which a person may sit and swing. **7.** In poetry, music, etc., steady, pulsing rhythm. **8.** *Slang, U. S.* The periodic fluctuation of interest rates, prices, or any business activity, between a high and a low point. **9.** In full, **swing music.** A style of playing dance music, esp. jazz, in which a basic melody and rhythm are always more or less present but submerged in individual interpretations of the theme, including impromptu variations, invented phrases, and contrapuntal improvisations, rhythmically synchronized. — **swing,** *adj.*

swinge (swĭnj), *v. t.;* SWINGED (swĭnjd); SWINGE′ING (swĭn′jĭng). [AS. *swengan* to shake, caus. of *swingan.* See SWING.] To beat; chastise. — **swing′er** (swĭn′jẽr), *n.*

swinge. Dial. var. of SINGE.

swinge′ing (swĭn′jĭng), *adj. Now Colloq.* **a** Strikingly large; whopping. **b** Strikingly good; capital.

swing′er (swĭng′ẽr), *n.* One who or that which swings.

swin′gle (swĭng′g'l), *n.* [AS. *swingel, swingele,* a stroke, blow, whip.] **1.** A wooden instrument like a large knife, used for beating and cleaning flax; a scutcher. **2.** The swiple of a flail. See FLAIL, *Illust.* — *v. t.;* SWIN′GLED (-g'ld); SWIN′GLING (-glĭng). To clean by beating with a swingle; to scutch.

swin′gle·tree′ (-trē′), *n.* Also **swin′gle·bar′** (-bär′), **swing′tree′** (swĭng′trē′). A whippletree. See SINGLETREE.

swing music. See SWING, *n.,* 9.

swing shift. The shift between the day and the night shifts in factories operating 24 hours a day, usually from 4 P.M. to midnight. — **swing shifter.**

swin′ish (swīn′ĭsh), *adj.* Of, pert. to, like, or befitting swine; beastly. — **swin′ish·ly,** *adv.* — **swin′ish·ness,** *n.*

swink (swĭngk), *v. i. & t.;* SWANK (swăngk), SWONK (swŭngk); SWONK′-EN (swŭngk′ĕn); SWINK′ING. [AS. *swincan.*] *Archaic.* To labor; toil; slave. — *n. Archaic.* Labor; drudgery.

swipe (swīp), *n.* [Var. of SWEEP.] **1.** A pump handle, a starting lever for a portable engine, or the like. **2.** *Slang.* A strong blow delivered with a sweeping motion. — *v. t.* **1.** To strike with a sweeping motion, as a ball. **2.** *Slang, U. S.* To snatch; pilfer.

swipes (swīps), *n. pl. Slang, Eng.* Poor, thin, or spoiled beer; small beer; also, beer in general.

swi′ple, swip′ple (swĭp′'l), *n.* [See SWIPE.] That part of a flail which strikes the grain in threshing; a swingle. See FLAIL, *Illust.*

swirl (swûrl), *v. i.* To move with an eddying or whirling motion; to whirl. — *v. t.* To cause to swirl, or whirl. — *n.* A whirling motion, or something characterized by such a motion; an eddy, whirl, twist, or the like.

swirl′y (swûr′lĭ), *adj. Scot.* Knotted; twisted.

swish (swĭsh), *v. i. & t.* [Imitative.] To move, strike, or lash, with a swish. — *n.* A thin prolonged sound such as that of a whip cutting the air; also, a light brushing sound of, or as of, a silk skirt in motion.

Swiss (swĭs), *adj.* [F. *suisse,* adj. & n.] Of, pertaining to, or characteristic of Switzerland or the Swiss. — *n. sing. & pl.* **1.** A native or inhabitant of Switzerland; the people of Switzerland. **2.** [*not cap.*] = SWISS MUSLIN.

Swiss chard. See CHARD.

Swiss cheese. Any cheese, esp. Gruyère, having the character of cheeses made in Switzerland.

Swiss franc. The monetary unit of Switzerland, equal to 0.290322 gram of fine gold. It is the equivalent of the former French franc, or $0.193 in U. S. currency when at par.

Swiss muslin. A thin sheer muslin usually with raised dots or small figures, used for curtains, dresses, etc.

switch (swĭch), *n.* **1.** A slender, flexible whip, rod, or twig. **2.** The end of the tail in some animals, as a cow or ox. **3.** A separate tress of hair worn to build up a coiffure. **4.** An act of switching; as: **a** A blow with a slender whip or twig. **b** A turn of a switch (defs. 5 & 6). **c** A changing or shifting, as of investments. **d** *Bridge.* A shift to another suit than that previously bid. **5.** *Elec.* A device for making, breaking, or changing the connections in an electric circuit. **6.** *Railroads.* A device, consisting usually of two movable rails and necessary connections, designed to turn a locomotive or train from one track to another. — *v. t.* **1.** To strike, beat, whip, or flog, with or as with a switch. **2.** To swing, whisk, or lash; as, to *switch* a cane. **3.** *U. S.* To turn aside; divert; shift. **4.** *Cards.* To change (suits) by bidding or playing from a suit other than that previously bid or played. **5.** *Elec.* **a** To shift to another circuit by means of a switch. **b** To operate a switch so as to turn (a light, current, etc.) *off* or *on.* **6.** *Railroads.* To turn from one track to another; to transfer by a switch. — *v. i.* **1.** To move off on, or as if on, a switch or spur track. **2.** To change or shift methods, places, suits (in cards, esp. in bidding), etc.

switch′back′ (-băk′), *n.* A zigzag road in a mountainous region, esp. an arrangement of zigzag railroad tracks for surmounting the grade of a steep hill.

switch′board′ (-bōrd′; 70), *n. Elec.* An apparatus consisting of a panel or panels, on which are mounted switching, measuring, controlling, and protective devices, with connections so arranged that a number of circuits may be combined, controlled, measured, and protected.

switch′er (swĭch′ẽr), *n.* One who or that which switches.

switch′man (-măn), *n.* One who attends a switch or switches; one employed, as on a railroad, in switching.

switch′yard′ (-yärd′), *n. Railroads.* The place where cars are switched from one track to another, where trains are made up, etc.

swith (swĭth), **swithe** (swīth), *adv.* [AS. *swīthe.*] *Archaic & Dial.* Instantly; quickly. — *v. i. Scot.* To hasten.

swith′er (swĭth′ẽr), *v. i. Scot.* To doubt; waver; hesitate.

Swit′zer (swĭt′sẽr), *n.* [MHG. (G. *Schweizer*).] A Swiss.

swiv′el (swĭv′'l), *n.* **1.** A part that swivels or turns on or as on a headed bolt or pin; specif., a compound link with one end turning on a headed bolt, pin, or the like in the other to permit rotation. **2.** *Mil.* A gun (**swivel gun**) fixed on a revolvable base so that it can be rotated horizontally and vertically. — *v. t.;* SWIV′ELED (-'ld) or SWIV′ELLED; SWIV′EL·ING or SWIV′EL·LING. **1.** To turn on or as on a swivel. **2.** To provide with, or secure by, a swivel. — *v. i.* To swing or turn on or as on a swivel.

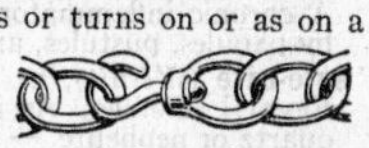
Swivel, 1, in Chain.

swivel chair. A chair that swivels on a stationary base.

swiz′zle (swĭz′'l), *n.* One of several intoxicating mixed drinks; specif., a short drink made with crushed ice, rum or other spirit, sugar, and bitters.

swob (swŏb), **swob′ber.** Vars. of SWAB, etc.

swol′len (swōl′ĕn), *past part.* of SWELL, *v.*

swoon (swōōn), *v. i.* [ME. *swonen, swounen,* fr. *swowening* swooning, fr. AS. *geswōgen* in a swoon.] To faint; — often with *away.* — *n.* **1.** A fainting fit; syncope. **2.** A spell, attack, etc., suggestive of a swoon.

swoop (swōōp), *v. i.* [ME. *swopen,* fr. AS. *swāpan* to sweep, rush.] To descend swiftly with closed wings, as a hawk; to pounce, in the manner of a bird of prey. — *v. t.* **1.** To seize, cut, etc., with a sweep; — often with *away, off, up,* etc. **2.** To pounce upon and seize; — sometimes with *up.* — *n.* The act or an instance of swooping, or pouncing, down upon.

swop (swŏp). Var. of SWAP.

sword (sōrd; 70), *n.* [AS. *sweord.*] **1.** A weapon having a long and usually sharp-pointed blade with a cutting edge or edges; — the general term, including the smallsword, rapier, saber, scimitar, etc. **2.** Something that kills, destroys, punishes, etc., as effectively as a sword. **3.** A symbol of power; as: **a** Judicial or legal authority. **b** Military power. **4.** War, esp. as a means of settling difficulties.

sword bayonet. *Mil.* A bayonet shaped like a sword.

sword′bill′ (sōrd′bĭl′), *n., or* **sword′-billed′ hum′ming·bird′.** A South American hummingbird (*Ensifera ensifera*) having a slender bill longer than the rest of the bird.

sword cane. A hollow cane which conceals a blade like that of a sword or dagger.

sword′craft′ (-kråft′; 9), *n.* **a** Knowledge of, or skill with, the sword. **b** The exercise of military force.

sword dance. A dance in which swords are used; esp., one performed over swords laid on, or set points up in, the ground, without touching them. — **sword dancer.**

sword fern. See BOSTON FERN.

sword′fish′ (sōrd′fĭsh′), *n.; pl.,* see FISH. A very large oceanic food fish (*Xiphias gladius*) having a long swordlike beak formed by the bones of the upper jaw.

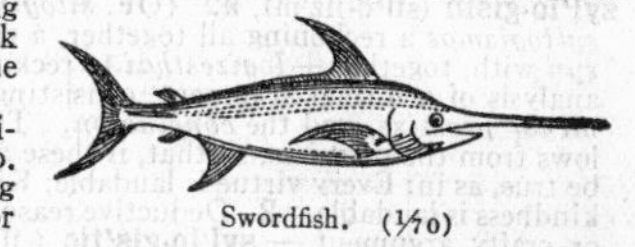
Swordfish. (1/70)

sword grass. Any of various grasses or sedges (esp. genus *Cladium*) having leaves with a sharp or toothed edge.

sword knot. Orig., a leather sling by which the hilt of a sword was attached to the wrist; later, an ornamental ribbon or tassel tied to the hilt.

sword′play′ (sōrd′plā′), *n.* The art or skill of wielding a sword, esp. in fencing. — **sword′play′er** (-ẽr), *n.*

swords′man (sōrdz′măn; 70), *n.* Also **sword′man.** **1.** One who fights with a sword; now, *Rhet.,* a soldier. **2.** One skilled in the use of the sword; a fencer.

sword′tail′ (sōrd′tāl′), *n.* A small brightly marked Central American fresh-water fish (*Xiphophorus helleri*) often kept as an aquarium fish and much used in genetic research.

swore (swōr; 70), **sworn** (swōrn). See SWEAR.

swot (swŏt), *v. i. Slang, Eng.* To sweat over a task; to grind. — **swot,** *n.*

swot. Variant of 1st SWAT.

swound (swound), *n. & v. i. Archaic.* Swoon.

'swounds (zwoundz; zwounz), *interj. Archaic.* Contr. of *God's wounds,* used as an oath.

swum (swŭm). Past part. & archaic & dial. past of SWIM.

swung (swŭng), *past & past part.* of SWING.

Syb′a·rite (sĭb′ȧ·rīt), *n.* [L. *Sybarita,* fr. Gr. *Sybaritēs,* fr. *Sybaris,* a Greek city of southern Italy.] One of the inhabitants of ancient Sybaris, noted for their love of luxury and pleasure; hence [*often not cap.*], a voluptuary.

Syb′a·rit′ic (-rĭt′ĭk), *adj.* Of, pert. to, or characteristic of Sybaris or the Sybarites; hence [*often not cap.*], luxurious; voluptuous. — **Syb′a·rit′i·cal** (-ĭ·kăl), *adj.* — **Syb′a·rit′i·cal·ly,** *adv.*

syc′a·mine (sĭk′ȧ·mĭn; -mīn), *n.* [L. *sycaminus,* fr. Gr. *sykaminos.*] = MULBERRY, 1.

syc′a·more (sĭk′ȧ·mōr; 70), *n.* [OF. *sicamor,* fr. L. *sycomorus,* fr. Gr. *sykomoros* fig mulberry.] **a** A tree (*Ficus sycomorus*) of Egypt and Asia Minor, often called **sycamore fig,** useful as a shade tree and having fruit that is sweet and edible. This is the sycamore of Scripture. **b** A Eurasian maple (*Acer pseudo-platanus*) with long racemes of showy yellow flowers and widely planted as a shade tree. **c** *U. S.* See 1st PLANE, *n.*

syce (sīs), *n.* [Ar. *sā'is,* colloq. *sāyis.*] *India.* A groom.

sy·cee′ (sī·sē′), *n.* [From Cant. pron. of Chin. (Pek.) *hsi⁴ssŭ¹* fine threads; — because if pure it may be drawn out into fine threads.] Silver in ingots, used in China as a medium of exchange, usually stamped.

sy·co′ni·um (sī·kō′nĭ·ŭm), *n.* [NL., fr. Gr. *sykon* the fig.] *Bot.* A collective fleshy fruit, in which the ovaries are borne upon an enlarged, more or less succulent, concave or hollow receptacle, as in the fig.

syc′o·phan·cy (sĭk′ō·făn·sĭ; sī′kō-), *n.* The character or characteristic of a sycophant; hence, servile flattery.

syc′o·phant (-fănt), *n.* [L. *sycophanta,* fr. Gr. *sykophantēs* a false accuser, false adviser, lit., a fig shower, fr. *sykon* a fig + *phainein* to show.] A parasite; flatterer, esp. of princes and great men. — **syc′o·phan′tic** (sĭk′ō·făn′tĭk; sī′kō-), **syc′o·phan′ti·cal** (-tĭ·kăl), *adj.* — **syc′o·phan′ti·cal·ly**, *adv.*

sy·co′sis (sī·kō′sĭs), *n.* [NL., fr. Gr. *sykōsis*, fr. *sykon* a fig.] *Med.* A chronic inflammatory disease involving the hair follicles, marked by papules, pustules, and crusts.

sy′e·nite (sī′ĕ·nīt), *n.* [L. *Syenites* (sc. *lapis*), fr. *Syene* (Aswan), Egypt.] *Petrog.* An igneous rock, chiefly feldspar, without notable quartz or nephelite. — **sy′e·nit′ic** (-nĭt′ĭk), *adj.*

syke (sīk). Var. of SIKE.

syl-. An assimilated form of *syn-* before *l*, as in *syll*able.

syl′la·bar′y (sĭl′ȧ·bĕr′ĭ *or, esp. Brit.,* -bẽr·ĭ), *n.; pl.* -IES (-ĭz). A table of syllables; specif., a set of characters each one of which is used to spell a syllable, and not a single sound as in an alphabet; as, the cuneiform *syllabary.*

syl·lab′ic (sĭ·lăb′ĭk), *adj.* **1.** Of, pertaining to, or denoting a syllable or syllables. **2.** Characterized by distinct enunciation or separation of syllables. **3.** *Pros.* Designating a type of verse distinguished primarily by regular count of syllables rather than by rhythmical arrangement of accents or quantities. — **syl·lab′i·cal·ly** (-ĭ·kăl·ĭ), *adv.*

syl·lab′i·cate (-ĭ·kāt), *v. t.* To syllabify. — **syl·lab′i·ca′tion** (-kā′shŭn), *n.*

syl·lab′i·fy (-ĭ·fī), *v. t.* To form or divide into syllables; syllabicate. — **syl·lab′i·fi·ca′tion** (-fĭ·kā′shŭn), *n.*

syl′la·bism (sĭl′ȧ·bĭz′m), *n.* Syllabic versification.

syl′la·bize (-bīz), *v. t.* To syllabify.

syl′la·ble (sĭl′ȧ·b′l), *n.* [OF. *sillabe*, fr. L. *syllaba*, fr. Gr. *syllabē* that which is held together, several letters taken together so as to form one sound, a syllable, deriv. of *syn* with + *lambanein* to take.] **1.** One or more speech sounds constituting an uninterrupted unit of utterance and forming either a whole word (*man*) or a division of a word (*A·mer·i·ca*); also, one or more letters representing a spoken syllable. **2.** In writing and printing, a part of a word separated from the rest and capable of being pronounced by a single impulse of the voice. It may or may not correspond to a syllable in the spoken language. **3.** The most trivial detail, mention, etc.; as, not to tell a *syllable* about it. — *v. t. & i.* To express in or by syllables.

syl′la·bub (sĭl′ȧ·bŭb). Var. of SILLABUB.

syl′la·bus (sĭl′ȧ·bŭs), *n.; pl.* SYLLABUSES (-ĕz; -ĭz), SYLLABI (-bī). [NL., fr. erron. reading of L. (Cicero) *sittybas*, acc. pl. of *sittyba*, fr. Gr. *sittyba, sittybē*, strip of parchment, label.] **1.** A compendium containing the heads of a discourse, treatise, course of study, etc.; an abstract. **2.** *Law.* The brief statement of the points of law determined prefixed to a reported case. — **Syn.** See COMPENDIUM.

syl·lep′sis (sĭ·lĕp′sĭs), *n.; pl.* -LEPSES (-sēz). [L., fr. Gr. *syllēpsis* a taking together, fr. *syllambainein*. See SYLLABLE.] *Gram.* The use of a word to modify or govern syntactically two (sometimes more) words, with only one of which it formally agrees in gender, number, etc.

syl′lo·gism (sĭl′ō·jĭz′m), *n.* [OF. *silogime, sillogisme*, fr. L., fr. Gr. *syllogismos* a reckoning all together, a reasoning, syllogism, deriv. of *syn* with, together + *logizesthai* to reckon.] **1.** A logical scheme or analysis of a formal argument, consisting of the *major premise*, the *minor premise*, and the *conclusion*. The conclusion necessarily follows from the premises, so that, if these are true, the conclusion must be true, as in: Every virtue is laudable; Kindness is a virtue; Therefore kindness is laudable. **2.** Deductive reasoning. **3.** A subtle, specious, or crafty argument. — **syl′lo·gis′tic** (-jĭs′tĭk), **syl′lo·gis′ti·cal** (-tĭ·kăl), *adj.* — **syl′lo·gis′ti·cal·ly**, *adv.*

syl′lo·gis′tic (-jĭs′tĭk), *n.* Also (*Rare*) **syl′lo·gis′tics** (-tĭks), see -ICS. The branch of logic dealing with the syllogism; also, the art of reasoning syllogistically.

syl′lo·gize (sĭl′ō·jīz), *v. i. & t.* To reason or infer by means of syllogisms. — **syl′lo·gi·za′tion** (-jĭ·zā′shŭn; -jī·zā′-), *n.* — **syl′lo·giz′er** (-jīz′ẽr), *n.*

sylph (sĭlf), *n.* [F. *sylphe.*] **1.** An imaginary being inhabiting the air; — a name given by Paracelsus to the elemental beings of the air, conceived as mortal but soulless. **2.** A slender, graceful woman. — **sylph′like′** (-līk′), *adj.*

sylph′id (sĭl′fĭd), *n.* [F. *sylphide.*] A young or diminutive sylph. — **sylph′id·ine** (-fĭ·dĭn; -dīn), *adj.*

syl′va (sĭl′vȧ), *n.; pl.* -VAS (-vȧz), -VAE (-vē). = SILVA.

syl′van, sil′van (sĭl′văn), *adj.* [L. *silva*, less correctly *sylva*, a wood or grove.] **1.** Of, pertaining to, living, located, or carried on in the woods; forest; as, *sylvan* deities, sports. **2.** Characteristic of the forest, esp. as disting. from the field or town; as, a *sylvan* landscape. **3.** Composed of, or abounding in, woods, groves, or trees. — *n.* A rustic; a woodsman.

syl′van·ite (sĭl′văn·īt), *n.* [From Tran*sylvania*, where first found.] *Mineral.* A telluride of gold and silver, $(Au,Ag)Te_2$, often occurring in crystals resembling written characters.

syl′vi·cul′ture (sĭl′vĭ·kŭl′tṳr). Var. of SILVICULTURE.

syl′vite (sĭl′vīt), *n.* Also **syl′vin, syl′vine** (sĭl′vĭn). [From NL. sal digestivus *sylvii*, potassium chloride.] *Mineral.* Native potassium chloride, KCl, occurring in colorless cubes or crystalline masses.

sym- (sĭm-). An assimilated form of *syn-*. See SYN-.

sym′bi·ont (sĭm′bĭ·ŏnt; sĭm′bī·ŏnt), *n.* [Gr. *symbiōn, symbiountos*, pres. part.] *Biol.* An organism living in symbiosis.

sym′bi·o′sis (-ō′sĭs), *n.* [NL., fr. Gr. *symbiōsis* a living together.] *Biol.* The living together in intimate association or even close union of two dissimilar organisms. In a broad sense the term includes parasitism, or ***antagonistic, or antipathetic, symbiosis***, in which the association is disadvantageous or destructive to one of the organisms, but ordinarily it is used of cases where the association is advantageous, or often necessary, to one or both, and not harmful to either. — **sym′bi·ot′ic** (-ŏt′ĭk), **sym′bi·ot′i·cal** (-ĭ·kăl), *adj.* — **sym′bi·ot′i·cal·ly**, *adv.*

sym′bol (sĭm′bŭl; -b′l), *n.* [F. and L.; F. *symbole*, fr. L. *symbolus, symbolum*, fr. Gr. *symbolon* a sign by which one knows or infers a thing, fr. *symballein* to throw together, compare, fr. *syn* with + *ballein* to throw.] **1.** That which suggests something else by reason of relationship, association, convention, etc.; esp., a visible sign of something invisible, as an idea, a quality; an emblem; as, the lion is the *symbol* of courage. **2.** In writing or printing, a conventional sign, such as a character, a letter, or an abbreviation, used instead of a word or words, as in mathematics, physics, chemistry, music, phonetics, or the like, to represent operations, quantities, spatial position, elements, relations, qualities, sounds, etc. See *Arbitrary Signs and Symbols*, in the Appendix. **3.** *Psychoanalysis.* An object or act representing a repressed desire of which the individual is unconscious. — *v. i.* To symbolize.

sym·bol′ic (sĭm·bŏl′ĭk), **sym·bol′i·cal** (-ĭ·kăl), *adj.* **1.** Of or pertaining to a symbol or symbols; that is or constitutes a symbol. **2.** Using or exhibiting a symbol or symbols; expressed in symbols; also, consisting of a symbol or mark; as, a *symbolic* signature. **3.** Characterized by symbolism; as, a *symbolic* dance, poem. **4.** *Gram.* = RELATIONAL, 3. — **sym·bol′i·cal·ly**, *adv.*

symbolic logic. = MATHEMATICAL LOGIC.

sym′bol·ism (sĭm′bŭl·ĭz′m), *n.* **1.** The practice or art of using symbols, as by investing things with a symbolic meaning or by expressing the invisible by means of visible or sensuous representations; specif., in literature and the fine arts: **a** The use of conventional or traditional signs, as, for example, the nimbus, in the representation of divine beings. **b** Artistic imitation or invention, not as an end in itself but as a method of revealing or suggesting immaterial, ideal, or otherwise intangible truth or states. **2.** A school of symbolists; also, the principles, methods, etc., of any one of these. **3.** A system of symbols, as in phonetics.

sym′bol·ist (-ĭst), *n.* **1.** One who employs symbols or symbolism. **2.** *Eccl.* **a** [*often cap.*] One who regards the elements of the Eucharist as mere symbols and not as the body and blood of Christ. **b** One who advocates or employs symbolism in religious worship. **3.** *Literature & Fine Arts.* One of a class of writers and artists prominent after 1880 in France and Belgium (including Verlaine, Mallarmé, and Maeterlinck), reactionists against realism. They concerned themselves with general truths instead of actualities, exalted the metaphysical and the mysterious, esp. the mystical power and charm of music, and aimed to unify and blend the arts and the functions of the senses. Also called *decadent.* — **sym′bol·ist**, *adj.*

sym′bol·is′tic (-ĭs′tĭk), *adj.* Of, belonging to, or characteristic of the symbolists; executed by, or in the manner of, a symbolist; symbolic.

sym′bol·ize (sĭm′bŭl·īz), *v. i.* To use symbols or symbolism. — *v. t.* **1.** To represent, express, or identify by a symbol or symbols; as, a nimbus enclosing a cross *symbolizes* Christ; also, to regard or treat as a symbol; as, to *symbolize* a rainbow. **2.** To serve as a symbol of. — **sym′bol·i·za′tion** (-ĭ·zā′shŭn; -ī·zā′-), *n.*

sym·bol′o·gy (sĭm·bŏl′ō·jĭ), *n.* [*symbol* + *-logy.*] The art of expression by symbols; also, the study or interpretation of symbols.

sym·met′al·lism (sĭm·mĕt′ăl·ĭz′m), *n.* That system of coinage in which the unit of currency consists of a certain weight of an amalgam of two or more metals, as gold and silver. Cf. BIMETALLISM, MONOMETALLISM.

sym·met′ric (sĭ·mĕt′rĭk), *adj.* Symmetrical.

sym·met′ri·cal (-rĭ·kăl), *adj.* **1.** Having or exhibiting symmetry, or, esp., correspondence in size and shape of parts. **2.** *Bot.* Specif.: **a** Capable of division by a longitudinal plane into similar halves; — said of a flower, shoot, or organ. The flower, etc., is said to be *monosymmetric*, or *zygomorphic*, when it is bilaterally symmetrical, that is, divisible by only a single such plane; *bisymmetrical* when doubly symmetrical, that is, divisible into two similar halves by either of two planes passing through the axis at right angles to each other; *radiosymmetrical*, or *actinomorphic*, when it is radially symmetrical, that is, divisible (as the buttercup) into equal symmetrical portions by any of three or more planes passing through the axis. **b** Having the same number of members in each whorl of floral leaves; — said of a flower. **3.** *Chem.* Exhibiting symmetry in the structural formula; specif., designating derivatives of benzene in which three or four substituting groups occupy positions (1, 3, 5) on alternate carbons or positions (1, 2, 4, 5) on opposite pairs of carbons. See BENZENE RING. Abbrs. *s-, sym-.* **4.** *Logic & Math.* Such that its terms may be interchanged without altering its value, character, or truth; — said of relations, equations, etc. **5.** *Med.* Affecting corresponding parts similarly. — **sym·met′ri·cal·ly**, *adv.* — **sym·met′ri·cal·ness**, *n.*

sym′me·trize (sĭm′ĕ·trīz), *v. t.* To make symmetrical. — **sym′me·tri·za′tion** (-trĭ·zā′shŭn; -trī·zā′-), *n.*

sym′me·try (sĭm′ĕ·trĭ), *n.* [F. or L.; F. *symmétrie* (now *symétrie*), fr. L., fr. Gr. *symmetria*, fr. *syn-* + *metron* a measure.] **1.** *Now Rare.* Due or balanced proportions; beauty of form arising from such harmony. **2.** Correspondence in size, shape, and relative position, of parts that are on opposite sides of a dividing line or median plane.

sym′pa·thet′ic (sĭm′pȧ·thĕt′ĭk), *adj.* **1.** Consonant with one's mood, disposition, etc.; congenial. **2.** Feeling, or inclined to feel, sympathy; sympathizing; also, pertaining to, manifesting, or expressive of, sympathy. **3.** *Colloq.* Favorably inclined or disposed; — with *to* or *toward.* **4.** *Anat. & Physiol.* **a** Designating or pertaining to that part of the autonomic nervous system which is made up of two gangliated cords, one on either side of the spinal column, and connected by nerve fibers with the peripheral blood vessels, glands, nonstriated muscles, etc., and which, in general, is opposite in effect to the *parasympathetic* system, as in accelerating the heart, etc. **b** Sometimes, designating or pertaining to the entire autonomic nervous system. Cf. PARASYMPATHETIC. **5.** *Music & Acoustics.* Designating a vibration produced in one body by the vibrations of exactly the same period in a neighboring body; also, produced by, or so tuned as to sound by, such vibration. — **Syn.** See CONSONANT. — **sym′pa·thet′i·cal·ly** (-ĭ·kăl·ĭ), *adv.*

sympathetic ink. A fluid for invisible writing to be made visible afterwards, as by application of heat.

sympathetic strike. A strike in which the strikers make no demands on their own employers, but try to bring pressure against the employers of other workers on strike.

sym′pa·thize (sĭm′pȧ·thīz), *v. i.* [F. *sympathiser.*] **1.** To react or respond in sympathy; as, a good eye often *sympathizes* with a diseased eye. **2.** To be in keeping, harmony, or agreement. **3.** To share in suffering, grieving, etc.; to commiserate; also, to express such sympathy; — often followed by *with.* **4.** To be in sympathy intellectually, to understand through fellow feeling. — **sym′pa·thiz′er** (-thīz′ẽr), *n.*

sym′pa·thiz′ing (-thīz′ĭng), *adj.* That sympathizes. — **sym′pa·thiz′ing·ly**, *adv.*

sym′pa·thy (sĭm′pȧ·thĭ), *n.; pl.* -THIES (-thĭz). [L. *sympathia*, fr. Gr. *sympatheia*, fr. *syn* with + *pathos* suffering, passion.] **1.** An affinity, association, or relationship between things so that whatever affects one, similarly affects the other or others; mutual or reciprocal susceptibility; hence, a reaction or response brought about by such relationship. **2.** Fitting or agreeable correspondence in qualities, properties, etc.; harmony. **3.** Reciprocal liking and understanding arising from community of interests, aims, etc., and compatibility of temperaments. **4.** The act or capacity of entering into or sharing the feelings, interests, etc., of another; also, the feeling or mental state so induced; specif., compassion; pity. **5.** *Physics & Acoustics.* The correlation existing between bodies capable of communicating their vibrational motion to one another through some medium. — **Syn.** See ATTRACTION; PITY.

sym·pet′al·ous (sĭm·pĕt′ăl·ŭs), *adj.* *Bot.* Gamopetalous.

sym·phon′ic (sĭm·fŏn′ĭk), *adj.* **1.** Relating to harmony of sound; symphonious; also, sounded alike; homophonous, as certain shorthand signs. **2.** *Music.* Of, relating to, or in the manner of a symphony.

symphonic poem. *Music.* An extended composition for a symphony orchestra differing from a symphony in being less restricted in form and based on a definite poetic subject or a program. It is usually in one continuous movement and has one or more principal themes.

sym·pho′ni·ous (sĭm·fō′nĭ·ŭs), *adj.* Agreeing, esp. in sound; accordant. — **sym·pho′ni·ous·ly,** *adv.*

sym′pho·nize (sĭm′fō·nīz), *v. i. & t.* To harmonize.

sym′pho·ny (-nĭ), *n.; pl.* -PHONIES (-nĭz). [OF. *simphonie,* fr. L. *symphonia,* fr. Gr. *symphōnia,* fr. *syn* with + *phōnē* a sound, the voice.] **1.** A consonance or harmony of sounds, esp. of instrumental sounds. **2.** Consonance or harmony of any kind. **3.** *Music.* **a** An instrumental passage in a vocal composition. **b** An instrumental movement in the midst of a choral work, as the "Pastoral Symphony" in *The Messiah* of Handel. **c** An elaborate instrumental composition in sonata form for a full orchestra. **4.** *Painting.* Consonance or harmony of color, or a picture marked by such.

symphony orchestra. *Music.* A large orchestra adapted for presenting symphonic works.

sym′phy·sis (sĭm′fĭ·sĭs), *n.; pl.* -SES (-sēz). [NL., fr. Gr. *symphysis* symphysis (in sense 1), deriv. of *syn* with + *phyein* to cause to grow, grow.] **1.** *Anat. & Zool.* **a** The articulation of certain bones in the median plane of the body, esp. that of the two halves of the lower jaw at the chin, and of the two pubic bones at the lower anterior point of the abdomen. **b** An articulation in which the bony surfaces are connected by fibrocartilage without a synovial membrane. See AMPHIARTHROSIS. **2.** *Bot.* A growing together into one body; coalescence. — **sym·phys′e·al** (sĭm·fĭz′ē·ăl), **sym·phys′i·al** (-ĭ·ăl), *adj.*

sym·po′di·um (sĭm·pō′dĭ·ŭm), *n.; pl.* -DIA (-*ȧ*). [NL., fr. *sym-* + *-podium.*] *Bot.* An apparent main axis not developed from a terminal bud, but made up of successive secondary axes, each of which represents one fork of a dichotomy, the other being of weaker growth or suppressed entirely as in the grapevine. Cf. MONOPODIUM.

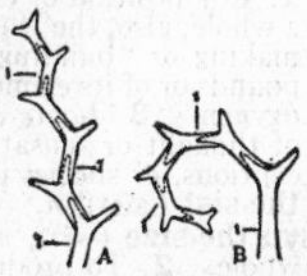

1, 1 Sympodia on Scorpioid (*A*) and Helicoid (*B*) Dichotomies.

sym·po′si·arch (sĭm·pō′zĭ·ärk), *n.* [Gr. *symposiarchēs, symposiarchos,* fr. *symposion* a symposium + *archein* to rule.] In Greek antiquity, the master of a feast; hence, one who presides over, or is the chief figure at, a symposium.

sym·po′si·um (-zĭ·ŭm), *n.; pl.* SYMPOSIA (-*ȧ*), SYMPOSIUMS (-ŭmz). [L., fr. Gr. *symposion* a drinking party, feast, fr. *syn* with + *posis* a drinking.] **1.** In ancient Greece, a drinking together, usually following the banquet proper, with music, singing, and conversation; hence, a banquet or social gathering at which there is free interchange of ideas. **2.** A conference at which a particular subject is discussed and opinions gathered; also, a collection of opinions on a subject; esp., such a collection published by a periodical.

symp′tom (sĭmp′tŭm), *n.* [F. *symptôme,* fr. Gr. *symptōma* anything that has befallen one, a chance, casualty, symptom, fr. *sympiptein* to fall together, fr. *syn* with + *piptein* to fall.] **1.** *Med.* Any perceptible change in the body or its functions indicating disease, or the kind or phases of disease. **2.** A sign; token; as, vice is a *symptom* of weakness. — **Syn.** See SIGN. — **symp′tom·less,** *adj.*

symp′to·mat′ic (sĭmp′tō·măt′ĭk), **symp′to·mat′i·cal** (-ĭ·kăl), *adj.* **1.** *Med.* Constituting a symptom of disease; indicative of the presence of a particular disease. **2.** Of or concerned with symptoms; as, a *symptomatic* treatment. **3.** Of the nature of a symptom or sign; characteristic; indicative. — **symp′to·mat′i·cal·ly,** *adv.*

symp′tom·a·tol′o·gy (sĭmp′tŭm·*ȧ*·tŏl′ō·jĭ), *n.* [Gr. *symptōma, symptōmatos,* symptom + *-logy.*] *Med.* That branch of medical science treating of symptoms of diseases; semeiology.

syn- (sĭn-). [Gr. *syn* with.] A prefix meaning *with, along with, together, at the same time,* as in *syn*chronize, *syn*thesis; also, *concurrent, associated, like,* as in *syn*esthesia, *syn*onym. *Syn-* becomes *sym-* before *p, b,* and *m,* and *syl-* before *l.*

syn·aer′e·sis, syn·er′e·sis (sĭ·nĕr′ē·sĭs *or, esp. Brit.,* sĭ·nēr′-), *n.* [NL., fr. Gr. *synairesis* a taking together.] *Pros.* **a** The union into one syllable of two consecutive vowels ordinarily pronounced separately (*seest* for seëst); — the opposite of *diaeresis.* **b** Also, often, synizesis.

syn′aes·the′si·a. Var. of SYNESTHESIA.

syn′a·gogue (sĭn′*ȧ*·gŏg; 74), *n.* Also **syn′a·gog.** [OF. *sinagoge,* fr. LL., fr. Gr. *synagōgē* a bringing together, assembly, synagogue, fr. *synagein* to bring together, fr. *syn* with + *agein* to lead.] *Jewish Relig.* **a** A local assembly of Jews organized chiefly for public worship. **b** The building or place of assembly used by Jewish communities primarily for religious worship. **c** The Jewish religion or communion. — **syn′a·gog′i·cal** (sĭn′*ȧ*·gŏj′ĭ·kăl), *adj.*

syn′a·loe′pha, syn′a·le′pha (sĭn′*ȧ*·lē′f*ȧ*), *n.* Also **syn′a·le′phe** (-lē′-fē). [L. *synaloepha,* fr. Gr. *synaloiphē,* lit., a melting together.] *Gram.* The blending into one syllable of two vowels of adjacent syllables, as by elision (*th′ army* for *the army*).

syn·apse′ (sĭ·năps′), *n.* [Gr. *synapsis* conjunction, union.] *Physiol.* The point at which the nervous impulse passes from one neuron to another.

syn·ap′sis (sĭ·năp′sĭs), *n.; pl.* SYNAPSES (-sēz). [NL.] **1.** *Biol.* Conjugation of pairs of homologous chromosomes, of maternal and paternal origin respectively. It is the primary step in meiosis. **2.** *Physiol.* = SYNAPSE. — **syn·ap′tic** (-tĭk), *adj.*

syn′ar·thro′sis (sĭn′är·thrō′sĭs), *n.; pl.* -SES (-sēz). [NL., fr. Gr. *synarthrōsis* a being jointed together, deriv. of *syn-* + *arthron* a joint.] *Anat.* An immovable articulation in which the bones are united by intervening fibrous connective tissues.

sync (sĭngk), *n. & v.* Also **synch** (sĭngk). *Motion Pictures & Television.* Short for SYNCHRONIZATION, SYNCHRONIZE.

syn′carp (sĭn′kärp), *n.* [NL. *syncarpium.*] *Bot.* A collective fruit.

syn·car′pous (sĭn·kär′pŭs), *adj.* *Bot.* **a** Having carpels united in a compound ovary; — opposed to *apocarpous.* **b** Pert. to, or characteristic of, a syncarp.

syn′chro–cy′clo·tron (sĭng′krō·sī′klō·trŏn; -sĭk′lō-), *n.* [*synchro-* (fr. *synchronize*) + *cyclotron.*] *Physics.* A modified cyclotron which achieves greater energies for the charged particles by compensating for the variation in mass that the particles experience with increasing velocity.

syn′chro·flash′ (sĭng′krō·flăsh′), *adj.* [*synchro*nized + *flash.*] *Photog.* Employing or produced with a synchronizing attachment that automatically opens the camera shutter at any chosen speed and fires a flashlight bulb at the same instant. — *n.* Synchroflash photography.

syn′chro·mesh′ (-mĕsh′), *adj.* [*synchro*nous + *mesh.*] Designating a device in a motor vehicle by which synchronized shifting is accomplished. Also, designating a gear system using this device. See SYNCHRONIZED SHIFTING. — *n.* A synchromesh gear or gear system.

syn′chro·nal (sĭng′krō·năl), **syn·chron′ic** (sĭn·krŏn′ĭk), **syn·chron′i·cal** (-ĭ·kăl), *adj.* Synchronous. — **syn·chron′i·cal·ly,** *adv.*

syn′chro·nism (sĭng′krō·nĭz′m), *n.* **1.** The fact of being synchronous; concurrence of events in time. **2.** Chronological arrangement of historical events and personages; also, a table showing such concurrences. **3.** *Physics.* The state of being synchronous. — **syn′chro·nis′tic** (-nĭs′tĭk), *adj.* — **syn′chro·nis′ti·cal** (-tĭ·kăl), *adj.*

syn′chro·nize (-nīz), *v. i.* [Gr. *synchronizein.*] To happen or take place at the same time or instant; to be synchronous. — *v. t.* **1.** To cause (events, acts, etc.) to be or to appear to be synchronous; to represent, arrange, tabulate, etc., so as to indicate coincidence or coexistence. **2.** To render synchronous in operation, etc.; as, to *synchronize* two alternating-current machines. **3.** *Motion Pictures.* To add (sound effects or dialogue) in time and harmony with the action of a picture; to add such effects to (a picture). — **syn′chro·ni·za′tion** (-nĭ·zā′shŭn; -nī·zā′-), *n.* — **syn′chro·niz′er** (-nīz′ẽr), *n.*

syn′chro·nized shift′ing (-nīzd). In a motor vehicle, a changing from one speed gear to another through a transmission with a device by which both gears are brought to the same speed before the shift is made.

syn′chro·nous (sĭng′krō·nŭs), *adj.* [LL. *synchronus,* fr. Gr. *synchronos,* fr. *syn-* + *chronos* time.] **1.** Happening at the same time; concurrent in time; simultaneous. **2.** *Physics.* Having the same period; also, having the same period and phase; as, *synchronous* vibrations. — **Syn.** See CONTEMPORARY. — **syn′chro·nous·ly,** *adv.* — **syn′chro·nous·ness,** *n.*

synchronous machine. *Elec.* A dynamoelectric machine whose normal operating speed is exactly proportional to the frequency of the current. Such a machine may be a generator, motor, or converter.

synchronous speed. *Elec.* A definite speed for an alternating-current machine, dependent on the frequency of the supply circuit.

syn′chro·scope (sĭng′krō·skōp), *n.* [*synchro*nism + *-scope.*] An instrument which indicates synchronism, as between two sources of alternating current, between two or more airplane engines, or between a camera shutter and flashlight apparatus.

syn′chro·tron (sĭng′krō·trŏn), *n.* [*synchro*nize + *-tron* as in elec*tron.*] *Physics.* An apparatus for imparting very high speeds to charged particles (electrons, protons, etc.) by means of a combination of a high-frequency electric field, as in the cyclotron, and a low-frequency magnetic field, as in the betatron.

syn·clas′tic (sĭn·klăs′tĭk), *adj.* [*syn-* + Gr. *klastos* broken, fr. *klan* to break.] *Math. Physics.* Curved toward the same side in all directions; — said of surfaces that in all directions around any point bend away from a tangent plane toward the same side, as the surface of a sphere. Cf. ANTICLASTIC.

syn·cli′nal (sĭn·klī′năl; -n′l; sĭng′klĭ-), *adj.* [Gr. *synklinein* to incline together.] **1.** Inclined down from opposite directions so as to meet. **2.** *Geol.* Formed by strata dipping toward a common line (**synclinal axis, synclinal line**) or plane. Cf. ANTICLINAL.

syn′cline (sĭng′klīn), *n.* *Geol.* A synclinal fold.

syn′co·pate (sĭng′kō·pāt), *v. t.* [LL. *syncopatus,* past part. of *syncopare* to syncopate, swoon. See SYNCOPE.] **1.** To contract by syncope; as, "Gloster" is a *syncopated* form of "Gloucester." **2.** *Music.* To modify or affect by syncopation. See SYNCOPATION, 3 **a.**

syn′co·pa′tion (-pā′shŭn), *n.* **1.** A syncopating; also, a rhythm, dance step, etc., in syncopated time. **2.** *Gram.* Syncope. **3.** *Music.* **a** A temporary displacing or shifting of the regular metrical accent. The commonest varieties of syncopation occur: (1) when a tone is begun on an unaccented beat and continued through the following accented beat (see *Illust.* **a**); (2) when a tone begins after the commencement of a beat and is continued into the following beat (see *Illust.* **b**). **b** Music, as ragtime, employing syncopation.

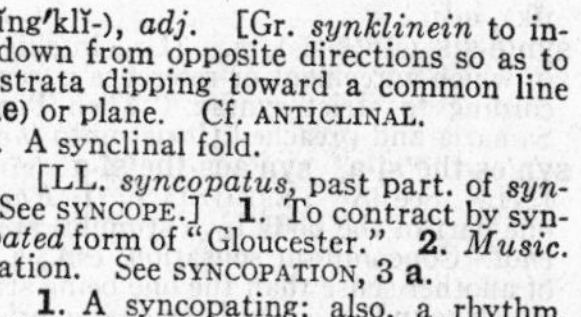

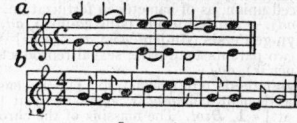

Syncopation.

syn′co·pa′tor (sĭng′kō·pā′tẽr), *n.* One who syncopates.

syn′co·pe (sĭng′kō·pē; -pē), *n.* [LL. *syncope, syncopa,* fr. Gr. *synkopē* a cutting up.] **1.** The loss or elision of one or more sounds or letters from the middle of a word (*ne′er* for *never*). **2.** *Med.* A swoon due to cerebral anemia. **3.** *Music.* = SYNCOPATION, 3 **a.**

syn′cre·tism (sĭng′krē·tĭz′m), *n.* [F. *syncrétisme,* fr. Gr. *synkrētismos,* fr. *synkrētizein* to combine.] **1.** The reconciliation or union of conflicting beliefs, esp. religious beliefs, or a movement or effort intending such. **2.** In the development of a religion, the process of growth through coalescence of different forms of faith and worship or through accretions of tenets, rites, etc., from those religions which are being superseded. **3.** *Philol.* The union or fusion into one of two or more originally different inflectional forms, as of two cases. — **syn·cret′ic** (sĭn·krĕt′ĭk), *adj.* — **syn′cre·tis′tic** (sĭng′krē·tĭs′tĭk), **syn′cre·tis′ti·cal** (-tĭ·kăl), *adj.*

syn′cre·tize (-tīz), *v. i. & t.* [Gr. *synkrētizein.*] To fuse or harmonize, as conflicting principles.

syn′cri·sis (sĭng′krĭ·sĭs), *n.* [NL., fr. Gr. *synkrisis* a comparison, fr. *syn-* + *krinein* to judge.] *Rhet.* Comparison, esp. of contraries or opposites.

syn·dac′tyl, syn·dac′tyle (sĭn·dăk′tĭl), *adj.* [*syn-* + Gr. *daktylos* finger, toe.] *Zool. & Med.* Having two or more digits wholly or partly united. — *n.* A syndactyl bird or mammal.

syn·dac′tyl·ism (sĭn·dăk′tĭ·lĭz′m), *n.* *Zool. & Med.* State of being syndactyl; union of two or more digits.

syn·des′mo- (sĭn·dĕs′mō-), **syndesm-**. [Gr. *syndesmos.*] A combining form meaning *ligament*, as in **syn′des·mot′o·my.**

syn′des·mo′sis (sĭn′dĕs·mō′sĭs), *n.; pl.* -SES (-sēz). [NL., fr. Gr. *syndesmos* a band.] *Anat.* An articulation in which the contiguous surfaces of the bones are united by a ligament. See AMPHIARTHROSIS. — **syn′des·mot′ic** (-mŏt′ĭk), *adj.*

syn·det′ic (sĭn·dĕt′ĭk), **syn·det′i·cal** (-ĭ·kăl), *adj.* [Gr. *syndetikos*, fr. *syndein* to bind together, fr. *syn-* + *dein* to bind.] Connecting; connective; also, indicated by a conjunctive; as, *syndetic* words. — **syn·det′i·cal·ly**, *adv.*

syn′dic (sĭn′dĭk), *n.* [F., fr. LL. *syndicus*, fr. Gr. *syndikos* helping in a court of justice, advocate, fr. *syn-* + *dikē* justice.] **1.** An officer of government, as a mayor of a town. **2.** An agent of a corporation or of any body of men engaged in business. — **syn′di·cal** (-dĭ·kăl), *adj.*

syn′di·cal·ism (sĭn′dĭ·kăl·ĭz′m), *n.* The theory, plan, or practice, of trade-union action which aims by the general strike and direct action to establish control over production by organizations of workers. — **syn′di·cal·ist** (-ĭst), *adj. & n.* — **syn′di·cal·is′tic** (-ĭs′tĭk), *adj.*

syn′di·cate (-kāt), *n.* [F. *syndicat.* See SYNDIC.] **1.** A body of syndics. **2.** An association of persons officially authorized to undertake some duty or to negotiate some business. **3.** *Finance.* An association of persons who combine to carry out a financial or industrial project, as the underwriting of an issue of bonds, the carrying out of a great industrial enterprise, etc. **4.** *Journalism.* A business concern which sells to the press such materials as special articles, photographs, or comic strips, for simultaneous publication in a number of newspapers. — **Syn.** See MONOPOLY.

— (-kāt), *v. t.* **1.** To subject to, or manage as, a syndicate; as, to *syndicate* (specified) newspapers. **2.** To sell (an article, etc.) for simultaneous publication in many newspapers or magazines. — *v. i.* To unite to form a syndicate.

syn′drome (sĭn′drōm), *n.* [NL., fr. Gr. *syndromē*, fr. *syn-* + *dramein* to run.] *Med.* A group of signs and symptoms that occur together and characterize a disease.

syne (sīn). Var. of SIN, *adv.*, since, ago.

syn·ec′do·che (sĭ·nĕk′dō·kē), *n.* [L. *synecdoche*, fr. Gr. *synekdochē*, fr. *synekdechesthai* to receive jointly.] *Rhet.* A figure of speech by which a part is put for the whole (fifty *sail* for fifty *ships*), the whole for a part (the smiling *year* for *spring*), the species for the genus (*cutthroat* for *assassin*), the genus for the species (a *creature* for a *man*), the name of the material for the thing made, etc. See TROPE. — **syn′ec·doch′ic** (sĭn′ĕk·dŏk′ĭk), **syn′ec·doch′i·cal** (-ĭ·kăl), *adj.*

syn·e′cious (sĭ·nē′shŭs). Var. of SYNOECIOUS.

syn·er′e·sis. Var. of SYNAERESIS.

syn′er·get′ic (sĭn′ĕr·jĕt′ĭk), *adj.* [Gr. *synergētikos*, deriv. of *syn-* + *ergon* work.] Working together; co-operating; as, *synergetic* muscles.

syn′er·gism (sĭn′ĕr·jĭz′m; sĭ·nûr′-), *n.* **1.** *Physiol.* Cooperative action of discrete agencies such that the total effect is greater than the sum of the two effects taken independently, as in the action of the mixtures of certain drugs. **2.** *Theol.* The doctrine that in regeneration there is a co-operation of divine grace and human activity. — **syn′er·gist** (-jĭst), *n.*

syn′er·gis′tic (-jĭs′tĭk), *adj.* **1.** Of or relating to synergism. **2.** Serving as a synergist; co-operating. **3.** Yielding to applied energy without resistance; — opp. to *antienergistic.*

syn′er·gy (sĭn′ĕr·jĭ), *n.* [Gr. *synergia.* See SYNERGETIC.] Combined action or operation, as of muscles, nerves, etc. Specif.: *Med.* **a** The combined healthy action of every organ of a system. **b** The combined effective action of two or more drugs. — **syn·er′gic** (sĭ·nûr′jĭk), *adj.*

syn′e·sis (sĭn′ē·sĭs), *n.* [Gr., intelligence.] *Gram.* A construction in which agreement or reference is according to sense rather than according to strict syntax ("Then Philip went down to the city of Samaria and preached Christ unto *them.*" *Acts* viii. 5).

syn′es·the′si·a, syn′aes·the′si·a (sĭn′ĕs·thē′zhĭ·ȧ; -zhȧ; -zĭ·ȧ), *n.* [NL. See SYN-; ESTHESIA.] **1.** *Physiol.* A sensation produced in one part of the body by a stimulus applied at another part. **2.** *Psychol.* Concomitant sensation; esp., a subjective sensation, or image, of another sense than the one being stimulated, as in color hearing, in which sounds seem to have characteristic colors.

syn′ga·my (sĭng′gȧ·mĭ), *n.* [*syn-* + *-gamy.*] *Biol.* Conjugation; cell union, as of gametes in fertilization. — **syn·gam′ic** (sĭn·găm′ĭk), *adj.* — **syn′ga·mous** (sĭng′gȧ·mŭs), *adj.*

syn·gen′e·sis (sĭn·jĕn′ē·sĭs), *n.* [NL.] *Biol.* Reproduction in which two parents take part; sexual reproduction. — **syn′ge·net′ic** (sĭn′jē·nĕt′ĭk), *adj.*

syn′i·ze′sis (sĭn′ĭ·zē′sĭs), *n.* [L. (in sense 2), fr. Gr. *synizēsis*, also, a settlement, collapse, fr. *synizein* to sit together, fr. *syn-* + *hizein* to sit.] **1.** *Biol.* The massing of the chromatin of the nucleus preceding the maturation division. **2.** *Pros.* Contraction of two syllables into one by uniting in pronunciation two adjacent vowels.

syn·kar′y·on (sĭn·kăr′ĭ·ŏn), *n.* *Biol.* A nucleus formed from two preexistent nuclei. See PRONUCLEUS.

syn′od (sĭn′ŭd), *n.* [L. and F.; F. *synode*, fr. LL. *synodus*, fr. Gr. *synodos* a meeting, fr. *syn* with + *hodos* a way.] **1.** An ecclesiastical council. **2.** An assembly or council; a meeting or convention.

syn·od′i·cal (sĭ·nŏd′ĭ·kăl), *adj.* Also **syn·od′ic** (-ĭk). **1.** *Eccl.* Of or pertaining to a synod. **2.** *Astron.* Pertaining to conjunction, esp. to the period between two successive conjunctions of the same bodies, as of the moon or a planet with the sun.

syn·oe′cious (sĭ·nē′shŭs), *adj.* [*syn-* + Gr. *oikos* house.] *Bot.* **a** Having staminate and pistillate flowers in the same head, as in many composites. **b** Often **syn·oi′cous** (sĭ·noi′kŭs). Having archegonia and antheridia in the same involucre, as certain mosses.

syn′o·nym (sĭn′ō·nĭm), *n.* Also **syn′o·nyme.** [LL. *synonyma*, pl. of *synonymum*, fr. Gr. *synōnymon.* See SYNONYMOUS.] **1.** One of two or more words of the same language having the same or nearly the same essential meaning in all or some of their senses. — contr. with *antonym.* **2.** A metonym. **3.** *Bot. & Zool.* A systematic name, as of a species or genus, regarded as incorrectly applied, or as incorrect in form. — **syn′o·nym′ic** (-nĭm′ĭk), **syn′o·nym′i·cal** (-ĭ·kăl), *adj.* — **syn′o·nym′i·ty** (-nĭm′ĭ·tĭ), *n.*

syn·on′y·mize (sĭ·nŏn′ĭ·mīz), *v. t.* To give the synonym or synonyms of (a word); also, to provide, as a dictionary, with synonymies.

syn·on′y·mous (-mŭs), *adj.* [ML. *synonymus*, fr. Gr. *synōnymos*, fr. *syn-* + *onoma*, *onyma*, name.] Having the character of a synonym; alike or nearly alike in meaning or significance. — **syn·on′y·mous·ly**, *adv.*

syn·on′y·my (sĭ·nŏn′ĭ·mĭ), *n.; pl.* -MIES (-mĭz). **1.** The study or discrimination of synonyms; hence, a list of synonyms, often defined and discriminated from each other. **2.** The scientific names (incorrect and correct), collectively, which have been used in different books to designate a species or other group; also, a list of these names. **3.** The quality of being synonymous; sameness of meaning.

syn·op′sis (sĭ·nŏp′sĭs), *n.; pl.* -SES (-sēz). [LL., fr. Gr. *synopsis*, fr. *syn-* + *opsis* a sight, view.] A general view, as of a treatise; condensed statement, often with headings and subheadings; abstract. — **Syn.** See ABRIDGMENT.

syn·op′tic (sĭ·nŏp′tĭk), *adj.* Also **syn·op′ti·cal** (-tĭ·kăl). **1.** Affording a synopsis, or general view of a whole; as, a *synoptic* presentation of a theory. **2.** [*often cap.*] Affording, presenting, or taking, the same or a common view; — applied to the first three Gospels (**Synoptic Gospels**) from their many agreements in subject, order, and language; hence, of or pertaining to the Synoptic Gospels; as, the *Synoptic* problem. **3.** *Meteorol.* Designating or pertaining to the branch of meteorology which deals with the analysis of observations taken in various places over a wide region at or near the same time. — **syn·op′ti·cal·ly** (-tĭ·kăl·ĭ), *adv.*

syn·o′vi·a (sĭ·nō′vĭ·ȧ), *n.* [NL.] *Anat.* A transparent, viscid, lubricating fluid secreted by membranes of articulations, bursae, and tendon sheaths. — **syn·o′vi·al** (-ăl), *adj.*

syn′o·vi′tis (sĭn′ō·vī′tĭs), *n.* [NL. See SYNOVIA; -ITIS.] *Med.* Inflammation of a synovial membrane.

syn·sep′al·ous (sĭn·sĕp′ăl·ŭs), *adj.* *Bot.* Gamosepalous.

syn·tac′ti·cal (-tăk′tĭ·kăl), *adj.* Also **syn·tac′tic** (-tĭk). Of, pertaining to, or according to the rules of syntax. — **-cal·ly**, *adv.*

syntactic construction. *Ling.* See CONSTRUCTION.

syn′tax (sĭn′tăks), *n.* [F. *syntaxe*, fr. LL. *syntaxis*, fr. Gr. *syntaxis*, deriv. of *syn-* + *tassein* to put in order.] **1.** Connected system or order; orderly arrangement. **2.** *Gram.* **a** Sentence structure; the due arrangement of word forms to show their mutual relations in the sentence. **b** That part of grammar which treats of the expression of predicative, qualifying, and other word relations, according to established usage in the language under study.

syn′the·sis (sĭn′thē·sĭs), *n.; pl.* -SES (-sēz). [L., a mixture, prop., a putting together, fr. Gr. *synthesis*, deriv. of *syn-* + *tithenai* to place.] **1.** Composition or combination of parts, elements, etc., so as to form a whole; also, the whole thus formed. **2.** *Chem.* The art or process of making or "building up" a compound by the union of simpler compounds or of its elements; as, the *synthesis* of water from hydrogen and oxygen. **3.** *Logic & Philos.* The combination of separate elements of thought or sensation into a whole, as of simple into complex conceptions, or species into genera; — the opposite of *analysis.* — **syn′the·sist** (-sĭst), *n.*

syn′the·size (-sīz), *v. t.* **1.** To combine by synthesis; to form into a whole. **2.** To produce by synthesis.

syn·thet′ic (sĭn·thĕt′ĭk), *adj.* [Gr. *synthetikos.*] **1.** Of, pert. to, or consisting in synthesis; specif., combining, or organizing, by logical synthesis; involving synthesis; — contrasted with *analytic.* **2.** Of, pert. to, or formed by artificial synthesis; as, *synthetic* dyes, drugs, or silk; hence, not genuine; artificial. — **Syn.** See ARTIFICIAL. — **syn·thet′i·cal** (-ĭ·kăl), *adj.* — **syn·thet′i·cal·ly**, *adv.*

synthetic philosophy. The philosophy of Herbert Spencer. See SPENCERIANISM.

syn′the·tize (sĭn′thē·tīz), *v. t.* To combine; synthesize.

syn·ton′ic (sĭn·tŏn′ĭk), *adj.* *Radio.* Of or pert. to resonance. — **syn·ton′i·cal** (-ĭ·kăl), *adj.* — **syn·ton′i·cal·ly**, *adv.*

syn′to·nize (sĭn′tō·nīz), *v. t.* [See SYNTONY.] *Radio.* To put (radio instruments or systems) in resonance with each other. — **syn′to·ni·za′tion** (-nĭ·zā′shŭn; -nī·zā′-), *n.*

syn′to·ny (-nĭ), *n.* [Cf. Gr. *syntonia* agreement. See SYN-; TONE.] *Radio.* Resonance.

sy′pher (sī′fĕr), *v. t.* [Var. of CIPHER, *v.*] *Carp.* To overlap the chamfered edges of (planks, etc.) to make a flush joint, as for a bulkhead.

syph′i·lis (sĭf′ĭ·lĭs), *n.* [NL., fr. the title of a Latin poem by Fracastoro, "*Syphilis* sive Morbus Gallicus," published in 1530, after the shepherd hero, *Syphilus.*] *Med.* A chronic, specific, contagious disease, ordinarily venereal, caused by a spirochete (*Treponema pallidum*); the pox. — **syph′i·lit′ic** (-lĭt′ĭk), *adj. & n.* — **syph′i·loid** (sĭf′ĭ·loid), *adj.* — **syph′i·lous** (-lŭs), *adj.*

syph′i·lol′o·gy (-lŏl′ō·jĭ), *n.* Medical knowledge of syphilis. — **syph′i·lol′o·gist** (-jĭst), *n.*

sy′phon (sī′fŏn; -fŭn). Var. of SIPHON.

Syr·ette′ (sĭr·ĕt′), *n.* A trade-mark applied to a patented injection unit comprising a small collapsible tube fitted with a hypodermic needle and containing a single dose of a medicinal agent.

Syr′i·ac (sĭr′ĭ·ăk), *adj.* [L. *Syriacus.*] Of or pertaining to Syriac. — *n.* An Aramaic dialect spoken in Edessa and western Mesopotamia, until superseded by the Arabic after the 13th century. The version of the Bible known as *Peshitta* is its most important monument.

sy·rin′ga (sĭ·rĭng′gȧ), *n.* [NL., fr. Gr. *syrinx*, *syringos*, a shepherd's pipe, tube.] **1.** Any of a genus (*Syringa*) of Old World shrubs of the olive family, the lilacs, having purple or white flowers in terminal, usually thyrsoid, panicles. **2.** [The stems were formerly used as pipe-stems.] In popular usage, any of a genus (*Philadelphus*) of garden shrubs with large white or cream, often fragrant, flowers; the mock orange. *P. lewisii* is the State flower of Idaho.

syr′inge (sĭr′ĭnj; sĭ·rĭnj′), *n.* [ML. *sirynga*, *siringa*, fr. Gr. *syrinx*, *syringos*, a pipe or tube, shepherd's pipe.] **a** A form of small hand pump used esp. for injecting liquids into animal bodies, for cleansing wounds, etc. **b** Hence, a device for a similar purpose, as a rubber bag connected with a nozzle by a long tube. — *v. t.;* -INGED (-ĭnjd; -rĭnjd′); -ING·ING (-ĭn·jĭng; -rĭn′jĭng). To wash by injections from a syringe; also, to inject (liquid) by a syringe.

sy·rin′ge·al (sĭ·rĭn′jē·ăl), *adj.* Of or pert. to the syrinx; as, *syringeal* muscles.

sy·rin′go·my·e′li·a (sĭ·rĭng′gō·mī·ē′lĭ·ȧ), *n.* [NL., fr. Gr. *syrinx* a tube + *myel-* + *-ia.*] *Med.* A chronic disease of the spinal cord occurring most often in young adults.

syr′inx (sĭr′ĭngks), *n.; pl.* SYRINGES (sĭ·rĭn′jēz). [NL., fr. Gr. *syrinx* a pipe.] **1.** The vocal organ of birds, a special modification of the lower part of the trachea or of the bronchi or of both. Cf. LARYNX. **2.** *Music.* A Panpipe.

syr'phus fly (sûr'fŭs). [NL. *Syrphus*, the generic name, fr. Gr. *syrphos* gnat.] Any of numerous dipterous flies (*Syrphus* and allied genera, constituting the family Syrphidae). The larvae of some species prey on plant lice. — **syr'phi·an** (-fĭ·ăn), **syr'phid** (-fĭd), *adj. & n.*

syr'up (sĭr'ŭp; sûr'-), *n.* Sirup. — **syr'up·y**, *adj.*

sys'sar·co'sis (sĭs'är·kō'sĭs), *n.* [NL., fr. Gr. *syssarkōsis* a being overgrown with flesh.] *Anat.* The junction of two or more bones by means of attached muscles.

sys·tal'tic (sĭs·tăl'tĭk), *adj.* [LL. *systalticus* drawing together, fr. Gr. *systaltikos*, fr. *systellein* to draw together.] Contractile; specif., *Physiol.*, capable of, or taking place by, alternate contraction and dilatation; as, the *systaltic* action of the heart.

sys'tem (sĭs'tĕm; -tĭm), *n.* [LL. *systema*, fr. Gr. *systēma*, fr. *synistanai* to place together, fr. *syn-* + *histanai* to place.] **1.** An assemblage of objects united by some form of regular interaction or interdependence; an organic or organized whole; as, the solar *system;* a new telegraph *system.* **2.** Specif.: **a** The universe. **b** The body considered as a functional unit. **3.** A complete exhibition of essential principles or facts, arranged in a rational dependence or connection; as, to reduce the dogmas to a *system;* also, a complex of ideas, principles, etc., forming a coherent whole; as, the American *system* of government; hence, a particular philosophy, religion, etc. **4.** A method of classification, codification, etc. **5.** Regular method or order; as, to have *system* in one's business. **6.** *Biol.* Those organs collectively which contribute toward one of the more important and complex vital functions; as, the alimentary or nervous *system.* **7.** *Geol.* A division of rocks, larger than a series and smaller than a group, formed during a period. Cf. PERIOD, 6. **8.** *Physical Chem.* An assemblage of substances in, or tending toward, equilibrium. Systems are classed as two-component, or binary; three-component, or ternary; etc. **9.** *Transportation.* A large group of lines under common ownership or control. — **Syn.** See METHOD.

sys'tem·at'ic (sĭs'tĕm·ăt'ĭk), **sys'tem·at'i·cal** (-ĭ·kăl), *adj.* **1.** That is or that forms a system; systematized. **2.** Reduced to, or presented or formulated as, a system, or coherent body of ideas, principles, etc. **3.** Methodical in conduct, performance, or habit; as, *systematic* investigations. **4.** Carried on, or carrying out a design, with thoroughness and regularity. **5.** Of, pertaining to, or concerned with systematics or classification; specif., *Biol.*, taxonomic. — **sys'tem·at'i·cal·ly**, *adv.*

sys'tem·at'ics (-ĭks), *n.*; see -ICS. The science of classification; classificatory method; also, classification; taxonomy.

sys'tem·a·tism (sĭs'tĕm·ȧ·tĭz'm), *n.* The reduction of facts, principles, etc., to a system.

sys'tem·a·tist (-tĭst), *n.* **1.** One who forms or adheres to a system; a systematizer. **2.** A taxonomist.

sys'tem·a·tize (-tīz), *v. t.* **1.** To make into a system; to render systematic. **2.** To reduce to system; to arrange methodically. — **Syn.** See ORDER. — **sys'tem·a·ti·za'tion** (-tĭ·zā'shŭn; -tī·zā'-), *n.* — **sys'tem·a·tiz'er** (-tīz'ẽr), *n.*

sys·tem'ic (sĭs·tĕm'ĭk), *adj.* Of, relating to, or common to a system; specif., *Anat. & Physiol.*, of or pertaining to the general system, or the body as a whole; as, *systemic* diseases.

sys'tem·ize (sĭs'tĕm·īz), *v. t.* To systematize. — **sys'tem·i·za'tion** (-ĭ·zā'shŭn; -ī·zā'-), *n.* — **sys'tem·iz'er** (-īz'ẽr), *n.*

sys'to·le (sĭs'tō·lē; -lē), *n.* [NL., fr. Gr. *systolē*, deriv. of *syn-* + *stellein* to set, place.] **1.** *Pros.* Shortening of a syllable naturally or by position long, as for metrical convenience; — opposed to *diastole.* **2.** *Physiol. & Biol.* The contraction of the heart by which the blood is forced onward and the circulation kept up; — correlative to *diastole.* — **sys·tol'ic** (sĭs·tŏl'ĭk), *adj.*

syz'y·get'ic (sĭz'ĭ·jĕt'ĭk), *adj.* Of, pert. to, or constituting a syzygy; syzygial. — **syz'y·get'i·cal·ly** (-ĭ·kăl·ĭ), *adv.*

syz'y·gy (sĭz'ĭ·jĭ), *n.; pl.* -GIES (-jĭz). [LL. *syzygia* conjunction, fr. Gr. *syzygia*, fr. *syn* with + *zeugnynai* to join.] **1.** *Astron.* The point of an orbit, as of the moon, at which the planet is in conjunction or opposition; — commonly in *pl.* **2.** *Gr. & Lat. Pros.* A group of two coupled feet; — applied by some to a dipody, but by others restricted to a combination of different feet. — **sy·zyg'i·al** (sĭ·zĭj'ĭ·ăl), *adj.*

T

T, t (tē), *n.; pl.* T's, T's, Ts, TS (tēz). **1.** The twentieth letter of the English alphabet. It comes through the Latin from the Greek (*tau*), which took it from the Phoenician (Hebrew *taw*). **2.** The sound of this letter. In modern English T usually represents the voiceless alveolar stop. With *h* it forms the digraph *th*, which has two simple continuant interdental sounds, one voiceless, as in *thin*, the other voiced, as in *then*. See *Pron.*, § 104. **3.** Anything having the shape of the letter T. Cf. TEE, *n.* **4.** As a *symbol*, used to denote or indicate esp. the nineteenth or (see K, 3) twentieth in order or class. — ***to a T.*** As if measured with a T square; hence, perfectly; precisely; exactly.

-t. [ME., fr. AS. *-t*, and fr. ME. *-d, -ed.*] A verbal suffix, forming past participles and participial adjectives, equivalent to (and most frequently from) *-ed*, as in *lost*, *dwelt.*

Taal (täl), *n.* [D., language.] South African Dutch.

tab (tăb), *n.* **1.** A slight flap, tag, strip, or the like, forming a pendant, as to a garment. **2.** A small loop for pulling or lifting something. **3.** *Colloq.* Account; reckoning; check; — esp. in to *keep tab* or *tabs on*, to keep count of or a check on. **4.** *Aeronautics.* A small auxiliary airfoil hinged to a control surface, esp. ***trimming tab***, a tab inset into the trailing edge of an aileron, rudder, or elevator and independently controlled, for holding the surface at a position suitable for stabilizing the airplane in a flight attitude, as for automatic piloting. See AIRPLANE, *Illust.* **5.** *Com.* A projection from a card, used as an aid in filing.

tab'a·nid (tăb'ȧ·nĭd), *n.* *Zool.* Any of a number of large biting flies, the horseflies. Cf. HORSEFLY, 1. — **tab'a·nid**, *adj.*

tab'ard (tăb'ẽrd), *n.* [OF. *tabart.*] **1.** Formerly, a short outer, usually closed, jacket with loose sleeves, or sometimes sleeveless, for outdoor wear. **2.** A type of cloak or mantle worn by knights. When worn over the armor it was usually blazoned with the bearer's arms. Hence, the garment of a herald, a cape or cloak blazoned with his lord's arms.

tab'a·ret (tăb'ȧ·rĕt), *n.* A strong upholstery silk with satin stripes.

Ta·bas'co (tȧ·băs'kō), *n.* A trade-mark applied to a pungent condiment sauce made of a species of pepper (genus *Capsicum*).

tab'by (tăb'ĭ), *n.; pl.* -BIES (-ĭz). [F. *tabis*, earlier *atabis*, fr. Ar. *'Attābi*, name of a quarter in Baghdad where it was made.] **1.** Any of several fabrics in plain, or taffeta, weave; as: **a** A watered, waved, or striped taffeta. **b** A moreen. **2.** **a** A yellowish-gray domestic cat banded and varied with black; hence, any domestic cat. **b** [Possibly fr. *Tabitha*, fem. prop. name.] An old maid or gossip. — *adj.* **1.** *Archaic.* Made of, or like, tabby; having a wavy or watered appearance. **2.** Brindled; as, a *tabby* cat. — *v. t.;* TAB'BIED (-ĭd); TAB'BY·ING. To water by calendering; to calender; as, to *tabby* silk.

ta'ber (tā'bẽr). Var. of TABOR.

tab'er·nac'le (tăb'ẽr·năk''l), *n.* [OF., fr. L. *tabernaculum*, dim. of *taberna* hut.] **1.** A transient shelter; a tent; hence, a place of abode; a habitation; esp., the human body conceived of as the temporary abode of the soul. **2.** **a** [*cap.*] *Jewish Hist.* A wooden framework covered with curtains, carried through the wilderness in the Exodus, as a place of sacrifice and worship. *Ex.* xxvi. **b** [*not cap.*] A Jewish temple. **3.** *Eccl.* A receptacle or safe for the consecrated elements of the Eucharist, as now generally, an ornamental locked box resting on the middle of the altar. **4.** A place of worship; — in England used derogatively of the meeting places of dissenters; now, esp., a church with a very large auditorium. **5.** [*cap.*] A domed Mormon structure at Salt Lake City, Utah, completed in 1867. — *v. i.;* -NAC'LED (-'ld); -NAC'LING (-lĭng). To reside temporarily; esp., to sojourn in the flesh or be incarnate. — **tab'er·nac'u·lar** (-năk'ū·lẽr), *adj.*

ta'bes (tā'bēz), *n.* [L., a wasting.] *Med.* **a** Formerly, progressive emaciation in any chronic disease, as tuberculosis. **b** Now, locomotor ataxia. — **ta·bet'ic** (tȧ·bĕt'ĭk; -bē'tĭk), *adj.* — **tab'id** (tăb'ĭd), *adj.*

‖**ta'bes dor·sa'lis** (tā'bēz dôr·sā'lĭs). [NL., tabes of the back.] *Med.* Locomotor ataxia.

ta'bet (tā'bĕt), *n.* *Scot.* Bodily feeling.

tab'la·ture (tăb'lȧ·tūr), *n.* [F.] *Archaic.* A tabular surface or a tablet, as for receiving an inscription.

ta'ble (tā'b'l), *n.* [OF., fr. L. *tabula* a board, tablet, painting.] **1.** Orig., a thin slab or flat piece of solid material with a smooth surface; a tablet; board; panel. **2.** **a** An article of furniture, consisting of a smooth flat slab, board, or the like, fixed on legs. **b** Such a table provided with food; as, a bountiful *table.* **3.** The company assembled round a table, as for eating, discussion, gaming, etc. **4.** Food; fare; entertainment; also, esp. in phrases, a meal; as, the pleasures of the *table.* **5.** Orig., a condensed tabulated statement; a synopsis; schedule; as, a *table* of contents. **6.** Any collection and arrangement in a condensed form, for ready reference, of many particulars or values, as of weights, measures, numbers, etc.; as, *tables* of logarithms. **7.** *Arch.* **a** A flat, distinctive, usually raised, surface on a wall. **b** A stringcourse; esp., a projecting band of stone or the like set where an offset is required. **8.** *Backgammon.* **a** Either leaf of a backgammon board, or either half of a leaf. **b** *pl. Obs.* Backgammon. **9.** *Geog. & Geol.* A tableland; also, a horizontal stratum. **10.** *Jewelry.* The upper flat facet of a precious stone. See BRILLIANT, *Illust.* **11.** *Palmistry.* The palm of the hand. — ***on the table.*** In parliamentary usage, on the table of the presiding officer, where a report, motion, bill, etc., may be laid by vote of an assembly to remove it temporarily or indefinitely from consideration.
— *v. t.;* TA'BLED (-b'ld); TA'BLING (-blĭng). **1.** To tabulate. **2.** To lay or place on a table, as money, a card, or the like. **3.** To lay (a motion, etc.) on the table.

tab'leau (tăb'lō; tȧ'blō'), *n.; pl.* TABLEAUX (tăb'lōz; tȧ'blō'), sometimes TABLEAUS (-lōz). [F., dim. See TABLET.] A vivid representation; picture; specif., a representation of some scene by the grouping of persons who remain silent and motionless in appropriate postures.

‖**ta'bleau' vi'vant'** (tȧ'blō' vē'väN'); *pl.* TABLEAUX VIVANTS (tȧ'blō' vē'väN'). [F.] A tableau of grouped persons.

ta'ble·cloth' (tā'b'l·klŏth'; 74), *n.* A cloth for covering a table, esp. before the dishes, etc., are set on for meals.

ta'ble d'hôte' (tȧ'blẽ dōt'; tā'b'l); *pl.* TABLES D'HÔTE (tȧ'blẽ; tā'b'lz). [F., lit., table of the landlord.] **1.** A common table for guests at a hotel. **2.** A meal in a restaurant, hotel, or the like, for which one pays a fixed price. Cf. À LA CARTE. — **ta'ble–d'hôte'** (*see Pron.*, § 2), *adj.*

ta'ble·land' (tā'b'l·lănd'), *n.* A broad elevated plateau.

table linen. Tablecloths, napkins, etc.

ta'ble·spoon' (-spōōn'), *n.* A large spoon, larger than a dessertspoon, having, in cookery, three times the capacity of a teaspoon, or one sixteenth of a standard measuring cup, and used esp. for serving at table.

ta'ble·spoon·ful' (-spōōn·fŏŏl'; -spōōn'fŏŏl), *n.; pl.* -FULS (-fŏŏlz'; -fŏŏlz). As much as a tablespoon will hold, ordinarily one-half fluid ounce.

tab'let (tăb'lĕt; -lĭt), *n.* [OF. *tablete*, dim. of *table.* See TABLE.] **1.** A flat thin slab of any hard or stiff material especially for writing, painting, drawing, etc.; specif.: **a** One of a portable set of smooth leaves or sheets used for writing, as memoranda; also, a set of such leaves. **b** Hence, a collection of sheets of writing paper, like a pad, but fastened at the top only. **2.** A flattish cake of compressed or molded solid matter, such as soap. **3.** *Pharm.* A small mass of medicated material, usually in the shape of a disk or flat square. Cf. TROCHE.

table tennis. An indoor game resembling tennis, played on a table.

ta'ble·ware' (tā'b'l·wâr'), *n.* Ware for table use.

Tab'loid (tăb'loid), *n.* A trade-mark applied to pharmaceuticals, chemicals, medicines, foods, and photographic supplies.

tab'loid, *adj.* [From *Tabloid* the trade-mark.] Compressed or condensed into small scope; as, *tabloid* criticism or plays. — *n.* A newspaper of about half the page size of the ordinary newspaper and containing news in condensed form and much photographic matter.

ta·boo′, ta·bu′ (tȧ·bōō′), *adj.* [Tongan *tabu;* akin to Maori, Samoan, Tahitian, etc., *tapu* sacred, under restriction, prohibited.] **1.** Set apart or sacred by religious custom, or forbidden to certain persons or uses; of persons, subject to a taboo. **2.** Forbidden by tradition or social usage or other authority. — *n.* **1.** A sacred interdiction laid upon the use of certain things or words or the performance of certain actions, commonly imposed by chiefs or priests, and found among most races of primitive culture. **2.** The system of interdictions based upon the principle of the taboo, most highly developed among the Polynesians. **3.** Similar restriction imposed by social convention. — *v. t.* **1.** To place under taboo. **2.** To debar from use, practice, or intercourse by authority of social or class convention.

ta′bor, ta′bour (tā′bẽr), *n.* [OF. *tabor, tabour* (F. *tambour*), fr. Ar. *ṭunbūr,* colloq. *ṭanbūr,* a drum.] *Music.* A small drum with one head (like a tambourine without jingles) used as an accompaniment to a pipe or fife, both being played by the same person. — *v. i.* To play on a tabor, or little drum; hence, to beat as one beats a tabor. — **ta′bor·er, ta′bour·er,** *n.*

tab′o·ret (tăb′ō·rĕt), **tab′ou·ret** (tăb′ōō-), *n.* [F. *tabouret.*] **1.** *Music.* A small tabor. **2. a** A seat without arms or back, or a stool; also, a small stand of similar form. **b** A light frame for holding material while it is being embroidered.

tab′o·rin′, tab′o·rine′ (tăb′ō·rēn′; tăb′ō·rĕn), *n.* Also **tab′ou·rine′** (-ōō-). [MF. *tabourin.*] A small tabor; a tabret.

tab′ret (tăb′rĕt; -rĭt), *n.* *Music.* A small tabor.

ta·bu′ (tȧ·bōō′). Var. of TABOO.

tab′u·lar (tăb′ū·lẽr), *adj.* [L. *tabularis,* fr. *tabula* a board, table.] Having the form of, or pertaining to, a table; specif.: **a** Having a flat surface. **b** Arranged or entered in a table or tabulated form; as, *tabular* statistics. **c** Derived from, or computed by, the use of tables. — **tab′u·lar·ly,** *adv.*

‖**ta′bu·la ra′sa** (tăb′ū·lȧ rā′sȧ). [L.] A smoothed tablet; hence, the mind before receiving impressions.

tab′u·lar·ize (tăb′ū·lẽr·īz), *v. t.* To tabulate.

tab′u·late (tăb′ū·lāt), *adj.* [L. *tabula* a table.] **1.** Shaped like a table; tabular. **2.** Having transverse septa, as certain corals. — (-lāt), *v. t.* To form into a table, or synopsis; to reduce to a table (senses 5, 6) or tables; as, to *tabulate* statistics. — **tab′u·la′tion** (-lā′shŭn), *n.*

tab′u·la′tor (-lā′tẽr), *n.* One that tabulates; specif., a typewriter attachment for tabulating figures, etc.

tac′a·ma·hac′ (tăk′ȧ·mȧ·hăk′), **tac′a·ma·hac′a** (-hăk′ȧ), *n.* [Sp. *tacamaca, tacamahaca,* fr. obs. Sp. *tecomahaca,* fr. Nahuatl *tecomahiyac,* lit., stinking pot tree.] **1.** An aromatic oleoresin used in ointments, and as incense. **2.** Any tree yielding this oleoresin; specif., the balsam poplar (see POPLAR).

tace (tās). Variant of TASSE.

‖**ta′cet** (tā′sĕt), *v. impers.* [L., it is silent, 3d pers. pres. of *tacere* to be silent.] *Music.* Literally, it is silent; — a direction for a part to be silent through a movement.

tache, tach (tăch), *n.* [OF. *tache* a fastening, nail.] *Archaic.* That by which a thing is attached, as a clasp.

tach′i·na fly (tăk′ĭ·nȧ). [NL. *tachina,* fr. Gr. *tachinos,* for *tachys* swift.] Any of numerous dipterous flies of the genus *Tachina* and allied genera. They are bristly, usually grayish or black flies, active in flight. Their larvae are parasitic, chiefly in caterpillars, and are important in checking the increase of noxious insects.

tach′i·ol (tăk′ĭ·ōl; -ŏl), *n.* Fluoride of silver, used as an antiseptic and disinfectant.

ta·chis′to·scope (tȧ·kĭs′tō·skōp), *n.* [Gr. *tachistos,* superl. of *tachys* swift + *-scope.*] *Psychol.* An apparatus for exposing colors, figures, or other visual stimuli for one fifth of a second or less.

tach′o·graph (tăk′ō·grȧf), *n.* [Gr. *tachos* speed + *-graph.*] A registering tachometer; also, its autographic record (**tach′o·gram** [-grăm]).

ta·chom′e·ter (tȧ·kŏm′ē·tẽr), *n.* [Gr. *tachos* speed + *-meter.*] A speed counter. — **ta·chom′e·try** (-trĭ), *n.*

tachy-. [Gr. *tachys.*] A combining form meaning *quick, swift,* as in *tachy*graphy.

tach′y·graph (tăk′ĭ·grȧf), *n.* An example of tachygraphy; a tachygraphic manuscript; also, a tachygrapher.

ta·chyg′ra·phy (tȧ·kĭg′rȧ·fĭ), *n.* Art or practice of rapid writing; shorthand writing; stenography, esp. that of the ancient Greeks and Romans; also, in paleography, cursive writing or the abbreviated form of Greek and Latin used in the Middle Ages. — **ta·chyg′ra·pher** (-fẽr), **ta·chyg′ra·phist** (-fĭst), *n.* — **tach′y·graph′ic** (tăk′ĭ·grăf′ĭk), **tach′y·graph′i·cal** (-ĭ·kăl), *adj.* — **tach′y·graph′i·cal·ly,** *adv.*

tach′y·lyte (tăk′ĭ·līt), *n.* Also **tach′y·lite.** [*tachy-* + Gr. *lyein* to dissolve.] A basaltic glass, formerly regarded as a mineral. It is decomposable by acids and readily fusible. — **-lyt′ic** (-lĭt′ĭk), *adj.*

ta·chym′e·ter (tȧ·kĭm′ē·tẽr), *n.* **1.** *Surveying.* An instrument, esp. a transit or theodolite, for determining quickly the distances, bearings, and elevations of distant objects. **2.** A speed indicator; tachometer.

ta·chym′e·try (-trĭ), *n.* The science or use of the tachymeter. — **tach′y·met′ric** (tăk′ĭ·mĕt′rĭk), *adj.*

ta·chys′ter·ol (tȧ·kĭs′tẽr·ōl; -ŏl), *n.* [*tachy-* + *sterol.*] *Biochem.* An isomer of ergosterol produced by irradiation, yielding calciferol on further irradiation.

tac′it (tăs′ĭt), *adj.* [F. or L.; F. *tacite,* fr. L. *tacitus,* past part. of *tacere* to be silent, pass over in silence.] **1.** Unspoken; silent; also, not speaking. **2.** Implied or indicated, but not actually expressed; as, *tacit* consent. **3.** *Law.* Arising without express contract or agreement; arising by operation of law. — **tac′it·ly,** *adv.* — **tac′it·ness,** *n.*

tac′i·turn (tăs′ĭ·tûrn), *adj.* [F. or L.; F. *taciturne,* fr. L. *taciturnus.*] Habitually silent; not given to conversation. — **Syn.** See SILENT. — **tac′i·turn·ly,** *adv.*

tac′i·tur′ni·ty (-tûr′nĭ·tĭ), *n.* Habitual reserve in speaking.

tack (tăk), *n.* [ONF. *taque,* OF. *tache,* a fastening, a nail.] **1.** A small, short, sharp-pointed nail, usually having a broad, flat head. **2.** *Naut.* **a** A rope used to hold in place the forward lower corner of a course. **b** A rope used to haul the outer lower corner of a studding sail to the end of the boom. **c** The lower forward corner of a fore-and-aft sail. **d** The corner of a sail to which a tack is fastened, as the weather clew of a square sail. **e** The direction of a vessel in regard to the trim of her sails; as, the starboard *tack,* when she has the wind on her starboard side; or the port *tack,* when the wind is on her port side; hence, the run of a vessel on one tack. **f** A change when close-hauled from the starboard to the port tack or vice versa; an act of tacking. **3.** Hence: **a** A zigzag movement on land. **b** A course or method of action, esp. one sharply divergent from that previously pursued. **4.** A slight sewing with long stitches; basting. — *v. t.* **1.** To fasten or attach by tacks. **2.** To attach or secure in a slight or hasty manner; as, to *tack* or baste together two pieces of cloth. **3.** In parliamentary usage, to add, as a rider, to a bill. **4.** *Naut.* To change the direction of (a vessel) when sailing close-hauled, by putting the helm alee and shifting the sails. — *v. i.* **1.** *Naut.* To tack a vessel; also (of a vessel), to have her direction changed by a tack. **2.** Hence, to pursue a zigzag course; to shift abruptly one's attitude or policy. — **tack′er,** *n.*

tack, *n.* *Scot. & Dial.* A lease; leased land.

tack, *n.* Stuff; — used of food, esp. contemptuously. Cf. HARDTACK.

tack′et (tăk′ĭt), *n.* *Scot. & Dial.* A hobnail.

tack′le (tăk″l; *obsolescent or naut.* tā′k′l), *n.* [ME. *takel,* fr. MLG. (& D.) *takel.*] **1.** Apparatus; equipment; gear; as, writing or fishing *tackle.* **2.** *Naut.* **a** Formerly, equipment for managing a ship. **b** The rigging of a ship. **c** Any purchase (def. 4) where more than one block is used. **3.** An assemblage of ropes and pulleys arranged for hoisting or pulling; — known as a ***single tackle or double tackle*** according to the number of sheaves in the blocks, or as a ***gun tackle*** when, as formerly, used for moving guns, or as a ***luff tackle*** when consisting of a double and a single block with the standing part of the fall attached to the single block. See PULLEY, *Illust.* **4.** Act of tackling, or seizing and holding or stopping, as in football. **5.** *Amer. Football.* One of two players, ***right tackle*** and ***left tackle,*** whose position is between guard and end. — (tăk″l), *v. t.;* -LED (-′ld); -LING (-lĭng). **1.** To secure with tackle; specif., to harness, as a horse. **2.** To seize or grapple, esp. with intent to stop or subdue; *Football,* to seize and stop (an opponent having the ball). **3.** To undertake to do, conquer, carry out, solve, etc., as a hard task. — (tăk″l), *v. i.* *Football.* To tackle an opposing player. — **tack′ler** (tăk′lẽr), *n.*

tack′ling (tăk′lĭng), *n.* *Rare.* Gear; tackle.

tack′y (tăk′ĭ), *adj.;* TACK′I·ER (-ĭ·ẽr); TACK′I·EST. Sticky; — of paint, glue, etc.

tack′y, *adj.* *Colloq., U. S.* Dowdy in appearance; shabby; of a party, made up of guests in ridiculous costume.

tac′ma·hack. Var. of TACAMAHAC.

tac′o·nite (tăk′ō·nīt), *n.* [*Taconic* Mountains, Mass., N. Y., and Vt. + 1st *-ite.*] A flintlike rock high enough in iron content to become commercially valuable as an ore.

tact (tăkt), *n.* [F., fr. L. *tactus* a touching, touch, fr. *tangere, tactum,* to touch.] **1.** *Rare.* The sense of touch; feeling. **2.** Sensitive mental perception; nice discernment of what is appropriate to do or say in dealing with others; peculiar ability to deal with others without giving offense.

Syn. **Tact, address, poise, savoir-faire** mean well-bred skill or grace in behavior. **Tact** implies delicate and sympathetic perception of what is fit or considerate in dealing with others; **address,** dexterity and grace in coping with new or difficult situations or persons; **poise,** self-possession in meeting embarrassing or upsetting situations; **savoir-faire,** a knowledge of the proper thing to say or do or of how to act under all circumstances.

tact′ful (-fŏŏl; -f′l), *adj.* Having or evincing tact (sense 2). — **tact′ful·ly,** *adv.* — **tact′ful·ness,** *n.*

tac′tic (tăk′tĭk), *n.* **a** Tactics. **b** A device or kind of tactics. — *adj.* Of or pert. to arrangement or order.

tac′tic, *adj.* *Biol.* Of, pert. to, or characteristic of taxis.

tac′ti·cal (-tĭ·kăl), *adj.* **1.** Of or pertaining to military or naval tactics. **2.** Skillful, or characterized by skill, in tactics. **3.** *Mil.* Designed or specially assigned to missions on the battlefield in supporting ground forces or units in contact with the enemy; — of bombing or air forces. Cf. STRATEGIC. — **tac′ti·cal·ly,** *adv.*

tac·ti′cian (tăk·tĭsh′ăn), *n.* One versed in tactics; hence, a skillful maneuverer or manager.

tac′tics (tăk′tĭks), *n.;* see -ICS. [Gr. *taktika,* pl., *taktikē* (sc. *technē*), sing., fr. *taktikos* fit for arranging, fr. *tassein, tattein,* to put in order, arrange.] **1.** [*usually construed as sing.*] The science and art of disposing and maneuvering troops or ships in action or in the presence of the enemy. **2.** [*usually construed as pl.*] Hence, any method of procedure; esp., adroit devices for accomplishing an end.

tac′tile (tăk′tĭl; *see* -ILE), *adj.* [L. *tactilis* tangible, fr. *tangere, tactum,* to touch.] **1.** Perceptible by the touch; tangible; as, *tactile* qualities. **2.** Of or pertaining or relating to the sense of touch. — **tac·til′i·ty** (tăk·tĭl′ĭ·tĭ), *n.*

tac′tion (tăk′shŭn), *n.* [L. *tactio.*] Touch; contact.

tact′less (tăkt′lĕs; -lĭs), *adj.* Having or showing no tact. — **tact′less·ly,** *adv.* — **tact′less·ness,** *n.*

tac′tu·al (tăk′tū·ăl), *adj.* Of or pertaining to the sense, or the organs, of touch; derived from, or producing the sensation of, touch; as, a *tactual* sense. — **tac′tu·al·ly,** *adv.*

tad (tăd), *n.* *U. S.* A small child.

Ta·djik′ (tä·jĭk′; -jēk′). Var. of TAJIK.

tad′pole′ (tăd′pōl′), *n.* [ME. *tadde, tade,* toad + *poll;* prob., a toad that is all head.] An aquatic, water-breathing, immature or larval amphibian with gills and a long tail, esp. one of the frogs and toads (Salientia) including the frogs and toads. The change to the adult form in frogs and toads is a rapid metamorphosis with loss of the gills, absorption of the tail, and many internal changes.

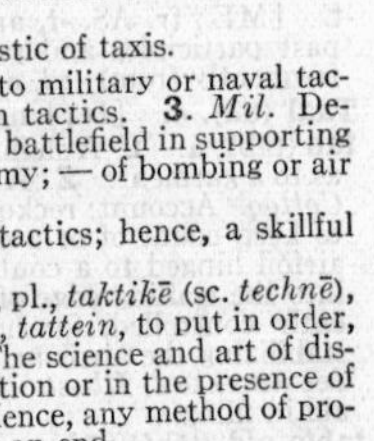
Tadpole of Frog in later stages of development.

tae (tā). *Scot.* To.

‖**tae′di·um vi′tae** (tē′dĭ·ŭm vī′tē). [L.] Weariness or loathing of life.

tael (tāl), *n.* [Pg., fr. Malay *tahil.*] **1.** A weight of Eastern Asia varying according to the locality; esp., the liang of China. **2.** A Chinese money of account, the value of a tael of silver. Formerly the haikwan tael (customs unit) was the basis for reckoning the value of other taels, but it is now officially superseded by the silver dollar (see YUAN).

ta′en (tān). Short for TAKEN.

tae′ni·a (tē′nĭ·ȧ), *n.; pl.* TAENIAE (-ē). Also **te′ni·a.** [L., fillet, tapeworm, fr. Gr. *tainia.*] **1.** *Gr. Antiq.* A headband; fillet. **2.** *Arch.* The fillet, or band, at the bottom of a Doric frieze, separating it from the architrave. Cf. ORDER, *Illust.* **3.** *Anat.* A band, esp. of nervous matter or muscle. **4.** A tapeworm.

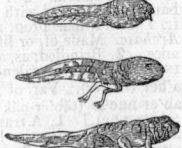

tae′ni·a·cide′ (tē′nĭ·*ȧ*·sīd′), *n.* Also **te′ni·a·cide′**. [*taenia* + *-cide.*] *Med.* A substance, esp. a remedy, destroying tapeworms. — **tae′ni·a·cid′al, te′ni·a·cid′al** (-sīd′ăl; -′l), *adj.*

tae′ni·a·fuge′ (-fūj′), *n.* Also **te′ni·a·fuge′**. [*taenia* + L. *fugare* to drive away.] A remedy to expel tapeworms.

tae·ni′a·sis (tē·nī′*ȧ*·sĭs), *n.* Also **te·ni′a·sis**. [NL., fr. *taenia.*] The condition characterized by the presence of taeniae, or tapeworms.

taf′fa·rel (tăf′*ȧ*·rĕl), **taf′fer·el** (tăf′ẽr-). Vars. of TAFFRAIL.

taf′fe·ta (tăf′ĕ·t*ȧ*), *n.* [OF. *taffetas*, fr. ML. *taffeta*, fr. Per. *tāftah*, orig., twisted, woven.] A fine, smooth, glossy silk or rayon fabric; loosely, any similar silk, rayon, or linen goods. — *adj.* Of or like taffeta; hence: **a** Excessively ornate; florid. **b** Dainty; delicate.

taff′rail (tăf′rāl; -rĭl), *n.* [From earlier *tafferel*, fr. D. *tafereel* a panel, picture, fr. *tafel* table, fr. L. *tabula*. In English confused with *rail.*] *Naut.* **a** *Rare.* The upper part of a ship's stern. **b** Rail around a ship's stern.

taf′fy (tăf′ĭ), *n.* [E. dial., also *toffee.*] **1.** A pulled candy made usually of molasses or brown sugar boiled down, often with butter. **2.** *Colloq.* Flattery; cajolery.

taf′i·a, taf′fi·a (tăf′ĭ·*ȧ*), *n.* [Creole.] A spirit obtained from distilled sugar-cane juice in the West Indies.

tag (tăg), *n.* **1.** A loose end, rag, or tatter, originally one of the flaps formed by slashing the skirt of a garment. **2.** Hence, a flap, tab, strip, or the like; as, to attach a *tag* to a trunk; specif.: **a** A large dungy lock of wool. **b** A stray lock of hair. **c** An added flourish made with the pen. **d** An insignificant remnant. **e** A loop by which a garment is hung or a boot pulled on. **3.** In angling, a small piece of tinsel or the like around the shank of the hook at the end of the body of an artificial fly. See FLY, *Illust.* **4.** A metallic binding, tube, or point, at the end of a string or lace to stiffen it, as for passing through an eyelet. **5.** A familiar saying or quotation added, as to a play, a book, a song, etc., for effect. **6.** The end, or catchword, of an actor's speech; cue. **7.** The rabble; — used in the phrases **tag and rag, and tag, rag, and bobtail.** — *v. t.*; TAGGED (tăgd); TAG′GING. **1.** To fit with a tag or tags; to append a tag or tags to. **2.** To attach a card or label to, as to a package. **3.** *Colloq.* To follow closely after; to dog. — *v. i. Colloq.* To follow closely, as if an appendage; as, to *tag* after a person.

tag, *n.* [Cf. TAG, *v.*, TAG an end.] A children's game in which one, called "it," chases others until he touches, or tags, a player, who in turn becomes "it." — *v. t.* To touch in or as if in this game.

Ta·ga′la (tä·gä′lä), *n.* = TAGALOG, 1. — *adj.* Designating, or pertaining to, a branch of the Austronesian languages including the Philippine idioms as a chief group. See LANGUAGE, *Table.*

Ta·ga′log (tä·gä′lŏg), *n.* Also **Ta·gal′** (tä·gäl′). **1.** One of a Malayan race, mainly of central Luzon, next to the Visayans the most numerous of the native peoples of the Philippines. **2.** The language of the Tagalogs, one of the most developed of the Austronesian languages.

tag day. A day on which contributions to some fund are publicly solicited, a tag being given to each contributor.

tag′ger (tăg′ẽr), *n.* **1.** One who tags. **2.** In form **tag′gers** (tăg′ẽrz). *Metalworking.* Very thin sheet metal, as thin tin plate.

Ta·hi′ti·an (t*ȧ*·hē′tĭ·ăn), *adj.* Of or pert. to Tahiti, its inhabitants, or their language. — *n.* One of the native Polynesians of Tahiti, a people noted for fine physique and intelligence; also, their language.

tah·sil′dar′ (t*ȧ*·sēl′där′), *n.* Also **tah·seel′dar′**. [Hind. & Per. *tahṣīldār*, fr. Ar. *taḥṣīl* gain, collection + Per. *dār* holder.] *India.* A revenue officer or tax collector, who is sometimes a magistrate.

Tai (tī). Var. of THAI.

tai′ga (tī′g*ȧ*), *n.* [Russ.] **a** The swampy, coniferous forests of Siberia between tundra and steppe. **b** *Ecol.* Any similar boreal forest.

tail (tāl), *n.* [AS. *tægel, tægl.*] **1.** The rear end, or a process or prolongation of the rear end, of the body of an animal. See HORSE, POULTRY, *Illusts.* **2.** Formerly, in Turkey, a horsetail (which see) as a mark of rank. **3.** Any long, flexible terminal appendage; an appendage resembling, in shape or position, the tail of an animal; as, the *tail* of a coat, dress, kite, letter, etc. **4.** The luminous train of a comet. **5.** The back, last, lower, or inferior part of anything; end; rear. **6.** Specif.: **a** *Often pl.* The side of a coin opposite to that bearing the head, effigy, or date; the reverse. **b** The part of a millrace below, or downstream from, the wheel. **7.** A relatively long line or series; specif.: **a** A long braid or tress, as a cue or switch. **b** A line of persons waiting; a cue. **c** A retinue. **8.** *pl. Colloq.* A swallow-tailed coat; also, full dress. **9.** *Aeronautics.* The rear part of an aircraft, in an airplane usually consisting of a group of stabilizing planes, or fins, to which are attached certain controlling instruments, as elevators and rudders. See AIRPLANE, *Illust.* **10.** *Print. & Bookbinding.* The bottom of a page. **11.** *Prosody.* A group of lines, often four, added to a sonnet; a coda. — *v. t.* **1.** To make or furnish with a tail; also, to follow, or be drawn behind, like a tail. **2.** To fasten by or at the tail or stern; as, to *tail* a ship to a dock; to connect by adding at the end. **3.** *Slang.* To follow and watch the movements of stealthily; to shadow. **4.** *Arch.* To fasten by one of the ends into a wall or other support; — with *in* or *on;* as, to *tail* in a timber. — *v. i.* **1.** To form a tail, train, or the like; to extend in a taillike line. **2.** *Colloq.* To follow close behind; to tag. **3.** To grow gradually smaller, fainter, or more scattered, so as to leave but a trace; as, her words would *tail* off into a murmur. **4.** *Arch.* To hold by the end; — said of a timber when its end is built into a support. **5.** *Naut.* To swing, or lie, with the stern in a certain direction, as downstream or against the wind; — said of a vessel at anchor. — *adj.* **1.** Hindmost. **2.** Coming from the rear; as, a *tail* wind. — **tail′less,** *adj.*

tail (tāl), *adj.* [OF. *taillié*, past part. of *taillier* to cut, also to decide, fix, settle.] *Law.* Limited; abridged; reduced; curtailed; entailed; as, an estate or fee *tail* (see FEE). — *n. Law.* Limitation; abridgment; entail.

tail beam. *Arch.* = TAILPIECE, 3. See HEADER, *Illust.*

tail′board′ (tāl′bōrd′; 70), *n.* The board at the rear end of a cart or wagon, which can be removed or let down.

tail′first′ (-fûrst′; 2), **tail′fore′most** (-fōr′mōst; -m*ŭ*st), *adv.* With the hinder part foremost; backwards.

tail′ing, *n.* **1.** *pl.* Refuse material separated as residue in the preparation of various products, as in milling grain or treating ores. **2.** *Arch.* The part of a projecting stone or brick inserted in a wall.

tail lamp. Also **tail′light′** (tāl′līt′), *n.* A lamp or light at the rear end of a vehicle, esp. an automobile.

taille (tāl; *F.* tä′y′), *n.* [OF. & F., fr. OF. *taillier* to cut.] *Fr. Hist.* A tax levied by the king, or a seigneur, on his subjects or on lands held of or under him.

tail′less air′plane′ (tāl′lĕs; -lĭs). An airplane consisting of a single wing, without conventional fuselage or tail.

tai′lor (tā′lẽr), *n.* [OF. *tailleor*, fr. F. *taillier* to cut, fr. L. *talea* rod, stick, cutting.] One whose occupation is to make men's or women's outer garments. — *v. i.* To follow the business of a tailor. — *v. t.* **1.** To make or fashion as the work of a tailor; as, a *tailored* suit. **2.** To make clothes for or fit clothes to; as, a faultlessly *tailored* man. **3.** To cut and fashion so as to suit a particular application, as armor plate to a tank or a play to an audience. **4.** To construct, produce, or modify so as to be suitable in qualifications; as, an architect *tailors* houses to the habits of the occupants. **5.** To fit or style (women's garments or items of interior décor) with trim, straight lines and finished handwork like that of a tailor's work on men's garments; — usually in the past participle *tailored;* as, a *tailored* shirtwaist or curtain.

tai′lor·bird′ (-bûrd′), *n.* Any of numerous Asiatic, East Indian, and African birds of the warbler group (esp. genus *Sutoria*) which stitch leaves together to hide their nests.

tai′lored (tā′lẽrd), *adj.* Cut and fitted by a tailor or as if by a tailor: **a** Custom-made. **b** Characteristic of a tailor's work; as, the *tailored* look of the hangings.

tai′lor·ing, *n.* Occupation of a tailor; work or workmanship of a tailor.

tai′lor-made′ (tā′lẽr·mād′; 2), *adj.* **1.** Fitted by a tailor or according to a tailor's fashion; tailored (cf. TAILOR, *v. t.*, 3, 4, and 5); specially made to order; as, *tailor-made* fuels; scores *tailor-made* for radio. **2.** *Colloq.* (Of a cigarette) factory-made, not hand-rolled. — *n. Colloq.* A factory-made cigarette.

tail′piece′ (tāl′pēs′), *n.* **1.** A piece added on at the end; an appendage. **2.** A triangular piece, as of ebony, fixed to the lower end of a violin or the like, to which the strings are fastened. See VIOLIN, *Illust.* **3.** *Arch.* A relatively shorter beam or rafter tailed in a wall and supported by a header. See HEADER, *Illust.* **4.** *Print.* An ornament at the bottom of a page or at the end of a chapter.

tail plane. *Aeronaut.* = STABILIZER, 2 **b**.

tail′race′ (tāl′rās′), *n.* **1.** A lower millrace. **2.** The channel into which the water from a water wheel or turbine is discharged. **3.** *Mining.* The channel in which tailings, in water, are carried off.

tail spin. *Aviation.* Same as SPIN, *n.*, 2; — a misnomer.

tail′stock′ (tāl′stŏk′), *n.* *Mach.* The adjustable or sliding head of a lathe, containing the dead center. Cf. HEADSTOCK.

tail wind. *Aeronautics.* A wind having the same general direction as the course of an airplane or a ship in motion.

tain (tān), *n.* [ME. *tein, teyne.*] Thin tin plate; also, tin foil for mirrors.

Tai′no (tī′nō), *n.* **a** An Indian of the extinct aborigines of the Greater Antilles and the Bahamas. **b** The language of the Tainos.

taint (tānt), *v. t.* [Partly fr. ATTAINT, *v.*, and partly fr. F. *teint*, past part. of *teindre* to dye, tinge, fr. L. *tingere, tinctum.*] **1.** *Obs.* To color; tinge. **2.** *Obs.* To affect so as to injure with or as with disease; to impair; to sully (one's honor). **3.** To imbue or impregnate with something odious, noxious, or poisonous; hence, to infect; poison. **4.** To affect with corrupting influence; to contaminate; corrupt. — *v. i.* To be or become imbued with something noxious; to be infected or corrupted. — **Syn.** See CONTAMINATE. — *n.* **1.** *Obs.* Tincture; tinge. **2.** A spot or stain; hence, a trace of some bad quality; esp., a blemish; a stain of disgrace. **3.** An infectious or corrupting tinge or trace; a contaminating influence. — **taint′less,** *adj.*

Tai′ping′ (tī′pĭng′), *adj.* [Chin. (Pek.) *t'ai⁴-p'ing²*, lit., great peace.] *Chinese Hist.* Pertaining to or designating a dynasty which Hung Hsiu Ch'üan, a religious enthusiast, attempted to substitute for the Manchu dynasty by the **Taiping rebellion** (1848–1865).

Tai′sho (tī′shō), *n.* The chronological name of the years (1912–26) of the reign of Yoshihito, emperor of Japan.

Ta·jik′ (tä·jĭk′; -jēk′), *n., sing. & pl.* Also **Ta·djik′**. One of a people of old Iranian blood, now living in and near the Tadzhik republic.

Taj Ma·hal′ (täj m*ȧ*·häl′). [Corrupt. of Per. *Mumtāz-i-Mahall*, lit., the distinguished one of the palace (title of the wife of Shah Jahan).] A marble mausoleum built (1631–45) at Agra, India, by the Mogul Emperor Shah Jahan, in memory of his favorite wife.

take (tāk), *v. t.*; TOOK (tŏŏk); TAK′EN (tāk′ĕn); TAK′ING. [AS. (late) *tacan*, fr. ON. *taka* (pret. *tōk*).] **1.** To lay or get hold of; to grip; grasp. **2.** To get possession or control of; specif.: **a** To seize or capture. **b** To catch by trapping, snaring, etc. **c** To secure by winning in competition, as a prize. **d** In many games, as chess, tennis, cards, etc., to capture, win, or secure; as, rook *takes* pawn. **e** To obtain by leasing, renting, etc. **f** To buy; as, I will *take* this coat. **3.** To catch or attack through the effect of a sudden force or influence; specif.: **a** To seize and affect; — of a disease, emotion, etc.; as, he was *taken* with a fit. **b** To catch or come upon (one) in a particular situation; as, to *take* one in the act. **c** To capture the fancy of; to charm or delight. **d** To cast a spell on. **4.** To derive; as, to *take* a name from a person or thing; specif.: **a** To extract and use; as, to *take* a line from Shakespeare. **b** To infer; deduce; as, arguments *taken* from false premises. **5.** To remove or abstract; as: **a** To subtract; as, to *take* two from four. **b** To remove from life; to cause to die; as, he was *taken* in the prime of life. **6.** To ascertain by inquiry, examination, etc.; as, to *take* a census; also, to measure or observe; as, to *take* the height of the sun. **7.** To pick out; to select or choose. **8.** To indulge in and enjoy; as, to *take* one's ease. **9.** To avail oneself of for use; specif.: **a** To employ; to use as a means of transportation; as, to *take* ship. **b** To have recourse to, for safety or refuge. **c** To proceed to occupy; as, to *take* a chair. **d** To consider in a certain relation; as, *taking* one poet with another. **e** To use, consume, or occupy; as, to *take* little room. **f** Hence, to require; need; as, it *takes* time. **10.** To adopt or lay hold of for oneself; specif.: **a** To assume (a property or attribute); as, a word *takes* a new meaning. **b** To absorb or become impregnated with or affected by; as, cloth *takes* a dye. **c** To catch or contract (a disease, etc.). **d** To assume (a task, duty); as, to *take* charge or office. **e** To adopt as one's point of argument or defense; as, a point well *taken*. **f** To assume (anything denoting an office or function); as, to *take* the veil. **g** *Gram.* To admit of; to be formed or used with; as, to *take* an accent or ending. **11.** To bring or receive (one) into a relation or connection; as, to *take* a wife. **12.** To introduce or receive into one's body; as, to *take* food. **13.** To receive or accept; as, to *take* a wager; to *take* advice. **14.** To submit to; undergo; as, to *take* punishment. **15.** To comprehend; understand. **16.** Hence: To understand to mean; as, to *take* a remark in the right sense. **17.** To convey or carry; to conduct or lead; — the opposite of *bring;* as, they *took* a plentiful lunch with them but brought most of it back. **18.** To begin to feel or experience; as, to *take* offense. **19.** To undertake and make, do, or perform; as, to *take* a walk; to *take* a resolution. **20.** To write down (notes, a record, etc.); to record (a speech), sometimes in shorthand. **21.** To draw or paint (a picture); to represent or portray in any artistic form (a figure, scene, etc.); to photograph. **22.** *Colloq.* To direct and make a specified motion such as a blow; as, to *take* a shot, swing, etc., at someone or something. — *v. i.* **1.** To lay hold; to take root or begin to grow, as a seed or shoot; to unite successfully, as a bud or graft in plant propagation or a surgical graft. **2.** To obtain possession; to capture. **3.** To take effect; operate; act. **4.** To charm; specif.: **a** *Obs.* To exert a spell. **b** *Colloq.* To win popular favor; as, a book *takes* well. **5.** To be, or admit of being, taken, in any sense; specif.: **a** *Dial.* To be seized or attacked so as to become; as, to *take* sick. **b** To be capable of being taken or moved in a specified way; as, the device *takes* to pieces. **c** To adhere or be absorbed; as, ink that *takes* well on cloth. **d** *Colloq.* To admit of being photographed; as, he *takes* well. **6.** To detract; as, it *takes* greatly from the pleasure. **7.** To betake oneself; to proceed; as, to *take* to the boats. **8.** *Law.* To receive property as one's own; as, he *takes* as heir.

Syn. (1) **Take, seize, grasp, clutch, snatch, grab** mean to get hold of as if by the arms, hands, or tentacles. **Take**, the most colorless term, may imply any one of several movements or operations in getting something into one's possession or power; **seize** implies a sudden and forcible movement in getting hold of something tangible, or a catching of something elusive or fleeting when intangible; **grasp**, a laying hold of with or as if with hands or claws so as to have it firmly in one's possession; **clutch**, more rush, more avidity, and often less success in holding; **snatch**, more suddenness but less force than *seize;* **grab**, more rudeness or roughness than *snatch.* (2) See RECEIVE.

take after. To resemble in features, build, etc. — ***take amiss.*** Orig., to mistake; hence, to impute a wrong motive or bad meaning to; to take offense at. — ***take breath.*** To stop, as from labor, in order to rest. — ***take down.*** To bring down; specif.: **a** To pull to pieces. **b** To take apart. **c** To humble. **d** To write down. — ***take heart.*** To gain confidence or courage. — ***take in.*** **a** To admit; receive. **b** To draw into a smaller compass; to brail or furl; as, to *take in* sail. **c** To comprise; comprehend. **d** To cheat; deceive. — ***take in vain.*** To use (a name) lightly or profanely. *Ex.* xx. 7. — ***take off.*** **a** To remove. **b** To deduct, as discount. **c** To take the life of. **d** To reproduce from some original; as, to *take off* another hundred copies. **e** *Colloq.* To mimic or burlesque. **f** To prepare; as, to *take off* a trial balance. **g** Of an airplane or bird, to leave the surface of the land or water; to begin flight. — ***take on.*** **a** To assume, as an appearance, quality, or function. **b** To undertake or tackle, as a new job or an opponent. **c** To engage or hire, as more hands. **d** *Colloq.* To show one's feelings demonstratively. **e** To behave haughtily; to put on airs. — ***take place.*** To happen; occur. — ***take stock.*** To take account of stock; to inventory. — ***take the field.*** **a** To go upon the playing field, as a football team. **b** *Mil.* To enter upon a campaign. — ***take the floor.*** To rise to make a more or less formal address, motion, or the like. — ***take to.*** **a** To care for; to become attached to. **b** To betake oneself to. — ***take to heart.*** To be deeply affected by. — ***take to task.*** To call to account for some shortcoming; to reprove. — ***take up.*** **a** To lift; raise; to pick up. **b** To begin; enter upon; specif., to resume, or resume a discourse, where another left off. **c** To employ; to occupy or fill. **d** To seize or arrest. **e** To reprimand. **f** To pay the amount of, as a note or loan. **g** To remove, as by adjustment of parts; as, to *take up* lost motion, as in a machine bearing. — ***take up the gauntlet** or **glove.*** To accept a challenge. — ***take up with.*** *Colloq.* To begin to associate with, esp. in courtship.

— *n.* The action of taking or that which is taken; specif.: **a** A portion of a scene filmed or televised at one time without stopping the camera; also, the taking of such a scene. **b** A trial recording.

take'down' (tāk'doun'), *adj.* Constructed so as to be readily taken apart; as, a *takedown* rifle. — *n.* Act of taking down; specif.: **a** *Colloq.* A humiliating. **b** Disassembly, as of an engine.

take'-home' pay *or* **wage.** Also **take'-home'**, *n.* The remainder of a person's gross salary or wages after deduction of such items as withholding tax, retirement insurance payments, and union dues.

take'-in', *n.* *Colloq.* An act of taking in, esp. of cheating.

take'-off', *n.* **1.** An action of taking off; specif.: **a** *Colloq.* An imitation, esp. in the way of caricature. **b** A rise or leap, esp. from the ground, in making a jump or flight. **2.** Spot at which one takes off.

tak'er (tāk'ẽr), *n.* One who takes; as: **a** A captor. **b** A thief. **c** One who accepts a bet. **d** One who collects, as tickets.

take'-up', *n.* **1.** The action of taking up or tightening. **2.** *Mach.* That which takes up or tightens.

tak'ing (tāk'ĭng), *n.* **1.** Act of one who or that which takes. **2.** *Colloq.* Agitation and distress. **3.** That which is taken or received; specif.: **a** *pl.* Receipts, esp. of money. **b** A catch or take, as of fish. — *adj.* **1.** Apt to take the fancy; captivating. **2.** *Colloq.* Infectious; contagious; catching.

tal'a·poin (tăl'á·poin), *n.* [Pg. *talapões*, pl. of *talapão*, fr. Burmese *tala poi* our lord.] **1.** *Indo-China.* A Buddhist monk. **2.** (*F. pron.* tȧ'lȧ'pwăɴ') [F.; — from some resemblance.] A West African guenon monkey (*Cercopithecus talapoin*), the smallest of the guenons.

tal'a·ri (tăl'á·rĭ), *n.* [Ar. *ṭalari*, fr. G. *t(h)aler.*] A silver coin of Ethiopia, equivalent to the Maria Theresa dollar; — now officially called the *thaler.*

ta·la'ri·a (tȧ·lā'rĭ·ȧ; 6), *n. pl.* [L., fr. *talaris* pertaining to the ankles, fr. *talus* ankle.] *Roman Myth.* Winged shoes fastened to the ankles.

talc (tălk), *n.* [F., fr. ML. *talcum*, fr. Ar. *ṭalq*, fr. Per. *talk.*] *Mineral.* A soft mineral of a soapy feel, in composition an acid magnesium metasilicate, $H_2Mg_3(SiO_3)_4$. Sp. gr., 2.6–2.9. H., 1 (for foliated talc). *Soapstone* and *French chalk* are varieties of talc. Other kinds are used in making soap, paper, lubricants, toilet powder, etc., or as inert pigment. — *v. t.;* TALCKED, TALCED (tălkt); TALCK'ING, TALC'ING (tăl'kĭng). To rub or treat with talc, as a photographic plate.

talc'ose (tăl'kōs; tăl·kōs'), **talc'ous** (tăl'kŭs), *adj.* Pertaining to or containing talc.

tal'cum pow'der (tăl'kŭm). **1.** Powdered talc. **2.** A toilet powder of perfumed talc, or perfumed talc and some mild antiseptic.

tale (tāl), *n.* [AS. *talu* speech, narrative.] **1.** *Obs.* Speech; talk. **2.** That which is told; an oral relation or recital. **3.** Hence, an account of some event or sequence of events, actual, legendary, or fictitious; narrative; story. **4.** An intentionally untrue recital; also, falsehood. **5.** A libelous report or piece of evil gossip. **6.** *Archaic & Poetic.* A reckoning by numbers; a count; enumeration. **7.** A sum; as, the yearly *tale* of plays at court.

tale'bear'er (-bâr'ẽr), *n.* Also **tale'car'ri·er** (-kăr'ĭ·ẽr), **tale'mon'ger** (-mŭng'gẽr). One who spreads gossip, etc. — **tale'bear'ing**, *adj. & n.*

tal'ent (tăl'ĕnt), *n.* [OF., fr. L. *talentum* a talent (sense 1), fr. Gr. *talanton* a balance, thing weighed, talent.] **1.** An ancient weight and money unit. The talent contained 60 minas of 60 or 50 shekels each, but its estimated money value varied greatly according to time and place. With the Hebrew gold shekel of 252⅔ grains valued at $10.88, a Hebrew gold talent would be equivalent to $32,640; a silver talent (1/15 of the gold) would be worth $2176. As a weight, the Attic talent was about 57.85 lb. av. (26.26 kg.). **2.** *Obs.* Disposition, esp. to do someone harm. **3.** *sing. & pl.* The abilities, powers, and gifts bestowed upon a man; natural endowments; — thought of as a divine trust. Cf. *Matthew* xxv. 14–30. **4.** Pre-eminent aptitude; superior intelligence and ability, as for business or artistic pursuits; — often distinguished from *genius.* **5.** A natural capacity or gift; as, musical *talent.* **6.** Collectively, persons of ability or skill; as, he engaged the best *talent* to sing. **7.** *Racing Slang.* Habitual betters, or takers of odds, on horses; — disting. from the bookmakers. — **Syn.** See GIFT.

tal'ent·ed, *adj.* Having talent; mentally gifted.

ta'ler (tä'lẽr), *n. sing. & pl.* Also **tha'ler** (tä'-). [G. *taler.* See DOLLAR.] An old German silver coin, made legal tender (1873–1920) at three marks (71.4 cents).

ta'les (tā'lēz), *n. pl.* [From the first word in the phrase *tales de circumstantibus*, such of the bystanders, in the Latin writ for summoning them, pl. of L. *talis* such (persons).] *Law.* **a** Persons added to a jury to make up any deficiency in the available number of jurors regularly summoned. **b** [*Construed as a singular.*] The writ for summoning them.

tales'man (tālz'măn; tā'lēz-), *n.* *Law.* A person summoned as one of the tales added to a jury.

tale'tell'er (tāl'tĕl'ẽr), *n.* One who tells tales or stories; esp., a talebearer. — **tale'tell'ing**, *adj. & n.*

tal'i·grade (tăl'ĭ·grād), *adj.* [L. *talus* ankle + *-grade.*] Bearing the weight on the outer side of the foot in walking.

tal'i·ped (tăl'ĭ·pĕd), *adj.* *Surg. & Zool.* Affected with talipes; clubfooted. — *n.* A clubfooted person.

tal'i·pes (-pēz), *n.* [NL., fr. L. *talus* an ankle + *pes, pedis*, a foot.] *Surg.* The deformity commonly called *clubfoot.* Two varieties are **talipes val'gus** (văl'gŭs), in which the foot is bent outward, often called simply *valgus*, and **talipes va'rus** (vā'rŭs), in which the foot is bent inward, often called simply *varus.*

tal'i·pot (-pŏt), *n., or* **talipot palm.** [Bengali *tālipāt* palm leaf, fr. Skr. *tālī* fan palm, talipot + *pattra* leaf.] A handsome fan palm (*Corypha umbraculifera*) of Ceylon and the Malabar coast. Its leaves are used as umbrellas and as fans and, cut into strips, as a substitute for writing paper.

tal'is·man (tăl'ĭs·măn; tăl'ĭz-), *n.; pl.* -MANS (-mănz). [F., through Sp. & It. fr. Ar. *ṭilasm, ṭilsam*, fr. Gr. *telesma* payment, completion, LGr., an initiation, incantation, fr. *telein* to complete, initiate.] **1.** A figure cut or engraved under certain superstitious observances of the heavens, supposed to act as a charm. **2.** Hence, something that produces extraordinary effects, esp. in averting evil; an amulet; charm. — **Syn.** See FETISH. — **tal'is·man'ic** (-măn'ĭk), **tal'is·man'i·cal** (-ĭ·kăl), *adj.*

talk (tôk), *v. i.* [ME. *talken.*] **1.** To express or exchange ideas by means of spoken words; to speak; converse. **2.** To communicate by any means; as, to *talk* by signs. **3.** To chatter or prate. **4.** To gossip. **5.** To confer; consult. **6.** To make sounds suggesting speech. — **Syn.** See SPEAK. — *v. t.* **1.** To deliver or express in speech; to utter. **2.** To discourse about; discuss; as, to *talk* business. **3.** To use, as a foreign tongue, for conversing; to speak; as, to *talk* French. **4.** To influence, as to induce or dissuade, or to affect by talking; as, to *talk* one into believing. — *n.* **1.** Act of talking; speech; esp., conversation. **2.** Hence, a conference or council. **3.** Report; rumor; gossip. **4.** Subject of discourse; a theme for conversation. **5.** Empty verbiage. **6.** *Colloq.* A dialect, tongue, or style of speech.

talk'a·tive (tôk'á·tĭv), *adj.* Given to talking; loquacious. — **talk'a·tive·ly**, *adv.* — **talk'a·tive·ness**, *n.*

Syn. **Talkative, loquacious, garrulous, voluble** mean given to talk or talking. **Talkative** may imply nothing more than a readiness to engage in talk, or an ease and fluency in talking, or a disposition to enjoy conversation; **loquacious**, the power of expressing oneself articulately, fluently, or glibly; **garrulous**, prosy, rambling, or tedious loquacity; **voluble**, a free, easy, and unending loquacity. — **Ant.** Silent.

talk'er (tôk'ẽr), *n.* A person who talks or is talkative.

talk'ie (tôk'ĭ), *n.* Also **talk film, talking film.** *Colloq.* A sound motion picture.

talk'ing (tôk'ĭng), *n.* Act of one who talks; discourse. — *adj.* That talks; esp., given to talking; talkative.

talking machine. A phonograph.

talking motion picture. = SOUND MOTION PICTURE.

talk'ing-to' (tôk'ĭng·tōō'), *n.* A reprimand or admonition.

tall (tôl), *adj.* [ME. *tal*, prob. fr. AS. *getæl* quick, ready, active.] **1.** *Archaic.* Comely; fine; excellent. **2.** *Archaic.* Brave; courageous. **3.** High in stature; high and slender; lofty. **4.** Of a specified height; as, a man six feet *tall.* **5.** **a** *Now Slang.* Grand; large; as, a *tall* order. **b** *Colloq.* Grandiloquent; as, *tall* talk. **c** *Colloq.* Unusual; incredible; as, *tall* stories. — **Syn.** See HIGH. — **Ant.** Short. — **tall'ish**, *adj.* — **tall'ness**, *n.*

tal'lage (tăl'ĭj), *n.* [OF. *taillage*, fr. *tailler*, v.] *Eng. Feudal Law.* A toll, fee, or render paid by a tenant to his lord; hence, a tax levied by a lord upon his tenants. — *v. t.* To tax.

tall'boy' (tôl'boi'), *n.* **1.** *Eng.* A highboy. **2.** A long sheet-metal pipe for a chimney top.

tall buttercup. See CROWFOOT, 1.

tall fescue. See MEADOW FESCUE.

tal'lith (tăl'ĭth; tăl'ĭs), *n.* [Late Heb. *ṭallīth* cover, sheet, cloak.] *Jewish Costume.* **a** An undergarment worn by orthodox Jews, over the chest and upper part of the back. **b** A tasseled shawl or scarf worn over the head or shoulders by men, usually during morning prayer.

tall oil (täl), *or* **tall'oel** (täl'ûl), *n.* [Partial trans. of G. *tallöl*, itself a partial trans. of Sw. *tallolja* pine oil.] A resinous by-product from the manufacture of chemical wood pulp. It is sometimes used in making soaps, etc.

tal'low (tăl'ō), *n.* [ME. *talgh*, fr. or akin to obs. D. *talgh*, MD. & MLG. *talch.*] The fat of animals of the ox and sheep kinds (***beef*** and ***mutton tallow*** respectively), extracted by melting and used in soap and candles, in oleomargarine, etc. — *v. t.* To grease or smear with tallow. — *adj.* Of tallow; dealing in tallow; as, a *tallow* chandler. — **tal′low·y** (tăl′ō·ĭ), *adj.*

tal′ly (tăl′ĭ), *n.; pl.* -LIES (-ĭz). [AF. *tallie,* fr. Anglo-Lat. *talia,* fr. L. *talea* a stick.] **1.** Formerly, a piece of wood (**tally stick**) on which notches were cut as marks of number, esp. a piece split lengthwise through the notches so that the parts exactly corresponded, the seller keeping one stick, and the purchaser the other. **2.** Any account or score kept by notches or marks; later, one of two books, sheets of paper, etc., on which accounts were kept correspondingly or in duplicate. **3. a** A notch, mark, or score made on or in a tally. **b** A reckoning, account or score. **4.** A mark connecting a group in counting, as a diagonal line through four vertical lines, made for each fifth count; hence, a number used as a unit of computation. **5.** A label, tag, or the like, with marks of identification. **6.** A counterpart; match. — *v. t.;* TAL′LIED (-ĭd); TAL′LY·ING. **1.** To register on or as on a tally; as, to *tally* six points in a game. **2.** To estimate; count; — esp. with *up.* **3.** To score with correspondent notches; hence, to make to correspond; to cause to agree. — *v. i.* **1.** To make a tally; to score. **2.** To be fitted; to correspond; match; as, his story *tallied* with mine. — **tal′li·er** (-ĭ·ẽr), *n.*

tal′ly·ho′ (tăl′ĭ·hō′; 2), *interj.* A huntsman's halloo at sight of the fox.

tal′ly·ho′ (tăl′ĭ·hō′), *n.* **1.** A calling of "Tallyho." **2.** A type of four-in-hand pleasure coach.

Tal′mud (tăl′mŭd), *n.* [Heb. *talmūdh* instruction, fr. *lāmadh* to learn.] The body of Jewish civil and canonical law, consisting of the combined Mishnah, or text, and Gemara, or commentary; also, restrictedly, the Gemara alone. — **Tal·mud′ic** (tăl·mŭd′ĭk), **Tal·mud′i·cal** (-ĭ·kăl), *adj.* — **Tal′mud·ist,** *n.*

tal′on (tăl′ŭn), *n.* [OF. *talon* heel, spur, fr. L. *talus* the ankle, heel.] **1.** The claw of an animal; esp., the claw of a bird of prey (see RAPTORIAL, *Illust.*); — chiefly *pl.;* hence, *pl.,* grasping human fingers or hands. **2.** *Arch.* An ogee molding. **3.** *Card Playing.* The stock. See STOCK, *n.,* 17. **4.** *Locksmithing.* The shoulder of the bolt of a lock on which the key acts to shoot the bolt. — **tal′oned** (-ŭnd), *adj.*

ta′luk (tä′lo͝ok; tä·lo͝ok′), *n.* [Ar. *ta'alluq* estate.] *India.* An estate including subtenants, somewhat like an English manor; esp., a subdivision of a revenue district.

ta′lus (tā′lŭs), *n.; pl.* TALI (-lī). [L., ankle, anklebone.] *Anat.* **a** The anklebone of man. See ASTRAGALUS, 1. **b** The entire ankle.

ta′lus, *n.* [F.] **1.** A slope. **2.** *Fort.* The slope of the face of a work. **3.** *Geol.* Rock debris at the base of a cliff.

tam (tăm), *n.* A tam-o'-shanter.

ta·ma′le (tȧ·mä′lē), *n.* [From Am. Sp. *tamales,* pl. of *tamal,* fr. Nahuatl *tamalli.*] A Mexican dish made of crushed maize mixed with minced meat, seasoned with red pepper, dipped in oil, and steamed.

ta′man·dua′ (tä′män·dwä′), *n.* Also **tam′an·du** (tăm′ăn·do͞o). [Pg. *tamanduá, tamenduá,* fr. Tupi *tamanduá,* lit., ant catcher.] An arboreal anteater (*Tamandua tetradactyla*) of Central and South America.

tam′a·rack (tăm′ȧ·răk), *n.* [Of Algonquian origin.] Any of several American larches (esp. *Larix laricina*); also, their wood.

ta′ma·rau′ (tä′mȧ·rou′), *n.* Also **ta′ma·rao′** (-rou′). A small dark sturdily built buffalo (*Bubalus mindorensis*) native to the Philippine island of Mindoro.

tam′a·rin (tăm′ȧ·rĭn), *n.* [F., fr. the Carib name in Guiana.] Any of numerous squirrellike South American marmosets (genus *Leontocebus*) having silky fur.

tam′a·rind (-rĭnd), *n.* [It., Sp., & Pg. *tamarindo,* fr. Ar. *tamr hindi,* lit., Indian date, fr. *tamr* a dried date + *Hind* India.] **a** A tropical tree (*Tamarindus indica*) of the senna family, with hard yellowish wood, pinnate leaves, and red-striped yellow flowers. **b** The fruit or pod of this tree, having an acid pulp, used for preserves, and also made into a cooling laxative drink.

tam′a·risk (-rĭsk), *n.* [LL. *tamariscus,* L. *tamarix, tamarice.*] Any of a genus (*Tamarix*) of shrubs or trees, typical of a family (Tamaricaceae, the tamarisk family) of chiefly desert shrubs and trees having narrow entire leaves, and flowers with five stamens and a one-celled ovary. Several species yield a manna.

ta·ma′sha (tȧ·mä′shȧ), *n.* [Ar. *tamāsha* a walking about.] *Anglo-Ind.* A spectacle; a pageant; excitement.

tam′bac (tăm′băk). Var. of TOMBAC.

tam′bour (tăm′bo͝or; -bōr; 70), *n.* [F. See TABOR.] **1.** *Music.* A drum. **2. a** A frame, usually circular, consisting of two parts fitting one within the other so as to hold a piece of cloth stretched over the smaller one for embroidering. **b** Embroidery done on such a frame. — *v. t. & i.* To embroider on a tambour.

tam′bou′rin′ (täɴ′bo͞o′răɴ′; *E.* tăm′bo͞o·rĭn), *n.* [F.] **1.** A long narrow drum, or tabor, used in Provence. **2.** A lively old Provençal dance; also, its music.

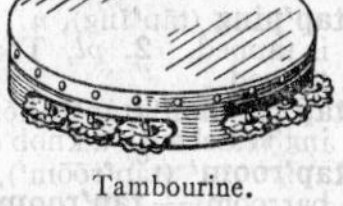
Tambourine.

tam′bou·rine′ (tăm′bo͞o·rēn′; -bŭ·rēn′), *n.* [F. *tambourin,* dim. of *tambour.*] A small drum; esp., a shallow one-headed drum with loose metallic disks or jingles at the sides.

tame (tām), *adj.* [AS. *tam.*] **1.** Reduced from native wildness; specif.: **a** Of animals, domesticated; made tractable and useful to man. **b** Not showing the ferocity, timidity, etc., characteristic of a wild state. **2.** Docile; hence, crushed; subdued; spiritless; also, harmless; gentle. **3.** Deficient in spirit, zest, etc.; dull; insipid; as, *tame* scenery. — *v. t.* To reduce from a wild to a domestic state; to make gentle, tractable, etc.; to domesticate. Hence, to deprive of spirit, courage, or the like; to humble, subdue; also, of colors, to soften; to tone down. — **tam′a·ble, tame′a·ble** (tām′ȧ·b'l), *adj.* — **tame′less,** *adj.* — **tame′ly,** *adv.* — **tame′ness,** *n.* — **tam′er** (tām′ẽr), *n.*

Tam′il (tăm′ĭl; tŭm′ĭl), *n.* **1.** A member of the most enterprising branch of the Dravidian race, mostly Hindus, numerous throughout southern India. **2.** The oldest and best known of the Dravidian languages.

Tam′ma·ny (tăm′ȧ·nĭ), *n.* [From Lenape *Tamanend,* name of a Delaware chief, lit., the affable.] The Tammany Society or Tammany Hall. See TAMMANY, SAINT.

Tammany, Saint. A Delaware chief (Tamanend or Tammany) of the 17th and 18th centuries, traditionally famous for wisdom in council and friendliness toward the whites. He was facetiously canonized as the patron saint of the republic, and his name was adopted by the **Tammany Society,** a fraternal and benevolent organization founded in New York City in 1789. The society's building, **Tammany Hall,** is leased to a nominally distinct political club (Democratic).

Tam′muz (tàm′mo͞oz; *Bib.* tăm′ŭz), *n.* [Heb. *Tammūz.*] **1.** *Babylon. Relig.* A god of agriculture, brought back from the lower world after having perished, his life thus symbolizing the dying of vegetation in the winter and its return in the spring. **2.** See JEWISH CALENDAR.

Tam′ o′ Shan′ter (tăm′ ŏ shăn′tẽr). **1.** The title and hero of a poem by Burns. **2.** [*not cap. and usually hyphened.*] A Scottish cap having a round, flattish top much wider than the headband, and usually a tassel.

tamp (tămp), *v. t.* **1.** To fill up (a drill hole) above the blasting charge with clay, earth, sand, or other material. **2.** To drive in or down by a succession of light or medium blows. — *n.* A tamper.

tamp′er (tămp′ẽr), *n.* One that tamps; esp., a metal-tipped timber used to tamp earth, etc.

tam′per (tăm′pẽr), *v. i.* [F. *tempérer* to temper. See TEMPER, *v.*] **1.** To deal secretly or unfairly; to plot; specif., to use bribery. **2.** To meddle so as to alter a thing; esp., to make corrupting changes. **3.** To meddle; to try trifling experiments; — commonly with *with.* — **tam′per·er,** *n.*

tam′pi·on (tăm′pĭ·ŭn), *n.* [F. *tampon.*] **1.** A plug for the upper end of an organ pipe. See FLUE PIPE, *Illust.* **2.** *Ordn.* A stopper, or plug, for the muzzle of a piece of ordnance not in use.

tam′pon (tăm′pŏn), *n.* [F. See TAMPION.] *Surg.* A plug of cotton or the like introduced into a cavity to arrest hemorrhage or absorb secretions. — *v. t.* To plug with a tampon.

tam′-tam′ (tŭm′tŭm′), *n.* [Hind.] A tom-tom.

tan (tăn), *v. t.;* TANNED (tănd); TAN′NING. [OF. *tanner,* fr. ML. *tannare,* whence AS. *getanned,* past part., tanned. See TAN, *n.*] **1.** To convert (hide or skin) into leather by treatment with an infusion of oak bark or some agent having a similar effect. **2.** To make brown or tan, as by exposure to the sun. **3.** *Colloq.* To thrash or beat. — *v. i.* To get or become tanned. — *n.* [F. *tan,* ML. *tanum,* perh. of Celt. origin.] **1. a** Tanbark. **b** Tannin. **2.** A brown color imparted to the skin by exposure to the sun. **3.** The color of tan (sense 1 **a**), red-yellow in hue, of high saturation and medium brilliance. See COLOR. **4.** *Chem.* A tanning substance. — *adj.* **1.** Of, pert. to, or for tan or tanning. **2.** Of the color tan.

tan′a·ger (tăn′ȧ·jẽr), *n.* [NL. *Tanagra,* fr. Pg. *tángara,* from Tupi *tangará.*] Any of a family (Thraupidae) of American oscine birds closely allied to the finches. The males usually are very bright-colored. Several species inhabit the United States, as the ***scarlet tanager*** (*Piranga erythromelas*) and the ***western,*** *or* ***Louisiana, tanager*** (*P. ludoviciana*), and the ***summer tanager*** (*P. rubra*) of the middle and southern United States.

tan′bark′ (tăn′bärk′), *n.* Any bark rich in tannin, bruised or cut into small pieces, and used in tanning. Spent tanbark is used for circus rings, race tracks, etc.

tan′dem (tăn′dĕm), *adv.* [L. *tandem* at length (of time only) taken, by way of a pun, as meaning lengthwise.] One after or behind another; — used in regard to two or more things so arranged, esp. and orig. of horses so harnessed and driven, instead of abreast. — *n.* **1.** A two-seated carriage drawn by horses harnessed one before the other; hence, a team so harnessed. **2.** A set of two or more persons or objects arranged one behind another. **3.** Short for TANDEM BICYCLE. — *adj.* Consisting of two arranged one behind the other.

tandem bicycle, tricycle, etc. A bicycle, etc., for two or more persons, one sitting before the other.

tang (tăng), *n.* [ON. *tangi* a projecting point.] **1.** A projecting shank, prong, fang, tongue, or the like, as on a knife or fork, file, chisel, sword, or the like, to connect with the handle. See FILE, SCYTHE, *Illusts.* **2. a** A strong or offensive lingering taste; as, cider with a *tang* of the cask. **b** A pungent odor. **c** A trace; smack; — with *of.* **d** A sharp specific flavor or tinge. — **Syn.** See TASTE.

tang (tăng), *n.* [Of imitative origin. Cf. TWANG.] A twang. — *v. t. & i.* To twang; clang; ring.

T'ang *or* **Tang** (täng), *n.* [Chin. (Pek.) *T'ang*².] A dynasty in Chinese history, A.D. 618–907, distinguished by wide conquests, great wealth, strength of Buddhism, and the invention of printing.

tan′ge·lo (tăn′jĕ·lō), *n.* [*tang*erine + pom*elo.*] A hybrid between the tangerine orange and the grapefruit, or pomelo; also, the fruit.

tan′gen·cy (tăn′jĕn·sĭ), *n.* State of being tangent.

tan′gent (tăn′jĕnt), *adj.* [L. *tangens, -entis,* pres. part. of *tangere* to touch.] Touching; touching at a single point; specif., *Geom.,* meeting a curve or surface at two or more consecutive points and hence having there the same direction as the curve or surface; — said of a straight line, curve, or surface. — *n.* **1.** A tangent line, curve, or surface (see CIRCLE, *Illust.*); specif.: **a** *Geom.* Portion (of the straight line tangent to a curve) between the point of tangency and a given line, as the axis of abscissas. **b** *Trig.* The tangent (in sense **a**) of the arc subtending or measuring the angle; the quotient of the sine divided by the cosine of the angle. Abbr. *tan* (no period). **2.** An abrupt change of course. **3.** *Music.* The small, upright, flat-ended metal pin at the inner end of a clavichord key, which strikes the string to produce the tone.

tan·gen′tal (tăn·jĕn′tăl), *adj.* Tangential. — **tan·gen′tal·ly,** *adv.*

tan·gen′tial (tăn·jĕn′shăl), *adj.* **1.** *Math.* Of, pertaining to, or of the nature of a tangent; in the direction of a tangent. **2. a** Divergent; digressive; hence, erratic. **b** Merely contiguous. — **tan·gen′tial·ly,** *adv.*

tan′ge·rine′ (tăn′jĕ·rēn′), *n.* [From *Tangier,* Morocco.] **1.** (*pron.* tăn′jĕ·rēn; -rēn′). = MANDARIN, 3. **2.** A color, yellowish-red in hue, of high saturation and medium brilliance. See COLOR.

tan′gi·ble (tăn′jĭ·b'l), *adj.* [LL. *tangibilis,* fr. *tangere* to touch.] **1.** Capable of being touched; also, perceptible to the touch; palpable. **2.** Capable of being realized by the mind; substantial; objective; as, *tangible* benefits. **3.** Capable of being appraised at an actual or approximate value; as, *tangible* assets. — **Syn.** See PERCEPTIBLE. — *n. pl.* Material things that can be appraised; tangible assets. — **tan′gi·bil′i·ty** (-bĭl′ĭ·tĭ), **tan′gi·ble·ness,** *n.* — **tan′gi·bly,** *adv.*

tan′gle (tăng′g'l), *n.* [Of Scand. origin.] Any large seaweed.

tan′gle, *v. t.;* -GLED (-g'ld); -GLING (-glĭng). [ME. *tangilen, tagilen.*] **1.** To involve so as to hamper, obstruct, or embarrass. **2.** To unite or knit together confusedly; entangle. **3.** To involve as in a mesh; ensnare; as, to be *tangled* in lies. — *v. i.* To be or become entangled. — *n.* **1.** A tangled mass, as of threads, hairs, etc.; a snarl. **2.** A tangled condition of affairs; complicated state; muddle. **3.** A state of perplexity; quandary. — **tan′gler** (-glẽr), *n.*

tan′gle·ber′ry (tăng′g'l·bĕr′ĭ), *n.* A species of huckleberry (*Gaylussacia frondosa*) of the eastern United States.

tan′go (tăng′gō), *n.; pl.* TANGOS (-gōz). [Argentine Sp., dance, fiesta, fr. Sp. *tango* a gypsy festival, dance, music.] Any of several dances of Spanish-American origin, commonly in 2/4 time and characterized by posturing and a variety of steps; specif., one distinguished by low dips and twisting steps on the toes. — **tan′go**, *v. i.*

tang′y (tăng′ĭ), *adj.* Having a tang, or taste.

tan′ist·ry (tăn′ĭst·rĭ; thôn′ĭst·rĭ), *n.* [Ir. *tānaiste* second, second person in rank.] *Hist.* The Irish law of succession, by which the successor (**tan′ist**) of a chief or king was elected by the people from among the chief's male relatives during his lifetime.

tank (tăngk), *n.* [Pg. *tanque,* for *estanque,* fr. L. *stagnum.* See STAGNATE.] **1.** A pond, pool, or small lake. **2.** A large basin, cistern, or other artificial receptacle for liquids; as, a swimming *tank.* **3.** *Mil.* A heavily armed and armored automotive combat vehicle which is driven by and travels upon two endless steel belts, one on each side, extending the full length of the vehicle and geared to an internal-combustion engine. — *v. t.* To place, store, treat, etc., in a tank.

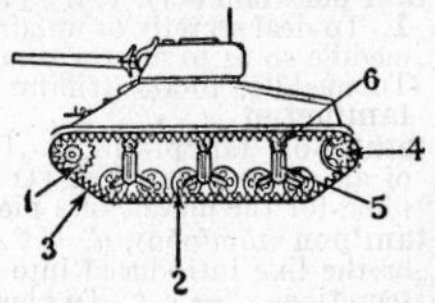

Tank, 3 (*U. S. Army,* M 4). 1 Drive Sprocket; 2 Bogie; 3 Track; 4 Idler; 5 Suspension Arm; 6 Support Roller.

tank′age (-ĭj), *n.* **1.** Act or process of storing in tanks; also, fees charged for such storage. **2.** The capacity or contents of a tank or tanks. **3.** *Agric.* Dried animal residues, usually freed from fat and gelatin, used as a fertilizer and feeding stuff.

tank′ard (-ẽrd), *n.* A tall, one-handled drinking vessel, esp. one of pewter with a lid.

tank destroyer. A highly mobile, lightly armored vehicle constructed of a half track or a tank chassis mounting a 75 mm. cannon or a 105 mm. howitzer. Often called *TD*

tank′er (tăngk′ẽr), *n.* A steel cargo boat fitted with tanks for the carrying of oil, molasses, etc.

tank farming. = HYDROPONICS.

tan′nage (tăn′ĭj), *n.* Act or process of tanning.

tan′nate (-āt), *n.* *Chem.* A salt or ester of tannin.

tanned (tănd), *past & past part.* of TAN.

tan′ner (tăn′ẽr), *n.* One whose occupation is to tan hides.

tan′ner, *n.* *Slang, Eng.* A sixpence.

tan′ner·y (-ĭ), *n.; pl.* -NERIES (-ĭz). A place where the work of tanning is carried on.

Tann′häu·ser (tän′hoi·zẽr; tăn′-), *n.* [G.] A German knight and minnesinger, identified with a legendary hero in Wagner's opera *Tannhäuser* who entered the enchanted cavern in the Venusberg. His escapes therefrom, his return, and his final release form the plot of the opera.

tan′nic (tăn′ĭk), *adj.* Of, like, or derived from tan.

tan′nin (-ĭn), *n.* [F. *tanin.*] Also **tannic acid.** *Chem.* **a** A strongly astringent substance obtained in scales from gallnuts, sumac, etc. It is used in tanning, dyeing, medicine, etc. **b** Any of a group of substances having similar uses.

tan′ning (tăn′ĭng), *pres. part.* of TAN. Specif.: *n.* Art or process by which a skin is tanned.

tan′sy (tăn′zĭ), *n.* [OF. *tanoisie, tanesie,* fr. ML., fr. Gr. *athanasia* immortality.] Any of a genus (*Tanacetum*) of plants of the aster family, esp. one species (*T. vulgare*) having an aromatic odor, a very bitter taste, and tonic properties.

tan′ta·late (tăn′tȧ·lāt), *n.* A salt of tantalic acid.

tan·tal′ic (tăn·tăl′ĭk), *adj.* *Chem.* Of, pertaining to, or derived from tantalum; specif., designating any of several acids derived from tantalum pentoxide and known chiefly in their salts, the tantalates.

tan′ta·lite (tăn′tȧ·līt), *n.* *Mineral.* A heavy iron-black mineral of submetallic luster, essentially iron tantalate, $Fe(TaO_3)_2$. H., 6. Sp. gr., up to 7.3.

tan′ta·lize (-līz), *v. t. & i.* [From TANTALUS.] To tease by keeping something desirable in view but out of reach. — **Syn.** See WORRY. — **tan′ta·li·za′tion** (-lĭ·zā′shŭn; -lī·zā′-), *n.* — **tan′ta·liz′er** (-līz′ẽr), *n.* — **tan′ta·liz′ing·ly,** *adv.*

tan′ta·lum (-lŭm), *n.* [NL.; — in ref. to the difficulties met in isolating it. See TANTALUS.] *Chem.* A hard, ductile, gray-white, acid-resisting metallic element of the vanadium family, found (combined) in tantalite, columbite, and other rare minerals. Symbol, *Ta;* at. no., 73; at. wt., 180.88.

Tan′ta·lus (-lŭs), *n.* [L., fr. Gr. *Tantalos.*] *Gr. Myth.* A wealthy king, son of Zeus and father of Pelops and Niobe. For an atrocious sin he was punished in the lower world by being placed in water up to his chin with fruit-laden branches over his head. The water or fruit receded whenever he sought to drink or eat.

tan′ta·mount′ (tăn′tȧ·mount′), *adj.* [From *tantamount,* n. & v., fr. AF. *tant amunter* to amount to as much. See AMOUNT.] Equivalent in value, meaning, or effect; as, his explanation was *tantamount* to a confession.

tan′ta·ra (tăn′tȧ·rȧ; tăn·tăr′ȧ; -tä′rȧ), *n.* [Imitative.] The blare of a trumpet or horn; a fanfare.

tan·tiv′y (tăn·tĭv′ĭ), *adv.* *Archaic.* Swiftly; headlong. — *adj.* Swift; speedy. — *n.; pl.* -TIVIES (-ĭz). **1.** An impetuous rush. **2.** *Hunting.* A call to signal full chase.

‖**tant mieux** (täɴ′ myû′). [F.] So much the better.

‖**tan′to** (tăn′tō), *adv.* [It.] So much; specif., *Music,* not too much; — a direction; as, allegro non *tanto,* brisk but not too brisk.

‖**tant pis** (täɴ′ pē′). [F.] So much the worse.

tan′trum (tăn′trŭm), *n.* *Colloq.* A fit of ill temper.

Tao′ism (tou′ĭz'm; dou′-), *n.* [Chin. (Pek.) *tao*⁴ road, way.] A religion and philosophy of China, traditionally founded by Lao-tzu (c. 604–531 B.C.), and teaching conformity to the cosmic order and simplicity of social and political organization. — **Tao′ist** (-ĭst), *n. & adj.* — **Tao·is′tic** (tou·ĭs′tĭk; dou-), *adj.*

tap (tăp), *v. t. & i.;* TAPPED (tăpt) or TAPT; TAP′PING. [ME. *tappen,* fr. OF. *taper,* of imitative origin.] **1.** To strike with a slight blow; rap lightly. **2.** To give a light blow or blows with (cane, feet, etc.). **3.** To make, as a hole, by tapping. **4.** To repair (a shoe) by putting a tap on. — *n.* **1.** A light blow; a rap; also, its sound. **2.** *pl.* A signal, by drum, bugle, or trumpet, to extinguish all lights in soldiers' or sailors' quarters, to go to bed and preserve silence. **3.** A partial sole put on over the worn sole of a boot or shoe.

tap, *n.* [AS. *tæppa.*] **1.** *Chiefly Brit.* A cock, faucet, or small valve, esp. for turning on water. See BIBCOCK, *Illust.* **2.** A hole or pipe through which liquor is drawn. **3.** A plug or spile to stop a hole, as in a cask; a spigot. **4.** Liquor drawn through a tap; hence: **a** A certain kind or quality of liquor; as, ale of the first *tap.* **b** *Colloq.* A taproom; bar. **5.** A tool for forming an internal screw thread. See DIE, *Illust.* **6.** In an electric circuit, a point where a connection may be made. — ***on tap.*** **a** Ready to be drawn; as, ale *on tap.* **b** Broached or furnished with a tap. **c** On hand. — *v. t.* **1.** To let out by piercing, or by drawing a plug from the containing vessel. **2.** Hence, to draw from (anything) in an analogous way; as, to *tap* telegraph wires. **3.** To pierce (a cask, a tree, tumor, etc.) so as to let out, or draw off, a fluid. **4.** To connect (a street, a water main) with a local supply. **5.** To form a female screw in by means of a tap. — *v. i.* To be, or act as, a tapster.

ta′pa (tä′pä), *n.* [Native name in Marquesas Isls.] **1.** The bark of a variety of mulberry tree, from which a cloth (**tapa cloth**) is made by steeping and beating. **2.** The cloth.

tap bond *or* **issue.** A U. S. government security of an issue unlimited in total amount, offered for sale for an unspecified period (often several weeks), and designed to tap idle funds from nonbanking sources.

tap dance. Any step dance, tapped out audibly with the feet, toes, or heels. — **tap′–dance′,** *v. i.* — **tap dancer.** — **tap dancing.**

tape (tāp), *n.* [AS. *tæppe.*] **1.** A narrow woven ribbon of cotton or linen. **2.** Hence, any narrow strip or band, as of paper, steel, or the like. **3.** Short for RED TAPE, TAPELINE. **4.** *Sports.* A string stretched breast-high above the finishing line to aid the judges in determining the winner of a race. — *v. t.* **1.** To furnish with tape; fasten, tie, bind, or the like, with tape. **2.** To measure with a tapeline; *Scot.,* to measure sparingly. — **tap′er** (tāp′ẽr), *n.*

tape grass. A submerged aquatic plant (*Vallisneria spiralis*) with long ribbonlike leaves; — in the southern United States called *wild celery,* a favorite food of canvasback ducks.

tape′line′ (tāp′līn′), *n.* Also **tape measure.** A tape marked with linear dimensions, as inches, feet, etc., and used for measuring.

ta′per (tā′pẽr), *n.* [AS. *taper, tapor, tapur,* fr. L. *papyrus* papyrus, in ML. also taper, wick.] **1.** Orig., a small wax candle; now esp., a long waxed wick; hence, any small light. **2.** A tapering form or figure, as a spire; hence, gradual diminution of thickness or width in an elongated object; as, the *taper* of a spire. — *adj.* Regularly narrowed toward a point; conical; pyramidical. — *v. i. & t.* To become or to make gradually smaller toward one end; hence, to diminish gradually. — **ta′per·ing·ly,** *adv.*

tape recorder. A device similar to a wire recorder but recording on a magnetizable tape (magnetic tape) instead of a wire.

tap′es·try (tăp′ĕs·trĭ), *n.; pl.* -TRIES (-trĭz). [F. *tapisserie,* fr. *tapis* a carpet, carpeting, fr. OF. *tapiz,* fr. Gr. *tapētion,* dim. of *tapēs* a carpet, rug.] A heavy, hand-woven, reversible textile, commonly figured and used as a wall hanging, carpet, or furniture covering; also, a machine-made imitation of it, of different weave and not reversible. — *v. t.;* -TRIED (-trĭd); -TRY·ING. To furnish or adorn with or as if with tapestry.

ta·pe′tum (tȧ·pē′tŭm), *n.* [LL., fr. L. *tapete* a carpet, a tapestry.] **1.** *Bot.* A layer of nutritive tissue commonly investing the archespore in a developing sporangium. **2.** *Anat. & Zool.* Any of certain membranous layers or areas, esp. of the chorioid and retina of the eye.

tape′worm′ (tāp′wûrm′), *n.* Any of numerous cestode worms (*Taenia* and allied genera) parasitic when adult in the intestine of man and various animals. Cf. BLADDER WORM, COENURUS, HYDATID.

tap′house′ (tăp′hous′), *n.* A tavern; a taproom.

tap′i·o′ca (tăp′ĭ·ō′kȧ), *n.* [Pg., Sp., F., fr. Tupi & Guarani *typyóca, tipyóca,* fr. *ty* juice + *pýa* heart, bowels + *ocô* to be removed.] A granular preparation of cassava starch, much used in puddings and as a thickening for soups.

ta′pir (tā′pẽr), *n.;* see PLURAL, *Note,* 3. [Sp., fr. Tupi *tapyra, tapira,* any large mammal.] Any of several large ungulates (family Tapiridae), all but one of which (the Malayan) inhabit South or Central America. They are chiefly nocturnal, shy, and gentle, and are the nearest living allies of horses and rhinoceroses.

tap′is (tăp′ē; tā′pĭs; tăp′ĭs; *F.* tȧ′pē′), *n.* [F. See TAPESTRY.] Tapestry; a floor or table cover; — now chiefly in ***on,*** *or* ***upon, the tapis*** (*pron. in this use perh. more often as F.* tȧ′pē′). [Transl. of F. *sur le tapis.*] On the floor; hence, under consideration.

tap′per (tăp′ẽr), *n.* [From 1st TAP.] One that taps; specif., a telegraph key, esp. one (in full, ***Morse tapper***) that makes one contact and breaks another by one movement.

tap′pet (-ĕt; -ĭt), *n.* *Mach.* A lever or projection moved by some other piece, as a cam, or intended to tap something else, to cause a certain motion, as in forms of internal-combustion-engine valve gear.

tap′ping (tăp′ĭng), *n.* **1.** Act, process, or means by which something is tapped. **2.** *pl.* That which is taken from a tap or from something tapped.

tap′pit-hen′ (tȧp′ĭt·hĕn′), *n.* *Scot.* **a** A crested hen. **b** A large drinking vessel with a knob on its lid.

tap′room′ (tăp′rōōm′), *n.* A room where liquors are kept on tap; a barroom. — **tap′room′,** *adj.*

tap′root′ (-rōōt′), *n.* A primary root which grows vertically downward, giving off small lateral roots.

taps (tăps), *n. pl.* = 1st TAP, *n.,* 2.

tap′sal-tee′rie (tȧp′săl·tēr′ĭ), *adv.* *Scot.* Topsy-turvy.

tap′ster (tăp′stẽr), *n.* [AS. *tæppestre* a female tapster.] Orig., a barmaid; later, anyone employed to tap, or draw, liquors. — **tap′-stress** (-strĕs; -strĭs), *n.*

Ta·pu′ya (tä·pōō′yä), *n. sing. & pl.* [Pg. *Tapuyo, Tapuya,* fr. Tupi *tapuya* savage, enemy.] An Indian of the Tapuyan stock.

Ta·pu′yan (-yăn), *adj.* Pertaining to or designating an important linguistic family of South American Indians, formerly of central Brazil.

tar (tär), *n.* [AS. *teru, teoru.*] **1.** A thick, dark-brown or black viscous liquid obtained by distillation of wood, coal, etc. **2.** [Abbr. fr. TARPAULIN.] A sailor; seaman. — *v. t.;* TARRED (tärd); TAR′RING. To smear with or as with tar. — *adj.* Of, from, or like tar.

tar′an·tass′, tar′an·tas′ (tăr′ăn·tăs′; *Russ.* tȧ·rŭn·tàs′), *n.* [Russ. *tarantas.*] A low four-wheeled carriage used in Russia.

tar′an·tel′la (tăr′ăn·tĕl′ȧ), *n.* [It., dim. fr. *Taranto.*] **a** A lively, passionate Neapolitan folk dance in 6/8 time, or a social dance evolved from it. **b** Music for such a dance.

tar′ant·ism (tăr′ăn·tĭz'm), *n.* Also **tar′ent·ism** (tăr′ĕn-). [NL. *tarantismus*, fr. It. *tarantismo*, fr. *Taranto*. See TARANTULA.] *Med.* A nervous affection characterized by melancholy, stupor, and an uncontrollable desire to dance. — **tar′ant·ist** (-tĭst), *n.*

ta·ran′tu·la (tȧ·răn′tū·lȧ), *n.; pl.* -LAS (-lȧz), -LAE (-lē). [ML. *tarantula*, It. *tarantola*, fr. L. *Tarentum*, now *Taranto*, in the south of Italy.] Any of several large venomous spiders; esp., a European species (*Lycosa tarentula*) whose bite was supposed to cause tarantism.

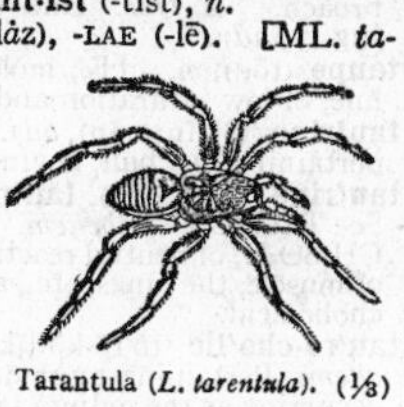

Tarantula (*L. tarentula*). (⅓)

ta·rax′a·cum (tȧ·răk′sȧ·kŭm), *n.* [NL., fr. Ar. *ṭarakhshaqūq*, -*aqūn*, of Per. origin.] *Pharm.* The dried rhizome and roots of the dandelion (*Taraxacum officinale*), used as a bitter and laxative.

tar·boosh′ (tär·bōōsh′), *n.* Also **tar·bush′** (tär·bōōsh′). [Ar. *ṭarbūsh*.] A red cap worn by Moslem men, and sometimes swathed as with linen to make a turban. A fez is one variety.

tar′di·grade (tär′dĭ·grād), *adj.* [F., fr. L. *tardigradus*, fr. *tardus* slow + *gradi* to step.] **1.** Moving or stepping slowly; slow-paced. **2.** Of or pertaining to a division (Tardigrada) of arthropods containing numerous microscopic creatures found in water, damp moss, etc. — **tar′di·grade**, *n.*

‖**tar′do** (tär′dō), *adj.* [It.] *Music.* Slow; — a direction.

tar′dy (tär′dĭ), *adj.; -*DI·ER (-dĭ·ẽr); -DI·EST. [F. *tardif*, fr. L. *tardus* slow.] **1.** Moving slowly; slow. **2.** Late; also, dilatory. — **tar′di·ly** (-dĭ·lĭ), *adv.* — **tar′di·ness** (-dĭ·nĕs; -nĭs), *n.*

tare (târ), *n.* **1.** Any of several vetches (esp. *Vicia sativa* and *V. hirsuta*); also, the seed. **2.** a *Bib.* A weed of grainfields, supposed to be the darnel. b First principle; source; seed; — in a bad sense.

tare, *n.* [F. *tare*, fr. Ar. *ṭarḥah* that which is thrown away, removed.] **1.** A deduction of weight, made in allowance for the weight of a container or vehicle. **2.** *Chem.* A counterweight; esp., an empty vessel similar to the container, used to counterpoise change in weight of the container due to temperature, moisture, etc. — *v. t.* To ascertain or mark the tare of.

tare (târ; tăr). Archaic & dial. past & past part. of TEAR.

targe (tärj), *n.* [OF.] *Archaic.* A shield or target.

tar′get (tär′gĕt; -gĭt), *n.* [OF. *targette*, later *targuete*, dim. of *targue*, *targe*, of Teut. origin.] **1.** *Hist.* A form of small shield or buckler, esp. one of circular form. **2.** A butt or mark to shoot at, as for practice; hence: a A butt that is marked by the shots fired at it. b Anything fired at. **3.** Any object of ridicule, criticisms, etc.; a butt. **4.** *Physics.* The metallic surface, usually of platinum or tungsten, upon which the stream of cathode rays within an X-ray tube is focused, the surface thus becoming the source from which the X rays emanate. **5.** *Railroads.* A day signal attached to a switch stand, indicating whether the switch is open or closed. **6.** *Surv.* The vane or sliding sight on a leveling staff.

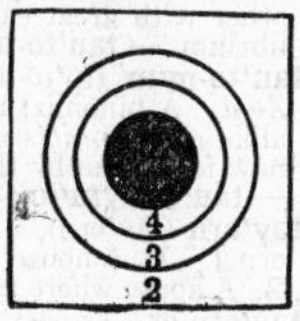

Target, showing scoring values. Cf. SIGHT, *Illust.*

tar′get·eer′ (-ēr′), *n.* One armed with a target, or shield.

Tar′gum (tär′gŭm; *Heb.* tär·gōōm′), *n.; pl.* -GUMS (-gŭmz), TARGUMIM (tär′gōō·mēm′). [Heb. *Targūm*, fr. Aram. *targūm* interpretation.] A translation or paraphrase of some portion of the Old Testament in the Aramaic of Judea.

Tar′heel′ (tär′hēl′), *n.* *Colloq., U. S.* A native of the pine barrens of North Carolina, the **Tarheel State**; — a nickname.

tar′iff (tăr′ĭf), *n.* [It. *tariffa*, fr. Ar. *ta'rīf* information, explanation.] **1.** A schedule, system, or scheme of duties imposed by a government on goods imported or exported, or esp., on imports. **2.** The duty, or rate of duty, imposed in a tariff (sense 1); as, the *tariff* on wool. **3.** A schedule of rates or charges, as of a railroad, bus line, etc. — *v. t.* **1.** To make a list of duties on, as goods. **2.** To list or schedule the tariff value of.

tar′la·tan (tär′lȧ·tăn), *n.* Also **tar′le·tan** (tär′lĕ-). [F. *tarlatane.*] A thin, stiff, transparent muslin.

Tar′mac (tär′măk), *n.* **1.** A trade-mark applied to a bituminous binder for roads. **2.** [*tar* + *macadam.*] *Brit.* a A road surfaced with a tar composition. b The apron in front of a hangar surfaced with this composition; also, a runway, flight strip, etc.

tarn (tärn), *n.* [ME. *terne.*] Small mountain lake or pool.

tar′nish (tär′nĭsh), *v. t.* [F. *ternir*, fr. *terne* dull, dim, wan.] To dull or destroy the luster of; to soil or dull by or as by the action of the air, dust, etc.; sully; smirch. — *v. i.* To lose luster; become dull. — *n.* State of being tarnished; discoloration; blemish; also, a tarnished surface or appearance. — **tar′nish·a·ble**, *adj.*

ta′ro (tä′rō), *n.; pl.* TAROS (-rōz). [Tahitian and Maori.] a A plant (*Colocasia esculenta*) of the arum family grown throughout the tropics for its edible starchy tuberous rootstocks and in temperate regions, under the name *elephant's-ear*, for ornament. b The rootstock of this plant.

tar·pau′lin (tär·pô′lĭn), *n.* [Prob. fr. *tar* + *palling* a covering, fr. *pall* cloth.] **1.** Canvas waterproofed with tar, paint, etc., used for covering hatches of a ship, boats, etc. **2.** A hat or coat of, or covered with, tarpaulin. **3.** *Now Rare.* A sailor; tar.

Tar·pe′ia (tär·pē′yȧ), *n.* [L.] In Roman legend, a maiden who betrayed the citadel to the Sabines for the promise of "what they wore on their arms," meaning their gold bracelets. They threw their shields on her and killed her.

Tar·pe′ian (-yăn), *adj.* [L. *Tarpeius.*] Pert. to or designating a peak of the Capitoline hill, Rome, from which condemned criminals were hurled as was Tarpeia.

tar′pon (tär′pŏn), *n.;* see PLURAL, *Note*, 3. [Origin uncert.] A marine fish (*Tarpon atlanticus*), common on the coast of Florida, in the West Indies, etc. It reaches a length of about six feet, has a silvery body, and is a noted game fish.

tar′ra·gon (tăr′ȧ·gŏn), *n.* [Sp. *taragona*, fr. Ar. *ṭarkhun*, fr. Gr. *drakōn* a dragon.] A European herb (*Artemisia dracunculus*) of the aster family, allied to wormwood; also, its aromatic herbage, used for seasoning.

tar′ri·ance (tăr′ĭ·ăns), *n.* *Archaic.* Tarrying; sojourn.

tar′ry (tär′ĭ), *adj.;* TAR′RI·ER (-ĭ·ẽr); TAR′RI·EST. Of, like, or covered with tar.

tar′ry (tăr′ĭ), *v. t.;* TAR′RIED (-ĭd); TAR′RY·ING. [ME. *tarien* to irritate, hinder, fr. AS. *tergan*, *tirgan*, to provoke, irritate.] *Archaic.* To wait or stop for; as, to *tarry* a reply. — *v. i.* **1.** To delay or be tardy; linger. **2.** To abide at or in a place; stay; specif., to rest in expectation; to wait. — **Syn.** See STAY. — *n.* Stay; sojourn.

tar′sal (tär′săl; -s'l), *adj.* *Anat. & Zool.* a Of or pertaining to the tarsus. b Designating, or pertaining to, plates of dense connective tissue which serve to stiffen the eyelids. — *n.* A tarsal bone or cartilage.

tar′si·er (tär′sĭ·ẽr), *n.* [F., fr. *tarse* tarsus.] Any of several nocturnal arboreal East Indian mammals (genus *Tarsius*) related to the lemurs.

tar′so- (tär′sō-), **tars-**. [From TARSUS.] A combining form denoting *tarsus;* also, *tarsal plate*, as in **tars·ec′to·my, tars·ot′o·my** (see -ECTOMY, -TOMY).

tar′so·met′a·tar′sus (-mĕt′ȧ·tär′sŭs), *n.* [NL.] The large bone of the shank, or *tarsus*, of a bird; also, the segment of the limb it supports.

tar′sus (tär′sŭs), *n.; pl.* TARSI (-sī). [NL., fr. Gr. *tarsos* the flat of the foot.] **1.** *Anat. & Zool.* The ankle; the part of the foot of a vertebrate between the metatarsus and the leg; the small bones collectively which support this part. **2.** *Zool.* a The tarsometatarsus, or shank, of a bird's leg. b The distal part of the limb in certain arthropods. **3.** *Anat.* The tarsal plate of the eyelid.

tart (tärt), *adj.* [AS. *teart* severe.] **1.** Sharp to the taste; sour. **2.** Pungent; keen; caustic; as, a *tart* reply. — **Syn.** See SOUR. — **tart′ly**, *adv.*

tart, *n.* [OF. *tarte.*] **1.** a A small pie or shell of pastry containing jelly, custard, etc. b *Eng.* A fruit pie. **2.** *Slang.* A girl or woman; — orig. a term of endearment; now usually, a woman of loose morals.

tar′tan (tär′tăn), *n.* [Origin uncert.] **1.** Woolen cloth, checkered or cross-barred with narrow bands of various colors, worn in the Scottish Highlands, where each clan had its distinctive tartan; hence, any such pattern. **2.** Plaid cloth resembling tartan. — **tar′tan**, *adj.*

tar′tan, *n.* [F. *tartane*, fr. It. *tartana.*] A coasting vessel, used in the Mediterranean, with one mast carrying a large lateen sail.

tar′tar (tär′tẽr), *n.* [OF. *tartre*, fr. ML. *tartarum*, fr. MGr. *tartaron.*] **1.** A substance, essentially acid potassium tartrate, existing in the juice of grapes and deposited in wine casks, with other suspended matter, as a reddish crust or sediment; specif., a recrystallized product, distinguished from *argol* (the crust), from *lees*, and from *cream of tartar*, obtained by further purification. **2.** An incrustation on the teeth, consisting of salivary mucus, food residue, and phosphate of lime.

Tar′tar, *n.* [Per. *Tātār*, of Tatar origin.] **1.** One of the people of Tatary (Tartary). See TATAR. **2.** [*often not cap.*] a A person of a violent or irritable temper. b A person who proves too strong for his assailant; — esp. in the phrase *to catch a tartar.* — *adj.* Also **Tar·tar′i·an** (tär·târ′ĭ·ăn). Of or pertaining to Tatary or the Tatars.

Tar′tar, *n.* *Obs.* Tartarus.

tartar emetic. A poisonous white crystalline salt, having a sweetish metallic taste, used in dyeing as a mordant and in medicine as a diaphoretic, expectorant, emetic, and counterirritant. Chemically it is potassium antimonyl tartrate, $KSbOC_4H_4O_6.\frac{1}{2}H_2O$.

tar′tare sauce (tär′tẽr). [F. *sauce tartare.*] Mayonnaise with chopped green herbs, pickles, olives, and capers.

tar·tar′ic (tär·tăr′ĭk; tär·tär′ĭk), *adj.* Of, pertaining to, derived from, or resembling tartar or tartaric acid.

tartaric acid. *Chem.* An acid, $C_2H_2(OH)_2(CO_2H)_2$, widely diffused among plants, and obtained chiefly from tartar. It is used in dyeing, calico printing, photography, medicine, esp. in the preparation of Seidlitz powders, and also as a substitute for lemon juice.

tar′tar·ous (tär′tẽr·ŭs), *adj.* Containing, or of the nature of, tartar.

Tar′ta·rus (tär′tȧ·rŭs), *n.* [L., fr. Gr. *Tartaros.*] *Gr. Myth.* The infernal regions, described in the *Iliad* as situated as far below Hades as heaven is above the earth, and by later writers as the place of punishment for the spirits of the wicked. In the later poets, also, Hades. — **Tar·tar′e·an** (tär·târ′ē·ăn), *adj.*

tart′let (tärt′lĕt; -lĭt), *n.* A small tart.

tart′ness (-nĕs; -nĭs), *n.* Tart flavor or nature.

tar′trate (tär′trāt), *n.* [F.] *Chem.* A salt or ester of tartaric acid.

tar′trat·ed (-trāt·ĕd; -ĭd), *adj.* *Pharm. Chem.* Containing, or derived from, tartar; combined with tartaric acid.

Tar·tufe′ (tär·tōōf′; *F.* tár′tüf′), **Tar·tuffe′** (tär·tōōf′), *n.* [F. *Tartufe*, *tartufe*, fr. It. *Tartufo*, *tartufo*, lit., truffle.] The title hero of a play (1664) by Molière, a hypocritical religious devotee; hence [*not cap.*], a hypocrite.

ta·sim′e·ter (tȧ·sĭm′ē·tẽr), *n.* [Gr. *tasis* stretching, extension (fr. *teinein* to stretch) + *-meter.*] A modification of the microphone for detecting or measuring minute extensions or movements of solid bodies (and hence changes of temperature) by the changes of pressure produced. — **tas′i·met′ric** (tăs′ĭ·mĕt′rĭk), *adj.*

task (tȧsk; 9), *n.* [ONF. *tasque*, for OF. *tasche*, fr. L. *taxare* to rate, appraise.] **1.** *Obs.* A tax; impost. **2.** Labor or study imposed by another, often in a definite quantity; broadly, an undertaking; work. **3.** An account or taxing; — chiefly in *to take*, or *call, to task*, that is, to censure.

Syn. **Task, duty, job, chore, stint, assignment** mean a piece of work to be accomplished. **Task** implies imposition by a teacher, employer, one's station in life, etc.; **duty**, an obligation to perform or a responsibility for performance; **job**, a piece of work which one is asked to do or accepts voluntarily; **chore**, one of the routine activities involved in the care of a home, of stock, or the like; **stint**, a piece of work allotted to one as one's share or prescribed for accomplishment within a given time; **assignment**, a definite limited task given by one in authority such as a teacher or editor.

— *v. t.* **1.** *Obs.* To tax. **2.** To impose a task upon; to assign a definite amount of business, labor, or duty to. **3.** To encumber, as with a load; burden; as, to *task* one's mind with details. **4.** To charge; to tax, as with a fault.

task force. *Mil. & Nav.* A tactical combat group specially made up of elements from one or more services, often naval, ground, and air forces, under a single commander, for fulfilling a single precisely defined mission.

task′mas′ter (tȧsk′mȧs′tẽr; 9), *n.* One who imposes a task, or burdens another with labor; an overseer.

Tas·ma′ni·an dev′il (tăz·mā′nĭ·ăn; -mān′yăn). A carnivorous burrowing Tasmanian marsupial (*Sarcophilus ursinus*, family Dasyuridae)

Tasmanian tiger *or* **wolf.** The thylacine.
tass (tȧs), *n.* [F. *tasse*, fr. Ar. *ṭass*, *ṭassah*, fr. Per. *tast* cup.] *Scot. & Dial.* A drinking cup or bowl.
Tass (tȧs), *n.* [Russ. abbr. fr. *T*elegraphnoye *A*gentstvo *S*ovetskovo *S*oyuza.] The Soviet News Agency.
tasse (tȧs), *n.* [ML., pocket, fr. MHG. *tasche.*] *Armor.* One of a series of steel splints forming a short skirt (called **tass'es** [tȧs'ĕz; -ĭz]). See ARMOR, *Illust.*
tas'sel (tăs''l), *n.* [ME., some part of a fastening of a mantle, fr. OF. *tassel, taisel.*] **1.** Orig., a clasp for a cloak; now, a pendent ornament, ending in a tuft of loose threads. **2.** Something likened to a tassel (def. 1); specif., the male inflorescence of some plants, as Indian corn. — *v. t.;* TAS'SELED (-'ld) or TAS'SELLED; TAS'SEL·ING, TAS'SEL·LING. To adorn with or make into tassels. — *v. i.* To put forth tassels or inflorescences.
tas'sel. Var. of TERCEL.
tas'set (-ĕt; -ĭt), *n.* = TASSE.
tass'ie (tȧs'ĭ), *n.* *Chiefly Scot.* A small cup.
taste (tāst), *v. t.* [OF. *taster* to feel, try, taste.] **1.** *Obs.* To try or test by or as by the touch. **2.** To try by the touch of the tongue; ascertain the relish or flavor of by taking a little into the mouth. **3.** To eat or drink a little of, as in testing. Cf. TASTER, 1. **4.** To perceive or recognize, as if by tasting; to become acquainted with by trial, experience, participation, or a foretaste; as, to *taste* deep joy. **5.** *Archaic & Dial.* To like; enjoy. — *v. i.* **1.** To eat or drink a little, esp. to test its flavor; partake (*of*) sparingly. **2.** To have a certain flavor or taste; savor; as, the milk *tastes* sour. **3.** To have a perception, experience, foretaste, etc. (*of*); as, to *taste* of death.
— *n.* **1.** *Obs.* **a** A test; an essay; a trial. **b** Act of tasting; gustation. **2.** A little piece tasted; a bit; a sample. **3.** The sense by which certain attributes (*taste, savor, flavor*) of substances are ascertained by contact with certain epithelial end organs (**taste buds**) occurring in the papillae on the surface of the tongue. **4.** The quality perceived by this sense or the sensation excited by stimulating it; savor; flavor. **5.** Intellectual relish; liking; inclination; as, he had no *taste* for study. **6.** The power of discerning and appreciating fitness, beauty, order, or whatever constitutes excellence, esp. in the fine arts and belles-lettres; critical judgment, discernment, or appreciation. **7.** Quality, as judged by persons with such qualifications; as, decorations in good *taste* or bad *taste.* **8.** Individual aesthetic preference or liking; as, there is no accounting for *tastes.*
Syn. (1) **Taste, sapidity, flavor, savor, tang, relish, smack** mean that property of a substance which makes it perceptible to the gustatory sense. **Taste**, the most inclusive term, carries no suggestion of specific character or quality; **sapidity** implies a highly perceptible taste; **flavor**, an appeal to the sense of smell as well as taste; **savor**, the quality that may be tasted or smelled, esp. when cooked or cooking; **tang**, a sharp, penetrating savor; **relish**, the peculiar flavor or taste of a thing; **smack**, a taste given by something added, often disguising its original taste.
(2) **Taste, palate, relish, gusto, zest** mean a liking for something that gives pleasure. **Taste** implies a natural or acquired liking or interest; **palate**, a liking dependent on pleasurable sensation; **relish**, a liking that evokes keen gratification; **gusto**, a hearty or vital relish; **zest**, eagerness and avidity in doing, making, encountering, etc.
taste'ful (tāst'fo͝ol; -f'l), *adj.* **1.** *Now Rare.* Savory. **2.** Having or exhibiting taste (sense 6) or conforming to good taste. — **taste'ful·ly,** *adv.* — **taste'ful·ness,** *n.*
taste'less, *adj.* **1.** Having no taste, or savor; insipid; flat; also, uninteresting; vapid. **2.** Not tasteful or in good taste; inartistic. — **taste'less·ly,** *adv.* — **taste'less·ness,** *n.*
tast'er (tās'tẽr), *n.* **1.** One who tastes, esp. one who tests, as tea, by tasting, for trade purposes. **2.** A device for tasting or sampling; as: **a** A shallow metal cup used in testing wine. **b** A pipette.
tast'y (tās'tĭ), *adj.;* TAST'I·ER (-tĭ·ẽr); TAST'I·EST. *Now Colloq.* **1.** Pleasing to the palate; savory. **2.** Having, or showing, good taste; tasteful. — **tast'i·ly,** *adv.* — **tast'i·ness,** *n.*
tat (tăt), *v. i.;* TAT'TED; TAT'TING. To work at tatting. — *v. t.* To make by tatting.
tat, *n.* A tap; — in ***tit for tat.***
Ta'tar (tä'tẽr), *n.* [See TARTAR.] A member of any of numerous tribes or hordes, mostly Turkic, inhabiting parts of Russia and of central and western Siberia; loosely, any Siberian Mongoloid. — *adj.* Also **Ta·tar'i·an** (tä·târ'ĭ·ăn), **Ta·tar'ic** (-tăr'ĭk). Of or pertaining to the Tatars.
tat'beb (tăt'bĕb), *n.* [Through F. (Théophile Gautier) fr. Egypt. *tebtebti*, dual.] *Egypt. Antiq.* A sandal.
tate (tāt), *n.* *Scot.* A small piece, as of wool.
tat'ou·ay (tăt'o͞o·ā; tä'to͞o·ī'), *n.* [Sp. *tatuay*, fr. Guarani *tatu-aí*, fr. *tatu* armadillo + *aí* worthless, vile; — because the flesh of this species is not edible.] A large armadillo (*Cabassous unicinctus*) of tropical South America.
tat'ter (tăt'ẽr), *n.* [Of Scand. origin.] A rag or a part torn and hanging; *pl.*, tattered clothing; shreds. — *v. t. & i.* To make or become ragged; shred. — **tat'tered** (-ẽrd), *adj.*
tat'ter·de·mal'ion (tăt'ẽr·dē·māl'yŭn; -măl'yŭn), *n.* A ragged fellow; a ragamuffin.
tat'ting (tăt'ĭng), *n.* A knotted lace made from cotton or linen thread wound on a shuttle; also, the act or process of making it. — **tat'ting,** *adj.*
tat'tle (tăt''l), *v. i.;* TAT'TLED (-'ld); TAT'TLING (-lĭng). [MD. *tatelen, tateren*, to stammer.] **1.** Orig., to prattle; now, to prate; chatter. **2.** To tell tales or secrets; be a talebearer. — *v. t.* To utter or disclose by tattling. — *n.* Idle talk or chat; gossip. — **tat'tler** (-lẽr), *n.* — **tat'tling·ly,** *adv.*
tat'tle·tale' (tăt''l·tāl'), *n.* A tattler; talebearer.
tat·too' (tă·to͞o'), *n.* [Earlier *taptoo*, fr. D. *taptoe*, fr. *tap* a tap, faucet + *toe* to shut.] *Mil. & Nav.* A call, as on drum and fife, trumpet, or bugle, shortly before taps, notifying soldiers or sailors to repair to quarters.
tat·too', *v. t.;* TAT·TOOED' (-to͞od'); TAT·TOO'ING. [Of Polynesian origin.] To mark or color (the skin) indelibly by pricking in coloring matter or by producing scars. — *n.* A mark or figure formed by tattooing. — **tat·too'er,** *n.*
tau (tô; tou), *n.* [Gr.] The nineteenth letter (**T, τ**) of the Greek alphabet, equivalent to English *t.*
tau cross. See CROSS, *Illust.* (10).
taught (tôt), *past & past part.* of TEACH.
taunt (tônt; tänt), *adj.* *Naut.* Very high or tall.
taunt, *v. t.* **1.** To reproach with scorn or insults; jeer at. **2.** *Dial.* To tease. — **Syn.** See RIDICULE. — *n.* **1.** Upbraiding language; reproach. **2.** *Obs.* One who is taunted. — **taunt'er,** *n.* — **taunt'ing·ly,** *adv.*
taupe (tōp), *n.* [F., mole.] The color of a mole's coat, yellow in hue, of low saturation and low brilliance. See COLOR.
tau'rine (tô'rīn; -rĭn), *adj.* [L. *taurinus*, fr. *taurus* a bull.] **1.** Of or pertaining to a bull; bovine. **2.** Relating to the zodiacal sign Taurus.
tau'rine (-rēn; -rĭn), **tau'rin** (-rĭn), *n.* [It was first found in ox bile. See TAURUS.] *Biochem.* A colorless crystalline compound, $H_2NCH_2CH_2SO_3H$, of neutral reaction, occurring in small quantity in the juices of muscle, the lungs, etc., and obtained as a cleavage product of taurocholic acid.
tau'ro·cho'lic (tô'rō·kō'lĭk; -kŏl'ĭk), *adj.* [*taurine* + *cholic.*] *Biochem.* Pertaining to or designating a deliquescent acid, $C_{26}H_{45}NO_7S$, occurring as the sodium salt in the bile of man, the ox, etc.
Tau'rus (tô'rŭs), *n.; gen.* TAURI (-rī). [L., a bull.] *Astron.* **a** A zodiacal constellation, containing the Pleiades and Hyades; the Bull; — represented pictorially by a bull's forequarters. **b** The second sign (♉) of the zodiac, which the sun enters about April 20. See ZODIAC.
taut (tôt), *adj.* [ME. *toght.*] **1.** *Obs.* Tough; firm; distended. **2.** Tightly drawn; not slack. **3.** Snug; tidy; in neat and proper condition. **4.** Tense; as, *taut* nerves. — **Syn.** See TIGHT. — **taut'ly,** *adv.* — **taut'ness,** *n.*
taut'ed (tăt'ĭt), *adj.* *Scot.* Tangled; matted.
taut'en (tôt''n), *v. t. & i.* To make, or become, taut.
tau'to- (tô'tō-). [Gr. *to auto.*] A combining form meaning *the same.*
tau·tog' (tô·tŏg'), *n.* [Amer. Ind. *tautauog*, pl. of *tautau* blackfish.] An edible fish (*Tautoga onitis*) of the wrasse family, found along the Atlantic coast of the United States; — called also *blackfish.*
tau·tol'o·gism (tô·tŏl'ō·jĭz'm), *n.* Use, or an instance, of tautology. — **tau·tol'o·gist** (-jĭst), *n. & adj.*
tau·tol'o·gize (-jīz), *v. i.* To write or speak tautologically.
tau·tol'o·gy (-jĭ), *n.; pl.* -GIES (-jĭz). [LL. *tautologia*, fr. Gr. *tautologia.*] Redundancy consisting of needless repetition of meaning in other words; also, an instance of this, as "audible to the ear." Cf. REDUNDANCY, PERIPHRASIS. — **tau'to·log'i·cal** (tô'tō·lŏj'ĭ·kăl), *adj.* — **tau'to·log'i·cal·ly,** *adv.*
tau·tom'er·ism (tô·tŏm'ẽr·ĭz'm), *n.* [*tauto-* + Gr. *meros* part.] *Chem.* A kind of isomerism in which the isomers change into one another with great ease, so that they ordinarily exist together in equilibrium. — **tau'to·mer'ic** (tô'tō·mĕr'ĭk), *adj.*
tau'to·nym (tô'tō·nĭm), *n.* [*tauto-* + Gr. *onyma* name.] *Bot. & Zool.* A binomial name in which the generic and specific names are alike as *Mephitis mephitis* (one species of skunk). Such names are now forbidden by the International Code of Botanical Nomenclature. — **tau'to·nym'ic** (-nĭm'ĭk), *adj.* — **tau·ton'y·my** (tô·tŏn'ĭ·mĭ), *n.*
tav'ern (tăv'ẽrn), *n.* [OF. *taverne*, fr. L. *taberna* a hut, booth, tavern.] **1.** A house where liquors are sold to be drunk on the premises. **2.** A house where transient guests are accommodated; an inn or hotel.
tav'ern·er (-ẽr·nẽr), *n.* [OF. *tavernier.*] *Archaic.* One who keeps or frequents a tavern.
taw (tô), *n.* **1.** A marble to be used as a shooter; also, a game at marbles. **2.** A line or mark from which players at marbles shoot. — **taw,** *v. i.*
taw (tô), *v. t.* [AS. *tawian.*] **1.** *Dial.* To prepare or dress, as hemp, by beating; hence, to scourge. **2.** To prepare, as sheepskin or goatskin, for gloves, by imbuing with alum, salt, etc. — **taw'er,** *n.*
taw'dry (tô'drĭ), *adj.;* TAW'DRI·ER (-drĭ·ẽr); TAW'DRI·EST. [From *Saint Audrey*, or *Etheldreda;* therefore, orig., bought at the fair of St. Audrey at Ely, where neckpieces, known as *St. Audrey's laces* or *tawdry laces* were sold.] Showy, without taste or elegance; as, *tawdry* clothing, jewelry; cheap and gaudy, as in dress; as, *tawdry* women. — **Syn.** See GAUDY. — **taw'dri·ly,** *adv.* — **taw'dri·ness,** *n.*
taw'ie (tô'ĭ), *adj.* *Scot.* Tractable.
taw'ny (tô'nĭ), *adj.;* TAW'NI·ER (-nĭ·ẽr); TAW'NI·EST. Also **taw'ney.** [OF. *tané, tanné*, past part. of *tanner* to tan.] Of the color of things tanned; specif., of a brown color, red-yellow in hue, of medium saturation and medium brilliance. See COLOR. — **Syn.** See DUSKY. — **taw'ni·ness,** *n.*
taw'pie (tô'pĭ), *n.* *Scot.* A giddy or slovenly girl.
taws, tawse (tôz; täz), *n.* *Scot.* A leather strap with thongs or a slit end. — *v. t.* *Scot.* To whip.
tax (tăks), *v. t.* [OF. *taxer*, fr. L. *taxare* to touch sharply, to censure, value, estimate; akin to L. *tangere, tactum*, to touch.] **1.** Orig., to estimate the worth of; now, *Law*, to assess or determine judicially the amount of; as, to *tax* the costs of a court action. **2.** To assess with, or subject to the payment of, a tax or taxes, specif. for the support of government; also, to lay any burden or demand upon; task; as, to *tax* one's strength. **3.** To charge; accuse; also, to censure; — often followed by *with.* — *n.* **1.** A charge, esp. a pecuniary burden imposed by authority; specif., a charge, usually pecuniary, laid upon persons or property for public purposes; a forced contribution of wealth to meet the public needs of a government. **2.** Something that taxes, or burdens; a strain or demand. — **Syn.** Impost, tribute, levy, duty, toll, assessment, rate.
☞ COMBINATIONS are:

tax-exempt	**taxgathering**	**taxpayer**
taxgatherer	**taxpaid**	**taxpaying**

— **tax'a·bil'i·ty** (tăk'sȧ·bĭl'ĭ·tĭ), **tax'a·ble·ness,** *n.* — **tax'a·ble,** *adj.* — **tax'a·bly,** *adv.* — **tax'er,** *n.*
tax·a'ceous (tăks·ā'shŭs), *adj.* [L. *taxus* yew.] Belonging to the yew family (Taxaceae). See YEW.
tax·a'tion (tăks·ā'shŭn), *n.* **1.** Act of laying a tax, or of imposing taxes. **2.** A tax; revenue from taxes.
tax'eme (tăk'sēm), *n.* [Gr. *tax*is arrangement + *phon*eme.] *Ling.* A grammatical feature; specif., order of words or morphemes; modulation, that is, stress and pitch; phonetic modification; selection, that is, choice of adjective, substantive, etc.
tax'i (tăk'sĭ), *n.; pl.* TAXIS (-sĭz). Short for TAXICAB. — *v. i.* Also **tax'y;** TAX'IED (-sĭd); TAX'I·ING *or* TAX'Y·ING. **1.** To ride in, or go by, taxicab. **2.** *Aviation.* To travel along the ground or on the water under the machine's own power, when picking out a starting place or coming in after a landing.
tax'i·cab' (tăk'sĭ·kăb'), *n.* A passenger-carrying vehicle, usually a motor vehicle with or without a taximeter, maintained for hire.

taxi dancer. [From *taxi*, for *taximeter, taxicab*, in the sense of employment by registered time.] A girl employed by a dance hall, café, cabaret, or the like, to dance with patrons who pay a certain amount for each dance.

tax′i·der′my (tăk′sĭ·dûr′mĭ), *n.* [Gr. *taxis* arrangement + *derma* a skin.] The art of preparing, stuffing, and mounting the skins of animals, esp. vertebrates, in lifelike form. — **tax′i·der′mal** (-dûr′măl), **tax′i·der′mic** (-mĭk), *adj.* — **tax′i·der′mist** (tăk′sĭ·dûr′mĭst), *n.*

tax′i·me′ter (tăk′sĭ·mē′tẽr; tăks·ĭm′ē·tẽr), *n.* [From F. or G. See TAX; -METER.] **1.** An instrument for use in a hired vehicle, as a taxicab, for automatically showing the fare due. **2.** A taxicab with a taximeter.

tax′is (tăk′sĭs), *n.* [NL., fr. Gr. *taxis* a division or arrangement, fr. *tassein* to arrange.] **1.** In technical uses, arrangement; order. **2.** *Biol.* Movement by freely motile (esp. small) organisms or organic bodies, as zoospores, toward or away from a source of stimulation, as light; — equivalent to *tropism* except in being usually applied to change of place as distinguished from simple orientation. **3.** *Gr. Antiq.* A division of troops, varying in size. **4.** *Surg.* Manual restoration of a displaced part or reduction of a hernia.

-tax′is. [NL., fr. Gr. *taxis*.] A combining form denoting *arrangement, taxis.*

tax′ite (tăk′sīt), *n.* [Gr. *taxis* arrangement.] *Petrog.* Any volcanic rock of clastic or schlieric appearance. — **tax·it′ic** (tăks·ĭt′ĭk), *adj.*

tax·on′o·my (tăks·ŏn′ō·mĭ), *n.* [F. *taxonomie*, fr. Gr. *taxis* arrangement + *nomos* law.] Classification, esp. of animals and plants according to their natural relationships; also, the laws and principles of such classification. See CLASSIFICATION, 2. — **tax·on′o·mer** (-mẽr), *n.* — **tax′o·nom′ic** (tăk′sō·nŏm′ĭk), *adj.* — **tax′o·nom′i·cal** (-ĭ·kăl), *adj.* — **tax′o·nom′i·cal·ly**, *adv.* — **tax·on′o·mist** (tăks·ŏn′ō·mĭst), *n.*

tax title. A title acquired under a sale of property for nonpayment of taxes.

tax′us (tăk′sŭs), *n.* [L., yew.] = YEW, 1.

-tax′y (-tăk′sĭ). = -TAXIS.

‖**taz′za** (tät′tsä), *n.* [It.] A somewhat goblet-shaped shallow cup or vase.

t.b. (tē′bē′). *Colloq.* See TUBERCULOSIS.

TD (tē′dē′). Short for TANK DESTROYER.

tea (tē), *n.* [From pron. of Chin. (Pek.) *ch'a*² in Fukien, better preserved in the earlier E. pron. (*tā*), and in that of G *tee, thee.*] **1. a** A shrub (*Camellia sinensis*) cultivated in China, Japan, India, etc. It is typical of a family (Theaceae, the tea family) of trees and shrubs having alternate divided leaves, pentamerous flowers, and a fleshy or capsular fruit. **b** The cured leaves, leaf buds, and internodes of this plant used in preparing a beverage. The chief teas of commerce are ***green tea***, made from leaves withered, rolled, and fired immediately (including *hyson* and *gunpowder*), ***black tea***, made from leaves fermented and oxidized before firing (including *congou, Souchong*, and *pekoe*), and ***oolong***, made from leaves partly oxidized before firing. **2.** An aromatic beverage prepared from tea leaves by infusion with boiling water. **3.** Any of numerous other plants more or less like tea; also, an infusion from their leaves used medicinally or as a beverage; as, sage *tea*. **4. a** A light collation, usually late in the afternoon, at which tea is commonly served; hence, the evening meal, when dinner is at midday; supper. **b** A reception at which tea is served. — **tea**, *adj.*

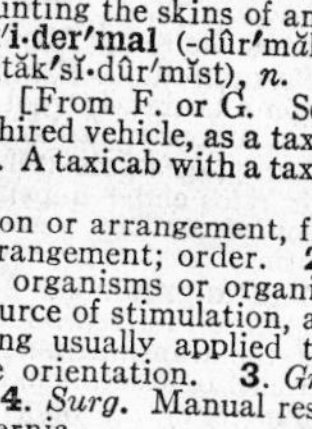

Tea Branch in Flower (*T. sinensis*). (⅕)

☞ COMBINATIONS are:

teabox	teakettle	teashop
teacake	tearoom	teatime

tea ball. A perforated metal ball to be filled with tea leaves and submerged in boiling water to make tea.

tea′ber′ry (tē′bĕr′ĭ; -bẽr·ĭ), *n.* The checkerberry.

tea biscuit. A short or sweet biscuit served with afternoon tea.

tea′cart′ (tē′kärt′), *n.* = TEA WAGON.

teach (tēch), *v. t.*; TAUGHT (tôt); TEACH′ING. [AS. *tǣcean*, pret. *tǣhte, tāhte*, to show, teach.] **1.** To make to know how; show how; hence, to train or accustom to some action. **2.** To direct as an instructor; guide the studies of. **3.** To impart the knowledge of; give lessons in; as, to *teach* Greek. **4.** To make aware by information, experience, or the like. — *v. i.* To give instruction; act as teacher.

Syn. **Teach, instruct, educate, train, discipline, school** mean to cause others to acquire knowledge or skill. **Teach** implies the imparting of information so that others may learn; **instruct**, the methodical furnishing of knowledge; **educate**, the bringing out of capacities latent in the individual; **train**, such subjection of the pupil as will fit him for the state in mind; **discipline**, subordination for the sake of controlling; **school**, a training or disciplining, esp. in that which is hard to bear.

teach′a·ble (-ȧ·b'l), *adj.* Capable of being taught; esp., apt or willing to learn; docile. — **teach′a·bil′i·ty** (-bĭl′ĭ·tĭ), **teach′a·ble·ness**, *n.* — **teach′a·bly**, *adv.*

teach′er (-ẽr), *n.* One who teaches, or instructs; esp., one whose occupation is to instruct; an instructor.

teacher bird. a = OVENBIRD, 2. **b** The red-eyed vireo.

teach′ing, *n.* The act or profession of instructing; also, that which is taught; instruction; doctrine.

tea′cup′ (tē′kŭp′), *n.* A cup for tea; also, a teacupful.

tea′cup·ful′ (tē′kŭp·fo͝ol′), *n.*; *pl.* -FULS (-fo͝olz′). Enough to fill a teacup, commonly estimated as four fluid ounces.

teak (tēk), *n.* [Pg. *teca*, fr. Malayalam *tēkka*.] A tall East Indian timber tree (*Tectona grandis*) of the verbena family; also, its hard, yellowish-brown wood (**teak′wood′**), used for shipbuilding, etc.

teal (tēl), *n.*; see PLURAL, *Note*, 3. [ME. *tele*.] Any of certain small short-necked river ducks (genera *Nettion* and *Querquedula*); esp., the ***green-winged teal*** (in Europe *N. crecca*, and in America *N. carolinense*). The ***blue-winged teal*** (*Q. discors*) is allied to the garganey.

team (tēm), *n.* [AS. *tēam* offspring, progeny, family, a line of animals harnessed together.] **1.** *Obs.* Progeny; lineage; race. **2.** *Now Dial.* A brood of young, esp. of pigs or ducks. **3. a** Two or more horses or other beasts harnessed to the same vehicle, the same plow, or the like. **b** The animals with their harness and attached vehicle; also, in popular use and in statutes, one or more draft animals, often with harness and vehicle (if any). **c** Erroneously, a wagon, carriage, or other vehicle. **4.** A number of persons associated together, as those on one side in a match. — *v. t.* **1.** To yoke or join in a team. **2.** To convey or haul with a team. — *v. i.* **1.** To be a teamster by occupation. **2.** To associate oneself in or as in a team; — with *up*. — **team**, *adj.*

team′mate′ (tēm′māt′), *n.* A fellow member of a team.

team′ster (tēm′stẽr), *n.* One who drives a team or is in the business of hauling with a team.

team′work′ (tēm′wûrk′), *n.* **1.** Work done with a team. **2.** Work done by a number of associates, all subordinating personal prominence to the efficiency of the whole.

tea′pot′ (tē′pŏt′), *n.* A vessel with a spout, in which tea is made and from which it is served.

tea′poy (tē′poi), *n.* [Hind. *tipāī*, fr. Hind. *tīn* three + Per. *pāē* foot.] Orig., an ornamental stand with three legs; hence, such a stand for a tea service; a tea table.

tear (tēr), *n.* [AS. *tēar, teagor, tæher.*] **1.** Also **tear′drop′** (-drŏp′). A drop of the saline fluid secreted by the lachrymal gland and diffused between the eye and the eyelids to moisten the parts and facilitate their motion. **2.** Something in the form of such a drop; also, a solid transparent tear-shaped drop, as of balsams. **3.** *Rare.* A lament. — **tear′less**, *adj.* — **tear′y**, *adj.*

tear (târ), *v. t.*; TORE (tōr; 70); TORN (tōrn); TEAR′ING. [AS. *teran*.] **1.** To separate parts of, or pull apart, by force; rend; also, to lacerate; as, to *tear* the skin. **2.** To divide or disrupt by the pull of contrary forces; as, a mind *torn* with doubts; also, to harrow; torture. **3.** To remove by force; wrench. **4.** To make, effect, or the like, by or as by tearing. — *v. i.* **1.** To separate on being pulled; be rent. **2.** To move or act with violence, excited haste, etc.

Syn. **Tear, rip, rend, split, cleave, rive** mean to separate forcibly. **Tear** implies pulling apart by main force, and leaving jagged edges, lacerations, etc.; **rip**, a breaking or pulling apart, sometimes but not always along a seam, a joint, etc.; **rend**, more poetical, a severing or sundering with violence; **split**, a fracturing through, esp. in the direction of grain or layers; **cleave**, a splitting by hewing asunder; **rive**, a poetical term for *cleave* or *rend*.

— *n.* **1.** Act or result of tearing; a rent. **2.** Specif.: **a** A violent passion, rage, or flurry. **b** *Slang, U.S.* A spree.

tear′ful (tēr′fo͝ol; -f'l), *adj.* Abounding with or causing tears; weeping. — **tear′ful·ly**, *adv.* — **tear′ful·ness**, *n.*

tear gas (tēr). A substance that, when dispersed in the atmosphere, blinds the eyes with tears; esp. in war, a liquid having this effect, used in shells, bombs, and grenades (**tear shells, tear bombs, tear grenades**).

tea rose. Any of various half-hardy hybrid garden roses, derived chiefly from *Rosa odorata* of China and valued for their abundant, large, fragrant, usually tea-scented blossoms. Tea roses have been largely supplanted in popularity by the hardier, more varied, richer colored ***hybrid tea roses*** often referred to as *R. dilecta*, but actually hybrids bred from crosses between tea or other roses and derivatives of *R. borboniana* or closely allied species.

tear sheet (târ). A sheet torn from a publication, esp. one to send to an advertiser whose advertisement appears on it.

tease (tēz), *v. t.* [AS. *tǣsan* to pluck, tease.] **1.** To disentangle and lay parallel, as fibers; comb or card, as wool or flax. **2.** To scratch, as cloth, to raise a nap; teasel. **3.** To tear in pieces; now, to shred finely (a tissue or specimen) for microscopic examination. **4.** To vex, harass, or irritate by petty requests, or by jests and raillery; plague; also, to importune; beg. — *v. i.* To practice teasing. — **Syn.** See WORRY. — *n.* **1.** Act of teasing or state of being teased. **2.** One who teases. — **teas′er**, *n.* — **teas′ing·ly**, *adv.*

tea′sel (tē′z'l), *n.* [AS. *tǣsel, tǣsl*, the fuller's herb.] **1.** Any of a genus (*Dipsacus*) typifying a family (Dipsacaceae, the teasel family) of Old World prickly herbs; esp. one, *D. fullonum*, the ***fuller's teasel***, with flower heads covered with stiff hooked bracts. **2.** A flower head of the fuller's teasel, formerly used, when dried, to raise a nap on cloth. **3.** Any contrivance used for teasels (in sense 2). — *v. t.*; -SELED or -SELLED (-z'ld); -SEL·ING or -SEL·LING. To subject to the action of teasels, to raise a nap. — **tea′sel·er, tea′sel·ler**, *n.*

tea′spoon′ (tē′spo͞on′), *n.* A spoon, used in stirring and sipping tea, coffee, etc. It is now generally reckoned in the United States as holding 1⅓ fluid drams (4.9 ml.), or one third of a tablespoon. — **tea′spoon·ful′** (-spo͞on·fo͝ol′), *n.*

teat (tēt; tĭt), *n.* [OF. *tete*, of Teut. origin.] The protuberance through which milk is drawn from the udder or breast of a mammal; a nipple or mammilla.

tea wagon. A small table on wheels, used in serving tea and light refreshments.

tea′zel, tea′zle (tē′z'l). Vars. of TEASEL.

Te·bet′ (tā·vāth′; tā′vĕs), *n.* Also **Te·beth′**. [Heb. *tebēth*.] See JEWISH CALENDAR.

tech·ne′ti·um (tĕk·nē′shĭ·ŭm), *n.* [NL., fr. Gr. *technētos* artificial + *-ium*.] *Chem.* A metallic element obtained by bombarding molybdenum with deuterons or neutrons and in the fission of uranium. Symbol, *Tc*; at. no., 43.

tech′nic (tĕk′nĭk), *n.* *Chiefly pl.* **a** Technique. **b** Technology.

tech′ni·cal (-nĭ·kăl), *adj.* Also **tech′nic**. [Gr. *technikos*, fr. *technē* an art.] **1.** Of or pertaining to the useful or mechanic arts, or to practice, method, procedure, etc., in any science, business, profession, sport, or the like; as, *technical* training or skill. **2.** Peculiar to or used only in a particular trade, profession, science, art, etc.; highly specialized, esp. in sense; as, *technical* words. **3.** *Stock Exchange.* Designating, or pert. to, a market in which prices are mainly determined by manipulation or speculative conditions. — **tech′ni·cal·ly**, *adv.*

tech′ni·cal′i·ty (-kăl′ĭ·tĭ), *n.*; *pl.* -TIES (-tĭz). **1.** Technical character or condition. **2.** Something which is technical; esp., a point of law, detail of procedure, rule, etc., of significance only to a technician.

tech·ni′cian (tĕk·nĭsh′ăn), *n.* One skilled in the technical details of a trade, profession, subject, art, etc.; a technical expert.

Tech′ni·col′or (tĕk′nĭ·kŭl′ẽr), *n.* A trade-mark applied to various products, including color motion pictures made by superposing the three primary colors to produce a final color print.

tech′nics (tĕk′nĭks), *n.*; see -ICS. The doctrine of arts in general; branches of learning relating to the arts.

tech·nique′ (tĕk·nēk′), *n.* [F.] The method or the details of procedure essential to expertness of execution in any art, science, etc.; hence, manner of performance with reference to such expertness; as, a violinist with bad *technique*; also, the formal elements, collectively, of an art; as, the *technique* of versification.

tech′no- (tĕk′nō-). [Gr. *technē.*] A combining form meaning: **a** *Art; skill; craft;* as in *techno*graphy. **b** *Technical; technological; applied;* as in **tech′no·chem′is·try, tech·non′o·my, tech′no·psy·chol′o·gy.**

tech·noc′ra·cy (tĕk·nŏk′rȧ·sĭ), *n.* [*techno-* + *-cracy.*] Government by technical experts. — **tech′no·crat** (tĕk′nō·krăt), *n.* — **tech′no·crat′ic** (-krăt′ĭk), *adj.*

tech·nog′ra·phy (tĕk·nŏg′rȧ·fĭ), *n.* [*techno-* + *-graphy.*] Description of arts and crafts; specif., the study of the geographical distribution of technological processes.

tech′no·log′i·cal (tĕk′nō·lŏj′ĭ·kăl), **tech′no·log′ic** (-ĭk), *adj.* **a** Pertaining or relating to technology; as, *technological* advance or problems. **b** Relating or due to advance in technology, esp. in application of scientific knowledge, methods, or research to the industrial arts and the fields of manufacture and building; as, advances in *technological* productivity. **c** *Econ.* Resulting from improvement in technical processes which increases the productiveness of machines, eliminates manual operations or old industries, or the like; as, *technological* unemployment. — **tech′no·log′i·cal·ly,** *adv.*

tech·nol′o·gy (tĕk·nŏl′ō·jĭ), *n.* [Gr. *technologia* systematic treatment. See TECHNO-; -LOGY.] **1.** Industrial science; systematic knowledge of the industrial arts. **2.** Terminology used in arts, sciences, or the like. **3.** Applied science. — **tech·nol′o·gist** (tĕk·nŏl′ō·jĭst), *n.*

tech′y (tĕch′ĭ), *adj.;* TECH′I·ER (-ĭ·ĕr); TECH′I·EST. [OF. *teche* a mark or quality (good or bad).] Unduly irritable; touchy. — **Syn.** See IRASCIBLE. — **tech′i·ly** (-ĭ·lĭ), *adv.* — **tech′i·ness** (-ĭ·nĕs; -nĭs), *n.*

tec·ton′ic (tĕk·tŏn′ĭk), *adj.* [L. *tectonicus,* fr. Gr. *tektonikos,* fr. *tektōn, -onos,* a builder.] Structural; constructional; esp.: **a** Architectural. **b** *Geol.* Of, pertaining to, or designating structures resulting from deformation of the earth's crust, esp. faulting.

tec·ton′ics (-ĭks), *n.;* see -ICS. **1.** The science or art of construction of implements, vessels, buildings, etc. **2.** *Geol.* Geology concerned with structure, esp. with folding and faulting.

tec′trix (tĕk′trĭks), *n.; pl.* TECTRICES (tĕk·trī′sēz; tĕk′trĭ·sēz). *Zool.* = COVERT, *n.,* 4. — **tec·tri′cial** (tĕk·trĭsh′ăl), *adj.*

ted (tĕd), *v. t.;* TED′DED; TED′DING. [From or akin to ON. *tethja* to dung, manure.] To spread, or turn from the swath and scatter, for drying, as new-mown grass.

ted′der (tĕd′ĕr), *n.* **1.** One who teds. **2.** A machine for tedding.

‖**Te De′um** (tē dē′ŭm). [L., fr. *te* (accus. of *tu* thou) + *Deum,* accus. of *Deus* God.] **1.** An ancient Latin hymn of praise to God; also, its English version "We praise thee, O God." **2.** Hence: **a** A musical setting of this hymn. **b** A religious service in which this hymn forms a principal part. **c** Loosely, any expression of praise or thanksgiving.

te′di·ous (tē′dĭ·ŭs; tĕd′yŭs; tē′jŭs), *adj.* [OF. & L.; OF. *tedieus,* fr. LL. *taediosus,* fr. *taedium.* See TEDIUM.] Involving tedium; tiresome; boring. — **te′di·ous·ly,** *adv.* — **te′di·ous·ness,** *n.*

te′di·um (tē′dĭ·ŭm), *n.* [L. *taedium,* fr. *taedet* it disgusts, it wearies one.] Tediousness; boredom; ennui.

‖**te′di·um vi′tae** (vī′tē). Var. of TAEDIUM VITAE.

tee (tē), *n.; pl.* TEES (tēz). **1.** The letter T, t. **2.** Anything having the shape of the letter T. — *adj.* T-shaped.

tee, *n.* [Prob. fr. the sign T to mark the exact place.] **1.** The mark aimed at in various games, as curling. **2.** An exact or precise point; — in the phrase ***to a tee,*** exactly; precisely. **3.** *Golf.* The place from which the ball is struck in starting play on a hole; also, specif., a small artificial elevation, as of sand, rubber, or wood, on which the ball is poised. — *v. t. & i.;* TEED (tēd); TEE′ING. *Golf.* To place (the ball) on a tee.

teel (tēl). Var. of TIL.

teem (tēm), *v. i.* [AS. *tēman, tȳman, tīeman.*] **1.** *Now Rare.* To bring forth young; bear. **2.** To be full, or ready to bring forth; to be prolific; abound. — *v. t.* To produce; generate. — **teem′er,** *n.*

teem, *v. t.* [ME. *temen,* fr. ON. *tœma.*] *Obs. exc. Dial.* To pour; empty.

teem′ing, *adj.* Prolific; crowding or crowded.

teen (tēn), *n.* [AS. *tēona* reproach, wrong, injury.] *Now Dial.* **a** Injury; pain. **b** Anger; vexation.

teen (tēn), *adj.* Within the teens; between thirteen and nineteen; as, boys of *teen* age. — **teen′-age′,** *adj.* — **teen′-ag′er** (-āj′ĕr), *n.*

teens (tēnz), *n. pl.* The years of one's age, or any numbers, having the termination *-teen;* as, a girl in her *teens.*

tee′ny (tē′nĭ), *adj.;* TEE′NI·ER (-nĭ·ĕr); TEE′NI·EST. *Colloq.* Very small; tiny.

tee′pee. Var. of TEPEE.

tee shirt. See T SHIRT.

tee′ter (tē′tĕr), *v. i. & t.* [E. dial. *titter* to tremble, seesaw.] To seesaw; hence, to waver. — **tee′ter,** *n.*

teeth (tēth), *n., pl.* of TOOTH.

teethe (tēth), *v. i.* To grow teeth; also, to cut one's teeth.

teeth′ing (tēth′ĭng), *n.* The first growth of teeth, or the phenomena attending their issue through the gums.

teething ring. A ring, usually of bone, ivory, or composition, for a teething infant to bite on.

teeth′ridge′ (tēth′rĭj′), *n.* The ridge of the jaw where the sockets for the teeth are situated; specif., *Phonet.,* the upper front alveolar process or ridge.

tee·to′tal (tē·tō′t'l), *adj.* [For *T-total,* used to emphasize the word.] **1.** *Colloq.* Entire; total. **2.** Of or pertaining to teetotalism. — **tee·to′tal·ly,** *adv.*

tee·to′tal·er, tee·to′tal·ler (-ĕr), *n.* A teetotalist.

tee·to′tal·ism (-ĭz'm), *n.* Principle or practice of entire abstinence from intoxicating drinks; total abstinence. — **tee·to′tal·ist** (-ĭst), *n.*

tee·to′tum (tē·tō′tŭm), *n.* [For *T-totum.* See TOTAL.] A child's toy, somewhat like a top, twirled by the fingers.

teg′men (tĕg′mĕn), *n.; pl.* TEGMINA (-mĭ·nȧ). [L., fr. *tegere, tectum,* to cover.] An integument, coating, or covering; — esp. in *Anat., Bot.,* and *Zool.* uses. — **teg′mi·nal** (-mĭ·năl), *adj.*

teg′u·lar (tĕg′ū·lĕr), *adj.* [L. *tegula* a tile.] Of, pert. to, or like a tile; of or arranged like tiles. — **teg′u·lar·ly,** *adv.*

teg′u·ment (-mĕnt), *n.* [L. *tegumentum,* fr. *tegere* to cover.] An integument. — **teg′u·men′ta·ry** (-mĕn′tȧ·rĭ), *adj.*

te ig′i·tur (tē ĭj′ĭ·tĕr). [L., thee therefore.] *R.C.Ch.* First words of the Canon of the Mass.

teil (tēl), *n., or* **teil tree.** [OF. & L.; OF. *til(le), teil(le),* fr. L. *tilia.*] A European linden, or lime tree.

teind, tiend (tēnd), *n.* [ME. *teind(e), tend(e),* tenth.] In Scotland, a tithe.

tek′tite (tĕk′tīt), *n.* [Gr. *tēktos* molten, soluble + 1st -ITE, 4.] A glassy body of rounded but indefinite shape and of unknown origin, found in the Netherlands Indies, Australia, and elsewhere.

tel-. **a** = TELE-. **b** = 2d TELO-.

tel′aes·the′si·a. Var. of TELESTHESIA.

tel′a·mon (tĕl′ȧ·mŏn), *n.; pl.* -MONES (-mō′nēz). [L., fr. Gr. *telamōn* a bearer, fr. root of *tlēnai* to bear.] *Arch.* A male figure used as a supporting column or pilaster. Cf. ATLANTES, CARYATID.

tel·an′gi·ec′ta·sis (tĕl·ăn′jĭ·ĕk′tȧ·sĭs), *n.; pl.* -SES (-sēz). [NL., fr. Gr. *telos* end + *angeion* vessel + *ektasis* dilatation.] *Med.* Dilatation of capillary vessels or terminal arteries, sometimes producing a form of angioma. — **tel·an′gi·ec·tat′ic** (-ĕk·tăt′ĭk), *adj.*

tel·au′to·graph (-ô′tō·grăf), *n.* [*tele-* + *autograph.*] A facsimile telegraph for reproducing writing, pictures, maps, etc. The motions of the transmitting pencil are reproduced by a receiving pen controlled by electromagnetic devices. — **tel·au′to·gram** (-grăm), *n.*

tel′e (tĕl′ē), *n.* Short for TELEVISION.

tel′e- (tĕl′ē-; tĕl′ĕ-), **tel-.** [Gr. *tēle* far, far off.] A combining form meaning: **a** *Far;* hence, *operating at a distance,* as in **tel′e·bar′o·graph, tel′e·ba·rom′e·ter.** **b** *Of, relating to, used in,* or *transmitted by television,* as in **tel′e·pic′ture.**

tel′e·cast′ (tĕl′ē·kăst′; tĕl′ĕ-; 9), *v. t. & i.;* -CAST′ or -CAST′ED; -CAST′ING. [*tele*vision + broad*cast.*] *Colloq.* To broadcast by television. — **tel′e·cast′,** *n.*

tel′e·com·mu′ni·ca′tion (-kŏ·mū′nĭ·kā′shŭn), *n.* Communication at a distance, as by telegraph, telephone, cable, or radio.

tel′e·du (tĕl′ē·do͞o), *n.* [Malay *tĕledu.*] A small dark-brown badger-like mammal (*Mydaus meliceps*) of Java, Borneo, and Sumatra, having a white stripe down the back and a very short tail. Like the skunk it ejects an evil-smelling secretion when alarmed.

te·le′ga (tĕ·lĕg′ȧ), *n.* [Russ.] A rude, four-wheeled, springless wagon, used among the Russians.

tel′e·gen′ic (tĕl′ē·jĕn′ĭk; tĕl′ĕ-), *adj.* [*tele-* + *-genic,* 2.] Eminently suitable for broadcast by television. Cf. RADIOGENIC.

te·leg′o·ny (tē·lĕg′ō·nĭ), *n.* [*tele-* + *-gony.*] The supposed carrying over of the influence of a sire to the offspring of subsequent matings of the dam with other males. — **tel′e·gon′ic** (tĕl′ē·gŏn′ĭk; tĕl′ĕ-), *adj.*

tel′e·gram (tĕl′ē·grăm; tĕl′ĕ-), *n.* A telegraphic dispatch.

tel′e·graph (-grăf; 9), *n.* [F. *télégraphe.* See TELE-; -GRAPH.] **1.** Orig., an apparatus for communication at a distance by signals; now,

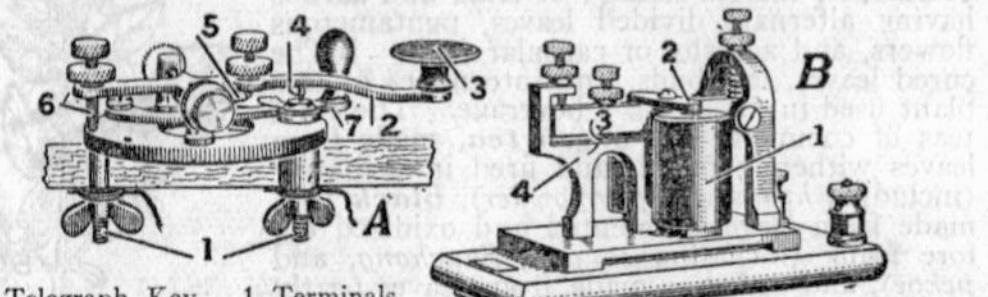

A Telegraph Key. 1 Terminals, connecting the ends of a break in the line wire; 2 Key Lever, depressed by its Button (3), thus bringing together the platinum Points (4) and closing the circuit. When not in use, the Spring (5) holds up 2, which then rests on its Backstop (6), the break being closed by setting the Lever (7) in the position shown. *B* Morse Telegraph Sounder. Currents from the line pass through the Magnet (1), causing it to draw down its Armature (2), which brings the Stop (3) against the Anvil (4) with a click for each current passing.

any apparatus, system, or process for communication at a distance by electric transmission. **2.** A telegram. — *v. t. & i.* To send or communicate by telegraph; also, to send a telegram to (a person). — **te·leg′ra·pher** (tē·lĕg′rȧ·fĕr; tĕl′ē·grăf′ĕr; tĕl′ĕ-), *n.* — **tel′e·graph′ic** (-grăf′ĭk), **tel′e·graph′i·cal** (-ĭ·kăl), *adj.* — **tel′e·graph′i·cal·ly,** *adv.* — **te·leg′ra·phist,** *n.*

te·leg′ra·phone (tē·lĕg′rȧ·fōn), *n.* [*tele-* + *-graph* + *-phone.*] An instrument for recording and reproducing sound by the local magnetization of a steel wire, disk, or ribbon, moved against the pole of a magnet connected electrically with a telephone receiver, or the like.

telegraph plant. An East Indian tick trefoil (*Desmodium gyrans*), whose lateral leaflets jerk up and down like the arms of a semaphore and also rotate on their axes.

te·leg′ra·phy (tē·lĕg′rȧ·fĭ), *n.* The use or operation of a telegraph apparatus or system for transmitting or receiving communications.

tel′e·ki·ne′sis (tĕl′ē·kĭ·nē′sĭs; -kī-; tĕl′ĕ-), *n.* [*tele-* + *kinesis.*] *Psychical Research.* The apparent production of motion in objects by a spiritualistic medium without contact or other physical means.

tel′e·lec′tric (tĕl′ē·lĕk′trĭk), *adj.* Of or pertaining to transmission, as of music, to a distance by electricity.

Te·lem′a·chus (tē·lĕm′ȧ·kŭs), *n.* [L., fr. Gr. *Tēlemachos.*] Son of Odysseus and Penelope who, failing to find his father, returns in time to help to slay Penelope's suitors.

Tel′e·mark (tĕl′ē·märk; tā′lĕ-), *n.* [From *Telemark,* southern Norway.] *Skiing.* A turn in which the ski which is to be on the outside of the turn is advanced considerably ahead of the other ski and then turned inward at a steadily widening angle until the actual turn. — **tel′e·mark,** *v. i.*

tel′e·me·chan′ics (tĕl′ē·mē·kăn′ĭks; tĕl′ĕ-), *n.;* see -ICS. The science of operating mechanisms, as motors, at a distance from the operator; specif., wireless transmission of electrical power.

te·lem′e·ter (tē·lĕm′ē·tĕr), *n.* **1.** An instrument for measuring the distance of an object from an observer. **2.** An electrical device for measuring strains. **3.** *Elec.* An electrical instrument for measuring a quantity, transmitting the result to a distant station, and there indicating or recording the quantity measured. — **tel′e·met′ric** (tĕl′ē·mĕt′rĭk; tĕl′ĕ-), *adj.* — **te·lem′e·try** (tē·lĕm′ē·trĭ), *n.*

tel′e·mo′tor (tĕl′ē·mō′tĕr; tĕl′ĕ-), *n.* *Naut.* A hydraulic device by which the movement of the wheel on the bridge operates the steering gear at the stern.

tel′en·ceph′a·lon (tĕl′ĕn·sĕf′ȧ·lŏn), *n.* See FOREBRAIN. — **tel′en·ce·phal′ic** (-sē·făl′ĭk), *adj.*

te·len′gi·scope (tē·lĕn′jĭ·skōp), *n.* [*tel-* + Gr. *engys* near + *-scope.*] An instrument that may be used as a telescope for objects close at hand or as a microscope.

tel′e·ol′o·gy (tĕl′ē·ŏl′ō·jĭ; tē′lē-), *n.* [NL. *teleologia,* fr. Gr. *telos, teleos,* end + *-logia* (see -LOGY).] **1.** The fact or the character of being directed toward an end or shaped by a purpose; — said esp. of natural processes, or of nature as a whole. **2.** The doctrine or belief that design is apparent or ends are immanent, in nature; esp., the vitalist doctrine that the processes of life are not exclusively determined by mechanical causes, but are directed to the realization of certain normal wholes or entelechies; — opposed to *mechanism.* — **tel′e·o·log′i·cal** (tĕl′ē·ō·lŏj′ĭ·kăl; tē′lē-), *adj.* — **tel′e·o·log′i·cal·ly,** *adv.* — **tel′e·ol′o·gist** (-ŏl′ō·jĭst), *n.*

tel′e·ost (tĕl′ē·ŏst; tē′lē-), *n.* [Gr. *teleos* complete, perfect + *osteon* bone.] *Zool.* A fish of a group (Teleostei), the bony fishes, including most living ordinary fishes, as distinguished from the ganoids, dipnoans, and elasmobranchs. — **tel′e·ost,** *adj.* — **tel′e·os′te·an** (-ŏs′tē·ăn), *adj.* & *n.*

te·lep′a·thy (tē·lĕp′ȧ·thĭ), *n.* [*tele-* + *-pathy.*] Apparent communication from one mind to another otherwise than through the channels of sense; thought transference. — **tel′e·path′ic** (tĕl′ē·păth′ĭk; tĕl′ĕ-), *adj.* — **tel′e·path′i·cal·ly** (-ĭ·kăl·ĭ), *adv.* — **te·lep′a·thist,** *n.*

tel′e·phone (tĕl′ē·fōn; tĕl′ĕ-), *n.* An instrument for reproducing sounds, esp. articulate speech, at a distance. — *v. t.* & *i.* To send or communicate by telephone; speak to (a person) by telephone. — **tel′e·phon′er** (-fōn′ẽr), *n.* — **tel′e·phon′ic** (-fŏn′ĭk), *adj.* — **tel′e·phon′i·cal·ly** (-ĭ·kăl·ĭ), *adv.*

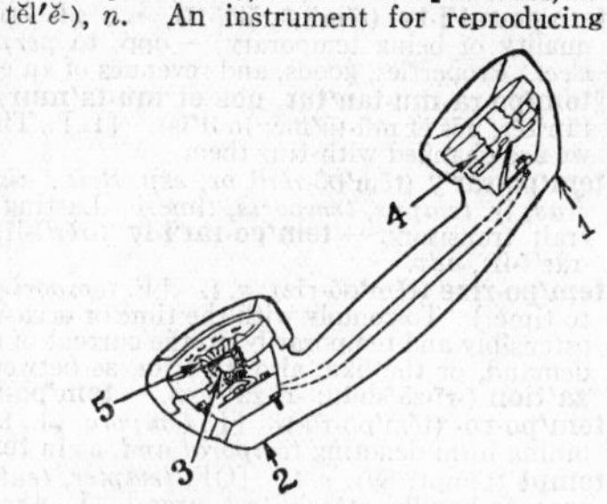

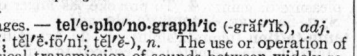

Telephone (Handset cross section). 1 Receiver; 2 Transmitter; 3 Carbon Granules; 4 Magnet; 5 Diaphragm.

telephone receiver. *Elec.* A device for converting electric impulses or varying current into sound.

tel′e·pho′no·graph (tĕl′ē·fō′nō·grăf; tĕl′ĕ-), *n.* A combination of a telephone receiver and a phonograph for recording and reproducing telephone messages. — **tel′e·pho′no·graph′ic** (-grăf′ĭk), *adj.*

te·leph′o·ny (tē·lĕf′ō·nĭ; tĕl′ē·fō′nĭ; tĕl′ĕ-), *n.* The use or operation of an apparatus for electrical transmission of sounds between widely removed points; as, wireless *telephony.*

tel′e·phote (tĕl′ē·fōt; tĕl′ĕ-), *n.* A telelectric apparatus for reproducing images photographically of distant objects.

tel′e·pho′to (-fō′tō), *adj.* **1.** Telephotographic. **2.** Pert. to or designating a compound lens giving a large image of a distant object in a camera of short focal length.

tel′e·pho′to·graph (-fō′tō·grăf), *n.* A photograph, image, or impression, reproduced by telephotography.

tel′e·pho·tog′ra·phy (-fō·tŏg′rȧ·fĭ), *n.* **1.** The photography of distant objects, usually by a camera provided with a telephoto lens or mounted in place of the eyepiece of a telescope. **2.** The art or process of transmitting and reproducing photographic or other pictures by telegraphic methods. — **tel′e·pho′to·graph′ic** (-fō′tō·grăf′ĭk), *adj.*

tel′e·print′er (tĕl′ē·prĭn′tẽr; tĕl′ĕ-), *n.* [*tele-* + *printer.*] A teletypewriter.

tel′e·ran (tĕl′ē·răn; tĕl′ĕ-), *n.* [*tele*vision + *ra*dar + *a*ir + *n*avigation.] A system of aerial navigation that utilizes a combination of television and radar for the guidance of aircraft.

tel′e·scope (tĕl′ē·skōp; tĕl′ĕ-), *n.* [NL. *telescopium,* fr. Gr. *tēleskopos* viewing afar, farseeing, fr. *tēle* far, far off + *skopos* a watcher.] An optical instrument used to aid the eye or camera in viewing or photographing distant objects, as the heavenly bodies. Telescopes having an object glass, which collects the beams of light and forms the image, are called ***refracting telescopes.*** If the light is collected by a mirror, the instrument is called a ***reflecting telescope.*** — *v. i.* To slide or pass one within another, like the sections of a small telescope; hence, force a way into, or enter, another lengthwise as the result of collision. — *v. t.* To cause to telescope.

tel′e·scop′ic (-skŏp′ĭk), **tel′e·scop′i·cal** (-ĭ·kăl), *adj.* **1.** Of or pertaining to a telescope; performed by a telescope. **2.** Seen or discoverable only by a telescope; as, *telescopic* stars. **3.** Able to discern objects at a distance; farseeing. **4.** Having parts that telescope; as, a *telescopic* drinking cup. — **tel′e·scop′i·cal·ly,** *adv.*

te·les′co·py (tē·lĕs′kō·pĭ; tĕl′ē·skō′pĭ; tĕl′ĕ-), *n.* Art or practice of using or making telescopes. — **te·les′co·pist** (-pĭst), *n.*

tel′e·sis (tĕl′ē·sĭs), *n.* [NL., lit., completion.] Intelligent direction of natural and social forces to a desired end; progress intelligently planned and directed.

tel′e·spec′tro·scope (tĕl′ē·spĕk′trō·skōp; tĕl′ĕ-), *n.* A spectroscope arranged to be attached to a telescope to obtain spectra of heavenly bodies.

tel′e·ster′e·o·scope′ (-stẽr′ē·ō·skōp′; -stēr′ē-), *n.* [*tele-* + *stereoscope.*] A binocular telescope used to obtain enhanced impressions of relief in distant objects.

tel′es·the′si·a (tĕl′ĕs·thē′zhĭ·ȧ; -zhȧ; -zĭ·ȧ), *n.* [NL., fr. *tel-* + *esthesia.*] An impression received at a distance without the normal operation of the sense organs.

te·les′tich (tē·lĕs′tĭk; tĕl′ē·stĭk), *n.* Also **te·les′tic.** [Gr. *telos* the end + *stichos* a line.] A poem in which the consecutive final letters of the lines spell a name. Cf. ACROSTIC.

tel′e·ther·mom′e·ter (tĕl′ē·thẽr·mŏm′ē·tẽr; tĕl′ĕ-), *n.* *Physics.* An apparatus for indicating the temperature of a distant point. — **tel′e·ther·mom′e·try** (-trĭ), *n.*

Tel′e·type (tĕl′ē·tīp; tĕl′ĕ-), *n.* **a** A trade-mark applied to a kind of teletypewriter. **b** [*often not cap.*] A system of communication in which the Teletype is used.

tel′e·type′writ′er (-tīp′rīt′ẽr), *n.* A form of printing telegraph, recording like a typewriter.

te·leu′to·spore (tē·lū′tō·spōr), *n.* [Gr. *teleutē* completion + *spore.*] A teliospore. — **te·leu′to·spor′ic** (-spŏr′ĭk), *adj.*

tel′e·view′ (tĕl′ē·vū′; tĕl′ĕ-), *v. t.* & *i.* To observe or watch by means of a television receiver. — **tel′e·view′er,** *n.*

tel′e·vise (-vīz), *v. t.* To transmit or receive (an image) by television.

tel′e·vi′sion (tĕl′ē·vĭzh′ŭn; tĕl′ĕ-; tĕl′ē·vĭzh′ŭn), *n.* The transmission and reproduction of a view or scene by any device which converts light rays into electrical waves and reconverts these into visible light rays. — **tel′e·vi′sion·al** (-ăl), **tel′e·vi′sion·ar′y** (-ẽr′ĭ *or, esp. Brit.,* -ẽr·ĭ), *adj.*

tel′e·vi′sor (tĕl′ē·vī′zẽr; tĕl′ĕ-), *n.* A television apparatus.

tel′fer, tel′fer·age. Vars. of TELPHER, etc.

tel′ford (tĕl′fẽrd), *adj.* [After T. *Telford* (1757–1834), Scot. road engineer.] Designating, or pertaining to, a road pavement having a hard, smooth surface of rolled stone.

tel′har·mo′ni·um (tĕl′här·mō′nĭ·ŭm), *n.* [NL., fr. *tele-* + *harmonium.*] An instrument for producing music at a distant point or points by alternating currents of electricity controlled by a keyboard.

te′li·al (tē′lĭ·ăl; tĕl′ĭ-), *adj.* Of or pertaining to a telium.

tel′ic (tĕl′ĭk), *adj.* [Gr. *telikos,* fr. *telos* the end.] Tending toward an end; purposive; teleological. — **tel′i·cal·ly** (-ĭ·kăl·ĭ), *adv.*

te′li·o·spore′ (tē′lĭ·ō·spōr′; tĕl′ĭ-), *n.* [*telium* + *spore.*] *Bot.* A thick-walled winter or resting spore developed in the final (telial) stage in the life cycle of rust fungi, and giving rise to the basidium.— **te′li·o·spor′ic** (-spŏr′ĭk), *adj.*

te′li·o·stage′ (tē′lĭ·ō·stāj′; tĕl′ĭ-), *n.* [*telium* the spore fruit, fr. Gr. *telos, teleos,* end + *stage.*] *Bot.* The final, or late summer, stage in the life cycle of the rust fungi.

te′li·um (tē′lĭ·ŭm; tĕl′ĭ-), *n.; pl.* TELIA (-ȧ). [NL., fr. Gr. *telos, teleos,* end, completion.] *Bot.* In the rust fungi, a teliospore-containing sorus, or pustule, on the host plant.

tell (tĕl), *v. t.;* TOLD (tōld); TELL′ING. [AS. *tellan.*] **1.** To mention one by one; enumerate; count; as, to *tell* money; to *tell* one's beads (in counting on a rosary the prayers said). **2.** To relate in detail; narrate; recount; as, to *tell* a yarn; also, to utter; say; as, to *tell* a lie. **3.** To make known or manifest; disclose; divulge; reveal; as, fossils *tell* much of the past. **4.** To inform; report to. **5.** To order; request; direct; as, he *told* her to go. **6.** To ascertain by observing; to find out; recognize; decide; as, how can I *tell* what to do? **7.** To assure emphatically; as, he did do it, I *tell* you. — **Syn.** See REVEAL. — *v. i.* **1.** To give an account; make report. **2.** To take effect; have a marked effect; as, every shot *tells.* **3.** *Colloq.* To act as a talebearer; inform. **4.** To serve as evidence or indication; — with *of.* — ***tell off.*** To number and set apart; esp., *Mil.,* to number and detail for special duty.

Tell, Wilhelm *or* **William.** See WILLIAM TELL.

tell′er (tĕl′ẽr), *n.* **1.** One who tells; an informer, narrator, or describer. **2.** One who reckons, counts, or the like; specif., one appointed to count the votes in a legislative body, assembly, etc. **3.** *Banking.* Any of several employees concerned with the direct handling of money received by, or paid out by, a bank.

tell′ing, *adj.* That tells; effective; as, a *telling* blow. — **Syn.** See VALID. — **tell′ing·ly,** *adv.*

tell′tale′ (tĕl′tāl′), *n.* **1.** A talebearer; informer; tattler. **2.** An outward sign of something kept secret; an indication. **3.** A device to keep a check on employees; esp., a time clock. **4.** *Music.* An indicator on an organ showing the wind pressure. **5.** *Naut.* A device showing the position of the helm or rudder. **6.** *Railroads.* A danger sign, as a row of strips hung over tracks to indicate approach to a low overhead bridge. **7.** *Squash, Rackets, etc.* A strip on the front wall of the court, 2 to 2½ ft. above the ground, over which the ball must be hit. — *adj.* That is or serves as a telltale.

tel·lu′ri·an (tĕ·lū′rĭ·ăn), *adj.* [L. *tellus, -uris,* the earth.] Of, pertaining to, or characteristic of the earth. — *n.* A dweller on the earth.

tel·lu′ri·an, *n.* Also **tel·lu′ri·on** (-ŏn). An apparatus to illustrate the causation of day and night by the rotation of the earth on its axis, the dependence of the seasons on the sun's declination, etc.

tel·lu′ric (-rĭk), *adj.* [L. *tellus, -uris,* the earth.] Tellurian; proceeding from the earth.

tel·lu′ric, *adj.* [From TELLURIUM.] *Chem.* Of, pertaining to, or containing tellurium, esp., designating compounds in which the element has a high valence. Cf. TELLUROUS.

tel′lu·ride (tĕl′ū·rīd; -rĭd), *n.* Also **tel′lu·rid.** *Chem.* A binary compound of tellurium with another element or a radical; — formerly called **tel′lu·ret** (-rĕt).

tel′lu·rite (-rīt), *n.* **1.** *Chem.* A salt of tellurous acid. **2.** *Mineral.* Native tellurium dioxide, TeO_2, occurring sparingly in tufts of white or yellowish crystals.

tel·lu′ri·um (tĕ·lū′rĭ·ŭm), *n.* [NL., fr. L. *tellus, -uris,* the earth.] *Chem.* A nonmetallic element analogous to sulfur and selenium, occasionally native as a crystalline substance of tin-white luster (sp. gr., 6.24), but usually combined with metals. Symbol, *Te;* at. no., 52; at. wt., 127.61.

tel′lu·rize (tĕl′ū·rīz), *v. t.* To combine, impregnate, or treat, with tellurium; — chiefly in *past part.*

tel′lu·rous (tĕl′ū·rŭs; tĕ·lū′-), *adj.* *Chem.* Of, pertaining to, or containing tellurium, esp., designating compounds in which the element has a low valence. Cf. TELLURIC.

tel′o- (tĕl′ō-). [Gr. *telo-,* fr. *tele* far, far off.] = TELE-, as in **tel′o·dy·nam′ic** (-dī·năm′ĭk; -dĭ-), relating to the transmission of power to a distance, specif. by a system of ropes or cables and pulleys.

tel′o- (tĕl′ō-; tē′lō-), **tel-.** [Gr. *telos.*] A combining form meaning *end,* as in **tel′o·phase** (-fāz), *Biol.,* the final stage of mitosis, following the anaphase in which the entire cell divides and the new nuclei are formed (cf. PROPHASE).

tel′pher (tĕl′fẽr), *n.* Also **tel′fer.** [Used instead of *telephore,* fr. *tele-* + Gr. *pherein* to bear.] A light car hung from, and run on, aerial cables, esp. one propelled by electricity. — *v. t.* To transport by telpher.

tel′pher·age (-ĭj), *n.* Also **tel′fer·age.** An electric transportation system, esp. one using telphers.

tel′son (tĕl′sŭn), *n.* [NL., fr. Gr. *telson* a boundary, limit.] *Zool.* The terminal segment of the body of an arthropod or segmented worm, esp. that of a crustacean. See KING CRAB, *Illust.*

Tel′u·gu (tĕl′ŏŏ·gōō), *n.* **1.** *sing.* & *pl.* One of a Dravidian people in Hyderabad, India. **2.** A Dravidian language of east central India. — **Tel′u·gu,** *adj.*

tem·blor′ (tĕm·blōr′), *n.; pl.* TEMBLORS (-blōrz′); -BLORES (-blō′rās). [Sp.] *U.S.* An earthquake.

tem′er·ar′i·ous (tĕm′ẽr·âr′ĭ·ŭs), *adj.* [L. *temerarius.*] Unreasonably venturous; rash. — **Syn.** See ADVENTUROUS. — **tem′er·ar′i·ous·ly,** *adv.*

te·mer′i·ty (tē·mĕr′ĭ·tĭ), *n.* [F. *témérité,* fr. L. *temeritas,* fr. *temere* by chance, rashly.] Unreasonable contempt of danger; rashness.

Syn. **Temerity, audacity, hardihood, effrontery, nerve, cheek, gall** mean flagrant boldness. **Temerity** suggests rashness and contempt of danger; **audacity**, a disregard of restraints imposed by prudence, convention, sound morals, etc.; **hardihood**, firmness in daring and defiance; **effrontery**, shameless disregard of courtesy, propriety, etc., or an arrogant assumption of a privilege; **nerve**, **cheek**, and **gall** are slang terms for *effrontery*.

tem′per (tĕm′pẽr), *v. t.* [From AS. *temprian*, but influenced by OF. *temprer*, F. *tempérer*; all fr. L. *temperare*.] **1.** *Archaic.* To mingle in due proportion; compound; blend. **2.** To regulate, esp. by moderating; qualify, as by an ingredient; mollify; assuage. **3.** *Now Rare.* To fit together; adjust. **4.** To bring to the desired consistency, texture, degree of toughness, etc., as clay by wetting and kneading, steel or glass by gradual heating and cooling, or artists' colors by mixing with oil. **5.** *Music.* To tune; esp., to adjust the pitch of (a note, chord, instrument, or the like) to a temperament. — *v. i.* To be or become tempered.

— *n.* **1.** State of being tempered; specif.: **a** Of a compound substance, due or just mixture of different qualities; as, the *temper* of mortar. **b** The state of a metal or other substance, esp. as to its hardness or toughness. Temper in steel is indicated either by its carbon content or its color in tempering. **2.** *Obs.* Constitution of body; temperament. **3.** Disposition or frame of mind, esp. as to the passions and affections; as, a fiery *temper*. **4.** Equanimity; composure. *Archaic*, exc. in the phrases, *to keep* or *lose one's temper*. **5.** Heat of mind or passion; proneness to anger. **6.** *Obs.* Mean; medium. **7.** A substance added to or mixed with something else to modify its properties. — **Syn.** See MOOD: DISPOSITION. — **tem′per·a·ble**, *adj.* — **tem′per·er**, *n.*

tem′per·a (tĕm′pẽr·ȧ; tĕm′pȧ·rä), *n.* [It.] A process of painting, in which an albuminous or colloidal medium, as white of egg, is employed as a vehicle instead of oil. Cf. 2d DISTEMPER, *n.*

tem′per·a·ment (tĕm′pẽr·ȧ·mĕnt), *n.* [L. *temperamentum* a mixing in due proportion, temperament.] **1.** Internal constitution with respect to balance or mixture of qualities or parts. **2.** The peculiar physical and mental character of an individual; as, the *sanguine*, *phlegmatic*, *choleric* (or *bilious*), or *melancholic temperament*, denoting types formerly believed to be due to the preponderance of one or other of these humors. See HUMOR, *n.*, 2. **3.** Frame of mind or type of mental reactions characteristic of an individual. **4.** Act, means, or result, of tempering, or modifying; adjustment. **5.** *Obs.* Temperature; also, climate. **6.** *Music.* The system or process of slightly modifying the intervals of the scale so as to admit of modulations without the use of an inconveniently large number of distinctions in pitch; also, the adjustment so made. ***equal temperament*** is a division of the octave into twelve equal parts, all keys being thus available for modulation. — **Syn.** See DISPOSITION.

tem′per·a·men′tal (-mĕn′tăl), *adj.* Of or pertaining to temperament; esp., having or showing a sensitive, easily excited temperament. — **tem′per·a·men′tal·ly**, *adv.*

tem′per·ance (tĕm′pẽr·ăns), *n.* [AF. *temperaunce*, fr. L. *temperantia*.] **1.** Habitual moderation in the indulgence of the appetites and passions; moderation; — one of the cardinal virtues. **2.** Specif., moderation in, or narrowly, abstinence from, the use of intoxicants. **3.** *Archaic.* Self-control; calmness.

tem′per·ate (-ĭt), *adj.* [L. *temperatus*, past part. of *temperare*.] **1.** Moderate; not excessive; as: **a** Moderate in the indulgence of the appetites or passions. **b** Self-controlled; restrained. **c** Abstemious in the use of intoxicating liquors. **2.** Neither excessively hot or cold; mild; as, a *temperate* climate. **3.** *Music.* Tempered; — of an interval or scale. — **Syn.** See MODERATE. — **tem′per·ate·ly**, *adv.* — **tem′per·ate·ness**, *n.*

Temperate Zone. See ZONE, *n.*

tem′per·a·ture (tĕm′pẽr·ȧ·tūr), *n.* [L. *temperatura* due measure, proportion, temperament.] **1.** *Obs.* **a** Constitution; temperament. **b** Moderation; mildness. **2.** Degree of hotness or coldness measured on a definite scale. See THERMOMETER. **3.** *Med.* The degree of heat, esp. of the human body; also, loosely, body heat above the normal, approximately 98.6° F.

temperature gradient. Rate of change of temperature with increase in height.

tem′pered (tĕm′pẽrd), *adj.* **1.** Having a temper. **2.** Moderated in intensity or the like by the mixture of an additional ingredient; as, *tempered* wisdom. **3.** *Music.* Conformed to temperament, esp. equal temperament.

temper pin. *Chiefly Scot.* **1.** The regulating pin of a spinning wheel. **2.** A peg of a violin.

tem′pest (tĕm′pĕst; -pĭst), *n.* [OF. *tempeste*, fr. L. *tempestas* a portion of time, a season, weather, storm.] **1.** An extensive violent wind, esp. one attended with rain, hail, or snow; a furious storm. **2.** Any violent tumult. — *v. t. & i.* To move forth like a tempest; to agitate.

tem·pes′tu·ous (tĕm·pĕs′tū·ŭs), *adj.* [OF. *tempestueus*, fr. LL. *tempestuosus*.] Involving or resembling a tempest; turbulent; violent. — **tem·pes′tu·ous·ly**, *adv.* — **tem·pes′tu·ous·ness**, *n.*

Tem′plar (tĕm′plẽr), *n.* [OF. *templier*, fr. ML. *templarius*. See TEMPLE church.] **1.** One of a religious and military order established at Jerusalem about A.D. 1118 for the protection of pilgrims and of the Holy Sepulcher. These ***Knights Templars*** were so named because for a time they occupied quarters next to the building known as *Solomon's Temple*. **2.** *Eng.* [*not cap.*] A barrister or student of law occupying chambers in the Temple, London. **3.** *Freemasonry.* = KNIGHT TEMPLAR, 2.

tem′plate (-plĭt), **tem′plet** (-plĕt; -plĭt), *n.* [F. *templet*, dim. of *temple*.] **1.** *Arch.* A short piece placed in a wall under a beam to distribute the pressure; also, a beam spanning a doorway or the like and supporting joists. **2.** *Mach.* A gauge, pattern, or mold, commonly a thin plate or board, used as a guide to the form of the work.

tem′ple (tĕm′p'l), *n.* [F.] *Weaving.* A device in a loom for keeping the web stretched transversely.

tem′ple, *n.* [OF., fr. dim. of L. *tempora*, pl. of *tempus*.] The flattened space on either side of the forehead of man and certain other mammals.

tem′ple, *n.* [From AS. *temp(e)l*, and fr. OF. *temple*, both fr. L. *templum* a space marked out, sanctuary.] **1.** An edifice dedicated to the worship of a deity. **2.** [*cap.*] One of three successive buildings in ancient Jerusalem for the worship of Jehovah. **3.** Among Christians, an edifice for public worship. **4.** [*cap.*] Two Inns of Court (***Inner*** and ***Middle Temple***) occupying the site of the original London establishment of Knights Templars. **5.** A local organization of Odd Fellows. — **tem′pled** (tĕm′p'ld), *adj.*

tem′plet (-plĕt; -plĭt), *n.* [F.] = TEMPLATE.

tem′po (tĕm′pō), *n.*; *pl.* TEMPI (-pē), TEMPOS (-pōz). [It., fr. L. *tempus*.] **1.** *Music.* The rate of speed at which a piece or passage moves, generally indicated by such adjectives as *adagio*, *andante*, *presto*, and by reference to the metronome. **2.** Rhythm; hence, rate of activity in general; as, the *tempo* of our age.

tem′po·ral (tĕm′pō·răl), *adj.* [LL. *temporalis*, fr. *tempora* the temples.] *Anat. & Zool.* Of or pertaining to the temple or temples or the sides of the skull behind the orbits.

tem′po·ral, *adj.* [L. *temporalis*, fr. *tempus*, *temporis*, time, portion of time.] **1.** Of, pertaining to, or limited by time. **2.** Pertaining to the present life, or this world; secular; also, transitory; temporary; — distinguished from *sacred* or *eternal*. **3.** Civil or political, as distinguished from *ecclesiastical*; as, *temporal* power. **4.** *Gram.* Expressive of time. — *n.* Anything temporal or secular; a temporality; — chiefly in *pl.* — **tem′po·ral·ly**, *adv.*

temporal bone. *Anat.* A compound bone of the side of the human skull.

tem′po·ral′i·ty (tĕm′pō·răl′ĭ·tĭ), *n.*; *pl.* -TIES (-tĭz). **1.** State or quality of being temporary; — opp. to *perpetuity*. **2.** *Usually pl. Eccl.* Properties, goods, and revenues of an ecclesiastical corporation.

‖**tem′po·ra mu·tan′tur, nos et mu·ta′mur in il′lis** (tĕm′pō·rȧ mū·tăn′tẽr, nōs ĕt mū·tā′mẽr ĭn ĭl′ĭs). [L.] The times are changed, and we are changed with (in) them.

tem′po·rar′y (tĕm′pō·rẽr′ĭ *or, esp. Brit.*, -rẽr·ĭ), *adj.* [L. *temporarius*, fr. *tempus*, *temporis*, time.] Lasting for a time only; ephemeral; transitory. — **tem′po·rar′i·ly** (-rẽr′ĭ·lĭ; -rẽr·ĭ·lĭ; *emphat. also* -râr′ĭ·lĭ), *adv.*

tem′po·rize (tĕm′pō·rīz), *v. i.* [F. *temporiser*. See TEMPORAL pert. to time.] To comply with the time or occasion; to yield, in reality or ostensibly and temporarily, to the current of opinion, circumstances, a demand, or the like; also, to trim, as between parties. — **tem′po·ri·za′tion** (-rĭ·zā′shŭn; -rī·zā′-), *n.* — **tem′po·riz′er** (-rīz′ẽr), *n.*

tem′po·ro- (tĕm′pō·rō-). [L. *tempora*, pl., temples.] *Anat.* A combining form denoting *temporal and*, as in **tem′po·ro·max′il·lar′y**.

tempt (tĕmpt; 89), *v. t.* [OF. *tempter*, *tenter*, fr. L. *temptare*, *tentare*, to handle, attack, test, urge.] **1.** *Archaic.* To put to trial; to test. **2.** To endeavor to persuade; to induce; incite. **3.** To lead, or endeavor to lead, into evil; to entice to what is wrong by promise of pleasure or gain. **4.** To provoke, as anger or a person to anger. — **Syn.** See LURE. — **tempt′a·ble**, *adj.*

temp·ta′tion (tĕmp·tā′shŭn), *n.* **1.** Act of tempting; seduction. **2.** State of being tempted, or enticed to evil. **3.** That which tempts, esp. to evil.

tempt′er (tĕmp′tẽr), *n.* One who tempts or entices; esp. [*cap.*], with *the*, the Devil. — **tempt′ress** (-trĕs; -trĭs), *n.*

tempt′ing, *adj.* Adapted to entice or allure; as, *tempting* pleasures. — **tempt′ing·ly**, *adv.* — **tempt′ing·ness**, *n.*

‖**tem′pus e′dax re′rum** (tĕm′pŭs ē′dăks rē′rŭm). [L.] Time devouring (all) things.

‖**tem′pus fu′git** (fū′jĭt). [L.] Time flies.

ten (tĕn), *n.* [AS. *tēn*, *tīen*, *tȳn*; akin to *-teen* in thir*teen*, four*teen*, etc.] **1.** See NUMBER, *Table*. **2.** A person or object distinguished by the number ten, often the tenth in a series, as a playing card having ten spots; *Colloq.*, a ten-dollar bill. — **ten**, *adj.*

ten-. = TENO-.

ten′a·ble (tĕn′ȧ·b'l; tē′nȧ-), *adj.* [F., fr. *tenir* to hold, fr. L. *tenere*.] Capable of being held, maintained, or defended. — **ten′a·bil′i·ty** (-bĭl′ĭ·tĭ), *n.* — **ten′a·bly**, *adv.*

ten′ace (tĕn′ĭs), *n.* [F., tenacious, *demeurer tenace* to hold the best and third-best cards and take both tricks, the adversary having to lead. See TENACIOUS.] *Bridge, Whist, etc.* A combination in one hand of the best and third-best cards unplayed, in any suit, as ace-queen called ***major tenace***; king-jack, ***minor tenace***.

te·na′cious (tē·nā′shŭs), *adj.* [L. *tenax*, *-acis*, fr. *tenere* to hold.] **1.** Holding fast, or inclined to hold fast; — with *of*. **2.** Apt to retain; retentive. **3.** Having parts apt to adhere to each other; cohesive; tough; as, a *tenacious* metal. **4.** Glutinous; viscous; sticking; adhesive. — **Syn.** See STRONG. — **te·na′cious·ly**, *adv.* — **te·na′cious·ness**, *n.*

te·nac′i·ty (tē·năs′ĭ·tĭ), *n.* **1.** Quality or state of being tenacious; as, persistency; also, cohesiveness; also, adhesiveness. **2.** *Physics.* Tensile strength. — **Syn.** See COURAGE.

te·nac′u·lum (tē·năk′ū·lŭm), *n.*; *pl.* TENACULA (-lȧ). [LL., a holder, fr. *tenere* to hold.] *Surg.* A slender sharp-pointed hook attached to a handle, for taking up arteries, etc.

te·naille′, te·nail′ (tĕ·nāl′), *n.* [F. *tenaille* a pair of pincers or tongs, a tenaille, fr. L. *tenaculum*, pl. *tenacula*. See TENACULUM.] *Fort.* An outwork in the main ditch between two bastions.

ten′an·cy (tĕn′ăn·sĭ), *n.*; *pl.* -CIES (-sĭz). **1.** *Law.* A holding, or a mode of holding, an estate; tenure; the temporary possession of what belongs to another. **2.** A piece of land held of another. **3.** The period of a tenant's occupancy or possession.

ten′ant (-ănt), *n.* [OF., orig. pres. part. of *tenir* to hold.] **1.** *Law.* **a** One who holds or possesses real estate, or sometimes personalty (as an annuity), by any kind of right. **b** One who has temporary possession of lands or tenements of another; — corr. of *landlord*. **2.** A dweller; an occupant. — *v. t.* To occupy as tenant. — **ten′ant·a·ble**, *adj.* — **ten′ant·less**, *adj.*

tenant farmer. A farmer who tills soil owned by another, paying rent either in cash or in shares of produce.

ten′ant·ry (tĕn′ănt·rĭ), *n.* Tenancy; also, the body of tenants.

tench (tĕnch), *n.* See PLURAL, *Note*, 3. [OF. *tenche*, fr. LL. *tinca*.] A European fresh-water fish (*Tinca tinca*) of the carp family, allied to the dace, noted for its tenacity of life.

Ten Commandments. The Decalogue, or summary of God's commands, given to Moses at Mount Sinai (*Ex.* xx).

tend (tĕnd), *v. i.* [Aphetic form of ATTEND.] **1.** To wait, as attendants; serve; attend; — with *on*. **2.** *Obs.* To be waiting or in readiness. *Shak.* — *v. t.* **1.** To apply oneself to the care of; as: **a** To minister to; to cultivate or foster, as a plant. **b** To have charge of as a caretaker or overseer. **c** To manage or oversee the operations of, as a store or a machine. **2.** *Archaic.* To attend as a retainer.

tend, *v. i.* [OF. *tendre*, fr. L. *tendere*, *tensum* and *tentum*, to extend, tend.] **1.** To move or direct one's course. **2.** To be directed or have a tendency, conscious or unconscious, to any end, object, or purpose; to serve as a means; conduce. — *v. t.* [F. *tendre*.] *Naut.* To stand by (a rope or the like) in readiness to prevent its fouling or suffering any mischance. Cf. MAN.

tend′ance (tĕn′dăns), *n.* **1.** Bestowal of attention; ministration; attendance. **2.** *Obs.* Attendants; retinue.

tend′en·cy (tĕn′dĕn·sĭ), *n.; pl.* -CIES (-sĭz). **1.** Direction or course toward any place, object, effect, or result; drift; hence, inclination; bias. **2.** Proneness to a certain course of thought or action; a propensity. **3.** [After G. *Tendenz.*] Directional presentation favoring a particular point of view, esp. a social or political thesis; — chiefly in attributive use, as in **tendency writings**.

Syn. **Tendency, trend, drift, tenor, current** mean direction taken by a course, a progression, or the like. **Tendency** specifically implies a driving force sending a person or thing in a given direction; **trend,** a direction maintained in spite of irregularities or windings, or one subject to change; **drift,** a tendency influenced by winds or the like, or an underlying meaning which may be inferred; **tenor,** a drift, esp. in the latter sense; **current,** a clearly defined but not necessarily unalterable direction or tendency.

ten·den′tious, ten·den′cious (tĕn·dĕn′shŭs), *adj.* Marked by an intruded reformatory intent or by an implicit purposive disposition to promote a point of view (cf. TENDENCY, 3); as, a novel, play, history, speech, or news dispatch may be *tendentious.* — **ten·den′tious·ly, ten·den′cious·ly,** *adv.* — **ten·den′tious·ness, ten·den′cious·ness,** *n.*

tend′er (tĕn′dẽr), *n.* [From TEND to attend.] **1.** One who tends or takes care. **2.** *Naut.* **a** A vessel employed to attend other vessels, to supply stores, provisions, etc. **b** A boat or small steamer for communication between shore and a larger vessel. **3.** *Railroads.* A vehicle attached to a locomotive, for carrying fuel and water.

ten′der (tĕn′dẽr), *v. t.* [F. *tendre* to stretch out, extend, fr. L. *tendere.*] **1.** *Law.* To make a tender of, as rent due. **2.** To offer; to present for acceptance, as one's resignation. — *n.* **1.** *Law.* An offer, either of money or of service in satisfaction of a debt or an obligation, made to save a penalty or forfeiture for nonpayment or nonperformance. **2.** Any offer or proposal made for acceptance; specif., an offer of a bid for a contract, usually for public supplies or work. **3.** The thing offered; esp., money offered in payment. — **ten′der·er,** *n.*

ten′der, *adj.;* TEN′DER·ER; TEN′DER·EST. [OF. *tendre,* fr. L. *tener.*] **1.** Easily impressed, broken, cut, masticated, or the like; soft; fragile; succulent. **2.** Physically weak; not hardy; delicate. **3.** Expressing, or expressive of, or susceptible to, the softer feelings, as love, compassion, kindness; affectionate; as, a *tender* lover, memory, caress. **4.** Considerate; careful; — with *of* or *over.* **5.** Feeble from immaturity. **6.** Adapted to, or conducive to, a delicate or sensitive constitution or character; gentle; as, *tender* breeding. **7.** Very susceptible to any impression, emotion, or the like, esp. to pain; impressionable; sympathetic. **8.** Delicate or soft in quality or tone; — of color. **9.** Fragile or delicate, so as to be easily injured or affected; as, a woman's *tender* honor. **10.** Requiring gentle or delicate handling; ticklish; as, a *tender* subject. **11.** *Naut.* Heeling over too easily when under sail; somewhat crank. — *v. t. & i.* To make or become tender; also, *Archaic,* to treat with tenderness. — *n. Obs.* Regard; care. — **ten′der·ly,** *adv.* — **ten′der·ness,** *n.*

ten′der·foot′ (-fo͝ot′), *n.; pl.* -FEET (-fēt′). **1.** *Orig. Western U.S.* A newcomer in a comparatively rough or newly settled region, esp. when not inured to hardship. **2.** A boy scout or girl scout of the beginning class.

ten′der·heart′ed (-här′tĕd; -tĭd; 2), *adj.* Easily moved to love, pity, or sorrow; compassionate; impressionable.

ten′der·loin′ (-loin′), *n.* **1.** A strip of tender flesh on either side of the vertebral column, sold as a separate cut of beef and pork. **2.** [*cap.*] In New York City, orig., a district that afforded the police profit through conniving at vice and lawbreaking; hence [*sometimes not cap.*], the region of a city which is largely devoted to vice and lawbreaking that encourage political and police corruption.

ten′di·nous (tĕn′dĭ·nŭs), *adj.* [F. *tendineux.*] **1** Of the nature of a tendon. **2.** Consisting of tendons; sinewy.

ten′don (tĕn′dŭn), *n.* [F. or ML.; F., fr. ML. *tendo,* fr. L. *tendere* to stretch.] *Anat.* A tough cord or band of dense, white, fibrous connective tissue uniting a muscle with some other part and transmitting the force exerted by the muscle; a sinew. A broad flat tendon is called an *aponeurosis.*

ten′dril (tĕn′drĭl), *n.* [Shortened fr. F. *tendrillon,* fr. *tendron,* fr. *tendre* tender.] *Bot.* A slender, leafless, spirally coiling organ of climbing plants serving as a means of attachment to a supporting body or surface. — **ten′dril·lar, ten′dril·ous,** *adj.*

Ten′e·brae (tĕn′ē·brē), *n. pl.* [L., pl., darkness.] A church service observed during the final part of Holy Week, commemorating the sufferings and death of Christ with the public chanting of psalms and the progressive extinguishing of all candles until only one remains burning behind or under the altar, leaving the church in darkness.

ten′e·brif′ic (-brĭf′ĭk), *adj.* [L. *tenebrae* darkness + *facere* to make.] Rendering dark or gloomy.

ten′e·brous (tĕn′ē·brŭs), *adj.* [OF. *tenebrus,* fr. L. *tenebrosus,* fr. *tenebrae* darkness.] Dark; gloomy; dusky.

1080, ten′–eight′y (tĕn′ā′tĭ), *n.* A poisonous substance (chemically, sodium fluoroacetate, $C_2H_2FNaO_2$) used as a rodenticide; — so called from its laboratory serial number.

ten′e·ment (tĕn′ē·mĕnt), *n.* [OF., a holding, a fief, fr. ML. *tenementum,* fr. L. *tenere* to hold.] **1.** *Law.* Orig., that which is the subject of tenure; hence, land, or any form of incorporeal property treated like land, held by a person of another. **2.** Hence: **a** A dwelling house; specif.: (1) A rented house or one intended to be rented. (2) = TENEMENT HOUSE. **b** An apartment, or a suite of rooms, for use by one tenant or family. **3.** Dwelling; abode; habitation. — **ten′e·men′ta·ry** (-mĕn′tȧ·rĭ), *adj.*

tenement house. A dwelling house for renting, esp. one divided into separate apartments, or tenements, for families; often, esp. in reference to large cities, such a building occupied as dwellings by the poorer classes.

te·nes′mus (tē·nĕz′mŭs; tē·nĕs′-), *n.* [NL., fr. Gr. *teinesmos,* fr. *teinein* to stretch.] *Med.* A sensation of the need to evacuate the bowels or the bladder, without result.

ten′et (tĕn′ĕt; -ĭt; tē′nĕt; -nĭt), *n.* [L. *tenet* he holds, fr. *tenere* to hold.] Any principle, dogma, belief, or doctrine, held as true, esp. by an organization. — **Syn.** See DOCTRINE.

ten′fold′ (tĕn′fōld′; 2), *adj. & adv.* See -FOLD.

te′ni·a, te′ni·a·cide′, etc. Vars. of TAENIA, TAENIACIDE, etc.

Ten′ite (tĕn′īt), *n.* A trade-mark applied to thermoplastic molding compositions made from a cellulose ester.

Ten′nes·see′ Val′ley Au·thor′i·ty (tĕn′ĕ·sē′; 2). *U.S.* A government agency created by Act of Congress, approved May 18, 1933, and amended Aug. 31, 1935, consisting of a board of three members with power to develop the Tennessee River system for the purposes of flood control, navigation, and the creation of water power, to generate and sell surplus electricity, to develop fertilizers, to aid in soil conservation, etc. Abbr. *TVA*

ten′nis (tĕn′ĭs), *n.* [ME. *tenys, tenetz.*] **1.** An ancient game played with a ball, which is struck with a racket (**tennis racket**) in an enclosed court; — often called ***court tennis.*** **2.** Short for LAWN TENNIS. Cf. TABLE TENNIS.

tennis shoes. Sneakers.

ten′o- (tĕn′ō-), **ten-, te·non′to-** (tē·nŏn′tō-), **tenont-.** [Gr. *tenōn, tenontos.*] Combining forms meaning *tendon,* as in **ten′o·si′tis,** inflammation of a tendon; **te·nor′rha·phy,** suture of a tendon; **te·not′o·my,** the division of, or the act of dividing, a tendon.

ten′on (tĕn′ŭn), *n.* [F., fr. *tenir* to hold.] *Carp.* A projecting member left by cutting away the wood around it for insertion into a mortise to make a joint. See DOVETAIL, *Illust.* — *v. t. & i.* **1.** To cut or fit for insertion into a mortise. **2.** To unite by a tenon.

ten′o·ni′tis (tĕn′ō·nī′tĭs), *n.* [NL., fr. Gr. *tenōn* tendon + *-itis.*] *Med.* Inflammation of a tendon.

ten′or (tĕn′ẽr), *n.* [OF. *tenour,* fr. L. *tenor,* fr. *tenere* to hold.] **1.** A holding on in a continuous course; general tendency; course; procedure; trend. **2.** The general drift of thought; purport; intent. **3.** Stamp; character; nature. **4.** *Law.* An exact copy of a writing; a transcript. **5.** [OF. *tenour* (F. *ténor,* fr. It. *tenore*), fr. L. *tenor* a holding; — because the tenor voice took and held the principal part.] *Music.* **a** The highest male voice (except the falsetto), having a compass between about the first c below middle c and the first c above middle c. **b** Hence, the part in the harmony adapted to this voice. **c** A person who sings the tenor, or the instrument that plays it, as the viola. **d** The lowest of a ring, or set, of bells. — **Syn.** See TENDENCY. — *adj.* Of, pertaining to, or adapted to the tenor (esp. voice or part); in compass between the bass and alto of its kind; as, *tenor* banjo.

ten′pence (tĕn′pĕns), *n.* The sum or value of, or a coin worth, ten pennies.

ten′pen′ny (tĕn′pĕn′ĭ; -pĕn·ĭ), *adj.* **1.** Valued at tenpence. **2.** (*pron.* tĕn′pĕn′ĭ) Designating a size of nails. See -PENNY.

ten′pin′ (-pĭn′), *n.* One of the pins used in tenpins.

ten′pins′ (-pĭnz′), *n., pl. in form but construed as sing.* A game played on a bowling alley, with ten wooden pins, usually arranged to form a triangle, at which a ball is bowled. In ***American tenpins,*** the pins are 15 ins. high, with a maximum circumference of 15 ins.

ten′rec (tĕn′rĕk), **ten′drac** (-drăk), *n.* [F. *tanrac, tenrec,* fr. Malagasy *tàndraka, tràndraka.*] Any of several insectivorous mammals, some spiny, of Madagascar; esp., a common tailless species (*Tenrec ecaudatus*).

tense (tĕns; 106), *n.* [OF. *tens,* fr. L. *tempus* time, tense.] *Gram.* Distinctive form in a verb for the expression of distinctions as to time; an inflectional form or phrase thus expressive of a time distinction.

tense, *adj.* [L. *tensus,* past part. of *tendere* to stretch.] **1.** Stretched tight; taut. **2.** Feeling or evincing nervous tension. **3.** *Phonet.* Uttered with the tongue and associated muscles in a relatively tense state, as ē, o͞o contrasted with ĭ, o͝o; narrow. — **Syn.** See TIGHT: STIFF. — *v. t. & i.* To make or become tense, as tendons. — **tense′ly,** *adv.* — **tense′ness,** *n.*

ten′sile (tĕn′sĭl; *see* -ILE), *adj.* [NL. *tensilis.* See TENSE, *adj.*] **1.** Capable of tension; ductile. **2.** Of or pertaining to tension. — **ten·sil′i·ty** (tĕn·sĭl′ĭ·tĭ), *n.*

tensile strength. *Physics.* The greatest longitudinal stress a substance can bear without tearing asunder.

ten·sim′e·ter (tĕn·sĭm′ē·tẽr), *n.* [*tension* + *-meter.*] Instrument for measuring gaseous tension. Cf. MANOMETER.

ten′si·om′e·ter (tĕn′sĭ·ŏm′ē·tẽr), *n.* A device for determining tautness, as in the wires of an airplane.

ten′sion (tĕn′shŭn), *n.* [F. or L.; F., fr. L. *tensio,* fr. *tendere.* See TENSE, *adj.*] **1.** Act of stretching, or tensing; state or degree of being strained to stiffness. **2.** Hence: **a** Mental strain; intensity of striving. **b** Nervous anxiety, with attendant muscular tenseness. **3.** A strained condition of relations, as between nations. **4.** A device to produce a desired tension, or pull, as in a loom. **5.** *Elec.* **a** The quality in consequence of which an electric charge tends to discharge itself, or to pass from a body of greater to one of less electrical potential. **b** Potential. **6.** *Mech.* **a** A force (either of two balancing forces) causing, or tending to cause, extension. **b** The stress or condition due to these forces. — **ten′sion·al** (-ăl), *adj.*

ten′si·ty (tĕn′sĭ·tĭ), *n.* Tenseness.

ten′sive (tĕn′sĭv), *adj.* [F. *tensif.*] Tending to or causing tension.

ten′sor (-sẽr; -sôr), *n.* [NL.] **1.** *Anat.* A muscle that stretches a part. **2.** *Geom.* A generalized concept of a vector, requiring for its description more than three components.

ten′–strike′ (tĕn′strīk′), *n.* *U.S.* **a** *Bowling.* A strike. **b** *Colloq.* Any successful and decisive stroke or act.

tent (tĕnt), *n.* [OF. *tente,* fr. L. *tenta,* fem. of *tentus* stretched out, past part. of *tendere, tentum,* to stretch.] **1.** A portable lodge of skins, canvas, or strong cloth, stretched and sustained by poles, used for shelter, esp. by soldiers in camp. **2.** *Med.* A tentlike screen for retaining vapors during administration; as, an oxygen *tent.* — *v. i.* To lodge in a tent. — *v. t.* To lodge in tents; to cover with a tent.

tent, *n.* [OF. *tente.*] *Surg.* A roll of lint or linen, or other absorbent, used to dilate a canal, to keep open a wound, etc. — *v. t.* To keep open with a tent, as a wound.

tent, *n.* *Now Scot.* Attention; heed; care. — *v. t.* **1.** To care for; tend; heed. **2.** To prevent. **3.** To teach.

ten′ta·cle (tĕn′tȧ·k'l; -tĭ·k'l), *n.* [NL. *tentaculum,* fr. L. *tentare* to handle, feel.] **1.** Any of various long, flexible processes, usually tactile or prehensile, borne by animals generally on the head, or about the mouth. See GASTROPOD, *Illust.* **2.** *Bot.* Any hair or emergence, as the insect-catching hairs on the leaves of the sundew, responding readily to stimuli. — **ten·tac′u·lar** (tĕn·tăk′ū·lẽr), *adj.*

tent′age (tĕn′tĭj), *n.* [From TENT a shelter.] Tents collectively.

ten′ta·tive (tĕn′tȧ·tĭv), *adj.* [ML. *tentativus,* fr. L. *tentare* to try.] Of the nature of an experiment; offered or undertaken provisionally. — **ten′ta·tive·ly,** *adv.* — **ten′ta·tive·ness,** *n.*

tent caterpillar. Any of several species of gregarious caterpillars (esp. *Malacosoma americanum*) which construct on trees large silken webs.

tent′ed (tĕn′tĕd; -tĭd), *adj.* Covered with a tent or tents.

ten′ter (tĕn′tẽr), *n.* [ME. *tenture, tentoure.*] A frame for stretching cloth by tenterhooks, so that it may dry even and square; also, a tenterhook. — *v. t.* To hang or stretch on or as on a tenter or tenters. — *v. i.* To admit of being tentered. — ***on tenters.*** = ON TENTERHOOKS.

ten'ter (tĕn'tẽr), *n.* One who has the care or charge of something, specif., *Chiefly Brit.*, of machines in a factory.

ten'ter·hook' (-ho͝ok'), *n.* A sharp hooked nail used for fastening cloth on a tenter. — ***on tenterhooks.*** In suspense, or under a distressing strain.

tenth (tĕnth; 106), *n. & adj.* See NUMBER, *Table.* — **tenth'ly,** *adv.*

tent stitch. A short slanting stitch in worsted work and embroidery, worked in even lines from left to right.

tent'y (tĕn'tĭ), *adj.*; TENT'I·ER (-tĭ·ẽr); TENT'I·EST. *Scot.* Attentive; watchful.

ten'u·is (tĕn'ū·ĭs), *n.*; *pl.* TENUES (-ēz). [L., thin, fine, weak; used to translate Gr. *psilos* bare, unaspirated (used of these consonants).] *Phonet.* One of the three surd mutes, or voiceless stops (*k, p, t*).

te·nu'i·ty (tĕ·nū'ĭ·tĭ), *n.* Tenuous quality or state; as: **a** Thinness; slenderness. **b** Rarity; — of fluids. **c** Poverty; meagerness. **d** Faintness, as of sound.

ten'u·ous (tĕn'ū·ŭs), *adj.* [L. *tenuis* thin.] **1.** Thin; slender. **2.** Rare; subtile; not dense; — of fluids. **3.** Unsubstantial; insignificant; flimsy. — **Syn.** See THIN. — **ten'u·ous·ly,** *adv.* — **ten'u·ous·ness,** *n.*

ten'ure (tĕn'ūr), *n.* [OF. *tenure, teneüre*, fr. *tenir* to hold.] **1.** Act or right of holding, esp. real estate, properly of a superior. **2.** The manner in, or the period for, which anything is had and enjoyed. — **ten·u'ri·al** (tĕn·ū'rĭ·ăl), *adj.* — **ten·u'ri·al·ly,** *adv.*

‖**te·nu'to** (tā·no͞o'tō), *adj.* [It., past part. of *tenere* to hold.] *Music.* Held firmly, as a tone or chord, to its full value; not staccato; — a direction. Abbr. *ten.* A **tenuto mark** is often used. Thus:

te'o·cal'li (tē'ō·kăl'ĭ; tā'ō·käl'yē), *n.*; *pl.* -LIS (-ĭz; -yēz). [Sp., also *teucali*, lit., house of the god, fr. Nahuatl *teocalli*.] *Archaeol.* A temple of Mexico or Central America, usually a structure built upon the summit of a truncated pyramidal mound.

te'o·sin'te (tē'ō·sĭn'tē), *n.* [Sp., fr. Nahuatl *teocentli*, lit., divine maize.] A large annual fodder grass (*Euchlaena mexicana*), native to Mexico and Central America, closely related to maize and grown for fodder and for cereal.

te'pee (tē'pē; tĕp'ē), *n.* [Dakota *tipi*, fr. *ti* to dwell + *pi* used for.] An American Indian conical tent, used by most of the tribes of the Great Plains. Cf. LODGE, *n.*, 5; WICKIUP; WIGWAM.

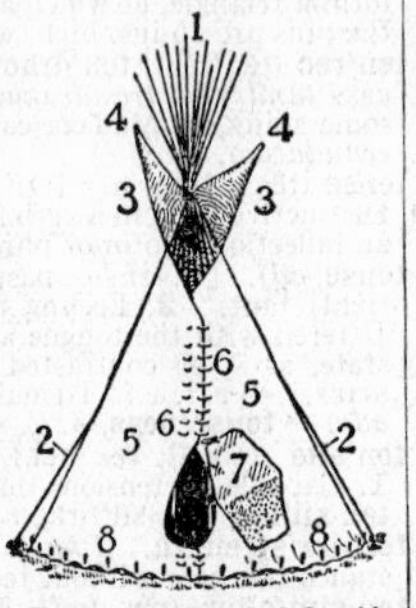

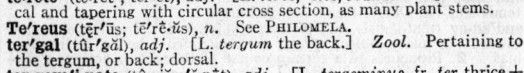

Tepee. 1 Poles; 2, 2 Outside Poles for supporting Flaps (3, 3) for regulating draft and escape of smoke; 4, 4 Ears of flaps, into which ends of outside poles are inserted; 5, 5 Cover (made of hides); 6, 6 Pins holding two sides of cover together; 7 Door (of skin stretched on a frame); 8, 8 Pegs.

teph'rite (tĕf'rīt), *n.* [Gr. *tephra* ashes.] A volcanic rock consisting of plagioclase, augite, and leucite or nephelite. — **teph·rit'ic** (tĕf·rĭt'ĭk), *adj.*

tep'id (tĕp'ĭd), *adj.* [L. *tepidus*, fr. *tepere* to be warm.] Moderately warm; lukewarm. — **te·pid'i·ty** (tē·pĭd'ĭ·tĭ), *n.* — **tep'id·ly,** *adv.* — **tep'id·ness,** *n.*

tep'i·dar'i·um (tĕp'ĭ·dâr'ĭ·ŭm), *n.*; *pl.* -IA (-*à*). [L., prop. neut. of *tepidarius* pertaining to a tepid bath. See TEPID.] A warm room for a bath.

te·qui'la (tā·kē'lä), *n.* [Sp., fr. the mt. town *Tequila*, Jalisco, Mexico.] A Mexican century plant (*Agave tequilana*); also, the distilled liquor made from the juices of the roasted stems of this plant.

te·rai' hat (tĕ·rī'). A wide-brimmed, ventilated, felt hat, such as one worn by explorers in the **Te·rai'**, a lowland belt in India north of the Ganges.

ter'a·phim (tĕr'*à*·fĭm), *n. pl.*; *sing.* TERAPH (tĕr'*ă*f), TERAPHIM. [Heb. *tĕrāphīm*.] Images representing the primitive household gods of the Jews and other Semitic peoples (*Gen.* xxxi. 19, 30).

ter'a·to- (tĕr'*à*·tō-), **terat-.** [Gr. *teras, teratos*.] A combining form meaning *wonder, monster*, as in **ter'a·to·gen'ic, ter'a·tog'e·ny.**

ter'a·toid (tĕr'*à*·toid), *adj.* [*terat-* + *-oid*.] Monstrous.

ter'a·tol'o·gy (-tŏl'ō·jĭ), *n.* The study of monstrosities, serious malformations, or deviations from the normal structure, esp. in man. — **ter'a·to·log'i·cal** (-tō·lŏj'ĭ·kăl), *adj.* — **ter'a·tol'o·gist** (-tŏl'ō·jĭst), *n.*

ter'bi·a (tûr'bĭ·*à*), *n.* [NL.] *Chem.* Terbium oxide, Tb_2O_3, a white solid, one of the rare earths.

ter'bi·um (-ŭm), *n.* [NL., fr. Yt*terby*, in Sweden.] *Chem.* A rare-earth metal resembling yttrium, found in certain minerals. Symbol, *Tb*; at. no., 65; at. wt., 159.2. — **ter'bic** (-bĭk), *adj.*

terbium metals. *Chem.* A group of related rare-earth metals: europium, gadolinium, and terbium.

ter'cel (tûr's'l), *n.* Also **terce'let** (tûrs'lĕt; -lĭt). [OF. *tercel, terçuel*, dim. fr. L. *tertius* the third.] *Falconry.* The male of various hawks, esp. of the peregrine falcon.

ter·cen'te·nar'y (tûr·sĕn'tē·nĕr'ĭ; tûr'sĕn·tĕn'*à*·rĭ; *or, esp. Brit.*, -sĕn-tē'n*à*·rĭ, -sĕn'tē·n*à*·rĭ), *adj.* [L. *ter* thrice + *centenary*.] Including, or relating to, an interval of three hundred years. — *n.* The three-hundredth anniversary of any event.

ter'cet (tûr'sĕt; -sĭt; tûr·sĕt'), *n.* [It. *terzetto*, dim. of *terzo* third, fr. L. *tertius*.] **1.** A group of three successive verses rhyming together or interlaced in rhyming with an adjoining tercet. **2.** *Music.* A triplet.

ter'e·bene (tĕr'ē·bēn), *n.* [See TEREBINTH; cf. TERPENE.] *Chem.* A mixture of terpenes from oil of turpentine.

te·reb'ic (tĕ·rĕb'ĭk; -rē'bĭk), *adj.* [*tereb*inth + *-ic*.] *Chem.* Designating, or pertaining to, a white crystalline acid, $C_7H_{10}O_4$, obtained by the oxidation of oil of turpentine with nitric acid, and otherwise.

ter'e·binth (tĕr'ē·bĭnth), *n.* [L. *terebinthus*, fr. Gr. *terebinthos*.] A small European tree (*Pistacia terebinthus*) of the sumac family, yielding Chian turpentine.

ter'e·bin'thic (-bĭn'thĭk), *adj.* Of or like turpentine.

ter'e·bin'thine (-thĭn), *adj.* **a** Of or pert. to the terebinth tree. **b** Of, consisting of, or like turpentine.

te·re'do (tĕ·rē'dō), *n.*; *pl.* -DOS (-dōz), -DINES (-dĭ·nēz). [L., a worm that gnaws wood, fr. Gr. *terēdōn*.] A shipworm (genus *Teredo*).

te·rete' (tē·rēt'; tĕr'ēt), *adj.* [L. *teres, -etis*, rounded off.] Cylindrical and tapering with circular cross section, as many plant stems.

Te'reus (tē'rūs; tē'rē·ŭs), *n.* See PHILOMELA.

ter'gal (tûr'găl), *adj.* [L. *tergum* the back.] *Zool.* Pertaining to the tergum, or back; dorsal.

ter·gem'i·nate (tûr·jĕm'ĭ·nāt), *adj.* [L. *tergeminus*, fr. *ter* thrice + *geminus* twin-born.] *Bot.* Forking with three pairs of leaflets.

ter'gi·ver·sate' (tûr'jĭ·vẽr·sāt'; tẽr·jĭv'ẽr·sāt), *v. i.* [L. *tergiversatus* past part. of *tergiversari* to turn one's back, shift, fr. *tergum* back + *versare*, freq. of *vertere* to turn.] To practice tergiversation; to become a renegade; apostatize; also, to use subterfuges; shuffle. — **ter'gi·ver·sa'tor** (-sā'tẽr), *n.*

ter'gi·ver·sa'tion (-sā'shŭn), *n.* **1.** Desertion of a cause, party, faith, etc.; also, a shifting; equivocation. **2.** A shift, subterfuge, or evasion.

ter'gum (tûr'gŭm), *n.*; *pl.* -GA (-g*à*). [L.] *Zool.* The back.

term (tûrm), *n.* [OF. *terme*, fr. L. *terminus* a boundary, limit, end.] **1.** *Archaic.* Limit; bound; also, end; goal. **2.** A limited or definite extent of time; the time for which anything lasts; duration; tenure. **3.** *pl.* Propositions, limitations, or provisions, stated or offered, for the acceptance of another and determining the nature and scope of the agreement; conditions. **4.** A word or expression having a precisely limited meaning or peculiar to a science, art, or the like; as, a technical *term.* **5.** *pl.* **a** Mutual relationship; footing; — often with *on* or *upon*; as, to be on good *terms.* **b** Good or even footing; agreement; as, to come to *terms.* **6.** *Obs. pl.* Conditions; circumstances. *Shak.* **7.** *Arch.* A boundary post; esp., a quadrangular pillar, adorned with a head or upper body. **8.** *Educ.* In universities, schools, etc., a definite continuous period during which instruction is regularly given to students. **9.** *Law.* **a** The time fixed for the payment of rents or interest; esp. in England, a quarter day. **b** The whole period for which an estate is granted; also, the estate thus granted. **c** A space of time granted to a debtor for discharging his obligation. **d** The time for which a court is held. **10.** *Logic.* One of the three substantive elements of a syllogism. **11.** *Math.* **a** *Alg.* A member of a compound quantity; as, *ab* or *cd* in $ab \pm cd$. **b** Any of the members composing a proportion or ratio. — *v. t.* To apply a term to; to name; call.

Ter'ma·gant (tûr'm*à*·gănt), *n.* [OF. *Tervagan, Trivigan(t)*.] **1.** An imaginary being, supposed by Christians to be a Mohammedan deity, represented in ancient moralities, farces, etc., as vociferous and tumultuous. **2.** [*not cap.*] A boisterous, brawling, turbulent woman; a virago. — [*not cap.*] *adj.* Tumultuous; boisterous; scolding. — **ter'ma·gan·cy** (-găn·sĭ), *n.*

term day. A day fixed as a term (sense 9); also, a special day set by scientists for making synoptic meteorological or other physical observations.

term'er (tûr'mẽr), *n.* A person serving for a term, esp. in prison; as, a third *termer.*

ter'mi·na·ble (tûr'mĭ·n*à*·b'l), *adj.* That may be terminated; limitable. — **ter'mi·na·bil'i·ty** (-bĭl'ĭ·tĭ), **ter'mi·na·ble·ness,** *n.* — **ter'mi·na·bly,** *adv.*

ter'mi·nal (-năl), *adj.* [L. *terminalis*.] **1.** Of or pertaining to a term, as an end, extremity, boundary, or terminus; forming the terminus or extremity. **2.** Of or pertaining to a term, or fixed period of time; occurring in a term or in every term. **3.** Occurring at the end of a period or series; concluding. **4.** *Bot.* Growing at the end of a branch or stem. **5.** *Transportation.* Connected with the receipt or delivery of freight; as, *terminal* charges. — **Syn.** See LAST. — *n.* **1.** The part which terminates; extremity; end. **2.** *Arch.* A terminating and usually ornamental detail, as the carved end of a church pew. Cf. FINIAL. **3.** *Elec.* A device attached to the end of a wire or cable or to an apparatus for convenience in making electrical connections. **4.** *Transportation.* **a** Either end of a carrier line, as a railroad, trucking, or shipping line or airline, with classifying yards, dock and lighterage facilities, management offices, storage sheds, and freight-loading and passenger station. **b** Any station central to a considerable area or junction station of a carrier line, for delivery and receipt of freight or embarkation of passengers. — **ter'mi·nal·ly,** *adv.*

terminal leave. A final leave granted to a member of the armed forces, consisting of accumulated unused leave, prior to his separation or discharge from service.

ter'mi·nate (tûr'mĭ·nāt), *v. t.* [L. *terminatus*, past part. of *terminare*.] **1.** To set or form a term or spatial limit to; to bound; limit. **2.** To put an end to; to end; as, to *terminate* an action or an argument; also, to form the conclusion of, as a story. — *v. i.* **1.** To be limited in space by a point, line, or surface. **2.** To come to a limit in time; to end. **3.** To have its end; — with *in*; as, words *terminating* in "-ism." — **Syn.** See CLOSE.

ter'mi·na'tion (-nā'shŭn), *n.* **1.** Act of terminating. **2.** Limit in space or extent; bound; also, end in time or existence; conclusion. **3.** The ending of a word; a final syllable or letter; esp., *Gram.*, the part added to a stem in inflection; ending; suffix. **4.** Outcome; completion; as, the dispute was brought to a satisfactory *termination.* — **Syn.** See END.

ter'mi·na'tion·al (-ăl), *adj.* **1.** Of or forming a termination, as of a word. **2.** *Gram.* Formed by inflectional suffixes; as, *terminational* comparison (*-er, -est*).

ter'mi·na'tive (tûr'mĭ·nā'tĭv; -n*à*·tĭv), *adj.* Tending or serving to terminate; determining. — **ter'mi·na'tive·ly,** *adv.*

ter'mi·na'tor (-nā'tẽr), *n.* **1.** One who or that which terminates. **2.** *Astron.* The line dividing the illuminated and the unilluminated part of the moon's or a planet's disk.

ter'mi·ner (tûr'mĭ·nẽr), *n.* *Law.* A determining. See OYER AND TERMINER.

ter'mi·nol'o·gy (tûr'mĭ·nŏl'ō·jĭ), *n.* [L. *terminus* term + *-logy*.] The technical or special terms or words used in any business, art, science, or the like; also, nomenclature as a field of study. Cf. NOMENCLATURE. — **ter'mi·no·log'i·cal** (-nō·lŏj'ĭ·kăl), *adj.* — **ter'mi·no·log'i·cal·ly,** *adv.*

term insurance. Insurance for a specified term providing for no payment to the insured except upon losses during the term, and becoming void upon its expiration.

ter'mi·nus (tûr'mĭ·nŭs), *n.*; *pl.* -NI (-nī), -NUSES (-nŭs·ĕz; -ĭz). [L.] **1.** A boundary; limit. **2.** A boundary stone or post. **3.** Termination; final goal. **4.** *Transportation.* **a** = TERMINAL, 4 **a**; also, the town or city at such a terminal. **b** *Chiefly Brit.* = TERMINAL, 4 **b.** — **Syn.** See END.

‖**ter'mi·nus ad quem** (ăd kwĕm'). [L.] Lit., end (or limit) to which; terminal point.

‖**ter'mi·nus a quo** (tûr'mĭ·nŭs ā kwō'). [L.] Lit., end (or limit) from which; starting point.

ter'mite (tûr'mīt), *n.* [L. *termes, tarmes, -itis,* a woodworm.] Any of numerous pale-colored, soft-bodied, social insects (order Isoptera); a white ant. Each colony consists of winged sexual forms (queen and king) and wingless sterile workers and, often, soldiers. Termites (which are not true ants) are found in temperate regions and abound in the tropics. They are highly destructive to buildings, furniture, books, etc.

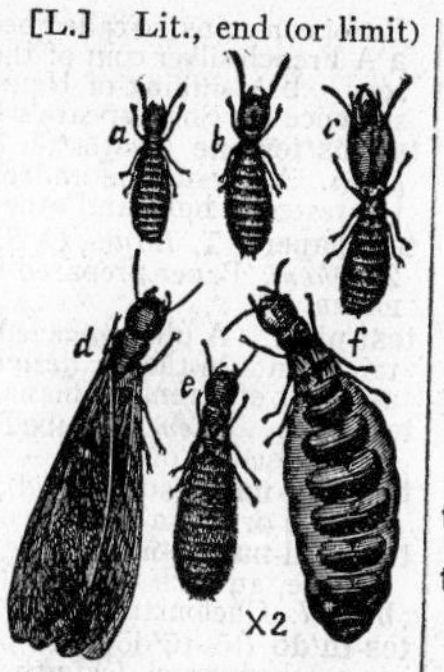

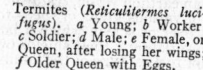

Termites (*Reticulitermes lucifugus*). *a* Young; *b* Worker; *c* Soldier; *d* Male; *e* Female, or Queen, after losing her wings; *f* Older Queen with Eggs.

term'less (tûrm'lĕs; -lĭs), *adj.* **1.** Having no term, or end; boundless. **2.** Unconditioned or unconditional.

term'or (tûr'mẽr), *n.* *Law.* One who has an estate for a term of years or for life.

tern (tûrn), *n.* [Of Scand. origin.] Any of numerous gull-like birds (see 2d GULL), mostly of the genus *Sterna,* including the ***common tern*** (*S. hirundo*) of both coasts of the Atlantic, pure white with a black cap and a pearl-gray mantle.

tern, *n.* [F. *terne,* fr. L. pl. *terni* three each, three.] A prize in a lottery resulting from the favorable combination of three numbers in the drawing; also, the three numbers.

ter'na·ry (tûr'nȧ·rĭ), *adj.* [L. *ternarius,* fr. *terni* three each.] **1.** Proceeding by threes; arranged in threes; consisting of three. **2.** Third in series, order, or rank. **3.** *Chem.* Containing or pertaining to three different parts, as elements, atoms, or groups. **4.** *Math.* Using three as the radix, or base; also, involving three variables. **5.** *Metal.* Consisting of an alloy of three elements. — *n.; pl.* -RIES (-rĭz). A set, group, or multiple, of three.

ter'nate (tûr'nāt), *adj.* Consisting of threes; arranged in threes; trifoliolate; — esp. of leaves. — **ter'nate·ly,** *adv.*

terne'plate' (tûrn'plāt'), *n.* [F. *terne* dull. See TARNISH.] Sheet iron or steel coated with an alloy of approximately 4 parts lead to 1 part tin.

ter'ni·on (tûr'nĭ·ŭn), *n.* [L. *ternio,* fr. *terni* three each.] **1.** A set of three. **2.** *Bibliog.* A section of three folio sheets.

ter'pene (tûr'pēn), *n.* [*terpentin* (old form of *turpentine*) + *-ene.*] *Chem.* Any one of a series of isomeric hydrocarbons, $C_{10}H_{16}$, prominent in many volatile oils obtained by distillation of plants, esp. conifers.

ter·pin'e·ol (tûr·pĭn'ē·ōl; -ŏl), *n.* [*terpin* (old form of *terpene*) + *-ol,* 2.] *Chem.* Any of certain isomeric alcohols, $C_{10}H_{17}OH$, occurring in natural essential oils and also made artificially. A liquid terpineol is used in perfumery.

Terp·sich'o·re (tûrp·sĭk'ō·rē), *n.* [L., fr. Gr. *Terpsichorē,* fr. *terpsis* enjoyment + *choros* dance, dancing.] *Gr. Myth.* The muse of dancing and choral song.

Terp'si·cho·re'an (tûrp'sĭ·kō·rē'ăn), *adj.* Of or pertaining to Terpsichore; hence [*not cap.*], of or pertaining to dancing. — *n.* [*not cap.*] *Colloq.* A dancer.

‖**ter'ra** (tĕr'rä; tĕr'ȧ), *n.* [It. & L.] The earth; earth.

ter'ra al'ba (tĕr'ȧ ăl'bȧ). [L., white earth.] *Com.* Any of several white mineral substances; as: **a** Gypsum, ground for a pigment. **b** Kaolin, used esp. as an adulterant of paints, etc. **c** Magnesia.

ter'race (tĕr'ĭs; -ȧs), *n.* [OF., fr. L. *terra* the earth, land, country, orig., dry land.] **1.** A raised level or platform of earth, supported on one or more faces by a wall, a bank of turf, or the like, often one of a series arranged one above the other on a slope; also, such bank of turf, etc., and the raised level collectively. **2.** A flat roof of a house, esp. a Spanish or Oriental house. **3. a** A row of houses along the side or top of rising ground, or a street with such a row of houses. **b** *U. S.* A strip of park in the middle of a street, usually planted with trees and shrubs. **4.** *Geol.* A level and rather narrow plain, usually with a steep front, bordering a river, a lake, or the sea. — *v. t.;* TER'RACED (-ĭst; -ȧst); TER'RAC·ING (-ĭs·ĭng). To form into or furnish with a terrace or terraces.

ter'ra cot'ta (tĕr'ȧ kŏt'ȧ). [It., fr. *terra* earth + *cotta,* fem. of *cotto* cooked.] **1.** Clayware having the surface coated with fine slip or glaze, used in the facing of large buildings and for relief ornament or for statuettes, vases, etc. **2.** The variable color of hard-baked clay, averaging reddish red-yellow in hue, of high saturation and medium brilliance. See COLOR. — **ter'ra-cot'ta,** *adj.*

‖**ter'rae fi'li·us** (tĕr'ē fĭl'ĭ·ŭs); *pl.* TERRAE FILII (fĭl'ĭ·ī). [L.] A son of the earth; a person of lowly birth.

ter'ra fir'ma (tĕr'ȧ fûr'mȧ). [L.] Firm or solid earth.

ter·rain' (tĕ·rān'; tĕr'ān), *n.* [F. See TERRANE.] **1.** A tract or region of ground immediately under observation; environment; milieu. **2.** *Geol.* Var. of TERRANE. **3.** *Mil.* An area of ground considered as to its use, as for a battlefield or for fortification.

ter'ra in·cog'ni·ta (tĕr'ȧ ĭn·kŏg'nĭ·tȧ); *pl.* TERRAE INCOGNITAE (tĕr'ē ĭn·kŏg'nĭ·tē). [L.] An unexplored country, field of knowledge, etc.

ter·rane' (tĕ·rān'; tĕr'ān), *n.* [F. *terrain,* fr. L. *terrenum,* fr. *terrenus* of earth, fr. *terra* earth.] *Geol.* A formation, or a group of formations.

ter'ra·pin (tĕr'ȧ·pĭn; tăr'-), *n.* [Of Algonquian origin.] Any of various edible North American turtles (family Testudinidae) living in fresh or brackish water, esp. the ***diamondback terrapin*** (genus *Malaclemys*) found in salt marshes along the U. S. Atlantic and Gulf coasts. Cf. TURTLE, 1.

ter·ra'que·ous (tĕr·ā'kwē·ŭs), *adj.* [L. *terra* the earth + E. *aqueous.*] Consisting of land and water.

ter·rar'i·um (tĕ·râr'ĭ·ŭm; 6), *n.; pl.* E. -IUMS (-ŭmz), L. -IA (-ȧ). [L. *terra* earth + *-arium* as in *aquarium.*] A vivarium without water.

ter·raz'zo (tĕr·rät'tsō), *n.* [It.] A type of flooring made of small chips of marble set irregularly in cement and polished.

ter·rene' (tĕ·rēn'), *adj.* [L. *terrenus.* See TERRANE.] **1.** Worldly. **2.** Earthy. — *n.* The earth; a terrain.

terre'plein' (târ'plān'), *n.* [F., fr. L. *terra* earth + *plenus* full.] *Fort.* The top or platform of a rampart, for the cannon, behind the parapet.

ter·res'tri·al (tĕ·rĕs'trĭ·ăl; tĕ-), *adj.* [L. *terrestris,* fr. *terra* the earth.] **1.** Of the earth; worldly; mundane; as, *terrestrial* delights; *terrestrial* magnetism. **2.** Representing, or constituting, the earth. **3.** Of or consisting of land, in distinction from water. **4.** Belonging to the land, in distinction from trees, water, etc. **5.** *Bot.* Growing in the ground. — **Syn.** See EARTHLY. — **Ant.** Celestial. — *n.* An earth dweller.

ter'ret (tĕr'ĕt; -ĭt), *n.* A ring for attaching a leash, chain, etc.; esp., one of the rings on top of a harness pad, through which the reins pass. Cf. HARNESS, *Illust.*

terre'–verte' (târ'vârt'), *n.* [F., fr. *terre* earth + *vert, verte,* green.] Glauconite, or a similar mineral, used as a green pigment by artists.

ter'ri·ble (tĕr'ĭ·b'l), *adj.* [F., fr. L. *terribilis,* fr. *terrere* to frighten.] **1.** Adapted, or likely, to excite terror, awe, or dread; dreadful; appalling. **2.** Afflicting severely. **3.** *Colloq.* Excessive. — **Syn.** See FEARFUL. — **ter'ri·ble·ness,** *n.* — **ter'ri·bly,** *adv.*

ter·ric'o·lous (tĕ·rĭk'ō·lŭs), *adj.* [L. *terricola* earth dweller, fr. *terra* earth + *colere* to inhabit.] *Zool. & Bot.* Living on or in the ground.

ter'ri·er (tĕr'ĭ·ẽr), *n.* [F. *terrier, chien terrier,* fr. *terre* the earth, fr. L. *terra.*] A dog, usually small, of any of several breeds (originally used by hunters to dig for small furred game), including *Airedale, Irish, Scottish, Sealyham, Skye,* and *Welsh terriers,* and *bull terrier, fox terrier,* and *schnauzer.*

ter'ri·er, *n.* [OF., fr. ML. *terrarius liber,* a book pert. to land or landed estates. See 1st TERRIER.] *Law.* A book or roll in which the interests of private persons or corporations in lands are described by site, boundaries, acreage, etc.

ter·rif'ic (tĕ·rĭf'ĭk), *adj.* [L. *terrificus,* fr. *terrere* to frighten + *facere* to make.] **1.** Exciting, or adapted to excite, great fear or dread; terrible; appalling. **2.** *Colloq.* Tremendous. — **Syn.** See FEARFUL. — **ter·rif'i·cal·ly** (-ĭ·kăl·ĭ), **ter·rif'ic·ly,** *adv.*

ter'ri·fy (tĕr'ĭ·fī), *v. t.;* -FIED (-fīd); -FY'ING. [L. *terrificare.*] **1.** To alarm or shock with terror or fear. **2.** To drive, impel, deter, etc., by such alarm or shock; as, to *terrify* the wits out of one.

ter·rig'e·nous (tĕ·rĭj'ē·nŭs), *adj.* [L. *terrigena, terrigenus,* fr. *terra* the earth + *genere, gignere,* to bring forth.] **1.** Earthborn; autochthonous. **2.** *Oceanography.* Designating or pertaining to oceanic muds and sediments derived directly from the waste of the land, as disting. from deep-sea oozes.

ter'ri·to'ri·al (tĕr'ĭ·tō'rĭ·ăl; 70), *adj.* **1.** Of or pertaining to territory or the territory of a state. **2.** Limited to or extending over a certain district; as, *territorial* rights. **3.** [*often cap.*] Of or pertaining to all or any one of the territories of the United States. **4.** *Mil.* Organized primarily for territorial defense; as, **territorial army, territorial force, territorial reserve.** — *n.* A member of a territorial force. — **ter'ri·to'ri·al·ly,** *adv.*

ter'ri·to'ri·al·ism (-ĭz'm), *n.* **1.** A system under which the landowning class predominates in a state; landlordism. **2.** *Eccl.* A system of church polity (established 1555) requiring all inhabitants of a territory to adhere to the religion of the civil ruler, or emigrate. — **ter'ri·to'ri·al·ist** (-ĭst), *n.*

ter'ri·to'ri·al'i·ty (-ăl'ĭ·tĭ), *n.* Territorial quality or status.

ter'ri·to'ri·al·ize (-tō'rĭ·ăl·īz), *v. t.* To make territorial; as: **a** To enlarge by extension of territory. **b** To reduce to a territory. **c** To distribute among territories or districts. — **ter'ri·to'ri·al·i·za'tion** (-ĭ·zā'shŭn; -ī·zā'-), *n.*

territorial system. = TERRITORIALISM, 2.

ter'ri·to'ry (tĕr'ĭ·tō'rĭ *or, esp. Brit.,* -tẽr·ĭ), *n.; pl.* -RIES (-ĭz). [L. *territorium,* fr. *terra* the earth.] **1.** An extent of land and waters or any given portion thereof, belonging to, or under the jurisdiction of, a prince, state, or government. **2.** Any definite portion of the area of a state considered by itself, as an area of a state not sovereign, but governed as a dependency, or having a legal system more or less peculiar to itself. **3.** A large extent or tract of land; a region; district. **4.** [*often cap.*] **a** In the United States, a portion of the country not included within any state, but organized with a separate legislature, under a territorial governor and other officers appointed by the President and U. S. Senate. **b** In Canada and Australia, a similarly organized area not yet formed into a province or state. **5.** An assigned or pre-empted area, as that assigned to a commercial traveler.

ter'ror (tĕr'ẽr), *n.* [OF. *terreur,* fr. L. *terror.*] **1.** State or instance of extreme fear; violent dread; fright. **2.** Terribleness; also, a person or thing that causes extreme fear. **3.** *Colloq.* One difficult to manage; a great nuisance. **4.** [*cap.*] A state of intense fear caused by the systematic use of violent means by a party or faction to maintain itself in power; as, ***the Terror,*** *or* ***the Reign of Terror,*** in France (1793–94); also, the party or movement itself. — **Syn.** See FEAR.

ter'ror·ism (tĕr'ẽr·ĭz'm), *n.* Act of terrorizing, or state of being terrorized; specif., a mode of governing, or of opposing government, by intimidation.

ter'ror·ist (-ĭst), *n.* [F. *terroriste.*] One who favors or practices terrorism; specif. [*often cap.*]: **a** An agent or partisan of the revolutionary tribunal during the Reign of Terror in France. **b** A member of a former Russian political party aiming to demoralize the government by violence and terror. — **ter'ror·is'tic** (-ĭs'tĭk), *adj.*

ter'ror·ize (-īz), *v. t.* To impress with terror; to coerce by intimidation. — **ter'ror·i·za'tion** (-ĭ·zā'shŭn; -ī·zā'-), *n.* — **ter'ror·iz'er** (-īz'ẽr), *n.*

ter'ry (tĕr'ĭ), *n.; pl.* TERRIES (-ĭz). **1.** Any loop formed for the pile in weaving velvet, plush, etc. **2.** Also **terry cloth.** Any fabric with such uncut loops.

terse (tûrs), *adj.* [L. *tersus,* past part. of *tergere* to rub or wipe off.] Elegantly concise; free of superfluous words; succinct. — **Syn.** See CONCISE. — **terse'ly,** *adv.* — **terse'ness,** *n.*

ter'tial (tûr'shăl), *adj.* [L. *tertius* third.] *Zool.* Designating the flight feathers borne on the basal joint or humerus of a bird's wing. — *n.* A tertial feather.

ter'tian (-shăn), *adj.* [L. *tertianus,* fr. *tertius* the third.] *Med.* Occurring every third day, reckoning inclusively (i. e., every other day). — *n.* [L. *tertiana* (sc. *febris*).] *Med.* A tertian disease, esp. an intermittent fever which returns every other day. Cf. QUARTAN, QUINTAN.

ter'ti·ar'y (tûr'shĭ·ĕr'ĭ *or, esp. Brit.,* -shȧ·rĭ), *adj.* [L. *tertiarius* containing a third part, fr. *tertius* third.] **1.** Of the third formation, order, or rank. **2.** *Chem.* **a** Characterized by replacement in the third degree; resulting from the substitution of three atoms or groups; as, a *tertiary* salt. **b** Designating or characterized by a carbon atom united by three valences to chain or ring members. **3.** *Eccl.* Of or pertaining to tertiaries. **4.** [*cap.*] *Geol.* Designating, or pertaining to, the earlier principal division (cf. QUATERNARY, 2) of the Cenozoic era, marked by widespread geographic changes, as in the Alps, and dominance of mammals on land. It includes the Eocene, Oligocene, Miocene, and Pliocene periods. — *n.; pl.* -IES (-ĭz). **1.** *Eccl.* A member of the third order in any monastic system. **2.** [*cap.*] *Geol.* The Tertiary division or its system of rocks. **3.** *Zool.* A tertial feather.

‖**ter′ti·um quid** (tûr′shĭ·ŭm kwĭd). [L.] **a** Something that escapes a division into two groups that are supposed to be exhaustive. **b** *Colloq.* A third someone or thing of ambiguous status.

ter·va′lent (tûr·vā′lĕnt), *adj.* [L. *ter* thrice + *valent.*] *Chem.* Trivalent.

‖**ter′za ri′ma** (tĕr′tsä rē′mä). [It., a third or triple rhyme.] *Pros.* A scheme of continuous verse (usually iambic pentameter in English poetry) arranged in tercets in which line 2 of each rhymes with 1 and 3 of the next, thus: *aba, bcb, cdc,* etc.

tes′sel·late (tĕs′ĕ·lāt), *v. t.* [L. *tessellatus* tessellated, fr. *tessella* little cube, dim. of *tessera.* See TESSERA.] To form into or adorn with mosaic; to lay with checkered work; as, *tessellated* floors. — (-lăt), *adj.* Tessellated.

tes′sel·la′tion (-lā′shŭn), *n.* Act of tessellating; state of being tessellated; also, the mosaic work so formed.

tes′ser·a (tĕs′ẽr·à), *n.; pl.* -SERAE (-ē). [L., a square piece, a die.] **1.** A small piece of marble, glass, or the like, having a square face, used in mosaic work, as for pavements, walls, etc. **2.** *Rom. Antiq.* **a** A small cube of ivory, bone, wood, etc., used as a die in gambling. **b** A similar piece, often modified in shape, used as a ticket, token, etc.

test (tĕst), *n.* [L. *testa* shell, pot. See TEST cupel.] *Zool.* The external shell or hard covering of many invertebrates, as mollusks, crustaceans, etc.

test, *n.* [OF., test, or cupel, potsherd, fr. L. *testum* an earthen vessel; akin to *testa* potsherd.] **1.** A cupel or cupeling hearth for refining precious metals. **2.** Examination or trial by the cupel; hence, any critical examination or decisive trial. **3. a** Means of trial; specif., subjection to conditions that show the real character of person or thing in a certain particular; as, the tuberculin *test* for tuberculosis. **b** That with which anything is compared for proof of genuineness; touchstone; standard. **4.** *Chem.* A procedure or reaction used to distinguish any particular substance or constituent; also, the reagent used or a positive result obtained. **5.** *Educ.* Any series of questions or exercises or other means of measuring the skill, knowledge, intelligence, capacities, or aptitudes of an individual or group. — *v. t.* **1.** To refine, as gold or silver, in a test, or cupel; to subject to cupellation. **2.** To put to the test or proof; to try. **3.** *Chem.* To examine or try, as by a reagent. — **test′a·ble,** *adj.*

tes′ta (tĕs′tà), *n.; pl.* -TAE (-tē). [L. *testa* a piece of burned clay, broken piece of earthenware, shell.] **1.** *Bot.* The hard external coating or integument of a seed. **2.** *Zool.* The test.

tes·ta′cean (tĕs·tā′shăn), *adj.* [L. *testaceum* a shelled animal, fr. *testa* a shell.] Of or pertaining to an order (Testacea) of rhizopods containing forms with shells.

tes·ta′ceous (-shŭs), *adj.* [L. *testaceus.*] **1.** Of or pertaining to a shell or shells; of the nature of, or having, a hard shell. **2.** *Zool.* & *Bot.* Dull red or brownish yellow.

tes′ta·cy (tĕs′tà·sĭ), *n.* *Law.* State or circumstance of being testate, or of leaving a valid will.

tes′ta·ment (-mĕnt), *n.* [L. *testamentum* (fr. *testari* to be a witness, make one's will, fr. *testis* a witness); in ref. to the Bible, translating Gr. *diathēkē* a last will, a covenant.] **1.** *Bib.* A solemn covenant: **a** [*caps.* with *Old* and *New.*] One of two general divisions of the Scriptures. See BIBLE. **b** [*cap.*] Colloquially, the New Testament. **2.** *Law.* An act by which a person determines the disposition of his property after his death; now, usually, a will.

tes′ta·men′ta·ry (tĕs′tà·mĕn′tà·rĭ), *adj.* **1.** Of or pert. to a will, or testament, or the administration of a will. **2.** Bequeathed by will; given by testament. **3.** Done or appointed by, or founded on, a testament, or will.

tes′tate (tĕs′tāt), *adj.* [L. *testatus,* past part. of *testari.*] *Law.* Having left a will; as, a person dying *testate.*

tes′ta·tor (tĕs′tā′tẽr), *n.* [F. and L.; F. *testateur,* fr. L. *testator.*] *Law.* A man who leaves a will, or testament, in force at his death. — **tes·ta′trix** (tĕs·tā′trĭks), *n. fem.; pl.* -TRICES (-trī′sēz).

test′er (tĕs′tẽr), *n.* One who or that which tests.

tes′ter (tĕs′tẽr), *n.* [OF. *testiere,* fr. *teste* the head, fr. L. *testa* an earthen pot, the skull.] The canopy over a bed or pulpit.

tes′ter, *n.* *Archaic.* = TESTON **b**.

tes′ti·cle (tĕs′tĭ·k'l), *n.* [L. *testiculus,* dim. of *testis* a testicle.] *Anat. & Zool.* A male genital gland; a testis. — **tes·tic′u·lar** (tĕs·tĭk′ū·lẽr), *adj.*

tes·tic′u·late (tĕs·tĭk′ū·lāt), *adj.* *Bot.* Shaped like a testicle, ovate and solid.

tes′ti·fi·ca′tion (tĕs′tĭ·fĭ·kā′shŭn), *n.* [MF. *testificacion,* fr. L. *testificatio.* See TESTIFY.] Act of testifying, or giving evidence; testimony.

tes′ti·fy (tĕs′tĭ·fī), *v. i.* -FIED (-fīd); -FY′ING. [L. *testificari,* fr. *testis* a witness + -*ficare* (in comp.) to make.] **1.** To make a solemn declaration to establish some fact. **2.** To bear witness; — with *against.* **3.** To serve as indication or evidence. **4.** *Law.* To make a solemn declaration under oath or affirmation, for establishing proof of some fact to a court. — *v. t.* **1.** To bear witness to; to affirm solemnly. **2.** To be indication of; as, acts *testify* intent. **3.** To declare or make known freely or publicly. **4.** *Law.* To affirm or declare under oath or affirmation before a tribunal, in order to prove some fact. — **tes′ti·fi′er** (-fī′ẽr), *n.*

tes′ti·mo′ni·al (-mō′nĭ·ăl), *n.* **1.** A writing or certificate in favor of one's character, ability, etc., or of the value of a thing. **2.** A token of regard or admiration, in acknowledgment of services rendered, or the like, presented to a person, or established in his memory. — *adj.* Of, comprising, or pertaining to, a testimonial (sense 2).

tes′ti·mo′ny (tĕs′tĭ·mō′nĭ *or,* *esp. Brit.,* -mŭn·ĭ), *n.; pl.* -NIES (-nĭz). [L. *testimonium,* fr. *testis* a witness.] **1.** A solemn declaration or affirmation made to establish some fact. **2.** Affirmation; declaration. **3.** Evidence, esp. validating evidence; attestation. **4.** Act of testifying; open attestation; profession. **5.** *Jewish Antiq.* **a** The tables of the law. *Ex.* xxv. 16. **b** Hence, the Scriptures.

tes′tis (tĕs′tĭs), *n.; pl.* TESTES (-tēz). [L.] *Anat. & Zool.* A testicle.

tes′ton (tĕs′tŏn; tĕs·tōon′), *n.* Also **tes·toon′** (tĕs·tōon′). [F. *teston,* fr. It. *testone,* aug. of *testa* the head.] *Obs. exc. Hist.* Any of several

European coins, so called because the obverse type was a head. Specif.: **a** A French silver coin of the 16th century, worth between 10 and 14½ sous. **b** A shilling of Henry VIII of England, which fell in value to sixpence (in Shakespeare's time); hence, a sixpence.

tes·tos′ter·one (tĕs·tŏs′tẽr·ōn), *n.* [*testes* + *sterol* + -*one*.] *Biochem.* A crystalline androgenic compound, $C_{19}H_{28}O_2$, obtained from the testes of bulls and otherwise.

test paper. 1. *Educ., U. S.* A paper containing a test or examination. **2.** *Chem.* Paper prepared for testing certain substances. See LITMUS PAPER.

test pilot. A pilot engaged to put newly built airplanes through certain stunts in the air designed to produce strains in excess of normal, as a test of strength, manageability, etc.

test tube. *Chem.* A tube for simple tests, usually a plain tube of thin glass closed at one end.

tes·tu′di·nal (tĕs·tū′dĭ·năl), **tes·tu′di·nar′i·ous** (-nâr′ĭ·ŭs), *adj. Zool.* Pert. to or like a tortoise or tortoise shell.

tes·tu′di·nate (-nāt), *adj.* [L. *testudinatus,* fr. *testudo,* -*inis,* a tortoise, an arch or vault.] **a** Like a tortoise shell; arched; vaulted. **b** *Zool.* Chelonian. — *n.* A turtle.

tes·tu′do (tĕs·tū′dō), *n.; pl.* -DINES (-dĭ·nēz). [L.; akin to L. *testu* an earthen vessel, *testa* the shell of shellfish.] **1.** *Rom. Antiq.* **a** Any of various kinds of sheds to protect soldiers in siege operations. **b** A cover or screen which a body of troops in close formation formed by overlapping their shields over their heads. **2.** [*cap.*] *Zool.* A genus of turtles, type of the family Testudinidae, comprising the typical land tortoises.

tes′ty (tĕs′tĭ), *adj.;* TES′TI·ER (-tĭ·ẽr); TES′TI·EST. [AF. *testif,* fr. *teste* head.] Easily irritated; snappish. — **Syn.** See IRASCIBLE. — **tes′ti·ly** (-tĭ·lĭ), *adv.* — **tes′ti·ness** (-tĭ·nĕs; -nĭs), *n.*

te·tan′ic (tē·tăn′ĭk), *adj.* Also **te·tan′i·cal** (-ĭ·kăl). *Physiol. & Med.* Of, pertaining to, having the character of, or tending to produce tetanus.

tet′a·nize (tĕt′à·nīz), *v. t.* *Physiol.* To throw, as a muscle, into a state of permanent contraction; to cause tetanus in.

tet′a·nus (-nŭs), *n.* [L., fr. Gr. *tetanos,* fr. *tetanos* stretched, fr. *teinein* to stretch.] **1. a** *Med.* A painful and often fatal infectious disease marked by tonic spasms of the voluntary muscles, caused by the toxin of a microorganism (*Clostridium tetani*), often introduced through wounds. When confined to the muscles of the lower jaw, it is called *lockjaw.* **b** Loosely, the microorganism causing this disease. **2.** *Physiol.* State of a muscle when undergoing continued contraction.

tet′a·ny (-nĭ), *n.* *Med.* A morbid state resembling tetanus, affecting chiefly the muscles in the extremities.

te·tar′to·he′dral (tē·tär′tō·hē′drăl), *adj.* [Gr. *tetartos* one fourth + *hedra* base.] *Cryst.* Having one fourth the number of planes requisite to symmetry. Cf. HEMIHEDRAL, HOLOHEDRAL.

tetch′y (tĕch′ĭ), *adj.;* TETCH′I·ER (-ĭ·ẽr); TETCH′I·EST. [See TECHY.] Irritable; touchy.

tête′ à tête′ (tāt′ à tāt′; tě′·tà tât′). Face to face; familiarly; — of two persons.

tête′–a–tête′ (tāt′à·tāt′; tě′-tà·tât′), *adj.* [F., head to head.] Being face to face with only two present; hence, sometimes, confidential or familiar with only two persons concerned. — *n.* **1.** Private conversation between two persons. **2.** A short sofa or the like intended to seat two persons, esp. so that they face each other.

‖**tête–bêche** (tât′bâsh′), *adj.* [F.] *Philately.* Of a pair of stamps, inverted in relation to one another. Tête-bêche stamps may be the result of an error in printing or they may be intentionally so printed.

‖**tête–de–pont** (tât′dĕ·pôn′), *n.; pl.* TÊTES-DE-PONT (tât′-). [F.] A bridgehead.

teth′er (tĕth′ẽr), *n.* [ME. *tether, tethir, tedir.*] **1.** A rope, chain, or the like, by which an animal is fastened so that it can range only within certain limits. **2.** The range of one's strength or resources; scope. — **at the end of one's tether.** At the limit of one's power or resources. — *v. t.* To confine by a tether.

Te′thys (tē′thĭs), *n.* [L., fr. Gr. *Tēthys.*] *Gr. Myth.* A Titaness, daughter of Uranus and wife of Oceanus.

tet′ra- (tĕt′rà-), **tetr-.** [Gr. *tessares, tettares.*] A combining form meaning *four, having four* or *four parts.* — **tet′ra** (-rà), *adj.*

tet′ra·bas′ic (-bās′ĭk), *adj.* *Chem.* **a** Having four hydrogen atoms capable of replacement by basic atoms or radicals. **b** Containing four atoms of a univalent metal, or their equivalent. **c** Having four basic hydroxyl groups; able to react with four molecules of a monoacid.

tet′ra·brach (tĕt′rà·brăk), *n.* [Gr. *tetrabrachys.* See TETRA-; TRIBRACH.] *Gr. & Lat. Pros.* A word or foot of four short syllables.

tet′ra·bran′chi·ate (-brăng′kĭ·āt), *adj.* Of or pertaining to a division (Tetrabranchia) of cephalopod mollusks, comprising the nautiluses. See NAUTILUS. — *n.* A nautilus.

tet′ra·chlo′ride (-klō′rīd; -rĭd), *n.* Also **tet′ra·chlo′rid.** *Chem.* A compound with four atoms of chlorine.

tet′ra·chord (tĕt′rà·kôrd), *n.* [Gr. *tetrachordon,* deriv. of *tetra-* + *chordē* a chord.] *Music.* A diatonic series of four tones, with an interval of a perfect fourth between the first and last. — **tet′ra·chor′dal** (-kôr′dăl; -d'l), *adj.*

te·trac′id (tē·trăs′ĭd), *adj.* [*tetr-* + *acid.*] *Chem.* **a** Able to react with four molecules of a monoacid, or two of a diacid, to form a salt or ester. **b** Having four hydrogen atoms replaceable by basic atoms or radicals.

tet′rad (tĕt′răd), *n.* [Gr. *tetras,* -*ados.*] **1.** The number four; a collection of four. **2.** *Biol.* A temporary grouping of chromosomes by fours in certain organisms due to the adjacent arrangement and longitudinal splitting of a pair of chromosomes during meiosis. **3.** *Bot.* A group of four cells, commonly arranged in the form of a tetrahedron, and produced by the successive divisions of a mother cell in two planes; as, a *tetrad* of pollen grains. **4.** *Chem.* A quadrivalent atom, radical, or element.

te·trad′y·mite (tē·trăd′ȳ·mīt), *n.* [Gr. *tetradymos* fourfold; — from its occurrence in compound twin crystals.] *Mineral.* A pale steel-gray mineral of metallic luster, essentially a telluride of bismuth, Bi_2Te_3.

tet′ra·dy′na·mous (tĕt′rà·dī′nà·mŭs; -dĭn′à·mŭs), *adj.* *Bot.* Having six stamens, four of which are longer than the others.

tet′ra·eth′yl lead′ (tĕt′rà·ĕth′ĭl·lĕd′), *n.* Also **tet′ra·eth′yl lead.** [*tetra-* + *ethyl.*] *Chem.* A heavy, colorless, poisonous liquid, Pb-$(C_2H_5)_4$, used as an antiknock agent.

tet′ra·gon (tĕt′rà·gŏn), *n.* [From LL., fr. Gr. *tetragōnon,* fr. *tetra-* +

gōnia corner, angle.] *Geom.* A (plane) figure having four angles; a quadrangle, such as a square, a rhombus, etc.
te·trag′o·nal (tĕ·trăg′ō·năl), *adj.* **1.** *Geom.* Of or pertaining to a tetragon; having four angles or sides. **2.** *Cryst.* Designating, or belonging to, a system (**tetragonal system**) having all three axes at right angles and the two lateral axes equal.
tet′ra·gram (tĕt′rȧ·grăm), *n.* [Gr. *tetragrammon.* See TETRA-; -GRAM.] A word of four letters; specif. [*often cap.*], the Tetragrammaton.
Tet′ra·gram′ma·ton (-grăm′ȧ·tŏn), *n.* [*sometimes not cap.*] [NL., fr. Gr. *tetragrammaton*, fr. *tetra-* (see TETRA-) + *gramma* a letter.] The four letters (variously written, without vowel points, *IHVH, JHVH, JHWH, YHVH, YHWH*) forming a Hebrew tribal name of the Supreme Being transliterated by modern scholars *Yahweh*, which the Jews about three centuries B.C. ceased to pronounce as too sacred and for fear of desecration, substituting for it in reading the word *Adonai*, My Lord, or *Elohim*, God. The three vowel points of *Adonai* often written with the Tetragrammaton as a direction to read it *Adonai*, being misinterpreted, gave rise to the Christian form *Jehovah.*
tet′ra·he′dral (tĕt′rȧ·hē′drăl), *adj.* [See TETRAHEDRON.] Pert. to a tetrahedron; having, or made up of, four sides.
tet′ra·he′drite (-drīt), *n.* [From TETRAHEDRON.] *Mineral.* A fine-grained gray mineral of metallic luster, essentially copper, antimony, and sulfur, $Cu_8Sb_2S_7$, often containing also other elements, occurring in tetrahedral crystals and also massive. It is often a valuable ore of silver.
tet′ra·he′dron (-drŭn), *n.; pl.* -HEDRONS (-drŭnz), -HEDRA (-drȧ). [NL., fr. LGr. *tetraedros* with four sides, fr. *tetra-* + *hedra* seat, base.] *Geom.* A polyhedron of four faces.
te·tral′o·gy (tĕ·trăl′ō·jĭ), *n.; pl.* -GIES (-jĭz). [Gr. *tetralogia.* See TETRA-; LOGIA.] **1.** *Gr. Drama.* A group or series of four dramatic pieces, represented consecutively on the Attic stage at the Dionysiac festival. **2.** Hence, any series of four connected works, as dramas, operas, etc.
te·tram′er·ous (tĕ·trăm′ẽr·ŭs), *adj.* Also **te·tram′er·al** (-ăl). [*tetra-* + *-merous.*] **1.** Having or characterized by the presence of four parts; specif., *Bot.*, having the parts arranged in sets of four or multiples of four: — often written *4-merous.* **2.** *Zool.* Having four (or apparently only four) joints in each of the tarsi.
te·tram′e·ter (-ē·tẽr), *adj.* [From LL., fr. Gr. *tetrametron*, fr. *tetra-* + *metron* a measure.] *Pros.* Consisting of four measures, either four dipodies (eight feet), as in ancient iambic, trochaic, and anapaestic verse, or four feet, as in modern verse. — *n.* A verse or line of four feet or dipodies.
te·tran′drous (tĕ·trăn′drŭs), *adj. Bot.* Having four stamens.
tet′ra·pet′al·ous (tĕt′rȧ·pĕt′ăl·ŭs), *adj. Bot.* Having four petals.
te·trap′o·dy (tĕ·trăp′ō·dĭ), *n.* [Gr. *tetrapodia.*] *Pros.* A verse or group of four feet.
te·trap′ter·ous (-tẽr·ŭs), *adj.* [Gr. *tetrapteros*, fr. *tetra-* + *pteron* wing.] *Biol.* Having four wings.
te′trarch (tē′trärk; tĕt′rärk), *n.* [LL. *tetrarcha*, fr. L., fr. Gr. *tetrarchēs, tetrarchos*, fr. *tetra-* + *archos* ruler.] *Class. Antiq.* A governor of the fourth part of a province, as in the Roman Empire; also, a petty king. — **te′trarch·ate** (tē′trär·kāt; tĕt′rär-), **te′trarch·y** (-kĭ), *n.*
tet′ra·spore (tĕt′rȧ·spōr; 70), *n. Bot.* In certain algae, one of the asexual nonmotile spores commonly produced in groups of four.
tet′ra·stich (tĕt′rȧ·stĭk; tĕ·trăs′tĭk), *n.* [L. *tetrastichon*, fr. Gr. *tetrastichon*, fr. *tetra-* + *stichos* a row, verse.] A stanza, epigram, or poem, consisting of four verses or lines. — **tet′ra·stich′ic** (tĕt′rȧ·stĭk′ĭk), *adj.*
te·tras′ti·chous (tĕ·trăs′tĭ·kŭs), *adj.* [Gr. *tetrastichos.* See TETRASTICH.] *Bot.* Four-ranked; — said esp. of flowers arranged in a spike in four vertical rows.
tet′ra·syl·lab′ic (tĕt′rȧ·sĭ·lăb′ĭk), **tet′ra·syl·lab′i·cal** (-ĭ·kăl), *adj.* Having four syllables.
tet′ra·syl′la·ble (-sĭl′ȧ·b'l), *n.* A word of four syllables.
tet′ra·tom′ic (-tŏm′ĭk), *adj.* [*tetr-* + *atomic.*] *Chem.* **a** Consisting of four atoms; having four atoms in the molecule, as phosphorus. **b** Quadrivalent. **c** Having four replaceable atoms or groups.
tet′ra·va′lent (tĕt′rȧ·vā′lĕnt; tĕ·trăv′ȧ-), *adj.* [*tetra-* + L. *valens, -entis*, pres. part.] *Chem.* Quadrivalent.
tet′rode (tĕt′rōd), *n.* [*tetr-* + 2d *-ode.*] *Elec.* A four-electrode vacuum tube containing two electrodes in addition to the cathode and anode.
te·trox′ide (tĕ·trŏk′sīd; -sĭd), *n.* Also **te·trox′id.** [*tetr-* + *oxide.*] *Chem.* A compound of an element or radical with four atoms of oxygen.
tet′ryl (tĕt′rĭl), *n.* [*tetr-* + *-yl.*] **1.** *Chem.* = BUTYL, 1. **2.** A pale-yellow crystalline explosive, $C_7H_5N_5O_8$, used esp. as a detonator.
tet′ter (tĕt′ẽr), *n.* [AS. *teter.*] Any of various vesicular skin diseases, as ringworm, eczema, and herpes.
teugh (tūk), **teugh′ly, teugh′ness.** Scot. vars. of TOUGH, TOUGHLY, TOUGHNESS.
Teu′ton (tū′tŏn; -t'n), *n.* [L. *Teutones, Teutoni*, pl.] **1.** One of the ancient German tribe **Teu′to·nes** (tū′tō·nēz). It is uncertain whether they were Teutonic or Celtic. **2.** A member of the Teutonic race (see TEUTONIC, 1); esp., a person of German nationality. — **Teu′ton,** *adj.*
Teu·ton′ic (tū·tŏn′ĭk), *adj.* **1.** Of or pertaining to the Teutons; designating, or pertaining to, the tall blond race characteristic of northern Europe and including the Burgundians, Goths, Franks, Vandals, Lombards, Angles, Saxons, Jutes, Danes, and Scandinavians. **2.** Pertaining to, belonging to, or designating the subfamily of Indo-European languages which includes the Scandinavian, Gothic, and the High and Low German tongues. See INDO-EUROPEAN LANGUAGES, *Table.* — *n.* The Teutonic languages.
Teu·ton′i·cism (-ĭ·sĭz'm), *n.* A mode of speech peculiar to the Teutons; a Teutonic idiom, phrase, or expression; also, a Teutonic mode or custom.
Teu′ton·ism (tū′tŏn·ĭz'm), *n.* **1.** Belief in the superiority of the Teutons, esp. of the German race. **2.** Teutonic civilization or culture. — **Teu′ton·ist** (-ĭst), *n.*
Teu′ton·ize (-īz), *v. t. & i.* To make or become Teutonic. — **Teu′ton·i·za′tion** (-ĭ·zā′shŭn; -ī·zā′-), *n.*
tew (*dial.* tē′ōō, tū), *v. i.* *Scot. & Dial.* **a** To work hard; strive. **b** To fuss. — *n. Chiefly Dial.* Laborious struggle; also, state of worry.
Tex′as (tĕk′sȧs), *n. sing. & pl.* **1.** An Indian of a large group of Texan tribes. **2.** [*not cap.*] [On Mississippi steamboats the staterooms were named after the states, and the officers' were the largest.] *Western U.S.* A structure on the hurricane deck of a steamer, containing officers' cabins, etc., with the pilothouse in front or on top.
Texas fever. *Veter.* An infectious disease of cattle transmitted by a tick and caused by a protozoan (*Babesia bigemina*) that multiplies in the blood and destroys the red blood cells.
Texas leaguer. [From the *Texas* (baseball) *League.*] *Baseball Cant.* A fly that falls too far out to be handled by an infielder and too close in to be caught by an outfielder.
Texas sparrow. A finch (*Arremonops rufivirgatus*) of southern Texas and Mexico. It is olive-green above with rufous stripes on the head and yellow on the wing.
text (tĕkst), *n.* [OF. *texte*, fr. L. *textus* texture, structure, context, fr. *texere, textum*, to weave, compose.] **1. a** The actual matter of an author's work, in distinction from a paraphrase, annotation, or commentary. **b** A composition on which a note or commentary is written. **2.** Any one of two or more written or printed versions of the matter of an author's work or works; as, the folio and quarto *texts* of Shakespeare. **3. a** The main body of matter on a printed or written page, as distinguished from notes, etc. **b** The letterpress, as distinguished from illustrations and the margins. **4.** Short for TEXTBOOK. **5.** A verse or passage of Scripture, esp. one chosen as the subject of a sermon, or in support of a doctrine. **6.** Hence, topic; theme. **7.** *Bib. Crit.* Any one of the various forms that have been assumed to represent the authentic reading of the Scriptures or a part of them. **8.** *Paleog.* Large writing; — so called because the text of a document was written in a larger hand than accompanying notes.
text′book′ (-bŏŏk′), *n.* Any manual of instruction; a book containing a presentation of the principles of a subject, used as a basis of instruction.
text hand. A large hand in writing; — from the practice of writing the text of a book in a large hand and the notes in a smaller hand.
tex′tile (tĕks′tĭl; -tīl; 56), *adj.* [L. *textilis*, fr. *texere* to weave.] **1.** Pertaining to weaving or to woven fabrics. **2.** Woven or capable of being woven; formed by weaving. — *n.* A woven fabric or a material for weaving.
tex′tu·al (tĕks′tū·ăl), *adj.* [ME. *textuel.*] Of, pertaining to, or contained in the text, specif. the text of the Scriptures; based on or adhering to the text; hence, sometimes, verbal or literal; as, *textual* criticism. — **tex′tu·al·ly**, *adv.*
tex′tu·al·ism (-ĭz'm), *n.* Rigid adherence to the letter of the text, specif. of the Scriptures. — **tex′tu·al·ist** (-ĭst), *n.*
tex′tu·ar′y (tĕks′tū·ĕr′ĭ *or, esp. Brit.,* -ẽr·ĭ), *adj.* Textual.
tex′tur·al (-tūr·ăl), *adj.* Of or pertaining to texture; as, *textural* change. — **tex′tur·al·ly**, *adv.*
tex′ture (-tūr), *n.* [L. *textura*, fr. *texere, textum*, to weave.] **1.** A woven fabric; a web. **2.** The characteristic disposition or connection of threads in woven fabric. **3.** The disposition or manner of union of the particles of a body or substance; as, the *texture* of minerals, plants, bones, etc. **4.** In general, manner of structure; in artistic composition, the structure or structural quality resulting from the artist's blending of elements, such as the parts in music, the pigment and brushwork in painting, etc.
-th. [AS.] A suffix forming nouns of *action* from verbs and of *state* or *quality* from adjectives, as in grow*th*, heal*th*.
-th. An ending of the 3d pers. sing. pres. indicative, as in do*th*, ha*th*, etc. See -ETH.
-th, or (*after a vowel*) **-eth** (-ĕth; -ĭth). [AS. -(*o*)*tha.*] A suffix forming ordinal numbers, as in four*th*, twenti*eth*.
thack (thăk; thȧk), *n. & v.* [AS. *thæc*, n., *thaccian*, v.] *Scot. & Dial.* Thatch; roof.
thae (thā), *adj. & pron.* [AS. *thā*, pl. of *se.* See THEY.] *Chiefly Scot.* Those; these.
Thai (tī), *adj.* Also **Tai** (tī). Designating, or pert. to, the chief linguistic stock of Indochina, including the peoples of Siamese and Shan speech. See LANGUAGE, *Table.* — *n.* A group of tribes in Burma and Thailand; also, their language.
thal′a·men·ceph′a·lon (thăl′ȧ·mĕn·sĕf′ȧ·lŏn), *n.* [NL., fr. Gr. *thalamos* chamber + *encephalon.*] *Anat.* The diencephalon. See FOREBRAIN.
tha·lam′ic (thȧ·lăm′ĭk), *adj.* Of or pertaining to the thalamus, esp., *Anat.*, the optic thalamus.
thal′a·mus (thăl′ȧ·mŭs), *n.; pl.* -MI (-mī). [L., fr. Gr. *thalamos* chamber.] **1.** *Anat.* The largest subdivision of the diencephalon (see FOREBRAIN) on either side, consisting chiefly of an ovoid nuclear mass. **2.** *Bot.* = TORUS, 3.
tha·las′sic (thȧ·lăs′ĭk), *adj.* [Gr. *thalassa* the sea.] Pertaining to the sea or ocean; — sometimes disting. from *oceanic*, as applying esp. to seas, gulfs, etc.
tha′ler (tä′lẽr), *n.* [G. *taler*, formerly *thaler.*] **1.** See TALER. **2.** The silver dollar of Ethiopia; — called also *talari.* **3.** The Maria Theresa dollar (see DOLLAR, 1 b).
Tha·li′a (thȧ·lī′ȧ), *n.* [L., fr. Gr. *Thaleia*, orig., blooming, luxuriant.] *Gr. Myth.* **a** The Muse of comedy and bucolic poetry. **b** One of the three Graces.
thal′lic (thăl′ĭk), *adj. Chem.* Of, pertaining to, or containing thallium, esp. in its valence of three.
thal′li·um (-ĭ·ŭm), *n.* [NL., fr. Gr. *thallos* a young shoot; — from the bright *green* line in its spectrum.] *Chem.* A sparsely but widely distributed metallic element, resembling lead in physical properties. Symbol, *Tl*; at. no., 81; at. wt., 204.39. Sp. gr., 11.8. Salts of it are used in making refractive glass.
thal′loid (-oid), *adj.* [*thallus* + *-oid.*] *Bot.* Pertaining to, resembling, or consisting of a thallus.
thal′lo·phyte (thăl′ō·fīt), *n.* [Gr. *thallos* young shoot + *-phyte.*] *Bot.* Any of a phylum (Thallophyta) of plants including the algae, bacteria, fungi, and lichens, and in some classifications the slime molds. The simpler forms are unicellular and reproduce vegetatively or by means of asexual spores. In the higher forms the plant body is a thallus, and both asexual and sexual reproduction occurs in these forms. — **thal′lo·phyt′ic** (-fĭt′ĭk), *adj.*
thal′lous (thăl′ŭs), *adj.* Also **thal′li·ous** (-ĭ·ŭs). *Chem.* Of, pert. to, or containing thallium, esp. in its valence of one.
thal′lus (-ŭs), *n.; pl.* -LI (-ī); -LUSES (-ŭs·ĕz; -ĭz). [NL., fr. Gr. *thallos* young shoot or branch, frond.] *Bot.* A plant body showing no differentiation into distinct members, as stem, leaves, and roots, and sometimes filamentous and sometimes consisting of plates of cells. It is characteristic of thallophytes.

Tham′muz (tȧm′mōōz; *Bib.* tăm′ŭz). Var. of TAMMUZ. See JEWISH CALENDAR.
than (thăn; 4), *conj.* [AS. *thanne, thonne, thænne,* then (the older sense), than.] Indicating the second member of a comparison expressive of inequality; used after: **a** Adjectives and adverbs of comparative degree; as, easier said *than* done. **b** Adjectives and adverbs expressing diversity, as *other, else,* etc.; as, none other *than* Pepys.
than′a·to- (thăn′ȧ·tō-), **thanat-**. [Gr. *thanatos.*] A combining form meaning *death,* as in **than′a·to·pho′bi·a**.
than′a·top′sis (-tŏp′sĭs), *n.* [NL., fr. *thanat-* + *-opsis.*] A view of death; a meditation on death.
thane (thān), *n.* Also, *esp. Hist.,* **thegn** (thān). [Prop. a Scot. form fr. ME. *thein, thegn,* fr. AS. *thegen, thegn,* a thane, man, warrior, follower, servant.] **1.** *O. Eng. Hist.* Among the Anglo-Saxons and Danes, one of a class of free attendants on a lord. There were two classes, the king's thanes, succeeded by the greater barons of later days, and the middle or lesser thanes, succeeded by the minor barons. **2.** *Scot. Hist.* One holding land of the king; the chief of a clan, who became one of the king's barons.
thank (thăngk), *n.* [AS. *thanc, thonc,* thanks, favor, thought.] **1.** *Archaic exc. in pl.* Kindly or grateful thought; gratitude; as, give *thanks* to God; also, grace; favor. **2.** *Now only in pl.* An expression of gratitude; an acknowledgment, as by words, for a favor or kindness received. — *v. t.* To express one's thanks to; sometimes, ironically, to hold responsible; to consider blameworthy.
thank′ful (-fōōl; -f'l), *adj.* **1.** Grateful. **2.** Expressive of thanks. — **Syn.** See GRATEFUL. — **thank′ful·ly,** *adv.* — **thank′ful·ness,** *n.*
thank′less, *adj.* **1.** Ungrateful. **2.** Not obtaining or deserving thanks; unappreciated; as, a *thankless* task. — **thank′less·ly,** *adv.* — **thank′less·ness,** *n.*
thanks·giv′ing (thăngks·gĭv′ĭng; thăngks′gĭv′ĭng; 2), *n.* **1.** Act of rendering thanks, esp. to God. **2.** A prayer expressing gratitude. **3. a** A public acknowledgment or celebration of divine goodness and mercies. **b** A day set apart for making this; specif. [*cap.*], *U. S.* In full, **Thanks·giv′ing Day** (thănks·gĭv′ĭng). A day (usually the fourth Thursday of November) set apart each year for thanksgiving and praise to God. See HOLIDAY, 3.
thank′wor′thy (thăngk′wûr′thĭ), *adj.* Worthy of thanks.
tharm (thärm), **thairm** (thārm), *n.* [AS. *thearm* a gut.] *Dial.* **a** The belly. **b** Catgut.
that (thăt; 4), *pron.* [AS. *thæt,* neut. nom. & acc. sing. of the demonstrative pron. and adj., also used as a relative pron.] **1.** As a demonstrative pronoun (*pl.* THOSE): The person, thing, or idea mentioned, indicated, or understood from the situation or context; as, the voice was *that* of Jacob; specif., in opposition or contradistinction to *this,* the more remote; also, the former of two foregoing words, phrases, etc. **2.** As a relative pronoun, equivalent to *who* or *which,* either sing. or pl.; as, books *that* are widely read.
☞ The relative *that* is now used only in restrictive clauses (the birds *that* were seen) and is never preceded by a preposition (the book *that* you refer to, *but* the book to *which* you refer). *Who* and *which* may be used to introduce either a descriptive clause (the older boys, *who* work, eat before the younger ones) or a restrictive clause (the boys *who* work eat first).
— *adj.* Of or pertaining to a person, thing, or idea indicated or understood from the situation or context; as, from *that* moment.
— *conj.* A connective derived by loss of stress from the demonstrative *that,* regarded as in apposition with a clause, as in "Before *that* thou shalt thrice deny." It is used: **1.** To introduce a clause employed as object, subject, or predicate nominative of a verb; as, tell them *that* you are afraid. **2.** To introduce a clause giving a reason, cause, purpose, result, etc.; as, he spoke plainly *that* they might be warned. **3.** In an elliptical sentence to introduce a sentence or clause expressing a wish, cause of surprise, etc.; as, Oh *that* he would come!
— *adv. Colloq.* To such a degree; so; so very.
thatch (thăch), *n.* [AS. *thæc* a roof.] **1.** The covering for a roof, grain stack, etc., made of straw, rushes, reeds, or leaves. **2.** In full, **thatch palm.** Any of several palms the leaves of which are used for thatch. — *v. t.* To cover with or as with thatch. — **thatch′er,** *n.*
thatch′ing, *n.* Act of, or material used by, one who thatches.
thau′ma·tol′o·gy (thô′mȧ·tŏl′ō·jĭ), *n.* [Gr. *thauma, thaumatos,* a wonder + *-logy.*] The study of miracles.
thau′ma·trope (thô′mȧ·trōp), *n.* [Gr. *thauma* a wonder + *tropos* turning.] An optical instrument or toy for showing the persistence of an impression upon the eye. It consists of a card having on its opposite faces different designs, which, when the card is whirled rapidly round a diameter by the strings that hold it, appear to the eye combined in a single picture.
thau′ma·turge (thô′mȧ·tûrj), *n.* Also **thau′ma·tur′gist** (-tûr′jĭst). A worker of miracles or wonders.
thau′ma·tur′gy (thô′mȧ·tûr′jĭ), *n.* [Gr. *thaumatourgia,* fr. *thauma* a wonder + *ergon* work.] The performance of miracles or wonders; specif., magic. — **thau′ma·tur′gic** (-tûr′jĭk), **thau′ma·tur′gi·cal** (-jĭ·kăl), *adj.*
thaw (thô), *v. i.* [AS. *thawian.*] **1.** To melt, dissolve, or become fluid or semifluid, as ice; also, to have its frozen contents melted or dissolved; as, the pipe *thawed.* **2.** To become so warm as to melt ice and snow; — impersonally of the weather. **3.** To be freed from coldness or reserve; grow genial; unbend. — *v. t.* To cause to thaw. — *n.* **1.** Act or process of thawing. **2.** A warmth of weather sufficient to thaw ice. **3.** State of growing less cold or reserved. — **thaw′er** (thô′ẽr), *n.*
the (thē, *unaccented before a consonant, as in "the man"*; thē *or* thĭ, *unaccented before a vowel, as in "the egg"*; thē, *emphatic or alone;* 4), *adj.,* or *definite article.* [AS. *thē,* a later form for earlier nom. sing. masc. *sē,* formed under the influence of *thæt* and the oblique cases. See THAT.] **1.** That (person or thing) in particular; as, to pick out *the* culprit. **2.** That (person or thing) close or at hand in space, time, thought, etc.; as, news of *the* hour; *the* heat is intense. **3.** That (one) so designated or distinguished; — used esp. in titles; as, *the* Duke of York; *the* Nile. **4.** That (one) having no fellow or equal; as, *the* poet of his day. **5.** Each; every; as, ten cents *the* copy. **6.** Any one (person or thing) typical of its genus, class, etc.; as, striped like *the* zebra. **7.** Her, his, its, one's, or the like; as, to lead her by *the* hand; pleasing to *the* eye. **8.** Before an adjective used substantively to indicate either a class or an abstract idea; as, *the* sublime; *the* pure in heart. — (thē; thē), *adv.* [AS. *thē, thȳ,* instrumental case of *sē, sēo, thæt,* masc. and neut.] By that; by so much; on that account; — before comparatives; as, *the* more, *the* merrier.
the-. = THEO-.
the·a′ceous (thē·ā′shŭs), *adj.* [From *Thea,* former generic name of the tea plant, taken by Linnaeus fr. Gr. *thea* goddess, as being a divine herb, but orig. fr. the source of E. *tea.*] Belonging to the tea family (Theaceae). See TEA.
the′an·throp′ic (thē′ăn·thrŏp′ĭk), *adj.* Having both a divine and a human nature; being God or a god incarnate.
the·an′thro·pism (thē·ăn′thrō·pĭz′m), *n.* [From Gr. *theanthrōpos,* fr. *theos* god + *anthrōpos* man.] **1.** *Theol.* The union of the divine and human natures in Christ. **2.** Anthropomorphism; also, belief in a theanthropic being or beings. — **the·an′thro·pist** (-pĭst), *n.*
the′ar·chy (thē′är·kĭ), *n.; pl.* -CHIES (-kĭz). [Gr. *theos* god + *-archy.*] **a** Government by God; divine sovereignty; theocracy. **b** A body or system of divine rulers.
the′a·ter, the′a·tre (thē′ȧ·tẽr; thē′-; 27; *obs. or dial.* thē·ā′tẽr), *n.* [OF. *theatre* (F. *théâtre*), fr. L. *theatrum,* fr. Gr. *theatron;* akin to Gr. *theasthai* to see, view.] **1.** An edifice for dramatic performances or spectacles. **2.** That which resembles a theater in form or use; as: **a** A place rising by steps or gradations. **b** A room adapted to any exhibition or performance before an assembly, as a lecture or surgical clinic. **3.** A place where events are enacted; a sphere of operation; as, the *theater* of war. **4.** The drama. **5.** Theatrical material or method with reference to its effectiveness; as, a certain play is good *theater.*
the′a·ter-in-the-round′, *n.* = ARENA THEATER.
the·at′ri·cal (thē·ăt′rĭ·kăl), *adj.* **1.** Of or pertaining to a theater or scenic or dramatic representations. **2.** Also **the·at′ric** (-rĭk). Histrionic; hence, in a bad sense, showy; artificial; affected. — **Syn.** See DRAMATIC. — **the·at′ri·cal·ism** (-ĭz′m), *n.* — **the·at′ri·cal·ly,** *adv.*
the·at′ri·cals (-kălz), *n. pl.* Dramatic performances, esp. by amateurs.
the·at′rics (-rĭks), *n., pl. in form but construed as sing.;* see -ICS. The art of producing effects suitable to theatrical presentation.
the′ba·ine (thē′bȧ·ēn; thē·bā′ēn; -ĭn), *n.* Also **the′ba·in** (-ĭn). [From a kind of Egyptian opium produced at Thebes, fr. L. *Thebae,* fr. Gr. *Thēbai, Thēbē,* Thebes.] *Chem.* A white, crystalline, poisonous alkaloid, $C_{19}H_{21}NO_3$, found in opium and having a tetanic action like strychnine.
the′ca (thē′kȧ), *n.; pl.* THECAE (-sē). [L., fr. Gr. *thēkē* a case to put anything in.] **1.** *Bot.* A sac, capsule, or spore case. **2.** *Zool. & Anat.* A sheath or case, as the cuticle enclosing an insect pupa or the dura mater of the spinal cord. — **the′cal** (-kăl), **the′cate** (-kāt), *adj.*
‖**thé dan′sant′** (tā′ däN′säN′); *pl.* THÉS DANSANTS (tā′ däN′säN′). [F.] An afternoon tea and dance.
thee (thē), *pron.* [AS. *thē,* acc. & dat. of *thū* thou.] **1.** The objective case of *thou.* **2.** Ungrammatically for *thou* in dialect or among Friends (Quakers).
thee′lin (thē′lĭn), *n.* [Gr. *thēlys* female + *-in.*] *Biochem.* Estrone.
thee′lol (-lōl; -lŏl), *n.* [Gr. *thēlys* female + *-ol,* 1.] *Biochem.* An oestrus-promoting hormone obtained from the urine of pregnant females.
theft (thĕft), *n.* [AS. *thēoft, thīefth.*] **1.** Act of stealing; specif., the felonious taking and removing of personal property, with intent to deprive the rightful owner of it; larceny. **2.** *Obs.* That which is stolen.
thegn (thān). Var. of THANE (esp. in sense 1).
the′ine (thē′ēn; -ĭn), *n.* Also **the′in** (-ĭn). [F. *théine,* fr. NL. *thea.* See THEACEOUS.] *Chem.* Caffeine; — from its occurrence in tea.
their (thâr; 4), *pron.* [ON. *theirra, theira,* of them, but prop. gen. pl. of the demonstrative pron. and article.] The possessive case of *they.* — *adj.* **1.** Of or belonging to them or themselves; as, *their* property. **2.** Of or relating to them as authors, doers, givers, etc., or as objects of an action; as, *their* poetry, donations; seeking *their* subjugation.
theirs (thârz), *pron.* The possessive form of *their* used absolutely; as, the book is *theirs.*
the′ism (thē′ĭz′m), *n.* [Gr. *theos* god.] Belief in the existence of a god or gods; specif.: **a** Monotheism. **b** Belief in the existence of one God, transcending, yet immanent in, the universe; — disting. from *pantheism* and *deism.* — **the′ist** (-ĭst), *n. & adj.* — **the·is′tic** (thē·ĭs′tĭk), **the·is′ti·cal** (-tĭ·kăl), *adj.* — **the·is′ti·cal·ly,** *adv.*
the·li′tis (thē·lī′tĭs), *n.* [NL., fr. Gr. *thēlē* nipple + *-itis.*] *Med.* Inflammation of the nipple.
them (thĕm; 4), *pron.* [AS. *thǣm,* dat. pl. of the demonstrative pron. and article.] The objective case of *they.*
theme (thēm), *n.* [OF. *teme,* fr. L. *thema,* fr. Gr. *thema,* fr. root of *tithenai* to set, place.] **1.** A subject or topic of discourse; a text. **2.** A brief dissertation as a scholastic exercise; essay; composition. **3. a** *Gram.* A noun or verb not modified by inflections. **b** *Philol.* A stem. **4.** *Music.* A short melody constituting the basis of variation, development, or the like, in a composition or movement. **5.** *Radio. & Television.* = SIGNATURE, 5. — **the·mat′ic** (thē·măt′ĭk), **the·mat′i·cal** (-ĭ·kăl), *adj.* — **the·mat′i·cal·ly,** *adv.*
theme song. A melody that so often recurs in a musical drama as to characterize it or a part in it.
them·selves′ (thĕm·sĕlvz′; 4), *pron.* An emphasized form for *they, them;* the plural of *himself, herself,* and *itself.*
then (thĕn), *adv.* [Orig. the same word as *than.*] **1.** At that time. **2.** Soon after this; next in order of time. **3.** In that case; as, keep it, *then.* **4.** Accordingly; evidently; consequently; therefore; as, if you did go, *then* you saw all. **5.** At another time; again; — chiefly as a correlative of *now.* — *adj.* Existing, acting at, or belonging to, the time mentioned; as, the *then* king. — *n.* That time.
the′nar (thē′när), *n.* [NL., fr. Gr. *thenar.*] *Anat.* **a** The palm of the hand. **b** The prominence at the base of the thumb; — sometimes the corresponding part of the foot.
thence (thĕns), *adv.* [ME. *thenne, thanne,* and (with adverbial *-s*) *thennes, thannes,* fr. AS. *thanon, thanan, thonan.*] **1.** From that place. **2.** *Obs.* Not there; elsewhere. **3.** From that time; thenceforth. **4.** Therefore.
thence′forth′ (thĕns′fōrth′; thĕns′fōrth′; 70), *adv.* From that time forward; thereafter.
thence′for′ward (thĕns′fôr′wẽrd), *adv.* Also **thence′for′wards** (-wẽrdz). Onward from that place or, esp., time.
the′o- (thē′ō-), **the-**. [Gr. *theos.*] A combining form meaning *god,* as in **the′o·cen′tric,** having God for its center; assuming divine sovereignty; as, a *theocentric* universe.
the′o·bro′mine (-brō′mēn; -mĭn), *n.* Also **the′o·bro′min.** [*theo-* + Gr. *brōma* food.] *Chem.* A bitter crystalline compound, $C_7H_8N_4O_2$, the principal alkaloid of cacao beans and chocolate. It is closely related to caffeine.

the·oc'ra·cy (thē·ŏk'rȧ·sĭ), *n.; pl.* -CIES (-sĭz). [Gr. *theokratia,* fr. *theos* God + *kratein* to rule.] **1.** Government of a state by the immediate direction of God; thearchy; hence, government by priests or ministers as representatives of God. **2.** A state so governed. — **the'o·crat** (thē'ō·krăt), *n.* — **-crat'ic** (-krăt'ĭk), **-crat'i·cal** (-ĭ·kăl), *adj.*

the·oc'ra·sy (thē·ŏk'rȧ·sĭ), *n.* [G. *theokrasia,* fr. *theos* God + *krasis* a mixing.] **1.** A mixture of the worship of different gods, as of Jehovah and idols. **2.** *Philos.* An intimate union of the soul with God in contemplation.

the·od'i·cy (thē·ŏd'ĭ·sĭ), *n.; pl.* -CIES (-sĭz). [F. *théodicée,* fr. Gr. *theos* God + *dikē* right, justice.] A vindication of the justice of God in permitting evil to exist.

the·od'o·lite (-ŏd'ō·līt), *n.* [Origin obscure.] *Surv.* An instrument for measuring horizontal, and, usually, vertical, angles. — **the·od'o·lit'ic** (-lĭt'ĭk), *adj.*

the·og'o·ny (-ŏg'ō·nĭ), *n.; pl.* -NIES (-nĭz). [Gr. *theogonia,* fr. *theos* a god + the root of *gignesthai* to be born.] The generation or genealogy of the gods. — **the'o·gon'ic** (thē'ō·gŏn'ĭk), *adj.*

the'o·lo'gi·an (thē'ō·lō'jĭ·ăn), *n.* A person well versed in theology, esp. Christian theology; a professor of, or a writer on, theology.

the'o·log'i·cal (-lŏj'ĭ·kăl), *adj.* Also **the'o·log'ic** (-ĭk). **1.** Of or pertaining to theology. **2.** Based upon the Bible, viewed as Word of God; — used in the phrase ***the theological virtues*** (faith, hope, and charity). — **the'o·log'i·cal·ly,** *adv.*

the·ol'o·gize (thē·ŏl'ō·jīz), *v. i. & t.* To frame or fit into a theology; to give divine character to. — **the·ol'o·gi·za'tion** (-jĭ·zā'shŭn; -jī·zā'-), *n.* — **the·ol'o·giz'er** (-jīz'ẽr), *n.*

the'o·logue (thē'ō·lŏg), **the'o·log,** *n.* *Colloq.* A theological student.

the·ol'o·gy (thē·ŏl'ō·jĭ), *n.; pl.* -GIES (-jĭz). [OF. *theologie,* fr. L., fr. Gr. *theologia,* fr. *theologos* a theologian, fr. *theos* a god + *legein* to speak.] **1.** Knowledge of God and the supernatural; religious knowledge and belief, esp. when methodically formulated. **2.** The critical, historical, and psychological study of religion and religious ideas. **3.** A system of religious theory or observance; as, Calvinistic *theology.*

the·om'a·chy (thē·ŏm'ȧ·kĭ), *n.; pl.* -CHIES (-kĭz). [Gr. *theomachia* a battle of the gods, fr. *theos* a god + *machē* a battle.] Battle or strife among or against the gods.

the'o·mor'phic (thē'ō·môr'fĭk), *adj.* [Gr. *theomorphos,* fr. *theos* god + *morphē* form.] Having the divine aspect.

the·op'a·thy (thē·ŏp'ȧ·thĭ), *n.; pl.* -THIES (-thĭz). [Gr. *theos* God + *-pathy.*] Mystical experience, or the capacity for it; religious ecstasy. — **the'o·pa·thet'ic** (thē'ō·pȧ·thĕt'ĭk), **the'o·path'ic** (-păth'ĭk), *adj.*

the·oph'a·ny (thē·ŏf'ȧ·nĭ), *n.; pl.* -NIES (-nĭz). [LL. *theophania,* fr. Gr. *theophaneia,* fr. *theos* God + *phainesthai* to appear.] Visible manifestation of God or a god.

the'o·phyl'line (thē'ō·fĭl'ēn; -ĭn), *n.* Also **the'o·phyl'lin.** [NL. *thea* tea, the tea plant + Gr. *phyllon* leaf.] *Chem.* A crystalline alkaloid, $C_7H_8N_4O_2$, extracted from tea leaves and closely related to theobromine and caffeine.

the·or'bo (thē·ôr'bō), *n.* [F. *théorbe, téorbe,* fr. It. *tiorba.*] *Music.* An obsolete form of lute with two necks.

the'o·rem (thē'ō·rĕm), *n.* [F. or L.; F. *théorème,* fr. L. *theorema,* fr. Gr. *theōrēma* a sight, theory, theorem, fr. *theōrein* to look at.] **1.** That which is considered and established as a principle or law. **2.** *Math.* **a** A general statement that has been proved or whose truth has been conjectured. **b** In analysis, a rule or statement of relations as expressed in a formula or by symbols; as, the binomial *theorem.* — **the'o·re·mat'ic** (-rē·măt'ĭk), *adj.*

the'o·ret'i·cal (thē'ō·rĕt'ĭ·kăl), *adj.* Also **the'o·ret'ic** (-ĭk). **1.** Pertaining to theory; depending on, or confined to, theory or speculation; speculative; not practical or applied. **2.** Given to theorizing. — **the'o·ret'i·cal·ly,** *adv.*

the'o·re·ti'cian (thē'ō·rĕ·tĭsh'ăn), *n.* A theorist.

the'o·ret'ics (-rĕt'ĭks), *n.;* see -ICS. The speculative part of a science.

the'o·rist (thē'ō·rĭst), *n.* One who theorizes.

the'o·rize (-rīz), *v. i.* To form a theory or theories; speculate. — **the'o·ri·za'tion** (-rĭ·zā'shŭn; -rī·zā'-), *n.* — **the'o·riz'er** (-rīz'ẽr), *n.*

the'o·ry (thē'ō·rĭ), *n.; pl.* -RIES (-rĭz). [F. or L.; F. *théorie,* fr. LL. *theoria,* fr. Gr. *theōria* a beholding, spectacle, speculation, fr. *theōrein* to look at.] **1.** Contemplation; speculation. **2.** The analysis of a set of facts in their ideal relations to one another; as, essays in *theory.* **3.** The general or abstract principles of any body of facts; pure, as distinguished from applied, science or art; as, the *theory* of music or of medicine. Cf. PRACTICE, 1. **4.** A more or less plausible or scientifically acceptable general principle offered to explain phenomena. **5.** Loosely, a hypothesis; a guess. **6.** *Math.* A body of theorems presenting a clear, rounded, and systematic view of a subject; as, the *theory* of equations. — **Syn.** See HYPOTHESIS.

the·os'o·phy (thē·ŏs'ō·fĭ), *n.* Also **the·os'o·phism** (-fĭz'm). [From ML., fr. LGr. *theosophia* knowledge of things divine, fr. *theosophos* wise in the things of God, fr. *theos* God + *sophos* wise.] **1.** Alleged knowledge of God and of the world as related to God obtained by direct mystical insight or by philosophical speculation or by a combination of both. **2.** [*often cap.*] The doctrines and beliefs of a modern school or sect following, in the main, Buddhistic and Brahmanic theories, esp. in teaching a pantheistic evolution and the doctrine of reincarnation. — **the'o·soph'ic** (thē'ō·sŏf'ĭk), **the'o·soph'i·cal** (-ĭ·kăl), *adj.* — **the'o·soph'i·cal·ly,** *adv.* — **the·os'o·phist** (thē·ŏs'ō·fĭst), *n.*

ther'a·peu'tic (thĕr'ȧ·pū'tĭk), **ther'a·peu'ti·cal** (-tĭ·kăl), *adj.* [Gr. *therapeutikos,* fr. *therapeutēs* attendant, servant, *therapeuein* to serve, take care of, treat medically, *theraps* attendant, servant.] *Med.* Of or pertaining to the healing art; concerned with remedies for diseases; curative. — **ther'a·peu'ti·cal·ly,** *adv.*

ther'a·peu'tics (-tĭks), *n.;* see -ICS. Medical science which treats of the application of remedies for diseases.

ther'a·peu'tist (thĕr'ȧ·pū'tĭst), **ther'a·pist** (thĕr'ȧ·pĭst), *n.* One skilled in therapeutics.

ther'a·py (thĕr'ȧ·pĭ), *n.* [Gr. *therapeia.*] **a** *Med.* Treatment of disease; therapeutics; — chiefly in compounds, as electro*therapy.* **b** Therapeutic quality; as, a *therapy* impaired by light.

there (thâr; 4), *adv.* [AS. *thǣr, thār, thēr.*] **1.** In or at that place; — opposed to *here.* **2.** Into or to that place; thither. **3.** At that point, stage, etc. **4.** In that matter, relation, or respect.

☞ *There* is sometimes used: in exclamation, as equal to *look there;* in phrases of encouragement or approval, as in *there's* (= that's) a good boy; with some intransitive verbs, frequently *to be,* as an anticipatory subject, as in once upon a time *there* lived a king who had three sons.

there'a·bouts' (thâr'ȧ·bouts'), *adv.* Also **there'a·bout'** (-bout'). **1.** Near that place. **2.** Near that number, degree, or quantity; as, a thousand people, or *thereabouts,* heard the speech.

there·aft'er (thâr·ăf'tẽr), *adv.* **1.** After that; subsequently. **2.** According to that; accordingly.

there'a·gainst' (thâr'ȧ·gĕnst'; *cf.* AGAINST), *adv.* Against that; against it; esp., in opposition; on the contrary.

there·at' (thâr·ăt'; 2), *adv.* **1.** At that place; there. **2.** At that occurrence; on that account.

there·by' (-bī'; 2), *adv.* **1.** By that; by that means. **2.** Connected with, or with reference to, that. **3.** Thereabouts; — of place, number, etc. **4.** By it; in possession of it; — used esp. in *come thereby.*

there·for' (thâr·fôr'), *adv.* [*there* + *for.*] For that; for it.

there'fore (thâr'fōr; 70), *adv.* [ME. *therfore.* See THERE; FORE, *adv.*] For that reason; because of that; to that end; consequently; hence. ∴ is the symbol.

there·from' (thâr·frŏm'; 2), *adv.* From that or it.

there·in' (-ĭn'; 2), *adv.* **1.** In or into that place, time, or thing. **2.** In that particular or respect.

there'in·aft'er (thâr'ĭn·ăf'tẽr), *adv.* In the following part of that (writing, document, speech, and the like).

there·in'to (thâr·ĭn'to͞o; -to͞o; -ĭn·to͞o'), *adv.* Into that or it.

there·of' (thâr·ŏv'; -ŏf'; 2), *adv.* **1.** Of that or it. **2.** From that cause or particular; therefrom.

there·on' (-ŏn'; 2), *adv.* **1.** On that. **2.** Thereupon.

there·out' (-out'), *adv.* *Archaic.* Out of that; therefrom.

there·to' (thâr·to͞o'; 2), *adv.* **1.** To that. **2.** Besides.

there'to·fore' (thâr'to͞o·fōr'; 70) *adv.* Up to that time.

there·un'der (thâr·ŭn'dẽr), *adv.* **a** Under that. **b** Fewer, as in number. **c** In a lower position, rank, etc.

there'un·to' (thâr'ŭn·to͞o'; -ŭn'to͞o), *adv.* Thereto. *Shak.*

there'up·on' (thâr'ŭ·pŏn'; 2), *adv.* **1.** Thereon. **2.** Therefore. **3.** Immediately after that; at once.

there·with' (thâr·wĭth'; -wĭth'; *cf.* HEREWITH), *adv.* **1.** With that. **2.** *Obs.* At the same time. **3.** Forthwith; thereupon.

there'with·al' (thâr'wĭth·ôl'; 2), *adv.* **1.** Over and above; besides. **2.** With that; therewith.

the·ri'a·ca (thē·rī'ȧ·kȧ), *n.* Also **the'ri·ac** (thēr'ĭ·ăk). [L. *theriaca* an antidote to snake bites.] **1.** *Old Med.* An antidote to poison, compounded of many drugs and honey. **2.** Treacle; molasses. — **the·ri'a·cal** (-kăl), *adj.*

the'ri·an·throp'ic (thēr'ĭ·ăn·thrŏp'ĭk), *adj.* [Gr. *thērion* beast + *anthrōpos* man.] Combining human and animal form, as the centaur; also, pertaining to religions in which deities of such form are worshiped.

the'ri·o·mor'phic (thēr'ĭ·ō·môr'fĭk), *adj.* Also **the'ri·o·mor'phous** (-fŭs). [Gr. *thēriomorphos,* fr. *thērion* wild beast + *morphē* form.] Having an animal form; as, *theriomorphic* gods.

therm (thûrm), *n.* Also **therme.** [Gr. *thermē* heat.] **1.** *Physics.* The great calorie; also: **a** The small calorie. **b** A practical unit equal to 1,000 great calories. See CALORIE. **2.** A unit of heat, equivalent to 100,000 British thermal units, used in the measurement of gas supplied for domestic or industrial use.

therm-. = THERMO-.

ther'mae (thûr'mē), *n. pl.* [L., hot springs, warm baths, fr. Gr. *thermai,* pl. of *thermē* heat.] Warm springs or baths; specif., *Rom. Antiq.,* the baths of a public establishment for bathing; also, the establishment.

ther'mal (-măl), *adj.* Also **ther'mic** (-mĭk). [Gr. *thermē* heat.] Of or pert. to heat; warm; hot; as, *thermal* springs. — **ther'mal·ly,** *adv.*

thermal spring. *Geol.* A spring whose water issues at a temperature higher than the mean temperature of the locality where the spring is situated. If its water temperature is above 98° F., it is termed a *hot spring.*

therm'es·the'si·a, therm'aes·the'si·a (thûrm'ĕs·thē'zhĭ·ȧ; -zhȧ; -zĭ·ȧ), *n.* [NL.] Sensitiveness to heat.

‖**Ther'mi·dor'** (tĕr'mē'dôr'; *E.* thûr'mĭ·dôr'), *n.* [F., fr. Gr. *thermē* heat + *dōron* gift.] See REVOLUTIONARY CALENDAR.

therm'i·on (thûrm'ī'ŏn), *n.* [*therm-* + *ion.*] *Physics.* An electrically charged particle emitted by an incandescent substance. Thermions are either negatively charged (electrons) or positively charged (ions). — **therm'i·on'ic** (-ī·ŏn'ĭk), *adj.*

therm'i·on'ic cur'rent. An electric current due to the directed movements of thermions.

therm'i·on'ics (-ī·ŏn'ĭks), *n.;* see -ICS. Science of thermionic phenomena.

thermionic tube. *Elec.* **a** A vacuum tube (sense **b**) in which electron emission is produced by the heating of an electrode. **b** Also **thermionic valve.** = ELECTRON TUBE.

Ther'mit (thûr'mĭt; -mĭt), *n.* A trade-mark for a mixture of aluminum in fine grains with an oxide of a chemically weaker metal, usually iron. It is used in welding.

ther'mo- (thûr'mō-), **therm-.** [Gr. *thermē.*] A combining form denoting: **a** *Heat,* as in:

thermocautery	**thermogenerator**	**thermology**
thermochemical	**thermogenic**	**thermomotive**
thermochemistry	**thermogeography**	**thermotherapy**
thermodiffusion	**thermokinematic**	**thermovoltaic**

b *Thermoelectric,* as in:

thermobattery	**thermocurrent**	**thermogalvanometer**

ther'mo·an'es·the'si·a, ther'mo·an'aes·the'si·a (-ăn'ĕs·thē'zhĭ·ȧ; -zhȧ; -zĭ·ȧ), *n.* [NL.] *Med.* Loss of power to distinguish heat or cold by touch.

ther'mo·bar'o·graph (-băr'ō·grăf), *n.* *Physics.* A combined thermograph and barograph.

ther'mo·ba·rom'e·ter (-bȧ·rŏm'ē·tẽr), *n.* *Physics.* **a** A hypsometer. **b** A siphon barometer adapted to be used also as a thermometer.

ther'mo·cou'ple (thûr'mō·kŭp''l), *n.* *Elec.* A thermoelectric couple used to measure temperature differences.

ther'mo·dy·nam'ics (-dī·năm'ĭks; -dĭ-), *n.;* see -ICS. The science which treats of the mechanical action or relations of heat. — **ther'mo·dy·nam'ic** (-ĭk), **ther'mo·dy·nam'i·cal** (-ĭ·kăl), *adj.*

ther'mo·e·lec'tric (thûr'mō·ē·lĕk'trĭk), **ther'mo·e·lec'tri·cal** (-trĭ·kăl), *adj.* Of or pertaining to thermoelectricity. — **ther'mo·e·lec'tri·cal·ly,** *adv.*

thermoelectric couple *or* **pair.** *Elec.* A union of two conductors, as bars or wires of dissimilar metals joined at their extremities, for producing a thermoelectric current.
ther′mo·e·lec′tric′i·ty (thûr′mō·ē·lĕk′trĭs′ĭ·tĭ; -ĕl′ĕk-), *n.* Electricity produced by the direct action of heat, as by the unequal heating of a circuit composed of two dissimilar metals.
thermoelectric thermometer. See THERMOMETER.
ther′mo·e·lec′trom′e·ter (thûr′mō·ē·lĕk′trŏm′ē·tẽr; -ĕl′ĕk-), *n.* An instrument to measure the strength of an electric current by the heat which it produces, or to determine the heat developed by it.
ther′mo·e·lec′tro·mo′tive (-ē·lĕk′trō·mō′tĭv), *adj.* Pert. to or designating the force causing thermoelectric currents.
ther′mo·gen′e·sis (-jĕn′ē·sĭs), *n.* [NL., fr. *thermo-* + *-genesis.*] Production of heat as in the body by oxidation, etc. — **ther′mo·ge·net′ic** (-jē·nĕt′ĭk), *adj.*
ther′mo·graph (thûr′mō·grăf), *n.* A self-registering thermometer.
ther′mo·kin′e·mat′ics (-kĭn′ē·măt′ĭks; -kī′nē-), *n.*; see -ICS. The study of the motion or motive power of heat.
ther′mo·la′bile (-lā′bĭl; -b′l; 56), *adj.* [*thermo-* + *labile.*] Unstable when heated; — said esp., *Biochem.*, of substances, as enzymes, which lose their characteristic properties on being heated to or above 55° C. Cf. THERMOSTABLE.
ther·mol′y·sis (thẽr·mŏl′ĭ·sĭs), *n.* [NL., fr. *thermo-* + *-lysis.*] **1.** *Chem.* Dissociation by heat. **2.** *Physiol.* The loss of heat from the body. — **ther′mo·lyt′ic** (thûr′mō·lĭt′ĭk), *adj.*
ther·mom′e·ter (thẽr·mŏm′ē·tẽr), *n.* An instrument used for determining the temperature of a body or space. It consists essentially of some confined substance, as mercury, the volume (or other measurable physical property) of which changes with a change in temperature. A ***clinical thermometer*** is a self-registering thermometer for determining body temperature; ***electric thermometers*** are: (1) ***resistance thermometers,*** based on increase in electric resistance of metals with increase in temperature, (2) ***thermoelectric thermometers,*** essentially thermoelectric couples. Cf. CENTIGRADE THERMOMETER, FAHRENHEIT, REAUMUR, WET-BULB THERMOMETER.
☞ To reduce degrees Fahrenheit to degrees centigrade, subtract 32° and multiply by 5/9; to reduce degrees centigrade to degrees Fahrenheit, multiply by 9/5 and add 32°. — **ther′mo·met′ric** (thûr′mō·mĕt′rĭk), **ther′mo·met′ri·cal** (-rĭ·kăl), *adj.* — **ther′mo·met′ri·cal·ly,** *adv.* — **ther·mom′e·try** (thẽr·mŏm′ē·trĭ), *n.*

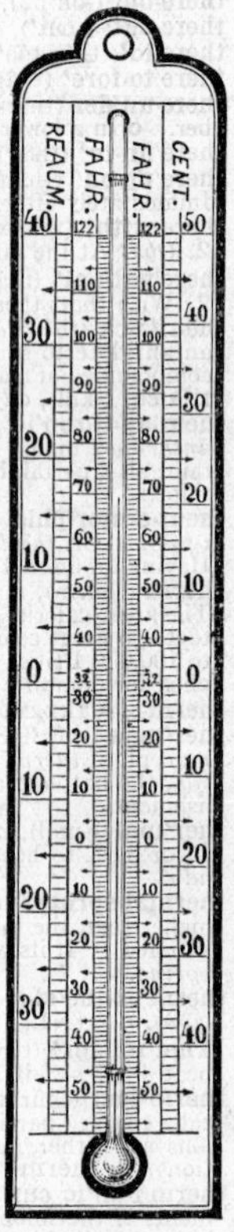

Thermometer with Centigrade, Fahrenheit, and Reaumur Scales.

ther′mo·mo′tor (thûr′mō·mō′tẽr), *n.* A heat engine.
ther′mo·nu′cle·ar (-nū′klē·ẽr), *adj.* [*thermo-* + *nuclear.*] Pert. to changes in the nucleus of atoms of low atomic weight (as hydrogen) that require a very high temperature for their inception, as in the hydrogen bomb; as, a *thermonuclear* weapon.
ther′mo·pile (thûr′mō·pīl), *n.* [*thermo-* + *pile* a heap.] *Physics.* An apparatus consisting of a number of thermoelectric couples, combined so as to multiply the effect. It is used, in a very sensitive form, for determining slight differences in temperature.
ther′mo·plas′tic (-plăs′tĭk), *adj.* [*thermo-* + *-plastic.*] Having the property of becoming plastic under application of heat, rigid at normal temperatures, and plastic on each reapplication of heat; not undergoing the thermosetting reaction; — said of natural or synthetic resins. — *n.* A thermoplastic substance.
Ther′mos bot′tle *or* **flask** (thûr′mŏs). A trademark applied to a kind of vacuum bottle.
ther′mo·scope (thûr′mō·skōp), *n.* An instrument for indicating changes of temperature without accurate measurement in degrees. — **ther′mo·scop′ic** (-skŏp′ĭk), *adj.*
ther′mo·set′ting (thûr′mō·sĕt′ĭng), *adj.* [*thermo-* + *set.*] Having the property of becoming permanently rigid by application of heat; undergoing, or designating, a chemical reaction of polymerization effected by heat, by which a substance previously plastic or fusible becomes infusible, as certain plastics. — *n.* Thermosetting act or property.
ther′mo·sta′ble (-stā′b′l), *adj.* Stable when heated; specif., *Biochem.*, capable of being heated to moderate temperatures without loss of special properties; — of enzymes, etc. Cf. THERMOLABILE. — **ther′mo·sta·bil′i·ty** (-stȧ·bĭl′ĭ·tĭ), *n.*
ther′mo·stat (thûr′mō·stăt), *n.* [*thermo-* + *-stat.*] An automatic device for regulating temperature by opening or closing the damper of a heating furnace, regulating supply of gas, or the like; also, one for actuating fire alarms, for controlling automatic sprinklers, etc. — **ther′mo·stat′ic** (-stăt′ĭk), *adj.* — **ther′mo·stat′i·cal·ly,** *adv.*
ther′mo·stat′ics (-stăt′ĭks), *n.*; see -ICS. That part of the science of heat treating of thermal equilibrium.
ther′mo·tax′is (-tăk′sĭs), *n.* [NL., fr. *thermo-* + *-taxis.*] *Biol. & Physiol.* **a** A taxis in which a temperature gradient constitutes the directive factor. **b** The regulation of body temperature. — **ther′mo·tax′ic** (-sĭk), *adj.*
ther′mo·ten′sile (-tĕn′sĭl; -sīl; 56), *adj.* Pertaining to the variation of tensile strength with the temperature.
ther·mot′ro·pism (thẽr·mŏt′rō·pĭz′m), *n.* [*thermo-* + *-tropism.*] *Biol.* A tropism in which a difference of temperature determines the movement. — **ther′mo·trop′ic** (thûr′mō·trŏp′ĭk), *adj.*
-ther′my (-thûr′mĭ). A combining form from Greek *thermē* heat, denoting *state* or *production of heat,* as in dia*thermy.*
the′roid (thē′roid), *adj.* [Gr. *thēr* wild beast + *-oid.*] Beastlike.
Ther·si′tes (thẽr·sī′tēz), *n.* [L., fr. Gr. *Thersitēs.*] The ugliest and most scurrilous of the Greeks before Troy. He reviled all, but chiefly Achilles and Odysseus.
ther·sit′i·cal (-sĭt′ĭ·kăl), *adj.* Characteristic of Thersites; loud-mouthed; scurrilous.
the·sau′rus (thē·sô′rŭs), *n.*; *pl.* -SAURI (-rī). [L. See TREASURE.] A treasury or storehouse; hence, a repository, esp. of words, as a dictionary.
these (thēz), *pron. & adj.* Plural of *this.*
The′seus (thē′sūs; -sē·ŭs), *n.* [L., fr. Gr. *Thēseus.*] *Gr. Myth.* The chief Attic hero, son of Aegeus, King of Athens. He rid Attica of Procrustes and other evildoers; slew the Minotaur, and carried off Minos's daughter Ariadne; conquered the Amazons, and married their queen, and after her death espoused Phaedra. He was one of the Argonauts, and took part in the Calydonian boar hunt.
the′sis (thē′sĭs *or, esp. in sense* 5, thĕs′ĭs), *n.*; *pl.* THESES (-sēz). [L., fr. Gr. *thesis,* fr. root of *tithenai* to place, set.] **1.** A proposition; specif., a position or proposition which a person advances and offers to maintain by argument. **2.** A theme, composition, essay, or the like; specif., a dissertation presented by a candidate for a degree or diploma. **3.** *Logic.* An affirmation to be proved, or advanced without proof; specif., a postulate. **4.** *Music.* The accented part of the measure, expressed by the downward beat; — opposite of *arsis.* **5.** *Pros.* **a** The stressed part of a foot, esp. in quantitative verse. **b** The unaccented syllable or syllables of a foot; — from misunderstanding of the Greek terms. Cf. ARSIS, *n.*
Thes′pi·an (thĕs′pĭ·ăn), *adj.* Of or pertaining to Thespis (fl. 535 B.C.), reputed founder of the Greek drama; hence [*sometimes not cap.*], relating to the drama; dramatic. — *n.* [*sometimes not cap.*] *Jocose.* An actor.
Thes′sa·lo′ni·ans (thĕs′ȧ·lō′nĭ·ănz), *n. pl., construed as sing.* Either of the two Epistles to the Thessalonians in the New Testament. See BIBLE.
the′ta (thē′tȧ; thā′tȧ), *n.* [Gr. *thēta,* of Sem. origin.] The eighth letter (Θ, θ, ϑ) of the Greek alphabet, corresponding to *th* in English, but pronounced in classic Greek about like *th* in ho*th*ouse.
thet′ic (thĕt′ĭk), *adj.* [Gr. *thetikos* fit for placing, fr. *thetos* placed, fr. root of *tithenai* to set, lay down.] **1.** Also **thet′i·cal** (-ĭ·kăl). Laid down; prescribed; arbitrary. **2.** *Gr. & Lat. Pros.* Constituting, or beginning with, the thesis; as, a *thetic* syllable. — **thet′i·cal·ly,** *adv.*
The′tis (thē′tĭs), *n.* [L., fr. Gr. *Thetis.*] *Gr. Myth.* A Nereid, mother of Achilles.
the′ur·gy (thē′ûr·jĭ), *n.*; *pl.* -GIES (-jĭz). [LL. *theurgia,* fr. Gr. *theourgia,* fr. *theourgos* doing the works of God, fr. *theos* God + *ergon* work.] **1. a** A divine work; a miracle. **b** The art or science of persuading or compelling a god or supernatural power to do, or refrain from doing, something. **2.** A form of occult art distinguished by certain Neoplatonists, in which the operator by means of self-purification and discipline, sacred rites, etc., is held capable of evoking or utilizing the aid of divine and beneficent spirits. — **the·ur′gic** (thē·ûr′jĭk), **the·ur′gi·cal** (-jĭ·kăl), *adj.* — **the·ur′gi·cal·ly,** *adv.* — **the′ur·gist** (thē′ûr·jĭst), *n.*
thew (thū), *n.* [AS. *thēaw* manner, habit.] A muscle; sinew; — usu. in the *pl.*; hence, *pl.*, muscular power; strength. — **thew′y** (thū′ĭ), *adj.*
thew′less (-lĕs; -lĭs), *adj. Scot.* Feeble; spiritless.
they (thā), *pron. pl.*; *poss.* THEIR (thâr) or THEIRS (thârz); *obj.* THEM (thĕm; 4). [ME. *thei, thai,* fr. ON. *their* they, prop. nom. pl. masc. of *sā, sū, that,* demonstrative pron.] **1.** The plural of *he, she,* or *it.* **2.** Indefinitely (like Ger. and ME. *man,* and the French *on*), people; men; as, *they* say (Ger. *man sagt,* French *on dit*).
thi-. = THIO-.
thi′a·mine (thī′ȧ·mēn; -mĭn), *n.* Also **thi′a·min.** [*thi-* + *amine.*] Vitamin B_1 (see VITAMIN).
thi′a·zine (thī′ȧ·zēn; -zĭn), *n.* Also **thi′a·zin.** [*thi-* + *az-* + *-ine.*] *Chem.* Any of a class of compounds, characterized by a ring composed of four carbon atoms, one sulfur atom, and one nitrogen atom.
thi′a·zole (-zōl), *n.* [*thi-* + *azole.*] Also **thi′a·zol** (-zōl; -zŏl). *Chem.* A colorless basic liquid, C_3H_3NS, consisting of a five-membered ring and having a pyridinelike odor; also, any of its various derivatives.
thick (thĭk), *adj.* [AS. *thicce.*] **1.** Having, or being of, relatively great depth or extent from one surface to its opposite; not thin or slender. **2.** Measuring in the third dimension (length and breadth being the other two), or from one surface to its opposite; — of a solid body; as, seven inches *thick.* **3.** Filled closely or compactly; dense; as, a *thick* forest; hence, numerous; abundant; crowded; as, where leaves are *thickest*; following in quick succession; as, *thick* snowflakes fell. **4.** Having, or being of, relatively great density or consistency; inspissated; as, *thick* sirup. **5.** Not clear; turbid; muddy; foggy. **6.** Dull; stupid; obtuse. **7.** Guttural, hoarse, husky, or the like. **8.** *Colloq.* **a** Intimate. **b** Beyond the bounds of one's patience; going too far, as in vulgarity or insolence. — **Syn.** See CLOSE. — **Ant.** Thin. — *n.* The thickest part, or the time when anything is thickest; as, in the *thick* of the fray. — *adv.* Thickly. — **thick′ish,** *adj.* — **thick′ly,** *adv.* — **thick′ness,** *n.*
thick and thin. Every conceivable or possible situation, no matter how distressing or difficult.
thick′en (thĭk′ĕn), *v. t. & i.* To make or become thick or thicker; specif.: **a** To render or become dense, in consistency, texture, etc. **b** To make or grow dull, obscure, turbid, or cloudy. **c** To make or grow complicated, intricate, intense, etc.; as, the plot *thickens.* — **thick′en·er,** *n.*
thick′en·ing, *n.* **1.** Act of making or becoming thick. **2.** Something used to thicken, as flour in a gravy. **3.** That which has thickened.
thick′et (thĭk′ĕt; -ĭt), *n.* [AS. *thiccet.*] A dense growth of shrubbery; a thick grove or coppice.
thick′head′ (thĭk′hĕd′), *n. Colloq.* A blockhead.
thick′leaf′ (-lēf′), *n.* Any of a genus (*Crassula*) of plants of the orpine family, with thick, succulent leaves.
thick′set′ (-sĕt′; 2), *adj.* **1.** Closely placed or planted; as, a *thickset* wood. **2.** Having a stout short body; stocky. — (-sĕt′), *n.* A thicket.
thick′-skinned′ (-skĭnd′; 2), *adj.* Having a thick skin; pachydermatous; hence, not sensitive; callous.
thick′-wit′ted (*see Pron.*, § 2), *adj.* Mentally slow.
thief (thēf), *n.*; *pl* THIEVES (thēvz) [AS. *thīof, thēof.*] One who steals, esp. stealthily; one who commits theft.
thieve (thēv), *v. t. & i.* [AS. *thēofian.*] To take by or practice theft; to steal.
thieve′less, *adj. Scot.* **a** Listless; also, aimless; bootless. **b** Bleak; cold; hence, forbidding.
thiev′er·y (thēv′ẽr·ĭ), *n.* Act or practice of stealing; theft.

thiev'ish (thēv'ĭsh), *adj.* **1.** Of, like, or characteristic of a thief; stealthy. **2.** Given to stealing; pilfering. — **thiev'ish·ly,** *adv.* — **thiev'ish·ness,** *n.*

thig (thĭg), *v. t. & i.* [ON. *thiggja* to take, receive.] *Chiefly Scot.* To beg; borrow.

thigh (thī), *n.* [AS. *thēoh, thēoh.*] **1.** The segment of the leg or hind limb, between the knee and the trunk. It has a single bone, the femur (**thigh'bone'**); loosely, the next lower segment in birds, and in certain quadrupeds, as the horse. **2.** *Zool.* In insects, the third segment of the leg (counting from the base).

thig'mo·tax'is (thĭg'mō·tăk'sĭs), *n.* [NL., fr. Gr. *thigma* touch + *-taxis.*] *Biol.* = STEREOTAXIS.

thig·mot'ro·pism (thĭg·mŏt'rō·pĭz'm), *n.* *Biol.* = STEREOTROPISM.

thill (thĭl), *n.* [AS. *thille* a board, plank, beam.] Either of two long pieces of wood between which a horse is hitched to a vehicle; a shaft.

thim'ble (thĭm'b'l), *n.* [AS. *thȳmel,* fr. *thūma* thumb.] **1.** A form of cap or cover, used in sewing to protect the finger when pushing the needle. **2.** A more or less thimble-shaped cup, appendage, or fixture; specif., a grooved ring of thin metal, as one to fit within a spliced loop in a rope and protect it from chafing. See CLEW, *Illust.*

thim'ble·ber'ry (-bĕr'ĭ), *n.; pl.* -RIES (-ĭz). Any of several American raspberries or blackberries having thimble-shaped fruit, esp. *Rubus occidentalis* and *R. parviflorus.*

thim'ble·ful (-fo͝ol), *n.* As much as a thimble will hold; hence, a very small quantity.

thim'ble·rig' (-rĭg'), *n.* **1.** A gambler's sleight-of-hand game played with three small cups and a small ball or pea. **2.** One who thimblerigs. — *v. t.;* -RIGGED' (-rĭgd'); -RIG'GING. To swindle by thimblerig; hence, to cheat by any trick. — **thim'ble·rig'ger** (-rĭg'ẽr), *n.*

thim'ble·weed' (-wēd'), *n.* **a** A rudbeckia. **b** Any of various American anemones, esp. *Anemone cylindrica* and *A. virginiana.*

thin (thĭn), *adj.;* THIN'NER (-ẽr); THIN'NEST. [AS. *thynne.*] **1.** Having or being of relatively little depth; not thick. **2.** Measuring little between opposite surfaces, or in diameter. **3.** Slim; slender; spare; lean; gaunt. **4.** Not dense in arrangement; not compact; sparse; scanty. **5.** Scanty or scanted in numbers or amount; as, a *thin* attendance; *thin* profits. **6.** Of little consistency, density, etc.; rare; rarefied; too fluid; as, *thin* air or sirup. **7.** Wanting substance, strength, or richness; weak; of liquors, small; as, *thin* broth. **8.** Wanting in body or volume; not full; somewhat shrill or metallic; as, a *thin* voice. **9.** Lacking in solidity, substance, or force; unsubstantial; inadequate; as, a *thin* argument. **10.** Transparent; flimsy; slight; as, a *thin* pretext. **11.** *Photog.* Lacking sufficient density or contrast; — of a negative, print, etc.

Syn. **Thin, slender, slim, slight, tenuous** mean not thick, broad, abundant, or dense. **Thin** implies comparatively little extension between the surfaces of a thing or in diameter, but it also implies, figuratively, lack of fullness, richness, and the like; **slender** implies leanness or spareness with grace and good proportion, but is often used figuratively; **slim,** slenderness that suggests fragility or scantiness; **slight,** thinness and smallness; **tenuous,** extreme thinness, esp. in diameter, or in qualities needed for compactness, firmness of texture, or the like. — **Ant.** Thick.

— *adv.* Thinly.

— *v. t. & i.;* THINNED (thĭnd); THIN'NING. To make or grow thin or thinner; specif.: **a** To draw or spread out thin; attenuate. **b** To make or grow less thick or viscid; to make or grow more fluid, tenuous, or the like. **c** To weaken. **d** To lose or cause to lose flesh. **e** To reduce numbers (in), as by removing units or surplus; as, to *thin* a forest. — **thin'ly,** *adv.* — **thin'ness** (thĭn'nĕs; -nĭs), *n.*

thine (thīn), *pron.* [AS. *thīn,* orig. same as the gen. of *thu, thū,* thou.] *Chiefly Archaic & Poetic.* The possessive case of *thou;* your. — *adj.* Thy; — now used only before a vowel or h, except when it follows its noun.

thing (thĭng), *n.* [AS., a thing, cause, assembly, judicial assembly.] **1.** An affair; matter; circumstance; — often in *pl.;* as, *things* will improve. **2.** Something done or to be done; a deed; as, to do great *things;* also, something said, thought, etc. **3.** That which is the product or the end of activity, or a step or moment in a round of activities; as, the *thing* was to get home; attend to this the first *thing.* **4.** Whatever exists, or is conceived to exist, as a separate entity; any separable or distinguishable object of thought; as, there is a name for every *thing.* **5.** More narrowly: **a** A concrete or tangible object; as, goodness is not a *thing,* but an attribute of a *thing.* **b** An inanimate object; hence, *pl.,* possessions; goods; also, clothes; apparel; as, put on your *things* and go for a walk. **c** Equipment; utensils. **6.** A detail; particular; item; as, not a *thing* escaped attention. **7.** *Colloq.* **a** A creature; a person; — often used in pity or the like. **b** Something not named because of forgetfulness, disdain, or the like; as, bring that *thing* here. **8.** *Law.* Whatever may be possessed or owned, or be the object of a right; — distinguished from *person.*

‖**thing** (thĭng), ‖**ting** (tĭng), *n.* [ON. *thing,* Dan., Nor., & Sw. *ting.*] [*often cap.*] In Scandinavian countries, a legislative or judicial assembly, held in a fixed place, the **thing'stead** (-stĕd); — used, esp. in composition, in titles of such bodies, as in Stor*ting.*

thing'a·ma·bob' (thĭng'ȧ·mȧ·bŏb'), **thing'a·ma·jig'** (-jĭg'). Vars. of THINGUMBOB, THINGUMAJIG.

thing'-in-it·self', *n.* [Trans. of G. *ding an sich.*] *Philos.* An ultimate reality, unqualified by the subjective modes of human perception and thought; a metaphysical reality.

thing'um·bob (thĭng'ŭm·bŏb), **thing'um·a·bob'** (-ȧ·bŏb'), **thing'um·a·jig'** (-ȧ·jĭg'), *n.* *Colloq.* A thing; — used instead of a specific name that one has forgotten or does not know.

think (thĭngk), *v. i.;* THOUGHT (thôt); THINK'ING. [ME. *thinken,* var. of *thinchen, thunchen,* fr. AS. *thync(e)an* (pret. *thūhte*). See THINK to reflect.] To seem or appear; — chiefly impersonal with indirect object. *Obs.* exc. in *methinks, methought.*

think, *v. t.* [ME. *thenken,* var. of *thenchen,* fr. AS. *thenc(e)an* (pret. *thōhte*), confused with the kindred ME. *thinken* (see THINK to seem).] **1.** To form in the mind; conceive; imagine; as, to *think* base thoughts. **2.** To have a judgment or opinion of; believe; esp., believe likely or possible; as, I *think* it will rain. **3.** To meditate or reflect upon; determine by reflection; as, to *think* one's way through a difficulty. **4.** To affect (in a specified way) or get rid of, by thinking. **5.** To have one's mind full of; as, to talk and *think* airplanes. — *v. i.* **1.** To exercise the powers of judgment, conception, or inference; to reflect for the purpose of reaching a conclusion; reason. **2.** To have in or call to one's mind a thought; to be or become conscious, mindful, or solicitous; — usually with *of.* **3.** To hold a (specified or implied) view or views; as, I don't *think* so. **4.** To have or form an opinion, mental picture, or notion; — now with *of.* **5.** To consider a matter; to reflect upon something; as, *think* twice before acting.

Syn. (1) **Think, conceive, imagine, fancy, realize, envisage, envision** mean to form an idea of. **Think** suggests consideration or reflection or, merely, entrance of an idea into one's mind; **conceive,** the bringing forth of an idea, plan, design, etc., and, usually, its development; **imagine,** a visualization; **fancy,** an imagining often unrestrained by facts; **realize,** a very vivid imagining; **envisage** and **envision,** a conceiving or imagining that is esp. clear or detailed.

(2) **Think, cogitate, reflect, reason, speculate, deliberate** mean to use one's powers of conception, judgment, or inference. **Think** implies mental activity as a means or as an end; **cogitate,** the process or appearance of thinking; **reflect,** a turning one's thoughts upon something that requires consideration, explanation, or the like; **reason,** consecutive logical thinking; **speculate,** reasoning about things which are theoretical; **deliberate,** slow or careful reasoning before forming an opinion, reaching a conclusion, or the like.

think better of. **a** To form a more favorable opinion of. **b** To reconsider (a thing) and alter for the better one's decision as to it. — ***think fit, good, proper,*** etc. To decide on good grounds or for good reasons.

think'a·ble (thĭngk'ȧ·b'l), *adj.* **1.** That can be thought, or conceived mentally; capable of being comprehended or reasoned about; as, persons who hold that a Supreme Being is not *thinkable.* **2.** Conceivably possible; capable of being realized; as, a *thinkable* project.

think'er (thĭngk'ẽr), *n.* One who or that which thinks.

think'ing, *adj.* That thinks; having the faculty of thought; rational; as, a *thinking* being; — often in combination; as, clear-*thinking,* hard-*thinking.* — **think'ing·ly,** *adv.*

thinking cap. Figuratively, mood of consideration or reflection.

thin'ner (thĭn'ẽr), *n.* One that thins; specif., a volatile liquid, as turpentine, used to thin paint.

thin'-skinned' (thĭn'skĭnd'; 2), *adj.* Having a thin skin; hence, sensitive; readily or unduly susceptible to criticism.

thi'o- (thī'ō-), **thi-.** [Gr. *theion* brimstone, sulfur.] *Chem. & Pharm.* A combining form denoting the *presence of sulfur;* — used specif. to indicate that the oxygen of a compound is more or less replaced by sulfur, as in **thi'o·al'de·hyde.** — **thi'o** (thī'ō), *adj.*

thi'o·a·ce'tic (-ȧ·sē'tĭk; *cf.* ACETIC), *adj.* [*thio-* + *acetic.*] *Chem.* Pertaining to or designating a colorless liquid acid, CH_3COSH, made by heating acetic acid with phosphorus pentasulfide and used as a chemical reagent; — better called **thi'ol·a·ce'tic** (thī'ŏl-; -ōl-).

thi'o·an'ti·mo·nate (-ăn'tĭ·mō·nāt), *n.* Also **thi'o·an'ti·mo'ni·ate** (-mō'nĭ·āt). *Chem.* Any of a series of compounds regarded as salts of the hypothetical **thi'o·an'ti·mon'ic ac'id** (-mŏn'ĭk), H_3SbS_4.

thi'o·an'ti·mo·nite (-ăn'tĭ·mō·nīt), *n.* *Chem.* Any of several compounds regarded as salts of the hypothetical **thi'o·an'ti·mo'ni·ous ac'ids** (-mō'nĭ·ŭs), H_3SbS_3, $HSbS_2$, $H_4Sb_2S_5$, and $H_2Sb_4S_7$.

thi'o·ar'se·nate (-är'sē·nāt), *n.* Also **thi'o·ar·se'ni·ate** (-är·sē'nĭ·āt). *Chem.* Any of a series of compounds regarded as salts of the **thi'o·ar·sen'ic ac'ids** (-är·sĕn'ĭk), H_3AsS_4, $HAsS_3$, and $H_4As_2S_7$, corresponding to the arsenic acids.

thi'o·ar'se·nite (-är'sē·nīt), *n.* *Chem.* Any of a series of compounds regarded as salts of hypothetical **thi'o·ar·se'ni·ous ac'ids** (-är·sē'nĭ·ŭs), H_3AsS_3, $HAsS_2$, $H_4As_2S_5$, $H_6As_4S_9$.

thi'o·car·bam'ide (-kär·băm'īd; -ĭd), *n.* Also **thi'o·car·bam'id.** = THIOUREA.

thi'o·cy'a·nate (-sī'ȧ·nāt), *n.* *Chem.* A salt or ester of thiocyanic acid.

thi'o·cy·an'ic (-sī·ăn'ĭk), *adj.* *Chem.* Pertaining to or designating a colorless unstable liquid acid, HSCN, of strong odor.

thi'o·cy'a·no- (thī'ō·sī'ȧ·nō-), **thiocyan-.** *Chem.* A combining form, *thio-* + *cyano-,* denoting the *presence of the univalent radical thiocyanogen,* CNS, esp. replacing hydrogen. — **thi'o·cy'a·no** (-nō), *adj.*

Thi'o·kol (thī'ō·kōl), *n.* A trade-mark for a series of synthetic rubber-like plastic materials made from halogenated organic compounds and metallic polysulfides.

thi'o·nate (thī'ō·nāt), *n.* *Chem.* A salt or ester of a thionic acid.

thi·on'ic (thī·ŏn'ĭk), *adj.* [See THIO-.] *Chem.* Pertaining to or containing sulfur.

thionic acid. *Chem.* Any of a series of unstable acids of the general formula $H_2S_xO_6$.

thi'o·nine (thī'ō·nēn; -nĭn), *n.* Also **thi'o·nin** [Gr. *theion* brimstone, denoting presence of sulfur + *-ine.*] *Chem.* A dark crystalline thiazine base, $C_{12}H_9N_3S$, artificially prepared, used esp. in microscopy as a violet dye.

thi'o·nyl (thī'ō·nĭl), *n.* *Inorg. Chem.* A bivalent radical, SO, of sulfur and oxygen.

thi'o·phene (-fēn), **thi'o·phen** (-fĕn), *n.* [*thio-* + *phenyl* + *-ene.*] *Chem.* A colorless liquid, C_4H_4S, occurring in coal tar.

thi'o·sin·am'ine (-sĭn·ăm'ĭn; -sĭn'ȧ·mēn'), *n.* Also **thi'o·sin·am'in.** [*thio-* + *sinamine* (see SINAPINE; AMINE).] *Chem.* A colorless crystalline compound, $C_3H_5NHCSNH_2$, of leeklike odor, obtained by action of ammonia on mustard oil.

thi'o·sul'fate (-sŭl'fāt), *n.* *Chem.* A salt of thiosulfuric acid; — formerly called *hyposulfite.* The sodium salt is still called, in photography, dyeing, etc., *sodium hyposulfite.*

thi'o·sul·fu'ric (-sŭl·fū'rĭk), *adj.* *Chem.* Pertaining to or designating an unstable acid, $H_2S_2O_3$, analogous to sulfuric acid, and formerly called *hyposulfurous* acid. It is known only in solution or in the form of its salts, the *thiosulfates.*

thi'o·u'ra·cil (thī'ō·ū'rȧ·sĭl), *n.* [*thio-* + *uracil,* a crystalline base, $C_4H_4N_2O_2$.] *Chem.* A white, odorless, bitter crystalline compound, $C_4H_4N_2OS$, that depresses the function of the thyroid gland.

thi'o·u·re'a (thī'ō·ū·rē'ȧ; -ū'rē·ȧ), *n.* [NL., fr. *thio-* + *urea.*] *Chem.* A colorless crystalline bitter compound, $CS(NH_2)_2$, analogous to and resembling urea, used esp. as a photographic fixative, and to remove stains from negatives.

thir (thĭr; thûr), *pron.* *Scot., N. of Eng., & Ir.* These.

third (thûrd), *adj.* [AS. *thridda,* fr. *thrī, thrēo,* three.] See NUMBER, *Table.* — *n.* **1.** See NUMBER, *Table.* **2.** A person or thing that is third, as in rank, numbering, place, grade, etc. **3.** The sixtieth part of a second of time or an arc. **4.** *pl. Law.* The third part of the personal estate of a deceased husband which goes under certain conditions absolutely to the widow upon the husband's dying intestate; loosely, a widow's dower. **5.** *Music.* **a** An interval of three diatonic degrees. **b** A tone at this interval. **c** The harmonic combination of two tones a third apart. **d** The third tone of the scale. — **third'ly,** *adv.*

third class. **1. a** The third group in a classification, specif., *Brit.*, of those passing an examination. **b** A place in or a member of such a group. **2.** The lowest class of accommodations in a passenger vessel having three classes; — now often called *tourist class* and formerly called *steerage.* — **third′-class′** (*see Pron.*, § 2), *adj. & adv.*

third degree. **1.** *Colloq., U. S.* Severe examination or treatment of a prisoner by the police to extort an admission. **2.** *Freemasonry.* The degree of master mason.

third estate. [often *caps.* when used specif.] The third of the political classes or orders in a kingdom, usually the commons, or common people. Cf. ESTATE, *n.*, 3.

third eyelid. = NICTITATING MEMBRANE.

third rail. A metal rail through which the electric current is led to the motors of an electric locomotive. — **third′-rail′**, *adj.*

third′-rate′ (*see Pron.*, § 2), *adj.* Belonging or pertaining to a third grade, quality, or the like; hence, very poor or inferior.

thirl (thûrl), *v. t.* [AS. *thyrlian, thyrelian*, fr. *thyrel* perforated, as n., a hole, fr. *thurh* through.] *Now Dial.* **a** To pierce; drill. **b** To thrill; cause to vibrate.

thirl′age (thûr′lĭj), *n.* Also **thirl.** A feudal servitude or obligation requiring tenants to use a certain mill for grinding their grain; also, the dues for such grinding.

thirst (thûrst), *n.* [AS. *thurst.*] **1.** A sensation of dryness in the mouth and throat with a craving for liquids; the condition producing this sensation; also, a strong desire for drink. **2.** Ardent desire; a craving or longing; as, a *thirst* for knowledge. — *v. i.* **1.** To feel thirsty; crave drink. **2.** To have a vehement desire; long. — **Syn.** See LONG. — **thirst′er**, *n.*

thirst′y (thûrs′tĭ), *adj.*; THIRST′I·ER (-tĭ·ẽr); THIRST′I·EST. **1.** Feeling thirst; hence, having an eager desire; avid. **2.** Deficient in moisture; dry; parched; arid; as, the *thirsty* earth. **3.** *Colloq.* Thirst-provoking. — **thirst′i·ly**, *adv.* — **thirst′i·ness**, *n.*

thir′teen′ (thûr′tēn′; 2), *n. & adj.* [AS. *thrēotēne, thrēotȳne.*] See NUMBER, *Table.* — **thir′teenth′** (-tēnth′; 2), *n. & adj.*

thir′ty (thûr′tĭ), *n. & adj.* [AS. *thrītig, thrittig.*] See NUMBER, *Table.* — **thir′ti·eth** (-tĭ·ĕth; -ĭth), *n. & adj.*

thir′ty·fold′ (-fōld′; 2), *adj. & adv.* See -FOLD.

thir′ty-sec′ond note. *Music.* See NOTE, *n.*, 11 **a.**

thirty-second rest. *Music.* See 2d REST, 9, *Illust.*

thir′ty-two′mo′ (thûr′tĭ·tōō′mō′), *adj.* [See -MO.] Having 32 leaves to a sheet; as, a *thirty-twomo*, or 32mo, book. — *n.* A size of a book, or of its pages, made of such sheets, measuring about 3½ × 5½ inches; also, a book of such size.

this (thĭs), *pron.*; *pl.* THESE (thēz). [AS. *thēs, thes*, masc., *thēos, thīos*, fem., *this*, neut.] A demonstrative word, referring particularly to what is present or near in place, time, or thought, or to something just mentioned or to be mentioned; the person, thing, or idea present, near in place, time, or thought, or just mentioned or being mentioned; specif., as opposed to or correlative of *that*, the latter. — *adj.* **1.** That is present, near, or just referred to. **2.** These; — taken collectively or as a whole. **3.** The nearer; — as opposed to *that.*

This′be (thĭz′bē), *n.* See PYRAMUS AND THISBE.

this′tle (thĭs′'l), *n.* [AS. *thistel.*] **1.** A prickly plant of any of various genera of the aster family (Carduaceae), as the Eurasian ***musk thistle*** (*Carduus nutans*), the European ***bull thistle*** and ***Canada thistle*** (*Cirsium lanceolatum* and *C. arvense*) naturalized in America as weeds, the ***blessed thistle*** (*Cnicus benedictus*), and the Eurasian ***cotton thistle*** (*Onopordon acanthium*). The flower of any of several European thistles (as the bull, cotton, and musk thistles) is the heraldic and national emblem of Scotland. **2.** Any of numerous other prickly plants, as the sow thistle (which see).

this′tle·down′ (-doun′), *n.* The down, or pappus, from the ripe flower head of a thistle.

thith′er (thĭth′ẽr; thĭth′ẽr), *adv.* [AS. *thider, thæder*, fr. stem of E. *that.*] **1.** To that place; — opposed to *hither.* **2.** *Rare.* To that point, end, or result. — *adj.* Being on the other and farther side; more remote.

thith′er·to′ (-tōō′; thĭth′ẽr·tōō′; thĭth′-), *adv.* Until that time.

thith′er·ward (thĭth′ẽr·wẽrd; thĭth′-), **thith′er·wards** (-wẽrdz), *adv.* Toward that place; in that direction.

tho (thō). Var. of THOUGH.

thole (thōl), *n.* Also **thole′pin′** (-pĭn′). [AS. *thol, tholl.*] A wooden or metal pin, set in the gunwale of a boat, to serve as a fixed rest against which the oar presses in rowing.

thole, *v. t. & i.* [AS. *tholian.*] *Archaic.* To endure; suffer; bear.

Thom′as (tŏm′ăs), *n.* *Bib.* One of the twelve apostles who, according to John xx. 24–29, doubted until he had proof of Christ's resurrection.

Tho′mism (tō′mĭz'm; thō′-), *n.* The philosophical and theological system of Thomas Aquinas, which though original in many ways, is a comprehensive summary of thirteenth-century thought (see SCHOLASTICISM, 1); specif., Thomas Aquinas's theory of the relation between grace and free will. — **Tho′mist** (-mĭst), *n. & adj.* — **Tho·mis′tic** (tō·mĭs′tĭk; thō-), *adj.*

Thomp′son (tŏmp′s'n; tŏm′-) *and* **Tom′my** (tŏm′ĭ), *n.* [After the coinventor, General John T. *Thompson* (1860–1940), U. S. Army officer.] Trademarks applied to a light portable weapon firing on the automatic principle and fed from a magazine or drum, which is provided with a pistol grip and a buttstock for firing from the shoulder or from the hip. See RIFLE, *Illust.*

thong (thŏng; 74), *n.* [AS. *thwang, thwong.*] A strap or strip of leather, esp. one used for fastening something.

Thor (thôr), *n.* [ON *Thōrr.* See THURSDAY.] *Norse Myth.* The god of thunder, as conceived in his character of a god of strength, as a helper in war, as a defender, etc., and in his person as a red-haired youth armed with a magic hammer that always returns to him after being cast.

tho·rac′ic (thō·răs′ĭk), *adj.* Of, pertaining to, or located within or near the thorax.

thoracic duct. *Anat.* The main trunk of the system of lymphatic vessels, lying along the front of the spinal column, and opening into the left subclavian vein.

tho·rac′i·co- (thō·răs′ĭ·kō-). A combining form denoting *thoracic and*, as in **tho·rac′i·co·lum′bar**, of or pertaining to the thoracic and lumbar regions.

tho′ra·co- (thō′rȧ·kō-; thō·rā′kō-), **thorac-.** [Gr. *thōrax, thōrakos*, chest.] A combining form, used to denote: **a** *The thorax* or *chest*, as in **tho′ra·cec′to·my, tho′ra·co·plas′ty** (see -ECTOMY, -PLASTY). **b** *Thoracic and*, as in **tho′ra·co·lum′bar.**

tho′rax (thō′răks; 70), *n.*; *pl.* THORAXES (-răk·sĕz; -sĭz), THORACES (thō′rȧ·sēz; thō·rā′sēz). [L., fr. Gr. *thōrax.*] **1.** *Anat. & Zool.* The part of the body of man and other mammals between the neck and the abdomen, in which the heart, lungs, esophagus, etc., are situated. **2.** In insects, the middle of the three chief divisions of the body. See INSECT, *Illust.*

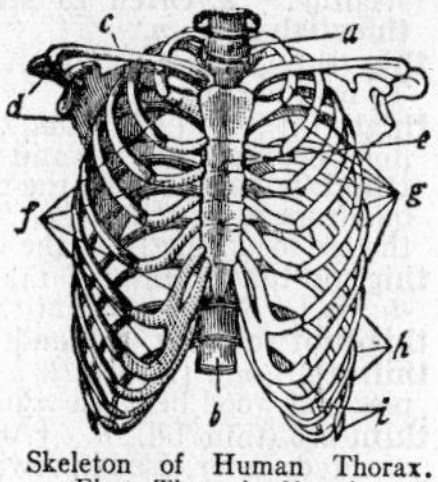

Skeleton of Human Thorax. *a* First Thoracic Vertebra; *b* Twelfth Thoracic Vertebra; *c* Clavicle; *d* Scapula; *e* Sternum, or Breastbone; *f* Costal Cartilages; *g* Sternal Ribs; *h*, *i* False Ribs; *i* Floating Ribs.

tho′ri·a (thō′rĭ·ȧ), *n.* [NL. See THORITE.] *Chem.* The oxide of thorium, thorium dioxide, ThO_2, a white earthy substance. See THORIUM.

tho′ri·a·nite (-nīt), *n.* [From THORIUM.] A mineral, in black cubic crystals, largely thorium oxide with the oxides of the cerium metals, uranium, etc. It is remarkable for its radioactivity.

tho′rite (thō′rīt), *n.* [*Thor* + *-ite.*] **1.** *Mineral.* A rare mineral usually of a brown to black color, essentially of thorium silicate, $ThSiO_4$. **2.** A high explosive used as a bursting charge for shell.

tho′ri·um (thō′rĭ·ŭm), *n.* [NL. See THORITE.] *Chem.* A radioactive element occurring in thorite, and certain other minerals, and isolated as a heavy, gray, difficultly fusible metal. Symbol, *Th*; at. no., 90; at. wt., 232.12. The oxide, ThO_2, is prepared from monazite on a large scale and used in gas mantles. See WELSBACH. — **thor′ic** (thŏr′ĭk; thō′rĭk), *adj.*

thorn (thôrn), *n.* [AS.] **1.** A sharp process or excrescence, as on a plant or an animal; specif., *Bot.*, a short, sharp-pointed, leafless branch, as of the hawthorn. Cf. SPINE, PRICKLE. **2.** That which pricks or hurts, as a thorn; a cause of distress, irritation, or anxiety. **3.** Any thorn-bearing shrub or small tree; specif., any of a genus (*Crataegus*) of plants of the apple family, esp. the hawthorn or blackthorn; also, the wood of any of these. **4.** Also **thorn letter.** The Anglo-Saxon letter þ (cap. Þ), used for either of the sounds of English *th*, as in *thin, then*; — so called because it was the initial letter of *thorn* (sense 1). See EDH. — **thorn′less**, *adj.*

thorn apple. **a** A haw; the fruit of the hawthorn. **b** The Jimson weed or any other plant of the same genus (*Datura*).

thorn′back′ (thôrn′băk′), *n.* **1.** A European ray (*Raja clavata*) having spines on its back. Cf. DEVILFISH, *Illust.* **2.** A large European spider crab (*Maia squinado*). See CRAB.

thorn′y (thôr′nĭ), *adj.*; THORN′I·ER (-nĭ·ẽr); THORN′I·EST. **1.** Full of thorns; spiny or brambly. **2. a** Beset with trials, vexations, obstacles, etc. **b** Beset with perplexities, points of controversy, etc.; as, the *thorny* question of states' rights. — **thorn′i·ness**, *n.*

tho′ron (thō′rŏn), *n.* [NL., fr. *thorium* + *-on* as in *neon.*] *Chem.* A gaseous radioactive element formed from thorium and isotopic with radon. Symbol, *Tn* or *Th-Em*; at. no., 86; at. wt., 220.

thor′ough (thûr′ō; 117), *prep. & adv.* [ME. *thoru, thuruh, thoruh.* See THROUGH.] *Archaic.* Through. — *adj.* **1.** *Now Rare.* Passing through. **2.** Carried through to completion or attainment; thoroughgoing. **3.** That is completely (such); through and through; as, a *thorough* gentleman. **4.** Painstakingly exact or careful about details. — *n.* [*cap.*] *Eng. Hist.* In the reign of Charles I, the tyrannical policy of Wentworth (Strafford) and Laud; — from their determination to carry their schemes "thorough" (i. e., through) every obstacle. — **thor′ough·ly**, *adv.* — **thor′ough·ness**, *n.*

thorough bass (bās). *Music.* **a** The representation of chords by figures under the bass; figured bass. **b** The system of figures so used.

thorough brace. A leather strap supporting the body of a carriage and attached to springs, or serving as a spring.

thor′ough·bred′ (thûr′ō·brĕd′), *adj.* **1.** *Now Rare.* Thoroughly trained or skilled. **2. a** [*sometimes cap.*] Being of the breed of horses called Thoroughbreds. **b** Bred from the best blood, through a long line; pure-blooded; — of horses, dogs, etc. **c** Having the characteristics of a Thoroughbred, as grace, elegance, high-spiritedness. — *n.* **1.** One that is thoroughbred. **2.** [*cap.*] A horse of a breed that originated in England, probably from crosses between the native mares and Arab or Turk stallions, and is kept for racing.

thor′ough·fare′ (-fâr′), *n.* **1.** A place or way for passing or travel; specif., a passage through; a public road or street open at both ends; esp., a street or way through which there is much passing. **2.** Passage; transit.

thor′ough·go′ing (-gō′ĭng; 2), *adj.* Characterized by great thoroughness; extremely thorough.

thor′ough·paced′ (-pāst′), *adj.* Thoroughly trained in all paces, as a horse; hence, thoroughgoing; out-and-out; as, a *thoroughpaced* impostor.

thor′ough·pin′ (-pĭn′), *n.* *Veter.* A synovial dilatation just above the hock of the horse on both sides of the leg and slightly anterior to the hamstring tendon.

thor′ough·wort′ (-wûrt′), *n.* = BONESET.

thorp, thorpe (thôrp), *n.* [AS. *thorp, throp.*] A group of houses in the country; hamlet; — chiefly in place names.

those (thōz), *pron. & adj.* [AS. *thās*, nom. and acc. pl. of *thēs* this.] Plural of *that.*

Thoth (thōth; tōt), *n.* [L., fr. Gr. *Thōth, Thōyth*, fr. Egypt. *Teḥuti.*] *Egypt. Relig.* The scribe of the gods, measurer of time, and inventor of numbers; hence, the god of wisdom and magic.

thou (thou), *pron.*; *singular: nom.* THOU; *poss.* THY (thī) OR THINE (thīn); *obj.* THEE (thē); *plural: nom.* YOU (yōō), YE (yē); *poss.* YOUR (yōōr) OR YOURS (yōōrz); *obj.* YOU, YE. [AS. *thū, thu.*] The personal pronoun of the 2d person singular, in the nominative case; — formerly often used with special implication of familiarity but now replaced by *you.* It is still found in solemn or poetical style, in dial. Eng., and in the language of Friends, or Quakers, who, however, instead of *thou*, usually say *thee* with a verb in the 3d person singular; as, "*Thee* tells no lies here." — *v. t.* To address as *thou*, as formerly in familiarity.

though (thō), *conj.* [ME. *thogh, thoh*, fr. Scand.] **1.** Granting or supposing that; notwithstanding that; although. **2.** In case that; if; *Obs.*, exc. in phrase *as though.* **3.** Even if, as a matter to be conceded; however; — introducing a concessive clause qualifying a main clause; as, we may escape, *though* I think not. — *adv. Colloq.* However; nevertheless; as, it was a good shot, *though.*

thought (thôt), *n.* [AS. *thōht, gethōht.*] **1.** Act or process of thinking; reflection; cogitation. **2.** Reasoning power; capacity to think and judge. **3.** The power to conceive or realize; conception; imagination; as, a beauty beyond *thought.* **4.** That which is thought; specif.: **a** That which is in one's mind; — often in *pl.;* as, to read one's *thoughts.* **b** A product of thinking; an idea, judgment, opinion, notion, fancy, or the like; as, second *thoughts* are best. **c** The views, principles, or systems, of a specified age, race, or school of thinkers; as, in modern *thought.* **5.** Solicitous attention; serious consideration; heed; as, give it no *thought.* **6.** Mental preoccupation; engrossment of mind; as, lost in *thought.* **7.** A little; a trifle; as, be a *thought* more courteous. — **Syn.** See IDEA.

thought (thôt), *past & past part.* of THINK.

thought'ful (-fo͝ol; -f'l), *adj.* **1.** Characterized by or manifesting depth or richness of thought; full of thought. **2.** Having thoughts (of); heedful; now esp., mindful of others; attentive to another's comfort; considerate. — **thought'ful·ly,** *adv.* — **thought'ful·ness,** *n.*

Syn. **Thoughtful, considerate, attentive** mean mindful of others. **Thoughtful** implies unselfish concern for others; **considerate,** concern for the feelings of others; **attentive,** repeated acts of kindness or courtesy.

thought'less (-lĕs; -lĭs), *adj.* **1.** Heedless; rash; reckless. **2.** Destitute of thought. **3.** Not thoughtful; inconsiderate. — **thought'less·ly,** *adv.* — **thought'less·ness,** *n.*

thou'sand (thou'zănd; -z'nd), *n. & adj.* [AS. *thūsend.*] See NUMBER, *Table.* — **thou'sandth** (-zăndth), *n. & adj.*

thou'sand·fold' (-fōld'; 2), *adj. & adv.* See -FOLD.

thow'less (thou'lĕs; -lĭs), *adj. Scot.* = THEWLESS.

Thra'cian (thrā'shăn), *adj.* Of or pertaining to Thrace. — *n.* A native or inhabitant of Thrace; also, the language of the ancient Thracians, an Indo-European language related to the Illyrian, supposed to be the parent of the Albanian. See INDO-EUROPEAN LANGUAGES, *Table.*

Thra'co-Il·lyr'i·an (thrā'kō-ĭ·lĭr'ĭ·ăn), *adj.* Designating or pertaining to a subfamily of Indo-European languages comprising the ancient Thracian and Illyrian and the modern Albanian. Little is known of the ancient tongues. See INDO-EUROPEAN LANGUAGES, *Table.* — **Thra'co-Il·lyr'i·an,** *n.*

Thra'co-Phryg'i·an (-frĭj'ĭ·ăn), *adj.* Of or pertaining to both Thrace and Phrygia; also, designating or pertaining to a subfamily of Indo-European languages including Phrygian and Armenian. See INDO-EUROPEAN LANGUAGES, *Table.* — **Thra'co-Phryg'i·an,** *n.*

thrall (thrôl), *n.* [AS. *thræl,* fr. ON. *thræll.*] *Archaic.* **a** A slave; bondman. **b** One in moral or mental bondage. **c** Thralldom. — *v. t.* To enslave; enthrall.

thrall'dom, thral'dom (thrôl'dŭm), *n.* State of servitude; slavery.

thrash (thrăsh), *v. t. & i.* [Dial. var. of THRESH.] Cf. THRESH. **1.** To thresh (wheat, etc.). **2.** To thresh, or go over again and again. **3.** To swing, beat, or strike in the manner of a rapidly moving flail; as, to *thrash* one's arms; also, to toss about; move violently; as, he *thrashed* about in bed with a high fever. **4.** To beat; flog. — **Syn.** See SWING. — *n.* A thrashing; specif., in swimming, a method of moving the legs employed in the crawl and the backstroke.

thrash'er (-ẽr), *n.* **1.** One who thrashes. **2.** Also **thrasher shark.** = THRESHER, 2.

thrash'er, *n.* [E. dial. *thresher.*] Any of numerous long-tailed thrushlike singing birds of the American family Mimidae, esp. those of the genus *Toxostoma.* The familiar eastern species is the ***brown thrasher*** (*T. rufum*).

thrash'ing, *n.* A whipping; beating.

thra·son'i·cal (thrā·sŏn'ĭ·kăl), *adj.* [From *Thraso,* a braggart soldier in Terence's *Eunuch.*] Bragging; boastful.

thrave (thrāv), *n.* [ME. *thrave, threve,* of Scand. origin.] *Dial.* **a** A measure containing twenty-four sheaves. **b** A bundle; a number; also, a crowd; throng.

thraw (thrô; thrä), *n. Scot.* **a** Throe. **b** A twist or wrench.

thraw. Scot. & dial. var. of THROW.

thrawn (thrôn; thrän), *adj.* [Dial. form of *thrown.*] *Scot.* Crooked; misshapen; perverse; unpleasant.

thread (thrĕd), *n.* [AS. *thrǣd.*] **1.** A very thin continuous filament, esp. one made by spinning the fibers of cotton, flax, silk, etc., and by combining the strands so produced. **2.** Something woven from thread; a garment; as, not a *thread* fit to wear. **3.** Any threadlike filament, as of metal or living tissue; a fiber, hair, etc.; hence: **a** A fine thin stream, ray, etc. **b** A thin seam or vein, as of coal. **4.** Something suggestive of a thread, as in length, tenuity, or use in sewing and weaving; as, a *thread* of humor; to lose the *thread* of one's story; his life hangs by a *thread.* **5.** = SCREW THREAD. **6.** In full, **thread of life.** The course of one's life, esp. as fabled in ancient times to be spun and cut by the Fates.

— *adj.* Of, made of, or like thread.

— *v. t.* **1.** To pass a thread through the eye of (a needle). **2.** To pass through in the manner of a thread; to make (one's way), esp. carefully, through or between obstacles. **3.** To connect by or as by passing a thread through; string together. **4.** *Elec.* To cause lines of force, or magnetic flux, to form around (an electric conductor). **5.** *Mach.* To form a thread or threads on or in. — *v. i.* **1.** To wind one's (or its) way. **2.** *Cookery.* To spin a fine hair or thread when dropped from a fork; — of boiling sirup tested at a certain point. — **thread'er** (-ẽr), *n.* — **thread'like'** (-līk'), *adj.*

thread'bare' (-bâr'), *adj.* Having the nap or pile worn off; shabby; hence, trite; hackneyed. — **Syn.** See TRITE.

thread'fin' (-fĭn'), *n.* Any fish of a family (Polynemidae) allied to the mullets, having the lower part of the pectoral fin divided into threadlike rays.

thread mark. In paper currency, a thin thread incorporated in the paper as a protection against counterfeiting.

thread'worm' (thrĕd'wûrm'), *n.* Any long slender nematode, esp. the pinworm, or a species of *Filaria* or an allied genus.

thread'y (thrĕd'ĭ), *adj.;* THREAD'I·ER (-ĭ·ẽr); THREAD'I·EST. Like a thread; slender; filamentous; very thin or slight, as in tone; also, containing, consisting of, or covered with thread; as, *thready* roots.

threap (thrēp), *v. t.* [AS. *thrēapian* to rebuke.] *Scot. & Dial.* **1.** To scold; chide. **2.** To maintain persistently.

threat (thrĕt), *n.* [AS. *thrēat* crowd, oppression.] The expression of an intention to inflict evil or injury on another; menace; threatening; denunciation. — *v. t. & i. Archaic & Dial.* To threaten.

threat'en (thrĕt''n), *v. t.* [AS. *thrēatnian.*] **1.** To utter threats against; promise punishment, reprisal, or the like, to. **2.** To give forewarning of, as by a threat, sign, etc.; hence, to hang over as a threat; as, famine *threatens* the city. — *v. i.* **1.** To utter threats. **2.** To have a menacing appearance; portend evil. — **threat'en·ing·ly,** *adv.*

Syn. **Threaten, menace** mean to forecast danger. **Threaten** implies warning in words, looks, or signs; **menace,** an alarming by hostile character or aspect.

three (thrē), *n. & adj.* [AS. *thrī, thrīe,* masc., *thrēo,* fem. and neut.] See NUMBER, *Table.*

three'-base' hit. Also **three'-bag'ger,** *n. Baseball.* A hit enabling the batter to reach third base without the aid of an error.

three'-col'or, *adj.* Designating or pertaining to a photomechanical process (**three-color photography** *or* **process**) wherein three primary colors are used to reproduce the color of the subject photographed.

three'-deck'er (-dĕk'ẽr; 2), *n.* **1.** *Naut.* A vessel with three decks; esp., a war vessel carrying guns on three decks. **2.** Any structure having three floors, stories, or tiers.

three'-di·men'sion·al, *adj.* Giving the illusion of depth or varying distances; — said of pictures, esp. photographs or stereoscopic motion pictures. Called also *3-D.*

three'fold' (-fōld'), *adj.* Consisting of three; thrice repeated; triple. — (-fōld'; 2), *adv.* Thrice; triply.

three'-mile', *adj.* Of or pertaining to three miles; as, the **three-mile limit,** the limit of the marine belt (the **three-mile belt** *or* **zone**) included in territorial waters of a state.

three'pence (thrĕp'ĕns; thrĭp'ĕns; thrŭp'-; thro͝op'-), *n.* The sum of three pence (about 6 cents U. S.); also, a silver coin of this value. See MONEY, *Tables.*

three'pen·ny (thrĕp'ĕn·ĭ; *see* THREEPENCE), *adj.* Costing or worth threepence; hence, worth but little; poor; mean.

three'-phase' (thrē'fāz'), *adj. Elec.* Pertaining to a combination of three circuits energized by alternating electromotive forces that differ in phase by 120 degrees.

three'-piece' (-pēs'; 2), *adj.* Designating a costume made of three separate parts, as coat, skirt, and blouse.

three'-ply' (-plī'; 2), *adj.* Consisting of three distinct parts or thicknesses, as of three webs interwoven, or of three veneers.

three'-point' land'ing. *Aviation.* A special mode of landing an airplane in which the two wheels of the landing gear and the tail skid touch the ground simultaneously.

three'-quar'ter, *n., or, in full,* **three-quarter back.** In Rugby football, one of the backs whose regular position is between the fullback and the halfbacks.

three'-quar'ter bind'ing. A bookbinding in which the material of the back extends upon the boards for one third of their width.

three R's, the. A jocose expression for reading, 'riting, and 'rithmetic, taken as the fundamentals of education.

three'score' (thrē'skōr'; 2; 70), *adj.* Thrice twenty; sixty.

three'some (thrē'sŭm), *adj.* [*three* + 1st *-some.*] Performed or engaged in by three persons. — *n.* A threesome game, dance, etc.; specif., *Golf,* a threesome match in which one plays his ball against the ball of the other two, the latter playing each stroke alternately.

three'-square' (-skwâr'; 2), *adj.* Having an equilateral triangular cross section; — said esp. of a kind of file.

threm'ma·tol'o·gy (thrĕm'ȧ·tŏl'ō·jĭ), *n.* [Gr. *thremma, -atos,* nursling + *-logy.*] *Biol.* The science of breeding animals and plants under domestication.

thre'node (thrē'nōd; thrĕn'ōd), *n.* [See THRENODY.] A threnody. — **thre·no'di·al** (thrē·nō'dĭ·ăl), **thre·nod'ic** (-nŏd'ĭk), *adj.* — **thren'o·dist** (thrĕn'ō·dĭst), *n.*

thren'o·dy (thrĕn'ō·dĭ), *n.; pl.* -DIES (-dĭz). [Gr. *thrēnoidia,* fr. *thrēnos* a dirge + *ōidē* a song.] A song of lamentation; a dirge or funeral song.

thre'o·nine (thrē'ō·nēn; -nĭn), *n.* Also **thre'o·nin.** [Irreg. fr. *threose* an artificial sugar + 2d -INE.] *Biochem.* A colorless crystalline amino acid, $C_4H_9NO_3$, believed essential to normal nutrition.

thresh (thrĕsh), *v. t.* [ME. *threschen,* fr. AS. *threscan, therscan.*] Cf. THRASH. **1.** To beat out grain from (wheat stalks, etc.) by treading, striking with a flail, etc. **2.** To go over again and again, as in discussion or argument; — with *over* or *out.* **3.** *Now Rare.* To thrash, or flog. — *v. i.* **1.** To thresh grain. **2.** To thrash or toss about. — *n.* A threshing.

thresh'er (-ẽr), *n.* **1.** One who or that which threshes. **2.** Also **thresher shark.** A large shark (*Alopias vulpinus*) of the American and European coasts, said to thresh or thrash the water with its great tail to round up the fish on which it feeds.

thresh'old (thrĕsh'ōld; -hōld), *n.* [AS. *therscwold, therscold;* akin to AS. *threscan* to thresh, orig., to tread.] **1.** The plank, stone, or piece of timber which lies under a door; the sill of a door; entrance. **2.** The entering or beginning point; outset. **3.** *Physiol. & Psychol.* The point at which a physiological or psychological effect begins to be produced, as that degree of stimulation of a nerve or nerve center which just produces a response; limen; as, the *threshold* of consciousness.

threw (thro͞o; 114), *past* of THROW.

thrice (thrīs), *adv.* [ME. *thries,* fr. *thrie* thrice (fr. AS. *thriga, thriwa*) + *-s,* adv. suff.] **1.** Three times. **2.** In a threefold manner or degree; hence, loosely, repeatedly; fully, as in **thrice'-blessed'.**

thrift (thrĭft), *n.* [ON. *thrift, thrif.*] **1.** *Obs.* A thriving condition; prosperity. **2.** Economical management; frugality. **3.** *Now Scot.* Work. **4.** Vigorous growth, as of a plant. **5.** Any of a genus (*Statice,* family Plumbaginaceae) of tufted acaulescent herbs; esp. one, a scapose herb (*S. armeria*) with pink or white flower heads. — **thrift'less,** *adj.*

thrift'y (thrĭf'tĭ), *adj.;* THRIFT'I·ER (-tĭ·ẽr); THRIFT'I·EST. **1.** Given to, or evincing, thrift; provident. **2.** Thriving by industry and frugality; prosperous. **3.** Growing vigorously; as, a *thrifty* plant. — **Syn.** See SPARING. — **thrift'i·ly** (-tĭ·lĭ), *adv.* — **thrift'i·ness,** *n.*

thrill (thrĭl), *v. t. & i.* [ME. *thrillen* to pierce, the same word as *thirlen* to pierce. See THIRL.] **1.** To affect or become affected emotionally as if by something that pierces; to shiver, throb, or tingle, or cause to become thus excited. **2.** To vibrate; tremble or make tremble. — *n.* **1.** A sensation as of being thrilled; a tremulous excitement. **2.** A vibration or tremor; esp., an abnormal fine tremor in the respiratory or circulatory systems. — **thrill'er,** *n.* — **thrill'ing·ly,** *adv.*

thrips (thrĭps), *n.* [L., a woodworm, fr. Gr. *thrips.*] Any of an order (Thysanoptera) of sucking insects of small, often minute, size, most species of which feed on plant juices, as of the onion or tobacco.

thrive (thrīv), *v. i.;* THROVE (thrōv) or THRIVED (thrīvd); THRIVED or THRIV'EN (thrĭv'ĕn); THRIV'ING (thrīv'ĭng). [ON. *thrīfast,* orig., to grasp for oneself, refl. of *thrīfa* to grasp.] **1.** To prosper by thrift. **2.** To prosper by any means; gain one's end. **3.** To grow vigorously or luxuriantly; flourish. — **thriv′er** (thrīv′ẽr), *n.* — **thriv′ing·ly**, *adv.*

thro′ (thrōō). Short for THROUGH.

throat (thrōt), *n.* [AS. *throte, throtu.*] **1.** The part of the neck in front of the spinal column; hence, the passage through it, containing the pharynx and upper part of the esophagus, the larynx, and the trachea; gullet. **2.** Something likened to the throat, as being a passageway, a constriction, or a narrowed place. — *v. t.* To mutter in one's throat; also, to sing or chant in a throaty voice.

throat′latch′ (-lăch′), *n.* A strap of a bridle or halter, passing under a horse's throat.

throat′y (thrōt′ĭ), *adj.;* THROAT′I·ER (-ĭ·ẽr); THROAT′I·EST. Uttered with a sound coming from the throat; guttural. — **throat′i·ly** (-ĭ·lĭ), *adv.* — **throat′i·ness** (-ĭ·nĕs; -nĭs), *n.*

throb (thrŏb), *v. i.;* THROBBED (thrŏbd); THROB′BING. [ME. *throbben,* of imitative origin.] **1.** To pulsate; to vibrate. **2.** To pulsate with abnormal force or rapidity; palpitate; — said of the heart, pulse, etc. — *n.* A beat, or pulsation, as of the heart and arteries. — **throb′ber** (-ẽr), *n.*

throe (thrō), *n.* [ME. *throwe, thrawe,* fr. AS. *thrauu,* var. of *thrēa* threatening, oppression, suffering.] **1.** Extreme pain; anguish; agony; esp., a pang in childbirth. **2.** Hence, agonized struggle or effort.

throm′bin (thrŏm′bĭn), *n.* [See THROMBUS.] *Biochem.* A substance present in serum, that unites with fibrinogen to form fibrin, as in blood clotting.

throm′bo·gen (thrŏm′bō·jĕn), *n.* [Gr. *thrombos* clot + *-gen.*] *Biochem.* The precursor of thrombin found in blood plasma; prothrombin.

throm′bo·kin′ase (-kĭn′ās; -kī′nās), *n.* [*thrombo-* (fr. Gr. *thrombos* clot) + *kinase.*] *Biochem.* A substance present in the tissues, which accelerates the clotting of blood.

throm′bo·plas′tic (-plăs′tĭk), *adj.* [*thrombo-* (fr. Gr. *thrombos* clot) + *-plastic.*] *Biochem.* Of, pertaining to, or causing acceleration of, the clotting of the blood.

throm′bo·plas′tin (-plăs′tĭn), *n.* [Gr. *thrombos* clot + *-plast* + *-in.*] *Biochem.* A clotting protein substance released by certain blood disks as they disintegrate or by tissue cells.

throm·bo′sis (thrŏm·bō′sĭs), *n.* [NL., fr. Gr. *thrombōsis* coagulation. See THROMBUS.] *Med.* The formation of a clot, or thrombus, in any part of the vascular or lymphatic system during life. — **throm·bot′ic** (-bŏt′ĭk), *adj.*

throm′bus (thrŏm′bŭs), *n.; pl.* -BI (-bī). [NL., fr. Gr. *thrombos* lump, clot.] A coagulum of blood elements or a growth of cells, as tumor cells, formed in the heart, a blood vessel, or a lymphatic during life.

throne (thrōn), *n.* [OF. *trone,* fr. L. *thronus,* fr. Gr. *thronos.*] **1.** A chair of state; esp., a royal seat on a dais with a canopy, as for a prince, bishop, etc. **2.** Sovereign power and dignity; sovereignty; also, the one invested therewith. **3.** *pl.* A high order of angels. — *v. t. & i.* To enthrone; to occupy a throne.

throng (thrŏng; 74), *n.* [AS. *thrang, gethrang;* akin to AS. *thringan* to crowd.] **1.** A multitude of persons congregated together; a crowd. **2.** Any great multitude. — **Syn.** See CROWD. — *v. i.* To crowd together; to move, pass, go, etc., in multitudes. — *v. t.* **1.** To crowd or press upon; to crush. **2.** To crowd into; to cram.

throng (thrŏng), *adj.* Also **thrang** (*dial.* thrăng). *Scot. & Dial.* **a** Crowded; thronged. **b** Busy.

thros′tle (thrŏs′'l), *n.* [AS.] **1.** *Scot.* A thrush. **2.** A machine for spinning wool, cotton, etc.

throt′tle (thrŏt′'l), *n.* [Dim. of THROAT.] **1.** The throat or windpipe. **2. a** In an internal-combustion engine, the valve (**throttle valve**) controlling the volume of vaporized fuel charge delivered to the cylinders. **b** The lever (**throttle lever**) controlling this valve. — *v. t.;* -TLED (-'ld); -TLING (-lĭng). **1.** To compress the throat of; to choke; strangle; hence, to check or suppress by or as if by choking. **2.** *Engin.* To obstruct the flow of, as steam to an engine, esp. by a throttle valve; hence, to reduce the speed of, as an engine, by such means; — often with *down.* — *v. i.* To choke; suffocate. — **throt′tler** (-lẽr), *n.*

through (thrōō), *prep.* [ME. *thurgh, thurh, thuruh, thoruh,* fr. AS. *thurh.*] **1.** In at one side and out at the opposite side of. **2.** Among or in the midst of. **3.** By way of; as, he left *through* the window. **4.** Over the whole surface or extent of. **5.** During; from the beginning to the end of. **6.** By means of; by the agency of. **7.** By reason of; in consequence of. — *adv.* **1.** From one end or side to the other. **2.** From beginning to end. **3.** Quite to the end or conclusion; as, to carry a project *through.* **4.** Thoroughly; entirely; as, wet *through.* — *adj.* **1.** Admitting free passage; as, a *through* way. **2.** Extending from one surface to the other; as, a *through* mortise, etc. **3.** *Colloq.* Arrived at completion; as, nearly *through* with the book. **4.** *Transportation.* **a** Extending or going from point of departure to destination, or from one end to the other of a route, without break, change, reshipment, etc. **b** Of or pertaining to such traffic or transportation; as, a *through* ticket.

through′ly, *adv. Archaic.* Thoroughly.

through′–oth′er (thrōō′ŭth′ẽr), *adv.* Also **throu′ther** (thrōō′thẽr). *Scot.* Confusedly.

through·out′ (thrōō·out′), *prep.* All the way from one end to the other of. — *adv.* In or to every part; everywhere; also, in all respects.

throve (thrōv), *past* of THRIVE.

throw (thrō), *v. t.;* THREW (thrōō); THROWN (thrōn); THROW′ING. [ME. *throwen, thrawen,* to throw, twist, fr. AS. *thrāwan* to twist, revolve.] **1.** *Obs. exc. Scot. & Dial.* To twist; wrench. **2.** To twist two or more filaments of, as silk, so as to form one thread. **3.** To fling, cast, or hurl, with a whirling motion of the arm; as, to *throw* a ball; hence, to propel; hurl; as, a gun *throws* a shell. **4.** To put in a (designated) position, condition, or situation; as, men *thrown* out of work. **5.** To drive or impel by violence; to dash. **6.** To cause to fall; to cast down; as, a wrestler *throws* his antagonist. **7.** To divest or strip oneself of; to shed; as, my horse *threw* a shoe. **8.** To put on hastily; to don; as, he *threw* on his coat. **9.** To move quickly; to advance; as, he *threw* a regiment across the river. **10.** To bring forth; to produce; — commonly said of animals; as, the mare *threw* a good colt. **11.** *Cant. or Colloq.* To allow an opponent to win; as, to *throw* a game. **12.** To cast, as dice. **13.** *Scot. & Dial.* To obstruct; thwart. **14.** *Card Playing.* To play (a card); esp., to discard. **15.** *Mach.* To move (a lever) so as to connect or disconnect parts of a clutch, switch, etc.; also, to connect or disconnect by such means. **16.** *Pottery.* To form or shape on a potter's wheel, as earthen vessels. — *v. i.* To cast, hurl, or fling. — **throw′er** (thrō′ẽr), *n.*

Syn. Throw, cast, fling, hurl, pitch, toss, sling mean to propel swiftly as through the air. Throw often is followed by an adverb to show destination or disposal; cast implies lightness in the thing thrown and, sometimes, a scattering; fling, violence in throwing; hurl, a driving force that makes for speed; pitch, a definite aim or direction; toss, light, careless, or aimless throwing; sling, sudden violent propulsion and directness of aim.

throw back. **a** To retort. **b** To revert to an ancestral type. — ***throw cold water on.*** Figuratively, to discourage by indifference. — ***throw down the glove or the gauntlet.*** To challenge; defy. — ***throw off.*** **a** To free oneself from. **b** To reject; discard. **c** *Colloq.* To make or utter offhand; as, to *throw off* a witty saying. **d** To abate (something from the price). **e** To cast or deflect to one side; also, to release or disconnect (a part in a machine, etc.). — ***throw up.*** **a** To cease to participate, use, engage, etc. **b** *Colloq.* To vomit. **c** To construct hastily; as, to *throw up* a breastwork. **d** To raise suddenly. **e** To mention repeatedly as a taunt.

— *n.* **1.** Act of throwing, hurling, or flinging; a cast. **2.** A cast of dice; hence, a venture; risk. **3.** A light scarf or coverlet. **4.** The distance which a missile may be thrown; — in the phrase a *stone's throw.* **5.** *Geol. & Mining.* The amount of vertical displacement produced by a fault. See FAULT, *Illust.* **6.** *Mach.* **a** The extreme movement given to a reciprocating piece by a cam, crank, eccentric, or the like; travel; stroke. **b** The length of the radius of a crank, or the virtual crank radius of an eccentric, cam, or the like. **7.** *Scot. & Dial. Eng.* Usually spelled **thraw** (thrô; thrä). *Wrestling.* A way of throwing one's opponent.

throw′a·way′ (thrō′ȧ·wā′), *n.* A handbill, advertising circular, booklet, shopping guide, or the like, distributed free to catch the brief attention of casual readers.

throw′back′ (thrō′băk′), *n.* Reversion to an ancestral type or to an earlier phase of civilization; atavism; also, an instance or product of such reversion.

throw′ster (thrō′stẽr), *n.* [*throw* + *-ster.*] One who throws silk.

thru (thrōō). Var. of THROUGH.

thrum (thrŭm), *n.* [ME. *thrum, throm.*] **1.** *Weaving.* **a** One of the ends of weavers' warp threads. **b** The fringelike row of such threads on the loom when the web has been cut free. **c** Any soft, short threads, tufts, or fringes. **2.** Any loose coarse yarn waste; — chiefly in *pl.* **3.** *Scot.* A particle; bit. **4.** *Scot.* A tangle. **5.** *pl. Naut.* Tufts, or short pieces, of rope yarn used in thrumming canvas. — *v. t.;* THRUMMED (thrŭmd); THRUM′MING. **1.** To furnish with, or make of, thrums; to tuft; fringe. **2.** *Naut.* To insert short pieces of rope yarn or spun yarn in (a piece of canvas), thus making a rough surface or a mat which can be wrapped about rigging to prevent chafing.

thrum, *v. i.* [Imitative.] **1.** To play monotonously or listlessly on or as on a stringed instrument; to strum. **2.** To sound with a repeated monotonous hum. **3.** To repeat monotonously. **4.** *Scot.* To purr. — *v. t.* **1.** To play, as a stringed instrument, in a monotonous or listless manner. **2.** *Scot.* To recite or repeat tiresomely. — *n.* A monotonous sound, as of thrumming.

thrush (thrŭsh), *n.* [D. *tröske,* Sw. *torsk,* and Dan. *trøske* rotten wood.] **1.** An affection of the mouth, fauces, etc., in infants, characterized by white patches and caused by a yeast. **2.** *Veter.* A suppurative affection of the feet in certain animals.

thrush, *n.* [AS. *thrysce, thrǣsce.*] Any of numerous small or medium-sized passerine birds (family Turdidae, esp. subfamily Turdinae). Typical thrushes are mostly of a plain color, but many have spotted under parts. See BILL, *Illust.* Among European species are the ***song thrush*** (*Turdus musicus*) and the ***missel, or missel thrush*** (*T. viscivorus*); American species are the ***robin*** (*T. migratorius*), the ***hermit thrush*** (*Hylocichla guttata faxoni*), the ***wood thrush*** (*H. mustelina*), etc.

thrust (thrŭst), *v. t.;* THRUST; THRUST′ING. [ME. *thrusten, thristen,* fr. ON. *thrȳsta* to thrust, press, compel.] **1.** To push or drive with force; to shove. **2.** To stab; pierce; — usually with *through.* **3.** To interpose; interject; as, to *thrust* a word in now and then. — *v. i.* **1.** To push; shove. **2.** To make a thrust as with a pointed weapon. **3.** To force an entrance or passage. — **Syn.** See PUSH. — *n.* **1.** A violent push, as with a pointed weapon. **2.** An attack; onset. **3.** Strong and continued pressure. **4.** *Engin.* **a** Force exerted endwise through a propeller shaft, as of a vessel or aircraft. **b** The forwardly directed reaction force produced by a jet (a high-speed stream of fluid) discharged rearwards from a nozzle or orifice, as in a jet airplane or a rocket. **5.** *Geol.* A form of fault that is nearly horizontal. **6.** *Mech.* The pressure of one part of a construction against another part; esp., *Arch.,* a horizontal or diagonal outward pressure, as of an arch against an abutment. — **thrust′er**, *n.*

thud (thŭd), *n.* **1.** A blow. **2.** A dull thump. — *v. i. & t.;* THUD′DED; THUD′DING. To move or strike so as to make a dull sound, or thud.

thug (thŭg; *Hind.* t'hŭg), *n.* [Hind. *ṭhag,* fr. Prakrit *ṭhaga,* Skr. *sthaga* a rogue, dishonest.] **1.** [*often cap.*] A member of a former religious fraternity of northern India among whose members murder was made a profession. **2.** A ruffian; assassin. — **thug′ger·y** (thŭg′ẽr·ĭ), *n.* — **thug′gish**, *adj.*

thug′gee (thŭg′ē; *Hind.* t'hŭg′ē), *n.* [Hind. *ṭhagī.* See THUG.] Practice of murder and robbery by the thugs.

thu′ja (thū′jȧ), *n.* [NL., fr. Gr. *thyia* an African tree.] *Bot.* Any of a genus (*Thuja*) of evergreen shrubs and trees of the pine family, esp. the arborvitae, which yields a medicinal oil (***oil of thuja***).

Thu′le (thū′lē; -lē), *n.* [L. *Thule, Thyle,* fr. Gr. *Thoulē, Thylē.*] Among the ancients, the northernmost part of the habitable world; — often in the phrase ***ultima Thule*** ("farthest Thule"). Norway, Iceland, or Mainland (largest of the Shetland Islands) may have been meant.

thu′li·a (thū′lĭ·ȧ), *n.* [NL.] *Chem.* Thulium oxide, Tm_2O_3, a greenish-white powder.

thu′li·um (-ŭm), *n.* [NL. See THULE.] *Chem.* A rare-earth metal. Symbol, *Tm;* at. no., 69; at. wt., 169.4.

thumb (thŭm), *n.* [AS. *thūma.*] **1.** The first digit of the human hand, apposable to the other fingers; the pollex. Also, the corresponding digit in animals. **2.** The part of a glove or mitten that covers the thumb. **3.** *Arch.* A type of molding; an ovolo. See MOLDING, *Illust.* (7). — *v. t.* **1.** To soil or wear with the thumb or the fingers by frequent handling. **2.** To run over the pages of (a book, etc.), as by turning with the thumb. **3.** *Colloq., U. S.* To request or to obtain (a ride) in a passing automobile by signaling with the thumb.

thumb′kin (thŭm′kĭn), *n.* Thumbscrew.

thumb′nail′ (thŭm′nāl′; 2), *n.* The nail of the thumb; hence, something of similar size. — *adj.* Of the size of the thumbnail; hence, small; complete in little space or in few words; as, a *thumbnail* sketch.
thumb′screw′ (-skrōō′), *n.* **1.** A screw having a flat-sided or knurled head, so that it may be turned by the thumb and forefinger. **2.** Also **thumb′kin** (-kĭn). An old instrument of torture for compressing the thumb.
thumb′tack′ (-tăk′), *n.* A short steel point with a broad flat head for pressing, with one's thumb, into a board.
Thum′mim, *n. pl.* See URIM.
thump (thŭmp), *n.* [Imitative.] A blow or knock, as with something blunt or heavy; also, the sound made by such a blow. — *v. t. & i.* To strike or beat as with something thick or heavy, or so as to cause a dull sound; loosely, to pound; also, to cudgel; thrash.
thun′der (thŭn′dẽr), *n.* [ME. *thunder, thonder, thoner,* fr. AS. *thunor.*] **1.** The sound following a flash of lightning, due to the sudden expansion of the air in the path of the discharge. International symbol, T. **2.** *Rare.* A discharge of lightning; a thunderbolt. **3.** Any noise likened to thunder; as, the *thunder* of cannon, of applause. **4.** An alarming or startling threat or denunciation. — *v. i.* **1.** To produce thunder; — often impersonal; as, it *thundered.* **2.** To give forth a sound likened to thunder, as a voice. **3.** To utter violent denunciation. — *v. t.* **1.** To emit with a noise of, or likened to, thunder; specif., to utter vehemently, as censure. **2.** To strike with a sound likened to thunder; as, to *thunder* blows upon an antagonist.
thun′der·bird′ (-bûrd′), *n.* Among North American Indians, a mythical bird supposed to cause thunder and lightning.
thun′der·bolt′ (-bōlt′), *n.* **1.** A single discharge of lightning with the accompanying thunder. **2.** An imaginary bolt conceived of as the missile cast to earth in the lightning flash. **3.** A person or thing likened to lightning in suddenness, effectiveness, and destructive power.
thun′der·clap′ (-klăp′), *n.* **a** A clap or crash of thunder. **b** Something sharp, loud, and sudden, like a crash of thunder.
thun′der·cloud′ (-kloud′), *n.* A cloud charged with electricity, and producing lightning and thunder.
thun′der·er (-ẽr), *n.* One who or that which thunders.
thun′der·head′ (-hĕd′), *n.* A rounded mass of cumulus cloud, often appearing before a thunderstorm.
thun′der·ing, *adj.* **1.** Emitting thunder or a sound likened to thunder. **2.** Big; unusual; as, a *thundering* lie. — **thun′der·ing·ly**, *adv.*
thun′der·ous (thŭn′dẽr·ŭs), *adj.* Producing thunder; also, making a noise like thunder. — **thun′der·ous·ly**, *adv.*
thun′der·peal′ (-pēl′), *n.* A thunderclap.
thun′der·show′er (-shou′ẽr), *n.* Also **thun′der·squall′** (-skwôl′), **thun′der·storm′** (-stôrm′). A shower, squall, or storm, accompanied with lightning and thunder.
thun′der·stick′ (-stĭk′), *n.* = BULL-ROARER, 1.
thun′der·stone′ (-stōn′), *n.* *Dial.* A thunderbolt; esp., a stone popularly supposed to be a thunderbolt. These stones may be fossil belemnite shells, prehistoric stone implements, meteorites, etc.
thun′der·stroke′ (thŭn′dẽr·strōk′), *n.* A stroke by or as by lightning with the attendant thunder.
thun′der·struck′ (-strŭk′), *adj.* Also **thun′der·strick′en** (-strĭk′ĕn). Literally, struck by a thunderbolt; hence, struck by astonishment, fear, or the like; astounded.
thu′ri·ble (thū′rĭ·b'l), *n.* [L. *thuribulum,* fr. *thus, thuris,* frankincense, fr. Gr. *thyos* incense.] *Eccl.* A censer.
thu′ri·fer (thū′rĭ·fẽr), *n.* [L. *thurifer,* fr. *thus* frankincense + *ferre* to bear.] *Eccl.* One who carries a thurible, formerly an acolyte, now usually an altar boy.
Thu·rin′gi·an (thū·rĭn′jĭ·ăn), *n.* A member of an ancient German tribe whose kingdom was overthrown by the Franks in the 6th century; also, one of the people of the part of Germany called Thuringia. — *adj.* Of or pertaining to Thuringia or the Thuringians; *Geol.*, designating the upper division of the European Permian.
Thurs′day (thûrz′dĭ; 13), *n.* [From AS. *Thunres dæg* day of Thunor, and ON. *Thōrsdagr,* fr. *Thōrr* Thor, the god of Thunder.] The fifth day of the week. Abbr. *Thurs., Thur., Th.*
thus (thŭs), *adv.* [AS.] **1.** In this or that manner, way, etc. **2.** To this degree or extent; so far; so. **3.** Because of this or that; consequently; hence.
thwack (thwăk), *v. t.* To strike with something flat or heavy; to whack. — *n.* A bang; a whack. — **thwack′er**, *n.*
thwart (thwôrt; *naut.* thôrt), *adj.* [ME. *thwert,* adv., fr. ON. *thvert,* orig. neut. of *thverr* athwart, transverse.] **1.** Situated or placed across something else; transverse; oblique. **2.** *Obs.* Perverse; intractable. — *adv.* Athwart. — *n.* *Naut.* A rower's seat reaching athwart a boat. — *v. t.* **1.** *Obs.* To pass through or across. **2.** To oppose or baffle, as a purpose; hence, to frustrate or defeat; block. — **Syn.** See FRUSTRATE. — **thwart′er**, *n.*
thy (thī), *pron.* [ME. *thy, thi,* shortened fr. *thin.* See THINE.] Historical possessive case of *thou.* See THINE. — *adj. Chiefly Archaic & Poetic.* **1.** Of or belonging to thee or thyself as possessor. **2.** Of or relating to thee as author, agent, etc.
Thy·es′te·an (thī·ĕs′tē·ăn; thī′ĕs·tē′ăn), *adj.* Also **Thy·es′ti·an** (thī·ĕs′tĭ·ăn). Of or pert. to Thyestes; as, **Thyestean banquet**, a banquet at which human flesh is eaten.
Thy·es′tes (thī·ĕs′tēz), *n.* [L., fr. Gr. *Thyestēs.*] A son of Pelops. See ATREUS.
thy′la·cine (thī′lȧ·sīn; -sĭn), *n.* [Gr. *thylax* a sack, pouch.] A carnivorous marsupial (*Thylacynus cynocephalus*) of Tasmania, of doglike appearance. It is destructive to sheep, and has been nearly exterminated. Called also *Tasmanian tiger* or *wolf.*
thyme (tīm), *n.* [OF. *tym,* fr. L. *thymum,* fr. Gr. *thymon.*] Any of a genus (*Thymus*) of plants of the mint family, with pungent, aromatic leaves used in seasoning and soups; esp., the common ***wild thyme*** (*T. serpyllum*).
thym′e·lae·a′ceous (thĭm′ē·lē·ā′shŭs), *adj.* [L. *thymelaea* a kind of plant, fr. Gr. *thymelaia.*] *Bot.* Belonging to the mezereon family (*Thymelaeaceae*). See MEZEREON.
thy′mic (thī′mĭk), *adj.* Of or pertaining to the thymus.
thy′mol (thī′mōl; -mŏl), *n.* [*thyme* + *-ol.*] *Chem.* A white crystalline phenol, $C_{10}H_{13}OH$, of aromatic odor and antiseptic properties, occurring in oil of thyme.
thy′mus (thī′mŭs), *n.* [NL., fr. Gr. *thymos.*] *Anat.* A gland of lymphoid character and uncertain function, present, at least in the young, in nearly all vertebrates. In man it lies in the upper part of the thorax and lower part of the throat. It disappears or becomes rudimentary in the adult. In lambs and calves it is one of the glands called *sweetbread.*
thy′re·o- (thī′rē·ō-), **thy′re-**, **thy′ro-** (thī′rō-). [Gr. *thyreoeidēs* thyroid.] Combining forms denoting: **a** *The thyroid,* as in **thy′re·ot′o·my** (see -TOMY). **b** *Thyroid and,* as in **thy′ro·ar′y·te′noid**, connecting the thyroid and arytenoid cartilages.
thy′re·oid (thī′rē·oid), *adj. & n. Anat.* Thyroid.
☞ *Thyreoid* is the spelling preferred by anatomists.
thy′roid (thī′roid), *adj.* [Gr. *thyreoeidēs* shield-shaped, fr. *thyreos* a large, oblong shield + *eidos* form.] **1.** Designating, pertaining to, or derived from, a large ductless gland (the **thyroid gland** *or* **body**) below the pharynx or in the neck, lying close to the larynx in man. The thyroid gland elaborates a hormone, thyroxine, having a profound influence on growth. Disturbed activity causes goiter, cretinism, etc. **2.** Designating, or pert. to, the chief cartilage (**thyroid cartilage**) of the larynx. — *n.* **1.** The thyroid gland, cartilage, or other part. **2.** *Pharm.* The prepared thyroid gland of certain food animals, used in treating goiter, cretinism, obesity, etc.
thy′roid·ec′to·my (thī′roid·ĕk′tō·mĭ), *n.* [*thyroid* + *-ectomy.*] The surgical removal of thyroid gland tissue.
thy′roid·i′tis (-ī′tĭs), *n.* [NL., fr. *thyroid* + *-itis.*] *Med.* Inflammation of the thyroid gland.
thy′ro·tox′i·co′sis (thī′rō·tŏk′sĭ·kō′sĭs), *n.* [NL., fr. *thyro-* + *toxicosis.*] *Med.* A morbid condition due to excessive or abnormal activity of the thyroid gland, and characterized by rapid heart action, tremors, structural abnormalities, etc. — **thy′ro·tox′ic** (-tŏk′sĭk), *adj.*
thy·rox′ine (thī·rŏk′sēn; -sĭn), *n.* Also **thy·rox′in.** [*thyroid* + *oxy-* + *-in.*] *Biochem.* The active principle, $C_{15}H_{11}I_4NO_4$, of the thyroid gland, used to treat goiter, cretinism, etc.
thyrse (thûrs), *n.* [F.] *Bot.* A thyrsus.
thyr′soid (thûr′soid), *adj.* Also **thyr·soi′dal** (thûr·soi′dăl; -d'l). [Gr. *thyrsoeidēs,* fr. *thyrsos* thyrsus + *eidos* form, shape.] *Bot.* Having somewhat the form of a thyrsus; as, a *thyrsoid* panicle.
thyr′sus (thûr′sŭs), *n.; pl.* -SI (-sī). [L., fr. Gr. *thyrsos.*] **1.** *Gr. Relig.* A staff surmounted by a pine cone, or by a bunch of vine or ivy leaves with grapes or berries. It is an attribute of Dionysus, satyrs, etc. **2.** *Bot.* A form of mixed inflorescence in which the main axis is racemose, and the secondary and later axes are cymose. See INFLORESCENCE, *Illust.* (10).
thy′sa·nu′ran (thī′sȧ·nū′răn; thĭs′ȧ-), *adj.* [Gr. *thysanos* tassel + *oura* tail.] *Zool.* Belonging to an order (Thysanura) of wingless insects (the bristletails) with setiform caudal appendages projecting as bristles. — **thy′sa·nu′ran**, *n.* — **thy′sa·nu′rous** (-rŭs), *adj.*
thy·self′ (thī·sĕlf′), *pron.* An emphasized form of the personal pronoun of the second person singular.
ti (tē), *n.* *Music.* A syllable applied to the seventh tone of the diatonic scale in solmization; — formerly called *si.*
ti (tē), *n.* [Maori and Samoan.] Also **ti palm.** Any of several species of Asiatic and Polynesian trees and shrubs (genus *Cordyline,* esp. *C. terminalis*).
ti·ar′a (tī·âr′ȧ; tē·ä′rȧ), *n.* [L., fr. Gr. *tiara, tiaras.*] **1.** The pope's triple crown. **2.** A crownlike head ornament; a frontlet or coronet.
Ti·bet′an (tĭ·bĕt′ăn; tĭb′ĕt-; -ĭt-), *adj.* Of or pertaining to Tibet or the Tibetans. — *n.* **1.** A member of the native race of Tibet, a distinct Mongolian type, modified in the west and south by intermixture with Indian peoples, and in the east with Chinese. Most are Lamaists. **2.** The Indo-Chinese language of the Tibetans. See LANGUAGE, *Table.*
tib′i·a (tĭb′ĭ·ȧ), *n.; pl.* TIBIAE (-ē), TIBIAS (-ȧz). [L.] **1.** *Anat. & Zool.* **a** The inner, and usually larger, of the two bones of the leg or hind limb between the knee and ankle. **b** The fourth joint of the leg of an insect. **2.** A type of ancient flute, originally fashioned from an animal's leg bone. — **tib′i·al** (-ăl), *adj.*
tic (tĭk), *n.* [F.] *Med.* A local and habitual spasmodic motion of certain muscles, esp. of the face; twitching.
ti·cal′ (tĭ·käl′; -kôl′; tē′kŭl), *n.; pl.* TICALS (-kälz′; -kôlz′; -kŭlz), TICAL. [Malay *tikal.*] *Thailand.* **a** The baht. **b** A weight (231.5 grains).
‖**tic dou′lou′reux′** (tĕk′ dōō′lōō′rû′; tĭk′ dōō′lōō·rōō′). [F., fr. *tic* a twitching + *douloureux* painful.] Spasmodic neuralgia of the face.
tick (tĭk), *n.* [ME. *tike, teke.*] **1.** Any of numerous arachnids (order Acarida), larger than ordinary mites, which attach themselves to man and many animals and birds, and suck their blood. **2.** Any of certain degraded parasitic dipterous insects, for example, the sheep *tick.*
tick, *n.* [Ult. fr. L. *theca* case, cover, fr. Gr. *thēkē.*] **1.** The stout cover, or case, which when filled with hair, feathers, or the like, forms a mattress, pillow, or bolster. **2.** *Colloq.* Ticking.
tick, *v. i.* [Prob. of imitative origin.] To make a tick or a continuous series of ticks, as a watch, the heart, or a meter. — *v. t.* **1.** To mark with a tick, or dot; also, check with a tick. **2.** To mark, note, count, record, etc., by or as by the ticks of a clock, a telegraph instrument, etc. — *n.* **1.** A light quick audible beat, as of a clock. **2.** Time taken by the tick of a clock; as, to do something in three *ticks.* **3.** A dot, dash, etc., esp. one to serve as a check.
tick, *n.* [Abbr. fr. TICKET.] *Colloq.* Credit; trust; also, a credit account; as, to buy or sell on *tick.*
tick′er (tĭk′ẽr), *n.* **1.** One who ticks. **2.** Something that ticks, as a clock, a telegraphic sounder, etc. **3.** *Slang.* The heart. **4.** *Stock Exchange.* A telegraphic receiving instrument that automatically prints off stock quotations (***stock ticker***) and other news on a paper ribbon or tape (**ticker tape**).
tick′et (tĭk′ĕt; -ĭt), *n.* [F. *étiquette* a ticket, label, inscription, fr. OF. *estiquet(te),* fr. *estiquer* to stick.] **1.** A notice, record, memorandum, or token, or a slip of paper or cardboard containing such a note or notice. **2.** A certificate, license, permit, or the like; specif., a master's, captain's, mate's, pilot's, or airman's certificate. **3.** A certificate, evidence, or token of a right, as of admission to a place of assembly, of passage in a public conveyance, of debt, etc. **4.** *Banking.* A record slip of sums, transactions, etc., to be entered. **5.** *Politics, U. S.* A list of candidates, esp. of one party only, to be voted for at an election; a ballot. — *v. t.* **1.** To distinguish by or as by a ticket; to put a label on. **2.** *U. S.* To furnish with a ticket or tickets; to book.
ticket of leave. *Brit.* A license or permit given to a convict under imprisonment to go at large, and to labor for himself, subject to certain specific conditions. Cf. PAROLE. — **tick′et-of-leave′**, *adj.*
tick fever. **a** *Med.* Any fever transmitted by ticks, as Rocky Mountain spotted fever. **b** *Veter.* Texas fever.
tick′ing (tĭk′ĭng), *n.* [From TICK a bed cover.] A strong woven linen or cotton fabric, of which ticks are made.

tic'kle (tĭk''l), *v. i.;* TICK'LED (-'ld); TICK'LING (-lĭng). To have a tingling or uneasy sensation; titillate. — *v. t.* **1.** To excite or stir up agreeably; to please; as, food that *tickles* the palate. **2.** To touch (one or a part of one's body) lightly so as to excite the surface nerves and to cause uneasiness, laughter, or spasmodic movements; titillate. **3.** To touch or stir gently; also, to move, take, do, operate, etc., by or as by light touches. **4.** To amuse; divert. — *n.* Act of tickling; a tickling sensation, device, etc.; a tickler. — *adj. Archaic & Dial.* Unsteady; unstable; insecure.

tick'ler (tĭk'lẽr), *n.* **1.** One who tickles. **2.** A device for tickling, esp. for jogging the memory. **3.** *Accounts.* A book, file, or the like, kept, as in a bank, to show the amounts due upon notes, etc., and the days of payment. **4.** *Elec.* A tickler coil.

tickler coil. *Elec.* A small coil connected in series with the plate circuit of an electron tube and inductively coupled with its grid circuit to return a part of the amplified signal for repeated amplification.

tick'lish (tĭk'lĭsh), *adj.* **1.** Sensitive to tickling. **2.** Easily unbalanced; unstable; of persons or their tempers, easily upset; touchy. **3.** Requiring careful handling; delicate; critical; as, a *ticklish* situation. — **tick'lish·ly**, *adv.* — **tick'lish·ness**, *n.*

tick'seed' (tĭk'sēd'), *n.* [*tick* the insect + *seed.*] **a** The coreopsis. **b** The tick trefoil.

tick'tack' (tĭk'tăk'), *n.* [Imitative.] **1.** A noise of ticking, as of a watch. **2.** A contrivance for making a tapping sound, as on a window, used esp. by children in play.

tick'tack·toe', tick'tack·too' (tĭk'tăk·tō', -tōō'), *n.* **1.** A game played by two players who alternately put crosses and ciphers in compartments of a crosslike figure, the object being to get a row of three crosses or three ciphers before the adversary does so. **2.** The prank of using a ticktack (def. 2).

tick trefoil. Any of certain plants (genus *Desmodium*) of the pea family, with trifoliolate leaves and roughened, sticky loments.

tid'al (tīd'ăl; -'l), *adj.* **1.** Of or pertaining to tides; periodically rising and falling, or flowing and ebbing; as, *tidal* waters. **2.** Dependent, as in regard to the time of arrival or departure, upon the tide; as, a *tidal* steamer.

tidal wave. **1.** **a** The great sea wave that sometimes follows an earthquake. **b** The great rise of water along shore due to exceptionally strong winds. **2.** An overwhelming impulse, burst of feeling, majority vote, or the like.

tid'bit' (tĭd'bĭt'), *n.* *U. S.* A titbit.

tid'dly·winks' (tĭd''l·ĭ·wĭngks'; tĭd'lĭ-), *n. pl.* Also **tid'dle·dy·winks'** (tĭd''l·dĭ-). A game in which the object is to snap small disks into a small cup.

tide (tīd), *n.* [AS. *tīd* time.] **1.** *Archaic.* A period of time; esp., an ecclesiastical anniversary; a festival or, often, its season. **2.** *Archaic.* Fit or opportune time; opportunity. **3.** The alternate rising and falling of the surface of the ocean, and of gulfs, bays, rivers, etc., connected with the ocean. The tide ebbs and flows twice in each lunar day (24 h. 51 m.). It is occasioned by the attraction of sun and moon. Hence, when sun and moon are in conjunction or opposition, as at new moon and full, their combined action produces a tide greater than usual, called ***spring tide.*** When the moon is at first or third quarter, the high tide (***neap tide***) is smaller than usual. The rising of the water is called ***flood tide;*** the reflux, ***ebb tide.*** **4.** The time during which something is at its height or best. **5.** *Chiefly Poetic.* A stream; current; flood. — *adj.* Tidal; as, a *tide* flow, hole, gauge. — *v. i.* **1.** To flow as a tide; to surge. **2.** To drift with the tide; esp., *Naut.*, to work into or out of a river or harbor by drifting with the tide. — *v. t.* **1.** To cause to float with the tide. **2.** To carry through or help along in the manner of a boat floated on a high tide; as, the gift *tided* us over that winter. **3.** To surmount, live through, endure, cover, etc.; — always with *over;* as, he *tided* over the difficulty.

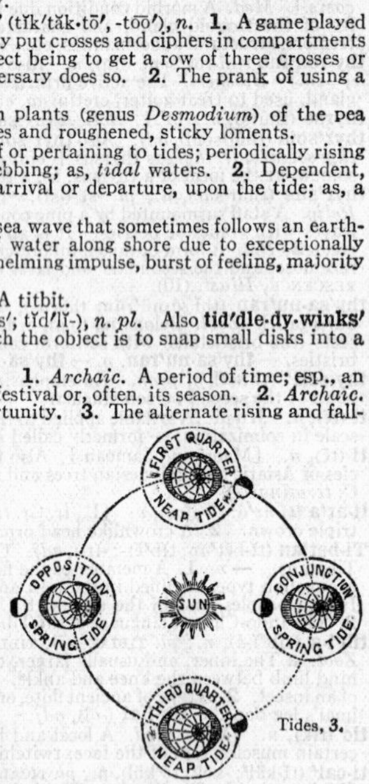

Tides, 3.

tide (tīd), *v. i.* [AS. *tīdan* happen.] *Archaic.* To betide; happen; befall.

tide'land' (tīd'lănd'), *n.* Land overflowed during flood tide.

tide'wait'er (tīd'wāt'ẽr), *n.* A customs officer who boards vessels and watches the landing of goods.

tide'wa'ter (-wô'tẽr; -wŏt'ẽr), *n.* Water overflowing land at flood tide; also, water affected by the ebb and flow of the tide; hence, broadly, the seaboard. — **tide'wa'ter**, *adj.*

tide'way' (-wā'), *n.* A channel in which the tide runs.

ti'ding (tī'dĭng), *n.* [ME. *tidinge, tithinge*, fr. or influenced by ON. *tīthindi*, pl.] A piece of news; a message; *pl.*, news; intelligence; as, good *tidings.*

ti'dy (tī'dĭ), *adj.;* TI'DI·ER (-dĭ·ẽr); TI'DI·EST. [ME. *tidy, tidi*, fr. *tid* time, season.] **1.** *Colloq.* Pretty good; fair. **2.** Neat in appearance, habits, or arrangement; orderly. **3.** *Colloq.* Not small in size, amount, extent, etc.; as, a *tidy* fortune. — **Syn.** See NEAT. — *v. t.;* TI'DIED (-dĭd); TI'DY·ING. To make neat or tidy. — *v. i.* To make things tidy; — with *up.* — *n.; pl.* TIDIES (-dĭz). A piece of fancywork used to protect the back, arms, or headrest of a chair, sofa, etc., from wear or dirt. — **ti'di·ly** (-dĭ·lĭ), *adv.* — **ti'di·ness** (-dĭ·nĕs; -nĭs), *n.*

ti'dy·tips' (-tĭps'), *n. sing. & pl.* An annual Californian herb (*Layia elegans*) of the aster family, having yellow-rayed flower heads often tipped with white.

tie (tī), *v. t.;* TIED (tīd); TY'ING (tī'ĭng) or TIE'ING. [AS. *tīgan*, fr. *tēag, tēah*, a rope.] **1.** To fasten or attach (one thing to another) by a connecting and knotted rope, band, cord, etc. **2.** To join firmly; *Colloq.*, to marry. **3.** To bind; restrict; confine. **4.** To bind, or confine, the parts, sides, or ends, of (a thing) by a cord, lace, etc., drawn around or through and knotted; as, to *tie* one's shoes. **5.** To form a knot or bow in; as, to *tie* one's scarf. **6.** To make or have an equal score with, in a contest; hence, *Slang*, to equal; beat. **7.** *Music.* To unite, as notes, by a tie. — *v. i.* To make a tie; specif.: **a** To make a bond or connection. **b** To make an equal score; to be equal. ***tie down.*** To secure, restrain, or confine by, or as by, fastening (to something); hence, to deprive of freedom of movement, range, choice, etc. — ***tie in.*** To make a connection; join in; hence, to be or make suitable or congruous. — ***tie the knot.*** *Colloq.* To perform the marriage ceremony; also, to get married. — ***tie up.*** **1.** To attach or fasten securely. **2.** To restrain or hinder from action, operation, etc. **3.** To place or invest so as to make unavailable for other use. — *n.* **1.** A band, cord, lace, etc., used for tying; specif., a shoelace. **2.** Something which serves as a connecting link. **3.** Figuratively, a bond; specif.: **a** A moral or legal obligation. **b** A bond of union or affection. **4.** Something that is knotted when worn; as: **a** A necktie. **b** *pl.* Low laced shoes; Oxfords. **5.** An equality in numbers, as of votes, scores, etc.; hence, a contest which ends in a draw. **6.** *Arch., Engin., etc.* A beam, post, rod, or angle, holding two pieces together. **7.** *Music.* A curved line joining two notes indicating the same pitch, to denote a single tone sustained through the time value of the two. **8.** *Railroads.* One of the transverse supports to which the rails are fastened; — called also (esp. *Brit.*) *sleeper.*

tie beam. A beam acting as a tie, as in a roof. See QUEEN POST, ROOF, *Illusts.*

tie'mann·ite (tē'măn·īt), *n.* [After W. *Tiemann*, a German, who discovered it.] *Mineral.* A compound of mercury and selenium, HgSe, occurring in dark masses of metallic luster.

tier (tēr), *n.* [OF. *tire* order, row, rank.] A row, rank, or layer; esp., one of two or more rows one above another; as, arranged *tier* upon *tier.* — *v. t. & i.* To place, arrange, or to be arranged, in tiers or layers.

tierce (tērs), *n.* [OF. *tierce, terce*, fr. L. *tertia*, fem. of *tertius* third.] **1.** *Obs.* A third. **2.** A liquid measure, formerly legal at 42 wine gallons, or one third of a pipe. Hence, a cask holding it, larger than a barrel and smaller than a hogshead. **3.** *Card Playing.* A sequence of three cards of the same suit. **4.** *Eccl.* The third of the canonical hours, or nine A.M.; also, the service or office for that hour; — called also *undernsong.* **5.** *Fencing.* A position in parrying, engaging, etc., in which the wrist is turned inward, the nails turned slightly downward, and the point of the weapon is about on the level of the eye and a little outside the line on the right.

‖**tiers é'tat'** (tyâr'-zā'tȧ'). [F.] *Hist.* The third estate, or commonalty, in France; — disting. from the nobles and the clergy.

tie'-up' (tī'ŭp'), *n.* *U. S.* A suspension of traffic or business, as by a strike, a breakdown of machinery, etc.

tiff (tĭf), *n.* [Perh. orig., a sniff, sniffing.] *Rare.* A small draft of liquor, esp. of punch.

tiff, *n.* [Prob. of imitative origin.] A slight fit of anger; a pet; a petty quarrel. — **Syn.** See QUARREL.

tiff, *v. i.* [See TIFFIN.] *India.* To take tiffin; to lunch.

tif'fa·ny (tĭf'ȧ·nĭ), *n.; pl.* -NIES (-nĭz). [OF. *tiphanie* Epiphany, fr. LL. *theophania;* — perh. so called with ref. to its transparency.] A species of gauze, originally of very thin silk, but now of muslin.

tif'fin (tĭf'ĭn), *n.* [Prop., *tiffing* a quaffing, a drinking.] *Orig. India.* Luncheon, esp. at midday. — *v. i. & t. Colloq.* To take or provide with tiffin; to lunch.

ti'ger (tī'gẽr), *n.; see* PLURAL, *Note*, 3. [OF. *tigre*, fr. L. *tigris*, fr. Gr. *tigris*, of Iranian origin.] **1.** **a** A large Asiatic carnivorous mammal (*Felis tigris*) of the cat family, of a tawny color transversely striped with black. **b** Any of certain other animals; as, in Spanish America, the jaguar; in South Africa, the leopard; and in Tasmania, the thylacine. **2.** A ferocious, bloodthirsty person. **3.** *Old Slang.* A groom in livery, esp. a boy. **4.** [*cap.*] An organization having a representation of a tiger as its emblem; as, the Tammany *tiger.* **5.** *U. S.* A howl or yell (sometimes the word *tiger*) at the end of a round of enthusiastic cheering. **6.** [*cap.*] See MARK.

tiger beetle. Any of numerous species of active carnivorous beetles (family Cicindelidae, mostly genus *Cicindela*) whose larvae live in tunnels in the soil.

tiger cat. **a** Any of certain wildcats of moderate size, as the serval, the ocelot, and the margay. **b** A domestic cat with tigerlike markings.

ti'ger-eye' (tī'gẽr·ī'), *n.* Also **ti'ger's-eye'** (tī'gẽrz-). A chatoyant stone, usually yellow-brown, much used for ornament. A blue variety is called *hawk's-eye.* It is a silicified crocidolite.

ti'ger·ish (tī'gẽr·ĭsh), *adj.* Of, pertaining to, or like a tiger or tigers; esp., fierce; bloodthirsty.

tiger lily. **a** A common Asiatic garden lily (*Lilium tigrinum*) having nodding orange-colored flowers densely spotted with black. **b** Any of various lilies having similar spotted flowers (as *L. pardalinum*, etc.).

tiger moth. A moth of a family (Arctiidae) typically stout-bodied with broad striped or spotted wings.

tight (tīt), *adj.* [ME. *tight, thight*, of Scand. origin.] **1.** So close in structure as not to admit liquid; often, watertight; as, a *tight* ship. **2.** **a** Held, bound, or fixed securely or firmly. **b** Hence, unmoved or steady; as, to sit *tight.* **3.** Not slack or loose; taut. **4.** Of persons: **a** *Now Dial.* Well-formed; shapely; also, neat; tidy. **b** Capable; alert. **5.** *Dial.* Snug; trim. **6.** Close-fitting; usually, too close for comfort; as, a *tight* coat. **7.** **a** Difficult to get through or out of; — chiefly in idiomatic colloquial expressions; as, to be in a *tight* spot or place; a *tight* squeeze. **b** Severe; exacting; as, a *tight* hand over him. **8.** *Colloq.* Close-fisted; stingy. **9.** Packed close; highly compressed; of language, style, etc., condensed. **10.** *Slang.* Intoxicated; tipsy. **11.** *Com. & Finance.* Scantily supplied or obtainable in proportion to the demand; — of money or of a commodity. Cf. EASY, 8. — *adv.* Tightly; firmly; hard. — **tight'ly**, *adv.* — **tight'ness**, *n.*

Syn. (1) **Tight, taut, tense** mean drawn or stretched to the limit. **Tight** implies a constriction or an impenetrability; **taut**, a pulling or stretching, as of a rope or fabric, until there is not the slightest give; **tense**, a tightness or tautness that involves great strain.
(2) See DRUNK.

-tight (-tīt). Combining form of the adjective *tight*, denoting *impervious to*, as in air*tight*, water*tight*, etc.

☞ Adjective compounds in *-tight* are formed freely, and their meanings can readily be understood from the above definition. Cf. -PROOF, *Note.*

tight'en (tīt''n), *v. t. & i.* To make or become tight or tighter. — **tight'en·er** (tīt''n·ẽr), *n.*

tight'fist'ed (-fĭs'tĕd; -tĭd; 2), *adj.* Closefisted; miserly.

tight'-lipped' (-lĭpt'), *adj.* **1.** Having the lips closed tightly, as in repression of emotion or in determination. **2.** Grudging of speech; uncommunicative; as, *tight-lipped* toward the inquisitive.

tight'rope' (-rōp'), *n.* A rope stretched taut on which acrobats perform. — **tight'rope'**, *adj.*

tights (tīts), *n. pl.* Skintight garments, usually for the hips and legs, worn esp. by performers in public.
tight′wad′ (tīt′wŏd′), *n.* [See 1st WAD, 5.] *Slang, U.S.* A miser; niggard.
tig′lic (tĭg′lĭk), *adj.* Also **tig·lin′ic** (tĭg·lĭn′ĭk). [NL. *tiglium* croton-oil plant.] *Chem.* Pertaining to or designating a crystalline, unsaturated acid, $C_4H_7CO_2H$, found as esters in croton oil, etc.
ti′gress (tī′grĕs; -grĭs), *n.* A female tiger; also, a tigerish woman.
ti′grish (tī′grĭsh). Var. of TIGERISH.
tike (tīk). Var. of TYKE.
til (tĭl; tēl), *n.* Also **teel.** [Hind. *til*, fr. Skr. *tila.*] Sesame.
til′bu·ry (tĭl′bĕr·ĭ), *n.; pl.* -RIES (-ĭz). [After its designer, *Tilbury*, a London coach builder.] A type of gig, or two-wheeled carriage, with or without a top.
til′de (tĭl′dĕ; -dĭ; *Sp.* tēl′dā), *n.* [Sp., fr. L. *titulus* a superscription, title, token, sign.] A diacritical mark over *n* in Spanish to form the letter *ñ*, which represents a simple palatal nasal, as in *cañon.* The same mark, called **til**, represents in Portuguese the nasalization of a vowel or diphthong, as in *lã, não, põe.*
tile (tīl), *n.* [AS. *tigle, tigele, tigule*, fr. L. *tegula* a tile.] **1.** A plate, or thin piece of fired clay, stone, concrete, or the like, used for roofing, floors, drains, etc., and often for ornamental work. Also, a piece of metal used for roofing. **2.** A plate, or thin piece of resilient material, as an asphalt composition, cork, linoleum, rubber, or the like, used for floors, walls, etc. **3.** Tiles collectively; tiling; also, an earthenware pipe used for a drain. **4.** *Colloq.* A stiff hat; esp., a high silk hat. — *v. t.* To cover with tiles.

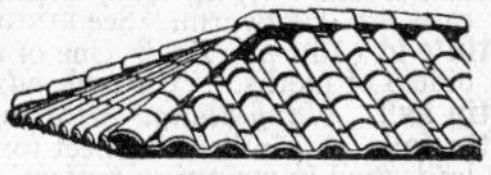
Tile Roof.

tile′fish′ (-fĭsh′), *n.; pl.*, see FISH. A large deepwater food fish (*Lopholatilus chamaeleonticeps*) covered with large yellow spots and having a fleshy appendage on the head.
til′er (tīl′ĕr), *n.* A maker or layer of tiles.
til′i·a′ceous (tĭl′ĭ·ā′shŭs), *adj.* [L. *tilia* linden.] *Bot.* Belonging to the linden family (Tiliaceae). See LINDEN.
til′ing (tīl′ĭng), *n.* **1.** The act of one who tiles. **2. a** Tiles collectively. **b** A surface of tiles. **c** Work done with tiles.
till (tĭl; 4), *prep.* [AS. (Northumbrian) *til.*] **1.** Up or down to (a specified time); as, *till* his return. **2.** *Obs. exc. Scot.* To; as far as. **3.** *Scot.* At; by; for; of; concerning. — *conj.* Up to the time when; until.
till (tĭl), *v. t. & i.* [AS. *tilian, teolian*, to aim, strive for, till.] To plow and prepare for seed, and to sow, dress, raise crops from, etc.; to cultivate. — **till′a·ble** (tĭl′ȧ·b′l), *adj.*
till, *n.* [ME. *tillen, tyllen*, to draw, pull, fr. AS. *tyllan* in *fortyllan* to draw away, lead astray.] A secret drawer or tray in a cabinet; specif., a drawer behind a counter for money, as in a shop or bank.
till, *n.* *Geol.* Unstratified glacial drift, consisting of clay, sand, gravel and boulders intermingled.
till′age (tĭl′ĭj), *n.* The operation of tilling land.
til·land′si·a (tĭ·lănd′zĭ·ȧ), *n.* [NL., after Elias *Tillands*, Sw. botanist.] *Bot.* Any of an immense genus (*Tillandsia*) of chiefly epiphytic plants of the pineapple family (Bromeliaceae), of tropical and subtropical America.
till′er (tĭl′ĕr), *n.* One who tills; a cultivator.
till′er, *n.* [OF. *tellier, telier*, fr. ML. *telarium* weaver's beam, fr. L. *tela* a web.] *Naut.* A lever used for turning the rudder from side to side.
till′er, *n.* [AS. *telgor* a small branch.] *Obs. exc. Dial.* A sprout or stalk, esp. one from the root. — *v. i. Agric.* To put forth new tillers, or shoots, as wheat and rye.
til′ly–val′ly (tĭl′ĭ·văl′ĭ; 2), *interj.* Also **til′ly–fal′ly** (-făl′ĭ). *Archaic.* Bosh; nonsense.
tilt (tĭlt), *n.* [ME. *telt*, var. of *teld*, fr. AS. *teld, geteld*, tent.] A canopy of a cart, boat, stall, etc. — *v. t.* To cover or provide with a tilt.
tilt, *v. t.* [ME. *tilten, tulten*, to totter, fall.] **1.** To cause to slope; to incline; tip. **2.** [From TILT encounter.] **a** To point or thrust in or as in a tilt. **b** To make a tilt or rush at; to charge against. — *v. i.* **1.** To move or shift so as to lean or incline; to tip; also, to slant; slope. **2.** [From TILT encounter.] To engage in a tilt, or combat with lances; to joust. — *n.* **1.** A military exercise on horseback, in which two combatants charging with lances, spears, or the like, try to unhorse each other; also, a tournament, or series of tilts. **2.** Hence: **a** Any encounter in which opponents attack each other in the manner of tilting knights. **b** Any of various sports resembling or suggesting tilting with lances. **c** A thrust; stroke. **d** An altercation; a dispute. **e** Speed; — in phrase ***at full tilt.*** **3.** The act or fact of tilting, or inclining; the state of being tilted; as, to give a board a *tilt.* **4.** Something which tilts, or slants. Specif.: **a** A slope. **b** *Local, U.S.* A seesaw. — **tilt′er**, *n.*
tilth (tĭlth), *n.* [AS., fr. *tilian* to till.] **1.** Act or occupation of tilling; cultivation of the soil. **2.** Cultivated, or tilled, land. **3.** The state of being tilled.
tilt hammer. A heavy drop hammer.
tilt′yard′ (tĭlt′yärd′), *n.* A yard or place for tilting.
tim′bal (tĭm′băl), *n.* [F. *timbale.*] A kettledrum; hence, *Zool.*, the vibrating membrane in the shrilling organ of a cicada.
tim′bale (tĭm′băl; tăN′bȧl′), *n.* [F., prop., a kettledrum; — so named from the form of the mold used.] *Cookery.* A seasoned preparation, as of chicken, lobster, cheese, or fish, cooked in a drum-shaped mold; a small pastry shell filled with a cooked mixture.
tim′ber (tĭm′bĕr), *n.* [AS., wood, building.] **1.** Material for construction; esp., wood suitable for building houses, bridges, ships, etc., whether on the tree or cut and seasoned. **2. a** A squared or dressed piece of wood, esp. one of comparatively large width and thickness, ready for use or already forming part of a structure. **b** *Eng.* Lumber (sense 2). **c** *Eng.* Sawed lumber more than 4½ in. thick and more than 6 in. wide. **3.** *U.S.* Land covered by trees from which timber (def. 1) is produced. **4.** *Shipbuilding.* A rib branching outward from the keel and bending upward in a vertical direction, usually composed of several pieces united. — *v. t.* To furnish with timber or timbers; to frame, cover, shore up, etc., with timbers. — *adj.* Of, pertaining to, or for timber. — **tim′ber·man** (-măn), *n.*
timber and a half hitch. See KNOT, *Illust.* (27).
timber cruiser. See CRUISER, *n.*, 5.
tim′bered (tĭm′bĕrd), *adj.* **1.** Furnished with, made of, or covered with, timber or timbers. **2.** Covered with growing timber; wooded.
tim′ber·head′ (tĭm′bĕr·hĕd′), *n.* *Naut.* **a** The top end of a timber, used above the gunwale, for belaying ropes, etc. **b** A bollard bolted to the deck where the end of a timber would come.
timber hitch. *Naut.* A hitch for temporarily securing a rope to a spar. See KNOT, *Illust.* (26). — **tim′ber–hitch′**, *v. t.*
tim′ber·ing, *n.* **1.** The action of one who timbers. **2.** Timbers collectively; timberwork; timber.
tim′ber·land′ (tĭm′bĕr·lănd′), *n.* Wooded land.
timber line. On mountains and in the frigid regions, the line above which there are no trees. — **tim′ber–line′**, *adj.*
timber wolf. See WOLF, 1 a.
tim′ber·work′ (tĭm′bĕr·wûrk′), *n.* Work made of timber.
tim′bre (tĭm′bĕr; *F.* tăN′br′), *n.* [OF., a bell to be struck with a hammer; hence, crest of a helmet, stamp, also (from bell), sound, tone.] **1.** Peculiar or distinctive character or tone. **2.** [F.] *Music.* The quality of tone distinguishing voices or instruments. **3.** *Phonet.* The resonance quality of a voiced speech sound, esp. a vowel.
tim′brel (tĭm′brĕl), *n.* [Dim. of ME. *timbre*, fr. OF. *timbre*, fr. L. *tympanum*, fr. Gr. *tympanon.*] *Music.* A small hand drum. See TAMBOURINE, *Illust.* — **tim′breled, tim′brelled** (-brĕld), *adj.*
time (tīm), *n.* [AS. *tīma.*] **1.** The period during which an action, process, etc., continues; measured or measurable duration. **2.** The period when something occurs; occasion; as, no one present at the *time.* **3.** The allotted, appointed, fixed, or customary moment or hour for something to happen, begin, or end. **4.** Proper season; favorable opportunity; as, now is the *time* to buy. **5.** A known, fixed, or anticipated period; hence, variously, a lifetime or the duration of gestation, a prison sentence, compulsory military service, apprenticeship, or the like. **6.** A period set apart in some way; hence, variously, a spell, a moment, a generation, an age, an era, an epoch, etc. **7.** A definite moment, hour, day, or year, as indicated or fixed by the clock or calendar. **8.** One of a number of recurring or multiplied instances, or repeated acts; a recurrent occasion; as, each *time* that it occurs; also, in *pl.*, a being multiplied or manifolded by a (specified) number; — often equivalent to a sign of multiplication (×), the number preceding it being the multiplier of the number following, or multiplicand; as, four *times* four is sixteen. **9.** Finite, as contrasted with infinite, duration; as, when *time* shall be no more. **10.** Leisure; opportunity; as, it is hard to find *time* for reading; also, in debt settlements, an extension of the customary term of credit; as, to buy goods on *time.* **11.** *Usually pl.* With *the.* Conditions prevalent at a specified period; often specif., the present state of advancement; as, behind the *times.* **12.** One's experience during a specified period or occasion; as, to have a hard *time* in a test. **13.** Reckoning of duration; system of reckoning the progress of time; as, astronomical, mean, sidereal, solar, or standard *time.* See STANDARD TIME; MEASURE, *Tables* 6 & 8. **14.** Rate of speed in marching, dancing, speaking, etc.; tempo. **15.** The length of the period required for, or consumed in, performing an action; as, the winner's *time* was 1.20. **16.** *Drama.* The unity of time. See UNITY, 6. **17.** *Geol.* Any division of geologic chronology. **18.** *Labor.* **a** The hours, days, etc., given to, or due to be given to, one's work; as, to make up *time.* **b** Amount of pay due, esp. according to the hourly rate; as, to get one's *time.* **19.** *Music.* The grouping of the successive rhythmic beats or pulses into equal measures; — called also *meter*, and *rhythm.* ***Simple time or measure*** groups the beats or time units by twos or threes and indicates this by a two or a three in the numerator of the signature, as $\frac{2}{4}$ or $\frac{3}{8}$. ***Two-part time*** (called also ***duple time or measure***) has two, or, in the United States, multiples of two units to the measure. It is simple duple time when $\frac{2}{2}$, $\frac{2}{4}$, or $\frac{2}{8}$; compound duple time when $\frac{4}{2}$, $\frac{4}{4}$, or $\frac{4}{8}$ (except in England where these are called ***quadruple time or measure*** and considered to be simple); $\frac{6}{4}$ and $\frac{6}{8}$ (***sextuple time or measure***); or $\frac{12}{8}$. ***Three-part time*** (called also ***triple time or measure***) has three units to the measure, the commonest signatures for simple triple time being $\frac{3}{2}$, $\frac{3}{4}$, and $\frac{3}{8}$, and for compound triple time $\frac{9}{4}$, $\frac{9}{8}$, and $\frac{9}{16}$. **20.** *Pros.* A unit of duration, as a basis for meter; esp., the mora. — ***at times.*** At intervals; now and then. — ***from time to time.*** Occasionally; once in a while. — ***in time.*** **a** In good or due season; sufficiently early. **b** In the course of time; eventually. **c** In correct rhythm or tempo.

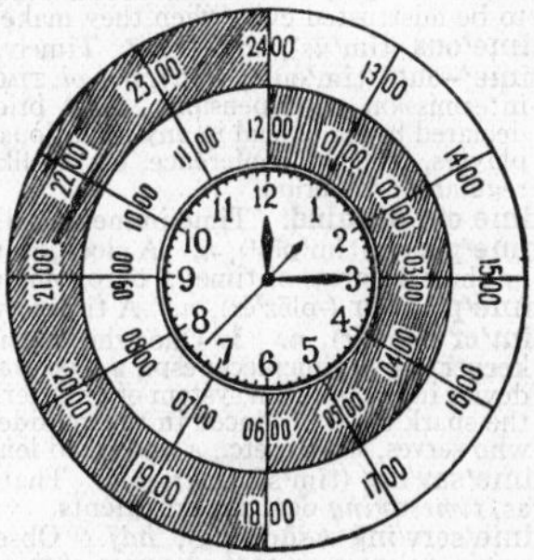
Time. A standard twelve-hour Dial surrounded by bands showing equivalent twenty-four-hour Military Time.

— *v. i. Rare.* To keep or beat time; to move in time.
— *v. t.* **1.** To arrange a time or times for; to schedule; as, he *timed* his appearance rightly. **2.** To regulate as to time; as, to *time* one's watch; to *time* one's steps to the music; also, to set the tempo for, as by beating; as, the conductor *timed* the performance admirably. **3.** To give metrical or rhythmical value to (syllables, notes, etc.). **4.** To ascertain or record the time, duration, or rate, of; as, to *time* the speed of horses.
— *adj.* **1.** Of or pertaining to time. **2.** Timed so as to ignite, explode, etc., at a given moment; as, a *time* fuse. **3.** *Com.* **a** Of a draft (**time draft**), note (**time note**), etc., payable on a future day or a certain length of time after sight. **b** Of a transaction, made with the understanding that time, or extended terms, will be given for settlement; as, a *time* purchase.
time bill. *Finance.* A bill of exchange payable at a definite future time.
time′card′ (tīm′kärd′), *n.* A card on which is kept a daily record of the time one has worked or the time of one's arrival and departure.
time clock. A clock with a device to record the times of arrival and departure of employees.
time deposit. *Banking.* A bank deposit payable at a definite future date, or upon advance notice to the bank.

time discount. *Com.* A reduction in an invoice price in consideration of payment within a specified time.
time exposure. *Photog.* Exposure for a definite time, usually more than one half second; also, a photograph taken by such exposure. — **time′-ex·po′sure,** *adj.*
time′-hon′ored, *or* **-hon′oured** (tīm′ŏn′ẽrd), *adj.* Honored or revered because of age or long-established usage.
time immemorial. **a** *Eng. Law.* A time antedating (legal) history, in 1276 fixed by statute as the beginning of the reign of Richard I (1189). **b** Time so long past as to be indefinite in history or tradition.
time′keep′er (tīm′kēp′ẽr), *n.* One who or that which keeps, marks, measures, regulates, or determines the time.
time′less, *adj.* **1.** *Archaic.* Untimely; premature. **2.** Having no beginning or end; unending; eternal. **3.** Not restricted to a particular time or date; undated; dateless.
time loan. *Finance.* A loan with a definite maturity date; — in contrast to a *demand loan.*
time′ly (tīm′lĭ), *adv.* *Archaic.* Early; soon; opportunely. — *adj.;* -LI·ER (-lĭ·ẽr); -LI·EST. **a** *Rare.* Showing itself in good time; early. **b** Seasonably or opportunely timed; as, a *timely* joke. — **Syn.** See SEASONABLE. — **time′li·ness,** *n.*
time money. A time loan.
||**ti′me·o Da′na·os et do′na fe·ren′tes** (tĭm′ē·ō dăn′ā·ŏs ĕt dō′nȧ fē·rĕn′tēz). [L.] I fear the Greeks even bringing gifts; hence, foes are to be mistrusted even when they make friendly advances.
time′ous (tīm′ŭs), *adj.* *Scot.* Timely.
time′-out′ (tīm′out′; -out′), *n.; pl.* TIME-OUTS (-outs′; -outs′). **1.** An intermission or suspension. **2.** A brief period of suspension of play declared by an official in any of various organized sports, as for rest of players, officials' conference, or the like. **3.** Time taken off from a regular work period.
time out of mind. Time immemorial.
time′piece′ (tīm′pēs′), *n.* A clock, watch, or other device to measure or show progress of time; a chronometer.
time′pleas′er (-plēz′ẽr), *n.* A timeserver.
tim′er (tīm′ẽr), *n.* **1.** One who or that which times; as: **a** A timekeeper. **b** A timepiece; esp., a stop watch for timing races, etc. **c** A device in the ignition system of an internal-combustion engine, causing the spark to be produced in the cylinder at the correct time. **2.** One who serves, works, etc., a (specified length of) time.
time′sav′ing (tīm′sāv′ĭng), *adj.* That expedites the matter in hand; as, *timesaving* devices, expedients.
time′serv′ing (-sûr′vĭng), *adj.* Obsequiously complying with the spirit of the times, or the humors of those in power. — **time′serv′er,** *n.* — **time′serv′ing,** *n.*
time signature. *Music.* A sign placed after the key signature to indicate the time.
time′ta′ble (tīm′tā′b'l), *n.* A tabular statement of the time at which, or within which, things are to take place; specif., a sheet giving times, etc., of trains.
time′work′ (-wûrk′), *n.* Work paid for by the hour or the day. — **time′work′er** (-wûr′kẽr), *n.*
time′worn′ (-wōrn′), *adj.* Worn or impaired by time; hence, antiquated; out-of-date.
time zone. A geographical region within which the same standard time is used. See STANDARD TIME.
tim′id (tĭm′ĭd), *adj.* [L. *timidus,* fr. *timere* to fear.] Feeling or evincing want of courage or self-confidence; not bold; fearful. — **tim′id·ly,** *adv.* — **tim′id·ness,** *n.*
Syn. Timid, timorous mean hesitating apprehensively. **Timid** implies fearfulness of venturing into the unknown or uncertain; **timorous,** a habitual shrinking from any action or activity which requires independence, self-assertiveness, etc.
ti·mid′i·ty (tĭ·mĭd′ĭ·tĭ), *n.* Quantity, state, or manifestation, of being timid.
tim′ing (tīm′ĭng), *n.* **1.** The art or practice of regulating the tempo in musical performance, utterance, etc., so as to heighten the effectiveness of certain moments; also, the effect so produced. **2.** *Athletics & Sports.* The regulating of the speed of a motion, stroke, blow, etc., so as to cause it to reach its maximum at the correct moment.
ti·moc′ra·cy (tī·mŏk′rȧ·sĭ), *n.* [OF. *tymocracie,* fr. ML., fr. Gr. *timokratia,* fr. *timē* honor, worth, value. See -CRACY.] *Polit. Sci.* **a** As defined by Plato, a state in which love of honor or glory is the ruling principle. **b** As derived from Aristotle, a state in which political and civil honors are distributed according to a rating of property. — **ti′mo·crat′ic** (tī′mō·krăt′ĭk), **ti′mo·crat′i·cal** (-ĭ·kăl), *adj.*
tim′or·ous (tĭm′ẽr·ŭs), *adj.* [OF. *timoureus, temerous,* fr. LL. *timorosus,* fr. L. *timor* fear.] **1.** Full of fear or fears; timid. **2.** Indicating, or caused by, timidity; as, *timorous* doubts. — **Syn.** See TIMID. — **tim′or·ous·ly,** *adv.* — **tim′or·ous·ness,** *n.*
Tim′o·thy (tĭm′ō·thĭ), *n.* [L. *Timotheus,* fr. Gr. *Timotheos.*] **1.** *Bib.* **a** A convert, and later a colleague, of St. Paul. **b** Either of the two Epistles to Timothy in the New Testament. See BIBLE. **2.** [*not cap.*] [After *Timothy* Hanson, who carried the seed from New York to Carolina about 1720.] A grass (*Phleum pratense*) with long cylindrical spikes, grown for hay; — called also **timothy grass.**
tim′pa·ni (tĭm′pȧ·nē), *n. pl.; sing.* TIM′PA·NO (-nō). [It. See TYMPANUM.] *Music.* Kettledrums; esp., a set of them played by the same performer. — **tim′pa·nist** (-nĭst), *n.*
tin (tĭn), *n.* [AS.] **1.** A soft, faintly bluish-white crystalline metal, malleable at ordinary temperatures, but brittle when heated. Symbol, *Sn* (Latin *stannum*); at. no., 50; at. wt., 118.70. Sp. gr., 7.3. **2.** Thin plates of iron or steel covered with tin; tin plate. **3.** A box, can, pan, or other vessel of tin plate; as, a pie *tin;* specif., *Brit.,* a hermetically sealed can of tin plate for foodstuffs such as preserves. **4.** *Slang.* Money. — *v. t.;* TINNED (tĭnd); TIN′NING. **1.** To cover or coat with tin. **2.** To put in a tin or tins; to preserve by sealing in tins. Cf. CAN, *v. t.,* 1. — **tin,** *adj.*
tin′a·mou (tĭn′ȧ·mōō), *n.* [F., fr. *tinamu,* the Carib name in Guiana.] Any of numerous birds (family Tinamidae, order Tinamiformes) resembling gallinaceous birds in habits, but related to the ratite birds. They are chiefly South American and are hunted as game birds.
tin′cal (tĭng′käl; -kôl), *n.* [Malay *tinkal.*] Crude native borax, formerly imported from Tibet.
tinct (tĭngkt), *adj.* [L. *tinctus,* past part. of *tingere* to tinge.] *Poetic.* Tinged; tinted; also, delicately flavored. — *v. t. Obs.* **a** To color or tinge; to tint. **b** To imbue, as with a substance, quality, etc.; to impregnate. — *n. Poetic.* Color; tint.
tinc·to′ri·al (tĭngk·tō′rĭ·ăl; 70), *adj.* [L. *tinctorius,* fr. *tinctor* a dyer, fr. *tingere, tinctum,* to dye.] Of or relating to color or colors, or to dyeing or staining.
tinc′ture (tĭngk′tụ̂r), *n.* [L. *tinctura* a dyeing, fr. *tingere.* See TINGE.] **1.** *Poetic.* A substance which colors, dyes, or stains. **2.** A slight trace; vestige. **3.** *Obs.* An active principle of a substance. **4.** *Her.* Any of the metals or colors used in armorial bearings. **5.** *Pharm.* A solution of a medicinal substance in an alcoholic menstruum. — *v. t.* **1.** To stain with a color; to tinge. **2.** To imbue (something) with a quality foreign to it; to impart a flavor, odor, etc., to.
tin′der (tĭn′dẽr), *n.* [AS. *tynder, tyndre.*] Something very inflammable, as esp. for kindling fire from a spark.
tin′der·box′ (-bŏks′), *n.* **1.** A metal box in which tinder is kept, usually with a flint and steel for striking a spark. **2.** A person or thing suggestive of a tinderbox in inflammability.
tin′der·y (tĭn′dẽr·ĭ), *adj.* Like tinder; highly inflammable.
tine (tīn), *n.* [AS. *tind.*] A tooth, as of a fork; a prong, as of an antler.
tine, *v. t. & i.; past & past part.* TINT. [ON. *tyna.*] *Now Dial.* To lose or be lost.
tin′e·a (tĭn′ē·ȧ), *n.* [L., worm, moth.] *Med.* Any fungus skin disease, esp. ringworm. See RINGWORM, SYCOSIS.
tin′e·id (-ĭd), *n.* *Zool.* One of a family (Tineidae, superfamily Tineoidea) of moths. — **tin′e·id,** *adj.*
tin fish. *Navy Slang.* A torpedo.
tin foil. **a** Tin in thin sheet form. **b** A similar thin sheet of tin and lead, used in wrapping confections, etc. — **tin′-foil′,** *adj.*
ting (tĭng), *n.* [Imitative.] A high-pitched sound, as is made by a light stroke on glass. — *v. t. & i.;* TINGED (tĭngd); TING′ING (tĭng′ĭng). To make, or cause to make, a ting or tings.
||**ting** (tĭng). Var. of 2d THING.
tinge (tĭnj), *v. t.;* TINGED (tĭnjd); TINGE′ING OR TING′ING (tĭn′jĭng). [L. *tingere, tinctum,* to dye, stain, wet.] **1.** To impart a tint to; to color slightly. **2.** To impart a trace of one's characteristic flavor, odor, etc., to. — *n.* A slight coloring, cast, flavor, quality, or the like, taken from or imparted by something else; a smack; trace; as, a *tinge* of red. — **Syn.** See COLOR.
tin′gle (tĭng′g'l), *v. i.;* TIN′GLED (-g'ld); TIN′GLING (-glĭng). [See TINKLE, TING.] **1.** To feel a ringing, stinging, prickling, or thrilling sensation, as from a shrill sound, cold, etc. **2.** To cause a thrilling, stinging, or prickling sensation. — *n.* A tingling sensation or condition; as, to feel a *tingle* in the cheek. — **tin′gler** (-glẽr), *n.*
tin hat. *Slang.* A soldier's steel helmet.
tin′horn′ (tĭn′hôrn′; 2), *adj.* *Slang.* Having little money, power, or ability, though often pretending to have these; cheap and flashy; as, a *tinhorn* gambler. — **tin′horn′,** *n.*
tink′er (tĭngk′ẽr), *n.* **1.** A mender of kettles, pans, etc., esp. an itinerant one. **2.** A botcher; a bungler. **3.** Act of tinkering; an unskillful attempt to mend or improve. **4.** Any of various fishes; as: **a** A young mackerel. **b** A silversides. — *v. i.* **1.** To work in the manner of a tinker. **2.** To make futile attempts to mend, repair, or improve; to potter fruitlessly. — *v. t.* To mend as a tinker, esp. in a makeshift, botching manner. — **tink′er·er,** *n.*
tink′er's damn *or* **dam** (tĭngk′ẽrz). [*tinker* + *damn,* n.] Something absolutely worthless; as, not worth a *tinker's damn.*
tin′kle (tĭng′k'l), *v. i.;* TIN′KLED (-k'ld); TIN′KLING (-klĭng). [Freq. of TINK.] To make, or emit, a series of short, thin, clinking notes, as of small bells. — *v. t.* **1.** To cause to give forth tinkles; as, to *tinkle* the keys of a piano. **2.** To sound or express with tinkles; as, small clocks *tinkled* the hours. — *n.* A tinkling sound, as from a small bell.
tin′kling (tĭng′klĭng), *n.* A tinkle, or series of tinkles.
tin′man (tĭn′măn), *n.* See TINSMITH.
tin′ner (tĭn′ẽr), *n.* **a** A tin miner. **b** A tinsmith.
tin·ni′tus (tĭ·nī′tŭs), *n.* [L., fr. *tinnire* to jingle.] *Med.* A ringing, whistling, or other sensation of noise, which is purely subjective.
tin′ny (tĭn′ĭ), *adj.;* TIN′NI·ER (-ĭ·ẽr); TIN′NI·EST. **1.** Of, abounding in, or yielding tin. **2.** Like tin; specif.: **a** Thin, hard, and brittle. **b** Thin in quality, as a voice. — **tin′ni·ly,** *adv.* — **tin′ni·ness,** *n.*
tin′-pan′, tin′-pan′ny, *adj.* Sounding like the noise made by striking a tin pan; harsh.
tin-pan alley. A street or district frequented by musicians, esp. theatrical musicians; hence, a district devoted to the interests of composers and players of popular music; also, the body of such musicians.
tin plate. Thin sheet iron or steel coated with tin.
tin′-plate′, *v. t.* To plate or coat with tin. — **tin plater.**
tin pyrites. See PYRITES.
tin′sel (tĭn′sĕl; -s'l), *n.* [F. *étincelle* a spark, OF. *estincelle.*] **1.** Also **tinsel cloth, satin,** etc. *Hist.* A fabric with a glittering surface of interwoven gold, silver, or other bright metallic threads. **2.** A shining, metallic or metal-coated, material used in thin strips, threads, etc., to produce a sparkling appearance at small expense, as in needlework. **3.** Something having the glitter but not the worth of gold; false show. — *adj.* **1.** Made of or covered with tinsel. **2.** Cheaply gaudy; tawdry. — *v. t.;* TIN′SELED (-sĕld; -s'ld) or TIN′SELLED; TIN′SEL·ING or TIN′SEL·LING. To interweave, overlay, or adorn, with or as with tinsel; to make tawdry or specious.
tin′smith′ (tĭn′smĭth′), *n.* Also **tin′man** (tĭn′măn), **tins′man** (tĭnz′măn). A worker in tin or tin plate.
tin spirit. *Dyeing.* Any of various solutions of tin compounds used as mordants.
tin′stone′ (tĭn′stōn′), *n.* The mineral cassiterite.
tint (tĭnt), *n.* [For older *tinct,* fr. L. *tinctus* a dyeing, dipping, fr. *tingere* to dye.] **1.** A slight coloring. **2.** A tinge; specif., a faint tinge of any hue. **3.** A color gradation with reference esp. to the amount of white in the mixture; as, to mix blue paint until it is several *tints* lighter. **4.** *Colors.* A color which, with respect to brilliance only, resembles white more closely than median gray resembles white; — contrasted with *shade* (def. 4 **a**). **5.** *Engraving.* A shaded effect produced by fine parallel lines close together. **6.** *Print.* A light-colored surface serving as a background. — **Syn.** See COLOR. — *v. t.* To impart or apply a tint to; to tinge. — **tint′er,** *n.*
tint, *past & past part.* of TINE.
tin′tin·nab′u·lar′y (tĭn′tĭ·năb′ū·lẽr′ĭ *or, esp. Brit.,* -lẽr·ĭ), *adj.* Also **tin′tin·nab′u·lar** (-lẽr). [L. *tintinnabulum* a little bell, fr. *tintinnare* to ring, jingle, fr. *tinnire* to jingle.] Of or pertaining to bells or their sounds; tinkling.
tin′tin·nab′u·la′tion (-lā′shŭn), *n.* The ringing of bells; a tinkling or jingling sound, as of a bell or bells.

tin′tin·nab′u·lous (tĭn′tĭ·năb′ū·lŭs), *adj.* Tintinnabulary.
tin′type′ (tĭn′tīp′), *n.* *Photog.* A ferrotype.
tin′ware′ (tĭn′wâr′), *n.* Articles made of tin plate.
tin′work′ (tĭn′wûrk′), *n.* **1.** Work in tin. **2.** *Usually pl. in form but construed as sing.* An establishment where tin is smelted, rolled, or otherwise treated.
ti′ny (tī′nĭ), *adj.*; TI′NI·ER (-nĭ·ẽr); TI′NI·EST. [ME. *tine.*] Very small or diminutive; minute. — **Syn.** See SMALL.
-tion (-shŭn). [F., OF., or L.; OF. *-cion* (F. *-tion*), fr. L. *-tio, -tionis.*] A suffix forming nouns from verbs and denoting *action, state,* and *concrete instance* or *result.* Corresponding adjectives are formed in **-tious** (see -IOUS). Of similar origin and meaning are **-sion** and **-xion.**
tip (tĭp), *v. t. & i.*; TIPPED (tĭpt); TIP′PING. [ME. *type,* of uncert. origin.] **1.** To overturn; upset. **2.** To incline or slant; to tilt. — *n.* **1.** A tipped position; a tilt. **2.** A place where material is dumped, as from wagons; as, a coal *tip;* a rubbish *tip.*
tip, *n.* [ME.] **1.** The pointed end of anything; an end; also, apex; summit. **2.** An end piece or part, as a cap, nozzle, ferrule, etc. — *v. t.*; TIPPED (tĭpt) or, *Rare,* TIPT; TIP′PING. To form a tip or point upon; to cover or adorn the tip or end of.
tip, *v. t.* [Cf. LG. *tippen* to tap, and TIP a point.] **1.** To strike lightly; to tap. **2.** In cricket, baseball, etc., to hit (the ball) a glancing blow with the edge of the bat; to snick. **3.** *Slang.* To perform, sing, or act, for; as, now *tip* us a song. **4.** *Colloq.* To give a tip, or hint, to, esp. secretly or stealthily. **5.** To give a fee, or gratuity, to. — *v. i.* To give a gratuity or gratuities. — *n.* **1.** A light blow; a tap. **2.** A bit of information such as a clue, hint, or warning; a pointer. **3.** A small gift of money; esp., a gratuity, as to a waiter.
ti palm. = 2d TI.
tip′cat′ (tĭp′kăt′), *n.* A game in which a small pointed stick (the *cat*) is struck lightly with a stick or bat, so as to fly into the air and while there is struck by the same player so as to drive it as far as possible; also, sometimes, the cat.
tip′cart′ (tĭp′kärt′), *n.*, **tip car, tip truck,** etc. A cart, car, truck, etc., whose body can be tipped on the frame to empty its contents.
ti′pi (tē′pē). Var. of TEPEE.
tip′-off′, *n.* A tipping off; esp., a timely warning.
tip′pet (tĭp′ĕt; -ĭt), *n.* [ME. *tipet, tippet,* prob. dim. of *tip, tippe,* a point.] **1.** *Hist.* A long hanging part or adjunct of the dress, as on a sleeve, cape, or hood. **2.** A scarf or scarflike garment of fur, cloth, etc. **3.** *Ch. of Eng.* A long black scarf, the distinguishing ecclesiastical vestment of the clergy in choir.
tip′ple (tĭp′′l), *v. t.*; -PLED (-′ld); -PLING (-lĭng). To drink, as liquor, often or in small quantities. — *v. i.* To indulge in intoxicating drinks habitually and often. — *n.* Liquor; drink. — **tip′pler** (-lẽr), *n.*
tip′ple, *n.* *U. S.* **1.** An apparatus by which loaded cars are emptied by tipping. **2.** The place where such tipping is done; specif., a coal-screening plant.
tip′staff′ (tĭp′stȧf′), *n.*; *pl.* -STAVES (-stāvz′; -stȧvz′). An officer who bears a staff; a constable or bailiff.
tip′ster (tĭp′stẽr), *n.* [*tip* a hint + *-ster.*] *Colloq.* One who gives or sells tips, esp. for gambling.
tip′sy (tĭp′sĭ), *adj.*; TIP′SI·ER (-sĭ·ẽr); TIP′SI·EST. [From TIP to lean, tilt.] **1.** Being under the influence of strong drink; unsteady, staggering, or foolish, from the effects of liquor, but not absolutely drunk; fuddled. **2.** Unsteady; askew; as, a *tipsy* angle. — **Syn.** See DRUNK. — **tip′si·ly,** *adv.* — **tip′si·ness,** *n.*
tip′toe′ (tĭp′tō′), *n.*; *pl.* -TOES (-tōz′). The tip, or end, of a toe; also, the ends of the toes collectively. — ***on tiptoe*** *or* ***a-tiptoe.*** Raised on the tips of the toes, esp. so as to see better; hence, roused; alert. — *v. i.*; TIP′TOED′ (-tōd′); TIP′TOE′ING. To go, step, or walk, on one's tiptoes. — *adj.* **1.** Standing or as if standing on tiptoe; hence, lifted up; exalted; also, alert; eager. **2.** Cautious; stealthy. — *adv.* On, or as on, tiptoe; expectantly; eagerly; also, quietly; warily.
tip′top′ (tĭp′tŏp′), *n.* [*tip* end + *top.*] The very top; the best. — (-tŏp′; 2), *adj.* At the top point; of highest station, quality, etc.; often, *Colloq.*, in the best of health, spirits, etc.; as, in *tiptop* condition. — **tip′top′** (-tŏp′; 2), *adv.*
ti′rade (tī′rād; tĭ·rād′; *now rarely* tĭ·räd′), *n.* [F., fr. It. *tirata* volley, drawing.] A long-drawn speech or declamatory passage, esp. one marked by intemperate language.
‖**ti′rail′leur′** (tē′rȧ′yûr′; *E.* tĭr′ȧ·lûr′), *n.* [F., fr. *tirailler* to skirmish, wrest, fr. *tirer* to draw, fire.] *Mil.* In the French army, an infantry skirmisher. See TURCO.
tire (tīr), *v. t.* [AS. *tȳrian, tīerian, tīorian.*] **1.** To exhaust or greatly decrease the physical strength of, as by exertion; to weary; fatigue. **2.** To wear out the patience, attention, or liking, of; to bore utterly. — *v. i.* To become weary.
Syn. **Tire, weary, fatigue, exhaust, jade, fag** mean to make or become disinclined or unable to continue. **Tire** implies a draining of one's strength or patience; **weary,** an incapacity for enduring more of the same thing; **fatigue,** great lassitude brought on by overstrain or undue effort; **exhaust,** a complete draining of one's strength; **jade,** a loss of all freshness and spirit; **fag,** a drooping with fatigue.
— *n. Dial.* Tiredness; fatigue; weariness.
tire, *v. t. & i.* [F. *tirer* to draw or pull.] *Obs.* **a** To seize, pull, or tear, as a hawk preying. **b** To be intent (upon) in thought.
tire, *v. t.* [Aphetic for *attire.*] *Archaic.* To attire; to dress, as the hair. — *n.* **1.** *Archaic.* Attire; dress. **2.** *Archaic.* A lady's headdress.
tire, *n.* Also, *Chiefly Brit.,* **tyre.** [So called as being an attire or covering for the wheel.] A hoop or band forming the tread of a vehicle wheel. The pneumatic tire for a bicycle or automobile serves primarily to reduce shock. — *v. t.* To put a tire on.
tire (tīr), *n.* [F. *tir.*] *Obs.* A discharge (of cannon).
tired (tīrd), *adj.* Weary; fatigued. — **tired′ly,** *adv.* — **tired′ness,** *n.*
tire′less (tīr′lĕs; -lĭs), *adj.* Untiring; unwearying. — **tire′less·ly,** *adv.* — **tire′less·ness,** *n.*

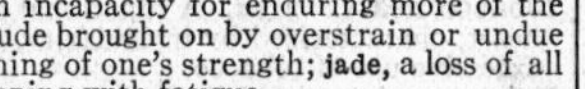

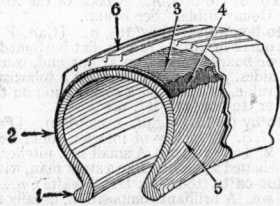

Fabric Tire (cross-section cutaway). 1 Bead; 2 Side Wall; 3 Breaker Strip; 4 Cushion; 5 Carcass; 6 Tread.

Ti·re′si·as (tī·rē′sĭ·ăs; -shĭ·ăs), *n.* [L., fr. Gr. *Teiresias.*] *Gr. Myth.* A blind Theban soothsayer to whom Athena gave knowledge of future events and of birds' language.
tire′some (tīr′sŭm), *adj.* Wearisome; tedious. — **tire′some·ly,** *adv.* — **tire′some·ness,** *n.*
tire′wom′an (-wŏŏm′ăn), *n.* *Archaic.* A lady's maid.
tir′ing room (tīr′ĭng). [For *attiring room.*] *Archaic.* A dressing room, esp. one in a theater.
tirl (tûrl), *v. t. & i.* *Scot.* To pluck a string; to vibrate. — *n.* *Scot.* A thrill or vibration.
ti′ro (tī′rō). Var. of TYRO.
tir′ri·vee (tûr′ĭ·vē), *n.* *Scot.* A tantrum; commotion.
'tis (tĭz; 4). A contraction of *it is.*
ti·sane′ (tē·zăn′; *F.* tē′zȧn′), *n.* [F.] *Pharm.* A decoction, or medicinal tea; a ptisan; — used in French pharmacy.
Tish′ah b'ab′ (tĭsh′ä bĕ·äv′) *or* **bov** (bŏv). See JEWISH HOLIDAYS.
Tish′ri (tĭsh′rē), *n.* [LHeb., fr. Aram. *Tishri.*] See JEWISH CALENDAR.
tis′sue (tĭsh′ū; -ōō), *n.* [OF. *tissu,* fr. *tissu,* past part. of *tistre* to weave, fr. L. *texere.*] **1.** A woven fabric; esp., a sheer fabric, usually of silk; a fine gauze. **2.** An interwoven number of things; a meshwork; a web; as, a *tissue* of lies. **3.** *Biol.* An aggregate of cells, with their intercellular substance, forming one of the structural materials of a plant or animal; as, epithelial *tissue;* nervous *tissue;* muscular *tissue;* connective *tissue.* **4.** *Paper Mfg.* Short for TISSUE PAPER. — *v. t.* *Rare.* To weave or interweave.
tissue paper. Gauzelike paper, used to protect engravings in books, to wrap up delicate articles, etc.
tit (tĭt), *n.* **1.** A small or inferior horse; a nag; jade. **2.** *Slang.* A girl or woman; — often in disrespect.
tit, *n.* [From TITMOUSE.] A titmouse; also, by extension, any of various other small birds, as the Asiatic ***hill tit*** (of the genus *Siva, Leiothrix,* or allied genera).
tit, *n.* A tap; a return blow; — chiefly in *tit for tat.*
tit, *n.* [AS. *tit, titt.*] A teat; nipple.
Ti′tan (tī′tăn), *n.* [L., fr. Gr. *Titan.*] **1.** *Gr. Myth.* One of the primeval deities, children of Uranus and Gaea. The great event in Titan history was the **Ti′tan·om′a·chy** (-ŏm′ȧ·kĭ), or war with the Olympian gods in Thessaly, which resulted in the overthrow of the Titan dynasty. **2.** The sun personified; — from Helios, the sun-god, being called *Titan* by Latin poets. **3.** [*not cap.*] One gigantic in size or power. — *adj.* [*often not cap.*] Titanic. — **Ti′tan·ess** (-ĕs; -ĭs), *n.*
ti′tan·ate (tī′tăn·āt), *n.* *Chem.* A salt or ester of titanic acid.
Ti′tan·esque′ (tī′tăn·ĕsk′), *adj.* Titanic.
Ti·ta′ni·a (tĭ·tā′nĭ·ȧ; tī-), *n.* The wife of Oberon, and queen of the fairies, in Shakespeare's *Midsummer Night's Dream.*
Ti·tan′ic (tī·tăn′ĭk), *adj.* **1.** Of, pertaining to, characteristic of, or like the Titans. **2.** [*usually not cap.*] Of enormous magnitude, force, or power.
ti·tan′ic (tī·tăn′ĭk; tĭ-), *adj.* *Chem. & Mineral.* Of, pert. to, or containing titanium, esp. in its higher valence. Cf. TITANOUS.
titanic acid. *Chem.* **a** Any of various feeble acids derived from titanium dioxide. **b** A compound, **titanium dioxide,** *or* **titanic oxide,** TiO_2, occurring as rutile, octahedrite, and brookite, and used as a pigment and mordant.
ti′tan·if′er·ous (tī′tăn·ĭf′ẽr·ŭs), *adj.* [*titanium* + *-ferous.*] Containing or affording titanium.
Ti′tan·ism (tī′tăn·ĭz′m), *n.* The quality or spirit of a Titan, esp. that of defiance and revolt, as against social or artistic conventions.
ti′tan·ite (tī′tăn·īt), *n.* [*titanium* + *-ite.*] *Mineral.* A mineral, essentially a calcium silicate and titanate, $CaTiSiO_5$, commonly a constituent of igneous rocks.
ti·ta′ni·um (tī·tā′nĭ·ŭm; tĭ-), *n.* [NL., fr. L. *Titani* or *Titanes,* fr. Gr. *Titanes,* the sons of earth.] *Chem.* A metal resembling silicon and found only in combination, in ilmenite and rutile. Symbol, *Ti;* at. no., 22; at. wt., 47.90; sp. gr., 4.5; melting point, 1800° C. (3272° F.).
ti′tan·o·saur′ (tī′tăn·ō·sôr′), *n.* [NL., fr. *Titan,* denoting *titanic* + *-saurus.*] *Paleontol.* Any of a genus (*Titanosaurus*) of large herbivorous, probably amphibious, dinosaurs widely distributed in the Cretaceous of South America, southern Asia, and, rarely, Europe.
ti·tan′ous (tī·tăn′ŭs; tī′tăn-), *adj.* *Chem.* Designating certain compounds of titanium in its lower valence. Cf. TITANIC.
tit′bit′ (tĭt′bĭt′), *n.* [See 1st TIT; BIT.] A delicate piece of anything eatable; a choice morsel; a tidbit.
ti′ter, ti′tre (tī′tẽr; tē′tẽr), *n.* [F. *titre.*] *Chem., Immunol., & Physiol.* **a** The strength of a solution or concentration of a substance in solution as determined by titration. **b** The minimum amount or volume required to bring about a given result in titration.
tit for tat. [Prob. for *tip for tap.*] Blow for blow; an equivalent; retaliation.
tith′a·ble (tīth′ȧ·b′l), *adj.* Subject to tithes.
tithe (tīth), *v. t.* [AS. *tēothian.* See TITHE, *n.*] **1.** To pay or give a tenth part of, esp. for the support of the church. **2.** To tax to the amount of a tenth. — *n.* [ME. *tithe, tethe,* properly an adj., tenth, fr. AS. *tēotha, tēogetha,* tenth.] A tenth part, or loosely, a small part; esp., *Brit.*, a tenth part of the yearly increase arising from the profits of land, stock, or personal industry, paid, in kind or money, to the church or for religious or charitable uses; hence, any small ratable tax or levy. — **tith′er** (tīth′ẽr), *n.*
tith′ing (tīth′ĭng), *n.* **1.** A paying, levying, or taking of tithes. **2.** A tithe. **3.** *English Law.* A small administrative division preserved in parts of England, apparently originally consisting of ten men with their families.
Ti·tho′nus (tĭ·thō′nŭs), *n.* [L., fr. Gr. *Tithōnos.*] *Gr. Myth.* Son of Laomedon, King of Troy, the favorite of Eos (Aurora), who prevailed on the gods to grant him immortality, but forgot to ask for him immortal youth. He grew old, and was finally changed by Eos into a grasshopper.
ti·ti′ (tē·tē′), *n.* [Sp. *tití,* fr. Guarani *titi.*] Any of various small South American monkeys (genus *Callicebus*).
ti′ti (tē′tē), *n.* **a** A tree (*Cliftonia monophylla,* family Cyrillaceae) of the southern United States, having glossy leaves and racemes of fragrant white flowers. **b** Any of a genus (*Cyrilla*) of related trees, often disting. as ***white titi.***
ti′tian (tĭsh′ăn; tĭsh′ĭ-), *n.* A color, used by Titian, red-yellow in hue, of high saturation and medium brilliance. See COLOR.

tit′il·late (tĭt′ĭ·lāt), *v. t. & i.* [L. *titillatus*, past part. of *titillare*.] To tickle; hence, to excite pleasurably. — **tit′il·la′tion** (-lā′shŭn), *n.* — **tit′il·la′tive** (-lā′tĭv), *adj.*

tit′i·vate, tit′ti·vate (tĭt′ĭ·vāt), *v. t. & i.* *Humorous.* To dress or smarten up; to spruce. — **tit′i·va′tion, tit′ti·va′tion** (-vā′shŭn), *n.*

tit′lark′ (tĭt′lärk′), *n.* [See 1st TIT; LARK.] A pipit.

ti′tle (tī′t'l), *n.* [OF., fr. L. *titulus* an inscription, label, title, sign, token.] **1.** *Archaic.* A placard. **2.** *Law.* **a** The union of all the elements which constitute ownership. **b** That which constitutes a just cause of exclusive possession. **c** The instrument which is evidence of a right. **3.** A claim; right; as, his services give him a *title* to our gratitude. **4.** A division of an instrument or book, usually one larger than a *section* or *article*, as of a statute or lawbook. **5.** The distinctive designation of a written or printed production, as a book, usually placed at the beginning, on a page by itself. **6.** A descriptive name; an appellation. **7.** An appellation of dignity, distinction, or pre-eminence given to persons by virtue of rank, office, or privilege, or as a mark of respect. **8.** *Eccl.* **a** *R.C.Ch.* A parish church or parish, esp. one in or near Rome, of which a cardinal is a titular head. **b** A sphere of work or source of income or maintenance, required by a bishop of a candidate for ordination. **9.** *Law.* **a** The heading forming the name of an act or statute. **b** *Pleading.* The heading which forms the distinctive designation of an action or proceeding. **10.** *Sports.* Championship; as, to win the *title.* — *v. t.;* TI′TLED (-t'ld); TI′TLING (-tlĭng). To call by a title; to name; designate.

ti′tled (tī′t'ld), *adj.* Having a title, esp. one of nobility.

title deed. *Law.* The deed constituting the muniments or evidences of a person's ownership.

ti′tle·hold′er (tī′t'l·hōl′dẽr), *n.* Also **ti′tlist** (tī′tlĭst). One who holds a title; specif., a champion.

title page. The page of a book, etc., on which is its title.

title role *or* **part.** The role that gives the title to a play, opera, etc.

tit′mouse′ (tĭt′mous′), *n.; pl.* -MICE (-mīs′). [ME. *titemose, titmase*, fr. *tit* small thing + AS. *māse* titmouse. The Eng. form has been influenced by the unrelated word *mouse.*] Any of numerous small oscine birds (genus *Parus* and allied genera, family Paridae) allied to the nuthatches but longer-tailed. The ***tufted titmouse*** (*Baeolophus bicolor*) of eastern United States, ashy gray with a pointed crest, and the chickadees are well-known species. Called also *tomtit.* Cf. 2d TIT.

Ti′to·ism (tē′tō·ĭz'm), *n.* National spirit and independence of action exercised by a communist state in resistance to domination by the U.S.S.R.; — after the stand taken by Yugoslavia under Tito (see BROZ, in *Biog.*).

ti′trate (tī′trāt; tĭt′rāt), *v. t. & i.* [F. *titrer*, fr. *titre* standard, title.] To subject to, or undergo, titration.

ti·tra′tion (tī·trā′shŭn; tĭ-), *n.* *Chem., Immunol., & Physiol.* A method, or the process, of determining the strength of a solution, or the concentration of a substance in solution, in terms of the smallest amount of it required to bring about a given effect in reaction with another known solution or substance.

ti′tre (tī′tẽr; tē′tẽr). Var. of TITER.

tit′tat·to′ (tĭt′tăt·tō′; -tōō′), **tit′tat·toe′, tit′tat·too′.** Vars. of TICKTACKTOE.

tit′ter (tĭt′ẽr), *v. i.* To laugh with convulsive efforts at suppression; snicker. — *n.* A tittering; partly stifled laugh. — **tit′ter·er,** *n.* — **tit′ter·ing·ly,** *adv.*

tit′tie, tit′ty (tĭt′ĭ), *n.* *Scot. & Dial.* Sister.

tit′tle (tĭt′'l), *n.* [L. *titulus* superscription, label, title.] **1.** A point or small sign used as a diacritical mark in writing or printing. **2.** A particle; a minute part; a jot.

tit′tle–tat′tle (-tăt′'l), *n.* [Redupl. of TATTLE.] **1.** Idle, trifling talk, esp. gossip. **2.** A tattler. — *v. i.* To talk idly; gossip.

tit′tup (tĭt′ŭp), *n.* [Imitative.] Lively, gay, or restless behavior; a prance, caper, etc. — *v. i.;* -TUPED (-ŭpt) or -TUPPED; -TUP·ING or -TUP·PING. To behave or move in a lively or restless manner; to caper; to frisk.

tit′u·ba′tion (tĭt′ū·bā′shŭn), *n.* [L. *titubatio.*] A staggering gait observed in certain nervous disturbances.

tit′u·lar (tĭt′ū·lẽr), *adj.* [L. *titulus* title.] **1.** Of, pertaining to, or bearing a title; related to a title. **2.** Existing in title or name only; nominal; as, *titular* sovereignty. **3.** *Eccl.* **a** Designating, pertaining to, or taking the name of a title (sense 8); as, a *titular* church at Rome. **b** Bearing a title derived from a defunct see, monastery, etc.; as, a *titular* abbot or bishop. — *n.* **1.** A person holding a title, esp. without obligation to perform its duties. **2.** *R.C.Ch.* An incumbent of a title (sense 8). — **tit′u·lar·ly,** *adv.*

tit′u·lar′y (-lẽr′ĭ *or, esp. Brit.*, -lẽr·ĭ), *adj.* Of, pert. to, arising from, or consisting in a title; titular. — *n.; pl.* -LARIES (-ĭz). A titular.

Ti′tus (tī′tŭs), *n.* [L. *Titus* or Gr. *Titos.*] The Epistle to Titus in the New Testament. See BIBLE.

Ti′u (tē′ōō), *n.* [AS. *Tīw.*] *Teut. Myth.* A sky-god and war-god, the Norse Tyr.

tiv′y (tĭv′ĭ), *adv.* [See TANTIVY.] With speed; quickly; — a huntsman's word or cry. Cf. TANTIVY.

tiz′zy (tĭz′ĭ), *n.* [Corrupt. of TESTON.] *Slang, Eng.* A sixpence.

tiz′zy, *n.* A highly excited and foolishly distracted or baffled state of mind, esp. over a petty matter.

Tlin′git (tlĭng′gĭt), *n. pl.* Also **Tlin′kit** (-kĭt). The Indians of a seafaring group of tribes of southern Alaska. They were expert stone carvers and copper workers.

tme′sis (t'mē′sĭs; mē′sĭs), *n.* [L., fr. Gr. *tmēsis* a cutting.] *Gram.* Separation of parts of a compound word by one or more words (*what place soever*, for *whatsoever place*).

TNT, *or* **T.N.T.** *Abbr.* Trinitrotoluene, or trinitrotoluol.

to (tōō; *unstressed*, tŏŏ, tŭ; 4), *prep.* [AS. *tō.*] Primarily *to* expresses the relation of direction of approach and arrival, making its governed word denote the terminus; as: **1.** Indicating the terminal point toward which movement is made or projected; as, to drive *to* town; ten feet *to* the ground. **2.** Indicating that which is in position of contact, proximity, connection, or opposition; as, applying soap *to* the surface; denounce him *to* his face. **3.** Indicating intention, purpose, or end; as, hastened *to* our aid; title *to* property. **4.** Indicating effect or resultant condition; as, burn *to* ashes; beaten *to* death; she was suddenly brought *to* herself. **5.** Indicating that which sustains addition, attachment, adherence, attribution, or harmonious accompaniment; as, to dance *to* a tune; a key *to* the desk; keep *to* the rules. **6.** Indicating the object of reverence or honor; as, to drink *to* one's country. **7.** Indicating that in respect of which there is accordance, correspondence, agreement, or the contrary; as, sixty pounds *to* the bushel; betting four *to* one; not *to* my knowledge. **8.** Indicating the end of a time period or interval; as, from seven *to* eight; the belief survives *to* this day. **9.** Indicating the final or full extent or degree; as, accurate *to* a hair. **10.** Indicating that which prompts or encounters an answering action or tendency; as, *to* this he said Amen; deaf *to* all entreaties. **11.** Indicating that in the direction of which as goal or limit there is application of activity; as, to fall *to* writing. **12.** Indicating relationship based on service or interest; as, that's all there is *to* it; tangent *to* a circle. **13.** Indicating the recipient affected by action causing benefit, disadvantage, and the like; as, a son born *to* them; that seems *to* me unwise; a room *to* myself. **14.** Indicating scope of percipience or participation; as, unbeknown *to* his parents; *to* their trained eyes the outcome was already determined. **15.** Introducing an infinitive; as, come *to* help; hence, used as a sign of the infinitive; as, *to* be or not *to* be.

— (tōō), *adv.* **1.** To or in the direction of something. **2.** To or into a certain position or state. **3.** To the matter or business in hand; as, they set *to* with their fists; come, men, buckle *to.* **4.** *Naut.* Close to the wind; — of a sailing vessel; as, keep her *to.* **5.** At hand; as, he was close *to.*

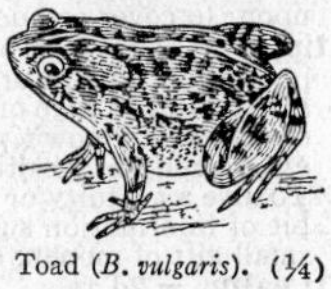
Toad (*B. vulgaris*). (¼)

toad (tōd), *n.* [AS. *tādie, tādige.*] **1.** Any of a genus (*Bufo* and allied genera, esp. of family Bufonidae) of tailless leaping amphibians. Toads are generally terrestrial in their habits, except during the breeding season, when they seek the water. They eat insects, worms, slugs, etc. Cf. FROG, 1; TREE TOAD. **2.** *Contemptuous.* A hateful person or thing.

toad′eat′er (-ēt′ẽr), *n.* A fawning parasite; a toady.

toad′fish′ (-fĭsh′), *n.; pl.*, see FISH. Any of certain marine fishes with jugular pelvic fins, a large head, and scaleless skin, constituting a family (Batrachoididae).

toad′flax′ (-flăks′), *n.* **a** A common Eurasian perennial herb (*Linaria vulgaris*) of the figwort family, widely naturalized as a weed in the United States. It has showy yellow-and-orange flowers, whence it is called also *butter-and-eggs*, etc. **b** Hence, any other plant of the same genus (*Linaria*).

toad spittle. = CUCKOO SPIT **a.**

toad′stone′ (tōd′stōn′), *n.* A stone, or stony substance, popularly supposed to have formed in the head or body of a toad. They were often worn formerly as charms, antidotes to poison, etc.

toad′stool′ (tōd′stōōl′), *n.* Any of various fungi having an umbrella-shaped cap or pileus; a mushroom, often (esp. in popular usage) one of the poisonous varieties. Cf. FUNGUS, *Illust.*

toad′y (tōd′ĭ), *n.; pl.* TOADIES (-ĭz). A toadeater; a truckler to the rich or powerful. — *v. t. & i.;* TOAD′IED (-ĭd); TOAD′Y·ING. To play the toady (to); to fawn (upon) with sycophancy. — **Syn.** See FAWN. — **toad′y·ism,** *n.*

to′–and–fro′ (tōō′ănd·frō′), *adj.* Forward and backward; as, *to-and-fro* motion or visiting.

toast (tōst), *v. t. & i.* [OF. *toster* to roast, toast, fr. L. *torrere, tostum*, to parch, roast.] **1.** To brown by heat as of the sun or a fire; usually, to brown (bread, cheese, bacon, etc.) by exposure to a flame. **2.** To warm thoroughly at a fire; as, to *toast* the feet. — *n.* Sliced bread dried and browned before a fire.

toast, *n.* [So called because toasts were formerly put into the liquor, as a delicacy.] **a** Any person whose health is drunk, or anything in honor of which persons drink; a sentiment that is drunk to. **b** The act of proposing, or of drinking in honor of, a toast. — *v. t.* To propose or drink to as a toast; to drink to the health or in honor of.

toast′er (tōs′tẽr), *n.* **1.** One who or that which toasts bread, cheese, etc. **2.** Any of various utensils for toasting.

toast′mas′ter (tōst′mȧs′tẽr), *n.* At a banquet, one who presides and introduces the after-dinner speakers. — **toast′mis′tress** (-mĭs′trĕs; -trĭs), *n.*

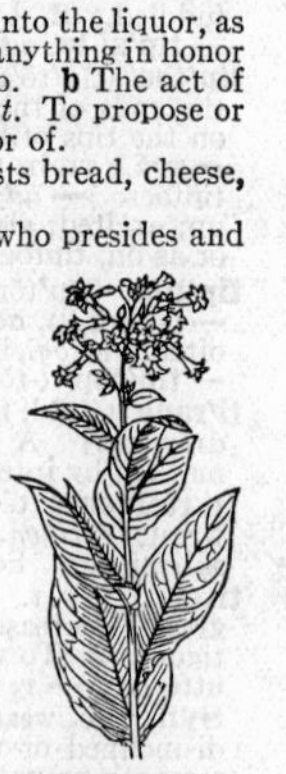
Tobacco. (1⁄20)

to·bac′co (tō·băk′ō; tŭ-), *n.; pl.* -COS, sometimes -COES (-ōz). [Sp. *tabaco*, fr. Taino *tabaco* a cigarlike roll of tobacco leaves, a Y-shaped pipe with which the Indians of the Antilles inhaled the smoke through the nostrils.] **1.** Any of a genus (*Nicotiana*) of American and Asiatic plants of the nightshade family (Solanaceae), having viscid foliage and tubular flowers; esp., any of the species (as *N. tabacum*) cultivated for their leaves, as distinguished from the ornamental species known usually as ***flowering tobacco.*** **2.** The leaves of this plant, prepared and used for smoking or chewing, or as snuff. **3.** The manufactured product from tobacco leaves; cigars, cigarettes, etc., collectively; also, smoking as a practice.

tobacco heart. *Med.* A functional disorder of the heart, characterized by irregularity, etc., caused by excessive use of tobacco.

to·bac′co·nist (tō·băk′ō·nĭst; tŭ-), *n.* A dealer in tobacco.

tobacco worm. Either of two species of large, green, obliquely white-striped caterpillars with a hornlike process near the posterior end, which feed on the tobacco plant. They are larvae of the hawk moths *Protoparce quinquemaculata* and *P. sexta.*

To·bi′as (tō·bī′ăs), *n.* In the Douay Bible, a book of the Old Testament; — called *Tobit* in the Protestant Apocrypha. See BIBLE.

To′bit (tō′bĭt), *n.* A book of the Apocrypha; — called *Tobias* in the Douay Bible. See BIBLE.

to·bog′gan (tō·bŏg′ăn), *n.* [Can. F. *tobagan, tabaganne*, of Algonquian origin.] A long, flat-bottomed, light sled made of a thin board or boards curved up at one end, usually having low handrails at the sides. — *v. i.* To coast on a toboggan; hence, to decline suddenly in value, as shares of a corporation on the stock market. — **to·bog′gan·er, to·bog′gan·ist,** *n.*

to′by (tō′bĭ), *n.; pl.* -BIES (-bĭz). [From *Tobias.*] **1.** *Slang. Local, U.S.* A variety of inferior, long, slender cigar, tapered at one end. **2.** [*often cap.*] A small jug, pitcher, or mug, generally used for ale, shaped somewhat like a stout man, with a cocked hat forming the brim.

toc·ca′ta (tō·kä′tȧ; *It.* tōk·kä′tä), *n.* [It., fr. *toccare* to touch.] *Music.* A brilliant composition, usually for organ or harpsichord, in free fantasia style.

To·char′i·an (tō·kâr′ĭ·ăn; -kär′ĭ-), *n.* **1.** One of a people of considerable culture dwelling in Central Asia in the first millennium of the Christian Era. **2.** Their language, recovered in 1904–08 from inscrip-

tions and manuscripts and established as an Indo-European tongue. — **To·char'i·an**, *adj.*
toch'er (tŏκ'ẽr), *n.* [Gael. *tochar, tochradh.*] *Scot.* Marriage portion; dot. — *v. t. Scot.* To dower.
to·col'o·gy (tō·kŏl'ō·jĭ), *n.* Also **to·kol'o·gy.** [Gr. *tokos* childbirth + *-logy.*] The science of obstetrics, or midwifery.
to·coph'er·ol (tō·kŏf'ẽr·ōl; -ŏl), *n.* [Gr. *tokos* offspring + *pherein* to bear + *-ol,* 1.] *Biochem.* Any of a number of alcohols having the properties of vitamin E in varying degrees, found in wheat-germ oil, cottonseed oil, and leaves of plants.
toc'sin (tŏk'sĭn), *n.* [F., fr. Pr. *tocasenh,* fr. *tocar* to touch, strike + *senh* bell, fr. L. *signum* a sign.] An alarm bell, or any warning signal.
tod (tŏd), *n.* [Origin unknown.] *Chiefly Scot.* A fox.
tod, *n.* [Appar. fr. LG. *tod, todde,* bundle, load.] **1.** An old weight for wool, usually 28 pounds (12.70 kg.). **2.** A bush; a bushy clump.
to·day', to–day' (tŏŏ·dā'; tŭ-), *adv.* [AS. *tō dæge.* See TO, *prep.;* DAY.] **1.** On or for this day. **2.** At the present time; nowadays. — *n.* The present day, time, or age.
tod'dle (tŏd''l), *v. i.;* -DLED (-'ld); -DLING (-lĭng). To walk with short tottering steps, as a child. — *n.* Act of toddling; a toddling gait. — **tod'dler** (-lẽr), *n.*
tod'dy (tŏd'ĭ), *n.* [Hind. *tāṛī* juice of the palmyra tree, fr. *tāṛ* palmyra tree, fr. Skr. *tāla.*] **1.** The fresh or fermented sap of various East Indian palms. **2.** A mixture of spirit and hot water sweetened; as, a rum *toddy.*
to–do' (tŏŏ·dōō'; tŭ-), *n.* *Colloq.* Bustle; stir.
to'dy (tō'dĭ), *n.; pl.* TODIES (-dĭz). [F. *todier,* fr. L. *todus* a kind of small bird.] Any of several tiny nonpasserine insectivorous West Indian birds (order Coraciiformes) constituting a genus (*Todus*). The ***green tody*** (*Todus todus*) of Jamaica is green with a crimson throat.
toe (tō), *n.* [ME. *too, taa,* fr. AS. *tā, tāhe.*] **1.** One of the terminal members or digits of the foot. **2.** The fore part of the foot; — opposed to *heel.* **3.** Any part of anything worn on, or attached to, the foot, corresponding to the toe; as, the *toe* of a skate. **4.** That part of a thing which, by its position, outline, etc., suggests a toe; as, the *toe* of Italy. **5.** *Mach.* **a** A journal or pivot supported in a bearing. **b** A lateral projection at one end, or between the ends, of a piece, as a rod or bolt, by which it is moved. — *v. t.;* TOED (tōd); TOE'ING (tō'ĭng). **1.** To furnish with a toe or toes; as, to *toe* a stocking. **2.** To touch, reach, or drive with the toes or with a toe; as, to *toe* a starting line. **3.** *Carp.* To drive slantingly (a nail, spike, etc.); also, to clinch or fasten by or with nails so driven. — *v. i.* To stand, walk, or be placed so that the toes are held or turned (in a specified position).
toe box. A piece of leather or fabric placed between the toecap and lining of a shoe and treated with a gum which hardens after the shoe is lasted permanently. See SHOE, *Illust.*
toe'cap' (tō'kăp'), *n.* A piece of leather covering the toe of a shoe.
toe crack. See SAND CRACK.
toed (tōd), *adj.* **1.** Having a toe or toes. **2.** *Carp.* Driven obliquely, as a nail; also, secured by diagonal or oblique nailing, as a board.
toe dance. A dance executed on the tips of the toes. — **toe'–dance',** *v. i.* — **toe dancer.**
toe hold. **1.** A hold, or place of support, for the toes, as in climbing; hence: **a** A means of gaining entry, surmounting barriers, etc. **b** A slight footing; as, at this time the Turks had only a *toe hold* in Europe. **2.** *Wrestling.* A hold in which the aggressor twists his opponent's foot.
toe'–in' (tō'ĭn'), *n.* Adjustment of the front wheels of an automobile so that they are closer together at the front than at the back.
toe'nail' (tō'nāl'; 2), *n.* A nail of a toe. — *v. t. Carp.* To clinch or fasten by toed nails.
toff (tŏf), *n.* *Brit. Slang.* A dandy; a swell.
tof'fee, tof'fy (tŏf'ĭ; 74), *n.* Taffy (the candy).
toft (tŏft; 74), *n.* [AS., homestead (ME. also, a knoll), fr. ON. *topt, tupt.*] **1.** *Now Dial.* **a** The site for a dwelling and outhouses. **b** An entire holding comprising a toft (sense **a**) and additional land; a messuage. **2.** *Dial. Eng.* A hill; knoll.
tog (tŏg), *n.* [From obs. *toge* cloak, fr. F. *toge,* fr. L. *toga.*] **1.** *Slang.* A coat. **2.** *pl. Colloq.* Clothes; esp., a set of clothes and accessories for a specified use; as, golf *togs.* — *v. t. & i.;* TOGGED (tŏgd); TOG'-GING *Colloq.* To put togs on; to dress.
to'ga (tō'gȧ), *n.; pl.* TOGAS (-gȧz), TOGAE (-jē). [L.] **1.** *Rom. Antiq.* The loose outer garment worn by citizens when appearing in public. **2.** A gown, garb, etc., associated with an office or profession; as, to don the *toga* of a judge. — **to'gaed** (-gȧd), *adj.*
to'gat·ed (tō'gāt·ĕd; -ĭd), *adj.* [L. *togatus,* fr. *toga* toga.] Togaed; hence, stately; dignified.
‖**to'ga vi·ri'lis** (tō'gȧ vĭ·rī'lĭs). [L. *virilis* manly.] *Rom. Antiq.* The toga of manhood, assumed by boys about the end of their fourteenth year.
to·geth'er (tŏŏ·gĕth'ẽr; tŭ-), *adv.* [AS. *tōgædere, tōgædre, tōgadore,* fr. *tō* to + *gador* together.] **1.** In or into one company, group, mass, or place. **2.** In or into contact or collision with each other; as, the foes rushed *together;* to live *together.* **3. a** At one time; coincidently. **b** In succession; without intermission; as, to work for hours *together.* **4.** By combined action; conjointly. **5.** In or into agreement, harmony, etc.; as, to get *together* in a policy. **6.** *Colloq.* As an intensive after *add, multiply, join, co-operate,* etc.
tog'ger·y (tŏg'ẽr·ĭ), *n.; pl.* -IES (-ĭz). *Colloq.* Clothes; togs.
tog'gle (tŏg''l), *n.* **1.** *Naut.* A pin or bolt fixed transversely in an eye of a rope or chain to be secured to any loop, bight, or ring. **2.** Any crosspiece attached to the end of, or to a loop in, a chain, rope, belt, etc., to prevent slipping, to serve in twisting or tightening, etc.; as, the *toggle* of a watch chain. **3.** *Mach.* A toggle joint. — *v. t.;* TOG'-GLED (-'ld); TOG'GLING (-lĭng). **1.** To fasten with or as with a toggle. **2.** To furnish with a toggle or toggles.
toggle joint. *Mach.* A device consisting of two bars jointed together end to end but not in line, so that when a force is applied to the knee tending to straighten the arrangement, the parts abutting or jointed to the ends of the bars will experience an endwise pressure.
toggle switch. *Elec.* A switch, originally containing a toggle, operated by pushing a projecting lever through a small arc.
togs (tŏgz), *n., pl.* of TOG. Clothes. See TOG, *n.,* 2.
toil (toil), *v. t.* [ME. *toilen* to pull about, toil, fr. OF. *tooillier, toeillier,* to pull or drag about, make dirty.] To accomplish by great labor. — *v. i.* **1.** To exert strength with pain and fatigue; to labor. **2.** To advance with laborious exertion or with much effort. — *n.* [AF., turmoil, struggle (OF. *tooil, toeil,* a struggling, a writhing or wallowing).] **1.** *Archaic.* Contention; struggle. **2.** A laborious effort. **3.** Labor with pain and fatigue. — **Syn.** See WORK. — **Ant.** Leisure.
toil, *n.* [F. *toiles,* pl., toils, nets, fr. *toile* cloth, spider web, fr. L. *tela* any woven stuff, a web.] **1.** *Archaic.* A net to trap game. **2.** *Chiefly pl.* Any snare or trap likened to a mesh or network.
toile (twäl), *n.* [F.] A variety of sheer linen, cotton, or silk; also, a kind of canvas.
toil'er (toil'ẽr), *n.* A laboring man.
toi'let (toi'lĕt; -lĭt), *n.* [F. *toilette,* dim. of *toile* cloth.] **1.** A dressing table. **2.** Act or process of dressing, esp. of dressing the hair; now, usually, a grooming of one's person. **3.** *Now Rare.* Toilette, or attire; also, a toilette, or costume. **4.** *U. S.* **a** A bathroom. **b** A water closet.
toi'let·ry (-rĭ), *n.; pl.* -RIES (-rĭz). [See -RY.] An article or preparation used in making one's toilet; — a general term in use in the trade.
toi·lette' (toi·lĕt'; *F.* twȧ'lĕt'), *n.* [F.] **1.** A lady's toilet including bathing, hairdressing, use of cosmetics, and costuming. **2.** Attire; esp., formal or fashionable attire; hence, a particular attire or costume.
toilet water. A perfumed liquid, usually weakly alcoholic, as cologne, used in or after a bath.
toil'ful (toil'fŏŏl; -f'l), *adj.* Full of, or involving toil; laborious. — **toil'ful·ly,** *adv.*
toil'some (-sŭm), *adj.* Attended with toil or fatigue; laborious. — **toil'some·ly,** *adv.* — **toil'some·ness,** *n.*
toil'worn' (-wōrn'; 70), *adj.* Worn out with toil.
toit (toit), *v. i. Scot.* To totter; saunter; dawdle.
To·kay' (tō·kā'), *n.* [From *Tokay,* Hungary.] **1.** A rich, sweet, whitish or purplish grape. **2.** A moderately strong wine, orig. of Tokay.
to'ken (tō'kĕn), *n.* [AS. *tācen, tācn.*] **1.** A visible sign; as, no *tokens* of his grief. **2.** Something that serves as a symbol; as, a white flag is a *token* of surrender. **3.** *Archaic.* A signal. **4.** A distinguishing feature; characteristic. **5.** Something given or shown as a guaranty of one's authority, right, identity, etc. **6.** A souvenir; keepsake. **7.** A piece of metal intended for currency issued at a nominal or face value in excess of its real value; hence, any piece of currency similarly issued or current. **8.** A metal fare or ticket issued by a transportation company. — **Syn.** See SIGN.
— *adj.* Done or given as a token (see TOKEN, *n.,* 5), esp. in partial fulfillment of an obligation or engagement; hence, having mere semblance or serving as a mere sign or sample of the real thing; simulated; minuscule; as, a *token* raid; *token* resistance.
token payment. A partial payment made upon a debt, as one between nations, to show the payer's good faith and to be an acknowledgment of the obligation.
to·kol'o·gy (tō·kŏl'ō·jĭ). Var. of TOCOLOGY.
to'la (tō'lä), *n.* [Hind. *tola.*] A unit of weight in India, the government standard being equal to 180 grains (11.664 grams), the weight of one rupee.
to'lan (tō'lăn), *n.* Also **to'lane** (-lān). [From TOLUENE.] *Chem.* A white crystalline hydrocarbon, $C_6H_5.C{:}C.C_6H_5$, obtained artificially; diphenyl-acetylene.
tol'booth', toll'booth' (tōl'bōōth'; -bōōth'), *n.* [ME. *tolbothe.*] *Scot.* A jail; hence, a prison.
told (tōld), *past & past part.* of TELL.
tole (tōl), *v. t. Dial.* To toll or entice; lure.
tole, tôle (tōl), *n.* [F. *tôle* sheet iron, plate, dial. var. of *table.*] A decorative lacquered or enameled metalware finished in various colors, originating as varnished sheet iron and, as used in the eighteenth century for cooking utensils, trays, etc., usually shiny black with gilt designs.
To·le'do (tō·lē'dō), *n.; pl.* -DOS (-dōz). A sword or sword blade famous for its fine temper, made at Toledo in Spain.
tol'er·a·ble (tŏl'ẽr·ȧ·b'l), *adj.* [L. *tolerabilis.*] **1.** Capable of being borne or endured. **2.** Moderately good or agreeable; satisfactory; passable. — **tol'er·a·bly,** *adv.*
tol'er·ance (tŏl'ẽr·ăns), *n.* **1.** *Rare.* Endurance. **2.** The act of tolerating; quality of being tolerant; specif., the disposition to tolerate beliefs, practices, or habits differing from one's own. **3.** A specified allowance for error in weighing, measuring, etc., or for variations from the standard or given dimensions, weight, or the like. **4.** *Coinage.* The amount which coins, either singly or in lots, are legally allowed to vary above or below the standard of weight or fineness. **5.** *Mach.* The difference between two limiting sizes as a means of specifying the degree of accuracy. **6.** *Med.* The constitutional or acquired capacity to endure shock, a poison, or, esp., a food or drug which may be harmful if taken in excess; also, the capacity to endure the effects of a drug or other substance.
tol'er·ant (-ănt), *adj.* **1.** Inclined to tolerate; forbearing. **2.** *Med.* Capable of enduring or resisting the action of a drug, shock, or the like; esp., capable, through long use, of enduring without injury large doses of a drug, as morphine. — **tol'er·ant·ly,** *adv.*
tol'er·ate (-āt), *v. t.* [L. *toleratus,* past part. of *tolerare,* fr. the same root as *tollere* to lift up, *tuli,* used as perf. of *ferre* to bear.] **1.** To bear up under; to endure; *Obs. exc. Med.,* to endure or resist, esp. without injurious effect, the action of, as a poison. **2.** To suffer to be, or to be done, without prohibition or hindrance; to allow or permit by not preventing. — **Syn.** See BEAR. — **tol'er·a'tive** (-ā'tĭv; -ȧ·tĭv), *adj.* — **tol'er·a'tor** (-ā'tẽr), *n.*
tol'er·a'tion (-ā'shŭn), *n.* Act or practice of tolerating; specif., policy of permitting the existence of all (or given) religious opinions and modes of worship contrary to, or different from, those of the established church or belief. — **tol'er·a'tion·ism** (-ĭz'm), *n.*
tol'i·dine (tŏl'ĭ·dēn; -dĭn), *n.* Also **tol'i·din.** [From TOLUENE.] *Chem.* Any of several isomeric bases, $C_{12}H_6(CH_3)_2(NH_2)_2$, dimethyl derivatives of benzidine.
toll (tōl), *n.* [AS. *toll,* also *tolne,* fr. LL. *tolonium,* fr. L. *teloneum* tollhouse, fr. Gr. *telōnion,* fr. *telōnēs* a tax collector, fr. *telos* a tax.] **1.** A tax or due paid for some liberty or privilege, as for passing over a highway or bridge. **2.** The right to take such taxes or dues. **3.** A compensation taken for services rendered; specif.: **a** *Now Dial.* A portion of grain taken by a miller as his fee. **b** A charge for transportation. **c** A charge for a long-distance call on a telephone. **4.** That which is exacted or taken, as if toll; specif., number of casualties; as, a battle's heavy *toll.* — **Syn.** Tax, custom, duty, impost. — *v. i. & t.* To collect or exact as toll or by way of toll.
☞ COMBINATIONS and PHRASES (in sense 1) are:

toll bridge	**tollgatherer**	**tollman**
toll collector	**tollhouse**	**toll road**

toll (tōl), *v. t.* [ME. *tollen, tullen.*] **1.** To allure; entice; invite. **2.** To entice (game, esp. ducks) to approach by arousing their curiosity, as by the antics of a trained dog. **3.** To pull (a bell) so as to sound a summons, signal, or the like, as slowly in announcement of a death. **4.** Hence: **a** To sound or strike by tolling or as if tolled; as, the clock *tolls* the hour. **b** To announce by tolling; as, to *toll* a friend's death. **5.** To draw or summon by or as by means of a tolling bell. — *v. i.* To sound or ring, as a bell, with strokes uniformly repeated at intervals, as to announce the death of a person. — *n.* The sound of a bell produced by strokes slowly and uniformly repeated.

toll′age (tōl′ĭj), *n.* Toll; also, payment or exaction of toll.

toll bar. A bar, beam, gate, or the like, used at a tollhouse to stop passengers, vehicles, etc., for collection of toll.

toll′booth′ (tōl′bōōth′; -bōōth′). Var. of TOLBOOTH.

toll call. A long-distance telephone call at charges above a local rate.

toll′er (tōl′ẽr), *n.* One who or that which tolls; specif.: **a** A dog trained for use in tolling. **b** One who tolls a bell; also, a bell suitable for tolling.

toll′gate′ (tōl′gāt′), *n.* A gate across a road, etc., where toll is taken.

toll′keep′er (tōl′kēp′ẽr), *n.* The keeper of a tollgate or tollhouse.

toll line. A long-distance telephone line.

Tol′tec (tŏl′tĕk), *n.* An Indian of the earliest of the Nahuatlan tribes to invade central and southern Mexico. Through contact with the Mayas, they derived much of their culture. — **Tol′tec, Tol′tec·an** (-ăn), *adj.*

to·lu′ (tō·lōō′), *n., or* **tolu balsam.** [Sp. *tolú,* fr. the seaport Santiago de *Tolú,* Colombia.] Balsam of Tolú. See BALSAM, *n.,* 1.

tol′u·ate (tŏl′ū·āt), *n. Chem.* A salt or ester of any of the toluic acids.

tol′u·ene (-ēn), *n.* [*tolu* + benz*ene.*] *Chem.* A hydrocarbon, $C_6H_5CH_3$, of the aromatic series, obtained chiefly from coke-oven vapors and by distillation of coal tar. It is used in the manufacture of dyes and other compounds.

to·lu′ic (tō·lū′ĭk; tŏl′ū·ĭk), *adj. Chem.* Pertaining to or designating any of four isomeric acids, $C_7H_7CO_2H$, carboxyl derivatives of toluene.

to·lu′i·dide (tō·lū′ĭ·dīd; -dĭd), **tol′u·ide** (tŏl′ū·īd; -ĭd), *n.* Also **to·lu′i·did, tol′u·id.** *Chem.* Any of a series of compounds, $RCONHC_6H_4CH_3$, analogous to the anilides and derived from toluidine by the substitution of an acid radical for hydrogen in the amino group.

to·lu′i·dine (tō·lū′ĭ·dēn; -dĭn), *n.* Also **to·lu′i·din.** *Chem.* Any of three isomeric amino derivatives of toluene, $CH_3C_6H_4NH_2$, analogous to aniline.

tol′u·ol (tŏl′ū·ōl; -ŏl), **tol′u·ole** (-ōl). [*tolu* + benz*ol.*] Toluene, esp. in crude commercial form.

tol′u·yl (-ĭl), *n.* [*tolu*ic + *-yl.*] *Chem.* The univalent acid radical C_7H_7CO.

tol′yl (tŏl′ĭl), *n.* [*tol*uic + *-yl.*] *Chem.* The univalent radical $CH_3C_6H_4$, of which toluene is the hydride.

Tom (tŏm), *n.* **1.** Short for, and diminutive of, *Thomas,* a masculine proper name. **2.** [*not cap.*] The male of certain animals; — often used adjectively or in composition; as, *tom* turkey, etc.; specif., a male cat; a tomcat.

tom′a·hawk (tŏm′ȧ·hôk), *n.* [Of Algonquian origin.] A light ax used both as a missile and as a hand weapon by the North American Indians. — *v. t.* To cut, strike, or kill with a tomahawk.

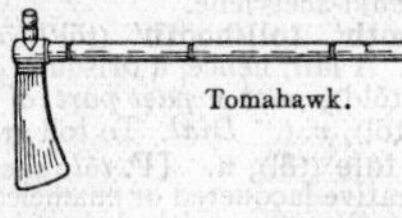
Tomahawk.

tom′al′ley (tŏm′ăl′ĭ), *n.* The liver of the lobster, which becomes green when boiled.

Tom and Jerry. A hot sweetened drink of rum and water spiced with cinnamon, etc., and beaten up with eggs.

to·ma′to (tō·mā′tō; tō·mä′tō), *n.; pl.* -TOES (-tōz). [Sp. *tomate,* fr. Nahuatl *tomatl.*] **a** A South American perennial herb (*Lycopersicon esculentum*) of the nightshade family, widely cultivated for its fruit. **b** Its large rounded edible pulpy berry, which is red or yellow when ripe.

tomb (tōōm), *n.* [AF. *tumbe,* OF. *tombe,* fr. LL. *tumba,* fr. Gr. *tymbos* sepulchral mound.] A grave; now, *Poetic,* any place of interment. — *v. t.* To bury; entomb.

tom′bac (tŏm′băk), *n.* Also **tom′back, tom′bak.** [F. and Pg.; F. *tombac,* fr. Pg. *tombaca,* fr. Malay *tĕmbaga* copper, fr. Skr. *tāmraka.*] An alloy, essentially of copper and zinc, used for cheap jewelry, gilding, etc. Cf. DUTCH FOIL, DUTCH METAL.

tom′boy′ (tŏm′boi′), *n.* [*Tom* + *boy.*] A romping girl; a hoyden. — **tom′boy′ish,** *adj.* — **tom′boy′ish·ness,** *n.*

tomb′stone′ (tōōm′stōn′), *n.* A gravestone.

tom′cat′ (tŏm′kăt′), *n.* A male cat.

tom′cod′ (-kŏd′), *n.* [*Tom* + *cod.*] Any of several small ganoid fishes (genus *Microgadus*) resembling the codfish.

Tom Col′lins (kŏl′ĭnz). A mixed drink of gin, sugar, lime or lemon juice, and soda or Seltzer water.

Tom, Dick, and Harry. Persons taken at random; the common run of humanity; when modified by *every,* everybody; everyone; — often derogatory.

tome (tōm), *n.* [F., fr. L. *tomus,* fr. Gr. *tomos* a piece cut off, part of a book, volume.] A volume forming part of a larger work; also, any book, esp. a large book.

-tome (-tōm). [Gr. *tomos* a cutting, the agent or result of cutting.] A combining form denoting: **a** *A part* or *section.* **b** *A cutting instrument.* Corresponding adjectives are formed with **-tom′ic** (-tŏm′ĭk).

to·men′tose (tō·mĕn′tōs; tō′mĕn·tōs), *adj.* [See TOMENTUM.] Covered with densely matted hairs.

to·men′tum (tō·mĕn′tŭm), *n.; pl.* -TA (-tȧ). [L., a stuffing of wool, hair, or feathers.] *Bot.* Pubescence composed of densely matted, woolly hairs.

tom′fool′ (tŏm′fōōl′), *n.* A great fool; blockhead. — (-fōōl′; 2), *adj.* Extremely foolish, stupid, or doltish.

tom′fool′er·y (tŏm′fōōl′ẽr·ĭ), *n.; pl.* -ERIES (-ĭz). Foolish trifling; nonsense.

tom′my (tŏm′ĭ), *n.* [From THOMAS.] **1.** *Mil. Slang.* A loaf or hunk of bread. **2.** Goods given to a workman instead of money wages; also, the exchange of labor for goods instead of money. **3.** A Tommy Atkins; a British soldier.

Tom′my (tŏm′ĭ). A trade-mark applied to a submachine gun. See THOMPSON; RIFLE, *Illust.*

Tom′my At′kins (ăt′kĭnz). [From *Thomas Atkins,* fictitious name used as model in official blank forms for private soldiers.] Any white regular soldier of the British Army.

tom′my·rot′ (tŏm′ĭ·rŏt′), *n. Slang.* Rank foolishness or nonsense.

to·mog′ra·phy (tō·mŏg′rȧ·fĭ), *n.* [Gr. *tomos* a cut, section + *-graphy.*] *Med.* A technique of diagnosis that uses X-ray photographs, **to′mo·grams** (tō′mō·grămz; tŏm′ō-), in which the shadows of structures before and behind the section under scrutiny do not show.

to·mor′row (tōō·mŏr′ō; tŭ-), *adv.* Also **to–mor′row.** [*to,* prep. + *morrow.*] On or for the day after today; on or for the morrow. — *n.* The day after the present.

tom′pi·on (tŏm′pĭ·ŭn). Var. of TAMPION.

Tom Thumb (thŭm). A legendary diminutive personage celebrated in English literature. Also, the pseudonym given by P. T. Barnum to a famous dwarf in his circus.

tom′tit′ (tŏm′tĭt′; tŏm′tĭt′), *n.* [See TOM; 2d TIT.] **a** *Local, Eng.* A titmouse. **b** *Local, Eng.* The wren.

tom′–tom′ (tŏm′tŏm′), *n.* [See TAM-TAM.] **1.** A type of drum of barbaric Eastern origin, commonly beaten with the hands. **2.** Any monotonous beating, rhythm, etc.

-tomy. [Gr. *tomē* a cutting; akin to Gr. *temnein* to cut. See TOME.] A combining form meaning *a cutting,* as in ana*tomy;* specif., *Surg., an operation of incision* or *section,* as in phlebo*tomy.* Corresponding adjectives are formed with **-tom′ic.**

ton (tŭn), *n.* [ME. *tonne.* See TUN.] **1. a** An avoirdupois weight of 2240 lb. (*long ton*) as commonly used in Great Britain, or 2000 lb. (*short ton*) as commonly used in U. S., Canada, South Africa, etc. See WEIGHT, *Table* 1. **b** A metric weight. See METRIC SYSTEM, *Table* 5. **2.** *Naut.* **a** A unit of internal capacity for ships; 100 cubic feet (2.8317 cu. m.); — called also ***register ton.*** **b** A unit approximately equal to the volume of a long-ton weight of sea water, used in reckoning the displacement of vessels, esp. war vessels; 35 cubic feet; — called ***displacement ton.*** **c** A unit of volume for cargo freight, usually reckoned at 40 cu. ft.; — called ***measurement ton*** *or* ***freight ton.***

‖**ton** (tôN), *n.* [F.] The vogue; also, smartness; style.

ton′al (tōn′ăl), *adj.* Of or pertaining to tone or tonality. — **ton′al·ly,** *adv.*

to·nal′i·ty (tō·năl′ĭ·tĭ), *n.; pl.* -TIES (-tĭz). Tonal quality: **a** *Music.* The character which a composition has by virtue of its key, or through the relationship of its tones and chords to the keynote, or tonic. **b** In the graphic arts, the arrangement or interrelation of the tones of a picture.

to′–name′ (tōō′nām′), *n.* [AS. *tōnama.* See TO, *prep.;* NAME.] *Scot.* A surname; also, a nickname.

tone (tōn), *n.* [OF. and L.; OF. *ton,* fr. L. *tonus* a sound, tone, a stretching, fr. Gr. *tonos* a stretching, straining, pitch, accent, meter.] **1.** Vocal or musical sound, or esp., sound quality. **2.** Accent, or inflection or modulation of the voice. **3.** In writing or speaking, style or manner of expression; as, a conciliatory *tone.* **4.** Healthy elasticity; resiliency; as, his mind has lost its *tone.* **5.** General trend, character, or quality; as, a city's low moral *tone.* **6.** Frame (of mind); temper; mood. **7.** Color quality or value; also, the color which modifies a hue or white or black; as, a light *tone* of blue. **8.** *Linguistics.* **a** The musical pitch or intonation of a sound, word, or sentence. **b** Specif., one of the four notes or keys in which Chinese (Pekingese) sounds are pitched. **9.** *Med.* That state of a body, or of its organs or parts, in which the animal functions are healthy and active. **10.** *Music & Acous.* **a** A sound having such regularity of vibration as to impress the ear with its individual character, esp. as regards pitch, and to enter into harmonic relations; musical sound; — opposed to *noise. Tone* is often used to designate a simple tone. But nearly all musical sounds are composed of two or more simple tones. These components are called *partial tones,* of which the lowest, which determines the pitch, is called the *fundamental tone,* or *fundamental,* and the others, *upper partial tones,* or *overtones.* See PITCH, *Illust.* **b** The larger interval between contiguous sounds in the diatonic scale, the smaller being a *semitone;* a whole step. **11.** *Painting.* The general effect of light and shade, together with color; — commonly implying harmony. **12.** *Phonet.* **a** Voice; vocal sound. **b** A particular pitch of voice. **13.** *Physiol.* The normal responsiveness to stimuli; tonicity.
— *v. t.* **1.** *Rare.* To intone. **2.** To give a particular intonation or inflection, character, color quality, etc., to. **3.** To change by treatment the tone, or color, of; to modify in color; specif., *Photog.,* to change the normal silver image of (a print, etc.) into a colored image. — *v. i.* **1.** To assume a tone, esp. a color quality or tint; as, shingles *tone* beautifully in the salt-laden air. **2.** To blend or harmonize in color.
tone down. **a** To give a lower tone to. **b** To become lower, softer, less emphatic, etc., in tone. **c** *Painting.* To modify, as color, by making it less brilliant or less crude. — ***tone up.*** To raise the tone of; to strengthen.

tone color. *Music.* Timbre.

to′ne·la′da (*Sp.* tō′nā·lä′thä; *Pg.* tōō′nĕ·lä′thȧ), *n.* [Sp. & Pg.] **a** In Spain and some Spanish-speaking countries, a weight of 2028.7 lb. (920.19 kg.). **b** In Brazil, a weight of 1748.79 lb. (793.24 kg.).

tone′less, *adj.* Without tone; devoid of tone or, often, expression. — **tone′less·ly,** *adv.* — **tone′less·ness,** *n.*

tone poem. *Music.* An orchestral composition based on or suggestive of poetic sentiments or images, a variety of the symphonic poem developed esp. by Richard Strauss. — **tone poet.** — **tone poetry.**

tong (tŏng; 74), *v. t. & i.* To take, gather, hold, or handle with tongs; to use tongs; as, to *tong* oysters.

tong (tŏng), *n.* [Chin. (Pek.) *t'ang*[2] (Cant. *t'ong*), lit., hall.] In China, an association, secret society, or organization of any kind; in the United States, usually, a secret association of Chinese. Cf. HIGHBINDER.

ton′ga (tŏng′gȧ), *n.* [Hind. *tāngā.*] *Anglo-Ind.* A light two-wheeled vehicle, usually for four persons.

tongs (tŏngz; 74), *n. pl.; sometimes construed as sing.* [AS. *tang, tange.*] Any of numerous instruments or devices for taking hold of something, as a hot coal or piece of metal from a forge.

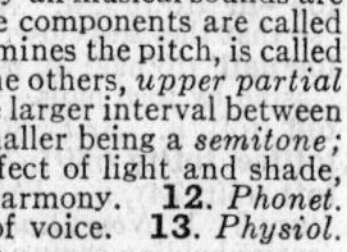
Tongs. 1 Fire Tongs; 2 Horseshoer's Tongs; 3 Pipe Tongs.

tongue (tŭng), *n.* [AS. *tunge.*] **1.** An organ or process (often protrusible and freely movable) of the floor of the mouth, present in most vertebrates. In man it serves as an organ of speech, and as the principal organ of taste. **2.** The flesh of the tongue of an animal, as the ox or sheep, used as an article of food. **3.** The power of communication through speech. **4.** Hence: **a** That which is uttered; speech. **b** Act of speaking; utterance. **5.** A language; esp., a spoken language. **6.** Manner or quality of utterance with respect to tone or sound, the sense of what is expressed, or the intention of the speaker. 7. The cry of or as of a hound pursuing or in sight of game, as in the phrase ***to give tongue,*** to bark, yelp, or howl. 8. Something like an animal's tongue in form, function, position, or motion; as: **a** The flap under the lacing or buckles of a shoe. See SHOE, *Illust.* **b** A bell clapper. See BELL, *Illust.* **c** A movable pin in a buckle. **d** The pole of a vehicle. **e** The rib on one edge of a board to fit into a groove in an edge of another board to make a flush joint (called a **tongue′-and-groove′ joint**). See MATCHBOARD, *Illust.* **f** *Mach.* A feather. **g** *Music.* The free, or vibrating end of a reed. 9. *Phys. Geog.* A long narrow strip of land, projecting into a body of water; a spit. 10. *Railroads.* The movable rail of a street railway switch. — *v. t.* 1. *Archaic.* To speak; utter; sometimes, to scold. 2. To give a voice or power of expression to (something). 3. To touch or lick (*up*) with or as with the tongue. 4. **a** To cut a tongue on; as, to *tongue* a board. **b** To join by means of a tongue and groove joint, as boards. 5. *Music.* To produce (tones) by tonguing (which see). — *v. i.* 1. *Rare.* To talk; prate. 2. To project like a tongue of land. 3. *Music.* To practice tonguing (which see). — **tongued** (tŭngd), *adj.* — **tongue′less,** *adj.*

tongue′-tie′ (tŭng′tī′), *n.* *Med.* Impeded motion of the tongue due to shortness of the frenum, or to its adhesion to the gums. — *v. t.* To deprive of speech or the power of distinct articulation. — **tongue′-tied′** (-tīd′), *adj.*

tongu′ing (tŭng′ĭng), *n.* *Music.* Modification or interruption of tone for a rapid staccato effect by the performer's tongue, in playing a wind instrument.

tonguing and grooving plane. See PLANE, *Illust.* (4).

ton′ic (tŏn′ĭk), *adj.* [Gr. *tonikos.*] 1. Pert. to tension, esp. muscular tension; hence, producing or adapted to produce healthy muscular condition and reaction. 2. Invigorating; refreshing; bracing. 3. Of or pert. to tones or sounds. 4. *Music.* Of or pert. to the keynote; as, the *tonic* chord. 5. *Painting.* Of or pert. to tone in a picture or scene. 6. *Philol.* Of or pert. to linguistic tones or languages using them; as, Chinese is a *tonic* language. 7. *Phonet.* **a** Voiced. **b** Of a sound or a syllable, stressed; accented. 8. *Physiol. & Med.* Of, pert. to, or characterized by tonus or tone; characterized by continuous muscular contraction; as, *tonic* convulsions. — *n.* 1. *Med.* A medicine having a tonic effect. 2. *Music.* The fundamental note or tone of a key; the keynote or key tone. 3. *Phonet.* A voiced sound.

tonic accent. **a** Syllabic accent; vocal accent as compared with a written, or graphic, accent. **b** *Phonet.* Prominence given to a syllable or word by means of raised pitch or change of pitch.

to·nic′i·ty (tō·nĭs′ĭ·tĭ), *n.* 1. The property of possessing tone; esp., vigor; health. 2. *Physiol.* The state of healthy tension or partial contraction of muscle fibers while at rest; tonus; tone.

tonic sol-fa. *Music.* A system of letter notation based on tonality, or key relationship, and replacing the usual staff symbols by the initial letters of the sol-fa syllables or the syllables themselves.

to·night′ (tŏŏ-nīt′; tŭ-), *adv.* Also **to-night′.** [*to,* prep. + *night.*] 1. On this present night or the night following this present day. 2. *Now Dial.* On the night just past; last night. — *n.* Also **to-night′.** The present or the coming night.

ton′ite (tōn′īt), *n.* [L. *tonare* to thunder.] An explosive consisting of a mixture of guncotton with a nitrate or nitro compound. It is used for blasting and in grenades.

ton′ka bean (tŏng′kȧ). [Appar. trans. of D. *tonquinboontjes* (pl.), lit., Tonkin berries.] **a** The seed of a tropical South American tree, species of the genus *Dipteryx,* esp. *D. odorata,* of the pea family, used in perfumes, as a flavor, etc. **b** The tree bearing this seed.

ton′kin′ (tŏn[g]′kĭn′), *n.* [From *Tonkin* (see *Gaz.*).] A firm bamboo from Indochina used for ski poles and fishing rods.

ton′nage (tŭn′ĭj), *n.* [From TON a measure.] 1. A duty or impost on vessels, based on tons carried; also, a duty, toll, or rate on goods per ton transported on canals. 2. Ships collectively, in terms of the number of tons registered or carried or of their carrying capacity. 3. The cubical content or burden of a vessel, or vessels, in tons. ***gross tonnage*** is such capacity of a vessel without deduction. ***register,*** or ***net, tonnage*** is the gross tonnage less certain deductions for space occupied by engines, crew's quarters, etc. 4. Total weight in tons shipped, carried, mined, etc.

ton·neau′ (tŭ·nō′; tō′nō′), *n.; pl.* TONNEAUS (tŭ·nōz′), TONNEAUX (tŭ·nōz′; *F.* tō′nō′). [F., lit., cask.] *Automobiles.* A type of after part of the body of a vehicle with sides enclosing the seat or seats, entered by a door now usually at the side; also, the entire body of an automobile having such an after part.

to·nom′e·ter (tō·nŏm′ē·tẽr), *n.* [Gr. *tonos* tone + *-meter.*] 1. *Acoustics & Music.* An instrument for determining the exact pitch or the vibration rate of tones. 2. *Med. & Physiol.* Any instrument for measuring tension or pressure, as blood pressure, the tension of the eyeball, etc. 3. *Physical Chem.* Device for measuring vapor pressure. — **ton′o·met′ric** (tŏn′ō·mĕt′rĭk; tō′nō-), *adj.*

ton′sil (tŏn′sĭl; -s'l), *n.* [L. *tonsillae,* pl.] *Anat.* Either of a pair of prominent masses of lymphoid tissue, one on each side of the throat between the anterior and posterior pillars of the fauces. — **ton′sil·lar, ton′sil·ar** (-sĭ·lẽr), *adj.*

ton′sil·lec′to·my (tŏn′sĭ·lĕk′tō·mĭ), *n.* [L. *tonsillae* tonsils + *-ectomy.*] The surgical removal of the tonsils.

ton′sil·li′tis (-lī′tĭs), *n.* [NL. See TONSIL; -ITIS.] *Med.* Inflammation of the tonsils. — **ton′sil·lit′ic** (-lĭt′ĭk), *adj.*

ton′sil·lot′o·my (-lŏt′ō·mĭ), *n.* [L. *tonsillae* tonsils + *-tomy.*] Operation of removing all or part of the tonsils.

ton·so′ri·al (tŏn·sō′rĭ·ăl; 70), *adj.* [L. *tonsorius,* fr. *tonsor* a shearer, barber, fr. *tondere, tonsum,* to shear.] Of or pertaining to a barber or his work; — generally used affectedly or humorously; as, *tonsorial* artist.

ton′sure (tŏn′shẽr; 117), *n.* [OF., fr. L. *tonsura* a shearing, fr. *tondere, tonsum,* to shear, shave.] Act of clipping the hair or of shaving the crown of the head; also, state of being shorn. *Rare, exc. Eccl.:* **a** The custom or, since the 7th century, the rite of shaving the head to denote admission as a candidate for orders in the Roman Catholic and Eastern churches. **b** The shaven crown or patch worn by monks and ecclesiastics. — *v. t.* To shave the head of. — **ton′sured** (-shẽrd), *adj.*

ton′tine (tŏn′tēn; tŏn·tēn′), *n.* [F., fr. It. *tontina,* after its inventor, Lorenzo *Tonti,* a Neapolitan.] 1. An annuity shared among a number, or a loan raised on life annuities, under a system whereby upon the death of each beneficiary of the annuity his share is enjoyed by the survivors, until at last the whole goes to the last survivor, or to the last two or three, according to the terms on which the money is advanced. Also, loosely, those who share the annuity; collectively, the share or right of each individual, or the system on which the annuity is shared. 2. Any similar arrangement whereby a group of persons share certain benefits or advantages, as in certain forms of insurance. 3. A tontine policy, risk, or the like.

to′nus (tō′nŭs), *n.* [L., a sound, tone.] 1. State of responding normally to stimuli; tonicity; tone. 2. *Med.* A spasm of continuous muscular contraction. 3. *Physiol.* The condition of mild steady activity characterizing normal protoplasm, as in a resting neuron or muscle fiber; as, muscular *tonus.*

too (tōō), *adv.* [The same word as *to,* prep.] 1. Likewise; also. 2. Over; more than enough; as, it is *too* long. 3. To such a degree as to be regrettable; as, *too* bad.

took (tŏŏk), *past* of TAKE.

tool (tōōl), *n.* [AS. *tōl.*] 1. **a** An instrument of manual operation, as a hammer, saw, plane, file, or the like, used to facilitate mechanical operations; an implement. **b** *Engineering.* The cutting or shaping part in a machine or a machine tool (which see); also, a machine for shaping metal in any way, often specifically, a machine tool. 2. Anything which serves as a means to an end. 3. A person used to accomplish another's ends; a dupe; as, a tyrant's *tool.* 4. *Law.* Any instrument necessary to a person in the efficient prosecution of his trade or calling. — **Syn.** See IMPLEMENT. — *v. t.* 1. To shape, form, or finish with a tool; specif., *Bookbinding, etc.,* to letter or ornament (a book cover) with or without gilding, inking, or coloring, by means of heated hand tools. 2. To equip (as a plant or industry) for volume production by designing, building, and integrating the machines, machine tools, precision instruments, etc., required for making and assembling products of manufacture. 3. *Slang.* To drive, as a coach; to convey in a vehicle. — *v. i.* 1. To use tools, as in bookbinding. 2. To tool a plant or industry; — often with *up.* 3. *Slang.* To drive or ride in a vehicle; as, to *tool* through the park.

tool engineering. A branch of engineering in industry whose function is to plan the processes of manufacture, design and supply the tools, and integrate the facilities required for producing given products with minimal expenditure of time, labor, and materials. — **tool engineer.**

tool′mak′er (tōōl′māk′ẽr), *n.* A machinist who specializes in the construction, repair, maintenance, and calibration of the tools, jigs, fixtures, and instruments of a machine shop.

toom (tōōm; *dial. also* tūm, tüm), *adj.* [AS. *tōm.*] *Scot., N. of Eng., & Ir.* Empty.

toon (tōōn), *n.* [Hind. *tun, tūn,* fr. Skr. *tunna.*] An East Indian and Australian tree (*Toona ciliata*) of the mahogany family, the flowers of which yield a dye; also, its soft reddish wood.

toot (tōōt), *v. i.* 1. To blow or sound a horn, etc., esp. so as to produce short rapid blasts. 2. To give forth a toot or toots. 3. To utter a similar sound, as certain birds. — *v. t.* To cause to sound, as a horn. — *n.* A short blast, as of a horn. — **toot′er,** *n.*

tooth (tōōth), *n.; pl.* TEETH (tēth). [AS. *tōth.*] 1. *Anat. & Zool.* **a** In most vertebrates, one of the hard bony appendages which are borne on the jaws, or in many of the lower vertebrates on other bones in the walls of the mouth or pharynx, and serve for the seizing and mastication of food, as weapons of offense and defense, etc. It is composed of *dentine,* surrounding a central *pulp cavity,* containing a vascular, sensitive *pulp,* and coated with *enamel* on the crown, and with *cement* on the root and sometimes also on parts of the crown. **b** In invertebrates, any of various hard or sharp processes about the mouth or on any jawlike part. 2. Any projection suggestive of the tooth of an animal in shape, arrangement, cutting power, etc.; as, a *tooth,* or tine, of a fork, of a comb, saw, or file. 3. Eating or appetite for eating; fondness or taste for (something); as, a sweet *tooth.* 4. Something that pierces, gnaws, cuts, poisons, etc., as a tooth, or often, a fang; as, the *teeth* of the wind. 5. *pl.* A threat of power, as legal or military power, to compel or constrain; hence, that which can or does compel submission, enforcement, etc.; as, to put *teeth* in a new law. 6. *Bot.* In general, any small sharp-pointed marginal lobe; specif., one of the processes forming the peristome in a moss. 7. *Mach.* One of the projections on the circumference of a wheel in a machine, etc., that engage with corresponding projections on another wheel, esp. to transmit force; a cog. — ***in the teeth of.*** **a** In or into direct contact or collision with. **b** In direct opposition to. — *v. t.* 1. To furnish with teeth. 2. To indent; jag; as, to *tooth* a saw. — **toothed** (tōōtht; tōōthd), *adj.*

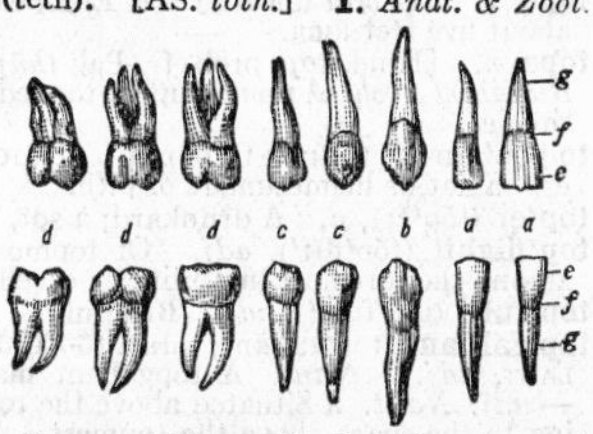

Permanent Human Teeth (right upper and lower). *a, a* Incisors; *b* Canines, or Eyeteeth; *c, c* Bicuspids, or Premolars; *d, d, d* Molars; *e* Crown; *f* Neck; *g* Fang, or Root.

tooth′ache′ (tōōth′āk′), *n.* Pain in a tooth or in the teeth.

tooth and nail. Gamely, fiercely, and desperately.

tooth′brush′ (tōōth′brŭsh′), *n.* A brush for cleaning the teeth.

tooth′less (-lĕs; -lĭs), *adj.* Having no teeth.

tooth′pick′ (-pĭk′), *n.* A pointed instrument, as a small, flat, tapering splinter, used for clearing the teeth of substances lodged between them.

tooth′some (-sŭm), *adj.* Pleasing, esp. to the taste; palatable. — **tooth′some·ly,** *adv.* — **tooth′some·ness,** *n.*

tooth′wort′ (-wûrt′), *n.* **a** A European parasitic plant (*Lathraea squamaria*) having a rootstock covered with tooth-shaped scales. **b** Any cress of the genus *Dentaria,* as the ***crinkleroot*** (*D. diphylla*) with succulent pungent rootstock.

too′tle (tōō′t'l), *v. i.;* TOO′TLED (-t'ld); TOO′TLING (-tlĭng). [Freq. of TOOT.] To toot gently, repeatedly, or continuously, as on a flute. — *n.* The noise produced by tootling.

top (tŏp; 73), *n.* [AS.] 1. *Now Dial.* A crowning tuft, esp. the hair on the head. 2. The crown; head; — in phrases, as *from top to toe.* 3. The upper end, edge, or surface; the uppermost part, or the part of anything regarded as uppermost. 4. The head of a plant; as, beet *tops.* 5. The highest degree or pitch conceivable or attained; the acme; pinnacle; as, the *top* of one's career, powers. 6. *Poetic.* The highest realization or example. 7. The highest place, as in rank or achievement. 8. One occupying the highest position; the head; chief; as, the *top* of his class. 9. The choicest part; the pick. 10. A fitted part which serves as an upper piece, lid, covering, etc. 11. *Cards.* At bridge, a card or (*pl.*) cards that will win the first or second round of the suit, such as an ace, or king and queen. **12.** *Chem.* The most volatile part (passing over first on distillation); — often in *pl.*; as, refinery *tops*. **13.** *Games.* A forward spin given to a ball, as in golf, tennis, cricket, etc., by striking it on or near the top or above the center; also, the stroke so given. **14.** *Naut.* A platform surrounding the head of the lower mast, which serves to spread the topmast rigging, and furnishes a standing place for men aloft; also, any comparable part of the superstructure, as, esp. on warships, a fire-control station or antiaircraft gun platform. Cf. CROW'S-NEST, 1.

— v. t.; TOPPED (tŏpt) or, *Poetic*, TOPT; TOP'PING. **1.** To remove or cut the top or tops of; to prune. **2.** To cover with a top or on the top; to provide, form, or serve as, a top for; to crown; cap. **3.** To reach or exceed in height, weight, amount, etc., of; as, a deer that *topped* 300 pounds. **4.** To be superior to; to excel. **5.** To gain ascendancy over; dominate. **6.** To rise to or reach the top of; also, to go over the top of; to surmount. **7.** *Chem.* To remove the top, or most volatile parts, from. **8.** *Dyeing.* To cover with another dye. **9.** *Games.* To strike (the ball) above the center; also, to make (as a stroke) by hitting the ball in this way. **— v. i. 1.** To top (in any sense) someone or something. **2.** To make an end, finish, or conclusion; to round (*off*). — ***top off.*** To complete by adding a top; also, to end or finish; as, to *top off* a meal with coffee.

— adj. Of, pertaining to, or at the top; highest; topmost.

top (tŏp; 73), *n.* [AS.] A child's toy having a tapering, usually steel-shod, point on which it is made to spin.

to'paz (tō'păz), *n.* [OF. *topace, topase* (F. *topaze*), fr. L. *topazos*, fr. Gr. *topazos, topazion.*] **1.** *Mineral.* **a** An orthorhombic mineral, occurring often in transparent prismatic crystals, and then classed as a semiprecious stone. Its characteristic color is yellow. Chemically, it is a fluosilicate of aluminum. H., 8. Sp. gr., 3.4–3.6. **b** In full, ***Oriental topaz.*** Yellow sapphire (see SAPPHIRE, 1 **b**). **c** A yellow variety of quartz, esp. citrine; — called specif. ***false topaz.*** **2.** Either of two large brilliantly colored South American hummingbirds (*Topaza pella* and *T. pyra*).

top boot. A high boot, often with light-colored leather bands around the upper part.

top'coat' (tŏp'kōt'), *n.* An outer lightweight overcoat.

top'-draw'er, *adj.* Also **out of the top drawer.** Of the highest social level; of the highest level of rank, excellence, or importance; topnotch; first-class.

top'-dress', *v. t.* To apply material to (land, a road, etc.), without working it in; as, to *top-dress* a road.

top'-dress'ing, *n.* The act of one who top-dresses, as soil with fertilizer, a road with crushed stone, etc.; also, the material so applied.

tope (tōp), *v. i. & t.* [F. *toper* to cover a stake at dice, accept an offer, *tope* agreed!, prop., I accept, fr. Sp. *topar.*] *Archaic.* To drink strong liquors to excess; to drink hard and often.

tope, *n.* [Origin uncert.] A European shark (*Galeorhinus galeus*) about five feet long.

tope, *n.* [Hind. *top*, prob. fr. Pali *thūpo*, fr. Skr. *stūpa* tope, stupa.] *Buddhist Arch.* A round cupola-topped building erected as a Buddhist shrine.

to·pee', to·pi' (tō·pē'; tō'pē), *n.* [Hind. *ṭopī.*] *India.* A hat or cap, esp. a hat or helmet made of pith.

top'er (tōp'ẽr), *n.* A drunkard; a sot.

top'flight' (tŏp'flīt'), *adj.* Of topmost rank or eminence; ranking among the foremost in ability or excellence.

top'full' (tŏp'fo͝ol'), *adj.* Brimful.

top'gal'lant (tŏp'găl'ănt; *naut.* tō·găl'ănt), *n.* [See 1st TOP, 14; GALLANT, *adj.*] *Naut.* A topgallant mast or sail. See SAIL, *Illust.* **— adj.** *Naut.* **a** Situated above the topmast; designating or pertaining to the spars above the topmast. **b** Raised above adjoining portions; — of a rail, bulwark, or deck.

top hamper, *or* **top'-ham'per,** *n.* *Naut.* **a** The upper rigging, spars, etc., of a ship. **b** Rigging, spars, etc., not needed for the time and hence in the way.

top hat. A man's hat, usually of beaver or silk, with tall crown, sometimes belled for formal wear.

top'-heav'y (tŏp'hĕv'ĭ), *adj.* **1.** Having the top part too heavy for the lower part; unstable. **2.** Of a financial structure, overcapitalized. — **top'-heav'i·ness,** *n.*

To'phet, To'pheth (tō'fĕt), *n.* [Heb. *tōpheth.*] **1.** A word of uncertain meaning and etymology, occurring in the Old Testament. Scholarly opinion holds it to have been a place in the valley, where human sacrifices by fire, esp. of children to Moloch, were performed. **2.** [*often not cap.*] Hell, or a place likened to it; utter chaos, darkness, etc.

top'-hole' (tŏp'hōl'; 2), *adj.* *Brit. Slang.* Excellent.

to'phus (tō'fŭs), *n.; pl.* TOPHI (-fī). [L., tufa. See TUFA.] *Med.* A concretion in the body, esp. about the joints, chiefly in gouty persons.

to'pi (tō'pĭ), *n.* [Of Bantu origin.] An antelope (*Damaliscus corrigum jimela*) of eastern central Africa.

to·pi' (tō·pē'; tō'pē). Variant of TOPEE.

to'pi·ar'y (tō'pĭ·ẽr'ĭ *or, esp. Brit.,* -ẽr·ĭ), *adj.* [L. *topiarius* belonging to ornamental gardening.] Designating the work or art of training and trimming trees or shrubs into odd or ornamental shapes; also, characterized, as a garden, by such work. **— n.; pl.** TOPIARIES (-ĭz). Topiary art or gardening; also, a topiary garden.

top'ic (tŏp'ĭk), *n.* [L. *topica*, title of a work of Aristotle, fr. Gr. *topika*, neut. pl., fr. *topikos* of or for place, concerning *topoi*, or commonplaces, fr. *topos* a place.] **1.** *Rhet. & Logic.* **a** One of the general forms of argument employed in probable reasoning. **b** *pl.* A treatise on forms of argument. **2.** A heading as in an outlined argument or exposition. **3.** The subject of a discourse or any section of it; subject matter.

top'i·cal (-ĭ·kăl), *adj.* **1.** Of or pertaining to a place; local or designed for local application; as, a *topical* remedy. **2.** Of or pert. to a topic, or heading or subject; as, a synopsis in *topical* form. **3.** Referring to the topics of the day; as, *topical* allusions in Ben Jonson's plays. — **top'i·cal·ly,** *adv.*

top'knot' (tŏp'nŏt'), *n.* **1.** A knot of ribbon or lace, a tuft of feathers, etc., forming an ornamental headdress. **2.** A crest of feathers or hair on the top of the head.

top'loft'y (-lŏf'tĭ; 2), *adj.* *Colloq.* Very haughty; contemptuous; disdainful. — **top'loft'i·ness,** *n.*

top'mast' (tŏp'măst'; -măst), *n.* The second mast from the deck.

top minnow. Any of numerous small viviparous surface-feeding fishes constituting a family (Poeciliidae).

top'most (tŏp'mōst; -mŭst), *adj.* Highest; uppermost.

top'notch' (tŏp'nŏch'; 2), *adj.* *Colloq.* Highest or best attained or attainable; tiptop; first-rate.

to·pog'ra·pher (tō·pŏg'rȧ·fẽr), *n.* One skilled in topography; one who describes, maps, etc., the topography of a region.

to·pog'ra·phy (-fĭ), *n.* [LL. *topographia*, fr. Gr. *topographia*, fr. *topos* place + *graphein* to write.] **1.** *Obs.* The description of a particular place. **2.** The art or practice of graphic and exact delineation in minute detail, usually on maps or charts, of the physical features of any place or region. **3.** The configuration of a surface, including its relief, the position of its streams, lakes, roads, cities, etc. **4.** Topographic surveying. — **top'o·graph'ic** (tŏp'ō·grăf'ĭk), **top'o·graph'i·cal** (-ĭ·kăl), *adj.* — **top'o·graph'i·cal·ly,** *adv.*

to·pol'o·gy (tō·pŏl'ō·jĭ), *n.* [*topo-* (fr. Gr. *topos* place) + *-logy.*] **1.** Topographical study of a particular place; specif., the history of a region as indicated by its topography. **2.** *Anat.* The anatomy of a particular region of the body. **3.** *Math.* The doctrine of those properties of a figure unaffected by any deformation without tearing or joining. — **top'o·log'ic** (tŏp'ō·lŏj'ĭk), **top'o·log'i·cal** (-ĭ·kăl), *adj.*

top'o·nym (tŏp'ō·nĭm), *n.* [From TOPONYMY.] A name of a place; in scientific terminology, a name designating a region, as of the body, or indicating the location or place of origin of the thing named, as of a plant.

top'o·nym'ic (-nĭm'ĭk), *adj.* Also **top'o·nym'i·cal** (-ĭ·kăl). Of or pertaining to toponyms or toponymy.

to·pon'y·my (tō·pŏn'ĭ·mĭ), *n.* [Gr. *topos* place + *onoma, onyma*, name.] **1.** The place names of a region or language. **2.** *Anat.* The nomenclature of regional anatomy.

top'per (tŏp'ẽr), *n.* **1.** One that tops; as, a turnip *topper*. **2.** *Slang.* Someone or something first-rate or surpassingly good. **3.** A top hat. **4.** A topcoat: usually, a woman's short, lightweight outer coat, esp. one loose-fitting, as for wearing over a suit.

top'ping (tŏp'ĭng), *n.* **1.** That which forms the top of anything; esp., a topknot, etc. **2.** Act of one who tops. **— adj. 1.** That tops; esp., that rises above; as, *topping* mountains. **2.** Topmost in rank, degree, etc.; *Slang*, tiptop. **3.** *Colloq.* Fine; gallant.

top'ple (tŏp''l), *v. i.;* TOP'PLED (-'ld); TOP'PLING (-lĭng). [From E. dial. *top* to tip, tilt.] **1.** To fall forward as from top-heaviness; to tumble down. **2.** To jut out or overhang, as if tottering. **— v. t.** To push over, causing to fall by its own weight; to upset.

tops, *or* **the tops** (tŏps). *Slang.* (Used predicatively.) Topmost or the topmost in excellence, in popularity, or the like; surpassing all others in ability, attainment, or quality.

top'sail' (tŏp'sāl'; *naut.* -s'l), *n.* *Naut.* In a square-rigged vessel, the sail next above the lowermost sail on a mast. See SAIL, *Illust.* In a fore-and-aft-rigged vessel, the sail set above, and sometimes on, the gaff. A ***jib topsail*** is a small jib set above all. A ***club topsail*** is a gaff topsail having its foot bent on a light spar, or *club* (see SLOOP, *Illust.*).

top'-se'cret, *adj.* Demanding, or labeled as demanding, inviolate secrecy among top officials or a select few.

top sergeant. *Colloq.* The first sergeant of a military company, battery, or troop.

top'side' (tŏp'sīd'; 2), *n.* **1.** *Eng.* Bottom of a round of beef. See ROUND OF BEEF. **2.** *Naut.* The portion of the outer surface of a vessel on either side above the water line; — usually in *pl.* **— adv.** On deck; above; figuratively, in a commanding position.

top'soil' (-soil'), *n.* Surface soil, as distinguished from subsoil. **— v. t.** To remove the topsoil from (land).

top'sy-tur'vy (tŏp'sĭ·tûr'vĭ), *adv.* With the top or head downward; upside down; hence, in confusion or disorder. **— adj.** Turned topsy-turvy; greatly disordered. **— n.** A topsy-turvy condition. — **top'sy-tur'vi·ly,** *adv.* — **top'sy-tur'vi·ness,** *n.* — **top'sy-tur'vy·dom,** *n.*

toque (tōk), *n.* [F.] **1.** Historically, a round, full-spreading cap of soft fabric, pleated into a snug headband and usually adorned with a short plume. **2.** A woman's small, round, brimless hat suggestive of the historical form. **3.** *U. S.* = TUQUE.

tor (tôr), *n.* [AS. *torr.*] A high, craggy hill.

to'rah, to'ra (tō'rä), *n.; pl.* -ROTH (-rōth). [Heb. *tōrāh.*] *Jewish Lit.* **a** A law; precept. **b** Divine instruction; revelation. **c** [*cap.*] The Pentateuch, or "Law of Moses."

torch (tôrch), *n.* [OF. *torche*, fr. L. *torques, torquis*, a twisted necklace or collar.] **1.** A flaming light, as from burning resinous wood or twisted tow soaked with tallow. **2.** Something that flames, illuminates, or enlightens, like a torch; as, the *torch* of knowledge. **3.** Any of various portable devices for emitting a hot flame; as, an acetylene *torch*. **4.** A small flashlight. — **torch'bear'er** (-bâr'ẽr), *n.* — **torch'light'** (-līt'), *n.*

tor'chon lace (tôr'shŏn; *F.* tôr'shôɴ'). [F. *torchon* a dishcloth.] A bobbin lace of coarse linen thread in simple geometrical patterns.

torch'wood' (tôrch'wo͝od'), *n.* Any of a genus (*Amyris*, family Burseraceae, the torchwood family) of tropical shrubs or trees with alternate, pinnately compound leaves, small greenish flowers, and drupaceous fruit, and with inflammable resinous wood; also, the wood.

tore (tōr; 70), *n.* [F., fr. L. *torus.*] **1.** *Arch.* = TORUS, 2. See MOLDING, *Illust.* **2.** *Geom.* **a** The surface described by a conic section, esp. a circle, rotating about a straight line in its own plane. **b** The solid of revolution enclosed by such a surface.

tore. Past & dial. past part. of TEAR.

tor'e·a·dor' (tŏr'ē·ȧ·dôr'; tōr'ē·ȧ·dôr'), *n.* [Sp., fr. *torear* to fight bulls, fr. *toro* bull, fr. L. *taurus.*] A bullfighter; esp., a mounted bullfighter. Cf. TORERO.

‖**to·re'ro** (tō·rā'rō), *n.; pl.* -ROS (-rōs). [Sp.] A bullfighter on foot.

to·reu'tic (tō·ro͞o'tĭk), *adj.* [Gr. *toreutikos*, fr. *toreuein* to bore through, work in relief.] *Sculp.* Pertaining to or designating work wrought, esp. in metal, by embossing, chasing, etc.

to·reu'tics (-tĭks), *n.;* see -ICS. *Sculp.* Art or process of making toreutic work.

tor'ic (tŏr'ĭk), *adj.* Pertaining to, resembling, or shaped like a tore, or segment; as, **toric lens,** a simple lens having for one of its surfaces a segment of an equilateral zone of a tore. Such a lens has different refracting power in different meridians and is often used in the lenses of eyeglasses.

to'ri·i (tō'rē·ē), *n. sing. & pl.* [Jap.] *Jap. Arch.* A gateway, or gateways, of light skeletonlike construction, built at the approach to a Shinto temple.

tor·ment' (tôr·mĕnt'), *v. t.* [OF. *to(u)rmenter.*] **1.** *Rare.* To torture. **2.** To cause acute physical suffering or mental anguish in; to distress. **3.** To agitate; stir up. **4.** To vex; harass. — **Syn.** See AFFLICT. — **tor·ment'ing·ly**, *adv.*

tor'ment (tôr'mĕnt), *n.* [OF. *tourment, torment*, fr. L. *tormentum* an instrument of torture, a rack, torture, fr. *torquere* to twist.] **1.** *Archaic.* A torturing device, as the rack. **2.** Anguish of body or mind; distress. **3.** That which gives pain, vexation, etc.

tor'men·til (tôr'mĕn·tĭl), *n.* [F. *tormentille*, fr. ML. *tormentilla*, fr. L. *tormentum* pain. It is said to allay pain.] A yellow-flowered Eurasian herb (*Potentilla tormentilla*) of the rose family, the root of which is used in medicine and in tanning.

tor·men'tor (tôr·mĕn'tẽr), *n.* Also **tor·ment'er** (-mĕn'tẽr). **1.** One that torments. **2.** *Motion Pictures.* A screen covered to prevent echo during the taking of scenes. **3.** *Theaters.* A fixed wing or curtain on each side of the stage directly behind the proscenium arch.

torn (tōrn; 70). Past part. of TEAR.

tor·na'do (tôr·nā'dō), *n.; pl.* -DOES (-dōz). [Sp. *tronada* thunderstorm, fr. *tronar* to thunder, fr. L. *tonare.*] **1.** *Obs.* A tropical thunderstorm. **2. a** A squall off the west coast of Africa in which a violent wind revolves beneath threatening clouds. **b** A whirling wind accompanied by a funnel-shaped cloud, very violent and destructive in a narrow path often for many miles over the land. **3.** Any violent or destructive windstorm; a whirlwind. — **tor·nad'ic** (-năd'ĭk), *adj.*

tor·nil'lo (tôr·nĭl'ō; -nē'yō), *n.* = SCREW BEAN **b**.

to'roid (tō'roid), *n.* [*tore* + *-oid.*] *Geom.* A surface generated by the rotation of a plane closed curve about an axis lying in its plane, a generalized form of the tore.

to'rose (tō'rōs; tō·rōs'), *adj.* Also **to'rous** (tō'rŭs). [L. *torosus* full of muscle, brawny, fleshy. See TORUS.] **a** Bulging, as with muscles; muscular. **b** Knobbed; esp., *Bot.*, cylindrical with alternate swellings and contractions.

tor·pe'do (tôr·pē'dō), *n.; pl.* -DOES (-dōz). [L. *torpedo, -inis*, stiffness, numbness, torpedo (the fish), fr. *torpere* to be stiff.] **1.** An electric ray (fish). See 1st RAY. **2.** An engine or machine for destroying ships by blowing them up. Specif.: **a** A submarine mine. **b** A dirigible, self-propelling, cigar-shaped submarine projectile carrying an explosive charge, and projected from one vessel, often designed for that purpose, against another vessel at a distance. **3.** *Fireworks.* A small firework which explodes when thrown against a hard object. **4.** *Mil.* A charge of explosive enclosed in a case. **5.** *Petroleum.* An explosive cartridge lowered into a bored oil well, and there exploded, to clear obstructions or to open communication with a supply of oil. **6.** *Railroading.* A kind of detonating cartridge placed on a rail, and exploded as an alarm or fog signal. — *v. t.;* -DOED (-dōd); -DO·ING (-dō·ĭng). **1.** To destroy by, or subject to the action of, a torpedo or torpedoes. **2.** To wreck; shatter; ruin; as, to *torpedo* a plan of action.

torpedo boat. A vessel designed for firing torpedoes; specif., a small, very fast, thinly plated vessel with one or more torpedo tubes, and carrying only light guns.

tor·pe'do-boat' de·stroy'er. A larger, swifter, and more powerfully armed type of torpedo boat, originally intended for the destruction of torpedo boats, but later used also as a more formidable torpedo boat.

torpedo body. *Cant.* An automobile body which is built so that the side surfaces are flush.

torpedo tube. *Nav.* A tube fixed below or near the water line, through which a torpedo is fired.

tor'pid (tôr'pĭd), *adj.* [L. *torpidus*, fr. *torpere* to be stiff, numb, or torpid.] **1.** Having lost motion, or the power of exertion and feeling, as a hibernating animal; dormant; numb. **2.** Lacking in energy or vim; inert; dull; stupid; apathetic. — **tor·pid'i·ty** (tôr·pĭd'ĭ·tĭ), *n.* — **Syn.** See LETHARGY. — **tor'pid·ly**, *adv.* — **tor'pid·ness**, *n.*

tor'pid (tôr'pĭd), *n.* *Oxford Univ.* **a** A clinker-built, eight-oared racing boat in which the races of the Lent term are rowed and which, orig., was the second boat of a college. **b** *pl.* The races rowed in such boats.

tor'por (tôr'pẽr), *n.* [L., fr. *torpere* to be torpid.] **1.** Suspended animation; dormancy; sluggishness or stagnation of function. **2.** Mental or spiritual sluggishness. — **Syn.** See LETHARGY. — **tor'por·if'ic** (-ĭf'ĭk), *adj.*

torque (tôrk), *n.* [L. *torques* a twisted neck chain.] **1.** A collar or neck chain, usually twisted. **2.** [L. *torquere* to twist.] **a** *Mech.* That which produces or tends to produce rotation or torsion; a moment (of forces); specif., the turning moment of a tangential effort. **b** *Optics.* The twisting or rotatory effect of certain crystals and liquids upon the plane of polarization of plane-polarized light traversing them.

tor'ques (tôr'kwēz), *n.* [L., a necklace.] *Zool.* A cervical ring of hair, feathers, or modified integument distinguished from the adjacent surface by color or structure; a collar. — **tor'quate** (tôr'kwāt), *adj.*

tor're·fy (tŏr'ē·fī), *v. t.;* -FIED (-fīd); -FY'ING. Also **tor'ri·fy** (-ĭ·fī). [F. *torréfier*, fr. L. *torrefacere*, fr. *torrere* to parch + *facere* to make.] To subject to heat; to roast by a fire; to parch; scorch. Specif., *Pharm.*, to parch (drugs) on a metallic plate until they are friable. — **tor're·fac'tion** (-făk'shŭn), *n.*

tor'rent (tŏr'ĕnt; 74), *n.* [F., fr. L. *torrens, -entis*, fr. *torrens* burning, roaring, boiling, pres. part.] **1.** A violent stream, as of water, lava, or the like. **2.** A violent or rapid flow; a strong current; a flood. — *adj.* Of or like a torrent; rolling or rushing in a rapid stream.

tor·ren'tial (tŏ·rĕn'shăl), *adj.* **1.** Pertaining to, or having the character of, a torrent; as, *torrential* rains; also, caused by, or resulting from, action of rapid streams; as, *torrential* gravel. **2.** Like a torrent in violence or rapidity of flow. — **tor·ren'tial·ly**, *adv.*

tor'rid (tŏr'ĭd; 74), *adj.* [L. *torridus.*] **1.** Parched; dried with, or exposed to, heat, esp. of the sun; arid and hot. **2.** So hot as to scorch, parch, or the like burning. — **tor·rid'i·ty** (tŏ·rĭd'ĭ·tĭ), *n.* — **tor'rid·ly**, *adv.* — **tor'rid·ness**, *n.*

Torrid Zone. See ZONE, *n.*

tor·sade' (tôr·sād'), *n.* [F.] A twisted cord; also, a molded or worked ornament of similar form.

tor'sion (tôr'shŭn), *n.* [F., fr. LL. *torsio, tortio*, fr. L. *torquere, tortum*, to twist.] **1.** Act of turning or twisting, or state of being twisted; the wrenching of a body by the exertion of a lateral force tending to turn one end or part of it about a longitudinal axis, while the other is held fast or turned in the opposite direction. **2.** *Mech.* The internal moment or couple of restitution which arises in a thread, wire, or rod when twisted. — **tor'sion·al** (-ăl), *adj.* — **tor'sion·al·ly**, *adv.*

torsion balance. An instrument used to measure minute forces, as electrostatic or magnetic attraction and repulsion, by the torsion of a wire or filament.

torsk (tôrsk), *n.; see* PLURAL, *Note*, 6. [Dan. & Sw.] **a** = CUSK **a**. **b** The codfish.

tor'so (tôr'sō), *n.; pl.* TORSOS (-sōz), TORSI (-sē). [It., also, stalk.] **1.** The trunk of a sculptured representation of a human body; esp. and usually, the trunk of a statue mutilated of head and limbs. **2.** An impressive fragment of an unfinished or mutilated work. **3.** The human trunk.

tort (tôrt), *n.* [OF., fr. L. *tortus* twisted, crooked.] *Law.* Any wrongful act (not involving a breach of contract) for which a civil action will lie.

‖**tor'te** (tôr'tĕ; *Angl.* tôrt), *n.; pl.* TORTEN (tôr'tĕn). [G.] Literally, cake, esp. of a rich variety; specif., a sticky cake made of nuts, fruits, white of egg, often crumbs, and very little, if any, flour.

tor'ti·col'lis (tôr'tĭ·kŏl'ĭs), *n.* [NL., fr. L. *tortus* twisted + *collum* neck.] *Med.* An affection causing twisting of the neck and an unnatural position of the head; wryneck.

tor'tile (tôr'tĭl; 56), *adj.* [L. *tortilis.*] Twisted; coiled.

‖**tor·til'la** (tôr·tē'yä), *n.* [Sp., dim.] *Sp. Amer.* A thin flat unleavened cake, as of maize, baked on a heated iron or stone.

tor'tious (tôr'shŭs), *adj.* [From TORT.] *Law.* Implying or involving tort. — **tor'tious·ly**, *adv.*

tor'toise (tôr'tŭs; -tĭs), *n.; see* PLURAL, *Note*, 3. [Earlier *tortose, tortuce, tortu*, fr. ML. *tortuca*, and fr. F. *tortue*, prob. fr. L. *testudo, testugo*, with influence of L. *tortus* crooked, twisted (with ref. to the feet).] **1.** Any of a subclass (Chelonia) of reptiles; a turtle; esp., a land turtle. See TURTLE. **2.** A person or animal that moves slowly.

tortoise beetle. Any of a family (Chrysomelidae) of small tortoise-shaped beetles.

tortoise shell. **1.** The mottled horny substance of the shell of certain turtles, esp. the hawksbill (see TURTLE, 1), used in inlaying and in making various ornamental articles. **2.** Short for **tortoise-shell butterfly**, a handsomely colored butterfly (genus *Aglais*).

tor'toise-shell', *adj.* Made of tortoise shell, or having a mottled coloration suggesting tortoise shell.

tor'tri·cid (tôr'trĭ·sĭd), *adj.* [From *Tortrix*, type genus, fr. L. *torquere, tortum*, to twist.] Belonging to a family (Tortricidae) of small, stout-bodied moths.

tor'tu·os'i·ty (tôr'tū̇·ŏs'ĭ·tĭ), *n.; pl.* -TIES (-tĭz). **1.** Quality or state of being tortuous; crookedness; deviousness. **2.** A bend or twist; winding.

tor'tu·ous (tôr'tū̇·ŭs), *adj.* [OF. *tortuous*, fr. L. *tortuosus*, fr. *tortus* a twisting, fr. *torquere, tortum*, to twist.] **1.** Bent in different directions; full of twists or curves; winding. **2.** Not straightforward; sometimes, deceitful. — **tor'tu·ous·ly**, *adv.* — **tor'tu·ous·ness**, *n.*

tor'ture (tôr'tūr), *n.* [F., fr. LL. *tortura*, fr. L. *torquere, tortum*, to twist, rack, torture.] **1.** Act or process of inflicting severe pain, esp. as a punishment, in order to extort confession, or in revenge. **2.** Extreme pain; agony; torment. **3.** Something that causes agony or pain. **4.** A violent straining, distorting, etc., as of sense, thought, text, etc. — *v. t.* **1.** To put to torture; to punish with torture; now, to inflict severe pain upon. **2.** To subject to undue strain; to wrench or twist; to distort. — **Syn.** See AFFLICT. — **tor'tur·er** (-tūr·ẽr), *n.*

to'rus (tō'rŭs), *n.; pl.* TORI (-rī). [L., a round, swelling, or bulging place.] **1.** *Anat.* A smooth rounded protuberance. **2.** *Arch.* A type of molding of convex profile, commonly the lowest molding in the base of a column, next above the plinth. See MOLDING, BASE, *Illusts.* **3.** *Bot.* That part of the axis of a flower which bears the floral leaves; the receptacle. Cf. PERIGYNOUS, *Illust.*

To'ry (tō'rĭ; 70), *n.* [Ir. *tōruidhe* pursued man, robber, prob., pursuer.] **1.** [*sometimes not cap.*] *Hist.* Any armed Irish Papist or Royalist. **2.** *Eng. Politics.* One who sought to maintain the extreme prerogatives of the crown; a member of the party of conservatism (*Conservative* party) as opposed to the progressive party formerly called the *Whig*, and now the *Liberal*, party. **3.** *Amer. Hist.* One who, in the time of the Revolution, favored submitting to the claims of Great Britain against the colonies; a loyalist. **4.** [*often not cap.*] An extreme conservative in any state or party. — **To'ry, to'ry**, *adj.*

To'ry·ism (-ĭz'm), *n.* Tory principles or practices.

tosh (tŏsh), *n.* *Brit. Slang.* Nonsense.

toss (tŏs; 74), *v. t.;* TOSSED (tŏst) or, *Obs. exc. Poetic & Ref. Sp.*, TOST; TOSS'ING. [Origin uncert.] **1.** To fling continuously about or to and fro; to buffet; as, a ship *tossed* by waves. **2.** To stir up; agitate; disturb. **3.** To throw with a quick, light, or careless motion or with a sudden jerk; as, to *toss* a ball to the pitcher. **4.** To fling, lift up, or raise with a sudden sharp motion; as, to *toss* one's head. — *v. i.* **1.** To be pitched, flung, or thrown to and fro, etc. **2.** To be restless; to fling oneself about as in sleep; as, to *toss* all night long. **3.** To move with a quick, spirited or disdainful gesture; as, to *toss* out of a room. **4.** To toss something; esp., to toss up a coin. — **Syn.** See THROW. — *n.* **1.** Act of tossing or state or fact of being tossed. **2.** Commotion; excitement. **3.** A wager; a chance. **4.** Tossing distance; as, within the *toss* of a ball.

toss, *n.* *Scot.* A toast; a belle.

toss'er (tŏs'ẽr), *n.* One who or that which tosses.

toss'pot' (-pŏt'), *n.* Toper; drunkard.

toss'up' (-ŭp'), *n.* Act of tossing up, as of a coin to determine a chance; hence, an even chance.

tot (tŏt), *n.* Short for TOTAL. — *v. t.;* TOT'TED (tŏt'ĕd; -ĭd); TOT'TING. *Colloq.* To make up the sum of; to total.

tot, *n.* [Origin uncert.] **1.** Anything small; — often, a little child. **2.** *Chiefly Dial.* A drink of liquor; an allowance of liquor.

to'tal (tō'tăl; -t'l), *adj.* [OF., fr. ML. *totalis*, fr. L. *totus* all, whole.] **1.** Comprising or constituting a whole; entire; as, the *total* amount. **2.** Complete; utter; absolute; as, a *total* failure. **3.** Co-ordinating the activities of all citizens and agencies and the use of all resources and methods in a concentrated national program; as, *total* defense. — **Syn.** See WHOLE. — *n.* The whole; the whole sum or amount. — **Syn.** See SUM. — *v. t.;* TO'TALED (-tăld; -t'ld) or TO'TALLED; TO'TAL·ING or TO'TAL·LING. To bring to a total; to ascertain the total of; to add. — *v. i.* To amount to altogether.

total depravity. *Theol.* The Calvinistic doctrine of a hereditary depravity which corrupts all parts of man's nature without necessarily corrupting the whole of any part; — often misinterpreted to mean that human nature is wholly depraved. See CALVINISM.

to·tal'i·tar'i·an (tō·tăl'ĭ·târ'ĭ·ăn), *adj.* Of or pertaining to a highly centralized government under the control of a political group which allows no recognition of or representation to other political parties, as in Fascist Italy or in Germany under the Nazi regime. — **to·tal'i·tar'i·an**, *n.* — **to·tal'i·tar'i·an·ism** (-ĭz'm), *n.*

to·tal′i·ty (tō·tăl′ĭ·tĭ), *n.* **1.** Quality or state of being total or a total; wholeness. **2.** The whole sum or quantity.

to′tal·i·za′tor, to′tal·i·sa′tor (tō′tăl·ĭ·zā′tẽr; tō′t'l-), *n.* A pari-mutuel.

to′tal·ize (-īz), *v. t.* To make total or a total; to combine into a whole. — **to′tal·i·za′tion** (-ĭ·zā′shŭn; -ī·zā′-), *n.*

to′tal·iz′er (-īz′ẽr), *n.* One who or that which totalizes; specif.: **a** A totalizator. **b** An adding machine.

to′tal·ly, *adv.* Altogether; wholly.

total war. War waged with simultaneous use of all available weapons of destruction and means of demoralization against enemy combatants and noncombatants.

to′ta·quine (tō′tȧ·kwēn; -kwĭn), *n.* Also **to′ta·qui′na** (tō′tȧ·kē′nȧ), **to′ta·quin.** [L. *totus* whole (quinine group of alkaloids) + Sp. *quina.* See QUININE.] *Pharm.* An antimalarial drug containing quinine and other alkaloids, obtained from American cinchona bark.

tote (tōt), *v. t.* [Origin uncert.] *Colloq., U. S.* To carry or bear; to transport; often, to carry in one's arms or on one's shoulders or back. — *n. Colloq., U. S.* Act of one who totes; also, a load; haul.

to′tem (tō′tĕm), *n.* [Of Algonquian origin; cf. Ojibway *ototeman* his relations.] **a** One of a class of objects regarded by a primitive people as having blood relationship to a specific family group or sib; esp., any animal or plant species so regarded. **b** A symbol or representation of the totemic being. — **to·tem′ic** (tō·tĕm′ĭk), *adj.*

to′tem·ism (tō′tĕm·ĭz'm), *n.* Belief in totems and totemistic relationships; esp., a system of distinguishing families, clans, etc., in a tribe by the totem; as, clan *totemism.*

to′tem·ist (-ĭst), *n.* One of a clan or tribe having a totem.

to′tem·is′tic (-ĭs′tĭk), *adj.* Of or pertaining to totemists or totemism.

totem pole *or* **post.** A pole or pillar, carved and painted with totemic symbols, set up before the houses of certain Indian tribes of the northwest coast of North America.

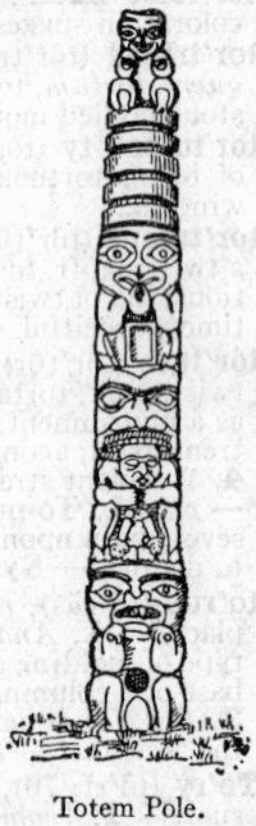

Totem Pole.

toth′er (tŭth′ẽr), *adj. & pron.* Also **t'oth′er.** [From ME. *the tother,* for *thet other, that other,* the other.] *Now Chiefly Dial.* That other; the other.

toti-. [L. *totus.*] A combining form meaning *whole, wholly,* as in *toti*palmate.

‖**to′ti·dem ver′bis** (tŏt′ĭ·dĕm vûr′bĭs). [L.] In so many words.

to′ti·pal′mate (tō′tĭ·păl′māt), *adj.* [L. *totus* all, whole + E. *palmate.*] *Zool.* Having all four toes united by a web, as pelicans, cormorants, etc. — **to′ti·pal·ma′tion** (-păl·mā′shŭn), *n.*

‖**to′tis vi′ri·bus** (tō′tĭs vĭr′ĭ·bŭs). [L.] With all one's might.

‖**to′to cae′lo** (tō′tō sē′lō). [L.] By the whole extent of the heavens; diametrically.

tot′ter (tŏt′ẽr), *v. i.* [ME. *toteren.*] **1.** To shake, tremble, or rock, as if falling or about to fall; to be unsteady. **2.** To be unsteady on the feet. — **tot′ter·y** (-ĭ), *adj.*

tot′ter·ing (-ĭng), *adj.* That totters; unsteady, esp. in gait. — **tot′ter·ing·ly,** *adv.*

tou·can′ (tōō·kăn′; tōō′kăn), *n.* [F., fr. Pg. *tucano,* fr. Tupi *tucano, tucan.*] Any of a family (Ramphastidae) of fruit-eating birds of tropical America. They have a very large but light and thin-walled beak, and brilliant coloring. See BILL, *Illust.*

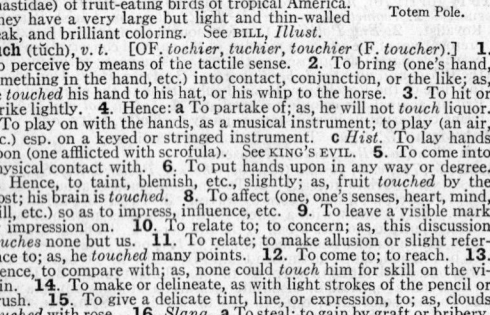

touch (tŭch), *v. t.* [OF. *tochier, tuchier, touchier* (F. *toucher*).] **1.** To perceive by means of the tactile sense. **2.** To bring (one's hand, something in the hand, etc.) into contact, conjunction, or the like; as, he *touched* his hand to his hat, or his whip to the horse. **3.** To hit or strike lightly. **4.** Hence: **a** To partake of; as, he will not *touch* liquor. **b** To play on with the hands, as a musical instrument; to play (an air, etc.) esp. on a keyed or stringed instrument. **c** *Hist.* To lay hands upon (one afflicted with scrofula). See KING'S EVIL. **5.** To come into physical contact with. **6.** To put hands upon in any way or degree. **7.** Hence, to taint, blemish, etc., slightly; as, fruit *touched* by the frost; his brain is *touched.* **8.** To affect (one, one's senses, heart, mind, will, etc.) so as to impress, influence, etc. **9.** To leave a visible mark or impression on. **10.** To relate to; to concern; as, this discussion *touches* none but us. **11.** To relate; to make allusion or slight reference to; as, he *touched* many points. **12.** To come to; to reach. **13.** Hence, to compare with; as, none could *touch* him for skill on the violin. **14.** To make or delineate, as with light strokes of the pencil or brush. **15.** To give a delicate tint, line, or expression, to; as, clouds *touched* with rose. **16.** *Slang.* **a** To steal; to gain by graft or bribery. **b** To induce to give or lend; to borrow from. **17.** *Geom.* To be tangent to. — **Syn.** See AFFECT.

— *v. i.* **1.** To touch (in any sense) someone or something. **2.** To be in contact. **3.** Hence, to approach near; verge; as, his remarks *touch* on blasphemy. **4.** To pertain; relate; as, this *touches* upon his well-being. **5.** To treat a topic, etc., in a slight or casual manner; as, he merely *touched* upon this. **6.** To make an incidental stop; as, the ship *touched* at many ports. — ***touch up.*** **a** To improve, as a picture by touches of the brush, or a literary work by emendations; to polish up. **b** To stimulate by or as by a flick of a whip.

— *n.* [From OF. *touche* (fr. the verb), and fr. E. *touch,* v. See TOUCH, *v.*] **1.** A light stroke, tap, or blow. **2.** Act, fact, or gesture of touching. **3.** The process, function, or power of perception by touching; the special sense by which pressure or traction exerted on the skin or mucous membrane is perceived; the tactile sense. **4.** Hence: **a** A (specified) sensation conveyed through the tactile nerves; feel; as, the velvety *touch* of a fabric. **b** Mental or moral sensitiveness, responsiveness, or tact. **5. a** A Touchstone, the stone. **b** Criterion; test; trial. **6.** Characteristic feature, trait, or quality; as, one *touch* of nature. **7.** An impression, mark, or stamp; a visible effect. **8.** A defect; a weakness; as, a *touch* in the brain. **9.** A suddenly aroused or transient emotion or impression; as, he had one *touch* of compunction. **10. a** A twinge, as of pain; a light attack, as of disease. **b** A trace; dash; as, a *touch* of summer. **11.** A delicate stroke in touching up an artistic composition; hence, any touching-up detail; also, an effect produced by or as if by the light stroke of a brush or the pencil. **12.** Distinctive manner or method; as, the *touch* of a master. **13.** A narrow escape; a near approach, as to death. **14.** The state of being in contact or communication; unbroken intercourse, intimate understanding or sympathy, etc. **15.** *Slang.* An act of touching, or borrowing, stealing, etc. **16.** *Change Ringing.* A set of changes less than the total number possible. **17.** *Music.* **a** The playing of an instrument, as a lute or piano, with the fingers; also, musical notes so produced. **b** A manner or method of touching or striking an instrument. **c** Particular action of a keyboard instrument with reference to the resistance of its keys to pressure; as, a piano with a stiff *touch.* **18.** *Rugby & Association Football.* That part of the ground lying immediately without the field of play on either side, in Rugby including the touch-lines.

touch′a·ble (tŭch′ȧ·b'l), *adj.* Capable of being touched.

touch and go. a Rapid movement from point to point. **b** A highly uncertain or precarious situation. — **touch′-and-go′,** *adj.*

touch′back′ (tŭch′băk′), *n.* *Amer. Football.* Act or an instance of being in possession of the ball behind one's own goal line when the ball is declared dead, the impetus which caused the ball to pass the goal line having been furnished by an opponent. Cf. SAFETY, *n.,* 6.

touch′down′ (-doun′), *n.* *Amer. Football.* The act of scoring by being lawfully in possession of the ball on, above, or behind, the opponents' goal line when the ball is declared dead.

‖**tou′ché′** (tōō′shā′), *adj.* [F.] Literally, touched, esp. by a fencing opponent's weapon; hence, scored on in argument; — used to acknowledge a successful point.

touched (tŭcht), *adj.* **1.** That has been subjected to touching. **2.** Slightly unbalanced mentally; cracked.

touch′er (tŭch′ẽr), *n.* One who or that which touches.

touch football. A variety of American football played usually without goal posts or protective clothing and usually with a ball slightly smaller than the regulation intercollegiate ball, in which forward and lateral passing, along with blocking, forms the basis of offensive play and the ball carrier is stopped for the down, not by tackling, but when a defensive player touches or tags him with two hands on or below the shoulders and above the waist.

touch′hole′ (tŭch′hōl′), *n.* In old-time cannons or firearms, the vent through which fire was communicated to the powder.

touch′ing (tŭch′ĭng), *adj.* That touches, esp. the emotions; pathetic. — **Syn.** See MOVING. — *prep. Archaic.* In reference to; concerning. — **touch′ing·ly,** *adv.*

touch′line′ (-līn′), *n.* *Rugby & Association Football.* Either of the sidelines bounding the field of play.

touch′-me-not′, *n.* **a** The garden balsam (*Impatiens balsamina*). **b** Squirting cucumber.

touch′stone′ (tŭch′stōn′), *n.* **1.** *Mineral.* A black siliceous stone allied to flint; — used to test the purity of gold and silver by the streak left on the stone when rubbed by the metal. **2.** Any test or criterion by which to try a thing's qualities. — **Syn.** See STANDARD.

touch′wood′ (-wŏŏd′), *n.* **1.** Wood decayed, dried, or prepared to serve for tinder; punk. **2.** Dried fungi used as tinder; punk; amadou.

touch′y (tŭch′ĭ), *adj.;* TOUCH′I·ER (-ĭ·ẽr); TOUCH′I·EST. [From *techy,* after *touch.*] **1.** Nervously sensitive to a touch, or open or covert criticism; easily offended; irascible. **2.** Acutely sensitive or irritable, as a part of the body; highly inflammable, as a chemical. — **Syn.** See IRASCIBLE. — **touch′i·ly,** *adv.* — **touch′i·ness,** *n.*

tough (tŭf), *adj.* [AS. *tōh.*] **1.** Strong or firm in texture, but flexible and not brittle. **2.** Specif., of meat, vegetables, etc., not easily chewed or masticated. **3.** Glutinous; sticky. **4.** Stiff; vigorous. **5.** Able to endure strain, hardship, or severe labor; robust. **6.** Very hard to influence; stubborn. **7.** *U. S.* Hence, unruly or vicious; often, rowdyish; ruffianly. **8.** Extremely difficult to cope with. **9.** Stubbornly fought; as, a *tough* contest. — **Syn.** See STRONG. — *n. U. S.* A tough person; esp., a rowdy. — **tough′ly,** *adv.* — **tough′ness,** *n.*

tough′en (tŭf′ĕn), *v. i. & t.* To grow or make tough or tougher. — **tough′en·er,** *n.*

‖**tou′jours′ per′drix′** (tōō′zhōōr′ pĕr′drē′). [F.] Literally, always partridge; hence, too much of a good thing.

tou·pee′ (tōō·pā′; -pē′), *n.* [F. *toupet,* dim. of OF. *top, toup,* tuft of hair.] **1.** *Hist.* A curl or lock of false hair worn at the crown of the head. **2.** Hence, a small wig or small patch of false hair covering a bald spot.

tour (tōōr; 84), *n.* [F. *tour,* OF. *tor, torn,* fr. L. *tornus* lathe, and fr. F. *tourner,* OF. *torner,* to turn. See TURN.] **1.** One's turn in an orderly schedule; a spell; also, a shift, as in a factory; as, three *tours* a day. **2.** A trip or excursion, esp. one in which one returns to one's starting point; a circular journey for business, pleasure, education, etc. — *v. i.* To make a tour; as, to *tour* through a country. — *v. t.* **1.** To make a tour of; as, to *tour* France. **2.** *Theater.* To present on a tour.

tou′ra·co′ (tōō′rȧ′kō′), *n.* [Prob. fr. a W. Afr. name.] Any of a family (Musophagidae) of African birds allied to the cuckoos.

tour·bil′lion (tōōr·bĭl′yŭn), *n.* [F. *tourbillon* a whirlwind, fr. L. *turbo, -inis,* a whirl, whirlwind.] Something resembling a whirlwind; sometimes, a vortex, as of a whirlwind or whirlpool; esp., a firework having a spiral flight.

tour de force (tōōr′ dē fôrs′). [F.] A feat of strength or skill; also, a merely adroit or ingenious accomplishment.

tour′ing (tōōr′ĭng), *adj.* That tours or is used for touring.

touring car. An automobile for touring; specif., an open car similar to a phaeton except that the body is longer, permitting the use of additional seats in the tonneau.

tour′ism (tōōr′ĭz'm; 84), *n.* **1.** The practice of touring; traveling for recreation. **2.** Tourists collectively; touring parties. **3.** The guidance or management of tourists, as a business.

tour′ist (tōōr′ĭst), *n.* One who makes a tour; esp., one who travels from place to place for pleasure or culture. — *adj.* Of, pertaining to, suitable for, or serving tourists.

tourist class. A class of accommodations in a passenger vessel, inferior to cabin class (which see). *Tourist class* was thus formerly applied to the second-best type of accommodations. — **tour′ist-class′,** *adj. & adv.*

tourist court. = MOTEL.

tour′ma·line (tōōr′mȧ·lĭn; -lēn), *n.* [F.] *Mineral.* A complex silicate, usually black, but sometimes blue, red, green, brown, or colorless. When transparent and cut, it makes a gem of great beauty. See BOROSILICATE.

tour′na·ment (tōōr′nȧ·mĕnt; tûr′-), *n.* [OF. *torneiement, tornoiement,* fr. *torneier.* See TOURNEY.] **1.** *Hist.* A knightly sport in which mounted armored combatants engaged one another to exhibit their skill and courage, and to win a prize bestowed by the "queen of beauty," or lady of the tournament. **2.** The whole series of knightly sports, jousts, and tilts occurring at a particular time and place. **3.** Hence, in modern usage, an athletic meeting, comprising contests in a large number of sports. **4.** An encounter; battle; contest. **5.** Any trial of skill in which there is a series of contests; as, a tennis or chess *tournament.*

tour′nay′ (to͝or′nā′), *n.* [From *Tournai,* Belgium.] A printed worsted fabric for upholstery.

tour′ney (to͝or′nĭ; tûr′nĭ), *n.; pl.* TOURNEYS (-nĭz). [OF. *tornei, tornoi,* fr. *torneier, tornoier, tournoier,* to tilt, tourney.] A tournament. — *v. i.* To perform in a tournament; to tilt; joust.

tour′ni·quet (to͝or′nĭ·kĕt; *now rarely* tûr′-), *n.* [F., fr. *tourner* to turn.] *Surg.* A device for arresting bleeding, originally a bandage twisted tight with a stick; now, any of various instruments, as a pad pressed down by a screw, or an elastic rubber bandage, for similar purposes.

touse (touz; *Scot.* to͞oz, to͞os), *v. t.* [ME. *tousen, tusen* (in comp.).] *Now Dial.* To tousle; rumple; dishevel. — *n. Dial.* Disturbance.

‖**tous frais faits** (to͞o′ frĕ′ fĕ′). [F.] All expenses defrayed.

tou′sle (tou′z'l), *v. t.;* TOU′SLED (-z'ld); TOU′SLING (-zlĭng). [Freq. of TOUSE.] *Colloq.* To dishevel; rumple. — *n.* A tousled mass or state; specif., a mop of hair.

‖**tous–les–mois** (to͞o′lā·mwȧ′), *n.* [F., all the months, i. e., every month, the tubers being edible at all seasons.] Starch from rootstocks of the edible canna (*Canna edulis*), often sold as arrowroot, and used in the preparation of foods for infants and as an adulterant of cocoa.

tout (tout; *Scot. & dial.* to͞ot), *v. i.* [ME. *tuten* to peep, look; akin to AS. *tōtian* to project.] **1.** *Colloq.* To canvass for customers, patronage, or votes, etc. **2.** *Horse Racing.* **a** *Slang, Eng.* To spy upon race horses at their trials, or to get by improper means the secrets of the stable, for betting purposes. **b** *Slang, U. S.* To act as a tout. — *v. t.* **1.** *Colloq.* To solicit; importune. **2.** *Horse Racing Slang.* **a** *Eng.* To spy out information about, as a racing stable or horse. **b** *U. S.* To give a tip on (a race horse) with the expectation of sharing in the winnings. — *n.* One who touts; specif., *Slang:* **a** A spy for a thief, or the like. **b** One who solicits custom, as a runner for a hotel, gambling place, etc. **c** *Eng.* One who secretly watches race horses in training, or gets racing information by improper means, for betting purposes. **d** *U. S.* One who gives a tip on a race horse for an expected compensation, esp. in hopes of a share in any winnings.

‖**tout à fait** (to͞o′-tȧ fĕ′). [F.] Entirely; quite.

‖**tout à vous** (to͞o′-tȧ vo͞o′). [F.] Wholly yours; at your service.

‖**tout com′pren′dre c'est tout par′don′ner** (to͞o′ kôN′präN′drĕ sĕ to͞o′ pȧr′dô′nā′). [F.] To understand all is to pardon all.

‖**tout de suite** (to͞ot′ swēt′). [F.] Immediately; also, successively.

‖**tout en′sem′ble** (to͞o′-täN′säN′bl′). [F.] All together; hence, in the fine arts, etc., the general effect of a work.

tout′er (tout′ẽr), *n.* One who touts or seeks customers, patronage, votes, etc.; a runner; a tout.

‖**tout le monde** (to͞ol′ môNd′). [F.] Literally, all the world; everybody.

tou′zle. Var. of TOUSLE.

to·va′rish, to·va′rich (tō·vä′rĭsh), *n.* [Russ. *tovarishch.*] Comrade; — applied to Russian Communist party members.

tow (tō), *v. t.* [AS. *togian* to pull, drag.] To draw or pull along after by a rope or chain; esp., to draw by a towline through water. — *n.* **1.** Act or instance of towing; the fact or state of being towed; — in the phrases *to take in tow,* that is, to tow, and *to take a tow,* that is, to avail oneself of towing. **2.** That which tows or is used for towing something, as a rope or chain or a towboat. **3.** That which is towed; esp., a barge.

tow, *n.* [AS. *toh-,* in *tohlīne* towline.] *Scot.* A rope.

tow, *n.* [AS. *tow* (in comp.) a spinning, weaving.] The coarse and broken part of flax, hemp, or jute, separated by the hatchel or swingle, and ready for spinning; also, yarn spun from tow, or cloth (**tow cloth**) made from such yarn.

tow′age (tō′ĭj), *n.* Act of towing; also, cost of towing.

to′ward (tō′ẽrd; tōrd; 70), *adj.* [AS. *tōweard* impending, future. See TO; -WARD.] **1.** Approaching; esp., imminent. **2.** *Archaic.* **a** Ready to learn; also, tractable; as, a *toward* youth. **b** Willing; obliging. **3.** Going on; in progress; — used predicatively. — (tō′ẽrd; tōrd; to͞o·wôrd′), *prep.* **1. a** In the direction of. **b** So as to face; as, his back was *toward* me. **2. a** Along a course which if pursued is bound to result in; as, efforts *toward* reconciliation. **b** In the presence, reception, or proximity of; in relation to; as, intolerance *toward* another sect. **3.** Approaching to; close upon; as, *toward* four o'clock. **4.** As a share or providing for the support or payment of; as, to save something *toward* an education.

to′ward·ly (tō′ẽrd·lĭ; tōrd′lĭ), *adj.* **1.** Favorable; timely. **2.** Compliant; tractable; docile. — **to′ward·li·ness** (-lĭ·nĕs; -nĭs), *n.*

to′wards (tō′ẽrdz; tōrdz; to͞o·wôrdz′; *see* TOWARD, *prep.*), *prep.* Toward (all senses). *Towards* is now the prevailing form in British usage.

tow′boat′ (tō′bōt′), *n.* **1.** A small, ruggedly built power vessel used for towing barges or towing and guiding large vessels; — more often called *tugboat.* **2.** *U. S.* A steam or diesel-powered flat-bottomed boat, strongly built and equipped with reinforced structures called "towing knees" at the bow for pushing forward barges lashed together, on inland waterways.

tow car. See WRECKER, *n.,* 4.

tow′el (tou′ĕl), *n.* [OF. *toaille* (F. *touaille*), of Teut. origin.] A cloth or absorbent paper used for wiping, esp. one used for drying anything wet. — *v. t.;* -ELED (-ĕld) or -ELLED; -EL·ING or -EL·LING. To rub or dry with a towel.

tow′el·ing, tow′el·ling (tou′ĕl·ĭng), *n.* Material for towels; specif., cloth in long pieces to be cut as desired.

tow′er (tou′ẽr), *n.* [ME. *towr, tour, tur, tor,* fr. AS. *torr* (fr. L.), and fr. OF. *tor, tur* (F. *tour*), fr. L. *turris.*] **1.** A building or structure typically higher than its diameter, or relatively high by its position. A tower may be isolated, as a campanile; or appended to a larger structure, as a church belfry. **2.** Such a structure used as a defense; hence, citadel; fortress. **3.** A towerlike structure, mast, or formation. — *v. i.* To reach or rise to a height above other objects; to be lofty. — **tow′ered** (-ẽrd), *adj.*

tow′er·ing (tou′ẽr·ĭng), *adj.* **1.** That towers; lofty. **2.** Hence: **a** Surpassing; extremely high or great. **b** Increasing in intensity; as, a *towering* rage. — **tow′er·ing·ly,** *adv.*

tow′head′ (tō′hĕd′), *n.* One having soft whitish hair; also, a head of such hair. — **tow′head′ed,** *adj.*

tow·hee′ (tō·hē′; tō·hwē′; tō′hē), *n.* Also **towhee bunting.** [Imitative.] Any of certain American finches (genera *Pipilo* and *Oberholseria*) related to the sparrows; esp., the common species (*P. erythrophthalmus*) of eastern North America, called also *chewink,* and the ***California towhee*** (*P. crissalis*) and the ***Oregon towhee*** (*P. maculatus oregonus*) of the western United States.

to wit. See 1st WIT.

tow′line′ (tō′līn′), *n.* A line used in towing.

tow′mond (tou′mŭnd), *n. Scot.* A twelvemonth.

town (toun), *n.* [AS. *tūn* enclosure, fence, manor, village, town.] **1.** *Dial.* Any cluster of houses recognized as a distinct place; a village. **2. a** A center of population, larger and more fully organized than a village, but not incorporated as a city. **b** *Eng.* A village with a periodical fair or market; — more fully ***market town.*** **c** Any large closely populated place, as a city, a borough, or an urban district. **3.** *U. S.* **a** In New England, a municipal corporation of a less complex character than a city, the sovereign authority generally being the **town meeting,** or general assembly of all the qualified voters, which elects all officers and decides all local governmental matters. **b** In other states, a unit of rural administration more or less like the New England town; a township (which see). **4. a** The body of inhabitants of a town; the townspeople. **b** The citizens, electorate, or qualified voters of a town. **5.** Usually with *the.* The city as contrasted with the country; urban life. — **town,** *adj.*

town clerk. An officer who keeps the records of a town.

town crier. A town officer who makes proclamations.

town hall. Sometimes **town′house′** (toun′hous′), *n.* Commonly, a public building belonging to a town and used for public offices and for the meetings of town council, courts, public assemblies, etc.

Town′send Re·cov′er·y Plan (toun′zĕnd). A proposal (1934), originated as **Townsend Old′–Age′ Re·volv′ing Pen′sion** by Dr. F. E. Townsend, to award to each person of sixty years or over, who retires from active employment, $200 per month to be spent within the month, funds to be provided by a 2% transaction tax.

towns′folk′ (tounz′fōk′), *n. pl.* Townspeople.

town′ship (toun′shĭp), *n.* [AS. *tūnscipe* the inhabitants of a *tūn.*] **1.** In England, an ancient unit of administration identical in area with, or a division of, a parish. **2.** In the United States, a primary unit of local government of varying character in different localities. In New England, where it is called *town* (which see), it exists in its primitive form except as modified and partly subordinated by the later-formed units, the county and state. In the northwestern states the county is the older unit and the township is a division of the county. In the southern states the county is generally the more important unit, and townships, where they exist, are mere local divisions. Abbr. *tp.* **3.** In surveys of U. S. public lands, a division of territory containing 36 sections, or 36 square miles. See MEASURE, *Table* 4. **4.** In Canada, a subdivision of certain of the provinces.

towns′man (tounz′măn), *n.; pl.* -MEN (-mĕn). **1.** An inhabitant of a town; hence, a town-bred man. **2.** One of the same town as another. **3.** In New England, a selectman.

towns′peo′ple (-pē′p'l), *n. pl.* Town-dwelling or town-bred persons.

tow′path′ (tō′pȧth′), *n.* A path along a canal, etc., traveled by men or animals towing boats.

tow′rope′ (-rōp′), *n.* A rope used in towing.

tox′al·bu·min (tŏk′săl·bū′mĭn), *n.* [*toxic* + *albumin.*] *Biochem.* Any of a class of toxic substances of protein nature.

tox·e′mi·a, tox·ae′mi·a (tŏks·ē′mĭ·ȧ), *n.; pl.* -AS (-ȧz). [NL., fr. *toxic* + *-emia.*] See BLOOD POISONING. — **tox·e′mic, tox·ae′mic** (-ē′mĭk; -ĕm′ĭk), *adj.*

tox′ic (tŏk′sĭk), *adj.* [ML. *toxicus,* fr. L. *toxicum* poison, fr. Gr. *toxikon* (sc. *pharmakon*) arrow poison, fr. *toxikos* of or for the bow, fr. *toxon* bow, arrow.] **1.** Of, pertaining to, or caused by poison or a toxin. **2.** Affected by a toxin. **3.** Poisonous.

tox′i·cant (tŏk′sĭ·kănt), *adj.* Poisonous; producing a toxic effect. — *n.* A poisonous agent or drug, as opium; also, an intoxicant.

tox′i·ca′tion (-kā′shŭn), *n.* Poisoning.

tox·ic′i·ty (tŏks·ĭs′ĭ·tĭ), *n.; pl.* -TIES (-tĭz). Quality, state, or degree of being toxic, or poisonous; poisonousness.

tox′i·co- (tŏk′sĭ·kō-), **toxic-.** [Gr. *toxikon.*] A combining form denoting *poison,* as in *toxicology,* **tox′i·co·pho′bi·a.**

tox′i·co·gen′ic (-jĕn′ĭk), *adj.* [*toxico-* + *-genic.*] *Physiol. & Med.* **a** Producing toxic products. **b** Produced by toxic substances.

tox′i·col′o·gy (tŏk′sĭ·kŏl′ō·jĭ), *n.* [*toxico-* + *-logy.* See TOXIC.] The science which treats of poisons, their antidotes, etc. — **tox′i·co·log′i·cal** (-kō·lŏj′ĭ·kăl), *adj.* — **tox′i·co·log′i·cal·ly,** *adv.* — **tox′i·col′o·gist** (-kŏl′ō·jĭst), *n.*

tox′i·co′sis (-kō′sĭs), *n.* [NL., fr. *toxic-* + *-osis.*] *Med.* A morbid condition caused by the action of a poison.

tox′in (tŏk′sĭn), *n.* Also **tox′ine** (-sĭn; -sēn). [See TOXIC.] *Biochem.* A poison formed as a specific secretion product in the metabolism of a vegetable or animal organism and chemically allied to proteins. True toxins (cf. EXOTOXIN) are elaborated by plants, esp. in seeds; by snakes; by insects, etc.; as well as by bacteria, as in tetanus, diphtheria, and botulism. See ENDOTOXIN.

tox′in–an′ti·tox′in, *n. Immunol.* A mixture of toxin and antitoxin, used in immunizing against the disease for which they are specific.

tox′i·pho′bi·a (tŏk′sĭ·fō′bĭ·ȧ), *n.* [NL., fr. *toxico-* + *-phobia.*] *Med.* Morbid fear of being poisoned.

tox′oid (tŏk′soid), *n. Immunol.* A toxin, as that of diphtheria, treated so as to destroy its toxicity but leave it still capable of inducing formation of antibodies on injection.

tox·oph′i·lite (tŏks·ŏf′ĭ·līt), *n.* [Gr. *toxon* bow + *philos* loving + *-ite.*] One fond of archery. — **tox·oph′i·lit′ic** (-lĭt′ĭk), *adj.*

tox′o·plas·mo′sis (tŏk′sō·plăz·mō′sĭs), *n.* [NL., fr. *toxo-* (fr. Gr. *toxikon* poison) + *plasm-* + *-osis.*] *Pathol.* The disease caused in human beings (in whom it is usually a highly fatal encephalitis), dogs, other mammals, and birds by infection with any of a genus (*Toxoplasma*) of parasitic microorganisms. — **tox′o·plas′mic** (-plăz′mĭk), *adj.*

toy (toi), *n.* [D. *tuig* tools, trash, speel*tuig* playthings, toys.] **1.** *Obs.* **a** Amorous dalliance; flirting. **b** Pastime; sport; antic. **2.** A paltry concern; a trifle. **3.** An ornament; gewgaw; trinket. **4.** A thing to play with; esp., something made for the amusement of a child or for his use in play. **5.** Hence, something diminutive; specif., any dog (**toy dog**), pigeon, etc., of various very small breeds. **6.** [Prob. the same word.] *Scot.* Formerly, a headdress of linen or woolen, that hangs down over the shoulders. — *v. i.* To trifle; play; dally. — **Syn.** See TRIFLE. — *adj.* Of the nature of, or made as, a toy; toylike. — **toy′er,** *n.*

toy fish. Any of various small fishes kept in aquariums as pets.

toy′on (toi′ŏn), *n.* [Sp. *toyon, tollon,* prob. of Mex. Ind. origin.] An ornamental evergreen shrub (*Heteromeles arbutifolia*) of the apple family, of the North American Pacific coast, having white flowers succeeded by bright-red berries.

tra′be·at′ed (trā′bē·āt′ĕd; -ĭd), *adj.* Also **tra′be·ate** (-āt). [L. *trabs, trabis,* beam, timber.] *Arch.* Designed or constructed of horizontal beams or lintels; not arcuate. — **tra′be·a′tion** (-ā′shŭn), *n.*

tra·bec′u·la (trȧ·bĕk′ū·lȧ), *n.; pl.* -LAE (-lē). [L., a little beam, dim. of *trabs* a beam.] **1.** *Anat. & Zool.* A small bar, rod, bundle of fibers, or septal membrane, in the framework of an organ or part. **2.** *Bot.* A row of cells bridging an intercellular space or, in mosses, extending across the cavity of a sporangium. — **tra·bec′u·lar** (-lẽr), **tra·bec′u·late** (-lāt), *adj.*

trace (trās), *n.* [ME., fr. OF. *trace.* See TRACE, *v.*] **1.** *Obs.* Course or path followed. **2.** A mark or line left by anything that has passed; footprint; track; also, *U. S.,* a beaten path; trail. **3.** A sign or evidence of some past thing; a vestige. **4.** Something traced or drawn; esp., a traced or lightly marked line. **5.** A barely discernible quantity, quality, or characteristic. **6.** *Chem.* A very small quantity of a constituent, esp. when not quantitatively determined because of minuteness. **7.** *Psychol.* An engram.

Syn. **Trace, vestige, track** mean a perceptible sign left by something that has passed. **Trace** may suggest any line or mark, material or immaterial; **vestige,** any trace, such as a fragment, a remnant, or any tangible or sensible reminder of what is past or gone; **track,** now more frequent than *trace,* means a continuous line that can be followed.

— *v. t.;* TRACED (trāst); TRAC′ING (trās′ĭng). [OF. *tracier,* fr. L. *tractus* a drawing, trailing, a track, fr. *trahere, tractum,* to draw.] **1.** To draw; specif.: **a** To draw; delineate; sketch. **b** To form, as letters, esp. carefully or with nicety. **c** To copy, as a drawing, by following the lines seen through a transparent superimposed sheet. **d** To impress or imprint (a design, pattern, etc.) as with a tracer. **e** To record in the form of a curved, wavy, or broken line; to make a tracing (sense 2 **b**) of; as, the cardiograph *traces* the heart action. **2.** To adorn with tracery, chasing, etc.; — chiefly in *past part.;* as, *traced* windows. **3.** *Archaic.* To traverse. **4.** To follow the footprints, track, or trail, of; to track down. **5.** To follow or study out in detail or step by step, esp. by going backward over the evidence; as, to *trace* one's descent; also, to discover or uncover by investigation; as, to *trace* the source of a play. **6.** To make out by examining vestiges or remains; as, to *trace* the former course of a river. — *v. i.* To make one's way; esp., to follow a track or trail. — **trace′a·bil′i·ty** (-ȧ·bĭl′ĭ·tĭ), **trace′a·ble·ness,** *n.* — **trace′a·ble,** *adj.* — **trace′a·bly,** *adv.*

trace, *n.* [ME. *trays,* pl., fr. OF. *traiz, trais* (F. *traits*), pl. of *trait.* See TRAIT.] **1.** One of two straps, chains, etc., of a harness, for attaching a horse to a vehicle; a tug. See HARNESS, *Illust.* **2.** *Mach.* A connecting rod or bar, pivoted at each end to another piece, for transmitting motion.

trace element. A chemical element, esp. a metal, used by organisms in minute quantities but believed essential to their physiology.

trac′er (trās′ẽr), *n.* **1.** One who or that which traces. **2.** Specif.: **a** A person engaged (esp. in the express or railroad service) in tracing missing articles. **b** An inquiry sent out (esp. in transportation service) for a missing article. **3.** A device used in tracing, such as a pointed wheel mounted in a handle, used in transferring patterns to cloth. **4.** *Chem.* An element or atom having a peculiarity (as the mass of an isotope or radioactivity) whereby it can be traced through chemical reactions or biological processes. **5.** *Mil.* A small firework attached to a projectile to mark its flight by a trail of smoke or fire. Hence, **tracer bullet.**

Tracery.

trac′er·y (trās′ẽr·ĭ), *n.; pl.* -ERIES (-ĭz). **1.** Ornamental work with branching lines, as in the head of a Gothic window or in some styles of vaulting. **2.** Any decorative interlacing of lines suggestive of such tracery.

tra′che·a (trā′kē·ȧ; trȧ·kē′ȧ), *n.; pl.* TRACHEAE (-ē). [ML., fr. LL. *trachia,* fr. Gr. *tracheia* (sc. *artēria* windpipe), fr. *trachys* rough, rugged.] **1.** *Anat. & Zool.* In vertebrates, the main trunk of the system of tubes by which air passes to and from the lungs; the windpipe. See BRONCHIAL TUBE, *Illust.* **2.** *Bot.* Orig., a duct or water-conveying vessel composed of a series of nonliving cells which have lost their end walls; now, also, one of the cells, or elements, which form such a series or duct. Tracheae are shorter and larger in diameter than tracheids. **3.** *Zool.* One of the air-conveying tubules forming the respiratory system of most insects, myriapods, many arachnids, etc.

tra′che·al (trā′kē·ăl; trȧ·kē′ăl), *adj.* Of, pertaining to, like, or having a trachea, tracheae, or tracheal tissue.

tracheal tissue. *Bot.* Conductive tissue made up of tracheae or tracheids or both; xylem tissue.

tra′che·id (trā′kē·ĭd), *n.* *Bot.* A tubelike water-conducting cell with tapering, closed ends and thickened, lignified walls. Tracheids serve also for support, being esp. characteristic of the wood of conifers. See TRACHEA, 2. — **tra·che′i·dal** (trȧ·kē′ĭ·dăl; trā′kē·ĭd′ăl), *adj.*

tra′che·i′tis (trā′kē·ī′tĭs), *n.* [NL., fr. *trache-* + *-itis.*] *Med.* Inflammation of the trachea, or windpipe.

tra′che·o- (trā′kē·ō-; trȧ·kē′ō-), **tra′che-** (trā′kē-). [From TRACHEA.] A combining form denoting: **a** *The trachea,* as in **tra′che·os′co·py, tra′che·ot′o·my** (see -SCOPY, -TOMY). Hence, **tra′che·o·scop′ic, tra′che·os′co·pist, tra′che·ot′o·mist.** **b** *Tracheal and;* — in adjectives, as in **tra′che·o·e′so·phag′e·al.**

tra′chle (trä′k′l), *v. t.* *Scot.* **a** To bedraggle. **b** To tire.

tra·cho′ma (trȧ·kō′mȧ), *n.* [NL., fr. Gr. *trachōma* roughness, fr. *trachys* rough.] *Med.* A chronic, contagious form of conjunctivitis, characterized by inflammatory granulations. — **tra·chom′a·tous** (-kŏm′ȧ·tŭs; -kō′mȧ·tŭs), *adj.*

tra′chy- (trā′kĭ-; trăk′ĭ-). [Gr. *trachys* rough, rugged.] A combining form meaning *rough,* as in **tra′chy·car′pous, tra′chy·sper′mous** (see -CARPOUS, -SPERMOUS).

tra′chyte (trā′kīt; trăk′īt), *n.* [F. *trachyte,* fr. Gr. *trachys.*] *Petrog.* A volcanic rock, usually light in color, consisting mainly of a feldspar; — so called from the roughness of the fractured surface.

tra·chyt′ic (trȧ·kĭt′ĭk), *adj.* *Petrog.* Relating to a texture of igneous rocks in which lath-shaped feldspar crystals are in almost parallel lines.

trac′ing (trās′ĭng), *n.* **1.** Act of one that traces. **2.** That which is traced; specif.: **a** A copy made through transparent paper. **b** A record made by a cardiograph, seismograph, etc.

track (trăk), *n.* [OF. *trac* track of horses, trace of animals.] **1.** A mark left by something that has passed; as, a wheel *track.* **2.** A vestige; a trace. **3.** The path along which something moves or has moved; course; trail; hence, a way of life, conduct, action, etc.; procedure; as, to leave the beaten *track.* **4.** A succession; the sequence in which things happen, ideas come, etc. **5.** Hence, awareness or cognizance of the sequence, count, etc. (of that specified); as, to keep *track* of current events. **6.** A path or course laid out for racing, exercise, etc.; as, a cinder *track.* **7.** A metal way for wheeled vehicles; specif., one or more pairs of parallel lines of rails with the fastenings, ties, etc., for a railroad, tramway, etc. **8.** Width between wheels, as of an automobile. **9.** *Sports.* **a** A running track (see sense 6) for athletic races. See FIELD, *n.,* 11 **b.** **b** Sports performed on such a track, as disting. from the field sports; also, track sports and field sports collectively. — **Syn.** See TRACE.

— *v. t.* **1.** To follow the tracks or traces of; trail; as, to *track* a deer; also, with *down, out,* or *up,* to trail until caught, discovered, etc. **2.** To trace, by following vestiges, remains, etc. **3.** To pass over; traverse; as, to *track* a desert. **4.** *U. S.* To make tracks upon, as with muddy shoes, or with, as mud or ashes. **5.** To furnish with tracks, or rails. — *v. i.* **1.** To span in width between a pair of wheels or runners; as, this car *tracks* 36 inches. **2.** To move in the same track as that which precedes; to be in alignment; as, the trailer *tracks* perfectly. **3.** To fit a track, or rails.

— *adj.* Of or pert. to a track, esp. a railway track or running track; performed or contested on a track; as, *track* repairs; *track* sports. — **track′er,** *n.* — **track′less,** *adj.*

track′age (trăk′ĭj), *n.* *Railroads.* **a** Lines of track, collectively. **b** A right to use the tracks of another road; also, the charge for such right.

track′lay′er (trăk′lā′ẽr), *n.* Any workman engaged in work involved in putting railway tracks in place.

trackless trolley. = TROLLEY BUS.

track′walk′er (-wôk′ẽr), *n.* *Railroads.* A person employed to walk over and inspect a section of tracks.

tract (trăkt), *n.* [Short for TRACTATE.] A treatise; now, a pamphlet issued for propaganda, esp. one containing a religious exhortation.

tract, *n.* [L. *tractus* a drawing, track, tract of land, fr. *trahere, tractum,* to draw.] **1.** *Now Poetic.* Duration; also, a period or space (of time). **2.** An expanse; an area; specif., a region, or stretch not definitely bounded. **3.** *Anat. & Zool.* A system of parts or organs serving some special purpose; as, the digestive *tract.* **4.** [ML. *tractus.*] *R.C.Ch.* Verses of Scripture sung or recited at Mass before the Gospel, in Lent, on Ember days, at requiems, etc.; — so called because sung, without a break, by one voice.

trac′ta·ble (trăk′tȧ·b′l), *adj.* [L. *tractabilis,* fr. *tractare* to draw violently, handle, treat.] **1.** Capable of being easily led, taught, or controlled; docile. **2.** Easily handled, wrought, or the like; malleable. — **Syn.** See OBEDIENT. — **trac′ta·bil′i·ty** (-bĭl′ĭ·tĭ), **trac′ta·ble·ness,** *n.* — **trac′ta·bly,** *adv.*

Trac·tar′i·an (trăk·târ′ĭ·ăn; 6), *n.* A founder or supporter of Tractarianism. — **Trac·tar′i·an,** *adj.*

Trac·tar′i·an·ism (-ĭz′m), *n.* A system of principles set forth in the ***Tracts for the Times,*** a series of pamphlets issued at Oxford (1833–41) by the early leaders of the movement toward Catholicism in the Church of England known as the ***Oxford movement.*** The tracts maintained that the Church of England was being led astray from its historic position as a branch of the Church Catholic, and that it was necessary to reaffirm its belief in the apostolic succession of its episcopate and in the sacraments as efficacious sources of Divine grace. The series came to an end when ***Tract No. 90,*** written by John Henry Newman, aroused bitter protests.

trac′tate (trăk′tāt), *n.* [L. *tractatus.*] A treatise; essay.

trac′tile (-tĭl; -tīl; 56), *adj.* Capable of being drawn out in length; tensile; ductile. — **trac·til′i·ty** (trăk·tĭl′ĭ·tĭ), *n.*

trac′tion (trăk′shŭn), *n.* [ML. *tractio,* fr. L. *trahere, tractum,* to draw.] **1.** Act of drawing or state of being drawn; also, the force exerted in drawing. **2.** The drawing of a vehicle by motive power; also, the (particular) motive power employed; as, steam or electric *traction.* **3.** The adhesive friction of a body on a surface on which it moves, as of a wheel on a rail. — **trac′tion·al** (-ăl), *adj.*

traction engine. A locomotive for drawing vehicles on highways or in the fields.

trac′tive (trăk′tĭv), *adj.* Serving to draw; tractional.

trac′tor (trăk′tẽr), *n.* [NL.] **1.** A self-propelled vehicle with large rear drive wheels for drawing plows, harrows, reapers, and other farm machines. **2.** A motor truck with very short chassis and no body for hauling a truck trailer or for hauling and carrying part of the weight of a semitrailer. **3.** A vehicle mounted upon and propelled by a single or twin continuous-chain mechanism of great tractive power, for crawling over rough terrain despite obstructions, as in the military tank, or for hauling or pushing, as in the bulldozer. **4.** Also **tractor airplane.** An airplane having a propeller (**tractor propeller**) that is forward of the main supporting surfaces.

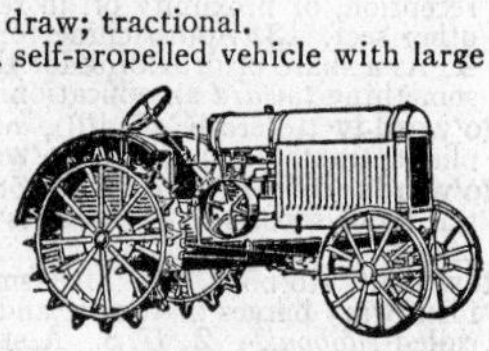

Farm Tractor.

trade (trād), *n.* [MLG., track, course.] **1.** *Obs.* **a** A track; course; path; way. **b** Customary action or course; practice. **2.** [*sometimes cap.*] A trade wind; — chiefly in *pl.* **3.** The business one practices or the work in which one engages regularly; occupation; means of livelihood. **4.** Specif.: **a** A pursuit requiring manual or mechanical training and dexterity; a craft. **b** *Chiefly Brit.* The occupation of a merchant, esp. a retail merchant. **5.** Act or business of exchanging commodities by barter or sale; commerce; traffic. **6.** *Obs.* Intercourse; dealing. **7.** Those engaged in a (specified or mutually understood) business or industry; — often in attributive use, as in **trade association, trade journal.** **8.** A firm's customers; the clientele of a business; as, those who wait on the *trade.* **9.** *U. S.* A purchase and sale; a deal. — **Syn.** See BUSINESS.

— *v. t. & i.* **1.** To barter or buy and sell; carry on a business of bartering or buying and selling. **2.** *Now Rare.* To resort (to) for trade. **3.** To have traffic, intercourse, or dealings (with). **4.** To profit by unethical, unfair, or venal dealings or by imposition; — with *in* or *on;* as, to *trade* on the credulity of a client. **5.** *Colloq.* To deal as a purchaser (with or at). — ***trade in.*** To turn in as payment or part payment for a purchase or bill.

— adj. **1.** Of, pert. to, or used in trade or commerce. **2.** Of or serving a particular trade or those engaged in it; as, *trade* journals. **3.** Also **trades** (trādz). Composed of or representing the trades or trade-unions; as, a *trade* (or *trades*) committee.
trade acceptance. *Com.* A bill of exchange arising out of a current transaction, drawn by the seller of goods on the buyer for the purchase price, and accepted by the buyer by a signed acknowledgment on the bill.
trade balance. = BALANCE OF TRADE.
trade discount. *Com.* A deduction from the retail or list price of goods allowed by a manufacturer or distributor to a merchant.
trade dollar. See DOLLAR, 1 **d.**
trade′–in′, *n.* That which is taken in trade; specif., an automobile, radio, etc., taken in trade as part of the purchase price of another.
trade′–last′ (trād′låst′; 9), *n.* *Colloq.* A complimentary remark by a third person that one offers to report to the person complimented if he will first similarly report a compliment to oneself. Abbr. *T.L.* — **trade′–last′,** *v. i.*
trade′–mark′, trade′mark′ (trād′märk′), *n.* A word, letter, device, or symbol, used in connection with merchandise and pointing distinctly to the origin or ownership of the article to which it is applied. **— v. t.** To label with a trade-mark; also, to register the trade-mark of.
trade name. **1. a** The name by which an article is called among traders, etc. **b** An arbitrarily adopted name given by a manufacturer or merchant to an article to distinguish it as one produced or sold by him. It is better called a **trade–mark name** and may be protected as a trade-mark. **2.** The name or style under which a concern does business.
trad′er (trād′ẽr), *n.* **1.** One who trades; a merchant. **2.** A vessel engaged in the coasting or foreign trade. **3.** *Stock Exchange.* **a** An exchange member who trades for himself, and not on commission for customers. **b** Anyone who trades extensively in securities.
trad′es·can′ti·a (trăd′ĕs·kăn′shĭ·ȧ), *n.* [NL., after John *Tradescant* (d. 1638), Eng. traveler and gardener.] Any of a genus (*Tradescantia,* family Commelinaceae) of American herbs; the spiderwort.
trade school. A school devoted to drill in the theory and practice of a trade or trades.
trades′man (trādz′măn), *n.* [*trade's* + *man.*] One who trades; a shopkeeper or one of his employees. Hence, **trades′folk′, trades′peo′ple, trades′wom′an.**
trade′–un′ion (trād′ūn′yŭn; trād′ūn′yŭn), *or* **trades′–un′ion** (trādz′-; trādz′-), *n.* A voluntary association of wage earners organized to further or maintain their rights and interests through collective bargaining with the employer, esp. for improving wages, hours, and conditions of employment. Originally, trade-unions were organized by craftsmen strictly by crafts (cf. CRAFT UNION); they have come to be organized also vertically through an industry (cf. INDUSTRIAL UNION) and some include unskilled, agricultural, and white-collar workers, hence are also called in the United States *labor unions,* though the universal term for all types is simply *union.* Cf. COMPANY UNION. — **trade′–un′ion·ism** (-ĭz′m), *or* **trades′–un′ion·ism,** *n.* — **trade′–un′ion·ist** (-ĭst), **trades′–un′ion·ist,** *n. & adj.*
trade wind. A drying wind blowing almost continually in the same course, or *trade,* toward the equator but from an easterly direction. The general direction of the trade winds is thus from N.E. to S.W. on the north side of the equator, and from S.E. to N.W. on the south side of the equator.
trad′ing post (trād′ĭng). A station of a trader or trading company established in a sparsely settled region where trade, usually in furs, etc., is carried on with the natives.
trading stamp. A printed stamp, with a certain value, given as a premium by a dealer to a customer and usable in procuring certain articles from the issuers of the stamps.
tra·di′tion (trȧ·dĭsh′ŭn), *n.* [OF. *tradicion,* fr. L. *traditio,* fr. *tradere* to give up, transmit.] **1.** *Now Rare.* **a** Delivery. **b** *Hist.* A surrender. **c** Oral delivery of something to be learned; instruction by word of mouth. **2.** The oral transmission of information, beliefs, customs, etc., from ancestors to posterity without written memorials; also, a belief, practice, etc., so transmitted. **3.** Something handed down from the past; an inherited culture, attitude, etc. **4.** *Theol.* **a** Among Jews, an unwritten code of law given by God to Moses on Sinai. **b** Among Christians, that body of doctrine and discipline, or any article thereof, put forth or revealed by Christ or his apostles, and not committed to writing.
tra·di′tion·al (-ăl), *adj.* Of, pertaining to, derived from, or conforming to tradition. — **tra·di′tion·al·ly,** *adv.*
tra·di′tion·al·ism (-ĭz′m), *n.* The doctrines, or practices, of those who follow or accept tradition; specif. [*often cap.*]: **a** Acceptance of tradition (def. 4), or orally transmitted revelation. **b** The beliefs of those opposed to modernism, liberalism, radicalism, etc.; sometimes, fundamentalism. — **tra·di′tion·al·ist** (-ĭst), *n. & adj.* — **tra·di′tion·al·is′tic** (-ĭs′tĭk), *adj.*
tra·di′tion·ar′y (trȧ·dĭsh′ŭn·ĕr′ĭ *or, esp. Brit.,* -ẽr·ĭ), *adj.* Of the nature of a tradition; traditional.
tra·di′tion·ist (-ĭst), *n. & adj.* **a** Traditionalist. **b** (One) versed in traditions.
trad′i·tive (trăd′ĭ·tĭv), *adj.* [L. *tradere, traditum,* to transmit, give up.] Traditionary.
trad′i·tor (-tẽr), *n.*; *pl.* -TORES (-tō′rēz). [L., fr. *tradere, traditum.* See TRAITOR.] A traitor among early Christians during the Roman persecutions.
tra·duce′ (trȧ·dūs′), *v. t.*; -DUCED′ (-dūst′); -DUC′ING (-dūs′ĭng). [L. *traducere, -ductum,* to lead across, lead along, disgrace, transfer, fr. *trans* across, over + *ducere* to lead.] To expose to contempt or shame by slander; calumniate; vilify; defame. — **Syn.** See MALIGN. — **tra·duc′er** (-dūs′ẽr), *n.* — **tra·duc′ing·ly,** *adv.*
traf′fic (trăf′ĭk), *n.* [F. *trafic, trafique,* fr. It. *traffico,* fr. *trafficare* to traffic.] **1.** *Archaic.* Trade between distant countries, communities, etc.; commerce. **2.** The business of transporting passengers, goods, merchandise, etc., as on railroad or steamship lines; — chiefly in attributive use; as, the *traffic* interests were represented. **3.** The business of bartering or buying and selling; trade; as, to carry on *traffic* with the Indians; — sometimes implying venality, etc.; as, *traffic* in votes. **4.** Dealings; intercourse; familiarity. **5.** That which is transported; hence: **a** The total of passengers or freight transported by a public carrier or carriers within a specified or implied period. **b** The total of communications, as of telephone calls or telegraphed messages. **6.** The flow of pedestrians and vehicles along a street or highway, of communications by wire, etc.; as, the *traffic* was diverted during the fire. — **Syn.** See BUSINESS.
— v. i.; -FICKED (-ĭkt); -FICK·ING (-ĭk·ĭng). To carry on traffic; to have traffic (*with*). — **traf′fick·er** (-ĭk·ẽr), *n.*
traffic circle. = ROTARY, *n.,* 2.
trag′a·canth (trăg′ȧ·kănth; *by pharmacists, freq.* trăj′-), *n.* [F. *tragacanthe,* the plant, fr. L. *tragacantha,* fr. Gr. *tragakantha,* fr. *tragos* he-goat + *akantha* a thorn.] **a** A gum obtained from various Asiatic or East European herbs (genus *Astragalus,* esp. *A. gummifer*) of the pea family. The gum swells up in water and is used in the arts and in pharmacy. **b** Any shrub or tree yielding this gum.
tra·ge′di·an (trȧ·jē′dĭ·ăn), *n.* A writer or an actor of tragedy.
tra·ge′di·enne′ (trȧ·jē′dĭ·ĕn′; *F.* trȧ′zhā′dyĕn′), *n.* [F. *tragédienne.*] An actress who plays tragedy.
trag′e·dy (trăj′ĕ·dĭ), *n.*; *pl.* -DIES (-dĭz). [OF. *tragedie,* fr. L. *tragoedia,* fr. Gr. *tragōidia,* appar. goat-song, prob. from the singers' being clothed in goatskins, fr. *tragos* he-goat + *ōidē* song.] **1.** A literary composition, esp. a dramatic composition, which excites pity and terror by a succession of unhappy events, and in which, typically, the leading character is by some passion or limitation brought to a catastrophe; also, generically, drama of this type, or the composing or acting of it. **2.** The theory or art of composing or of acting tragedies. **3.** An event or a series of events like those of a tragedy; a tragic happening or series of happenings; as, his life was a *tragedy.* **4.** Tragic lot, fate, or end.
trag′ic (trăj′ĭk), *adj.* **1.** Of, pert. to, of the nature of, or having the character of tragedy or the tragic. **2.** Characterized by, or involving, death or calamity or the suffering implied in tragedy. **3.** Appropriate to, or in the manner of, tragedy, esp. as performed; as, *tragic* accents. **— n.** Usually with *the.* That quality in art or nature which excites the emotions of pity and terror.
trag′i·cal (-ĭ·kăl), *adj.* Tragic (esp., sense 3). — **trag′i·cal·ly,** *adv.* — **trag′i·cal·ness,** *n.*
trag′i·com′e·dy (trăj′ĭ·kŏm′ĕ·dĭ), *n.* [Through F. and LL., fr. L. *tragicocomoedia.*] A drama, or by extension, a situation, blending tragic and comic elements. — **trag′i·com′ic** (-ĭk), **trag′i·com′i·cal** (-ĭ·kăl), *adj.*
trag′o·pan (trăg′ō·păn), *n.* [NL., fr. L. *tragopan* a fabulous Ethiopian bird, fr. Gr. *tragopan,* lit. goat-Pan.] Any of several brilliantly colored Asiatic pheasants (genus *Tragopan*) having the back and breast usually covered with white or buff ocelli.
tra′gus (trā′gŭs), *n.*; *pl.* TRAGI (-jī). [NL., fr. Gr. *tragos* a part of the inner ear.] *Anat.* The prominence in front of the external opening of the ear. See EAR, *Illust.*
traik (trāk), *v. i.* *Chiefly Scot.* To trudge; tramp. **— n.** A fatiguing tramp; a stroll.
trail (trāl), *v. t.* [OF. *trailler* to tow, fr. L. *tragula* dragnet, sledge, fr. root of *trahere* to draw, drag.] **1.** To draw or drag along a surface, as something loosely held or attached; also, to carry or bring along as an addition, burden, or the like. **2.** To make a track or trail in; to tread down in a line or path, as grass. **3.** To hunt by tracking. **4.** To follow in one's track; hence, to lag or fall behind. **5.** *Mil.* To carry, as a firearm, at the position **trail arms,** that is, with butt end near the ground and muzzle inclined forward. — **Syn.** See FOLLOW.
— v. i. **1.** To hang down so as to be drawn along or to sweep the ground, etc. **2.** To walk, move, or proceed, heavily, wearily, etc.; lag; crawl. **3.** To grow to such length as to droop over, or rest or creep upon, the ground. **4.** To form a trail or wake behind; as, smoke *trailed* from the chimney. **5.** To extend in an erratic or uneven course or line; straggle. **6.** To follow a trail, as hounds; to track game.
— n. **1.** Something that trails or is trailed, as a train of a gown. **2.** A track left by something that has passed or has been trailed; as, to follow the *trail* of blood. **3.** Hence: **a** A scent left by man or beast. **b** A track worn by passage through a wilderness or wild region; as, an Indian *trail;* also, a blazed or otherwise marked path through such a region; as, the Santa Fe *trail.* **c** [*cap.*] In names of highways, a road approximately following a trail or series of trails left as by Indians or pioneers. **4.** *Mil.* **a** The position *trail arms* (see TRAIL, *v. t.,* 5, above). **b** That part of the stock of a gun carriage which rests on the ground when the piece is unlimbered. Cf. STOCK, *n.,* 19 **c.**
trail′er (trāl′ẽr), *n.* **1.** One who or that which trails. **2.** A highway vehicle designed to be hauled, esp. by an automotive vehicle, as a truck trailer or a semitrailer; specif., one equipped for use as a dwelling, to be drawn by a passenger automobile.
trail′ing arbutus. = ARBUTUS, 2.
trailing edge. *Aeronautics.* The rearmost edge of an airfoil or a propeller blade. See AIRPLANE, *Illust.*
train (trān), *n.* [From OF. *train, trahin,* F. *train,* and in some senses fr. OF. *traine,* F. *traine,* both fr. OF. *trainer* to draw. See TRAIN, *v.*] **1.** Something which trails or is trailed after or along; specif., an elongated piece of a gown which trails behind the wearer or is carried by pages. **2.** A number of followers or attendants; retinue; suite. **3.** A moving or continuous line or file; a procession. **4.** Orderly arrangement; regular or proper order. **5.** A connected succession or series; a sequence; as, a *train* of events. **6.** Results or accompanying circumstances viewed as a sequence; as, war brings many evils in its *train.* **7.** A line of gunpowder laid to lead fire to a charge. **8.** *Gun.* The movement or line of direction of the axis of a piece in a horizontal plane. **9.** *Mach.* A series of moving pieces, as wheels and pinions, for transmitting and modifying motion. **10.** *Mil.* The vehicles, men, and animals, accompanying a military body to transport its baggage, supplies, etc. **11.** *Railroads.* A connected line of cars, etc.
— v. t. [OF. *trahiner, trainer,* fr. root of L. *trahere* to draw, drag.] **1.** *Now Rare.* To trail; drag. **2.** To lead or direct the growth of; to form by bending, pruning, etc. **3.** To form by instruction, discipline, drill, etc.; educate; narrowly, to teach so as to be fitted, qualified, proficient, etc. **4.** To make prepared for a test, contest, etc., as by exercise, dieting, etc. **5.** To aim at an object; bring to bear; as, to *train* guns on the enemy. **— v. i.** **1.** To subject oneself or be subjected to instruction, drilling, regular exercise, dieting, etc. **2.** To form habits or impart proficiency by teaching, drilling, etc. **3.** *Colloq.* To associate, or be on friendly terms; as, he *trains* with a fast crowd. — **Syn.** See TEACH. — **train′a·ble,** *adj.* — **train·ee′** (trān·ē′), *n.* — **train′er,** *n.*
train (trān), *v. t.* To entice; allure.
train′band′ (-bănd′), *n.* [For *trained band.*] *Eng. Hist.* One of the bands of trained citizen soldiers first raised in the counties and London in the 16th century. These bands developed into the militia.
train′ing, *n.* Act, process, or method of one who trains; state of being trained. **— adj.** That trains; used in or for training; as, a *training* ship for sailors.

train'man (trān'măn), *n.; pl.* -MEN (-mĕn). A brakeman or, on a passenger train, an employee subordinate to the conductor.

train oil. [From earlier *train, trayne, trane,* fr. MLG. *trān;* akin to D. *traan* train oil.] Oil from the whale or other marine animal.

traipse, trapes (trāps), *v. i. & t. Colloq.* **a** To walk; trudge. **b** To wander about idly; to gad. — *n.* A fatiguing walk.

trait (trāt; *in British use commonly* trā), *n.* [F., fr. L. *tractus* a dragging, a stretch, extent, tract of land, fr. *trahere* to draw.] **1.** A stroke; hence, a touch; a note, as of sarcasm or humor. **2.** A distinguishing quality of character, mind, etc.; a characteristic; a peculiarity.

trai'tor (trā'tẽr), *n.* [OF. *traïtor, traïtur,* through VL., fr. L. *traditor,* fr. L. *tradere, traditum,* to deliver, give up, betray, fr. *trans* across, over + *dare* to give.] One who betrays a confidence or trust; one who acts perfidiously or treacherously; specif., one who violates his allegiance and betrays his country; one guilty of treason. — *adj.* Traitorous. — **trai'tress** (-trĕs; -trĭs), *n.*

trai'tor·ous (-ŭs), *adj.* **1.** Guilty or capable of treason; treacherous; perfidious; faithless. **2.** Consisting in treason; of the nature of treason. — **Syn.** See FAITHLESS. — **trai'tor·ous·ly,** *adv.* — **-ness,** *n.*

tra·ject' (trȧ·jĕkt'), *v. t.* [L. *trajectus,* past part. of *trajicere, traicere,* to throw across, fr. *trans-* + *jacere* to throw.] To transmit by or as by projecting or impelling through space or a different medium. — **tra·jec'tion** (-jĕk'shŭn), *n.*

tra·jec'to·ry (trȧ·jĕk'tō·rĭ), *n.; pl.* -RIES (-rĭz). The curve which a body describes in space, as a planet or comet in its orbit, or a projectile in passing from the muzzle to the first point of impact.

tram (trăm), *n.* Also **trame.** [F. *trame,* fr. L. *trama.*] A silk thread, used esp. for the weft of the best velvets and silks.

tram, *n.* [E. dial. *tram* a coal wagon, shaft of a cart, beam, bar.] **1.** Any of various vehicles; specif.: **a** A boxlike wagon running on a railway, as in a mine. **b** *Brit.* A passenger car of a street railway; a streetcar. **c** The carriage of an overhead conveyor. **2.** Short for TRAMWAY, TRAMROAD, etc. — *v. t.* To haul in a tram or over a tramway.

tram, *n.* **1.** Short for TRAMMEL, *n.,* 5 **b**. **2.** *Mach.* Correct relative position or adjustment; — in the phrases *in tram, out of tram.* — *v. t. & i.;* TRAMMED (trămd); TRAM'MING. To measure, align, or adjust, with a trammel (sense 5 **b**).

tram'car' (trăm'kär'), *n.* = 2d TRAM, *n.,* 1 **a** & **b**.

tram'line' (-līn'), *n. Brit.* A streetcar line.

tram'mel (trăm'ĕl; -'l), *n.* [OF. *tramail* (F. *trémail*), fr. LL. *tremaculum* a fish net, fr. L. *tres* three + *macula* a mesh.] **1.** A form of net; esp., one (**trammel net**) made of three layers, the middle one finemeshed and slack, so that fish passing through either outer coarse net are pocketed in the center. **2.** A form of shackle used for making a horse amble. **3.** *Often pl.* Something impeding activity, progress, or freedom; toil; restraint; check. **4.** An adjustable pothook for the fireplace crane. **5.** *Mach.* **a** An instrument for drawing ellipses. **b** Any of various gauges used for aligning or adjusting machine parts, etc. — *v. t.;* -MELED (-ĕld; -'ld) or -MELLED; -MEL·ING or -MEL·LING. **1.** To hold as in a net; intercept; — with *up.* **2.** To prevent or impede the free play of; hamper; confine. — **Syn.** See HAMPER. — **tram'mel·er, tram'mel·ler,** *n.*

tra·mon'tane (trȧ·mŏn'tān; trăm'ŏn·tān), *adj.* [It. *tramontano,* fr. L. *transmontanus,* fr. *trans* across + *mons, montis,* mountain.] Lying, being beyond, or coming from the other side of, the mountains, esp. the Alps; — chiefly from the Italian point of view. — *n.* One dwelling in a tramontane region; hence, a foreigner; a stranger.

tramp (trămp), *v. i.* [ME. *trampen.*] **1.** To walk, step, or tread, esp. heavily. **2.** To travel about on foot; also, to journey as a tramp. — *v. t.* **1.** To tread on forcibly and repeatedly; trample. **2.** To travel or wander through on foot. — *n.* **1.** A foot traveler; often, a begging or thieving vagrant. Cf. HOBO, *Illust.* **2.** A journey on foot; a hike. **3.** The succession of sounds made by the beating of feet on a pavement, floor, etc. **4.** An iron plate attached to the sole of a shoe. **5.** *Naut.* A vessel not making regular trips but taking a cargo when and where it offers and to any port. — **tramp'er,** *n.*

tram'ple (trăm'p'l), *v. i.;* TRAM'PLED (-p'ld); TRAM'PLING (-plĭng). [ME. *trampelen,* freq. of *trampen.*] To tramp or tread heavily so as to bruise, crush, or injure; also, to inflict injury; to make encroachments in a contemptuous or ruthless fashion; — with *on* or *upon.* — *v. t.* To tread underfoot; stamp upon. — *n.* Act or sound of trampling. — **tram'pler** (-plẽr), *n.*

tram'po·line (trăm'pō·lĭn), *n.* [Prob. fr. Sp. *trampolín* springboard, fr. It. *trampolino.*] A resilient canvas bed or net mounted on a metal frame, used as a springboard in tumbling.

tram'road' (trăm'rōd'), *n.* A road made for trams or wagons with tracks of beams of wood (usually metal-faced), blocks of stone, or rails; esp., a railway in a mine.

tram'way' (-wā'), *n.* A way for trams; as: **a** A tramroad. **b** *Eng.* A streetcar line.

trance (tràns; 9), *n.* [OF. *transe* fear, trance, swoon, fr. *transir* to pass (usually from life), fr. L. *transire* to pass over. See TRANSIENT.] **1.** A state of partly suspended animation or of inability to function; a daze; a stupor. **2.** A state of profound abstraction of mind or spirit, as in religious contemplation; ecstasy. **3.** A sleeplike state such as that of deep hypnosis. — *v. t.;* TRANCED (trànst); TRANC'ING (tràn'sĭng). To entrance; enrapture.

trance, *n.* [Origin uncert.] *Scot.* A passage or passageway.

tran'gam (trăng'găm), *n.* Also **tran'kum** (-kŭm). *Obs.* Knickknack; gewgaw; trinket.

tran'quil (trăng'kwĭl; trăn'-), *adj.;* TRAN'QUIL·ER, TRAN'QUIL·LER (-ẽr); TRAN'QUIL·EST, TRAN'QUIL·LEST. [L. *tranquillus,* fr. *trans-* + a word akin to *quies* calm, rest.] Quiet; calm; undisturbed; not agitated. — **Syn.** See CALM. — **tran'quil·ly,** *adv.* — **tran'quil·ness,** *n.*

tran'quil·ize, tran'quil·lize (trăng'kwĭ·līz), *v. t. & i.* To render or become tranquil; to quiet or have a quieting effect. — **tran'quil·i·za'tion** (-ĭ·zā'shŭn; -ī·zā'-), *n.* — **tran'quil·iz'er** (-īz'ẽr), *n.*

tran·quil'li·ty, tran·quil'i·ty (trăn·kwĭl'ĭ·tĭ; trăng-), *n.* Quality or state of being tranquil; calmness; composure.

trans- (trăns-; *before a voiced sound often* trănz-; 9). [L. *trans* across, over.] A prefix meaning *over, across, beyond, through;* specif.: **a** *On* or *to the other side of;* — with adjectives and nouns of place, and opp. to *cis-;* as in **trans'con·ti·nen'tal,** being on or crossing to the other side of the continent; **trans'–An·de'an,** located on the other side of the Andes; and in the words in the list below:

trans-American, **transarctic**, **trans-Canadian**, **transequatorial**, **transisthmian**, **trans-Jordan**, **transmarine**, **trans-Mississippi**, **transoceanic**, **transpolar**, **trans-Siberian**, **trans-Ural**

b *Through and through; so as to change completely;* as in **trans·fash'ion,** to fashion into something else; and in:

transcolor, **transmold**, **transshape**

c *Transcending; surpassing;* as in **trans·hu'man,** surpassing or exceeding the human; and in:

transconscious, **transempirical**, **transexperiential**, **transfinite**, **transmental**, **transmundane**, **transphysical**, **transrational**, **transsensual**

trans·act' (trăns·ăkt'; trăn·zăkt'), *v. i.* [L. *transactus,* past part. of *transigere.* See TRANSACTION.] To deal; negotiate. — *v. t.* To carry through; bring about; esp., to carry on, or conduct, as business. — **trans·ac'tor** (trăns·ăk'tẽr; trăn·zăk'-), *n.*

trans·ac'tion (trăns·ăk'shŭn; trăn·zăk'-), *n.* [L. *transactio,* fr. *transigere, -actum,* to drive through, accomplish, fr. *trans-* + *agere* to drive.] **1.** A transacting. **2.** That which is transacted or in the process of being transacted; specif.: **a** A business deal. **b** *pl.* The records, esp. the published records, of action taken, addresses read, etc., at the meeting or meetings of a society or association. — **trans·ac'tion·al** (-ăl), *adj.*

trans·al'pine (trăns·ăl'pĭn; -pīn), *adj.* Being on the farther side of the Alps, esp. from Rome; also, of, pertaining to, or characteristic of regions or peoples on the farther side of the Alps. — **trans·al'pine,** *n.*

trans'at·lan'tic (trăns'ăt·lăn'tĭk), *adj.* Lying or belonging across the Atlantic Ocean; crossing the Atlantic Ocean.

trans·ca'lent (trăns·kā'lĕnt), *adj.* [*trans-* + L. *calens,* pres. part. of *calere* to grow warm.] Pervious to, or permitting the passage of, heat. — **trans·ca'len·cy** (-lĕn·sĭ), *n.*

trans·ceiv'er (trăns·sēv'ẽr), *n.* [*trans*mitter + *receiver.*] A radio transmitter-receiver that uses the same tubes for transmission as for reception.

tran·scend' (trăn·sĕnd'), *v. t.* [L. *transcendere, -censum,* fr. *trans-* + *scandere* to climb.] **1.** To rise above or beyond the limits or powers of; to overpass; exceed. **2.** To surpass (in some quality, way, etc.); excel; outstrip. **3.** *Philos. & Theol.* To be transcendent to. — *v. i.* To be transcendent; to excel. — **Syn.** See EXCEED.

tran·scend'ent (-sĕn'dĕnt), *adj.* **1.** Transcending; surpassing; extraordinary. **2.** *Philos.* Transcending or going beyond what is given or presented in experience; specif., *Kantianism,* beyond the limits of all possible experience and hence beyond knowledge; — contrasted with *transcendental* (sense 2). **3.** *Theol.* Of God, being prior to and exalted above the universe, and having being apart from it. Cf. IMMANENT. — **tran·scend'ence** (-dĕns), **tran·scend'en·cy** (-dĕn·sĭ) *n.* — **tran·scend'ent·ly,** *adv.*

tran'scen·den'tal (trăn'sĕn·dĕn'tăl; -t'l), *adj.* **1.** Transcendent; now, usually, marked by or characteristic of transcendentalism; hence, being beyond the natural or rational; remote from practical affairs or from human comprehension. **2.** In Kantianism, of or pertaining to the a priori and necessary conditions of human experience, as determined by the constitution of the mind itself; hence, transcending what is determined by the contingent particularity of experience, but not transcending all human knowledge; — contrasted with *transcendent.* — **tran'scen·den'tal·ly,** *adv.*

tran'scen·den'tal·ism (trăn'sĕn·dĕn'tăl·ĭz'm; -t'l·ĭz'm), *n.* **a** Any philosophy, as that of Kant, which emphasizes a priori conditions of knowledge and experience, or the unknowable character of ultimate reality; also, a doctrine, as that of Fichte and Hegel, which emphasizes what transcends sense experience as being fundamental in reality. **b** Hence, more widely, any philosophy, as that of Ralph Waldo Emerson, which asserts the primacy of the spiritual and superindividual as against the material and empirical. — **-tal·ist** (-ĭst), *n. & adj.*

tran·scribe' (trăn·skrīb'), *v. t.* [L. *transcribere, -scriptum,* fr. *trans-* + *scribere* to write.] **1.** To write a copy of; hence, to make a long-hand or typewritten copy from shorthand notes of. **2.** *Music.* To make a transcription of. **3.** *Phonet.* To represent (speech sounds) by means of phonetic symbols. **4.** *Radio.* To broadcast by electrical transcription. — **tran·scrib'er** (-skrīb'ẽr), *n.*

tran'script (trăn'skrĭpt), *n.* [L. *transcriptum,* neut. past part. of *transcribere.*] **1.** A transcribed letter, document, etc. **2.** A copy of any kind; a representation.

tran·scrip'tion (trăn·skrĭp'shŭn), *n.* **1.** A transcribing. **2.** A copy; transcript; specif., reproduction, as over a radio system, of material previously specially prepared for the purpose. See ELECTRICAL TRANSCRIPTION. **3.** *Music.* An arrangement of a composition, for some other instrument or voice than that for which it was written. — **tran·scrip'tive** (-tĭv), *adj.*

transcription machine. = TURNTABLE, 2.

trans·duc'er (trăns·dūs'ẽr), *n.* [L. *transducere* to lead across.] *Physics.* A device actuated by power from one system and supplying power to a second system.

tran·sect' (trăn·sĕkt'), *v. t.* [*trans-* + L. *secare, sectum,* to cut.] To cut transversely. — **tran·sec'tion** (-sĕk'shŭn), *n.*

tran'sept (trăn'sĕpt), *n.* [ML. *transseptum,* for L. *transversum septum,* fr. *transversus* transverse + L. *septum, saeptum,* an enclosure.] *Arch.* The part of a cruciform church which crosses at right angles to the greatest length and between the nave and the apse or choir; loosely, one of the arms, or projecting ends, of a transept. — **tran·sep'tal** (trăn·sĕp'tăl; -t'l), *adj.* — **tran·sep'tal·ly,** *adv.*

trans'e·unt (trăn'sē·ŭnt), *adj.* [L. *transiens, -euntis,* pres. part. of *transire* to go over.] Passing from one to another; operating, or efficient in producing results, beyond itself; as, a *transeunt* cause; — opposed to *immanent.*

trans·fer' (trăns·fûr'; trăns'fûr), *v. t.;* -FERRED (-fûrd'; -fûrd); -FER'RING. [OF. or L.; OF. *transferer,* fr. L. *transferre,* fr. *trans-* + *ferre* to bear.] **1.** To convey from one place, person, or thing, to another; transport, remove, or cause to pass, to another. **2.** To make over the possession or control of; to convey, as a title to land. **3.** To print or otherwise copy from one surface to another. — *v. i.* To change from one car, line, or the like, to another. — **trans·fer'a·bil'i·ty** (trăns·fûr'ȧ·bĭl'ĭ·tĭ; trăns'fẽr-), *n.* — **trans·fer'a·ble** (trăns·fûr'ȧ·b'l; trăns'fẽr-), *adj.* — **trans·fer'rer** (trăns·fûr'ẽr), *n.*

trans'fer (trăns'fûr), *n.* **1.** A transferring, or state of being transferred. **2.** One who or that which is transferred. **3.** An order transferring shares of stock, money, etc. **4.** A drawing or writing printed in reverse from one surface on another, as in ceramics. **5.** *U. S.* In some public transportation systems, a ticket given with or without extra charge to a passenger entitling him to continue on his journey on another route. **6.** *Law.* The conveyance of right, title, or property, from one person (the **trans·fer'or** [trăns·fûr'ẽr]) to another (the **trans'fer·ee'** [trăns'fẽr·ē']). **7.** *Railroading.* A place where a transfer is made, as of trains to ferries, where one form of power is changed to another, etc.

trans·fer′ence (trăns·fûr′ĕns; trăns′fĕr-), *n.* **1.** Act of transferring; conveyance; passage; transfer; as, ***thought transference*** (i. e., telepathy). **2.** *Psychoanalysis.* Direction of feelings and desires, esp. as unconsciously retained from childhood, toward a new object.

trans′fer·en′tial (trăns′fĕr·ĕn′shăl), *adj.* Pertaining to, or involving, a transfer.

trans·fig′u·ra′tion (trăns·fĭg′ū·rā′shŭn), *n.* A transfiguring; esp. [*cap.*], the supernatural change in the appearance of Jesus on the mountain (*Matt.* xvii.; *Mark* ix.), or a church feast (August 6) commemorating this.

trans·fig′ure (trăns·fĭg′ūr; *cf.* FIGURE, *n.*), *v. t.* [OF. *transfigurer*, fr. L. *transfigurare.*] **1.** To change the form or appearance of; metamorphose. **2.** To exalt, glorify, illumine, in appearance or character; idealize; irradiate; — orig. with allusion to the Transfiguration. — **Syn.** See TRANSFORM.

trans·fix′ (-fĭks′), *v. t.;* -FIXED′ (-fĭkst′); -FIX′ING. [L. *transfixus*, past part. of *transfigere* to transfix, fr. *trans-* + *figere* to fix, fasten.] To pierce through with or as with a pointed weapon; impale. — **trans·fix′ion** (-fĭk′shŭn), *n.*

trans·form′ (trăns·fôrm′), *v. t.* [OF. *transformer*, fr. L. *transformare, -formatum*, fr. *trans-* + *formare* to form.] **1.** To change the form of; specif.: **a** To change in outward shape or semblance. **b** To change in structure or composition; rarely, to transmute. **c** To change in nature, disposition, heart, or the like; convert. **2.** *Elec.* To change (a current) in potential or in type. **3.** *Math.* To change the form of, as an algebraic expression or geometrical figure, without altering the meaning or value. **4.** *Physics.* To change (one form of energy) into another, as mechanical energy into electricity. — *v. i.* To be or become transformed. — **trans′for·ma′tion** (trăns′fôr·mā′shŭn), *n.* — **trans·form′a·tive** (trăns·fôr′mȧ·tĭv), *adj.*

Syn. Transform, metamorphose, transmute, convert, transmogrify, transfigure mean to change something into a different thing. Transform implies a change in form, shape, nature, function, or the like; metamorphose, a change induced supernaturally, magically, or as if by magic; transmute, a change involving a transformation from a lower to a higher element or thing; convert, a change more in details which fit it for a new or different use or function; transmogrify, a grotesque, preposterous, or thoroughgoing metamorphosis; transfigure, a supernatural or preternatural change involving glorification.

trans·form′er (trăns·fôr′mĕr), *n.* **1.** One who or that which transforms. **2.** *Elec.* An apparatus for transforming an electric current from a high to a low potential (***step-down transformer***) or vice versa (***step-up transformer***) without changing the current energy; a converter. The term is now usually limited to a stationary apparatus for transforming alternating currents.

trans·fuse′ (trăns·fūz′), *v. t.* [L. *transfusus*, past part. of *transfundere*, fr. *trans-* + *fundere* to pour.] **1.** To pour, as a liquid, from one vessel into another. **2.** To cause to pass from one through another; diffuse itself through; transmit by infusing; as, air *transfused* with sunshine. **3.** *Med.* **a** To transfer, as blood, from the veins or arteries of one man or animal to those of another. **b** To subject (a patient) to transfusion. — **trans·fus′er** (-fūz′ĕr), *n.* — **trans·fus′i·ble** (-ĭ·b'l), *adj.* — **trans·fu′sive** (-fū′sĭv), *adj.*

trans·fu′sion (-fū′zhŭn), *n.* [L. *transfusio.*] A transfusing; specif., *Med.*, the operation of transfusing blood.

trans·gress′ (trăns·grĕs′), *v. t.* **1.** To go beyond the limits set by; to break, as a law. **2.** To pass over (limits, boundaries, etc.); exceed. — *v. i.* To break a law; to sin. — **trans·gres′sor** (-ĕr), *n.*

trans·gres′sion (-grĕsh′ŭn), *n.* [F., fr. L. *transgressio* a going across, fr. *transgredi, -gressus*, to step across, go over, fr. *trans-* + *gradi* to step, walk.] A transgressing; trespass; sin; a violation of a command, a law, etc.

tran·ship′, tran·ship′ment. Variants of TRANSSHIP, TRANSSHIPMENT.

tran′sience (trăn′shĕns), *n.* Also **tran′sien·cy** (-shĕn·sĭ). Quality or state of being transient; transitoriness.

tran′sient (-shĕnt), *adj.* [L. *transiens* (gen. *-euntis*), pres. part. of *transire, -itum*, to go or pass over, fr. *trans* + *ire* to go.] **1.** Passing quickly from existence; ephemeral; transitory; short-lived. **2.** Transeunt; effective or efficient in producing results beyond itself. **3.** Shifting; changing in form, appearance, etc. **4.** Not settled, established, or permanent; staying for a short time; as, a *transient* boarder. **5.** *Music.* Of a modulation, introduced casually. — *n.* One that is transient; esp., a transient guest. — **-sient·ly**, *adv.* — **-sient·ness**, *n.*

Syn. Transient, transitory, ephemeral, momentary, fugitive, fleeting, evanescent mean lasting or staying briefly. Transient applies to that which is actually short in duration or stay; transitory, to that which by its nature or essence is bound to pass or go; ephemeral, to that which has marked brevity of life or duration; momentary, to that which lasts but a moment or incredibly short time; fugitive and fleeting, to that which passes swiftly and is gone, but *fugitive* usually suggests a catching and fixing in mind; evanescent, to that which vanishes almost as it comes.

trans′il·lu′mi·nate (trăns′ĭ·lū′mĭ·nāt), *v. t.* To pass light through, as through an organ for medical examination.

tran·sis′tor (trăn·zĭs′tĕr; trăn·sĭs′-), *n.* [*trans*fer + res*istor.*] A nonvacuum electronic device similar in uses to the electron tube, whose control of an electron current is effected by the conducting properties of a semiconductor, as germanium.

trans′it (trăn′sĭt; -zĭt), *n.* [L. *transitus*, fr. *transire* to go across.] **1.** Passage through or over; as, rapid *transit* from city to city; also, figuratively, change; transition. **2.** Act or process of causing to pass; conveyance; as, *transit* of goods. **3.** *Astron.* **a** The passage of a celestial body over the meridian of a place, or through the field of a telescope. **b** The passage of a smaller body across the disk of a larger, as of Venus across the sun's disk. **4.** *Surv.* A variety of theodolite with the telescope mounted so that it can be transited; — called in full, **transit theodolite.** — *v. t.* **1.** To make a transit across or over. **2.** *Surv.* To turn (a telescope) over, about its horizontal transverse axis. — *v. i.* **1.** To make a transit. **2.** To be transited; also to transit a telescope.

transit instrument. **1.** A telescope mounted at right angles to a horizontal axis, and used with a clock and chronograph for observing the time of transit of a celestial body over the meridian of a place. **2.** = TRANSIT, *n.*, 4.

tran·si′tion (trăn·zĭsh′ŭn; -sĭzh′-; -sĭsh′-), *n.* [L. *transitio.*] **1.** Passage from one place, state, stage of development, type, etc., to another; change; also, the period, place, passage, etc., in which such a change is effected. **2.** *Music.* **a** A modulation, esp. a transient modulation. **b** A sudden change of key. — **tran·si′tion·al** (-ăl), *adj.* — **tran·si′tion·al·ly**, *adv.*

tran′si·tive (trăn′sĭ·tĭv), *adj.* **1.** Characterized by or involving transition; transitional. **2.** *Gram.* Passing over to an object; expressing an action as not limited to the agent or subject, but directed upon an object. Abbr. *tr., trans.* — *n. Gram.* A verb or construction expressive of transitive force. — **tran′si·tive·ly**, *adv.* — **tran′si·tive·ness**, *n.*

tran′si·to′ry (-tō′rĭ *or, esp. Brit.*, -tĕr·ĭ), *adj.* Continuing only for a short time; not enduring; fleeting; evanescent; temporary. — **Syn.** See TRANSIENT. — **tran′si·to′ri·ly**, *adv.* — **tran′si·to′ri·ness**, *n.*

trans·late′ (trăns·lāt′), *v. t.* [L. *translatus*, used as past part. of *transferre* to transfer, but from a different root.] **1.** To bear or change from one place, condition, etc., to another; to transfer. **2.** Specif.: **a** To remove to heaven; — originally implying without death. **b** To remove (remains) for reinterring. **c** To transfer (a bishop) from one see to another. **3.** To turn into one's own or another language; broadly, to carry over from one medium or sphere (into another). **4.** To transport or ravish; enrapture. **5.** *Mech.* To impart translation to. **6.** *Teleg.* To repeat or forward (a message) by translation. — *v. i.* To translate books, articles, messages, etc.; to admit of translation. — **trans·lat′a·ble** (-lāt′ȧ·b'l), *adj.* — **trans·la′tor** (-lā′tĕr), *n.*

trans·la′tion (trăns·lā′shŭn), *n.* **1.** Act, process, or an instance of translating. **2.** That produced by one who translates into another language or medium; a version resulting from translation. **3.** *Mech.* Motion in which all the points of the moving body have at any instant the same velocity and direction of motion; — in contrast to or as distinct from *rotation.* **4.** *Teleg.* The automatic repeating or forwarding of messages, as by means of a relay connected with a further section of the line. — **trans·la′tion·al** (-ăl), *adj.*

trans′light′ (trăns′līt′), *n.* A transparency (def. 2), as one bearing advertising.

trans·lit′er·ate (trăns·lĭt′ĕr·āt), *v. t.* [*trans-* + L. *litera, littera*, letter.] To represent or spell in the characters of another alphabet. — **trans·lit′er·a′tion** (-ā′shŭn), *n.*

trans·lo′cate (-lō′kāt), *v. t.* [*trans-* + *locate.*] To change the location or position of; to dislocate; displace; specif., *Plant Physiol.*, to subject to translocation.

trans′lo·ca′tion (trăns′lō·kā′shŭn), *n.* **1.** Act or fact of translocating; displacement. **2.** *Plant Physiol.* Transfer of food materials or products of metabolism from one part to another.

trans·lu′cent (trăns·lū′sĕnt), *adj.* [L. *translucens, -entis*, pres. part. of *translucere* to shine through, fr. *trans-* + *lucere* to shine.] **1.** Shining or glowing through; as, the *translucent* rays of the sun. **2.** *Now Rare.* Transparent. **3.** Admitting passage of light but diffusing it so that objects beyond cannot be clearly distinguished; partly transparent. — **Syn.** See CLEAR. — **trans·lu′cence** (-sĕns), **trans·lu′cen·cy** (-sĕn·sĭ), *n.* — **trans·lu′cent·ly**, *adv.*

trans·lu′cid (-sĭd), *adj.* [L. *translucidus.*] Translucent.

trans·mi′grant (trăns·mī′grănt; trăns′mĭ·grănt), *n.* [L. *transmigrans*, pres. part. See TRANSMIGRATE.] One who transmigrates; specif., an emigrant passing through a country en route to another country in which he will be an immigrant.

trans·mi′grate (-grāt), *v. i.* [L. *transmigrare, -migratum*, fr. *trans-* + *migrare* to migrate.] To pass from one place, condition, body (as in transmigration), or country to another. — **trans·mi′gra·tor** (-grā-tĕr; -grā′tĕr), *n.* — **trans·mi′gra·to′ry** (trăns·mī′grȧ·tō′rĭ *or, esp. Brit.*, -tĕr·ĭ), *adj.*

trans′mi·gra′tion (trăns′mī·grā′shŭn; -mĭ-), *n.* Act or instance of transmigrating; specif., the passing of the soul at death into another body or successive bodily forms, either human or animal; also (often **transmigration of souls**), the doctrine that souls so pass.

trans·mis′si·ble (trăns·mĭs′ĭ·b'l), *adj.* Capable of being transmitted. — **trans·mis′si·bil′i·ty** (-bĭl′ĭ·tĭ), *n.*

trans·mis′sion (-mĭsh′ŭn), *n.* [L. *transmissio.* See TRANSMIT.] **1.** Act, operation, or process, of transmitting. **2.** Something that is transmitted. **3.** *Mach.* The gear, including the propeller shaft or driving chain (or chains), by which the power is transmitted from the engine of an automobile to the live axle; sometimes, any one of these parts. **4.** *Radio.* Passage of radio waves in the space between transmitting and receiving stations. — **trans·mis′sive** (-mĭs′ĭv), *adj.*

trans·mit′ (-mĭt′), *v. t.;* -MIT′TED; -MIT′TING. [L. *transmittere, -missum*, fr. *trans-* + *mittere* to send.] **1.** To send or transfer from one person or place to another; to forward by rail, post, wire, etc. **2.** To pass on or down to others; specif., to impart hereditarily. **3.** To cause (as light, force, etc.) to pass or be conveyed through space or a medium. **4.** To admit the passage of; to conduct; as, metals *transmit* electricity. **5.** *Radio & Television.* To send out (a signal) by means of radio waves. — **trans·mit′tal** (-mĭt′ăl; -'l), *n.* — **trans·mit′tance** (-ăns; -'ns), *n.* — **trans·mit′ti·ble** (-ĭ·b'l), *adj.*

trans·mit′ter (-mĭt′ĕr), *n.* **1.** One who or that which transmits. **2.** Specif.: **a** On a telephone, a part into which one speaks and which contains a mechanism for converting sound waves into electric waves. See TELEPHONE, *Illust.* **b** That portion of a telegraph instrument by which the message is sent. **c** *Radio & Television.* Also **trans·mit′ting set.** Apparatus for transmitting radio waves; esp., that part of the equipment which produces and modulates radio-frequency current and delivers it to the antenna.

trans·mog′ri·fy (trăns·mŏg′rĭ·fī), *v. t.;* -FIED (-fīd); -FY′ING. [A humorous coinage; cf. TRANSMIGRATE.] To change, often with absurd effect; to transform. — **Syn.** See TRANSFORM. — **trans·mog′ri·fi·ca′tion** (-fĭ·kā′shŭn), *n.*

trans·mon′tane (-mŏn′tān), *adj.* Tramontane.

trans′mu·ta′tion (trăns′mū·tā′shŭn), *n.* **1.** Fluctuation; alternation, as in states of mind. **2.** A transmuting; esp.: **a** *Alchemy.* The conversion of base metals into gold or silver; — more fully **transmutation of metals.** **b** *Chem. & Physics.* The conversion of one element or isotope into another either naturally or artificially. — **trans′mu·ta′tion·al** (-ăl), **trans·mut′a·tive** (trăns·mūt′ȧ·tĭv), *adj.*

trans·mute′ (trăns·mūt′), *v. t.* [L. *transmutare, -mutatum*, fr. *trans-* + *mutare* to change.] **a** To change from one nature, form, substance, or species, into another; convert. **b** *Chem. & Physics.* To subject to transmutation (sense 2 **b**). — **Syn.** See TRANSFORM. — **trans·mut′a·bil′i·ty** (-mūt′ȧ·bĭl′ĭ·tĭ), **trans·mut′a·ble·ness** (-mūt′ȧ·b'l·nĕs; -nĭs), *n.* — **trans·mut′a·ble**, *adj.* — **trans·mut′a·bly**, *adv.* — **trans·mut′er** (-mūt′ĕr), *n.*

tran′som (trăn′sŭm), *n.* [Prob. fr. L. *transtrum* a crossbeam, transom, fr. *trans* across.] **1.** A transverse piece in a structure. Specif.:

a A lintel. **b** The horizontal bar of a cross, gallows, etc. **c** The seat of a throne, swing, etc. **d** *Arch.* A horizontal crossbar in a window, over a door, or between a door and a window or fanlight above it. See MULLION, *Illust.* **e** *Shipbuilding.* Any of several transverse timbers or beams secured to the sternpost. **2.** *Chiefly U. S.* A window above a door or other window, built on, and commonly hinged to, a transom (def. 1 **d**).

tran·son′ic (trăn·sŏn′ĭk), *adj.* [*trans-* + L. *sonans, -antis,* pres. part. of *sonare* + *-ic.*] *Physics.* Of, pertaining to, or designating a speed approximating that of sound in air, that is, about 1087 feet per second (or about 738 miles per hour); — often used in referring to speeds from 600 miles to 900 miles per hour.

trans′pa·cif′ic (trăns′pȧ·sĭf′ĭk), *adj.* Lying or dwelling beyond or across the Pacific Ocean; crossing the Pacific.

trans′pa·dane′ (trăns′pȧ·dān′; trăns·pā′dān), *adj.* [L. *transpadanus,* fr. *trans* across + *Padus* the Po.] On the farther (north) side of the Po from Rome.

trans·par′en·cy (trăns·pâr′ĕn·sĭ; 6), *n.; pl.* -CIES (-sĭz). **1.** Also **trans·par′ence** (-ĕns). Quality or state of being transparent. **2.** Something transparent; esp., a picture or the like, as on glass, viewed by light shining through it; hence, a framework covered with thin cloth or paper bearing a device for public display, as for advertisement, and lighted from within.

trans·par′ent (-ĕnt), *adj.* [F. and ML.; F., fr. ML. *transparens, -entis,* pres. part. of *transparere* to be transparent, fr. L. *trans* across, through + *parere* to appear.] **1.** Having the property of transmitting rays of light, so that bodies can be seen through; pervious to light; diaphanous; pellucid; — opposed to *opaque.* **2.** *Poetic.* Luminous; bright. **3.** So fine in texture or open in mesh as not to conceal what lies beyond; sheer; gauzy. **4. a** Readily understood; clear. **b** Easily detected; perfectly evident. **c** Guileless; free from pretense. — **Syn.** See CLEAR. — **trans·par′ent·ly,** *adv.*

tran·spic′u·ous (trăn·spĭk′ū·ŭs), *adj.* [L. *transpicere* to see or look through.] Transparent.

trans·pierce′ (trăns·pērs′), *v. t.* [F. *transpercer.*] To pierce through; penetrate.

tran′spi·ra′tion (trăn′spĭ·rā′shŭn), *n.* Act, fact, or process of transpiring, as in exhalation of vapor through the skin or from the surface of green tissues in plants. Perspiration is a form of transpiration. — **tran·spir′a·to′ry** (trăn·spīr′ȧ·tō′rĭ *or, esp. Brit.,* -tẽr·ĭ), *adj.*

tran·spire′ (trăn·spīr′), *v. t.* [F. *transpirer,* fr. L. *trans* across, through + *spirare* to breathe.] To exhale or cause to pass through the pores of a tissue or substance, as a gas or a liquid; specif.: **a** *Physiol.* To excrete, as through the skin; to perspire. **b** *Plant Physiol.* To evaporate (moisture) from living cells. — *v. i.* **1.** To exhale moisture, vapor, perfume, etc.; to pass off in the form of vapor, perspiration, etc. **2.** To leak out; come to light; become known. **3.** To come to pass; happen; occur; — a sense disapproved by most authorities but found in writings of authors of good standing. — **Syn.** See HAPPEN.

trans·plant′ (trăns·plȧnt′; 9), *v. t.* [LL. *transplantare,* fr. *trans-* + *plantare* to plant.] **1.** To remove and plant in another place; to lift and reset in another soil or situation. **2.** To transport as for colonization; cause to emigrate. **3.** *Surg.* To remove tissue from one part or individual and plant for growth in another. — (trăns′plȧnt), *n.* A transplanting; a transplanted seedling, tissue, etc. — **trans′plan·ta′tion** (trăns′plăn·tā′shŭn), *n.* — **trans·plant′er** (trăns·plȧn′tẽr), *n.*

trans·pon′tine (-pŏn′tĭn; -tīn), *adj.* [*trans-* + L. *pons, pontis,* bridge.] Being on the other side of a bridge; esp., of or characteristic of London south of the Thames.

trans·port′ (trăns·pōrt′; 70), *v. t.* [OF. *transporter,* fr. L. *transportare,* fr. *trans-* + *portare* to carry.] **1.** To convey; esp., to carry or convey from one place to another, as by boat or rail. **2.** To carry away with vehement emotion; ravish. **3.** To remove by death. **4.** To banish to or as to a penal colony. — **Syn.** See CARRY; BANISH. — **trans·port′a·bil′i·ty** (-bĭl′ĭ·tĭ), *n.* — **trans·port′a·ble** (-pōr′tȧ·b′l), *adj.* — **trans·port′er,** *n.*

trans′port (trăns′pōrt; 70), *n.* **1.** Transportation; conveyance. **2.** Vehement emotion; ecstasy; rapture. **3. a** A vessel employed in transportation, esp. of soldiers. **b** An airplane used in transporting mail, passengers, etc. **4.** A transported convict. — **Syn.** See ECSTASY.

trans′por·ta′tion (trăns′pōr·tā′shŭn), *n.* **1.** Act of transporting, or state of being transported; specif., systems and modes of conveyance of persons or goods from place to place. **2.** *U. S.* A ticket, pass, or the like, required to secure passage on a public conveyance. **3.** Banishment to a penal colony.

trans·pose′ (trăns·pōz′), *v. t.* [OF. *transposer* (for L. *transponere, -positum*), fr. *trans-* (L. *trans-*) + *poser* to put.] **1.** *Now Rare.* To transfer; transport; also, transmute. **2.** To change the relative, usual, or natural place or order of; exchange in position; reverse or rearrange the sequence of; as, to *transpose* letters or words. **3.** *Alg.* To bring, as a term of an equation, from one side to the other, with change of its sign. **4.** *Music.* To change to a different key. — **Syn.** See REVERSE. — **trans·pos′al** (-pōz′ăl), *n.* — **trans·pos′er** (-ẽr), *n.* — **trans′po·si′tion** (trăns′pō·zĭsh′ŭn), *n.* — **trans′po·si′tion·al** (-ăl), *adj.*

trans·ship′ (trăns·shĭp′), *v. t.* Also **tran·ship′** (trăn-). To transfer for further transportation from one ship or conveyance to another. — **trans·ship′ment,** *also* **tran·ship′ment,** *n.*

tran′sub·stan′ti·ate (trăn′sŭb·stăn′shĭ·āt), *v. t.* [ML. *transubstantiatus,* past part. of *transubstantiare* to transubstantiate, fr. L. *trans* over + *substantia* substance.] **1.** To change into another substance; transmute. **2.** *Theol.* To effect transubstantiation in (sacramental bread and wine).

tran′sub·stan′ti·a′tion (-ā′shŭn), *n.* A transubstantiating; specif., *R. C. & Eastern Churches,* the change, by and at the consecration of the elements in the Eucharist, of the substance of the bread and wine into the body and blood of Christ, only the appearances of the bread and wine remaining; also, the doctrine that such a change occurs; — distinguished from *consubstantiation* and *impanation.* — **tran′sub·stan′ti·a′tion·al·ist** (-ăl·ĭst), *n.*

tran′su·date (trăn′sū·dāt), *n.* A transuded substance.

tran′su·da′tion (-dā′shŭn), *n.* **1.** Act or process of transuding. **2.** A transudate.

tran·sude′ (trăn·sūd′), *v. i.* [F. *transsuder,* fr. L. *trans* through + *sudare* to sweat.] To pass as or like sweat through the pores of tissues or textures.

trans′u·ra′ni·um (trăns′ū·rā′nĭ·ŭm), *n. Chem.* Any element having an atomic number greater than that of uranium (92). — **trans′u·ran′ic** (-răn′ĭk), **trans′u·ra′ni·an** (-rā′nĭ·ăn), *adj.*

trans·val′ue (trăns·văl′ū), *v. t.* To value on a different basis; to evaluate according to a novel principle, esp. one repudiating conventional standards. — **trans′val·u·a′tion** (trăns′văl·ū·ā′shŭn), *n.*

trans·ver′sal (-vûr′săl; -s'l), *adj.* [See TRANSVERSE.] Running or lying across; transverse. — *n. Geom.* A line that traverses or intersects any system of lines. — **trans·ver′sal·ly,** *adv.*

trans·verse′ (trăns·vûrs′; 2), *adj.* [L. *transversus,* past part. of *transvertere* to turn or direct across, fr. *trans-* + *vertere* to turn.] Lying or being across; athwart. Cf. LONGITUDINAL, 2. — **trans·verse′ly,** *adv.*

trans·verse′ (trăns·vûrs′; trăns′vûrs), *n.* **1.** A transverse piece, muscle, etc. **2.** *Geom.* The longer, or transverse, axis of an ellipse.

transverse process. A lateral process of a vertebra.

trap (trăp), *n.* [AS. *treppe, træppe.*] **1.** A device, as a pitfall, snare, or machine that shuts suddenly as with a spring, for taking game, etc.; a gin. **2.** A condition, device, expedient, place, etc., for entrapping the unwary; as, a *trap* for speeders; a sand *trap* on a golf course. **3.** Any of various devices permitting one kind of thing to pass through while restraining another, as a bend or partitioned chamber in a drainpipe in which liquid forms a seal preventing escape of sewer gas, etc. **4.** *Music.* A percussion instrument, or *pl.,* a group of them. **5.** *Sports.* A machine for throwing into the air balls, clay pigeons, etc., to be shot at. **6.** [Cf. RATTLETRAP.] A light, usually two-wheeled, one-horse carriage with springs. **7.** A trap door.
— *v. t.;* TRAPPED (trăpt) or, *Rare,* TRAPT; TRAP′PING. **1.** To catch or take in or as in a trap; ensnare; entrap. **2.** To provide with a trap or traps. **3.** To stop, hold, or separate by a trap, as water from steam; — sometimes with *out.* — **Syn.** See CATCH. — *v. i.* To set traps for game; to make a business of trapping game or, esp., fur-bearing animals. — **trap′per** (trăp′ẽr), *n.*

trap, *n.* [See TRAPPING, TRAP to adorn.] **1.** *Obs.* A trapping, as for a horse. **2.** *pl. Colloq.* Personal belongings; luggage. — *v. t.* [ME. *trappen,* fr. ME. *trappe, trappure,* trappings, fr. OF. *drap* cloth, *drapure* a covering for a horse.] To adorn with traps or trappings.

trap, *n.* [Sw. *trapp.*] Also **trap′rock′** (trăp′rŏk′). *Geol. & Petrog.* Any of various dark-colored, fine-grained, igneous rocks, including esp. basalt, amygdaloid, etc.

tra·pan′ (trȧ·păn′), **tra·pan′ner.** Var. of TREPAN, etc.

trap door. A lifting or sliding door covering an opening in a roof or floor. — **trap′-door′,** *adj.*

trapes (trāps). Var. of TRAIPSE.

tra·peze′ (tră·pēz′), *n.* [F. *trapèze.*] **1.** A horizontal bar suspended at a height by two parallel ropes, for use by gymnasts and acrobats. **2.** *Geom.* A trapezium.

tra·pe′zi·form (trȧ·pē′zĭ·fôrm), *adj.* [*trapezium* + *-form.*] Like a trapezium in form.

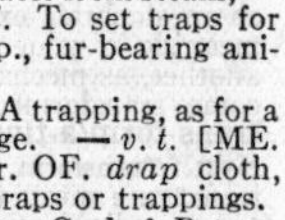

Trapezium.

tra·pe′zi·um (-zĭ·ŭm), *n.; pl.* -ZIUMS (-ŭmz), -ZIA (-ȧ). [NL., fr. Gr. *trapezion* a little table, an irregular four-sided figure, deriv. of *tetra-* (see TETRA-) + *peza* foot; hence, orig., a table with four feet.] **1.** *Geom.* **a** A plane figure formed by four right lines, of which no two are parallel. **b** *Chiefly Eng.* A trapezoid. **2.** *Anat.* A bone in the wrist at the end of the thumb.

trap′e·zo·he′dron (trăp′ē·zō·hē′drŭn; trȧ·pē′zō-), *n.* [NL., fr. *trapezium* + Gr. *hedra* a seat, base.] *Cryst.* A form whose faces are trapeziums. See TRISOCTAHEDRON, 2.

trap′e·zoid (trăp′ē·zoid), *n.* [Gr. *trapezoeidēs* trapezoid-shaped, fr. *trapeza* table + *eidos* shape, likeness.] **1.** *Geom.* **a** A plane four-sided figure with two parallel sides. **b** *Eng.* = TRAPEZIUM, 1 **a.** **2.** *Anat. & Zool.* A bone in the wrist at the end of the forefinger. — **trap′e·zoid, trap′e·zoi′dal** (-zoi′dăl; -d'l), *adj.*

trap′pe·an (trăp′ē·ăn; tră·pē′ăn), *adj. Geol., etc.* Of or pert. to trap.

trap′ping, *n.* [See 2d TRAP, *n. & v.*] *Commonly pl.* An ornamental housing for a horse; hence, *pl.,* ornaments; dress; superficial decorations. See 2d HOUSING.

Trap′pist (trăp′ĭst), *n.* [F. *trappiste.*] *R.C.Ch.* A monk of a reformed branch of the Cistercian Order established in 1664, at the monastery of La Trappe, in Normandy. The discipline is extremely austere. The order was introduced into the United States in 1848.

trap′rock′ (trăp′rŏk′), *n.* = 3d TRAP.

trap′shoot′ing (-shōōt′ĭng), *n.* Shooting at pigeons liberated, or glass balls or clay pigeons sprung into air, from a trap.

trap shot. *Tennis, etc.* = HALF VOLLEY.

tra·pun′to (trȧ·pōōn′tō), *n.* [It.] Ornamental single-outline design raised into high relief on a fabric or garment by inserting cotton or yarn with a steel crochet hook into the design from the underside; as, *trapunto* quilting.

trash (trăsh), *n.* [Of Scand. origin.] **1.** Worn-out, broken up, or worthless things; refuse; rubbish. **2.** Loppings, twigs, and leaves of trees, bruised sugar cane, corn husks, etc. **3.** Someone, something, or a class of persons or things, condemned as of no account, despicable, or the like; riffraff. — *v. t.* **1.** To free from trash; hence, to lop; crop; as, to *trash* trees. **2.** To treat as trash; discard.

trash, *v. t.* [OF. *trachier,* var. of *tracier* to trace, track.] To hold back by a leash, as a dog pursuing game; hence, to retard or restrain. — *n.* A leash or halter used to trash a dog; hence, any hindrance.

trash′y (trăsh′ĭ), *adj.;* -I·ER (-ĭ·ẽr); -I·EST. Like trash; worthless; useless. — **trash′i·ly,** *adv.* — **trash′i·ness,** *n.*

trass (trăs), *n.* [D. *tras* (whence G. *trass*).] *Petrog.* A light-colored volcanic tuff resembling pozzuolana in composition, sometimes ground for use as a hydraulic cement.

trau′ma (trô′mȧ), *n.; pl.* -MATA (-mȧ·tȧ), -MAS (-mȧz). [NL., fr. Gr. *trauma.*] An injury, wound, shock, or the resulting condition.

trau·mat′ic (trô·măt′ĭk), *adj.* [LL. *traumaticus,* fr. Gr. *traumatikos,* fr. *trauma, traumatos,* a wound.] *Med.* Of, pertaining to, or resulting from a trauma; caused by a wound, injury, or shock.

traumatic neurosis. A neurosis marked by disturbances especially incidental to active warfare, caused by injuries and fear.

trau′ma·tism (trô′mȧ·tĭz'm), *n. Med.* The morbid condition of the system due to a trauma; improperly, a trauma.

trau′ma·tize (-tīz), *v. t.* To wound or injure, esp. in surgical operation.

trav′ail (trăv′āl; -'l), *n.* [OF., fr. *travaill(i)er.* See TRAVAIL, *v.*] **1.** Toil; esp., painful effort or exertion. **2.** Parturition; labor. **3.** Agony; racking pain. — **Syn.** See WORK. — *v. i.* [OF. *traveillier, travaillier,* to labor, toil, be in labor, torment, deriv. of LL. *trepalium* an instrument of torture, fr. L. *tripalis* having three stakes.] **1.** To toil; labor. **2.** To suffer the pangs of childbearing; to be in labor.

trave (trāv), *n.* [OF. *trave* a beam, *travée* space between two beams, fr. L. *trabs* a beam.] **1.** *Arch.* A crossbeam; hence, a division or bay, as in a ceiling, made by crossbeams. **2.** A frame to confine an unruly horse or ox while shoeing.

trav'el (trăv'ĕl; -'l), *v. i.;* -ELED (-ĕld; -'ld) or -ELLED; -EL·ING or -EL·LING. [Prop., to labor, and the same word as *travail.*] **1.** To journey to a distant place or to many places; make a journey including many places. **2.** Specif.: **a** *Now Dial.* To walk. **b** To journey from place to place selling, taking orders, etc. **3.** To pass; move from point to point. **4.** *Mach.* To move in a given direction or path, or through a given distance. — *v. t.* To journey over or through; traverse. — *n.* **1.** Act of traveling. **2.** A journey; trip; tour; — now chiefly *pl.;* also, a literary account of such travels. **3.** The number of those traveling; amount of traffic. **4.** *Mach.* Motion, esp. reciprocating motion; the length of stroke, as of a piston.

trav'eled, trav'elled (-ĕld; -'ld), *adj.* **1.** Having done much traveling. **2.** Used by travelers; as, a *traveled* road.

trav'el·er, trav'el·ler (-ĕl·ẽr), *n.* **1.** One who or that which travels; specif., a commercial traveler. **2.** A sales ticket on which a customer's purchases in various departments are entered so that all may be paid for together. **3.** *Mach.* Any of various devices for transporting laterally. **4.** *Naut.* **a** An iron ring sliding along a rope, bar, or the like. **b** A rod on the deck on which such a ring slides.

trav'el·er's check *or* **cheque** (trăv'ĕl·ẽrz). A draft issued by a banker and payable by any of the correspondents of the issuing banker.

trav'el·ing sales'man (-ĕl·ĭng). = COMMERCIAL TRAVELER.

trav'e·logue, trav'e·log (trăv'ĕ·lŏg; 74), *n.* [*travel* + *-logue.*] A lecture, usually illustrated, on travel.

trav'erse (trăv'ẽrs; -ûrs; trȧ·vûrs'), *v. t.* [OF. *traverser*, fr. (assumed) VL. *transversare.* See TRAVERSE, *n.*] **1.** To pass through or across; esp., to cross in traveling; also, to move backwards and forwards over; as, a patrolman *traversing* his beat. **2.** To cross by way of opposition; run or go counter to; thwart. **3.** To survey or study carefully. **4.** *Chiefly Technical.* To move or turn laterally. **5.** *Law.* In pleading, to deny formally (an allegation of fact made by the opposite party); specif.: **a** To take issue upon (an indictment). **b** To impeach the validity of (an inquest of office). **6.** *Skiing.* To ski up or down (a slope) at an angle to the straight line of ascent or descent. — **Syn.** See DENY. — *v. i.* **1.** To move across or over; cross over; also, to cross to and fro; pace, step, or run back and forth. **2.** To swivel; pivot. **3.** *Fencing.* To slide one's blade toward the opponent's hilt while exerting pressure on his blade. **4.** *Skiing.* To traverse a slope. — ***traverse a yard.*** *Naut.* To brace a yard fore and aft.

— (trăv'ẽrs; -ûrs), *n.* [OF. *travers*, fr. L. *transversum* cross direction or position (see TRANSVERSE, *adj.*); OF. *traverse*, fr. *traverser* to traverse (see TRAVERSE, *v.*).] **1.** Something that traverses or crosses; a crosspiece, as a rung, a crossbeam, transom, etc.; specif., *Arch.:* **a** A screen, railing, etc., used as a barrier. **b** A gallery or communicating loft between sides of a large building. **2.** *Now Rare.* Something that traverses, or thwarts; an obstacle; reverse. **3.** The action or an instance of traversing; a passage or journey across. **4.** A route or way across; often, a zigzag course. **5.** *Fort.* Formerly, a parapet for attackers; now, a projecting wall or bank of earth in a trench for protection. **6.** *Law.* A formal traversing, or denial. **7.** *Mach.* A lateral movement, as of a saddle of a lathe carriage; also, a device for imparting such movement. **8.** *Mil.* The swiveling of a gun in the horizontal plane so as to point it in any direction. **9.** *Surv.* A line surveyed across a plot of ground.

— (trăv'ẽrs; -ûrs), *adj.* Lying across; transverse.

— **trav'ers·a·ble** (trăv'ẽr·sȧ·b'l; trȧ·vûr'-), *adj.* — **trav'ers·al** (trăv'ẽr·săl; -s'l; trȧ·vûr'-), *n.* — **trav'ers·er** (-sẽr), *n.*

trav'er·tine (trăv'ẽr·tĭn; -tēn), *n.* Also **trav'er·tin.** [It. *travertino, tivertino*, fr. L. lapis *Tiburtinus*, fr. *Tibur* (now Tivoli) in Latium.] *Mineral.* Crystalline calcium carbonate, either aragonite or calcite formed by deposition from spring waters.

trav'es·ty (trăv'ĕs·tĭ; -ĭs·tĭ), *n.; pl.* -TIES (-tĭz). [From obs. *travesty*, adj., fr. F. *travesti*, past part. of *travestir* to disguise, travesty, fr. It., fr. L. *trans* across + *vestire* to dress.] A burlesque translation or imitation; a grotesque parody or likeness. — **Syn.** See CARICATURE. — *v. t.;* TRAV'ES·TIED (-tĭd); TRAV'ES·TY·ING. To make a travesty of; parody; burlesque.

tra·vois' (trȧ·voi'), **tra·voise'** (-voiz'), *n.; pl.* TRAVOIS (-voiz'), TRAVOISES (-voiz'ĕz; -ĭz). [Can. F.] A primitive vehicle of the Indians of the Great Plains consisting of two trailing poles (**travois poles**) serving as shafts, and bearing a platform or net for the load.

trawl (trôl), *n.* **1.** A large bag net dragged at the bottom in sea fishing. **2.** A very long fishing line anchored at the ends, having many short lines bearing hooks. — *v. i. & t.* To fish or catch with a trawl; also, erroneously, to troll.

trawl'er (-ẽr), *n.* A person or craft that fishes or dredges by trawling.

tray (trā), *n.* [AS. *trēg, trieg, trīg.*] **1.** *Chiefly Dial.* A shallow wooden bowl, trough, hod, etc. **2.** A flat-bottomed open receptacle with a low rim for holding, carrying, or displaying, articles. **3.** Such a receptacle and its contents; esp., a tray holding food.

tray agriculture. = HYDROPONICS.

treach'er·ous (trĕch'ẽr·ŭs), *adj.* **1.** Characterized by or manifesting treachery; traitorous; perfidious. **2.** Having an appearance that belies; untrustworthy; unreliable; esp., providing insecure footing or support; as, the *treacherous* sands. — **Syn.** See FAITHLESS. — **treach'er·ous·ly**, *adv.* — **treach'er·ous·ness**, *n.*

treach'er·y (-ĭ), *n.; pl.* -ERIES (-ĭz). [OF. *trecherie, tricherie*, deceit, trickery, fr. *trichier, trechier*, to cheat, trick.] Violation of allegiance or of faith and confidence; perfidious character or act; treason.

trea'cle (trē'k'l), *n.* [OF. *triacle*, fr. L. *theriaca* an antidote against venom, fr. Gr. *thēriakē*, fr. *thērion* a wild beast, dim. of *thēr* a beast.] **1.** *Old Med.* A remedy against poison. See THERIACA. **2.** *Obs.* A sovereign remedy; a cure. **3.** *Eng.* Molasses; specif., molasses which drains from sugar-refining molds. — **trea'cly** (-klĭ), *adj.*

tread (trĕd), *v. t.;* TROD (trŏd); TROD'DEN (trŏd''n), TROD; TREAD'ING. [AS. *tredan.*] **1.** *Now Poetic.* To step on; walk on or over. **2.** To execute by stepping, or dancing; as, to *tread* a measure. **3.** To beat or press with the feet; trample. **4.** To subdue or repress as if by trampling; crush. **5.** To copulate with; to cover; — said of male birds. — *v. i.* **1.** To walk; move on foot. **2.** To set foot; put one's foot; step. **3.** To trample; stamp; — with *on* or *upon.* **4.** To copulate. — *n.* **1.** A mark left by treading or made by a tread. **2.** Act, manner, or sound, of treading; as, a nimble or a cautious *tread.* **3.** That part of a thing which treads or is trodden upon; specif.: **a** The part of a sole that touches the ground. **b** The part of a wheel that bears on a road or rail, as, in automobiles, the thickened face of the tire (see TIRE, *Illust.*); also, the part of a rail on which the car wheels bear. **c** *Arch.* The upper horizontal part of a step; also, the width of this. See STAIR, *Illust.* **4.** *Embryol.* **a** = CICATRICLE **b.** **b** = CHALAZA. See EGG, *Illust.* **5.** *Vehicles.* The distance between the points of contact with the ground of the two front wheels or the two rear wheels. — ***tread water.*** To keep oneself nearly upright in water, with the head above water, by a treading motion of the feet, usually aided by the hands. — **tread'er**, *n.*

trea'dle (trĕd''l), *n.* [AS. *tredel.*] A swiveling or lever device pressed by the foot to drive a machine. Where the treadle is attached directly to the end of a crank, as in a bicycle, it is usually called a *pedal.* — *v. i.;* TREAD'LED (-'ld); TREA'DLING (-lĭng). To operate a treadle.

tread'mill' (trĕd'mĭl'), *n.* **1.** **a** A mill worked by persons treading on steps on the periphery of a wide wheel having a horizontal axis, and used, formerly, chiefly in prison discipline. **b** A mill worked by horses, dogs, etc., treading an endless belt. **2.** Any wearisome routine.

trea'son (trē'z'n), *n.* [OF. *traïson*, fr. L. *traditio* a delivering up, fr. *tradere* to give up, betray.] **1.** *Now Rare.* The betrayal of any trust or confidence; breach of faith. **2.** The offense of attempting by overt acts to overthrow the government of the state to which the offender owes allegiance, or (in monarchies) to kill or personally injure the sovereign or his family. Treason against the United States is defined by the Constitution (Art. III, sec. 3) to consist "only in levying war against them, or in adhering to their enemies, giving aid and comfort to them." — **Syn.** See SEDITION.

trea'son·a·ble (-ȧ·b'l), *adj.* Pertaining to, consisting of, or involving treason. — **trea'son·a·bly**, *adv.*

trea'son·ous (-ŭs), *adj.* Treasonable. — **trea'son·ous·ly**, *adv.*

treas'ure (trĕzh'ẽr), *n.* [OF. *tresor*, fr. L. *thesaurus*, fr. Gr. *thēsauros* a store laid up, treasure.] **1.** Money, jewels, or the like hoarded up; esp., a store of money in reserve. **2.** A thing of great worth; something rare or precious. — *v. t.* To collect and deposit, as valuables, for future use; hoard; hence, to cherish; prize. — **Syn.** See APPRECIATE.

treas'ur·er (trĕzh'ẽr·ẽr), *n.* One trusted with charge of a treasure or treasures; specif.: **a** A guardian of a collection of treasures; a curator. **b** An officer who receives the public money, takes charge of it, and disburses it upon orders made by the proper authority. **c** A similar official in charge of the funds of an organization, society, or corporation. Abbr. *treas.* — **treas'ur·er·ship'**, *n.*

treas'ure-trove' (trĕzh'ẽr·trōv'; 2), *n.* [*treasure* + OF. *trové* (F. *trouvé*), past part. of *trover* to find.] **1.** *Law.* Any money, bullion, or the like, found hidden, the owner of which is not known. **2.** Figuratively, any discovery that yields treasure.

treas'ur·y (trĕzh'ẽr·ĭ), *n.; pl.* -IES (-ĭz). **1.** A place in which stores of wealth are deposited; esp., a place where public revenues are deposited, kept, and disbursed; hence, the place of deposit and disbursement of any funds. **2.** [*often cap.*] That department of a government which has charge of the finances. **3.** A repository for treasures; also, a thesaurus.

treasury note. *U. S. Finance.* A currency note or bill issued from the Treasury Department, and receivable in payment of dues to the government.

treat (trēt), *v. i.* [OF. *tretier, traitier*, fr. L. *tractare* to draw violently, handle, manage, treat, v. intens. fr. *trahere, tractum*, to draw.] **1.** To negotiate; to consider terms of settlement, or the like. **2.** To handle a subject, esp. in writing or speaking; discourse; — now usually with *of.* **3.** To bear the expense of another's entertainment. — *v. t.* **1.** To deal with (a subject, theme, etc.); discuss, represent, present, etc., in a specified manner, style, etc. **2.** To bear oneself toward; as, to *treat* a horse cruelly; also, to regard (as such) and act toward or deal with accordingly; as, to *treat* life as a joke. **3.** To give gratification to; provide a treat for; specif., to pay the cost of entertaining, dining, supplying with drinks, etc.; — often with *to.* **4.** To care for medically or surgically; also, to seek cure or relief of (a disease, etc.) by treatment. **5.** To subject to some action, as of a chemical reagent; as, to *treat* a substance with sulfuric acid; often, to subject to some process to improve appearance, taste, etc.

— *n.* **1.** The act or an instance of treating. **2.** A repast; a feast; now usually, a free entertainment. **3.** That which affords gratification or pleasure; a cause of joy, delight, or, sometimes, amusement.

— **treat'a·ble**, *adj.* — **treat'er**, *n.*

trea'tise (trē'tĭs *or, esp. Brit.,* -tĭz), *n.* [AF. *tretiz*, either fr. (assumed) OF. *traiteïz*, fr. *traitier* to treat, or fr. OF. *traitiz, traitis*, well made, fr. L. *trahere, tractum*, to draw.] **1.** A systematic exposition or argument in writing; a methodical discussion of the facts and principles involved and conclusions reached. **2.** *Obs.* An account; a narration.

treat'ment (trēt'mĕnt), *n.* Act, manner, or an instance of treating, as a patient, a subject, or a substance in processing; handling; usage.

trea'ty (trē'tĭ), *n.; pl.* -TIES (-tĭz). [ME. *tretee*, fr. OF. *traité, traitié*, fr. L. *tractatus* a handling, treatment.] **1.** *Now Rare.* **a** Act of treating, esp. of negotiating. **b** Entreaty; proposal for agreement. **2.** An agreement made by negotiation or diplomacy; specif., an agreement, league, or contract, between two or more states or sovereigns, formally signed and usually ratified.

treaty port. A port opened by treaty to foreign trade; — formerly used esp. [*often caps.*] of certain ports in China, Japan, and Korea.

tre'ble (trĕb''l), *adj.* [OF. *treble, treible*, fr. L. *triplus* threefold.] **1.** Threefold; triple. **2.** **a** Of, pertaining to, or having the range of a treble; playing or singing treble. **b** Hence, high-pitched; acute; shrill. — *n.* **1.** *Music.* **a** The highest of the four voice parts; the part sung esp. by boys or women; soprano. **b** A singer or instrument taking this part. **c** The highest bell of a ring. **2.** A high-pitched or shrill voice, tone, or sound. — *v. t. & i.;* TRE'BLED (-'ld); TRE'BLING (-lĭng). **1.** To make or become threefold. **2.** To sing treble. — **tre'bly** (trĕb'lĭ), *adv.*

treble clef. See CLEF.

treble staff. *Music.* The staff carrying the G clef. See CLEF.

treb'u·chet (trĕb'ū·shĕt), *n.* Also **tre'buck·et** (trē'bŭk·ĕt; -ĭt). [OF. *trebuchet, trabuchet*, fr. *trebuchier, trabucher*, to stumble, trip, fall.] A military engine of the Middle Ages for throwing stones, etc. Cf CATAPULT.

‖**tre·cen'to** (trā·chĕn'tō), *n.* [It., three hundred. Cf. CINQUECENTO.] The fourteenth century, esp. with reference to Italian literature, art, etc.

tre'de·cil'lion (trē'dē·sĭl'yŭn), *n.* See NUMERATION, *Table.*

tree (trē), *n.* [AS. *trēo, trēow*, tree, wood.] **1.** A woody perennial plant having a single main axis or stem (trunk), commonly exceeding 10 feet in height. **2.** Hence, a shrub or bush formed like a tree; as, a rose *tree;* a banana *tree.* **3.** A piece of timber; a stick, stake, post, pole, or the like. **4.** *Archaic.* **a** The cross on which Jesus was crucified. **b** A gibbet; gallows. **5.** Something in the form of, or suggesting, a tree; specif.: **a** A diagrammatic representation, which indicates a branching from an original stem; as, a genealogical *tree.* **b** *Chem.* A treelike aggregation of crystals. **6.** Short for: **a** BOOT TREE, SADDLETREE, etc. **b** CHRISTMAS TREE. — *v. t.* **1.** To drive to or up a tree; as, a dog *trees* a squirrel. **2.** *Colloq.* Hence, to corner. **3.** To place upon or fit with a boot tree. — **tree,** *adj.* — **tree′less,** *adj.*

tree crab. = PURSE CRAB.

tree fern. Any fern (chiefly of families Cyatheaceae and Marattiaceae) of arborescent habit, having a woody trunk.

tree frog. = TREE TOAD.

tree heath. A shrubby heath (*Erica arborea*) of the Mediterranean and Caucasian region, cultivated for its nearly globular white flowers.

tree kangaroo. Any of a number of active, lightly built arboreal kangaroos (genus *Dendrolagus*) of northern Australia and parts of New Guinea.

tree′nail′, tre′nail′ (trē′nāl′; *colloq. or cant* trĕn′'l, trŭn′'l), *n.* [*tree* + *nail.*] A wooden peg, ordinarily of dry compressed timber so as to swell in its hole when moistened.

tree of heaven. An ornamental Asiatic tree (*Ailanthus glandulosa*) having ill-scented staminate flowers.

tree of knowledge of good and evil. Also **tree of knowledge.** The tree in the Garden of Eden whose fruit Adam and Eve tasted in spite of God's prohibition.

tree of life. *Bib.* In Genesis, a tree growing in the midst of the Garden of Eden, eating of which gave everlasting life; in Revelation xxii. 2, a tree in the heavenly Jerusalem whose leaves are for the healing of the nations.

Tree Planters State. Nebraska; — a nickname.

tree shrew. Any member of a family (Tupaiidae) of arboreal insectivorous mammals sometimes regarded as true insectivores and sometimes as primitive primates.

tree sparrow. See SPARROW.

tree surgery. Operative treatment of diseases of trees, esp. for decay. — **tree surgeon.**

tree toad. Any of many toadlike or froglike amphibians of arboreal habits (esp. family Hylidae, genus *Hyla*); a tree frog; hyla.

tree′top′ (trē′tŏp′), *n.* The top branches or part of a tree; also, *pl.,* the height or line marked by the tops of a row or group of trees.

tre′foil (trē′foil), *n.* [OF. and L.; OF. *trefueil,* fr. L. *trifolium.* See TRI-; FOIL leaf.] **1.** The clover; any of a genus (*Trifolium*) of plants including the clovers; hence, any of various related trifoliolate herbs, as the bird's-foot trefoil (which see); esp. (in England) the black medic (*Medicago lupulina*). **2.** *Arch.* An ornamental foliation of three divisions, or foils. See FOIL, *Illust.*

trefoil arch. See ARCH, *Illust.*

tre′ha·lose (trē′hȧ·lōs), *n.* *Chem.* A crystalline sugar, $C_{12}H_{22}O_{11}$, stored instead of starch by many fungi.

treil′lage (trāl′ĭj), *n.* [F., fr. *treille* vine arbor, fr. L. *trichila.*] Latticework for vines, etc.; trellis.

trek (trĕk), *v. t.;* TREKKED (trĕkt); TREK′KING. Also **treck.** [D. *trekken.*] *S. Africa.* To draw or pull; as, the oxen *trekked* the wagon. — *v. i.* To travel by ox wagon; to migrate; hence, loosely, to make one's way arduously. — *n.* **1.** *Chiefly S. Africa.* The act of trekking; a journey by ox wagon. **2.** A migration, esp. of a group in wagons, to a new home. **3.** Loosely, a journey. — **trek′ker** (trĕk′ẽr), *n.*

trel′lis (trĕl′ĭs), *n.; pl.* TRELLISES (-ĕz; -ĭz). [OF. *treliz, tresliz,* woven fabric (F. *treillis* trellis, lattice, sackcloth), fr. L. *trilix, -icis,* triple-twilled.] A structure or frame of latticework; also, a bower, summerhouse, or the like, of latticework. — *v. t.* **1.** To provide with a trellis; esp., to train on a trellis, as vines. **2.** To cross or interlace as in a trellis; to interweave.

trel′lis·work′ (-wûrk′), *n.* Latticework.

trem′a·tode (trĕm′ȧ·tōd; trē′mȧ-), *n.* [Gr. *trēmatōdēs,* fr. *trēma, trēmatos,* hole + *eidos* form.] *Zool.* Any of a class (Trematoda) of flatworms including the flukes and their allies. — **trem′a·tode,** *adj.*

trem′ble (trĕm′b'l), *v. i.;* -BLED (-b'ld); -BLING (-blĭng). [OF. *trembler,* fr. L. *tremulus* trembling, tremulous, fr. *tremere* to shake, tremble.] **1.** To shake involuntarily, as with fear, cold, excitement, fatigue, etc.; to shiver. **2.** Hence, to vibrate; totter; quake. **3.** To feel fear, etc. — *n.* A trembling; a fit or spell of involuntary shaking or quivering. — **trem′bler** (-blẽr), *n.* — **trem′bling·ly,** *adv.*

trem′bly (trĕm′blĭ), *adj.* *Colloq.* Trembling; tremulous.

tre·men′dous (trē·mĕn′dŭs), *adj.* [L. *tremendus* that is to be trembled at, fearful, fr. *tremere* to tremble.] **1.** Fitted to excite trembling; terrifying. **2.** *Colloq.* Astonishingly large, powerful, or the like; extraordinary. — **Syn.** See MONSTROUS. — **tre·men′dous·ly,** *adv.*

trem′o·lant (trĕm′ō·lănt), *adj.* [It. *tremolante.*] Having a vibrant, tremolo note, as certain organ pipes. — *n.* An organ pipe having a tremolant note.

trem′o·lite (-līt), *n.* [From *Tremola,* a valley in the Alps.] *Mineral.* A white or gray variety of amphibole, essentially a calcium magnesium silicate, $CaMg_3(SiO_3)_4$.

trem′o·lo (trĕm′ō·lō), *n.; pl.* -LOS (-lōz). [It., fr. L. *tremulus.*] *Music.* **a** The rapid fluttering reiteration of a tone or chord without apparent breaks, producing a tremulous effect. **b** A mechanical contrivance in an organ causing a tremulous effect. — **trem′o·lo,** *adj.*

trem′or (trĕm′ẽr; trē′mẽr), *n.* [OF. *tremour,* fr. L. *tremor,* fr. *tremere* to tremble.] **1.** A trembling, esp. from disease or weakness; a shivering or shaking. **2.** A quivering or vibratory motion. **3.** A nervous thrill.

trem′u·lant (trĕm′ū·lănt), *adj.* Also **trem′u·lent** (-lĕnt). Tremulous; trembling.

trem′u·lous (-lŭs), *adj.* [L. *tremulus.*] **1.** Quivering; palpitating; shaking. **2.** Affected with timidity; timorous. **3.** Such as is caused or affected by trembling or tremors; as, *tremulous* handwriting. — **trem′u·lous·ly,** *adv.* — **trem′u·lous·ness,** *n.*

tre′nail′. Var. of TREENAIL.

trench (trĕnch), *v. t.* [OF. *trenchier* to cut.] **1.** To cut; also, to make, form, or shape, by cutting; to carve; gash; slash. **2.** To cut a trench or trenches in; to ditch; as, to *trench* land to drain it. **3.** To protect or surround by or as by trenches. — *v. i.* **1.** To cut; esp., to cut its way, as a torrent. **2.** To dig a trench or trenches; to entrench. **3.** *Archaic.* To extend so as to pertain, pass, tend, penetrate, etc.; — with *to* or *into.* **4.** To encroach; trespass. — **Syn.** See TRESPASS. — *n.* A long cut, as in land; specif., a ditch; esp., *Mil.,* a narrow ditch, the earth thrown up from which serves as a parapet to protect soldiers under fire; also, *pl.,* the works consisting of such excavations and embankments.

trench′an·cy (trĕn′chăn·sĭ), *n.* Quality of being trenchant.

trench′ant (-chănt), *adj.* **1.** Having a sharp edge or point; cutting. **2.** Incisive; penetrating; sharply clear; as, a *trenchant* analysis of a situation. **3.** Keen; mentally energetic; as, a *trenchant* critic. — **Syn.** See INCISIVE. — **trench′ant·ly,** *adv.*

trench coat. **1.** *Mil.* A waterproof overcoat, with a removable woolen lining, originally for wear in the trenches. **2.** Hence, a type of lined waterproof overcoat.

trench′er (trĕn′chẽr), *n.* [OF. *trencheor, trencheoir,* fr. *trenchier* to cut.] **1.** *Obs.* **a** A knife. **b** *Hist.* A slice of bread used to hold meat being eaten. **2.** *Hist.* A board or wooden platter on which to carve or serve food; also, any platter. **3.** *Archaic.* A trencher of food; hence, food. — **trench′er,** *adj.*

trench′er, *n.* One who trenches; specif.: **a** *Obs.* One who carves at table. **b** One who digs ditches.

trench′er·man (-măn), *n.* **1.** A hearty eater. **2.** One frequenting his patron's table; a sponger.

trench fever. *Med.* A form of relapsing fever, affecting soldiers in the trenches and spread by lice.

trench foot *or* **feet.** *Med.* An affection resembling that attending chilblains, due to the effect of cold and wet.

trench mouth. *Med.* Inflammation of the mouth common among soldiers in the trenches; Vincent's infection.

trend (trĕnd), *v. i.* [ME. *trenden* to roll or turn about, fr. AS. *trendan.*] **1.** To have or take a particular direction; to turn in a specified or implied direction; to tend. **2.** Hence, to manifest a trend, tendency, or drift. — *n.* **1.** General direction taken by a stream, a shore line, etc. **2.** Underlying or prevailing tendency or inclination; drift; as, modern *trends* in poetry. — **Syn.** See TENDENCY.

‖**trente et qua′rante′** (träɴ′-tā kȧ′räɴt′). [F., lit., thirty and forty.] A gambling game of cards; rouge et noir.

tre·pan′ (trē·păn′), *n.* [F. *trépan,* fr. ML. *trepanum,* fr. Gr. *trypanon* a borer, trepan, fr. *trypan* to bore.] **1.** *Surg.* A crown saw or cylindrical saw for perforating the skull. See TREPHINE. **2.** *Civil Engin. & Mining.* A heavy tool used in boring shafts. — *v. t.;* TRE·PANNED′ (-pănd′); TRE·PAN′NING. **1.** *Surg.* To perforate (the skull) with a trepan, so as to remove a portion of the bone; to operate upon with the trepan. **2.** *Mach.* To cut a disk out of (a solid plate, ingot, etc.), as by means of a saw. — **trep′a·na′tion** (trĕp′ȧ·nā′shŭn), *n.*

tre·pan′, *n.* Also **tra·pan′** (trȧ-). **a** A deceiver. **b** A snare. — *v. t.* To snare; entrap; swindle. — **tre·pan′ner,** *also* **tra·pan′ner,** *n.*

tre·pang′ (trē·păng′), *n.* [Malay *tĕripaṅ.*] Any of several large holothurians (sea cucumbers) mostly of the genera *Actinopyga* and *Holothuria.* They are caught in northern Australia and the East Indies, boiled, dried, and smoked, and then shipped to China for making soup. Called also *bêche-de-mer.*

tre·phine′ (trē·fīn′; -fēn′), *n.* [Alteration of 1st *trepan.*] *Surg.* An improved kind of trepan. — *v. t.* To operate upon with a trephine.

trep′i·da′tion (trĕp′ĭ·dā′shŭn), *n.* [L. *trapidatio,* fr. *trepidare* to hurry with alarm, tremble, fr. *trepidus* agitated, alarmed.] **1.** A quaking; esp., an involuntary trembling. **2.** A state of alarm, or trembling agitation; fear; perturbation; also, a time or spell of such alarm. — **Syn.** See FEAR.

trep′o·ne′ma (trĕp′ō·nē′mȧ), *n.* [NL., fr. Gr. *trepein* to turn + *nēma* thread.] *Bacteriol.* Any of a genus (*Treponema*) of spirochetes parasitic in warm-blooded animals and man, including the organisms causing syphilis and yaws.

tres′pass (trĕs′pȧs), *v. i.* [OF. *trespasser* to go across or over, transgress, die, fr. *tres-* (L. *trans* across) + *passer* to pass.] **1.** To exceed the bounds of what is lawful, right, or just; to sin; to offend. **2.** Hence, to encroach, as on another's privileges, rights, privacy, etc.; to intrude. **3.** *Law.* To commit a trespass.

Syn. **Trespass, encroach, trench, entrench** (*or* **intrench**), **infringe, invade** mean to make inroads upon territory or rights of another. **Trespass** implies intrusion, esp. one that is unwarranted, offensive, or illegal; **encroach,** gradual or stealthy entrance upon another's territory or assumption of another's rights or possessions; **trench,** and the now more common **entrench,** a cutting or digging one's way into what belongs to another, what is outside one's sphere, etc.; **infringe,** an encroachment that is illegal and that violates a right or prerogative; **invade,** a definite entrance into the territory, or a clear assumption of the rights, of another.

— *n.* **1.** An act or instance of trespassing; specif., a transgression; offense; sin. **2.** *Law.* An unlawful act committed with force and violence on the person, property, or relative rights of another; also, the action for injuries done by such an act.

tres′pass·er (-ẽr), *n.* One who trespasses; *Law,* one who commits a trespass against another or his property.

tress (trĕs), *n.* [OF. *trece* (F. *tresse*).] Originally, a braid or plait, esp. of hair; now, a long lock of hair; *pl.,* the hair of a woman, esp. when unbound.

-tress (-trĕs; -trĭs; 30). An ending in feminine nouns corresponding to masculine agent nouns in *-er, -or,* usually short for *-eress, -oress,* as in ac*tress,* mis*tress,* etc.

tressed (trĕst), *adj.* Arranged in tresses; braided.

tres′sure (trĕsh′ẽr), *n.* Also **tres′sour.** [OF. *tressure, tresseor, treceor,* fillet or band for the hair, or headdress.] *Her.* A charge like a double orle, usually enriched with fleurs-de-lis.

tres′-tine′ (trĕs′tīn′), *n.* A royal antler. See ANTLER, *Illust.*

tres′tle (trĕs′'l), *n.* [OF. *trestel,* fr. L. *transtillum* a little crossbeam.] **1.** A form of stool or horse, usually a horizontal piece with three or four braced legs, which is commonly used in pairs to support a horizontal board, plank, etc., as for a table. **2.** A braced frame forming the whole support for a table top or the like. **3.** *Engin.* A braced framework of timbers, piles, or steelwork for carrying a road, railroad, etc., over a depression.

tres′tle·tree′ (-trē′), *n.* *Naut.* A strong timber fixed on the masthead to support the crosstrees, the frame of the top, and the topmast through the fid; — chiefly in *pl.*

tres′tle·work′ (-wûrk′), *n.* The system of connected, usually high, trestles supporting a viaduct, pier, scaffold, etc.

tret (trĕt), *n.* [AF. *tret,* F. *trait* turn or pull of the scale, fr. OF. *traire* to draw, fr. L. *trahere.*] *Com.* Formerly, an allowance to purchasers of certain articles for waste or refuse, after the tare was deducted.

trews (trōōz), *n. pl.* *Scot.* Close-fitting breeches.

trey (trā), *n.* [OF. *trei, treis,* fr. L. *tres* three.] Three, at cards, dice, or dominoes; a card, die, or domino of three spots or pips.

tri- (trī-). [F. or L. or Gr.; F. *tri-,* fr. L. *tri-;* akin to Gr. *tri-,* L. *tres* three, and E. THREE.] A combining form meaning: **1.** *Characterized by,* or *having, three,* or *three parts,* as in *tri*cycle. **2.** *Three times* or *in three ways;* also, *into three,* as in *tri*sect. **3.** *Thrice; every third;* as in *tri*weekly. **4.** *Chem.* Denoting the presence of *three* atoms, groups, or equivalents of that signified by the term to which it is prefixed. — **tri** (trī), *adj.*

tri'a·ble (trī'ȧ·b'l), *adj.* [From TRY.] **1.** That may or can be tried or tested. **2.** *Law.* Liable or subject to undergo a judicial examination or trial. — **tri'a·ble·ness,** *n.*

tri·ac'id (trī·ăs'ĭd), *n.* *Chem.* An acid having three acid hydrogen atoms, as phosphoric acid; a triacid acid. — *adj.* *Chem.* **a** Able to react with three molecules of a monoacid, or one of a triacid, to form a salt or ester; — of bases and alcohols. **b** Having three hydrogen atoms replaceable by basic atoms or radicals; — of acids and acid salts.

tri'ad (trī'ăd), *n.* [L. *trias, -adis,* fr. Gr. *trias, -ados,* fr. *treis, tria,* three.] **1.** A union or group of three, esp. of three closely related persons, beings, or things; a trinity. **2.** *Music.* A chord of three notes or tones, esp. the common chord, consisting of a given tone, or *root,* with its third and fifth. A ***major triad*** has a major third and perfect fifth; a ***minor triad*** has a minor third and perfect fifth.

tri·ag'o·nal (trī·ăg'ō·năl; -n'l), *adj.* [From *trigonal,* after *tetragonal.*] Triangular.

‖**tri'a junc'ta in u'no** (trī'ȧ jŭngk'tȧ ĭn ū'nō). [L.] Three joined in one; — motto of the Order of the Bath.

tri'al (trī'ăl), *n.* [AF., fr. *trier* to try.] **1.** The action or process of trying or putting to the proof; test. **2.** The state or fact of being tried by suffering; hence, that which so tries or afflicts; a cross; tribulation; as, their son's conduct was a severe *trial;* loosely, a source of vexation or annoyance. **3.** A trying out to test efficacy, or the like; as, give this soap a *trial.* **4.** An effort; attempt. **5.** *Law.* The formal examination of the matter in issue in a case before a competent tribunal for the purpose of determining such issue. — *adj.* **1.** Of, pert. to, or employed in a trial or trials. **2.** Made or done by way of trial or test. **3.** Used in trying or testing, or as a sample, specimen, etc.

trial and error. A finding out the best way to reach a desired result, a correct solution, or the like, by trying out one or more ways or means, and by noting and eliminating errors or causes of failure; sometimes, a trying this and that until something succeeds. — **tri'al–and–er'ror,** *adj.*

trial balance. *Bookkeeping.* A list of the debit and credit balances (or debit and credit totals) of all open accounts in a double-entry ledger at a given date prepared primarily for the purpose of testing their equality.

trial balloon. A balloon sent up to test air currents, wind velocity, etc.; hence, a project or scheme tentatively announced in order to test public opinion.

trial jury. A jury impaneled to try a cause; petit jury.

tri'an'gle (trī'ăng'g'l), *n.* [OF. or L.; OF. *triangle,* fr. L. *triangulum,* fr. *triangulus* triangular, fr. *tri-* + *angulus* angle.] **1.** *Geom.* A figure (formerly the area, now commonly the three bounding lines) formed by three lines intersecting by twos in three points, and so forming three angles (or sets of angles). **2.** A triangular object, marking, area, etc.,

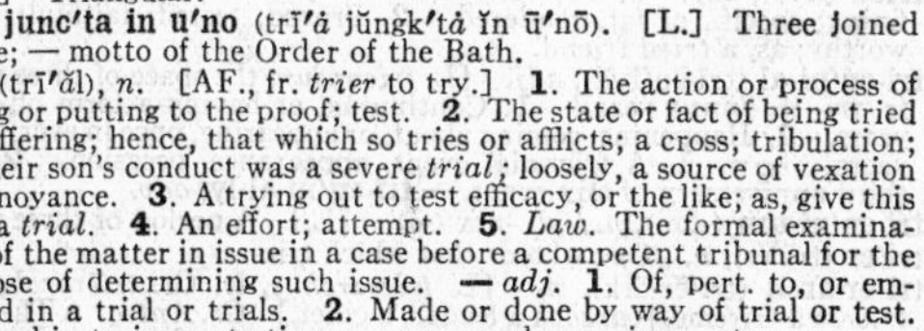

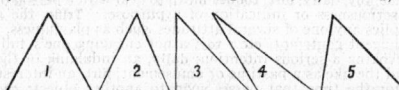

Triangles. 1 Equilateral; 2 Isosceles; 3 Right-angled; 4 Obtuse-angled; 5 Scalene. 1, 2, and 5 are also Acute-angled.

as a thin, flat, right-angled, triangular instrument used in drafting. **3.** A set of three; a situation involving three persons; specif., the love of two men for one woman or of two women for one man, and the resulting complications. **4.** *Music.* An instrument of percussion, usually made of a rod of steel, bent into the form of a triangle, open at one angle.

tri·an'gu·lar (trī·ăng'gū·lẽr), *adj.* **1.** Of, relating to, or consisting of a triangle. **2.** Of, relating to, or involving three parts, elements, factions, or the like; as, a *triangular* agreement. **3.** *Mil.* Of an army division, organized for flexibility on a basis of three infantry regiments, two in advance and one in support, roughly 9000 men, and for mobility equipped with armored scout cars and motorcycles and motorized artillery and antitank guns. — **tri·an'gu·lar'i·ty** (-lăr'ĭ·tĭ), *n.* — **tri·an'gu·lar·ly,** *adv.*

tri·an'gu·late (-lāt), *adj.* Consisting of, or marked with, triangles. — (-lāt), *v. t.* **1.** To divide into triangles; specif., to survey by triangulation. **2.** To make triangular.

tri·an'gu·la'tion (-lā'shŭn), *n.* *Surv.* The series of triangles into which any portion of the earth's surface is divided in a trigonometrical survey; the operation of measuring the elements necessary to determine these triangles.

tri'arch·y (trī'är·kĭ), *n.; pl.* -ARCHIES (-kĭz). [Gr. *triarchia.* See TRI-; -ARCHY.] **a** Government by three persons; a triumvirate. **b** A country under three rulers.

Tri'as (trī'ăs), *n.* *Geol.* The Triassic period or system.

Tri·as'sic (trī·ăs'ĭk), *adj.* [L. *trias* triad; — from its threefold division in Germany.] *Geol.* Of, pertaining to, or designating the earliest period of the Mesozoic era, or the system of rocks (largely red sandstone) formed during this period. — **Tri·as'sic,** *n.*

tri·at'ic (trī·ăt'ĭk), *adj.* *Naut.* A term used in: ***triatic stay,*** a rope secured to the heads of the foremast and mainmast.

tri'a·tom'ic (trī'ȧ·tŏm'ĭk), *adj.* *Chem.* **a** Preferably, consisting of three atoms; having three atoms in the molecule. **b** Trivalent. **c** Having three replaceable atoms or groups.

tri·ax'i·al (trī·ăk'sĭ·ăl), *adj.* Having three axes.

tri'a·zine (trī'ȧ·zēn; -zĭn; trī·ăz'ēn; -ĭn), *n.* Also **tri'a·zin.** [*tri-* + *az-* + *-ine, -in.*] *Chem.* Any of three parent compounds, $C_3H_3N_3$, containing a ring of three carbon and three nitrogen atoms; also, any of various derivatives of these.

tri'a·zo'ic (trī'ȧ·zō'ĭk), *adj.* = HYDRAZOIC.

tri'a·zole (trī'ȧ·zōl; trī·ăz'ōl), *n.* *Chem.* Any of four parent ring compounds, $C_2H_3N_3$, regarded as derived from pyrrole by replacement of two CH groups by nitrogen atoms.

trib'al (trīb'ăl), *adj.* Of, pertaining to, or characteristic of a tribe or tribes; as, *tribal* customs. — **trib'al·ly,** *adv.*

tri·bas'ic (trī·bās'ĭk), *adj.* *Chem.* **a** Having three hydrogen atoms capable of replacement by basic atoms or radicals; — said of acids. **b** Containing three atoms of a univalent metal, or their equivalent. **c** Having three basic hydroxyl groups; able to react with three molecules of a monoacid; — of bases and basic salts.

tribe (trīb), *n.* [OF. and L.; OF. *tribu,* fr. L. *tribus,* one of the three, later more, divisions of the Roman people, a tribe.] **1.** A social group comprising a series of families, clans, or generations, together with slaves, adopted strangers, etc. **2.** *Anc. Hist.* **a** In ancient Rome, one of the three divisions of the Roman people, traditionally of Latin, Sabine, and Etruscan origin respectively. Later the tribes were constituted on a territorial basis, four belonging to the city. **b** One of the phylae of ancient Athens. **3.** More loosely, any aggregation of people, esp. in a primitive or nomadic state, believed to be of a common stock and acting under a central authority, as of a chief. **4.** A group of persons having a common character or occupation; as, the scribbling *tribe.* **5.** A category of classification usually equivalent to, or ranking just below, a suborder; also, often, any natural group, irrespective of taxonomic rank; as, the cat *tribe.* **6.** *Stock Breeding.* A group of animals descended from some particular female progenitor, through the female line.

tribes'man (trībz'măn), *n.* A member of a tribe.

tri'bo- (trī'bō-; trĭb'ō-). [Gr. *tribein* to rub.] A combining form meaning *pertaining to,* or *resulting from, friction,* as in **tri'bo·e·lec'·tric'i·ty, tri'bo·flu'o·res'cence, tri'bo·lu'mi·nes'cence.**

tri'brach (trī'brăk; trĭb'răk), *n.* [L. *tribrachys,* fr. Gr. *tribrachys* consisting of three short syllables, fr. *tri-* + *brachys* short.] *Pros.* A poetic foot of three short syllables, two belonging to the thesis and one to the arsis.

tri·bro'mo·eth'a·nol (trī·brō'mō·ĕth'ȧ·nōl; -nŏl), *n.* [*tribromo-* (*tri-* + *bromine*) + *ethanol.*] *Chem.* A bromine derivative, CBr_3CH_2OH, of ethyl alcohol, used in solution for basal anesthesia by rectal administration.

trib'u·la'tion (trĭb'ū·lā'shŭn), *n.* [OF. *tribulacion,* fr. LL. *tribulatio,* fr. *tribulare* to press, afflict, fr. *tribulum* a threshing sledge.] Distress or suffering, as from oppression, persecution, etc.; also, an instance of such suffering.

tri·bu'nal (trī·bū'năl; -n'l; trĭ-), *n.* [L., fr. *tribunus* a tribune who administered justice.] **1.** A tribune; specif., the seat of a judge. **2.** Hence, a court or forum of justice. **3.** That which decides or judges; as, the *tribunal* of public opinion.

trib'u·nate (trĭb'ū·nāt), *n.* [F. *tribunat,* fr. L. *tribunatus.*] State, office, or function of a tribune; tribuneship.

trib'une (trĭb'ūn; *as the name of American newspapers, often pronounced* trĭ·būn'), *n.* [L. *tribunus,* prop., the chief of a tribe, fr. *tribus* tribe.] **1.** *Rom. Hist.* An official or magistrate of any of several classes; esp., a magistrate whose specific function was to protect the individual plebeian citizen from the arbitrary action of the patrician magistrates. **2.** Hence, any defender of the people. — **trib'une·ship,** *n.* — **trib'u·ni'tial, trib'u·ni'cial** (trĭb'ū·nĭsh'ăl), *adj.*

trib'une (trĭb'ūn; trĭ·būn'), *n.* [F. and It.; F., fr. It. *tribuna,* fr. L. *tribunal.*] *Arch.* Any dais or platform from which an assembly is addressed, as the rostrum in the French Chamber of Deputies.

trib'u·tar'y (trĭb'ū·tĕr'ĭ *or, esp. Brit.,* -tẽr·ĭ), *adj.* **1.** Paying tribute to another; hence, subject; subordinate; as, *tributary* nations. **2.** Paid or owed as tribute; of the nature of tribute. **3.** Yielding or carrying supplies or accretions of any kind; contributory; as, a *tributary* stream. — *n.; pl.* -TARIES (-ĭz). **1.** A ruler or state that pays tribute. **2.** A stream feeding a larger stream or a lake. — **trib'u·tar'i·ly,** *adv.*

trib'ute (trĭb'ūt), *n.* [L. *tributum,* fr. *tribuere, tributum,* to bestow, grant, pay, allot, fr. *tribus* tribe.] **1.** A payment paid by one ruler or nation to another, either as an acknowledgment of submission, or as the price of protection, or by virtue of some treaty; also, the tax levied for such a payment. **2.** *Hist.* A tax paid by a subject vassal to his sovereign or lord. **3.** Liability or obligation to pay such tax. **4.** An offering, gift, service rendered, or the like, manifesting respect, allegiance, gratitude, etc.; specif., praise; encomium. — **Syn.** See ENCOMIUM.

tri·car'pel·lar'y (trī·kär'pĕ·lĕr'ĭ *or, esp. Brit.,* -lẽr·ĭ), *adj.* See TRI-, 1.

trice (trīs), *v. t.;* TRICED (trīst); TRIC'ING (trīs'ĭng). [MD. *trīsen* to hoist by block and tackle, fr. *trīse* windlass, pulley.] *Chiefly Naut.* To haul up or in and lash, or secure, with a small rope, as a sail; — usually with *up.*

trice, *n.* [From *at a trice,* lit., at one pull. See TRICE, *v.*] A single pull or effort; hence, an instant; a moment; — in the phrase *in a trice.*

tri'cen·ten'ni·al (trī'sĕn·tĕn'ĭ·ăl), *adj. & n.* Tercentenary.

tri'ceps (trī'sĕps), *n.; pl.* TRICEPSES (-sĕp·sĕz; -sĭz). [NL., fr. L. *triceps* having three heads, fr. *tres, tria,* three + *caput* head.] *Anat.* The three-headed extensor muscle along the back of the upper arm.

tri·chi'a·sis (trĭ·kī'ȧ·sĭs), *n.* [NL., fr. Gr. *trichiasis,* fr. *thrix, trichos,* hair.] *Med.* **a** A condition in which the eyelashes turn in. **b** The appearance of hairlike filaments in the urine.

tri·chi'na (trĭ·kī'nȧ), *n.; pl.* TRICHINAE (-nē). [NL., fr. Gr. *trichinos,* hairy, made of hair, fr. *thrix, trichos,* hair.] *Zool.* A small slender nematode worm (*Trichinella,* or, incorrectly, *Trichina, spiralis*) which, in the larval state, is parasitic in the voluntary muscles of man, the hog, and many other animals.

trich'i·nize (trĭk'ĭ·nīz), *v. t.* To render trichinous; to affect with trichinae; — chiefly used in past participle; as, *trichinized* pork. — **trich'i·ni·za'tion** (-nĭ·zā'shŭn; -nī·zā'-), *n.*

trich'i·no'sis (-nō'sĭs), **trich'i·ni'a·sis** (-nī'ȧ·sĭs), *n.* [NL.] *Med.* The disease caused by trichinae in the intestinal tract and the muscles.

trich'i·nous (trĭk'ĭ·nŭs), *adj.* Also **trich'i·nosed** (trĭk'ĭ·nōzd; trĭk'ĭ·nōst'). Of or pertaining to trichinae or trichinosis; affected with, or containing, trichinae.

trich'ite (trĭk'īt), *n.* [Gr. *thrix, trichos.*] *Petrog.* A hairlike crystallite, occurring singly or in clusters.

tri·chlo'ride (trī·klō'rīd; -rĭd), *n.* Also **tri·chlo'rid.** *Chem.* A compound of an element or radical with three atoms of chlorine.

trich'o- (trĭk'ō-; trī'kō-), **trich-.** [Gr. *thrix, trichos.*] A combining form meaning *hair,* as in **tri·chol'o·gy** (trĭ·kŏl'ō·jĭ), science treating of the hair; **tri·chol'o·gist** (-jĭst).

trich′o·cyst (trĭk′ō·sĭst), *n.* [*tricho-* + *-cyst.*] *Zool.* Minute lasso-ing or stinging organs on the body of many infusorians. — **trich′o·cys′tic** (-sĭs′tĭk), *adj.*

trich′o·gyne (trĭk′ō·jīn; -jĭn), *n.* [*tricho-* + Gr. *gynē* woman, female.] *Bot.* The filamentous receptive portion of a procarp or an archicarp. Cf. CARPOGONIUM.

trich′oid (trĭk′oid), *adj.* Hairlike; capillary.

tri′chome (trī′kōm; trĭk′ōm), *n.* [Gr. *trichōma* a growth of hair.] *Bot.* Any epidermal hair structure. — **tri·chom′ic** (trī·kŏm′ĭk), *adj.*

trich′o·mon′ad (trĭk′ō·mŏn′ăd), *n.* [From *Trichomonas* (*tricho-* + *monas*).] *Zool.* A flagellate protozoan of a genus (*Trichomonas*) parasitic in many vertebrates and invertebrates including man. — **trich′o·mon′ad,** *adj.*

trich′o·mo·ni′a·sis (-mō·nī′ȧ·sĭs), *n.* [NL., fr. *Trichomonas* + *-iasis.*] Infection with trichomonads, esp. ***bovine trichomoniasis,*** inducing abortion in cattle, and ***avian trichomoniasis,*** a disease of pigeons and turkeys resembling blackhead.

tri·cho′sis (trĭ·kō′sĭs), *n.* [NL. See TRICHO-; -OSIS.] *Med.* Any disease of the hair.

tri·chot′o·my (trī·kŏt′ō·mĭ), *n.* [Gr. *tricha* threefold, in three parts + *-tomy.*] Division into three parts, elements, or classes; specif., the division of the nature of man into body, soul, and spirit. — **trich′o·tom′ic** (trĭk′ō·tŏm′ĭk), **tri·chot′o·mous** (trī·kŏt′ō·mŭs), *adj.*

tri′chro·ism (trī′krō·ĭz′m), *n.* [*tri-* + Gr. *chrōs* color.] *Physics.* The property of some crystals of presenting different colors in three different directions. — **tri·chro′ic** (trī·krō′ĭk), *adj.*

tri′chro·mat′ic (trī′krō·măt′ĭk), *adj.* Also **tri·chro′mic** (trī·krō′mĭk). Of, pertaining to, consisting of, or employing three colors, as in the three-color process in printing. — **tri·chro′ma·tism** (trī·krō′mȧ·tĭz′m), *n.*

trick (trĭk), *n.* [ONF. *trique,* fr. *trikier* to trick, cheat.] **1.** An artifice or stratagem; crafty procedure or practice; a cheating device. **2. a** A mischievous or roguish act; a prank; also, a foolish or silly action. **b** A sly or ingenious feat fitted to puzzle or amuse. **3.** Knack; specif.: **a** A quick or effective way of getting a result. **b** An artful expedient; sometimes, a mere convention, as in art; as, to learn all the *tricks* of the stage. **c** Instant or skillful effecting of a result; as, that does the *trick.* **d** A feat demanding skill; as, the *trick* is to land the fish. **4.** A mannerism; as, a *trick* of gesturing. **5.** An illusion, as one caused by art or legerdemain. **6.** A turn or spell of duty; shift. **7.** *Dial., U.S.* Creature; child; — usually *little,* or *pretty, trick.* **8.** *Card Playing.* The cards played in one round, collectively, often used as a unit of score.

Syn. **Trick, ruse, stratagem, maneuver, artifice, wile, feint** mean an indirect, ingenious, and often cunning means used to gain an end. **Trick** may imply deception, roguishness, illusion, or the like, and an evil or a harmless end; **ruse** implies an attempt to give a false impression; **stratagem,** a ruse by means of which one wishes to entrap, outwit, circumvent, or surprise another, esp. an enemy; **maneuver,** adroit and skillful handling of others for one's own ends; **artifice,** a means that seems to be invented or manufactured; **wile,** an attempt to entrap or ensnare by allurements or false and deceptive appearances; **feint,** a stratagem or maneuver that distracts attention from one's real end until it is achieved.

— *v. t.* **1.** To deceive by cunning or artifice; to defraud; cheat. **2.** To dress; adorn, esp. fancifully; — often with *up, off,* or *out.* — **Syn.** See DUPE.

— *adj.* Of or pertaining to a trick or tricks; skilled in or used for tricks.

trick′er (trĭk′ẽr), *n.* One who tricks; a trickster.

trick′er·y (trĭk′ẽr·ĭ), *n.; pl.* -IES (-ĭz). Tricking; the use of tricks, esp. fraudulent tricks. — **Syn.** See DECEPTION.

trick′ing, *n.* Trickery; deceit; also, embellishment; *Rare,* dress; costumes.

trick′ish, *adj.* Given to, or characterized by, tricks or trickery; tricky. — **trick′ish·ly,** *adv.* — **trick′ish·ness,** *n.*

trick′le (trĭk′'l), *v. i.;* TRICK′LED (-'ld); TRICK′LING (-lĭng). To run or fall in drops; to flow in a thin gentle stream. — *n.* Something that trickles or seems to trickle; a thin slow stream; a drip.

trick′ster (trĭk′stẽr), *n.* One who tricks or cheats; one given to trickery; as, political *tricksters.*

trick′sy (trĭk′sĭ), *adj.* **1.** Tricked out; esp., nattily attired. **2.** Given to tricks or pranks; prankish. **3.** Having the craftiness of a trickster; hence, uncertain; deceptive. — **trick′si·ness** (-sĭ·nĕs; -nĭs), *n.*

trick′track′ (-trăk′), *n.* [F. *trictrac.*] Backgammon.

trick′y (trĭk′ĭ), *adj.;* -I·ER (-ĭ·ẽr); -I·EST. **1.** Of or characteristic of a trickster. **2.** *Colloq.* **a** Deceptively safe, easy, etc.; ticklish; as, a *tricky* situation. **b** Intricate; manifesting or requiring skill or knack in doing, making, etc.; as, *tricky* clothes or rhymes. — **Syn.** See SLY. — **trick′i·ly** (-ĭ·lĭ), *adv.* — **trick′i·ness** (-ĭ·nĕs; -nĭs), *n.*

tri·clin′ic (trī·klĭn′ĭk), *adj.* [*tri-* + Gr. *klinein* to incline.] *Cryst.* Having, or characterized by, three unequal axes intersecting at oblique angles.

tri·clin′i·um (-ĭ·ŭm), *n.* [L., fr. Gr. *triklinion, triklinos,* fr. *tri-* (see TRI-) + *klinē* couch.] *Rom. Antiq.* A couch for reclining at meals, extending round three sides of a table; also, a room having such a couch.

tric′o·lette′ (trĭk′ō·lĕt′), *n.* A knitted fabric resembling jersey cloth, but made of cotton, rayon, or silk.

tri′col′or, tri′col′our (trī′kŭl′ẽr), *n.* [F. *tricolore,* in *drapeau tricolore* a tricolored flag.] **1.** The national flag of France, consisting of three nearly equal vertical stripes, blue, white, and red, in order from the hoist. **2.** Hence, any flag of three colors in nearly equal masses; as, the Mexican *tricolor.* — **tri′col′or, tri′col′our,** *adj.*

tri′corn (trī′kôrn), *adj.* [F. *tricorne,* fr. L. *tricornis.*] Having three horns or corners.

tri′corn (trī′kôrn), *n.* Also **tri′corne.** A three-cornered cocked hat.

tri·cor′nered (trī·kôr′nẽrd), *adj.* Three-cornered.

tri·cos′tate (trī·kŏs′tāt), *adj.* *Bot. & Zool.* Three-ribbed; having three ribs, or costae.

tri′cot (trē′kō; *F.* trē′kō′), *n.* [F., fr. *tricoter* to knit.] **1.** A fabric of woolen, silk, cotton, or rayon, knitted, or so woven as to resemble knitting. **2.** A soft ribbed wool or mixed fabric for dresses. **3.** A skintight garment or tights worn by ballet dancers.

tric′o·tine′ (trĭk′ō·tēn′; *F.* trē′kô′tēn′), *n.* A worsted dress fabric with a double twill.

tri′cro·tism (trī′krō·tĭz′m; trĭk′rō-), *n.* [*tri-* + Gr. *krotein* to beat.] *Physiol.* That condition of the arterial pulse in which there is a triple beat. — **tri·crot′ic** (trī·krŏt′ĭk), *adj.*

tric′trac′ (trĭk′trăk′). Var. of TRICKTRACK.

tri·cus′pid (trī·kŭs′pĭd), *adj.* [L. *tricuspis, -idis,* fr. *tri-* + *cuspis* a point.] Having three cusps.

tri·cus′pi·date (-pĭ·dāt), *adj.* Three-pointed; tricuspid.

tricuspid valve. *Anat.* The valve of three flaps which prevents reflux of blood from the right ventricle to the right auricle.

tri′cy·cle (trī′sĭk·'l), *n.* [F. See TRI-; CYCLE.] **a** A light three-wheeled vehicle, for one or more riders, propelled by treadles or hand levers. See VELOCIPEDE, *Illust.* **b** A three-wheeled motorcycle.

tri·cy′clic (trī·sī′klĭk; -sĭk′lĭk), *adj.* Having three cycles.

tri·dac′tyl (trī·dăk′tĭl), *adj.* [Gr. *tridaktylos,* fr. *tri-* + *daktylos* digit.] Having three fingers or toes.

tri′dent (trī′dĕnt), *n.* [L. *tridens, -entis,* fr. *tri-* + *dens* tooth.] **1.** *Gr. & Rom. Myth.* A three-pronged spear, the attribute of Poseidon, or Neptune. **2.** *Rom. Antiq.* A three-pronged spear used by retiarii. **3.** A three-pronged fish spear. — *adj.* Having three teeth or points.

tri·den′tate (trī·dĕn′tāt), *adj.* Also **tri·den′tat·ed** (-tāt·ĕd; -ĭd). [NL. *tridentatus.*] Having three teeth, processes, or points.

Tri·den′tine (trī·dĕn′tĭn; trĭ-; -tīn), *adj.* [ML. *Tridentinus,* fr. *Tridentum,* Italy.] Of or pert. to Trent, Italy (formerly in Austria), or to a church council (***Council of Trent***) held in that city (1545–1563).

tri′di·men′sion·al (trī′dĭ·mĕn′shŭn·ăl; -'l), *adj.* Of three dimensions. — **tri′di·men′sion·al′i·ty** (-ăl′ĭ·tĭ), *n.*

tri·e′cious, tri·e′cious·ly. Vars. of TRIOECIOUS, etc.

tried (trīd), *adj.* **1.** *Obs.* Freed from impurities, as by sifting or refining; specif., of fat, rendered. **2.** Proved; tested; faithful; trustworthy; as, a *tried* friend.

tri·en′ni·al (trī·ĕn′ĭ·ăl), *adj.* [L. *triennium* the space of three years, fr. *tri-* + *annus* year.] **1.** Continuing, or having a term of, three years. **2.** Happening, coming about, or appearing, once in every three years. — *n.* **1.** A triennial event, appearance, occasion. **2.** The third anniversary of any event. — **tri·en′ni·al·ly,** *adv.*

tri·en′ni·um (-ŭm), *n.; pl.* -NIA (-ȧ). [L.] A period of three years.

tri′er (trī′ẽr), *n.* One who or that which tries.

tri′er·arch (trī′ẽr·ärk), *n.* [L. *trierarchus,* fr. Gr. *triērarchos,* fr. *triērēs* a trireme + *archos* a leader, a chief.] *Gr. Antiq.* **a** The commander of a trireme. **b** At Athens, one who had to fit out a trireme for the public service.

tri′er·arch′y (-är′kĭ), *n.; pl.* -ARCHIES (-kĭz). [Gr. *triērarchia.*] **1.** The office or duty of a trierarch. **2.** Trierarchs collectively. **3.** The Athenian plan whereby citizens furnished triremes.

tri·fa′cial (trī·fā′shăl), *adj. & n.* Trigeminal.

tri′fid (trī′fĭd), *adj.* [L. *trifidus,* fr. *tri-* + root of *findere* to split.] Three-cleft; tridentate.

tri′fle (trī′f'l), *n.* [OF. *trufle, trufe,* mockery, raillery, trickery.] **1.** A thing of little value or importance; a paltry or trivial affair, object, etc.; also, a small amount, as of money. **2.** A dessert made of spongecake soaked in wine or liqueur, with macaroons, jam, and whipped cream. **3.** A variety of pewter used for small utensils, as beer measures. — *v. i.;* TRI′FLED (-f'ld); TRI′FLING (-flĭng). **1.** To talk jestingly or mockingly; to indulge in beguiling or misleading talk. **2.** To toy (with some object); fidget. **3.** To act, or to speak, write, etc., with levity or flippancy; to dally, play, toy, or flirt. — *v. t.* To spend or waste in trifling or on trifles. — **tri′fler** (trī′flẽr), *n.*

Syn. **Trifle, toy, dally, flirt, coquet** mean to deal with a person or thing without seriousness or indication of a purpose. **Trifle,** the general term, implies any one of several attitudes, such as playfulness, unconcern, indulgent contempt, etc.; **toy,** a not engaging one's full attention or evoking a serious intention; **dally,** an indulging in thoughts, plans, and the like as a pastime or amusement; **flirt,** an interest or attention for the time that passes soon to another object; **coquet,** a catching of one's interest without coming to terms with it.

tri′fling, *adj.* **1.** That trifles; frivolous. **2.** Trivial; insignificant. — *n.* **a** Light talk; badinage. **b** Wasting of time; activity without value. — **tri′fling·ly,** *adv.*

tri·fo′cal (trī·fō′kăl), *adj.* [*tri-* + *focal.*] Having three foci; — used specifically of an eyeglass lens having one part that corrects for near vision, one for intermediate vision (commonly at arm's length), and one for distant vision. — *n.* A trifocal glass or lens; specif., *pl.,* eyeglasses with such lenses.

tri·fo′li·ate (trī·fō′lĭ·āt), *adj.* Also **tri·fo′li·at′ed** (-āt′ĕd; -ĭd). [*tri-* + *foliate.*] *Bot.* **a** Having three leaves; as, a *trifoliate* plant. **b** Sometimes, loosely, trifoliolate.

tri·fo′li·o·late (-fō′lĭ·ō·lāt; trī′fō·lī′ō·lāt), *adj. Bot.* Having three leaflets, as the leaf of a clover. See LEAF, *Illust.* (24).

tri·fo′li·um (trī·fō′lĭ·ŭm), *n.* [L., trefoil.] *Bot.* Any of a genus (*Trifolium*) of herbs, the clovers, of the pea family.

tri·fo′ri·um (trī·fō′rĭ·ŭm; 70), *n.; pl.* -RIA (-ȧ). [ML., appar. fr. L. *tri-* + *foris* a door.] The gallery forming an upper story to the aisle of a church, often having three openings to each bay. See GOTHIC, *Illust.*

tri′form (trī′fôrm), *adj.* Also **tri′formed** (-fôrmd). [L. *triformis.*] Having a triple form, constitution, or nature.

tri′fur·cate (trī′fẽr·kāt; trī·fûr′kāt), *adj.* Also **tri′fur·cat′ed** (-kāt′ĕd; -ĭd). [L. *trifurcus,* fr. *tri-* + *furca* fork.] Having three branches or forks; trichotomous.

trig (trĭg), *adj.* [ON. *tryggr.*] **1.** Trim; neat; spruce; smart. **2.** Sound; in good condition. **3.** Very precise; stiff; prim. — **Syn.** See NEAT. — *v. t. & i. Dial.* To put in order; to tidy; — usually with *up.*

trig, *v. t. Dial.* To stop, as a wheel, by placing something under it; also, sometimes, to prop or support. — *n. Dial.* Something used in trigging, as a stone or block.

tri·gem′i·nal (trī·jĕm′ĭ·năl), *adj.* [L. *trigeminus* born three together, fr. *tri-* + *geminus* twin.] *Anat. & Zool.* Of, pertaining to, or designating the fifth pair of cranial nerves. — *n.* A trigeminal nerve.

trig′ger (trĭg′ẽr), *n.* [For older *tricker,* fr. D. *trekker,* fr. *trekken* to draw, pull.] A piece, as a lever, connected with a catch or detent as a means of releasing it; specif., *Firearms,* the part of a lock moved by the finger to release the cock in firing. See GUNLOCK, *Illust.*

trig′ger·fish′ (trĭg′ẽr·fĭsh′), *n.; pl.,* see FISH. Any of numerous plectognath fishes (*Balistes* and allied genera) having two or three stout spines on the anterior dorsal fin. They inhabit chiefly warm seas.

tri′glyph (trī′glĭf), *n.* [L. *triglyphus,* fr. Gr. *triglyphos,* fr. *tri-* + *glyphē* carving.] *Arch.* In a Doric frieze, a rectangular tablet, slightly projecting, and having two vertical channels of V section, called *glyphs,* and two chamfers or half channels on the vertical sides. — **tri·glyph′ic** (trī·glĭf′ĭk), **tri·glyph′i·cal** (-ĭ·kăl), *adj.*

‖**tri′go** (trē′gō), *n.* [Sp.] Wheat.

tri′gon (trī′gŏn), *n.* [L. *trigonum*, fr. Gr. *trigōnon*, fr. *trigōnos* three-cornered, fr. *tri-* + *gōnia* a corner, angle.] **1.** A triangle. **2.** *Astrol.* **a** = TRIPLICITY, 3. **b** = TRINE, *n.*, 1. **3.** *Gr. & Rom. Antiq.* A form of triangular lyre or harp.

trig′o·nal (trĭg′ō·năl), *adj.* **1.** Of or pertaining to a triangle; triangular. **2.** Of or pertaining to a, or the, trigon.

trig′o·nom′e·ter (trĭg′ō·nŏm′ē·tẽr), *n.* [Gr. *trigōnos* triangular + *-meter.*] A device for solving graphically any plane right-angled triangle.

trig′o·nom′e·try (-trĭ), *n.; pl.* -TRIES (-trĭz). [Gr. *trigōnon* triangle + *-metry.*] That branch of mathematics treating of the relations holding among the sides and angles of triangles and among closely related magnitudes, and esp. of methods of deducing from given parts other required parts. Also, a treatise on this science. — **trig′o·no·met′ric** (-nō·mĕt′rĭk), **trig′o·no·met′ri·cal** (-rĭ·kăl), *adj.* — **trig′o·no·met′ri·cal·ly**, *adv.*

trig′o·nous (trĭg′ō·nŭs), *adj.* [L. *trigonus*, fr. Gr. *trigōnos.* See TRIGON.] Having three angles; triangular.

tri′graph (trī′grăf), *n.* [*tri-* + *-graph.*] Three letters spelling a single consonant, vowel, or diphthong, as *sch* (schism), *eau* (*beau*). — **tri·graph′ic** (trī·grăf′ĭk), *adj.*

tri·he′dron (trī·hē′drŭn), *n.; pl.* -DRONS (-drŭnz), -DRA (-drȧ). [NL., fr. *tri-* + Gr. *hedra* a seat, base.] *Geom.* A figure formed by three planes meeting in a point. — **tri·he′dral** (-drăl), *adj.*

tri′hy·drox′y (trī′hī·drŏk′sĭ), *adj.* *Chem.* Containing three hydroxyl groups, esp. replacing hydrogen.

tri′ju·gate (trī′jōō·gāt; trī·jōō′gāt; 114), *adj.* Also **tri′ju·gous** (-gŭs). [L. *trijugus* threefold, fr. *tri-* + *jugum* a yoke.] *Bot.* Having three pairs of leaflets; — said of a pinnate leaf.

tri·lat′er·al (trī·lăt′ẽr·ăl), *adj.* [L. *trilaterus*, fr. *tri-* + *latus, lateris*, side.] *Geom.* Having three sides. — **tri·lat′er·al·ly**, *adv.*

tri·lin′e·ar (-lĭn′ē·ẽr), *adj.* *Math.* Of, pertaining to, or included by three lines; as, *trilinear* co-ordinates.

tri·lin′gual (-lĭng′gwăl), *adj.* [L. *trilinguis*, fr. *tri-* + *lingua* tongue, language.] Consisting of, having, or expressed in, three languages; also, familiar with three languages.

tri·lit′er·al (-lĭt′ẽr·ăl), *adj.* Consisting of three letters. — *n.* A triliteral word.

tri·lit′er·al·ism (-ĭz′m), *n.* Quality of being triliteral; as, *triliteralism* is characteristic of the Semitic languages.

trill (trĭl), *v. i. & t.* [ME. *trillen* to roll, turn round, of Scand. origin.] **1.** *Obs.* To turn, twirl, roll, or rock; also, to quiver. **2.** To trickle, as a tear.

trill, *v. t.* [It. *trillare*, prob. of imitative origin.] To impart the quality of a trill to; to utter as, or with, a trill. — *v. i.* To utter trills or a trill; to play or sing with a trill; to quaver. — *n.* **1.** *Phonet.* The rapid vibration of one speech organ against another, as of the tip of the tongue against the teethridge; also, a speech sound so made, as a trilled *r.* **2.** A letter or a word pronounced with a trill (sense 1). **3.** *Music.* **a** The alternation of two tones a degree apart; a shake. See SHAKE, *Illust.* **b** = VIBRATO. **4.** A sound likened to a musical trill; a warble.

tril′lion (trĭl′yŭn), *n. & adj.* [F., formed fr. *tri-* in imitation of *million.*] In French and American notation, a thousand billions, or in English and German notation, a million billions. See NUMERATION, *Table.* — **tril′lionth** (-yŭnth), *n. & adj.*

tril′li·um (trĭl′ĭ·ŭm), *n.* [NL., fr. *tri-*; — so called because all species have leaves in sets of three.] Any of a genus (*Trillium*) of herbs of the lily-of-the-valley family, with short rootstocks and an erect stem bearing a whorl of three leaves and a large solitary flower. Cf. GREAT WHITE TRILLIUM.

tri·lo′bate (trī·lō′bāt; trī′lō-), *adj.* Also **tri·lo′bal** (-băl), **tri·lo′bat·ed** (-bāt·ĕd; -ĭd), **tri′lobed′** (trī′lōbd′). Having three lobes.

tri′lo·bite (trī′lō·bīt), *n.* [NL. *Trilobites, Trilobita.* See TRI-; LOBE.] Any of numerous extinct marine arthropods (group Trilobita) so called from the division of the segments of the body by furrows on the dorsal surface into three lobes. Trilobites lived during the Paleozoic, becoming extinct in the Permian. Most of them were an inch or two long, some one or even two feet. — **tri′lo·bit′ic** (-bĭt′ĭk), *adj.*

tri·loc′u·lar (trī·lŏk′ū·lẽr), *adj.* [*tri-* + *locular.*] Having three cells or cavities.

tril′o·gy (trĭl′ō·jĭ), *n.; pl.* -GIES (-jĭz). [Gr. *trilogia*, fr. *tri-* + *logos* speech, discourse.] A series of three dramas or, by extension, three literary or musical compositions, which, although each is in one sense complete, have a close mutual relation, and form one theme.

trim (trĭm), *v. t.;* TRIMMED (trĭmd); TRIM′MING. [AS. *trymian, trymman*, to make strong, set in order, array, fr. *trum* firm, strong.] **1.** To put in order; to make neat or trim. **2.** To make trim, neat, or right, by cutting, clipping, etc.; hence, often with *off* or the like, to cut, clip, or lop. **3.** *Obs.* To equip; furnish; dress. **4.** To decorate; adorn; as, to *trim* a hat. **5.** *Colloq.* **a** To rebuke. **b** To chastise. **c** To defeat, as in a game; sometimes, to cheat. **6.** *Aeronautics.* To alter the attitude of an aerostat to a longitudinal horizontal plane. **7.** *Carp.* To dress, as timber; to make smooth. **8.** *Naut.* **a** To adjust to a position in the water, as a ship, by arranging the ballast, cargo, etc. **b** To arrange in due order for sailing; as, to *trim* the sails.

— *v. i.* **1.** To preserve a balance; specif., to maintain a middle position between parties or the like, so as to appear to favor each equally, or to be neutral; sometimes, to act according to expediency. **2.** *Naut.* Of a vessel, to assume, or, of a person, to cause a boat or other vessel to assume, a certain position, or *trim*, in the water.

— *n.* **1.** Order; condition; as, in good *trim.* **2.** *Obs.* Character; disposition. **3.** Dress; gear; as, in hunting *trim.* **4.** That which is cut out for rejection, as in motion-picture film, etc. **5.** *Advertising.* Window dressing. **6.** *Aeronautics.* The attitude of an aerostat relative to a longitudinal horizontal plane. **7.** *Arch.* The lighter woodwork in the finish of a building, esp. around openings. **8.** *Automobiles.* The interior furnishings of an automobile body collectively. **9.** *Naut.* **a** The state of a ship or her cargo, masts, etc., in reference to her fitness for sailing. **b** The position of a vessel in the water, esp. with reference to the horizontal plane. **c** The buoyancy status of a submarine.

— *adj.;* TRIM′MER (-ẽr); TRIM′MEST. **1.** *Obs.* Excellent; also, gay. **2.** *Archaic.* In good order; made ready for service. **3.** Neat and compact or well ordered; of clean lines and good proportions. — **Syn.** See NEAT. — **Ant.** Frowzy. — *adv.* Trimly. — **trim′ly**, *adv.* — **trim′ness**, *n.*

trim′er·ous (trĭm′ẽr·ŭs), *adj.* [See TRI-; -MEROUS.] **a** *Bot.* Having the parts in threes; — said of a flower. Often written *3-merous.* **b** *Zool.* Having three (or apparently three) joints in each tarsus.

tri·mes′ter (trī·mĕs′tẽr), *n.* [F. *trimestre*, fr. L. *trimestris* of three months, fr. *tri-* + *mensis* month.] **1.** A term or period of three months. **2.** One of three terms into which an academic year is sometimes divided. — **tri·mes′tral** (-trăl), **tri·mes′tri·al** (-trĭ·ăl), *adj.*

trim′e·ter (trĭm′ē·tẽr), *adj.* [L. *trimetrus*, fr. Gr. *trimetros*, fr. *tri-* + *metron* measure.] Consisting of three measures; specif., *Pros.*, consisting of three dipodies (six feet), as in ancient iambic, trochaic, and anapaestic verse, or of three feet, as in modern verse. — *n.* A verse or line of three feet or three dipodies.

tri·met′ric (trī·mĕt′rĭk), *adj.* **a** *Pros.* = TRIMETER, *adj.* **b** *Cryst.* Orthorhombic.

tri·met′ri·cal (-rĭ·kăl), *adj.* Trimeter.

trimetric projection. *Geom.* A form of projection (resembling isometric projection) in which each of the three dimensions is measured by a different scale, the angles being chosen arbitrarily.

tri·met′ro·gon (trī·mĕt′rō·gŏn), *n.* [*tri-* + Gr. *metron* measure + Gr. *gōnon* angle.] A system of aerial mapping involving the use of one vertical and two oblique aerial photographs taken simultaneously at regular intervals over the area being mapped.

trim′mer (trĭm′ẽr), *n.* **1.** One who trims articles, as a man employed on shipboard to stow coal or freight so as to distribute the weight properly. **2.** A machine with which trimming, as of lumber, is done. **3.** One who for the sake of expediency will modify his policy, position, etc. **4.** *Arch.* A beam which receives the end of a header in floor framing. See HEADER, *Illust.*

trim′ming (trĭm′ĭng), *n.* **1.** The act of one who trims; specif., *Colloq.*, thrashing, defeating, etc.; as, a sound *trimming.* **2.** That which serves to trim; esp., fittings, as of a garment; hence, *Colloq.*, any accessories, as of a dish; — usually in *pl.*; as, *trimmings* for a hat. **3.** *pl.* Parts or pieces removed by trimming. — **trim′ming**, *adj.*

tri′mo·lec′u·lar (trī′mō·lĕk′ū·lẽr), *adj.* *Chem.* Of, pertaining to, or formed from three molecules.

tri·month′ly (trī·mŭnth′lĭ), *adj.* Occurring, done, or coming once in three months.

tri′morph (trī′môrf), *n.* *Cryst.* A substance which crystallizes in three distinct forms; also, any of these forms. See TRIMORPHISM, 3.

tri·mor′phism (trī·môr′fĭz′m), *n.* [From Gr. *trimorphos* three-formed, fr. *tri-* + *morphē* form.] **1.** *Biol.* Polymorphism in which there are three distinct forms of a species. Cf. DIMORPHISM, 1. **2.** *Bot.* Occurrence of three distinct forms of organs, as leaves, flowers, etc., on individuals of the same species. **3.** *Cryst.* The property of crystallizing in three forms fundamentally distinct. — **tri·mor′phic** (-fĭk), **tri·mor′phous** (-fŭs), *adj.*

Tri·mur′ti (trĭ·mōōr′tĭ), *n.* [Skr. *trimūrti*, fr. *tri* three + *mūrti* shape.] *Hindu Relig.* The triad, or trinity, of Hindu gods (Brahma, Vishnu, and Siva).

Tri·nac′ri·an (trĭ·năk′rĭ·ăn; trī-), *adj.* [L. *Trinacria* Sicily.] Sicilian.

tri′nal (trī′năl; -n'l), *adj.* [See TRINE.] Threefold.

tri′na·ry (trī′nȧ·rĭ), *adj.* Ternary.

trin′dle (trĭn′d'l; *dial. also* trĕn′'l), *n.* [AS. *trendel* a circle, ring, disk.] *Dial.* A round object; a trundle; specif., a wheel, as of a wheelbarrow. — *v. t. & i. Dial.* To roll; trundle; bowl along.

trine (trīn), *adj.* [OF. *trin, trine*, fr. L. *trinus* triple, fr. *trini* three each, fr. *tres, tria*, three.] **1.** Threefold; triple. **2.** *Astrol.* Being in trine (see TRINE, *n.*, 1); hence, auspicious. — *n.* **1.** *Astrol.* The (favorable) aspect of planets 120 degrees apart; trigon. **2.** A triad; trinity; specif. [*cap.*], the Trinity.

Trin′i·tar′i·an (trĭn′ĭ·târ′ĭ·ăn), *adj.* **1.** [*sometimes not cap.*] Of or pert. to the Trinity, the doctrine of the Trinity, or believers in that doctrine. **2.** [*not cap.*] Involving three; triple. — *n.* One who believes the doctrine of the Trinity.

Trin′i·tar′i·an·ism (-ĭz′m), *n.* The doctrine of the Trinity.

tri·ni′tro·cre′sol (trī·nī′trō·krē′sōl; -sŏl), *n.* [*trinitro-* (*tri-* + *nitro-*) + *cresol.*] *Chem.* A high explosive, $C_7H_5N_3O_7$, similar to picric acid.

tri·ni′tro·tol′u·ene (-tŏl′ū·ēn), *n.* Also **tri·ni′tro·tol′u·ol** (-ōl; -ŏl). [*trinitro-* (*tri-* + *nitro-*) + *toluene.*] *Chem.* Any of several derivatives, $CH_3C_6H_2(NO_2)_3$, of toluene; specif., a high explosive resembling picric acid, made by nitrating toluene. Abbr. *TNT* or *T.N.T.*

trin′i·ty (trĭn′ĭ·tĭ), *n.; pl.* -TIES (-tĭz). [OF. *trinité*, fr. L. *trinitas* triad, in LL., Trinity, fr. *trini* three each.] **1.** [*cap.*] *Theol.* The union of three persons or hypostases (the Father, the Son, and the Holy Ghost) in one Godhead, so that all the three are one God as to substance, but three persons or hypostases as to individuality. **2.** Any symbol of the Trinity in art. **3.** Any union of three in one; a triad; as, the Hindu *trinity*, or Trimurti.

Trinity Sunday. The Sunday next after Whitsunday, observed as a feast in honor of the Holy Trinity.

trin′ket (trĭng′kĕt; -kĭt), *n.* [ONF. *trenquet*, OF. & F. *tranchet* a sort of knife.] **1.** A small article of equipment. **2.** A small ornament, as a jewel, ring, or the like. **3.** A thing of little value; a trifle.

trin′kums (trĭng′kŭmz), *n. pl.* Rarely in *sing.*, TRINKUM, exc. in composition. *Scot.* Trinkets; frippery.

tri·nod′al (trī·nōd′ăl), *adj.* [L. *trinodis* three-knotted, fr. *tri-* + *nodus* knot.] *Anat. & Bot.* Having three nodes.

tri·no′mi·al (-nō′mĭ·ăl), *adj.* [*tri-* + *-nomial* as in bi*nomial.*] **1.** *Math.* Consisting of three terms; of or pertaining to trinomials; as, a *trinomial* root. **2.** *Biol.* Consisting of names composed of three words or terms; as, a *trinomial* scientific name, the first name being that of the genus, the second that of the species, and the third that of the subspecies or variety. — *n.* **1.** *Math.* An expression consisting of three terms connected by the sign plus (+) or minus (−) or both. **2.** *Biol.* A trinomial name.

tri′o (trē′ō; trī′ō), *n.; pl.* TRIOS (-ōz). [F., fr. It. *trio*, fr. L. *tres, tria*, three.] **1.** Three, considered collectively; a set of three. **2.** *Music.* **a** A composition for three voice parts or three instruments; also, the performers of such a composition. **b** The secondary, or episodical, division of a minuet or scherzo, or of a march, or of various dance forms.

tri′ode (trī′ōd), *n.* [*tri-* + *-ode* as in cath*ode.*] A vacuum tube with an anode, a cathode, and a control grid.

tri·oe′cious, tri·e′cious (trī·ē′shŭs), *adj.* Also **tri·oi′cous** (-oi′kŭs). [*tri-* + Gr. *oikos* house.] *Bot.* Having staminate, pistillate, and hermaphrodite flowers on different plants. — **tri·oe′cious·ly, tri·e′cious·ly,** *adv.*

tri′o·let (trī′ō·lĕt), *n.* [F., dim. of *trio.*] A stanza of eight lines, in which the first is repeated as the fourth and seventh, and the second as the eighth. Its rhyme scheme is *abaaabab.*

tri·ox′ide (trī·ŏk′sīd; -sĭd), *n.* Also **tri·ox′id.** *Chem.* An oxide with three atoms of oxygen in the molecule.

trip (trĭp), *v. i.;* TRIPPED (trĭpt), or, *Rare,* TRIPT; TRIP′PING. [OF. *tripper, triper, treper,* of Teut. origin.] **1.** To move with light quick steps; to skip. **2.** *Rare.* To make a journey. **3.** To stumble. **4.** To offend against morality, propriety, accuracy, etc.; to err. **5.** *Horol.* To run past the pallet of the escapement; — said of a tooth of the scape wheel. — *v. t.* **1.** To perform lightly or nimbly, as a dance. **2.** To cause to stumble. **3.** To cause to fail; to obstruct; halt. **4.** To detect in a misstep, error, etc. **5.** *Mach.* To release, let fall, set free, etc., as a weight or compressed spring, as by removing a catch or detent. **6.** *Naut.* **a** To raise (an anchor) from the bottom so that it hangs free. **b** To pull (a yard) into a perpendicular position for lowering it. **c** To hoist (a topmast) far enough to enable the fid to be withdrawn, preparatory to housing it or sending it down. — *n.* **1.** A quick, light step. **2.** A journey, esp. a short journey; an excursion; also, a voyage. **3.** A false step or misstep; a stumble; hence, an error; mistake. **4.** A stroke, or catch, by which one, esp. a wrestler, causes his antagonist to lose footing. **5.** *Mach.* Act of releasing, or tripping; also, a pawl or other device for tripping a catch or detent.

tri·par′tite (trī·pär′tīt; trĭp′ẽr·tīt), *adj.* [L. *tripartitus,* fr. *tri-* + *partitus,* past part. of *partiri* to part, divide.] **1.** Divided into three parts; as, a *tripartite* leaf. **2.** Having three corresponding parts or copies; as, indentures *tripartite.* **3.** Made between, or involving, three parties; as, a *tripartite* treaty. — **tri·par′tite·ly,** *adv.*

tri′par·ti′tion (trī′pär·tĭsh′ŭn; trĭp′ẽr-), *n.* A division by threes, or into three parts; also, the taking of a third part.

tripe (trīp), *n.* **1.** A part of the stomach of a ruminant, esp. of the ox kind, used as food. The parts used are the walls of the rumen (***plain tripe***) and of the reticulum (***honeycomb tripe***). **2.** *Slang.* Any poor, worthless (usually offensive) thing, matter, or person.

tri′pe·dal (trī′pē·dăl; trī·pē′-; trĭp′ē·dăl), *adj.* [L. *tripedalis,* fr. *tri-* + *pes, pedis,* a foot.] Having three feet.

tri·per′son·al (trī·pûr′sŭn·ăl), *adj.* Consisting of three persons.

tri·pet′al·ous (-pĕt′ăl·ŭs), *adj.* *Bot.* Having three petals.

trip hammer. Also **trip′ham′mer** (trĭp′hăm′ẽr), *n.* *Mach.* A massive power hammer that is tripped, and allowed to fall, by cam or lever action. — **trip′ham′mer,** *adj.*

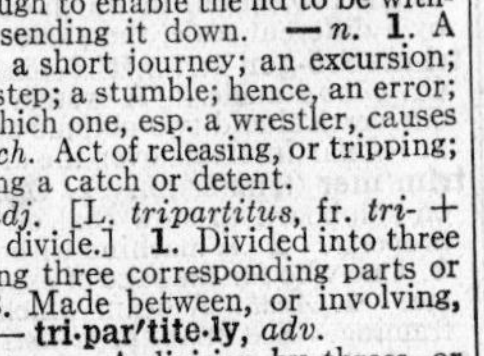

Trip Hammer. *a* Lever, or Helve, pivoted at *b*; *c* Hammer Head; *d* Anvil; *f* Shaft carrying Collar *e* with Cams for lifting the Hammer Head; *g* Prop to hold up the Hammer Head when not in use.

tri·phen′yl·meth′ane (trī·fĕn′ĭl·mĕth′ān; trī·fē′nĭl-), *n.* [*triphenyl-* (*tri-* + *phenyl*) + *methane.*] *Chem.* A colorless crystalline hydrocarbon, $CH(C_6H_5)_3$, the parent substance of many synthetic dyes.

tri·phib′i·an (trī·fĭb′ĭ·ăn), *adj.* [*tri-* + am*phibian.*] **1.** Adept at warfare alike on land, at sea, and in the air; — coined by Prime Minister Winston Churchill August 31, 1943. **2.** = TRIPHIBIOUS. — *n.* A triphibian commander.

tri·phib′i·ous (-ŭs), *adj.* [*tri-* + am*phibious.*] Employing land, naval, and air forces, often including air-borne troops, in co-ordinated attack; — used in 1941 by Leslie Hore-Belisha, then British Secretary for War (1937–40).

triph′thong (trĭf′thŏng; 74), *n.* [*tri-* + *-phthong* as in di*phthong.*] *Phonet.* **1.** Three vowel sounds united in one syllable, as in *fire, sour* (approximately fäēr, säōr). Such groups tend to become dissyllabic. **2.** Incorrectly, three letters spelling a single vowel or diphthong.

triph′y·lite (trĭf′ĭ·līt), *n.* Also **triph′y·line** (-lĭn; -lēn). [*tri-* + Gr. *phylē* a family, class; — in allusion to its three bases.] *Mineral.* A grayish-green or bluish mineral, a phosphate of lithium and iron, with a little manganese, $Li(Fe,Mn)PO_4$.

tri·pin′nate (trī·pĭn′āt), *adj.* Also **tri·pin′nat·ed** (-āt·ĕd; -ĭd). *Bot.* Thrice pinnate; bipinnate with each division pinnate, as the leaves of many ferns, etc. — **tri·pin′nate·ly,** *adv.*

tri′plane′ (trī′plān′), *n.* An airplane with three main supporting surfaces superposed.

tri′ple (trĭp′'l), *adj.* [F. or L.; F., fr. L. *triplus,* fr. *tri-* + *-plus* as in du*plus* double.] **1.** Consisting of three, usually united or in series; threefold; as, a *triple* difficulty. **2.** Three times repeated; treble. — *n.* **1.** A group of three. **2.** *Baseball.* A three-base hit. — *v. t.;* TRI′PLED (-'ld); TRI′PLING (-lĭng). To make threefold, or thrice as much or as many. — *v. i.* **1.** To increase threefold; to treble. **2.** *Baseball.* To make a triple.

Triple Alliance. *Hist.* **a** An alliance between England, Sweden, and the Netherlands, against France, in 1668. **b** An alliance between France, Great Britain, and the Netherlands, against Spain, in 1717. **c** An alliance between Austria, Great Britain, and Russia, against France, in 1795. **d** The Dreibund.

Tri′ple En′tente′ (trĭp′'l äN′täNt′). *Hist.* An entente constituting a virtual alliance between France, Great Britain, and Russia, counterbalancing the Dreibund; also, the nations party to this understanding.

tri′ple-ex·pan′sion en′gine. A form of compound engine in which the working fluid is expanded successively in three cylinders.

triple measure *or* **time.** *Music.* A measure of three beats, the first being accented; also, the rhythm derived from use of this measure, as in the waltz.

tri′ple-nerved′ (trĭp′'l·nûrvd′; 2), *adj.* *Bot.* Having three nerves; — said of a leaf.

triple play. *Baseball.* A play during which three men are put out.

tri′plet (trĭp′lĕt; -lĭt), *n.* [From TRIPLE.] **1.** A combination of three of a kind or three united. **2.** One of three offspring born at one birth; *pl.,* a group of three offspring born at one birth. **3.** *Music.* A group of three notes performed in the time of two of the same value. **4.** *Poetry.* A metrical unit of three verses, often rhymed.

tri′ple·tail′ (trĭp′'l·tāl′), *n.* A large edible marine fish (*Lobotes surinamensis*) inhabiting warm waters. The long dorsal and anal fins extend backward, and with the caudal fin appear like a three-lobed tail.

tri′plex (trĭp′lĕks; trī′plĕks), *adj.* [L.] Triple; threefold. — *n.* Something which is triplex; specif., *Music,* triple measure.

trip′li·cate (trĭp′lĭ·kāt), *adj.* [L. *triplicatus,* past part. of *triplicare* to triple, fr. *triplex* threefold.] Threefold; triple; made in three identical copies or the like; as, a *triplicate* agreement. — *n.* A third thing corresponding to two others of the same kind. — ***in triplicate.*** Made in three identical copies. — (-kāt), *v. t.* **1.** To treble; to reproduce twice. **2.** *Ling.* To form by triplication.

trip′li·ca′tion (trĭp′lĭ·kā′shŭn), *n.* **1.** Act of tripling, or making threefold, or adding three together; also, that which is triplicated. **2.** *Ling.* Formation of a word by tripling the stem; also, a word so formed.

tri·plic′i·ty (trĭ·plĭs′ĭ·tĭ), *n.; pl.* -TIES (-tĭz). **1.** Quality or state of being triple, or threefold. **2.** A group of three; specif., *Astrol.,* any of the groups of three signs into which the signs of the zodiac are divided; a trigon.

trip′lite (trĭp′līt), *n.* [See TRIPLE.] *Mineral.* A dark-brown mineral, principally a fluophosphate of iron and manganese, containing also calcium and magnesium.

trip′loid (trĭp′loid), *adj.* [See -OID.] *Biol.* Having three times the haploid chromosome number. Cf. HAPLOID, DIPLOID. — *n.* A triploid individual. — **trip·loi′dy** (trĭp·loi′dĭ), *n.*

tri′ply (trĭp′lĭ), *adv.* In a triple degree; to a triple amount.

tri′pod (trī′pŏd), *n.* [L. *tripus, -odis,* fr. Gr. *tripous,* fr. *tri-* + *pous, podos,* foot.] **1.** Any utensil or vessel, as a stool or caldron, on three feet or legs. **2.** A three-legged stand for a camera, theodolite, etc.

trip′o·dal (trĭp′ō·dăl), *adj.* Having three feet or legs.

tri·pod′ic (trī·pŏd′ĭk), *adj.* Having or using three feet; three-footed.

trip′o·dy (trĭp′ō·dĭ), *n.; pl.* -DIES (-dĭz). [*tri-* + *-pody* as in di*pody.*] *Pros.* A verse or group, consisting of three metrical feet.

trip′o·li (trĭp′ō·lĭ), *n.* [From *Tripoli,* Africa.] **a** Friable, soft, schistose deposits of silica, including diatomite and kieselguhr. **b** Deposits (not diatomaceous in origin) of friable and dustlike silica.

tri′pos (trī′pŏs), *n.; pl.* TRIPOSES (-ĕz; -ĭz). [L. *tripus* or Gr. *tripous.* See TRIPOD.] **1.** *Obs.* A tripod. **2.** *Cambridge Univ., Eng.* Any of the honor examinations, orig. for honors in mathematics.

trip′per (trĭp′ẽr), *n.* **1.** One who trips; hence, *Colloq., Brit.,* a tourist. **2.** *Mach.* A tripping device or mechanism, as for operating a signal on a railroad.

trip′pet (-ĕt; -ĭt), *n.* [From TRIP.] *Mach.* A cam, wiper, or projecting piece that strikes another piece at definite times.

trip′ping (-ĭng), *adj.* Quick; nimble; stepping lightly and quickly. — *n.* **1.** Act of one who or that which trips. **2.** A light dance. — **trip′ping·ly,** *adv.*

trip′tane (trĭp′tān), *n.* [*tri-* + *p* (for *b*) + but*ane.*] *Chem.* A liquid motor fuel (2, 2, 3-tri-methyl-butane) of high antiknock properties, used esp. to increase the power of aviation gasolines.

trip′ter·ous (trĭp′tẽr·ŭs), *adj.* [*tri-* + Gr. *pteron* wing.] *Bot.* Three-winged, as certain fruits or seeds.

trip′tych (trĭp′tĭk), *n.* [Gr. *triptychos* consisting of three layers, or plates, fr. *tri-* + *ptyx, ptychos,* a fold, layer.] **1.** A folding writing tablet in three parts. **2.** A picture or carving in three compartments side by side, esp. for an altar. Cf. DIPTYCH.

tri·que′trous (trī·kwē′trŭs; -kwĕt′rŭs), *adj.* [L. *triquetrus.*] Triangular; trigonous.

tri·ra′di·ate (-rā′dĭ·āt), *adj.* Having three rays, or radiating branches. — **tri·ra′di·ate·ly,** *adv.*

tri′reme (trī′rēm), *n.* [L. *triremis,* fr. *tri-* + *remus* an oar.] *Gr. & Rom. Antiq.* A galley having three banks of oars. — **tri′reme,** *adj.*

tri·sac′cha·ride (trī·săk′ȧ·rīd; -rĭd), *n.* Also **tri·sac′cha·rid.** *Chem.* Any of a group of sugars, as raffinose, yielding on complete hydrolysis three monosaccharide molecules.

tri′sect′ (trī′sĕkt′), *v. t.* [*tri-* + L. *sectus,* past part. of *secare* to cut.] To cut or divide into three parts, specif., *Geom.,* three equal parts. — **tri·sec′tion** (trī·sĕk′shŭn), *n.* — **tri·sec′tor** (-tẽr), *n.*

tri′seme (trī′sēm), *n.* *Pros.* A syllable or foot of three morae.

tri·se′mic (trī·sē′mĭk), **tri′seme** (trī′sēm), *adj.* [LL. *trisemus,* fr. Gr. *trisēmos,* fr. *tri-* + *sēma* sign.] *Pros.* Equal to, or having the length of, three times, or morae.

tri·sep′al·ous (-sĕp′ăl·ŭs), *adj.* *Bot.* Having three sepals.

tri·sep′tate (-sĕp′tāt), *adj.* *Bot. & Zool.* Having three partitions, or septa.

tri·se′ri·al (-sēr′ĭ·ăl), *adj.* Arranged in three series; specif.: *Bot.* **a** Arranged in three vertical or spiral rows. **b** Having only three floral whorls, as some flowers.

tris·kel′i·on (trĭs·kĕl′ĭ·ŏn), *or* **tris′kele** (trĭs′kēl), *n.* [Gr. *triskelē* three-legged. See TRI-; ISOSCELES.] A figure composed of three branches, usually curved, radiating from a center.

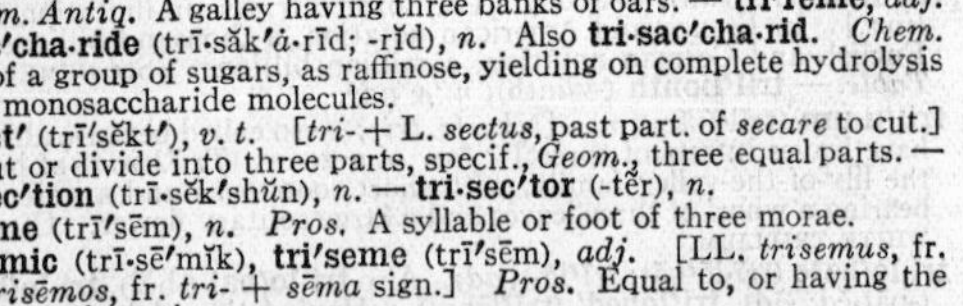

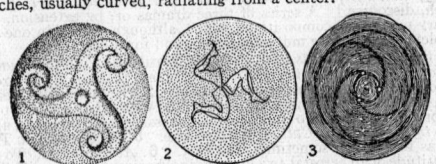

Triskelion. 1 On Fragment of Bronze from Ireland; 2 On a Shield pictured on a Greek Vase from Sicily; 3 On a Shell Disk from a Mound in Tennessee.

tris′mus (trĭz′mŭs; trĭs′-), *n.* [NL., fr. Gr. *trismos* gnashing of the teeth.] *Med.* Lockjaw. — **tris′mic** (-mĭk), *adj.*

tris·oc′ta·he′dron (trĭs·ŏk′tȧ·hē′drŭn), *n.* [Gr. *tris* thrice + E. *octahedron.*] **1.** *Math.* A polyhedron of 24 congruent faces meeting on the edges of a (regular) octahedron. **2.** *Cryst.* The solid described in sense 1 (fig. 2), frequently called a ***trigonal trisoctahedron*** in distinction from a related solid, bounded by 24 quadrilateral faces, the ***tetragonal trisoctahedron,*** or (more frequently) the ***trapezohedron.*** — **tris·oc′ta·he′dral** (-drăl), *adj.*

Trisoctahedrons. 1 Tetragonal; 2 Trigonal.

tri·so′mic (trī·sō′mĭk), *adj.* [*tri-* + Gr. *sōma* body.] *Genetics.* Having one or more chromosomes triploid in an otherwise diploid set. — **tri′some** (trī′sōm), *n.* — **tri′so′my** (trī′sō′mĭ), *n.*

tri·sper′mous (trī·spûr′mŭs), *adj.* [*tri-* + Gr. *sperma* seed.] Three-seeded.

tri·spor'ic (trī·spŏr'ĭk), **tri·spor'ous** (-spō'rŭs), *adj.* *Biol.* Three-spored.
Tris'tan (trĭs'tăn), *n.* = TRISTRAM.
‖**triste** (trēst), *adj.* [F.] Sad; dismal; dull; depressing.
‖**tris'tesse'** (trēs'tĕs'), *n.* [F.] Sadness; also, dullness.
tris·te'za (trĭs·tā'zȧ), *n.* [Pg. & Sp., lit., grief.] *Plant Pathol.* A fatal virus disease of citrus trees evidenced by rotting of the rootlets and wilting, and appearing only when certain cions, as sweet orange, tangerine, or grapefruit, are grafted on bitter-orange rootstalks.
trist'ful (trĭst'fo͝ol; -f'l), *adj.* Sad. — **trist'ful·ly**, *adv.*
tris'tich (trĭs'tĭk), *n.* [See TRISTICHOUS.] *Pros.* A group or stanza of three lines, or verses.
tris'tich·ous (-tĭ·kŭs), *adj.* [Gr. *tristichos* in three rows, fr. *tri-* + *stichos* a row.] In three rows; specif., *Bot.*, arranged in three vertical rows.
Tris'tram (trĭs'trăm), *n.* [AF. & OF. *Tristran*, *Tristan*, fr. OW., fr. a Pictish name *Drostan*. The initial *t* was perh. due to influence of L. *tristis* sad.] The hero of a medieval romance. Tristram is sent to Ireland by King Mark of Cornwall, his uncle, to fetch the king's bride, *Isolde the Beautiful*, and on the return voyage he and Isolde partake of a love potion. Tristram is stabbed by King Mark, who surprised him with Isolde. According to another version, he marries another Isolde, called *Isolde of the White Hand*. Being wounded, he sends for Isolde the Beautiful to come and cure him. The messenger is to hoist a white sail if Isolde returns with him. He does so; but Tristram's wife tells him the sail is black, and at this he dies.
tri·sty'lous (trī·stī'lŭs), *adj.* [*tri-* + Gr. *stylos* style.] *Bot.* Three-styled.
tri·sul'fide (-sŭl'fīd; -fĭd), *n.* Also **tri·sul'fid, tri·sul'phide, tri·sul'phid.** *Chem.* A compound containing three atoms of sulfur combined with an element or radical.
tri·syl'la·ble (trĭ·sĭl'ȧ·b'l; trī-), *n.* A word of three syllables, as *pho·no·graph*. — **tris'yl·lab'ic** (trĭs'ĭ·lăb'ĭk; trī'sĭ-), **tris'yl·lab'i·cal** (-ĭ·kăl), *adj.* — **tris'yl·lab'i·cal·ly**, *adv.*
trite (trīt), *adj.* [L. *tritus*, past part. of *terere* to rub, wear out.] Used until so common as to have lost novelty and interest; hackneyed; stale. — **trite'ly**, *adv.* — **trite'ness**, *n.*
Syn. **Trite, hackneyed, stereotyped, threadbare** mean without the freshness that evokes attention or interest. **Trite** implies a being spoiled for use, as a phrase or theme, by long familiarity with it; **hackneyed**, a being worn out in service so that it (esp. a word or phrase) has become dulled or meaningless in ordinary use; **stereotyped**, a falling invariably into the same pattern or form; **threadbare**, a being used so much that it has no longer any power to evoke interest.
tri'the·ism (trī'thē·ĭz'm), *n.* [*tri-* + Gr. *theos* God.] The opinion or doctrine that the Father, Son, and Holy Spirit are three distinct Gods. — **tri'the·ist** (-ĭst), *n.* & *adj.* — **tri'the·is'tic** (-ĭs'tĭk), **tri'the·is'ti·cal** (-tĭ·kăl), *adj.*
tri'thing (trī'thĭng), *n.* [For *thriding*. See 1st RIDING.] *Eng.* = 1st RIDING.
trit'i·um (trĭt'ĭ·ŭm; trĭsh'ĭ·ŭm), *n.* [NL., fr. Gr. *tritos* third + *-ium*.] The hydrogen isotope of mass number 3. Symbol, H^3 or *T*
Tri'ton (trī'tŏn), *n.* [L., fr. Gr. *Tritōn*.] **1.** *Gr. Myth.* A sea demigod, son of Poseidon and Amphitrite, represented as having the lower part of his body fishlike. His special attribute is a trumpet made of a conch shell. **2.** *Zool.* [*not cap.*] Any of a genus (*Triton*) of marine snails (suborder Taenioglossa) having a stout spiral shell, often handsomely colored; also, the shell.
tri'ton (trī'tŏn), *n.* [Gr. *triton*, neut., third.] The nucleus of tritium.
tri'tone' (trī'tōn'), *n.* [Gr. *tritonos* of three tones, fr. *tri-* + *tonos* a tone.] *Music.* An interval of three tones, or whole steps.
trit'u·ra·ble (trĭt'ū·rȧ·b'l), *adj.* Capable of being triturated.
trit'u·rate (-rāt), *v. t.* [LL. *trituratus*, past part. of *triturare* to thresh (grain), deriv. of *terere*, *tritum*, to rub, rub to pieces.] **1.** To rub, grind, bruise, or thrash. **2.** To rub or grind to a very fine or impalpable powder; to pulverize. — *n.* A triturated substance; *Pharm.*, a trituration. — **trit'u·ra'tor** (-rā'tẽr), *n.*
trit'u·ra'tion (-rā'shŭn), *n.* **1.** Act of triturating, or state of being triturated; comminution. **2.** *Pharm.* A triturated powder; esp., a powder made by triturating a substance with lactose as a diluent.
tri'umph (trī'ŭmf), *n.* [OF. *triumphe*, fr. L. *triumphus*.] **1.** *Rom. Antiq.* An imposing ceremonial in honor of a general who had gained a decisive victory over a foreign enemy. **2.** *Obs.* Hence, any triumphal procession. **3.** A state of joy or exultation for success. **4.** Victory; conquest; as, the *triumph* of knowledge. — **Syn.** See VICTORY. — *v. i.* **1.** To receive the honor of a triumph; hence, to celebrate victory; to exult. **2.** To obtain victory; to be successful. — *v. t.* *Obs.* To conquer.
tri·um'phal (trī·ŭm'făl), *adj.* Of, pertaining to, or used in a triumph; indicating, or in honor of, a triumph.
tri·um'phant (-fănt), *adj.* [MF. *triumphant*, fr. L. *triumphans*, pres. part.] **1.** *Obs.* Triumphal. **2.** Rejoicing for, or celebrating, victory; exultant. **3.** Graced with conquest; victorious. **4.** *Obs.* Magnificent. — **tri·um'phant·ly**, *adv.*
tri·um'vir (trī·ŭm'vẽr), *n.*; *pl.* -VIRS (-vẽrz), -VIRI (-vĭ·rī). [L., fr. *trium virorum* of three men.] *Rom. Antiq.* One of three men united in public office or authority; a member of a triumvirate. — **tri·um'vi·ral** (-vĭ·răl), *adj.*
tri·um'vi·rate (-vĭ·rāt), *n.* [L. *triumviratus*.] **1.** The office or term of a triumvir. **2.** Government by three in coalition or association; the term of such a government. **3.** A coalition or association of three in office or authority.
tri'une (trī'ūn), *adj.* [*tri-* + L. *unus* one.] Being three in one; — used esp. of unity of the Trinity in the Godhead. — *n.* A triad; esp. [*cap.*], the Trinity.
tri·u'ni·tar'i·an (trī·ū'nĭ·târ'ĭ·ăn), *n.* A Trinitarian.
tri·u'ni·ty (trī·ū'nĭ·tĭ), *n.* Quality or state of being triune; trinity.
tri·va'lent (trī·vā'lĕnt; trĭv'ȧ·lĕnt), *adj.* [*tri-* + L. *valens*, *-entis*, pres. part. See VALENCE.] *Chem.* Having a valence of three. — **tri·va'lence** (-lĕns), **tri·va'len·cy** (-lĕn·sĭ), *n.*
tri'valve' (trī'vălv'), *adj.* Having three valves.
triv'et (trĭv'ĕt; -ĭt), *n.* [AS. *trefet*, fr. L. *tripes*, *-pedis*, three-footed.] **1.** A three-legged stand or support; a tripod. **2.** An ornamental metal plate on very short legs, used under a hot dish to protect the table.
triv'i·a (trĭv'ĭ·ȧ), *n. pl.* [NL.] Trifles; unimportant matters.
triv'i·al (-ăl), *adj.* [F., fr. L. *trivialis*, prop., that belongs to the crossroads, hence, that may be found everywhere, common, fr. *trivium* a place where three roads meet, a crossroad, fr. *tri-* + *via* a way.] **1.** *Archaic.* Commonplace; trite. **2.** Of little importance; trifling; petty. — **triv'i·al·ly**, *adv.*
triv'i·al·ism (-ĭz'm), *n.* A trivial matter.
triv'i·al'i·ty (trĭv'ĭ·ăl'ĭ·tĭ), *n.*; *pl.* -TIES (-tĭz). **1.** Quality or state of being trivial. **2.** That which is trivial; a trifle.
triv'i·um (trĭv'ĭ·ŭm), *n.*; *pl.* TRIVIA (-ȧ). [ML. See TRIVIAL.] The three "liberal" arts, grammar, logic, and rhetoric, classified in medieval schools as the lower group of the liberal arts. Cf. QUADRIVIUM.
tri·week'ly (trī·wēk'lĭ), *adj.* Occurring or appearing every three weeks or three times a week. — *adv.* Three times a week.
-trix (-trĭks). [L. *-trix* as in bella*trix* a female warrior.] A suffix in feminine agent nouns, corresponding to masculines ending in *-or* (see -OR; -TRESS), as in avia*trix*, execu*trix*, etc.
tro'car (trō'kär), *n.* Also **tro'char.** [F. *trocart* (or *troisquarts*, i. e., three quarters), fr. *trois* three (fr. L. *tres*) + *carre* the side of a sword blade; — from its triangular point.] *Surg.* A stylet to explore tissues or to insert drainage tubes.
tro·cha'ic (trō·kā'ĭk), *adj.* [L. *trochaïcus*, fr. Gr. *trochaïkos*.] *Pros.* Of, pertaining to, or consisting of a trochee or trochees. — *n.* *Pros.* A trochaic measure or verse.
tro'chal (trō'kăl), *adj.* [Gr. *trochos* a wheel.] *Zool.* Resembling a wheel.
tro·chan'ter (trō·kăn'tẽr), *n.* [NL., fr. Gr. *trochantēr*, fr. *trechein* to run.] *Anat. & Zool.* In many vertebrates, a prominence at the upper part of the femur.
tro'che (trō'kē), *n.* [Gr. *trochos* anything round or circular, a wheel, prop., a runner, fr. *trechein* to run.] *Pharm.* A medicinal tablet or lozenge, esp. one used as a demulcent; strictly, one of circular form.
tro'chee (trō'kē), *n.* [L. *trochaeus*, fr. Gr. *trochaios* (sc. *pous*), fr. *trochaios* running, fr. *trechein* to run.] *Pros.* A foot of two syllables, the first long and the second short.
troch'el·minth (trŏk'ĕl·mĭnth), *n.* *Zool.* Any of a phylum (Trochelminthes) of invertebrates, including the rotifers.
troch'i·lus (trŏk'ĭ·lŭs), *n.*; *pl.* -ILI (-lī). [L., a kind of small bird, an annular molding, etc., fr. Gr. *trochilos*, fr. *trechein* to run.] **a** A crocodile bird. **b** Any of several Old World warblers. **c** A hummingbird.
troch'le·a (trŏk'lē·ȧ), *n.* [L., a case or sheaf containing one or more pulleys, fr. Gr. *trochilia*.] *Anat.* A structure likened to a pulley, as that part of the surface of the humerus which articulates with the ulna.
troch'le·ar (-ẽr), *adj.* **1.** *Anat.* Shaped like, or resembling, a pulley; pertaining to a trochlea. **2.** *Bot.* Pulley-shaped; round, and narrow in the middle, like the wheel of a pulley.
tro'choid (trō'koid), *n.* [Gr. *trochos* a wheel + *-oid*.] The path in a fixed plane of any point in a moving coincident plane when a given curve in the latter plane rolls without sliding on a straight line or an arc or circle in the former plane; — used in naval architecture in apportioning the displacement in the after part of the body of a vessel. — *adj.* *Anat.* Admitting of rotation on a longitudinal axis. — **tro·choi'dal** (trō·koi'dăl), *adj.* — **tro·choi'dal·ly**, *adv.*
troch'o·phore (trŏk'ō·fōr; 70), *n.* [Gr. *trochos* wheel + *-phore*.] *Zool.* A free-swimming ciliate larva typical of marine annelid worms but occurring in several invertebrate groups.
trod (trŏd), *past* & *past part.* of TREAD.
trod'den (trŏd''n), *past part.* of TREAD.
trode (trōd). Archaic past of TREAD.
trog'lo·dyte (trŏg'lō·dīt), *n.* [L. *troglodytae*, pl., fr. Gr. *trōglodytēs* one who creeps into holes, fr. *trōglē* a hole, cavern (fr. *trōgein* to gnaw) + *dyein* to enter.] **1.** *Ethnol.* One of any savage race that dwells in caves; a cave dweller. **2.** Hence, any person of primitive or degraded ways of living. **3.** An anthropoid ape, as the chimpanzee. — **trog'lo·dyt'ic** (-dĭt'ĭk), **trog'lo·dyt'i·cal** (-ĭ·kăl), *adj.*
tro'gon (trō'gŏn), *n.* [NL., fr. Gr. *trōgōn*, pres. part. of *trōgein* to gnaw.] Any of numerous nonpasserine tropical birds (family Trogonidae) noted for brilliant plumage.
troi'ka (troi'kȧ), *n.* [Russ.] *Russia.* A vehicle drawn by three horses abreast; also, a team of three horses abreast.
Tro'i·lus (trō'ĭ·lŭs; troi'lŭs), *n.* See CRESSIDA.
tro'i·lus but'ter·fly' (trō'ĭ·lŭs). A large American butterfly (*Papilio troilus*), black, with yellow marginal spots on the front wings, and blue on the rear.
Tro'jan (trō'jăn), *adj.* [L. *Trojanus*, fr. *Troja*, *Troia*, Troy, fr. *Tros*, fr. Gr. *Trōs*, *Trōos*, Tros, founder of Troy.] Of or pertaining to ancient Troy or its inhabitants. — *n.* **1.** A native or inhabitant of Troy. **2.** One who shows pluck, endurance, or determined energy. **3.** *Old Slang.* A gay or somewhat disreputable companion.
Trojan horse. **1.** *Class. Myth.* = WOODEN HORSE, 1. **2.** A device, used by German Nazis, of placing espionage and propaganda agents inside the country of an intended victim for purposes of sabotage and direction of native subversive groups. Cf. FIFTH COLUMN.
Trojan War. See APPLE OF DISCORD.
troke (trōk), *v.* & *n.* *Scot.* Barter; exchange.
troll (trōl), *n.* [ON. & Sw. *troll*, Dan. *trold*.] *Teut. Myth.* A supernatural being, conceived sometimes as a dwarf, sometimes as a giant, fabled to inhabit caves, hills, and like places.
troll, *v. t.* [ME. *trollen* to roll, wander.] **1.** *Obs.* To revolve; turn; wag. **2.** To send about; to circulate, as a vessel in drinking. **3.** **a** To sing the parts of in succession, as of a round or catch. **b** To sing loudly. **c** To celebrate in song. **4.** To angle for with a hook drawn along or through the water; hence, to allure; entice. **5.** To angle in; as, to *troll* a lake. — *v. i.* **1.** *Archaic.* To roll, ramble, or walk about; to circulate; as, to *troll* in a coach. **2.** To speak rapidly. **3.** To sing or play in a jovial manner; to sound with a rolling tone. **4.** To fish, esp. by drawing the hook along or through the water, as with a long line behind a moving boat. — *n.* **1.** Act of moving round; routine. **2.** A song sung in parts successively; a catch; round. **3.** The lure, as a spoon, used in trolling; also, the line with its lure and hook, used in trolling. — **troll'er**, *n.*
trol'ley, trol'ly (trŏl'ĭ), *n.*; *pl.* -LEYS, -LIES (-ĭz). [Prob. fr. TROLL to roll.] **1.** *Local, Eng.* Any of various vehicles of the cart type. **2.** A wheeled carriage running on an overhead rail or track, as on a parcel railway in a store. **3.** *Elec. Railways.* **a** A current collector operating in connection with a trolley wire. **b** An electric car; a trolley car. — *v. t.* & *i.* *Colloq.* To convey by, or to ride on, a trolley car.
trolley bus *or* **coach.** A bus electrically propelled by power through two overhead wires, otherwise like a motorbus.
trolley car. An electric car running on tracks with power derived through a trolley; — in English use called *tramcar* or *tram*.

trol'lop (trŏl'ŭp), *n.* A slattern; also, a loose woman.

trom'bi·di'a·sis (trŏm'bĭ·dī'ȧ·sĭs), *n.* [NL., fr. *Trombidium*, a genus of red mites + *-iasis*.] *Veter.* Infestation with chiggers.

trom'bone (trŏm'bōn; trŏm·bōn'), *n.* [It., aug. of *tromba* trumpet.] *Music.* A powerful brass wind instrument with a cupped mouthpiece; — called also ***slide trombone***. It consists of a long cylindrical metal tube bent twice upon itself and ending in a bell. The first crook (the *slide*) is movable and by it the player can control the length of the vibrating column and thus produce any pitch within the compass of the instrument. — **trom'bon·ist** (trŏm'bōn·ĭst; trŏm·bōn'ĭst), *n.*

Trombone.

trom'mel (trŏm'ĕl), *n.* *Ore Dressing.* A screen used for screening, or sizing, rock, ore, coal, etc.

tro·mom'e·ter (trō·mŏm'ē·tẽr), *n.* [Gr. *tromos* trembling + *-meter.*] An instrument for measuring or detecting minute earth tremors.

trompe (trŏmp), *n.* [F.] An apparatus, as for a forge, in which air is sucked through holes in the upper end of a vertical tube by a stream of falling water. The water is discharged below, and the air is led to the furnace. A fall of 30 feet gives an air pressure of about 2 lb. per square inch.

tro'na (trō'nȧ), *n.* [Sw., fr. reduced form of Ar. *naṭrūn.* See NATRON.] *Mineral.* A gray-white, or yellowish-white, monoclinic combination of normal and acid sodium carbonate, $Na_2CO_3NaHCO_3.2H_2O$.

trone (trōn), *n.* [OF., fr. L. *trutina* a balance, fr. Gr. *trytanē.*] *Scot. & Dial.* A weighing machine for heavy wares.

troop (trōōp), *n.* [F. *troupe*, fr. *troupeau*, fr. LL. *troppus* herd, of Teut. origin.] **1.** A collection of people or, formerly, also of things. **2.** Loosely, a quantity; a lot. **3.** Soldiers collectively; an armed force; — usually in *pl.* **4.** *Rare.* A company of actors; a troupe. **5.** *Mil.* A body of cavalry, a division of a squadron, commanded by a captain; — corresp. to the *company* in infantry. **6.** A group of boy scouts consisting typically of sixteen to thirty-two boys, in two to four patrols. — **Syn.** Company, party, band. — *v. i.* **1.** To move or gather in crowds or troops; as, *trooping* to school. **2.** To march on, esp. as one of a throng. **3.** *Archaic.* To associate; to consort in company.

troop carrier. A troop-carrying plane.

troop'er (trōōp'ẽr), *n.* [Cf. F. *troupier* soldier.] **1.** A cavalryman; also, his horse. **2.** *Rare in U. S.* A troopship. **3.** *Australia.* A mounted policeman. **4.** *U. S.* A private in a state constabulary. **5.** = PARATROOPER.

troop'ship' (-shĭp'), *n.* A vessel for carrying troops; transport.

troost'ite (trōōst'īt), *n.* [After Gerard *Troost*, of Nashville, Tenn.] *Mineral.* A variety of willemite having large reddish crystals, the zinc being partly replaced by manganese.

‖**trop** (trō), *adv.* [F.] Too much; too. Cf. DE TROP.

tro·pae'o·lin, tro·pe'o·lin (trō·pē'ō·lĭn), *n.* Also **tro·pae'o·line, tro·pe'o·line** (-lĭn; -lēn). Any of a series of orange or orange-yellow azo dyes, so called because colored like nasturtium flowers.

tro·pae'o·lum (-lŭm), *n.* [NL., dim. fr. Gr. *tropaion* trophy. See TROPHY. So named because likened to ancient trophies.] *Bot.* Any of a genus (*Tropaeolum*) of tropical American diffuse or climbing pungent herbs with lobed or dissected peltate leaves and showy, variously colored flowers; esp., a garden species (*T. majus*), the nasturtium.

-tro·pal (-trō·păl). A combining form denoting *turning.* See -TROPIC.

trope (trōp), *n.* [F. or L.; F., fr. L. *tropus*, fr. Gr. *tropos* a turning, turn; akin to Gr. *tropē* a turn, *trepein* to turn.] **1.** Formerly, a phrase or clause, with which the sung parts of the Mass (Introit, Kyrie, etc.) were interpolated in the Middle Ages. **2.** A topical head or heading. **3.** *Rhet.* The use of a word or expression in a figurative sense; also, an instance of such use; a figure of speech.

-trope. [Gr. *tropos.*] An adjectival combining form meaning *turning*, equivalent to *-tropic.*

troph'ic (trŏf'ĭk), *adj.* Also, rarely, **troph'i·cal** (-ĭ·kăl). [Gr. *trophikos* nursing.] *Physiol. & Plant Physiol.* Pertaining to nutrition; as, *trophic* nerves, those believed to influence nutrition. — **troph'i·cal·ly**, *adv.*

tro'phied (trō'fĭd), *adj.* Adorned with trophies.

troph'o- (trŏf'ō-), **troph-.** [Gr. *trophos* feeder, or *trophē* nutrition, fr. *trephein* to nourish.] A combining form used to denote *connection with*, or *relation to, nutrition*, as in **tro·phop'a·thy** (see -PATHY).

troph'o·blast (-blăst), *n.* [*tropho-* + *-blast.*] *Embryol.* A layer of ectodermic tissue developed on the outer surface of the blastodermic vesicle of many mammals.

troph'o·plasm (-plăz'm), *n.* [*tropho-* + *-plasm.*] *Biol.* **a** The nutritive or vegetative cell substance; — disting. from the *idioplasm.* **b** The less active substance of the cytoplasm; — disting. from the *archoplasm.*

troph'o·zo'ite (-zō'īt), *n.* [*tropho-* + Gr. *zōion* animal + *-ite.*] *Zool.* A protozoan during its vegetative stage.

tro'phy (trō'fĭ), *n.; pl.* -PHIES (-fĭz). [F. *trophée*, fr. L. *tropaeum, trophaeum*, fr. Gr. *tropaion* a monument of the enemy's defeat, prop., neut. adj., fr. *tropē* a turn.] **1.** *Gr. & Rom. Antiq.* A memorial of a victory raised on the field of battle, or, in case of a naval victory, on the nearest land, and sometimes in the chief city. **2.** The representation of such a memorial, as on a medal; esp., *Arch.*, an ornament representing a group of weapons. **3.** Any memorial of victory or conquest; as, *trophies* of the chase. **4.** Any memorial or memento; as, *trophies* of an earlier civilization.

-tro·phy (-trō·fĭ). [Gr. *-trophia*, fr. *trephein* to nourish.] A combining form denoting *nutrition, nurture.*

trop'ic (trŏp'ĭk), *n.* [L. *tropicus* of a turn, i. e., of the sun, fr. Gr. *tropikos* of the solstice, *tropikos* (sc. *kyklos*) the tropic or solstice, fr. *tropē* a turning.] **1.** *Astron.* Either of the two small circles of the celestial sphere, on each side of and parallel to the equator, at a distance of 23° 27′, which the sun reaches at its greatest declination north or south. The northern circle is called the ***Tropic of Cancer***, and the southern the ***Tropic of Capricorn***, from the two signs at which the tropics touch the ecliptic. **2.** *Geog.* **a** Either of the two parallels of terrestrial latitude corresponding to the celestial tropics. See ZONE, *Illust.* **b** [*often cap.*] *pl.* The region lying between these parallels of latitude; as, life in the *tropics.* — *adj.* Of or pertaining to the tropics; tropical.

-trop'ic. [Gr. *-tropos* turning. See TROPE.] A combining form used to denote *turning, changing*, or *tending to turn* or *change*, esp., *in a* (specified) *manner* or *in response to a* (specified) *stimulus*, as in photo*tropic*, iso*tropic*, etc. Cf. -TROPISM.

trop'i·cal (trŏp'ĭ·kăl), *adj.* [See TROPIC.] **1.** Of, pertaining to, characteristic of, or incident to the tropics; being within the tropics. **2.** [L. *tropicus*, fr. Gr. *tropikos*, orig., of turning. See TROPE.] Figurative; metaphorical. — **trop'i·cal·ly**, *adv.*

tropical fish. Any of various small, often brightly marked or bizarrely formed fishes of tropical origin which are kept in aquariums as pets.

tropic bird. Any of several web-footed birds (genus *Phaëthon*) found chiefly in tropical seas, often far from land. The plumage is mostly white with a few black markings. The central pair of tail feathers is greatly elongated and the bill is bright-colored.

tro'pine (trō'pēn; -pĭn), *n.* Also **tro'pin.** [From ATROPINE.] *Chem.* A poisonous, colorless, crystalline base, $C_8H_{15}NO$, formed by hydrolysis of atropine and other alkaloids derived from plants of the nightshade family.

tro'pism (trō'pĭz'm), *n.* [Gr. *tropē* a turning.] **1.** *Biol.* Involuntary movement of an organism or any of its parts involving turning or curvature and induced either automatically or in response to stimuli, as a chemical agent, light, etc. **2.** Any innate tendency to react in a definite manner to stimuli. — **tro·pis'tic** (trō·pĭs'tĭk), *adj.*

-tro·pism (-trō·pĭz'm). A combining form, *-trope* + *-ism*, denoting *tendency to turn, affinity for tropism*, as in helio*tropism*, photo*tropism*, geo*tropism*, chemo*tropism*, hydro*tropism*, thermo*tropism.*

tro·pol'o·gy (trō·pŏl'ō·jĭ), *n.; pl.* -GIES (-jĭz). [Through LL. & LGr., fr. Gr. *tropos* a trope + *logos* discourse.] A figurative mode of speech or writing; also, a method of interpreting Scripture in which great stress is laid on the figurative sense of the language. — **trop'o·log'ic** (trŏp'ō·lŏj'ĭk), **trop'o·log'i·cal** (-ĭ·kăl), *adj.* — **trop'o·log'i·cal·ly**, *adv.*

trop'o·pause (trŏp'ō·pôz), *n.* [Gr. *tropos* (as in *troposphere*) + *paucis* a ceasing.] *Meteorol.* The top of the troposphere.

tro·poph'i·lous (trō·pŏf'ĭ·lŭs), *adj.* [Gr. *tropos* turn + *-philous.*] *Ecology.* Thriving under alternating periods of dryness and moisture or of heat and cold; adapted to seasonal changes.

trop'o·phyte (trŏp'ō·fīt), *n.* [Gr. *tropos* turn + *-phyte.*] *Ecology.* A tropophilous plant, as the deciduous trees of temperate regions. — **trop'o·phyt'ic** (-fĭt'ĭk), *adj.*

trop'o·sphere (-sfēr), *n.* [F. *troposphère*, fr. Gr. *tropos* a turn, but in sense as if fr. *tropē* a turn or change + F. *sphère* sphere.] *Meteorol.* All that portion of the atmosphere below the stratosphere. In it temperature generally rapidly decreases with altitude, clouds form, and convection is active.

-tro·pous (-trō·pŭs). [See TROPE.] *Bot.* A combining form, denoting *turned* or *curved in a* (specified) *way.* Corresponding nouns denoting *state* are formed in **-tro·py** (-trō·pĭ).

‖**trop'po** (trŏp'pō), *adv.* [It.] Too much; — chiefly in musical directions, as in *non troppo presto*, not too fast.

-tro·py (-trō·pĭ). [Gr. *tropē.*] A combining form meaning *turning*, used to denote: **a** See -TROPOUS. **b** = -TROPISM.

trot (trŏt), *v. i. & t.*; TROT'TED; TROT'TING. [OF. *troter*, fr. OHG. *trottōn* to tread.] **1.** To ride, drive, or proceed at a trot. **2.** To run; jog; hurry. — *n.* **1.** A gait of the horse and other quadrupeds in which the legs move in diagonal pairs. In a fast trot all four feet are off the ground twice during each stride. **2.** Hence, the sound made by a horse going at this gait; also, a race between trotters. **3.** A jogging pace, as of one hurrying. **4.** *Now Rare.* A toddler; a child. **5.** *Archaic.* An old woman; — in contempt. **6.** *Slang, U. S.* A translation; a "pony."

trot, *n.* *Fishing.* A trotline (which see) or one of the short lines with hooks which are attached to it at intervals.

troth (trŏth; trōth; 74), *n.* [AS. *trēowth.*] **1.** Faith; fidelity; pledged faith; as, plighted *troth.* **2.** Truth; verity. **3.** *Archaic.* Betrothal. — *v. t.* To pledge; betroth.

troth'plight' (-plīt'), *n.* Betrothal. — *adj.* Betrothed; pledged. — *v. t.* To betroth. *All Archaic.*

trot'line' (trŏt'līn'), *n.* *Fishing.* A stout line reaching across a stream or for some distance from one bank, bearing at frequent intervals single hooks hung by short lines.

trot'ter (trŏt'ẽr), *n.* **1.** One who or that which trots; esp., a horse trained for trotting matches. **2.** The foot of a pig, etc., used for food.

tro'tyl (trō'tĭl; -tēl), *n.* *Chem.* The high explosive trinitrotoluene.

trou'ba·dour (trōō'bȧ·dōōr; -dôr; -dōr), *n.* [F., fr. Pr. *trobador*, fr. *trobar* to find, compose in verse (F. *trouver*).] One of a class of lyric poets and poet-musicians who flourished from the 11th to the end of the 13th century, chiefly in Provence, the south of France, and the north of Italy.

trou'ble (trŭb''l), *v. t.*; TROU'BLED (-'ld); TROU'BLING (-lĭng). [OF. *trubler, troubler, tourbler*, deriv. of L. *turba* disorder, crowd.] **1.** To agitate; disturb. **2.** To agitate mentally or spiritually; worry. **3.** To afflict physically; ail. **4.** To put to inconvenience; as, I will not *trouble* you. — *v. i.* **1.** To take trouble; make an effort. **2.** To worry or be agitated. — *n.* **1.** State of being troubled; also, an affliction, misfortune, etc. **2.** A person, situation, event, etc., that troubles or provokes worry. **3.** Civil disorder; unrest or agitation or an instance of it. **4.** Exertion; pains; as, he took the *trouble* to call. **5.** An ailment; as, lung *trouble.* — **Syn.** See EFFORT. — **trou'bler** (-lẽr), *n.* — **trou'bling·ly**, *adv.*

trouble man. Also, *Colloq.*, **trouble shooter.** A man employed to locate causes of trouble and to correct troubles, as on light and power circuits and gas lines, in automobile repair shops, etc.

trou'ble·some (trŭb''l·sŭm), *adj.* **1.** Provoking worry or anxiety; vexatious. **2.** *Archaic.* Characterized by disturbance; turbulent. **3.** Burdensome; bothersome. — **trou'ble·some·ly**, *adv.* — **trou'ble·some·ness**, *n.*

trou'blous (trŭb'lŭs), *adj.* **1.** Troubled; agitated; turbulent. **2.** Causing trouble, disturbance, or disquiet.

‖**trou-de-loup** (trōōd'lōō'), *n.; pl.* TROUS-DE-LOUP (trōōd'-). [F., fr. *trou* hole + *de* of + *loup* wolf.] *Mil.* One of a group of sloping pits with a pointed stake in the middle, built as an obstacle to enemy movements; — usually in *pl.*

trough (trŏf; *dial.* trŏth *is widespread in America, and known in England; by Amer. bakers, often* trō; *by Brit. bakers, often* trou; 74), *n.* [AS. *trog, troh.*] **1.** An open boxlike or basinlike receptacle, often of wood, esp. one for water or fodder for livestock. **2.** A bowl or basin, often of wood in which something is kneaded, washed, or the like. **3.** A gutter for rain water under the eaves of a roof. **4.** Any long, narrow or shallow channel or depression, as between waves.

trounce (trouns), *v. t.*; TROUNCED (trounst); TROUNC'ING (troun'sĭng). To thrash or punish severely; flog.

troupe (tro͞op), *n.* [F.] A company or troop, esp. of traveling actors. Hence **troup'er** (tro͞op'ẽr).

troup'i·al (tro͞op'ĭ·ăl), *n.* [F. *troupiale*, fr. *troupe* flock, troop; — from their habit of congregating in large flocks.] Broadly, any bird of the family Icteridae, including the American blackbirds, grackles, and orioles; specif., one of the larger brilliant orioles of Central and South America; esp., *Icterus icterus.*

trou'sers (trou'zẽrz), *n. pl.* [Formed, on model of *drawers*, fr. *trouse* (*trews*), fr. Ir. & Gael. *triubhas.*] A garment extending from the waist to the ankles and covering each leg separately, for outer wear by men and women; typically, in western style a fitted but not tight-fitting garment; in Mohammedan countries, large and baggy, but also loose-fitting, as the lower garment of pajamas; also, a young boy's similar outer garment extending to the knees. Called also in the United States *pants.*

trous'seau' (tro͞o'sō'; tro͞o'sō), *n.*; *pl.* TROUSSEAUX (-sō'), TROUSSEAUS (-sōz'; -sōz). [From OF. *trousseau* a bundle and F. *trousseau* bundle, bride's outfit, dim. of *trousse* a bundle, truss.] **1.** *Obs.* A bundle. **2.** A bride's personal outfit, as of clothes, jewelry, etc.

trout (trout), *n.* See PLURAL, *Note*, 6. [AS. *truht*, fr. LL. *tructa*, *tructus*, fr. Gr. *trōktēs* a sea fish with sharp teeth, from *trōgein* to gnaw.] **1.** Any of certain highly esteemed food and game fishes, most of which live in fresh water, though some are anadromous. The trouts belong to the family Salmonidae and to the genus *Salmo* (cf. SALMON), and in America also to the genera *Salvelinus* (the chars: see 2d CHAR) and *Cristivomer* (see NAMAYCUSH). Well-known trouts include: the ***brown, or river, trout*** (*Salmo fario*), and the ***sea trout*** (specif., the European *S. trutta*); in the western U. S., the ***cutthroat trout*** (*S. clarkii*), the steelhead *S. gairdneri* (see STEELHEAD **a**), ***rainbow trout*** (the anadromous *S. irideus* of California, and the closely allied *S. shasta* of California and Oregon widely introduced elsewhere), ***Dolly Varden trout*** (*Salvelinus malma spectabilis* of streams west of the Cascade range); in the eastern U. S., the ***brook, or speckled, trout*** (*Salvelinus fontinalis*) and the oquassa (which see). **2.** Any of various more or less troutlike fishes.

trou'vère' (tro͞o'vâr'), *n.* Also **trou'veur'** (-vûr'). [F., fr. OF. *trovere*, fr. *trover* to compose. See TROUBADOUR.] One of a school of poets who flourished in northern France from the 11th to the 14th century. Their works are of a prevailingly narrative character.

tro'ver (trō'vẽr), *n.* [OF. *trover* to find (F. *trouver*); inf. as n.] *Law.* Originally an action of trespass against one who found goods, and would not restore them to the owner; hence, an action to recover the value of goods wrongfully converted.

trow (trō), *v. i. & t.* [AS. *trēowan*, *trēowian*; akin to AS. *trūwian* to trust, and to AS. *trēow* faith, belief.] **1.** *Obs.* To believe. **2.** *Archaic.* To think or suppose.

trow'el (trou'ĕl), *n.* [OF. *troele*, *truele*, fr. LL. *truella*, dim. of L. *trua* a ladle.] Any of various hand implements, used for spreading, shaping, or smoothing loose or plastic material; also, a scooplike or flat-bladed implement for taking up and setting small plants, etc. — *v. t.*; TROW'ELED (-ĕld) or TROW'ELLED; TROW'EL·ING or TROW'EL·LING. To smooth, dress, shape, etc., with or as with a trowel. — **trow'el·er**, *n.*

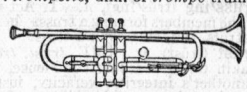

Trowels. 1 Gardener's Trowel; 2 Plasterer's Trowel; 3 Bricklayer's Trowel.

troy (troi), *adj.* Pertaining to or designating the system (**troy weight**) of weights commonly used in England and the United States for gold, silver, etc.; — so named from Troyes in France. See WEIGHT, *Tables* 2 & 4. — *n.* Troy weight.

tru'ant (tro͞o'ănt), *n.* [OF., a vagrant, beggar, of Celt. origin.] One who stays away from business, school, etc., without leave; one who shirks his duty. — *v. i.* To play truant. — *adj.* Being, like, or characteristic of, a truant. — **tru'an·cy** (-ăn·sĭ), *n.* — **tru'ant·ry**, *n.*

truce (tro͞os), *n.* [ME. *trewes*, pl. of *trewe* a truce, prop., pledge of fidelity, truth, fr. AS. *trēow* fidelity, troth.] **1.** A suspension of arms by agreement; an armistice. **2.** Hence, respite; brief quiet.

truck (trŭk), *v. t. & i.* [F. *troquer.*] To exchange; barter; traffic (in); peddle. — *n.* **1.** Barter. **2.** *Colloq.* Intercourse; dealing. **3.** Small commodities; esp., *U. S.*, vegetables raised for the market. Hence **truck farm, truck farmer, truck farming, truck garden,** etc. **4.** Payment of wages in goods instead of cash. Hence **truck system.** **5.** *Colloq.* Small articles of little value; hence, rubbish.

truck (trŭk), *n.* [Prob. fr. L. *trochus* hoop, fr. Gr. *trochos* a wheel, fr. *trechein* to run.] **1.** A small wheel; specif., a small strong wheel for a gun carriage. **2.** A small wooden disk; esp., a small wooden cap at the summit of a flagstaff or a masthead, usually having holes in it for reeving flag or signal halyards. **3.** Any of numerous vehicles for transporting heavy articles; esp.: **a** A form of two-wheeled handbarrow without sides used for trunks, boxes, etc. **b** A heavy rectangular frame supported on four small wheels used in rolling heavy objects. **c** Any of various small flat-topped cars propelled by pulling or pushing, and used in shops, stores, etc. **d** Any strong horse-drawn or automotive vehicle for heavy or long-distance hauling. **e** *Brit.* An open railroad freight car. **4.** A swiveling carriage, consisting of a frame with one or more pairs of wheels, springs, etc., to carry and guide one end of a locomotive or a railroad car, and facilitate the turning of sharp curves. — *v. t.* To transport on a truck or trucks. — *v. i.* **1.** To truck goods. **2.** To be employed in driving a truck. — **truck**, *adj.*

truck'age (trŭk'ĭj), *n.* Transportation by truck or the cost of it.

truck'er (trŭk'ẽr), *n.* One who trucks; esp., one who raises or peddles truck.

truck'er, *n.* Also **truck'man** (trŭk'măn). One who drives a truck, or whose business it is to convey goods on trucks.

truck'le (trŭk''l), *n.* [Dim. of *truck* a wheel; or from the kindred L. *trochlea* a block (see TROCHLEA).] A small wheel, as of a pulley; *Dial.*, a caster. — *v. t. & i.* To roll or move on casters; trundle.

truck'le, *v. i.*; -LED (-'ld); -LING (-lĭng). [From *truckle* in *truckle bed.*] To yield obsequiously to the will of another; — in allusion to the custom of rolling a pupil's truckle bed under his master's bed. — **Syn.** See FAWN. — **truck'ler** (-lẽr), *n.* — **truck'ling·ly**, *adv.*

truckle bed. [*truckle*, n. + *bed.*] A low bed on wheels, that may be pushed under another bed; a trundle bed.

truck tractor. = TRACTOR, 2.

truck trailer. A nonautomotive trucking vehicle to be drawn by a motor truck or truck tractor.

truc'u·lent (trŭk'ū·lĕnt; tro͞o'kū-), *adj.* [MF. or L.; MF. *truculent*, fr. L. *truculentus*, fr. *trux*, *trucis*, wild, fierce.] **1.** Feeling or displaying fierceness; savage; cruel. **2.** *Rare.* Destructive. — **Syn.** See FIERCE. — **truc'u·lence** (-lĕns), **truc'u·len·cy** (-lĕn·sĭ), *n.* — **truc'u·lent·ly**, *adv.*

trudge (trŭj), *v. i.*; TRUDGED (trŭjd); TRUDG'ING (trŭj'ĭng). [Orig., to pack, to be off, possibly fr. F. *trousser* to pack.] To walk or march steadily, esp. toilsomely or wearily. — *n.* A tramp or walk, esp. a weary one. — **trudg'er**, *n.*

trudg'en stroke, *or* **trudg'en** (trŭj'ĕn), *n.* *Swimming.* A racing stroke in which a double overarm motion is used and the legs execute a scissors kick; — from its use by an amateur named Trudgen.

true (tro͞o; 114), *adj.* [AS. *trēowe* faithful, trusty; akin to AS. *trēow* fidelity, faith, troth.] **1.** Faithful to friends, promises, allegiance, etc.; loyal. **2.** *Archaic.* Honest; upright. **3.** To be relied upon; certain; as, a *true* indication. **4.** Conformable to fact; correct; not erroneous, inaccurate, or the like. **5.** Truthful. **6.** Properly so called; ideally or typically such; genuine; as, a *true* Christian. **7.** Legitimate; rightful. **8.** Conformable to a standard, rule, pattern or original; exact; as, a *true* likeness. **9.** *Biol.* Not deviating from the essential characters of a class; as, a lizard is a *true* reptile. **10.** *Geol. & Surveying.* Determined with reference to the earth's axis rather than the Magnetic Poles; as, *true* north; a *true* bearing. Cf. VARIATION, *Illust.* — **Syn.** See REAL. — *adv.* **1.** Truly; in accordance with truth. **2.** *Biol.* Conformably to parental type; without change. — *n.* **1.** That which is true; — usually with *the.* **2.** State of being true or accurate, as in phrases *in true, out of true.* — *v. t.*; TRUED (tro͞od); TRU'ING (tro͞o'ĭng) or TRUE'ING. To make true; bring to its exact form, angle, adjustment, etc. — **true'ness**, *n.*

true bill. *Law.* A bill of indictment returned so endorsed by the grand jury.

true blue. **1.** Originally, some especially fast blue dye or color. **2.** The blue color adopted by the Covenanters, or Scottish Presbyterians; hence, Presbyterianism. **3.** Thoroughgoing or uncompromising loyalty, fidelity, or orthodoxy. — **true'-blue'** (-blo͞o'; 2), *adj.*

true level. See LEVEL, *n.*, 7.

true'love' (tro͞o'lŭv'), *n.* One truly beloved or loving; a sweetheart.

true'love', *or* **true'-lov'er's, knot.** A complicated knot not readily untying, emblem of mutual love.

true'pen'ny (tro͞o'pĕn'ĭ), *n.* An honest or trusty fellow.

true ribs. *Anat.* Ribs whose costal cartilages connect directly with the sternum, in man the first seven pairs. See THORAX, *Illust.*

true time. Mean time, or solar time.

truf'fle (trŭf''l; tro͞o'f'l; tro͝of''l), *n.* [MF. *trufle*, *truffe*, fr. Pr. *trufa* or It. *truffa.*] Any of various subterranean fungi (genus *Tuber*) or the edible blackish fruit.

tru'ism (tro͞o'ĭz'm), *n.* An undoubted or self-evident truth, esp. one too obvious or trifling to mention.

trull (trŭl), *n.* A trollop; strumpet.

tru'ly (tro͞o'lĭ), *adv.* **1.** In a true manner; honestly, genuinely, accurately, etc. **2.** In fact; in reality.

trump (trŭmp), *n.* [OF. *trompe*, of Teut. origin.] **1.** *Chiefly Poetic.* A trumpet. **2.** *Scot. & Ir.* A jew's-harp. — *v. i. & t.* To make a sound like, or proclaim by, a trumpet.

trump, *n.* [A corruption of *triumph*; cf. F. *triomphe* a triumph, a game of cards, a trump.] **1.** *Card Playing.* One of a suit any card of which takes any card of the other suits; the suit itself. **2.** *Colloq.* A good fellow (man or woman). — *v. t. & i.* **1.** To play a trump (on) so as to make high cards of the suit led useless. **2.** To nonplus; outdo; beat; cap. — ***trump up.*** To devise unfairly; fabricate; as, to *trump up* a charge.

trump'er·y (-ẽr·ĭ), *n.*; *pl.* -ERIES (-ĭz). [F. *tromperie* deceit, fr. *tromper* to deceive.] Something deceptively showy; hence, vain or valueless things; rubbish. — **trump'er·y**, *adj.*

trum'pet (trŭm'pĕt; -pĭt), *n.* [OF. *trompette*, dim. of *trompe* trump.] **1.** A wind instrument consisting of a long metal tube, commonly once or twice curved, and ending in a bell. **2.** A trumpeter. **3.** A trumpet-shaped instrument for collecting, directing, or intensifying, sounds; as, an ear *trumpet*; a speaking *trumpet.* **4.** *pl. Southern U. S.* Any of several pitcher plants having long trumpet-shaped leaves (esp. *Sarracenia flava*). **5.** A sound as of a trumpet; esp., an elephant's cry. — *v. t. & i.* To sound or proclaim on or as on a trumpet; to sound, bellow, utter, etc., with a trumpetlike tone.

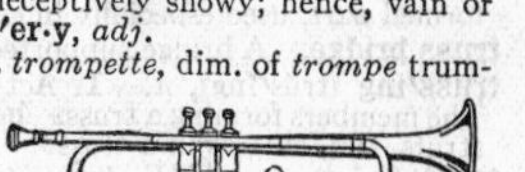
Trumpet, with Pistons.

trumpet creeper. A North American woody vine (*Campsis radicans*) having pinnate leaves and large, red, trumpet-shaped flowers. It belongs to a family (Bignoniaceae, the trumpet-creeper family; see BIGNONIA) of chiefly tropical trees, shrubs, and herbs, including the calabash and the catalpa, having opposite leaves and irregular flowers with 2 to 4 stamens.

trum'pet·er (trŭm'pĕt·ẽr; -pĭt-), *n.* **1.** One who trumpets; specif., a soldier, sailor, or herald, who signals with a trumpet. **2. a** Any of several long-legged, long-necked South American birds (genus *Psophia*, esp. *P. crepitans*) often domesticated to protect poultry. **b** Also **trumpeter swan.** A North American wild swan (*Cygnus buccinator*) noted for its sonorous voice. **c** A pigeon of a breed having a rounded crest and heavily feathered feet.

trumpet flower. **1.** Any of several plants having trumpet-shaped flowers; also, its flower. **2.** Specif.: **a** Also **trumpet vine.** The trumpet creeper. **b** In full, **trumpet honeysuckle.** An American honeysuckle (*Lonicera sempervirens*) with coral-red or orange flowers.

trum'pet·weed' (trŭm'pĕt·wēd'; -pĭt-), *n.* Any of several herbs; as: **a** The boneset *Eupatorium perfoliatum.* **b** The joe-pye weed *E. maculatum.*

trum'pet·wood' (-wo͝od'), *n.* A tropical American tree (*Cecropia peltata*) of the mulberry family, having hollow stems used for wind instruments, and large peltate leaves.

trun'cate (trŭng'kāt), *v. t.* [L. *truncatus*, past part. of *truncare* to cut off, mutilate.] To cut off; lessen by cutting; lop. — *adj.* Truncated; as: **a** *Bot. & Zool.* Having the end square or even. **b** *Zool.* Lacking the apex; — of certain spiral shells. — **trun·ca'tion** (trŭng·kā'shŭn), *n.*

trun′cat·ed cone *or* **pyr′a·mid** (trŭng′kāt·ĕd; -ĭd). *Geom.* The part left of a cone or pyramid whose vertex is cut off by a plane. See UNGULA, *Illust.*

trun′cheon (trŭn′chŭn), *n.* [ME. *tronchoun* broken spear shaft, fr. OF. *tronchon*, deriv. of L. *truncus* stem, trunk.] **1.** *Archaic.* A short staff or cudgel; a spear shaft. **2.** A baton; now esp., a policeman's club. **3.** *Obs.* A trunk or stem, esp. one with branches lopped off to hasten growth. — *v. t.* To beat with a truncheon.

trun′dle (trŭn′d'l), *n.* [For *trendle*, fr. AS. *trendel* a circle, ring, disk.] **1.** (*pron. also* trŭn′'l, trōōn′d'l, trōōn′'l) A round or circular object as a small wheel, caster, or hoop. **2. a** A low-wheeled cart or truck. **b** Also **trundle bed.** A truckle bed. **3.** A rolling motion or the sound due to it. **4.** *Mach.* A lantern pinion; also, any of its bars. — *v. t. & i.*; TRUN′DLED (-d'ld); TRUN′DLING (-dlĭng). **1.** To roll along, as a hoop or bed on casters. **2.** To revolve; rotate. — **trun′dler** (-dlẽr), *n.*

trun′dle-tail′ (-tāl′), *n.* *Archaic.* A curly-tailed dog; a cur.

trunk (trŭngk), *n.* [F. *tronc*, fr. L. *truncus*, fr. *truncus* mutilated.] **1. a** The main stem, or body, of a tree; bole. **b** The body of an animal or a man, apart from head and limbs. **c** The main body of anything. **2.** [Confused with *trump*, fr. F. *trompe* proboscis, trumpet.] A proboscis, esp. of an elephant. **3.** A box or chest for containing clothes or other goods, esp. of a traveler. **4.** A long, large box, pipe, etc., serving as a conduit or conveyer. **5.** *Arch.* The shaft of a column or pilaster. **6.** *pl. Costume.* **a** In full, **trunk hose.** Short, full breeches reaching halfway down the thigh, worn by gentlemen in the 16th and early 17th centuries. **b** Close-fitting short breeches, worn by athletes, swimmers, etc. **7.** *Mach.* See TRUNK ENGINE. **8.** *Naut.* **a** The part of a cabin projecting above the upper deck. **b** A box or funnel around an opening in the bottom of a vessel, as for a centerboard. **c** The casing around a hatch continued between two decks to a hatch above or below, making a shaft. **9.** *Teleph.* A circuit between two telephone exchanges for making connections between subscribers. **10.** *Zool.* The thorax of an insect. — *adj.* Designating, or pertaining to, a main railroad, telegraph, telephone, or other line; as, *trunk* call (in telephony), operator, etc.

trunk engine. *Mach.* **a** A steam engine the piston rod of which is a pipe (called a *trunk*) of sufficient diameter to enable one end of the connecting rod to be attached to the crank and the other end to pass within the pipe and be pivoted to the piston, giving compactness. **b** An engine having an elongated hollow piston (**trunk piston**) to the open end of which the connecting rod is pivoted. Most internal-combustion engines are of this type.

trunk′fish′ (trŭngk′fĭsh′), *n.; pl.*, see FISH. Any of a family (Ostraciidae) of plectognath fishes having an angular body covered with bony plates so that only the jaws, fins, eyes, and tail are free to move.

trunk line. *U. S. & Canada.* **a** A line connecting an inland commercial center or centers with the seaboard; also, a system handling long-distance through traffic. **b** Any similar main line, as a telegraph or telephone system.

trun′nel (trŭn′'l). Var. of TREENAIL.

trun′nion (trŭn′yŭn), *n.* [F. *trognon* a core, stalk.] Either of two opposite projecting pivots, journals, or gudgeons, that provide a means of swiveling or turning a cannon, engine cylinder, etc.

truss (trŭs), *v. t.* [OF. *trusser, trousser.*] **1.** To pack into a bundle; — often with *up.* **2.** Hence, to bind or fasten closely; to tighten, tie, etc., the clothing, laces, etc., of; specif., to skewer, as a fowl's wings to its body in cooking; — often with *up.* **3.** To support by a truss; strengthen or stiffen, as a girder, by a brace or braces. — *n.* **1.** A bundle; pack; package. **2.** A measured quantity of hay (56 or 60 lb.) or straw (36 lb.). **3.** *Arch.* A bracket or modillion. **4.** *Engin.* An assemblage of members, such as beams, bars, rods, etc., forming a rigid framework. See BRIDGE, *Illust.* **5.** *Hort.* A compact flower cluster at the top of a stem. **6.** *Naut.* An iron band around a lower mast. **7.** *Surg.* An appliance to support a weakened, injured, or deformed part, used especially in cases of hernia. — **truss′er**, *n.*

truss bridge. A bridge supported mainly by trusses.

truss′ing (trŭs′ĭng), *n.* **1.** Act of one who trusses. **2.** *Engin.* **a** The members forming a truss. **b** Trusses collectively. **c** Bracing with struts, ties, etc., as in a truss.

trust (trŭst), *n.* [ME. *trust, trost* (also *trist, trest*), fr. (or perh. akin to) ON. *traust* confidence, security.] **1.** Assured reliance on another's integrity, veracity, justice, etc.; confidence. **2.** Assured anticipation; confident hope. **3.** *Now Rare.* Trustworthiness. **4.** The person or thing trusted; ground of reliance, faith, or hope. **5.** Responsible charge or office. **6.** Custody; keeping. **7.** Credit given; esp., reliance on future payment for merchandise or other property delivered; as, to sell on *trust.* **8.** That which is committed or entrusted to one, as a duty, task, or charge. **9.** *Law.* An equitable right or interest in property distinct from the legal ownership thereof; also, a property interest held by one person for the benefit of another. **10.** A combination of firms or corporations formed by an agreement legally establishing a trust (sense 9), and managed and operated by trustees. **11.** A permanent organization controlling the commercial policy of a number of establishments operated independently, esp. when such an organization is strong enough to control prices by suppressing or disregarding competition. — **Syn.** See MONOPOLY.
— *v. i.* **1.** To have trust, confidence, or hope. **2.** To give trust, or credit. — **Syn.** See RELY. — *v. t.* **1.** To place confidence in; rely on. **2.** To commit, or consign, as to one's care; entrust. **3.** To allow (one) to go, act, etc., without fear or misgiving. **4.** To give credence to; believe. **5.** To hope or expect confidently. **6.** To invest with a trust; commission confidentially. **7.** To give trust, or credit, to.
— *adj.* Held in trust; as, *trust* property; *trust* funds.
— **trust′er**, *n.* — **trust′ing·ly**, *adv.*

trust company. **a** Any corporation formed for the purpose of acting as trustee. **b** *U. S.* A bank organized under state laws for handling trusts and also performing all the ordinary banking functions except the issuing of bank notes.

trus·tee′ (trŭs·tē′), *n.* *Law.* **a** A person, real or juristic, holding property in trust. **b** *U. S.* One holding the effects of another taken by the **trustee process**, or attachment by garnishment. — *v. t.* **a** To commit (property) to the care of a trustee. **b** *U. S.* To attach by the trustee process.

trus·tee′ship, *n.* **1.** The office or function of a trustee. **2.** Authorized supervisory control by a country or countries as trustee of the administration of a trust territory under the international system of the United Nations, through an agreement approved by its General Assembly, or, in the case of a strategic area, by its Security Council.

trust′ful (trŭst′fōōl; -f'l), *adj.* Full of trust; confiding. — **trust′ful·ly**, *adv.* — **trust′ful·ness**, *n.*

trust fund. Money, securities, or other like property, settled or held in trust.

trust′ing, *adj.* That trusts; trustful.

trust territory. A non-self-governing territory placed under an administrative authority by the Trusteeship Council of the United Nations as belonging to one of three classes: a former mandate under the League of Nations, a territory taken from an ex-enemy state as a result of World War II, or a territory voluntarily placed under the international system by the state responsible for its administration.

trust′wor′thy (trŭst′wûr′thĭ), *adj.* Worthy of trust or confidence; reliable. — **trust′wor′thi·ness** (-thĭ·nĕs; -nĭs), *n.*

trust′y (trŭs′tĭ), *adj.;* TRUST′I·ER (-tĭ·ẽr); TRUST′I·EST. **1.** Trustful. **2.** Deserving trust, or confidence; trustworthy; dependable. — *n.* A trusty or trusted person; specif., *U. S.*, a convict considered trustworthy and allowed special privileges. — **trust′i·ly** (trŭs′tĭ·lĭ), *adv.* — **trust′i·ness** (-tĭ·nĕs; -nĭs), *n.*

truth (trōōth; 114), *n.; pl.* TRUTHS (trōōthz; trōōths). [AS. *trēowth, trīewth.*] **1.** Quality or state of being true; hence: **a** *Archaic.* Fidelity; constancy. **b** Veracity; sincerity; genuineness. **c** Agreement with that which is represented; correspondence to reality; verisimilitude. **d** Conformity to rule; exactness; correctness. **2.** That which is true; that which conforms to fact or reality; that which is or is characterized by being in accord with what is, has been, or must be; as, to seek the *truth.* **3.** *Christian Science.* A synonym for God.
Syn. **Truth, veracity, verity, verisimilitude** mean the quality of adhering to facts or reality. **Truth** may represent an abstraction that is an ideal construction or a quality manifested in statements, acts, feelings, etc.; **veracity**, a quality of persons as manifested esp. in their utterances or of the utterances themselves; **verity**, the quality of a thing that is exactly what it purports to be, or is in complete accordance with the facts; **verisimilitude**, a quality of representations (esp. artistic or literary) that convinces one of their truth to life either as it actually is or as it universally is.

truth′ful (-fōōl; -f'l), *adj.* Characterized by truth; veracious; rendering reality accurately. — **truth′ful·ly**, *adv.* — **truth′ful·ness**, *n.*

try (trī), *v. t.*; TRIED (trīd); TRY′ING. [OF. *trier* to sift, cull, pick out.] **1.** *Archaic.* To cull (out) or separate. **2.** To essay; attempt; endeavor. **3.** To test or make trial of; put to proof. **4.** To settle by a test as by an appeal to arms; as, to *try* conclusions. **5.** To use, test, or treat experimentally; as, to *try* a new remedy or a convalescent's appetite with dainties. **6.** To subject to strain, affliction, annoyance, etc.; as, the poor light *tries* his eyes; to *try* one's patience. **7.** To refine by rendering or melting; — often with *out.* **8.** *Carp. & Mech.* To fit or finish with accuracy; specif., to plane with a trying plane; — usually with *up.* **9.** *Law.* To examine or investigate judicially; to conduct the trial of; as, to *try* a criminal. — *v. i.* **1.** To prove something by experiment; make trial. **2.** To endeavor; make an attempt. — **Syn.** See ATTEMPT: AFFLICT.
— *n.; pl.* TRIES (trīz). **1.** An attempt; an experimental trial. **2.** In Rugby football, a score (counting three points) made by grounding the ball on or behind the opponents' goal line.

try′ing (trī′ĭng), *adj.* Hard to endure; distressing; as, these are *trying* times.

try′ing, *adj.* Fitted for or used in trying.

trying plane. A long finishing plane used especially on the edges of pieces to be accurately joined. See PLANE, *Illust.* (7).

try′ma (trī′mȧ), *n.* [Gr., hole.] *Bot.* A nutlike drupe, in which the epicarp and mesocarp separate from the hard 2-valved endocarp, as in the walnut and hickory.

try′out′ (trī′out′), *n.* **a** In sports, a test by which the fitness of a contestant to remain in a certain class is determined. **b** *Colloq., U. S.* A performance or an opportunity for demonstration given as a test.

tryp′a·no·so′ma (trĭp′ȧ·nō·sō′mȧ), **tryp′a·no·some′** (trĭp′ȧ·nō·sōm′; trĭ·păn′ō·sōm), *n.* [NL. *trypanosoma*, fr. Gr. *trypanon* auger + *sōma* body.] *Zool.* Any of a genus (*Trypanosoma*) of parasitic flagellate protozoans infesting the blood of various animals, including man, being usually transferred by the bite of an insect. Some cause serious or fatal diseases such as sleeping sickness and nagana. See TSETSE.

tryp′a·no·so·mi′a·sis (-sō·mī′ȧ·sĭs), *n.* *Med.* Disease due to infection with trypanosomes.

Tryp′ars·am′ide (trĭp′ärs·ăm′ĭd; -īd; trĭp·ärs′ȧ·mĭd; -mīd), *n.* A trade-mark for a drug used in the treatment of sleeping sickness (def. 1) and syphilis of the central nervous system.

tryp′sin (trĭp′sĭn), *n.* [G., fr. Gr. *tryein* to rub down, wear out (hence, to digest) + *pepsin.*] *Biochem.* **a** A proteolytic enzyme present in the pancreatic juice. **b** Any of several similar enzymes. — **tryp′tic** (-tĭk), *adj.*

tryp′to·phan (trĭp′tō·făn), **tryp′to·phane** (-fān), *n.* [*tryptic* + *-phane.*] *Biochem.* A crystalline amino acid, $C_{11}H_{12}N_2O_2$, a product of tryptic digestion, essential to animal life.

try′sail′ (trī′sāl′; *naut.* trī′s'l), *n.* *Naut.* A fore-and-aft sail bent to a gaff, hoisted on a lower mast or a small mast (**trysail mast**) close abaft a lower mast.

try square. An instrument for marking or measuring off right angles, and testing work for squareness.

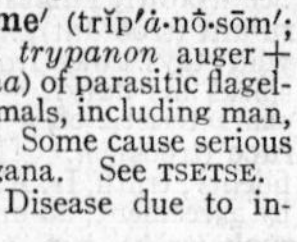

Try Square.

tryst (trĭst; trīst; *in Scot. & Dial.* trīst *only*), *n.* [OF. *triste, tristre*, a place for watching or waiting (in hunting), an ambush.] **1.** An appointment to meet; a meeting; also, an appointed place (**tryst′ing place**) of meeting. **2.** *Now Scot. & Dial.* A market or fair. — *v. t. & i. Scot.* **1.** To agree to meet. **2.** To appoint; fix; agree upon. — **tryst′er**, *n.*

tsar (zär; tsär), **czar** (zär), *n.* [Russ. *tsar'*, fr. *tsesar'*, through OSlav. and Goth., fr. L. *Caesar* Caesar.] A king; an emperor; specif.: **a** The popular title of the former emperors of Russia; officially, their title as kings of Poland and some other parts of their empire. **b** The title of the former kings of Bulgaria, from 1908. — **tsar′dom, czar′dom** (-dŭm), *n.*

tsar′e·vitch (zär′ĕ·vĭch; tsär′-), **czar′e·vitch** (zär′ĕ·vĭch), *n.* [Russ. *tsarevich.*] A son of a tsar of Russia; — orig. a title, later replaced by *grand duke.* Cf. CESAREVITCH.

tsa·rev′na (zä·rĕv′nȧ; tsä-), **cza·rev′na** (zä·rĕv′nȧ). [Russ. *tsarevna.*] A daughter of a tsar of Russia; also, the wife of a tsarevitch; — originally a title.

tsa·ri′na (zä·rē′nȧ; tsä-), **cza·ri′na** (zä·rē′nȧ), *n.* [G. *Zarin, Czarin,* fem.; in Russ., *tsaritsa.*] The title of an empress of Russia, corresponding to the emperor's title of *tsar.*

tsar′ism (zär′ĭz'm; tsär′-), **czar′ism** (zär′ĭz'm), *n.* Autocratic government; absolutism.

tsa·rit′sa, tsa·rit′za (zä·rēt′sȧ; tsä-), **cza·rit′za** (zä·rēt′sȧ), *n.* = TSARINA.

tset′se (tsĕt′sē), *n., or,* **tsetse fly.** [S. Afr. D. *tsetse,* of Bantu origin.] Any of several African muscid flies (genus *Glossina*), as *G. morsitans* the vector of the nagana parasite (*Trypanosoma brucei*) of cattle and horses or *G. palpalis* which carries the parasite *T. gambiense* of human sleeping sickness.

Tshi (chwē), *adj.* Designating a linguistic stock of Negroes of the Gold Coast of West Africa. — *n.* The Tshi language, the chief language of the Gold Coast.

T shirt *or* **tee shirt.** A man's or boy's cotton undershirt with very short sleeves and collarless neck; also, a similarly styled knit jersey or shirt for outer wear.

T square. A ruler having a crosspiece or head at one end, used in making parallel lines.

tsu·na′mi (tsōō·nä′mē), *n.* [Jap., storm wave.] A great sea wave produced by submarine earth movement or volcanic eruption.

tsu′tsu·ga·mu′shi dis·ease′ (tsōō′tsŭ·gȧ·mōō′shĭ). [Jap. *tsutsugamushi,* fr. *mushi* bug.] *Med.* A typhuslike acute febrile disease, originally observed in Japan, caused by microorganisms of a certain genus (*Rickettsia*) that are transmitted by the bite of a larval mite (*Trombicula akamushi*); — called also *scrub typhus.*

Tua′reg (twä′rĕg), *n.* [From *Touareg,* Berber pron. of Ar. *Ṭawāriq,* pl. of *Ṭāriq.*] One of the dominant nomads of the central and western Sahara who have preserved their Hamitic speech in great purity but are of the Moslem faith.

tu′a·ta′ra (tōō′ȧ·tä′rä), *n.* A large iguanalike reptile (*Sphenodon punctatum*) of certain islands off the coast of New Zealand. It is the only surviving rhynchocephalian.

tub (tŭb), *n.* [MD. (& MLG.) *tubbe, tobbe* (D. *tobbe*).] **1.** A wide, low bucketlike vessel, originally formed with wooden staves, round bottom, and hoops. **2.** *Slang.* A slow-moving boat or vessel; also, a short fat person. **3.** The amount which such a bucketlike vessel will hold; as, a *tub* of butter. **4.** A bathtub; hence, *Colloq.,* a bath in a bathtub. **5.** A small cask; esp., a keg or cask holding about four gallons. **6.** *Obs.* A sweating in a bathtub. **7.** *Mining.* **a** A box or bucket in which coal or ore is sent up a shaft. **b** A tram used underground. — *v. t. & i.;* TUBBED (tŭbd); TUB′BING. To wash, bathe, plant, etc., in a tub. — **tub′ba·ble** (tŭb′ȧ·b'l), *adj.* — **tub′ber** (-ẽr), *n.* — **tub′bing,** *n.*

tu′ba (tū′bȧ), *n.; pl.* TUBAE (-bē), TUBAS (-bȧz). [L., trumpet.] **1.** An ancient trumpet. **2.** A large, deep-toned saxhorn. **3.** A powerful organ reed stop of 8-foot pitch.

tub′al (tūb′ăl), *adj.* Of or pertaining to a tube, esp. a Fallopian tube. — *n.* A Fallopian tube.

tu′bate (tū′bāt), *adj.* Having or forming a tube or tubes.

tube (tūb; 114), *n.* [F., fr. L. *tubus.*] **1.** A hollow cylinder to convey liquids, gases, etc.; also, a round metal container from which pastes may be squeezed; as, a *tube* of tooth paste. **2.** Something with a tube or tubelike part as its chief feature, as a gun or telescope. **3.** *Bot.* The narrow basal portion of a gamopetalous corolla or a gamosepalous calyx. **4.** *Elec.* = ELECTRON TUBE. **5.** *Elec. & Magnetism.* A space, usually assumed to be tubular in form, bounded by lines of force or induction; — called specif. **tube of force** *or* **tube of induction. 6.** A tunnel for an underground railway; also, *Colloq.,* the railway itself (**tube railway**). — *v. t.* To furnish with, enclose in, or pass through, a tube or tubes; also, to make tubular.

tu′ber (tū′bẽr), *n.* [L., a hump, knob, truffle.] **1.** *Bot.* A short, fleshy, usually underground, stem or shoot bearing minute scale leaves with buds or "eyes" in their axils, as the potato. Cf. BULB, CORM. **2.** *Anat.* A tuberosity, tubercle, or protuberance.

tu′ber·cle (tū′bẽr·k'l), *n.* [L. *tuberculum,* dim. of *tuber.*] **1.** A small knoblike prominence or excrescence, esp. on an animal or plant; a nodule; specif.: **a** *Anat.* An eminence near the head of a rib which articulates with the transverse process of a vertebra. See VERTEBRA, *Illust.* **b** *Bot.* A nodule on the root of a leguminous plant. **2.** *Med.* A small rounded morbid growth in an organ or in the skin; esp., the specific lesion of tuberculosis.

tubercle bacillus. The microorganism (*Mycobacterium tuberculosis*) which causes tuberculosis. Cf. BACILLUS, 2.

tu·ber′cu·lar (tū·bûr′kū·lẽr), *adj.* Of, pertaining to, or like a tubercle or tubercles; having tubercles; specif.: *Med.* **a** Nodular; as, *tubercular* leprosy. **b** Loosely, tuberculous. — *n.* A person having tuberculosis.

tu·ber′cu·late (-lāt), *adj.* [NL. *tuberculatus.*] Tuberculated; also, tubercular. — **tu·ber′cu·la′tion** (-lā′shŭn), *n.*

tu·ber′cu·lat′ed (-lāt′ĕd; -ĭd), *adj.* Having, or characterized by, a tubercle or tubercles.

tu·ber′cu·lin (-lĭn), *n.* Also **tu·ber′cu·line** (-lĭn; -lēn). A sterile liquid containing the growth products of, or specific substances extracted from, the tubercle bacillus, used in the diagnosis and treatment of tuberculosis, esp. in children and cattle; as, **tuberculin test,** the injection of tuberculin into the skin to determine by the reaction the presence of tuberculosis.

tu·ber′cu·lo- (tū·bûr′kū·lō-), **tubercul-.** [L. *tuberculum* tubercle.] A combining form denoting: **a** *Tuberculous,* as in **tu·ber′cu·lo·cele′.** **b** *The tubercle bacillus.* **c** *Tuberculosis,* as in **tu·ber′cu·lo·ther′a·py.**

tu·ber′cu·loid (-loid), *adj.* *Med.* Resembling a tubercle.

tu·ber′cu·lo′sis (tū·bûr′kū·lō′sĭs; tū′bẽr-), *n.* [NL. See TUBERCLE; -OSIS.] *Med.* An infectious disease caused by the tubercle bacillus and characterized by the production of tubercles, or lesions. The commonest seat of human tuberculosis is the lungs (***pulmonary tuberculosis, consumption,*** *or* ***phthisis***). Often, *Colloq.,* abbreviated to *t.b.*

tu·ber′cu·lous (tū·bûr′kū·lŭs), *adj.* **a** Orig., having, or characterized by, tubercles; tubercular. **b** *Med.* Affected with, or of the nature of, tuberculosis; caused by, or due to the bacillus of, tuberculosis.

tube′rose′ (tūb′rōz′; tū′bẽr·ōs), *n.* [See TUBEROUS.] A bulbous herb (*Polianthes tuberosa*) of the amaryllis family, cultivated for its spike of fragrant white lilylike flowers.

tu′ber·os′i·ty (tū′bẽr·ŏs′ĭ·tĭ), *n.; pl.* -TIES (-tĭz). An obtuse prominence; specif., *Anat. & Zool.,* any of certain large prominences on bones, usually serving for the attachment of muscles or ligaments.

tu′ber·ous (tū′bẽr·ŭs), *adj.* Also **tu′ber·ose** (-ōs). [F. *tubéreux,* fr. L. *tuberosus.* See TUBER.] **1.** Covered with knobby or wartlike prominences. **2.** *Bot.* Consisting of, bearing, or like a tuber or tubers.

tuberous root. A thick fleshy root like a tuber, but having no buds or scale leaves, as in the dahlia. — **tu′ber·ous–root′ed,** *adj.*

tubi-. [L. *tubus.*] A combining form meaning *tube,* as in **tu′bi·form.**

tub′ing (tūb′ĭng), *n.* **1.** Act of making tubes. **2.** A series of tubes; tubes, collectively; a length or piece of a tube; also, material for tubes.

tu′bu·lar (tū′bū·lẽr), *adj.* [L. *tubulus,* dim. of *tubus* tube, pipe.] **1.** Having the form of, or consisting of, a tube or tubes; fistulous; also, made or provided with tubes. **2.** Of, pert. to, or sounding as if produced through tubes.

tu′bu·late (-lāt), *adj.* Tubulated. — (-lāt), *v. t.* To form into, or to provide with, a tube or a tubulure; as, a *tubulated* bottle or retort. — **tu′bu·la′tion** (-lā′shŭn), *n.*

tu′bule (tū′būl), *n.* [F. or L.; F., fr. L. *tubulus,* dim. of *tubus* tube, pipe.] A small tube or fistular body.

tubuli-. [L. *tubulus* a small tube.] A combining form meaning tubule, as in **tu′bu·li·flo′rous,** having all the flowers with tubular corollas, as plants of the aster family.

tu′bu·lous (tū′bū·lŭs), *adj.* [See TUBULE.] Like, or in the form of, a tube; specif.: **a** Tubular. **b** *Bot.* Having, or made up of, tubular florets.

tu′bu·lure (-lūr), *n.* [F.] *Chem.* A short tubular opening, as at the top of a retort.

‖**tu′chun′** (dōō′jün′), *n.* [Chin. (Pek.) *tu^{1}-chün^{1},* lit., overseer of troops.] In China, 1916–1923, the title of the military governor of a province; a war lord.

tuck (tŭk), *v. t.* [AS. *tūcian* to ill-treat; akin to MD. & MLG. *tucken, tocken,* to tug.] **1.** To pull up in a fold or folds and fasten; to shorten or tighten by drawing up or together in folds; — usually with *up.* **2.** To secure (something) by pushing its edges under; also, to cover or wrap snugly or tightly; — with *in, up,* etc.; as, to *tuck* a child in bed. **3.** To put (something) where it will be held tightly or snugly; to press, cram, or poke. **4.** To make a tuck or tucks in. — *v. i.* **1.** To draw up or together in or as in folds. **2.** To make tucks. — *n.* **1.** A sewed fold, as in a garment, for decoration or shortening. **2.** [Perh. a different word.] *U. S.* Vital spirit; energy; life. **3.** *Fancy Diving.* In a dive of the somersault type, a series of movements in which a diver clasps his ankles with his hands and rolls himself into a ball in order to increase the rate of his spin. **4.** *Shipbuilding.* The part of a vessel where the ends of the lower planks meet under the stern.

tuck (tŭk; to͝ok), *v. t. & n.* *Chiefly Scot.* Sound; beat.

tuck (tŭk), *n.* [F. *estoc.*] *Hist.* A rapier.

tuck′a·hoe (tŭk′ȧ·hō), *n.* [Of Algonquian origin.] The edible sclerotium of a subterranean fungus (*Poria cocos*).

tuck′er (tŭk′ẽr), *n.* **1.** One who or that which tucks. **2.** Orig., a neckerchief; now, a chemisette.

tuck′er, *v. t.* *Colloq.* To tire; fatigue to exhaustion.

tuck′et (tŭk′ĕt; -ĭt), *n.* [From *tuck* sound, fr. ONF. *toquer* to touch, strike.] A trumpet flourish or fanfare.

-tude (-tūd). [F. *-tude* and L. *-tudo.*] A suffix forming nouns and equivalent to *-ness,* as in promptit*ude.*

Tu′dor (tū′dẽr), *adj.* Of or pertaining to an English royal family descended from Owen Tudor of Wales, who married Catherine, the widow of Henry V, or to the period (1485–1603) of the Tudor sovereigns, Henry VII, Henry VIII, Edward VI, Mary, and Elizabeth. — *n.* A Tudor sovereign, poet, etc.

Tudor architecture *or* **style.** The latest style of English Gothic, that under the Tudors, characterized by a particular type of arch (**Tudor arch**), by shallow moldings, and by much paneling. See ARCH, *Illust.*

‖**tu·e′bor** (tū·ē′bôr). [L.] I will defend; — motto of Michigan.

Tues′day (tūz′dĭ; 13; 114), *n.* [AS. *Tīwesdæg.*] The third day of the week; the day following Monday. Abbr. *Tues., Tu.*

tu′fa (tōō′fȧ; tū′fȧ), *n.* [It. *tufo* soft, sandy stone, fr. L. *tofus, tophus, tufus.*] *Geol.* **a** A porous rock formed as a deposit from springs or streams; — usually in phrase ***calcareous tufa.*** **b** Tuff. — **tu·fa′ceous** (tōō·fā′shŭs; tū-), *adj.*

tuff (tŭf), *n.* [F. *tuf,* fr. It. *tufo.*] A rock composed of the finer kinds of volcanic detritus, usually stratified. — **tuff·a′ceous** (tŭf·ā′shŭs), *adj.*

tuft (tŭft), *n.* [OF. *tufe, tofe, toffe* (F. *touffe*).] **1.** A small cluster of elongated flexible parts or outgrowths, as hairs, feathers, blades of grass, etc., close together or attached at the base. **2.** A cluster; clump; esp. any of the clusters of threads drawn tightly through a mattress, quilt, etc., to secure the padding; also, a button or leather disk used in the place of such a tuft. **3.** *Slang.* A gold tassel formerly worn by titled students at Cambridge and Oxford; also, the wearer of such a tuft. — *v. t.* **1.** To provide, adorn, secure, etc., with a tuft or tufts. **2.** To fasten padding in (a quilt, mattress, etc.) by stitching at intervals and sewing on tufts. — **tuft′er,** *n.* — **tuft′y,** *adj.*

tuft′ed (tŭf′tĕd; -tĭd), *adj.* **1.** Having a tuft or tufts; finished or decorated with tufts. **2.** Growing in tufts.

tuft′hunt′er (tŭft′hŭn′tẽr), *n.* One who seeks association with tufts (see TUFT, 3); a snob; toady; sycophant. — **tuft′hunt′ing,** *adj.*

tug (tŭg), *v. t. & i.;* TUGGED (tŭgd); TUG′GING. [ME. *tuggen, toggen,* intens.] **1.** To ply or pull (at) strenuously; strain (at). **2.** To drag; haul. **3.** To strive; toil; labor; drudge. **4.** To tow with a tugboat. — **Syn.** See PULL. — *n.* **1.** A tugging; a violent or strong pull or strain. **2.** A supreme effort. **3.** A trace of a harness; any rope, chain, etc., used in pulling something along. **4.** *Naut.* Also **tug′boat′** (tŭg′bōt′). A strongly built steam or power vessel, used for towing; — called also ***towboat.*** — **tug′ger** (tŭg′ẽr), *n.*

tug of war. a A struggle for supremacy. **b** An athletic contest in which a number of men pull on a rope against an equal number.

tu′i (tōō′ē), *n.* [Maori.] A New Zealand bird (*Prosthemadera novaeseelandiae*) having glossy black plumage, with a white tuft on each side of the throat and white streaks on the back of the neck and on the shoulder, noted for its powers of mimicry; — called also *parson bird.*

tuille (twēl), *n.* [F. *tuile* tile, fr. L. *tegula.*] In plate armor, one of the hinged plates before the thigh. See ARMOR, *Illust.*

tu·i′tion (tū·ĭsh′ŭn), *n.* [OF. *tuicion,* MF. *tuition,* fr. L. *tuitio -onis,* protection, fr. *tueri, tuitus,* to watch, guard, protect.] **1.** *Now Rare.* Protection; guardianship. **2.** The act or profession of teaching; instruction. **3.** The price of, or payment for, instruction. — **tu·i′tion·al** (-ăl), **tu·i′tion·ar′y** (-ẽr′ĭ *or, esp. Brit.,* -ẽr·ĭ), *adj.*

tu′la·re′mi·a, tu′la·rae′mi·a (tōō′lȧ·rē′mĭ·ȧ), *n.* [NL., fr. *Tulare* Co., Calif. + *-emia, -aemia.*] A disease of rodents, man, and some domestic animals, caused by a microorganism (*Pasteurella tularensis*) transmitted chiefly by insects, esp. horseflies, and producing in man a fever.

tu′le (to͞o′lē), *n.* [Sp., fr. Nahuatl *tollin* rush.] Either of two large bulrushes (*Scirpus lacustris* and *S. acutus*) growing on overflowed land in the southwestern United States.

tu′lip (tū′lĭp), *n.* [Obs. D. *tulipa* (D. *tulp*), obs. F. *tulipan* (F. *tulipe*), fr. colloq. Turk. *tülbend* turban; — so called (in Europe) from the resemblance of the flower to a turban.] Any of a genus (*Tulipa*) of Eurasian bulbous herbs of the lily family with linear or broadly lanceolate leaves and, commonly, a single showy flower; also, its flower or bulb.

tu′lip·o·ma′ni·a (tū′lĭp·ō·mā′nĭ·ȧ), *n.* [NL., fr. *tulip* + *-mania*.] A mania for acquiring or growing tulips, as in Holland about 1634.

tulip tree. A tree (*Liriodendron tulipifera*) which bears tuliplike greenish-yellow flowers; hence, any of various other trees with tulip-shaped flowers.

tu′lip·wood′ (tū′lĭp·wo͝od′), *n.* **1.** The soft white wood of the tulip tree (*Liriodendron*) used for cabinetmaking, etc.; whitewood. **2.** The striped or variegated wood of any of several trees; also, any of the trees yielding such wood.

tulle (to͞ol; tōōl; *F.* tül), *n.* [F., fr. the town *Tulle*, France.] A thin fine net, commonly of silk, for veils, dresses, etc.

tul′li·bee (tŭl′ĭ·bē), *n.* [Can. F. *toulibi*, fr. Cree *otonabi*, lit., mouth water; — from its insipid taste.] A food fish (genus *Leucichthys*) of the north-central United States and adjacent Canada. It is closely allied to the whitefishes.

tum′ble (tŭm′b'l), *v. i.*; TUM′BLED (-b'ld); TUM′BLING (-blĭng). [Freq. of ME. *tumben* to dance, jump, fr. AS. *tumbian* to somersault, dance violently.] **1.** To leap, spring, etc., rhythmically; now, usually, to perform acrobatic feats, such as somersaults, handsprings, etc. **2.** To fall suddenly and violently. **3.** To roll over, or to and fro; roll or toss about. **4.** To move, go, come, pass, jump, etc., in a hasty disorderly manner. — *v. t.* **1.** To cause to tumble, or fall or roll (over or down). **2.** To disorder or throw into disorder; toss recklessly here and there, or the like. **3.** To whirl in a tumbler or tumbling barrel, as for polishing (metal), softening (leather), etc. — *n.* A tumbling; a tumbled state; disorder.

tum′ble·bug′ (-bŭg′), *n.* Also **tum′ble·dung′** (-dŭng′). Any of various scarabaeid beetles (as species of the genera *Scarabaeus*, *Canthon*, *Copris*, and *Phanaeus*) which form masses of dung, which they bury in the ground, and in which they lay their eggs.

tum′ble–down′ (-doun′), *adj.* Ready to fall; dilapidated.

tum′bler (tŭm′blẽr), *n.* **1.** One who tumbles; esp., a tumbling acrobat. **2.** A dog of a breed formerly used in coursing rabbits. **3.** A drinking glass without a foot or stem, orig. made with a pointed or convex base; also, the contents of a tumbler. **4.** *Chiefly Dial.* A variety of cart; a tumbrel. **5.** Any of certain domestic pigeons having the habit of tumbling, or somersaulting backward in flight. **6.** A movable obstruction in a lock, consisting of a lever, slide, pin, or the like, which must be adjusted to a particular position, as by a key, before the bolt can be thrown. See LOCK, *Illust.* **7.** A device or mechanism for tumbling (see TUMBLE, *v. t.*, 3), as a drum in which hides are washed and softened; also, the one who operates a tumbler. **8.** A type of toy, so formed and weighted as to rock or tumble at a slight touch. **9.** In a gunlock, a piece on which the mainspring acts. **10.** *Mach.* **a** A projecting piece on a revolving shaft or rockshaft, for actuating another piece. **b** The movable part of a reversing or speed-changing gear (**tumbler gear**).

tum′ble·weed′ (tŭm′b'l·wēd′), *n.* *U. S.* Any plant, as the bugseed, certain amaranths, etc., which breaks away from its roots in the autumn, and is driven about by the wind.

tum′bling bar′rel (tŭm′blĭng). A revolving cask in which small metal parts are polished, as by mutual attrition.

tum′brel (tŭm′brĕl), **tum′bril** (-brĭl), *n.* [OF. *tomberel*, *tumerel*, a tipcart, fr. *tomber* to fall, tumble, and *tumer* to dance, turn somersaults.] **1.** *Hist.* An instrument of torture; specif., a cucking stool. **2.** A cart; esp., a farmer's cart or wagon. **3.** In the French Revolution, such a cart or any vehicle used to convey the condemned to the guillotine. **4.** *Mil.* A two-wheeled cart carrying tools, cartridges, etc.

tu′me·fa′cient (tū′mē·fā′shĕnt), *adj.* [L. *tumefaciens*, *-entis*, pres. part. of *tumefacere* to tumefy, fr. *tumere* to swell + *facere* to make.] *Med.* Producing swelling.

tu′me·fac′tion (-făk′shŭn), *n.* **1.** Act of tumefying; state of being swollen. **2.** A tumor; swelling.

tu′me·fy (tū′mē·fī), *v. t. & i.*; TU′ME·FIED (-fīd); TU′ME·FY′ING. [F. *tuméfier*, fr. L. *tumere* to swell + *-ficare* (in comp.) to make.] To swell or become swelled.

tu·mes′cent (tū·mĕs′ĕnt; -'nt), *adj.* [L. *tumescens*, *-entis*, pres. part. of *tumescere* to swell up, fr. *tumere* to swell.] Slightly tumid or swollen. — **tu·mes′cence** (-ĕns; -'ns), *n.*

tu′mid (tū′mĭd), *adj.* [L. *tumidus*, fr. *tumere* to swell.] **1.** Swollen, enlarged, or distended. **2.** Bulging; protuberant. **3.** Figuratively: **a** Pompous; inflated; bombastic; — of style, etc. **b** Teeming; bursting. — **Syn.** See INFLATED. — **tu·mid′i·ty** (tū·mĭd′ĭ·tĭ), *n.* — **tu′mid·ly**, *adv.* — **tu′mid·ness**, *n.*

tu′mor, tu′mour (tū′mẽr), *n.* [OF. or L.; OF. *tumour* (F. *tumeur*), fr. L. *tumor*.] **1.** A swollen or distended part; specif., *Med.*, an abnormal mass of tissue, not inflammatory, arising without obvious cause from cells of pre-existent tissue, possessing no physiological function. **2.** *Now Rare.* Tumidity. — **tu′mor·ous** (-ŭs), *adj.*

tump (tŭmp; to͞omp), *n.* *Eng.* **a** A hillock. **b** A clump of trees on a height. **c** A heap.

tu′mu·lar (tū′mū·lẽr), *adj.* [L. *tumulus* a mound.] Consisting of, pertaining to, or resembling a tumulus.

tu′mu·lose (-lōs), **tu′mu·lous** (-lŭs), *adj.* [L. *tumulosus*, fr. *tumulus* a mound.] Full of small hills or mounds.

tu′mult (tū′mŭlt *or, esp. Brit.*, -mŭlt), *n.* [OF. or L.; OF. *tumulte*, fr. L. *tumultus*.] **1.** Commotion or agitation of a multitude, usually with great uproar and confusion of voices. **2.** Turbulence combined with din. **3.** Violent agitation of mind or feelings; a violent outburst.

tu·mul′tu·ar′y (tū·mŭl′tū·ĕr′ĭ *or, esp. Brit.*, -ẽr·ĭ), *adj.* Attended or characterized by tumult, mob action, lawlessness, confusion, or impetuosity.

tu·mul′tu·ous (-ŭs), *adj.* Characterized by tumult; full of turbulence, commotion, agitation, etc. — **tu·mul′tu·ous·ly**, *adv.* — **tu·mul′tu·ous·ness**, *n.*

tu′mu·lus (tū′mū·lŭs), *n.*; *pl.* -LI (-lī). [L., hillock, sepulchral mound.] An artificial hillock or mound, as over a grave, esp. an ancient grave; a barrow.

tun (tŭn), *n.* [AS. *tunne* a tun, tub, a large vessel.] **1.** A large cask, esp. for wine. **2.** Hence, the capacity of a tun as a varying liquid measure, in England formerly equivalent to two pipes (see PIPE, *n.*, 7) and legal at 252 wine gallons.

tu′na (to͞o′nȧ), *n.* [Sp., fr. Taino *tuna*.] Any of various flat-jointed prickly pears of the genus *Opuntia*, esp. *O. tuna*, common in tropical America; also, the edible fruit.

tu′na, *n.*; see PLURAL, *Note*, 3. Also **tuna fish.** [Am. Sp., fr. Sp. *atún*, after E. *tunny*.] A tunny, esp., a Pacific-coast species (*Thunnus* saliens), and a Florida-coast species (*Neothunnus allisoni*).

tun′a·ble (tūn′ȧ·b'l), *adj.* Also **tune′a·ble.** **1.** Tuneful; melodious. **2.** Being in tune; agreeable. **3.** Capable of being tuned. — **tun′a·ble·ness**, *n.* — **tun′a·bly**, *adv.*

tun′dra (to͝on′drȧ; tŭn′-), *n.* [Russ.] One of the level or undulating treeless plains of northern arctic regions.

tune (tūn; 114), *n.* [ME. *tun*, *tune*, vars. of *tone*. See TONE.] **1.** *Now Rare.* A sound; tone. **2.** A succession of musical tones constituting a melody; an air. **3.** The state or capacity of giving tones of proper pitch; agreement of a voice or instrument in pitch. **4.** Harmony or concord in mind or mood; right frame of mind or attitude. — *v. t.* **1.** To adjust (a voice or instrument) to a given musical pitch or temperament. **2.** To put in tune with itself or another; attune. **3.** To adapt in pitch, tone, or esp., mood. **4.** To utter musically or in song. — *v. i.* To sound in tune; harmonize. — ***tune in.*** *Radio.* To adjust the receiving apparatus to resonance with the frequency of a particular transmitting station from which signals are to be received. — ***tune out.*** *Radio.* To adjust a receiving apparatus so as not to receive (unwanted signals). — ***tune up.*** **1.** To adjust instruments for playing together; to tune an instrument to the proper pitch. **2.** *Mach.* To adjust an engine, as of an automobile, so that it is in first-class running condition. — **tun′er** (tūn′ẽr), *n.*

tune′ful (tūn′fo͝ol; -f'l), *adj.* Harmonious; melodious; musical. — **tune′ful·ly**, *adv.* — **tune′ful·ness**, *n.*

tune′less (-lĕs; -lĭs), *adj.* **1.** Not tuneful; unmelodious. **2.** Not producing music.

tung oil (tŭng). [From Chin. (Pek.) *yu²-t'ung²*, in which *yu²* means oil.] A poisonous, fixed oil got from the seeds of a Chinese tree, the **tung tree** (*Aleurites fordii*) and allied species, the most powerful drying oil known.

tung′state (tŭng′stāt), *n.* *Chem.* A salt or ester of tungstic acid.

tung′sten (-stĕn), *n.* [Sw., fr. *tung* heavy + *sten* stone.] *Chem.* A metallic element of the chromium family, white and ductile when pure. Symbol, *W* (wolfram); at. no., 74; at. wt., 183.92. It has the highest melting point (about 3370° C.) of any of the metals and is used for electric-light filaments, for alloying steel, etc. Called also *wolfram*. — **tung·sten′ic** (tŭng·stĕn′ĭk), *adj.*

tungsten lamp. An electric glow lamp having filaments of metallic tungsten and very low watt expenditure.

tungsten steel. Steel containing tungsten and noted for its tenacity, hardness, and resistance to heat.

tung′stic (tŭng′stĭk), *adj.* Of, pertaining to, or containing tungsten, esp. in its valence of six.

tungstic acid. **a** Tungsten trioxide, WO_3, a yellow crystalline powder. **b** Any of various acids corresponding to the above oxide.

tung′stite (tŭng′stīt), *n.* *Mineral.* Native tungsten trioxide, WO_3, a yellow or yellowish-green pulverulent mineral.

Tun·gus′, Tun·guz′ (to͝on·go͞oz′), *n.* **1.** *sing. & pl.* One of a Mongoloid people widely spread over Eastern Siberia. **2.** Also **Tun·gus′ic** (-ĭk). The language of the Tungus, a subfamily of the Ural-Altaic. — **Tun·gus′**, *adj.* — **Tun·gus′ic** (-ĭk), *adj.*

tu′nic (tū′nĭk), *n.* [F. or L.; F. *tunique*, fr. L. *tunica*.] **1.** *Rom. Antiq.* A knee-length or longer girdled undergarment worn by both sexes. **2.** A hip-length or longer blouse or coat, usually belted. **3.** *Bot.* A natural integument. **4.** *Eccl.* A bishop's tunicle. **5.** *Mil. Colloq.* Any undress coat worn by British soldiers. **6.** *Zool. & Anat.* A mantle; a tunica.

‖**tu′ni·ca** (tū′nĭ·kȧ), *n.*; *pl.* -CAE (-sē). [NL.] *Anat. & Zool.* An enveloping membrane or layer of tissue; a mantle.

tu′ni·cate (tū′nĭ·kāt), *n.* Any of a subphylum and class (Tunicata) of marine chordates, as the ascidians; — so called from the characteristic cuticular outer covering (test, or tunic) of the body.

tu′ni·cate (-kāt), *adj.* Also **tu′ni·cat′ed** (-kāt′ĕd; -ĭd). [L. *tunicatus*, past part. of *tunicare* to clothe with a tunic, fr. *tunica* tunic.] **1.** *Bot.* Covered with a tunic; coated with layers, as an onion. **2.** *Zool.* Having a tunica or mantle.

tu′ni·cle (tū′nĭ·k'l), *n.* [L. *tunicula*, dim. of *tunica* a tunic.] *R.C.Ch.* A short vestment, esp. a close-fitting one worn by a bishop under the dalmatic. See VESTMENT, *Illust.*

tun′ing fork (tūn′ĭng). *Music.* A steel instrument consisting of two prongs and a handle, which, being struck, gives a certain fixed tone that serves as a standard for tuning instruments.

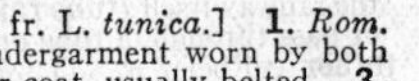

Tuning Fork.

tun′nage (tŭn′ĭj). Var. of TONNAGE.

tun′nel (tŭn′ĕl; -'l), *n.* [OF. *tonel*, *tonnel*, tun, cask, F. *tonnelle* a semicircular vault, a tunnel net, an arbor, dim. of *tonne* a tun.] **1.** *Now Rare.* **a** A smokestack; flute; pipe. **b** A funnel. **2.** A subterranean passageway, esp. one for a road, railroad, canal, etc., or for a sewer or drain. **3.** A tunnellike excavation; specif., a burrow. **4.** *Mining.* A horizontal or nearly level passage in a mine; loosely, any drift, level, crosscut, or gangway. — *v. t.*; TUN′NELED (-ĕld; -'ld) or TUN′NELLED; TUN′NEL·ING or TUN′NEL·LING. **1.** *Obs.* To form into or like a tunnel. **2.** To make a tunnel or tunnellike opening through or under. — *v. i.* To construct a tunnel. — **tun′nel·er, tun′nel·ler**, *n.*

tun′ny (tŭn′ĭ), *n.*; see PLURAL, *Note*, 3. [F. *thon*, fr. Pr. *ton*, fr. L. *thunnus*, *thynnus*, fr. Gr. *thynnos*, *thynos*.] Any of several mackerellike, edible, coarse-fleshed, oily fishes (family Thunnidae); a tuna; esp. the ***great tunny*** (*Thunnus thynnus*) found in all warm seas and sometimes weighing a thousand pounds. The common tunny (*T. secundodorsalis*) of the northern American Atlantic coast is called *horse mackerel*, and a Pacific-coast species (*T. saliens*) is sought as a game fish.

tup (tŭp), *n.* [ME. *tuppe*, *tupe*.] **1.** A ram (male of the sheep). **2.** Any of various devices acting by impact, as the weight in a pile driver. — *v. t.*; TUPPED (tŭpt); TUP′PING. To cover; — of a ram.

tu′pe·lo (to͞o′pĕ·lō), *n.*; *pl.* -LOS (-lōz). Also **tupelo gum.** [Creek *eto opelwv*, lit., swamp tree.] See GUM, *n.*, 5.

Tu·pi′ (to͞o·pē′), *n.* **a** Any Indian of the group of Tupian tribes dwelling in central and northern Brazil. **b** The language of the Tupis, esp., the northern dialect, widely used as a lingua franca in the valley of the Amazon.

Tu·pi′an (to͞o·pē′ăn), *adj.* Pertaining to or designating an important linguistic family occupying many scattered areas in central South America, but esp. the valley of the Amazon. Its two main branches are the Tupi, its northern dialect, and the Guarani, its southern dialect. See LANGUAGE, *Table.*

tup′pence (tŭp′ĕns), **tup′pen·ny** (tŭp′ĕn·ĭ). *Colloq.* for TWOPENCE, TWOPENNY.

tuque (tūk), *n.* [Can. F. See TOQUE.] **1.** A type of warm cap for winter wear, made from a knit bag with closed tapered ends by pushing one end up in the other. **2.** A similar tight-fitting knitted cap of a single thickness gathered in at the peak and worn with the bottom folded back. Cf. WATCH CAP.

‖**tu quo′que** (tū kwō′kwē). [L.] Thou also; — a retort charging an adversary with being or doing the same as oneself.

Tu·ra′ni·an (tū·rā′nĭ·ăn), *adj.* [Per. *Tūrān* the region north of the Oxus, Turkestan.] Ural-Altaic. — *n.* **1.** A member of any of the peoples of Ural-Altaic stock. **2.** The Ural-Altaic languages collectively. — **Tu·ra′ni·an·ism** (-ĭz′m), *n.*

tur′ban (tûr′băn), *n.* [Turk. and F.; F. *turban*, earlier *turbant, tulban*, fr. Turk. *dülbend*, colloq. *tülbend*, a length or square of muslin, a turban, fr. Per. *dulband* turban, sash.] **1.** A headdress worn by men in the Levant and by most male Moslems, consisting of a cap, with a sash, scarf, or shawl, wound about it. **2.** A headdress resembling the Oriental turban. **3.** A type of woman's or child's hat with no brim or with brim turned up close to the crown.

tur′ba·ry (tûr′bȧ·rĭ), *n.; pl.* -RIES (-rĭz). [OF. *turberie, tourberie*, peat bog, fr. *tourbe* peat, of Teut. origin.] *Eng. Law.* An easement to dig turf or peat on another's land; also, the ground where turf is dug.

tur′bel·lar′i·an (tûr′bĕ·lâr′ĭ·ăn), *n.* [L. *turbellae* a bustle, stir, dim. fr. *turba* disturbance; — because the cilia cause tiny currents in the water.] Any member of a class (*Turbellaria*) of flatworms consisting of the planarians. — **tur′bel·lar′i·an**, *adj.*

tur′beth (tûr′bĕth; -bĭth), **tur′bith** (-bĭth). Vars. of TURPETH.

tur′bid (tûr′bĭd), *adj.* [L. *turbidus*, fr. *turbare* to disturb, fr. *turba* a disorder, tumult, crowd.] **1.** Having the lees or sediment disturbed; roiled. **2.** Clouded or cloudy; not clear or translucent. **3.** Muddled; not lucid. — **tur·bid′i·ty** (tûr·bĭd′ĭ·tĭ), **tur′bid·ness**, *n.*

Syn. **Turbid, muddy, roily** mean clouded with or as with sediment. **Turbid** specifically implies a disturbance or stirring up until darkened, obscured, confused, or the like; **muddy**, the presence of mud, or something suggesting mud, which darkens, discolors, muddles, or the like; **roily**, turbidness and agitation.

tur′bi·dim′e·ter (tûr′bĭ·dĭm′ē·tẽr), *n.* [ML. *turbiditas* turbidity + *-meter.*] An instrument for comparing the turbidity of liquids by viewing light through them and determining how much light is cut off by them; also, loosely, a nephelometer. — **tur′bi·dim′e·try** (-trĭ), *n.* — **tur′bi·di·met′ric** (-dĭ·mĕt′rĭk), *adj.*

tur′bi·nal (tûr′bĭ·năl; -n'l), *adj.* [L. *turbo, turben, -inis*, a top, whirl.] *Anat. & Zool.* Rolled in a spiral; scroll-like; turbinate; — applied to the thin, plicated, bony or cartilaginous plates on the walls of the nasal chambers. — *n.* Also **tur′bi·nat′ed bone** (-nāt′ĕd; -ĭd). A turbinal bone or cartilage.

tur′bi·nate (-nāt), **tur′bi·nat′ed** (-nāt′ĕd; -ĭd), *adj.* [L. *turbinatus.*] **1.** *Anat. & Zool.* Turbinal. **2.** *Bot.* Shaped like a top, or inverted cone. **3.** *Zool.* Spiral with whorls decreasing rapidly from base to apex; — said of certain shells. — **tur′bi·na′tion** (-nā′shŭn), *n.*

tur′bine (tûr′bĭn; -bīn), *n.* [F., fr. L. *turbo, -inis*, that which spins, or whirls round, whirl.] A rotary engine actuated by the reaction, impulse, or both, of a current of fluid subject to pressure. A turbine usually consists of a series of curved vanes on a central rotating spindle.

tur′bit (tûr′bĭt), *n.* A pigeon of a fancy breed having a short head and beak and a frilled breast.

tur′bo- (tûr′bō-). A combining form for *turbine*, meaning: **a** *Coupled directly to a driving turbine*, as **tur′bo·blow′er, tur′bo·com·pres′sor. b** *Consisting of a turbine*, as **tur′bo·ven′ti·la′tor.**

tur′bo·fan′ (-făn′), *n.* *Aeronautics.* A fan directly connected to and driven by a turbine, usually by means of a common shaft. It is used to supply air for cooling, for ventilation, or for combustion.

tur′bo·jet′ en′gine (tûr′bō·jĕt′). *Aeronautics.* A jet engine having a turbine-driven air compressor for supplying compressed air to the combustion chamber and a discharge nozzle for directing the heated air and exhaust gases rearward. This engine produces thrust only by means of a high-speed jet of hot gases.

tur′bo–pro·pel′ler en′gine (-prō·pĕl′ẽr). *Aeronautics.* A jet engine having a turbine-driven propeller, designed to produce thrust principally by means of a propeller, although additional thrust is usually obtained from the hot exhaust gases which issue in a jet; — called also **tur′bo·prop′** (-prŏp′), *or* **tur′bo·prop′–jet′** (-prŏp′jĕt′), **en′gine.**

tur′bo–ram′–jet′ en′gine. *Aeronautics.* A jet engine consisting essentially of a turbojet engine with provisions for burning additional fuel in the tail pipe, or portion of the engine to the rear of the turbine, thus making it possible to obtain higher gas temperatures in the exhaust jet than can be tolerated by the turbine blades.

tur′bo·su′per·charge′ (tûr′bō·sū′pẽr·chärj′), *v. t.* To equip with a turbosupercharger.

tur′bo·su′per·charg′er (-sū′pẽr·chär′jẽr), *n.* A supercharger driven by a turbine that is operated by the hot exhaust gases of an airplane engine, for increasing engine efficiency. See SUPERCHARGER, *Illust.*

tur′bot (tûr′bŭt), *n. sing. & pl.* [OF. *tourbout*, fr. OSw. *törnbut.*] **a** A European flatfish (*Psetta maxima*) highly esteemed as a food fish and often weighing from 30 to 40 pounds. **b** Any of many somewhat similar flounders.

tur′bu·lence (tûr′bū·lĕns), *n.* Also **tur′bu·len·cy** (-lĕn·sĭ). Quality or state of being turbulent; a situation or event characterized by tumult.

tur′bu·lent (-lĕnt), *adj.* [F. or L.; F., fr. L. *turbulentus*, fr. *turba* disorder, tumult.] **1.** Causing or inciting violence, unrest, or disturbance. **2.** Characterized by agitation or tumult; tempestuous. — **tur′bu·lent·ly**, *adv.*

turbulent flow. Fluid flow in which the velocity at a given point changes constantly in magnitude and direction; — contrasted with *laminar flow.*

Tur′co (tûr′kō), *n.; pl.* -COS (-kōz). [F. or It. *turco* a Turk.] A member of the force of French Algerian infantry (technically *Algerian tirailleurs*) composed chiefly of natives, the chief officers being French.

Tur′co- (tûr′kō-). Var. of TURKO-.

Tur′co·man (tûr′kō·măn), *n.; pl.* -MANS (-mănz). Var. of TURKOMAN.

tur′di·form (tûr′dĭ·fôrm), *adj.* [L. *turdus* a thrush + *-form.*] *Zool.* Having the form or structure of a thrush.

tur′dine (tûr′dīn; -dĭn), *adj.* [L. *turdus* thrush.] Belonging to a widely distributed family (Turdidae) of singing birds including the true thrushes which constitute a subfamily (Turdinae).

tu·reen′ (tū·rēn′; to͞o-), *n.* [F. *terrine*, fr. L. *terrenus*, fr. L. *terra* earth.] A large deep vessel from which soup is served at the table.

turf (tûrf), *n.; pl.* TURFS (tûrfs), *sometimes* TURVES (tûrvz). [AS.] **1.** The upper stratum of earth and vegetable mold filled with the roots of grass and other small plants, so as to form a kind of mat; sward; sod; also, a piece or slab of this; a sod. **2.** Peat, esp. when used or ready for fuel. **3.** Usually with *the.* The course for, or the sport of, horse racing. Hence, **turf′man.** — *v. t.* To cover with turf or sod.

turf′y (tûr′fĭ), *adj.;* TURF′I·ER (-fĭ·ẽr); TURF′I·EST. **1.** Abounding with turf; made of, or covered with, turf. **2.** Having the nature or appearance of turf. **3.** Of, pertaining to, or smacking of the turf, or horse racing. — **turf′i·ness** (tûr′fĭ·nĕs; -nĭs), *n.*

tur·ges′cent (tûr·jĕs′ĕnt; -'nt), *adj.* [L. *turgescens, -entis*, pres. part. of *turgescere.*] Becoming turgid, distended, or inflated; swelling. — **tur·ges′cence** (-ĕns; -'ns), **tur·ges′cen·cy** (-ĕn·sĭ; -'n·sĭ), *n.*

tur′gid (tûr′jĭd), *adj.* [L. *turgidus*, fr. *turgere* to swell.] **1.** Distended by some internal agent or expansive force; inflated; swollen; bloated. **2.** Swelling in style or language; vainly ostentatious; bombastic; pompous. — **Syn.** See INFLATED. — **tur·gid′i·ty** (tûr·jĭd′ĭ·tĭ), **tur′gid·ness**, *n.* — **tur′gid·ly**, *adv.*

tur′gite (tûr′jīt), *n.* [From *Turginsk*, copper mine, Ural Mts.] *Mineral.* An iron ore, consisting of hydrous ferric oxide, $2Fe_2O_3.H_2O$.

tur′gor (tûr′gẽr; -gôr), *n.* [LL., a swelling, fr. *turgere* to swell.] **1.** Turgescence; also, turgidity. **2.** *Physiol.* The state of normal turgidness and tension in living cells; specif., *Plant Physiol.*, the distention of the protoplasmic layer and cell wall by the fluid contents.

Turk (tûrk), *n.* [OF. *turc*, fr. ML. *Turcus*, fr. Turk., Ar., & Per. *Turk.*] **1.** A member of any of the groups of Asiatic peoples speaking Turkic languages who dwell in the region ranging from the Adriatic to the Okhotsk. **2.** A native or inhabitant of Turkey or the Turkish republic, esp. a member of the dominant race. **3. a** *Now Rare.* One of the Moslem faith. **b** One exhibiting any quality attributed to Turks. **4.** A Turkish horse; specif., a race of horses related to the Arabs.

tur′key (tûr′kĭ), *n.* See PLURAL, *Note*, 3. [From *turkey cock*, first applied to the guinea cock, which was imported from Africa through *Turkey* into Europe and with which the Am. bird was for a time identified.] **1.** Either of two species of large American birds of a family (Meleagridae), one of which (*Meleagris gallopavo*) is of wide range in North America, and is domesticated in most parts of the world. **2.** *Orig. Theat. Slang.* A failure; a "flop."

turkey buzzard. An American vulture (*Cathartes aura*) common in South and Central America and in the southern United States.

turkey cock. A male turkey; also, a strutting, pompous person.

Turkey red. A brilliant, durable red produced upon cotton by means of alizarin (or, formerly, madder) in connection with an aluminum mordant and fatty matter.

turkey trot. A ragtime dance of the period of the first World War, danced with the feet well apart and with a rise on the ball of the foot, followed by a drop upon the heel. — **tur′key–trot′**, *v. i.*

Tur′ki (to͝or′kē), *adj.* [Per., fr. *Turk.* See TURK.] **1.** Designating or pertaining to the groups of Turkic languages, as Turkish, or Osmanli. **2.** Designating, or pertaining to, the peoples of Turkic speech, as the Osmanlis in Europe and the Uigurs, Seljuks, Uzbeks, Turkomans, and other Tatar tribes in Asia.

Tur′kic (tûr′kĭk), *adj.* **1.** Designating or pertaining to a subfamily of the Ural-Altaic languages, or the peoples speaking these languages, esp. the Turki groups. See LANGUAGE, *Table.* **2.** Loosely, equivalent to TURKISH.

Turk′ish (tûr′kĭsh), *adj.* Of or pertaining to Turkey or the Turks. — *n.* The language spoken by Turks, esp. by those of Turkey. Since 1928 it has been written in the Roman alphabet. See LANGUAGE, *Table.*

Turkish bath. A type of bath introduced from the East, in which after a profuse perspiration has been induced in a superheated room, the body is washed, rubbed, kneaded, etc.

Turkish delight *or* **paste.** A confection of jellylike consistency, usually cut in cubes and dusted with sugar.

Turkish tobacco. A very aromatic tobacco grown in certain districts of Turkey, Greece, Syria, and other parts of the Levant and used in cigarettes.

Turkish, *or* **turkish, towel** *or* **toweling.** A cotton or linen towel or towel fabric having rough surfaces formed by raised loops or a thick pile.

Turk′ism (tûr′kĭz′m), *n.* Turkish customs, beliefs, institutions, and principles; also, *Rare*, a Turkish idiom.

Turk′man (tûrk′măn), *n.; pl.* -MEN (-mĕn). A native or inhabitant of the Turkmen Soviet Socialist Republic. — **Turk·me′ni·an** (tûrk-mē′nĭ·ăn), *adj.*

Tur′ko- (tûr′kō-). Also **Tur′co-.** [ML. *Turcus* Turk.] A combining form, meaning *Turkic, Turki, Turkish, Turkish and*, as in:

Turko-Bulgar	**Turko-Italian**	**Turkophobe**
Turko-Greek	**Turkophile**	**Turko-Tatar**

Tur′ko·man (tûr′kō·măn), *n.; pl.* -MANS (-mănz). [Per. *Turkmān* Turklike.] A member of any of a group of tribes of East Turkic stock dwelling in the Turkmen, Uzbek, and Kazakh, Soviet Socialist Republics of western Asia. They are chiefly Mohammedan.

Turk's′–head′, *n.* *Naut.* A knot of turbanlike form worked on a rope with a piece of small line.

tur′ma·line (tûr′mȧ·lĭn; -lēn). Var. of TOURMALINE.

tur′mer·ic (tûr′mẽr·ĭk), *n.* [Earlier *tormerik, tarmaret*, fr. F. *terre-mérite*, fr. ML. *terra merita*, lit., deserved, or deserving, earth.] **1.** An East Indian herb (*Curcuma longa*) of the ginger family; also, its aromatic rootstock, used as a condiment, yellow dye, and medicine. **2.** Any of several other plants yielding colored juices, as the bloodroot.

turmeric paper. Paper impregnated with turmeric, used as a test for alkaline substances, which turn it from yellow to brown, and for boric acid, which turns it red-brown.

tur′moil (tûr′moil), *n.* [Origin uncert.] Harassing confusion of sounds, movements, thoughts, etc.; turbulence; tumult; also, *Rare*, harassing labor.

turn (tûrn), *v. t.* [AS. *turnian, tyrnan*, combined with OF. *torner, turner*, both fr. L. *tornare* to turn in a lathe, to round off, fr. *tornus* a lathe, fr. Gr. *tornos* a turner's chisel.] **1.** To cause to revolve; rotate. **2. a** To revolve mentally; ponder; — often with *over*. **b** To execute by revolving, as handsprings. **3.** To shape by applying a cutting tool while revolving; form in a lathe; hence, to give a finished or well-rounded form to; as, to *turn* a phrase. **4.** To cause to move around so as to open, close, tighten, etc., something; as, to *turn* a cock; release, lower, etc. (something) by such a movement; as, to *turn* on the gas. **5.** To cause to change position, posture, or part exposed; as, to *turn* a chair to the light; to *turn* the pages of a book. **6.** To invert; reverse the sides or surfaces of; specif.: **a** To dig or plow so as to bring the lower soil to the surface. **b** To make over (a dress, coat, etc.) by reversing the material. **7.** To reverse the order of or arrangement in; as, to *turn* things topsy-turvy. **8.** To upset; derange; unsettle; specif., nauseate; as, the sight *turned* his stomach. **9.** To divert; deflect; to bend or change the course of; specif.: **a** To convert; as, to *turn* one to religion. **b** To pervert. **c** To prejudice; as, to *turn* a child against his father. **10.** To make go or move back; specif.: **a** To repel; as, to *turn* attackers by sharp fire. **b** To make rebound or recoil; as, to *turn* a joke against one. **c** To make look back; avert; as, *turn* your eyes. **11.** To move, so as to aim, point, make play, etc.; direct; as, to *turn* a hose on a fire. **12.** To direct the employment or use of; as, to *turn* everything to account. **13.** To drive; dismiss; as, to *turn* one adrift. **14.** To cause to rise, fall, etc.; — in set phrases; as, ***turn a hair,*** show a sign of discomposure. **15.** To keep (money, goods, etc.) moving, circulating, or passing in trade; also, to earn; as, to *turn* a penny. **16.** To take a circular course around; pass around; as, to *turn* the enemy's flank. **17.** To pass or go beyond (an age, amount, etc.). **18.** To change; transform; also, translate. **19.** To ferment, sour, curdle, etc.; as, to *turn* milk. **20.** To affect (a person or thing) so as to be or become; as, to *turn* one sick. **21.** To dispose of by exchanging for an equivalent; as, to *turn* stock into cash; also, to transfer. **22.** To cause to curve, bend, fold back, etc., as by pressure or meeting resistance; hence, ***to turn the edge or point of,*** to blunt, dull, etc. — **Syn.** See CURVE.

— *v. i.* **1.** To move circularly or in a circle; revolve; rotate; swing; pivot; as, to *turn* on one's heels. **2.** Hence: **a** To reel. **b** To hinge; depend; as, the decision *turns* on one fact. **c** To center; concentrate. **3.** To operate a lathe. **4.** To reverse one's or its course or direction; go backward or in the opposite direction; hence: **a** To recoil. **b** To redound. **5.** To reverse one's policy, attitude, etc.; hence: **a** To rebel; as, the worm will *turn*. **b** To make retaliation; as, to *turn* upon an accuser. **6.** To direct oneself or itself; as, his genius *turned* to painting. **7.** To change one's or its direction; shift; as, the wind has *turned*. **8.** Specif.: **a** To face about; glance back or to the side; as, he heard but did not *turn*. **b** To avert one's eyes; as, to *turn* from a sight. **c** To incline; move from a point of rest; as, these scales will *turn* on the weight of a hair. **d** To be variable or inconstant. **9.** To be changed, altered, or transformed; also, to become (such) by a change or changes; as, to *turn* sour or pale. **10.** Specif.: **a** To become acid, rancid, or putrid; sour. **b** To become mentally deranged. **c** To be nauseated; — of the stomach. **d** To change color; — esp. of leaves. **e** *Chiefly Ir.* To change one's religion. **11.** To become curved or bent; hence, of an edge, to be blunted. — **Syn.** See CURVE.

turn down. To reject; decline; as, to *turn down* an offer. — ***turn in.*** *Colloq.* To go to bed. — ***turn out.*** **a** To drive out; expel. **b** To produce as the result of labor; as, to *turn out* a poem. **c** To extinguish, as by turning a switch. **d** To prove (to be); to become; as, he *turned out* a failure. **e** To come or go out; as, all *turned out* for the parade. — ***turn over a new leaf.*** To make a radical change, usually for the better, in one's way of living or doing. — ***turn tail.*** To run away; flee. — ***turn the corner.*** To pass the crisis safely; begin to improve, succeed, etc. — ***turn the head of.*** To make foolish or foolishly conceited. — ***turn the tables.*** **a** To bring about a reversal of the relative conditions or fortunes of two contending persons or parties. **b** To show that an argument advanced for or against a thesis actually favors the other side. — ***turn to.*** **a** To set to work. **b** To have recourse or resort to. **c** To use, employ, etc., so as to acquire (profit, advantage, etc.). — ***turn turtle.*** Of a vessel, to capsize bottom upward; loosely, to overturn. — ***turn up.*** **a** To find or be found; as, the book *turned up*. **b** To happen or occur unexpectedly.

— *n.* **1.** A turning around; revolution; rotation. **2.** A round, wind, twist, or coil; also, a convolution. **3.** A reeling; a spell of faintness, dizziness, etc.; *Colloq.*, a nervous start or shock. **4.** A single trip including the return; as, take a *turn* in the park. **5.** A changing of course, position, etc.; a turning aside, back, face about, etc.; as, the *turn* of the tide. **6.** Hence: **a** A change in tendency, drift, policy, trend, or the like; as, a *turn* in one's luck. **b** An occasion; an exigency; — chiefly in ***at every turn,*** that is, constantly. **7.** Turning point; specif.: **a** A bend in a road. **b** A crisis. **8.** An unusual or unexpected deed, service, office, or the like; as, to do one a good *turn*. **9.** One's place, time, or opportunity in a scheduled or alternating order; as, to wait one's *turn*. **10.** Hence: **a** A spell; as, to get a *turn* of work on the harvest. **b** *Colloq.* A job; a piece of work; — often a ***hand's turn,*** an act of manual labor. **c** *Brit.* A shift, or tour of duty. **11.** A try or trial; specif., a bout; as, a *turn* at wrestling. **12.** A variation; a difference in type, kind, etc. **13.** Distinctive or characteristic quality, form, fashion, appearance, etc.; as, the *turn* of her neck; to give a story a new *turn*. **14.** Something well-turned or skillfully fashioned. **15.** Natural or special ability or aptitude; bent; as, to have a *turn* for mechanics. **16.** *Mil.* A drill maneuver in which troops in line change direction without preserving their alignment. **17.** *Music.* An ornament consisting of four tones, the first a degree above and the third a degree below the principal tone which comes in the second and fourth positions. When the auxiliary tones are reversed in order the grace is called an ***inverted turn.*** **18.** *Stock Exchange.* A complete transaction involving purchase and sale of securities. **19.** *Theater.* A short act, esp. for a variety show.

— ***by turns.*** **a** Alternately; in succession. **b** At intervals. — ***in turn.*** In due order of succession. — ***to a turn.*** Exactly; perfectly; as, done *to a turn;* — from the practice of cooking on a revolving spit.

turn′a·bout′ (tûrn′*a*·bout′), *n.* **1.** Also **turn′–a·bout′–face′.** A changing from one side, allegiance, etc., to another. **2.** A person who changes or advocates change. **3.** *U. S.* A merry-go-round.

turn′buck′le (tûrn′bŭk′'l), *n.* *Mach.* A loop or sleeve with a screw thread at one end and swivel at the other, or a right-and-left screw link, to tighten a rod, stay, etc.

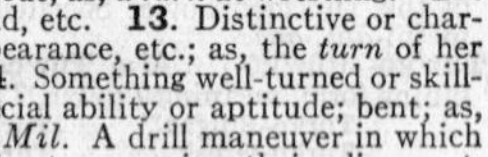

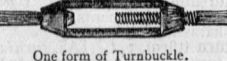

One form of Turnbuckle.

turn′coat′ (-kōt′), *n.* A renegade; apostate.

turn′down′ (-doun′), *adj.* **1.** Capable of being turned down. **2.** Worn with the upper part turned down; as, a *turndown* collar.

turned comma (tûrnd). *Print.* An inverted comma.

turn′er (tûr′nẽr), *n.* One who or that which turns; specif., one who forms articles with a lathe.

turn′er (tûr′nẽr; *G.* tōōr′nẽr), *n.* [G., fr. *turnen*, v., fr. F. *tourner.*] Literally, a gymnast; specif., a member of a Turnverein.

turn′er·y (tûr′nẽr·ĭ), *n.; pl.* -IES (-ĭz). The work, the products, or the shop of a turner or turners.

turn′ing (tûr′nĭng), *n.* **1.** The act or course of one that turns; a rotation, winding, bending, wheeling around, etc. **2.** The place of a turn; angle or corner, as of a road. **3.** A shaping or forming by the use of a lathe; turnery; hence, a fashioning; as, the neat *turning* of a phrase.

tur′nip (tûr′nĭp), *n.* [Formerly *turnep*, appar. fr. *turn*, or F. *tour* a turn + ME. *nepe* a turnip, fr. AS. *nǣp*, fr. L. *napus.*] **1.** The thick edible root of either of two biennial herbs (*Brassica rapa* and *B. napobrassica*) of the mustard family; also, either of these plants. The second species comprises forms more properly called *rutabaga* or *Swedish turnip*. **2.** The roots of these plants cooked and prepared for eating.

tur′nix (tûr′nĭks), *n.* [NL., fr. L. *coturnix* a quail.] Any of a genus (*Turnix*) of small three-toed birds of southern Europe, Asia, and northern Africa that are mostly solitary and live on grassy plains.

turn′key′ (tûrn′kē′), *n.; pl.* TURNKEYS (-kēz′). A person who has charge of the keys of a prison; a warder.

turn′out′ (-out′), *n.* **1.** A coming forth. **2.** *Colloq.* **a** *Chiefly Eng.* A labor strike or striker. **b** A gathering of persons for a special purpose. **c** Act of getting up (from bed). **d** An equipage; a carriage, with its horses, attendants, and equipment. **e** Costume, dress, garb, or the like. **3.** Net yield; output. **4. a** A railroad siding, or sidetrack. **b** A widened space in a road to allow vehicles to pass one another.

turn′o′ver (tûrn′ō′vẽr), *adj.* Admitting of being turned over; turndown. — *n.* **1.** An upset; spill. **2.** A shift from one side, place, opinion, etc., to another. **3.** A pie or tart made by turning one half of a circular crust over the other. **4.** The amount of business done, of work accomplished, etc. **5.** *Econ.* **a** A cycle of purchase, sale, and replacement, of a stock of goods; as, a *turnover* four times a year; also, the rate at which this process takes place. **b** The number of persons hired within a given period to replace those leaving or dropped; also, the ratio of this number to that of the average force maintained; — called, specif., ***labor turnover.***

turn′pike′ (-pīk′), *n.* [*turn* + *pike* a sharp point, or *pike* a weapon.] **1.** *Hist.* = TURNSTILE, 1. **2.** A toll bar or tollgate; also, a road (**turnpike road**) having, or formerly having, a tollgate.

turn′plate′ (-plāt′), *n.* A turntable.

turn′sole′ (-sōl′), *n.* [F. *tournesol*, fr. Sp. *tornasol*, or fr. It. *tornasole*, fr. *tornare* to turn + *sole* the sun, fr. L. *sol.*] **1.** Any of several plants whose flowers or stems are supposed to turn with the sun, as the heliotrope or sunflower. **2.** A European herb (*Chrozophora tinctoria*) of the spurge family, the juice of which is turned blue by ammonia; also, a purple dye obtained from it.

turn′spit′ (-spĭt′), *n.* **1.** One who turns a spit. **2.** A small dog of a breed with long body and short crooked legs, formerly used to turn a spit.

turn′stile′ (-stīl′), *n.* **1.** Orig., a post with four arms pivoted on the top, set in a passageway so that persons may pass by turning the arms, but not cattle, horses, etc. **2.** A similar device, as at a doorway, to register the number of persons passing through.

turn′stone′ (-stōn′), *n.* A migratory shore bird (genus *Arenaria*), ploverlike in form and habits, but allied also to the sandpipers; esp., the common turnstone (*A. interpres*) of the Old World, or the similar American species, the ***ruddy turnstone*** (*A. i. morinella*) and the ***black turnstone*** (*A. melanocephala*).

turn′ta′ble (-tā′b'l), *n.* **1.** A revolvable platform; as: **a** A platform with a track for turning a locomotive. **b** The rotating platform of a phonograph which carries the record. **2.** A machine that reproduces speech, music, etc., from records and transcriptions for radiobroadcasting; — called also *transcription machine* or *playback machine*.

turn′up′ (-ŭp′), *adj.* Turned up; made or fitted to be turned up. — *n.* Something turned up.

‖**Turn′ver·ein′** (tōōrn′fĕr·īn′), *n.* [G. fr., *turnen* to exercise + *verein* a club.] An association of gymnasts and athletes.

tur′pen·tine (tûr′pĕn·tīn), *n.* [OF. *turbentine*, *terbentine*, fr. L., fr. Gr. *terebinthos* the turpentine tree.] **1. a** A yellow to brown semifluid oleoresin, the exudation of the terebinth; — called specif. ***Chian turpentine.*** **b** An oleoresin derived from various coniferous trees, as the Georgia pine and the loblolly. **2.** Popularly: **a** The essential oil (***oil of turpentine*** or ***spirits of turpentine***) obtained from the various turpentines by distillation. **b** A similar oil obtained from pine and other resinous woods. — *v. t.* **1.** To saturate or rub with turpentine; to apply turpentine to. **2.** To extract turpentine from (pine trees).

tur′peth (tûr′pĕth; -pĭth), *n.* [ML. *turpethum*, deriv. of Ar. & Per. *tirbid.*] **1.** The root of a tropical Asiatic and Australian vine (*Ipomoea turpethum*) of the morning-glory family, formerly used as a purgative; also, the plant. **2.** Also **turpeth mineral.** A basic mercuric sulfate, $HgSO_4.2HgO$, used as a purgative.

tur′pi·tude (tûr′pĭ·tūd), *n.* [F., fr. L. *turpitudo*, fr. *turpis* foul, base.] Inherent baseness; depravity.

tur′quoise (tûr′koiz; tûr′kwoiz), *n.; pl.* TURQUOISES (-ĕz; -ĭz), sometimes TURQUOISE. [F., prop. fem. of OF. *turcois*, *turquois*, *turqueis*, Turkish; — because first brought from or through Turkey.] **1.** *Mineral.* A blue, bluish-green, or greenish-gray, hydrous basic phosphate of aluminum, $Al_2(OH)_3PO_4.H_2O$, containing a little copper. H., 6. Sp. gr., 2.60–2.83. It takes a high polish, and when blue is valued as a gem; hence, the gem. **2.** Also **turquoise blue.** The color of the turquoise, greenish green-blue in hue, of medium saturation and high brilliance. See COLOR.

tur′ret (tûr′ĕt; -ĭt; 117), *n.* [OF. *torete*, *tourete*, dim. of *tur*, *tor*, *tour*, tower, fr. L. *turris.*] **1.** A little tower, often a merely ornamental structure at an angle of a larger structure. **2.** *Mach.* A pivoted and revolving toolholder; — called also ***tur′ret·head′.*** **3.** *Mil. Antiq.* A movable tall building, usually moved on wheels, and carrying soldiers, engines, rams, etc., for breaching or scaling a wall. **4.** *Nav. & Mil.* **a** A towerlike structure, heavily armored and usually revolving, within which heavy guns are mounted. **b** A gunner's enclosed compartment in an airplane, usually power-driven for raising or lowering so as to protrude fully from the fuselage only when in use. **c** The cylindrical armored structure surmounting a tank, rotatable for swinging the gun mounted within it.

tur'ret·ed (tûr'ĕt·ĕd; -ĭd; tûr'ĭt-), *adj.* **1.** Furnished with a turret or turrets; turret-shaped. **2.** *Zool.* Designating shells in which the whorls form a high conical spiral.

tur·ric'u·late (tŭ·rĭk'ů·lāt), **tur·ric'u·lat'ed** (-lāt'ĕd; -ĭd), *adj.* [L. *turricula* little tower, turret.] **a** Having or like a small turret or turrets. **b** *Zool.* Of shells, turreted.

tur'ri·lite (tûr'ĭ·līt), *n.* [L. *turris* tower + Gr. *lithos* stone.] *Paleontol.* Any of a genus (*Turrilites*) of Cretaceous cephalopods having a spiral, sinistral, turreted shell with the later whorls more or less separate.

tur'tle (tûr't'l), *n.* [AS. *turtle*, masc. *turtla*, fr. L. *turtur*.] *Archaic.* A turtledove.

tur'tle, *n.*; see PLURAL, Note, 3. [Corrupt. by sailors (after *turtle-dove*) of F. *tortue*. See TORTOISE.] **1.** Any of an order (Chelonia) of land, fresh-water, and marine reptiles having a toothless horny beak, and a bony shell (see CARAPACE, PLASTRON) which encloses the trunk, and into which in many species the head, limbs, and tail, may be withdrawn. The restriction of the term *turtle* to the aquatic or, more narrowly, marine forms is not warranted by modern usage, though sea turtles are rarely called *tortoise* and land turtles are oftener called *tortoise* than *turtle*. Land turtles include: the North American *box tortoise* or *box turtle* (3 species of genus *Terrapene*), which can withdraw entirely within its shell and close the shell by hinged joints on the bottom; the common *Greek tortoise* (*Testudo graeca*) of southern Europe, Asia Minor, etc.; and the *giant tortoise* (*Testudo*, including many extinct species) of the Galápagos Islands and islands of the Indian Ocean. Fresh-water turtles include: the *mud turtles*, *terrapins*, or *tortoises* of U. S. (esp. of genus *Kinosternon*), the *snapping turtles*, which seize their prey with a snap of the jaws, esp. the common U. S. species (*Chelydra serpentina*) and the edible *alligator snapper*, *terrapin*, *tortoise*, or *turtle* (*Macrochelys temminckii*) of the rivers of the Gulf states; the *soft-shelled turtle* (of the family Tryonychidae), with soft leathery skin, found in parts of Africa, Asia, and North America, esp. in the Great Lakes and Mississippi Valley; and some species of *terrapin* (see TERRAPIN). Marine turtles include: the *bastard turtle* (*Colpochelys kempii*) of the U. S. Atlantic coast; the large edible *green turtle* (*Chelonia mydas*) found widely in warm seas; the large *hawksbill turtle*, *hawksbill*, or *tortoise-shell turtle* (*Eretmochelys imbricata*), whose shell, with large overlapping horny plates, furnishes the best commercial tortoise shell; the *leatherback* (*Dermochelys coriacea*), the largest existing marine species, sometimes reaching 9 feet and weighing over 1000 pounds, with flexible shell composed of a mosaic of small bones embedded in a leathery skin; and the large *loggerhead* or *loggerhead turtle* (*Caretta* or a closely related genus, esp. *Caretta caretta*) of the warmer parts of the Atlantic Ocean. **2.** The flesh of certain of these reptiles, as the terrapin, cooked and served for food. — *v. i.; Turt'led* (-'ld); *Tur'tling* (-tlĭng). To catch turtles, esp. as an occupation.

Hawksbill Turtle. (½₀)

tur'tle·back' (tûr't'l·băk'), *n.* A part rounded similarly to the back of a turtle; specif., *Shipbuilding*, a convex deck at the bow or stern, so made to shed the seas quickly; — called also *turtle deck*.

tur'tle·dove (-dŭv'; 2), *n.* [See 1st TURTLE.] Any Old World wild dove (*Streptopelia* or allied genus), esp. the common European species (*S. turtur*), noted for its plaintive cooing and affectionate disposition.

tur'tle·head' (-hĕd'), *n.* Any of a genus (*Chelone*, esp. *C. glabra*) of American herbs.

turtle neck. Something resembling or suggesting the neck of a turtle, as a type of collar on some sweaters. — **tur'tle-neck'**, *adj.*

turtle peg. A detachable sharp steel spearhead, attached to a cord, used in harpooning sea turtles.

turves (tûrvz), *n.*, *pl.* of TURF.

Tus'can (tŭs'kăn), *adj.* **1.** Of or pertaining to Tuscany in Italy. **2.** *Arch.* Of, pertaining to, or designating one of the five classical orders. It is of Roman origin and is rudely plain in style. See ORDER, *Illust.* — *n.* **a** A native or inhabitant of Tuscany. **b** The standard dialect of Italian. See INDO-EUROPEAN LANGUAGES, *Table.*

Tus'ca·ro'ra (tŭs'kà·rō'rà), *n.*; *pl.* -RORA, -RORAS (-ràz). One of a tribe of Iroquoian Indians formerly living in northeastern North Carolina.

tusch'e (tōōsh'ĕ), *n.* [G. *tusche*, fr. F. *toucher* to touch.] A lithographic drawing or painting material of the same nature as lithographic ink. It is also used as a resistant in the etching process.

tush (tŭsh), *n.* [AS. *tusc*.] A tusk; specif., a horse's canine. — **tushed** (tŭsht), *adj.*

tush, *interj.* An exclamation expressing impatient reprobation or contempt.

tusk (tŭsk), *n.* [AS. *tux*, var. of *tusc*.] **1.** In many animals, as the elephant, walrus, narwhal, wild boar, etc., an elongated greatly enlarged tooth which serves to dig up food, as a weapon, etc. **2.** Hence, any long protruding tooth. **3.** *Carp.* A form of small tenon. See TUSK TENON. — *v. t.* To dig or turn up with the tusk; also, to gash or gore with the tusk; — **tusked** (tŭskt), *adj.*

tusk'er (tŭs'kẽr), *n.* An elephant, or a wild boar, having large tusks.

tusk tenon. *Carp.* A tenon strengthened by one or more smaller tenons underneath forming a steplike outline.

tus'sah (tŭs'à), **tus'seh** (-ĕ), *n.* [Hind. *tasar*, fr. Skr. *tasara*, *trasara*, a shuttle.] **1.** An Oriental silkworm (*Antheraea paphia*, family Saturniidae), producing a brownish silk (also, the TUSSAH SILK); also, the silk itself. Other spellings are **tus'sa**, **tus'sar**, **tus'ser**, **tus'sor**, **tus'sore**, **tus'sur**.

tussah, or **tusseh**, **silk.** The strong, coarse fiber produced by various undomesticated Asiatic silkworms, esp. the tussahs; also, cloth which is woven from it.

tus'sal (tŭs'ăl), *adj.* [L. *tussis* cough.] *Med.* Pertaining to or manifested by cough.

tus'sis (tŭs'ĭs), *n.* [L.] *Med.* A cough.

tus'sive (-ĭv), *adj.* Pert. to or caused by a cough.

tus'sle (tŭs''l), *v. i.*; TUS'SLED (-'ld); TUS'SLING (-lĭng). [Freq. of ME. *tusen*, *tousen* (in comp.).] To struggle, as in sport; to scuffle; wrestle. — *n.* A scuffle; figuratively, a rough argument or controversy.

tus'sock (tŭs'ŭk), *n.* A tuft, as of grass, twigs, hair, or the like; esp., a dense tuft or bunch of grass or sedge.

tussock moth. Any of numerous dull-colored moths (family Lymantriidae) whose larvae (**tussock caterpillars**) are covered with long tufts of hair.

tut (tŭt; t'-*suction click*), *interj.* An exclamation expressing: **a** Impatience at something trivial. **b** Mild rebuke.

tu'te·lage (tū'tḗ·lĭj), *n.* [L. *tutela* protection. See TUITION.] **1.** Act of guarding or protecting; guardianship. **2.** State of being under a guardian or tutor. **3.** Teaching; instruction.

tu'te·lar·y (-lẽr'ĭ or, esp. Brit., -lẽr·ĭ), *adj.* Also **tu'te·lar** (-lẽr). [L. *tutelarius*.] **1.** Having the guardianship of a person or a thing; guardian; as, *tutelary* goddesses. **2.** Of or pertaining to a guardian; as, *tutelary* authority.

tu'te·nag (tū'tḗ·năg), *n.* Also **tu'te·nague.** [Pg. *tutenaga*, *tutanaga*, fr. Tamil *tuttanāgam* impure zinc.] *Com.* Crude zinc; also, an alloy rich in zinc.

tu'tor (tū'tẽr; 114), *n.* [OF. *tutour*, fr. L. *tutor*, fr. *tueri*, *tuitus*, to watch; protect.] **1.** One who has charge of the instruction of another in any branch, or in various branches, of learning; specif.: **a** A private teacher. **b** *Eng. Univ.* A college officer (usually a fellow) who supervises the study, discipline, etc., of undergraduates assigned to him. **c** In some American colleges and universities, a teacher ranking below an instructor. **2.** *Roman & Civil Law.* One who has the charge of the person and estate of a pupil, or child under the age of puberty. — *v. t.* **1.** To have the guardianship, tutelage, or care, of. **2.** To teach; instruct. **3.** To treat sternly, as a tutor might. — *v. i.* **1.** To do the work of a tutor, or instructor. **2.** *Colloq., U. S.* To be tutored, or instructed, esp. privately.

tu'tor·age (-ĭj), *n.* Office, function, or work, of a tutor; tutorship; also, a charge made for tutoring.

tu·to'ri·al (tū·tō'rĭ·ăl; 70), *adj.* Of or pert. to, or exercised by, a tutor.

tutorial system. A system of instruction, usually collegiate, in which each student's work is supervised by a tutor, who often acts also as advisor and intermediary in official business with the school or college.

tu'tor·ship, *n.* Office, duty, care, or practice, of a tutor.

tu'toy·er' (tü'twä·yā'), *v. t.* [F., fr. *tu* thou.] To address familiarly by the pronoun *tu*; hence, to treat with or show familiarity.

tut'ti (tōōt'tē), *adj.*, *masc. pl.* of TUTTO. [It.] *Music.* For all voices or instruments together; — opposed to *solo*.

tut'ti (tōō'tē), *n.*; *pl.* -TIS (-tēz). *Music.* **a** A passage performed by all the players or singers. **b** The total tonal effect produced by an orchestra or chorus performing together.

tut'ti-frut'ti (tōō'tē·frōō'tē), *n.* [It., lit., all fruits.] A confection consisting of different kinds of preserved fruits. — *adj.* Flavored with, or containing, various fruits.

tut'to (tōōt'tō), *adj. masc.*; *pl.* -TI (-tē). [It.] All; entire; — chiefly in musical directions.

tut'ty (tŭt'ĭ), *n.* [F. *tutie*, through Ar. fr. Per. *tūtiyā'*, fr. Skr. *tuttha*.] A crude zinc oxide obtained from the flues of smelting furnaces.

tu'tu (tōō'tōō; F. tü'tü'), *n.* [F.] A very short projecting skirt worn by a ballet dancer.

tu'um (tū'ŭm), *n.* [L.] See MEUM.

tu–whit' (tōō·hwĭt'), **tu–whoo'** (-hwōō'), *n. & interj.* Words imitating notes of the owl. — *v. i.* To utter the cry *tu whit* or *tu whoo.*

tux·e'do (tŭk·sē'dō), *n.*; *pl.* -DOS, -DOES (-dōz). Often shortened to **tux** (tŭks). [From a country club at *Tuxedo* Park, N. Y.] An evening dress for men's wear, distinguished chiefly by a short coat instead of the swallowtail coat of fully formal dress.

tu'yère' (twē'yâr'; tü'yâr'; twēr'), *n.* [F., fr. stem of *tuyau* a pipe.] A nozzle that delivers the air blast to a forge, blast furnace, etc.

twa (twä; twô). *Scot. & dial.* Var. of TWO.

twad'dle (twŏd''l), *v. i. & t.*; TWAD'DLED (-'ld); TWAD'DLING (-lĭng). To talk in a weak and silly manner; to prattle; gabble. — *n.* **a** Silly talk; gabble; also, bombastic talk; fustian. **b** A twaddler. — **twad'dler** (-lẽr), *n.*

twain (twān), *adj. & n.* [AS. *twēgen*, masc.] *Chiefly Poetic.* Two.

twang (twăng), *v. i. & t.* [Of imitative origin.] **1.** To sound with a quick, harsh, ringing noise. **2.** To speak with or have a nasal twang, as a person's voice. — *n.* **1.** A harsh, quick, ringing sound, like that of a tense bowstring pulled and suddenly released. **2.** Hence: **a** A sharp vibrant nasal tone; also, enunciation or utterance characterized by such a tone. **b** A sound likened to or suggesting the nasal twang or the twang of a bowstring.

Twan'kay tea (twăng'kā). [From Chin. (Pek.) *T'un²ch'i* (or -*hsi¹*), town in Anhwei province.] A variety of green tea (see TEA, 1 **b**).

twat'tle (twŏt''l), *v. i. & t. & n.* Twaddle.

tway'blade (twā'blād'), *n.* [*tway* (ME. *twei*) two + *blade*.] Any of several orchids (esp. of genera *Listera* or *Liparis*) having a pair of leaves.

tweak (twēk), *v. t. & i.* [ME. *twikken*, orig. the same word as *twitch*.] To pinch and pull with a sudden jerk and twist; to twitch. — *n.* Act of tweaking; a sharp pinch.

tweed (twēd), *n.* [By error fr. *tweel*, Scot. form of *twill*, but associated with the River Tweed.] **1.** A soft flexible fabric, usually of wool, dyed before weaving, and used esp. for suits and coats. **2.** A tweed suit or, in *pl.*, clothing.

twee'dle·dum' and twee'dle·dee' (twē'd'l·dŭm', -dē'). **1.** Two things practically alike; — a phrase used by John Byrom in his satire *On the Feuds between Handel and Bononcini.* **2.** [*caps.*] Characters in *Alice's Adventures in Wonderland.*

'tween (twēn), *prep.* Contr. of BETWEEN.

tweet (twēt), *n.* A low chirping note; — often reduplicated, **tweet'-tweet'.** — *v. i.* To utter a tweet.

tweet'er (twēt'ẽr), *n.* [*tweet* + 1st *-er*.] A small loud-speaker responsive only to the higher acoustic frequencies, used for reproducing sounds of high pitch. Cf. WOOFER.

tweeze, tweese (twēz), *n.* [For *twees*, *etwees*, pl. of *etwee*, fr. F. *étui* a case, sheath, box.] *Obs.* A surgeon's case of instruments.

tweez'ers (twēz'ẽrz), *n. pl.* [See TWEEZE.] A small pincerlike implement for grasping or extracting.

twelfth (twĕlfth), *adj. & n.* See NUMBER, *Table.*

Twelfth'-night' (twĕlfth'nīt'), *n.* The evening of January 6, the feast of Epiphany, or Twelfth-day, the concluding period of medieval Christmas festivities.

Twelfth′tide′ (twĕlfth′tīd′), *n.* The twelfth day after Christmas; Epiphany; — called also **Twelfth′–day′**.
twelve (twĕlv), *adj.* & *n.* [AS. *twelf.*] See NUMBER, *Table.*
Twelve Apostles, *or* **the Twelve.** *Bib.* See APOSTLE, 1.
twelve′fold′ (twĕlv′fōld′; 2), *adj.* & *adv.* See -FOLD.
twelve′mo (twĕlv′mō), *n.* & *adj.* = DUODECIMO.
twelve′month′ (-mŭnth′), *n.* A year.
twelve′–tone′ (-tōn′), *adj.* [Transl. of G. *zwölfton* in *zwölftonmusik.*] *Music.* Based on a series of twelve notes and thus disregarding the major-minor system; atonal; as, he uses the *twelve-tone* technique in a piano suite.
twen′ty (twĕn′tĭ), *adj.* & *n.* [AS. *twēntig, twentig.*] See NUMBER, *Table.* — **twen′ti·eth** (-tĭ·ĕth; -ĭth), *n.* & *adj.*
twen′ty·fold′ (-fōld′; 2), *adj.* & *adv.* See -FOLD.
twen′ty–one′, *n.* *Cards.* = VINGT-ET-UN.
twen′ty–twen′ty, *or* **20/20**; **twen′ty–for′ty**, *or* **20/40**; etc. See VISUAL ACUITY.
twi- (twī-). [AS.] A prefix used with nouns and adjectives, and meaning *two, double, doubly, twice.*
twi′bil′, twi′bill′ (twī′bĭl′), *n.* [AS. *twibill*, fr. *twi-* two + *bill, bil,* an ax, hoe, bill.] *Hist.* A double-headed battle-ax.
twice (twīs), *adv.* [ME. *twies* (where *s* is adv. ending), *twie*, fr. AS. *twigea, twiga, twiwa.*] **1.** Two times; once and again; as, he tried *twice.* **2.** Doubly; in twofold quantity or degree; as, *twice* the sum.
twice′–laid′ (-lād′; 2), *adj.* **a** Made from the ends of a rope and strands of used rope; as, *twice-laid* rope. **b** Hence, made from odds and ends, refuse, etc.
twi′–col′ored, twi′col′oured, *adj.* Twice colored; varicolored.
twid′dle (twĭd′′l), *v. t.*; TWID′DLED (-′ld); TWID′DLING (-lĭng). [Prob. imitative.] To touch lightly, or play with; to twirl; as, to *twiddle* one's thumbs. — *v. i.* **1.** To play or trifle with anything; hence, to be busied with trifles; to fiddle. **2.** To quiver or shake lightly; to tremble. — *n.* A slight twist or twirling motion with the fingers.
twi′er (twī′ĕr). Corrupt. of TUYÈRE.
twig (twĭg), *v. t.*; TWIGGED (twĭgd); TWIG′GING. [Gael. *tuig*, or Ir. *tuigim* I understand.] *Colloq.* **1.** To understand; to comprehend. **2.** To observe slyly; also, to perceive; discover.
twig, *n.* [AS. *twig, twigge.*] A small shoot or branch. Hence: **twig blight, twig borer, twig gall**, etc.
twig, *n.* *Colloq., Eng.* & *Ir.* Fashion; mode; style.
twi′light′ (twī′līt′), *n.* [ME., fr. AS. *twi-* two + *lēoht* light.] **1.** The light from the sky between full night and sunrise, or between sunset and full night. Twilight is sunlight scattered once or (the fainter) twice by the atmosphere and its dust. **2.** Hence, a faint light or obscure medium through which anything is viewed. — *adj.* Of, pertaining to, or characteristic of the twilight.
Twilight of the Gods. = RAGNAROK.
twilight sleep. [Trans. of G. *dämmerschlaf.*] A condition of partial anesthesia, or subconsciousness, which dulls awareness to pain and softens or effaces memory of pain, as from childbirth. It is produced by hypodermic injection of morphine and scopolamine.
twill (twĭl), *n.* [ME. *twile*, fr. AS. *twili*, fr. *twi-.*] **1.** An appearance of diagonal lines or ribs in textile fabrics. **2.** A fabric woven with a twill. — *v. t.* To weave, as cloth, so as to produce a twill.
twin (twĭn), *adj.* [AS. *twinn.*] **1.** Made up of two distinct, nearly related, and equal, members; double; twofold. **2.** Specif.: **a** Consisting of, or being, twins, or a pair; as, *twin* boys. **b** Composed of two alike or nearly related parts or factors. **3.** Standing in the relation of a twin; esp., being one of two born at a birth; as, a *twin* brother or sister. See FRATERNAL, *adj.*, 3; IDENTICAL, *adj.*, 3. — *n.* **1. a** One of two persons or things closely related by ties of birth, resemblance, or the like. **b** Specif., one of two produced at a birth. **2.** *pl.* [*cap.*] *Astron.* = GEMINI **a**. **3.** *Cryst.* A compound crystal composed of two or more crystals, or parts of crystals, in reversed position with reference to each other. — *v. i.*; TWINNED (twĭnd); TWIN′NING. **1.** To bring forth twins. **2.** To be mated, or coupled, with another; specif., to be born at the same birth. — *v. t.* To bring forth as twins; to couple; match; as, eye and hand are *twinned* in action.
twin′ber′ry (twĭn′bĕr′ĭ; -bĕr·ĭ), *n.* **a** A shrubby North American honeysuckle (*Lonicera involucrata*) with purple involucrate flowers. **b** = PARTRIDGEBERRY, 1.
twin′born′ (-bôrn′; 2), *adj.* Born at the same birth.
twine (twīn), *n.* [AS. *twīn*, prop., a twisted or double thread.] **1.** A strong thread of two or three strands twisted together. **2.** Act of twining, or winding, round; a twining. **3.** *Rare.* A twist, as formed by winding; a convolution. **4.** An entwining, or interlacing; hence, a snarl, or tangle; also, an interlaced branch or spray of a plant, ivy, etc. — *v. t.* **1.** To twist together; also, to form by twisting; loosely, to weave. **2.** To wind, as any flexible substance around another body; to wreathe. **3.** To embrace; entwine; encircle. — *v. i.* **1.** To intertwine; twist. **2.** To wind; bend; coil. — **twin′er** (twīn′ĕr), *n.*
twine (twīn), **twin** (twĭn), *v. t.* & *i.* *Scot.* To part; sunder.
twin′flow′er (twĭn′flou′ĕr), *n.* Either of two low, prostrate, vinelike plants (*Linnaea borealis* of northern Europe and Asia, and *L. americana* of northern North America) of the honeysuckle family, having opposite leaves and fragrant flowers in pairs on slender, upright stalks.
twinge (twĭnj), *v. t.*; TWINGED (twĭnjd); TWING′ING (twĭn′jĭng). [AS. *twengan* to pinch, squeeze.] **1.** *Rare.* To tweak; twitch. **2.** To affect with a sharp, sudden pain. — *v. i.* To have a sudden, sharp, local pain. — *n.* **1.** A tweak; twitch. **2.** A sudden, sharp, local pain.
twink (twĭngk), *n.* & *v.* [See TWINKLE.] Wink; twinkle.
twink, *v. i.* *Obs.* To tinkle; clink.
twin′kle (twĭng′k′l), *v. i.*; TWIN′KLED (-k′ld); TWIN′KLING (-klĭng). [AS. *twinclian.*] **1.** To blink; wink; also, of the eyelids, to open and close rapidly and twitchingly. **2.** To shine with an intermittent light; to sparkle; scintillate. **3.** To appear at intervals while moving rapidly to and fro; as, feet *twinkling* in a dance. — *v. i.* **1.** To cause to twinkle; to blink; wink. **2.** To discharge in quick intermittent gleams; as, fireflies *twinkle* a faint light. — *n.* **1.** A closing or opening, or a quick motion, of the eye; a wink or sparkle of the eye. **2.** A brief or intermittent flash or gleam; a glimmer; sparkle. **3.** The time occupied by a single wink; a twinkling. — **twin′kler** (-klĕr), *n.*
twin′kling (twĭng′klĭng), *n.* **1.** A wink; twinkle. **2.** A scintillation. **3.** The time occupied by a single wink; a moment.
twinned (twĭnd), *adj.* *Cryst.* Formed by twinning.
twin′ning (twĭn′ĭng), *pres. part.* & *verbal n.* of TWIN. Hence: *n.* **1.** The bearing of twins. **2.** Loosely, the coupling of two related persons or objects. **3.** *Cryst.* The assemblage of two or more crystals, or parts of crystals, in reversed position with reference to each other.
twin′–screw′, *adj.* *Shipbuilding.* Having two propeller screws, one on each side of the plane of the keel, one right-handed and one left-handed.
twirl (twûrl), *v. t.* & *i.* To move or turn round rapidly; to whirl round, as with the fingers; in baseball, to pitch. — *n.* **1.** A twirling; a rapid circular motion; a whirl. **2.** A twist; coil; convolution. — **twirl′er** (twûr′lĕr), *n.*
twist (twĭst), *v. t.* & *i.* [ME. *twisten* to twist, strip of leaves, fr. AS. *twist* (in comp.) a rope, as made of two (twisted) strands.] **1.** To unite by winding one thread or strand round another. **2.** Hence, to wreathe; twine; wind. **3.** To wrench; contort; specif.: **a** To crook spirally; to writhe. **b** To subject to torsion; as, to *twist* a shaft. **c** To compress, constrain, or bring by or as by torsion; hence, to wring; torment; also, to confuse; perplex. **d** To turn from the true form or meaning; to pervert; as, to *twist* a passage. — **Syn.** See CURVE. — *n.* **1.** That which is formed by twisting or winding together parts; specif.: **a** A cord, thread, etc., formed by winding strands round each other. **b** A form of closely twisted, strong sewing silk. **c** A form of tightly twisted cotton yarn. **d** A roll of twisted dough, baked. **e** Tobacco in a thick twisted roll. **2.** Act or manner of twisting, or state of being twisted; hence, a knot, web, or the like, formed by twisting; also, a bending; flexure; deviation; turning; in persons, a marked natural tendency or bent; a bias. **3. a** Act of imparting a turning or twisting motion, as to a pitched ball; a twirl; spin; also, the motion thus imparted. **b** A wrenching or distorting; as, he fell and gave his knee a bad *twist.* **4. a** Torque or torsional stress applied to a body, as a shaft. **b** Torsional strain. **5.** *Slang.* A woman; a "skirt."
twist drill. A drill having deep helical grooves extending from the point to the smooth portion of the shank. See DRILL, *Illust.*
twist′er (twĭs′tĕr), *n.* **1.** One who twists, as in joining warp threads in weaving. **2.** One that twists, as in baseball a curve, in cricket a break. **3.** *Local, U. S.* A tornado, waterspout, dust whirl, or the like.
twit (twĭt), *v. t.*; TWIT′TED; TWIT′TING. [AS. *ætwītan* to reproach, blame, fr. *æt* at + *wītan* to blame; orig. to observe, see; hence, to observe what is wrong.] To reproach, taunt, or upbraid, esp. by reminding of a fault, defect, etc. — **Syn.** See RIDICULE. — *n.* Act of twitting; a taunting allusion.
twitch (twĭch), *v. t.* & *i.* [ME. *twicchen*; akin to AS. *twiccian.*] To pull or move with a jerk or quick motion; to snatch; pluck. — *n.* **1.** Act of twitching; a short, sudden, quick pull; as, a *twitch* at the sleeve. **2.** A short spastic contraction of the fibers or muscles; a twinge. — **twitch′ing·ly**, *adv.*
twitch grass. [See QUITCH.] See COUCH GRASS.
twit′ter (twĭt′ĕr), *v. i.* [ME. *twiteren*, of imitative origin.] **1.** To make a succession of small, tremulous, intermitted noises. **2.** To titter; giggle. **3.** [Perhaps influenced by *twitch.*] To have a slight trembling of the nerves; to be excited or agitated. — *v. t.* To utter with a twitter. — *n.* **1.** A small, tremulous, intermitted noise, as that made by a swallow. **2.** A titter; giggle. **3.** A slight agitation of the nerves.
twit′ter, *v. t.* To twit; taunt.
′twixt (twĭkst), *formerly* **twixt.** *Poet.* & *Dial.* Contr. of BETWIXT.
two (tōō), *adj.* & *n.* [ME. *two, twa*, prop. fem. & neut., *twei, twein, tweien*, prop. masc. (whence E. *twain*), fr. AS. *twā*, fem. & neut., *twēgen*, masc., *tū*, neut.] See NUMBER, *Table.*
two′–base′ hit, *or* **two′–bag′ger** (tōō′băg′ĕr; 2), *n.* *Baseball.* A hit on which the batter reaches second base without the aid of an error.
two′–by–four′ (tōō′bī·fōr′), *adj.* Measuring two units by four; hence, *Colloq.*, small; petty; also, cramped. — *n.* Something, as a board, that is two-by-four.
two′–cy′cle, *n.* *Thermodyn.* A two-stroke cycle for an internal-combustion engine. Cf. FOUR-CYCLE. — **two′–cy′cle**, *adj.*
two′–faced′ (tōō′fāst′; 2), *adj.* Having two faces; hence, practicing double-dealing; false. — **two′–fac′ed·ly** (-fās′ĕd·lĭ; -ĭd·lĭ; -fāst′lĭ), *adv.*
two′–fist′ed (*see Pron.*, § 2), *adj.* *Colloq., U. S.* Virile; vigorous; as, a *two-fisted* story of the Wild West.
two′fold′ (tōō′fōld′), *adj.* Consisting of two things or parts; twice as much or as many. — (-fōld′; 2), *adv.* To twice as much or as many; doubly.
2,4–D, 2–4–D (tōō′fōr′dē′). *Chem.* A white crystalline compound (chemically, 2,4-dichlorophenoxy-acetic acid, $C_8H_6Cl_2O_3$) used as a weed killer.
two′–hand′ed (*see Pron.*, § 2), *adj.* **1.** Having two hands; — often equivalent to *large, stout*, or *strong.* **2.** Used with both hands; as, a *two-handed* sword. **3.** Using either hand equally well; ambidextrous. **4.** Requiring two persons for operation, as some saws.
two′–mast′er, *n.* A ship having two masts.
two′–name′, *adj.* *Colloq., Banking.* Having or bearing two names; as, ***two-name paper***, that is, negotiable paper on which at least two persons are severally liable as separate makers, or, usually, one as maker and one as endorser.
two′pence (tŭp′ĕns; *in England pron′d* tōō pĕns *only when two words*), *n.* The sum of two pence; also, *Brit.*, a small silver coin of this value, now issued only on special occasions.
two′pen·ny (tŭp′ĕn·ĭ; *cf.* TWOPENCE), *adj.* Of the value of, or costing, twopence; hence, cheap; mean.
two′–phase′, *adj.* *Elec.* = DIPHASE.
two′–ply′ (tōō′plī′), *adj.* **1.** Consisting of two thicknesses. **2.** Woven double, as cloth, by incorporating two sets of warp thread and two of filling. **3.** Of two strands.
two′some (tōō′sŭm), *adj.* [*two* + 1st *-some.*] Consisting of, or done by, two. — *n.* *Golf.* Incorrectly, a match between two players; — properly called a *single.*
two′–step′, *n.* A ballroom dance executed with a sliding step in march or polka time; also, music for this dance.
two′–thirds′ rule. *U. S. Politics.* In Democratic presidential conventions, the rule requiring a vote of at least two thirds of the delegates for nomination.
two′–way′, *adj.* Literally, having two ways; in *Math.*, having two ways of variation; as, a *two-way* series. Specif.: **a** Passing or allowing passage in two directions. **b** *Mech.* Designating a cock or valve that will connect a pipe or channel with either of two others at will.
-ty. [AS. *-tig.*] A suffix in numbers, denoting *tens, times ten*, as in twen*ty*. In ordinal numbers *-ty* appears as *-ti-*, as in twen*ti*eth.

-ty. [OF. *-té*, fr. L. *-tas, -itas*.] A suffix forming abstract nouns of *quality, state, condition*, and the like.

Ty'burn (tī'bẽrn), *n.* A former place of public execution in London, England.

ty-coon' (tī-kōōn'), *n.* [Jap. *taikun*, lit., great lord.] **1.** Great Prince; — an incorrect title applied to the shogun of Japan to impress foreigners. **2.** A businessman of extraordinary wealth, power, and influence; also, a masterful political leader.

Ty'deus (tī'dūs; tĭd'ẹ̄·ŭs), *n.* [L., fr. Gr. *Tydeus*.] *Gr. Lit.* One of the "Seven against Thebes" (which see).

Ty·di'des (tĭ·dī'dēz), *n.* [L., fr. Gr. *Tydeidēs*.] Son of Tydeus; — a patronymic of Diomedes.

ty'ing (tī'ĭng), *pres. part.* of TIE.

tyke, tike (tīk), *n.* [ON. *tīk* a bitch.] **1.** A dog; cur. **2.** *Now Scot.* A clumsy or churlish person; a country bumpkin. **3.** *Colloq.* A lively child.

tym'bal (tĭm'băl). Var. of TIMBAL.

tym'pan (tĭm'păn), *n.* [OF., fr. L. *tympanum* a kettledrum, panel of a door.] **1.** *Arch.* A panel; tympanum. **2.** *Printing Presses.* The sheet of paper, cloth, or other material, placed between the impression surface (platen, impression cylinder, or the like) and the paper to be printed. **3.** *Music.* A drum.

tym'pa·ni (tĭm'pȧ·nē), **tym'pa·no** (-nō). Vars. of TIMPANI, TIMPANO.

tym·pan'ic (tĭm·păn'ĭk), *adj.* **1.** Like a tympanum, or drum; as, a *tympanic* membrane. **2.** *Anat. & Zool.* Of or pertaining to the tympanum.

tympanic bone. *Anat. & Zool.* In mammals, a bone which encloses a part of the tympanum and supports the tympanic membrane.

tympanic membrane. *Anat. & Zool.* A thin membrane closing externally the cavity of the middle ear. See EAR, *Illust.*

tym'pa·nist (tĭm'pȧ·nĭst), *n.* One who beats a drum; a member of an orchestra who plays percussion instruments.

tym·pa·ni'tes (-nī'tēz), *n.* [LL., fr. Gr. *tympanitēs*, fr. *tympanon* a kettledrum.] *Med.* A distention of the abdomen, caused by accumulation of air or gas. — **tym'pa·nit'ic** (-nĭt'ĭk), *adj.*

tym·pa·ni'tis (-nī'tĭs), *n.* [NL. See TYMPANUM; -ITIS.] *Med.* Inflammation of the middle ear.

tym'pa·num (tĭm'pȧ·nŭm), *n.; pl.* -NUMS (-nŭmz), -NA (-nȧ). [L., a drum.] **1.** *Anat. & Zool.* **a** The drum, or middle ear. See EAR, *Illust.* **b** The tympanic membrane. **2.** *Arch.* **a** The recessed face of a pediment within the frame made by the upper and lower cornices, being usually triangular. **b** The space within an arch, and above a lintel or a subordinate arch. **3.** *Elec.* The diaphragm of a magneto-telephone. **4.** = TYMPAN, 3.

tym'pa·ny (tĭm'pȧ·nĭ), *n.; pl.* -PANIES (-nĭz). [ML. *tympanias*, fr. Gr. *tympanias*, fr. *tympanon* a kettledrum.] Inflation; distention; hence, conceit; bombast; turgidness.

tyne (tīn). Var. of TINE.

typ'al (tīp'ăl; -'l), *adj.* Relating to a type or types; belonging to types; serving as a type; typical.

type (tīp), *n.* [L. *typus* a figure, image, a form, type, character, fr. Gr. *typos* the mark of a blow, impression, model.] **1.** The distinctive stamp; sign; emblem. **2.** A person or thing regarded as the symbol of someone or something that is yet to appear; as, in medieval poetry, Jerusalem is the *type* of heaven. Cf. ANTITYPE. **3.** A particular kind, class, or order; as, the seedless *type* of orange; also, *Colloq.*, kind; sort; as, he won't stand for that *type* of thing. **4.** A model; standard; exemplar; as, a *type* of chivalry. **5.** *Agric.* Of livestock, the combination of characters appropriate to a special kind of use; as, beef *type*; hence, an animal or group having such a combination of characters. **6.** *Biol.* **a** A form of being having the morphological and physiological characteristics by which a number of individuals may be classified together. **b** An individual, species, genus, etc., considered as typical of a higher group. **7.** *Biol. & Physiol.* A group classified according to the physiological and morphological characters of the individuals and to their specific interreaction; as, **blood type**, one of several groups into which blood may be divided on the basis of its compatibility with the blood of other individuals. In blood transfusions, nonidentity of blood types leads to serious results. **8.** *Math.* The simplest of the forms equivalent with respect to a group of transformations. **9.** *Print.* **a** A rectangular block, usually of metal or wood, having its face so shaped as to produce, in printing, a letter, figure, or other character; — often used attributively; as, *type* matter; *type* body; *type* face. **b** Such blocks, or the letters or characters impressed, collectively. The different alphabets of body type used in book composition consist of roman CAPITALS, SMALL CAPITALS, and lower-case letters, and *italic CAPITALS* and *lower-case* letters, with accompanying figures, points, accents, etc., in all over 230 characters. A single type consisting of two or more letters or characters united (as æ, fi, ffl) is a ligature. The three classes of type are these:

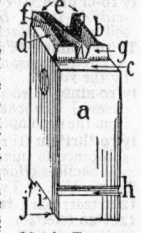

Metal Type. *a* Body; *b* Face; *c* Shoulder; *d* Counter; *e* Serifs; *f* Stem, or Shank; *g* Beard, or Neck; *h* Nick; *i* Groove; *j* Feet.

black letter   roman   *italic*

Black letter is in England sometimes called *gothic*, or *Gothic*. Among the derivations and variations of the original three classes are:

old-style roman   modern roman
old-style italic   *modern italic*
cursive   sans-serif (Gothic)

Movable types of clay were in use in China in the 11th century, and were followed by tin types, strung on a wire, and by individual wooden types (a kind still widely used). Type made from metal, cast molten into a matrix and cooled (essentially the process by which most modern type is made), was known in Europe in the 15th century. Early European type makers produced much black letter, but this declined in favor of more readable faces, notable examples being the old style of William Caslon, and the prototype "modern" faces of Giambattista Bodoni, both of the 18th century. Notable American contributions are Cheltenham and Goudy. Modern advertising typography has developed a profusion of styles. See POINT SYSTEM.

The following table shows the old names and the sizes of type used in bookwork; the black squares show the sizes of the corresponding em quad, and the numbers refer to the nearest equivalent in the American point system.

Name	Specimen	Em quad	Point
Diamond	abcdefghijklmnopqrstuvwxyz	■	4½
Pearl	abcdefghijklmnopqrstuvwxyz	■	5
Agate	abcdefghijklmnopqrstuvwx	■	5½
Nonpareil	abcdefghijklmnopqrstuvw	■	6
Minion	abcdefghijklmnopqrstu	■	7
Brevier	abcdefghijklmnopqrstu	■	8
Bourgeois	abcdefghijklmnopqrs	■	9
Long Primer	abcdefghijklmnopqr	■	10
Small Pica	abcdefghijklmnop	■	11
Pica	abcdefghijklmn	■	12
English	abcdefghijklm	■	14
Columbian	abcdefghijk	■	16
Great Primer	abcdefghij	■	18

Excelsior (3-point type) and *brilliant* (3½-point) are seldom used. Today, type sizes are almost universally indicated in points, as 8-, 12-, 18-, 24-, 36-, 48-, 60-point, etc. The standard height of type, technically called *height-to-paper*, is 0.9186 of an inch. According to its width, type is described as *standard* or *normal, condensed, extra-condensed*, and *extended*.

standard   condensed
extra-condensed   **extended**

The weight of a type face (lightness or heaviness of tone) is stated as *standard, lightface, boldface, extrabold*.

standard   lightface
boldface   **extrabold**

Examples of some representative types follow:

This is Brevier O. S. ANTIQUE

𝕿𝖍𝖎𝖘 𝖎𝖘 10=point 𝕭𝖑𝖆𝖈𝖐 𝕷𝖊𝖙𝖙𝖊𝖗*

This is 8-point Bodoni

This is 10-point Bradley Text*

This is 8-point CASLON OLD STYLE

This is 8-point CENTURY

This is 8-point Cheltenham Old Style

This is 6-point Clarendon

This is 8-point Elzevir

This is 10-point FUTURA Medium†

This is 8-point GARAMOND

This is 8-point GOTHIC †

This is 10-point GOUDY OLD STYLE

This is 8-point JANSON

This is 8-point Kabel LIGHT†

This is 14-point Kaufmann Script

𝕮𝖍𝖎𝖘 𝖎𝖘 8=point 𝕺𝖑𝖉 𝕰𝖓𝖌𝖑𝖎𝖘𝖍 *

This is 12=point Outline

This is 8-point SCOTCH ROMAN

This is 12-point script

This is 10=point 𝕿𝖀𝕯𝕺𝕽 Black *

* Each of these is a form of *black letter* (in England, sometimes called *gothic*, or *Gothic*).

† Each of these is a form of *gothic* (or *Gothic*), or *sans-serif* (called also, in England, *grotesque*).

Syn. Type, kind, sort, nature, description, character mean a group thought of as a class because of close resemblances. **Type** is the preferred term when the resemblances are so clearly marked that the distinction between that group and related groups cannot be questioned; **kind**, when the group equals a biological species or genus or a similar scientific class: *kind* sometimes implies, and *sort* generally implies, a group with less explicit resemblances; **nature**, in discriminating use, implies a group marked by inherent or innate likenesses; **description**,

one marked by agreement in all details that belong to a type as described or defined; **character**, one marked by likenesses that are distinctive or peculiar to the type.
— *v. t.* **1.** To represent beforehand as a type; to prefigure. **2.** To produce a copy of; also, to represent; typify. **3.** To typewrite. **4.** *Med.* To determine the type of (a sample of blood). See TYPE, *n.*, 7. — *v. i.* To typewrite.

-type (-tīp). [Gr. *typos* impression.] A combining form signifying: **a** *Typical* form; type; representative; as in arche*type*, proto*type*. **b** [From *type*.] *Impressed* form, stamp, print, as in daguerreo*type*, lino*type*.

type founder. One who casts or makes type. — **type founding.** — **type foundry.**

type genus. *Biol.* That genus from which the name of the family or subfamily is formed and which theoretically most perfectly typifies the family.

type′-high′, *adj.* *Print.* Exactly as high as type (usually 0.9186 of an inch).

type metal. An alloy, consisting essentially of lead, antimony, and tin, used esp. in making type.

type page. The part of a printed page that is covered by the type or letterpress.

type′script′ (tīp′skrĭpt′), *n.* Typewritten matter.

type′set′ter (-sĕt′ẽr), *n.* One who or that which sets type; specif.: **a** A compositor. **b** A typesetting machine.

type′set′ting, *n.* Act or process of setting type. — **type′set′ting,** *adj.*

type species. *Biol.* That species (theoretically the most typical) upon which a generic name depends; genotype (def. 1).

type specimen. *Biol.* The specimen or individual on which the original scientific description of a given species or subspecies is based.

type′write′ (-rīt′), *v. t. & i.* To write with a typewriter.

type′writ′er (-rīt′ẽr), *n.* **1.** Any of various instruments or machines for writing in characters similar to those produced by printers' types. **2.** One who operates a typewriter. **3.** *Print.* A style of type imitating typewriting.

type′writ′ing (-rīt′ĭng), *n.* Act or art of using a typewriter; also, a print made with a typewriter.

SPACE BAR

Typewriter Keyboard.

typh·li′tis (tĭf-lī′tĭs), *n.* [NL., fr. Gr. *typhlos* blind, closed (of the caecum) + *-itis*.] *Med.* Inflammation of the caecum. — **typh·lit′ic** (-lĭt′ĭk), *adj.*

typh·lol′o·gy (-lŏl′ō·jĭ), *n.* [Gr. *typhlos* blind + *-logy.*] The science that deals with blindness.

typh·lo′sis (-lō′sĭs), *n.* [Gr. *typhlōsis.*] *Med.* Blindness.

ty′pho- (tī′fō-), *typh-.* [Gr. *typhos* vapor, fever stupor.] A combining form used for *typhus* and *typhoid.*

Ty·pho′ë·an (tī-fō′ē·ăn), *adj.* Of, pert. to, or like Typhoeus.
☞ Sometimes incorrectly written and pronounced *Ty·phoe′an* or *Ty·phe′an* (tī·fē′ăn).

Ty·pho′eus (tī-fō′ūs), *n.* [Gr. *Typhōeus, Typhōs.*] *Gr. Myth.* A monster, having a hundred heads with fearful eyes and voices. He was conquered by Zeus and buried in Tartarus under Mt. Etna. See TYPHON.

ty·pho·gen′ic (tī′fō·jĕn′ĭk), *adj.* [*typho-* + *-genic.*] *Med.* Producing typhus or typhoid fever.

ty′phoid (tī′foid), *adj.* [*typh-* + *-oid.* See TYPHUS.] *Med.* Of or pertaining to typhus or, now, typhoid fever; resembling typhus; stuporous, as in typhus. — *n.* Typhoid fever.

typhoid fever. *Med.* An infectious febrile disease caused by the **typhoid bacillus** (*Eberthella typhi*, syn. *Bacillus typhosus*), introduced with food or drink, and marked by intestinal catarrh, an eruption on the abdomen and chest, diarrhea, and a pronounced stupor.

Ty′phon (tī′fŏn), *n.* [L., fr. Gr. *Typhōn.*] *Gr. & Rom. Myth.* A monster, orig. the son of Typhoeus, but later identified with Typhoeus.

ty·phoon′ (tī·fōōn′), *n.* [From Chin. (Cant.) *tai-fung,* (Pek.) *ta′-feng*, lit., great wind, but influenced in E. by earlier *tuphan, tufan, toofan,* fr. Ar. *tūfān,* fr. Gr. *typhōn, typhōs.*] A tropical cyclone in the region of the Philippines or China Sea. See CYCLONE, *n.*, 2.

ty′phus (tī′fŭs), *n.* [NL., fr. Gr. *typhos* smoke, cloud, stupor arising from fever.] *Med.* A serious rickettsial fever transmitted by body lice, with great prostration, cerebral disorder and eruption of red spots on the body. — **ty′phous** (-fŭs), *adj.*

typ′ic (tĭp′ĭk), *adj.* Typical.

typ′i·cal (-ĭ-kăl), *adj.* **1.** Of the nature of a type; emblematic. **2. a** Exhibiting the essential characteristics of a group. **b** Conforming to a type; as, a *typical* species. — **Syn.** See REGULAR. — **typ′i·cal·ly,** *adv.* — **typ′i·cal·ness,** *n.*

typ′i·fy (-ĭ-fī), *v. t.;* -FIED (-fīd) -FY′ING. [L. *typus* type + *-fy.*] **1.** To represent by an image, form, or resemblance; to prefigure. **2.** To embody the essential or salient characteristics of. — **typ′i·fi·ca′tion** (-fĭ-kā′shŭn), *n.* — **typ′i·fi′er** (-fī′ẽr), *n.*

typ′ist (tīp′ĭst), *n.* A person who operates a typewriter.

ty·pog′ra·pher (tī-pŏg′rà·fẽr; tī-), *n.* A printer, or one who designs or arranges printing.

ty′po·graph′ic (tī′pō-grăf′ĭk; tĭp′ō-), **ty′po·graph′i·cal** (-ĭ-kăl), *adj.* Of, pertaining to, expressed by or in, or concerning typography or printing; as, *typographic* art; a *typographical* error. — **ty′po·graph′-i·cal·ly,** *adv.*

ty·pog′ra·phy (tī-pŏg′rà·fĭ; tĭ-), *n.* [ML. *typographia.* See TYPE; -GRAPHY.] Art of printing with type; also, the style, arrangement, or appearance of printed matter.

ty·poth′e·tae (tī-pŏth′ē·tē; tĭ-; tī′pō·thē′tē), *n. pl.* [NL., fr. Gr. *typos* type, model + *tithenai* to put, set.] Printers; — used in the names of associations of master printers.

Tyr (tür), *n.* [ON. *Tȳr.*] In Norse mythology, a war-god, the son of Odin, by whom he is largely replaced.

ty·ran′nic (tĭ-răn′ĭk; tī-), *adj.* Tyrannical.

ty·ran′ni·cal (-ĭ-kăl), *adj.* [L. *tyrannicus,* fr. Gr. *tyrannikos.*] Of or pertaining to a tyrant; unjustly severe in government; despotic. — **ty·ran′ni·cal·ly,** *adv.* — **ty·ran′ni·cal·ness,** *n.*

ty·ran′ni·cide (-ĭ·sīd), *n.* [F., fr. L. *tyrannicidium* the killing of a tyrant, *tyrannicida* killer of a tyrant, fr. *tyrannus* tyrant + *caedere* to kill.] Act of killing a tyrant; also, one who kills a tyrant.

tyr′an·nize (tĭr′ă·nīz), *v. i.* To act the tyrant; to rule with unjust and oppressive severity. — *v. t.* To oppress. — **tyr′an·niz′er** (-nīz′ẽr), *n.*

ty·ran′no·saur (tĭ·răn′ō·sôr; tī-), *n.* *Paleontol.* A very large, bipedal, carnivorous dinosaur (*Tyrannosaurus rex*) of the Upper Cretaceous of North America.

tyr·an·nous (tĭr′ă·nŭs), *adj.* Tyrannical; unjustly severe; despotic. — **tyr′an·nous·ly,** *adv.*

tyr·an·ny (tĭr′ă·nĭ), *n.; pl.* -NIES (-nĭz). [OF. *tirannie.* See TYRANT.] **1.** The government or authority of a tyrant; the office, tenure, or system of administration, of an absolute ruler called a tyrant. **2.** Hence, arbitrary or despotic exercise of power; despotism. **3.** A tyrannical act. **4.** Severity; rigor.

ty′rant (tī′rănt), *n.* [OF. *tiran* (F. *tyran*), tyrant, fr. L. *tyrannus,* Gr. *tyrannos,* orig., lord.] **1.** An absolute ruler; a sovereign unrestrained by law or constitution; a usurper of sovereignty. **2.** Specif.: **a** A monarch, or other ruler, who exercises absolute power oppressively or brutally; a despot. **b** A cruel master; an oppressor.

tyrant flycatcher. See FLYCATCHER.

tyre (tīr). Chiefly Brit. Var. of TIRE (of a wheel).

Tyr′i·an (tĭr′ĭ·ăn), *adj.* [L. *Tyrius,* fr. *Tyrus* Tyre, fr. Gr. *Tyros.*] **1.** Of or pertaining to ancient Tyre or its people. **2.** Of the color Tyrian purple. — *n.* A native of Tyre.

Tyrian blue. = TYRIAN PURPLE **a.**

Tyrian purple. **a** A crimson or purple dye used by the Greeks and Romans, prepared from certain mollusks. **b** A color, bluish-red in hue, of very high saturation and low brilliance. See COLOR. — **Tyr′i·an-pur′ple,** *adj.*

ty′ro, ti′ro (tī′rō), *n.; pl.* -ROS (-rōz). [ML., fr. L. *tiro* a recruit, a beginner.] A beginner in learning; one who is in the rudiments of any branch of study; a novice. — **Syn.** See AMATEUR.

ty′ro·ci′dine (tī′rō·sī′dēn; -dĭn), *n.* Also **ty′ro·ci′din.** [*tyrosine* + *-cide* + *-ine.*] *Biochem.* An antibacterial substance produced by a soil bacillus (*Bacillus brevis*).

Ty′ro·li·enne′ (tē′rō·lyĕn′), *n.* [F., prop., fem. of *tyrolien* Tirolese.] A Tirolese peasants' dance, or the song or melody for it, characterized by the yodel.

ty′ro·sine (tī′rō·sēn; -sĭn; tĭr′ō-), *n.* Also **ty′ro·sin.** [Gr. *tyros* cheese.] *Biochem.* A crystalline amino acid, $C_9H_{11}NO_3$, formed from the decomposition of protein by various means, as by putrefaction.

ty′ro·thri′cin (tī′rō·thrī′sĭn; -thrĭs′ĭn), *n.* *Biochem.* An antibacterial substance (a mixture of gramicidin and tyrocidine) extracted from a soil bacillus (*Bacillus brevis*).

Tyrr. Var. of TYR.

tzar (zär; tsär), **tza·ri′na,** etc. Vars. of TSAR, TSARINA, etc.

tzet′ze (tsĕt′sĕ). Var. of TSETSE.

‖tzi′gane′ (tsē·gàn′), *n.* [F.] A gypsy, esp. one of Hungary. — **tzi′gane′,** *adj.*

U

U, u (ū), *n.; pl.* U's, u's, Us, us (ūz). **1.** The twenty-first letter of the English alphabet. It is a cursive form of the letter V (see V). In dictionaries of English, U and V were not given separate alphabetical positions until about 1800. **2.** The sound, or any sound, of the letter U. See *Pron.,* § 112. **3.** Anything having the shape of the letter U. **4.** As a *symbol,* used to denote or indicate anyone or anything arbitrarily or conveniently so designated, esp. as the twentieth or (see K, 3) the twenty-first in order or class.

‖u′a ma′u ke e′a o ka a′i·na i ka po′no (ōō′ä mä′ōō kä ā′ä ō kä ä′ē·nä ē kä pō′nō). (Hawaiian.) The life of the land is established in righteousness; — motto of Hawaii.

u·bi′e·ty (ū·bī′ē·tĭ), *n.* [NL. *ubietas,* fr. L. *ubi* where.] **a** The state of being placed in a definite local relation; position. **b** The abstract quality of being in position.

u·biq′ui·tar′y (ū·bĭk′wĭ·tĕr′ĭ or, esp. Brit., -tẽr·ĭ), *adj.* [L. *ubique* everywhere.] Ubiquitous.

u·biq′ui·tous (-tŭs), *adj.* [See UBIQUITY.] Existing or being everywhere at the same time; omnipresent. — **Syn.** See OMNIPRESENT. — **u·biq′ui·tous·ly,** *adv.* — **u·biq′ui·tous·ness,** *n.*

u·biq′ui·ty (-tĭ), *n.* [L. *ubique* everywhere, fr. *ubi* where.] Pres-

ence in more than one place, or in an indefinite number of places, at the same time; omnipresence.

‖u′bi su′pra (ū′bĭ sū′prà). [L.] Where above (mentioned).

U′-boat′ (ū′bōt′), *n.* [G. *U-boot,* for *unterseeboot,* lit., undersea boat.] A submarine; — generally restricted to German submarines in World Wars I and II.

ud′der (ŭd′ẽr), *n.* [AS. *ūder.*] A mammary gland or milk gland, when large, pendent, and provided with two or more nipples or teats, as in cows.

u′do (ōō′dō), *n.* [Jap.] A stout Japanese herb (*Aralia cordata*), the blanched young shoots of which are edible.

u·dom′e·ter (ū·dŏm′ē·tẽr), *n.* [L. *udus* wet, moist + *-meter.*] *Meteorol.* A rain gauge. — **u′do·met′ric** (ū′dō·mĕt′rĭk), *adj.* — **u·dom′e·try** (ū·dŏm′ē·trĭ), *n.*

ugh (ŭ; ōō; ŭk), *interj.* [Imitative.] An exclamation expressing disgust, horror, or recoil.

ug′li·fy (ŭg′lĭ·fī), *v. t.* [*ugly* + *-fy.*] To make ugly. — **ug′li·fi·ca′tion** (-fĭ·kā′shŭn), *n.*

ug′ly (ŭg′lĭ), *adj.;* UG′LI·ER (-lĭ·ẽr); UG′LI·EST. [ME. *ugly, uglike,* fr. ON. *uggligr* fearful, dreadful.] **1.** Offensive to the sight; contrary to beauty; hideous. **2.** Offensive from a moral aspect; repulsive. **3.** *Colloq., U.S.* Ill-natured; quarrelsome. **4.** *Colloq.* Unpleasant; disagreeable; likely to cause trouble or loss. **5.** Threatening; — applied to the weather. — **ug′li·ly,** *adv.* — **ug′li·ness,** *n.*

ugly duckling. An unpromising child who develops into a person of unusual beauty, intelligence, or the like; — from a fable by Hans Andersen of a swan hatched by a duck.

U′gri·an (ōō′grĭ·ăn; ū′-), *n.* A member of the eastern division of the Finno-Ugric peoples. — **U′gri·an,** *adj.*

U′gric (-grĭk), *adj.* Designating or pertaining to the languages of the Ugrians. See FINNO-UGRIC.

U′gro- (ōō′grō-; ū′-). A combining form denoting *Ugrian and,* as in **U′gro-Al·ta′ic** (= URAL-ALTAIC), **U′gro-Finn′ic** (= FINNO-UGRIC).

ug′some (ŭg′sŭm; ōōg′-), *adj.* [From ME. *uggen,* fr. ON. *ugga* to fear.] *Scot. & N. of Eng.* Frightful; abhorrent.

uh′lan (ōō′län; ōō·län′; ū′lăn), *n.* [G. *uhlan, ulan,* fr. Pol., fr. Turk. *oghlān* a youth, lad.] **1.** One of a certain kind of Tatar militia. **2.** *Mil.* One of a kind of lancers of Tatarian origin, especially prominent in the Prussian armies.

Ui′gur (wē′gōōr), *n.* **1.** A member of a Turkic people powerful in Mongolia and East Turkestan between the 8th and 12th centuries A.D. **2.** The language of the Uigurs, a tongue of the eastern branch of the Turkic. See LANGUAGE, *Table.* — **Ui′gur, Ui·gu′ri·an** (wē-gōōr′ĭ·ăn), **Ui·gu′ric** (-gōōr′ĭk), *adj.*

u·in′ta·ite, u·in′tah·ite (ū·ĭn′tȧ·īt), *n.* [From *Uinta* Mts., Utah.] *Mineral.* A black lustrous kind of asphalt, occurring on a large scale in Utah; — called also *gilsonite.*

‖**uit′land′er** (oit′län′dẽr; *Angl.* āt′lăn′dẽr), *n.* [D.] [*often cap.*] *S. Africa.* A foreigner; outlander.

u·kase′ (ū·kās′; ū′kās; *esp. Brit.,* ū·kāz′), *n.* [Russ. *ukaz,* lit., a command.] **1.** In Russia, formerly, a proclamation or imperial order, having the force of law. **2.** Hence, any official decree.

U·krain′i·an (ū·krān′ĭ·ăn; ū·krīn′-), *adj.* Of or pertaining to the Ukraine, its people, or their language. — *n.* **a** An inhabitant of the Ukraine. **b** The Ukrainian language; Little Russian. See RUSSIAN, *n.,* 2; INDO-EUROPEAN LANGUAGES, *Table.*

u′ku·le′le (ū′kŭ·lā′lē; *Hawaiian* ōō′kōō·lā′lā), *n.* [Hawaiian, fr. *ukulele* a flea, fr. *uku* insect + *lele* to jump, leap; — from the movement of the fingers.] *Music.* A small guitar of Portuguese origin which became popular in Hawaii about 1877. It has, typically, four strings.

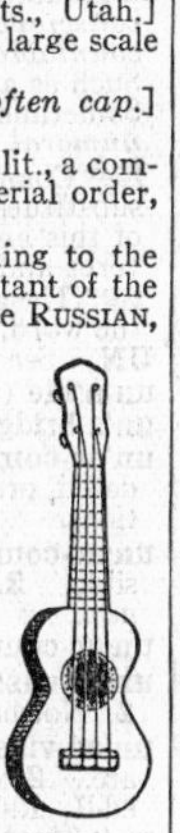

Ukulele.

ul′cer (ŭl′sẽr), *n.* [L. *ulcus, ulceris.*] **1.** *Med.* A superficial sore discharging pus; — distinguished from an abscess, which has its beginning deep in the tissues. **2.** Figuratively, anything that festers and corrupts like an open sore.

ul′cer·ate (-āt), *v. t.;* -AT′ED (-āt′ĕd; -ĭd); -AT′ING. [L. *ulceratus,* past part. of *ulcerare* to make sore, fr. *ulcus* ulcer.] To affect with or as with an ulcer or ulcers; as, *ulcerated* sore throat. — *v. i.* To undergo ulceration.

ul′cer·a′tion (-ā′shŭn), *n.* *Med.* The process of forming an ulcer or becoming ulcerated; state of being ulcerated; also, an ulcer.

ul′cer·a′tive (ŭl′sẽr·ā′tĭv; -ȧ·tĭv), *adj.* Of or pertaining to ulcers.

ul′cer·ous (-ŭs), *adj.* **1.** Having the nature or character of an ulcer. **2.** Affected with an ulcer or ulcers; ulcerated. — **ul′cer·ous·ly,** *adv.* — **ul′cer·ous·ness,** *n.*

-ule (-ūl). [F. or L.; F. *-ule,* fr. L. *-ulus, -ula, -ulum.*] A suffix forming diminutives, as in caps*ule,* spic*ule,* tub*ule.*

u′le·ma′ (ōō′lĕ·mä′), *n.* [Turk. *'ulema,* fr. Ar. *'ulamā'* learned men.] **a** *Moslem Law.* A body of scholars trained in Moslem religion and law. **b** Sometimes, erroneously, a Moslem learned man or theologian.

-ulent. [F. or L.; F. *-ulent,* fr. L. *-ulentus.*] A suffix, denoting *abounding in,* as in fraud*ulent.*

ul′lage (ŭl′ĭj), *n.* [OF. *eullage, ouillage,* fr. *ouillier, oillier,* to fill a wine cask, prop., to fill up to the bunghole, lit., eye, deriv. of L. *ad* to + *oculus* eye.] *Com.* The amount which a vessel of liquor, as a cask, lacks of being full; also, loss of commodities by sifting through bags, as seed, grain, etc.

ul·ma′ceous (ŭl·mā′shŭs), *adj.* [L. *ulmus* elm.] *Bot.* Belonging to the elm family (Ulmaceae). See ELM.

ul′na (ŭl′nȧ), *n.; pl.* -NAE (-nē), -NAS (-nȧz). [L., elbow.] *Anat. & Zool.* The inner of the two bones of the forearm or like part of the forelimb of vertebrates above fishes. — **ul′nar** (-nẽr), *adj.*

ul′no- (ŭl′nō-). [From ULNA.] A combining form denoting *ulnar and,* as in **ul′no·ra′di·al.**

-u·lose (-ū·lōs). [L. *-ulosus,* fr. *-ulus* + *-osus.* See -ULE; -OSE.] A suffix denoting *characterized by* or *having in marked degree,* as in gran*ulose.* Cf. -ULOUS.

U·lot′ri·chi (ū·lŏt′rĭ·kī), *n. pl.* [NL., fr. Gr. *oulothrix, oulotrichos,* woolly-haired, fr. *oulos* woolly + *thrix, trichos,* hair.] *Anthropol.* In Huxley's classification, the races having woolly or crispy hair. — **u·lot′ri·chous** (-kŭs), *adj.*

-u·lous (-ū·lŭs). [See -ULE, -ULOSE.] An adjectival suffix denoting: **a** [L. *-ulus.*] *Tending* or *addicted to; -ive;* as in cred*ulous,* garr*ulous.* **b** [L. *-ulosus.*] = -ULOSE, as in fab*ulous,* pop*ulous.*

ul′ster (ŭl′stẽr), *n.* A long, loose overcoat, worn by both sexes, orig. made of frieze in Belfast, Ulster, Ireland.

ul·te′ri·or (ŭl·tēr′ĭ·ẽr), *adj.* [L., compar. of *ulter* (preserved in adv. abl., *ultra, ultro,* beyond, on the other side).] **1.** Situated beyond or on the farther side. **2.** Further; remoter; often specif., beyond what is manifest or avowed; as, *ulterior* motives. — **ul·te′ri·or·ly,** *adv.*

ul′ti·ma (ŭl′tĭ·mȧ), *n.* [L., fem. of *ultimus* last.] *Gram. & Pros.* The last syllable of a word.

‖**ul′ti·ma ra′ti·o re′gum** (ŭl′tĭ·mȧ rā′shĭ·ō rē′gŭm). [L.] The final argument of kings (i. e. war).

ul′ti·mate (ŭl′tĭ·mĭt), *adj.* [LL. *ultimatus,* past part. of *ultimare* to come to or be at an end, fr. *ultimus* the farthest, last, superl. of *ulter.* See ULTERIOR; cf. ULTIMATUM.] **1.** Farthest; most remote in space or time; extreme. **2.** Last in a train of progression or consequences. **3.** Incapable of further analysis, division, or separation; elemental. **4.** *Mech.* Maximum; as, *ultimate* strain. — **Syn.** See LAST. — *n.* That which is ultimate; something final. — **ul′ti·mate·ly,** *adv.* — **ul′ti·mate·ness,** *n.*

ultimate constituent. *Ling.* See CONSTITUENT.

ul′ti·ma Thu′le (ŭl′tĭ·mȧ thū′lē). [L.] See THULE.

ul′ti·ma′tum (ŭl′tĭ·mā′tŭm), *n.; pl.* -TUMS (-tŭmz), -TA (-tȧ). [NL., fr. LL. neut. past part. See ULTIMATE.] A final proposition or condition; esp., the final terms offered by either of the parties in a diplomatic negotiation.

ul′ti·mo (ŭl′tĭ·mō), *adv.* [L. *ultimo* (*mense*) in the last month.] In the month preceding the present. Abbr. *ult.*

ul′ti·mo·gen′i·ture (ŭl′tĭ·mō·jĕn′ĭ·tūr), *n.* [L. *ultimus* last + *genitura* a begetting.] *Law.* A system of inheritance by which the youngest son succeeds to the estate; borough-English; — opposed to *primogeniture.*

ul′tra (ŭl′trȧ), *adj.* [L., adv. & prep., beyond, on the other side.] Going beyond others, or beyond due limit; extreme. — *n.* An extremist; radical.

ul′tra- (ŭl′trȧ-). [See ULTRA, *adj.*] A prefix meaning *beyond,* used to signify: **a** *Beyond in space; on the other side; trans-;* as in *ultra*montane. **b** *Beyond the range or limits of; transcending; super-;* as in *ultra*microscopic. **c** *Excessively, exceedingly, beyond what is common, ordinary, natural, right, proper,* or the like; *hyper-;* as in *ultra*modern.

☞ The meanings of the following can be understood by reference to their elements.

ultra-ambitious	**ultraexclusive**	**ultramodest**
ultraconfident	**ultrafashionable**	**ultrareligious**
ultraconservative	**ultraliberal**	**ultraroyalist**
ultracredulous	**ultraloyal**	**ultratropical**

ul′tra·cen′tri·fuge (-sĕn′trĭ·fūj), *n.* *Physical Chem.* A very high-speed centrifuge. — **ul′tra·cen′tri·fuge,** *v. t.* — **ul′tra·cen·trif′u·gal** (-sĕn·trĭf′ū·găl), *adj.* — **ul′tra·cen·trif′u·ga′tion** (-sĕn·trĭf′ū·gā′shŭn), *n.*

ul′tra·crit′i·cal (-krĭt′ĭ·kăl), *adj.* Hypercritical.

ul′tra·high′-fre′quen·cy, *adj.* *Elec.* Of a frequency between 300 and 3000 megacycles per second. Abbr. *U.H.F., UHF, u.h.f., uhf,* etc.

ul′tra·ism (ŭl′trȧ·ĭz′m), *n.* [See ULTRA-.] **a** The principles of those who advocate extreme measures, as radicalism. **b** An instance or example of radicalism. — **ul′tra·ist** (-ĭst), *n. & adj.* — **ul′tra·is′tic** (-ĭs′tĭk), *adj.*

ul′tra·ma·rine′ (ŭl′trȧ·mȧ·rēn′), *adj.* [ML. *ultramarinus.* See ULTRA-; MARINE.] Beyond the sea. — *n.* [Cf. Sp. *ultramarino.* So called because the lapis lazuli was orig. brought from beyond the sea, from Asia.] **1. a** A costly blue pigment, prepared by powdering lapis lazuli; also, a similar artificial pigment, prepared from a mixture of kaolin, soda ash, sulfur, and charcoal. **b** Any of several artificial pigments, as, *ultramarine* violet; yellow *ultramarine.* **2.** The color ultramarine blue.

ultramarine blue. **1.** A color, blue in hue, of very high saturation and low brilliance. See COLOR. **2.** The pigment ultramarine.

ul′tra·mi′cro·chem′is·try (ŭl′trȧ·mī′krō·kĕm′ĭs·trĭ), *n.* Chemistry dealing with minute quantities of substances, as a millionth of a gram. — **ul′tra·mi′cro·chem′ist** (-ĭst), *n.* — **ul′tra·mi′cro·chem′i·cal** (-ĭ·kăl), *adj.*

ul′tra·mi·crom′e·ter (-mī·krŏm′ē·tẽr), *n.* An extremely sensitive micrometer.

ul′tra·mi′cro·scope (-mī′krō·skōp), *n.* *Optics.* An apparatus for rendering visible, by scattered light, particles too small to be perceived by the ordinary microscope.

ul′tra·mi′cro·scop′ic (-skŏp′ĭk), **ul′tra·mi′cro·scop′i·cal** (-ĭ·kăl), *adj.* **1.** Too small to be seen with an ordinary microscope. **2.** Of or pertaining to an ultramicroscope. — **ul′tra·mi·cros′co·py** (-mī·krŏs′kō·pĭ; -mī′krō·skō′pĭ), *n.*

ul′tra·mod′ern (ŭl′trȧ·mŏd′ẽrn), *adj.* Beyond the norm of the modern; extreme in typically modern ideas or tendencies. — **ul′tra·mod′ern·ism** (-ẽr·nĭz′m), *n.* — **ul′tra·mod′ern·ist** (-nĭst), *n.* — **ul′tra·mod′ern·is′tic** (-nĭs′tĭk), *adj.*

ul′tra·mon′tane (-mŏn′tān), *adj.* [ML. *ultramontanus,* fr. L. *ultra* beyond + *mons, montis,* mountain.] Beyond the mountains; esp., beyond the Alps; specif., favoring the Italian party (upholding papal supremacy) in the Roman Catholic Church. — *n.* **1.** One who lives beyond the mountains, esp. the Alps. **2.** One who lives south of the Alps; hence, one identified with the Italian party in the Roman Catholic Church, which favored papal supremacy; now, a Roman Catholic who takes an exaggerated view of papal supremacy. — **ul′tra·mon′ta·nism** (-mŏn′tȧ·nĭz′m), *n.*

ul′tra·mun′dane (-mŭn′dān), *adj.* [L. *ultramundanus.*] Being beyond the world, or beyond the limits of our system.

ul′tra·na′tion·al·ism (-năsh′ŭn·ăl·ĭz′m), *n.* Great or excessive devotion to, or advocacy of, national interests, rights, etc., esp. as opposed to international considerations. — **ul′tra·na′tion·al,** *adj.* — **ul′tra·na′tion·al·ist** (-ĭst), *n. & adj.*

ul′tra·red′ (-rĕd′), *adj.* Infrared.

ul′tra·son′ic (-sŏn′ĭk), *adj.* [*ultra-* + *sonic.*] Supersonic.

ul′tra·son′ics (-sŏn′ĭks), *n.;* see -ICS. Supersonics.

ul′tra·vi′o·let (-vī′ō·lĕt; -lĭt), *adj.* *Physics.* Outside the visible spectrum at its violet end; — said of rays more refrangible than the extreme violet rays, and opp. to *infrared.*

‖**ul′tra vi′res** (vī′rēz). [Law L., fr. L. *ultra* beyond + *vires,* pl. of *vis* strength.] Beyond power; transcending authority; esp., exceeding legal power or authority; — used often in relation to acts by corporations in excess of their chartered or statutory rights.

ul′tra·vi′rus (ŭl′trȧ·vī′rŭs), *n.* [NL.] *Bacteriol.* An ultramicroscopic or filtrable virus.

ul′u·lant (ŭl′ū·lănt; ūl′-), *adj.* [L. *ululans,* pres. part.] Howling; wailing.

ul′u·late (-lāt), *v. i.* [L. *ululatus,* past part. of *ululare,* of imitative origin.] To howl, as a dog or a wolf; to wail; also, to hoot, as an owl.

ul′u·la′tion (-lā′shŭn), *n.* A howling, as of a dog or wolf.

U·lys′ses (ū·lĭs′ēz), *n.* [L., better *Ulixes,* fr. Gr. *Odysseus.*] Odysseus.

um′bel (ŭm′bĕl; -b'l), *n.* [L. *umbella* parasol, umbrella. See UMBRELLA.] *Bot.* A racemose inflorescence in which the axis is very much contracted, so that the pedicels (known as *rays*) appear to spring from the same point, forming a flat or rounded flower cluster. See INFLORESCENCE, *Illust.* (3); INVOLUCRE, *Illust.* — **um′bel·lar** (ŭm′bĕl·ẽr), *adj.*

um′bel·late (ŭm′bĕl·āt), *adj.* Also **um′bel·lat′ed** (-āt′ĕd; -ĭd). *Bot.* Bearing, or consisting of, umbels; arranged in umbels. — **um′bel·late·ly,** *adv.*

um′bel·lif′er·ous (ŭm′bĕ·lĭf′ẽr·ŭs), *adj.* [*umbel* + *-ferous.*] *Bot.* Producing umbels.

um·bel′lu·late (ŭm·bĕl′ū·lāt), *adj.* Disposed in umbellules.

um′bel·lule (ŭm′bĕl·ūl; ŭm·bĕl′ūl), *n.* [NL. *umbellula*, dim. of *umbella*. See UMBEL.] *Bot.* One of the small or secondary umbels in a compound umbel.

um′ber (ŭm′bẽr), *n.* [F. *ombre, terre d'ombre*, It. *terra d'ombra*, prob. orig., earth from *Umbria*, fr. L. *Umbria*, but confused with It. *ombra* shade.] **1.** A brown earth valued as a pigment and used either in the raw state, or calcined or burnt, in which case it has a slight reddish hue. Its color is due to manganese and iron oxides. **2.** A brown, red-yellow in hue, of medium saturation and low brilliance (***burnt umber***) or of low saturation and low brilliance (***raw umber***). See COLOR. — *adj.* Of, pertaining to, or resembling umber; of the color raw umber or burnt umber. — *v. t.* To make umber, as by staining.

um′ber, *n.* [OF. *umbre*, fr. L. *umbra.*] **1.** The European grayling (*Thymallus thymallus*). **2.** Also **umber bird.** The umbrette.

um·bil′i·cal (ŭm·bĭl′ĭ·kăl), *adj.* [ML. *umbilicalis*, fr. L. *umbilicus* navel.] Of or pertaining to, from, or used at the navel.

umbilical cord. *Anat. & Embryol.* The cord or stalk arising from the navel, which connects the fetus of a mammal with the placenta.

um·bil′i·cate (ŭm·bĭl′ĭ·kāt), *adj.* Also **um·bil′i·cat′ed** (-kāt′ĕd; -ĭd), *adj.* Depressed in the middle, like a navel; navel-shaped; having an umbilicus.

um·bil′i·ca′tion (-kā′shŭn), *n.* **a** A navellike depression. **b** The state of being umbilicated.

um·bil′i·cus (ŭm·bĭl′ĭ·kŭs; ŭm′bĭ·lī′kŭs), *n.; pl.* -ICI (-sī). [L.] **1.** *Anat. & Zool.* The scar on the abdomen where the umbilical cord was attached; the navel. **2.** *Bot.* The hilum.

um·bil′i·form (ŭm·bĭl′ĭ·fôrm), *adj.* [*umbilicus* + *-form.*] Shaped like an umbilicus, or navel.

um′ble pie (ŭm′b'l). [See UMBLES.] A pie made of umbles.

um′bles (ŭm′b'lz), *n.* [Var. of NUMBLES.] *Obs.* Numbles, or certain entrails, as of a deer, used for food, as the heart, lights, and liver.

um′bo (ŭm′bō), *n.; pl.* UMBONES (ŭm·bō′nēz), UMBOS (ŭm′bōz). [L.] **1.** The boss of a shield. **2.** Any elevation suggestive of the boss, as in the tympanic membrane of the ear where the malleus is attached. **3.** *Zool.* One of the lateral prominences just above the hinge of a bivalve shell. — **um′bo·nal** (ŭm′bō·năl; ŭm·bō′năl), *adj.* — **um′bo·nate** (-nāt), *adj.* — **um·bon′ic** (ŭm·bŏn′ĭk), *adj.*

um′bra (ŭm′brȧ), *n.; pl.* UMBRAE (-brē). [L., a shadow.] **1.** Shade; shadow. **2.** *Astron.* **a** The conical shadow projected from a planet or satellite, on the side opposite the sun, within which a spectator could see no portion of the sun's disk. Cf. PENUMBRA, 1. **b** The central dark portion, or nucleus, of a sunspot. **3.** A complete shadow, within which no light is received from a given source. Cf. PENUMBRA, 2.

um′brage (-brĭj), *n.* [OF. (F. *ombrage*), fr. L. *umbraticus* pert. to shade, fr. *umbra* shadow.] **1.** *Obs.* Shade; shadow. **2.** Hence, that which casts shade, esp. foliage. **3.** *Archaic.* Shadowy indication; semblance; trace. **4.** Offense; resentment; as, to take *umbrage* at another's advancement. — **Syn.** See OFFENSE.

um·bra′geous (ŭm·brā′jŭs), *adj.* **1.** Forming or affording a shade, or being shaded; shady; shaded; as, *umbrageous* trees, caves. **2.** Feeling umbrage; taking, or disposed to take, umbrage; suspicious. — **um·bra′geous·ly,** *adv.* — **um·bra′geous·ness,** *n.*

um·brel′la (ŭm·brĕl′ȧ), *n.* [It. *ombrella* (after It. *ombra* shade), fr. L. *umbella*, in glosses *umbrella* (after *umbra* shade), a little shadow, parasol, umbrella, dim. of *umbra* shade.] **1.** A shade, screen, or guard, carried in the hand for sheltering one from rain, sun, etc. **2.** A protective force of fighter aircraft, and sometimes bombers, maintained directly over and surrounding naval or ground forces or operations, for preventing enemy bombing and observation. **3.** *Zool.* The bell-shaped or saucer-shaped structure chiefly of jellylike substance which forms the chief part of the body of most jellyfishes.

umbrella bird. Any of several South American and Central American birds (genus *Cephalopterus;* esp., *C. ornatus* of Guiana and Brazil). The male is black with a radiating crest curving forward over the head.

umbrella leaf. A North American herb (*Diphylleia cymosa*) with two large peltate stem leaves and a solitary lobed basal one.

umbrella palm. A pinnate-leaved palm (*Hedyscepe canterburyana*) native to Lord Howe's Island, but common in cultivation.

umbrella tree. **a** An American magnolia (*Magnolia tripetala*) having large leaves clustered at the ends of the branches. **b** Any of various other trees or shrubs so called from the shape of their leaves or the position of their crown of foliage.

um·brette′ (ŭm·brĕt′), *n.* [F. *ombrette.*] An African wading bird (*Scopus umbretta*) allied to the storks and herons; umber bird.

Um′bri·an (ŭm′brĭ·ăn), *adj.* Of or pertaining to Umbria, in central Italy, or its inhabitants; as, the *Umbrian* school of painters. — *n.* One of the people of Umbria; also, the language of the ancient Umbrians, an Italic tongue of Oscan origin. See INDO-EUROPEAN LANGUAGES, *Table.*

um·brif′er·ous (ŭm·brĭf′ẽr·ŭs), *adj.* [L. *umbrifer*, fr. *umbra* a shade + *ferre* to bear.] Casting a shade; umbrageous.

u′mi·ak (ōō′mĭ·ăk), *n.* Also **u′mi·ack.** [Eskimo *umiak.*] An open Eskimo boat about 30 feet long and 8 feet wide, consisting of a wooden frame covered with skins, and propelled, usually with broad paddles, by women.

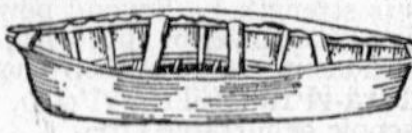
Umiak.

um′laut (ŏŏm′lout), *n.* [G., fr. *um* about + *laut* sound.] **1.** *Philol.* The change of a vowel caused by partial assimilation to a succeeding sound, esp. the palatalization of a back vowel, as *a*, *o*, or *u*, caused by a (front) *i* or *j* originally standing in the following syllable, but now generally lost or altered; vowel mutation; also, the vowel resulting from such partial assimilation. Umlaut, though occurring in other Indo-European languages, is esp. characteristic of the Teutonic languages. **2.** Loosely, the two dots used in German to indicate a vowel affected by umlaut. — *v. t.* To affect, form, or sound with umlaut.

um′pir·age (ŭm′pīr·ĭj; ŭm′pĭ·rĭj), *n.* The office or power of an umpire; also, the act of umpiring; arbitrament.

um′pire (ŭm′pīr), *n.* [OF. *nomper, nonper*, uneven (i. e., third) person, fr. *non* not + *per* even, equal, peer. *Umpire*, without initial *n-*, arose through the incorrect division of *a numpire* as *an umpire.*] **1.** A person to whose sole decision a controversy or question between parties is referred; now specif., one chosen to rule on the plays of a game, as cricket, baseball, etc. Cf. REFEREE **b.** **2.** That by which a matter is decided. — *v. t.* To decide or supervise as umpire. — *v. i.* To act as umpire.

un- (ŭn-; *usually unaccented or under secondary accent only, except when in direct contrast; see Pron.*, § 2). [AS. *un-, on-*, the unaccented form of the accented prefix *and-* against.] A prefix used: **a** With verbs to express the *contrary*, or reversal of the action, as in *uncoil, unfold.* **b** With nouns to form verbs expressing *removal* or *privation of* (or *release from*) the thing, quality, or state expressed, as in *unman, unsex, unyoke;* also, *removal from*, as in *unearth, unhorse.* **c** Merely intensifying a negative sense, as in *unloose.*

un- (ŭn-; *see 2d note below*). [AS. *un-.*] A prefix, signifying *not; in-; non-*, attached to almost any adjective or adverb, and less freely to nouns, and to their adjective derivatives in *-able, -ive, -ory, -ful, -some, -like*, etc. Definitions are given in the Vocabulary for compounds: **a** Such as have acquired an opposing or contrary meaning, as *unfriendly, unbelief*, or else a special intensive sense, as *unending, undoubted.* **b** Such as have the value of independent words, as *unconscionable, unruly.* **c** Such as have a special sense, as *unaccountable*, or are felt as positive rather than negative, as *uneven.* **d** Such as are anomalous or provincial, etc., as *unpure*, for *impure.* **e** Sometimes confined to a *neutral* rather than *contrary* meaning, as in *unmoral* (contrast *immoral*).

☞ Compounds that are mere negations are sufficiently explained by substituting *not* for *un-;* of these a selected list is provided at the foot of this and succeeding pages, without inclusion of corresponding adverbs and nouns in *-ly* and *-ness*, which may be freely formed.

☞ The accent in compounds of *un-* often varies with the position of the word, as an *un′born′* child, a child *un′born′*, etc. See *Pron.*, § 2.

UN. See UNITED NATIONS.

un·a′ble (ŭn·ā′b'l; 2), *adj.* Not able.

un′a·bridged′ (ŭn′ȧ·brĭjd′), *adj.* Not abridged; complete.

un′ac·com′mo·dat′ed (ŭn′ă·kŏm′ō·dāt′ĕd; -ĭd), *adj.* Not accommodated, provided, equipped, or furnished; also, not having accommodations.

un′ac·count′a·ble (-koun′tȧ·b'l), *adj.* **1.** Not accountable or responsible. **2.** Inexplicable; strange; mysterious. — **un′ac·count′a·bly,** *adv.*

un′ac·count′ed–for′, *adj.* Not accounted for; unexplained.

un′ac·cus′tomed (ŭn′ă·kŭs′tŭmd), *adj.* **1.** Not usual; uncommon. **2.** Not habituated; unfamiliar; — with *to.*

un′ad·vised′ (-ăd·vīzd′), *adj.* **1.** Indiscreet. **2.** Rash; inconsiderate. **3.** Without counsel or consultation. — **un′ad·vis′ed·ly** (-vīz′ĕd·lĭ; -ĭd·lĭ), *adv.*

un′af·fect′ed (-ă·fĕk′tĕd; -tĭd), *adj.* **1.** Free from affectation; natural; sincere; genuine. **2.** Not influenced, moved, altered, or the like. — **un′af·fect′ed·ly,** *adv.* — **un′af·fect′ed·ness,** *n.*

un′al·loyed′ (-ă·loid′), *adj.* Not alloyed; unmixed; unqualified; pure; as, *unalloyed* metals, happiness.

un′–A·mer′i·can, *adj.* Not American; not characteristic of, or consistent with, American customs, principles, etc.

un′a·neled′ (ŭn′ȧ·nēld′), *adj.* *Archaic.* Not having received extreme unction.

u′na·nim′i·ty (ū′nȧ·nĭm′ĭ·tĭ), *n.* State or quality of being unanimous.

u·nan′i·mous (ū·năn′ĭ·mŭs), *adj.* [L. *unanimus, unanimis*, fr. *unus* one + *animus* mind.] **1.** Being of one mind; agreeing; consentient; as, the assembly was *unanimous* in approval. **2.** Formed with or indicating the agreement and consent of all; as, a *unanimous* opinion, vote. — **u·nan′i·mous·ly,** *adv.* — **u·nan′i·mous·ness,** *n.*

un′ap·peal′a·ble (ŭn′ă·pēl′ȧ·b'l), *adj.* Not appealable; not to be appealed against.

un·apt′ (ŭn·ăpt′; 2), *adj.* **1.** Unsuitable. **2.** Not accustomed and not likely. **3.** Inapt. — **un·apt′ly,** *adv.* — **un·apt′ness,** *n.*

un·ar′gued (-är′gūd), *adj.* **1.** Not argued or debated. **2.** Not argued against; undisputed.

un·arm′ (-ärm′), *v. t.* [1st *un-* + *arm.*] To disarm.

un·armed′ (-ärmd′; 2), *adj.* [*un-* not + *armed.*] Not armed or armored; having no weapons.

un′ar·tis′tic (ŭn′är·tĭs′tĭk), *adj.* Not conforming to art.

un′as·sum′ing (-ă·sūm′ĭng), *adj.* Modest; retiring. — **un′as·sum′ing·ly,** *adv.*

u·nau′ (ū·nô′; ōō·nou′), *n.* [F., of Tupian origin.] The two-toed sloth *Choloepus hoffmanni.* See SLOTH.

un′aus·pi′cious (ŭn′ôs·pĭsh′ŭs), *adj.* Inauspicious.

un′a·void′a·ble (-ȧ·void′ȧ·b'l), *adj.* **1.** Not avoidable; inevitable. **2.** Not voidable.

un′a·ware′ (ŭn′ȧ·wâr′; 6), *adj.* Not aware; ignorant; also, giving no heed; unwary. — *adv. Poetic.* Unawares.

un′a·wares′ (-wârz′), *adv.* Without design or preparation; without premeditation; also, suddenly; unexpectedly.

un·backed′ (ŭn·băkt′; 2), *adj.* **1.** Never mounted by a rider; unbroken. **2.** Not supported. **3.** Not backed by bets.

un·baked′ (-bākt′; 2), *adj.* Not baked; hence, immature.

un·bal′ance (ŭn·băl′ăns), *v. t.* To put out of balance.

un·bal′anced (-ănst), *adj.* [In senses 1 and 2, *un-* not + *balanced;* in sense 3, 1st *un-* + *balance.*] **1.** Not in equipoise. **2.** *Com.* Not adjusted or brought to an equality of debt and credit. **3.** Being out of equilibrium; hence, disordered or deranged in sense; as, an *unbalanced* mind.

☞ See 2d UN-, *Note.*
un′a·bashed′
un′a·bat′ed
un′ab·solved′
un′ac·a·dem′ic
un′ac·cent′ed
un′ac·cept′a·ble
un′ac·cli′mat·ed
un′ac·cli′ma·tized
un′ac·com′mo·dat′ing
un′ac·com′pa·nied
un′ac·com′plished
un′ac·cred′it·ed
un′ac·knowl′edged
un′ac·quaint′ed
un′a·dapt′a·ble
un′ad·just′ed
un′a·dorned′
un′a·dul′ter·at′ed
un′a·fraid′
un·aid′ed
un′al·le′vi·at′ed
un′al·lied′
un′al·low′a·ble
un′al·loyed′
un·al′ter·a·ble
un·al′tered
un′am·big′u·ous
un′am·bi′tious
un·a′mi·a·ble
un·an′i·mat′ed
un′an·nounced′
un·an′swer·a·ble
un′ap·par′ent
un′ap·peas′a·ble
un′ap·peased′
un·ap′pe·tiz′ing
un′ap·proach′a·ble
un′ap·proached′
un′ap·pro′pri·at′ed
un′ap·proved′
un·ar′mored, un·ar′moured
un′ar·rest′ed
un′a·shamed′
un·asked′
un·as′pi·rat′ed
un′as·sail′a·ble
un′as·sist′ed
un′at·tached′
un′at·tain′a·ble
un′at·tempt′ed
un′at·tend′ed
un′at·trac′tive
un′au·then′tic
un′au·then′ti·cat′ed
un·au′thor·ized
un′a·vail′a·ble
un′a·vail′ing
un′a·vowed′

un·bar' (ŭn·bär'), v. t. & i. To unbolt; to open.

un·bat'ed (-bāt'ĕd; -ĭd), adj. 1. Unabated. 2. Archaic. Not blunted, as a sword without a button.

un·bear' (-bâr'), v. t. [1st un- + bear to support.] To loose the bearing rein of (a horse).

un·be·com'ing (ŭn'bē·kŭm'ĭng), adj. Not becoming; unsuitable; indecorous; improper. — Syn. See INDECOROUS. — un'be·com'ing·ly, adv. — un'be·com'ing·ness, n.

un·be·known' (-nōn'), adj. Also, Dial., un'be·knownst' (-nōnst'). Unknown; — often with to.

un·be·lief' (ŭn'bē·lēf'), n. Withholding of belief; incredulity or skepticism, esp. in matters of religious faith.

Syn. Unbelief, disbelief, incredulity mean the attitude of one who does not believe. Unbelief stresses the lack or absence of belief, esp. but not always in religion or revelation; disbelief, a positive rejection of what is stated or asserted; incredulity, an indisposition to believe.

un·be·liev'er (-lēv'ẽr), n. 1. One who does not believe; a doubter; a skeptic. 2. A disbeliever, esp. in some given divine revelation; an infidel. 3. One who has not exercised saving faith in Christ. — Syn. See ATHEIST.

un·be·liev'ing (-lēv'ĭng), adj. 1. Incredulous; distrusting; skeptical. 2. Disbelieving, esp. some given divine revelation. — un'be·liev'ing·ly, adv.

un·belt' (ŭn·bĕlt'), v. t. To ungird; also, to remove, by loosing the belt.

un·bend' (-bĕnd'), v. t.; see BEND. 1. To free from flexure; to make, or allow to become, straight; to loosen. 2. To relax, as the mind. 3. Naut. a To unfasten, as sails, from the spars or stays. b To cast loose or untie, as a rope. — v. i. 1. To cease to be bent. 2. To relax in stiffness, austerity, or the like; to become affable.

un·bend'ing (see Pron., § 2), adj. Unyielding, esp. in will; inflexible; resolute. — un·bend'ing·ly, adv. — un·bend'ing·ness, n.

un·be·seem'ing (ŭn'bē·sēm'ĭng), adj. Not beseeming; not befitting. — un'be·seem'ing·ly, adv. — un'be·seem'ing·ness, n.

un·bi'ased, un·bi'assed (ŭn·bī'ăst), adj. Free from bias; esp., unprejudiced; impartial. — Syn. See FAIR.

un·bid'den (ŭn·bĭd'n; 2), adj. Also un·bid' (-bĭd'). 1. Not commanded. 2. Uninvited.

un·bind' (-bīnd'), v. t.; see BIND. [AS. unbindan. See 1st UN-; BIND.] To remove a band from; to free from fastenings; to untie; unfasten; loose.

un·bit'ted (-bĭt'ĕd; -ĭd), adj. Not bitted or bridled.

un·blenched' (-blĕncht'), adj. Not disconcerted; undaunted; also, unstained.

un·blessed', un·blest' (-blĕst'; 2), adj. a Unconsecrated. b Unholy; accursed. c Wretched; unfortunate. d Excluded from religious blessing.

un·blush'ing (-blŭsh'ĭng), adj. Not blushing; shameless. — un·blush'ing·ly, adv.

un·bod'ied (-bŏd'ĭd; 2), adj. Having no body; incorporeal; also, disembodied.

un·bolt' (ŭn·bōlt'), v. t. & i. To withdraw a bolt (from); to unbar; to open. — un·bolt'ed (-bōl'tĕd; -tĭd; 2), adj.

un·bolt'ed, adj. Not bolted or sifted; hence, coarse; gross.

un·bon'net·ed, adj. Uncovered; bareheaded.

un·born' (ŭn·bôrn'; 2), adj. Not yet brought into life; still to appear; future.

un·bos'om (ŭn·bŏŏz'ŭm; cf. BOSOM), v. t. [1st un- + bosom.] To disclose, as secrets; to confess. — v. i. To make a disclosure.

un·bound', adj. Having no limit; unchecked.

un·bowed' (ŭn·boud'; 2), adj. [un- not + bowed.] Not bent; not bowed down; hence, unsubdued.

un·brace' (-brās'), v. t. To free from the braces of clothing or armor; to undo; hence, to relax or loosen, as a drum, the nerves; also, to enfeeble.

un·braid' (-brād'), v. t. To separate the strands of; unravel.

un·breathed' (-brēthd'; 2), adj. Not breathed; unuttered.

un·bred' (-brĕd'; 2), adj. Not well-bred; ill-bred.

un·bri'dle (-brī'd'l), v. t. To free or loose from the bridle.

un·bri'dled (-d'ld; 2), adj. Not confined by a bridle; hence, unrestrained; licentious; violent.

un·broke' (ŭn·brōk'), adj. Archaic & Dial. Unbroken.

un·bro'ken (-brō'kĕn; 2), adj. Not broken; as: a Whole; intact. b Unsubdued; untamed. c Not interrupted; continuous. d Not disorganized.

un·buck'le (-bŭk''l), v. t. To unfasten; to detach.

un·build' (-bĭld'), v. t.; see BUILD. To demolish; to raze.

un·bur'den (-bûr'd'n), v. t. To relieve as from a burden.

un·but'ton (-bŭt'n), v. t. & i. To loose the buttons (of).

un·called'—for', adj. Not called for or needed; gratuitous; also, rude; impertinent. — Syn. See SUPEREROGATORY.

un·can'ny (ŭn·kăn'ĭ), adj. 1. Scot. & N. of Eng. Dangerous; also, severe, as a blow. 2. Ghostly; eery; mysterious. — Syn. See WEIRD. — un·can'ni·ly, adv. — un·can'ni·ness, n.

un·cap' (ŭn·kăp'), v. t. & i. To remove the cap from, as from a bottle; also, to doff the cap, esp. in respect.

un·caused' (-kôzd'; 2), adj. Uncreated; self-existent.

un'cer·e·mo'ni·ous (ŭn'sĕr·ē·mō'nĭ·ŭs), adj. Lacking, or acting without, formality or ordinary courtesy; abrupt. — un'cer·e·mo'ni·ous·ly, adv.

un·cer'tain (ŭn·sûr'tĭn; -t'n; 2), adj. 1. Indeterminate. 2. Not certain to occur; indefinite; problematical. 3. Not reliable; untrustworthy. 4. a Not known beyond doubt; dubious. b Not having

certain knowledge; doubtful. c Not clearly identified or defined. 5. Not constant; variable; fitful. — un·cer'tain·ly, adv. — un·cer'tain·ness, n.

un·cer'tain·ty (-tĭ), n.; pl. -TIES (-tĭz). 1. Lack of certainty; doubt. 2. That which is uncertain.

Syn. Uncertainty, doubt, dubiety, dubiosity, skepticism, suspicion, mistrust mean lack of sureness about someone or something. Uncertainty may imply a falling short of certainty or so far a remove from it that one can only guess or surmise; doubt suggests not only uncertainty but an inability to make a decision; dubiety and dubiosity suggest uncertainty, the former implying wavering and the latter, vagueness or mental confusion; skepticism suggests incredulity while any plausible evidence to the contrary exists; suspicion, a lack of faith in the truth, reality, fairness, etc., of someone or something; mistrust, genuine doubt based upon suspicion.

un·chain' (ŭn·chān'), v. t. To set free; to liberate.

un·chanc'y (ŭn·chăn'sĭ), adj. [un- not + Scot. chancy fortunate, safe.] Scot. a Ill-fated. b Dangerous. c Unseasonable.

un·charge' (-chärj'), v. t. To unload; to acquit.

un·char'i·ta·ble (-chăr'ĭ·tà·b'l), adj. Severe in judging; censorious. — un·char'i·ta·ble·ness, n. — un·char'i·ta·bly, adv.

un·chaste' (ŭn·chāst'; 2), adj. a Not continent; lewd. b Not chaste in style or taste. — un·chaste'ly, adv. — un·chas'ti·ty (-chăs'tĭ·tĭ), n.

un·chris'tian (ŭn·krĭs'chăn; -krĭst'yăn), adj. Not Christian; specif.: a Heathen; pagan. b Contrary to the Christian spirit or character. c Uncivilized; barbarous.

un·church' (ŭn·chûrch'), v. t. 1. To expel from a church; to excommunicate. 2. To deprive of a church.

un·churched' (-chûrcht'; 2), adj. Not belonging to or connected with any church.

un'ci·al (ŭn'shĭ·ăl; -shăl; 58), adj. [L. uncialis inch-high, fr. uncia inch. See INCH.] Pertaining to or written in form of majuscule script, with somewhat rounded letters, seldom used after the 10th century A.D. — n. An uncial letter, or uncial writing.

NON hABEMUS REGEM NISI CAESAREM

Uncial Letters from a Latin Bible.

un'ci·form (ŭn'sĭ·fôrm), adj. [L. uncus a hook + -form.] Hook-shaped. — n. A bone on the ulnar side of the carpus in mammals.

unciform process. Anat. a The hook-shaped process on the unciform. b The uncinate process of the ethmoid bone.

un'ci·na·ri'a·sis (ŭn'sĭ·nà·rī'à·sĭs), n. [NL., fr. Uncinaria (fr. L. uncinus hook, barb) + -iasis.] Ancylostomiasis; hookworm disease.

un'ci·nate (ŭn'sĭ·nāt), adj. Also un'ci·nal (-năl). [L. uncinatus, fr. uncinus a hook, uncus a hook.] Hooked; bent at the tip like a hook.

un·cir'cum·cised (ŭn·sûr'kŭm·sīzd), adj. Not circumcised; hence, not of the Israelites; hence, irreligious; heathen.

un'cir·cum·ci'sion (ŭn'sûr·kŭm·sĭzh'ŭn), n. 1. Absence or want of circumcision. 2. Bib. People not circumcised; the Gentiles.

un·civ'il (ŭn·sĭv'ĭl; -'l), adj. a Barbarous; uncivilized. b Not civil or courteous; ill-mannered. — un·civ'il·ly, adv.

un·civ'i·lized (-sĭv'ĭ·līzd), adj. Not civilized; barbarous.

un·clasp' (-klȧsp'), v. t. & i. To loose the clasp (of); to release from a clasp.

un'cle (ŭng'k'l), n. [OF. oncle, uncle, fr. L. avunculus maternal uncle; akin to L. avus grandfather.] 1. The brother of one's father or mother; also, the husband of one's aunt. Cf. CONSANGUINITY, Illust. 2. Elderly man; — in address. 3. Slang. A pawnbroker.

un·clean' (ŭn·klēn'), adj. [AS. unclǣne.] a Foul; filthy. b Ceremonially impure. c Unchaste; obscene. — un·clean'ness, n.

un·clean'ly (-klĕn'lĭ), adj. Not cleanly; filthy; also, unchaste. — un·clean'li·ness, n.

un·clench' (ŭn·klĕnch'), un·clinch' (-klĭnch'), v. t. & i. To relax or force open (the clenched, or clinched, hand).

Uncle Sam. Colloq. The United States government.

un·cloak' (ŭn·klōk'), v. t. & i. To remove a cloak or cover (from); hence, to unmask; reveal.

un·close' (-klōz'), v. t. & i. To open; hence, to disclose.

un·clothe' (-klōth'), v. t. To strip of clothes or cloths.

un'co (ŭng'kō), adj. [Scot., fr. UNCOUTH.] Scot. & N. of Eng. Strange; specif.: a Unknown; foreign. b Uncanny; weird. c Extraordinary; great. — adv. Remarkably; uncommonly; extremely. — n. Anything strange; a stranger; pl., news.

un·coil' (ŭn·koil'), v. t. & i. To unwind.

un·com'fort·a·ble (ŭn·kŭm'fẽrt·à·b'l), adj. a Feeling discomfort; uneasy. b Causing discomfort; unpleasant.

un'com·mit'ted (ŭn'kŏ·mĭt'ĕd; -ĭd), adj. Not committed; as: a Not imprisoned. b Not bound by previous decision.

un·com'mon (ŭn·kŏm'ŭn), adj. Unusual; rare; hence, remarkable. — Syn. See INFREQUENT. — un·com'mon·ly, adv. — un·com'mon·ness, n.

un'com·mu·ni·ca·tive (ŭn'kŏ·mū'nĭ·kā'tĭv; -kà·tĭv), adj. Not disposed to talk or to impart information; reserved.

un'com·pro·mis'ing (ŭn·kŏm'prŏ·mīz'ĭng), adj. Not making or admitting of compromise; unyielding; inflexible. — un·com'pro·mis'ing·ly, adv.

un·con·cern' (ŭn'kŏn·sûrn'), n. Want of concern; freedom from solicitude or anxiety; also, indifference.

un'con·cerned' (ŭn'kŏn·sûrnd'), adj. Not concerned; as: a Not involved or implicated. b Not anxious or solicitous; easy in mind. — Syn. See INDIFFERENT. — un'con·cern'ed·ly (-sûr'nĕd·lĭ; -nĭd·lĭ), adv. — un'con·cern'ed·ness, n.

un'con·di'tion·al (ŭn'kŏn·dĭsh'ŭn·ăl), adj. Not conditional or conditioned; absolute; unreserved; as, *unconditional* surrender. — **un·con·di′tion·al·ly**, *adv.*

un′con·di′tioned (ŭn′kŏn·dĭsh′ŭnd), *adj.* **1.** Not conditioned; unconditional. **2.** *Educ.* Admitted or promoted without a condition. **3.** *Metaph.* Infinite; absolute. **4.** *Psychol.* Not acquired or learned; natural; — of a response, etc.

un′con·form′a·ble (ŭn′kŏn·fôr′mȧ·b'l), *adj.* Not conformable; specif., *Geol.*, exhibiting unconformity.

un′con·form′i·ty (-fôr′mĭ·tĭ), *n.; pl.* -TIES (-tĭz). **1.** Lack of conformity; incongruity; inconsistency. **2.** *Geol.* **a** Lack of continuity in deposition between strata in contact, corresponding to a gap in the stratigraphic record. **b** The surface of contact between unconformable strata.

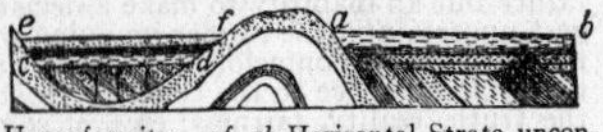

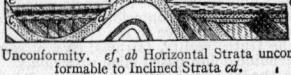

Unconformity. *ef, ab* Horizontal Strata unconformable to Inclined Strata *cd.*

un·con′scion·a·ble (ŭn·kŏn′shŭn·ȧ·b'l), *adj.* **1.** Not conscionable; unreasonable; as, an *unconscionable* charge. **2.** Not guided or controlled by conscience; unscrupulous; as, an *unconscionable* rascal. — **un·con′scion·a·bly**, *adv.*

un·con′scious (ŭn·kŏn′shŭs), *adj.* **1.** In a state unaccompanied by conscious experience; also, with *of*, not aware. **2.** Not known or apprehended by consciousness, esp. by self-consciousness; as, an *unconscious* mistake; *unconscious* humor. **3.** Not possessed of mind or consciousness. — *n. Psychoanalysis.* With *the:* That part of the individual psyche inaccessible to consciousness, and consisting of repressed desires and their associated ideas. It often disturbs the course of conscious life, in dreams, phobias, etc. — **un·con′scious·ly**, *adv.* — **un·con′scious·ness**, *n.*

un′con·sti·tu′tion·al (ŭn′kŏn·stĭ·tū′shŭn·ăl; -'l), *adj.* Not constitutional; contrary to the constitution. — **un′con·sti·tu′tion·al′i·ty** (-ăl′ĭ·tĭ), *n.*

un·cork′ (ŭn·kôrk′), *v. t.* To draw a cork from.

un·count′ed (-koun′tĕd; -tĭd; 2), *adj.* Not counted; also, innumerable.

un·cou′ple (-kŭp′'l), *v. t.* To loose, as dogs, from their couples; also, to disconnect (something coupled).

un·couth′ (ŭn·ko͞oth′; 2), *adj.* [AS. *uncūth* unknown, strange, fr. *un-* not + *cūth* known, old past part. of *cunnan* to know.] **1.** Unfamiliar or strange; hence, mysterious; uncanny. **2.** Outlandish; awkward in appearance or bearing; rude; boorish; of speech, manners, etc., rugged and untrained; harsh or blunt; unrefined. — **un·couth′ly**, *adv.* — **un·couth′ness**, *n.*

un·cov′e·nant·ed (ŭn·kŭv′ĕ·năn·tĕd; -tĭd), *adj.* **1.** Not granted or sanctioned by a covenant. **2.** Not having assented to a covenant.

un·cov′er (-kŭv′ẽr), *v. t.* **1.** To lay bare; to disclose; reveal. **2.** To expose to view by removing some covering. **3.** To take the cover from. **4.** To divest of the hat or cap; esp. in token of reverence. — *v. i.* **1.** To take off the hat in respect. **2.** To remove the covers.

un·cov′ered (-kŭv′ẽrd), *adj.* **a** Devoid or divested of a covering. **b** Not covered by collateral, as a note, or by insurance.

un·crown′ (ŭn·kroun′), *v. t.* To deprive or divest of a crown; to dethrone.

unc′tion (ŭngk′shŭn; 68), *n.* [L. *unctio*, fr. *ungere, unctum*, to anoint.] **1.** Act of anointing, esp. for medical purposes, or as a symbol of consecration. Cf. EXTREME UNCTION. **2.** An unguent; an ointment. **3.** That quality in language, address, or the like, which expresses or excites sober and fervent emotion; religious fervor; sometimes, a simulated fervor or emotional gush; unctuousness.

unc′tu·os′i·ty (ŭngk′tụ̈·ŏs′ĭ·tĭ), *n.* Unctuous quality.

unc′tu·ous (ŭngk′tụ̈·ŭs), *adj.* [ML. *unctuosus*, fr. L. *unctus* an ointment, fr. *ungere, unctum*, to anoint.] **1.** Fatty; oily. **2.** Hence: **a** Rich in organic matter and easily workable, as soil. **b** Plastic, as clay. **c** Greasy to the touch or having a soapy feel, as certain minerals. **3.** Bland or fervid; esp. characterized by a smugly or ingratiatingly sentimental pretense of spirituality in speech or attitude; gushing. — **unc′tu·ous·ly**, *adv.* — **unc′tu·ous·ness**, *n.*

un·curl′ (ŭn·kûrl′), *v. t. & i.* To straighten out from a curled or coiled position; to unroll.

un·daunt′ed (ŭn·dôn′tĕd; -tĭd; ŭn·dän′-; 2), *adj.* Courageous with an undiminished resolution; undismayed. — **Syn.** Bold, intrepid. — **un·daunt′ed·ly**, *adv.* — **un·daunt′ed·ness**, *n.*

un′dé, un′dée (ŭn′dā), *adj.* [OF. (F. *ondé*), fr. L. *unda* a wave.] *Her.* Waving or wavy.

un·dec′a·gon (ŭn·dĕk′ȧ·gŏn), *n.* [L. *undecim* eleven + *-gon.*] *Geom.* A figure having eleven angles and eleven sides.

un′de·ceive′ (ŭn′dē·sēv′), *v. t.* To free from deception.

un′de·cil′lion (ŭn′dē·sĭl′yŭn), *n.* See NUMERATION, *Table.*

un′de·mon′stra·tive (ŭn′dē·mŏn′strȧ·tĭv), *adj.* Restrained or reserved as to expression of feeling; not effusive.

un′de·ni′a·ble (ŭn′dē·nī′ȧ·b'l), *adj.* **1.** Incapable of denial; indisputable; incontestable. **2.** Unquestionably excellent. — **un′de·ni′a·bly**, *adv.*

un′der (ŭn′dẽr), *prep.* [AS., prep. & adv.] **1.** In or to a position lower in elevation and in the same vertical line or plane, so as to be overhung, surmounted, enveloped, protected, or concealed by; — opposed to *over;* as, *under* sunny skies; to swim *under* water; *under* separate cover; *under* pretense of ignorance. **2.** Subject to the authority, guidance, or instruction of; as, to fight *under* Cromwell; controlled, limited, weighed upon, or oppressed by, either physically or as by affliction, obligation, or the like; as, *under* quarantine; brave *under* trials; undergoing the action or effect of; as, *under* ether. **3.** As part of by assignment or inclusion or by association with a name or title; as, classified *under* Reptilia; sustaining by way of limiting circumstance, or in conformity with; as, *under* the contract; with the sanction or guarantee of; as, *under* one's seal. **4.** Bearing or assuming outwardly, esp. for the sake of concealment or disguise; as, *under* an incognito. **5.** Inferior or subordinate to or exceeded by, as in size, amount, etc.; as, all weights *under* twelve ounces; inferior to the standard or requisite degree of; as, *under* age.

— *adv.* **1.** In a position under something; beneath; underneath. **2.** In or into a condition of subjection or subordination. **3.** So as to be covered or concealed; as, snowed *under* in the election. **4.** Short of or less than the appointed sum, period, etc.

— *adj.* **1.** Lying or moving below or beneath something else or on the ventral side. **2.** Facing or protruding downwards. **3.** Lower in rank or authority; subordinate. **4.** Lower or less than usual or proper; short; as, an *under* dose. **5.** Used predicatively: **a** Held in subjection; as, to keep his passions *under.* **b** Lower in amount; as, he finds my estimates far *under.*

un′der- (ŭn′dẽr-; 2). A prefix meaning: **a** *Below in position; to* or *from a lower position; against* or *on the underside;* as in:

undercellar	underprop	understratum
undercurve	underspecified	undersurface

b *Placed,* or *to be placed, below* or *inside; lower;* also, *on the side beneath;* hence, *covert;* as in:

underbud	underfur	underskirt
undercrust	undergarment	undersoil
underfeathering	undershirt	undertitle

c *One subordinate* or *subsidiary to; sub-;* as in:

underagent	underofficer	understeward
underclerk	underofficial	underteacher
underhint	undersecretary	undertenant

d *Below standard; imperfectly; deficient;* as in:

undercapitalize	underconsumption	underpay
underclothed	underofficered	underripe

un′der·act′ (ŭn′dẽr·ăkt′), *v. t. & i.* **1.** To perform without the required force or expedition. **2.** To perform (a dramatic part) with insufficient insight, passion, emphasis, and business for a full interpretation. **3.** To perform or act with restraint for greater dramatic impact or personal force.

un′der·age′ (ŭn′dẽr·āj′; 2), *adj.* Of less than mature age.

un′der·arm′ (ŭn′dẽr·ärm′), *adj.* **1.** Placed under, or on the underside of, the arm; as, *underarm* seams. **2.** = UNDERHAND, 1. — *adv.* With an underarm motion.

un′der·bel′ly (-bĕl′ĭ), *n.* The belly; hence, the underside. See BELLY, *n.*, 5.

un′der·bid′ (-bĭd′), *v. t.;* -BID′; -BID′DING. **1.** To offer to contract, sell, or do, for a less price than. **2.** To bid less than the value of. — **un′der·bid′der** (-bĭd′ẽr), *n.*

un′der·bred′ (-brĕd′; 2), *adj.* **1.** Not of, or marked by, good breeding; ill-bred. **2.** Not of pure breed.

un′der·brush′ (ŭn′dẽr·brŭsh′), *n.* Shrubs, bushes, small trees, etc., growing beneath large trees in a wood; brush.

un′der·buy′ (-bī′), *v. t.;* see BUY. **1.** To buy at less than the real value or worth. **2.** To buy cheaper than.

un′der·car′riage (ŭn′dẽr·kăr′ĭj), *n.* **1.** The supporting framework, as of an automobile. **2.** The landing gear of an aircraft.

un′der·charge′ (-chärj′), *v. t.* **1.** To charge less than is usual or suitable for; also, to charge (a person) too little. **2.** To load with too small an explosive charge, as a gun. — **un′der·charge′** (ŭn′dẽr·chärj′), *n.*

un′der·class′ (ŭn′dẽr·klȧs′), *n.* *Usually pl.* The freshman or the sophomore class. — **un′der·class′man** (-klȧs′măn), *n.*

un′der·clothes′ (-klōthz′; *see* CLOTHES), *n. pl.* Also **un′der·cloth′ing** (ŭn′dẽr·klōth′ĭng). Clothes worn under others, esp. those worn next the skin.

un′der·cov′er (-kŭv′ẽr), *adj.* Acting or executed in secret.

un′der·croft′ (ŭn′dẽr·krŏft′; 74), *n.* [*under* + *croft* a vault.] *Arch.* A subterranean room; esp., a vaulted chamber under a church; a crypt.

un′der·cur′rent (-kûr′ĕnt), *n.* **1.** A current below the upper currents or surface. **2.** A hidden tendency of feeling or opinion, often contrary to that publicly shown.

un′der·cut′ (-kŭt′), *v. t.;* see CUT. **1.** To cut away the under part of; as, to *undercut* a vein of ore. **2.** To cut away or shape, so as to leave an overhanging portion in relief, as in carving and sculpture. **3.** To offer to sell at lower prices, or to work for lower wages, than (another). **4.** *Golf.* To strike obliquely down against (the ball) so as to impart backspin. **5.** *Lawn Tennis.* To cut (the ball) with an underhand stroke. — *v. i.* To undercut a surface, a ball, a rival, etc.

un′der·cut′ (ŭn′dẽr·kŭt′), *n.* **1.** An undercutting or a part so cut away. **2.** *Cooking.* **a** *Eng.* The tenderloin. **b** *U.S.* A piece of beef for roasting boned out from under the shoulder blade. **3.** *Golf.* Backspin. **4.** *Lawn Tennis.* A cut made with an underhand stroke.

un′der·do′ (-do͞o′), *v. i. & t.* To do less thoroughly than one can, or less than is requisite, as in cooking meat rare.

un′der·dog′ (ŭn′dẽr·dŏg′; 2; 74), *n.* The losing dog in a fight; hence, the loser in any struggle; esp., a victim of social injustice.

un′der·done′ (ŭn′dẽr·dŭn′; ŭn′dẽr·dŭn′; 2), *adj.* Not thoroughly cooked; rare.

un′der·drain′age (ŭn′dẽr·drān′ĭj), *n.* The drainage of soil by means of drains placed beneath the surface.

un′der·es′ti·mate (-ĕs′tĭ·māt), *v. t. & i.* To set too low a value on; to estimate below the truth; underrate. — **un′der·es′ti·mate** (-māt), **un′der·es′ti·ma′tion** (-mā′shŭn), *n.*

un′der·ex·pose′ (-ĕks·pōz′; -ĭks·pōz′), *v. t.* *Photog.* To expose for less time than is needed. — **un′der·ex·po′sure** (-pō′zhẽr), *n.*

un′der·feed′ (-fēd′), *v. t.;* see FEED. **1.** To feed with too little food. **2.** To feed, as a furnace, with fuel from the underside.

☞ See 2d UN-, *Note.*
un′con·fined′
un′con·firmed′
un′con·geal′a·ble
un′con·gealed′
un′con·gen′ial
un′con·nect′ed
un·con′quer·a·ble
un·con′quered
un′con·sci·en′tious
un·con′se·crat′ed
un′con·sid′ered
un·con′stant
un′con·strained′
un′con·sumed′
un′con·tam′i·nat′ed
un′con·test′ed
un′con·tra·dict′ed
un′con·trol′la·ble
un′con·trolled′
un′con·ven′tion·al
un′con·ven′tion·al′i·ty
un′con·vert′ed
un′con·vinced′
un′con·vinc′ing
un·cooked′
un′-co·or′di·nat′ed
un·corked′
un′cor·rect′ed
un′cor·rob′o·rat′ed
un′cor·rupt′ed
un·count′a·ble
un·cour′te·ous
un′cre·at′ed
un·cred′it·ed
un·crip′pled
un·crit′i·cal
un·crowned′
un·crys′tal·line
un·crys′tal·liz′a·ble
un·cul′ti·va·ble
un·cul′ti·vat′ed
un·cul′tured
un·curbed′
un·cur′dled
un·cured′
un·cu′ri·ous
un·cur′rent
un·cur′tained
un·cut′
un·dam′aged
un·damped′
un·dat′ed
un·daz′zled
un′de·ceived′
un′de·cid′ed
un′de·ci′pher·a·ble
un′de·ci′phered
un·decked′
un′de·clared′
un′de·clin′a·ble
un·dec′o·rat′ed
un′de·duc′i·ble
un′de·face′a·ble
un′de·feat′ed
un′de·fend′ed
un′de·fen′si·ble
un′de·filed′
un′de·fin′a·ble
un′de·fined′
un′de·layed′
un′de·liv′er·a·ble
un′de·liv′ered
un′dem·o·crat′ic
un′de·mon′stra·ble
un′de·nom′i·na′tion·al
un′de·pend′a·ble
un′de·pre′ci·at′ed

un′der·foot′ (ŭn′dẽr·fo͝ot′), *adv.* Under the feet, esp. against the ground; below at one's feet; *Colloq.*, in the way.

un′der·glaze′ (ŭn′dẽr·glāz′), *adj.* Applied before the glaze is put on; fitted to be so applied; — of colors in porcelain decoration.

un′der·go′ (-gō′), *v. t.;* see GO. To be subjected or submit to; to bear up against; to endure; suffer; sustain.

un′der·grad′u·ate (-grăd′ū·āt), *n.* A student in a university, a college, etc., who has not taken a degree.

un′der·ground′ (-ground′), *adv.* **1.** Beneath the surface of the earth. **2.** In secret; surreptitiously; into hiding and secrecy of operation.

un′der·ground′ (ŭn′dẽr·ground′), *adj.* Being, occurring, operating, or to be done or used underground; conveyed by secret means. — *n.* **1.** A subterranean space or channel. **2.** An underground railway, running in a subway, esp. one beneath the street level in a city. **3.** A movement or group organized in strict secrecy among citizens in an occupied or totalitarian country for maintaining communications, popular solidarity, and concerted resistive action pending liberation; also, any clandestine conspiratorial cell or organization set up for revolutionary or other disruptive purposes, esp. against a civil order.

Underground Railroad. Formerly, a system of co-operation among certain antislavery people in the United States, whereby fugitive slaves were secretly helped to reach the North or Canada.

un′der·growth′ (ŭn′dẽr·grōth′), *n.* **1.** Underbrush. **2.** Fine hair underlying the outer hair of a pelt.

un′der·hand′ (-hănd′; 2), *adv.* **1.** By secret means; in a clandestine manner; slyly; hence, by fraud. **2.** With an underhand motion.

un′der·hand′, *adj.* **1.** Performed with the hand swinging downward always lower than the shoulders. **2.** Secret; sly; clandestine; hence, unfair; fraudulent. — **Syn.** See SECRET. — **Ant.** Aboveboard.

un′der·hand′ed (*see Pron.*, § 2), *adj.* Underhand; clandestine. — **un′der·hand′ed·ly**, *adv.* — **un′der·hand′ed·ness**, *n.*

un′der·hung′ (ŭn′dẽr·hŭng′; 2), *adj.* **1.** Projecting beyond the upper jaw; — said of the lower jaw; also, having the lower jaw projecting beyond the upper jaw. **2.** Underslung.

un′der·laid′ (-lād′; 2), *adj.* **1.** Laid or placed underneath. **2.** Having something laid or lying underneath.

un′der·lay′ (-lā′), *v. t.;* -LAID′ (-lād′); -LAY′ING. [AS. *underlecgan.*] **1.** To cover or traverse the bottom of. **2.** To raise or support by something laid under. **3.** To place or interpose in an under or supporting position.

un′der·lay′ (ŭn′dẽr·lā′), *n.* A thickness of paper placed under type, etc., to bring it to the proper height for printing.

un′der·let′ (-lĕt′), *v. t.* **1.** To let below the real value. **2.** To sublet.

un′der·lie′ (-lī′), *v. t.;* -LAY′ (-lā′); -LAIN′ (-lān′); -LY′ING (-lī′ĭng). [AS. *underlicgan.*] **1.** To be subject or amenable to, as a challenge. **2.** To lie or be situated under. **3.** To be at the basis of; to form the foundation of; to support. **4.** *Finance.* To exist as a claim or security anterior and prior to (another).

un′der·line′ (-līn′), *v. t.* **1.** To draw a line under; to underscore. **2.** To emphasize. — (ŭn′dẽr·līn′), *n.* **1.** A line underneath. **2.** The outline of the lower part of an animal's body; also, the lower border of the flank of a domestic animal, as a sheep. See SHEEP, *Illust.*

un′der·ling (ŭn′dẽr·lĭng), *n.* [Late AS. See UNDER; 1st -LING.] One who is under another's orders; a subordinate; an underofficial.

un′der·ly′ing (-lī′ĭng; 2), *adj.* **1.** Lying beneath; fundamental; also, evident only on close inspection. **2.** *Finance.* Anterior and prior in claim.

un′der·mine′ (ŭn′dẽr·mīn′), *v. t.* **1.** To excavate beneath; to form a mine under. **2.** To subvert or weaken insidiously or secretly; to ruin underhandedly; as, to *undermine* a person's reputation; also, to ruin or weaken by degrees, as one's health. — **Syn.** See WEAKEN. — **un′der·min′er** (-mīn′ẽr), *n.*

un′der·most (ŭn′dẽr·mōst), *adj.* Lowest, as in place, rank, etc.

un′der·neath′ (ŭn′dẽr·nēth′; -nēth′), *adv.* [AS. *underneothan, undernythan.* See UNDER; BENEATH.] **1.** Under or below a surface or object; beneath. **2.** On the lower side. — *prep.* **1.** Directly beneath. **2.** Under subjection to. **3.** Under the guise or aspect of.

un′der·nour′ish (-nûr′ĭsh), *v. t.* To supply with insufficient nourishment, or less than the minimum necessary for sound health and growth. — **un′der·nour′ish·ment**, *n.*

un′dern·song′ (ŭn′dẽrn·sŏng′; 74), *n.* *Eccl.* Tierce; — an old name.

un′der·pass′ (ŭn′dẽr·pås′), *n.* A passage beneath, esp. a passageway for highway traffic under a railway. Cf. OVERPASS, GRADE CROSSING.

un′der·pin′ (-pĭn′), *v. t.* **1.** To lay stones, masonry, etc., under, as under the sills of a building, as a support. **2.** To place struts, props, or the like, underneath for support. **3.** To maintain, vindicate, or substantiate.

un′der·pin′ning (ŭn′dẽr·pĭn′ĭng), *n.* **1.** *Arch.* The material and construction used for support, introduced beneath a wall already constructed. **2.** *Colloq.* A person's legs.

un′der·plot′ (ŭn′dẽr·plŏt′), *n.* A series of events in a play, collateral with the main story but subservient to it.

un′der·priv′i·leged (-prĭv′ĭ·lĭjd), *adj.* Deprived, as through social or economic oppression, of some of the fundamental rights of all members of a civilized society.

un′der·pro·duc′tion (-prō·dŭk′shŭn), *n.* The production of less than enough to satisfy the demand, or of less than the usual supply.

un′der·proof′ (ŭn′dẽr·pro͞of′; 2), *adj.* Containing less alcohol than proof spirit. See PROOF SPIRIT.

un′der·quote′ (-kwōt′), *v. t.* To quote at a lower price than another; to quote a lower price than.

un′der·rate′ (-rāt′), *v. t.* To rate too low; to undervalue.

un′der·run′ (-rŭn′), *v. t.;* see RUN. **1.** To run or pass under. **2.** *Naut.* To pass along and under, as in a boat under a cable or net, to take it in or examine it.

un′der·score′ (-skōr′; 70), *v. t.* **1.** To draw a line under; to underline. **2.** To emphasize. — **un′der·score′** (ŭn′dẽr·skōr′), *n.*

un′der·sea′ (ŭn′dẽr·sē′), *adj.* Being, or carried on, beneath the surface of the sea; designed for use under the surface of the sea; as, an *undersea* boat.

un′der·sea′ (-sē′), **un′der·seas′** (-sēz′), *adv.* Under the sea; beneath the surface of the sea; as, a submarine moving *undersea.*

un′der·sell′ (-sĕl′), *v. t.;* see SELL. **1.** To sell cheaper than. **2.** To sell for less than the intrinsic value.

un′der·shap′en (-shāp′ĕn; 2), *adj.* Imperfectly shaped.

un′der·shot′ (ŭn′dẽr·shŏt′), *adj.* **1.** Having the lower incisor teeth projecting beyond the upper ones when the mouth is closed, as in a bulldog; also, having a projecting lower jaw. Cf. UNDERHUNG. **2.** Moved by water passing beneath; — of a water wheel (**undershot wheel**). Cf. OVERSHOT.

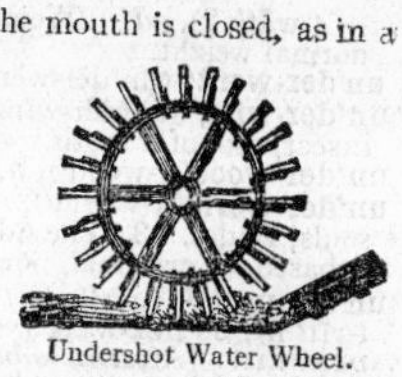

Undershot Water Wheel.

un′der·shrub′ (-shrŭb′), *n.* A low-growing shrubby plant.

un′der·side′ (-sīd′; 2), *n.* The side or surface lying underneath. — **un′der·side′**, *adj.*

un′der·sign′ (-sīn′), *v. t.* To write one's name at the foot or end of, as a letter. — ***the un′der·signed′*** (-sīnd′). The subscriber or subscribers.

un′der·sized′ (ŭn′dẽr·sīzd′; 2), *adj.* Also **un′der·size′**. Of a size less than is common, proper, normal, or average.

un′der·slung′ (-slŭng′; 2), *adj.* Suspended below the axles; — of the frame of an automotive vehicle.

un′der·song′ (ŭn′dẽr·sŏng′; 74), *n.* **1.** The burden of a song; an accompanying strain. **2.** Underlying meaning.

un′der·sparred′ (-spärd′; 2), *adj.* *Naut.* Having spars too small to spread the proper amount of canvas.

un′der·stand′ (ŭn′dẽr·stănd′), *v. t.;* -STOOD′ (-sto͝od′); -STAND′ING. [AS. *understandan* to understand, lit., to stand under.] **1.** To apprehend the purport or meaning of, as by knowing what is conveyed by the words or signs used, or by way of information or explanation; as, I did not *understand* the wink; I *understand* why he came; to have thorough or technical acquaintance with or expertness in the practice of, as finance. **2.** To gather or infer; to accept as the signification. **3.** To take or take to mean, according to one's individual interpretation; to interpret; explain. **4.** To take or accept as the signification; also, in the passive, to signify. **5.** To accept as established or laid down as a condition. **6.** To imply tacitly; to assume; as, conditions expressed or *understood.* **7.** *Chiefly Gram.* To supply in thought as if present.

Syn. Understand, comprehend, appreciate mean to have a clear or complete idea of. Understand and comprehend differ in precise use in that *understand* implies a result, and *comprehend* a mental process of arriving at a result (as, to come to *understand* a person in spite of difficulties in *comprehending* his peculiarities); appreciate implies a just estimation of a thing's true or exact value (as, to *appreciate* the strength of public opinion).

— *v. i.* **1.** To have understanding. **2.** To gain full mental grasp of the nature, significance, or explanation, of something. **3.** *Archaic.* To learn or be informed. **4.** To believe or infer to be the case; — usually parenthetically. **5.** To comprehend fully the implications of a situation and have a consequently tolerant or sympathetic attitude. — **un′der·stand′a·bil′i·ty** (-stăn′då·bĭl′ĭ·tĭ), *n.* — **un′der·stand′a·ble**, *adj.* — **un′der·stand′a·bly**, *adv.*

un′der·stand′ing, *n.* [AS.] **1.** Discernment, comprehension, or interpretation. **2.** Power to understand; capability of comprehending and judging; the rational powers taken collectively. **3.** *Philos.* The power to render experience intelligible by bringing perceived particulars under appropriate concepts. **4.** The intellectual power or the capacity of a particular person to form reasoned judgments; as, to despise one's *understanding.* **5. a** An agreement of opinion; an adjustment of differences; as, to reach an *understanding.* **b** A mutual agreement, informal but having definite engagements.

un′der·stand′ing, *adj.* Knowing; intelligent. — **un′der·stand′ing·ly**, *adv.*

un′der·state′ (ŭn′dẽr·stāt′), *v. t. & i.* To represent as less, or less strongly, than may be done truthfully. — **un′der·state′ment**, *n.*

un′der·stock′ (ŭn′dẽr·stŏk′), *n.* *Hort.* A plant or portion of a plant upon which a graft is made.

un′der·stood′ (-sto͝od′), *past & past part.* of UNDERSTAND. — *adj.* **1.** Fully apprehended. **2.** Agreed upon. **3.** Implied.

un′der·strap′per (ŭn′dẽr·străp′ẽr), *n.* An underling; an inferior or subordinate agent.

un′der·stud′y (-stŭd′ĭ), *v. i. & t.* *Theater.* To study another actor's part, in order to be his substitute in an emergency. — *n.* One who is prepared to act another's part.

un′der·take′ (-tāk′), *v. t.;* see TAKE. **1.** To take upon oneself; to engage in; to enter upon; to take in hand; set about, as a task. **2.** To enter into stipulations to perform or to execute; to covenant; contract. **3.** Hence, to guarantee; promise. **4.** To take over as a charge. **5.** Formerly, to engage with, as in combat. *Shak.* — *v. i.* *Archaic.* To guarantee or assume responsibility; to be surety; — usually with *for.*

un′der·tak′er (ŭn′dẽr·tāk′ẽr; ŭn′dẽr·tāk′ẽr), *n.* **1.** One who undertakes; specif., an entrepreneur. **2.** (*pron.* ŭn′dẽr·tāk′ẽr) One whose business is to prepare the dead for burial and to take the charge and management of funerals.

un′der·tak′ing (ŭn′dẽr·tāk′ĭng), *n.* **1.** Act of one who undertakes, or engages in, any project or business; specif. (*pron.* ŭn′dẽr·tāk′ĭng) the business of an undertaker. **2.** Anything undertaken; an enterprise. **3.** A promise or guarantee.

un′der·ten′ant (ŭn′dẽr·tĕn′ănt), *n.* The tenant of a tenant; one who holds land or tenements by sublease.

un′der·tone′ (-tōn′), *n.* **1.** A low or subdued tone or utterance. **2.** A subdued color; specif.: **a** A color seen through and modifying another or other colors. **b** The color of the light transmitted, as by a paint or varnish film. Cf. OVERTONE, 2. **3.** *Stock Exchanges.* An underlying stability in price level of a stock or commodity.

un′der·tow′ (-tō′), *n.* The current beneath the surface that sets seaward when waves are breaking upon the shore.

un′der·trick′ (-trĭk′), *n.* *Card Playing.* A trick, or any of the tricks, by which a player fails to make his contract.

un′der·trump′ (-trŭmp′), *v. t. & i.* *Card Playing.* To trump with a lower trump; to trump lower than (one's partner).

un′der·val′ue (-văl′ū), *v. t.* **1.** To value, rate, or estimate, below the real worth. **2.** To esteem lightly. — **un′der·val′u·a′tion** (ŭn′dẽr·văl′ū·ā′shŭn), *n.*

un′der·waist′ (ŭn′dẽr·wāst′), *n.* A waist for wear under another waist.

un′der·wa′ter (-wô′tẽr; -wŏt′ẽr), *adj.* **1.** Lying, growing, etc., below the surface of the water. **2.** That is below the water line of a ship.

under way. Into motion from a standstill.

un′der·wear′ (ŭn′dẽr·wâr′), *n.* Underclothes.

un′der·weight′ (-wāt′), *n.* Weight below normal or requisite weight.

— (-wāt'; 2), *adj.* Weighing less than the normal amount; below the normal weight.

un'der·went' (ŭn'dẽr·wĕnt'), *past* of UNDERGO.

un'der·wing' (ŭn'dẽr·wĭng'), *n.* *Zool.* One of the posterior wings of an insect, esp. of a moth.

un'der·wood' (-wŏŏd'), *n.* Undergrowth; underbrush.

un'der·world' (-wûrld'), *n.* **1.** The earth. **2.** The place of departed souls; Hades. **3.** The side of the globe opposite to one. **4.** The lower, debased, or criminal, portion of humanity.

un'der·write' (-rīt'), *v. t.*; UN'DER·WROTE' (-rōt'); UN'DER·WRIT'TEN (-rĭt''n); UN'DER·WRIT'ING (-rīt'ĭng). *Obs. past* and *past part.* UNDERWRIT. [After L. *subscribere* to subscribe; cf. AS. *underwrītan* to sign.] **1.** To write under something else; to subscribe. **2.** To write one's name under, or set one's name to (a policy of insurance), for the purpose of thereby becoming answerable for a designated loss or damage; hence, to insure on life or property; also, to assume (a certain sum or risk) by way of insurance. **3.** *Finance.* **a** To agree to purchase on a fixed date at a fixed price (normally an entire issue of bonds, capital stock, or the like). **b** Sometimes, loosely, to subscribe to (any large business enterprise). — *v. i.* To do the business of an underwriter.

un'der·writ'er (ŭn'dẽr·rīt'ẽr), *n.* **1.** One who underwrites a slip or policy of insurance; an insurer; *Colloq., U. S.*, one who determines the risks to be solicited and plans programs of insurance; as, a fire *underwriter.* **2.** *Finance.* One who shares in underwriting a loan, stock issue, or the like.

un'de·sign'ing (ŭn'dē·zīn'ĭng), *adj.* Having no artful, ulterior, or fraudulent, purpose; sincere; artless; simple.

un'de·sir'a·ble (ŭn'dē·zīr'ȧ·b'l), *adj.* **1.** Not desirable. **2.** Objectionable or unwanted, for example on grounds of alien race, radical views, or social amenities. — *n.* An objectionable person. — **un'de·sir'a·bil'i·ty** (-bĭl'ĭ·tĭ), *n.* — **un'de·sir'a·ble·ness,** *n.* — **un'de·sir'a·bly,** *adv.*

un·dine' (ŭn·dēn'; ŭn'dēn), *n.* [G. *undine,* F. *ondine,* fr. NL. *Undina,* fr. L. *unda* a wave, water.] A fabled female water spirit who might receive a human soul by marrying a mortal.

un'di·rect'ed (ŭn'dĭ·rĕk'tĕd; -tĭd; -dī-), *adj.* **1.** Not guided. **2.** Not addressed; not superscribed, as a letter.

un·do' (ŭn·dōō'), *v. t.*; UN·DID' (-dĭd'); UN·DONE' (-dŭn'); UN·DO'ING. [AS. *undōn, ondōn.*] **1.** To open or loose by releasing a lock, lacing, or other binding device, or by uncovering; to unfasten; untie; to release. **2.** To unravel or solve, as a riddle. **3.** To render null or as if not done, decided, imposed, etc., as a jury's findings; to reverse by restoring the original condition or form. **4.** To bring to ruin or disaster; to ruin, as in property, morals, hopes, or the like. — **un·do'er** (-dōō'ẽr), *n.*

un·do'ing (-dōō'ĭng), *n.* **1.** The reversal of what is done; annulment. **2.** Ruin or cause of ruin.

un·dou'ble (-dŭb''l), *v. t.* To unfold; to unclench.

un·doubt'ed (-dout'ĕd; -ĭd), *adj.* Not doubted or called in question; indubitable. — **un·doubt'ed·ly,** *adv.*

un·drape' (-drāp'), *v. t.* To strip of drapery; to unveil.

un·draw' (-drô'), *v. t.*; see DRAW. To draw aside, back, or open, as a curtain.

un·dress' (-drĕs'), *v. t.*; see DRESS. **1.** To divest of clothes; to strip. **2.** To divest of formal garments; to disrobe. **3.** To take the dressing from (a wound). — *v. i.* To strip.

un'dress' (ŭn'drĕs'; ŭn·drĕs'), *n.* **1.** A loose, informal dress. **2.** Ordinary dress as opposed to *full dress.*

‖und so wei'ter (ŏŏnt zō vī'tẽr). [G.] And so forth; et cetera. Abbr. *usw.*

un·due' (ŭn·dū'; ŭn'dū'; 2), *adj.* **1.** Not yet payable. **2.** Inappropriate; unsuitable. **3.** Not right; not lawful or legal; as, *undue* influence over another. **4.** Not agreeable to a standard; excessive; immoderate; inordinate.

un'du·lant (ŭn'dụ̈·lănt), *adj.* Undulating.

undulant fever. *Med.* A long-persisting bacterial disease characterized by an undulating, or remittent, fever, profuse perspiration, pain and swelling in the joints and an enlarged spleen. The disease is contracted from cattle, swine, and goats, and is transmitted esp. through milk; — called also *Mediterranean fever, Malta fever, brucellosis.*

un'du·late (ŭn'dụ̈·lāt), **un'du·lat'ed** (-lāt'ĕd; -ĭd), *adj.* [L. *undulatus* undulated, wavy, fr. *unda* a wave.] Having a wavy surface or margin or wavelike markings.

un'du·late (-lāt), *v. i.* **1.** To move in, or have, undulations. **2.** To rise and fall as if on waves; to surge. — *v. t.* To cause to move backward and forward, or up and down, in undulations or waves. — **Syn.** See SWING.

un'du·la'tion (-lā'shŭn), *n.* **1.** The action of rising and falling on or as if on waves; of sound, pulsation or a pulsation. **2.** A wavy appearance or outline. **3.** *Physics.* A continuously propagated motion to and fro, in any fluid or elastic medium, with no permanent translation of the particles themselves; a vibration; a wave.

un'du·la·to'ry (ŭn'dụ̈·lȧ·tō'rĭ; -tẽr·ĭ; 3), *adj.* Of or pertaining to undulation; moving in the manner of undulations; resembling waves; also, undulating.

undulatory theory. *Physics.* A theory that light is transmitted from luminous objects to the eye and other objects by an undulatory, or vibrational, movement; — called also *wave theory.*

un·du'ly (ŭn·dū'lĭ), *adv.* **1.** Not in accord with law or right. **2.** Beyond a proper degree; excessively.

un·dy'ing (ŭn·dī'ĭng), *adj.* Not dying; unending.

un·earned' (-ûrnd'; 2), *adj.* Not gained by labor or service.

unearned increment. *Econ.* An increase in the value of land due to no labor or outlay of the owner, but to natural causes making an increased demand for it, as increased population.

un·earth' (ŭn·ûrth'), *v. t.* To drive or draw from the earth; to exhume; hence, to bring to light. — **Syn.** See DISCOVER.

un·earth'ly (-lĭ), *adj.* **a** Not terrestrial; supernatural; preternatural; hence, weird; appalling; terrific. **b** Outlandish; preposterous. — **unearth'li·ness,** *n.*

un·eas'y (ŭn·ēz'ĭ), *adj.*; -EAS'I·ER (-ĭ·ẽr); -EAS'I·EST. **1.** Occasioning want of ease; constraining; cramping. **2.** Constrained; stiff; awkward. **3.** Restless or disturbed by pain, anxiety, or the like. — **un·eas'i·ly,** *adv.* — **un·eas'i·ness,** *n.*

un'em·ploy'a·ble (ŭn'ĕm·ploi'ȧ·b'l), *adj.* Not employable. — *n.* An unemployable person.

un'em·ployed' (-ploid'), *adj.* **1.** Not employed at any paid labor. **2.** Not invested. — *n.* An unemployed person; with *the,* unemployed persons collectively.

un'em·ploy'ment (-ploi'mĕnt), *n.* Unemployed state.

un·e'qual (ŭn·ē'kwăl), *adj.* Not equal; as: **1.** Not of the same size, length, talents, age, station, or the like; as, *unequal* in rank. **2.** Illbalanced or ill-matched; uneven. **3.** Not uniform; variable; irregular; as, *unequal* pulsations. **4.** Not adequate or sufficient; as, timber *unequal* to the strain. — **un·e'qual·ly,** *adv.*

un·e'qualed, un·e'qualled (-kwăld), *adj.* Not equaled; unmatched; unparalleled; unrivaled; surpassing.

un'e·quiv'o·cal (ŭn'ē·kwĭv'ō·kăl), *adj.* Not doubtful; not ambiguous; clear; sincere. — **un'e·quiv'o·cal·ly,** *adv.*

un·err'ing (ŭn·ûr'ĭng; -ẽr'ĭng), *adj.* Committing no mistake; certain; unfailing; infallible. — **un·err'ing·ly,** *adv.*

un'es·sen'tial (ŭn'ĕ·sĕn'shăl), *adj.* Not indispensable; unimportant.

un·e'ven (ŭn·ē'vĕn), *adj.* [AS. *unefen.*] **1.** Not level; not uniform; rough; rugged. **2.** **a** Not of equal length. **b** Not parallel. **3.** Odd; — of numbers. — **Syn.** See ROUGH. — **un·e'ven·ly,** *adv.* — **un·e'ven·ness,** *n.*

un'ex·am'pled (ŭn'ĕg·zăm'p'ld; ŭn'ĭg-; 9), *adj.* Having no example or similar case; unprecedented; unparalleled.

un'ex·cep'tion·a·ble (ŭn'ĕk·sĕp'shŭn·ȧ·b'l; ŭn'ĭk-), *adj.* Not liable to any exception or objection; beyond reproach. — **un'ex·cep'tion·a·ble·ness,** *n.* — **un'ex·cep'tion·a·bly,** *adv.*

un'ex·pect'ed (ŭn'ĕks·pĕk'tĕd; ŭn'ĭks·pĕk'tĭd; 30), *adj.* Not expected. — **un'ex·pect'ed·ly,** *adv.* — **un'ex·pect'ed·ness,** *n.*

un'ex·pres'sive (-prĕs'ĭv), *adj.* **1.** Inexpressive. **2.** *Obs.* Ineffable.

un·fail'ing (ŭn·fāl'ĭng), *adj.* **a** Unflagging. **b** Inexhaustible. **c** Infallible. — **un·fail'ing·ly,** *adv.*

un·fair' (ŭn·fâr'; 2), *adj.* [AS. *unfæger* unlovely.] **1.** Disingenuous; using or involving trick or artifice; dishonest; unjust. **2.** Not equitable in business dealings, esp. as regards competition, wages, or attitude toward labor unions. — **un·fair'ly,** *adv.* — **un·fair'ness,** *n.*

un·faith'ful (ŭn·fāth'fŏŏl; -f'l), *adj.* **a** Not observant of vows, allegiance, or duty. **b** Wanting in good faith; dishonest. **c** Inaccurate; untrustworthy; as, an *unfaithful* copy. **d** Not faithful to marriage vows. — **un·faith'ful·ly,** *adv.* — **un·faith'ful·ness,** *n.*

un'fa·mil'iar (ŭn'fȧ·mĭl'yẽr), *adj.* Not well known or not knowing well. — **un'fa·mil'i·ar'i·ty** (-ĭ·ăr'ĭ·tĭ; -yăr'ĭ·tĭ), *n.* — **un'fa·mil'iar·ly,** *adv.*

un·fas'ten (ŭn·făs''n), *v. t.* & *i.* To make or become loose.

un·fa'thered (-fä'thẽrd), *adj.* **a** Fatherless; hence, illegitimate; bastard. **b** Unauthenticated; spurious.

un·fa'vor·a·ble, un·fa'vour·a·ble (-fā'vẽr·ȧ·b'l), *adj.* Not propitious; adverse; contrary. — **un·fa'vor·a·ble·ness,** *n.* — **un·fa'vor·a·bly,** *adv.*

un·feel'ing (-fēl'ĭng), *adj.* **1.** Destitute of feeling; insensible; insensate. **2.** Cruel; hardhearted; callous. — **un·feel'ing·ly,** *adv.* — **un·feel'ing·ness,** *n.*

un·feigned' (-fānd'; 2), *adj.* Not counterfeit; not hypocritical; genuine. — **Syn.** See SINCERE. — **un·feign'ed·ly** (-fān'ĕd·lĭ; -ĭd·lĭ), *adv.* — **un·feign'ed·ness,** *n.*

un·fet'ter (ŭn·fĕt'ẽr), *v. t.* To unshackle; liberate.

un·fil'i·al (ŭn·fĭl'ĭ·ăl; -fĭl'yăl; 58), *adj.* Not observing, or according to, the obligations of a son or daughter.

un·fin'ished (ŭn·fĭn'ĭsht), *adj.* **1.** Not finished; incomplete; imperfect. **2.** Subjected to no other processes after coming from the loom; — of wool fabrics.

un·fit' (-fĭt'; 2), *adj.* [*un-* not + *fit.*] **1.** Having inherent or natural want of suitability. **2.** Not fitted; insufficiently adapted. — **un·fit'ly,** *adv.* — **un·fit'ness,** *n.*

un·fit' (ŭn·fĭt'), *v. t.* [1st *un-* + *fit.*] To make unsuitable or incompetent; to disable; incapacitate; disqualify.

un·fix' (ŭn·fĭks'), *v. t.* To loosen; to detach; unsettle.

un·fledged' (-flĕjd'; 2), *adj.* Not feathered; hence, not fully developed; immature.

un·flesh'ly (-flĕsh'lĭ), *adj.* Not of the flesh; spiritual.

☞ See 2d UN-, *Note.*

un'de·served'
un'de·serv'ing
un·des'ig·nat'ed
un'de·signed'
un'de·sired'
un'de·tach'a·ble
un'de·tect'ed
un'de·ter'mi·na·ble
un'de·ter'mined
un'de·terred'
un'de·vel'oped
un·de'vi·at'ing
un'dif·fer·en'ti·at'ed
un'di·gest'ed
un·dig'ni·fied
un'di·lut'ed
un'di·min'ished
un·dimmed'
un'dip·lo·mat'ic
un'dis·cern'i·ble
un'dis·cern'ing
un'dis·charged'
un·dis'ci·plined
un'dis·closed'
un'dis·cov'er·a·ble
un'dis·cov'ered
un'dis·crim'i·nat'ing
un'dis·guised'
un'dis·heart'ened
un'dis·mayed'
un'dis·posed'
un'dis·put'ed
un'dis·solved'
un'dis·tilled'
un'dis·tin'guish·a·ble
un'dis·tin'guished
un'dis·trib'ut·ed
un'dis·turbed'
un'di·ver'si·fied
un'di·vid'ed
un'di·vulged'
un'do·mes'tic
un'do·mes'ti·cat'ed
un·done'
un·dou'bled
un·doubt'ing
un·drained'
un'dra·mat'ic
un·draped'
un·dreamed', un·dreamt'
un·dressed'
un·drilled'
un·drink'a·ble
un·du'ti·ful
un·dyed'
un·eat'a·ble
un·eat'en
un'e·co·nom'i·cal
un·ed'i·fy'ing
un·ed'u·ca·ble
un·ed'u·cat'ed
un'ef·faced'
un'e·lim'i·nat'ed
un'em·bar'rassed
un'em·bel'lished
un'e·mo'tion·al
un'em·phat'ic
un'en·closed'
un'en·cum'bered
un'en·dan'gered
un·end'ing
un'en·dorsed'
un'en·dur'a·ble
un'en·dur'ing
un'en·force'a·ble
un'en·forced'
un'en·gaged'
un'en·joy'a·ble
un'en·light'ened
un'en·rolled'
un·en'ter·pris'ing
un'en·ter·tain'ing
un'en·thu'si·as'tic
un·en'vi·a·ble
un·en'vied
un·en'vi·ous
un'e·quipped'
un'es·cap'a·ble
un·es'ti·mat'ed
un·eth'i·cal
un'e·vent'ful
un'ex·ag'ger·at'ed
un'ex·celled'
un'ex·cep'tion·al
un'ex·change'a·ble
un'ex·cit'ing
un·ex'e·cut'ed
un'ex·haust'ed
un'ex·pend'ed
un'ex·pe'ri·enced
un'ex·pired'
un'ex·plain'a·ble
un'ex·plained'
un'ex·plod'ed
un'ex·plored'
un'ex·pressed'
un·ex'pur·gat'ed
un'ex·tin'guishod
un·fad'a·ble
un·fad'ing
un·fal'ter·ing
un·fash'ion·a·ble
un·fas'tened
un·fath'om·a·ble
un·fath'omed
un·fea'si·ble
un·fed'
un·fed'er·at'ed
un·felt'
un·fem'i·nine
un·fenced'
un'fer·ment'ed
un·fer'ti·lized
un·fet'tered
un·filled'
un·fired'
un·fit'ting
un·flag'ging
un·flat'ter·ing
un·fla'vored, -voured

un·flinch′ing (ŭn·flĭn′chĭng), *adj.* Not flinching or shrinking; unyielding. — **un·flinch′ing·ly**, *adv.*

un·fold′ (ŭn·fōld′), *v. t.* [AS. *unfealdan.*] **1.** To open the folds of; to expand or spread out. **2.** To lay open to view or contemplation; to bring out in the details, or by successive development; to display; disclose; reveal. **3.** To remove from the folds of; to unwrap. — *v. i.* To open; to become disclosed or developed, as buds. — **un·fold′er** (-fōl′dẽr), *n.*

un′for·get′ta·ble (ŭn′fŏr·gĕt′ȧ·b′l), *adj.* Not forgettable; enduring in memory. — **un′for·get′ta·bly**, *adv.*

un·formed′ (ŭn·fôrmd′; 2), *adj.* Not arranged in regular shape, order, or relations; shapeless; amorphous; specif., *Biol.*, unorganized, as a ferment.

un·for′tu·nate (ŭn·fôr′tū·nĭt), *adj.* Unsuccessful; not prosperous; unlucky; attended with or resulting in misfortune. — *n.* An unfortunate person; specif.: **a** A prostitute. **b** *Irish.* An insane person. — **un·for′tu·nate·ly**, *adv.*

un·found′ed (-foun′dĕd; -dĭd), *adj.* **1.** Not established. **2.** Having no foundation; baseless; vain; groundless.

un′fre·quent′ed (ŭn′frē·kwĕn′tĕd; -tĭd), *adj.* Rarely visited; seldom or never resorted to by human beings.

un·friend′ed (ŭn·frĕn′dĕd; -dĭd), *adj.* Having no friends; not befriended.

un·friend′ly (-frĕnd′lĭ), *adj.* **1.** Not friendly; not kind or benevolent; hostile. **2.** Not favorable; unpropitious. — **un·friend′li·ness**, *n.* — **un·friend′ly**, *adv.*

un·frock′ (-frŏk′), *v. t.* To divest of a frock; specif., to deprive (a priest or minister) of the right to exercise the functions of his office.

un·fruit′ful (ŭn·fro͞ot′fo͝ol; -f′l), *adj.* Not producing fruit or offspring; infertile; barren; unproductive; not remunerative. — **Syn.** See STERILE. — **un·fruit′ful·ly**, *adv.* — **un·fruit′ful·ness**, *n.*

un·fund′ed (-fŭn′dĕd; -dĭd), *adj.* Not funded (see FUND, *v. t.*, 2); floating; as, *unfunded* debt.

un·furl′ (-fûrl′), *v. t. & i.* To loose from a furled state.

un·gain′ly (ŭn·gān′lĭ), *adj.* [ME. *ungeinliche*, adv., fr. *ungein* inconvenient. See UN- not; GAINLY.] Clumsy; awkward; uncouth. — *adv.* In an ungainly manner. — **un·gain′li·ness**, *n.*

un·gen′er·ous (-jĕn′ẽr·ŭs), *adj.* Not generous; illiberal; exacting, harsh, or mean. — **un·gen′er·ous·ly**, *adv.*

un·gird′ (ŭn·gûrd′), *v. t.* [AS. *ungyrdan.*] To loose the girdle of; to unbind.

un·girt′ (-gûrt′; 2), *adj.* Having the girdle off or loose; hence, slack; loose; not braced.

un·glue′ (ŭn·glo͞o′; 114), *v. t. & i.* To part or open (anything fastened with or as with glue).

un·god′ly (ŭn·gŏd′lĭ), *adj.* **1.** Disobedient to God; wicked; impious. **2.** *Colloq.* Atrocious. — **un·god′li·ness** (-lĭ·nĕs; -nĭs), *n.*

un·got′ten (-gŏt′'n), *adj.* Also **un·got′** (-gŏt′). **1.** Not begotten. **2.** Not got or obtained.

un·gov′ern·a·ble (-gŭv′ẽr·nȧ·b′l), *adj.* Not capable of being governed, ruled, or restrained; licentious; unbridled. — **Syn.** See UNRULY.

un·grace′ful (-grās′fo͝ol; -f′l), *adj.* Inelegant; awkward; clumsy. — **un·grace′ful·ly**, *adv.* — **un·grace′ful·ness**, *n.*

un·gra′cious (-grā′shŭs), *adj.* **a** Not acceptable; unpleasant; unattractive. **b** Not courteous; rude. — **un·gra′cious·ly**, *adv.* — **un·gra′cious·ness**, *n.*

un·grate′ful (-grāt′fo͝ol; -f′l), *adj.* **1.** Not thankful for favors; making no return or an ill return. **2.** Unpleasing; disagreeable. — **un·grate′ful·ly**, *adv.* — **un·grate′ful·ness**, *n.*

un′gual (ŭng′gwăl), *adj.* [L. *unguis* a nail, claw, or hoof.] Pertaining to, resembling, or bearing a nail, claw, or hoof.

un·guard′ (ŭn·gärd′), *v. t.* To remove the guard from.

un′guent (ŭng′gwĕnt), *n.* [L. *unguentum*, fr. *unguere* to anoint.] A salve for sores, burns, or the like; ointment.

un′guen·tar′y (ŭng′gwĕn·tẽr′ĭ; -tẽr·ĭ), *adj.* Like an unguent; for or connected with unguents.

un·guic′u·late (ŭng·gwĭk′ū·lāt), *adj.* [L. *unguiculus* finger nail.] Furnished with nails, claws, or hooks. — *n.* A mammal having claws or nails, as distinguished from hoofed animals (ungulates) and cetaceans.

un′guis (ŭng′gwĭs), *n.; pl.* UNGUES (-gwēz). [L., nail, claw, or hoof.] **1.** A nail, claw, or hoof, as on a digit of a vertebrate. **2.** *Bot.* A claw-like base of a petal.

un′gu·la (ŭng′gū·lȧ), *n.; pl.* -LAE (-lē). [L., a claw, hoof, fr. *unguis* nail, claw, hoof.] **1.** A hoof; also, a claw, or nail. **2.** *Bot.* = UNGUIS, 2. **3.** *Geom.* A section or part of a cylinder, cone, or other solid of revolution, cut off by a plane oblique to the base.

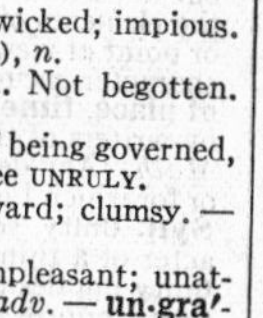

Ungula, 3.

un′gu·lar (-lẽr), *adj.* Pertaining to or like a hoof; ungual.

un′gu·late (-lāt), *adj.* [LL. *ungulatus.* See UNGULA.] **1.** Shaped like a hoof; having hoofs. **2.** Of or pertaining to the ungulates. — *n.* Any of a group (Ungulata) consisting of the hoofed mammals, as the ruminants, swine, horses, tapirs, rhinoceroses, elephants, and conies, nearly all exclusively herbivorous and many having horns.

un·hair′ (ŭn·hâr′), *v. t. & i.* To deprive of or lose the hair; to scrape the hair from (hides), as with a blunt two-handled knife.

un·hal′low (ŭn·hăl′ō), *v. t.* To profane; desecrate.

un·hal′lowed (-ōd), *adj.* Not consecrated; unholy.

un·hand′ (ŭn·hănd′), *v. t.* To loose from the hand; to let go.

un·hand′some (ŭn·hăn′sŭm), *adj.* Not handsome; as: **a** Not beautiful; homely. **b** Unbecoming or unseemly; discourteous. **c** Lacking noble or liberal qualities; mean.

un·hand′y (-hăn′dĭ), *adj.* Clumsy; awkward; inconvenient. — **un·hand′i·ly**, *adv.*

un·hap′py (ŭn·hăp′ĭ), *adj.* **1.** Not fortunate; unlucky; as, an *unhappy* event. **2.** Not cheerful or glad; sad; sorrowful; wretched. **3.** Marked by infelicity; calamitous; inappropriate. **4.** *Obs.* Mischievous; evil. — **un·hap′pi·ly**, *adv.* — **un·hap′pi·ness**, *n.*

un·har′ness (-här′nĕs; -nĭs), *v. t.* **1.** To strip of or loose from harness or gear. **2.** To disarm; to divest of armor.

un·health′y (ŭn·hĕl′thĭ), *adj.* **a** Unwell; diseased. **b** Not evincing health; as, an *unhealthy* complexion. **c** Not conducive to health; unwholesome. **d** Morally unsound; unwholesome. — **un·health′i·ly**, *adv.* — **un·health′i·ness**, *n.*

un·heard′ (ŭn·hûrd′), *adj.* **1.** Not heard; not perceived by the ear. **2.** Not granted a hearing; unheeded. **3.** Not known to fame; unknown.

un·heard′-of′, *adj.* Not heard of; unprecedented.

un·hinge′ (-hĭnj′), *v. t.* **1.** To take from the hinges. **2.** To render unstable; to unsettle, as one's mind.

un·hitch′ (ŭn·hĭch′), *v. t.* To free from or as if from being hitched; to unfasten; loose.

un·ho′ly (ŭn·hō′lĭ), *adj.* [AS. *unhālig.*] Unhallowed; not consecrated; hence, profane; wicked; also, *Colloq.*, frightful. — **un·ho′li·ly**, *adv.* — **un·ho′li·ness**, *n.*

un·hood′ (ŭn·ho͝od′), *v. t.* To remove a hood or disguise from.

un·hook′ (-ho͝ok′), *v. t. & i.* **1.** To loose, or to become loosed, from a hook. **2.** To disengage from being hooked.

un·hoped′ (-hōpt′; 2), *adj.* Not hoped or expected.

un·horse′ (-hôrs′), *v. t.* To throw from a horse; also, to take a horse from; by extension, to overthrow; dislodge.

un·hou′seled, un·hou′selled (-hou′z'ld), *adj.* Not having had the Eucharist administered.

un·hur′ried (ŭn·hûr′ĭd), *adj.* Not hurried; leisurely.

u′ni- (ū′nĭ-). [L. *unus* one.] A combining form meaning *one, single*, as in *uni*form; *characterized by, consisting of*, or *having, but one*, as in *uni*corn.

uniaxial	**unifoliate**	**unipersonal**
unicolor	**uniglobular**	**unipetalous**
unicostate	**unilingual**	**uniseptate**
unidirectional	**unilobed**	**unispinose**
uniflagellate	**unilocular**	**unispiral**
uniflorous	**uniocular**	**univalvular**

U′ni·at (ū′nĭ·ăt), *n.* Also **U′ni·ate** (-āt). [Russ. *uniyat*, fr. *uniya* union (i. e., with the Roman Church).] A Christian of an Eastern rite acknowledging the pope's primacy, and agreeing with the Latin Church in matters of faith, but differing from it in liturgy, in discipline, etc.

u′ni·cam′er·al (ū′nĭ·kăm′ẽr·ăl), *adj.* Having, or consisting of, a single chamber, or legislative house.

u′ni·cel′lu·lar (-sĕl′ū·lẽr), *adj.* *Biol.* Of a single cell.

unicellular animals. The protozoans.

u′ni·corn (ū′nĭ·kôrn), *n.* [OF. *unicorne*, fr. L. *unicornis*, lit., one-horned (fr. *unus* one + *cornu* a horn).] **1.** A fabulous animal resembling a horse with one horn. **2.** *Bib.* A two-horned animal called *rĕ'ēm* in Hebrew. See A.V. Deut. xxxiii. 17.

un′i·de′aed (ŭn′ī·dē′ăd), *adj.* Having no ideas; senseless.

u′ni·fi′a·ble (ū′nĭ·fī′ȧ·b′l), *adj.* Capable of being unified.

u′ni·fi·ca′tion (ū′nĭ·fĭ·kā′shŭn), *n.* Act, process, or result of unifying; state of being unified.

u′ni·fi′er (ū′nĭ·fī′ẽr), *n.* One who or that which unifies.

u′ni·fi′lar (ū′nĭ·fī′lẽr), *adj.* [*uni-* + L. *filum* a thread.] Having, or involving use of, only one thread, wire, or fiber.

u′ni·fo′li·ate (-fō′lĭ·āt), *adj.* *Bot.* Having only one leaf; — often used erron. for *unifoliolate.*

u′ni·fo′li·o·late (-fō′lĭ·ō·lāt; -fō·lī′ō·lāt), *adj.* *Bot.* Compound with but a single leaflet, as the leaf of the orange.

u′ni·form (ū′nĭ·fôrm), *adj.* [F. *uniforme*, fr. L. *uniformis*, fr. *unus* one + *forma* form.] **1.** Having always the same form, manner, or degree; not varying or variable; homogeneous; as, the temperate is *uniform.* **2.** Of the same form with others; conforming to one rule or mode; consonant. **3.** Presenting an undiversified appearance of surface, pattern, color, etc. **4.** Consistent in conduct, opinion, etc. — **Syn.** See SIMILAR; STEADY. — *n.* Dress of a particular style or fashion worn by persons in the same service, order, etc. — *v. t.* To clothe with a uniform. — **u′ni·form′ly**, *adv.* — **u′ni·form′ness**, *n.*

u′ni·formed (ū′nĭ·fôrmd), *adj.* Dressed in uniform.

u′ni·form′i·ty (ū′nĭ·fôr′mĭ·tĭ), *n.* State of being uniform.

u′ni·fy (ū′nĭ·fī), *v. t.* [F. or ML.; F. *unifier*, fr. ML. *unificare.*] To cause to be one; to make into a unit; to unite.

u′ni·ju′gate (ū′nĭ·jo͞o′gāt; ū·nĭj′o͞o·gāt; 114), *adj.* [*uni-* + L. *jugum* yoke, pair.] *Bot.* Having but one pair of leaflets; — of a pinnate leaf.

u′ni·lat′er·al (ū′nĭ·lăt′ẽr·ăl), *adj.* **1.** One-sided; done, made, undertaken, or shared by one of two or more persons or parties. **2.** *Bot. & Zool.* Produced or arranged on one side. **3.** *Law.* Pertaining to a contract or engagement imposing an express obligation on but one party. **4.** *Med.* Affecting but one side of the body. **5.** *Sociol.* Tracing descent through or from one side or line only.

un′im·peach′a·ble (ŭn′ĭm·pēch′ȧ·b′l), *adj.* Exempt from liability to accusation; irreproachable; blameless; unquestionable. — **un′im·peach′a·bly**, *adv.*

un′im·proved′ (-pro͞ovd′), *adj.* Not improved; as: **a** Not used or employed. **b** Not tilled, cultivated, or built upon, as land. **c** Not improved in health.

un′in·tel′li·gent (ŭn′ĭn·tĕl′ĭ·jĕnt), *adj.* Lacking intelligence; unwise;

☞ See 2d UN-, *Note.*

un·forced′
un′fore·see′a·ble
un′fore·seen′
un′for·get′ting
un′for·giv′a·ble
un′for·giv′en
un′for·giv′ing
un′for·got′ten
un·for′mu·lat′ed
un·for′ti·fied
un·framed′
un·free′
un′ful·filled′
un·fur′nished
un·gal′lant
un·gar′nished
un·gath′ered
un·gen′tle
un·gen′tle·man·ly
un·gift′ed
un·glazed′
un·glossed′
un·gov′erned
un·grad′ed
un·grained′
un′gram·mat′i·cal
un′gram·mat′i·cal·ly
un·ground′ed
un·grudg′ing
un·guard′ed
un·guid′ed
un·hack′neyed
un·ham′pered
un·hand′i·capped
un·hanged′
un·har′assed
un·hard′ened
un·harmed′
un′har·mo′ni·ous
un·har′nessed
un·hatched′
un·health′ful
un·heed′ed
un·heed′ful
un·heed′ing
un·her′ald·ed
un′he·ro′ic
un·hes′i·tat′ing
un·hin′dered
un·hon′ored, un·hon′oured
un·hoped′-for′
un·housed′
un·hurt′
un·hurt′ful
un′hy·gi·en′ic
un·hy′phen·at′ed
un·hy′phened
un′i·de′al
un′i·den′ti·fied
un′id·i·o·mat′ic
un′il·lu′mi·nat′ed
un′im·ag′i·na·ble
un′im·ag′i·na′tive
un′im·paired′
un′im·pas′sioned
un′im·ped′ed
un′im·por′tance
un′im·por′tant
un′im·pos′ing
un′im·press′i·ble
un′im·pres′sion·a·ble
un′im·pres′sive
un′in·closed′
un′in·cor′po·rat′ed
un′in·cum′bered
un′in·fect′ed
un′in·flam′ma·ble
un′in·flect′ed
un·in′flu·enced
un′in·formed′
un′in·hab′it·a·ble
un′in·hab′it·ed
un′in·i′ti·at′ed
un·in′jured
un′in·spired′
un′in·spir′ing
un′in·struct′ed
un′in·struc′tive

ignorant. — **un′in·tel′li·gence** (ŭn′ĭn·tĕl′ĭ·jĕns), *n.* — **un′in·tel′li·gent·ly,** *adv.*

un·in′ter·est·ed (ŭn·ĭn′tĕr·ĕs·tĕd; *see* INTERESTED), *adj.* **a** Not having or owning an interest (*in*). **b** Not interested; inattentive; apathetic; indifferent; — now the usual sense.

un′ion (ūn′yŭn), *n.* [F., fr. L. *unio* oneness, union, a single large pearl, fr. *unus* one.] **1.** Act or instance of uniting two or more things into one; state of being so united; junction; coalition; combination. **2.** A spiritual uniting to bring about concord; also, the unity so produced. **3.** A uniting into a nation, political body, or association, as the political change of 1706, uniting the kingdoms of England and Scotland on and after May 1, 1707. **4.** A uniting in marriage. **5.** That which is united, or made one; something formed by a combination or coalition of parts or members; a confederation; a consolidated body; as, the United States of America is often called ***the Union***. **6.** A device emblematic of union, used on a national flag or ensign, sometimes covering the whole field, as the three crosses in the British ensign, sometimes occupying an upper inner corner, as, in the U. S. ensign, the cluster of white stars on a blue field. **7.** *Eng.* **a** Two or more parishes united for administration of poor relief, etc. **b** A workhouse maintained by such a union. **8.** A league or association for a common purpose, as for religious or debating purposes. **9.** A trade-union (which see). **10.** *Mach.* Any of various devices for connecting machine parts, etc., esp., a coupling for pipes, and/or fittings, facilitating connection or disconnection. — **Syn.** See UNITY.

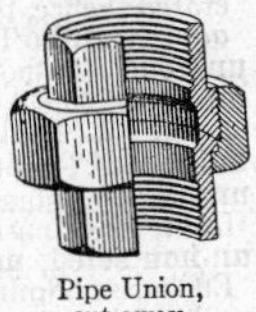
Pipe Union, cut away.

union card. A card certifying personal membership in good standing in a labor union.

un′ion·ism (ūn′yŭn·ĭz′m), *n.* **1.** Principle of, or sentiment of attachment to, a union; specif. [*cap.*], to the federal union of the United States, esp. at the time of the Civil War. **2.** The principles or system of trade-unions. — **un′ion·ist** (-ĭst), *n.*

un′ion·ize (-īz), *v. t.* **1.** To form into a union. **2.** To cause to become a member of, or subject to the rules of, a trade-union. — **un′-ion·i·za′tion** (-ĭ·zā′shŭn; -ī·zā′-), *n.*

union jack. A jack (def. 13) consisting of the union of a national ensign; hence, a flag symbolizing union of two or more states; specif. [*caps.*]: **a** The national flag of the United Kingdom, combining the crosses of St. George, St. Andrew, and St. Patrick. **b** *U.S.* A blue flag charged with one white star for each state of the Union.

union shop. An establishment in which the employer by agreement is free to hire nonmembers as well as members of the union but retains nonmembers on the payroll only on condition of their becoming members of the union within a specified time.

u·nip′a·rous (ū·nĭp′ȧ·rŭs), *adj.* [*uni-* + *-parous.*] **1.** *Zool.* Producing but one egg or offspring at a time. **2.** *Bot.* Producing but one axis at each branching.

u′ni·pla′nar (ū′nĭ·plā′nẽr), *n.* *Mech.* Lying or occurring in one plane; as, *uniplanar* motion.

u′ni·pod (ū′nĭ·pŏd), *n.* [*uni-* + *pod*, after *tripod.*] A one-legged support, as for a camera. — **u′ni·pod,** *adj.*

u′ni·po′lar (-pō′lẽr), *adj.* **a** *Physics.* Having, produced by, or acting by one pole only. **b** *Anat.* Designating nerve cells having but one process, as in spinal ganglia.

u·nique′ (ū·nēk′), *adj.* [F., fr. L. *unicus;* akin to L. *unus* one.] **1.** Single; sole. **2.** Being without a like or equal; single in kind or excellence; unequaled; matchless. — **Syn.** See SINGLE: STRANGE. — **u·nique′ly,** *adv.* — **u·nique′ness,** *n.*

u′ni·sex′u·al (ū′nĭ·sĕk′shŏŏ·ăl; -sĕks′ū·ăl), *adj.* Of one sex; as: **a** *Bot.* Diclinous. **b** *Zool.* Either male or female; not hermaphrodite.

u′ni·son (ū′nĭ·sŭn; -s′n; -zŭn; -z′n), *n.* [F. *unisson*, fr. ML. *unisonus* having the same sound, fr. L. *unus* one + *sonus* a sound.] **1.** *Music.* **a** Identity in pitch; the interval of a perfect prime. **b** State of being so tuned or sounded. Parts played or sung in octaves are also loosely said to be in *unison;* a piece or passage is said to be sung or played in *unison* when all the voices or instruments perform the same part. **2.** Harmony; agreement; concord.

u·nis′o·nous (ū·nĭs′ō·nŭs), *adj.* Also, **u·nis′o·nal** (-năl), **u·nis′o·nant** (-nănt). Being in unison; sounded alike in pitch.

u′nit (ū′nĭt), *n.* [From UNITY.] **1.** A distinct part or member analyzable in an aggregate or whole. **2.** Any determinate amount or quantity (as of length, time, heat, value) adopted as a standard of measurement. **3.** A single thing or person, or a group regarded as an individual member of a number of groups. **4.** *Biol., Immunol., etc.* The amount of a drug, serum, or antigen required to produce a certain result; as, a clinical *unit;* specif., the quantity required to produce a particular effect upon a particular animal or upon animal tissues. **5.** *Educ.* A basic amount of work used in calculating credits, as in secondary schools approximately 120 hours of classroom work in a course. **6.** *Math.* **a** *Arith.* The least whole number; one. **b** A single thing, as a magnitude or number, regarded as an undivided whole.

u′nit·age (ū′nĭ·tĭj), *n.* Specification of the amount or quantity constituting a unit in any system of measure.

U′ni·tar′i·an (ū′nĭ·târ′ĭ·ăn; 6), *n.* **1.** One who denies the doctrine of the Trinity, believing that God exists only in one person. **2.** One of a religious denomination holding the belief that God exists only in one person. — *adj.* **1.** [*not cap.*] Unitary. **2.** [*cap.*] Of or pertaining to Unitarians or their doctrines. — **U′ni·tar′i·an·ism** (-ĭz′m), *n.*

u′ni·tar′y (ū′nĭ·tĕr′ĭ *or, esp. Brit.,* -tẽr·ĭ), *adj.* **1.** Of or pertaining to a unit or units; relating to, based upon, or characterized by unity. **2.** Having the character of a unit; not divided; integrated.

‖**U′ni·tas Fra′trum** (ū′nĭ·tăs frā′trŭm). [L., unity of brethren.] See BOHEMIAN BRETHREN.

unit character. *Biol.* A trait inherited singly in accord with Mendel's law; a Mendelian character.

u·nite′ (ū·nīt′), *v. t.* [L. *unitus*, past part. of *unire* to unite, fr. *unus* one.] **1.** To put together so as to make one; to combine; connect; to cause to adhere. **2.** To join by a legal or moral bond, as families by intermarriage, nations by treaty, men by opinions; to join in interest, fellowship, or the like. **3.** To amalgamate; consolidate. **4.** To have in union or combinations, as qualities. — *v. i.* **1.** To become one or as one; to become cemented or consolidated or incorporated together; to coalesce. **2.** To act in concert. — **Syn.** See JOIN. — **Ant.** Divide.

u′nite (ū′nīt; ū·nīt′), *n.* An English gold coin of James I, current at 20 shillings; — from the union (1603) of England and Scotland.

u·nit′ed (ū·nīt′ĕd; -ĭd), *adj.* **1.** Combined; made one. **2.** Pertaining to or produced by joint action. **3.** In agreement; harmonious. — **u·nit′ed·ly,** *adv.*

United Nations. Also **UN** (ū′ĕn′). An international organization growing out of the association of the nations allied against the Axis powers in World War II (Declaration by the United Nations at Washington, Jan. 1, 1942, by 26 nations) and formed on the basis of a charter drafted and adopted at San Francisco, Apr. 25–June 26, 1945, by representatives of 50 nations binding them to maintain international peace and security and to achieve international co-operation in solving economic, social, cultural, or humanitarian problems. The charter came into force on the 29th ratification Oct. 24, 1945.

United Nations Relief and Rehabilitation Administration. An organization set up by agreement of 44 nations, Nov. 9, 1943, for assisting in furnishing the medicine, food, clothing, and other basic necessities and essential services required to restore the strength of the liberated peoples. Terminated June 30, 1947, except in China. Abbr. *UNRRA* (ŭn′rȧ; -rä).

united states. A federation of states, esp.: [*cap.*] One forming a nation in some (specified) territory; specif., the United States of America.

United States Employment Service. A bureau of the U. S. Department of Labor (from 1933) for co-ordinating a nationwide system of employment offices, made a federal war agency (Dec. 1941), transferred to the Federal Security Agency (July 1, 1948). Abbr. *USES*

unit factor. *Biol.* A gene, or factor, responsible for the inheritance of a unit character.

u′ni·tive (ū′nĭ·tĭv), *adj.* [ML. *unitivus.*] Characterized by, or tending to produce, union.

unit magnetic pole. A magnetic pole which will repel an equal and like pole at a distance of one centimeter in a vacuum with a force of one dyne.

unit rule. *U. S. Politics.* The rule, adopted by some delegations in a political convention, that the entire vote of the delegation shall be cast as a unit as determined by a majority vote.

u′ni·ty (ū′nĭ·tĭ), *n.; pl.* -TIES (-tĭz). [OF. *unité*, fr. L. *unitas*, fr. *unus* one.] **1.** State of being one; singleness; absence of diversity. **2.** Concord; harmony; accord; uniformity; as, a *unity* of sentiment. **3.** A uniting or being united into one body; unification. **4.** A totality of related parts; a complex or systematic whole. **5.** Continuity without deviation or change, as in purpose or action. **6.** The reference of the elements of a literary or artistic composition to a single main idea or point of view; also, the singleness of effect or consistency of style and character secured. **7.** *Drama.* Any of the three principles (**unities of place, time, and action**) governing the structure of drama derived by writers of the French classical school from Aristotle's *Poetics.* **8.** *Math.* Any definite quantity, or aggregate of quantities, taken as one, or for which 1 is made to stand in calculation; often the unit 1.

Syn. **Unity, solidarity, integrity, union** mean the property or character of a thing that is a whole composed of many elements or parts. **Unity** implies oneness, esp. of that which is varied and diverse rather than uniform in its elements or its parts; **solidarity** implies that unity in a group, class, community, etc., that enables it to express its opinions, manifest its strength, or exert its influence as one; **integrity** implies that unity, esp. of a built-up or created thing, which indicates the interdependence of parts and the completeness and perfection of the whole; **union**, now somewhat rare in this sense, implies a thorough integration of parts and their harmonious co-operation.

u′ni·va′lent (ū′nĭ·vā′lĕnt; ū·nĭv′ȧ·lĕnt), *adj.* [*uni-* + L. *valens, -entis*, pres. part. See VALENCE.] **1.** *Biol.* Single; — said esp. of a chromosome which fails to unite with, or lacks, a synaptic mate. **2.** *Chem.* Having a valence of one. — **u′ni·va′lence** (-lĕns), **u′ni·va′len·cy** (-lĕn·sĭ), *n.*

u′ni·valve′ (ū′nĭ·vălv′), *adj.* Also **u′ni·valved′** (-vălvd′). *Zool. & Bot.* Having one valve only. — *n.* A mollusk shell consisting of one piece; also, any mollusk with a univalve shell; specif., any gastropod. — **u′ni·val′vu·lar** (-văl′vū·lẽr), *adj.*

u′ni·ver′sal (ū′nĭ·vûr′săl; -s'l), *adj.* [OF. *universal, universel*, fr. L. *universalis.*] **1.** Including or covering the whole or all, either collectively or distributively; unlimited; as, *universal* suffrage. **2.** Of or pertaining to the universe; present everywhere or in all. **3.** Constituting, or considered as, a whole; entire; as, the *universal* world. **4.** Versed or interested in, or embracing, a wide range of subjects, pursuits, etc.; as, a *universal* genius. **5.** Used or for use among all, esp. all peoples; as, a *universal* language. **6.** *Logic.* Generic; relatively unrestricted in application; (of a proposition) affirming or denying something of every member of a class. "No man is omniscient" is a *universal* negative. **7.** *Mach., Elec., etc.* Adapted or adaptable to all or to various uses, shapes, sizes, etc.; as, a *universal* bevel.

Syn. **Universal, general, generic** mean of or relating to all or the whole. **Universal**, used chiefly in logic and philosophy, implies reference to every one without exception in the class, category, or genus considered; **general**, a more common term, reference to all or nearly all not only of a class or category but of any group considered (as, the idea has met with *general* but not *universal* acceptance); **generic**, chiefly a biological term, reference to every member of a genus (as, there are *generic* likenesses between all animals called dogs).

— *n.* **1** *Logic.* **a** A universal proposition. **b** One of the five predicables, namely genus, species, difference, property, accident, named collectively ***the universals***. **c** A general concept or that in reality to which it corresponds; an abstract and general term or what such a term denotes; an abstraction. **2.** *Metaph.* Any metaphysical being which preserves or evinces an identity of nature through a series of changes or as embodying different relations, as the ego or self.

— **u′ni·ver′sal·ly,** *adv.* — **u′ni·ver′sal·ness,** *n.*

U′ni·ver′sal·ism (-ĭz′m), *n.* *Theol.* The doctrine that all men will eventually be saved. — **U′ni·ver′sal·ist** (-ĭst), *n. & adj.*

u′ni·ver·sal′i·ty (ū′nĭ·vûr·săl′ĭ·tĭ), *n.; pl.* -TIES (-tĭz). **1.** Quality or state of being universal. **2.** Universal comprehensiveness in range; unrestricted versatility.

u′ni·ver′sal·ize (-vûr′săl·īz), *v. t.* To make universal.

☞ See 2d UN-, *Note.*	un′in·tel′li·gi·bly	un′in·ten′tion·al·ly	un′in·ter·mit′tent	un′in·ven′tive	un′in·vit′ed
un′in·tel′li·gi·bil′i·ty	un′in·tend′ed	un·in′ter·est·ing	un′in·ter·mit′ting	un′in·vert′ed	un′in·vit′ing
un′in·tel′li·gi·ble	un′in·ten′tion·al	un′in·ter·mit′ted	un′in·ter·rupt′ed	un′in·vest′ed	un·is′sued

universal joint *or* **coupling.** *Mach.* Any of various joints or couplings permitting swiveling or turning at any angle within defined limits, as in the ball-and-socket joint.

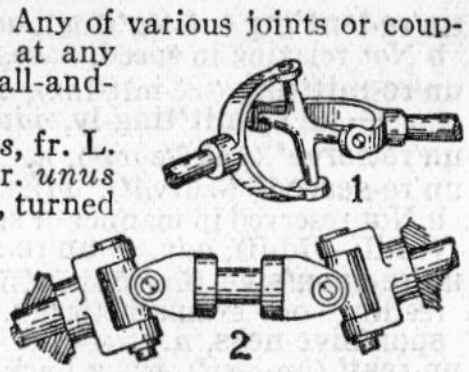

u′ni·verse (ū′nĭ·vûrs), n. [F. *univers*, fr. L. *universum*, fr. *universus* universal, fr. *unus* one + *vertere*, *versum*, to turn, that is, turned into one, combined into one whole.] **1.** All created things viewed as constituting one system or whole; the creation; the cosmos. **2.** Any distinct field or province of thought or reality conceived as forming a closed system or self-inclusive and independent organization. **3.** *Astron.* Properly, the entire celestial cosmos; the totality of the observed or postulated physical whole. — **Syn.** See EARTH.

1 Single, and 2 Double, Universal Joint.

universe of discourse. *Logic.* That collection of facts or ideas which is tacitly implied and understood in a given statement or discussion.

u′ni·ver′si·ty (ū′nĭ·vûr′sĭ·tĭ), n.; pl. -TIES (-tĭz). An institution organized for teaching and study in the higher branches of learning, and empowered to confer degrees in special departments, as theology, law, medicine, and the arts. In the United States, a university typically comprises a college and one or more graduate or professional schools.

un·just′ (ŭn·jŭst′; 2), adj. **1.** Contrary to justice and right; wrongful. **2.** *Now Rare.* Dishonest; faithless. — **un·just′ly,** adv. — **un·just′ness,** n.

un·kempt′ (ŭn·kĕmpt′; 2), adj. [*un-* not + *kempt*, past part. of *kemb*, Scot. or dial. var. of COMB.] **1.** Not combed; disheveled; as, *unkempt* hair. **2.** Unrefined; unpolished; rough. — **un·kempt′ness,** n.

un·kenned′ (-kĕnd′; *Scot.* -kĕnt′), adj. *Dial.* Strange.

un·ken′nel (ŭn·kĕn′ĕl; -'l), v. t. & i. **1.** To drive, take, or come from a kennel or hole. **2.** To discover; disclose.

un·kind′ (ŭn·kīnd′; 2), adj. Wanting in kindness, sympathy, or the like; cruel; harsh. — **un·kind′ly,** adv. — **un·kind′ness,** n.

un·kind′ly, adj. Ungracious; harsh. — **un·kind′li·ness,** n.

un·knit′ (ŭn·nĭt′), v. t. & i.; see KNIT. [AS. *uncnyttan* to untie.] To undo or unravel.

un·know′a·ble (ŭn·nō′á·b'l), adj. That cannot be known or comprehended; specif., *Philos.*, beyond the limits of human experience or of human powers of apprehension or understanding. — *the Unknowable.* Absolute reality, conceived as lying beyond human experience or understanding.

Un·known′ Sol′dier (ŭn·nōn′; 2). [*also not cap.*] An unidentified soldier whose body has been selected, as a representative of all of the same nation who died in World War I, to receive national honors, esp. on Armistice Day.

un·lace′ (ŭn·lās′), v. t. **1.** To loose by undoing a lacing. **2.** To loose the dress; to undress.

un·lade′ (-lād′), v. t.; see LADE. **1.** To take the load from; to take out the cargo of (a ship, etc.). **2.** To unload or discharge (cargo, etc.).

un·lash′ (-lăsh′), v. t. To untie the lashing of; to undo.

un·latch′ (-lăch′), v. t. To open or loose by lifting the latch. — v. i. To become loosed or opened.

un·law′ful (ŭn·lô′fŏŏl; -f'l), adj. **1.** Not lawful; illegal. **2.** Illegitimate. — **un·law′ful·ly,** adv. — **un·law′ful·ness,** n.

un·lay′ (-lā′), v. t. & i.; see LAY. *Naut.* To untwist, as a rope.

un·lead′ed (-lĕd′ĕd; -ĭd), adj. **1.** Stripped of lead; not weighted or covered with lead. **2.** *Print.* Not having leads between the lines; solid (see SOLID, adj., 9).

un·learn′ (ŭn·lûrn′), v. t.; see LEARN. To put out of memory or to teach the contrary of or to disbelieve (something one has learned).

un·learn′ed (ŭn·lûr′nĕd; -nĭd), adj. **1.** Untaught; illiterate. **2.** (pron. -lûrnd′). Not gained by study or experience. **3.** Not exhibiting learning. — **Syn.** See IGNORANT.

un·leash′ (-lēsh′), v. t. To free from or as from a leash.

un·less′ (ŭn·lĕs′; ŭn-), conj. [Formerly, *onles*, *onlesse*, *onlesse that*, that is, in less, in a less case than. See ON; LESS.] If not; supposing that not; except that. — prep. Except; excepting; — now only preceding elliptical adverbial clauses; as, *unless* on occasions, nobody rides.

un·let′tered (ŭn·lĕt′ẽrd), adj. Not marked with letters; not lettered; also, illiterate. — **Syn.** See IGNORANT.

un·like′ (ŭn·līk′; 2), adj. **1.** Having no resemblance; dissimilar; diverse; as, brothers having *unlike* traits; as *unlike* as day and night; also, unequal; as, contributing *unlike* amounts. **2.** In this sense also prep. Not characteristic of; differing from in character or appearance or unbefitting; as, this neglect, or this photograph, is *unlike* him; it is *unlike* him to refuse. — adv. & prep. In a manner dissimilar to or unbefitting; as, to behave *unlike* a soldier. — **un·like′ness,** n. — **Syn.** See DISSIMILARITY.

un·like′ly, adj. **1.** Improbable. **2.** Not holding out a prospect of success; likely to fail. — **un·like′li·hood,** n. — **un·like′li·ness,** n.

un·lim′ber (ŭn·lĭm′bẽr), v. t. & i. To detach the limber (from) and so make ready; hence, to get ready for action.

un·lim′it·ed (-lĭm′ĭt·ĕd; -ĭd), adj. **1.** Boundless. **2.** Undefined; not bounded by proper exceptions. **3.** Unconfined; unrestricted.

un·link′ (ŭn·lĭngk′), v. t. To separate or undo the links of.

un·list′ed (ŭn·lĭs′tĕd; -tĭd), adj. *Stock Exchange.* Not listed; not admitted to trading on an exchange.

un·live′ (ŭn·lĭv′), v. t. **a** To live in a manner contrary to. **b** To live down; to annul, as a memory or reputation gained from some experience.

un·load′ (-lōd′), v. t. **1.** To take the load or cargo from; to disburden. **2.** To relieve from anything onerous. **3.** To discharge or remove, as a burden or one's resentment. **4.** To draw the charge from (a gun). **5.** *Stock Exch.* To sell in large quantities, as stock; to get rid of. — v. i. To perform the act of unloading something. — **un·load′er,** n.

un·lock′ (ŭn·lŏk′), v. t. **1.** To unfasten as what is locked. **2.** To open; to undo; hence, to disclose.

un·looked′ (-lŏŏkt′), adj. Not observed or foreseen; unexpected; — generally **un·looked′-for′.**

un·loose′ (ŭn·lōōs′), v. t. To loosen; to set free.

un·loos′en (-lōōs′'n), v. t. To loosen; to unloose.

un·love′ly (ŭn·lŭv′lĭ), adj. Not amiable; having qualities that excite dislike; disagreeable. — **un·love′li·ness,** n.

un·luck′y (-lŭk′ĭ), adj. **1.** Unfortunate; ill-fated. **2.** Bringing bad luck; ill-omened. — **un·luck′i·ly,** adv. — **un·luck′i·ness,** n.

un·make′ (ŭn·māk′), v. t.; see MAKE. **1.** To destroy the form and qualities of; to deprive of being. **2.** To depose from a rank, position, etc.; to reduce to a lower grade. **3.** To destroy; ruin.

un·man′ (-măn′), v. t. **1.** To emasculate. **2.** To deprive of the courage and fortitude of a man; to make womanish. **3.** To deprive of men. — **Syn.** See UNNERVE.

un·man′ly (-lĭ), adj. **a** Not having a man's character or qualities. **b** Unbecoming a man. — **un·man′li·ness,** n.

un·manned′ (ŭn·mănd′; 2), adj. Deprived of virility.

un·manned′, adj. **a** Without its complement of men. **b** Unpeopled.

un·manned′ (ŭn·mănd′), adj. [*un-* not + *man* + *-ed*.] *Obs. Falconry.* Not tamed.

un·man′nered (ŭn·măn′ẽrd), adj. Rude; discourteous.

un·man′ner·ly (ŭn·măn′ẽr·lĭ), adj. Not mannerly; rude. — adv. Uncivilly. — **un·man′ner·li·ness,** n.

un·mask′ (ŭn·másk′; 9), v. t. To strip of a mask or disguise; to lay open; to expose. — v. i. To put off a mask.

un·mean′ing (-mēn′ĭng), adj. **1.** Having no meaning. **2.** Not indicating intelligence; senseless.

un·meant′ (-mĕnt′), adj. Not meant; unintentional.

un·meet′ (ŭn·mēt′), adj. [AS. *unmǣte.*] Not fit; unbecoming; unsuitable.

un·men′tion·a·ble (-mĕn′shŭn·á·b'l), adj. Not of a fit nature to be talked about. — n. pl. Unmentionable things; as, humorously, various articles of clothing. — **un·men′tion·a·ble·ness,** n.

un·mer′ci·ful (-mûr′sĭ·fŏŏl; -f'l), adj. Cruel; inhuman; merciless. — **un·mer′ci·ful·ly,** adv.

un·mew′ (ŭn·mū′), v. t. [1st *un-* + *mew* to confine.] To release from confinement.

un·mind′ful (-mīnd′fŏŏl; -f'l), adj. Not mindful; forgetful. — **Syn.** See FORGETFUL.

un·mis·tak′a·ble (ŭn′mĭs·tāk′á·b'l), adj. Not capable of being mistaken or misunderstood; clear; obvious; evident. — **un′mis·tak′a·bly,** adv.

un·mi′ter, un·mi′tre (ŭn·mī′tẽr), v. t. To depose or degrade from the rank of a bishop.

un·mit′i·gat′ed (-mĭt′ĭ·gāt′ĕd; -ĭd), adj. **1.** Not softened or lessened; stark; as, the desert in its *unmitigated* reality. **2.** Unqualified; downright; as, an *unmitigated* falsehood; *unmitigated* impudence; also, absolute; out-and-out; as, an *unmitigated* liar, ass, or fraud. — **un·mit′i·gat′ed·ly,** adv.

un·moor′ (ŭn·mŏŏr′; 84), v. t. & i. To loose (a vessel) from moorings or anchorage.

un·mor′al (ŭn·mŏr′ăl), adj. Having no moral perception, quality, or relation; not involving morality. — **un′mo·ral′i·ty** (ŭn′mō·răl′ĭ·tĭ), n. — **un·mor′al·ly,** adv.

un·mor′tise (ŭn·môr′tĭs), v. t. To loosen, unfix, or separate, as a mortise, or things mortised together.

un·muf′fle (-mŭf′'l), v. t. **1.** To take a covering from. **2.** To remove the muffling of, as a drum.

un·muz′zle (-mŭz′'l), v. t. To remove a muzzle from.

un·nail′ (-nāl′), v. t. To remove the nails from.

un·nat′u·ral (ŭn·năt′ũ·răl), adj. **a** Contrary to the order of nature; hence, artificial. **b** Without, or acting contrary to, natural traits or instincts. **c** Abnormally cruel or wicked; also, strange; abnormal. — **Syn.** See IRREGULAR. — **un·nat′u·ral·ly,** adv. — **un·nat′u·ral·ness,** n.

un·nec·es·sar′y (ŭn·nĕs′ē·sĕr′ĭ *or*, esp. Brit., -sĕr′ĭ), adj. Not required under the circumstances; useless; needless. — **un·nec′es·sar′i·ly** (-ĭ·lĭ), adv.

un·nerve′ (ŭn·nûrv′), v. t. To deprive of nerve; hence, of courage, steadiness, etc.; to cause to lose self-control.

Syn. Unnerve, enervate, unman, emasculate mean to deprive of vigor. Unnerve implies marked loss of courage or self-control or of power to act or fight; enervate, a gradual dissipation of one's strength until one is too feeble to make effort; unman, a loss of manly fortitude or spirit; emasculate, a loss of virile power which has made for the strength of a person, a group, or the like.

un·num′bered (ŭn·nŭm′bẽrd), adj. Innumerable.

un·oc′cu·pied (-ŏk′ū·pīd), adj. **a** Not occupied; empty. **b** Not busy; unemployed.

un·or′gan·ized (-ôr′găn·īzd), adj. Not organized; without organic structure; as: **a** Not brought into a coherent or well-ordered whole. **b** Not having the characteristics of a living organism.

un·pack′ (ŭn·păk′), v. t. To separate and remove, as things packed; to open and remove the contents of (a trunk, crate, etc.). — v. i. To unpack a trunk, crate, or the like.

☞ See 2d UN-, *Note.*

un·jus′ti·fi′a·ble	un·light′ed	un·marked′	un·mer′it·ed	un·moved′	un′ob·served′
un·kept′	un·lik(e)′a·ble	un·mar′ket·a·ble	un′me·thod′i·cal	un′mu′si·cal	un′ob·serv′ing
un·know′ing	un·lined′	un·mar′riage·a·ble	un·mil′i·tar′y	un·nam(e)′a·ble	un′ob·struct′ed
un·known′	un·liq′ue·fi′a·ble	un·mar′ried	un·milled′	un·named′	un′ob·tain′a·ble
un·la′beled, un·la′-belled	un·liq′ue·fied	un·mas′tered	un·min′gled	un·nat′u·ral·ized	un′ob·tru′sive
	un·lit′	un·matched′	un′mis·tak′en	un·nav′i·ga·ble	un·of·fi′cial
un·la′bored, un·la′-boured	un·lov′a·ble	un·meas′ur·a·ble	un·mixed′, un·mixt′	un′ne·go′ti·a·ble	un·of·fi′cious
un·la′dy-like′	un·lov′ing	un·meas′ured	un·mod′i·fied	un·neigh′bor·ly, un-neigh′bour·ly	un·o′pen
un·laid′	un·mag′ni·fied	un′me·chan′i·cal	un·mod′u·lat′ed	un·no′tice·a·ble	un′op·posed′
un′la·ment′ed	un·mail′a·ble	un·med′i·tat′ed	un·mo·lest′ed	un·no′ticed	un′or·dained′
un·leav′ened	un·mal′le·a·ble	un·mel′o′di·ous	un·mort′gaged	un′ob·jec′tion·a·ble	un·or′tho·dox
un·let′tered	un·man′age·a·ble	un·melt′ed	un·mo′ti·vat′ed	un′o·blig′ing	un·os·ten·ta′tious
un·li′censed	un′man·u·fac′tured	un·men′tioned	un·mount′ed	un′ob·scured′	un·owned′
		un·mer′chant·a·ble	un·mov′a·ble	un′ob·serv′ant	

un·par′al·leled (ŭn·păr′ă·lĕld), *adj.* Having no parallel, or equal; unmatched; peerless; nonpareil.
un′par·lia·men′ta·ry (ŭn′pär·lĭ·mĕn′tȧ·rĭ), *adj.* Contrary to the practice of parliamentary bodies.
un·peg′ (ŭn·pĕg′), *v. t.* To remove a peg from; to unfasten.
un·peo′ple (-pē′p'l), *v. t.* To depopulate.
un·per′fo·rat′ed (-pûr′fō·rāt′ĕd; -ĭd), *adj.* *Philately.* Imperforate.
un·pile′ (-pīl′), *v. t.* To take from a pile. — *v. i.* To become disentangled from a pile.
un·pin′ (-pĭn′), *v. t.* To loose from pins; also, to remove the pins from; unfasten.
un·pleas′ant (ŭn·plĕz′ănt; -'nt), *adj.* Not amiable or agreeable; disagreeable; offensive. — **un·pleas′ant·ly**, *adv.*
un·pleas′ant·ness, *n.* Quality of being unpleasant; also, an unpleasant situation, experience, or the like.
un·plumbed′ (ŭn·plŭmd′), *adj.* **a** Not sealed with lead. **b** Not supplied with plumbing. **c** Not measured with a plummet; never explored as to depth, intensity, etc.; as, *unplumbed* depths of human emotion.
un·pol′i·tic (-pŏl′ĭ·tĭk), *adj.* Impolitic.
un·pop′u·lar (-pŏp′ū·lẽr), *adj.* Not popular; viewed or received unfavorably. — **un′pop·u·lar′i·ty** (ŭn′pŏp·ū·lăr′ĭ·tĭ), *n.* — **un·pop′u·lar·ly**, *adv.*
un·prec′e·dent′ed (-prĕs′ē·dĕn′tĕd; -tĭd), *adj.* Having no precedent; novel; unexampled. — **un·prec′e·dent′ed·ly**, *adv.*
un·prej′u·diced (-prĕj′ŏŏ·dĭst; 114), *adj.* Not prejudiced; free from undue bias or prepossession; impartial.
un·priced′ (ŭn·prīst′; 2), *adj.* Being without a fixed value; also, priceless.
un·prin′ci·pled (-prĭn′sĭ·p'ld), *adj.* Being without right moral principles.
un·print′a·ble (-prĭn′tȧ·b'l), *adj.* Unfit to be printed.
un·priz′a·ble (-prīz′ȧ·b'l), *adj.* Beneath valuation.
un′pro·fes′sion·al (ŭn′prō·fĕsh′ŭn·ăl; -'l), *adj.* Not professional; esp., designating language, action, or method not befitting one's profession. — **un′pro·fes′sion·al·ly**, *adv.*
un·qual′i·fied (ŭn·kwŏl′ĭ·fīd), *adj.* **a** Not having requisite qualifications. **b** Not modified or restricted by reservations. — **un·qual′i·fied·ly**, *adv.*
un·ques′tion·a·ble (-kwĕs′chŭn·ȧ·b'l), *adj.* **1.** Not questionable; indisputable. **2.** Acknowledged as beyond question or doubt. — **un·ques′tion·a·bly**, *adv.*
un·qui′et (-kwī′ĕt), *adj.* **a** Agitated; disturbed; also, disturbing. **b** Physically restless; uneasy.
un′quote′ (ŭn′kwōt′), *v. t.* To end a quotation.
un·rav′el (ŭn·răv′ĕl; -'l), *v. t.* **1.** To disentangle; to disengage or separate the threads of. **2.** To clear from complication or difficulty; to unfold; solve. — *v. i.* To become unraveled.
un·read′ (-rĕd′), *adj.* **1.** Not read, as a book. **2.** Not versed in literature.
un·read′y (-rĕd′ĭ), *adj.* Not prepared; unfit for action.
un·re′al (-rē′ăl; -rē′ăl), *adj.* Unsubstantial; illusive; fanciful; ideal. — **un·re′al·ly**, *adv.*
un′re·al′i·ty (ŭn′rē·ăl′ĭ·tĭ), *n.; pl.* -TIES (-tĭz). **1.** The quality or state of being unreal; lack of reality; also, something unreal or visionary. **2.** Tendency toward being visionary.
un·rea′son (ŭn·rē′z'n), *n.* Want of reason; unreasonableness; irrationality; absurdity.
un·rea′son·a·ble (-ȧ·b'l), *adj.* **a** Not conformable to reason; irrational; also, not governed by reason. **b** Immoderate; exorbitant. — **Syn.** See IRRATIONAL. — **un·rea′son·a·ble·ness**, *n.* — **un·rea′son·a·bly**, *adv.*
un·rea′son·ing, *adj.* Giving away to emotions without the guidance of reason and judgment; as, *unreasoning* fear, panic. — **un·rea′son·ing·ly**, *adv.*
un′re·con·struct′ed (ŭn′rē·kŏn·strŭk′tĕd; -tĭd), *adj.* Not reconstructed; specif.: **1.** *U. S. Hist.* **a** Not yet having undergone reconstruction (which see). **b** *Colloq.* Of a secessionist, not reconciled to the political results of the Civil War. **2.** Stubbornly tenacious of the political and economic tenets of an outmoded period.
un·reel′ (ŭn·rēl′), *v. t. & i.* To unwind from or as from a reel.
un·reeve′ (-rēv′), *v. t.* *Naut.* To withdraw (a rope) from a block or thimble. — *v. i.* To become unrove.
un′re·gen′er·ate (ŭn′rē·jĕn′ẽr·ĭt), *adj.* Also **un′re·gen′er·at′ed** (-āt′ĕd; -ĭd). Not regenerated; not renewed in heart; remaining or being at enmity with God. — **un′re·gen′er·a·cy** (-ȧ·sĭ), *n.* — **un′re·gen′er·ate·ly**, *adv.*
un′re·lent′ing (-rē·lĕn′tĭng), *adj.* **a** Unyielding; inexorable; rigorous. **b** Not relaxing in speed, pace, etc. — **un′re·lent′ing·ly**, *adv.*
un′re·mit′ting (-rē·mĭt′ĭng), *adj.* Not remitting; incessant; persevering. — **un′re·mit′ting·ly**, *adv.*
un′re·serve′ (ŭn′rē·zûrv′), *n.* Absence of reserve; frankness.
un′re·served′ (-zûrvd′), *adj.* **a** Unrestricted; not withheld in part. **b** Not reserved in manner or speech; frank. — **un′re·serv′ed·ly** (-zûr′vĕd·lĭ; -vĭd·lĭ), *adv.* — **un′re·serv′ed·ness**, *n.*
un′re·spon′sive (ŭn′rē·spŏn′sĭv), *adj.* Not responsive; not reacting readily or sympathetically. — **un′re·spon′sive·ly**, *adv.* — **un′re·spon′sive·ness**, *n.*
un·rest′ (ŭn·rĕst′), *n.* **a** Lack of repose. **b** Uneasiness; esp., disquiet, sometimes amounting to insurgency.
un′re·strained′ (ŭn′rē·strānd′), *adj.* Free from restraint. — **un′re·strain′ed·ly** (-strān′ĕd·lĭ; -ĭd·lĭ), *adv.*
un·rid′dle (ŭn·rĭd′'l), *v. t.* To read the riddle of; solve.
un·rig′ (-rĭg′), *v. t.* To strip of rigging, as a ship.
un·right′eous (ŭn·rī′chŭs), *adj.* [AS. *unrihtwīs*.] **1.** Not righteous; wicked; sinful. **2.** Unjust; not merited. — **un·right′eous·ly**, *adv.* — **un·right′eous·ness**, *n.*
un·rip′ (-rĭp′), *v. t.* To slit apart; to strip off.
un·ripe′ (ŭn·rīp′; 2), *adj.* **1.** Not yet mature. **2.** Precocious; premature. — **un·ripe′ness**, *n.*
un·ri′valed, un·ri′valled (-rī′văld), *adj.* Having no rival; without a competitor; peerless.
un·robe′ (-rōb′), *v. t. & i.* To disrobe; undress.
un·roll′ (ŭn·rōl′), *v. t.* **1.** To open, as what is rolled. **2.** To display; spread forth to view; disclose. **3.** *Rare.* To remove from a register. *Shak.* — *v. i.* To become unrolled; to unfold.
un·roof′ (-rōōf′), *v. t.* To strip off the roof or covering of.
un·root′ (-rōōt′), *v. t.* To eradicate; uproot.
un·round′ (-round′), *v. t.* *Phonet.* **a** To spread (the lips) laterally, as in the pronunciation of ē. **b** To pronounce (a sound usually rounded) without lip rounding, or with decreased rounding. See ROUND, *v. t.*, 6. — **un·round′ed**, *adj.*
un·rove′ (ŭn·rōv′), *adj.* *Naut.* Taken out from a block.
un·ruf′fled (ŭn·rŭf′'ld), *adj.* Not ruffled or agitated; calm. — **Syn.** See COOL.
un·rul′y (-rōōl′ĭ), *adj.* Not submissive to rule or restraint; turbulent; ungovernable; refractory. — **un·rul′i·ness**, *n.*
Syn. **Unruly, ungovernable, intractable, refractory, recalcitrant, willful** (*or* **wilful**), **headstrong** mean not submissive to control. **Unruly** suggests a lack of, or an incapacity for, discipline; **ungovernable**, an incapacity for, or an escape from, guidance or control; **intractable** and **refractory**, resistance to all attempts to control, manage, or mold; **recalcitrant**, violent resistance, as of another's will or authority; **willful**, an obstinate determination to have one's own way; **headstrong**, a violently willful attitude that makes for refractoriness.
un·sad′dle (-săd′'l), *v. t.* **1.** To strip of a saddle. **2.** To throw from the saddle; to unhorse.
un·safe′ty (-sāf′tĭ), *n.* Want of safety; insecurity.
un·san′i·tar′y (-săn′ĭ·tĕr′ĭ *or, esp. Brit.*, -tẽr·ĭ), *adj.* Not sanitary; unhealthy; liable to promote disease.
un·sat′u·rat′ed (-săt′ū·rāt′ĕd; -ĭd), *adj.* **a** Capable of dissolving to a greater degree; as, an *unsaturated* solution. **b** *Chem.* Capable, as ethylene and ammonia are, of uniting with certain other elements or compounds, without the elimination of any side product.
un·sa′vor·y, un·sa′vour·y (ŭn·sā′vẽr·ĭ), *adj.* **1.** Insipid; tasteless. **2.** Unpleasant to taste or smell; figuratively, morally offensive.
un·say′ (-sā′), *v. t.;* see SAY. To recant, recall, or retract.
un′sci·en·tif′ic (ŭn′sī·ĕn·tĭf′ĭk), *adj.* Not scientific; as: **a** Not used in scientific work. **b** Not in accord with the principles and methods of science. **c** Not showing scientific knowledge, or familiarity with scientific methods. — **un′sci·en·tif′i·cal·ly** (-ĭ·kăl·ĭ), *adv.*
un·scram′ble (ŭn·skrăm′b'l), *v. t.* To resolve into its original elements; — originally in the phrase "You can't *unscramble* eggs," attributed to J. P. Morgan referring to trusts.
un·screw′ (-skrōō′), *v. t.* To draw the screws from; to loosen or withdraw by turning. — *v. i.* To admit of being unscrewed.
un·scru′pu·lous (-skrōō′pū·lŭs), *adj.* Not scrupulous; unprincipled. — **un·scru′pu·lous·ly**, *adv.* — **un·scru′pu·lous·ness**, *n.*
un·seal′ (-sēl′), *v. t.* To remove the seal of; to open.
un·seam′ (-sēm′), *v. t.* To open the seam or seams of.
un·search′a·ble (-sûr′chȧ·b'l), *adj.* Not to be searched or explored; inscrutable. — **un·search′a·bly** (-blĭ), *adv.*
un·sea′son·a·ble (ŭn·sē′z'n·ȧ·b'l), *adj.* Out of the proper season; untimely. — **un·sea′son·a·ble·ness**, *n.* — **un·sea′son·a·bly**, *adv.*

☞ See 2d UN-, *Note.*
un·paid′
un·paired′
un·pal′at·a·ble
un·par′don·a·ble
un·par′doned
un·par′ti·san, un·par′ti·zan
un·pas′teur·ized
un′pa·tri·ot′ic
un·paved′
un·ped′i·greed
un·peo′pled
un′per·ceiv′a·ble
un′per·ceived′
un′per·ceiv′ing
un′per·suad′a·ble
un′per·suad′ed
un′per·sua′sive
un′per·turbed′
un′pe·rused′
un′phil·o·soph′ic
un′phil·o·soph′i·cal
un′pho·net′ic
un·picked′
un·pierced′
un·pit′ied
un·pit′y·ing
un·placed′
un·plagued′
un·planned′
un·plant′ed
un·played′
un·pleas′ing
un·pledged′
un·plowed′
un′po·et′ic
un′po·et′i·cal
un·poised′
un·po′lar·ized
un·polled′
un′pol·lut′ed
un·prac′ti·cal
un·prac′ticed
un′pre·dict′a·ble
un′pre·med′i·tat′ed
un′pre·oc′cu·pied
un′pre·pared′
un′pre·par′ed·ness
un′pre·pos·sess′ing
un′pre·scribed′
un′pre·sent′a·ble
un·pressed′
un′pre·tend′ing
un′pre·ten′tious
un′pre·vail′ing
un′pre·vent′a·ble
un·print′ed
un·priv′i·leged
un·prized′
un·proc′essed
un′pro·cur′a·ble
un′pro·duc′tive
un′pro·faned′
un′pro·fes′sion·al
un·prof′it·a·ble
un·prof′it·a·ble·ness
un′pro·gres′sive
un′pro·hib′it·ed
un·prom′is·ing
un·prompt′ed
un′pro·nounce′a·ble
un′pro·nounced′
un′pro·pi′ti·a·ble
un′pro·pi′tious
un′pro·por′tion·ate
un′pro·por′tioned
un·pros′per·ous
un′pro·tect′ed
un·proved′
un·prov′en
un′pro·vid′ed
un′pro·voked′
un′pro·vok′ing
un·pruned′
un·pub′lished
un·punc′tu·al
un·pun′ished
un′pur·chas′a·ble
un·pure′
un·quail′ing
un·qual′i·fy′ing
un·quench′a·ble
un·quenched′
un·ques′tioned
un·ques′tion·ing
un·quot′a·ble
un·raised′
un·ran′somed
un·rat′i·fied
un·read′a·ble
un·re′al·ized
un·rea′soned
un′re·buked′
un′re·ceived′
un′re·claimed′
un·rec′og·niz′a·ble
un·rec′og·nized
un·rec′om·pensed
un·rec′on·cil′a·ble
un·rec′on·ciled
un′re·cord′ed
un′re·deemed′
un·reel′a·ble
un′re·fined′
un′re·flect′ing
un′re·flec′tive
un′re·flec′tive·ly
un′re·form′a·ble
un′re·formed′
un′re·gard′ed
un·reg′is·tered
un·reg′u·lat′ed
un′re·lat′ed
un′re·lat′ed·ness
un′re·laxed′
un′re·lax′ing
un′re·li′a·ble
un′re·liev′a·ble
un′re·lieved′
un′re·li′gious
un′re·mem′bered
un′re·mit′ted
un′re·mov′a·ble
un′re·moved′
un′re·mu′ner·at′ed
un′re·mu′ner·a′tive
un′re·nowned′
un·rent′ed
un′re·paid′
un′re·paired′
un′re·pealed′
un′re·pent′ant
un′re·pent′ing
un′re·port′ed
un′rep·re·sent′a·tive
un′rep·re·sent′ed
un′re·pressed′
un′re·proved′
un′re·quit′ed
un′re·signed′
un′re·sist′ant
un′re·sist′ed
un′re·sist′ing
un·res′pit·ed
un·rest′ful
un′re·straint′
un′re·strict′ed
un′re·ten′tive
un′re·tract′ed
un′re·trieved′
un′re·vealed′
un′re·venged′
un′re·voked′
un′re·ward′ed
un·rhymed′
un·rhyth′mic
un·right′ful
un·rimed′
un·rinsed′
un·rip′ened
un′ro·man′tic
un·ruled′
un·sac′ri·fic′ing
un·safe′
un·said′
un·saint′ly
un·sal(e)′a·ble
un·sal′a·ried
un·salt′ed
un·sanc′ti·fied
un·sanc′tioned
un·sa′ti·at′ed
un′sat·is·fac′to·ry
un·sat′is·fied
un·sat′is·fy′ing
un·scaled′
un·scarred′
un·scathed′
un·scent′ed
un·schol′ar·ly
un·schooled′
un·scorched′
un·scoured′
un·scratched′
un·screened′
un·scrip′tur·al
un·sculp′tured

un·seat′ (ŭn·sēt′), *v. t.* **1.** To throw from one's seat. **2.** To deprive of the right to sit in a legislative or like body.

un·seem′ly (-sēm′lĭ), *adj.* Not seemly; unbecoming; indecent. — **un·seem′li·ness**, *n.* — **Syn.** See INDECOROUS. — *adv.* Not seemly.

un·seen′ (-sēn′; 2), *adj.* Not seen or discovered; invisible.

un·set′tle (-sĕt′'l), *v. t.* To move or loosen from a settled position or state; to displace; disorder. — *v. i.* To become unsettled or unfixed; to be disordered.

un·sew′ (-sō′), *v. t.;* see SEW. To undo, as something sewn; to rip.

un·sex′ (-sĕks′), *v. t.* To deprive of sex, or of qualities becoming one's sex; esp., to make unfeminine.

un·shack′le (-shăk′'l), *v. t.* To loose from shackles.

un·shaped′ (-shāpt′; 2), *adj.* Shapeless; misshapen.

un·shap′en (-shāp′ĕn), *adj.* Unshaped.

un·sheathe′ (-shēth′), *v. t.* To draw or remove from or as from sheath or scabbard, as a sword.

un·ship′ (-shĭp′), *v. t.* **1.** To take out of a ship or vessel; hence, to unload. **2.** *Naut.* To remove, as an oar, from its proper position when in use.

un·sick′er (-sĭk′ẽr), *adj.* *Obs. exc. Scot.* Untrustworthy.

un·sight′ (-sīt′), *adj.* Not seen or examined; — in **unsight, unseen,** that is, without seeing it.

un·skilled′ (ŭn·skĭld′; 2), *adj.* Not skilled; not requiring skill; specif., not dependent on training and experience for its efficacy; as, *unskilled* labor; — opposed to *skilled.*

un·skill′ful, un·skil′ful (-skĭl′fŏŏl; -f'l), *adj.* Not skillful; inexperienced; awkward. — **un·skill′ful·ly**, *adv.* — **un·skill′ful·ness**, *n.*

un·sling′ (-slĭng′), *v. t.;* see SLING. **a** To take, as a rifle, from where it has been slung. **b** *Naut.* To take off the slings of; to release from slings, as a yard, a cask, etc.

un·snap′ (-snăp′), *v. t.* To loosen or free by undoing a snap.

un·snarl′ (-snärl′), *v. t.* To undo the entanglement of.

un·so′cia·ble (ŭn·sō′shȧ·b'l), *adj.* **a** Not inclined to society or conversation; solitary; reserved. **b** Not conducive to sociability. — **un′so·cia·bil′i·ty** (ŭn′sō·shȧ·bĭl′ĭ·tĭ), **un·so′cia·ble·ness**, *n.* — **un·so′cia·bly**, *adv.*

un·sol′der (ŭn·sŏd′ẽr; *cf.* SOLDER, *n.*), *v. t.* To disunite (what has been soldered); hence, to divide; sunder.

un·son′sy (ŭn·sŏn′sĭ), *adj.* *Scot. & Dial.* [*un-* not + *sonsy.*] Ominous; fatal; ill-favored.

un′so·phis′ti·cat′ed (ŭn′sō·fĭs′tĭ·kāt′ĕd; -ĭd), *adj.* **a** Not worldly-wise. **b** Simple; ingenuous; innocent; genuine. — **un′so·phis′ti·cat′ed·ness**, *n.* — **Syn.** See NATURAL. — **Ant.** Sophisticated.

un′so·phis′ti·ca′tion (-fĭs′tĭ·kā′shŭn), *n.* Lack of, or freedom from, sophistication.

un·sound′ (ŭn·sound′; 2), *adj.* Not sound; as: **a** Not healthy or whole. **b** Not valid or true. **c** Not mentally normal; not wholly sane. **d** Not firmly made, fixed or the like. **e** Of sleep, not profound. — **un·sound′ly**, *adv.* — **un·sound′ness**, *n.*

un·spar′ing (-spâr′ĭng), *adj.* **1.** Profuse; lavish. **2.** *Rare.* Not merciful or forgiving. — **un·spar′ing·ly**, *adv.*

un·speak′ (ŭn·spēk′), *v. t.;* see SPEAK. To unsay.

un·speak′a·ble (-ȧ·b'l), *adj.* Inexpressible; unutterable; sometimes, inexpressibly bad. — **un·speak′a·bly**, *adv.*

un·sphere′ (-sfẽr′), *v. t.* To remove from its sphere.

un·spot′ted (-spŏt′ĕd; -ĭd), *adj.* Free from spot or stain; esp., free from moral stain; immaculate.

un·sprung′ (-sprŭng′), *adj.* Without springs; as, *unsprung* weight, weight not supported by springs.

un·sta′ble (ŭn·stā′b'l), *adj.* Not firm, fixed, or constant; hence: **a** Fluctuating; irregular. **b** Fickle; vacillating. **c** Unsteady. **d** *Chem.* Of compounds, readily decomposing or changing into other compounds. **e** Characterized by emotional instability. — **Syn.** See INCONSTANT. — **un·sta′ble·ness**, *n.* — **un·sta′bly**, *adv.*

un·state′ (ŭn·stāt′), *v. t.* To deprive of state or dignity.

un·steel′ (-stēl′), *v. t.* To disarm; soften.

un·step′ (-stĕp′), *v. t.* *Naut.* To remove, as a mast, from its step.

un·stick′ (-stĭk′), *v. t.;* see STICK. To release, as something stuck.

un·stop′ (-stŏp′), *v. t.* **1.** To take the stopple or stopper from. **2.** To free from any obstruction; to open.

un·strap′ (-străp′), *v. t.* To remove or loose a strap from.

un·string′ (-strĭng′), *v. t.;* see STRING. **1.** To deprive of a string or strings; also, to take from a string. **2.** To remove the strings of, as a harp. **3.** To relax the tension of; to loosen. **4.** To render weak or disordered; — usually passive; as, nerves *unstrung* by fear.

un·strung′ (ŭn·strŭng′; 2), *adj.* **a** Having the strings loose or detached. **b** Nervously tired, anxious, or fearful.

un·stud′ied (-stŭd′ĭd), *adj.* Not studied; as: **a** Not acquired by study. **b** Unlabored; unforced; natural.

un′sub·stan′tial (ŭn′sŭb·stăn′shăl), *adj.* Not substantial; as: **a** Wanting substance; not of solid matter. **b** Having no physical or real existence; visionary. — **un′sub·stan′ti·al′i·ty** (-shĭ·ăl′ĭ·tĭ), *n.* — **un′sub·stan′tial·ly**, *adv.*

un·suit′a·ble (ŭn·sūt′ȧ·b'l), *adj.* Unfitting; unbecoming. — **un′suit·a·bil′i·ty** (ŭn′sūt·ȧ·bĭl′ĭ·tĭ), *n.* — **un·suit′a·ble·ness**, *n.* — **un·suit′a·bly**, *adv.*

un·sung′ (ŭn·sŭng′; 2), *adj.* **1.** Not sung. **2.** Not celebrated in song or verse; as, *unsung* heroes.

un·swathe′ (ŭn·swāth′), *v. t.* To take a swathe from.

un·swear′ (-swâr′), *v. t. & i.;* see SWEAR. To recant or recall (an oath), esp. by a second oath; to abjure.

un·tan′gle (-tăng′g'l), *v. t.* To disentangle; resolve. — **Syn.** See EXTRICATE.

un·teach′ (ŭn·tēch′), *v. t.* To cause to forget, disbelieve, or believe the opposite of; to teach the contrary of.

un·tent′ed (-tĕnt′ĕd; -tĭd), *adj.* [*un-* not + *tented,* past part. of *tent* to probe.] Not probed or kept open with a tent. *Shak.*

un·think′ (-thĭngk′), *v. t.;* see THINK. To retract in the mind, as a thought; to change the mind about.

un·think′ing, *adj.* **1.** Thoughtless; inconsiderate. **2.** Not indicating thought or reflection. **3.** Not having the power of thought. — **un·think′ing·ly**, *adv.*

un·thread′ (ŭn·thrĕd′), *v. t.* **1.** To draw or take out a thread from. **2.** To make one's way through.

un·throne′ (-thrōn′), *v. t.* To dethrone.

un·ti′dy (ŭn·tī′dĭ), *adj.* Not neat; careless; slovenly. — **un·ti′di·ly** (-dĭ·lĭ), *adv.* — **un·ti′di·ness** (-dĭ·nĕs; -nĭs), *n.*

un·tie′ (ŭn·tī′), *v. t.;* see TIE. [AS. *untīgan.*] **1.** To loosen, as something interlaced or knotted. **2.** To free from fastening or restraint; to unbind. **3.** To resolve; to unfold; to clear. — *v. i.* To become untied.

un·til′ (ŭn·tĭl′; ŭn-), *prep.* [ME. *until, ontil,* fr. *un-* (as in *unto*) + *til* till.] **1.** Up to the time of; as, to remain *until* evening. **2.** At any time before; — after a negative expression; as, not available *until* tomorrow. — *conj.* **1.** Up to the time that or when. **2.** After negatives, *hardly,* etc., before the time that. **3.** To the point or degree that; as, he struggled *until* he loosed the knot.

un·time′ly (ŭn·tīm′lĭ), *adj.* Not timely; as: **a** Unseasonable; inopportune. **b** Esp., premature; occurring unexpectedly early. — *adv.* Inopportunely; prematurely; unseasonably. — **un·time′li·ness**, *n.*

un·time′ous (-tīm′ŭs), *adj.* *Scot.* Untimely.

un·ti′tled (-tī′t'ld), *adj.* **1.** Having no title of dignity or distinction. **2.** Being without title or right.

un′to (ŭn′tōō; -tŏŏ; 4), *prep.* *Archaic & Poetic.* [ME. *unto,* fr. *un-* (only in *unto, until*) unto, as far as + *to* to.] = TO (except as introducing infinitives).

un·told′ (ŭn·tōld′; 2), *adj.* **1.** Not related; not revealed. **2.** Not numbered or counted; too great for computation; incalculable.

un′touch·a·bil′i·ty (ŭn′tŭch·ȧ·bĭl′ĭ·tĭ), *n.* **1.** Quality of being untouchable. **2.** The character of very low-caste persons or non-Hindus of being regarded as defiling to a strict Hindu of high caste, esp. a Brahman.

un·touch′a·ble (ŭn·tŭch′ȧ·b'l), *adj.* That cannot be touched; as: **a** Beyond the reach. **b** Intangible. **c** Forbidden to the touch. **d** Not inviting handling; as, *untouchable* lepers. — *n.* In India, one of the lowest classes, whose touch is a defilement to members of the higher castes, esp. to Brahmans.

un·to′ward (ŭn·tō′ẽrd; -tōrd′; 70: *see* TOWARD, *prep.*), *adj.* [*un-* not + *toward.*] **1.** Froward; perverse; difficult to guide or manage. **2.** Awkward; ungraceful. **3.** Inconvenient; vexatious; unlucky. — **un·to′ward·ly**, *adv.* — **un·to′ward·ness**, *n.*

un·tread′ (ŭn·trĕd′), *v. t.;* see TREAD. To tread back; to retrace.

un·tried′ (ŭn·trīd′; 2), *adj.* **a** Not tested, as by experience; not proved by actual trial. **b** Not tried in court.

un·true′ (ŭn·trōō′; 2), *adj.* [AS. *untrēowe.*] Not true; as: **a** False; contrary to fact. **b** Not accordant with a standard of correctness; as, an *untrue* note. **c** Not faithful; disloyal. — **un·tru′ly** (-trōō′lĭ), *adv.*

un·truss′ (ŭn·trŭs′), *v. t.* To loose from a truss; to untie or unfasten, as one's points (see POINT, *n.,* 11) or lower garments; to undress.

un·trust′ful (-trŭst′fŏŏl; -f'l), *adj.* Not trusting; distrustful.

un·truth′ (ŭn·trōōth′), *n.* [AS. *untrēowth.*] **1.** Quality of being untrue; want of veracity; also, disloyalty. **2.** That which is untrue; a falsehood; a lie.

un·truth′ful (-fŏŏl; -f'l), *adj.* Not truthful; unveracious; not in accord with the truth or the fact. — **Syn.** See DISHONEST. — **un·truth′ful·ly**, *adv.* — **un·truth′ful·ness**, *n.*

un·tuck′ (ŭn·tŭk′), *v. t.* To release from a tuck or fold.

un·tune′ (ŭn·tūn′), *v. t.* To put out of tune; hence, to disarrange; discompose.

un·tu′tored (-tū′tẽrd), *adj.* **a** Untaught; unschooled. **b** Unsophisticated; naïve. — **Syn.** See IGNORANT.

un·twine′ (-twīn′), *v. t.* To undo (that which is twined); to disentangle; unwind. — *v. i.* To become untwined.

☞ See 2d UN-, *Note.*
un·sea′soned
un·sea′wor′thy
un·sec′ond·ed
un′sec·tar′i·an
un′se·cured′
un·see′ing
un·seg′ment·ed
un′se·lec′tive
un·self′ish
un·self′ish·ly
un·self′ish·ness
un′sen·ti·men′tal
un·serv′ice·a·ble
un·set′
un·set′tled
un·shad′ed
un·shak(e)′a·ble
un·shak′en
un·shape′ly
un·shav′en
un·shed′
un·shel′tered
un·shod′
un·shorn′
un·shrink′a·ble
un·shrink′ing
un·sift′ed
un·sight′ed
un·sight′ly
un·signed′
un·sing′a·ble
un·sink′a·ble
un·sis′ter·ly
un·sized′
un·slaked′, un·slacked′
un·so′cial
un·soiled′
un·sold′
un·sol′dier·ly
un′so·lic′it·ed
un′so·lic′it·ous
un·sol′u·ble
un·solv′a·ble
un·sort′ed
un·sought′
un·sound′ed
un·sowed′
un·sown′
un·spe′cial·ized
un·spec′i·fied
un·spent′
un·spir′it·u·al
un·spoiled′, un·spoilt′
un·spo′ken
un·sports′man·like′
un·squared′
un·stain′a·ble
un·stained′
un·stamped′
un·stand′ard·ized
un·states′man·like′
un·stead′fast
un·stead′i·ly
un·stead′i·ness
un·stead′y
un·stig′ma·tized
un·stint′ed
un·stitched′
un·stopped′
un·strained′
un·strat′i·fied
un·stressed′
un·stri′at·ed
un·striped′
un·stud′ied
un·stuffed′
un′sub·dued′
un′sub·mis′sive
un′sub·stan′ti·at′ed
un′suc·cess′
un′suc·cess′ful
un′sug·ges′tive
un·suit′ed
un·sul′lied
un′sup·port′a·ble
un′sup·port′ed
un′sup·pressed′
un·sure′
un′sur·passed′
un′sus·cep′ti·ble
un′sus·pect′ed
un′sus·pect′ing
un′sus·pi′cious
un′sus·tained′
un·sweet′ened
un·swept′
un·swerv′ing
un·swerv′ing·ly
un′sym·met′ri·cal
un′sym·pa·thet′ic
un·sym′pa·thiz′ing
un′sys·tem·at′ic
un·tact′ful
un·taint′ed
un·tal′ent·ed
un·tam(e)′a·ble
un·tamed′
un·tanned′
un·tar′nished
un·taught′
un·tax′a·ble
un·taxed′
un·teach′a·ble
un·tech′ni·cal
un·tem′pered
un·ten′a·ble
un·ten′ant·ed
un·tend′ed
un·ter′ri·fied
un·test′ed
un·thanked′
un·thank′ful
un·think′a·ble
un·thought′-of′
un·thrift′y
un·tied′
un·till′a·ble
un·tilled′
un·tired′
un·tir′ing
un·touched′
un·trace′a·ble
un·traced′
un·tracked′
un·tract′a·ble
un·trained′
un·tram′meled, un·tram′melled
un′trans·act′ed
un′trans·fer′a·ble
un′trans·lat′a·ble
un′trans·lat′ed
un′trans·mit′ted
un·trav′eled, un·trav′elled
un·trav′ers·a·ble
un·trav′ersed
un·treat′ed
un·trimmed′
un·trod′, un·trod′den
un·trou′bled
un·trust′wor′thy
un·tuft′ed
un·tun′a·ble
un·twilled′

un·twist' (ŭn·twĭst'), *v. t. & i.* To separate and open, as twisted threads; to untwine; disentangle.
un·used' (ŭn·ūzd'; 2), *adj.* **1.** Not used; as, an *unused* room. **2.** (*before* to, *usu.* ŭn·ūs[t]') Unaccustomed; not habituated.
un·u'su·al (ŭn·ū'zhōō·ăl), *adj.* Not usual; uncommon; rare. — **un·u'su·al·ly,** *adv.* — **un·u'su·al·ness,** *n.*
un·ut'ter·a·ble (-ŭt'ẽr·à·b'l), *adj.* **a** Unpronounceable. **b** Inexpressible; unspeakable. — **un·ut'ter·a·bly,** *adv.*
un·val'ued (ŭn·văl'ūd), *adj.* Not appraised; not prized; hence, disregarded.
un·var'nished (-vär'nĭsht), *adj.* Not varnished; hence, not embellished; as, the *unvarnished* truth.
un·veil' (ŭn·vāl'), *v. t.* To remove a veil from; to disclose to view; reveal. — *v. i.* To remove a veil; to reveal oneself.
un·vo'cal (-vō'kăl), *adj.* Not vocal; esp., not given to expressing one's emotions in language.
un·voice' (ŭn·vois'), *v. t.* To utter without voice (sense 9); to pronounce as surd instead of sonant. Thus, the *-sed* in *used,* ordinarily pronounced zd (ūzd), is usually unvoiced to st (ūst) before *to.* — **un·voic'ing** (-vois'ĭng), *n.*
un·voiced' (-voist'; 2), *adj.* **1.** Not expressed; unspoken. **2.** *Phonet.* Uttered without voice (see UNVOICE).
un·war'rant·a·ble (-wŏr'ăn·tà·b'l), *adj.* Indefensible; not justifiable. — **un·war'rant·a·bly,** *adv.*
un·war'y (ŭn·wâr'ĭ; 6), *adj.* Not vigilant against danger; unguarded; rash. — **un·war'i·ly,** *adv.* — **un·war'i·ness,** *n.*
un·wea'ried (-wẽr'ĭd), *adj.* Indefatigable.
un·weave' (-wēv'), *v. t.* To ravel, as anything woven.
un·weight' (-wāt'), *v. t. Skiing.* To shift the larger part of the burden of weight from; as, to *unweight* a ski.
un·well' (ŭn·wĕl'; 2), *adj.* **1.** Not well; indisposed; ailing. **2.** Specif., menstruous.
un·whole'some (ŭn·hōl'sŭm), *adj.* Not wholesome; as: **a** Not healthy. **b** Not conducive to good health. **c** Not conducive to good morals; also, morally corrupt; immoral.
un·wield'y (-wēl'dĭ), *adj.* Not wieldy; as: **a** Awkward; clumsy. **b** Not easily wielded; unmanageably bulky or ponderous. — **un·wield'i·ness,** *n.*
un·willed' (-wĭld'; 2), *adj.* Unintended; involuntary.
un·will'ing (-wĭl'ĭng), *adj.* **a** Not willing; loath; reluctant; averse. **b** Done or given reluctantly. — **un·will'ing·ly,** *adv.* — **un·will'ing·ness,** *n.*
un·wind' (-wīnd'), *v. t.;* see WIND. [AS. *unwindan.*] To wind off; to loose, as what is wound or convolved; hence: **a** To uncoil. **b** To straighten out (something involved). — *v. i.* To be, or admit of being, unwound.
un·wis'dom (-wĭz'dŭm), *n.* Lack of wisdom; folly.
un·wise' (ŭn·wīz'; 2), *adj.* [AS. *unwīs.*] Injudicious; foolish. — **un·wise'ly,** *adv.*
un·wish' (-wĭsh'), *v. t.* **1.** *Obs.* To destroy by wishing. **2.** To stop wishing (something).
un·wit'ting, *adj.* **1.** Not knowing; unconscious; unaware. **2.** Unintentional. — **un·wit'ting·ly,** *adv.*
un·wont'ed (ŭn·wŭn'tĕd; -tĭd; *see* WONT), *adj.* **1.** Unaccustomed; not made familiar by practice. **2.** Uncommon; unusual; rare. — **un·wont'ed·ly,** *adv.* — **un·wont'ed·ness,** *n.*
un·world'ly (-wûrld'lĭ), *adj.* **a** Not moved by worldly considerations; not sordid. **b** Not of this world; unearthly; esp., spiritual. — **un·world'li·ness,** *n.*
un·wor'thy (-wûr'thĭ), *adj.* Not worthy; as: **a** Wanting merit, value, or the like. **b** Not deserving; — often with *of.* **c** Not fit; unbecoming; — usually with *of.* **d** Despicable. — **un·wor'thi·ly,** *adv.* — **un·wor'thi·ness,** *n.*
un·wrap' (-răp'), *v. t. & i.* To undo, or become undone, as what is wrapped or folded; to free from wrappings.
un·wreathe' (-rēth'), *v. t.* To untwist, uncoil, or untwine.
un·wrin'kle (-rĭng'k'l), *v. t.* To free from wrinkles.
un·writ'ten (ŭn·rĭt''n; 2), *adj.* [AS. *unwriten.*] **1.** Not reduced to writing; oral; traditional. **2.** Containing no writing; blank.
unwritten law. **a** *Law.* Law not committed to writing at its origin, but originated in custom, as the common law of England. **b** The assumed rule or custom that a measure of immunity shall be given to those guilty of certain criminal acts of revenge, esp. in avenging injury to family honor arising from seduction or adultery.
un·yoke' (ŭn·yōk'), *v. t.* **1.** To loose or free from a yoke. **2.** To part; disjoin. — *v. i.* To become loosed from or as from a yoke.
up (ŭp), *adv.* [AS. *up, upp,* up, *uppe* on high, up.] Primarily *up* denotes direction of movement contrary to the direction of gravity, that is, radially away from the center of the earth. Specific uses of *up* are: **1.** With respect to movement, position, or direction in space, toward or at a point above or overhead; from a lower to a higher level in space. **2.** From a lower to a higher or better condition or status; also, into existence or evidence; so as to be seen, heard, etc.; as, to draw *up* a will; scare *up* a bird. **3.** In or near to; as, close *up* to the wall; into the hands of; as, to yield *up* the prisoner; into a close or constricted area; as, tie *up* the package. **4.** Aside; by; as, lay *up* treasure. **5.** So as to approach, arrive at, or overtake, the person, point, or time at present under consideration; as, to catch *up* with the enemy. **6.** To a state of or approaching completion, totality, or finality; — used as an intensive after certain verbs; as, eat *up,* burn *up,* clean *up,* dress *up,* reckon *up,* etc. **7.** In a direction conventionally or temporarily considered as the opposite of down; as, going *up* to college. **8.** *Baseball.* At bat; as, three hits in four times *up.* **9.** *Naut.* Toward the point from which the wind blows; as, to put the helm *up.* **10.** *Colloq. Sports.* In tennis, etc., each; apiece; also, ahead (of one's opponent); as, two (games) *up.*
— *prep.* In its primary signification *up* expresses the relation of approach to the highest point or a higher point or part. Specific uses are: **1.** From a lower to a higher place on or along. **2.** From the mouth toward the source of; as, to sail *up* the Hudson; in a direction contrary to that of; as, *up* the wind. **3.** Toward or near to the inner part or interior of. **4.** In the direction of the higher end or the end regarded as higher; as, *up* a street.
— *adj.* **1.** Dwelling or situated in inland country or at high altitude. **2.** Inclining, moving, or directed up; tending upward. **3.** Bound in a direction regarded as up. **4.** In a position higher than before or than any given level; in a higher status or condition. **5.** Hence, *Colloq.,* in a state of activity, agitation, or excitement; as, his temper was *up;* in progress; going on; as, what was *up?* **a** Exerting pressure; as, the wind is *up.* **b** Advanced in measure, scale, etc.; as, prices are *up.* **c** Informed; as, he is *up* on chemistry. **d** Expired; as, his term is *up.* **e** Presented or considered publicly; as, his name is *up* for election. **f** *Colloq.* Confronting; meeting; as, he is *up* against opposition. **g** *Colloq.* Before a court; as, he was *up* for trial. **6.** *Gambling.* At stake; as, money *up* on a game. **7.** *Games.* **a** Necessary for completion or winning; as, the game is fifteen points *up.* **b** Ahead of one's opponent; as, in spite of being set four tricks they were still *up.* **8.** *Golf.* **a** In advance of one's opponent; as, to be one *up;* — opposed to *down.* **b** On the green; as, the ball was well *up.*
— *n.* One who or that which is up; as: **a** One enjoying a rise of fortune, high rank, prosperity, or the like. **b** A slope toward higher ground; an elevation. **c** An upward course. **d** An upbound train, bus, or the like. — ***ups and downs.*** Upward and downward movements; hence, fluctuations, as in one's fortunes.
— *v. i.;* UPPED (ŭpt); UP'PING (ŭp'ĭng). To raise oneself up; to arise or rouse oneself, esp. in readiness for action. — *v. t.* **1.** To raise or lift up. **2.** *Colloq.* To cause to rise; as, to *up* prices, production.
up- (ŭp-). [AS. *up-, upp-.* See UP, *adv.*] The adv., adj., and preposition *up* used in composition, as in *up*raise, *up*heaval, *up*land, and in the words in the following list:

upbear	upfold	upsurge
upborne	upgather	upswell
upbound	upreach	uptilt
upburst	uprouse	uptorn
upcrop	upstretch	upwhirl

U·pan'i·shad (ōō·păn'ĭ·shăd), *n.* [Skr. *upaniṣad.*] One of a class of speculative treatises, concerned with the nature of man and the universe, forming a late part of the Vedic literature.
u'pas (ū'pàs), *n.* [Malay *pohon upas* tree of poison.] **1.** **a** A tall Javanese tree (*Antiaris toxicaria*) of the mulberry family, the *upas tree,* which yields an intensely poisonous milky juice used as an arrow poison. **b** A shrub or tree (*Strychnos tieuté*) of the same region, also yielding an arrow poison. **2.** The sap or juice of either of these trees. **3.** Figuratively, a poisonous or harmful influence or institution.
up'-bow' (ŭp'bō'), *n. Music.* In playing a bowed instrument, a stroke toward the lower end of the bow; — indicated by the sign (V). Cf. DOWN-BOW.
up·braid' (ŭp·brād'), *v. t.* [AS. *upbregdan,* fr. *upp, ūp,* up + *bregdan* to draw, twist, weave.] To charge, accuse, or reprove reproachfully; — followed by *with* or *for,* and formerly *of,* before the thing imputed; as, he *upbraided* me for my statement. — *v. i.* To utter upbraidings. — **Syn.** See SCOLD. — **up·braid'er,** *n.* — **up·braid'ing·ly,** *adv.*
up·braid'ing, *n.* A reproof or reproach.
up'bring'ing (ŭp'brĭng'ĭng; 2), *n.* Rearing; nurture.
up·build' (ŭp·bĭld'), *v. t.;* -BUILT' (-bĭlt'); -BUILD'ING. To build up, in any sense. — **up·build'er,** *n.*
up'cast' (ŭp'kàst'), *n.* Act of casting upward, or state of being cast up; also, anything cast up. — (-kàst'; 2), *adj.* Cast up; directed upward; as, with *upcast* eyes.
up'chuck' (ŭp'chŭk'), *v. t. & i. Colloq.* To vomit.
up'coun'try (ŭp'kŭn'trĭ; 2), *adj.* Living or lying in the interior; as, an *upcountry* residence. — *n.* The interior of the country.
up'coun'try (-kŭn'trĭ; 2), *adv. Colloq.* In an upcountry direction or region; as, to live *upcountry.*
up·date' (ŭp·dāt'), *v. t.* To bring up to date.
up'do' (ŭp'dōō'), *n. Colloq.* A dressing of the hair on the top of the head; often specif., an upsweep.
up·end' (ŭp·ĕnd'), *v. t. & i.* To set, stand, or rise, on end.
up'grade' (ŭp'grād'; 2), *n.* An upward grade or slope.
up·grade' (ŭp·grād'), *v. t.* To raise or step up in grade; specif.: **a** To advance (a workman) to a job requiring a higher level of skill, esp. as part of a training program. **b** In merchandising, to substitute (a lower-grade product) for a product of higher quality on which a higher price is allowed.
up'growth' (ŭp'grōth'), *n.* The process or a result of growing up; development; also, a thing grown up.
up·heav'al (ŭp·hēv'ăl), *n.* Act or instance of upheaving, esp. of part of the earth's crust; hence, a violent social commotion or agitation.
up·heave' (-hēv'), *v. t.;* see HEAVE. To heave or lift up from beneath; to raise. — *v. i.* To rise.
up·held' (-hĕld'), *past & past part.* of UPHOLD.
up'hill' (ŭp'hĭl'; 2), *n.* An ascent; rising ground.
up'hill' (ŭp'hĭl'; 2), *adv.* Upwards on or as on a hillside.
up'hill' (ŭp'hĭl'; 2), *adj.* **1.** Elevated in situation. **2.** Ascending; going up; hence, laborious; difficult.
up·hold' (ŭp·hōld'), *v. t.;* see HOLD. **1.** To hold up; to raise. **2.** To keep erect; to support; sustain; maintain. **3.** To aid by approval or encouragement; to countenance. — **Syn.** See SUPPORT. — **up·hold'er,** *n.*
up·hol'ster (ŭp·hōl'stẽr), *v. t.* [From UPHOLSTERER.] **1.** To furnish (a room) with hangings, curtains, etc. **2.** To stuff (chairs, etc.) and to cover (the stuffed parts) with fabric.
up·hol'ster·er (-ẽr), *n.* [From *upholster, upholdster,* for older *upholder,* in ME., a tradesman.] One who provides upholstery; one who upholsters.
up·hol'ster·y (-ĭ), *n.* **1.** Furniture or interior fittings, as hangings, cushions, curtains, coverings, etc., covered or made with textile materials, leather, etc.; esp., material used to stuff or cover furniture. **2.** The art or business of an upholsterer.

☞ See 2d UN-, *Note.*

un·twist'ed	un·var'ied	un·vexed'	un·wa'ver·ing	un·weld'ed	un·work'a·ble
un·us'a·ble	un·var'y·ing	un·vis'it·ed	un·weaned'	un·wept'	un·work'man·like'
un·u'ti·liz'a·ble	un·veiled'	un·vit'ri·fied	un·wea'ry·ing	un·wife'like'	un·wound'
un·ut'tered	un·ven'ti·lat'ed	un·want'ed	un·weath'ered	un·wife'ly	un·wound'ed
un·vac'ci·nat'ed	un've·ra'cious	un·war'like'	un·wed'	un·winc'ing	un·wo'ven
un·vac'il·lat'ing	un·ver'i·fi'a·ble	un·war'rant·ed	un·wed'ded	un·wink'ing	un·wrin'kled
un·val'i·dat'ed	un·ver'i·fied	un·washed'	un·weed'ed	un·wit'nessed	un·wrought'
	un·versed'	un·watched'	un·wel'come	un·wom'an·ly	un·yield'ing

up′keep′ (ŭp′kēp′), *n.* Act or cost of keeping up, or maintaining; maintenance; also, state of being kept up; repair.

up′land′ (ŭp′lănd′; -lănd), *n.* High land, esp. far from the sea; ground elevated above the lowlands along rivers or between hills. — *adj.* Of, pertaining to, or living on upland.

upland cotton. See COTTON.

upland plover. A large sandpiper (*Bartramia longicauda*) of eastern North America, which frequents fields and uplands.

up·lift′ (ŭp·lĭft′), *v. t.* **1.** To lift or raise aloft; to elevate. **2.** To improve the condition of, esp. morally, socially, or intellectually; as, to *uplift* the drama. — **up·lift′er,** *n.*

up′lift′ (ŭp′lĭft′), *n.* Act, process, or result of uplifting; as: **a** An elevation; esp., *Geol.*, upheaval. **b** A bettering in condition, esp. mentally or emotionally. **c** A social movement to uplift morally, aesthetically, etc.

up′most (ŭp′mōst), *adj.* Uppermost.

up·on′ (ŭ·pŏn′; 4), *prep.* [ME. *upon, uppon*, fr. *up* up + *on, an*, on.] On; — in all its senses. See ON. — *adv. Obs.* On or upon one; also, thereon.

up′per (ŭp′ẽr), *adj.; orig., compar. of* UP, *adj.* **1.** Being farther up; farther inland, above, etc. **2.** Designating strata relatively near the earth's surface; hence [*cap.*], *Geol.*, designating a later period or formation (of a specified period); — so called because the strata are normally above those of the earlier formations; as, *Upper* Cambrian. **3.** Of clothes, worn above or outside another garment; also, covering a part above the waist. — *n.* A part that is upper; specif., *Shoemaking*, one of the uppers (which see); also, *Colloq.*, an upper berth, as in a sleeping car.

upper case. *Print.* See 2d CASE, *n.*, 6. — **up′per-case′** (-kās′; 2), *adj.*

up′per-class′ (-klȧs′; 2), *adj.* Of, pertaining to, or characteristic of a class regarded as socially superior, or the junior and senior classes in a college or secondary school. — **up′per·class′man,** *n.*

upper crust. **a** The top crust, as on a pie. **b** *Colloq.* The highest upper-class social circles.

up′per·cut′ (ŭp′ẽr·kŭt′), *n.* In boxing, a short-arm swinging blow directed upward. — *v. t. & i.;* see CUT. To strike, or hit, with an uppercut.

upper hand. The advantage; mastery; dominion.

Upper House. [*often not cap.*] In a legislature, the house of more restricted membership, as the House of Lords in Great Britain, or the Senate in the United States.

up′per·most (ŭp′ẽr·mōst), *adj.* Highest in place, position, rank, power, or the like; upmost; topmost.

up′pers (ŭp′ẽrz), *n. sing. & pl.* **1.** The parts of a shoe or boot above the sole. See SHOE, *Illust.* **2.** Gaiters of cloth buttoned over the ankle. — ***on one's uppers.*** Having worn out one's shoe soles; hence, at the end of one's means; in hard luck.

up′ping (ŭp′ĭng), *n.* [From UP.] Act or process of marking a swan or swans by cuts on the beak. See SWAN-UPPING.

up′pish (-ĭsh), *adj.* [From UP.] *Colloq.* Proud; arrogant. — **up′pish·ly,** *adv.* — **up′pish·ness,** *n.*

up·raise′ (ŭp·rāz′), *v. t.* To raise or lift up; elevate.

up·rear′ (-rēr′), *v. t.* To raise; hence, to erect; exalt; bring up. — *v. i.* To rise.

up′right′ (ŭp′rīt′; *sometimes also* ŭp·rīt′; 2), *adj.* [AS. *upriht, upp-riht.*] **1.** Erect in position or posture. **2.** Erect in bearing or carriage. **3.** Morally correct; honest; just.

Syn. **Upright, honest, just, conscientious, scrupulous, honorable** (*or* **honourable**) mean strictly regarding what is morally right. **Upright** implies an uncompromising adherence to high moral principles; **honest**, strict adherence to virtues, esp. such as truthfulness, fairness, and the like; **just**, now archaic in this sense, strict adherence to moral principles; **conscientious** and **scrupulous**, an active moral sense which governs all one's actions; **honorable**, the guidance of a high sense of honor or of the dictates of the code of one's profession, etc.

— *adv.* Uprightly.

— (ŭp′rīt′), *n.* **1.** State of being upright or perpendicular; as, a pillar out of *upright*. **2.** Something standing upright, as a piece of timber in a building. **3.** *pl. Football.* The goal posts. **4.** *Music.* Short for **upright piano** (see PIANO).

— **up′right′ly,** *adv.* — **up′right′ness,** *n.*

up·rise′ (ŭp·rīz′), *v. i.;* see RISE. **1.** To rise, as from sleep; to get up. **2.** To ascend; to rise or seem to rise into view. **3.** To have an upright direction or inclination. **4.** To swell up, as a sound.

up′rise′ (ŭp′rīz′; ŭp·rīz′), *n.* **1.** Act or process of rising; rising or ascent. **2.** A slope upward.

up·ris′ing (ŭp·rīz′ĭng; ŭp′rīz′-), *n.* **1.** Act of rising; also, a steep place; ascent. **2.** An insurrection; revolt. — **Syn.** See REBELLION.

up′roar′ (ŭp′rōr′; 2; 70), *n.* [D. *oproer.*] Great tumult; bustle and clamor.

up·roar′i·ous (ŭp·rōr′ĭ·ŭs), *adj.* Making, or accompanied by, uproar, or noise and tumult. — **up·roar′i·ous·ly,** *adv.*

up·root′ (ŭp·ro͞ot′), *v. t.* To tear up by or as by the roots; hence, to remove utterly; extirpate. — **Syn.** See EXTERMINATE. — **up·root′al** (-ăl; -'l), *n.* — **up·root′er** (-ẽr), *n.*

up·set′ (ŭp·sĕt′; 2), *adj.* **a** Set up; as: (1) Erected. (2) Fixed; determined. **b** Overturned; disordered; capsized. **c** Mentally distressed or perturbed.

up·set′ (ŭp·sĕt′), *v. t.;* see SET. **1.** To overturn, overthrow, or capsize. **2.** To discompose; disturb the self-possession of. **3.** *Mach.* **a** To thicken and shorten, as a heated bar of iron, by hammering on the end; to swage. **b** To shorten (a tire) in the process of resetting, as by cutting it and hammering on the ends. — **Syn.** See DISCOMPOSE. — *v. i.* To become upset or overturned.

up′set′ (ŭp′sĕt′), *n.* **1.** Act or result of upsetting, or state of being upset; overturn. **2.** A derangement of plans or ideas; also, a physical disorder; as, a stomach *upset*. **3.** *Mach.* **a** A swage used in upsetting. **b** A part of a rod or the like that is upset.

up′set′ price. The price fixed on as the minimum for property offered in a public sale.

up′shot′ (ŭp′shŏt′), *n.* [Orig., the last shot in an archery contest.] Final issue; conclusion.

up′side′ (-sīd′), *n.* The upper side; the uppermost part.

upside down. [A corruption of ME. *up so down*, lit., up as down.] With the upper part undermost; hence, in confusion; topsy-turvy. — **up′side′-down′,** *adj.*

up′si·lon (ūp′sĭ·lŏn *or, esp. Brit.*, ūp·sī′lŏn), *n.* [Gr. *y psilon* bare, mere, simple *y*.] The twentieth letter (Υ, υ) of the Greek alphabet.

up·spring′ (ŭp·sprĭng′), *v. i.;* see SPRING. To spring up; rise; to come into existence.

up′spring′ (ŭp′sprĭng′), *n.* A spring or leap into the air.

up′stage′ (ŭp′stāj′), *adv.* Toward or at the rear of the stage; backstage; — the rear being orig. higher than the front. — *adj.* Of or pertaining to the rear of the stage; hence, *Colloq.*, backward or shy; also, offish; snobbish.

up′stairs′ (ŭp′stârz′; 2), *adv.* **1.** Up the stairs; in or toward an upper story; hence, to a higher position, authority, etc. **2.** *Aviation.* At high elevation.

up′stairs′ (ŭp′stârz′; 2), *adj.* Being above stairs; pertaining to an upper story; as, an *upstairs* room. — *n.* The portion of a building above the ground story.

up·stand′ing (ŭp·stăn′dĭng), *adj.* Erect; hence, straightforward; having integrity.

up·start′ (ŭp·stärt′), *v. i. & t.* To start or cause to start up.

up′start′ (ŭp′stärt′), *n.* One who has risen suddenly, as from humble position to wealth, power, or honor, esp. such a one who presumes on his success; a parvenu. — *adj.* Characteristic of, or of the nature of, a parvenu.

up′state′ (ŭp′stāt′; 2), *adj.* *U. S.* Of or from that part of a state outside of some large city, esp. to the north. — *n.* *U. S.* An upstate region, esp. northern New York. — **up′stat′er** (-stāt′ẽr), *n.*

up′stream′ (ŭp′strēm′), *adv.* At or toward a location nearer the source of a stream.

up′stroke′ (ŭp′strōk′), *n.* An upward stroke; esp., a stroke or line made by a pen, or the like, moving upward.

up·sweep′ (ŭp·swēp′), *v. t. & i.;* see SWEEP. To sweep, brush, curve, or slope upward. — (ŭp′swēp′), *n.* A sweeping upward or position of being swept, brushed, curved, or sloped upward; specif.: **a** The upward curving of the underjaw of certain animals, as the bulldog. **b** A style of hairdressing in which the hair is brushed up to the top of the head.

up·swept′ (ŭp·swĕpt′; 2), *adj.* Brushed, curved, or sloped upward; as, an *upswept* tail of an airplane; specif., having the hair brushed up to the top of the head; as, an *upswept* hairdo.

up·swing′ (ŭp·swĭng′), *v. i.;* see SWING. To swing up; improve. — (ŭp′swĭng′), *n.* A swinging upward; improvement; as, an *upswing* in the stock market.

up′take′ (ŭp′tāk′), *n.* **1.** Act of taking up; a lifting. **2.** Understanding; comprehension; as, quick in the *uptake*. **3.** **a** In steam boilers, the pipe leading upward to the chimney from the chamber below it. **b** A shaft or tube up which a current of air passes, esp. for ventilation.

up the wind. *Aviation.* Into the wind; as, the airplane landed *up the wind*.

up′throw′ (ŭp′thrō′), *n.* Upheaval; a casting up.

up′thrust′ (-thrŭst′), *n.* An upward thrust; specif., *Geol.*, an uplift of part of the earth's crust.

up′-to-date′, *adj.* Extending to the present time; abreast of the times in style, manners, information, etc. — **up′-to-date′ness,** *n.*

up′town′ (ŭp′toun′), *adv.* To or in the upper part of a town, specif., the part distant from the main business section.

up′town′ (ŭp′toun′; 2), *adj.* Situated in, or belonging to, the upper part of a city or the part distant from the main business section.

up′trend′ (ŭp′trĕnd′), *n.* An incipient upward swing.

up·turn′ (ŭp·tûrn′), *v. t. & i.* **1.** To turn over, as in digging. **2.** To direct or turn upward.

up′turn′ (ŭp′tûrn′), *n.* A turning upward; esp., a turn toward better conditions, higher prices, etc.

up′ward (ŭp′wẽrd), *adv.* [AS. *upweard.*] **1.** In a direction from lower to higher. **2.** Toward the source or origin; toward the interior. **3.** Toward a higher degree, rank, etc. **4.** In a higher position; as, lying with the face *upward*. **5.** In the upper parts; above; toward the head. **6.** Toward or into later years, esp. of age; as, from his youth *upward*. **7.** Indefinitely more; above; over. **8.** Toward a higher price; as, from five dollars *upward*. — ***upward of.*** Upwards of. — *adj.* Directed or moving toward, or situated in, a higher place; ascending. — **up′ward·ly,** *adv.*

up′wards (ŭp′wẽrdz), *adv.* Upward (in all senses).

upwards of. More than; in excess of; above.

ur-. = URO-.

ur- (o͝or-). [G.] A prefix signifying *primitive, primeval, original*.

u·rae′mi·a (ū·rē′mĭ·ȧ), **u·rae′mic.** Var. of UREMIA, etc.

u·rae′us (ū·rē′ŭs), *n.* [NL., fr. Gr. *ouraios.*] *Egypt. Relig.* The representation of the sacred asp appearing on the headdress of rulers, esp. just over the forehead, as a symbol of sovereignty.

U′ral-Al·ta′ic (ū′răl·ăl·tā′ĭk), *adj.* **1.** Of or pertaining to the Urals and the Altai. **2.** Designating or pertaining to a great family of agglutinative languages or the peoples whose mother tongues are comprised in it. Physically these peoples vary from the pure Mongolian type of eastern Siberia to the Caucasian Finn and Magyar. See LANGUAGE, *Table.*

u′ral·ite (ū′răl·īt), *n.* [From the *Ural* Mts.] *Mineral.* Amphibole, usually fibrous and dark green, resulting from alteration of pyroxene. — **u′ral·it′ic** (-ĭt′ĭk), *adj.*

u′ra·nal′y·sis (ū′rȧ·năl′ĭ·sĭs), *n.* Chemical analysis of urine; urinalysis.

U·ra′ni·a (ū·rā′nĭ·ȧ), *n.* [L., fr. Gr. *Ourania*, fr. *ouranios* heavenly, fr. *ouranos* heaven.] **a** *Gr. Myth.* The Muse of astronomy. **b** An epithet of Aphrodite.

u·ran′ic (ū·răn′ĭk), *adj.* [Gr. *ouranos* heaven.] Of or pertaining to the heavens; celestial; astronomical.

u·ran′ic, *adj.* [From URANIUM.] *Chem.* Of, pertaining to, or containing uranium, esp. in its higher valence. Cf. URANOUS.

u·ran′i·nite (ū·răn′ĭ·nīt), *n.* [From URANIUM.] *Mineral.* A mineral commonly occurring in black octahedrons. It consists largely of an oxide of uranium but contains also thorium, the cerium and yttrium metals, and lead; further, it often yields when heated a gas consisting chiefly of helium.

u′ra·nite (ū′rȧ·nīt), *n.* *Mineral.* A general term for the uranium phosphates, autunite, or lime uranite, and copper uranite, formerly classed as a single species. The **uranite group** includes these and a few related minerals. — **u′ra·nit′ic** (-nĭt′ĭk), *adj.*

u·ra′ni·um (ū·rā′nĭ·ŭm), *n.* [NL., fr. *Uranus* the planet + *-ium.*] *Chem.* A radioactive element of the chromium group, found in combination in pitchblende and certain other rare minerals, and reduced as a heavy, hard, nickel-white metal. Symbol, *U* or *Ur;* at. no., 92; at. wt., 238.07. Natural uranium consists of the isotope of mass number 238 (99.3 per cent), 235 (0.7) and 234 (minute amount). U 238 can be converted into plutonium which, as well as U 235, is used as a source of atomic energy (which see).

u′ra·nog′ra·phy (ū′rȧ·nŏg′rȧ·fĭ), *n.* [Gr. *ouranographia*, fr. *ouranos* heaven + *graphein* to write.] The science of describing the heavens and the celestial bodies; the construction of celestial maps, globes, etc. — **u′ra·nog′ra·pher** (-fẽr), *n.* — **u′ra·no·graph′ic** (-nō·grăf′ĭk), **u′ra·no·graph′i·cal** (-ĭ·kăl), *adj.* — **u′ra·nog′ra·phist** (-nŏg′rȧ·fĭst), *n.*

u′ra·nol′o·gy (-nŏl′ō·jĭ), *n.* [Gr. *ouranos* heaven + *-logy.*] A treatise on the heavens and the celestial bodies; the study of the heavens. — **u′ra·no·log′i·cal** (-nō·lŏj′ĭ·kăl), *adj.*

u′ra·nom′e·try (-nŏm′ē·trĭ), *n.* [Gr. *ouranos* heaven + *-metry.*] *Astron.* **a** A chart or catalogue of celestial bodies, esp. of visible fixed stars. **b** The measurement of the heavens.

u′ra·nous (ū′rȧ·nŭs), *adj.* *Chem.* Pertaining to or containing uranium, esp. in its lower valence. Cf. 2d URANIC.

U′ra·nus (-nŭs; 114), *n.* [LL., fr. Gr. *Ouranos* Uranus, *ouranos* heaven, sky.] **1.** *Gr. Myth.* The personification of Heaven, husband (or son) of Gaea (Earth) and father of the Titans, the Cyclopes, the Furies, etc. See CRONUS. **2.** *Astron.* One of the most remote known major planets. It is nearly 1,800,000,000 miles from the sun, about 32,000 miles in diameter, and its period of revolution round the sun is about 84 of our years. Symbol, ⛢, ♅, or ♅. See PLANET, *Table.*

u′ra·nyl (ū′rȧ·nĭl), *n.* [*uranium* + *-yl.*] *Chem.* The bivalent radical UO_2, which behaves as an element in many uranium compounds. — **u′ra·nyl′ic** (-nĭl′ĭk), *adj.*

u′rase (ū′rās; -rāz), *n.* *Biochem.* Urease.

u′rate (ū′rāt; 114), *n.* [F.] *Chem.* A salt of uric acid.

ur′ban (ûr′băn), *adj.* [L. *urbanus* belonging to the city or town, refined, polished, fr. *urbs, urbis*, a city.] Characteristic of, constituting, or pertaining to, a city or town.

urban district. In England, Wales, and Northern Ireland, a subdivision of an administrative county, disting. from a *borough* in not possessing a borough charter, and governed by an urban district council having local jurisdiction.

ur·bane′ (ûr·bān′), *adj.* Courteous; polite; polished. — **Syn.** See SUAVE. — **ur·bane′ly**, *adv.* — **ur·bane′ness**, *n.*

ur·ban′i·ty (-băn′ĭ·tĭ), *n.; pl.* -TIES (-tĭz). [L. *urbanitas.*] Quality or state of being urbane; courtesy; suavity.

ur′ban·ize (ûr′băn·īz), *v. t.* **1.** To render urbane; to refine; polish. **2.** To cause to have the characteristics of a city; as, electric railways *urbanize* rural districts. — **ur′ban·i·za′tion** (-ĭ·zā′shŭn; -ī·zā′-), *n.*

‖**ur′bi et or′bi** (ûr′bī ĕt ôr′bī). [L.] To the city (i. e. Rome) and the world; that is, to everyone; — used esp. in publishing papal bulls.

ur′ce·o·late (ûr′sē·ō·lāt), *adj.* [L. *urceolus*, dim. of *urceus* pitcher, waterpot.] Urn-shaped; as, an *urceolate* corolla.

ur′chin (ûr′chĭn), *n.* [ME. *urchon, irchoun*, fr. OF. *irechon, ireçon, heriçon*, fr. L. *ericius*, fr. *er* hedgehog.] **1.** A hedgehog. **2.** A pert or roguish youngster. **3.** *Obs.* A mischievous elf. **4.** A sea urchin.

Ur′du (ŏŏr′dōō; ŏŏr·dōō′; ûr-), *n.* [Prop., (the language of) the camp, fr. Hind. *urdū*, fr. Per. *urdū.*] Hindustani as spoken by Mohammedans in India. See INDO-EUROPEAN LANGUAGES, *Table.*

-ure. [F. or L.; F. *-ure*, fr. L. *-ura.*] A suffix denoting: **a** *Act, process*, or *being*, as in culture, exposure. **b** *Result* (of an act), as in picture. **c** *State, rank, etc.*, as in judicature, prefecture; also, *a constituted body*, as in legislature. **d** *An agent* or *means of action*, as in signature.

u·re′a (ū·rē′ȧ; ū′rē·ȧ; *see note below*), *n.* [NL., fr. F. *urée*, fr. Gr. *ouron* urine.] *Biochem.* A very soluble, crystalline, nitrogenous compound, $CO(NH_2)_2$, the chief solid constituent of the urine of man and other mammals. It is synthesized, as from carbon dioxide and ammonia; condensed with formaldehyde it forms thermosetting **u·re′a-form·al′de·hyde res′ins** used in wood-bonding adhesives, for molded articles, etc. — **u′re·al** (ū′rē·ăl; ū·rē′ăl), *adj.*

☞ Although most general dictionaries accent **u′rea**, practically all medical dictionaries and chemists favor **ure′a**.

u′re·ase (ū′rē·ās; -āz), *n.* [*urea* + *-ase.*] *Biochem.* An enzyme that accelerates the hydrolysis of urea into ammonium carbonate.

u·re′do (ū·rē′dō), *n.* [L., a blast, blight, a burning itch, fr. *urere* to burn.] Urticaria; hives.

u·re′do·stage′ (ū·rē′dō·stāj′), *n.* [*uredo* + *stage.*] *Bot.* The stage in the life cycle of a typical rust characterized by the production of spore fruit consisting of spore-bearing hyphae forming spore pustules which become exposed by rupture of the cuticle.

u′re·ide (ū′rē·īd; -ĭd), *n.* Also **u′re·id.** *Chem.* Any of various compounds derived from urea and an acid by eliminating water. Many ureides are cyclic.

u·re′mi·a, u·rae′mi·a (ū·rē′mĭ·ȧ), *n.* [NL., fr. Gr. *ouron* urine + *-emia.*] *Med.* Accumulation in the blood of constituents which should have been eliminated in the urine, producing a toxic condition. It is due to insufficient secretion of urine. — **u·re′mic, u·rae′mic** (-mĭk), *adj.*

-u·ret (-ū·rĕt). [For earlier *-ure*, fr. F. *-ure*, in *sulfure, phosphure*, used to express compounds with metals.] *Chem.* A suffix formerly used with the same meaning as *-ide.* Corresponding participial adjectives were formed in *-eted, -etted*, as in carbur*eted*, phosphor*eted*.

u·re′ter (ū·rē′tẽr), *n.* [NL., fr. Gr. *ourētēr.*] *Anat. & Zool.* The duct which carries away the urine from a kidney to the bladder or cloaca. — **u·re′ter·al** (ū·rē′tẽr·ăl), **u′re·ter′ic** (ū′rē·tẽr′ĭk), *adj.*

u·re′ter·o- (ū·rē′tẽr·ō-), **ureter-.** [Gr. *ourētēr.*] A combining form denoting: **a** *The ureter*, as in **u·re′ter·ec′to·my, u·re′ter·o·li·thot′o·my, u·re′ter·os′to·my, u·re′ter·ot′o·my. b** *Ureteral and;* — in adjectives, as in **u·re′ter·o·cer′vi·cal**, pertaining to a ureter and the cervix, **u·re′ter·o·gen′i·tal, u·re′ter·o·in·tes′ti·nal, u·re′ter·o·vag′i·nal.**

u′re·than′ (ū′rē·thăn′; ū·rĕth′ăn), *n.* Also **u′re·thane′** (-thān′; -ăn). [F. *uréthane.* See UREA; ETHER.] *Chem.* **a** A colorless crystalline compound, $NH_2COOC_2H_5$, used as a hypnotic, antispasmodic, and sedative; ethyl carbamate. **b** Any ester of carbamic acid.

u·re′thra (ū·rē′thrȧ), *n.; pl.* URETHRAE (-thrē); URETHRAS (-thrȧz). [LL., fr. Gr. *ourēthra.*] The canal which in most mammals carries off the urine from the bladder and in the male serves also as a genital duct. — **u·re′thral** (-thrăl), *adj.*

u′re·thri′tis (ū′rē·thrī′tĭs), *n.* [NL. See URETHRA; -ITIS.] Inflammation of the urethra. — **u′re·thrit′ic** (-thrĭt′ĭk), *adj.*

u·re′thro- (ū·rē′thrō-), **urethr-.** [Gr. *ourēthra.*] A combining form denoting: **a** *The urethra*, as in **u′re·threc′to·my, u′re·thros′to·my, u′re·throt′o·my. b** *Urethral and;* — in adjectives, as in **u·re′thro·bulb′ar.**

u·re′thro·scope (-skōp), *n.* [*urethro-* + *-scope.*] *Med.* An instrument for viewing the interior of the urethra.

u′re·thros′co·py (ū′rē·thrŏs′kō·pĭ), *n.* *Med.* Examination of the urethra by means of a urethroscope.

u·ret′ic (ū·rĕt′ĭk), *adj.* [LL. *ureticus*, fr. Gr. *ourētikos.* See URINE.] Of or pert. to the urine; diuretic; urinary.

urge (ûrj), *v. t.;* URGED (ûrjd); URG′ING (ûr′jĭng). [L. *urgere.*] **1.** To present in an earnest manner; to press upon attention; to plead or allege; to advocate or demand with importunity. **2.** To force onward; prosecute energetically, as an enterprise. **3.** To solicit earnestly. **4.** To force or impel in an indicated direction, esp. onward; to drive. **5.** To ply hard; as, to *urge* one's oars. — *v. i.* To declare, advance, or press earnestly, a statement, argument, charge, or the like. — *n.* Act of urging; a force or impulse that urges; esp., a continuing impulse toward some activity or goal.

ur′gen·cy (ûr′jĕn·sĭ), *n.* Quality or state of being urgent; insistence; pressure, as of necessity.

ur′gent (-jĕnt), *adj.* [F., fr. L. *urgens, -entis*, pres. part. of *urgere.*] Urging; pressing; plying with importunity; calling for immediate attention; instantly important. — **ur′gent·ly**, *adv.*

-urgy. [Gr. *-ourgia*, fr. *-ourgos* worker. See DEMIURGE.] A combining form denoting a *technical art of working a* (specified) *product*, as in zym*urgy*.

-u′ri·a (-ū′rĭ·ȧ). [NL., fr. Gr. *-ouria*, fr. *ouron* urine.] A combining form meaning *a condition of the urine*, esp. implying *an abnormal* or *diseased condition caused by the presence of a* (specified) *substance*, as in albumin*uria*.

u′ric (ū′rĭk; 114), *adj.* [Gr. *ouron* urine.] Of or pertaining to urine; obtained from urine.

uric acid. *Chem.* A white, odorless and tasteless, nearly insoluble diacid, $C_5H_4N_4O_3$, present in small quantity in urine. — **u′ric-ac′id**, *adj.*

u′ri·co- (ū′rĭ·kō-), **uric-.** A combining form for *uric*, denoting *uric acid*, as in **u′ri·col′y·sis, u′ri·co·lyt′ic.**

U′ri·el (ū′rĭ·ĕl), *n.* [Heb. *Ūrī'ēl.*] In Semitic angelology, an archangel. Milton makes him "regent of the sun."

U′rim (ū′rĭm), *n. pl., and* **Thum′mim** (thŭm′ĭm), *n. pl.* [Heb. *ūrīm; tummīm.*] *Bib.* Certain objects mentioned in the Old Testament (*Exodus* xxviii. 30; etc.) as being mediums for the revelation of the will of God to his people or as being placed in the breastplate by the high priest on certain occasions.

u′ri·nal (ū′rĭ·năl), *n.* **1.** A vessel for holding urine. **2.** A building or enclosure for urinating purposes.

u′ri·nal′y·sis (ū′rĭ·năl′ĭ·sĭs), *n.* [NL.] Chemical analysis of the urine.

u′ri·nar′y (ū′rĭ·nĕr′ĭ *or, esp. Brit.*, -nẽr·ĭ), *adj.* **1.** Pertaining to, occurring in, or designating the organs for the excretion and removal of urine. **2.** Of, pertaining to, or for urine. — *n.; pl.* -IES (-ĭz). A urinal.

urinary bladder. In many vertebrates, a bladder serving for the temporary retention of urine.

urinary calculus. *Med.* A concretion of some constituents of urine, occurring in the urinary passages.

u′ri·nate (ū′rĭ·nāt), *v. i.* To discharge urine. — **u′ri·na′tion** (-nā′shŭn), *n.*

u′rine (ū′rĭn), *n.* [OF. *urine*, fr. L. *urina.*] *Physiol.* In mammals, a fluid excretion from the kidneys; in birds and reptiles, a solid or semisolid excretion. In man, the urine is a clear, transparent fluid of an amber color and peculiar odor, with an average density of 1.02.

u′ri·nif′er·ous (ū′rĭ·nĭf′ẽr·ŭs), *adj.* Carrying urine, as the **uriniferous tubules** (see KIDNEY).

u′ri·no- (ū′rĭ·nō-), **urin-.** [L. *urina* urine.] A combining form equivalent to URO-, as in **u′ri·no·gen′i·tal, u′ri·nos′co·py.**

u′ri·nous (ū′rĭ·nŭs), *adj.* Also **u′ri·nose** (-nōs). Of, pertaining to, like, or having the qualities or odor of urine; containing urine.

urn (ûrn), *n.* [L. *urna.*] **1.** A vessel of various forms, usually a vase with a pedestal. **2.** Esp., such a vessel used for preserving the ashes of the dead after cremation, and anciently for holding lots to be drawn. **3.** Figuratively, the grave. **4.** A closed vessel, usually with a spout, for serving beverages, as tea and coffee.

u′ro- (ū′rō-), **ur-.** [Gr. *ouron* urine.] *Chem. & Med.* A combining form denoting: **a** *Urine*, as in *urology, uranalysis.* **b** *Urinary tract*, as in **u′ro·gen′i·tal** (-jĕn′ĭ·tăl; -t'l), relating to the organs or functions of excretion (production or removal of urine) and reproduction. **c** *Urination.*

u′ro·chord (-kôrd), *n.* [Gr. *oura* tail + *chord.*] *Zool.* The notochord of larval ascidians, etc.; — so called because chiefly confined to the caudal region. — **u′ro·chor′dal** (-kôr′dăl; -d'l), *adj.*

u′ro·chrome (-krōm), *n.* [*uro-* + *-chrome.*] *Biochem.* A yellow pigment to which the yellow color of normal urine is principally due.

u·rog′e·nous (ū·rŏj′ē·nŭs), *adj.* [*uro-* + *-genous.*] *Physiol.* **a** Producing urine. **b** Derived from urine.

u′ro·lith (ū′rō·lĭth), *n.* [*uro* + *-lith.*] *Med.* A urinary calculus. — **u′ro·lith′ic** (-lĭth′ĭk), *adj.*

u·rol′o·gy (ū·rŏl′ō·jĭ), *n.* [*uro-* + *-logy.*] Medical science relating to the urine or urinary organs, specif., to diseases of the urogenital organs. — **u′ro·log′ic** (ū′rō·lŏj′ĭk), **u′ro·log′i·cal** (-ĭ·kăl), *adj.* — **u·rol′o·gist** (ū·rŏl′ō·jĭst), *n.*

u′ro·pod (ū′rō·pŏd), *n.* [Gr. *oura* tail + *-pod.*] *Zool.* Any of the abdominal appendages of a crustacean or other arthropod, as in the lobster.

u′ro·pyg′i·al (-pĭj′ĭ·ăl), *adj.* [See UROPYGIUM.] *Zool.* Of or pertaining to the uropygium. — **u′ro·pyg′i·al**, *n.*

uropygial gland. *Zool.* A large gland opening on the back at the base of the tail feathers in most birds, secreting an oily fluid which the bird uses in preening its feathers.

u′ro·pyg′i·um (-ŭm), *n.* [NL., fr. Gr. *ouropygion*, for *orrhopygion*, fr. *orrhos* the end of the os sacrum + *pygē* rump.] *Zool.* The fleshy and bony prominence at the posterior extremity of a bird's body, which supports the tail feathers.

u·ros′co·py (ū·rŏs′kō·pĭ), *n.* [*uro-* + *-scopy.*] The diagnosis of diseases by inspection of urine. — **u′ro·scop′ic** (ū′rō·skŏp′ĭk), *adj.* — **u·ros′co·pist** (ū·rŏs′kō·pĭst), *n.*

u′ro·xan′thin (ū′rō·zăn′thĭn), *n.* [*uro-* + *xanthin.*] = INDICAN, 2.

Ur'sa (ûr'sȧ), *n.* [L. *ursa* a she-bear, also, a constellation, fem. of *ursus* a bear.] *Astron.* Either one of the Bears, Ursa Major or Ursa Minor.

Ur'sa Ma'jor (mā'jẽr); *gen.* URSAE MAJORIS (ûr'sē mȧ·jō'rĭs). [L.] The most conspicuous of the northern constellations. It is situated near the pole, and contains the stars which form the *Dipper*, two of which are the *Pointers*, or stars which point toward the North Star. Called also *Great Bear.*

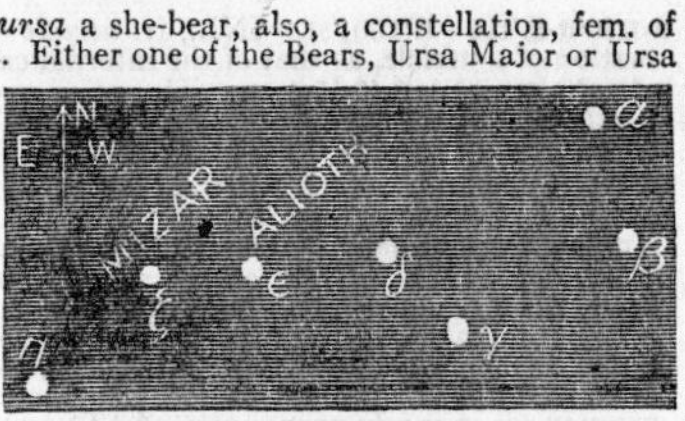

Ursa Major. *β*, *α* The Pointers. Greek letters distinguish the various Stars, the names of two of which (*ε* and *ζ*) are shown.

Ur'sa Mi'nor (mī'nẽr); *gen.* URSAE MINORIS (ûr'sē mĭ·nō'rĭs). [L.] The Little Bear (sometimes also the Little Dipper), the constellation including the north pole of the heavens, and the North Star, or polestar (Polaris), situated in the tip of the tail of the Bear.

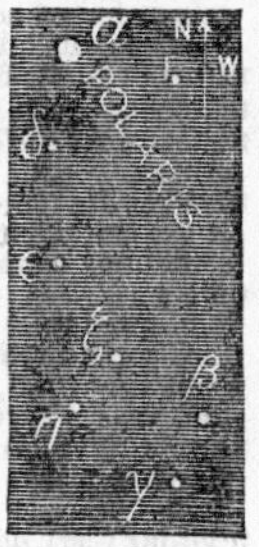

Ursa Minor.

ur'sine (ûr'sīn; -sĭn), *adj.* [L. *ursinus*, fr. *ursus* a bear.] Of, pertaining to, or like a bear or the bear family; having bearlike characteristics.

ursine howler. See HOWLING MONKEY.

‖**Ur'spra'che** (o͞or'shprä'kĕ), *n.* [G., fr. *ur-* primitive, original + *sprache* language.] A parent language; the original tongue, esp. primitive Indo-European.

Ur'su·line (ûr'sū·lĭn; -līn; -lēn), *n.* [NL. *Ursulinus.*] *R.C.Ch.* One of an order of women, founded c. 1537; — so called from its patron, ***St. Ur'su·la*** (ûr'sū·lȧ), a British princess martyred, according to legend, at Cologne (c. 300). Its work is chiefly educational. — **Ur'su·line,** *adj.*

ur'ti·ca'ceous (ûr'tĭ·kā'shŭs), *adj.* [L. *urtica* nettle.] *Bot.* Belonging to the nettle family (Urticaceae). See NETTLE.

ur'ti·car'i·a (-kâr'ĭ·ȧ; 6), *n.* [NL., fr. L. *urtica* nettle.] *Med.* An inflammatory disease of the skin, characterized by wheals, accompanied with itching; hives; uredo. The cause may be external, or it may follow ingestion of some foods, such as shellfish or strawberries. — **ur'ti·car'i·al** (-kâr'ĭ·ăl), *adj.*

ur'ti·cate (ûr'tĭ·kāt), *v. t. & i.* To sting with or as with nettles.

ur'ti·ca'tion (-kā'shŭn), *n.* *Med.* **a** Act or process of whipping or stinging with nettles, for its stimulating effect. **b** An itching and stinging sensation.

u'rus (ū'rŭs), *n.* [L., of Teut. origin.] A large, long-horned wild ox (*Bos primigenius*) of the German forests, now extinct; — so called by Julius Caesar.

u·ru'shi·ol (o͞o·ro͞o'shē·ōl; -ŏl), *n.* [Jap. *urushi* lacquer + *-ol.*] *Chem.* A poisonous, liquid, phenolic substance, $C_{21}H_{32}O_2$, constituent of Japanese and Chinese lacquer.

us (ŭs; 4), *pron.* [ME., fr. AS. *ūs.*] The objective case of *we*, used: **1.** As dative of indirect object. **2.** As direct object of a verb or preposition. **3.** As *pl.*, of royalty and editorially in the same way as *we.*

us'a·ble (ūz'ȧ·b'l), *adj.* **a** That can be used. **b** That is convenient and practicable for use. — **us'a·bil'i·ty** (-bĭl'ĭ·tĭ), *n.* — **us'a·ble·ness,** *n.*

us'age (ūs'ĭj; ūz'ĭj), *n.* [F., fr. ML. *usaticum.* See USE, *n.*] **1.** Long-continued practice; customary procedure or action. **2.** Act of using; mode of using or treating; treatment. **3.** Customary use or employment, as of a word or phrase in a particular sense. — **Syn.** See HABIT.

us'ance (ūz'ăns), *n.* [OF.] **1.** *Obs.* **a** Use; employment. **b** Custom; usage. **c** Interest paid for money. **2.** *Com.* The time allowed (exclusive of grace) for the payment of a bill of exchange or note. **3.** *Econ.* The flow of benefits coming from the use of any form of wealth.

Us'bek (ŭs'bĕk), **Us'beg** (-bĕg). Vars. of UZBEK, UZBEG.

use (ūz), *v. t.* [OF. *user* to use, make use of, fr. L. *uti*, past part. *usus*, to use.] **1.** To make use of, esp. habitually or customarily; as, to *use* diligence in business. **2.** To convert to one's service; to avail oneself of; to employ; as, to *use* a plow, a chair, a book. **3.** To behave toward; to act with regard to; to treat; as, to *use* a beast cruelly. **4.** To partake of; also, to smoke (tobacco); as, he had *used* tobacco all his life. **5.** To accustom; habituate; inure; as, men *used* to cold and hunger. — *v. i.* To be wont or accustomed; as, he *used* to ride daily. — ***use up.*** **a** To consume or exhaust by using. **b** *Colloq.* To exhaust; to leave no capacity of force or use in.

Syn. Use, employ, utilize mean to make serviceable. **Use** suggests availing oneself of a thing as a means or instrument to one's end; **employ**, the use of a person or thing that is idle, inactive, disengaged, or the like; **utilize**, the discovery of a profitable use or of employment for a practical purpose.

use (ūs), *n.* [OF. *us* use, usage, fr. L. *usus*, fr. *uti*, past part. *usus*, to use.] **1.** Act of employing anything or state of being employed; application; employment; as, the *use* of a pen. **2.** The fact of being used or employed habitually; usage; as, the wear and tear from ordinary *use.* **3.** **a** Continued or repeated exercise or employment; as, a habit is strengthened by *use.* **b** A practice, habit, or custom. **4.** Occasion or need to employ; necessity; — often with *for;* as, no further *use* for a book. **5.** Method or way of using; as, he knew the *use* of various herbs. **6.** Quality of being suitable for employment; usefulness; utility; as, there is small *use* in anger; also, the end served; the object; as, he put his knowledge to good *use.* **7.** Function; as, everything in nature seems to have its *use.* **8.** *Rare.* Common occurrence; ordinary experience. **9.** *Law.* That enjoyment of property which consists in its employment, occupation, exercise, or practice. **10.** [Due to confusion with OF. *ues* profit, advantage, fr. L. *opus* need, business, work.] *Law.* Advantage; benefit; specif., the benefit or profit of lands and tenements the legal title to which is given to a person other than the one entitled to the occupation or use (in sense 9); a trust of real estate. **11.** [*often cap.*] *Liturgics.* The special form of ritual or liturgy or of any liturgical form or observance, used in some particular church, diocese, etc.; as, the Roman or Anglican *use.*

Syn. (1) **Use, usefulness, utility** mean ability to serve one's end or purpose. **Use** implies suitability, often for any conceivable purpose; **usefulness**, capacity, as of concrete things, to serve a practical purpose; **utility** is more formal than either and is often used abstractly as well as concretely.
(2) See HABIT.

use'a·ble (ūz'ȧ·b'l), **use'a·ble·ness,** etc. Vars. of USABLE, etc.

used (ūzd; *see sense* 3), *adj.* **1.** Employed in doing something, especially customarily or repeatedly; hence, usual; customary. **2.** That has had use; hence, worn; secondhand. **3.** (*pron.* ūzd; ūz; ūst; ūs) Accustomed; habituated; as, he is *used* to working late.

use'ful (ūs'fo͝ol; -f'l), *adj.* Full of use; serviceable for any object; helpful; having utility; beneficial; advantageous. — **use'ful·ly,** *adv.* — **use'ful·ness,** *n.* — **Syn.** See USE.

use'less (ūs'lĕs; -lĭs), *adj.* Having, or being of, no use; unserviceable; ineffectual or inefficient. — **use'less·ly,** *adv.* — **use'less·ness,** *n.*

us'er (ūz'ẽr), *n.* One who or that which uses.

us'er, *n.* *Law.* Enjoyment of a right of use; a right to use, resulting from long-continued use.

U'shas (o͞o'shȧs; o͞o·shȧs'), *n.* [Skr. *Uṣas.*] *Vedic Myth.* The goddess of the dawn, to whom are addressed some of the noblest hymns in the Vedas.

ush'er (ŭsh'ẽr), *n.* [OF. *uissier* (F. *huissier*), fr. VL. *ustiarius*, fr. *ustium*, for L. *ostium*, door, entrance.] **1.** An officer or servant who has the care of the door of a court, hall, chamber, or the like. Also, one who escorts persons to seats in a church, theater, etc. **2.** *Brit.* An underteacher, or assistant, in a school. — *v. t.* To introduce or escort, as an usher, forerunner, or harbinger.

‖**us'que ad a'ras** (ŭs'kwē ăd ā'răs). [L.] Even to the altars, i. e., in everything except what is contrary to one's religion. See AMICUS USQUE AD ARAS.

us'que·baugh (ŭs'kwē·bä; -bô), *n.* Also **us'que·bae, us'que.** [Ir. & Gael. *uisge beatha*, lit., water of life.] Whisky, as made in Ireland or Scotland.

us'tu·late (ŭs'tū·lāt), *adj.* [L. *ustulatus*, past part. of *ustulare* to scorch, fr. *urere* to burn.] Discolored as if burned.

us'tu·la'tion (-lā'shŭn), *n.* *Pharm.* The roasting or drying of moist substances to prepare them for pulverizing.

u'su·al (ū'zho͞o·ăl), *adj.* [OF. *usual, usuel*, fr. LL. *usualis*, fr. *usus* use.] Such as is in common use; such as occurs in ordinary practice, or in the ordinary course of events; ordinary. — **u'su·al·ly,** *adv.* — **u'su·al·ness,** *n.*

Syn. Usual, customary, habitual, wonted, accustomed mean familiar through frequent or regular repetition. **Usual** stresses the absence of strangeness or unexpectedness; **customary**, a following the practices, conventions, usages, etc., of a particular community; **habitual**, a settled or established practice, as of an individual confirmed in a habit; **wonted** approximates *habitual* or *customary;* **accustomed**, more familiar than *wonted*, is weaker in its suggestion of a fixed habit or of custom than either.

u'su·fruct (ū'zū·frŭkt), *n.* [LL. *usufructus*, fr. L. *ususfructus, usus et fructus*, fr. *usus* use + *fructus* fruit.] *Roman & Civil Law.* The right of using and enjoying the fruits or profits of an estate or other thing belonging to another, without impairing the substance.

u'su·fruc'tu·ar'y (-frŭk'tū·ĕr'ĭ *or, esp. Brit.*, -ẽr·ĭ), *n.; pl.* -ARIES (-ĭz). [LL. *usufructuarius.*] *Roman & Civil Law.* One having the usufruct of property. — *adj.* *Law.* Of or pertaining to a usufruct; having the nature of a usufruct.

u'su·rer (ū'zho͞o·rẽr; 118), *n.* [OF. *usureor, usurier*, fr. ML. *usurarius.* See USURY.] **1.** One who lends money and takes interest for it; a moneylender. **2.** Specif., one who lends money at an exorbitant rate of interest.

u·su'ri·ous (ū·zho͝or'ĭ·ŭs; 118), *adj.* **1.** Practicing usury; taking illegal or exorbitant interest for the use of money. **2.** Partaking of or involving usury; of the nature of usury. — **u·su'ri·ous·ly,** *adv.* — **u·su'ri·ous·ness,** *n.*

u·surp' (ū·zûrp'; -sûrp'), *v. t.* [OF. *usurper*, fr. L. *usurpare, -patum*, to make use of, enjoy, usurp, fr. *usus* use + *rapere* to seize.] To seize and hold in possession by force, or without right; — applied to seizure of office, place, functions, powers, rights, etc. — *v. i.* To commit forcible seizure of place, power, functions, or the like, without right; to be, or act as, a usurper. — **Syn.** See ARROGATE.

u'sur·pa'tion (ū'zẽr·pā'shŭn; ū'sẽr-), *n.* Act of usurping; specif., the illegal seizure of sovereign power.

u·surp'er (ū·zûr'pẽr; -sûr'-), *n.* One who usurps, or seizes and holds, as sovereign power, without proper authority.

u'su·ry (ū'zho͞o·rĭ; 118), *n.; pl.* USURIES (-rĭz). [OF. *usure*, fr. L. *usura* use, usury, fr. *uti*, past part. *usus*, to use.] **1.** *Obs.* A premium paid for a loan of money or goods; interest. **2.** The lending out of money with an interest charge for its use. **3.** An unconscionable or exorbitant rate or amount of interest; specif., *Law*, interest in excess of a legal rate charged to a borrower for the use of money.

ut (ŭt; *in solmization*, o͞ot), *n.* [L. See GAMUT.] *Music.* The first syllable in a system of solmization invented by Guido d'Arezzo, now usually superseded by *do.*

Ute (ūt; ū'tē), *n.* An Indian of a group of Shoshonean tribes, of extremely primitive culture, formerly ranging in Colorado, Utah, and New Mexico.

u·ten'sil (ū·tĕn'sĭl; -s'l), *n.* [OF. *utensile*, fr. L. *utensile*, fr. *utensilis* that may be used, fit for use, fr. *uti*, past part. *usus*, to use.] **1.** An instrument or vessel, esp. one used in a kitchen or dairy. **2.** Any useful tool or implement; as, farming *utensils.* — **Syn.** See IMPLEMENT.

uter-. = UTERO-, as in **u'ter·al'gi·a, u'ter·ec'to·my.**

u'ter·ine (ū'tẽr·ĭn; -īn), *adj.* [LL. *uterinus* born of the same mother, fr. *uterus* womb.] **1.** Of or pertaining to the uterus, or womb. **2.** Born of the same mother, but by a different father.

u'ter·o- (ū'tẽr·ō-), **uter-.** A combining form from *uterus* denoting: **a** *The uterus*, as in **u'ter·ol'o·gy.** **b** *Uterine and;* — in adjectives, as in **u'ter·o·ab·dom'i·nal,** pert. to the uterus and abdomen.

u'ter·us (ū'tẽr·ŭs), *n.; pl.* UTERI (-ī). [L., womb, belly, abdomen.] *Anat. & Zool.* In female mammals, an organ for containing, and usually for nourishing, the young during the development previous to birth; the womb.

U'ther (ū'thẽr), *n.* One of the three principal magicians of Britain, later regarded as king of Britain and father of King Arthur. See IGRAINE.

u'tile (ū'tĭl; *see* -ILE), *adj.* [F., fr. L. *utilis*, fr. *uti* to use.] Practical; profitable; useful.

u·til'i·tar'i·an (ū·tĭl'ĭ·târ'ĭ·ăn; ū'tĭl-), *adj.* **1.** Of, pertaining to, or consisting in utility; aiming at utility as distinguished from beauty, ornament, etc.; sometimes, derogatorily, marked by a sordid spirit.

2. Of or pert. to utilitarianism; supporting utilitarianism. — *n.* One who believes in utilitarianism.

u·til′i·tar′i·an·ism (ū·tĭl′ĭ·târ′ĭ·ăn·ĭz′m; ū′tĭl-), *n.* *Ethics.* The doctrine that the useful is the good, and that the determining consideration of right conduct is the usefulness of its consequences; esp., the doctrine that the aim of moral action is the largest possible balance of pleasure over pain, or the greatest happiness of the greatest number. Cf. BENTHAMISM.

u·til′i·ty (ū·tĭl′ĭ·tĭ), *n.; pl.* -TIES (-tĭz). [OF. *utilité*, fr. L. *utilitas*, fr. *utilis* useful.] **1.** Quality or state of being useful; usefulness. **2.** *Econ.* Power to satisfy human wants; — opp. to *disutility*. **3.** Happiness; the greatest good or happiness of the greatest number, — the foundation of utilitarianism. **4.** Short for PUBLIC UTILITY. **5.** *pl.* Shares of stock in public utility companies. — **Syn.** See USE. — *adj.* Adapted or available for general utility; as, a *utility* table or actor.

u′ti·lize (ū′tĭ·līz), *v. t.* To make useful; to turn to profitable account or use; to make use of. — **Syn.** See USE. — **u′ti·liz′a·ble** (-līz′ȧ·b'l), *adj.* — **u′ti·li·za′tion** (-lĭ·zā′shŭn; -lī·zā′-), *n.* — **u′ti·liz′er** (-līz′ẽr), *n.*

‖**ut in′fra** (ŭt ĭn′frȧ). [L.] As below.

‖**u′ti pos′si·de′tis** (ū′tī pŏs′ĭ·dē′tĭs). [L., as you possess.] *Internat. Law.* The principle that a conclusion or treaty of peace between belligerents vests in them respectively as absolute property the territory under their actual control.

ut′most (ŭt′mōst; -mŭst), *adj.* [AS. *ūtmest, ūtemest, ȳt(e)mest*, double superl. fr. *ūt, ūte*, out.] **1.** Situated at the farthest point; most distant; extreme. **2.** Of the greatest or highest degree, quantity, number, or the like; greatest; as, the *utmost* assiduity. — *n.* The most possible; the uttermost.

U′to–Az′tec·an (ū′tō·ăz′tĕk·ăn), *adj.* Pertaining to or designating an important American Indian linguistic family, including the Shoshonean, Piman, and Nahuatlan. See LANGUAGE, *Table.*

U·to′pi·a (ū·tō′pĭ·ȧ), *n.* [NL., fr. Gr. *ou* not + *topos* a place.] **1.** A book (1516) by Sir Thomas More, describing an ideal commonwealth. Utopia is an imaginary island, enjoying perfection in politics, law, etc. **2.** [*often not cap.*] Hence, any place of ideal perfection; also, an impracticable scheme of social regeneration.

U·to′pi·an (-ăn), *adj.* Of, pertaining to, or like Utopia; hence [*often not cap.*], involving imaginary perfections; ideal; visionary. — *n.* **1.** An inhabitant of Utopia. **2.** Hence [*not cap.*], one who believes in the perfectibility of human society; a visionary.

u·to′pi·an·ism (-ĭz′m), *n.* The ideas, views; aims, etc., of a utopian; impracticable schemes of human perfection.

u′tri·cle (ū′trĭ·k'l), *n.* [L. *utriculus*, dim. of *uter, utris*, a bag or bottle made of an animal's hide.] **1.** A little sac or vesicle, as the air cell of a fucoid seaweed. **2.** *Bot.* A small, one-celled, usually indehiscent, one-seeded or few-seeded achene with thin, membranous pericarp.

u·tric′u·lar (ū·trĭk′ū·lẽr), *adj.* **1.** Of or pertaining to a utricle, or utriculus; containing a utricle. **2.** Resembling a utricle or bag, whether large or minute.

u·tric′u·late (-lāt), *adj.* Resembling a bladder; swollen like a bladder; inflated; utricular.

u·tric′u·li′tis (-lī′tĭs), *n.* [NL., fr. *utricle* + *-itis.*] *Med.* Inflammation of a utricle, as that of the internal ear.

u·tric′u·lus (ū·trĭk′ū·lŭs), *n.* [L. See UTRICLE.] A utricle, esp. *Anat.*, that of the ear.

‖**ut su′pra** (ŭt sū′prȧ). [L.] As above.

ut′ter (ŭt′ẽr), *adj.* [AS. *ūttra, ūtera, ȳtera;* compar. adj. to AS. *ūt* out.] **1.** Complete; total; as, *utter* ruin. **2.** Extreme to the point of strangeness; unusual. **3.** Peremptory; unqualified; as, an *utter* denial.

ut′ter, *v. t.* [ME. *uttren, outren*, fr. *utter(e)* outside, adv. (fr. AS. *ūtter, ūttor*, compar. of *ūt* out), and fr. *out, ut*, out, adv.] **1.** *Obs.* **a** To put forth or out; to emit. **b** To sell or vend. **2.** To put in circulation, as money or currency; — often used, specif., of counterfeit notes or coins, forged or fraudulent documents, etc. **3.** To give public expression to; to speak; pronounce. **4.** To reveal; divulge. — **Syn.** See EXPRESS. — **ut′ter·a·ble** (-ȧ·b'l), *adj.*

ut′ter·ance (ŭt′ẽr·ăns), *n.* [OF. *outrance.*] *Obs.* The last extremity; esp., the point of death.

ut′ter·ance, *n.* [From UTTER, *v.*] **1.** Act of uttering. Specif.: **a** *Obs.* Sale or disposal to the public. **b** Putting in circulation, as false coin or forged notes. **2.** Vocal expression; style or power of speaking. **3.** That which is uttered, or spoken or published.

ut′ter·er (ŭt′ẽr·ẽr), *n.* One who utters (in various senses).

ut′ter·ly, *adv.* In an utter manner; fully; totally.

ut′ter·most (ŭt′ẽr·mōst; -mŭst), *adj.* [From UTTER, *adj.*] Extreme; utmost. — *n.* The utmost.

u·va′rov·ite (o͞o·vä′rŭf·īt), *n.* [After Count S. S. *Uvarov* (1786–1855), Russ. statesman.] *Mineral.* An emerald-green variety of garnet containing chromium. Chemically it is $Ca_3Cr_2(SiO_4)_3$.

u′ve·a (ū′vē·ȧ), *n.* [ML., fr. L. *uva* grape.] *Anat.* The posterior pigmented layer of the iris; also, the iris and ciliary body together with the chorioid coat. — **u′ve·al** (-ăl), *adj.* — **u′ve·ous** (-ŭs), *adj.*

u′ve·i′tis (-ī′tĭs), *n.* [NL., fr. *uvea* + *-itis.*] *Med.* Inflammation of the uvea. — **u′ve·it′ic** (-ĭt′ĭk), *adj.*

u′vu·la (ū′vū·lȧ), *n.; pl.* -LAS (-lȧz), -LAE (-lē). [ML., dim. fr. L. *uva* grape, uvula.] *Anat.* The pendent fleshy lobe in the middle of the posterior border of the soft palate.

u′vu·lar (-lẽr), *adj.* Of or pertaining to the uvula; specif., *Phonet.*, pronounced with the aid of the uvula, as in trilling. — *n.* *Phonet.* A uvular sound.

u′vu·li′tis (-lī′tĭs), *n.* [NL., fr. *uvula* + *-itis.*] *Med.* Inflammation of the uvula.

ux·o′ri·al (ŭks·ō′rĭ·ăl; ŭg·zō′-; 70), *adj.* *Rare.* Of, pertaining to, or characteristic of a wife.

ux·or′i·cide (ŭks·ŏr′ĭ·sīd), *n.* [L. *uxor* wife + *-cide.*] The murder of a wife by her husband; also, one who murders his wife. — **ux·or′i·cid′al** (-sīd′ăl), *adj.*

ux·o′ri·ous (ŭks·ō′rĭ·ŭs; ŭg·zō′-; 70), *adj.* [L. *uxorius*, fr. *uxor* wife.] Excessively or dotingly fond of, or submissive to, a wife. — **ux·o′ri·ous·ly,** *adv.* — **ux·o′ri·ous·ness,** *n.*

Uz′bek (ŭz′bĕk), **Uz′beg** (-bĕg), *n.* A member of the most civilized of the Turkic peoples of Turkestan, esp. in the Uzbek republic.

V

V, v (vē), *n.; pl.* V's, v's, Vs, vs (vēz). **1.** The twenty-second letter of the English alphabet. V and U are varieties of the same character, and were formerly used indiscriminately (see U). The letter W, a doubled V called "double U," is a survival of this use. V is from the Latin alphabet, where it was used both as a vowel and as a consonant (first with the value of English *w*, and later with that of *v*). The Latin derived the letter from a western form (V) of the Greek upsilon (see Y). **2.** The sound of this letter. In English *v* represents a labiodental continuant, the voiced correlative of *f*. See *Pron.* § 123. **3.** [*cap.*] In Roman numerals, 5 or, in the form V̄, 5000. In this use V was only the upper part of X, the symbol for 10. **4.** Anything having the shape of the letter V. **5.** *Colloq., U. S.* A five-dollar bill. **6.** **a** As a *symbol*, used to denote or indicate anyone or anything arbitrarily or conveniently so designated, esp. as the twenty-first or (see K, 3) twenty-second in order or class. **b** Symbol for *Victory* much used in World War II, often represented by the Morse code letter (. . .—) or musically by the first four notes of Beethoven's Fifth Symphony or by the gesture of the index and middle fingers spread to form a V. Cf. V DAY.

V–1 (vē′wŭn′), *n.* [Abbr. of G. *Vergeltungswaffe eins* vengeance weapon one.] A robot bomb.

V–2 (vē′to͞o′), *n.* [Abbr. of G. *Vergeltungswaffe zwei* vengeance weapon two.] A rocket of German invention that contained about a ton of explosive, was over 45 feet long and about 5½ feet in diameter, ascended to an altitude of over 60 miles, and descended at a speed far greater than that of sound. It was used against London in World War II.

va′can·cy (vā′kăn·sĭ), *n.; pl.* -CIES (-sĭz). **1.** *Archaic.* Leisure or an interval of leisure. **2.** A vacating of an office, post, etc., or the state of such office, etc., when vacated or vacant; also, the time such office, etc., is vacant. **3.** A vacant office, post, tenancy, etc. **4.** Empty space; the void; also, a vacuum; blank. **5.** State of being empty or void; also, vacuity.

va′cant (vā′kănt), *adj.* [OF., fr. L. *vacans, -antis*, pres. part. of *vacare* to be empty, to be free or unoccupied.] **1.** Not occupied by an incumbent, possessor, or officer; as, a *vacant* throne, office. **2.** Without contents or content; as, a *vacant* room; of the mind, free from preoccupation, cares, etc. **3.** Characterized by freedom from occupation; leisure; disengaged; free; as, few *vacant* hours. **4.** **a** Vacuous; foolish. **b** Marked by or enjoying a respite from thought; unreflecting. **5.** *Law.* **a** Not put to use, as land. **b** Of an estate or the like, abandoned; having no heir or claimant. — **Syn.** See EMPTY. — **va′cant·ly,** *adv.*

va′cate (vā′kāt), *v. t.* [L. *vacare, vacatum*, to be empty.] **1.** To annul; to make void; as, to *vacate* a charter; — now in legal use only. **2.** To make vacant, as an office, house, etc.; also, to give up the occupancy of. — *v. i.* **1.** To vacate an office, post, etc. **2.** *Slang.* To leave; go away.

va·ca′tion (vā·kā′shŭn; vȧ-), *n.* [OF. *vacacion, vacation*, fr. L. *vacatio* a being free from a duty, service, etc., fr. *vacare* to be empty.] **1.** Respite or a time of respite; an intermission or rest. **2.** A scheduled period during which activity or work is suspended; as: **a** *Law.* Intermission of judicial proceedings; recess. **b** In educational institutions, an intermission of the regular studies and exercises, as between terms or during the summer. **c** In industry or business, a period of exemption from work granted to employees. **3.** A period for rest and recreation; a holiday. **4.** *Rare.* Act or an instance of vacating, esp. of vacating an office.

va·ca′tion·ist (-ĭst), *n.* Also **va·ca′tion·er** (-ẽr). A person taking a vacation, esp. one traveling for pleasure or staying at a summer resort.

vac′ci·nal (văk′sĭ·năl), *adj.* *Med.* Of or pertaining to vaccine or vaccination.

vac′ci·nate (văk′sĭ·nāt), *v. t.* [From VACCINE, *adj.*] To inoculate with cowpox vaccine, esp. in order to prevent or mitigate an attack of smallpox; hence, to inoculate with any vaccine, or, loosely, any antigen, esp. as a preventive measure. — *v. i.* To perform or practice vaccination.

vac′ci·na′tion (-nā′shŭn), *n.* Act, art, or practice of vaccinating.

vac′ci·na′tor (văk′sĭ·nā′tẽr), *n.* *Med.* One who vaccinates; also, an instrument used in vaccinating.

vac′cine (văk′sēn; -sĭn), *adj.* [L. *vaccinus*, fr. *vacca* a cow.] **1.** Of, pertaining to, or derived from cows, or, esp. in technical use, cows afflicted with vaccinia or inoculated with its virus; as, *vaccine* lymph. **2.** Of or pertaining to vaccinia or vaccination. — *n.* **1.** Matter or a preparation containing the virus of cowpox, or vaccinia, in a form used for vaccination. **2.** In general, any substance for preventive inoculation, esp. a suspension of sensitized, attenuated, or killed, bacteria, called preferably ***bacterial vaccine,*** injected into the body to induce immunity to the same species of bacteria or their toxins.

vac·cin′i·a (văk·sĭn′ĭ·ȧ), *n.* [NL.] *Med.* Cowpox.

vac·cin′i·a′ceous (-ā′shŭs), *adj.* [L. *vaccinium* the blueberry.] *Bot.* Belonging to the huckleberry family (Vacciniaceae). See HUCKLEBERRY.

vac′il·late (văs′ĭ·lāt), *v. i.* [L. *vacillare, -latum.*] **1.** To waver; totter; hence, to fluctuate; oscillate. **2.** To waver in mind, will, or feeling. — **Syn.** See HESITATE.

vac′il·lat′ing (-lāt′ĭng), **vac′il·la·to′ry** (-lȧ·tō′rĭ *or, esp. Brit.,* -tẽr·ĭ), *adj.* Inclined to vacillate; wavering. — **vac′il·lat′ing·ly,** *adv.*

vac′il·la′tion (-lā′shŭn), *n.* **1.** Act or an instance of vacillating; a wavering in conduct, purpose, etc. **2.** Changeableness; irresolution.

vac′u·a (văk′ū·ȧ), *n., pl.* of VACUUM.

va·cu′i·ty (vă·kū′ĭ·tĭ), *n.; pl.* -TIES (-tĭz). [L. *vacuitas.*] **1.** An empty space; vacancy; void. **2.** The condition, fact, or quality of being empty; emptiness; hollowness. **3.** Vacancy of mind; mental emptiness or inactivity. **4.** Inanity; vacuousness. **5.** A vacuous or inane thing; as, to fill up a speech with *vacuities.*

‖**va′cu·o** (văk′ū·ō). Ablative of Latin *vacuum,* empty space, used esp. in: ***in vacuo,*** in an empty space; specif., in a space from which the air has been exhausted.

vac′u·o·lat′ed (văk′ū·ō·lāt′ĕd; -ĭd), *adj.* Also **vac′u·o·late** (-lāt). *Biol.* Containing one or more vacuoles. — **vac′u·o·la′tion** (-lā′shŭn), *n.*

vac′u·ole (văk′ū·ōl), *n.* [F., fr. L. *vacuus* empty.] *Biol.* **a** A small cavity or space in the tissues of an organism, containing air or fluid. **b** In modern usage, a cavity or vesicle in the protoplasm of a cell, containing a watery fluid. See CELL, 4, *Illust.*

vac′u·ous (văk′ū·ŭs), *adj.* [L. *vacuus.*] **1.** Empty; unfilled. **2.** Dull; stupid; inane. **3.** Devoid of serious occupation; spent in inanities; idle. — **Syn.** See EMPTY. — **vac′u·ous·ly,** *adv.* — **vac′u·ous·ness,** *n.*

vac′u·um (-ŭm), *n.; pl.* -UMS (-ŭmz), -A (-ȧ). [L., prop. neut. of *vacuus* empty.] **1.** A space entirely devoid of matter; hence, a space exhausted to a high degree by an air pump. Cf. PLENUM, 1. **2.** A degree of rarefaction well below atmospheric pressure; as, to get a fair or good *vacuum.* **3.** A void; a gap; as, his death has left a *vacuum* in their lives. — *adj.* **1.** Of, pertaining to, or used in producing a vacuum. **2.** Operated by suction or by a device producing a partial vacuum; — of a mechanism; as, a *vacuum* sweeper. **3.** Exhausted or partly exhausted of air or gas; — of a vessel, bulb, etc.; as, a *vacuum* tube, tank.

☞ PHRASES are:

vacuum cleaner	vacuum fan	vacuum jar
vacuum drier	vacuum gauge	vacuum sweeper

vac′u·um, *v. t. Colloq.* To use a vacuum cleaner, drier, or the like, upon; as, to *vacuum* a rug.

vacuum bottle *or* **flask.** A bottle-shaped vessel with a double wall, and a vacuum between the inner and outer wall, used to keep liquids either hot or cold for considerable periods.

vacuum pump. An air pump (for exhaustion only).

vacuum tube. *Elec.* **a** A sealed tube with the contained gas exhausted to a pressure low enough to permit the passage of electric discharges between metallic electrodes projecting into the tube from the outside. **b** An electron tube.

vacuum valve. An electron tube.

va′de me′cum (vā′dē mē′kŭm). [L., go with me.] Something, esp. a book, carried as a constant companion; hence, a manual; handbook.

‖**vae vic′tis** (vē vĭk′tĭs). [L.] Woe to the vanquished.

vag′a·bond (văg′ȧ·bŏnd), *adj.* [OF., fr. L. *vagabundus,* fr. *vagari* to stroll about, wander.] **1.** Moving from place to place without a settled habitation; wandering. **2.** Of, characteristic of, or leading the life of a vagrant or tramp; hence, unsettled and irresponsible. **3.** Following an irregular or vagrant course, path, line, etc. — *n.* One who wanders from place to place, having no fixed dwelling; esp., such a person who is lazy and without means of honest livelihood; vagrant; tramp; *Colloq.,* a scamp; rascal.

vag′a·bond′age (-bŏn′dĭj), *n.* [F.] The condition of a vagabond; vagrancy; also, vagabonds as a class.

va·gar′y (vȧ·gâr′ĭ; -gā′rĭ; 6), *n.; pl.* -IES (-ĭz). [Formerly used also as a verb, to wander, fr. L. *vagari* to stroll about.] An eccentric manifestation, action, notion, etc.; a caprice; as, the *vagaries* of his imagination; a *vagary* of fashion. — **Syn.** See CAPRICE.

va·gi′na (vȧ·jī′nȧ), *n.; pl.* -NAE (-nē), -NAS (-nȧz). [L., prop., a scabbard, sheath.] **1.** *Anat. & Zool.* **a** A sheath or sheathlike part or tube; a theca. **b** Specif., in female mammals, a canal which leads from the uterus to the external orifice of the genital canal, or to the cloaca. **2.** *Bot.* The expanded or sheathing part of some leaf bases.

vag′i·nal (văj′ĭ·năl; vȧ·jī′năl; -n′l), *adj. Anat. & Zool.* **a** Resembling or pertaining to a sheath; thecal. **b** Of, pertaining to, supplying, or used in treating the vagina of the genital canal; as, the *vaginal* plexus of nerves or veins.

vag′i·na·lec′to·my (văj′ĭ·nȧ·lĕk′tō·mĭ), *n.* [NL. tunica *vaginalis* + *-ectomy.*] *Surg.* Dissection and removal of the serous membrane covering the testis.

vag′i·nate (văj′ĭ·nāt), *adj.* Invested with or as with a sheath, or vagina.

vag′i·ni′tis (-nī′tĭs), *n.* [NL.] *Med.* Inflammation of the vagina or of any sheath.

vag′i·no- (văj′ĭ·nō-), **vagin-.** [From *vagina.*] A combining form denoting: **a** *The vagina,* as in **vag′i·nec′to·my, vag′i·not′o·my.** See -ECTOMY, -TOMY. **b** *Vaginal and;* — as in **vag′i·no·ab·dom′i·nal.**

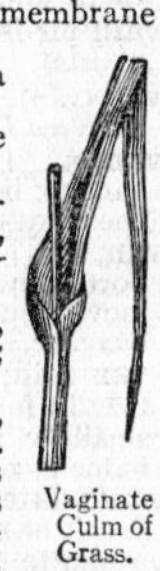

Vaginate Culm of Grass.

va′gran·cy (vā′grăn·sĭ), *n.* The condition, quality, or fact, of being vagrant; also, a vagrant act, thought, etc.; a vagary; as, the *vagrancies* of genius.

va′grant (vā′grănt), *n.* [Prob. fr. OF. *waucrant, wacrant,* pres. part. of *waucrer, wacrer,* to wander, influenced by F. *vagant,* pres. part. of *vaguer* to stray.] One who strolls from place to place; an idle wanderer; specif., one who has no settled habitation; a vagabond. — *adj.* **1.** Of, pertaining to, or characteristic of, a vagrant; as, *vagrant* beggars. **2.** Vagabond; nomadic; tied to no home, country, abode, or the like; roving. **3.** Having no fixed course, direction, aim, etc.; wayward; capricious; as, *vagrant* breezes, fancies. — **va′grant·ly,** *adv.* — **va′grant·ness,** *n.*

va′grom (vā′grŭm), *adj. Humorous.* A corruption of VAGRANT. *Shak.*

vague (vāg), *adj.* [F., fr. L. *vagus* wandering.] **1.** Not clearly expressed; stated so as to be indefinite; as, a *vague* accusation. **2.** Hence: **a** Lacking in precision; as, *vague* phrases. **b** Not clearly defined, grasped, or understood; indistinct; as, a *vague* idea. **c** Not clearly felt; more or less subconscious; as, a *vague* unrest. **d** Not sharply outlined; hazy. — **Syn.** See OBSCURE. — **Ant.** Definite. — **vague′ly,** *adv.* — **vague′ness,** *n.*

va′gus (vā′gŭs), *n.; pl.* VAGI (-jī). Also **vagus nerve.** [L. *vagus* wandering.] *Anat. & Zool.* Either of the tenth pair of cranial nerves arising from the medulla and supplying branches to various organs, including the lungs and stomach.

vail (vāl), *v. i.* [Aphetic form of AVAIL.] *Archaic.* To avail; to be of profit or benefit; — often with *it.* — *n. Archaic.* A gratuity, esp. to a servant; a tip.

vail, *v. t.* [Aphetic form of obs. *avale,* fr. F. *avaler* to lower.] *Archaic.* **1.** To lower; to let fall; to allow or cause to sink. **2.** To lower, as a banner, or take off, as a cap, in token of submission, inferiority, reverence, etc.

vail. Obs. var. of VEIL.

vain (vān), *adj.* [OF. *vain, vein,* fr. L. *vanus* empty, void, vain.] **1.** Empty; devoid of real value; useless; worthless. **2.** Hence: **a** Fruitless; futile; as, *vain* discussion. **b** *Rare.* Petty. **c** Of persons, foolish; silly. **3.** Having or manifesting undue or excessive pride in one's appearance, attainments, etc.; conceited. — **vain′ly,** *adv.* — **vain′ness,** *n.*

Syn. (1) **Vain, nugatory, otiose, idle, empty, hollow** mean devoid of worth or significance. **Vain** implies absence of all value or, in comparison, implies of very little value; **nugatory,** a triviality and, often, inoperativeness; **otiose,** a lack of excuse for being, as serving no purpose or as being an encumbrance or superfluity; **idle,** a being incapable of having any worthwhile effects; **empty** and **hollow,** a being destitute of substance or reality and therefore deceptive in its soundness, genuineness, or the like.
(2) See FUTILE.
(3) See PROUD.

— ***for vain.*** In vain. *Shak.* — ***in vain.*** To no purpose; ineffectually; as, he has not lived *in vain.*

vain′glo′ri·ous (vān′glō′rĭ·ŭs; 70), *adj.* Feeling or manifesting vainglory; elated by vanity; boastful. — **Syn.** See PROUD. — **vain′glo′ri·ous·ly,** *adv.* — **vain′glo′ri·ous·ness,** *n.*

vain′glo′ry (-rĭ), *n.* Excessive pride in one's own performances, attainments, etc., as shown in undue elation, boasting, etc.; a vaunting of oneself.

vair (vâr), *n.* [OF., fr. L. *varius* various, variegated.] The skin of a species of squirrel, much used in the 14th century as fur for costly apparel.

Vai′sya (vī′syȧ), *n.* [Skr. *vaiśya.*] One belonging to the mercantile and agricultural caste, third of the four great Hindu castes. Cf. BRAHMAN, KSHATRIYA, SUDRA.

val′ance (văl′ăns), *n.* [Prob. from the town of *Valence,* France.] Drapery hanging from an edge, as of an altar table, a shelf, a bed, etc.; specif., a short decorative drapery across the top of a window. — **val′anced** (-ănst), *adj.*

vale (vāl), *n.* [OF. *val,* fr. L. *vallis.*] *Chiefly Poetic.* A valley.

‖**va′le** (vā′lē). [L., fr. *valere.*] Farewell; a farewell.

val′e·dic′tion (văl′ē·dĭk′shŭn), *n.* [L. *valedicere, -dictum,* to say farewell, fr. *vale* farewell (imper. of *valere* to be strong or well) + *dicere* to say.] A farewell; a bidding farewell.

val′e·dic·to′ri·an (-dĭk·tō′rĭ·ăn; 70), *n.* In American colleges and high schools, the student of the graduating class who pronounces the valedictory oration at commencement, usually the student who ranks first in scholarship. Cf. SALUTATORIAN.

val′e·dic′to·ry (-dĭk′tō·rĭ), *adj.* Bidding farewell; delivered as a valediction; as, Washington's *valedictory* address. — *n.; pl.* -RIES (-rĭz). A valedictory oration.

va′lence (vā′lĕns), *n.* Also **va′len·cy** (-lĕn·sĭ). [L. *valens, -entis,* pres. part. of *valere* to have power, to be strong.] **1.** *Chem. & Physics.* **a** The degree of combining power of an element (or radical) as shown by the number of atomic weights of hydrogen (chlorine, sodium, or the like, with which the atomic weight of the element (or the partial molecular weight of the radical) will combine, or for which it can be substituted, or with which it can be compared. An element or radical having a valence of one is said to be univalent; of two, bivalent; of three, trivalent, etc. The valence of certain elements varies in different compounds. **b** A unit of valence; as, the four *valences* of carbon. **2.** The degree of power which exists between certain bodies or substances, causing them to unite or produce a specific effect upon each other; — used, specif., *Biol.,* of chromosomes, serums, or the like, as in bi*valence,* poly*valence.*

Va′len′ciennes′ (vȧ′län′syĕn′; vȧ·lĕn′sĭ·ĕnz′), *n.* Also **Valenciennes lace.** [From *Valenciennes,* France.] A type of fine bobbin lace formerly made at Valenciennes, France.

va′lent (vā′lĕnt; *in compounds, also* -vȧ·lĕnt), *adj.* [L. *valens, valentis,* pres. part.] Having valence. Cf. BIVALENT, TRIVALENT.

val′en·tine (văl′ĕn·tīn), *n.* [OF. *valentin, valentine,* after St. *Valentine.*] **1.** A sweetheart complimented on St. Valentine's Day; hence, one's beloved. **2.** Something, as an ornamental greeting of a sentimental, or by extension, comic character, sent, usually anonymously, on St. Valentine's Day.

va·le′ri·an (vȧ·lēr′ĭ·ăn), *n.* [OF. *valeriane,* fr. ML. *valeriana,* fr. L. *valere* to be strong, powerful; — from its medicinal virtues.] **1.** *Bot.* Any of a genus (*Valeriana*) of perennial herbs, typifying a family (Valerianaceae, the valerian family) most of the species of which possess tonic properties. The dried rootstock and roots of one species (*V. officinalis*) constitute a drug, used as a carminative and sedative. **2.** The drug derived from *Valeriana officinalis.*

va·le′ri·a·na′ceous (-ȧ·nā′shŭs), *adj.* [LL. *valeriana* valerian.] *Bot.* Belonging to the valerian family (Valerianaceae). See VALERIAN.

va·ler′ic (vȧ·lĕr′ĭk; -lēr′ĭk), *adj.* Also **va·le′ri·an′ic** (-lēr′ĭ·ăn′ĭk). [See VALERIAN.] *Chem.* Pertaining to or designating any of four isomeric acids, $C_4H_9CO_2H$, two of which occur in the valerian root, etc.; specif., designating the normal acid, $CH_3(CH_2)_3CO_2H$. All may be made synthetically.

val′et (văl′ĕt; -ĭt; văl′ā), *n.* [F. *valet,* fr. OF. *vallet, varlet, vaslet.* See VARLET.] **1.** A manservant; a valet de chambre. **2.** Hence, an attendant, as in a hotel, etc., who performs the services of a valet (sense 1) for patrons. — *v. t. & i.* To serve as a valet.

‖**va′let′ de cham′bre** (vȧ′lĕ′ dē shäN′br′); *pl.* VALETS DE CHAMBRE (vȧ′lĕ′). [F.] A manservant serving as a personal attendant.

val′e·tu′di·nar′i·an (văl′ē·tū′dĭ·nâr′ĭ·ăn), *n.* A person of a weak or sickly constitution. — *adj.* Sickly; infirm.

val′e·tu′di·nar′i·an·ism (-ĭz′m), *n.* The condition or state of mind of a valetudinarian.

val′e·tu′di·nar′y (-tū′dĭ·nĕr′ĭ *or, esp. Brit.,* -nĕr·ĭ), *adj.* [L. *valetudinarius,* fr. *valetudo* state of health, ill health, fr. *valere* to be strong or well.] Infirm; sickly. — *n. Rare.* A valetudinarian.

val′gus (văl′gŭs), *n.* [L.] *Med.* **a** Also ***talipes valgus.*** See TALIPES. **b** Also ***spurious valgus.*** Splayfoot; extreme flat-footedness. — *adj.* Turned abnormally outward; twisted; — used esp. of the lower extremities; hence, loosely, bowlegged or knock-kneed.

Val·hal′la, Val·hall′ (văl·hăl′ȧ, văl·hăl′), *n.* [ON. *valhöll,* lit., hall of the slain, fr. *valr* the slain + *höll* a royal hall.] *Norse Myth.* The hall of Odin, into which he receives the souls of heroes slain in battle.

val′iance (văl′yăns), *n.* [F. *vaillance.*] *Archaic.* Valiancy.

val′ian·cy (-yăn·sĭ), *n.* The quality or state of being valiant; bravery; valor; also, an instance of it.

val′iant (văl′yănt), *adj.* [OF. *vailant, vaillant, valant,* pres. part. of

OF. *valoir* to be worth, fr. L. *valere* to be strong.] **1.** *Dial.* Vigorous; robust. **2.** Stouthearted; brave; courageous; valorous. **3.** Performed with valor; heroic. — **val′iant·ly,** *adv.* — **val′iant·ness,** *n.*

val′id (văl′ĭd), *adj.* [F. *valide,* fr. L. *validus* strong, fr. *valere* to be strong.] **1.** *Rare.* Strong; healthy. **2.** Founded on truth or fact; capable of being justified, supported, or defended; well-grounded; sound. **3.** Efficient; effective. **4.** *Law.* Having legal strength or force. — **val′id·ly,** *adv.* — **val′id·ness,** *n.*

Syn. Valid, sound, cogent, convincing, telling mean correct, well-grounded, and effective, as in argument. Valid implies the impossibility of breaking down because conforming to law, correct reasoning, etc.; sound, flawlessness in reasoning and solidity in the grounds upon which it is based; cogent, a power to compel assent because of the validity and soundness of its reasoning; convincing, a power to overcome doubt, opposition, reluctance, or the like; telling, a power to produce immediately the desired effect by an argument, word, phrase, etc.

val′i·date (văl′ĭ·dāt), *v. t.* **1.** To make valid; to give legal force to. **2.** To test or prove the validity of; to confirm. — **Syn.** See CONFIRM. — **val′i·da′tion** (-dā′shŭn), *n.*

va·lid′i·ty (vȧ·lĭd′ĭ·tĭ), *n.* The state, status, or fact of being valid; soundness.

va·lise′ (vȧ·lēs′ *or, esp. Brit.,* -lēz′), *n.* [F., fr. It. *valigia,* or ML. *valisia.*] A case for the clothes, toilet articles, etc., of a traveler; a traveling bag.

Val·kyr′ie (văl·kĭr′ĭ; -kī′rĭ; văl′kĭ·rĭ), *n.* [ON. *valkyrja,* fr. *valr* the slain + a stem akin to *kjōsa* to choose.] *Norse Myth.* [*sometimes not cap.*] One of the maidens of Odin, awful and beautiful, who hover over the field of battle choosing those to be slain, and conducting the worthy to Valhalla. — **Val·kyr′i·an** (văl·kĭr′ĭ·ăn), *adj.*

val·la′tion (vă·lā′shŭn), *n.* [LL. *vallatio,* deriv. of *vallum* rampart.] A rampart; an earthwork wall; also, the act or art of laying out ramparts.

val·lec′u·la (-lĕk′ū·lȧ), *n.; pl.* -LAE (-lē). [NL., dim. fr. L. *vallis, valles,* valley.] *Anat. & Bot.* A groove; a channel, as one of the depressions between the base of the tongue and the epiglottis. — **val·lec′u·lar** (-lẽr), **val·lec′u·late** (-lāt), *adj.*

val′ley (văl′ĭ), *n.* [OF. *valee* (F. *vallée*), fr. *val.* See VALE.] **1.** An elongate depression, usually with an outlet, between bluffs, or between ranges of hills or mountains. **2.** A valleylike depression; specif.: **a** The trough between waves. **b** *Arch.* The place of meeting of two slopes of a roof which form on the plan a re-entrant angle.

Va′lois′ (vȧ′lwȧ′; *Angl.* văl′wä), *n.* [F.] The house of Valois, a French royal family reigning from 1328 to 1589. — **Va′lois′,** *adj.*

va·lo′ni·a (vȧ·lō′nĭ·ȧ), *n.* [It. *vallonia, vallonea,* through NGr., fr. Gr. *balanos* acorn.] The dried acorn cups of the **valonia oak** (*Quercus aegilops*), used esp. in tanning and dressing leather.

val′or, val′our (văl′ẽr), *n.* [OF. *valor, valur, valour,* fr. LL. *valor,* fr. L. *valere* to be strong, or worth.] Strength of mind or spirit which enables a man to encounter danger with firmness; personal bravery. — **Syn.** See HEROISM.

val′or·i·za′tion (văl′ẽr·ĭ·zā′shŭn; -ī·zā′shŭn), *n.* [Pg. *valorização.*] Act or process of attempting to give an arbitrary market value or price to a commodity, usually by governmental interposition, as by maintaining a purchasing fund, making loans to producers to enable them to hold their products, etc.

val′or·ize (văl′ẽr·īz), *v. t. & i.* To determine prices or the price of by valorization; as, to *valorize* coffee.

val′or·ous (-ŭs), *adj.* [OF. *valeureux.*] Possessing, exhibiting, or characteristic of valor; brave; courageous. — **val′or·ous·ly,** *adv.* — **val′or·ous·ness,** *n.*

valse (vȧls; vôls), *n.* [F.] *Music.* A waltz; specif., a concert waltz. — *v. i.* To waltz.

val′u·a·ble (văl′ū·ȧ·b′l), *adj.* **1.** Having monetary value; as, during a period in Egyptian history, silver was so scarce as to be more *valuable* than gold. **2.** Having relatively great monetary value; worth a good price; as, a *valuable* horse. **3.** Highly useful or serviceable; worthy; precious. — **Syn.** See COSTLY. — *n.* A precious possession; a thing of value, esp. a small thing, as a jewel; — used mostly in *pl.* — **val′u·a·ble·ness,** *n.* — **val′u·a·bly,** *adv.*

val′u·a′tion (văl′ū·ā′shŭn), *n.* **1.** Act of valuing; appraisal; as, the *valuation* of an estate. **2.** Value set upon a thing; appraised price. **3.** Estimation, usually personal estimation, as of the merit, standing, or character of something; as, to take one at his own *valuation.*

val′u·a′tor (văl′ū·ā′tẽr), *n.* An appraiser.

val′ue (văl′ū), *n.* [OF., fr. *valoir,* past part. *valu,* to be worth, fr. L. *valere* to be strong, be worth.] **1.** A fair return in money, goods, services, etc., for something exchanged. **2.** Monetary worth of a thing; marketable price. **3.** The quality or fact of being excellent, useful, or desirable; worth in a thing. **4.** Estimated or assessed worth; valuation. **5.** Precise signification; import; as, the *value* of a word. **6.** Distinctive character or quality of sound, esp. in speech; as, phonetic *value.* **7.** That property of a color by which it is distinguished as light or dark; luminosity; brilliance. **8.** *Art.* Hence, in painting and other graphic arts, the relation of one part or detail in a picture to another with respect to lightness and darkness. **9.** *Com.* A valuable consideration, as in *value received,* a phrase often used, esp. on negotiable paper, to denote that it was given for a valuable consideration. **10.** *Econ.* **a** Efficiency in exchange; purchasing power. **b** Proper price; the quantity of money, goods, or services, which an article is likely to command in the long run, as distinct from its price in an individual instance. **c** The estimate which an individual places upon some of his possessions as compared with others, independently of any intent to sell. **11.** *Music.* The relative length or duration of a tone or note, corresponding to *quantity* in prosody; thus, a quarter note has the *value* of two eighth notes. — **Syn.** See WORTH.

— *v. t.* **1.** To estimate the value or worth of; to appraise. **2.** To rate in usefulness, excellence, etc.; to place in a scale of values; as, to *value* honor above riches. **3.** To hold in high esteem; to prize. — **Syn.** See ESTIMATE: APPRECIATE.

val′ued (văl′ūd), *adj.* Highly regarded; esteemed.

val′ue·less, *adj.* Of no value; worthless; not valued.

val′u·er (văl′ū·ẽr), *n.* *Chiefly Brit.* An appraiser.

||**va·lu′ta** (vä·lo͞o′tä), *n.* [It., fr. *valere* to be worth, fr. L. *valere.*] Value; worth; specif., value of any currency, as of certain European countries, as agreed upon, or its exchange value with reference to the currency of another (specified) country.

val′vate (văl′vāt), *adj.* [L. *valvatus* having folding doors.] Having valves or valvelike parts; specif.: *Bot.* **a** Meeting at the edges without overlapping; — said of sepals or petals in estivation, and of leaves in vernation. **b** Opening as if by valves, as most capsules, some anthers, etc.

valve (vălv), *n.* [L. *valva* the leaf, fold, or valve of a door.] **1.** *Archaic.* One of a pair of folding doors, or one of the leaves of such a door. **2.** *Anat.* A structure which temporarily closes a passage or orifice or permits movement in one direction only. **3.** *Bot.* **a** One of the segments or pieces into which a dehiscing capsule or legume separates. **b** The lidlike portion of certain anthers, as of the barberry. **4.** *Elec.* Any device, as a kind of vacuum tube or electrolytic cell, that permits a flow of current in one direction only; specif., *Chiefly Brit.,* an electron tube. **5.** *Mach.* Any device by which the flow of liquid, air or other gas, loose material in bulk, etc., may be started, stopped, or regulated, by a movable part which opens or obstructs passage; also, the movable part of such a device. **6.** *Music.* A device in instruments of the horn and trumpet class for quickly varying the tube length in order to change the fundamental tone by some definite interval. It is usually either a form of piston or rotary valve. **7.** *Zool.* One of the distinct pieces, usually movably articulated, of which the shell of lamellibranch mollusks, brachiopods, barnacles, and some other shell-bearing animals consists. — *v. t. & i.* To furnish with a valve or valves; to control the flow or escape (of) by means of a valve.

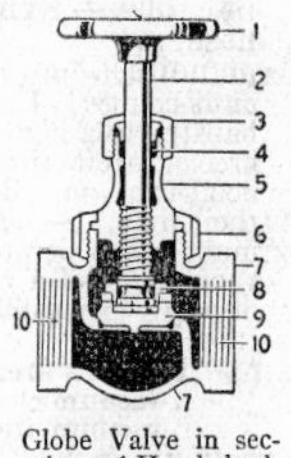

Globe Valve in section. 1 Handwheel; 2 Stem, or Spindle; 3 Stuffing Nut; 4 Stuffing Box; 5 Bonnet; 6 Bonnet Ring; 7, 7 Body, or Case; 8 Lock Nut; 9 Disk; 10, 10 Pipe Ends.

valve′-in-head′ en′gine. *Mach.* An internal-combustion engine in which both inlet and exhaust valves are located in the cylinder head.

valve′less, *adj.* Having no valve or valves.

valve′let, *n.* A little valve; a valvule.

val′vu·lar (văl′vū·lẽr), *adj.* **1.** Of or pertaining to a valve or valves; specif., *Med.,* of or pertaining to the valves of the heart. **2.** Containing, or opening by, valves; serving as a valve.

val′vule (-vūl), *n.* [F.] A small valve or valvelike structure.

val′vu·li′tis (văl′vū·lī′tĭs), *n.* [NL., fr. *valvula* a little valve + *-itis.*] *Med.* Inflammation of a valve, esp. of the heart.

va·moose′ (vă·mo͞os′), *v. i. & t.* Also **va·mose′** (vă·mōs′; văm′ōs). [Sp. *vamos* let us go.] *Slang.* To leave or go away quickly.

vamp (vămp), *n.* [OF. *avanpié* (F. *avant-pied*), fr. *avant* before, fore + *pié, pied,* foot.] **1.** The part of a boot or shoe above the sole and welt, and in front of the ankle seam; an upper. See SHOE, *Illust.* **2.** [From VAMP, *v.*] Something vamped or patched up; specif., *Music,* a simple accompaniment improvised for the occasion. — *v. t.* **1.** To provide, as a shoe, with a new vamp; to revamp; hence, to piece, as any old thing, with a new part; to patch; — with *together* or *up.* **2.** *Music.* To make a vamp to; to improvise. — **vamp′er,** *n.*

vamp (vămp), *n.* *Slang.* **a** Short for VAMPIRE, *n.,* 2. **b** One who uses her charm or wiles to gain admiration and attentions from the opposite sex. — *v. t. Slang.* To play the vamp with; to beguile into admiration or attentions. — *v. i. Slang.* To play vampire parts or the part of a vamp.

vam′pire (văm′pīr), *n.* [F., fr. G. *vampir,* fr. Slavic.] **1.** A bloodsucking ghost or reanimated body of a dead person believed to come from the grave and wander about by night sucking the blood of persons asleep. **2.** One who lives by preying on others; a bloodsucker; commonly, a woman who uses her attractions to bring her lover to a debased or impoverished condition; also, an actress who plays such parts. **3.** Also **vampire bat.** **a** Any of various bats popularly but erroneously believed to suck the blood of animals. **b** Any member of a South American family (Desmodontidae) of small specialized bats that live entirely on fresh blood. In certain areas they are highly destructive to cattle and are reputed to transmit rabies.

vam′pir·ism (văm′pīr·ĭz′m; -pĭ·rĭz′m), *n.* **1.** Belief in vampires (the ghosts). **2.** The actions of a vampire.

van (văn), *n.* [F., fr. L. *vannus* a van, or fan, or dial. form of E. *fan.*] **1.** *Now Dial.* A fan or other winnowing device. **2.** *Poetic.* A wing.

van, *n.* [Abbr. fr. VANGUARD.] The front of an army, fleet, or advancing body; specif., in a military formation, the leading unit; hence, the front or those at the front of any line, movement, etc.

van, *n.* [Abbr. fr. CARAVAN.] **1.** *Eng.* A light wagon for the transportation of goods. **2.** *Chiefly U. S.* A large covered vehicle used for moving furniture, for trucking, etc. **3.** *Eng.* A closed railway car for baggage.

||**van** (vän; *Eng.* văn), *prep.* [D. Cf. VON.] Of; from.

☞ In foreign practice, the *van* of personal names is written with a small "v"; in American and British usage the style of the owner of the name is generally followed.

van′a·date (văn′ȧ·dāt), *n.* Also **va·na′di·ate** (vȧ·nā′dĭ·āt). *Chem.* A salt or ester of vanadic acid.

va·nad′ic (vȧ·năd′ĭk; -nā′dĭk), *adj.* *Chem.* Pertaining to or containing vanadium, esp. in its higher valence. Cf. VANADOUS.

vanadic acid. *Chem.* Any of a number of acids (known with certainty only in their salts) regarded as hydrates of vanadium pentoxide, V_2O_5.

va·nad′i·nite (vȧ·năd′ĭ·nīt), *n.* *Mineral.* A mineral occurring in yellowish, brownish, and ruby-red hexagonal crystals. It consists of lead vanadate with some lead chloride.

va·na′di·um (vȧ·nā′dĭ·ŭm), *n.* [NL., fr. ON. *Vanadīs,* a name of the goddess Freya.] *Chem.* An element of the phosphorus group, isolated as a steel-white metal, malleable, soft, and ductile. Symbol, *V;* at. no., 23; at. wt., 50.95. Vanadium is both basic and acid.

vanadium steel. **a** Steel alloyed with vanadium (usually about 0.10 to 0.15 per cent), which strengthens the steel and serves to remove oxygen and possibly nitrogen. **b** Steel alloyed with vanadium and other elements, esp. chromium.

van′a·dous (văn′ȧ·dŭs), **va·na′di·ous** (vȧ·nā′dĭ·ŭs), *adj.* *Chem.* Pertaining to or containing vanadium, esp. in its lower valence. Cf. VANADIC.

Van′dal (văn′dăl), *n.* [L. *Vandalus, Vandalius,* of Teut. origin.] **1.** One of a Germanic people anciently dwelling south of the Baltic between the Vistula and the Oder. In the 4th and 5th centuries they overran Gaul, Spain, and northern Africa, and in 455 sacked Rome. **2.** [*usually not cap.*] One who willfully or ignorantly destroys, damages, or defaces property belonging to another or to the public. Cf. HUN. — **Van′dal, van′dal, Van·dal′ic, van·dal′ic** (văn·dăl′ĭk), *adj.*

van′dal·ism (-ĭz′m), *n.* The spirit or conduct of, or like that of, the

Vandals; hostility to, or willful destruction or defacement of, things of beauty.

Van de Graaff generator (văn′ dĕ grăf′). [After Robert Jemison *Van de Graaff* (b. 1901), American physicist.] *Physics.* An electrostatic generator for producing extremely high voltages that are used esp. for accelerating charged particles in nuclear bombardment.

van der Waals forces (văn′ dẽr wôlz′). *Physical Chem.* The relatively weak forces operative between neutral atoms or molecules, arising from the interaction of dipoles or stray electric fields.

Van·dyke′ (văn·dīk′), *adj.* Of or pert. to the style of Van Dyck, or Vandyke, the painter; represented by Van Dyck. — *n.* A Vandyke beard, collar, or cape.

Vandyke beard. A trim, pointed beard, as in pictures by Van Dyck.

Vandyke brown. A deep-brown pigment of uncertain identity, used by the painter Van Dyck; hence, any of various brown pigments.

Vandyke collar *or* **cape.** A broad collar or shoulder cape of fine linen and lace with a deep pointed or indented edge.

vane (vān), *n.* [ME., dial. form of *fane* weathercock, banner, fr. AS. *fana* a banner, flag.] **1.** A contrivance attached to some elevated object so as to be moved by the wind, to show which way the wind blows; weathercock. **2.** Any flat extended surface attached to an axis and moved by the wind; as, the *vane* of a windmill; hence, a similar fixture of any form moved in or by water, air, or other fluid; as, the *vane* of a propeller. **3.** The web or flat expanded part of a feather; *Archery*, a feather fastened to the shaft of an arrow near the nock. **4.** *Surv.* **a** The target of a leveling staff. **b** One of the sights of a compass, quadrant, etc. — **vaned** (vānd), *adj.*

vang (văng), *n.* [D. *vang* a catch, curb, fr. *vangen* to catch, seize.] *Naut.* Either of two ropes extending from the peak of a gaff to steady it when the sail is not set.

van′guard′ (văn′gärd′), *n.* [For *vantguard, avantguard*, fr. OF. *avant-garde*, fr. *avant* before, fore + *garde* guard.] **1.** *Mil.* The troops who march in front of an army; the van. **2.** Hence, one who or that which is in the forefront.

va·nil′la (vȧ·nĭl′ȧ), *n.; pl.* VANILLAS (-ȧz). [NL., fr. Sp. *vainilla*, dim. of *vaina* sheath, pod, fr. L. *vagina;* — because its grains, or seeds, are contained in little pods.] **1.** *Bot.* Any of a genus (*Vanilla*) of tropical American climbing orchids. **2. a** The long podlike capsule of a species (*Vanilla planifolia*) of these plants. **b** A flavoring extract made from the capsules, used in confectionery, perfumery, etc.

va·nil′lic (-ĭk), *adj.* Of or derived from vanilla or vanillin.

van′il·lin (văn′ĭ·lĭn; vȧ·nĭl′ĭn), *n.* Also **van′il·line** (-lĭn; -lēn). *Chem.* A white crystalline compound, $(OH)(CH_3O)C_6H_3CHO$, the fragrant constituent of vanilla.

Va′nir (vä′nĭr; *class. Icel.* wä′-), *n. pl.* [ON., pl. of *Vanr.*] *Norse Myth.* An early race of gods, who became gods of the weather, of crops, and of commerce. The three whose names survive, Njorth, Frey, and Freya, are later associated with the Aesir.

van′ish (văn′ĭsh), *v. i.* [OF. *esvanir, esvanuir*, to evanish, fr. L. *evanescere* to vanish.] To pass quickly or entirely from sight or existence; to disappear utterly. — *n.* A vanishing; specif., *Phonet.*, the relatively faint latter part of a speech sound, esp. of such falling diphthongs as ā in *ale* (ending in a slight ĭ) or ō in *go* (ending in a slight ŏŏ). — **van′ish·er**, *n.*

van′i·ty (văn′ĭ·tĭ), *n.; pl.* -TIES (-tĭz). [OF. *vanité*, fr. L. *vanitas*, fr. *vanus* empty, vain.] **1.** That which is vain or empty, idle, or useless; a vain or futile thing or things. **2.** Quality or fact of being vain, or devoid of worth, use, truth, etc.; emptiness; falsity; futility. **3.** The quality of being vain; also, vainglory; conceit. **4.** A vanity box or case. **5.** Also **vanity table.** In the trade, a dressing table.

vanity box *or* **case.** A small box containing a mirror, powder puff, and other small toilet articles for a woman.

Vanity Fair. 1. In Bunyan's *Pilgrim's Progress*, a fair which was held all the year long in the town of Vanity (the world). **2.** Hence, the world as a place where vanity and ostentation obtain; also, the world of fashion. **3.** Title of a novel (1847–48) by Thackeray.

van′quish (văng′kwĭsh; văn′-), *v. t.* [OF. *vainquir*, var. of *veintre*, fr. L. *vincere* to conquer.] **1.** To overcome in battle; to subdue completely; to rout. **2.** Hence: **a** To overcome; suppress; as, love *vanquished* his pride. **b** To get the better of, as in a debate. — **Syn.** See CONQUER. — **van′quish·a·ble**, *adj.* — **van′quish·er**, *n.*

van′tage (vȧn′tĭj; 9), *n.* [For *advantage.*] **1.** Superiority in position, equipment, etc.; advantage; also, a position giving an advantage. **2.** A favorable opportunity. **3.** *Tennis.* = ADVANTAGE, 5.

vantage point. A point giving advantage; vantage ground.

vantage ground. Superiority of state or place; the place or condition which gives one an advantage over another.

van′ward (văn′wẽrd), *adj.* Being on, or toward, the van, or front.

vap′id (văp′ĭd), *adj.* [L. *vapidus* having lost its life and spirit, vapid.] Having lost its life, spirit, or zest; insipid; as, *vapid* beer; hence, dull; spiritless; inane. — **Syn.** See INSIPID. — **va·pid′i·ty** (vă·pĭd′ĭ·tĭ), *n.* — **vap′id·ly**, *adv.* — **vap′id·ness**, *n.*

va′por, va′pour (vā′pẽr), *n.* [OF. *vapour, vapor, vapeur*, fr. L. *vapor.*] **1.** Any diffused matter suspended floating in the air and impairing its transparency, as smoke, fog, etc. **2.** *Physics.* Any substance in the gaseous state, thought of with some reference to the liquid or solid form; a gasified liquid or solid. **3.** Hence, a substance, as gasoline, alcohol, mercury, benzoin, etc., vaporized for industrial, therapeutic, or other uses; also, a mixture of such a vapor with air, as the explosive mixture in an internal-combustion engine. **4.** Something unsubstantial, fleeting, or transitory. **5.** *Old Med. pl.* Hypochondria or melancholy; the blues. — *v. i.* **1.** To rise in vapor, as a mist; to be emitted or exhaled in vaporous form, as fumes; to pass off as vapor or to evaporate, as liquid alcohol; to emit vapors, to send forth steam, fumes, etc. **2.** To brag; bluster; to speak or write in a pompous, inflated, or extravagant manner. — *v. t.* **1.** *Now Rare.* To send in or as in vapor; to reduce to vapor. **2.** To affect with vapors, or blues. — **va′por·er, va′pour·er**, *n.*

vapori-, vapouri-. A combining form from *vapor*, vapor, as in **va′por·if′er·ous, va′por·i·form′.**

va′por·if′ic, va′pour·if′ic (vā′pẽr·ĭf′ĭk; văp′ẽr-), *adj.* [L. *vapor* vapor + *facere* to make.] Producing vapor; tending to pass, or to cause to pass, into vapor; also, vaporous.

va′por·im′e·ter, va′pour·im′e·ter (-ĭm′ē·tẽr), *n.* [*vapori-* + *-meter.*] An instrument for measuring the volume or the tension of a vapor.

va′por·ing, va′pour·ing (vā′pẽr·ĭng), *adj.* That vapors; spouting forth vapors; vaunting. — *n.* Act or speech of one that vapors; an idle or high-flown expression or speech. — **-ing·ly**, *adv.*

va′por·ish, va′pour·ish (vā′pẽr·ĭsh), *adj.* **1.** Of the nature of vapor; full of vapors. **2.** Affected by the vapors; given to fits of depression.

va′por·i·za′tion, va′pour·i·za′tion (vā′pẽr·ĭ·zā′shŭn; văp′ŏ·rĭ-; -ī·zā′-), *n.* [Cf. F. *vaporisation.*] **1.** Act or process of vaporizing, or state of being vaporized; artificial formation of vapor; specif., conversion of water into steam, as in a steam boiler. **2.** *Med.* Treatment with vapor.

va′por·ize, va′pour·ize (vā′pẽr·īz), *v. t.* **1.** To convert into vapor, either naturally or artificially, as by the application of heat, by spraying, etc. **2.** To reduce to a vaporous state or form. — **va′por·iz′a·ble, va′pour·iz′a·ble** (-īz′ȧ·b'l), *adj.*

va′por·iz′er, va′pour·iz′er (-īz′ẽr), *n.* That which vaporizes; specif.: **a** An atomizer. **b** An apparatus for vaporizing a heavy oil, as petroleum, for the explosive charge of an internal-combustion engine.

va′por·ous (vā′pẽr·ŭs), *adj.* **1.** Consisting or characteristic of vapor or vapors. **2.** Full of vapors, esp. of exhalations; foggy, misty, or the like. **3.** Vaporlike; ethereal; unsubstantial; more narrowly, consisting of, of the nature of, or indulging in vaporings, or high-flown expressions. — **va′por·os′i·ty** (-ŏs′ĭ·tĭ), *n.* — **va′por·ous·ly**, *adv.* — **va′por·ous·ness**, *n.*

vapor pressure *or* **tension.** *Physics.* The pressure of a confined body of vapor. The pressure of a given saturated vapor is a function of the temperature only.

va′por·y, va′pour·y (vā′pẽr·ĭ), *adj.* **1.** Full of, or of the nature of, a vapor; vaporous. **2.** Hypochondriacal; peevish; also, vaporing.

va·que′ro (vä·kâr′ō), *n.; pl.* -ROS (-ōz). [Sp., cowherd, fr. *vaca* a cow, fr. L. *vacca.*] *Southwestern U. S.* A herdsman; cowboy.

va′ra (vä′rȧ), *n.* [Sp. & Pg., prop., staff, wand, fr. L. *vara* forked pole.] A Spanish and Portuguese measure of length, varying in different localities from about 32 in. to about 43 in.; also, a measure of area (***square vara***). In Texas it is 33.33 inches.

Va·ran′gi·an (vȧ·răn′jĭ·ăn), *n.* [ML. *Varangus, Varingus*, through MGr. & Slav. fr. ON. *Væringi* a Varangian, a Scandinavian, prop., a confederate, fr. *vārar*, pl., pledge, troth.] One of the Northmen who founded a dynasty in Russia in the 9th century.

var′i·a·bil′i·ty (vâr′ĭ·ȧ·bĭl′ĭ·tĭ; 6), *n.* Quality or fact of being variable or subject to variation; variableness.

var′i·a·ble (vâr′ĭ·ȧ·b'l; 6), *adj.* **1.** Able or apt to vary or change; susceptible or subject to variation; changeable. **2.** Fickle; inconstant. **3.** *Biol.* Not true to type; aberrant; inconstant; — of a species or of a specific character. — *n.* **1.** That which is variable; a thing which may vary or is liable to vary. **2.** *Math.* **a** A quantity that may assume a succession of values, which need not be distinct; — opposed to *constant.* Cf. PARAMETER. **b** A symbol standing for any one of a class of things. **3.** *Naut.* **a** A shifting wind, or one that varies in force. **b** *pl.* Those parts of the sea where a steady wind is not expected, esp. the parts between the tradewind belts. **4.** *Science & Statistics.* Any magnitude which has different values under different conditions. — **var′i·a·ble·ness**, *n.* — **var′i·a·bly**, *adv.*

variable star. *Astron.* A star that varies in its apparent magnitude, the variation being due to internal changes, or to external causes such as eclipse by a dark companion.

variable timing fuze. See PROXIMITY FUZE.

Variable Zone. See ZONE.

var′i·ance (vâr′ĭ·ăns; 6), *n.* **1.** The fact, quality, or state of being variable or variant; variation or a degree of it; difference; deviation; discrepancy. **2.** Dissension; discord; a dispute; quarrel. **3.** *Law.* A disagreement between two parts of the same legal proceeding, which, to be effectual, ought to agree, as the writ and the declaration, or the allegation and the proof. — **Syn.** See DISCORD.

var′i·ant (-ănt), *adj.* [OF., fr. L. *varians*, pres. part. of *variare* to change.] **1.** *Rare.* Variable; changeable. **2.** *Rare.* Manifesting diversity; variegated; varied. **3.** Different from others of its kind or class; more narrowly, varying from the norm, standard, type, or the like; as, a *variant* spelling; a *variant* reading, as of a passage in Chaucer. **4.** Being at variance; discrepant. — *n.* Something that is variant, as a variant spelling of a word.

var′i·ate (-āt), *n.* *Science & Statistics.* **a** A particular value of a variable. **b** Less precisely, a variable.

var′i·a′tion (vâr′ĭ·ā′shŭn; 6), *n.* **1.** Act or an instance of varying; change in the form, position, state, or qualities of a thing; modification, mutation, or deviation, or an instance or example thereof. **2.** Extent to which a thing varies; amount or rate of change. **3.** *Aeronautics.* The angle between true north and magnetic north. **4.** *Alg.* One of the different linear arrangements that can be made of any number of objects taken from a set. **5.** *Astron.* A change in the mean motion, mean orbit, etc., of a planet or other celestial body. **6.** *Biol.* In an organism, divergence in characters from those typical or usual in the group (esp. the species) to which it belongs; also, divergence in the characters of the offspring from those of the parents producing it. Esp., an organism differing from a type or from its parents. **7.** *Music.* Repetition of a theme or melody with embellishments or modifications in rhythm, tune, harmony, or key; the presentation of a musical thought in new and varied aspects, yet keeping the essential features of the original. — **var′i·a′tion·al**, *adj.*

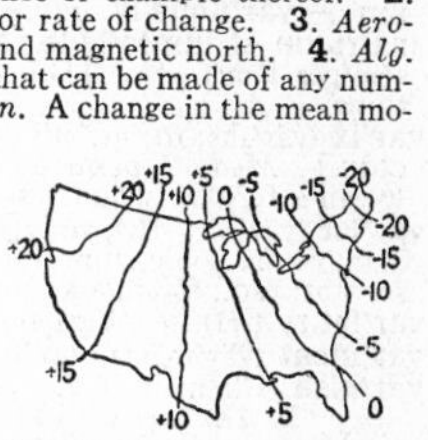

Variation, 3. Agonic Line (0–0) and Isogonic Lines across the U. S.

var′i·cel′la (văr′ĭ·sĕl′ȧ), *n.* [NL., dim. fr. VARIOLA.] *Med.* Chicken pox.

var′i·cel′late (-āt), *adj.* [Dim. of *varix* + 2d *-ate*, 2.] *Zool.* Having small or indistinct varices; — of certain shells.

var′i·cel′loid (-oid), *adj.* [*varicella* + *-oid.*] *Med.* Resembling chicken pox (varicella); as, *varicelloid* smallpox.

var′i·ces (văr′ĭ·sēz; vâr′-), *n., pl.* of VARIX.

var′i·co- (văr′ĭ·kō-), **varic-.** [L. *varix.* See VARICOSE.] A combining form denoting *a dilated vein.*

var′i·co·cele′ (văr′ĭ·kō·sēl′), *n.* [*varico-* + *-cele.*] A varicose enlargement of the veins of the spermatic cord.

var′i·col′ored, var′i·col′oured (vâr′ĭ·kŭl′ẽrd; 6), *adj.* Having various colors; hence, figuratively, diversified.

var′i·cose (văr′ĭ·kōs), *adj.* [L. *varicosus*, fr. *varix, -icis*, a dilated vein.] Irregularly swollen; affected with, containing, or pertaining to varices or varicosities; cirsoid; as, a *varicose* vein.

var'i·co'sis (văr'ĭ·kō'sĭs), *n.* [NL., fr. *varic-* + *-osis.*] *Med.* **a** The formation of varices. **b** Varicosity.

var'i·cos'i·ty (-kŏs'ĭ·tĭ), *n.; pl.* -TIES (-tĭz). Quality or state of being varicose; also, a varicose part or a varix.

var'i·cot'o·my (-kŏt'ō·mĭ), *n.* [*varico-* + *-tomy.*] *Surg.* Incision of a varicose vein; cirsotomy.

var'ied (vâr'ĭd; 6), *adj.* **1.** Changed; altered. **2.** Various; diverse; as, *varied* scenery. **3.** Marked with several colors, as many animals.

var'i·e·gate (vâr'ĭ·ĕ·gāt; vâr'ĭ·gāt), *v. t.* [L. *variegatus,* past part. of *variegare* to variegate.] **1.** To diversify in external appearance, esp. with different colors; to dapple. **2.** Hence, to diversify; to enliven by variety. — **var'i·e·gat'ed** (-gāt'ĕd; -ĭd), *adj.*

var'i·e·ga'tion (-gā'shŭn), *n.* Act of variegating, or state of being variegated; diversity of colors.

var'i·er (vâr'ĭ·ẽr), *n.* One who varies.

va·ri'e·tal (vȧ·rī'ĕ·tăl; -t'l), *adj.* Of or pert. to, or characterizing, a variety; constituting a variety, in distinction from an individual or species. — **va·ri'e·tal·ly,** *adv.*

va·ri'e·ty (-tĭ), *n.; pl.* -TIES (-tĭz). [F. or L.; F. *variété,* fr. L. *varietas.*] **1.** State or quality of being various or varied; diversity. **2.** Variation; difference. **3.** That which is various; as: **a** A collection of different things; a varied assortment. **b** Something varying or differing from others of the same general kind; a sort; as, *varieties* of wood. **4.** Entertainment of the kind given in variety shows; variety performances, collectively; vaudeville. **5.** *Biol.* A group of animals or plants related by descent, but distinguished from other similar groups only by characters considered too inconstant or too trivial to entitle it to recognition as a species; often, any group of lower rank than a species.

☞ This Dictionary has followed the frequent practices of writing all botanical specific names without capitalization and of omitting the abbreviation "var." before varietal names in trinomials.

variety show. A stage entertainment of successive separate performances, usually songs, dances, acrobatic feats, etc. Cf. VAUDEVILLE, 2.

var'i·form (vâr'ĭ·fôrm; 6), *adj.* [L. *varius* various + *-form.*] Having various forms; varied in form; diversiform.

var'i·o·cou'pler (vâr'ĭ·ō·kŭp'lẽr), *n.* [L. *varius* various + *coupler.*] *Elec.* An inductive coupler, of which the mutual inductance is adjustable by rotating one of the coils.

va·ri'o·la (vȧ·rī'ō·lȧ), *n.* [ML., fr. L. *varius* various.] *Med.* Smallpox.

va·ri'o·lar (-lẽr), *adj. Med.* Variolous.

var'i·o·late (vâr'ĭ·ō·lāt; 6), *v. t.;* -LAT'ED (-lāt'ĕd; -ĭd); -LAT'ING. [See VARIOLA.] *Med.* To inoculate with the virus of smallpox. — **var'i·o·la'tion** (-lā'shŭn), *n.*

var'i·ole (vâr'ĭ·ōl; 6), *n.* **1.** A foveola. **2.** *Petrog.* A spherule of a variolite.

var'i·o·lite (-ō·līt), *n.* [G. *variolit,* fr. ML. *variola* smallpox; — from its variegated color.] *Petrog.* Any basic rock embedded with whitish spherules.

var'i·o·lit'ic (-ō·lĭt'ĭk), *adj.* **1.** Thickly marked with small round specks; spotted. **2.** *Petrog.* Of, pertaining to, or resembling variolite.

var'i·o·loid (vâr'ĭ·ō·loid; văr'-; 6), *adj.* [*variola* + *-oid.*] *Med.* **a** Resembling smallpox. **b** Pertaining to varioloid. — *n. Med.* A modified mild form of smallpox, or variola, occurring in persons who have been vaccinated or who have had smallpox.

va·ri'o·lous (vȧ·rī'ō·lŭs), *adj.* **1.** *Med.* Of, pertaining to, or suffering from smallpox; having pits like those of smallpox. **2.** *Zool.* Foveate.

var'i·om'e·ter (vâr'ĭ·ŏm'ē·tẽr; 6), *n.* [L. *varius* various + *-meter.*] *Elec.* **a** An instrument for comparing magnetic forces, esp. in the earth's magnetic field. **b** A variable inductor consisting of two coils of wire one rotating within the other and connected in series or parallel.

var'i·o'rum (-ō'rŭm; 70), *n.* [Abbr. fr. L. *cum notis variorum* with notes of various persons.] **1.** An edition or text (**variorum edition** *or* **text**), esp. of a classical author, with notes by different persons; as, Furness's Shakespeare *Variorum.* **2.** An edition of a publication containing variant readings, or versions, of the text. — **var'i·o'rum,** *adj.*

var'i·ous (vâr'ĭ·ŭs; 6), *adj.* [L. *varius.*] **1.** Different; diverse; several; manifold. **2.** Changeable; inconstant; variable. **3.** Many-sided; diversiform; also, variegated; diversified. — **Syn.** See DIFFERENT. — **var'i·ous·ly,** *adv.* — **var'i·ous·ness,** *n.*

‖**va'ri·um et mu·ta'bi·le sem'per fe'mi·na** (vâ'rĭ·ŭm ĕt mū·tăb'ĭ·lē sĕm'pẽr fĕm'ĭ·nȧ). [L.] Woman is ever a fickle and changeable thing.

var'ix (vâr'ĭks; 6), *n.; pl.* VARICES (vâr'ĭ·sēz; văr'-). [L. See VARICOSE.] *Med.* A permanent uneven or tortuous dilatation of a vein (or an artery or lymph vessel); a varicose vein.

var'let (vär'lĕt; -lĭt), *n.* [OF., var. of *vaslet, vallet,* servant, young man, young noble, dim. fr. source of *vassal.*] **1.** *Obs.* An attendant; servant; esp., *Hist.,* a knight's page. **2.** A scoundrel; a knave.

var'let·ry (-rĭ), *n.* Varlets, collectively; hence, rabble.

var'ment (vär'mĕnt), **var'mint** (-mĭnt). Dial. var. of VERMIN.

var'nish (vär'nĭsh), *v. t.* [OF. *vernir, vernisser,* fr. the n., OF. *vernis.*] **1.** To cover with varnish. **2.** To coat over with something likened to varnish, as giving a fair or glossy appearance. **3.** To furbish or polish up. — *n.* **1.** A liquid preparation which, when spread upon a surface, dries forming a hard, lustrous coating. ***oil varnishes*** are essentially solutions of resins (natural or artificial) or of asphalt in drying oils, esp. linseed oil and tung oil. ***spirit varnishes*** are solutions of resins (natural or artificial), asphalt, cellulose esters (as pyroxylin), etc., in volatile solvents, as alcohol, spirits of turpentine, or amyl acetate. **2.** The covering or glaze given by the application of varnish (sense 1). **3.** That which suggests varnish by its gloss. **4.** Outside show; gloss. — **var'nish·er,** *n.*

varnish tree. Any of various trees yielding a milky juice from which in some cases varnish or lacquer is prepared; esp., the ***Japanese varnish tree*** (*Rhus verniciflua*).

var'si·ty (vär'sĭ·tĭ), *adj.* A colloquial short form of UNIVERSITY; as, the *varsity* crew, baseball team. — *n.* The team, in any sport, chosen to represent a university, or, by extension, a school, etc.

Var'u·na (vär'ŏŏ·nȧ; vŭr'-). [Skr. *Varuna.*] *Hinduism.* The supreme cosmic deity, creator and ruler, and especially guardian of cosmic order.

var'us (vâr'ŭs; 6), *n.* [NL., fr. L. *varus* bent, grown inwards.] *Med.* Also ***talipes varus.*** See TALIPES. — *adj.* Turned abnormally inward; — used esp. of the lower extremities; hence, loosely, bowlegged.

varve (värv), *n.* [Sw. *varv* layer.] *Geol.* An annual layer of silt as deposited in a lake or other body of still water.

var'y (vâr'ĭ; 6), *v. t.;* VAR'IED (-ĭd); VAR'Y·ING. [OF. *varier,* fr. L. *variare,* fr. *varius* various.] **1.** To alter in form, appearance, substance, position, etc.; to modify. **2.** To make different or change from one another; as, to *vary* one's meals. **3.** To diversify; as, to *vary* one's diet. **4.** *Music.* To present under new aspects, as of rhythm, interval, harmonic treatment, etc. — *v. i.* **1.** To alter, or be altered, in any manner; to change. **2.** To differ; to be diverse; as, the laws of France *vary* from those of England. **3.** To deviate; swerve. **4.** To alter or change in succession; to alternate; as, one mathematical quantity may *vary* inversely as another. **5.** *Biol.* To exhibit or undergo variation. — **Syn.** See CHANGE. — **var'y·ing·ly,** *adv.*

‖**vas** (văs), *n.; pl.* VASA (vā'sȧ). [L., a vessel. See VASE.] *Anat.* A vessel; a duct.

vas-. = VASO-.

vas'cu·lar (văs'kū·lẽr), *adj.* [L. *vasculum* a small vessel, dim. of *vas* vessel.] **1.** *Biol., Med., etc.* **a** Of or pertaining to a vessel or vessels for the conveyance of a fluid, esp. (in animals) a nutritive fluid, as blood or lymph, or (in plants) the sap; designating, or pertaining to, the system of vessels having this function. **b** Supplied with, or containing, vessels or ducts, esp. blood vessels. **2.** Hence, hot-blooded, high-spirited. — **vas'cu·lar'i·ty** (-lăr'ĭ·tĭ), *n.*

vascular bundle. *Bot.* See BUNDLE, *n.,* 4.

vascular plants. *Bot.* Plants with specialized conductive tissues in organs distinguished as roots, stems, and leaves, — as opposed to lower plants without such organs.

vascular tissue. *Bot.* Any conductive tissue in plants, esp. the specialized tissue found in the higher plants, forming a continuous system (**vascular system**) throughout the plant body.

vas'cu·lose (văs'kū·lōs), *adj.* Also **vas'cu·lous** (-lŭs). Vascular.

vas'cu·lum (-lŭm), *n.; pl.* -LA (-lȧ). [L., a small vessel.] A tin box used in collecting plants.

‖**vas de'fe·rens** (văs dĕf'ĕ·rĕnz); *pl.* VASA DEFERENTIA (vā'sȧ dĕf'ĕ·rĕn'shĭ·ȧ). [L. *deferens* carrying down.] *Anat. & Zool.* The excretory duct of a testicle; a spermatic duct, which is, in man, a small but thick-walled tube about two feet long, greatly convoluted in its proximal portion.

vase (vās; vāz; *or, esp. Brit.,* väz, vôz), *n.* [F., fr. L. *vas,* also *vasum.*] A vessel, usually rounded and of greater depth than width, commonly decorative though adapted for domestic purposes, and used anciently in sacrifices.

vas·ec'to·my (văs·ĕk'tō·mĭ), *n.* [*vas* + *-ectomy.*] *Surg.* Resection or removal of the vas deferens.

Vas'e·line (văs'ĕ·lēn; -lĭn), *n.* A trade-mark for petrolatum and certain other products.

vas'o- (văs'ō-), **vas-.** [From VAS.] *Biol. & Physiol.* A combining form used to signify: **a** *The blood vessels,* as in *vaso*motor. **b** *Surg. The vas deferens,* as in **vas'o·lig'a·ture, va·sot'o·my.** See LIGATURE, -TOMY. **c** *Vasomotor,* as in **vas'o·stim'u·lant.**

vas'o·con·stric'tor (-kŏn·strĭk'tẽr), *adj.* [*vaso-* + *constrictor.*] *Physiol.* Causing constriction of the blood vessels.

vas'o·di·la'tor (-dī·lā'tẽr; -dĭ-), *adj.* [*vaso-* + *dilator.*] *Physiol.* Causing dilatation or relaxation of the blood vessels.

vas'o·mo'tor (-mō'tẽr), *adj.* [*vaso-* + *motor.*] *Physiol. & Anat.* Pertaining to the nerves or centers controlling the size of the blood vessels.

vas'sal (văs'ăl), *n.* [OF., fr. ML. *vassallus,* fr. LL. *vassus,* of Celt. origin.] **1.** *Early Law.* One who has placed himself under the protection of another as his lord and has vowed homage and fealty; later, a feudal tenant; a feudatory. **2.** A subject; dependent; servant; sometimes, a slave. — *adj.* Like a vassal; servile; subservient.

vas'sal·age (-ĭj), *n.* **1.** State of being a vassal; homage, fealty, or services due from the vassal. **2.** Servitude; esp., political dependence. **3.** A territory held in political dependence.

vast (vȧst; 9), *adj.* [L. *vastus* empty, waste, immense.] **1.** *Obs.* Waste; desert. **2.** Of great extent; also, huge in bulk; immense. **3.** Very great in numbers, quantity, or amount. **4.** Very great in degree, intensity, range, or the like. — **Syn.** See ENORMOUS. — *n.* **1.** A waste; immensity. **2.** *Dial. Eng.* A great quantity. — **vast'ly,** *adv.* — **vast'ness,** *n.*

vas'ti·tude (văs'tĭ·tūd), *n.* Vastness.

vas'ti·ty (-tĭ), *n.; pl.* -TIES (-tĭz). [F. or L.; F. *vastité,* fr. L. *vastitas.*] *Rare.* Vastness; a vast.

vast'y (vȧs'tĭ), *adj.* [From VAST.] Vast; immense.

vat (văt), *n.* [Dial. for *fat,* fr. ME. *fat,* fr. AS. *fæt.*] **1.** A large vessel, cistern, tub, or barrel, esp. for holding liquors in an immature state, preparations for dyeing or tanning, etc. **2.** A liquor containing a dye which has been converted into a soluble, nondyeing form. When textile material steeped in the liquor is exposed to the air, the dye is re-formed by oxidation and precipitated in the fiber. Dyes so used are called **vat dyes.** — *v. t.;* VAT'TED (-ĕd; -ĭd); VAT'TING. To put into, or treat in, a vat.

vat'ic (văt'ĭk), **vat'i·cal** (-ĭ·kăl), *adj.* [L. *vates* a prophet.] Of or pertaining to a prophet; prophetical.

Vat'i·can (văt'ĭ·kăn), *n.* [L. *Vaticanus* (sc. *mons,* or *collis*), the Vatican hill, in Rome, on the western bank of the Tiber.] **1.** The pope's palace, an assemblage of buildings at Rome, beside the Church of St. Peter, including museums, art galleries, library, the Sistine Chapel, etc. Here was held the **Vatican Council** (1869–70), which promulgated the dogma of papal infallibility. **2.** The papal authority or government. See VATICAN CITY in *Gaz.*

Vat'i·can·ism (-ĭz'm), *n.* The doctrine of absolute papal supremacy; — used opprobriously.

vat'i·cide (văt'ĭ·sīd), *n.* The murder, or the murderer, of a prophet.

va·tic'i·nal (vȧ·tĭs'ĭ·năl), *adj.* Prophetic.

va·tic'i·nate (-nāt), *v. i. & t.* [L. *vaticinatus,* past part. of *vaticinari* to prophesy, fr. *vates* a prophet.] To prophesy; foretell. — **vat'i·ci·na'tion** (văt'ĭ·sĭ·nā'shŭn), *n.* — **va·tic'i·na'tor** (vȧ·tĭs'ĭ·nā'tẽr), *n.*

vau'de·ville (vōd'vĭl; vô'dĕ·vĭl; *or, esp. Brit.,* vō'dĕ·vĭl), *n.* [F., fr. *Vau-de-Vire,* lit., valley of Vire (a village in Normandy), where such songs were composed.] **1.** A popular song, often satirical; a topical song. **2.** *Now Rare.* A theatrical piece, usually comic, consisting of dialogue or pantomime intermingled with light songs and, sometimes, dances. **3.** Variety (def. 4); — now the usual meaning in America.

Vau'dois' (vō'dwȧ'; *Angl.* vō'dwä), *n. pl.* [F., fr. ML. *Valdenses.*] The Waldenses.

vault (vôlt), *n.* [OF. *vaute, vaulte, voute, volte,* fr. L. *volutus,* past part. of *volvere* to roll, to turn about.] **1.** An arched structure of masonry, usually forming a ceiling, or roof, but sometimes carrying a separate roof, a floor, staircase, or the like. **2.** a A room or space covered by a vault (sense 1), esp. when underground, as a part of a cellar devoted to a special purpose, as the storage of wine or valuables. **b** By extension, such a compartment even when not covered by a vault, as a room for the safekeeping of valuables. **3.** The canopy of heaven; the sky. **4.** A burial chamber. **5.** *Anat.* Any arched or dome-shaped structure. — *v. t.* To form with, or to cover with, a vault.

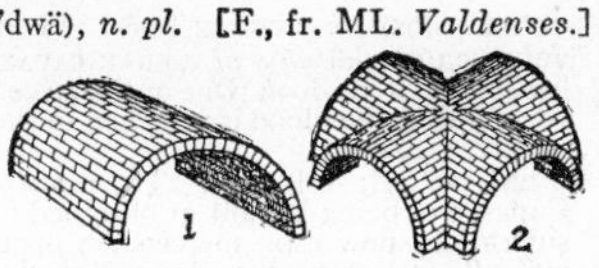

Vaults, 1. 1 Barrel Vault; 2 Cylindrical Intersecting, or Cross Vault. Type 2 is an example of a Groined Vault.

vault, *n.* [F. *volte,* prop., a turn, fr. It. *volta* turn, arch. See 1st VAULT.] A leap or bound; specif.: a A leap over or upon something, made by aid of the hands, or of a pole. Cf. POLE VAULT. **b** *Manège.* The bound or leap of a horse; a curvet. — *v. i.* **1.** To leap; bound; spring. **2.** Specif., to execute a vault (which see) or leap. — *v. t.* To leap over, esp. by aid of the hands or a pole; as, to *vault* a fence; also, to leap on, as the back of a horse; to mount with a leap.

vault'ed, *adj.* **1.** Built as a vault; arched. **2.** Having a vault or vaults.

vault'er (vôl'tẽr), *n.* One who vaults.

vault'ing, *n.* Act, practice, or art of building vaults; also, vaulted construction.

vault'ing, *adj.* **1.** That overleaps; also, overweening; as, *vaulting* ambition. **2.** That is used in vaulting, as in gymnastic exercises.

vaunt (vônt; vänt), *v. i.* [OF. *vanter,* fr. LL. *vanitare,* fr. L. *vanus* vain.] To talk vaingloriously; to brag; boast. — *v. t.* To boast of; to make a vainglorious display of. — **Syn.** See BOAST. — *n.* A vainglorious display of what one is, or has, or has done; ostentation; brag. — **vaunt'er,** *n.* — **vaunt'ing·ly,** *adv.*

vaunt'-cour'i·er (vänt'ko͝or'ĭ·ẽr; vônt'-), *n.* [F. *avant-courrier.*] **1.** *Obs.* One sent in advance, as of a body of troops. **2.** Hence, a precursor; forerunner.

vaunt'y (vôn'tĭ), *adj. Scot.* Proud; boastful; vain.

vav'a·sor, vav'a·sour (văv'ȧ·sōr, -so͞or), *n.* [OF. *vavassor, vavassour,* fr. LL. *vassus vassorum* vassal of vassals.] *Feud. Law.* Any of a certain class of feudal lords next in rank to a knight banneret.

va'ward' (vä'wôrd'), *n.* [For *avantward,* fr. ONF. *avantwarde.* See VANGUARD.] *Archaic.* Vanguard, as of troops; hence, the forefront.

V Day (vē). Victory Day. See V-E DAY, V-J DAY.

Ve'a·dar' (vē'ȧ·där'; vā'-), *n.* [Heb. *wĕ-Adhār,* lit., and Adar, i. e., the second Adar.] See JEWISH CALENDAR.

veal (vēl), *n.* [OF. *veel* (F. *veau*), fr. L. *vitellus,* dim. of *vitulus* a calf.] **1.** *Obs. exc. Dial.* A calf. **2.** The flesh of a calf used for food.

veal'er (-ẽr), *n. Cant.* A calf suitable for veal.

vec'tion (vĕk'shŭn), *n.* [L. *vectio,* fr. *vehere, vectum,* to carry.] *Med.* Transference of disease germs from an infected to a well person.

vec'tor (vĕk'tẽr), *n.* [L., a bearer, carrier, fr. *vehere, vectum,* to carry.] **1.** *Astron.* = RADIUS VECTOR, 2. **2.** *Biol.* An organism, usually an insect, which carries and transmits disease-causing microorganisms. **3.** *Math.* A complex entity representative of a directed magnitude, as of a force or a velocity, and represented by any of a system of equal and parallel line segments; — distinguished from *scalar.* — **vec·to'ri·al** (vĕk·tō'rĭ·ăl; 70), *adj.*

Ve'da (vā'dȧ; vē'dȧ), *n.* [Skr. *veda* knowledge, sacred lore.] The most ancient sacred literature of the Hindus, comprising more than one hundred extant books; specif. (*singular* or *collective; pl.* VEDAS [-dȧz]), one or all of the four canonical collections of hymns, prayers, and liturgical formulas which are the foundation of Vedic literature and religion: viz., ***Rig-Veda*** the oldest and most important, comprising over a thousand hymns; the ***Yajur-Veda, Sama-Veda,*** and ***Atharva-Veda.*** The language of the Vedas, *Vedic Sanskrit,* is usually distinguished from the *classical Sanskrit.* See SANSKRIT. — **Ve·da'ic** (vā·dā'ĭk; vē-), *adj.* — **Ve'da·ism** (vā'dȧ·ĭz'm; vē'dȧ-), *n.*

Ve·dan'ta (vā·dän'tȧ; vē·dăn'tȧ), *n.* [Skr. *Vedānta,* fr. *Veda* Veda + *anta* end.] *Hinduism.* A system of monistic or pantheistic philosophy, based on the Upanishads, — primarily so called as being an investigation of the latter part of the Vedas, afterwards interpreted as embodying the ultimate aim or end of the Vedas. — **Ve·dan'tism** (-tĭz'm), *n.* — **Ve·dan'tist** (-tĭst), *n.*

Ve·dan'tic (-tĭk), *adj.* Of or pertaining to the Vedanta philosophy; also, of or pertaining to the Vedas; Vedic.

V-E Day (vē'ē'). The day of victory in Europe (May 8, 1945), the day of Germany's surrender in World War II.

Ved'da, Ved'dah (vĕd'ȧ), *n.* [Singhalese *vedda* a hunter.] One of an aboriginal people of Ceylon.

ve·dette' (vē·dĕt'), *n.* [F., fr. It. *vedetta* (after *vedere* to see), fr. *veletta,* fr. Sp. *vela,* fr. L. *vigilare* to keep watch.] a *Mil.* A mounted sentinel, stationed in advance of the pickets. **b** *Nav.* A small vessel used to watch an enemy; — usually called **vedette boat**; *Fr. Navy,* a motor torpedo boat.

Ve'dic (vā'dĭk; vē'dĭk), *adj.* Of or pertaining to the Vedas. — *n.* Also **Vedic Sanskrit.** See SANSKRIT, VEDA.

vee (vē), *n.; pl.* VEES (vēz). **1.** The letter V, v. **2.** Anything having the shape of the letter V. **3.** A five-dollar bill (= V, *n.,* 5). — *adj.* Having the form of a capital V; V-shaped.

veep (vēp), *n.* [From abbr. *v.p.*] *Colloq.* Vice-president.

veer (vēr), *v. i.* [F. *virer.*] **1.** To change direction; shift, as from one direction, condition, position, etc., to another. **2.** *Meteorol.* To shift in a clockwise direction; — said of the wind. Opposed to *back.* **3.** *Naut.* To wear ship; to alter the course by turning away from the direction of the wind. — **Syn.** See SWERVE. — *v. t.* To direct to a different course; to shift; specif., *Naut.,* to wear; as, to *veer,* or wear, a vessel. — *n.* A change in course, direction, etc.; a swerve.

veer, *v. t.* [MD. *vieren* to slacken.] *Naut.* To let or pay out, as a rope, anchor chain, etc.

veer'y (-ĭ), *n.; pl.* VEERIES (-ĭz). [Prob. imitative of one of its notes.] A thrush (*Hylocichla fuscescens*) of the eastern United States. Called also *Wilson's thrush.*

Ve'ga (vē'gȧ), *n.* [ML., fr. Ar. (*al-Nasr*) *al-Waqi'* the falling (vulture).] *Astron.* A star of the first magnitude, brightest in the constellation Lyra; Alpha (α) Lyrae.

veg'e·ta·ble (vĕj'ē·tȧ·b'l; vĕj'tȧ-), *adj.* [See VEGETABLE, *n.*] **1.** Of or pert. to plants; having the nature of, or produced by, plants; growing in the manner of a plant; as, a *vegetable* nature; *vegetable* growths, juices, etc.; consisting of plants; as, the *vegetable* kingdom. **2.** Made from vegetables or their substance; as, *vegetable* silk, butter, pigments. — *n.* [OF., fr. *vegeter* to vegetate, fr. ML. *vegetare,* fr. L. *vegetus* lively, active, fr. *vegere* to be active.] A plant; specif., in common usage, a herbaceous plant cultivated for food, as the cabbage, potato, bean, etc.; also, the edible part or parts of such plants, as prepared for market or table.

vegetable butter. Any fixed vegetable oil that is solid at ordinary temperatures, as cacao butter.

vegetable ivory. a See IVORY NUT. **b** The shell of the coquilla nut.

vegetable marrow. A large, tender, cylindrical squash (a form of *Cucurbita pepo*), a popular vegetable in England.

vegetable silk. A cottonlike fibrous material obtained from the coating of the seeds of a Brazilian tree (*Chorisia speciosa* of the silk-cotton family). It is used for stuffing cushions, etc.

vegetable tallow. Any fatty tallowlike substance obtained from plants, used in soap and candles, for burning, etc.

vegetable wax. Any waxy product secreted by various plants, commonly in thin flakes by the walls of the epidermal cells of leaves, fruits, etc.

veg'e·ta·bly (-blĭ), *adv.* In the manner of or like a vegetable.

veg'e·tal (vĕj'ē·tăl), *adj.* **1.** Pertaining to vegetables, or the vegetable kingdom; of the nature of a vegetable. **2.** Being, resembling, or suggesting, a vegetable in lack of sense responses and reasoning power. **3.** *Biol.* Pertaining to vegetation; vegetative.

veg'e·tant (-tănt), *adj.* [LL. & ML. *vegetans, -antis,* pres. part.] a Inspiring growth and vigor; invigorating. **b** Of the nature of vegetation, in lack of sense response and power of reason; vegetative.

veg'e·tar'i·an (vĕj'ē·târ'ĭ·ăn; 6), *n.* One who believes that plants afford the only proper food for man. Strict vegetarians eat no butter, eggs, or milk. — *adj.* Of or pertaining to vegetarianism; also, consisting wholly of vegetables; as, a *vegetarian* diet.

veg'e·tar'i·an·ism (-ĭz'm), *n.* The theory or practice of living solely upon vegetables and fruits.

veg'e·tate (vĕj'ē·tāt), *v. i.* [ML. *vegetatus,* past part. of *vegetare.* See VEGETABLE, *n.*] **1.** To grow after the fashion of plants. **2.** Hence, to lead a passive existence; to do little but eat and grow. **3.** *Med.* To grow exuberantly; to produce fleshy or warty outgrowths; as, a *vegetating* papule. **4.** To produce vegetation; as, a field permitted to *vegetate* for several years. — *v. t.* To establish vegetation on or in; as, to *vegetate* a hillside or a ravine.

veg'e·ta'tion (-tā'shŭn), *n.* **1.** Act or process of vegetating; vegetable growth, development, or activity. **2.** Hence, inert existence; dull and stagnant living. **3.** The sum of vegetable life; plants in general. **4.** *Med.* A morbid outgrowth upon any part. — **veg'e·ta'tion·al** (-ăl), *adj.*

veg'e·ta'tive (vĕj'ē·tā'tĭv), *adj.* **1.** Growing, or having the power of growing, as plants; designating functions (as metabolism, nutrition, etc.) most directly concerned with the maintenance of life; — often, esp. in *Bot.,* in specif. sense opposed to *reproductive;* as, *vegetative* stage. **2.** Having the power to produce growth in plants; fertile; productive; as, the *vegetative* properties of soil. **3.** Designating the division of nature which includes the vegetable kingdom. **4.** Leading a passive existence; plantlike; as, he led a *vegetative* life. — **veg'e·ta'tive·ly,** *adv.* — **veg'e·ta'tive·ness,** *n.*

veg'e·tism (vĕj'ē·tĭz'm), *n.* Vegetal state or characteristic.

veg'e·tive (-tĭv), *adj.* Vegetable; vegetative.

ve'he·mence (vē'ē·mĕns; vē'hē-), *n.* Also, *Rare,* **ve'he·men·cy** (-mĕn·sĭ). Quality or state of being vehement; as: a Impetuous force; fury. **b** Violent ardor; fervor.

ve'he·ment (-mĕnt), *adj.* [F. *véhément,* fr. L. *vehemens, -entis,* fr. *vehere* to carry.] **1.** Acting with great force; furious; impetuous. **2.** Deeply felt; as, a *vehement* suspicion. **3.** Very ardent; very eager or urgent; passionate; as, a *vehement* protest. — **ve'he·ment·ly,** *adv.*

ve'hi·cle (vē'ĭ·k'l; vē'hĭ-), *n.* [F. *véhicule,* fr. L. *vehiculum,* fr. *vehere* to carry.] **1.** That in or on which a person or thing is or may be carried; any moving support or container for the conveyance of bulky objects. **2.** That which is used as the instrument of conveyance or communication; as, matter is the *vehicle* of energy. **3.** An art form or device used to convey an effect. **4.** a *Painting.* The liquid medium, as oil, with which a pigment is applied. **b** *Paints.* The liquid portion, as oil, of a paint or the like. **5.** *Pharm.* A medium in which medicine is administered, as a sirup.

ve·hic'u·lar (vē·hĭk'ū·lẽr), *adj.* Of or pertaining to a vehicle; also, serving as a vehicle, transported by vehicle, or intended for use by vehicles; as, *vehicular* traffic; a *vehicular* tunnel.

‖**Vehm'ge·richt** (fām'gē·rĭKt), *n.; pl.* -GERICHTE (-rĭK'tē). [G. *vehme, fehme, feme,* criminal tribunal + *gericht* court, judgment.] One of certain late medieval tribunals common in Germany, chiefly in Westphalia. They met in secret and usurped many functions of government.

veil (vāl), *n.* [ONF. *veile* (OF. & F. *voile*), fr. L. *vela,* pl. of *velum* a sail, curtain, veil.] **1.** A fabric hung up, or spread out, to intercept the view, and hide an object; a curtain; esp., a piece of stuff, usually diaphanous, worn to hide or protect the face. **2.** Hence, a cover; disguise; mask; — in phrases, as *veil of silence, veil of darkness,* etc. **3.** The state accepted or the vows made by a nun when she assumes the white veil of a novice or the black veil on making solemn profession of her vows; hence, the cloistered life; as, to take the black *veil;* to renounce the *veil.* **4.** *Anat.* A caul; as, born with a *veil.* **5.** *Bot. & Zool.* A velum. — *v. t.* **1.** To throw a veil over; to cover as with a veil. **2.** To cloak; mask. — **veiled** (vāld), *adj.*

veil'ing, *n.* **1.** Act of covering with a veil. **2.** A veil; also, gauzy material, as for veils.

vein (vān), *n.* [OF. *veine,* fr. L. *vena.*] **1.** A fissure or cavity, as in any substance. **2.** A crevice or narrow water channel in rock, earth, or ice. **3.** A streak or wave appearing in wood, marble, etc. **4.** Anything of distinctive character considered as running through something else; a strain; as, a *vein* of humor; specif., a particular disposition or turn of mind, or a manner of speech or of conduct expressive of it; as, a satirical *vein.* **5.** *Anat. & Zool.* One of the tubular branching vessels which carry the blood back to the heart. Cf. ARTERY, 1; see HEART, *Illust.* **6.** *Bot.* One of the vascular bundles forming the

framework of fibrous tissue of a leaf; — called also *nerve.* See VENATION, *Illust.* **7.** *Geol. & Mining.* **a** A fissure in rock filled by mineral matter, usually by deposition from solution by underground water. **b** A lode. **c** A bed of useful mineral material; as, a *vein* of coal. **8.** *Zool.* One of the thickened ribs, nervures, or nerves, which serve to stiffen the wings of insects. — **Syn.** See MOOD.
— *v. t.* To form or mark with veins; as: **a** To fill or cover with veins. **b** To extend in or over in a manner like or suggestive of veins. **c** To decorate with narrow stripes suggesting veins.

veined (vānd), *adj.* Full of veins; showing venation; streaked; variegated; specif., *Bot.*, having veins.

vein′let (vān′lĕt; -lĭt), *n.* A small vein.

vein′stone′ (-stōn′), *n.* *Mining.* Valueless material surrounding the ore in a lode; gangue; matrix.

vein′ule (vān′ūl), *n.* Also **vein′u·let** (-ū·lĕt; -lĭt). [Dim. of *vein;* cf. F. *veinule.*] A small vein; a veinlet.

vein′y (vān′ĭ), *adj.;* VEIN′I·ER (-ĭ·ẽr); VEIN′I·EST. Full of veins; veined, as marble.

ve′la (vē′lȧ), *n., pl.* of VELUM.

ve·la′men (vē·lā′mĕn), *n.; pl.* VELAMINA (vē·lăm′ĭ·nȧ). [L., fr. *velare* to cover.] **1.** *Anat.* A membrane; a velum. **2.** *Bot.* The thick corky epidermis covering the aerial roots of epiphytic orchids.

ve′lar (vē′lẽr), *adj.* [L. *velaris* pert. to a veil or curtain, fr. *velum.*] **1.** Of or pertaining to a velum, esp. that of the palate (the soft palate). **2.** *Phonet.* Formed with the back of the tongue touching or near the velum, or soft palate (the *k* sound in *coop, g* in *good, ng* in *song,* or the vowels ä, ô, ō, o͞o); guttural; back. — *n.* A velar sound.

ve·lar′i·um (vē·lâr′ĭ·ŭm; 6), *n.; pl.* -IA (-ȧ). [L., covering.] *Rom. Antiq.* An awning over a theater or amphitheater.

ve′lar·ize (vē′lẽr·īz), *v. t.* *Phonet.* To modify in utterance by simultaneously raising the back of the tongue toward the velum, as in the *l* of *pool,* and in English *w.* — **ve′lar·i·za′tion** (-ĭ·zā′shŭn; -ī·zā′-), *n.*

ve′late (vē′lāt), *adj.* [L. *velatus,* past part. of *velare* to veil.] *Bot. & Zool.* Having a veil or velum.

veld, veldt (vĕlt; *in S. Africa,* fĕlt), *n.* [D. *veld.*] *S. Afr.* A grassland, in which there may be also scattered shrubs or trees.

vel′i·ta′tion (vĕl′ĭ·tā′shŭn), *n.* [L. *velitatio,* fr. *velitari, -tatus,* to skirmish, fr. *veles, -itis,* light-armed soldier.] A dispute or skirmish.

‖**ve′li·tes** (vē′lĭ·tēz), *n. pl.* [L., pl. of *veles, velitis.*] *Rom. Antiq.* Light-armed foot soldiers.

vel·le′i·ty (vĕ·lē′ĭ·tĭ), *n.; pl.* VELLEITIES (-tĭz). [ML. *velleitas,* fr. L. *velle* to will, to be willing.] **1.** The lowest degree of desire; imperfect or incomplete volition. **2.** Hence, a slight wish; a faint desire, inclination, or the like.

vel′li·cate (vĕl′ĭ·kāt), *v. t.* [L. *vellicatus,* past part. of *vellicare* to twitch, fr. *vellere* to pluck.] To twitch; nip; pinch. — *v. i.* To move spasmodically; to twitch. — **vel′li·ca′tion** (-kā′shŭn), *n.* — **vel′li·ca′tive** (-kā′tĭv), *adj.*

vel′lum (vĕl′ŭm), *n.* [OF. *velin, veelin,* orig. adj., fr. *veel* calf. See VEAL.] **1.** A fine-grained lambskin, kidskin, or calfskin prepared for writing upon, binding books, etc. **2.** A manuscript written or printed on such material. **3.** Loosely, a type of paper so made as to resemble parchment. — *adj.* Of, like, or bound in vellum.

‖**ve·lo′ce** (vā·lō′chā), *adj.* [It., swift.] *Music.* Rapid and dashing in tempo; — a direction.

ve·loc′i·pede (vē·lŏs′ĭ·pēd), *n.* [F. *vélocipède,* fr. L. *velox, -ocis,* swift + *pes, pedis,* foot.] Any of various light vehicles propelled by the rider or riders; — applied esp. to early forms of bicycle and tricycle, and later to a form of railroad handcar.

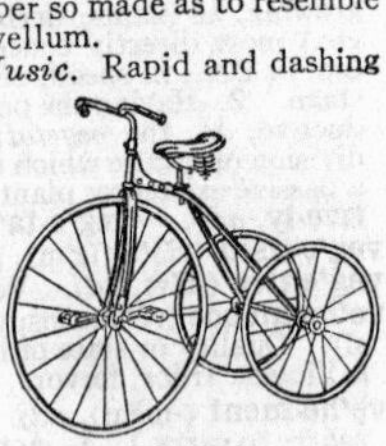

Velocipede.

ve·loc′i·ty (-ĭ·tĭ), *n.; pl.* -TIES (-tĭz). [F. *vélocité,* fr. L. *velocitas,* fr. *velox, -ocis,* swift, quick.] **1.** Quickness of motion; swiftness; speed. **2.** *Mech.* Time rate of motion in a given direction and sense.

ve′lo·drome (vē′lō·drōm), *n.* [F. *vélodrome.*] A building with a specially designed cycle track.

ve·lours′ (vĕ·lo͞or′) *or* **ve·lour′,** *n.* [F. See VELURE.] **1.** Any of various fabrics finished to present a velvetlike surface, chiefly of two characteristic types: a heavy cut-pile cotton, jute, worsted, or other fabric having a dense, stiff pile, as of cotton or ramie, similar to plush and used for example for draperies, upholsteries, and couch covers; or a soft fabric woven in satin or twill weave with an open, erect, furry nap, similar to duvetyn and used for coats, suits, and dresses. **2.** A felt made from the fur of rabbit, hare, or nutria. — *adj.* Made of velours or resembling velours as regards texture, surface, or appearance.

ve′lum (vē′lŭm), *n.; pl.* VELA (-lȧ). [L., an awning, a veil.] *Anat. & Zool.* A membranous partition likened to a veil or curtain; specif., the soft palate.

ve·lure′ (vĕ·lūr′), *n.* [F. *velours,* through OF. & Pr. fr. L. *villosus,* fr. *villus* shaggy hair.] **1.** Velvet, or some fabric resembling it, esp. one of linen, silk, or jute. **2.** A silk or plush pad used as a brush for silk hats. — *v. t.* To brush with a velure.

ve·lu′ti·nous (vē·lū′tĭ·nŭs), *adj.* [It. *velluto* velvet. See VELVET.] Covered with a silky pubescence; velvety.

vel′vet (vĕl′vĕt; -vĭt), *n.* [ME. *velvet, veluet,* dim. fr. OF. *velu* shaggy, fr. L. *villus* shaggy hair.] **1. a** A silk fabric having a thick soft pile of short erect threads. It is called ***pile velvet*** when the loops of the pile are uncut, and ***cut velvet*** when the loops are cut so that the pile is of single threads. **b** A piece of this fabric. **c** A similar fabric with a cotton or linen back. **2.** Something like or suggesting velvet, as in softness, luster, etc. **3.** The soft skin on the antlers of deer during their rapid growth. **4.** Short for VELVET SPONGE. **5.** *Slang.* Surplus; the cash or chips a player is ahead in any game; as, he is gambling on *velvet;* hence, loosely, any profit or gain. — *adj.* **1.** Made of or covered with velvet. **2.** Like or suggesting velvet; velvety.

vel′vet·een′ (vĕl′vĕ·tēn′; 2), *n.* [From VELVET.] **1.** An all-cotton velvet. **2.** *pl.* Clothes, esp. trousers, of this fabric. — **vel′vet·een′, vel′vet·eened′** (-tēnd′), *adj.*

velvet sponge. A fine, soft commercial sponge (*Hippospongia equina meandriformis*) of more or less cakelike form, occurring in the Gulf of Mexico and off the West Indies.

vel′vet·y (vĕl′vĕ·tĭ; -vĭ·tĭ), *adj.* **1.** Velvetlike; soft and smooth, as in appearance, or to the sight, hearing, or touch. **2.** Mild; smooth to the taste; as, *velvety* rum; hence, giving a contact like that of velvet; as, a *velvety* touch.

‖**ve′na** (vē′nȧ), *n.; pl.* VENAE (-nē). [L.] *Anat.* A vein.

‖**ve′na ca′va** (kā′vȧ); *pl.* VENAE CAVAE (vē′nē kā′vē). [L. *cava* hollow.] *Anat. & Zool.* One of the large veins by which, in air-breathing vertebrates, the blood is returned to the right atrium of the heart. See HEART, *Illust.*

ve′nal (vē′năl; -n'l), *adj.* [L. *venalis,* fr. *venus, venum,* sale.] **1.** Capable of being bought or obtained for money or other valuable consideration; now esp., mercenary; open to corrupt influence, bribery, etc. **2.** Originating in, or characterized by, corrupt bargaining; as, a *venal* arrangement. — **ve′nal·ly,** *adv.*

ve·nal′i·ty (vē·năl′ĭ·tĭ), *n.; pl.* -TIES (-tĭz). Quality or state of being venal, or purchasable; prostitution of talents, offices, or services for reward; willingness to be influenced by bribery or corrupt measures.

ve·nat′ic (vē·năt′ĭk), *adj.* Also **ve·nat′i·cal** (-ĭ·kăl). [L. *venaticus,* fr. *venatus* hunting, fr. *venari,* past part. *venatus,* to hunt.] Of or pert. to or used in hunting; also, fond of or living by hunting. — **ve·nat′i·cal·ly,** *adv.*

ve·na′tion (vē·nā′shŭn), *n.* [L. *vena* a vein.] **1.** The arrangement or system of veins, as in the wing of an insect; veins, collectively. **2.**

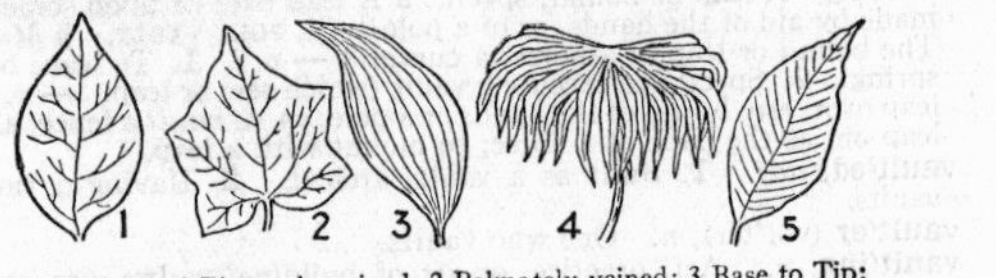

Venation. 1 Pinnately veined; 2 Palmately veined; 3 Base to Tip; 4 Base to Midrib; 5 Midrib to Margin.

Bot. The arrangement and disposition of the veins or vascular bundles in the green tissue of a leaf blade; — called also *nervation.* — **ve·na′tion·al** (-ăl), *adj.*

vend (vĕnd), *v. t. & i.* [F. *vendre,* fr. L. *vendere,* fr. *venum dare,* fr. *venus, venum,* sale + *dare* to give.] **1.** To sell; as, to *vend* fruit. **2.** To utter publicly; to publish abroad.

ven′dace (vĕn′dās), *n. sing. & pl.* [OF. *vendoise* dace, of Celt. origin.] A whitefish (*Coregonus vandesius*) native to certain lakes in Scotland and England.

vend·ee′ (vĕn·dē′), *n.* The person to whom a thing is vended, or sold; — correl. of *vendor,* and chiefly legal.

‖**Ven′dé′miaire′** (văN′dā′myâr′), *n.* [F., fr. L. *vindemia* vintage.] See REVOLUTIONARY CALENDAR.

vend′er (vĕn′dẽr), *n.* A vendor; seller.

ven·det′ta (vĕn·dĕt′ȧ), *n.; pl.* -DETTAS (-ȧz). [It., fr. L. *vindicta* revenge.] A feud for blood revenge, as in Corsica, where this ancient custom has continued to recent times. The obligation rests upon the relatives of a dead or injured man to take vengeance on the person who has caused his death or injury. — **ven·det′tist** (-ĭst), *n.*

vend′i·ble (vĕn′dĭ·b'l), *adj.* **a** Capable of being vended; salable. **b** Venal. — *n.* A vendible article; — usually in *pl.* — **vend′i·bil′i·ty** (-bĭl′ĭ·tĭ), *n.* — **vend′i·bly,** *adv.*

vend′ing ma·chine′. A slot machine for vending merchandise.

ven·di′tion (vĕn·dĭsh′ŭn), *n.* Act of vending, or selling.

ven′dor (vĕn′dẽr; *in contrast with* vendee *often* vĕn·dôr′), *n.* [AF. (F. *vendeur*).] **1.** One who vends; a seller; vender. **2.** A vending machine.

ven′due (vĕn′dū; -do͞o; văn′do͞o; vĕn′do͞o; *also accented* ven·due′), *n.* [D. *vendu,* fr. MF. *vendue,* fr. *vendre,* past part. *vendu,* to sell.] A public sale by auction.

ve·neer′ (vĕ·nēr′), *n.* [G. *furnier* or *fournier.* See VENEER, *v. t.*] **1.** A thin sheet of a material; specif.: **a** A layer of valuable or beautiful material for overlaying an inferior one, esp. such a thin leaf of wood to be glued to a cheaper wood. **b** Any one of the layers glued together to impart stiffness and strength to plywood. **2.** Superficial or meretricious show; gloss. — *v. t.* [G. *furnieren, fourniren,* fr. F. *fournir* to furnish.] **1.** To overlay or plate, as a common sort of wood, with a thin layer of finer wood for outer finish or decoration; as, to *veneer* furniture with mahogany; hence, to coat or face with any material giving a superior surface; also, to glue together (thin pieces of wood) into plywood. **2.** To cover over with a veneer; to give an attractive appearance to. — **ve·neer′er,** *n.*

ve·neer′ing, *n.* Thin material used as a veneer or in plywood; also, a surface made by veneer.

ven′e·punc′ture (vĕn′ē·pŭngk′tŭr; vē′nē-), *n.* [L. *vena* vein + E. *puncture.*] *Med.* Puncture of a vein, specif. with a hypodermic needle.

ven′er·a·ble (vĕn′ẽr·ȧ·b'l), *adj.* [OF., fr. L. *venerabilis.*] **1.** Capable of being venerated; worthy of veneration; — generally implying an advanced age. *Venerable* is used in the churches of the Anglican Communion as a title for an archdeacon. In the Roman Catholic Church *venerable* is applied to those who have attained to the lowest of the three recognized degrees of sanctity, but are not among the *beatified* or the *canonized.* **2.** Rendered sacred by religious, historic, or other associations. — **Syn.** See OLD. — **ven′er·a·bil′i·ty** (-bĭl′ĭ·tĭ), **ven′er·a·ble·ness,** *n.* — **ven′er·a·bly,** *adv.*

ven′er·ate (vĕn′ẽr·āt), *v. t.* [L. *veneratus,* past part. of *venerari* to venerate.] To regard with reverential respect, or with admiration and deference. — **Syn.** See REVERE.

ven′er·a′tion (-ā′shŭn), *n.* **1.** Act of venerating, or state of being venerated; respect mingled with awe, excited by the dignity, wisdom, or superiority of a person, by sacredness of character, etc. **2.** Act of expressing reverent feeling; worship.

ven′er·a′tor (vĕn′ẽr·ā′tẽr), *n.* [L.] One who venerates.

ve·ne′re·al (vē·nēr′ē·ăl), *adj.* [L. *venereus, venerius,* fr. *Venus, Veneris,* Venus, the goddess of love.] **1.** Of or pertaining to venery, or sexual love; relating to sexual intercourse. **2.** *Med.* **a** Arising from sexual intercourse with an infected person, as in **venereal disease** (abbr. *VD, V.D.*), any of several diseases transmitted chiefly by sexual intercourse, as syphilis, gonorrhea, and lymphogranuloma. **b** Adapted to the cure of venereal diseases. **c** Infected with venereal disease; as, a *venereal* patient.

ve·ne′re·ol′o·gy (-ŏl′ō·jĭ), *n.* *Med.* That branch of medical science concerned with venereal diseases. — **ve·ne′re·ol′o·gist** (-jĭst), *n.*

ven′er·y (vĕn′ẽr·ĭ), *n.* [L. *Venus, Veneris,* the goddess of love.] Sexual intercourse; coition.

ven′er·y (vĕn′ẽr·ĭ), *n.* [OF. *venerie,* fr. *vener* to hunt, fr. L. *venari.*] Art, act, or practice of hunting; the sports of the chase; hunting.

ven′e·sec′tion (vĕn′ē·sĕk′shŭn; vē′nē-), *n.* [NL. *venaesectio,* fr. L. *vena* vein, gen. *venae* + *sectio* a cutting.] *Med.* Phlebotomy.

Ve·ne′tian (vē·nē′shăn), *adj.* Of or pertaining to Venice in Italy. — *n.* **1.** A native or inhabitant of Venice. **2.** Any of various things suggesting, or named in allusion to, Venice; as: **a** *Colloq.* A Venetian blind. **b** *pl.* A heavy tape or braid used especially on Venetian blinds.

Venetian blind. A blind (capable of being raised or lowered) having numerous thin parallel slats that can be set simultaneously at any desired angle.

Venetian glass. A dainty, delicate, and artistic glassware made at Murano near Venice.

Venetian red. **1.** A red pigment consisting of ferric oxides, artificially prepared. **2.** A brown, reddish red-yellow in hue, of medium saturation and low brilliance. See COLOR.

Venetian school. Painting as practiced in and near Venice in the 15th and 16th centuries, noted for its richness and beauty of color, culminating in the work of Giorgione, Titian, Paul Veronese, and Tintoretto.

venge (vĕnj), *v. t. & i.* [OF. *vengier.*] *Archaic.* = AVENGE.

venge′ance (vĕn′jăns), *n.* [OF., fr. *vengier, venchier,* to avenge, fr. L. *vindicare* to claim, defend, avenge, fr. *vindex* a claimant, avenger.] Punishment inflicted in return for an injury or an offense; retribution; often, passionate or unrestrained revenge.
— ***with a vengeance.*** **a** With great violence, force, or the like. **b** Extremely. **c** In great or excessive amount.

venge′ful (vĕnj′fo͝ol; -f'l), *adj.* Revengeful; as: **a** Vindictive; seeking to avenge. **b** Serving to gain vengeance. — **venge′ful·ly,** *adv.* — **venge′ful·ness,** *n.*

ve′ni·al (vē′nĭ·ăl; 58), *adj.* [OF. *venial,* fr. LL. *venialis,* fr. *venia* forgiveness, grace, favor.] **1.** Capable of being forgiven; excusable; as, a *venial* sin. **2.** *Obs.* Allowed; unobjectionable. — **ve′ni·al′i·ty** (-ăl′ĭ·tĭ), *n.* — **ve′ni·al·ly,** *adv.* — **ve′ni·al·ness,** *n.*

venial sin. *R.C.Ch.* A slight offense against divine law in unimportant matters, or, in grave matters, an offense committed without reflection or full consent.

ven′in (vĕn′ĭn; vē′nĭn), *n.* [L. *venenum* poison.] *Biochem.* Any of a class of toxic substances in snake venom.

ven′i·punc′ture (vĕn′ĭ·pŭngk′tūr; vē′nĭ-), *n.* *Med.* = VENEPUNCTURE.

ve·ni′re fa′ci·as (vē·nī′rē fā′shĭ·ăs), *or* **ve·ni′re,** *n.* [L., make, or cause, to come.] *Law.* A judicial writ or precept used in summoning persons to appear in court to serve as jurors.

ve·ni′re·man (vē·nī′rē·măn; vē·nẽr′ē-), *n.; pl.* -MEN (-mĕn). *Law.* A juror summoned by a venire.

ven′i·son (vĕn′ĭ·z'n; -s'n; *Brit.* vĕn′z'n), *n.* [OF. *veneison,* fr. L. *venatio* hunting, the chase, game, fr. *venari,* past part. *venatus,* to hunt.] The flesh of an animal of the deer kind.

Ve·ni′te (vē·nī′tē), *n.* [L., come, imper. 2d pers. pl.; — so called from its opening word in the Latin version.] The 94th Psalm (Vulgate, in A.V., the 95th), which in the form of a response is said or sung at matins.

‖**ve′ni, vi′di, vi′ci** (vē′nī, vī′dī, vī′sī; wā′nē, wē′dē, wē′kē). I came, I saw, I conquered; — the words with which Julius Caesar announced to the Roman Senate his victory at Zela, 47 B.C.

ven′om (vĕn′ŭm), *n.* [OF. *venim, venin,* fr. L. *venenum* poison.] **1.** *Archaic.* Matter fatal or injurious to life; poison in general. **2.** The poisonous matter which certain animals, such as serpents, scorpions, bees, etc., secrete and communicate by biting or stinging. **3.** That which poisons, embitters, or blights; spite; malice; malignity. — *v. t.* To envenom. — **ven′om·er,** *n.*

ven′om·ous (-ŭs), *adj.* **1.** Full of venom; poisonous; also, virulent; baneful. **2.** Malignant; spiteful; as, a *venomous* writer. **3.** *Zool.* Having a gland or glands for the secretion of venom; able to inflict a poisoned bite, sting, or wound. — **ven′om·ous·ly,** *adv.* — **ven′om·ous·ness,** *n.*

ve′nose (vē′nōs), *adj.* [See VENOUS.] Venous; specif., *Bot.,* having numerous or conspicuous veins.

ve·nos′i·ty (vē·nŏs′ĭ·tĭ), *n.* Quality or state of being venous or venose.

ve′nous (vē′nŭs), *adj.* [L. *venosus,* fr. *vena* a vein.] **1.** Of or pertaining to a vein or veins. **2.** *Physiol.* Designating blood, as that in the veins, which has passed through the capillaries, given up oxygen, and become charged with carbon dioxide. Venous blood in the higher animals is dark red. Cf. ARTERIAL. — **ve′nous·ly,** *adv.*

vent (vĕnt), *n.* [From *fent, fente,* a slit, cleft, fissure, fr. *fendre* to split, fr. L. *findere;* confused with F. *vent* wind, fr. L. *ventus.*] **1.** A small aperture; a hole or opening for passage or escape, as of a fluid. **2.** Opportunity of escape or passage; outlet, as from confinement or privacy; passage; escape; hence, utterance, expression, or publication; as, to give *vent* to one's wrath. **3.** *Ordn.* The opening at the breech of a gun through which fire is communicated to the powder. **4.** *Zool.* **a** The anus. **b** The opening of the cloaca or of the intestine on the surface of the body; esp., that of the lower vertebrates, as fishes.
— *v. t.* **1.** To let out at a vent, or small aperture; give passage or outlet to. **2.** To give vent or expression to; as, to *vent* one's anger; also, to utter; publish; as, to *vent* a grievance. **3.** To furnish with a vent; make a vent in. **4.** To relieve by giving vent; as, to *vent* oneself in grief. — **Syn.** See EXPRESS. — **vent′er,** *n.*

vent′age (vĕn′tĭj), *n.* A small hole; a vent.

ven′tail (vĕn′tāl), *n.* [OF. *ventaille* (F. *ventail*). See VENTILATE.] *Hist.* The lower movable front of a helmet.

ven′ter (vĕn′tẽr), *n.* [L.] **1.** Something suggesting a vent; specif.: *Anat. & Zool.* **a** The belly. **b** A protuberant part, as of a muscle. **c** A broad shallow concavity as in a bone. **2.** *Law.* Womb (of wife or mother).

ven′ti·duct (vĕn′tĭ·dŭkt), *n.* [L. *ventus* wind + *ductus* a leading, conduit, fr. *ducere, ductum,* to lead.] A passage or pipe for wind or air, as for ventilation.

ven′ti·late (vĕn′tĭ·lāt), *v. t.* [L. *ventilatus,* past part. of *ventilare* to toss, fan, winnow, fr. *ventus* wind.] **1.** *Now Rare.* To winnow; fan. **2.** To cause fresh air to circulate through (a room, mine, etc.) so as to replace foul air simultaneously removed; also, of air, to circulate through so as to freshen and replace foul air, gas, etc. **3.** To oxygenate, as blood. **4.** To give vent to; utter; as, to *ventilate* one's grievances; also, to discuss freely and openly; expose by publicity. **5.** To provide with a vent, or escape. — **ven′ti·la′tion** (-lā′shŭn), *n.* — **ven′ti·la′tive** (-lā′tĭv), *adj.*

ven′ti·la′tor (-lā′tẽr), *n.* One who or that which ventilates; esp., a contrivance for drawing off or expelling foul or stagnant air, or for introducing fresh air. — **ven′ti·la·to′ry** (-lȧ·tō′rĭ *or, esp. Brit.,* -tẽr·ĭ), *adj.*

‖**Ven′tôse′** (văN′tōz′), *n.* [F., fr. L. *ventosus* windy.] See REVOLUTIONARY CALENDAR.

ven′tral (vĕn′trăl), *adj.* [F. or L.; F., fr. L. *ventralis,* fr. *venter* the belly.] **1.** Of or pertaining to the belly; abdominal; hence, in *Zool. & Anat.,* designating, pertaining to, or situated on or toward that surface of the body which in man is anterior, but in most other animals is the lower surface; — the opposite of *dorsal.* **2.** *Bot.* **a** Pertaining to or designating that surface of a carpel, petal, etc., which faces toward the center of a flower. **b** Pertaining to the lower side or surface of a dorsiventral organ or thallus; — opposed to *dorsal.* — **ven′tral·ly,** *adv.*

ven′tri·cle (vĕn′trĭ·k'l), *n.* [F. or L.; F. *ventricule,* fr. L. *ventriculus* the stomach, a ventricle, dim. of *venter* the belly.] *Anat. & Zool.* A cavity of an organ; esp.: **a** Either of the chambers of the heart that receive the blood from an auricle (atrium), and deliver it to the arteries. See HEART, *Illust.* **b** In the brain, one of the communicating cavities continuous with the central canal of the spinal cord. See BRAIN, *Illust.*

ven′tri·cose (-kōs), *adj.* Also **ven′tri·cous** (-kŭs). [NL. *ventricosus,* fr. L. *venter* belly.] Having a large belly; *Bot. & Zool.,* swelling out on one side or unequally. — **ven′tri·cos′i·ty** (-kŏs′ĭ·tĭ), *n.*

ven·tric′u·lar (vĕn·trĭk′ū·lẽr), *adj.* **1.** Of or pertaining to a ventricle or ventriculus. **2.** Bellied; bulging out.

ven·tric′u·lus (-lŭs), *n.; pl.* -ULI (-lī). [L. See VENTRICLE.] *Zool.* A ventricle; specif., a division of a compound stomach, as the digestive portion of an insect stomach or the gizzard of a bird.

ven′tri·lo′qui·al (vĕn′trĭ·lō′kwĭ·ăl), *adj.* Also **ven·tril′o·qual** (vĕn·trĭl′ō·kwăl). Of, pertaining to, resembling, or using ventriloquism.

ven·tril′o·quism (vĕn·trĭl′ō·kwĭz'm), *n.* Also **ven·tril′o·quy** (-kwĭ). [From LL. *ventriloquus* a ventriloquist, fr. *venter* the belly + *loqui,* past part. *locutus,* to speak.] Act, art, or practice of speaking in such a manner that the voice appears to come from some source other than the vocal organs of the speaker. — **ven·tril′o·quist** (-kwĭst), *n.* — **ven·tril′o·quis′tic** (-kwĭs′tĭk), *adj.*

ven·tril′o·quize (-kwīz), *v. i. & t.* To utter ventriloquially.

ven′tro- (vĕn′trō-). [L. *venter* belly, paunch.] A combining form denoting: **a** *The abdomen,* as in **ven·trot′o·my** (see -TOMY). **b** *Ventral and,* as in **ven′tro·dor′sal.**

ven′ture (vĕn′tūr; 118), *n.* [Aphetic form of ME. *aventure.* See ADVENTURE.] **1.** An undertaking involving chance or danger; a hazard; risk; specif., a speculative business enterprise. **2.** *Now Rare.* Fortune; chance; contingency. **3.** The thing put to hazard, as in gambling; a stake; a risk; esp., something sent to sea in trade. — ***at a venture*** (orig. *at aventure*). At hazard; at random.
— *v. t.* **1.** To expose to hazard; risk. **2.** To undertake the risk of; to brave; dare, as a voyage. **3.** To put or send on a venture or chance, as a business speculation. **4.** *Rare.* To confide in; rely on. **5.** To dare to advance or put forward, or to expose to criticism or refutation, as an opinion. — *v. i.* **1.** To hazard oneself; dare. **2.** To make a venture; run a risk; as, to *venture* ashore. — **ven′tur·er** (-tūr·ẽr), *n.*

venture capital. Money invested in stocks, esp. new or expanding private enterprises, with the expectation of repayment in profits and dividends but subject to the hazards of ownership, as distinguished from capital loaned by banks; — called also *risk capital* or *equity capital.*

ven′ture·some (-sŭm), *adj.* **1.** Inclined to venture; venturous; daring. **2.** Risky; involving hazard; dangerous. — **Syn.** See ADVENTUROUS. — **ven′ture·some·ly,** *adv.* — **ven′ture·some·ness,** *n.*

Ven·tu′ri (vĕn·to͞o′rē; văn·to͞o′rē). A trade-mark applied to a meter, using a venturi tube, to measure the flow of liquids in pipes.

venturi tube, *or* **venturi,** *n.* [After G. B. *Venturi* (1746–1822), It. physicist, who noted the effect of constriction.] **1.** *Hydraulics.* A short tube, inserted in a pipeline, whose internal surface consists of two truncated cones connected at the small ends by a very short cylinder. As the velocity of flow of the liquid increases in the throat, the pressure decreases. The tube is used to measure the quantity of fluid flowing or, by joining a branch tube at the throat, to produce suction. **2.** *Aeronautics.* A short tube with flaring ends and constricted connecting portion, placed parallel to the air flow, with a branch tube entering at the throat, and used, by virtue of the diminished pressure in the throat, to furnish power, for example, to operate an injector or a gyroscopic instrument.

ven′tur·ous (vĕn′tūr·ŭs), *adj.* **1.** Courting danger; ready to meet risks; daring; bold. **2.** Involving danger or risk; hazardous; dangerous; risky. — **Syn.** See ADVENTUROUS. — **ven′tur·ous·ly,** *adv.* — **ven′tur·ous·ness,** *n.*

ven′ue (vĕn′ū), *n.* [OF., a coming, fr. *venir* to come, fr. L. *venire.*] *Law.* **a** The place or county in which the alleged events from which an action arises took place; also, the place from which the jury is taken, and where the trial is held. **b** The statement in a pleading, laying the place for the trial; also, sometimes, the clause in an affidavit indicating the place where it was sworn to.

ven′ule (-ūl), *n.* [L. *venula,* dim. fr. *vena* vein.] A small vein; a veinlet; specif., *Zool.,* one of the small branches of the veins of the wings in insects. — **ven′u·lar** (-ū·lẽr), *adj.*

ven′u·lose (-ū·lōs), **ven′u·lous** (-lŭs), *adj.* Full of venules.

Ve′nus (vē′nŭs), *n.* [L. *Venus, -eris.*] **1.** *Rom. Relig.* An ancient Italian goddess of bloom and beauty, protectress of gardens, who became identified with the Greek *Aphrodite;* also, a statue or picture of Venus; a very beautiful woman. **2.** A planet moving in an orbit between that of Mercury and that of the earth, at a mean distance from the sun of about 67,000,000 miles. Venus passes through phases similar to those of the moon, and at its brightest is far more brilliant than any fixed star. As morning star, it was called by the ancients *Lucifer;* as evening star, *Hesperus.* Its period of rotation is not exactly known. Symbol, ♀. See PLANET, *Table.* **3.** *Alchem.* The metal copper.

Ve′nus·berg (vē′nŭs·bûrg; *G.* vā′no͝os·bĕrK), *n.* [G., mountain of Venus.] A mountain between Eisenach and Gotha in Germany, in a cave of which, according to medieval legend, Venus held court and kept her victims prisoner by means of sensuous pleasures. The name was also given to various other mountains. See TANNHÄUSER.

Ve′nus of Mi′lo (mē′lō; *It.* -lō) *or* **Me′los** (mē′lŏs). A Hellenistic marble statue representing Venus undraped above the thighs and without arms, found on Melos in 1820, and now in the Louvre.

Ve′nus's–fly′trap′, *n.* An insectivorous plant (*Dionaea muscipula*) of the sundew family, found on the Carolinian coast, having the apex of its leaf modified into an insect trap.

Ve′nus's–hair′, *n.* A maidenhair fern (*Adiantum capillus-veneris*) having a slender black stipe and branches.

ver′a (vĕr′ȧ; văr′ȧ), *adj. & adv.* *Scot.* Very.

ve·ra′cious (vĕ·rā′shŭs), *adj.* [L. *verax, -acis,* fr. *verus* true.] **1.** Observant of truth; truthful; honest. **2.** Characterized by truth; true; accurate; as, a *veracious* story. — **ve·ra′cious·ly,** *adv.* — **ve·ra′cious·ness,** *n.*

ve·rac′i·ty (vĕ·răs′ĭ·tĭ), *n.; pl.* -TIES (-tĭz). **1.** Quality of being veracious; specif.: **a** Truthfulness; honesty. **b** Correctness; accuracy. **c** Trueness; precision. **2.** That which is true; a truth; the truth. — **Syn.** See TRUTH.

ve·ran′da, ve·ran′dah (vĕ·răn′dȧ), *n.* [Anglo-Indian (also cf. forms in Bengali, Hind., etc.), but some forms doubtless fr. Pg. *varanda,* an earlier Ind. borrowing.] An open gallery or portico, usually roofed, attached to the exterior of a building; — in the United States often called a *porch* or *piazza.* See LOGGIA.

ve·rat′ric (vē·răt′rĭk), *adj.* [L. *veratrum* hellebore.] *Chem.* Pertaining to or designating a white crystalline acid, $(CH_3O)_2C_6H_3CO_2H$, occurring in sabadilla seed and also formed by decomposition of veratridine.

ve·rat′ri·dine (-rĭ·dēn; -dĭn), *n.* Also **ve·rat′ri·din.** *Chem.* An amorphous alkaloid, $C_{37}H_{53}NO_{11}$, occurring in sabadilla seed.

ver′a·trine (vĕr′ȧ·trēn; -trĭn), *n.* Also **ver′a·trin** (-trĭn), **ver′a·tri′na** (-trī′nȧ), **ve·ra′tri·a** (vē·rā′trĭ·ȧ; -răt′rĭ·ȧ). **1.** *Pharm.* A mixture of alkaloids obtained as a white or grayish powder from sabadilla seeds and used in the local treatment of neuralgia and arthritis. **2.** *Chem.* Veratridine.

verb (vûrb), *n.* [OF. *verbe,* fr. L. *verbum* a word, verb.] *Grammar.* A word expressing an action performed by or suffered by the subject, or a state experienced by the subject, and having the force of a predicate, — specif. called a *transitive* verb when requiring an object to complete its meaning; an *intransitive* verb when expressing a state or action without connection with any subject. See AUXILIARY VERB, LINK VERB.

ver′bal (vûr′băl; -b'l), *adj.* **1.** Of or pertaining to words; consisting in, or having to do with, words only; esp., dealing with words rather than with the ideas to be conveyed; as, a *verbal* change. **2.** Expressed in words, whether spoken or written, but commonly in spoken words; hence, by confusion, spoken; oral; not written; as, a *verbal* contract. **3.** Word for word; literal; as, a *verbal* translation. **4.** *Gram.* Of or pertaining to a verb; as, a *verbal* group; comprising a verb or verbs; as, a *verbal* predicate; derived directly from a verb; like a verb in sense and constructions; as, a *verbal* adjective; used in forming verbs; as, a *verbal* prefix. — **Syn.** See ORAL. — *n. Gram.* A word form that combines something of verb meaning and use with the uses of a noun or adjective; in English, specif., infinitive, gerund, participle. — **ver′bal·ly,** *adv.*

ver′bal·ism (-ĭz'm), *n.* **1.** Verbal expression. **2.** An empty form of words. **3.** Verboseness; wordiness.

ver′bal·ist (-ĭst), *n.* **1.** A literalist. **2.** One given to verbalism or verbalisms.

ver′bal·ize (-īz), *v. t. & i.* **1.** To express (oneself or something) precisely, skillfully, verbosely, or the like. **2.** To convert into a verb; verbify. — **ver′bal·i·za′tion** (-ĭ·zā′shŭn; -ī·zā′-), *n.* — **ver′bal·iz′er** (-īz′ĕr), *n.*

verbal noun. *Gram.* A noun derived directly from a verb or verb stem and, in certain uses, partaking of the sense and constructions of a verb; in English, a noun in *-ing* meaning in general the act or process of doing something; specif., an infinitive or gerund.

ver·ba′tim (vûr·bā′tĭm), *adv.* [ML., fr. L. *verbum* word.] Word for word; in the same words. — **ver·ba′tim,** *adj.*

‖**ver·ba′tim ac lit′te·ra′tim** (ăk lĭt′ĕ·rā′tĭm). [L.] Word for word and letter for letter.

ver·be′na (vĕr·bē′nȧ), *n.* [L. See VERVAIN.] A garden plant (genus *Verbena*) of numerous varieties, with large, often fragrant flowers ranging from white through pink and red to purple, or sometimes variegated. It is typical of a family (Verbenaceae) of herbs, shrubs, and trees, the verbena family, distinguished by the opposite leaves, chiefly irregular flowers, and entire ovary, and including the verbena, the vervain, the lantana, and also some timber trees. — **ver′be·na′ceous** (vûr′bē·nā′shŭs), *adj.*

ver′bi·age (vûr′bĭ·ĭj), *n.* [F. See VERB.] Use of many words without necessity, or with little sense; verbosity; wordiness.

verb′i·fy (vûr′bĭ·fī), *v. t.* To make into or use as a verb.

ver·bose′ (vûr·bōs′), *adj.* [L. *verbosus,* fr. *verbum* word.] Abounding in words; given to or marked by verbiage; prolix; wordy. — **Syn.** See WORDY. — **ver·bose′ly,** *adv.* — **ver·bose′ness,** *n.*

ver·bos′i·ty (-bŏs′ĭ·tĭ), *n.* Verboseness; prolixity; wordiness.

‖**ver·bo′ten** (fĕr·bō′tĕn; *Angl.* vĕr·bō′t'n), *adj.* [G., past part. of *verbieten.*] Literally, forbidden; prohibited by authority; — often used satirically.

‖**ver′bum sat sa′pi·en′ti (est)** (vûr′bŭm săt săp′ĭ·ĕn′tī (ĕst)). [L.] A word to the wise (is) sufficient. Abbr. *verbum sap.*

ver′dan·cy (vûr′dăn·sĭ), *n.* Verdant appearance or state.

ver′dant (-dănt), *adj.* [From *verdure,* or fr. F. *verdoyant,* pres. part. of *verdoyer* to be verdant, grow green, ult. fr. L. *viridis* green.] **1.** Green with growing plants or grass; covered with fresh vegetation. **2.** *Colloq.* Unsophisticated; raw; green; as, a *verdant* youth. — **ver′dant·ly,** *adv.*

verd an·tique′ (vûrd′ ăn·tēk′). [F. *vert antique* a kind of marble, fr. *verd, vert,* green + *antique* ancient.] *Petrog.* **a** A green mottled or veined serpentine marble, or calcareous serpentine, much used for indoor decoration, esp. by the ancient Romans. **b** An andesite porphyry showing crystals of feldspar in a dark-green groundmass; — called ***Oriental verd antique.***

ver′der·er, ver′der·or (vûr′dĕr·ĕr), *n.* [For *verder,* fr. F. *verdier,* fr. L. *viridis* green.] *Early Eng. Law.* A judicial officer having charge of the king's forest.

ver′dict (vûr′dĭkt), *n.* [OF. *veirdit, voirdit,* prop., a true saying, fr. *veir, voir,* true (fr. L. *verus*) + *dit* a saying (fr. L. *dictum* a thing said).] **1.** *Law.* The finding or decision of a jury on the matter submitted in trial. **2.** Decision; judgment; opinion pronounced.

ver′di·gris (vûr′dĭ·grēs; -grĭs; -grē), *n.* [OF. *vert de Grice* or *Grece,* lit., green of Greece.] **1. a** A green or greenish-blue poisonous pigment and drug, obtained by the action of acetic acid on copper, consisting of one or more basic copper acetates. **b** Normal copper acetate, $Cu(C_2H_3O_2)_2H_2O$. **2.** A green or bluish deposit, esp. of copper carbonate, formed on copper, brass, or bronze surfaces.

ver′din (vûr′dĭn), *n.* [F., yellowhammer.] A very small yellow-headed titmouse (*Auriparus flaviceps*) found from Texas to California and southward.

ver′di·ter (vûr′dĭ·tĕr), *n.* [F. *vert-de-terre,* lit., green of earth.] **a** *Obs.* Verdigris. **b** Either of two basic carbonates of copper used as pigments, and prepared by grinding azurite (giving ***blue verditer***) and malachite (giving ***green verditer***) or artificially; bice.

ver′dure (vûr′dŭr), *n.* [OF., fr. *verd* green. See VERDANT.] **1.** Greenness, esp. of vegetation; also, such vegetation itself; a green growth. **2.** Hence, vigorous condition; good health; freshness and strength. — **ver′dur·ous** (-dŭr·ŭs), *adj.* — **ver′dur·ous·ness,** *n.*

ver′e·cund (vĕr′ē·kŭnd), *adj.* [L. *verecundus.*] Bashful.

‖**Ver·ein′** (fĕr·īn′), *n.* [G.] An association; a society.

verge (vûrj), *n.* [OF. *verge,* fr. L. *virga.*] **1.** A rod or staff carried as an emblem of authority or as a symbol of office. **2.** The stick or wand with which persons were formerly admitted tenants, they holding it and swearing fealty. **3.** The shaft of a column, or a small ornamental shaft. **4.** [From sense 8.] A border, limit, or boundary; edge, margin, or brink. **5.** A circumference; hence, an enclosing or encircling thing, as a ring. **6.** The edge of the tiling projecting over a gable. **7.** *Horol.* The spindle of a watch balance, esp. one with pallets. **8.** *Law.* The area or limit within which certain high officials, as the marshal, of the king's household had special jurisdiction. — **Syn.** See BORDER. — *v. i.;* VERGED (vûrjd); VERG′ING (vûr′jĭng). **1.** To be on the verge, or border. **2.** To be contiguous; as, streets *verging* on Fifth Avenue.

verge, *v. i.* [L. *vergere* to bend, turn.] **1.** To tend; incline; as, a hill *verges* to the north. **2.** To be passing (*into*); approach in transition, gradation, etc.; as, a dark red *verging* on purple.

ver′ger (vûr′jĕr), *n.* [F., fr. *verge* rod.] One who carries a verge, or emblem of office; specif.: **a** *Eng.* An attendant on a bishop, a dean, a justice, etc. **b** An official who takes care of the interior of a church building.

ve·rid′i·cal (vē·rĭd′ĭ·kăl), *adj.* [L. *veridicus,* fr. *verus* true + *dicere* to say, tell.] **a** Veracious; accurate. **b** Genuine. — **ve·rid′i·cal′i·ty** (-kăl′ĭ·tĭ), *n.* — **ve·rid′i·cal·ly,** *adv.*

ver′i·fy (vĕr′ĭ·fī), *v. t.;* -FIED (-fīd); -FY′ING. [OF. *verifier,* fr. ML. *verificare,* fr. L. *verus* true + *-ficare* to make.] **1.** To prove to be true; to confirm; substantiate. **2.** To check or test the accuracy or exactness of. **3.** To authenticate; specif., *Law,* to confirm or substantiate by oath or proof; also, to add a verification, or statement that the pleader is ready to prove his allegations, to (a pleading, etc.). — **Syn.** See CONFIRM. — **ver′i·fi′a·ble** (-fī′ȧ·b'l), *adj.* — **ver′i·fi·ca′tion** (-fĭ·kā′shŭn), *n.* — **ver′i·fi·ca′tive** (vĕr′ĭ·fĭ·kā′tĭv), *adj.* — **ver′i·fi′er** (-fī′ĕr), *n.*

ver′i·ly (vĕr′ĭ·lĭ), *adv.* [From VERY.] **1.** In very truth; beyond question; certainly. **2.** Truly; confidently.

ver′i·sim′i·lar (vĕr′ĭ·sĭm′ĭ·lĕr), *adj.* [L. *verisimilis, veri similis,* fr. *verus* true (gen. *veri*) + *similis* like.] Having the appearance of truth or reality; probable; likely. — **ver′i·sim′i·lar·ly,** *adv.*

ver′i·si·mil′i·tude (-sĭ·mĭl′ĭ·tūd), *n.* [L. *verisimilitudo.*] Quality or state of being verisimilar; appearance of truth; also, something, as a statement, that is verisimilar. — **Syn.** See TRUTH.

ver′ism (vēr′ĭz'm), *n.* [L. *verus* true.] The theory that in art and literature the ugly and the vulgar have their place on the grounds of truth and aesthetic value. — **ver′ist** (-ĭst), *n. & adj.* — **ve·ris′tic** (vē·rĭs′tĭk), *adj.*

ver′i·ta·ble (vĕr′ĭ·tȧ·b'l), *adj.* [F. *véritable.*] Agreeable to truth or to fact; actual; real; true; genuine. — **Syn.** See AUTHENTIC. — **ver′i·ta·ble·ness,** *n.* — **ver′i·ta·bly,** *adv.*

ver′i·ty (vĕr′ĭ·tĭ), *n.; pl.* -TIES (-tĭz). [OF. *verité, veritet,* fr. L. *veritas,* fr. *verus* true.] **1.** Quality or state of being true, or real; consonance of a statement, proposition, or the like, with fact; truth; reality. **2.** That which is true; a truth; a reality. — **Syn.** See TRUTH.

ver′juice′ (vûr′jōōs′; 114), *n.* [OF. *verjus, vert jus,* lit., green juice juice of green fruits, fr. *vert* green + *jus* juice.] **1.** The sour juice of crab apples, unripe grapes, apples, etc., or an acid liquor made from it. **2.** Tartness; sourness, as of disposition.

ver′meil (vûr′mĭl; -m'l), *n.* [OF., vermilion, fr. L. *vermiculus* a little worm, fr. *vermis* worm.] **1.** *Now Poetic.* Vermilion, or its bright red color. **2.** Gilded silver, bronze, or copper. — **ver′meil,** *adj.*

vermi-. [L. *vermis.*] A combining form meaning *worm,* as in **ver′mi·cide, ver′mi·cule.**

ver′mi·cel′li (vûr′mĭ·sĕl′ĭ; -chĕl′ĭ), *n.* [It., pl. of *vermicello,* lit., a little worm, dim. of *verme* a worm, fr. L. *vermis.*] A paste like spaghetti, but made in finer cords.

ver·mic′u·lar (vûr·mĭk′ū·lĕr), *adj.* [L. *vermiculus* a little worm, dim. of *vermis* worm.] **1.** Wormlike in form or motion. **2.** Vermiculate, or vermiculated. — **ver·mic′u·lar·ly,** *adv.*

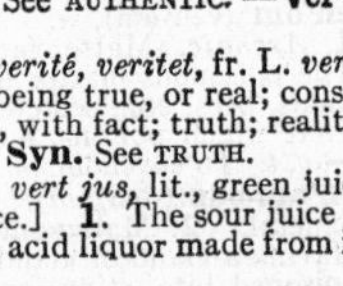
Vermiculated Work.

ver·mic′u·late (-lāt), *v. t.* [L. *vermiculatus* inlaid so as to resemble the tracks of worms, deriv. of *vermiculus* a little worm.] **1.** To infest with worms; cause to become worm-eaten. **2.** To form or work, as by inlaying, with irregular lines or impressions like worm tracks. — (-lāt), *adj.* **1.** Vermiculated in markings or design. **2.** Crawling or twisting like a worm; hence, insinuating; sophistical. **3.** Full of worms; worm-eaten. — **ver·mic′u·la′tion** (-lā′shŭn), *n.*

ver·mic′u·lite (-līt), *n.* [L. *vermiculus,* dim. of *vermis* worm.] *Mineral.* Any of a number of micaceous minerals, hydrous silicates derived generally from alteration of mica.

ver′mi·form (vûr′mĭ·fôrm), *adj.* [*vermi-* + *-form.*] Resembling a worm in shape.

vermiform appendix. *Anat.* A narrow blind tube about three or four inches long and about ⅓ inch in diameter, extending from the caecum (of which it represents an atrophied terminal part), in the lower right-hand part of the abdomen. Cf. APPENDICITIS.

vermiform process. *Anat.* **a** The part of the median lobe of the cerebellum which appears on the upper or lower surface of the cerebellum. **b** The median lobe or part of the cerebellum. **c** The vermiform appendix.

ver′mi·fuge (vûr′mĭ·fūj), *adj. & n.* [*vermi-* + *-fuge.*] *Med.* Anthelmintic.

ver·mil′ion (vĕr·mĭl′yŭn), *n.* [OF. *vermillon,* fr. *vermeil.* See VERMEIL.] **1. a** A bright-red pigment consisting of mercuric sulfide. **b** Any of certain other red pigments. **2.** A red color like the pigment; one of several colors yellowish-red in hue, that vary in degree of yellow, but are, on the average, of very high saturation and medium brilliance. See COLOR. — *adj.* Of the color vermilion. — *v. t.* To color or tint with or as with vermilion.

ver′min (vûr′mĭn), *n. sing. & pl.; chiefly as pl.* [OF. *vermin, vermine,* fr. L. *vermis* worm.] **1.** Any noxious or disgusting animal; esp., such an animal, or such animals collectively, when of small size, of common occurrence, and difficult to control, as flies, lice, bedbugs, rats, mice, weasels, etc.; also, *Eng.*, birds and animals which prey upon game. **2.** A noxious or offensive person, or such persons collectively.

ver′mi·na′tion (vûr′mĭ·nā′shŭn), *n.* **1.** Infestation with worms or vermin. **2.** Growth or multiplication of vermin by breeding; — esp. of parasites.

ver′min·ous (vûr′mĭ·nŭs), *adj.* **1.** Consisting of vermin; of the nature of vermin. **2.** Tending to breed vermin; infested by vermin. **3.** Caused by vermin; as, *verminous* disease. — **ver′min·ous·ly,** *adv.* — **ver′min·ous·ness,** *n.*

ver·mouth′ (vẽr·mo͞oth′; vûr′mo͞oth), *n.* [F. *vermout*, fr. G. *wermut(h).*] A white wine highly flavored with aromatic herbs and sometimes sweetened.

ver·nac′u·lar (vẽr·năk′ū·lẽr), *adj.* [L. *vernaculus* born in one's house, native, fr. *verna* a slave born in his master's house, a native.] **1.** Belonging to or developed in a particular place, region, or country; native; indigenous; esp., spoken or used by the people of a particular place, country, etc.; as, English is our *vernacular* tongue. **2.** Belonging to, or written in, or using, the native, as opposed to the literary, language; as, *vernacular* poets or poetry; *vernacular* words. **3.** Characteristic of a locality; local; as, a *vernacular* disease. **4.** Applied to a plant or animal in the common native speech, as distinguished from the Latin nomenclature of scientific classification; as, winterberry is a *vernacular* name of *Ilex verticillata.* — *n.* **1.** The vernacular language; one's mother tongue; often, the common mode of expression in a particular locality, or, by extension, in a particular trade, etc. **2.** A vernacular word or term; specif., a vernacular name of a plant or animal. — **Syn.** See DIALECT. — **ver·nac′u·lar·ly,** *adv.*

ver·nac′u·lar·ism (-ĭz′m), *n.* **1.** A vernacular word or idiom. **2.** Use of vernacular language.

ver′nal (vûr′năl; -n'l), *adj.* [L. *vernalis*, fr. *vernus* vernal, fr. *ver* spring.] **1.** Of, pertaining to, appearing, or occurring in the spring; as, the *vernal* equinox or point (see EQUINOX, 1). **2.** Springlike as in freshness; hence, youthful. — **ver′nal·ly,** *adv.*

ver′nal·ize (-īz), *v. t.* *Chiefly Agric.* To induce premature flowering and fruiting of (a plant) by artificial treatment of the seed or bulb to delay seed germination, as by exposure for a fixed period to low temperature in darkness. — **ver′nal·i·za′tion** (-ĭ·zā′shŭn; -ī·zā′-), *n.*

ver·na′tion (vûr·nā′shŭn), *n.* [NL. *vernatio*, fr. L. *vernare* to flourish, be verdant.] *Bot.* The disposition or method of arrangement of foliage leaves within the bud. Cf. ESTIVATION.

Ver′ner's law (vĕr′nẽrz). *Philol.* A statement, propounded by the Danish philologist Karl Verner in 1875, explaining certain apparent exceptions to Grimm's law by the original position of the accent. For example, the Germanic *h, th, f,* resulting by Grimm's law from Indo-European *k, t, p,* became voiced and ultimately gave *g, d, b,* if the principal accent did not originally rest on the immediately preceding syllable.

ver′ni·er (vûr′nĭ·ẽr), *n.* [After Pierre *Vernier* (1580–1637), French mathematician.] **1.** Also **vernier scale.** A short scale made to slide along the divisions of a graduated instrument, to indicate parts of divisions. **2.** *Physics.* A small auxiliary device used with a main device, to obtain fine adjustment, as a variable condenser of very small capacity in parallel with another condenser. — *adj.* Having or comprising a vernier, as in **vernier compass, gauge,** *or* **telescope.**

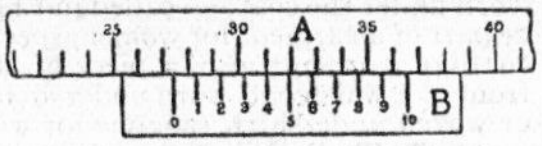

Vernier. *A* Regular Scale; *B* Vernier Scale, indicating a measurement of 27.4.

vernier caliper *or* **calipers.** *Mech.* A caliper rule with vernier attachment and adjusting screw, for very fine measurement.

Ver′o·nal (vĕr′ō·năl), *n.* A trade-mark applied to the hypnotic barbital.

ve·ron′i·ca (vē·rŏn′ĭ·kȧ), *n.* [ML.] **1.** An image of the face of Christ on a cloth; — from the legend that Veronica, one of the women following Christ up Calvary, wiped his bleeding face and found his image impressed on her handkerchief. **2.** [*often cap.*] The supposed handkerchief of Veronica, preserved at Rome.

ve·ron′i·ca, *n.* [NL., from the name of the saint.] The speedwell.

ver·ru′ca (vĕ·ro͞o′kȧ), *n.; pl.* -CAE (-sē). [L.] **a** *Med.* A wart. **b** *Zool.* A wartlike elevation.

ver′ru·cose (vĕr′o͝o·kōs), *adj.* [L. *verrucosus*, fr. *verruca* wart.] Covered with wartlike elevations; warty; as, a *verrucose* capsule. — **ver′ru·cos′i·ty** (-kŏs′ĭ·tĭ), *n.*

ver′ru·ca′no (vĕr′o͝o·kä′nō), *n.* [It., fr. Mt. *Verruca* near Pisa, Italy.] *Geol.* A stratified rock (Carboniferous in part) in the Alps, the age of which is not definitely known.

ver′sant (vûr′sănt), *n.* [F.] The slope of a side of a mountain chain; hence, general slope of a country; inclination.

ver′sa·tile (vûr′sȧ·tĭl; -tīl; 56), *adj.* [F. or L.; F., fr. L. *versatilis*, fr. *versare* to turn around.] **1.** *Now Rare.* **a** Capable of being turned round. **b** Changeable; variable; fickle. **2.** Turning with ease from one thing to another; having many aptitudes; many-sided; as, *versatile* genius. **3.** *Bot.* Attached at or near the middle, so as to swing freely; as, a *versatile* anther. **4.** *Zool.* **a** Capable of turning forward or backward; reversible; as, a *versatile* toe of a bird. **b** Capable of moving laterally and up and down, as antennae. — **ver′sa·tile·ly,** *adv.* — **ver′sa·tile·ness,** *n.*

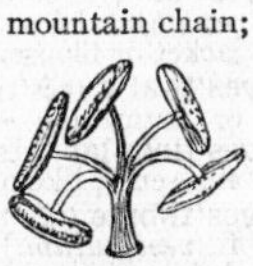
Versatile Anthers of Passionflower.

ver′sa·til′i·ty (vûr′sȧ·tĭl′ĭ·tĭ), *n.; pl.* VERSATILITIES (-tĭz). Quality or state of being versatile; esp., ability along many lines of effort; many-sidedness.

Syn. **Versatile, many-sided, all-round** mean having several skills or abilities. **Versatile** implies aptitude for many employments and facility in turning to any of these; **many-sided,** breadth of interests as well as variety of gifts; **all-round,** completeness and symmetry of development as a human being and as an individual.

‖**vers de so′cié′té′** (vâr′ dē sô′syā′tā′). [F.] = SOCIETY VERSE.

verse (vûrs), *n.* [AS. *fers*, combined with F. *vers*, both fr. L. *versus* a furrow, a row, a line in writing, and, in poetry, a verse, fr. *vertere, versum,* to turn, to turn round.] **1.** *Pros.* **a** A line of poetry having, usually, a determined metrical or rhythmical pattern. **b** Metrical writing; that which is composed in measured rhythms; hence, poetry; a poem. **c** Metrical structure or form; versification; type of meter; as, heroic *verse.* **2.** A short division of any composition; specif., a stanza. **3.** *Bib.* One of the short divisions of the chapters in the Old and New Testaments. Abbr. *v.*

versed (vûrst), *adj.* Acquainted or familiar from experience, study, practice, etc.; skilled; practiced.

versed, *adj.* [L. *versus* turned, past part. of *vertere.*] *Math.* Turned; as, a **versed sine,** that part of the diameter of a unit circle between the foot of the sine and the arc; the remainder on subtracting the cosine of an angle from unity.

ver′si·cle (vûr′sĭ·k'l), *n.* [L. *versiculus*, dim. of *versus.*] A little verse; specif., a short verse or sentence said or sung by the priest or minister, and followed by a response from the people; — indicated by the sign ℣.

ver′si·col′or, ver′si·col′our (-kŭl′ẽr), *adj.* [L. *versicolor*, fr. *versare* to change + *color* color.] **1.** Having various colors; variegated; parti-colored. **2.** Changeable in color; iridescent; as, *versicolor* silk.

ver·sic′u·lar (vûr·sĭk′ū·lẽr), *adj.* [See VERSICLE.] Of or pertaining to verses, esp. verses of a book as the Bible; designating distinct divisions of a writing.

ver′si·fi·ca′tion (vûr′sĭ·fĭ·kā′shŭn), *n.* **1.** The making of verses; the act, art, or practice of metrical composition. **2.** Metrical structure; prosody.

ver′si·fy (vûr′sĭ·fī), *v. i.;* -FIED (-fīd); -FY′ING. [OF. *versifier*, fr. L. *versificare*, fr. *versus* a verse + *-ficare* to make.] To make verses; write verse. — *v. t.* **1.** To turn into verse; esp., to turn from prose form to verse form. **2.** To relate or describe in verse. — **ver′si·fi′er** (-fī′ẽr), *n.*

ver′sine (vûr′sīn), *n.* Also **ver′sin** (-sīn). *Math.* = VERSED SINE.

ver′sion (vûr′shŭn; *in senses* 3 & 4 *commonly* -zhŭn *in U. S.*), *n.* [F., fr. ML. *versio*, fr. L. *vertere, versum,* to turn, change, translate.] **1.** *Obs.* A change of form, direction, or the like. **2.** Act of translating; translation, as of a word, a passage, a book. **3.** A translation; specif., a translation or rendering of the Bible or a part of it; as, the Authorized and Douay *versions.* **4.** An account or description from a particular point of view, esp. as contrasted with another account; as, two *versions* of an affair. **5.** *Med.* A condition of the uterus in which its axis is deflected from its normal position without being bent upon itself. — **ver′sion·al** (-ăl), *adj.*

vers li′bre (vâr′ lē′br′). [F.] Literally, free verse; rhythmical or cadenced, as distinguished from metrical and rhymed, verse.

vers li′brist (lē′brĭst), *or* ‖**vers li′briste′** (lē′brēst′). [F. *vers-libriste.*] A writer of vers libre.

ver′so (vûr′sō), *n.; pl.* -SOS (-sōz). [L., abl. of *versus*, past part. of *vertere* to turn.] **1.** The reverse, or left-hand, page of a book or a folded sheet of paper; — opposed to *recto.* **2.** The reverse, as of a coin; — opposed to *obverse.*

verst (vûrst; vĕrst), *n.* [Russ. *versta* verst, row, line.] A Russian measure of length, equal to 0.6629 mile, or 1.067 kilometers.

ver′sus (vûr′sŭs), *prep.* [L., toward, turned in the direction of, fr. *vertere, versum,* to turn.] Against, as in legal action, a contest, etc.; as, the case of John Doe *versus* (or *v.* or *vs.*) Richard Roe; Harvard *versus* Yale at football; hence, as considered in contrast to or as the alternative of; as, to debate the question of free trade *versus* protection. Abbr. *v.* or *vs.*

vert (vûrt), *n.* [OF., green, fr. L. *viridis.*] **1.** *Eng. Forest Law.* **a** Everything that bears a green leaf within the forest, esp. great and thick coverts. **b** The right or privilege of cutting growing wood in a forest. **2.** *Her.* The color green.

ver′te·bra (vûr′tē·brȧ), *n.; pl.* -BRAE (-brē), -BRAS (-brȧz). [L., fr. *vertere* to turn, change.] One of the segments composing the spinal column. In some of the lower vertebrates each vertebra consists of several distinct elements or pieces which never become united. In the higher vertebrates a typical vertebra has a short, more or less cylindrical, body or *centrum,* whose ends articulate by means of disks or pads of elastic fibrous or cartilaginous tissue with the centra of the adjacent vertebrae.

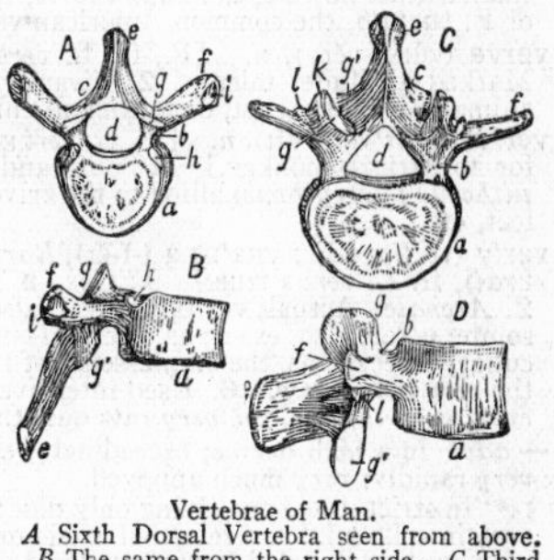
Vertebrae of Man.
A Sixth Dorsal Vertebra seen from above. *B* The same from the right side. *C* Third Lumbar Vertebra from above. *D* The same from the right side. *a* Centrum, or Body; *b* Pedicle forming the Side of the Neural Arch; *c* Lamina forming the Top of the Neural Arch; *d* Spinal Foramen; *e* Spinous Process; *f* Transverse Process; *g* Anterior Articular Process; *g′* Posterior Articular Process; *h* Flat Surface of Head of Rib; *i* Facet for Tubercle of Rib; *k* Projecting Tubercle; *l* a Dorsal Process. See also THORAX, *Illust.*

ver′te·bral (-brăl), *adj.* *Anat. & Zool.* **a** Of or pertaining to a vertebra, vertebrae, or the vertebral column; spinal. **b** Composed of, or having, vertebrae.

vertebral column. The spinal column; the backbone.

ver′te·brate (vûr′tē·brāt), *adj.* [L. *vertebratus.*] Having a backbone, or spinal column; also, of, pertaining to, found in, or characteristic of vertebrates. — *n.* *Zool.* One of a comprehensive division (Vertebrata, now usually regarded as a subphylum) of animals, containing all those with a segmented spinal column together with a few more primitive forms in which the backbone is represented by a notochord.

ver′te·bra′tion (-brā′shŭn), *n.* Segmentation into vertebrae or divisions like vertebrae.

ver′te·bro- (vûr′tē·brō-), **vertebr-.** [For *vertebra.*] A combining form denoting: **a** *The vertebrae.* **b** *Vertebral and,* as **ver′te·bro·cos′tal.**

ver′tex (vûr′tĕks), *n.; pl.* VERTEXES (-tĕk·sĕz; -sĭz), VERTICES (-tĭ·sēz). [L. *vertex, -icis,* a whirl, the pole of the heavens, top, fr. *vertere* to turn.] **1.** The principal or highest point; top; summit; apex. **2.** *Anat. & Zool.* The top of the head. **3.** *Astron.* The zenith. **4.** *Craniom.* The highest point on the skull. **5.** *Math.* In any figure having a base, the point opposite to, and farthest from, the base; the top; the terminating point of some particular line or lines in a figure or curve, as where the sides of an angle meet, or where a curve (or surface) meets its axis.

ver'ti·cal (vûr'tĭ·kăl), *adj.* **1.** Of or pertaining to the vertex; situated at the vertex, or highest point; directly overhead, or in the zenith. **2.** Perpendicular to the plane of the horizon; upright; plumb. **3.** *Bot.* **a** At right angles to the plane of the supporting surface. **b** In the direction of the axis; lengthwise. **4.** *Econ.* Composed of or consolidating concerns engaged in different stages of manufacture or distribution of a product, such as steel, as in **vertical combination, merger,** *or* **trust.**

Syn. Vertical, perpendicular, plumb mean located actually or seemingly at a right angle to the plane of the horizon. Though **vertical** suggests an upward rising as to the zenith, and **perpendicular** a downward falling as to the center of the earth, the former is more often used abstractly or figuratively, and the latter in application to concrete things; **plumb,** an artisan's term, is used when testing the exact perpendicularity of something.

— *n.* **1.** A vertical line, plane, or circle; esp., a perpendicular. **2.** A vertical member in a truss. — **ver'ti·cal'i·ty** (-kăl'ĭ·tĭ), **ver'ti·cal·ness,** *n.* — **ver'ti·cal·ly,** *adv.*

vertical circle. *Astron.* Any great circle of the celestial sphere whose plane is perpendicular to that of the horizon. See CIRCLE, *n.,* 10.

vertical envelopment. *Mil.* Seizure by paratroops and air-borne infantry of airports, bridges, and other strategic points and communication centers behind the enemy defense line, in conjunction with infiltration of the line by mechanized ground forces.

vertical union. = INDUSTRIAL UNION.

ver'ti·ces (vûr'tĭ·sēz), *n., pl.* of VERTEX.

ver'ti·cil (vûr'tĭ·sĭl), *n.* [L. *verticillus,* dim. of *vertex* whirl.] *Bot.* A circle of similar parts, as leaves, flowers, or inflorescences, about the same point on the axis; a whorl. See INVOLUCRE, *Illust.*

ver'ti·cil·las'ter (vûr'tĭ·sĭ·lăs'tẽr), *n.* [NL., fr. L. *verticillus* a whirl + 2d *-aster.*] *Bot.* A mixed inflorescence consisting of a pair of much-condensed, nearly sessile cymes, disposed around the axis like a true verticil, as in many mints. See INFLORESCENCE, *Illust.* (11).

ver·tic'il·late (vûr·tĭs'ĭ·lāt; vûr'tĭ·sĭl'āt), *adj.* Also **ver·tic'il·lat'ed** (-lāt'ĕd; -ĭd). Disposed in verticils; whorled; arranged in a transverse whorl or whorls like the spokes of a wheel; as, *verticillate* leaves; a *verticillate* shell. — **ver·tic'il·late·ly,** *adv.* — **ver·tic'il·la'tion** (-lā'shŭn), *n.*

ver·tic'i·ty (vûr·tĭs'ĭ·tĭ), *n.* Tendency to turn toward a magnetic pole, as shown by a magnetized needle.

ver·tig'i·nous (-tĭj'ĭ·nŭs), *adj.* [L. *vertiginosus,* fr. *vertigo* a whirling around, giddiness.] **1.** Turning round; rotary; revolving. **2.** Affected with vertigo; giddy; dizzy. **3.** Causing, or tending to cause, dizziness.

ver'ti·go (vûr'tĭ·gō; *by some, as Lat.,* vẽr·tī'gō *or* -tē'gō), *n.; pl.* -GOES (-gōz), VERTIGINES (vẽr·tĭj'ĭ·nēz). [L., fr. *vertere* to turn.] **1.** *Med.* Dizziness or swimming of the head; giddiness. **2.** *Veter.* Staggers (in horses), gid (in sheep), or the like.

ver·tim'e·ter (vûr·tĭm'ē·tẽr), *n.* [*vertical* + *-meter.*] An instrument which indicates the rate of rise and fall of an aircraft.

ver·tu' (vûr·tōō'; vûr'tōō). Var. of VIRTU.

Ver·tum'nus (vẽr·tŭm'nŭs), *or* **Vor·tum'nus** (vôr-), *n.* [L., fr. *vertere* to turn.] *Rom. Relig.* God of the changing season and of developing vegetation.

ver'vain (vûr'vān), *n.* [OF. *verveine,* fr. L. *verbena,* pl. *verbenae* sacred boughs of laurel, olive, or myrtle, a class of plants.] Any of a genus (*Verbena*) of plants of the verbena family; esp., any species with small spicate flowers, as *V. officinalis,* the common vervain of Europe, or *V. hastata,* the common American vervain.

verve (vûrv; vĕrv), *n.* [F., fr. L. *verba,* pl. of *verbum* word.] **1.** Marked aptitude; talent. **2.** Vivacity of imagination, esp. such as animates a poet, artist, or musician; enthusiasm; spirit.

ver'vet (vûr'vĕt; -vĭt), *n.* [F., fr. *vert* green + *grivet,* an earlier name for an African monkey.] A South and East African guenon (*Cercopithecus pygerythrus*) allied to the grivet, but with black chin, hands, feet, etc.

ver'y (vĕr'ĭ), *adj.;* VER'I·ER (-ĭ·ẽr), *Rare;* VER'I·EST. [OF. *verai* (F. *vrai*), fr. L. *verus* true.] **1.** *Obs.* **a** True. **b** Truthful; veracious. **2.** *Archaic.* Actual; veritable; real; also, lawful; legitimate. **3.** Absolute; utter; also, exact; as, the *veriest* fool; the *very* truth. **4.** Peculiar; especial; as, the *very* essence of truth. **5.** Identical; same; as, the *very* man I saw. **6.** Used intensively in a sense corresponding to *even, even the;* as, the *very* rats quit the ship. — **Syn.** See SAME.

— *adv.* In a high degree; exceedingly; extremely; as, a *very* cold day; *very* rapidly; *very* much annoyed.

☞ In strict usage qualifying only descriptive adjectives and adverbs, *very* in colloquial and informal use is made to qualify also participles with weakened verbal force that denote a physical or mental state; as, in a *very* torn condition [strictly, badly or severely torn]; his look became *very* troubled [strictly, much or deeply troubled].

Ver'y's, *or* **Ver'y, night signals** (vĕr'ĭz, vĕr'ĭ). [After Edward W. *Very,* who invented it in 1877.] *Mil. & Naut.* A system of signaling in which balls of red and green fire (**Very lights**) are fired from a pistol.

‖**ve·si'ca** (vē·sī'kȧ), *n.; pl.* -CAE (-sē). [L.] *Anat.* A bladder.

ves'i·cal (vĕs'ĭ·kăl), *adj.* Of or pertaining to a bladder, esp., *Anat.,* the urinary bladder.

ves'i·cant (-kănt), *adj. & n.* [L. *vesica* blister.] *Med.* Vesicatory.

ves'i·cate (-kāt), *v. t. & i.* *Med.* To blister. — **ves'i·ca'tion** (-kā'shŭn), *n.*

ves'i·ca·to'ry (vĕs'ĭ·kȧ·tō'rĭ; *by some,* vē·sĭk'ȧ·tō'rĭ; -tẽr·ĭ), *adj.* Tending, or having the power, to blister. — *n.; pl.* -RIES (-rĭz). A blistering application or plaster.

ves'i·cle (vĕs'ĭ·k'l), *n.* [F. or L.; F. *vésicule,* fr. L. *vesicula,* dim. of *vesica* a bladder, blister.] **1.** A bladderlike vessel; a membranous cavity; a cyst; a cell. **2.** *Anat. & Zool.* A cavity or sac, esp. one filled with fluid. **3.** *Bot.* A small bladderlike air cavity within the tissues. **4.** *Med.* A small circular elevation of the cuticle, containing a clear watery fluid; a blister. **5.** *Geol.* A small cavity in a mineral or rock.

ves'i·co- (vĕs'ĭ·kō-). [L. *vesica* bladder, blister.] A combining form denoting: **a** *The bladder,* as in **ves'i·cot'o·my.** **b** *Vesical and,* as in **ves'i·co·ab·dom'i·nal.**

ve·sic'u·lar (vē·sĭk'ū·lẽr), *adj.* **1.** Of or pertaining to a vesicle or vesicles; specif., *Med.,* of or pertaining to the air cells (alveoli) of the lungs. **2.** Having the form or structure of a vesicle. **3.** Containing, composed of, or characterized by vesicles; vesiculate. — **ve·sic'u·lar·ly,** *adv.*

ve·sic'u·late (-lāt), *adj.* Containing, or covered with, vesicles; also, vesicular in structure. — (-lāt), *v. t.* To form vesicles in, as lava. — *v. i.* To become vesicular. — **ve·sic'u·la'tion** (-lā'shŭn), *n.*

ves'per (vĕs'pẽr), *n.* [L.] **1.** [*cap.*] The evening star; Hesperus; Venus, as evening star. **2.** The evening; eventide. **3.** A vesper prayer, hymn, or service; also, a vesper bell. **4.** *pl.* See VESPERS. — *adj.* Of or pertaining to the evening or the service of vespers.

ves'per·al (-ăl), *n.* **1.** A book containing the office and music for vespers. **2.** A cover for an altar cloth between ceremonies.

ves'pers (vĕs'pẽrz), *n. pl.* [OF. *vespres,* fr. ML. *vesperae,* fr. L. *vespera* evening.] **1.** *Eccl.* [*often cap.*] The sixth and next to the last of the canonical hours; the office or service for this time. **2.** [*often cap.*] A late afternoon or evening service; specif.: **a** *R.C.Ch.* A public chanting of vespers (sense 1) in the later afternoon or the evening of Sundays and holydays. **b** *Anglican Communion.* A service of evening prayer; evensong.

ves'per·til'i·o·nine (vĕs'pẽr·tĭl'ĭ·ō·nīn; -nĭn), *adj.* [L. *vespertilio* a bat.] Belonging to a family (Vespertilionidae) of bats, including the majority of the common bats of temperate regions. — **ves'per·til'i·o·nid** (-nĭd), *n. & adj.*

ves'per·tine (vĕs'pẽr·tĭn; -tīn), *adj.* Also **ves'per·ti'nal** (-tī'năl; -n'l). [L. *vespertinus.*] **1.** Of or pertaining to the evening; active at, or flourishing in, the evening. **2.** *Bot.* Blossoming in the evening. **3.** *Zool.* Active or flying in early evening; crepuscular.

ves'pi·ar'y (vĕs'pĭ·ẽr'ĭ *or, esp. Brit.,* -ẽr·ĭ), *n.; pl.* -IES (-ĭz). [From L. *vespa* wasp, after *apiary.*] A nest of any of the social wasps, or the colony of wasps inhabiting it.

ves'pid (vĕs'pĭd), *n.* [NL., fr. L. *vespa* wasp + *-id.*] *Zool.* A member of a cosmopolitan family (Vespidae) comprising the social wasps, which live in colonies like bees. The type genus (*Vespa*) includes the common hornets and yellow jackets (see these terms). — *adj.* Of or pertaining to a vespid.

ves'pine (vĕs'pīn; -pĭn), *adj.* *Zool.* Of, like, or pertaining to a wasp, esp. to a vespid wasp.

ves'sel (vĕs''l), *n.* [OF. *vessel, vessele,* fr. L. *vascellum,* pl. *vascella,* dim. of *vas* vessel.] **1.** A hollow or concave utensil for holding anything; a hollow receptacle, as a hogshead, barrel, bottle, kettle, cup, bowl, etc. **2.** Any structure, esp. a hollow one, made to float upon the water for navigation; a craft for navigating the water, usually, specif., one larger than a common rowboat; as, a war *vessel;* a passenger *vessel.* **3.** Hence, any of various types of aircraft; an airship. **4.** A person regarded, esp. in scriptural language, as one into whom something is poured, infused, etc.; as, a *vessel* of grace. **5.** *Anat. & Zool.* A tube or canal in which a fluid is contained and circulated, as one of the veins. **6.** *Bot.* A tube or duct for water conduction.

vest (vĕst), *n.* [F. *veste,* fr. It. *veste,* fr. L. *vestis* a garment, vesture.] **1.** *Archaic.* A robe; sometimes, an ecclesiastical vestment. **2.** Any outer covering; array; garb; dress. **3.** A garment for men, varying in style at different times; specif.: **a** *Obs. exc. Hist.* A long cassocklike garment worn in the time of Charles II. **b** A sleeveless body garment worn under the coat; — called in England a *waistcoat.* **4.** A garment or part of a garment for women; specif.: **a** A type of jacket. **b** A waistcoatlike garment; also, a piece of facing or trimming resembling the front of a waistcoat, worn under an open bodice or coat. **5.** A knitted or woven undershirt, esp. one for women.

— *v. t.* **1.** To clothe; dress; robe; esp., to garb or dress in ecclesiastical vestments. **2.** To clothe (with authority, power, or the like); invest; endow; as, to *vest* a court with power to try cases of life and death. **3.** To place or give into the possession or discretion of some person or authority; commit to another; as, power of life and death is *vested* in the courts. — *v. i.* **1.** To put on vestments or garments. **2.** To become vested; to be fixed; to take effect or pass, as a title or right so that there is a present right of enjoyment or future enjoyment; — often followed by *in;* as, upon the death of the father, the estate *vests* in the heir-at-law.

Ves'ta (vĕs'tȧ), *n.* [L.] **1.** *Rom. Relig.* The goddess of the hearth and its fire, and hence of cookery. Her temple symbolized the hearth of the city and contained a fire, rekindled on the day (March 1) beginning the new year, by friction of wood and in charge of the vestal virgins. Cf. HESTIA. **2.** [*not cap.*] A short match with a shank of thin wax taper; also, later, a short wooden match.

ves'tal (-tăl; -t'l), *adj.* **1.** Of or pertaining to Vesta. **2.** Pertaining to, characteristic of, or befitting, a vestal virgin; hence, chaste; pure. — *n.* Also **vestal virgin.** [L. *Vestalis* (sc. *virgo*).] **1.** *Rom. Relig.* A virgin consecrated to Vesta, and to the service of watching the sacred fire, which was to be perpetually kept burning upon her altar. **2.** A virgin; a woman pure and chaste; also, a nun.

vest'ed (vĕs'tĕd; -tĭd), *adj.* **1.** Clothed; robed, esp. in vestments. **2.** *Law.* That has become a complete and consummated right; as, *vested* rights.

vest'ee' (vĕs'tē'), *n.* [*vest* + *-ee* as in coatee, with dim. force.] An ornamental front piece showing between the open edges of a woman's jacket or blouse.

ves'ti·ar'y (vĕs'tĭ·ẽr'ĭ *or, esp. Brit.,* -ẽr·ĭ), *adj.* Pertaining to clothes, or vestments. — *n.* A vestry; robing room.

ves·tib'u·lar (vĕs·tĭb'ū·lẽr), *adj.* Of or pertaining to a vestibule, in any sense; like or of the nature of a vestibule.

ves'ti·bule (vĕs'tĭ·būl), *n.* [F. and L.; F. *vestible,* now *vestibule,* fr. L. *vestibulum.*] **1.** A passage, hall, or chamber between the outer door and the interior of a building. **2.** On trains, the enclosed entrance to a passenger car. Cars with such vestibules (**vestibule cars**), when joined, form a **vestibule train,** in which there is free and protected passage from one end to the other. **3.** *Anat. & Zool.* Any of various cavities or fossae; esp., one serving as, or resembling, an entrance to some other, as the central cavity of the bony labyrinth of the ear or the part of the left ventricle below the aortic orifice. See EAR, *Illust.*

vestibule school. A school organized in an industrial plant to introduce new workers into the industry by means of a few weeks of training along specific lines.

ves'tige (vĕs'tĭj), *n.* [F., fr. L. *vestigium* footprint, sign.] **1.** *Now Rare.* A track or footprint. **2.** A trace, mark, or visible sign left by something lost, perished, or no longer existent; remains. **3.** *Biol.* A small, degenerate, or imperfectly developed part or organ which has been more fully developed in an earlier stage of the individual or in a past generation. — **Syn.** See TRACE. — **ves·tig'i·al** (vĕs·tĭj'ĭ·ăl), *adj.* — **ves·tig'i·al·ly,** *adv.*

ves·tig'i·um (vĕs·tĭj'ĭ·ŭm), *n.; pl.* VESTIGIA (vĕs·tĭj'ĭ·ȧ). [L.] A vestige; trace.

vest′ing (vĕs′tĭng), *n.* Cloth for vests; esp., a heavy silk or mixed fabric used chiefly for evening waistcoats.

vest′ment (vĕst′mĕnt), *n.* [OF. *vestement, vestiment,* fr. L. *vestimentum,* fr. *vestire* to clothe, fr. *vestis* a garment.] **1.** A garment; esp., a garment or robe of ceremony or office; also, clothing; garb; dress. **2.** *Eccl.* A liturgical garment; any article of the ceremonial attire and insignia worn by officiants and assistants during divine service as appropriate to the rite and indicative of their hierarchical rank.

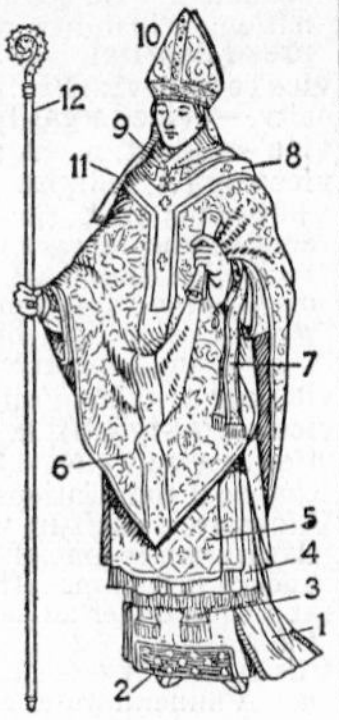

Vestment, 2, of 16th-cent. archbishop. 1 Alb; 2 Embroidered edging; 3 Stole; 4 Tunicle; 5 Dalmatic; 6 Chasuble; 7 Maniple; 8 Pallium; 9 Amice; 10 Miter; 11 Lappet; 12 Crosier, or Pastoral Staff.

vest′-pock′et (*see Pron.,* § 2), *adj.* Adapted to fit into the vest, or waistcoat, pocket; hence, of very small size.

ves′try (vĕs′trĭ), *n.; pl.* -TRIES (-trĭz). [ME. *vestrye,* prob. for *vestery,* fr. OF. *vestier,* fr. ML. *vestiarium,* in L. a clothespress, wardrobe.] **1.** *Obs.* A repository for clothes or vestments; a wardrobe. **2.** *Eccl.* **a** A room within or attached to a church building in which the vestments of the clergy, the altar linen and hangings, and the sacred vessels are kept; — often called a *sacristy.* **b** Such a room used as a chapel, Sunday-school room, prayer-meeting room, etc. **3.** In the Church of England and in the Protestant Episcopal Church, a body of persons entrusted with the administration of the temporal affairs of a parish; also, in England, a parish meeting or a meeting of a vestry. In the Protestant Episcopal Church the vestry is composed of the rector, two wardens, and a variable number of vestrymen elected annually by the parish meeting.

ves′try·man (-măn), *n.* One of a vestry.

ves′ture (vĕs′tūr), *n.* [OF. *vesture, vesteüre,* fr. LL. *vestitura,* fr. L. *vestire* to clothe, dress.] **1.** That with which one is clothed; a garment or garments; dress; apparel. **2.** That which invests, or covers; a covering. — *v. t.* To cover with vesture; clothe; envelop.

ve·su′vi·an (vē·sū′vĭ·ăn), *n.* **1.** *Mineral.* Vesuvianite. **2.** A type of match or fuse for lighting cigars, etc.

ve·su′vi·an·ite (-īt), *n.* *Mineral.* A brown-to-green mineral, a basic silicate of aluminum and calcium with some iron and magnesium. It is common at Vesuvius. Also called *idocrase.*

vet (vĕt), *n.* *Colloq.* Short for VETERAN, VETERINARIAN, VETERINARY.

vet, *v. t.;* VET′TED; VET′TING. [From 1st *vet.*] *Veter.* To submit (an animal) to medical examination and treatment. — *v. i.* *Veter.* To be or to act as a veterinary surgeon.

vetch (vĕch), *n.* [OF. *veche,* var. of *vece,* fr. L. *vicia.*] Any of a genus (*Vicia*) of plants, some species of which are valuable for fodder. The common vetch (*V. sativa*) of Europe is naturalized in N. Am.

vetch′ling (-lĭng), *n.* [*vetch* + 1st *-ling.*] Any of a genus (*Lathyrus,* esp. L. *pratensis*) of small herbs of the pea family.

vet′er·an (vĕt′ēr·ăn), *n.* [See VETERAN, *adj.*] **1.** One who has had long experience and practice in any service, profession, industry, or art, or originally and commonly, in military service; as, a *veteran* of the South Pacific, of the law, the Congress, or the stage. **2.** *U. S. Statutes.* An ex-member of the military or naval service who by length and type of service or degree of disablement, honorable discharge or release, and otherwise, meets statutory requirements precedent to the extension of benefits provided by law for ex-servicemen.

vet′er·an (vĕt′ēr·ăn), *adj.* [L. *veteranus,* fr. *vetus, veteris,* old.] **1.** Grown old in experience; long exercised or practiced in anything, esp. in military life; seasoned; as, a *veteran* officer. **2.** Of, pertaining to, or characteristic of a veteran. **3.** Extending over a great period; long.

Vet′er·ans′ Ad·min′is·tra′tion. An independent office established by executive order (July 21, 1930) consolidating and co-ordinating all hospitals and agencies charged with administering laws relative to relief, pensions, education, insurance, and other benefits provided by law for veterans. See VETERAN, 2. Abbr. *VA*

Veterans Day. November 11 as a legal holiday; — replacing Armistice Day by Act of Congress June 1, 1954.

Veterans of Foreign Wars of the United States. A society, founded in 1899, of men formerly in the armed services who have taken part in the wars or campaigns conducted by the United States on foreign soil or in foreign waters. Abbr. *V. F. W.*

vet′er·i·nar′i·an (vĕt′ēr·ĭ·nâr′ĭ·ăn; 6), *n.* One skilled in, or treating, diseases and injuries of animals; a veterinary.

vet′er·i·nar′y (vĕt′ēr·ĭ·nĕr′ĭ *or, esp. Brit.,* -nĕr·ĭ; vĕt′′n·rĭ), *n.; pl.* -IES (-ĭz). A veterinarian; a veterinary surgeon. — *adj.* [L. *veterinarius* of or pert. to beasts of burden and draft, fr. *veterinus,* prob. fr. *vetus, veteris,* old (hence, good for nothing else).] Of or pertaining to **veterinary medicine,** the science and art dealing with the prevention, cure, or alleviation of disease and injury in animals, esp. domestic animals.

vet′i·ver (vĕt′ĭ·vēr), *n.* [F. *vétiver,* fr. Tamil *veṭṭivēru,* lit., the root which is dug up, fr. *vēr* root.] An East Indian grass (*Vetiveria zizanioides*) cultivated in the tropics and in Louisiana; also, its fragrant roots, used for making mats and screens, and yielding an essential oil (**vetiver oil**) used for perfumes.

ve′to (vē′tō), *n.; pl.* -TOES (-tōz). [L., I forbid, inf. *vetare.*] **1.** An authoritative prohibition; interdiction. **2.** Specif.: A right or power (**veto power**) possessed by one department or branch of a government to forbid or prohibit finally or provisionally the carrying out of projects attempted by another department; esp., a power vested in the chief executive to prevent permanently or temporarily the enactment of measures passed by the legislature. **3.** The exercise of such authority; as, a *veto* is probable if the bill passes; also, *Chiefly U. S.,* a document or message (**veto message**) communicating the reasons of the executive for not officially approving a proposed law. — *v. t.;* VE′TOED (-tōd); VE′TO·ING. To prohibit; to refuse to admit or approve; to negative; also, to refuse assent to, as a legislative bill, so as to prevent its enactment or cause its reconsideration. — **ve′to·er** (-ēr), *n.*

vex (vĕks), *v. t.;* VEXED (vĕkst), or, *Chiefly Rare & Poetic,* VEXT; VEX′ING. [OF. *vexer,* fr. L. *vexare, vexatum,* to vex, agitate.] **1.** To shake or toss about; agitate. **2.** By extension, to discuss; dispute; moot; — chiefly in phrases; as, a *vexed* question, point, etc. **3.** To annoy or anger, as by petty provocations; to irritate; as, *vexed* by ridicule; by extension, to trouble grievously; to harass; afflict, as with disease. — **Syn.** See ANNOY.

vex·a′tion (vĕks·ā′shŭn), *n.* **1.** A state of being vexed; trouble; irritation. **2.** Act of harassing or vexing; troubling. **3.** A cause of trouble or disquiet; affliction.

vex·a′tious (-shŭs), *adj.* **1.** Causing vexation; annoying; sometimes, harassing by process of law; of actions, instituted chiefly to cause annoyance; as, a *vexatious* action. **2.** Full of vexation, trouble, or disquiet; disturbed; as, a *vexatious* hour in court. — **vex·a′tious·ly,** *adv.* — **vex·a′tious·ness,** *n.*

vexed (vĕkst), *adj.* Harassed; afflicted; disturbed; agitated. — **vex′ed·ly** (vĕk′sĕd·lĭ; -sĭd·lĭ), *adv.*

vex′il·lar′y (vĕk′sĭ·lĕr′ĭ *or, esp. Brit.,* -lĕr·ĭ), *n.* [See VEXILLARY, *adj.*] In the Roman army, a veteran under a special standard; hence, a standard-bearer. — *adj.* [L. *vexillarius* a standard-bearer. See VEXILLUM.] **1.** Of or pertaining to an ensign or standard. **2.** *Bot.* Pertaining to or designating the vexillum.

vex′il·late (vĕk′sĭ·lāt), *adj.* *Bot. & Zool.* Having a vexillum.

vex·il′lum (vĕk·sĭl′ŭm), *n.; pl.* -ILLA (-ȧ). [L., a standard, a flag.] **1.** *Rom. Antiq.* **a** A square flag, used esp. by the cavalry. **b** A company of troops serving under one standard. **2.** The web or vane of a feather. **3.** *Bot.* The large upper posterior petal in a pea flower.

vi′a (vī′ȧ; vē′ȧ), *prep.* [L., abl. of *via* way.] By the way of; as, shipped to New York *via* the Panama Canal.

vi′a·ble (vī′ȧ·b'l), *adj.* [F., fr. *vie* life, fr. L. *vita.*] **1.** Capable of living; born alive and with such form and development of organs as to be normally capable of living; — said of a newborn infant. **2.** Capable of growing or developing; as, *viable* seeds. — **vi′a·bil′i·ty** (-bĭl′ĭ·tĭ), *n.*

vi′a·duct (-dŭkt), *n.* [L. *via* a way, road + *-duct* as in aque*duct.*] A bridge, esp. one on narrow reinforced concrete or masonry arches, having high supporting towers or piers, for carrying a road or railroad over a valley, gorge, etc. Also, esp. *U. S.,* a steel structure of short spans carried on high steel towers.

vi′al (vī′ăl), *n.* [ME. *viole,* var. of *fiole.* See PHIAL.] A small vessel for liquids; a phial. — ***to pour out the vials of wrath on*** *or* ***upon.*** To visit vengeance or anger on. — *v. t.;* VI′ALED (-ăld) or VI′ALLED; VI′AL·ING or VI′AL·LING. To put into a vial or vials.

‖**vi′a me′di·a** (vī′ȧ mē′dĭ·ȧ). [L.] A middle way; a mean.

vi′and (vī′ănd), *n.* [OF. *viande,* fr. L. *vivenda,* neut. pl. gerundive of *vivere* to live.] An article of food; — chiefly in *pl.,* provisions; food; fare.

vi·at′ic (vī·ăt′ĭk), *adj.* Also **vi·at′i·cal** (-ĭ·kăl). [L. *viaticus,* fr. *via* a way.] Of or pertaining to a road, or a journey or traveling.

vi·at′i·cum (-ĭ·kŭm), *n.; pl.* VIATICA (-kȧ), VIATICUMS (-kŭmz). [L., fr. *viaticus,* adj.] **1.** Orig., at Rome, traveling money or supplies; later, generally, an allowance, as of transportation or supplies and money for traveling expenses. **2.** Provisions for a journey. **3.** *Eccl.* The Communion, or Eucharist, when given to one dying.

vi·a′tor (vī·ā′tôr), *n.; pl.* VIATORES (vī′ȧ·tō′rēz; 70). [L., fr. *viare* to journey, fr. *via* way.] Traveler; wayfarer.

vi·brac′u·lum (vī·brăk′ū·lŭm), *n.; pl.* VIBRACULA (-lȧ). [NL. dim. fr. L. *vibrare* to vibrate.] *Zool.* One of the movable, slender, spinelike organs or parts with which certain bryozoans are furnished. — **vi·brac′u·lar** (-lẽr), *adj.* — **vi·brac′u·loid** (-loid), *adj.*

vi′bran·cy (vī′brăn·sĭ), *n.; pl.* -CIES (-sĭz). Quality or state of being vibrant; resonance; vibration.

vi′brant (-brănt), *adj.* [L. *vibrans, -antis,* pres. part.] **a** Vibrating; pulsing; as, cities *vibrant* with life and energy. **b** Imparting an impression of activity and energy; as, a *vibrant* personality. **c** Thrilling; as, *vibrant* feelings. **d** Sounding as a result of vibration; hence, resonant; sonorous; resounding; as, a *vibrant* drum or voice. — **vi′brant·ly,** *adv.*

vi′brate (vī′brāt), *v. t.* [L. *vibratus,* past part. of *vibrare* to shake, vibrate.] **1.** To swing or move to and fro. **2.** To mark or measure by oscillation, or moving or swinging to and fro; as, a pendulum *vibrating* seconds. **3.** To set in vibration. — *v. i.* **1.** To move to and fro, or from side to side; esp., to swing like a pendulum; to oscillate. **2.** To be in a state of vibration; to quiver. **3.** Hence: **a** To thrill; throb; as, his heart *vibrates* to the call. **b** To waver; fluctuate; as, to *vibrate* between two opinions. **4.** To produce an oscillating or quivering effect or sound; as, a whisper *vibrates* on the ear. — **Syn.** See SWING.

vi′bra·tile (vī′brȧ·tĭl; -tīl; 56), *adj.* Adapted to, or used in, vibratory motion; as, the *vibratile* organs of insects; characterized by vibration; vibratory; oscillating. — **vi′bra·til′i·ty** (-tĭl′ĭ·tĭ), *n.*

vi·bra′tion (vī·brā′shŭn), *n.* **1.** Act of vibrating, or state of being vibrated, or in vibratory motion; specif., oscillation, as of a pendulum; also, a quivering or trembling motion; quiver. **2.** **a** Figuratively, vacillation; changeableness. **b** A pulsing, throbbing, or thrilling, effect or appearance, as of a living body. **3.** *Physics.* A periodic motion of the particles of an elastic body or medium in alternately opposite directions from the position of equilibrium, when that equilibrium has been disturbed, as when a stretched cord produces musical tones, or particles of air transmit sounds to the ear. Cf. NODE, *Illust.* — **vi·bra′tion·al** (-ăl; -'l), *adj.* — **vi·bra′tion·less** (-lĕs; -lĭs), *adj.*

vi′bra·tive (vī′brȧ·tĭv), *adj.* Vibratory.

vi·bra′to (vē·brä′tō), *n.* [It., past part. of *vibrare* to vibrate.] *Music.* A slightly tremulous or pulsating effect (but not a tremolo) for adding warmth and beauty to the tone or for expressing changes in emotional intensity.

vi′bra·tor (vī′brā·tẽr), *n.* One who or that which vibrates, or causes vibration of any kind; as: **a** A vibrating electrical apparatus used in massage. **b** A vibrating hammer, as of an electric bell. **c** In electricity, an oscillator.

vi′bra·to′ry (vī′brȧ·tō′rĭ *or, esp. Brit.,* -tẽr·ĭ), *adj.* Consisting in, capable of, or causing, vibration or oscillation; vibrant.

vib′ri·o (vĭb′rĭ·ō), *n.* [NL., fr. L. *vibrare* to vibrate.] *Bacteriol.* Any of a genus (*Vibrio*) of short, rigid, motile bacteria typically shaped like a comma or an S. — **vib′ri·oid** (-oid), *adj.*

vib′ri·oid (-oid), *n.* A vibrioid body.

vibrioid body. *Bot.* One of certain slender cylindrical bodies found abundantly in the superficial layers of the cytoplasm of some fungi and algae. They resemble in appearance and size certain common bacilli.

vi·bris′sa (vī·brĭs′ȧ), *n.; pl.* -SAE (-ē). [L. *vibrissae,* pl., fr. *vibrare* to vibrate.] **1.** *Anat. & Zool.* One of the stiff hairs about the nostrils or on other parts of the face, in many animals, as the so-called whiskers of the cat. **2.** *Zool.* One of the bristlelike feathers near the mouth of many birds; — chiefly in *pl.* They occur chiefly in insectivorous birds and may help to prevent the escape of insects.

vi′bro·scope (vī′brō·skōp), *n.* [L. *vibrare* to vibrate + *-scope.*] An instrument for observing or tracing vibrations.

vi·bur′num (vī·bûr′nŭm), *n.* [L., the wayfaring tree.] *Bot.* Any of a genus (*Viburnum*) of widely distributed shrubs or trees of the honeysuckle family, having simple leaves and white or rarely pink cymose flowers, including a black haw (*V. prunifolium*), sheepberry, withe rod (*V. cassinoides* and *V. nudum*), dockmackie, etc.

vic′ar (vĭk′ẽr), *n.* [OF. *vicaire,* fr. L. *vicarius.* See VICARIOUS.] **1.** A substitute in office; a deputy or vicegerent. **2.** Hence, proxy; deputy; as, God's *vicar.* **3.** *Eng. Eccl. Law.* The priest of a parish the owner of the tithes of which is a layman (or formerly a spiritual corporation); any incumbent of a parish not a rector. **4.** *Prot. Episc. Ch.* A clergyman in charge of a dependent chapel as the deputy of another clergyman. **5.** *R.C.Ch.* An ecclesiastic who acts as substitute for, or representative of, another; — used with a qualifying word, as in *vicar-general.* — **vic′ar·ly,** *adv.* — **vic′ar·ship,** *n.*

vic′ar·age (-ĭj), *n.* **1.** The benefice of a vicar. **2.** The house, residence, or household of a vicar. **3.** *Rare.* The office, function, or duty of a vicar.

vicar apostolic, *or* **apostolic vicar.** *R.C.Ch.* **a** Formerly, a bishop or archbishop to whom the pope delegated a portion of his jurisdiction. **b** A prelate commissioned by the Holy See to administer a diocese which is vacant or in which the ordinary is incapacitated. **c** A titular bishop, acting as delegate of the Holy See in regions where the ordinary hierarchy has not been established.

vic′ar·ate (vĭk′ẽr·āt), *n.* A vicariate.

vic′ar fo·rane′ (fō·rān′). [See FOREIGN.] *R.C.Ch.* An ecclesiastic or parish priest appointed by a bishop to exercise a limited jurisdiction in a particular town or district of his diocese.

vic′ar–gen′er·al, *n.; pl.* VICARS-GENERAL. **1.** *Ch. of Eng.* A lay legal officer who acts as deputy of the archbishop of Canterbury or York in certain matters. **2.** *Eng. Hist.* The king's ecclesiastical vicegerent. The only vicar-general was Thomas Cromwell (d. 1540). **3.** *R.C.Ch.* [*sometimes cap.*] The deputy of a bishop in the discharge of his jurisdictional functions.

vi·car′i·al (vī·kâr′ĭ·ăl; vĭ-; 6), *adj.* **1.** Of, pert. to, being, or acting as a vicar; as, *vicarial* duties. **2.** Vicarious; delegated; as, *vicarial* power.

vi·car′i·ate (-āt), *n.* **1.** The office, authority, or jurisdiction of a vicar; vicarship. **2.** A governmental or administrative office held by a deputy; also, a district administered by a deputy.

vi·car′i·ous (-ŭs), *adj.* [L. *vicarius,* fr. *vicis* change, the place or office of one person as assumed by another.] **1.** Of or pertaining to a vicar, substitute, or deputy; deputed; delegated; as, *vicarious* authority. **2.** Acting on behalf of or as representing another; as, a *vicarious* agent. **3.** Performed or suffered by one person with results accruing to the benefit or advantage of another; substitutional; as, a *vicarious* sacrifice; also, enjoyed by one person through his sympathetic participation in the experience of another person; as, *vicarious* pleasure. **4.** *Med.* Acting as or being a substitute; also, occurring in an abnormal situation; replacing a discharge from a usual part; as **vicarious menstruation,** a discharge of blood from some part or organ other than the uterus, with suppression of the menses. — **vi·car′i·ous·ly,** *adv.* — **vi·car′i·ous·ness,** *n.*

Vicar of (Jesus) Christ. *R.C.Ch.* The pope, regarded as head of the church and representative on earth of Christ.

vice (vīs), *n.* [OF., fr. L. *vitium.*] **1.** A moral fault or failing; esp., immoral conduct or habit, as in the indulgence of degrading appetites; as, the *vice* of gluttony. **2.** State of being given up to evil conduct or habit; depravity; wickedness. **3.** A physical defect, deformity, taint, or imperfection. **4.** *Hist.* [*cap.*] The buffoon of old English moralities, often named from some particular vice. **5.** A fault; blemish; defect; as, a *vice* of style. — **Syn.** See FAULT: OFFENSE (**Ant.** virtue).

vice, *n.* [See VISE.] **1.** A vise. **2.** *Obs.* A grip, or grasp. — *v. t.;* VICED (vīst); VIC′ING (vīs′ĭng). *Rare.* To hold, force, or squeeze, with or as if with a vice (vise).

vi′ce (vī′sē), *prep.* [L., abl. of *vicis* change, turn.] In the place of; in the stead of.

vice– (vīs-). [See VICE, *prep.*] A prefix used with nouns (and their derivatives) which designate persons, esp. by their title of office, meaning in general *one who takes the place of;* specif., denoting one who in certain cases may assume the office or duties of a superior having a (specified) title; also, denoting one delegated to act as deputy or substitute for another, as in *vice*roy, *vice*-chancellor, *vice*-presidency, and words in the following list:

vice-governor	**vice-principal**
vice-governorship	**vice-principalship**

vice′–ad′mi·ral, *n. Nav.* A commissioned officer ranking above a rear admiral and below an admiral.

vice′–ad′mi·ral·ty, *n.* The office of a vice-admiral.

vice′–chan′cel·lor, *n.* **1.** A deputy for, or an officer next below in rank to, an official holding the title of chancellor; as, the *vice-chancellor* of a university. **2.** *Law.* A judge appointed to act for, or as the assistant of, the chancellor.

vice′–con′sul, *n.* A consular officer subordinate to a consul general or to a consul. — **vice′–con′su·lar,** *adj.* — **vice′–con′su·late,** *n.* — **vice′–con′sul·ship,** *n.*

vice′ge′ral (vīs′jēr′ăl), *adj.* Of or pertaining to a vicegerent.

vice′ge′ren·cy (vīs′jēr′ĕn·sĭ), *n.* The office, authority, or administration of a vicegerent; also, a district governed by a vicegerent.

vice′ge′rent (-jēr′ĕnt), *n.* [ML. *vicegerens, -entis.* See VICE-; GERENT.] An officer deputed by a superior, as a monarch, to exercise the powers of another; a vicar. — *adj.* Having or exercising delegated power.

vic′e·nar′y (vĭs′ē·nĕr′ĭ *or, esp. Brit.,* -nẽr·ĭ), *adj.* [L. *vicenarius,* fr. *viceni* twenty each.] **a** Of or pertaining to twenty; consisting of twenty. **b** Using 20 as radix or base; — said of a system of notation.

vi·cen′ni·al (vī·sĕn′ĭ·ăl), *adj.* [L. *vicennium* a period of twenty years, fr. *vicies* twenty times + *annus* year.] **a** Lasting or comprising twenty years. **b** Happening once in twenty years; as, a *vicennial* celebration.

vice′–pres′i·den·cy, *n.* The office of vice-president.

vice′–pres′i·dent, *n.* Also **vice president.** [Cf. F. *vice-président.*] An officer next in rank below a president, acting as president in case of that officer's absence or disability. The vice-president of the United States (who has no part in the executive function, but acts as president of the Senate) is elected at the same time and in the same way as the president. He becomes president in case of the removal, death, resignation, or inability, of that officer (Const. Art. II, sec. 1, 5). — **vice′–pres·i·den′tial,** *adj.*

vice′re′gal (vīs′rē′găl), *adj.* Of or pertaining to a viceroy or viceroyalty. — **vice′re′gal·ly,** *adv.*

vice′–re′gent, *n.* A deputy regent. — **vice′–re′gent,** *adj.*

vice′roy (vīs′roi), *n.* [F. *vice-roi,* fr. *vice-* in the place of (fr. L. *vice*) + *roi* king, fr. L. *rex.*] **1.** The governor of a country or province who acts as the representative of his king or sovereign; as, the former *viceroy* of India. **2.** A handsome American butterfly (*Basilarchia archippus*), closely mimicking the monarch butterfly (*Danaüs archippus*) in coloration, but of smaller size. The larvae feed on willow, poplar, and apple trees. — **vice′roy·ship,** *n.*

vice′roy′al (vīs′roi′ăl), *adj.* Viceregal.

vice′roy′al·ty (-tĭ), *n.* The dignity, office, or jurisdiction of a viceroy.

vi′ce ver′sa (vī′sē vûr′sȧ). [L.] The alternation or order being changed; the relations being reversed; conversely.

Vi′chy·ite (vĭsh′ĭ·īt; vē′shē-), *n.* An adherent or advocate of the authoritarian regime of Marshal Henri Pétain, Chief of State, governing unoccupied France (from July, 1940 to Nov., 1942), from headquarters at Vichy, under an agreement calling for economic collaboration with the Nazis.

Vi′chy wa′ter (vĭsh′ĭ; *F.* vē′shē′), *or* [*also not cap.*], *Colloq.,* **Vi′chy,** *n.* A mineral water at Vichy, France; also, by extension, any artificial or natural water resembling this.

vic′i·nage (vĭs′ĭ·nĭj), *n.* [OF. *visenage, voisinage,* fr. L. *vicinus.*] The place or places adjoining or near; neighborhood; vicinity.

vic′i·nal (-năl), *adj.* [L. *vicinalis.*] **1.** Neighboring; adjacent; nearby. **2.** Designating a local road as disting. from a highway. **3.** *Mineral.* Designating subordinate forms or faces on a crystal, sometimes taking the place of the fundamental ones.

vi·cin′i·ty (vĭ·sĭn′ĭ·tĭ; *by some, esp. in Brit. usage, also* vī-), *n.; pl.* -TIES (-tĭz). [L. *vicinitas,* fr. *vicinus* neighboring, near, fr. *vicus* a group of houses, a village.] **1.** Quality or state of being near; nearness; proximity; as, towns in close *vicinity.* **2.** A region about, near, or adjacent; neighborhood; vicinage; as, the *vicinity* of London.

vi′cious (vĭsh′ŭs), *adj.* [OF., fr. L. *vitiosus,* fr. *vitium* vice.] **1.** Addicted to vice or immorality; depraved; wicked. **2.** Characterized by vice, or defect; defective; faulty; as, *vicious* reasoning, pronunciation. **3.** Impure; foul; noxious; as, *vicious* air, water, etc. **4.** *Colloq.* Spiteful; malignant; as, a *vicious* slander. **5.** Not well tamed or broken; refractory; as, a *vicious* horse. — **vi′cious·ly,** *adv.* — **vi′cious·ness,** *n.*

Syn. **Vicious, villainous, iniquitous, nefarious, flagitious, infamous, corrupt, degenerate** mean highly reprehensible or offensive. **Vicious** usually suggests moral depravity and is the diametrical opposite of *virtuous;* **villainous,** usually an intensive of *vicious,* any characteristic or conduct worthy of a villain; **iniquitous,** absence of all signs of justice and fairness; **nefarious,** breach of all laws and traditions which have immemorially been observed; **flagitious** and **infamous,** shameful and scandalous wickedness; **corrupt,** a lack or loss of moral integrity or probity that makes one go contrary to sworn obligations; **degenerate,** descent or deterioration from an earlier high type or condition so as to be extremely low in the moral scale. — **Ant.** Virtuous.

vicious circle. **1.** A chain of circumstances constituting a situation in which the process of solving one difficulty creates a new problem involving increased difficulty in the original situation. **2.** *Logic.* An argument or definition which is valueless because it assumes as true or as understood something which is to be proved or defined. See CIRCLE, *n.,* 11. **3.** *Med.* A chain of morbid processes in which a primary disorder leads to a second which aggravates the first.

vi·cis′si·tude (vĭ·sĭs′ĭ·tūd), *n.* [F., fr. L. *vicissitudo.*] **1.** Regular succession from one thing to another; alternation; as, the *vicissitude* of night and day. **2.** Irregular change; mutation; hence, commonly, changes of fortune, condition, etc.; as, after many *vicissitudes* he enjoyed a prosperous old age. — **Syn.** See CHANGE: DIFFICULTY. — **vi·cis′si·tu′di·nar′y** (-tū′dĭ·nĕr′ĭ *or, esp. Brit.,* -nẽr·ĭ), *adj.* — **vi·cis′si·tu′di·nous** (-nŭs), *adj.*

vic′tim (vĭk′tĭm), *n.* [L. *victima.*] **1.** A living being sacrificed to some deity, or in the performance of a religious rite. **2.** One injured, destroyed, or sacrificed under any of various conditions; as, a *victim* of ambition or jealous rage; a *victim* of a defaulter; a *victim* of the pestilence. **3.** *Colloq.* Hence, dupe; gull; as, the *victim* of a gambler.

vic′tim·ize (-īz), *v. t.* To make a victim of; esp., to make a victim of by deception; to dupe; cheat. — **vic′tim·i·za′tion** (-ĭ·zā′shŭn; -ī·zā′-), *n.* — **vic′tim·iz′er** (-īz′ẽr), *n.*

vic′tor (vĭk′tẽr), *n.* [L., fr. *vincere, victum,* to vanquish.] The winner in a contest or in any struggle; conqueror. — *adj.* Victorious; triumphant; conquering.

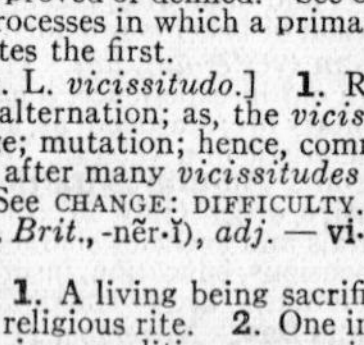

Victoria.

vic·to′ri·a (vĭk·tō′rĭ·ȧ; 70), *n.* [L., prop., victory.] **1.** A type of low four-wheeled pleasure carriage, with a calash top, designed for two passengers, with a raised seat in front for the driver. **2.** *Automobiles.* An open passenger car equipped with a calash top that usually extends over the rear seat only. **3.** [NL.] *Bot.* Any of a genus (*Victoria*) of remarkable South American aquatic plants of the water-lily family. They have large spreading leaves often over 5 feet in diameter, and immense rose-white flowers.

Victoria Cross. A bronze Maltese cross, awarded for remarkable valor to members of the British armed services. Abbr. *V. C.*

Victoria Day. = EMPIRE DAY. See HOLIDAY, 3.

Vic·to′ri·an (vĭk·tō′rĭ·ăn; 70), *adj.* Of or pertaining to the reign of Queen Victoria of England (1837–1901); as, the *Victorian* poets; pertaining to English life and sentiment during the reign of Queen Victoria; esp. fastidious, prudish, or narrow in opinion or expression, particularly regarding conduct. — *n.* **1.** One who lived in the Victorian era; esp., an author who reached prominence in this era. **2.** Anything identified with the Victorian age, as a habit, article of dress, etc.

Vic·to′ri·an·ism (-ĭz′m), *n.* Quality of being Victorian, as in habit, expression, style, etc.; also, an example of Victorian habit, expression, style.

vic·to′ri·ous (vĭk·tō′rĭ·ŭs; 70), *adj.* **1.** Having gained victory; conquering. **2.** Of, pertaining to, or characteristic of victory. **3.** Effective in causing or bringing about victory; as, *victorious* strategy. — **vic·to′ri·ous·ly,** *adv.*

vic′to·ry (vĭk′tō·rĭ), *n.; pl.* -RIES (-rĭz). [OF. *victorie,* fr. L. *victoria.*] The overcoming of an enemy in battle, or of an antagonist in any contest; conquest; triumph; — opposite of *defeat.*

Syn. Victory, conquest, triumph mean a successful outcome in a contest or struggle. Victory implies the winning of any contest or struggle; conquest, subjugation of one's opponents and bringing them under control; triumph, a brilliant and decisive victory or an overwhelming conquest.

vic′tress (vĭk′trĕs; -trĭs), *n.* Also, *Rare,* **vic′trix** (-trĭks). A female victor.

Vic·tro′la (vĭk·trō′lȧ), *n.* A trade-mark applied to a kind of phonograph.

vict′ual (vĭt′'l), *n.* [OF. *vitaille,* fr. *victuaille,* pl. *victuailles,* fr. L. *victualia,* neut. pl. of *victualis* belonging to living or nourishment, fr. *victus* nourishment, fr. *vivere, victum,* to live.] Food; specif., chiefly in *pl.,* food for human beings, esp. when prepared for eating; viands.

☞ This word is common in dialect, but in the standard language is now seldom used, except depreciatively or jocosely. Cf. VITTLE.

— *v. t.;* -UALED (-'ld) or -UALLED; -UAL·ING or -UAL·LING. To supply with provisions; to provide or store with food. — *v. i.* **a** To eat; feed. **b** To supply or take in stores of provisions.

vict′ual·er, vict′ual·ler (vĭt′'l·ẽr; vĭt′lẽr), *n.* **1.** One who furnishes victuals or provisions; specif.: **a** One who supplies an army with provisions; a sutler. **b** A tavernkeeper; innkeeper. **2.** A provision ship.

vi·cu′ña (vĭ·ko͞on′yȧ; vĭ·kū′nȧ), *n.;* see PLURAL, *Note,* 3. [Sp., fr. Quechua *huik' uña.*] **1.** A wild ruminant (*Lama vicugna*) of the Andes from Ecuador to Bolivia, allied to the domesticated llama and alpaca. **2.** Short for **vicuña cloth,** a very soft woolen fabric, made from the wool of the vicuña, or an imitation of it.

‖**vi′de** (vī′dē), *imperative sing.* of L. *videre,* to see; — used to direct attention or refer; as, ‖**vi′de an′te** (ăn′tē), see before. Hence, loosely, for example; for instance; as, mere numbers will not win, *vide* the coalition. Abbr. *v.*

‖**vi′de in′fra** (vī′dē ĭn′frȧ). [L.] See herein; see below.

‖**vi·de′li·cet** (vĭ·dĕl′ĭ·sĕt), *adv.* [L., contr. fr. *videre licet,* lit., it is easy to see, one may or can see.] To wit; scilicet; namely; — often abbreviated to *viz.*

vid′e·o (vĭd′ē·ō), *adj.* [L. *videre* to see.] *Television.* Pertaining to or used in the transmission or reception of the image; as, *video* channel; *video* frequency; — contrasted with *audio.* — *n.* Television; — sometimes contrasted with radio concerned with sound only.

vid′e·o·gen′ic (vĭd′ē·ō·jĕn′ĭk), *adj.* [*video* + *-genic,* 2.] = TELEGENIC.

‖**vi′de post** (vī′dē pōst′). [L.] See after this; see the following.

‖**vi′de su′pra** (vī′dē sū′prȧ). [L.] See hereinbefore; see above.

vi·dette′ (vĭ·dĕt′), *n.* = VEDETTE.

‖**vi′de ut su′pra** (vī′dē ŭt sū′prȧ). [L.] See as (stated) above.

vie (vī), *v. i.;* VIED (vīd); VY′ING (vī′ĭng). [ME. *vien,* shortened fr. *envien,* fr. OF. *envier* to invite, challenge, fr. L. *invitare* to invite.] To strive for superiority; to contend. — *v. t.* **1.** *Obs.* To stake; wager. **2.** *Now Rare.* To do or produce in emulation or competition; to match.

‖**vi et ar′mis** (vī′ ĕt är′mĭs). [L.] *Law.* Literally, with force and arms; — said of a trespass to person or property which is the immediate cause of damage.

Vi·et′nam·ese′ (vē·ĕt′nä·mēz′; -mēs′; -nȧ-; vĕt′-; vē′ĕt-), *n. sing. & pl.* **1.** An inhabitant of Vietnam, in Indochina. **2.** The Vietnamese language. — **Vi·et′nam·ese′,** *adj.*

view (vū), *n.* [OF. *veüe* (F. *vue*), fr. *veoir* to see, past part. *veü,* fr. L. *videre* to see.] **1.** Act of seeing; inspection by the eye; survey. **2.** Mental survey; intellectual perception or examination; as, a just *view* of the arguments. **3.** Power of seeing, either physically or mentally; reach or range of sight; extent of prospect. **4.** That which is seen; scene; prospect. **5.** The pictorial representation of a scene; a sketch. **6.** Mode of looking at anything; esp., manner of regarding any subject of thought; judgment; as, to state one's *views* of a policy. **7.** That which is looked towards or kept in sight, as an object; aim; end; as, he did it with a *view* of escaping; hence, prospect; expectation. **8.** *Obs. exc. Dial.* Appearance; show; aspect. — **Syn.** See OPINION. — ***in view of.*** In regard to; in consideration of. — ***on view.*** On exhibition; open to public inspection. — ***with a view to.*** With the purpose or aim of. — *v. t.* **1.** To see; behold; esp., to look at with attention; to scrutinize; examine; as, to *view* property prior to renting or leasing it. **2.** To survey or examine mentally; to consider. — **view′er** (vū′ẽr), *n.*

view halloo. Also **view hallo, view halloa.** The shout uttered by a hunter on seeing the fox start from covert.

view′less, *adj.* **a** Affording no view. **b** Expressing no views, or opinions. **c** Not perceivable by the eye; invisible; unseen. — **view′less·ly,** *adv.*

view′point′ (vū′point′), *n.* Point of view; standpoint.

view′y (vū′ĭ), *adj. Colloq.* **1.** Having peculiar views; visionary; unpractical. **2.** Spectacular; sometimes, *Slang,* speciously attractive; showy.

vi·ges′i·mal (vī·jĕs′ĭ·măl), *adj.* [L. *vigesimus,* var. of *vicesimus,* fr. *viceni* twenty each.] Twentieth; divided into, or consisting of, twenties or twenty parts; proceeding by twenties.

vig′il (vĭj′ĭl), *n.* [OF. *vigile,* fr. L. *vigilia,* fr. *vigil* awake, watchful.] **1.** *Eccl.* **a** Orig., the watch kept on the night before a feast, spent in prayer or other devotions. **b** Later, the eve of a feast; esp., an eve which is a fast. **c** A religious service on the eve of a feast. **2.** Devotional watching; hence, *pl.,* evening or nocturnal devotions, prayers, etc. **3.** Act of keeping awake, or state of being awake, at times when sleep is customary or needed; wakefulness; sleeplessness. **4.** Hence, a watching; watch; wakeful attention; as, to keep *vigil.*

vig′i·lance (vĭj′ĭ·lăns), *n.* **1.** Wakefulness; sleeplessness. **2.** Quality or state of being vigilant; watchfulness in respect of danger or hazard; caution.

vigilance committee. *U. S.* A volunteer committee of citizens for the oversight and protection of any interest, esp. one organized to suppress and punish crime summarily, as when the processes of law appear inadequate.

vig′i·lant (vĭj′ĭ·lănt), *adj.* [F. or L.; F., fr. L. *vigilans, -antis,* pres. part. of *vigilare* to watch, fr. *vigil* awake.] Alertly watchful as one keeping vigil; circumspect; alert. — **Syn.** See WATCHFUL. — **vig′i·lant·ly,** *adv.* — **vig′i·lant·ness,** *n.*

vig′i·lan′te (vĭj′ĭ·lăn′tē), *n.* [Sp., prop., vigilant.] *U. S.* A member of a vigilance committee.

vig′i·lan′tism (-tĭz'm), *n.* The policy or practice of vigilantes.

vi·gin′ti- (vī·jĭn′tĭ-). [L. *viginti.*] A combining form meaning *twenty,* as in **vi·gin′ti·an′gu·lar.**

vig′in·til′lion (vĭj′ĭn·tĭl′yŭn), *n.* See NUMERATION, *Table.*

vi·gnette′ (vĭn·yĕt′), *n.* [F., fr. *vigne* a vine. See VINE.] **1.** Orig., a running ornament of vine leaves, tendrils, etc., as used in decoration. **2.** Hence, now: **a** A small decorative design or illustration of any kind put on or just before the title page, at the beginning or end of a chapter, etc., of a manuscript or book. **b** Hence, as such pictures are often without a definite bounding line, any picture, as an engraving, photograph, or the like, which shades off gradually into the surrounding ground or the unprinted paper. **3.** In general, a picture, illustration, or depiction in words, esp. one of a small or dainty kind. — *v. t.* To finish, as a photograph, in the manner of a vignette; to make a vignette of. — **vi·gnett′er** (vĭn·yĕt′ẽr), **vi·gnett′ist** (-ĭst), *n.*

vig′or, vig′our (vĭg′ẽr), *n.* [OF. *vigor,* fr. L. *vigor,* fr. *vigere* to be lively or strong.] **1.** Active strength or force of body or mind; effective energy or power; strength. **2.** Strength or force in animal or vegetable nature or action; as, a plant grows with *vigor.* **3.** Intensity of action or effect; force; as, the *vigor* of his argument. **4.** Effective legal status; validity; as, laws still in *vigor.*

‖**vi·go·ro′so** (vē·gō·rō′sō), *adj.* [It.] *Music.* Vigorous; energetic in style; — a direction.

vig′or·ous (vĭg′ẽr·ŭs), *adj.* **1.** Possessing vigor; full of physical or mental strength or active force; strong; lusty; robust. **2.** Exhibiting strength, either of body or mind; strong; forcible; energetic. **3.** Done with vigor; carried out forcefully and energetically. — **vig′or·ous·ly,** *adv.* — **vig′or·ous·ness,** *n.*

Syn. Vigorous, energetic, strenuous, lusty, nervous mean having great vitality and force. Vigorous further implies no signs of depletion of freshness or robustness of body or mind; energetic, the display of abundant force or a capacity for intense activity; strenuous, no flagging of ardor nor avoidance of the arduous; lusty, exuberance in vigor or energy; nervous, a display of forcibleness, compactness, and strength that result from mental vigor.

vi′king (vī′kĭng), *n.* [ON. *vīkingr.*] One of the pirate Northmen who plundered the coasts of Europe in the 8th to 10th centuries; a sea rover. *Viking* is sometimes confounded with *sea king.*

vi′la·yet′ (vē′lä·yĕt′; vē·lä′yĕt), *n.* [Turk. *vilāyet,* fr. Ar. *wilāyat,* fr. Ar. *wāli* governor.] One of the chief administrative divisions or provinces of Turkey.

vile (vīl), *adj.* [OF. *vil,* fr. L. *vilis* cheap, vile, base.] **1.** Of small account; low; mean; worthless; base. **2.** Morally base; wicked; sinful. **3.** Hence, unclean; repulsive; odious. **4.** Loosely, objectionable for any reason; bad; as, *vile* weather. — **Syn.** See BASE. — **vile′ly,** *adv.* — **vile′ness,** *n.*

vil′i·fy (vĭl′ĭ·fī), *v. t.;* -FIED (-fīd); -FY′ING. [LL. *vilificare.* See VILE; -FY.] **1.** To make vile; debase; degrade. **2.** To degrade or debase by report; to defame; asperse. — **Syn.** See MALIGN. — **vil′i·fi·ca′tion** (-fĭ·kā′shŭn), *n.* — **vil′i·fi′er** (-fī′ẽr), *n.*

vil′i·pend (vĭl′ĭ·pĕnd), *v. t.* [F. *vilipender,* fr. L. *vilipendere,* fr. *vilis* vile, cheap + *pendere* to weigh, value.] To hold or express a low opinion of; to depreciate; to slight; despise; belittle; disparage.

vill (vĭl), *n.* [OF. *ville, vile,* a village, town, fr. L. *villa.*] *O. Eng. Law.* **a** A township or division of a hundred. **b** Hence, a village.

vil′la (vĭl′ȧ), *n.* [L. & It.; It., fr. L. *villa,* LL. also village, dim. fr. L. *vicus* a village.] Originally, a country property; as, Cicero had a *villa* at Baiae; hence, a somewhat pretentious rural or suburban residence.

vil′la·dom (-dŭm), *n.* The world constituted by villas and their occupants; hence, the world of smug, financially independent mediocrity.

vil′lage (vĭl′ĭj), *n.* [OF., fr. L. *villaticus* belonging to a country house or villa. See VILLA.] **1.** Any small aggregation of houses in the country, in general less in number than in a town or city and more than in a hamlet. **2.** *U. S.* Such a community incorporated as a municipality and governed by a board of three or more trustees and a president, locally elected. **3.** Any of various territorial divisions incorporated as "villages" under statutory authority, as under various civil codes in the United States, in some Provinces of Canada, etc., or officially or conventionally called "villages." **4.** An aggregation of nests, burrows, etc., considered as suggesting a village (sense 1); as, a prairie-dog *village.* **5.** The residents, collectively, of a village; the villagers. — *adj.* Of, pertaining to, or characteristic of, a village.

village community. A primitive organized agricultural community, a term used in the middle of the 19th century to designate the free, autonomous, communistic group unit considered to be the political unit at the base of modern states, and believed by some to be represented in the early self-dependent agricultural communities of England, Germany, India, Russia (the *mir*), etc.

vil′lag·er (vĭl′ĭj·ẽr), *n.* An inhabitant of a village.

vil′lain (vĭl′ĭn), *n.* [OF. *vilain,* fr. LL. *villanus,* fr. *villa* village, fr. L. *villa* a farm, country house.] **1.** = VILLEIN. **2.** *Obs.* A baseborn or clownish person; a boor. **3.** **a** One capable or guilty of great crimes; a deliberate scoundrel; — often used playfully; as, the little *villain* has stolen my hat. **b** Hence, a character drawn to represent such a person, as in a novel or play; specif., *Theat.,* an actor regularly cast in such a role. — **vil′lain·ess** (-ĕs; -ĭs), *n. fem.*

vil′lain·age (-ĭj), *n.* = VILLENAGE.

vil′lain·ous (-ŭs), *adj.* **1.** Befitting a villain, or scoundrel; depraved; evil. **2.** Highly objectionable; bad; wretched; detestable; as, *villainous* weather; a *villainous* jargon. — **Syn.** See VICIOUS. — **vil′lain·ous·ly,** *adv.* — **vil′lain·ous·ness,** *n.*

vil′lain·y (-ĭ), *n.; pl.* -LAINIES (-ĭz). **1.** A villainous act, action, or conduct; a deed of deep depravity; a crime. **2.** Quality or state of being villainous, or evil; extreme depravity. **3.** *Obs.* **a** = VILLENAGE. **b** Humble or miserable condition.

vil′lan·age (vĭl′ăn·ĭj), *n.* **1.** Var. of VILLENAGE. **2.** *Obs.* Infamy; villainy.

vil′la·nel′la (vĭl′ȧ·nĕl′ȧ), *n.; pl.* -NELLE (-ē). [It., prop. fem. dim. See VILLAIN.] *Music.* **a** An old rustic dance, and the accompanying song. **b** An Italian rustic part song, unaccompanied and in free form.

vil′la·nelle′ (vĭl′ȧ·nĕl′), *n.* [F., fr. It. *villanella.*] A fixed form of verse, chiefly French, having normally five tercets and a quatrain, the second lines of which have one rhyme, and the remaining lines another.

vil·lat′ic (vĭ·lăt′ĭk), *adj.* [L. *villaticus* of a country house. See VILLAGE.] Rural; rustic.

vil′lein (vĭl′ĭn), *n.* [AF. See VILLAIN, *n.*] Originally, any free common villager of any of the classes lower in rank than the thegn; a churl; specif., in a restricted sense, a free peasant of a class lower than a sokeman and higher in rank than the cotters. Later, by about the 13th century, the term *villein* was applied to a class of unfree peasants, or serfs, who as regards their lord were slaves, but were free in their legal relations with respect to all others. From this status they gradually improved in condition, becoming the free peasants of later days, their precarious tenure of land developing into the customary copyhold tenures.

vil′len·age (vĭl′ĕn·ĭj), *n.* Also **vil′lein·age.** [OF. *villenage, vilenage.*] *Feudal Law.* **a** Tenure on the terms by which a villein held of his lord; tenure at the will of the lord by villein services. **b** The status of a villein.

vil′li·form (vĭl′ĭ·fôrm), *adj.* [*villus* + *-form.*] Having the form or appearance of villi; like the pile of velvet.

vil·los′i·ty (vĭ·lŏs′ĭ·tĭ), *n.* **1.** State of being villous. **2.** *Anat.* A villus. **3.** *Bot.* A coating of long, slender hairs.

vil′lous (vĭl′ŭs), *adj.* [L. *villosus.*] **1.** Covered with fine hairs, or a woolly substance; shaggy with soft hairs; specif., *Bot.*, pubescent, with soft hairs. **2.** *Anat.* Furnished, or clothed, with villi. — **vil′lous·ly,** *adv.*

vil′lus (-ŭs), *n.*; *pl.* VILLI (-ī). [L., shaggy hair, a tuft of hair.] **1.** *Anat. & Embryol.* A small slender vascular process; esp., one of the minute fingerlike processes of the mucous membrane of the small intestine which serve in the absorbing of nutriment. **2.** Any of the fine, straight, soft hair on villous plants.

vim (vĭm), *n.* [L., acc. of *vis* strength, force.] Energetic or active power; force; energy; spirit; vigor.

vi′men (vī′mĕn), *n.*; *pl.* VIMINA (vĭm′ĭ·nȧ). [L., a twig.] *Bot.* A long, slender, flexible shoot or branch.

Vim′i·nal (vĭm′ĭ·năl), *n.* [L. *Viminalis.*] One of the Seven Hills of ancient Rome. See SEVEN HILLS.

vi·min′e·ous (vĭ·mĭn′ē·ŭs), *adj.* [L. *vimineus*, fr. *vimen* pliant twig.] **1.** Of or pertaining to twigs; woven of pliant twigs. **2.** *Bot.* Of or producing long slender twigs.

vi′na (vē′nä), *n.* [Skr. *vīṇā.*] *Music.* An ancient Hindu instrument, originally a seven-stringed harp; later, after about A.D. 700, an instrument of the guitar type, still used in India. It has a long bamboo finger board with movable frets and a gourd resonator at each end.

vi·na′ceous (vī·nā′shŭs), *adj.* [L. *vinaceus.* See VINE.] **1.** Pertaining to, or like, wine or grapes. **2.** Wine-colored.

vin′ai·grette′ (vĭn′ā·grĕt′), *n.* [F., fr. *vinaigre* vinegar.] **1.** Vinaigrette sauce. **2.** A small box or, now usually, a bottle, of ornamental design, having a perforated top or cover, for holding aromatic vinegar, smelling salts, etc.

vinaigrette sauce. A sauce made of vinegar, oil, shallots, parsley, etc., used esp. on cold meats, as calf's head.

Vin′cent's an·gi′na (vĭn′sĕnts; văN′säNz′). [After H. *Vincent* (b. 1862), French physician.] *Med.* A painful disease of the tonsils and pharynx, marked by ulceration and the formation of a membrane, and held to be caused by two species of bacteria, which in the mouth produce **Vincent's infection,** *or* **Vincent's stomatitis,** commonly known as *trench mouth.*

vin′ci·ble (vĭn′sĭ·b'l), *adj.* [L. *vincibilis*, fr. *vincere* to vanquish, conquer.] Capable of being overcome or subdued; conquerable. — **vin′ci·bil′i·ty** (-bĭl′ĭ·tĭ), *n.*

‖**vin′cit om′ni·a ve′ri·tas** (vĭn′sĭt ŏm′nĭ·ȧ vĕr′ĭ·tăs). [L.] Truth conquers all things.

vin′cu·lum (vĭng′kū·lŭm), *n.*; *pl.* -LA (-lȧ). [L., fr. *vincire, vinctum* to bind.] **1.** A bond of union; a tie. **2.** *Math.* A straight, horizontal mark placed over two or more members of a compound quantity, equiv. to parentheses or brackets about them, as $a-\overline{b-c}=a-(b-c)$.

‖**vin′cu·lum ma′tri·mo′ni·i** (măt′rĭ·mō′nĭ·ī). [L.] The bond of marriage.

vin′di·ca·ble (vĭn′dĭ·kȧ·b'l), *adj.* Capable of being vindicated; justifiable.

vin′di·cate (vĭn′dĭ·kāt), *v. t.* [L. *vindicatus*, past part. of *vindicare* to lay claim to, defend, avenge.] **1.** To support or maintain as true or correct, against denial, censure, or objections; to sustain; justify; as, to *vindicate* one's honor; to *vindicate* a claim. **2.** To defend or secure against assault; to defend. **3.** To lay claim to; to assert a right to. **4.** To serve as, or provide, justification for. **5.** *Obs.* **a** To set free; deliver. **b** To avenge. **c** To punish. **6.** *Roman & Civil Law.* To assert one's legal right to (a thing); to recover by legal process. — **Syn.** See MAINTAIN; EXCULPATE. — **vin′di·ca′tor** (vĭn′dĭ·kā′tēr), *n.*

vin′di·ca′tion (-kā′shŭn), *n.* Act of vindicating, or state of being vindicated; specif., defense; justification against denial or censure.

vin·dic′a·tive (vĭn·dĭk′ȧ·tĭv; vĭn′dĭ·kā′tĭv), *adj.* Tending to, or intended to, vindicate; vindicating.

vin′di·ca·to′ry (vĭn′dĭ·kȧ·tō′rĭ *or, esp. Brit.*, -kā′tēr·ĭ, -kȧ·tēr·ĭ), *adj.* **1.** Tending or serving to vindicate; specif., justificatory. **2.** Inflicting punishment; avenging.

vin·dic′tive (vĭn·dĭk′tĭv), *adj.* [For *vindicative*, confused with L. *vindicta* revenge, punishment, fr. *vindicare* to vindicate.] Disposed to revenge; prompted or characterized by revenge; retaliatory; as, a *vindictive* spirit, punishment, man. — **vin·dic′tive·ly,** *adv.* — **vin·dic′tive·ness,** *n.*

‖**vin du pays** (văN′ dü pā′ē′). [F.] Wine of the country or the locality.

vine (vīn), *n.* [OF. (F. *vigne*), fr. L. *vinea* a vineyard, vine, fr. *vineus* of or belonging to wine, fr. *vinum* wine, grapes.] **1.** A grapevine. **2.** Any plant whose stem requires support, and which climbs by tendrils or other means, or which creeps along the ground; as, a squash *vine;* a honeysuckle *vine.* Also, the stem of such plant.

vine′dress′er (vīn′drĕs′ēr), *n.* One who cultivates, prunes, or cares for grapevines.

vin′e·gar (vĭn′ē·gēr), *n.* [OF. *vinaigre*, fr. *vin* wine (fr. L. *vinum*) + *aigre* sour (fr. L. *acer*).] **1.** A sour liquid containing acetic acid, used as a condiment, or as a preservative, obtained by the fermentation of dilute alcoholic liquids, as beer, cider, malt, wine, etc. **2.** Sharp, sour, crabbed speech.

vinegar eel. See EELWORM.

vin′e·gar·ette′ (vĭn′ē·gēr·ĕt′), *n.* = VINAIGRETTE, 2.

vin′e·gar·roon′ (vĭn′ē·gȧ·rōōn′), *n.* [Sp. *vinagre* vinegar.] A whip scorpion, esp. a large species (*Mastigoproctus giganteus*) of Mexico and the southwestern United States, which is popularly supposed to be very venomous; — so called from the odor that it emits when alarmed.

vinegar worm. The vinegar eel. See EELWORM.

vin′e·gar·y (vĭn′ē·gēr·ĭ), *adj.* Of the nature of vinegar; hence, sour; unamiable; crabbed.

vin′er·y (vīn′ēr·ĭ), *n.*; *pl.* -ERIES (-ĭz). A building used for the growing of grapevines; a grapery.

vine′yard (vĭn′yērd), *n.* [From *vine* + *yard*, after earlier *wineyard*, fr. AS. *wīngeard.*] **1.** A plantation of grapevines. **2.** A field of labor, esp. of spiritual endeavor. — **vine′yard·ist,** *n.*

‖**vingt-et-un** (văN′-tā·ûN′), *n.* [F., twenty and one.] A game at cards, in which the aim of each player is to obtain from the dealer such cards that the sum of their pips, or spots, is as near as possible to twenty-one, without exceeding it.

vini-. [L. *vinum.*] A combining form meaning *wine* or *wine grapes.* as in **vin′i·cul′tur·al, vin′i·cul′ture, vin′i·cul′tur·ist, vi·nif′er·ous.**

vi′nic (vī′nĭk; vĭn′ĭk), *adj.* [L. *vinum* wine.] Of, pertaining to, or derived from wine or alcohol; as, *vinic* ether.

vin·om′e·ter (vĭn·ŏm′ē·tēr; vī·nŏm′-), *n.* [L. *vinum* wine + *-meter.*] A hydrometer for determining the strength or purity of wine.

‖**vin or′di′naire′** (văN′ ôr′dē′nâr′). [F., lit., common wine.] Wine for ordinary table use, esp. a cheap claret.

vi·nos′i·ty (vī·nŏs′ĭ·tĭ), *n.* [LL. *vinositas.*] **1.** Quality or state of being vinous. **2.** Addiction to wine.

vi′nous (vī′nŭs), *adj.* [L. *vinosus*, fr. *vinum* wine.] **1.** Of, pertaining to, produced by, or having the qualities of wine. **2.** Habitually given to wine; also, affected by wine.

vin′tage (vĭn′tĭj), *n.* [Corrupt. by influence of *vintner*, fr. ME. *vindage, vendage*, for *vendange*, fr. OF. *vendenge*, fr. L. *vindemia*, fr. *vinum* wine, grapes + *demere* to take off.] **1.** A season's produce of the vine, in grapes or, now usually, in wine. **2.** Act or time of gathering grapes, or of making wine. **3.** Wine; specif., a wine of a particular type or district in a specified year, esp. one (**vintage wine**) prized for distinctive qualities. **4.** *Humorous.* The type fashionable or popular in some season or period; as, a drama of prewar *vintage.*

vin′tag·er (vĭn′tĭj·ēr), *n.* One who gathers the vintage.

vint′ner (vĭnt′nēr), *n.* [OF. *vinetier, vinotier.*] A wine seller, or wine merchant, esp. at wholesale.

vi′nyl (vī′nĭl; vĭn′ĭl), *adj.* [L. *vinum* wine + *-yl.*] *Chem.* Pertaining to, designating, or containing the univalent radical CH_2:CH-; as, **vinyl alcohol,** a compound, CH_2:CHOH, known only in the form of its polymer *polyvinyl alcohol;* **vinyl resin** (called also *polyvinyl resin*), any of a group of thermoplastic resins formed by the polymerization of a vinyl compound, as vinyl acetate, with or without some other substance. Resins of this group are resistant to chemical agents, and are used for surface coatings, molded articles, etc.

vi·nyl′i·dene (vī·nĭl′ĭ·dēn), *adj.* [*vinyl* + *-idene*, a suffix for naming radicals attached with a double bond.] *Chem.* Pertaining to, designating, or containing the bivalent radical CH_2:C=; as, **vinylidene resin** (called also *polyvinylidene resin*), any of a group of thermoplastic resins formed by the polymerization of a vinylidene compound, as vinylidene chloride, with or without some other substance. **vinylidene chloride,** a derivative of ethylene, polymerizes to form *polyvinylidene chloride*, a resin used for filaments, molded articles, etc.

vi′ol (vī′ŭl), *n.* [OF. *vielle* (in Pr., *viola*), of Teut. origin.] Any of the class of stringed instruments including the violin, viola, violoncello, and contrabass. Specif., a medieval stringed instrument, with a flat tapering back, a broad neck (originally fretted), low-arched bridge, and, usually, six strings. It was made in four sizes, treble, alto or tenor, bass, and contrabass.

vi·o′la (vē·ō′lȧ; vĭ-; *It.* vyô′lä), *n.* [It.] **a** A viol instrument, intermediate in size and compass between the violin and violoncello, tuned a fifth lower than the former. **b** A string-toned labial organ stop of 8-foot or 4-foot pitch. See STOP, *n.*

vi′o·la (vī′ō·lȧ; vē·ō′lȧ; vĭ·ō′lȧ), *n.* [L., a violet.] Any of a genus (*Viola*) of low-growing plants, typifying a family (Violaceae, the violet family), having solitary white, yellow, or purple flowers, often variegated as in the pansies, esp. any of certain garden hybrids with flowers resembling but smaller than pansies.

vi′o·la·ble (vī′ō·lȧ·b'l), *adj.* [L. *violabilis.*] That may be violated. — **vi′o·la·bil′i·ty** (-bĭl′ĭ·tĭ), *n.* — **vi′o·la·bly,** *adv.*

vi′o·la′ceous (vī′ō·lā′shŭs), *adj.* [L. *violaceus*, fr. *viola* a violet.] **1.** Of the color violet. **2.** Belonging to the violet family (Violaceae). See 2d VIOLA.

vi·o′la da brac′cio (*It.* vyô′lä dä brät′chō). [It., viol for the arm.] The tenor viol, predecessor of the viola.

vi·o′la da gam′ba (gäm′bä). [It., viol for the leg.] **a** The bass viol, predecessor of the violoncello. **b** A string-toned organ stop of 8-foot pitch. See STOP, *n.*, 10.

vi·o′la d'a·mo′re (dä·mō′rā). [It., viol of love.] **a** A tenor viol, whose tone is peculiarly sweet and tender. **b** A soft string-toned organ stop of 8-foot or 4-foot pitch. See STOP, *n.*, 10.

vi′o·late (vī′ō·lāt), *v. t.* [L. *violatus*, past part. of *violare* to violate. See VIOLENT.] **1.** To trench or infringe on; also, to break or disregard, as a promise. **2.** To ravish; outrage. **3.** To profane; desecrate. **4.** *Obs.* To treat roughly or harshly; abuse. **5.** To interrupt; disturb. — **vi′o·la′tive** (-lā′tĭv), *adj.* — **vi′o·la′tor** (-lā′tēr), *n.*

vi′o·la′tion (-lā′shŭn), *n.* [OF. or L.; OF. *violacion* (F. *violation*), fr. L. *violatio.*] Act or instance of violating, or state of being violated; specif.: **a** Infringement; transgression; nonobservance; as, the *violation* of law, covenants, promises, etc. **b** An act of irreverence or desecration; profanation; as, the *violation* of a church. **c** Interruption; disturbance. **d** Ravishment; rape.

vi′o·lence (vī′ō·lĕns), *n.* [OF., fr. L. *violentia.*] **1.** *Chiefly Law.* **a** Broadly, exertion of any physical force considered with reference to its effect on another than the agent, as in effecting an entrance into a house in burglary; sometimes, the overcoming or prevention of resistance by threats of violence. **b** An instance of violent treatment or procedure. **2.** Profanation; infringement; outrage; assault. **3.** Strength or energy actively displayed or exerted; vehement, forcible, or destructive action; force. **4.** Hence: **a** Intensity; severity. **b** Vehemence in feeling; passion; ardor; fury; fervor. **5.** Unjustified alteration of wording or sense; as, to do *violence* to a Scriptural text.

vi′o·lent (-lĕnt), *adj.* [OF. *violent*, fr. L. *violentus;* akin to L. *violare* to violate, *vis* strength, force.] **1.** Moving, acting, or characterized by physical force, esp. by extreme and sudden or by unjust or improper force; furious; as, a *violent* assault. **2.** That commits or is characterized or accompanied by violence (sense 1); as, to lay *violent* hands on one. **3.** Extreme; intense; as, a *violent* contrast in colors; *violent* pain. **4.** Extremely convincing; nearly conclusive, as in the legal phrase, *violent* presumption. **5.** Produced or effected by force; not spontaneous or natural; as, a *violent* death. **6.** Evincing, or due to, strong mental excitement; vehement; passionate; as, *violent* words. **7.** That wrests meaning unduly; as, a *violent* interpretation. — **vi'o·lent·ly**, *adv.*

vi'o·let (vī'ō·lĕt; -lĭt), *n.* [OF. *violete* a violet, dim. of *viole* a violet, fr. L. *viola.*] **1. a** A plant or flower of the genus *Viola* (see 2d VIOLA); esp. the common purple-flowered species (*V. cucullata*) of eastern North America. See SEED, *Illust.* The violet is the State flower of Illinois, New Jersey, and Rhode Island. The bird's-foot violet (which see) is the State flower of Wisconsin. **b** With a qualifying word, any of various unrelated plants or their flowers; as, dogtooth *violet.* **2.** Any of the colors resembling those of certain violets, averaging bluish blue-red in hue, of medium saturation and low brilliance. See COLOR. — *adj.* Of the color violet.

violet ray. **a** The shortest ray of the visible spectrum, producing violet color. **b** Erroneously, the ultraviolet ray.

vi'o·lin' (vī'ō·lĭn'; *attrib. often* vī'ō·lĭn'; 2), *n.* [It. *violino*, dim. of *viola.*] **1.** The modern treble instrument of the viol class, distinguished in its developed form by having the back scooped out and slightly rounded like the belly, a low bridge, four strings, etc.; a fiddle. **2.** A violin player, esp. in an orchestra; as, the first *violin.* — **vi'o·lin'mak'er**, *n.*

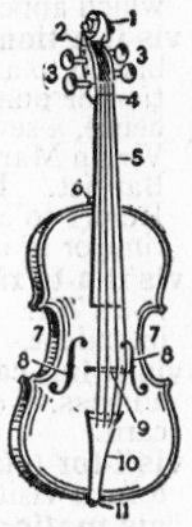

Violin. 1 Scroll; 2 Setting for Pegs (3,3); 4 Nut; 5 Finger Board; 6 Neck Plate; 7, 7 Curves forming the Waist; 8, 8 Sound Holes; 9 Bridge; 10 Tailpiece; 11 Button.

vi'o·lin'ist (vī'ō·lĭn'ĭst), *n.* A player on the violin.

vi'ol·ist (vī'ŭl·ĭst), *n.* A player on the viol.

vi'o·lon·cel'list (vē'ō·lŏn·chĕl'ĭst; vī'ō·lŏn·sĕl'ĭst), *n.* A player on the violoncello; — often shortened to *cellist.*

vi'o·lon·cel'lo (vē'ō·lŏn·chĕl'ō; vī'ō·lŏn·sĕl'ō), *n.; pl.* -LOS (-ōz). [It., dim. of *violone* contrabass.] A bass instrument of the viol class, developed from the viola da gamba, with its four strings tuned an octave lower than the viola; — commonly shortened to *cello.*

vio·lo'ne (vyō·lō'nā), *n.* [It., aug. of *viola* a viol.] *Music.* **1.** The contrabass. **2.** An open, labial, string-toned stop of 16-foot pitch. See STOP, *n.*

vi·os'ter·ol (vī·ŏs'tẽr·ōl; -ŏl), *n.* [ultra*violet* + ergo*sterol.*] *Pharm.* A preparation of irradiated ergosterol dissolved in neutral oil.

vi'per (vī'pẽr), *n.* [OF. or L.; OF. *vipre, vipere,* fr. L. *vipera.*] **1. a** A common European venomous snake (*Vipera berus*) attaining a length of two feet and varying in color from red, brown, or gray, with dark markings, to black; also, any snake of the same genus or, by extension, of allied genera of the family Viperidae; an adder (which see); as, the ***horned viper*** or ***sand viper*** (see CERASTES). **b** Any of a group of very venomous, mostly American snakes (***pit vipers***) constituting a family (Crotalidae, sometimes included in the family Viperidae) including the rattlesnake, copperhead, water moccasin, and fer-de-lance, and characterized by having, between the eye and the nostril, a hollow or pit. See FANG, *Illust.* **c** Loosely, any of various venomous or supposedly venomous snakes. **2.** A treacherous or malignant person. — **vi'per·ine** (-ĭn; -īn), *adj.*

vi'per·ous (-ŭs), *adj.* **1.** Viperine. **2.** Venomous.

vi'per's bu'gloss (vī'pẽrz). A coarse, bristly weed (*Echium vulgare*) of Europe and Asia, naturalized in North America, having showy blue, tubular flowers with exserted stamens.

vi·ra'go (vĭ·rā'gō; vī-), *n.; pl.* -GOES, -GOS (-gōz). [L., fr. *vir* man.] **1.** *Archaic.* A large powerful woman; an amazon. **2.** A turbulent, quarrelsome woman; a termagant.

vi'ral (vī'răl), *adj.* Of, pertaining to, or caused by a virus.

vir'e·lay (vĭr'ĕ·lā), *n.* Also ‖**vire'lai'** (vēr'lĕ'). [OF. *virelai* (influenced by *lai* lay), fr. earlier *vireli,* orig. a mere refrain.] An old French verse form having a refrain and composed wholly in two rhymes; also, one composed of stanzas each of which has two rhymes, one new and one repeated from the preceding stanza. The unused rhyme of the first stanza takes the place of the new rhyme in the last.

vir'e·o (vĭr'ē·ō), *n.; pl.* -OS (-ōz). [L., a species of bird.] Any of certain small insectivorous oscine American birds (family Vireonidae) chiefly olivaceous and grayish in color. Common species are: ***red-eyed vireo*** (*Vireo olivaceus*); ***warbling vireo*** (*V. gilvus*); ***solitary, or blue-headed, vireo*** (*V. solitarius*); ***white-eyed vireo*** (*V. griseus*); ***yellow-throated vireo*** (*V. flavifrons*). — **vir'e·o·nine** (-ō·nīn; -nĭn), *adj.* & *n.*

vi·res'cence (vī·rĕs'ĕns; -'ns), *n.* [L. *virescens,* pres. part. of *virescere* to grow green.] State or condition of becoming or growing green, specif., *Bot.*, through the development of chloroplasts in organs normally white or colored, as petals. — **vi·res'cent** (-ĕnt; -'nt), *adj.*

vir'gate (vûr'gāt), *n.* [ML. *virgate, virgata terrae,* so much land as *virga terrae,* a land measure, contains, fr. L. *virga* a twig, rod.] *Early Eng. Law.* A measure of land equal to one quarter of an acre or, more commonly, one quarter of a hide.

vir'gate, *adj.* [L. *virgatus* made of twigs, fr. *virga* a twig, rod.] *Bot.* **a** Rodlike; wand-shaped. **b** Bearing many small twigs.

vir'gin (vûr'jĭn), *n.* [OF. *virgine, virgene, virge* (F. *vierge*), fr. L. *virgo, -inis.*] **1.** *Eccl.* **a** An unmarried woman devoted to religion and asceticism; — chiefly in designations of saints. **b** [*cap.*, usually with *the.*] The Virgin Mary. **2.** An unmarried woman, esp., a girl. **3.** One who has not had sexual intercourse; esp.: **a** A maid. **b** A female animal before copulation. **4.** [*cap.*] *Astron.* The constellation Virgo. — *adj.* **1.** Being a virgin; chaste; of, pertaining to, or befitting a virgin; virginal. **2.** Pure; undefiled; unsullied; as, *virgin* snow. **3.** Undisturbed; fresh; new; unadulterated; unalloyed; as, *virgin* soil or gold. **4. a** Hitherto unused; as, his *virgin* sword. **b** Initial; first, as, a *virgin* cruise. **c** Not yet trained (to) or having experience (of); as, a team *virgin* to harness. **5. a** Of elements, naturally uncombined; native; as, *virgin* sulfur. **b** Of oils, obtained from the first light pressing (of olives, walnuts, etc.) in the cold. **c** Produced directly from ore, or by primary smelting; — of metal.

vir'gin·al (vûr'jĭ·năl; -n'l), *adj.* [OF., fr. L. *virginalis.*] Virgin; esp., maidenly; modest; pure.

vir'gin·al, *n.* [Cf. F. *virginale;* — prob. so called from being used by young girls, or *virgins.*] A small rectangular spinet, without legs, popular in the 16th and 17th centuries. Also *pl.*, and sometimes called a ***pair of virginals.*** — *v. i.* To tap with the fingers, as if on a virginal.

virgin birth. **a** Birth from a virgin; parthenogenesis. **b** *Theol.* The doctrine that Jesus was miraculously begotten of God and born of a virgin mother.

Vir·gin'ia creep'er (vẽr·jĭn'yȧ; -jĭn'ĭ·ȧ). A common North American tendril-climbing vine (*Parthenocissus quinquefolia*) of the grape family, with bluish-black berries; — called also *woodbine* and *American ivy.*

Virginia deer *or* **white-tailed deer.** The most widely distributed deer of the United States (*Odocoileus virginianus* and allied species), with long tail white on the underside, and forward-arching **antlers;** — in its summer coat called also *red deer.* Cf. DEER.

Virginia, *or* **Virginia rail, fence.** A worm fence.

Vir·gin'ian (vẽr·jĭn'yăn; -jĭn'ĭ·ăn), *adj.* **1.** Of or pertaining to Virginia. **2.** Designating the language of certain Algonquian Indians, formerly of eastern Virginia and vicinity. — *n.* A native or inhabitant of Virginia.

Virginia reel. A variety of country-dance.

Virginia trumpet flower. The trumpet creeper.

‖**vir·gi'ni·bus pu'er·is'que** (vẽr·jĭn'ĭ·bŭs pū'ẽr·ĭs'kwē). [L.] For boys and girls.

vir·gin'i·ty (vẽr·jĭn'ĭ·tĭ), *n.* **1.** Virgin quality or state; maidenhood. **2.** The unmarried life; spinsterhood. **3.** State of being virgin, or fresh, new, etc.

vir·gin'i·um (vẽr·jĭn'ĭ·ŭm), *n.* [NL., fr. the State *Virginia.*] *Chem.* A name given to the element of at. no. 87, supposedly detected in sea water and other materials. Cf. FRANCIUM.

Virgin Mary. The mother of Jesus.

vir'gin's-bow'er (vûr'jĭnz·bou'ẽr), *n.* See CLEMATIS.

virgin wool. Wool not used before in manufacture.

Vir'go (vûr'gō), *n.; genitive* VIRGINIS (-jĭ·nĭs). [L. *virgo* a virgin, the constellation Virgo.] *Astron.* **a** A zodiacal constellation on the celestial equator, due south of the handle of the Dipper, pictured as a woman holding a spike of grain. **b** The sixth sign (♍) of the zodiac. See ZODIAC.

vir'gu·late (vûr'gū·lāt), *adj.* Rod-shaped.

vir'gule (vûr'gūl), *n.* [F., fr. L. *virgula,* dim. of *virga* a rod.] A short slanting stroke between two words (thus, and/or) indicating that either may be used in interpreting the sense.

vir'i·des'cent (vĭr'ĭ·dĕs'ĕnt; -'nt), *adj.* [LL. *viridescens,* pres. part. of *viridescere* to grow green.] Slightly green; greenish. — **vir'i·des'cence** (-ĕns; -'ns), *n.*

vi·rid'i·an (vĭ·rĭd'ĭ·ăn), *n.* [L. *viridis* green.] A chrome green held to be chromic oxide, Cr_2O_3.

vi·rid'i·ty (-ĭ·tĭ), *n.* [OF. *viridité,* fr. L. *viriditas,* fr. *viridis* green.] Greenness; hence, freshness.

vir'ile (vĭr'ĭl; vī'rĭl; *or, esp. Brit.*, vĭr'īl; vī'rīl; 56), *adj.* [F. *viril,* fr. L. *virilis,* fr. *vir* man.] **1.** Having the nature, properties, or qualities of an adult man; characteristic of manhood; specif., capable of procreation. **2.** Masterful; forceful. **3.** Masculine; male. — **Syn.** See MALE.

vir'i·lism (vĭr'ĭ·lĭz'm), *n.* *Med.* An abnormality in a woman marked by male secondary sexual characters, as hair distribution, skeletal form, etc.

vi·ril'i·ty (vĭ·rĭl'ĭ·tĭ; vī-), *n.; pl.* -TIES (-tĭz). Quality or state of being virile; manhood; manly vigor. Cf. MULIEBRITY.

virl (vûrl), *n.* *Obs. exc. Scot.* Ferrule; ring.

vi·rol'o·gy (vī·rŏl'ō·jĭ), *n.* The science dealing with viruses and virus diseases. — **vi'ro·log'i·cal** (vī'rō·lŏj'ĭ·kăl), *adj.* — **vi·rol'o·gist** (vī·rŏl'ō·jĭst), *n.*

vi·ro'sis (vī·rō'sĭs), *n.; pl.* VIROSES (-sēz). [NL., fr. *virus* + *-osis.*] Disease due to a virus, specif. a filtrable virus, as the virus of smallpox.

vir·tu' (vûr·tōō'; vûr'tōō), *n.* [It. *virtù* virtue, excellence, fr. L. *virtus.* See VIRTUE.] **1.** A love of, or a taste for, curios or objets d'art. **2.** Productions of art, esp. curios or antiques, collectively; as, an article or piece of *virtu.*

vir'tu·al (vûr'tū·ăl), *adj.* **1.** *Archaic.* Of or relating to a virtue, or efficacious power; energizing. **2.** Being in essence or effect, but not in fact; as, the *virtual* rulers of a country. — **vir'tu·al'i·ty** (-ăl'ĭ·tĭ), *n.* — **vir'tu·al·ly**, *adv.*

vir'tue (vûr'tū), *n.* [OF. *vertu,* fr. L. *virtus* strength, courage, virtue, fr. *vir* a man.] **1.** *pl.* One of the orders of angels. **2.** Moral practice or action; moral excellence; rectitude; morality. **3.** A particular moral excellence; any moral quality conceived as a good; also, such virtues collectively. Plato distinguished four ***cardinal virtues,*** prudence, fortitude, temperance, and justice. Christian moralists called these the ***natural virtues*** (see NATURAL, 4 **a**) and added the ***supernatural, theological, or Christian virtues*** of faith, hope, and charity, or virtues infused by God. **4.** Active quality or power; power adequate to the production of a given effect; potency; efficacy; as, a medicine without *virtue;* also, a particular instance of such virtue; as, the *virtue* of a given remedy. **5.** Manly strength or courage; valor. **6.** Excellence or an excellence of any kind; as, to make a *virtue* of necessity. **7.** Chastity; esp., the chastity of women. — ***in, or by virtue of.*** Through the force of; by authority of.

vir'tu·os'i·ty (vûr'tū·ŏs'ĭ·tĭ), *n.; pl.* -TIES (-tĭz). **1.** Taste for or interest in virtu. **2.** Great technical skill in the practice of the fine arts, esp. in music; as, a pianist noted for his *virtuosity.* **3.** Virtuosos collectively.

vir'tu·o'so (vûr'tū·ō'sō; vĭr'tōō·ō'sō), *n.; pl.* -SOS (-sōz), -SI (-sē). [It. (in senses 2 & 3).] **1.** *Hist.* **a** An experimental philosopher; an empiricist. **b** A savant; scholar. **2.** A collector or ardent admirer of virtu. **3.** One who exhibits virtuosity, esp. in playing a musical instrument.

vir'tu·ous (vûr'tū·ŭs), *adj.* [OF. *vertuos, vertuous,* fr. LL. *virtuosus.*] **1.** Having or exhibiting virtue, esp. moral virtue; specif., chaste, pure. **2.** Efficacious; potent. — **Syn.** See MORAL. — **Ant.** Vicious. — **vir'tu·ous·ly**, *adv.* — **vir'tu·ous·ness**, *n.*

‖**vir·tu'te et ar'mis** (vûr·tū'tē ĕt är'mĭs). [L.] By valor and arms; — motto of Mississippi.

vir'u·lent (vĭr'ū·lĕnt; vĭr'ōō-; 118), *adj.* [L. *virulentus,* fr. *virus* poison.] **1.** Extremely venomous; noxious; deadly; as, a *virulent* poison. **2.** Bitter in enmity; malignant; as, *virulent* invective. **3.** *Bacteriol.* Infectious; able to overcome or break down the defensive mechanism of the host; — of microorganisms. **4.** *Med.* Characterized by rapid course and malignancy; — of diseases, infections, etc. — **vir'u·lence** (-lĕns), **vir'u·len·cy** (-lĕn·sĭ), *n.* — **vir'u·lent·ly**, *adv.*

vi'rus (vī'rŭs), *n.* [L., slimy liquid, poison.] **1.** Venom. **2. a** Any of a group of submicroscopic infective agents, thought by some to be living organisms, and by others to be complex proteins capable of multiplication in living cells. Viruses cause a number of diseases in animals and plants, as rabies, smallpox, mumps, and tobacco mosaic. **b** In full, ***filtrable virus.*** Loosely, any minute infective agent capable of passing through a filter too fine to pass bacteria. Filtrable viruses include undoubted living organisms as well as agents of undetermined character. **c** The fluid exudates from the vesicles, esp. of cowpox, used in vaccination for smallpox. **3.** Something that corrupts or poisons the mind or the soul.

‖**vis** (vĭs), *n.; pl.* VIRES (vī'rēz). [L.] Force; vigor.

vi'sa (vē'zȧ), **vi'sé** (vē'zā; vē·zā'), *n.* [F., fr. L. *visa*, fem. sing. or neut. pl. of *visus*, past part. of *videre* to see.] **1.** An endorsement made on a passport by the proper authorities, denoting that it has been examined, and that the bearer may proceed. **2.** A signature of formal approval by a superior upon a document.

☞ The original form *visé* is widely used. The United States Department of State prefers *visa*.

— *v. t.;* VI'SAED (vē'zȧd), VI'SÉED (vē'zād; vē·zād'); VI'SA·ING, VI'SÉ·ING. To give a visa to.

vis'age (vĭz'ĭj; vĭs'-), *n.* [OF., fr. *vis* face, fr. L. *visus* a seeing, a look, fr. *videre, visum,* to see.] The face, countenance, or look, of a person or an animal; — chiefly applied to the human face; hence, aspect; appearance. — **Syn.** See FACE.

vis'ard (vĭz'ẽrd). Var. of VIZARD.

vis'-à-vis' (vē'-zȧ·vē'), *n. sing. & pl.* [F., opposite, face to face.] **1.** One who or that which is face to face with another, esp. in dancing. **2.** = TÊTE-À-TÊTE, *n.*, 2. **—** *adv. & adj.* Face to face; opposite.

Vi·sa'yan (vē·sä'yăn), **Bi·sa'yan** (bē-), *n.* [Cf. Sp. *Bisayo* a Visayan.] A member of the most numerous of the native races of the Philippines; also, their language.

vis·ca'cha (vĭs·kä'chȧ), *n.* [Sp., fr. Quechua *uiscacha, huiscacha.*] A burrowing South American rodent (*Lagostomus maximus*) allied to the chinchillas, but much larger.

vis'cer·a (vĭs'ẽr·ȧ), *n. pl.; sing.* VISCUS (-kŭs). [L. *viscus*, pl. *viscera.*] The internal organs, esp. those of the cavities of the body, as the heart, liver, intestines, etc. — **vis'cer·al** (-ăl), *adj.*

vis'cid (vĭs'ĭd), *adj.* [LL. *viscidus*, fr. L. *viscum* the mistletoe, birdlime.] **1.** Sticking or adhering, and having a ropy or glutinous consistency; viscous; glutinous; sticky. **2.** Overlaid with a sticky layer; — esp. of leaves. — **vis·cid'i·ty** (vĭ·sĭd'ĭ·tĭ), **vis'cid·ness**, *n.* — **vis'cid·ly**, *adv.*

vis·com'e·ter (vĭs·kŏm'ē·tẽr), **vis'co·sim'e·ter** (vĭs'kō·sĭm'ē·tẽr), *n.* A device to measure viscosity. — **vis'co·met'ric** (vĭs'kō·mĕt'rĭk), **vis'co·si·met'ric** (-sĭ·mĕt'rĭk), *adj.*

vis'cose (vĭs'kōs; vĭs·kōs'), *adj.* [LL. *viscosus.*] **a** Viscous; viscid. **b** Of, pertaining to, or made from viscose. **—** (vĭs'kōs), *n.* A viscous orange solution made by treating cellulose with caustic alkali solution and carbon disulfide, and used in making rayon, transparent paper, etc.

vis·cos'i·ty (vĭs·kŏs'ĭ·tĭ), *n.; pl.* -TIES (-tĭz). **1.** Quality, state, or degree of being viscous. **2.** *Physics.* **a** That property of a body in virtue of which, when flow occurs inside it, forces arise in such a direction as to oppose the flow. **b** In a solid, power of yielding continually under stress.

vis'count' (vī'kount'), *n.* [OF. *visconte, vezconte*, fr. ML. *vicecomes*, fr. L. *vice* (see VICE, *prep.*) — *comes* a companion, ML., a count. See COUNT nobleman.] **1.** *Hist.* An officer who formerly acted in place of the count, or earl; later, a sheriff. **2.** A nobleman next below an earl or count and next above a baron. — **vis'count'cy** (-sĭ), **vis'count'y** (vī'koun'tĭ), *n.* — **vis'count'ess** (-koun'tĕs; -tĭs), *n.*

vis'cous (vĭs'kŭs), *adj.* [LL. *viscosus.* See VISCID.] **1.** Viscid. **2.** *Physics.* Possessing or characterized by viscosity. — **vis'cous·ly**, *adv.* — **vis'cous·ness**, *n.*

vis'cus (vĭs'kŭs), *n., sing.* of VISCERA.

vise, vice (vīs), *n.* [OF. *vis, viz*, a screw, winding stair, fr. L. *vitis* a vine, pl. *vites.*] Any of various devices having two jaws, closing by a screw, lever, cam, or the like, for holding work. **— *v. t.;*** VISED or VICED (vīst); VIS'ING or VIC'ING (vīs'ĭng). To hold, force, or squeeze, with or as with a vise.

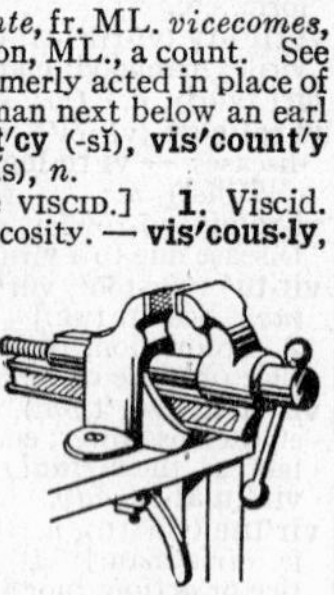

Vise.

vi'sé (vē'zā; vē·zā'), *n. & v. t.* [F., past part. of *viser* to put a visa to. See VISA.] Visa.

Vish'nu (vĭsh'nōō), *n.* [Skr. *Viṣṇu.*] *Hindu Relig.* The second god of the Hindu triad, called *the Preserver.* He has many avatars, or incarnations, as Rama and Krishna, under which forms he has millions of worshipers. See TRIMURTI.

vis'i·bil'i·ty (vĭz'ĭ·bĭl'ĭ·tĭ), *n.; pl.* -TIES (-tĭz). **1.** Quality, state, or degree, of being visible. **2.** *Meteorol. & Aeronautics.* **a** The degree of clearness of the atmosphere. **b** The greatest horizontal distance at which prominent objects can be recognized. **3.** The relative efficiency of radiant energy in evoking brilliance.

vis'i·ble (vĭz'ĭ·b'l), *adj.* [OF. or L.; OF., fr. L. *visibilis*, fr. *videre, visum,* to see.] **1.** Capable of being seen; as, a *visible* star. **2.** Exposed to view; as, the *visible* horizon; manifest; apparent; as, no *visible* means of support; also, available; as, the *visible* supply. **3.** Constructed, presented, etc., so as to make something (formerly hidden, not perceptible, etc.) visible or graphic; as, a *visible* typewriter. — **vis'i·ble·ness**, *n.* — **vis'i·bly**, *adv.*

Vis'i·goth (vĭz'ĭ·gŏth), *n.* [LL. *Visigothi*, pl., lit., the good, or noble, Goths; later, the western Goths. See GOTH.] One of the West Goths. See GOTH, 1. — **Vis'i·goth'ic** (-gŏth'ĭk), *adj.*

vi'sion (vĭzh'ŭn), *n.* [OF., fr. L. *visio*, fr. *videre, visum,* to see.] **1.** Something seen otherwise than by ordinary sight; something beheld as in a dream or ecstasy, or revealed, as to a prophet. **2.** A visual image without corporeal presence; also, an object of imaginative contemplation; as, to have *visions* of wealth. **3.** Power or activity of the imagination; as, a poet with *vision.* **4.** Unusual discernment or foresight; as, a man of *vision.* **5.** Actual sight; ocular perception. **6.** That which is seen; as, she was a *vision* of delight; also, a lovely or charming sight. **7.** The sense by which light and color are apprehended; as, the organ of *vision* is the eye. **— *v. t & i.*** To see in or as if in a vision. — **vi'sion·al** (-ăl), *adj.* — **vi'sion·al·ly**, *adv.*

vi'sion·ar'y (-ĕr'ĭ *or, esp. Brit.,* -ẽr·ĭ), *adj.* **1.** Seeing, or disposed to see, visions; given to dreaming or imagining. **2.** Of the nature of a vision; existing in imagination only; hence, impracticable; chimerical. **3.** Of, pert. to, or favorable for visions. — **Syn.** See IMAGINARY. **—** *n.; pl.* -IES (-ĭz). One who sees visions; specif., one whose ideas or projects are impractical.

vis'it (vĭz'ĭt), *v. t.* [OF. *visiter*, fr. L. *visitare*, fr. *visere* to go to see, visit, fr. *videre, visum,* to see.] **1.** To go or come to see in order to comfort or help. **2.** Hence: **a** To pay a call upon as an act of friendship or courtesy. **b** To go or come to see in an official or professional capacity; to inspect. **c** To dwell with temporarily as a guest. **3.** To come to or upon, as to reward, afflict, punish, etc.; hence: **a** To bless. **b** To inflict. **— *v. i.*** **1.** To visit punishment or vengeance. **2.** To make a visit; to make frequent or regular visits. **3.** *Colloq.* To chat or converse; as, to *visit* over the telephone.

— *n.* **1.** A visiting; specif.: **a** A call. **b** A stay as a guest. **c** A formal call, as for inspection, professional service, etc. **d** *Colloq.* A chat; a conversation. **2.** *Marine Law.* The act of a naval officer of one state in boarding a neutral merchant vessel of another state in the exercise of the right of search.

vis'it·a·ble (-ȧ·b'l), *adj.* **1.** Subject to, or allowing, visitation or inspection. **2.** Socially eligible to receive visits.

vis'it·ant (vĭz'ĭ·tănt), *n.* **1.** A visitor; esp., one who visits from, or as if from, outside one's own sphere. **2.** *Ornith.* A migratory bird which appears at intervals for a limited period.

vis'it·a'tion (-tā'shŭn), *n.* **1.** A visit; esp., an official visit, as of a bishop to a church, college, etc., in his diocese. **2.** A visiting of affliction or punishment, or rarely, blessing, esp. as a divine dispensation; hence, a severe trial or affliction. **3.** [*cap.*] *Eccl.* **a** The visit of the Virgin Mary to Elisabeth before the birth of Elisabeth's son, John the Baptist. **b** The church feast (July 2) commemorating this visit. **4.** Resort to a place by birds, mammals, or other animals, at an unusual time or in unusual numbers. — **vis'it·a'tion·al** (-ăl; -'l), *adj.*

vis'it·a·to'ri·al (vĭz'ĭ·tȧ·tō'rĭ·ăl; 70), *adj.* Also **vis'i·to'ri·al** (vĭz'ĭ·tō'rĭ·ăl; 70). Of or pertaining to visitation, or a judicial visitor or superintendent.

vis'it·ing card. A small card bearing the name, and sometimes the address, of a person or married couple, presented when calling; a calling card.

vis'i·tor (vĭz'ĭ·tẽr), *n.* One who makes a visit; specif., one who makes formal visits of inspection.

‖**vis ma'jor** (vĭs mā'jŏr). [L. *major* greater.] *Law.* A superior force which under certain circumstances is held to exempt from contract obligations.

vi'sor, vi'zor (vī'zẽr; vĭz'ẽr), *n.* [AF. *viser* (F. *visière*), fr. *vis* face.] **1.** A face mask; a disguise. **2.** The front piece of a helmet, esp. a movable upper piece. See HELMET, *Illust.* **3.** The projecting front of a cap, to protect the eyes. **— *v. t.*** To cover with a visor; mask.

vis'ta (vĭs'tȧ), *n.* [It., sight, view, fr. *vedere*, past part. *visto, veduto*, to see, fr. L. *videre, visum.*] **1.** A long view, or prospect, esp. one through or along an avenue, as between rows of trees; also, the trees or other objects forming the avenue. **2.** A mental view, or prospect, extending over a series of events, or the like; as, *vistas* of memory.

vis'u·al (vĭzh'ū·ăl; 118), *adj.* [LL. *visualis*, fr. L. *visus* a seeing, sight.] **1.** Of, pertaining to, or used in sight; ocular; as, the *visual* nerve. **2.** Perceived, attained, performed, etc., by vision; as, *visual* impressions or tests. **3.** Optic; as, the *visual* focus of a lens. **4.** Produced as, or conveying, a mental vision; as, a *visual* image or epithet. — **vis'u·al·ly**, *adv.*

visual acuity. Sharpness of vision in respect to the ability to distinguish detail. For human beings it is commonly tested by means of letters or other characters graduated in size according to the maximum distance at which they can be distinguished by the normal eye. According to one common scale, the visual acuity of the normal eye, which can distinguish at 20 feet characters one-third inch in diameter, is designated as ***twenty-twenty*** (*or* ***20/20***), the acuity of an eye that can distinguish at 20 feet only characters of twice this size is designated as ***twenty-forty*** (*or* ***20/40***), and so on.

visual aid. Any device or means using vision as the chief medium to aid instruction, for example, a chart, map, model, perspective drawing, or projector, but especially a documentary or other expository motion picture or a filmstrip. Hence, **visual instruction** *or* **education.**

vis'u·al·ize (vĭzh'ū·ăl·īz), *v. t. & i.* To make or become visible; esp., to see or form a mental image of. — **vis'u·al·i·za'tion** (-ĭ·zā'shŭn; -ī·zā'-), *n.*

vis'u·al·iz'er (-īz'ẽr), *n.* One that visualizes; esp., one whose mental imagery is prevailingly visual. Cf. AUDILE, MOTILE.

visual purple *or* **red.** *Biochem.* A purple-red pigment contained in the retinal rods in human eyes and those of most other animals. It is quickly bleached by light to another pigment, **visual yellow,** another pigment, and finally to the white compound **visual white.** It is said to function in vision at night.

vi'ta (vī'tȧ), *n.* [L.] Literally, life; specif., a brief autobiographical sketch.

vi·ta'ceous (vī·tā'shŭs), *adj.* [L. *vitis* a vine.] Belonging to the grape family (Vitaceae). See GRAPE.

vi'tal (vī'tăl; -t'l), *adj.* [OF., fr. L. *vitalis*, fr. *vita* life.] **1.** Of, pertaining to, or existent as a manifestation of life; as, *vital* functions or energy. **2.** Essential to the continuance of life or full physical vigor; necessary to life; as, wounded in a *vital* part; *vital* blood. **3. a** *Now Rare.* Living; animate. **b** Animated; full of life and vigor; as, a *vital* personality. **4.** Fatal; mortal; as, a *vital* wound. **5.** Fundamentally affecting the continuation, value, efficiency, or the like, of anything; basic; as, a *vital* error in reasoning; hence, indispensable; requisite; as, his support is *vital* to us; loosely, highly important. **6.** Relating to lives, or data concerning births, deaths, etc.; as, *vital* statistics. — **Syn.** See LIVING: ESSENTIAL. **—** *n. pl.* **a** Vital organs, as the heart, brain, etc. **b** Parts essential to a thing's life, maintenance, etc. — **vi'tal·ly**, *adv.*

vi'tal·ism (vī'tăl·ĭz'm), *n.* *Philos. & Biol.* **a** The doctrine that the functions of a living organism are due to a vital principle or force. **b** The doctrine that the processes of life are not explicable by the laws of physics and chemistry alone and that life is in some part self-determining; — opposed to *mechanism.* See TELEOLOGY, 2; ORGANICISM. — **vi'tal·ist** (-ĭst), *n. & adj.* — **vi'tal·is'tic** (-ĭs'tĭk), *adj.*

vi·tal'i·ty (vī·tăl'ĭ·tĭ), *n.* State or quality of being vital; specif.: **a** Life; animate existence; the principle of life. **b** Power of enduring or continuing; as, the *vitality* of slang. **c** Animation; vigor; liveliness.

vi'tal·ize (vī'tăl·īz), *v. t.* To endow with life; make alive; impart vigor or energy to; animate. — **vi'tal·i·za'tion** (-ĭ·zā'shŭn; -ī·zā'-), *n.*

Vi·tal'li·um (vī·tăl'ĭ·ŭm), *n.* A trade-mark applied to a cobalt-chromium alloy for cast dentures, bone surgical appliances, etc.

vi'ta·mer (vī'tȧ·mẽr), *n.* [From *vitamin* + iso*mer.*] A compound that relieves a particular vitamin deficiency; as, a D *vitamer.* — **vi'ta·mer'ic** (-mĕr'ĭk), *adj.*

vi′ta·min (vī′tȧ·mĭn; vĭt′ȧ-), *n.* Also **vi′ta·mine** (vī′tȧ·mĭn; -mēn; vĭt′ȧ-). [L. *vita* life + E. *amine.*] *Biochem.* Any of a number of constituents of foods in their natural state, of which very small quantities are essential for the normal nutrition of animals, and possibly of plants. **vitamin A**, $C_{20}H_{29}OH$, occurs esp. in fish-liver oils, butter, and eggs, and is synthesized in the animal; its lack causes hardening of certain tissues, as in the eye, and failure of young animals to grow. **vitamin B**, a group of substances (the **vitamin–B complex**), includes: (1) **vitamin B₁**, **vitamin F**, *aneurin*, or *thiamine*, $C_{12}H_{17}ClN_4OS$, the antineuritic or antiberiberi factor, found esp. in cereals, nuts, yeast, and animal food products. (2) **vitamin B₂**, **vitamin G**, (D-)*riboflavin*, or *lactoflavin*, $C_{17}H_{20}N_4O_6$, a growth-promoting factor, found esp. in whey, eggs, and green leaves. (3) *Nicotinic acid*, or *niacin*, a crystalline acid, $C_6H_5NO_2$, and its amide *nicotinamide*, or *niacin amide*, $C_6H_6N_2O$, preventing pellagra, found in meats, milk, leafy green vegetables, peas, and beans; — called also the "*P.P.* (pellagra-preventive) *factor.*" (4) **vitamin B₆**, *adermin*, *pyridoxine*, or the "rat antidermatitis factor," $C_8H_{11}NO_3$, essential to human nutrition, found in meat, fish liver, wheat germs, etc. (5) The "chick antidermatitis factor," or *pantothenic acid*, $C_9H_{17}NO_5$, a substance extracted from various organic tissues, and promoting growth, as of yeast. (6) *Biotin* (formerly called **vitamin H**), $C_{10}H_{16}N_2O_3S$, an acid that is a growth-promoting factor, occurring esp. in yeast and liver. (7) **para-** (*or* **p-**) **aminobenzoic acid**, the "anti-gray-hair vitamin," $C_7H_7NO_2$, a growth-promoting factor, found esp. in yeast and bran. (8) *Choline.* (9) *Folic acid.* (10) *Inositol.* **vitamin C**, (L-)*ascorbic acid*, or *cevitamic acid*, $C_6H_8O_6$, the antiscorbutic vitamin, is abundant in fresh fruits, esp. citrus fruits, tomatoes, and vegetables, and occurs in animal products. Of **vitamin D**, which is antirachitic and regulates the phosphorus-calcium metabolism, there are several varieties, prepared or occurring naturally in fish-liver oils, egg yolk, etc., as **vitamin D₁** and **vitamin D₂**, or *calciferol*, $C_{28}H_{43}OH$, an alcohol formed by irradiating ergosterol. **vitamin E** (formerly called **vitamin X**), whose lack causes infertility and muscular atrophy, is abundant in the leaves of many plants and in oils from seeds. It includes *α-tocopherol*, $C_{29}H_{50}O_2$, and other varieties of tocopherol. **vitamin K** is the antihemorrhagic vitamin, the variety **vitamin K₁**, $C_{31}H_{46}O_2$, occurring in the leaves of alfalfa and other plants, vegetables, fish meal, etc. **vitamin K₂** is similar to it. The terms **vitamin P** and *citrin* have been applied to a substance (now believed to be a mixture of flavones) isolated from lemons and paprika, thought to promote the resistance of the capillaries to hemorrhage. — **vi′ta·min,** *adj.* — **vi′ta·min′ic** (-mĭn′ĭk), *adj.*

vi′ta·scope (vī′tȧ·skōp), *n.* [L. *vita* life + *-scope.*] A motion-picture projector. — **vi′ta·scop′ic** (-skŏp′ĭk), *adj.*

vi·tel′lin (vĭ·tĕl′ĭn; vī-), *n.* [See VITELLUS.] *Biochem.* A protein in the yolk of egg.

vi·tel′line (-ĭn), *adj.* Of, pertaining to, or like the yolk of an egg; esp., yellow in color. — *n.* The yolk of an egg.

vi·tel′lus (vĭ·tĕl′ŭs; vī-), *n.* [L., the yolk of an egg.] *Embryol.* The yolk of an egg.

vi′ti·a·ble (vĭsh′ĭ·ȧ·b′l), *adj.* That can be vitiated.

vi′ti·ate (vĭsh′ĭ·āt), *v. t.* [L. *vitiatus*, past part. of *vitiare* to vitiate, fr. *vitium* a fault, vice.] **1.** To contaminate; spoil; corrupt; pollute; as, sewer gas *vitiates* the air. **2.** To debase; pervert; as, plays that *vitiate* one's taste. **3.** To render ineffective, either wholly or in part; invalidate; as, fraud *vitiates* a contract. — **Syn.** See DEBASE. — **vi′ti·a′tion** (-ā′shŭn), *n.* — **vi′ti·a′tor** (-ā′tẽr), *n.*

vi′ti·at′ed (-āt′ĕd; -ĭd), *adj.* Made defective, ineffective, etc.; contaminated; invalidated.

vit′i·cul′ture (vĭt′ĭ·kŭl′tūr; vī′tĭ-), *n.* [L. *vitis* vine + E. *culture.*] The cultivation of the vine; grape growing. — **vit′i·cul′tur·al** (-kŭl′tūr·ăl), *adj.* — **vit′i·cul′tur·er** (-ẽr), **vit′i·cul′tur·ist** (-ĭst), *n.*

vit′i·li′go (vĭt′ĭ·lī′gō), *n.* [L., a kind of tetter.] A skin disease manifested by smooth, milk-white spots, on various parts of the body.

vit′re·ous (vĭt′rē·ŭs), *adj.* [L. *vitreus*, fr. *vitrum* glass, orig., woad.] **1.** Of, pertaining to, or derived from glass. **2.** Like glass, as in color, brittleness, luster, etc.; glassy; as, *vitreous* rocks. **3.** Of or pertaining to the vitreous humor. — **vit′re·os′i·ty** (-ŏs′ĭ·tĭ), **vit′re·ous·ness,** *n.*

vitreous electricity. Electricity of the kind excited by rubbing glass with silk; positive electricity.

vitreous humor. *Anat.* The clear colorless transparent jelly which fills the posterior chamber of the eyeball. See EYE, *Illust.*

vi·tres′cent (vĭ·trĕs′ĕnt; -′nt), *adj.* [See VITREOUS; -ESCENT.] Capable of being formed into glass; tending to become glass. — **vi·tres′cence** (-ĕns; -′ns), *n.*

vi·tres′ci·ble (-ĭ·b′l), *adj.* Vitrifiable.

vit′ric (vĭt′rĭk), *adj.* [L. *vitrum* glass.] Of the nature of glass; glasslike; — disting. from *ceramic.*

vit′ri·fac′tion (vĭt′rĭ·făk′shŭn), *n.* Vitrification.

vit′ri·form (vĭt′rĭ·fôrm), *adj.* [L. *vitrum* glass + *-form.*] Having the form or appearance of glass; glasslike.

vit′ri·fy (-fī), *v. t. & i.* [F. *vitrifier*, fr. L. *vitrum* glass + *-ficare* to make.] To change into glass or a glassy substance, by heat and fusion; to make or become vitreous. — **vit′ri·fi′a·ble** (-fī′ȧ·b′l), *adj.* — **vit′ri·fi·ca′tion** (-fĭ·kā′shŭn), *n.*

vit′ri·ol (vĭt′rĭ·ŭl), *n.* [OF. *vitriol*, fr. ML. *vitriolum*, fr. *vitreus* vitreous.] **1.** *Chem.* **a** A sulfate of various metals in its crystallized form, esp. of copper (***blue vitriol*** $CuSO_4 5H_2O$), iron (***green vitriol*** *or* ***copperas*** $FeSO_4 7H_2O$), zinc (***white vitriol*** $ZnSO_4 7H_2O$); — from the glassy appearance of many of these salts. Blue vitriol is used in dyeing and calico printing, germicides, fungicides (as Bordeaux mixture), electric batteries, etc.; green vitriol, as a mordant, in medicine, and in making ink and pigments; white vitriol, in dyes, varnishes, medicines, etc. **b** Oil of vitriol. See SULFURIC ACID. **2.** Hence, anything likened to vitriol as being caustic; figuratively, virulence. — *v. t.;* -OLED (-ŭld) or -OLLED; -OL·ING or -OL·LING. *Metal.* To dip in dilute sulfuric acid; pickle. — **vit′ri·ol′ic** (-ŏl′ĭk), *adj.*

vit′ri·ol·ize (-īz), *v. t.* **1.** To convert into, or subject to the action of, vitriol. **2.** To injure (a person) with vitriol, as by throwing it upon the face. — **vit′ri·ol·i·za′tion** (-ĭ·zā′shŭn; -ī·zā′-), *n.*

vit′ta (vĭt′ȧ), *n.; pl.* -TAE (-ē). [L., ribbon, fillet.] **1.** *Class. Antiq.* A headband or fillet. **2.** *Bot.* One of the oil tubes in the fruits of plants of the carrot family. **3.** *Zool. & Bot.* A stripe of color.

vit′tate (vĭt′āt), *adj.* **1.** *Bot.* Bearing or containing vittae. **2.** *Bot. & Zool.* Striped longitudinally.

vit′tle (vĭt′′l). Dial. var. of VICTUAL.

vit′u·line (vĭt′ū·lĭn; -lĭn), *adj.* [L. *vitulinus*, fr. *vitulus* a calf.] Of, pert. to, or like a calf or veal.

vi·tu′per·ate (vī·tū′pẽr·āt; vĭ-), *v. t. & i.* [L. *vituperatus*, past part. of *vituperare* to blame, vituperate.] To abuse in words; censure severely or abusively; berate. — **Syn.** See SCOLD. — **vi·tu′per·a′tive** (-ā′tĭv), *adj.* — **vi·tu′per·a′tive·ly,** *adv.* — **vi·tu′per·a′tor** (-ā′tẽr), *n.*

vi·tu′per·a′tion (-ā′shŭn), *n.* Act or instance of vituperating; wordy abuse. — **Syn.** See ABUSE.

‖**vi′va** (vē′vä), *interj.* [It.] Literally, (long) live; — an exclamation of well-wishing, etc. — *n.* A shouted *viva.*

‖**vi·va′ce** (vē·vä′chā), *adj.* [It.] *Music.* Brisk; spirited; — a direction.

vi·va′cious (vī·vā′shŭs; vĭ-), *adj.* [L. *vivax*, *-acis*, fr. *vivere* to live.] **1.** *Archaic.* Tenacious of life; long-lived. **2.** Lively in temper or conduct; sprightly. — **Syn.** See LIVELY. — **vi·va′cious·ly,** *adv.* — **vi·va′cious·ness,** *n.*

vi·vac′i·ty (vī·văs′ĭ·tĭ; vĭ-), *n.* Vivaciousness; sprightliness.

vi′van′dière′ (vē′väɴ′dyâr′), *n.* [F., fem. of *vivandier* a sutler.] *Hist.* A woman accompanying troops, esp. of the French army, and selling provisions and liquor.

vi·var′i·um (vī·vâr′ĭ·ŭm), *n.; pl.* -IUMS (-ŭmz), -IA (-ȧ). [L., fr. *vivarius* belonging to living creatures, fr. *vivus* alive, living.] An enclosure for keeping or raising indoors plants or animals, esp. terrestrial animals.

vi′va vo′ce (vī′vȧ vō′sē). [L.] By word of mouth; orally; as, an examination conducted *viva voce.*

vi′va–vo′ce, *adj.* Expressed or conducted by word of mouth; oral; as, *viva-voce* voting.

‖**vive** (vēv). [F., subjunctive sing. pres. fr. *vivre* to live, fr. L. *vivere.*] Long live, that is, success to; as in **vive le roi** (lẽ rwä′), long live the king.

vi·ver′rine (vī·vĕr′ĭn; -īn; vĭ-), *adj.* [L. *viverra* a ferret.] Belonging to a family (Viverridae) of small catlike carnivores, the civet family. — *n.* A civet.

vi′vers (vē′vẽrz), *n. pl.* *Scot.* Victuals; food.

vives (vīvz), *n.* [F., fr. *avives*, fr. Sp., fr. Ar. *al-dhībah.*] Inflammatory swelling of the submaxillary glands of a horse.

Viv′i·an (vĭv′ĭ·ăn; vĭv′yăn), **Viv′i·en** (-ĕn; -yĕn), *n.* In Arthurian legend, the mistress of Merlin; — called also *Lady of the Lake.*

viv′id (vĭv′ĭd), *adj.* [L. *vividus*, fr. *vivere* to live.] **1.** Having the appearance of vigorous life or freshness; animated; lively; as, a *vivid* sketch or portrait. **2.** Of colors: brilliant; intense; bright; technically, having a very high saturation. **3.** Of a sensation, an impression, a mental image, etc.: sharp and clear; distinctly felt, conceived, etc.; as, *vivid* recollections. **4.** Evoking lifelike mental images; as, *vivid* description. — **Syn.** See GRAPHIC. — **viv′id·ly,** *adv.* — **viv′id·ness,** *n.*

viv′i·fy (vĭv′ĭ·fī), *v. t.;* -FIED (-fīd); -FY′ING. [F. *vivifier*, fr. LL. *vivificare.* See VIVID, -FY.] **1.** To endue with life; quicken; animate. **2.** To make vivid. — **Syn.** See QUICKEN. — **viv′i·fi·ca′tion** (-fĭ·kā′shŭn), *n.* — **viv′i·fi′er** (-fī′ẽr), *n.*

vi·vip′a·rous (vī·vĭp′ȧ·rŭs), *adj.* [L. *viviparus*, fr. *vivus* alive + *parere* to bear, bring forth.] **1.** Producing living young (instead of eggs) from within the body, as nearly all mammals; — contrasted with *oviparous.* **2.** *Bot.* **a** Germinating while still attached to the parent plant. **b** Proliferous. — **viv′i·par′i·ty** (vĭv′ĭ·păr′ĭ·tĭ), **vi·vip′a·rous·ness,** *n.* — **vi·vip′a·rous·ly,** *adv.*

viv′i·sect (vĭv′ĭ·sĕkt; vĭv′ĭ·sĕkt′), *v. t. & i.* To perform or practice vivisection (on). — **viv′i·sec′tor** (-sĕk′tẽr; -sĕk′tẽr), *n.*

viv′i·sec′tion (-sĕk′shŭn), *n.* [L. *vivus* alive + E. *section.*] The cutting of, or operation on, a living animal, esp. for physiological or pathological investigation; also, an instance of this. — **viv′i·sec′tion·al** (-ăl), *adj.* — **viv′i·sec′tion·ist** (-ĭst), *n. & adj.*

vix′en (vĭk′s′n), *n.* [Dial. form of *fixen*, fr. AS. *fyxen*, fem. of *fox.*] **1.** A she-fox. **2.** A shrewish, ill-tempered person; — now only of a woman. — **vix′en·ish, vix′en·ly,** *adj.*

viz. (*usually read* "namely"). Abbrev. of VIDELICET.

viz′ard (vĭz′ẽrd), *n.* [See VISOR.] Mask; visor.

vi·zier′ (vĭ·zēr′; vĭz′yẽr; -ĭ·ẽr), *n.* Also **vi·zir′** (vĭ·zēr′). [Turk. *vezīr*, fr. Ar. *wazīr*, prop., a bearer of burdens, porter.] A high executive officer of various Mohammedan countries, esp. of the former Turkish empire; a minister or councilor of state. — **vi·zier′ate, vi·zir′ate** (-āt), *n.* — **vi·zier′i·al, vi·zir′i·al** (vĭ·zēr′ĭ·ăl), *adj.* — **vi·zier′ship, vi·zir′ship,** *n.*

vi′zor. Var. of VISOR.

V–J Day (vē′jā′). The day of victory over Japan in World War II, either the day of Japan's surrender (August 14, 1945) or the day of formal surrender aboard the U.S.S. Missouri (September 2, 1945).

V′–mail′ (vē′māl′), *n.* [*V* as symbol for *Victory.*] A mailing system by which a letter is reproduced on photographic microfilm to be forwarded and enlarged on photographic paper for delivery.

vo′ca·ble (vō′kȧ·b′l), *n.* [F., fr. L. *vocabulum* an appellation, name, fr. *vocare* to call.] A word; term; name; specif., a word regarded as composed of certain sounds or letters without regard to its meaning. — *adj.* Utterable.

vo·cab′u·lar′y (vō·kăb′ū·lẽr′ĭ *or, esp. Brit.,* -lẽr·ĭ), *n.; pl.* -IES (-ĭz). [ML. *vocabularium*, *vocabularius.* See VOCABLE.] **1.** A list or collection of words or of words and phrases, usually alphabetically arranged and explained or defined; a dictionary or lexicon. **2.** A sum or stock of words used in a language, by a class, individual, etc., or in a field of knowledge.

vocabulary entry. An entry of a word or term in a vocabulary; specif., in dictionary usage, any term (word or entry) listed alphabetically or as part of a related or associated group of terms, for the purpose of definition or identification, and printed in type that is readily distinguishable from that of the definitions or explanations. Inflectional forms, run-on and run-in entries, and self-explanatory combinations or phrases are included in vocabulary entries (see Explanatory Notes, §§ 4, 8–10).

vo′cal (vō′kăl), *adj.* [L. *vocalis*, fr. *vox*, *vocis*, voice.] **1.** Of, pertaining to, or having voice or speech; as, *vocal* sounds or cavities. **2.** Full of voice or voices; as, air *vocal* with the song of birds. **3.** Uttered by the voice; oral; as, *vocal* prayer. **4.** Expressing, or given to expressing, oneself in speech; hence, expressing oneself insistently; clamorous; as, *vocal* persons. **5.** *Music.* Made or rendered by, or composed or arranged for, the human voice; as, *vocal* music. **6.** *Phonet.* **a** Consisting of, or characterized by, voice, or tone produced in the larynx; voiced; sonant; intonated. **b** Of or pertaining to a vowel; having the character of a vowel; vowel. — *n.* A vocal sound. — **vo·cal′i·ty** (vō·kăl′ĭ·tĭ), *n.* — **vo′cal·ly,** *adv.*

vocal cords. *Anat.* Either of two pairs of folds of mucous membrane which project into the cavity of the larynx. The upper pair (***superior, or false, vocal cords***) are thick and are not directly concerned in the production of voice. The passage of breath between the edges of the lower pair (***inferior, or true, vocal cords;*** — called also **vocal folds**) when drawn tense and approximated together produces the voice.
vo·cal′ic (vō·kăl′ĭk), *adj.* Of, pertaining to, of the nature of, or containing vowel sounds.
vo′cal·ism (vō′kăl·ĭz'm), *n.* **1.** Vocalization. **2.** Act, technique, or art of singing. **3.** The vowel system of a language or dialect.
vo′cal·ist (-ĭst), *n.* A singer. Cf. INSTRUMENTALIST.
vo′cal·ize (-īz), *v. t.* **1.** To form into voice; to make vocal, or sonant; voice. **2.** To change into, or use as, a vowel; as, to *vocalize* the letter *w.* **3.** To give utterance or expression to. — *v. i.* **1.** To vocalize sounds. **2.** To sing; specif., to practice singing upon vowel sounds. — **vo′cal·i·za′tion** (-ĭ·zā′shŭn; -ī·zā′-), *n.* — **vo′cal·iz′er** (-īz′ẽr), *n.*
vo·ca′tion (vō·kā′shŭn), *n.* [L. *vocatio* a bidding, a calling, invitation, fr. *vocare* to call.] **1.** A call; a summons; specif., a calling to a particular state, business, or profession; as, a *vocation* to the religious life. **2.** Regular employment; occupation; profession; as, to change one's *vocation.* Cf. AVOCATION, 2.
vo·ca′tion·al (-ăl; -'l), *adj.* **1.** Of, pertaining to, or concerned with vocation; also, pursued as a vocation. **2.** Guiding in the choice, or training for the pursuit, of a vocation; also, concerned with or skilled in such guidance or training; as, a *vocational* adviser. — **vo·ca′tion·al·ly,** *adv.*
voc′a·tive (vŏk′ȧ·tĭv), *adj.* [F. or L.; F. *vocatif,* fr. L. *vocativus,* fr. *vocare* to call.] Of, pertaining to, or used in calling; specif., *Gram.,* designating, or pertaining to, the case denoting that which is addressed. — *n.* The vocative case, a word in it, or the relation denoted by it. Abbr. *voc.* — **voc′a·tive·ly,** *adv.*
‖**vo′ces** (vō′sēz), *n., pl.* of VOX.
vo·cif′er·ant (vō·sĭf′ẽr·ănt), *adj.* Vociferous; clamorous. — *n.* One who is vociferant. — **vo·cif′er·ance** (-ăns), *n.*
vo·cif′er·ate (-āt), *v. i. & t.* [L. *vociferatus,* past part. of *vociferari* to vociferate, fr. *vox, vocis,* voice + a deriv. of *ferre* to bear.] To cry out loudly; clamor. — **vo·cif′er·a′tion** (-ā′shŭn), *n.* — **vo·cif′er·a′tor** (-ā′tẽr), *n.*
vo·cif′er·ous (-ŭs), *adj.* Making a loud outcry; clamorous; noisy. — **vo·cif′er·ous·ly,** *adv.* — **vo·cif′er·ous·ness,** *n.*
Syn. **Vociferous, clamorous, blatant, strident, boisterous, obstreperous** mean conspicuously loud and noisy. **Vociferous** implies vehement shouting that is deafening; **clamorous,** insistency and vociferousness; **blatant,** a tendency to bellow or be offensively noisy or clamorous; **strident,** not always of sounds, so harsh and disagreeable as to force itself upon one's attention; **boisterous,** extreme noisiness and turbulence; **obstreperous,** resistance to or defiance of any efforts to restrain not only noise but excitement.
vod′ka (vŏd′kȧ), *n.* [Russ., lit., little water.] A Russian distilled alcoholic liquor commonly made from rye.
vo′gie (vō′gĭ; vŏg′ĭ), *adj. Scot.* Proud; vain; also, elated; merry.
vogue (vōg), *n.* [F. *vogue* a rowing, vogue, fashion, fr. *voguer* to row, fr. It. *vogare* to row, sail.] **1.** With *the,* the way or fashion of people at any period; accepted mode or style. **2.** Popular repute, acceptation, or favor; popularity; as, to acquire *vogue;* also, a period of popularity; as, a short-lived *vogue.* **3.** That which is in fashion at a particular time; as, stripes were then the *vogue.* — **Syn.** See FASHION.
voice (vois), *n.* [OF. *vois, voiz* (F. *voix*), fr. L. *vox, vocis.*] **1.** Sound uttered by living beings, esp. by human beings in speech or song, crying, shouting, etc. **2.** Faculty or power of utterance; speech. **3.** Any sound regarded as, or likened to, vocal utterance; as, the *voice* of the sea. **4.** Anything likened to human speech as an instrument or medium of expression; as, the ballot is the *voice* of the people. **5.** Expressed wish, choice, or opinion; hence, right to express one's wish, etc.; vote; as, to have no *voice* in the matter. **6.** *Obs.* Rumor; also, fame; reputation. **7.** *Gram.* Distinction of form in a verb, or a particular system of verbal inflections, to indicate the relation of the subject of the verb to the action which the verb expresses; also, the relation so indicated; as, the active and passive *voices.* **8.** *Music.* **a** Musical sound produced by the vocal cords and resonated by the various cavities of head and throat; tones delivered in singing. **b** The ability to sing; as, to have a *voice.* **c** Condition of the vocal organs with respect to the production of musical tones; as, to be in good *voice.* **9.** *Phonet.* Vocal sound of the kind heard in the vowels and in such consonants as *l, v, n;* sonant or intonated utterance; tone; — distinguished from mere breath sound as heard in *f, s, sh,* etc., and also from whisper. — ***with one voice.*** Unanimously. — *v. t.;* VOICED (voist); VOIC′ING. **1.** To give voice or expression to; utter; also, announce; divulge. **2.** *Music.* To regulate the tone of; as, to *voice* the pipes of an organ. **3.** *Phonet.* To utter with voice. See VOICE, *n.,* 9. — **Syn.** See EXPRESS.
voiced (voist), *adj.* **1. a** Furnished with a voice. **b** Expressed by the voice. **2.** *Phonet.* Uttered with voice; sonant; vocal. See VOICE, *n.,* 9.
voice′ful (vois′fōōl; -f'l), *adj.* Having a voice or vocal quality; having a loud voice or many voices; vocal.
voice′less, *adj.* **1.** Having no voice, utterance, or vote; mute. **2.** *Phonet.* Sounded without voice; not voiced; surd.
voice part. One of the parts in a vocal or instrumental composition.
void (void), *adj.* [OF. *voit, voide,* dial. form of *vuit, vuide* (F. *vide*), fr. VL. *vocitare* to empty, fr. *vocuus* empty, for L. *vacuus.*] **1.** Containing nothing; empty. **2.** Unoccupied; vacant; — of offices, etc. **3.** Being without; destitute; wanting; devoid; as, *void* of common sense. **4.** Not producing any effect; useless. **5.** *Law.* **a** Properly, of no legal force or effect (and hence incapable of confirmation or ratification); null. **b** Improperly, voidable. — **Syn.** See EMPTY. — *n.* That which is void; an empty or unfilled space; a vacuum; also, a feeling of emptiness. — *v. t.* **1.** To make or leave void, or empty; clear; also, to vacate; leave. **2.** To throw or send out; evacuate; discharge. **3.** To render void; annul; nullify. — **void′er,** *n.*
void′a·ble (void′ȧ·b'l), *adj.* Capable of being voided; specif., *Law,* capable of being adjudged void. A *voidable* contract must be *avoided* to render it null. See AVOID, 2. — **void′a·ble·ness,** *n.*
void′ance (-ăns), *n.* A voiding; vacancy, esp. of a benefice.
void′ed (void′ĕd; -ĭd), *adj.* **a** Made void, empty, vacant, invalid, etc. **b** Having a void or opening; specif., *Her.,* having the inner part cut away or left vacant, a narrow border being left at the sides; — said of a charge.
‖**voi′là′** (vwȧ′lȧ′). [F.] See there! Behold! There!
‖**voi′là′ tout** (tōō′). [F.] That's all.
voile (voil; *F.* vwȧl), *n.* [F., a veil.] A sheer dress material of silk, cotton, or wool.
‖**voir dire** (vwär dẽr). [OF., to say the truth, fr. L. *verus* true + *dicere* to say.] *Law.* An oath administered to a witness requiring him to speak the truth in reference to matters inquired of to ascertain his competency.
voix cé′leste′ (vwä′ sā′lĕst′). [F.] A labial stop of 8-foot pitch with a soft tremulous tone. See STOP, *n.*
vo′lant (vō′lănt), *adj.* [F. or L.; F., fr. L. *volans, -antis,* pres. part. of *volare* to fly.] **1.** Flying; capable of flying. **2.** Nimble; light and quick. **3.** *Her.* Represented as if flying, as a bird.
‖**vo·lan′te** (vō·län′tā), *adj.* [It.] *Music.* Flying; moving with light rapidity; — a direction.
Vo′la·pük′ (vō′lȧ·pük′), *n.* Also **Vol′a·puk** (vŏl′ȧ·pŏŏk). Literally, world's speech; a language, intended to be international, invented by Johann Martin Schleyer, of Konstanz, Baden, about 1879. Cf. ESPERANTO. — **Vo′la·pük′ist** (-ĭst), *n.*
vo′lar (vō′lẽr), *adj.* [L. *vola* palm of the hand, sole of the foot.] *Anat.* Pertaining to the palm or sole.
vo′lar, *adj.* [L. *volare* to fly.] Pert. to or used in flight.
vol′a·tile (vŏl′ȧ·tĭl; -tīl; 56), *adj.* [OF. *volatil,* fr. L. *volatilis,* fr. *volare* to fly.] **1.** *Now Rare.* Flying; volant. **2.** Readily vaporizable; as, *volatile* oils. **3.** Lighthearted; airy; lively; hence, changeable; fickle.
volatile oil. A readily vaporizable oil; an oil that is volatile; specif., an essential oil; — disting. from *fixed oil.*
volatile salt. = SAL VOLATILE.
vol′a·til′i·ty (vŏl′ȧ·tĭl′ĭ·tĭ), *n.* Volatile quality or state. — **Syn.** See LIGHTNESS.
vol′a·til·ize (vŏl′ȧ·tĭl·īz), *v. t. & i.* To render or become volatile; exhale or evaporate. — **vol′a·til·i·za′tion** (-ĭ·zā′shŭn; -ī·zā′-), *n.* — **vol′a·til·iz′er** (-īz′ẽr), *n.*
‖**vol-au-vent** (vō′-lō′väɴ′), *n.* [F.] A large case of light puff paste with a raised border, filled, after baking, with a ragout of meat, fowl, game, fish, or the like.
vol·can′ic (vŏl·kăn′ĭk), *adj.* **1.** Of, pert. to, like, or characteristic of a volcano; characterized by or composed of volcanoes. **2.** *Geol.* Formed by solidification of a molten magma that has poured out as lava over the earth's surface from a volcano or from any surface eruption. Cf. PLUTONIC. — **vol·can′i·cal·ly** (-ĭ·kăl·ĭ), *adv.*
volcanic glass. Natural glass produced by the cooling of molten lava too rapidly to permit of crystallization.
vol′can·ism (vŏl′kăn·ĭz'm), *n.* Volcanic power or action; — used esp. in physical geography and geology.
vol′can·ist (-ĭst), *n.* A volcanologist.
vol′can·ize (-īz), *v. t.* To subject to, or affect by, volcanic heat. — **vol′can·i·za′tion** (-ĭ·zā′shŭn; -ī·zā′-), *n.*
vol·ca′no (vŏl·kā′nō), *n.; pl.* -NOES or -NOS (-nōz). [It. *volcano, vulcano,* fr. L. *Vulcanus* Vulcan.] A vent in the earth's crust from which molten or hot rock, steam, etc., issue; also, a hill or mountain composed wholly or in part of the ejected material. A volcano is called ***active*** while it is in eruption, ***dormant*** during a long cessation of activity, and ***extinct*** after eruptions have altogether ceased.
vol′can·ol′o·gy (vŏl′kăn·ŏl′ō·jĭ), *n.* [*volcano* + *-logy.*] The science treating of volcanic phenomena. — **vol′can·o·log′i·cal** (-ō·lŏj′ĭ·kăl), *adj.* — **vol′can·ol′o·gist** (-ŏl′ō·jĭst), *n.*
vole (vōl), *n.* [From dial. *volemouse,* of Scand. origin.] Any of a genus (*Microtus*) and various allied genera of mouselike or ratlike rodents; esp., the ***field mouse*** (*M. agrestis*) and the ***meadow mouse*** (*M. pennsylvanicus* or one of its subspecies) of eastern North America.
vole, *n.* [F.] *Card Playing.* A slam; hence, ***to go the vole,*** to hazard all for great gains.
vol′er·y (vŏl′ẽr·ĭ), *n.; pl.* -ERIES (-ĭz). [F. *volerie* a flying, fr. *voler* to fly, fr. L. *volare.*] An aviary; also, *Rare,* the birds in it.
vol′i·tant (vŏl′ĭ·tănt), *adj.* [L. *volitans, -antis,* pres. part.] Flying; able to fly; also, moving about.
vol′i·ta′tion (-tā′shŭn), *n.* [ML. *volitatio,* fr. L. *volitare, volitatum,* to fly to and fro, v. freq. fr. *volare* to fly.] Act or power of flying; flight. — **vol′i·ta′tion·al** (-ăl), *adj.*
vo·li′tion (vō·lĭsh′ŭn), *n.* [F., fr. ML. *volitio,* fr. L. *volo* I will, *velle* to will.] **1.** Act of willing or choosing; exercise of the will. **2.** Termination of an act of choosing or willing; a state of decision or choice. **3.** The power of willing or determining; will. — **vo·li′tion·al** (-ăl), *adj.* — **vo·li′tion·al·ly,** *adv.*
vol′i·tive (vŏl′ĭ·tĭv), *adj.* [See VOLITION.] **1.** Of or pert. to the will. **2.** *Gram.* Used in expressing a wish or permission.
‖**Volks′lied′** (fôlks′lēt′), *n.; pl.* VOLKSLIEDER (-lē′dẽr). [G.] A folk song.
‖**Volks′wa′gen** (fôlks′vä′gĕn), *n. sing. & pl.* [G., fr. *volk* people + *wagen* vehicle.] A small passenger automobile put into production by the Nazis as the people's car.
vol′ley (vŏl′ĭ), *n.; pl.* -LEYS (-ĭz). [F. *volée* a flight, volley, fr. *voler* to fly, fr. L. *volare.*] **1.** A flight of missiles, as arrows, bullets, or the like; simultaneous discharge of a number of missile weapons. **2.** Hence: A burst or emission of many things at once; as, a *volley* of words or oaths. **3. a** *Tennis.* The flight of the ball, or its course before striking the ground; hence, a return of the ball before it touches the ground. **b** *Cricket.* A bowled ball aimed to hit the wicket without first touching the ground. **c** *Association Football.* A kick of the ball before it rebounds. — *v. t. & i.* **1.** To discharge or be discharged, in or as in a volley; to make a volley or volleys. **2. a** *Tennis.* To hit (the ball) or return it on the volley. **b** *Cricket.* To bowl (a ball) aimed to hit the wicket before touching the ground. **c** *Association Football.* To kick (the ball) before it rebounds. — **vol′ley·er,** *n.*
vol′ley·ball′ (vŏl′ĭ·bôl′), *n.* A game played by volleying a large inflated ball, with the hands, over a net.
vo′lost (vō′lŏst), *n.* [Russ. *volost′.*] In Russia: **a** Formerly, a canton (sense 2). **b** A rural soviet (see SOVIET).
vol′plane′ (vŏl′plān′), *v. i.* [F. *vol plané,* fr. *vol* flight (fr. *voler* to fly) + *plané,* past part. of *planer* to glide, soar, fr. *plan* a plane.] To glide in an airplane. — *n.* A glide in an airplane. — **vol′plan′ist** (-plān′ĭst), *n.*
Vol′sci (vŏl′sī), *n. pl.* [L.] A people of ancient Italy dwelling in Latium.

Vol′scian (vŏl′shăn), *n.* **a** One of the Volsci. **b** The language of the Volsci, belonging to the Sabellian branch and closely akin to the Umbrian. See INDO-EUROPEAN LANGUAGES, *Table.* — **Vol′scian,** *adj.*
Vol′stead·ism (vŏl′stĕd·ĭz′m), *n.* The doctrine or the enforcement of prohibition; — from the Prohibition Enforcement Act, introduced by Representative A. J. Volstead and passed by Congress in October, 1919, repealed 1933.
Vol′sun·ga Sa′ga (vŏl′sŏŏng·gȧ sä′gȧ). [ON. *Völsunga saga.*] An Icelandic saga, probably of Norwegian origin, giving a variant form of the Nibelungenlied legend.
volt (vōlt), *n.* [F. *volte,* fr. It. *volta* a turn.] **1.** *Manège.* **a** A tread or gait in which a horse going sideways makes a turn round a center. **b** A circle traced by a horse so turning. **2.** *Fencing.* A leaping movement to avoid a thrust.
volt, *n.* [After Alessandro *Volta,* It. physicist.] *Elec.* The unit of electromotive force; — defined by the International Electrical Congress in 1893 and by United States statute as that electromotive force which steadily applied to a conductor whose resistance is one ohm will produce a current of one ampere. It is practically equiv. to 10^8 C.G.S. electromagnetic units. Abbr. *v* or *V*
‖**vol′ta** (vôl′tä; vŏl′tȧ), *n.; pl.* -TE (-tā). [It., a turn, turning, time. See VOLT a tread.] *Music.* A turning; a time; — chiefly in directions; as, ***una volta,*** once. ***seconda volta,*** second time, points to certain modifications in the close of a repeated strain.
vol′ta- (vŏl′tȧ-). [From the name *Volta.* See 2d VOLT.] A combining form meaning *voltaic,* as in **vol′ta·e·lec′tric, vol′ta·e·lec′tric′i·ty.**
volt′age (vōl′tĭj), *n.* *Elec.* Electric potential or potential difference expressed in volts.
voltage divider. *Elec.* A source of adjustable voltage, consisting of a resistor through which current is flowing, provision being made to connect to any desired point along the resistor.
vol·ta′ic (vŏl·tā′ĭk), *adj.* **1.** Of or pertaining to, or discovered by, Alessandro Volta, who first devised apparatus for chemically developing electric currents. **2.** Of or pertaining to voltaism, or voltaic electricity; galvanic; as, a **voltaic couple,** a pair of (usually metallic) substances capable of acting together as an electric source when dipped in an electrolyte. — **voltaic battery.** — **voltaic cell.**
voltaic electricity. Dynamical electricity. See ELECTRICITY, 2.
voltaic pile. *Elec.* See 2d PILE, 3 **a.**
vol′ta·ism (vŏl′tȧ·ĭz′m), *n.* Voltaic or current electricity; also, electrical science dealing with this.
vol·tam′e·ter (vŏl·tăm′ē·tẽr), *n.* [*voltaic* + *-meter.*] *Physics.* An instrument for measuring the quantity of electricity passed through a conductor by the amount of electrolysis produced. — **vol′ta·met′ric** (vŏl′tȧ·mĕt′rĭk), *adj.*
volt′am′me·ter (vōlt′ăm′mē·tẽr), *n.* [2d *volt* + *ammeter.*] *Physics.* A combined voltmeter and ammeter.
volt′–am′pere, *n.* [2d *volt* + *ampere.*] *Elec.* A unit of electric measurement equal to the product of a volt and an ampere. For direct current it is a measure of power and is the same as a watt; for alternating current it is a measure of apparent power.
Vol′ta's pile (vŏl′tȧz). = 2d PILE, 3 **a.**
‖**volte–face** (vôlt′fȧs′; vōlt′fās′), *n.* [F.] A change of front; a facing about; a reversal, as of one's policy.
‖**vol′ti** (vôl′tē), *imperative.* [It.] Turn; specif., *Music,* turn over the leaf.
volt′me′ter (vōlt′mē′tẽr), *n.* [2d *volt* + *-meter.*] *Elec.* Any instrument for measuring in volts the differences of potential between different points of an electrical circuit.
vol′u·ble (vŏl′ū·b′l), *adj.* [F. or L.; F., fr. L. *volubilis,* fr. *volvere, volutum,* to roll, turn round.] **1.** Easily rolling or turning; apt to roll; rotating. **2.** Fluent and smooth in utterance; glib; garrulous. **3.** *Bot.* Having the power or habit of twining. — **Syn.** See TALKATIVE. — **vol′u·bil′i·ty** (-bĭl′ĭ·tĭ), **vol′u·ble·ness,** *n.* — **vol′u·bly,** *adv.*
vol′ume (vŏl′yŭm), *n.* [OF., fr. L. *volumen* a roll of writing, a book, volume, fr. *volvere, volutum,* to roll.] **1.** *Now Rare.* A roll; a scroll; also, a scroll-like form or mass. **2.** A collection of printed sheets bound together, whether a single work, a part of a work, or more than one work; a book, esp., that part of an extended work bound up together in one cover. Abbr. *vol.* **3.** Sufficient matter of discourse to fill a volume or volumes. **4.** Space occupied, as measured by cubic units, that is, cubic inches, feet, etc.; compass; as, the *volume* of a container. See MEASURE, *Table* 5. **5.** Hence, a mass; bulk; often, a considerable quantity; as, the total *volume* of sales. **6.** *Music.* Fullness or quantity of tone. — **Syn.** See BULK. — **vol′umed** (-yŭmd), *adj.*
vo·lu′me·ter (vō·lū′mē·tẽr), *n.* *Physics.* **a** An instrument for measuring volumes, as of gases or liquids directly, or of solids by displacement. **b** A form of hydrometer.
vol′u·met′ric (vŏl′ū·mĕt′rĭk), *adj.* Also **vol′u·met′ri·cal** (-rĭ·kăl). [*volume* + *metric.*] Of or pertaining to the measurement of volume. — **vol′u·met′ri·cal·ly,** *adv.* — **vo·lu′me·try** (vō·lū′mē·trĭ), *n.*
volumetric analysis. *Chem.* **a** Quantitative analysis by the use of definite volumes of standard solutions of reagents. **b** Analysis of gases by volume, as by the eudiometer.
vo·lu′mi·nous (vō·lū′mĭ·nŭs), *adj.* [LL. *voluminosus* full of folds.] **1.** Of or pertaining to volume or volumes. **2.** Winding or full of windings; consisting of many folds or convolutions. **3.** Of great volume, or bulk; large; swelling; specif., of low density. **4.** Filling, or capable of filling, a large volume or several volumes; as, a *voluminous* treatise; *voluminous* remarks. **5.** Writing or, figuratively, speaking much or at great length; as, a *voluminous* essayist. — **vo·lu′mi·nous·ly,** *adv.* — **vo·lu′mi·nous·ness,** *n.*
vol′un·ta·rism (vŏl′ŭn·tȧ·rĭz′m), *n.* *Philos.* Any theory which conceives will to be the dominant factor in experience or in the constitution of the world; — applied to doctrines of Fichte, Schopenhauer, etc. — **vol′un·ta·rist** (-rĭst), *n. & adj.* — **vol′un·ta·ris′tic** (-rĭs′tĭk), *adj.*
vol′un·tar′y (vŏl′ŭn·tĕr′ĭ *or, esp. Brit.,* -tẽr·ĭ, -trĭ), *adj.* [L. *voluntarius,* fr. *voluntas* will, choice, fr. the root of *velle* to will, pres. part. *volens.*] **1.** Proceeding from the will, or from one's own choice or full consent. **2.** Unconstrained by interference; self-impelled; freely given, done, etc. **3.** Done by design or intention; intentional; not accidental; as, *voluntary* manslaughter. **4.** Of or pertaining to the will; subject to, or regulated by, the will; as, the *voluntary* muscles. **5.** Able to will; having power of free choice; as, man is a *voluntary* agent. **6.** Provided or supported by voluntary action; not established, state-supported, etc.; as, *voluntary* churches. **7.** *Law.* Acting, or done, of one's own free will without valuable consideration or legal obligation. — **vol′un·tar′i·ly,** *adv.* — **vol′un·tar′i·ness,** *n.*

Syn. Voluntary, intentional, deliberate, willful, willing mean done or brought about of one's own will. **Voluntary,** though it may apply to movements, etc., subject to the control of the will, more often suggests that in spite of contrary influences the decision to make, do, etc., resulted from free choice; **intentional** implies an awareness of an end to be achieved; **deliberate** implies a full consciousness of the nature of one's act and its consequences; **willful** implies a refusal to be taught, advised, or commanded; **willing** implies a ready and eager disposition to accede to or anticipate the wishes of another.
— *n.* **1.** A voluntary action or piece of work. **2.** *Music.* A piece of music, often improvised, serving usually as a prelude; esp., an organ solo, played in a religious service.
vol′un·tar′y·ism (-ĭz′m), *n.* The principle of supporting anything by reliance upon voluntary action; specif.: **a** In education, a system under which schools (***voluntary schools***) are supported by voluntary subscriptions. **b** *Eccl.* The principle of supporting a religious system and its institutions by voluntary association and effort. — **vol′un·tar′y·ist** (-ĭst), *n.*
vol′un·teer′ (vŏl′ŭn·tēr′), *n.* [F. *voluntaire,* now *volontaire,* orig. adj., fr. L. *voluntarius.* See VOLUNTARY.] **1.** One who enters into, or offers himself for, any service of his own free will. **2.** *Law.* **a** A voluntary actor, performer, or agent, in any transaction. **b** The grantee in a conveyance made without valuable consideration. **3.** *Mil.* One who enters into service voluntarily; — opposed to *conscript.* — *adj.* **1.** Of or pertaining to a volunteer or volunteers; voluntary. **2.** Growing spontaneously or from self-sown seed; as, a *volunteer* crop. — *v. t.* To offer or bestow voluntarily. — *v. i.* To enter into, or offer oneself for, any service voluntarily.
Vol′un·teers′ of A·mer′i·ca. A religious and philanthropic organization, similar to the Salvation Army, founded in 1896 by Commander and Mrs. Ballington Booth.
Volunteer State. Tennessee; — a nickname.
vo·lup′tu·ar′y (vō·lŭp′tū·ĕr′ĭ *or, esp. Brit.,* -ẽr·ĭ), *n.; pl.* -IES (-ĭz). [L. *voluptuarius* for *voluptarius,* fr. *voluptas* pleasure.] A voluptuous person; one who makes luxury and the gratification of sensual appetites his chief care; a sensualist. — **vo·lup′tu·ar′y,** *adj.*
vo·lup′tu·ous (-ŭs), *adj.* [OF. *voluptueux,* fr. L. *voluptuosus,* fr. *voluptas* pleasure.] **1.** Full of delight or pleasure, esp. to the senses; ministering or inclining to, or arising from, sensuous or sensual gratification. **2.** Given to, or spent in, enjoyments of luxury, pleasure, or sensual gratifications. — **Syn.** See SENSUOUS. — **vo·lup′tu·ous·ly,** *adv.* — **vo·lup′tu·ous·ness,** *n.*
vo·lute′ (vō·lūt′), *n.* [F., fr. It. *voluta,* fr. L. *voluta,* fr. *volvere, volutum,* to roll.] **1.** A spiral or scroll-like conformation; esp., that ornament forming the chief feature of the Ionic capital. See IONIC, *Illust.* **2.** *Zool.* A turn, or whorl, of a spiral shell. — *adj.* Spiral; rolled up; also, *Mach.,* having a part of spiral form or operating with a rotary action. — **vo·lu′tion** (-lū′shŭn), *n.*
volute spring. See SPRING, *Illust.*
vol′va (vŏl′vȧ), *n.* *Bot.* A cup-shaped structure around the base of the stipe of some mushrooms, as agarics and stinkhorns.
vol′vu·lus (vŏl′vū·lŭs), *n.* [NL., fr. L. *volvere* to turn about, roll.] *Med.* Any twisting of the intestines causing obstruction.
vo′mer (vō′mẽr), *n.* [L., a plowshare.] *Anat. & Zool.* A bone of the skull of most vertebrates, situated below the ethmoidal region. In man it forms part of the nasal septum. — **vo′mer·ine** (vō′mẽr·ĭn; vŏm′ẽr-), *adj.*
vom′i·ca (vŏm′ĭ·kȧ), *n.* [L., an abscess.] *Med.* **a** A cavity in the lungs, as from suppuration or tuberculosis. **b** An abscess in any other parenchymatous organ.
vom′it (vŏm′ĭt), *n.* [L. *vomitus,* fr. *vomere, vomitum,* to vomit.] **1. a** A vomiting. **b** That which is vomited. **2.** An emetic. **3.** A sickness characterized by vomiting; as, the black *vomit.* — *v. i.* **1.** To eject the contents of the stomach by the mouth; spew. **2.** To be ejected or emitted; come forth violently. — *v. t.* **1.** To throw up; eject from the stomach through the mouth; — often with *up.* **2.** To belch forth; as, volcanoes *vomit* lava. — **vom′it·er,** *n.*
vom′i·tive (vŏm′ĭ·tĭv), *adj. & n.* Emetic.
vom′i·to (vŏm′ĭ·tō), *n.* Also **vom′i·to ne′gro.** [Sp. *vómito,* fr. L. *vomitus.*] *Med.* Black vomit.
vom′i·to′ry (vŏm′ĭ·tō′rĭ *or, esp. Brit.,* -tẽr·ĭ), *adj.* Emetic; vomitive. — *n.; pl.* -RIES (-rĭz). **1.** An emetic. **2.** An opening, vent, or the like, for discharging or emitting. **3.** [LL. *vomitorium.*] *Arch.* An entrance piercing the banks of seats of a theater or amphitheater.
vom′i·tu·ri′tion (-tū·rĭsh′ŭn), *n.* *Med.* **a** Ineffectual attempts at vomiting; retching. **b** Vomiting of little matter; also, vomiting effected with little effort.
‖**von** (fôn), *prep.* [G.] Of, from; — often a prefix in German and Austrian personal names, formerly and still often the sign of nobility of birth.
V′–one′ (vē′wŭn′), *n.* See V-1.
voo′doo (vōō′dōō; vōō·dōō′), *n.* [Creole F. *voudou,* fr. Ewe (a Negro language of the Slave Coast) *vodu.*] **1.** Voodooism. **2.** One who practices voodooism; a Negro sorcerer. **3.** Voodoo magic; as, to work *voodoo;* also, a voodoo charm, fetish, or the like. — *adj.* Of or pertaining to voodoos or voodooism. — *v. t.* To affect by voodoo sorcery.
voo′doo·ism (-ĭz′m), *n.* [*often cap.*] A Negro religion, orig. African and barbaric, but now found chiefly among Haitian Negroes and consisting largely of sorcery; also, belief in or practice of this religion. — **voo′doo·ist** (-ĭst), *n.* — **voo′doo·is′tic** (-ĭs′tĭk), *adj.*
vo·ra′cious (vō·rā′shŭs), *adj.* [L. *vorax, -acis,* fr. *vorare* to devour.] **a** Greedy in eating; ravenous; gluttonous; rapacious. **b** Excessively eager; immoderate; insatiable; as, a *voracious* reader. — **vo·ra′cious·ly,** *adv.* — **vo·rac′i·ty** (vō·răs′ĭ·tĭ), *n.*
‖**Vor′la′ge** (fōr′lä′gĕ), *n.* [G.] *Skiing.* A position in which one leans forward from the ankles without lifting the heels from the skis, keeping the body, as a rule, at least perpendicular to the slope.
-vorous. [L. *-vorus,* fr. *vorare* to devour.] A combining form signifying *eating, feeding on, consuming,* as in carni*vorous.* Corresponding nouns in **-vora** denote *orders* and *genera,* and in **-vore** denote *an individual member,* as in carni*vora,* carni*vore.*
vor′tex (vôr′tĕks), *n.; pl.* -TEXES (-tĕk·sĕz; -sĭz), -TICES (-tĭ·sēz). [L. *vortex,* var. of *vertex, -icis.* See VERTEX.] A mass of fluid, esp. of a liquid, having a whirling or circular motion tending to form a cavity or vacuum in the center of the circle, and to draw toward this cavity or vacuum bodies subject to its action; a whirlpool; eddy.
vor′ti·cal (vôr′tĭ·kăl), *adj.* Of, pertaining to, or like a vortex or vortexes; whirling. — **vor′ti·cal·ly,** *adv.*

vor′ti·cel′la (vôr′tĭ·sĕl′*ȧ*), *n.; pl.* -LAE (-ē). [NL., dim. fr. L. *vortex;* see VORTEX.] *Biol.* A one-celled ciliated animal with a bell-shaped body, occurring in fresh and salt water.

vor′ti·cose (vôr′tĭ·kōs), *adj.* [L. *vorticosus.*] Vortical; whirling.

vor·tig′i·nous (vôr·tĭj′ĭ·nŭs), *adj.* [See VERTIGINOUS.] Vortical; whirling.

Vor·tum′nus (vôr·tŭm′nŭs), *n.* See VERTUMNUS.

vot′a·ble, vote′a·ble (vōt′*ȧ*·b'l), *adj.* **a** Capable, or having the right, of voting. **b** Capable of being submitted to a vote.

vo′ta·ress (vō′t*ȧ*·rĕs; -rĭs), *n.* Also **vo′tress** (vō′trĕs; -trĭs). A woman votary.

vo′ta·rist (-rĭst), *n.* A votary.

vo′ta·ry (-rĭ), *n.; pl.* -RIES (-rĭz). [L. *vovere, votum,* to vow.] One devoted, consecrated, or engaged, by a vow or promise; hence, a devoted adherent, student, worshiper, etc.; as, a *votary* of science. — **vo′ta·ry,** *adj.*

vote (vōt), *n.* [L. *votum* a vow, wish, will.] **1.** *Obs.* **a** A vow. **b** A prayer. **c** An ardent wish or desire. **2.** A wish, choice, or opinion, of a person or a body of persons, expressed by a ballot, viva voce, or the like; a suffrage; also, the ballot, ticket, the voice or other medium of expressing one's choice, opinion, etc.; as, to cast a *vote;* to count the *votes.* **3.** The decision reached by voting; as, the *vote* was unanimous. **4.** Votes collectively; as, the prohibition *vote.* **5.** The right of suffrage; a voice; as, to have the *vote.* **6.** A voter.
— *v. i.* To express or signify the mind, will, or preference, viva voce, by ballot or the like, in order to reach a decision; to cast or give a vote.
— *v. t.* **1.** To enact, bring about, effect, etc., by a formal vote; as, to *vote* an appropriation. **2.** *Colloq.* To declare by general opinion or common consent; as, he was *voted* a bore. — **vot′er** (vōt′ẽr), *n.*

vot′ing ma·chine′ (vōt′ĭng). A mechanical device for recording and counting the votes of the electorate.

vo′tive (vō′tĭv), *adj.* [L. *votivus,* fr. *votum* a vow.] Given by vow, or in fulfillment of a vow or promise, or in devotion; as, *votive* offerings. — **vo′tive·ly,** *adv.* — **vo′tive·ness,** *n.*

vouch (vouch), *v. t.* [OF. *voucher, vochier,* fr. L. *vocare* to call. The E. word is in part a shortening of *avouch.*] **1.** *Archaic.* To call; esp., to call to witness. **2.** To attest, as a statement or its truth or accuracy; bear witness to; also, to answer or stand sponsor for. **3.** *Rare.* To back; support. **4.** *Law.* To support or maintain, as a claim; *Obs. exc.* specif., to authenticate, as a claim, by vouchers.
— *v. i.* **1.** To bear witness; give testimony or full attestation. **2.** To make assertion; affirm. **— *n.*** Assertion; attestation.

vouch′er, *n.* **1.** One who vouches. **2.** A book, paper, etc., which serves to vouch the truth of something; specif., any receipt or the like showing payment of a debt; as, paid checks are his *vouchers.* **3.** *Early English Law.* One who vouches another to establish his warranty of title.

vouch·safe′ (vouch·sāf′), *v. t.* [*vouch* + *safe,* i. e., to vouch or answer for as safe.] **1.** *Obs.* To guarantee as safe; guarantee. **2.** To condescend to grant; concede; bestow. **— *v. i.*** To condescend; deign; yield. — **Syn.** See GRANT. — **vouch·safe′ment,** *n.*

vous′soir′ (vōō′swȧr′), *n.* [F.] *Arch.* Any of the wedge-shaped pieces of which an arch or vault is composed. See ARCH, *Illust.;* KEYSTONE, 1.

vow (vou), *n.* [OF. *vou,* fr. L. *votum,* orig. past part. neut. of *vovere, votum,* to vow.] **1.** A solemn promise, esp. one made to God or to some deity; an act by which one consecrates or devotes himself to some act, service, or condition. **2.** A promise of fidelity or constancy; as, the marriage *vow.* **3.** A solemn assertion; an asseveration. **— *v. t.*** **1.** To bind oneself by a vow to do, give, etc.; promise solemnly. **2.** To assert solemnly; to asseverate. **— *v. i.*** To make a vow. — **vow′er** (vou′ẽr), *n.*

vow′el (vou′ĕl), *n.* [OF. *vouel* (F. *voyelle*), fr. L. *vocalis* (sc. *littera*), fr. *vocalis* sounding, fr. *vox, vocis,* a voice, sound.] A speech sound in the articulation of which the oral part of the breath channel is not blocked and is not narrowed enough to cause audible friction; also, a letter (in English, *a, e, i, o, u,* and, sometimes, *y*) representing such a sound. Distinguished from *consonant.* **— *adj.*** Of or pertaining to a vowel; vocal.

vow′el·ize (-īz), *v. t.* To furnish with vowel signs or points; as, to *vowelize* a Hebrew text. — **vow′el·i·za′tion** (-ĭ·zā′shŭn; -ī·zā′-), *n.*

vowel point. In Hebrew and certain other Eastern languages, a mark placed above or below a consonant, or attached to it, as in Ethiopic, representing the vowel sound.

‖**vox** (vŏks), *n.; pl.* VOCES (vō′sēz). [L.] Voice.

‖**vox an·ge′li·ca** (ăn·jĕl′ĭ·k*ȧ*). [L., angelic voice.] = VOIX CÉLESTE.

‖**vox, et prae·te′re·a ni′hil** (ĕt prē·tĕr′ē·*ȧ* nī′hĭl). [L.] A voice, and nothing more; sound without sense.

‖**vox hu·ma′na** (hū·mā′n*ȧ*). [L., human voice.] *Music.* An organ reed stop of 8-foot pitch made to give a sound imitative of the human voice. See STOP, *n.*

‖**vox po′pu·li, vox De′i** (pŏp′ū·lī, dē′ī). [L.] The voice of the people (is) the voice of God; — often shortened to **vox populi** (abbr. *vox pop.*).

voy′age (voi′ĭj), *n.* [OF. *veage, viage, voiage* (F. *voyage*), fr. L. *viaticum* traveling money, fr. *viaticus* belonging to a road or journey, fr. *via* way.] **1.** Formerly, a passage either by sea or land; a journey; now: **a** A journey by sea or water, from one place, port, or country, to another; also, a round trip by water. **b** A journey by air, as in an airship. **2.** An account of, or a work dealing with, a voyage or voyaging. **3.** *Obs.* **a** An undertaking; enterprise. **b** Act or practice of traveling; travel. **— *v. i. & t.;*** -AGED (-ĭjd); -AG·ING (-ĭj·ĭng). To take, make, or traverse by a voyage; travel (through). — **voy′ag·er** (-ĭj·ẽr), *n.*

‖**voy′a′geur′** (vwȧ′yȧ′zhûr′), *n.; pl.* -GEURS (*F.* -zhûr′). [F., fr. *voyager* to travel.] A traveler; in Canada, specif., a man employed by the fur companies in transporting goods and men to and from the remote stations; also, any boatman and trapper of those regions.

‖**vrai′sem′blance′** (vrĕ′säN′bläNs′), *n.* [F.] The appearance of truth; exact appearance; verisimilitude.

‖**vrouw** (vrou; *S. Afr. pron.* frou), *n.* [D.] A woman; housewife; frow.

VT fuze (vē′tē′). See PROXIMITY FUZE.

V′-two′ (vē′tōō′), *n.* See V-2.

vug, vugg, vugh (vŭg; vōōg), *n.* [Corn. *vooga* a cavern.] *Petrog.* A small unfilled cavity in a lode or in the rock.

Vul′can (vŭl′k*ă*n), *n.* [L. *Vulcanus, Volcanus.*] *Rom. Relig.* The god of fire, esp. in its fearful aspects. Later he was identified with the Greek *Hephaestus* and represented as consort of Venus and god of metalworking.

Vul·ca′ni·an (vŭl·kā′nĭ·*ă*n), *adj.* **1.** Of, pertaining to, or made by Vulcan; hence, of or pertaining to ironworking or metalworking. **2.** [*not cap.*] **a** Volcanic. **b** Plutonic.

vul′can·ism (vŭl′k*ă*n·ĭz'm), *n.* Volcanism.

vul′can·ite (-īt), *n.* A variety of hard rubber. — **vul′can·ite,** *adj.*

vul′can·i·za′tion (-ĭ·zā′shŭn; -ī·zā′shŭn), *n.* Process of treating crude rubber, rubber latex, gutta-percha, etc., chemically to improve its strength, hardness, elasticity, etc.

vul′can·ize (vŭl′k*ă*n·īz), *v. t. & i.* To subject to or undergo vulcanization. — **vul′can·iz′a·ble** (-īz′*ȧ*·b'l), *adj.* — **vul′can·iz′er** (-īz′ẽr), *n.*

Vul′can·ized Fi′ber (-īzd). A trade-mark for a tough substance made by a treatment of cellulose.

vul′can·ol′o·gy (-ŏl′ō·jĭ), *n.* Volcanology. — **vul′can·o·log′i·cal** (-ō·lŏj′ĭ·k*ă*l), *adj.* — **vul′can·ol′o·gist** (-ŏl′ō·jĭst), *n.*

vul′gar (vŭl′gẽr), *adj.* [L. *vulgaris,* fr. *vulgus, volgus,* the multitude, the common people.] **1.** Of or pertaining to the common people, or general public; general; public; popular; as, a *vulgar* superstition. **2.** Vernacular; also, written in or translated into the vernacular; as, poems in the *vulgar* tongue. **3.** Belonging or relating to the common people as distinguished from the cultivated or educated; plebeian; boorish; also, offensive to good taste or refined feelings; low; coarse; as, *vulgar* ostentation; *vulgar* manners. **4.** Obscene; profane; low; as, a *vulgar* joke. — **Syn.** See COMMON: COARSE. **— *n.*** *Archaic.* The vernacular. — **vul′gar·ly,** *adv.* — **vul′gar·ness,** *n.*

vulgar fraction. = *common fraction* (see FRACTION).

vul·gar′i·an (vŭl·gâr′ĭ·*ă*n; 6), *n.* A vulgar person; esp., a rich, pretentious person of vulgar standards.

vul′gar·ism (vŭl′gẽr·ĭz'm), *n.* **1.** Grossness; rudeness; vulgarity. **2.** A vulgar phrase or expression, or one used only in colloquial speech, or, esp., in the speech of the ill-bred or uneducated.

vul·gar′i·ty (vŭl·găr′ĭ·tĭ), *n.; pl.* -TIES (-tĭz). **1.** Quality or state of being vulgar; commonness. **2.** Grossness or coarseness of manners or language; also, an instance of this.

vul′gar·ize (vŭl′gẽr·īz), *v. t.* To make vulgar. — **vul′gar·i·za′tion** (-ĭ·zā′shŭn; -ī·zā′-), *n.* — **vul′gar·iz′er** (-īz′ẽr), *n.*

Vulgar Latin. A popular or colloquial form of Latin used concurrently with the standard Latin and forming the chief source of the Romance languages.

Vul′gate (vŭl′gāt), *n.* [ML. *vulgata editio,* fr. L. *vulgatus* usual, common.] **1.** A Latin version of the Scriptures, in the main the work of St. Jerome in the 4th century, used as the standard for the services of the Roman Catholic Church. The standard text of the Vulgate is that of Pope Clement VIII of 1592. It is being superseded by a new revision ordered by Pius X in 1908. See BIBLE, DOUAY BIBLE. **2.** [*not cap.*] Any vulgate, or commonly accepted, text or reading. **— *adj.*** **1.** [*cap.*] Of or pertaining to the Vulgate. **2.** Commonly accepted; as, a *vulgate* text.

vul′gus (vŭl′gŭs), *n.; pl.* -GUSES (-ĕz; -ĭz). [L. See VULGAR.] **1.** The common people. **2.** In some English public schools, a short composition in Latin verse on a given subject.

vul′ner·a·ble (vŭl′nẽr·*ȧ*·b'l), *adj.* [LL. *vulnerabilis* wounding, injurious, fr. *vulnerare* to wound, *vulnus* a wound.] **1.** Capable of being wounded. **2.** Liable to attack or injury; assailable; as, a *vulnerable* reputation. **3.** *Contract Bridge.* Liable to greater penalties or bonuses; — of a side that has won one game. — **vul′ner·a·bil′i·ty** (-bĭl′ĭ·tĭ), **vul′ner·a·ble·ness,** *n.* — **vul′ner·a·bly,** *adv.*

vul′ner·ar′y (-ẽr′ĭ *or, esp. Brit.,* -ẽr·ĭ), *adj.* Used for or useful in healing wounds; as, *vulnerary* plants. **— *n.*** A vulnerary remedy.

vul·pec′u·lar (vŭl·pĕk′ū·lẽr), *adj.* Of or pertaining to a fox, esp. a young one; vulpine.

vul′pi·cide (vŭl′pĭ·sīd), *n.* [L. *vulpes* a fox + *-cide.*] *Eng.* One who kills a fox, except in hunting; also, the act of so killing a fox. — **vul′pi·cid′al** (-sīd′*ă*l; -'l), *adj.*

vul′pine (vŭl′pīn; -pĭn), *adj.* [L. *vulpinus,* fr. *vulpes* a fox.] Of, pertaining to, or like a fox or foxes; foxy; cunning; crafty.

vul′pi·nite (-pĭ·nīt), *n.* [From *Vulpino,* Italy.] *Mineral.* A scaly granular grayish-white variety of anhydrite.

vul′ture (vŭl′tūr), *n.* [OF. *voltour, voutour,* fr. L. *vulturius,* fr. *vultur.*] **1.** Any of certain large raptorial birds of temperate and tropical regions, allied to the hawks, eagles, and falcons, but having weaker claws, and the head usually naked. Cf. RAPTORIAL, *Illust.* They subsist chiefly on carrion. They constitute two families: Vulturidae, the Old World vultures, including the small, largely white ***Egyptian vulture*** (*Neophron percnopterus*) common in Egypt and India; Cathartidae, the American vultures, including the ***black vulture*** (*Coragyps atratus*), ***king vulture*** (*Sarcorhamphus papa*) ranging from Mexico to Paraguay, and the *condor* and *turkey buzzard* (which see). Cf. LAMMERGEIER. **2.** A meanly or unscrupulously rapacious person. — **vul′tur·ine** (-tūr·īn; -ĭn), **vul′tur·ous** (-ŭs), *adj.*

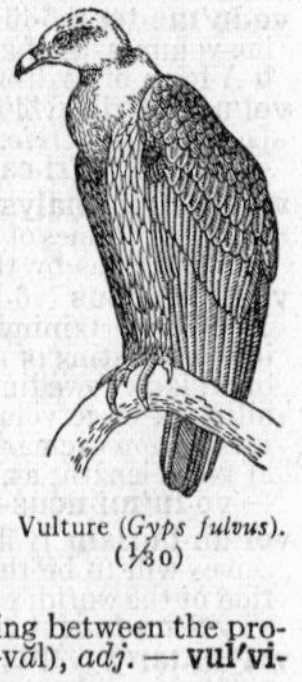

Vulture (*Gyps fulvus*). (1/30)

vul′va (vŭl′v*ȧ*), *n.* [L. *vulva, volva,* covering, integument, womb.] *Anat.* The external parts of the female genital organs; sometimes, the opening between the projecting parts of the external organs. — **vul′val** (-v*ă*l), *adj.* — **vul′vi·form** (-vĭ·fôrm), *adj.*

vul′vo- (vŭl′vō-), **vulv-.** [From VULVA.] A combining form denoting: **a** *The vulva,* as in *vulvitis.* **b** *Vulvar and;* — in adjectives, as in **vul′vo·u′ter·ine, vul′vo·vag′i·nal.**

vy′ing (vī′ĭng), *adj.* That vies. — **vy′ing·ly,** *adv.*

W

W, w (dŭb′'l·ū), *n.; pl.* W's, w's, Ws, ws (-ūz). **1.** The twenty-third letter of the English alphabet. In form and origin W is a ligatured combination, VV or UU, called "double U," which was introduced into English by French scribes in the 11th century to replace the Anglo-Saxon runic wen (see V, *n.*, 1; 2d WEN). **2.** The sound of the letter *w*. The sound of *w* is usually a consonant as in *we*, a voiced bilabial sound formed by raising the back of the tongue as for o͞o while rounding the lips as for this vowel. In English the letter *w* represents a vowel only in diphthongs, as in *few, how*. Written *w* is silent in some words, as *wrist, answer*. See *Pron.*, § 124. **3.** As a *symbol*, used to indicate anyone or anything so designated, esp. as the twenty-second or (see K, 3) twenty-third in order or class.

wa′ (wô; wä). Scot. var. of WALL.

WAAF, Waaf (wăf), *n.; pl.* WAAFs, WAAFS (wăfs). A member of the Women's Auxiliary Air Force (**WAAF**), an auxiliary of the British Royal Air Force in World War II incorporated into the Air Force in 1949 as the Women's Royal Air Force (WRAF).

wab (wȧb). Scot. & Dial. Eng. var. of WEB.

wab′ble (wŏb′'l), *n.* Var. of WARBLE, tumor. Hence, the larva of a botfly (*Bogeria emasculator*) which infests squirrels.

wab′ble, *v. i.* To wobble. — **wab′bler** (-lẽr), *n.*

wab′bly (wŏb′lĭ), *adv.* Wobbly; waveringly.

WAC, Wac (wăk), *n.; pl.* WACs, WACS (wăks). A member of the Women's Army Corps (**WAC**) of the U. S. Army, established by acts of Congress (July 1, 1943, and June 12, 1948); formerly the Women's Army Auxiliary Corps (**WAAC** [wăk]).

wack′e (wăk′ĕ), *n.* [G.] *Petrog.* Rock similar to sandstone in texture, but derived from disintegrated basic rocks.

wack′y (wăk′ĭ), *adj.;* WACK′I·ER (-ĭ·ẽr); WACK′I·EST. Also **whack′y** (hwăk′ĭ). *Slang, U. S.* Crazy; screwy. — **wack′i·ness** (wăk′ĭ·nĕs; -nĭs), *n.*

wad (wŏd), *n.* [From F. *ouate, houatte,* prop. the cotton or silk obtained from the Syrian swallowwort.] **1.** A little mass, tuft, or bundle, as of hay or tow; also, loosely, a lump; a small compact heap; as, paper *wads*. **2.** Specif.: A relatively soft plug or stopper, to retain a charge of powder, to keep the powder and shot close, or to avoid windage, in a muzzle-loading cannon or gun or in a cartridge. See CARTRIDGE, *Illust.* **3.** A soft mass, esp. of some loose fibrous substance, variously used, as to stop an aperture, pad a garment, etc. **4.** *Dial.* A considerable amount; a mass. **5.** *Slang, U. S.* A roll of paper money; hence, wealth in general; money. — *v. t.;* WAD′DED (-ĕd; -ĭd); WAD′DING. **1.** To form into a wad, or mass, or into wadding; as, to *wad* tow; esp., *U. S.*, to roll into a tight wad, as a piece of paper. **2.** To insert or crowd a wad into; as, to *wad* a gun; to hold in by a wad; as, to *wad* a bullet in a gun. **3.** To stuff or line with some soft substance, as cotton; to pad, as a cloak. — **wad′der** (-ẽr), *n.*

wad, *n.* [ML. *vadium.*] *Scots Law.* A pledge. Hence, ***in wad,*** pledged.

wad (wäd; wȧd). Scot. & Dial. var. of WED, WOULD.

wad′ding (wŏd′ĭng), *n.* **1.** Wads collectively, or material for making wads. **2.** Any soft padding, esp. prepared sheets of carded cotton.

wad′dle (wŏd′'l), *v. i.;* WAD′DLED (-'ld); WAD′DLING (-lĭng). [Freq. of WADE.] To walk with short steps, swaying from one side to the other, like a duck; to move clumsily and totteringly along, as a baby; to toddle; hence, to proceed with a clumsy motion suggesting a waddle. — *n.* Act of waddling; a toddle; an awkward, clumsy, swaying gait. — **wad′dler** (-lẽr), *n.*

wad′dy (wŏd′ĭ), *n.; pl.* -DIES (-ĭz). *Australia.* An aboriginal war club. — *v. t. Australia.* To attack or beat with a waddy.

wade (wād), *v. i.* [AS. *wadan* to go, proceed, wade.] **1.** *Obs.* To go; pass. **2.** To move by stepping in or through a medium, as water, mud, sand, that offers more resistance than air. **3.** Hence, to move, pass, go, or get forward, with difficulty or labor; as, to *wade* through a dull book. **4.** *Slang.* To set to work or attack with determination or vigor; — with *in* or *into;* as, to *wade* into the morning's mail. — *v. t.* To pass or cross by wading; as, he *waded* the swamps. — *n. Colloq.* Act of wading; also, a ford.

wad′er (wād′ẽr), *n.* **1.** One who or that which wades. **2.** Any of many long-legged birds that wade in water in search of food, including the shore birds, as sandpipers and snipe, and the inland water birds, as cranes, herons, etc **3.** *pl.* High waterproof boots for wading.

wa′di, wa′dy (wä′dĭ), *n.; pl.* WADIES (-dĭz). [Ar. *wādī.*] In the Near East and northern Africa, a valley; a river; a ravine through which a stream flows; the channel or bed of a watercourse which is dry except in the rainy season; also, an oasis.

wad′mal (wŏd′măl), *n.* Also **wad′maal, wad′mol, wad′moll.** [ON. *vathmāl* a woolen stuff, for *vāthmāl,* fr. *vāth* stuff + *māl* measure.] *Chiefly Hist.* A coarse, often hairy, woolen fabric, used in England, Scotland, Ireland, and Scandinavia, for stout warm clothing, protective coverings, etc.

wad′na (wȧd′nȧ). Scot. contraction of *would not.*

wad′set′ (wŏd′sĕt′), *n.* [From WADSET, *v.*] *Scots Law.* A mortgage; also, a pledge or pawn. — *v. t.* [Scot. var. of *wedset,* fr. *wed* a pledge + *set,* v.] *Scots Law.* To mortgage; pledge. — **wad′set′ter** (-ẽr), *n.*

wa′dy (wä′dĭ). Var. of WADI.

wae (wā). Dial. var. of WOE.

wae′suck (wā′sŭk), **wae′sucks** (-sŭks), *interj.* [Dial. *wae* woe + a slurred form of *sake, sakes.*] *Scot. & N. of Eng.* An exclamation expressing grief or pity; alas!

WAF, Waf (wăf), *n.; pl.* WAFs, WAFS (wăfs). A member of the women's component of the U. S. Air Force (authorized by act of Congress June 12, 1948), called Women in the Air Force (**WAF**).

wa′fer (wā′fẽr), *n.* [ONF. *waufre,* of Teut. origin.] **1.** A thin, crisp cake or biscuit. **2.** Hence, anything resembling a wafer (sense 1), as in thinness, size, shape, etc. **3.** An adhesive disk of dried paste, made of flour, gelatin, isinglass, or the like, and coloring matter, used as a seal. **4.** *Eccl.* A thin cake or piece of bread (commonly unleavened, circular, and stamped with a crucifix or with the sacred monogram; see XP) used in the Eucharist, as in the Roman Catholic Church. **5.** *Mach.* A thin disk or ring resembling a wafer, often used as a valve, diaphragm, or the like. **6.** *Hist. Ordnance.* A form of old-time primer. — *v. t.* To seal, close, or fasten, with a wafer.

waff (wȧf), *n.* [See WAVE to waver.] *Scot. & N. of Eng.* **a** A waving motion; a signal, as from a boat. **b** A puff; whiff, as of perfume. **c** A slight attack or affection. **d** A glimpse. **e** A wraith. — *v. t. & i. Scot.* To wave; flutter; wag; flap.

waff, waf (wȧf), *adj.* [Var. of WAIF.] *Scot.* **1.** Solitary; woebegone. **2.** Worthless. — *n. Scot.* A vagrant.

waff′ie (wȧf′ĭ), *n. Scot.* A vagrant; vagabond.

waf′fle (wŏf′'l), *n.* [D. *wafel.*] A soft but crisped indented cake of batter cooked in a waffle iron.

waffle iron. A utensil for cooking waffles, having two metal parts hinged together and shutting upon each other, with projecting studs on the insides.

waft (wȧft; 9), *v. t.* [From *wafter* a convoy, fr. D. & LG. *wachter* a guard.] **1.** To cause to move or go by or as by the impulse of waves, as of water or air; as, a balloon was *wafted* over the channel. **2.** [From confusion with *waff* to wave.] *Obs.* To signal to, or summon, as by waving the hand; to beckon. **3.** *Obs.* To turn; direct; as, to *waft* the eyes. — *v. i.* To be moved, or to pass, on or as on a buoyant medium; to float. — *n.* **1.** Act of wafting; a signal made by waving. **2.** A floating; waving; a wave or current, as of wind; a puff; gust. **3.** *Naut.* A pennant or a flag, used, now rarely, in signaling or sometimes to show the direction of the wind to the steersman.

waft. Scot. var. of WEFT.

waft′age (wȧf′tĭj), *n.* Act of wafting, or state of being wafted; hence, in general, conveyance; carriage.

waft′er (-tẽr), *n.* One who or that which wafts; specif., *Mach.*, a form of revolving disk or fan for a blower.

waf′ture (wȧf′tūr), *n.* Act of wafting or waving; also, something wafted or conveyed as by a breeze, by the waves of the sea, etc.

wag (wăg), *v. t.;* WAGGED (wăgd); WAG′GING (wăg′ĭng). [ME. *waggen;* akin to AS. *wagian* to move, wag.] To sway or swing shortly to and fro, esp. from side to side, with jerky or quick turns, as a small body attached to a larger body; as, a dog *wags* its tail. To *wag* the tongue implies rapid and continuous talking. — *v. i.* **1.** To move one way and the other; to oscillate; sway. **2.** To be in action or motion; to move; stir. **3.** *Colloq.* Of the tongue, to keep moving in chatter or gossip; as, his tongue *wags* incessantly. **4.** To waddle. **5.** *Colloq.* To go; to pack off. **6.** *School Slang.* To play truant from school. **7.** To signal, as with a wag of the head or finger. — *n.* **1.** *Colloq.* Act of wagging; a shake; as, a *wag* of the head or hand. **2.** [Perh. shortened fr. *waghalter* a rogue, joker.] One full of sport and humor; a wit; a joker.

wage (wāj), *v. t.;* WAGED (wājd); WAG′ING (wāj′ĭng) [ONF. *wagier* (OF. *gagier,* F. *gager*). See GAGE to pledge.] **1.** *Archaic or Hist.* To pledge; to put down as a security; hence, to stake; wager. **2.** *Obs.* To expose oneself to, as a risk; to venture; attempt. **3.** To engage in, as a contest; to carry on, as a war. **4.** *Chiefly Dial. Eng.* To hire; employ. — *v. i. Rare.* To engage in, or carry on, war; to contend. — *n* **1.** *Obs. exc. Hist.* A pledge; a security that one will do something or will abide by the result of something, as a duel or combat. **2.** *Obs.* State of being pledged; pledge; pawn; as, to lay one's life in *wage.* **3.** That which is pledged or paid for work or other services; hire; pay. See WAGES. **4.** Figuratively, produce; yield.

☞ The plural form *wages* was formerly often, and is still sometimes, construed as a singular; as, "The *wages* of sin is death." *Rom.* vi. 23.

Syn. **Wage** (*or* **wages**), **salary, stipend, fee, pay, hire, emolument** mean the price paid for services. **Wage** or **wages** applies chiefly to the amount paid daily or weekly for labor, esp. labor that involves physical effort; **salary** and **stipend** (the latter more common in British use), to the fixed compensation paid for services which require training or ability; **fee,** to the amount, often fixed, paid to a physician, lawyer, etc., for professional services; **pay,** to wages or salaries but often, specifically, in reference to those of military men; **hire,** now archaic, the pay given for services or for use of one's talents; **emolument,** now often bookish, the financial reward of one's work or one's office.

wage earner. A person who works for wages.

wa′ger (wā′jẽr), *n.* [ONF. *wageüre,* fr. *wagier,* v. See WAGE, *v.*] **1.** *Obs.* A gage, or pledge. **2.** That which is risked on an uncertain event; a bet. **3.** Act of wagering. **4.** That on which bets are laid; the subject of a bet. **5.** *Obs. exc. Hist.* [ONF. *wagier* (OF. *gagier*), inf. as n.] Act of giving a pledge to do something or to abide the event of something; as, *wager* of battle. — *v. t.* To hazard; risk; venture; also, to stake; bet. — *v. i.* To make a bet; to lay a wager. — **wa′ger·er,** *n.*

wag′es (wāj′ĕz; -ĭz; 30), *n., pl.* of WAGE, *n.* (see WAGE, *n., Note*). **1.** Pay given for labor, usually manual or mechanical, at short stated intervals, as distinguished from salaries or fees. **2.** *Theoretical Econ.* The share of the annual product or national dividend which goes as a reward to labor, as distinct from the remuneration received by capital in its various forms. This economic or technical sense of the word *wages* is broader than the current sense, and includes **wages of management** *or* **superintendence** which are earned by skill in directing the work of others. Cf. PROFIT, 5; RENT, 4. — **Syn.** See WAGE.

wage scale. **1.** A series of rates of wages paid for related tasks. **2.** The level of wages paid by an employer.

wage′work′er (wāj′wûr′kẽr), *n.* A person who works for wages. — **wage′work′ing,** *adj. & n.*

wag′ger·y (wăg′ẽr·ĭ), *n.; pl.* WAGGERIES (-ĭz). **1.** The manner or action of a wag; mischievous merriment; pleasantry; waggishness. **2.** A jest, esp. a practical joke.

wag′gish (wăg′ĭsh), *adj.* **1.** Like or characteristic of a wag; mischievous. **2.** Done, made, or laid in waggery or for sport; sportive. — **wag′gish·ly,** *adv.* — **wag′gish·ness,** *n.*

wag′gle (wăg′'l), *v. i.;* WAG′GLED (-'ld); WAG′GLING (-lĭng). [Freq. of *wag.*] To reel, sway, or move, from side to side; to wag. — *v. t.* To move frequently one way and the other; to wag. — *n.* A wagging or waggling. — **wag′gling·ly,** *adv.* — **wag′gly** (-lĭ), *adj.*

wag′gon, wag′gon·er, etc. Brit. vars. of WAGON, etc.

Wag·ne′ri·an (väg·nẽr′ĭ·ăn), *adj.* Of, pertaining to, characterized by, or resembling the theories or style of Richard Wagner (1813–1883), German composer of opera and music drama. — *n.* An admirer of the musical theories and style of Wagner.

Wag′ner·ism (väg′nẽr·ĭz'm), *n.* **1.** Richard Wagner's theory and practice in the composition of opera, or, esp., music drama, his chief aim being to free opera from the conventions of the Italian school, and make dramatic fitness dominate the ensemble of text, music, action, and scene. 2. The influence of the work of Wagner in the world of music. — **Wag′ner·ist** (väg′nẽr·ĭst), *n.*

wag′on *or, British,* **wag′gon** (wăg′ŭn), *n.* [D. *wagen,* MD. *waghen.*] **1.** A four-wheeled vehicle for carrying heavy loads of produce, goods, military supplies, etc., and drawn by beasts of burden, variously having only a flat bed, a box, high sides, a canvas covering as in a prairie schooner for moving effects cross-country. Cf. WAIN, DRAY, VAN. By extension, *Chiefly U. S.:* **a** A light one-horse business vehicle for delivering baggage, groceries, etc. **b** Loosely, a carriage, carryall, or buggy. **c** A child's four-wheeled cart; — in full, ***express wagon.*** **d** A hand-propelled stand on wheels or casters for serving hors d'oeuvres, tea things, etc.; — in full, ***tea wagon.*** **2.** *Brit.* A railway freight car. **3.** An automobile, with covered wooden body of a light delivery wagon, for carrying passengers and luggage (in full, ***beach,*** *or* ***station, wagon***), or with closed body of a police carryall for conveying apprehended persons (***police,*** *or* ***patrol, wagon***; usually, ***the wagon***). **4.** *Colloq.* A baby carriage or perambulator. **5.** *Slang.* **a** A warship. **b** A firearm. **c** An automobile. — ***on the*** **(*water*)** ***wagon.*** See WATER WAGON. — *v. t. & i.* To convey or travel by wagon.

wag′on·age, wag′gon·age (-ĭj), *n.* **1.** Transportation by wagon or wagons; also, money paid for carriage or conveyance in a wagon. **2.** A collection of wagons.

wag′on·er, wag′gon·er (-ẽr), *n.* **1.** One who drives a wagon, esp., as a business. **2.** *Obs.* A charioteer. **3.** [*cap.*] *Astron.* **a** Auriga. **b** Charles's Wain.

wag′on·ette′, wag′gon·ette′ (wăg′ŭn·ĕt′), *n.* [*wagon* + *-ette.*] A type of wagon with two facing seats along the sides behind a transverse seat in front.

‖**wa′gon′-lit′** (và′gôN′lē′), *n.* [F., fr. *wagon* railway coach (fr. E. *wagon*) + *lit* bed.] Railway sleeping car.

wagon train. A train of wagons; esp., *Mil.,* a train of provision or service wagons.

wag′some (wăg′sŭm), *adj. Rare.* Waggish.

wag′tail′ (wăg′tāl′), *n.* **a** Any of numerous mostly Old World birds (subfamily Motacillinae) allied to the pipits. They have a trim slender body and a very long tail which they habitually jerk up and down. **b** A similar bird, as an American water thrush.

Wa·ha′bi, Wa·ha′bee, Wah·ha′bi (wä·hä′bē), *n.* [Ar. *wahhābī.*] A follower of Abdul-Wahhab (1691–1787), reformer who sought to restore the primitive form of Mohammedanism. The Wahabis, a sect of purists that arose in Arabia, are a warlike people and under ibn-Saud have by a revival of power since 1910 enlarged their state from Nejd to nearly all of Arabia (Saudi Arabia). — **Wa·ha′bi·ism** (-bē·ĭz′m), **Wa·ha′bism** (-bĭz′m), *n.* — **Wa·ha′bite** (-bīt), *adj.*

Wa·ha′bit (wä·hä′bĭt), **Wa·ha′bite** (-bīt), *n.* A Wahabi.

wa·hoo′ (wä·hōō′; wä′hōō), *n.* [Dakota *wanhu* (*wāhu*), lit., arrowwood.] A shrub (*Evonymus atropurpureus*) having purple capsules which in dehiscence expose the scarlet-ariled seeds; — called also *burning bush.*

wa·hoo′, *n.* [Creek *ûhawhu* cork elm.] Any of various American trees or shrubs; specif.: **a** Either of two elms (*Ulmus racemosa* and *U. alata*). **b** The cascara buckthorn. **c** The basswood (*Tilia*).

waif (wāf), *n.* [ONF. *waif,* OF. *guaif, gaif,* adj., lost, unclaimed, *chose gaive* a waif.] **1.** *Eng. Law.* Stolen goods thrown away by a thief in his flight. **2.** Hence, anything found, or without an owner; a stray article. **3.** A stray person or beast, as a homeless child or a lost sheep. **4.** *Naut.* = WAFT, *n.,* 3. — *adj. Chiefly Scot.* Stray; vagrant; as, a *waif* word or expression.

wail (wāl), *v. t. & i.* [ON. *væla, vāla.*] To lament; bewail; to grieve over; as, to *wail* one's death. — *n.* Act of wailing; also, a mournful, usually prolonged, cry or sound arising from grief or pain. — **wail′er,** *n.*

wail′ful (-fŏŏl; -f'l), *adj.* **1.** Sorrowful; mournful; wailing. **2.** Giving utterance to wailing, mournful sounds; as, the *wailful* sough of the wind. — **wail′ful·ly,** *adv.*

Wail′ing Place of the Jews, *or* **Wail′ing Wall.** An enclosed area in Jerusalem, near the Moslem Mosque of Omar, one wall of which is 59 feet high and supposed to contain some of the stones of Solomon's temple. In front of this wall Jews gather on Fridays to lament and pray.

wail′some (wāl′sŭm), *adj.* Deplorable; productive of grief and lamentation; also, lamenting; plaintive.

wain (wān), *n.* [AS. *wæn, wægn, wægen.*] **1.** *Archaic.* A wagon, esp. a heavy wagon or two-wheeled cart for farm use. **2.** [*cap.,* with *the.*] *Astron.* Charles's Wain.

wain′rope′ (-rōp′), *n. Rare.* A cart rope; a trace.

wain′scot (wān′skŭt; -skŏt; -skōt; *formerly commonly, still often in Brit. use,* wĕn′skŭt), *n.* [MLG. *wagenscot,* appar. fr. *wagen* wagon + *schot* wooden partition, crossbar.] **a** In British usage, a fine grade of oak imported for woodwork; also, a piece of such wood. **b** Hence, a wooden lining of an interior wall, usually paneled; also, by extension, any lining of an interior wall, irrespective of material; as, a tile *wainscot.* **c** The lower three or four feet of an interior wall when finished differently from the remainder of the wall. — *v. t.;* -SCOT·ED or -SCOT·TED; -SCOT·ING or -SCOT·TING. To line with or as with boards or paneling; as, to *wainscot* a hall.

wain′scot·ing, wain′scot·ting, *n.* The material used to wainscot a house, or the wainscot as a whole.

wain′wright′ (wān′rīt′), *n.* [*wain* a wagon + *wright.*] A builder of wagons.

wair (wâr). Scot. & N. of Eng. var. of WARE, to spend.

waist (wāst), *n.* [ME. *wast;* orig., growth, akin to AS. *weaxan* to grow, *wæstm* growth.] **1.** The small part of the body between the thorax and hips. **2.** That part of anything which resembles in some way the human waist; the middle part, esp. when less thick than the ends; as, the *waist* of a violin (see VIOLIN, *Illust.*). **3.** A garment, or that part of a garment, which covers the body from the neck or shoulders to, or about to, the waistline. Specif.: **a** The bodice, or upper part, of a woman's dress. **b** An undergarment for children, worn similarly, to which other clothing may be buttoned. **4.** *Naut.* That part of a vessel's deck between the quarter-deck and forecastle; the middle part of the ship. **5.** *Zool.* The greatly constricted basal part of the abdomen of certain wasps, flies, and other insects.

waist′band′ (wāst′bănd′; -bănd), *n.* A band, sash, or the like, which encompasses the waist; specif., one on the upper part of breeches, trousers, skirts, or the like, serving often as an inner belt.

waist′cloth′ (-klŏth′; 74), *n.* A cloth or wrapper worn about the waist; esp., a loincloth.

waist′coat′ (wās(t)′kōt′; wĕs′kŭt; 105), *n.* **a** A man's garment of ornamental character, formerly worn under the doublet. **b** A sleeveless garment for men, worn under the coat, now extending a little below the waist; — in U. S. commonly called *vest.* **c** A similar garment or a front resembling a man's waistcoat, worn by women. — **waist′coat′ed** (-ĕd; -ĭd), *adj.*

waist′coat′ing, *n.* A fabric designed for waistcoats.

waist′er (wās′tẽr), *n. Now Rare. Naut.* A seaman, usually an inexperienced or broken-down man, stationed in the waist of a whaler or, formerly, of a vessel of war.

waist′line′ (wāst′līn′), *n.* A line surrounding, or thought of as surrounding, the waist where it is most contracted; also, in dressmaking, the line at which the waist and skirt of a dress meet.

wait (wāt), *v. i.* [ONF. *waitier* (OF. *guaitier, gaitier,* to watch, attend), of Teut. origin.] **1.** To look (mentally); to be in expectation; — usually with *for.* **2.** To stay or remain in readiness for action. **3.** To act as attendant or servant; esp., to attend or wait upon persons at table; to serve. — **Syn.** See STAY. — *v. t.* **1.** To stay for; to remain stationary in expectation of; to await; as, to *wait* orders. **2.** To attend on; escort; esp., to attend with ceremony or respect; as, to *wait* a funeral. **3.** To serve as a waiter or attendant upon; as, to *wait* table. **4.** *Obs.* To attend as a consequence; to follow upon. **5.** *Colloq.* To cause to wait; to defer; postpone; — said of a meal; as, we shall *wait* dinner for you. — ***wait on*** *or* ***upon.*** **a** To attend as a servant; to serve. **b** To go and see; to visit on business or for ceremony. **c** To follow as a consequence. — *n.* **1.** *Obs.* A watchman. **2.** **a** *Hist.* One of a band of public musicians who, in England, were once employed to play for entertainments. **b** One of a group of street or rustic serenaders who play or sing at night for small gratuities, esp. around the Christmas season; also, music provided by these. **3.** An ambush; trap; as, to lie in *wait* for the enemy. **4.** Act of waiting; a delay; also, interval of waiting, as between acts of a play.

wait′-a-bit′, *n.* [Trans. of S. Afr. D. *wacht-en-beetje, -bitje,* a variety of wattle.] Any of several plants, as the greenbrier and hawthorn, bearing thorns or stiff hooked appendages.

wait′er (wāt′ẽr), *n.* **1.** A watcher; watchman. *Obs.* exc. in composition, as in tide*waiter.* **2.** One who waits (in various senses); specif., a man who waits at table, as at a restaurant, etc. **3.** A tray on which something is carried; a salver.

wait′ing, *n.* A period during which one waits (in various senses). — *adj.* That waits (in various senses). — **wait′ing·ly,** *adv.* — ***in waiting.*** **a** *Eng.* In attendance; as, lords *in waiting.* **b** *Brit. Mil. & Nav.* Next in turn for a service, tour of duty, etc. — **waiting maid.** — **waiting man.** — **waiting woman.**

waiting room. A room for the use of persons waiting, as at a railroad station or other public place.

wait′ress (wāt′rĕs; -rĭs), *n.* A female waiter or attendant at table; a maidservant who waits on table.

waive (wāv), *v. t.* [AF. *weyver,* fr. ONF. var. of OF. *gaiver, guever,* to abandon, prob. of Scand. origin.] **1.** *Obs.* To remove; reject; leave. **2.** To put away, or give up, a claim to; to forgo. **3.** To refrain from taking advantage of; to neglect; disregard; as, he *waived* his rights to the property. **4.** To postpone; defer; as, let's *waive* this question until later. **5.** *Law.* To relinquish voluntarily, as a right which one may enforce if he chooses. — **Syn.** See RELINQUISH.

waive, *v. t. & i. Now Rare.* To wave.

waiv′er (wāv′ẽr), *n.* [AF. *weyver,* inf. as n.] *Law.* Act of waiving, or intentionally relinquishing or abandoning some known right, claim, or privilege; also, the instrument evidencing such an act.

wake (wāk), *n.* [Of Scand. origin.] The track left by a vessel in the water; by extension, any track; as, the *wake* of an army; the *wake* of a meteor.

wake (wāk), *v. i.;* WAKED (wākt) or WOKE (wōk); WAKED or, sometimes, WOK′EN (wōk′ĕn); WAK′ING (wāk′ĭng). [AS. *wacan* to wake, be born (pret. *wōc,* past part. *wacen*), combined with the kindred *wacian* (pret. *wacode*), var. of *wæccan* to watch, be awake.] **1.** To be or to continue awake; not to sleep; specif., to keep watch or vigil, as over a corpse; to hold a wake. **2.** *Obs.* To sit up late for festivities or revel. **3.** To be roused from sleep; to awake; — often with *up.* **4.** To be stirred up from a dormant, torpid, or inactive state; also, to be alert. **5.** To become alive again; to undergo resurrection. — *v. t.* **1.** To rouse from sleep; to awake. **2.** To put in motion or action; to arouse; excite. **3.** To bring to life again, as if from the sleep of death; to revive; as, to *wake* sad memories. **4.** To watch; guard; specif., to watch, or sit up with, at night, as a dead body; to hold a wake over.

— *n.* **1.** *Obs. exc. Poetic.* Act of waking or being awaked; also, sleeplessness. **2.** State of forbearing sleep, esp. for solemn or festive purposes; vigil. **3.** *Ch. of Eng.* An annual parish festival formerly held in commemoration of the dedication of a church; also, the ceremonies attending such a festival. **4.** The sitting up of persons with a dead body, formerly often attended with festivity.

wake′ful (wāk′fŏŏl; -f'l), *adj.* **1.** Not sleeping; sleepless; indisposed to sleep; hence, watchful; vigilant. **2.** *Now Rare.* That wakes; awakening. — **wake′ful·ly,** *adv.* — **wake′ful·ness,** *n.*

wake′less (-lĕs; -lĭs), *adj.* Of sleep, sound; unbroken.

wak′en (wāk′ĕn), *v. i.* [AS. *wæcnan, wæcnian.*] To wake: **a** To become awake; to cease to sleep; to be awakened. **b** *Obs.* To continue awake; to keep vigil; to watch. **c** To become active or animated. — *v. t.* **1.** To excite or rouse from sleep; to wake. **2.** To excite; to move to action. **3.** *Scot.* To watch as a protection; to guard.

wak′en·er (-ẽr), *n.* One who or that which wakens.

wak′en·ing, *n.* Act of one who wakens; an awakening.

wak′er (wāk′ẽr), *n.* One who wakes.

wake′rife (wāk′rīf), *adj.* [See WAKE, *v.;* RIFE, *adj.*] Wakeful; alert. — **wake′rife·ness,** *n. Both Scot.*

wake′-rob′in (wāk′rŏb′ĭn), *n.* **a** *Eng.* Any of various arums, esp. the cuckoopint; also, the European orchid *Orchis maculata.* **b** *U. S.* Any of various trilliums; also, the jack-in-the-pulpit.

wake′-up′ (-ŭp′), *n. Local, U. S.* The flicker.

Wal·den′ses (wŏl·dĕn′sēz), *n. pl.* [ML. *Waldenses, Valdenses,* after Peter *Waldo,* or *Valdo.*] *Eccl.* A sect of dissenters from the system of the Roman Catholic Church, founded about 1179 by Petrus Waldus, or Peter Waldo, a merchant of Lyon. Waldo and his followers sought to revive primitive pureness of living. — **Wal·den′si·an** (-sĭ·ăn; -shăn), *adj. & n.*

wald′grave (wŏld′grāv), *n.* [G. *waldgraf.*] In the old German empire, the head forest keeper; also, formerly, in the Rhine districts, a noble of a certain rank.

Wal'dorf sal'ad (wôl'dôrf). [From the old *Waldorf*-Astoria Hotel, N. Y. City.] A salad made commonly of diced apples, celery, and nuts, and dressed with mayonnaise.

wale (wāl), *n.* [ME., fr. ON. *val* choice.] *Scot., N. of Eng., & Ir.* A choosing; a choice; a field for choice; also, the choicest or best; the pick. — *v. t. Scot., N. of Eng., & Ir.* To choose; select for oneself.

wale, *n.* [AS. *walu* a ridge, a mark of stripes or blows.] **1.** A streak made on the skin by a rod or whip; a wheal; by extension, any ridge, or narrow raised surface. **2.** A rib or heavy twill in a fabric; hence, texture, as of cloth; grain. **3.** *pl. Shipbuilding.* Certain strakes of the outside planking of a vessel; the bends; as, channel *wales*, or strakes along the upper deck, etc. — *v. t.* To mark with wales, or stripes; to manufacture, as a fabric, with a rib or a heavy twill.

Wal'er (wāl'ẽr), *n.* [From *Wales*, i. e., New South Wales.] *Colloq.* A horse, esp. for cavalry, imported from New South Wales; also, any Australian horse.

☞ The term originated in India, whither many horses are exported from Australia (esp. New South Wales).

Wal·hal'la (wŏl·hăl'ȧ), *n.* = VALHALLA.

walk (wôk), *v. i.* [AS. *wealcan, wealcian*, to roll, turn, revolve.] **1.** *Obs.* To be or to keep in motion; hence, of the tongue, to move incessantly; wag. **2.** *Obs.* To go forth or about; to roam. **3.** To go restlessly about contrary to the normal course of nature, as a somnambulist or a specter. **4.** To move along on foot; to advance by steps; specif., of two-legged creatures, to proceed without running, or lifting one foot entirely before the other touches the ground; of four-legged creatures, to proceed with a gait in which at least two feet are always on the ground; sometimes, specif., to move or go on foot for exercise or amusement. **5.** To make slow progress, as at a walk. **6.** To pursue a course of life; to conduct oneself. **7.** To move in a manner likened to walking, as a chimney swaying through the action of winds. **8.** *Baseball Slang.* To go to first base as the result of a base on balls. — *v. t.* **1.** To pass through, over, or upon; as, to *walk* the streets. **2.** To bring to a (specified) state by walking; as, to *walk* one's companion to exhaustion. **3.** To follow on foot for the purpose of measuring, surveying, etc.; as, to *walk* a boundary. **4.** To cause to walk; as, to *walk* one's horses. **5.** To take for a walk; also, to force to keep moving on foot. **6.** *Colloq.* To move in a manner likened to walking. **7.** *Baseball Slang.* To give a base on balls to.

walk Spanish. *Colloq., U. S.* To walk on tiptoe involuntarily through another's lifting one by the seat of the trousers, etc., as in boys' sports; hence, to walk gingerly; also, to get discharged. — ***walk the plank.*** To walk along a plank laid across the bulwark of a ship, until one overbalances it and falls into the sea, — a method of disposing of captives practiced by pirates; hence, to vacate a position under compulsion.

— *n.* **1.** Act of walking, specif. for recreation or exercise; hence, peregrination; wandering. **2.** Manner of walking; gait. Specif., a gait of a horse in which there are always at least two feet on the ground. **3.** Distance as measured in time required by a walker to cover; as, ten minutes' *walk* to the station. **4.** Conduct; behavior. **5.** Habitual or proper place, range, or sphere of action; — esp. in the phrase *walk of life.* **6.** That in or through which one walks, or a place designed for walking; specif.: **a** A haunt. **b** A path specially arranged or paved for walking. **c** An avenue for promenading; a promenade. **d** = ROPEWALK. **7.** A plantation of coffee, coconut, or other trees, arranged in rows with wide spaces between them. **8.** A place or region in which animals may graze or exercise; range; pasture land; — now only in the combination sheep*walk*. **9.** The route regularly served by a vendor; hence, in general, a beat; round. **10.** *Athletics.* A trial of speed in walking over a given course; a walking race. **11.** *Slang. Baseball.* A base on balls.

walk'a·way' (wôk'ȧ·wā'), *n.* An easily won contest.

walk'er (wôk'ẽr), *n.* One who walks (in any sense).

walk'ie-talk'ie (wôk'ĭ·tôk'ĭ), *n.* Also **walk'y-talk'y.** A compact battery-operated radiotelephonic transmitting and receiving set that is carried like a knapsack to provide two-way communication in the field.

walk'ing (wôk'ĭng), *adj.* That walks. Specif.: **a** *Agric. Mach.* Drawn by animal power and guided by a man on foot; as, a *walking* cultivator. **b** That oscillates to and fro; as, a *walking* beam. **c** That moves itself forward in the manner of, or suggesting that of, a walker; as, a *walking* crane. — *n.* **1.** Act of one who walks; also, manner of walking; gait. **2.** Condition of the track, sidewalk, or road for one going on foot; as, the *walking* is slippery.

walking delegate. A business representative of a union, appointed to visit members and their places of employment, to secure the enforcement of union rules and agreements, and, at times, to represent the union in dealing with employers.

walking leaf. **a** Also **walking fern.** Any of a genus (*Camptosorus*, esp. *C. rhizophyllus*) of ferns. **b** Any of a family (Phasmatidae, order Orthoptera) of insects with wings and legs resembling leaves.

walking papers *or* **ticket.** *Colloq.* An order to leave; dismissal.

walking stick. **a** A staff carried when walking; a cane. **b** A stick insect (as *Aplopus mayeri*).

walk'out' (wôk'out'), *n.* Act of walking out, or leaving; specif., *Colloq., U. S.*, a labor strike.

walk'o'ver (-ō'vẽr), *n.* In racing, the going over a course by a horse which is the only starter; hence, *Colloq.*, a one-sided contest; an easy victory.

walk'-up' (wôk'ŭp'), *n.* An apartment house without an elevator. — **walk'-up'**, *adj. Both Colloq., U. S.*

‖**Wal·kü're, Die** (dē väl·kü'rĕ). [G., the Valkyrie.] The second part (1869) of Wagner's tetralogy of music dramas *Der Ring des Nibelungen.* See RING OF THE NIBELUNG.

walk'way' (wôk'wā'), *n.* **1.** A passage for walking, esp. one connecting sections of a ship, a factory, or the like. **2.** *U. S.* A broad path, as in a garden.

Wal·kyr'ie (wŏl·kĭr'ĭ), *n.* [AS. *wælcyrie.*] = VALKYRIE.

walk'y-talk'y, *n.* See WALKIE-TALKIE.

wall (wôl), *n.* [AS. *weall*, fr. L. *vallum* a wall set with palisades, fr. *vallus* a stake, pale, palisade.] **1.** A work or structure of stone, brick, or other materials, intended for defense or security, or for an enclosure; esp.: **a** A solid fence, as around a field, a park, etc. **b** One of the upright enclosing parts of a building or a room. **c** A levee, sea wall, or the like. **2.** A defense; rampart; in *pl.*, fortifications. **3.** Something that is like, or suggestive of, a wall; esp., something conceived of as a separating barrier; as, language differences form a *wall* between peoples. **4.** The bounding side or inside surface of a cavity or vessel; as, the *walls* of a boiler. — ***to drive, push,*** *or* ***thrust to the wall.*** To force or push aside or to an extreme position; to compel to give way; to crush. — ***to go to the wall.*** To be hard pressed or driven; hence, to become bankrupt; fail. — *adj.* Of or pertaining to a wall; growing on or placed against a wall. — *v. t.* **1.** To enclose with a wall or as with a wall; to immure; also, to provide with walls, as a room. **2.** To defend by walls or as if by walls; to fortify. **3.** To separate by, or as by, a wall.

wal'la·by (wŏl'ȧ·bĭ), *n.; pl.* -BIES (-bĭz), sometimes -BY. See PLURAL, *Note*, 3. [From a native name, *wolabā* a kind of kangaroo.] Any of various small and medium-sized kangaroos (esp. of the genus *Macropus*).

wal'lah (wäl'ä), *n.* Also **wal'la.** [Hind. *-vālā*, suff. like L. *-arius* (cf. -ER).] *Anglo-Ind.* Agent; a master or owner; a servant or worker; also, *Colloq.*, a person.

wal'la·roo' (wŏl'ȧ·rōō'), *n.* [In an Australian native dialect, *wolarū* mountain kangaroo.] Any of several large kangaroos, esp. a formerly common species (*Macropus robustus*).

wall'board' (wôl'bōrd'; 70), *n.* Board or other material for use as or against a wall; specif., an artificial board of wood fiber, cane fiber, or the like, made in large sheets and used for the interior sheathing of walls of rooms.

walled (wôld), *adj.* Furnished or enclosed with a wall or walls; specif., fortified; as, a *walled* town.

wal'let (wŏl'ĕt; -ĭt), *n.* [ME. *walet.*] **1.** A bag or sack for carrying about the person; knapsack; pack. **2.** *Obs.* Anything hanging loose like a bag; as, *wallets* of flesh. **3.** A pocketbook, esp. one of some size for papers, paper money unfolded, etc.

wall'eye' (wôl'ī'), *n.* [See WALLEYED.] **1. a** An eye, as of a horse, in which the iris is whitish. **b** An eye in which the cornea is opaque and white. **c** Leucoma of the cornea. **d** An eye which turns outward showing an undue amount of white. **e** See STRABISMUS. **2.** Any of various fishes: **a** The walleyed pike. **b** The walleyed surf fish. **c** = ALEWIFE, 2. **d** The walleyed pollack.

wall'eyed' (-īd'), *adj.* [ON. *vagleygr*, fr. *vagl* a beam, a beam in the eye + *eygr* having eyes (fr. *auga* eye).] **1. a** Having a very light gray or whitish eye. **b** Affected with leucoma of the cornea. **c** Affected with strabismus. **2.** Having a blank or staring appearance, as of a person affected with walleye. **3.** Having glaring eyes; fierce-eyed.

walleyed herring. = ALEWIFE, 2.

walleyed pike *or* **perch.** An American fresh-water food fish (*Stizostedion vitreum*) having large prominent eyes.

walleyed pollack. A large sooty-black pollack (*Theragra fucensis*) of the Pacific coast of North America.

walleyed surf fish. A common California fish (*Hyperprosopon argenteus*), of a nearly uniform sooty color.

wall fern. The common polypody (*Polypodium vulgare*).

wall'flow'er (wôl'flou'ẽr), *n.* **1.** Any of a genus (*Cheiranthus*) of herbs, esp. a perennial herb (*C. cheiri*) with sweet-scented flowers. In Europe it is common on old walls. **2.** In Australia, a desert shrub (*Gastrolobium grandiflorum*). **3.** *Colloq.* A woman or man who remains by the wall as a spectator at a dance, either by choice or because not chosen as a partner.

wal'lie (wŏl'ĭ), *n.* [From VALET.] *Scot.* A valet.

Wal·lo'ni·an (wŏ·lō'nĭ·ăn), *adj.* Of or pertaining to the Walloons or their language. — *n.* The language of the Walloons; Walloon.

Wal·loon' (wŏ·lōōn'), *n.* [F. *Wallon.*] **a** One of a people, primarily of Celtic race, inhabiting southern Belgium. **b** Their language, Belgian French. — **Wal·loon'**, *adj.*

wal'lop (wŏl'ŭp), *v. i.* [ONF. *waloper* (F. *galoper*).] **1.** *Scot. & Dial. Eng.* To move quickly, but with great effort; to gallop. **2.** To move in a rolling, cumbersome manner; to flounder; waddle. **3.** *Chiefly Scot.* To dangle, flutter, or flap, as rags. — *v. t.* **1.** *Dial. & Colloq.* To beat soundly; thrash. **2.** *Slang.* To strike hard; as, to *wallop* a baseball for a home run. — *n.* **1.** *Scot. & Dial. Eng.* A quick, rolling movement; a gallop. **2.** *Scot.* An awkward, heavy leap, jump, or plunge. **3.** *Slang.* A powerful blow; also, the ability, as of a pugilist, to deliver such a blow; as, he packs a *wallop* in either hand. — *adv.* With a heavy thud.

wal'lop (wŏl'ŭp), *v. i.* [Prob. imitative, but perh. same as *wallop* to move.] *Scot. & Dial.* To boil with a continued bubbling noise.

wal'lop·er (-ẽr), *n.* One that wallops. Cf. POT-WALLOPER.

wal'lop·er, *n. Colloq.* = WHOPPER, something enormous.

wal'lop·ing, *adj. Dial.* Large; whopping. — *n. Colloq.* A beating; thrashing; licking.

wal'low (wŏl'ō), *v. i.* [AS. *wealwian.*] **1.** To roll oneself about, as in mire; to welter; flounder; as, swine *wallow* in the mud. **2.** To live or continue in animal satisfaction in some condition or mode of life; as, to *wallow* in luxury, in money. **3.** To surge, as waves; to billow, as smoke; to gush forth in eddies, as flame or a spring. — *n.* **1.** Act of wallowing, in various senses. **2.** A place to which an animal comes to wallow; also, the depression made by its wallowing; as, a buffalo *wallow.* **3.** A depression suggesting a place where animals have wallowed; as, sunk in the *wallow* of despondency. — **wal'low·er** (-ō·ẽr), *n.*

wall'pa'per (wôl'pā'pẽr), *n* Paper for walls of rooms; paper hangings. — **wall'pa'per,** *v. t. & i.*

wall pellitory. A European herb (*Parietaria officinalis*) of diuretic properties, growing on old walls.

wall plate. **a** *Arch.* A continuous plate on a wall to support posts, joists, or the like; a plate. See ROOF, *Illust.* **b** *Mach.* A metal plate or bracket secured flat against the wall to support a bearing, machinery, etc.

wall rock. *Geol. & Mining.* The rock through which a fault or vein runs.

wall rocket. A plant (*Diplotaxis tenuifolia*) of the mustard family of Europe, with large yellow flowers, adventive in North America.

wall rue. A small delicate spleenwort (*Asplenium rutamuraria*) found on walls, cliffs, etc.

Walls'end' (wôlz'ĕnd'), *n.* [From *Wallsend*, Eng.] A grade, or a size, of coal.

Wall Street. A street toward the southern end of New York City, extending from Broadway to the East River. It is the chief financial center of the United States, and the name is often used for the money market and the financial interests. Cf. LOMBARD STREET.

wal'ly (wāl'ĭ), *adj.* [ME. *wale*, adj. & n., choice.] **a** Excellent; fine. **b** Ample; robust. **c** Pleasant; jolly. — *n.* An ornament or toy; a gewgaw; *pl.*, finery. *All Scot.*

wal'ly·drag' (wăl'ĭ-drăg'; wŏl'ĭ-), *n.* Also **wal'ly·drai'gle** (-drā'g'l). *Scot.* A feeble, undergrown, or slovenly creature; the youngest of a brood.

wal'nut (wôl'nŭt; -nŭt), *n.* [AS. *wealh-hnutu* a Celtic or foreign nut, a walnut, fr. *wealh* foreign, strange, *n.*, a Welshman, Celt + *hnutu* a nut.] **1. a** The fruit or nut of any of a genus (*Juglans*) of trees, esp. of one species (*J. regia*) distinguished in the United States as the ***English walnut.*** **b** A tree of this genus; also, its wood. The walnuts are ornamental shade trees, and the wood of several species, notably the ***black walnut*** (*J. nigra*), is valuable for furniture, indoor finishings, etc. The genus is typical of a family (Juglandaceae, the walnut family). **2.** *Local, U.S.* The shagbark; also, its nut. **3.** The color of the heartwood of the black walnut, reddish red-yellow in hue, of saturation and brilliance varying from low to medium. See COLOR.

Wal·pur'gis Night (väl-pōōr'gĭs). Ger. **Wal·pur'gis·nacht'** (-näkt'). The eve of May Day, or the feast of Walburga (Walpurgis), the saint, on which, according to German superstition, a witches' Sabbath took place on the Brocken, a peak of the Harz Mountains.

wal'rus (wôl'rŭs; wŏl'-), *n.*; see PLURAL, *Note*, 3. [D. *walrus, walros*, of Scand. origin.] **1.** A very large marine mammal (*Odobenus rosmarus*) of the Arctic Ocean, allied to the seals but forming a distinct family (Odobenidae). In the male the upper canine teeth form greatly elongated protruding tusks. The skin makes valuable leather, the tusks are fine ivory, and the blubber yields oil. **2.** *Colloq.* A walrus mustache. — *adj.* Of or pertaining to a walrus; specif., designating a type of mustache with long downward-curving ends.

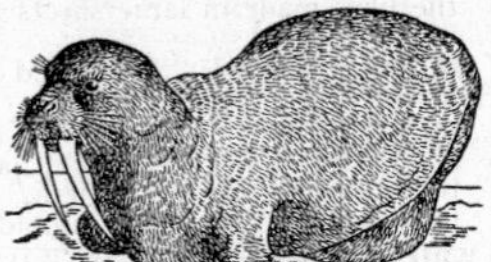
Walrus. (1/120)

waltz (wôlts *or, esp. Brit.*, wôls), *n.* [G. *walzer*, fr. *walzen* to roll, dance, fr. OHG. *walzan* to roll.] **a** A form of round dance performed to music in triple measure. **b** Music for this dance or in its characteristic triple measure. — *adj.* Of, pertaining to, or characteristic of the waltz; as, *waltz* time; a *waltz* tune. — *v. i. & t.* To dance a waltz or in a waltz movement or step; hence, to move nimbly or quickly as in a waltz; to whirl. — **waltz'er**, *n.*

wal'y (wăl'ĭ; wôl'ĭ), *interj. Scot. & N. of Eng.* An exclamation, usually of grief.

wal'y (wăl'ĭ). Scot. var. of WALLY.

wam'ble (wŏm''l; wăm'-), *v. i.*; WAM'BLED (-'ld); WAM'BLING (-lĭng). [ME. *wamlen.*] *Now Chiefly Dial.* **1. a** *Obs.* To feel nausea. **b** To rumble; — said of the stomach. **2.** To move unsteadily; as: **a** To writhe; wriggle; twist. **b** To quiver; shake. **c** To revolve; spin. **d** To stagger; totter. **e** To turn topsy-turvy; to tumble. **f** To ramble. — *n. Now Dial.* **1.** A wambling; esp., a rumbling of the stomach. **2.** A reeling gait. — **wam'bling·ly**, *adv.* — **wam'bly** (wŏm'lĭ; wăm'-), *adj.*

wame (wām), *n.* [Dial. var. of WOMB.] *Scot. & Dial.* **a** The womb. **b** The belly; stomach.

wame'fou, wame'fu' (wām'fōō), **wame'ful** (-fŏŏl; -fōō), *n. Scot. & N. of Eng.* A bellyful.

wamp'ish (wămp'ĭsh), *v. i. & t. Scot.* To fluctuate; to swing; wave.

wam'pum (wŏm'pŭm; wôm'-), *n.* [Of Algonquian origin; cf. Massachuset Indian *wanpanpiag*, fr. *wab* white + *umpe* string + *-ag*, pl. suff. E. *wampum* and *peag* are abbrs. of earlier *wampumpeag.*] **1.** Beads made of shells, used by the North American Indians as money, as ceremonial pledges, or as ornaments. There were two kinds, black, or dark purple, and white, the black having double the value of the white. From its convenience in the fur trade with the Indians, wampum was largely used by the earlier settlers of the Eastern colonies, as far south as Virginia, and imitation wampum of white porcelain was made for sale to the Indians. **2.** *Slang.* Money.

wam'pum·peag' (-pēg'), *n.* [See WAMPUM.] Strictly, the white kind of shell beads used as money, etc., by the aborigines of North America; hence, by extension, any shell money used by them; wampum.

wam'pus (wŏm'pŭs), *n. Slang.* A heavy, stupid, sluggish person; sometimes, a person objectionable for any reason.

wa'mus (wô'mŭs; wŏ'mŭs), *n.* Also **wam'mus** (wŏm'ŭs), **wam'pus** (-pŭs). [D. *wammes, wambuis*, fr. OF. *wambais.*] *U.S.* A type of cardigan; also, an outer jacket made of strong, rough cloth.

wan (wŏn), *adj.* [AS. *wann, wonn, wan, won*, dark, lurid, livid.] **1.** Dark; gloomy; dusky; — now chiefly of water. **2.** *Obs.* **a** Sad; sorrowful. **b** Faint; dim; as, a *wan* hope. **3.** Having a pale or sickly hue; livid; pallid; as, his face was *wan* and drawn; hence, sickly; languid; as, a *wan* smile. — *v. i.*; WANNED (wŏnd); WAN'NING. To grow or make wan; to become or make pale or sickly in looks.

wan (wăn). Archaic & dial. past tense of WIN.

wan- (wŏn-). [AS. *wan-, won-*. See WANE.] A prefix formerly in use, meaning *deficient, wanting*, as in **wan·rest'ful**, *Scot.*, restless; **wan·chanc'y**, *Scot.*, dangerous.

wand (wŏnd), *n.* [ME. *wand, wond*, fr. ON. *vöndr.*] **1.** *Now Dial.* A slender switch or stick cut from a tree; a supple twig; also, a young shoot, esp. of willow; an osier. **2.** Specif., a slender flexible rod used, esp. waved, by one who enchants, conjures, or performs feats of legerdemain; a magician's rod. **3.** A staff of authority, as a scepter. **4.** *Archery.* In America, a slat 6 feet by 2 inches, stood, at 100 yards for men and 60 for women, as a mark.

wan'der (wŏn'dẽr; 73), *v. i.* [AS. *wandrian.*] **1.** To move about without a fixed course, aim, or objective; to rove; ramble. **2.** To take a roundabout or leisurely course; to meander; stroll. **3.** To deviate, as from a path; to stray; specif., to go astray morally; to err. **4.** To be or become irrational or delirious; to rave. — *v. t.* To travel over without a certain course; to stroll through. — *n.* Act of wandering; a rambling; a stroll.

wan'der·er (-ẽr), *n.* One who wanders.

wan'der·ing, *adj.* That wanders (in any sense). — *n.* A roaming at will; traveling. — **wan'der·ing·ly**, *adv.*

wandering albatross. A large black-winged white albatross (*Diomedea exulans*) of southern oceans.

Wandering Jew. **1.** In medieval legend, a Jew who treated Christ contemptuously on His way to the crucifixion, and was condemned by Him to wander upon the earth until the Second Advent. **2.** Spelled **wandering Jew.** Either of two trailing or creeping plants of cultivation (*Zebrina pendula* and *Tradescantia fluminensis*).

‖**Wan'der·jahr'** (vän'dẽr-yär'), *n.*; *pl.* WANDERJAHRE (-yä'rĕ). [G.] A year of wandering or of travel, esp. before settling down to one's permanent occupation; — also in English form **wan'der·year'** (wŏn'dẽr-yēr').

wan'der·lust' (vän'dẽr-lŏŏst'; wŏn'dẽr-lŭst'), *n.* [G.] Strong longing for, or impulse toward, wandering.

wan'der·oo' (wŏn'dẽr-ōō'), *n.* [Singhalese *vanduru*, pl. of *vandurā*, fr. Skr. *vānara* monkey.] **a** The purple-faced langur (*Presbytis cephalopterus*) of Ceylon. **b** A monkey (*Macaca albibarbata*) of the Indian peninsula.

wan'dle (wăn'd'l; -'l), *adj. Scot.* Supple; agile.

wane (wān), *v. i.* [AS. *wanian, wonian*; akin to AS. *wan, won*, deficient, wanting.] **1.** To be diminished; to decrease; specif., to undergo gradual diminution after being at the full; — chiefly of the moon, and contrasted with *wax*. **2.** Hence: **a** To fall from power, prosperity, influence, etc.; as, when its commerce decreased, the nation *waned*. **b** Of a season, life, etc., to draw to its end; as, summer is *waning*. **c** To grow dim or faint. — **Syn.** See ABATE. — **Ant.** Wax. — *n.* **1.** The missing or defective part of an imperfect board or plank. **2.** The act, process, or fact, of waning; also, the period in which something, as the moon, is waning; — chiefly in phrases *at, in, on,* or *upon, the wane*; as, the year is on the *wane*.

wan'gle (wăng'g'l; -'l), *v. i.*; -GLED (-g'ld; -'ld); -GLING (-glĭng; -lĭng). *Colloq.* **1.** To wriggle; to extricate oneself from a crowd, a difficulty, etc. **2.** To resort to trickery or indirect methods. — *v. t.* **1.** To shake; wiggle. **2.** To adjust or manipulate for personal or fraudulent ends; as, to *wangle* the records so as to show a profit. **3.** To make or get by manipulating, contriving, etc.; as, to *wangle* an invitation to a ball. — **wan'gler** (-glẽr), *n.*

wan'ion (wŏn'yŭn), *n.* [From ME. *waniand*, pres. part. of *wanien* to wane.] *Archaic.* A plague; a vengeance; — in the phrase *with a wanion.*

wan'ly (wŏn'lĭ), *adv.* In a wan manner.

wan'ness (wŏn'nĕs; -nĭs), *n.* Quality or state of being wan.

want (wŏnt; wônt; 73), *v. t.* [ME. *wanten*, fr. ON. *vanta* to want, lack.] **1.** To be without; to lack. **2.** To fall short (of) by; as, it *wants* three minutes to six. **3.** To feel or suffer the need of; loosely, to require; need. **4.** To desire; wish; long for. — *v. i.* **1.** *Archaic.* To be lacking, needed, or nonexistent; to fail to be available; as, there *wants* only a spark to set all aflame. **2.** To be in want; to be needy. **3.** To long; to have need or a need; to suffer a lack; — with *of* (*Obs.*) or *for*; as, he never *wants* for friends. — **Syn.** See LACK: DESIRE. — *n.* [From *want*, v., and, orig., fr. ON. *vant*, neut. of *vanr* lacking, wanting.] **1.** State or fact of not having, or of not having enough; lack; shortage. **2.** Specif., lack of necessaries; destitution; indigence. **3.** A wish for something; a desire; craving. **4.** That which is wanted; a need. — **Syn.** See POVERTY.

want ad. *Colloq.* An advertisement, as in a newspaper, stating one's want of an employee, employment, etc.

want'age (wŏn'tĭj; wôn'-), *n.* Amount wanting; shortage.

want'ing, *adj.* **1.** Absent; lacking; as, not *wanting* in zeal. **2.** Falling below a standard, an expectation, or a need. **3.** In quasi-prepositional uses: **a** Lacking (something); without; as, a book *wanting* a cover. **b** Less; minus; as, a month *wanting* two days. **4.** *Dial.* Feeble-minded; mentally defective.

wan'ton (wŏn'tŭn), *adj.* [ME. *wanton, wantoun*, contr. fr. *wantowen*, fr. *wan-* wanting + *towen*, past part., fr. AS. *togen*, lit., drawn.] **1.** Orig., undisciplined; unruly. **2.** *Chiefly Poetic.* Excessively merry or gay. **3.** Unchaste; lewd; also, licentious. **4.** Marked by arrogant recklessness of justice, of the feelings of others, or the like; as, *wanton* cruelty; also, having no just provocation; willfully malicious; as, a *wanton* insult. **5.** Unrestrained; specif.: **a** *Poetic.* Luxuriant in growth; rank; — of vegetation. **b** Extravagant; unduly lavish; — of speech, imagination, etc. — **Syn.** See SUPEREROGATORY. — *n.* A wanton person or thing; specif.: **a** *Obs.* A pampered pet. **b** A frolicsome child or animal. **c** One given to dalliance or trifling; — in the phrase *to play the wanton*. **d** A lewd or lascivious person. — *v. i.* To be or grow wanton; to act wantonly. — *v. t. Now Rare.* To pass or waste wantonly or in wantonness. — **wan'ton·ly**, *adv.* — **wan'ton·ness**, *n.*

wan'y, wane'y (wān'ĭ), *adj.* Waning or diminished in some parts; — chiefly of timbers cut too near the outside of the log.

wap (wăp; wŏp), *v. t. & i.* [See WHOP, *v.*] *Now Dial.* To whop, or strike; to pull or throw roughly. — *n. Now Dial.* **1.** A blow; a whop. **2. a** A blast; storm. **b** A fight.

wap, *v. t.* [ME. *wappen.*] *Now Dial.* To wrap or fold up; to bind. — *n. Now Dial.* A wrapping.

wap'en·take (wŏp'ĕn-tāk; wăp'-), *n.* [AS. *wǣpengetæc, wǣpentac*, fr. ON. *vāpnatak*, lit., a weapon taking or touching. See WEAPON; TAKE. This name had its origin in a custom of touching lances or spears when the chief entered on his office.] *Hist.* In some northern counties of England, a division corresponding to the *hundred* and *ward* of other English counties.

wap'i·ti (wŏp'ĭ-tĭ), *n.*; see PLURAL, *Note*, 3. [Of Algonquian origin; cf. Shawnee *wapiti*, Cree *wâpitiu* pale, white.] The American stag or elk (*Cervus canadensis*), allied to the European red deer, but larger.

wap'pen·schaw (wăp'ĕn-shô), *n.* Also **wap'in·schaw.** [Scot. See WEAPON; SHOW.] = WAPPENSCHAWING.

wap'pen·schaw'ing (-shô'ĭng), *n.* Also **wap'in·schaw'ing.** *Scot.* An exhibition of arms formerly held at certain seasons in each district; a muster or review.

wap'per–jawed' (wŏp'ẽr-jôd'), *adj. Local, U.S.* Having crooked or wry jaws; sometimes, having an undershot jaw.

war (wôr), *n.* [ME. & (late) AS. *werre*, fr. ONF. *werre* (OF. & F. *guerre*) fr. OHG. *werra* scandal, quarrel, sedition.] **1.** The state or fact of exerting violence or force against another, now only against a state or other politically organized body; esp., a contest by force between two or more nations or states. **2.** Hostility; strife; also, a contest or struggle. **3.** *Poetic.* **a** A battle. **b** Instruments of war. **c** Armed or fighting forces. **4. a** The military profession or science. **b** [*often cap.*] In titles, esp., the department having charge of military forces; the army, often as distinct from the navy; as, the secretary of *war*. — *v. i.*; WARRED (wôrd); WAR'RING. **1.** To make or wage war. **2.** To contend; to strive violently; to fight. — *adj.* Of, pertaining to, or resulting from war.

war (wär), **waur** (wôr; wär), *adv. & adj.* [ON. *verri*, adj., *verr*, adv.] *Scot. & N. of Eng.* Worse.

war. Dial. var. of WARE, goods; WARE, beware.

War between the States. The American Civil War (1861–65).
war'ble (wôr'b'l), *v. t. & i.;* -BLED (-b'ld); -BLING (-blĭng). [ONF. *werbler* to sing, play on a musical instrument, of Teut. origin.] **1.** To sing in a trilling manner, or with many turns and variations. **2.** *U. S.* To yodel. **3.** To be uttered, sounded, or produced with trills, quavers, etc. — *n.* Act or instance of warbling; a musical trill; a song; a carol; as, a linnet's *warble.*
war'ble, *n.* **1.** *Veter.* A small hard tumor produced on a horse by heat or pressure of the saddle. **2. a** A swelling caused by the maggot of a botfly or warble fly under the hide (esp. of the back) of cattle, deer, rabbits, etc. **b** The maggot of the warble fly; a wormil. — **war'bled** (wôr'b'ld), *adj.*
warble fly. Any of several dipterous flies (family Oestridae) whose larvae live under the skin of cattle and other mammals.
war'bler (wôr'blẽr), *n.* **1.** One that warbles; songster; — applied chiefly to birds. **2.** Any of a family (Sylviidae) of Old World singing birds, including the whitethroat. **3.** Any of about a hundred species (collectively called ***wood warbler***) of small bright-colored American songsters constituting a family (Compsothlypidae). See GOLDEN WARBLER; REDSTART, 2; YELLOWTHROAT; YELLOW WARBLER.
war cry; *pl.* WAR CRIES. **1.** A cry used by a body of fighters in war. **2.** A slogan; an identifying phrase used by a group, as in a political campaign.
ward (wôrd), *v. t.* [AS. *weardian* to keep, protect.] **1.** *Archaic.* To keep watch over; to guard. **2.** To fend off (a blow, a weapon, etc.); to repel; avert; as, to *ward* off an attack. **3.** To put in or assign to a ward, esp. a hospital ward. — **Syn.** See PREVENT. — *n.* [AS. *weard,* masc., a warder, watchman.] *Obs.* One who guards; a warden.
ward, *n.* [AS. *weard,* fem., a guarding, watch, body of men keeping watch.] **1.** Act of guarding; guard. **2.** *Archaic.* A garrison; the watch. **3.** State of being under guard or guardianship; esp., confinement under guard; custody. **4.** A guarded place: **a** *Obs.* A defensive station. **b** A jail; prison; now, a division, as a cell, block, or wing, of a prison. **c** A division of a hospital; as, a fever *ward.* **5.** A division; specif.: **a** *Scot.* An enclosure for cattle. **b** A district of a town or city, esp. the latter, for representative, executive, or magisterial, purposes. **c** *Eng. Hist.* In certain northern counties a division corresponding to the *hundred* and *wapentake.* **6.** A person who is under protection; esp., one under the care of a guardian. **7.** Means of guarding; defense; protection. **8.** A guarding or defensive motion or position in fencing, etc.; guard. **9.** [OF. *warde.*] *Locksmithing.* A projecting ridge of metal in a lock casing or keyhole, or any of several, permitting only the insertion of keys with corresponding notches; also, a corresponding notch in a bit of a key. See LOCK, *Illust.* **10.** *Feudal Law.* A minor who is subject to wardship. **11.** *Law.* A person who, by reason of minority, lunacy, or other incapacity, is under the protection of a court.
-ward (-wẽrd; *formerly* -ērd, *now dial., or, as in* eastward, windward, *etc., naut.;* 126), **-wards** (-wẽrdz). [AS. *-weard, -weardes.* The *s* in *-wards* was orig. a gen. ending. See 2d -s.] Suffixes denoting *course* or *direction to; motion* or *tendency toward.* They are added to adverbs, as in up*ward,* up*wards,* etc., and to nouns indicating a direction or terminal point, as in home*ward,* home*wards,* etc. The forms in *-ward* are primarily adjectives often used as adverbs, as in down*ward.* Those in *-wards* are usually adverbs.
☞ Some writers have tried to make distinctions of usage between for*ward,* back*ward,* down*ward,* etc., and the corresponding forms in *-wards;* but the choice between them is in general influenced simply by euphony, sometimes perhaps by the fact that *-wards* is adverbial only.
war dance. A dance among savages preliminary to war.
ward'ed (wôr'dĕd; -dĭd), *adj.* Having wards, as a lock.
ward'en (wôr'd'n), *n.* [ONF. *wardein* (OF. & F. *gardien*).] **1.** Watchman; specif., a gatekeeper. **2.** A chief executive officer. Specif.: **a** *Hist.* A governor, as of a town, district, or fortress. **b** The officer in charge of a port or market. **c** *Eng.* The head of a college, guild, or conventual church. **d** In Connecticut, the chief executive of a borough. **3.** An official charged with special supervisory duties; as, a game *warden.* Specif.: **a** *Eng.* One of certain officers of the crown or royal household; as, *warden* of the mint. **b** A chief or principal keeper; as, the *warden* of a prison. **4. a** An officer in certain colleges, usually having the duties of a dean. **b** A churchwarden; — used chiefly in the Protestant Episcopal Church. — **ward'en·ship,** *n.*
Ward'en, *n.* [ME. *wardon,* fr. ONF. *warder* to keep.] A variety of winter pear.
ward'en·ry (-rĭ), *n.; pl.* -RIES (-rĭz). *Now Rare.* Office or jurisdiction of a warden.
ward'er (wôr'dẽr), *n.* [AF. *wardere, wardour.*] **1.** Watchman; also, a stronghold. **2.** *Brit.* A warden; esp., a custodian, as in museums; also, a prison guard. — **ward'er·ship,** *n.*
ward'er (wôr'dẽr), *n.* [ME.] *Hist.* A truncheon or staff of a king or commander, used in signaling his will.
ward heeler. *Colloq.* See HEELER, 2.
ward'ress (wôr'drĕs; -drĭs), *n.* A woman warden.
ward'robe' (wôrd'rōb'), *n.* [ONF. *warderobe* (F. *garderobe*), of Teut. origin. See WARD, *v.;* ROBE.] **1.** A closet where clothes are kept; a clothes closet; now, often, a form of portable closet for clothes. **2.** Wearing apparel, in general; (one's) clothes or clothing; as, to add to one's *wardrobe.* **3.** In a noble household, the department entrusted with the care of wearing apparel, jewels, etc.; — chiefly in titles; as, gentleman of the *wardrobe.*
ward'room' (-ro͞om'; 85), *n. Nav.* **a** The space in a war vessel allotted for living quarters to the commissioned officers above the rank of ensign, excepting the captain, who has quarters to himself. **b** More specifically, the room assigned to these officers for meals. **c** These officers considered collectively.
ward'ship (-shĭp), *n.* **1.** Office of a ward or keeper; care and protection of a ward; guardianship. **2.** State of being under a guardian; pupilage.
ware (wâr), *adj.* [ME. *ware, war.* See WARY.] **1.** *Archaic.* Aware; cognizant; conscious. **2.** *Archaic.* Wary; cautious; also, prudent; shrewd. — *v. t.* [AS. *warian.*] To take heed of or to; to beware of; — now chiefly in the imperative; as, *ware* the dog.
ware, *n.* [AS. *waru.*] **1.** Collectively, articles of merchandise; products of handicraft or manufacture; utensils of everyday use; — now rare except with a qualifying word or in compounds, as in mahogany *ware,* plated *ware,* hard*ware,* silver*ware.* **2.** *pl.* **wares** (wârz). Articles of merchandise; goods; commodities; merchandise; as, exports of iron and steel *wares.* **3.** One's own product offered for compensation; as, Robert Burns wrote that he was sending some of his rhyming *ware;* artists showing their *wares;* also, satirically, goods or stuff offered as if for some return; as, "Work's my *ware,* but what's it worth?" (*Robert Browning*); peddling his gossipy *wares.* **4.** Collectively, pottery; — usually with a qualifying word or in compounds; as, enameled *ware;* stone*ware.* **5.** A particular make or type of pottery. **6.** *Archaeology.* A large division in a grouping of ceramic types.
ware (wār; wâr), *v. t.* [ON. *verja.*] *Scot. & Dial. Eng.* **a** To spend; bestow. **b** To squander; waste.
ware'house' (wâr'hous'), *n.* **1.** A storehouse for wares, or merchandise. **2.** *Chiefly Eng.* A wholesale, or sometimes retail, shop. — (-houz'; -hous'), *v. t.* To deposit or secure in a warehouse; esp., to place in the government or customhouse stores, or bonded warehouse, to be kept until duties are paid. — **ware'house'man** (-hous'măn), *n.*
warehouse receipt. A certificate issued by a warehouseman, containing a description of goods stored with him. Such a receipt is usually negotiable and must be surrendered to the warehouseman to procure delivery of the goods.
ware'room' (wâr'ro͞om'), *n.* A room in which goods are exhibited for sale; a shop; a store.
wares (wârz), *n. pl.* See WARE, merchandise.
war'fare' (wôr'fâr'), *n.* [*war* + *fare* a going. See FARE, *n.*] **1.** Military operations between enemies; armed contest; war. **2.** Hence, contest; struggle; conflict.
war footing. Condition of being at war or ready to go to war; as, to keep the army on a *war footing.*
war game. **1.** An umpired training maneuver imitative of war, in which opposed forces engage in attack and defense with actual personnel and equipment. **2.** Mimic warfare by staff officers with markers on a map, sand table, or the like, as a tactical exercise; for example, kriegspiel.
war'head' (wôr'hĕd'), *n.* The forward section of a torpedo or a jet-propelled or rocket-propelled weapon containing the explosive.
war horse. **1.** A horse used in war; a charger. **2.** *Colloq.* A veteran soldier or public person, esp. a politician; an old campaigner.
war'i·ly (wâr'ĭ·lĭ; 6), *adv.* In a wary manner.
war'i·ness (-ĭ·nĕs; -nĭs), *n.* Quality or state of being wary.
war'i·son (wăr'ĭ·sŭn), *n.* [ONF., fr. *warir* to heal.] *Pseudoarchaic.* A note of assault; a battle cry.
wark (wärk), *n. & v.* [AS. *wærc,* n., *wærcan,* v.] *Dial.* Pain; ache; throb.
wark. Dial. var. of WORK.
War Labor Board. *U. S.* = NATIONAL WAR LABOR BOARD. Abbr. *WLB*
war'like' (wôr'līk'), *adj.* **1.** Fit or disposed for, or fond of war; bellicose; as, a *warlike* disposition. **2.** Belonging or relating to war; military; martial. **3.** Presaging or threatening war; belligerent; hostile. — **Syn.** See MARTIAL. — **war'like'ness,** *n.*
war'lock (wôr'lŏk), *n.* [AS. *wærloga* a breaker of his word, fr. *wær* covenant, troth + *loga* a liar (in comp.).] A sorcerer or wizard; now, also, a conjuror.
war lord. A general or military commander; — used sometimes to translate foreign military titles, esp. the Chinese *tuchun.*
warm (wôrm), *adj.* [AS. *wearm.*] **1.** Having heat in a moderate degree; as, *warm* milk; a *warm* climate. **2.** Sending out or imparting heat; warming; as, a *warm* fire or sun. **3.** Making one feel heat (to such a degree) or suffer no loss of bodily heat; as, *warm* clothing; also, glowing, flushed, or perspiring, from heat; as, to be *warm* from exercise. **4.** Hence: **a** Genial; grateful. **b** Affecting or intended to affect one disagreeably; hot; as, they made things *warm* for him. **5.** *Colloq.* Well-to-do; rich. **6. a** Marked by or revealing passion, anger, or the like; irascible; as, his *warm* temper. **b** Sympathetic; cordial; as, a *warm* welcome. **c** Characterized by enthusiasm; fervent; as, *warm* support. **d** Lively; sprightly; as, a *warm* imagination. **e** Amorous; passionate. **7.** Newly made; fresh; — said of a scent or trail; hence: **a** *Colloq.* Near the discovery of something concealed, esp. in play. **b** *Slang.* At a point where realization seems possible or likely; as, to keep a business prospect *warm.* **8.** Of colors, producing a sense of warmth; specif., of a hue near red or yellow; — opposed to *cool.* — **Ant.** Cool.
— *v. t. & i.* **1.** To communicate heat to; to become warm; to keep warm, as over a fire, by exercise, etc. **2.** To make or become ardent or interested.
— *n. Colloq.* Act of warming, or state of being warmed; a warming; a heating.
— **warm'ly,** *adv.* — **warm'ness,** *n.*
War Manpower Commission. *U. S.* A commission established by executive order April 18, 1942, for the purpose of "assuring the most effective mobilization and utilization of the national manpower." It was terminated by executive order Sept. 19, 1945, and all its functions, agencies, etc., transferred to the Department of Labor. Abbr. *WMC*
warm'–blood'ed (wôrm'blŭd'ĕd; -ĭd; 2), *adj.* **1.** Having warm blood; having a relatively high and constant body temperature, as birds and mammals. **2.** Fervent or ardent in spirit.
warm'er (wôr'mẽr), *n.* One who or that which warms; as, a foot *warmer;* a vegetable *warmer.*
warm'heart'ed (wôrm'här'tĕd; -tĭd; 2), *adj.* Having or indicating strong affection; cordial; hearty; sympathetic. — **warm'heart'ed·ly,** *adv.* — **warm'heart'ed·ness** *n.*
warm'ing pan. A long-handled covered pan into which live coals are put, formerly used for warming beds.
warm'ish, *adj.* Somewhat warm.
war'mon'ger (wôr'mŭng'gẽr), *n.* One who stirs up war. — **war'-mon'ger·ing,** *n.*
warmth (wôrmth; 89), *n.* **1.** Quality or state of being warm; gentle heat. **2.** Emotional intensity; zeal, ardor, fervor, anger, etc. **3.** *Paint.* A glowing effect such as is produced by the use of warm colors.
warn (wôrn), *v. t.* [AS. *warnian, wearnian,* to take heed, warn.] **1.** To put on guard; to give notice to beforehand (of approaching danger or evil); to caution. **2.** To admonish; counsel; as, you should *warn* him. **3.** To notify or apprise, esp. in advance; to inform. **4.** To bid to go or leave; as, to *warn* a tenant out of a house. — **warn'er,** *n.*
Syn. **Warn, forewarn, caution** mean to let one know of possible danger or risk. **Warn** implies a timely notification that makes avoidance of any situation possible whether it threatens one's safety or merely makes one prepare; **forewarn** heightens the implication of advance

notification and suggests impending, sometimes imminent, danger or peril; **caution** stresses advice that puts one on one's guard or suggests need of precaution.

warn'ing, *n.* **1.** The act of one that warns; notice in advance; also, the fact or state of being warned. **2.** Something that warns or serves to warn. **— *adj.*** That warns; as, a *warning* signal. **— warn'ing·ly**, *adv.*

war nose. The active, live end of a projectile, as a shell or torpedo, loaded with explosive. Cf. WARHEAD.

War of Independence. = REVOLUTIONARY WAR.

warp (wôrp), *n.* [AS. *wearp* a warp in weaving.] **1.** *Weaving.* **a** The threads lengthwise in the loom, crossed by the woof. **b** In a pneumatic tire, the cords, collectively, which form the carcass. **2.** [From the verb.] The state or fact of being warped, or not true in plane or line; also, an instance of warping; as, a *warp* in a panel. **3.** A mental twist or aberration. **4.** *Naut.* A rope used in warping a vessel.

warp, *v. t.* [ME. *warpen, werpen*, pret. *warp*, fr. AS. *weorpan*, pret. *wearp.*] **1.** To turn or twist out of shape, as by contraction, curving, cooking, etc. **2.** Hence: **a** To give a warp, or mental twist, to; as, his misfortunes *warped* his mind. **b** To pervert; lead astray. **3.** To misinterpret; distort; as, to *warp* the sense of a passage. **4.** *Aeronautics.* To change the form of (a wing) by twisting. Warping is sometimes used to maintain the lateral equilibrium of an airplane. **5.** *Naut.* To move (a vessel, etc.) by hauling on a line, or warp, attached to a buoy, anchor, or other fixed object; as, the tugs *warped* the steamer into its slip. **6.** *Weaving.* To arrange (yarns) so as to form a warp. **— Syn.** See DEFORM. **— *v. i.*** **1.** To be or become twisted out of shape as by contraction or shrinkage. **2.** To turn from a straight course; to swerve. **3.** *Naut. Rare.* To warp a vessel; to move by a warp.

war paint. **1.** Paint put on the face and other parts of the body by savages, as a token of going to war. **2.** *Colloq.* Ceremonial or official dress; regalia; finery.

war'path' (wôr'päth'), *n.* **1.** The route taken by a party of American Indians going on a warlike expedition. **2.** Hence, a hostile course of action, frame of mind, or the like.

warp beam. A roller on which the warp is wound in a loom.

warp'er (wôr'pẽr), *n.* One who or that which warps.

war'plane' (wôr'plăn'), *n.* Any airplane attached to the military or naval service, esp. one for war.

War Production Board. *U. S.* A government agency established by executive order Jan. 16, 1942 (and terminated Nov. 3, 1945), responsible for war procurement and production. Abbr. *WPB*

war'rant (wŏr'ănt; 74), *n.* [ONF. *warant* (OF. *guarant, garant*) a warrant, a defender, partly fr. OHG. *werēnto* guarantor, prop. pres. part. of *werēn* to guarantee, and partly fr. ONF. *warir* to preserve, defend.] **1.** Authorization; sanction of law or of a superior. **2.** A guaranty; security. **3.** A document giving authority to do something. Specif.: **a** A writing which authorizes a person to pay or deliver to another and the other to receive money or other thing; as, a *warrant* on a city treasurer. **b** *Eng.* A form of receipt given to a person who has deposited goods in a warehouse, by assignment of which the title to the goods is transferred. **c** *Law.* A precept or writ issued by a competent magistrate authorizing an officer to make an arrest, a seizure, or a search, or the like. **d** *Mil. & Nav.* An official certificate of appointment issued usually to an officer of lower rank than a commissioned officer. See WARRANT OFFICER, NONCOMMISSIONED OFFICER; cf. COMMISSION, *n.*, 8. **4.** Justification; foundation; as, there is no *warrant* for such a belief.

— *v. t.* **1.** *Now Colloq.* To declare with little or no fear of being contradicted or belied; as, I *warrant* this is the truth. **2.** To guarantee against harm, loss, damage, etc. **3.** To give (one) authority or power to do or forbear to do something; to authorize; as, the law *warrants* this procedure. **4.** To attest; as, the genuineness is *warranted* by several facts. **5.** To justify; as, his need *warrants* the expenditure. **6.** *Law.* **a** To secure to, as a grantee, an estate granted; to assure. **b** To secure to, as a purchaser of goods, the title to the same; to indemnify against loss. **c** To secure to, as a purchaser, the quality or quantity of goods sold, as represented. **d** To assure, as a thing sold, to the purchaser; that is, to engage that the thing is what it appears, or is represented, to be, which implies a covenant to make good any defect or loss incurred by it. **— war'rant·a·ble**, *adj.* **— war'rant·a·bly**, *adv.*

war'ran·tee' (wŏr'ăn·tē'), *n.* *Law.* The person to whom a warranty is made.

war'rant·er (wŏr'ăn·tẽr), *n.* One who warrants.

warrant officer. **a** *U. S. Army.* A subordinate officer occupying a grade between that of commissioned officer and enlisted man by virtue of a warrant issued by the secretary of war. Cf. NONCOMMISSIONED OFFICER; INSIGNIA, *Illust.* **b** *U. S. Navy.* A subordinate officer appointed, or warranted, by the president, including boatswain, gunner, machinist, electrician, radio electrician, carpenter, pay clerk, or pharmacist.

war'ran·tor (wŏr'ăn·tôr; wŏr'ăn·tôr'; 2), *n.* *Law.* One who warrants.

war'ran·ty (wŏr'ăn·tĭ), *n.*; *pl.* -TIES (-tĭz). [ONF. *warantie.* See WARRANT.] **1.** *Real Estate Law.* A real covenant whereby the grantor of an estate of freehold and his heirs were bound to warrant and defend the title. A ***covenant of warranty***, often called simply a *warranty*, runs with the land, and is in the nature of a real covenant, breach of which gives a claim for damages only. **2.** *Law.* A collateral engagement that a certain fact regarding the subject of a contract is, or shall be, as it is expressly or by implication declared or promised to be. **3. a** That which authorizes, sanctions, supports, or justifies. **b** *Dial.* A guarantee; also, a warrant, or writ.

warranty deed. A deed containing a covenant of warranty. See WARRANTY, 1.

war'ren (wŏr'ĕn; -ĭn; 74), *n.* [OF. *warenne, garenne, warende*, fr. *varenne* waste land, enclosure, preserve (of Celt. origin), but influenced by *garer* to make safe, secure.] **1.** *Eng. Law.* **a** A place privileged, by grant from the king, for keeping certain animals (as hares, conies, partridges, pheasants, etc.) called beasts and fowls of *warren.* **b** An exclusive privilege which one has in lands, by royal grant, of hunting and taking game. **2.** A piece of ground for the breeding of rabbits, etc. **3.** A tenement or district as crowded and as full of life as a rabbit warren.

war'ren·er (wŏr'ĕn·ẽr), *n.* **1.** *Hist.* The keeper of a warren (def. 1); a gamekeeper. **2.** One who maintains a rabbit warren.

war'ri·or (wŏr'ĭ·ẽr; wôr'yẽr; 74), *n.* [ONF. *werreieor*, fr. *werreier* to make war, fr. *werre* war.] A man engaged or experienced in war, or in military life. **— *adj.*** Martial.

war risk insurance. Term insurance written by the U. S. Government for members of the military and naval forces.

war'saw (wôr'sô), *n.* [Corrupt. of Sp. *guasa.*] A very large grouper (*Garrupa nigrita*).

war'ship' (wôr'shĭp'), *n.* Also **war vessel.** A government vessel employed for war purposes, esp. one armed for attack.

war'sle, wars'tle (wär's'l), *v. i. & t.* To wrestle; struggle; flounder. **— war'sle, wars'tle**, *n.* **— war'sler, wars'tler** (-slẽr), *n.* *All Scot., N. of Eng., & Ir.*

wart (wôrt), *n.* [AS. *wearte.*] **1.** *Med.* A small tumor on the skin, usually hard; verruca. **2.** *Bot.* A glandular excrescence or hardened protuberance on plants. **— wart'y** (wôr'tĭ), *adj.*

wart hog. Any of a genus (*Macrocephalus*, esp. *M. aethiopicus* of South Africa and *M. africanus* of northeast Africa) of wild hogs having two pairs of rough warty excrescences on the face, and large protruding tusks.

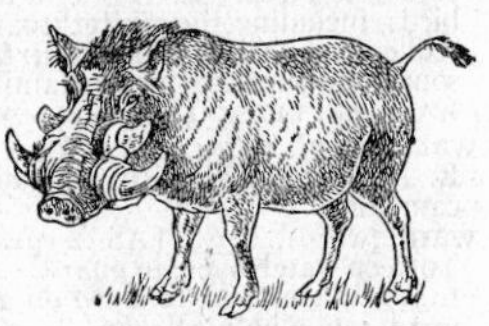
Wart Hog (*M. aethiopicus*). (1/40)

war'time' (wôr'tīm'), *n.* A period during which a war is in progress. **— *adj.*** Of, characteristic of, or occurring in wartime.

war whoop. A war cry, esp. that of American Indians.

war'y (wâr'ĭ; 6), *adj.*; WAR'I·ER (-ĭ·ẽr); WAR'I·EST. [ME. *ware, war*, fr. AS. *wær.*] **1.** Cautious of danger; careful; circumspect. **2.** Characterized by caution; guarded. **— Syn.** See CAUTIOUS. **— Ant.** Foolhardy.

was (wŏz; 4). [AS. *wæs*]. See BE.

wash (wŏsh; 73), *v. t.*; WASHED (wŏsht) or WASHT; WASH'ING. [AS. *wascan, wæscan.*] **1.** To cleanse by ablution, or by dipping, rubbing, or scrubbing, in water. **2.** To cleanse or purify in the religious sense. **3.** To cover, drench, flush, or wet thoroughly, with water or any liquid. **4.** To pass (a gas or gaseous mixture) through or over a liquid for the purpose of purifying it, esp. by removing soluble constituents. **5.** To flow or flood along the border of; to lave; as, waves *wash* the shore. **6.** To move or remove by or as if by the use of water; as, a man *washed* overboard; to *wash* away the dirt. **7.** To cover or daub lightly with an application of a liquid, as whitewash, varnish, or pigment. **8.** To overlay with a thin coat of metal by deposit from a solution; as, steel *washed* with silver. **9.** *Mining.* To subject, as earth, gravel, or crushed ore, to the action of water to separate the valuable material from the worthless; as, to *wash* gravel for gold. **— *v. i.*** **1.** To perform the act of ablution; often specif., to cleanse the body or face and hands with water. **2.** To perform the operation of cleansing clothes, ore, etc., in water; as, to *wash* for gold. **3.** To pour, sweep, or flow, in a stream or current, as over a barrier, against a cliff, etc. **4.** To bear without injury the operation of being washed; as, some calicoes do not *wash*; hence, *Colloq.*, to undergo successfully submission to a testing or proving; as, his story will not *wash.* **5.** To be eroded or worn away by water, as by a stream or by the sea; — said of a road, etc.

wash one's hands of. To disclaim or renounce interest in, responsibility for, or further connection with. **— *wash out.*** To reject or be rejected; specif., to reject as unqualified or to fail to qualify, for military flight training.

— *n.* **1.** Act of washing; ablution. **2.** A collection of articles, as of clothing, set apart for washing, in process of being washed, or a quantity washed at one time; a washing. **3.** Waste liquid, refuse food, etc., from a kitchen. **4.** That with which anything is washed, or wetted, smeared, tinted, etc.; specif.: **a** A liquid cosmetic, dentifrice, etc. **b** A liquid mixture of slight consistency for coating a surface thinly. **c** *Painting.* A thin coat of paint, esp. water color. **5.** The flow, dash, rush, swash, or breaking, of a body of water, as a wave; erosion by action of waves, esp. of the sea. **6.** The sound of water, esp. waves, surging, swishing, lapping, etc., against or over a surface. **7.** = BACKWASH. **8.** *Aeronautics.* The disturbance in the air produced by the passage of an airfoil. **9.** A piece of ground washed by the action of a sea or river; also: **a** A bog; marsh. **b** *Eng.* An estuary; as, the *Wash* between Lincolnshire and Norfolk. **c** A shallow body of water. **10.** Debris, detritus, or other matter collected and deposited by the action of water; as, the *wash* of a river, etc. **11.** *Western U. S.* The dry bed of an intermittent stream, often at the bottom of a canyon.

— *adj.* Capable of being washed without injury; washable; as, *wash* fabrics or silk; *wash* gloves.

wash'a·ble (wŏsh'ȧ·b'l), *adj.* That may be washed, esp. without damage; as, a *washable* silk.

wash'board' (wŏsh'bōrd'; 70), *n.* **1.** A fluted, or ribbed, board on which clothes are rubbed in washing them. **2.** *U. S.* = BASEBOARD. **3.** *Naut.* A broad thin plank fixed along a gunwale to keep out the sea, or a plank on the sill of a lower deck port for that purpose.

wash'bowl' (-bōl'), *n.* A large bowl for water to wash one's hands, face, etc.

wash'cloth' (-klŏth'; 74), *n.* A cloth used for washing, esp. one's face.

washed'-out' (wŏsht'out'; 2), *adj.* **1.** Faded in color. **2.** *Colloq.* Depleted in vigor or animation; played out.

washed'-up' (-ŭp'; 2), *adj.* **a** *Colloq.* = WASHED-OUT, 2. **b** *Slang.* Discarded; done with; done for.

wash'er (wŏsh'ẽr; 73), *n.* **1.** One who washes. **2.** A ring of metal, leather, or other material, or a perforated plate, used for various purposes, as around a bolt or screw to form a seat for the head or nut, or around a wagon axle to prevent endwise motion of the hub and relieve friction, in a joint as a packing, etc. See GROMMET, *Illust.* **3.** A machine for washing anything, as clothes, or coal. **4.** An apparatus in which gases are washed; a scrubber.

wash'er·man (-măn), *n.* A man who works at washing clothes, esp. for hire; a laundryman.

wash'er·wom'an (-wŏŏm'ăn), *n.* A woman who works at washing clothes or who takes in washing.

wash goods. Material, as fabrics, which may be easily washed without loss of color or impairment of quality.

wash'ing, *n.* **1.** Act of one who or that which washes, esp. for cleansing; ablution. **2.** The operation of bathing, drenching, or coating with a liquid, for a particular purpose. **3.** The erosion or removal of material by running water. **4.** The clothes or other articles washed or to be washed, esp. at one time; a wash. **5.** A thin covering or coat; as, a *washing* of silver. **6.** *Mining.* Metal, esp. gold dust, procured by washing; also, a place where this is done. **7.** *Stock Exchange.* The execution of a wash sale. — *adj.* Used or designed for washing or to facilitate washing; as, a *washing* powder.

washing machine. A machine for washing cloth in a manufactory, or clothes, household linen, etc.

washing soda. A form of sodium carbonate.

Wash′ing·ton palm (wŏsh′ĭng·tŭn). A fan palm (see PALM, 1) of California (*Washingtonia filamentosa*).

Washington pie. *U.S.* Layer cake with a cream filling or with a fruit-jam filling.

Wash′ing·ton's Birth′day′ (wŏsh′ĭng·tŭnz). February 22, date of the birth of George Washington (1732–1799).

wash′out′ (wŏsh′out′), *n.* **1.** The washing out or away of earth, etc., esp. in the bed of a road or railroad by a freshet; also, a place where the earth is washed away. **2.** *Slang.* **a** One that fails utterly to fulfill expectations or requirements; specif., a person who fails in a qualifying test. **b** Failure to pass a qualifying test, as for military flight training or for academic promotion.

wash′rag′ (-răg′), *n.* A washcloth.

wash′room′ (-ro͝om′; 85), *n.* A room for washing.

wash sale. *Stock Exchange.* A prearranged fictitious sale of a given security to influence the market. The transaction is prohibited because there is no intent to make delivery or change ownership.

wash′stand′ (wŏsh′stănd′), *n.* A stand holding the requisites for washing, esp. for cleansing one's face and hands.

wash′wom′an (-wo͝om′ăn), *n.* A washerwoman.

wash′y (wŏsh′ĭ), *adj.*; WASH′I·ER (-ĭ·ẽr); WASH′I·EST. **1.** *Now Rare.* **a** Watery or wet so as to wash about; slippery with moisture. **b** Moisture-bearing; — of weather, wind, etc. **2.** Lacking substance, strength, or the like; weak; thin; watery. **3.** Lacking body or firmness of color or outline.

wasp (wŏsp; 73), *n.* [AS. *wæsp, wæps, waefs.*] Any of numerous winged insects (order Hymenoptera) characterized by having a slender body, the abdomen attached by a narrow stalk or petiole, well-developed wings, biting mouth parts, and (in the females and workers) a formidable sting. Unlike bees, wasps are largely carnivorous. Some species, as the ***digger wasp*** and ***sand wasp,*** build their nests in burrows; ***mud wasps*** build nests of mud on the woodwork of buildings, etc.; some social species, as the *hornet* and the *yellow jacket* (see these terms), build nests of a paperlike material in hollow trees or suspended from tree branches. — **wasp′y,** *adj.*

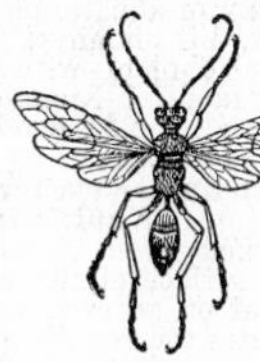

Wasp. (½)

WASP, Wasp (wŏsp), *n.*; *pl.* WASPs, WASPS (wŏsps). A noncombat flier of the Women's Air Force Service Pilots (**WASP**) of the U. S. Army Air Forces, disbanded in December, 1944.

wasp′ish, *adj.* **1.** Resembling a wasp in form; having a slender waist, like a wasp. **2.** Wasplike in nature; irascible; snappish. — **wasp′ish·ly,** *adv.* — **wasp′ish·ness,** *n.*

wasp waist. A waist suggesting by its slenderness that of a wasp. — **wasp′-waist′ed,** *adj.*

was′sail (wŏs′'l; -āl; wăs′-), *n.* [ME. *wæs hæil,* lit., be thou well, fr. ON. *ves heill;* akin to AS. *wes hāl.*] **1.** An ancient expression of good wishes on a festive occasion, esp. when drinking a health. **2.** The liquor used for a wassail; esp., a beverage of ale (or wine) flavored with spices, sugar, toast, roasted apples, etc. **3.** A drinking bout; carouse. **4.** *Dial. Eng.* A drinking song. — *v. i.* To hold a wassail; to carouse. — *v. t.* To drink to the health or thriving of. — **was′sail·er,** *n.*

Was′ser·mann re·ac′tion (väs′ẽr·män; *Angl.* wŏs′ẽr·măn). [After A. von *Wassermann* (1866–1925), Ger. bacteriologist.] A complement-fixing reaction occurring with the serum of syphilitic patients, and used as a test (***Wassermann test***) for syphilis.

wast (wŏst). See BE.

wast (wȧst). Scot. var. of WEST.

wast′age (wās′tĭj), *n.* Loss by use, decay, etc.; waste.

waste (wāst), *adj.* [ONF. *wast* (OF. *guast, gast*), fr. L. *vastus,* but influenced by a kindred G. word.] **1.** Wild and uninhabited; desert; hence, bare; empty; also, dreary; gloomy. **2.** Lying unused for pasture, tilling, or planting. **3.** Thrown away as worthless after being used or spent; as, a *waste* product. **4.** Serving to conduct or hold refuse material; as, a *waste* pipe. **5.** Excreted by a human or animal body. **6.** *Obs.* Unneeded; excess; lavish.

— *v. t.* **1.** To lay waste; devastate. **2.** To use up; consume; to wear out. **3.** To emaciate; to cause to be consumed or weakened, as by overuse, disease, or the like; to enfeeble. **4.** To expend needlessly, carelessly, or without valuable result; to squander. — **Syn.** See RAVAGE. — *v. i.* **1.** To lose bulk, substance, strength, value, or the like, gradually; to be used up or worn away by degrees. **2.** To fall away in flesh, health, or vitality; to become gradually feebler; — often with *away.* **3.** To be consumed without serving its purpose; to produce no adequate result; as, men of ability *wasting* in routine positions. **4.** To spend or consume money or property lavishly or without proper return; as, *waste* not, want not.

— *n.* **1.** That which is waste; a desert; wilderness; also, an uncultivated tract. **2.** The action of wasting, or state of being wasted; useless expenditure; as, *waste* of time. **3.** Gradual loss or decrease, by use, wear, or decay; specif., loss through breaking down of bodily tissue. **4.** *Archaic.* Ruin, or devastation, as by war. **5.** Superfluous or rejected matter; refuse. Specif.: **a** Remnants of cops, etc., from the working of cotton, wool, hemp, etc.; used for wiping machinery, absorbing oil, as in axle boxes of railroad cars, etc. **b** Fluid, as steam, allowed to escape without being utilized. **c** = SCRAP, *n.,* 4. **6.** Garbage; ashes; rubbish; sewage. **7.** *Phys. Geog.* Material derived by erosion from the land, carried by streams to the sea.

waste′bas′ket (wāst′bȧs′kĕt; -kĭt), *n.* A basket for odds and ends, esp. wastepaper.

waste′ful (-fo͝ol; -f'l), *adj.* **1.** Full of, occasioning, or involving waste. **2.** Lavish; squandering. — **waste′ful·ly,** *adv.* — **waste′ful·ness,** *n.*

waste′ness, *n.* *Now Rare.* Desolation; barrenness.

waste′pa′per (wāst′pā′pẽr), *n.* Also **waste paper.** Paper rejected as not fit for use. — **waste′pa′per** (*see Pron.,* § 2), *adj.*

wastepaper basket. = WASTEBASKET.

waste pipe. A pipe for carrying off waste fluid.

wast′er (wās′tẽr), *n.* One who wastes; esp., a prodigal.

wast′ing (wās′tĭng), *adj.* **1.** Laying waste; devastating. **2.** Enfeebling; as, a *wasting* disease.

wast′rel (wās′trĕl), *n.* [From *waste,* v.] One who wastes; a waster; spendthrift; also, a profligate.

wast′ry (wās′trĭ), *n.* Also **wast′rie, wast′er·y.** *Scot.* Waste; prodigality.

wat (wät; wŏt). Scot. & dial. var. of WET; of WOT, know.

watch (wŏch; 73), *v. i.* [AS. *wæccan, wacian.*] **1.** To be awake; to keep vigil, often as a devotional exercise. **2. a** To be attentive; to heed; to be on the lookout. **b** To take measures or precautions; as, *watch* that he does not fall. **3.** To keep guard. **4.** To be expectant; to wait; as, *watching* for a signal. — *v. t.* **1. a** To attend with alert vigilance; to observe. **b** To pay heed to. **2.** To tend; guard; to have in keeping. **3.** To lie in wait for, esp. in order to take advantage of; to bide, as one's time. — **Syn.** See SEE.

— *n.* **1.** *Obs.* State of being awake; watching; also, wakefulness. **2.** A keeping awake for purposes of guarding, protecting, attending, or the like; vigil. **3.** *Hist.* One of the definite divisions of the night made by ancient peoples. Hence, usually *pl.,* one of the indeterminate wakeful intervals marking the passage of night; as, through the silent *watches* of the night. **4.** Close observation; as, keeping a better *watch* over the prisoner. **5.** *Archaic.* The office of sentinel or guard; service as a watchman. **6.** *Obs.* Wakeful attention; vigilance. **7.** One who watches, or those who watch, for purposes of guarding; a guard. **8.** *Chiefly Scot.* A hill used as a lookout station. **9.** The time during which a guard does duty. **10.** *Naut.* **a** An allotted portion of time, usually four hours, for being on duty, or being on deck ready for duty. **b** That part, usually one half, of the officers and crew, who together attend to the working of a vessel during the same watch. **11.** Something which measures the progress of time; specif.: **a** *Obs.* A candle marked out into sections, each of which burned a known length of time. *Shak.* **b** *Obs.* The cry of a watchman. **c** A ship's chronometer. **12.** A pocket timepiece with a spring-driven movement.

— *adj.* Used while or for watching.

watch cap. A knitted close-fitting navy-blue cap worn by enlisted men in the United States Navy in cold or storm.

watch′case′ (wŏch′kās′), *n.* The case, or outside metal covering, of a watch.

watch′dog′ (-dŏg′; 74), *n.* A dog kept to guard property; hence, any watchful guardian against loss, waste, etc.

watch′er (wŏch′ẽr), *n.* One who watches.

watch fire. A fire lighted at night, as a signal, or for the use of a watch or guard.

watch′ful (wŏch′fo͝ol; -f'l), *adj.* **1.** *Archaic.* Wakeful; causing wakefulness; spent in watching. **2.** Vigilant; attentive. **3.** Characterized by vigilance; as, *watchful* care. — **watch′ful·ly,** *adv.* — **watch′ful·ness,** *n.*

Syn. **Watchful, vigilant, wide-awake, alert** mean on the lookout, esp. for danger or opportunity. **Watchful** is the general, least explicit term; **vigilant** implies keen, courageous, often wary watchfulness; **wide-awake,** watchfulness of opportunities more often than dangers, and a knowledge of all events or factors affecting a situation; **alert,** readiness or promptness in apprehending and meeting a danger, an opportunity, or an emergency.

watch′mak′er (wŏch′māk′ẽr), *n.* One who makes or repairs watches. — **watch′mak′ing** (-ĭng), *n.*

watch′man (-măn), *n.* One set to watch; a guard.

watch night. A devotional exercise lasting until after midnight, held originally each month by Wesleyan Methodists, later by them and others on New Year's Eve.

watch′tow′er (wŏch′tou′ẽr), *n.* A tower for a lookout.

watch′word′ (-wûrd′), *n.* **1.** A secret word used as a countersign; now, chiefly, a password or sign of recognition among members of the same society or class. **2.** A sentiment or motto as embodying a principle or guide to action, esp one used as a rallying cry or a signal.

wa′ter (wô′tẽr; wŏt′ẽr; 10), *n.* [AS. *wæter.*] **1.** The liquid which descends from the clouds in rain, and which forms rivers, lakes, seas, etc. Pure ordinary water (H_2O) consists of hydrogen (11.188 per cent by weight) and oxygen (88.812 per cent). It has a slightly blue color and is very slightly compressible. At its maximum density, 39.2° F. or 4° C., it is the standard for specific gravities, one cubic centimeter weighing one gram. It is also the standard for specific heats. It freezes at 32° F. or 0° C. and boils at 212° F. or 100° C. Ordinary water is a mixture of molecules containing hydrogen of at. wt. 1 with a small proportion of a chemically different kind of water, ***heavy water,*** consisting of molecules containing deuterium, or hydrogen of mass number 2. Heavy water differs from ordinary water in physical properties (as, sp. gr. about $\frac{1}{10}$ greater, freezing point about 8° C.), biological effect, etc. **2.** This liquid substance occurring not chemically combined; specif.: **a** Springs, rivers, lakes, or rain; often, this liquid as impregnated with mineral salts; as, to take the *waters* at Karlsbad. **b** Depth of a stream, esp. for navigating purposes; as, a boat draws twelve feet of *water.* **c** Leakage into the hull of a vessel; as, the boat is making *water* fast. **d** The surface or level of any body of this liquid; as, above or below the *water.* **e** *Now pl.* A flood or inundation; as, the *waters* have fallen. **3. a** A liquid containing or resembling water, esp. one for pharmaceutical or cosmetic purposes; as, lavender *water.* **b** *Pharm.* A solution in water of a gaseous or readily volatile substance; as, ammonia *water.* **4.** Any organic liquid, secretion, effusion, humor, or the like, suggestive of water, esp.: **a** Urine. **b** With *the* or in *pl.* The amniotic fluid; as, the *water* broke, that is, before expulsion of the fetus. **c** Saliva. **5.** The limpidity and luster of a precious stone, esp. a diamond; as, a diamond of the first *water;* hence, ***of the first water,*** of the highest excellence. **6.** Hence, a specified degree of excellence or thoroughness; as, a scoundrel of the purest *water.* **7.** A wavy lustrous pattern such as is imparted to linen, silk, metals, etc. **8.** A water-color painting. **9.** *Finance.* An addition to the securities issued by a stock company not representing a corresponding increase in assets. — ***above water.*** Floating; hence, out of difficulty, as of a financial nature.

— *v. t.* **1.** To moisten, sprinkle, or soak with water; as, to *water* the street. **2.** To supply with water for drink; as, to *water* horses. **3.** To supply water to, esp. through the soil; as, land *watered* by the Missouri. **4.** To wet and calender, as cloth, so as to impart to it a lustrous appearance in wavy lines; as, to *water* silk. **5.** To add water to (anything), thus increasing quantity while reducing strength; to

dilute. **6.** [From the practice of (salting and then) watering live stock before selling it by weight.] *Finance.* To add to the aggregate par value of (stock or other securities) without a corresponding addition to the assets represented by the security. — *v. i.* **1.** To shed, secrete, or fill with, water or liquid matter; as, his eyes *water;* also, to secrete saliva in anticipation of food; as, the mouth *waters.* **2.** To get or take in water; specif., usually of animals, to drink water; to take fresh water aboard; as, the ship put into port to *water.*
— *adj.* **1.** Of, pertaining to, or for water or its storage, distribution, or transport. **2.** Worked or driven by water; as, a *water* turbine. **3.** Used in or on the water. **4.** Prepared with water, esp. by hardening with water or by mixing with water; as, *water* biscuit; *water* lime. **5.** Placed or performed on, in, or near, water; as, *water* beacons; *water* sports. **6.** Dwelling in or on, or having dominion over, water; as, *water* police, spirits. **7.** Growing or living in water; as, *water* birds, reeds.

wa′ter·age (wô′tẽr·ĭj; wŏt′ẽr-), *n. Eng.* Transportation of goods, etc., by water; also, money paid for this service.

water back. A water heater set in the back of a stove.

Water Bearer. *Astron.* Aquarius.

water beetle. Any of numerous aquatic beetles (esp. of *Dytiscus* and allied genera, family Dytiscidae). They are dark, and have fringed hind legs that act as oars.

water bird. Any aquatic bird; a waterfowl.

water biscuit. A biscuit or cracker made of flour, fat, and water.

water blister. *Med.* A vesicle with a clear, watery content, not filled with pus or blood.

wa′ter–borne′, *adj.* **1.** Floated or floating upon the water. **2.** Conveyed by water or by boat.

wa′ter·brain′ (wô′tẽr·brān′; wŏt′ẽr-), *n. Veter.* = GID.

water brash. *Med.* Pyrosis.

wa′ter·buck′ (-bŭk′), *n.;* see PLURAL, *Note,* 6. [Trans. of D. *waterbok.*] **a** Either of two large, coarse-haired, reddish-brown or grayish-brown antelopes (genus *Kobus*) of eastern Africa, which frequent rivers and swim easily. **b** Any of various other antelopes, as the reedbuck.

water buffalo. See BUFFALO, 1.

water bug. **a** The Croton bug. **b** Any of numerous aquatic hemipterous insects (esp. of *Lethocerus, Benacus, Zaitha,* and other genera of the family Belostomatidae). Their hind legs are long and fringed and act like oars.

water caltrop, water chestnut. Any of a genus (*Trapa*) of aquatic plants (esp. *T. natans* and *T. bicornis*); also, their edible nutlike fruit.

water chinquapin. A lotus (*Nelumbo lutea*) of North America; also, its edible nutlike seed.

water clock. An instrument or machine to measure time by the fall, or flow, of a quantity of water, as a clepsydra.

water closet. A closet or room containing a hopper for defecation fitted with some device for flushing the bowl with water; also, the hopper itself, with accessories. Sometimes, loosely, any privy.

water color. **1.** A paint whose liquid is a water dispersion of the binding material, which may be glue, casein, gums, etc.; — so called in distinction from *oil.* **2.** The art or method of painting with water colors. **3.** A picture or design executed in water colors. — **wa′ter–col′or,** *adj.*

wa′ter–cool′, *v. t.* To cool by means of water, as circulating water, esp. in a water jacket; as, a *water-cooled* gas-engine cylinder. — **wa′ter–cooled′,** *adj.* — **wa′ter–cool′ing,** *adj.* — **water cooling,** *or* **wa′ter–cool′ing,** *n.*

wa′ter·course′ (wô′tẽr·kōrs′; wŏt′ẽr-; 70), *n.* **1.** A stream of water; also, the bed of a stream. **2.** A natural channel for water; also, a canal for the conveyance of water.

wa′ter·craft′ (-krȧft′; 9), *n.* **1.** Skill in managing boats or in swimming, diving, etc. **2.** Any vessel or boat; vessels and boats, collectively.

water crake. **a** The water ouzel. **b** The spotted crake.

water cress. See CRESS.

water culture. = HYDROPONICS.

water cure. **1.** *Med.* Hydropathy; hydrotherapeutics. **2.** *Slang.* A form of torture consisting of forcing a person to drink large quantities of water in a short time.

water dog. **1.** A dog accustomed to the water, trained to retrieve waterfowl. **2.** A person who is quite at ease in or on water; specif.: **a** *Jocose.* A sailor; an old salt. **b** A good swimmer.

wa′ter·er (wô′tẽr·ẽr; wŏt′ẽr-), *n.* One who waters.

wa′ter·fall′ (-fôl′), *n.* **1.** A perpendicular or very steep descent of the water of a stream. See CASCADE, 1; CATARACT, 1. **2.** *Colloq.* A chignon likened to a waterfall.

wa′ter·find′er (-fīn′dẽr), *n.* One who tries to locate subterranean water with a divining rod; a dowser.

water flea. Any of numerous small dark aquatic entomostracans (genera *Cyclops, Daphnia,* etc.); — so called because they swim with sudden leaps, or starts.

wa′ter·fowl′ (wô′tẽr·foul′; wŏt′ẽr-), *n.;* see PLURAL, *Note,* 6. Any bird that frequents the water; esp., a swimming bird; collectively, swimming game bird as distinguished from upland game birds and shore birds.

water front. Land, or land with buildings, or a section of a town, fronting or abutting on a body of water.

water gap. A pass in a mountain ridge through which a stream runs; as, the Delaware *Water Gap.*

water gas. A gas made by forcing steam over incandescent carbon (usually coke), whereby there results a mixture of hydrogen and carbon monoxide, according to the reaction: $C + H_2O = H_2 + CO$. Water gas is sometimes used uncarbureted as a fuel but usually is carbureted with illuminating constituents from oil. It is much more poisonous than coal gas. — **wa′ter–gas′,** *adj.*

water gauge. An instrument to measure or find the depth or quantity of water, or to indicate the height of its surface, esp. in a steam boiler.

water glass. **1.** A water clock; a clepsydra. **2.** A glass bowl, globe, or other vessel, containing water; also, a drinking glass. **3.** Often **wa′ter–glass′** (wô′tẽr·glȧs′; wŏt′ẽr-), *n.* An instrument consisting of an open box or tube with a glass bottom, used for examining objects in or under the water. **4.** A substance consisting usually of sodium silicate, but sometimes of potassium silicate, or of both ("double" water glass), found in commerce as a glassy mass, a stony powder, or dissolved in water as a viscous sirupy liquid. It is used as a cement, as a protective coating and fireproofing agent, and in preserving eggs, etc. **5.** A water gauge for a steam boiler, etc.

water gum. In the U. S., the sour gum or tupelo. See GUM, 5 **a.**

water hammer. The concussion of moving water against the sides of a containing pipe or vessel, as in a steam pipe. — **wa′ter–ham′mer,** *v. i.*

water hemlock. See HEMLOCK, 1.

water hen. Any of various ralline birds, as a coot or gallinule; esp.: **a** = MOOR HEN **b.** **b** The American coot *Fulica americana.*

water ice. **1.** A frozen dessert consisting of sweetened diluted fruit juice. **2.** Massive ice formed by the downward freezing of water.

wa′ter–inch′, *n.* A former unit of hydraulic measure, being the discharge from a round hole one inch in diameter. It is commonly estimated at fourteen pints per minute.

wa′ter·i·ness (wô′tẽr·ĭ·nĕs; wŏt′ẽr-; 30), *n.* Watery state or quality.

wa′ter·ing, *n.* The action of one who or that which waters. — *adj.* **1.** That waters, or waters something. **2.** Having medicinal springs, a place for sea bathing, etc., and often equipped as a resort; as, a **watering place,** a resort for bathing, boating, etc.

watering pot. A vessel, esp. a can with a spout having a perforated nozzle, to sprinkle water on plants, clothes, etc.

wa′ter·ish, *adj.* Watery. — **wa′ter·ish·ly,** *adv.*

water jacket. An outer casing holding water, or through which water circulates, to cool the interior; specif., the enclosed space surrounding the cylinder block of an internal-combustion engine and containing the cooling liquid. — **wa′ter–jack′et,** *v. t.* — **wa′ter–jack′et·ing,** *n.*

water jump. A pool, stream, or ditch of water, to be jumped over by a horse, as in a steeplechase.

wa′ter·less (wô′tẽr·lĕs; wŏt′ẽr-; -lĭs), *adj.* Destitute of water; dry.

water level. **1.** The surface of still water; specif., *Hydraulics,* a water table (sense 2). **2.** The level assumed by a particular body of water. **3.** The water line of a vessel. **4.** An instrument to show the level by means of the surface of water in a trough, or in a tube.

water lily. Any of a genus (*Nymphaea*) of aquatic plants typifying a family of aquatic plants (Nymphaeaceae, the water-lily family); hence, in general, any aquatic plant with showy flowers (esp. of the families Nymphaeaceae and Nelumbonaceae); esp., the ***white water lily*** (*Nymphaea odorata*).

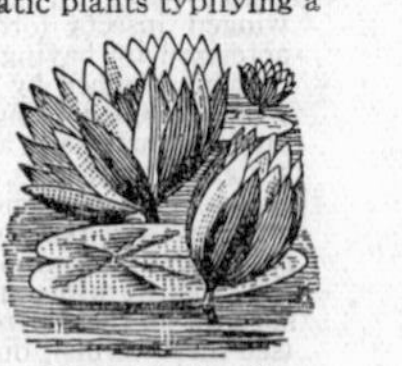
Water Lily (*N. odorata*). (1/6)

water line *or* **wa′ter·line′** (wô′tẽr·līn′; wŏt′ẽr-), *n. Naut.* Any one of several lines marked upon a vessel, corresponding with the surface of the water when the vessel is afloat on an even keel. The lowest line indicates the vessel's proper submergence when not loaded; the highest, the vessel's proper submergence when loaded.

wa′ter·log′ (-lŏg′), *v. t.;* -LOGGED′ (-lŏgd′); -LOG′GING. **1.** To render unmanageable by flooding or leakage of water, as a boat. **2.** To deprive of buoyancy by saturation with water, as floating timber. — **wa′ter·logged′,** *adj.*

Wa′ter·loo′ (wô′tẽr·lōō′; wŏt′ẽr-; wô′tẽr·lōō′; wŏt′ẽr-), *n.* [In allusion to Napoleon's defeat at *Waterloo,* June 18, 1815.] A decisive defeat or reverse.

water main. A pipe or conduit for conveying water.

wa′ter·man (wô′tẽr·măn; wŏt′ẽr-), *n.* A man who lives and works mostly in or near water; esp., one who plies for hire, esp. as a boatman or ferryman, on rivers, harbors, etc.

wa′ter·man·ship′, *n.* **a** The business or skill of a waterman. **b** Art of, or skill in, rowing; oarsmanship.

water marigold. A North American aquatic herb (*Megalodonta beckii*) of the aster family, having finely dissected leaves, and heads of yellow flowers.

wa′ter·mark′ (wô′tẽr·märk′; wŏt′ẽr-), *n.* **1.** A mark indicating the height to which water has risen. **2.** A marking in paper produced by pressure of a projecting design on the dandy roll, in the mold, etc., and visible when the paper is held up to the light. Also, the design or the metal pattern producing the marking. In philately, watermarks are important in distinguishing varieties of stamps. Abbr. *wmk.* — *v. t.* To mark (paper) with a watermark; to impress (a given design) as a watermark.

wa′ter·mel′on (-mĕl′ŭn), *n.* **a** The large oblong or roundish fruit of a vine (*Citrullus vulgaris*) of the cucumber family. It has a hard green or white rind, and a pink or red pulp with a copious sweet juice. **b** The plant or vine which bears this fruit.

water meter. An instrument for recording the quantity of water passing through a particular outlet.

water milfoil. Any of a genus (*Myriophyllum*) of aquatic plants, with finely pinnate submersed leaves.

water mill. A mill whose machinery is moved by water.

water moccasin. See MOCCASIN, 2.

water nymph. *Class. Myth.* A goddess of any body of water, as one of the naiads, Nereids, or Oceanids.

water oak. **a** An oak (*Quercus nigra*) of the southeastern United States. **b** Any of several other American oaks.

water of crystallization. *Chem.* Water which is regarded as present (chemically combined) in many crystallized substances, and which is expelled from them by heat, usually with loss by the substance of its crystalline properties.

water of hydration. *Chem.* Water chemically combined with some substance to form a hydrate.

wa′ter ou′zel (ōō′z'l). Any of a genus (*Cinclus*) of birds allied to the thrushes; esp., the European water ouzel (*C. cinclus*), and the American water ouzel (*C. mexicanus*). They have the peculiar habit of diving into swift mountain streams and walking on the bottom in search of food.

water ox. A water buffalo. See BUFFALO, 1.

water parting. A divide or watershed.

water pepper. Any of a genus (*Persicaria,* esp. *P. hydropiper*) of acrid plants growing in wet places.

water pimpernel. **a** Any of a species (*Samolus floribundus*) of small, white-flowered herbs growing in wet places. **b** The common pimpernel (*Anagallis arvensis*).

water plantain. Any of a genus (*Alisma,* esp. *A. plantago-aquatica* of the Old World, and *A. subcordatum* of America) of plants with acrid, plantainlike leaves.

water polo. A game played in a swimming pool by teams of swimmers with a ball like an association football.
water power. The power of water employed to move machinery, etc.; also, a fall of water which may be used to drive machinery; loosely, a water privilege for a mill.
water pox. *Med.* A variety of chicken pox, or varicella.
wa′ter·proof′ (wô′tẽr·pro͞of′; wŏt′ẽr-; 2), *adj.* Impervious to water; coated with a material, as a solution of rubber, to prevent permeation by water. — (-pro͞of′), *n.* Something made waterproof; specif., an outer garment made of waterproof material. — (-pro͞of′), *v. t.* To make waterproof.
water purslane. A plant (*Isnardia palustris*) of the evening-primrose family (Onagraceae).
water rat. **1.** **a** Any of a genus (*Arvicola*, esp. the large British species *A. amphibius*) of voles. **b** The muskrat. **2.** *Cant & Slang.* A vagabond or thief who loafs or thieves on the water or about water fronts.
water sapphire. [Equiv. to F. *saphir d'eau.*] A deep-blue variety of iolite, sometimes used as a gem.
wa′ter·scape (wô′tẽr·skāp; wŏt′ẽr-), *n.* [After LANDSCAPE.] A water or sea view; a seascape.
water scorpion. Any of numerous aquatic hemipterous insects (of *Nepa*, *Ranatra*, and allied genera). The end of their abdomen bears a long, taillike breathing tube.
wa′ter·shed′ (wô′tẽr·shĕd′; wŏt′ẽr-), *n.* [See WATER; SHED to part.] **1.** A ridge dividing one drainage area from another; a divide. **2.** The whole region or area contributing to the supply of a river or lake; drainage area.
water shield. **a** An American aquatic plant (*Brasenia schreberi*) having floating oval leaves, with a jellylike coating, and small dull-purple flowers. **b** Any plant of a related genus (*Cabomba*).
wa′ter–sick′, *adj.* Of land, uncultivable and unproductive because of overirrigation.
wa′ter·side′ (wô′tẽr·sīd′; wŏt′ẽr-), *n.* The land bordering a body of water. — *adj.* **a** Of, pertaining to, or located on the waterside; as, *waterside* trees. **b** Employed along the waterside, as stevedores, watermen, etc.
water snake. Any of numerous snakes (of *Natrix* and related genera) which live more or less in fresh water and feed largely on aquatic animals. See MOCCASIN, 2.
wa′ter–soak′ (-sōk′), *v. t.* To soak in water.
wa′ter–sol′u·ble, *adj.* Soluble in water; — specif., *Biochem.*, used with a letter (with or without the word *vitamin*) in designating certain vitamins; as, *water-soluble* vitamin B, or *water-soluble* B.
water spaniel. See SPANIEL.
water speedwell. A very common speedwell (*Veronica anagallis-aquatica*) found in wet places.
wa′ter·spout′ (wô′tẽr·spout′; wŏt′ẽr-), *n.* **1.** A pipe, duct, or orifice, from which water is spouted. **2.** A funnel-shaped or tubular column of rotating, cloud-filled wind extending from an ordinary cumulus or cumulo-nimbus cloud down to a cloud of spray torn up by whirling winds from an ocean or lake.
water sprite. A sprite supposed to inhabit or haunt the water; a water nymph. Cf. KELPIE, NIXIE, NAIAD, NEREID.
water starwort. Any of a genus (*Callitriche*) of small aquatic weeds.
water strider. Any of a family (Gerridae) of long-legged bugs which move about on the surface of fresh waters.
water supply. Supply of water, or process of supplying water, as for communities by means of reservoirs, tunnels, and pipe lines. — **wa′ter–sup·ply′** (*see Pron.*, § 2), *adj.*
water system. **a** A river with its tributaries. **b** = WATER SUPPLY.
water table. **1.** *Arch.* A stringcourse or similar member when projecting so as to throw off the water. **2.** The upper limit of the ground saturated with water.
water thrush. **a** Any of several North American warblers (genus *Seiurus*), as the ovenbird (*S. aurocapillus*) and allied forms, usually found in the vicinity of streams. **b** The European water ouzel.
wa′ter·tight′ (wô′tẽr·tīt′; wŏt′ẽr-; 2), *adj.* **a** So tight as to be impermeable by water. **b** Figuratively, sealed tight against the permeation of anything; of a legal document, so phrased as to leave no possibility of misconstruction or of a defeat of its purpose.
water tower. **1.** A tower or standpipe serving as a reservoir to deliver water at a required head, as to a fountain. **2.** A fire apparatus having a vertical pipe which can be extended to various heights, and supplied with water under high pressure.
water vapor. The vapor of water; — so called esp. when below boiling temperature and in diffused form (as in the atmosphere), as distinguished from *steam.*
water wagon. A wagon used to carry water. — ***on the water wagon.*** *Slang, U. S.* In a condition of abstention from alcoholic liquor.
water wave. **1.** Lit., a wave of water. **2.** A type of wave made when the hair is damp, and now usually formed with combs and set with heat. Cf. FINGER WAVE.
wa′ter–wave′, *v. t.* To make a water wave in (hair).
wa′ter·way′ (wô′tẽr·wā′; wŏt′ẽr-), *n.* **1.** A way or channel for water; also, a navigable body of water. **2.** Amount of opening for the passage of water; specif., *Naut.*, a drainage hole on each side of a vessel's deck.
wa′ter·weed′ (-wēd′), *n.* Any aquatic plant with inconspicuous flowers, as the pondweed, etc.
water wheel. **1.** Any wheel made to rotate by direct action of water. A turbine operated by water is often called a water wheel. See UNDERSHOT, *Illust.* **2.** A wheel for raising water, as a noria.
water wing. *pl.* A pneumatic device to give support to a person's body when he is swimming or learning to swim.
water witching. The finding of water by means of a divining rod, as a hazel wand. — **water witch.**
wa′ter·work′ (wô′tẽr·wûrk′; wŏt′ẽr-), *n.* **1.** A pageant presented, or designed to be presented, on boats or floats on the water. **2.** Chiefly *pl.* and often written **water works.** A hydraulic apparatus, or a system of works or fixtures, by which a supply of water is furnished. **3.** *Slang.* A fountain; also, *pl.*, the source of tears; hence, tears.
wa′ter·worn′ (-wōrn′; 70), *adj.* Worn, smoothed, or polished, by the action of water.
wa′ter·y (wô′tẽr·ĭ; wŏt′ẽr-), *adj.* **1.** Of, pertaining to, or connected with water. **2.** Containing or discharging water; as, *watery* clouds; soaked with or washed by water; as, a *watery* shore; wet; as, *watery* garments; hence, tearful; as, *watery* complaints. **3.** Resembling water; thin or transparent, as a liquid; weak; vapid; pale; as, a *watery* style in writing. **4.** Soft, soggy, flabby, or the like.
watt (wŏt), *n.* [After James *Watt*, Scot. inventor.] *Physics.* A unit of power or activity equal to 10^7 C.G.S. units of power, or to work done at the rate of one joule a second or to the rate of work represented by a current of one ampere (one coulomb per second) under a pressure of one volt; a volt-ampere. An English horsepower is approximately equal to 746 watts. Abbr., *w* or *W* (no period).
watt′age (wŏt′ĭj), *n.* *Elec.* Amount of electric power expressed in watts.
Wat·teau′ (wŏ·tō′ *or, esp. Brit.*, wŏt′ō; *Fr.* vȧ′tō′), *adj.* Of or pert. to Antoine Watteau, French painter (1684–1721); of a kind represented in Watteau's pictures; — esp. of women's garments.
Watteau back. A style of back for a woman's gown, in which broad folds or plaits are carried from the neck to the floor without being held in at the waist.
watt′–hour′, *n.* Work done in an hour at the steady rate of one watt; — a unit of energy.
wat′tle (wŏt′'l), *n.* [AS. *watel, watul, watol*, interwoven twigs, wattle.] **1.** A twig or flexible rod; a withe; wand; hence, a framework or hurdle made of such rods. **2.** *pl.* Rods laid on a roof to support the thatch. **3.** Material consisting of wattled twigs, withes, etc., used for walls, fences, etc. **4.** [Perh. a different word.] **a** A naked, fleshy, and usually wrinkled and highly colored, process of the skin hanging from the chin or throat of a bird or reptile. See POULTRY, *Illust.* **b** A barbel of a fish. **5.** In Australia, any acacia (genus *Acacia*), either tree or shrub; — so called from the *wattles*, or hurdles, which the early settlers made of the long, pliable branches. — *adj.* Made of, or covered with, wattle or wattles. — *v. t.*; WAT′TLED (-'ld); WAT′TLING (-lĭng). **1.** To bind, fence, etc., with wattles; to hurdle; also, to cover or support with or as with wattle. **2.** To twist or interweave, one with another, as twigs; to plat. **3.** To form by interweaving or platting twigs. — **wat′tled** (wŏt′'ld), *adj.*
wat′tle·bird′ (wŏt′'l·bûrd′), *n.* Any of several Australasian honey eaters (genus *Coleia*) having ear wattles.
watt′less (wŏt′lĕs; -lĭs), *adj.* *Elec.* Without any power (cf. WATT); — said of an alternating current or component of current when it differs in phase by ninety degrees from the electromotive force which produces it, or of an electromotive force or component thereof when the current which it produces differs from it in phase by ninety degrees.
watt′me′ter (-mē′tẽr), *n.* [*watt* + *-meter.*] *Elec.* An instrument for measuring electric power in watts.
waucht, waught (*Scot.* wäᴋt, wôᴋt; *dial. Eng.* wȧft), *n.* A copious draft. — *v. t. & i.* To drink deeply; to quaff. *Both Scot. & N. of Eng.*
waugh (wôf), *adj.* [AS. *wealg* lukewarm.] *Scot.* Insipid; nauseous; damp and stale; also, faint; weak.
wauk (wôk; wäk). Scot. var. of WAKE.
wauk′rife (-rīf). Scot. & N. of Eng. var. of WAKERIFE.
waul (wôl). Var. of WAWL, WAIL.
waur (wôr; wär), *adj.* *Scot.* Worse.
wav′a·ble (wāv′ȧ·b'l), *adj.* That can be waved.
wave (wāv), *v. i.* [AS. *wafian* to wave.] **1.** To play loosely; move one way and the other; flutter; as, the flags *wave* in the breeze. **2.** To be moved to and fro as a signal; to signal in this way; as, the lights are *waving;* he *waved* to us. **3.** To be sinuous like a wave; undulate; as, his hair *waves.* — *v. t.* **1.** To move one way and the other; swing, sway, brandish, or the like; as, to *wave* a sword. **2.** To shake or vibrate (something) as a signal; as, to *wave* lights; also, to convey (some message or signal) by a wave, as of the hand or head; as, we *waved* them good-by. **3.** To call, order, etc., by a waving motion; beckon; as, to *wave* one aside. **4.** To give an undulating form or surface to; as, to *wave* hair. **5.** To water, as silk. — **Syn.** See SWING.
— *n.* **1.** A moving ridge or swell on the surface of a liquid, as of the sea; an undulation. **2.** *Poetic.* Water; a body of water. **3.** An undulation or one of a series of undulations formed or impressed on a surface, as the wavy line on a watered fabric, or a wavelike curl or curls in hair. **4.** A waving or undulating motion; esp., a signal made by waving. **5.** Something that swells, has a crest, rises and falls, etc., like a wave; specif.: **a** A period of intensity, unusual activity, etc.; as, a *wave* of buying. **b** One of a series (as of successive stages or of events, groups, etc., representative of such stages) marked by fluctuation, or rising and falling; as, the last *wave* of settlers to come to our shores. **6.** *Meteorol.* An oscillation or change of atmospheric pressure, temperature, etc.; as, a cold *wave* (specif., an unusual fall of temperature to or below the freezing point); a hot *wave*, etc. **7.** *Physics.* Any disturbance that advances through a medium (solid, gas, liquid, space) with a speed that is completely determined by properties of that medium, as in the transmission of sound, light, etc.; the disturbance included in the space of a single wave length. In a ***longitudinal wave*** the motion of the particles of the medium is always parallel to the direction of propagation of the wave. In a ***transverse wave*** the motion of the particles of the medium is always in a plane perpendicular to the direction of propagation of the wave. — **wav′er** (wāv′ẽr), *n.*
wave front. *Physics.* A surface composed at any instant of all the points just reached by a vibrational disturbance in its propagation through a medium.
wave guide. A metal pipe of circular or rectangular cross section, or a dielectric cylinder, of such dimensions that it will propagate electromagnetic waves of a given frequency, used for channeling ultra-high-frequency waves.
wave length. *Physics.* The distance in the line of advance of a wave from any one point to the next point at which, at the same instant, there is the same phase.
wave′let (wāv′lĕt; -lĭt), *n.* A little wave; a ripple.
wave mechanics. *Physics.* A theory of matter holding that electrons have wave properties and seeking a mathematical interpretation of the structure of matter on the basis of these properties.
wa′ver (wā′vẽr), *v. i.* [ME. *waveren;* akin to AS. *wæfre* wavering, restless.] **1.** To play or move to and fro; sway; hence: **a** To totter; reel. **b** To quiver; flicker. **2.** To be unsettled in opinion; vacillate. **3.** To falter; as, the front line *wavered* under fire. — **Syn.** See SWING; HESITATE. — *n.* A wavering. — **wa′ver·er**, *n.* — **wa′ver·ing·ly**, *adv.*
WAVES, Waves (wāvz). A branch of the armed forces comprising

from July 30, 1942, to June 12, 1948, the Women's Reserve, U.S.N.R. (*Women Accepted for Volunteer Emergency Service*), after June 12, 1948, part of the regular navy. Hence, **WAVE, Wave** (wāv), *n.*, a member of the WAVES.

wave theory. = UNDULATORY THEORY.

wav'y (wāv'ĭ), *adj.*; WAV'I·ER (-ĭ·ẽr); WAV'I·EST. **1.** Rising or swelling in waves; abounding in waves. **2.** Undulating; fluctuating; wavering; sinuous; as, *wavy* hair. **3.** Undulatory; rolling; as, a *wavy* terrain. — **wav'i·ly** (-ĭ·lĭ), *adv.* — **wav'i·ness** (-ĭ·nĕs; -nĭs), *n.*

wawl (wôl), *v. i. Scot. & Dial. Eng.* To wail; howl. — **wawl,** *n.*

wax (wăks), *v. i.*; WAXED (wăkst); WAXED, *Poetic* WAX'EN (wăk'sĕn; -s'n); WAX'ING. [AS. *weaxan.*] **1.** To increase in size, numbers, strength, etc.; specif., of the moon, to increase apparently in size, as when approaching the period of full moon; — opposed to *wane.* **2.** To pass from one state to another; to grow; as, to *wax* strong.

wax, *n.* [AS. *weax.*] **1.** A substance secreted by bees for constructing the honeycomb; beeswax. It is a dull-yellow solid of agreeable odor, plastic when warm, and melting at about 62–66° C. (143–151° F.). Sp. gr., usually 0.958–0.967 at 15° C. **2.** Any of various substances resembling beeswax; specif.: **a** Any of a class of substances of plant or animal origin, containing esters and often free fatty acids, free alcohols, and higher hydrocarbons, and including, beside beeswax, spermaceti, carnauba wax, etc. Waxes typically are harder and of less greasy feel than fats. **b** Any of certain solid substances of mineral origin, as ozocerite and paraffin wax. **c** A pliable composition for uniting surfaces, for excluding air, etc.; as, sealing *wax.* **d** A resinous preparation used by shoemakers for rubbing their thread. **3.** *Bot.* Any waxlike product secreted by plants. **4.** *Physiol.* Earwax, or cerumen. **5.** *Zool.* A substance similar to beeswax, secreted by several species of scale insects. — *v. t.* To treat, smear, rub, etc., with wax. — **wax,** *adj.* — **wax'er,** *n.*

wax, *n. Colloq.* A fit of temper; a rage.

wax bean. See STRING BEAN.

wax'ber'ry (wăks'bĕr'ĭ; -bẽr·ĭ), *n.*; *pl.* -RIES (-ĭz). **a** The wax-covered fruit of the wax myrtle, or bayberry; also, the shrub itself. **b** = SNOWBERRY.

wax'bill' (-bĭl'), *n.* Any of numerous Old World birds of the weaver-bird family (esp. genus *Estrilda*), having white, pink, or reddish bills of a waxy appearance. Many are common cage birds, as the Java sparrow.

wax'en (wăk'sĕn; -s'n), *adj.* **1.** Made of wax. **2.** Covered with wax; waxed; as, a *waxen* tablet; also, appearing as if covered with wax; hence, smooth and shining; sometimes, pallid. **3.** Resembling wax; hence, pliable; impressionable.

wax insect. Any of various homopterous insects that secrete a wax-like substance, as a Chinese scale insect (*Ericerus pela*) which produces wax in commercially important quantities.

wax myrtle. Any of a genus (*Myrica*, esp. *M. cerifera* and *M. carolinensis*, family Myricaceae) of shrubs or trees having aromatic foliage, and small hard berries with a thick coating of white wax used for candles. The shrub and its fruit are also called *bayberry* and *candleberry.*

wax palm. **a** A pinnate-leaved palm (*Ceroxylon andicolum*) of the Andes, the stem of which yields a resinous wax. **b** A Brazilian palm (*Copernicia cerifera*) the young leaves of which are covered with a waxy secretion. See CARNAUBA.

wax paper. Paper with a coating of white wax and other ingredients.

wax'weed' (wăks'wēd'), *n.* A small purple-flowered herb (*Cuphea petiolata*, of the loosestrife family) having a viscid pubescence.

wax'wing' (-wĭng'), *n.* Any of several American and Asiatic passerine birds (genus *Bombycilla*), chiefly brown, with a showy crest and velvety plumage. The ***cedar waxwing*** (*B. cedrorum*) and the similar but larger ***Bohemian waxwing*** (*B. garrula pallidiceps*) of northern North America are the best-known species. See BIRD, *Illust.*

wax'work' (-wûrk'), *n.* **1.** Work made of wax; esp., a figure or figures formed wholly or partly of wax, in imitation of living beings. **2.** (*Usually pl. in form but construed as sing.*) An exhibition of wax figures.

wax'y (wăk'sĭ), *adj.*; WAX'I·ER (-sĭ·ẽr); WAX'I·EST. **1.** Waxen; viscid; adhesive; hence, yielding; impressible. **2.** Made of, or abounding in, wax; waxed. **3.** *Med.* Designating, or affected with, a waxlike degeneration produced by the deposit of a white insoluble substance in an organ. — **wax'i·ness,** *n.*

way (wā), *n.* [AS. *weg.*] **1.** Direction of motion, progress, facing, etc.; route; as, what *way* do we go? **2.** That along which one passes or progresses to reach some place; a road, street, tract, or path; as, all *ways* lead to the metropolis. **3.** Room to advance, pass, or progress; hence, freedom of action or opportunity; as, give him *way* to work his will. **4.** Length of space; distance; as, a great *way;* — in dial. and colloq. form, *ways;* as, he ran a long *ways.* **5.** A moving; passage; progression; as, to make one's *way* through a crowd. **6.** Manner; mode; fashion; style; as, her *way* of doing her hair. **7.** Means to a particular end; method; procedure; as, let us try this *way* to persuade him. **8.** Respect; point; as, a plan good in every *way.* **9.** Regular course; habitual method of life or action; as, it is the *way* of the world. **10.** Individual characteristic or peculiarity; esp., *pl.*, idiosyncrasies; as, I do not mind his *ways.* **11.** *Colloq.* **a** Line of business; occupation. **b** Condition, as of health; as, in a bad *way.* **c** District or region in which one lives; as, his home is out your *way.* **12.** Determined course; that which one wills to do or be; as, to have one's *way.* **13.** Sphere, scope, or range, as of observation or experience; as, nothing came my *way.* **14.** Advance; progress; headway; as, the ship on starting gathers *way;* also, course of advance or progress; as, nothing stood in his *way;* hence, career; as, he has his *way* to make. **15.** *pl.* An inclined structure upon which a vessel is built or supported in launching. **16.** The direction of the weave in cloth; as, to cut silk the *way* of the goods. **17.** *Law.* A right of way. **18.** *Mach.* The surface, as on the bed of a planer, along which a table or carriage moves during operation. — **Syn.** See METHOD.
— ***by the way.*** By way of incident or digression; in passing. — ***by way of.*** **a** For the purpose of; as being; as, to send flowers *by way of* apology. **b** Through; via. — ***out of the way.*** **a** In a position making contact or obstruction impossible. **b** Away from the beaten track; hence, unusual; extraordinary; as, to buy books that are *out of the way.* **c** Out of the proper course or place; astray; hence, improper; wrong; as, nothing *out of the way.* — ***under way.*** In motion; making progress.

way'bill' (wā'bĭl'), *n.* A document issued with every shipment of freight, giving details regarding the goods, route, and charges.

way'far'er (-fâr'ẽr), *n.* A traveler, esp. on foot; hence, a transient patron of an inn or hotel.

way'far'ing, *adj. & n.* Traveling, esp. on foot.

way'go'ing (wā'gō'ĭng), *adj.* Going away; departing. — *n.* Leave-taking; farewell.

waygoing crop. *Law.* A crop removable under certain conditions by a tenant at the end of his tenancy.

Way'land (wā'lănd), *n.* Also **Wayland (the) Smith.** [AS. *Wēland.*] A supernatural and invisible smith of Teutonic and English legend.

way'lay' (wā'lā'; 2), *v. t.*; see LAY. [From *way* + *lay*, after MLG. or MHG. *wegelagen*, fr. *wegelage* an ambush, lit., a belaying of the roads.] To lie in wait for in the way; to take steps to meet or encounter in the way, esp. with a view of seizing, robbing, etc. — **way'lay'er** (-ẽr), *n.*

-ways (-wāz). [*way* + adverbial *-s* (see -WARD).] A suffix forming adverbs from adjectives (no*ways*) and nouns (end*ways*) denoting *in* (such) *manner, direction, position;* — usually equivalent to adverbs in *-wise.* The *-ways* and *-wise* forms are practically indistinguishable except that *-ways* lends especially a literal signification of extension in space, and *-wise* that of manner, means, respect, degree. By some the forms in *-wise* are preferred indiscriminately.

ways and means. Methods and resources for accomplishing something, esp. for defraying expenses; specif., *Legislation,* methods of raising the necessary revenues for the expenses of the state.

way'side' (wā'sīd'; 2), *n.* The side, edge, or border of a road. — **way'side',** *adj.*

way station. *U. S.* An intermediate station between principal stations on a line of travel, esp. on a railroad.

way train. A train which stops at way stations; a local.

way'ward (wā'wẽrd), *adj.* [ME. *weiward*, for *aweiward*, i. e., turned away.] **1.** Taking one's own way; disobedient. **2.** Fluctuating; irregular; unsteady. **3.** Contrary to expectation or wish; as, a *wayward* fate. — **Syn.** See CONTRARY. — **way'ward·ly,** *adv.* — **way'ward·ness,** *n.*

way'worn' (wā'wōrn'; 70), *adj.* Wearied by traveling.

we (wē; 4), *pron.*; *pl.* of I; *poss.* OUR (our) or OURS (ourz); *obj.* US (ŭs). See I. [AS. *wē.*] The personal pronoun of the 1st person pl., nominative case. *We* is used for the singular *I*, by kings and other sovereigns, and by editors and other writers to keep an impersonal character or to avoid the egotistical sound of a repeated *I.*

weak (wēk), *adj.* [ME. *weik*, fr. ON. *veikr;* akin to AS. *wāc* weak, soft, pliant.] **1.** Lacking physical strength; feeble; infirm; debilitated. **2.** Not able to sustain or exert a great weight, pressure, or strain; as, a *weak* bridge. **3.** Easily impressed, molded, or the like; pliable; as, a *weak* will; — often in combination, as in **weak'-brained', weak'-mind'ed, weak'-willed'.** **4.** Not able to resist attack; easily subdued; as, a *weak* fortress. **5.** Lacking force of utterance or sound; not sonorous; faint; as, a *weak* voice. **6.** Not containing a given ingredient or ingredients in full, usual, or proper amount; of less than the usual strength; as, *weak* tea; a *weak* decoction. **7.** Lacking in power to perform properly a function or office; as, *weak* eyes. **8.** Mentally or intellectually deficient; lacking judgment or discernment; simple; foolish; as, to put *weak* men in office. **9.** Resulting from, or indicating, lack of judgment, discernment, or firmness; specif.: **a** Vacillating; wavering; as, *weak* in faith. **b** Not able to withstand temptation, urgency, etc.; as, *weak* resolution. **c** Powerless in convincing, persuading, etc.; as, a *weak* argument. **d** Wanting in point or vigor of expression; as, a *weak* style. **10.** Impotent politically or in governing; as, a *weak* state. **11.** Faulty or defective or indicating faults or defects as from lack of experience, skill, proper manufacture or organization, etc.; as, *weak* players or plays; a *weak* spot in a fabric. **12.** Of flour or wheat, relatively low in gluten content. **13.** *Gram.* As opposed to *strong:* pertaining to or designating a verb, or its conjugation (**weak conjugation**), which forms the past tense and past participle by adding to the present the suffix *-ed, -d,* or the variant *-t* (*abash, abashed; abate, abated; deny, denied; deal, dealt*). **14.** *Phonet.* **a** Of a sound or a syllable, unstressed; unaccented; light. **b** Of accent or stress, relatively slight or low; not strong. **15.** *Photog.* Lacking contrast; thin; as, a *weak* negative. **16.** *Pros.* Designating a verse ending in which the accent falls on a word naturally unstressed, esp. one where it falls on a word (such as *of, as, to*) which in utterance tends to connect itself with the beginning of the next line. **17.** *Stock Exchange.* Tending toward a lower price or lower prices; as, a *weak* market. — **weak'ly,** *adv.* — **weak'ness,** *n.*

Syn. **Weak, feeble, frail, fragile, infirm, decrepit** mean not strong enough to endure strain, pressure, or the like. **Weak** implies a deficiency or inferiority in strength and is applicable not only to man but to any of his powers, creations, etc., or to any structure, any product, or the like; **feeble** is not only more narrowly applied but suggests a lamentable or pitiable weakness; **frail** suggests delicacy or slightness, as in constitution or structure; **fragile** suggests a frailty that cannot cope with destructive forces; **infirm** suggests instability, unsoundness, and insecurity due to old age or other weakness that cripples; **decrepit** suggests a condition of being broken down by use or old age.

weak'en (wēk'ĕn), *v. t. & i.* To make or become weak or weaker; to lessen, as in strength, spirit, or determination. — **weak'en·er,** *n.*

Syn. **Weaken, enfeeble, debilitate, undermine, sap, cripple, disable** mean to lose or cause to lose strength or vigor. **Weaken** may imply loss of health, soundness, stability, force, or the like, by anything material or immaterial; **enfeeble** implies a more obvious and pitiable condition than *weaken* and often a helpless condition; **debilitate** usually suggests a less marked or a less prolonged impairment of vitality; **undermine** and **sap** suggest a weakening by something working surreptitiously and insidiously; **cripple** suggests a loss of strength or in power to work by something that literally or figuratively maims or mutilates; **disable** suggests a crippling or enfeebling that renders one unable to carry on work, esp. the work for which one is trained.

weak'fish' (wēk'fĭsh'), *n.*; *pl.*, see FISH. Any of several marine food fishes (genus *Cynoscion* and allied genera, family Otolithidae), esp. the common species (*C. regalis*), which occurs along the eastern coast of the United States.

weak'-kneed' (-nēd'; 2), *adj.* Having weak knees; hence, easily yielding; lacking will power or resolution; irresolute.

weak'ling (wēk'lĭng), *n.* [*weak* + 1st *-ling.*] One that is physically or mentally weak. — **weak'ling,** *adj.*

weak'ly (-lĭ), *adj.*; -LI·ER (-lĭ·ẽr); -LI·EST. Not strong or robust; feeble; weak. — **weak'li·ness,** *n.*

weal (wēl), *n.* [AS. *wela, weola;* akin to AS. *wel* well.] **1.** *Obs.* Wealth. **2.** *Archaic.* A sound, healthy, or prosperous state; well-being; prosperity. **3.** *Obs.* The body politic; the state.

weal, *n.* [Var. of WALE stripe.] A wheal; wale, as on the skin.

weald (wēld), *n.* [AS. See WOLD.] A wold.

wealth (wĕlth), *n.* [ME. *welthe,* fr. *wele.* See 1st WEAL.] **1.** *Obs.* Weal; welfare. **2.** Large possessions, collectively; an abundance of things desired, esp. of worldly estate; affluence; riches. **3.** *Econ.* **a** In the private sense, all property which has a money value. **b** In the public sense, all objects, esp. material objects, which have economic utility. **c** Those energies, faculties, and habits, directly contributing to make people industrially efficient; — called specif. ***personal wealth.***

wealth'y (wĕl'thĭ), *adj.;* WEALTH'I·ER (-thĭ·ēr); WEALTH'I·EST. **1.** Having wealth; affluent; rich. **2.** Characterized by abundance; ample; opulent. — **Syn.** See RICH. — **wealth'i·ly,** *adv.* — **wealth'i·ness,** *n.*

Wealth'y, *n.* A bright-red apple of a fall-bearing American variety.

wean (wēn), *v. t.* [AS. *wenian* to accustom, wean.] **1.** To accustom (a child or other young animal) to loss of mother's milk. **2.** Hence, to detach or alienate the affections of; to reconcile to a severance; — with *from;* as, to *wean* one from a life of ease. — **Syn.** See ESTRANGE. — **wean'er,** *n.*

wean (wēn; wăn), *n.* [Contr. of Scot. *wee ane.* See WEE; ONE.] *Scot. & Ir.* An infant; child.

wean'ling (wēn'lĭng), *n.* [*wean* + 1st *-ling.*] A child or animal newly weaned. — *adj.* Recently weaned.

weap'on (wĕp'ŭn), *n.* [AS. *wǣpen.*] **1.** An instrument of offensive or defensive combat; something to fight with. **2.** Any means by which one contends against another; as, argument was his only *weapon.*

weap'on·eer' (-ēr'), *n.* One who activates an atomic bomb into readiness for release upon a target.

weap'on·shaw, weap'on·show, weap'on·show'ing. Vars. of WAPPENSCHAW, WAPPENSCHAWING.

wear (wâr), *v. t.* [AS. *werian.*] *Chiefly Scot. & Dial. Eng.* **1.** To defend; ward off. **2.** To collect and drive. — *n.* Defense; guard.

wear (wâr), *v. t.;* WORE (wōr; 70); WORN (wōrn; 70); WEAR'ING. Before the 15th century *wear* was a weak verb, the *past tense & past part.* being WEARED. [AS. *werian* to carry, wear, as arms or clothes.] **1.** To carry or bear upon the person as an article of clothing, decoration, etc. **2.** To use or affect in dressing or personal adornment; as, to *wear* white; to *wear* one's hair in a braid. **3.** To bear; to carry on or as on the person; as, he *wears* his honors gracefully. **4.** To exhibit, as in one's expression, manner, etc.; display; as, to *wear* a smile. **5.** Of a vessel, to show or fly (its flag, its colors). **6.** To use up by wearing (sense 1); as, to *wear* out a dress; hence, to consume or cause to deteriorate by use, esp. personal use; as, the luggage is *worn.* **7.** To impair, waste, or diminish, by continual attrition, scraping, or the like; as, the rocks are *worn* by water; hence, to exhaust or lessen the strength of; fatigue; weary; use up; as, to be *worn* with disease. **8.** To cause or make by friction or wasting; as, to *wear* a channel or hole. **9.** *Rare.* To bring or lead gradually, as by making accustomed. **10.** [Orig. corrupt. of 1st VEER.] *Naut.* To cause to go about, as a vessel, by putting the helm *up,* instead of *down* as in tacking, so that the vessel's bow is turned away from, and her stern is presented to, the wind in turning from one tack to the other. Cf. 1st JIBE.
— *v. i.* **1.** *Obs.* To be commonly worn or used; be fashionable. **2.** *Rare.* To become adapted as clothes do to the wearer. **3.** To endure or suffer use (well, ill, or the like); last under use or, by extension, increasing familiarity, or the like; as, the coat *wore* badly; he *wears* well; also, to become under use, familiarity, passage of time, etc.; as, the coin has *worn* thin. **4.** To be wasted, consumed, or diminished, by use; to suffer injury, loss, or extinction, by use or time; — often with *out, off, on,* etc.; as, the day *wore* on. **5.** *Naut.* To go about by turning the head away from the wind; — said of a vessel. See WEAR, *v. t.,* 10.
— *n.* **1.** Act of wearing, or state of being worn; use; as, clothes for everyday *wear.* **2.** That which is worn or proper to be worn; esp., the fashion; as, men's *wear;* — also in combination, as in neck*wear.* **3.** The result of wearing or use; impairment due to use; as, a coat that shows *wear.* **4.** Wearing quality; lasting quality. — **wear'a·ble,** *adj. & n.* — **wear'er,** *n.*

wear and tear. The loss or injury to which anything is subjected by, or in the course of, use.

wea'ri·ful (wēr'ĭ·fo͝ol; -f'l), *adj.* Tedious; dreary; vexatious. — **wea'ri·ful·ly,** *adv.* — **wea'ri·ful·ness,** *n.*

wea'ri·less (-lĕs; -lĭs), *adj.* Tireless; untiring.

wear'ing (wâr'ĭng), *adj.* **1.** Pertaining to, or designed for, wear. **2.** Subjecting to, or inflicting, wear; esp., fatiguing; as, a *wearing* journey. — **wear'ing·ly,** *adv.*

wear'ish (wâr'ĭsh; wĕr'-), *adj.* Also *Scot.* **wersh** (wĕrsh). *Scot. & Dial.* **a** Unsavory. **b** Sickly. **c** Squeamish.

wea'ri·some (wēr'ĭ·sŭm), *adj.* Causing weariness; tiresome; tedious. — **wea'ri·some·ly,** *adv.* — **wea'ri·some·ness,** *n.*

wea'ry (wēr'ĭ; 27), *adj.;* WEA'RI·ER (-ĭ·ēr); WEA'RI·EST. [AS. *wērig.*] **1.** Having the strength much impaired by toil, suffering, etc.; tired; fatigued. **2.** Expressing, or characteristic of, weariness; as, a *weary* gait. **3.** Having one's patience, tolerance, or liking, exhausted; — usually with *of;* as, *weary* of reading. — *v. t. & i.;* WEA'RIED (-ĭd); WEA'RY·ING. To make or become weary. — **Syn.** See TIRE. — **wea'ri·ly,** *adv.* — **wea'ri·ness,** *n.*

wea'sand (wē'zănd), *n.* Also, *Scot.,* **wea'son.** [AS. *wǣsend, wāsend.*] The throat; gullet; also, the windpipe.

wea'sel (wē'z'l), *n.;* see PLURAL, *Note,* 3. [AS. *wesole, wesle.*] Any of certain small slender-bodied carnivorous mammals (genus *Mustela*) allied to the minks and true polecats. They kill many birds and great numbers of mice, rats, and other vermin. They are mostly reddish brown with white or yellowish under parts and black-tipped tail, but northern species (see ERMINE) turn white in winter.

weasel words. Words that destroy the force of a statement by equivocal qualification as a weasel ruins an egg by sucking out its contents while leaving it superficially intact; — a phrase given currency by Theodore Roosevelt.

weath'er (wĕth'ēr), *n.* [AS. *weder.*] **1.** State of the air or atmosphere with respect to heat or cold, wetness or dryness, calm or storm, clearness or cloudiness, or any other meteorological phenomena. **2.** Storm; tempest. — ***under the weather.*** *Colloq., U. S.* **a** Ill. **b** Financially embarrassed. **c** More or less intoxicated. — *v. t.* **1.** To expose to the air; to season, dry, pulverize, discolor, etc., by exposure to air. **2.** To bear up against and come safely through, as a storm, trials, etc. **3.** *Naut.* To sail or pass to the windward of: as, to *weather* a cape. — *v. i.* To undergo or endure the action of the atmosphere. — *adj. Naut.* Windward; — opposed to *lee.*

weath'er-beat'en, *adj.* Also, **weath'er·worn'** (wĕth'ēr·wōrn'; 70). Worn or damaged by exposure to the weather; also, toughened, tanned, or bronzed by the weather.

weath'er·board' (wĕth'ēr·bōrd'; 70), *n.* **1.** A board shaped so as to be especially adapted to shed water by forming lapped joints with the boards above and below; a clapboard. **2.** *Naut.* The weather, or windward, side of a vessel. — *v. t. & i.* To nail boards upon so as to lap one over another in order to exclude rain, etc.

weath'er·board'ing, *n.* **a** The covering or siding of a weatherboarded building. **b** Weatherboards collectively.

weath'er-bound', *adj.* Kept in port or at anchor, and hence from travel, sport, etc., by bad weather.

weath'er·cock' (wĕth'ēr·kŏk'), *n.* **1.** A vane, originally often in the figure of a cock, turning, as on the top of a spire, with the wind, and showing its direction. **2.** Any thing or person that turns easily and often; one who veers with every change of current opinion.

weath'ered (wĕth'ērd), *adj.* **1.** Seasoned by exposure to the weather; altered in color, texture, etc., by such exposure or by artificial means producing a similar effect; as, *weathered* oak. **2.** *Arch.* Made sloping, so as to throw off water.

weather gauge. **a** *Naut.* The position of a vessel to the windward of another, in the case of sailing vessels giving an advantage in maneuvering. **b** A position of advantage or superiority.

weath'er·glass' (wĕth'ēr·glȧs'), *n.* An instrument to indicate the state of the atmosphere, esp. changes of pressure, and hence of weather, as a barometer or baroscope.

weath'er·ing (wĕth'ēr·ĭng), *n.* Action of the elements in altering the color, texture, composition, or form of exposed objects; also, alteration so effected.

weath'er·ly (wĕth'ēr·lĭ), *adj. Naut.* Able to sail close to the wind with little leeway. — **weath'er·li·ness** (-lĭ·nĕs; -nĭs), *n.*

weath'er·man' (-măn'), *n.* Originally, one who notes the weather; now, *Colloq.,* a meteorologist, esp. one who gives out reports on the weather.

weather map. A map or chart showing the principal meteorological elements at a given hour and over an extended region.

weath'er·proof' (wĕth'ēr·pro͞of'; 2), *adj.* Able to withstand exposure to weather without sensible depreciation. See -PROOF. — **weath'er-proof',** *v. t.*

weather strip. Also **weather stripping.** A strip of material to cover the joint of a door, window, etc., with the sill, casing, or threshold, to exclude rain, drafts, etc. — **weath'er-strip',** *v. t.*

weather vane. = VANE, 1.

weath'er-wise', *adj.* Skillful in forecasting the changes of the weather, or, by extension, changes in opinion or feeling.

weave (wēv), *v. t.;* WOVE (wōv), *Rare* WEAVED (wēvd); WO'VEN (wō'vĕn), WOVE; WEAV'ING. [AS. *wefan* (pret. *wæf*).] **1.** To form, as a textile, by interlacing yarns; specif., to make or manufacture (cloth, a kind of cloth) on a loom by interlacing warp and filling yarns. **2.** To fabricate by or as by interlacing; contrive; as, to *weave* a plot. **3.** To unite so as to form a texture, design, etc.; as, words *woven* into song. **4.** To move to and fro, up and down, or in an intricate course; as, to *weave* one's way through a crowd. **5.** To spin (a web), as spiders, etc. — *v. i.* **1.** To work at weaving; to make cloth on a loom. **2.** To become interwoven; to interlace. **3.** To move from side to side repeatedly; to move in a devious and intricate course; as, to *weave* through a crowd. — *n.* A particular method or pattern of weaving; as: ***plain, or taffeta, weave,*** in which the threads interlace alternately; ***basket weave,*** in which double threads are interlaced as in plain weave; ***satin weave,*** in which warp threads interlace with filling threads at points distributed over the surface, thereby producing a smooth-faced fabric; ***twill weave,*** in which the filling threads pass over one and under two or more warp threads, thereby giving an appearance of diagonal lines, or ribs.

weav'er (wēv'ēr), *n.* **1.** One who weaves, or whose occupation is weaving. **2.** A weaverbird.

weav'er·bird' (-bûrd'), *n.* Also **weav'er.** Any of many Asiatic and African birds (family Ploceidae) resembling finches, that construct elaborate nests of interlaced grass and other vegetation.

weav'er's hitch *or* **knot** (wēv'ērz). A sheet bend. See KNOT, *Illust.* (34).

web (wĕb), *n.* [AS. *webb.*] **1.** A textile fabric, esp. one on a loom, or coming from a loom. **2.** The cobweb of a spider or other insect. **3.** Formerly, an affection of the eye, as in ***pin and web,*** an eye disease named after the occurrence of a small excrescence (*pin*) and a film (*web*). **4.** Anything like a web, as in interlacing of threads, complexity, etc.; a network; as, a *web* of railroads; also, anything flimsy, entangling, etc., as a cobweb; as, a *web* of lies. **5.** The membrane uniting fingers or toes, either at their bases, as in man, or for a greater part of their length, as in many water birds and amphibians. Hence, **web'-fin'gered, web'-foot'ed, web'-toed'.** **6.** A thin metal plate, sheet, or strip, as the blade of a saw, the bit of a key, etc.; specif., *Mach. & Engin.,* a plate or thin portion between stiffening ribs or flanges. See CRANK, *Illust.* **7.** Paper from the roll in a printing press, or in process of manufacture in a paper machine. **8.** *Anat. & Med.* A tissue or membrane. **9.** *Arch.* The portion of a ribbed vault between the ribs. **10.** *Zool.* The series of barbs implanted on each side of the shaft of a feather; the vane or vexillum. See FEATHER, *Illust.* — *v. t.;* WEBBED (wĕbd); WEB'BING. To unite or surround with a web, or as if with a web; envelop; entangle. — **webbed** (wĕbd), *adj.*

web'bing (wĕb'ĭng), *n.* A stout close-woven tape used for reins, straps, as in upholstery, etc.

web defense. *Mil.* A system of defense for dissipating blitzkrieg attack, featuring tankproof islands of defense, or hedgehogs, in pairs, forward and reserve, separated by a zone from ten to twenty miles deep scattered with smaller islands of defense.

we'ber (vā'bēr; wē'bēr), *n.* [After W. E. *Weber,* Ger. physicist.] *Elec.* **a** A unit of magnetic flux equal to 10^8 maxwells. **b** Formerly, a coulomb; later, a maxwell.

web'foot' (wĕb'fo͝ot'), *n.* **1.** A foot having toes connected by a web. **2.** A web-footed animal.

web press. A rotary printing press using a paper roll or rolls.

web′ster (wĕb′stẽr), *n.* *Archaic.* A weaver.
Web·ste′ri·an (wĕb·stēr′ĭ·ăn), *adj.* Of or pertaining to Webster, either Daniel Webster the statesman (1782–1852), or Noah Webster the lexicographer (1758–1843).
web′worm′ (wĕb′wûrm′), *n.* Any of various caterpillars which are more or less gregarious and spin large webs.
wecht (wĕKt). Scot. var. of WEIGHT.
wed (wĕd), *v. t.*; WED′DED; WED′DED or WED; WED′DING. [AS. *weddian* to covenant, promise, to wed, marry; akin to AS. *wed(d)* a pledge.] **1.** To take for wife or husband; marry. **2.** To join in marriage; give in wedlock. **3.** To unite as if by the bond of marriage; attach firmly or indissolubly; — chiefly in *past part.*; as, *wedded* to art. — *v. i.* To contract matrimony; marry. — **wed′der** (wĕd′ẽr), *n.*
wed′ding (wĕd′ĭng), *n.* [AS. *weddung.*] **1.** Nuptial ceremony; nuptial festivities; marriage. **2.** A wedding anniversary or its celebration. Such anniversaries are named according to the kind of gifts customarily presented. Thus the fifth is called ***wooden wedding;*** tenth, ***tin wedding;*** fifteenth, ***crystal wedding;*** twentieth, ***china wedding;*** twenty-fifth, ***silver wedding;*** fiftieth, ***golden wedding;*** sixtieth (or seventy-fifth), ***diamond wedding.***
wedge (wĕj), *n.* [AS. *wecg.*] **1.** A piece of wood, metal, etc., tapering to a thin edge, used in splitting wood, rocks, etc., in raising heavy bodies, and the like. See SIMPLE MACHINE, *Illust.* **2.** Anything wedge-shaped; as, a *wedge* of cheese; specif.: **a** An array or military formation in the form of a wedge. **b** The wedge-shaped stroke in cuneiform characters. See CUNEIFORM, *Illust.* **3.** An action, policy, move, etc., that serves to open a way for a breach, change, intrusion, etc.; — more fully ***entering wedge.*** **4.** [Trans. of G. *keil* wedge.] A German military tactic in which a wedge-shaped shock force with a spearhead of panzers, followed by motorized divisions, then by infantry, each widening the wedge, creates a gap in an enemy line.
— *v. t.*; WEDGED (wĕjd); WEDG′ING (wĕj′ĭng). **1.** To cleave or separate with or as with a wedge; rive. **2.** To fasten with a wedge or wedges. **3.** To force or drive as a wedge is driven; crowd. — *v. i.* To push or be forced or fixed as or as if a wedge; — with *in* or *into.*
Wedg′ie (wĕj′ĭ), *n.* A trade-mark applied to a woman's shoe, variously an oxford, sandal, or pump, having in place of a heel a thick wedge-shaped block that tapers forward, filling the arch of the instep, and joins the halfsole to form a continuous flat undersurface.
Wedg′wood ware, *or* **Wedg′wood** (wĕj′wo͝od), *n.* The fine hard porcelainlike ware first produced by Josiah Wedgwood (see *Biog.*) and characteristically of a tinted clay ground with small cameo reliefs in white paste, applied before firing.
wed′lock (wĕd′lŏk), *n.* [AS. *wedlāc* a pledge, betrothal, fr. *wed* a pledge + *-lāc*, akin to ON. *-leikr*, forming abstract nouns, AS. *lāc* play, sport.] The ceremony, or the state, of marriage; matrimony.
Wednes′day (wĕnz′dĭ; 13), *n.* [AS. *Wōdnes dæg*, i. e., Woden's day.] The fourth day of the week. Abbr. *Wed.*
wee (wē), *adj.*; WE′ER (wē′ẽr); WE′EST (wē′ĕst; -ĭst). [ME. *we* a bit, in a *little we, a little wei; we, wei* being finally taken as synonymous with *little.*] Very small; little. — **Syn.** See SMALL. — *n. Chiefly Scot.* A little; a mite; as, bide a *wee.*
weed (wēd), *n.* [AS. *wǣde, wǣd.*] **1.** A garment; — now commonly in *pl.* and used esp. of mourning garments; as, a widow's *weeds.* **2.** A band of crape worn on a man's hat.
weed, *n.* [AS. *wēod.*] **1.** *Archaic.* Wild growth, as rank grass, undergrowth, etc. **2.** Any plant growing in cultivated ground to the detriment of the crop or to the disfigurement of the place; an economically useless or unsightly plant, esp. of wild growth. **3.** *Colloq.* **a** Tobacco; esp., tobacco prepared for use; — usually with *the.* **b** A cigar. **4.** Something of little value; specif., *Stock Breeding*, an animal unfit to breed from. — *v. t.* **1.** To free from noxious plants; clear of weeds. **2.** To free from anything that is hurtful or offensive; also, *Colloq.*, to dispose of the less desirable portions of; as, to *weed* a stock of goods. **3.** To remove, eradicate, reject, etc., as a weed, or something harmful, valueless, etc.; — often with *out* or *up.* — *v. i.* To remove weeds or something harmful. — **weed′er,** *n.* — **weed′less,** *adj.*
weed′y (wēd′ĭ), *adj.*; -I·ER (-ĭ·ẽr); -I·EST. **1.** Abounding with weeds; as, a *weedy* garden. **2.** Of, pertaining to, or like a weed or weeds. **3.** Weedlike, esp. in growth or ready propagation. **4.** *Colloq.* Scraggy; ungainly; as, a *weedy* youth. — **weed′i·ly,** *adv.* — **weed′i·ness,** *n.*
week (wēk), *n.* [AS. *wice, wicu, wucu.*] **1.** A period of seven days, usually reckoned from one Sunday or Sabbath to the next. See MEASURE, *Table* 6. **2.** The series of regular working days, business days, or days of class attendance during each seven-day period; as, the banking *week* is Monday through Friday; also, a workweek. **3.** A time seven days before or after a specified day.
week′day′ (-dā′), *n.* Any day of the week except Sunday; a working day. — **week′day′,** *adj.*
week end. The end of the week; specif., the period from Saturday noon or Friday night to Monday; also, a house party during a week end. — **week′-end′** (-ĕnd′; 2), *adj.*
week′-end′ (wēk′ĕnd′; 2), *v. i.* To spend the week end, esp. in visiting.
week′ly (wēk′lĭ), *adv.* Once a week; once every seven days. — *adj.* **1.** Of or pertaining to a week or weekdays. **2.** Coming, happening, or done weekly. — *n.*; *pl.* -LIES (-lĭz). A publication issued weekly.
ween (wēn), *v. i. & t.* [AS. *wēnan*; akin to AS. *wēn* hope, expectation, opinion.] *Archaic.* To suppose; imagine.
weep (wēp), *n.* The lapwing; — so called from its cry.
weep (wēp), *v. i.*; WEPT (wĕpt); WEEP′ING. [AS. *wēpan* (pret. *wēop*); akin to AS. *wōp* lamentation.] **1.** Formerly, to express sorrow, grief, or anguish, by outcry; lament; in modern use, to show grief or other passion by shedding tears; cry. **2.** To drop water, or the like; to drip; as, *weeping* skies. **3.** *Plant Physiol.* To exude water under pressure; bleed, as the stem of a plant. — *v. t.* **1.** To weep for; lament; bewail. **2.** To shed, or pour forth, as tears. **3.** To affect in a specified way by, or to spend in, weeping; as, to *weep* life away. **4.** To exude; — esp. of trees. — *n.* Weeping or, *Colloq.*, a fit of weeping.
weep′er (wēp′ẽr), *n.* **1.** One who weeps; esp., a professional mourner. **2.** A badge of mourning, as a white cuff band or border formerly worn.
weep′ing, *adj.* **1.** That weeps; tearful; also, rainy. **2.** Having slender, pendent branches; as, a *weeping* willow.
wee′ver (wē′vẽr), *n.* [ONF. *wivre* (F. *vive*). See WIVERN.] Any of several edible marine fishes (genus *Trachinus* or family Trachinidae) having a broad spinose head, with the eyes looking upward.

wee′vil (wē′v'l; -vĭl), *n.* [AS. *wifel.*] Any of numerous (mostly small) beetles of a group (Rhynchophora) with snoutlike heads. The larvae eat out the interior of nuts, fruit, and grain, as the ***nut weevil*** and ***seed weevil***, or bore into the pith of trees and other plants, as the ***white pine weevil.*** See BOLL WEEVIL, *Illust.* — **wee′vil·y, wee′vil·ly** (wē′v'l·ĭ), *adj.*

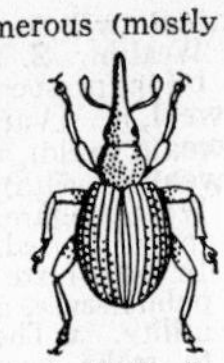

Seed Weevil (*Apion sayi*). (× 5)

weft (wĕft), *n.* [AS. *wefta, weft.*] **1.** In weaving, the woof; also, yarn for the shuttle. **2.** A web; a thing woven.
‖**Wehr′macht′** (vār′mäKt′), *n.* [G., fr. *wehr* defense + *macht* force.] Germany's armed forces, collectively.
wei·ge′la (wī·jē′là; wī·gē′là), *n.* [NL., after C. E. *Weigel* (1748–1831), Sw. physician.] Any Asiatic species of a genus (*Diervilla*) of shrubs of the honeysuckle family; esp., the pink or reddish-flowered *D. florida* of China, cultivated in American gardens. See HONEYSUCKLE, 3.
weigh (wā), *v. t.* [AS. *wegan* to bear, move, weigh.] **1.** To hoist; — now only in to *weigh* anchor. **2.** To examine by the balance; to ascertain the weight of; to measure out on or as on scales; also, to balance in one's hands to determine weight. **3.** To ponder in the mind; consider carefully, as before speaking or deciding; as, to *weigh* one's words or one's chances of success. **4.** To outweigh; — with *down* or *out.* **5.** To consider as worthy of notice; regard; esteem. — **Syn.** See CONSIDER. — *v. i.* **1.** To have weight; to be heavy; to have a certain weight; as, he *weighs* 200 pounds. **2.** To have weight, or importance; to be influential; carry weight. **3.** To bear heavily; press hard; — with *on* or *upon.* **4.** *Obs.* To judge; estimate; consider. **5.** *Naut.* To weigh anchor. — **Syn.** See DEPRESS. — ***weigh down.*** To bear heavily down on someone or something. — ***weigh in.*** To weigh (a jockey or a boxer), or to be weighed, before a contest. — ***weigh one's words.*** To choose one's words carefully before speaking. — **weigh′er** (wā′ẽr), *n.*
weigh, *n.* *Orig. Naut.* Erroneous for WAY, used in the phrase *under weigh*, by assoc. with *aweigh.*
weight (wāt), *n.* [AS. *wiht, gewiht.*] **1.** A quantity or thing weighing a fixed, usually specified, amount; as, equal *weight* of water and air. **2. a** A unit of weight or mass; as, a table of *weights.* **b** A mass, as of iron, brass, etc., having the weight of one (or a multiple of one) of these units and used in weighing; as, an ounce *weight.* **c** A mode of estimating weight or mass; a system of weights (sense 2 **a**); as, apothecaries' *weight.* See *Table*, below; METRIC SYSTEM. **3.** A ponderous mass; a heavy object for pressing, counterbalancing, etc.; as, a paper-*weight.* **4.** Burden; as, the *weight* of care or business; pressure, as of onslaught. **5.** Quantity of heaviness; the amount which a given thing weighs, or should weigh. Abbr. *wt.* **6.** Relative heaviness; ponderability, regarded as a property of matter. **7.** Importance; consequence; influence; as, a consideration of vast *weight.* **8.** The force with which a body is attracted toward the earth. It is equal to the mass of a body multiplied by the acceleration due to gravity. **9.** Of garments, the relative heaviness suited to the season; as, winter *weight.* **10.** *Athletics.* A heavy object, usually a ball of metal, thrown, put, or lifted as an athletic exercise. **11.** *Statistics.* The frequency of an item in a frequency distribution; also, a number assigned to express its relative importance. — **Syn.** See IMPORTANCE: INFLUENCE. — *v. t.* **1.** To load with a weight or weights; make heavy. **2.** To oppress, as with a burden; weigh down. **3.** To increase in heaviness, as a fabric, by adding barite. **4.** To assign a value to (each of several related things) as a measure of their relative importance; as, to *weight* factors. **5.** *Skiing.* To shift the burden of weight upon; as, to *weight* the inside ski. **6.** *Statistics.* To assign a weight (sense 11) to.

TABLES
(with metric equivalents)

1. Avoirdupois Weight (Ordinary Commodities)

16 drams (dr.)	= 1 ounce (oz.)
16 ounces or 7000 grains	= 1 pound (lb.)
14 pounds	= 1 stone (st.)
100 (in Eng. 112) pounds	= 1 hundredweight (cwt.)
2000 pounds or 20 hundredweights	= 1 ton (tn. or t.) or short ton (s. t.)
2240 pounds or 20 hundredweights	= 1 long ton (l. t.)

Metric Equivalents: 1 dr. = 1.772 g.; 1 oz. = 28.3495 g.; 1 lb. = 453.59 g. or 0.4536 kg.; 1 st. = 6.35 kg.; 1 cwt. (U. S.) = 45.36 kg.; 1 short ton = 907.18 kg. or 0.9072 M. T.; 1 long ton = 1016.05 kg. or 1.0160 M. T.

2. Troy Weight (Precious Metals, Jewels, etc.)

3.086 grains (gr.)	= 1 carat (car.)	= 200 mg.
24 grains	= 1 pennyweight (dwt.)	= 1.555 g.
20 pennyweights	= 1 ounce (oz. t.)	= 31.1035 g.
12 ounces or 5760 grains	= 1 pound (lb. t.)	= 373.24 g. or 0.3732 kg.

Metric Equivalents: 1 grain = 0.0648 gram; in weighing pearls, etc., a grain = ¼ carat (0.77 troy grains) or 50 mg.

3. Apothecaries' Weight (Drugs, etc.)

20 grains (gr.)	= 1 scruple (s. ap. or ℈)
3 scruples	= 1 dram (dr. ap. or ʒ)
8 drams	= 1 ounce (oz. ap. or ℥)
12 ounces	= 1 pound (lb. ap. or ℔)

Metric Equivalents: 1 s. ap. = 1.296 g.; 1 dr. ap. = 3.888 g.

4. Comparison of Weights

	Grain	Ounce	Pound
Avoirdupois	1	437½ gr.	7000 gr.
Troy	1	480 gr.	5760 gr.
Apothecaries'	1	480 gr.	5760 gr.
175 lb. troy			= 144 lb. av.

weight′y (wāt′ĭ), *adj.*; -I·ER (-ĭ·ẽr); -I·EST. **1.** Having much weight; heavy; ponderous; hence, burdensome. **2.** Momentous; serious; also, influential; as, *weighty* reasons. — **Syn.** See HEAVY. — **weight′i·ly** (-ĭ·lĭ), *adv.* — **weight′i·ness** (-ĭ·nĕs; -nĭs), *n.*
Wei′mar Re·pub′lic (vī′mär). The German federated republic founded (1919) upon the Weimar Constitution and succeeded by the Third Reich (1933).
weir (wēr; *locally* wâr), *n.* [AS. *wer.*] **1.** A dam in a river to stop

and raise the water, as for the purpose of conducting it to a mill. **2.** A fence, as of stakes, set in a stream, tideway, etc., for taking fish.

weird (wērd), *n.* [AS. *wyrd* fate, destiny; akin to AS. *weorthan* to become.] *Chiefly Scot.* **a** Fate; destiny; lot; esp., ill fortune. **b** [*cap.*] One of the Fates; Fate. **c** A prophecy; prediction; also, an omen. **d** A spell; charm. **e** A soothsayer. **f** A fateful tale. **g** The inevitable event. — *adj.* **1.** Of, pertaining to, or dealing with fate or the Fates. **2.** Of or pertaining to witchcraft; hence, unearthly; uncanny; as, a *weird* sound. — **weird′ly**, *adv.* — **weird′ness**, *n.*

Syn. **Weird, eerie, uncanny** mean mysteriously strange or fantastic. **Weird**, in stricter use, often implies an unearthly or preternatural mysteriousness; **eerie**, a vague consciousness that unearthly or mysterious and, often, malign powers or influences are at work; **uncanny**, in its prevailing but looser sense, unpleasant mysteriousness or strangeness, as of persons, places, sensations, thoughts, etc.

Weird Sisters. **a** *Scot.* The Fates. **b** The witches in *Macbeth.*

Weis′mann·ism (vīs′män·ĭz′m), *n.* *Biol.* The theories and teachings as to heredity of the German biologist August Weismann, esp. in regard to germ plasm as the basis of heredity and the impossibility of transmitting acquired characters. Cf. NEO-DARWINISM.

weiss beer (wīs). [G. *weissbier* white beer.] A light-colored highly effervescent beer.

we′jack (wē′jăk), *n.* [Of Algonquian origin.] = FISHER, 2.

we′ka (wā′kä; wē′kȧ), *n.* [Maori.] Any of several flightless New Zealand rails (genus *Gallirallus*).

welch (wĕlch; wĕlsh), **welch′er.** Vars. of WELSH, WELSHER.

Welch (wĕlch; wĕlsh), **Welch′man.** Vars. of WELSH, etc.

wel′come (wĕl′kŭm), *adj.* [AS. *wilcuma* a welcome guest, fr. *wil-* (akin to *willa* will, and *wel* well) + *cuma* a comer, fr. *cuman* to come; hence, prop., one who comes so as to please another's will; influenced by ME. *wel* well.] **1.** Received gladly into one's presence or companionship; as, a *welcome* visitor. **2.** Giving pleasure; grateful; pleasing; as, *welcome* news. **3.** Willingly permitted or admitted; as, you are *welcome* to enter or to the use of my library. — **Syn.** See PLEASANT. — *n.* A cordial greeting to, or reception of, a guest or newcomer; as, we found a ready *welcome.* — *v. t.* **1.** To greet (a visitor, or the like) with cordiality or courtesy; make welcome. **2.** To accept with an expression of pleasure; as, he *welcomes* honest criticism. — **wel′com·er** (-kŭm·ẽr), *n.* — **wel′come·ly**, *adv.* — **wel′come·ness**, *n.*

weld (wĕld), *n.* Also **woald** (wōld), **wold** (wōld), and **would** (wōld). [ME. *welde.*] A European mignonette (*Reseda luteola*) yielding a yellow dye; also, the dye.

weld, *v. t.* [From past part. of *well,* fr. ME. *wellen.* See WELL, *v.*] **1.** To unite metallic parts by (1) heating the surfaces of the parts to be joined and then allowing the metals to flow together, or (2) by hammering or compressing with or without previous softening by heat. **2.** To unite closely or intimately; join so as to form a single or integrated whole. — *v. i.* To be, or be capable of being, welded. — *n.* State of being welded; also, a welded joint; as, a butt *weld.* — **weld′a·ble**, *adj.* — **weld′er**, *n.*

weld′ment (wĕld′mĕnt), *n.* **a** Act or process of welding. **b** A unit formed by welding together an assembly of pieces.

wel′dor (wĕl′dẽr), *n.* One whose work is welding; one skilled in welding; — preferred to *welder* by some authorities on welding.

wel′fare′ (wĕl′fâr′), *n.* [ME. *wel fare,* fr. *wel* well + *fare* to go.] **1.** State of faring, or doing, well; esp., condition of health, prosperity, etc.; negatively, exemption from evil or calamity. **2.** In full, **welfare work.** Organized community or corporate efforts for social betterment of a class or group; as, engaged in child *welfare.*

welfare state. A state that by legislation directly concerned with safeguarding health, providing insurance against sickness and unemployment, and other measures looking to social security assumes a major share of responsibility for the individual and social welfare of its citizens.

wel′kin (wĕl′kĭn), *n.* [AS. *wolcen,* pl. *wolcnu,* a cloud.] *Archaic.* The sky; loosely, the air.

well (wĕl), *n.* [AS. *wella, wiella, wylla.*] **1.** An issue of water from the earth; a spring with its accompanying pool; a fountain. **2.** A pit or hole sunk into the earth to reach a supply of water. **3.** A shaft or hole sunk to obtain oil (***oil well***), brine (***salt well***), gas (***gas well***), etc. **4.** A source of supply; fountain; wellspring; as, a *well* of knowledge. **5.** Any of various hollowed vessels; as, the *well* of a fountain pen. **6.** Any space so enclosed, or shaped, as to suggest a well; specif.: **a** In English law courts, a space before the judge's bench, usually for lawyers, esp. solicitors. **b** An open space extending vertically through floors, as for a staircase or an elevator. **c** An enclosure in the middle of a vessel's hold, around the pumps, to preserve them from damage and facilitate their inspection. **d** A compartment in the hold of a fishing vessel, with tight sides but holes in the bottom to admit water, in which fish are kept alive. — *v. i. & t.* [ME. *wellen* to well up, boil, fr. AS. *wiellan, wellan,* caus.] To issue or pour forth from or as from a well; flow.

well, *adv.; compar.* BET′TER (bĕt′ẽr); *superl.* BEST (bĕst). [AS. *wel.*] **1.** In such manner as is desirable or pleasing; as one could wish; satisfactorily; favorably; fortunately; as, to turn out *well.* **2.** In a good or proper manner; rightly; worthily; hence, excellently; expertly; as, to cook, sing, or talk *well.* **3.** To a good, proper, or suitable degree; abundantly; adequately; as, to be *well* pleased; a *well*-watered region. **4.** With reason, propriety, or the like; properly; as, I cannot *well* refuse. **5.** Fully; quite; as, he was *well* out of sight. **6.** Intimately; closely; as, I knew him *well.* **7.** Considerably; far; as, *well* ahead.

☞ *Well* is often combined with (1) an adjective; (2) a participle, as in:

well-acted	well-defined	well-informed
well-balanced	well-disposed	well-made
well-behaved	well-dressed	well-preserved
well-chosen	well-established	well-timed
well-content	well-grounded	well-worn

(3) a word or suffix consisting of a noun + *-ed*, as in **well′-man′nered.** All such expressions are hyphened when used attributively (a *well-acted* play). When used predicatively they are, however, treated as separate words (the play was *well acted*), except for combinations of the third type (he is *well-mannered*), and a few others that have from long usage become hyphened (*well-read*) or, rarely, solid words (*wellborn*).

— *adj.* **1.** Good or desirable in any way; fortunate; advantageous; satisfactory; suitable; proper; — now only predicative; as, all is *well.* **2.** Being in health; not ailing, diseased, or sick. **3.** Being in satisfactory circumstances or condition. — **Syn.** See HEALTHY.

well (wĕl), *interj.* An exclamation, orig. an ellipsis for *it is well,* but now used in expressing surprise, expostulation, assent, etc.

we'll (wēl). Contraction of *we will;* — often used for *we shall.*

well′a·way′ (wĕl′ȧ·wā′; 2), *interj.* [ME. *weilawey,* fr. *wei* wo! + *la* lo! (AS. *lā*) + *wei* wo!] An exclamation expressing lament.

well′-be′ing (-bē′ĭng; 2), *n.* Condition of being well, comfortable, happy, etc.; welfare.

well′born′ (-bôrn′; 2), *adj.* Born of good stock, esp. socially or physically.

well′-bred′ (-brĕd′; 2), *adj.* **1.** Having good breeding; refined in manners. **2.** Of good breed, as an animal.

well′-do′er (-do͞o′ẽr), *n.* One who does well; esp., one known for good life or deeds. — **well′do′ing** (-do͞o′ĭng; 2), *n. & adj.*

well′-fa′vored, *or* **well′-fa′voured** (-fā′vẽrd; 2); *adj.* Handsome.

well′-found′ (-found′; 2), *adj.* Well or thoroughly found, or provided; as, a *well-found* ship.

well′-found′ed (-foun′dĕd; -dĭd; 2), *adj.* Based on excellent reasoning, information, judgment, etc.; as, a *well-founded* charge.

well′-groomed′ (-gro͞omd′; 2), *adj.* **a** Carefully tended, curried, etc., as a horse. **b** Of a person, well-dressed and scrupulously neat.

well′-han′dled (-hăn′d'ld; 2), *adj.* Managed efficiently.

well′head′ (wĕl′hĕd′), *n.* A source, spring, or fountain.

Wel′ling·ton boot *or* **Wel′ling·ton** (wĕl′ĭng·tŭn), *n.* [After the 1st duke of *Wellington.*] A loose-topped boot for men, the front coming above the knee.

well′-known′ (wĕl′nōn′; 2), *adj.* Fully or widely known.

well′-mean′ing (-mēn′ĭng; 2), *adj.* Having good intentions.

well′-nigh′ (-nī′; 2), *adv.* Almost; nearly.

well off. Also **well′-off′,** *adj.* In good condition; esp., thriving; prosperous.

well′-read′ (wĕl′rĕd′; 2), *adj.* Of extensive reading; deeply versed through reading; — often followed by *in.*

wells′ite (wĕlz′īt), *n.* [After H. L. *Wells* (1855–1924), Am. chemist.] *Mineral.* A silicate of aluminum, calcium, barium, and potassium, $(Ba,Ca,K_2)Al_2Si_3O_{10}.3H_2O$, occurring in glassy, colorless, or white crystals.

well′-spo′ken (wĕl′spō′kĕn; 2), *adj.* **1.** Speaking well, fitly, or courteously. **2.** Spoken with propriety; as, *well-spoken* words.

well′spring′ (wĕl′sprĭng′), *n.* **1.** A fountainhead; a spring. **2.** A source of continual supply.

well′-thought′-of′, *adj.* Being of good repute.

well′-to-do′ (*see Pron.,* § 2), *adj.* Also **well to do.** Prosperous.

well′-wish′ing, *adj.* Hoping for another's success. — **well′-wish′er,** *n.* — **well′-wish′ing,** *n.*

Wels′bach (wĕlz′băk; -bäk; *G.* vĕls′bäκ), *n.* [After C. Auer von *Welsbach,* Austrian chemist.] A trade-mark for gaslight appliances and accessories, applied esp. to a burner (**Welsbach burner**) in which the combustion of a mixture of air and gas or vapor is employed to heat a mantle (**Welsbach mantle**) to incandescence.

welsh (wĕlsh), *v. t. & i.* *Slang.* To cheat by avoiding payment of bets. — **welsh′er,** *n.*

Welsh (wĕlsh), *adj.* [AS. *wælisc, welisc,* fr. *wealh* a foreigner, not of Saxon origin, a Welshman.] Of or pertaining to Wales, its inhabitants, or their language. — *n.* **1.** The language of Wales or of the Welsh people, possessing an extensive literature in prose and poetry. See INDO-EUROPEAN LANGUAGES, *Table.* **2.** (*Used only as a pl.*) The natives or inhabitants of Wales. The Welsh call themselves *Cymry.* See CYMRIC.

Welsh cor′gi (kôr′gĭ). [W. *corgi,* fr. *corr* dwarf + *ci* dog.] A short-legged, long-backed dog with foxlike head, belonging to either of two Welsh breeds: the ***Car′di·gan*** (kär′dĭ·găn), marked by rounded ears, slightly bowed forelegs, long tail; the ***Pem′broke*** (pĕm′bro͝ok), by pointed-erect ears, straight legs, and short tail.

Welsh′man (wĕlsh′măn), *n.* One of the Welsh.

Welsh rabbit. A dish, variously made, of melted or toasted cheese, often mixed with ale or beer, poured over toasted bread or crackers; — a jocose term, like "Cape Cod turkey" (codfish), that through failure to recognize the joke is commonly modified in cookbooks to **Welsh rarebit.**

Welsh terrier. A wiry-coated terrier of a breed supposed to have originated two centuries ago in Wales.

welt (wĕlt), *n.* [ME. *welte, walte.*] **1.** A cord, fold, etc., sewed or otherwise fastened to an edge or border, to guard, strengthen, or adorn it; specif., the narrow strip of leather between a shoe upper and the sole to which each part is in turn stitched. **2.** *Colloq.* A wale, or ridge raised on the flesh or skin by a blow; also, a heavy stroke or blow. — *v. t.* **1.** To furnish with a welt. **2.** *Colloq.* To beat or lash, esp. so as to raise a welt.

‖**Welt′an′schau′ung** (vĕlt′än′shou′o͝ong), *n.* [G.] Literally, a world view; specif., a philosophy, esp. a personal or racial one, explaining history in general or the purpose of the world as a whole.

‖**Welt′an′sicht** (vĕlt′än′zĭκt), *n.* [G.] A world view; a special view or apprehension of reality as a whole.

wel′ter (wĕl′tẽr), *v. i.* [ME. *weltren,* fr. MD. & MLG. *welteren,* freq.] **1.** To tumble about or wallow, as a hog in mire; to roll while prostrate, esp. in a liquid; hence, to wallow in something regarded as sinful or degraded. **2.** To rise and fall tumultuously; hence, to be in a turmoil. — *n.* A weltering; hence, confusion; turmoil.

wel′ter, *adj.* *Horse Racing.* Of, pertaining to, or designating a race in which welterweights are carried. — *n.* *Colloq.* A welterweight.

wel′ter·weight′ (-wāt′), *n.* [From earlier *welter* a heavyweight, prob. fr. *welt* to thrash, beat.] **1.** *Horse Racing.* A weight of 28 pounds (one of 40 pounds is called a ***heavy welterweight***) sometimes imposed in addition to weight for age. **2.** A boxer or wrestler whose weight does not exceed 147 pounds.

‖**Welt′po·li·tik′** (vĕlt′pō·lē·tēk′), *n.* [G.] Literally, world politics or policy; international politics.

‖**Welt′schmerz′** (vĕlt′shmĕrts′), *n.* [G., fr. *welt* world + *schmerz* pain.] Sorrow or sadness over the present or future woes of the world; sentimental pessimism.

wen (wĕn), *n.* [AS. *wenn.*] *Med.* An indolent, encysted tumor of the skin; esp., a sebaceous cyst. — **wen′nish** (wĕn′ĭsh), **wen′ny** (-ĭ), *adj.*

wen, *n.* [AS.] A rune (ƿ) adopted into the Old English alphabet. See W.

wench (wĕnch), *n.* [ME. *wenche,* for *wenchel* child, fr. AS. *wencel, wincel,* child.] **1.** A girl or maiden. **2.** A peasant girl; also, a female servant. **3.** *Archaic.* A lewd woman; a strumpet. — *v. i.* To consort with wenches (sense 3). — **wench′er** (wĕn′chẽr), *n.*

wend (wĕnd), *v. i.* [AS. *wendan* to turn, go.] To betake oneself or direct one's course; travel. — *v. t.* To direct; proceed on; — used esp. in phrase *to wend one's way*. See WENT.
Wend (wĕnd), *n.* [G. *Wende.*] One of a Slavic people of eastern Germany, chiefly peasants of Lusatia. See SORB.
Wend'ish (wĕn'dĭsh), *adj.* Also **Wend'ic** (-dĭk). Of or pertaining to the Wends or their language. — *n.* The language of the Wends; Sorbian. See SORBIAN.
went (wĕnt), *past tense & past part.* of WEND; — now used only as a past tense of *go*. See GO.
wen'tle·trap' (wĕn't'l·trăp'), *n.* [D. *wenteltrap* a winding staircase.] Any of a genus (*Epitonium*) or family (Epitonidae) of elegant, usually white, marine shells.
wept (wĕpt), *past tense & past part.* of WEEP.
were (wûr; *also, esp. Brit.,* wâr; 4). [AS. *wǣre* (thou) wast, *wǣron* (we, you, they) were, *wǣre*, imp. subj.] See BE.
weren't (wûr''nt; wâr'-). Colloquial contraction of *were not.*
were'wolf' (wēr'wo͝olf'; wûr'-), *n.; pl.* -WOLVES (-wo͝olvz'). [AS. *werewulf*, fr. *were, wer,* man + *wulf* wolf.] *Folklore.* A person transformed into a wolf in form and usually in appetite, or a person capable of assuming a wolf's form; a lycanthrope.
wer'gild' (wûr'gĭld'; wĕr'-), **were'gild'** (wēr'gĭld'; wĕr'-), *n.* [AS., fr. *wer, were,* man + *gild* payment.] *Law.* In Anglo-Saxon and Germanic law, the price to be paid by the kindred of a manslayer to the kindred of the slain person as compensation to avoid the blood feud.
wer'ner·ite (wûr'nẽr·īt), *n.* Scapolite.
wert (wûrt; *unstressed* wẽrt; 4). See BE.
Wes'ley·an (wĕs'lĭ·ăn; wĕs·lē'ăn; *esp. Brit.,* wĕz['']-), *adj.* Of or pert. to the Wesley family or a member of it, esp. John Wesley (1703–91), founder of Methodism; specif., Methodist. — *n. Eccl.* A follower of John Wesley; a Methodist. — **Wes'ley·an·ism** (-ĭz'm), *n.*
west (wĕst), *n.* [AS., adv.] **1.** The point in the heavens where the sun is seen to set at the equinox; that one of the four cardinal points which is in a direction at right angles to that of north and south, and on the left of a person facing north. See COMPASS CARD, *Illust.* **2.** A quarter, region, locality, country, section, or the like, lying to the west. **3.** [*cap.*] Specif.: **a** The Western Hemisphere or New World so called, it having been discovered by sailing westward from Europe; also, the Occident. **b** *U. S. Hist. & Geog.* Formerly, that part of the United States west of the Allegheny Mountains; now, commonly, the whole region west of the Mississippi River, esp. that part north of Arkansas, New Mexico, etc.; — usually with the definite article. **c** *Hist.* The Western Roman Empire after the division of the Roman Empire (A.D. 395) into two parts. — *adj.* **1.** Lying toward, situated in, or proceeding toward the west; western. **2.** Facing toward the west; as, a porch with a *west* exposure. **3.** Coming from the west; — said chiefly of the wind. **4.** *Eccl.* Designating, or situated in, that part of a church directly opposite the altar or apse. Cf. EAST, *adj.*, 2. — *adv.* To or toward, or in, the west; westward.
west by north. *Navig. & Surv.* One point, or 11° 15', north of due west; N. 78° 45' W. Abbr. *Wb* (or *by*) *N.* See COMPASS CARD, *Illust.*
west by south. *Navig. & Surv.* One point, or 11° 15', south of due west; S. 78° 45' W. Abbr. *Wb* (or *by*) *S.* See COMPASS CARD, *Illust.*
West End. The western portion of London, England, including the aristocratic residence sections; hence, the fashionable quarter of any large city.
west'er (wĕs'tẽr), *v. i.* To turn or move westward. — *n.* A westerly wind, esp. a storm.
west'er·ing, *adj.* That westers, or turns westward; esp., of the sun that lies in or is descending in the west.
west'er·ly (wĕs'tẽr·lĭ), *n.; pl.* -LIES (-lĭz). A wind blowing from the west. — *adj.* Western; west. — *adv.* **1.** Toward the west; westward. **2.** From the west; as, the winds blew *westerly.* — **west'er·li·ness** (-lĭ·nĕs; -nĭs), *n.*
west'ern (wĕs'tẽrn), *adj.* **1.** Of, pertaining to, situated in, or from the west; west. **2.** [*cap.*] Of or characteristic of a region specifically called the West, as the Occident, or the part of the United States west of the Mississippi. **3.** [*cap.*] Of or pertaining to the Western Church or churches; as, *Western* liturgies. — *n.* **1.** A westerner; specif., *U. S.*, a native or resident of one of the states west of the Mississippi. **2.** *U. S.* A story, novel, or esp., motion picture, dealing with frontier or cowboy life in the West.
Western Church. **a** The portion of the Catholic Church which recognizes the pope as both pope and patriarch; the Latin Church (which see). **b** All the churches of western Christendom or of western Europe and the Americas.
west'ern·er (wĕs'tẽr·nẽr), *n.* A native or inhabitant of the west, esp. [*cap.*] of the West in the United States.
west'ern·most (wĕs'tẽrn·mōst), *adj.* Farthest west.
Western Ocean. Among the ancients, the ocean lying to the west of the then known world.
western paper birch. See BIRCH.
West Indian corkwood. = BALSA, 1.
west'ing (wĕs'tĭng), *n.* *Navig.* Departure in a westerly direction.
Wes'ting·house' brake (wĕs'tĭng·hous'). [After George *Westinghouse*, Am. inventor.] A continuous brake worked by compressed air from a pump on the engine, first used on passenger trains in 1868.
west'lins (wĕst'lĭnz), *adv.* *Scot.* Westward.
West'min'ster Ab'bey (wĕst'mĭn'stẽr). A famous church in London, orig. the abbey church of a monastery. It is a national sanctuary.
Westminster Assembly. [From *Westminster*, borough in London, where it met.] An assembly (1643–1649) which framed certain formulae of faith now accepted as authoritative by Presbyterian churches.
west'–north'west', *n., adj., & adv.* Two points, or 22° 30', north of due west; N. 67° 30' W. Abbr. *WNW.* See COMPASS CARD, *Illust.*
West Saxon, *n.* **a** A dialect of Anglo-Saxon. See ANGLO-SAXON, 3. **b** A native of the West Saxon kingdom; also, one whose native tongue was West Saxon (sense **a**). — **West Saxon,** *adj.*
west'–south'west', *n., adj., & adv.* Two points, or 22° 30', south of due west; S. 67° 30' W. Abbr. *WSW.* See COMPASS CARD, *Illust.*
West'wall' (wĕst'wôl'; *G.* vĕst'väl'), *n.* = LIMES, 2.
west'ward (wĕst'wẽrd), *adj.* Moving, lying, or facing toward the west. — *adv.* Also **west'wards** (-wẽrdz). Toward the west. — **west'ward·ly,** *adv.*
wet (wĕt), *adj.*; WET'TER (-ẽr); WET'TEST. [ME. *wet, wete, wett,* fr. past part. of the v., and fr. AS. *wǣt.*] **1.** Consisting of, covered with, or soaked with water or other liquid. **2.** Rainy. **3.** Not yet dry; as, *wet* paint. **4.** *Chiefly U. S.* **a** Not prohibiting or marked by the prohibition of traffic in intoxicating liquor; as, a *wet* town; also, opposed to prohibition; as, *wet* candidates. **b** *Slang.* Crazy; misguided; wrong; as, his ideas are all *wet.* **5.** Preserved, as by bottling, in a liquid. **6.** *Chem., Metal., etc.* Employing, or done by means of or in the presence of, water or other liquid.
Syn. Wet, damp, dank, moist, humid mean more or less soaked with water or liquid. Wet usually implies saturation but may suggest a covering of a surface with water or something not yet dry; damp implies a slight or moderate absorption or covering and often connotes an unpleasant degree of wetness; dank, a disagreeable, penetrating, often dangerous dampness; moist, absence of dryness or a slight dampness; humid, presence of sensible moisture in the air.
— *n.* [AS. *wǣt, wǣta.*] **1.** Water or wetness; moisture. **2.** Rainy or drizzly weather; rain. **3.** *U. S.* One in favor of allowing the sale of intoxicating liquors.
— *v. t. & i.*; WET or WET'TED; WET'TING. To make or become wet.
— ***wet one's whistle.*** *Colloq.* To take a drink.
— **wet'ly,** *adv.* — **wet'ness,** *n.* — **wet'ta·ble,** *adj.* — **wet'ter,** *n.*
wet blanket. A person or thing that quenches or dampens enthusiasm, pleasure, or the like.
wet'–blan'ket, *v. t.* To discourage; dispirit; depress.
wet'–bulb' ther·mom'e·ter. In a psychrometer, the thermometer whose bulb is kept moistened while making determinations of humidity; also, the entire instrument.
weth'er (wĕth'ẽr), *n.* [AS.] A castrated ram.
wet nurse. A nurse who suckles a child. Cf. DRY NURSE. — **wet'–nurse',** *v. t.*
wet pack. *Med.* A form of bath, in which a patient is wrapped in wet sheets, used esp. to reduce fever.
wet'ting, *or* **wet'ting–out', a'gent.** A substance that by becoming adsorbed renders a surface nonrepellent to a wetting liquid, used in mixing solids with liquids and in spreading liquids on surfaces.
whack (hwăk), *v. t. & i.* **1.** *Colloq.* **a** To strike, esp. with a smart or resounding blow. **b** To beat, as in a game. **2.** *Slang.* To make division; — often with *up.* — *n.* **1.** A smart or resounding blow or its sound. **2. a** A stroke; an attempt or trial. **b** A portion; share. — **whack'er,** *n.*
whack'ing (hwăk'ĭng), *adj.* *Colloq.* Very large; whopping.
whack'y (hwăk'ĭ), *adj.* See WACKY.
whale (hwāl; 127), *n.*; see PLURAL, *Note,* 3. [AS. *hwæl.*] **1.** *Zool.* Any of numerous cetaceans, esp. those of large size, in distinction from the smaller porpoises and dolphins. Whales are true air-breathing, warm-blooded, viviparous mammals. The act of spouting, or blowing, is the exhalation of air from the lungs. There are two living groups: the ***whalebone,*** *or* ***baleen, whales*** (suborder Mysticeti), including the *right whale, sulphur-bottom,* etc., which have no teeth in the adult but horny plates (see WHALEBONE) suspended from the upper jaw; and the ***toothed whales*** (Odontoceti), including *porpoises, dolphins, killers, narwhals, belugas, blackfish, sperm whales,* etc., which have numerous simple conical teeth. **2.** *Chiefly U. S.* Something impressive as in size or qualities, or superlatively good of its kind; as, a *whale* of a story. — *v. i.*; WHALED (hwāld); WHAL'ING (hwāl'ĭng). To engage in whale fishing.

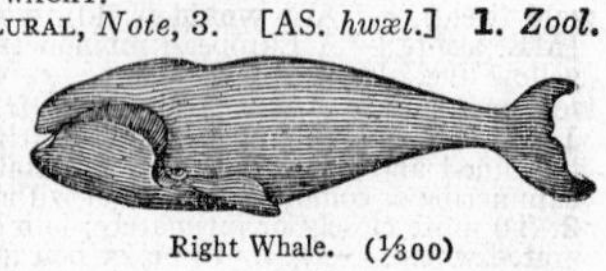

Right Whale. (1/300)

whale, *v. t.* [Var. of WALE to mark with wales.] *Colloq.* To lash; thrash; to strike hard.
whale'back' (hwāl'băk'), *n.* Something shaped like the back of a whale; specif., a freight steamer with a convex upper deck.
whale'boat' (-bōt'), *n.* A long narrow rowboat, sharp and raking at both ends, and often steered with an oar, originally used by whalers.
whale'bone' (hwāl'bōn'), *n.* **a** A horny substance growing in independent plates, from 2 to 12 feet long, attached in two rows along the upper jaw of certain whales (see WHALE, 1); baleen. It is used to stiffen stays, fans, etc. **b** Something made of this substance.
whal'er (hwāl'ẽr), *n.* **1.** A vessel or person employed in the whale fishery. **2.** A whaleboat.
whang (hwăng; *dial. also* wăng, wäng), *v. t.* **1.** *Dial.* To beat; thrash. **2.** *Scot. & Dial.* To throw or fling about violently. **3.** *Scot.* To slice; chop. — *v. i.* To strike or assail with force or violence. — *n.* **1.** *Dial.* A whack. **2.** *Scot.* A slice; chunk.
whang·ee' (hwăng·ē'), *n.* [Prob. fr. Chin. (Pek.) *huang²-li²*, fr. *huang²* yellow + *li²* bamboo cane.] **1.** A Chinese bamboo (genus *Phyllostachys*). **2.** A walking stick of whangee (sense 1).
whap (hwŏp; wŏp; wäp), **whap'per,** etc. Vars. of WHOP, WHOPPER, etc.
wharf (hwôrf; 127), *n.; pl.* WHARVES (hwôrvz), also WHARFS (hwôrfs). [AS. *hwerf, hwearf,* a bank, shore.] **1. a** A structure built on the shore of a harbor, river, canal, etc., so that vessels may lie alongside to receive and discharge cargo, passengers, etc. **b** Any structure, as a pier or dock, alongside which a vessel may lie. **2.** *Obs.* The bank of a river, or the shore of the sea. — *v. t.* **1.** To furnish with a wharf or wharves. **2.** To place upon or bring to a wharf. — *v. i.* Of a vessel, to dock.

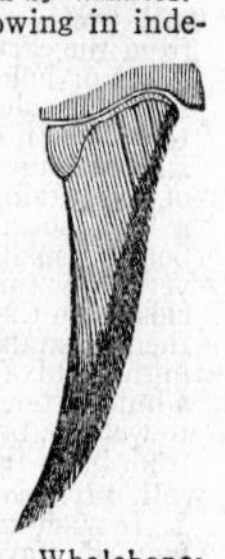

Whalebone; or Baleen, much reduced. A single plate showing articulation with upper jaw.

wharf'age (hwôr'fĭj), *n.* **1.** The use of a wharf, as for handling goods; also, fee or duty for using a wharf. **2.** A place's wharves, collectively; wharf accommodations.
wharf'in·ger (hwôr'fĭn·jẽr), *n.* [For *wharfager*, with an intrusive *n*, as in *passenger.*] An owner or manager of a wharf.
wharve (hwôrv), *n.* [AS. *hweorfa.*] *Spinning.* Orig., the small flywheel on the lower end of a spindle used for momentum; in modern spinning machinery, the small grooved pulley on a spindle, by which the spindle is driven.
what (hwŏt; 4; 127), *pron.* [AS. *hwæt*, neuter of *hwā* who.] A pronominal word used both as singular and plural. It is: **1.** An interrogative, referring to the nature or identity of an object or matter (sometimes a person in reference to his character, occupation, etc.) in question; as, *what* is this? *what* did you say? *what* is that man?; specif., of *what* value, consequence, etc. (is it)?; — sometimes followed by *if, though,* etc.; as, *what* if it be true? **2.** A compound relative, equivalent

to *which* with an antecedent demonstrative, used of both persons and things for: **a** *That which,* or *those* [persons] *who,* or *those* [things] *which;* as, you may have *what* is left. *But what* has the force of *who,* or *that, . . . not;* as, he never had any money *but what* he absolutely needed, that is, that he did not need. **b** *The kind* or *amount that; such as; as much as;* as, very much *what* we might expect. **3.** An indefinite relative: whatever; whatsoever; what thing soever; as, call it *what* you please. **4.** An indefinite pronoun: something; anything; — now only in such phrases as *I tell you what,* where *what* anticipates the following statement, being elliptical for *what I think, what it is, how it is,* etc. **—** *adj.* **1.** An interrogative, referring to the nature or identity of a person, object, or matter, in question; as, *what* child is lost? **2.** A relative, equivalent to: **a** *The . . . which* or *who; the sort* or *kind of . . . which; such . . . as;* as, we know *what* men are responsible. **b** *Any . . . which* or *that; whatever;* as, take *what* things you need. **3.** How remarkable; how great; as, *what* folly! *what* a size! **—** *n.* **a** An interrogation of "what?" **b** An exclamation of "what!" **—** *adv.* **1.** *Obs.* Why? **2. a** How? in what respect?; as, *what* does it benefit him? **b** *Obs.* How great; to what degree; — with exclamatory or intensive force. **3.** In part; partly; somewhat; — followed by a preposition, esp. *with,* and often repeated with distributive force; as, *what* with war and *what* with famine, the country was desolated. **4.** Prefixed to adjectives, as nearly equivalent to *how;* as, *what* happy boys! **—** *conj.* **1.** *Now Dial.* As much as; so far as; as, he helped them *what* he could. **2.** That; — in *but what,* but that; that . . . not; as, never fear but *what* we shall go. **—** *interj.* An exclamation expressing surprise or excitement; — often with the force of an uncompleted question.

what·ev′er (hwŏt·ĕv′ẽr), *pron.* An emphasized equivalent of *what,* used: **1.** *Colloq.* Interrogatively, expressing surprise or perplexity; as, *whatever* do you want? **2.** Relatively: **a** Anything or everything that; as, take *whatever* you want. **b** No matter what; as, *whatever* you do, take care; also, notwithstanding anything that. **—** *adj.* Of any kind soever that it may be; — often following its noun; as, no food *whatever.*

what′not′ (hwŏt′nŏt′), *n.* **1.** A nondescript object or article. **2.** A light open set of shelves used for bric-a-brac, etc.

what′so·ev′er (hwŏt′sō·ĕv′ẽr), *pron. & adj.* A more formal or intensive form of *whatever.*

whaup (hwäp; hwôp), *n.* [From one of its notes.] *Scot. & Dial.* The curlew *Numenius arquatus.*

wheal (hwēl), *n.* [ME. *whele.*] **1.** A pustule; a whelk. **2.** *Med.* A flat burning or itching eminence on the skin.

wheal, *n.* [From *weal* a wale, confused with *wheal* a pustule.] A wale.

wheat (hwēt; 127), *n.* [AS. *hwǣte.*] Any grass of the genus *Triticum,* esp. *T. aestivum;* also, the cereal grain produced by these plants, the most important food of temperate climates, and next to rice the most largely used of any grain. Some varieties of wheat (***bearded wheat***) have awned seed spikes; others (***bald,*** *or* ***beardless, wheat***) have awnless spikes. Some varieties (***soft wheat***) have soft, starchy, usually pale-colored kernels yielding a flour esp. suitable for pastry and breakfast foods; others (***hard wheat***) have flinty, usually dark-colored kernels yielding a flour esp. suitable for bread and macaroni. Specific wheats include: ***club wheat*** (*T. compactum*) with thick club-shaped spikes; ***durum wheat*** *or* ***durum*** (*T. durum*) grown esp. in southern Russia, North Africa, and north-central America, used esp. in making macaroni, etc.; ***einkorn*** (*T. monococcum*), a one-grained wheat with a short flat barleylike spike; ***emmer*** (*T. dicoccum*), or any of its varieties, grown in Russia, Germany, and in north-central North America, esp. as a stock feed; ***Polish wheat*** (*T. polonicum*), or any of its varieties, not grown extensively in the United States; ***poulard wheat*** (*T. turgidum*), or any of its varieties, suitable only for stock feed and little grown in the United States; ***spelt*** (*T. spelta*), or any of its varieties.

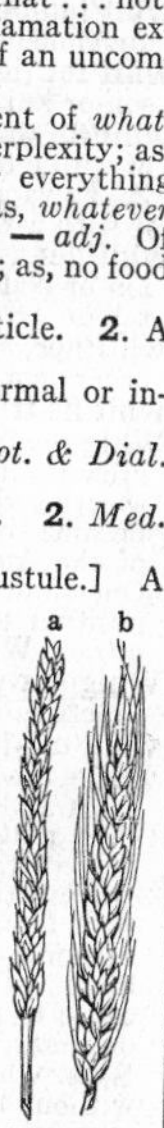

Wheat. *a* Bald, or Beardless, Wheat; *b* Bearded Wheat. (1/3)

wheat′ear′ (-ēr′), *n.* A small bird (*Oenanthe,* syn. *Saxicola, oenanthe*) of northern Europe, Asia, and America, allied to the stonechat and whinchat.

wheat′en (hwēt′'n), *adj.* Of, pert. to, or made of wheat.

Wheat′stone's, *or* **Wheat′stone, bridge** (hwēt′stōn[z]; -stŭn[z]). *Elec.* A device for the measurement of resistances, named after Sir Charles Wheatstone, English physicist. The balance between the resistances to be measured is indicated by the absence of a current in a certain wire forming a bridge or connection between two branches of the circuit.

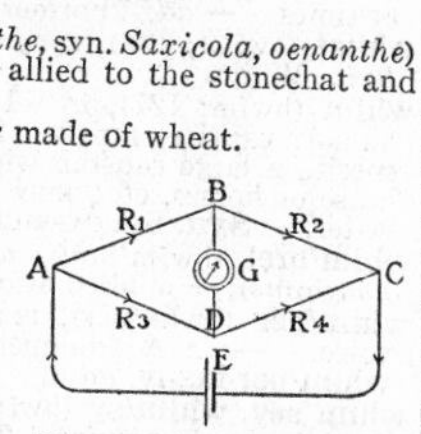

Diagram of Wheatstone's Bridge. R_1, R_2, Arms of known resistance; R_3 Resistance to be measured; R_4 Variable Resistance Arm; *G* Galvanometer; *E* Battery. When *G* shows no current, $R_1{:}R_2 = R_3{:}R_4$.

wheat′worm′ (hwēt′wûrm′), *n.* A small nematode worm (*Tylenchus tritici*) which attacks wheat.

whee′dle (hwē′d'l), *v. t. & i.;* -DLED (-d'ld); -DLING (-dlĭng). **1.** To entice by soft words or the like; cajole; flatter; coax. **2.** To gain, or get something, by flattery or coaxing. **— whee′dler** (-dlẽr), *n.* **— whee′dling·ly,** *adv.*

wheel (hwēl; 127), *n.* [AS. *hwēol, hweogul, hweowol.*] **1.** A disk, or a circular frame or body, whether solid or built up, capable of turning on a central axis. **2.** Any of various things resembling or likened to a wheel, or, *Chiefly Poetic,* shaped like an orb or disk. **3.** An instrument or device in which the chief essential consists of a wheel or wheels; specif., a bicycle; rarely, a tricycle. **4.** An obsolete instrument of torture or execution in which the limbs of a victim attached to a wheel were broken. **5.** The emblematic wheel of the personified Fortune, symbolizing the rapid alternations of human fate. **6.** A turn or revolution; rotation. **7.** Figuratively: **a** *pl.* The machinery which operates anything; the moving power; as, the *wheels* of government. **b** The directing or controlling force or element. **8.** The refrain or burden of a song. **9.** A firework which rotates while burning. **10.** *Mil. & Nav.* A movement of troops or vessels in line in which the units preserve alignment and relative positions but change direction. **11.** *Naut.* A circular frame with handles, for controlling the rudder. **—** *v. t.* **1.** To convey or move on wheels, or in a wheeled vehicle. **2.** To cause to turn; rotate; revolve. **3.** To make or perform in a circle. **—** *v. i.* **1.** To turn on or as on an axis; to revolve; also, to pivot. **2.** To go on or as if on wheels; roll forward. **— wheel,** *adj.* **— wheeled** (hwēld), *adj.*

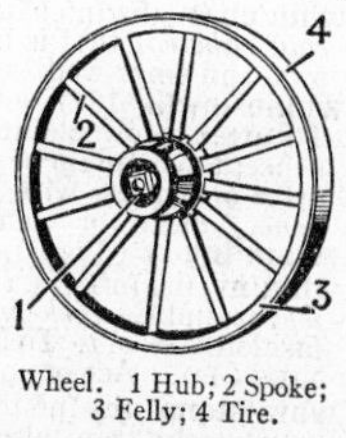

Wheel. 1 Hub; 2 Spoke; 3 Felly; 4 Tire.

wheel and axle. A device consisting of a grooved wheel (turned by a cord or chain) with a rigidly attached axle (for winding up a weight by a cord or chain), together with the supporting standards. See SIMPLE MACHINE, *Illust.*

wheel animalcule *or* **animal.** A rotifer.

wheel′bar′row (hwēl′băr′ō), *n.* A small vehicle, or barrow, with handles and, usually, one wheel for conveying small loads. Cf. HANDBARROW. **— wheel′bar′row,** *v. t.*

wheel base. In automotive vehicles, the distance in inches between the front and rear axles.

wheel bug. A large North American hemipterous insect (*Arilus cristatus*) which sucks blood of other insects; — so called from a high serrated crest on its prothorax.

wheel chair. A chair mounted on wheels, to be propelled by an attendant or by its occupant, as a Bath chair.

wheel′er (hwēl′ẽr), *n.* **1.** One who wheels. **2.** That which has wheels, as a vehicle or vessel; — now chiefly in compounds; as, a side-*wheeler;* a four-*wheeler.* **3.** A wheel horse.

wheel horse. **1.** A horse in a tandem, or one of the horses in a similar arrangement, nearest to the wheels. **2.** One in any labor or enterprise who does especially steady and effective work.

wheel′house′ (hwēl′hous′), *n.* *Naut.* A pilothouse.

wheel′ing (hwēl′ĭng), *n.* **1.** Act of one that conveys, travels, etc., on wheels; specif., cycling. **2.** A turning or circular movement. **3.** Condition of a road, or roads, which admits of passing on wheels.

wheel lock. A former kind of gunlock in which sparks were struck from a flint, or the like, by a revolving wheel.

wheel′man (hwēl′măn), *n.* One who makes wheels or tends a wheel; also, a cyclist.

wheels′man (hwēlz′măn), *n.; pl.* -MEN (-mĕn). A steersman; strictly, one who steers by turning a wheel.

wheel′work′ (hwēl′wûrk′), *n.* *Mach.* Wheels in gear, and their connections, etc., in a machine or mechanism.

wheel′wright′ (-rīt′), *n.* A man whose occupation is to make or repair wheels and wheeled vehicles.

wheen (hwēn), *n.* [AS. *hwēne, hwǣne,* a little, somewhat, fr. *hwōn* little, few.] *Scot.* A few; a group.

wheep (hwēp), *n.* Also **whee′ple** (hwē′p'l). [Imitative.] A curlew's whistle. **— wheep, whee′ple,** *v. i. & t.*

wheeze (hwēz; 127), *v. i.* [ME. *whesen,* fr. or akin to ON. *hvæsa* to hiss.] To breathe hard, and with an audible piping or whistling; to make a sound like asthmatic breathing. **—** *n.* **1.** A sound of wheezing. **2.** *Slang.* Orig., a theatrical gag, esp. one used repeatedly; hence, a familiar saying, adage, or tale; a joke or witticism, esp. an old one. **— wheez′er** (hwēz′ẽr), *n.* **— wheez′ing·ly,** *adv.*

wheez′y (hwēz′ĭ), *adj.;* WHEEZ′I·ER (-ĭ·ẽr); WHEEZ′I·EST. Wheezing, or making or having a sound like wheezing. **— wheez′i·ly,** *adv.* **— wheez′i·ness,** *n.*

whelk (hwĕlk; wĭlk; 127), *n.* [AS. *weoloc, wioloc.*] Any of numerous large marine snails (*Buccinum* and allied genera); esp., one (*B. undatum*) much used as food in Europe. See GASTROPOD, *Illust.*

whelk (hwĕlk), *n.* [AS. *hwylca,* fr. *hwelian* to suppurate.] A papule; a pustule.

whelm (hwĕlm), *v. t. & i.* [ME. *hwelmen* to turn over.] To overwhelm; engulf; hence, overpower; crush.

whelp (hwĕlp; 127), *n.* [AS. *hwelp.*] **1.** One of the young of a dog or a beast of prey; a puppy; a cub. **2.** *Contemptuous.* A youth; child; "cub." **3.** *Mach.* **a** Any of the longitudinal ribs or ridges on a capstan, windlass, etc.; — usually in *pl.* **b** = SPROCKET **a.** **—** *v. i. & t.* To bring forth young; give birth to; — said of the female of the dog or of some beasts of prey.

when (hwĕn; 127), *adv.* [AS. *hwænne, hwanne, hwonne.*] **1.** At what time? in what period? how long ago? how soon? **2.** At which time; at the same time or moment that; whereupon; as, *when* he at once consented. **—** *conj.* **1.** At the time that; at, during, or after the time that; at, or just after, the moment that; while; as, come *when* you please. **2.** In the event that; on condition that; as, *when* in doubt, win the trick. **3.** Whereas; although; — introducing a clause having a causal, conditional, or adversative relation to the principal proposition; as, he removed the tree *when* it was the best in the ground. **—** *pron.* What or which time; the or a time at which; as, Till *when* will you wait? **—** *n.* The time of a happening or action.

-when. A combining form of the adverb *when,* as in **some′when′.**

when·as′ (hwĕn·ăz′), *conj.* *Archaic.* **a** When. **b** For the reason that; as. **c** Whereas; while.

whence (hwĕns), *adv.* [ME. *whennes, whens* (with adverbial *s,* prop. a gen. ending), also *whenne, whanene,* fr. AS. *hwanan, hwonan.*] From what place; hence, from what or which source, origin, cause, etc.; — used interrogatively and relatively.

whence′so·ev′er (hwĕns′sō·ĕv′ẽr), *adv. & conj.* From what place soever; from what cause or source soever.

when·ev′er (hwĕn·ĕv′ẽr), *adv. & conj.* At whatever time.

when′so·ev′er (hwĕn′sō·ĕv′ẽr), *adv. & conj.* At what time soever; whenever.

where (hwâr; 127), *adv.* [AS. *hwǣr.*] **1.** At or in what place? hence, in what situation, position, or circumstances?; as, *where* can we expect a welcome, if not among our kin? **2.** At or in which place; at the place in which; as, the place *where* he was born. **3.** At which part, stage, or passage; — used interrogatively and relatively; as, I forget *where* we were reading; *where* do I come in? **4.** To what place? to which place; in what direction? in which direction; hence, to what goal, result, or issue? whither? whither. **5.** From what place or source; as, *where* did he get his suspicions? **—** *conj.* **1. a** At or in the place in which; as, I shall stay *where* you stay. **b** In the or a case, situation, or respect in which; as, *where* others are weak, he is strong. **2.** To the place at, in, or to which; in or to whatever place; as, let me take you *where* you live. **—** *pron.* What or which place? which place; the or a place in or to which; the or a particular or respect in which; as, *where* does he hail from? (*Colloq.*); that is *where* he made his mistake. — *n.* A place or spot; also, the place in which something is or occurs; as, all the *wheres* and hows of an event.

where′a·bouts′ (hwâr′*à*·bouts′; 2), *adv.* Now rarely **where′a·bout′** (-bout′). **1.** About where? near what place? **2.** *Obs.* About or around which, concerning which.

where′a·bouts′, *n. sing.* Also **where′a·bout′**. The place where a person or thing is.

where·as′ (hwâr·ăz′), *conj.* **1.** Considering that; it being the case that; since; — implying a recognition of facts, and often used to introduce a preamble. **2.** When in fact; while on the contrary; the case being in truth that; — implying opposition or contrast to what precedes. — *n.; pl.* WHEREASES (-ăz′ĕz; -ĭz). An introductory consideration; also, a clause, document, etc., beginning "Whereas."

where·at′ (hwâr·ăt′), *adv.* **1.** At or toward which. **2.** On which occasion; on which account; whereupon.

where·by′ (-bī′), *adv.* **1.** By or through which; by the help of which; in accordance with which; as, the truth *whereby* one lives. **2.** *Now Rare.* By what? how? why?

where′fore (hwâr′fōr; 70), *adv.* [*where* + *for.*] **1.** For what reason? for what end or object? why? **2.** *Archaic.* By reason, or in consequence, of which; why. **3.** For which reason; therefore; so; — used conjunctively. — *n.* The reason; cause.

where·from′ (hwâr·frŏm′), *adv.* From which; from which place; from what place?

where·in′ (hwâr·ĭn′), *adv.* **1.** In what? in what particular or regard? **2.** In which; in the course of or during which; as, the book *wherein* these things are found.

where·in′to (hwâr·ĭn′tōō; -tŏŏ; hwâr′ĭn·tōō′), *adv.* Into which.

where·of′ (hwâr·ŏv′; -ŏf′), *adv.* **1.** Of what; — esp., of what material, subject, etc.; as, he knows *whereof* he speaks. **2** Of which; of whom; formerly, also, with or by which; as, the persons *whereof* he speaks.

where·on′ (-ŏn′), *adv.* **1.** On what? **2.** On which; as, a foundation *whereon* to build.

where′so·ev′er (hwâr′sō·ĕv′ẽr), *adv. & conj.* In, to (or, in former use, from) whatsoever place; wherever.

where·through′ (hwâr·thrōō′), *adv.* Through which.

where·to′ (-tōō′), *adv.* **1.** To what? to what place, purpose, end, or the like? **2.** To which.

where′un·to′ (hwâr′ŭn·tōō′), *adv. Archaic.* Whereto.

where′up·on′ (-ŭ·pŏn′), *adv.* **1.** Upon or concerning what? **2.** Upon which; whereon; in consequence of which fact, happening, etc.

wher·ev′er (hwâr·ĕv′ẽr), *adv.* **1.** *Now Colloq.* Where; — used in questions expressing astonishment or puzzlement; — also written **where ever.** **2.** At, in, or to whatever place; hence, in whatever instance or situation; as, *wherever* there is need, he is lending aid. **3.** Regardless of the place where; as, he will do well, *wherever* he goes.

where·with′ (hwâr·wĭth′; -wĭth′), *adv.* **1.** With what. **2.** With which; by means of which; as, he had not the money *wherewith* to buy food. — *pron.* That with or by which; — followed by *to* and an infinitive; as, he had not *wherewith* to buy food.

where′with·al′ (hwâr′wĭth·ôl′), *adv. & pron.* Wherewith. — *n.* Also, less commonly **where·with′**. That with which anything can be purchased or done; — generally with *the;* as, he had the *wherewithal* for a dinner.

wher′ry (hwĕr′ĭ), *n.; pl.* -RIES (-ĭz). [Origin unknown.] Any of various light boats; as: **a** A long light rowboat, sharp at both ends, used, esp. in England, to carry passengers and freight on rivers and harbors. **b** A racing scull for one person. **c** *Eng.* A large light barge, lighter, or fishing boat, varying in type in different parts of Great Britain. — *v. t. & i.;* WHER′RIED (-ĭd); WHER′RY·ING. To carry in, or to sail or propel, a wherry.

whet (hwĕt), *v. t.;* WHET′TED; WHET′TING. [AS. *hwettan.*] **1.** To sharpen by rubbing on or with some substance, as a piece of stone. **2.** To make sharp, keen, or eager; excite; stimulate; as, to *whet* the appetite. — *n.* **1.** A whetting. **2.** That which whets or sharpens. **3.** *Now Dial.* A turn of work; hence, an attempt; try; also, a time; occasion. — **whet′ter** (hwĕt′ẽr), *n.*

wheth′er (hwĕth′ẽr; 127), *conj.* [See WHETHER, *pron.*] Indicating that the elements which follow are alternatives in an interrogation or statement of choice, doubt, hesitancy, etc.; — followed usually by *or,* or by *or whether.* Used: **1.** *Now Rare.* To introduce a direct question involving alternatives. **2.** To introduce an indirect question; if it be the fact, true, better, etc., that; as, ask *whether* he is going or not. **3.** To introduce alternative condition: **a** In case that; in either case, namely if . . . (or) if; as, *whether* we escape or not, we must make an attempt. **b** Either; as, to win, *whether* by hook or by crook. — *pron.* [AS. *hwether, hwæther.*] *Archaic.* Which (of two); which one (of two); — used interrogatively and relatively.

whet′stone′ (hwĕt′stōn′), *n.* A stone for whetting edge tools.

whew (hwū; hū), *interj.* An exclamation expressing astonishment mingled with scorn, relief, admiration, etc. — *n.* An utterance of "whew"; or sound like it.

whey (hwā; 127), *n.* [AS. *hwæg, hweg.*] The serum, or watery part, of milk, separated from the more thick or coagulable part, or curd, esp. in the process of making cheese. — **whey′ey** (hwā′ĭ), *adj.*

whey′face′ (-fās′), *n.* A face pale or pallid, as from fear, or one having such a face. — **whey′faced′** (-fāst′), *adj.*

which (hwĭch; 127), *pron.* [ME. *which, whilk,* fr. AS. *hwilc, hwylc, hwelc,* from the stem of *hwā* who + that of *līc* body, hence prop., of what sort or kind.] An indeclinable pronominal word, used as singular or plural, and for either persons or things. It is: **1.** An interrogative, used in both direct and indirect questions to ask for or concerning one or more of a group or number, esp. among several individuals of a class; as, *which* is the house? he asked *which* he should take; formerly, what sort of? **2.** A simple relative, introducing an added qualification or statement, sometimes a restriction of its antecedent. See THAT, *pron., Note.* It is used: **a** *Archaic & Dial.* For *who, whom, that,* referring to persons; as, "Our Father, *which* art in heaven." **b** Now referring chiefly to animals, things, or ideas, its antecedent being sometimes a phrase or clause; as, a letter *which* he wrote; a subject of *which* he knew little.

☞ *Which,* referring to a series of preceding sentences, or members of a sentence, may have *all* joined to it adjectively; as, all *which,* it may be seen, is harmful.

3. A compound relative or indefinite pronoun, standing for *any one which, whichever, that which, those which,* and the like; as, take *which* you will. — *adj.* **1.** What one or ones of (two or more); as, *which* men are guilty? **2.** That already named or referred to; as, after three days, during *which* time he had not eaten. **3.** Whichever; whatever; as, it will not fit, turn it *which* way you like.

which·ev′er (hwĭch·ĕv′ẽr), *pron. & adj.* Also **which′so·ev′er** (hwĭch′sō·ĕv′ẽr). An emphasized form of *which* implying choice among a number, used relatively and interrogatively; any (undetermined) one that; no matter which; as, *whichever* road you take it will lead you to town.

whick′er (hwĭk′ẽr; wĭk′-), *v. i. Colloq.* To neigh; whinny. — **whick′er,** *n.*

whid (hwĭd; hwŭd), *v. i. Scot. & Ir.* To whisk; frisk.

whid′ah (hwĭd′*à*), *n.* In full, **whidah bird, whidah finch.** [Alteration of *widow bird,* on assumption that it was prop. named from *Whydah* (now *Ouidah*) in Dahomey.] Any of various African weaverbirds (subfamily Viduinae) the males of which have drooping tail feathers often a foot in length during the breeding season.

whiff (hwĭf; 127), *n.* [Partly imitative, and partly fr. ME. *wheffe* vapor, whiff.] **1.** A quick puff or slight gust of air, smoke, vapor, etc.; esp., an exhalation as of tobacco smoke from the mouth. **2.** An inhalation of tobacco smoke or the like. — *v. t. & i.* **1.** To expel or puff out in a whiff or whiffs; to exhale, as tobacco smoke; hence, to smoke, as a pipe. **2.** To carry or convey by or as by a whiff; to puff or blow away. — **whiff′er,** *n.*

whif′fen·poof′ (hwĭf′ĕn·pōōf′), *n. Slang.* **a** A mythical creature of undefined character. **b** A gadget.

whif′fet (hwĭf′ĕt; -ĭt), *n. Colloq., U. S.* A small or insignificant person or animal.

whif′fle (hwĭf′'l), *v. i.;* WHIF′FLED (-'ld); WHIF′FLING (-lĭng). [Freq. of WHIFF to puff.] **1.** To blow unsteadily or in gusts; — of the wind. **2.** To vacillate. — *v. t.* To blow, disperse, emit, or expel, with or as if with a whiff or puff.

whif′fler (-lẽr), *n.* One who whiffles, or frequently changes his opinion or course; one who uses shifts and evasions in argument; an idle talker; trifler. — **whif′fler·y,** *n.*

whif′fler, *n. Hist.* A soldier or officer who instructed recruits and kept order on a march; hence, one of those clearing the way for a procession.

whif′fle·tree′ (hwĭf′'l·trē′; -trĭ), *n.* A whippletree.

Whig (hwĭg; 127), *n.* **1.** *Eng. Politics.* One of a political party which grew up in England in the 17th century during the great contests respecting the royal prerogatives and the rights of the people, and later became the Liberal party. **2.** *Amer. Hist.* **a** A friend and supporter of the American Revolution; — opposed to *Tory* and *Royalist.* **b** One of a political party in the United States formed about 1834 in opposition to the Democrats. — **Whig,** *adj.* — **Whig′gish** (hwĭg′ĭsh), *adj.* — **Whig′gism** (-ĭz'm), *n.*

Whig′ger·y (hwĭg′ẽr·ĭ), *n.; pl.* -GERIES (-ĭz). The principles or practices of Whigs, esp. of the English Whigs.

whig′ma·lee′rie (hwĭg′m*à*·lē′rĭ), *n. Scot.* A gimcrack; also, a whim.

while (hwīl; 127), *n.* [AS. *hwīl.*] **1.** A space of time, esp. when short and marked by some action or happening; a time; as, stay here (for) a *while.* **2.** Time used in doing something; labor; pains; — now only in the phrase *worth while* or *worth one's while.* — *conj.* **1.** During the time that; as long as; as, *while* I write, you sleep. **2.** *Now Dial.* Until. **3.** At the same time that; — sometimes having the force of *although,* sometimes *whereas;* as, *while* respected, he is not liked. This use of *while* is often regarded as improper. — *v. t.* To cause to pass away, esp. pleasantly or without irksomeness; to spend or pass; — usually followed by *away.*

Syn. While, wile, beguile, fleet mean to pass time, esp. leisure time, without being bored. **While** or **wile** (with *away*) implies a filling it with something pleasant, diverting, or amusing; **beguile,** an avoidance of tedium by agreeable and, usually, not time-wasting employments; **fleet,** a causing of time to pass quickly or imperceptibly.

whiles (hwīlz), *adv. Now Dial.* Sometimes; meantime. — *conj.* During the time that; while.

whi′lom (hwī′lŭm), *adv.* [AS. *hwīlum,* prop. at times, dat. pl. of *hwīl.* See WHILE, *n.*] *Archaic.* Formerly; once; of old; erewhile; at times. — *adj.* Former; sometime; as, his *whilom* friends.

whilst (hwīlst; 127), *conj.* [From WHILES; cf. AMONGST.] *Chiefly Brit.* While.

whim (hwĭm; 127), *n.* **1.** A sudden turn or start of the mind; a humor; caprice; fancy. **2.** Any of various machines for hoisting; specif., a large capstan with one or more radiating arms to which a horse or horses, etc., may be yoked, used in mines for raising ore or water. — **Syn.** See CAPRICE.

whim′brel (hwĭm′brĕl), *n.* A small European curlew (*Phaeopus phaeopus*); — applied also to other small curlews.

whim′per (hwĭm′pẽr), *v. i.* To cry with a low, whining, broken voice. — *n.* A whimpering cry or sound. — **whim′per·er,** *n.* — **whim′per·ing·ly,** *adv.*

whim′sey, whim′sy (hwĭm′zĭ), *n.; pl.* -SEYS (-zĭz), -SIES (-zĭz). **1.** A whim; freak; caprice. **2.** Whimsicality; oddity; fantastic speech or action; as, *whimsey* characterized his plays.

whim′si·cal (hwĭm′zĭ·k*ă*l), *adj.* [From *whimsey.*] **1.** Full of whims; actuated or characterized by a whim or whims; freakish. **2.** Odd; queer; fantastic. — **whim′si·cal′i·ty** (-kăl′ĭ·tĭ), **whim′si·cal·ness,** *n.* — **whim′si·cal·ly,** *adv.*

whin (hwĭn), *n.* [Of Scand. origin.] Gorse; furze.

whin, *n.* [See WHINSTONE.] Any particularly hard rock, especially one which, on weathering, cumbers the ground with large fragments; whinstone.

whin′chat′ (hwĭn′chăt′), *n.* A small European singing bird (*Saxicola rubetra*) that is brown and buff in color, frequents grassy meadows, and sings well. See CHAT, *n.,* 3.

whine (hwīn; 127), *v. i.* [AS. *hwīnan* to make a whizzing sound.] To utter a low plaintive nasal sound, esp. in complaint or distress; hence, to complain or to beg in a mean or unmanly way. — *v. t.* To utter or express with a whine. — *n.* A whining or the sound of it; hence, mean or unmanly complaint. — **whin′er** (hwīn′ẽr), *n.* — **whin′ing·ly** (-ĭng·lĭ), *adv.* — **whin′y** (-ĭ), *adj.*

whin′ny (hwĭn′ĭ), *v. i.;* WHIN′NIED (-ĭd); WHIN′NY·ING. [Akin to E. *whine* and G. *wiehern.*] Of a horse, to neigh, esp. in a low or gentle fashion. — *v. t.* To utter with or as with a whinny. — *n.; pl.* WHINNIES (-ĭz). Act or sound of whinnying.

whin′stone′ (hwĭn′stōn′), *n.* [Perh. fr. *whin* gorse + *stone.*] Basaltic rock; trap; also, any of various other dark resistant rocks, as chert.

whip (hwĭp; 127), *v. t.;* WHIPPED (hwĭpt) or WHIPT; WHIP'PING. [ME. *whippen, wippen.*] **1.** To move, take, pull, snatch, jerk, or the like, suddenly and forcibly; — usually followed by *into, out, up, off,* and the like; as, he *whipped* out a gun. **2.** To strike with a lash, whip, rod, or the like; lash; beat. **3.** Specif.: **a** To punish by lashing; flog. **b** To force, urge, or drive, by use of a whip, rod, etc. **c** To belabor with stinging or biting words. **d** To strike as a lash does; as, the rain *whips* the pavement. **4.** To overlay (a cord, rope, or the like) with other cords, rope, or the like, going round and round it; wrap; — often with *about, around,* or *over.* **5.** To wind, wreathe, or bind about something. **6.** *Colloq.* To conquer; to defeat, as in a contest. **7.** To gather together or hold together for united action, in the manner of a party whip. See WHIP, *n.*, 10 **a**. **8.** To fish (water) with rod, line, and artificial fly. **9.** To beat (eggs, cream, or the like) into a froth, as with a whisk, fork, or the like. **10.** *Naut.* To hoist or purchase by a whip (sense 5). **11.** *Sewing.* To overhand lightly; specif., to form (a fabric) into gathers by loosely overcasting the rolled edge with fine stitches and drawing up the thread. — *v. i.* **1.** To move nimbly; to start, turn, go, pass, or the like, quickly or suddenly; whisk. **2.** To thrash about in the manner of a whiplash; swish; as, flags *whipping* in the wind. — ***whip in.*** To keep from scattering, as hounds in a hunt; hence, to collect or to keep together, as members of a party, for legislative action.

— *n.* **1.** An instrument consisting usually of a lash attached to a handle used in whipping. **2.** A stroke or cut with or as with a whip. **3.** *Obs.* A sudden rush or start. **4.** One of the arms of a windmill. See WINDMILL, *Illust.* **5.** A hoisting apparatus; esp., a purchase consisting of a single block and a small rope, for lifting light articles. See BLOCK, *Illust.* **6.** One who handles a whip; specif.: **a** A coachman; a driver of horses; as, a good *whip.* **b** A huntsman who whips in the hounds. **7.** A whipping motion; a thrashing about. **8.** *Cookery.* A dish made light with whipped cream, eggs, etc. **9.** *Mach.* Any of various pieces that operate with a quick vibratory motion, as a spring in certain electrical devices for making a circuit. **10.** *Politics.* **a** Also ***party whip.*** A person, as a member of a legislature, appointed to enforce party discipline, and secure the attendance of the members of a party at any important session. **b** A call made on members of a legislative party to be in their places at a given time.

whip'cord' (hwĭp'kôrd'), *n.* **1.** A type of hard-twisted or braided cord. **2.** A cord made of animal intestines; catgut. **3.** A hard-woven worsted fabric with fine close diagonal cords or ribs.

whip hand. The hand holding the whip in driving; hence, advantage; control; as, to have or get the *whip hand.*

whip'lash' (hwĭp'lăsh'), *n.* The lash of a whip.

whip'per (hwĭp'ẽr), *n.* One who or that which whips.

whip'per–in', *n.; pl.* WHIPPERS-IN (hwĭp'ẽrz-ĭn'). **1.** A huntsman's assistant who whips in the hounds. **2.** A parliamentary whip.

whip'per·snap'per (-snăp'ẽr), *n.* A diminutive, insignificant, or presumptuous person. — **whip'per·snap'per,** *adj.*

whip'pet (hwĭp'ĕt; -ĭt; 127), *n.* [From WHIP to move nimbly.] **1.** A small swift dog of a breed developed from a cross between a greyhound and a terrier. **2.** Someone or something as small or as swift as a whippet; specif., also ***whippet tank,*** a type of small mobile and speedy armored tank, used in World War I.

whip'ping (hwĭp'ĭng), *n.* **1.** Act of one that whips; as: **a** A beating; flogging. **b** In sewing, overcasting. **2.** Material used to whip, or bind.

whipping boy. Formerly, a boy educated with a prince and punished in his stead; hence, figuratively, scapegoat.

whipping post. *Hist.* A post to which offenders are tied to be legally whipped.

whip'ple·tree' (hwĭp''l·trē'; -trĭ), *n.* [From WHIP.] The pivoted or swinging bar to which the traces, or tugs, of a harness are fastened; whiffletree; swingletree; singletree.

whip'poor·will' (hwĭp'po͝or·wĭl'; -ẽr·wĭl'; 2), *n.;* see PLURAL, *Note,* 3. [From its call.] A nocturnal bird (*Antrostomus vociferus*) of the eastern United States and Canada, allied to the European nightjar.

whip'saw' (hwĭp'sô'), *n.* A type of narrow pit saw, tapering from butt to point, with hook teeth, and from 5 to 7½ feet in length. — *v. t.* **1.** To saw with a whipsaw. **2.** To defeat in, or to cause to lose, two different bets at the same turn or in one play, as at faro; hence, to worst in two ways at once; esp., in speculation, to cause to buy high and sell low, or vice versa.

whip scorpion. Any of numerous arachnids (*Thelyphonus* and allied genera) somewhat resembling true scorpions, but usually having a long slender taillike organ, and no sting.

whip'stall' (hwĭp'stôl'), *n.*, *or* **whip stall.** *Aeronautics.* A stall during a vertical climb in which the nose of the plane whips violently forward and then downward. — *v. i.* To slip into a whipstall. — *v. t.* To put into a whipstall.

whip'stitch' (hwĭp'stĭch'), *v. t.* To sew by passing the thread over and over; to overcast; whip.

whip'stock' (-stŏk'), *n.* The handle of a whip.

whip'worm' (-wûrm'), *n.* [So called from its shape.] A roundworm (*Trichuris trichiura*) often found parasitic in the human intestine.

whir (hwûr; 127), *v. i.;* WHIRRED (hwûrd); WHIR'RING. [Cf. WHIRL.] To move, fly, revolve, etc., quickly with a buzzing or whizzing sound. — *n.* **1.** Hurry; commotion. **2.** A buzzing or whizzing sound due to rapid motion.

whirl (hwûrl; 127), *v. i.* [ME. *whirlen,* fr. ON. *hvirfla.*] **1.** To revolve or rotate with great speed; to gyrate. **2.** To move, go, pass, or the like, hastily or swiftly. **3.** To feel giddiness; to reel; as, my head *whirls.* — *v. t.* **1.** To turn round rapidly; to rotate or revolve with velocity; as, to *whirl* a top. **2.** To remove or carry quickly with or as with a revolving motion; as, the wind *whirls* along the dead leaves. **3.** *Obs.* To hurl with or as with a revolving motion. — *n.* **1.** Rapid rotation, gyration, or circumvolution; as, the *whirl* of a top, or of a wheel. **2.** Anything that moves with a whirling motion; as, a *whirl* of wind, dust, etc. **3.** Commotion; bustle; tumult. **4.** A mental state of dizziness, confusion, or distraction; as, a *whirl* of passion. — **whirl'er,** *n.*

whirl'a·bout' (-ȧ·bout'), *n.* Act of whirling about; also, a whirligig. — **whirl'a·bout',** *adj.*

whirl'i·gig' (hwûr'lĭ·gĭg'), *n.* [See WHIRL; GIG.] **1.** A child's toy having a whirling motion, as a teetotum. **2. a** A carrousel, or merry-go-round. **b** A whirligig beetle. **3.** Anything having a whirling course or motion; also, a whirling motion. **4.** *Obs. exc. Scot.* A fanciful trifle or notion.

whirligig beetle. Any of numerous beetles (family Gyrinidae) which live mostly on the surface of water and move swiftly about in curves.

whirl'pool' (hwûrl'po͞ol'), *n.* An eddy or vortex of water; water moving rapidly in a circle so as to produce a depression in the center, into which floating objects may be drawn.

whirl'wind' (-wĭnd'), *n.* [After ON. *hvirfilvindr.* See WHIRL; WIND, *n.*] **1.** A rotating windstorm of limited extent, marked by an inward and upward spiral motion of the lower air, followed by an outward and upward spiral motion, and usually a progressive motion at all levels. **2.** A rush or thing rushing likened to such a windstorm.

whirr (hwûr). Var. of WHIR.

whir'ry (hwûr'ĭ), *v. t. & i.* *Scot.* To whir; to whirl.

whish (hwĭsh; 127), *v. i.* To move with a whizzing or swishing sound; to whiz or swish. — *n.* A whizzing sound.

whisht (hwĭsht; wĭsht; *Scot. also* hwŭsht), *interj.* An exclamation equivalent to *whist.* — *adj.* Silent; hushed. — *v. t. & i.* To silence; to be silent. — *n.* A faint sound; a whisper. *All Chiefly Scot.*

whisk (hwĭsk; 127), *n.* [ME. *wisk, wysk,* of Scand. origin.] **1. a** A quick sweeping or brushing motion, as of something light; a quick light stroke, as of a brush. **b** Act of whisking. **2.** A small culinary instrument for whisking or beating eggs, cream, etc. **3.** A small bunch of grass, straw, twigs, hair, as used for brushing or lightly sweeping; hence, a small brush or broom (**whisk broom**), as for brushing clothes, etc. — *v. i.* To move nimbly and quickly; as, to *whisk* away. — *v. t.* **1.** To move, pass, carry, etc., with a quick sweeping motion; as, to *whisk* out a handkerchief. **2.** To beat or whip lightly; as, to *whisk* eggs into froth. **3.** To brush with a light rapid motion; as, to *whisk* dust, a coat.

whisk'er (hwĭs'kẽr; 127), *n.* **1.** *Dial.* A thing that whisks, as a whisk broom. **2.** *Chiefly in pl.* **a** Formerly, a mustache. **b** That part of the beard which grows on the sides of the face, or on the chin, or on both. **3. a** A hair of the beard. **b** One of the long projecting hairs or bristles growing near the mouth of a cat, bird, or other animal. **4.** *Naut. Usually in pl.* Either of two bars or rods extending on either side of the bowsprit, to spread the jib and flying jib guys; — called also **whisker boom.** — **whisk'ered** (-kẽrd), *adj.*

whis'ky, whis'key (hwĭs'kĭ), *n.* *Whisky,* pl. WHISKIES (-kĭz), is the usual spelling for imported spirits; *whiskey,* pl. WHISKEYS (-kĭz), for spirits made in the United States. [Ir. & Gael. *uisge* water, in *uisgebeatha* whisky, prop., water of life.] **1.** A distilled alcoholic liquor made from any of various grains, esp. in Scotland, Ireland, and the United States and Canada. In the United States whisky has been generally distilled from rye and maize or corn. In Scotland and Ireland whisky is often made from malted barley. **2.** A drink of whisky. — *adj.* Of, pertaining to, or like whisky; made of whisky.

whis'per (hwĭs'pẽr; 127), *v. i.* [AS. *hwisprian.*] **1.** To speak softly, or under the breath; to utter words or sounds in a whisper. **2.** To speak covertly, esp. in conspiracy or criticism. **3.** To make a low sibilant rustling sound, as of a whisper. — *v. t.* **1.** To say under the breath; hence, to mention privately and confidentially in or as in a whisper. **2.** To address or speak to in a whisper, or undertone, as in privacy or secrecy. — *n.* **1.** A low soft sibilant utterance, which can be heard only by those near at hand; speech without voice. **2.** Act of communicating, or something communicated, by or as by whispering; a secret or private utterance, word, hint, etc. **3.** A low, sibilant, rustling sound, as of whispered speech; as, the *whisper* of leaves in the wind. — **whis'per·er,** *n.*

whis'per·ing, *n.* Act of one who whispers; whispered sound, talk, rumor, etc. — *adj.* That whispers. — **whis'per·ing·ly,** *adv.*

whis'per·ous (hwĭs'pẽr·ŭs), *adj.* Also **whis'per·y** (-ĭ). Like a whisper; full of whispers.

whist (hwĭst; 127), *interj.* *Now Chiefly Dial.* An exclamation enjoining silence and attention; be still; hush. — *n.* *Ir.* Silence; as, hold your *whist.* — *adj.* *Archaic & Dial.* Silent; mute; still; quiet. — *adv.* Silently.

whist, *n.* [Earlier *whisk,* from *whisking* up the tricks, but later accommodated to *whist,* from the silence observed during play.] A card game for four players, the forerunner of bridge. See BRIDGE, *n.*, 5.

whis'tle (hwĭs''l; 127), *v. i.;* WHIS'TLED (-'ld); WHIS'TLING (-lĭng). [AS. *hwistlian* to hiss.] **1.** To make a kind of shrill musical sound, or series of sounds, by forcing the breath through the teeth or compressed lips. **2.** To emit or utter from the mouth or beak a sound like a whistle, as birds. **3.** To move, pass, go, or the like, with a sharp shrill sound; as, a bullet *whistled* past. **4.** To sound a wind or steam whistle; to blow on a whistle. — *v. t.* **1.** To form, utter, express, or modulate by whistling; as, to *whistle* a tune. **2.** To send, bring, signal, or call by or as by a whistle. — *n.* [AS. *hwistle* a pipe, flute.] **1.** An instrument for producing a shrill whistling sound; specif., an instrument in which air, steam, or the like, is forced into a cavity, or against a thin edge; as, a steam *whistle.* **2.** *Colloq.* The mouth and throat. **3.** A sharp, shrill sound, made by the expulsion of the breath in whistling or by blowing through an instrument. **4.** An act of whistling. **5.** A call or summons, as by a whistling sound. **6.** A sound likened to a whistling sound, as of wind through trees, of a bullet through the air, etc.

whis'tler (hwĭs'lẽr), *n.* **1.** One who whistles. **2.** Any of various birds; as: **a** A goldeneye. **b** *Local, Eng.* The widgeon. **3.** A thing that makes a sound like whistling. **4.** A large mountain marmot (*Marmota caligata*) of northwestern North America.

whis'tling (hwĭs'lĭng), *n.* [AS. *hwistlung.*] Act or noise of one that whistles; a whistle.

whistling buoy. See BUOY, 1.

whit (hwĭt), *n.* [For *wit,* ME. *wight, wiht,* fr. AS. *wiht* a creature, a thing.] The smallest part or particle; a bit; jot; iota; as, he cared not a *whit.*

white (hwīt; 127), *adj.* [AS. *hwīt.*] **1.** Of the color of pure snow; reflecting to the eye all the rays of the spectrum combined; — the opposite of *black* or *dark.* **2.** Hence, light or relatively light in color; as, *white* wine; *white* hair; lips *white* with fear; the snow made it a *white* Christmas. **3.** Free from spot or blemish; hence, innocent; pure. **4.** Light gray and lustrous; — of metal or metal objects, esp. silver; hence, made of silver. **5.** Clothed or habited in white; as, *white* friars. **6.** Without evil in intent; relatively harmless; as, a *white* lie; *white* magic. **7.** *Now Rare.* Fortunate; auspicious. **8. a** Having a light-colored skin; Caucasian; as, a *white* man. **b** Composed of or controlled by the white race; as, the policy of a *white* Australia. **c** *Orig. Slang, U.S.* Honest; square-dealing; honorable. **9.** Being at white heat (which see).

— *n.* **1.** The achromatic color of highest brilliance. See COLOR. **2.** Whiteness; figuratively, purity; innocence. **3.** Something white or

light-colored; as, the *white* of an egg, of the eye; dressed in *white*. **4.** A white-colored breed or variety; esp. [*cap.*], of swine, an animal of a pure-white breed distinguished, according to size, as ***Large, Middle, or Small White.*** **5.** A person with a white skin; a member of the white, or Caucasian, races of men. **6.** *Archery.* **a** *Archaic.* A white target. **b** The fifth or outermost circle of a target; also, a shot that hits it. **7.** *Chess & Checkers.* The light-colored men; also, the player having them.
— *v. t.*; WHIT′ED (hwīt′ĕd; -ĭd); WHIT′ING (hwīt′ĭng). **1.** To make white; to whiten; bleach. **2.** Hence, to give a deceptive gloss to; to gloss over; as, a *whited* sepulcher. **3.** *Print.* To make blank spaces in; — often with *out.*

white alkali. **a** *Agric.* A mixture of salts (sodium sulfate, magnesium sulfate, sodium chloride), forming a white crust on some alkali soils. **b** *Com.* Refined soda ash.

white ant. A termite.

white′bait′ (hwīt′bāt′), *n.* **a** The young of several European species of herrings, esp. of the common herring (*Clupea harengus*) and of the sprat (*C. sprattus*), esteemed a delicacy. **b** Any of various other small fishes likened to the European whitebait and used as food.

white bear. The polar bear (see 2d BEAR, 1).

white′beard′ (hwīt′bērd′), *n.* An old man; a graybeard.

white birch. See BIRCH.

white book. An official report of government affairs bound in white.

white bryony. See BRYONY.

white′cap′ (hwīt′kăp′), *n.* **1.** A wave crest breaking into white foam. **2.** **a** One who wears a white cap. **b** [*cap.*] *U.S.* A member of a self-appointed vigilance committee attempting by lynch-law methods to drive away or coerce persons obnoxious to it.

White′chap′el (hwīt′chăp′ĕl; -′l; 127), *n.* Also **Whitechapel district.** A quarter of London just east of the City, now largely Jewish.

white′-col′lar (-kŏl′ẽr; 2), *adj.* *Colloq.* Designating or pertaining to the class of salaried workers, whose duties permit a well-groomed appearance; as, *white-collar* jobs.

whit′ed sep′ul·cher (hwīt′ĕd; -ĭd). A person inwardly corrupt or wicked, but outwardly or professedly virtuous or holy; a hypocrite.

white elephant. **1.** An Indian elephant of a pale color. Such elephants are rare, and are venerated in India, Ceylon, Siam, and Burma. **2.** *Colloq.* Something requiring much care and expense and yielding little profit; any burdensome possession.

white′-eye′ (hwīt′ī′), *n.* Any of several small Old World singing birds (genus *Zosterops* or related genera, as *Z. palpebrosa* of India, or *Z. lateralis* of Australia and New Zealand). The eyes are encircled by white feathers.

white′-faced′ (-fāst′; 2), *adj.* **1.** Having a wan pale face. **2.** Having a white mark on the forehead, as a horse.

white feather. A mark or symbol of cowardice, a white feather in the tail of a cock being considered an indication that he is not a true gamecock; hence, a coward.

white′fish′ (hwīt′fĭsh′), *n.*; *pl.*, see FISH. **1.** Any of various freshwater food fishes (family Coregonidae), esp. one species (*Coregonus clupeiformis*) of northern and eastern lakes in the U. S. The ***Rocky Mountain whitefish*** (*Prosopium williamsoni*) ranges from Colorado to Vancouver Island; the ***Menominee whitefish*** (*P. quadrilaterale*) from the lakes of Maine to the Great Lakes and northward. The ***lavaret*** (*Coregonus lavaretus*) and the ***schnabel*** (*C. oxyrhynchus*) are European whitefishes. See CISCO. **2.** **a** Any of various other fishes, as the menhaden, or the young of the bluefish. **b** The beluga, or white whale.

white flag. A flag of plain white, esp. used as a flag of truce or surrender. Hence, in phrases as ***to hoist, show, or wave the white flag,*** the sign of cowardice or yielding.

white fox. See FOX.

White Friar. *R.C.Ch.* A Carmelite friar.

White′fri′ars (hwīt′frī′ẽrs), *n.* A Carmelite monastery (c. 1241–1538) in Fleet Street, London; hence, its precincts (a sanctuary till 1697) and neighborhood.

white gold. Gold alloyed with 25 per cent of nickel and zinc, causing it to resemble platinum in appearance; hence, any similar white alloy of gold.

white gum. See GUM, 5 **a.**

White′hall′ (hwīt′hôl′; 2), *n.* **1.** Also **White′hall′ Pal′ace.** A former palace in London, which stood to the north of Westminster Abbey. **2.** A thoroughfare in the Westminster section of London which is bordered by government offices; hence, figuratively, the British imperial government, or its policies.

white′-head′ed (*see Pron.*, § 2), *adj.* **1.** Having a head with white hair, plumage, etc. **2.** Fair-haired; flaxen-haired. **3.** *Ir.* Favorite; as, my *white-headed* boy.

white heat. **a** The temperature, higher than red heat (for copper and iron, from 1500° to 1600° C.), at which a body becomes brightly incandescent. **b** A state of intense mental or physical strain, emotion, etc.

white′-hot′ (*see Pron.*, § 2), *adj.* Radiating or feeling white heat.

White House, the. **a** In the United States, the executive or presidential mansion at Washington, a large freestone building, built in 18th-century colonial style, and painted white. **b** *Colloq.* The office of president of the United States; the federal executive.

white lead. **a** A heavy, white, poisonous powder consisting of basic lead carbonate, usually having the composition $2PbCO_3.Pb(OH)_2$, and forming an important pigment; ceruse; also, paste formed by grinding it with oil (**white lead in oil**). **b** Native lead carbonate; cerussite.

white leather. Leather prepared with alum and salt; tawed leather.

white lie. A lie without evil intent or in a matter of slight importance; a fib.

white line. A band or edge of something white; as: **a** A stripe painted on a road and used to guide traffic. **b** The cross section of the leafy layer of the wall of a horse's hoof. See HOOF, *Illust.*

white′-liv′ered (hwīt′lĭv′ẽrd; 2), *adj.* Having a pale look; feeble; hence, cowardly; pusillanimous.

white lupine. A Eurasian white-flowered lupine (*Lupinus albus*) widely cultivated in Europe for forage.

white′ly (hwīt′lĭ), *adv.* of WHITE.

white man's burden. The supposed duty of the white peoples to manage the affairs of the so-called backward, colored races; — originated (1899) by Rudyard Kipling.

white matter. *Anat.* White nervous tissue (esp. of the brain and spinal cord) which consists largely of medullated nerve fibers. Cf. GRAY MATTER.

white meat. Any light-colored flesh, as breast of chicken.

white metal. **a** Any of several lead-base or tin-base bearing metals. **b** Any of several white alloys, as pewter.

whit′en (hwīt′′n), *v. t. & i.* To make or become white or whiter; to blanch, bleach, etc. — **whit′en·er** (-′n·ẽr), *n.*

Syn. **Whiten, blanch, bleach** mean to change in color to white. **Whiten** implies a making white commonly by the application or addition of something from without; **blanch,** by the removal or withdrawal of color; **bleach,** by exposure or by chemical processes.

white′ness (hwīt′nĕs; -nĭs), *n.* **1.** Quality or state of being white; as: **a** White color. **b** Paleness. **c** Freedom from stain; cleanness. **2.** White substance.

whit′en·ing (hwīt′′n·ĭng), *n.* **1.** Act or process of making or becoming white. **2.** Something used to render white; whiting.

white oak. **a** A British species of oak (*Quercus sessiliflora*). **b** An American oak (*Quercus alba*) of the eastern United States, having characteristic leaves with usually seven deep, rounded, entire lobes. See OAK, *Illust.* **c** Any species of oak of the group of which the above is typical. **d** The wood of any of various species of oak.

white paper. **a** Paper of white color. **b** An official report of government affairs. Cf. WHITE BOOK, BLUE BOOK.

white pepper. See PEPPER, *n.*, 1 **a.**

white perch. A small silvery anadromous food fish (*Morone americana,* the family Serranidae) of the coast and coastal streams of the eastern United States.

white person. A person of the Caucasian race.

white pine. See PINE.

white plague. Tuberculosis, esp. of the lungs.

white poplar. **a** See POPLAR. **b** The wood of the tulip tree.

white potato. The common, or Irish, potato.

white race. The Caucasian race of mankind.

white rat. An albino rat; specif., an albino form of the Norway rat (*Rattus norvegicus*), used extensively as a laboratory animal in biological experimentation.

White Russian. See RUSSIAN, *n.*, 1 & 2; INDO-EUROPEAN LANGUAGES, *Table.*

whites (hwīts), *n. pl.* **1.** *Med.* Leucorrhea. **2.** The finest flour made from white wheat.

white sauce. Milk thickened with a mixture of flour and butter, with or without seasonings.

white slave. A woman held unwillingly for purposes of commercial prostitution. — **white′-slave′,** *adj.*

white slaver. One engaged in white-slave traffic. — **white slavery.** — **white′-slav′ing,** *n. & adj.*

white′smith′ (hwīt′smĭth′), *n.* **1.** A tinsmith. **2.** A worker in iron who finishes or polishes the work, in distinction from one who forges it.

white′tail′ (hwīt′tāl′), *n.* The white-tailed deer.

white′-tailed′ deer (-tāld′). See VIRGINIA DEER.

white′throat′ (hwīt′thrōt′), *n.* Any of several Old World warblers (genus *Sylvia*). They are white below with grayish-brown upper parts.

white′-throat′ed spar′row. A common brown sparrow (*Zonotrichia albicollis*) of eastern North America, having a square white patch on the throat.

white′wash′ (hwīt′wŏsh′), *v. t.* **1.** To whiten with whitewash. **2.** *Colloq.* **a** To gloss over or cover up, as vices, crimes, etc.; esp., to exonerate by an investigation or trial of a perfunctory character. **b** *U.S.* In various games, to defeat (an opponent) so that he fails to score or to reach a given score. **— *n.*** **1.** Any wash or liquid composition for whitening something; as: **a** A wash for making the skin fair. **b** A composition of lime and water, whiting, size, and water, or the like, used for whitening walls, etc. **2.** *Colloq.* **a** The act or an instance of whitewashing; specif., a book, verdict, investigation, etc., that whitewashes somebody or something. **b** A defeat in a game in which the loser fails to score. — **white′wash′er,** *n.*

white whale. The beluga.

white′wing′ (hwīt′wĭng′), *n.* A person, esp. a street sweeper, wearing a white uniform.

white′wood′ (-wŏŏd′), *n.* Any of numerous trees having white or light-colored wood; also, the wood itself. Specif.: *U.S.* (1) The wood of the tulip tree, used largely for house finishings, boatbuilding, woodenware, etc.; also, the tree. (2) The linden, or basswood; also, the wood. (3) The cottonwood.

whith′er (hwĭth′ẽr; 127), *adv.* [AS. *hwider.*] **1.** To what place; — used interrogatively. **2.** To what or which place; — used relatively. **3.** To what point, degree, end, conclusion, or design; whereto; — used interrogatively.

whith′er·so·ev′er (-sō·ĕv′ẽr), *adv.* To whatever place.

whith′er·ward (hwĭth′ẽr·wẽrd), **whith′er·wards** (-wẽrdz), *adv.* In what direction; toward what or which place.

whit′ing (hwīt′ĭng), *n.*; see PLURAL, *Note,* 3. [MD. *wijting.*] **a** A common European marine food fish (*Merlangus merlangus*) of the cod family. **b** The silver hake. See HAKE. **c** Any of several North American sciaenoid food fishes (esp. genus *Menticirrhus*), as the ***northern whiting*** (*M. saxatilis*), found from Cape Ann to southern Florida.

whit′ing, *n.* [From WHITE, *v.*] Chalk (calcium carbonate) prepared as an impalpable powder by pulverizing and washing, used as a pigment, esp. in putty and cold-water paints, for polishing metals, etc.

whit′ish (hwīt′ĭsh), *adj.* Somewhat white. — **whit′ish·ness,** *n.*

whit′low (hwĭt′lō), *n.* [Perh. fr. dial. *whickflaw,* for *quickflaw,* i. e., a flaw or sore at the quick.] *Med.* An inflammation of a finger or toe, esp. of the periosteal structures of the last phalanx or of the cuticle at the edge of the nail, usually terminating in suppuration; a felon.

Whit′mon′day (hwĭt′mŭn′dĭ; 2), *n.* The day after Whitsunday. It is a bank holiday in England and Ireland.

whit′rack′ (hwĭt′răk′), *n.* [ME. *whitratt, whytrat.* See WHITE; RAT.] *Scot. & Dial.* The common weasel (*Mustela vulgaris*).

Whit′sun (hwĭt′sŭn; -s′n), *adj.* Of, pertaining to, or observed at Whitsunday or Whitsuntide; as, *Whitsun* eve.

Whit′sun′day (hwĭt′sŭn′dĭ; hwĭt′sŭn·dā′; -s′n-), *n.* Erroneously, **Whitsun Day.** [AS. *hwīta sunnandæg,* lit., white Sunday; — prob. from white robes worn at baptism.] *Eccl.* The seventh Sunday, and fiftieth day, after Easter, observed as a festival in commemoration of the descent of the Holy Spirit on the day of Pentecost (*Acts* ii. 1–4); Pentecost.

Whit′sun·tide′ (hwĭt′sŭn·tīd′; -s′n-), *n.* Also **Whitsun Tide, Whit′-sun, Whit′-week′.** *Eccl.* The week beginning with Whitsunday, esp. the first three days (***Whitsunday, Whitmonday,*** and ***Whit-Tuesday***).

whit′ter (hwĭt′ẽr; wĭt′ẽr), *n.* *Scot.* A heavy draft (of liquor).

whit′tle (hwĭt′'l), *n.* [ME. *thwitel,* fr. AS. *thwītan* to cut.] *Obs. exc. Scot.* A large knife. — *v. t.;* WHIT′TLED (-'ld); WHIT′TLING (-lĭng). **1.** To pare or cut off chips from the surface of (wood) with a knife; to cut or shape by so paring or cutting. **2.** Hence, to reduce, remove, destroy, etc., gradually, as if by cutting off bits with a knife; to pare; — with *away, down, off, up,* etc.; as, to *whittle* down expenses. — *v. i.* **1.** To cut or shape wood by slowly paring it with a knife. **2.** *Dial.* To wear one or oneself out fretting. — **whit′tler** (-lẽr), *n.*

whit′tling (-lĭng), *n.* A chip made by whittling.

whiz, whizz (hwĭz), *v. i.;* WHIZZED (hwĭzd); WHIZ′ZING. [Imitative.] To hum, whir, or hiss like a speeding arrow, ball, etc. — *v. t.* To cause to whiz; esp., to rotate very rapidly. — *n.* A hissing or buzzing sound.

whiz′-bang′, whizz′-bang′, *n.* A form of small shell of such high velocity that the sound it makes in passing through the air is almost simultaneous with its explosion; also, a firecracker resembling such a shell.

whiz′zer (hwĭz′ẽr), *n.* Something that whizzes; specif.: **a** A toy that whizzes. **b** A centrifugal machine for drying grain, sugar, nitrated cotton, etc.

who (hōō; 4), *pron.; possessive* WHOSE (hōōz); *objective* WHOM (hōōm). [ME. *who, wha,* fr. AS. *hwā,* interrog. pron., neut. *hwæt.*] A substantive pronoun, either singular or plural. It is used: **1.** As an interrogative: What or which person or persons? **2.** As a simple relative; — now properly used of persons (corresponding to *which* as applied to things). See THAT, *pron., Note.* **3.** As a compound or indefinite relative, with its antecedent implied: **a** Whoever; the person or persons that. **b** One who; one that; — now only in the archaic phrase, *as who should say.*

whoa (hwō; wō), *interj.* [Var. of 1st HO.] An exclamation ordering a draft animal to stand still; hence, *Jocular,* stop!

who′dun′it (hōō′dŭn′ĭt), *n.* *Slang, U. S.* A detective story, play, or motion picture.

who·ev′er (hōō·ĕv′ẽr), *pron.* Whatever person; no matter who.

whole (hōl), *adj.* [ME. *hole, hoole, hale,* complete, all, well, fr. AS. *hāl* well, sound, healthy.] **1.** Being uninjured or without signs of injury; of a wound, healed; more widely, sound and healthy, or restored to soundness and health. **2.** Not broken or defective; unimpaired; undamaged; intact. **3.** Not divided into smaller parts or particles; not broken or cut up. **4.** Containing all its constituent parts or elements; entire. **5.** Representing the sum or aggregate of its parts, members, etc.; total; hence, undivided; not scattered, diffused, distracted, etc. **6.** Of blood (family or racial blood), unmixed with any other; now usually, having the same mother and father; as, a *whole* brother. **7.** *Colloq.* All; each one of the; as, he fought through the *whole* series of battles.

Syn. (1) See PERFECT.

(2) **Whole, entire, total, all, gross** mean including everything or everyone without exception. **Whole** implies the omission, ignoring, or abating of nothing (or no one); **entire,** often interchangeable with *whole,* sometimes distinctively implies a completeness or perfection from which nothing has been taken and to which nothing can be added; **total** implies that everything without exception has been counted, measured, weighed, etc.; **all** (usually followed by *the* or a possessive pronoun) may equal *whole,* or *entire,* or *total;* **gross,** used esp. in financial statements in place of *total,* implies that deductions, as for costs or expenses, have not been made.

— *n.* **1.** The entire thing; the whole amount, collection, body, structure, extent, etc. **2.** All that is comprehended under some concept, generic term, or abstraction of any sort; as, the *whole* of arithmetic. **3.** A totality, sum, or entirety; a complete assemblage or organization of parts or elements. — **Syn.** See SUM. — **Ant.** Part.

whole′heart′ed (-här′tĕd; -tĭd; 2), *adj.* Singlehearted; hence, sincere; earnest; as, a *wholehearted* man, effort. — **Syn.** See SINCERE. — **whole′heart′ed·ly,** *adv.* — **whole′heart′ed·ness,** *n.*

whole hog. *Slang.* Altogether; the whole way; without reservation; — in the phrase *to go the whole hog.*

whole milk. Milk from which no constituent has been removed; — distinguished esp. from *skim milk.*

whole′ness (hōl′nĕs; -nĭs), *n.* State or quality of being whole.

whole note. *Music.* See NOTE, *n.*

whole number. *Math.* An integer.

whole′sale′ (hōl′sāl′), *n.* Sale of goods by the piece or in large quantity; — opposed to *retail.* — ***by wholesale.*** In the mass; in large quantities; hence, without distinction or discrimination. — *adj.* **1.** Of, pertaining to, or engaged in the business of selling to retailers or jobbers rather than consumers. **2.** Extensive and indiscriminate; as, *wholesale* slaughter. — **Syn.** See INDISCRIMINATE. — (*see Pron.,* § 2), *adv.* In a wholesale manner; by wholesale. — *v. t. & i.;* -SALED′ (-sāld′); -SAL′ING (-sāl′ĭng). To sell or dispense by wholesale. — **whole′sal′er** (-sāl′ẽr), *n.*

whole′some (hōl′sŭm), *adj.* [ME. *holsum.* See WHOLE; 1st -SOME.] **1.** Promoting spiritual or mental health or well-being; salutary; as, *wholesome* advice. **2.** Promoting physical well-being; salubrious; healthful. **3.** Healthy; sound in body, mind, and morals. **4.** Indicative or characteristic of health, esp. physical health; robust; vigorous; hearty. **5.** *Rare.* Favorable; propitious. *Shak.* **6.** *Slang.* Safe for one to remain in, as a place, or to face, as a situation. — **Syn.** See HEALTHY. — **whole′some·ly,** *adv.* — **whole′some·ness,** *n.*

whole′-souled′ (hōl′sōld′; 2), *adj.* Noble; high-minded; sincere and zealous.

whole step. *Music.* An interval comprising two half steps, as C–D, F♯–G♯, etc.; a major second.

whole tone. *Music.* A whole step.

whole′-wheat′ (hōl′hwēt′; 2), *adj.* Made of the whole kernel of the wheat, containing all the constituents of the cleaned grain in their natural proportions.

whol′ly (hōl′lĭ; hōl′ĭ), *adv.* **1.** In entirety; fully. **2.** Totally; completely. **3.** Solely; exclusively.

whom (hōōm), *pron.* [ME. *whom, wham,* fr. AS. dative *hwām, hwǣm.*] The objective of *who.*

whoop (hōōp), *interj.* A loud exclamation or shout expressing exultation, incitement, etc. — *v. i.* [OF. *houper,* fr. *houp,* interj.] **a** To utter a loud cry; to shout. **b** To hoot, as an owl. **c** To make the sonorous inspiration which characteristically follows a paroxysm of coughing in whooping cough. — *v. t.* **1.** To utter, express, cheer, etc., with a whoop, or whoops. **2.** To call, incite, insult, drive, chase etc., with whoops. — ***whoop it,*** *or* ***her,*** *or* ***things, up.*** *Slang.* To raise a disturbance with or as if with whoops, or shouts. — *n.* **1.** The sound or utterance of "whoop"; a whooping; specif.: **a** A loud cry or shout of war, pursuit, enthusiasm, etc. **b** A hoot. **c** The sonorous intake of breath following a paroxysm in whooping cough. **2.** *Colloq.* A whooping up or about; — chiefly in *not worth a whoop;* hence, the least possible amount, degree, etc.

whoop′ee (hwōōp′ē; hwŏŏp′ē; wŏŏp′ē; hōōp′ē), *interj.* [From WHOOP.] An exclamation expressing exuberant or hilarious delight, or the like. — *n.* **a** An utterance of "whoopee." **b** A gay or lively time; hilarity. *All Slang.* — ***to make whoopee.*** To have a gay or hilarious time.

whoop′ing cough (hōōp′ĭng; hŏŏp′-). *Med.* An infectious disease, usually of children, characterized by a violent convulsive cough, returning by fits, and consisting of several expirations, followed by a sonorous inspiration, or whoop; pertussis.

whop (hwŏp; wŏp), **whap** (hwŏp; wŏp; wăp), *v. i. & t.* [Prob. partly imitative; cf. ME. *quappen* to palpitate.] *Now Dial.* **1. a** To strike quickly. **b** To move quickly. **2.** *U. S.* To throw or plump oneself; to flop. — *n.* *Now Dial.* **a** A stroke; knock. **b** A bump; fall. **c** The noise of a blow.

whop′per, whap′per (-ẽr), *n.* [See WHOP.] *Colloq.* Something huge of its kind; specif., a monstrous lie.

whop′ping, whap′ping (-ĭng), *adj.* *Colloq.* That whops or is a whopper; thumping.

whore (hōr; 70), *n.* [AS. *hōre,* fr. ON. *hōra.*] A prostitute; harlot. — *v. i.* **1.** To have unlawful sexual intercourse, esp. for hire; to be promiscuously lewd. **2.** *Bib.* To commit idolatry. **3.** To stray in a false devotion. — *v. t.* To corrupt by lewd intercourse.

whore′dom (hōr′dŭm), *n.* **1.** The practice of harlotry. **2.** Idolatry or unfaithfulness to God; hence, sinful desire.

whore′mas′ter (-mȧs′tẽr; 9), *n.* A man given to whoring; a lecher; whoremonger. — **whore′mas′ter·y** (-ĭ), *n.*

whore′mon′ger (-mŭng′gẽr), *n.* A whoremaster; a lecher. — *Now Rare.* **whore′mon′ging,** *n.*

whore′son (hōr′sŭn), *n.* *Archaic.* A bastard; *Colloq.,* a low, scurvy fellow — **whore′son,** *adj.*

whor′ish (hōr′ĭsh; 70), *adj.* That is or is like a whore; lewd. — **whor′ish·ly,** *adv.* — **whor′ish·ness,** *n.*

whorl (hwûrl; hwôrl), *n.* [Also *wharl,* fr. ME. *wharwyl, whorlwyl, wharle,* the whorl of a spindle.] **1.** The wharve, or small flywheel, of a spindle. **2.** Something that whirls or seems to whirl as a wharve; a convoluted line or convoluted lines; a coil. **3.** A type of fingerprint in which the central papillary ridges turn through at least one complete circle. **4.** *Bot.* A verticil. See INVOLUCRE, *Illust.* **5.** *Zool.* One of the volutions, or turns, of a univalve shell. — **whorled** (hwûrld; hwôrld), *adj.*

whort (hwûrt), **whor′tle** (hwûr′t'l), *n.* The whortleberry of Europe.

whor′tle·ber′ry (hwûr′t'l·bĕr′ĭ), *n.* [Earlier *hurtleberry* (also, *whortle, whort, hurt*), prob. fr. AS. *horte* whortleberry.] **a** A European species of blueberry (*Vaccinium myrtillus*); also, its glaucous blackish edible berry. **b** The huckleberry. See HUCKLEBERRY.

whose (hōōz), *pron.* [ME. *whos, whas,* fr. AS. *hwæs,* gen. of *hwā.*] The possessive of *who,* originally also of *what,* and sometimes of *which.*

who′so (hōō′sō), *pron.* Whosoever.

who′so·ev′er (hōō′sō·ĕv′ẽr), *pron.* Whatsoever person.

why (hwī; 127), *adv.* [ME. *whi, why,* fr. AS. *hwī, hwȳ,* instrumental case of *hwā, hwæt.* See WHO.] **1.** For what cause, reason, or purpose; wherefore; — used interrogatively and as a compound relative. **2.** For which; on account of which; — used relatively; as, I know no reason *why* he opposes me. — (wī; hwī), *interj.* An exclamation used in expressing surprise, impatience, hesitation, etc.; as, *why,* this is the very book I want. — (hwī; 127), *n.* **1.** That which constitutes a reason or cause. **2.** A baffling problem; enigma.

whyd′ah (hwĭd′ȧ). Var. of WHIDAH.

wick (wĭk), *n.* [AS. *wēoce, wēoc.*] A bundle of fibers, or a loosely twisted cord, tape, or tube of soft spun cotton threads, which by capillary attraction draws up a steady supply of the oil in lamps, the melted tallow or wax in candles, etc., to be burned.

wick′ed (wĭk′ĕd; -ĭd), *adj.* [ME., fr. *wicke* wicked.] **1.** Morally bad; evil; iniquitous. **2.** Bad; — with little or no moral connotation, used variously, as: **a** Fierce; vicious; — of animals. **b** That does or may harm; causing or likely to cause trouble; as, *wicked* wounds. **c** Vile; disgustingly unpleasant; as, a *wicked* odor. **d** Disposed to mischief; roguish. — **Syn.** See BAD. — **wick′ed·ly,** *adv.* — **wick′ed·ness,** *n.*

wick′er (wĭk′ẽr), *n.* [ME. *wyker, wekir,* osier, of Scand. origin.] **1.** A small pliant osier; a withe. **2.** Wickerwork; also, a piece of wickerwork, as a basket. — *adj.* Made or consisting of wicker; incased in wickerwork.

wick′er·work′ (-wûrk′), *n.* Work consisting of a texture of osiers, twigs, or rods; work made of wicker.

wick′et (wĭk′ĕt; -ĭt), *n.* [ONF. *wiket* (OF. & F. *guichet*).] **1.** A small gate or door, esp. one forming part of, or placed near, a larger gate or door. **2.** A windowlike opening; esp., a grilled or grated window, as at a ticket office, teller's desk, etc. **3.** A small gate by which the chamber of a canal lock is emptied, or by which the amount of water passing through a channel, as to a water wheel, is regulated. **4.** *Cricket.* **a** Either of the two frameworks at which the ball is bowled, now consisting of three vertical stumps stuck in the ground less than a bail's length apart from each other and spaced by two bails placed in grooves on top of them. **b** The playing pitch included between the wickets; as, a fast *wicket.* **c** The stay or turn of a batsman at the wicket; also, the period during which two men bat together; as, the fourth *wicket* added 58 runs. **d** An innings (of a batsman) that is not completed or never begun. **5.** *Croquet.* A hoop.

wick′et·keep′er (-kēp′ẽr), *n.* *Cricket.* The player who stands behind the wicket to prevent byes and if possible to catch, stump, or put out the batsmen.

wick′ing (wĭk′ĭng), *n.* Material made esp. for wicks; a loosely braided or woven cord, tape, or tube, of cotton.

wick′i·up′, wik′i·up′ (wĭk′ĭ·ŭp′), *n.* [Of Algonquian origin.] The hut used by the nomadic Indian tribes of the arid regions of the western and southwestern United States, typically elliptical in form, with a rough frame covered with reed mats or grass or brushwood (cf. LODGE, *n.*, 5; TEPEE; WIGWAM); hence, any rude temporary shelter or hut.

wic'o·py (wĭk'ō·pĭ), *n.* [Of Algonquian origin.] **a** The leatherwood. **b** The basswood *Tilia glabra*. **c** Any of various species of willow herb (genera *Epilobium* and *Chamaenerion*).

wid'dy (wĭd'ĭ), *n.* [Var. of WITHY.] *Scot.* **a** A rope of osiers; a withy. **b** A noose, or halter.

wid'dy. Dial. var. of WIDOW.

wide (wīd), *adj.* [AS. *wīd.*] **1.** Extending over a vast area; extensive; as, the *wide* world. **2.** Of a specified measure in a direction at right angles to that of length; of a designated width, or breadth; as, a table three feet *wide*. **3.** Having considerable distance or extent between the sides; not narrow; broad; as, a *wide* table. **4.** Roomy; loose; as, *wide* breeches. **5.** Distended; opened to full width; as, eyes *wide* with wonder. **6.** Of large scope or range; comprehensive; all-inclusive; as, *wide* reading. **7.** *Now Rare.* Far apart in nature, etc., from something specified; being different; — with *of*; as, views *wide* of ours. **8.** Deviating or diverging from a point aimed at, the real issue, the truth, etc.; as, a conclusion *wide* of the mark. **9.** *Agric.* Containing a relatively small amount of protein as compared with the carbohydrates and fats; — said of a feed ration. Cf. NARROW, *adj.*, 7. **10.** *Phonet.* = LAX, 5. **11.** *Stock Exchanges.* Having or showing a large fluctuation between the highest and lowest prices, amount of supply, etc.; as, a *wide* opening; *wide* prices. — **Syn.** See BROAD. — **Ant.** Strait.

— *adv.* **1.** Over or to a great distance or extent; far; widely. **2.** So as to have or leave a wide space or distance between; as, the issues are *wide* apart. **3.** So as to be wide of the mark; so as to strike far from or aside from the aim, objective, subject, truth, etc.; astray; as, the ball went *wide*; also, not cogently; discursively.

— *n.* **1.** *Chiefly Poet.* Width; a wide space or extent. **2.** That which goes wide, or to one side of the mark; specif., *Cricket*, a bowled ball that goes out of the batsman's reach. It counts as a run to the batting side. **3.** A wide, or lax, vowel. See LAX, *adj.*, 5.

— **wide'ly**, *adv.* — **wide'ness**, *n.*

wide'–an'gle, *adj.* *Photog. & Optics.* Having or covering an angle wider than the ordinary; — of certain lenses.

wide'–a·wake' (*see Pron.*, § 2), *adj.* Fully awake; hence, keen; alert. — **Syn.** See WATCHFUL. — (wīd'*à*·wāk'), *n.* Also **wide–awake hat.** A low-crowned soft felt hat.

wid'en (wīd''n), *v. t. & i.* To make or become wide or wider; to extend in width, range, etc.; as, to *widen* a path; the gulf between them *widened.* — **wid'en·er** (-'n·ẽr), *n.*

wide'–o'pen (*see Pron.*, § 2), *adj.* Opened wide; specif., lax in enforcing laws regulating or prohibiting the sale of liquors, etc.; tolerating gambling, vice, etc.; as, a *wide-open* town.

wide'spread' (wīd'sprĕd'; 2), *adj.* **1.** Widely extended; spread far or as far as possible. **2.** Widely distributed, scattered, communicated, effective, etc. — **wide'–spread'ing**, *adj.*

widg'eon, wi'geon (wĭj'ŭn), *n.; see* PLURAL, *Note*, 3. **1.** Any of several fresh-water ducks (genus *Mareca*) in size between the teal and the mallard. **2.** *Obs.* A simpleton.

wid'ow (wĭd'ō), *n.* [AS. *weoduwe, widuwe, wuduwe.*] **1. a** A woman who has lost her husband by death; the female survivor of a marital union. Cf. GRASS WIDOW. **b** A woman who has not remarried after the death of her husband. **2.** *Card Playing.* In various games, any extra hand or part of a hand, as one dealt to the table. **3.** *Print.* A short line or a single word carried over from the foot of one column or page to the top of the next. — *v. t.* **1.** To reduce to the state of a widow; to bereave of a husband; as, thousands *widowed* by the war. *Now Rare*, except in past participle. **2.** *Rare.* **a** To endow with a widow's right. **b** To survive as the widow of. **3.** To deprive of anything esteemed; to bereave. — *adj. Now Dial.* Widowed.

widow bird. [*widow* + *bird*; — from the somber color of its plumage and long black tail feathers.] A whidah bird.

wid'ow·er (wĭd'ō·ẽr), *n.* A man who has lost his wife by death, and has not married again. Cf. GRASS WIDOWER.

wid'ow·hood (-hŏŏd), *n.* State of being a widow or, *Rare*, a widower; time during which one is widowed.

wid'ow's cruse (wĭd'ōz). An inexhaustible supply; — from the story in 2 Kings iv. 1–7. Cf. 1 Kings xvii. 10–16.

widow's mite. A small contribution, willingly given, that is all one can afford; — in allusion to Mark xii. 42.

widow's peak. See PEAK, *n.*, 5.

width (wĭdth), *n.* **1.** The dimension of an object measured across from side to side or in a direction at right angles to the length. **2.** The fact, state, or property of being wide or having breadth; wideness. **3.** Something that has width; specif., one of the breadths, or measured and cut pieces, which are sewed together to make a skirt.

width'way' (-wā'), *n.* The direction of the width. — *adv.* Also **width'ways'** (-wāz'). Along the width.

width'wise' (-wīz'), *adv.* Widthway.

wield (wēld), *v. t.* [AS. *wyldan, wieldan, wealdan.*] **1.** *Obs.* **a** To govern; rule. **b** To manage; to deal with. **2.** To use (an implement, etc.) with full command or power; to handle with skill, effectiveness, etc.; as, to *wield* a sword or a spade; to *wield* a pen or a brush. **3.** To exercise one's power or authority by means of (a staff, scepter, etc.); hence, to exercise (power, sovereignty, etc.). — **Syn.** See HANDLE. — **wield'a·ble**, *adj.* — **wield'er**, *n.*

wield'y (wēl'dĭ), *adj.* Capable of being wielded; manageable; wieldable; — opposed to *unwieldy.*

Wie'ner schnit'zel (vē'nẽr shnĭt'sĕl). = SCHNITZEL.

wie'ner·wurst' (wē'nẽr·wûrst'; -wŏŏrst'), *n.* [G., fr. *Wiener* of Vienna + *wurst* sausage.] *U. S.* A variety of sausage, usually of mixed beef and pork, made in a shorter and more slender link than a frankfurter; — often shortened to **wie'ner.**

wife (wīf), *n.; pl.* WIVES (wīvz). [ME. *wif* wife, woman, fr. AS. *wīf.*] **1.** A woman; an adult female. *Rare*, exc. in dialect and in certain compounds and phrases; as, old *wives'* tales. **2.** A woman united to a man in lawful wedlock; spouse; — correl. of *husband.* — **wife'dom**, *n.* — **wife'hood**, *n.*

wife'less, *adj.* Without a wife, as a bachelor or widower. — **wife'less·ness**, *n.*

wife'ly (wīf'lĭ), *adj.;* -LI·ER (-lĭ·ẽr); -LI·EST. Befitting, like, or pertaining to a wife.

wig (wĭg), *n.* [From PERIWIG.] A manufactured covering of hair for the head, either imitating a natural growth, or supplying a coiffure; a periwig; peruke. Cf. TOUPEE. — *v. t.;* WIGGED (wĭgd); WIG'GING (wĭg'ĭng). **1.** To supply or provide with a wig or wigs. **2.** *Colloq.* To censure or rebuke; to scold severely. — **wigged** (wĭgd), *adj.*

wig'an (wĭg'ăn), *n.* [From *Wigan*, Lancashire, Eng.] A canvas-like cotton fabric, used to stiffen parts of garments.

wig'ger·y (wĭg'ẽr·ĭ), *n.; pl.* -GERIES (-ĭz). A wig; a peruke; also, wigs collectively; the use of wigs.

wig'ging (wĭg'ĭng), *n.* *Colloq.* A scolding.

wig'gle (wĭg''l), *v. i.;* WIG'GLED (-'ld); WIG'GLING (-lĭng). [ME. *wigelen* to totter, reel.] Originally, to wobble; stagger; now chiefly, to move to and fro with a quick jerky or shaking motion; to waggle; wriggle. — *v. t.* To cause to wiggle, or shake or move jerkily; as, a dog *wiggles* his tail.

— *n.* **1.** Act of wiggling; a wriggle. **2.** A dish of creamed shellfish or fish with peas. — **wig'gly** (wĭg'lĭ), *adj.*

wig'gler (wĭg'lẽr), *n.* **1.** One who or that which wiggles. **2.** The larva or pupa of the mosquito; a wriggler. **3.** *Angling.* A type of casting lure that makes a jerky to-and-fro motion. See LURE, *Illust.*

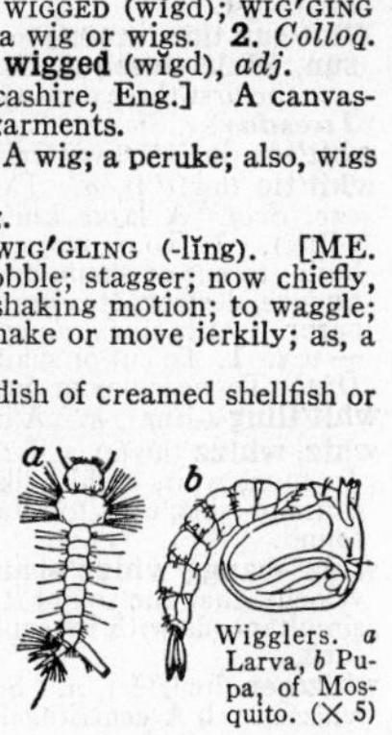

Wigglers. *a* Larva, *b* Pupa, of Mosquito. (× 5)

wight (wīt), *n.* [AS. *wiht* creature, thing.] *Now Jocose or Archaic.* A creature; a living being.

wight, *adj.* [ME. *wight, wiht*, fr. ON. *vīgr* in fighting condition, neut. *vīgt;* akin to ON. *vīg* war.] *Archaic & Dial.* **1.** Brave; valiant; also, strong; powerful. **2.** Loud; rough; also, active; nimble.

wig'wag' (wĭg'wăg'), *v. t. & i.;* -WAGGED' (-wăgd'); -WAG'GING (-wăg'ĭng). [See WAG, *v.*] **1.** To move to and fro; to wag. **2.** *Mil. & Nav.* To signal by means of a flag, or portable light, waved according to a code. — *n. Mil. & Nav.* Act or art of wigwagging; also, a message wigwagged; — used chiefly attributively; as, the *wigwag* system or code. See SEMAPHORE, *Illust.* — **wig'wag'ger**, *n.*

wig'wam (wĭg'wŏm; -wôm), *n.* [Of Algonquian origin; cf. Ojibway *wigiwam* lodge, tent, prop., their dwelling.] **1.** A cabin or hut of the Indians of the region of the Great Lakes and eastward, formed of a framework of poles overlaid with bark, rush mats, or hides. Cf. LODGE, *n.*, 5; TEPEE; WICKIUP. **2.** *Slang, U. S.* **a** Any large structure, formerly often temporary and of rude construction, used for political conventions, etc. **b** [*cap., with the.*] = TAMMANY HALL.

wik'i·up' (wĭk'ĭ·ŭp'). Var. of WICKIUP.

wild (wīld), *adj.* [AS. *wilde.*] **1.** Living in a state of nature; not domesticated; as, a *wild* boar; a *wild* ox. **2.** Growing, produced, or prepared without the aid and care of man; not cultivated; as, *wild* honey. **3.** Not inhabited or cultivated; hence, waste; desolate; as, *wild* land. **4.** Savage; uncivilized; as, the *wild* tribes of Africa; of animals, destructive; ferocious. **5.** Impatient of, or not subjected to, restraint or regulation; as: **a** Turbulent; stormy; as, a *wild* coast. **b** Inordinate; unrestrained; as, *wild* passions. **c** Boisterous; gay. **d** Fantastic in appearance or in nature; as, his *wild* garb; of ideas, plans, or the like, visionary; crazy; as, a *wild* project. **e** *Colloq.* Licentious; dissolute. **6.** *Colloq.* Eager, as with desire, enthusiasm, or anticipation; keen; as, horses *wild* to start; also, angry; vexed; as, when he heard the news, he was *wild*. **7.** Erratic; as, a *wild* remark; deviating from an intended aim or object; as, a *wild* pitch in baseball. **8.** *Cards.* Having its denomination determined by the will of the holder; — said of a card; as, to play with deuces *wild*.

— *adv.* **1.** Wildly; as, to talk *wild*. **2.** Without regulation or control; as, an engine running *wild*.

— *n.* An uninhabited, uncultivated tract or region, as a forest or desert; a wilderness; waste. — ***the wild.*** The wilderness or, by extension, wild, or free, natural life; as, the call of *the wild*.

wild allspice. The spicebush (see BENZOIN, 2).

wild boar. See BOAR, 2.

wild brier. Any uncultivated species of brier; specif.: **a** The dog rose. **b** The sweetbrier.

wild carrot. A Eurasian plant (*Daucus carota*), the original of the cultivated carrot; Queen Anne's lace. It is widely naturalized as a weed. Its root is acrid and unpleasant.

wild'cat' (wīld'kăt'), *adj.* **1.** Not sound or safe; as, a *wildcat* scheme; *wildcat* currency, such as was issued by a *wildcat* bank (see WILDCAT BANK). **2.** Designating any business, promotion, procedure, or the like, considered outside the bounds of legitimate practice; as, *wildcat* brands of canned goods. **3.** Started by a local union or small group of workers without authorization from responsible union officers or in violation of contract; as, a *wildcat* strike or walkout. — *n.; see* PLURAL, *Note*, 3. Also **wild cat, wild'–cat'.** **1.** A European native cat (*Felis sylvestris*), similar in color to the domestic tabby cat, but larger, stronger, and having a shorter, blunter tail. That it is the parent stock of domestic cats is doubtful. **2.** Any of the small or medium-sized undomesticated cats, as a lynx. **3.** Figuratively, any savage, quick-tempered, hard-fighting person. **4.** An unsound business, promotion, etc. **5.** *Petroleum.* Any well drilled for oil or gas in territory which is not known to be productive. — *v. t.* In petroleum exploration, to prospect and drill experimental wells in (some territory not known to be productive).

wildcat bank. *Colloq., U. S.* Before the enactment of the National Bank Act of 1863–64, a bank which issued notes in excess of its capacity to redeem them.

wild'cat'ter (wīld'kăt'ẽr), *n.* *Colloq., U. S.* **a** One who drills wells in the hope of finding oil in territory not known to be an oil field. **b** One who promotes unsafe and unreliable enterprises. — **wild'cat'ting**, *n. & adj.*

wild celery. The tape grass.

wil'de·beest' (wĭl'dĕ·bēst'; vĭl'dĕ·bāst'), *n.; see* PLURAL, *Note*, 3. [S. Afr. D., fr. D. *wild* wild + *beeste* beast.] A gnu.

wil'der (wĭl'dẽr), *v. t.* [Prob. fr. *wilderness.*] *Now Chiefly Poetic.* To lead astray; to bewilder; perplex. — *v. i.* To stray; wander. — **wil'der·ment**, *n.*

wil'der·ness (-nĕs; -nĭs), *n.* [ME. *wilderness*, fr. *wilderne* wild, wilderness, fr. AS. *wilddēoren*, fr. *wilddēor* wild beast, fr. *wildor.*] **1.** A tract or region uncultivated and uninhabited by human beings; a wild; waste; hence, a pathless waste of any kind; as, a *wilderness* of sea. **2.** *Obs.* Quality or state of being wild; wildness. **3.** A confusing multitude or mass; as, such a *wilderness* of things to do.

wild fig. Caprifig.

wild′fire′ (wīld′fīr′), *n.* **1.** A destructive conflagration. **2.** An inflammable composition very hard to quench when kindled; Greek fire; — chiefly in the phrase, *to spread like wildfire*, to spread, or be diffused, rapidly; — of news, rumor, etc. **3.** The ignis fatuus, and similar phosphorescent appearances. **4. a** *Now Rare.* Erysipelas. **b** A disease of sheep, attended with inflammation of the skin.
wild flax. a The gold-of-pleasure. **b** The toadflax *Linaria vulgaris.*
wild flower, *or* **wild′flow′er** (wīld′flou′ẽr), *n.* The flower of a wild or uncultivated plant; also, the plant.
wild fowl, *or* **wild′fowl′** (wīld′foul′), *n.* Wild game and water birds; now, esp., wild ducks and geese; also, one of these birds. — **wild′-fowl′er,** *n.* — **wild′-fowl′ing,** *n. & adj.*
wild goose. Any undomesticated goose; esp., in England, the graylag; in America, the Canada goose. Cf. BRANT.
wild′-goose′ chase. A pursuit after something as unlikely to be caught as a wild goose; hence, a futile chase.
wild honeysuckle. See AZALEA, 3.
Wild Hunt. In European folklore, a nighttime chase or rushing of spectral hunters through the wilderness or athwart the sky, led by the **Wild Huntsman,** who was probably originally Odin, or Woden.
wild hyacinth. a A North American bulbous plant (*Camassia esculenta*) with linear basal leaves and white racemose flowers. **b** The wood hyacinth.
wild indigo. Any of a genus (*Baptisia*) of American plants; esp., a tumbleweed (*B. tinctoria*) having bright-yellow flowers and trifoliolate leaves with cuneate leaflets.
wild′ing (wīl′dĭng), *n.* **1. a** A wild or uncultivated plant; esp., a wild apple or crab-apple tree; also, the fruit of such a tree. **b** An escape. **2.** Hence, a variant from the mass of persons or things. — *adj.* Not tame, domesticated, or cultivated; wild.
wild lettuce. Any uncultivated species of lettuce which becomes a weed; specif., a species (*Lactuca virosa*) with prickly stems and yellow flower heads.
wild′ling (wīld′lĭng), *n.* [*wild*, adj. + 1st *-ling.*] **a** A wild flower or plant. **b** A wild animal.
wild′ly (-lĭ), *adv.* In a wild manner.
wild madder. a = MADDER, 1 & 2. **b** Either of two species of bedstraw (*Gallium mollugo* or *G. tinctorium*).
wild mandrake. The May apple.
wild mustard. The charlock.
wild′ness, *n.* **1.** Quality or state of being wild (in any sense). **2.** *Obs.* A wild, or waste, place.
wild oat *or* **oats.** Any of a genus (*Avena*) of wild grasses, esp. a European species (*A. fatua*), a common weed in meadows and pastures. — ***sow one's wild oats.*** To commit follies in youth.
wild olive. Any of many trees more or less like the olive, or having olivelike fruit.
wild pansy. See PANSY.
wild parsley. Any of numerous wild plants of the carrot family with parsleylike foliage.
wild parsnip. The wild original form of the cultivated parsnip, found as a weed in both Europe and America.
wild pink. Any of certain American plants of the genus *Silene*, esp. *S. pennsylvanica* of the eastern United States. Cf. ANTHOPHORE, *Illust.*
wild rice. A tall aquatic North American perennial grass (*Zizania aquatica*) yielding a grain used for food.
wild rose. Any of various roses, as the sweetbrier, growing without cultivation in the North Temperate Zone. See ROSE.
wild rubber. Rubber derived from uncultivated trees (esp. *Hevea brasiliensis* in Brazil).
wild rye. Any of several grasses (genus *Elymus*) like rye.
wild vanilla. A perennial herb (*Trilisa odoratissima*) of the southeastern United States, the leaves of which have the fragrance of vanilla.
wild West. The western United States in its frontier and lawless period; — often used attributively.
wild′wood′ (wīld′wo͝od′), *n.* A wild or unfrequented wood.
wild yam. Any of various uncultivated species of yam (genus *Dioscorea*), as *D. paniculata* of eastern North America.
wile (wīl), *n.* [ME. *wile, wil*, prob. fr. ONF. var. of OF. *guile*, fr. AS. *wigle* divination, sorcery.] **1.** A trick or stratagem; a sly artifice; also, loosely, a beguiling or playful trick; as, coquettish *wiles.* **2.** Trickery; deceit; as, a man of *wile* and subtlety. — **Syn.** See TRICK. — *v. t.* **1.** To lure by or as by a magic spell; to beguile; allure. **2.** [Confused with *while.*] To while; to pass or spend pleasurably; — often with *away.* — **Syn.** See WHILE.
wil′ful, wil′ful·ly, wil′ful·ness. Vars. of WILLFUL, etc.
wil′i·ly (wīl′ĭ·lĭ), *adv.* In a wily manner.
wil′i·ness (-ĭ·nĕs; -nĭs), *n.* Quality or state of being wily.
will (wĭl), *n.* [AS. *willa, will.*] **1.** Wish or desire; specif.: **a** Inclination; pleasure. **b** Appetite or passion. **c** Purpose; choice; intention. **2.** What is wished by another; esp., the choice or determination of one who has authority. Hence, a request, command, or decree. **3.** Power coupled with desire or intention; specif.: **a** Arbitrary power to control, dispose, or determine. **b** Self-control; as, a man of iron *will.* **4.** The act or experience of willing; specif.: **a** The settlement of mental uncertainty or indecision; a volition (in sense 2). **b** The total conscious process involved in effecting a decision. **5.** The power of choosing; also, the power of choosing and of acting in accordance with choice; as, freedom of the *will;* sometimes, in a broader sense, a disposition to act according to certain principles or ideals; as, the *will* to power, success; the *will* to live, to do. **6.** *Law.* The legal declaration of a person's mind as to the manner in which he would have his estate disposed of after his death; the written instrument, legally executed, by which a man makes disposition of his estate, to take effect after his death.
— *v. t.* Indic. present, I *will*, thou *willest*, he *wills* or *willeth;* we, you, they *will.* [AS. *willian.*] **1.** *Archaic.* To wish or long for; to desire. **2.** *Obs.* To enjoin or command; to order. **3.** To determine by an act of choice; hence, to ordain; decree. **4.** To influence by one's will, as through hypnotism. **5.** To give or direct the disposal of by will or testament; to bequeath; devise. — *v. i.* To exercise volition; to choose.
will, *v. t. & auxiliary; pres. indic., sing.*, 1st & 3d pers. WILL, 2d WILT (wĭlt), *pl.* WILL; *past* WOULD (wo͝od); *past part.* (*Obs.*) WOLD (wōld), WOULD. Infinitive and imperative lacking. [AS. *willan*, pres. indic., 1st pers. *wille*, 2d pers. *wilt*, 3d pers. *wil(l)e*, pret. *wolde.*] **1.** As *verb transitive:* Wish; desire; — now chiefly in the form *would* (which see). **2.** As an auxiliary verb followed by the infinitive without *to:* **a** Am (is, are, etc.) willing or desirous to, or, emphatically, determined to; choose to. Hence, simply, am (is, are, etc.) to; — forming future-tense phrases (see SHALL). **b** Am (is, are, etc.) accustomed to; have a practice or habit to. **c** Can; as, the word *will* bear that construction. — *v. i.* To be willing; to be inclined or disposed; to be pleased; to wish; desire.
☞ This word has been confused with 1st *will, v. i.*, to choose, which, unlike this, is entirely of the weak conjugation.
will I, nill I, or will ye, nill ye, or will he, nill he. [See NILL, *v.*] Whether I, you, or he will it or not; hence, without choice; compulsorily; — sometimes corrupted into *willy-nilly.*
will′a·ble (wĭl′ȧ·b'l), *adj.* That may be willed, wished, determined by will, etc.
willed (wĭld), *adj.* Having a will; — chiefly in composition; as, strong-*willed;* weak-*willed.*
wil′lem·ite (wĭl′ĕm·īt), *n.* [After *Willem* I, King of the Netherlands.] *Mineral.* Native zinc orthosilicate, Zn_2SiO_4, occurring in hexagonal prisms and also in massive or granular forms, and varying in color. H., 5.5. Sp. gr., 3.89–4.18. Cf. TROOSTITE.
wil′let (wĭl′ĕt; -ĭt), *n.; see* PLURAL, *Note*, 3. [Imitative.] A large shore bird (*Catoptrophorus semipalmatus*) of central North America. Its loud whistle resembles the syllables *pilly-will-willet.*
will′ful, wil′ful (wĭl′fo͝ol; -f'l), *adj.* [*will* + *full.*] **1.** Self-determined; intentional; as, *willful* murder. **2.** Governed by will without yielding to reason; obstinate; stubborn; as, a *willful* man or horse. — **Syn.** See VOLUNTARY: UNRULY. — **will′ful·ly, wil′ful·ly,** *adv.* — **will′ful·ness, wil′ful·ness,** *n.*
Wil′liam, *or* **Wil′helm, Tell** (wĭl′yăm, vĭl′hĕlm, tĕl). A legendary Swiss patriot sentenced by an Austrian governor to shoot an apple from his own son's head.
wil′lies (wĭl′ĭz), *n. pl. Slang, U. S.* A fit of nervousness; — usually with *the.*
will′ie-waucht′, will′ie-waught′ (wĭl′ĭ·wäKt′; -wôKt′; wŭl′ĭ-), *n. Scot.* A deep draft, as of ale.
will′ing, *adj.* **1.** Inclined or favorably disposed in mind; desirous; ready. **2.** Ready to act; prompt to do, give, grant, etc.; not slow, lazy, or reluctant. **3.** Accepted, done, given, etc., of choice, or without reluctance; voluntary; as, a *willing* sacrifice. **4.** Of or pertaining to the will or power of choosing; volitional. — **Syn.** See VOLUNTARY. — **will′ing·ly,** *adv.* — **will′ing·ness,** *n.*
will′-o′-the-wisp′ (wĭl′ō·thē·wĭsp′), *n.* Ignis fatuus; hence, figuratively, a misleading or elusive object. — **will′-o′-the-wisp′,** *adj.*
wil′low (wĭl′ō), *n.* [ME. *wilowe, wilwe*, fr. AS. *welig.*] **1.** Any of a genus (*Salix*) of trees and shrubs typifying a family (Salicaceae, the willow family) characterized by small apetalous flowers in aments. The willow has tough pliable shoots used in basketry, etc. The ***weeping willow*** (*S. babylonica*) has long slender hanging branches, is a native of Asia, and is widely cultivated as an ornamental tree. **2.** The wood of the willow; hence, *Colloq.*, something made of that wood, as a cricket bat. **3.** *Textile Mfg.* A machine in which cotton or wool is opened and cleansed by long spikes projecting from a drum or drums revolving in a box studded (internally) with spikes. — *adj.* Of or pert. to the willow; made of willow wood. — *v. t.* [See WILLOW, 3.] To open and cleanse, as cotton, flax, or wool, with or as with a willow. — **wil′low·er** (wĭl′ō·ẽr), *n.*
willow herb. a A perennial herb (*Chamaenerion angustifolium*) of the North Temperate Zone, having narrow willowlike leaves and showy rose-purple flowers; — called also *great willow herb;* also, any other species of this genus or of a related genus (*Epilobium*). **b** The loosestrife *Lythrum salicaria.*
willow oak. A medium-to-large-sized oak (*Quercus phellos*) of moist locations in the eastern United States, with willowlike, linear, entire leaves. See OAK, *Illust.*
willow pattern. [From the *willow* tree in the design.] *Pottery.* A design used in decorating china, orig. the blue china of Nanking, introduced in English earthenware by Thomas Turner of Caughley, England, about 1780. Hence **wil′low-ware′** (wĭl′ō·wâr′).
wil′low·y (wĭl′ō·ĭ), *adj.* **1.** Abounding with willows; edged, as a walk, with willow trees. **2.** Resembling a willow; pliant; of persons, tall and graceful.
wil′ly (wĭl′ĭ), *v. t.;* WIL′LIED (-ĭd); WIL′LY·ING. To willow, as cotton, flax, or wool.
wil′ly (wĭl′ĭ), *n.* [AS. *wilige.*] = WILLOW, *n.*, 3.
will′yard (wĭl′yẽrd; wŭl′-), **will′yart** (-yẽrt), *adj. Chiefly Scot.* **a** Wild; willful. **b** Bewildered; also, shy.
wil′ly-nil′ly (wĭl′ĭ·nĭl′ĭ), *adv. & adj.* Having no regard for one's wishes; without choice; compulsorily. See *will I, nill I*, etc., under 2d WILL.
Wil′son's thrush (wĭl′s'nz). The veery.
Wilson's warbler. A small North American fly-catching warbler (*Wilsonia pusilla*), yellow with a black crown.
wilt (wĭlt), *v. i.* [Also *welt*, dial. var. of *welk* to fade.] **1.** To lose freshness and become flaccid, as a plant on a dry day, or when cut; to droop. **2.** To grow weak or faint; to languish; flag; as, she *wilted* for shame and grief; hence, *Colloq.*, to lose courage, spirit, or the like; as, to *wilt* before an accuser's gaze. — *v. t.* **1.** To cause to droop; to make flaccid, as a plant. **2.** To cause to languish; to lower in spirit, force, or vigor. — *n.* **1.** Act of wilting; in persons, a state of depression, weakness, or faintness. **2.** Also **wilt disease. a** A disease of certain caterpillars, highly infectious, with great mortality, aiding greatly in reducing the abundance of many species, such as the gypsy moth. When the caterpillar dies its body liquefies and becomes flaccid, hence the name. **b** *Plant Pathol.* Any of numerous fungous and bacterial diseases characterized by wilting and withering of the leaves.
wilt (wĭlt), *2d pers. sing.* of WILL, *v. t. & auxiliary.*
Wil′ton, *n.*, *or* **Wil′ton car′pet** *or* **rug** (wĭl′t'n; -tŭn). A type of carpet or rug woven with loops like the Brussels carpet, but having the loops cut, forming an elastic velvet pile; — so called because first made at Wilton, Eng.
Wilt′shire (wĭlt′shĭr; -shẽr), *n.* [From *Wiltshire*, England.] A pure-white sheep of an old English breed having long spirally curved horns and a long arched head.
Wiltshire cheese. An English variety of Cheddar cheese.
wil′y (wīl′ĭ), *adj.;* WIL′I·ER (-ĭ·ẽr); WIL′I·EST. [From WILE.] Full of wiles; crafty. — **Syn.** See SLY.
wim′ble (wĭm′b'l), *n.* [ME., through ONF., fr. MD. *wimpel*, MLG.

wimmel.] Any of various instruments for boring holes; as: **a** A gimlet. **b** A form of brace. **c** An auger for boring in earth; a scoop to clear out a bored hole. — *v. t.;* WIM′BLED (-b'ld); WIM′BLING (-blĭng). To bore or pierce, as with a wimble.

wim′ple (wĭm′p'l), *n.* [AS. *wimpel.*] **1.** A covering of silk, linen, or other material, formerly worn by women over the head and around the neck and chin as an outdoor protection, and still retained in the dress of some nuns. **2.** *Scot.* **a** A fold; plait. **b** A winding turn; a curve; bend, as in a road. **c** A crafty or wily act. — *v. t.;* WIM′PLED (-p'ld); WIM′PLING (-plĭng). **1.** To clothe with or as with a wimple; to veil. **2.** *Obs.* To confuse; hoodwink; deceive. **3.** To draw down, or to lay in folds or plaits, as a veil; hence, to cause to appear as if folded or plaited; to cause to ripple or undulate; as, the wind *wimples* the lake. — *v. i.* **1.** To lie in folds; also, to appear as if folded or plaited; to ripple. **2.** *Chiefly Scot.* **a** To meander, as a stream. **b** To wriggle.

win (wĭn), *v. i.;* WON (wŭn), *Obs.* WAN (wăn); WON; WIN′NING. [AS. *winnan* to strive, labor, endure.] **1.** To gain the victory in any contest; to triumph; prevail; succeed. **2.** To succeed by effort in reaching a specified place or state (often expressed by an adverb or preposition); to succeed in getting; as, to *win* across, away, back, by, down, forward, off, out, over, through, etc.; as, then he *won* through the tacklers and scored a touchdown. — *v. t.* **1.** To get possession of by or as by labor or effort; hence, to get; gain; obtain; secure; as, to *win* praise. **2.** Specif., to gain in competition or contest; to obtain by victory; as, to *win* the prize; also, to be successful in (a competition of any kind); to come off victor in; as, to *win* a race or an election. **3.** To acquire as a compensation for service done; to earn; as, to *win* a livelihood. **4.** To effect or achieve by or as by effort; as, to *win* one's way by pluck. **5.** To come to by toil or effort; to reach; as, they *won* the hut just at nightfall. **6.** To persuade; influence; also, to entice; allure. **7.** To influence so as to gain the favor of; as: **a** To render friendly or favorable to one's cause; as, tears *won* the jury. **b** To gain the affection of; esp., to induce to accept one in marriage. **8.** *Metal.* To recover (metal, etc.) from ore. **9.** *Mining.* To obtain, as ore or coal, by mining; hence, also, to prepare, as a vein or bed, by shafts, gangways, levels, etc., for the operation of regular removal of ore. — **Syn.** See GET. — **Ant.** Lose.

— *n. Colloq.* **a** A success; victory, as in a game or competition. **b** Gain; profit; winnings.

win (wĭn), *v. t.* *Chiefly Scot.* To dry, as hay, esp. by exposure; also, to winnow (grain).

win. Scot. & dial. var. of WIND.

wince (wĭns; 106), *v. i.;* WINCED (wĭnst); WINC′ING (wĭn′sĭng). [ME. *wincen* (also *winchen, wenchen*).] To shrink, as from a blow, or from pain; to draw back; to flinch. — **Syn.** See RECOIL. — *n.* Act or fact of wincing.

wince, *n.* [Var. of WINCH an instrument.] *Dyeing & Calico Printing.* A reel used in dyeing, steeping, or washing cloth. It is placed over the wall between two tanks (**wince pits**) so as to allow the cloth to descend into either.

winch (wĭnch), *n.* [ME. *wynch*, fr. AS. *wince* a winch, a reel.] **1.** A crank with a handle, for giving motion to a machine, a grindstone, etc. **2.** Any of various machines or instruments to turn or strain something more or less forcibly; as: **a** A powerful machine having one or more barrels or drums on which to coil a rope, etc., for hauling or hoisting; a more or less elaborate form of windlass. See WINDLASS, *Illust.* **b** *Local, Eng.* A screw vise. **c** A reel for a fishing rod. **3.** *Weaving, Eng.* A divided roller for warps. — *v. t.* To hoist by means of a winch; to haul as with a winch. — **winch′er** (wĭn′chẽr), *n.*

winch, *v. & n.* *Obs. exc. Dial.* Wince; flinch.

Win′ches′ter (wĭn′chĕs′tẽr; -chĭs·tẽr), *n.* A trade-mark applied originally to a breech-loading repeating rifle having a tubular magazine under the barrel and a horizontal bolt operated by a lever on the underside of the stock, which was made (first about 1866) by, and named after, Oliver Fisher Winchester (1810–1880), American manufacturer, and applied subsequently to firearms of various types and other products of the manufacturer of this rifle.

wind (wīnd), *v. t.;* WOUND (wound), rarely, exc. in nautical senses, WIND′ED (wīn′dĕd; -dĭd); WIND′ING (wīn′dĭng). [AS. *windan.*] **1.** To turn completely, or repeatedly, esp. about something fixed; to cause to form convolutions about anything; to twist; twine; coil; wreathe; as, to *wind* thread on a spool. **2.** To move in a curved path or course; to curve. **3.** To cover, surround, infold, or the like, with something coiled, twisted, or otherwise wrapped around; to entwine; entwist; as, to *wind* a rope with twine. **4.** To vary or alter at will the course of; hence, to manage; control; govern. **5.** To effect by or as by bending or turning. **6.** To introduce sinuously or stealthily; to insinuate; as, to *wind* oneself into power. **7.** To wind up; as, to *wind* a watch; to *wind* the strings of a mandolin. **8.** To hoist or haul by a rope, etc., pulled by machinery, as coal from a pit or a vessel to her wharf. — *v. i.* **1.** To go or move in a devious or sinuous course; to curve; meander, as a stream; also, to double on one's course; as, a hare pursued turns and *winds.* **2.** To work, progress, or gain an end by sinuous, stealthy, or indirect methods; as, to *wind* into favor. **3.** To coil, as about something; to assume a convolved or spiral form; twine; as, vines *wind* around a pole. **4.** To warp, as a board. **5.** Of a horse or horses, to exhibit the defective gait of winding. See WINDING, *n.*, 5.

wind up. **a** To coil into a ball or small compass, as a skein of thread. **b** To bring to a conclusion; as, to *wind up* one's affairs. **c** To put in a state of renewed or continued motion, as a clock, a watch, etc., by winding the spring; hence, to prepare for continued movement or action. **d** To make tense or tight; to subject to strain; hence, to arouse; excite. **e** To tighten, as the strings of a musical instrument, so as to tune it. **f** To hoist, as water from a well, by or as by a windlass. **g** *Colloq.* To come to a finish; to conclude; finish. **h** *Baseball.* To give a preliminary swing to the arm before delivering a pitched ball. — *n.* Act of winding, or state of being wound; a turn; bend; twist; coil.

wind (wĭnd; *orig., and now poet., archaic, or dial.,* wīnd), *n.* [AS.] **1.** Any movement of air, usually restricted to natural, horizontal movements; air in motion with any degree of velocity. Cf. BEAUFORT'S SCALE, *Illust.* **2.** Hence, a strong or destructive movement of air; a wind storm. **3.** A direction from which the wind may blow; a point of the compass; esp., one of the cardinal points, which are often called the *four winds.* **4.** Air artificially put in motion by any force or action; as, the *wind* of a cannon ball; he pumped some *wind* into the tire. **5.** Air impregnated with a scent, as of game; hence, scent or, figuratively, intimation of something; — used in phrases; as, he caught *wind* of their plans. **6.** Power of respiration; breath; as, he had the *wind* knocked out of him. **7.** Mere breath or talk; idle words; as, his arguments are but *wind;* also, conceit; vain self-satisfaction. **8.** A current of air conceived as imparting motion to something, or influencing or carrying along something; as, it's an ill *wind* that blows nobody good. **9.** *Often pl.* Wind instruments, collectively; also, the players of these instruments. See WIND INSTRUMENT; cf. STRING, *n.*, 4 **b**; PERCUSSION INSTRUMENT. **10.** Air or gas generated in the stomach or bowels; flatulence. **11.** *Boxing Cant.* The pit of the stomach, where a blow may paralyze the diaphragm and cause temporary loss of breath or other injury.

— ***in the wind*** **a** Stirring; moving; afoot. **b** *Slang.* Intoxicated; — esp. in the nautical phrase, *three sheets in the wind.* — ***to have in the wind, to have the wind of.*** To be on the scent of. — ***to sail close to the wind.*** **a** To sail with the head directed as nearly as possible to the point from which the wind blows. **b** To manage economically. **c** To approach vulgarity, indecency, indiscretion, or the like, in speech or conduct. — ***up the wind.*** In a direction counter to the wind.

— (wĭnd), *v. t.* **1.** To expose to the wind; to dry by exposing to the wind or air; to ventilate; *Dial. Eng.*, to winnow. **2.** To perceive or follow by the scent; to scent; as, the hounds *winded* the game. **3.** To render scant of wind by violent exertion; to put out of breath. **4.** To rest, as a horse, in order to allow the breath to be recovered.

wind (wīnd; wĭnd), *v. t.;* WOUND (wound), rarely WIND′ED; WIND′ING. [From WIND air, but confused in sense and in conjugation with *wind* to turn.] To blow; to sound by blowing, as a horn, trumpet, etc.

wind′age (wĭn′dĭj), *n.* **1.** The disturbance of the air caused by a passing projectile. **2. a** The influence of the wind in deflecting the course of a projectile; also, the amount of deflection due to wind. **b** In gunnery, the amount of sight deflection necessary to compensate for wind displacement. **3.** *Naut.* The surface exposed by a vessel to the wind. **4.** *Ordn.* **a** The space between the projectile of a smoothbore gun and the surface of the bore. **b** In a muzzle-loading rifled cannon, the difference between the diameter of the bore and that of the projectile cylinder.

wind′bag′ (wĭnd′băg′), *n.* A bag of wind; as: **a** A bellows. **b** *Jocose.* The chest, considered as containing the lungs. **c** *Slang.* One who talks much to little effect.

wind′-blown′, *adj.* **1.** Blown by the wind; also, of trees, having a set or character of growth determined by the prevailing winds. **2.** Designating a type of bob haircut in which the hair (usually waved) is cut and brushed so that its ends turn outward and to the front.

wind′break′ (wĭnd′brāk′), *n.* A clump of trees or shrubs serving to break the force of wind; hence, any protective shelter from the wind, as a fence or the like.

Wind′break′er (-brāk′ẽr), *n.* A trade-mark for a sports jacket of leather, heavy wool, or the like, commonly lined and having a fitted band at the waist.

wind′-bro′ken, *adj.* Having the power of breathing impaired by the rupture, dilatation, or running together of air cells of the lungs; affected with pulmonary emphysema or with heaves; — said of a horse.

wind cone. *Aviation & Meteorol.* A cone-shaped sleeve of cloth attached aloft to a support, as a pole, to show the direction of the wind.

wind′ed (wĭn′dĕd; -dĭd), *adj.* **1.** Exposed to the wind or air; also, tainted by such exposure. **2.** Having lost one's wind, or breath, as from exertion.

wind′er (wīn′dẽr), *n.* One who or that which winds; as: **a** A twining plant or vine. **b** A person who winds yarn or the like for a weaver. **c** A device used in the winding of thread, yarn, etc. **d** A key for winding up a spring, as a watch key. **e** Any one of the steps in a winding staircase.

wind′fall′ (wĭnd′fôl′), *n.* **1.** Anything blown down or off by the wind, as fruit from a tree or the tree itself. **2.** An unexpected legacy, or other gain.

wind′flaw′ (-flô′), *n.* A gust of wind; a flaw.

wind′flow′er (-flou′ẽr), *n.* [Trans. of Gr. *anemōnē.*] An anemone; also, the related rue anemone.

wind′gall′ (-gôl′), *n.* *Veter.* In horses, a soft tumor or synovial swelling generally found on the fetlock joint; — so called from having formerly been supposed to contain air. — **wind′galled′** (-gôld′), *adj.*

wind gap. *Phys. Geog.* A notch in the crest of a mountain ridge; a pass not occupied by a stream.

wind harp. *Music.* = AEOLIAN HARP *or* LYRE.

wind′hov′er (wĭnd′hŭv′ẽr), *n.* [From its habit of hovering over one spot.] *Local, Eng.* The kestrel.

wind′i·ly (wĭn′dĭ·lĭ), *adv.* In a windy manner.

wind′i·ness (wĭn′dĭ·nĕs; -nĭs), *n.* Quality or state of being windy.

wind′ing (wīn′dĭng), *n.* **1.** Act of one who or that which winds; a turn or turning; also, sinuous, intricate, or sometimes dishonest, movements, devices, or methods of thought or action. **2.** The coiling, twisting, or twining of some pliable material about itself or about some object; as, the *winding* of thread on a spool. **3.** The material, as wire or rope, wound or coiled about anything, or a single round or turn of the material; also, the manner in which anything is wound; as, *Elec.*, a series *winding;* a shunt *winding.* **4.** State, quality, or fact of being twisted or warped out of a plane; as, in *winding;* out of *winding.* **5.** In horses, a defective gait in which there is a twisting of one leg around the other. — *adj.* That winds, curves, coils, etc. — **wind′ing·ly,** *adv.*

winding frame. A machine which winds yarn.

winding sheet. A sheet in which a corpse is wrapped.

wind instrument (wĭnd). *Music.* Any instrument sounded by wind, esp. by the breath; as: ***wood-wind instruments,*** *or* ***wood winds,*** as the flute, oboe, bassoon, clarinet; and ***brass-wind instruments,*** *or* ***brass winds,*** as the trumpet, horn, trombone, tuba. Cf. WIND, *n.*, 9.

wind′jam′mer (wĭnd′jăm′ẽr), *n.* **1.** *Naut. Colloq.* A sailing vessel or one of its crew; — orig. so called contemptuously by sailors on steam vessels. **2.** *Slang.* A very talkative person.

wind′lass (wĭnd′lȧs), *n.* [Icel. *vindilāss.*] Any of various machines for hoisting or hauling. The simplest form consists of a horizontal barrel for the hoisting rope, supported in vertical standards and turned by a crank with a handle. — *v. t. & i.* To hoist or haul with a windlass; to use a windlass for hoisting or hauling.

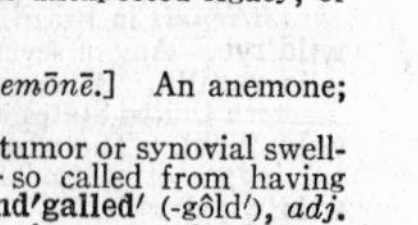

Windlass.

win′dle (wĭn′d'l; wĭn″'l), *v. i.;* -DLED (-d'ld; -'ld); -DLING (-dlĭng; -lĭng). [From WIND to turn.] *Scot.* **a** To wind yarn. **b** To whirl around; to meander; also, to drift, as snow.

win′dle·strae′ (wĭn′d'l·strā′; wĭn′'l-), **win′dle·straw′** (-strô′), *n.* [AS. *windelstrēaw*, fr. *windel* a basket + *strēaw* straw.] *Scot. & Dial.* A grass or grass stalk used for making ropes or for plaiting; hence, a trifling, feeble person or object.

wind′mill′ (wĭnd′mĭl′; wĭn′mĭl′; 25), *n.* **1.** A mill operated by the wind, usually by the wind acting on oblique vanes or sails which radiate from a horizontal shaft. Also, the wind-driven wheel of such a mill. **2.** Something resembling or suggesting a windmill. **3.** An imaginary wrong, evil, or opponent; — esp. in the phrases *to fight windmills, to tilt at windmills,* etc., in allusion to those which Don Quixote took for giants.

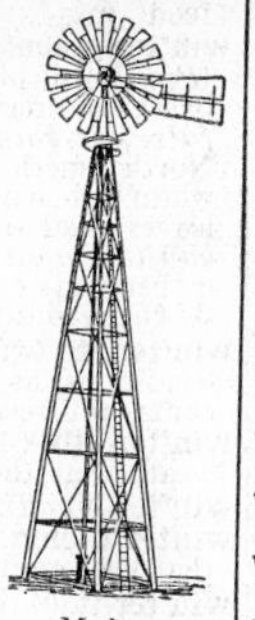

Modern Windmill.

win′dow (wĭn′dō; 87), *n.* [ME. *windowe, windoge,* fr. ON. *vindauga* window, prop., wind eye.] **1.** An opening in the wall of a building for admission of light and air, usually closed by casements or sashes containing transparent material, as glass, and capable of being opened and shut. **2.** A windowpane; as, to wash *windows.* **3.** An opening like, or suggestive of, a window (sense 1), as a shutter, slot, valve, or the like. **4.** The transparent portion, usually of celluloid, of a window envelope. **5.** *Arch.* The shutter, sash with its fittings, or other framework, which closes a window opening. — *v. t.* **1.** To furnish with a window or windows. **2.** To fill with holes suggestive of windows.

window box. 1. One of the hollows in the sides of a window frame for the weights which counterbalance a lifting sash. **2.** A box on a window sill designed to hold soil for growing plants, etc.

window dressing. The arrangement of trim and commodities attractively in retail store windows; hence, a specious statement of facts, as of financial condition, giving a misleadingly favorable appearance. — **window dresser.** — **win′dow-dress′ing,** *adj.*

window envelope. An envelope having a transparent panel through which the address on the enclosure is visible.

win′dow·pane′ (wĭn′dō·pān′), *n.* *Arch.* A pane in a window.

window seat. A seat built in the recess of a window.

window shade. A shade or curtain for a window.

win′dow–shop′, *v. i.* To inspect the window displays of goods in stores without entering the stores. — **win′dow–shop′per,** *n.* — **win′dow–shop′ping,** *adj. & n.*

window sill. = SILL, *n.,* **b.**

wind′pipe′ (wĭnd′pīp′), *n.* The passage for the breath from the larynx to the lungs; the trachea; weasand. See BRONCHIAL TUBE, *Illust.*

wind′–pol′li·nat′ed, *adj.* *Bot.* Fertilized by pollen carried by the wind; anemophilous. — **wind′–pol′li·na′tion,** *n.*

wind rose. A diagram showing, for a given place, the relative frequency, or frequency and strength, of winds from different directions.

wind′row′ (wĭnd′rō′; wĭn′rō′), *n.* [*wind* + *row.*] **1.** A row of hay raked up to dry before being rolled or pitched into cocks; also, any similar row for drying, as of grain. **2.** By extension, a wind-swept line or row, as of dry leaves or dust, of foam, surf, etc. **3.** A deep furrow, esp. for sugar-cane planting. Stalks are cut off and laid in it and covered with soil. — *v. t.* To arrange (as hay, grain sheaves, peat, etc.) or store (as sugar cane) in windrows.

wind scale. A systematic arrangement of words or numbers used for recording the velocity or force of the wind, as *hurricane,* above 75 m per hour, *whole gale,* between 55 and 75 m. per hour, etc. See BEAUFORT'S SCALE, *Illust.*

wind′screen′ (wĭnd′skrēn′), *n.* *Brit.* A windshield.

wind shake. *Forestry.* Shake attributed to the action of high winds.

wind′–shak′en (-shāk′ĕn), *adj.* Shaken by the wind; specif., *Forestry,* affected by wind shake.

wind′shield′ (wĭnd′shēld′; 25), *n.* In automotive vehicles, a shield or screen, as of glass, in front of the occupants to protect them from wind, rain, etc. — **wind′shield′,** *adj.*

wind sleeve, wind sock. = WIND CONE.

Wind′sor, House of (wĭn′zẽr). [From *Windsor* Castle, Berkshire, Eng.] The royal family of Great Britain from 1917, when the name was changed by proclamation from *House of Saxe-Coburg and Gotha.*

Windsor chair. A type of wooden chair popular esp. in 18th-century England and the American colonies.

Windsor tie. A kind of broad silk necktie, tied in a double bow.

wind′storm′ (wĭnd′stôrm′; 25), *n.* A storm characterized by high wind with little or no precipitation.

wind sucking. *Veter.* The swallowing of air, as during the act of crib biting. — **wind′suck′er** (wĭnd′sŭk′ẽr), *n.* — **wind′–suck′ing,** *adj.*

wind′–swept′, *adj.* Swept by winds.

wind tee. *Aviation.* A large weather vane on or near a landing field.

wind tunnel. A tunnellike passage through which air is blown at a known velocity to determine the action of wind pressure on structures, airplanes, etc., that are often in the form of models of reduced dimensions.

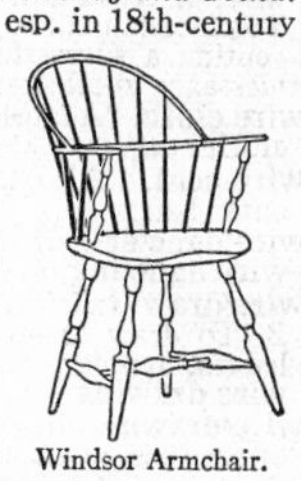

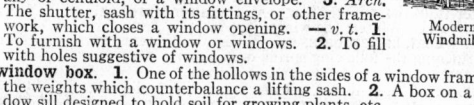

Windsor Armchair.

wind′up′ (wĭnd′ŭp′), *n.* **1.** Act of winding up or closing. **2.** A concluding act or part; the end. **3.** *Baseball.* A preliminary swing of the arm before pitching the ball.

wind′ward (wĭnd′wẽrd; *colloq., chiefly naut.,* wĭn′dẽrd), *n.* The point or side from which the wind blows; as, to sail to the *windward;* — opposed to *leeward.* — ***to windward of.*** Into or in an advantageous position with respect to. — *adv.* Toward the wind; in the direction from which the wind blows. — *adj.* **1.** Moving windward. **2.** On the side toward the point from which the wind blows.

wind′way′ (wĭnd′wā′), *n.* A passage for air; esp., *Music,* the slit between the languet and lower lip of a flue pipe. See FLUE PIPE, *Illust.*

wind′y (wĭn′dĭ), *adj.;* WIND′I·ER (-dĭ·ẽr); WIND′I·EST. [AS. *windig.*] **1.** Consisting of or pertaining to wind; accompanied or characterized by wind; as, *windy* spray. **2.** Specif.: **a** Exposed to wind; swept by wind. **b** Tempestuous; boisterous; as, *windy* weather. **c** Like the wind; swift; stormy; changeable; as, *windy* passion. **3.** Producing, or tending to produce, wind or gas in the stomach or intestines; also, due to, attended with, or affected by flatulence; flatulent; as, *windy* food. **4.** Moving by means of, or so as to produce, a wind; as, a *windy* reed. **5.** Given to, or characterized by, vain or empty talk; esp.: **a** Verbose; bombastic. **b** Given to boasting. **6.** Airy; unsubstantial.

wine (wīn), *n.* [AS. *wīn,* fr. L. *vinum.*] **1.** Fermented juice of grapes. Wine is essentially a dilute solution of alcohol, to which its stimulating properties are due, together with small quantities of certain ethers and esters, which impart to it the bouquet. *Red* wine is made by allowing the juice of dark-colored grapes to ferment in contact with the skins so as to extract their coloring matter; wine made in other ways is yellow or colorless and is termed *white* wine. **2.** The fermented, or, loosely, the unfermented, juice of any fruit or plant used as a beverage; as, currant *wine.* **3.** The effect of drinking wine in excess; intoxication. **4.** *Eng.* A social gathering, as at a meal where wine is served; esp., at English universities, a wine party. **5.** Any of several colors resembling those of wines, esp. red wines.

wine, *v. t. & i.* To supply with wine, or to drink wine.

wine′bib′ber (wīn′bĭb′ẽr), *n.* One who drinks wine to excess; a tippler. — **wine′bib′bing** (-ĭng), *n. & adj.*

wine card. A card with a list of wines that may be ordered, as in a restaurant.

wine cellar. A cellar adapted or used for storing wine; loosely, a stock of wines.

wine′glass′ (wīn′glȧs′), *n.* A small glass from which to drink wine, the form often varying with the wine.

wine′glass·ful′ (-glȧs·fŏŏl′), *n.; pl.* -GLASSFULS (-fŏŏlz′). As much as a wineglass will hold, usually reckoned at 2 fluid ounces or 4 tablespoonfuls (59.1 ml.).

wine′grow′er (-grō′ẽr), *n.* One who cultivates a vineyard, and makes wine. — **wine′grow′ing,** *n. & adj.*

wine measure. A system of measures for wine; specif., an old system by which wine and spirits were sold.

wine palm. Any palm from the sap of which wine is made.

wine press. a A vat for treading out the juice from grapes. **b** A machine for expressing the juice from grapes. — **wine presser.**

win′er·y (wīn′ẽr·ĭ), *n.; pl.* -ERIES (-ĭz). A wine-making establishment.

Wine′sap′ (wīn′săp′), *n.* A medium-sized variety of deep-red winter apple, much grown in the United States.

wine′skin′ (-skĭn′), *n.* A large bag made of the skin of an animal, used esp. in the Orient for holding wine.

wing (wĭng), *n.* [ME. *winge, wenge,* fr. ON. *vængr.*] **1. a** An organ of aerial flight; one of the movable paired appendages by means of which certain animals, as most birds, bats, and many insects, are able to fly; also, such an appendage, even though rudimentary, if possessed by an animal belonging to a group characterized by the power of flight. See BIRD, *Illust.* **b** Any of various winglike structures, as of the flying fish, flying lemur; esp., the broad thin anterior lobes of the foot of a pteropod. **c** *Humorous.* A human arm. **2. a** Means or instrument of flight; means of travel. **b** Act or manner of flying; passage by flying; flight. **3.** An appendage or part likened to a wing in shape, appearance, or position, as one, or either of a pair, attached to a side or the sides of something; specif.: **a** A device to be attached at the shoulders, as for flight or swimming. **b** An ornament worn on the shoulder. **c** Either of the parts of a double door or screen. **d** A curved mudguard for a vehicle; a fender. **4.** A side or outlying region or district. **5.** Anything which agitates the air as a wing does, as a fan or vane to winnow grain, the sail of a windmill, etc. **6.** A faction; either of two opposing groups within an organization. **7.** *Aeronautics.* The portion of a main supporting surface of an airplane on either side of the plane of symmetry. See AIRPLANE, *Illust.* **8.** *Agric. Mach.* The outside corner of the share of a moldboard plow. See PLOW, *Illust.* **9.** *Anat.* An ala; as, the *wings* of the nose. **10.** *Arch.* A part or feature of a building projecting from and subordinate to the main or central part; as, one of the *wings* of a palace. **11.** *Baseball Slang.* An arm, esp. a throwing or pitching arm. **12.** *Bot.* **a** Any foliaceous, membranous, or woody expansion, as that along the sides of certain stems and petioles, of samaras, etc. Cf. SAMARA, *Illust.* **b** Either of the two lateral petals of a flower of the pea family. **13.** *Fort.* In an outwork, either of the longer sides connecting it with the main work. **14.** *Furniture.* In an armchair, a sidepiece at the top. **15.** *Mil. & Nav.* The right or left division of an army, fleet, or any command. **16.** *Mil. Aviation.* **a** A unit of aircraft, chiefly tactical, consisting of a varying number and combination of squadrons. **b** *pl.* See WINGS. **17.** *Sports.* In certain team games, one of the positions, or one of the players in such positions, on either side of a center position, called ***left wing or right wing,*** respectively, looking in a direction towards the opponents' goal; esp., such a position or player on the forward line of a team. **18.** *Theater.* **a** One of the side scenes. **b** A chamber or platform at either side of the stage proper; also, one of the sidepieces of scenery. — ***on the wing.*** **a** Supported by, or flying with, the wings; flying. **b** Moving from one place to another; traveling. — ***under the wing, or wings, of.*** Under the care or protection of; in the charge of.

— *v. t.* **1. a** To fit with or as with wings; hence, to enable to fly or to move swiftly. **b** To supply with wings; as, a wide-*winged* house. **2. a** To pass through in flight; to traverse with or as with wings; as, an arrow *wings* the sky. **b** To transport by flight; — chiefly used reflexively. **3.** To effect or achieve by wings or by flying; as, the aviator *winged* his flight over the enemy trenches. **4.** To let fly; send off; dispatch; as, to *wing* a shaft. **5.** To wound in the wing; to disable a wing of; as, to *wing* a bird; hence, *Colloq.,* to wound, as with a bullet, without killing; as, the duelist *winged* his adversary. — *v. i.* To go with or as if with wings; to fly.

wing and wing. *Naut.* With sails boomed out on either side; — said of a schooner or her sails.

wing back formation. *Am. Football.* A formation on the offense by which one of the backs is placed just behind, or slightly beyond and to the rear of, the end; — called also ***single wing back formation.*** In a ***double wing back formation,*** two of the backs are thus placed, one behind each end of the line.

wing bow (bō). The lesser coverts of the bend of a bird's wing when distinctively colored; — esp. of poultry. See POULTRY, *Illust.* (13).

wing case *or* **cover.** = ELYTRUM.

wing chair. An upholstered easy chair with high solid back and sides, the latter turned at such an angle that they provide a rest for the head and protection from drafts.

wing covert. Any one of the coverts of the wing quills. See BIRD, POULTRY, *Illusts.*

winged (wĭngd; *also, esp. rhetorical or poet.,* wĭng′ĕd, -ĭd), *adj.* **1.** Furnished with wings. **2.** Using wings in flight; hence: **a** Lofty; sublime. **b** Swift; rapid. **3.** Wounded in the wing; hence, *Colloq.*, of persons, wounded; hurt; also, killed. **4.** Swarming with birds.

winged chair. A wing chair.

wing′-foot′ed, *adj.* Having winged feet; swift; fleet.

wing′less, *adj.* Without wings; also, having very rudimentary wings, as an apteryx.

wing′let (wĭng′lĕt; -lĭt), *n.* A very small wing or winglike appendage; also, a bastard wing, or alula.

wing loading *or* **load.** *Aeronautics.* The gross weight of an airplane fully loaded, divided by the area of the supporting surface. The area used in computing the wing loading should include ailerons, but not the stabilizer or elevators.

wing over. *Aviation.* Half a loop. See LOOP, *n.*, 3.

wings (wĭngz), *n. pl.* Insignia consisting of an outspread pair of stylized bird's wings, which are awarded on completion of prescribed training to a qualified pilot, bombardier, gunner, navigator, observer, flight surgeon, or other crew member, or a balloon pilot; — in U. S. Air Force called officially *aviation badge.*

Wings. 1–4 *U.S. Air Force:* 1 Pilot, 2 Aircrew, 3 Bombardier, 4 Navigator; 5 Naval Aviator (*U. S. Navy, Marine Corps, and Coast Guard*); 6 Aircrew (*U. S. Navy*).

wing shooting. Act or practice of shooting birds on the wing.

wing′spread′ (wĭng′sprĕd′), *n.* The spread of the wings; specif., the extreme measurement between the tips or outer margins of the wings, as of a bird or insect or of an airplane.

wing′-wea′ry, *adj.* Weary from flight or traveling.

wink (wĭngk), *v. i.;* WINKED (wĭngkt) or, *Rare,* WINKT; WINK′ING. [AS. *wincian.*] **1.** To close and open the eyelids quickly; to blink. **2.** To avoid seeing or noting, as if by shutting the eyes; to connive at anything; to be tolerant; — usually with *at.* **3.** To gleam or flash fitfully or intermittently; to twinkle. **4.** To give a hint or sign by a wink, often of one eye only. — *v. t.* **1.** To cause (the eyes) to wink. **2.** To affect or influence in any way by or as if by winking; as, to *wink* back one's tears.

Syn. **Wink, blink** mean to move one's eyelids. **Wink** implies closing and opening them rapidly and, usually, involuntarily; **blink**, an involuntary winking with eyes nearly shut, as if dazzled or partly asleep. Figuratively, *wink* implies connivance, and *blink* evasion or shirking. — *n.* **1.** Act of closing the eyelids in or as in sleep; hence, a sleep; nap. Hence, *Colloq.*, ***forty winks,*** a short nap. **2.** An instant; twinkling; as, gone in a *wink.* **3.** Act of winking; a blink, esp. with one eye, as in conveying a hint or sign; hence, a hint thus given. **4.** A twinkle.

wink′er (wĭngk′ẽr), *n.* One who or that which winks; hence: **a** A horse's blinder; a blinker. **b** *Colloq.* An eye or eyelash; — chiefly *pl.* **c** *pl. Colloq.* Spectacles.

win′kle (wĭng′k'l), *n.* [AS. *wincle* (in comp.).] **a** Any periwinkle. **b** Any of various large marine spiral whelklike snails, esp. of a genus (*Busycon*) of the United States.

win′ner (wĭn′ẽr), *n.* One who or that which wins.

win′ning (wĭn′ĭng), *n.* **1.** Act of one that wins; victory. **2.** That which one wins; esp., the money, etc., won by success in any competition; any gain; — chiefly *pl.* **3.** *Coal Mining.* A shaft or pit opening made to win coal; also, a portion of a coal bed ready for mining, or a more or less isolated section of a mine, etc. — *adj.* That wins; being a winner; hence, attractive; charming; as, a *winning* address. — **win′ning·ly,** *adv.*

winning gallery. *Court Tennis.* The netted opening farthest from the dedans; — so called because a ball played into it is counted as winning.

winning opening. *Court Tennis.* The dedans, grille, or winning gallery; — so called because a stroke into any of these openings is a winning stroke.

winning post. The post, or goal, at the end of a racecourse.

win′nock (wĭn′ŭk), *n.* *Scot.* A window.

win′now (wĭn′ō; 87), *v. t.* [AS. *windwian.*] **1.** To separate, and drive off the chaff from, by means of wind; to fan; as, to *winnow* grain. **2.** To treat in a way likened to fanning out the chaff from the good grain; to sift; to analyze and assort; hence, to eliminate; also, to select. **3.** To blow on, as for fanning out chaff from grain; hence, to disperse or scatter by or as if by wind; as, the breeze *winnowed* the leaves. **4.** To beat with or as with wings; to make (one's way) by flying. — *v. i.* **1.** To separate chaff from grain by fanning. **2.** To move or pass through the air with wings; to fly. — *n.* **1.** A device for winnowing. **2.** Act of winnowing; also, a motion like, or likened to, that of winnowing. — **win′now·er** (-ō·ẽr), *n.*

win′some (wĭn′sŭm), *adj.* [AS. *wynsum;* akin to AS. *wynn* joy.] **1.** Causing joy or pleasure; pleasant; winning; as, a *winsome* voice. **2.** Cheerful; merry; gay. — **win′some·ly,** *adv.* — **win′some·ness,** *n.*

wint (wĭnt). Scot. var. of *wound,* past of WIND.

win′ter (wĭn′tẽr), *n.* [AS.] **1.** The season of the year, in any region, in which the noonday sun shines most obliquely; the coldest season of the year; hence, cold weather. North of the equator, winter is popularly taken to include the months of December, January, and February; but astronomically winter may be considered as lasting from the winter solstice about December 22d until the vernal equinox about March 21st. **2.** A year as marked by the winter season; as, a man of seventy *winters.* **3.** A period likened to winter, as being marked by dreariness, decay, old age, death, or the like. — *v. i.* To pass the winter; as, to *winter* in Florida. — *v. t.* To keep, feed, or manage during the winter; as, to *winter* young cattle on straw. — **win′ter,** *adj.*

winter aconite. A small Old World perennial herb (*Eranthis hyemalis*) producing its bright-yellow flowers often before snow is off the ground. It is often cultivated.

win′ter·ber′ry (wĭn′tẽr·bĕr′ĭ), *n.* Any of various American species of holly (*Ilex*), having bright-red berries persistent through the winter.

win′ter·bourne′ (-bōrn′; -bo͝orn′; 70), *n.* A stream which flows only or chiefly in winter.

winter cress. See CRESS.

win′ter·er (wĭn′tẽr·ẽr), *n.* One who winters or spends the winter in a (specified) place.

win′ter-feed′ (-fēd′), *v. t. & i.* To feed through the winter. — **win′ter-feed′,** *n.*

win′ter·green′ (wĭn′tẽr·grēn′), *n.* **1.** In Great Britain, any of a genus (*Pyrola*) of plants, esp. a species (*P. minor*) which has small round basal evergreen leaves. In the United States these plants are called ***false,*** or ***English, wintergreen,*** or more often ***shinleaf.*** **2.** In North America, a low evergreen herb (*Gaultheria procumbens*) with white bell-shaped flowers followed by spicy red berries. The aromatic leaves yield ***oil of wintergreen*** or ***wintergreen oil*** (called also *gaultheria oil*) used in flavoring and in medicine. Both the plant and its berry are called also *checkerberry* and, incorrectly, *partridgeberry.* **3.** Oil of wintergreen; also, its flavor, or a lozenge, etc., flavored with it.

win′ter·ize (wĭn′tẽr·īz), *v. t.* To make ready or safe for use in winter conditions, as an airplane or automobile with special deicers, lubricants, antifreeze, etc.

win′ter·kill′ (-kĭl′), *v. t. & i.* *U. S.* To kill or die by exposure to winter weather; as, the wheat was *winterkilled.* — **win′ter·kill′ing,** *adj. & n.*

win′ter·ly, *adj.* Wintry; hence, cheerless.

winter melon. A variety (*Cucumis melo inodorus*) of muskmelon that keeps well. See MUSKMELON.

win′ter·tide′ (wĭn′tẽr·tīd′), *n.* Also **win′ter·time′** (-tīm′). Cf. AS. *wintertīd.*] Winter; the winter season.

winter wheat, barley, oats, etc. Wheat, barley, etc., sown in autumn, and ripening the following spring or summer.

win′ter·y (wĭn′tẽr·ĭ; -trĭ). Var. of WINTRY.

win′tle (wĭn′t'l), *n. & v. i.* *Scot.* Stagger; wriggle; roll.

win′try (wĭn′trĭ), *adj.;* WIN′TRI·ER (-trĭ·ẽr); WIN′TRI·EST. **1.** Suitable to winter; resembling winter; cold; stormy. **2.** Figuratively, aged; white; chilling; cheerless. — **win′tri·ly,** *adv.* — **win′tri·ness,** *n.*

win′y (wīn′ĭ), *adj.* Having the taste or qualities of wine; like wine; vinous.

winze (wĭnz), *n.* [Flem. & D. *wensch* a wish.] *Scot.* A curse.

winze, *n.* [From *winds,* pl. of *wind* a turn.] *Mining.* A steeply inclined passageway driven to connect one mine working place with another at a lower level.

wipe (wīp), *v. t.* [AS. *wīpian.*] **1.** To rub with or as with something soft for cleaning; to clean or dry by rubbing; as, to *wipe* the hands. **2.** To remove by or as by rubbing or cleansing; to rub off; hence, to obliterate; — usually followed by *away, off,* or *out;* as, to *wipe* out a regiment. **3.** To draw, pass, or the like, for or as for rubbing or cleaning; as, he *wiped* a cloth over the dusty table. **4.** *Plumbing.* To form (a joint between pieces of lead piping) by applying semifluid solder and shaping the joint by rubbing with a greased cloth pad or the like. — *n.* **1. a** A blow; swipe; as, to fetch one a *wipe.* **b** *Now Dial. & Slang.* A gibe; jeer. **2.** Act of rubbing, esp. in order to clean. **3.** *Thieves' Slang.* A handkerchief. **4.** *Mach.* A wiper, or cam.

wip′er (wīp′ẽr), *n.* **1.** One who or that which wipes. **2.** Something used for wiping, as a towel or rag. **3.** *Slang.* A handkerchief. **4.** *Elec.* A moving contact for making connections with the terminals of an electrical device, such as a rheostat. **5.** *Mach.* A projecting tooth, tumbler, eccentric, tappet, or cam, on a rotating or oscillating piece, esp. for raising a stamper, the helve of a power hammer, or the like, to fall by its own weight.

wir′a·ble (wīr′ȧ·b'l), *adj.* Capable of being wired.

wire (wīr), *n.* [AS. *wīr.*] **1.** Metal in the form of a thread or slender rod, usually very flexible, and circular in cross section; also, such a thread or rod. **2.** Wirework, esp. wire netting. **3.** A thing made of wire or wirework; — chiefly *pl.* Specif.: **a** A bar of a cage. **b** A metal snare, as for rabbits. **c** Fencing or a fence of barbed wire. **d** A telegraph wire or cable. **4.** *Chiefly in pl.* The system of wires used to operate the puppets in a puppet show; hence, *Colloq.*, the network of hidden influences controlling the action of a person or organization; as, to pull the *wires* for office. **5.** The telegraph system; as, to send a message by *wire;* also, *Colloq.*, a message thus sent; a telegram. **6.** *Horse Racing.* An imaginary line marking the finish. — *v. t.* **1.** To provide with wire or to use wire on for any purpose; to furnish, bind, attach, string, set up, mount, etc., with wire; as, to *wire* a skeleton, beads, a fence; to *wire* a house for electric lights, etc. **2.** To snare by means of a wire or wires. **3.** *Colloq.* To send, or send word to, by wire, or telegraph; to telegraph; as, *wire* me the news. **4.** *Croquet.* To place (a ball) so that it will be behind the wire of an arch, thus preventing a successful shot. — *v. i.* *Colloq.* To send a telegraphic message; to telegraph.

wire cloth. A fabric of woven metallic wire, as for strainers. — **wire′-cloth′,** *adj.*

wire coat. A coat, as of certain dogs, of extremely harsh and dense outer hair.

wire′danc′er (wīr′dȧn′sẽr), *n.* One who performs feats on a wire. — **wire′danc′ing,** *n.*

wire′draw′ (wīr′drô′), *v. t.;* see DRAW. **1.** To draw (metal) into wire. **2.** To draw or stretch forcibly; also, to draw or spin out to great length, tenuity, or overrefinement. — **wire′draw′er** (-drô′ẽr), *n.* — **wire drawing.**

wire′drawn′ (-drôn′), *adj.* Drawn out fine and long, like wire; hence, of theories, distinctions, etc., very minute and finely spun.

wire entanglement. *Fort.* Strong barbed wire stretched on supports or over the ground to impede the advance of assaulting troops.

wire gauge. A gauge for measuring the diameter of wire, thickness of sheet metal, etc. See GAUGE, *Illust.*

wire gauze. A gauzelike texture of fine wires.

wire glass. Glass in which wire netting is embedded.

wire grass. Any of certain grasses having wiry culms or leaves; esp., a European slender-stemmed meadow grass (*Poa compressa*) widely naturalized in the United States.

wire′hair′ (wīr′hâr′), *n.* A rough-coated fox terrier.

wire′-haired′ (-hârd′), *adj.* Having short, crisp, and slightly curly hair.

wire-haired terrier. A wirehair.

wire′less (wīr′lĕs; -lĭs), *adj.* **1.** Having no wire or wires. **2.** *Chiefly Brit.* Radio. — *n.* **a** Short for WIRELESS TELEGRAPHY, WIRELESS TELEPHONY, etc. **b** *Chiefly Brit.* Radio. — *v. t. & i.* *Chiefly Brit.* To radio.

wireless telegraphy *or* **telegraph.** Any system of telegraphy employing no connecting wire or wires between the transmitting and receiving stations. See RADIO.

wireless telephone. An apparatus or contrivance for wireless telephony; a radiotelephone.

wireless telephony. Telephony without wires.

wire′man (wīr′măn), *n.* A maker of or worker in wire; now, esp., a lineman. See LINEMAN, 2.

wire netting. A texture of woven wire coarser than wire gauze.

Wire′pho′to (wīr′fō′tō; 2), *n.* A trade-mark applied to news photographs transmitted by electrical signals over telephone wires.

wire′pull′ing (wīr′po͝ol′ĭng), *n.* The use of wires, as in operating a puppet show; hence, use of means to influence secretly the acts of a person or organization, esp. in politics. — **wire′pull′**, *v. i. & t.* — **wire′pull′er**, *n. All Colloq.*

wir′er (wīr′ẽr), *n.* One who wires, or uses wire; a wireman; esp., a trapper who uses a wire trap.

wire recorder. A device that records sounds magnetically upon a fine steel or other magnetic wire by actuating in an electromagnet the variations in electric current from a microphone as the wire is uncoiled between the poles, and that reproduces the sound as the magnetized wire passes again between the poles, with a loud-speaker replacing the microphone.

wire rope. A rope formed of wires.

wire′spun′ (wīr′spŭn′), *adj.* Spun or drawn long and fine like wire; wiredrawn; figuratively, excessively fine.

wire tapper. One who taps, or cuts in on, telephone or telegraph wires to get messages. — **wire tapping.**

wire′work′ (wīr′wûrk′), *n.* Work, esp. openwork, of wires; wire netting, grilled work, or the like.

wire′works′ (-wûrks′), *n. pl.; sometimes construed as sing.* A factory where wire is made, or where wire is used in making other articles. — **wire′work′er** (-wûr′kẽr), *n.*

wire′worm′ (-wûrm′), *n.* **a** One of the larvae of various snapping beetles, or elaters; — from their slenderness and the hardness of the integument. **b** A millepede.

wire′-wove′, *adj.* **a** Designating a superior smooth and fine paper, esp. for letter writing. **b** Of woven wire.

wir′ing (wīr′ĭng), *n.* **1.** Act of one who wires. **2.** A system of wires or wirework; esp., an arrangement of wires used for electric distribution; as in a building. — *adj.* That wires; employed in wiring.

wir′ra (wĭr′ȧ), *interj.* [Ir. *a* O + *Muire* Mary.] *Ir.* An exclamation expressing lament, grief, etc.

wir′y (wīr′ĭ), *adj.;* WIR′I·ER (-ĭ·ẽr); WIR′I·EST. **1.** Made of, or like, wire; drawn out like wire. **2.** Capable of endurance; sinewy. **3.** Produced by or suggestive of the vibration of wire; — of sound; as, a *wiry* twang. — **wir′i·ly** (-ĭ·lĭ), *adv.* — **wir′i·ness** (-ĭ·nĕs; -nĭs), *n.*

wis (wĭs), *v. t.* [From ME. *iwis* certainly, erron. taken as *I wis* I know. See IWIS.] *Archaic.* To think; suppose; imagine; — used chiefly in *I wis.*

wis′dom (wĭz′dŭm), *n.* [AS. *wīsdōm.* See WISE, *adj.;* -DOM.] **1.** Quality of being wise; ability to judge soundly and deal sagaciously with facts, esp. as they relate to life and conduct; discernment and judgment; discretion; sagacity. **2.** *Hist.* Scientific or philosophical knowledge; erudition; learning. **3.** *Rare.* A wise saying, act, or course of procedure. **4.** [*cap.*] A book of the Old Testament in the Douay Bible or (more fully **Wisdom of Solomon**) of the Apocrypha. See BIBLE. — **Syn.** See SENSE. — **Ant.** Folly.

Wisdom of Jesus, Son of Si′rach (sī′răk). Ecclesiasticus. See BIBLE.

Wisdom of Solomon. See WISDOM, 4.

wisdom tooth. The back tooth of the full set on each half of each jaw in man; — familiarly so called, because appearing late (from the 17th to the 22d year).

wise (wīz), *n.* [AS. *wīse.*] Way of being or acting; manner; mode; fashion; — chiefly in phrases, as *in any* (or *no*) *wise, on this wise,* etc.

-wise (-wīz). [From *wise,* n., as in *likewise,* fr. *in like wise.*] An adverbial suffix denoting *way, manner, respect.* Combinations with certain common nouns and pronouns (length*wise;* any*wise*), having similar meaning to *-ways* compounds, have come to be used interchangeably with them. See -WAYS. *-wise* is now used freely in combination with nouns, signifying *in the characteristic manner* or *fashion of a* (thing specified), as in clock*wise.*

wise (wīz), *adj.* [AS. *wīs.*] **1.** Discerning and judging soundly concerning what is true or false, proper or improper; discreet; — opposed to *foolish.* **2.** Dictated or guided by wisdom; judicious; sage; as, a *wise* saying, plan. **3.** Cognizant; aware; informed; — now chiefly in the slang phrase *to be,* or *get, wise to* (something). **4.** Calculating; shrewd; subtle; cunning; sophisticated. **5.** *Obs. exc. Dial.* Skilled in magic, divination, etc. **6.** *Obs.* **a** Versed in some art, science, or skill; skillful. **b** Having knowledge; learned. — **wise′ly**, *adv.*

Syn. **Wise, sage, sapient, judicious, prudent, sensible, sane** mean having the power to recognize the best ends and means to those ends. **Wise** suggests great understanding of persons, conditions, and situations, and unusual discernment and discrimination in dealing with them; **sage** suggests wide experience, great learning, and wisdom; **sapient**, in older and learned use, suggests sageness but, in current ironical use, the appearance of it; **judicious** suggests a capacity for arriving at wise decisions or just conclusions; **prudent** suggests a wisdom that enables one to keep himself, his passions, and his actions under guidance by what he knows to be right and necessary; **sensible** suggests a capacity for not exceeding the dictates of good sense in his words or acts; **sane** suggests a healthy-mindedness and levelheadedness shown in words and acts.

wise, *v. t.* [AS. *wīsian.*] **1.** *Obs. exc. Dial.* **a** To guide; direct. **b** To instruct; show; inform. **c** To beguile; persuade. **d** To explain. **e** To employ; use. **2.** To make wise, esp., *Slang,* in senses 3 and 4. — ***wise up.*** *Slang.* To make or become informed, sophisticated, etc.

wise′a′cre (wīz′ā′kẽr), *n.* [MD. *wijssegger,* corrupt. (as if from the words for *wise* and *sayer*) fr. OHG. *wīzzago* prophet.] **1.** One making undue pretensions to wisdom; hence, in contempt, a simpleton; dunce. **2.** A wise person; — usually ironical.

wise′crack′ (-krăk′), *n.* A jocular smart remark. — **Syn.** See JEST. — **wise′crack′**, *v. i.* — **wise′crack′er**, *n. All Slang.*

wish (wĭsh), *v. t.* [AS. *wȳscan.*] **1.** To long for; to crave; to desire. **2.** To frame or express a desire concerning; to desire (one) to be (in some specified place or condition); as, to *wish* the day over. **3.** To invoke in favor of, or against, anyone; to invoke; as, to *wish* one happiness or harm. **4.** In weakened sense, to bid; — used in the phrases, *to wish one good morning, good-by, welcome,* etc. **5.** To request; command; as, I *wish* you to go now. — *v. i.* **1.** To have a desire or yearning; to long. **2.** To frame or express a wish. — **Syn.** See DESIRE. — *n.* **1.** An act or instance of wishing; a desire; longing; as, if *wishes* were horses beggars would ride. **2.** A thing desired; an object of desire. **3.** Expression of desire; request; hence, invocation or imprecation; also, an expressed desire; as, I shall go if it is your *wish.* **4.** *pl.* A desire for welfare, good fortune, etc.; as, you have my best *wishes.*

wish′bone′ (wĭsh′bōn′), *n.* The forked bone in front of the breastbone in most birds; furculum; merrythought.

wish′er (wĭsh′ẽr), *n.* One who wishes.

wish′ful (-fo͝ol; -f'l), *adj.* **1.** Having desire or yearning; longing. **2.** Showing desire; wistful. — **wish′ful·ly**, *adv.* — **wish′ful·ness**, *n.*

wish′-wash′ (wĭsh′wŏsh′), *n.* Any weak, thin drink.

wish′y-wash′y (wĭsh′ĭ·wŏsh′ĭ), *adj.* [Redupl. of WASHY.] Thin and pale; weak; — orig. of liquids; hence, feeble; sickly.

wisp (wĭsp), *n.* [ME.] **1.** A small bunch or bundle, as of hay, straw, or the like. **2.** A slender, twisted piece of something, as of paper or grass; hence, a torch; figuratively, a fragment; shred; as, a *wisp* of smoke; a mere *wisp* of a woman. **3.** A will-o'-the-wisp; an ignis fatuus. **4.** A whisk, or small broom. — *v. t.* To roll into a wisp.

wisp′y (wĭs′pĭ), *adj.* Like a wisp; hence, slender; filmy.

wist (wĭst), *past* of WIT, to know.

wis·ta′ri·a (wĭs·tā′rĭ·ȧ; 6), *n.* [NL., after Caspar *Wistar* (1761–1818), Am. anatomist. The spelling *Wisteria* is the one originally published by Nuttall.] *Bot.* Any of a genus (*Wistaria*) of handsome woody vines of the pea family, with two species in the southeastern United States and the rest Asiatic. They have pinnately compound leaves, showy, racemose, blue, purple, or white flowers, and elongated pods. It is usually spelled **wis·te′ri·a** (wĭs·tẽr′ĭ·ȧ). Especially, either of two species, the ***Chinese wisteria*** (*W. chinensis*) with racemes of handsome purple flowers, or the ***Japanese wisteria*** (*W. floribunda*), which blooms later than the Chinese species.

wist′ful (wĭst′fo͝ol; -f'l), *adj.* [For *wishful.*] **1.** *Obs.* Intent. **2.** Feeling or evincing yearning with little expectation of gratification. — **wist′ful·ly**, *adv.* — **wist′ful·ness**, *n.*

wit (wĭt), *v. t. & i.; pres. sing.* WOT, *pl.* WITE; *past* WIST(E); *past part.* WIST; *pres. part.* WIT′(T)ING. (See the *Note* below.) [ME. *witen,* pres. *ich wot, wat,* I know (wot), pret. *wiste,* fr. AS. *witan,* pres. *wāt,* pret. *wiste, wisse.*] *Archaic,* except in the phrase *to wit.* To know or have knowledge of; to learn; to be or become aware (of).

☞ The present tense was originally inflected as follows: sing. 1st pers. *wot;* 2d pers. *wost,* or *wot(t)est;* 3d pers. *wot,* or *wot(t)eth; pl. witen,* or *wite.* Variant or corrupt forms are found, as, in Shakespeare, 3d pers. sing. pres. *wots,* and, in dialect, I *wit.*

— ***to wit.*** That is to say; namely; scilicet; — used esp. in legal language, to call attention to a more particular specification of what has preceded.

wit, *n.* [AS.] **1.** *Obs.* Activity of mind. **2.** *Archaic.* The power of conceiving, judging, or reasoning; intellectual power; sense; as, in *wit,* a man. **3.** **a** A mental faculty, or power of the mind; — chiefly *pl.,* and in certain phrases; as, to lose one's *wits.* **b** Powers of mind in a specified condition of balance or soundness, esp. in a sane state; — now only in *pl.;* as, in or out of one's *wit* or *wits.* **4.** Practical good judgment; wisdom; — now rare except in the phrase *to have the wit to.* **5.** Mental alertness; esp., such capacity along with lively fancy and aptness or talent for clever expression; as, a man with little *wit* in conversation. **6.** Felicitous perception or expression of associations between ideas or words not usually connected, such as to produce an amusing surprise. **7.** A person quick in perception of felicitous and amusing associations of ideas or words and apt in expressing them. **8.** One distinguished for clever and amusing sayings, for bright repartee, etc. — ***at one's wit's end.*** Wholly at a loss for a means of extrication from a perplexing situation; at the limit of one's mental resource.

Syn. **Wit, humor, irony, sarcasm, satire, repartee** mean expression that arouses sharp interest accompanied by amusement or laughter. **Wit** now usually suggests the power to evoke laughter by remarks showing swift perception, esp. of the incongruous, and verbal felicity; **humor**, an ability to perceive the ludicrous, the comical, and the absurd in human life or situations, usually without bitterness, and to express these so that others may see them; **irony**, a way of speaking or writing in which the meaning intended is contrary to that seemingly expressed; **sarcasm**, a form of humor intended to wound feelings; **satire**, a type of writing that holds up vices or follies for ridicule and reprobation; **repartee**, the power of answering quickly, pointedly, and often wittily or humorously.

wit′an (wĭt′ăn), *n. pl.* [AS., pl. of *wita* sage, councilor.] Literally, wise men; specif., *A.-S. Hist.,* the members of the national, or king's, council which sat to assist the king in administrative and judicial matters; also, the council.

witch (wĭch), *n.* [AS. *wicce,* fem., *wicca,* masc.] **1.** One who practices the black art, or magic; one regarded as possessing supernatural or magical power by compact with an evil spirit, esp. with the Devil; a sorcerer or sorceress; — now applied to women only. **2.** An ugly old woman; a hag; crone. **3.** *Colloq.* One who exercises more than common power or attraction; a charming or bewitching person. — *v. t.* **1.** To work a spell, esp. an evil spell, upon by sorcery. **2.** To effect by sorcery, or witchcraft. **3.** To bewitch; fascinate. — **witch**, *adj.*

witch broom. = WITCHES'-BROOM.

witch′craft′ (wĭch′krăft′; 9), *n.* **1.** The practices or art of witches; black magic; sorcery; intercourse with evil spirits; also, an instance of such practice. **2.** Power more than natural; irresistible influence or charm.

witch doctor. **1.** Among Africans, esp. Kaffirs, one whose business it is to detect or "smell out" witches and to counteract magic spells and influences. **2.** Loosely, any medicine man or practitioner of magic.

witch′-elm′. Var. of WYCH-ELM.

witch′er·y (wĭch′ẽr·ĭ), *n.; pl.* -ERIES (-ĭz). **1.** The practice of witchcraft; sorcery; also, usually *pl.,* a deed of witchcraft. **2.** Fascination; irresistible influence; enchantment.

witch′es′-be′som (wĭch′ĕz·bē′zŭm; wĭch′ĭz-), *n.* = WITCHES'-BROOM.

witch′es′-broom′, *n.* **a** Any abnormal brushlike growth of small branches on trees or shrubs; — called also *hexenbesen.* They are caused mostly by various fungi. **b** *Plant Pathol.* A virus disease of the potato characterized by the formation of bushy clusters of slender sprouts.

witches' Sabbath. In medieval demonology, a midnight assembly in which demons, sorcerers, and witches were thought to celebrate their orgies.

witch grass. [Cf. QUITCH GRASS.] **a** See COUCH GRASS. **b** A common North American panic grass (*Panicum capillare*) with slender brushlike panicles.

witch hazel. **a** A shrub (*Hamamelis virginiana*) of eastern North America, having leaves like those of the hazel and small yellow flowers appearing after the leaves have fallen. It typifies a family (Hamamelidaceae, the witch-hazel family) of shrubs and trees having small, often clustered, flowers with separate petals. **b** An alcoholic solution of a distillate of the bark of this plant, widely used as a remedy for bruises, sprains, etc., but not recognized in pharmacy as a valuable therapeutic.

witch hunt. A searching out of victims professedly for exposure on charges of subversion, disloyalty, or the like, but ulteriorly for harassing proponents of an incompatible political philosophy. — **witch′–hunt′**, *v. i.* — **witch hunter.**

witch′ing, *n.* Witchcraft; also, enchantment. — *adj.* That enchants; bewitching. — **witch′ing·ly**, *adv.*

witch moth. Any of various noctuid moths (*Erebus* and allied genera).

wite (wīt), *v. t. & n.* [AS. *wītan* to see to, keep, impute.] *Scot. & Dial.* Blame; censure.

wite, *pres. pl.* of WIT, to know.

wit′e·na·ge·mot′, wit′e·na·ge·mote′ (wĭt′ĕ·nȧ·gĕ·mōt′), *n.* [AS. *witena gemōt.* See WITAN; GEMOT.] *A.-S. Hist.* The assembly or council of the witan. It was chiefly advisory, but also elected the king, sat as the highest court of judicature, authorized new laws, the levying of taxes, granting of land, raising of military forces, etc.

with (wĭth; *often* wĭth, *esp. if accented or before a voiceless consonant; 108*), *prep.* [AS. *with* with, against, towards, opposite.] In general, *with* denotes a relation of proximity, contiguity, or association. In various applications *with* may indicate: **1.** Opposition; as, to fight *with* one's neighbor. **2.** Association of a reciprocal kind; as, to talk *with* friends. **3.** Association as object of attention or concern; as, patient *with* children. **4.** Association in the way of comparison, equality, or sameness; as, on equal terms *with* another. **5.** Association by way of alliance, assistance, or harmony; as, on friendly terms *with* all nations. **6.** Association in respect of sphere of activity; hence, in the estimation, sight, or opinion of; as, their arguments had weight *with* him. **7.** Causal connection; as, eyes dim *with* tears. **8.** Attendance by way of manner, purpose, result, condition, etc., upon action or expression; as, dismissed *with* thanks. **9.** Association by way of addition; as, an astronomer, *with* his students, is taking observations. **10.** Association in the way of possession, care, or attribute; as, to arrive *with* good news. **11.** Association in the way of simultaneousness; as, grief moderates *with* the years. **12.** Association in respect of accompaniment; hence, alongside of; in the company of; as, he went *with* his friends. **13.** Conjunction or contiguity; as, one week *with* another. **14.** That from which, as being formerly near or closely connected, there is separation; as, he parted *with* them at the crossroad. — ***with that.*** **a** *Obs.* Provided; if. **b** *Obs.* Moreover. **c** Thereupon; after that.

with- (wĭth-; wĭth-; 108: *see the prep.*). A combining form of the preposition *with*, prefixed to verbs, meaning: **a** *Back, away*, as in *with*draw. **b** *Against*, as in *with*stand.

with·al′ (wĭth·ôl′), *adv.* [*with* + *all.*] *Archaic.* **a** Together with this; besides. **b** By means of or on account of this. **c** Immediately thereupon. **d** On the other hand; for all that; still. — *prep. Archaic.* With; — put after its object, often at the end of a clause with an implied relative pronoun as object; as, "a potsherd to scrape himself *withal.*" *Job* ii. 8.

with·draw′ (wĭth·drô′; wĭth-; 108), *v. t.*; see DRAW. [*with-* + *draw.*] **1.** To take back or away. **2.** To recall or retract; as, to *withdraw* a threat. — *v. i.* **1.** To retire; retreat; to go away. **2.** In parliamentary practice, to recall a motion from consideration. — **Syn.** See GO. — **with·draw′al** (-ăl; -'l), *n.*

with·draw′ing room. A room for retirement from another room, as from a dining room; a drawing room.

withe (wĭth; wĭth; wīth), *n.* [AS. *withthe.*] A flexible, slender twig or branch, esp. one used as a band or rope; a willow or osier twig; a withy. — *v. t. Now Dial.* **1.** To twist like a withe. **2.** To bind or fasten with withes.

with′er (wĭth′ẽr), *v. i. & t.* [ME. *wideren*, var. of *wederen* to weather.] **1.** To dry; to lose, or cause to lose, freshness, vigor, force, etc. **2.** To shrink, wrinkle, or decay, as for want of moisture.

with′er·ite (wĭth′ẽr·īt), *n.* [After W. *Withering* (1741–99), Eng. physician.] *Mineral.* Native barium carbonate, $BaCO_3$, which occurs in white or gray crystals, and also in columnar or granular masses.

withe rod. A North American shrub (*Viburnum nudum*) with osierlike shoots. Also, the closely related species *V. cassinoides.*

with′ers (wĭth′ẽrz), *n. pl.* [Prop., the parts which resist the pull in drawing, fr. ME. *wither* resistance, from AS. *wither*, fr. *wither* against.] **1.** The ridge between the shoulder bones of a horse. See HORSE, *Illust.* **2.** The corresponding part in other animals. See DOG, SHEEP, *Illusts.*

with′er·shins (wĭth′ẽr·shĭnz), *adv.* [AS. *withersȳnes* backward.] *Scot.* In a direction contrary to the apparent course of the sun; contrariwise.

with·hold′ (wĭth·hōld′; wĭth-; 108), *v. t.*; see HOLD. [*with-* + *hold.*] **1.** To hold back; to check; restrain. **2.** To refrain from granting, allowing, or the like; as, to *withhold* assent. — **Syn.** See KEEP. — *v. i.* To refrain from action. — **with·hold′er**, *n.*

withholding tax. A deduction levied as a tax upon income at the source, as upon salaries, wages, fees, dividends, etc.

with·in′ (wĭth·ĭn′; 108), *adv.* [AS. *withinnan*, adv. & prep.] **1.** In or into the interior; as: **a** On the inside or inner side. **b** Inside the bounds, as of a region; as, besieged *within.* **c** Inside the body. **d** In the house, room, etc.; indoors. **2.** In or into the inner thought or character; as, outwardly calm but raging *within.* — *prep.* **1.** In the inner part of. **2.** In the limits or compass of; specif.: **a** Not farther in length than; as, *within* five miles. **b** Not longer in time than; as, *within* an hour. **c** Not exceeding in quantity or degree; as, expenses *within* one's income. **3.** Hence, inside the limits or influence of; as, *within* call, sight.

with·in′doors′ (wĭth·ĭn′dōrz′; 70; 108), *adv.* Indoors.

with·in′–named′ (-nāmd′), *adj.* Named in this writing.

with·out′ (wĭth·out′; 108), *adv.* [AS. *withūtan.*] **1.** On or at the outside; externally. **2.** Outside of the house; out of doors. — *prep.* **1.** At, to, or on, the outside of; out of; — opposed to *within.* **2.** Out of the limits of; beyond; as, *without* our reach. **3.** Not with; specif.: **a** Dissociated or separated from; not having or using; lacking. **b** Exempt or free from; as, *without* end, fail, fear. **c** In absence of the act of; as, looking *without* seeing. **4.** With the lack or absence of something indicated in the context; as, if no lunch comes, we must go *without.* **5.** *Obs.* Exclusive of; besides. — *conj. Dial.* Unless; except; — often followed by *that.* — ***without day.*** Sine die.

with·out′doors′ (-dōrz′; 70), *adv.* Out of doors.

with·stand′ (wĭth·stănd′; wĭth-), *v. t. & i.*; see STAND. [AS. *withstandan.* See WITH, *prep.*; STAND.] To stand against; to oppose or resist, with either physical or moral force; specif., to be proof against the weight, pressure, influence, etc., of; as, to *withstand* the force of a storm; to *withstand* temptation. — **Syn.** See OPPOSE.

with′y (wĭth′ĭ; wĭth′ĭ), *n.*; *pl.* WITHIES (-ĭz). [AS. *wīthig* willow, willow twig.] A flexible slender twig; a withe. — *adj.* Flexible and tough; of a person, wiry and agile.

wit′less (wĭt′lĕs; -lĭs), *adj.* Destitute of wit, or understanding; foolish. — **wit′less·ly**, *adv.* — **wit′less·ness**, *n.*

wit′ling (wĭt′lĭng), *n.* [*wit* + 1st *-ling.*] A person of little wit or understanding; a pretender to wit.

wit′ness (wĭt′nĕs; -nĭs), *n.* [AS. *witness, gewitness*, knowledge, testimony, a witness (person).] **1.** Attestation of a fact or an event; testimony. **2.** One who beholds, or otherwise has personal knowledge of, anything. **3.** That which serves as or furnishes evidence, or proof. **4.** *Law.* **a** One who testifies in a cause, or gives evidence before a judicial tribunal. **b** One called on to be present at some transaction so as to be able to testify to its having taken place. — *v. t.* **1.** To testify to; attest. **2.** To give or be evidence of. **3.** To establish by evidence. **4.** To have direct cognizance of; to observe with one's own eyes or ears. **5.** To be the scene of; as, western Europe has *witnessed* many wars. **6.** *Law.* To act as a witness of, as a signature, writing, etc.; as, to *witness* a will. — *v. i.* To bear testimony; to give evidence. — **wit′ness·er**, *n.*

witness stand *or* **box.** A stand, or an enclosure, from which a witness gives evidence in a court.

wit′ted (wĭt′ĕd; -ĭd), *adj.* Having wit, or understanding; — used esp. in combination; as, quick-*witted*; thick-*witted.*

wit′ti·cism (wĭt′ĭ·sĭz'm), *n.* [From *witty*, after *criticism.*] A witty saying, sentence, or phrase. — **Syn.** See JEST.

wit′ting (wĭt′ĭn; -'n), *n.* *Obs. exc. Dial.* Information; news.

wit′ting (-ĭng), *adj.* Done with the knowledge of the doer, or knowingly; not unintentional. — **wit′ting·ly**, *adv.*

wit′tol (wĭt′ŭl; -'l), *n.* [From *witwall*, the bird, associated with the cuckoo (cf. CUCKOLD).] *Archaic.* A man who knows his wife's infidelity and submits to it.

wit′ty (wĭt′ĭ), *adj.*; WIT′TI·ER (-ĭ·ẽr); WIT′TI·EST. [AS. *witig, wittig.*] **1.** Possessed of wit, or intelligence. **2.** Quick or ready in the perception or expression of amusing congruities and incongruities; cleverly facetious. **3.** Marked by wit; as, a *witty* remark. — **wit′ti·ly**, *adv.* — **wit′ti·ness**, *n.*

Syn. **Witty, humorous, facetious, jocular, jocose** mean provoking laughter or smiles. **Witty** usually suggests cleverness and quickness and, often, a caustic tongue; **humorous**, often applied to anything that evokes (esp. consciously) laughter, in contrast to *witty*, usually suggests sensibility, whimsicality, or the like; **facetious** implies a delight in saying things that make people laugh; **jocular** implies a jolliness that disposes one to keep others laughing or amused; **jocose**, a waggish facetiousness.

wive (wīv), *v. i.* [AS. *wīfian.*] To marry a woman; to take a wife. — *v. t.* **1.** To marry to a wife; to provide with a wife. **2.** To take for a wife; to marry.

wi′vern (wī′vẽrn), *n.* [ONF. *wivre* (OF. *guivre*) wivern, fr. L. *vipera* viper.] *Her.* A fabulous two-legged winged creature, like a cockatrice, but having a dragon's head.

wives (wīvz), *n., pl.* of WIFE.

wiz′ard (wĭz′ẽrd), *n.* [ME. *wysard*, fr. *wys, wis*, wise + *-ard.*] **1.** *Obs.* A sage. **2.** A sorcerer. **3.** *Colloq.* A very clever or skillful person. — *adj.* **1.** Possessed of magical influence. **2.** Enchanting. — **wiz′ard·ly**, *adj.*

wiz′ard·ry (-rĭ), *n.* Magical skill; magic; witchcraft.

wiz′en (wĭz′'n; *dial. also* wē′z'n), *v. i. & t.* [AS. *wisnian, weosnian*, to wither.] To wither; shrivel. — *adj.* Wizened; thin.

wiz′ened (wĭz′'nd; *dial. also* wē′z'nd), *adj.* Dried; shriveled; withered; as, *wizened* old men.

woad (wōd), *n.* [AS. *wād.*] A European herb (*Isatis tinctoria*) of the mustard family, formerly grown for the blue dyestuff yielded by its leaves; also, the dyestuff.

woad′wax′en (-wăk′sĕn; -s'n), *n.* = WOODWAXEN.

woald (wōld). Var. of 1st WELD.

wob′ble, wab′ble (wŏb′'l), *v. i.*; -BLED (-'ld); -BLING (-lĭng). **1.** To move or move along with an irregular rocking or staggering motion or unsteadily and clumsily from one side to the other. **2.** To waver; vacillate; to show indecision. — *n.* A hobbling or rocking unequal motion, as of a wheel unevenly hung. — **wob′bler, wab′bler** (-lẽr), *n.* — **wob′bly, wab′bly** (-lĭ), *adj.*

wob′ble pump (wŏb′'l). An auxiliary hand pump used to supply fuel to the carburetor of an airplane engine when the power-driven pump fails, or for forcing fuel from an extra tank.

wob′bling, wab′bling (wŏb′lĭng), *adj.* That wobbles, permits a vacillating motion, or operates with such motion. — **wob′bling·ly, wab′bling·ly**, *adv.*

Wo′den (wō′d'n), *n.* Also **Wo′dan** (-d'n). [AS. *Wōden.*] *Teut. Myth.* Odin. *Wednesday* is named for him.

woe (wō), *interj.* Also **wo.** Alas!

woe, *n.* Also **wo.** [ME. *wo, wa, woo*, fr. AS. *wā*, interj.] **1.** *Archaic.* Grief; sorrow. **2.** A miserable or sorrowful state; also, an affliction. — **Syn.** See SORROW.

woe′be·gone′, wo′be·gone′ (wō′bē·gŏn′; 74), *adj.* **1.** *Archaic.* Beset or overwhelmed with woe; woeful. **2.** Indicating woe, sorrow, or misery; hence, desolate.

woe′ful, wo′ful (wō′fo͝ol; -f'l), *adj.* **1.** Full of woe; afflicted. **2.** Involving, bringing, or pert. to woe; as, *woeful* want. **3.** Paltry; miserable. — **woe′ful·ly, wo′ful·ly**, *adv.* — **woe′ful·ness, wo′ful·ness**, *n.*

woe′some, wo′some (wō′sŭm), *adj.* Woeful.

woe worth. Woe be to. See WORTH, *v. i.*

woke (wōk), *past* of WAKE.

wok′en (wōk′ĕn). Archaic & dial. past part. of WAKE.

wold (wōld), *n.* [AS. *wald, weald*, a wood, forest.] **1.** *Obs.* A wood; forest. **2.** An upland plain; a region without woods.

wold (wōld). Var. of 1st WELD.

wold. Obs. past part. of 2d WILL.

wolf (wo͝olf), *n.; pl.* WOLVES (wo͝olvz), sometimes WOLF. [AS. *wulf.*] **1. a** Any of certain large doglike carnivorous mammals of the genus *Canis,* including: the European species (*C. lupus*), yellowish or brownish gray with rather coarse fur, erect, pointed ears and a bushy tail; the similar but larger ***gray, or timber, wolf*** (*C. occidentalis*) of northern North America; the smaller ***prairie wolf,*** or *coyote,* of western North America; and the ***Indian wolf*** (*C. pallipes*) and ***Japanese wolf*** (*C. hodophylax*) of Asia. Cf. THYLACINE. **b** The fur or pelt of one of these animals. **2.** Any of various larvae of certain small beetles or moths which infest granaries. **3.** A fierce, rapacious, or destructive person. **4.** A man forward, direct, and zealous in amatory attentions to women. **5.** *Music.* **a** Dissonance in some chords on organs, pianos, etc., tuned by unequal temperament; also, an instance of such dissonance. **b** In bowed instruments, a harshness due to faulty vibration in certain tones. — *v. t.* To eat greedily as does a wolf; to devour. — ***to keep the wolf from the door.*** To keep away poverty; to prevent starvation.

wolf'ber'ry (-bĕr'ĭ; -bẽr·ĭ), *n.* A western American shrub (*Symphoricarpos occidentalis*) with white berries.

wolf cub. See CUB, *n.*, 4.

wolf dog. Any of several breeds of large dogs formerly kept in Ireland for hunting wolves.

Wolff'i·an (wo͝ol'fĭ·ăn; vôl'-), *adj.* *Anat.* Discovered, or first described, by Kaspar Friedrich Wolff.

Wolffian body. *Embryol.* One of a pair of functional renal organs found in most vertebrate embryos, and becoming the kidneys in fishes and amphibians; the mesonephros.

wolf fish. Any of several large marine blennies notable for their strong teeth and ferocity.

wolf'hound' (wo͝olf'hound'), *n.* A dog of any of several breeds, esp. one of gigantic proportions, originally used in hunting the wolf and other large animals. The ***Irish wolfhound*** resembles the deerhound but is larger and stronger, its height being from 28 to 34 inches and its weight from 90 to 135 pounds. The ***Russian wolfhound,*** or *borzoi,* is from 26 to 31 inches high and weighs between 60 and 105 pounds.

wolf'ish (wo͝ol'fĭsh), *adj.* Of or characteristic of a wolf or wolves; ferocious. — **wolf'ish·ly,** *adv.* — **wolf'ish·ness,** *n.*

wolf pack. A flotilla of submarines that surface simultaneously at night in the midst of an enemy convoy, to loose torpedoes in every direction.

wolf'ram (wo͝ol'frăm; vôl'-), *n.* [G.] **1.** Tungsten. Symbol, *W* (no period). **2.** = WOLFRAMITE.

wolf'ram·ite (-īt), *n.* [G. *wolframit, wolfram,* said to be fr. *wolf* wolf + *rahm* cream, soot.] *Mineral.* A tungstate of iron and manganese ($(Fe,Mn)WO_4$), usually of a brownish or grayish-black color and submetallic luster; — called also *wolfram.* It occurs in monoclinic crystals and in granular or columnar masses. It is a source of tungsten.

wolfs'bane' (wo͝olfs'bān'), *n.* Aconite, or monkshood.

woll. Obs. var. of WILL.

wol'las·ton·ite (wo͝ol'ăs·tŭn·īt), *n.* [After W. H. *Wollaston* (1766–1828), Eng. chemist and physicist.] *Mineral.* A native calcium silicate, $CaSiO_3$, a monoclinic mineral of varying color, usually in cleavable masses.

wolv'er (wo͝ol'vẽr), *n.* One who hunts wolves.

wol'ver·ine', wol'ver·ene' (wo͝ol'vẽr·ēn'), *n.; see* PLURAL, *Note,* 3. [From WOLF; — prob. so called from its supposed wolfish qualities.] **1.** An American carnivorous mammal (*Gulo luscus,* family Mustelidae) very similar to the glutton (*Gulo gulo*) of Europe. **2** *U.S.* [*cap.*] A native or an inhabitant of Michigan, the **Wolverine State**; — a nickname.

wolves (wo͝olvz), *n., pl.* of WOLF.

wom'an (wo͝om'ăn), *n.; pl.* WOMEN (wĭm'ĕn; -ĭn). [ME. *woman, womman, wumman, wimman, wifmon,* fr. AS. *wīfmann, wimmann,* fr. *wīf* woman, wife + *mann* a human being, man.] **1.** An adult female person. **2.** Womankind. **3.** With *the.* Distinctively feminine nature; womanhood; womanliness. **4.** A female attendant. **5.** A paramour; mistress. — **Syn.** See FEMALE. — *v. t. Obs.* To associate (one) with a woman. *Shak.* — *adj.* **1.** Belonging or becoming to a woman; feminine. **2.** [with a plural noun, usually WOMEN.] Female; as, a *woman* physician. **3.** Of or for or affecting a woman or women; as, a *woman* hater.

wom'an·hood (-ho͝od), *n.* **1.** State of being a woman; the distinguishing character or qualities of a woman, or of womankind. **2.** Women collectively; womankind.

wom'an·ish (-ĭsh), *adj.* Resembling or suitable to a woman; effeminate. — **Syn.** See FEMALE. — **Ant.** Mannish. — **wom'an·ish·ly,** *adv.* — **wom'an·ish·ness,** *n.*

wom'an·ize (-īz), *v. t.* To make effeminate.

wom'an·kind' (wo͝om'ăn·kīnd'; 2), *n.* Women collectively.

wom'an·like' (-līk'), *adj.* Womanly. — **Syn.** See FEMALE. — **Ant.** Unwomanlike.

wom'an·ly (-lĭ), *adj.* Possessed of the qualities characteristic of women, as gentleness, compassion, modesty; feminine. — **Syn.** See FEMALE. — **Ant.** Unwomanly. — *adv.* In a distinctively feminine manner. — **wom'an·li·ness** (-lĭ·nĕs; -nĭs), *n.*

woman suffrage. The suffrage possessed and exercised by women. — **wom'an–suf'frage,** *adj.* — **wom'an–suf'fra·gist,** *n.*

womb (wo͞om), *n.* [AS. *wamb, womb.*] **1.** *Obs.* The belly. **2.** The uterus. **3.** Any cavity like a womb in containing and enveloping.

wom'bat (wŏm'băt), *n.* [From native name in Australia.] Any of a genus (*Phascolomys*) of burrowing marsupials resembling a small bear.

wom'en (wĭm'ĕn; -ĭn), *n., pl.* of WOMAN.

wom'en·folk', wom'en·folks' (-fōk', -fōks'), *n. pl.* Women, collectively.

wom'er·a (wŏm'ẽr·*ȧ*), *n.* Also **wom'er·ah, wom'ma·la, wom'mer·ah, wom'mer·a, woo'mer·a, woo'mer·ah, woo'mer·ang,** etc. [Native name in New South Wales.] A spear thrower used by the Australian aborigines.

won (wŭn; wo͝on; wōn), *v. i.* [AS. *wunian.*] *Archaic & Dial.* To dwell; live; abide.

won (wŭn), *past & past part.* of WIN.

won'der (wŭn'dẽr), *n.* [AS. *wundor.*] **1.** A cause of surprise or astonishment; a marvel; prodigy. **2.** A miracle. **3.** The emotion excited by novelty, or by something strange or not well understood; astonishment. — *v. i.* **1.** To be affected with astonishment; to marvel. **2.** To feel doubt and curiosity; to query in the mind. — *v. t.* To feel doubt and curiosity about; as, he *wondered* why they came. — **won'der·er,** *n.*

won'der·ful (-fo͝ol; -f'l), *adj.* [AS. *wundorfull.*] Adapted to excite wonder; marvelous; astonishing. — **-ful·ly,** *adv.* — **-ful·ness,** *n.*

won'der·ing, *adj.* Marveling or admiring. — **won'der·ing·ly,** *adv.*

won'der·land' (wŭn'dẽr·lănd'), *n.* **1.** A fairylike imaginary realm. **2.** A place abounding in natural features and phenomena, scientific apparatus, or art objects, etc., that excite admiration or wonder.

won'der·ment (-mĕnt), *n.* **1.** Surprise; astonishment. **2.** An object, deed, etc., exciting wonder; a miracle; marvel.

won'der–strick'en (-strĭk'ĕn), **won'der–struck'** (-strŭk'), *adj.* Struck with wonder, admiration, or surprise.

won'der·work' (-wûrk'), *n.* [AS. *wundorweorc.*] A wonderful work or act; a wonder; miracle. — **won'der–work'er,** *n.* — **won'der–work'ing,** *adj.*

won'drous (wŭn'drŭs), *adj.* [As if *wonder* + *-ous,* but orig. fr. *wonders,* adv.] Wonderful; marvelous. — *adv.* In a surprising manner or degree; wonderfully. — **won'drous·ly,** *adv.* — **won'drous·ness,** *n.*

won'ky (wŏng'kĭ), *adj.;* WON'KI·ER (-ĭ·ẽr); WON'KI·EST. [E. dial. *wanky.*] *Brit. Slang.* Unsteady; shaky; feeble; awry; off.

won'na (wŭn'*ȧ*). *Scot.* Contraction of *will not.*

won'ner (wŭn'ẽr). Scot. & dial. var. of WONDER.

wont (wŭnt; wōnt; wŏnt), *adj.* [ME. *wunt, woned,* past part. of *wonien, wonen, wunien, wunen,* to dwell, be accustomed, fr. AS. *wunian.*] Used predicatively with *be:* Using or doing customarily; accustomed; as, he slept longer than he was *wont* (to sleep). — *n.* Custom; habit; usage. — **Syn.** See HABIT. — *v. t.; past* WONT; *past part.* WONT or WONT'ED; *pres. part.* WONT'ING. To accustom. — *v. i.* To be accustomed; to be used.

won't (wōnt; wŭnt). Will not; — colloquial contraction of *woll not.*

wont'ed (wŭn'tĕd; wōn'-; wŏn'-; -tĭd), *adj.* **1.** Accustomed; customary. **2.** *U.S.* Habituated to new surroundings. — **Syn.** See USUAL. — **wont'ed·ly,** *adv.* — **wont'ed·ness,** *n.*

woo (wo͞o), *v. t. & i.;* WOOED (wo͞od); WOO'ING. [AS. *wōgian.*] **1.** To sue for the affection of, and usually, marriage with; to court. **2.** To solicit or entreat; to court solicitously.

wood (wo͝od; wōd; wo͞od), *adj.* [AS. *wōd.*] *Archaic.* Mad; violent.

wood (wo͝od), *n.* [AS. *wudu, wiodu, widu.*] **1.** *Often pl.* A dense growth of trees; a forest; grove. **2.** The hard fibrous substance which makes up the greater part of the stems and branches of trees or shrubs beneath the bark and is found to a limited extent in herbaceous plants. **3.** Timber or lumber. **4.** Something made of wood; pieces of wood cut or shaped for some particular use; specif., firewood. **5.** *Golf.* Any club having a wooden head; specif., the driver, brassie, and spoon. Cf. IRON, *n.*, 6. **6.** *pl. Music.* The wood winds (see WIND INSTRUMENT). — ***out of the woods*** (*or, now Brit.,* ***wood***). *Colloq.* Escaped from a situation of perplexity, anxiety, peril, or difficulty; safe after hazard. — *adj.* **1.** Wooden. **2.** Suitable for holding or cutting wood. **3.** Living or growing in woods; as, a *wood* thrush. — *v. t.* **1.** To cover with a growth of trees; to plant with trees. **2.** To supply with wood; as, to *wood* a steamboat. — *v. i.* To take or get a supply of wood.

wood alcohol. *Chem.* Methanol; methyl alcohol.

wood anemone. Any of several anemones (as *Anemone quinquefolia* of the United States, and *A. memorosa* of Europe).

wood betony. **a** See BETONY. **b** A lousewort (*Pedicularis canadensis*) of eastern North America, with red or yellowish flowers in bracted spikes.

wood'bin' (wo͝od'bĭn'), *n.* A bin for holding firewood.

wood'bine' (-bīn'), *n.* Also **wood'bind'** (-bīnd'). [With *bine,* dial. var. of *bind,* fr. AS. *wudubind, widubindae;* — so named as binding or winding about trees.] **a** The honeysuckle *Lonicera periclymenum* of Europe; also, any of several other honeysuckles. **b** *New Eng.* The Virginia creeper.

wood block. **1.** A solid block of wood, as for paving. **2.** A die for printing, cut in relief on wood; a woodcut; also, a print from such a cut. — **wood'–block',** *adj.*

wood'chat' (wo͝od'chăt'), *n.* **a** Any of several Asiatic birds of the thrush family (genera *Ianthia* and *Larvivora*). **b** A European shrike (*Lanius rutilus*).

wood'chuck' (-chŭk'), *n.* [From *wejack,* or from one of the northern Algonquian names for the wejack or fisher, assimilated to *wood* and *chuck.*] A thickset marmot (*Marmota monax*) of the northeastern United States and Canada. See MARMOT.

wood coal. **a** Charcoal. **b** Lignite.

wood'cock' (wo͝od'kŏk'), *n.; see* PLURAL, *Note,* 3. [AS. *wuducoc.*] **1.** An Old World limicoline bird (*Scolopax rusticola*); hence, also, a similar and related American bird (*Philohela minor*). **2.** *Archaic.* A simpleton.

wood'craft' (-kråft'; 9), *n.* **1.** Skill in anything pertaining to the woods, esp. in making one's way, in hunting or trapping, etc. **2.** Skill in constructing articles from wood. — **wood'crafts'man** (-kråfts'măn), *n.*

wood'cut' (-kŭt'), *n.* **1.** An engraving on wood; also, a print from such an engraving. **2.** = WOOD BLOCK, 2.

wood'cut'ter (-kŭt'ẽr), *n.* One who cuts wood. — **wood'cut'ting,** *n.*

wood'ed (wo͝od'ĕd; -ĭd), *adj.* Covered with trees.

wood'en (wo͝od''n), *adj.* **1.** Made or consisting of wood. **2.** Stiff, clumsy, awkward, as if made of wood. **3.** Spiritless; stupid. — **wood'en·ly,** *adv.* — **wood'en·ness,** *n.*

wood engraving. **a** The art or process of engraving designs upon wood for printing. **b** A woodcut. — **wood engraver.**

wood'en·head' (wo͝od''n·hĕd'), *n.* *Colloq.* A blockhead. — **wood'en·head'ed** (-hĕd'ĕd; -ĭd), *adj.*

wooden horse. **1.** *Class. Myth.* A huge wooden horse filled with Greek soldiers, accepted by the Trojans as a present from the Greeks. The soldiers, stealing out at night, admitted the Greek army, and Troy was sacked. See TROJAN HORSE. **2.** = HORSE, 4 & 8.

wooden Indian. A standing wooden image of an American Indian brave formerly used for advertising before a cigar store; hence, *Colloq.*, a person without animation or change of expression.

wood'en·ware' (wo͝od''n·wâr'), *n.* A general name for buckets, bowls, and other domestic articles made of wood.

wood hyacinth. A European squill (*Scilla nonscripta*) bearing racemes of drooping bell-shaped flowers; — called also *harebell* or *bluebell.*

wood ibis. A large wading bird (*Mycteria americana,* family Ciconiidae) of wooded swamps of South and Central America and the southern United States.

wood'i·ness (wŏŏd'ĭ·nĕs; -nĭs), *n.* State or quality of being woody.

wood'land' (wŏŏd'lănd'; -lănd), *n.* Land covered with wood or trees; timberland. — *adj.* Of, pertaining to, or of the nature of woodland; growing in woodland. — **wood'land·er** (-lăn·dẽr), *n.*

wood lot. An area devoted to the growing of forest trees.

wood louse. Any of numerous small terrestrial isopod crustaceans (*Oniscus, Cubaris,* or a related genus). They have a flattened body, sometimes capable of being rolled into a ball. See LOUSE, 2; PILL BUG; 1st SLATER, 2; SOW BUG.

wood'man (wŏŏd'măn), *n.* **1.** *Eng.* A forester. **2.** A hunter of forest game. **3.** A woodcutter. **4.** One who dwells in the woods. — **wood'man·craft'** (-krȧft'; 9), *n.*

wood'-note', *n.* A wild or natural note, as of a forest bird.

wood nymph. **1.** A nymph of the woods; dryad or hamadryad. **2. a** Any of several handsome moths (genus *Euthisanotia*). **b** Any of several South American hummingbirds (genus *Thalurania*). **c** = SATYR, *n.,* 3.

wood'peck'er (wŏŏd'pĕk'ẽr), *n.* Any of more than 300 species of climbing zygodactyl birds (family Picidae) having stiff, spiny tail feathers to aid in climbing or resting on tree trunks, and a chisellike bill used to drill into trees for insects. American species include the ***downy woodpecker*** (*Dryobates pubescens;* small, black and white), ***ivory-billed woodpecker*** (*Campephilus principalis;* large, glossy black with white on wings and neck, ivory-white bill, scarlet crest in male), ***pileated woodpecker*** (*Ceophloeus pileatus;* black, with red crest and white markings on wings and sides of neck), ***redheaded woodpecker*** (*Melanerpes erythrocephalus;* black, with white underparts and wing patches and red head and neck), and *flicker.*

wood pigeon. **a** The ringdove *Columba palumbus* of Europe; also, any of certain related eastern pigeons. **b** *Local, U.S.* A wild pigeon (*Columba fasciata*) of western North America.

wood'pile' (wŏŏd'pīl'), *n.* A pile of wood, esp. firewood.

wood'print' (wŏŏd'prĭnt'), *n.* = WOODCUT.

wood pulp. Pulp from wood, used in making paper.

wood pussy. *Local, U.S.* A skunk.

wood rat. Any of numerous native rats of the genus *Neotoma,* of the southern United States and western North America. They have soft fur, light gray to ocherous above and white below.

wood ray. See MEDULLARY RAY.

wood'ruff' (wŏŏd'rŭf'), *n.* [AS. *wudurofe.*] A small European sweet-scented herb (*Asperula odorata*) sometimes used in perfumery and for flavoring wine.

wood'shed' (wŏŏd'shĕd'), *n.* A shed for wood, esp. for firewood.

wood'si·a (wŏŏd'zĭ·ȧ), *n.* [NL., after Joseph *Woods* (1776–1864), Eng. botanist.] *Bot.* Any of a genus (*Woodsia*) of rock-inhabiting ferns (family Polypodiaceae).

woods'man (wŏŏdz'măn), *n.* A woodman, esp. one who frequents the forest; one skilled in woodcraft.

wood sorrel. **a** Any herb of the genus *Oxalis,* esp. *O. acetosella,* having usually compound leaves with obcordate leaflets and acid sap. See SHAMROCK, *Illust.* This genus typifies a family (Oxalidaceae, the wood-sorrel family). **b** = SHEEP SORREL (see SORREL **a**).

wood spirit. Any supernatural being believed to live in or among trees, esp. in a forest.

wood spirit. Methanol (wood alcohol).

wood sugar. Dextroxylose (see XYLOSE).

woods'y (wŏŏd'zĭ), *adj.* Of or pertaining to the woods, or forest; suggesting the woods; dwelling in, or coming from, the woods.

wood tar. Tar obtained by the dry distillation of wood, either as a deposit from pyroligneous acid or as a residue from the distillation of the acid or of wood turpentine.

wood thrush. **a** A large thrush (*Hylocichla mustelina*) of eastern North America, noted for its loud clear song. **b** *Local, Eng. & Scot.* The missel thrush. See THRUSH.

wood turning. The art or process of fashioning wooden pieces or blocks into various forms and shapes by means of a lathe. — **wood turner.** — **wood'-turn'ing,** *adj.*

wood vinegar. Pyroligneous acid or crude acetic acid.

wood'wax'en (wŏŏd'wăk'sĕn; -s'n), *n.* Also formerly **wood'wax'** (-wăks'). [AS. *wuduweaxe.*] A low, bushy, yellow-flowered Eurasian shrub (*Genista tinctoria*) formerly the source of a yellow dye.

wood winds (wĭndz). *Music.* See WIND INSTRUMENT. — **wood'-wind',** *adj.*

wood'work' (wŏŏd'wûrk'), *n.* Work made of wood; esp., interior fittings of wood, as moldings, stairways, etc.

wood'work'ing, *adj.* Working or shaping things of wood. — **wood'work'er,** *n.* — **wood'work'ing,** *n.*

wood'worm' (wŏŏd'wûrm'), *n.* A larva that bores in wood.

wood'y (wŏŏd'ĭ), *adj.;* WOOD'I·ER (-ĭ·ẽr); WOOD'I·EST. **1.** Abounding with wood or woods. **2.** Of or containing wood or woody fiber; ligneous. **3.** *Rare.* Of or pert. to woods; sylvan. **4.** Like, or characteristic of, wood; as, a *woody* taste.

wood'y (wŭd'ĭ; wŏŏd'ĭ). Scot. var. of WITHY.

woo'er (wōō'ẽr), *n.* One who woos; a suitor.

woof (wōōf), *n.* [ME. *oof,* fr. AS. *ōwef,* fr. *on* on + *wefan* to weave. The initial *w* is due to the influence of E. *weave.*] **1.** The threads that cross the warp in a woven fabric; the thread carried by the shuttle; the weft; filling. **2.** Texture; cloth.

woof'er (wōōf'ẽr), *n.* [*woof,* v., to make a low gruff sound as of a suppressed bark + 1st *-er.*] A loud-speaker, larger than a tweeter, responsive only to the lower acoustic frequencies, used for reproducing sounds of low pitch. Cf. TWEETER.

wool (wŏŏl), *n.* [AS. *wull.*] **1.** The soft and curled, or crisped, covering or coat of domesticated sheep and some other animals; esp., that of sheep, which constitutes, next to cotton, the most important material of clothing. **2.** Material, esp. clothing, made with wool. **3.** Short, thick hair, esp. when crisped or curled. **4.** Any substance light and fleecy like wool. **5.** Short for WOOL SPONGE. — *adj.* Of, pertaining to, or concerned with wool or woolen goods, esp. in their manufacture, storage, transportation, or sale.

wool clip. The annual production or crop of wool.

wool'en, wool'len (wŏŏl'ĕn; -ĭn), *adj.* **1.** Of or like wool. **2.** Pert. to wool or woolen cloths; as, a *woolen* mill. — *n.* Any fabric of wool.

wool'er (wŏŏl'ẽr), *n.* An animal bred for its wool, as an Angora rabbit.

wool fat *or* **grease.** A fatlike wax coating the surface of the fibers of sheep's wool; lanolin.

wool'fell' (wŏŏl'fĕl'), *n.* [*wool* + *fell* a skin.] A skin from which the wool has not been sheared or pulled.

wool'gath'er·ing (-găth'ẽr·ĭng), *n.* Act of gathering wool, as that found in tufts caught on bushes, etc.; figuratively, act of indulging in vagrant fancies. — *adj.* Indulging in idle fancies. — **wool'gath'er·er,** *n.*

wool'grow'er (-grō'ẽr), *n.* One who raises sheep for the production of wool. — **wool'grow'ing,** *n.*

wool'ly (wŏŏl'ĭ), *adj.;* WOOL'LI·ER (-ĭ·ẽr); WOOL'LI·EST. Also **wool'y.** **1.** Consisting of, of the nature of, or like wool. **2.** Clothed with wool; bearing wool. **3.** *Colloq., U.S.* Characterized by the spirit of the West in frontier times; hence, attended with unusual excitement. — *n.; pl.* WOOLLIES (-ĭz). **1.** *Western U.S.* A sheep. **2.** *Slang.* A garment made from wool. — **wool'li·ness, wool'i·ness,** *n.*

woolly bear. The hairy larva of several bombycid moths.

wool'pack' (wŏŏl'păk'), *n.* **1.** A wrapper of canvas, cotton, wool, etc., for holding wool; also, the wool so wrapped. **2.** *Meteorol.* A rounded cumulus cloud springing from a horizontal base.

wool'sack' (-săk'), *n.* A sack for or of wool; specif., the seat of the English lord chancellor in the House of Lords, a sack of wool in shape like a divan.

wool'sort'ers' dis·ease' (-sôr'tẽrz). Pulmonary anthrax, an occupational hazard due to inhalation of bacterial spores (*Bacillus anthracis*) from contaminated wool.

wool sponge. A soft-fibered durable commercial sponge, esp. *Hippospongia canaliculata gossypina,* occurring in the Gulf of Mexico, the Caribbean Sea, and off the southeast coast of Florida.

wool stapler. A dealer in wool. — **wool'-sta'pling,** *adj.*

woo'mer·a (wōō'mẽr·ȧ), **woo'mer·ah, woo'mer·ang.** Vars. of WOMERA.

wooz'y (wōōz'ĭ; wŏŏz'ĭ), *adj. Slang.* Befuddled.

Worces'ter chi'na *or* **por'ce·lain** (wŏŏs'tẽr). China or porcelain made at Worcester, England, from 1751; — now called also *Royal Worcester* by reason of a royal warrant.

Worces'ter·shire sauce (wŏŏs'tẽr·shĭr; -shẽr), *also* **Worces'ter sauce.** A pungent sauce, orig. made in Worcester, England, consisting of soy, vinegar, and many other ingredients.

word (wûrd), *n.* [AS.] **1.** That which is said; esp., a brief remark or expression. **2.** A declaration; promise; as, he pledged himself on his *word* to be present. **3.** *Archaic.* A saying; adage. **4.** Account; tidings; also, communication; information; — used only in the singular. **5.** A password, watchword, or verbal signal; also, an order; command. **6.** *Chiefly pl.* Talk; discourse; in a vocal musical composition, the text as distinguished from the notes. **7.** *pl.* Verbal contention; dispute. **8.** An articulate sound or series of sounds which symbolizes and communicates an idea; the smallest unit of speech that has meaning when taken by itself. Words are *notional* when they present ideas as terms of thought (as *white*); *relational,* when they express relationships between terms of thought (as *to*). **9.** Hence, the written or printed character or characters expressing such a unit of discourse; as, the *words* on a page. **10.** *Theol.* Often with *the:* **a** The gospel message; esp. [*sometimes cap.*], the Scriptures, as a revelation of God. **b** [*cap.*] The Logos (which see); the divine Wisdom, esp. as finding manifestation in the world and man, and above all in Jesus Christ (*John* i. 1–5, 9–14); the Second Person of the Trinity. — *v.t.* **1.** To express in words; to phrase. **2.** *Obs.* To flatter with words; to cajole. — *v.i. Archaic & Dial.* To speak; discourse.

word'age (wûr'dĭj), *n.* Words, collectively.

word blindness. A condition, sometimes found after brain injuries, in which the patient is no longer able to recognize the words that he sees. — **word'-blind',** *adj.*

word'book' (wûrd'bŏŏk'), *n.* **1.** A vocabulary; dictionary. **2.** A libretto, as of an opera.

word class. *Gram.* Part of speech.

word for word. In the exact words; verbatim. — **word'-for-word',** *adj.*

word'ing (wûr'dĭng), *n.* Expression in words; phrasing; as, the happy *wording* of an idea.

word'less (wûrd'lĕs; -lĭs), *adj.* Without words; silent.

word order. The order of arrangement of words in a phrase, clause, or sentence.

word square. A series of words so arranged that their letters read alike vertically and horizontally.

H E A R T
E M B E R
A B U S E
R E S I N
T R E N D

Word Square.

word'y (wûr'dĭ), *adj.;* WORD'I·ER (-dĭ·ẽr); WORD'I·EST. **1.** Of or pertaining to words; verbal; as, a *wordy* war. **2.** Using or containing many words; verbose. — **word'i·ly,** *adv.* — **word'i·ness,** *n.*

Syn. **Wordy, verbose, prolix, diffuse, redundant** mean using more words than needed to express thought. **Wordy** may also (but not necessarily) imply loquaciousness or garrulousness; **verbose** suggests resulting dullness, obscurity, lack of incisiveness, grandiloquence, or the like; **prolix,** such attention to minute details as to extend one's expression unduly and, often, tediously; **diffuse,** verbosity with lack of the compactness or condensation needed for pointedness and strength of style; **redundant,** indulgence in repetitious or unnecessary words or statements.

wore (wōr; 70). Past & Scot. & dial. past part. of WEAR.

work (wûrk), *n.* [AS. *worc, werc, weorc.*] **1.** Exertion of strength or faculties to accomplish something; toil; labor; also, employment; occupation; as, to be out of *work.* **2.** The matter on which one is working; task; duty. **3.** Material which is or is to be operated upon at any stage in the process of manufacture. **4.** That which is produced or accomplished by exertion or toil; product; also, anything accomplished; act; deed; feat; as, a bad night's *work;* a man of good *works.* **5.** Specif.: **a** That which is produced by mental labor, as a book, poem, etc. **b** Embroidery; needlework. **c** *pl.* Structures in engineering, as docks, bridges, etc.; in mining, a shaft or working. **6.** A place where industrial labor of any kind is carried on; now, esp. in plural form (*works*) but often used with singular construction, the structures, grounds, machinery, etc., of a manufacturing establishment. **7.** *pl.* The working or moving parts of a mechanism; as, the *works* of a watch. **8.** Manner of working; workmanship. **9.** Ability to work. **10.** The foam or froth caused by fermentation, as in cider, in making vinegar, etc. **11.** *pl. Bib.* Performance of moral duties or prescribed ceremonial acts, or both. **12.** *Fort.* A fortified structure of any kind

13. *Mech.* The transference of energy by a process involving the motion of the point of application of a force, as when there is movement against a resisting force or when a body is given acceleration; it is measured by the product of the force and the displacement of its point of application in the line of action.

Syn. (1) **Work, labor** (*or* **labour**), **travail, toil, drudgery, grind** mean any activity which involves effort or exertion. **Work** may imply activity of body, of mind, of a machine, etc., or be applied to the effort or the thing produced by effort; **labor** usually applies to physical or intellectual work involving great and often strenuous exertion; **travail**, now bookish, implies labor involving pain or suffering; **toil**, prolonged and fatiguing labor; **drudgery**, dull, irksome, and distasteful labor; **grind**, labor exhausting to mind or body.
(2) **Work, employment, occupation, calling, pursuit, métier, business** mean the specific activity engaged in, esp. in earning one's living; **work** applies to any activity engaged in, whether remunerative or not; **employment**, one in which one employs or uses one's time; **occupation**, one in which one engages regularly, esp. as a result of training; **calling** applies to an occupation to which one feels called by nature, by tastes, etc.; **pursuit**, a trade, profession, or the like, which one pursues; **métier**, a calling or pursuit for which one believes oneself fitted; **business**, loosely, means any employment or occupation.

— *adj.* Of or pertaining to work; used in work.

— *v. i.*; WORKED (wûrkt) or WROUGHT (rôt); WORK'ING. [AS. *wyrc(e)an, wircan* (pret. *worhte, wrohte,* past part. *geworht*).] **1.** To exert oneself for a purpose; to labor; toil. **2.** Hence, to operate; act; as, a machine *works* well; esp., to operate effectively; to have a desired effect or influence. **3.** To be engaged or employed customarily in some occupation, trade, business, etc. **4.** To move, progress, proceed, or penetrate slowly or with effort. **5.** To respond to work expended; to react (in a specified way) to being worked; as, butter *works* more easily in certain weathers. **6.** To ferment, as a liquid. **7.** To be tossed or agitated; to strain; labor; as, a ship *works* in a heavy sea.

— *v. t.* 1. To fashion by or as if by labor; to shape; form. **2.** Hence, to bring to pass; to effect; accomplish; as, the frost *worked* havoc with the crop. **3.** To prepare for use by manipulation with the hands or with an implement; as, to *work* butter. **4.** To set or keep in motion, operation, or activity; to operate; manage; as, to *work* a machine, a ship. **5.** To cause to labor or toil; as, to *work* one's horses. **6.** To cover (a district) in one's operations; as, the trapper *worked* the stream from its source. **7.** To make, effect, or bring into some condition, by slow degrees or as if laboriously; as, a stream will *work* itself clear after rain. **8.** To make or ornament by weaving, knitting, or needlework of any kind; as, to *work* a shawl. **9.** To solve, as a problem in mathematics. **10.** *Colloq.* To make use of; to use; as, to *work* one's social relations in business. **11.** To influence by acting upon; to induce. **12.** To practice trickery upon (one) for one's own ends; as, he *worked* the management for a ticket. **13.** To excite; provoke; — often with *up;* as, to *work* oneself into a rage. **14.** To cause to ferment, as liquor.

work one's passage. To pay for a passage by doing work on board or about the conveyance. — ***work out.*** **a** To effect by labor and exertion. **b** To solve, as a problem; also, to develop or arrange; as, to *work out* a plan. **c** To exhaust, as a mine, by working. **d** To make its way out; as, a nail that *worked out* from the sole of my shoe. **e** To make payment of in labor rather than in money; as, to *work out* one's taxes. **f** To show itself or be shown to be practicable, effective, or the like; as, a plan that will not *work out.*

work'a·ble (wûr'kȧ·b'l), *adj.* Capable of being worked. — **work'a·bil'i·ty** (-bĭl'ĭ·tĭ), **work'a·ble·ness,** *n.*

work'a·day' (-dā'), *adj.* Pertaining to, or suited for, working days; hence, sometimes, prosaic; ordinary.

work'bag' (wûrk'băg'), *n.* A bag for holding implements or materials for work; esp., a reticule for needlework.

work'bench' (-bĕnch'), *n.* A bench on which work is performed, as by mechanics, machinists, etc.

work'book' (-bo͝ok'), *n.* **a** A booklet outlining a course of study. **b** A workman's handbook or manual. **c** A record book of work done. **d** A schoolchild's or student's individual exercise book made up of a progressive series of problems to be solved directly on the pages.

work'box' (-bŏks'), *n.* A box for working instruments or materials.

work'day' (-dā'), *n.* **1.** A day on which work is performed, as distinguished from Sunday, festivals, etc.; a working day. **2.** The period of time in one day during which work is performed. — *adj.* Workaday.

worked (wûrkt), *adj.* That has been subjected to some process of treatment, manufacture, or the like.

work'er (wûr'kẽr), *n.* **1.** One who or that which works; laborer; toiler. **2.** Any citizen of Soviet Russia, other than a soldier or sailor, who works either with hand or brain for his living; — used in contrast to *capitalist* or *bourgeois.* **3.** *Print.* An electrotype for printing purposes, as distinguished from one used for making molds for other electrotypes. **4.** *Zool.* One of the neuter, or sterile, individuals of the social ants, bees, and termites. The workers are generally (except in termites) females having the sexual organs imperfectly developed. See HONEYBEE, TERMITE, *Illusts.*

work'folk' (wûrk'fōk'), **work'folks'** (-fōks'), *n. pl.* Workpeople.

work'house' (-hous'), *n.* **1.** *Obs.* A workshop. **2.** In England, a poorhouse. **3.** *U. S.* A house of correction for petty offenders, as drunkards or vagrants.

work'ing (wûr'kĭng), *adj.* **1.** Doing work; engaged in labor; as, a *working* woman. **2.** Of, relating to, occupied by, or taken up with work; as, *working* hours. **3.** Adequate to permit work to be done or to accomplish necessary results; as, they had a *working* majority in the legislature. **4.** Twitching spasmodically, as if moved by great feeling; said esp. of the face or the muscles of the face. **5.** Fermenting; — said of liquor, cider, vinegar, etc. **6.** Assumed or adopted to facilitate other or further work; as, a *working* arrangement, hypothesis. — *n.* **1.** *Now Rare.* The doing of work; also, the making of something by labor; sometimes, the craft, skill, or manner of making something. **2.** Manner of functioning or operating; operation. **3.** The process of shaping or fashioning things, esp. with skill. **4.** The act or process of solving, as a mathematical problem; calculation. **5.** Agitated movement or contortion. **6.** Progress slowly or gradually made by or as if by effort; as, his *working* against the current. **7.** Any excavation made in mining, tunneling; etc.; — chiefly in *pl.* **8.** Fermentation, as of liquor or yeast.

working assets; *sing.* WORKING ASSET. *Accounting.* Invested capital of a nonpermanent character; — a term rather loosely applied.

working capital. **1.** *Accounting.* Excess of quick assets over current liabilities. **2.** *Finance.* The portion of the capital of a business which is not invested in plant, etc., but remains liquid.

working day. **a** A workday. **b** The number of hours, determined by law or custom, during which a workman, hired at a stated price per day, must work to be entitled to a day's pay.

work'ing-day', *adj.* Pert. to, or characteristic of, working days; workaday; hence, plodding.

working drawing. *Arch. & Mech.* A drawing made to scale intended to be followed by the workmen.

work'ing·man' (wûr'kĭng·măn'), *n.* A laboring man.

working papers. Official documents, such as an age certificate legalizing the employment of a minor.

working substance. *Mech.* The substance, usually a fluid (**working fluid**) under pressure, that actuates the piston, vanes, etc., in an engine or the like.

work'less (wûrk'lĕs; -lĭs), *adj.* Without work; unemployed.

work'man (wûrk'măn), *n.* A man employed for wages in labor; often, a skilled artificer or laborer.

work'man·like' (wûrk'măn·līk'), *adj.* Also **work'man·ly** (-lĭ). Befitting a workman, esp. a skillful one; skillful.

work'man·ship, *n.* **1.** The art or skill of a workman; craftsmanship; also, the quality imparted to anything in the process of making; as, a vase of exquisite *workmanship.* **2.** That which is effected, made, or produced; work.

work'men's com'pen·sa'tion (wûrk'mĕnz). The compensation, fixed by statute, that workmen may recover from an employer in case of accident (and sometimes of occupational disease) arising out of their employment.

work of art. A production of art; specif., a production in one of the fine arts, esp. in painting or sculpture.

work'out' (wûrk'out'), *n. Slang.* A test or trial to determine ability or capacity for some special position, work, competition, race, etc.

work'peo'ple (-pē'p'l), *n. pl.* People who work, esp. at manual labor; laboring people.

work'room' (-ro͞om'), *n.* A room in which work is done.

works (wûrks), *n., pl.* of WORK. See WORK, *n.*, 5 **c**, 6, 7, & 11.

works council. A body or committee formed by an employer among workers within his organization for the discussion of problems of industrial relations.

work'shop' (wûrk'shŏp'), *n.* A shop where any manufacture or handiwork is carried on.

Works Progress Administration. *U. S.* A government agency established by government order, May 6, 1935, as a branch of the Federal Emergency Relief Administration (later superseding it) to investigate wages, hours, and working conditions and to provide work for the unemployed by means of grants to the several states. Abbr. *WPA*

work'ta'ble (wûrk'tā'b'l), *n.* A table for holding working materials and implements; esp., a small table with drawers and other conveniences for needlework, etc.

work'-up' (wûrk'ŭp'), *n. Print.* An unintended mark on a printed sheet caused by the rising of something not meant to print, as a space, lead, or the like.

work'week' (-wēk'), *n.* The aggregate number of hours worked per week.

work'wom'an (-wo͝om'ăn), *n.* A woman who works.

world (wûrld), *n.* [AS. *weorold, worold.*] **1.** The earth and the heavens; the universe. **2.** The earth and its inhabitants, with their affairs and interests; hence, humanity; mankind; also, people in general; the public; as, all the *world* loves a lover. **3.** A sphere or scene of life and action; as, the present *world.* **4.** Individual experience of, or concern with, life on earth; course of life; career; as, to fail, and begin the *world* anew. **5.** The customs, practices, and interests of men as social beings; — usually with *the;* as, to withdraw from the *world.* **6.** The section of mankind engrossed in the concerns of this present life. **7.** Concerns of this life as distinguished from those of the life to come; hence, secular affairs or interests. **8.** As an emblem of immensity, a great multitude or quantity. **9.** A division, or section, of the earth, its concerns, inhabitants, etc., regarded as a separate, independent unit; as, the Old *World;* the medieval *world.* **10.** One of the three grand divisions or primary groups of natural objects; a kingdom; as, the animal, mineral, or vegetable *world.* **11.** A class of persons regarded as a body and distinguished by some characteristic; as, the heathen *world;* the musical *world;* hence, the peculiar interests of such a body or the realm of such interests; as, the *world* of art and letters. **12.** Any whole likened to the world, as by reason of completeness, variety, complexity, or the like; a domain. **13.** Any planet or heavenly body, esp. when regarded as inhabited, and as the scene of interests analogous to human interests. — **Syn.** See EARTH.

world island. In geopolitics, the land mass consisting of Europe, Asia, and Africa.

world'ling (wûrld'lĭng), *n.* [*world* + 1st *-ling.*] A person engrossed in the concerns of this present world.

world'ly (-lĭ), *adj.;* WORLD'LI·ER (-lĭ·ẽr); WORLD'LI·EST. **1.** Of or belonging to this world or existence in this world; not heavenly or spiritual. **2.** Specif., of or relating to the concerns of this life as distinguished from those of the life to come; secular; as, *worldly* pleasures. **3.** Wise in the ways of this present world; sophisticated. — **Syn.** See EARTHLY. — **Ant.** Spiritual. — **world'li·ness,** *n.* — **world'ly,** *adv.*

world'ly-mind'ed (*see Pron.*, § 2), *adj.* Devoted to, or engrossed in, worldly interests. — **world'ly-mind'ed·ly,** *adv.* — **world'ly-mind'ed·ness,** *n.*

world'ly-wise' (*see Pron.*, § 2), *adj.* Wise as to things and ways of this world.

world power. A state or organization powerful enough to affect world politics by its influence or actions.

world, *or* **world's, series.** *Baseball.* A series of baseball games played in the fall of each year between the champion teams of the two major leagues to decide the professional championship of the United States.

world soul. An animating spirit or creative principle of the universe related to the world as the human soul is to the body.

world spirit. **a** = WORLD SOUL. **b** Ultimate reality.

World War. One of the international conflicts which ultimately involved the principal nations of the world; specif.: **World War I,** 1914–1919; **World War II,** 1939–1946.

world'-wea'ry, *adj.* Weary of the world, or wearied by the life of the world; esp., bored by overindulgence in material pleasures. — **world'-wea'ri·ness,** *n.*

world′–wide′ (*see Pron.*, § 2), *adj.* Extended throughout the world.

worm (wûrm), *n.* [AS. *wyrm, wurm,* serpent, worm.] **1.** An earthworm or angleworm; also, a larva; grub; maggot. **2.** Any of numerous small, elongate and slender creeping or crawling animals, usually soft-bodied, naked, and limbless or nearly so. See BLINDWORM, EARTHWORM, SILKWORM. **3.** A being likened to a worm by reason of its humility, debasement, etc. **4.** Anything spiral, vermiculated, or conceived of as like a worm, as the thread of a screw. **5.** Something that inwardly torments or devours in a way suggesting the gnawing of a worm. **6.** *pl.* Any disorder due to the presence of parasitic worms in the body, as in the intestines; helminthiasis. **7.** The spiral condensing tube of a still. **8.** *Anat.* = VERMIFORM PROCESS **a** & **b**. **9.** *Distilling.* A spiral condensing tube. See STILL, *Illust.* **10.** *Mach.* A short revolving screw, the threads of which gear with the teeth of a worm wheel or a rack. See WORM GEAR, *Illust.* **11.** *Mech.* An Archimedean screw, or a conveyer working on the same principle. **12.** *Zool.* = LYTTA. — *v. t.* **1.** To work or effect by slow, devious, and insidious means. **2.** To free of worms; as, to *worm* dogs. **3.** To cut the lytta from, as from a dog, to check a disposition to gnaw. **4.** *Naut.* To wind rope, yarn, etc., spirally round and between the strands of (a cable or rope), before serving. — *v. i.* To move, go, or work slowly, deviously, and insidiously. — **worm′er,** *n.*

worm′–eat′en (wûrm′ēt′'n), *adj.* Eaten, or eaten into, by worms.

worm fence. A zigzag fence of rails crossing at their ends; snake fence; Virginia rail fence.

worm gear. *Mach.* **a** A worm wheel. **b** A gear of a worm and a worm wheel working together.

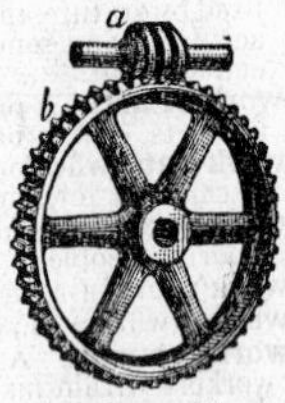

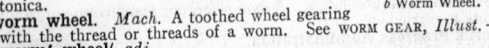

Worm Gear. *a* Worm; *b* Worm Wheel.

worm′hole′ (wûrm′hōl′), *n.* The burrow of a worm.

wor′mil (wôr′mĭl), *n.* A warble or other fly larva which burrows beneath the skin of animals.

worm′root′ (wûrm′rōōt′), *n.* An herb (genus *Spigelia,* esp. *S. marilandica,* the ***American wormroot***) used as an anthelmintic.

worm′seed′ (-sēd′), *n.* **1.** Any of several plants, as santonica and certain species of goosefoot (esp. *Chenopodium ambrosioides*), whose seeds are anthelmintic. **2.** *Pharm.* The drug santonica.

worm wheel. *Mach.* A toothed wheel gearing with the thread or threads of a worm. See WORM GEAR, *Illust.* — **worm′–wheel′,** *adj.*

worm′wood′ (wûrm′wŏŏd′), *n.* [AS. *wermōd.*] **1.** A European woody herb (genus *Artemisia*); esp., one species (*A. absinthium*) yielding a bitter, slightly aromatic dark-green oil used in making absinthe. **2.** Anything bitter or grievous; bitterness.

worm′y (wûr′mĭ), *adj.;* WORM′I·ER (-mĭ·ẽr); WORM′I·EST. **1.** Of, pertaining to, containing, or abounding with worms; also, worm-eaten. **2.** Infested with worms. **3.** Resembling a worm; hence, groveling; humble.

worn (wōrn; 70), *past part.* of WEAR.

worn′–out′ (-out′; 2), *adj.* Exhausted or used up by wear.

wor′ry (wûr′ĭ; 117), *v. t.;* WOR′RIED (-ĭd); WOR′RY·ING. [ME. *worowen, wirien,* to strangle, fr. AS. *wyrgan.*] **1.** To harass with or as if with continual snapping or biting; also, to shake and mangle with the teeth; as, the dog was *worrying* the rat. **2.** To torment; trouble; plague. **3.** To bother; annoy. — *v. i.* **1.** To be engaged in worrying, or mangling, something by tearing it with the teeth. **2.** To feel or express great care and anxiety; to fret.

Syn. **Worry, annoy, harass, harry, plague, pester, tease, tantalize** mean to torment with disturbing effects. **Worry** strictly implies an incessant attacking or goading with the intention or, now, the effect of driving one to desperation; **annoy** (see also ANNOY), a molestation, interference, or intrusion to the point of becoming a nuisance; **harass,** persecution or petty and continued exactions that drive one to distraction; **harry,** a harassing by maltreatment or oppression; **plague,** an infliction comparable to that of a devastating epidemic disease; **pester,** the power to annoy past endurance; **tease,** an attempt to break down one's resistance or to rouse one's wrath; **tantalize,** the awakening of expectation and, then, its frustration.

— *n.; pl.* -RIES (-ĭz). **1.** Act of worrying. **2.** Undue solicitude; vexation; anxiety. **3.** A cause of anxiety. — **Syn.** See CARE. — **wor′ri·er** (wûr′ĭ·ẽr), *n.* — **wor′ri·ment** (-mĕnt), *n.* — **wor′ri·some** (-sŭm), *adj.*

worse (wûrs), *adj.*, used as *compar.* of BAD. [AS. *wiersa, wyrsa,* a compar. with no corresponding positive.] **1.** Bad, ill, evil, or corrupt, in a greater degree; less good; specif., in poorer health; more sick. **2.** More unfavorable, unpleasant, or the like. — *n.* That which is worse (in various senses). — *adv.* In a manner more evil, severe, careless etc.

wors′en (wûr′s'n), *v. t. & i.* To make or become worse.

wors′er (wûr′sẽr), *adj.* Worse; — a redundant comparative formerly often used. — *adv.* Worse.

wor′set (wûr′sĭt). Scot. & N. of Eng. var. of WORSTED.

wor′ship (wûr′shĭp), *n.* [AS. *weorthscipe,* fr. *weorth* worth + *-scipe* -ship.] **1.** Courtesy or reverence paid to worth; hence, honor; respect. **2.** *Obs.* Dignity; worthiness; also, repute; renown. **3.** A title of honor, used in addresses to certain magistrates and others of rank or station. **4.** Act of paying divine honors to a deity; religious reverence and homage. **5.** Obsequious respect or devotion. **6.** An object of worship. — *v. t.;* -SHIPED (-shĭpt) or -SHIPPED; -SHIP·ING or -SHIP·PING. **1.** To pay divine honors to; to adore; venerate. **2.** To idolize. — *v. i.* To perform acts of homage or adoration; esp., to perform religious service. — **Syn.** See REVERE. — **wor′ship·er, wor′ship·per,** *n.*

wor′ship·ful (-fōōl; -f'l), *adj.* **1.** Entitled to worship, reverence, or high respect. **2.** Honorable; esteemed; — used in formal address. **3.** Rendering reverence or adoration; adoring. — **wor′ship·ful·ly,** *adv.* — **wor′ship·ful·ness,** *n.*

worst (wûrst), *adj.*, used as *superl.* of BAD. [AS. *wyrsta, wersta, wurresta.*] Bad, unpleasant, inferior, in the highest degree. — *n.* That which is most bad, unpleasant, etc. — *adv.* To the extreme degree of badness, unpleasantness, etc. — *v. t.* To gain advantage over; to defeat.

wor′sted (wŏŏs′tĕd; -tĭd), *n.* [From *Worsted,* now spelled *Worstead,* Norfolk, Eng.] A smooth-surfaced yarn for weaving, knitting, etc., spun from long-stapled wool; also, a fabric woven from such yarn. — **wor′sted,** *adj.*

wort (wûrt), *n.* [AS. *wyrt* herb, root.] *Bot.* A plant or herb of any kind; esp., a potherb.

wort, *n.* [AS. *wyrt.*] An infusion of malt unfermented (***sweetwort***), or in fermentation; the sweet infusion of malt which ferments and forms beer; hence, any similar liquid in incipient fermentation.

worth (wûrth), *v. i.* [AS. *weorthan.*] To be; become; betide; — in archaic phrases with *woe;* as, woe *worth* the day.

worth (wûrth), *adj.* [AS. *weorth, wurth.*] **1.** Deserving of; meriting; as, this issue is *worth* your attention. **2.** Equal in value to; of the value of; as, it is *worth* five dollars. **3.** Having wealth to the value of.

worth, *n.* **1.** That quality or sum of qualities of a thing rendering it valuable or useful; value; hence, often, value as expressed in a standard, as money; equivalent in exchange; price. **2.** Moral or personal excellence; merit. **3.** Wealth; riches.

Syn. **Worth, value,** as here compared, mean the quality of being useful, important, excellent, or the like. **Worth** implies intrinsic excellence, importance, and the like; **value,** often influenced by *valuation,* an imputed importance, excellence, etc. (as, "*worth* makes the man" — *Pope;* to give an inflated *value* to a poem).

worth′less (wûrth′lĕs; -lĭs), *adj.* Destitute of worth; useless; waste. — **worth′less·ly,** *adv.* — **worth′less·ness,** *n.*

worth′while′ (wûrth′hwīl′; 2; 127), *adj.* When used predicatively, **worth′while′** *or* **worth while.** Being worth the time spent; of sufficient value to repay the effort. — **worth′while′ness,** *n.*

wor′thy (wûr′thĭ), *adj.;* WOR′THI·ER (-thĭ·ẽr); WOR′THI·EST. **1.** Having worth; valuable; estimable. **2.** Having adequate merit; meriting; fit; as, *worthy* of promotion. **3.** *Archaic.* Deserved; merited. — *n.; pl.* -THIES (-thĭz). A person of eminent worth. — **wor′thi·ly,** *adv.* — **wor′thi·ness,** *n.*

wot (wŏt), *Archaic exc. Dial. 1st & 3d pers. sing. pres.* of WIT, to know.

would (wŏŏd; 4), *past tense & (obs.) past part.* of WILL, *v t. & auxiliary & 2d v. i.* [ME. & AS. *wolde.* See WILL, *v. t. & auxiliary.*] For use of *would* as auxiliary, see SHOULD. Special uses of *would* are: **a** In expressions of desire or wish; as, I *would* I were young again. **b** In expressing what might be expected; as, that *would* make talk.

would (wōld). Var. of 1st WELD.

would′–be′ (wŏŏd′bē′), *adj.* Desiring or professing to be.

wound (wōōnd; *now rarely,* wound), *n.* [AS. *wund.*] **1.** An injury of a person or animal in which the skin or other membrane is broken, as by violence or surgery. **2.** A cut or breach due to external violence in any part of a plant. **3.** An injury to feelings, reputation, etc. — *v. t. & i.* To inflict a wound or wounds (on) — **wound′less,** *adj.*

wound (wound), *past & past part.* of WIND, to twist, and WIND, to blow.

wove (wōv), *past & occasional past part.* of WEAVE.

wo′ven (wō′vĕn), *past part.* of WEAVE.

wove paper. Paper bearing the impression of the weave of fine wire gauze. Cf. LAID PAPER.

wow (wou; wō), *n. & v. Scot.* Howl; wail; mew; whine.

wow (wou), *n. Slang, U. S.* A striking success.

wow′ser (wou′zẽr), *n.* [Origin obscure.] *Colloq., Orig. Australia.* One who is censoriously hostile to minor vices; one who disapproves of certain forms of popular amusement, as Sunday sports.

WRAC (dŭb′'l·ū·är′ā′sē′). The Women's Royal Army Corps, formerly the ATS (which see).

wrack (răk), *n.* [MD. & MLG. *wrak* unsound, damaged, a shipwreck, a wreck.] **1.** Wreck; ruin. *Archaic & Scot.*, except in the phrase *wrack and ruin.* **2.** A wrecked vessel; also, wreckage. **3.** Any marine vegetation cast up or growing on the shore, as eelgrass (grass *wrack*), seaweeds, etc. **4.** *Scot. & Dial.* Weeds. — *v. t.* To wreck. — *v. i.* To be wrecked or ruined.

wrack. Var. of RACK, thin flying clouds.

WRAF (dŭb′'l·ū·är′ā′ĕf′). The Women's Royal Air Force, formerly the WAAF (which see).

wraith (rāth), *n.* [Scot. *wraith, warth,* orig., a guardian angel, fr. ON. *vörthr* a warden, guardian.] An apparition of a living person in his exact likeness, thought to be seen usually just before his death; hence, an apparition.

wran′gle (răng′g'l), *v. i.;* -GLED (-g'ld); -GLING (-glĭng). [ME. *wranglen,* v. freq.] **1.** To dispute angrily; to brawl. **2.** To argue; dispute. — *v. t.* **1.** To argue or debate. **2.** *Western U. S.* To herd or round up (livestock), esp. on the range. — *n.* Angry dispute; a noisy quarrel. — **Syn.** See QUARREL.

wran′gler (-glẽr), *n.* **1.** One who wrangles; esp., a bickering disputant. **2.** *Cambridge Univ., Eng.* An honors man placed in the first class in the mathematical tripos. **3.** *Western U. S.* A herdsman, esp. on the range.

wrap (răp), *v. t.;* WRAPPED (răpt); WRAP′PING. [ME. *wrappen.*] **1.** To cover by winding or folding; to infold. **2.** Hence, to envelop or enclose; as, darkness *wraps* him round; specif., to ensnare; entangle; as, *wrapped* in conspiracy; also, to infold or involve in that which soothes; as, *wrapped* in slumber. **3.** To envelop, as with paper, and secure, as with string, for protection, transportation, or storage; to enclose in a package. **4.** To conceal by enveloping or infolding; to hide. **5.** To fold, as a napkin. — *v. i.* To wind, coil, or twine so as to encircle or cover something. — *n.* **1.** A blanket. **2.** An article of dress intended to be wrapped round the person; esp., an outer garment, as a cloak, fur, shawl, etc.

wrap′per (răp′ẽr), *n.* **1.** That in which anything is wrapped, or enclosed; an envelope; covering; specif.: **a** The paper cover put on a book to protect the binding. **b** The tobacco leaf used for the outside covering of a cigar or plug or twist of tobacco. **c** A paper wrapping used to hold a newspaper, magazine, or the like, during delivery by post or otherwise. **2.** One whose work is wrapping articles. **3.** A loose outer garment; an article of dress fitted loosely round the person.

wrap′ping (-ĭng), *n.* That in which something is wrapped.

wrasse (răs), *n.* [Corn. *wrach.*] Any of numerous edible, usually brilliantly colored, spiny-finned fishes (family Labridae) of warm and temperate seas. They are allied to the parrot fishes.

wrath (răth; räth; *or, esp. Brit.,* rôth; 9), *n.* [AS. *wrǣththu, wrǣththo,* fr. *wrāth* wroth.] **1.** Violent anger; rage. **2.** Retributory punishment for an offense or a crime; divine chastisement. — **Syn.** See ANGER. — *adj. Archaic.* Moved to deep anger.

wrath′ful (răth′fōōl; -f'l; *see* WRATH), *adj.* **1.** Full of wrath; very angry. **2.** Springing from, expressing, or marked by wrath. — **Syn.** See ANGRY. — **wrath′ful·ly,** *adv.* — **wrath′ful·ness,** *n.*

wrath′y (-ĭ), *adj.* Wrathful. — **wrath′i·ly,** *adv.* — **wrath′i·ness,** *n.*

wreak (rēk), *v. t.* [AS. *wrecan.*] **1.** To give free play or free course to (wrath); as, to *wreak* one's resentment on the innocent. **2.** To inflict or exact (vengeance); as, to *wreak* vengeance on an enemy.

wreath (rēth), *n.; pl.* WREATHS (rēthz). [ME. *wrethe*, fr. AS. *writha;* akin to AS. *wrīthan* to twist.] **1.** Something intertwined into a circular shape; as, a *wreath* of smoke, of flowers. **2.** Now esp., a garland, as of flowers; a chaplet, esp. for a victor.

wreathe (rēth), *v. t. & i.;* WREATHED (rēthd); WREATHED, *Archaic* WREATH'EN (rēth'ĕn); WREATH'ING (-ĭng). [From ME. *wrethen*, *writhen*, past part. of *writhen* to writhe. Partly fr. *wreath*, n.] **1.** To twist; contort so as to show folds or creases; as, his face was *wreathed* in smiles; to form or combine by twisting together; to entwine. **2.** To form into a wreath or the shape of a wreath; to twine or twist about; to encircle. **3.** To encircle as with a wreath.

wreck (rĕk), *n.* [AF. *wrek, wrec*, of Scand. origin.] **1.** *Law.* Goods, etc., which, after a shipwreck, are cast upon the land by the sea. **2.** A hulk or the ruins of a wrecked ship. **3.** The broken remains of anything wrecked or otherwise ruined; hence, the emaciated form of a person. **4.** The destruction or injury of a vessel by being cast on shore, or on rocks, etc.; shipwreck. **5.** Act of wrecking, or the state of being wrecked; ruin; as, the *wreck* of a train, of one's hopes. — *v. t.* **1.** To shipwreck. **2.** To ruin, damage, or imperil by wreck. **3.** To reduce to a wreck or ruinous state by any kind of violence. **4.** To bring to a condition of complete physical impairment or to an unsound condition; as, to *wreck* one's nervous system. **5.** To demolish, as a building. — *v. i.* **1.** To suffer wreck or ruin. **2.** To work upon a wreck, as for rescue or plunder.

wreck'age (-ĭj), *n.* **1.** Act of wrecking; state of being wrecked; also, remains of a wreck. **2.** Broken, disrupted, and disordered parts or material from a wrecked structure.

wreck'er (rĕk'ĕr), *n.* **1.** One who wrecks, or ruins; one who disrupts, shatters, or frustrates. **2.** One who searches for, or works upon, the wrecks of vessels, etc., as for rescue or for plunder. **3.** One whose work is the demolition and removal of buildings, etc. **4.** An autotruck equipped to hoist and tow wrecked or disabled cars, free cars stuck in mud or snow, or make minor repairs; — called also *tow car.*

wreck'ing (rĕk'ĭng), *n.* Act or occupation of one who wrecks, esp. of one who saves wrecked vessels or cargoes, or of one whose work is to demolish buildings. — *adj.* Engaged, used, or adapted or equipped for use in wrecking or demolishing something or in salvaging shipwrecks or otherwise removing wrecks or recovering ships, railroad rolling stock, or automobiles from a wrecked or disabled condition.

wren (rĕn), *n.* [AS. *wrenna, wrænna, werna.*] **1.** Any of numerous small singing birds (family Troglodytidae), including the European wren (*Nannus troglodytes*) and the American ***house wren*** (*Troglodytes aedon*). **2.** Any of numerous small singing birds resembling true wrens.

Wren, WREN (rĕn), *n.; pl.* WRENS, WRENS (rĕnz). A member of the Women's Royal Naval Service, an auxiliary of the British Navy (1917–1919), which was reorganized in 1939 and made part of the regular Navy in 1949.

wrench (rĕnch), *n.* [AS. *wrenc* deceit, a twisting.] **1. a** A violent twisting, or a pull with or as with twisting. **b** A sprain, an injury by twisting, as in a joint. **c** A distortion of the original meaning (of a word, passage, etc.). **2.** An instrument for exerting a twisting strain, as in turning bolts, nuts, screw taps, etc.; a spanner. — *v. t.* **1.** To twist violently; to pull jerk, or wrest by a violent wrench or sudden twist. **2.** To injure by a twisting of a bodily part; to sprain. **3.** To distort from its original meaning; to pervert.

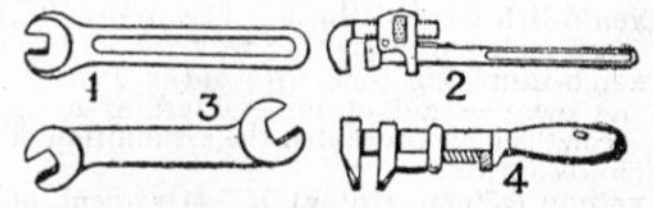

Wrenches. 1 Single-head Wrench; 2 Pipe, or Stillson, Wrench; 3 Double-head Wrench; 4 Monkey Wrench. See also DIE, *Illust.*

wrest (rĕst), *v. t.* [AS. *wrǣstan.*] **1.** To turn; twist; esp., to pull or force away by or as if by violent wringing or twisting. **2.** To snatch or wrench forcibly, esp. by usurpation, extortion, etc.; as, to *wrest* the throne from the heir. **3.** To twist from its natural or proper use or meaning by violence; to distort (the words or sense of a text). — *n.* **1.** Act of wresting; a wrench; twist. **2.** A key or wrench to tune a stringed instrument of music, as a harp or piano, by turning pins (**wrest pins**). — **wrest'er**, *n.*

wres'tle (rĕs''l), *v. i.;* -TLED (-'ld); -TLING (-lĭng). [AS. *wrǣstlian*, freq.] **1.** To contend by grappling with, and striving to trip or throw down, an opponent. **2.** To struggle for mastery; to strive earnestly. — *v. t.* To engage in (a match, bout, fall, etc.) in wrestling; to wrestle with; to seek to throw in wrestling. — *n.* The action of wrestling; a wrestling bout; a struggle. — **wres'tler** (-lĕr), *n.*

wres'tling (rĕs'lĭng), *n.* The sport consisting of the hand-to-hand combat between two unarmed contestants who seek to throw each other.

wretch (rĕch), *n.* [AS. *wrecca, wræcca*, exile, stranger, wretched person, fr. *wrecan* to drive out, punish.] **1.** A miserable person; one profoundly unhappy. **2.** One sunk in vice or degradation; a vile person.

wretch'ed (rĕch'ĕd; -ĭd), *adj.* **1.** Deeply afflicted, dejected, or distressed; very miserable. **2.** Woeful; grievous; as, a *wretched* accident. **3.** Hatefully contemptible; despicable. **4.** Very poor in quality or ability; mean, unsatisfactory, or worthless. — **wretch'ed·ly**, *adv.* — **wretch'ed·ness**, *n.*

wri'er, wri'est, *compar. & superl.* of WRY.

wrig'gle (rĭg''l), *v. i. & t.;* WRIG'GLED (-'ld); WRIG'GLING (-lĭng). [MLG. *wriggeln.*] **1.** To move to and fro with short writhing motions, like a worm; to squirm; wiggle. **2.** To proceed by crooked, dodging, or evasive ways, by equivocation, or by shifts; as, to *wriggle* out of expressing an opinion; to *wriggle* into court favor. — *n.* Act of wriggling; wiggle. — **wrig'gly** (-lĭ), *adj.*

wrig'gler (rĭg'lĕr), *n.* **1.** One that wriggles. **2.** Specif., the larva or pupa of a mosquito. See WIGGLER, *Illust.*

wright (rīt), *n.* [AS. *wryhta, wyrhta.*] A workman; an artificer; — now chiefly in compounds; as, mill*wright.*

wring (rĭng), *v. t.;* WRUNG (rŭng), formerly sometime WRINGED (rĭngd); WRING'ING. [AS. *wringan.*] **1.** To extract or obtain by twisting and compressing; to squeeze or press (*out*), as moisture from wet clothes. **2.** To twist round or wrest forcibly or violently; as, to *wring* his neck. **3.** To twist and compress, esp. so as to expel moisture; to turn and strain with violence. **4.** To torment; torture, as by twisting and squeezing. **5.** To subject to extortion. **6.** To acquire by extortion; to exact by violence or against resistance; as, to *wring* a confession from the prisoner. — *v. i.* To perform the action of wringing; to strain with a writhing motion; to squirm. — **wring**, *n.*

wring'er (-ĕr), *n.* **1.** One who or that which wrings. **2.** Specif., a machine or device for pressing water out of anything, as from clothes after they have been washed; also, its attendant or operator.

wrin'kle (rĭng'k'l), *n.* [AS. *wrincle.*] **1.** A corrugation; a small ridge or furrow formed on a surface by the shrinking or contraction of any smooth substance; a crease; a pucker; a slight fold. **2.** Specif.: **a** A small crease or ridge of the skin; as, the *wrinkles* on his face. **b** A ripple on the surface of a liquid. **3.** [Prob. a different word, and a dim. of ME. *wrenk*, var. of *wrench* deceit.] *Colloq.* A clever notion, fancy, or device; a little trick or novelty, as in dress; as, the latest *wrinkle.* — *v. i.;* -KLED (-k'ld); -KLING (-klĭng). To be or become marked with, or contracted into, wrinkles. — *v. t.* To contract into wrinkles; to pucker. — **wrin'kly** (-klĭ), *adj.*

wrist (rĭst), *n.* [AS.] **1.** The joint, or the region of the joint, between the hand and the arm, or a corresponding part on an animal; carpus. **2.** The part of a garment or glove covering the wrist. **3.** *Brit.* = WRIST PIN.

wrist'band' (rĭst'bănd'; -bŏnd; rĭz'bŭnd), *n.* The band of a sleeve, as of a shirt, which covers the wrist; a cuff.

wrist'-drop' (rĭst'drŏp'), *n., or* **wrist drop**. *Med.* Paralysis of the extensor muscles of the hand, commonly due to poisoning by lead.

wrist'let (-lĕt; -lĭt), *n.* **1.** A band worn around the wrist, as for protection or ornament. **2.** A handcuff.

wrist'lock' (-lŏk'), *n.* A wrestling hold in which one contestant is rendered helpless by a twisting grip on the wrist.

wrist pin. *Mach.* A stud or pin which forms a journal, as in a crosshead or trunk piston, for the connecting rod.

wrist watch. A small watch attached to a bracelet or strap to fasten about the wrist.

writ (rĭt), *n.* [AS. *writ, gewrit.*] **1.** That which is written; writing; — now rare except in *Holy Writ.* **2.** *Law.* Orig., in English law, any of various instruments in epistolary form issued under seal in the king's name; hence, in general, an order or mandatory process under seal, issued, in the name of the sovereign or in the name of a court or judicial officer, commanding the performance or nonperformance of some act. Cf. HABEAS CORPUS.

write (rīt), *v. t.;* WROTE (rōt); WRIT'TEN (rĭt''n); WRIT'ING (rīt'ĭng). *Archaic past & past part.* WRIT (rĭt). [AS. *wrītan*, orig., to scratch, score.] **1.** To inscribe, as by cutting, carving, etc.; as, hieroglyphics *written* on the pyramids. **2.** To form, as characters, letters, or words, on paper, parchment, etc., with a pen or pencil. **3.** To set down, esp. for others to read; also, to pen or indite; by extension, to typewrite or dictate. **4.** Specif.: **a** To draw up; to draft; as, get a lawyer to *write* your will. **b** To spell in writing; as, words *written* alike but pronounced differently. **c** To fill, or fill in, by writing; as, to *write* a check. **d** To pen, typewrite, or the like, a letter or note to. **e** To communicate (a message) by letter; as, to *write* that I am leaving today. **f** To write contracts, or the like, for; specif., to underwrite; as, to *write* insurance upon a person's life. **5.** To compose; to be the author or composer of. **6.** To express in literary form. — *v. i.* **1.** To make significant characters or inscriptions as by incising, engraving, or, esp., penning; also, of things, to be adapted to such writing; as, to *write* on stone tablets; this pen *writes* well. **2.** To form letters, words, or sentences with a pen, pencil, or the like; as, immigrants who cannot *write.* **3.** To produce poems, books, plays, etc. **4.** To communicate by a letter or letters. **5.** To be regularly employed or occupied in writing, as a clerk, journalist, etc. — ***write off.*** **a** *Accounting.* To deduct for depreciation. **b** *Bookkeeping.* To take off the books or to cancel, as by debiting the profit-and-loss account; as, we shall *write off* those claims. — ***write up.*** **a** To write an account of. **b** To bring up to date the writing of. **c** To praise highly in the public press. **d** *Accounting.* To set down an unduly high value for an asset.

writ'er (rīt'ĕr), *n.* **1.** One who writes. **2.** One who practices writing as an occupation, as an author, journalist, etc. **3.** *Law, Scot.* A lawyer; a solicitor.

writ'er's cramp, palsy, *or* **spasm** (rīt'ĕrz). *Med.* A painful spasmodic cramp of the finger muscles, brought on by excessive use in writing.

write'-up', *n.* **1.** *Slang.* A writing up; a press report, esp. a laudatory article. **2.** *Finance, U. S.* An unwarranted increase in the book value or alleged assets of a corporation.

writhe (rīth), *v. t. & i.; past* WRITHED (rīthd); *past part.* WRITHED, *Obs. exc. Poetic* WRITH'EN (rĭth'ĕn); *pres. part.* WRITH'ING (rīth'ĭng). [AS. *wrīthan* to twist.] To twist into coils or folds; now, usually, to twist or turn so as to distort; to twist violently, as the body in pain; to contort. — *n.* Act or an instance of writhing; a contortion; twist. — **writh'er** (rīth'ĕr), *n.*

writh'en (rĭth'ĕn), *adj.* *Poet.* Writhed; contorted.

writ'ing (rīt'ĭng), *n.* **1.** The act of one who writes (in any sense). **2.** Something written, as a letter, notice, etc.; specif.: **a** An inscription. **b** Any written or printed paper or document, as a deed, contract, etc. **c** Any written composition; book; as, the *writings* of Addison. **3.** Handwriting; chirography. **4.** The occupation of a writer. **5.** The practice of composition, esp. literary composition; also, style or form in composition.

writ of extent. See EXTENT, 3 **a**.

writ of prohibition. *Law.* A writ issued by a superior tribunal, directed to an inferior court, commanding the latter to cease from the prosecution of a suit depending before it.

writ of right. *Law.* **a** *Eng. Law.* Either of two original writs which lay to protect feudal tenants in the enjoyment of their freehold property by trial of the rights of the parties in the manorial court. **b** In the United States, an analogous common-law writ for restoring to its owners freehold property unjustly withheld.

writ'ten (rĭt''n), *past part.* of WRITE. Hence: *adj.* That is in writing or in print; — esp. as opposed to *spoken.*

wrong (rŏng; 74), *adj.* [ME. *wrong, wrang*, adj. & n., fr. AS. *wrang*, n., fr. ON. *rangr* awry, wrong.] **1.** Not according to the moral standard; sinful; immoral. **2.** That is not right or proper according to a code, standard, or convention; improper. **3.** Not suitable or appropriate; as, to do right things at the *wrong* times. **4.** Not according to truth or facts; incorrect; as, a *wrong* statement. **5.** Not satisfactory, as in condition, results, health, or temper. **6.** Designed to be placed inward, downward, under, or the like; as, the *wrong* side of a fabric. — **Syn.** See FALSE. — **Ant.** Right. — *adv.* In a wrong direction, place, manner, etc.; astray. — *n.* [AS. *wrang.* See WRONG, *adj.*] **1.** That which is wrong; any departure from duty, truth, or fact, or from moral rectitude. **2.** *Law.* A violation of the legal rights of another; an invasion of right to the damage of the party who suffers it; esp., a tort. — **Syn.** See INJUSTICE. — *v. t.* To do wrong to. Hence: **a** To treat disrespectfully, dishonorably, etc. **b** To defraud; deprive wrongfully; — with *of*. **c** To dishonor; malign. **d** To seduce (a woman). **e** *Now Scot.* To injure. — **wrong′er** (rŏng′ẽr), *n.*

Syn. **Wrong, oppress, persecute, aggrieve** mean to inflict injury upon unjustly or outrageously. **Wrong** implies unjustifiable injury either as unmerited or entirely out of proportion to one's deserts; **oppress**, the inhumane laying on of burdens one cannot endure or exacting of more than one can possibly perform; **persecute**, a relentless and unremitting subjection to annoyance or suffering; **aggrieve**, a giving cause for remonstrance by wronging, oppressing, or persecuting.

wrong′do′er (rŏng′do͞o′ẽr; rŏng′do͞o′ẽr), *n.* One who does wrong; esp., a transgressor of the moral law. — **wrong′do′ing**, *n.*

wrong font. Also **wrong fount.** The incorrect font of type; — used on printers' proofs. Abbr. *w. f.*

wrong′ful (rŏng′fo͝ol; -f'l), *adj.* **1.** Full of wrong; injurious; unjust; unfair. **2.** Not rightful, esp. in law; unlawful. — **wrong′ful·ly**, *adv.* — **wrong′ful·ness**, *n.*

wrong′head′ed (-hĕd′ĕd; -ĭd; 2), *adj.* Stubborn in adherence to wrong opinion; perverse; obstinately wrong. — **wrong′head′ed·ly**, *adv.* — **wrong′head′ed·ness**, *n.*

wrong′ly, *adv.* In a wrong fashion or way; wrong.

wrong′ness (rŏng′nĕs; -nĭs), *n.* State or quality of being wrong.

wrote (rōt). Past & obs. exc. illit. & dial. past part. of WRITE.

wroth (rôth *or, esp. in Brit. usage,* rŏth), *adj.* [AS. *wrāth* wroth, crooked, bad.] Full of wrath; angry.

wrought (rôt), *past & past part.* of WORK. Hence: *adj.* **1.** Fashioned; formed; as, a curiously *wrought* ring. **2.** Elaborated; ornamented; as, *wrought* tapestries. **3.** Manufactured; processed; of leather, etc., dressed. **4.** Of metals or metalwork, hammered; beaten into shape by tools; as, dishes of *wrought* silver.

wrought iron. *Metal.* A commercial form of iron, tough, malleable, and relatively soft. It contains less than 0.3 per cent carbon and has 1 or 2 per cent of slag mixed with it. It is distinguished from ingot iron and low-carbon steel by its slag content and its process of manufacture. Cf. STEEL, CAST IRON, INGOT IRON. — **wrought′-i′ron**, *adj.*

wrought′-i′ron cast′ing. = MITIS CASTING.

wrought′-up′ (rôt′ŭp′; 2), *adj.* Greatly stirred up; excited.

wrung (rŭng), *past & past part.* of WRING.

wry (rī), *v. i. & t.*; WRIED (rīd); WRY′ING. [ME. *wrien*, fr. AS. *wrīgian* to turn, go, move.] To twist; writhe; contort. — *adj.*; WRI′ER (rī′ẽr); WRI′EST. **1.** Turned to one side; twisted; contorted; also, made by twisting the features out of shape; as, a *wry* face or smile. **2. a** Marked by perversity or contrariness; wrongheaded; as, *wry* notions. **b** Distorted; warped. — **wry′ly**, *adv.* — **wry′ness**, *n.*

wry′neck′ (rī′nĕk′), *n.* **1.** *Colloq.* One with a wry, or twisted, neck; one afflicted with torticollis. **2.** *Med.* Torticollis. **3.** *Zool.* A bird (genus *Jynx*) allied to the woodpeckers, but having soft tail feathers and a peculiar manner of writhing its head and neck.

wud (wo͝od). Dial. var. of WOOD, *adj.*, mad.

wul′fen·ite (wo͝ol′fĕn·īt), *n.* [After F. X. von *Wulfen* (1728–1805), Austrian mineralogist.] *Mineral.* A tetragonal mineral, $PbMoO_4$, bright orange-yellow to red, gray, green, or brown, usually in tabular crystals.

Wy′an·dot (wī′ăn·dŏt), *n.* An Indian of an Iroquoian tribe once powerful in the Middle West.

Wy′an·dotte (-dŏt), *n.* **1.** Var. of WYANDOT. **2.** One of an American breed of medium-sized domestic fowls derived in part from the dark Brahma and spangled Hamburg.

wych′-elm′ (wĭch′ĕlm′), *n.* [ME. *wyche*, fr. AS. *wice*.] **a** A Eurasian elm (*Ulmus glabra*), a common species in England, Scotland, and Ireland. **b** The wood of this tree.

wych′-ha′zel (-hā′z'l), *n.* **a** Witch hazel. **b** = WYCH-ELM **a.**

Wyc′lif·fite, Wyc′lif·ite (wĭk′lĭf·īt), *adj.* Of or pert. to John Wycliffe (d. 1384), English religious reformer, or his doctrines. — *n.* A follower of Wycliffe; Lollard.

wye (wī), *n.*; *pl.* WYES (wīz). [See Y.] The letter Y, or something shaped like it.

wyle (wīl). Scot. var. of WILE, to lure.

wy′lie·coat′ (wī′lĭ·kōt′; wĭl′ĭ-; wŭl′ĭ-), *n.* *Scot.* An undervest or petticoat.

wyte (wīt). Obs. exc. Scot. var. of WITE, to blame.

wy′vern (wī′vẽrn). Var. of WIVERN.

X

X, x (ĕks), *n.*; *pl.* X's, x's, Xs, xs (ĕk′sĕz; -sĭz). **1.** The twenty-fourth letter of the English alphabet. Its form and value are from the Latin, as is its name, *ex* (Latin *ix*). The letter came into Latin from a western Greek alphabet, in which it had the value of *ks.* **2.** The sound of this letter. In English, *x* stands for six sounds: *ks, gz, ksh, gzh, z,* and *sh* (see *Pron.*, § 128). **3.** [*cap.*] In Roman numerals, 10 or, in the form ⋈, 1,000 or, in the form X̄, 10,000. XX stands for 20 and XXX for 30. When placed before another Roman numeral, X denotes that 10 is to be subtracted from the value of that numeral, and when placed after, that 10 is to be added; thus, XL stands for 40, LX for 60. See NUMBER, *Table.* **4.** Anything having the shape of the letter X. **5.** [*cap.*] The word *Christ*, alone or in combination (chiefly in *X*mas). **6.** [*not cap.*] *Math.* **a** An unknown quantity. **b** Usually in the form ×, the sign of multiplication; as, 2 × 2 = 4; in measurements, equiv. to *by*; as, a room 20 × 30 feet. **7.** As a *symbol*, used to denote: **a** Anyone or anything arbitrarily or conveniently so designated, esp. as the twenty-third or (see K, 3) twenty-fourth, or, when V and W are not used, the twenty-first, in order or class. **b** Anything marked with an *x*; specif., *Colloq., U. S.*, a ten-dollar bill; hence, **XX**, a twenty-dollar bill. **c** All the letters save the first letter of a word, as in D*X* for *distance.*

xanth-. = XANTHO-.

xan′thate (zăn′thāt), *n.* A salt or ester of xanthic acid.

xan′the·in (zăn′thē·ĭn), *n.* [Gr. *xanthos* yellow.] *Chem.* A soluble yellow coloring matter found in yellow flowers.

xan′thic (zăn′thĭk), *adj.* [F. *xanthique*, fr. Gr. *xanthos* yellow.] **1.** Pert. to, or tending toward, a yellow color; specif., *Bot.*, designating flowers with some tint of yellow. Cf. CYANIC, 2. **2.** *Chem.* **a** Of or pertaining to xanthin or xanthine. **b** Pert. to or designating any of a series of thio acids, as, specif., a colorless unstable oil, C_2H_5OCSSH.

xan′thin (-thĭn), *n.* [Gr. *xanthos* yellow.] *Chem.* A yellow insoluble coloring matter extracted from yellow flowers.

xan′thine (-thēn; -thĭn), *n.* Also **xan′thin.** [Gr. *xanthos* yellow.] *Biochem.* A white microcrystalline nitrogenous compound, $C_5H_4N_4O_2$, present in muscle tissue, urine, and certain plants, and closely related to uric acid.

Xan·thip′pe (zăn·tĭp′ē; -thĭp′ē) *or* **Xan·tip′pe** (-tĭp′ē), *n.* [Gr. *Xanthippē.*] Socrates's wife, whose peevish scolding and quarrelsome temper have become proverbial.

xan′tho- (zăn′thō-), **xanth-.** [Gr. *xanthos.*] A combining form meaning *yellow*, as in *xantho*phyll.

xan′tho·chroid (-kroid), *adj.* [*xantho-* + Gr. *chroa* color + *-oid.*] *Ethnol.* Having light-colored hair and fair complexion. — *n.* A person having xanthochroid traits.

xan′tho·phyll (-fĭl), *n.* Also **xan′tho·phyl.** [*xantho-* + *-phyll.*] *Biochem.* **a** A crystalline, unsaturated compound, $C_{40}H_{56}O_2$, found in plants, having a golden-yellow color in dilute solution; — called also *lutein.* **b** Any of several related natural yellow pigments.

xan′thous (zăn′thŭs), *adj.* [Gr. *xanthos* yellow.] Yellow; specif., *Ethnol.*, of or pert. to those races with yellowish, red, auburn, or brown hair; also, designating or pert. to races (esp. the Mongolian) with yellow complexion.

X chromosome. *Biol.* See SEX CHROMOSOME.

xe′bec (zē′bĕk), *n.* [From earlier *chebec* (with influence of Sp. *xabeque*, now *jabeque*), through F. & It., fr. Ar. *shabbāk.*] *Naut.* A Mediterranean vessel, usually three-masted, with long overhanging bow and stern.

xe′ni·a (zē′nĭ·ȧ), *n.* [NL., fr. Gr. *xenia* hospitality, fr. *xenos* guest.] *Bot.* The direct influence of pollen upon the seed in the cross-pollination of certain plants, whereby hybrid characters are manifested in the form, color, etc., of the fruit or seed in the same generation.

xen′o- (zĕn′ō-), **xen-.** [Gr. *xenos.*] A combining form meaning: **a** *Guest, stranger.* **b** *Strange; foreign.*

xe·nog′a·my (zē·nŏg′ȧ·mĭ), *n.* [*xeno-* + *-gamy.*] *Bot.* Cross-fertilization. — **xe·nog′a·mous** (-mŭs), *adj.*

xen′o·gen′e·sis (zĕn′ō·jĕn′ē·sĭs), *n.* [NL., fr. *xeno-* + *-genesis.*] *Biol.* **a** Spontaneous generation. **b** Alternation of generations. **c** The fancied production of an organism altogether and permanently unlike the parent. — **xen′o·ge·net′ic** (-jē·nĕt′ĭk), **xen′o·gen′ic** (-jĕn′ĭk), *adj.*

xen′o·lith (zĕn′ō·lĭth), *n.* [*xeno-* + *-lith.*] *Petrog.* A fragment of a rock included in another rock.

xen′o·mor′phic (-môr′fĭk), *adj.* *Petrog.* Having a form other than its own; — said of mineral grains of igneous rocks whose mutual growths have prevented the assumption of outward crystal form. Cf. IDIOMORPHIC.

xe′non (zē′nŏn; zĕn′ŏn), *n.* [Gr., neut. of *xenos* strange.] *Chem.* A heavy, colorless, inert gaseous element occurring in air (about one part in 170 millions by volume). Symbol, *Xe* or *X*; at. no., 54; at. wt., 131.3.

xen′o·pho′bi·a (zĕn′ō·fō′bĭ·ȧ), *n.* [NL., fr. *xeno-* + *-phobia.*] Hatred of foreigners.

xe′ric (zē′rĭk; zēr′ĭk), *adj.* [Gr. *xēros* dry.] *Bot.* Characterized by deficiency of moisture, or aridity.

xe′ro- (zē′rō-), **xer-.** [Gr. *xēros.*] A combining form meaning *dry*, as in **xe′ro·der′ma**, a disease of the skin, characterized by dryness, roughness, and the peeling off of flakes of skin.

xe·roph′i·lous (zē·rŏf′ĭ·lŭs), *adj.* [*xero-* + *-philous.*] *Bot.* Drought-resistant, as desert plants. — **xe·roph′i·ly** (-lĭ), *n.*

xe′roph·thal′mi·a (zē′rŏf·thăl′mĭ·ȧ), *n.* [LL., fr. Gr. *xērophthalmia*, fr. *xēros* dry + *ophthalmos* the eye.] *Med.* A dry and thickened condition of the conjunctiva, leading to a lusterless condition of the eyeball. — **xe′roph·thal′mic** (-mĭk), *adj.*

xe′ro·phyte (zē′rō·fīt), *n.* [*xero-* + *-phyte.*] *Ecology.* A xerophilous plant. — **xe′ro·phyt′ic** (-fĭt′ĭk), *adj.*

xi (zī; ksī; ksē), *n.* [Gr.] The fourteenth letter (Ξ, ξ) of the Greek alphabet, equivalent to English *x.*

-xion. See -TION.

xiph′i·ster′num (zĭf′ĭ·stûr′nŭm), *n.*; *pl.* -NA (-nȧ). [NL., fr. Gr. *xiphos* a sword + *sternum.*] *Anat. & Zool.* The posterior or inferior segment of the sternum; — in man usually called *xiphoid.*

xiph′oid (zĭf′oid), *adj.* [Gr. *xiphoeidēs* sword-shaped, fr. *xiphos* sword + *eidos* form, shape.] *Anat.* Ensiform; sword-shaped. — *n.* The xiphisternum.

xiph′o·su′ran (zĭf′ō·sū′răn), *adj.* [Gr. *xiphos* sword + *oura* tail.] *Zool.* Of or designating an order (Xiphosura) of arthropods made up of the king crabs. See KING CRAB, *Illust.* — **xiph′o·su′ran**, *n.*

Xmas. See X, *n.*, 5.

XP (kī rō; kē rō). [The Greek letters chi (X) and rho (P), not the Eng. XP.] The first two letters of the Greek word ΧΡΙΣΤΟΣ, Christ; — an abbreviation used with the letters in a monogram.

X particle. = MESON.

X ray. **1.** *Physics.* Any of the radiations of the same nature as light radiation, but of an extremely short wave length, emitted primarily as the result of a sudden change in the velocity of a moving electric charge (as when rapidly moving cathode rays strike a solid obstacle, or target, in a vacuum tube), and as the result of changes in the atoms of the target due to this impact. The most notable properties of these rays are: (a) ionization of a gas through which they pass; (b) penetration through various thicknesses of all solids; (c) production of secondary X rays by impinging on material bodies; and (d) action on photographic plates, fluorescent screens, etc., like that of light. See ROENTGEN. **2.** A photograph obtained by use of X rays. — **X′-ray′**, *adj.*

X′–ray′ (*see Pron.*, § 2), *v. t.* To expose to the action of X rays; to examine, treat, or photograph with X rays.
X′–ray′ pho′to·graph. A shadow picture made with X rays.
X–ray therapy. *Med.* Treatment, as of a cancer, by controlled application of X rays.
X–ray tube. *Physics.* A vacuum tube designed to produce X rays copiously.
xy′lan (zī′lăn), *n.* [Gr. *xylon* wood.] *Chem.* A yellow gummy substance of the pentosan class, present in woody tissue, as straw.
xy′la·ry ray (zī′lȧ·rĭ). See MEDULLARY RAY.
xy′lem (zī′lĕm), *n.* [G., fr. Gr. *xylon* wood.] *Bot.* A complex tissue in higher plants, consisting of tracheids or tracheae (or both) and usually also of wood fibers and parenchyma cells; woody tissue; — disting. from *phloem.* It conveys water and minerals, serves as mechanical support, and (in many plants) stores food during dormant periods. Xylem originating from apical meristem is called ***primary xylem,*** while that produced by the cambium is called ***secondary xylem.*** Xylem constitutes the wood of timber trees.
xy′lene (zī′lēn), *n.* [Gr. *xylon* wood.] *Chem.* Any of three isomeric colorless hydrocarbons, $C_6H_4(CH_3)_2$, derivatives of benzene, found in coal and wood tar and certain kinds of petroleum. Commercial xylene, a mixture of the three, is used as a solvent.
xy′lic (zī′lĭk; zĭl′ĭk), *adj.* *Chem.* Pertaining to or designating any of six isomeric crystalline acids, $(CH_3)_2C_6H_3CO_2H$, carboxyl derivatives of xylene.
xy′li·dine (zī′lĭ·dēn; zĭl′ĭ-; -dĭn), *n.* Also **xy′li·din.** [From XYLENE.] Any one of six isomeric compounds, $(CH_3)_2C_6H_3NH_2$, amino derivatives of xylene, resembling aniline. Commercial xylidine, used in making certain dyes, is a liquid consisting of a mixture of five of the above compounds.
xy′lo- (zī′lō-), **xyl-.** [Gr. *xylon.*] A combining form meaning *wood,* as in *xylo*phone.
xy·log′ra·phy (zī·lŏg′rȧ·fĭ), *n.* [*xylo-* + *-graphy.*] The art of engraving on wood or of taking impressions from engravings so made. — **xy′lo·graph** (zī′lō·grăf), *n.* — **xy·log′ra·pher** (zī·lŏg′rȧ·fẽr), *n.* — **xy′lo·graph′ic** (zī′lō·grăf′ĭk), **xy′lo·graph′i·cal** (-ĭ·kăl), *adj.*
xy′loid (zī′loid), *adj.* [*xyl-* + *-oid.*] Resembling wood.
xy′lol (zī′lōl; -lŏl), *n.* [*xyl-* + *-ol,* 2.] Xylene.
xy·loph′a·gous (zī·lŏf′ȧ·gŭs), *adj.* [Gr. *xylophagos* eating wood, fr. *xylon* wood + *phagein* to eat.] *Zool.* Eating, boring in, or destroying wood; — said esp. of certain insect larvae, crustaceans, and mollusks. — **xy′lo·phage** (zī′lō·fāj), *n.*
xy′lo·phone (zī′lō·fōn; zĭl′ō-), *n.* [*xylo-* + Gr. *phōnē* sound.] *Music.* A percussion instrument consisting of a series of wooden bars, graduated in length to sound the musical scale, and sounded by striking with two small wooden hammers. Cf. GLOCKENSPIEL. — **xy′lo·phon′ist** (-fōn′ĭst; zī·lŏf′ō·nĭst; zī-), *n.*

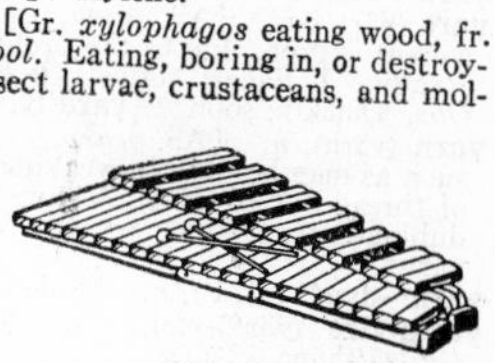

Xylophone.

xy′lose (zī′lōs), *n.* [*xyl-* + *-ose.*] *Chem.* A crystalline nonfermentable sugar, $C_5H_{10}O_5$, one form of which, dextroxylose (called also *wood sugar*), is made by hydrolysis of xylan.
xy·lot′o·mous (zī·lŏt′ō·mŭs), *adj.* [*xylo-* + root of Gr. *temnein* to cut.] *Zool.* Capable of boring or cutting wood; — said of many insects.
xy·lot′o·my (-mĭ), *n.* [*xylo-* + *-tomy.*] Art of preparing sections of wood, esp. by means of a microtome, for microscopic examination. — **xy·lot′o·mist** (-mĭst), *n.*
xys′ter (zĭs′tẽr), *n.* [NL., fr. Gr. *xystēr* a scraper, fr. Gr. *xystos,* fr. *xyein* to scrape, polish.] *Surg.* An instrument for scraping bones.

Y

Y, y (wī), *n.; pl.* Y's, y's, Ys, ys (wīz). **1.** The twenty-fifth letter of the English alphabet. It comes from the Latin, which borrowed it, after the Roman conquest, from the Greek *upsilon* and used it as a vowel in the writing of Greek words. *Y* is ultimately from the same Semitic source as *U, V,* and *W.* **2.** The sound of this letter. In English, *y* has both consonantal and vocalic value. At the beginning of a word or syllable, except when a prefix (see Y-), it is usually pronounced as a voiced palatal spirant consonant, but with slight or no audible friction (as in *yes*); as a prefix, and usually in the middle or at the end of a syllable, it is a vowel, with various values (as in *myth, happy, my, myrrh, martyr*). See *Pron.*, § 129. **3.** Anything having the shape of the letter **Y**. **4.** As a *symbol,* used to denote or indicate anyone or anything arbitrarily or conveniently so designated, esp. as the twenty-fourth or (see K, 3) twenty-fifth, or, when V and W are not used, the twenty-second, in order or class.
y- (ĭ-). Also **i-** (ĭ-). [ME. *y-, i-,* fr. AS. *ge-.*] A prefix originally denoting *association,* but by Spenser and later archaists used chiefly with past participles in a vaguely perfective sense, as in *y*-clept, *y*-wrought.
-y (-ĭ; 53). [F. or L. or Gr.; F. *-ie,* fr. L. *-ia,* often fr. Gr. *-ia, -eia.*] A suffix of nouns, esp. of abstract nouns, as in courtes*y,* glor*y,* jealous*y,* victor*y.* It often forms abstract nouns corresponding to adjectives in *-ous,* as in *-geny, -gamy, -phagy,* etc.
-y (-ĭ; 53). Also **-ie** (-ĭ). [Origin obscure.] A noun suffix forming diminutives, as in Johnn*y,* lass*ie.*
-y (-ĭ; 53). Also, *esp. after y,* **-ey** (-ĭ). [AS. *-ig.*] An adjective suffix, Anglo-Saxon *-ig,* signifying: **a** *Characterized by; having; full of;* as in angr*y,* ston*y,* clay*ey.* **b** *Tending* or *inclined to; -ive;* as in chatt*y,* sleep*y.* **c** *Somewhat; rather; -ish;* as in chill*y,* lank*y.* **d** *Chiefly Colloq. Somewhat like; suggesting;* as in bump*y,* mess*y.*
-y. [AF. or L.; AF. *-ie,* fr. L. *-ium.*] A noun suffix, denoting *result of action,* as in augur*y,* perjur*y.*
yab′ber (yăb′ẽr), *v. i. & n.* [From native *yabba* language, talk.] *Australia.* Talk; jabber.
yacht (yŏt), *n.* [D. *jacht,* fr. MD. *jaght, jaghtschip,* lit., a pursuit ship (orig. against pirates), fr. *jaght* pursuit, chase, hunting.] *Naut.* Any one of various types of relatively small vessels, characteristically with sharp prow and graceful lines, and ordinarily used for pleasure. — *v. i.* To race or cruise in a yacht.
yacht′ing, *n.* The action, fact, or pastime of cruising in or navigating a yacht.
yachts′man (yŏts′măn), *n.* One who owns or sails a yacht for pleasure; one devoted to yachting. — **yachts′man·ship, yacht′man·ship,** *n.* — **yachts′wom′an** (-wo͝om′ăn), *n.*
yaff (yăf), *n. & v. i.* [Imitative.] *Scot.* Bark; yelp; scold.
ya′ger (yä′gẽr). Var. of JÄGER.
ya′gi (yä′gĭ; yăg′ĭ), *n.; pl.* YAGIS (-gĭz; -ĭz). [After H. *Yagi* (b. 1886), Jap. electrical engineer.] A highly directional, selective antenna consisting of horizontal, parallel, tubular rods whose length equals that of the radio or television channel for which it is used.
Ya′hoo (yä′ho͞o; yä·ho͞o′; yā′-), *n.* **1.** In Swift's *Gulliver's Travels,* one of a filthy race of brutes having the form and all the vices of man. See HOUYHNHNM. **2.** Hence [*not cap.*]: **a** Any degraded or vicious man. **b** *U. S.* A lout; bumpkin.
Yah′ve (yä′vĕ), **Yah′veh, Yah′vism, Yah·vis′tic.** Vars. of YAHWEH, etc.
Yah′weh (yä′wĕ), **Yah′we,** *n.* Also **Jah′veh, Jah′ve** (yä′vĕ), etc. A modern transliteration of the Hebrew word translated *Jehovah* in the Bible; — used by some critics to discriminate the tribal god of the ancient Hebrews from the Christian *Jehovah.* See TETRAGRAMMATON.
Yah′wism (-wĭz′m), *n.* Also **Jah′vism** (-vĭz′m). **1.** The worship of Yahweh (Jehovah), or the system of doctrines, etc., connected with it. **2.** Use of *Yahweh* as a name for God.
Yah·wis′tic (yä·wĭs′tĭk), *adj.* Also **Jah·vis′tic, Jah·wis′tic** (yä-), older **Je′ho·vis′tic** (jē′hō·vĭs′tĭk). Characterized by the use of *Yahweh,* or *Jehovah,* as a name of God; — said of certain parts of the Old Testament, esp. of the Hexateuch. Cf. ELOHISTIC.
yak (yăk), *n.;* see PLURAL, *Note,* 3. [Tibetan *gyag.*] A large wild or domesticated ox (*Bos grunniens*) of Tibet and adjacent elevated parts of central Asia.
yam (yăm), *n.* [Pg. *inhame,* fr. Senegal (Guinea) *nyami* to eat.] **1.** The edible, starchy root of various plants (genus *Dioscorea,* as *D. sativa, D. alata,* etc.). It largely replaces the potato as a food in tropical climates. The genus is typical of a family (Dioscoreaceae, the yam family) of monocotyledonous twining herbs having netted-veined leaves and small dioecious flowers. **2. a** *Scot.* The potato. **b** *Southern U. S.* The sweet potato.
ya′men (yä′mĕn), *n.* [Chin. (Pek.) ya^2-men^2, lit., flag gate; — because flags were placed in front of the buildings.] In China, the official headquarters or residence of a mandarin or tuchun.
yam′mer (yăm′ẽr), *n. & v.* [AS. *gēomrian, gēomerian,* fr. *gēomor* sad, sorrowful.] *Now Dial. & Colloq.* **a** Whimper. **b** Yell; cry; — of birds. **c** Chatter; stammer.
yank (yăngk), *n.* [Origin uncert.] *Colloq., U. S.* A jerk or twitch. — *v. t. & i.* *Colloq.* To jerk.
Yank (yăngk), *n. & adj.* *Slang.* Short for YANKEE.
Yan′kee (yăng′kē), *n.* [Often derived, through an early *Yengee(s),* fr. Am. Ind. corrupt. of *English,* or F. *Anglais,* but prob. fr. a D. dim. of *Jan* John, as applied by the Dutch of N. Y. to the English of Conn.] A nickname for a native of New England, or, by extension, of the northern part of the United States; also, as sometimes used by foreigners, any inhabitant of the United States. — *adj.* Of, pert. to, or characteristic of the Yankees; loosely, *Brit.,* American. — **Yan′kee·dom** (-dŭm), *n.* — **Yan′kee·ism** (-ĭz′m), *n.*
Yan′kee–Doo′dle (-do͞o′d'l), *n.* A song and air, popularly recognized as quasi-national in the United States. The words, which are doggerel and of which there are several versions, are said to have been written originally in 1755 in derision of the provincial troops, by Dr. Schuckburgh, a surgeon in Lord Amherst's army.
yap (yăp; yȧp), *n.* [Imitative.] **1.** A snappish bark; yelp. **2.** *Chiefly Slang.* **a** Talk; gab. **b** A hoodlum. **c** A bumpkin. — *v. i.;* YAPPED (yăpt; yȧpt); YAP′PING. **1.** To bark snappishly; to yelp. **2.** *Slang.* To talk noisily.
ya·pok′, ya·pock′ (yȧ·pŏk′), *n.* [From *Oyapok, Oyapock,* river in Guiana, prob. fr. Tupi *oyapuça, oaiapussá,* a monkey of the genus *Callicebus.*] A small semiaquatic South and Central American opossum (*Chironectes minimus*). Cf. OPOSSUM.
Ya′qui (yä′kē), *n.* An Indian of one of the most important of the Piman tribes, now living in Sonora, Mexico.
Yar′bor′ough (yär′bûr′ō; -bŭ·rŭ), *n.* *Whist.* A hand containing no card higher than a nine; — so called because a former Lord Yarborough used to offer 1,000 to 1 before a deal that the taker would not hold such a hand.
yard (yärd), *n.* [AS. *gierd, gyrd,* rod, measure, yard.] **1.** A measure of length, the standard of English and American linear measure. Abbr. *yd.;* pl. *yd.* or *yds.* See MEASURE, *Tables* 1 & 3. **2.** *Naut.* A long spar, tapering toward the ends, to support and extend a square, lateen, or lug sail.
yard, *n.* [AS. *geard.*] **1.** An enclosure; specif.: **a** A small enclosed place in front of or around a house, barn, or other building. **b** An enclosure within which any work or business is carried on; — usually in combinations; as, a brick*yard.* **2.** The grounds of a building or group of buildings, as the campus of a university. **3.** A locality in a forest where moose or deer herd in winter for feeding and protection; as, a moose *yard.* **4.** *Railroads.* A system of tracks within prescribed limits used for making up trains, storing cars, etc. — *v. t.* To confine, enclose, or store in a yard; to shut up, or keep, in a yard; — often with *up.*
yard′age (yär′dĭj), *n.* The aggregate number of yards (linear, square, or cubic); also, the length, extent, or volume of something as measured in yards.
yard′age, *n.* Use of a yard, as for keeping cattle received at a railroad station; also, the charge for such use.
yard′arm′ (yärd′ärm′), *n.* *Naut.* Either end of a square-rigged vessel's yard.
yard grass. A coarse annual grass (*Eleusine indica*) having digitate spikes, common in dooryards, etc.
yard′man (yärd′măn), *n.; pl.* -MEN (-mĕn). *Naut.* A sailor assigned to the yards.
yard′man (-măn), *n.* A man employed in or about a yard; specif., *Railroads,* an employee engaged in yard service.

yard′mas′ter (yärd′más′tẽr), *n.* *Railroads.* The man in charge of, and directing operations in, a yard.

yard′stick′ (yärd′stĭk′), *n.* **1.** A stick three feet, or a yard, in length, used as a measure of cloth, etc. **2.** A test or criterion by which something intangible is measured. — **Syn.** See STANDARD.

yard′wand′ (-wŏnd′), *n.* A yardstick.

yare (yâr), *adj.* [AS. *gearu, gearo,* ready, complete. The initial consonant is prob. due to the prefix *ge-* (see Y-).] *Archaic & Dial.* **a** Ready. **b** Eager; active. **c** Easily worked; manageable. — *adv. Obs.* Quickly; soon. — **yare′ly**, *adv.*

yarn (yärn), *n.* [AS. *gearn.*] **1.** Spun wool, flax, silk, cotton, etc., such as may be used in weaving, in knitting, and in the manufacture of thread. **2.** *Colloq.* A story of adventure; an exciting and, often, dubiously true story. — *v. i. Colloq.* To tell yarns; to spin a yarn or yarns.

yarn′-dyed′ (-dīd′), *n.* Made of yarn dyed before being woven.

yar′o·vize (yär′ō·vīz), *v. t.* Var. of JAROVIZE. — **yar′o·vi·za′tion** (-vĭ·zā′shŭn; -vī-), *n.*

yar′row (yăr′ō), *n.* [AS. *gearwe.*] **a** A strong-scented Eurasian herb (*Achillea millefolium*) of the aster family, widely naturalized in North America, having small white corymbose flowers. **b** Any of several related American species.

yash·mak′ (yäsh·mäk′; yăsh′măk), *n.* Also **yash·mac′**. [Ar. *yashmaq.*] A form of double veil worn by Mohammedan women when not in their private apartments.

yat′a·ghan (yăt′*à*·găn), *n.* Also **yat′a·gan**. [Turk. *yātāghan.*] A long knife, or short saber, without a crosspiece, common among Mohammedans.

yaud (yôd; yäd), *n.* *Scot.* A work horse, esp. a mare.

yauld (yôd; yäd; yäld), *adj.* *Scot.* Alert; active.

yaup (yôp; yäp), **yaup′er**. Vars. of YAWP, etc.

yau′pon (yô′pŏn), *n.* [Am. Ind. *yopún.*] A species of holly (*Ilex vomitoria*) native to the southern United States. The smooth elliptical leaves are used as a substitute for tea.

yaw (yô), *v. i. & t.* [Origin uncert.] **1.** *Naut.* To steer wild, or out of the line of her course, as when struck by a heavy sea; — said of a vessel. **2.** *Aeronautics.* To turn or deviate from the line of flight by angular motion about the normal, or vertical, axis of an airplane. — **yaw**, *n.*

yawl (yôl), *n. & v.* *Now Dial.* Howl; scream.

yawl, *n.* [MLG. *jolle,* D. *jol.*] *Naut.* **1.** A ship's small boat; jolly boat. **2.** A fore-and-aft rigged vessel carrying a mainsail and one or more jibs, with mizzenmast far aft.

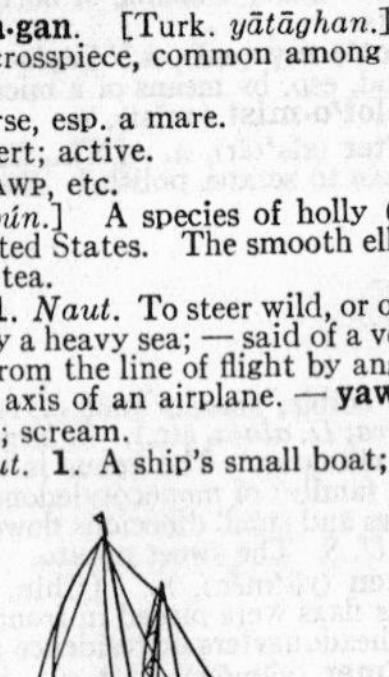

Yawl, 2.

yaw′me′ter (yô′mē′tẽr), *n.* An instrument for measuring the angle of yaw of an aircraft.

yawn (yôn), *v. i.* [ME. *ȝanien,* prob. for *ganien, gonien,* fr. AS. *gānian,* influenced by the kindred ME. *yonen, ȝeonien,* AS. *geonian* to yawn.] **1.** To open the mouth wide, esp. involuntarily through drowsiness, dullness, or fatigue. **2.** To open wide; to gape. — *v. t.* **1.** To open wide. **2.** To utter with a yawn. — *n.* **1.** Act of yawning, opening wide, or gaping. **2.** A chasm, mouth, or opening. — **yawn′er**, *n.*

yawp, yaup (yôp; yäp), *v. i.* *Dial.* **a** To yelp; bawl; to scream as a bird. **b** *Also Slang.* To talk noisily; yap. **c** To yawn audibly; gape. — **yawp, yaup**, *n.* — **yawp′er, yaup′er**, *n.*

yaws (yôz), *n. pl.* [Of Cariban origin.] *Med.* Frambesia.

Y chromosome. *Biol.* See SEX CHROMOSOME.

y-clad′ (ĭ·klăd′). Archaic past part. of CLOTHE.

y-clept′, y-cleped′ (ĭ·klĕpt′), *past part.* [AS. *geclipod,* past part. of (*ge*)*clipian* to call.] *Archaic.* Called; named.

ye (yē; 4), *pron.* [ME. *ye, ȝe,* nom. pl., fr. AS. *ge, gē.*] *Archaic.* The personal pronoun of the second person, used: **1.** As nominative plural; — orig. its only construction. **2.** As nominative singular. **3.** (*pron.* yē, yĭ) As objective singular & plural. **4.** Disjunctively, by way of address or emphasis.

ye (thē; *cf.* THE, *def. art.*). An old method of printing the article *the* (AS. *þe*), "y" being used for the Anglo-Saxon, or Old English, and Middle English character thorn (*þ*). It is often printed *y*ᵉ as if a contraction, like *y*ᵗ for *that,* and is sometimes incorrectly pronounced *yē.*

yea (yā; *obs. or archaic* yē), *adv.* [ME. *ye, ya,* fr. AS. *gēa, gē.*] **1.** Yes; — an affirmative answer now superseded by *yes.* **2.** Indeed; truly; — introducing a question or assertion. **3.** *Archaic.* More than this; not only so, but; — marking the addition of something more emphatic. — *n.* The word "yea" uttered in assent; specif., an affirmative vote; one who votes in the affirmative.

yeal′ing (yēl′ĭn), *n.* *Scot.* A contemporary in age.

yean (yēn), *v. t. & i.* [AS., fr. *ge-* + *ēanian* to yearn.] To bring forth young, as a goat or a sheep; lamb.

yean′ling (-lĭng), *n.* [*yean* + 1st *-ling.*] A lamb or a kid. — *adj.* Newborn; young.

year (yẽr), *n.* [ME. *yer, yeer,* fr. AS. *gēar.*] **1.** The time of one apparent revolution of the sun around the ecliptic; the period occupied by the earth in making its revolution around the sun, called the ***astronomical, equinoctial, natural, solar,*** *or* ***tropical year,*** whose length is 365 days, 5 hours, 48 minutes, 45.51 seconds. The ***lunar year*** is a period of 354 days divided into 12 lunar months. **2.** A period of 365 days (***common year***) or, in leap year (which see), 366 days. See MEASURE, *Table* 6. Abbr. *yr.,* or *y.;* pl. *yr., yrs.,* or *y.* The ***calendar year, civil year,*** *or* ***legal year*** begins Jan. 1 and ends Dec. 31. Formerly, in England, the legal year began on Annunciation (Day), March 25; the change to January 1 took place on that day in 1752; in Scotland in 1600. Hence, dates between January 1 and March 25 are sometimes written thus: February 21, 1574–5, that is, 1575 according to present reckoning. **3.** A period having the same length as the civil year, but having different limits fixed by a special calendar or schedule; as, the school *year.* **4.** *pl.* Age; also, old age; as, a man in *years.* **5.** *Chiefly pl.* In vague use: **a** A period of time; as, in *years* to come. **b** A long time; as, *years* before. **6.** The time in which any planet completes a revolution about the sun.

year′book′ (yẽr′bo͝ok′), *n.* A book, as of the statistics or facts of a year, published yearly; an annual.

year′ling (yẽr′lĭng; yûr′-), *n.* [*year* + 1st *-ling.*] **1.** One that is a year old; usually, an animal one year old, or in the second year of its age. The racing and trotting rules provide that the age of a horse shall be reckoned from January 1st of the year when it was foaled. **2.** A member of the next to the lowest class in the United States Military Academy at West Point. — *adj.* A year old.

year′long′ (yẽr′lŏng′), *adj.* Lasting through a year.

year′ly (yẽr′lĭ; yûr′-), *adj.* Recurring every year; made, done, observed, produced, received, etc., every year or during each year; annual. — *adv.* Annually; once a year.

yearn (yûrn), *v. i.* [AS. *geornian, gyrnan, giernan;* akin to AS. *georn* desirous, eager.] **1.** To be filled with longing. **2.** To feel pity or sympathy. — **Syn.** See LONG. — **yearn′ing** (yûr′nĭng), *adj. & n.* — **yearn′ing·ly**, *adv.*

yeast (yēst), *n.* [AS. *gist.*] **1.** A substance consisting of the aggregated cells of certain minute sac fungi, and appearing as a surface froth or as a thick sediment in fruit juices, malt worts, and other saccharine liquids, in which it induces alcoholic fermentation through the agency of an enzyme (see ZYMASE). Yeast is used in making alcoholic liquors, esp. beer, and in baking as a means of leavening. **2.** Any of a family (Saccharomycetaceae) of minute unicellular fungi. **3.** A commercial product (***yeast′cake′***) consisting of meal or the like impregnated with living yeast (see sense 1, above). **4.** Spume, or foam, as of water. **5.** **a** That which causes ferment; a leaven. **b** Ferment; agitation. — *v. i.* To ferment; froth.

yeast′y (yēs′tĭ), *adj.* **1.** Consisting of or like yeast. **2.** **a** Frothy; frivolous. **b** Foaming; spumy; — esp. of water.

yegg (yĕg), *n.* Also **yegg′man** (-măn), *n.* *Slang.* A safebreaker or burglar; broadly, any burglar.

yeld (yĕld), *adj.* Also **yell** (yĕl). [AS. *geld.*] *Scot.* Of an animal, esp. a cow or ewe: **a** Barren. **b** Giving no milk.

yelk (yĕlk). Var. of YOLK.

yell (yĕl), *v. i. & t.* [AS. *giellan, gillan, gyllan.*] To shriek; scream. — *n.* **a** A shriek. **b** *U. S. & Canada.* A shout or cheer, usually rhythmic, used esp. by college students, as to encourage contestants in athletic sports, etc.; as, the college *yell.* — **yell′er**, *n.*

yel′low (yĕl′ō), *adj.* [ME. *yelow, yelwe,* fr. AS. *geolu* (gen. masc. & neut. *geolwes*).] **1.** Of the color yellow. **2.** **a** Changed to a sallow hue through age, disease, etc.; yellowed; as, *yellow* parchment, skin. **b** Having a yellow complexion, as a Mongolian. **3.** Figuratively: **a** Jaundiced, or jealous, melancholy, etc. **b** Cowardly or treacherous. **c** Sensational; — of some newspapers, etc. Hence, **yellow journal, yellow journalism, yellow journalist, yellow press.** — *n.* **1.** **a** Any of several colors the hues of which resemble those of ripe lemons, or of butter, or of sunflowers; any color the hue of which is that of the portion of the color spectrum lying between red and green. **b** That one of the four psychological primaries which is seen when energy of wave length 574.5 mμ is employed as a stimulus. **2.** Any pigment or dye that colors yellow (sense 1). **3.** The yolk of an egg. **4.** Short for YELLOW SPONGE. **5.** **a** *pl.* Jaundice, esp. of domestic animals. **b** *Obs.* A jaundiced humor; jealousy. **6.** *pl. Plant Pathol.* Any of several unrelated plant diseases occurring in aster, cabbage, celery, peach, etc., in which growth is stunted and there is a yellowing of the foliage. — *v. t. & i.* To make or turn yellow.

yel′low-billed′ cuck′oo. See CUCKOO.

yellow birch. See BIRCH.

yel′low·bird′ (yĕl′ō·bûrd′), *n.* **a** The American goldfinch. **b** *Local, U. S.* The yellow warbler.

yellow daisy. The black-eyed Susan *rudbeckia hirta.*

yellow fever. *Med.* An acute, infectious, often fatal, febrile disease, characterized by jaundice, hemorrhages, vomiting, etc. It occurs in certain tropical and semitropical regions. The **yel′low-fe′ver mos·qui′to** (*Aëdes aegypti:* see AËDES) is the usual agent for transmitting the virus that produces it. Cf. MALARIA.

yel′low-green′, *n.* The hue of the color cycle exactly intermediate between yellow and green. See COLOR. — **yel′low-green′**, *adj.*

yellow-green algae. See ALGA.

yellow gum. See GUM, 5 **a**.

yel′low·ham′mer (yĕl′ō·hăm′ẽr), *n.* [For *yellowammer,* fr. AS. *amore* a kind of bird.] **a** A common European finch (*Emberiza citrinella*). The male is mostly bright yellow. **b** *Local, U. S.* The flicker.

yel′low·ish (yĕl′ō·ĭsh), *adj.* Somewhat yellow.

yellow jack. **a** Yellow fever. **b** The quarantine flag. **c** A silvery and golden food fish (*Caranx,* or *Elaphotoxon, bartholomaei*) of Florida and the West Indies.

yellow jacket. Any of several American social wasps (genus *Vespa*), having the body partly bright yellow. They are noted for their irritability and their painful stings.

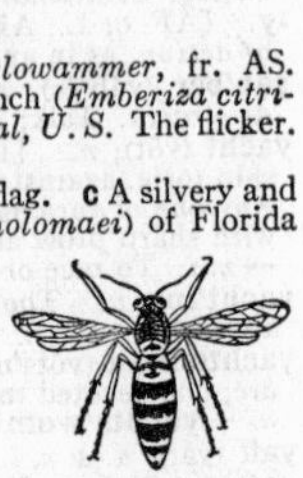

Yellow Jacket. (3/4)

yellow lead ore (lĕd). Wulfenite.

yel′low-legs′ (yĕl′ō·lĕgz′), *n. sing. & pl.* Either of two American shore birds allied to the greenshank but having long yellow legs. The ***lesser yellowlegs*** (*Totanus flavipes*) is about eleven inches long, and the ***greater, or winter, yellowlegs*** (*T. melanoleucus*) is about fourteen inches long.

yellow metal. Gold.

yel′low·ness, *n.* Quality or state of being yellow.

yellow peril. The supposed danger to people of a white race imminent in the dominance of races, like the Chinese and Japanese, having yellow or yellowish-brown skin.

yellow pine. Any of various American pines or their timber, as the Georgia pine, the loblolly, etc. See PINE.

yellow race. The Mongolian race.

yel′lows (yĕl′ōz), *n.* = YELLOW, *n.,* 5.

yellow sponge. A yellow or brownish short-fibered commercial sponge (*Euspongia agaricina corlosia*) occurring in the Gulf of Mexico and in the Atlantic Ocean off the West Indies.

yellow spot. *Anat.* The most sensitive area on the human retina. See EYE, *Illust.*

yellow streak. A streak of cowardice or timidity.

yel′low·tail′ (yĕl′ō·tāl′), *n.;* see PLURAL, *Note,* 3. Any of various fishes having a yellow or yellowish tail; as: **a** A carangoid fish (genus *Seriola*), esp. one (*S. dorsalis*) of the coast of California and southward. **b** The menhaden. **c** A California rockfish (*Sebastodes flavidus*).

yel′low·throat′ (-thrōt′), *n.* Any of several American warblers (genus *Geothlypis*); esp., the ***Maryland yellowthroat*** (*G. trichas*).

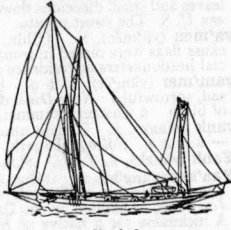

yellow warbler. A small, mostly yellow, North American warbler (*Dendroica aestiva*).

yellow water lily. Any of a genus (*Nuphar*) of aquatic plants usually having yellow flowers.

yel′low·weed′ (yĕl′ō·wēd′), *n.* **a** = SNEEZEWEED. **b** *Local, U.S.* Any of several species of goldenrod. **c** *Dial. Eng.* Weld, the plant. **d** The European ragwort *Senecio jacobaea.*

yel′low·wood′ (-wo͝od′), *n.* The wood of any of various trees having light-colored or yellowish wood; also, any of the trees themselves; specif.: *U.S.* **a** A southern tree (*Cladrastis lutea*) having showy white fragrant flowers and yielding a yellow dye. **b** Locally, the Osage orange, the smoke tree, etc.

yelp (yĕlp), *v. i. & t.* [ME. *yelpen* to boast, boast noisily, fr. AS. *gielpan, gilpan, gylpan.*] To utter a sharp, quick cry, as a hound; to bark or cry shrilly. — *n.* A sharp quick cry, bark, etc. — **yelp′er,** *n.*

yen (yĕn), *n. sing. & pl.* [Jap., fr. Chin. (Pek.) *yüan*[2] round, a circle.] The monetary unit of Japan, divided into 100 sen, equivalent to 0.75 gram of pure gold. See MONEY, *Tables.*

yen, *n.* [Chin. (Pek.) *yen*[1], opium, lit., smoke.] *Slang.* An intense desire; a longing; an urge; as, he has a *yen* to travel. — *v. i. Slang.* To desire intensely; to long; to yearn.

yeo′man (yō′măn), *n.* [ME. *yoman.*] **1.** *Hist.* An attendant; esp., a gentleman attendant in a royal or noble household, subordinate in rank to an esquire, who performed menial services; retainer. **2.** *Hist.* A subordinate or assistant. **3.** A man of the commonalty of the first or most respectable class; a freeholder; a man free born. **4.** *Eng.* **a** A yeoman of the guard. **b** *Mil.* A member of the yeomanry (sense 2). **5.** *Nav.* A petty officer enlisted to perform clerical duties.

yeo′man·ly (yō′măn·lĭ), *adj.* Pertaining to a yeoman; of yeoman's rank; becoming to a yeoman; sturdy. — *adv.* As a yeoman; bravely.

yeoman of the (royal) guard. One of the bodyguard of the English sovereign, consisting of one hundred yeomen habited in a uniform dating from the 15th century; beefeater.

yeo′man·ry (yō′măn·rĭ), *n.* **1.** The body of yeomen, esp. of small landed proprietors. **2.** [*cap.*] A British volunteer cavalry force, created in 1761 orig. as a home defense force, since 1907 a part of the territorial force.

yeo′man's serv′ice (yō′mănz) *or* **yeoman service.** Great and loyal service, assistance, or support.

-yer (-yẽr). = -IER.

yerk (yûrk), *v. t. Obs. exc. Dial.* **1.** To lash. **2.** To jerk; wrench. **3.** To bind tightly. — *v. i. Obs. exc. Dial.* **1.** To move hastily. **2.** To work or think hard. **3.** Of a whip, to crack. **4.** To kick, as a horse. **5.** To draw stitches tight. — *n. Obs. exc. Dial.* **1.** A lashing; kick; also, a stab. **2.** A jerk.

yes (yĕs; *dial. or obs.* yĭs), *adv.* [ME. *yis, ȝes, ȝise,* fr. AS. *gese, gise,* prob. fr. *gēa, gē,* yea + *swā* so, or perh. fr. *gēa sī* so be it.] **1.** Aye; yea; — used to express affirmation, assent, or confirmation in answer to a question. **2.** More than this; what is more; — used to mark the addition of something more emphatic. — *n.; pl.* YESES (yĕs′ĕz; -ĭz). An affirmative reply; a yea.

ye′se (yēs). *Scot. & Dial.* Ye shall.

yes man. *Slang, U.S.* A person who agrees with everything that is said to him; one who endorses or supports, without criticism, every opinion or proposal of an associate or superior.

yes′ter (yĕs′tẽr), *adj.* [See YESTERDAY.] *Poetic.* Of, pert. to, or designating yesterday; — often in combination, as in **yes′ter·eve′, yes′ter·eve′ning, yes′ter·morn′, yes′ter·morn′ing, yes′ter·night′, yes′ter·noon′, yes′ter·week′, yes′ter·year′.** — **yes′ter,** *adv.*

yes′ter·day (yĕs′tẽr·dĭ; -dā; 13), *n.* [ME. *ȝisterdai,* fr. AS. *geostran dæg,* fr. *geostran, giestran,* yesterday + *dæg* day.] **1.** The day last past; the day next before the present. **2.** Figuratively, a recent time. — *adv.* **1.** On the day last past. **2.** At a time not long past. — *adj.* Of or belonging to yesterday, or to a very recent time.

yes′treen′ (yĕs′trēn′), *n. Chiefly Poetic & Scot.* Yestereve; yesternight. — *adv.* On yesterday evening.

yet (yĕt), *adv.* [AS. *gīt, gȳt, gīet.*] **1.** At any time up to the present, or a specified time; as soon as now. **2.** In addition; further. **3.** Before all is done; eventually. **4.** Although such be the case; nevertheless. — *conj. Obs.* Though; — sometimes followed by *that.*

yet. Dial. var. of GATE, an opening.

yeuk, yewk (yo͞ok), *n. & v. Scot.* Itch. — **yeuk′y,** *adj.*

yew (yo͞o; 113), *n.* [ME. *ew, ewe,* fr. AS. *ēow, īw.*] **1.** Any of a genus (*Taxus*) of coniferous shrubs and trees, esp. one species (*T. baccata*) often called ***English yew.*** Also, the fine-grained wood of any of these trees. The genus is typical of a family (Taxaceae, the yew family) of widely distributed trees and shrubs distinguished by dioecious flowers and, commonly, fleshy fruit. The ***Japanese yew*** (*T. cuspidata*) is widely grown as an ornamental tree. Cf. CONIFER. **2.** *Archaic.* A bow for shooting made of the yew.

Y·gerne′ (ē·gẽrn′). Var. of IGRAINE.

Ygg′dra·sill (ĭg′drȧ·sĭl; ŭg′-), *n.* Also **Yg′dra·sil.** [ON.] *Norse Myth.* The great ash tree symbolizing the universe.

YHVH, YHWH. See TETRAGRAMMATON.

Yid′dish (yĭd′ĭsh), *n.* [G. *jüdisch,* prop., Jewish.] A High German dialect developed under Hebrew and Slavic influence, spoken by Jews in Russia, in central European countries, and elsewhere. It is written in Hebrew characters. — **Yid′dish,** *adj.*

yield (yēld), *v. t.* [AS. *gieldan, gildan,* to pay, give, restore, make an offering.] **1.** *Archaic.* To pay or repay. **2.** To produce, give, or bring, as fruit, profit, or other return or result. **3.** To produce as payment or interest on what is expended or invested; as, an investment that *yields* five per cent. **4.** To give up possession of as claimed or demanded; as, to *yield* a military stronghold. **5.** To admit to be true; to concede. — *v. i.* **1.** To produce; bear. **2.** To give way; surrender; succumb. **3.** To give place, as to something superior; to give precedence. — **yield′er,** *n.*

Syn. (1) See RELINQUISH.
(2) **Yield, submit, capitulate, succumb, relent, defer** mean to give way when one can no longer resist. **Yield** implies a being overcome by force, argument, entreaty, etc.; **submit,** surrender after opposing or resisting; **capitulate,** submission to a force or power that one has not the strength, the skill, or the will to overcome; **succumb,** a giving way in weakness or helplessness, often suggesting death or subjugation; **relent,** a yielding, as through pity or mercy, by one who has the upper hand; **defer,** a yielding or submitting as through respect or reverence.

— *n.* That which is yielded; amount or quantity yielded; product.

yield′ing, *adj.* That yields. — **yield′ing·ly,** *adv.*

yill (yĭl). Scot. & N. of Eng. var. of ALE.

yin (yĭn). Chiefly Scot. var. of ONE.

yip (yĭp), *v. i.* [Imitative.] *Colloq.* To yelp; — said esp. of a dog. — **yip,** *n.*

yird (yûrd). Scot. & N. of Eng. var. of EARTH.

yirr (yûr), *n. & v.* [Prob. imitative.] *Scot.* Growl; snarl.

-yl (-ĭl; -ēl; *see note below*). [Gr. *hylē* wood, material.] *Chem.* A combining form, used in names of radicals, esp. univalent ones, as in ethyl, hydroxyl, etc.

☞ Chemists generally prefer the pron. -ĭl to -ēl.

y′lang-y′lang (ē′läng·ē′läng). *Phil. I.* Var. of ILANG-ILANG.

Y′mir (ē′mĭr; ü′mĭr), *n.* [ON. *Ymir.*] *Norse Myth.* The giant from whose body the gods created the world.

yo′del, yo′dle (yō′d'l), *v. t. & i.;* -DELED or -DELLED, -DLED (-d'ld); -DEL·ING or -DEL·LING (-d'l·ĭng; -dlĭng), -DLING (-dlĭng). [G. *jodeln.*] To sing with sudden changes from chest voice to head voice, or falsetto, and the reverse; to warble. — **yo′del, yo′dle,** *n.* — **yo′del·er, yo′del·ler** (yō′d'l·ẽr; yō′dlẽr), **yo′dler** (-dlẽr), *n.*

yo′ga (yō′gȧ), *n.* [*often cap.*] [Skr., lit., union.] *Hinduism.* Mental discipline consisting in the direction of attention exclusively upon any object with a view to the identification of consciousness with the object. The object of attention may be, but need not be, the deity.

yogh (yōk), *n.* [ME. *yogh, ȝok.*] The name of the letter ȝ, used in Middle English to represent the guttural (ME. *laȝe, laghe,* law) and the palatal voiced spirant (ME. *ȝernen, yernen,* yearn).

yo′ghurt (yō′go͝ort), *n.* Also **yo′ghourt, yo′gurt, yoh′ourt** (yō′o͝ort). [Turk. *yōghurt.*] A semisolid cheeselike or, sometimes, thickly fluid or jellylike preparation from milk partly evaporated and then fermented by action of a bacterium (*Lactobacillus bulgaricus*) used as food, esp. in the Levant.

yo′gi (yō′gē), *n.* Also **yo′gin** (-gĭn). [Hind. *yogī,* fr. Skr. *yogin.*] One who practices yoga; an ascetic.

yoicks (yoiks), *interj.* [Var. of HOICKS.] *Hunting.* A cry of encouragement to foxhounds.

yoke (yōk), *n.* [AS. *geoc.*] **1.** A bar or frame of wood by which two draft animals, esp. oxen, are joined at the heads or necks for working together, as for drawing a plow or a load. **2.** In ancient times, an arched device laid upon the necks of the vanquished. **3.** Hence, servitude; bondage. **4.** A frame like a yoke (sense 1), as in use or shape; specif.: **a** A frame of wood fitted to a person's shoulders for carrying pails, etc., suspended on each side. **b** A band or shaped piece cut to fit the shoulders or the hips, and intended to support the gathered or plaited hanging parts of a garment, as a skirt. **c** A bar by which the end of the tongue of a wagon or carriage is suspended from the collars of the harness. **d** A frame by which a bell is hung for ringing it. See BELL, *Illust.* **e** *Mach.* A clamp that embraces two other parts to hold them in place. **f** *Mach.* A slotted crosshead used in donkey engines, steam fire engines, etc., in place of a connecting rod. **g** *Naut.* A crosspiece on the head of a boat's rudder. **5.** *sing. & pl.* Two animals yoked together; as, a *yoke* of oxen. **6.** A tie; bond; as, the *yoke* of matrimony. **7.** *Scot.* The time during which a plowman and his team work continuously; hence, a portion of the working day.
— *v. t.* **1.** To put a yoke on; to join in or with a yoke. **2.** To couple; link; hence, to marry. **3.** *Now Rare.* To bring into bondage; oppress; restrain. **4.** To attach a draft animal to; as, to *yoke* a cart; to *yoke* a horse to a cart. — *v. i.* To be joined or intimately associated.

yoke′fel′low (yōk′fĕl′ō), *n.* A close companion; mate.

yo′kel (yō′kĕl; -k'l), *n.* [Perh. connected with *yoke* (of oxen).] *Contemptuous.* A plowboy; a rustic.

yol′dring (yŏl′drĭn; yōl′-), *n. Scot. & Dial.* The European yellowhammer (*Emberiza citrinella*).

yolk (yōk; yōlk), *n.* [AS. *geolca, geoleca,* fr. *geolu* yellow.] **1. a** The yellow spheroidal mass of food material in the egg of a bird or reptile. See EGG, *Illust.* **b** *Embryol.* The contents of the ovum, or egg cell, of an animal. **2.** The oily fat in sheep's wool; suint. — **yolk′y,** *adj.*

yom (yōm; *colloq. Eng.* yŏm), *n.* [Heb. *yōm.*] Day; — a Hebrew word used in the names of various Jewish feasts.

Yom Kip′pur (kĭp′ẽr; kĭ·po͞or′). [Heb. *yōm kippūr* day of atonement.] See JEWISH HOLIDAYS.

yon (yŏn), *adj. & adv.* [AS. *geon.*] Yonder. — *pron.* That or those yonder. *All Archaic & Dial.*

yond (yŏnd), *adv. & adj.* [AS. *geond,* adv. & prep., through, over, yonder.] *Archaic & Dial.* Yonder.

yon′der (yŏn′dẽr), *adv.* [ME. *yonder, ȝonder.* See YON, *adj.*] At or in that (indicated and more or less distant) place. — *adj.* **1.** With *the,* farther removed; more distant. **2.** Being at a distance within view, or conceived of as within view; that or those there.

yop′on (yŏp′ŏn). Var. of YAUPON.

yore (yōr; 70), *adv.* [AS. *gēara* formerly, of old, fr. *gēar* year.] *Obs.* In time long past. — *n.* Time long since past; as, days of *yore.*

york′er (yôr′kẽr), *n. Cricket.* A bowled ball which first hits the ground at, or just short of, the spot where the end of the bat rests.

York′ist (yôr′kĭst), *n. Eng. Hist.* A member or supporter of the English royal house of York, founded by Richard, Duke of York, in the time of Henry VI. Edward IV, Edward V, and Richard III were the reigning members. Its symbol was the white rose. Cf. LANCASTRIAN.

York rite. *Freemasonry.* The rite or ceremonial observed by one of the Masonic systems; also, the system itself, which, in America, confers 13 degrees, the last three in commanderies of Knights Templar. Cf. SCOTTISH RITE.

York′shire pud′ding (yôrk′shĭr; -shẽr). A batter pudding baked with roasting meat or its drippings, orig. in a pan under a spit, but now commonly in a roaster with the meat.

Yo′ru·ba (yō′ro͞o·bä), *n.* A Negro of an extensive linguistic family of the West African coast, mainly between Dahomey and the Niger; also, their language. — **Yo′ru·ban** (-băn), *adj.*

you (yo͞o; 4), *pron.; poss.* YOUR (yo͞or; 84) or YOURS (yo͞orz); *dat. & obj.* YOU. [ME. *you, eou, eow,* dat. & acc., fr. AS. *ēow,* used as dat. & acc. of *ge, gē,* ye.] A personal pronoun of the second person, used: **1.** As objective case of *ye,* pl., orig. its only use: **a** As dative of indirect object; as, we give *you* greeting. **b** As direct object. **2.** As nominative pl.; — now usually replacing *ye.* **3.** As nominative or objective sing.; — now usually replacing *thou, thee,* but taking, as subject, a plural verb. **4.** *Colloq.* Indefinitely (in the same way as *your, we, they, one*); as, so sudden as to make *you* jump.

young (yŭng), *adj.* [AS. *geong, gung.*] **1.** Being in the first or early period of life or growth. **2.** Youthfully fresh or vigorous in body, mind, or feeling. **3.** Immature; inexperienced; ignorant; weak. **4.** Of, pert. to, or relating to early life. **5.** Not having existed long; lately come into being. **6.** Representing a new tendency, movement, etc.; — esp. of a progressive or radical society of young men; as, *Young* Turks. **7.** Junior; — used of the younger of two persons having the same name or title; as, *young* Mr. Smith. **8.** *Phys. Geog.* = YOUTHFUL, 5. — *n.* **1.** Young persons, collectively. **2.** The offspring of animals; offspring, collectively. — ***with young.*** With child; pregnant.

young′ber′ry (yŭng′bĕr′ĭ), *n.* [After B. M. *Young*, Louisiana fruit-grower.] The large sweet reddish-black fruit of a hybrid between a trailing variety of blackberry and a southern dewberry, grown in the western and southern United States.

young blood. Young people; youthful vigor.

young′–eyed′ (yŭng′īd′), *adj.* Having the bright eyes of youth; also, having a youthful or fresh vision.

young′ish (yŭng′ĭsh), *adj.* Somewhat young.

young′ling (yŭng′lĭng), *n.* [AS. *geongling.*] A young person; a youth; also, an animal, plant, etc., in its early life; any young thing. — *adj.* Young.

Young Pretender. Also **Young Adventurer, Young Chevalier.** Charles Edward Stuart (1720–88), affectionately called Bonnie Prince Charlie, who nominally led the insurrection of 1745 in England.

young′ster (yŭng′stẽr), *n.* **1.** *Colloq.* A young person, esp. one not of age; sometimes, a colt or filly. **2.** A member of the next to lowest class in the U. S. Naval Academy at Annapolis.

youn′ker (yŭng′kẽr), *n.* [D. *jonker, jonkheer*, fr. *jong* young + *heer* a lord, gentleman.] **1.** A young gentleman. **2.** *Colloq.* A youngster; child.

your (yo͝or; 4; 84), *pron.* [AS. *ēower*, orig. used as the gen. of *ge, gē*, ye.] The possessive case of *you;* of you; of yourself. — *adj.* **1.** Of or belonging to you; inherent in you; associated with you. **2.** Of or relating to you as author, doer, giver, agent, etc. **3.** Preceding a title of honor in address; as, *your* Highness.

yours (yo͝orz; 84), *pron.* The form of the possessive *your* used absolutely, that is, with no noun following; as, what's mine is *yours.*

your·self′ (yo͝or·sĕlf′), *pron.; pl.* -SELVES (-sĕlvz′). An emphasized form of the pronoun of the second person, used: **1.** For emphasis: **a** As a simple objective. **b** In apposition with *ye, you;* as, you *yourself* said so. **c** As a predicate nominative, often with the force of *by yourself, alone;* as, shall you go *yourself?* **2.** Your true, normal self.

yours truly. A conventional phrase used just before one's signature in a letter and sometimes, esp. humorously, used substantively by a person in allusion to himself.

youth (yo͞oth), *n.; pl.* YOUTHS (yo͞oths; yo͞othz) or, *collectively*, YOUTH. [AS. *geoguth, geogoth.*] **1.** Quality or state of being young. **2.** The part of life that succeeds childhood; the period usually from puberty to maturity; adolescence. **3.** Hence, the early period of existence or growth, as of a flower, crop, or movement. **4.** Young persons, collectively. **5.** A young person of either sex; esp., a young man.

youth′ful (yo͞oth′fo͝ol; -f'l), *adj.* **1.** Possessing youth; not yet mature; young. **2.** Of or pertaining to the early part of life; suited to youth; as, *youthful* sports. **3.** Fresh; vigorous; as, *youthful* spirits. **4.** Early; new; as, the *youthful* season of the year. **5.** *Phys. Geog.* Having accomplished or undergone little erosion; — said of rivers, drainage, topography, etc. — **youth′ful·ly**, *adv.* — **youth′ful·ness**, *n.*

youth hostel. = HOSTEL, 2.

yow (yō; you). Dial. var. of EWE.

yowl (youl), *v. i. & t.* [ME. *ȝoulen.*] To utter, or utter with, a yowl. — *n.* A loud, long, mournful cry, as of a dog or wildcat.

Yo′–yo′ (yō′yō′), *n.* A trade-mark for a disk-shaped top manipulated up and down a cord one end of which is looped around its grooved middle and the other end attached to the operator's hand or finger.

y′per·ite (ē′pẽr·īt), *n.* [F. *ypérite*, fr. *Ypres*, Belgium.] Mustard gas; — the French name.

Y potential, *or* **Y′–po·ten′tial**, *n.* *Elec.* The potential difference between a terminal and the neutral point of a three-phase armature.

Y′quem′ (ē′kĕm′), *n.* [From Château *Yquem*, in southwestern France.] The finest sauterne wine.

Y·seult′ (ĭ·so͞olt′). Var. of ISOLDE.

-yte (-īt). Variant of -ITE as a suffix in names of rocks.

yt·ter′bi·a (ĭ·tûr′bĭ·ȧ), *n.* [NL.] *Chem.* Ytterbium oxide, Yb_2O_3, obtained as a heavy white powder.

yt·ter′bi·um (-ŭm), *n.* [NL., fr. *Ytterby*, Sweden.] *Chem.* A trivalent metallic element of the rare-earth series resembling yttrium, and occurring with it and other related elements in certain minerals, as gadolinite. Symbol, *Yb;* at. no., 70; at. wt., 173.04. — **yt·ter′bic** (-bĭk), *adj.*

ytterbium metals. *Chem.* A group of related rare-earth metals: dysprosium, holmium, erbium, thulium, ytterbium, lutecium.

yt′tri·a (ĭt′rĭ·ȧ), *n.* [NL. See YTTRIUM.] *Chem.* Yttrium oxide, Y_2O_3, obtained as a heavy white powder.

yt′tric (ĭt′rĭk), *adj.* Of, pert. to, or containing yttrium.

yt·trif′er·ous (ĭ·trĭf′ẽr·ŭs), *adj.* Bearing or containing yttrium or the allied elements.

yt′tri·um (ĭt′rĭ·ŭm), *n.* [NL., fr. *Ytterby*, Sweden.] *Chem.* A trivalent metallic element, found (combined) in gadolinite, euxenite, etc. Symbol, *Y* or *Yt;* at. no., 39; at. wt., 88.92.

yu·an′ (yo͞o·än′), *n. sing. & pl.* Also **yuan dollar.** [See YEN.] The monetary unit of China, established in 1914; also, a silver coin containing 23.4934 grams of pure silver. See MONEY, *Tables;* HAIKWAN TAEL.

yuc′ca (yŭk′ȧ), *n.* [NL., fr. Sp. *yuca.*] *Bot.* **a** Any of a genus (*Yucca*) of plants of the lily family, sometimes arborescent, having long, often rigid, fibrous-margined leaves on a woody base, and bearing a large panicle of white blossoms. **b** A flower of this genus; — designated as the State flower of New Mexico.

Yu′ga (yo͝o′gȧ), *n.* [Skr., an age, a yoke.] *Hindu Cosmogony.* One of the four ages of the world: ***Krita Yuga***, or golden age; ***Treta Yuga***, darker and less righteous; ***Dvapara Yuga***, still darker and briefer; ***Kali Yuga***, the present age, darkest and briefest of all.

Yu′go·slav′, Ju′go·slav′ (yo͞o′gō·släv′; -släv′), *n.* [Serbo-Croatian *jugo-*, fr. *jug* the south. See SLAV.] **1.** A native or inhabitant of Yugoslavia; one of the south, or southern, Slavs (Serbians, Croats, and Slovenes). **2.** The Serbo-Croatian language. — **Yu′go·slav′, Ju′go·slav′** (2), *adj.* — **Yu′go·slav′i·an, Ju′go·slav′i·an**, *adj. & n.* — **Yu′go·slav′ic, Ju′go·slav′ic**, *adj.*

yule (yo͞ol), *n.* [AS. *gēol, geohhol.*] Christmas or Christmastide.

yule block, clog, *or* **log.** A large log formerly put on the hearth on Christmas Eve, as the foundation of the fire.

yule′tide′ (yo͞ol′tīd′), *n.* Christmas time; Christmastide.

Yu′man (yo͞o′măn), *adj.* Naming or pert. to an American Indian linguistic family of southwestern United States and northern Mexico.

y·wis′ (ĭ·wĭs′). Var. of IWIS.

Z

Z, z (zē; *in British usage, in America sometimes, called* zĕd; *formerly also* ĭz′ẽrd), *n.; pl.* Z's, z's, Zs, zs (zēz). **1.** The twenty-sixth and last letter of the English alphabet. It comes from the Latin, which borrowed it from the Greek *zeta* and used it to render that letter in words from the Greek. **2.** The sound of this letter. In English, *z* represents a voiced fricative consonant, the sonant correlative of *s.* See *Pron.*, § 132. **3.** [*usually cap.*] Anything having the shape of the letter Z. **4.** As a *symbol*, used to denote or indicate anyone or anything arbitrarily or conveniently so designated, esp. as the twenty-fifth or (see K, 3) twenty-sixth, or, when V and W are not used, the twenty-third, in order or class.

Zab′u·lon (zăb′ū·lŏn; zȧ·bū′lŭn), *n.* *Douay Bib.* Zebulun. See JACOB.

‖za·ca·tón′ (thä′kä·tōn′; sä′-), *n.* [Sp.] Any of several tough, wiry grasses, native to or cultivated in dry regions of the United States and adjacent Mexico. Cf. SACATON.

Zach′a·ri′ah (zăk′ȧ·rī′ȧ), **Zach′a·ri′as** (-ăs), **Zach′a·ry** (zăk′ȧ·rĭ), *n.* *Bib.* **1.** A man referred to as a martyr by Jesus. **2.** Father of John the Baptist.

Zach′a·ri′as (zăk′ȧ·rī′ăs), *n.* **1.** Zachariah. **2.** In the Douay Bible, Zechariah. See BIBLE.

zaf′fer (zăf′ẽr), *n.* Also **zaf′fre**, and formerly **zaf′free, zaf′far, zaf′fir**, etc. [F. *zafre, safre*, or It. *zaffera*, fr. Ar. *ṣufr* yellow copper.] An impure oxide of cobalt, used in the manufacture of smalt, and in coloring pottery, glass, etc., blue.

zai·ba′tsu (zī·bät′so͞o), *n. sing. & pl.* [Jap., fr. *zai* property + *batsu* family.] The few, esp. four, wealthy families owning and controlling most of Japanese industry before and during World War II.

za′mi·a (zā′mĭ·ȧ), *n.* [NL., fr. L. *zamiae*, pl., erron. reading in Pliny for *azaniae* (*nuces*) pine nuts.] *Bot.* Any of a genus (*Zamia*) of cycadaceous plants having a short thick trunk or woody base, a crown of palmlike leaves, and oblong cones or strobiles.

za·min′dar′ (zȧ·mēn′där′), **ze·min′dar′** (zĕ-), *n.* [Hind. *zamīndār*, fr. Per. *zamīn* land + *-dār* suffix of agent.] *India.* A landowner; also: **a** Formerly, a collector of the land revenue of a specified district for the government. **b** Now, usually, a kind of feudatory paying the government a fixed revenue.

zan′der (zăn′dẽr), *n.* [G.] A pike perch (*Sander*, syn. *Lucioperca, lucioperca*) of central Europe, allied to the walleyed pike.

za′ny (zā′nĭ), *n.; pl.* ZANIES (-nĭz). [F. *zani*, fr. It. *zanni* a buffoon, merry-andrew, orig. dial. form of *Giovanni* John.] **1.** In old comedies, a subordinate clown or acrobat who aped ludicrously the acts of his principal; a merry-andrew. **2.** One who acts the buffoon for the amusement of others; esp., one who acts an amusing role of crack-brained whimsy or capers in giddy antics. **3.** *Archaic.* A slavish follower or imitator or a toady. **4.** *Dial.* A simpleton or idiot. — **za′ny**, *adj.;* ZA′NI·ER (-nĭ·ẽr); ZA′NI·EST (-ĕst; -ĭst). Being or characteristic of a zany; esp., utterly irrational, mildly insane, or fantastically ludicrous. — **za′ni·ness**, *n.* — **za′ny·ish**, *adj.* — **za′ny·ism**, *n.*

za′ra·tite (zä′rȧ·tīt), *n.* [Sp. *zaratita*, after G. (?) *Zarate* of Spain.] *Mineral.* A basic nickel carbonate, $NiCO_3.2Ni(OH)_24H_2O$, occurring in emerald-green incrustations or compact masses.

za·re′ba (zȧ·rē′bä), *n.* Also **za·ree′ba.** [Ar. *zarībah* cattle pen, camp.] An improvised stockade, esp. of thorn bushes, etc.; — orig. an African use.

zarf (zärf; zûrf), *n.* [Ar. *ẓarf* sheath, case.] *Art.* A metallic cuplike stand for a small coffee cup.

zax (zăks), *n.* [AS. *seax* a knife.] A tool for trimming and puncturing roofing slates.

zeal (zēl), *n.* [OF. or LL.; OF. *zele*, fr. LL. *zelus*, fr. Gr. *zēlos* zeal, emulation.] Ardor in the pursuit of anything; ardent and active interest; enthusiasm; fervor. — **Syn.** See PASSION.

zeal′ot (zĕl′ŭt), *n.* [LL. *zelotes*, fr. Gr. *zēlōtēs.*] **1.** One who is zealous; esp., one who is overzealous; a fanatical partisan. **2.** [*cap.*] *Jewish Antiq.* One of a fanatical Jewish sect which bitterly opposed the Roman domination of Palestine.

zeal′ot·ry (-rĭ), *n.* Character and behavior of a zealot; excess of zeal; fanatical devotion.

zeal′ous (zĕl′ŭs), *adj.* [ML. *zelosus*, fr. LL. *zelus* zeal.] Filled with, characterized by, or due to zeal. — **zeal′ous·ly**, *adv.* — **zeal′ous·ness**, *n.*

ze′bec (zē′bĕk), **ze′beck.** Vars. of XEBEC.

Zeb′e·dee (zĕb′ē·dē), *n.* *Bib.* The father of the disciples James and John.

ze′bra (zē′brȧ), *n.;* see PLURAL, *Note*, 3. [From Amharic *zebrā*, partly through Pg. & D. *zebra.*] Any of several fleet African equine mammals, allied to the horse and the ass, but with dark stripes on a white or buffy ground. The ***true, or mountain, zebra*** (*Equus zebra*) of the mountains of Cape Province has the body and legs striped, but the belly plain. — **ze′brine** (zē′brĭn; -brīn), *adj.*

ze′bra·wood′ (zē′brȧ·wo͝od′), *n.* Any of several trees or shrubs having marked or striped wood; also, the wood itself; specif., a tropical American tree (*Connarus guianensis*) with hard wood used in cabinetwork.

ze'bu (zē'bū), *n.*; see PLURAL, *Note*, 3. [F. *zébu*, its name at the Paris fair of 1752, prob. fr. Tibetan *zeu, zeba*, the hump of a zebu or camel.] A bovine mammal (*Bos indicus*) widely domesticated in India, China, the East Indies, and East Africa. It usually has short horns, large pendulous ears, a large dewlap, and a large hump over the shoulders, and ranges in size from that of the common ox to that of a large mastiff.

Zeb'u·lun (zĕb'ū·lŭn; zĕ·bū'lŭn), *n.* *Bib.* See JACOB.

zec·chi'no (tsĕk·kē'nō), **zech'in** (zĕk'ĭn). = SEQUIN.

Zech'a·ri'ah (zĕk'ȧ·rī'ȧ), *n.* **a** A Hebrew prophet (about 520 B.C.), who, with Haggai, persuaded the Jews to rebuild the temple. **b** The Old Testament Book of Zechariah. See BIBLE.

zed (zĕd), *n.*; *pl.* ZEDS (zĕdz). [F. *zède*, perh. through It. *zeta*, fr. L. *zeta*.] The letter Z, z. *Zed* is the name used throughout the British Empire. Cf. ZEE.

zed'o·ar'y (zĕd'ō·ĕr'ĭ; -ĕr·ĭ), *n.* [ML. *zedoaria*, fr. Ar. *jadawār*, fr. Per. *zadwār*.] A perennial herb (*Curcuma zedoaria*) with pale-yellowish or white flowers and crimson bracts, grown in India for its tuberous rhizomes which yield a spice and are used in medicine, perfumery, and cosmetics.

zee (zē), *n.*; *pl.* ZEES (zēz). The letter Z, z. *Zee* is the usual name in the United States. Cf. ZED.

ze'in (zē'ĭn), *n.* Also **ze'ine** (-ĭn; -ēn). [From *Zea*, a genus of grasses, fr. L. *zea* a kind of grain, fr. Gr. *zea, zeia* + *-in*.] *Biochem.* A protein obtained from Indian corn, deficient in the amino acids tryptophan and lysine.

‖**Zeit'geist'** (tsīt'gīst'), *n.* [G., fr. *zeit* time + *geist* spirit.] The spirit of the time; the general intellectual and moral state or the trend of culture and taste characteristic of an era.

ze·min'dar' (zĕ·mēn'där'). Var. of ZAMINDAR.

zem'stvo (zĕmst'vō; *Russ.* zyĕm'stfŭ), *n.*; *pl.* -STVOS (-vōz). [Russ., fr. *zemlya* land.] In Russia, an elective local district and provincial administrative assembly, superseded since 1917 by the soviet system.

ze·na'na (zĕ·nä'nȧ), *n.* [Hind. *zenāna, zanāna*, fr. Per. *zanāna*, fr. *zan* woman.] *India & Persia.* The harem or seraglio.

Zend'-A·ves'ta (zĕnd'ȧ·vĕs'tȧ), *n.* [Prop., the *Avesta*, or sacred text, and its *zend*, or interpretation.] See AVESTA.

ze'nith (zē'nĭth; *also, esp. Brit.*, zĕn'ĭth), *n.* [OF. *cenit, cenith*, fr. Sp. & ML. *cenit*, by scribal error (*senit* for *semt*) fr. Ar. *samt* (*al-ra's*) the way of (the head).] **1.** That point of the heavens vertically above one; the upper pole of the horizon; — opposed to *nadir*. **2.** Summit; peak. — **Syn.** See SUMMIT.

ze'nith·al (-ăl), *adj.* Of or pertaining to the zenith; of a map, drawn to show correct directions from the center.

zenithal equidistant projection. = AZIMUTHAL EQUIDISTANT PROJECTION.

ze'o·lite (zē'ō·līt), *n.* [NL. *zeolites*, fr. Gr. *zein* to boil + *-lite*.] *Mineral.* Any of a family of hydrous silicates, occurring as secondary minerals in cavities of lavas.

Zeph'a·ni'ah (zĕf'ȧ·nī'ȧ), *n.* [Heb. *Tsĕphanyāh*.] *Bib.* **a** A Hebrew prophet (c. 640 B.C.). **b** Book of the Old Testament. See BIBLE.

Zeph'i·ran (zĕf'ĭ·răn), *n.* A trade-mark applied to an antiseptic (chemically a mixture of ammonium chloride derivatives) used esp. as a skin disinfectant.

zeph'yr (zĕf'ẽr), *n.* [L. *zephyrus*, fr. Gr. *zephyros*.] **1. a** The west wind. **b** Hence, any soft, gentle breeze. **2.** Any of various articles of wear made of light material, as a light shawl. **3.** Short for ZEPHYR CLOTH, YARN, etc.

zephyr cloth. A thin kind of cassimere for women's wear.

zeph'y·rus (zĕf'ĭ·rŭs), *n.* [L.] The west wind, or zephyr; — usually personified [*cap.*], and made the most mild and gentle of all the sylvan deities.

zephyr yarn *or* **worsted.** A fine, soft yarn or worsted, used for knitting and embroidery.

Zep'pe·lin *or, often*, **zep'pe·lin** (zĕp'ĕ·lĭn; *G.* tsĕp'ĕ·lēn', tsĕp'ĕ·lēn), *n.* Any rigid airship of a type first constructed in 1899–1900 by Ferdinand Count von Zeppelin (1838–1917).

ze'ro (zẽr'ō; 27), *n.*; *pl.* ZEROS, ZEROES (-ōz). [F. *zéro*, fr. It. *zero*, fr. Ar. *ṣifr* empty, a cipher.] **1.** *Arith.* A cipher; naught. **2.** The point of departure in reckoning; specif., the point from which the graduation of a scale, as of a thermometer, commences. See THERMOMETER, *Illust.* **3.** The lowest point. **4.** [*cap.*] A type of light, single-seated, highly maneuverable Japanese fighter plane; — from markings with the last two figures of the date of its introduction, the Japanese year 2600 (A.D. 1940). — *adj.* *Meteorol.* **a** Designating a ceiling (base of a cloud or other obstruction to vision in a vertical direction) that is limited to fifty feet or less. **b** Designating visibility (in a horizontal direction) that is limited to 165 feet (1/32 mile) or less by any obstruction to vision. **zero–zero** indicates visibility limited both horizontally and vertically; as, *zero-zero* conditions.

zero hour. a *Mil. Brit.* The hour at which a previously planned movement is started. **b** The moment at which any ordeal is to begin; the moment of crisis.

zest (zĕst), *n.* [F. *zeste*.] Something that gives or enhances a pleasant taste or relish; also, the relish or taste enhanced or imparted; piquancy; hence, keen enjoyment; relish; gusto. — **Syn.** See TASTE. — *v. t.* To give a relish or flavor to. — **zest'ful**, *adj.* — **zest'ful·ly**, *adv.* — **zest'ful·ness**, *n.*

ze'ta (zē'tȧ; zā'tȧ), *n.* [Gr. *zēta*.] The sixth letter (Z, ζ) of the Greek alphabet, probably pronounced in classical Greek either *zd* or *dz*, later as *z*.

zeug'ma (zūg'mȧ), *n.* [L., fr. Gr. *zeugma*, fr. *zeugnynai* to yoke, join.] *Gram. & Rhet.* The use of a word (as an adjective or verb) to modify or govern two (sometimes more) words, with only one of which it makes sense.

Zeus (zūs; zōōs), *n.* [Gr. (gen. *Dios*); akin to L. *Jupiter*.] *Gr. Relig.* The chief of the Olympian gods, son of Cronus and Rhea and husband of Hera, identified by the Romans with Jupiter. The most primitive character of Zeus is probably as god of the elements; the thunderbolt is his sign, the rainbow, *Iris*, his messenger. Zeus is also god of moral law and order, protector of suppliants and punisher of guilt.

zib'el·ine, zib'el·line (zĭb'ĕ·lĭn; -līn), *n.* [F. *zibelline*, fr. It. *zibellino*, of Slav. origin.] **1.** *Now Rare.* The fur or pelt of a sable. **2.** (*pron.* -lēn). A type of soft woolen dress fabric having long silky hairs on the right side. — **zib'el·ine, zib'el·line**, *adj.*

zib'et, zib'eth (zĭb'ĕt; -ĭt), *n.* [ML. *zibethum*, It. *zibetto*.] The Indian civet (*Viverra zibetha*), inhabiting India, southern China, and the Malay Peninsula.

zig'gu·rat (zĭg'ōō·răt), **zik'u·rat** (zĭk'-), *n.* [Assyr.-Bab. *ziqquratu* pinnacle, top of a mountain.] *Babylon. Antiq.* A temple tower of the Babylonians, consisting of a lofty pyramidal structure, built in successive stages, with outside staircases, and a shrine at the top.

zig'zag' (zĭg'zăg'), *n.* [F.] One of a series of short sharp turns or angles in a course; also, something characterized by such a series; a zigzag path, pattern, etc. — *adj.* Having short sharp turns or angles. — *adv.* In or by a zigzag path or course. — *v. t. & i.*; -ZAGGED' (-zăgd'); -ZAG'GING. To form or move with zigzags.

zil'lah (zĭl'ȧ), *n.* [Hind. *ḍil'* (pron. *zil'*), fr. Ar. *ḍil'* rib, part.] *India.* A district or administrative division.

Zil'pah (zĭl'pȧ), *n.* *Bib.* Mother of Gad.

zinc (zĭngk), *n.* [G. *zink*, of unknown origin.] **1.** *Chem.* A bluish-white crystalline metallic element, brittle when cold, malleable at 110–210° C. (230–410° F.), and brittle at 260° C. Symbol, *Zn*; at. no., 30; at. wt., 65.38. Sp. gr. (of pure zinc), 7.14; weight of a cubic foot, 445 lbs. Zinc melts at 419.4° C. (787° F.) and boils at 907° C. It tarnishes only slightly in moist air at ordinary temperatures. At high temperatures it burns in air with a brilliant bluish-green flame, forming the oxide. In contact with almost any other metal, it dissolves readily in dilute acids. **2.** A piece of zinc for use in a voltaic cell. — *v. t.*; ZINCKED or ZINCED (zĭngkt); ZINCK'ING or ZINC'ING (zĭngk'ĭng). To treat or coat with zinc; galvanize. — **zinc'ic** (zĭngk'ĭk), *adj.* — **zinck'y, zinc'y, zink'y**, *adj.*

zinc'ate (zĭngk'āt), *n.* *Chem.* A salt of zinc hydroxide, $Zn(OH)_2$, in its capacity of a weak acid.

zinc blende. *Mineral.* Sphalerite.

zinc·if'er·ous (zĭngk·ĭf'ẽr·ŭs; zĭn·sĭf'-), *adj.* [*zinc* + *-ferous*.] Containing or yielding zinc.

zinc'i·fy (zĭngk'ĭ·fī), *v. t.*; -FIED (-fīd); -FY'ING. [*zinc* + *-fy*.] To coat or impregnate with zinc; to zinc; galvanize.

zinc'ite (zĭngk'īt), *n.* *Mineral.* Native zinc oxide, ZnO, a brittle, deep-red to orange-yellow hexagonal mineral usually occurring in massive or granular form; — called also *red zinc ore*, and *red oxide of zinc*.

zinck'en·ite. Var. of ZINKENITE.

zin'co·graph (zĭng'kō·grȧf), *n.* A zinc plate prepared for printing by zincography; also, a print from such a plate.

zin·cog'ra·phy (zĭng·kŏg'rȧ·fĭ), *n.* The art or process of engraving or etching on zinc. — **zin·cog'ra·pher** (-fẽr), *n.* — **zin'co·graph'ic** (zĭng'kō·grăf'ĭk), **zin'co·graph'i·cal** (-ĭ·kăl), *adj.*

zinc ointment. *Pharm.* An ointment containing 20 per cent of zinc oxide, mixed with a petrolatum or lard base, used in the treatment of skin diseases.

zinc'ous (zĭngk'ŭs), *adj.* *Chem.* **a** Zincic. **b** Hence, formerly, electropositive; basic.

zinc oxide. *Chem.* An infusible solid, ZnO, used as a pigment (see ZINC WHITE), in compounding rubber, in ointments, etc.

zinc white. Zinc oxide, used as a white pigment, esp. in house paints, water colors, etc. See CHINESE WHITE.

zin'fan·del (zĭn'făn·dĕl), *n.* **a** The leading wine grape of California, notable for productivity and adaptability. **b** A red or white dry wine made from grapes of this variety.

zing (zĭng), *n.* [Imitative.] A shrill humming noise. — **zing**, *v. i.* — **zing**, *interj.* *All Slang.*

‖**zin'ga·ro** (tsēng'gä·rō), *n.*; *fem.* ‖**zin'ga·ra** (-rä); *pl.* -RI (-rē). [It.] A gypsy.

zin'gi·ber·a'ceous (zĭn'jĭ·bẽr·ā'shŭs), *adj.* Also **zin'zi·ber·a'ceous** (zĭn'zĭ-). [L. *zingiber* ginger.] *Bot.* Of or belonging to a family (Zingiberaceae) of tropical monocotyledonous plants (order Musales) consisting of leafy perennial herbs with aromatic rootstocks, including ginger, turmeric, etc.

zin'ken·ite (zĭng'kĕn·īt), *n.* [After J. K. L. *Zinken*, director of the Anhalt mines.] *Mineral.* A steel-gray mineral of metallic luster, chemically $PbSb_2S_4$.

zink'y (zĭngk'ĭ). Var. of ZINCKY.

zin'ni·a (zĭn'ĭ·ȧ), *n.* [NL., after J. G. *Zinn* (1727–59), professor of medicine at Göttingen.] *Bot.* Any of a small genus (*Zinnia*) of tropical American herbs of the aster family, with very showy flowers. The flower of *Z. elegans*, the common zinnia, is the State flower of Indiana.

Zi'on (zī'ŭn), *n.* [Heb. *Tsīyōn*, orig. the name of a stronghold of Jerusalem.] **1.** *Jewish Antiq.* A hill in Jerusalem, site of the royal palace of David and his successors, the place of the temple, the center of Hebrew government, worship, and national life. **2.** Hence: **a** The Israelites. **b** The theocracy, or church directly administered by God. **c** The heavenly city of God.

Zi'on·ism (-ĭz'm), *n.* Also **Zion movement.** Among modern Jews, a movement for colonizing Jews in Palestine, either for religious or nationalizing purposes. — **Zi'on·ist** (-ĭst), *n. & adj.* — **Zi'on·is'tic** (-ĭs'tĭk), *adj.* — **Zi'on·ite** (zī'ŭn·īt), *n.*

zip (zĭp), *n.* [Imitative.] **a** A sudden sharp hissing or sibilant sound such as that made by a flying bullet. **b** *Colloq.* Energy; vim. — *v. i.*; ZIPPED (zĭpt); ZIP'PING. To make, or move with, a zip; also, *Colloq.*, to be full of vim. — **zip'per** (zĭp'ẽr), *n.*

Zip'per (zĭp'ẽr), *n.* **1.** A trade-mark for a boot fastened by a slide fastener designed to replace buttons or lacings by drawing together or loosing the folds with a single pull of an attached tab. **2.** [*not cap.*] Loosely, any slide fastener suggesting that on the Zipper.

zip'py (zĭp'ĭ), *adj.* *Colloq.* Brisk; snappy.

zir'con (zûr'kŏn), *n.* [F., orig. the same word as *jargon*.] *Mineral.* A silicate of zirconium, $ZrSiO_4$, a tetragonal mineral occurring usually in square brown or grayish prisms or pyramids. Transparent varieties are used as gems, esp. reddish kinds called *hyacinth*. Colorless, pale-yellow, or smoky varieties from Ceylon are called *jargon*.

zir'con·ate (-kŏn·āt), *n.* *Chem.* A salt of zirconium hydroxide, $Zr(OH)_4$ or $ZrO(OH)_2$, in its capacity of an acid.

zir·co'ni·a (zẽr·kō'nĭ·ȧ), *n.* [NL.] *Chem.* Zirconium dioxide, ZrO_2, usually obtained artificially as a white amorphous powder. Because of its infusibility, and brilliant luminosity, it has been used in lighting, in making refractory crucibles, etc.

zir·co'ni·um (-ŭm), *n.* [NL.] *Chem.* A metallic element found (combined only) in zircon and certain other minerals. Symbol, *Zr*; at. no., 40; at. wt., 91.22. It is quadrivalent, and has both basic and acid properties. — **zir·con'ic** (-kŏn'ĭk), *adj.*

zith′er (zĭth′ẽr), *n.* Also **zith′ern** (-ẽrn). [G. *zither*, fr. L. *cithara.*] *Music.* An instrument having from thirty to forty strings over a shallow horizontal sounding box, and played with plectrum and fingers. — **zith′er·ist** (zĭth′ẽr·ĭst), *n.*

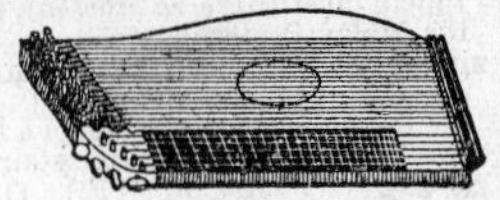

Zither.

zit′tern (zĭt′ẽrn). Var. of CITTERN.
‖**zi·zith′** (tsē·tsēt′; tsĭ′tsĭs), *n. pl.* [Heb. *tsītsīth.*] The tassels, or "fringes" (*Deut.* xxii. 12), of twisted cords or threads on the corners of the tallith (which see) or of an upper garment worn by strict Jews.
zlo′ty (zlô′tĭ), *n.; pl.* ZLOTYS (-tĭz), *collectively*, ZLOTY. [Pol. *zloty*, lit., golden.] The monetary unit of Poland. See MONEY, *Tables.*
-zo′a (-zō′ȧ). [NL. See ZOON.] A combining form used in names of zoological groups, as in Bryo*zoa*, Proto*zoa.*
zo′di·ac (zō′dĭ·ăk), *n.* [OF. *zodiaque*, fr. L. *zodiacus*, fr. Gr. *zōdiakos* (sc. *kyklos*), prop., circle of animals, deriv. of *zōion* an animal.] **1.** *Astron.* **a** An imaginary belt in the heavens, 16° broad, including the paths of the moon and all the principal planets and, as its middle line, the ecliptic, or sun's path. The zodiac has twelve divisions, or signs. **b** A figure representing the signs, symbols, etc., of the zodiac.

NO.	NAME & SYMBOL	SUN ENTERS	NO.	NAME & SYMBOL	SUN ENTERS
1	**Aries**, Ram ♈	Mar. 21	8	**Scorpio**, Scorpion ♏	Oct. 24
2	**Taurus**, Bull ♉	Apr. 20	9	**Sagittarius**, Archer ♐	Nov. 22
3	**Gemini**, Twins ♊	May 21	10	**Capricornus**, Goat ♑	Dec. 22
4	**Cancer**, Crab ♋	June 22	11	**Aquarius**, Water Bearer ♒	Jan. 20
5	**Leo**, Lion ♌	July 23	12	**Pisces**, Fishes ♓	Feb. 19
6	**Virgo**, Virgin ♍	Aug. 23			
7	**Libra**, Balance ♎	Sept. 23			

2. *Rare.* A circuit; zone; also, a girdle. — **zo·di′a·cal** (zō·dī′ȧ·kăl), *adj.*
zo·di′a·cal light (zō·dī′ȧ·kăl). *Astron.* A nebulous light seen in the west after twilight and in the east before dawn.
‖**zo′e mou, sas a′ga·po′** (zô′ĕ mōō′, säs′ ä′gȧ·pô′). [NGr.] My life, I love thee. *Byron* (*Maid of Athens*).
zois′ite (zois′īt), *n.* [After Baron *Zois* von Edelstein (1747–1819).] *Mineral.* A silicate of calcium and aluminum, $HCa_2Al_3Si_3O_{13}$, the aluminum sometimes being replaced by iron.
‖**Zoll′ver·ein′** (tsôl′fẽr·īn′), *n.* [G., fr. *zoll* duty + *verein* union.] [*also not cap.*] A customs union; specif., any of the several customs unions formed, as in 1834 and 1867, under the leadership of Prussia among certain German states.
zom′bi (zŏm′bĭ), *n.; pl.* ZOMBIS (-bĭz). Also **zom′bie** (-bĭ); *pl.* ZOMBIES (-bĭz). **1. a** Orig., in West African voodoo cults, the deity of the python; hence, in Haiti and the southern United States, the snake deity of the voodoo rite. **b** The supernatural power or essence which it is believed may enter into and reanimate a dead body. **c** A corpse so reanimated. **d** In the West Indies, a will-less and speechless being capable only of automatic, trancelike movement, supposed to have died and been reanimated but often suspected to have been drugged into a catalepsy for the hours of interment. **2.** Spelled **zom′bie.** **a** *Slang.* A person of the lowest order of intelligence suggestive of the so-called walking dead. **b** *Canada.* A home-defense army conscript unwilling to volunteer for overseas service. **c** A quite tall mixed drink made of several different kinds of rum with fruit juices and dashes of different brandies. — **zom′bi·ism** (-ĭz′m), *n.*
zon′al (zōn′ăl; -′l), *adj.* Also **zon′a·ry** (zōn′ȧ·rĭ). Of or pertaining to a zone; having the form of a zone or zones; also, arranged or living in zones.
zon′ate (zōn′āt), *adj.* Also **zon′at·ed** (-āt·ĕd; -ĭd). **a** Marked with zones; ringed or belted. **b** *Bot.* Arranged in a single row, as certain tetraspores.
zo·na′tion (zō·nā′shŭn), *n.* **a** State of being zoned or zonate. **b** *Biogeog.* Arrangement or distribution in zones.
zone (zōn), *n.* [F., fr. L. *zona*, fr. Gr. *zōnē.*] **1.** *Obs. exc. Poetic.* A girdle; belt. **2.** Any encircling band, stripe, or girdle; as, a *zone* of trees; more broadly, any encircling line, course, or the like; circuit. **3.** Any of five great divisions of the earth's surface with respect to latitude and temperature; the ***Torrid Zone***, extending 46° 54′, or 23° 27′ on each side of the equator; two ***Temperate, or Variable, Zones***, situated between the tropics and the polar circles, which are 23° 27′ from the poles; and two ***Frigid Zones***, between the polar circles and the poles. **4.** An area or region set off or characterized as

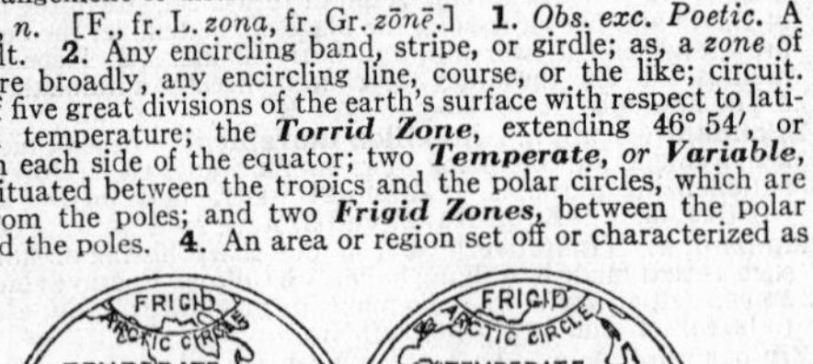

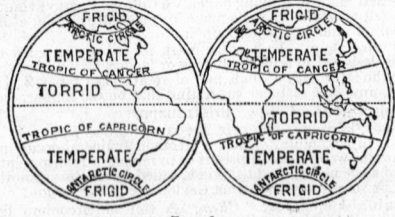

Zone, 3.

distinct from adjoining parts; as, the wheat *zone;* the Canal *Zone.* **5.** A section of a city that has been zoned. **6.** In the United States postal system: **a** For parcel-post purposes, any of the areas about any point of shipment for which but one rate of postage is charged for a parcel-post shipment from that point. Called specifically ***parcel post zone.*** **b** One of the numbered sections into which a large city or metropolitan area is divided so that affixing of the appropriate number to each street address on mail matter will expedite the delivery of mail to patrons. Called specifically ***postal delivery zone.*** **7.** *Biogeog.* **a** An area or part of a region characterized by uniform or similar animal and plant life. **b** A similar area dominated by a particular form or forms of plant or animal life. **8.** *Geol. & Paleontol.* A belt, layer, or series of layers of rock, characterized by some particular property, action, or content. **9.** *Railroad Econ.* **a** The aggregate of stations, in whatsoever direction or on whatsoever railroad, situated between certain maximum and minimum limits from a point at which a shipment of traffic originates. **b** Any circular or ring-shaped area within which the streetcar companies make no differences of fare. — *v. t.* **1.** To encircle or embrace; to mark off into zones. **2.** *City Planning.* To partition (a city, etc.) by ordinance into zones reserved for different purposes, as residence, business, etc. — **zoned** (zōnd), *adj.*
Zon′ta In′ter·na′tion·al (zŏn′tȧ). [From Sioux *zon′-ta* honest, trustworthy.] An organization of service clubs (**Zonta Clubs**) made up of executive women, each a sole representative of one business or profession in a community, which was established in 1919 for "the advancement of understanding, good will, and peace through a world fellowship." — **Zon′ti·an** (zŏn′tĭ·ăn), *n. & adj.*
zon′ule (zōn′ūl), *n.* [L. *zonula.*] A little zone; belt.
zoo (zōō), *n.* A zoological garden or collection.
zo′o- (zō′ō-), **zo-.** [Gr. *zōion* animal.] A combining form denoting *animal, animals, animal kingdom, zoological* (*and*), as in:

zoochemical	**zoolatry**	**zoophile**
zoochemistry	**zoomechanical**	**zoophobia**
zoogeology	**zoomechanics**	**zoophysiology**

zo′o·ge·og′ra·phy (zō′ō·jē·ŏg′rȧ·fĭ), *n.* [*zoo-* + *geography.*] Study or description of the geographical distribution of animals; esp., determination of the land and marine areas characterized by special groups of animals and the study of the causes and significance of such groups. — **zo′o·ge·og′ra·pher** (-fẽr), *n.* — **zo′o·ge′o·graph′ic** (-jē′ō·grăf′ĭk), **zo′o·ge′o·graph′i·cal** (-ĭ·kăl), *adj.* — **zo′o·ge′o·graph′i·cal·ly**, *adv.*
zo′o·gloe′a (zō′ō·glē′ȧ), *n.* [NL., fr. *zoo-* + Gr. *gloios* a glutinous substance.] *Bacteriol.* A colony or mass of bacteria embedded in a jellylike substance formed by the swelling of cell membranes through absorption of water.
zo·og′ra·phy (zō·ŏg′rȧ·fĭ), *n.* [*zoo-* + *-graphy.*] Description or depiction of animals, esp. their forms and habits. — **zo′o·graph′ic** (zō′ō·grăf′ĭk), **zo′o·graph′i·cal** (-ĭ·kăl), *adj.* — **zo·og′ra·pher** (-fẽr), *n.*
zo′oid (zō′oid), *n.* [*zo-* + *-oid.*] *Biol.* An entity which resembles but is not wholly the same as a separate individual animal; specif.: **a** An organic body or cell having locomotion, as a sperm cell. **b** *Zool.* A more or less independent animal produced by fission, proliferation, or the like, and not by direct sexual methods. Cf. ZOON **a.** **c** *Zool.* Any of the individuals which, in alternation of generations, come between the products of true sexual reproduction, as the free-swimming medusa of a hydroid colony. — **zo·oi′dal** (zō·oi′dăl), *adj.*
zo′o·log′i·cal (zō′ō·lŏj′ĭ·kăl), *adj.* Also **zo′o·log′ic** (-ĭk). Of, pert. to, or engaged in zoology. — **zo′o·log′i·cal·ly**, *adv.*
zoological garden. A garden or park where wild animals are kept for exhibition.
zo·ol′o·gist (zō·ŏl′ō·jĭst), *n.* One who is versed in zoology.
zo·ol′o·gy (-jĭ), *n.; pl.* -GIES (-jĭz). [*zoo-* + *-logy.*] **1.** The science which treats of animals; the branch of biology dealing with the animal kingdom and its members (as individuals and classes) and with animal life. Cf. CLASSIFICATION, 2. **2.** A treatise on zoology. **3.** Animal life, as of a region.
zoom (zōōm), *v. i.* [Imitative.] To move with a loud but low hum; specif., *Aviation*, to climb for a short time at an angle greater than that which can be maintained in steady flight, the machine being carried upward at the expense of its stored kinetic energy. — *v. t.* To cause to zoom. — *n.* Act of zooming.
zo·om′e·try (zō·ŏm′ē·trĭ), *n.* Scientific measurement of animals. — **zo′o·met′ric** (zō′ō·mĕt′rĭk), *adj.*
zo′o·mor′phism (zō′ō·môr′fĭz′m), *n.* The representation of God, or of gods, in the form, or with the attributes, of the lower animals. — **zo′o·mor′phic** (-fĭk), *adj.*
zo′on (zō′ŏn), *n.; pl.* ZOA (-ȧ). [NL., fr. Gr. *zōion* an animal.] *Zool.* **a** An animal which is the sole product of a single egg; — opposed to *zooid.* **b** Any of the perfectly developed individuals of a compound animal.
zo·oph′i·lous (zō·ŏf′ĭ·lŭs), *adj.* [*zoo-* + *-philous.*] Animal-loving; specif., *Bot.*, adapted to pollination by animals.
zo′o·phyte (zō′ō·fīt), *n.* [NL. *zoophyton*, fr. Gr. *zōophyton*, fr. *zōion* animal + *phyton* plant.] *Zool.* Any of numerous invertebrate animals resembling plants in appearance or mode of growth, as the corals, sea anemones, hydroids, bryozoans, sponges, etc. — **zo′o·phyt′ic** (-fĭt′ĭk), **zo′o·phyt′i·cal** (-ĭ·kăl), *adj.*
zo′o·plas′ty (-plăs′tĭ), *n.* [*zoo-* + *-plasty.*] *Surg.* Act or process of grafting animal tissue into the human body. — **zo′o·plas′tic** (-plăs′tĭk), *adj.*
zo′o·sperm (zō′ō·spûrm), *n.* *Biol.* **a** One of the spermatic particles; a spermatozoid. **b** = ZOOSPORE, 1. — **zo′o·sper·mat′ic** (-spẽr·măt′ĭk), *adj.*
zo′o·spo·ran′gi·um (-spō·răn′jĭ·ŭm), *n.; pl.* -SPORANGIA (-ȧ). [NL.] *Bot.* A spore case, or sporangium, with zoospores. — **zo′o·spo·ran′gi·al** (-ăl), *adj.*
zo′o·spore (zō′ō·spōr; 70), *n.* **1.** *Bot.* An asexual spore with slender cilia, by the vibration of which it swims. Zoospores are produced by many algae and by many of the lower phycomycetous fungi (subclass Oömycetes). **2.** *Zool.* One of the minute motile flagellate or amoeboid bodies into which the protoplasm of a sporocyst divides. — **zo′o·spor′ic** (-spŏr′ĭk), *adj.* — **zo·os′po·rous** (zō·ŏs′pō·rŭs; zō′ō·spō′rŭs), *adj.*
zo·ot′o·my (zō·ŏt′ō·mĭ), *n.* [*zoo-* + *-tomy.*] The science dealing with the anatomy of animals, esp. other than man. — **zo′o·tom′ic** (zō′ō·tŏm′ĭk), **zo′o·tom′i·cal** (-ĭ·kăl), *adj.* — **zo′o·tom′i·cal·ly**, *adv.* — **zo·ot′o·mist** (zō·ŏt′ō·mĭst), *n.*
zoot suit (zōōt). [Origin obscure.] *Slang, U. S.* A flashy suit made up of knee-length coat with broad, square, padded shoulders, form-fitted waist, leg-of-mutton sleeves, and diagonal pockets, and peg-top trousers reaching to the armpits, ballooning at the knee, and tapering to narrow cuffs. — **zoot′-suit′er, zoot′er** (zōōt′ẽr), *n.*
zor′il (zŏr′ĭl), *n.* Also **zo·ril′la** (zō·rĭl′ȧ). [F. *zorille*, fr. Sp. *zorrilla*, *zorrillo*, dim. of *zorra, zorro*, fox.] A South African musteline mammal (*Ictonyx striata*) about the size and form of the common skunk.
Zo′ro·as′tri·an (zō′rō·ăs′trĭ·ăn), *adj.* Of or pertaining to Zoroaster or his religious system. — *n.* A follower of Zoroaster; one who accepts Zoroastrianism.

Zo'ro·as'tri·an·ism (zō'rō·ăs'trĭ·ăn·ĭz'm), *n.* Also **Zo'ro·as'trism** (-trĭz'm). The religion of Persia previous to the conversion of the Persians to Mohammedanism. It is traditionally derived from its great prophet, Zoroaster, or Zarathustra (fl. early in the first millennium B.C.), and its sacred literature is the Zend-Avesta. The religion teaches that Ormazd, lord of light and goodness, wars ceaselessly against Ahriman and the hosts of evil. Ormazd created man to aid him, and finally the good kingdom will be attained.

zos'ter (zŏs'tẽr), *n.* [L. (in sense 2), fr. Gr. *zōstēr* girdle, herpes zoster.] **1.** *Gr. Costume.* A girdle. **2.** *Med.* Herpes zoster; shingles.

Zou·ave' (zōō·äv'; zōō-), *n.* [F., fr. *Zouaoua*, or *Zawia*, name of a tribe of Kabyles in Algeria.] *Mil.* **a** One of a body of infantry in the French service, originally Algerians, wearing a brilliant uniform and noted for dash and valor. **b** Hence, one of a body of soldiers adopting the dress and drill of the Zouaves, as was done by some volunteer regiments in the Army of the United States in the Civil War.

zounds (zoundz), *interj. Archaic.* An abbreviation of *God's wounds;* — used as a mild oath.

zuc·chet'to (tsōōk·kāt'tō; *Angl.* zōō·kĕt'ō), *n.* [It.] A small round skullcap worn by Roman Catholic ecclesiastics, the colors varying as for the biretta (which see); a calotte.

zuc·chi'ni (zōō·kē'nē), *n.* [It. *zucchino, pl. zucchini,* dim. of *zucca* squash.] *Hort.* A cultural form of summer squash (derived from *Cucurbita pepo*), having a bushy growth and long, dark-green, cylindrical to slightly curved fruit with thick, tender flesh.

Zu'l·hij'jah (zōōl'hĭj'ä), *n.* [Ar. *dhu-al-ḥijjah,* lit., the one (the month) of pilgrimage.] See MOHAMMEDAN CALENDAR.

Zu'l·ka·dah' (zōōl'kà·dä'), *n.* [Ar. *dhu-al-qa'dah,* lit., the one (the month) of staying home.] See MOHAMMEDAN CALENDAR.

Zu'lu (zōō'lōō), *n.; pl.* ZULUS (-lōōz), sometimes ZULU. One of a great Bantu nation of Natal, in type and culture identical with the Kaffirs; also, their language. — **Zu'lu,** *adj.*

Zu'ñi (zōō'nyĕ; sōō'-), *n.* [Sp.] An Indian of the Zuñi pueblo, in western New Mexico. The Zuñi constitute a linguistic family. — **Zu'ñi·an** (zōō'nyĭ·ăn; sōō'-), *adj. & n.*

zwie'back' (tsvē'bäk'; tswē'-; *called also* swī'bäk', zwī'-), *n.* [G., fr. *zwie-* two, twice + *backen* to bake.] [*often cap.*] A form of toasted biscuit or rusk.

Zwing'li·an (zwĭng'glĭ·ăn; tsvĭng'lĭ-), *adj. Theol.* Of or pert. to Ulrich Zwingli (1484–1531), reformer, of German Switzerland, who maintained that in the Lord's Supper there is an influence of Christ upon the soul, but that the true body of Christ is present by the contemplation of faith, and not in essence or reality. — **Zwing'li·an,** *n.* — **Zwing'li·an·ism** (-ĭz'm), *n.* — **Zwing'li·an·ist** (-ĭst), *n. & adj.*

zwit'ter i'on, or **zwit'ter·i·on** (tsvĭt'ẽr·ī'ŏn; 2), *n.* [G. *zwitter* hybrid.] *Physical Chem.* An ion charged both positively and negatively, as that of an amino acid in solution. — **zwit'ter·i·on'ic** (-ĭ·ŏn'ĭk), *adj.*

zyg'a·poph'y·sis (zĭg'à·pŏf'ĭ·sĭs; zī'gà-), *n.; pl.* -SES (-sēz). [NL., fr. Gr. *zygon* yoke + NL. *apophysis.*] *Anat. & Zool.* One of the articular processes of the neural arch of a vertebra. — **zyg'ap·o·phys'e·al,** **zyg'ap·o·phys'i·al** (zĭg'ăp·ō·fĭz'ē·ăl, -ī·ăl), *adj.*

zy'go- (zī'gō-; zĭg'ō-). [Gr. *zygon.*] A combining form meaning *yoke, pair,* as in *zygo*spore.

zyg'o·dac'tyl (-dăk'tĭl), *adj.* [*zygo-* + Gr. *daktylos* finger.] Having the toes arranged in pairs, two in front and two behind, as in a woodpecker or parrot. Cf. PARROT, *Illust.* — **zyg'o·dac'tyl,** *n.*

zy·go'ma (zī·gō'mà), *n.; pl.* -MATA (-mà·tà). [NL., fr. Gr. *zygōma,* fr. *zygoun* to yoke, fr. *zygon* yoke.] *Anat. & Zool.* **a** The whole zygomatic arch. **b** A process (**zygomatic process**) of the temporal bone helping to form the zygomatic arch. **c** The zygomatic bone, or cheekbone.

zy'go·mat'ic (zī'gō·măt'ĭk; zĭg'ō-), *adj. Anat. & Zool.* Of or pertaining to the zygoma. — *n.* The zygomatic bone.

zygomatic arch. *Anat.* The arch of bone which extends along the front or side of the skull beneath the orbit. See RODENT, *Illust.*

zygomatic bone. *Anat.* A bone of the side of the face below the eye; the malar bone.

zy'go·mor'phic (zī'gō·môr'fĭk; zĭg'ō-), *adj.* Also **zy'go·mor'phous** (-fŭs). [*zygo-* + *-morphic.*] *Biol.* Monosymmetric. See SYMMETRICAL, 2 a. — **zy'go·mor'phism** (-fĭz'm), *n.*

zy'go·phyl·la'ceous (-fĭ·lā'shŭs), *adj.* [*zygo-* + Gr. *phyllon* leaf.] *Bot.* Belonging to the bean-caper family (Zygophyllaceae). See BEAN CAPER.

zy'go·phyte (zī'gō·fīt; zĭg'ō-), *n.* [*zygo-* + -*phyte.*] *Bot.* A plant in which reproduction consists in the union of two similar cells.

zy·go'sis (zī·gō'sĭs; zī-), *n.* [NL., fr. Gr. *zygōsis* a balancing, fr. *zygon* yoke.] *Bot. & Zool.* = CONJUGATION, 2.

zy'go·spore (zī'gō·spōr; zĭg'ō-; 70), *n.* [*zygo-* + *spore.*] *Bot.* A spore formed by conjugation of two similar gametes or sexual cells. Cf. OÖSPORE.

zy'gote (zī'gōt; zĭg'ōt), *n.* [Gr. *zygōtos* yoked.] *Biol.* A cell formed by the union of two gametes; a zygospore.

zy'mase (zī'mās), *n.* [From ZYME.] *Biochem.* Any of a group of enzymes (originally found in yeasts and bacteria) which, in the presence of oxygen, convert glucose and a few other carbohydrates into carbon dioxide and water or, in the absence of oxygen, into alcohol and carbon dioxide or into lactic acid.

zyme (zīm), *n.* [Gr. *zymē* leaven.] A ferment; as, *Med.,* the morbific principle of a zymotic disease.

zy'mo- (zī'mō-), **zym-**. [Gr. *zymē* leaven.] A combining form denoting *relation to a ferment* or *fermentation.*

zy'mo·gen (zī'mō·jĕn), **zy'mo·gene** (-jĕn), *n.* [F. *zymogène.*] **1.** *Biol.* Any microorganism deriving energy chiefly from zymase fermentation of carbohydrates. **2.** *Biochem.* The inactive form of an enzyme.

zy'mo·gen·e·sis (-jĕn'ē·sĭs), *n.* [NL.] *Biochem.* Transformation of a zymogen into an enzyme.

zy'mo·gen'ic (-jĕn'ĭk), *adj.* **1.** Producing fermentation. **2.** Of or pertaining to a zymogen.

zymogenic organism. *Biol.* A microorganism, as a yeast plant, which sets up fermentative processes.

zy·mol'o·gy (zī·mŏl'ō·jĭ), *n.* [*zymo-* + -*logy.*] The science of, or a treatise on, fermentation. — **zy'mo·log'ic** (zī'mō·lŏj'ĭk), *adj.* — **zy·mol'o·gist** (zī·mŏl'ō·jĭst), *n.*

zy·mol'y·sis (-ĭ·sĭs), *n.* [NL., fr. *zymo-* + -*lysis.*] *Biochem.* Action of enzymes; also, the changes produced by such action. — **zy'mo·lyt'ic** (zī'mō·lĭt'ĭk), *adj.*

zy·mom'e·ter (zī·mŏm'ē·tẽr), *n.* [*zymo-* + -*meter.*] An instrument for measuring fermentation.

zy·mo'sis (zī·mō'sĭs), *n.* [NL., fr. Gr. *zymōsis* fermentation, fr. *zymē* ferment.] **a** Fermentation; hence, *Med.,* an analogous process by which an infectious disease is believed to be developed. **b** *Rare.* A zymotic disease.

zy·mot'ic (-mŏt'ĭk), *adj.* [Gr. *zymōtikos* causing to ferment.] **1.** Of, pertaining to, causing, or caused by fermentation. **2.** *Med.* Designating, pert. to, or causing any infectious or contagious disease.

zy'mur·gy (zī'mûr·jĭ), *n.* [*zym-* + -*urgy.*] Applied chemistry dealing with fermentation processes, as in brewing.

ABBREVIATIONS
USED IN WRITING AND PRINTING

For a list of special abbreviations used in this dictionary see pages xxi–xxii preceding the Vocabulary.

A

A, argon. *Chem.*

A., absolute (temperature); Academician; Academy; America; American.

A., a., acre; answer; artillery.

A., Å., A, angstrom unit.

a., about; accepted (*Com.*); acting; adjective; after; afternoon; alto; amateur; ampere; anno (L., in the year); anode; anonymous; ante; approved (*Com.*); are (*metric system*); area; argent (*Her.*); at.

a, @, ad (L., at, or to). *Com.*

ā, aa, Ā, or **ĀĀ**, ana. *Med.*

AA, Airman Apprentice. *U.S. Navy.*

AA, A.A., achievement age (*Psychol.*); Alcoholics Anonymous; antiaircraft.

AAA, Agricultural Adjustment Agency, *formerly* Agricultural Adjustment Administration; antiaircraft artillery.

AAA, A.A.A., Amateur Athletic Association; American Automobile Association; Automobile Association of America.

AAAA, A.A.A.A., Amateur Athletic Association of America.

A.A.A.L., American Academy of Arts and Letters.

A.A.A.S., AAAS, American Association for the Advancement of Science.

AACS, Army Air Communications System; Airways and Air Communications Service.

AAF, Army Air Forces.

A. and M., Agricultural and Mechanical.

A.A.U., Amateur Athletic Union.

A.A.U.P., AAUP, American Association of University Professors.

Ab, alabamine. *Chem.*

AB, Aviation Boatswain's Mate. *U.S. Navy.*

A.B., Artium Baccalaureus (L., Bachelor of Arts).

A.B., a.b., able-bodied (seaman).

abbr., abbrev., abbreviated; abbreviation.

ABC, American Broadcasting Company; Argentina, Brazil, and Chile.

A.B.C., (Alphabetical) Railway Guide. *Brit.*

ABCD, America, Britain, China, Dutch East Indies.

ab init., ab initio (L., from the beginning.)

abl., ablative.

abn, airborne.

Abp., Archbishop.

abr., abridged; abridgment.

abs., absent; absolute (temperature); absolutely; abstract.

abstr., abstract; abstracted.

AC, Air Controlman (*U.S. Navy*); Air Corps.

Ac, actinium (*Chem.*); alto-cumulus.

AC, A.C., a.c., alternating current. *Elec.*

A.C., after Christ; Athletic Club.

A/C, a/c, account current.

A/C, a/c, ac., account.

ac., acre.

acad., academic; academy.

ACC, Air Co-ordinating Committee.

acc., acceptance; accompanied; according; account; accountant.

acc., accus., accusative.

accel., accelerando.

acct., account; accountant.

ack., acknowledge; acknowledgment.

A.C.L.S., ACLS, American Council of Learned Societies.

A.C.P., American College of Physicians.

acpt., acceptance. *Banking.*

A/cs Pay., accounts payable.

A/cs Rec., accounts receivable.

Act, actinium. *Chem.*

actg., acting.

AD, Aviation Machinist's Mate. *U.S. Navy.*

A.D., A.D., anno Domini.

ad., add; advertisement.

a.d., after date.

ADC, ADC, a.d.c., aide-de-camp.

add., addenda; addendum; addition; additional; address.

ad inf., ad infinitum (L., to infinity).

ad init., ad initium (L., to, or at, the beginning).

ad int., ad interim (L., in the meantime).

adj., adjacent; adjective; adjourned; adjunct; adjustment (*Banking*).

Adj., Adjt., Adjutant.

ad lib., ad libit., ad libitum (L., at one's pleasure, to the amount desired).

Adm., Admiral; Admiralty.

Adm., adm., administrative; administrator.

admin., administration; administrator.

A.D.S., American Dialect Society.

adv., ad valorem; advance; adverb; adverbial; adverbially; adversus; advertisement; advocate.

ad val., ad valorem (L., according to value).

advt., advertisement.

AE, Aviation Electrician's Mate. *U.S. Navy.*

ae., aet., aetat., aetatis (L., of age).

A.E. and P., Ambassador Extraordinary and Plenipotentiary.

AEC, Atomic Energy Commission.

A.E.F., AEF, American Expeditionary Force, *or* Forces.

AF, Air Force; Aviation Photographer's Mate (*U.S. Navy*).

AF, AF, Anglo-French.

Af., Africa; African.

A.F., a.f., a–f, audio frequency.

A.F. & A.M., A.F. & A.M., Ancient Free and Accepted Masons.

AFL, A.F. of L., American Federation of Labor.

Afr., Africa; African.

Ag, argentum (silver). *Chem.*

Ag., August.

AG, Aerographer's Mate. *U.S. Navy.*

A.G., Adjutant General; Attorney General.

agcy., agency.

agr., agri., agriculture; -ural.

agric., agricultural; agriculture; agriculturist.

Agt., agt., agent; agreement.

a.h., ampere-hour.

AK, Aviation Storekeeper. *U.S. Navy.*

AKC, American Kennel Club.

AL, Aviation Electronicsman. *U.S. Navy.*

Al, aluminum, *or* aluminium.

Ala., Alabama.

A.L.A., ALA, American Library Association; Automobile Legal Association.

Alas., Alaska.

Alb., Albanian; Albany; Albert; Alberta.

Alba., Alberta (Canada).

Ald., Aldm., Alderman.

Alex., Alexander; Alexandre.

Alf., Alfonso; Alfred.

Alg., Algernon; Algiers.

alg., algebra.

ALP, American Labor Party.

alt., alternate; alternating; alternations; altitude; alto.

Alta., Alberta (Canada).

alum., aluminum.

Am, alabamine; americium.

Am., America; American.

AM, Aviation Structural Mechanic. *U.S. Navy.*

AM, A.M., a–m, a.m., amplitude modulation.

A.M., Artium Magister (L., Master of Arts).

A.M., A.M., a.m., ante meridiem.

A.M.A., AMA, American Medical Association.

Amb., Ambassador.

Amer., America; American.

AMG, Allied (*also*, American) Military Government.

amp., ampere; amperage.

amp.–hr., ampere-hour.

amt., amount.

AMVETS, American Veterans (of World War II).

AN, Airman. *U.S. Navy.*

AN, AN, Anglo-Norman.

anal., analogous; analogy; analysis; analytic.

anat., anatomical; anatomy.

anc., ancient; anciently.

and., andante.

Angl., Anglian, Anglican.

anim., animato.

ann., anni (L., years); annual; annuity.

anon., anonymous.

ans., answer; answered.

ant., antenna; antiquarian; antonym.

anthrop., anthropol., anthropological; anthropology.

antiq., antiquarian; antiquities.

ANZAC, Australian and New Zealand Army Corps.

AO, Aviation Ordnanceman. *U.S. Navy.*

AOL, absent over leave.

aor., aorist.

AP, A.P., antipersonnel; armor-piercing.

A P, airplane. *Mil.*

Ap., Apostle; April.

AP, A.P., AP, Associated Press.

apmt., appointment.

APO, Army Post Office.

Apoc., Apocalypse; Apocrypha; Apocryphal.

app., apparent; apparently; appended; appendix; appointed; apprentice.

appar., apparent; apparently.

approx., approximately.

Apr., Apr, April.

apt(s)., apartment(s).

A.Q., AQ, achievement quotient, *sometimes* accomplishment *or* attainment quotient.

Aq, aq, aqua.

AR, Airman Recruit. *U.S. Navy.*

Ar, argon. *Chem.*

Ar., Arabian; Arabic; Aramaic; argentum (L., silver).

ar., argent (*Her.*); aromatic; arrival; arrive; arrives.

ARA, Agricultural Research Administration.

A.R.A., Associate of the Royal Academy.

Arab., Arabian; Arabic.

ARC, A.R.C., American (National) Red Cross.

Arch., Archbishop; Archibald.

arch., archaic; archaism; archery; archipelago; architect(ure).

archaeol., archaeological; archaeology.

Archd., Archduke.

archeol., archeological; archeology.

archit., architecture.

archt., architect.

arg., argent (*Her.*); argentum.

arith., arithmetic; arithmetical.

Ariz., Arizona.

Ark., Arkansas.

Arm., Armen., Armenian.

Ar.M., Architecture Magister (L., Master of Architecture).

ARP, A.R.P., air-raid precautions. *Orig. Brit.*

arr., arranged; arrangements; arrival; arrive; arrived.

art., article; artificial; artillery; artist.

Arty., Artillery.

A.R.V., American Standard Revised Version (of the Bible).

As, alto-stratus; arsenic. *Chem.*

AS, AS., A.–S., A.S., Anglo-Saxon.

as, asymmetric. *Org. Chem.*

ASA, American Standards Association.

asb., asbestos.

ASC, A.S.C., Air Service Command; Army Service Corps.

ASCAP, A.S.C.A.P., American Society of Composers, Authors and Publishers.

ASCE, A.S.C.E., American Society of Civil Engineers.

ASF, Army Service Forces.

asgd., assigned.

ass., assistant; association.

assd., assigned.

assn., association.

assoc., associate; association.

asst., assistant.

Assyr., Assyrian.

A.S.T.M., ASTM, American Society for Testing Materials.

ASTP, Army Specialized Training Program.

astr., astronomer; astronomical; astronomy.

astrol., astrologer; astrological; astrology.

astron., astronomer, astronomical; astronomy.

AT, Aviation Electronics Technician. *U.S. Navy.*

AT, A.T., antitank.

At, astatine.

at., atmosphere(s); atomic.

ATC, Air Transport Command.

athl., athletics.

Atl., Atlantic.

atm., atmosphere(s); atmospheric.

at. no., atomic number.
ATS, A.T.S., Army Transport Service.
ats., at suit of. *Law.*
Att., attorney.
att., attn., atten., attention.
attrib., attribute; attributive; attributively.
Atty., Attorney.
Atty. Gen., Attorney General.
at. wt., atomic weight.
Au, aurum (gold). *Chem.*
A.U., Å.U., a.u., å.u., angstrom unit.
A.U.C., ab urbe condita. See in *Foreign Words and Phrases.*
aud., auditor.
Aug., Aug, August.
AUS, A.U.S., Army of the United States.
Aus., Austl., Australia.
Aust., Austria; Austrian.
Austral., Australia; Australasia.
auth., authentic; author; authoress; authorized.
Auth. Ver., Authorized Version (of the Bible).
auto., automatic; automotive.
aux., auxil., auxiliary.
A.V., Authorized Version (of the Bible).
Av., Avenue.
a.v., A/V., ad valorem.
av., average.
av., avdp., avoir., avoirdupois.
AVC, A.V.C., American Veterans Committee.
AVC, a.v.c., automatic volume control.
Ave., Avenue.
avg., average.
avn., aviation.
A/W., actual weight; all water. *Transp.*
AWL, A.W.L., a.w.l., absent with leave.
AWOL, A.W.O.L., a.w.o.l., absent without leave.
AWVS, American Women's Volunteer Services.
ax., axiom.
az., azure.

B

B, Bishop (*Chess*); boron (*Chem.*).
B., Bacillus; Bible; Boston; British; Brotherhood.
B., b., bachelor; base; bass; basso; bat; battery; bay; bicuspid; bolivar; boliviano; book; born; breadth; brother.
B/–, bag; bale. *Com.*
Ba, barium. *Chem.*
B.A., Baccalaureus Artium (L., Bachelor of Arts); British Association (for the Advancement of Science); Buenos Aires.
bach., bachelor.
bact., bacteriology.
BAE, Bureau of Agricultural Economics; Bureau of American Ethnology.
B.Ag., B.Agr., Baccalaureus Agriculturae (L., Bachelor of Agriculture).
BAL, British anti-lewisite.
bal., balance; balancing.
B. and S., brandy-and-soda.
Bap., Bapt., Baptist.
bapt., baptized.
BAR, Browning automatic rifle.
bar., barometer; barrel; barrister.
B.Ar., B.Arch., Bachelor of Architecture.
barit., baritone.
Bart., Baronet.
bat., batt., battalion; battery.
Bav., Bavarian.
B.B.A., Bachelor of Business Administration.
B.B.C., BBC, British Broadcasting Corporation.
bbl., barrel; barrels.
bbls., barrels.
B.C., Bachelor of Chemistry; British Columbia.
B.C., b.c., before Christ.
B.C., b.c., bass clarinet; boat club.
B.C.E., Bachelor of Chemical Engineering; Bachelor of Civil Engineering.

B.C.L., Bachelor of Civil Law.
B.D., Bachelor of Divinity.
B/D, bank draft.
bd., board; bond; bound.
bd., bdl., bdle., bundle.
bd. ft., board feet; board foot.
B.D.S., Bachelor of Dental Surgery.
bds., bundles; (bound in) boards.
Be, beryllium. *Chem.*
B.E., Bachelor of Education; Bachelor of Engineering.
B.E., B/E, b.e., bill of exchange.
B.E.E., Bachelor of Electrical Engineering.
B.E.F., BEF, British Expeditionary Force, *or* Forces.
Belg., Belgian; Belgium.
B.E.M., British Empire Medal.
Beng., Bengali.
Benj., Benjamin.
B. ès L., Bachelier ès Lettres (F., Bachelor of Letters).
B. ès S., Bachelier ès Sciences (F., Bachelor of Sciences).
bet., between.
B/F, brought forward.
bf, b.f., bold-faced (type).
BFDC, Bureau of Foreign and Domestic Commerce.
bg., bag.
Bglr, Bugler.
bgs., bags.
Bi, bismuth. *Chem.*
Bib., Bible; Biblical.
Bibl., bibl., Biblical; bibliographical.
bibliog., bibliography.
bicarb., sodium bicarbonate.
biog., biographer; biographical; biography.
biol., biologist; biology.
B.I.S., Bank for International Settlements.
B.J., Bachelor of Journalism.
bk., bank; block; book.
bkg., banking.
bklr., black letter. *Bibliog.*
bks., barracks; books.
bkt., basket; bracket.
B.L., Bachelor of Laws.
B/L, bill of lading.
bl., bale; barrel; black.
b.l., bill of lading; breech-loading.
bldg., blg., building.
B.L.E., Brotherhood of Locomotive Engineers.
B.Lit(t)., Baccalaureus Lit(t)erarum (L., Bachelor of Literature, *or* of Letters).
blk., black; block.
Bln., bln., balloon.
BLS, Bureau of Labor Statistics.
B.L.S., Bachelor of Library Science.
bls., bales; barrels.
blvd., boulevard.
BM, Boatswain's Mate. *U. S. Navy.*
B.M., Baccalaureus Medicinae (L., Bachelor of Medicine); British Museum.
BMI, Broadcast Music, Inc.
BMR, basal metabolic rate.
B.Mus., Bachelor of Music.
Bn., bn., battalion.
b.o., bad order. *Transp.*
Boh., Bohem., Bohemian.
bor., boron; borough.
bot., botanical; botanist; botany; bottle.
boul., boulevard.
bp., birthplace; bishop.
b.p., below proof; boiling point.
B/P, bills payable.
B.Pd., B.Pe., Bachelor of Pedagogy.
B.P.E., Bachelor of Physical Education.
BPI, Bureau of Public Inquiries.
B.P.O.E., BPOE, Benevolent and Protective Order of Elks.
Br, bromine. *Chem.*
Br., British.
br., branch; brig; bronze; brother.
b.r., B/R, bills receivable.
Braz., Brazil; Brazilian.
brev., brevet; brevetted.
Brig., Brigade; Brigadier.
Brig. Gen., Brigadier General.
Brit., Britain; Britannia; Britannica; British.

bro., brother.
bros., brothers.
B.S., Bachelor of Science.
B/s, bags; bales.
b.s., balance sheet.
b.s., B/S, bill of sale.
B.S.A., BSA, Boy Scouts of America; British South Africa.
B.Sc., Baccalaureus Scientiae (L., Bachelor of Science).
B.S.Ed., Bachelor of Science in Education.
Bt., Baronet.
BT, Boilerman. *U. S. Navy.*
B.T., B.Th., Baccalaureus Theologiae (L., Bachelor of Theology).
BTRY, btry., battery.
B.T.U., B.Th.U., b.t.u., btu, British thermal unit.
BU, Builder. *U. S. Navy.*
Bu., Bureau.
bu., bureau; bushel; bushels.
buck., buckram.
bul., bull., bulletin.
Bulg., Bulgaria; Bulgarian.
bvt., brevet; brevetted.
B.W.I., British West Indies.
bx., box.
bxs., boxes.
Bz., benzene.

C

C, carbon. *Chem.*
C., Catholic; Celsius; Celtic.
C., c., calends; candle; capacity (*Elec.*); cape; carbon; carton; case; cathode; cent; center; centime; centigrade; chancellor; chancery; chapter; chief; church; circa; circum (L., about); cirrus (*Meteor.*); companion (in titles); congius (L., gallon); congress; conservative; consul; copper; corps; cost; court; cubic; current.
C., C, c, centimeter.
Ca, calcium. *Chem.*
C.A., Central America; Coast Artillery.
C.A., c.a., Catholic Action; chartered accountant; chief accountant; commercial agent; consular agent; controller of accounts.
CA, C.A., chronological age. *Psychol.*
C/A, capital account; credit account; current account.
ca., cathode; centiare; circa.
CAA, Civil Aeronautics Administration, *or* Authority.
CAB, Civil Aeronautics Board; Consumers' Advisory Board; Cooperative Analysis of Broadcasting.
Cal., California; large calorie.
cal., calendar; caliber; calorie(s).
Calif., California.
Cam, camouflage. *Mil.*
Camb., Cambridge.
Can., Canada; Canadian.
can., canon; canto.
canc., canceled; cancellation.
Cant., Canterbury; Canticles.
Cantab., Cantabrigiensis (L., of Cambridge).
CAP, Civil Air Patrol.
cap., capital; capitalize; capitulum, caput (L., chapter).
caps., capital letters.
Capt., Captain.
CAR, C.A.R., Civil Air Regulations.
car., carat.
Card., Cardinal.
CARE, Co-operative for American Remittances to Everywhere.
carp., carpentry.
cat., catalogue; catechism.
Cath., Catherine; Catholic.
cath., cathedral.
cav., cavalier; cavalry.
CAVU, C.A.V.U., ceiling and visibility unlimited. *Aviation.*
Cb, columbium. *Chem.*
C.B., Chirurgiae Baccalaureus (L., Bachelor of Surgery); Companion of the Bath.
c.b., confined to barracks.
CBC, Canadian Broadcasting Corporation.
C.B.D., cash before delivery.
CBI, China, Burma, India.

CBS, Columbia Broadcasting System.
Cc, cirro-cumulus.
C.C., c.c., carbon copy; cashier's check; chief clerk; city council; city councilor; common councilman; compte courant (F., current account); consular clerk; county clerk.
cc., chapters.
cc., cc, c.c., cubic centimeters.
CCA, Commission for Conventional Armaments.
CCC, Civilian Conservation Corps; Commodity Credit Corporation.
C.C.F., CCF, Cooperative Commonwealth Federation (of Canada).
CCS, Combined Chiefs of Staff.
CD, Driver. *U. S. Navy.*
Cd, cadmium. *Chem.*
cd., cord. cd. ft., cord foot.
CDR, Cdr., Commander.
Ce, cerium. *Chem.*
CE, Construction Electrician's Mate. *U. S. Navy.*
C.E., Chief Engineer; Christian Endeavor; Church of England; Civil Engineer.
CEA, Council of Economic Advisers.
CED, Committee for Economic Development.
Cels., Celsius.
Celt., Celtic.
cen., central; century.
cent., centered; centigrade; centimeter; central; century.
ceram., ceramics.
cert., certificate; certify.
certif., certificate; certificated.
cet. par., ceteris paribus (L., other things being equal).
cf., calf (binding); confer (L., compare).
C.F.I., c.f.i., cost, freight, and insurance.
c.f.m., cfm, cubic feet a minute.
C.G., Coast Guard.
C.G., c.g., center of gravity; commanding general; consul general.
cg., cg, centigram; centigrams.
CGT, Confédération Générale du Travail (F., General Confederation of Labor).
Ch., Chaplain; Charles; China; Chinese.
Ch., ch., chain; champion; chapter; check (*Chess*); chervonets; chervontsi; chestnut; chief; child; children; chirurgeon; chirurgiae (L., of surgery); church.
C.H., clearinghouse; Companion of Honor (Order).
c.h., courthouse; customhouse.
Chanc., Chancellor; Chancery.
chap., chaplain; chapter.
Chas., Charles.
Ch.B., Chirurgiae Baccalaureus (L., Bachelor of Surgery).
Ch. Clk., Chief Clerk.
Ch.D., Doctor of Chemistry.
Ch.E., Chemical Engineer.
chem., chemical; chemist; chemistry.
chg., charge. **chgd.**, charged.
Chin., China; Chinese.
chm., chairman; checkmate.
Chr., Christian; Christopher.
Chron., Chronicles.
chron., chronol., chronological; chronology.
chs., chapters.
Ci, cirrus.
CIA, Central Intelligence Agency.
CIAA, Coordinator of Inter-American Affairs.
C.I.D., Criminal Investigation Department. *Brit.*
cie., compagnie (F., company).
C.I.F., c.i.f., cost, insurance, and freight.
C. in C., C in C, Commander in Chief.
CINC, Cinc, Commander in Chief. Used also in combinations, as **CINCLANT** (Commander in Chief of the Atlantic [Fleet]). *All U. S. Navy.*
CIO, C.I.O., Congress (formerly Committee) of Industrial Organizations.

cir., circ., circa; circular; circum (L., about).
cit., citation; cited; citizen.
civ., civil; civilian.
ck., cask; check; cook.
Cl, chlorine. *Chem.*
cl., claim; class; clause; clearance; clergyman; clerk; cloth.
c.l., carload; carload lots.
cl., cl, centiliter.
clar., clarinet.
class., classic; classical; classification.
clk., clerk; clock.
C.L.U., Chartered Life Underwriter.
CM, Mechanic. *U.S. Navy.*
Cm, curium. *Chem.*
cm., cm, centimeter.
c.m., church missionary; corresponding member; court-martial.
Cmdr., Commander.
C.M.G., Companion (of the Order) of St. Michael and St. George.
cml., commercial.
CMTC, C.M.T.C., Citizens' Military Training Camp.
CN, Constructionman. *U.S. Navy.*
Cn, cumulo-nimbus.
C.N.S., CNS, central nervous system. *Med.*
Co, cobalt. *Chem.*
CO, C.O., Commanding Officer; conscientious objector.
Co., co., company; county.
c.o., c/o, care of; carried over.
coad., coadjutor.
C.O.D., c.o.d., cash on delivery; collect on delivery.
C. of S., Chief of Staff.
cog., cognate.
Col., Colonel; Colorado; Colossians; Columbia.
col., collected; collector; college; colonel; colonial; colony; color; colored; column.
coll., colleague; collect; collection; collective; collector; college; collegiate; colloquial.
collab., collaborated; collaboration; collaborator.
collat., collateral.
colloq., colloquial; colloquialism; colloquially.
Colm, column. *Mil.*
Colo., Colorado.
com., comedy; comma; commerce; commercial; commission; commissioner; committee; common; commonly; communication; community.
Com., Commander; Commodore.
comdg., commanding.
Comdr., Commander.
Comdt., Commandant.
Com. in Ch., Commander in Chief.
coml., commercial.
comm., commander; commerce; commissary; commission; committee; commonwealth.
COMO, Como., Commodore.
comp., comparative; comparison; compilation; compiled; composition; compositor; compound; comprising.
compar., comparative.
Comr., Commissioner.
con., concerto; conclusion; conjunx (L., wife) (*Law*); connection; consolidated; consul; contra (L., against).
conc., concentrate; concentrated; concentration; concerning.
conch., conchology.
cond., conducted (*Mus.*); conductivity; conductor.
conf., confer (L., compare); conference; confessor.
Confed., Confederate.
Cong., Congregational; Congress; Congressional.
cong., congius (L., gallon).
conj., conjugation; conjunction; conjunctive.
Conn., Connecticut.
cons., consecrated; consolidated; consonant; constable; constitution; constitutional; construction; consul; consulting.
consol., consolidated.

Const., const., constable; constant; constitution.
constr., construction.
Cont., Continental.
cont., containing; contents; continent; continue; continued.
contd., continued.
contemp., contemporary.
contr., contract; contraction; contralto; contrary.
contrib., contribution; contributor.
co-op., co-operative.
cop., copper; copyrighted.
Cor., Corinthians.
cor., corner; cornet; coroner; corrected; correction; correspondence; correspondent; corresponding.
corol., coroll., corollary.
Corp., Corporal; Corporation.
corp., corpn., corporation.
corr., correspond; correspondence; correspondent; corresponding; corrected.
corresp., correspondence.
C.O.S., c.o.s., cash on shipment.
cos, cosine.
cos., companies; counties.
cosec, cosecant.
cot, cotangent.
cp., compare.
c.p., candle power.
CP, command post; Communist Party; Construction Apprentice (*U.S. Navy*).
C.P., Chief Patriarch; Common Prayer.
C.P., c.p., chemically pure; court of probate.
C.P.A., CPA, Certified Public Accountant.
cpd., compound.
Cpl., Corporal.
CPO, C.P.O., Chief Petty Officer.
cps., coupons.
CPTP, C.P.T.P., Civil Pilot Training Program.
CQ, Charge of Quarters (*Mil.*).
C Q, General call preceding certain radiograms.
CR, Construction Recruit. *U.S.N.*
C.R., Costa Rica.
Cr, chromium. *Chem.*
Cr., credit; creditor; creek.
craniol., craniology.
craniom., craniometry.
cres., cresc., crescendo.
crim. con., criminal conversation.
crit., critical; criticism.
cryst., crystallized; crystalline; crystallography.
Cs, cesium (*Chem.*); cirro-stratus.
CS, Commissaryman. *U.S. Navy.*
C.S., Christian Science; Christian Scientist.
C.S., c.s., capital stock; civil service.
C/S, cs., cases.
C.S.A., Confederate States of America.
C.S.C., Conspicuous Service Cross.
CSC, Civil Service Commission.
csc, cosecant.
csk., cask.
CSO, CSigO, C.S.O., Chief Signal Officer.
CST, C.S.T., Central Standard Time.
CT, Communications Technician. *U.S. Navy.*
Ct., Connecticut.
ct., cent(s); county; court.
ctn., cotangent.
ctr., center.
cts., centimes; cents.
Cu, cumulus; cuprum (copper).
cu., cubic.
cu. cm., cubic centimeter.
cu. in., cubic inch.
cur., currency; current.
cv., cvt., convertible (bonds).
CW, continuous wave.
CWA, Civil Works Administration.
CWAC, C.W.A.C., Canadian Women's Army Corps.
C.W.O., c.w.o., cash with order.
CWS, Chemical Warfare Service.
cwt., hundredweight.
cyc., cyclopedia; cyclopedic.
cyl., cylinder; cylindrical.

CYO, Catholic Youth Organization.
C.Z., Canal Zone (Panama).
Czech., Czechoslovakia.

D

D., December; Department (*U.S. Army*); Deus (L., God); Doctor; Dominus (L., Lord); Don; Duchess; Duke; Dutch.
D. d., da (L., give) (*Pharm.*); dam (in pedigrees); date; daughter; day, *or* days; dead; decretum (L., decree); degree; democrat; democratic; denarii; denarius; density (*Physics*); deputy; diameter; died; dinar; dollar; door (*Theat.*); dose; dowager; drachma.
D, deuterium. *Chem.*
d, dextro. *Chem.*
d-, dextro-. *Chem.*
DA, Dental Apprentice. *U.S.N.*
D.A., District Attorney.
da., daughter; day; days.
D.A.B., DAB, Dictionary of American Biography.
dal., dal, decaliter.
Dan., Danish.
Dan., Danl., Daniel.
D.A.R., DAR, Daughters of the American Revolution.
dat., dative.
dau., daughter.
DAV, D.A.V., Disabled American Veterans.
db, decibel.
d.b.a., doing business as.
d.b.h., diameter breast high *or* at breast height. *Forestry.*
D. Bib., Douay Bible.
dbl., double.
DC, Damage Controlman. *U.S. Navy.*
D.C., da capo; District of Columbia; Doctor of Chiropractic.
DC, D.C., direct current.
D.C.L., Doctor of Canon Law; Doctor of Civil Law.
D.C.M., Distinguished Conduct Medal. *British Army.*
D.D., Divinitatis Doctor (L., Doctor of Divinity).
D.D., D/D, demand draft.
dd., d/d, delivered.
D/D, D/d, d.d., days after date, *or* days' (day's) date.
D.D.S., Doctor of Dental Surgery.
DE, destroyer escort.
deb., deben.; debenture.
Dec., Dec, December.
dec., decim., decimeter.
dec., deceased; declaration; declension; declination; decrease; decrescendo.
decd., deceased.
decl., declension.
decresc., decrescendo.
def., defendant; deferred; defined; definite; definition.
deg., degree; degrees.
D.E.I., Dutch East Indies.
Del., Delaware.
del., delegate.
Dem., Democrat; Democratic.
Den., Denmark.
denom., denomination.
dent., dentist; dentistry.
Dep., dep., deposit. *Banking.*
dep., department; departs; departure; deponent; depot; deputy.
dept., department; deputy.
der., deriv., derivation; derivative; derive; derived.
desc., descendant.
D. ès L., Docteur ès Lettres (F., Doctor of Letters).
D. ès S., Docteur ès Sciences (F., Doctor of Sciences).
det., detachment. *Mil.*
Deut., Deuteronomy.
DF, D/F, D.F., direction finding.
D.F.C., DFC, Distinguished Flying Cross. *U.S. & Brit.*
dg., dg, decigram.
d.h., das heisst (G., that is to say); deadhead (*Colloq.*).
Di, didymium. *Chem.*
di., dia., diam., diameter.
dial., dialect; dialectal.
dict., dictator; dictionary.
diff., difference; different.

dig., digest.
dim., dimin., diminuendo; diminutive.
din., dinar.
dipl., diplomatic.
dir., director.
disc., discount; discovered.
disch., discharged.
dist., distance; distinguish; distinguished; district.
Dist. Atty., District Attorney.
distr., distribute; distribution; distributor.
div., divided; dividend; division; divisor; divorced.
DK, Disbursing Clerk. *U.S. Navy.*
dkg., dkg, decagram.
dkl., dkl, decaliter.
dkm., dkm, decameter.
D/L, demand loan.
dl., dl, deciliter.
D.Lit., D.Litt., Doctor Lit(t)erarum (L., Doctor of Literature, *or* of Letters).
D.L.S., Doctor of Library Science.
DM, Draftsman. *U.S. Navy.*
DM., Dm, Deutsche mark.
D.M., Deputy Master.
dm., dm, decameter; decimeter.
D.M.D., Dentariae Medicinae Doctor (NL., Doctor of Dental Medicine).
D.Mus., Doctor of Music.
DN, Dentalman. *U.S. Navy.*
D.N.B., DNB, Dictionary of National Biography (British).
D.O., Doctor of Osteopathy.
do., ditto (It., the same).
doc., document.
dol., dollar; dollars.
dom., domestic; dominion.
doz., dozen; dozens.
DP, D.P., degree of polymerization; diametrical pitch; displaced person.
dpt., department; deponent.
DR, Dental Recruit. *U.S. Navy.*
D.R., D/R, d.r., dead reckoning; deposit receipt.
Dr., Dr, debit; debtor; Doctor.
dr., debit; debtor; drachma; dram; drams; drawer.
dram. pers., dramatis personae.
Ds, dysprosium. *Chem.*
d.s., days after sight. *Com.*
D.S., D.Sc., Doctor of Science.
D.S.C., DSC, Distinguished Service Cross. *U.S. & Brit.*
D.S.M., DSM, Distinguished Service Medal. *U.S. & Brit.*
D.S.O., (Companion of the) Distinguished Service Order; District Staff Officer.
DST, D.S.T., Daylight Saving Time.
DT, Dental Technician. *U.S.N.*
d.t., delirium tremens.
D.Th., D.Theol., Doctor of Theology.
Du., Duke; Dutch.
dup., duplicate.
D.V., Deo volente (L., God willing); by God's will); Douay Version.
D.V.M., Doctor of Veterinary Medicine.
D/W, dock warrant.
dwt., denarius weight, i. e., pennyweight.
DX, D.X., distance. *Radio.*
Dy, dysprosium. *Chem.*
dyn., dynam., dynamics.
dz., dozen.

E

E, E., e., east; eastern.
E., Earl; Earth; English.
e., engineer; engineering; entrance (*Theat.*).
e, erg.
E.A., EA, educational age.
ea., each.
EAM, Ethnikon Apeleftherotikon Metopon (Gr., National Liberation Front).
e. & o. e., errors and omissions excepted.
ECA, Economic Cooperation Administration.
eccl., eccles., ecclesiastical; ecclesiology.
Eccles., Eccl., Ecclesiastes.

Ecclus., Ecclesiasticus.

ecol., ecological; ecology.

econ., economic; economics; economy.

Ecua., Ecuador.

ed., edited; edition; editor.

Ed.B., Bach. of Education.

Ed.D., Doctor of Education.

EDES, Ellinikos Dimokratikos Ethnikos Stratos (Gr., Hellenic National Democratic Party).

edit., edited; edition.

Ed.M., Master of Education.

educ., education; educational.

Edw., Edward.

E.E., Electrical Engineer.

e.e., errors excepted.

EEG, electroencephalogram.

Eg., Egypt; Egyptian.

e.g., exempli gratia (L., for example).

Egyptol., Egyptology.

E.I., East Indian; East Indies.

EKG, electrocardiogram.

ELAS, Ellinikos Laikos Apeleftherotikos Stratos (Gr., Hellenic People's Army of Liberation).

elec., elect., electric; electrical; electrician; electricity.

elem., elementary; element(s).

elev., elevation.

Eliz., Elizabeth; Elizabethan.

E. long., east longitude.

EM, Electrician's Mate (U.S. Navy); enlisted man or men.

Em., emanation (Chem.); Emily; Emma.

embryol., embryology.

E.M.F., e.m.f., emf, electromotive force.

Emp., Emperor; Empress.

e.m.u., electromagnetic unit(s).

EN, Engineman. U.S. Navy.

enc., encl., enclosure.

ency., encyc., encycl., encyclopedia.

Ency. Brit., Encyc. Brit., Encyclopaedia Britannica.

ENE, east-northeast.

Eng., England; English.

eng., engine; engineer; engineering; engraved; engraver; engraving.

Eng. D., Doctor of Engineering.

engin., engineering.

engr., engineer; engraved; engraver; engraving.

Ens., Ensign.

entom., entomology.

env., envelope.

Eph., Ephes., Ephesians.

Epis., Episc., Episcopal.

E.Q., EQ, educational quotient.

eq., equal; equalizer; equalizing; equation; equivalent.

equiv., equivalent.

Er, erbium. Chem.

E.R., Eduardus Rex (L., King Edward).

ERA, Emergency Relief Administration.

ERP, European Recovery Program.

erron., erroneous; -ously.

E.R.V., English Revised Version (of the Bible).

ES, Specialist (emergency service). U.S. Navy.

ESC, Economic and Social Council.

Esd., Esdras.

ESE, east-southeast.

ESP, extrasensory perception.

esp., espec., especially.

Esq., Esqr., Esquire.

EST, E.S.T., Eastern Standard Time.

Est., Estonia.

est., established; estimated.

estab., established.

Esth., Esther.

e.s.u., esu, electrostatic unit(s).

ET, Electronics Technician. U.S. Navy.

ETA, estimated time of arrival.

et al., et alibi (L., and elsewhere); et alii (L., and others).

etc., et cetera.

Eth., Ethiopia; Ethiopic.

ethnol., ethnology.

ETO, European Theater of Operations.

et seq., et sequens (L., and the following); et sequentes or sequentia (L., and those that follow).

etym., etymol., etymological; etymology.

Eu, europium. Chem.

Eur., Europe; European.

e.v., ev, electron volt(s).

evang., evangelical.

Ex., Exodus.

ex., examined; example; exception; exchange; excursion; executed; executive.

exam., examination.

exc., excellency; excellent; except; excepted; exception.

exch., exchange; exchequer.

excl., exclam., exclamation.

excl., exclusive.

exec., executive; executor.

ex lib., ex libris (L., from the books [of]).

Exod., Exodus.

exp., expenses; export; express.

expt., experiment.

exptl., experimental.

ext., extension; externally; extinct; extra; extract.

Ez., Ezr., Ezra.

Ezek., Ezekiel.

F

F, Fahrenheit; farad; fathom; fluorine (Chem.); function (Math.).

F., Fahrenheit; February; Fellow; France; French.

f., f., farad; farthing; fathom; feminine; fine; fluid (ounce); folio; following; franc; frequency.

f, forte. Music.

FA, Fireman Apprentice. U.S. Navy.

FA, F.A., field artillery.

f.a., free alongside. Shipping.

F.A.A.A.S., Fellow of the American Association for the Advancement of Science.

fac., facsim., facsimile.

F.A.C.D., Fellow of the American College of Dentists.

F.A.C.P., Fellow of the American College of Physicians.

F.A.C.S., Fellow of the American College of Surgeons.

F.A.G.O., Fellow of the American Guild of Organists.

Fahr., Fahrenheit.

F.A.I.A., Fellow of the American Institute of Architects.

F.A.M., F. and A.M., Free and Accepted Masons.

fam., familiar; family.

FAO, Food and Agriculture Organization.

F.A.P.S., Fellow of the American Physical Society.

F.A.S., Fellow of the Actuarial Society (Canada); Fellow of the Antiquarian Society (Brit.); Fellow of the Anthropological Society (Brit.).

f.a.s., free alongside ship.

F.A.S.A., Fellow of the Acoustical Society of America.

F.A.S.B., Fellow of the Asiatic Society of Bengal.

fath., fathom.

F.B.A., Fellow of the British Academy.

FBI, Federal Bureau of Investigation.

F.B.O.A., Fellow of the British Optical Association.

F.B.O.U., Fellow of the British Ornithologists' Union.

F.B.S., Fellow of the Botanical Society.

f.c., follow copy. Print.

FC, Fire Controlman. U.S. Navy.

FCA, Farm Credit Administration.

F.C.A., Fellow of the (Institute of) Chartered Accountants. Brit.

FCC, Federal Communications Commission.

F.C.C., First Class Certificate.

FCIC, Federal Crop Insurance Corporation.

F.C.I.C., Fellow of the Canadian Institute of Chemistry.

F.C.I.S., Fellow of the Chartered Institute of Secretaries. Brit.

F.C.P., Fellow of the College of Preceptors. Brit.

fcp., foolscap.

F.C.S., Fellow of the Chemical Society.

FDA, Food and Drug Administration.

FDIC, Federal Deposit Insurance Corporation.

Fe, ferrum (iron). Chem.

FEB, Fair Employment Board.

Feb., Feb, February.

fec., fecit (L., He [or she] made [or executed] it).

fed., federal; federated; federation.

F.E.I.S., Fellow of the Educational Institute of Scotland.

fem., feminine.

FEPC, Fair Employment Practice Committee.

FERA, Federal Emergency Relief Administration.

F.E.S., Fellow of the Entomological Society; Fellow of the Ethnological Society.

ff, fortissimo. Music.

ff., folios; following (pages).

F.F.A., Fellow of the Faculty of Actuaries. Brit.

F.F.A., f.f.a., free from alongside.

FFC, Foreign Funds Control.

F.F.P.S., Fellow of the Faculty of Physicians and Surgeons.

F.F.R., Fellow of the Faculty of Radiologists.

F.F.Sc., Fellow of the Faculty of Sciences. Brit.

F.F.V., First Families of Virginia.

F.G.S., Fellow of the Geological Society (of London).

F.G.S.A., Fellow of the Geological Society of America.

FHA, Farmers Home Administration; Federal Housing Administration.

F.H.S., Fellow of the Horticultural Society.

F.I., Falkland Islands.

F.I.A., Fellow of the Institute of Actuaries. Brit.

F.I.C., Fellow of the Institute of Chemistry. Brit. & Ir.

fid., fiduciary.

fig., figurative; figuratively; figure; figures.

F.I.Inst., Fellow of the Imperial Institute. Brit.

F.I.J., Fellow of the Institute of Journalists. Brit.

Fin., Finland; Finnish.

fin., financial.

f.i.o., free in and out (shipping).

fir., firkin.

Fl, fluorine. Chem.

Fl., Flanders; Flemish.

fl., florin; floruit (L., he flourished); flourished.

FLA, Federal Loan Agency.

F.L.A., Fellow of the Library Association. Brit.

Fla., Flor., Florida.

fld., field.

Flem., Flemish.

flex., flexible.

flor., floruit (L., he flourished).

fl. oz., fluid ounce, or ounces.

F.L.S., Fellow of the Linnaean Society.

FM, F.M., f–m, f.m., frequency modulation.

fm., fathom; from.

FMCS, Federal Mediation and Conciliation Service.

F.M.S.A., Fellow of the Mineralogical Society of America.

FN, Fireman. U.S. Navy.

fn., footnote.

F.N.A.O., Fellow of the National Association of Opticians.

FNMA, Federal National Mortgage Association.

F.O., Foreign Office.

F.O., f.o., field officer.

F.O.B., f.o.b., free on board.

F.O.E., Fraternal Order of Eagles.

fol., folio; following.

foll., following.

for., foreign; forestry.

F.O.R., f.o.r., free on rail.

fort., fortification; fortified.

FP, Pipefitter. U.S. Navy.

F.P., f.p., foot-pound; freezing point.

fp, forte piano. Music.

FPC, Federal Power Commission.

f.p.m., fpm, feet per minute.

FPO, Fleet Post Office.

F.P.S., Fellow of the Philharmonic Society (Brit.); Fellow of the Philological Society; Fellow of the Philosophical Society.

f.p.s., fps, feet per second.

FR, Fireman Recruit. U.S. Navy.

Fr, francium. Chem.

Fr., Father (Eccl.); France; Francis; Frater (L., Brother); French; Friar; Friday.

fr., fragment; franc; from.

F.R.A.I., Fellow of the Royal Anthropological Institute.

F.R.A.M., Fellow of the Royal Academy of Music.

F.R.A.S., Fellow of the Royal Astronomical Society.

F.R.B.S., Fellow of the Royal Botanic Society (of London).

FRC, Federal Radio Commission.

F.R.C.I., Fellow of the Royal Colonial Institute.

F.R.C.M., Fellow of the Royal College of Music.

F.R.C.O., Fellow of the Royal College of Organists.

F.R.C.P., Fellow of the Royal College of Physicians.

F.R.C.S., Fellow of the Royal College of Surgeons.

Fredk., Frederick.

freq., frequent; frequentative; frequently.

F.R.G.S., Fellow of the Royal Geographical Society.

F.R.H.S., Fellow of the Royal Horticultural Society.

Fri., Friday.

F.R.I.B.A., Fellow of the Royal Institute of British Architects.

Fris., Frs., Frisian.

F.R.S., Fellow of the Royal Society (scientific).

F.R.S.A., Fellow of the Royal Society of Arts.

F.R.S.C., Fellow of the Royal Society of Canada.

F.R.S.E., Fellow of the Royal Society, Edinburgh.

F.R.S.L., Fellow of the Royal Society of Literature; Fellow of the Royal Society, London.

F.R.S.N.Z., Fellow of the Royal Society of New Zealand.

frt., freight.

FSA, Federal Security Agency.

F.S.A., Fellow of the Society of Antiquaries. Brit.

FSH, follicle-stimulating hormone.

FSR, F.S.R., Field Service Regulations.

F.S.S., Fellow of the (Royal) Statistical Society.

FT, Fire Control Technician. U.S. Navy.

ft., feet; foot; fort; fortification.

FTC, Federal Trade Commission.

fth., fthm., fathom.

ft–lb, foot-pound.

furn., furnished.

fut., future.

f.v., folio verso (L., on the back of the page).

FWA, Federal Works Agency.

fwd., forward.

fz, forzando. Music.

F.Z.S., Fellow of the Zoological Society.

G

G, gun. Mil.

G., German; specific gravity.

G., g., conductance (Elec.); gauge; gourde; grain; guinea; gulf.

g, general intelligence (Psychol.); gravity.

g., g, gram.

Ga, gallium. Chem.

Ga., Gallic; Georgia.

G.A., GA, General Agent; General Assembly.

G.A., g.a., general average.
Gael., Gaelic.
Gal., Galatians; Galen.
gal., gall., gallon; gallons.
gals., gallons.
galv., galvanic; galvanism; galvanized.
GAO, General Accounting Office.
G.A.R., GAR, Grand Army of the Republic.
gaz., gazette; gazetteer.
G.B., Great Britain.
GCA, ground control approach.
G.C.B., (Knight) Grand Cross of the Bath.
gcd, g.c.d., G.C.D., greatest common divisor.
gcf, g.c.f., G.C.F., greatest common factor.
G.C.L.H., Grand Cross of the Legion of Honor.
gcm, g.c.m., G.C.M., greatest common measure.
GCT, G.C.T., Greenwich civil time.
G.C.V.O., (Knight) Grand Cross of the (Royal) Victorian Order.
G.D., Grand Duchess; Grand Duchy; Grand Duke.
Gd, gadolinium. *Chem.*
gde., gourde.
gds., goods.
Ge, germanium. *Chem.*
g.e., gilt edges. *Bookbinding.*
geb., geboren (G., born).
Gen., General (*Army*); Genesis; Geneva; Genevan.
gen., gender; genera; general; generally; genitive; genus.
geneal., genealogy.
genit., genitive.
genl., general.
gent., gentleman.
Geo., George.
geod., geodesy; geodetic.
geog., geographer; geographic; geographical; geography.
geol., geologic; geological; geologist; geology.
geom., geometer; geometric; geometrical; geometry.
Ger., German; Germany.
ger., gerund.
gest., gestorben (G., died).
Gestapo, Geheime Staatspolizei (G., Secret State Police).
g.gr., great gross.
GHA, Greenwich hour angle. *Navigation.*
GHQ, G.H.Q., General Headquarters. *Mil.*
gi., gill; gills.
GI, G.I. See in *Vocab.*
Gib., Gibraltar.
Gk., Greek.
Gl, glucinum, *or* glucinium.
gld., guilder.
gloss., glossary.
glt. gilt. *Bookbinding.*
GM, Gunner's Mate. *U.S. Navy.*
G.M., General Manager; George Medal (*Brit.*); Grand Master.
gm., gram; grams.
GMT, G.M.T., Greenwich mean time.
GO, general orders. *Mil.*
G.O.P., GOP, Grand Old Party (a rhetorical name for the Republican party).
Goth., goth, Gothic.
Gov., gov., governor.
Govt., govt., government.
G.P., general paresis; general practitioner.
GPM, g.p.m., gpm, gallons per minute.
G.P.O., GPO, General Post Office; Government Printing Office.
G.P.U. See GAY-PAY-OO, in *Vocab.*
GQ, G.Q., g.q., general quarters. *Nav.*
Gr., Grecian; Greece; Greek.
gr., grain; grains; gram; grams; gross.
grad., graduate; graduated.
gram., grammar; grammarian; grammatical.
Gr. Br., Gr. Brit., Great Britain.
gro., gross.
gr. wt., gross weight.
GS, G.S., General Staff; Girl Scouts.

G.S.A., GSA, Girl Scouts of America.
GSC, G.S.C., General Staff Corps.
GSO, General Staff Officer.
gt., great.
G.T.C., g.t.c., good till canceled, *or* countermanded.
guar., guaranteed.
gun., gunnery.

H

H, henry (*Elec.*); hydrogen (H², deuterium) (*Chem.*); intensity of magnetic field (*Physics*).
H., h., harbor; hard; hardness; height; high; hour; husband.
H¹, protium.
H²⁺, proton.
H³, tritium.
HA, Hospital Apprentice. *U.S. Navy.*
ha., hectare(s).
h.a., hoc anno (L., in this year).
Hab., Habakkuk.
Hag., Haggai.
Hal., halogen. *Chem.*
Hants, Hampshire.
Hb, hemoglobin.
H.C., House of Commons.
hcf, h.c.f., highest common factor.
h.c.l., high cost of living. *Colloq.*
hd., head.
hdkf., handkerchief.
hdqrs., headquarters.
He, helium. *Chem.*
HE, high explosive.
H.E., His Eminence; His Excellency.
Heb., Hebr., Hebrew(s).
Hen., Henry.
her., heraldry.
H.F., HF, h.f., hf, high-frequency.
Hf, hafnium. *Chem.*
hf., half.
hf. bd., half-bound.
hf. cf., half-calf.
hf. mor., half-morocco.
Hg, hydrargyrum (mercury).
hg., hectogram; heliogram.
H.H., His, or Her, Highness; His Holiness (the Pope).
hhd., hogshead.
HHFA, Housing and Home Finance Agency.
H.I., Hawaiian Islands.
H.I.H., His (Her) Imperial Highness.
H.I.M., His (Her) Imperial Majesty.
Hind., Hindu; Hindustan; Hindustani.
hist., historian; historical; history.
H.J., hic jacet (L., here lies); — used in epitaphs.
hl., hl, hectoliter.
HLBB, Home Loan Bank Board.
HM, Hospital Corpsman. *U.S. Navy.*
H.M., His (Her) Majesty.
hm., hm, hectometer.
H.M.S., His (Her) Majesty's Service, Ship, or Steamer.
HN, Hospitalman. *U.S. Navy.*
Ho, holmium. *Chem.*
ho., house.
HOLC, Home Owners' Loan Corporation.
Hon., Honorable.
hon., honorably; honorary.
Hor., Horace.
hor., horizon; horizontal.
horol., horology.
hort., horticultural; -culture.
Hos., Hosea.
hosp., hospital.
H.P., HP, h.p., hp, high pressure; horsepower.
HQ, H.Q., hq, h.q., headquarters.
Hq. Co., Headquarters Company.
HR, Hospital Recruit. *U.S. Navy.*
H.R., Home Rule, *or* Ruler; House of Representatives.
hr., hour; hours.
H.R.H., His (Her) Royal Highness.
hrs., hours.
Ht., Harriet.
ht., height; heat.
Hts., Heights.
Hung., Hungarian; Hungary.

Hy., Henry.
hyd., hydros., hydrostatics.
hydraul., hydraulics.
hyp., hypoth., hypothesis.

I

I, iodine. *Chem.*
I., Island(s), Isle(s).
i., intransitive; island.
Ia., Iowa. *Not Official.*
IADB, Inter-American Defense Board.
IAS, indicated air speed. *Aviation.*
ib., ibid., ibidem (L., in the same place).
IC, Interior Communications Electrician. *U.S. Navy.*
ICAO, International Civil Aviation Organization.
ICC, Interstate Commerce Commission.
Ice., Icel., Iceland; Icelandic.
ichth., ichthyology.
ICI, I.C.I., Imperial Chemical Industries (*Brit.*); International Committee on Illumination.
ICJ, International Court of Justice.
I.C.S., Indian Civil Service.
Id., Idaho. *Not Official.*
id., idem.
ID, I.D., i.d., inside diameter.
I.D., Intelligence Department; Iraqi dinar.
Ida., Idaho. *Not Official.*
IE, I.E., Indo-European.
i. e., id est (L., that is).
I.F., i.f., i–f, intermediate frequency.
IFF, Identification, Friend or Foe.
I.F.S., Irish Free State.
I.G., Indo-Germanic; Inspector General.
ign., ignition.
IHP, I.H.P., ihp, i.h.p., indicated horsepower.
IHS, I.H.S., see in *Vocab.*
Il, illinium. *Chem.*
Ill., Illinois.
ill., illus., illust., illustrated; illustration.
ILO, I.L.O., International Labor Organization.
I.L.P., Independent Labour Party. *Brit.*
ILS, instrument landing system.
IM, Instrumentman. *U.S. Navy.*
I.M., Isle of Man.
imit., imitation; imitative.
Imp., Imperator.
imp., imperative; imperfect; imperial; impersonal; import; imported; importer; imprimatur (L., let it be printed).
imper., imperative.
imperf., imperfect; imperforate.
impers., impersonal.
impf., imperfect.
imp. gal., imperial gallon.
impv., imperative.
In, indium. *Chem.*
in., inch; inches.
inc., inclosure; including; inclusive; income; incorporated; increase.
inch., incho., inchoative.
incl., inclosure; inclusive.
incog., incognito.
incor., incorp., incorporated.
incr., increased; increasing.
Ind., India; Indian; Indiana; Indies.
ind., independent; index; indicative; indigo; industrial.
indecl., indeclinable.
indef., indefinite.
indic., indicating; indicative.
individ., individual.
induc., induction.
inf., infinitive; information.
inf., Inf., infantry.
infin., infinitive.
init., initial.
in loc. cit., in loco citato (L., in the place cited).
inorg., inorganic.
I.N.R.I., Iesus (Jesus) Nazarenus, Rex Iudaeorum (Judaeorum) (L., Jesus of Nazareth, King of the Jews).

INS, I.N.S., International News Service.
ins., inches; inspector; insular; insulated; insulator; insurance.
insep., inseparable.
insp., inspector.
Inst., Institute; Institution.
inst., instant (the present month); instrumental.
instr., instructor; instrument; instruments; instrumental.
int., intelligence; interest; interior; interjection; internal; international; intransitive.
interj., interjection.
internat., international.
interrog., interrogative.
intr., intrans., intransitive.
Int. Rev., Internal Revenue.
introd., introduction; introductory.
inv., inventor; invoice.
invt., inventory.
Io, ionium. *Chem.*
I.O.F., Independent Order of Foresters.
I.O.O.F., Independent Order of Odd Fellows.
I.O.R.M., Improved Order of Red Men.
IOU, I.O.U., I owe you.
I.O.W., Isle of Wight.
IPA, International Phonetic Association *or* Alphabet.
IQ, I.Q., intelligence quotient.
i.q., idem quod (L., the same as).
Ir, iridium. *Chem.*
Ir., Ireland; Irish.
Iran., Iranian.
Ire., Ireland.
IRO, International Refugee Organization.
irreg., irregular; irregularly.
Is., Isaiah.
Is., is., island; islands; isle.
Isa., Isaiah.
Isl(s)., isl(s)., island(s).
Isr., Israel.
It., Ital., Italian; Italy.
ital., italic (type).
ITO, International Trade Organization.
IU, I.U., international unit(s). *Biol., Immunol., etc.* (Measuring amount and effect of a vitamin. Cf. UNIT, 4.)
I.W., Isle of Wight.
IWW, I.W.W., Industrial Workers of the World.

J

J, joule. *Physics.*
J., Judge, Justice.
Ja, Ja, January.
JA, J.A., Judge Advocate.
J.A.G., Judge Advocate General.
Jam., Jamaica.
Jan., Jan, January.
Jap., Japan; Japanese.
Jas., James.
Jav., Javanese.
J.C.D., Juris Canonici Doctor (L., Doctor of Canon Law); Juris Civilis Doctor (L., Doctor of Civil Law).
jct., jctn., junction.
J.D., Jurum Doctor (L., Doctor of Laws).
Je, Je, June.
Jer., Jeremiah; Jeremy.
jg, j.g., junior grade.
Jl, July.
Jno., John.
JO, Journalist. *U.S. Navy.*
Jo., Josephine.
Jon., Jona, Jonathan.
Jos., Joseph; Josiah.
Josh., Joshua.
jour., journal; journeyman.
J.P., justice of the peace.
Jr., jr., junior.
Judg., Judges.
Jul., Jules; Julius; July.
Jun., jun., junior.
Junc., junc., junction.
Jur. D., Juris Doctor (L., Doctor of Law).
jurisp., jurisprudence.
jus., just., justice.
juv., juvenile. *Cataloguing.*
Jy, July.

K

K, kalium (*L.,* potassium); king (*Chess*); koruna (*Czech.*).
K, k., kalendae (*L.,* calends); kilogram; king; knight; kopeck; krone.
k., capacity (*Elec.*); carat (*Assaying*); constant.
k, kilo- (thousand).
ka., kathode, *or* cathode.
kal., kalends.
Kan., Kans., Kas., Kansas.
Kath., Katharine.
KB, king's bishop. *Chess.*
K.B., King's Bench; Knight Bachelor.
K.C., King's Counsel; Knights of Columbus.
kc., kc, kilocycle(s).
Kč, korun; koruna; koruny. *Czech.*
kcal., kilocalorie.
K.C.B., Knight Commander (of the Order) of the Bath.
Kčs, korun; koruny. *Czech.*
K.C.V.O., Knight Commander of the (Royal) Victorian Order.
K.D., knocked down. *Com.*
K.G., Knight (of the Order) of the Garter.
kg., kg, keg(s); kilogram(s).
kil., kilometer(s).
kilo., kilogram; kilometer.
kilog., kilogram.
kilol., kiloliter.
kilom., kilometer.
K.K.K., KKK, Ku Klux Klan.
K Kt, king's knight. *Chess.*
kl., kl, kiloliter.
km., km, kilometer; kingdom.
kn., kronen.
knt., knight.
KO, K.O., k.o., knockout. *Pugilism.*
K. of C., Knight, *or* Knights, of Columbus.
K. of P., Knight, *or* Knights, of Pythias.
kop., kopeck(s). *U.S.S.R.*
KP, king's pawn. *Chess.*
K.P., Knight (of the Order) of St. Patrick; Knights of Pythias.
K.P., KP, see KITCHEN POLICE in *Vocab.*
KR, king's rook. *Chess.*
Kr, krypton. *Chem.*
kr, kreutzer; krone.
Krs, kuruş. *Turkey.*
K.T., Knight Templar; Knight (of the Order) of the Thistle (*Scotland*).
Kt, knight.
kt., carat.
kw., kilowatt.
K.W.H., kw-h, kw-hr, kilowatt-hour.
Ky., Kentucky.

L

£, L, l., libra (*L.,* pound).
L, length (*Physics*); (terrestrial) longitude (*Geod.*).
L, l, coefficient of inductance (*Elec.*).
L., Latin; Licentiate; Linnaeus; Lodge (*Fraternal*).
L., l., lake; land; latitude; law; leaf; league; left; lempira; length; leu; lev; lex; liber (*L.,* book); line; link; lira, lire (*It.*); low.
l., l, liter.
l-, l., levo-. *Chem.*
La, lanthanum. *Chem.*
La., Louisiana.
L.A., Library Association; Local Agent.
Lab., Labrador.
lab., laboratory.
Lam., Lamentations.
lang., language.
Lat., Latin.
lat., latitude.
Latv., Latvia.
L.B., Lit(t)erarum Baccalaureus (*L.,* Bachelor of Letters); Local Board.
lb., ℔, libra (*L.,* pound); librae (*L.,* pounds).
lb. ap., pound (apothecaries' weight).

lbs., pounds.
lb. t., pound troy.
LC-, landing craft (with type specified by following letter), *for example,* **LCI,** Landing Craft Infantry; **LCP,** Landing Craft Personnel.
L.C., Library of Congress.
L/C, l/c, letter of credit.
l.c., left center; loco citato (*L.,* in the place cited); lower case (*Typog.*).
L.C.L., l.c.l., less than carload lot. *Com.*
L.C.M., l.c.m., lowest, *or* least, common multiple.
LCT, L.C.T., local civil time.
LD, LD., L.D., Low Dutch.
L.D.S., Licentiate in Dental Surgery.
Ld., Lord.
L. Div., Licentiate in Divinity.
£E, Egyptian pound.
lea., league; leather.
lect., lecture.
leg., legal; legate; legato; legislative; legislature.
legis., legislation; legislative; legislature.
L. ès Sc., Licencié ès Sciences (*F.,* Licentiate in Sciences).
Lev., Levit., Leviticus.
lex., lexicon.
lexicog., lexicographer; lexicographical; lexicography.
L.F., LF, l.f., lf, low-frequency.
LG, LG., L.G., Low German.
lg., lge, large.
LH, luteinizing hormone.
LH, L.H., l.h., left hand.
LHA, local hour angle. *Navig.*
L.H.D., Litterarum Humaniorum, *or* In Litteris Humanioribus, Doctor (*L.,* Doctor of Humanities).
LI, Lithographer. *U.S. Navy.*
Li, lithium. *Chem.*
li, link. See MEASURE table in *Vocab.*
L.I., Long Island.
Lib., Liberal.
lib., liber (*L.,* book); librarian; library.
Lieut., Lieutenant.
lin., lineal; linear.
ling., linguistics.
liq., liquid; liquor.
lit., liter; literal; literally; literary; literature.
Lit.B., Litt.B., Lit(t)erarum Baccalaureus (*L.,* Bachelor of Letters, Bachelor of Literature).
Lit.D., Literarum Doctor (*L.,* Doctor of Literature).
Lith., Lithuania; Lithuanian.
lith., litho., lithog., lithograph; lithography.
Litt.D., Litterarum Doctor (*L.,* Doctor of Letters).
LL, LL., Late Latin; Low Latin.
ll., lines.
LL.B., Legum Baccalaureus (*L.,* Bachelor of Laws).
LL.D., Legum Doctor (*L.,* Doctor of Laws).
L.M., Licentiate in Medicine, *or* in Midwifery.
LMT, local mean time.
loc. cit., loco citato (*L.,* in the place cited).
log., logarithm.
lon., long., longitude.
L.O.O.M., Loyal Order of Moose.
loq., loquitur (*L.,* he (she, it) speaks).
£P, Palestine pound.
L.P.S., Lord Privy Seal.
LS-, landing ship (of specified type), *for example,* **LST,** Landing Ship Tank.
L.S., Licentiate in Surgery; locus sigilli (*L.,* the place of the seal).
L.S.S., (*U.S.***)** Lifesaving Service.
Lt., Lieutenant.
l.t., long ton.
£T, Turkish pound.
Ltd., ltd., limited.
L.Th., Licentiate in Theology.
Lt. Inf., Light Infantry.
Lu, lutecium. *Chem.*
Luth., Lutheran.
lv., leave; livre(s).

M

M, thousand; mobilization.
M., Manitoba; Monday; Monsieur.
M., m., majesty; male; manual; mark (*Currency*); marquis; married; masculine; mass; medicine; medium; meridian; meridies (*L.,* noon); mile; mill; minim; minute; modulus; month; moon; morning; mountain.
m., m, meter.
Ma, masurium. *Chem.*
MA, Machine Accountant. *U.S. Navy.*
MA, M.A., mental age. *Psychol.*
M.A., Magister Artium (*L.,* Master of Arts); Military Academy.
ma, ma., mA, milliampere.
Macc., Mac., Maccabees.
mach., machine; machinery; machinist.
Mad., Madm., Madam.
mag., magazine; magnetism; magnitude (of a star).
M.Agr., Master of Agriculture.
Maj., Major.
Mal., Malachi; Malayan.
Man., Manila (paper); Manitoba.
manuf., manufacture; manufactured; manufacturer; manufacturing.
Mar., Mar, March.
mar., maritime.
March., Marchioness.
marg., margin; marginal.
Marq., Marquis.
mas., masc., masculine.
Mass., Massachusetts.
mat., matins
math., mathematical; mathematician; mathematics.
MATS, Military Air Transport Service.
Matt., Matthew; Matthias.
max., maximum.
M.B., Medicinae Baccalaureus (*L.,* Bachelor of Medicine); Militia Bureau.
M.B.A., Master in, *or* of, Business Administration.
MBS, Mutual Broadcasting System.
M.C., Master Commandant; Master of Ceremonies; Medical Corps; Member of Congress.
mc, mc., m.c., megacycle.
M.C.L., Master of Civil Law.
M.D., Medical Department; Medicinae Doctor (*L.,* Doctor of Medicine).
Md., Maryland.
M/D, m/d, months' date.
M.D.S., Master of Dental Surgery.
mdse., merchandise.
ME, Metalsmith. *U.S. Navy.*
ME, ME., M.E., Middle English.
Me, methyl. *Chem.*
Me., Maine. *Not Official.*
M.E., Methodist Episcopal; Mining, *or* Mechanical, Engineer.
m.e., marbled edges.
meas., measure.
mech., mechanical; mechanics; mechanism.
M.Ed., Master of Education.
med., medical; medicine; medieval; medium.
Medit., Mediterranean.
meg., megacycle.
mem., member; memoir; memorandum; memorial.
memo., memorandum.
mer., meridian; meridional.
Messrs., Messrs, Messieurs.
met., metaphor; metaphysics; metropolitan.
metal., metallurgy.
metaph., metaphor; metaphysics.
meteorol., meteorology.
Meth., Methodist.
meton., metonymy.
mev, Mev, m.e.v., million electron volts.
Mex., Mexican; Mexico.
mf, mezzo forte (*Music*); millifarad.
mf, mfd, microfarad.
mfg., manufacturing.
mfr., manufacture; manufacturer.

MG, Military Government.
Mg, magnesium. *Chem.*
mg., mg, mgm, milligram(s).
MGB, see in *Vocab.*
Mgr., Mgr, Manager; Monseigneur; Monsignor.
MH, Medal of Honor.
MHG, MHG., M.H.G., Middle High German.
mi., mile; mill.
Mic., Micah.
Mich., Michael; Michigan.
micros., microscopy.
mid., middle; midshipman.
mil., military; militia.
milit., military.
min., mineralogical; mineralogy; minim; minimum; mining; minor; minute(s).
mineral., mineralogy.
Minn., Minnesota.
misc., miscellaneous.
Miss., Mississippi.
mk., mark; markka (*Finland*).
mks, m.k.s., meter-kilogram-second (system).
ML, Molder. *U.S. Navy.*
ML, ML., M.L., Medieval, *or* Middle, Latin.
ml., ml, milliliter.
MLA, M.L.A., Modern Language Association.
M.L.D., MLD, m.l.d., minimum lethal dose.
MLG, MLG., M.L.G., Middle Low German.
Mlle., Mlle, Mademoiselle.
Mlles., Mlles, Mesdemoiselles.
MM, Machinist's Mate. *U.S. Navy.*
MM., Their Majesties; Messieurs (*F.,* Sirs).
mm., mm, millimeter; millimeters; millia (*L.,* thousands).
Mme., Mme, Madame.
Mmes., Mmes, Mesdames.
MN, Mineman. *U.S. Navy.*
Mn, manganese. *Chem.*
Mo, molybdenum. *Chem.*
Mo., Missouri; Monday.
MO, M.O., Medical Officer.
M.O., m.o., money order.
mo., month(s).
mod., moderate; moderato.
Moham., Mohammedan.
M.O.I., Ministry of Information (*Brit.*).
Mon., Monday; Monsignor.
mon., monastery; monetary.
monogr., monograph.
Mons., Monsieur.
Monsig., Monsignor.
Mont., Montana.
mor., morocco.
morphol., morphology.
MOS, military occupational specialty (duty classification by serial number).
mos., months.
MP, M.P., military police.
M.P., Member of Parliament.
M.P., m.p., melting point.
mp, mezzo piano. *Music.*
M.Pd., Master of Pedagogy.
M.P.E., Master of Physical Education.
mph, m.p.h., miles per hour.
MR, Machinery Repairman. *U.S. Navy.*
Mr., Mr, Mister. *Title.*
MRC, Metals Reserve Company.
MRP, Mouvement Republicain Populaire (*F.,* Popular Republican Movement).
Mrs., Mrs, Mistress. *Title.*
Ms, MS., ms., ms, manuscript.
M.S., Master of Science.
m.s., M/S, months after sight (*Com.*).
M.Sc., Master of Science.
Msgr., Monsignor.
M/Sgt, M.Sgt., Master Sergeant.
m.s.l., mean sea level.
MSS, MSS., mss., mss, manuscripts.
MST, M.S.T., Mountain Standard Time.
Ms-Th, mesothorium. *Chem.*
M.T., metric ton.
Mt., mt., mount; mountain.
mtg., meeting; mortgage.
mtge., mortgage.

mtn., mountain.
MTO, Mediterranean Theater of Operations.
Mt. Rev., Most Reverend.
Mts., mts., mountains.
MU, Musician. *U.S. Navy*.
mun., municipal.
mus., museum; music; musician.
Mus.B., Mus.Bac., Musicae Baccalaureus (L., Bachelor of Music).
Mus.D., **Mus.Doc.**, **Mus.Dr.**, Musicae Doctor (L., Doctor of Music).
mut., mutilated; mutual.
MVA, Missouri Valley Authority.
MVD, see in *Vocab*.
M.W., Most Worshipful; Most Worthy.
M.W.A., Modern Woodmen of America.
M.W.G.M., Most Worthy Grand Master.
My., May.
mycol., mycology.
myg., myriagram.
mym., myriameter.
mythol., **myth.**, mythology.

N

N, nitrogen. *Chem*.
N, N., n., north; northern.
N., Nationalist; Norse; November.
N., n., navy; noon; normal (strength solution) (*Chem*.).
n., natus (L., born); nephew; neuter; new; nominative; note; noun; number.
Na, natrium (sodium). *Chem*.
N.A., National Academician; National Army; North America.
NAA, N.A.A., National Aeronautic Association.
NAACP, National Association for the Advancement of Colored People.
NACA, National Advisory Committee for Aeronautics.
NAB, National Association of Broadcasters.
N.A.D., National Academy of Design.
Nah., Nahum.
NAM, National Association of Manufacturers.
nat., national; native; natural; naturalist.
Nath., Nathaniel.
nat. hist., natural history.
natl., national.
NATS, Naval Air Transport Service.
naut., nautical.
nav., naval; navigation.
navig., navigation.
Nb, niobium. *Chem*.
N.B., New Brunswick.
N.B., n.b., nota bene (L., note well).
NBA, N.B.A., National Boxing Association.
NBC, National Broadcasting Company.
NBS, N.B.S., National Bureau of Standards.
NC, Nurse Corps.
N.C., North Carolina.
N.C., n.c., nitrocellulose.
NCAA, N.C.A.A., National Collegiate Athletic Association.
NCO, N.C.O., n.c.o., noncommissioned officer.
Nd, neodymium. *Chem*.
N.D., North Dakota.
N.D., n.d., no date.
N.Dak., North Dakota.
NE, N.E., n.e., northeast.
Ne, neon. *Chem*.
N.E., New England.
NEA, N.E.A., National Education Association; Newspaper Enterprise Association.
Nebr., Neb., Nebraska.
N.E.D., NED, New English Dictionary (the Oxford English Dictionary).
neg., negative; negatively.
Neh., Nehemiah.
N.E.I., NEI, Netherlands East Indies.

nem. con. See NEMINE CONTRADICENTE in *Vocab*.
nem. diss. See NEMINE DISSENTIENTE in *Vocab*.
NEP, Nep. See NEW ECONOMIC POLICY in *Vocab*.
Neth., Netherlands.
neut., neuter.
Nev., Nevada.
Newf., Newfoundland.
New M., New Mexico.
New Test., New Testament.
N.F., Newfoundland; Norman French.
N.F., n/f., no funds. *Banking*.
NG, N.G., National Guard.
N.G., n.g., no good.
NGr, NGr., N.Gr., New Greek.
N.H., New Hampshire.
NHA, National Housing Agency.
NHG, NHG., N.H.G., New High German.
NHI, National Health Insurance. *Brit*.
Ni, nickel. *Chem*.
NIA, National Intelligence Authority.
Nicar., Nicaragua.
N.J., New Jersey.
NKVD, N.K.V.D. See in *Vocab*.
NL, NL., N.L., New Latin.
n l., new line (*Print*.); non licet (L., it is not permitted *or* lawful); non liquet (L., it is not clear).
NLRB, National Labor Relations Board.
N.M., New Mexico.
N. Mex., New Mexico.
NNE, north-northeast.
NNW, north-northwest.
No., Noah; north; northern.
No., no., numero (L., by number); number.
nol. pros. See NOLLE PROSEQUI in *Vocab*.
nom., nominative.
noncom., noncommissioned officer.
non obst., non obstante (L., notwithstanding).
non pros., non prosequitur (L., he does not prosecute).
non seq., non sequitur (L., it does not follow).
Nor., Norman; North; Norway; Norwegian.
Northum(b)., Northumberland.
Norw., Norway; Norwegian.
Nos., nos., numbers.
Nov., Nov, November.
nov., novelist.
NP, neuropsychiatric.
N.P., nisi prius (L., unless before — used of certain actions, trials, etc.); no protest (*Banking*); Notary Public.
Np, neptunium. *Chem*.
n.p., no place (of publication).
NPN, N.P.N., nonprotein nitrogen.
n.p. or d., no place or date.
n.p.t., normal pressure and temperature.
nr., near.
NRA, N.R.A., National Recovery Administration.
NRAB, National Railroad Adjustment Board.
N.S., New Style (see GREGORIAN CALENDAR in *Vocab*.); Nova Scotia.
N.S., n.s., not specified.
Ns, nimbo-stratus.
NSC, National Security Council.
N.S.P.C.A., National Society for the Prevention of Cruelty to Animals.
N.S.P.C.C., National Society for the Prevention of Cruelty to Children.
NSRB, National Security Resources Board.
N.S.W., New South Wales.
NT, N.T., New Testament.
nt. wt., net weight.
num., numeral; numerals.
Num., Numb., Numbers.
numis., numism., numismatic, *or* numismatics.
NW, N.W., n.w., northwest.

NWLB, National War Labor Board.
N.W.T., Northwest Territories. *Can*.
N.Y., New York.
NYA, National Youth Administration.
N.Y.C., New York City.
N.Z., N.Zeal., New Zealand.

O

O, oxygen. *Chem*.
O., Ocean; October; Ohio (*Not Official*); Ontario; Order.
O., o., octavo; old; order.
o, ohm.
o-, ortho. *Chem*.
o., octarius (L., pint) (*Pharm*.); off; only.
ob., obiit (L., he (she) died); obiter (L., in passing, i. e. incidentally); oboe.
Obad., Obadiah.
obb., obbligato.
obdt., obedient.
O.B.E., Officer (of the Order of) the British Empire.
obj., object; objective.
obl., oblique; oblong.
obs., observation; obsolete.
obstet., obstetrical.
Oc., oc., ocean.
O.C., Officer Commanding; original cover (*Philately*).
o.c., opere citato (L., in the work cited).
o/c, overcharge.
OCD, Office of Civilian Defense.
OCIAA, Office of Co-ordinator of Inter-American Affairs.
OCS, Office of Contract Settlement; Officer Candidate School.
Oct., Oct, October.
O.D., Officer of the Day; ordinary seaman; overdraft, *or* overdrawn.
OD, O.D., o.d., olive drab; outside diameter.
ODT, Office of Defense Transportation.
OE, OE., O.E., Old English.
o.e., omissions excepted.
O.E.D., OED, Oxford English Dictionary.
OEM, Office for Emergency Management.
O.E.S., Order of the Eastern Star.
OF, OF., O.F., Old French.
off., offered; officer; official; official.
O.G., Officer of the Guard; original gum (*Philately*).
Ogpu, see in *Vocab*.
OHG, OHG., O.H.G., Old High German.
O.H.M.S., On His (Her) Majesty's Service.
O.K., see in *Vocab*.
Okla., Oklahoma.
Old Test., Old Testament.
OM, Opticalman. *U.S. Navy*.
O.M., Order of Merit (*Brit*.).
ON., O.N., Old Norse.
ONI, Office of Naval Intelligence.
Ont., Ontario.
OP, observation post. *Mil*.
O.P., OP, o.p., op, out of print; overprint (*Philately*); overprinted.
op., operation; opposite; opus.
OPA, Office of Price Administration.
op. cit., opere citato (L., in the work cited).
opp., opposed; opposite.
opt., optative; optics.
o.r., owner's risk. *Transp*.
ORC, Officers' Reserve Corps.
orch., orchestra.
ord., order; ordinal; ordinance; ordinary; ordnance.
ordn., ordnance.
Ore., Oreg., Oregon.
org., organic; organized.
orig., original; originally.
ornith., ornithol., ornithological; ornithology.
OS, OS., O.S., Old Saxon.
O.S., Old Style (see GREGORIAN CALENDAR in *Vocab*.); ordinary seaman.
Os, osmium. *Chem*.
OSS, Office of Strategic Services.

OSSR, Office of Selective Service Records.
O.T., Old Testament.
OTC, O.T.C., Officers' Training Camp, *or* Corps.
OTS, O.T.S., Officers' Training School.
O.U.A.M., Order of United American Mechanics.
OWI, Office of War Information.
Oxf., Ox., Oxford.
oxon., Oxonia (L., Oxford, Oxfordshire).
oz., [From old It. abbr. of *onza*, pl. *onze*, L. *uncia*, with n represented as a stroke over *o*, ōz.], ounce(s).
oz. ap., ounce (apothecaries' weight).
oz. av., ounce (avoirdupois weight).
ozs., ounces.
oz. t., ounce troy.

P

P, parental (*Biol*.); phosphorus (*Chem*.); pressure (*Phys*.); prisoner (*Mil*.).
P., p., pater (L., father); pawn (*Chess*); père (F., father); post; president; priest; prince; prompter (*Theat*.).
p, piano (It., softly). *Music*.
p., page; part; participle; past; penny; per (L., by); perch (the measure); perishable; peseta; peso; pint; pole (the measure); population; post (L., after); pro (L., for).
p-, para-. *Chem*.
Pa, protoactinium.
Pa., Pennsylvania.
P.A., Passenger Agent; Post Adjutant; public address (system); Purchasing Agent.
P.A., P/A, power of attorney; private account.
p.a., participial adjective; per annum.
PABA, paba, para-aminobenzoic acid. See AMINOBENZOIC ACID in *Vocab*.
PAC, Political Action Committee.
Pac., Pacif., Pacific.
paleog., paleography.
paleontol., paleontology.
pam., pamph., pamphlet.
Pan., Panama.
P. and L., profit and loss.
PAPA, Philippine Alien Property Administration.
par., paragraph; parallel.
Para., Paraguay.
paren., parenthesis.
parens., parentheses.
parl., parliamentary.
part., participle; particular.
part. adj., participial adjective.
pass., passenger; passive.
pat., patent; patented.
patd., patented.
path., pathol., pathology.
Pat. Off., Patent Office.
P.A.U., PAU, Pan American Union.
P.A.Y.E., pay as you earn; pay as you enter.
payt., payment.
Pb, plumbum (lead). *Chem*.
P.B., Pharmacopoeia Britannica (L., British Pharmacopoeia); Prayer Book.
PBA, Public Buildings Administration.
PBX, P.B.X., private branch (telephone) exchange.
PC, Preparatory Commission (of the United Nations).
P.C., Past Commander; Philippine Constabulary; Police Constable; Post Commander; Privy Council, *or* Councilor.
P/C, p/c, petty cash; prices current.
pc., piece; price(s).
p.c., per cent; post card.
PCA, Progressive Citizens of America.
Pd, palladium. *Chem*.
P.D., Police Department.
P.D., p.d., per diem (L., by the day).

pd., paid.
Pd.B., Pedagogiae Baccalaureus (L., Bachelor of Pedagogy).
Pd.D., Doctor of Pedagogy.
Pd.M., Master of Pedagogy.
P.E., Presiding Elder; probable error (*Statistics*); Protestant Episcopal.
ped., pedal; pedestal.
P.E.I., Prince Edward Island.
P.E.N., (International Association of) Poets, Playwrights, Editors, Essayists and Novelists.
Pen., pen., peninsula.
Penn., Penna., Pennsylvania.
per., period; person.
per an., per ann., per annum.
perf., perfect; perforated.
perh., perhaps.
perm., permanent.
Pers., Persia; Persian.
pers., person; personal.
pert., pertaining.
Peruv., Peruvian.
Pet., Peter.
petrog., petrography.
petrol., petrology.
pf., pfennig; preferred.
Pfc, Pfc., Private, First Class.
pfd., preferred.
pfg., pfennig.
Pg., Portugal; Portuguese.
P.G., Past Grand; postgraduate.
PGA, Professional Golfers Association.
pH, pH, see in *Vocab*.
PH, Photographer's Mate. *U.S. Navy.*
P.H., Purple Heart.
Ph, phenyl. *Chem.*
PHA, Public Housing Authority.
Phar., Pharm., pharmaceutical; pharmacopoeia; pharmacy.
Phar.B., Pharmaciae Baccalaureus (L., Bachelor of Pharmacy).
Phar.D., Pharm.D., Doctor of Pharmacy.
Pharm.M., Master of Pharmacy.
Ph.B., Philosophiae Baccalaureus (L., Bachelor of Philosophy).
Ph.C., Pharmaceutical Chemist.
Ph.D., Philosophiae Doctor (L., Doctor of Philosophy).
Phil., Philemon; Philip; Philippians; Philippine.
phil., philosophy.
Phila., Philadelphia.
Philem., Philemon.
Phil. I., Phil. Is., Philippine Islands.
philol., philology.
philos., philosophy.
phon., phonet., phonetics.
photo., photograph.
photog., photography.
photom., photometry.
phr., phrase.
phren., phrenol., phrenology.
PHS, Public Health Service.
phys., physical; physician; physics.
physiol., physiological; physiology.
PI, Printer. *U.S. Navy.*
P.I., Philippine Islands.
Pi., pias., piaster.
PICAO, Provisional International Civil Aviation Organization.
pinx., pinxit (L., he (she) painted it).
pizz., pizzicato.
pk., pack; park; peak; peck.
pkg., package, *or* packages.
pkt., packet.
pl., plural.
plat., platoon.
plu., plural.
plupf., pluperfect.
plur., plural; plurality.
PM, Patternmaker. *U.S. Navy.*
P.M., Past Master; Paymaster; Police Magistrate; Postmaster; Provost Marshal.
P.M., p.m., p.m., post meridiem.
p.m., post-mortem.
PMA, Production and Marketing Administration.
pmk., postmark.
pmkd., postmarked.
PN, Personnel Man. *U.S. Navy.*
p.n., P/N, promissory note.
pneum., pneumatic.

pnxt., pinxit (L., he (she) painted it).
Po, polonium. *Chem.*
P.O., p.o., petty officer; postal order; post office.
po., p.o., put-out. *Baseball.*
P.O.D., Post Office Department.
Pod.D., Doctor of Podiatry.
poet., poetic; poetical; poetry.
P. of H., Patrons of Husbandry.
Pol., Poland; Polish.
pol. econ., polit. econ., political economy.
polit., political; politics.
pop., popularly; population.
Port., Portugal; Portuguese.
pos., positive; possessive.
poss., possession; possessive; possible; possibly.
pot., potential.
POW, P.O.W. See in *Vocab*.
P.P., p.p., parcel post; parish priest; past participle; postpaid.
pp., pages; privately printed.
pp, pianissimo.
ppd., postpaid; prepaid.
pph., pamphlet.
PPI, see in *Vocab*.
p.p.m., ppm, ppm, part(s) per million.
p.pr., ppr., participle present.
P.P.S., p.p.s., post postscriptum (L., an additional postscript).
P.Q., Province of Quebec.
p.q., previous question.
PR, Parachute Rigger. *U.S. Navy.*
Pr, praseodymium. *Chem.*
Pr., Provençal.
Pr., pr., preferred (stock).
P.R., Puerto Rico; Proportional Representation.
pr., pair; pairs; paper; power; present; price; priest; prince; printing; pronoun.
PRA, Public Roads Administration.
prec., preceding.
precanc., precanceled.
pred., predicate.
pref., preface; preference; preferred; prefix.
prelim., preliminary.
prep., preparation; preparatory; prepare; preposition.
Pres., President.
pres., present; presidency.
Presb., Presbyterian.
pret., preterit.
prim., primary; primitive.
prin., principal; principally; principle.
print., printing.
priv., privative.
P.R.O., PRO, public relations officer.
prob., probably; problem.
proc., proceedings; process.
prod., produced.
Prof., prof., professor.
prom., promontory.
pron., pronominal; pronoun; pronounced; pronunciation.
prop., properly; property; proposition.
propr., proprietor.
pros., prosody.
Prot., Protestant.
pro tem., pro tempore.
Prov., Provençal; Proverbs.
prov., province; provincial; provisional; provost.
prox., proximo (mense) (L., next [month]).
prs., pairs.
Prus., Pruss., Prussia; Prussian.
P.S., Privy Seal; public sale; Public School.
P.S., p.s., passenger steamer; permanent secretary; post scriptum (L., postscript).
Ps., Psa., Psalm; Psalms.
ps., pieces.
pseud., pseudonym.
p.s.f., psf, pounds per square foot.
p.s.i., psi, pounds per square inch.
P.SS., postscripta (L., postscripts).
PST, P.S.T., Pacific Standard Time.
psychol., psych., psychological; psychology.

Pt, platinum. *Chem.*
pt., part; payment; pint; pints; point; port.
p.t., pro tempore.
P.T.A., PTA, Parent-Teacher Association.
pta., peseta.
PT boat, see in *Vocab*.
Pte., Private. *Brit.*
Ptg., ptg., printing.
P.T.O., p.t.o., please turn over (a leaf).
pts., parts; pints.
pty. ltd., proprietary limited.
Pu, plutonium. *Chem.*
pub., public; published; publisher; publishing.
publ., published; publisher.
Pvt., Private. *U.S. Army.*
PW, Prisoner of War.
PWA, Public Works Administration.
P.W.D., PWD, Public Works Department.
pwt., pennyweight.
PX, see in *Vocab*.
pxt., pinxit (L., he painted it).

Q

Q., Quebec.
Q., q., quarto; question.
q., quadrans (L., farthing); quart; quarter (of a hundredweight); quarterly; quasi; queen; query; quetzal; quintal; quire.
QB, queen's bishop. *Chess.*
Q.B., Queen's Bench.
Q.C., Queen's Counsel.
Q.E.D., quod erat demonstrandum (L., which was to be demonstrated).
Q.E.F., quod erat faciendum (L., which was to be done).
Q.F., quick-firing.
QKt, queen's knight. *Chess.*
ql., quintal.
QM, Q.M., Quartermaster.
QMC, Q.M.C., Quartermaster Corps.
QMG, Q.M.G., Q. M. Gen., Quartermaster-General.
Q.P., q.pl., quantum placet (L., as much as you please).
Qq, quartos.
qr., quadrans (L., farthing); quarter; quire.
QR, queen's rook. *Chess.*
qrs., quadrantes (L., farthings); quarters; quires.
q.s., quantum sufficit (L., as much as suffices); quarter section (of land).
qt., quantity; quart; quarts.
q.t., quiet. *Slang.*
qto., quarto.
qts., quarts.
qu., quart; queen; query; question.
qu., quar., quart., quarter; quarterly.
Que., Quebec.
ques., question.
quot., quotation.
q.v., quod vide (L., which see).

R

R, radical, *or* resp. hydrocarbon radical (*Chem.*); radius; ratio (*Math.*); rook (*Chess*); gas constant (*Phys. Chem.*).
R, r, resistance (*Elec.*); royal; ruble.
℟, **R,** respond, *or* response. *Church Service.*
R., Reaumur; Republican; ring (*Org. Chem.*).
R., r., rabbi; railroad; railway; rector; redactor; regina; rex; right; river; road; royal; rupee.
r, roentgen(s).
r., rare; received (*Com.*); recipe; resides; retired; right; rises; rod; rook (*Chess*); rubber; ruble.
Ra, radium. *Chem.*
R.A., Rear Admiral; right ascension (*Astron.*); Royal Academy, *or* Academician; Royal Artillery.
RA, R.A., Regular Army.
R.A.A.F., RAAF, Royal Australian Air Force.
rad., radical; radix.
R.A.F., RAF, Royal Air Force.

rall., rallentando.
R.A.M., Royal Academy of Music; Royal Arch Mason.
Rb, rubidium. *Chem.*
r.b.i., rbi, RBI, run(s) batted in.
R.C., RC, Red Cross; Reserve Corps; Roman Catholic.
R.C.A.F., RCAF, Royal Canadian Air Force.
R.C.Ch., Roman Catholic Church.
Rct., Recruit. *U.S. Army.*
Rd, radium. *Chem.*
RD, Radarman. *U.S. Navy.*
R.D., Rural Delivery.
R/D, refer to drawer. *Banking.*
Rd., rd., rix-dollar; road.
rd., rod; round.
RDB, Research Development Board.
Re, rhenium. *Chem.*
R.E., Right Excellent; Royal Engineers.
Re., rupee.
Réaum., Réaumur.
rec., receipt; recipe; record; recorded; recorder.
recd., received.
recit., recitative.
rec. sec., recording secretary.
rect., receipt; rector; rectory.
ref., referee; reference; referred; reformed; refunding.
Ref.Ch., Reformed Church.
refl., reflection; reflective; reflectively; reflex; reflexive.
Ref. Sp., Reformed Spelling.
reg., regent; regiment; region; register; registered; registrar; registry; regular; regularly; regulation; regulator.
regt., regent; regiment.
rel., relating; relative; relatively; religion; religious.
rel. pron., relative pronoun.
Rep., Republican.
rep., report; reporter; representative; republic.
Repub., Republic; Republican.
req., required; requisition.
res., reserve; residence; resides; resigned.
resp., respective; respectively; respiration; respondent.
restr., restaurant.
Resurr., Resurrection.
ret., retired; returned.
retd., retained; returned.
Rev., Revelation; Reverend.
rev., revenue; reverse; review; reviewed; revise; revised; revision; revolution; revolving.
Rev. Ver., Revised Version (of the Bible).
R.F., r.f., radio frequency; rapid-fire.
R.F.A., Royal Field Artillery.
RFC, Reconstruction Finance Corporation.
R.F.C., Royal Flying Corps.
R.F.D., Rural Free Delivery.
Rh, rhodium. *Chem.*
Rh, see RH FACTOR in *Vocab*.
RH, R.H., r.h., right hand.
R.H., Royal Highness.
r.h., relative humidity.
rheo., rheostat, *or* rheostats.
rhet., rhetoric; rhetorical.
R.I., Rhode Island.
Rich., Richard.
R.I.I.A., Royal Institute of International Affairs.
R.I.P., requiescat, *or* requiescant, in pace (L., may he (she), *or* they, rest in peace).
rit., ritard., ritardando. *Music.*
riv., river.
RJ, road junction.
RM, Radioman. *U.S. Navy.*
RM, r.m., reichsmark(s).
rm., ream. *Paper.*
R.M.A., Royal Military Academy (Woolwich).
R.M.C., Royal Military College (Sandhurst).
rms, r.m.s., root mean square.
rms., rooms.
R.M.S., Royal Mail Service, *or* Steamship.
Rn, radon. *Chem.*
R.N., Registered Nurse; Royal Navy.

R.N.R., Royal Naval Reserve.
R.N.V.R., Royal Naval Volunteer Reserve.
R.N.Z.A.F., **RNZAF**, Royal New Zealand Air Force.
ro., recto; roan; rood.
Rob., **Robt.**, Robert.
Rom., Roman; Romance; Romania; Romanian; Romans.
Rom. Cath., Roman Catholic.
R.O.P., record of production; run of paper.
rot., rotating; rotation.
ROTC, **R.O.T.C.**, Reserve Officers' Training Corps, or Camp.
roul., roulette. *Philately.*
Roum., Roumania; Roumanian.
R.P., Regius Professor.
RPF, Rassemblement du Peuple Français (F., Reunion of the French People).
rpm, **r.p.m.**, revolutions per minute.
R.P.O., Railway Post Office.
rpt., report.
R.Q., respiratory quotient.
R.R., railroad; Right Reverend.
RRB, Railroad Retirement Board.
Rs, **Rs**, **rs.**, rupees.
Rs., reis.
R.S., Revised Statutes.
R.S.F.S.R., **RSFSR**, Russian Socialist Federated Soviet Republic.
R.S.V.P., **r.s.v.p.**, Répondez, s'il vous plaît (F., please reply).
rt., right.
Rt. Hon., Right Honorable.
Rt. Rev., Right Reverend.
Rts., rights. *Stocks & bonds.*
Ru, ruthenium. *Chem.*
rub., ruble.
Rum., Rumania; Rumanian.
Rus., **Russ.**, Russia; Russian.
R.V., Revised Version (of the Bible).
R.W., Right Worshipful, or Worthy.
Rx, **Rx**, **rx**, **R**, abbr. of *rupee* + x, for *ten.*
Ry., Railway.

S

S, sulfur. *Chem.*
S, **S.**, **s.**, south.
S., Sabbath; Saturday; Saxon; Seaman; September; Signor; Sunday.
S., **s.**, saint; school; scribe; senate; socialist; society; soprano; southern; steel.
s., sacral (*Anat.*); second; section; see; semi-; series; set; shilling; sign; signed; silver; singular; sire (*Pedigree*); solo; son; sou; steamer; stem; substantive; sucre; sun; surplus.
s-, symmetrical. *Chem.*
Sa, samarium. *Chem.*
SA, Seaman Apprentice. *U.S. Navy.*
SA, S.A., see STURMABTEILUNG in *Vocab.*
S.A., Salvation Army; Société Anonyme; South Africa; South America; South Australia.
S.A., sex appeal. *Slang.*
s.a., sine anno (L., without year); semiannual.
S.A.E., **SAE**, Society of Automotive Engineers.
S.Afr., South Africa.
Salv., Salvador; Salvator.
S.Am., **S.Amer.**, South America, or American.
Sam., **Saml.**, Samuel.
Sans., **Sansk.**, Sanskrit.
s.ap., scruple (apothecaries' weight).
S.A.R., **SAR**, Sons of the American Revolution.
Sask., Saskatchewan.
Sat., Saturday; Saturn.
Sax., Saxon; Saxony.
Sb, stibium (L., antimony).
S.B., Scientiae Baccalaureus (L., Bachelor of Science).
sb., substantive.
s.b., **sb**, stolen base(s).
Sc, scandium (*Chem.*); stratocumulus.

Sc., science; Scotch; Scots; Scottish.
SC, Security Council (of United Nations).
S.C., Sanitary Corps; Signal Corps; South Carolina; Supreme Court.
sc., scale; scene; science; scilicet; screw; scruple.
s.c., small capitals (*Print.*); super-calendered.
Scan., **Scand.**, Scandinavia.
SCAP, Supreme Commander Allied Powers.
s. caps., small capitals.
Sc.B., Scientiae Baccalaureus (L., Bachelor of Science).
Sc.D., Scientiae Doctor (L., Doctor of Science).
Sch., School.
sci., science; scientific.
scil., scilicet (L., to wit).
Sc.M., Scientiae Magister (L., Master of Science).
Scot., Scotch; Scotland; Scottish.
scr., scruple.
Script., Scripture.
SCS, Soil Conservation Service.
sculp., **sculpt.**, sculpsit (L., he (she) carved it); sculptor; sculptural; sculpture.
S.C.V., Sons of Confederate Veterans. *U.S.*
SD, Steward. *U.S. Navy.*
S.D., Scientiae Doctor (L., Doctor of Science).
S.D., **s.d.**, standard deviation. *Statistics.*
s.d., sine die.
S.Dak., South Dakota.
SE, **S.E.**, **s.e.**, southeast.
Se, selenium. *Chem.*
SEC, Securities and Exchange Commission.
sec., secant; second; secondary; seconds; secretary; section; sections; sector.
secs., seconds; sections.
sect., section.
secy., secretary.
seismol., seismology.
sel., selected; selections.
Sem., Seminary; Semitic.
Sen., **sen.**, senate; senator; senior.
Sep., Septuagint.
sep., sepal; separate.
Sept., **Sept**, September.
seq., sequel.
seq., **seqq.**, sequentia (L., the following).
ser., series; sermon.
Serb., Serbia; Serbian.
Serg., **Sergt.**, Sergeant.
serv., servant; service.
sf, **sfz**, sforzando. *Music.*
sg, **s.g.**, senior grade.
s.g., specific gravity.
sgd., signed.
Sgt., Sergeant.
SH, Ship's Serviceman. *U.S. Navy.*
sh., share; sheep (*Bookbinding*); sheet; shilling, or shillings.
SHA, sidereal hour angle. *Navigation.*
SHAEF, Supreme Headquarters, Allied Expeditionary Forces.
Shak., Shakespeare.
shpt., shipment.
shr., share; shares.
shtg., shortage.
Si, silicon. *Chem.*
S.I., Sandwich Islands; Staten Island (N.Y.).
Sib., Siberia; Siberian.
Sic., Sicilian; Sicily.
Sig., **sig.**, signature; signor; signore; signori.
sigill, sigillum (L., seal).
sin, sine.
sing., singular.
S.J., Society of Jesus.
S.J.D., Scientiae Juridicae Doctor (L., Doctor of Juridical Science).
SK, Storekeeper. *U.S. Navy.*
sk., sack.
Skr., Sanskrit.
Skt., Sanskrit.
S. lat., south latitude.
Slav., Slavic; Slavonian.
sld., sailed; sealed.
Sm, samarium. *Chem.*

S.M., Scientiae Magister (L., Master of Science); Sergeant Major; Soldier's Medal; State Militia.
sm.c., **sm.caps.**, small capitals.
SN, Seaman. *U.S. Navy.*
Sn, stannum. *Chem.*
Sn., sanitary.
So, Sonarman. *U.S. Navy.*
So., South; Southern.
Soc., **soc.**, society.
sociol., sociology.
S. of Sol., Song of Solomon.
Sol., Solicitor; Solomon.
sol., soluble; solution.
sop., soprano.
SP, shore patrol, or police. *U.S. Navy.*
Sp., Spain; Spaniard; Spanish.
sp., special; species; specific; specimen; spelling; spirit.
s.p., sine prole (L., without issue); supraprotest.
SPARS [from Coast Guard motto "Semper Paratus — Always Ready"], Women's Coast Guard Reserves.
S.P.C.A., Society for Prevention of Cruelty to Animals.
S.P.C.C., Society for Prevention of Cruelty to Children.
spec., special; specification.
specif., specifically.
sp. gr., specific gravity.
sp. ht., specific heat.
spp., species (*pl.*).
S.P.Q.R., Senatus Populusque Romanus (L., the Senate and People of Rome).
S.P.R., Society for Psychical Research.
spt., seaport.
Sq., Squadron.
sq., square; sequence; sequentia (L., the following); also in compounds, as **sq.ft.**, **sq.in.**, etc.
SR, Seaman Recruit. *U.S. Navy.*
Sr, strontium. *Chem.*
Sr., Senior; Señor; Sir; Sister.
S.R., Sons of the Revolution.
Sra., Señora.
S.R.O., standing room only.
Srta., Señorita.
SS, **S.S.**, Schutzstaffel.
SS., Sancti (L., Saints); Saints.
SS., **ss.**, scilicet.
S.S., Silver Star; Sunday School; supra scriptum (L., written above).
SS, **S.S.**, **S/S**, steamship.
SSE, south-southeast.
S/Sgt., **S.Sgt.**, Staff Sergeant.
SSR, **S.S.R.**, Soviet Socialist Republic.
SSS, Selective Service System.
SSW, south-southwest.
St, stratus.
St., Saint; Strait; stratus; Street.
St., **st.**, statute, statutes.
st., stanza; stere; stet; stitch; stone (weight); strophe.
s.t., short ton.
Sta., Santa; Station.
sta., stationary; stator.
stacc., staccato. *Music.*
stat., statuary; statue; statute (miles); statutes.
S.T.B., Sacrae Theologiae Baccalaureus (L., Bachelor of Sacred Theology).
S.T.D., Sacrae Theologiae Doctor (L., Doctor of Sacred Theology).
Ste., Sainte (F., *fem.* of saint); Stephen.
ster., **stg.**, sterling.
stereo., stereotype.
St. Ex., Stock Exchange.
stg., sterling.
stge., storage.
stk., stock.
str., steamer; string, or strings (*Mus.*).
stud., student.
sub., subaltern; submarine; substitute; suburb; suburban.
subj., subject; subjective; subjectively; subjunctive.
subst., substantive; substitute.
suf., **suff.**, suffix.
Suff., **Suffr.**, Suffragan.
Sun., **Sund.**, Sunday.

sup., superior; superlative; supplement; supplementary; supply; supra (L., above); supreme.
super., superfine; superior.
superl., superlative.
supp., **suppl.**, supplement.
supr., supreme.
Supt., **supt.**, superintendent.
sur., surcharged; surplus.
surg., surgeon; surgery.
surv., survey; surveying; surveyor.
SV, Surveyor. *U.S. Navy.*
s.v., sub verbo, or sub voce (L., under the word).
SW, Steelworker. *U.S. Navy.*
SW, **S.W.**, **s.w.**, southwest; southwestern.
Sw., **Swed.**, Sweden; Swedish.
Swtz., **Swit.**, **Switz.**, Switzerland.
sym-, **sym.**, symmetrical. *Chem.*
sym., symbol; symphony.
syn., synonym; synonymy.
synop., synopsis.
Syr., Syria; Syriac; Syrian.
syr., syrup. *Pharm.*
syst., system.

T

T, tantalum (*Chem.*); temperature (on the absolute scale); (surface) tension; tritium.
T., Testament; Tuesday; Turkish; Turkish (pounds).
t., tare; target; telephone; temperature; tempo; tempore (L., in the time of); tenor; tense (*Gram.*); territorial; territory; thaler or talari (money, Ethiopia); time; tome; ton, or tons; tonneau (F. [metric] ton); town; township; transit; transitive; troy (wt.).
T-, triple bond. *Chem.*
TA, Steward Apprentice. *U.S. Navy.*
Ta, tantalum. *Chem.*
tab., tables.
tal. qual., talis qualis (L., as they come; average quality).
tan, **tan**, tangent.
Tasm., Tasmania.
Tass, **TASS**, Telegraphnoye Agentstvo Sovyetskovo Soyuza (Russ., The Soviet News Agency).
Tb, terbium. *Chem.*
T.B., **Tb**, **Tb**, **t.b.**, tubercle bacillus; tuberculosis.
t.b., trial balance.
tbs., **tbsp.**, tablespoon.
TC, Trusteeship Council (of the United Nations).
Tc, technetium.
tc., tierce; tierces.
TCCA, Textile Color Card Association (of the U.S.).
TCS, traffic control station.
TD, tank destroyer; touchdown; Tradeyman (*i.e.*, training devices man) (*U.S. Navy*).
t.d.n., total digestible nutrients.
TE, Teleman. *U.S. Navy.*
Te, tellurium. *Chem.*
tech., technical; technology.
technol., technology.
Tech. Sgt., Technical Sergeant.
tel., telegram; telegraph; telegraphic; telephone.
teleg., telegram; telegraph; telegraphic; telegraphy.
temp., temperature; temporary; tempore (L., in the time of).
ten., tenor; tenuto.
Tenn., Tennessee.
ter., terrace; territory.
term., terminal; termination.
terr., terrace; territorial; territory.
Test., Testament.
Teut., Teuton; Teutonic.
Tex., Texan; Texas.
T.F., Territorial Force.
tfr., transfer. *Finance.*
t.g., type genus.
Th., thorium. *Chem.*
Th., Thomas; Thursday.
T.H., Territory of Hawaii.
Thad., Thaddeus.
Th.D., Theologiae Doctor (L., Doctor of Theology).
theat., theatrical.
Th—Em, thoron. *Chem.*
Theo., Theodore; Theodosia.

theol., theologian; theological; theology.

theor., theorem.

therm., thermometer.

Thess., Thessalonians.

Tho., Thos., Thomas.

Thur., Thurs., Thursday.

Ti, titanium. *Chem.*

Tim., Timothy.

tinct., tincture.

Tit., Titus.

tit., title.

tk., truck.

TKO, T.K.O., t.k.o., technical knockout. *Pugilism.*

T.L., TL, trade-last.

Tl, thallium. *Chem.*

TM, Torpedoman's Mate. *U.S. Navy.*

Tm, thulium. *Chem.*

T Mort, trench mortar.

TN, Stewardsman. *U.S. Navy.*

Tn, thoron. *Chem.*

tn., ton; train.

tng., training.

TNT, T.N.T., trinitrotoluene; trinitrotoluol.

t.o., turn over; turnover.

Tob., Tobit.

tonn., tonnage.

top., topographical.

topog., topography; -ical.

tox., toxicol., toxicology.

t.p., title page.

tp., township.

TR, Steward Recruit. *U.S. Navy.*

Tr, terbium. *Chem.*

Tr., Troop.

tr., transitive; translated; translation; translator; transpose; treasurer.

trag., tragedy; tragic.

trans., transactions; transferred; transitive; translated; translation; translator; transportation; transpose; transverse.

transf., transferred.

transl., translated; translation, *or* translations.

transp., transportation.

trav., traveler; travels.

treas., treasurer; treasury.

treasr., treasurer.

t.r.f., t-r-f, T.R.F., tuned radio frequency.

trfd., transferred.

trig., trigon., trigonometric; trigonometry.

trit., triturate.

trop., tropic; tropical.

T/Sgt, T.Sgt., Technical Sergeant.

tsp., teaspoon.

T.T., Tanganyika Territory.

Tu, thulium; tungsten.

Tu., Tues., Tuesday.

T.U.C., TUC, Trades Union Congress. *Brit.*

Turk., Turkey; Turkish.

TV, television; terminal velocity.

TVA, Tennessee Valley Authority, *or* Administration.

Ty., Territory.

typ., typo., typog., typographer; typographic; typographical; typography.

U

U, uranium. *Chem.*

U., u., uncle; university; upper.

u., und (G., and).

UAW, U.A.W., United Auto, Aircraft and Agricultural Implements Workers.

u.c., upper case. *Printing.*

U.C.V., United Confederate Veterans. *U.S.*

U.D.C., United Daughters of the Confederacy. *U.S.*

U.H.F., UHF, u.h.f., uhf, ultrahigh-frequency.

U.K., United Kingdom (of Great Britain and Northern Ireland).

Ukr., Ukraine.

ult., ultimate; ultimately.

ult., ulto., ultimo.

UM, Underwater Mechanic. *U.S. Navy.*

UMT, Universal Military Training.

UMW, U.M.W., United Mine Workers.

UN, U.N., United Nations.

UNCIO, United Nations Conference on International Organization.

UNESCO, United Nations Educational, Scientific and Cultural Organization.

Unit., Unitarian.

Univ., Universalist.

univ., universal; universally; university.

UNRRA, United Nations Relief and Rehabilitation Administration.

U. of S. Afr., Union of South Africa.

UP, U.P., United Press.

up., upper.

Ur, uranium. *Chem.*

Uru., Uruguay.

U.S., US, United States.

u.s., ubi supra (L., in the place above mentioned); ut supra (L., as above).

U.S.A., USA, Union of South Africa; United States Army; United States of America.

USAF, United States Air Force.

USAFI, United States Armed Forces Institute.

USCC, United States Commercial Company.

USCG, U.S.C.G., United States Coast Guard.

USDA, United States Department of Agriculture.

USES, United States Employment Service.

U.S.M., United States Mail.

U.S.M.A., USMA, United States Military Academy.

USMC, U.S.M.C., United States Marine Corps.

USN, U.S.N., United States Navy.

U.S.N.A., USNA, United States National Army; United States Naval Academy.

USNG, U.S.N.G., United States National Guard.

USNR, U.S.N.R., United States Naval Reserve.

USO, United Service Organizations.

U.S.P., USP, U. S. Pharm., United States Pharmacopoeia.

U.S.S., United States Senate.

USS, U.S.S., United States Ship, *or* Steamer.

U.S.S.R., USSR, Union of Soviet Socialist Republics.

usu., usual; usually.

U.S.V., United States Volunteers.

usw., und so weiter (G., and so forth).

UT, Utilities Man. *U.S. Navy.*

Ut., Utah. *Not Official.*

ut dict., ut dictum (L., as directed).

V

V, vanadium (*Chem.*); vector (*Math.*); velocity; victory.

V, v, volt; volume.

V., Venerable; Viscount.

v., valve; ventral; verb; verse; version; versus; verse-; vide; village; vocative; voce; voice; volti; voltage; volume; volunteers; von (G., of) (*in names*).

VA, Veterans' Administration.

Va., Virginia.

V.A., Vicar Apostolic; Vice-Admiral; (order of) Victoria and Albert.

v.a., verb active.

var., variant; variation; variety; variometer; various.

Vat., Vatican.

v. aux., verb auxiliary.

vb., verb.

vb. n., verbal noun.

V.C., Veterinary Corps; Vice-Chancellor; Vice-Consul; Victoria Cross.

Vd, vanadium. *Chem.*

VD, V.D., v.d., venereal disease.

v.d., various dates.

vel., vellum.

Ven., Venerable; Venice.

Venez., Venezuela.

ver., verse, *or* verses.

verb. sap., verbum sap., verbum sat, verbum sat sapienti (est) (L., a word to the wise (is) sufficient).

Ver. St., Vereinigte Staaten (G., United States).

Vet., vet., veteran; veterinarian; veterinary.

veter., veterinary.

VFW, V.F.W., Veterans of Foreign Wars (of the U. S.).

V.H.F., VHF, v.h.f., very high frequency.

Vi, virginium. *Chem.*

V.I., Virgin Islands.

v.i., verb intransitive; vide infra (L., see herein, *or* below).

Vic., Vict., Victoria.

vid., vide.

vil., village.

v. imp., verb impersonal.

VIP, V.I.P., very important person. *Informal.*

v. irr., verb irregular.

Vis., Visc., Visct., Viscount, *or* Viscountess.

viz., videlicet (L., namely).

V.M.D., Veterinariae Medicinae Doctor (L., Doctor of Veterinary Medicine).

v.n., verb neuter.

voc., vocative.

vocab., vocabulary.

vol., volcano; volume.

vols., volumes.

vox pop., vox populi (L., voice of the people).

V.P., Vice-President.

v.p., various places.

V.Rev., Very Reverend.

V.S., Veterinary Surgeon.

vs., versus.

v.s., vide supra (L., see above).

VSS, versions.

Vt., Vermont.

v.t., verb transitive.

VT fuze, variable timing fuze. See PROXIMITY FUZE in *Vocab.*

Vulg., Vul., Vulgate.

vulg., vulgar; vulgarly.

vv., verses; violins.

v.v., vice versa.

W

W, wolfram (G., tungsten). *Chem.*

W, w, watt.

W., W., w., west.

W., Wales; Washington; Wednesday; Welsh.

W., w., warden; warehousing; weight; western; width; won; work (*Physics*).

w., wanting; week, *or* weeks; wide; wife; with.

W.A., West Africa; Western Australia.

WAA, War Assets Administration.

WAAC, Women's Army Auxiliary Corps. *U.S. Army.*

WAAF, Women's Auxiliary Air Force. *Brit.*

WAAS, Women's Auxiliary Army Service. *Brit.*

WAC, Women's Army Corps. *U.S.*

WAF, Women in the Air Force. *U.S.*

WAFS, Women's Auxiliary Ferrying Squadron. *U.S. Army.*

Wal., Walloon.

Wal., Walach., Walachian.

Wash., Washington.

WASP, Women's Air Force Service Pilots.

watt-hr., watt-hour.

WAVES, Women Accepted for Volunteer Emergency Service. *U.S. Navy.*

W.b., W/b, waybill.

w.b., warehouse book; water ballast; westbound.

W.C.T.U., Woman's Christian Temperance Union.

WD, W.D., War Department.

Wed., Wednesday.

Westm., Westminster.

w.f., wrong font. *Printing.*

WFTU, World Federation of Trade Unions.

W. Ger., West Germanic.

wh., whr., watt-hour.

whf., wharf.

WHO, World Health Organization.

W.I., West India; West Indian; West Indies.

w.i., when issued. *Stocks.*

Wis., Wisc., Wisconsin.

Wisd., Wisdom (Book of).

wk., week; work.

wks., weeks; works.

WL, w.l., water line; wave length.

WLB, War Labor Board.

W. long., west longitude.

Wm., William.

W.M., Worshipful Master.

WMC, War Manpower Commission.

wmk., watermark.

WNW, west-northwest.

WO, W.O., wait order; Warrant Officer.

WOWS, Women Ordnance Workers.

W.P., Worthy Patriarch.

WPA, Works Progress Administration.

WPB, War Production Board.

WRAC, Women's Royal Army Corps.

WRAF, Women's Royal Air Force.

WRENS, W.R.N.S., Women's Royal Naval Service. *Brit.*

wrnt., warrant.

WSW, west-southwest.

wt., weight.

W. Va., West Virginia.

WVS, Women's Voluntary Service. *Brit.*

Wyo., Wy., Wyoming.

X

X, Christ, Christian; xenon.

x, an abscissa; an unknown quantity.

X.C., x.c., x-cp., ex coupon.

X.D., x.d., x-div., ex dividend. (See EX, *prep.*)

Xe, xenon. *Chem.*

X.i., x-i., x-int., ex interest.

Xmas, Christmas.

Xn., Christian.

Xnty., Xty., Christianity.

X-rts., ex-rights.

Xtian., Christian.

Y

Y, yttrium. *Chem.*

Y., Young Men's Christian Association.

y, an ordinate (see ABSCISSA); an unknown quantity.

y., yard; yards; year; years.

Yb, ytterbium. *Chem.*

yd., yard; yards.

yds., yards.

yeo., yeomanry.

Y.M.C.A., YMCA, Young Men's Christian Association.

Y.M.H.A., YMHA, Young Men's Hebrew Association.

YN, Yeoman. *U.S. Navy.*

Y.P.S.C.E., Young People's Society of Christian Endeavor.

yr., year(s); younger; your.

yrs., years; yours.

Yt, yttrium. *Chem.*

Yuc., Yucatán.

Y.W., Young Women's Christian Association.

Y.W.C.A., YWCA, Young Women's Christian Association.

Y.W.H.A., YWHA, Young Women's Hebrew Association.

Z

Z, atomic number (*Chem.*); zenith distance (*Astron.*).

Z., z., zone.

z, an unknown quantity.

Zech., Zechariah.

Zeph., Zephaniah.

zl., zloty.

Zn, zinc. *Chem.*

zoochem., zoochemistry.

zoogeog., zoogeography.

zool., zoological; zoology.

Zr, zirconium. *Chem.*

ARBITRARY SIGNS AND SYMBOLS

I. ASTRONOMY

1. SUN, GREATER PLANETS, ETC.

☉ *or* ☼ The Sun; Sunday.
◐, ☾, *or* ☽ The Moon; Monday.
● New Moon.
☽, ◐, ☽, ☽ First Quarter.
○ *or* ☺ Full Moon.
☾, ◑, ☾, ☾ Last Quarter.
☿ Mercury; Wednesday.
♀ Venus; Friday.
⊕, ⊖, *or* ♁ The Earth.
♂ Mars; Tuesday.
♃ Jupiter; Thursday.
♄ *or* ♄ Saturn; Saturday.
♅, H, *or* ♅ Uranus.
♆, ♆, *or* ♆ Neptune.
♇ Pluto.
☄ Comet.
✳ *or* ✱ Fixed Star.

2. SIGNS OF THE ZODIAC

Spring Signs:
1. ♈ Aries, *the Ram.*
2. ♉ Taurus, *the Bull.*
3. ♊, ☐, *or* ♊ Gemini, *the Twins.*

Summer Signs:
4. ♋ *or* ♋ Cancer, *the Crab.*
5. ♌ Leo, *the Lion.*
6. ♍ *or* ♍ Virgo, *the Virgin.*

Autumn Signs:
7. ♎ Libra, *the Balance.*
8. ♏ Scorpio, *the Scorpion.*
9. ♐ *or* ♐ Sagittarius, *the Archer.*

Winter Signs:
10. ♑ *or* ♑ Capricorn, *the Goat.*
11. ♒ *or* ♒ Aquarius, *the Water Bearer.*
12. ♓ *or* ♓ Pisces, *the Fishes.*

3. ASPECTS AND NODES

☌ Conjunction; — indicating that the bodies have the same longitude, or right ascension.

✱ Sextile; — indicating a difference of 60° in longitude, or right ascension.

□ Quadrature; — indicating a difference of 90° in longitude, or right ascension.

△ Trine; — indicating a difference of 120° in longitude, or right ascension.

☍ Opposition; — indicating a difference of 180° in longitude, or right ascension; as, ☍ ♆ ☉, opposition of Neptune to the sun.

☊ Ascending Node; — called also *dragon's head.*

☋ Descending Node; — called also *dragon's tail.*

II. BIOLOGY

○, ⊙, *or* ① An annual plant.
②, ♂, *or* ⊙⊙ A biennial plant.
♃ A perennial herb.
♀ Female.
♂ *or* ♁ Male.

III. CHEMISTRY

\+ signifies "plus," "and," "together with," and is used between the symbols of substances brought together for, or produced by, a reaction. Placed above a symbol or to its right above the line, it signifies a unit charge of positive electricity. Thus: Ca^{++} denotes the ion of calcium, which carries two positive charges. The plus sign is also used to indicate dextrorotation; as, +143°. It is sometimes used to indicate a base or alkaloid, when placed above the initial letter of the name of the substance; as, $\overset{+}{M}$, morphine; $\overset{+}{Q}$, quinine.

— signifies a single "bond," or unit of attractive force or affinity, and is used between the symbols of elements or groups which unite to form a compound; thus, H—Cl for HCl, H—O—H for H_2O. Placed above a symbol, or to its right above the line, it signifies a unit charge of negative electricity; thus, Cl^- denotes a chlorine ion carrying a negative charge. The dash indicates levorotation; as, —92°. It also indicates an acid, when placed above the initial letter of the name of the acid; as, $\bar{C}$, citric acid. It is also used to indicate the removal of a part from a compound.

′ often indicates valence; as, Fe'' denotes bivalent iron; Fe''', trivalent iron. Sometimes its use is restricted to negative ions, so that it is equivalent to —.

. is often used: (1) To indicate a bond; as, H.Cl for H—Cl. (2) To denote a unit positive charge of electricity; as, Ca.. denotes two positive charges. (3) To separate parts of a compound regarded as loosely joined; as, $CuSO_4.5H_2O$.

⬡ denotes the benzene ring.

= indicates a double bond. Placed above a symbol or to its right above the line, it signifies two unit charges of negative electricity; as, $SO_4{=}$, the negative ion of sulfuric acid, carrying two negative charges.

≡ signifies a triple bond or negative charge.

: indicates a double bond.

⋮ indicates a triple bond.

( ) mark groups or radicals within a compound, as in $C_6H_4(CH_3)_2$, the formula for xylene which contains two methyl radicals (CH_3).

⌐ *or* ⌙ join separated atoms or groups in structural formulas, as in that for glucose:

$$\overbrace{CH_2OHCH(CHOH)_3CHOH}^{\quad O \quad}$$

= Give or form.

→ Give, pass over to, or lead to.

⇄ Forms and is formed from.

↓ indicates precipitation of the substance.

↑ indicates that the substance passes off as a gas.

≡ *or* ⇌ Is equivalent; — used in statements to show how much of one substance will react with a given quantity of another so as to leave no excess of either.

1-, 2-, etc., used initially in names, referring to the positions of substituting groups, attached to the first, etc., of the numbered atoms of the parent compound.

☞ Every element is represented by a symbol consisting of the initial or the abbreviation of its name, or, sometimes, its Latin name. (See ELEMENT, *Table*, in *Vocab.*)

IV. MATHEMATICS

RELATIONS OF QUANTITIES

\+ Plus; and; more; — indicating addition; as, $a + b = c$. Used also to indicate that figures have been omitted from the end of a number, or that the latter is approximately exact; as, the square root of 2 is 1.4142135+.

− Minus; less; — indicating subtraction; as, $a - b = c$. Used also in a similar manner to + to indicate approximate exactness.

±, ∓, ±, *or* ∓ Plus or minus; — indicating that the number or quantity to which it is prefixed may have either of the signs + or −; as, the square root of $4a^2$ is $\pm 2a$.

× Multiplied by; times; into; as, $a \times b = ab$; $6 \times 4 = 24$.

☞ Multiplication is also indicated by placing a raised dot between the factors (as, 4·5·6 = 120), or by writing the latter, when not numerals, one after another without any sign.

÷ *or* : Divided by; as, $a \div b$; that is, a divided by b; $6 \div 3 = 2$.

☞ Division is also indicated by writing the divisor under the dividend, with a line between, or by writing the divisor after the dividend, with an oblique line between; as, $\frac{a}{b}$; 3/8.

= Is equal to; equals; as, $(a + b) \times c = ac + bc$; $6 + 2 = 8$.

≠ *or* ∓ Is not equal to; as, $a \neq b$.

\> Is greater than; as, $a > b$; that is, a is greater than b; $6 > 5$.

< Is less than; as, $a < b$; that is, a is less than b; $3 < 4$.

∼ *or* ∽: Difference.

∝ Varies directly as; is directly proportional to; as, $a \propto b$.

: Is to; the ratio of.

: : As; equals.

$a/b = c/d$ is now the preferred way of writing geometrical proportions.

∴ Therefore.

∵ Since, or because.

∞ Infinity.

0 Zero; also, infinitesimal; a quantity less than any assignable value.

∠ Angle; the angle; as, ∠ ABC.

∟ Right angle; as, ∟ ABC.

⊥ The perpendicular; perpendicular to; as, draw AB ⊥ CD.

‖ Parallel; parallel to; is parallel to; as, AB ‖ CD.

⊙ *or* ○ Circle; circumference; 360°.

⌒ Arc of a circle; arc.

△ Triangle; as, △ ABC.

□ Square; as, □ ABCD.

▭ Rectangle; as, ▭ ABCD.

√ *or* √ Root; — the *radical sign,* indicating, when used without a figure placed above it, the square root; as, $\sqrt{4} = 2$; $\sqrt{4a^2} = 2a$. To denote any other than the square root, a figure (the *index*), expressing its degree, is placed above the sign; as, $\sqrt[3]{a}$, $\sqrt[5]{a}$, etc.; that is, the cube root, fifth root, etc., of a.

☞ The root of a quantity is also denoted by a fractional index at the right-hand side of the quantity and above it, the denominator of the index expressing the degree of the root; as, $a^{\frac{1}{2}}$, $a^{\frac{1}{3}}$, $a^{\frac{1}{5}}$; that is, the square, cube, and fifth roots, respectively, of a.

—— Vinculum, ( ) Parentheses, [ ] Brackets, { } Braces — Indicate that the quantities to which they are applied, or which are enclosed by them, are to be taken together.

f or *F* Function; function of; as, $y = f(x)$; that is, y is, or equals, a function of x.

☞ Other letters or signs are frequently used to indicate functions; as, ϕ, ϕ', ψ, π, and the like.

d Differential; as, dx; that is, the differential of x.

δ Variation; as, δx; that is, the variation of x.

Δ Finite difference.

D Differential coefficient; derivative.

☞ The letters d, δ, Δ, D, and sometimes others, prefixed to quantities, are variously employed, by different mathematicians, to denote that the differentials, variations, finite differences, or differential coefficients of these quantities are to be taken; but the ordinary significations are those given above.

∫ Integral; integral of; — denoting that the following expression is to be integrated; as, $\int 2xdx = x^2$; that is, the integral of $2xdx$ is x^2.

☞ If integration is to be performed more than once, the sign is repeated once for each time. For a number of times greater than three, an index is commonly written at the right hand above. The variable, with respect to which the integral is taken, is sometimes indicated by writing the letter designating it at the right hand below; as, $\int_x \phi$; that is, the integral of ϕ with respect to x.

$\int_b^a$ or $\int_b^a$ denotes that the integral is to be taken between the value b of the variable and its value a. $\int^a$ denotes that the integral ends at the value a of the variable, and $\int_b$ that it begins at the value b. These forms must not be confounded with that indicating repeated integration or with that indicating the integral with respect to a particular variable.

Σ Sum; algebraic sum; — commonly used to indicate the sum or summation of finite differences, thus having a sense somewhat like ∫.

π Pi; the number 3.14159265+; the ratio of the circumference of a circle to its diameter, of a semicircle to its radius, and of the area of a circle to the square of its radius.

e or ϵ **a** The number 2.7182818+; the base of the natural system of logarithms. **b** The eccentricity of a conic section.

G Constant of gravitation.

° Degrees; as, 60°, sixty degrees.

′ Minutes of arc; as, 30′, thirty minutes; also, minutes of time; also, feet.

″ Seconds of arc; as, 20″, twenty seconds; also, seconds of time; also, inches.

\# Pounds, if it follows a numeral; number, if it precedes the numeral.

′ A prime, or accent, is added to distinguish between different values of the same variable or between different variables; as, a', a'', a''', etc., which are usually read a prime, *a* second prime, or *a* double prime, *a* third prime, or *a* triple prime, etc.

², ³, etc. Exponents, placed above and at the right hand of quantities to denote that they are raised to powers whose degree is indicated by the figure; as, a^2, the square of *a*.

log Common logarithm.

log, *or* ln Natural logarithm.

i Imaginary unit, $\sqrt{-1}$.

V. MEDICINE

$\overline{AA}$, $\overline{A}$, *or* $\overline{aa}$ (Gr. *ává*.) Of each.

℞ (L. *Recipe*.) Take.

S *or* Sig. Write; — used in a prescription to indicate directions to be put on the medicine package.

APOTHECARIES' WEIGHTS

℔ Pound.

℥ Ounce; as, ℥ i *or* ℥ j, one ounce; ℥ ss, half an ounce; ℥ iss *or* ℥ jss, one ounce and a half; ℥ ij, two ounces, etc.

ʒ Dram; as, ʒ i, one dram; ʒ ss, half a dram; ʒ iss, one dram and a half; ʒ ij, two drams, etc.

℈ Scruple; as, ℈ i, one scruple; ℈ ss, half a scruple; ℈ iss, one scruple and a half; ℈ ij, two scruples, etc.

APOTHECARIES' MEASURES

C (L. *Congius*.) Gallon.

O *or* 0 (L. *Octarius*.) Pint.

℥ Ounce. f℥ Fluid ounce.

fʒ Fluid dram.

♏, ℟, ℔, *or* min. Minim.

VI. MISCELLANEOUS

&, &, & And.

&c. (*Et caetera*.) And the rest; and so forth; and so on; and the like.

℞ Response; — indicating the part repeated by the congregation in a responsive religious service.

℣, V, *or* ℣ Versicle; — indicating the part recited or sung by the choir.

✱ A character used in Roman Catholic service books to divide each verse of a psalm into two parts, and show where the response begins.

✠ *or* + A sign of the cross used by the pope, and by Roman Catholic bishops and archbishops, immediately before the subscription of their names. In some service books, it is used in those places where the sign of the cross is to be made.

☧ See LABARUM, also XP, in *Vocabulary*.

✕ *or* + A character customarily made by persons unable to write, when they are required to execute instruments of any kind. The name of the person is added by another, *John* ✕ *Smith* as shown: _{his} / _{mark}

♀ Ankh, or Crux Ansata.

⌐ *or* ⌐⌐ Gammadion.

f° Folio.

4to *or* 4° Quarto; four leaves, or eight pages, to a sheet.

8vo *or* 8° Octavo; eight leaves, or sixteen pages, to a sheet.

12mo *or* 12° Duodecimo; twelve leaves, or twenty-four pages, to a sheet.

16mo *or* 16° Sextodecimo; sixteen leaves, or thirty-two pages, to a sheet.

18mo *or* 18° Octodecimo; eighteen leaves, or thirty-six pages, to a sheet.

☞ Other sizes are 24mo *or* 24°, 32mo *or* 32°, 36mo *or* 36°, 48mo *or* 48°, etc. These are commonly called twenty-four-mo, thirty-two-mo, etc., or twenty-fours, thirty-twos, etc. Sizes above 48mo are rare.

7ber; September; 8ber, October; 9ber, November; 10ber, December.

† Died. Used in genealogies, etc.

h Hour(s).

m Minute(s).

s Second(s).

lb. *or* ℔ Pound(s).

< Derived from.

> Whence derived. } Used in

+ And. } etymologies.

✱ Assumed.

VII. MONEY AND COMMERCE

$ *or* $ Dollar, or dollars; peso, or pesos.

¢ Cent, or cents; as, 12¢; 33¢.

₱ Peso, or pesos. *Philippines.*

/ *or* s. Shilling, or shillings (British). See SOLIDUS, in *Vocabulary.*

£ Pound, or pounds (sterling).

£T, £E *or* LE, etc. Pound, or pounds, of Turkey, of Egypt, etc.

¥ *or* Y Yen.

℔ Pound, or pounds.

@ At, or to; as, silk @ $2 per yard; flour per bbl. $8 @ $10.50.

Number, or numbered; as, #60 thread. After figures # sometimes means "pounds."

℔ Per; as, sheep $4 ℔ head.

% Per cent; as, discount 6% = $10.21. Also, order of.

a/c Account; as, J. Smith in a/c with J. Jones.

c/o Care of; also, carried over.

B/E Bill of exchange.

B/L Bill of lading.

B/s Bill of sale.

L/c Letter of credit.

c/d *or* c/D Carried down.

c/f *or* c/F Carried forward.

VIII. MUSIC

Staff with notes; — whole note, half note, quarter, eighth, sixteenth, thirty-second (or semibreve, minim, crotchet, quaver, semiquaver, and demisemiquaver). A dot after a note adds to it half the length of the note without the dot.

☞ When it is desired to extend the compass of the staff, short lines called *ledger lines* are added above or below.

Breve, or double whole note.

Rests; — whole, half, quarter, eighth, etc.

Brace connecting two or more staffs indicating that the parts on these staffs are to be performed simultaneously.

Bar; — a vertical line across the staff, dividing it into equal measures of time.

Double bar; — marking the end of a division, movement, or entire composition.

Single heavy bar; — marking the end of a verse or sentence in hymn tunes, chorals, etc.

G clef, or treble clef; — indicating that the second line is to represent the first G above middle C.

F clef, or bass clef; — indicating that the fourth line is to represent the first F below middle C.

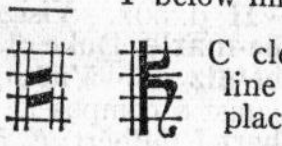

C clefs; — indicating that any line or space on which it was placed represented middle C.

♯ Sharp. ♭ Flat.

♮ Natural; — used to annul the effect of a previous ♯ or ♭.

☞ The *sharps* or *flats* placed at the beginning of a composition or of one of its sections are called collectively the *key signature.*

✕ *or* ✕ Double sharp; — raising a note two half steps.

♭♭ Double flat; — lowering a note two half steps.

♮♯ Single sharp; — used after a double sharp.

♮♭ Single flat; — used after a double flat.

Repeat; — indicating that a passage is to be played or sung twice. When found at two points, the first time as in lower symbol, repeat only the part between the two sets of marks.

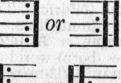

𝄋 *or* :�: Segno, or Sign; — used to mark the beginning or end of a passage to be repeated.

:𝄐:, +, ※ Presa; — indicates where successive voice parts are to take up the theme.

𝄴 Common measure, $= \frac{4}{4}$.

𝄵 (*alla breve*) $= \frac{4}{2}$ *or* $\frac{2}{2}$

♪ *or* ♩ Long appoggiatura; — an embellishing note a degree above or below the principal note.

♫ Acciaccatura, or short appoggiatura, performed very quickly.

∼ ∾ Turn; — a grace consisting of four tones: (1) the one above the principal tone; (2) the principal tone; (3) the one below the principal tone; (4) the principal tone.

↊ ↊ Inverted turn; — a grace of four tones like the turn but beginning with the *tone below* instead of the *tone above.*

tr∿ Trill, or shake.

Arpeggio.

8va All' ottava; — at the octave. When above the staff it indicates that the tone or tones are to be sounded an octave higher than written; when below the staff that they are to be an octave lower.

⌢ *or* ⌣ Pause, or hold; — placed over or under a note. When placed over a double bar it denotes the conclusion of the piece.

< ◁ Crescendo.

> ▷ Decrescendo, or diminuendo.

<> ◁▷ Swell; — crescendo and decrescendo combined.

> < ∧ Accent marks; — indicate that a tone or chord is to be given an additional amount of stress.

‾ Tenuto mark; — indicates that a note is to be held to its full value.

' *or* . Staccato; — placed over or under a note.

⌢ *or* ⌣ Slur or tie.

⊓ ⊓ ∧ Down-bow } in music for stringed
∨ Up-bow } instruments.

IX. PHYSICS, ETC.

Å Angstrom unit.

A Mass number.

α Alpha particle.

β Beta ray.

C Capacitance.

c Velocity of light.

e Electronic charge.

g Acceleration due to gravity.

h Planck's constant.

k Susceptibility to magnetism.

L Inductance.

λ Wave length.

μ Micron, or microns; permeability; modulus (used with a specifying subscript); coefficient of viscosity; index of refraction.

mμ Millimicron; micromillimeter.

μμ Micromicron.

m₀ Rest mass of a particle.

n Neutron.

ν Frequency.

p Proton.

R Resistance.

ρ Density.

T Kinetic energy.

V Potential energy.

X Reactance.

Z Impedance.

X. PROOFREADERS' MARKS

See page 1158.

XI. PUNCTUATION

See page 1148.

BIOGRAPHICAL NAMES

OVER FIVE THOUSAND NAMES WITH PRONUNCIATIONS

The aim of this section is to give dates, nationality, and status or occupation of the persons included and to indicate the syllabification and pronunciation of their names. Alternative spellings and pronunciations are shown, if supported by usage. Pronunciations of prenames not here pronounced may be found in their alphabetical place in this section, or in "A Pronouncing Vocabulary of Common English Given Names" (pages 1131 ff.), or in the main vocabulary.

Names containing connectives like *d'*, *de*, *di*, *van*, or *von* are alphabetized usually under the part of the name

following the connective; exceptions are chiefly American or British names.

Dates of birth and death follow the name. A doubtful or approximate date is indicated by a question mark; in some instances only the years of principal activity are given, preceded by the abbreviation *fl.* (flourished). The dates of a reign or other term of office are also given, in parentheses.

Most of the abbreviations used will be found in the list on pages xxi–xxii; for others consult the longer list of Abbreviations on pages 998 ff.

A

Ab′bey (ăb′ĭ), Edwin Austin, 1852–1911. Am. painter & illustrator.
Ab′bott (ăb′ŭt), Jacob, 1803–1879. Am. clergyman & author.
—, Lyman, 1835–1922. *Son of Jacob.* Am. clergyman & author.
Abd (äbd) (Arabic, *servant*), an initial word in Semitic proper names.
Abd-el-Ka′der *or* **Abd-al-Ka′dir** (ăb·dōōl·kä′dĭr), 1807?–1883. Arab leader in Algeria.
Abd′-er-Rah·man′ Khan (äb′dĕr·rŭ·män′ kän′), 1830?–1901. Amir of Afghanistan (1880–1901).
Abd′ul-A·ziz′ (äb′dül·ä·zēz′), 1830–1876. Sultan of Turkey (1861–76).
Abd′ul Ba·ha′ (äbd′ōōl bä·hä′), 1844–1921. *Ab·bas′ Ef·fen′di* (ăb·bäs′ ĕ·fĕn′dĭ). Pers. Bahai leader.
Abd′ul-Ha·mid′ II (äb′dül·hä·mēd′), 1842–1918. Sultan of Turkey (1876–1909; dep.).
Abd·ul·lah′ ibn-Hu·sein′ (ăb·dōōl·lä′ ĭb″n·hŏŏ·sīn′), 1882–1951. Ruler of Transjordan (amir 1921–46; king 1946–51).
Abd′ul-Me·djid′ I *or* **Abd′ul Me·jid′** (äb′dül mĕ·jēd′), 1823–1861. Sultan of Turkey (1839–61).
A′bel (ā′bĕl), Sir Frederick Augustus, 1827–1902. Eng. chem.
Ab′e·lard (ăb′ē·lärd), Peter; *Fr.* Pierre **A′bé′lard′** *or* **A′bai′lard′** (à′bä′lär′), 1079–1142. Fr. philos. & theol.
Ab′er·corn (ăb′ĕr·kôrn), James Albert Edward Hamilton, 3d Duke of, 1869–1953. Gov. of N. Ireland (1922–45).
Ab′er·crom′bie *or* **-crom′by** (ăb′ĕr·krŏm′bĭ; -krŭm′bĭ), James, 1706–1781. Brit. gen. in Am.
Ab′er·crom′by (ăb′ĕr·krŏm′bĭ; -krŭm′bĭ), Sir Ralph, 1734–1801. Brit. gen.
Ab′ing·ton (ăb′ĭng·tŭn), Frances *or* Fanny, 1737–1815. Nee *Bar′ton* (bär′t'n). Eng. actress.
A·bruz′zi (ä·brōōt′tsē), Duke of the, 1873–1933. Prince *Lui′gi of Sa·voy′-A·o′sta* (lwē′jē, sä·voi′ä·ôs′tä). Ital. naval officer & explorer.
a·bu′-Bakr′ (ä·bōō′bäk′ĕr), *also* **Abu Bekr** (bĕk′ĕr), 573–634. 1st caliph of Mecca.
A·bul′ Ka′sim (ä·bōōl′ kä′sĭm), *Lat.* **Al′bu·ca′sis** (ăl′bū·kā′sĭs), d. ?1013. Arab surgeon & medical writer.
Ac′ton (ăk′tŭn), John Emerich Edward Dal′berg-Ac′ton (dôl′bûrg-), 1st Baron, 1834–1902. Eng. hist.
Ad′am (ăd′ăm), Robert, 1728–1792, & his bro. James, 1730–1794. Eng. architects & furniture designers.
Ad′ams (ăd′ămz), Charles Francis, 1807–1886. *Son of J. Q.* Am. lawyer & diplomat.
—, Franklin Pierce, 1881– . *F. P. A.* Am. journalist.
—, Henry Brooks, 1838–1918. *Son of C. F.* Am. hist.
—, James Trus′low (trŭs′lō), 1878–1949. Am. hist.
—, John, 1735–1826. Lawyer & 2d pres. of the U. S. (1797–1801).
—, John Quin′cy (kwĭn′zĭ; -sĭ), 1767–1848. *Son of John.* 6th pres. of the U. S. (1825–29).
—, Maude, 1872–1953. *Maude Kis·kad′den* (kĭs·kăd′n). Am. actress.
—, Samuel, 1722–1803. Am. Revolutionary patriot.
Ad′dams (ăd′ămz), Jane, 1860–1935. Am. social worker.
Ad′di·son (ăd′ĭ·s'n), Joseph, 1672–1719. Eng. essayist & poet.
Ade (ād), George, 1866–1944. Am. humorist.
A′de·nau′er (ä′d'n·ou′ĕr; äd′n-), Kon′rad (kŏn′räd), 1876– . Chancellor of West Germany (1949–).
Ad′ler (äd′lĕr), Alfred, 1870–1937. Austrian psychiatrist.
Ad′ler (ăd′lĕr), Cyrus, 1863–1940. Am. educ. & author.
—, Felix, 1851–1933. Am. educ. & reformer.
A′dri·an (ā′drĭ·ăn) *or* **Ha′dri·an** (hā′-). A name of 6 popes: esp. **IV** (*Nicholas Break′spear* [brāk′spēr]), 1100?–1159; the only Eng. pope (1154–59).
— Rom. emp. See HADRIAN.
A′dri·an (ā′drĭ·ăn), Edgar Douglas, 1889– . Eng. physiol.
Æ *or* **A.E.** See George William RUSSELL.
Æl′fric (ăl′frĭk), ab. 955–ab. 1020. *Gram·mat′i·cus* (grä·măt′ĭ·kŭs). Eng. abbot & writer.
Ae·ne′as Sil′vi·us *or* **Syl′vi·us.** See PIUS II.
Aes′chi·nes (ĕs′kĭ·nēz; *esp. Brit.*, ēs′-), 389–314 B.C. Athenian orator.
Aes′chy·lus (ĕs′kĭ·lŭs; *esp. Brit.*, ēs′-), 525–456 B.C. Greek dram.

Ae′sop (ē′sŏp), ab. 620–ab. 560 B.C. Greek fabulist.
A′ga Khan III (ä′gä kän′), 1877–1957. *Aga Sultan Sir Ma·hom′ed* (má·hŏm′ĕd; -ĭd) *Shah.* Head of Ismailian Mohammedans (1885–1957).
Ag′as·siz (ăg′á·sē), Alexander, 1835–1910. *Son of J. L. R.* Am. zool.
—(ä·á·sē; *Fr.* à′gà′sē′), (Jean) Louis (Ro′dolphe′ [rô′dôlf′]), 1807–1873. Am. (Swiss-born) naturalist.
A·gath′o·cles (á·găth′ō·klēz), 361–289 B.C. Tyrant of Syracuse.
A·ges·i·la′us II (á·jĕs′ĭ·lā′ŭs), d. ab. 360 B.C. King of Sparta (ab. 400–360).
Ag′nes (ăg′nĕs; -nĭs), Saint, d. 304 A.D. R.C. virgin martyr.
A·gric′o·la (á·grĭk′ō·lá), Gnae′us (nē′ŭs) Julius, 37–93. Rom. gen.
A·grip′pa (á·grĭp′á), Marcus Vip·sa′ni·us (vĭp·sā′nĭ·ŭs), 63–12 B.C. Rom. statesman.
Ag′rip·pi′na (ăg′rĭ·pī′ná) the elder, 13 B.C.?–33 A.D. *Dau. of Agrippa, wife of Germanicus Caesar, mother of Caligula & of Agrippina the younger.*
— the younger, 15?–59. *Mother of Emp. Nero.*
A′gui·nal′do (ä′gē·näl′dō), E·mi′lio (ā·mē′lyō), 1870?– . Filipino leader.
Ah·mad′ Qa·vam′-i Sal·ta·na′ (à·h′·mäd′ kà·väm′ē sŏŏl·tä·nà′), 1881–1955. Iranian polit.
Ah·med′ III (ä·mĕt′), 1673–1736. Sultan of Turkey (1703–30).
Ai′ken (ā′kĕn), Conrad Pot′ter (pŏt′ĕr), 1889– . Am. poet.
Ains′worth (ānz′wûrth; -wĕrth), William Harrison, 1805–1882. Eng. nov.
A′i·sha *or* **A′ye·sha** (ä′ĭ·shä), 611–678. *Favorite wife of Mohammed.*
Ait′ken (āt′kĕn), Robert Ingersoll, 1878–1949. Am. sculptor.
Ak′bar (ăk′bär; *in Eng., also* -bär), 1542–1605. *The Great.* Emp. of Hindustan (1556–1605).
Ak′bar Khan (ŭk′bär kän′), d. 1849. Afghan leader.
a Kem′pis, Thomas. See THOMAS A KEMPIS.
A′ken·side (ā′kĕn·sīd), Mark, 1721–1770. Eng. poet & physician.
Akh·na′ton, A′khe·na′ton, Akh·na′ton. Vars. of IKHNATON.
A′lar·cón′, de (thä ä′lär·kôn′), Pe′dro (pā′thrō) An·to′nio (än·tō′nyō), 1833–1891. Span. author.
Al′a·ric (ăl′á·rĭk), 370?–410. Visigoth king; conqueror of Rome.
— **II**, d. 507. Visigoth king; issued legal code.
Al′be·marle, Duke of. See George MONCK.
Al·bé′niz (äl·vā′nēth; 17), I′sa·ac′ (ē′sä·äk′), 1860–1909. Span. pianist & composer.
Al′bert I (ăl′bĕrt; *F.* àl′bâr′; *Flem.* äl′bĕrt), 1875–1934. King of the Belgians (1909–34).
Al′bert of Saxe′-Co′burg-Go′tha (ăl′bĕrt, săks′kō′bûrg·gō′thà [-tà]; *Ger.* -tä), Prince, 1819–1861. *Consort of Queen Victoria of Gr. Britain.*
Al·ber′tus Mag′nus (ăl·bûr′tŭs măg′nŭs), Saint, 1193? (or 1206?)–1280. *Al′bert* (*Ger.* äl′bĕrt), Count *von Boll′städt* (fôn bŏl′shtĕt). Ger. philos. & theol.
Al′boin (ăl′boin; ŏl·ĭn), d. 573. King of the Lombards (ab. 565–573).
Al·bu·ca′sis. See ABUL KASIM.
Al·bu·quer′que, de (thĕ äl′bŏŏ·kĕr′kĕ; *Angl.* ăl′bū·kûr′kĕ), Af·fon′so (ä·fôn′sōō), 1453–1515. Port. viceroy & conqueror in India.
Al·cae′us (ăl·sē′ŭs), fl. ab. 600 B.C. Greek poet.
Al′ci·bi′a·des (ăl′sĭ·bī′á·dēz), ab. 450–404 B.C. Athenian gen. & polit.
Al′cott (ôl′kŭt), Amos Bron′son (brŏn′s'n), 1799–1888. Am. teacher & philos.
—, Louisa May, 1832–1888. *Dau. of A. B.* Am. author.
Al′cuin (ăl′kwĭn), 735–804. Eng. theol. & scholar.
Al′da (äl′dä), Frances, 1885–1952. N. Z.-born soprano.
Al′den (ôl′dĕn), John, 1599?–1687. *Mayflower* pilgrim.
Al′drich (ôl′drĭch), Thomas Bailey, 1836–1907. Am. author.
Al′dus Ma·nu′ti·us. See MANUTIUS.
A·le′khine *or* **A·lje′chin** (ŭ·lyä′kĭn), Alexander, 1892–1946. Fr. (Russ.-born) world chess champion.
A·le·mán′ (ä′lä·män′), Ma·te′o (mä·tā′ō), 1547?–?1610. Span. nov.
— **Val·dés′** (väl·dās′), Mi·guel′ (mē·gĕl′), 1902– . Mex. lawyer; pres. of Mexico (1946–52).

(1010)

A'lem·bert', d' (då·län·bâr'), Jean Le Rond (lē rôn'), 1717?–1783. Fr. math. & philos.

Al'ex·an'der (ăl'ĕg·zăn'dẽr; ăl'ĭg·; *Brit. also* -zän'-). Name of 8 popes; esp. **VI** (*Ro·dri'go* [rrô·thrē'gō] *Lan·zol' y Bor'ja* [län·thôl'ē vôr'hä; län·sôl']), 1431?–1503 (pope 1492–1503).

— **III of Mac'e·don** (măs'ĕ·dŏn), 356–323 B.C. *The Great.* King (336–23).

—, *Russ.* **A·le·ksan'dr** (ŭ·lyĭ·ksän'dẽr). Name of 3 emps. of Russia: **I**, 1777–1825 (reigned 1801–25); **II**, 1818–1881 (reigned 1855–81); **III**, 1845–1894 (reigned 1881–94).

— **I O·bre'no·vich** (ô·brĕ'nô·vĭch), 1876–1903. King of Serbia (1889–1903).

— **I**, 1888–1934. King of Yugoslavia (1921–34).

—, Albert Victor, 1885– . Brit. polit.

— **Nev'ski** (nĕv'skĭ; nĕf'-; *Russ.* ŭ·lyĭ·ksän'dẽr nyäf'skĭ), 1220?–1263. Russ. saint & mil. hero.

— **Se·ve'rus** (sē·vēr'ŭs), 208?–235. Rom. emp. (222–235).

— of Tu'nis (tū'nĭs), 1st Viscount, 1891– . *Harold Rupert Le·of'ric* (lē·ŏf'rĭk) *George Alexander.* Brit. field marshal; gov. gen. of Canada (1946–52).

A·lex'is I Mi·khai'lo·vich (å·lĕk'sĭs, *Russ.* myĭ·κī'lŭ·vyĭch), 1629–1676. *Father of Peter the Great.* Tsar of Russia (1645–76).

A·lex'is Pe·tro'vich (*Russ.* pyĭ·trô'vyĭch), 1690–1718. *Son of Peter the Great.* Tsarevitch of Russia.

A·lex'i·us I Com·ne'nus (å·lĕk'sĭ·ŭs, kŏm·nē'nŭs), 1048–1118. Eastern Rom. emp. (1081–1118).

Al·fie'ri (äl·fyā'rē), Vit·to'rio (vēt·tô'ryô), Count, 1749–1803. Ital. dram.

Al·fon'so (äl·fŏn'sō; -zō), *Port.* **A·fon'so**, *older* **Af·fon'so** (å·fôn'sōō). Name of 6 kings of Portugal; esp. **I**, 1112–1185 (1st king; 1139–85); **V**, 1432–1481 (reigned 1438–81).

Al·fon'so *or* Al·phon'so XIII (äl·fŏn'sō; -zō; *Span.* äl·fôn'sō), 1886–1941. King of Spain (1886–1931; dep.).

Al'fred *or* Æl'fred (äl'frĕd; -frĭd), 849–899. *The Great.* King of the West Saxons (871–899).

Al'ger (ăl'jẽr), Horatio, 1834–1899. Am. author.

A·li' (ä·lī'), *Arab.* 'A·li ibn-abi-Ṭālib, 600?–661. *Cousin & son-in-law of Mohammed.* 4th orthodox caliph (656–661).

A'li' *or* A'li Pa·sha' (ä'lē' pä·shä'), 1741–1822. *The Lion of Ja'ni·na* (yä'·nē·nä). Turk. pasha.

Al'len (ăl'ĕn; -ĭn), (Charles) Grant (Blair·fin'die [blâr·fĭn'dĭ]), 1848–1899. Brit. author.

—, Ethan, 1738–1789. Am. Revolutionary soldier.

—, William, 1532–1594. Eng. cardinal.

Al'len·by (ăl'ĕn·bĭ), Edmund Henry Hyn'man (hĭn'măn), 1st Viscount, 1861–1936. Brit. field marshal.

Al'leyn (ăl'ĭn; äl'ån; ă·lēn'), Edward, 1566–1626. Eng. actor.

Al'li·son (ăl'ĭ·s'n), Samuel King, 1900– . Am. physicist.

All'ston (ôl'stŭn), Washington, 1779–1843. Am. painter. (Du.-born) painter.

Al'ma-Tad'e·ma (äl'må·tăd'ĕ·må), Sir Lawrence, 1836–1912. Eng.

Al'va *or* *Span.* äl'vä) *or* Al'ba (äl'bå; *Span.* äl'vä), Fer·nan'do (fĕr·nän'dô) Ál'va·rez de To·le'do (äl'vä·rāth thä tô·lā'thô), Duke of, 1508–1582. Span. gen.

Al'va·ra'do, de (thä äl'vä·rä'thô), Alonso, 1490?–1554. Span. soldier in Mexico (under Cortes) & Peru.

—, Pe'dro (pā'thrô), 1495?–1541. Span. soldier; companion of Cortes in Mexico.

Al've·ar', de (thä äl'vā·är'), Car'los (kär'lōs) Ma·rí'a (mä·rē'ä), 1789–1853. Argentine revolutionist.

A·ma'ti (ä·mä'tē). Family of Ital. violinmakers of Cremona; esp. Ni·co·lò' (nē·kô·lô') *or* Ni·co'la (nē·kô'lä), 1596–1684.

Am'brose (ăm'brōz), Saint, 340?–397. Bishop of Milan.

A'men·ho'tep (ä'mĕn·hô'tĕp) *or* Am'e·no'phis (ăm'ĕ·nō'fĭs). Name of 4 kings of Egypt; esp. **III** (reigned ab. 1411–1375 B.C.); **IV** = IKH·NATON.

A'me·ri'go Ves·puc'ci. See VESPUCCI.

Ames (āmz), Winthrop, 1871–1937. Am. theater producer.

Am'herst (ăm'ẽrst; -ûrst), Jeffrey *or* Jeffery, Baron, 1717–1797. Brit. gen.; gov. gen. of Brit. N. Am. (1760–63).

Am'père (äN·pâr'; *Angl.* ăm'pẽr, ăm·pâr'), An'dré' (äN'drā') Ma'rie' (mä'rē'), 1775–1836. Fr. physicist.

A'mund·sen (ä'mōōn·sĕn), Ro'ald (rō'äl), 1872–1928. Norw. polar explorer; disc. South Pole (1911).

A·nac're·on (å·năk'rē·ŏn), 572?–?488 B.C. Greek poet.

An'ax·ag'o·ras (ăn'ăk·săg'ô·răs), 500?–428 B.C. Greek philos. & astron.

An'ax·i·man'der (å·năk'sĭ·măn'dẽr), 611–547 B.C. Greek philos. & astron.

An'ders (än'dẽrs), Wla·dy'slaw (vlä·dĭ'släf), 1892– . Pol. gen.

An'der·sen (än'dẽr·s'n); *Dan.* än'ẽr·s'n), Hans Chris'tian (hănz [häns] krĭs'chǎn [krĭst'yän]; *Dan.* häns krēs'tyän), 1805–1875. Dan. author.

An'der·son (än'dẽr·s'n), Carl David, 1905– . Am. physicist.

—, Clinton Pres'ba (prĕz'bå), 1895– . Am. polit. & admin.

—, Sir John, 1882–1958. 1st Viscount *Wa'ver·ley* (wā'vẽr·lĭ). Brit. polit.

—, Sir Kenneth Arthur Noel, 1891– . Brit. gen.

—, Marian, 1908– . Am. contralto.

—, Max'well (mǎks'wĕl; -wĕl), 1888– . Am. dram.

—, Sherwood, 1876–1941. Am. poet & story writer.

An'drás·sy (ŏn'drä·shĭ), Gyu'la (dyōō'lŏ), Count, father, 1823–1890, & son, 1860–1929. Hung. statesmen.

An'dré (än'drā; ăn'drĭ), John, 1751–1780. Brit. major, spy in Am. Rev.; hanged.

An·dre'a del Sar'to (än·drā'ä dĕl sär'tô), 1486–1531. *Andrea Do·me'ni·co* (dō·mā'nē·kô) *d'A'gno·lo di Fran·ce'sco* (dä'nyô·lô dē frän·chās'kô). Florentine painter.

An·dre'ev (ŭn·dryā'yĕf), *Am·dre' An·dre'e·vich* (ŭn·dryā'ĭ ŭn·dryā'yĕ·vyĭch), 1895– . Russ. polit.

— *or* An·dre'yev, Le·o·nid' Ni·ko·la'e·vich (lyĭ·ŭ·nyēt' nyĭ·kŭ·lä'yĕ·vyĭch), 1871–1919. Russ. nov., story writer & dram.

An'drews (ăn'drōōz), Roy Chapman, 1884– . Am. naturalist.

An'dros (ăn'drŏs), Sir Edmund, 1637–1714. Brit. colonial gov. in Am.

An·ge·la Me·ri'ci (än'jå·lä må·rē'chē), Saint, 1474?–1540. Ital. religious, founder of Ursuline order (1535).

An·ge'li·co, Fra. See Giovanni da FIESOLE.

An·gell' (än'jĕl), James Bur'rill (bûr'ĭl), 1829–1916. Am. educ.; pres. U. of Michigan (1871–1909).

—, James Row'land (rō'lånd), 1869–1949. *Son of J. B.* Am. educ.; pres. of Yale U. (1921–37).

—, Sir Norman, 1874– . *Ralph Norman Angell Lane.* Eng. author & lecturer.

Ång'ström (ông'strŭm; *Angl.* ăng'strŭm), An'ders Jo'nas' (än'dẽrs yōō'nås'), 1814–1874. Swed. physicist.

An'na I·va'nov·na (än'nå ĭ·vä'nŭv·nå), 1693–1740. Empress of Russia (1730–40).

Anne (ăn), 1665–1714. *Dau. of James II.* Queen of Gr. Britain (1702–14).

— of Aus'tri·a (ôs'trĭ·å), 1601–1666. *Consort of Louis XIII of France.* Regent (1643–61) for her son Louis XIV.

— of Cleves (klēvz), 1515–1557. *4th wife of Henry VIII of Eng.*

An·nun'zi·o, D', Gabriele. See D'ANNUNZIO.

An'selm (ăn'sĕlm), Saint, 1033–1109. Archbishop of Canterbury.

An'son (ăn's'n), George, Baron, 1697–1762. Eng. admiral.

An'tho·ny (ăn'thô·nĭ; -tô·nĭ), Saint, ab. 250–350. Egyptian monk, regarded as founder of Christian monachism.

—, Mark. See Marcus ANTONIUS.

—, Susan Brow·nell' (brou·nĕl'; brou'nĕl), 1820–1906. Am. suffragist.

— of Pad'u·a (păd'ū·å), Saint, 1195–1231. Franciscan monk.

An·tig'o·nus I (ăn·tĭg'ô·nŭs), 382–301 B.C. *Cy'clops* (sī'klŏps). Gen. of Alexander the Great & king of Macedonia (306–301).

An·ti'o·chus (ăn·tī'ô·kŭs). Name of 13 Seleucid kings of Syria; esp. **III** (*the Great*), 242–187 B.C. (reigned 223–187); **IV** (*E·piph'a·nes* [ē·pĭf'å·nēz]), d. 163 B.C. (reigned 175–163).

An·tip'a·ter (ăn·tĭp'å·tẽr), 398?–319 B.C. Macedonian gen. & statesman.

An·tis'the·nes (ăn·tĭs'thē·nēz), 444?–after 371 B.C. Athenian philos.; founder of Cynic school.

An'toine' (äN'twän'), Père (pâr'), 1748–1829. *An·to'nio de Se·dil'la* (än·tô'nyô thä sä·thē'lyä). Span. Capuchin priest in New Orleans.

An'to·ne'scu (än'tô·nĕs'kōō), Ion (yōn), 1882–1946. Romanian gen.; dictator (1940–44); executed.

An·to·ni'nus (ăn'tô·nī'nŭs), Marcus Aurelius, 121–180. *Nephew, son-in-law, & adopted son of Antoninus Pius.* Rom. emp. (161–180) & Stoic philos.

— Pi'us (pī'ŭs), 86–161. Rom. emp. (138–161).

An·to'ni·us (än·tô'nĭ·ŭs), Marcus; *Eng.* Mark *or* Marc An'to·ny (märk ăn'tô·nĭ) *or* An'tho·ny (ăn'thô·nĭ; -tô·nĭ), 83?–30 B.C. Rom. orator, triumvir, & gen.

A·o·ki (ä·ô·kē), Shu·zo (shōō·zō), Viscount, 1844–1914. Jap. diplomat; 1st Jap. amb. to U. S. (1905–09).

A·o'sta (ä·ôs'tä), Prince A'me·de'o (ä'mä·dā'ô) Um·ber'to (ōōm·bĕr'tô), Duke of, 1898–1942. Ital. gen. & viceroy (1937–41) in East Africa.

A·pel'les (å·pĕl'ēz), 4th cent. B.C. Greek painter.

Ap·ol·lo'ni·us (ăp'ŏ·lō'nĭ·ŭs) of Rhodes (rōdz), 3d–2d cent. B.C. Greek poet.

Ap'pi·us Clau'di·us. See CLAUDIUS.

Ap'ple·seed', Johnny. See John CHAPMAN.

Ap'ple·ton (ăp'l·tŭn; -t'n), Sir Edward Victor, 1892– . Eng. physicist.

A·prak'sin *or* A·prax'in (ŭ·prä'ksyĭn), Fĕ'dor (fyô'dẽr) Mat·ve'e·vich (mŭt·vyä'yĕ·vyĭch), 1671–1728. Russ. admiral.

Ap·u·le'ius (ăp'ū·lē'yŭs), Lucius, 2d cent. A.D. Rom. philos. & satirist.

A·qui'nas (å·kwī'nås), Saint Thomas, 1225–1274. Ital. theol.

Ar'am (âr'ăm), Eugene, 1704–1759. Eng. philologist & murderer.

A·ra'nha (å·rä'nyå), Os·wal'do (ôzh·wäl'dōō), 1894– . Brazilian lawyer & polit.

Ar'ber (är'bẽr), Edward, 1836–1912. Eng. editor.

Ar'blay, d', Madame. See Fanny BURNEY.

Ar·buth'not (är·bŭth'nŭt; är'bŭth·nŏt), John, 1667–1735. Scot. physician & author.

Ar'cher (är'chẽr), William, 1856–1924. Scot. critic & dram.

Ar·chi·me'des (är'kĭ·mē'dēz), 287?–212 B.C. Greek math. & inventor.

A·re'ti·no (ä'rå·tē'nô), Pie'tro (pyā'trô), 1492–1556. Ital. satirist.

— *or* d'A·rez'zo, Guido. See GUIDO D'AREZZO.

A·ré'va·lo (ä'rā·vä·lô), Juan (hwän) Jo·sé' (hô·sā'), 1904– . Guatemalan educ.; pres. of Guatemala (1945–51).

Ar'gall (är'gôl; -g'l), Sir Samuel, fl. 1609–1625. Eng. mariner.

Ar·gyll' (är·gīl'), 9th Duke of, 1845–1914. *John Douglas Sutherland Campbell.* Gov. gen. of Canada (1878–83).

A·ri·os'to (ä'rē·ôs'tô), Lo·do·vi'co (lô·dô·vē'kô), 1474–1533. Ital. poet.

Ar'is·tar'chus (ăr'ĭs·tär'kŭs), 220?–?150 B.C. Greek grammarian.

— of Sa'mos (sā'mōs), 3d cent. B.C. Greek astron.

Ar·is·ti'des *or* Ar'is·tei'des (ăr'ĭs·tī'dēz), 530?–?468 B.C. *The Just.* Athenian statesman.

Ar·is·tip'pus (ăr'ĭs·tĭp'ŭs), 435?–?356 B.C. Greek philos.

Ar·is·toph'a·nes (ăr'ĭs·tŏf'å·nēz), 448?–?380 B.C. Athenian dram.

— of By·zan'ti·um (bĭ·zăn'shĭ·ŭm; bĭ-; -shŭm; -tĭ·ŭm), 257?–?180 B.C. Greek scholar.

Ar'is·tot'le (ăr'ĭs·tŏt'l), 384–322 B.C. Greek philos.

A·ri'us (å·rī'ŭs; âr'ĭ·ŭs), d. 336 A.D. Greek theol.

Ark'wright (ärk'rīt), Sir Richard, 1732–1792. Eng. inventor.

Ar'len (är'lĕn), Michael, 1895–1956. *Di·kran' Kou·youm'djian* (dĭ·krän' kōō·yōōm'jyän). Brit. (Armenian-born) nov.

Ar'liss (är'lĭs), George, 1868–1946. Eng. actor.

Ar·min'i·us (är·mĭn'ĭ·ŭs; *Ger.* är·mē'nĕ·ōōs) *or* Ar·min' (är·mēn'), 17 B.C.?–21 A.D. Sometimes *Her'mann* (hĕr'män). Ger. hero.

— (pron. är·mĭn'ĭ·ŭs; *Du.* är·mē'nĕ·ŭs), Ja·co'bus (jå·kō'bŭs; *Du.* yä·kô'bŭs), 1560–1609. *Ja'cob Har'men·sen* (yä'kŏp här'mĕn·sĕn; *Angl.* jā'kŭb) *or* Her'mansz (hĕr'mäns). Du. theol.

Ar'mour (är'mĕr), Norman, 1887– . Am. diplomat.

Arm'strong (ärm'strŏng), William George, 1810–1900. Baron *Armstrong of Crag'side* (krăg'sīd). Eng. inventor & industrialist.

Arne (ärn), Thomas Augustine, 1710–1778. Eng. composer.

Ar'nim, von (fôn är'nĭm), Jür'gen (yür'gĕn), 1889?– . Ger. gen.

Ar'nold (är'n'ld), Benedict, 1741–1801. Am. Revolutionary gen. & traitor.

—, Sir Edwin, 1832–1904. Eng. poet.

—, Henry Harley, 1886–1950. Am. gen. of the army.

—, Matthew, 1822–1888. *Son of Thomas.* Eng. poet & critic.

—, Thomas, 1795–1842. Eng. educ.

Ar'nold·son (är'nŏŏld·sôn), Klas (kläs) Pon'tus (pôn'tŭs), 1844–1916. Swed. pacifist.

A'rou·et', François Marie. See VOLTAIRE.

Ár'påd (är'päd), d. 907. Hung. national hero.

Ar·rhe'ni·us (är·rā'nĭ·ŭs), Svan'te' (svän'tĕ') Au'gust (ou'gŭst), 1859–1927. Swed. physicist & chem.

Ar'son'val', d' (där'sôn'väl'), Jacques (zhäk) Ar'sène' (är'sân'), 1851–1940. Fr. physicist.

Ar'ta·xer'xes (är'tăg·zûrk'sēz; -tăk·sûrk'-; -tå·zûrk'-). Name of 3 Pers. kings: **I**, d. 424 B.C. (reigned 464–424); **II**, d. 359 B.C. (reigned 404–359); **III**, d. 338 B.C. (reigned 359–338).

Ar'te·vel'de, van (vän är'tĕ·vĕl'dĕ), Ja'cob (yä'kôp), 1290?–1345, & his son Phi'lip (fē'lĭp), 1340?–1382. Flem. leaders.

Ar'thur (är'thĕr), 6th cent. Real or legendary Brit. king.

—, Chester Alan, 1830–1886. 21st pres. of the U. S. (1881–85).

Ar·tzy·ba·sheff (ŭr·tsĭ·bä'shĕf), Boris, 1899– . Am. (Russ.-born) illustrator.

As'bur'y (ăz'bĕr'ĭ; -bĕr·ĭ; -brĭ), Francis, 1745–1816. 1st Methodist bishop in Am.

Asch (ăsh; *Angl.* ăsh), Sho'lem (shō'lĕm) or Sha·lom' (shä·lōm') or Sho'lom (shō'lăm), 1880–1957. Am. (Pol.-born) Yiddish nov. & dram.

As'cham (ăs'kăm), Roger, 1515–1568. Eng. scholar & author.

Ash'bur'ton, Baron. See Alexander BARING.

A'shur·ba'ni·pal (ä'shŏŏr·bä'nĕ·päl), *also* **A(s)'sur·ba'ni·pal** (ä'sŏŏr-). King of Assyria (669–626 B.C.).

A·so'ka (*Pali; pron.* ä·sō'kä) or **A·ço'ka** (*Skr.; pron.* å·shō'kä), d. 232 B.C. King of Magadha, India (273–232).

As·pa'si·a (ăs·pā'shĭ·å; -zhĭ·å), 470?–410 B.C. *Consort of Pericles.*

As'quith (ăs'kwĭth), Herbert Henry, 1852–1928. 1st Earl of *Ox'ford* (ŏks'fĕrd) *and Asquith.* Brit. statesman.

As'ser (ăs'ĕr), To·bi'as (tô·bē'ăs) Mi'cha·el (mē'kå·ĕl) Ca'rel (kä'rĕl), 1838–1913. Du. jurist.

As'ton (ăs'tŭn), Francis William, 1877–1945. Eng. physicist.

As'tor (ăs'tĕr), John Jacob, 1763–1848. Am. (Ger.-born) fur trader & capitalist.

—, Nancy Lang'horne (lăng'ĕrn), Viscountess, 1879– . 1st woman member of Brit. Parliament (1919–45).

At'a·hual'pa (ät'å·wäl'på; *Span.* ä'tä·wäl'pä), 1500?–1533. Last Inca king of Peru.

Ath·a·na'si·us (ăth'å·nā'shĭ·ŭs; -sĭ'ŭs; -shŭs), Saint, 293?–373. Greek church father.

Ath'el·stan *or* Æth'el·stan (ăth'ĕl·stăn), 895–940. King of Eng.

Ath'er·ton (ăth'ĕr·tŭn; -t'n), Gertrude Franklin, 1857–1948. Nee *Horn* (hôrn). Am. nov.

Ath·lone' (ăth·lōn'), 1st Earl of, 1874–1957. Gov. gen. of S. Africa (1923–31), of Canada (1940–45).

At'tar (ä'tĕr), 1119–?1229. Pers. poet.

At'ti·la (ăt'ĭ·lå), 406?–453. *The Scourge of God.* King of the Huns.

At'tlee (ăt'lē), Clement Richard, 1883– . Brit. polit.

Au'ber (ō'bâr'), Da'niel' (dá'nyĕl') Fran'çois' (frän'swä') Es'prit' (ĕs'prē'), 1782–1871. Fr. composer.

Au'brey (ô'brĭ), John, 1626–1697. Eng. antiquary.

Au'chin·leck' (ô'kĭn·lĕk'; ô'kĭn-), Sir Claude John Eyre (âr), 1884– . Brit. statesman.

Au'den (ô'd'n), Wys'tan (wĭs'tăn) Hugh, 1907– . Am. (Eng.-born) poet.

Au'du·bon (ô'dŏŏ·bŏn; -dŭ-; -bŭn), John James, 1785–1851. Am. ornithologist.

Au'er·bach (ou'ĕr·bäk), Berthold, 1812–1882. Ger. nov.

Au'gier' (ō'zhyä'), É'mile' (ā'mēl'), 1820–1889. Fr. poet & dram.

Au'gus·tine (ô'gŭs·tēn; ô·gŭs'tĭn), Saint, 354–430. Church father; bishop of Hippo (396–430).

—, *also* Aus'tin (ôs'tĭn), Saint, d. 604. *Apostle of the English.* 1st archbishop of Canterbury.

Au·gus'tus (ô·gŭs'tŭs), 63 B.C.–14 A.D. *Ga'ius* (gā'yŭs) *Julius Caesar Oc·ta'vi·a'nus* (ŏk·tā'vĭ·ā'nŭs). Rom. emp. (27 B.C.–14 A.D.).

Au'rang·zeb or Au'rung·zeb (ô'rŭng·zĕb; ou'-; *Hindustani* ä'ŏŏ·rŭng·zäb) or Au'rung·zebe (ô'rŭng·zēb; ou'-; *Hindustani* ä'ŏŏ·rŭng·zēb), 1618–1707. Emp. of Hindustan (1658–1707).

Au·re'li·an (ô·rē'lĭ·ăn; -rēl'yăn), 212?–275. *Lucius Do·mi'ti·us* (dô·mĭsh'ĭ·ŭs; -mĭsh'ŭs) *Au·re'li·a'nus* (ô·rē'lĭ·ā'nŭs). Rom. emp. (270–275).

Au'riol' (ô'ryôl'), Vin'cent' (văn'sän'), 1884– . Fr. lawyer; 1st pres. of 4th Republic (1947–54).

Aus'ten (ôs'tĕn; -tĭn), Jane, 1775–1817. Eng. nov.

Aus'tin (ôs'tĭn), Alfred, 1835–1913. Eng. poet; poet laureate (1896–1913).

—, John, 1790–1859. Eng. jurist.

—, Mary, 1868–1934. Nee *Hun'ter* (hŭn'tĕr). Am. nov.

—, Stephen Fuller, 1793–1836. Am. colonizer in Texas.

—, Warren Robinson, 1877– . Am. lawyer & polit.

Ave'bury, 1st Baron. See under LUBBOCK.

Av'en·zo'ar (ăv'ĕn·zō'ĕr; -zō·är'), 1091?–1162. Also *ibn-Zuhr* (ĭb''n-zŏŏr') or *-Zohr* (-zōr'). Arab physician in Spain.

A·ver'ro·ës or A·ver'rho·ës (å·vĕr'ō·ēz; ăv'ĕr·ō'ēz), 1126–1198. Also *ibn-Rushd* (ĭb''n-rŏŏsht'). Span.-Arab philos. & physician.

Av'i·cen'na (ăv''ĭ·sĕn'å), 980–1037. Also *ibn-Si'na* (ĭb''n-sē'nä). Arab physician & philos.

Á'vi·la Ca·ma'cho, Manuel. See CAMACHO.

A'vo·ga'dro (ä'vō·gä'drō), Count A'me·de'o (ä'mä·dâ'ō), 1776–1856. Ital. chem. & physicist.

Ay'de·lotte (ā'dĕ·lŏt), Frank, 1880–1956. Am. educ.

A·za'ña (ä·thä'nyä), Ma·nuel' (mä·nwĕl'), 1880–1940. Span. lawyer; pres. of Spain (1936–39).

B

Bab'bitt (băb'ĭt), Irving, 1865–1933. Am. scholar & educ.

—, Isaac, 1799–1862. Am. inventor.

Ba'ber or Ba'bur or Ba'bar (bä'bĕr), 1483–1530. *Zahir ud-Din Muhammad.* Founder of Mogul dynasty of India; emp. (1526–30).

Ba'beuf' or Ba'bœuf' (bä'bûf'), Fran'çois' (frän'swä') É'mile' (ā'mĕl'), 1760–1797. Fr. Communist.

Bab'ing·ton (băb'ĭng·tŭn), Anthony, 1561–1586. Eng. R.C. conspirator against Queen Elizabeth.

Bab'son (băb's'n), Roger Ward, 1875– . Am. statistician.

Bach (bäk), Jo·hann' (yō·hän' [yō'hän]) Se·ba'sti·an (zä·bäs'tē·än), 1685–1750. Ger. organist & composer.

Ba'con (bā'k'n), Francis, 1561–1626. 1st Baron *Ver'u·lam* (vĕr'ŏŏ·lăm; vĕr'ū-), Viscount *St. Al'bans* (sânt ôl'bănz). Eng. philos. & author.

—, Roger, Friar, 1214?–1294. Eng. philos.

Ba'den-Pow'ell (bā'd'n-pō'ĕl), Robert Ste'phen·son Smyth (stē'vĕn·s'n smĭth), 1857–1941. 1st Baron of Gil'well (gĭl'wĕl). Brit. gen.; founder of Boy Scout movement (1908).

Ba·do'glio (bä·dō'lyō), Pie'tro (pyä'trō), 1871–1956. Ital. gen.; premier (1943–44).

Bae'yer, von (fôn bā'yĕr), A'dolf (ä'dôlf), 1835–1917. Ger. chem.

Baf'fin (băf'ĭn), William, 1584–1622. Eng. navigator.

Bage'hot (băj'ŭt), Walter, 1826–1877. Eng. econ. & journalist.

Ba·gram·ian' (bá·grŭm·yän'), Ivan Khri·sto·fo'ro·vich (krўĭ·stŭ·fô'rŭ·vўĭch), 1895– . Russ. marshal.

Ba·gra·ti·on' (bä·grä·tyē·ôn'), Prince Pëtr (pyô'tĕr) I·va'no·vich (ĭ·vä'nŭ·vўĭch), 1765–1812. Russ. gen.

Ba·ha'ul·lah' (bä·hä'ŏŏl·lä') 1817–1892. Mir·za' (mēr·zä') *Husayn Ali.* Pers. founder of Bahaism.

Bai'ley (bā'lĭ), Lib'er·ty (lĭb'ĕr·tĭ) Hyde (hīd), 1858–1954. Am. botanist.

—, Nathan or Nathaniel, d. 1742. Eng. lexicographer.

Bail'lie (bāl'ĭ), Joanna, 1762–1851. Scot. dram. & poet.

Bain (bān), Alexander, 1818–1903. Scot. psychol.

Baird (bârd), John Lo'gie (lō'gĭ), 1888–1946. "*Father of Television.*" Scot. inventor.

Bairns'fa'ther (bârnz'fä'thĕr), Bruce, 1888– . Eng. soldier & cartoonist.

Baj'er (bī'ĕr), Fred'rik (frĭth'rĭk), 1837–1922. Dan. statesman & writer.

Ba'ker (bā'kĕr), Ernest Albert, 1869– . Eng. librarian & author.

—, George Pierce, 1866–1935. Am. educ. & editor.

—, Newton Diehl (dēl), 1871–1937. Am. lawyer & statesman.

—, Ray Stan'nard (stăn'ĕrd), 1870–1946. Pseud. *David Gray'son* (grā's'n). Am. author.

—, Sir Samuel White, 1821–1893. Eng. explorer in Africa.

Bakst (bäkst), Lé'on' (lā'ôn') Ni·ko·la'ie·vich (nyĭ·kô·lä'yĕ·vўĭch), 1866?–1924. Russ. painter.

Ba·ku'nin (bŭ·kŏŏ'nyĭn), Mi·kha·il' (myĭ·kŭ·ēl') A·le·ksan'dro·vich (ŭ·lyĭ·ksän'drŭ·vўĭch), 1814–1876. Russ. anarchist.

Bal'bo (bäl'bō), I'ta·lo (ē'tä·lō), 1896–1940. Ital. aviator & polit.

Bal·bo'a (bäl·bō'ä; *Span.* bäl·vō'ä; 17), Vas'co (bäs'kō) Nu'ñez de (nŏŏ'nyäth thä), 1475–1517. Span. explorer; disc. Pacific Ocean.

Balch (bôlch), Emily Greene, 1867– . Am. econ. & sociol.

Bald'win (bôld'wĭn) **I**, 1058–1118. *Bro. of Godfrey of Bouillon.* King of Jerusalem (1100–18).

—, James Mark, 1861–1934. Am. psychol.

—, Stanley, 1867–1947. 1st Earl *Baldwin of Bewd'ley* (būd'lĭ). Brit. statesman.

Balfe (bălf), Michael William, 1808–1870. Irish composer & singer.

Bal'four (băl'fŏŏr), Arthur James, 1st Earl of, 1848–1930. Brit. philos. & statesman.

Bal'iol, de (bāl'yŭl), John, 1249–1315. King of Scot. (1292–96).

Ball (bôl), John, d. 1381. Eng. priest & social agitator.

—, Thomas, 1819–1911. Am. sculptor.

Bal'lan·tyne (băl'ăn·tīn), James, 1772–1833. Scot. printer.

Bal'ti·more, Lord. See George CALVERT.

Bal'zac', de (bäl'zäk'; *Angl.* bôl'zăk, băl'zăk), Ho'no·ré' (ô'nô'rā'), 1799–1850. Fr. nov.

Ban'croft (băn'krôft; băng'-), George, 1800–1891. Am. hist.

—, Richard, 1544–1610. Eng. prelate.

Ban·del'lo (bän·dĕl'lō), Mat·te'o (mät·tā'ō), 1480?–1562. Ital. writer.

Bangs (băngz), John Ken'drick (kĕn'drĭk), 1862–1922. Am. humorist.

Banks (băngks), Sir Joseph, 1743–1820. Eng. naturalist.

Ban'ting (băn'tĭng), Sir Frederick Grant, 1891–1941. Canadian physician; disc. insulin treatment of diabetes.

Ban'ville', de (dĕ bän'vēl'), Thé'o·dore' (tā'ô·dôr'), 1823–1891. Fr. poet & writer.

Ba·ra'nov (bŭ·rä'nŭf), A·le·ksan'dr (ŭ·lyĭ·ksän'dĕr) An·dre'e·vich (ŭn·dryä'yĕ·vўĭch), 1747–1819. Russ. fur trader; 1st gov. of Russ. Am.

Bá'rány (bä'rän·y'), Ro'bert (Ger. rō'bĕrt), 1876–1936. Austrian physician.

Bar·ba·ros'sa (bär'bä·rōs'ä). See FREDERICK I.

—. Name of 2 Algerian corsairs, brothers: **I**, 1473?–1518; **II**, 1466?–1546.

Bar'busse' (bär'büs'), Hen'ri' (än'rē'), 1873–1935. Fr. editor & author.

Bar'clay (bär'klĭ; -klä), Robert, 1648–1690. Scot. Quaker author.

Barc'lay' de Tol'ly (bärk·lī' dĕ tô'lўĭ), Prince Mi·kha·il' (myĭ·kŭ·ēl'), 1761–1818. Russ. field marshal.

Ba'rents (bä'rĕnts), Wil'lem (vĭl'ĕm), d. 1597. Du. navigator.

Ba·ret'ti (bä·rāt'tē), Giu·sep'pe (jŏŏ·zĕp'pä) Marc'An·to'nio (märk'än·tô'nyō), 1719–1789. Ital. critic.

Bar′ing (bâr′ĭng), Alexander, 1774–1848. 1st Baron *Ash′bur′ton* (ăsh′bûr′t'n). Brit. financier & diplomat.

—, Evelyn, 1841–1917. 1st Earl of *Cro′mer* (krō′mẽr). Brit. diplomat.

—, Maurice, 1874–1945. Eng. writer.

Bark′la (bärk′là), Charles Glov′er (glŭv′ẽr), 1877–1944. Eng. physicist.

Bar′kley (bär′klĭ), Al′ben (ăl′bĕn) William, 1877–1956. Am. lawyer & polit.

Bar′low (bär′lō), Joel, 1754–1812. Am. poet & diplomat.

Bar′nard (bär′nẽrd), George Grey, 1863–1938. Am. sculptor.

Barnes (bärnz), Harry Elmer, 1889– . Am. sociol. & educ.

Bar′ne·veldt or **Bar′ne·veld** (bär′nẽ·vĕlt), Jan (yän) van Ol′den (vän ōl′dĕn), 1547–1619. Du. statesman.

Bar′num (bär′nŭm), Phineas Taylor, 1810–1891. Am. showman.

Ba·roc′chio or **Ba·roz′zi**, Giacomo. See VIGNOLA.

Ba·ro′ja (bä·rō′hä), Pi′o (pē′ō), 1872–1956. Span. nov. & essayist.

Bar′rès (bà′rĕs′), Au′guste′ (ō′güst′) Mau′rice′ (mō′rēs′), 1862–1923. Fr. nov. & polit.

Bar′rie (bär′ĭ), Sir James Matthew, 1860–1937. Scot. nov. & dram.

Bar′ros, de (thĕ bär′rōōsh), João (zhwoUN), 1496–1570. Port. hist.

Bar′row (bär′ō), Isaac, 1630–1677. Eng. math. & theol.

Bar′ry (bär′ĭ), Philip, 1896–1949. Am. dram.

Bar′ry·more (bär′ĭ·mōr). Family of Am. actors: Maurice, 1847–1905, real name *Herbert Blythe* (blīth); his wife Georgiana Emma, 1856–1893, *dau. of John Drew;* their children, Lionel, 1878–1954, Ethel, 1879– , & John Blythe, 1882–1942.

Bart (bär) or **Barth** (bärt), Jean (zhäN), 1651?–1702. Fr. naval hero.

Barth (bärt), Karl, 1886– . Swiss theol.

Bar′thol′di (bär′tōl′dē′; *Angl.* bär·thŏl′dĭ), Fré′dé′ric′ (frā′dā′rēk′) Au′guste′ (ō′güst′), 1834–1904. Fr. sculptor.

Bart′lett (bärt′lĕt; -lĭt), John, 1820–1905. Am. publisher.

—, Robert Abram, 1875–1946. Newfoundland arctic explorer.

Bar′tók (bôr′tŏk), Bé′la (bā′lō), 1881–1945. Hung. composer.

Bar′to·lom·me′o (bär′tō·lŏm·mā′ō), Fra (frä), 1475–1517. *Bac′cio del′la Por′ta* (bät′chō däl′lä pōr′tä). Florentine painter.

Bar′ton (bär′t'n), Clara, *in full* Cla·ris′sa (klà·rĭs′à) Har′lowe (här′lō), 1821–1912. Founder of American Red Cross Society.

—, Fanny. See Frances ABINGTON.

Bar′tram (bär′trăm), John, 1699–1777. Am. botanist.

Ba·ruch′ (bà·rōōk′; bär′ōōk [*his own pron.*]), Bernard Man′nes (măn′ĕs), 1870– . Am. businessman & statesman.

Bas′il (băz′ĭl; băs′-; bā′z'l) or **Ba·sil′i·us** (bà·sĭl′ĭ·ŭs; -zĭl′-), Saint, 330?–?379. *The Great.* Church father; bishop of Caesarea.

Bas′ker·ville (băs′kẽr·vĭl), John, 1706–1775. Eng. typographer.

Bas′ti·en′-Le·page′ (bàs′tyăN′lĕ·pàzh′), Jules, 1848–1884. Fr. painter.

Bates (bāts), Katharine Lee, 1859–1929. Am. poet & educ.

Ba·tis′ta y Zal·dí′var (bä·tēs′tä ē säl·dē′vär), Ful·gen′cio (fōōl·hän′syō), 1901– . Cuban soldier; pres. of Cuba (1940–44; 1952–).

Bat·ta′ni, al- (ăl′bät·tä′nē), c. 850–929. *Al′ba·teg′ni·us* (ăl′bà·tĕg′nĭ·ŭs) or *Al′ba·te′ni·us* (ăl′bà·tē′nĭ·ŭs). Arab astron.

Bau′de·laire′ (bō′dlâr′), Charles Pierre, 1821–1867. Fr. poet.

Bau′douin′ (bō′dwăN′), 1930– . King of Belgium (1951–).

Bau′er (bou′ẽr), Harold, 1873–1951. Eng. pianist.

Baum (bäm), Lyman Frank, 1856–1919. Am. journalist & story writer.

— (boum), Vick′i (vĭk′ē), 1888– . Am. (Austrian-born) nov.

Bau′mé′ (bō′mā′), An′toine′ (än′twàn′), 1728–1804. Fr. chem.

Bax′ter (băks′tẽr), Richard, 1615–1691. Eng. Puritan theol.

Ba′yard′, de (dĕ bà′yàr′; *Angl.* dĕ bā′ẽrd), Pierre Ter′rail′ (tĕ′rà′y′), Sei′gneur′ (sĕ′nyûr′), 1473?–1524. Fr. mil. hero. See *Vocab.*

Bayle (bäl), Pierre, 1647–1706. Fr. philos. & critic.

Bay′lor (bā′lẽr), Robert Em′met (ĕm′ĕt; -ĭt) Bled′soe (blĕd′sō), 1793?–1873. Am. jurist.

Ba′zaine′ (bà′zân′), A′chille′ (à′shēl′), 1811–1888. Fr. gen.

Ba′zin′ (bà′zăn′), René, 1853–1932. Fr. nov.

Bea′cons·field, Earl of. See Benjamin DISRAELI.

Beard (bẽrd), Charles Austin, 1874–1948, & his wife Mary, *nee* Rit′ter (rĭt′ẽr), 1876–1958. Am. historians.

—, Daniel Carter, 1850–1941. Am. painter & illustrator; organizer of Boy Scouts in U. S. (1910).

Beards′ley (bẽrdz′lĭ), Aubrey Vincent, 1872–1898. Eng. illustrator.

Beat′tie (bē′tĭ), James, 1735–1803. Scot. poet.

Beat′ty (bē′tĭ), David, 1871–1936. 1st Earl of *the North Sea & of Brooks′by* (brōōks′bĭ). Brit. admiral.

Beau′fort (bō′fẽrt), Sir Francis, 1774–1857. Brit. admiral.

—, Henry, 1377?–1447. Eng. cardinal & statesman.

Beau′har·nais′, de (dĕ bō′àr′nĕ′). Fr. family including: Vicomte A′lex′an′dre (à′lĕk′säN′dr′), 1760–1794, gen.; his wife Jo′sé′phine′ (zhō′zā′fēn′), 1763–1814, later the first wife of Napoleon I; their son Eu′gène′ (ü′zhân′), 1781–1824, Prince of Eich′stätt (īK′shtĕt); their daughter Hor′tense′ (ôr′täNs′), 1783–1837, wife of Louis Bonaparte & mother of Napoleon III.

Beau′mar′chais′, de (dĕ bō′màr′shĕ′; *Angl.* dĕ bō′mär·shā′), Pierre Au′gus′tin′ (ō′güs′tăN′) Ca′ron′ (kà′rôn′), 1732–1799. Fr. dram.

Beau′mont (bō′mŏnt), Francis, 1584–1616. Eng. dram.

—, William, 1785–1853. Am. surgeon.

Beau′re·gard, de (dĕ bō′rē·gärd; Fr. dĕ bōr′gàr′), Pierre Gus′tave′ (güs′tàv′) Tou′tant′ (tōō′tänt′), 1818–1893. Am. Confed. gen.

Beaux (bō), Cecilia, 1863–1942. Am. painter.

Bea′ver·brook (bē′vẽr·brŏok), 1st Baron, 1879– . *William Maxwell Aitken.* Brit. (Canadian-born) newspaper publisher.

Be′bel (bā′bĕl), Au′gust (ou′gŏōst), 1840–1913. Ger. socialist.

Beck′et, à (à [*or* ä] bĕk′ĕt; -ĭt), Thomas, Saint, 1118?–1170. Archbishop of Canterbury.

Beck′ford (bĕk′fẽrd), William, 1760–1844. Eng. author.

Bec′que·rel′ (bĕ′krĕl′). Family of Fr. physicists including: An′toine′ (än′twàn′) Cé′sar′ (sā′zàr′), 1788–1878; his son A′lex′an′dre (à′lĕk′säN′dr′) Ed′mond′ (ĕd′môN′), 1820–1891; the latter's son Antoine Hen′ri′ (än′rē′), 1852–1908.

Bed′does (bĕd′ōz), Thomas Lov′ell (lŭv′ĕl), 1803–1849. Eng. poet & dram.

Bede (bēd) or **Bae′da** (bē′dà) or **Be′da** (bē′dà), Saint, 673–735. *The Venerable Bede.* Eng. scholar, hist., & theol.

Bed′ford (bĕd′fẽrd), Duke of, 1389–1435. *John of Lan′cas·ter* (lăng′kăs·tẽr; *in U. S., also* lăn[g]′kăs′tẽr); *son of Henry IV of Eng.* Regent for Henry V.

Bee′be (bē′bē), Charles William, 1877– . Am. naturalist.

Bee′cham (bē′chăm), Sir Thomas, 1879– . Eng. conductor.

Bee′cher (bē′chẽr), Henry Ward, 1813–1887. Am. clergyman.

—, Lyman, 1775–1863. *Father of H. W. & of Harriet Beecher Stowe.* Am. clergyman.

Beer′bohm (bẽr′bōm), Max (măks), 1872–1956. Eng. critic & caricaturist.

Beer′naert (bär′nàrt), Au′guste′ (ō′güst′) Ma′rie′ (mà′rē′) Fran′çois′ (fräN′swà′), 1829–1912. Belg. statesman.

Bee′tho·ven, van (vän [or fän] bā′tō′vĕn; *Ger.* bāt′hō′-), Lud′wig (*Ger.* lōōt′vĭK, lōōd′-; *Angl.* lŭd′wĭg, lōōd′-), 1770–1827. Ger. composer.

Beh′ring, von (fôn bā′rĭng), E′mil (ā′mēl), 1854–1917. Ger. bacteriol.

Beith (bēth), John Hay, 1876–1952. Pseud. *Ian Hay.* Scot. writer.

Be·las′co (bĕ·läs′kō), David, 1854–1931. Am. dram. & producer.

Bel′i·sar′i·us (bĕl′ĭ·sâr′ĭ·ŭs), 505?–565. Gen. of the Eastern Rom. Empire.

Bell (bĕl), Alexander Graham, 1847–1922. Am. (Scot.-born) inventor of the telephone.

Bel′la·my (bĕl′à·mĭ), Edward, 1850–1898. Am. author.

Bel′lay′, du (dü bĕ′lā′), Jo′a′chim′ (zhō′à′kēm′), 1522–1560. Fr. poet.

Bel·li′ni (bāl·lē′nē). Family of Venetian painters including: Ia′co·po (yä′kō·pō), ab. 1400–ab. 1470, and his sons Gen·ti′le (jān·tē′lä), 1429?–1507, and Gio·van′ni (jō·vän′nē), 1430?–1516.

—, Vin·cen′zo (vēn·chĕn′tsō), 1801–1835. Ital. composer.

Bel′loc (bĕl′ŏk; -ŭk), Hil·a·ry (hĭl′à·rĭ), *pen name* Hi·laire′ (hĭ·lâr′), 1870–1953. Eng. author.

Bel′lows (bĕl′ōz), Albert Fitch, 1829–1883. Am. painter.

—, George Wesley, 1882–1925. Am. painter & lithographer.

Be′na·ven′te y Mar·ti′nez (bā′nä·vän′tä ē mär·tē′näth), Ja·cin′to (hä·thēn′tō), 1866–1954. Span. dram.

Ben′bow (bĕn′bō), John, 1653–1702. Eng. admiral.

Bench′ley (bĕnch′lĭ), Robert Charles, 1889–1945. Am. humorist.

Ben′da′ (băn′dà′), Ju′lien′ (zhü′lyäN′), 1867–1956. Fr. philos.

Ben′dix (bĕn′dĭks), Vincent, 1882–1945. Am. inventor & industrialist.

Ben′e·dict (bĕn′ē·dĭkt). Name of 15 popes: esp. **XIV** (*Pro′spe·ro Lam′ber·ti′ni* [prōs′pā·rō läm′bẽr·tē′nē]), 1675–1758 (pope 1740–1758); **XV** (*Gia′co·mo del′la Chie′sa* [jä′kō·mō däl′lä kyä′zä]), 1854–1922 (pope 1914–22).

— **of Nur′si·a** (nûr′shĭ·à; -shà), Saint, 480?–?543. Ital. founder of Benedictine order.

Be′neš (bĕ′nĕsh), E′du·ard (ĕ′dŏō·ärt), 1884–1948. Czechoslovak statesman; pres. (1935–38, 1939–48).

Be·nét′ (bĕ·nā′), Stephen Vincent, 1898–1943. Am. poet & story writer.

—, William Rose (rōz), 1886–1950. Am. poet & nov.

Ben′-Gur′ion (bĕn′gŏōr·yôn′), David, 1886– . Israeli (Pol.-born) laborite; prime min. of Israel (1948–53).

Ben′ja·min (bĕn′jà·mĭn), Judah Philip, 1811–1884. Am. Confed. statesman.

Ben′nett (bĕn′ĕt; -ĭt), (Enoch) Arnold, 1867–1931. Eng. nov.

—, James Gordon, 1795–1872. Am. (Scot.-born) journalist; founder of New York *Herald* (1835).

—, Richard Bed′ford (bĕd′fẽrd), Viscount, 1870–1947. Canadian prime min. (1930–35).

Be·noit′ de Sainte′-Maure′ (bĕ·nwà′ dĕ sănt′môr′), 12th cent. Fr. trouvère.

Ben′son (bĕn′s'n), Arthur Christopher, 1862–1925. Eng. educ. & author.

—, Edward Frederic, 1867–1940. *Bro. of A. C.* Eng. nov.

—, Frank Wes′ton (wĕs′tŭn), 1862–1951. Am. painter.

—, Godfrey Rathbone. See Baron CHARNWOOD.

—, William Shep′herd (shĕp′ẽrd), 1855–1932. Am. admiral.

Ben′tham (bĕn′thăm; -tăm), Jeremy, 1748–1832. Eng. jurist & philos.

Ben′tinck (bĕn′tĭngk), Lord William Cav′en·dish (kăv′ĕn·dĭsh), 1774–1839. *Son of W. H. C.* 1st gov. gen. of India (1833).

—, William Henry Cavendish, 1738–1809. 3d Duke of *Port′land* (pôrt′lănd). Brit. prime min. (1783, 1807–09).

Bent′ley (bĕnt′lĭ), Richard, 1662–1742. Eng. clergyman & scholar.

Ben′ton (bĕn′t'n; -tŭn), Thomas Hart, 1889– . Am. painter.

Bé′ran′ger′, de (dĕ bā′räN′zhä′), Pierre Jean, 1780–1857. Fr. poet.

Ber·dya′ev (byĭr·dyà′yĕf), Ni·ko·lai′ (nyē′kŭ·lī′) A·le·ksan′dro·vich (ŭ·lyĭ·ksän′drŭ·vyĭch), 1874–1948. Russ. philos.

Ber′ge·rac′, de, Cyrano. See CYRANO DE BERGERAC.

Ber′gi·us (bĕr′gē·ŏōs), Fried′rich (frē′drĭK), 1884–1949. Ger. chem.

Berg′son′ (bĕrg′sôN′; *Angl.* bĕrg′s'n), Hen′ri′ (än′rē′), 1859–1941. Fr. philos.

Be′ri·a or **Be′ri·ya** (byä′ryĭ·yà), Lav·ren′ti (lŭv·ryän′tyĭ) Pa·vlo′vich (pŭ·vlō′vyĭch), 1899–1953. Russ. polit.

Be′ring (bā′rĭng; *Angl.* bẽr′ĭng, bâr′-), Vi′tus (vē′tŏōs), 1680–1741. Dan. navigator; discoverer of Bering Strait & Bering Sea.

Berke′ley (bûrk′lĭ; *Brit. usu.* bärk′-), George, 1685–1753. Irish bishop & philos.

—, Sir William, 1606–1677. Colonial gov. of Virginia.

Ber′le (bûr′lĭ), Ad′olf (ăd′ŏlf) Augustus, 1895– . Am. diplomat.

Ber′lich·ing·en, von (fôn bẽr′lĭK·ĭng·ĕn), Götz (gŭts) or Gott′fried (gŏt′frēt), 1480–1562. Ger. knight.

Ber′li·ner (bûr′lĭ·nẽr), E′mile (ā′mĭl), 1851–1929. Am. (Ger.-born) inventor.

Ber′lioz′ (bẽr′lyôz′; *Angl.* bẽr′lĭ·ōz), (Louis) Hec′tor′ (ĕk′tôr′), 1803–1869. Fr. composer.

Ber′na·dette′ of Lourdes (bẽr′nà′dĕt′, lōōrd; *Angl.* bûr′nà·dĕt′), 1844–1879. *Bernadette Sou′bi′rous′* (sōō′bē′rōō′). Fr. religious.

Ber′na·dotte (bûr′nà·dŏt; *Fr.* bẽr′nà′dŏt′), Jean Bap′tiste′ (bà′tēst′) Jules, 1763?–1844; king (1818–44) of Sweden as Charles XIV John, founding present Swed. dynasty.

Ber′nard′ (bẽr′nàr′), Claude (klōd), 1813–1878. Fr. physiol.

Ber·nard' of Clair'vaux' (bĕr-närd' ŭv klâr'vō'; bĕr'nàr'-dŭv), Saint, 1091–1153. Fr. ecclesiastic.

Ber'nar·din' de Saint'-Pierre' (bĕr'nàr'dăn' dĕ săn'pyâr'), Jacques (zhàk) Hen'ri' (än'rē'), 1737–1814. Fr. nov. & author.

Bern·har'di, von (fôn bĕrn-här'dē), Frie'drich (frē'drĭk), 1849–1930. Ger. gen. & mil. writer.

Bern'hardt (bûrn'härt; Fr. bĕr'nàr'), Sar'ah (sâr'à; sä'rà; Fr. sà'rà'), 1844–1923. Orig. Ro'sine' Ber'nard' (rō'zēn' bĕr'nàr'). Fr. actress.

Ber·ni'ni (bâr-nē'nĕ), Gio·van'ni (jō·vän'nē) Lorenzo, 1598–1680. Ital. sculptor, architect, & painter.

Bern'stein' (bĕrn'stēn'), Hen'ry' (än'rē'), 1876–1953. Fr. dram.

Bern'storff, von (fôn bĕrn'shtôrf), Count Jo'hann-Hein'rich (yō'hän-hīn'rĭk), 1862–1939. Ger. diplomat.

Ber'til'lon' (bĕr'tē'yôn'; Angl. bûr'tĭ·lŏn), Al'phonse' (àl'fôns'), 1853–1914. Fr. anthropologist.

Ber·ze'li·us (bĕr-zē'lĭ·ŭs; bûr-; Swed. bĕr-sä'lĭ·ŭs), Baron Jöns (yûns) Ja'kob (yä'kŏp), 1779–1848. Swed. chem.

Bes'ant (bĕz'nt), An'nie (ăn'ĭ), 1847–1933. Nee Wood. Eng. theosophist.

— (bĕ·zănt'; bĕ-; orig. bĕz'nt), Sir Walter, 1836–1901. Eng. nov.

Bes'se·mer (bĕs'ē·mēr), Sir Henry, 1813–1898. Eng. engineer.

Beth'mann-Holl'weg, von (fôn bāt'män-hôl'vāk), The'o·bald (tā'ō·bält), 1856–1921. Ger. statesman; chancellor (1909–17).

Bet'ter·ton (bĕt'ēr·tŭn; -t'n), Thomas, 1635?–1710. Eng. actor.

Bev'er·idge (bĕv'ēr·ĭj), Albert Jeremiah, 1862–1927. Am. polit. & hist.

—, Sir William Henry, 1879– . Eng. econ.

Bev'in (bĕv'ĭn), Ernest, 1884–1951. Brit. labor leader & polit.

Beyle, Marie Henri. See STENDHAL.

Bi'dault' (bē'dō'), Georges (zhôrzh), 1899– . Fr. statesman; provisional pres. (1946).

Bid'dle (bĭd'l), Francis, 1886– . Am. lawyer.

—, John, 1615–1662. Founder of Eng. Unitarianism.

Bien'ville', de (dĕ byän'vēl'; Angl. dĕ bĭ·ĕn'vĭl, byĕn'-), Sieur (syûr) Jean Bap'tiste' (bà'tēst') Le·moyne' (lĕ·mwän'), 1680–1768. Fr. colonial gov. of Louisiana.

Bierce (bērs), Ambrose Gwi·nett' (gwĭ·nĕt'), 1842–?1914. Am. author.

Bie'rut (byĕ'rŏot), Bo·le'slaw (bō·lĕ'släf), 1892–1956. Pol. polit.; pres. of Poland (1947–54).

Big'gers (bĭg'ērz), Earl Derr (?dĕr), 1884–1933. Am. author.

Bi'net' (bē'nĕ'; Angl. bē·nā'), Alfred, 1857–1911. Fr. psychol.

Bi'on (bī'ŏn), 2d cent. B.C. Greek poet.

Birk'beck (bûr[k]'bĕk), George, 1776–1841. Eng. physician; founder of mechanics' institutions.

Bir'ken·head (bûr'kĕn·hĕd), 1st Earl of, 1872–1930. Frederick Edwin Smith. Eng. jurist & statesman.

Bi'ron (Russ. byē'rŭn), Ernst (ĕrnst) Jo·hann' (yō·hän'), 1690–1772. Orig. Büh'ren (Ger. bü'rĕn); Duke of Kur'land (kŏor'länd). Russ. statesman.

Bir'rell (bĭr'ĕl), Augustine, 1850–1933. Eng. author.

Bis'marck, von (fôn bĭz'märk; Ger. bĭs'-), Prince Ot'to (ŏt'ō) E'du·ard (ā'dŏo·ärt) Le'o·pold (lā'ō·pōlt), 1815–1898. In full Bis'marck-Schön'hau'sen (-shün'hou'zĕn). 1st chancellor of Ger. Empire.

Bis'sell (bĭs'l), Clayton Lawrence, 1896– . Am. gen.

Bi'zet' (bē'zĕ'), A'lex'an·dre (à'lĕk'sän'dr') Cé'sar' (sā'zàr') Lé'o'pold' (lā'ō'pōld'), 1838–1875. Called Georges (zhôrzh). Fr. composer.

Björn'son (byûrn'sôn), Björn'stjer'ne (byûrn'styâr'nĕ), 1832–1910. Norw. poet, dram., & nov.

Björns'son (byût''n·sôn), Sveinn (svāt''n), 1881–1952. Icelandic statesman; pres. of Iceland (1945–52).

Black (blăk), Hugo La Fayette, 1886– . Am. jurist.

Black Hawk (blăk' hôk'), 1767–1838. Ma-ka-tae-mish-kia-kiak. Am. Indian (Sac) chief.

Black'more (blăk'mōr), Richard Dod'dridge (dŏd'rĭj), 1825–1900. Eng. nov.

Black'stone (blăk'stōn; Brit. -stŭn), Sir William, 1723–1780. Eng. jurist.

Black'wood (blăk'wŏod), William, 1776–1834. Scot. publisher.

Blaine (blān), James Gil·les'pie (gĭ·lĕs'pĭ), 1830–1893. Am. statesman.

Blake (blāk), Robert, 1599–1657. Eng. admiral.

—, William, 1757–1827. Eng. artist, poet, & mystic.

Bla'mey (blā'mĭ), Sir Thomas Albert, 1884–1951. Australian gen.

Blan'dy (blăn'dĭ), William Henry Pur·nell' (pûr·nĕl'), 1890–1954. Am. admiral.

Blas'co-I·bá'ñez (bläs'kō-ē·vä'nyăth; 17), Vi·cen'te (bē·thän'tā), 1867–1928. Span. nov.

Bla·vat'sky (Angl. blà·văt'skĭ, -vät'-), E·le'na Pe·trov'na (Russ. yĭ·lyĕ'nà pyĭ·trôv'nà), 1831–1891. Nee (He'le·na) Hahn (hä'là·nä hän). Russ. traveler & theosophist.

Blé'riot' (blā'ryō'; Angl. blâ'rĭ·ō, blĕr'ĭ·ō), Louis, 1872–1936. Fr. engineer & pioneer aviator.

Bligh (blī), William, 1754–1817. Eng. naval officer.

Bliss (blĭs), Tas'ker (tăs'kĕr) Howard, 1853–1930. Am. gen.

Bloch (Fr. blôk; Angl. blŏk), Er'nest' (Fr. ĕr'nĕst'; Angl. ûr'nĕst, -nĭst), 1880– . Am. (Swiss-born) composer.

Blü'cher, von (fôn blü'kĕr), Geb'hard (gĕp'härt) Le'be·recht (lā'bĕ·rĕkt), 1742–1819. Prussian field marshal.

Blum (blŏom), Lé'on' (lā'ôn'), 1872–1950. Fr. polit.; provisional pres. (1946).

Blu'men·bach (blŏo'mĕn·bäk), Jo'hann' (yō'hän' [yō'hän]) Frie'drich (frē'drĭk), 1752–1840. Ger. anthropologist.

Bluntsch'li (blŏonch'lĭ), Jo'hann' (yō'hän' [yō'hän]) Kas'par (käs'pär), 1808–1881. Swiss legal scholar.

Bo·ab·dil' (bō'äv·thēl'; 17), d. 1533 or 1534. Last Moorish king of Granada.

Bo·a·di·ce'a (bō'àd·ĭ·sē'à), d. 62. Queen of the Iceni.

Bo'as (bō'ăs), Franz (fränts), 1858–1942. Am. (Ger.-born) anthropologist.

Bo·ba·dil'la, de (thä vō'vä·thē'[l]yä; 17), Fran·cis'co (frän·thēs'kō; -sēs'kō), d. 1502. Span. viceroy of Indies.

Boc·cac'cio (bŏk·kät'chō; Angl. bō·kä'chē·ō, -chō), Gio·van'ni (jō·vän'nē), 1313–1375. Ital. author.

Bock, von (fôn bŏk), Fe'dor (fā'dôr; -dôr), 1880–1945. Ger. gen.

Bod'ley (bŏd'lĭ), Sir Thomas, 1545–1613. Eng. diplomat & founder of Bodleian library.

Bo·do'ni (bō·dō'nē), Giam'bat·ti'sta (jäm'bät·tēs'tä), 1740–1813. Ital. printer.

Bo·e'thi·us (bō·ē'thĭ·ŭs), A·ni'ci·us Man'li·us Sev'er·i'nus (à·nĭsh'ĭ·ŭs măn'lĭ·ŭs sĕv'ēr·ī'nŭs), 480?–?524. Rom. philos.

Böh'me (bû'mĕ) or Böhm (bûm), Ja'kob (yä'kŏp), 1575–1624. Ger. mystic.

Bohr (bōr), Niels (nēls), 1885– . Dan. physicist.

Bo·iar'do (bō·yär'dō), Mat·te'o (mät·tā'ō) Ma·ri'a (mä·rē'ä), 1434–1494. Ital. poet.

Boi'leau'-Des'pré'aux' (bwà'lō'dā'prä'ō'), Ni'co'las' (nē'kō'lä'), 1636–1711. Fr. critic & poet.

Bo'jer (boi'ēr), Jo·han' (yō·hän'), 1872– . Norw. nov. & dram.

Bok (bŏk), Edward William, 1863–1930. Am. (Du.-born) editor.

Bol'eyn (bŏŏl'ĭn; Angl. boŏl·lēn'), Anne, 1507–1536. 2d wife of Henry VIII of Eng. & mother of Queen Elizabeth.

Bol'ing·broke (bŏl'ĭng·brŏŏk; in U. S., also bō'lĭng-), 1st Viscount, 1678–1751. Henry St. John (sĕn'jŭn; in U. S., also sănt jŏn'). Eng. statesman.

Bo·li'var (bō·lē'vär; Angl. bŏl'ĭ·vēr, -vär), Si·món' (sē·môn'; Angl. sī'mŭn), 1783–1830. S. Am. liberator.

Bo'na·parte (bō'nà·pärt; Fr. bô'nà'pàrt'); Ital. Buo'na·par'te (bwô'nä·pär'tä). Corsican family including Na·po'le·on I (nà·pō'lē·ŭn; -pōl'yŭn) (q.v.) & his bros.: Jo'seph (jō'zĕf; -zĭf; Fr. zhô'zĕf'), 1768–1844, King of Naples & Spain; Lu'cien (lū'kĕn; Fr. lü'syän'), 1775–1840, Prince of Ca·ni'no (kä·nē'nō); Lou'is (lŏō'ĭ; Fr. lwē; Du. lŏō·ē'), 1778–1846, King of Holland & father of Napoleon III; Jé'rôme' (zhā·rōm'; Angl. jĕ·rōm'), 1784–1860, King of Westphalia.

Bon'ar Law. See under LAW.

Bon·a·ven·tu'ra (bŏn'à·vĕn·tū'rà; It. bô·nä·vän·tōō'rä) or Bon'a·ven'ture (bŏn'à·vĕn'tūr), Saint, 1221–1274. The Seraphic Doctor. Ital. philos.

Bone (bōn), Sir Muir'head (mūr'hĕd), 1876–1953. Scot. etcher & painter.

Bon'heur' (bô'nûr'), Ro'sa' (rō'zä'; Angl. rō'zà), 1822–1899. Ma'rie' Ro'sa'lie' (mà'rē' rō'zà'lē'). Fr. painter.

Bon'i·face (bŏn'ĭ·fās), Saint, 680?–755. Win'frid (wĭn'frĭd) or Wyn'frith (wĭn'frĭth). Eng. missionary in Germany.

— Name of 9 popes; esp. VIII (Be·ne·det'to Ca'e·ta'ni [bā·nā·dāt'tō kä'ā·tä'nē]), 1235?–1303 (pope 1294–1303).

Bon'ner or Bon'er (bŏn'ēr), Edmund, 1500?–1569. Eng. bishop.

Bon'net' (bô'nĕ'), Georges (zhôrzh), 1889– . Fr. polit. & diplomat.

—, Hen'ri' (än'rē'), 1888– . Fr. hist. & diplomat.

Boone (bŏon), Daniel, 1734–1820. Am. pioneer in Kentucky & Missouri.

Booth (bŏoth; Brit. usu. bŏŏth). Family of Am. actors: Junius Bru'tus (brŏō'tŭs), 1796–1852, b. in Eng., & his sons Edwin Thomas, 1833–1893, & John Wilkes, 1838–1865, assassin of Lincoln.

—, William, 1829–1912. Founder of Salvation Army & father of: William Bram'well (brăm'wĕl; -wĕl), 1856–1929, Salv. Army gen.; Bal'ling·ton (băl'ĭng·tŭn), 1859–1940, founder of Volunteers of America; Evangeline Co'ry (kō'rĭ), 1865–1950, Salv. Army gen.

Boothe (bŏoth), Clare. See Clare Boothe LUCE.

Bo'rah (bō'rà), William Edgar, 1865–1940. Am. lawyer & polit.

Bor'den (bôr'd'n), Sir Robert Laird (lârd), 1854–1937. Canadian lawyer & statesman; prime min. (1911–20).

Bor'det' (bôr'dĕ'), Jules, 1870– . Belg. bacteriol.

Bor'gia (bôr'jä), Ce'sa·re (chā'zä·rä), 1475 (or 1476)–1507. Son of Rodrigo. Ital. cardinal & mil. leader.

—, Lu·cre'zia (lōō·krā'tsyä), 1480–1519. Dau. of Rodrigo. Duchess of Fer·ra·ra (fär·rä'rä).

—, Ro·dri'go, 1431?–1503. See Pope ALEXANDER VI.

Bor'glum (bôr'glŭm), (John) Gut'zon (gŭt's'n) (de la Mothe [dĕl'à·mōt']), 1871–1941. Am. sculptor.

Bo'ri (bō'rē), Lu·cre'zia (lōō·krā'tsyä), 1888– . Span. soprano in U. S.

Bo'ris III (bō'rĭs; Bulg. bô·rĭs', bō'rĭs), 1894–1943. Tsar of Bulgaria (1918–1943).

Bo·ro·din' (bŭ·rō·dyēn'), A·le·ksan'dr (ù·lyĭ·ksän'dĕr) Por·fir'e·vich (pûr·fyēr'yĕ·vyĭch), 1834–1887. Russ. composer & chem.

Bor'row (bŏr'ō), George, 1803–1881. Eng. author, linguist, & traveler.

Bosch (bôsh), Karl, 1874–1940. Ger. chem.

Bose (bōs; bôs; bŏsh), Sir Ja·ga·dis' (jà·gà·dēs') Chan'dra (chŭn'drà), 1858–1937. Indian physicist.

Bos'suet' (bô'sü·ē'), Jacques (zhàk) Bé'nigne' (bā'nēn'y'), 1627–1704. Fr. bishop.

Bos'well (bŏz'wĕl; -wĕl), James, 1740–1795. Boz'zy (bŏz'ĭ). Scot. lawyer & author; biographer of Samuel Johnson.

Bo'tha (bō'tà), Lou·is (lŏō·ē'), 1862–1919. Boer gen.; 1st prime min. of Transvaal (1907) & of Union of S. Africa (1910–19).

Bot·ti·cel'li (bŏt·tē·chĕl'ĭ; Angl. bŏt'ĭ·chĕl'ē), San'dro (sän'drō), 1444?–1510. A'les·san'dro di Ma·ri'a·no dei Fi·li·pe'pi (ä'läs·sän'drō dĕ mä·ryä'nō dā'ē fē·lē·pā'pē). Ital. painter.

Bou·cher (bŏō·shā'), Fran'çois' (frän'swä'), 1703–1770. Fr. painter.

Bou·ci·cault (bŏō'sĭ·kō) or Bour'ci·cault (bŏŏr'sĭ·kō), Dion, 1820?–1890. Dionysius Lardner Bour'si·quot (bŏŏr'sĭ·kō). Irish actor & dram.

Bou·gain·ville', de (dĕ bŏō'găn'vēl'), Louis An'toine' (än'twàn'), 1729–1811. Fr. navigator.

Bou'gue·reau' (bŏō'grō'), A'dolphe' (à'dôlf') Wil'liam (wēl'yàm'), 1825–1905. Fr. painter.

Bou·lan'ger (bŏō'län'zhā'), Georges (zhôrzh) Er'nest' (ĕr'nĕst') Jean Ma'rie' (mà'rē'), 1837–1891. Fr. gen.

Bour'bon, de (dĕ bŏŏr'bŏn'; Fr. bŏŏr'bôn'), Duc (dük) Charles, 1490–1527. Fr. gen.; constable of France.

Bour'ci·cault, Dion. See BOUCICAULT.

Bour'geois' (bŏŏr'zhwä'), Lé'on' (lā'ôn') Vic'tor' (vēk'tôr') Au'guste' (ō'güst'), 1851–1925. Fr. statesman.

Bour'get' (bōōr'zhĕ'), (Charles Jo'seph' [zhō'zĕf']) Paul, 1852–1935. Fr. poet, critic, & nov.

Bow'ditch (bou'dĭch), Nathaniel, 1773–1838. Am. math. & astron.

Bowles (bōlz), Samuel, father, 1797–1851, & son, 1826–1878. Am. newspaper editors & publishers.

Boy'den (boi'd'n), Seth, 1788–1870. Am. inventor.

Boyle (boil), Robert, 1627–1691. Brit. physicist & chem.

Boz'za·ris (bŏt'sä·rĕs; often Angl. bŏ·zăr'ĭs, -zăr'ĭs), Mar'co (mär'kō), 1788?–1823. Greek patriot.

Brab'a·zon of Tar'a, Baron. See MOORE-BRABAZON.

Brad'dock (brăd'ŭk), Edward, 1695–1755. Brit. gen. in Am.

Brad'ford (brăd'fērd), Gamaliel, 1863–1932. Am. biographer.

—, Roark (rōrk), 1896–1948. Am. writer.

—, William, 1590–1657. Pilgrim father; 2d gov. of Plymouth Colony.

—, William, 1663–1752. Am. printer.

Brad'ley (brăd'lĭ), Francis Herbert, 1846–1924. Eng. philos.

—, Henry, 1845–1923. Eng. philologist & lexicographer.

—, O'mar (ō'mär) Nelson, 1893– . Am. gen. of the army.

Brad'street (brăd'strēt), Anne, 1612?–1672. Nee Dud'ley; wife of Simon. Am. poet.

—, Simon, 1603–1697. Colonial gov. of Massachusetts.

Bragg (brăg), Brax'ton (brăks'tŭn), 1817–1876. Am. Confed. gen.

—, Sir William Henry, 1862–1942. Eng. physicist.

—, Sir William Lawrence, 1890– . Son of prec. Eng. physicist.

Bra'he (brä'ē), Ty'cho (tü'kō), 1546–1601. Dan. astron.

Brahms (bräms; freq. Angl. brämz), Jo·han'nes (yō·hän'ĕs; -ĕs), 1833–1897. Ger. composer & pianist.

Braille (brä'y; Angl. brāl), Louis, 1809–1852. Fr. blind teacher of the blind.

Bra·man'te (brä·män'tā), 1444–1514. Do·na'to (dō·nä'tō) d'A'gno·lo (dä'nyō·lō) or d'An'ge·lo (dän'jā·lō). Ital. architect.

Bran'deis (brăn'dīs), Louis Dem'bitz (dĕm'bĭts), 1856–1941. Am. jurist.

Bran'des (brän'dĕs), Ge·org' (gĭ·ôr[g]') Mor'ris (mō'rĕs), 1842–1927. Orig. Co'hen (kō'ĕn). Dan. literary critic & hist.

Brang'wyn (brăng'wĭn), Sir Frank, 1867–1956. Eng. artist.

Bran'nan (brăn'ăn), Charles Franklin, 1903– . Am. lawyer & administrator.

Bran'ting (brăn'tĭng'), Karl (kärl) Hjal'mar (yàl'màr), 1860–1925. Swed. statesman.

Braque (bråk), Georges (zhôrzh), 1882– . Fr. painter; a founder of cubism.

Brau'chitsch, von (fôn brou'kĭch), Hein'rich (hīn'rĭk) Alfred Hermann Wal'ther (väl'tĕr), 1881–1948. Ger. gen.

Braun (broun), Karl Fer'di·nand (fĕr'dĕ·nänt), 1850–1918. Ger. physicist.

Breas'ted (brĕs'tĕd; -tĭd), James Henry, 1865–1935. Am. archaeologist.

Breck'in·ridge (brĕk'ĭn·rĭj), John Cab'ell (kăb'ĕl), 1821–1875. Am. lawyer; vice-pres. of the U. S. (1857–61).

Breit (brīt), Gregory, 1899– . Am. (Russ.-born) physicist.

Brere'ton (brâr't'n), Lewis Hyde, 1890– . Am. gen.

Bresh·kov'sky (Angl. brĕsh·kôf'skĭ), Catherine, 1844–1934. Russ. revolutionist.

Brett (brĕt), George Howard, 1886– . Am. gen.

Brew'ster (brōō'stĕr), William, 1567–1644. Pilgrim father.

Brian Bo·ru' (brēn [Angl. bō·rōō'] bō·rōō'; bō·rōō'); Irish **Brian Bo·ram'ha** or **Bo·raim'he** (bō·rō'; -rōō'), 926–1014. King of Ireland (1002–1014).

Bri'and' (brē'äN'), A'ris'tide' (à'rēs'tēd'), 1862–1932. Fr. statesman.

Brick'er (brĭk'ĕr), John William, 1893– . Am. lawyer & polit.

Bridg'es (brĭj'ĕz; -ĭz), Robert Seymour, 1844–1930. Eng. poet; poet laureate (1913–30).

Bridg'man (brĭj'măn), Percy Williams, 1882– . Am. physicist.

Bri'eux' (brē'ö'), Eu'gène' (ü'zhän') (ü'zhän'), 1858–1932. Fr. dram.

Briggs (brĭgz), Lyman James, 1874– . Am. physicist.

Bright (brīt), John, 1811–1889. Eng. orator & statesman.

Brig'id (brĭj'ĭd; brē'ĭd), also **Bridg'et** (brĭj'ĕt; -ĭt), **Brig'it** (brĭj'ĭt; brē'ĭt), **Brighid** (brēd), or **Bride** (brīd), of Kil·dare' (kĭl·dâr'), Saint, 453–523. A patron saint of Ireland.

Bril'lat·Sa'va'rin' (brē'yà'sä'và'răN'), An'thelme' (äN'tĕlm'), 1755–1826. Fr. polit. & gastronomist.

Brit'ten (brĭt'''n), Edward Benjamin, 1913– . Eng. composer.

Brit'ton (brĭt'''n), Nathaniel Lord (lôrd), 1859–1934. Am. botanist.

Bro·glie', de (dĕ brō·glē'), Louis Vic'tor' (vēk'tôr'), 1892– . Fr. physicist.

Brom'field (brŏm'fēld), Louis, 1896–1956. Am. nov.

Bron'të (brŏn'tē), Charlotte, 1816–1855, Emily, 1818–1848, & Anne, 1820–1849. Pseud. Cur'rer (kûr'ĕr) Bell, Ellis Bell, Acton Bell, resp. Eng. nov., sisters.

Brooke (brōōk), Alan Francis, 1883– . 1st Viscount Al'an·brooke' (ăl'ăn·brōōk'). Brit. gen.

—, Sir Basil Stan'lake (stăn'lāk), 1888– . Prime min. of N. Ireland (1943–).

—, Rupert, 1887–1915. Eng. poet.

Brooks (brōōks), Phillips, 1835–1893. Am. bishop.

—, Van Wyck (văn wīk), 1886– . Am. author.

Brown (broun), Charles Brock'den (brŏk'dĕn), 1771–1810. Am. nov.

—, Ford Mad'ox (măd'ŭks), 1821–1893. Eng. painter.

—, John, of O'sa·wat'o·mie (ō'sà·wŏt'ō·mĭ; ŏs'à-), 1800–1859. Am. abolitionist.

—, John, 1810–1882. Scot. physician & author.

Browne (broun), Charles Far'rar (făr'ĕr), 1834–1867. Pseud. Ar'te·mus (är'tĕ·mŭs) Ward. Am. humorist.

—, Sir Thomas, 1605–1682. Eng. physician & author.

Brown'ing (broun'ĭng), Elizabeth Bar'rett (băr'ĕt; -ĭt), 1806–1861. Wife of Robert. Eng. poet.

—, Robert, 1812–1889. Eng. poet.

Broz (brōz) or **Bro'zo·vich** (brō'zō·vĭch; Yugo. -vĕt'y'), Jo'sip (yō'sēp), 1892– . Ti'to (tē'tō). Yugoslav marshal; premier (1945–).

Bruce (brōōs), Sir David, 1855–1931. Brit. physician & bacteriol.

—, Robert, 1274–1329. Liberator & king (as Robert I, 1306–29) of Scot.

—, Stanley Mel'bourne (mĕl'bĕrn; -bôrn), Viscount, 1883– . Australian statesman; prime min. (1923–29).

Brue'ghel or **Breu'ghel** (brö'gĕl). Family of Flem. painters including: Pie'ter (pē'tĕr), 1520?–1569, & his sons Pieter, 1564?–?1638, & Jan (yän), 1568–1625.

Brum'mell (brŭm'ĕl), George Bryan, 1778–1840. Beau (bō) Brum'mell. Eng. dandy. Cf. BEAU BRUMMELL in Vocab.

Bru'nel·le'schi (brōō'nĕl·lās'kē) or **Bru'nel·le'sco** (-kō), Fi·lip'po (fē·lĕp'pō), 1377?–1446. Ital. architect.

Bru'ne·tière' (brü'nĕ·tyâr'), Ferdinand, 1849–1906. Fr. critic.

Brü'ning or **Brue'ning** (brü'nĭng), Hein'rich (hīn'rĭk), 1885– . Chancellor of Germany (1930–32).

Bru'no (brōō'nō), Gior·da'no (jôr·dä'nō), 1548?–1600. Ital. philos.

Bru·si'lov (brōō·syē'lŭf), A·le·ksei' (ä·lyĭ·ksyā'ĭ) A·le·kse'e·vich (ŭ·lyĭ·ksyā'yĕ·vyĭch), 1853–1926. Russ. gen.

Bru'tus (brōō'tŭs), Marcus Junius, 85?–42 B.C. Rom. polit.; one of Caesar's assassins.

Bry'an (brī'ăn), William Jen'nings (jĕn'ĭngz), 1860–1925. Am. lawyer & polit.

Bry'ant (brī'ănt), William Cul'len (kŭl'ĕn), 1794–1878. Am. poet & editor.

Bryce (brīs), James, Viscount, 1838–1922. Brit. jurist, hist., & diplomat.

Buch'an (bŭk'ăn; Scot. bŭk'ăn), John, 1875–1940. 1st Baron Tweeds'muir (twēdz'mŭr). Scot. author; gov. gen. of Canada (1935–40).

Bu·chan'an (bū·kăn'ăn; bū-), James, 1791–1868. Am. polit. & diplomat; 15th pres. of the U. S. (1857–61).

Buch'man (bōōk'măn), Frank Nathan Daniel, 1878– . Am. evangelist.

Buch'ner (bōōk'nĕr), E'du·ard (ĕd'ōō·ärt), 1860–1917. Ger. chem.

Buck (bŭk), Pearl, 1892– . Nee Sy'den·strick'er (sī'd'n·strĭk'ĕr). Am. nov.

Buck'ing·ham (bŭk'ĭng·ăm; -hăm), 1st & 2d Dukes of. See George VILLIERS.

Buck'le (bŭk''l), Henry Thomas, 1821–1862. Eng. hist.

Buck'ner (bŭk'nĕr), Simon Bol'i·var (bŏl'ĭ·vĕr), 1823–1914. Am. Confed. gen. & polit.

—, Simon Bolivar, 1886–1945. Son of S. B. Am. gen.

Bud'dha. See GAUTAMA BUDDHA.

Bu·dën'ny (bōō·dyôn'nü·ĭ; Angl. bōō·dĕn'ĭ), Se·mën' (syĭ·myôn') Mi·khai'lo·vich (myĭ·kī'lŭ·vyĭch), 1883– . Russ. gen.

Buf'fa·lo Bill. See William Frederick CODY.

Buf'fon', de (dĕ bü'fôn'), Georges (zhôrzh) Louis Le·clerc' (lĕ·klâr'), Comte (kônt), 1707–1788. Fr. naturalist.

Bu·is'son' (bü·ē'sôn'), Ferdinand, 1841–1932. Fr. educ.

Bul·ga'nin (bōōl·gä'nyĭn), Ni·ko·lai' (nyĭ·kŭ·lī') A·le·ksan'dro·vich (ŭ·lyĭ·ksän'drō·vĭch), 1895– . Russ. polit. & marshal.

Bull (bōōl), O'le Bor'ne·mann (ō'lĕ bôr'nĕ·män), 1810–1880. Norw. violinist.

Bul'litt (bōōl'ĭt), William Christian, 1891– . Am. diplomat.

Bü'low, von (fôn bü'lō), Bern'hard (bĕrn'härt), Prince, 1849–1929. Ger. diplomat & statesman; chancellor of Ger. (1900–09).

Bul'wer (bōōl'wĕr), William Henry Lytton Earle (ûrl), 1801–1872. Sir Henry Bulwer; Baron Dal'ling (dôl'ĭng) and Bulwer. Bro. of 1st Baron Lytton (q.v.). Brit. diplomat.

Bul'wer-Lyt'ton. See LYTTON.

Bu'nin (bōō'nyĭn), Ivan A·le·kse'e·vich (ŭ·lyĭ·ksyā'yĕ·vyĭch), 1870–1953. Russ. poet & nov.

Bun'ner (bŭn'ĕr), Henry Cuy'ler (kī'lĕr), 1855–1896. Am. writer.

Bun'sen (bōōn'sĕn; Angl. bŭn's'n), Ro'bert (rō'bĕrt) Wil'helm (vĭl'hĕlm), 1811–1899. Ger. chem.

Bun'yan (bŭn'yăn), John, 1628–1688. Eng. preacher & author.

Buo'na·par'te. Ital. spelling of BONAPARTE.

Bur'bage (bûr'bĭj), Richard, 1567?–1619. Eng. actor.

Bur'bank (bûr'băngk), Luther, 1849–1926. Am. horticulturist.

Bür'ger (bür'gĕr), Gott'fried (gôt'frēt) Au'gust (ou'gŏōst), 1747–1794. Ger. poet.

Bur'gess (bûr'jĕs; -jĭs), (Frank) Ge·lett' (jĕ·lĕt'), 1866–1951. Am. humorist.

—, Thornton Waldo, 1874– . Am. writer.

Burgh'ley or **Bur'leigh**, 1st Baron. See under CECIL.

Bur·goyne' (bûr·goin'; bûr'goin), John, 1722–1792. Brit. gen. in Am.

Burke (bûrk), Edmund, 1729–1797. Brit. statesman.

Bur'lin·game (bûr'lĭn·gām; -lĭng·gām), Anson, 1820–1870. Am. lawyer & diplomat.

Burne'-Jones' (bûrn'jōnz'), Sir Edward Co'ley (kō'lĭ), 1833–1898. Orig. Jones. Eng. painter & designer.

Bur·nett' (bûr·nĕt'; bĕr-), Frances Eliza, 1849–1924. Nee Hodg'son (hŏj's'n). Am. (Eng.-born) writer.

Bur'ney (bûr'nĭ), Fanny, 1752–1840. Orig. Frances; Madame d'Ar'blay (där'blā; Fr. där'blä'). Eng. nov. & diarist.

Burns (bûrnz), Robert, 1759–1796. Scot. poet.

Burn'side (bûrn'sīd), Ambrose Everett, 1824–1881. Am. gen.

Burr (bûr), Aaron, 1756–1836. 3d vice-pres. of the U. S. (1801–05).

Bur'roughs (bûr'ōz), Edgar Rice, 1875–1950. Am. writer.

—, John, 1837–1921. Am. naturalist.

Bur'ton (bûr't'n), Harold Hitz, 1888– . Am. jurist.

—, Sir Richard Francis, 1821–1890. Brit. explorer & orientalist.

—, Robert, 1577–1640. Eng. clergyman & author.

Bush (bōōsh), Van·ne'var (vă·nē'vär), 1890– . Am. electrical engineer.

Bus'ta·man'te y Ri·ve'ro (bōōs'tä·män'tā ē rē·vā'rō), Jo·sé' (hō·sā') Lu·is' (lōō·ēs'), 1894– . Peruvian lawyer & diplomat; pres. of Peru (1945–48).

Bu'te·nandt (bōō'tĕ·nänt), A'dolph (ä'dôlf), 1903– . Ger. chem.

But'ler (bŭt'lĕr), Benjamin Franklin, 1818–1893. Am. lawyer, gen., & polit.

—, Joseph, 1692–1752. Eng. theol.

—, Nicholas Murray, 1862–1947. Am. educ.

—, Samuel, 1612–1680. Eng. satirical poet.

—, Samuel, 1835–1902. Eng. nov. & satirist.

Buys′ Bal·lot′ (bois′ bä·lŏt′), Chris′toph (krĭs′tôf) Hen′drik (hĕn′drĭk) Di′de·ri′cus (dē′dĕ·rē′kŭs), 1817–1890. Du. meteorologist.

Byng (bĭng), George, 1663–1733. Brit. admiral.

—, Julian Hed′worth (hĕd′wŭrth; -wẽrth) George, 1862–1935. 1st Baron *Byng of Vi′my* (vē′mĭ; *Fr.* vē′mē′). Brit. gen.; gov. gen. of Canada (1921–26).

Byrd (bûrd), Richard E′ve·lyn (ĕ′vĕ·lĭn), 1888–1957. Am. admiral & polar explorer.

Byrnes (bûrnz), James Francis, 1879– . Am. polit. & jurist.

By′ron (bī′rŭn), George Gordon, 6th Baron, 1788–1824. Eng. poet.

C

Ca′bal·le′ro, Francisco Largo. See LARGO CABALLERO.

Cab′ell (kăb′ĕl), James Branch (brănch), 1879–1958. Am. nov.

Ca·be′za de Va′ca (kä·vā′thä thä vä′kä), Ál′var (äl′vär) Nú′ñez (nōō′nyäth), 1490?–1557? Span. explorer.

Ca′ble (kā′b'l), George Washington, 1844–1925. Am. nov.

Cab′ot (kăb′ŭt), John, 1450–1498. *Gio·van′ni Ca·bo′to* (jō·vän′nē kä·bō′tō). Venetian navigator in service of Eng.; disc. N. Am.

—, Sebastian, 1476?–1557. *Son of John.* Eng. navigator.

Ca·bral′ (kȧ·vräl′), Pe′dro (pā′thrōō) Ál′va·res (äl′vȧ·rĕsh), 1460?–?1526. Port. navigator; claimed Brazil for Portugal.

Ca·bri′ni (kȧ·brē′nē), Saint Frances Xavier, 1850–1917. 1st. Am. citizen canonized (1946).

Cade (kād), Jack, d. 1450. Eng. rebel.

Cad′il·lac (kăd′ĭ·lȧk; *Fr.* kȧ·dē′yȧk′), An′toine′ (äN′twän′) de la Mothe (dē lȧ mŏt′), Sieur (syûr), 1658–1730. Fr. founder of Detroit.

Ca·dor′na (kä·dôr′nä), Lui′gi (lwē′jē), Count, 1850–1928. Ital. gen.

Caed′mon (kăd′mŭn), fl. 670. Anglo-Saxon poet.

Cae′sar (sē′zẽr), Ga′ius (gā′yŭs; gī′ŭs) Julius, 102 or 100–44 B.C. Rom. gen., statesman, & writer.

Caf′fer·y (kăf′rĭ; kăf′ẽr·ĭ), Jefferson, 1886– . Am. diplomat.

Ca·glio′stro, di (dē kä·lyōs′trō), Count A′les·san′dro (ä′läs·sän′drō), 1743–1795. Real name *Giu·sep′pe* (jōō·zĕp′pā) *Bal′sa·mo* (bäl′sä·mō). Ital. impostor.

Caine (kān), Sir (Thomas Henry) Hall, 1853–1931. Eng. nov.

Cal·am′i·ty Jane (kȧ·lăm′ĭ·tĭ jān′), 1852?–1903. *Martha Jane Burke,* nee *Can′a·ry* (kăn′ȧ·rĭ). Am. frontier markswoman.

Cal′de·rón′ de la Bar′ca (käl′dā·rôn′ thä lä vär′kä; 17), Pe′dro (pā′thrō), 1600–1681. Span. dram. & poet.

Cald′well (kôld′wĕl; -wĕl; kŏld′-), Erskine, 1903– . Am. nov.

Cal·houn′ (kăl·hōōn′), John Caldwell, 1782–1850. Am. lawyer; vice-pres. of the U. S. (1825–32).

Ca·lig′u·la (kȧ·lĭg′ū·lȧ), 12–41. *Ga′ius* (gā′yŭs; gī′ŭs) *Caesar.* Rom. emp. (37–41).

Cal′les (kä′yäs), Plu·tar′co (plōō·tär′kō) E·lí′as (â·lē′äs), 1877–1945. Mex. gen.; pres. of Mexico (1924–28).

Cal·lim′a·chus (kă·lĭm′ȧ·kŭs), 5th cent. B.C. Greek sculptor.

—, b. ab. 310 B.C. Greek scholar & Alexandrian librarian.

Cal·lis′the·nes (kă·lĭs′thĕ·nēz), 360?–?328 B.C. Greek philos. & hist.

Cal·lis′tra·tus (kă·lĭs′trȧ·tŭs), d. 355 B.C. Athenian orator & gen.

Cal·vé′ (kȧl′vā′), Em′ma (ĕm′ȧ; *Fr.* ĕm′mä′), 1858–1942. Nee *de Ro′quer′* (dē rō′kā′). Fr. soprano.

Cal′vert (kăl′vẽrt), George, 1580?–1632. 1st Baron *Bal′ti·more* (bôl′tĭ·mōr). Eng. statesman; proprietor in Am.

—, Leonard, 1606–1647. *Son of George.* Gov. of Maryland province (1634–47).

Cal′vin (kăl′vĭn; *Fr.* käl′văN′), John, 1509–1564. Orig. *Jean Chau′vin′* (shō′văN′) or *Caul′vin′* (kōl′văN′). Fr. Protestant at Geneva.

Ca·ma′cho (kä·mä′chō), Ma·nuel′ (mä·nwĕl′) Á′vi·la (ä′vē·lä), 1897–1955. Mex. gen.; pres. of Mexico (1940–46).

Cam′ba·cé′rès′, de (dē käN′bȧ′sā′rĕs′), Duc (dük), 1753–1824. *Jean Jacques* (zhäk) *Ré′gis′* (rā′zhēs′). Fr. jurist; counselor of Napoleon I.

Cam·by′ses (kăm·bī′sēz), d. 522 B.C. *Son of Cyrus the Great.* King of Persia (529–522).

Cam′den (kăm′dĕn), William, 1551–1623. Eng. antiquary & hist.

Cam′er·on of Loch·iel′ (kăm′ẽr·ŭn ŭv lŏk·ēl′), 1629–1719. Sir *Ew′en* (ū′ĕn) *Cameron.* Scot. chieftain.

—, 1695?–1748. *Donald Cameron; the Gentle Lochiel.* Chieftain.

Cam′maerts (käm′ärts), É·mile′ (ȧ·mēl′), 1878–1953. Belg. writer & patriot.

Ca·mões′, Vaz de (vazh thĕ kȧ·mōēnsh′), *Eng.* **Cam′o·ens** (kăm′ō·ĕnz; kȧ·mō′ĕnz), Lu·iz′ (lōō·ēsh′), 1524–1580. Port. poet.

Camp (kămp), Walter Chauncey, 1859–1925. Am. football coach.

Camp′bell (kăm′bĕl; *in U.S., also* kăm′ĕl), Alexander, 1788–1866. Am. (Irish-born) founder of Disciples of Christ.

—, Colin, 1792–1863. Orig. *Mac·li′ver* (măk·lē′vẽr); Baron *Clyde* (klīd). Brit. field marshal.

—, John, 1705–1782. 4th Earl of *Lou′doun* (lou′d'n). Brit. gen. in Am.

—, Thomas, 1777–1844. Brit. poet.

—**-Ban′ner·man** (-băn′ẽr·măn), Sir Henry, 1836–1908. Brit. statesman; prime min. (1905–08).

Cam′pi (käm′pē). Ital. family of painters in Cremona, including Ga′le·az′zo (gä′lä·ät′tsō), 1477–1536, and his three sons, Giu′lio (jōō′lyō), ab. 1502–1572, An·to′nio (än·tō′nyō), d. 1591?, and Vin·cen′zo (vēn·chĕn′tsō), 1536–1591.

Cam′pi·on (kăm′pĭ·ŭn; -ŏn), Thomas, 1567–1620. Eng. poet & musician.

Can′by (kăn′bĭ), Henry Sei′del (sī′d'l), 1878– . Am. editor & educ.

Can′dolle′, de (dē käN′dôl′), Au′gus′tin′ Py′rame′ (ô′güs′tăN′ pē′räm′), 1778–1841. Swiss botanist.

Can′ning (kăn′ĭng), Charles John, Earl, 1812–1862. Gov. gen. of India (1856–62).

—, George, 1770–1827. *Father of C. J.* Brit. statesman; prime min. (1827).

—, Strat′ford (străt′fẽrd), 1786–1880. 1st Viscount *Stratford de Red′cliffe* (dē [dĕ] rĕd′klĭf). Brit. diplomat.

Can′non (kăn′ŭn), Joseph Gur′ney (gûr′nĭ), 1836–1926. *Uncle Joe.* Am. lawyer & polit.

Ca·no′va (kä·nō′vä), An·to′nio (än·tō′nyō), 1757–1822. Ital. sculptor.

Cá′no·vas del Cas·til′lo (kä′nō·väs thĕl kȧs·tēl′yō), An·to′nio (än·tō′nyō), 1828–1897. Span. statesman & writer.

Can′ro′bert′ (käN′rō′bĕr′), Fran′çois′ (frän′swä′) Cer′tain′ (sĕr′tăN′), 1809–1895. Fr. marshal.

Ca·nute′ (kȧ·nūt′), **Cnut** (k'nōōt), or **Knut** (k'nōōt), 994?–1035. *The Great.* King of Eng. (1016–35) & of Denmark (1018–35).

Ca′pa·blan′ca (kä′pä·vläng′kä; 17), Jo·sé′ Ra·oul′ (hō·sā′ rä·ōōl′), 1888–1942. *Capablanca y Gran·per′ra* (ē gräm·pĕr′rä). Cuban world chess champion.

Ča′pek (chä′pĕk), Ka′rel (kä′rĕl), 1890–1938. Czech nov. & dram.

Ca′pet, Hugh. See HUGH CAPET.

Car′a·cal′la (kăr′ȧ·kăl′ȧ), 188–217. *Marcus Aurelius An′to·ni′nus* (ăn′tō·nī′nŭs); orig. *Bas·si·a′nus* (băs′ĭ·ā′nŭs). Rom. emp. (211–217).

Ca·rac′ta·cus (kȧ·răk′tȧ·kŭs) or **Ca·rat′a·cus** (kȧ·răt′ȧ·kŭs); *Eng.* **Ca·rad′oc** (kȧ·răd′ŭk), fl. 43–50. Brit. chieftain.

Cár′de·nas (kär′thā·näs), Lá′za·ro (lä′sä·rō), 1895– . Mex. gen. & polit.; pres. of Mexico (1934–40).

Car·do′zo (kär·dō′zō), Benjamin Nathan, 1870–1938. Am. jurist.

Car·duc′ci (kär·dōōt′chē), Gio·sue′ (jō·zwē′), 1835–1907. Ital. poet.

Ca·rew′ (kȧ·rōō′; kȧr′ōō; kâr′ĭ), Thomas, 1595?–?1645. Eng. poet.

Ca·rí′as An·dí′no (kä·rē′äs än·dē′nō), Ti·bur′cio (tē·vōōr′syō), 1876– . Honduran gen.; pres. of Honduras (1933–49).

Carle′ton (kärl′tŭn; -t'n), Guy, 1724–1808. 1st Baron *Dor′ches′ter* (dôr′chĕs′tẽr; -chĭs·tẽr). Brit. gen. & administrator in Am.

Car′los (kär′lōs; *Span.* -lōs), Don (dŏn; *Span.* dôn), 1788–1855. Infante & pretender to Span. throne.

— **de Aus′tri·a** (thä ous′trē·ä), 1545–1568. Prince of Asturias & heir to Span. throne.

Car·lo′ta (kär·lō′tä); *Eng.* **Char′lotte** (shär′lŏt), 1840–1927. Incorrectly *Car·lot′ta* (kär·lŏt′ä). Empress of Mexico (1864–67).

Carl′son (kärl′s'n), Evans For′dyce (fôr′dīs), 1896–1947. Am. gen.

Car·lyle′ (kär·līl′; kär′līl), Thomas, 1795–1881. Scot. essayist & hist.

Car′man (kär′măn), (William) Bliss, 1861–1929. Canadian poet.

Car·mo′na (kẽr·mō′nä), An·to′nio (änn·tō′nyō) Os·car′ (ôsh·kär′) de Fra·go′so (dē frä·gō′zōō), 1869–1951. Port. gen.; pres. of Portugal (1926–51).

Car·ne′gie (kär·nā′gĭ; -nĕg′ĭ; *being the first was his own pron.*), Andrew, 1835–1919. Am. (Scot.-born) industrialist & philanthropist.

Car′not′ (kär′nō′), La′zare′ (lȧ′zär′) Ni′co·las′ (nē′kô′lä′) Mar′gue·rite′ (mär′gĕ·rēt′), 1753–1823. Fr. statesman & gen.

—, Ma′rie′ (mȧ′rē′) Fran′çois′ (frän′swä′) Sa′di′ (sȧ′dē′), 1837–1894. Pres. of France (1887–94).

Ca′rol II (kä′rŏl; *Angl.* kăr′ŭl), 1893–1953. King of Romania (1930–40).

Car·ran′za (kär·rän′sä; *Angl.* kȧ·răn′zȧ), Ve′nus·tia′no (bā′nōōs·tyä′nō; 17), 1859–1920. Pres. of Mexico (1915–20).

Car′rel (kăr′ĕl; *Fr.* kȧ′rĕl′), A·lex′is (ȧ·lĕk′sĭs; *Fr.* ȧ′lĕk′sē′), 1873–1944. Fr. surgeon & biologist.

Car·rère′ (kȧ·râr′), John Mer′ven (mûr′vĕn), 1858–1911. Am. architect.

Car′roll (kăr′ŭl), Charles, 1737–1832. *Carroll of Car′roll·ton* (kăr′ŭl·tŭn; -t'n). Am. patriot.

—, Lewis. See Charles Lutwidge DODGSON.

Car′son (kär′s'n), Christopher, 1809–1868. *Kit.* Am. trapper & frontiersman.

—, Edward Henry, 1854–1935. Baron *Carson of Dun·cairn′* (dŭn·kârn′; dŭn-). Brit. jurist & statesman.

Carte, D′Oy′ly (doi′lĭ kärt′), Richard, 1844–1901. Eng. opera impresario.

Car′ter (kär′tẽr), Howard, 1873–1939. Eng. archaeologist.

Car′ter·et (kär′tẽr·ĕt; -ĭt), John, 1690–1763. Earl *Gran′ville* (grän′vĭl). Eng. statesman.

Car′tier′ (kär′tyā′), Jacques (zhäk), 1491–1557. Fr. navigator & explorer; disc. St. Lawrence River.

Cart′wright (kärt′rīt), Edmund, 1743–1823. Eng. inventor.

Ca·ru′so (kä·rōō′zō; *Angl.* kȧ·rōō′sō, -zō), En·ri′co (ân·rē′kō), 1873–1921. Orig. *Er·ri′co* (är·rē′kō). Ital. tenor.

Car′ver (kär′vẽr), George Washington, 1864–1943. Am. botanist.

—, John, 1576?–1621. Eng. *Mayflower* pilgrim; 1st gov. of Plymouth colony.

Car′y (kâr′ĭ), Henry Francis, 1772–1844. Eng. clergyman; trans. of Dante.

Ca′sa′bian′ca′, de (dē kȧ′zȧ′byäN′kȧ′), Louis, 1755?–1798. Fr. naval officer.

Ca·sals′ (kä·säls′), Pa′blo (pä′vlō), 1876– . Span. violoncellist.

Ca′sa·no′va (kä′sä·nō′vä; *Angl.* kăs′ȧ·nō′vȧ, kăz′ȧ-) or **Ca′sa·no′va de Sein′galt′** (dĕ săN′gäl′), Gio·va′mo (jō·vä′mō) Gi·ro′la·mo (jē·rō′lä·mō), 1725–1798. Also *Gio·van′ni* (jō·vän′nē) *Ja′co·po* (yä′kō·pō). Ital. adventurer.

Ca·sau′bon (kȧ·sô′bŭn; *Fr.* kȧ′zō′bôN′), I′saac′ (ē′zäk′), 1559–1614. Fr. theol. & scholar.

Case′ment (kās′mĕnt), Sir Roger David, 1864–1916. Irish rebel, hanged by British.

Ca′si·mir′-Pé′rier′ (kȧ′zē′mēr′pā′ryä′), Jean Paul Pierre, 1847–1907. Fr. statesman; pres. of France (1894–95).

Cas′lon (kăz′lŏn), William, 1692–1766. Eng. type founder.

Cass (kăs), Lewis, 1782–1866. Am. statesman.

Cas·satt′ (kȧ·săt′), Mary, 1845–1926. Am. painter.

Cas′si·o·do′rus (kăs′ĭ·ō·dō′rŭs), Fla′vi·us (flä′vĭ·ŭs) Mag′nus (măg′nŭs) Aurelius, d. 575 A.D. Rom. statesman & author.

Cas′si·us Lon·gi′nus (kăsh′ĭ·ŭs lŏn·jī′nŭs; kăsh′ŭs; kăs′ĭ·ŭs), Ga′ius (gā′yŭs; gī′ŭs), d. 42 B.C. Rom. gen. & conspirator.

Cas′te·lar′ y Ri·poll′ (käs′tā·lär′ ē rē·pōl′y′), E·mi′lio (â·mē′lyō), 1832–1899. Span. statesman & writer.

Ca·stel′ve′tro (käs·tĕl′vā′trō), Lo·do·vi′co (lō·dō·vē′kō), 1505–1571. Ital. critic.

Ca·sti·glio′ne (käs′tē·lyō′nä), Con′te (kōn′tā) Bal′das·sa′re (bäl′däs·sä′rä), 1478–1529. Ital. statesman & author.

Cas·ti'lho, de (thē kảsh·tē'lyōō), Vis·con'de (vĕsh·kōnn'dĕ) An·tô'nio (ănn·tô'nyōō) Fe·li·cia'no (fĕ·lē·syä'nōō), 1800–1875. Port. poet.

Cas'tle·reagh, Viscount. See Robert STEWART.

Cas'tri·o'ta, George. See SCANDERBEG.

Cas'tro (käs'trō), Ci'pri·a'no (sē'prē·ä'nō), 1858?–1924. Venezuelan gen.; pres. of Venezuela (1902–08).

—, de (thả), I·nés' (ē·nās'); *Eng.* Agnes, 1320?–1355. Span. noble-woman.

Cates (kāts), Clifton Bled'soe (blĕd'sō), 1893– . Am. marine corps gen.

Cates'by (kāts'bĭ), Mark, 1679?–1749. Eng. naturalist.

—, Robert, 1573–1605. Eng. rebel.

Cath'er (kăth'ẽr), Wil'la (wĭl'ả) Si'bert (sī'bẽrt), 1873–1947. Am. nov.

Cath'er·ine (kăth'ẽr·ĭn). Name of 1st, 5th, & 6th wives of Henry VIII of Eng.: Catherine of Ar'a·gon (ăr'ả·gŏn), 1485–1536; Catherine How'ard (hou'ẽrd), 1520?–1542; Catherine Parr (pär), 1512–1548.

— I, 1684?–1727. *Wife of Peter the Great.* Empress of Russia (1725–27).

— II, 1729–1796. *The Great.* Empress of Russia (1762–96).

— of Bra·gan'za (brả·gǎn'zả), 1638–1705. Queen of Charles II of Eng.

Ca'the·rine' de Mé'di·cis' (kả'trēn' dĕ mã'dē'sēs'); *Ital.* **Ca'te·ri'na de' Me'di·ci** (kä'tả·rē'nä dä mä'dē·chē; *Angl.* mĕd'ĭ-, mã'dē-), 1519–1589. Queen of Henry II of France.

Cat'i·line (kăt'ĭ·līn; -'l·ĭn), 108?–62 B.C. *Lucius Ser'gi·us* (sûr'jĭ·ŭs) *Cat'i·li'na* (kăt'ĭ·lī'nả). Rom. polit. & conspirator.

Ca'to (kā'tō), Marcus Por'ci·us (pôr'shĭ·ŭs; pôr'shŭs), 234–149 B.C. *The Elder; the Censor.* Rom. statesman.

—, Marcus Porcius, 95–46 B.C. *The Younger; great-grandson of prec.* Rom. Stoic philos.

Catt (kăt), Car'rie (kăr'ĭ) Chapman, 1859–1947. Nee *Lane.* Am. suffragist.

Cat·tell' (kă·tĕl'), James Mc·Keen' (mả·kēn'), 1860–1944. Am. psychol. & editor.

Ca·tul'lus (kả·tŭl'ŭs), Ga'ius (gā'yŭs [gī'ŭs]) Va·le'ri·us (vả·lēr'ĭ·ŭs), 84?–54 B.C. Rom. poet.

Cau·lain'court', de (dĕ kō'lăn'kōōr'), Marquis Armand Au'gus'tin' (ō'güs'tăn') Louis, 1772–1827. Fr. gen. & diplomat.

Ca'val·le'ro (kä'väl·lâ'rō), Con'te (kôn'tả) U'go (ōō'gô), 1880–1943. Ital. gen.

Cav'an (kăv'ăn), 10th Earl of, 1865–1946. *Frederic Rudolph Lam'bart* (lăm'bärt). Brit. field marshal.

Cav·ell' (kăv'l), Edith Louisa, 1865–1915. Eng. nurse, executed by Germans.

Cav'en·dish (kăv'ĕn·dĭsh), Henry, 1731–1810. Eng. scientist.

—, Spencer Compton, 1833–1908. 8th Duke of *Dev'on·shire* (dĕv'ăn·shĭr; -shẽr). Eng. statesman.

—, Sir William, 1505?–1557. Eng. statesman.

—, William, 1640–1707. 1st Duke of *Devonshire.* Eng. statesman.

Ja·vour', di (dĕ kä·vōōr'), Con'te (kôn'tả) Ca·mil'lo (kä·mēl'lō) Ben'so (bĕn'sō), 1810–1861. Ital. statesman.

Ca·xi'as, de (thĕ kả·shē'ảs), Du'que (dōō'kĕ), 1803–1880. *Lu·iz' Al'ves* (lōō·ēz' äl'vĕz) *de Li'ma e Sil'va* (thĕ lē'mả ē sĭl'vả). Brazilian gen. & statesman.

Cax'ton (kăks'tŭn), William, 1422?–1491. 1st Eng. printer.

Cec'il (sĕs'l; sĕs'ĭl; sĭs''l), (Edgar Algernon) Robert, 1864– . 1st Viscount *Cecil of Chel'wood* (chĕl'wŏŏd). Eng. statesman.

—, (Edward Christian) David, Lord, 1902– . Eng. biographer.

—, Robert, 1563?–1612. 1st Earl of *Salis'bur·y* (sôlz'bẽr·ĭ; -brĭ) and 1st Viscount *Cran'borne* (krăn'bôrn). Eng. statesman.

—, Gas'coyne- (găs'koin-), Robert Arthur Tal'bot (tôl'bŭt), 1830–1903. 3d Marquis of *Salisbury.* Eng. statesman.

—, William, 1520–1598. 1st Baron *Burgh'ley* or *Bur'leigh* (bûr'lĭ). Eng. statesman.

Cel·li'ni (chĕ·lē'nē; *Ital.* chäl·lē'nē), Ben·ve·nu'to (bĕn·vả·nōō'tō), 1500–1571. Ital. goldsmith & sculptor.

Cel'si·us (sĕl'sĭ·ŭs; -shĭ·ŭs; *Swed.* sĕl'sĭ·ŭs), An'ders (än'dẽrs), 1701–1744. Swed. astron.

Cen'ci (chĕn'chē), Be·a·tri'ce (bā·ä·trē'chä), 1577–1599. Ital. woman, executed for parricide.

Cer·van'tes Sa'a·ve'dra, de (dä thẽr·vän'täs sä'ä·vä'thrä), Mi·guel' (mē·gĕl'), 1547–1616. Span. nov.

Cer·ve'ra y To·pe'te (thẽr·vä'rä ē tô·pā'tä), Pas·cual' (päs·kwäl'), 1839–1909. Con·de (kôn'dä) *de Je·rez'* (thä hä·rāth'); Mar·qués' (mär·kās') *de San'ta A'na* (thä sän'tä ä'nä). Span. admiral.

Cé'zanne' (sā'zän'), Paul, 1839–1906. Fr. painter.

Chad'wick (chăd'wĭk), Sir James, 1891– . Eng. physicist.

Chain (chān), Ernst (ẽrnst) Boris, 1906– . Brit. (Ger.-born) biochem.

Cha·lia'pin (shǔ·lyä'pyĭn), Fe·o'dor (fyĭ·ô'dẽr) I·va'no·vitch (ĭ·vä'nŭ·vyĭch), 1873–1938. Russ. basso.

Chal'mers (chä'mẽrz), Alexander, 1759–1834. Scot. biographer & editor.

Cham'ber·lain (chăm'bẽr·lĭn), Joseph, 1836–1914, and his sons Sir (Joseph) Austen, 1863–1937, and (Arthur) Neville, 1869–1940. Brit. statesmen.

Cham'ber·lin (chăm'bẽr·lĭn), Thomas Chrow'der (krou'dẽr), 1843–1928. Am. geologist.

—, William Henry, 1897– . Am. journalist & author.

Cham'bers (chăm'bẽrz), Robert, 1802–1871. Scot. publisher & editor.

Cham'bord, de (dĕ shän'bôr'), Comte (kônt), 1820–1883. Duc (dük) *de Bor'deaux'* (dĕ bôr'dō'). Bourbon claimant to Fr. throne.

Cha'mi'nade' (shá'mē'nád'), Cé'cile' (sā'sēl') Lou·ise' (lwēz) Sté'pha'nie' (stā'fá'nē'), 1861–1944. Fr. composer & pianist.

Cha·mor'ro Var'gas (chä·môr'rō vär'gäs), E'mi·lia'no (ā'mē·lyä'nō), 1871– . Nicaraguan gen. & polit.; pres. of Nicaragua (1917–20; 1926).

Cham·plain', de (dĕ [dĕ] shăm·plān'; *Fr.* dĕ shän'plăn'), Sam'u·el (săm'û·ĕl; *Fr.* sà'mü·ĕl'), 1567?–1635. Fr. explorer in Am.; founder of Quebec.

Cham'pol'lion' (shän'pŏ'lyôn'), Jean Fran'çois' (frän'swä'), 1790–1832. Fr. Egyptologist.

— -Fi'geac' (-fē'zhàk'), Jean Jacques (zhàk), 1778–1867. *Bro. of prec.* Fr. archaeologist.

Chan'dra·gup'ta (chŭn'drả·gŏŏp'tả), 4th cent. B.C. Also *San'dro·cot'tus* (săn'drō·kŏt'ŭs) or *San'dra·cot'tus* (săn'drả-). Indian ruler (Maurya dynasty).

— II, Indian ruler (383?–413; Gupta dynasty).

Chang Hsueh-liang (jäng' shü·ē'lyäng'), 1898– . *Son of Chang Tso-lin.* Chin. gen.

Chang Tso-lin (jäng' tsō'lĭn'), 1873–1928. Chin. gen.

Chan'ning (chăn'ĭng), William El'ler·y (ĕl'ẽr·ĭ), 1780–1842. Am. Unitarian clergyman & author.

Chao K'uang-yin (jou'kwäng'yĭn'), d. 976. *Kao Tsu* (gou' dzōō'). Chin. emp. (960–976); founder of Sung dynasty.

Chap'man (chăp'măn), Frank Mich'ler (mĭk'lẽr), 1864–1945. Am. ornithologist.

—, George, 1559?–1634. Eng. dram. & trans.

—, John, 1775?–1847. *John'ny Ap'ple·seed'* (jŏn'ĭ ăp''l·sēd'). Am. pioneer.

Char'cot' (shàr'kō'), Jean Mar'tin' (màr'tăn'), 1825–1893. Fr. neurologist.

Char'le·magne (shär'lĕ·mān; *Fr.* shàr'lĕ·màn'y'), 742–814. *Charles the Great* (chärlz) or *Charles I.* Frankish king (768–814) & emp. of the West (800–814).

Charles (chärlz) **I**, 1600–1649. *Charles Stuart.* King of Gr. Britain (1625–49); executed.

— II, 1630–1685. *Son of Charles I.* King of Gr. Britain (1660–85).

— I, 1887–1922. *Charles Francis Joseph. Nephew of Francis Ferdinand.* Emp. of Austria & (as Charles IV) king of Hungary (1916–18).

— (chärlz; *Fr.* shàrl) I or II, 823–877. *The Bald.* King of France, as Charles I (840–877); emp. as Charles II (875–877).

— IV, 1294–1328. *The Fair.* King of France (1322–28).

— V, 1337–1380. *The Wise.* King of France (1364–80).

— VI, 1368–1422. *The Mad* or *the Beloved.* King of France (1380–1422).

— VII, 1403–1461. *The Victorious.* King of France (1422–61).

— IX, 1550–1574. King of France (1560–74).

— X, 1757–1836. King of France (1824–30).

— V (chärlz), 1500–1558. Holy Rom. emp. (1519–56); king of Spain as Charles I (1516–56).

— XII, 1682–1718. King of Sweden (1697–1718).

—, Prince, 1903– . *Bro. of King Leopold.* Regent of Belgium (1944–50).

— XIV John. See BERNADOTTE.

— Ed'ward Stu'art, 1720–1788. *The Young Pretender.* (*Bonnie*) *Prince Charlie.* Eng. prince.

—, or Karl Lud'wig (lōōt'vĭk; lōōd'-), 1771–1847. Archduke of Austria.

— Mar·tel' (chärlz' mär·tĕl'; *Fr.* shàrl' màr'tĕl'), 689?–741. *Grandfather of Charlemagne.* Frankish ruler (715–741).

Char'lotte, Empress of Mexico. See CARLOTA.

Charn'wood (chärn'wŏŏd), 1st Baron, 1864–1945. *Godfrey Rath'bone* (răth'bōn; -bŭn) *Benson.* Eng. biographer.

Char'pen'tier' (shàr'pän'tyā'), Gus'tave' (güs'tàv'), 1860–1956. Fr. composer.

Chase (chās), Mary Ellen, 1887– . Am. educ. & author.

—, Salm'on Port'land (săm'ŭn pōrt'lănd), 1808–1873. Am. statesman.

Cha'teau'bri'and', de (dĕ shä'tō'brē'än'), Fran'çois' (frän'swä') René, Vi'comte' (vē'kônt'), 1768–1848. Fr. author.

Chat'ham, 1st Earl of. See William PITT.

Cha'tri'an', Alexandre. See ERCKMANN-CHATRIAN.

Chat'ter·ji (chä'tĕr·jē), Ban'kim (bŏng'kĭm) Chan'dra (chŏn'drô), 1838–1894. Indian nov.

Chat'ter·ton (chăt'ẽr·t'n; -tŭn), Thomas, 1752–1770. Eng. poet.

Chau'cer (chô'sẽr), Geoffrey, 1340?–1400. Eng. poet.

Chau'temps' (shō'tän'), Ca'mille' (kä'mē'y'), 1885– . Fr. lawyer & polit.; premier (1930; 1933–34; 1937–38).

Cha'vannes', de. See PUVIS DE CHAVANNES.

Chá'vez (chä'vãs), Car'los (kär'lōs), 1899– . Mex. conductor & composer.

Che'khov (chĕ'kǔf; *Angl.* chĕk'ôf), An·ton' (ǔn·tôn') Pa·vlo'vich (pǔ·vlô'vyĭch), 1860–1904. Also *Che'kov* or *Tche'khov.* Russ. dram. & story writer.

Ché'nier' (shē'nôlt'), An'dré' (än'drā') Ma'rie' (mà'rē'), 1762–1794. Fr. poet.

Chen·nault' (shē·nôlt'), Claire (klâr) Lee, 1891– . Am. gen.

Che'ops. See KHUFU.

Cher·nya·khov'sky (chĭr·nyü·kôf'skĭ; *Angl.* chẽrn'yả·kôf'skĭ), Ivan Da·nil'o·vich (dä·nyēl'ô·vyĭch), 1908?–1945. Russ. gen.

Cher·ny·shev'ski (chĭr·nĭ·shĕf'skĭ), Ni·ko·lai' (nyĭ·kù·lī') Ga·vri'lo·vich (gǔ·vryē'lǔ·vyĭch), 1829–1889. Russ. revolutionist & author.

Che·ru·bi'ni (kā·rōō·bē'nē), Ma·ri'a (mä·rē'ä) Lui'gi (lwē'jē) Car'lo (kär'lō) Ze·no'bio (dzä·nô'byō) Sal'va·to're (säl'vä·tō'rä), 1760–1842. Ital. composer.

Ches'ter·field (chĕs'tẽr·fēld), 4th Earl of, 1694–1773. *Philip Dor'mer* (dôr'mẽr) *Stan'hope* (stăn'ŭp). Eng. statesman & author.

Ches'ter·ton (chĕs'tẽr·t'n; -tŭn), Gilbert Keith, 1874–1936. Eng. journalist & author.

Chiang Kai-shek (jē·äng' kī'shĕk'), 1886– . *Chiang Chungcheng.* Chin. gen. & statesman; pres. of China (1943–49; 1950–).

Ch'ien Lung *or* **Kien Lung** (chē·ĕn' lōōng'), 1711–1799. Dynastic name *Kao Tsung* (gä'ô dzôông'). Chin. emp. (1736–96).

Chif'ley (chĭf'lĭ), Joseph Benedict, 1885–1951. Australian labor polit.

Chi·ka·ma·tsu Mon·za·e·mon (chē·kä·mä·tsōō mŏn·zä·ĕ·mŏn), 1653–?1724. *The Shakespeare of Japan.* Jap. dram.

Child (chīld), Francis James, 1825–1896. Am. philologist.

Chip'pen·dale (chĭp'ĕn·dāl), Thomas, 1718?–1779. Eng. cabinetmaker.

Chit'ty (chĭt'ĭ), Joseph, 1776–1841. Eng. lawyer & legal writer.

Choate (chōt), Joseph Hodg'es (hŏj'ĕz; -ĭz), 1832–1917. Am. lawyer & diplomat.
—, Rufus, 1799–1859. Am. jurist.
Choi'seul', de (dĕ shwä'zûl'), Duc (dük) É'tienne' (ā'tyĕn') Fran'çois' (frän'swä'), 1719–1785. Fr. statesman.
Cho'pin' (shō'păN'; *Angl.* shō'păn), Fré'dé'ric' (frā'dā'rēk') Fran'çois' (frän'swä'), 1810–1849. Pol. pianist & composer.
Chou En-lai (jō' ĕn'lī'), 1898– . Chin. Communist.
Chré'tien' de Troyes' (krā'tyäN' dĕ trwä'), 12th cent. Also *Chres'-tien'* (krā'tyäN'). Fr. trouvère.
Christ, Je'sus. See JESUS.
Chris'tian X (krĭs'chăn; krĭst'yăn), 1870–1947. King of Denmark (1912–47).
Chris·ti'na (krĭs·tē'nà), 1626–1689. *Dau. of Gustavus Adolphus.* Queen of Sweden (1632–54).
Chris'tophe' (krēs'tôf'), Hen'ri' (äN'rē'), 1767–1820. King of Haiti (1811–20).
Chris'ty (krĭs'tĭ), Howard Chan'dler (chăn'dlēr), 1873–1952. Am. painter & illustrator.
Chrys'os·tom (krĭs'ŭs·tŭm; krĭ·sŏs'tŭm), Saint John, 345?–407. Church father & patriarch of Constantinople (398–404).
Church'ill (chûrch'[h]ĭl), John, 1650–1722. 1st Duke of *Marl'bor-ough* (môl'bŭ·rŭ; -brŭ; märl'-). Eng. gen.
—, Randolph Henry Spencer, 1849–1895. Lord *Randolph Churchill.* Brit. statesman.
—, Winston, 1871–1947. Am. nov.
—, Winston Leonard Spencer, 1874– . *Son of Lord Randolph.* Brit. statesman; prime min. (1940–45; 1951–55).
Chu Yüan-chang (jōō' yü·än'jäng'), 1328–1398. *Hung Wu* (hōong' wōō'). Chin. emp. (1368–98); founder of Ming dynasty.
Cia'no (chä'nō), Con'te (kōn'tä) Ga'le·az'zo (gä'lā·ät'tsō), 1903–1944. *Ciano di Cor·tel·laz'zo* (dĕ kōr·tāl·lät'tsō); *son-in-law of Mussolini.* Ital. statesman.
Cib'ber (sĭb'ēr), Col'ley (kŏl'ĭ), 1671–1757. Eng. dram. & actor; poet laureate (1730–57).
Cic'er·o (sĭs'ēr·ō), Marcus Tul'li·us (tŭl'ĭ·ŭs), 106–43 B.C. Rom. statesman, orator, & author.
Cid, the (thĕ sĭd'), 1040?–1099. *Ro·dri'go* (rrō·thrē'gō) or *Ruy* (rōō·ē') *Di'az de Bi·var'* (thē'äth thä vē·vär'). Span. soldier & hero.
Ci·ma·bu'e (chē·mä·bōō'ā), Gio·van'ni (jō·vän'nē), ab. 1240–ab. 1302. Properly *Cen'ni di Pe'po* (chän'nē dĕ pā'pō). Florentine painter.
Ci'mon (sī'mŏn), 507?–449 B.C. Athenian gen. & statesman.
Cin·cin·na'tus (sĭn'sĭ·nā'tŭs; -nā'tŭs), Lucius Quinc'ti·us (kwĭngk'-shĭ·ŭs; -shŭs), 5th cent. B.C. Rom. gen. & statesman.
Clar'en·don, Earl of. See Edward HYDE.
Clark (klärk), Champ (chămp), 1850–1921. *James Beau'champ* (bē'-chăm) *Clark.* Am. polit.
—, George Rogers, 1752–1818. Am. soldier & frontiersman.
—, Mark Wayne, 1896– . Am. gen.
—, Thomas Campbell, 1899– . Am. jurist.
—, William, 1770–1838. Am. explorer (with Meriwether Lewis).
Clarke (klärk), Charles Cow'den (kou'd'n), 1787–1877, and his wife Mary Victoria Cow'den-Clarke', 1809–1898. Eng. Shakespearean scholars.
—, Samuel, 1675–1729. Eng. philos.
Clau'di·us (klô'dĭ·ŭs). Rom. gens, including: **Ap'pi·us** (ăp'ĭ·ŭs) **Clau'di·us Cras'sus** (krăs'ŭs), consul (471 & 451 B.C.) & decemvir (451–450); **Ap'pi·us Clau'di·us Cae'cus** (sē'kŭs), censor (312–307 B.C.), consul (307 & 296), & dictator, who began building of the Appian Way (312 B.C.).
— **I**, 10 B.C.–54 A.D. *Ti·be'ri·us* (tĭ·bēr'ĭ·ŭs) *Clau'di·us Dru'sus* (drōō'sŭs) *Ne'ro* (nē'rō; nēr'ō) *Ger·man'i·cus* (jûr·măn'ĭ·kŭs; jēr-). Rom. emp. (41–54).
— **II**, 214–270. *Marcus Aurelius Claudius Gothicus.* Rom. emp. (268–270).
Clau'se·witz, von (fôn klou'zĕ·vĭts), Karl, 1780–1831. Prussian gen. & writer on military science.
Clay (klā), Henry, 1777–1852. Am. statesman & orator.
—, Lucius Du·Bi'gnon (dōō·bĭn'yŭn), 1897– . Am. gen.
Cle·an'thes (klē·ăn'thēz), 3d cent. B.C. Greek Stoic philos.
Cle·ar'chus (klē·är'kŭs), fl. 408–401 B.C. Greek soldier; gov. of Byzantium.
Cleis'the·nes (klīs'thĕ·nēz) or **Clis'the·nes** (klĭs'-), fl. ab. 507 B.C. Athenian statesman.
Cle'men'ceau' (klā'mäN'sō'; *Angl.* klĕm'ĕn·sō), Georges (zhôrzh), 1841–1929. *The Tiger.* Fr. statesman.
Clem'ens (klĕm'ĕnz), Samuel Lang'horne (lăng'hôrn), 1835–1910. Pseud. *Mark Twain* (märk twān). Am. humorist.
Clem'ent (klĕm'ĕnt). Name of 14 popes; esp. **VII** (Giu'lio [jōō'lyō] de' Me'di·ci [dä mâ'dē·chē; *Angl.* mĕd'ē-, mā'dē-]), 1478–1534 (pope 1523–34).
— **of Al'ex·an'dri·a**, 150?–?220. *Titus Fla'vi·us* (flā'vĭ·ŭs) *Clem'ens* (klĕm'ĕnz; klē'mĕnz). Greek Christian theol. & church father.
Cle·om'e·nes (klē·ŏm'ĕ·nēz). Name of 3 kings of Sparta; esp. **III** (reigned 235–219 B.C.).
Cle'o·pat'ra (klē'ō·păt'rà; -pā'trà; -pä'trà), 69–30 B.C. Queen of Egypt (51–49; 48–30).
Clerk'-Max'well, James. See James Clerk MAXWELL.
Cleve'land (klēv'lănd), (Stephen) Gro'ver (grō'vēr), 1837–1908. 22d & 24th pres. of the U. S. (1885–89; 1893–97).
Clin'ton (klĭn't'n; -tŭn), De Witt (dĕ wĭt'), 1769–1828. Am. statesman.
—, George, 1739–1812. Vice-pres. of the U. S. (1805–12).
—, Sir Henry, 1738?–1795. Eng. gen. in Am. Revolution.
Clis'the·nes. See CLEISTHENES.
Clive (klīv), Robert, 1725–1774. Baron *Clive of Plas'sey* (plăs'ĭ). Brit. gen.; founder of the empire of Brit. India.
Cloots, de (dĕ klōts'), Baron, 1755–1794. *Jean Bap'tiste'* (bà'tēst') *du Val'-de-Grâce'* (dü väl'dĕ·gräs') *An'a·char'sis* (ăn'à·kär'sĭs; *Fr.* à'nä'kär'sēs') *Cloots.* Prussian-Fr. revolutionist.

Clough (klŭf), Arthur Hugh, 1819–1861. Eng. poet.
Clo'vis I (klō'vĭs; *Fr.* klô'vēs'); *Ger.* **Chlod'wig** (klōt'vĭk), 466?–511. Frankish king (481–511 Merovingian dynasty).
Clyde, Baron. See Colin CAMPBELL.
Cnut. See CANUTE.
Coates (kōts), Joseph Gordon, 1878–1943. N. Z. statesman.
Cobb (kŏb), Ir'vin (ûr'vĭn) Shrews'bur·y (shrōōz'bĕr·ĭ; shrōz'-; -brĭ), 1876–1944. Am. journalist & humorist.
Cob'bett (kŏb'ĕt; -ĭt), William, 1763–1835. *Peter Por'cu·pine* (pôr'-kū·pīn). Eng. polit. writer.
Cob'den (kŏb'dĕn), Richard, 1804–1865. Eng. statesman & econ.
Cob'ham, Lord. See Sir John OLDCASTLE.
Coc'teau' (kŏk'tō'), Jean, 1891– . Fr. author.
Co'dy (kō'dĭ), William Frederick, 1846–1917. *Buf'fa·lo Bill* (bŭf'à·lō bĭl'). Am. scout, Indian fighter, & showman.
Coen (kōōn), Jan (yän) Pie'ters·zoon (pē'tēr·sŭn; -sôn; -sōn), 1587–1629. Du. colonial gov.; founder of Du. East Indian empire.
Cœur' de Li'on'. See RICHARD I of Eng.
Cof'fin (kôf'ĭn), Robert Peter Tristram, 1892–1955. Am. author.
Co·han' (kō·hăn'), George Michael, 1878–1942. Am. actor, dram., & producer.
Cohn (kōn), Fer'di·nand (fĕr'dĕ·nänt) Ju'li·us (yōō'lĕ·ŏŏs), 1828–1898. Ger. botanist; called founder of bacteriology.
Coke (kōōk), Sir Edward, 1552–1634. *Lord Coke.* Eng. jurist.
Col'bert' (kôl'bâr'), Jean Bap'tiste' (bà'tēst'), 1619–1683. Fr. statesman & financier.
Col'cord (?kŏl'kĕrd), Lincoln Ross, 1883–1947. Am. writer.
Cole (kōl), Thomas, 1801–1848. Am. (Eng.-born) painter.
Cole'pep'er (kŭl'pep'ēr) or **Cul'pep'er** (kŭl'-), Thomas, 1635–1689. 2d Baron *Colepeper of Thores'way* (thôrz'wā). Eng. colonial administrator; gov. of Virginia.
Cole'ridge (kōl'rĭj), Samuel Taylor, 1772–1834. Eng. poet.
Col'et (kŏl'ĕt; -ĭt), John, 1466?–1519. Eng. theol. & scholar.
Col'fax (kŏl'făks), Schuy'ler (skī'lēr), 1823–1885. Vice-pres. of the U. S. (1869–73).
Co'li'gny' or **Co'li'gni', de** (dĕ kô'lē'nyē'), Gas'pard' (gàs'pär') (II), 1519–1572. Fr. admiral & Huguenot leader.
Col'lier (kŏl'yēr; kŏl'ĭ·ēr), Jeremy, 1650–1726. Eng. clergyman & reformer.
—, John Payne, 1789–1883. Eng. editor.
—, Peter Fen'e·lon (fĕn''l·ŭn), 1849–1909. Am. publisher.
Col'lins (kŏl'ĭnz), Michael, 1890–1922. Irish revolutionist.
—, William, 1721–1759. Eng. poet.
—, (William) Wil'kie (wĭl'kĭ), 1824–1889. Eng. nov.
Col'man (kŏl'mŭn), George, 1732–1794. Eng. dram.
Co·lum'ba (kō·lŭm'bà); *Irish* **Col'um** (kŭl'ŭm) or **Col'um·cille** (kŭl'ŭm·kĭl), Saint, 521–597. *Apostle of Cal'e·do'nia* (kăl'ē·dōn'yà; -dō'nĭ·à). Irish missionary in Scot.
Co·lum'bus (kō·lŭm'bŭs), Christopher; *Ital.* Cri·sto'fo·ro (krēs·tô'-fō·rō) **Co·lom'bo** (kō·lōm'bō); *Span.* Cris·tó'bal (krēs·tō'väl) **Co·lón'** (kō·lôn'), 1451–1506. Ital. navigator; disc. Am.
Col'vin (kŏl'vĭn), Sir Sidney, 1845–1927. Eng. author & critic.
Co·me'ni·us (kō·mē'nĭ·ŭs); *Czech* **Ko'men·ský** (kô'mĕn·skē), John Amos, 1592–1670. Czech theol. & educ.
Co'mines' or **Com'mines'** or **Com'mynes'** or **Co'mynes', de** (dĕ kô'-mēn'), Phi'lippe' (fē'lēp'), 1447?–?1511. Sire (sēr) *d'Ar'gen'ton'* (där'zhäN'tôN'). Fr. chronicler.
Com'mo·dus (kŏm'ō·dŭs), Lucius Ae'li·us (ē'lĭ·ŭs) Aurelius, 161–192. Rom. emp. (180–192).
Comp'ton (kŏmp'tŭn), Arthur Hol'ly (hŏl'ĭ), 1892– . Am. physicist.
—, Karl Taylor, 1887–1954. *Bro. of A. H.* Am. physicist.
Com'stock (kŭm'stŏk), Anthony, 1844–1915. Am. reformer.
Comte (kôNt), Au'guste' (ō'güst'), 1798–1857. *I'si'dore'* (ē'zē'dôr') Auguste Ma'rie' (mä'rē') Fran'çois' (frän'swä') Comte. Fr. math. & philos.
Co'mynes'. See COMINES.
Co'nant (kō'nănt), James Bryant, 1893– . Am. chem.; pres. of Harvard U. (1933–53); ambassador to West Germany (1955–).
Con·dé', de (dĕ kôN'dā'), Prince, 1621–1687. *Louis II de Bour'bon'* (dĕ bōōr'bôN'); *the Great Condé;* Duc (dük) *d'En'ghien'* (däN'găN'). Fr. gen.
Con'don (kŏn'dŭn), Edward Uh'ler (ū'lēr), 1902– . Am. physicist.
Con'dor'cet', de (dĕ kôN'dôr'sĕ'), Mar'quis' (mär'kē'), 1743–1794. *Ma'rie' (mä'rē') Jean An'toine' (äN'twän') Ni'cho'las' (nē'kô'lä') de Ca'ri'tat' (dĕ kä'rē'tà'). Fr. math., philos., & polit.
Con·fu'cius (kŏn·fū'shŭs; -shĭ·ŭs); *Chin.* **K'ung Fu-tzŭ** or **Kung Fu-tse** (kōōng' fōō'dzū'), ab. 551–479 B.C. Chin. philos.
Con'greve (kŏn'grēv; kŏng'grēv), William, 1670–1729. Eng. dram.
Con'ing·ham (kŭn'ĭng·ăm; *in U. S., also* -hăm), Sir Arthur, 1895–1948. Brit. air marshal.
Con'rad (kŏn'răd), Joseph, 1857–1924. Orig. *Te·o'dor* (tĕ·ô'dôr) *Jó'zef* (yōō'zĕf) *Kon'rad* (kôn'rät) *Kor'ze·niow'ski* (kôr'zĕ·nyôf'-skē). Brit. (Ukrainian-born) nov.
Con'sta·ble (kŭn'stà·b'l; kŏn'-), John, 1776–1837. Eng. painter.
Cons'tant' (kôNs'täN'), Ben'ja·min' (băN'zhà'măN'), 1845–1902. Fr. painter.
— **de Re·becque'** (dĕ rĕ·bĕk'), Benjamin, 1767–1830. Fr. writer & polit.
Con'stan·tine I (kŏn'stăn·tīn; -tēn), 280?–337. *The Great.* Rom. emp. (306–337).
— **I**, 1868–1923. King of Greece (1913–17; 1920–22).
Con·ta·ri'ni (kôn·tä·rē'nē). Venetian family, including esp. Ga'spa·ro (gäs'pä·rō), 1485–1542, cardinal (1535) & diplomat.
Con'ti, de' (dä kôn'tē), Nic'co·lo (nēk'kô·lô), 15th cent. Venetian traveler & writer.
Cook (kōōk), Capt. James, 1728–1779. Eng. navigator & explorer.
Cooke (kōōk), Jay (jā), 1821–1905. Am. financier.
Coo'lidge (kōō'lĭj), (John) Calvin, 1872–1933. 30th pres. of the U. S. (1923–29).
—, Julian Lowell, 1873–1954. Am. math.

Coo′per (kŏŏ′pẽr; kŏŏp′ẽr), Anthony Ashley. See SHAFTESBURY.

—, Hugh Lincoln, 1865–1937. Am. engineer.

—, James Fen′i·more (fĕn′ĭ·mōr), 1789–1851. Am. nov.

—, Peter, 1791–1883. Am. manuf. & philanthropist.

Co·per′ni·cus (kṓ·pûr′nĭ·kŭs), Nic′o·la′us (nĭk′ṓ·lā′ŭs); *Pol.* Mi·kō′laj (mē·kō′lĭ) Ko·per′nik (kṓ·pĕr′nĕk) *or* Ni′klas (nē′kläs) Kop′per·nigk (kŏp′ẽr·nĭk), 1473–1543. Pol. (or Prussian) astron.; founder of modern astronomy.

Cop′ley (kŏp′lĭ), John Sin′gle·ton (sĭng′g'l·tŭn), 1738–1815. Am. portrait painter.

—, John Singleton, 1772–1863. *Son of prec.* Baron *Lynd′hurst* (lĭnd′hûrst). Eng. statesman.

Cop′pée′ (kŏ′pā′), Fran′çois′ (frän′swä′) É′dou·ard′ (ā′dwär′) Jo′a′chim′ (zhō′à·kĕm′), 1842–1908. Fr. author.

Co′que·lin′ (kŏ′klăn′), Be·noît′ (bĕ·nwä′) Cons′tant′ (kôNs′tän′), 1841–1909. Fr. actor.

Cor′co·ran (kôr′kŏ·răn), Thomas Gardiner, 1900– . Am. lawyer.

Cor′day′ (kôr′dā′), Char′lotte′ (shär′lŏt′), 1768–1793. *Marie Anne* (än) *Charlotte Corday d'Ar′mont′* (där′môN′). Fr. patriot; assassinated Marat.

Co′ri (kō′rĭ), Carl (kärl) Fer′di·nand (fĕr′dĭ·nänt), 1896– , and his wife, Ger′ty (gĕr′tĭ) The·re′sa (tẽ·rē′sà), *nee* Rad′nitz (rät′nĭts), 1896–1957. Am. (Czechoslovakian-born) biochemists.

Cor′i·o·la′nus (kôr′ĭ·ō·lā′nŭs; kŏ·rĭ′ō·lăn′ŭs), Ga′ius (gā′yŭs; gī′ŭs) *or* Gnae′us (nē′ŭs) Mar′ci·us (mär′shĭ·ŭs; -shŭs), 5th cent. B.C. Legendary Rom. hero.

Cor′neille′ (kôr′nā′y; -nāl′), Pierre, 1606–1684. Fr. dram.

Cor·ne′lia (kôr·nēl′yà; -nē′lĭ·à), 2d cent. B.C. *Mother of the Gracchi.* Rom. matron.

—, d. 67? B.C. *Wife of Julius Caesar.*

Cor·ne′li·us, von (fôn kôr·nā′lē·ŏŏs), Pe′ter (pā′tẽr), 1783–1867. Ger. painter.

Cor·nell′ (kôr·nĕl′), Ezra, 1807–1874. Am. financier & philanthropist.

—, Katharine, 1898– . Am. actress.

Corn·wal′lis (kôrn·wŏl′ĭs), Charles, 1st Marquis, 1738–1805. Brit. gen. & statesman.

Co′ro·na′do (kō′rŏ·nä′thō; *Angl.* kŏr′ō·nä′dō), Fran·cis′co (frän·thēs′kō; -sēs′kō) Vás′quez (väs′kăth; -kās), 1510–1554. Span. explorer in New Mexico.

Co′rot′ (kō′rō′), Jean Bap′tiste′ (bà′tēst′) Ca′mille′ (kà′mē′y′), 1796–1875. Fr. painter.

Cor·reg′gio (kôr·rĕd′jō; *Angl.* kŏ·rĕj′ō, -rĕj′ĭ·ō), 1494–1534. *An·to′nio* (än·tō′nyō) *Al·le′gri da Correggio* (äl·lā′grē dä). Ital. painter.

Cor′tes (kôr′tĕz) *or* Cor′tez, Her·nan′do (hẽr·nän′dō), 1485–1547. Span. conqueror of Mexico.

Cos′grave (kŏz′grāv), William Thomas, 1880– . Irish statesman.

Cos′ta Ca·bral′, da (thä kŏsh′tà kà·vräl′), An·tô′nio (äNn·tô′nyŏŏ) Ber·nar′do (vẽr·när′dŏŏ), 1803–1889. Con′de (kŏNn′dễ) *de Tho·mar′* (thễ tŏŏ·mär′). Port. statesman.

Cos′tel·lo (kŏs′tĕl·ō), John Aloysius, 1891– . Irish lawyer; prime min. of Eire (1948–51).

Cot′ton (kŏt′ʼn), Charles, 1630–1687. Eng. author & trans.

—, John, 1584–1652. Eng. Puritan clergyman in Am.

Co′ty′ (kŏ′tē′), Re·né′ (rẽ·nā′), 1882– . Fr. lawyer; 2d pres. of 4th Republic (1947–).

Cou′lomb′, de (dễ kŏŏ′lôN′; *Angl.* kŏŏ·lŏm′), Charles Au′gus′tin′ (ō′gŭs′tăn′), 1736–1806. Fr. physicist.

Cour′bet′ (kŏŏr′bĕt′), Gus′tave′ (gŭs′tàv′), 1819–1877. Fr. painter.

Cou′sin′ (kŏŏ′zăn′), Vic′tor′ (vēk′tôr′), 1792–1867. Fr. philos.

Co′var·ru′bias (kō′vär·rŏŏ′vyäs), Mi·guel′ (mē·gĕl′), 1904–1957. Mex. illustrator.

Cov′er·dale (kŭv′ẽr·dāl), Miles, 1488?–1569. Eng. Bible trans.

Cow′ard (kou′ẽrd), Noel Pierce, 1899– . Eng. actor & dram.

Cowl (koul), Jane, 1884–1950. Orig. *Cowles* (koulz). Am. actress.

Cow′ley (kou′lĭ), Abraham, 1618–1667. Eng. poet.

Cow′per (kŏŏ′pẽr), William, 1731–1800. Eng. poet.

Cox′ey (kŏk′sĭ), Jacob Sech′ler (sĕk′lẽr), 1854–1951. Am. polit. reformer.

Crabbe (krăb), George, 1754–1832. Eng. poet.

Craig·av′on (krāg·ăv′ŭn), 1st Viscount, 1871–1940. *James Craig* (krāg). Brit. statesman; 1st prime min. of N. Ireland (1921–40).

Crai′gie (krā′gĭ), Sir William Alexander, 1867–1957. Brit. philologist & lexicographer.

Craik (krāk), Dinah Maria, 1826–1887. Nee *Mu′lock* (mū′lŏk). Eng. nov.

Cram (krăm), Ralph Adams, 1863–1942. Am. architect & author.

Cran′borne, Viscount. See under CECIL.

Crane (krān), (Robert) Bruce, 1857–1937. Am. painter.

—, Stephen, 1871–1900. Am. writer.

—, Walter, 1845–1915. Eng. painter & illustrator.

Cran′mer (krăn′mẽr), Thomas, 1489–1556. Eng. reformer; archbishop of Canterbury.

Crash′aw (krăsh′ô), Richard, 1613?–1649. Eng. poet.

Cras′sus (krăs′ŭs), Marcus Li·cin′i·us (lĭ·sĭn′ĭ·ŭs), 115?–53 B.C. *Di′ves* (dī′vēz). Rom. polit.

Craw′ford (krô′fẽrd), Francis Marion, 1854–1909. Am. nov.

—, Thomas, 1813?–1857. Am. sculptor.

Cré′bil′lon′ (krā′bē′yôN′), 1674–1762. Pseud. of *Pros′per* (prôs′pâr′) *Jo′lyot′* (zhō′lyō′). Fr. dram.

Cre′mer (krē′mẽr), Sir William Ran′dal (răn′d'l), 1838–1908. Eng. pacifist.

Crève′cœur′, de (dễ krĕv′kûr′), Mi′chel′ (mē′shĕl′) Guil′laume′ (gē′yōm′) Jean, 1735–1813. Am. (Fr.-born) essayist.

Crich′ton (krī′t′n), James, 1560?–1582. *The Admirable Crichton.* Scot. prodigy.

Crile (krīl), George Washington, 1864–1943. Am. surgeon.

Cripps (krĭps), Sir Richard Staf′ford (stăf′ẽrd), 1889–1952. Brit. lawyer & socialist statesman.

Cri′spi (krēs′pē), Fran·ce′sco (frän·chās′kō), 1819–1901. Ital. statesman; premier (1887–91; 1893–96).

Cro′ce (krō′chä), Be·ne·det′to (bā·nā·dāt′tō), 1866–1952. Ital. philos. & statesman.

Crock′ett (krŏk′ĕt; -ĭt), David, 1786–1836. *Davy.* Am. frontiersman & polit.

Croe′sus (krē′sŭs), d. 546 B.C. King of Lydia (560–546); amassed vast wealth.

Cro′ker (krō′kẽr), John Wilson, 1780–1857. Brit. essayist & editor.

Cro′mer, 1st Earl of. See Evelyn BARING.

Cromp′ton (krŭmp′tŭn), Samuel, 1753–1827. Eng. inventor of the spinning mule.

Crom′well (krŏm′wĕl; -wĕl; krŭm′-), Oliver, 1599–1658. Eng. gen. & statesman; lord protector of Eng. (1653–58).

—, Richard, 1626–1712. *Son of Oliver.* Lord protector (1658–59).

—, Thomas, 1485?–1540. Earl of *Es′sex* (ĕs′ĕks; -ĭks). Eng. statesman.

Cro′nin (krō′nĭn), Archibald Joseph, 1896– . Eng. physician & nov.

Cron·jé′ (krôn·yā′), Piet (pēt) Ar·nol′dus (är·nôl′dŭs), 1840?–1911. Boer leader & gen.

Crookes (krŏŏks), Sir William, 1832–1919. Eng. physicist & chem.

Cross (krŏs), Wilbur Lucius, 1862–1948. Am. educ. & polit.

Croth′ers (krŭth′ẽrz), Samuel Mc·Chord′ (mà·kôrd′), 1857–1927. Am. clergyman & essayist.

Cru′den (krŏŏ′d′n), Alexander, 1701–1770. Scot. concordist.

Cruik′shank (krŏŏk′shăngk), George, 1792–1878. Eng. caricaturist & illustrator.

Cud′worth (kŭd′wûrth; -wẽrth), Ralph, 1617–1688. Eng. philos.

Cul′pep′er. See COLEPEPER.

Cu′nha, da (dá kŏŏ′nyà), Tris·tão′ (trẽsh·toun′), 1460?–?1540. Port. navigator & explorer.

Cun′ning·ham (kŭn′ĭng·ăm; *in U.S., also* -hăm), Sir Alan Gordon, 1887– . *Bro. of A.B.* Brit. gen.

—, Allan, 1784–1842. Scot. author.

—, Andrew Browne, 1883– . 1st Viscount *Cunningham of Hynd′hope* (hīnd′hōp). Brit. admiral.

—, Sir John Henry Da′cres (dā′kẽrz), 1885– . Brit. admiral.

Cu′rie′ (kü′rē′; *Angl.* kū·rē′), Ève (âv), 1904– . *Dau. of Marie & Pierre.* Fr. author.

—, Marie, 1867–1934. Nee (*Ma′rja* [mä′ryä]) *Sklo·dow′ska* (sklô·dôf′skà). Fr. (Pol.-born) chem.

—, Pierre, 1859–1906. *Husband of Marie.* Fr. chem.

—Jo′liot′. See JOLIOT-CURIE.

Cur′ri·er (kûr′ĭ·ẽr), Nathaniel, 1813–1888. Am. lithographer.

Cur′ry (kûr′ĭ), John Steu′art (stū′ẽrt), 1897–1946. Am. painter.

Cur′tin (kûr′tĭn), John, 1885–1945. Australian polit.; prime min. (1941–45).

Cur′tis (kûr′tĭs), Charles, 1860–1936. Vice-pres. of the U. S. (1929–33).

—, Cyrus Her′mann (hûr′măn) Kotzsch′mar (kŏch′mär), 1850–1933. Am. publisher.

—, George Tick′nor (tĭk′nẽr; -nôr), 1812–1894. Am. lawyer & writer.

—, George William, 1824–1892. Am. author.

Cur′tiss (kûr′tĭs), Glenn Hammond, 1878–1930. Am. aviator & inventor.

Cur′ti·us (kŏŏr′tsē·ŏŏs), Ernst (ĕrnst), 1814–1896. Ger. philologist & archaeologist.

Cur′wen (kûr′wĕn), John, 1816–1880. Eng. music teacher.

Cur′zon (kûr′z′n), George Nathaniel, 1859–1925. 1st Baron & 1st Marquis *Curzon of Ked′le·ston* (kĕd′'l·stŭn; kĕl′stŭn). Eng. statesman; viceroy of India (1899–1905).

Cush′ing (kŏŏsh′ĭng), Caleb, 1800–1879. Am. lawyer & diplomat.

—, Harvey, 1869–1939. Am. surgeon.

Cush′man (kŏŏsh′măn), Charlotte Saunders, 1816–1876. Am. actress.

Cus′ter (kŭs′tẽr), George Armstrong, 1839–1876. Am. gen.

Cuth′bert (kŭth′bẽrt), Saint, 635?–687. Eng. monk.

Cu′vier′ (kü′vyä′; *Angl.* kū′vĭ·ā, kŏŏ′vĭ·ā), Baron Georges (zhôrzh) Lé′o′pold′ (lā′ō′pôld′) Chré′tien′ (krā′tyăN′) Fré′dé′ric′ (frā′dā′rēk′) Da′go′bert′ (dä′gō′bär′), 1769–1832. Fr. naturalist.

Cyn′e·wulf (kĭn′ễ·wŏŏlf; *A.-S.* kün′ễ-) *or* Cyn′wulf (kĭn′wŏŏlf) *or* Kyn′e·wulf, fl. 750. Anglo-Saxon poet.

Cyp′ri·an (sĭp′rĭ·ăn), Saint, d. 258. *Thas′ci·us* (thăsh′ĭ·ŭs) *Cae·cil′i·us* (sễ·sĭl′ĭ·ŭs; -sĭl′yŭs) *Cyp′ri·a′nus* (sĭp′rĭ·ā′nŭs). Christian martyr; bishop of Carthage (248–258).

Cy′ran·kie′wicz (tsĭ′rän·kyễ′vĕch), Jó′zef (yŏŏ′sĕf), 1911?– . Pol. polit.

Cy′ra′no′ de Ber′ge·rac′, de (dễ sễ′rà′nō′ dễ bĕr′zhễ·räk′), Sa′vi′nien′ (sà′vē′nyäN′), 1619–1655. Fr. poet & soldier.

Cyr′il (sĭr′ĭl), Saint, 827–869. *Con′stan·tine* (kŏn′stăn·tĭn; -tēn). Slavic apostle.

Cy′rus (sī′rŭs), 600?–529 B.C. *The Great* or *the Elder.* King of Persia (550–529).

—, 424?–401 B.C. *The Younger.* Pers. prince & satrap.

D

☞ D′, De, Du, etc. For many names beginning with these elements, see the specific family names.

Da′guerre′ (dà′gĕr′), Louis Jacques (zhàk) Man′dé′ (mäN′dā′), 1789–1851. Fr. painter; inventor of the daguerreotype.

Dahl′gren (däl′grĕn), John Adolphus Bernard, 1809–1870. Am. admiral.

Da′kin (dā′kĭn), Henry Drys′dale (drĭz′dāl), 1880–1952. Am. chem.

Da′la′dier′ (dà′lä′dyā′), É′dou·ard′ (ā′dwär′), 1884– . Fr. statesman.

D′Al′bert (*Ger.* däl′bĕrt; *Eng.* dăl′bẽrt), Eu·gen′ (oi·gān′), 1864–1932. Scot. pianist & composer.

D′Al′bi·ac (dôl′bĭ′ăk), John Henry, 1894– . Brit. air marshal.

Dale (dāl), Sir Henry Hal′lett (hăl′ĕt; -ĭt), 1875– . Eng. physiol.

—, Sir Thomas, d. 1619. Eng. colonial administrator in Virginia (1611–16).

Da·lén′ (dá·lān′), Nils (nĭls) Gus′taf (gŭs′täv), 1869–1937. Swed. inventor.

Dal·hou′sie, Earl and Marquis of. See under RAMSAY.

Da'li (dä'lē), Sal'va·dor' (säl'vä·thôr'), 1904– . Span. painter; leader of surrealist school.

Dal'las (dăl'ăs), George Mifflin, 1792–1864. Vice-pres. of the U. S. (1845–49).

Dal·rym'ple (dăl·rĭm'p'l; dăl'rĭm'p'l), Sir James, 1619–1695. 1st Viscount *Stair* (stâr). Scot. jurist.

—, Sir John, 1673–1747. 2d Earl of *Stair*. Brit. gen. & diplomat.

Dal'ton (dôl't'n; -tŭn), Hugh, 1887– . Brit. lawyer & polit.

—, John, 1766–1844. Eng. chem. & physicist.

Da'ly (dā'lĭ), (John) Augustin, 1838–1899. Am. dram. & theater manager.

Dam (dăm), (Carl Pe'ter [kärl pĕ'tĕr]) Hen'rik (hĕn'rĕk), 1895– . Dan. biochem.

Da'mien' de Veus'ter' (dà·myăn' dĕ vûs'târ'; *Angl.* dā'mĭ·ĕn), Jo'seph' (zhō'zĕf'; *Angl.* jō'zĕf, -zĭf), 1840–1889. *Father Da'mi·en* (dā'mĭ·ĕn). Belg. R.C. missionary to lepers on Molokai.

Dam'o·cles (dăm'ō·klēz), 4th cent. B.C. Syracusan courtier.

Dam'pi·er (dăm'pĭ·ĕr; dămp'yĕr), William, 1652–1715. Eng. buccaneer & navigator.

Dam'rosch (dăm'rŏsh), Walter Jo·han'nes (jō·hän'ĕs), 1862–1950. Am. (Ger.-born) musician & conductor.

Da'na (dā'nà), Charles Anderson, 1819–1897. Am. newspaper editor.

—, Edward Salis'bur·y (sôlz'bĕr·ĭ; -brĭ), 1849–1935. Am. mineralogist.

—, James Dwight, 1813–1895. Am. geologist.

—, Richard Henry, 1815–1882. Am. lawyer & author.

Dane (dān), Clemence, 20th cent. Pseud. of *Winifred Ash'ton* (ăsh'tŭn). Eng. nov.

Dan'iel (dăn'yĕl), Samuel, 1562–1619. Eng. poet; poet laureate (1599–1619).

Dan'iels (dăn'yĕlz), Jo·se'phus (jō·sē'fŭs), 1862–1948. Am. journalist & statesman.

D'An·nun'zi·o (dän·nōōn'tsyō), Ga'bri·e'le (gä'brĕ·â'lâ), 1863–1938. Ital. author & soldier.

Dan'te (dăn'tē; *Ital.* dän'tā), 1265–1321. *Dante* (orig. *Du·ran'te* [dōō·rän'tā]) *A'li·ghie'ri* (ä'lē·gyâ'rē). Ital. poet.

Dan'ton' (dän'tôn'), Georges (zhôrzh) Jacques, 1759–1794. Fr. revolutionist.

Dare (dâr), Virginia, 1587–? 1st child born in Am. of Eng. parents.

Da·ri'us (dà·rī'ŭs). Name of 3 kings of Persia; esp. **I**, 558?–486 B.C. (reigned 521–486). *Darius Hys·tas'pis* (hĭs·tăs'pĭs); *the Great.*

Dar'lan' (där'län'), Jean Louis Xa'vier' (gzà'vyà') Fran'çois' (frän'swä'), 1881–1942. Fr. admiral.

Darn'ley (därn'lĭ), Lord, 1545–1567. *Henry Stewart* or *Stuart*; husband of Mary, Queen of Scots.

Dar'row (dăr'ō), Clarence Seward, 1857–1938. Am. lawyer & author.

Dar'win (där'wĭn), Charles Robert, 1809–1882. Eng. naturalist.

—, Erasmus, 1731–1802. *Grandfather of C. R.* Eng. physiol. & poet.

Dau'bi'gny' (dō'bē'nyē'), Charles (shàrl) Fran'çois' (frän'swä'), 1817–1878. Fr. painter.

Dau'det' (dō'dĕ'), Al'phonse' (àl'fôns'), 1840–1897. Fr. nov.

—, Lé'on' (lā'ôn'), 1867–1942. *Son of Alphonse.* Fr. journalist & writer.

Dav'e·nant or **D'Av'e·nant** (dăv'ĕ·nănt), Sir William, 1606–1668. Eng. poet & dram.; poet laureate (1638–68).

Dav'en·port (dăv'ĕn·pôrt), John, 1597–1670. Eng. clergyman; founder of New Haven colony.

Da'vid (dā'vĭd) **I**, 1084–1153. King of Scotland.

—, (dà'vēt'), Ge'rard (kā'rärt), 1450? or 1460?–1523. Du. painter.

Da'vid' (dā'vēd'), Jacques (zhàk) Louis, 1748–1825. Fr. painter.

— **d'An'gers'** (dän'zhà'), Pierre Jean, 1788–1856. Fr. sculptor.

Da'vid·son (dā'vĭd·s'n), Jo, 1883–1952. Am. sculptor.

Dá'vi·la y Pa·dil'la (dà've·lä ē pä·thē'[l]yä), A'gus·tín' (ä'gōōs·tēn'), 1562–1604. Mex. monk & hist.

Da'vis (dā'vĭs), Jefferson, 1808–1889. Am. statesman; pres. of Confed. States (1861–65).

—, Norman Hezekiah, 1878–1944. Am. financier & diplomat.

—, Owen, 1874–1956. Am. dram.

—, Richard Harding, 1864–1916. Am. author.

—, William Stearns (stûrnz), 1877–1930. Am. educ. & hist.

Da'vis·son (dā'vĭ·s'n), Clinton Joseph, 1881–1958. Am. physicist.

Da'vout' (dā'vōō'), Louis Ni'co·las' (nē'kō·lä'), 1770–1823. Duc (dük) *d'Au'er'staedt'* (dà'wĕr'stàt') & Prince *d'Eck'mühl'* (dĕk'mül'). Marshal of France.

Da'vy (dā'vĭ), Sir Hum'phry (hŭm'frĭ), 1778–1829. Eng. chem.

Dawes (dôz), Charles Gates, 1865–1951. Am. lawyer & financier; vice-pres. of the U. S. (1925–29).

Daw'son (dô's'n), Sir John William, 1820–1899. Canadian geologist.

— **of Penn** (pĕn), 1st Viscount, 1864–1945. *Bertrand Edward Dawson.* Eng. physician.

Day (dā), Edmund Ezra, 1883–1951. Am. educ.; pres., Cornell U. (1937–49).

—, Thomas, 1748–1789. Eng. author.

—, William Rufus, 1849–1923. Am. statesman & jurist.

De'ák (dĕ'äk), Fe'rencz (fĕ'rĕnts), 1803–1876. Hung. statesman.

Deane (dēn), Silas, 1737–1789. Am. lawyer & diplomat.

De·be·ney' (dĕ·bĕ·nā'), Ma'rie' (mà'rē') Eu'gène' (û'zhân'; ü'zhân'), 1864–1943. Fr. gen.

De·bierne' (dĕ·byern'), An'dré' (än'drā') Louis, 1874–1949. Fr. chem.

Debs (dĕbz), Eugene Victor, 1855–1926. Am. socialist.

De·bus'sy' (dĕ·bü'sē'; *Angl.* dĕ·bū'sĭ), Claude (klōd) A'chille' (à'shēl'), 1862–1918. Fr. composer.

De·bye' (dĕ·bī'), He'man (*sic?*) . . . *(illegible)* . . . Jo'seph (yō'sĕf) Wil'helm (vĭl'hĕlm), 1884– . Du.-born physicist in Am.

De Cas'se·res (dĕ kăs'ĕr·ĕs; -ĭs), Benjamin, 1873–1945. Am. journalist & poet.

De·ca'tur (dĕ·kā'tēr), Stephen, 1779–1820. Am. naval officer.

De·cazes' (dĕ·käz'), Duc (dük) É'lie' (ā'lē'), 1780–1860. Fr. jurist & statesman.

De Chair (dĕ shâr'), Sir Dudley Raw'son (rô's'n) Strat'ford (străt'fĕrd), 1864–1958. Brit. admiral; gov. of New S. Wales (1923–30).

De·ci·us (dē'shĭ·ŭs; -shŭs), 201–251. *Ga'ius* (gā'yŭs; gī'ŭs) *Mes'si·us* (mĕs'ĭ·ŭs) *Quin'tus* (kwĭn'tŭs) *Tra·ja'nus* (trà·jā'nŭs) *Decius.* Rom. emp. (249–251).

Deck'er, Thomas. See DEKKER.

Deep'ing (dēp'ĭng), George Warwick, 1877–1950. Eng. nov.

Def'fand', **du** (dü dĕ'fän'), Mar'quise' (mär'kēz'), 1697–1780. Nee (*Ma'rie'* [mà'rē']) *de Vi'chy'-Cham'rond'* (dĕ vē'shē'shän'rôn'). Fr. noblewoman.

De·foe' (dĕ·fō'; dē-), Daniel, ab. 1660–1731. Eng. journalist & nov.

De For'est (dĕ fŏr'ĕst; -ĭst), Lee, 1873– . Am. inventor.

De·gas' (dĕ·gä'), Hi'laire' (ē'lâr') Ger'main' (zhĕr'măN') Ed'gar' (ĕd'gär'), 1834–1917. Fr. impressionist painter.

de Gaulle (dĕ gōl'), Charles An'dré' (än'drā') Jo'seph' (zhō'zĕf') Ma'rie' (mà'rē'), 1890– . Fr. gen.; interim pres. of France (1945–46).

De·grelle' (dĕ·grĕl'), Lé'on' (lā'ôn'), 1906– . Belg. polit.

Dek'ker or **Deck'er** (dĕk'ĕr), Thomas, 1572?–?1632. Eng. dram.

De Ko'ven (dĕ kō'vĕn), (Henry Louis) Reginald, 1859–1920. Am. composer.

de Kruif (dĕ krīf'), Paul, 1890– . Am. bacteriol. & author.

De·la·croix' (dĕ·là·krwä'), Ferdinand Vic'tor' (vēk'tôr') Eu'gène' (û'zhân'; ü'zhân'), 1799–1863. Fr. painter.

De la Mare (dĕ là mâr'), Walter John, 1873–1956. Eng. poet & nov.

De·land' (dĕ·lănd'), Margaret, 1857–1945. Nee (*Mar'ga·ret'ta Wade* [mär'gà·rĕt'à wād]) *Campbell.* Am. nov.

De La Rey (dĕ là rī'), Ja·co'bus (yà·kō'bŭs) Her'cu·les (hĕr'kŭ·lēz), 1847–1914. Boer gen. & statesman.

De·la·roche' (dĕ·là·rôsh'), (Hip'po·lyte' [ē'pō'lēt']) Paul, 1797–1856. Fr. painter.

de la Roche (dĕ là rôsh'), Ma'zo (mā'zō), 1885– . Canadian nov.

De·la·vigne' (dĕ·là·vēn'y'), Ca'si'mir' (kà'zē'mēr'), 1793–1843. Fr. poet & dram.

De La Warr (dĕl'à·wĕr'), Baron, 1577–1618. *Thomas West*; Lord *Del'a·ware* (dĕl'à·wâr'). Eng. colonial administrator in Am.

Del'cas·sé' (dĕl'kà·sā'), The'o'phile' (tā'ō'fēl'), 1852–1923. Fr. statesman.

De·led'da (dà·lĕd'dä), Gra'zia (grä'tsyä), 1875–1936. Ital. nov.

De'li·us (dē'lĭ·ŭs; dēl'yŭs), Frederick, 1863–1934. Eng. composer.

Del'lin·ger (dĕl'ĭn·jēr), John Howard, 1886– . Am. radio engineer.

De Long (dĕ lŏng'), George Washington, 1844–1881. Am. naval officer & explorer.

De·lorme' or **de l'Orme** (dĕ·lôrm'), Phi'li'bert' (fē'lē'bâr'), 1515?–1570. Fr. architect.

De·mar'çay' (dĕ·màr'sā'), Eu'gène' (û'zhân'; ü'zhân'), 1852–1903. Fr. chem.

De Mille (dĕ mĭl'), Cec'il (sĕs''l) Blount (blŭnt), 1881– . Am. motion-picture producer.

De·moc'ri·tus (dē·mŏk'rĭ·tŭs), b. ab. 460 B.C. *The Laughing Philosopher.* Greek philos.

De Mor'gan (dĕ môr'găn), William Frend (frĕnd), 1839–1917. Eng. artist & nov.

De·mos'the·nes (dē·mŏs'thĕ·nēz), 385?–322 B.C. Athenian orator & statesman.

Den'feld (dĕn'fĕld), Lou'is (lōō'ĭ) E'mil (ā'mĭl), 1891– . Am. admiral.

De'ni'ker' (dā'nē'kâr'), Jo'seph' (zhō'zĕf'), 1852–1918. Fr. anthropologist.

Den'is or **Den'ys** (sänt dĕn'ĭs; *Fr.* săN' dĕ·nē'), Saint, 3d cent. A.D. 1st bishop of Paris; patron saint of France.

Dent (dĕnt), Joseph Mal'a·by (măl'à·bĭ), 1849–1926. Eng. publisher.

De·pew' (dĕ·pū'), Chauncey Mitchell, 1834–1928. Am. lawyer & polit.

De Quin'cey (dĕ kwĭn'sĭ; -zĭ), Thomas, 1785–1859. Eng. author.

De·rain' (dĕ·răN'), An'dré' (än'drā'), 1880–1954. Fr. painter.

d'Er'lan'ger' (dĕr'län'zhä'), Baron Frederic A., 1868–1943. Brit. composer.

Der·vish' Pa·sha' (dĕr·vĕsh' pä·shä'), Ib·ra·him' (ĭb·rä·hĭm'), 1817–1896. Turk. gen.

Der·zha'vin (dyĕr·zhä'vyĭn), Ga·vri·il' (gá·vryĭ·ēl') Ro·ma'no·vich (rŭ·mä'nŭ·vyĭch), 1743–1816. Russ. poet.

De·saix' de Vey'goux' (dĕ·zĕ' dĕ vä'gōō'), Louis Charles (shàrl) An'toine' (äN'twän'), 1768–1800. Fr. gen.

Des·argues' (dā'zärg'), Gé'rard' (zhā'rär'), 1593–1662. Fr. math.

Des·cartes' (dā·kärt'; *Fr.* dā'kärt'), René, 1596–1650. Lat. *Re·na'tus* (rē·nā'tŭs) *Car·te'si·us* (kär·tē'zhĭ·ŭs; -zhŭs). Fr. math. & philos.

de Se·ver'sky (dĕ sĕ·vĕr'skĭ), Alexander Pro·cof'ieff (*Russ.* prŭ·kôf'yĕf), 1894– . Am. (Russ.-born) aeronautical engineer.

Des'mond (dĕz'mŭnd), Shaw, 1877– . Irish author.

Des'mou'lins' (dā'mōō'läN'), Ca'mille' (kà'mēy'), 1760–1794. *Lu'cie'* (lü'sē') *Sim'plice'* (săN'plēs') *Camille Be·noît'* (bĕ·nwä') *Desmoulins.* Fr. revolutionist.

de So'to (dĕ sō'tō; *Span.* dā sō'tō), Her·nan'do (ĕr·nän'dō) or Fer·nan'do (fĕr·nän'dō), 1500?–1542. Span. explorer in Am.

Des'saix' (dā'sĕ'), Comte (kôNt) Jo'seph' (zhō'zĕf') Ma'rie' (mà'rē'), 1764–1834. Fr. gen. under Napoleon.

Des'sa'lines' (dā'sà'lēn'), Jean Jacques (zhàk), 1758–1806. Emp. as Jacques I of Haiti (1804–06).

De·taille' (dĕ·tä'y'), (Jean Bap'tiste' [bà'tēst']) É'dou·ard' (ā'dwàr'), 1848–1912. Fr. painter.

Deus Ra'mos (dĕ'ōōs rä'mōōsh), João (zhwouN), 1830–1896. Port. poet.

de Va·le'ra (dĕv'à·lâr'à), Ea'mon (ā'mŭn), 1882– . Irish polit.; prime min. of Ireland (1937–48; 1951–54).

de Vere (dĕ vēr'), Aubrey Thomas, 1814–1902. Irish poet.

Dev'er·eux (dĕv'ĕr·ōō; -ōōks), Robert, 1566–1601. 2d Earl of *Es'sex* (ĕs'ĕks; -ĭks). Eng. soldier & courtier.

Dev'ers (dĕv'ĕrz), Jacob Loucks (louks), 1887– . Am. gen.

De Vin'ne (dĕ vĭn'ē), Theodore Low (lō), 1828–1914. Am. printer.

De Vo'to (dĕ vō'tō), Bernard Augustine, 1897–1955. Am. author.

De Vries (dĕ vrēs'), Hu'go (hü'kō), 1848–1935. Du. botanist.

Dew'ar (dū'ĕr), Sir James, 1842–1923. Scot. chem.

De Wet (dĕ vĕt'), Chris'ti·aan (krĭs'tē·än') Ru'dolph (rü'dôlf'), 1854–1922. Boer soldier & polit.

Dew'ey (dū'ĭ), George, 1837–1917. Am. admiral.
—, John, 1859–1952. Am. philos. & educ.
—, Mel'vil (mĕl'vĭl), 1851–1931. Am. librarian.
—, Thomas Edmund, 1902– . Am. lawyer & polit.
De Witt (dĕ vĭt'), Jan (yän), 1625–1672. Du. statesman.
Dia'ghi·lev (dyä'gĭ-lyĕf'), Ser·gei' (sylĭr-gā'ĭ) Pa·vlo'vich (pŭ·vlô'vyĭch), 1872–1929. Russ. ballet producer & art critic.
Di'as or **Di'az** (dē'ásh), Bar'tho·lo·meu' (bär'tōō·lōō·mā'ōō), 1450?–1500. Port. navigator; disc. Cape of Good Hope.
Dí'az (dē'äts), Ar·man'do (är·män'dō), 1861–1928. Du'ca del'la Vit·to'ria (dōō'kä däl'lä vēt·tô'ryä). Ital. gen.; marshal of Italy (1920).
Dí'az (dē'äs), Por·fi'rio (pôr·fē'ryō), 1830–1915. Jo·sé' de la Cruz (hō·sā' thä lä krōōs') Porfirio. Mex. gen.; pres. of Mexico (1877–80; 1884–1911).
Dí'az de Bi·var'. See CID.
Dick (dĭk), George Frederick, 1881– . Am. physician.
Dick'ens (dĭk'ĕnz; -ĭnz), Charles John Huf'fam (hŭf'm), 1812–1870. Boz (bŏz). Eng. nov.
Dick'in·son (dĭk'ĭn·s'n), Emily Elizabeth, 1830–1886. Am. poet.
—, John, 1732–1808. Am. statesman.
Di'de·rot' (dē'drō'), De·nis' (dē·nē'), 1713–1784. Fr. encyclopedist.
Die'sel (dē'zĕl), Ru'dolf (rōō'dôlf), 1858–1913. Ger. mechanical engineer.
Diez (dēts), Frie'drich (frē'drĭk) Chri'sti·an (krĭs'tē·än), 1794–1876. Ger. philologist.
Dig'by (dĭg'bĭ), Sir Ken'elm (kĕn'ĕlm), 1603–1665. Eng. naval commander, diplomat, & author.
Dill (dĭl), Sir John Greer (grēr), 1881–1944. Brit. gen.
Dil'lon (dĭl'ŭn), John, 1851–1927. Irish nationalist polit.
Di·mi'trov (dĭ·mē'trôf), Ge·or'gi (gā·ôr'gĭ), 1882–1949. Bulgarian Communist.
Dim'net' (dēm'nĕ'), Er'nest' (ĕr'nĕst'), 1866–1954. Fr. abbé & writer.
Din·wid'die (dĭn·wĭd'ĭ; dĭn'wĭd'ĭ), Robert, 1693–1770. Eng. colonial administrator in Am.
Di'o·cle'tian (dī'ō·klē'shăn), 245–313. Ga'ius (gā'yŭs; gī'ŭs) Au·relius Va·le'ri·us (vä·lēr'ĭ·ŭs) Di'o·cle'ti·a'nus (dī'ō·klē'shĭ·ā'nŭs). Rom. emp. (284–305).
Di·og'e·nes (dī·ŏj'ē·nēz), 412?–323 B.C. Greek Cynic philos.
Di·o·ny'si·us (dī'ō·nĭsh'ĭ·ŭs; -nĭsh'ŭs; -nĭs'ĭ·ŭs; -nī'sĭ·ŭs), 430?–?367 B.C. The Elder. Greek tyrant of Syracuse (405–367).
— The Younger. Tyrant of Syracuse (367–356; 347–344 B.C.).
— **Ex·ig'u·us** (ĕg·zĭg'ū·ŭs; ĕks·ĭg'-), 6th cent. Christian monk; introduced method of reckoning the Christian era.
— **of Al'ex·an'dri·a** (ăl'ĕg·zăn'drĭ·à; ăl'ĭg-; Brit. also -zän'-), Saint, 3d cent. Theol. & bishop of Alexandria (247).
— **of Hal'i·car·nas'sus** (hăl'ĭ·kär·năs'ŭs), d. ab. 7 B.C. Greek scholar.
Di·rac' (dĭ·răk'), Paul Adrien Maurice, 1902– . Eng. physicist.
Dis'ney (dĭz'nĭ), Walter Elias, 1901– . Am. producer of animated motion-picture cartoons.
Dis·rae'li (dĭz·rā'lĭ), Benjamin, 1804–1881. 1st Earl of Bea'cons·field (bē'kŭnz·fēld; bĕk'ŭnz-; the former appears to have been the earl's own pron.; the latter is the local pron. for the town in Buckinghamshire from which the title comes); Diz'zy (dĭz'ĭ). Brit. polit. & author; prime min. (1868; 1874–80).
Dit'mars (dĭt'märz), Raymond Lee, 1876–1942. Am. naturalist.
Dix, Dorothy. See Elizabeth Meriwether GILMER.
Dix (dĭks), Dorothea Lynde, 1802–1887. Am. humanitarian.
Dix'on (dĭk's'n), Jeremiah, fl. 1763–1767. Eng. surveyor in Am.
Dmow'ski (d'môf'skē), Roman, 1864–1939. Pol. statesman.
Dö'be·rei'ner (dö'bĕ·rī'nĕr), Jo·hann' (yō·hän' yō'hän) Wolf'gang (vôlf'gäng), 1780–1849. Ger. chem.
Do'bie (dō'bĭ), James Frank, 1888– . Am. folklorist.
Do'brée (dō'brē), Bon'a·my (bŏn'à·mĭ), 1891– . Eng. scholar.
Dob'son (dŏb's'n), (Henry) Austin, 1840–1921. Eng. poet & essayist.
Dodds (dŏdz), Harold Willis, 1889– . Am. educ.; pres., Princeton U. (1933–).
Dodge (dŏj), Mary Elizabeth, 1831–1905. Nee Mapes (māps). Am. author.
Dodg'son (dŏj's'n), Charles Lut'widge (lŭt'wĭj), 1832–1898. Pseud. Lewis Carroll. Eng. math. & story writer.
Dods'ley (dŏdz'lĭ), Robert, 1703–1764. Eng. author & bookseller.
Doe'nitz (dö'nĭts), Karl, 1891– . Ger. grand admiral.
Doi'sy (doi'zĭ), Edward Adelbert, 1893– . Am. biochem.
Dole (dōl), San'ford (săn'fĕrd) Bal'lard (băl'ĕrd), 1844–1926. Am. jurist; pres. (1894–98) & gov. (1900–03) of Hawaii.
Doll'fuss (dôl'fōōs), Eng'el·bert (ĕng'ĕl·bĕrt), 1892–1934. Austrian statesman.
Do'magk (dō'mäk), Ger'hard (gĕr'härt), 1895– . Ger. chem.
Do·me·ni·chi'no, Il (ēl dō·bē·nē·kē'nō), 1581–1641. Do·me'ni·co (dō·mā'nē·kō) Zam·pie'ri (tsäm·pyā'rē). Ital. painter.
Dom'i·nic (dŏm'ĭ·nĭk), Saint, 1170–1221. Do·min'go (dō·mēng'gō) de Guz·mán' (thä gōōth·män'). Span.-born founder of the Dominican order of friars.
Do·mi'tian (dō·mĭsh'ăn; -ĭ·ăn), 51–96. Ti'tus (tī'tŭs) Fla'vi·us (flā'vĭ·ŭs) Do·mi'ti·a'nus (dō·mĭsh'ĭ·ā'nŭs) Augustus. Rom. emp. (81–96).
Don'ald·son (dŏn'l·ds'n), Jesse Monroe, 1885– . Am. government administrator.
Don·a·tel'lo (dŏn'à·tĕl'ō; Ital. dō·nä·tĕl'lō), 1386?–1466. Do·na'to di (dō·nä'tō dē) Nic'co·lò' di Bet'to Bar'di (nēk'kō·lō' dē bāt'tō bär'dē). Ital. sculptor.
Don·i·zet'ti (dŏn'ĭ·zĕt'ĭ; Ital. dō·nē·dzät'tē), Ga'e·ta'no (gä'ē·tä'nō), 1797–1848. Ital. composer.
Donne (dŭn; dŏn), John, ab. 1572–1631. Eng. divine & poet.
Don'o·van (dŏn'ō·văn), William Joseph, 1883– . Wild Bill. Am. lawyer & gen.
Doo'lit'tle (dōō'lĭt''l), James Harold, 1896– . Am. aviator & gen.
Dopp'ler (dŏp'lĕr), Chri'sti·an (krĭs'tē·än) Jo·hann' (yō·hän' yō'hän), 1803–1853. Austrian physicist & math.
Do'ré' (dō'rā'), Paul Gus'tave' (güs'täv'), 1833–1883. Fr. illustrator & painter.

Dor·nier' (dôr·nyä'), Claude (klōd), 1884– . Ger. airplane builder.
Dorr (dôr), Thomas Wilson, 1805–1854. Am. lawyer & polit.
Dor'set, 1st Earl of. See Thomas SACKVILLE.
Dos Pas'sos (dŭs päs'ŭs), John Rod·er·i'go (rŏd·rē'gō), 1896– . Am. writer.
Do'sto·ev'ski (dŏs'tŭ·yĕv'skĭ; -yĕf'skĭ; Russ. dŭ·stŭ·yĕf'skĭ), Fë'dor (fyŏ'dĕr) Mi·khai'lo·vich (myĭ·kī'lŭ·vyĭch), 1821–1881. Russ. nov.
Dou, Dow, or **Douw** (dou), Ge'rard (kā'rärt), 1613–1675. Du. painter.
Dou'gher·ty (dō'hĕr·tĭ), Denis J., 1865–1951. Am. cardinal (1921).
Dough'ty (dou'tĭ), Charles Montagu, 1843–1926. Eng. poet & traveler.
Doug'las (dŭg'lăs), John Shol'to (shŏl'tō), 1844–1900. 8th Marquis & Earl of Queens'ber'ry (kwēnz'bĕr'ĭ; -bĕr·ĭ; -brĭ). Scot. boxing patron.
—, Lewis Williams, 1894– . Am. polit. & diplomat.
—, Norman, 1868–1952. Eng. author.
—, Stephen Arnold, 1813–1861. Am. polit.
—, William Orville, 1898– . Am. jurist.
—, (William) Sholto, Baron, 1893– . Brit. air marshal.
Doug'lass (dŭg'lăs), Frederick, 1817?–1895. Orig. Frederick Augustus Washington Bailey. Am. abolitionist.
Dou'mer' (dōō'mâr'), Paul, 1857–1932. Pres. of France (1931–32).
Dou'mergue' (dōō'mĕrg'), Gas'ton' (gàs'tôn'), 1863–1937. Fr. statesman; pres. of France (1924–31).
Douw or **Dow,** Gerard. See Gerard DOU.
Dow'den (dou'd'n), Edward, 1843–1913. Irish literary critic.
Dow'ie (dou'ĭ), John Alexander, 1847–1907. Scot.-born religious leader in Am.
Downes (dounz), (Edwin) O'lin (ō'lĭn), 1886–1955. Am. music critic.
Dow'son (dou's'n), Ernest Christopher, 1867–1900. Eng. lyric poet.
Doyle (doil), Sir Arthur Co'nan (kō'năn), 1859–1930. Brit. physician, nov., & detective-story writer.
D'Oy'ly Carte. See CARTE.
Drach'mann (dräk'män), Hol'ger (hōl'gĕr) Hen'rik (hĕn'rĕk) Her'holdt (här'hōlt), 1846–1908. Dan. author.
Dra'co (drā'kō), late 7th cent. B.C. Athenian lawgiver.
Drake (drāk), Sir Francis, 1540?–1596. Eng. navigator & admiral.
Dra'per (drā'pĕr), Henry, 1837–1882. Am. astron.
—, John William, 1811–1882. Am. (Eng.-born) scientist & writer.
Dray'ton (drā't'n), Michael, 1563–1631. Eng. poet.
—, William Henry, 1742–1779. Am. Revolutionary polit.
Drei'ser (drī'sĕr; -zĕr; the first was his own pron.), Theodore, 1871–1945. Am. editor & nov.
Drew (drōō), John, 1827–1862. Am. (Irish-born) actor.
—, John, 1853–1927. Son of prec. Am. actor.
Drey'fus (drā'fŭs; drī'fŭs; Fr. drā'füs'), Alfred, 1859–1935. Fr. army officer.
Driesch (drēsh), Hans A'dolf (ä'dôlf) E'du·ard (ā'dōō·ärt), 1867–1941. Ger. biologist & philos.
Drink'wa'ter (drĭngk'wô'tĕr; -wôt'ĕr), John, 1882–1937. Eng. poet & dram.
Drou'et' d'Er'lon' (drōō'ĕ' dĕr'lôn'), Comte (kônt) Jean Bap'tiste' (bà'tēst'), 1765–1844. Fr. gen.; marshal of France.
Drum (drŭm), Hugh Aloysius, 1879–1951. Am. gen.
Drum'mond (drŭm'ŭnd), Henry, 1851–1897. Scot. clergyman & writer.
—, William, 1585–1649. 1st Laird of Haw'thorn'den (hô'thôrn'dĕn). Scot. poet.
—, William Henry, 1854–1907. Canadian (Irish-born) poet.
Dru'sus (drōō'sŭs), 38–9 B.C. Ne'ro (nē'rō; nĕr'ō) Claudius Drusus Ger·man'i·cus (jŭr·măn'ĭ·kŭs). Rom. gen.
Dry'den (drī'd'n), John, 1631–1700. Eng. poet & dram.; poet laureate (1670–89).
Du Bar'ry (dū bär'ĭ; Fr. dü bà'rē'), Com'tesse' (kôn'tĕs'), 1746 (or 1743?)–1793. Marie Jeanne Bé'cu' (bā'kü'). Mistress of Louis XV of France.
Du'bois' (dü'bwä'; -bwà'), Paul, 1829–1905. Fr. sculptor.
—, Thé'o'dore' (tā'ō'dôr'), 1837–1924. Fr. composer.
Du Bois (dōō bois'), William Edward Burg'hardt (bûrg'härd), 1868– . Am. educ. & writer.
Du Cange (dü känzh'), Charles du Fresne (dü frân'), Sieur (syûr), 1610–1688. Fr. scholar & glossarist.
Du Chail'lu' (dü shä'yü'; Angl. dŭ shăl'ū), Paul (pôl) Bel'lo'ni' (bĕ'lō'nē'), 1831–1903. Am. (Fr.-born) explorer in Africa.
Du'com'mun' (dü'kô'mûn'), É'lie' (ā'lē'), 1833–1906. Swiss journalist.
Du'de·vant', Aurore. See George SAND.
Dud'ley (dŭd'lĭ), Robert, 1532?–1588. 1st Earl of Leices'ter (lĕs'tĕr). Eng. courtier.
—, Thomas, 1576–1653. Colonial administrator in Massachusetts Bay colony.
Duf'fer·in and A'va (dŭf'ĕr·ĭn, ä'vä), 1st Marquis of, 1826–1902. Frederick Temple Hamilton-Temple-Black'wood (-blăk'wŏod). Brit. diplomat & administrator.
Duff'–Gor'don (dŭf'gôr'd'n), Lady Lu'cie (lū'sĭ) or Lucy, 1821–1869. Eng. author.
Duf'fy (dŭf'ĭ), Sir Charles Gav'an (găv'ăn), 1816–1903. Irish nationalist & Australian polit.
—, Francis Patrick, 1871–1932. Father Duffy. Am. (Canadian-born) R.C. clergyman.
Du'for, Earl of. See David LLOYD GEORGE.
Du Gard (dü gàr'), Ro'ger' (rô'zhā') Mar'tin' (màr'tăn'), 1881– . Fr. nov.
Du Gues'clin' (dü gĕ'klăn'), Ber'trand' (bĕr'trän'), 1320?–1380. Constable of France.
Du'ha'mel' (dü'à'mĕl'), Georges (zhôrzh), 1884– . Pseud. De·nis' (dē·nē') Thé've·nin' (tāv'năn'). Fr. writer.
Duke (dūk), Benjamin Newton, 1855–1929, & his bro., James Buchanan, 1856–1925. Am. tobacco industrialists.
Dul'les (dŭl'ĕs), John Foster, 1888– . Am. lawyer & diplomat.
Du'mas' (dü'mä'; Angl. dōō·mä', dōō'mä), A'lex·an'dre (à'lĕk'sän'dr'), 1802–1870. Dumas père (pâr). Fr. nov. & dram.
—, Alexandre, 1824–1895. Dumas fils (fēs). Fr. nov. & dram.

du Mau'ri·er (dŭ mô'rĭ·ā; *Fr.* dü mô'ryā'), Daphne, 1907–
. *Granddaughter of George.* Eng. nov.
—, George Louis Pal·mel'la (păl·mĕl'à) Bus'son' (bü·sôn'), 1834–1896. Brit. artist & nov.
Du'mou'riez' (dü'mōō'ryā'), Charles Fran'çois' (frän'swà'), 1739–1823. Fr. gen.
Du'nant' (dü'näN'), Jean Hen'ri' (äN'rē'), 1828–1910. Swiss philanthropist; founder of Red Cross.
Dun'bar (dŭn'bär), Paul Laurence, 1872–1906. Am. poet.
Dun·bar' (dŭn·bär'), William, 1460?–?1520. Scot. poet.
Dun'can (dŭng'kăn), Isadora, 1878–1927. Am. dancer.
Dun·das' (dŭn·dăs'; dŭn'dăs), Henry, 1742–1811. 1st Viscount *Melville* and Baron *Dun·i'ra* (dŭn·ēr'à). Brit. statesman.
Dun·lop' (dŭn·lŏp'; dŭn'lŏp), John Boyd (boid), 1840–1921. Scot. inventor.
Dun·more' (dŭn·mōr'), 4th Earl of, 1732–1809. *John Murray.* Scot. colonial administrator in Am.
Dunne (dŭn), Fin'ley (fĭn'lĭ) Peter, 1867–1936. Am. humorist.
Du·nois', de (dü·nwà'), Jean, Comte (kôNt), 1403?–1468. *The Bastard of Or·lé'ans'* (ôr'lā'äN'; *Angl.* ôr'lē·ănz). Fr. gen.
Dun·sa'ny (dŭn·sā'nĭ), 18th Baron, 1878–1957. *Edward John More'ton* (môr't'n) *Drax* (drăks) *Plun'kett* (plŭng'kĕt; -kĭt); Lord *Dunsany.* Irish poet & dram.
Duns Sco'tus (dŭnz skō'tŭs), John, 1265?–?1308. Scot. scholastic theol.
Dun'stan (dŭn'stăn), Saint, 925?–988. Archbishop of Canterbury (961).
Du'pleix' (dü'plĕks'; *Angl.* dū·plĕks', -plāks'), Marquis Jo'seph' (zhô'zĕf') Fran'çois' (fräN'swà'), 1697–1763. Fr. colonial administrator in India.
Du·ples'sis'-Mor'nay'. See Philippe de MORNAY.
Du Pont (dü pôN'; *Angl.* dū pŏnt'), É'leu'thère' (ā'lû'târ') I're'née' (ē'rā·nā'), 1771–1834. *Son of P. S. Du Pont de Nemours.* Am. (Fr.-born) industrialist.
—, Samuel Francis, 1803–1865. *Nephew of prec.* Am. admiral.
Du Pont de Ne·mours' (dü pôN' dĕ nĕ·mōōr'; *Angl.* dū pŏnt' dĕ nĕ·mōōr'), Pierre Sa'mu·el' (sà'mü·ĕl'), 1739–1817. Fr. econ. & statesman.
Du·pré' (dü'prā'), Jules, 1811–1889. Fr. painter.
Du·quesne' (dü'kān'; *Angl.* dū·kān'), Marquis A'bra'ham' (à'brà'âm'), 1610–1688. Fr. naval officer.
Du·rant' (dū·rănt'), William James, 1885–
. Am. educ. & writer.
Dü'rer (dü'rẽr), Al'brecht (äl'brĕkt), 1471–1528. Ger. painter & engraver.
D'Ur'fey (dûr'fĭ), Thomas, 1653–1723. Eng. song writer & dram.
Du·roc' (dü·rôk'), Gé'raud' (zhā'rō') Chris'tophe' (krēs'tôf') Mi'chel' (mē'shĕl'), 1772–1813. Duc (dük) *de Fri'u·li* (dē frē'ōō·lē; frē·ōō'lē). Fr. gen. under Napoleon.
Du'ruy' (dü'rü·ē'), Vic'tor (vĕk'tôr'), 1811–1894. Fr. hist.
Du'se (dōō'zā), E·le·o·no'ra (ā·lā·ô·nō'rà), 1859–1924. Ital. actress.
Du'tra (dōō'trà), Eu·ri'co (ā·ōō·rē'kōō) Gas·par' (gàs·pär'), 1885–
. Brazilian gen.; pres. of Brazil (1946–51).
Du'val' (dü'väl'), Paul, 1850?–1906. *Pseud. Jean Lor'rain'* (lô'răN'). Fr. author.
Du've·neck (dōō'vĕ·nĕk), Frank, 1848–1919. *Orig. Frank Deck'er* (dĕk'ẽr). Am. artist.
Dvo'řák (dvôr'zhäk), An'ton (än'tôn), 1841–1904. Czech composer.
Dwight (dwīt), Timothy, 1752–1817. Am. clergyman; pres., Yale U. (1795–1817).
—, Timothy, 1828–1916. *Grandson of prec.* Am. clergyman; pres., Yale U. (1886–98).
Dyce (dīs), Alexander, 1798–1869. Scot. editor.
Dy'er (dī'ẽr), John, 1700?–1758. Brit. poet.
Dyk'stra (dĭk'strà), Clarence Addison, 1883–1950. Am. educ.; pres., U. of Wisconsin (1937–45).
Dzer·zhin'ski (dyĭr·zhĕn'skĭ), Fe'liks (fyä'lyĭks) Ed·mun'do·vich (ĕd·mōōn'dŭ·vyĭch), 1877–1926. Russ. polit.

E

Eads (ēdz), James Buchanan, 1820–1887. Am. engineer.
Ea'ker (ā'kẽr), Ira Clarence, 1896–
. Am. aviator & gen.
Eames (āmz), Emma, 1865–1952. Am. soprano.
Ear'hart (âr'härt), Amelia, 1898–1937. Am. aviator.
Ear'ly (ûr'lĭ), Ju'bal (jōō'băl) Anderson, 1816–1894. Am. Confed. gen.
East'man (ēst'măn), George, 1854–1932. Am. inventor & industrialist.
—, Max For'res·ter (fŏr'ĕs·tẽr; -ĭs·tẽr), 1883–
. Am. editor & writer.
Ea'ton (ē't'n), Theophilus, 1590–1658. Eng. colonial administrator in Am.; gov. of New Haven colony (1638–58).
—, Walter Prich'ard (prĭch'ẽrd), 1878–1957. Am. author & educ.
E'bert (ā'bẽrt), Frie'drich (frē'drĭk), 1871–1925. Ger. polit.; pres. of the Reich (1919–25).
Ec'cles (ĕk'l'z), Mar'ri·ner (măr'ĭ·nẽr) Stoddard, 1890–
. Am. banker & econ.
E'che·ga·ray' y Ei'za·guir're (ā'chä·gä·rä'ē ē ē'ē·thä·gēr'rē), Jo·sé' (hō·sā'), 1832–1916. Span. dram.
Eck (ĕk), Jo·hann' (yō·hän'; yō'hän), 1486–1543. *Orig. surname May'er* (mī'ẽr). Ger. R.C. theol.
Eck'er·mann (ĕk'ẽr·män), Jo·hann' (yō·hän'; yō'hän) Pe'ter (pā'tẽr), 1792–1854. Ger. writer.
Eck'hart (ĕk'härt); Eck'art, Eck'ardt, or Ec'card (ĕk'ärt); or Eck'e·hart (ĕk'ē·härt), Jo·han'nes (yō·hän'ĕs; -ĕs), 1260?–?1327. Ger. Dominican theol.; founder of Ger. mysticism.
Ed'ding·ton (ĕd'ĭng·tŭn), Sir Arthur Stanley, 1882–1944. Eng. astron.
Ed'dy (ĕd'ĭ), Mary Morse, 1821–1910. *Née Baker.* Founder of the Christian Science Church.
E'den (ē'd'n), (Robert) Anthony, 1897–
. Eng. statesman; prime min. (1955–57).
Edge'worth (ĕj'wûrth; -wẽrth), Maria, 1767–1849. Brit. nov.

Ed'in·burgh, Duke of. See under PHILIP.
Ed'i·son (ĕd'ĭ·s'n), Thomas Al'va (ăl'va), 1847–1931. Am. inventor.
Ed'mund (ĕd'mŭnd) *or* Ead'mund (*A.-S.* ā'àd·mŏŏnd) II, 980?–1016. *I'ron·side'* (ī'ẽrn·sīd'). King of the Eng. (1016).
Ed'ward (ĕd'wẽrd). Name of 8 post-Norman Eng. (Brit.) kings:
—— I, 1239–1307 (reigned 1272–1307). *Long'shanks'* (lŏng'shăngks').
—— II, 1284–1327 (reigned 1307–27).
—— III, 1312–1377 (reigned 1327–77).
—— IV, 1442–1483 (reigned 1461–70; 1471–83).
—— V, 1470–1483 (reigned 1483).
—— VI, 1537–1553 (reigned 1547–53). *Son of Henry VIII & Jane Seymour.*
—— VII, 1841–1910 (reigned 1901–10). *Albert Edward; son of Victoria.*
—— VIII, 1894–
 (reigned 1936; abdicated). Duke of *Wind'sor* (wĭn'zẽr); *son of George V.*
—, 1330–1376. *The Black Prince; son of Edward III.* Prince of Wales.
— *or* Ead'ward (*A.-S.* ā'àd·wärd), 1002?–1066. *The Confessor.* King of the Eng. (1042–66).
Ed'wards (ĕd'wẽrdz), Jonathan, 1703–1758. Am. theol.
Ed'win (ĕd'wĭn) *or* Ead'wi'ne (â'àd·wī'nē), 585?–633. King of Northumbria (617–633).
Eg'bert (ĕg'bẽrt), 775?–839. King of the West Saxons (802–839) & 1st king of the Eng. (828–839).
Eg'gle·ston (ĕg'l·stŭn), Edward, 1837–1902. Am. writer.
—, George Cary, 1839–1911. *Bro. of Edward.* Am. writer.
Eg'mont, d' (dĕk'mônt; *Angl.* dĕg'mŏnt, -mŭnt), La'mo'ral' (là'mô'ràl'), Comte (kôNt), 1522–1568. Flem. gen. & statesman.
Eh'ren·burg (ā'rĕn·bŏŏrk), Il·ya' (ĭl·yà') Gri·gor'ie·vich (gryĭ·gôr'yĕ·vyĭch), 1891–
. Russ. writer.
Ehr'lich (âr'lĭk), Paul (poul), 1854–1915. Ger. bacteriol.
Ei'chel·ber'ger (ī'kĕl·bûr'gẽr), Robert Lawrence, 1886–
. Am. gen.
Eif'fel' (ē'fĕl'; *Angl.* ī'fĕl), A'lex'an'dre (à'lĕk'säN'dr') Gus'tave' (güs'tàv'), 1832–1923. Fr. engineer.
Eijk'man (īk'män), Chris'ti·aan (krĭs'tē·än), 1858–1930. Du. hygienist.
Ein'stein (īn'stīn; *Ger.* īn'shtīn), Al'bert (ăl'bẽrt; *Ger.* äl'bẽrt), 1879–1955. Am. (Ger.-born) physicist.
Eint'ho'ven (īnt'hō'vĕn), Wil'lem (vĭl'ĕm), 1860–1927. Du. physiol.
Ei'sen·how'er (ī'z'n·hou'ẽr), Dwight David, 1890–
. Am. gen. of the army; 34th pres. of the U. S. (1953–
).
El'a·gab'a·lus. See HELIOGABALUS.
El'don (ĕl'dŭn), 1st Earl of, 1751–1838. *John Scott.* Eng. jurist.
El'ea·nor (ĕl'à·nẽr) of Aq'ui·taine (ăk'wĭ·tān'; ăk'wĭ·tān'; *Fr.* à'kē'tĕn'), 1122?–1204. Queen of Louis VII of France (divorced 1152) and of Henry II of Eng.
— of Cas·tile' (kăs·tēl'), d. 1290. Queen of Edward I of Eng.
— of Pro'vence' (prō'väNs'), d. 1291. Queen of Henry III of Eng.
El'gar (ĕl'gẽr; -gär), Sir Edward, 1857–1934. Eng. composer.
El'i·ot (ĕl'ĭ·ŭt; ĕl'yŭt), Charles William, 1834–1926. Am. educ.; pres., Harvard U. (1869–1909).
—, George, 1819–1880. *Pseud. of Mary Ann (or Marian) Evans.* Eng. nov.
—, Sir John, 1592–1632. Eng. statesman.
—, John, 1604–1690. *Apostle to the Indians.* Am. clergyman & missionary.
—, Thomas Stearns (stûrnz), 1888–
. Brit. (Am.-born) poet & critic.
E·liz'a·beth (ē·lĭz'à·bĕth) I, 1533–1603. *Dau. of Henry VIII & Anne Boleyn.* Queen of Eng. (1558–1603).
—— II, 1926–
. Elizabeth Al'ex·an'dra (ăl'ĕg·zăn'drà; ăl'ĭg-; Brit. also -zän'-) Mary; *dau. of George VI; wife of Prince Philip; mother of Prince Charles (b. 1948), heir apparent.* Queen of Gr. Britain (1952–
).
—, 1596–1662. *Queen of Hearts.* Queen of Frederick V of Bohemia.
—, 1900–
. *Elizabeth Angela Marguerite Bowes'-Ly'on* (bōz'-lī'ŭn). Queen of George VI of Gr. Britain.
—, 1843–1916. *Pseud. Car'men Syl'va (Romanian kär'mĕn sĕl'và; Ger.* kär'mĕn zül'và; *Angl.* kär'mĕn sĭl'và). Queen of Romania & writer.
—, *Pseud. of Countess Elizabeth Mary* RUSSELL.
— Pe·trov'na (pyĭ·trôv'nà), 1709–1762. Empress of Russia (1741–62).
El'len·bor'ough, 1st Baron. See under LAW.
El'li·ott (ĕl'ĭ·ŭt; ĕl'yŭt), Maxine, 1871–1940. *Pseud. of Jessie Der'mot* (dûr'mŭt). Am. actress.
El'lis (ĕl'ĭs), Alexander John, 1814–1890. *Orig. surname Sharpe* (shärp). Eng. philologist.
—, (Henry) Have'lock (hăv'lŏk; -lŭk), 1859–1939. Eng. psychol. & writer.
Ells'berg (ĕlz'bûrg), Edward, 1891–
. Am. engineer & naval officer.
Ells'worth (ĕlz'wûrth; -wẽrth), Lincoln, 1880–1951. Am. explorer.
—, Oliver, 1745–1807. Am. jurist.
El'man (ĕl'măn), Mi'scha (mē'shà), 1891–
. Am. (Russ.-born) violinist.
El'phin·stone (ĕl'fĭn·stōn; *Brit.* -stŭn), Mount·stu'art (mount·stū'ẽrt), 1779–1859. Brit. statesman in India.
—, William, 1431–1514. Scot. bishop & statesman.
El'y·ot (ĕl'ĭ·ŭt; ĕl'yŭt), Sir Thomas, 1490?–1546. Eng. scholar & diplomat.
El'ze·vir (ĕl'zĕ·vĭr; -vẽr) *or* El'ze·vier (ĕl'zĕ·vēr). Family of Du. printers, including esp. Louis, 1540?–1617, his son Bonaventure, 1583–1652, and his grandson Abraham, 1592?–1652.
Em'er·son (ĕm'ẽr·s'n), Ralph Waldo, 1803–1882. Am. essayist & poet.
Em'met (ĕm'ĕt; -ĭt), Robert, 1778–1803. Irish nationalist & rebel; hanged.
Em'mons (ĕm'ŭnz), De·los' (dĕ'lŏs') Carleton, 1888–
. Am. gen.
Em·ped'o·cles (ĕm·pĕd'ô·klēz), 5th cent. B.C. Greek philos. & statesman.

En·de·cott, En'di·cott (ĕn'dĭ·kŭt), John, 1589?–1665. Colonial gov. of Massachusetts.

Eng'els (ĕng'ĕls), Frie'drich (frē'drĭk), 1820–1895. Ger. socialist; collaborator with Karl Marx.

En·ver' Pa·sha' (ĕn·vĕr' pä·shä'), 1881?–1922. *Enver Bey* (bā). Turk. soldier & polit.

E·pam'i·non'das (ē·păm'ĭ·nŏn'dăs), 418?–362 B.C. Theban gen. & statesman.

Ep'ic·te'tus (ĕp'ĭk·tē'tŭs), 1st–2d cent. A.D. Greek Stoic philos. in Rome.

Ep'i·cu'rus (ĕp'ĭ·kū'rŭs), 342?–270 B.C. Greek philos.

Ep'stein (ĕp'stīn), Jacob, 1880– . Am. sculptor.

E·ras'mus (ē·răz'mŭs), Des'i·de'ri·us (dĕs'ĭ·dēr'ĭ·ŭs), 1466?–1536. *Ger'hard* (kā'rärt) *Ger'hards* (kā'rärts; kĕr'härts) or *Geert* (kärt) *Geerts* (kärts). Du. scholar.

Er'a·tos'the·nes (ĕr'ȧ·tŏs'thē·nēz), 3d cent. B.C. Greek astron. & geographer.

Erck'mann'-Cha'tri'an' (ĕrk'män'shä'trē'än'). Joint pseud. of *É'mile'* (ā'mēl') Erckmann, 1822–1899, and *A'lex'an'dre* (ȧ'lĕk'sän'dr') Chatrian, 1826–1890. Fr. authors.

Er'ic (ĕr'ĭk; ĕr'-; *Norw.* ā'rĕk), 10th cent. *The Red.* Norw. navigator; explored Greenland coast.

Er'ic·son (ĕr'ĭk·s'n), Leif (lāv); *Old Norse* **Leifr Eiriksson**, fl. 1000. *Son of Eric the Red.* Norw. mariner; disc. "Vinland."

Er'ics·son (ĕr'ĭk·s'n; *Swed.* ā'rĭk·sôn'), John, 1803–1889. Am. (Swed.-born) engineer & inventor.

E·rig'e·na (ē·rĭj'ē·nȧ), Jo·han'nes (jō·hăn'ēz; -ĕs) Sco'tus (skō'tŭs), 815?–?877. Scot.-Irish(?) philos. & theol.

Er·lan'der (ĕr·län'dĕr), Ta'ge (tä'gĕ) Frit'hiof (frĭt'yôf), 1901– . Swed. polit.

Er'lang·er (ûr'lăng'ĕr), Joseph, 1874– . Am. physiol.

Er'len·mey'er (ûr'lĕn·mī'ĕr), E'mil (ā'mēl), 1825–1909. Ger. chem.

Er'skine (ûr'skĭn), John, 1695–1768. Scot. jurist.

—, John, 1879–1951. Am. educ. & writer.

Er'vine (ûr'vĭn), St. John (*Brit.* sĭn'jŭn) Greer (grēr), 1883– . Irish dram. & nov.

Erz'ber'ger (ĕrts'bĕr'gĕr), Mat·thi'as (mä·tē'äs), 1875–1921. Ger. statesman.

E·se'nin (yĭ·syā'nyĭn), Ser·gei' (syĭr·gā'ĭ) A·le·ksan'dro·vich (ŭ·lyĭ·ksän'drŭ·vyĭch), 1895–1925. Russ. poet.

Es'par·te'ro (äs'pär·tā'rō), Bal'do·me'ro (bäl'dō·mā'rō), 1792–1879. Con'de (kôn'dā) *de Lu·cha'na* (thä lōō·chä'nä). Span. gen. & statesman.

Es·que'me·ling (ĕs·kwā'mĕ·lĭng). See EXQUEMELIN.

Es'sen, von (fôn ĕs'sĕn), Count Hans (häns) Hen'rik (hĕn'rĭk), 1755–1824. Swed. field marshal & statesman.

Es'sex, 2d Earl of. See DEVEREUX.

Es'taing', d' (dĕs'tăN'), Comte (kôNt) Jean Bap'tiste' (bȧ'tēst') Charles Hen'ri' (äN'rē') Hec'tor' (ĕk'tôr'), 1729–1794. Fr. admiral.

E'ste (ĕs'tā). Ital. princely family, beginning with *Al·ber'to* (äl·bĕr'tō) *Az'zo II* (äd'dzō), 996–1097, and ending with *Er'co·le III* (ĕr'kō·lā) *Ri·nal'do* (rē·näl'dō), 1727–1803.

Es'ter·ha'zy' (ĕs'tĕr·ä'zē'), Ma'rie' (mȧ'rē') Charles Fer'di'nand' (rō'bär'), Wal'sin' (väl'săN'), 1847–1923. Fr. army officer.

Es'tienne' (ĕs'tyĕN') or **É'tienne'** (ā'tyĕN'). Fr. family of printers and bookdealers, including esp. Hen'ri' I (äN'rē'), d. 1520, his son Ro'bert' (rō'bär'), 1503–1559, and Robert's son Henri II, 1528?–1598.

Es'ti'mé' (ĕs'tē'mā'), Du'mar'sais' (dü'mär'sē'), 1900–1953. Pres. of Haiti (1946–50).

Es'tour'nelles' de Cons'tant', d' (dĕs'tōōr'nĕl' dē kôNs'täN'), Baron Constant de Re·becque' (dē rē·bĕk'), 1852–1924. *Paul* (pôl) *Hen'ri'* (äN'rē') *Ben'ja'min'* (băN'zhä'măN') *Bal'luat'* (bȧ'lü·ȧ'). Fr. diplomat & polit.

Eth'el·bert (ĕth'ĕl·bĕrt) or **Æ'thel·bert** (äth'ĕl·bĕrt), 552?–616. King of Kent.

Eth'el·red (ĕth'ĕl·rĕd) or **Æ'thel·red** (äth'ĕl·răd') II, 968?–1016. *The Unready.* King of Eng. (978–1016).

Eth'er·ege (ĕth'ĕr·ĭj), Sir George, 1635?–?1691. Eng. dram.

Euck'en (oi'kĕn), Ru'dolf (rōō'dôlf) Chri'stoph (krĭs'tôf), 1846–1926. Ger. philos.

Eu'clid (ū'klĭd), fl. ab. 300 B.C. Greek geometer.

Eu·gene' (ū·jēn'; ū'jēn) *or* **Eu'gène'** (ū'zhäN'; ū'-), 1663–1736. *Fran'çois'* (fräN'swä') *Eugène de Sa'voie'-Ca'ri'gnan'* (dē sȧ'vwä'kȧ'rē'nyäN'), Prince of Savoy & Austrian gen.

Eu·gé'nie' (ū'zhā·nē'; ū'-), 1826–1920. *Eugénie Marie de Mon·ti'jo de Guz·mán'* (thä môn·tē'hō thä gōōth·män'). Wife of Napoleon III. Empress of Fr. (1853–71).

Eu'ler (oi'lẽr), Le'on·hard (lā'ōn·härt), 1707–1783. Swiss math. & physicist.

Eu'ler-Chel'pin, von (fôn oi'lẽr·kĕl'pĭn), Hans Au'gust (ou'gōōst) Si'mon (zē'mōn), 1873– . Swed. (Ger.-born) chem.

Eu·rip'i·des (ū·rĭp'ĭ·dēz), 480?–?406 B.C. Greek dram.

Eus'den (ūz'dĕn), Laurence, 1688–1730. Eng. poet; poet laureate (1718–30).

Eu·se'bi·us of Cae'sa·re'a (ū·sē'bĭ·ŭs, sē'zȧ·rē'ȧ; sĕs'ȧ·; sĕz'ȧ·), 260?–?340. Theol. & church hist.

Eu·sta'chio (ā·ōō·stä'kyō), Bar'to·lom·me'o (bär'tō·lōm·mā'ō), 1524?–1574. Lat. *Eu·sta'chi·us* (ū·stā'kĭ·ŭs). Ital. anatomist.

Ev'ans (ĕv'ănz), Sir Arthur John, 1851–1941. Eng. archaeologist.

—, Herbert Mc·Lean' (măk·lān'), 1882– . Am. anatomist & embryologist.

—, Mau'rice (mŏr'ĭs), 1901– . Eng. actor.

—, Rob'ley (rŏb'lĭ) Dun'gli·son (dŭng'glĭ·s'n), 1846–1912. Am. admiral.

—, Ru'dulph (rōō'dŭlf), 1878– . Am. sculptor.

Ev'arts (ĕv'ẽrts), William Maxwell, 1818–1901. Am. lawyer & statesman.

Ev'att (ĕv'ăt), Herbert Vere (vẽr), 1894– . Australian lawyer & statesman.

Eve'lyn (ēv'lĭn), John, 1620–1706. Eng. diarist.

Ev'er·ett (ĕv'ẽr·ĕt; -ĭt; ĕv'rĕt; -rĭt), Edward, 1794–1865. Am. clergyman & statesman.

E'vill (ē'v'l; -vĭl), Sir Douglas Claude Stra·thern' (strȧ·thĕrn'; strȧ·thûrn'), 1892– . Brit. air marshal.

E'wald *or* **E'vald** (ī'väl), Jo·han'nes (yōō·hän'ĕs), 1743–1781. Dan. poet & dram.

Ew'ell (ū'ĕl), Richard Stod'dert (stŏd'ĕrt), 1817–1872. Am. Confed. gen.

Ex'que·me·lin' (ĕks'kĕm·lăn'), A'lex'an'dre (ȧ'lĕk'sän'dr') O'li'vier' (ō'lē'vyä'), 1645?–1707. Fr. pirate, surgeon, & author.

Eyck, van (vän īk'), Hu'bert (hü'bĕrt) *or* Huy'brecht (hoi'brĕkt), 1366?–1426, and his bro. Jan (yän), 1370?–?1440. Flem. painters.

E·zek'iel (ē·zēk'yĕl; ē·zē'kĭ·ĕl), Moses Jacob, 1844–1917. Am. sculptor.

F

Fa'bi·us (fā'bĭ·ŭs; făb'yŭs), d. 203 B.C. *Quin'tus* (kwĭn'tŭs) *Fabius Max'i·mus* (măk'sĭ·mŭs) *Ver'ru·co'sus* (vĕr'ū·kō'sŭs; vĕr'ōō-) *Cunc·ta'tor* (kŭngk·tā'tẽr; -tôr). Rom. gen. against Hannibal.

Fa'bre (fä'br'), Jean Hen'ri' (äN'rē'), 1823–1915. Fr. entomologist.

Fad'i·man (făd'ĭ·măn), Clifton, 1904– . Am. writer & editor.

Fah'ren·heit (fä'rĕn·hīt; *Angl.* făr'ĕn-), Ga'bri·el (gä'brē·ĕl) Da'ni·el (dä'nē·ĕl), 1686–1736. Ger. physicist.

Fair'banks (fâr'băngks), Douglas, 1883–1939. Am. actor.

Fair'fax (fâr'făks), Thomas, 3d Baron, 1612–1671. Eng. gen.

—, Thomas, 6th Baron, 1692–1782. Proprietor in Virginia.

Fai'sal (fī'sắl) *or* **Fei'sal** (fī'sắl) *or* **Fei'sul** (fī's'l) I, 1885–1933. King of Syria (1920) and Iraq (1921–33).

— II, 1935–1958. King of Iraq (1939–1958).

Fa·lie'ri (fä·lyä'rē) *or* **Fa·lie'ro** (-rō), Ma·ri'no (mä·rē'nō), 1278?–1355. Doge of Venice (1354–55).

Fal'ken·hau'sen, von (fôn fäl'kĕn·hou'zĕn), Baron Lud'wig (lōōt'vĭk; lōōd'-), 1844–1936. Ger. gen.

Fal'ken·hayn, von (fôn fäl'kĕn·hīn), E'rich (ā'rĭk), 1861–1922. Ger. gen.

Fal'ken·horst, von (fôn fäl'kĕn·hôrst), Ni'ko·la'us (nē'kō·lä'ōōs; nē'kō·lous), 1885– . Ger. gen.

Falk'ner (fôk'nẽr), William. See FAULKNER.

Fal'la, de (dä fä'lyä), Ma·nuel' (mä·nwĕl'), 1876–1946. Span. composer.

Fal'lières' (fȧ'lyâr'), Clé'ment' (klā'mäN') Armand, 1841–1931. Fr. statesman; pres. of France (1906–13).

Fan'euil (făn''l; făn'yĕl; -ū·ĭl; *old-fashioned*, fŭn''l), Peter, 1700–1743. Am. merchant.

Far'a·day (făr'ȧ·dā; -dĭ), Michael, 1791–1867. Eng. chem. & physicist.

Fa·ri'na (fä·rē'nä), Sal'va·to're (säl'vä·tō'rä), 1846–1918. Ital. nov.

Fa'ri·nac'ci (fä'rē·nät'chē), Ro·ber'to (rō·bĕr'tō), 1892–1945. Ital. Fascist polit.

Far'man' (fär'mäN'), Hen'ri' (äN'rē'), 1874–1958. Fr. pioneer aviator & airplane manuf.

Far'mer (fär'mẽr), Fannie Merritt, 1857–1915. Am. cookery expert.

Far·ne'se (fär·nā'sā), A'les·san'dro (ä'läs·sän'drō), 1545–1592. Duke of *Par'ma* (pär'mä; *Ital.* -mä). Ital. gen. in Span. service.

Far'nol (fär'n'l), (John) Jef'fer·y (jĕf'rĭ; jĕf'ĕr·ĭ), 1878–1952. Eng. nov.

Fa·rouk' I. See FARUK I.

Far'quhar (fär'kwẽr; -kẽr), George, 1678–1707. Brit. dram.

Far'ra·gut (făr'ȧ·gŭt), David Glasgow, 1801–1870. Am. admiral.

Far'rand (făr'ănd), Livingston, 1867–1939. Am. educ.; pres., Cornell U. (1921–37).

Far'rar (făr'ẽr), Frederic William, 1831–1903. Eng. clergyman & writer.

Far·rar' (fȧ·rär'), Geraldine, 1882– . Am. soprano.

Far'rell (făr'ĕl), James Thomas, 1904– . Am. nov.

Fa·ruk' *or* **Fa·rouk' I** (fä·rōōk'), 1920– . King of Egypt (1936–52; abdicated).

Fat'i·ma (făt'ĭ·mä; *in U.S., usu.* fȧ·tē'mä), 606–632. *Dau. of Mohammed.*

Faulk'ner (fôk'nẽr), William, 1897– . Sometimes *Falk'ner.* American novelist.

Faunce (fôns), William Herbert Perry, 1859–1930. Am. clergyman; pres., Brown U. (1899–1929).

Faure (fôr), Fran'çois' (fräN'swä') Fé'lix' (fā'lēks'), 1841–1899. Fr. statesman; pres. of France (1895–99).

Faust (foust), Dr. Jo·hann' (yō·hän'; yō'hän), 1480?–?1540. *Jo·han'nes* (jō·hän'ēz; -ĕs) *Faus'tus* (fôs'tŭs). Ger. magician & astrologer.

Faus'ta (fôs'tä), 289–326. *Flavia Max·im'i·a'na* (măk·sĭm'ĭ·ä'nä) *Fausta. Wife of Constantine the Great.* Rom. empress.

Fawkes (fôks; *Brit. also* fŏks), Guy, 1570–1606. Eng. R.C. conspirator.

Faÿ (fä'y'), Ber'nard' (bĕr'nàr'), 1893– . Fr. hist.

Fa'yolle' (fȧ·yôl'), Ma'rie' (mȧ'rē') É'mile' (ā'mēl'), 1852–1928. Fr. gen.; marshal of France (1921).

Fech'ner (fĕk'nẽr), Gu'stav (gōōs'täf) The'o·dor (tā'ō·dōr), 1801–1887. Ger. physicist & psychol.

Fei'sal *or* **Fei'sul.** See FAISAL.

Fell'tham (fĕl'thăm) *or* **Felt'ham** (fĕl'thăm), Owen, 1602?–1668. Eng. writer.

Fé'ne·lon' (fān'lôN'), Fran'çois' (fräN'swä') de Sa'li'gnac' de La Mothe- (dē sȧ'lē'nyàk' dē là môt'-), 1651–1715. Fr. prelate & writer.

Fêng Yü-hsiang (fŭng' yü'shē·äng'), 1880–1948. *The Christian general.* Chin. gen.

Fer'ber (fûr'bẽr), Edna, 1887– . Am. writer.

Fer'di·nand (fûr'dĭ·nănd; -d'n·änd; *Ger.* fĕr'dē·nänt) I, 1503–1564. Holy Rom. emp. (1556–64).

— II, 1578–1637. King of Bohemia (1617–19) and of Hungary (1621–25); Holy Rom. emp. (1619–37).

— III, 1608–1657. King of Hungary (1625–55); Holy Rom. emp. (1637–57).

— I, 1861–1948. *Ma'xi·mi'li·an* (măk'sē·mē'lē·än) *Karl Le'o·pold* (lā'ō·pôlt) *Ma·ri'a* (mä·rē'ä). King of Bulgaria (1908–18).

—**I,** d. 1065. *The Great.* King of Navarre (1037–65); of Castile (1033); of León (1037); emp. of Spain (1056).

—**V** of Castile *or* **II** of Aragon, 1452–1516. *The Catholic.* King of Castile (1474–1504); of Aragon (1479–1516); of Naples (1504–16); founder of the Span. monarchy.

—**VII,** 1784–1833. King of Spain (1808; 1814–33).

Fe·rish·tah' (fẽ·rĭsh·tä'), Mo·ham'med (mŏ·hăm'măd) Ka'sim (kä'sĭm), 1550?–?1626. Pers. hist.

Fer'mat', de (dĕ fẽr'mà'), Pierre, 1601–1665. Fr. math.

Fer'mi (fãr'mē), En·ri'co (ãn·rē'kō), 1901–1954. Ital. physicist.

Fer·nán'dez (*Span.* fẽr·nän'dãth; *Angl.* fẽr·năn'dĕz), Juan (*Span.* hwän; *Angl.* jōō'ăn), 1536–?1602. Span. navigator.

Fer·re'ro (fãr·rā'rō), Gu·gliel'mo (gōō·lyĕl'mō), 1871–1942. Ital. hist. & author.

Fer'ry' (fẽ'rē'), Jules Fran'çois' (frän'swä') Ca'mille' (kà'mē'y'), 1832–1893. Fr. statesman; premier (1880–81; 1883–85).

Fes'sen·den (fĕs''n·dĕn), William Pitt, 1806–1869. Am. polit.; secy. of the treas. (1864–65).

Fes'tus (fĕs'tŭs), Por'ci·us (pôr'shĭ·ŭs; -shŭs), d. ab. 62 A.D. Rom. procurator of Judea (58 or 60–62).

Feucht'wang'er (foikt'väng'ẽr), Li'on (lē'ôn), 1884– . Ger. nov. & dram.

Feuil'let' (fû'yĕ'), Oc'tave' (ôk'tàv'), 1821–1890. Fr. nov. & dram.

Fey (fī), E'mil (ā'mēl), 1888–1938. Austrian soldier & polit.

Fi'bi·ger (fē'bĕ·gẽr), Jo·han'nes (yōō·hän'ĕs), 1867–1928. Dan. pathologist.

Fich'te (fĭ'tĕ), Jo·hann' (yō·hän'; yō'hän) Gott'lieb (gôt'lēp), 1762–1814. Ger. philos.

Field (fēld), Cyrus West, 1819–1892. Am. financier.

—, Eugene, 1850–1895. Am. poet & journalist.

—, Marshall, 1834–1906. Am. merchant.

Fiel'ding (fēl'dĭng), Henry, 1707–1754. Eng. nov.

—, Sarah, 1710–1768. *Sister of prec.* Eng. writer.

Fie'so·le, da (dä fyā'zō·lä), Gio·van'ni (jō·vän'nē), 1387–1455. Fra An·ge'li·co (frä än·jā'lē·kō); orig. *Gui'do* (gwē'dō) *di Pie'tro* (dē pyä'trō). Ital. painter.

Figl (fē'g'l), Le'o·pold (lā'ô·pôlt), 1902– . Austrian agrarian & polit.

Fi'gue·ro'a, de (thä fē'gā·rō'ä), Fran·cis'co (frän·thēs'kō), 1536?–1620. Span. poet.

Fill'more (fĭl'mōr), Mil'lard (mĭl'ẽrd), 1800–1874. 13th pres. of the U. S. (1850–53).

Fin·lay' (*Span.* fēn·lī'), Car'los (kär'lōs) Juan (hwän), 1833–1915. Cuban physician & biologist.

Fin'sen (fĭn's'n), Niels (nēls) Ry'berg (rü'bẽrg), 1860–1904. Dan. physician.

Fir·dau'si (fĭr·dou'sē) *or* **Fir·du'si** (-dōō'sē), 940?–?1020. *Abul Qasim Mansur or Hasan.* Pers. epic poet.

Fi'scher (fĭsh'ẽr), E'mil (ā'mēl), 1852–1919. Ger. chem.

—, Hans, 1881–1945. Ger. chem.

Fish (fĭsh), Hamilton, 1808–1893. Am. statesman.

Fish'bein (fĭsh'bīn), Morris, 1889– . Am. physician & editor.

Fish'er (fĭsh'ẽr), Dorothy, 1879– . *Dorothea Frances,* nee *Can'field* (kăn'fēld). Am. nov.

—, Herbert Albert Lau'rens (lô'rĕnz, -rĕns; lôr'ĕnz, -ĕns), 1865–1940. Eng. hist.

—, Irving, 1867–1947. Am. econ.

—, John Arbuthnot, 1841–1920. 1st Baron *Fisher of Kil'ver·stone* (kĭl'vẽr·stŭn). Brit. admiral.

Fiske (fĭsk), John, 1842–1901. Orig. *Edmund Fisk* (fĭsk) *Green.* Am. philos. & hist.

—, Minnie Mad'dern (măd'ẽrn), 1865–1932. Nee *Da'vey* (dā'vĭ). Am. actress.

Fitch (fĭch), John, 1743–1798. Am. inventor.

—, (William) Clyde, 1865–1909. Am. dram.

Fitz·Ger'ald (fĭts·jẽr'ăld), Edward, 1809–1883. Eng. poet & trans.

Fitz·ger'ald (fĭts·jẽr'ăld), Francis Scott Key (kē), 1896–1940. Am. nov.

Fitz·her'bert (fĭts·hûr'bẽrt), Maria Anne, 1756–1837. Nee *Smythe* (smīth; smĭth). *Wife of George IV of Eng.*

Flagg (flăg), James Montgomery, 1877– . Am. painter, illustrator, & writer.

Flag'stad (fläg'stä), Kir'sten (kĭrsh't'n, kĭr'st'n), 1895– . Norw. soprano.

Fla·min'i·us (flå·mĭn'ĭ·ŭs), Ga'ius (gā'yŭs; gī'ŭs), d. 217 B.C. Rom. gen. & statesman.

Flam'ma'rion' (flä'mä'ryôn'), (Ni'co'las' [nē'kô'lä']) Ca'mille' (kà'mē'y'), 1842–1925. Fr. astron. & writer.

Flan'a·gan (flăn'å·găn; -ĭ·găn), Edward Joseph, 1886–1948. Am. (Irish-born) R.C. priest & founder of Boys Town.

Flan'din' (flän'dăn'), Pierre É'tienne' (ā'tyĕn'), 1889–1958 Fr. lawyer; premier (1934–35).

Flau'bert' (flō'bâr'), Gus'tave' (güs'tàv'), 1821–1880. Fr. nov.

Flax'man (flăks'măn), John, 1755–1826. Eng. sculptor.

Fleck'er (flĕk'ẽr), Herman James El'roy (ĕl'roi), 1884–1915. Eng. poet.

Fleet'wood (flēt'wŏod), Charles, d. 1692. Eng. gen.

Flem'ing (flĕm'ĭng), Sir Alexander, 1881–1955. Brit. bacteriol.

—, Sir John Ambrose, 1849–1945. Eng. electrical engineer.

Fletch'er (flĕch'ẽr), John, 1579–1625. Eng. dram.

—, John Gould, 1886–1950. Am. poet & critic.

Fleu'ry', de (dĕ flû'rē'), An'dré' (än'drā') Her'cule' (ẽr'kül'), 1653–1743. Fr. cardinal & statesman.

—, Claude (klōd), 1640–1723. Fr. ecclesiastical hist.

Flex'ner (flĕks'nẽr), Simon, 1863–1946. Am. pathologist.

Flint (flĭnt), Austin, father, 1812–1886, and son, 1836–1915. Am. physicians.

Flo'res (flō'rās), Juan (hwän) Jo·sé' (hō·sā'), 1800–1864. Ecuadorian soldier; pres. of Ecuador (1830–35; 1839–45).

—, Ve·nan'cio (bä·nän'syō), 1809–1868. Uruguayan soldier; pres. of Uruguay (1854–55; 1866–68).

Flo'rey (flō'rĭ), Sir Howard Walter, 1898– . Brit. pathologist.

Flo'ri·o (flō'rē·ō; *in Eng., also* flō'-), John, 1553?–1625. Eng. lexicographer & trans.

Flo'tow, von (fôn flō'tō), Baron Frie'drich (frē'drĭk), 1812–1883. Ger. composer.

Foch (fôsh), Fer'di/nand' (fẽr'dē'nän'), 1851–1929. Fr. gen.; marshal of France (1918).

Fo'kine (fō'kĭn; *Fr.* fô'kēn'), Mi'chel' (mē'shĕl'), 1880–1942. Am. (Russ.-born) choreographer.

Fok'ker (fŏk'ẽr), Anthony Herman Ge'rard (*Du.* kā'rärt), 1890–1939. Am. (Du.-born) aircraft designer & builder.

Fo'ley (fō'lĭ), John Henry, 1818–1874. Irish sculptor.

Fonck (fônk), René, 1894–1953. Fr. aviator.

Fon'tanne' (fôn'tăn'; *Angl.* fŏn·tän'), Lynn (lĭn), 1887?– . *Wife of Alfred Lunt.* Am. (Eng.-born) actress.

Foote (fŏot), Andrew Hull, 1806–1863. Am. admiral.

Forbes'-Rob'ert·son (fôrbz'rŏb'ẽrt·s'n), Sir Johnston, 1853–1937. Eng. actor.

Ford (fōrd), Ford Mad'ox (măd'ŭks), 1873–1939. Orig. *Huef'fer* (hŭf'ẽr). Eng. author.

—, Henry, 1863–1947. Am. automobile manuf.

—, John, 1586?–after 1638. Eng. dram.

—, Paul Leices'ter (lĕs'tẽr), 1865–1902. Am. hist. & nov.

For'es·ter (fŏr'ĕs·tẽr; -ĭs·tẽr), Cecil Scott, 1899– . Eng. nov.

For'rest (fŏr'ĕst; -ĭst), Edwin, 1806–1872. Am. actor.

—, Nathan Bed'ford (bĕd'fẽrd), 1821–1877. Am. Confed. gen.

For'res·tal (fŏr'ĕs·t'l), James Vincent, 1892–1949. Am. banker; 1st U. S. secy. of defense (1947–49).

For'ster (fôr'stẽr), Edward Morgan, 1879– . Brit. nov.

For·syth' (fôr·sīth'), John, 1780–1841. Am. statesman.

Fos'dick (fŏz'dĭk), Harry Emerson, 1878– . Am. clergyman.

Fos'ter (fŏs'tẽr), Stephen Collins, 1826–1864. Am. song writer.

—, William Zeb'u·lon (zĕb'ū·lŏn), 1881– . Am. Communist.

Fou·cault' (fōō'kō'), Jean Ber'nard' (bẽr'nàr') Lé'on' (lā'ôn'), 1819–1868. Fr. physicist.

Fou·qué'. See LA MOTTE-FOUQUÉ.

Fou'quet' *or* **Fouc'quet'** (fōō'kĕ'), Ni'co'las' (nē'kô'lä'), 1615–1680. Fr. superintendent of finance.

Fou·quier'-Tin'ville' (fōō'kyä'tăN'vēl'), An'toine' (äN'twän') Quen'tin' (käN'tăN'), 1746–1795. Fr. polit.

Four·drin'i·er (fōōr·drĭn'ĭ·ẽr), Henry, 1766–1854, and his bro. Sea'ly (sē'lĭ), d. 1847. Eng. papermakers & inventors.

Fou'rier' (fōō'ryä'), Fran'çois' (frän'swä') Ma'rie' (mà'rē') Charles, 1772–1837. Fr. sociol. & reformer.

Four'nier d'Albe (fōōr'nyä dălb'), Edmund Edward, 1868–1933. Eng. physicist.

Fowl'er (foul'ẽr), Henry Watson, 1858–1933. Eng. lexicographer.

Fox (fŏks), Charles James, 1749–1806. Eng. statesman & orator.

—, Dixon Ry'an (rī'ăn), 1887–1945. Am. educ. & hist.

—, George, 1624–1691. Eng. preacher; founder of Society of Friends (Quakers).

—, Henry, 1705–1774. 1st Baron *Hol'land* (hŏl'ănd). Brit. statesman.

—, John William, 1863–1919. *John Fox, Jr.* Am. nov.

Foxe (fŏks), John, 1516–1587. Eng. martyrologist.

—, *or* Fox, Richard, 1448?–1528. Eng. prelate & statesman.

Fra'go'nard' (frà'gô'nàr'), Jean Ho'no'ré' (ô'nô'rā'), 1732–1806. Fr. painter & engraver.

France (fräns; *Angl.* frăns), A'na'tole' (à'nà'tôl'), 1844–1924. Pseud. of *Jacques* (zhäk) *Anatole Fran'çois'* (frän'swä') *Thi'bault'* (tē'bō'). Fr. nov. & satirist.

Fran·ce'sca, del'la (dăl'lä frän·chäs'kä), Pie'ro (pyâ'rō), 1420?–1492. *Piero de'i Fran·ce'schi* (dā'ē frän·chäs'kē). Ital. painter.

Fran·ce'sca da Ri'mi·ni (frän·chäs'kä dä rē'mē·nē), d. 1285? Ital. lady immortalized by Dante.

Fran'chet' d'Es'pe·rey' (frän'shĕ' dĕs'prā'), Louis Fé'lix' (fā'lēks') Ma'rie' (mà'rē') Fran'çois' (frän'swä'), 1856–1942. Fr. gen.; marshal of France (1921).

Fran'cis (frăn'sĭs) **I,** 1494–1547. King of France (1515–47).

—**II,** 1768–1835. Last Holy Rom. emp. (1792–1806); emp. of Austria (as Francis I, 1804–35).

—**Fer'di·nand,** 1863–1914. Archduke of Austria; assassinated.

—**Jo'seph I,** 1830–1916. Emp. of Austria (1848–1916).

—**of As·si'si** (à·sē'zē; *Ital.* äs·sē'zē), Saint, 1182–1226. *Gio·van'ni* (jō·vän'nē) *Fran·ce'sco* (frän·chäs'kō) *Ber·nar·do'ne* (bãr·när·dō'nā). Ital. friar; founder of Franciscan order.

—**of Sales** (sälz; *Fr.* säl), Saint, 1567–1622. Fr. R.C. bishop of Geneva.

Franck (fräNk), Cé'sar' (sā'zàr') Au'guste' (ô'güst'), 1822–1890. Belg.-Fr. organist & composer.

—(frängk), James, 1882– . Ger. physicist.

Franck'e (fräng'kĕ), Ku'no (kōō'nō), 1855–1930. Am. (Ger.-born) hist. & educ.

Fran'co (fräng'kō), Fran·cis'co (frän·thēs'kō), 1892– . *Francisco Pau·li'no* (pou·lē'nō) *Her'me·ne·gil'do* (ẽr'mä·nä·hēl'dō) *Te·ó'du·lo* (tä·ō'thōō·lō) *Franco-Ba'ha·mon'de* (-vä'ä·môn'dä). Span. gen. & dictator.

Frank (frăngk), Glenn, 1887–1940. Am. educ.

Frank'furt·er (frăngk'fẽr·tẽr), Felix, 1882– . Am. (Austrianborn) jurist.

Frank'lin (frăngk'lĭn), Benjamin, 1706–1790. Am. statesman & philos.

—, Sir John, 1786–1847. Eng. arctic explorer.

Franks (frăngks), Sir Oliver Shewell (shōōl; shōō'ĕl), 1905– . Eng. philos. & diplomat.

Fra'ser (frā'zẽr), Bruce Austin, 1888– . 1st Baron *Fraser of North Cape.* Brit. admiral.

—, James Earle (ûrl), 1876–1953. Am. sculptor.

—, Peter, 1884–1950. N. Z. statesman; prime min. (1940–49).

—, Simon, 1667?–1747. 12th Baron *Lov'at* (lŭv'ăt). Scot. Jacobite.

Fraun'ho'fer, von (fôn frouN'hō'fẽr). Jo'seph (yō'zĕf). 1787–1826. Bavarian optician & physicist.

Fra'zer (frā'zĕr), Sir James George, 1854–1941. Scot. anthropologist.

Fré'chette' (frā'shĕt'), Louis Ho'no'ré' (ô'nô'rā'), 1839–1908. Canadian journalist & poet.

Fred'er·ick (frĕd'rĭk; frĕd'ēr-ĭk) **I**, 1123?–1190. *Frederick Bar'ba-ros'sa* (bär'bȧ·rŏs'ȧ). Holy Rom. emp. (1152–90).

— **II**, 1194–1250. Holy Rom. emp. (1215–50); king of Sicily (1198–1212).

— **I**, 1657–1713. King of Prussia (1701–13).

— **II**, 1712–1786. *Frederick the Great.* King of Prussia (1740–86).

— **IX**, 1899– . King of Denmark (1947–).

Fred'er·ick Wil'liam (wĭl'yăm), 1620–1688. *The Great Elector.* Elector of Brandenburg (1640–88).

—. Name of 4 kings of Prussia: **I**, 1688–1740 (reigned 1713–40); **II**, 1744–1797 (reigned 1786–97); **III**, 1770–1840 (reigned 1797–1840); **IV**, 1795–1861 (reigned 1840–61).

Free'man (frē'măn), Douglas Sou'thall (sou'thôl), 1886–1953. Am. editor & hist.

—, Edward Augustus, 1823–1892. Eng. hist.

—, Mary Eleanor, 1852–1930. Nee *Wilkins.* Am. writer.

Fre'ling·huy'sen (frē'lĭng-hī'z'n), Frederick Theodore, 1817–1885. Am. statesman.

Fré'mont (frē'mŏnt), John Charles, 1813–1890. Am. gen. & explorer.

Frem'stad (frĕm'städ), Anna Olivia, 1872–1951. *Olive.* Am. (Swed.-born) soprano.

French (frĕnch), Alice, 1850–1934. Pseud. *Oc'tave Than'et* (ŏk'tăv thăn'ĕt; -ĭt). Am. nov.

—, Daniel Chester, 1850–1931. Am. sculptor.

—, John Den'ton (dĕn't'n; -tŭn) Pink'stone (pĭngk'stōn; -stŭn), 1852–1925. 1st Earl of *Y'pres* (ē'pr'). Brit. field marshal.

Fre·neau' (frē·nō'; frē'nō), Philip Mo'rin' (mō'răn'), 1752–1832. Am. poet.

Fres'nel' (frā'nĕl'), Au'gus'tin' (ô'güs'tăn') Jean, 1788–1827. Fr. physicist.

Freud (froit; *Angl.* froid), Sig'mund (zēĸ'mŏŏnt; *Angl.* sĭg'mŭnd), 1856–1939. Austrian neurologist; founder of psychoanalysis.

Frey'berg (frī'bûrg), Sir Bernard Cyril, 1890– . N. Z. gen.

Frey'ci'net', de (dē frā'sē'nĕ', Charles Louis de Saulces (dē sōls'), 1828–1923. Fr. statesman; premier (1879–80; 1882; 1886; 1890–92).

Frey'tag (frī'täk), Gu'stav (gŏŏs'täf), 1816–1895 Ger. nov., dram., & critic.

Frick (frĭk), Henry Clay, 1849–1919. Am. industrialist.

Fried (frēt), Alfred Her'mann (hĕr'män), 1864–1921. Austrian pacifist.

Pro'bish·er (frō'bĭsh-ĕr; frŏb'ĭsh-), Sir Martin, 1535?–1594. Eng. navigator.

Froe'bel *or* Frö'bel (frû'bĕl), Frie'drich (frē'drĭĸ), 1782–1852. Ger. educ.

Froh'man (frō'măn), Charles, 1860–1915. Am. theater manager.

Frois'sart' (frwä'sär'; *Angl.* froi'särt), Jean, 1333?–?1400. Fr. chronicler.

Fron'te·nac', de (dē frŏnt'năk'; *Angl.* frŏn't'n-ăk), Comte (kônt) *de Pal'lu·au' et* (dē pȧ'lü·ō' ā), 1620–1698. *Louis de Bu·ade'* (dē bü·åd'). Fr. gen. & colonial administrator.

Frost (frŏst), Robert Lee, 1874– . Am. poet.

Froude (frŏŏd), James Anthony, 1818–1894. Eng. hist.

Fu·ad' I (fŏŏ·äd'), 1868–1936. Orig. *Ah'med Fuad Pa'sha* (ä'măd, pȧ'shä). Sultan (1917–22) & king (1922–36) of Egypt.

Fuer'tes (fūr'tēz; *Span.* fwĕr'tȧs), Louis Agassiz, 1874–1927. Am. naturalist illustrator.

Ful'da (fŏŏl'dä), Lud'wig (lŏŏt'vĭĸ; lŏŏd'-), 1862–1939. Ger. writer.

Ful'ler (fŏŏl'ēr), Melville Wes'ton (wĕs'tŭn), 1833–1910. Am. jurist.

—, (Sarah) Margaret, 1810–1850. Marchioness *Os'so·li* (ŏs'sô·lē). Am. critic & reformer.

—, Thomas, 1608–1661. Eng. divine & author.

Ful'ton (fŏŏl't'n; -tŭn), Robert, 1765–1815. Am. engineer & inventor.

Funk (fŏŏngk), Cas'i·mir (kăz'ĭ·mĭr), 1884– . Am. (Pol.-born) biochem.

— (füngk), Isaac Kauff'man (kôf'măn), 1839–1912. Am. editor & publisher.

— (fŏŏngk), Wal'ther (väl'tĕr), 1890– . Ger. journalist & econ.

Fun'ston (fŭn'stŭn), Frederick, 1865–1917. Am. gen.

Fur'ness (fûr'nĕs; -nĭs), Horace Howard, father, 1833–1912, and son, 1865–1930. Am. Shakespearean scholars.

Fur'ni·vall (fûr'nĭ·văl), Frederick James, 1825–1910. Eng. philologist.

G

Ga'bo'riau' (gȧ'bô'ryō'), É'mile' (ā'mēl'), 1835–1873. Fr. writer.

Ga'bri·ló'witsch (*Angl.* gȧ'brĭ·lŭ'vĭch; *Russ.* gȧ·vryĭ·lô'vĭch), Os'sip (ô'syĭp), 1878–1936. Russ. pianist & composer in Am.

Gads'den (gădz'dĕn), James, 1788–1858. Am. army officer & diplomat.

Gad'ski (gät'skē), Jo·han'na (yō·hän'ä), 1872–1932. Ger. soprano.

Gage (gāj), Thomas, 1721–1787. Brit. gen. & colonial gov. in Am.

Gail·lard' (gĭ·yärd'), David Du Bose (dü bōz'; dōō; dŭ), 1859–1913. Am. army officer & engineer.

Gaines (gānz), Edmund Pen'dle·ton (pĕn'd'l·tŭn), 1777–1849. Am. gen.

Gains'bor'ough (gānz'bûr'ō; *esp. Brit.,* -bȧ·rȧ, -brȧ), Thomas, 1727–1788. Eng. painter.

Ga'ius (gā'yŭs; gī'ŭs) *or* Ca'ius (kā'yŭs; kī'ŭs), 2d cent. A.D. Rom. jurist.

Gal'ba (găl'bȧ; gôl'bȧ), Ser'vi·us (sûr'vĭ·ŭs) Sul·pi'ci·us (sŭl·pĭsh'ĭ·ŭs; -pĭsh'ŭs), 5 B.C.?–69 A.D. Rom. emp. (68–69).

Gale (gāl), Zona, 1874–1938. Am. nov.

Ga·le'ri·us (gȧ·lēr'ĭ·ŭs), d. 311. *Ga'ius* (gā'yŭs; gī'ŭs) *Galerius Va·le'ri·us Max·im'i·a'nus* (vȧ·lēr'ĭ·ŭs măk·sĭm'ĭ·ā'nŭs). Rom. emp. (305–311).

Ga·li·le'i (gä'lē·lā'ē), Ga'li·le'o (gä'lē·lā'ō; *Angl.* găl'ĭ·lē'ō), 1564–1642. *Galileo.* Ital. astron. & physicist.

Ga·lits'ky (gŭ·lyĭts'kĭ), Kuz·ma' (kŏŏz·y'·mȧ'), 1898– . Russ. gen.

Gal'land' (gȧ'län'), An'toine' (äɴ'twàn'), 1646–1715. Fr. orientalist & trans.

Gal'la·tin (găl'ȧ·tĭn), (Abraham Al'fonse [ăl'fŏns; -fŏnz] Albert, 1761–1849. Am. (Swiss-born) financier & statesman.

Gal'lau·det' (găl'ŭ·dĕt'), Thomas Hopkins, 1787–1851. Am. teacher of the deaf & dumb.

Gal·le'gos (gä·yā'gōs) Frei're (frā'ĕ·rä), Ró'mu·lo (rrô'mŏŏ·lô), 1884– . Venezuelan nov.; pres. of Venezuela (1948).

Gal'li·Cur'ci (găl'lē·kŏŏr'chē; *Angl.* găl'ĭ·kûr'chĭ), A'me·li'ta (ä'mä·lē'tä), 1889– . Nee *Galli.* Am. (Ital.-born) soprano.

Gal'lie'ni' (gȧ'lyä'nē'), Jo'seph' (zhô'zĕf') Si'mon' (sē'môɴ'), 1849–1916. Fr. gen. & colonial administrator.

Gal·lie'nus (găl'ĭ·ē'nŭs), Pub'li·us (pŭb'lĭ·ŭs) Li·cin'i·us (lĭ·sĭn'ĭ·ŭs) Va·le'ri·a'nus (vȧ·lēr'ĭ·ā'nŭs) Eg·na'ti·us (ĕg·nā'shĭ·ŭs; -shŭs), d. 268. Rom. emp. (253–268).

Gal'lup (găl'ŭp), George Horace, 1901– . Am. statistician.

Ga'lois' (gȧ'lwä'), É'va'riste' (ā'vȧ'rēst') 1811–1832. Fr. math.

Gals'wor'thy (gôlz'wûr'thĭ), John, 1867–1933. Eng. nov. & dram.

Galt (gôlt), John, 1779–1839. Scot. nov.

Gal'ton (gôl't'n; -tŭn), Sir Francis, 1822–1911. Eng. scientist.

Gal·va'ni (gäl·vä'nē), Lui'gi (lwē'jē) *or* A'lo·i'sio (ä'lō·ē'zyō), 1737–1798. Ital. physician & physicist.

Gál'vez (gäl'vāth; -väs), Jo·sé' (hō·sā'), 1729–1787. Mar·qués' (mär·kās') *de la So·no'ra* (thä lä sō·nō'rä). Span. jurist & colonial administrator.

Gal'way (gôl'wä), 8th Viscount, 1882–1943. *George Vere* (vĕr) *Arun·dell Monck'ton·Ar'un·dell* (mŭngk'tŭn·är'ŭn·dĕl). Brit. gen.; gov. gen. of N. Z. (1935–41).

Ga'ma, da (thä gä'mä), Vas'co (väsh'kŏŏ), 1469?–1524. Port. navigator.

Ga·mar'ra (gä·mär'rä), A'gus·tín' (ä'gŏŏs·tēn'), 1785–1841. Peruvian gen.; pres. of Peru (1829–33; 1839–41).

Gam·bet'ta (găm·bĕt'ȧ; *Fr.* gäɴ'bĕ'tä), Lé'on' (lā'ôɴ'), 1838–1882. Fr. lawyer & statesman.

Ga'me·lin' (gȧm'lăɴ'), Mau'rice' (mô'rēs') Gus'tave' (güs'täv'), 1872–1958. Fr. gen.

Gan'dhi (gän'dē; *Angl.* -dĭ), Mo'han·das (mō'hän·däs) Ka'ram·chand (kŭ'rȧm·chŭnd), 1869–1948. Ma·hat'ma (mȧ·hät'mä; *Angl.* mȧ·hät'mä) *Gandhi.* Hindu nationalist leader.

Gar'a·mond (gär'ȧ·mŏnd; *Fr.* gȧ'rȧ'môɴ'), Claude (klōd), d. 1561. Fr. typefounder.

Gar'and (găr'ŏnd), John Can'tius (kăn'tyüs), 1888– . Am. (Canadian-born) inventor.

Gar·cí'a Gu·tiér'rez (gär·thē'ä gŏŏ·tyĕr'räth), An·to'nio (än·tō'nyō), 1813–1884. Span. dram.

Gar·cí'a Í'ñi·guez (gär·sē'ä ē'nyē·gäs; *Angl.* gär'shȧ, -shĭ·ȧ, -sĭ·ȧ), Ca·lix'to (kä·lē[k]s'tō), 1836?–1898. Cuban lawyer & revolutionist.

Gar·cí'a Mo·re'no (gär·sē'ä mō·rä'nō), Ga'bri·el' (gä'vrē·ĕl'), 1821–1875. Ecuadorian journalist; pres. of Ecuador (1861–65; 1869–75).

Gar·ci·la'so de la Ve'ga (gär·sē·lä'sō thä lä vā'gä), 1539?–1616. *El In'ca* (ĕl ēng'kä). Peruvian hist.

Gar'den (gär'd'n), Mary, 1877– . Am. (Scot.-born) soprano.

Gar'di·ner (gärd'nēr; gär'd'n-ēr), Samuel Raw'son (rô's'n), 1829–1902. Eng. hist.

—, Stephen, 1483?–1555. Eng. prelate & statesman.

Gar'field (gär'fēld), James Abram, 1831–1881. 20th pres. of the U. S. (1881).

Gar'i·bal'di (găr'ĭ·bôl'dĭ; -bäl'dĭ; *Ital.* gä'rē·bäl'dē), Giu·sep'pe (jŏŏ·zĕp'pä), 1807–1882. Ital. patriot.

Gar'land (gär'lănd), Hamlin, 1860–1940. Am. nov.

Gar'ner (gär'nēr), John Nance (năns), 1868– . Am. polit.; vice-pres. of the U. S. (1933–41).

Gar'nett (gär'nĕt; -nĭt), Constance, 1862–1946. Nee *Black* (blăk). Eng. trans.

Gar'rick (găr'ĭk), David, 1717–1779. Eng. actor.

Gar'ri·son (găr'ĭ·s'n), Mabel, 1886– . Am. soprano.

—, William Lloyd, 1805–1879. Am. abolitionist.

Gar'ros' (gȧ'rôs'), Ro'land' (rô'läɴ'), 1888–1918. Fr. aviator.

Gar'shin (gär'shĭn), Vse'vo·lod (fsyĕ'vŭ·lŭt) Mi·khai'lo·vich (myĭ·ĸī'lŭ·vyĭch), 1855–1888. Russ. writer.

Gar'y (gär'ĭ), Elbert Henry, 1846–1927. Am. lawyer & industrialist.

Gas'coigne (găs'koin), George, 1525?–1577. Eng. poet.

Gas'kell (găs'kĕl; -kĭl), Elizabeth Cleg'horn (klĕg'hôrn; ?-ĕrn), 1810–1865. Nee *Ste'ven·son* (stē'vĕn·s'n). Eng. nov.

Gas'ser (găs'ēr), Herbert Spencer, 1888– . Am. physiol.

Gas·set'. See José ORTEGA Y GASSET.

Gates (gāts), Horatio, 1728?–1806. Am. gen. in Rev.

Gau'guin' (gō'găn'), Eu'gène' (û'zhän'; ü'-) Hen'ri' (äɴ'rē') Paul, 1848–1903. Fr. painter.

Gauss (gous), Karl Frie'drich (frē'drĭĸ), 1777–1855. Ger. math. & astron.

Gau'ta·ma Bud'dha (Skr. gä'ŏŏ·tȧ·mȧ bŏŏd'dȧ; *Angl.* gou'tȧ·mȧ bŏŏd'ȧ), 563?–?483 B.C. Orig. Prince *Sid·dhar'tha* (sĭd·där'tȧ). Indian philos.; founder of Buddhism.

Gau'tier' (gō'tyā'), Thé'o'phile' (tā'ô'fēl'), 1811–1872. Fr. author.

Gay (gā), John, 1685–1732. Eng. poet & dram.

Gay'·Lus·sac' (gā'lŭ·săk'; *Fr.* -lü'sàk'), Jo'seph' (zhô'zĕf') Louis, 1778–1850. Fr. chem. & physicist.

Ge'ber (*Lat.* jē'bĕr), fl. 721–766. Arab scholar.

Ged'des (gĕd'ĭs), Sir Eric Campbell, 1875–1937, & his bro., Sir Auck'land (ôk'lănd), 1879–1954. Eng. statesmen.

— (gĕd'ĕz), Norman Bel (bĕl), 1893–1958. Am. designer.

Gei'kie (gē'kĭ), Sir Archibald, 1835–1924. Scot. geologist.

Ge·lée' *or* Gel'lée', Claude. See Claude LORRAIN.

Ge·nêt' (zhĕ·nā'), Ed'mond' (ĕd'môɴ') Charles É'dou·ard' (ā'dwär'), 1763–1834. Fr. diplomat in U. S.

Gen'ghis Khan (jĕng'gĭs kän') *or* Jen'ghiz Khan (jĕng'gĭz), 1162–1227. Mongol conqueror.

Gen'se·ric (gĕn'sĕ·rĭk; jĕn'-), d. 477. King of the Vandals (428–477).

Gen·ti'le da Fa'bri·a'no (jän·tē′lä dä fä′brē·ä′nō), 1370?–?1427. *Gentile Mas'si* (mäs′sē). Ital. painter.

Geof'frey of Mon'mouth (jĕf′rĭ ŭv mŏn′mŭth), 1100?–1154. Eng. ecclesiastic & chronicler.

George (jôrj), Saint, d. ab. 303. Christian martyr & patron saint of Eng.

—. Name of 6 kings of Gr. Britain: **I**, 1660–1727 (reigned 1714–27); **II**, 1683–1760 (reigned 1727–60); **III**, 1738–1820 (reigned 1760–1820); **IV**, 1762–1830 (reigned 1820–30); **V**, 1865–1936 (reigned 1910–36); **VI**, 1895–1952 (reigned 1936–52).

— I, 1845–1913. King of Greece (1863–1913).

— II, 1890–1947. King of Greece (1922–23; 1935–47).

—, David Lloyd. See LLOYD GEORGE.

—, Harold Lee, 1893– . Am. gen.

—, Henry, 1839–1897. Am. econ.

Ge·rard' (jĕ·rärd′; *esp. Brit.*, jĕr′ärd, jĕr′ĕrd), Charles, 1618?–1694. 1st Baron *Gerard of Bran'don* (brän′dŭn); Viscount *Brandon*. Eng. Royalist commander.

—, James Watson, 1867–1951. Am. lawyer & diplomat.

Gé·rard' (zhā′rär′), Comte (kônt) É′tienne′ (ā′tyĕn′) Mau′rice′ (mô′rēs′), 1773–1852. Fr. Napoleonic gen.; marshal of France.

Ger'hard·sen (gĕr′här·sĕn), Ei′nar (ī′i·när), 1897– . Norw. polit.

Ger'lach, von (fôn gĕr′läk), Hell′muth (hĕl′mōōt), 1866–1935. Ger. polit.; a founder of National Socialist party.

Ger·man'i·cus Cae'sar (jûr·măn′ĭ·kŭs sē′zĕr), 15 B.C.–19 A.D. Rom. gen.

Gé·rôme' (zhā′rōm′), Jean Lé′on′ (lā′ôn′), 1824–1904. Fr. painter.

Ge·ron'i·mo (jĕ·rŏn′ĭ·mō), 1829–1909. Apache chieftain.

Ger'ry (gĕr′ĭ), El′bridge (ĕl′brĭj), 1744–1814. Am. statesman; vice-pres. of the U. S. (1813–14).

Gersh'win (gûrsh′wĭn), George, 1898–1937. Am. composer.

Ge·sell' (gĕ·zĕl′), Arnold Lucius, 1880– . Am. psychol. & pediatrician.

Ges'ner, von (fôn gĕs′nĕr), Kon′rad (kôn′rät), 1516–1565. Swiss naturalist.

Get'ty (gĕt′ĭ), George Washington, 1819–1901. Am. gen.

Ghaz·za'li or **Gha·za'li, al-** (äl′gä[z]·zä′lē), 1058–1111. Arab philos.

Ghi·ber'ti (gē·bĕr′tē), Lorenzo, 1378–1455. Florentine goldsmith, painter, & sculptor.

Ghir·lan·da'jo (gēr·län·dä′yō), Do·me′ni·co (dō·mā′nē·kō), 1449–1494. Florentine painter & mosaicist.

Ghorm'ley (gôrm′lĭ), Robert Lee, 1883–1958. Am. admiral.

Ghose (gōs), Sri (shrē; srē) Au′ro·bin′do (ô′rô·bĭn′dô), 1872–1950. Indian philos. & nationalist statesman.

Giar·di'no (jär·dē′nō), Ga′e·ta′no (gä′ä·tä′nō), 1864–1935. Ital. gen.

Gib'bon (gĭb′ŭn), Edward, 1737–1794. Eng. hist.

Gib'bons (gĭb′ŭnz), James, 1834–1921. Am. cardinal.

Gibbs (gĭbz), Josiah Willard, 1839–1903. Am. math. & physicist.

—, Sir Philip, 1877– . Eng. journalist & nov.

Gib'son (gĭb′s'n), Charles Dana, 1867–1944. Am. illustrator.

—, Wilfrid Wilson, 1878– . Eng. poet.

Gide (zhēd), An′dré′ (än′drā′), 1869–1951. Fr. nov., critic, & essayist.

—, Charles, 1847–1932. Fr. econ.

Gie'se·king (gē′zĕ·kĭng), Wal′ter (väl′tĕr; *Angl.* wôl′tĕr) Wil′helm (vĭl′hĕlm), 1895–1956. Ger. (Fr.-born) pianist.

Gi'gli (jē′lyē), Be·nia·mi′no (bâ·nyä·mē′nō), 1890–1957. Ital. tenor.

Gil'bert (gĭl′bĕrt), Cass (käs), 1859–1934. Am. architect.

—, Sir Humphrey, 1539?–1583. Eng. navigator.

—, William, 1540–1603. Eng. physician & physicist.

—, Sir William Schwenck (shwĕngk), 1836–1911. Eng. librettist & poet; collaborator with Sir Arthur Sullivan.

Gil'der (gĭl′dĕr), Richard Watson, 1844–1909. Am. poet & editor.

Gil·lette' (jĭ·lĕt′), King Camp (kămp), 1855–1932. Am. inventor & manuf.

—, William, 1855–1937. Am. actor.

Gil'man (gĭl′măn), Arthur, 1837–1909. Am. educ.; developed Radcliffe College.

—, Daniel Coit (koit), 1831–1908. Am. educ.; pres., Johns Hopkins U. (1875–1901).

Gil'mer (gĭl′mĕr), Elizabeth, 1870–1951. Nee *Mer'i·weth'er* (mĕr′ĭ·wĕth′ĕr); pseud. *Dorothy Dix* (dĭks). Am. journalist.

Gil'pin (gĭl′pĭn), Charles Sidney, 1878–1930. Am. actor.

Gior·gio'ne, Il (ēl jôr·jō′nā), ab. 1478–1511. *Giorgione da Ca·stel'fran'co* (dä käs·tĕl′fräng′kō); orig. *Gior'gio* (jôr′jō; jôr′-) *Bar'ba·rel'li* (bär′bä·rĕl′lē). Venetian painter.

Giot'to (jôt′tō), 1276?–?1337. *Giotto di Bon·do'ne* (dē bōn·dō′nä). Florentine painter, architect, & sculptor.

Gipps (gĭps), Sir George, 1791–1847. Brit. gov. of New S. Wales (1838–46).

Gi'rard' (zhē′rär′), Jean Bap′tiste′ (bä′tēst′), 1765–1850. Swiss Franciscan & educ.

Gi·rard' (jĭ·rärd′; *Fr.* zhē′rär′), Stephen, 1750–1831. Am. (Fr.-born) financier & philanthropist.

Gi'raud' (zhē′rō′), Hen′ri′ (än′rē′) Ho′no′ré′ (ô′nô′rā′), 1879–1949. Fr. gen.

Gi·rau'doux' (zhē′rō′dōō′), Jean, 1882–1944. Fr. writer.

Gir'tin (gûr′tĭn), Thomas, 1775–1802. Eng. founder of art of modern water-color painting.

Gis'sing (gĭs′ĭng), George Robert, 1857–1903. Eng. nov.

Gjel'le·rup (gĕl′lĕ·rōōp), Karl (kärl), 1857–1919. Dan. writer.

Glad'stone (glăd′stŏn; *Brit. usu.* -stŭn), William Ew′art (ū′ĕrt), 1809–1898. Brit. statesman; prime min. (1868–74; 1880–85; 1886; 1892–94).

Glas'gow (glăs′gō), Ellen Anderson Ghol′son (gōl′s'n), 1874–1945. Am. nov.

Glas'pell (glăs′pĕl), Susan, 1882–1948. Am. nov. & dram.

Glass (glàs), Carter, 1858–1946. Am. statesman.

Glass'ford (glăs′fĕrd), William Alexander, 1886–1958. Am. admiral.

Glen·dow'er (*Eng.* glĕn′dou′ĕr; glĕn′dou′ĕr), Owen, 1359?–?1416. Welsh chieftain & rebel against Henry IV of Eng.

Glin'ka (glĭng′kà; *Russ.* glēn′kà), Mi·kha·il′ (myĭ·kü·ēl′) I·va′no·vich (ĭ·vä′nŭ·vyĭch), 1803–1857. Russ. composer.

Glouces'ter, Duke of. See HUMPHREY.

Glov'er (glŭv′ĕr), John, 1732–1797. Am. Revolutionary gen.

—, Sarah Ann, 1785–1867. Eng. music teacher; invented tonic sol-fa system of notation.

Gluck (glōōk), Al′ma (äl′mä), 1884–1938. Nee (*Re'ba* [rē′bà]) *Fier'sohn* (fēr′zōn). Am. (Romanian-born) soprano.

—, Chri′stoph (krĭs′tôf) Wil′li·bald (vĭl′ē·bält), 1714–1787. Ger. composer.

Glyn (glĭn), Elinor, 1864–1943. Nee *Sutherland*. Brit. (Jersey-born) nov.

Go'bat' (gō′bà′), Charles Al′bert′ (àl′bâr′), 1843–1914. Swiss statesman.

God'dard (gŏd′ĕrd), Robert Hutch′ings (hŭch′ĭngz), 1882–1945. Am. physicist.

God'frey of Bouil'lon (gŏd′frĭ ŭv bōō′yôn′); *Fr.* **Go'de·froy' de Bouil'lon** (gŏd′frwä′ dĕ bōō′yôn′), 1061?–1100. Fr. crusader.

Go·dol'phin (gô·dŏl′fĭn), Sidney, 1645–1712. 1st Earl of *Godolphin*. Eng. statesman.

Go·doy', de (dä gô·thoi′), Ma·nuel′ (mä·nwĕl′), 1767–1851. Span. statesman.

Go·du·nov' (gŭ·dōō·nôf′; *Angl.* gō′d′n·ôf, gŏd′n-), Boris Fë′do·ro′vich (fyô′dŭ·rô′vyĭch), 1551?–1605. Tsar of Russia (1598–1605).

God'win (gŏd′wĭn), d. 1053. Earl of the West Saxons.

—, William, 1756–1836. Eng. philos. & nov.

God'win-Aus'ten (gŏd′wĭn-ôs′tĕn; -tĭn), Henry Hav′er·sham (hăv′ĕr·shăm; här′shăm), 1834–1923. Eng. explorer & geologist.

Goeb'bels (gûb′ĕls), Jo′seph (yō′zĕf) Paul, 1897–1945. Ger. Nazi propagandist.

Goe'ring. See GÖRING.

Goes (kōōs), Hu′go (hü′kō) van der (vän dĕr), 1440?–1482. Du. painter.

Goe'thals (gō′thälz), George Washington, 1858–1928. Am. gen. & engineer.

Goe'the, von (fôn gû′tĕ; *Angl.* gā′tĕ), Jo′hann (yō′hän) Wolf′gang (vôlf′gäng), 1749–1832. Ger. poet & dram.

Gogh, van (vän kôx′), Vin·cent′ (vĭn·sĕnt′), 1853–1890. Du. painter.

Go'gol (gō′gŭl·y; *Angl.* gō′gŏl), Ni·ko·lai′ (nyĭ·kŭ·lī′) Va·sil′ie·vich (vŭ·syēl′yĕ·vyĭch), 1809–1852. Russ. writer.

Gol'den·wei'ser (gōl′dĕn·vī′zĕr), Alexander A., 1880–1940. Am. (Russ.-born) anthropologist & sociol.

Gol·do'ni (gōl·dō′nē), Car′lo (kär′lō), 1707–1793. Ital. dram.

Gold'smith (gōld′smĭth), Oliver, 1728–1774. Brit. author.

Gol'gi (gōl′jē), Ca·mil′lo (kä·mēl′lō), 1844–1926. Ital. physician.

Go'li·kov (gō′lyĭ·kŭf), Fi·lipp′ (fyĭ·lyĕp′) I·va′no·vich (ĭ·vä′nŭ·vyĭch), 1900?– . Russ. gen.

Gol'lancz (gō′länts), Sir Her′mann (hûr′măn), 1852–1930. Eng. Semitic scholar.

Goltz, von der (fôn dĕr gôlts′), Baron Kol′mar (kôl′mär), 1843–1916. Ger. gen.

Gó'mez (gō′mäs), Juan Vi·cen′te (hwäm bē·sän′tä), 1857?–1935. Venezuelan gen. & polit.; dictator (1908–35).

Gom'pers (gŏm′pĕrz), Samuel, 1850–1924. Am. (Brit.-born) labor leader.

Gon·çal'ves Di'as (gōN·säl′vĕz thē′às), An·tô′ni·o (ăNn·tô′nyōō), 1823–1864. Brazilian poet.

Gon'court', de (dĕ gôN′kōōr′), Ed′mond′ (ĕd′môN′) Louis An′toine (än′twän′), 1822–1896, and his bro. Jules Alfred Hu′ot′ (ü′ō′), 1830–1870. Fr. novelists & collaborators.

Gon'do·mar' (gôn′dō·mär′), Count of, 1567–1626. *Die'go* (dyä′gō) *Sar·mien'to de A·cu'ña* (sär·myän′tô thä ä·kōō′nyä). Span. diplomat.

Gon·za'ga (gōn·dzä′gä; *Angl.* gŏn·zăg′à, -zä′gà, -zä′gà), Saint Aloysius, 1568–1591. Ital. Jesuit cleric.

Gon·zá'lez (gōn·sä′läs), Ma·nuel′ (mä·nwĕl′), 1833–1893. Mex. gen.; pres. of Mexico (1880–84).

— Vi·de'la (vē·thä′lä), Ga′bri·el′ (gä′vrē·ĕl′), 1898– . Chilean lawyer; pres. of Chile (1946–52).

Gon·za'lo de Cór'do·ba (gōn·thä′lō thä kôr′thō·vä), Her·nán′dez (ĕr·nän′däth), 1453–1515. *El Gran Ca'pi·tán'* (ĕl grän kä′pē·tän′). Span. soldier.

Good'hue (gŏŏd′hū), Bertram Grosvenor, 1869–1924. Am. architect.

Good'rich (gŏŏd′rĭch), Samuel Gris′wold (grĭz′wŭld; -wōld; -wôld), 1793–1860. Pseud. *Peter Par'ley* (pär′lĭ). Am. writer.

Good'year (gŏŏd′yēr), Charles, 1800–1860. Am. inventor.

Gor·cha·kov' (gĕr·chŭ·kôf′; *Angl.* gôr′chä·kôf), Prince A·le·ksan'dr (ŭ·lyĭ·ksän′dĕr) I·va′no·vich (ĭ·vä′nŭ·vyĭch), 1764–1825. Russ. gen. & statesman.

—, Prince Aleksandr Mi·khai'lo·vich (myĭ·KI′lŭ·vyĭch), 1798–1883. Russ. statesman & diplomat.

Gor'din (gôr′dĭn; -d'n), Jacob, 1853–1909. Am. (Russ.-born) Yiddish dram.

Gor'don (gôr′d'n), Charles George, 1833–1885. *Chinese Gordon; Gordon Pa'sha* (pà′shä). Brit. soldier.

—, Charles William, 1860–1937. Pseud. *Ralph Con'nor* (kŏn′ĕr). Canadian clergyman & nov.

—, Lord George, 1751–1793. Eng. polit. agitator.

Go·re·my'kin (gŭ·ryĕ·mĭ′kĭn), Ivan Lon′gi·no·vich (lôn′gĭ·nŭ·vyĭch), 1839–1917. Russ. statesman; prime min. (1906; 1914–16).

Gor'gas (gôr′gǎs), William Crawford, 1854–1920. Am. army surgeon & sanitation expert.

Gö'ring (gû′rĭng), Her′mann (hĕr′män) Wil′helm (vĭl′hĕlm), 1893–1946. Ger. Nazi polit.

Gor'ki (*Angl.* gôr′kĭ; *Russ.* gôr′y·kĭ), Mak·sim′ (mŭk·syēm′); also Maxim Gor'ky, 1868–1936. Pseud. of *A·le·ksei'* (ŭ·lyĭ·ksyā′ĭ) *Mak'si·mo·vich* (mŭk·syē′mŭ·vyĭch) *Pesh'kov* (pyäsh′kŭf). Russ. writer.

Gort (gôrt), 6th Viscount, 1886–1946. *John Standish Surtees Pren'der·gast* (prĕn′dĕr·gäst) *Ver'e·ker* (vĕr′ĭ·kĕr). Eng. field marshal.

Go'schen (gō′shĕn), George Jo′a·chim (jō′à·kĭm), 1st Viscount, 1831–1907. Brit. statesman.

Gos'sage (gŏs′ĭj), Sir (Ernest) Leslie, 1891–1949. Brit. air marshal.

Gosse (gŏs), Sir Edmund William, 1849–1928. Eng. poet & critic.

Go'ta·ma Bud'dha (*Pali* gō'tȧ·mȧ). See GAUTAMA BUDDHA.

Gou'dy (gou'dĭ), Frederic William, 1865–1947. Am. printer & type designer.

Gough (gŏf), Hubert de la Poer (dē'lȧ·pōōr'), 1870– . Eng. gen.
—, Sir Hugh, 1st Viscount, 1779–1869. Eng. field marshal.

Gould (gōōld), Jay, *orig.* Jason, 1836–1892. Am. financier.

Gou'nod' (gōō'nō'; *Angl.* gōō'nō), Charles Fran'çois' (frän'swä'), 1818–1893. Fr. composer.

Gou'raud' (gōō'rō'), Hen'ri' (än'rē') Jo'seph' (zhō'zĕf') Eu'gène' (û'zhän'; ü'-), 1867–1946. Fr. gen.

Gour'mont', de (dē gōōr'môN'), Re'my' (rā'mē'), 1858–1915. Fr. writer.

Gow'er (gou'ẽr), John, 1325?–1408. Eng. poet.

Go'ya y Lu·cien'tes, de (thä gō'yä ē lōō·thyän'tãs), Fran·cis'co (frän·thēs'kō) Jo·sé' (hō·sā'), 1746–1828. Span. painter.

Grac'chus (grăk'ŭs), Ga'ius (gā'yŭs; gī'ŭs) Sem·pro'ni·us (sĕm·prō'nĭ·ŭs), 153–121 B.C., and Ti·be'ri·us (tĭ·bē'rĭ·ŭs) Sempronius, 163–133, bros. *The Grac'chi* (grăk'ī). Rom. statesmen.

Gra'ham (grā'ăm; *Scot.* grä'ăm), John, 1649?–1689. *Graham of Clav'er·house* (klăv'ẽrz; klä'vẽrz; klăv'ẽr·hous); 1st Viscount *Dun·dee'* (dŭn·dē'); *Bonny Dundee.* Scot. Royalist.

Gra'ham, Stephen, 1884– . Eng. writer.
—, Thomas, 1805–1869. Scot. chem.

Gra'hame (grā'ăm; grä'ăm), Kenneth, 1859–1932. Brit. writer.

Grain'ger (grān'jẽr), Percy Al'dridge (ôl'drĭj), 1882– . Brit. (Australian-born) pianist & composer.

Gramme (grăm), Zé'nobe' (zā'nōb') Thé'o'phile' (tā'ō'fēl'), 1826–1901. Belg. electrician.

Gra'mont', de (dē grȧ'môN'), Comte (kôNt) Phi'li'bert' (fē'lē'bâr'), 1621?–1707. Fr. soldier & courtier.

Gran'di (grän'dē), Di'no (dē'nō) di Mor·da'no (dē môr·dä'nō), 1895– . Ital. Fascist polit.

Grant (grȧnt), He'ber (hē'bẽr) Jed·e·di'ah (jĕd'ĭ·dī'ȧ), 1856–1945. Am. Mormon; pres. of the church (1918–45).
—, Ulysses Simpson, 1822–1885. *Ulysses Hiram* (baptized *Hiram Ulysses*) *Grant.* Am. gen.; 18th pres. of the U. S. (1869–77).

Gran'ville (grăn'vĭl), 4th Earl. See LEVESON GOWER.
— ·Bar'ker (-bär'kẽr), Har'ley (här'lĭ) Granville, 1877–1946. Eng. actor-manager & dram.

Grasse, de (dē gräs'), Comte (kôNt) Fran'çois' (frän'swä') Jo'seph' (zhō'zĕf') Paul, 1722–1788. Marquis *de Grasse'-Til'ly'* (-tē'yē'). Fr. naval officer.

Gra'tian (grā'shĭ·ăn; -shȧn; *Lat.* Fla'vi·us (flā'vĭ·ŭs) **Gra'ti·a'nus** (grā'shĭ·ā'nŭs), 359–383. Rom. emp. (375–383).

Grat'tan (grăt'ʼn), Henry, 1746–1820. Irish orator & statesman.

Grau San Mar·tin' (grou' sän mär·tēn'), Ra·món' (rä·mōn'), 1887– . Cuban physician & polit.; pres. of Cuba (1944–48).

Graves (grāvz), Robert Ran'ke (räng'kĕ), 1895– . Irish author.

Gray (grā), Asa, 1810–1888. Am. botanist.
—, Carl Raymond, 1889–1955. Am. railroad executive & gen.
—, Thomas, 1716–1771. Eng. poet.

Gray'son, David. See under BAKER.

Gra·zia'ni (grä·zyä'nē), Jean Cé'sar' (sā'zàr'), 1859–1932. Fr. gen.

Gra·zia'ni (grä·tsyä'nē), Ro·dol'fo (rō·dōl'fō), 1882–1955. Mar·che'se (mär·kā'zĕ) *di Neghel'li* (dē nā·gĕl'lē). Ital. marshal & colonial administrator.

Gre'co, El (ĕl grā'kō; *Angl.* grĕk'ō, grē'kō), 1548?–?1614 or ?1625. *Do·me'ni·co* (dō·mā'nē·kō) *Te·o·to·co'pu·lo* (tā·ō·tō·kō'pōō·lō). Span. (Cretan-born) painter.

Gree'ley (grē'lĭ), Horace, 1811–1872. Am. journalist & polit.

Gree'ly (grē'lĭ), Adolphus Washington, 1844–1935. Am. gen. & arctic explorer.

Green (grēn), Anna Katharine, 1846–1935. Am. writer.
—, John Richard, 1837–1883. Eng. hist.
—, Julian, 1900– . Am. nov.
—, William, 1873–1952. Am. labor leader.

Green'a·way (grĕn'ȧ·wā), Catherine, 1846–1901. *Kate.* Eng. painter & illustrator.

Greene (grēn), Nathanael, 1742–1786. Am. Revolutionary gen.
—, Robert, 1560?–1592. Eng. poet & dram.

Gree'nough (grē'nō), Horatio, 1805–1852. Am. sculptor.

Green'wood (grēn'wŏŏd), Arthur, 1880–1954. Brit. polit.

Greg'o·ry (grĕg'ō·rĭ; grĕg'rĭ). Name of 16 popes; esp.: **I** (*the Great*), Saint, 540?–604 (pope 590–604); **VII** (*Hil'de·brand* (hĭl'dĕ·brănd]), Saint, 1020?–1085 (pope 1073–85); **XIII** (*U'go Buon'com·pa'gni* [ōō'gō bwŏn'kŏm·pä'nyē]), 1502–1585 (pope 1572–85).
—, Lady Augusta, 1859?–1932. Nee *Persse* (pûrs). Irish dram.
—, Edmund Bris'tol (brĭs't'l), 1882– . Am. gen.
— **of Nys'sa** (ĭv nĭs'ȧ), Saint, 331?–?396. Eastern church father.
— **of Tours** (tŏŏr; *Fr.* tōōr), Saint, 538?–593. Frankish ecclesiastic & hist.

Gren'fell (grĕn'fĕl), Sir Wilfred Thomason, 1865–1940. Eng. medical missionary to Labrador.

Gren'ville (grĕn'vĭl), George, 1712–1770. Eng. statesman.
— **or Greyn'ville** (grăn'vĭl; grĕn'-), Sir Richard, 1541?–1591. Brit. admiral.

Gresh'am (grĕsh'ăm), Sir Thomas, 1519?–1579. Eng. financier.

Greuze (grûz), Jean Bap'tiste' (bȧ'tēst') 1725–1805. Fr. painter.

Gré'vy' (grā'vē'), Fran'çois' (frän'swä') Paul Jules, 1807–1891. Fr. lawyer; 3d pres. of the Republic (1879–87).

Grey (grā), Charles, 2d Earl, 1764–1845. Eng. statesman; prime min. (1830–34).
—, Edward, 1862–1933. Viscount *Grey of Fal'lo·don* (făl'ō·d'n; -dŭn). Eng. statesman.
—, Lady Jane, 1537–1554. Eng. noblewoman beheaded as a possible rival for the throne.
—, Zane (zān), 1875–1939. Am. nov.

Grieg (grēg; *Angl.* grēg), Ed'vard (ĕd'värt; äd'-), 1843–1907. Norw. composer.

Grier'son (grēr's'n), Sir Herbert John Clifford, 1866– . Brit. scholar.

Grif'fin (grĭf'ĭn), Walter Bur'ley (bûr'lĭ), 1876–1937. Am. architect.

Grif'fith (grĭf'ĭth), Arthur, 1872–1922. Irish polit.
—, David Lew·el'yn (lŏŏ·ĕl'ĭn) Wark (wôrk), 1875–1948. Am. motion-picture producer.

Gri'gnard' (grē'nyàr'), Vic'tor' (vĕk'tôr'), 1871–1934. Fr. chem.

Grill'par'zer (grĭl'pär'tsĕr), Franz (fränts), 1791–1872. Austrian dram. & poet.

Grimm (grĭm), Ja'cob (jä'kŭb; *Ger.* yä'kôp), 1785–1863, and his bro. Wil'helm (vĭl'hĕlm), 1786–1859. Ger. philologists & fairy tale collaborators.

Gris'wold (grĭz'wŭld; -wōld; -wôld), Dwight Palmer, 1893–1954. Am. polit. & administrator.

Groe'ner (grû'nẽr), Wil'helm (vĭl'hĕlm), 1867–1939. Ger. gen.

Gro'lier' de Ser'vières' (grō'lyä' dĕ sĕr'vyâr'), Jean, 1479–1565. Fr. bibliophile.

Gro·my'ko (grō·mē'kō; *Russ.* grû·mĭ'kŭ), An·drei' (ŭn·dryä'ī) A., 1909– . Russ. econ. & diplomat.

Groo'te (krō'tĕ), Ger'hard (kā'rärt), 1340–1384. *Ge·rar'dus Mag'nus* (jē·rär'dŭs mäg'nŭs). Du. religious reformer.

Gro'pi·us (grō'pĭ·ŭs; *Ger.* -pē·ōōs), Wal'ter (wôl'tĕr; *Ger.* väl'-), 1883– . Ger.-born architect in America.

Grop'per (grŏp'ẽr), William, 1897– . Am. painter.

Gros (grō), Baron An'toine' (än'twàn'), Jean, 1771–1835. Fr. painter.

Gros've·nor (grōv'nẽr), Gilbert Hovey, 1875– . Am. geographer.

Grote (grōt), George, 1794–1871. Eng. hist.

Gro'ti·us (grō'shĭ·ŭs), Hu'go (hū'gō), 1583–1645. *Huig de Groot* (hoik' dĕ krōt'). Du. jurist & statesman.

Grou'chy', de (dē grōō'shē'), Marquis Em'ma'nu·el' (ĕ'mȧ'nü·ĕl'), 1766–1847. Fr. gen.

Grove (grōv), Sir George, 1820–1900. Eng. writer on music.

Groves (grōvz), Leslie Richard, 1896– . Am. gen.

Grü'ne·wald (grü'nĕ·vält), Mat'thi·as (mä·tē'äs) *or* Ma·thä'us (mä·tä'ŏŏs), fl. 1500–1530. Ger. painter.

Gryph'i·us (grĭf'ĭ·ŭs; *Ger.* grü'fē·ōŏs), An'dre·as (än'drĕ·äs; *Ger.* än·drä'äs), 1616–1664. Lat. *Greif* (grīf). Ger. poet & dram.

Guar·ne'ri (gwär·nä'rē; *Lat.* **Guar·ne'ri·us** (gwär·nē'rĭ·ŭs). Family of Italian violinmakers; esp. Giu·sep'pe (jōō·zĕp'pā) An·to'nio (än·tō'nyō), 1683–1745.

Gu·de'ri·an (gōō·dā'rē·än), Heinz (hīnts), 1886–1954. Ger. gen.

Gue·dal'la (gwĕ·dăl'ȧ), Philip, 1889–1944. Eng. writer.

Gué'rard' (gā'rär'; *Angl.* gȧ·rärd'), Al'bert' (àl'bâr'; *Angl.* ăl'bẽrt) Lé'on' (lā'ôn'), 1880– . Am. (Fr.-born) educ. & writer.

Gue'rin' (gā'rän'), Jules, 1866–1946. Am. painter.

Guesde (gĕd), Jules, 1845–1922. *Ma'thieu'* (mȧ'tyû') *Ba'sile'* (bȧ'zēl'). Fr. socialist.

Guest (gĕst), Edgar Albert, 1881– . Am. journalist & poet.

Gui'do d'A·rez'zo (gwē'dō dä·rät'tsō) *or* **Gui'do A're·ti'no** (ä'rä·tē'nō), 995?–?1050. Benedictine monk & music reformer.

Guil·laume' (gē'yōm'), Charles É'dou·ard' (ā'dwàr'), 1861–1938. Fr. physicist.

Guis'card' (gēs'kàr'), Ro'bert' (rō'bâr'), 1015?–1085. Norman conqueror in Italy.

Guise, de (dē gēz' *or*, *less often*, gwēz'; *Fr.* gü·ēz' *or* gēz'), 1st Duc (dük), 1519–1563. *Fran'çois'* (frän'swä') *de Lor'raine'* (dĕ lô'rân'); *le Ba'la'fré'* (lĕ bȧ'lȧ'frē'). Fr. soldier & polit.
—, 3d Duc, 1550–1588. *Hen'ri'* (än'rē') *I de Lorraine; also* le *Balafré.* Fr. soldier & polit.

Gui·te'ras (gē·tä'räs), Juan (hwän), 1852–1925. Cuban physician.

Gui'try' (gē'trē') Sa'cha' (sȧ'shä'), 1885–1957. Fr. actor & dram.

Gui'zot' (gē'zō'), Fran'çois' (frän'swä') Pierre Guil'laume' (gē'yōm'), 1787–1874. Fr. hist. & statesman.

Gull'strand (gŭl'stränd), All'var (äl'vàr), 1862–1930. Swed. ophthalmologist.

Gun'nars·son (gŭn'närs·sŏn), Gun'nar (gŭn'när), 1889– . Icelandic poet & nov.

Gun'ter (gŭn'tẽr), Edmund, 1581–1626. Eng. math.

Gürt'ner (gürt'nẽr), Franz (fränts), 1881–1941. Ger. Nazi jurist.

Gus·ta'vus (gŭs·tā'vŭs; -tä'vŭs). Name of 5 kings of Sweden: **I** (*Gustavus Va'sa* [vä'sä]), 1496–1560 (reigned 1523–60); **II** (*Gustavus A·dol'phus* [ȧ·dōl'fŭs]), 1594–1632 (reigned 1611–32); **III**, 1746–1792 (reigned 1771–92); **IV** (*Gustavus Adolphus*), 1778–1837 (reigned 1792–1809); **V** (*Gus'taf* [gŭs'täv]), 1858–1950 (reigned 1907–50); **VI**, 1882– (reigned 1950–).

Gu'ten·berg (gōō'tĕn·bẽrk; *Angl.* gōō't'n·bûrg), Jo·hann (yō·hän'; yō'hän), 1400?–?1468. *Johann Gens'fleisch* (gĕns'flīsh). Ger. inventor of printing from movable type.

Gutz'kow (gōŏts'kō), Karl, 1811–1878. Ger. journalist, nov., & dram.

Guz·mán' Blan'co (gōōs·män' bläng'kō), An·to'ni·o (än·tō'nyō), 1829–1899. Venezuelan soldier & statesman; pres. of Venezuela (alternate terms of two years 1870–89).

Gwin·nett' (gwĭ·nĕt'), But'ton (bŭt'ʼn), 1735?–1777. Am. Revolutionary leader.

Gwyn *or* **Gwynne** (gwĭn), Eleanor, 1650–1687. *Nell.* Eng. actress; mistress of Charles II.

H

Haa'kon VII (hô'kŏn), 1872–1957. King of Norway (1905–57).

Ha'ber (hä'bẽr), Fritz (frĭts), 1868–1934. Ger. chem.

Há'cha (hä'kȧ), E'mil (ē'mĭl), 1872–1945. Czech jurist & statesman.

Had'field (hăd'fēld), Sir Robert Abbott, 1858–1940. Eng. metallurgist.

Had'ley (hăd'lĭ), Arthur Twi'ning (twī'nĭng), 1856–1930. Am. econ.; pres., Yale U. (1899–1921).
—, Henry Kim'ball (kĭm'b'l), 1871–1937. Am. composer.

Had'ow (hăd'ō), Sir William Henry, 1859–1937. Eng. educ. & writer on music.

Ha'dri·an (hā'drĭ·ăn), Pope. See ADRIAN.
— *or* **A'dri·an** (ā'drĭ·ăn), 76–138. Rom. emp. (117–138).

Haeck'el (hĕk'ĕl), Ernst (ẽrnst) Hein'rich (hīn'rĭk), 1834–1919. Ger. biologist & philos.

Ha·fiz' (hä·fēz'), 14th cent. *Shams ud·din Mohammed.* Pers. poet.

Hag'e·dorn (hăg'ĕ·dôrn), Her'mann (hûr'măn), 1882– . Am. poet, nov., & critic.
Hag'gard (hăg'ĕrd), Sir Henry Ri'der (rī'dĕr), 1856–1925. Eng. nov.
Hag'gin (hăg'ĭn), Ben (bĕn) Al'i (ăl'ĭ), 1882–1951. Am. painter & stage designer.
Hahn (hän), Ot'to (ôt'ō), 1879– . Ger. physical chem.
Hah'ne·mann (hä'nĕ·män; Angl. -măn), (Chri'sti·an Frie'drich [krĭs'tē·än frē'drĭk]) Sam'u·el (zä'mōō-ĕl; Angl. săm'ū·ĕl), 1755–1843. Ger. physician; founder of homeopathy.
Hai'dar (or Hy'der) A·li' (hī'där [hī'dĕr] ä·lĭ'), 1722–1782. Mohammedan ruler of Mysore, India.
Haig (hāg), Douglas, 1861–1928. 1st Earl Haig. Brit. field marshal.
Hai'le Se·las'sie (hī'lĕ sĭl·lä'syĕ; freq. Angl. hī'lĕ sĕ·lăs'ĭ or -lä'sĭ), 1891– . Ras Taffari or Tafari. Emp. of Ethiopia (1930–).
Hak'luyt (hăk'lōōt), Richard, 1552?–1616. Eng. geographer & hist.
Hal'dane (hôl'dān), John Bur'don (bûr'd'n) San'der·son (săn'dĕr·s'n), 1892– . Brit. scientist.
—, John Scott, 1860–1936. Brit. physiol.
—, Richard Burdon, 1856–1928. Viscount Haldane of Cloan (klōn). Bro. of J. S. Brit. lawyer, philos., & statesman.
Hal'der (häl'dĕr), Franz, 1884– . Ger. gen.
Hale (hāl), Edward Everett, 1822–1909. Am. Unitarian clergyman & writer.
—, George El'ler·y (ĕl'ĕr·ĭ), 1868–1938. Am. astron.
—, Sir Matthew, 1609–1676. Eng. jurist.
—, Nathan, 1755–1776. Am. Revolutionary officer, executed as a spy.
Ha·lé·vy' (hȧ·lā'vē'), 1799–1862. Pseud. of Jacques (zhȧk) Fro'men'tal' (frō'mäⁿ'tȧl') É'lie' (ā'lē') Lé'vy' (lā'vē'). Fr. composer.
—, Lu'do'vic' (lü'dō'vēk'), 1834–1908. Nephew of prec. Fr. dram. & nov.
Hal'i·fax (hăl'ĭ·făks), Earl of, 1881– . Edward Frederick Lind'ley (lĭn[d]'lĭ) Wood. Eng. statesman & diplomat.
Hall (hôl), Charles Francis, 1821–1871. Am. arctic explorer.
—, Charles Martin, 1863–1914. Am. chem. & manuf.
—, Granville Stanley, 1844–1924. Am. psychol. & educ.
—, James Norman, 1887–1951. Am. nov.
Hal'lam (häl'ăm), Henry, 1777–1859. Eng. hist.
Hal'leck (hăl'ĕk), Fitz'-Greene' (fĭts'grēn'; fĭts·grēn'), 1790–1867. Am. poet.
—, Henry Wa'ger (wā'jĕr), 1815–1872. Am. gen.
Hal'ler (häl'lĕr), Jó'zef (yōō'zĕf), 1873– . Pol. soldier.
Hal'ley (hăl'ĭ), Edmund, 1656–1742. Eng. astron.
Hals (häls), Frans (fräns), 1580?–1666. Du. painter.
Hal'sey (hôl'sĭ), William Frederick, 1882– . Am. admiral of the fleet.
Hal'sted (hôl'stĕd; -stĭd), William Stewart, 1852–1922. Am. surgeon.
Ham'bro (häm'brō), Carl (kärl) Jo'a·chim (yō'ä·kĭm), 1885– . Norw. statesman.
Ha·mil'car Bar'ca (hȧ·mĭl'kär bär'kȧ; hăm'ĭl·kär), 270?–228 B.C. Father of Hannibal. Carthaginian gen.
Ham'il·ton (hăm'ĭl·tŭn; -t'n), Alexander, 1755–1804. Am. statesman.
—, Lady Emma, 1761?–1815. Nee Lyon. Mistress of Lord Nelson.
—, Sir Ian Standish Mon·teith' (mŏn·tēth'), 1853–1947. Brit. gen.
Ham'lin (hăm'lĭn), Hannibal, 1809–1891. Vice-pres. of the U. S. (1861–65).
Ham'mar·skjöld' (häm'är·shûld'), Dag (däg) Hjal'mar (yäl'mär) Ag'ne (äng'nĕ) Carl, 1905– . Swedish U.N. official; sec'y gen. (1953–).
Ham'mer·stein (häm'ĕr·stīn), Oscar, 1847?–1919. Ger.-born theater manager in Am.
—, Oscar, 1895– . Grandson of prec. Am. dram.
Ham'mond (hăm'ŭnd), John Hays, 1855–1936. Am. mining engineer.
—, John Hays, 1888– . Son of prec. Am. electrical engineer & inventor.
—, Percy, 1873–1936. Am. dramatic critic.
Ham'mu·ra'bi (häm'ŏŏ·rä'bē; häm'-). King of Babylon (ab. 1955–1913 B.C., or earlier).
Hamp'den (hăm[p]'dĕn), John, 1594–1643. Eng. statesman.
—, Walter, 1879–1955. Stage name of W. H. Dough'er·ty (dŏk'ĕr·tĭ). Am. actor.
Hamp'ton (hăm[p]'tŭn), Wade (wād), 1752?–1835. Am. gen.
—, —, 1818–1902. Grandson of prec. Am. polit. & Confed. gen.
Ham'sun (häm'sŏŏn), Knut (k'nōōt), 1859–1952. Pseud. of Knut Pe'der·sen (pā'dĕr·sĕn). Norw. writer.
Han'cock (hăn'kŏk), John, 1737–1793. Am. Revolutionary statesman.
—, Win'field (wĭn'fēld) Scott, 1824–1886. Am. gen.
Han'del (hăn'd'l), George Frederick, 1685–1759. Brit. (Ger.-born) composer.
Han'na (hăn'ȧ), Marcus Alonzo, 1837–1904. Mark. Am. businessman & polit.
Han'nay (hăn'ā), James Owen, 1865–1950. Irish clergyman & nov.
Han'ne·gan (hăn'ĕ·găn), Robert Em'met (ĕm'ĕt; -ĭt), 1903–1949. Am. lawyer & polit.
Han'ni·bal (hăn'ĭ·băl), 247–183 B.C. Son of Hamilcar Barca. Carthaginian gen.
Han'no (hăn'ō), 3d cent. B.C. Carthaginian statesman.
Ha'no'taux' (à'nō'tō'), (Al'bert' Au'guste' [ăl'bâr' ō'güst']) Ga'bri·el' (gä'brē'ĕl'), 1853–1944. Fr. hist. & statesman.
Han'sard (hän'sĕrd; -särd), Luke, 1752–1828. Eng. printer.
Hans'son (hän'sôn), Per (pâr) Al'bin (äl'bĭn), 1885–1946. Swed. statesman.
Han Yü (hän' yü'), 768–824. Han Wên-Kung (hän' wŭn'gŏŏng'). Chin. poet, essayist, & philos.
Har'bach (här'bäk), Otto A'bels (ā'bĕlz), 1873– . Am. dram. & musical comedy librettist.
Har'bord (här'bĕrd), James Guth'rie (gŭth'rĭ), 1866–1947. Am. gen. & businessman.
Har'court (här'kĕrt; -kôrt), Sir Cecil Hal'li·day (hăl'ĭ·dā) Jep'son (jĕp's'n), 1892– . Brit. admiral.

Har'de·ca·nute' (här'dĭ·kȧ·nūt'), 1019?–1042. King of Denmark (1035–42) and of Eng. (1040–42).
Har'den (här'd'n), Sir Arthur, 1865–1940. Eng. chem.
— (här'dĕn), Ma'xi·mil'li·an (mäk'sē·mē'lē·än), 1861–1927. Orig. Wit·kow'ski (vĭt·kôf'skē). Ger. journalist & writer.
Har'den·berg, von (fôn här'dĕn·bĕrk), Prince Karl Au'gust (ou'gŏŏst), 1750–1822. Prussian statesman.
Har'ding (här'dĭng), Warren Gamaliel, 1865–1923. 29th pres. of the U. S. (1921–23).
Har'dinge (här'dĭng), Henry, 1785–1856. 1st Viscount Hardinge of La·hore' (lȧ·hōr'). Brit. field marshal; gov. gen. of India (1844–47).
Hard'wicke (härd'wĭk), Sir Ce'dric (sē'drĭk) Webster, 1893– . Eng. actor.
Har'dy (här'dĭ), Thomas, 1840–1928. Eng. nov. & poet.
Har'greaves (här'grēvz), James, d. 1778. Eng. inventor of the spinning jenny.
Har'ing·ton or Har'ring·ton (här'ĭng·tŭn), Sir John, 1561–1612. Eng. writer & trans.
Ha·ri'ri, al- (äl'hä·rē'rē), 1054–1122. Arab scholar & poet.
Har'ley (här'lĭ), Robert, 1661–1724. 1st Earl of Ox'ford (ŏks'fĕrd). Eng. statesman.
Har'mon (här'mŏn), Mil'lard (mĭl'ĕrd) Fillmore, 1888–1945. Am. gen.
Harms'worth (härmz'wûrth; -wĕrth), Alfred Charles William, 1865–1922. Viscount North'cliffe (nôrth'klĭf). Eng. publisher & polit.
—, Harold Sidney, 1868–1940. 1st Viscount Roth'er·mere (rŏth'ĕr·mĕr). Bro. of A. C. W. Eng. publisher & polit.
Har'old (här'ŭld) I, d. 1040. Harold Hare'foot' (hâr'fŏŏt'). King of Eng. (1035–40).
— II, 1022?–1066. King of Eng. (1066).
—. Name of 3 kings of Norway; esp. III (Haard'raa'de [hôr'rô'dĕ]), 1015–1066 (reigned 1047–66).
Har'per (här'pĕr), William Rai'ney (rā'nĭ), 1856–1906. Am. educ.; pres., U. of Chicago (1891–1906).
Har'ri·man (här'ĭ·măn), William A'ver·ell (ā'vĕr·ĭl), 1891– . Am. businessman, diplomat, & polit.
Har'ris (här'ĭs), Sir Arthur Trav'ers (trăv'ĕrz), 1892– . Brit. air marshal.
—, Frank, 1854–1931. Am. (Irish-born) writer.
—, Joel Chan'dler (chăn'dlĕr), 1848–1908. Am. writer.
—, William Tor'rey (tôr'ĭ), 1835–1909. Am. philos. & educ.
Har'ri·son (här'ĭ·s'n), Benjamin, 1833–1901. 23d pres. of the U. S. (1889–93).
—, Frederic, 1831–1923. Eng. writer & philos.
—, William Henry, 1773–1841. 9th pres. of the U. S. (1841).
Hart (härt), Albert Bush'nell (bŏŏsh'nĕl), 1854–1943. Am. hist. & editor.
—, Moss, 1904– . Am. librettist & dram.
—, Sir Robert, 1835–1911. Brit. diplomat.
—, William Shakespeare, 1872–1946. Am. actor.
Harte (härt), Francis Brett (brĕt), 1836–1902. Bret (brĕt). Am. writer.
Ha·run' al-Ra·shid' (Arab. hä·rōōn' är'rä·shēd'; sometimes Angl. här'ŏŏn äl·räsh'ĭd), 764?–809. Caliph of Baghdad (786–809).
Har'vard (här'vĕrd), John, 1607–1638. Eng. clergyman in Am.
Har'vey (här'vĭ), George Brin'ton (brĭn't'n; -tŭn) McClellan, 1864–1928. Am. journalist & diplomat.
—, Sir John Martin, 1863–1944. Eng. actor & producer.
—, William, 1578–1657. Eng. physician & anatomist.
Har'wood (här'wŏŏd), Sir Henry Harwood, 1888–1950. Brit. admiral.
Has'dru·bal (hăz'drŏŏ·băl; hăz'drŏŏ·băl; häz·drōō'băl), d. 207 B.C. Bro. of Hannibal. Carthaginian gen.
Has'sam (hăs'ăm), Childe (chīld), 1859–1935. Am. painter & etcher.
Hass'ler (häs'lĕr), Hans Le'o (lā'ō), 1564–1612. Ger. composer.
Has'tings (häs'tĭngz), 1st Marquis of, 1754–1826. Francis Raw'don-Hastings (rô'd'n-). Brit. gen. & colonial administrator.
—, Thomas, 1860–1929. Am. architect.
—, Warren, 1732–1818. Eng. statesman & administrator in India.
Ha·ta (hä·tä), Shun·ro·ku (shōōn·rō·kŏō), 1879– . Jap. gen.
Haupt'mann (houpt'män), Ger'hart (gär'härt), 1862–1946. Ger. writer.
Haus'ho'fer (hous'hō'fĕr), Karl, 1860–1946. Ger. gen. & geographer.
Hauss'mann' (ōs'män'), Baron Georges (zhôrzh) Eu'gène' (ü'zhän'; ü'-), 1809–1891. Fr. administrator; improver of Paris.
Have'lock (hăv'lŏk; -lŭk), Sir Henry, 1795–1857. Brit. gen.
Hawke (hôk), Edward, 1st Baron, 1705–1781. Eng. admiral.
Haw'kins (hô'kĭnz), Sir Anthony Hope (hōp), 1863–1933. Pseud. Anthony Hope. Eng. nov. & dram.
— or Haw'kyns (hô'kĭnz), Sir John, 1532–1595. Eng. admiral.
Ha'worth (härth), Sir Walter Norman, 1883–1950. Eng. chem.
Haw'thorne (hô'thôrn), Nathaniel, 1804–1864. Am. author.
Hay (hā), Ian. See John Hay BEITH.
—, John Milton, 1838–1905. Am. statesman.
Hay'dn (hī'd'n; Angl. hā'd'n), (Franz [fränts]) Jo'seph (yō'zĕf), 1732–1809. Austrian composer.
Hayes (hāz), Carl'ton (kärl't'n; -tŭn) Joseph Hunt'ley (hŭnt'lĭ), 1882– . Am. hist. & diplomat.
—, Helen, 1900– . Helen Hayes Brown; wife of Charles Mac-Arthur. Am. actress.
—, Isaac Israel, 1832–1881. Am. arctic explorer.
—, Patrick Joseph, 1867–1938. Am. cardinal.
—, Roland, 1887– . Am. tenor.
—, Ruth'er·ford (rŭth'ĕr·fĕrd) Bir'chard (bûr'chĕrd), 1822–1893. 19th pres. of the U. S. (1877–81).
Haynes (hānz), El'wood (ĕl'wŏŏd), 1857–1925. Am. inventor.
Hays (hāz), Will Harrison, 1879–1954. Am. lawyer & polit.
Haz'ard (hăz'ĕrd), Caroline, 1856–1945. Am. educ.; pres., Wellesley Coll. (1899–1910).
Ha'zard' (à'zàr'), Paul Gus'tave' (güs'tàv') Ma'rie' (mà'rē') Ca'mille' (kà'mē'y'), 1878–1944. Fr. literary hist.
Ha'zen (hā'z'n), Charles Dow'ner (dou'nĕr), 1868–1941. Am. hist.
Haz'litt (hăz'lĭt), William, 1778–1830. Eng. essayist.

Hea′ly (hē′lĭ), Timothy Michael, 1855–1931. Irish nationalist statesman.

Hearn (hûrn), Laf·cad′i·o (?lăf·kăd′ĭ·ō), 1850–1904. *Ya·ku·mo Ko·i-zu·mi* (yä·kōō·mō kō·ē·zōō·mē). Jap. (Irish-Greek-born) writer.

Hearst (hûrst), William Randolph, 1863–1951. Am. newspaper publisher.

Heav′i·side (hĕv′ĭ·sīd), Oliver, 1850–1925. Eng. physicist & electrician.

Heb′bel (hĕb′ĕl), Frie′drich (frē′drĭк), 1813–1863. Ger. dram.

He′ber (hē′bēr), Reginald, 1783–1826. Eng. prelate & hymn writer.

Hé′bert′ (ā′bâr′), Jacques (zhäk) René, 1755–1794. Fr. Revolutionary journalist.

He·din′ (hĕ·dēn′), Sven (svĕn) An′ders (än′dĕrs), 1865–1952. Swed. explorer.

He′gel (hā′gĕl), Ge·org′ (gĕ·ôrк′) Wil′helm (vĭl′hĕlm) Frie′drich (frē′drĭк), 1770–1831. Ger. philos.

Hei′den·stam, von (fôn hē′ĭ·dĕn·stäm), Ver′ner (văr′nĕr), 1859–1940. Swed. writer.

Hei′fetz (hī′fĕts), Ja′scha (yä′shä), 1901– . Russ. violinist.

Hei′ne (hī′nĕ), Hein′rich (hīn′rĭк), 1797–1856. Ger. poet & critic.

Hei′sen·berg (hī′zĕn·bĕrк), Wer′ner (vĕr′nĕr), 1901– . Ger. physicist.

Hei′ser (hī′zēr), Victor George, 1873– . Am. public health physician & writer.

He′li·o·gab′a·lus (hē′lĭ·ō·găb′à·lŭs) or **El′a·gab′a·lus** (ĕl′à·găb′à·lŭs), 204–222. *Var′i·us* (vâr′ĭ·ŭs) *A·vi′tus Bas′si·a′nus* (à·vī′tŭs băs′ĭ·ā′nŭs). Rom. emp. (218–222).

Helm′holtz, von (fôn hĕlm′hōlts), Her′mann (hĕr′män) Lud′wig (lōōt′vĭк; lōōd′-) Fer′di·nand (fĕr′dĕ·nänt), 1821–1894. Ger. physicist, anatomist, & physiol.

Hé·lo′ïse′ (ā′lō′ēz′), 1101?–1164. *Wife of Abelard.* Fr. abbess.

Hel′vé′tius′ (ĕl′vā′syüs′), Claude (klōd) Adrien, 1715–1771. Fr. philos.

Hem′ans (hĕm′ănz), Felicia Dorothea, 1793–1835. Nee *Browne.* Eng. poet.

Hem′ing or **Hem′minge** (hĕm′ĭng), John, 1556?–1630. Eng. actor.

Hem′ing·way (hĕm′ĭng·wā), Ernest, 1898– . Am. story writer & journalist.

Hé′mon′ (ā′môN′), Louis, 1880–1913. Fr. nov.

Hem′pel (hĕm′pĕl), Frieda, 1885–1955. Ger. soprano.

Hen′der·son (hĕn′dēr·s′n), Arthur, 1863–1935. Brit. labor leader & statesman.

—, Leon, 1895– . Am. econ. & administrator.

—, Sir Nev′ile (nĕv′′l; -ĭl) Mey′rick (mĕr′ĭk; mā′rĭk; mī′rĭk), 1882–1942. Brit. diplomat.

Hen′gist (hĕng′gĭst) *and* **Hor′sa** (hôr′sà), d. 488 and 455 A.D. resp. *Bros.* Jute invaders of Britain (ab. 449).

Hen′ley (hĕn′lĭ), William Ernest, 1849–1903. Eng. editor & author.

Hen′ne·pin (hĕn′ē·pĭn; *Fr.* ĕn′păn′), Louis, 1640–?1701. Belg. friar & explorer in Am.

Hen′ri (hĕn′rĭ), Robert, 1865–1929. Am. painter.

Hen′ry (hĕn′rĭ). Name of 8 kings of Eng.: **I**, 1068–1135 (reigned 1100–35); **II**, 1133–1189 (reigned 1154–89); **III**, 1207–1272 (reigned 1216–72); **IV**, 1367–1413 (reigned 1399–1413); **V**, 1387–1422 (reigned 1413–22); **VI**, 1421–1471 (reigned 1422–61 & 1470–71); **VII**, 1457–1509 (reigned 1485–1509); **VIII**, 1491–1547 (reigned 1509–47).

—. Name of 4 kings of France: **I**, 1008–1060 (reigned 1031–60); **II**, 1519–1559 (reigned 1547–59); **III**, 1551–1589 (reigned 1574–89); **IV**, *of Na·varre′* (nà·vär′), 1553–1610 (reigned 1589–1610).

—, 1394–1460. *The Navigator.* Port. prince; promoter of navigation.

—, Joseph, 1797–1878. Am. physicist.

—, O. See under PORTER.

—, Patrick, 1736–1799. Am. statesman & orator.

Hens′lowe (hĕnz′lō), Philip, d. 1616. Eng. theater manager & diarist.

Hen′ty (hĕn′tĭ), George Alfred, 1832–1902. Eng. nov.

Hep′burn (hĕp′bērn), Katharine, 1909– . Am. actress.

Hep′ple·white (hĕp′′l·hwīt), George, d. 1786. Eng. cabinetmaker.

Her′a·cli′tus (hĕr′à·klī′tŭs), 6th–5th cent. B.C. Greek philos.

Her′a·cli′us (hĕr′à·klī′ŭs; hĕ·răk′lĭ·ŭs), 575?–641. Byzantine emp. (610–641).

Her′bart (hĕr′bärt), Jo·hann′ (yō·hän′; yō′hän) Frie′drich (frē′drĭк), 1776–1841. Ger. philos. & educ.

Her′bert (hûr′bērt), George, 1593–1633. Eng. divine & poet.

—, Victor, 1859–1924. Am. (Irish-born) composer & conductor.

—, William, 1580–1630. 3d Earl of *Pem′broke* (pĕm′brŏŏk). Eng. statesman & poet.

Her′der, von (fôn hĕr′dēr), Jo·hann′ (yō·hän′; yō′hän) Gott′fried (gôt′frēt), 1744–1803. Ger. philos. & writer.

He·re′dia, de (thä ā·rā′thyä), Jo·sé′ (hō·sā′) Ma·ri′a (mä·rē′ä), 1842–1905. Fr. (Cuban-born) poet.

Her′ford (hûr′fērd), Oliver, 1863–1935. Eng. writer & illustrator.

Her′ges·hei′mer (hûr′gĕs·hī′mēr), Joseph, 1880–1954. Am. nov.

He′ring (hā′rĭng), E′wald (ā′vält), 1834–1918. Ger. physiol. & psychol.

Her′ki·mer (hûr′kĭ·mēr), Nicholas, 1728–1777. Am. Revolutionary gen.

Hern′don (hûrn′dŭn), William Henry, 1818–1891. Am. lawyer.

He′ro (hē′rō) or **He′ron** (hē′rŏn), 3d cent. A.D. Greek scientist.

Her′od (hĕr′ŭd), 73?–4 B.C. *The Great.* Rom. king of Judaea (37–4).

— **An′ti·pas** (ăn′tĭ·păs), d. after 40 A.D. *Son of prec.* Rom. tetrarch of Galilee (4 B.C.–40 A.D.).

He·rod′o·tus (hē·rŏd′ō·tŭs), 5th century B.C. Greek hist.

Her·re′ra, de (thä ĕr·rā′rä), Fran·cis′co (frän·thēs′kō), 1576–1656. *El Vie′jo* (ĕl vyĕ′hō). Span. painter.

Her′rick (hĕr′ĭk), My′ron (mī′rŭn) Timothy, 1854–1929. Am. diplomat.

—, Robert, 1591–1674. Eng. poet.

—, Robert, 1868–1938. Am. nov.

Her′ri·ot′ (ĕ′ryō′), É′dou·ard (ā′dwär′) 1872–1957. Fr. statesman.

Her′schel (hûr′shĕl; *Ger.* hĕr′shĕl), Sir John Frederick William, 1792–1871, and his father, Sir William, 1738–1822. Eng. astronomers.

Her′shey (hûr′shĭ), Lewis Blaine, 1893– . Am. gen.

Her′ty (hûr′tĭ), Charles Holmes, 1867–1938. Am. chem.

Hertz (hĕrts), Gu′stav (gōōs′täf), 1887– . Ger. physicist.

—, Hein′rich (hīn′rĭк) Ru′dolph (rōō′dôlf), 1857–1894. Ger. physicist.

Her′tzog (ĕr′sôg), En·ri′que (ĕn·rē′kä), 1897?– . Pres. of Bolivia (1947–49).

— (hĕr′tsŏк), James Barry Mun′nik (*Du.* mûn′ŭk), 1866–1942. S. African gen. & statesman.

Herzl (hĕr′ts′l), The′o·dor (thē′ō·dōr; *Ger.* tā′ō·dōr), 1860–1904. Austrian (Hung.-born) Zionist.

He′si·od (hē′sĭ·ŏd; hĕs′ĭ-), 8th cent. B.C. Greek poet.

Hess (hĕs), Myra, 1890– . Eng. pianist.

—, Vic′tor (vĭk′tôr) Franz (fränts), 1883– . Austrian physicist.

—, (Wal′ter Ri′chard (väl′tēr rĭк′ärt]) Ru′dolf (rōō′dôlf), 1894– . Ger. Nazi polit.

Hes′se (hĕs′ĕ), Her′mann (hĕr′män), 1877– . Ger. author.

He′ve·sy, von (fôn hĕ′vĕ·shĭ), Georg (gā·ôrк′), 1885– . Hung. chem.

Hey′drich (hī′drĭк), Rein′hard (rīn′härt), 1904–1942. *The Hangman.* Ger. Nazi administrator.

Hey′mans (hī′mäns), Cor′neille′ (kôr′nā′y′), 1892– . Belg. physiol.

Hey′se, von (fôn hī′zĕ), Paul, 1830–1914. Ger. nov., dram., & poet.

Hey′ward (hā′wērd), Du·Bose′ (dŭ·bōz′), 1885–1940. Am. author.

Hey′wood (hā′wŏŏd), John, 1497?–?1580. Eng. author.

—, Thomas, 1574?–1641. Eng. dram.

Hib′ben (hĭb′ĕn), John Grier (grēr), 1861–1933. Am. educ.; pres., Princeton U. (1912–32).

Hich′ens (hĭch′ĕnz), Robert Smythe (smīth; smĭth), 1864–1950. Eng. nov.

Hick′ok (hĭk′ŏk), James Butler, 1837–1876. *Wild Bill.* Am. scout & U. S. marshal.

Hi′er·o I (hī′ĕr·ō) or **Hi′er·on** (hī′ĕr·ŏn), d. 466 B.C. Tyrant of Syracuse (478–466).

Hi′er·on′y·mus, Saint Eusebius. See JEROME.

Hig′gin·son (hĭg′ĭn·s′n), Thomas Wentworth Stor′row (stŏr′ō), 1823–1911. Am. clergyman & writer.

Hil′de·brand. See Pope GREGORY VII.

Hill (hĭl), Ambrose Powell, 1825–1865. Am. Confed. gen.

—, Archibald Vivian, 1886– . Eng. physiol.

—, James Jerome, 1838–1916. Am. financier & railway promoter.

—, Sir Row′land (rō′lănd), 1795–1879. Eng. postal reformer.

Hill′man (hĭl′măn), Sidney, 1887–1946. Am. labor leader.

Hill′quit (hĭl′kwĭt), Morris, 1869–1933. Am. (Latvian-born) lawyer & socialist.

Hil′precht (hĭl′prĕкt), Her′mann (hĕr′män) Vol′rath (fōl′rät), 1859–1925. Am. (Ger.-born) Assyriologist.

Hil′ton (hĭl′t′n; -tän), James, 1900–1954. Eng. nov.

Himm′ler (hĭm′lēr), Hein′rich (hīn′rĭк), 1900–1945. Ger. Nazi polit.

Hin′de·mith (hĭn′dĕ·mĭt), Paul, 1895– . Ger. violist & composer.

Hin′den·burg, von (fôn hĭn′dĕn·bŏŏrk; *Angl.* -bûrg), Paul, 1847–1934. *Paul Lud′wig* (lōōt′vĭк; lōōd′-) *Hans An′ton* (än′tōn) *von Be′neck-en·dorff* (bā′nĕ·kĕn·dôrf) *und von Hindenburg.* Ger. field marshal; pres. of Germany (1925–34).

Hip·par′chus (hĭ·pär′kŭs), 6th cent. B.C. Tyrant of Athens (527–514).

—, fl. 130 B.C. Greek astron.

Hip′pi·as (hĭp′ĭ·ăs), 6th cent. B.C. *Bro. of Hipparchus.* Ruled Athens with his bro.

Hip·poc′ra·tes (hĭ·pŏk′rà·tēz), 460?–?377 B.C. *Father of medicine.* Greek physician.

Hi·ra·nu·ma (hē·rä·nōō·mä), Baron Ki·i·chi·ro (kē·ē·chē·rō), 1867–1952. Jap. statesman.

Hi·ro·hi·to (hē·rō·hē·tō; *Angl.* hē′rō·hē′tō, hĭr′ō-), 1901– . Emp. of Japan (1926–).

Hi·ro·shi·ge (hē·rō·shē·gĕ), An·do (än·dō), 1797–1858. Jap. painter.

Hitch′cock (hĭch′kŏk), Edward, 1793–1864. Am. geologist & educ.

—, Ethan Allen, 1835–1909. Am. diplomat & administrator.

Hit′ler (hĭt′lēr), Ad′olf (ăd′ôlf; ä′dôlf; *Ger.* ä′dôlf), 1889–1945. Ger. chancellor & Führer.

Hit′ti (hĭt′ĭ), Philip Khu′ri (kōō′rē), 1886– . Am. (Syrian-born) orientalist.

Hit′torf (hĭt′ôrf), Jo·hann′ (yō·hän′; yō′hän) Wil′helm (vĭl′hĕlm), 1824–1914. Ger. physicist.

Hoare (hōr), Samuel John Gur′ney (gûr′nĭ), 1880– . Viscount *Tem′ple·wood* (tĕm′p′l·wŏŏd′). Eng. statesman.

Hob′be·ma (hŏb′ĕ·mä), Mein′dert (mīn′dĕrt), 1638–1709. Du. painter.

Hobbes (hŏbz), Thomas, 1588–1679. Eng. philos.

Hob′son (hŏb′s′n), Rich′mond (rĭch′mŭnd) Pearson, 1870–1937. Am. naval officer.

Hoc′cleve (hŏk′lēv) or **Oc′cleve** (ŏk′-), Thomas, 1370?–?1450. Eng. poet.

Hock′ing (hŏk′ĭng), William Ernest, 1873– . Am. philos.

Hodg′es (hŏj′ĕz; -ĭz), Court′ney (kōrt′nĭ) H., 1887– . Am. gen.

Hoe (hō), Richard March (märch), 1812–1886. *Son of Robert.* Am. manuf. & inventor.

—, Robert, 1784–1833. Am. (Eng.-born) printing press manuf.

Ho′fer (hō′fēr), An·dre′as (än·drā′äs), 1767–1810. Tyrolese patriot.

Hoff′man (hôf′măn), Mal·vi′na (măl·vē′nà), 1887– . Am. sculptor.

—, Paul Gray, 1891– . Am. industrialist & administrator.

Hoff′mann (hôf′män), Au′gust (ou′gŏŏst) Hein′rich (hīn′rĭк), 1798–1874. Ger. poet, philologist, & hist.

—, Ernst (ĕrnst) The′o·dor (tā′ō·dōr) Wil′helm (vĭl′hĕlm), 1776–1822. *Ernst Theodor A′ma·de′us* (ä′mä·dā′ŏŏs). Ger. composer, writer, & illustrator.

Hof′mann (hōf′män; *Pol.* hôf′män), Jo′sef (jō′zĕf; -zĭf) Cas′i·mir (kăz′ĭ·mĭr), 1876–1957. Pol. pianist.

Hof′mann, von (fôn hōf′män; hôf′-), Au′gust (ou′gŏŏst) Wil′helm (vĭl′hĕlm), 1818–1892. Ger. chem.

Hof′manns·thal, von (fôn hôf′mäns·täl; hôf′-), Hu′go (hōō′gō), 1874–1929. Austrian poet & dram.

Ho'garth (hō'gärth), William, 1697–1764. Eng. painter & engraver.

Hog'ben (hŏg'bĕn), Lancelot Thomas, 1895– . Eng. scientist & writer.

Hogg (hŏg), James, 1770–1835. *The Ett'rick Shepherd* (ĕt'rĭk). Scot. poet.

Ho'hen·zol'lern, Michael. See MICHAEL.

Ho·ku·sai (hō·kŏŏ-sī), Ka·tsu·shi·ka (kä·tsŏŏ-shē·kä), 1760–1849. Jap. artist.

Hol'bein (hŏl'bīn; *Angl.* hŏl'-), Hans, father, 1465?–1524, and son, 1497?–1543. Ger. painters.

Hol'comb (hŏl'kŭm), Thomas, 1879– . Am. marine corps gen.

Hol'ins·hed (hŏl'ĭnz-hĕd; *often* -ĭn-shĕd) *or* **Hol'lings·head** (hŏl'ĭngz-hĕd), Raphael, d. ab. 1580. Eng. chronicler.

Hol'land (hŏl'ănd), John Philip, 1840–1914. Irish-born inventor in Am.

Hol'man-Hunt', William. = Holman HUNT.

Holmes (hōmz), Elias Burton, 1870– . Am. traveler.

—, John Haynes, 1879– . Am. clergyman.

—, Oliver Wendell, 1809–1894. Am. physician & author.

—, Oliver Wendell, 1841–1935. *Son of prec.* Am. jurist.

Holst, von (fôn hôlst'), Her'mann (hĕr'män; *Angl.* hûr'măn) E'du·ard (ā'dŏŏ-ärt), 1841–1904. Russ.-born hist. in Am.

Holt (hōlt), Luther Em'mett (ĕm'ĕt; -ĭt), 1855–1924. Am. pediatrician.

Ho Lung (hō' lŏŏng'), 1886?– . Chin. Communist gen.

Home (hūm), Daniel Dun·glas' (dŭn-glâs'), 1833–1886. Scot. spiritualist medium.

Ho'mer (hō'mēr), fl. 850 B.C. or earlier. Traditional Greek epic poet.

—, Winslow, 1836–1910. Am. painter.

Ho'neg'ger (hō'nĕg'ĕr; *Fr.* ô'ne'gâr'), Ar'thur' (àr'tür'), 1892–1955. Fr. composer.

Ho·no'ri·us (hō-nō'rĭ-ŭs), Fla'vi·us (flā'vĭ-ŭs), 384–423. Rom. emp. of the West (395–423).

Hood (hŏŏd), John Bell, 1831–1879. Am. Confed. gen.

—, Samuel, 1st Viscount, 1724–1816. Brit. admiral.

—, Thomas, 1799–1845. Eng. poet.

Hooke (hŏŏk), Robert, 1635–1703. Eng. experimental philos.

Hook'er (hŏŏk'ēr), Joseph, 1814–1879. Am. army officer.

—, Sir Joseph Dalton, 1817–1911. Eng. botanist.

—, Richard, 1554?–1600. Eng. theol.

—, Thomas, 1586?–1647. Eng. Puritan clergyman; a founder of Connecticut.

Hoo'ton (hŏŏ't'n), Ear'nest (ûr'nĕst; -nĭst) Albert, 1887–1954. Am. anthropologist.

Hoo'ver (hŏŏ'vēr), Herbert Clark, 1874– . 31st pres. of the U. S. (1929–33).

—, John Edgar, 1895– . Am. criminologist; director, Federal Bureau of Investigation (1924–).

Hope (hōp), Anthony. See Sir Anthony Hope HAWKINS.

—, John Adrian Louis, 1860–1908. 7th Earl of *Hope'toun* (hōp'-tŭn; -toun) and 1st Marquis of *Lin·lith'gow* (lĭn-lĭth'gō). Brit. statesman; gov. gen. of Australia (1901–02).

—, Victor Alexander John, 1887–1951. *Son of prec.* 8th Earl of *Hopetoun* and 2d Marquis of *Linlithgow.* Brit. soldier; viceroy of India (1936–43).

Hop'kins (hŏp'kĭnz), Sir Frederick Gow'land (gou'lănd), 1861–1947. Eng. biochem.

—, Gerard Man'ley (măn'lĭ), 1844–1889. Eng. poet.

—, Harry Lloyd, 1890–1946. Am. polit. & administrator.

—, Johns (jŏnz), 1795–1873. Am. financier.

—, Mark, 1802–1887. Am. educ.

Hop'kin·son (hŏp'kĭn-s'n), Francis, 1737–1791. Am. lawyer & satirist.

Hop'pe (hŏp'ē), William Frederick, 1887– . Am. billiardist.

Hop'per (hŏp'ēr), (William) De Wolf (dĕ wŏŏlf'), 1858–1935. Am. actor.

Hop'wood (hŏp'wŏŏd), (James) Avery, 1882–1928. Am. dram.

Hor'ace (hŏr'ĭs), 65–8 B.C. *Quin'tus* (kwĭn'tŭs) *Ho·ra'tius Flac'cus* (hō-rā'shŭs [-shĭ-ŭs] flăk'ŭs). Rom. poet & satirist.

Hore'-Be·li'sha (hôr'bē-lē'shà), Leslie, 1893–1957. Eng. polit.

Hor'na·day (hôr'nà-dā), William Temple, 1854–1937. Am. zool.

Ho'ro·witz (hô'rō-wĭts), Vla·di'mir (*Russ.* vlŭ-dyē'myĭr), 1904– . Russ.-born pianist.

Hor'sa. See HENGIST.

Hor'tense' de Beau·har'nais'. See BEAUHARNAIS.

Hor'thy (hôr'tĭ), Mi'klós (mĭ'klōsh) von Nagy'bá'nya (fôn nŏd'y'-bä'nyŏ), 1868–1957. Hung. admiral; regent of Hungary (1920–44).

Hos'kins (hŏs'kĭnz), Roy Graham, 1880– . Am. physiol.

Hou·di'ni (hŏŏ-dē'nĭ; -dĭn'ĭ), Harry, 1874–1926. *Eh'rich* (ā'rĭk) *Weiss* (wīs). Am. magician.

Hou'don' (hŏŏ'dôn'; *Angl.* hŏŏ'dŏn), Jean An'toine' (än'twän'), 1741–1828. Fr. sculptor.

Hou'dry (hŏŏ'drē; -drĭ; *Fr.* ŏŏ'drē'), Eugene J., 1892– . Am. (Fr.-born) engineer.

House (hous), Edward Man'dell (măn'd'l), 1858–1938. *Colonel House.* Am. diplomat.

Hous'man (hous'măn), Alfred Edward, 1859–1936. Eng. classical scholar & poet.

—, Laurence, 1865– . *Bro. of prec.* Eng. writer & illustrator.

Hous·say' (ŏŏ-sī'), Ber·nar'do (bĕr·när'thô) Al·ber'to (äl·vĕr'tô), 1887– . Argentine physiol.

Hous'ton (hūs'tŭn), Samuel, 1793–1863. *Sam.* Am. gen.; pres. of the Republic of Texas (1836–38; 1841–44).

Hov'ey (hŭv'ĭ), Richard, 1864–1900. Am. poet.

How'ard (hou'ērd), Catherine. See under CATHERINE.

—, Henry, 1517?–1547. Earl of *Sur'rey* (sûr'ĭ; sŭr'ĭ). Eng. soldier & poet.

—, Sidney Coe (kō), 1891–1939. Am. dram.

Howe (hou), Ed, 1853–1937. *Edgar Watson.* Am. journalist.

—, Elias, 1819–1867. Am. inventor.

—, Julia, 1819–1910. Nee *Ward.* Am. suffragist & reformer.

—, Richard, Earl, 1726–1799. Eng. admiral of the fleet.

—, William, 5th Viscount, 1729–1814. Eng. gen. in Am.

How'ells (hou'ĕlz), William Dean (dēn), 1837–1920. Am. author.

Hoyt (hoit), Charles Hale, 1860–1900. Am. dram.

Hr'dlič·ka (hûr'dlĭch-kà), A'leš (à'lĕsh), 1869–1943. Am. (Bohemian-born) anthropologist.

Hsian T'ung (shü·än' dzŏŏng'), 1906– . *Henry Pu-yi* (pŏŏ'ē'). Chin. emp. (1908–12), last of Manchu dynasty; puppet emp. (as *K'ang Tê* [käng' dŭ']) of Manchukuo (1934–45).

Hsü Hai·tung (shü' hī'dŏŏng'), 1900– . Chin. Communist.

Hsü Shih-ch'ang (shü' shīr'chäng'), 1858–1939. Chin. gen.; pres. of China (1918–22).

Huás'car (wäs'kär), 1495?–1533. Inca prince.

Hub'bard (hŭb'ērd), Elbert Green, 1856–1915. Am. writer, editor, & printer.

Hud'son (hŭd's'n), Henry, d. 1611. Erroneously *Hen'drick* (hĕn'-drĭk). Eng. navigator & explorer.

—, Man'ley (măn'lĭ) Ott'mer (ŏt'mēr), 1886– . Am. jurist.

—, William Henry, 1841–1922. Eng. naturalist & writer.

Huer'ta (wĕr'tä), Vic'to·ria'no (bĕk'tō·ryä'nō), 1854–1916. Mex. gen.; provisional pres. of Mexico (1913–14).

Hug'gins (hŭg'ĭnz), Sir William, 1824–1910. Eng. astron.

Hugh Ca'pet (hū' kā'pĕt, -pĭt; kăp'ĕt, -ĭt); *Fr.* **Hugues Ca'pet'** (üg' kà'pĕ'), 940?–996. King of France (987–996).

Hughes (hūz), Charles Evans, 1862–1948. Am. jurist; chief justice of the U. S. (1930–41).

—, (James) Lang'ston (lăng'stŭn), 1902– . Am. writer.

—, Rupert, 1872–1956. Am. writer.

—, Thomas, 1822–1896. Eng. jurist, reformer, & writer.

—, William Morris, 1864–1952. Australian statesman.

Hu'go (hū'gō; *Fr.* ü'gō'), Vic'tor (vĭk'tēr; *Fr.* vēk'tôr') Ma·rie' (mà·rē'; *Fr.* mà'rē'), 1802–1885. Fr. poet, nov., & dram.

Hu·la'gu (hŏŏ·lä'gŏŏ; hŏŏ'lä-gŏŏ'), 1217–1265. *Grandson of Genghis Khan.* Mongol ruler.

Hull (hŭl), Cor'dell (kôr'dĕl; kôr-dĕl'), 1871–1955. Am. statesman; U. S. secy. of state (1933–44).

—, Isaac, 1773–1843. Am. naval officer.

—, William, 1753–1825. Am. gen.

Hu·ma'yun (hŏŏ-mä'yŏŏn), 1508–1556. Emp. of Hindustan (1530–56).

Hum'bert (hŭm'bērt) **I**; *Ital.* **Um·ber'to** (ŏŏm-bĕr'tō), 1844–1900. King of Italy (1878–1900).

— **II**, 1904– . Prince of *Pied'mont* (pēd'mŏnt); count of *Sar're* (sär'rā). King of Italy (1946).

Hum'boldt, von (fôn hŏŏm'bôlt; *Angl.* hŭm'bōlt), Baron (Frie'drich Hein'rich [frē'drĭk hīn'rĭk]) A'le·xan'der (ä'lĕ·ksän'dēr; *Angl.* ăl'ĕg-zăn'dēr; äl'ĭg-), 1769–1859. Ger. naturalist, traveler, & statesman.

—, Baron Wil'helm (vĭl'hĕlm), 1767–1835. *Bro. of prec.* Ger. philologist & diplomat.

Hume (hūm), David, 1711–1776. Scot. philos. & hist.

Hum'per·dinck (hŏŏm'pēr-dĭngk), Eng'el·bert (ĕng'ĕl-bĕrt), 1854–1921. Ger. composer.

Hum'phrey (hŭm'frĭ), 1391–1447. *Son of Henry IV;* Duke of *Glouces'ter* (glŏs'tēr; glŏs'-) ("*the Good Duke*") & Earl of *Pem'broke* (pĕm'brŏŏk). Eng. statesman & book collector.

Hun'e·ker (hŭn'e·kĕr; -ĭ·kēr), James Gibbons, 1860–1921. Am. musician & critic.

Hung Wu. See CHU YÜAN-CHANG.

Hunt (hŭnt), (James Henry) Leigh, 1784–1859. Eng. essayist & poet.

—, (William) Hol'man (hŏl'măn), 1827–1910. Eng. painter.

Hun'ter (hŭn'tēr), John, 1728–1793. Brit. anatomist & surgeon.

Hun'ting·ton (hŭn'tĭng-tŭn), Col'lis (kŏl'ĭs) Pot'ter (pŏt'ēr), 1821–1900. Am. pioneer railroad builder.

—, Ellsworth, 1876–1947. Am. geographer & explorer.

—, Samuel, 1731–1796. Am. Revolutionary polit.

Hun'tzi·ger' (ŭn'tsē'zhâr'), Charles Lé'on' (lā'ôn') Clé'ment' (klā'män'), 1880–1941. Fr. gen.

Hu'nya·di *or* **Hu'nya·dy** (hŏŏ'nyŏ-dĭ), Já'nos (yä'nŏsh), 1387?–1456. Hung. soldier & hero.

Hur'ley (hûr'lĭ), Patrick Jay, 1883– . Am. lawyer & diplomat.

Hurst (hûrst), Sir Cecil James Bar'ring·ton (băr'ĭng-tŭn), 1870– . Eng. jurist.

—, Fannie, 1889– . Am. writer.

Hu·sein' ibn-A·li' (hŏŏ-sīn' ĭb'n-ä·lī'), 1856–1931. First king of the Hejaz (1916–24).

Hu Shih (hŏŏ' shīr'), 1891– . Chin. philos., diplomat, & writer.

Huss *or* **Hus** (hŭs; *Ger. & Czech,* hŏŏs), John *or* Jan (*Czech* yän), ab. 1374–1415. *Jo·han'nes* (yō·hän'ĕs; -ēs) *Hus von Hu'si·netz* (fôn hŏŏ'zĕ-nĕts). Bohemian religious reformer.

Hu'szár (hŏŏ'sär), Ká'roly (kä'rôl·y'), 1882– . Hung. journalist & polit.

Hutch'ins (hŭch'ĭnz), Robert May'nard (mā'nērd; -närd), 1899– . Am. educ.; pres. (1929–45) & chancellor (1945–51), U. of Chicago.

Hutch'in·son (hŭch'ĭn-s'n), Anne, 1591–1643. Nee *Mar'bur·y* (mär'bĕr-ĭ). Religious liberal in Am.

—, Arthur Stuart-Men·teth' (-mĕn·tēth'), 1879– . Eng. nov.

—, Ray Cor'y·ton (kŏr'ĭ·tŭn), 1907– . Eng. nov.

—, Thomas, 1711–1780. Am. colonial administrator.

Hut'ten, von (fôn hŏŏt'ĕn), Ul'rich (ŏŏl'rĭk), 1488–1523. Ger. humanist & supporter of Luther.

Hut'ton (hŭt'n), Sir Thomas Ja'comb (jā'kŭm), 1890– . Brit. gen.

Hux'ley (hŭks'lĭ), Al'dous (ôl'dŭs) Leonard, 1894– . *Bro. of J. S.* Eng. nov. & critic.

—, Julian So·rell' (sō·rĕl'), 1887– . *Grandson of T. H.* Eng. biologist.

—, Thomas Henry, 1825–1895. Eng. biologist.

Huy'gens *or* **Huy'ghens** (hoi'kĕns; *Angl.* hī'gĕnz), Chris'ti·an (Du. krĭs'tē·än'), 1629–1695. Du. math., physicist, & astron.

Huys'mans (*Du.* hois'mäns; *Fr.* ü·ēs'mäns'), Ca'mille' (kà'mē'y'), 1871– . Belg. polit.

—, Jo'ris (yō'rĭs) Karl (kärl), 1848–1907. *Orig. Charles Ma'rie'* (mà'rē') *Georges* (zhôrzh). Fr. nov.

Hy'att (hī'ăt), Al'phe·us (ăl'fē·ŭs), 1838–1902. Am. naturalist.

J

Hyde (hīd), Douglas, 1860–1949. Irish author; pres. of Eire (1938–45).
—, Edward, 1609–1674. 1st Earl of *Clar'en·don* (klär'ĕn·dŭn). Eng. statesman & hist.
Hy'der A·li' (hī'dẽr ä·lī'). = HAIDAR ALI.
Hy'mans (hī'mäns), Paul (pôl), 1865–1941. Belg. statesman.
Hy'pse·lan'tes. See YPSILANTI.

I

I·bá'ñez, Vicente Blasco-. See BLASCO-IBÁÑEZ.
I'ber'ville', d' (dē'bẽr'vēl'; *Angl.* dē'bẽr·vĭl *or* dī'-), Sieur (syûr), 1661–1706. *Pierre Le·moyne'* (lĕ·mwän'). Fr.-Canadian explorer; founder of Louisiana.
ibn-Khal·dun' (ĭb'n·kăl·dōōn'), 1332–1406. Arab hist.
ibn-Rushd'. See AVERROËS.
ibn-Sa·ud' (ĭb'n·sǒō·ōōd'), Abd·ul'-A·ziz' (ăb·dǒōl'ä·zēz'), 1880–1953. King of Saudi Arabia (1932–53).
ibn-Zuhr' *or* **ibn-Zohr'.** See AVENZOAR.
Ib·ra'him' Pa'sha (ĭb·rä'hēm' pä'shä), 1789–1848. Egyptian gen. & viceroy.
Ib'sen (ĭb's'n; *Norw.* ĭp'sĕn), Hen'rik (hĕn'rĭk), 1828–1906. Norw. poet & dram.
Ick'es (ĭk'ĕs), Harold Le Claire (lĕ klâr'), 1874–1952. Am. lawyer & administrator.
Ic·ti'nus (ĭk·tī'nŭs), 5th cent. B.C. Greek architect.
Ig·na'ti·us (ĭg·nā'shǐ·ŭs; -shŭs), Saint, 1st–2d cent. A.D. *The·oph'o·rus* (thē·ŏf'ō·rŭs). Bishop of Antioch & church father.
— **of Loy·o'la**, Saint. See LOYOLA.
Ikh·na'ton (ĭk·nä't'n) *or* **A'khe·na'ten** (ä'kĕ·nä't'n). *A'men·ho'tep IV* (ä'mĕn·hō'tĕp). King of Egypt (ab. 1375–1358 B.C.); religious reformer.
Im'mel·mann (ĭm'ĕl·män; *Angl.* -măn), Max (mäks; *Angl.* măks), 1890–1916. Ger. aviator.
In'dy', d' (dăN'dē'), Vin'cent' (văn'säN'), 1851–1931. Fr. composer.
I·nês' de Cas'tro. See under CASTRO.
Inge (ĭng), William Ralph, 1860–1954. Eng. prelate & author; dean of St. Paul's (1911–34).
In'ger·soll (ĭng'gẽr·sŏl; -s'l), Robert Green, 1833–1899. Am. lawyer & agnostic.
—, Roy'al (roi'ăl) Ea'son (ē's'n), 1883–   . Am. admiral.
In'gram (ĭng'grăm), Arthur Foley Win'ning·ton (wĭn'ĭng·tŭn), 1858–1946. Eng. prelate; bishop of London (1901–39).
—, Jonas Howard, 1886–1952. Am. admiral.
In'gres (äN'gr'), Jean Au'guste' (ō'güst') Do'mi'nique' (dô'mē'nēk'), 1780–1867. Fr. painter.
In'ness (ĭn'ĕs; -ĭs), George, father, 1825–1894, and son, 1854–1926. Am. painters.
In'no·cent (ĭn'ō·sĕnt; -s'nt). Name of 13 popes; esp.: **II**, d. 1143 (pope 1130–43); **III**, 1161–1216 (pope 1198–1216); **IV**, d. 1254 (pope 1243–54); **XI**, 1611–1689 (pope 1676–89).
Ï·nö·nü' (ĭ·nû·nü'), Is·met' (ĭs·mĕt'), 1884–   . Turk. statesman; pres. of Turkey (1938–50).
In'sull (ĭn's'l), Samuel, 1859–1938. Am. (Eng.-born) utilities executive.
In'ver·chap'el, 1st Baron. See KERR.
I·pa'tieff *or* **I·pa'tiev** (ĭ·pä'tyĕf), Vla·di'mir (vlŭ·dyē'myĭr) Ni·ko·la'e·vich (nyĭ·kŭ·lä'yĕ·vyĭch), 1867–1952. Russ.-born chem. in Am.
Ire'dell (īr'dĕl), James, 1751–1799. Am. jurist.
Ire'ton (īr't'n), Henry, 1611–1651. Eng. Parliamentary commander & regicide.
I'ri·go'yen (ē'rē·gō'yän), Hi·pó'li·to (ē·pō'lē·tō), 1850–1933. Pres. of Argentina (1916–22; 1928–30).
I'ron·side' (ī'ẽrn·sīd'), William Edmund, 1st Baron, 1880–   . Brit. field marshal.
Ir'ving (ûr'vĭng), Sir Henry, 1838–1905. Orig. *John Henry Brod'ribb* (brŏd'rĭb). Eng. actor.
—, Washington, 1783–1859. Am. essayist, nov., & hist.
Ir'win (ûr'wĭn), Wallace, 1875–   . Am. journalist & humorist.
—, William Henry, 1873–1948. *Will.* Am. journalist & writer.
I'saacs (ī'zăks; -zĭks), Sir Isaac Alfred, 1855–1948. Australian jurist & statesman; gov. gen. of Australia (1931–36).
—, Rufus Daniel. See Marquis of READING.
Is·a·bel'la I (ĭz'à·bĕl'à), 1451–1504. *Wife of Ferdinand II of Aragon.* Queen of Castile (1474–1504); aided Columbus.
Ish'er·wood (ĭsh'ẽr·wǒōd), Christopher William Brad'shaw- (brăd'shô-), 1904–   . Eng. author.
I·shi·i (ē·shē·ē), Viscount Ki·ku·ji·ro (kē·kǒō·jē·rō), 1866–   . Jap. diplomat.
Is'i·dore of Se·ville' (ĭz'ĭ·dōr ŭv se·vĭl'; *esp. Brit.*, sĕv''l, -ĭl), Saint, ab. 570–636. *I·do'rus His'pa·len'sis* (ĭz'ĭ·dō'rŭs hĭs'pà·lĕn'sĭs). Span. prelate & scholar.
Is·ken·der' Bey. See SCANDERBEG.
Is·ma'il' Pa'sha (ĭs·mä'ēl' pä'shä), 1830–1895. *Ismail I.* Khedive of Egypt (1863–79).
I·soc'ra·tes (ī·sŏk'rà·tēz), 436–338 B.C. Athenian orator.
I·to (ē·tō), Marquis Hi·ro·bu·mi (hē·rō·bǒō·mē), 1841–1909. Jap. statesman.
—, Yu·ko (yōō·kō) *or* Su·ke·no·ri (sǒō·kĕ·nō·rē), 1843–1914. Jap. admiral.
I·tur'bi (ĭ·tōōr'bē; *Span.* ē·tōōr'vē), Jo·sé' (hō·sā'), 1895–   . Span.-born pianist & conductor in Am.
I'tur·bi'de, de (dä ē'tōōr·vē'thä), A'gus·tín' (ä'gǒōs·tēn'), 1783–1824. Mex. soldier; emp. of Mexico (1822–23).
I·van' (ī·văn'; *Angl.* ī·văn', ī'văn, ī'văn) **III Va·sil'ie·vich** (vŭ·syēl'yĕ·vyĭch), 1440–1505. *Ivan the Great.* Grand duke of Russia (1462–1505).
— **IV Vasilievich**, 1530–1584. *Ivan the Terrible.* Ruler of Russia (1533–84).
Ives (īvz), James Merritt, 1824–1895. Am. lithographer.
I·ye·ya·su (ē·yĕ·yä·sǒō) *or* **I·e·ya·su** (ē·yĕ-), 1542–1616. Jap. gen.; founder (1603) of Tokugawa shogunate.
Iz'ard (ĭz'ẽrd), Ralph, 1742–1804. Am. Revolutionary leader.

Ja'bir. See GEBER.
Jack'son (jăk's'n), Andrew, 1767–1845. Am. gen.; 7th pres. of the U. S. (1829–37).
—, Helen Maria Hunt, 1830–1885. Nee *Fiske.* Am. poet & nov.
—, Robert Hough'wout (hou'ŭt), 1892–1954. Am. jurist.
—, Thomas Jonathan, 1824–1863. *Stone'wall'* (stōn'wôl') *Jackson.* Am. Confed. gen.
Ja'cobs (jā'kŭbz), William Wy'mark (?wī'märk), 1863–1943. Eng. writer.
Jac'quard' (zhà'kàr'; *Angl.* jă·kärd'), Jo'seph' (zhō'zĕf') Ma'rie' (mà'-rē'), 1752–1834. Fr. inventor.
Jacques I, Emp. See Jean Jacques DESSALINES.
Jag'a·tai' (jäg'à·tī'), d. 1242. *2d son of Genghis Khan.* Mongol ruler.
Ja·han'gir (jà·hän'gēr), 1569–1627. Emp. of Hindustan (1605–27).
Ja·lal'-ud-din' Ru'mi (jä·lä'lōōd·dēn' rōō'mē), 1207–1273. Pers. poet.
James (jāmz). Name of 6 kings of Scot.; and 2 kings of Gr. Britain: **I,** 1566–1625 (reigned 1603–25); **II,** 1633–1701 (reigned 1685–88).
—, Henry, 1811–1882. Am. philos.
—, Henry, 1843–1916. *Son of prec.* Brit. writer.
—, William, 1842–1910. *Bro. of prec.* Am. psychol. & philos.
—, Sir William Mil'burne (mĭl'bẽrn), 1881–   . Brit. admiral.
— **Edward.** See James Francis Edward STUART.
Jame'son (jām's'n), Sir Leander Starr (stär), 1853–1917. *Doctor Jameson.* Scot. physician & administrator in S. Africa.
Ja'mi (jä'mĭ), 1414–1492. Pers. poet & mystic.
Ja'ná·ček (yä'nä·chĕk), Le'oš (lĕ'ôsh), 1854–1928. Czech composer.
Jan'sen (jän's'n; *Du.* yän'sĕn), Cor·ne'lis (kôr·nā'lĭs), 1585–1638. *Cornelius Jan·se'ni·us* (jän·sē'nĭ·ŭs; -sĕn'yŭs). Du. R.C. theol.
Ja·rir' (jà·rēr'), d. 729? Arab poet.
Jas'trow (jăs'trō; yäs'trō), Morris, 1861–1921. Am. (Pol.-born) Semitic scholar.
Jau·rès' (zhō'râs'), Jean Lé'on' (lā'ôN'), 1859–1914. Fr. socialist.
Jay (jā), John, 1745–1829. Am. jurist & statesman; 1st chief justice of the U. S. (1789–95).
Jeanne d'Arc. See JOAN OF ARC.
Jeans (jēnz), Sir James Hop'wood (hŏp'wǒōd), 1877–1946. Eng. physicist, astron., & author.
Jebb (jĕb), Sir Richard Clav'er·house (klăv'ẽr·hous), 1841–1905. Scot. Greek scholar.
Jef'fers (jĕf'ẽrz), (John) Robinson, 1887–   . Am. poet.
Jef'fer·son (jĕf'ẽr·s'n), Joseph, 1829–1905. Am. actor.
—, Thomas, 1743–1826. Am. statesman; 3d pres. of the U. S. (1801–09).
Jef'frey (jĕf'rĭ), Francis, Lord, 1773–1850. Scot. critic & jurist.
Jef'freys (jĕf'rĭz), George, 1648–1689. 1st Baron *Jeffreys of Wem* (wĕm). Eng. jurist.
Jel'li·coe (jĕl'ĭ·kō), John Rush'worth (rŭsh'wûrth; -wẽrth), 1st Earl, 1859–1935. Brit. admiral of the fleet.
Jen'ghiz Khan. Variant of GENGHIS KHAN.
Jen'ner (jĕn'ẽr), Edward, 1749–1823. Eng. vaccinationist.
—, Sir William, 1815–1898. Eng. physician.
Jen'sen (yĕn's'n), Jo·han'nes (yōō·hän'ĕs) Vil'helm (vĭl'hĕlm), 1873–1950. Dan. poet & nov.
Jep'son (jĕp's'n), Helen, 1907–   . Am. singer.
Je'ri·tza (yĕ'rē·tsä), Ma·ri'a (mä·rē'ä), 1887–   . *Wife of Irving P. See'ry* (sēr'ĭ). Am. (Austrian-born) soprano.
Je·rome' (jĕ·rōm'; *Brit. usu.* jĕr'ŭm), Saint, 340?–420. *Eu·se'bi·us Hi'er·on'y·mus* (ū·sē'bǐ·ŭs hī'ẽr·ŏn'ĭ·mŭs). Latin church father.
Jer'vis (jẽr'vĭs; jûr'-), John, 1735–1823. Earl of *St. Vin'cent* (sänt vĭn's'nt). Eng. admiral.
Jes'per·sen (yĕs'pẽr·s'n), (Jens [yĕns]) Ot'to (ŏt'ō) (Har'ry [här'ē]), 1860–1943. Dan. philologist.
Je'sus (jē'zŭs) *or* **Jesus Christ** (krīst) *or* **Christ Jesus,** 4–8? B.C.–?29 A.D. *Jesus of Naz'a·reth* (năz'à·rĕth). *The son of Mary.* Source of the Christian religion & Saviour in the Christian faith.
Jev'ons (jĕv'ŭnz), William Stanley, 1835–1882. Eng. econ. & logician.
Jew'ett (jōō'ĕt; -ĭt), Sarah Orne (ôrn), 1849–1909. Am. writer.
Ji·mé'nez de Cis·ne'ros (hē·mā'näth thä thēs·nā'rôs), Fran·cis'co (frän·thēs'kō), 1436–1517. Span. prelate & statesman.
Jin'nah (jĭn'nä), Mo·ham'med (mǒō·häm'mäd) A·li' (ä·lī'), 1876–1948. Moslem lawyer; 1st gov. gen. of dominion of Pakistan (1947–48).
Jo'a·chim (yō'à·kĭm; yō·ä'kĭm), Jo'seph (yō'zĕf), 1831–1907. Hung. violinist.
Joan of Arc (jōn [jō'ăn, jō·än'] ŭv ärk'; *Fr.* **Jeanne d'Arc** (zhän dàrk'), Saint, 1412–1431. *The Maid of Or'le·ans* (ôr'lē·ănz). Fr. national heroine.
Jodl (yō'd'l), Alfred, 1892?–1946. Ger. gen.
Jof'fre (zhô'fr'), Jo'seph' (zhō'zĕf') Jacques (zhàk) Cé'saire' (sā'zâr'), 1852–1931. Fr. field marshal; marshal of France (1917).
John XXIII (jŏn) (*An'ge·lo Giu·sep'pe Ron·cal'li* [än'jà·lō jōō·zĕp'pä rŏng·käl'lē]), 1881–   . Pope (1958–   ).
John (jŏn), 1167?–1216. *John Lack'land'* (lăk'lănd'). King of England (1199–1216).
— **I,** 1357–1433. *The Great.* King of Portugal (1385–1433).
—, Augustus Edwin, 1878–   . Brit. painter & etcher.
— **of Aus'tri·a** (ôs'trĭ·à), 1547–1578. *Don John* (dŏn jŏn). Sp. gen.
— **of Gaunt** (gônt; gänt), 1340–1399. Duke of *Lan'cas·ter* (lăng'kăs·tẽr; *in U. S., also* lăn[g]'kăs'tẽr). *Son of Edward III of Eng.*
— **of Lan'cas·ter.** See Duke of BEDFORD.
— **of Lei'den** (lī'd'n), 1509–1536. Du. Anabaptist fanatic.
— **of Salis'bur·y** (sôlz'bẽr·ĭ; -brĭ), d. 1180. Eng. ecclesiastic.
— **III So·bies'ki** (sô·byĕs'kē; *Pol.* sô-), 1624–1697. King of Poland (1674–96).
John'son (jŏn's'n), Andrew, 1808–1875. 17th U. S. pres. (1865–69).
—, Edward, 1881–   . Am. tenor.
—, James Wel'don (wĕl'dŭn), 1871–1938. Am. author.
—, Samuel, 1709–1784. *Dr. Johnson.* Eng. lexicographer & author.
—, Sir William, 1715–1774. Brit. administrator in Am.

John'ston (jŏn'stŭn; -s'n), Albert Sidney, 1803–1862. Am. Confed. gen.
—, Joseph Eggleston, 1807–1891. Am. Confed. gen.
—, Mary, 1870–1936. Am. nov.
Join'ville', de (dĕ zhwăⁿ'vēl'), Jean, 1224?–1317. Fr. chronicler.
Jō'kai (yō'koi), Mau'rus (mou'rŏŏs) or Mó'ricz (mō'rĭts), 1825–1904. Hung. nov. & dram.
Jo'liot'-Cu'rie' (zhō'lyō'kü'rē'), Fré'dé'ric' (frā'dā'rēk'), 1900–1958. Orig. Joliot. Fr. physicist.
—, I'rène' (ē'rĕn'), 1897–1956. Formerly Irène Curie-Joliot; dau. of Marie & Pierre Curie & wife of prec. Fr. physicist.
Jol'li·et' (jŏl'ĭ·ĕt'; Fr. zhō'lyĕ') or **Jo'li·et'** (jō'lĭ·ĕt'; Fr. zhō'lyĕ'), Louis, 1645–1700. Fr.-Canadian explorer in Mississippi valley.
Jo'mi'ni' (zhō'mē'nē'), Baron Hen'ri' (än'rē'), 1779–1869. Swiss-born soldier & writer on military science.
Jones (jōnz), An'son (ăn's'n), 1798–1858. Pres. of Republic of Texas (1844–46).
—, Daniel, 1881– . Eng. phonetician
—, Henry Arthur, 1851–1929. Eng. dram.
—, In'i·go (ĭn'ĭ·gō), 1573–1652. Eng. architect.
—, Jesse Hol'man (hōl'măn), 1874–1956. Am. financier & administrator.
—, John Paul, 1747–1792. Orig. in full John Paul. Am. (Scot.-born) naval officer.
—, Thomas Hudson, 1892– . Am. sculptor.
Jon'son (jŏn's'n), Ben (bĕn), 1573?–1637. Orig. Benjamin. Eng. dram.; poet laureate (1619–37).
Jor'dan (jôr'd'n), David Starr (stär), 1851–1931. Am. biologist & educ.
Joseph II (jō'zĕf; -zĭf), 1741–1790. King of Germany (1764–90); Holy Rom. emp. (1765–90).
Jo'se·phine (jō'zĕ·fēn; jō'zĕ·fēn'), Empress. See under de BEAU-HARNAIS.
Jo·se'phus (jō·sē'fŭs), Fla'vi·us (flā'vĭ·ŭs), 37–?100. Jewish hist.
Jou'bert' (zhōō'bâr'), Jo'seph' (zhō'zĕf'), 1754–1824. Fr. essayist & moralist.
—, Pe'trus (pā'trŭs) Ja·co'bus (yà·kō'bŭs), 1834–1900. Piet (pēt). Boer gen. & statesman.
— de la Fer'té' (dĕ lä fĕr'tā'), Sir Philip Ben'net (bĕn'ĕt; -ĭt), 1888– . Brit. air marshal.
Joule (jōōl), James Prescott, 1818–1889. Eng. physicist.
Jour'dan' (zhōōr'däⁿ'), Comte (kôⁿt) Jean Bap'tiste' (bä'tēst'), 1762–1833. Fr. soldier; marshal of France (1804).
Jo'vi·an (jō'vĭ·ăn), 331?–364. Fla'vi·us (flā'vĭ·ŭs) Claudius Jo'vi·a'nus (jō'vĭ·ā'nŭs). Rom. emp. (363–364).
Jow'ett (jou'ĕt; -ĭt), Benjamin, 1817–1893. Eng. Greek scholar.
Jow'itt (jou'ĭt), William Allen, 1st Viscount, 1885–1957. Brit. jurist.
Joyce (jois), James, 1882–1941. Irish writer.
Juan Ma·nuel (hwän' mä·nwĕl'), Don (dôn), 1282–1349. Span. soldier, polit., & writer.
Juá'rez (hwä'rĕs), Be·ni'to (bā·nē'tō) Pa'blo (pä'vlō), 1806–1872. Mex. lawyer; pres. of Mexico (1857–72).
Ju'das Mac'ca·bae'us (jōō'dăs măk'à·bē'ŭs), d. 160 B.C. Jewish patriot; with 4 bros. (the Mac'ca·bees [măk'à·bēz]) revolted against Antiochus Epiphanes.
Judd (jŭd), Charles Hubbard, 1873–1946. Am. psychol. & educ.
Ju·gur'tha (jōō·gûr'thà), d. 104 B.C. King of Numidia (113–104).
Jul'ian (jōōl'yăn), 331–363. Fla'vi·us (flā'vĭ·ŭs) Claudius Ju'li·a'nus (jōō'lĭ·ā'nŭs). The Apostate. Rom. emp. (361–363).
Ju'li·an·a (jōō'lĭ·ăn'à; -ä'nà; Du. yü'lē·ä'nä), 1909– . Dau. of Wilhelmina. Queen of the Netherlands (1948–).
Jung (yŏŏng), Carl Gu'stav (gōōs'täf), 1875– . Swiss psychol. & psychiatrist.
Jun'ius (jōōn'yŭs; jōō'nĭ·ŭs; Ger. yōō'nĕ·ŏŏs), Fran·cis'cus (frăn·sĭs'kŭs), 1589–1677. Eng. (Ger.-born) philologist.
Jun'kers (yŏŏng'kĕrs), Hu'go (hōō'gō), 1859–1935. Ger. airplane engineer & builder.
Ju'not' (zhü'nō'), An'doche' (äⁿ'dôsh'), 1771–1813. Duc (dük) d'A'bran'tès' (Fr. dà'bräⁿ'tĕs'; Port. dà·vrăⁿn'tēsh). Fr. gen. under Napoleon.
Jus'se·rand' (zhüs'rän'), Jean Jules, 1855–1932. Jean Adrien An'toine' (äⁿ'twän') Jules. Fr. scholar & diplomat.
Jus'tin (jŭs'tĭn), Saint, 100?–?165. Justin (the) Martyr. Church father.
Jus·tin'i·an I (jŭs·tĭn'ĭ·ăn), 483–565. The Great. Byzantine emp. (527–565).
Ju've·nal (jōō'vĕ·n'l), 60?–?140. Dec'i·mus (dĕs'ĭ·mŭs) Jun'ius (jōōn'yŭs; jōō'nĭ·ŭs) Ju've·na'lis (jōō'vĕ·nā'lĭs). Rom. poet & satirist.

K

Ka·ga·no'vich (kȧ·gŭ·nô'vychˌ), La'zar (lȧ'zĕr·y') Moi·se'e·vich (mŭ·ĭ·syä'yĕ·vychˌ), 1893– . Russ. polit.
Ka·ga·wa (kä·gä·wä), To·yo·hi·ko (tō·yō·hē·kō), 1888– . Jap. social reformer.
Kai'ser (kī'zĕr), Henry J., 1882– . Am. industrialist.
Kalb (kälp; Angl. kălb), Jo·hann' (yō·hän'; yō'hän), 1721–1780. Baron de Kalb (dĕ kälb'). Ger. gen. in Am.
Ka'li·da·sa (kä'lĭ·dä'sä), 5th cent. A.D. Hindu dram. & poet.
Ka·li'nin (kä·lyē'nyĭn), Mi·kha·il' (myĭ'·kŭ·ēl') I·va·no'vich (ĭ·vȧ'nŭ·vychˌ), 1875–1946. Russ. polit.; pres., U. S. S. R. (1923–46).
Ka'mer·lingh On'nes (kä'mĕr·lĭng ôn'ĕs), Hei'ke (hī'kĕ), 1853–1926. Du. physicist.
Kane (kān), Elisha Kent, 1820–1857. Am. arctic explorer.
K'ang-hsi (käng'shē'), 1654–1722. Shéng-tsu (shŭng'dzōō'). Chin. emp. (1662–1722).
K'ang Tê. See HSÜAN T'UNG.
Kant (känt; Angl. känt), Im·ma'nu·el (ĭ·mä'nōō·ĕl; Angl. ĭ·măn'û·ĕl), 1724–1804. Ger. philos.
Kao Tsung. See CH'IEN LUNG.
Kar'a·george' (kär'à·jôrj'), 1766?–1817. Orig. George Pe'tro·vić (pĕ'-

trô·vēt'y'; Angl. -vĭch). Serbian nationalist; founder of Kar'a·geor'·ge·vich (kär'à·jôr'jĕ·vĭch) dynasty.
Karl'feldt (kärl'fĕlt), E'rik' (ā'rĭk') Ax'el (äk'sĕl), 1864–1931. Swed. poet.
Ká'ro·lyi (kä'rō·lyĭ), Count Mi'hály (mĭ'häl·y'), 1875–1955. Hung. polit.
Kar'rer (kär'ĕr), Paul, 1889– . Swiss chem.
Kauf'man (kôf'măn), George Simon, 1889– . Am. dram.
Kau'nitz, von (fôn kou'nĭts), Count Wen'zel (vĕn'tsĕl) An'ton (än'tōn), 1711–1794. Prince von Kaunitz-Riet'berg (-rēt'bĕrĸ). Austrian statesman.
Kaut'sky (kout'skĕ), Karl Jo·hann' (yō·hän'; yō'hän), 1854–1938. Ger. socialist writer.
Kaye'-Smith' (kā'smĭth'), Sheila, 1887–1956. Eng. nov.
Kean (kēn), Edmund, 1787–1833. Eng. actor.
Kear'ny (kär'nĭ), Philip, 1814–1862. Am. gen.
Keats (kēts), John, 1795–1821. Eng. poet.
Ke'ble (kē'b'l), John, 1792–1866. Eng. clergyman & poet.
Kee'ley (kē'lĭ), Leslie En'raught (ĕn'rôt), 1834–1900. Am. physician & founder of a sanitarium for alcoholics.
Kei'tel (kī'tĕl), Wil'helm (vĭl'hĕlm), 1882–1946. Ger. field marshal.
Keith (kēth), Sir Arthur, 1866–1955. Brit. anthropologist.
Kel'land (kĕl'ănd), Clarence Bud'ing·ton (bŭd'ĭng·tŭn), 1881– . Am. nov.
Kel'ler (kĕl'ĕr), Helen Adams, 1880– . Am. deaf and blind lecturer.
Kel'ler'mann' (kĕ'lĕr'màn'), Fran'çois' (fräⁿ'swä') Chris'tophe' (krēs'tôf'), 1735–1820. Duc (dük) de Val'my' (dĕ väl'mē'). Fr. soldier; marshal of France.
Kel'logg (kĕl'ŏg; -ŭg), Frank Bil'lings (bĭl'ĭngz), 1856–1937. Am. statesman.
Kel'ly (kĕl'ĭ), George Edward, 1887– . Am. actor & dram.
—, James Edward, 1855–1933. Am. sculptor.
Kel'vin (kĕl'vĭn), 1st Baron, 1824–1907. William Thom'son (tŏm'-s'n). Brit. math. & physicist.
Ke·mal' A·ta·türk' (kĕ·mäl' ä·tä·türk'), 1881–1938. Mus·ta·fa' or Mus·ta·pha' (mōōs·tä·fä') Kemal. Turk. gen.; pres. of Turkey (1923–38).
Kem'ble (kĕm'b'l), Frances Anne, 1809–1893. Fanny. Eng. actress.
—, John Philip, 1757–1823. Eng. actor.
Kem'pis, Thomas a. See THOMAS A KEMPIS.
Ken or **Kenn** (kĕn), Thomas, 1637–1711. Eng. prelate & hymn writer.
Ken'dall (kĕn'd'l), (William) Ser'geant (sär'jĕnt), 1869–1938. Am. painter & sculptor.
Ken'ne·dy (kĕn'ĕ·dĭ), Charles Rann (răn), 1871–1950. Am. (Eng.-born) actor & dram.
—, Joseph Patrick, 1888– . Am. businessman & diplomat.
Ken'nel·ly (kĕn'l·ĭ), Arthur Edwin, 1861–1939. Am. electrical engineer.
Ken'ney (kĕn'ĭ), George Churchill, 1889– . Am. gen.
Ken'ny (kĕn'ĭ), Elizabeth, 1886–1952. Australian nurse & physiotherapist.
Kent (kĕnt), James, 1763–1847. Am. jurist.
—, Rock'well (rŏk'wĕl; -wĕl), 1882– . Am. painter.
Ken'wor'thy (kĕn'wûr'thĭ), Joseph Montague, 1886–1953. 10th Baron Stra·bol'gi (strȧ·bō'gĭ). Brit. naval officer.
Ken'yon (kĕn'yŭn), John Samuel, 1874– . Am. phonetician.
Kep'ler (kĕp'lĕr), Jo·han'nes (yō·hän'ĕs; -ĕs), 1571–1630. Ger. astron.
Kep'pel (kĕp'ĕl), Augustus, 1st Viscount, 1725–1786. Brit. admiral.
Ker (kâr), William Pa'ton (pā't'n), 1855–1923. Brit. scholar.
Ke·ren'ski (kĕ·rĕn'skĭ; Russ. kĭ·ryĕn'skĭ), A·le·ksan'dr (ü·lyĭ·ksän'dĕr) Fe·o'do·ro'vich (fyĭ·ō'dŭ·rō'vychˌ), 1881– . Russ. revolutionist.
Kern (kûrn), Jerome David, 1885–1945. Am. composer.
Kerr (kär), Archibald John Kerr Clark, 1882–1951. 1st Baron In'ver·chap'el (ĭn'vĕr·chăp'ĕl; -'l). Brit. diplomat.
Kes'sel·ring (kĕs'ĕl·rĭng), Al'bert (äl'bĕrt), 1887– . Ger. field marshal.
Ket'ter·ing (kĕt'ĕr·ĭng), Charles Franklin, 1876– . Am. electrical engineer & inventor.
Key (kē), Francis Scott, 1779–1843. Am. lawyer; author of "The Star-Spangled Banner."
Keyes (kēz), Geoffrey, 1888– . Am. gen.
—, Sir Roger John Brown'low (broun'lō), 1872–1945. Brit. admiral.
Keynes (kānz), John May'nard (mā'nĕrd; -närd), 1883–1946. Eng. econ.
Key'ser·ling (kī'zĕr·lĭng), Count Her'mann (hĕr'män; Angl. hûr'măn) A'le·xan'der (ä'lĕ·ksän'dĕr; Angl. ăl'ĕg·zăn'dĕr, äl'ĭg-), 1880–1946. Ger. philos. & writer.
Khe·ra'skov (kĕ·rä'skŭf), Mi·kha·il' (myĭ'·kŭ·ēl') Mat·ve'e·vich (mȧt·vyä'yĕ·vychˌ), 1733–1807. Russ. poet.
Khru·shchev' (krōōsh·chôf'), Ni·ki'ta (nyĭ·kē'tà) Ser·ge'e·vich (syĭr·gä'yĕ·vychˌ), 1894– . Russ. polit.
Khu'fu (kōō'fōō); Greek **Che'ops** (kē'ŏps). King of Egypt (ab. 2900–2877 B.C.) & pyramid builder.
Khwa'riz·mi', al- (äl·nwä'rĭz·mē'), 780–?850. Arab math.
Kidd (kĭd), William, 1645?–1701. Captain Kidd. Scot. navigator & pirate.
Kien Lung. = CH'IEN LUNG.
Kier'an (kēr'ăn), John Francis, 1892– . Am. journalist.
Kier'ke·gaard (kĭr'kĕ·gôr), Sö'ren (sü'rĕn) Aa'bye (ô'bü), 1813–1855. Dan. philos. & theol.
Kil'mer (kĭl'mĕr), (Alfred) Joyce, 1886–1918. Am. poet.
Kil·pat'rick (kĭl·păt'rĭk), Hugh Jud'son (jŭd's'n), 1836–1881. Am. gen.
Kim'mel (kĭm'ĕl), Hus'band (hŭz'bănd) Edward, 1882– . Am. admiral.
Kin'di, al- (äl·kĭn'dē), 9th cent. A.D. Arab philos.
King (kĭng), Ernest Joseph, 1878–1956. Am. admiral of the fleet.
—, Rufus, 1755–1827. Am. polit. & diplomat.
—, William Lyon Mackenzie, 1874–1950. Canadian statesman; prime min. (1921–26; 1926–30; 1935–48).

King'lake (kǐng'lāk), Alexander William, 1809–1891. Eng. hist.

Kings'ley (kǐngz'lǐ), Charles, 1819–1875. Eng. clergyman & nov.

Kin·kaid' (kǐn·kād'), Thomas Cas'sin (kǎs'ǐn), 1888– . Am. admiral.

Kip'ling (kǐp'lǐng), Rud'yard (rŭd'yẽrd), 1865–1936. Eng. author.

Kir'by-Smith' (kûr'bǐ·smǐth'), Edmund, 1824–1893. Am. Confed. gen.

Kirch'hoff (kǐrK'hôf), Gu'stav (gōōs'täf) Ro'bert (rō'bẽrt), 1824–1887. Ger. physicist.

Ki'rov (kē'rŭf), Ser·gei' (syǐr·gā'ǐ) Mi·ro'no·vich (myǐ·rô'nŭ·vyǐch), 1888–1934. Russ. revolutionist.

Kitch'e·ner (kǐch'ē·nẽr), Horatio Herbert, 1850–1916. 1st Earl *Kitchener of Khar·toum'* (kär·tōōm') *and of Broome* (broom; brōōm). Brit. field marshal.

Kit'tredge (kǐt'rǐj), George Lyman, 1860–1941. Am. philologist & educ.

Klé·ber' (klā'bâr'), Jean Bap'tiste' (bà'tēst'), 1753–1800. Fr. gen. under Napoleon.

Klee (klā), Paul, 1879–1940. Swiss painter.

Klein (klīn), Charles, 1867–1915. Eng. dram. in Am.

—, Fe'lix (fā'lǐks), 1849–1925. Ger. math.

Kleist, von (fôn klīst'), Hein'rich (hīn'rǐk), 1777–1811. Ger. dram.

—, Paul Lud'wig (lōōt'vǐk; lōōd'-) E'wald (ā'vält), 1881–1954. Ger. gen.

Kling'er (klǐng'ẽr), Max (mäks), 1857–1920. Ger. etcher, painter, & sculptor.

Klop'stock (klôp'shtôk), Frie'drich (frē'drǐk) Gott'lieb (gôt'lēp), 1724–1803. Ger. poet.

Kluck, von (fôn klŏŏk'), A'le·xan'der (ä'lĕ·ksän'dẽr), 1846–1934. Ger. army officer.

Klu'ge, von (fôn klōō'gĕ), Gün'ther (gün'tẽr), 1882–1944. Ger. field marshal.

Knel'ler (nĕl'ẽr; *Ger.* k'nĕl'ẽr), Sir Godfrey, 1646–1723. Orig. *Gott'fried* (gôt'frēt) *Knil'ler* (k'nǐl'ẽr). Ger.-born portrait painter in Eng.

Knob'lock (nŏb'lŏk), Edward, 1874–1945. Brit. dram. & nov.

Knox (nŏks), Frank, 1874–1944. *William Franklin.* Am. newspaper publisher & administrator.

—, Henry, 1750–1806. Am. Revolutionary gen.

—, John, 1505–1572. Scot. reformer & statesman.

— *Philander Chase*, 1853–1921. Am. statesman.

Knud'sen (nōōd's'n; *orig. Dan. pron.* k'nōō'ṡ'n), William S., 1879–1948. Am. (Dan.-born) industrialist & administrator.

Knut. See CANUTE.

Koch (kōK), Ro'bert (rō'bẽrt), 1843–1910. Ger. physician & bacteriologist.

Ko'cher (kō'Kẽr), E'mil (ā'mēl) The'o·dor (tā'ō·dōr), 1841–1917. Swiss surgeon.

Kock, de (dē kôk'), Paul, 1794–1871. Fr. nov. & dram.

Koe'nig' (kû'nĕg'), Pierre, 1898– . Fr. gen.

Ko·ga (kō·gä), Mi·nei·chi (mĕ·nā·chē), 1885?–1944. Jap. admiral.

Ko·i·so (kō·ē·sō), Ku·ni·a·ki (kōō·nē·ä·kē), 1880–1950. Jap. gen. & statesman.

Kol·chak' (kŭl·chàk'), A·le·ksan'dr (ŭ·lyǐ·ksàn'dẽr) Va·sil'ie·vich (vŭ·syĕl'yĕ·vyǐch), 1874–1920. Russ. admiral & counterrevolutionist.

Kol·lon·tai' (kŭl·lŭn·tī'), A·le·ksan'dra (ŭ·lyǐ·ksàn'drà) Mi·khai'lov·na (myǐ·Kī'lŭv·nà), 1872–1952. Russ. diplomat.

Kol·tsov' (kŭl·y·tsôf'), A·le·ksei' (ŭ·lyǐ·ksā'ǐ) Va·sil'ie·vich (vŭ·syĕl'yĕ·vyǐch), 1808–1842. Russ. poet.

Ko·mu·ra (kō·mōō·rä), Marquis Ju·ta·ro (jōō·tä·rō), 1855–1911. Jap. diplomat.

Kon·do (kôn·dō), No·bu·ta·ke (nō·bōō·tä·kĕ), 1886–1953. Jap. admiral.

Kon·dy'les (kôn·thē'lyĕs), Ge·or'gi·os (yâ·ôr'yē·ôs), 1879–1936. Greek gen. & statesman.

Kon'ev (kôn'yĕf), Ivan Ste·pa'no·vich (styĕ·pá'nŭ·vyǐch), 1897– . Russ. gen. & marshal of Soviet Union.

Ko·no·ye (kō·nō·yĕ), Prince Fu·mi·ma·ro (fōō·mē·mä·rō), 1891–1945. Jap. statesman.

Koo (gōō; *Angl.* kōō), Vi Kyuin (wā' jün') Wel'ling·ton (wĕl'ǐng·tŭn), 1887– . Orig. *Ku Wei·chün* (gōō' wā'jün'). Chin. statesman & diplomat.

Ko·per'nik *or* **Kop'per·nigk.** See COPERNICUS.

Ko'ri·zes' (kō'rē·zĕs'), A·le'xan·dros (ä·lā'ksän·thrôs), 1885–1941. Greek premier (1941).

Korn'gold (kôrn'gôlt), E'rich (ā'rǐk) Wolf'gang (vôlf'gäng), 1897–1957. Austrian composer, conductor, & pianist.

Kor·ni'lov (kŭr·nyē'lŭf), Lavr (lä'vẽr) Ge·or'gi·e·vich (gǐ·ôr'gǐ·yĕ·vyǐch), 1870–1918. Russ. gen.

Ko·rob'kov (kŭ·rüp·kôf'), Fē'dor (fyô'dẽr), 1898– . Russ. gen.

Ko·ro·len'ko (kŭ·rŭ·lyĕn'kŭ), Vla·di'mir (vlŭ·dyē'myǐr) Ga·lak·ti·o'no·vich (gà·làk·tyǐ·ô'nŭ·vyǐch), 1853–1921. Russ. nov.

Kor·zyb'ski (kôr·zǐp'skē), Alfred Hab'dank (häb'dängk) Skar'bek (skär'bĕk), 1879–1950. Am. (Pol.-born) scientist & writer.

Kos'ci·us'ko (kŏs'ǐ·ŭs'kō), Thaddeus, 1746–1817. Pol. patriot.

Kos'sel (kôs'ĕl), Al'brecht (äl'brĕkt), 1853–1927. Ger. physiological chem.

Kos'suth (kŏ'shōōt; *Angl.* kŏs'ōōth), Fe'renc (fĕ'rĕnts), 1841–1914. *Son of Lajos.* Hung. polit.

—, La'jos (lŏ'yōsh), 1802–1894. Hung. patriot & statesman.

Ko·sy'gin (kŭ·sǐ'gǐn), A·le·ksei' (ŭ·lyǐ·ksyā'ǐ) Ni·ko·la'e·vich (nyǐ·kŭ·lä'yĕ·vyǐch), 1905– . Russ. polit.

Kot'ze·bue, von (fôn kôt'sĕ·bōō), Au'gust (ou'gŏŏst) Frie'drich (frē'drǐk) Fer'di·nand (fĕr'dē·nänt), 1761–1819. Ger. dram.

Koun'dou·rio'tes (kōōn'dōō·ryō'tĕs), Pav'los (päv'lôs), 1855–1935. Greek admiral & statesman.

Kous'se·vitz'ky (*Angl.* kōō'sĕ·vǐts'kǐ; *Russ.* kōō·syǐ·vyĕts'kǐ), Serge (sûrj; sĕrzh), 1874–1951. *Ser·gei'* (syǐr·gā'ǐ) *A·le·xan'dro·vich* (ŭ·lĕ·ksàn'drŭ·vyǐch). Russ.-born conductor.

Krafft'-E'bing, von (fôn kräft'ā'bǐng), Baron Ri'chard (rǐk'ärt), 1840–1902. Ger. neurologist.

Kreis'ler (krīs'lẽr), Fritz (frǐts), 1875– . Am. (Austrian-born) violinist.

Kreym'borg (krām'bôrg), Alfred, 1883– . Am. poet.

Krogh (krôg), Au'gust (ou'gŏŏst), 1874–1949. Dan. physiol.

Kroll (krōl), Leon, 1884– . Am. painter.

Kro·pot'kin (krŭ·pôt'kǐn), Prince Pĕtr (pyô'tẽr) A·le·kse'e·vich (ŭ·lyǐ·ksyä'yĕ·vyǐch), 1842–1921. Russ. geographer & revolutionist.

Krue'ger (krōō'gẽr), Walter, 1881– . Am. gen.

Krug (krōōg), Julius Albert, 1907– . Am. power engineer & administrator.

Kru'ger (krü'[k]ẽr; *Angl.* krōō'gẽr), Ste·pha'nus (stä·fä'nûs) Jo·han'nes (yō·hän'ĕs) Pau'lus (pô'ōō·lûs), 1825–1904. *Oom Paul* (ōōm pô'ōōl). S. African statesman.

Krupp (krōōp; *Angl.* krŭp). Family of Ger. munition makers, including: Frie'drich (frē'drǐk), 1787–1826; his son Alfred, 1812–1887; Alfred's son Friedrich Alfred, 1854–1902; and Friedrich Alfred's daughter Ber'tha (bĕr'tä), 1886–1957.

Krup'ska·ya (krōōp'skà·yà), Na·dezh'da (nŭ·dyäzh'dà) Kon·stan·ti'nov·na (kŭn·stŭn·tyē'nŭv·nà), 1869–1939. *Wife of Nikolai Lenin.* Russ. social worker.

Ku'blai Khan (kōō'blī kän'), 1216–1294. Founder of Mongol dynasty in China.

Kuhn (kōōn), Ri'chard (rǐk'ärt), 1900– . Ger. chem.

Kui'by·shev (kōō'ǐ·bǐ·shĕf), Va·le·ri·an' (vä·lyǐ·ryǐ·än') Vla·di'mi·ro'vich (vlŭ·dyē'myǐ·rô'vyǐch), 1888–1935. Russ. Bolshevik.

Ku·lik' (kōō·lyĕk'), Gri·go'ri (gryǐ·gô'ryǐ) I·va'no·vich (ǐ·vä'nŭ·vyǐch), 1890– . Russ. marshal.

Kun (kōōn), Bé'la (bā'lŏ), 1885–1937. Hung. Communist.

Kung (gŏŏng), Prince, 1833–1898. Manchu statesman.

— (kŏŏng), H. H., 1881– . Orig. *K'ung Hsiang-hsi* (kŏŏng' shĕ·äng'shē'). Chin. statesman.

Ku·ro·ki (kōō·rō·kē), Count Ta·me·mo·to (tä·mĕ·mô·tō) Ta·me·sa·da (tä·mĕ·sä·dä), 1844–1923. Jap. gen.

Ku·ro·pat'kin (kōō·rŭ·pät'kǐn), A·le·ksei' (ŭ·lyǐ·ksyā'ǐ) Ni·ko·la'e·vich (nyǐ·kŭ·lä'yĕ·vyǐch), 1848–1925. Russ. gen.

Ku·ru·su (kōō·rōō·sōō), Sa·bu·ro (sä·bōō·rō), 1888–1954. Jap. diplomat.

Ku·tu'zov (kōō·tōō'zŭf), Mi·kha·il' (myǐ·Kŭ·ēl') I·la·ri·o'no·vich (ǐ·lä·ryǐ·ô'nŭ·vyǐch), 1745–1813. Prince of *Smo·lensk'* (smô·lĕnsk'; *Russ.* smū·lyĕnsk'). Russ. field marshal.

Kyd *or* **Kid** (kǐd), Thomas, 1558–1594. Eng. dram.

Kyne (kīn), Peter Bernard, 1880–1957. Am. writer.

Kyn'e·wulf. See CYNEWULF.

L

La'biche' (lä'bēsh'), Eu'gène' (û'zhân'; ü'-) Ma'rin' (mà'rǎn'), 1815–1888. Fr. dram.

La'bou'laye', de (dē lä'bōō'lā'), É'dou·ard' (ā'dwär') René Le·feb'vre (lĕ·fä'vr'), 1811–1883. Fr. journalist & polit.

La Bru'yère', de (dē lä brü'yâr'), Jean, 1645–1696. Fr. moralist.

La Chaise, de (dē lä shâz'), Fran'çois' (frän'swä') d'Aix (dĕks'), 1624–1709. Fr. Jesuit.

La Farge (lä färzh'), John, 1835–1910. Am. painter.

La'fa·yette', de (dē lä'fī·ĕt'; läf'ĭ-; *Fr.* là'fà'yĕt'), Marquis, 1757–1834. *Ma'rie'* (mà'rē') *Jo'seph'* (zhō'zĕf') *Paul Yves* (ēv) *Roch* (rôk) *Gil'bert'* (zhēl'bâr') *du Mo'tier'* (dü mô'tyä'). Fr. gen. & statesman; served in Am.

Laf·fite' *or* **La·fitte'** (là·fēt'; *Fr.* là'fēt'), Jean, ab. 1780–ab. 1826. Fr. pirate in Gulf of Mexico.

La Fol'lette (là fŏl'ĕt; -ǐt), Robert Marion, 1855–1925. Am. polit.

La·fon'taine' (là'fôn'tĕn'), Hen'ri' (än'rē'), 1854–1943. Belg. lawyer & statesman.

La Fon'taine', de (dē lä fôn'tĕn'), Jean, 1621–1695. Fr. fabulist.

La'ger·löf' (lä'gĕr·lûv'), Sel'ma (sĕl'mä) Ot'ti·li·a'na' (ôt'tǐ·lǐ·ä'nà') Lo'vi·sa' (lōō'vǐ·sà'), 1858–1940. Swed. nov. & poet.

La'grange' (là'gränzh'), Comte (kônt) Jo'seph' (zhō'zĕf') Louis, 1736–1813. Fr. geometer & astron.

La Guar'di·a (lä gwär'dǐ·à; lä gär'dǐ·à), Fi'o·rel'lo (fē'ô·rĕl'ō) Henry, 1882–1947. Am. lawyer & polit.

Lahm (läm), Frank Pur'dy (pûr'dǐ), 1877– . Am. aeronaut.

Lake (lāk), Simon, 1866–1945. Am. naval architect & submarine builder.

La'marck', de (dē là'märk'), Che·va'lier' (shĕ·và'lyä'), 1744–1829. *Jean Bap'tiste'* (bà'tēst') *Pierre An'toine'* (än'twän') *de Mo'net'* (dē mô'nĕ'). Fr. naturalist.

La'mar'tine', de (dē là'màr'tēn'), Al'phonse' (àl'fôns') Ma'rie' (mà'rē') Louis de Prat (dē prä'), 1790–1869. Fr. poet.

Lamb (läm), Charles, 1775–1834. Eng. essayist & critic.

—, William, 1779–1848. 2d Viscount *Mel'bourne* (mĕl'bẽrn; -bôrn). Eng. statesman.

Lam'bert (läm'bẽrt), John, 1619–1683. Eng. Parliamentary gen.

Lam'masch (läm'äsh), Hein'rich (hīn'rǐk), 1853–1920. Austrian jurist & statesman.

La·mont' (là·mônt'), Thomas William, 1870–1948. Am. banker.

La Motte'-Fou·qué' (lä môt'fōō·kā'), Baron Frie'drich (frē'drǐk) Hein'rich (hīn'rǐk) Karl, 1777–1843. Ger. nov.

Lamp'son (läm[p]'s'n), Sir Miles Wed'der·burn (wĕd'ẽr·bûrn), 1880– . Brit. diplomat.

Land (länd), Emory Scott, 1879– . Am. admiral.

Lan'dis (län'dǐs), Ken'e·saw Moun'tain (kĕn'ĕ·sô moun'tǐn; -tĕn), 1866–1944. Am. jurist & baseball commissioner.

Lan'don (län'dŭn), Alfred Moss'man (môs'măn), 1887– . Am. polit.

Lan'dor (län'dôr; -dẽr), Walter Savage, 1775–1864. Eng. author.

Lan·dow'ska (län·dôf'skä), Wan'da (vän'dä), 1879– . Pol. pianist.

Land'seer (län[d]'sẽr; -syẽr), Sir Edwin Henry, 1802–1873. Eng. painter.

Land'stei'ner (länd'stī'nẽr; *Ger.* länt'shtī'nẽr), Karl, 1868–1943. Austrian-born pathologist in Am.

Lane (lān), Edward William, 1801–1876. Eng. orientalist.

Lan'franc (län'frăngk), 1005?–1089. Ital.-born prelate & scholar in Eng.

Lang (lăng), Andrew, 1844–1912. Scot. scholar & author.

—, Cos'mo (kŏz'mō) Gordon, 1864–1945. Brit. prelate; archbishop of Canterbury.

Lang'e (läng'ĕ), Chris'tian (krĭs'tyän) Lou'is (lōō'ĭ; -ĭs), 1869–1938. Norw. pacifist & hist.

Lang'land (läng'lănd) *or* **Lang'ley** (läng'lĭ), William, 1332?–?1400. Eng. poet.

Lang'ley (läng'lĭ), Samuel Pier'pont (pēr'pŏnt), 1834–1906. Am. astron. & airplane pioneer.

Lang'muir (läng'mūr), Irving, 1881–1957. Am. chem.

Lang'ton (läng'tŭn), Stephen, d. 1228. Eng. theol., hist., & poet.

Lang'try (läng'trĭ), Lily, 1852–1929. Nee (*Emily Charlotte*) *Le Bret'on* (lĕ brĕt''n). *The Jersey Lily.* Eng. actress.

La·nier' (là·nēr'), Sidney, 1842–1881. Am. poet.

Lan'kes·ter (läng'kĕs·tēr; -kĭs-), Sir Edwin Ray, 1847–1929. Eng. zool.

Lannes (län), Jean, 1769–1809. Duc (dük) *de Mon'te·bel'lo* (dĕ mŏn'tā·bĕl'lō). Fr. soldier under Napoleon; marshal of France (1804).

Lans'bur·y (länz'bĕr·ĭ; -brĭ; *in U. S., also* -bĕr'ĭ), George, 1859–1940. Brit. labor leader.

Lan'sing (län'sĭng), Robert, 1864–1928. Am. lawyer & statesman.

Lan'son' (län'sôn'), Gus'tave' (güs'tàv'), 1857–1934. Fr. literary hist. & critic.

Lao-tzu *or* **Lao-tse** *or* **Lao-tze** (lou'dzŭ'), 604?–?531 b.c. Chin. philos.

La Pé'rouse', de (dĕ là pā'rōōz'), Comte (kônt), 1741–1788. *Jean Fran'çois'* (frän'swä') *de Ga'laup'* (dĕ gà'lō'). Fr. navigator & explorer.

La'place', de (dĕ là'plàs'), Marquis Pierre Si'mon' (sē'môN'), 1749–1827. Fr. astron. & math.

Lard'ner (lärd'nēr), Ring (rĭng), 1885–1933. *Ring'gold* (rĭng'gōld) *Wil'mer* (wĭl'mĕr). Am. humorist & writer.

La·re'do Brú (lä·rā'thō vrōō'), Fe'de·ri'co (fā'thā·rē'kō), 1875–1946. Cuban soldier; pres. of Cuba (1936–40).

Lar'go Ca'bal·le'ro (lär'gō kä'väl·yā'rō), Fran·cis'co (frän·thēs'kō), 1869–1946. Span. labor leader; prime min. (1936–37).

La Roche'fou'cauld', de (dĕ là rŏsh'fōō'kō'), Duc (dük) Fran'çois' (frän'swä'), 1613–1680. Fr. writer & moralist.

La'rousse' (là'rōōs'; *Angl.* là-), Pierre A'tha'nase' (à'tà'nàz'), 1817–1875. Fr. grammarian & lexicographer.

Lar'tet' (làr'tĕ'), É'dou·ard' (ā'dwär') Armand I'si'dore' (ē'zē'dôr') Hip'po'lyte' (ē'pō'lēt'), 1801–1871. Fr. archaeologist.

La Salle, **de** (dĕ là säl'; *Fr.* là säl'), Sieur (syûr), 1643–1687. *Ro'bert' Ca've·lier'* (kȧ've·lyā'). Fr. explorer in Am.

Las Ca'sas, **de** (thä läs kä'säs), Bar'to·lo·mé' (bär'tō·lō·mā'), 1474–1566. Span. Dominican missionary & hist.

Las'ki (läs'kĭ), Harold Joseph, 1893–1950. Eng. polit. scientist.

Las·salle' (là·säl'), Fer'di·nand (fĕr'dĕ·nänt), 1825–1864. Ger. socialist.

Lat'i·mer (lăt'ĭ·mēr), Hugh, 1485?–1555. Eng. Protestant martyr.

La·trobe' (là·trōb'), Benjamin Henry, 1764–1820. Am. (Eng.-born) architect & engineer.

Lat'ti·more (lăt'ĭ·mōr), Owen, 1900– . Am. orientalist.

Latz'ko (läts'kō), An·dre'as (än·drā'äs), 1876– . Hung.-born writer in Austria.

Laud (lôd), William, 1573–1645. Eng. prelate; archbishop of Canterbury; executed.

Lau'der (lô'dēr), Sir Harry, 1870–1950. Orig. *MacLen'nan* (măk·lĕn'ăn). Scot. singer.

Lau'e, von (fôn lou'ĕ), Max (mäks), 1879– . Ger. physicist.

Laugh'ton (lô'tŭn), Charles, 1899– . Am. (Eng.-born) actor.

Lau'ri·er (lô'rĭ·ā; *Fr.* lô'ryā'), Sir Wilfrid, 1841–1919. Canadian statesman.

La'val' (là'väl'; *Angl.* là·väl'), Pierre, 1883–1945. Fr. lawyer & polit.

La Val·lière', **de** (dĕ là vȧ'lyâr'), Du'chesse' (dü'shĕs'), 1644–1710. Mistress of Louis XIV of France.

Lav'a·rack (lăv'à·răk), Sir John Dudley, 1885–1957. Australian gen.

La've·ran' (là'vrän'), Charles Louis Al'phonse' (àl'fôNs'), 1845–1922. Fr. physiol. & bacteriol.

La Vé'ren'drye', **de** (dĕ là vā'räN'drē'), Sieur (syûr), 1685–1749. *Pierre Gaul'tier' de Va'rennes'* (gō'tyā' dĕ vȧ'rĕn'). Canadian explorer in Am.

La'ver·y (lā'vēr·ĭ; läv'ēr·ĭ), Sir John, 1856–1941. Brit. painter.

La'voi'sier' (là'vwà'zyā'), An'toine' (äN'twàn') Lau'rent' (lō'räN'), 1743–1794. Fr. chem.

Law (lô), (Andrew) Bon'ar (bŏn'ēr), 1858–1923. Brit. statesman.

—, Edward, 1750–1818. 1st Baron *El'len·bor'ough* (ĕl'ĕn·bûr'ō; *esp. Brit.,* -bŭr'ō, -brŭ). Eng. jurist.

—, John, 1671–1729. Scot. financier & speculator.

—, William, 1686–1761. Eng. devotional writer.

Lawes (lôz), Henry, 1596–1662. Eng. composer.

—, Lewis Edward, 1883–1947. Am. penologist.

Law'rence (lô'rĕns; lŏr'ĕns), David, 1888– . Am. journalist.

—, David Herbert, 1885–1930. Eng. nov.

—, Ernest Orlando, 1901–1958. Am. physicist.

—, Gertrude, 1901–1952. Orig. *Ger'trud* (gĕr'trōōth) *A'lex·an'dra* (à'lĕk·săn'drä) *Dag'mar* (dăg'mär) *Lawrence Kla'sen* (klä's'n). Eng. actress.

—, James, 1781–1813. Am. naval officer.

—, Sir Thomas, 1769–1830. Eng. painter.

—, Thomas Edward, 1888–1935. *Lawrence of Arabia;* later surname *Shaw* (shô). Brit. archaeologist, soldier, & writer.

Law'rie (lô'rĭ; lŏr'ĭ), Lee, 1877– . Am. sculptor.

Lay'a·mon (lä'à·mŭn; -mŏn; *Angl.* lī'yà-; lī'à-), fl. 1200. Eng. poet.

Lay'ard (lârd; lā'ērd), Sir Austen Henry, 1817–1894. Eng. archaeologist & diplomat.

Lay'ton (lā't'n), Sir Geoffrey, 1884– . Brit. admiral.

Lea'cock (lē'kŏk), Stephen Butler, 1869–1944. Canadian econ. & humorist.

Leaf (lēf), Walter, 1852–1927. Eng. banker & scholar.

Lea'hy (lā'hĭ), William Daniel, 1875– . Am. admiral of the fleet.

Lear (lēr), Ben (bĕn), 1879– . Am. gen.

—, Edward, 1812–1888. Eng. painter & nonsense poet.

Lea'ry (lēr'ĭ), Herbert Fairfax, 1885–1957. Am. admiral.

Le·brun' (lĕ·brûN'), Al'bert' (àl'bâr'), 1871–1950. Fr. statesman; pres. of France (1932–40).

—, Mme. Vigée-. See VIGÉE-LEBRUN.

Le Brun *or* **Le·brun'** (lĕ·brûN'), Charles, 1619–1690. Fr. painter.

Leck'y (lĕk'ĭ), William Edward Hart'pole (?härt'pōl), 1838–1903. Irish hist. & essayist.

Le·conte' de Lisle (lĕ·kôNt' dĕ lēl'), Charles Ma'rie' (mȧ'rē'), 1818–1894. Orig. *Leconte.* Fr. poet.

Lee (lē), Ann, 1736–1784. Eng. mystic; founder of Shaker society in U. S.

—, Charles, 1731–1782. Am. (Eng.-born) gen.

—, Fitz'hugh' (fĭts'hū'; fīts·hū'), 1835–1905. *Nephew of R. E. Lee.* Am. gen.

—, Francis Light'foot (līt'fŏŏt), 1734–1797. Am. Revolutionary statesman.

—, Henry, 1756–1818. *Light-Horse Harry.* Am. gen.

—, John Clifford Hodges, 1887–1958. Am. gen.

—, Richard Henry, 1732–1794. Am. Revolutionary statesman.

—, Robert Edward, 1807–1870. Am. Confed. gen.

—, Sir Sidney, 1859–1926. Eng. editor & scholar.

Leeb, **von** (fôn lāp'), Wil'helm (vĭl'hĕlm) Jo'seph (yō'zĕf) Franz (fränts), 1876–1956. Ger. field marshal.

Leeu'wen·hoek *or* **Leu'wen-hoek**, **van** (vän lā'vĕn·hŏŏk), An'ton (än'tŏn), 1632–1723. Du. naturalist.

Le·feb'vre (lĕ·fâ'vr'), Fran'çois' (frän'swä') Jo'seph' (zhō'zĕf'), 1755–1820. Duc (dük) *de Dant'zig'* (dĕ dänt'sĕk'). Fr. gen.; marshal of France (1807).

Le Gal·lienne' (lĕ găl·yĕn'; găl'yĕn), Eva, 1899– . *Dau. of Richard.* Actress in Am.

—, Richard, 1866–1947. Eng. writer.

Le·gen'dre (lĕ·zhäN'dr'), Adrien Ma'rie' (mȧ'rē'), 1752–?1833. Fr. math.

Le·guí'a y Sal·ce'do (lā·gē'ä ē säl·sā'thō), Au·gus'to (ou·gōōs'tō) Ber'nar·di'no (vĕr'när·thē'nō; 17), 1863–1932. Peruvian banker; pres. of Peru (1908–12; 1919–30).

Le'hár (lĕ'här; *Angl.* lā'här), Franz (fränts), 1870–1948. Hung. composer.

Leh'man (lē'măn), Herbert Henry, 1878– . Am. banker & polit.

Leh'mann (lā'män), Lot'te (lŏt'ĕ), 1888– . Ger. soprano.

—, Rosamond, 1904?– . Eng. nov.

Leib'nitz, *or more correctly* **Leib'niz**, **von** (fôn līp'nĭts), Baron Gott'fried (gŏt'frēt) Wil'helm (vĭl'hĕlm), 1646–1716. Ger. philos. & math.

Leices'ter, 1st Earl of. See Robert DUDLEY; see also under de MONTFORT.

Leif Er'ic·son. See ERICSON.

Leigh'-Mal'lo·ry (lē'măl'ō·rĭ), Sir Traf'ford (trăf'ērd) Leigh, 1892–1944. Brit. air marshal.

Leigh'ton (lā't'n), Frederick, 1830–1896. Baron *Leighton of Stret'ton* (strĕt''n). Eng. painter.

Leins'dorf (līns'dôrf), E'rich (ā'rĭk), 1912– . Am. (Austrian-born) conductor.

Leith'-Ross' (lēth'rŏs'), Sir Frederick William, 1887– . Brit. econ. & financier.

Le·jeune' (lĕ·zhūn'), John Archer, 1867–1942. Am. marine corps gen.

Le'land *or* **Ley'land** (lē'lănd), John, 1506?–1552. Eng. antiquary.

Le'ly (lē'lĭ; *Du.* lā'lĕ), Sir Peter, 1618–1680. Orig. *Pie'ter* (pē'tēr) *Van der Faes* (vän dēr fäs'). Du. painter in Eng.

Le·maî'tre (lĕ·mâ'tr'), (Fran'çois' É'lie' [frän'swä' ā'lē']) Jules, 1853–1914. Fr. writer & literary critic.

—, Ab'bé' (à'bā') Georges (zhôrzh) É'dou·ard' (ā'dwàr'), 1894– . Belg. astrophysicist & math.

Le·moyne', Pierre. See IBERVILLE.

Le'nard (lā'närt), Phi'lipp (fē'lĭp; fīl'ĭp), 1862–1947. Ger. physicist.

Len'clos' (läN'klō'), Anne (än; äN), 1620–1705. *Ni'non' de* (nē'nôN' dĕ) *Lenclos.* Fr. wit & lady of fashion.

L'En'fant' (läN'fäN'), Pierre Charles, 1754–1825. Fr. engineer in Am.

Le'nin (lyā'nyĭn; *Angl.* lĕn'ĭn), Ni·ko·lai' (nyē·kŭ·lī'), 1870–1924. *Vla·di'mir* (vlŭ·dyē'myĭr) *Il·ich'* (ĭl·yēch') *Ul·ya'nov* (ŏŏl·yä'nŭf). Russ. Communist.

Le'o (lē'ō). Name of 13 popes; esp.: **I**, Saint, 390?–461 (pope 440–461); **III**, Saint, 750?–816 (pope 795–816); **XIII**, 1810–1903 (pope 1878–1903).

Leon'ard (lĕn'ērd), William El'ler·y (ĕl'ēr·ĭ), 1876–1944. Am. educ. & poet.

Le·o·nar'do da Vin'ci. See Leonardo da VINCI.

Le·on·ca·val'lo (lĕ·ŏn'kä·väl'lō), Rug·gie'ro (rōōd·jâ'rō), 1858–1919. Ital. composer & librettist.

Le·on'i·das (lē·ŏn'ĭ·dăs), 5th cent. b.c. Greek hero; king of Sparta (490?–480).

Le·o·par'di (lā·ō·pär'dĕ), Con'te (kŏn'tä) Gia'co·mo (jä'kō·mō), 1798–1837. Ital. poet.

Le'o·pold (lē'ō·pōld) **I**, 1640–1705. King of Hungary (1655–87) and Holy Rom. emp. (1658–1705).

— **II**, 1747–1792. Holy Rom. emp. (1790–92).

— **I**, 1790–1865. King of Belgium (1831–65).

— **II**, 1835–1909. King of Belgium (1865–1909).

— **III**, 1901– . King of Belgium (1934–51).

Lep'i·dus (lĕp'ĭ·dŭs), Marcus Ae·mil'i·us (ē·mĭl'ĭ·ŭs; ē·mĭl'yŭs), d. 13 b.c. Rom. triumvir.

Ler'mon·tov (lyĕr'mŏn·tŭf), Mi·kha·il' (myĭ·κŭ·ēl') Yur'ie·vich (yŏŏr'yĕ·vyĭch), 1814–1841. Russ. poet & nov.

Le·sage' (lĕ·sàzh'), A'lain' (à'lăN') René, 1668–1747. Fr. nov. & dram.

Le'sche·tiz'ky (*Ger.* lā'shä·tĭts'kē), The'o·dor (*Ger.* tā'ō·dōr), 1830–1915. Pol. pianist & composer.

Les'seps', de (lĕs'ĕps'; *Angl.* lĕs'ĕps), Vi'comte' (vē'kôNt') Fer'di·nand' (fĕr'dĕ'näN') Ma'rie' (mȧ'rē'), 1805–1894. Fr. diplomat; promoter of Suez Canal.

Les'sing (lĕs'ĭng), Gott'hold (gŏt'hōlt) E'phra·im (ā'frä·ĭm; ā·frä'ĭm), 1729–1781. Ger. critic & dram.

Les'ter (lĕs'tēr), Seán (shŏn; shăn) J. E., 1889– . Irish journalist & diplomat; last secy.-gen. of League of Nations (1940–46).

L'Es·trange' (lĕs·trānj'; lĕs-), Sir Roger, 1616–1704. Eng. journalist & trans.

Leut'ze (loi'tsĕ), E·ma'nu·el (ā·mä'nōō·ĕl), 1816–1868. Ger.-born painter.

Le·vas'seur' (lĕ·vȧ·sûr'), Pierre É'mile' (ā'mēl'), 1828–1911. Fr. econ.

Le'ver (lē'vẽr), Charles James, 1806–1872. Brit. nov.

Leve'son Gower (lōō's'n gōr'; lū'-; gôr'), William Spencer, 1880–1953. 4th Earl Gran'ville (grăn'vĬl). Brit. admiral; gov. of N. Ireland (1945–52).

Lew'es (lū'Ĭs), George Henry, 1817–1878. Eng. philos. & critic.

Lew'is (lū'Ĭs; lōō'-), Cecil Day, 1904– . Eng. poet.

—, Isaac Newton, 1858–1931. Am. army officer & inventor.

—, John Llewellyn, 1880– . Am. labor leader.

—, Matthew Gregory, 1775–1818. *Monk* (mŭngk) *Lewis.* Eng. author.

—, Mer'i·weth'er (mĕr'Ĭ·wĕth'ẽr), 1774–1809. Am. explorer.

—, (Percy) Wyndham, 1884–1957. Brit. painter & writer.

—, Sin'clair (sĬn'klâr), 1885–1951. Am. nov.

Lew'i·sohn (lū'Ĭ·sŭn), Lud'wig (lŭd'wĬg), 1883–1955. Ger.-born nov. & critic.

Ley (lī), Ro'bert (rō'bẽrt), 1890–1945. Ger. Nazi leader.

Lhé·vinne' (lā·vēn'), Jo'sef (jō'zĕf; -zĬf), 1874–1944. Russ. pianist.

Lib'bey (lĬb'Ĭ), Laura Jean, 1862–1924. Am. nov.

Li·cin'i·us (lĬ·sĬn'Ĭ·ŭs), 270?–325. *Va·le'ri·us* (vȧ·lēr'Ĭ·ŭs) *Li·cin'i·a'nus* (lĬ·sĬn'Ĭ·ā'nŭs) *Licinius.* Rom. emp. (308–324).

Lid'dell Hart (lĬd'l härt'), Basil Henry, 1895– . Eng. military scientist.

Lie (lē), Jo'nas (jō'näs; *Norw.* yō'näs), 1833–1909. Norw. nov. & dram.

—, Jonas, 1880–1940. *Nephew of prec.* Norw.-born painter in Am.

—, Tryg've (trüg'vĕ; *Angl.* trĬg'vē), 1896– . Norw. lawyer & statesman; secy.-gen. of UN (1946–53).

Lie'big, von (fôn lē'bĬk), Baron Ju'stus (yōōs'tōōs), 1803–1873. Ger. chem.

Lig'gett (lĬg'ĕt; -Ĭt), Hun'ter (hŭn'tẽr), 1857–1935. Am. gen.

Li Hung-chang (lē' hŏŏng'jäng'), 1823–1901. Chin. statesman.

Lil'ien·thal (lĬl'yĕn·thôl), David Eli, 1899– . Am. lawyer & administrator.

Li'li·en·thal' (lē'lĬ·ĕn·täl'), Ot'to (ôt'ō), 1848–1896. Ger. aeronautical engineer.

Li·li'uo·ka·la'ni (lē·lē'wō·kä·lä'nē), Lyd'i·a (lĬd'Ĭ·ȧ) Ka'me·ke·ha (kä'mä·kā'hä), 1838–1917. Queen of the Hawaiian Islands (1891–93).

Lil'lo (lĬl'ō), George, 1693?–1739. Eng. dram.

Lin'a·cre (lĬn'ȧ·kẽr), Thomas, 1460?–1524. Eng. humanist & physician.

Lin'coln (lĬng'kŭn), Abraham, 1809–1865. 16th pres. of the U. S. (1861–65).

—, Benjamin, 1733–1810. Am. Revolutionary gen.

—, Joseph Cros'by (krôz'bĬ·krôs'-), 1870–1944. Am. nov.

Lind (lĬnd), Jen'ny (jĕn'Ĭ), 1820–1887. *Jo·han'na'* (yō·hän'nä') *Ma·ri'a* (mȧ·rē'ȧ). *The Swedish Nightingale.* Swed. soprano.

Lind'bergh (lĬn[d]'bûrg), Anne Spencer, 1907– . *Nee Mor'row* (mŏr'ō); *wife of C. A.* Am. aviator & author.

—, Charles Augustus, 1902– . Am. aviator.

Lind'ley (lĬn[d]'lĬ), John, 1799–1865. Eng. botanist.

Lind'say (lĬn'zĬ), Howard, 1889– . Am. dram. & actor.

—, (Nicholas) Va'chel (vā'chĕl), 1879–1931. Am. poet.

—, Sir Ronald Charles, 1877–1945. Brit. diplomat.

Link'la·ter (lĬngk'lā·tẽr), Eric, 1899– . Brit. writer.

Lin·lith'gow, Marquis of. See under HOPE.

Lin·nae'us (lĬ·nē'ŭs), Car'o·lus (kăr'ō·lŭs), 1707–1778. *Carl* (kärl) *von Lin·ne'* (fôn lĬn·nā'). Swed. botanist.

Lin Sên (lĬn' sĕn') *or* **Lin Shen** (lĬn' shĕn'), 1867?–1943. Chin. statesman; pres. of the National government (1932–43).

Lin Yutang (lĬn' yü'täng'), 1895– . Chin. author & philologist.

Li Po (lē' bô') *or* **Li T'ai-po** (lē' tī'bô'), fl. 762 A.D. Chin. poet.

Lip'pi (lēp'pē), Fra (frä) Fi·lip'po (fē·lēp'pō) *or* Lip'po (lēp'pō), 1406?–1469. Florentine painter.

—, Filippo *or* Fi·lip·pi'no (fē·lēp·pē'nō), 1457?–1504. *Son of prec.* Florentine painter.

Lipp'mann (lēp'màn'), Ga'bri·el' (gȧ'brē'ĕl'), 1845–1921. Fr. physicist.

Lipp'mann (lĬp'mǎn), Walter, 1889– . Am. journalist & author.

Lip'ton (lĬp'tǔn), Sir Thomas John'stone (jŏn'stǔn; -s'n), 1850–1931. Eng. merchant & yachtsman.

Lisle, de. See (1) LECONTE DE LISLE, (2) ROUGET DE LISLE.

List (lĬst), Sieg'mund (zēk'mŏŏnt) Wil'helm (vĬl'hĕlm) Wal'ther (väl'tẽr), 1880– . Ger. field marshal.

Lis'ter (lĬs'tẽr), Joseph, 1827–1912. 1st Baron *Lister of Lyme Re'gis* (līm rē'jĬs). Eng. surgeon.

Liszt, von (fôn lĬst'), Franz (fränts), 1811–1886. Hung. pianist & composer.

Li T'ai-po. See LI PO.

Lit'tle (lĬt'l), Sir Charles James Cole'brooke (kōl'brŏŏk), 1882– . Brit. admiral.

Lit'tle·ton (lĬt'l·tǔn), Sir Thomas, 1407?–1481. Eng. jurist.

Lit'tré' (lē'trā'), Max'i'mi'lien' (mȧk'sē'mē'lyăn') Paul É'mile' (ā'mēl'), 1801–1881. Fr. lexicographer.

Lit·vi'nov (lyĬt·vyē'nǔf; *Angl.* lĬt·vē'nôf), Mak'sim' (mŭk·syēm') Mak·si'mo·vich (mŭk·syē'mŭ·vy'Ĭch), 1876–1951. Russ. Communist.

Liv'ing·ston (lĬv'Ĭng·stǔn), Robert R., 1746–1813. Am. statesman.

Liv'ing·stone (lĬv'Ĭng·stǔn), David, 1813–1873. Scot. explorer in Africa.

Liv'y (lĬv'Ĭ), 59 B.C.–17 A.D. *Titus Liv'i·us* (lĬv'Ĭ·ŭs). Rom. hist.

Lloyd George (loid' jôrj'), David, 1863–1945. 1st Earl of *Du'for* (dōō'vôr). Brit. statesman; prime min. (1916–22).

Lo·ba·chev'ski (lŏ·bȧ·chĕf'skĬ; *Angl.* lŏ'bȧ·chĕf'skĬ), Ni·ko·lai' (nyĬ·kŏ·lī') I·va'no·vich (ē·vä'nŭ·vy'Ĭch), 1793–1856. Russ. math.

Lo'ben·gu'la (lō'bĕng·gū'lȧ; lŏ·bĕng'gŏŏ·lȧ), 1833–1894. Zulu king of the Matabele.

Locke (lŏk), John, 1632–1704. Eng. philos.

—, William John, 1863–1930. Brit. nov.

Lock'er-Lamp'son (lŏk'ẽr·lăm[p]'s'n), Frederick, 1821–1895. Eng. poet.

Lock'hart (lŏk'ẽrt; -härt), John Gibson, 1794–1854. Scot. nov. & biographer.

Lock'yer (lŏk'yẽr), Sir Joseph Norman, 1836–1920. Eng. astron.

Lodge (lŏj), Henry Cabot, 1850–1924. Am. statesman & author.

—, Sir Oliver Joseph, 1851–1940. Eng. physicist.

—, Thomas, 1558?–1625. Eng. poet & dram.

Loeb (lōb), Jacques (zhäk), 1859–1924. Ger.-born biophysiol. in Am.

Loe'wi (lū'vē), Ot'to (ôt'ō), 1873– . Ger. pharmacologist.

Löff'ler (lûf'lẽr), Frie'drich (frē'drĬk) Au'gust (ou'gŏŏst) Jo·han'nes (yō·hän'es; -ĕs), 1852–1915. Ger. bacteriol.

Lo'max (lō'măks), John Avery, 1872–1948. Am. folklorist.

Lom'bard (lŏm'bẽrd; -bärd; lǔm'-), Peter, 1100?–1160 or 1164. *Pe'trus* (pē'trǔs) *Lom·bar'dus* (lŏm·bär'dǔs). Ital. theol.

Lom·bro'so (lŏm·brō'sō), Ce'sa·re (chā'zä·rā), 1836–1909. Ital. physician & psychiatrist.

Lon'don (lǔn'dǔn), Jack, 1876–1916. Am. writer.

Long (lŏng), Hu'ey (hū'Ĭ) Pierce, 1893–1935. Am. lawyer & polit.

—, Stephen Harriman, 1784–1864. Am. army officer & explorer.

Long'fel'low (lŏng'fĕl'ō), Henry Wads'worth (wŏdz'wûrth; -wẽrth), 1807–1882. Am. poet.

Lon·gi'nus (lŏn·jī'nǔs), Dionysius Cas'si·us (kăsh'Ĭ·ŭs; kăsh'ŭs; kăs'Ĭ·ŭs), d. 273 A.D. Greek philos.

Long'street' (lŏng'strēt'), James, 1821–1904. Am. Confed. gen.

Lönn'rot (lûn'rŏt), E'li·as (ē'lyȧs), 1802–1884. Finnish scholar.

Lons'dale (lŏnz'dāl), Frederick, 1881–1954. Brit. dram.

Ló'pez (lō'pās), Car'los (kär'lōs) An·to'nio (än·tō'nyō), 1790–1862. Pres. of Paraguay (1844–62).

—, Fran·cis'co (frän·sēs'kō) So·la'no (sō·lä'nō), 1827–1870. *Son of prec.* Pres. of Paraguay (1862–70).

Lo'rentz (lō'rĕnts), Hen'drik (hĕn'drĬk) An'toon (än'tōn), 1853–1928. Du. physicist.

Lo'renz (lō'rĕnts), A'dolf (ä'dôlf), 1854–1946. Austrian orthopedic surgeon.

Lor·rain' (lŏ·răn'; lô-; *Fr.* lô'răn'), Claude (klôd; *Fr.* klōd), 1600–1682. Pseud. of *Claude Gel·lée'* (zhĕ'lā') or *Ge·lée'* (zhĕ-). Fr. painter.

Lo·thair' (lō·thâr'; -târ') **I**, 795?–855. King of Germany (840–843) & Holy Rom. emp. (840–855).

— **II** (or **III**), 1070?–1137. *The Saxon.* King of Germany & Holy Rom. emp. (1125–37).

Lo'ti' (lō'tē'), Pierre, 1850–1923. Pseud. of *Louis Ma'rie'* (mȧ'rē') *Ju'lien'* (zhü'lyăn') *Viaud* (vyō). Fr. naval officer & nov.

Lou'bet' (lōō'bĕ'), É'mile' (ā'mēl'), 1838–1929. Fr. statesman; pres. of France (1899–1906).

Lou'doun, 4th Earl of. See John CAMPBELL.

Lou'is (lōō'Ĭs; lōō'Ĭ; *Fr.* lwē). Name of 18 kings of France; esp.: **I** (*Le Dé'bon'naire'* [lĕ dā'bô'nâr']), 778–840 (reigned 814–840); **V** (*Le Fai'né'ant'* [lĕ fā'nā'äṅ'], 966?–987 (reigned — last Carolingian — 986–987); **IX** (*Saint*), 1214–1270 (reigned 1226–70); **XI**, 1423–1483 (reigned 1461–83); **XII**, 1462–1515 (reigned 1498–1515); **XIII**, 1601–1643 (reigned 1610–43); **XIV**, 1638–1715 (reigned 1643–1715); **XV**, 1710–1774 (reigned 1715–74); **XVI**, 1754–1793 (reigned 1774–92; guillotined); **XVII**, 1785–1795 (nominally reigned 1793–95); **XVIII**, 1755–1824 (reigned 1814–15, 1815–24).

— **IV**, 1287?–1347. *Duke of Bavaria.* King of Germany & Holy Rom. emp. (1314–47).

— **II de Bour'bon'**. See under CONDÉ.

— **Napoleon.** See NAPOLEON III.

— **Phi'lippe'** (lwē' fē'lēp'; *Angl.* lōō'Ĭ fĬ·lēp'), 1773–1850. *The Citizen King.* King of the French (1830–48).

Louns'bur'y (lounz'bĕr'Ĭ; -bẽr·Ĭ), Thomas Raynes'ford (rānz'fẽrd), 1838–1915. Am. scholar & educ.

Louÿs (lwē), Pierre, 1870–1925. Fr. writer.

Lov'at, 12th Baron. See under FRASER.

Love'lace (lŭv'lās), Richard, 1618–1658. Eng. Cavalier poet.

Lov'er (lŭv'ẽr), Samuel, 1797–1868. Irish nov.

Low (lō), David, 1891– . Brit. cartoonist.

Low'ell (lō'ĕl), Abbott Lawrence, 1856–1943. Am. educ.; pres., Harvard U. (1909–33).

—, Amy, 1874–1925. *Sister of A. L.* Am. poet & critic.

—, James Russell, 1819–1891. Am. poet, essayist, & diplomat.

—, Percival, 1855–1916. *Bro. of A. L.* Am. astron.

Lowes (lōz), John Livingston, 1867–1945. Am. educ.

Lowndes (loundz), William Thomas, 1798–1843. Eng. bibliographer.

Loy·o'la (*Angl.* loi·ō'lȧ), Saint Ignatius of, 1491–1556. *Í'ñi·go* (ē'nyē·gō) *de O'ñez' y Lo·yo'la* (thä ō·nyäth' ē lō·yō'lä). Span. soldier & ecclesiastic; founder of the Society of Jesus.

Lub'bock (lŭb'ǔk), Sir John, 1834–1913. 1st Baron *Ave'bur·y* (āv'bẽr·Ĭ; ā'bẽr·Ĭ). *Son of Sir J. W.* Eng. financier & author.

—, Sir John William, 1803–1865. Eng. astron. & math.

Lu'can (lū'kǎn), 39–65. *Marcus An·nae'us* (ǎ·nē'ŭs) *Lu·ca'nus* (lū·kā'nŭs). Rom. poet.

Luce (lūs), Clare, 1903– . *Nee Boothe* (bōōth). *Wife of H. R.* Am. dram., polit., & diplomat.

—, Henry Robinson, 1898– . Am. editor & publisher.

Luck'ner, von (fôn lŏŏk'nẽr), Count Fe'lix (fā'lĬks; *Angl.* fē'lĬks), 1881– . Ger. naval officer.

Lu·cre'ti·us (lū·krē'shĬ·ŭs; -shǔs), 96?–55 B.C. *Titus Lucretius Car'us* (kār'ŭs; kä'rŭs). Rom. poet & philos.

Lu·cul'lus (lū·kŭl'ŭs), Lucius Li·cin'i·us (lĬ·sĬn'Ĭ·ŭs), fl. 79?–?57 B.C. Rom. gen. & epicure.

Lu'den·dorff (lōō'dĕn·dôrf), E'rich (ā'rĬk) Frie'drich (frē'drĬk) Wil'helm (vĬl'hĕlm), 1865–1937. Ger. gen.

Lud'wig (lōōt'vĬk; lōōd'-), E'mil (ā'mēl), 1881–1948. Orig. *Cohn* (kōn). Swiss (Ger.-born) author.

— Ot'to (ôt'ō), 1813–1865. Ger. nov. & dram.

Lul'ly (lü'lē'), Jean Bap'tiste' (bȧ'tēst'), 1633?–1687. Fr. (Ital.-born) composer.

Lul'ly (lŭl'ĭ), Raymond, 1235?–1315. Span. ecclesiastic & philos.

Lunt (lŭnt), Alfred, 1893– . Am. actor.

Lu'ther (lōōt'ĕr; *Angl.* lū'thĕr), Mar'tin (mär'tēn; *Angl.* mär'tĭn), 1483–1546. Ger. Reformation leader.

Lyau'tey' (lyō'tā'), Louis Hu'bert' (ü'bâr') Gon'zalve' (gôn'zàlv'), 1854–1934. Fr. soldier; marshal of France (1921).

Ly·cur'gus (lī·kûr'gŭs), 9th cent. B.C. Spartan lawgiver.

Lyd'gate (lĭd'gāt; -gĭt), John, 1370?–?1451. Eng. poet.

Ly'ell (lī'ĕl), Sir Charles, 1797–1875. Brit. geologist.

Lyl'y (lĭl'ĭ), John, 1554?–1606. Eng. author.

Lynd (lĭnd), Robert Staugh'ton (stô't'n), 1892– , & his wife, Helen, *nee* Mer'rell (mĕr'ĕl), 1897– . Am. sociologists.

Ly'on (lī'ŭn), Mary, 1797–1849. Am. educ.

Ly'ons (lī'ŭnz), Joseph Aloysius, 1879–1939. Australian statesman; prime min. (1932–39).

Ly·san'der (lī·săn'dĕr), d. 395 B.C. Spartan commander.

Ly·sen'ko (lĭ·sĕng'kō), Tro·fim' De·ni'so·vich (trŭ·fyēm' dyĭ·nyē'sŭ·vyĭch), 1898– . Russ. scientist.

Lys'i·as (lĭs'ĭ·ăs), 450?–?380 B.C. Athenian orator.

Ly·sim'a·chus (lī·sĭm'á·kŭs), 361?–281 B.C. Macedonian gen. under Alexander the Great; king of Thrace (306).

Ly·sip'pus (lī·sĭp'ŭs), 4th cent. B.C. Greek sculptor.

Lyt'ton (lĭt''n), 1st Baron, 1803–1873. *Edward George Earle* (ûrl) *Lytton Bul'wer-Lytton* (bŏōl'wĕr-). *Bro. of Sir Henry Bulwer* (*q.v.*). Eng. nov. & dram.

—, 1st Earl of, 1831–1891. *Edward Robert Bulwer Lytton.* Pseud. *Owen Meredith. Son of prec.* Brit. statesman & poet.

—, 2d Earl of, 1876–1947. *Victor Alexander George Robert Lytton. Son of 1st earl.* Brit. administrator & author.

M

☞ **M'-, Mc-.** Names beginning with these prefixes are alphabetized as if spelled MAC-.

Mc'A·doo (măk'á·dōō), William Gibbs, 1863–1941. Am. lawyer & administrator.

Mc'A·fee (măk'á·fē), Mildred Helen, 1900– . *Wife of Douglas Horton.* Am. educ.; pres., Wellesley Coll. (1936–49).

Mac·Ar'thur (măk·är'thĕr), Arthur, 1845–1912. Am. gen.

—, Charles, 1895–1956. Am. dram.

—, Douglas, 1880– . *Son of Arthur.* Am. gen. of the army.

Ma·cau'lay (má·kô'lĭ), Rose, 1889?– . Eng. nov.

—, Thomas Babington, 1st Baron, 1800–1859. Eng. hist., author, & statesman.

Mac·beth' (măk·bĕth'), d. 1057. King of Scot. (1040–57).

Mc·Bur'ney (măk·bûr'nĭ), Charles, 1845–1913. Am. surgeon.

Mc·Cain' (má·kān'), John Sidney, 1884–1945. Am. admiral.

M'Car'thy (má·kär'thĭ), Justin, 1830–1912. Irish writer & polit.

—, Justin Hunt'ly (hŭnt'lĭ), 1861–1936. *Son of Justin.* Irish dram., nov., & hist.

Mc·Clel'lan (má·klĕl'ăn), George Brin'ton (brĭn't'n; -tŭn), 1826–1885. Am. gen.

Mc·Clos'key (má·klŏs'kĭ), John, 1810–1885. 1st Am. cardinal.

Mc·Clure' (má·klŏōr'), Samuel Sidney, 1857–1949. Am. (Irish-born) editor & publisher.

Mc·Cor'mack (má·kôr'măk), John, 1884–1945. Am. (Irish-born) tenor.

Mc·Cor'mick (má·kôr'mĭk), Cyrus Hall, 1809–1884. Am. reaping machine inventor.

—, Joseph Me·dill' (mĕ·dĭl'), 1877–1925, and his bro. Robert Ruth'er·ford (rŭth'ĕr·fĕrd), 1880–1955. Am. newspaper publishers.

Mc·Cosh' (má·kŏsh'), James, 1811–1894. Am. (Scot.-born) educ.; pres., Princeton U. (1868–88).

Mac·Crack'en (má·krăk'ĕn), Henry Noble, 1880– . Am. educ.

Mc·Crae' (má·krā'), John, 1872–1918. Canadian physician & poet.

Mc·Cutch'eon (má·kŭch'ŭn), George Barr (bär), 1866–1928. Am. nov.

Mac·don'ald (măk·dŏn''ld), George, 1824–1905. Scot. nov. & poet.

—, Sir John Alexander, 1815–1891. Canadian statesman; prime min. (1867–73; 1878–91).

Mac·Don'ald (măk·dŏn''ld), James Ramsay, 1866–1937. Brit. statesman; prime min. (1924; 1929–31; 1931–35).

Mac·don'ough (măk·dŏn'ŭ), Thomas, 1783–1825. Am. naval officer.

Mac·Dow'ell (măk·dou'ĕl), Edward Alexander, 1861–1908. Am. composer.

Mc·Dow'ell (măk·dou'ĕl), Ir'vin (ûr'vĭn), 1818–1885. Am. gen.

Mc·Fee' (măk·fē'), William, 1881– . Eng. writer.

Mc·Gill' (má·gĭl'), James, 1744–1813. Canadian (Scot.-born) businessman & philanthropist.

Mc·Guf'fey (má·gŭf'ĭ), William Holmes, 1800–1873. Am. educ.

Ma·cha'do y Mo·ra'les (mä·chä'thō ē mō·rä'lās), Ge·rar'do (hā·rär'thō), 1871–1939. Pres. of Cuba (1925–33).

Ma'chia·vel'li (mä'kyä·vĕl'lē; *Angl.* măk'ĭ·á·vĕl'ĭ), Nic·co·lò' (nēk·kō·lô'), 1469–1527. Ital. statesman & polit. philos.

Mac·Kay' (má·kī'), Sir I'ven (ī'vĕn) Gif'fard (gĭf'ĕrd), 1882– . Australian gen.

Mac·Kaye' (má·kī'), Percy, 1875–1956. Am. poet & dram.

Mack'en·sen, von (fôn măk'ĕn·zĕn), Au'gust (ou'gŏŏst), 1849–1945. Ger. field marshal.

Mac·Ken'zie (má·kĕn'zĭ), Alexander, 1822–1892. Canadian (Scot.-born) statesman; prime min. (1873–78).

—, Sir Alexander Campbell, 1847–1935. Brit. composer & conductor.

—, Compton, 1883– . Eng. nov.

—, William Lyon, 1795–1861. Canadian (Scot.-born) insurgent leader.

Mc·Kim' (má·kĭm'), Charles Fol'len (fŏl'ĕn), 1847–1909. Am. architect.

Mc·Kin'ley (má·kĭn'lĭ), William, 1843–1901. 25th pres. of the U.S. (1897–1901).

Mack'in·tosh (măk'ĭn·tŏsh), Sir James, 1765–1832. Scot. philos. & hist.

Mac·lar'en, Ian. See John WATSON.

Mc·Laugh'lin (măk·läf'lĭn), Andrew Cunningham, 1861–1947. Am. hist.

Mac·Leish' (măk·lēsh'), Archibald, 1892– . Am. poet & administrator.

Mac·leod' (măk·loud'), Fiona. See William SHARP.

—, John James Rick'ard (rĭk'ĕrd), 1876–1935. Scot. physiol.

Mac'Ma'hon', de (dē māk'má'ôn'), Comte (kônt) Ma'rie' (má'rē') Edme Pa'trice' (ĕd'mĕ pá'trēs') Mau'rice' (mô'rēs'), 1808–1893. Marshal (1859) & pres. (1873–79) of France.

Mc·Mas'ter (măk·màs'tĕr), John Bach (băch), 1852–1932. Am. hist.

Mac·Mil'lan (măk·mĭl'ăn), Donald Baxter, 1874– . Am. arctic explorer.

Mac·Mon'nies (măk·mŏn'ĭz), Frederick William, 1863–1937. Am. sculptor.

Mc·Nair' (măk·nâr'), Les'ley (lĕs'lĭ) James, 1883–1944. Am. gen.

Mc·Nar'ney (măk·när'nĭ), Joseph Tag'gart (tăg'ĕrt), 1893– . Am. gen.

Mc·Naugh'ton (măk·nô't'n), Andrew George Lat'ta (lăt'á), 1887– . Canadian gen.

Mac·Neice' (măk·nēs'), Louis, 1907– . Brit. poet & classical scholar.

Mac·Neil' (măk·nēl'), Her'mon (hûr'mŭn) At'kins (ăt'kĭnz), 1866–1947. Am. sculptor.

Mc·Nutt' (măk·nŭt'), Paul Vo'ries (vō'rēz), 1891–1955. Am. lawyer & administrator.

Mac·pher'son (măk·fûr's'n), James, 1736–1796. Scot. writer.

Mac·rea'dy (măk·rē'dĭ), William Charles, 1793–1873. Eng. actor.

Ma'da·ria'ga y Ro'jo, de (thä mä'thä·ryä'gä ē rrô'hō), Sal'va·dor' (säl'vä·thôr'), 1886– . Span. writer & diplomat.

Ma'de·lin' (má'dlăn'), Louis, 1871–1956. Fr. hist.

Ma·de'ro (mä·thā'rō), Fran·cis'co (frän·sēs'kō) In'da·le'cio (ēn'dä·lā'syō), 1873–1913. Pres. of Mexico (1911–13).

Mad'i·son (măd'ĭ·s'n), Dolley, 1768–1849. Nee (*Dorothea*) *Payne. Wife of James.* Am. hostess.

—, James, 1751–1836. 4th pres. of the U.S. (1809–17).

Mae·ce'nas (mē·sē'năs), Ga'ius (gā'yŭs; gī'ŭs) Cil'ni·us (sĭl'nĭ·ŭs), 70?–8 B.C. Rom. statesman & patron of literature.

Maes *or* **Maas** (mäs), Ni'co·laes (nē'kō·läs), 1632–1693. Du. painter.

Mae'ter·linck (*Flem.* mä'tĕr·lĭngk; *Fr.* mĕ'tĕr'lăngk'; *Angl.* mā'tĕr·lĭngk, mĕt'ĕr-, mä'tĕr-), Count Mau'rice' (mô'rēs'), 1862–1949. Belg. poet, dram., & essayist.

Ma·gel'lan (má·jĕl'ăn; *Brit.* -gĕl'ăn), Ferdinand, 1480?–1521. *Fernan'do* (fēr·nänn'dōō) *de Ma·ga·lhães'* (thĕ mä·gä·lyãēnsh'). Port. navigator.

Ma'gi'not' (má'zhē·nō'; *Angl.* măzh'ĭ·nō), An'dré' (än'drā'), 1877–1932. Fr. polit.; min. of war (1922–24; 1926–29; 1929–30; 1931).

Ma·han' (má·hăn'), Alfred Thayer, 1840–1914. Am. admiral & hist.

Mah·mud' II (mä·mōōd'), 1785–1839. Sultan of Turkey (1808–39).

Ma·hom'et *or* **Ma·hound** (má·hound'). See MOHAMMED.

Mai·mon'i·des (mī·mŏn'ĭ·dēz), 1135–1204. Rabbi *Moses ben Maimon'* (bĕn mī·mōn'). Span.-born philos.

Maine (mān), Sir Henry James Sumner, 1822–1888. Eng. jurist.

Main'te·non', de (dē mănt·nôn'), Mar'quise' (màr'kēz'), 1635–1719. *Fran'çoise'* (frän'swäz') *d'Au'bi'gné'* (dō'bē'nyā'). Consort of Louis XIV.

Mait'land (māt'lănd), Frederic William, 1850–1906. Eng. jurist & hist.

Ma·ki·no (mä·kē·nō), Count No·bu·a·ki (nō·bōō·ä·kē), 1861–1949. Jap. statesman.

Ma·lan' (má·län'), Daniel Fran'çois' (frän'swä'), 1874– . S. African editor; prime min. (1948–54).

Male'branche', de (dē mál'bränsh'), Ni'co'las' (nē'kō'lä') 1638–1715. Fr. philos.

Ma·len'kov (mŭ·lyĕn'kŭf), Ge·or'gi (gĭ·ôr'gĭ) Mak·si·mi·li·a'no·vich (mák·syĭ·myĭ·lĭ·à'nô·vyĭch), 1901– . Russ. polit.

Mal'herbe', de (dē má·lĕrb'), Fran'çois' (frän'swä'), 1555–1628. Fr. poet.

Ma·li·nov'sky (má·lyĭ·nôf'skĭ), Ro·di·on' (rŭ·dyĭ·ôn') Ya'kov·le·vich (yä'kʌv·lyĕ·vyĭch), 1899– . Russ. gen.

Ma·li·now'ski (mä'lē·nôf'skē), Bro·ni'slaw (brô·nē'släf) Kas'per (käs'pĕr), 1884–1942. Pol.-born anthropologist.

Mal'lar'mé' (má'lär'mā'), Sté'phane' (stā'fán'), 1842–1898. Fr. poet.

Ma·lone' (má·lōn'), Edmund *or* Edmond, 1741–1812. Irish Shakespearean scholar.

Mal'o·ry (măl'ō·rĭ), Sir Thomas, fl. 1470. Eng. trans. & compiler.

Mal·pi'ghi (mäl·pē'gē), Mar·cel'lo (mär·chĕl'lō), 1628–1694. Ital. anatomist.

Mal'thus (măl'thŭs), Thomas Robert, 1766–1834. Eng. econ.

Man'del' (män'dĕl'), Georges (zhôrzh), 1885–1943. Orig. *Jé'ro'bo'am' Roth'schild'* (zhā'rō'bō·àm' rôt'shēld'). Fr. polit.

Man'de·ville (măn'dĕ·vĭl), Bernard, 1670?–1733. Du.-born physician & satirist in Eng.

—, Sir John, d. 1372. Pseud. of unidentified author of travel books.

Ma'net' (má'nĕ'), É'dou·ard' (ā'dwär'), 1832–1883. Fr. painter.

Ma·nil'i·us (má·nĭl'ĭ·ŭs), Ga'ius (gā'yŭs; gī'ŭs), 1st cent. B.C. Rom. polit.

Ma·niu' (mä·nyōō'), Iu'liu (yōō'lyōō), 1873–1951. Romanian statesman.

Mann (măn), Horace, 1796–1859. Am. educ.

— (măn; *Angl.* măn), Tho'mas (*Ger.* tō'mäs), 1875–1955. Am. (Ger.-born) author.

Man'ner·heim, von (fôn män'nĕr·hām), Baron Carl (kärl) Gus'taf (gōōs'täf) E'mil (ē'mĭl), 1867–1951. Finnish gen. & statesman.

Man'ning (măn'ĭng), Henry Edward, 1808–1892. Eng. cardinal & author.

—, William Thomas, 1866–1949. Am. clergyman; bishop of New York (1921–46).

Mann'stein, von (fôn män'shtīn), Fritz (frĭts) E'rich (ā'rĭk), 1887– . Orig. *von Le·win'ski* (fôn lä·vĭn'skē). Ger. field marshal.

Mans'field (mănz'fēld; *Angl.* -), Katherine, 1888–1923. Pseud. of *Kathleen,* nee *Beau'champ* (bē'chăm), *Mur'ry* (mûr'ĭ). Brit. writer.

—, Richard, 1854–1907. Eng. actor in Am.

Man·son (măn's'n), Sir Patrick, 1844–1922. Brit. parasitologist.
Man·sur′, al- (ăl/măn·sŏŏr′), 712?–775. Arab caliph (754–775); founder of Baghdad.
Man·te′gna (män·tē′nyä), An·dre′a (än·drä′ä), 1431–1506. Ital. painter & engraver.
Man·tell′ (măn·tĕl′), Robert Bruce, 1854–1928. Scot.-born actor in Am.
Man′tle (măn′t'l), (Robert) Burns, 1873–1948. Am. journalist.
Ma·nuel′, Don Juan. See JUAN MANUEL.
Ma·nu′ti·us (má·nū′shǐ·ŭs), Al′dus (ôl′dŭs; ăl′-), 1450–1515. Te·o·bal′do (tā·ô·bäl′dō) Man·nuc′ci (män·nōōt′chē) or Ma·nu′zi·o (mä·nōō′tsyō). Ital. printer & classical scholar.
Man·zo′ni (män·dzō′nē), A′les·san′dro (ä′läs·sän′drō) Fran·ce′sco (frän·chās′kō) Tom·ma′so (tôm·mä′zō) An·to′nio (än·tô′nyō), 1785–1873. Ital. nov. & poet.
Mao Tse-tung (mä′ō dzū′dŏong′), 1893– . Chin. Communist.
Map (măp), Walter, 1140?–?1209. Welsh writer.
Ma′rat′ (má′rä′), Jean Paul, 1743–1793. Fr. (Swiss-born) Revolutionist.
Mar·cel′lus (mär·sĕl′ŭs), Marcus Claudius, 268?–208 B.C. Rom. gen.
March, 1st Earl of. See Roger de MORTIMER.
Mar·co′ni (mär·kō′nē), Mar·che′se (mär·kä′zā) Gu·gliel′mo (gōō·lyĕl′mō), 1874–1937. Ital. electrical engineer & inventor.
Mar′co Po′lo. See POLO.
Mar′cus Au·re′li·us (mär′kŭs ô·rē′lǐ·ŭs; ô·rēl′yŭs). See Marcus Aurelius ANTONINUS.
Mar′ga·ret (mär′gá·rĕt; -rǐt) **of An′jou** (ăn′jōō; Fr. äN′zhōō′), 1430–1482. Queen of Henry VI of Eng.
— **of Na·varre′** (ná·vär′; Fr. ná/vàr′), 1492–1549. Queen of Navarre (1544–49) & writer.
— **of Va′lois′** (vá/lwä′; Angl. văl′wä), 1553–1615. Queen of Navarre.
Ma·ri′a The·re′sa (Eng. má·rē′á [má·rī′á] tĕ·rē′sá; -zá), 1717–1780. Wife of Emp. Francis I. Queen of Hungary and Bohemia.
Ma·rie′ (Eng. má·rē′ or Brit. mä′rǐ; mô′rǐ), 1875–1938. Queen of Romania (1914–27; queen dowager 1927–38).
— **An′toi·nette′** (ăn′t[w]ô·nĕt′; Fr. mà′rē′ äN′twà′nĕt′), 1755–1793. Dau. of Maria Theresa & wife of Louis XVI of France. Executed.
— **Lou·ise′** (lōō·ēz′; Fr. mà′rē′ lwēz′); Ger. **Ma·ri′a Lu·i′sa** (mä·rē′á lōō·ē′zä), 1791–1847. Dau. of Francis I of Austria. 2d wife of Napoleon I.
Ma·rie′ de Mé′di·cis′ (mà′rē′ dĕ mä′dē′sēs′), 1573–1642. 2d wife of Henry IV of France.
Ma·ri′net′ti (mä′rē·nät′tē), E·mi′lio (ā·mē′lyō) Fi·lip′po (fē·lēp′pō) Tom·ma′so (tôm·mä′zō), 1876–1944. Ital. poet.
Ma·ri′ni (mä·rē′nē) or **Ma·ri′no** (-nō), Giam′bat·ti′sta (jäm′bät·tēs′tä), 1569–1625. Ital. poet.
Mar′i·on (măr′ǐ·ŭn; măr′-), Francis, 1732?–1795. The Swamp Fox. Am. Revolutionary commander.
Ma·ri′tain′ (má′rē′tăN′), Jacques (zhàk), 1882– . Fr. philos. & diplomat.
Mar′i·us (mâr′ǐ·ŭs), Ga′ius (gā′yŭs; gī′ŭs), 155?–86 B.C. Rom. gen.
Ma′ri′vaux′, de (dĕ mà′rē′vō′), Pierre Car′let′ de Cham′blain′ (kär/lĕ′ dĕ shäN′blăN′), 1688–1763. Fr. dram. & nov.
Mark An′to·ny or **An′tho·ny.** See Marcus ANTONIUS.
Mark′ham (mär′kăm), (Charles) Edward, 1852–1940. Am. poet.
Marl′bor·ough, 1st Duke of. See John CHURCHILL.
Mar′lowe (mär′lō), Christopher, 1564–1593. Eng. dram.
—, Julia, 1866–1950. Pseud. of Sarah Frances Frost (frôst). Am. (Eng.-born) actress.
Mar′mont′, de (dĕ màr′môN′), Au′guste′ (ô′güst′) Fré′dé·ric′ (frä′dā′rēk′) Louis Viesse (vyĕs), 1774–1852. Duc (dük) de Ra′guse′ (dĕ rà′güz′). Fr. gen. under Napoleon; marshal of France (1809).
Mar′mon′tel′ (mär′môN′tĕl′), Jean Fran′çois′ (fräN′swä′), 1723–1799. Fr. author.
Ma′rot′ (mà′rō′), Clé′ment′ (klä′mäN′), 1495?–1544. Fr. poet.
Mar·quand′ (mär·kwŏnd′), John Phillips, 1893– . Am. writer.
Mar′quette′ (mär′kĕt′; Angl. mär·kĕt′), Jacques, 1637–1675. Père Marquette (pâr; Angl. pĕr). Jesuit missionary & explorer in Am.
Mar′quis (mär′kwĭs), Donald Robert Perry, 1878–1937. Don (dŏn). Am. humorist.
Mar′ry·at (măr′ǐ·ăt), Frederick, 1792–1848. Eng. naval commander & nov.
Mar′shall (mär′shăl), Alfred, 1842–1924. Eng. econ.
—, George Cat′lett (kăt′lĕt; -lĭt), 1880– . Am. gen. of the army & diplomat.
—, John, 1755–1835. Am. jurist.
—, Thomas Riley, 1854–1925. Vice-pres. of the U. S. (1913–21).
Mar·sil′i·us of Pad′u·a (mär·sĭl′ĭ·ŭs, păd′ū·á), 1290?–?1343. Ital. scholar.
Mar′ston (mär′stŭn), John, 1575?–1634. Eng. dram.
Mar·tel′ (mär·tĕl′), Charles. See CHARLES MARTEL.
—, Sir Gif′fard (gĭf′ērd) Le Quesne (lĕ kān′), 1889– . Brit. gen.
Mar′tens (mär′tyĕns; Angl. mär′t'nz), Fë′dor (fyô′dĕr) Fë′do·ro′vich (fyô′dŭ·rô′vўch), 1845–1909. Russ. jurist.
Mar′tial (mär′shăl), ab. 40–ab. 102. Marcus Va·le′ri·us (vá·lēr′ĭ·ŭs) Mar′ti·a′lis (mär′shĭ·ā′lĭs). Rom. epigrammatist.
Mar′tin (mär′tĭn; -t'n; Fr. màr′tăN′), Saint, 315?–?399. Martin of Tours (tōōr). Patron saint of France.
Mar′tin (mär′tĭn; -t'n), Glenn Luther, 1886–1955. Am. airplane manuf.
—, Homer Dodge, 1836–1897. Am. painter.
—, Joseph William, 1884– . Am. publisher & polit.
—, Sir Theodore, 1816–1909. Brit. author.
Mar′tin′ du Gard′, Roger. See DU GARD.
Mar′ti·neau (mär′tĭ·nō; -t′n·ō), Harriet, 1802–1876. Eng. nov. & econ.
—, James, 1805–1900. Eng. theol. & philos.
Mar′ti·nel′li (mär′tē·nĕl′lē; Angl. mär′tĭ·nĕl′ĭ, -t′n·ĕl′ĭ), Gio·van′ni (jô·vän′nē), 1885– . Am. (Ital.-born) tenor.
Mar·ti′ni (mär·tē′nē), Si·mo′ne (sē·mō′nā), 1283?–1344. Ital. painter.
Mar′vell (mär′vĕl; -v'l), Andrew, 1621–1678. Eng. poet & satirist.
Marx (märks), Karl, 1818–1883. Ger. polit. philos. & socialist.

Mar′y (mâr′ĭ), 1867–1953. Princess Victoria Mary of Teck (tĕk). Queen of George V of Eng.
— **I,** 1516–1558. Mary Tu′dor (tū′dĕr). Bloody Mary. Queen of Eng. (1553–58).
— **II,** 1662–1694. Joint Brit. sovereign with William III.
— **Stu′art** (stū′ĕrt), 1542–1587. Mary, Queen of Scots. Queen of Scot. (1542–67); beheaded.
Ma·sac′cio (mä·zät′chō), 1401–1428. Orig. Tom·ma′so (tôm·mä′zō) Gui′di (gwē′dē). Ital. painter.
Ma′sa·ryk (mä′sá·rĭk), Jan (yän) Gar·rigue′ (gä·rēg′), 1886–1948. Son of T. G. Czechoslovak diplomat & polit.
—, To′máš (tô′mäsh) Garrigue, 1850–1937. Czechoslovak philos.; 1st pres. of Czechoslovakia (1918–35).
Ma·sca′gni (mäs·kä′nyē), Pie′tro (pyä′trō), 1863–1945. Ital. composer.
Mase′field (mās′fēld), John, 1878– . Eng. author; poet laureate (1930–).
Mas′i·nis′sa or **Mas′si·nis′sa** (mäs′ĭ·nĭs′á), 238?–149 B.C. King of Numidia.
Ma′son (mā′s'n), Charles, 1730–1787. Eng. astron. & surveyor.
Mas′pe·ro′ (mäs′pĕ·rō′), Sir Gas′ton′ (gàs′tôN′) Ca′mille′ (kà′mē′y) Charles, 1846–1916. Fr. Egyptologist.
Mas′sa·soit′ (mäs′á·soit′), d. 1661. Sachem of Wampanoag Indians in eastern Massachusetts.
Mas·sé′na′ (mà·sā′nä′), An′dré′ (äN′drā′), 1758–1817. Duc (dük) de Ri′vo·li (dĕ rē′vô·lē). Prince d′Ess′ling (dĕs′lĭng). Fr. soldier under Napoleon; marshal of France (1804).
Mas′se·net′ (màs′nĕ′; Angl. măs′n·ā′), Jules É′mile′ (ā′mēl′) Fré′dé·ric′ (frä′dā′rēk′), 1842–1912. Fr. composer.
Mas′sey (măs′ĭ), Raymond, 1896– . Am. (Canadian-born) actor & producer.
—, William Fer′gu·son (fûr′gŭ·s'n), 1856–1925. N. Z. statesman.
Mas′sin·ger (măs′ĭn·jēr), Philip, 1583–1640. Eng. dram.
Mas′son (măs′n), David, 1822–1907. Scot. editor & scholar.
Mas′ters (màs′tērz), Edgar Lee, 1869–1950. Am. author.
Math′er (măth′ēr; măth′ēr), Cotton, 1663–1728. Am. clergyman & author.
—, In′crease (ĭn′krēs), 1639–1723. Father of Cotton. Am. clergyman & author; pres., Harvard U. (1685–1701).
Ma′tisse′ (mà′tēs′), Hen′ri′ (äN′rē′), 1869–1954. Fr. painter.
Ma·tsu·o·ka (mä·tsŏō·ô·kä), Yo·su·ke (yō·sŏō·kĕ), 1880–1946. Jap. statesman.
Mat′te·ot′ti (mät′tā·ôt′tē), Gia′co·mo (jä′kô·mō), 1885–1924. Ital. socialist.
Mat′thews (măth′ūz), (James) Bran′der (brăn′dēr), 1852–1929. Am. educ. & author.
Maugham (môm), William Som′er·set (sŭm′ēr·sĕt; -sĭt), 1874– . Eng. nov. & dram.
Mau′nou′ry′ (mō′nōō′rē′), Mi′chel′ (mē′shĕl′) Jo′seph′ (zhō′zĕf′), 1847–1923. Fr. gen.
Mau′pas′sant′, de (dĕ mō′pá′säN′), (Hen′ri′ Re·né′ Al′bert′ [äN′rē′ rĕ·nā′ àl′bâr′]) Guy (gē), 1850–1893. Fr. short-story writer.
Mau′rice (mô′rĭs; mŏr′ĭs); Ger. **Mo′ritz** (mō′rĭts), 1521–1553. Elector of Saxony (1547–53) & gen.
— **of Nas′sau** (năs′ô; năs′ou), 1567–1625. Prince of Or′ange (ŏr′ĕnj; -ĭnj). Du. gen. & statesman.
Mau′rois′ (mō′rwä′), An′dré′ (äN′drā′), 1885– . Pseud. of É′mile′ (ā′mēl′) Sa′lo′mon′ (sà′lô′môN′) Wil′helm′ (vē′lĕlm′) Her′zog′ (ĕr′zôg′). Fr. writer.
Mau′ry (mô′rĭ), Matthew Fon·taine′ (fŏn·tān′), 1806–1873. Am. naval officer & oceanographer.
Mau′ser (mou′zĕr), Pe′ter (pā′tĕr) Paul (poul), 1838–1914, and his bro. Wil′helm (vĭl′hĕlm), 1834–1882. Ger. inventors.
Maw′son (mô′s'n), Sir Douglas, 1882– . Brit. antarctic explorer & geologist.
Max′im (măk′sĭm), Sir Hiram Stevens, 1840–1916. Brit. (Am.-born) inventor.
—, Hudson, 1853–1927. Bro. of Sir Hiram. Am. inventor & explosives expert.
Max·i·mil′ian (măk/sĭ·mĭl′yăn; -mĭl′ĭ·än; Ger. mäk/sē·mē′lē·än), 1832–1867. Bro. of Francis Joseph I of Austria. Emp. of Mexico (1864–67); executed.
— **I,** 1459–1519. Holy Rom. emp. (1493–1519).
— **II,** 1527–1576. Holy Rom. emp. (1564–76).
Max′well (măks′wĕl; -wĕl), James Clerk (klärk), 1831–1879. Scot. physicist.
May (mā), Sir Thomas Erskine, 1815–1886. 1st Baron Farn′bor·ough (färn′bûr′ō; esp. Brit., -bŭ·rŭ, -brŭ). Eng. constitutional jurist.
May′o (mä′ō), Charles Horace, 1865–1939, and his bro. William James, 1861–1939. Am. surgeons.
—, Henry Thomas, 1856–1937. Am. admiral.
Ma′za′rin′ (mà′zà′răN′; Angl. măz′á·rĭn, măz′á·rēn′), Jules, 1602–1661. Fr. cardinal & statesman.
Maz·zi′ni (mät·tsē′nē; mäd·dzē′nē), Giu·sep′pe (jōō·zĕp′pā), 1805–1872. Ital. patriot.
Mc-. See under Mac-.
Meade (mēd), George Gordon, 1815–1872. Am. gen.
Med′hurst (mĕd′hûrst), Sir Charles Edward Hastings, 1896–1954. Brit. air marshal.
Me′di·ci, de′ (dā mä′dĕ·chē; Angl. mĕd′ĕ-, mā′dĕ-), Catherine. See CATHERINE DE MÉDICIS.
—, Co′si·mo (kô′zē·mō) or Cos′mo (kôz′mō), 1389–1464. Florentine financier & polit.
—, Cosimo I, 1519–1574. Cosimo the Great. Duke of Flor′ence (flôr′ĕns); Grand Duke of Tuscany.
—, Giulio. See CLEMENT VII.
—, Lo·ren′zo (lô·rĕn′tsō; Angl. lô·rĕn′zō), 1449–1492. Lorenzo the Magnificent. Florentine statesman, ruler, & patron.
Me·di·na-Si·do′nia (mä·thē′nä·sē·thō′nyä), 7th Duke of, 1550–1615. A·lon′so (ä·lôn′sō) Pé′rez de Guz·mán′ (pā′rāth thä gōōth·män′). Span. admiral.
Meer van Delft, van der. See Jan VERMEER.

Me·he·met' A·li' (mě·mět' ä·lĭ') or Mo·ham'med Ali (mō·hăm'ĕd; -Ĭd), 1769-1849. Viceroy of Egypt (1805-48).

Meigh'en (mē'ĕn), Arthur, 1874- . Canadian statesman; prime min. (1920-21, 1926).

Mei'kle·john (mĭk'l·jŏn), Alexander, 1872- . Am. (Eng.-born) educ.

Meil'hac' (mě'yàk'), Hen'ri' (än'rē'), 1831-1897. Fr. dram.

Meis·so'nier' (mā'sō'nyā'), Jean Louis Er'nest' (ěr'něst'), 1815-1891. Fr. painter.

Meit'ner (mīt'nēr), Li'se (lē'zě), 1878- . Ger. physicist.

Me·lanch'thon (mě·lăngk'thŭn; Ger. mā·länk'tōn), 1497-1560. Phi'lipp (fē'lĭp; fĭl'ĭp) Schwarz'ert' (shvärts'ärt'). Ger. scholar & religious reformer.

Mel'ba (měl'bá), Nellie, 1861-1931. Orig. Helen Porter Mitchell. Australian soprano.

Mel'bourne (měl'bērn; -bôrn), 2d Viscount, 1779-1848. William Lamb (lăm). Eng. statesman.

Mel'chers (měl'chěrz), Gar'i (gär'ĭ), 1860-1932. Am. painter.

Mel'chior (měl'kyôr), Lau'ritz (lou'rěts) Leb'recht (lĭb'rěkt) Hommel (hŏm'ěl), 1890- . Am. (Dan.-born) tenor.

Mel'lon (měl'ŭn), Andrew William, 1855-1937. Am. financier.

Mel'ville (měl'vĭl), Herman, 1819-1891. Am. nov.

Mem'ling (měm'lĭng) or Mem'linc (-lĭngk), Hans (häns), 1430?-1495. Flem. painter.

Me·nan'der (mě·năn'dēr), 343?-?291 B.C. Greek dram.

Men'ci·us (měn'shĭ·ŭs), 372?-?289 B.C. Měng-tzŭ or Meng-tse (mŭng'dzŭ'). Chin. philos.

Menck'en (měng'kěn), Henry Louis, 1880-1956. Am. editor.

Men'del (měn'děl), Gre'gor (grā'gôr; grä·gôr') Jo·hann' (yō·hän'; yō'hän), 1822-1884. Austrian botanist.

Men·de·le'ev (myěn·dyĭ·lyā'yěf; Angl. měn'dě·lā'[y]ěf), Dmi'tri (d'myē'trĭ) I·va'no·vich (ĭ·vä'nŭ·vyĭch), 1834-1907. Russ. chem.

Men'dels·sohn (měn'děls·zōn; Angl. -děl·s'n), Mo'ses (mō'zěs; Angl. mō'zěz, -zĭz), 1729-1786. Ger. philos.

Men'dels·sohn-Bar·thol'dy (-bär·tōl'dē), Ja'kob (yä'kŏp) Lud'wig (lōōt'vĭk; lōōd'-) Fe'lix (fā'lĭks; Angl. fē'lĭks), 1809-1847 Grandson of Moses Mendelssohn. Ger. composer, pianist, & conductor.

Men·do'za, de (thä mān·dō'sä), An·to'nio (än·tō'nyō), 1485?-1552. Span. colonial administrator.

Men'e·lik II (Angl. měn'ě·lĭk), 1844-1913. Emp. of Abyssinia (1889-1913).

Me·nén'dez de A'vi·lés' (mā·nän'dāth thä ä'vē·lās'), Pe'dro (pā'thrō), 1519-1574. Span. admiral; colonizer of Florida.

Me'nes (mē'nēz), fl. 3400 (3500?) B.C. Egyptian king; uniter of north and south kingdoms.

Men·u·hin (měn'ū·ĭn), Ye·hu·di (yě·hōō'dĭ), 1916- . Am. violinist.

Men'zies (měn'zēz), Robert Gordon, 1894- . Australian statesman.

Mer·ca'tor (mûr·kā'tēr; Flem. měr·kà'tôr), Ger·har'dus (jûr·här'dŭs; jēr-), 1512-1594. Ger'hard (gā'rärt) Kre'mer (krā'měr). Flem. geographer.

Mer'cier' (měr'syā'), Dé'si'ré' (dā'zē'rā') Jo'seph' (zhō'zěf'), 1851-1926. Belg. cardinal; primate of Belgium.

Mer'e·dith (měr'ě·dĭth), George, 1828-1909. Eng. nov. & poet.

—, Owen. See E. R. Bulwer LYTTON.

Me·rets·kov' (myĭ·ryěts·kôf'), Ki·rill' (kĭ·ryěl') A·fa·na'se·vich (ŭ·fü·nä'syě·vyĭch). Russ. marshal (World War II).

Mer'gen·tha'ler (měr'gěn·tä'lēr), Ott'mar (ôt'mär), 1854-1899. Am. (Ger.-born) inventor.

Mé'ri·mée' (mā'rē'mā'), Pros'per' (prôs'pâr'), 1803-1870. Fr. nov. & hist.

Mer'ritt (měr'ĭt), Wesley, 1834-1910. Am. gen.

Mer'ry del Val, de (thä měr'rē thěl väl'), Mar·qués' (mär·kās') Al·fon'so (äl·fōn'sō), 1864-1943. Span. diplomat.

Mes'mer (měs'měr; Angl. měz'-), Franz (fränts) or Frie'drich (frē'drĭk) An'ton (än'tōn), 1734-1815. Austrian physician.

Mes·sa'la Cor·vi'nus (mě·sā'là [-săl'á] kôr·vī'nŭs), Marcus Va·le'ri·us (vá·lēr'ĭ·ŭs), 1st cent. B.C. Rom. gen. & statesman.

Mes·sa·li'na (měs·á·lī'ná), Va·le'ri·a (vá·lēr'ĭ·á), d. 48 A.D. 3d wife of Emp. Claudius.

Mes'ser·schmitt (měs'ěr·shmĭt), Wil'helm (vĭl'hělm), 1898- . Ger. aircraft designer & manuf.

Mes'sier' (mě'syā'), Charles, 1730-1817. Fr. astron.

Meš'tro·vić (měsh'trô·vēt'y'; Angl. -vĭch), I'van (ē'vän), 1883- . Yugoslav sculptor.

Me'ta·xas' (mě·tăk'săs; Angl. jō·ăn'ēz; -ēs), Jo·an'nes (yō·ä'nyěs; Angl. jō·ăn'ēz; -ēs), 1871-1941. Greek gen. & dictator.

Metch'ni'koff (Fr. měch'nē'kôf'), É'lie' (ā'lē'), 1845-1916. Russ. zool. & bacteriol.

Met'ter·nich, von (fôn mět'ěr·nĭk), Prince Kle'mens (klā'měns) Wen'zel (věn'tsěl) Ne'po·muk (nā'pō·mŏŏk) Lo'thar (lō'tär; lō'tär'), 1773-1859. Austrian statesman.

Mey'er (mī'ěr), Annie (ăn'ĭ), 1867-1951. Nee Na'than (nā'thăn; -th'n). Am. educ. & writer.

Mey'er·beer (mī'ěr·bâr; sometimes Angl. to -bēr), Gia'co·mo (jä'kō·mō), 1791-1864. Ja'kob (yä'kŏp) Lieb'mann (lēp'män) Beer (bär). Ger. composer.

Mey'er·hof (mī'ěr·hôf), Ot'to (ôt'ō), 1884-1951. Ger. physiol.

Meyn'ell (měn'l), Alice Christiana Gertrude, 1847-1922. Nee Thomp'son (tŏm[p]'s'n). Wife of Wilfrid. Eng. poet & essayist.

—, Wilfrid, 1852-1948. Eng. journalist & biographer.

Mi'chael (mī'kěl; -k'l); Romanian Mi·hai' (mě·hī'), 1921- . Michael Ho'hen·zol'lern (hō'ěn·tsôl'ěrn). King of Romania (1927-30, 1940-47).

Mi'chel·an'ge·lo Buo'nar·ro'ti (mī'kěl·ăn'jě·lō; mĭk'ěl-; Ital. mē'kěl·än'jā·lō bwō'när·rō'tē), 1475-1564. Ital. sculptor, painter, architect, & poet.

Mi'che·let' (mēsh'lě'), Jules, 1798-1874. Fr. hist.

Mi'chel·son (mī'kěl·s'n), Albert Abraham, 1852-1931. Am. (Ger.-born) physicist.

Mic·kie'wicz (mēts·kyě'věch), A'dam (ä'däm), 1798-1855. Pol. poet.

Mid'dle·ton (mĭd'l·tŭn), Thomas, 1570?-1627. Eng. dram.

Miff'lin (mĭf'lĭn), Thomas, 1744-1800. Am. Revolutionary gen. & statesman.

Mi·haj'lo·vić or Mi·khai'lo·vitch (mě·hī'lō·vět'y'; mě·kī'-; Angl. -vĭch), Dra'ža or Dra'ja (drä'zhä), 1893?-1946. Yugoslav gen.

Mi'klas (mĭk'läs), Wil'helm (vĭl'hělm), 1872-1956. Austrian polit.

Mi·ko·yan' (myĭ·kŭ·yàn'), A·na·stas' (ŭ·nŭ·stäs') I·va'no·vich (ĭ·vä'nŭ·vyĭch), 1895- . Russ. polit.

Milch (mĭlk), Er'hard (ār'härt), 1892- . Ger. field marshal.

Miles (mīlz), Nelson Appleton, 1839-1925. Am. gen.

Mil'haud' (mē'yō'), Da'rius' (dä'ryüs'), 1892- . Fr. composer.

Mill (mĭl), James, 1773-1836. Scot. philos., hist., & econ.

—, John Stuart, 1806-1873. Son of James. Eng. philos. & econ.

Mil·lais' (mĭ·lā'), Sir John Everett, 1829-1896. Eng. painter.

Mil·lay' (mĭ·lā'), Edna St. Vin'cent (sănt vĭn'sěnt), 1892-1950. Am. poet.

Mil'ler (mĭl'ěr), Alice, 1874-1942. Nee Duer (dūr). Am. nov.

—, Cin'cin·nat'us (sĭn'sĭ·nät'ŭs) Hi'ner (hī'něr), 1839-1913. Pseud. Joa·quin' (wä·kēn') Miller. Am. poet.

—, William, 1782-1849. Am. Adventist.

Mil'le·rand' (mēl'rän'), A'lex'an'dre (à'lěk'sän'dr'), 1859-1943. Fr. statesman; pres. of France (1920-24).

Mil'let' (mě'lě'; Angl. mĭl·lā', mĭl'ä), Jean Fran'çois' (frän'swä'), 1814-1875. Fr. painter.

Mil'li·kan (mĭl'ĭ·kăn), Robert Andrews, 1868-1953. Am. physicist.

Mills (mĭlz), Darius Ogden, 1825-1910. Am. financier.

Mil'man (mĭl'măn), Henry Hart, 1791-1868. Eng. poet & hist.

Milne (mĭln), Alan Alexander, 1882- . Eng. poet & dram.

Mil'ner (mĭl'něr), Alfred, 1st Viscount, 1854-1925. Brit. administrator in S. Africa.

Mil·ti'a·des (mĭl·tī'à·dēz), 540?-?489 B.C. Athenian gen.

Mil'ton (mĭl't'n; -tŏn), John, 1608-1674. Eng. poet.

Mi·lyu·kov' (myĭ·lyōō·kôf'), Pa'vel (pä'vyěl) Ni·ko·la'e·vich (nyĭ·kŭ·lä'yě·vyĭch), 1859-1943. Russ. polit. & hist.

Mi'nié' (mē'nyā'; Angl. mĭn'ĭ·ā), Claude (klōd) É'tienne' (ā'tyěn'), 1814-1879. Fr. army officer & inventor.

Mi'not (mī'nŭt), George Richards, 1885-1950. Am. physician.

Min'ton (mĭn't'n; -tŭn), Sherman, 1890- . Am. jurist.

Min·u·it (mĭn'ū·ĭt; mē'nwē') or Min'ne·wit (mĭn'ě·wĭt), Peter, 1580-1638. Du. colonial administrator in Am.

Mi·ra'beau, de (dě mē'rà'bō'; Angl. mĭr'à·bō), Comte (kônt), 1749-1791. Ho'no'ré' (ō'nō'rā') Ga'bri'el' (gä'brē'ěl') Vic'tor' (vēk'tôr') Ri'que·ti' (rēk'tē'). Fr. orator & revolutionist.

Mis'tral' (mēs·träl'), Fré'dé'ric' (frā'dā'rēk'), 1830-1914. Provençal poet.

Mis·tral' (mēs·träl'), Ga·bri·e'la (gä'vrē·ā'lä), 1889-1957. Lu·ci'la (lōō·sē'lä) Go·doy' de Al'ca·ya'ga (gō·thoi' thä äl'kä·yä'gä). Chilean poet & educ.

Mitch'el (mĭch'ěl), John, 1815-1875. Irish patriot.

Mitch'ell (mĭch'ěl), Donald Grant, 1822-1908. Pseud. Ik (ĭk) Mar'vel (mär'věl; -v'l). Am. author.

—, John, 1870-1919. Am. labor leader.

—, Maria, 1818-1889. Am. astron.

—, Silas Weir, 1829-1914. Am. physician & writer.

—, William, 1879-1936. Am. gen.

Mit'ford (mĭt'fērd), Mary Russell, 1787-1855. Eng. nov. & dram.

—, William, 1744-1827. Eng. hist.

Mith'ri·da'tes VI (mĭth'rĭ·dā'tēz), ab. 132-63 B.C. The Great. King of Pontus (120-63).

Mo·djes'ka (mô·jěs'kà), He·le'na (hě·lā'nà), 1840-1909. Orig. Mo'drze·jew'ska (mō'jě·yěf'skä); nee O'pid (ô'pět). Pol.-born actress in Am.

Mo·ham'med (mô·hăm'ěd; -Ĭd), Ma·hom'et (mà·hŏm'ět; -Ĭt; mä'ō·mět, -mĭt), or Mu·ham'mad (mŏŏ·hăm'măd), 570-632. Arab prophet & founder of Mohammedanism.

Mo·ham'med II, 1430-1481. Turk. sultan (1451-81).

Mo·ham'med Ri·za' Pah'la·vi or Pah'le·vi (Pers. mŏ·hăm'măd rĭ·zä' pä'lä·vē), 1919- . Shah of Iran (1941-).

Mo'holy-Nagy' (mō'hoi·nŏd'y'), Lász'ló (läs'lō) or La'dis·laus (Ger. lä'dĭs·lous), 1895-1946. Hung. painter, designer, & photographer.

Mois'san' (mwä'sän'), Hen'ri' (än'rē'), 1852-1907. Fr. chem.

Mo'la (mō'lä), E·mi'lio (ā·mē'lyō), 1887-1937. Span. gen.

Mo'ley (mō'lĭ), Raymond, 1886- . Am. educ.

Mo·lière' (mō'lyâr'), 1622-1673. Pseud. of Jean Bap'tiste' (bà'tēst') Po'que·lin' (pō'klän'). Fr. actor & dram.

Mo·li'na, de, Tirso. See TIRSO DE MOLINA.

Mol'li·son (mŏl'ĭ·s'n), James Allan, 1905- . Brit. aviator.

Mol'nár (mŏl'när), Fe'renc (fě'rěnts), 1878-1952. Hung. author.

Mo'lo·tov (mō'lŭ·tŭf), Vya·che·slav' (vyĭ·chě·släf') Mi·khai'lo·vich (myĭ·kī'lŭ·vyĭch), 1890- . Orig. Skrya'bin (skryä'byĭn). Russ. statesman.

Molt'ke, von (fôn mōlt'kě), Count Hel'muth (hěl'mōōt), 1800-1891. Prussian field marshal.

—, Helmuth, 1848-1916. Nephew of prec. Ger. gen.

Momm'sen (mŏm'zěn; Angl. mŏm'sěn), The'o·dor (Ger. tā'ō·dōr), 1817-1903. Ger. classical scholar & hist.

Monck or Monk (mŭngk), George, 1608-1670. 1st Duke of Al'be·marle (ăl'bě·märl). Eng. gen.

Mon'dri·aan (mŏn'drē·än), Pie'ter (pē'těr) Cor·ne'lis (kôr·nā'lĭs), 1872-1944. Du. painter.

Mo'net' (mō'ně'), Claude (klōd), 1840-1926. Fr. painter.

Mo·ne'ta (mō·nā'tä), Er·ne'sto (ār·něs'tō) Te·o·do'ro (tā·ō·dō'rō), 1833-1918. Ital. journalist & pacificist.

Mon'i·er-Wil'liams (mŭn'ĭ·ēr·wĭl'yămz; mŏn'-), Sir Monier, 1819-1899. Eng. Sanskrit scholar.

Monk, George. See MONCK.

Mon'mouth (mŏn'mŭth; mŭm'-), Duke of, 1649-1685. James Scott (skŏt). Son of Charles II of Eng. Eng. rebel & claimant to the throne.

Mon·roe' (mŭn·rō'), Harriet, 1861?-1936. Am. poet & editor.

—, James, 1758-1831. 5th pres. of the U. S. (1817-25).

Mon·ta′gna (mŏn·tä′nyä), Bar′to·lom·me′o (bär′tṓ·lŏm·mâ′ṓ), 1450?–1523. Ital. painter.

Mon′ta·gu (mŏn′tá·gū; mŭn′-), Lady Mary Wort′ley (wûrt′lĭ), 1689–1762. Eng. letter writer.

Mon′taigne′, de (dĕ mŏn′tĕn′y; -tän′y′; Angl. mŏn·tān′), Mi′chel′ (mē′shĕl′) Ey′quem′ (ĕ′kĕm′), 1533–1592. Fr. essayist.

Mont′calm′ de Saint′-Vé′ran′, de (dĕ mŏn′kȧlm′ dĕ săn′vä′rän′; Angl. mŏnt·käm′), Marquis Louis Jo′seph′ (zhṓ′zĕf′), 1712–1759. Fr. field marshal in Canada.

Mon′tes·pan′, de (dĕ mŏn·tĕs′pän′; Angl. mŏn′tĕs·păn′), Mar′quise′ (mȧr′kēz′), 1641–1707. Nee (Fran′çoise′ A′thé′na′ïs′ [frän′swäz′ä′tā′nä′ēs′]) Roche′chou·art′ (rŏsh′shwär′). Mistress of Louis XIV.

Mon′tes′quieu′, de (dĕ mŏn′tĕs′kyū′; Angl. mŏn′tĕs·kū′), Baron de La Brède et (dĕ lȧ brĕd′ ā), 1689–1755. Charles de Se·con′dat′ (dĕ sĕ·gŏn′dä′). Fr. lawyer & polit. philos.

Mon·tes·so′ri (mŏn·tĕs·sō′rē; Angl. mŏn′tĕ·sō′rē), Ma·ri′a (Ital. mä·rē′ä), 1870–1952. Ital. physician & educ.

Mon′teux′ (mŏn′tû′), Pierre, 1875–   . Fr. conductor.

Mon′te·zu′ma II (mŏn′tĕ·zōō′mä; Span. môn′tā·sōō′mä), 1480?–1520. Last Aztec emp. of Mexico.

Mont′fort, de (dĕ mŏnt′fĕrt; Fr. dĕ mŏn′fôr′), Simon, 1208?–1265. Earl of Leices′ter (lĕs′tĕr). Eng. soldier & statesman.

— l′A′mau′ry′ (dĕ mŏn′fôr′ lȧ′mō′rē′), Simon IV, 1160?–1218. Earl of Leicester and Comte (kônt) de Tou′louse′ (dĕ tōō′lōōz′). Father of prec. Fr. crusader.

Mont′gol′fier′ (mŏn′gŏl′fyä′; Angl. mŏnt·gŏl′fĭ·ẽr), Jo′seph′ (zhṓ′zĕf′) Mi′chel′ (mē′shĕl′), 1740–1810, and his bro. Jacques (zhàk) É′tienne′ (ā′tyĕn′), 1745–1799. Fr. inventors & pioneer aeronauts.

Mont·gom′er·y (mŏn[t]·gŭm′ẽr·ĭ; -gŭm′rĭ; -gŏm′-), Bernard Law, 1887–   . 1st Viscount Montgomery of A′la·mein′ (ăl′á·mān′). Brit. field marshal.

—, Richard, 1736–1775. Am. (Irish-born) Revolutionary gen.

Mont·gom′er·y-Mas′sing·berd (-măs′ĭng·bûrd; Sir Archibald Ar′mar (är′mẽr), 1871–1947. Brit. field marshal.

Mont′mo′ren′cy′, de (dĕ mŏn′mô′rän′sē′; Angl. mŏnt′mô·rĕn′sĭ), Duc (dük) Anne (än; än), 1493–1567. Fr. soldier; constable (1537).

Mont·rose′ (mŏnt·rōz′; mŏn·trōz′), James Graham, 1st Marquis of, 1612–1650. Scot. Royalist.

Moo′dy (mōō′dĭ), Dwight Lyman, 1837–1899. Am. evangelist.

—, William Vaughn, 1869–1910. Am. poet & dram.

Mook, van (vän mōk′), Hu·ber′tus (hū·bĕr′tŭs) Jo·han′nes (yō·hän′ĕs), 1895–   . Du. East Indian administrator.

Moo′ney (mōō′nĭ), Edward, 1882–   . Am. cardinal.

Moore (mōōr; mōr), George, 1852–1933. Irish author.

—, Sir John, 1761–1809. Brit. gen. in Am.

—, John Bas′sett (băs′ĕt; -ĭt), 1860–1947. Am. jurist.

—, Thomas, 1779–1852. Irish poet.

—·Brab′a·zon (-brăb′á·z′n), John Theodore Cuthbert, 1884–   . 1st Baron Brabazon of Tar′a (tär′á). Brit. aviator & administrator.

More (mōr), Hannah, 1745–1833. Eng. religious writer.

—, Henry, 1614–1687. Eng. philos.

—, Paul Elmer, 1864–1937. Am. essayist & critic.

—, Sir Thomas, 1478–1535. Saint. Eng. statesman & author.

Mo′reau′ (mô′rō′), Jean Vic′tor′ (vĕk′tôr′), 1763–1813. Fr. soldier.

Mor′gan (môr′găn), Con′way (kŏn′wā) Lloyd, 1852–1936. Eng. zool. & psychol.

—, Daniel, 1736–1802. Am. Revolutionary gen.

—, Sir Henry, 1635?–1688. Brit. buccaneer.

—, John Hunt, 1825–1864. Am. Confed. cavalry officer.

—, John Pier′pont (pẽr′pŏnt), 1837–1913. Am. financier.

—, John Pierpont, 1867–1943. Son of J. P. Am. financier.

—, Thomas Hunt, 1866–1945. Am. zool.

Mor′gen·thau (môr′gĕn·tou), Henry, 1856–1946. Am. diplomat.

— (-thô), Henry, 1891–   . Son of prec. U. S. secy. of the treas. (1934–45).

Mor′i·son (mŏr′ĭ·s′n), Samuel Eliot, 1887–   . Am. hist.

Mor′land (môr′lănd), Sir Thomas Leth′bridge (lĕth′brĭj) Napier, 1865–1925. Brit. (Canadian-born) gen.

Mor′ley (môr′lĭ), Christopher Dar′ling·ton (där′lĭng·tŭn), 1890–1957. Am. writer.

—, John, 1838–1923. Viscount Morley of Black′burn (blăk′bẽrn; -bûrn). Eng. statesman and writer.

Mor′nay′, de (dĕ môr′nā′), Phi′lippe′ (fē′lēp′), 1549–1623. Sei′gneur′ (sĕ′nyûr′) du Ples′sis′-Mar′ly′ (dü plĕ′sē′mȧr′lē′); Duplessis-Mornay. Fr. Huguenot.

Mor′ris (mŏr′ĭs), Gou′ver·neur′ (gŭv′ẽr·nẽr′), 1752–1816. Am. statesman & diplomat.

—, Robert, 1734–1806. Am. financier & statesman.

—, William, 1834–1896. Eng. poet, artist, & socialist.

Mor′ri·son (mŏr′ĭ·s′n), Herbert Stanley, 1888–   . Eng. labor leader & polit.

—, Robert, 1782–1834. Scot. missionary in China.

Morse (môrs), Samuel Fin′ley (fĭn′lĭ) Breese (brēz), 1791–1872. Am. artist & inventor.

Mor′ti·mer, de (dĕ môr′tĭ·mẽr), Roger (IV), 1287–1330. 1st Earl of March (märch). Welsh rebel & paramour of Isabella, queen of Edward II of Eng.

Mor′ton (môr′t′n), William Thomas Green, 1819–1868. Am. dentist.

Mos′by (mŏz′bĭ), John Sin′gle·ton (sĭng′g′l·tŭn), 1833–1916. Am. lawyer & Confed. cavalry officer.

Mos·cic′ki (mŏsh·chēts′kĕ), Ig·na′cy (ĕg·nä′tsĭ), 1867–1946. Pol. chem.; pres. of Poland (1926–39).

Mos′ley (mŏz′lĭ), Sir Oswald Er′nald (ûr′n′ld), 1896–   . Eng. polit.

Mosz·kow′ski (mŏsh·kôf′skĕ), Mo′ritz (mō′rĭts), 1854–1925. Pol. pianist & composer.

Mo Ti (mô′ dē′) or Mo-tzŭ (mô′dzŭ′), 5th–4th cent. B.C. Chin. philos.

Mot′ley (mŏt′lĭ), John Lo′throp (lŏ′thrŭp), 1814–1877. Am. hist.

Mo′ton (mô′t′n), Robert Rus′sa (rŭs′á), 1867–1940. Am. educ.

Mott (mŏt), John Ra′leigh (rô′lĭ), 1865–1955. Am. Y.M.C.A. leader.

—, Lucretia, 1793–1880. Nee Cof′fin (kŏf′ĭn). Am. social reformer.

Mot′ta (môt′tä), Giu·sep′pe (jōō·zĕp′pā), 1871–1940. Swiss lawyer & statesman.

Mot′teux′ (mô′tû′), Peter Anthony, 1660 or 1663–1718. Eng. (Fr.-born) dram. & trans.

Moul′ton (mōl′t′n; -tŭn), For′est (fŏr′ĕst; -ĭst) Ray, 1872–1952. Am. astron.

Moul′trie (mōōl′trĭ), William, 1730–1805. Am. Revolutionary gen.

Mount·bat′ten (mount·băt′′n), Louis, Earl, 1900–   . Prince Louis of Bat′ten·berg (băt′′n·bûrg; Ger. bät′ĕn·bĕrk). Brit. admiral; 1st gov. gen. of dominion of India (1947–48).

—, Philip, Duke of Edinburgh. See under PHILIP.

Mous·sorg′sky. See MUSORGSKI.

Mo′zart (mō′tsärt; Angl. mō′zärt), Wolf′gang (vôlf′gäng) A′ma·de′us (ä′mä·dā′ōōs), 1756–1791. Austrian composer.

Muck (mōōk), Karl, 1859–1940. Ger. conductor.

Mu·ham′mad. Variant of MOHAMMED.

Muh′len·berg (mü′lĕn·bĕrk; Angl. mū′lĕn·bûrg), Henry Mel′chi·or (mĕl′kē·ôr), 1711–1787. Ger.-born Lutheran clergyman in Am.

Muir (mūr), John, 1838–1914. Am. (Scot.-born) naturalist.

Mu′ker·ji′ (mōō′kĕr·jē′), Dhan (Bengali dôn, dô′nô; Angl. dŭn) Go·pal′ (Bengali gô·pô′lô; Angl. gô·pôl′), 1890–1936. East Indian writer in Am.

Mül′ler (mül′ẽr), Hermann Joseph, 1890–   . Am. geneticist.

Mül′ler (mül′ẽr; Angl. mül′ẽr, mĭl′-), Frie′drich (frē′drĭk) Max (mäks; Angl. mäks), 1823–1900. Brit. (Ger.-born) philologist.

— (mül′ẽr), Jo·hann′ (yō·hän′; yō′hän), 1436–1476. Re′gi·o·mon·ta′nus (rē′jĭ·ô·mŏn·tä′nŭs; Ger. rā′gĕ·ō·mŏn·tä′nōōs). Ger. astron.

— (mül′ẽr), Wil′helm (vĭl′hĕlm), 1794–1827. Father of F. M. Ger. poet.

Mun′lock, Dinah Maria. See CRAIK.

Münch′hau′sen, von (fôn münk′hou′zĕn), Baron Karl Frie′drich (frē′drĭk) Hi′e·ro′ny·mus (hē′á·rô′nü·mōōs), 1720–1797. Baron Mun·chau′sen (mŭn·chô′z′n). Ger. hunter & soldier.

Mun′de·lein (mŭn′dĕ·līn), George William, 1872–1939. Am. cardinal.

Mundt (mōōnt), Kla′ra (klä′rä), 1814–1873. Nee Mül′ler (mül′ẽr); pseud. Lu·i′se (lōō·ē′zĕ) Mühl′bach (mül′bäk). Ger. nov.

Mun′ká·csy, von (fôn mōōn′kä·chĭ), Mi′kály (mĭ′häl·y′), 1844–1900. Mi′cha·el Lieb (mĭ′kä·ĕl lēp). Hung. painter.

Mun′sey (mŭn′sĭ), Frank Andrew, 1854–1925. Am. publisher.

Mün′ster·berg (mün′stẽr·bĕrk), Hu′go (hōō′gō; Eng. hū′gō), 1863–1916. Ger.-born psychol. in Am.

Mun′the′ (mün′tĕ′), Ax′el (äk′sĕl) Mar′tin (mȧr′tĭn) Fre′drik (frā′drĭk), 1857–1949. Swed. physician & author.

Mu·ra·sa·ki (mōō·rä·sä·kê), Baroness, 11th cent. Murasaki Shi·ki·bu (shĕ·kê·bōō). Jap. poet.

Mu′rat′ (mü′rȧ′), Jo′a′chim′ (zhō′á′kēm′), 1767?–1815. Fr. gen.; marshal of France (1804); king of Naples (1808–1815).

Mur′free (mûr′frē), Mary No·ailles′ (nô·ī′), 1850–1922. Pseud. Charles Egbert Crad′dock (krăd′ŭk). Am. nov.

Mu·ril′lo (mōō·rē′lyō; Angl. mū·rĭl′ō), Bar′to·lo·mé′ (bär′tô·lô·mā′) Es·te′ban (äs·tā′vän), 1617–1682. Span. painter.

Mur′phy (mûr′fĭ), Frank, 1890–1949. Am. jurist.

—, Robert Daniel, 1894–   . Am. diplomat.

—, William Parry, 1892–   . Am. physician.

Mur′ray (mûr′ĭ), (George) Gilbert (Ai′mé′ [ā′mā′]), 1866–1957. Brit. classical scholar.

—, Sir James Augustus Henry, 1837–1915. Brit. lexicographer.

—, Lindley, 1745–1826. Am. grammarian.

—, Philip, 1886–1952. Am. labor leader.

Mur′ry (mûr′ĭ), John Middleton, 1889–1957. Eng. writer.

—, Kathleen. Wife of J. M. See Katherine MANSFIELD.

Mu·sorg′ski or Mous·sorg′sky (mōō·sôrg′skĭ; Angl. mōō·sôrg′skĭ), Mo·dest′ (mŭ·dyäst′) Pe·tro′vich (pyĭ·trô′vyĭch), 1835–1881. Russ. composer.

Mus′set′, de (dĕ mü·sĕ′), (Louis Charles) Alfred, 1810–1857. Fr. poet.

Mus·so·li′ni (mōōs·sō·lē′nē; Angl. mōōs′l·ē′nē, mōōs′l-), Be·ni′to (bā·nē′tō), 1883–1945. Il Du′ce (ēl dōō′chä). Ital. Fascist premier & dictator (1922–45).

Mus·ta·fa′ (or Mus·ta·pha′) Ke·mal′ Pa·sha′ (pä·shä′). See KEMAL ATATÜRK.

Mu·tsu·hi·to (mōō·tsōō·hē·tô), 1852–1912. Mei·ji (mā·jē). Emp. of Japan (1867–1912).

Muz′zey (müz′ĭ), David Sav′ille (săv′ĭl), 1870–   . Am. hist.

My′ers (mī′ẽrz), Frederic William Henry, 1843–1901. Eng. poet & essayist.

My′ron (mī′rŏn), 5th cent. B.C. Greek sculptor.

N

Na·ga·no (nä·gä·nô), O·sa·mi (ō·sä·mē), 1888–1947. Jap. admiral.

Nai′du (nä′ĭ·dōō), Sa·ro′ji·ni (sá·rô′jĭ·nē), 1879–1949. Hindu poet & reformer.

Nan′sen (nän′sĕn), Fridt′jof (frĭt′yŏf), 1861–1930. Norw. arctic explorer, zool., & statesman.

Na′pi·er (nā′pĭ·ẽr; Angl. nä·pēr′), Sir Charles James, 1782–1853. Brit. gen.

—, John, 1550–1617. Laird of Mer′chis·ton (mûr′kĭs·tŭn). Scot. math.

—, Robert Cor·ne′lis (kôr·nē′lĭs), 1810–1880. 1st Baron Napier of Mag′da·la (măg′dá·lá). Brit. field marshal.

Na·po′le·on (ná·pō′lē·ŭn; -pōl′yŭn) I or Napoleon Bo′na·parte (bō′ná·pärt; Fr. bô′nà·pärt′), 1769–1821. Emp. of the French (1804–15). See BONAPARTE, BEAUHARNAIS.

— II, 1811–1832. L′Ai′glon′ (lĕ′glôn′). Duc (dük) de Reich′stadt (dĕ rīk′shtät). Son of Napoleon I and Marie Louise.

— III, 1808–1873. Louis Napoleon. Son of Louis Bonaparte and Hortense de Beauharnais. Emp. of the French (1852–70). See EUGÉNIE.

Nar·vá′ez, de (thä när·vä′äth; -äs), Pán′fi·lo (päm′fē·lô), 1480?–1528. Span. soldier in Am.

Nash (năsh), Ogden, 1902–   . Am. poet.

Nash or Nashe (năsh), Thomas, 1567–1601. Eng. satirist & dram.

Nas'myth (năz'mĭth; nā'smĭth; năz'mĭth), Alexander, 1758–1840. Scot. painter.

Nast (năst), Thomas, 1840–1902. Am. (Ger.-born) cartoonist.

Na'than (nā'thăn; -th'n), George Jean (jēn), 1882–1958. Am. editor & dramatic critic.

—, Robert, 1894– . Am. nov.

Na'tion (nā'shŭn), Car'ry (kăr'ĭ) Amelia, 1846–1911. Nee *Moore.* Am. temperance agitator.

Na·zi'mo·va (nŭ·zyē'mu·và; *Angl.* nà·zĭm'ŏ·và), Al'la (ăl'là), 1879–1945. Am. (Russ.-born) actress.

Neb'u·chad·nez'zar (nĕb'ů·kăd·nĕz'ẽr) or **Neb'u·chad·rez'zar** (-rĕz'-ẽr), d. 562 B.C. Chaldean king of Babylon (605–562).

Nec'ker' (nĕ'kâr'; *Angl.* nĕk'ẽr), Jacques (zhăk), 1732–1804. Father of *Mme. de Staël.* Fr. (Swiss-born) financier & statesman.

Neh'ru (nā'rōō), Ja·wa'har·lal (jà·wä'hăr·läl), 1889– . Son of *Motilal.* Indian nationalist; 1st prime min. of dominion of India (1947–).

—, Pundit Mo'ti·lal (mō'tĭ·läl), 1861–1931. Indian nationalist.

Neil'son (nēl's'n), William Allan, 1869–1946. Am. (Scot.-born) educ.; pres., Smith Coll. (1917–39).

Nel'son (nĕl's'n), Donald Marr (mär), 1888– . Am. businessman & administrator.

—, Horatio, Viscount, 1758–1805. Brit. admiral.

Ne'pos (nē'pŏs; nĕp'ŏs), Cornelius, 1st cent. B.C. Rom. hist.

Ne'ri, de' (dā nā'rē), San Fi·lip'po (säm' fē·lēp'pō), 1515–1595. Saint *Philip Neri.* Ital. founder (1564) of "Fathers of the Oratory."

Nernst (nĕrnst), Wal'ther (väl'tĕr) Her'mann (hĕr'män), 1864–1941. Ger. physicist & chem.

Ne'ro (nē'rō; nĕr'ō), 37–68. *Nero Claudius Caesar Dru'sus* (drōō'sŭs) *Ger·man'i·cus* (jŭr·măn'ĭ·kŭs). Orig. *Lucius Do·mi'ti·us A·he'no·bar'bus* (dŏ·mĭsh'ĭ·ŭs [-mĭsh'ŭs] à·hē'nŏ·bär'bŭs; à·hĕn'ŏ-). Rom. emp. (54–68).

Ner'va (nûr'và), Marcus Coc·ce'ius (kŏk·sē'yŭs), 35?–98. Rom. emp. (96–98).

Nes·sel·ro'de (nyĕs·sĭl·y'·rô'dyĕ; *Angl.* nĕs'l·rōd), Count Karl (kärl) Ro·bert' (rŭ·byârt'; rô'byĕrt), 1780–1862. Russ. statesman.

Nes·to'ri·us (nĕs·tō'rĭ·ŭs), d. ab. 451. Patriarch of Constantinople (428–431).

Neu'rath, von (fôn noi'rät), Baron Kon'stan·tin' (kôn'stän·tēn'; kôn'-stän·tēn), 1873–1956. Ger. diplomat.

Nev'in (nĕv'ĭn), Ethelbert Wood'bridge (wŏŏd'brĭj), 1862–1901. Am. composer.

New'all (nū'ăl), Sir Cyril Louis Norton, 1886– . Brit. air marshal & gov. gen. of N. Z. (1941–46).

New'bolt (nū'bōlt), Sir Henry John, 1862–1938. Eng. author.

New'comb (nū'kŭm), Simon, 1835–1909. Am. astron.

New'man (nū'măn), Cardinal John Henry, 1801–1890. Eng. theol. & writer.

New'ton (nū't'n), Sir Isaac, 1642–1727. Eng. math. & natural philos.

Ney (nā), Mi'chel (mē'shĕl'), 1769–1815. Duc (dük) *d'El'ching·en* (dĕl'kĭng·ĕn). Prince de la Mos'ko'va (dĕ là môs'kŏ'và'). Fr. soldier; marshal of France (1804); executed.

Nich·o·las (nĭk'ô·lăs), Saint, 4th cent. Christian prelate; patron saint of children.

— **I,** 1796–1855. Tsar of Russia (1825–55).

— **II,** 1868–1918. Tsar of Russia (1894–1917).

—, Grand Duke, 1856–1929. Russ. gen. & monarchist.

— **of Cu'sa** (kū'sà), 1401–1464. R.C. prelate, math., & philos.

Nich'ols (nĭk'ŭlz; -'lz), Anne, 20th cent. Am. dram.

Nich'ol·son (nĭk'ŭl·s'n; -'l·s'n), Sir Francis, 1655–1728. Eng. administrator in Am.

—, Francis, 1753–1844. Eng. water-colorist.

—, Meredith, 1866–1947. Am. nov. & diplomat.

Ni'ci·as (nĭsh'ĭ·ăs), d. 413 B.C. Athenian gen. & statesman.

Nic'o·lay' (nĭk'ô·lā'), John George, 1832–1901. Am. biographer.

Ni'colle' (nē'kôl'), Charles Jean Hen'ri' (än'rē'), 1866–1936. Fr. physician & bacteriol.

Nic'ol·son (nĭk'ŭl·s'n; -'l·s'n), Harold, 1886– . Eng. biographer & diplomat.

Nie'buhr (nē'bŏŏr), Bar'thold (bär'tôlt) Ge·org' (gã·ôrk'), 1776–1831. Ger. hist., statesman, & philologist.

Niem·ce'wicz (nyĕm·tsĕ'vĕch), Ju'lian (yōō'lyän) Ur'syn (ŏŏr'sĭn), 1758–1841. Pol. patriot & writer.

Nie'möl'ler (nē'mŭl'ẽr), Mar'tin (mär'tēn; *Angl.* -tĭn), 1892– . Ger. anti-Nazi Protestant theol.

Nietz'sche (nē'chĕ), Frie'drich (frē'drĭk) Wil'helm (vĭl'hĕlm), 1844–1900. Ger. philos.

Nieu'port' (nyü'pôr'), É'dou·ard' (ā'dwär'), 1875–1911. Fr. aviator & airplane builder.

Night'in·gale (nīt'ĭn·gāl; nīt''n-; -ĭng·gāl), Florence, 1820–1910. Eng. nurse & philanthropist.

Ni·jin'sky (*Angl.* nĭ·zhĭn'skĭ; *Russ.* nyĭ·zhēn'skĭ), Was·law' (vŭts·läf'), 1890–1950. Russ. ballet dancer.

Nim'itz (nĭm'ĭts), Chester William, 1885– . Am. admiral of the fleet.

Nit'ti (nēt'tē), Fran·ce'sco (frän·chās'kŏ) Sa·ve'rio (sä·vâ'ryŏ), 1868–1953. Ital. econ. & statesman.

Ni'velle' (nē'vĕl'), Ro'bert' (rô'bâr') Georges (zhôrzh), 1856–1924. Fr. gen.

Nix'on (nĭk's'n), Richard Mil'hous' (mĭl'hous'), 1913– . Am. lawyer; vice-pres. of the U. S. (1953–).

No·bel' (nŏ·bĕl'), Al'fred (ăl'frĕd) Bern'hard (bär'närd), 1833–1896. Swed. manuf., inventor, & philanthropist.

No'bi·le (nō'bē·lā), Um·ber'to (ōōm·bĕr'tŏ), 1885– . Ital. arctic explorer & aeronautical engineer.

No'ble (nō'b'l), Sir Percy Lockhart Har'nam (här'năm), 1880–1955. Brit. admiral.

No·gu·chi (nō·gŏŏ·chē; *Angl.* nŏ·gŏō'chē), Hi·de·yo (hē·dĕ·yŏ), 1876–1928. Jap.-born bacteriol. in Am.

No'guès' (nŏ·gās'), Au'guste' (ŏ'güst'), 1876– . Fr. gen.

No·mu·ra (nō·mōō·rä), Ki·chi·sa·bu·ro (kē·chē·sä·bŏŏ·rō), 1877– . Jap. admiral & diplomat.

Nor'dau (nôr'dou), Max (mäks) Si'mon (zē'môn), 1849–1923. Orig. *Süd'feld* (züt'fĕlt). Ger. physician, author, & Zionist.

Nor'den·skjöld' (nŏōr'dĕn·shŭld'), Baron Nils (nĭls) A'dolf' (ä'dôlf') E'rik' (ā'rĭk'), 1832–1901. Swed. arctic explorer.

—, Nils Ot'to' (ŏt'tōō') Gus'taf (gŭs'täv), 1869–1928. Swed. explorer.

Nor'di·ca (nôr'dĭ·kà), Lillian, 1859–1914. Pseud. of *Lillian Norton.* Am. soprano.

Nor'man (nôr'măn), Montagu Col'let (kŏl'ĕt; -ĭt), 1st Baron, 1871–1950. Eng. banker.

Nor'ris (nŏr'ĭs), Charles Gilman, 1881–1945. Am. nov.

—, Frank, 1870–1902. *Bro. of C. G.* Am. nov.

—, George William, 1861–1944. Am. statesman.

—, Kathleen, 1880– . *Wife of C. G.* Am. nov.

North (nôrth), Christopher. See John WILSON.

—, Frederick, 1732–1792. *Lord North.* Eng. statesman; prime min. (1770–82).

—, Sir Thomas, 1535?–?1601. Eng. trans.

North'cliffe, Viscount. See HARMSWORTH.

Nor'throp (nôr'thrŭp), John Howard, 1891– . Am. scientist.

Nor'ton (nôr't'n), Charles Eliot, 1827–1908. Am. author & educ.

—, Thomas, 1532–1584. Eng. lawyer & poet.

Nos'tra·da'mus (nŏs'trà·dā'mŭs), 1503–1566. Fr. physician & astrologer.

No'vi·kov (nô'vyĭ·kŭf), A·le·ksan'dr (ŭ·lyĭ·ksän'dĕr) A·le·ksan'dro·vich (ŭ·lyĭ·ksän'drŭ·vyĭch), 1905– . Russ. air marshal.

—, Ni·ko·lai' (nyĭ·kŭ·lī') Va·sil'ie·vich (vŭ·syĕl'yĕ·vyĭch), 1903– . Russ. diplomat.

Noyes (noiz), Alfred, 1880– . Eng. poet.

Nun'ges'ser' (nûn'zhä'sär'), Charles, 1892–1927. Fr. aviator.

Nut'ting (nŭt'ĭng), Wallace, 1861–1941. Am. clergyman & antiquarian.

Nye (nī), Edgar Wilson, 1850–1896. *Bill.* Am. humorist.

O

Oates (ōts), Lawrence Edward Grace (grās), 1880–1912. Eng. antarctic explorer.

—, Titus, 1649–1705. Eng. fabricator of the Popish Plot.

O'ber·holt'zer (ō'bĕr·hōlt'sẽr), Ellis Pax'son (păk's'n), 1868–1936. Am. hist.

O·bre'no·vić, Alexander I. See under ALEXANDER.

O'Bri'en (ô·brī'ĕn), Edward Joseph Har'ring·ton (hăr'ĭng·tŭn), 1890–1941. Am. editor.

—, Frederick, 1869–1932. Am. writer.

O'Ca'sey (ô·kā'sĭ), Sean (shôn; shän), 1884– . Irish dram.

Oc'cam, William of. See OCKHAM.

Ochs (ŏks), A'dolph (ā'dôlf) Simon, 1858–1935. Am. newspaper publisher.

Ock'ham or **Oc'cam** (ŏk'ăm), William of, 1300?–?1349. Eng. philos.

O'Con'nell (ô·kŏn''l), Daniel, 1775–1847. Irish orator & polit. agitator.

—, William Henry, 1859–1944. Am. cardinal.

O'Con'nor (ô·kŏn'ẽr), Thomas Pow'er (pou'ẽr), 1848–1929. *Tay Pay* (tā' pā'). Irish journalist & nationalist.

Oc·ta'vi·an or **Oc·ta'vi·a'nus.** See AUGUSTUS.

O'do·a'cer (ō'dô·ā'sẽr), 434?–493. 1st barbarian ruler of Italy (476–493).

Oeh'len·schlä'ger (û'lĕn·shlä'gĕr), A'dam (ä'däm) Gott'lob (gôt'lŏp), 1779–1850. Dan. poet & dram.

Of'fen·bach (ŏf'ĕn·bäk; *Fr.* ô'fĕn'bâk'), Jacques (zhăk), 1819–1880. Fr. composer.

O'Fla'her·ty (ô·flä'hẽr·tĭ), Li'am (lē'äm), 1896– . Irish nov.

Og'a·dai' (ŏg'à·dī'), 1185–1241. Mongol khan (1229–41).

Og'den (ŏg'dĕn), Charles Kay (kā), 1889–1957. Brit. psychol. & educ.

O'gle·thorpe (ō'g'l·thôrp), James Edward, 1696–1785. Eng. philanthropist & gen.; founder of Georgia.

O'Hig'gins (*Eng.* ô·hĭg'ĭnz; *Span.* ô·ē'gēns), Ber·nar'do (bĕr·när'thŏ), 1778–1842. *Liberator of Chile.* Chilean soldier & statesman.

Ohm (ōm), Ge·org' (gã·ôrk') Si'mon (zē'môn), 1787–1854. Ger. physicist.

O'Keeffe' (ô·kēf'), Georgia, 1887– . Am. muralist & painter.

O'Kel'ly (ô·kĕl'ĭ), Seán (shôn; shän) Thomas, 1883– . Irish journalist; pres. of Eire (1945–).

—, Seumas (shā'măs), d. 1920. Irish writer.

O·ku·ma (ô·kōō·mä), Marquis Shi·ge·no·bu (shē·gĕ·nŏ·bŏō), 1838–1922. Jap. statesman.

O'laf (ō'läf; *Angl.* ō'läf) **I,** 969–1000. *Olaf Trygg'ves·son* (trüg'vĕ·sŏn). King of Norway (995–1000).

— **II,** 995?–1030. Saint *Olaf.* King of Norway (1016–28).

Old'cas'tle (ōld'kăs''l), Sir John, 1377?–1417. Baron *Cob'ham* (kŏb'ăm). Eng. Lollard; executed.

Ol'li·vant (ŏl'ĭ·vănt), Alfred, 1874–1927. Eng. nov.

O'man (ō'măn), Sir Charles William Chadwick, 1860–1946. Brit. hist.

O'mar Khay·yám' (ō'mär [ō'mẽr] kī·[y]äm' [kī-]), d. ab. 1123. Pers. poet & astron.

O·ne'gin (ŭ·nyä'gĭn), Ev·ge'ni (yĭv·gã'nyĭ) B., 1883–1919. Russ. composer.

O'Neill' (ô·nēl'), Eugene Gladstone, 1888–1953. Am. dram.

On'ions (ŭn'yŭnz), Charles Tal'but (tôl'bŭt), 1873– . Eng. philologist & lexicographer.

Oost, van (vän ōst'), Ja'cob (yà'kôp), father, 1600–1671, and son, 1639–1713. Flem. painters.

Op'pen·heim (ŏp'ĕn·hīm), Edward Phillips, 1866–1946. Eng. nov.

Op'pen·hei'mer (ŏp'ĕn·hī'mẽr), J. Robert, 1904– . Am. physicist.

Or·ca'gna (ôr·kä'nyä), 1308?–?1368. An·dre'a (än·drā'ä) di Cio'ne (dē chō'nā). Florentine painter, sculptor, & architect.

Or'czy (ôr'tsĭ; *Hung.* ôr-), Baroness Em'mus·ka (ĕm'mōōsh·kŏ), 1865–1947. Eng. (Hung.-born) nov. & dram.

Or'i·gen (ŏr'ĭ·jĕn; -jĕn), 185?–?254. Greek writer, teacher, & church father.

Or·lan'do (ôr·län'dō), Vit·to'rio (vēt·tô'ryŏ) E·ma·nue'le (ä·mä·nwâ'lā), 1860–1952. Ital. statesman.

O·roz′co (ō·rōs′kō), Jo·sé′ (hō·sā′) Cle·men′te (klā·mān′tā), 1883–1949. Mex. painter.

Or′pen (ôr′pĕn), Sir William New′en·ham (nū′ĕn·ăm) Montague, 1878–1931. Brit. painter.

Or·te′ga y Gas·set′ (ôr·tā′gä ē gä·sĕt′), Jo·sé′ (hō·sā′), 1883–1955. Span. philos., writer, & statesman.

Or·tiz′ Ru′bio (ôr·tēs′ rōō′vyō), Pas·cual′ (päs·kwäl′), 1877– . Pres. of Mexico (1930–32).

Os′born (ŏz′bĕrn), Henry Fair′field (fâr′fēld), 1857–1935. Am. paleontologist.

Os′borne (ŏz′bĕrn), Thomas Mott, 1859–1926. Am. penologist.

Os′car II (ŏs′kẽr), 1829–1907. King of Sweden (1872–1907) and of Norway (1872–1905).

Os′ce·o′la (ŏs′ē·ō′lȧ), 1800?–1838. Chief of the Seminole Indians.

Os′ler (ōs′lẽr), Sir William, 1849–1919. Canadian physician.

Os·man′ (*Turk.* ŏs·män′) *or* **Oth·man′** (*Arab.* ōōth·män′), 1259–1326. Founder of the Ottoman Empire.

Os·me′ña (ŏs·mā′nyä), Ser′gio (sẽr′hyō), 1878– . Pres. of Philippine Commonwealth (1944–46).

Os′si·etz′ky, von (fŏn ŏs′ē·ĕts′kē), Carl, 1889–1938. Ger. writer & pacificist.

Os′so·li, Marchioness. See Margaret FULLER.

Os′ten·so′ (ŏs′tĕn·sō′), Martha, 1900– . Norw.-born nov.

Ost′wald (ôst′vält), Wil′helm (vĭl′hĕlm), 1853–1932. Ger. physical chem. & philos.

Oth·man′. See OSMAN.

O′tis (ō′tĭs), El′well (ĕl′wĕl; -wĕl) Stephen, 1838–1909. Am. gen.

—, Harrison Gray, 1837–1917. Am. gen. & journalist.

—, James, 1725–1783. Am. Revolutionary statesman.

Ot′ter·bein (ŏt′ẽr·bīn; *Ger.* ôt′-), Philip William, 1726–1813. Ger.-born clergyman in Am.

Ot′to I (ŏt′ō; *Ger.* ôt′ō), 912–973. *The Great.* Holy Rom. emp. (936–973).

Ot′way (ŏt′wā), Thomas, 1652–1685. Eng. dram.

Ou′di·not′ (ōō′dē′nō′), Ni′co′las′ (nē′kô′lä′) Charles, 1767–1847. Duc (dük) *de Reg′gio* (dĕ rād′jō). Fr. gen. under Napoleon; marshal of France (1809).

Oui′da. See Marie Louise de la RAMÉE.

Ov′id (ŏv′ĭd), 43 B.C.–?17 A.D. *Pub′li·us* (pŭb′lĭ·ŭs) *O·vid′i·us Na′so* (ō·vĭd′ĭ·ŭs nā′sō). Rom. poet.

Ow′en (ō′ĕn; -ĭn), Robert, 1771–1858. Brit. social reformer.

Ox′en·stier′na *or* **Ox′en·stjer′na** (ōōk′sĕn·shâr′nä) *or* **Ox′en·stiern** (ŏk′s′n·stẽrn), Count Ax′el (äk′sĕl) Gus′tafs·son (gŭs′täv·sôn), 1583–1654. Swed. statesman.

Ox′ford, Earl of. See Robert HARLEY.

O·ya·ma (ō·yä·mä), Prince I·wa·o (ē·wä·ō), 1842–1916. Jap. field marshal.

P

Paa′si·ki′vi (pä′sĭ·kĭ′vĭ), Ju′ho (yōō′hŏ) K., 1870–1956. Finnish businessman; pres. of Finland (1946–).

Pach′mann, de (dȳe päk′màn), Vla·di′mir (vlŭ·dyē′myĭr), 1848–1933. Russ. pianist.

Pa′de·rew′ski (pä′dĕ·rĕf′skē; *Angl.* păd′ĕ-), I′gnace′ (*Fr.* ē′nyás′) Jan (*Pol.* yän), 1860–1941. Pol. pianist & statesman.

Pa′ga·ni′ni (pä′gä·nē′nē), Ni·co·lò′ (nē·kô·lô′), 1782–1840. Ital. violinist.

Page (pāj), Thomas Nelson, 1853–1922. Am. nov. & diplomat.

—, Walter Hines (hīnz), 1855–1918. Am. journalist & diplomat.

Pag′et (păj′ĕt; -ĭt), Sir James, 1814–1899. Eng. surgeon & pathologist.

Paine (pān), Albert Big′e·low (bĭg′ē·lō), 1861–1937. Am. author.

—, Thomas, 1737–1809. Am. (Eng.-born) polit. philos. & author.

Pain′le·vé′ (păN′lvā′), Paul, 1863–1933. Fr. math. & statesman.

Pa·la′cio Val·dés′ (pä·lä′thyō väl·dās′), Ar·man′do (är·män′dō), 1853–1938. Span. nov.

Pa′le·stri′na, da (dä pä′lās·trē′nä; *Angl.* päl′ĕs·trē′nȧ), Gio·van′ni (jō·vän′nē) Pier·lui′gi (pyĕr·lwē′jē), 1526?–1594. Ital. composer.

Pa′ley (pā′lĭ), William, 1743–1805. Eng. theol. & philos.

Pal′grave (pȧl′grāv; pôl′-), Francis Turner, 1824–1897. Eng. poet & anthologist.

Pal·la′dio (päl·lä′dyō), An·dre′a (än·drā′ä), 1518–1580. Ital. architect.

Pal′ma (päl′mä), To·más′ (tō·mäs′) Es·tra′da (ās·trä′thä), 1835–1908. 1st pres. of Cuba (1902–06).

Palm′er (päm′ẽr), Alice Elvira, 1855–1902. Nee *Free′man* (frē′măn). *Wife of G. H.* Am. educ.

—, Daniel David, 1845–1913. Canadian-born founder of chiropractic.

—, George Herbert, 1842–1933. Am. scholar & educ.

Palm′er·ston (päm′ẽr·stŭn), 3d Viscount, 1784–1865. *Henry John Temple.* Eng. statesman; prime min. (1855–58, 1859–65).

Palm′gren (palm′grän), Se′lim (sā′lĭm), 1878–1951. Finnish pianist & composer.

Pan·fi′lov (pŭn·fyē′lŭf), Ivan, d. 1941. Russ. gen.

Pank′hurst (păngk′hûrst), Emmeline, 1858–1928. Nee *Goul′den* (gōōl′dĕn). Eng. suffragist.

Pa·nyush′kin (pŭ·nyōōsh′kĭn), A·le·ksan′dr (ŭ·lyĭ·ksän′dẽr) Se·myo′no·vich (syĭ·myô′nô·v* ↑vĭch), 1905?– . Russ. diplomat.

Pa′o·li, di (dē pä′ō·lē), Pa·squa′le (päs·kwä′lā), 1725–1807. Corsican patriot.

Pa′pen, von (fŏn pä′pĕn), Franz (fränts), 1879– . Ger. diplomat.

Pap′pen·heim, zu (tsōō päp′ĕn·hīm), Count Gott′fried (gôt′frēt) Hein′rich (hīn′rĭk), 1594–1632. Ger. gen.

Par′a·cel′sus (păr′ȧ·sĕl′sŭs), Phi·lip′pus (fĭ·lĭp′ŭs) Au·re′o·lus (ô·rē′-ō·lŭs), 1493–1541. *The′o·phra′stus* (thē′ō·fräs′tŏŏs) *Bom·ba′stus* (bŏm·bäs′tŏŏs) *von Ho′hen·heim* (fŏn hō′ĕn·hīm). Swiss-born alchemist & physician.

Pares (pârz), Sir Bernard, 1867–1949. Eng. hist.

Pa·re′to (pä·rā′tō), Vil·fre′do (vēl·frā′dō), 1848–1923. Ital. econ. & sociol.

Pa′ris′ (pä′rēs′), Gas′ton′ (gȧs′tôN′), 1839–1903. Fr. philologist.

Par′is (păr′ĭs), Matthew, 1200?–1259. Eng. monk & hist.

Park (pärk), Mun′go (mŭng′gō), 1771–1806. Scot. explorer in Africa.

Par′ker (pär′kẽr), Dorothy, 1893– Nee *Roths′child* (?rŏths′-chĭld). Am. writer.

—, Sir Gilbert, 1862–1932. Canadian author.

—, Matthew, 1504–1575. Eng. theol.

—, Theodore, 1810–1860. Am. Unitarian clergyman.

Parkes (pärks), Sir Henry, 1815–1896. Australian statesman.

Park′man (pärk′măn), Francis, 1823–1893. Am. hist.

Par′ley, Peter. See Samuel Griswold GOODRICH.

Par·men′i·des (pär·mĕn′ĭ·dēz), 5th cent. B.C. Greek philos.

Par·nell′ (pär·nĕl′; pär′n′l), Charles Stewart, 1846–1891. Irish nationalist.

Parr, Catherine. See under CATHERINE.

Par′ring·ton (pär′ĭng·tŭn), Vernon Louis, 1871–1929. Am. literary hist.

Par′rish (păr′ĭsh), Max′field (măks′fēld), 1870– . Am. painter & illustrator.

Par′ry (păr′ĭ), Sir William Edward, 1790–1855. Eng. arctic explorer.

Par′sons (pär′s′nz), William, 1800–1867. 3d Earl of *Rosse* (rŏs). Eng. astron.

Pas′cal′ (päs·kȧl′; *Angl.* păs′kȧl′, păs′kăl), Blaise (blâz), 1623–1662. Fr. math. & philos.

Pa′šić (pä′shĕt·y′; *Angl.* -shĭch), Ni′ko·la (nē′kô·lä), 1845?–1926. Serbian & Yugoslav statesman.

Pass′field, 1st Baron. See under WEBB.

Pas′sy′ (pȧ′sē′), Fré′dé′ric′ (frā′dā′rēk′), 1822–1912. Fr. econ. & statesman.

—, Paul É′dou·ard′ (ā′dwȧr′), 1859–1940. *Son of prec.* Fr. phonetician.

Pas′teur′ (päs·tûr′), Louis, 1822–1895. Fr. chem.

Patch (păch), Alexander Mc·Car′rell (mȧ·kăr′ĕl), 1889–1945. Am. gen.

Pa′ter (pā′tẽr), Walter Horatio, 1839–1894. Eng. essayist & critic.

Pa·ti′ño (pä·tē′nyō), Si·món′ (sē·môn′) I·tu′ri (ē·tōō′rē), 1862–1947. Bolivian industrialist & diplomat.

Pat′more (păt′mōr), Cov′en·try (kŏv′ĕn·trĭ; kŭv′-) Ker′sey (kûr′zĭ) Digh′ton (dī′t′n), 1823–1896. Eng. poet.

Pa′tri (pä′trē), An′ge·lo (ä′n′jä·lō), 1877– . Am. (Ital.-born) educ. & author.

Pat′rick (păt′rĭk), Saint, 389?–?461. Apostle & patron saint of Ireland.

Pat′ter·son (păt′ẽr·s′n), Robert Porter, 1891–1952. Am. lawyer & statesman.

Pat′ti (pät′tē; *Angl.* păt′ĭ), A′de·li′na (ä′dä·lē′nä), 1843–1919. Coloratura soprano, of Ital. descent.

Pat′ti·son (păt′ĭ·s′n), Mark, 1813–1884. Eng. scholar & author.

Pat′ton (păt′′n), George Smith, 1885–1945. Am. gen.

Pau′ker (pou′kẽr), A′na (ä′nä), 1889?– . Nee *Ra′bin·sohn* (rä′bēn·sŏn). Romanian Communist.

Paul (pôl). Name of 5 popes; esp.: **III,** 1468–1549 (pope 1534–49); **V,** 1552–1621 (pope 1605–21).

— **I,** 1754–1801. Emp. of Russia (1796–1801); assassinated.

— **I,** 1901– . King of Greece (1947–).

— (poul). Jean. See RICHTER.

Paul′-Bon′cour′ (pôl′bôN′kōōr′), Jo′seph′ (zhō′zĕf′), 1873– . Fr. lawyer & statesman.

Paul′ding (pôl′dĭng), James Kirke (kûrk), 1778–1860. Am. author.

Pau′li (pou′lē), Wolf′gang (vôlf′gäng), 1900– . Austrian-born physicist in Am.

Pau′lus (pou′lŏŏs), Frie′drich (frē′drĭk), 1890–1957. Ger. field marshal (1943).

— (pô′lŭs), Julius, 2d–3d cent. A.D. Rom. jurist.

Pau·sa′ni·as (pô·sā′nĭ·ŭs), 2d cent. A.D. Greek traveler & geographer.

Pa′vlov (pȧ′vlŭf), Ivan Pe·tro′vich (pyĭ·trô′vyĭch), 1849–1936. Russ. physiol.

Pa′vlo·va (pȧ′vlŭ·vȧ), An′na (än′nä), 1885–1931. Russ. ballerina.

Payne (pān), John Howard, 1791–1852. Am. actor & dram.

Pea′bod′y (pē′bŏd′ĭ; -bŭd·ĭ), En′di·cott (ĕn′dĭ·kŭt), 1857–1944. Am. educ.

—, George, 1795–1869. Am. merchant & philanthropist.

—, Josephine Pres′ton (prĕs′tŭn), 1874–1922. Am. poet & dram.

Pea′cock (pē′kŏk), Thomas Love (lŭv), 1785–1866. Eng. nov. & poet.

Peale (pēl), Charles Will′son (wĭl′s′n), 1741–1827, his bro. James, 1749–1831, and Charles's son Rem′brandt (rĕm′brănt), 1778–1860. Am. painters.

Pear′son (pẽr′s′n), Karl, 1857–1936. Eng. scientist.

Pea′ry (pēr′ĭ), Robert Edwin, 1856–1920. Am. arctic explorer.

Pe·co′ra (pĕ·kō′rȧ), Ferdinand, 1882– . Am. jurist.

Peel (pēl), Sir Robert, 1788–1850. Eng. statesman.

Peele (pēl), George, 1558?–?1597. Eng. dram. & poet.

Pe′gram (pē′grăm), George Brax′ton (brăks′tŭn), 1876– . Am. physicist.

Peirce (pûrs), Charles San′ders (săn′dẽrz), 1839–1914. Am. math. & logician.

Peirse (pẽrs), Sir Richard Edmund Charles, 1892– . Brit. air marshal.

Pei·xot′to (pȧ·shō′tō), Ernest Clifford, 1869–1940. Am. painter & illustrator.

Pe·ker′ (pĕ·kẽr′), Re·cep′ (rĕ·jĕp′), 1888–1950. Turk. soldier & polit.

Pe·la′gi·us (pĕ·lā′jĭ·ŭs), 360?–?420. Brit. monk & theol.

Pe·lop′i·das (pĕ·lŏp′ĭ·dȧs), d. 364 B.C. Theban gen.

Penn (pĕn), Sir William, 1621–1670. Eng. admiral.

—, William, 1644–1718. *Son of prec.* Eng. Quaker; founder of Pennsylvania.

Pen′nell (pĕn′′l), Joseph, 1857–1926. Am. etcher.

Pep′in the Short (pĕp′ĭn), 714?–768. King of the Franks (751–768).

Pepys (pēps; pĕps; pĕp′ĭs), Samuel, 1633–1703. Eng. diarist.

Per′cy (pûr′sĭ), Sir Henry, 1364–1403. *Hot′spur′* (hŏt′spûr′). Eng. soldier.

—, Thomas, 1729–1811. Eng. antiquary & poet.

Pé′rez Gal·dós′ (pā′rāth gäl·dōs′), Be·ni′to (bā·nē′tō), 1843–1920. Span. nov. & dram.

Per′i·cles (pĕr′ĭ·klēz), d. 429 B.C. Athenian statesman.

Per'kins (pûr'kĭnz), Frances, 1882– . Am. social worker & administrator.
Pe·rón' (pā·rôn'), Juan (hwän) Do·min'go (dō·mēng'gō), 1895– . Argentine polit.; pres. of Argentina (1946–55).
Per'rault' (pĕ'rō'), Charles, 1628–1703. Fr. fairy tale writer.
Per'rin' (pĕ'răN'), Jean Bap'tiste' (bå'tēst'), 1870–1942. Fr. physicist & chem.
Per'ry (pĕr'ĭ), Bliss, 1860–1954. Am. educ. & critic.
—, Matthew Cal'braith (kăl'brĕth), 1794–1858. Am. commodore.
—, Oliver Hazard, 1785–1819. *Bro. of prec.* Am. naval officer.
—, Ralph Barton, 1876–1957. Am. philos. & educ.
Per'shing (pûr'shĭng), John Joseph, 1860–1948. Am. gen. of the armies.
Per'sius (pûr'shŭs; -shĭ-ŭs), 34–62. *Au'lus* (ô'lŭs) *Persius Flac'cus* (flăk'ŭs). Rom. satirist.
Pe·ru·gi'no, Il (ēl på·rōō·jē'nō), 1446–1523. *Pie'tro* (pyā'trō) *Van·nuc'ci* (vän·nōōt'chē). Ital. painter.
Pe·ruz'zi (på·rōōt'tsē), Bal'das·sa're (bäl'däs·sä'rā), 1481–1536. Ital. architect & painter.
Pes'ta·loz'zi (pĕs'tå·lŏt'sē; *Ger.* -tä·lŏt'sē), Jo·hann' (yō·hän'; yō'hän) Hein'rich (hīn'rĭk), 1746–1827. Swiss educ.
Pé'tain' (pā'tăn'), Hen'ri' (äN'rē') Phi'lippe' (fē'lēp'), 1856–1951. Fr. gen.; marshal of France (1918).
Pe'ter, Saint, d. 67? A.D. Disciple of Jesus; by some, esp. R.C., regarded as vicar of Christ on earth (*Matthew* xvi. 16–19).
— I, 1672–1725. *The Great.* Tsar of Russia (1682–1725).
— I Kar'a·geor'ge·vich (kär'å·jôr'jĕ·vĭch), 1844–1921. King of Serbia (1903–21).
— II, 1923– . King of Yugoslavia (1934–45).
— the Hermit, 1050?–?1115. Fr. preacher of the 1st Crusade.
Pe'ters (pā'tĕrs), Carl, 1856–1918. Ger. explorer in Africa.
Pe'tő·fi (pĕ'tû·fĭ), Sán'dor (shän'dôr), 1823–1849. Hung. poet.
Pe'trarch (pē'trärk) *or* **Pe·trar'ca** (på·trär'kä), Fran·ce'sco (frän·chās'kō), 1304–1374. Ital. poet.
Pe'trie (pē'trĭ), Sir (William Matthew) Flin'ders (flĭn'dĕrz), 1853–1942. Eng. Egyptologist.
Pe·tro'ni·us (pē·trō'nĭ·ŭs), Ga'ius (gā'yŭs; gī'ŭs), 1st cent. A.D. *Ar'bi·ter El'e·gan'ti·ae* (är'bĭ·tēr ĕl'ē·găn'shĭ·ē). Rom. satirist.
Pet'ty (pĕt'ĭ), Sir William, 1623–1687. Eng. polit. econ.
Pey'rou'ton' (pā'rōō'tôN'), Mar'cel' (mär'sĕl') B., 1888?– . Fr. polit. & administrator.
Phae'drus (fē'drŭs), 5th cent. B.C. Greek philos.
—, 1st cent. A.D. Rom. fabulist.
Phelps (fĕlps), William Lyon, 1865–1943. Am. educ.
Phid'i·as (fĭd'ĭ·ŭs), 5th cent. B.C. Greek sculptor.
Phil'ip (fĭl'ĭp), d. 1676. *Met'a·com'et* (mĕt'å·kŏm'ĕt; -ĭt). Sachem of the Wampanoag Indians.
—. Name of 6 kings of France; esp.: **II**, *or* **Philip Augustus**, 1165–1223 (reigned 1180–1223); **IV** (*the Fair*), 1268–1314 (reigned 1285–1314); **VI**, 1293–1350 (reigned 1328–50).
—. Name of 5 kings of Spain; esp.: **II**, 1527–1598 (reigned 1556–98); **V**, 1683–1746 (reigned 1700–46).
— II, 382–336 B.C. King of Macedon (359–336).
—, Prince, 1921– . *Consort of Queen Elizabeth II of Gr. Britain.* 3d Duke of Edinburgh (from 1947).
— the Good, 1396–1467. Duke of Burgundy (1419–67).
Phil'ips (fĭl'ĭps), Ambrose, 1675?–1749. *Nam'by-Pam'by* (năm'bĭ-păm'bĭ). Eng. poet & dram.
Phil'lips (fĭl'ĭps), Stephen, 1868–1915. Eng. poet & dram.
—, Sir Tom Spencer Vaughan, 1888–1941. Brit. admiral.
—, Wendell, 1811–1884. Am. orator & reformer.
Phil'potts (fĭl'pŏts), Eden, 1862– . Eng. nov. & dram.
Phi'lo Ju·dae'us (fī'lō jōō·dē'ŭs), 1st cent. B.C.–1st cent. A.D. Hellenistic Jewish philos. of Alexandria.
Pho'ci·on (fō'shĭ·ŏn), 402?–317 B.C. Athenian gen. & statesman.
Phu·mi·phon A·dul·det (p'hōō·mē·p'hŏn å·dōōn·lå·dāt), 1927– . *Ra'ma IX* (rä'må). King of Thailand (1946–).
Phyfe (fīf), Duncan, 1768–1854. Am. (Scot.-born) cabinetmaker.
Pi'card' (pē'kär'), Jean, 1620–1682. Fr. astron.
Pi·cas'so (pē·kä'sō), Pa'blo (pä'vlō), 1881– . Span. painter & sculptor.
Pic'card' (pē'kär'), Au'guste' (ō'güst'), 1884– . Swiss physicist & aeronaut.
Pick'ens (pĭk'ĕnz), Andrew, 1739–1817. American Revolutionary gen.
Pick'er·ing (pĭk'ĕr·ĭng), Edward Charles, 1846–1919, and his bro. William Henry, 1858–1938. Am. astronomers.
Pick'ett (pĭk'ĕt), George Edward, 1825–1875. Am. Confed. gen.
Pi'co del'la Mi·ran'do·la (pē'kō dăl'lä mē·rän'dō·lä), Count Gio·van'ni (jō·vän'nē), 1463–1494. Ital. humanist.
Pieck (pēk), Wil'helm (vĭl'hĕlm), 1876– . Ger. Communist.
Pierce (pērs), Franklin, 1804–1869. 14th pres. of the U. S. (1853–57).
Pike (pīk), Zeb'u·lon (zĕb'û·lŭn) Montgomery, 1779–1813. Am. gen. & explorer.
Pił·sud'ski (pēl·sōōt'skē), Jó'zef (yōō'zĕf), 1867–1935. Pol. gen. & statesman.
Pin'chot (pĭn'shō), Gif'ford (gĭf'fĕrd), 1865–1946. Am. forester & polit.
Pinck'ney (pĭngk'nĭ), Charles Cotes'worth (kōts'wûrth; -wêrth), 1746–1825. Am. statesman.
Pin'dar (pĭn'dĕr), 522?–443 B.C. Greek poet.
Pi·ne'ro (pĭ·nēr'ō), Sir Arthur Wing (wĭng), 1855–1934. Eng. dram.
Pin'ker·ton (pĭng'kĕr·t'n; -tŭn), Allan, 1819–1884. Scot.-born detective in Am.
Pin·tu·ric'chio (pēn·tōō·rēk'kyō), 1454–1513. *Ber·nar·di'no* (bär·när·dē'nō) *Bet'ti* (bāt'tē). Ital. painter.
Pin·zón' (pēn·thôn'), Mar·tín' (mär·tēn') A·lon'so (ä·lôn'sō), 1440?–1493, and his bro. Vi·cen'te (vē·chĕn'tā) Yá'ñez (yä'nyäth), 1460?–?1524. Span. navigators with Columbus.
Pioz'zi (pyŏt'tsē), Hester Lynch (lĭnch), 1741–1821. Mrs. *Thrale* (thrāl). Eng. writer.
Pi·ran·del'lo (pē·rän·dĕl'lō), Lui'gi (lwē'jē), 1867–1936. Ital. nov. & dram.

Pi·sa'no (pē·sä'nō), Gio·van'ni (jō·vän'nē), 1245–1314, and his father Ni·co'la (nē·kô'lä), 1220–1284. Ital. sculptors.
Pi·sis'tra·tus *or* **Pei·sis'tra·tus** (pī·sĭs'trå·tŭs), d. 527 B.C. Tyrant of Athens.
Pis'sar'ro' (pē'sä'rō'), Ca'mille' (kå'mē'y'), 1830–1903. Fr. painter.
Pit'man (pĭt'măn), Sir Isaac, 1813–1897. Eng. phonographer.
Pitt (pĭt), William, 1708–1778. Earl of *Chat'ham* (chăt'ăm). *The Elder Pitt.* Eng. statesman.
—, William, 1759–1806. *The Younger Pitt.* Son of prec. Eng. statesman.
Pi'us (pī'ŭs). Name of 12 popes; esp.: **II** (*E·ne'a Sil'vio de Pic·co·lo'mi·ni* [ā·nā'ä sēl'vyō dā pēk·kô·lō'mē·nē] *or Ae·ne'as Sil'vi·us or Syl'vi·us* [ē·nē'ăs sĭl'vĭ·ŭs]), 1405–1464 (pope 1458–64); **VII**, 1742–1823 (pope 1800–23); **IX**, 1792–1878 (pope 1846–78); **X**, 1835–1914 (pope 1903–14); **XI** (*A·chil'le Rat'ti* [ä·kēl'lā rät'tē]), 1857–1939 (pope 1922–39); **XII** (*Eu·ge'nio Pa·cel'li* [ā·ōō·jā'nyō pä·chĕl'lē]), 1876–1958 (pope 1939–58).
Pi·zar'ro (pĭ·zär'ō; *Span.* pē·thär'rō, -sär'rō), Fran·cis'co (frän·thēs'kō; -sēs'-), 1470?–1541. Span. conqueror of Peru.
Planck (plängk), Max (mäks) Karl Ernst (ĕrnst) Lud'wig (lōōt'vĭk; lōōd'-), 1858–1947. Ger. physicist.
Plan'çon' (plän'sôn'), Pol (pŏl), 1854–1914. Fr. basso profundo.
Pla'to (plā'tō), 427?–347 B.C. Greek philos.
Plau'tus (plô'tŭs), Titus Mac'ci·us (măk'sĭ·ŭs), 254?–184 B.C. Rom. dram.
Plim'soll (plĭm's'l; -sōl), Samuel, 1824–1898. *The Sailors' Friend.* Eng. shipping reformer.
Plin'y (plĭn'ĭ), 23–79. *Ga'ius* (gā'yŭs; gī'ŭs) *Plin'i·us Se·cun'dus* (plĭn'ĭ·ŭs sē·kŭn'dŭs). *The Elder.* Rom. scholar.
—, 62–113. *Gaius Plinius Cae·cil'i·us* (sē·sĭl'ĭ·ŭs) *Secundus. The Younger.* Nephew of prec. Rom. author.
Plo·ti'nus (plō·tī'nŭs), 205?–270. Rom. (Egyptian-born) philos.
Plu'mer (plōō'mēr), Herbert Charles Ons'low (ŏnz'lō), 1st Viscount, 1857–1932. Eng. field marshal.
Plu'tarch (plōō'tärk), 46?–?120. Greek biographer & moralist.
Po'ca·hon'tas (pō'kå·hŏn'tås), 1595?–1617. *Dau. of Powhatan.* Am. Indian princess.
Poe (pō), Edgar Allan, 1809–1849. Am. poet & story writer.
Po·ga'ny (pō·gä'nĭ; *Hung.* pō'gän·y'), William Andrew, 1882–1955. *Wil'ly* (wĭl'ĭ; *Hung.* vĭl'lĭ). Hung.-born painter, illustrator, & designer.
Poin·ca·ré' (pwăN'kå'rā'), Jules Hen'ri' (äN'rē'), 1854–1912. Fr. math.
—, Ray'mond' (rā'môN'), 1860–1934. *Cousin of J. H.* Fr. statesman; pres. of France (1913–20).
Pole (pōl), Reginald, 1500–1558. Eng. cardinal; archbishop of Canterbury.
Po·li'tian (pō·lĭsh'ăn), 1454–1494. *An'ge·lo* (än'jå·lō) *Po·li·zia'no* (pō·lē·tsyä'nō). Ital. classical scholar & poet.
Polk (pōk), James Knox, 1795–1849. 11th pres. of the U. S. (1845–49).
Pol'li·o (pŏl'ĭ·ō), Ga'ius (gā'yŭs; gī'ŭs) A·sin'i·us (å·sĭn'ĭ·ŭs), 75 B.C.–5 A.D. Rom. soldier, orator, & polit.
Pol'lock (pŏl'ŭk), Channing, 1880–1946. Am. nov., dram., & lecturer.
—, Sir Frederick, 1845–1937. Eng. jurist.
Po'lo (pō'lō; *Ital.* pô'lō), Mar'co (mär'kō; *Ital.* -kō), 1254?–?1324. Ital. traveler.
Po·lyb'i·us (pō·lĭb'ĭ·ŭs), 205?–?125 B.C. Greek hist.
Pol'y·carp (pŏl'ĭ·kärp), Saint, 69?–?155. Christian martyr & Apostolic Father; bishop of Smyrna.
Pol'y·cli'tus *or* **Pol'y·clei'tus** (pŏl'ĭ·klī'tŭs), 5th cent. B.C. Greek sculptor & architect.
Po·lyc'ra·tes (pō·lĭk'rå·tēz), d. ab. 522 B.C. Tyrant of Samos.
Pol'y·do'rus (pŏl'ĭ·dō'rŭs), 1st cent. B.C. Rhodian sculptor.
Pol'yg·no'tus (pŏl'ĭg·nō'tŭs), 5th cent. B.C. Greek painter.
Pom·pa'dour', de (dĕ pôn'på'dōōr'; *Angl.* pŏm'på·dōor, -dōr), Mar'quise' (mär'kēz'), 1721–1764. *Jeanne Antoinette Pois'son'* (pwä'sôN'). Mistress of Louis XV of France.
Pom'pey (pŏm'pĭ), 106–48 B.C. *Gnae'us* (nē'ŭs) *Pom·pe'ius Mag'nus* (pŏm·pē'[y]ŭs măg'nŭs). *The Great.* Rom. gen. & statesman.
Pon'ce de Le·ón' (pŏn'thä thā lå·ôn'; pŏn'sä; *Angl.* pŏns' dē lē'ŭn), Juan (hwän), 1460?–1521. Span. explorer; disc. Florida.
Pons (pôNs), Li'ly' (lē'lē'; *Angl.* lĭl'ĭ), 1904– . Fr. soprano.
Pon·selle' (pŏn·sĕl'), Rosa Mel'ba (mĕl'bå), 1897– . Am. soprano.
Pon'ti·ac (pŏn'tĭ·ăk), d. 1769. Ottawa Indian chief.
Pon·top'pi·dan (pŏn·tŏp'ē·dän), Hen'rik (hĕn'rēk), 1857–1943. Dan. nov.
Pope (pōp), Alexander, 1688–1744. Eng. poet.
—, John, 1822–1892. Am. gen.
Pop'ham (pŏp'ăm; pŏp'm), Sir Henry Robert Moore Brooke- (brŏŏk-), 1878–1953. Brit. air marshal.
Por'son (pôr's'n), Richard, 1759–1808. Eng. scholar.
Por'tal (pôr't'l; pôr'-), Charles Frederick Algernon, 1893– . 1st Viscount *Portal of Hun'ger·ford* (hŭng'gĕr·fĕrd). Brit. air marshal.
Por'ter (pôr'tĕr; pôr'-), Cole, 1893– . Am. composer & song writer.
—, David, 1780–1843, and his son David Dixon, 1813–1891. Am. naval officers.
—, Eleanor, 1868–1920. Nee *Hodg'man* (hŏj'măn). Am. nov.
—, Gene, 1868–1924. Nee *Strat'ton* (străt'n). Am. nov.
—, Noah, 1811–1892. Am. philos. & lexicographer; pres., Yale U. (1871–86).
—, William Sydney, 1862–1910. Pseud. *O. Hen'ry* (ō' hĕn'rĭ). Am. short-story writer.
Port'land, Duke of. See BENTINCK.
Post (pōst), Emily, 1873?– . Nee *Price* (prīs). Am. columnist & writer.
Po·tëm'kin (pŭ·tyŏm'kĭn), Gri·go'ri (gryē'gô'ryē) A·le·ksan'dro·vich (ŭ·lyĕ·ksän'drŭ·vyĭch), 1739–1791. Russ. field marshal & statesman.
Pot'ter (pŏt'ĕr), Paul (poul), 1625–1654. Du. painter.
Pound (pound), Sir (Alfred) Dudley (Pick'man [pĭk'măn] Rogers), 1877–1943. Brit. admiral of the fleet.
—, Ezra Loo'mis (lōō'mĭs), 1885– . Am. poet.
—, Roscoe, 1870– . Am. jurist.

Pous'sin' (pōō'săN'), Ni'co'las' (nē'kô'lä'), 1594–1665. Fr. painter.

Pow'ell (pou'ĕl), Maud, 1868–1920. Am. violinist.

Pow'ha·tan' (pou'á·tăn'), 1550?–1618. *Father of Pocahontas.* Am. Indian chief.

Pow'nall (pou'n'l), Sir Henry Royds (roidz), 1887– . Brit. gen.

Pow'ys (pō'ĭs), John Cow'per (kōō'pĕr), 1872– , and his bros. Theodore Francis, 1875–1953, and Llewelyn, 1884–1939 Eng. authors.

Pra'do U'gar·te'che (prä'thô ōō'gär·tā'chă), Ma·nuel' (mä·nwĕl'), 1889– . Peruvian banker; pres. of Peru (1939–45).

Praed (prād), Winthrop Mack'worth (?măk'wûrth; -wĕrth), 1802–1839. Eng. poet.

Pra·ja'dhi·pok (prá·chä'tĭ·pŏk), 1893–1941. King of Siam (1925–35).

Pratt (prăt), Be'la (bē'lá) Lyon, 1867–1917. Am. sculptor.

Prax·it'e·les (prăk·sĭt''l·ēz), 4th cent. B.C. Athenian sculptor.

Pre'ble (prĕb''l), Edward, 1761–1807. Am. naval officer.

Pregl (prā'g'l), Fritz (frĭts), 1869–1930. Austrian chem.

Pres'cott (prĕs'kŏt), William Hick'ling (hĭk'lĭng), 1796–1859. Am. hist.

Pre·to'ri·us (prĕ·tōō'rē·ŭs), An'dries (än'drēs) Wil·hel'mus (vĭl·hĕl'mŭs) Ja·co'bus (yá·kō'bŭs), 1799–1853, and his son Mar·thi'nus (mär·tē'nŭs) Wes'sels (vĕs'ĕls), 1819–1901. S. African Du. colonizers & soldiers.

Pré'vost' (prā'vō'), Mar'cel' (màr'sĕl'), 1862–1941. Fr. nov.

— d'Ex'iles' (dāg'zēl'), An'toine' (än'twän') Fran'çois' (fräN'swà'), 1697–1763. Fr. abbé & writer.

Price (prīs), Byron, 1891– . Am. journalist.

Pride (prīd), Thomas, d. 1658. Eng. Parliamentary commander.

Priest'ley (prēst'lĭ), John Boyn'ton (boin't'n; -tŭn), 1894– . Eng. author.

—, Joseph, 1733–1804. Eng. clergyman & chem.

Pri'mo de Ri·ve'ra y Or'ba·ne'ja. See RIVERA Y ORBANEJA.

Pri'or (prī'ēr), Matthew, 1664–1721. Eng. poet.

Pris'cian (prĭsh'án; prĭsh'ĭ·án), fl. 500. *Pri'sci·a'nus Cae·sar'i·en'sis* (prĭsh'ĭ·ā'nŭs sē·zär'ĭ·ĕn'sĭs). Latin grammarian at Constantinople.

Pro'clus (prō'klŭs; prŏk'lŭs), 410?–485. Greek philos.

Pro·co'pi·us (prō·kō'pĭ·ŭs), 6th cent. A.D. Byzantine hist.

Pro·kof'iev (prŭ·kôf'yĕf), Ser·gei' (syĭr·gā'ī) Ser·ge'e·vich (syĭr·gā'yĕ·vĭch), 1891–1953. Russ. composer.

Pro·per'tius (prō·pûr'shŭs; -shĭ·ŭs), Sex'tus (sĕks'tŭs), 50?–?15 B.C. Rom. poet.

Pro·tag'o·ras (prō·tăg'ō·răs), 5th cent. B.C. Greek philos.

Prou'dhon' (prōō'dôN'), Pierre Jo'seph' (zhō'zĕf'), 1809–1865. Fr. journalist & polit.

Proust (prōōst), Mar'cel' (màr'sĕl'), 1871–1922. Fr. nov.

Prynne (prĭn), William, 1600–1669. Eng. Puritan pamphleteer.

Przhe·val'ski (pĕr·zhĕ·väl'y·skī), Ni·ko·lai' (nyĭ·ků·lī') Mi·khai'lo·vich (myĭ·kī'lŭ·vyĭch), 1839–1888. Russ. explorer.

Ptol'e·my (tŏl'ĕ·mĭ). Name of 14 kings of Egypt; esp.: I (*So'ter* [sō'tĕr]), 367?–283 B.C. (reigned 323–285); II (*Phil'a·del'phus* [fĭl'á·dĕl'fŭs]), 309–246 B.C. (reigned 285–246).

—, 2d cent. A.D. *Claudius Ptol'e·mæ'us* (tŏl'ĕ·mā'ŭs). Alexandrian astron., math., & geographer.

Puc·ci'ni (pōōt·chē'nē; *Angl.* pōō·chē'-), Gia'co·mo (jä'kô·mô), 1858–1924. Ital. composer.

Pu·las'ki (pů·lăs'kĭ; -kī), Cas'i·mir (kăz'ĭ·mĭr), 1748?–1779. Pol. soldier in Am. Rev.

Pul'itz·er (pōōl'ĭt·sĕr), Joseph, 1847–1911. Am. (Hung.-born) journalist.

Pull'man (pŏōl'măn), George Mortimer, 1831–1897. Am. inventor.

Pu'pin (pōō'pēn; *Angl.* pů·pēn'), Michael Id·vor'sky (ĕd·vôr'skē), 1858–1935. Am. (Yugoslavian-born) physicist & inventor.

Pur'cell (pûr's'l; -sĕl), Henry, 1658?–1695. Eng. composer.

Pur'chas (pûr'chăs), Samuel, 1575?–1626. Eng. compiler.

Pur'kin·je (*Ger.* pŏŏr'kĭn·yĕ), Jo·han'nes (*Ger.* yō·hän'ĕs; -ĕs) E'van·ge·li'sta (*Ger.* ā'väng·gā·lĭs'tä), 1787–1869. Czech physiol.

Pu'sey (pū'zĭ), Edward Bou'ver·ie (bōō'vĕr·ĭ), 1800–1882. Eng. theol.

Push'kin (pŏōsh'kĭn; *Angl.* pŏōsh'kĭn), A·le·ksan'der (ŭ·lyĭ·ksän'dĕr) Ser·ge'e·vich (syĭr·gā'yĕ·vyĭch), 1799–1837. Russ. poet.

Put'nam (pŭt'năm), Israel, 1718–1790. Am. Revolutionary gen.

—, Rufus, 1738–1824. *Cousin of Israel.* Am. Revolutionary gen. & pioneer in Ohio region.

Pu'vis' de Cha'vannes' (pü'vē' dĕ shà'vàn'), Pierre, 1824–1898. Fr. painter & muralist.

Pu-yi, Henry. See HSÜAN T'UNG.

Pye (pī), Henry James, 1745–1813. Eng. poet laureate (1790–1813).

Pym (pĭm), John, 1584–1643. Eng. Parliamentary statesman.

Pyn'chon (pĭn'chŏn), William, 1590?–1662. Eng. pioneer in Am.

Pyr'rhus (pĭr'ŭs), 318?–272 B.C. King of Epirus (306–272).

Py·thag'o·ras (pĭ·thăg'ō·răs; pī-), d. ab. 497 B.C. Greek philos. & math.

Q

Qa·vam', Ahmad. See AHMAD QAVAM-I SALTANA.

Quan'trill (kwŏn'trĭl), William Clarke, 1837–1865. Am. Confed. guerrilla commander.

Quarles (kwôrlz; kwärlz), Francis, 1592–1644. Eng. poet.

Queens'ber'ry, Marquis of. See under DOUGLAS.

Quer'cia, del'la (dāl'lä kwĕr'chä), Ja'co·po (yä'kô·pô), 1378?–1438. Sienese sculptor.

Ques'nay' (kĕ'nā'), Fran'çois' (fräN'swà'), 1694–1774. Fr. physician & econ.

Que'zon y Mo·li'na (kā'sôn ē mô·lē'nä), Ma·nuel' (mä·nwĕl') Lu·is' (lōō·ēs'), 1878–1944. Pres. of the Philippine Commonwealth (1935–44).

Quid'de (kvĭd'ĕ), Lud'wig (lōōt'vĭk; lōōd'-), 1858–1941. Ger. hist. & pacifist.

Quil'ler-Couch' (kwĭl'ĕr·kōōch'), Sir Arthur Thomas, 1863–1944. Eng. author.

Quin'cy (kwĭn'zĭ; -sĭ), Josiah, 1744–1775. Am. lawyer & polit.

Quin·te'ro, Ál'va·rez (äl'vä·räth kēn·tā'rō), Se'ra·fín' (sā'rä·fēn') 1871–1938, and his bro. Joa·quín' (wä·kēn'), 1873–1944. Span. dramatists.

Quin·til'ian (kwĭn·tĭl'yăn), 1st cent. A.D. *Marcus Fa'bi·us* (fā'bĭ·ŭs) *Quin·til'i·a'nus* (kwĭn·tĭl'ĭ·ā'nŭs). Rom. rhetorician.

Qui·ri'no (kē·rē'nô), El·pi'dio (âl·pē'thyô), 1891?–1956. Pres. of the Philippine Republic (1948–53).

Quis'ling (kvĭs'lĭng; *Angl.* kwĭz'-), Vid'kun (vĭd'kŏŏn), 1887–1945. Norw. polit.; Nazi collaborator.

Quo Tai-chi (gwô' tī'chē'), 1889–1952. Chin. diplomat.

R

Ra'be·lais' (răb'ĕ·lä'; răb'ĕ·lā; *Fr.* rà'blĕ'), Fran'çois' (fräN'swà'), 1494?–1553. Fr. humorist & satirist.

Ra'bi (rä'bī), Isidor Isaac, 1898– . Am. (Austrian-born) physicist.

Ra'chel' (rà'shĕl'), Mlle., 1820–1858. Pseud. of *É'li·sa'* (ā'lē'zà') *Fé'lix'* (fā'lēks'). Fr. actress.

Rach·ma'ni·noff (rŭk·mä'nyĭ·nŏf), Ser·gei' (syĭr·gā'ī) Was·sil'ie·vitch (vŭ·syĕl'yĕ·vyĭch), 1873–1943. Russ. composer, pianist, & conductor.

Ra'cine' (rà'sēn'), Jean Bap'tiste' (bà'tēst'), 1639–1699. Fr. dram.

Rack'ham (răk'ăm), Arthur, 1867–1939. Brit. illustrator.

Rad'cliffe (răd'klĭf), Ann, 1764–1823. Nee *Ward* (wôrd). Eng. nov.

Ra'dek (rà'dyĕk), Karl (kàrl) Ber·nar'do·vich (byĕr·när'dŭ·vyĭch), 1885– . Russ. Communist.

Ra·detz'ky (rä·dĕts'kē), Jo'seph (yō'zĕf) Wen'zel (vĕn'tsĕl), 1766–1858. Count *Radetzky von Ra'detz* (fôn rä'dĕts). Austrian field marshal.

Rae (rā), John, 1813–1893. Scot. arctic explorer.

Rae'burn (rā'bĕrn; -bûrn), Sir Henry, 1756–1823. Scot. painter.

Rae'der (rà'dĕr), E'rich (ā'rĭk), 1876– . Ger. admiral.

Rae'mae'kers (rà'mä'kĕrs), Lou·is' (lōō·ē'), 1869–1956. Du. cartoonist.

Rag'lan (răg'lăn), 1st Baron, 1788–1855. *Fitz'roy'* (fĭts'roi'; fĭts·roi') *James Henry Som'er·set* (sŭm'ĕr·set; -sĭt). Brit. field marshal.

Rai·mon'di (rī·môn'dē), Marc'an·to'nio (màr'kän·tô'nyô), 1475?–?1534. Ital. engraver.

Rai·su'li (rä·sōō'lĭ), Ah'med ibn-Mu·ham'med (ä'mĕd ĭb'n·mŏŏ·hăm'mĕd), 1875?–1925. Moroccan brigand.

Ra'ja·go·pa'la·cha'ria (rä'jà·gō·pä'lä·chä'ryà), Cha'kra·var'ti (chŭ'krà·vûr'tĭ), 1879– . Indian lawyer; gov. gen. of India (1948–50).

Ra'leigh or Ra'legh (rô'lĭ; rä'lĭ; râl'ī), Sir Walter, 1552?–1618. Eng. courtier, navigator, & hist.

Ra'ma'dier' (rà'mà'dyä'), Paul, 1888– . Fr. lawyer & polit.

Ra'ma·krish'na (rä'mà·krĭsh'nà), 1834–1886. Hindu yogi.

Ra'man (rä'màn), Sir Chan'dra·se'kha·ra (chŭn'drà·shä'kà·rà) Ven'ka·ta (văng'kà·tà), 1888– . Indian physicist.

Ra·mée', de la (dĕl'à·rà·mā'), Marie Louise, 1839–1908. Pseud. *Oui'da* (wē'dà). Eng. nov.

Ram'e·ses. See RAMSES.

Ra·mi'rez (rä·mē'rĕs), Pe'dro (pā'thrô), 1884– . Argentine gen.; pres. of Argentina (1943–44).

Ra·món' y Ca·jal' (rä·môn' ē kä·häl'), San·tia'go (sän·tyä'gô), 1852–1934. Span. histologist.

Ram'say (răm'zĭ), Allan, 1686–1758. Scot. poet.

—, James Andrew Broun (brōōn), 1812–1860. 10th Earl & 1st Marquis of *Dal·hou'sie* (dăl·hōō'zĭ; -hou'zĭ). Brit. colonial administrator.

—, Sir William, 1852–1916. Brit. chem.

Ram'ses (răm'sēz) or Ram'e·ses (răm'ĕ·sēz). Name of 12 kings of Egypt; esp.: II (reigned 1292–1225 B.C.); III (reigned 1198–1167 B.C.).

Ran'dolph (răn'dŏlf; -d'lf), Edmund Jen'nings (jĕn'ĭngz), 1753–1813. Am. statesman.

—, John, 1773–1833. Am. statesman.

Ran'jit Singh (rŭn'jĭt sĭN'hà), Maharaja, 1780–1839. Founder of Sikh kingdom.

Ran'ke, von (fôn räng'kĕ), Le'o·pold (lā'ô·pôlt), 1795–1886. Ger. hist.

Raph'a·el (răf'ā·ĕl, -ĭ·ĕl; rä'fā·ĕl, -fĭ·ĕl), 1483–1520. *Raf'fa·el'lo* (räf'·fä·ĕl'lô) *San'ti* (sän'tē) or *San'zio* (sän'tsyô). Ital. painter.

Rask (răsk), Ras'mus (räs'mŏŏs) Chris'ti·an (krĭs'tē·än), 1787–1832. Dan. philologist & orientalist.

Ras'mus·sen (räs'mŏŏ·s'n), Knud (k'nōōth) Jo·han' (yō·hàn') Vic'tor (vĭk'tôr), 1879–1933. Dan. arctic explorer & ethnologist.

Ras·pu'tin (rŭs·pōō'tyĭn; *Angl.* răs·pū't'n), Gri·go'ri (grĭ·gō'ryĭ) E·fi'mo·vich (yĭ·tyĕ'mô·vyĭch), 1871?–1916. Russ. holy man & polit.

Ra'the·nau (rä'tĕ·nou), E'mil (ā'mēl), 1838–1915. Ger. industrialist & statesman.

Rausch'ning (roush'nĭng), Her'mann (hĕr'män), 1887– . Ger. anti-Nazi polit. & writer.

Ra'vel' (rà'vĕl'), Mau'rice' (mô'rēs') Jo'seph' (zhō'zĕf'), 1875–1937. Fr. composer.

Raw'lin·son (rô'lĭn·s'n), George, 1812–1902. Eng. orientalist & hist.

—, Sir Henry Cres'wicke (krĕz'ĭk), 1810–1895. *Bro. of prec.* Eng. Assyriologist.

Ray (rā), John, 1627?–1705. Eng. naturalist.

Ray'burn (rā'bĕrn), Sam, 1882– . Am. lawyer & polit.

Ray'leigh (rā'lĭ), 3d Baron, 1842–1919. *John William Strutt* (strŭt). Eng. math. & physicist.

Read (rēd), George, 1733–1798. Am. lawyer & Revolutionist.

—, Thomas Buchanan, 1822–1872. Am. poet & painter.

Reade (rēd), Charles, 1814–1884. Eng. nov.

Read'ing (rĕd'ĭng), 1st Marquis of, 1860–1935. *Rufus Daniel I'saacs* (ī'zàks; -zĭks). Brit. statesman; viceroy of India (1921–26).

Ré'au'mur', de (dĕ rā'ô'mür'), René An'toine' (än'twän') Fer'chault' (fĕr'shô'), 1683–1757. Fr. naturalist & physicist.

Ré'ca'mier' (rā'kà'myä'), Jeanne Fran'çoise' (fräN'swàz') Ju'lie' (zhü'lē') A'dé'la'ïde' (à'dā'là'ēd'), 1777–1849. Fr. society wit.

Red'mond (rĕd'mŭnd), John Edward, 1856–1918. Irish polit.

Reed (rēd), John, 1887-1920. Am. journalist, poet, & Communist.
—, Stanley Forman, 1884– . Am. jurist.
—, Thomas Brack'ett (brăk'ĕt; -ĭt), 1839-1902. Am. polit.
—, Walter, 1851-1902. Am. army surgeon.
Ré·gnier', de (dĕ rā'nyā'), Hen'ri' (än'rē'), 1864-1936. Fr. author.
Reg'u·lus (rĕg'ū·lŭs), Marcus A·til'i·us (à·tĭl'ĭ·ŭs), d. ab. 250 B.C. Rom. gen.
Rei'che·nau, von (fôn rī'kĕ·nou), Wal'ther (väl'tĕr), 1884-1942. Ger. field marshal.
Reid (rēd), Thomas, 1710-1796. Scot. philos.
—, White'law (hwīt'lô), 1837-1912. Am. journalist & diplomat.
Rei'nach' (rē'näk'), Sa'lo'mon' (sà'lô'môN'), 1858-1932. Fr. archaeologist.
Rein'hardt (rīn'härt), Max (mäks; Angl. mäks), 1873-1943. Orig. Gold'mann (gôlt'män). Austrian theater director.
Ré'jane' (rā'zhàn'), 1856-1920. Pseud. of Ga'bri'elle' (gà'brē'ĕl') Char'lotte' (shàr'lôt') Ré'ju' (rā'zhü'). Fr. actress.
Re·marque' (rĕ·märk'), E'rich (Ger. ā'rĭk) Ma·ri'a (mä·rē'ä), 1898– . Am. (Ger.-born) nov.
Rem'brandt van Rijn or **Ryn** (rĕm'brănt [Du. rĕm'bränt] vän rīn'), 1606-1669. Du. painter.
Rem'ing·ton (rĕm'ĭng·tŭn), Frederic, 1861-1909. Am. artist.
Rem'sen (rĕm's'n), Ira, 1846-1927. Am. chem.
Re·nan' (rĕ·nän'), Jo'seph' (zhō'zĕf') Er'nest' (ĕr'nĕst'), 1823-1892. Fr. philologist & hist.
Re·nault' (rĕ·nō'), Louis, 1843-1918. Fr. jurist & pacifist.
Re'ni (râ'nē), Guido (gwē'dō), 1575-1642. Ital. painter.
Ren'ner (rĕn'ĕr), Karl, 1870-1950. Austrian statesman; pres. of Austria (1945-50).
Re·noir' (rĕ·nwàr'), Pierre Au'guste' (ō'güst'), 1841-1919. Fr. painter.
Rep'plier (rĕp'lēr), Agnes, 1855-1950. Am. essayist.
Re·spi'ghi (rās·pē'gē), Ot·to·ri'no (ôt·tō·rē'nō), 1879-1936. Ital. composer.
Resz'ke, de (dĕ rĕsh'kĕ), É'dou·ard' (ā'dwàr'), 1855-1917. Bro. of Jean. Pol. basso.
—, Jean (zhän), 1850-1925. Jan (yän) Mie·czi'slaw (myĕ·chē'släf). Pol. tenor.
Reth'berg (Angl. rĕth'bûrg; Ger. rĕt'bĕrk), E·lis'a·beth (ê·lĭz'à·bĕth; Ger. ā·lē'zä·bĕt), 1894– . Pseud. of Lis'beth (lēs'bĕt) Sätt'ler (zĕt'lēr). Am. (Ger.-born) soprano.
Retz, de (dĕ rĕts), Cardinal, 1614-1679. Jean Fran'çois' (frän'swà') Paul de Gon'di' (dĕ gôn'dē'). Fr. ecclesiastic & polit.
Reuch'lin (roik'lēn; roik·lēn'), Jo·hann' (yō·hän'; yō'hän), 1455-1522. Cap'ni·o (kăp'nĭ·ō; Ger. käp'nē·ō). Ger. humanist.
Reu'ter, von (fôn roi'tēr), Lud'wig (lōōt'vĭk; lōōd'-), 1869-1943. Ger. admiral.
—, Paul Julius, Baron, 1816-1899. Orig. Israel Beer (bār) Jo'sa·phat (yō'zä·fät). Brit. (Ger.-born) news agent.
Reu'ter·dahl (Swed. rĕ'ŏŏ·tĕr·däl), Henry, 1871-1925. Swed.-born painter in Am.
Reu'ther (rōō'thĕr), Walter Philip, 1907– . Am. labor leader.
Re·vere' (rĕ·vēr'), Paul, 1735-1818. Am. patriot & silversmith.
Rey'bold (rī'bōld), Eugene, 1884– . Am. gen.
Rey'mont (rā'mônt), Wła·dy'slaw (vlä·dĭ'släf) Sta·ni'slaw (stä·nē'släf), 1867-1925. Pol. nov.
Rey'naud' (rā'nō'), Paul, 1878– . Premier of France (1940).
Reyn'olds (rĕn'ŏldz), Sir Joshua, 1723-1792. Eng. painter.
Rhodes (rōdz), Cecil John, 1853-1902. Brit. administrator & financier in S. Africa.
—, James Ford, 1848-1927. Am. hist.
Rhon'dda (rŏn'dä; Welsh r'hŏn'thà), Viscount, 1856-1918. David Alfred Thomas. Brit. industrialist & administrator.
Rib'ben·trop, von (fôn rĭb'ĕn·trôp), Jo'a·chim (yō'ä·kĭm; yō·ä'kĭm), 1893-1946. Ger. diplomat.
Ri·be'ra (rē·vā'rä), Jo·sé' (hō·sā'), 1588-1652. Lo Spa'gno·let'to (lō spä'nyō·lāt'tō). Span. painter & etcher.
Ri·car'do (rĭ·kär'dō), David, 1772-1823. Eng. econ.
Rice (rīs), Alice Caldwell, 1870-1942. Nee He'gan (hē'găn). Wife of Cale. Am. writer.
—, Cale (kāl) Young, 1872-1943. Am. poet & dram.
—, Elmer L., 1892– . Orig. Rei'zen·stein (rī'z'n·stīn). Am. dram.
Rich'ard (rĭch'ĕrd). Name of 3 kings of Eng.: **I** (Cœur' de Li'on [kûr' dē lē'ŏn; Fr. kûr' dē lyôn']), 1157-1199 (reigned 1189-99); **II**, 1367-1400 (reigned 1377-99); **III**, 1452-1485 (reigned 1483-85).
Rich'ards (rĭch'ĕrdz), Theodore William, 1868-1928. Am. chem.
Rich'ard·son (rĭch'ĕrd·s'n), Henry Han'del (hăn'd'l), 1870-1946. Pseud. of Ethel Florence Linde'say Richardson. Australian nov.
—, Owen Wil'lans (wĭl'ănz), 1879– . Eng. physicist.
—, Samuel, 1689-1761. Eng. nov.
Ri'che·lieu', de (dĕ rē'shĕ·lyū'; Angl. rĭsh'ĕ·lōō), Duc (dük), 1585-1642. Armand Jean du Ples'sis' (dü plĕ'sē'). Fr. cardinal & statesman.
Ri'chet' (rē'shĕ'), Charles Ro'bert' (rō'bâr'), 1850-1935. Fr. physiol.
Rich'ter (rĭk'tēr), Jean (zhän) Paul (poul) Frie'drich (frē'drĭк), 1763-1825. Pseud. Jean Paul. Ger. writer.
Ric'i·mer (rĭs'ĭ·mēr), d. 472. Rom. gen.
Rick'en·back'er (rĭk'ĕn·băk'ēr), Edward Vernon, 1890– . Am. aviator.
Rid'ley (rĭd'lĭ), Nicholas, 1500?-1555. Eng. reformer & martyr.
Rid'path (rĭd'päth), John Clark, 1840-1900. Am. hist.
Riel (ryĕl), Louis, 1844-1885. Canadian insurgent.
Rie'mann (rē'män), Ge·org' (gā·ôrk') Frie'drich (frē'drĭк) Bern'hard (bĕrn'härt), 1826-1866. Ger. math.
Rien'zi, di (dē ryĕn'tsē), or **Rien'zo** (-tsō), Co'la (kō'lä), 1313-1354. Nic'co·lo (nĭk'ō·lō) Ga·bri'ni (gä·brē'nē). Last of the Romans. Ital. patriot; tribune of Rome.
Riis (rēs), Ja'cob (jā'kŭb; Dan. -yä'kŏp) Au'gust (ô'gŭst; Dan. ou'gŏŏst), 1849-1914. Am. (Dan.-born) social worker & writer.
Ri'ley (rī'lĭ), James Whit'comb (hwĭt'kŭm), 1849-1916. Am. poet.

Ril'ke (rĭl'kĕ), Rai'ner (rī'nĕr) Ma·ri'a (mä·rē'ä), 1875-1926. Ger. poet.
Ri'mi·ni, Francesca da. See FRANCESCA DA RIMINI.
Rim'ski-Kor·sa·kov' (ryĕm'skĭ-kŭr·sŭ·kôf'; Angl. rĭm'skĭ-kôr'sà·kôf), Ni·ko·lai' (nyī·kŭ·lī') An·dre'e·vich (ŭn·dryā'yĕ·vyĭch), 1844-1908. Russ. composer.
Rin·cón', del (thĕl rēng·kôn'), An·to'nio (än·tō'nyō), 1446-1500. Span. painter.
Rine'hart (rīn'härt), Mary, 1876– . Nee Rob'erts (rŏb'ĕrts). Am. nov. & dram.
Rí'os (rē'ōs), Juan (hwän) An·to'nio (än·tō'nyō), 1888-1946. Chilean lawyer; pres. of Chile (1942-46).
Rip'ley (rĭp'lĭ), George, 1802-1880. Am. literary critic & socialist.
—, William Ze·bi'na (zĕ·bī'nà), 1867-1941. Am. econ.
Rist (rēst), Charles, 1873-1955. Fr. econ.
Ri·sto'ri (rēs·tō'rē), A'de·la'i·de (ä'dā·lä'ē·dä), 1822-1906. Ital. actress.
Ritch'ie (rĭch'ĭ), Sir Neil (nēl) Meth'u·en (mĕth'ū·ĭn), 1897– . Brit. gen.
Rit'ten·house (rĭt'n·hous), Jessie Belle, 1869-1948. Am. critic & poet.
Ri·ve'ra (rē·vä'rä), Die'go (dyā'gō), 1886-1957. Mex. painter & muralist.
Ri·ve'ra y Or'ba·ne'ja, de (thä rē·vä'rä ē ôr'vä·nĕ'hä), Mi·guel' (mē·gĕl') Pri'mo (prē'mō), 1870-1930. Mar·qués' (mär·kās') de Es·tel'la (thä äs·tā'lyä). Span. gen.; dictator (1925-30).
Ri·zal' (rē·zäl'; Span. -säl'), Jo·sé' (hō·sā'), 1861-1896. Filipino patriot.
Ri·za' Shah Pah'la·vi or **Pah'le·vi** (rĭ·zä' shä' pä'lá·vē), 1877-1944. Shah of Iran (1925-41).
Riz'zio (rĕt'tsyō; Angl. rĭt'sĭ·ō) or **Ric'cio** (rĕt'chō; Angl. rĭch'ĭ·ō), Da'vid (dä'vēd; Angl. dā'vĭd), 1533?-1566. Ital. musician.
Rob'bia, del'la (däl'lä rŏb'byä), Lu'ca (lōō'kä), 1400?-1482. Florentine sculptor.
Rob'ert (rŏb'ĕrt). See Robert BRUCE.
—, **I**, d. 1035. Duc (dük) de Nor'man'die' (dĕ nôr'män'dē'). Le Dia'ble (lĕ dyà'bl'). Duke (1028-35).
Ro'bert' Guis'card'. See GUISCARD.
Rob'erts (rŏb'ĕrts), Frederick Sleigh (slā), 1832-1914. 1st Earl Roberts of Kan'da·har, Pre·to'ri·a, and Wa'ter·ford (kăn'dà·här [native kän·dà·här'], prē·tō'rĭ·à, wô'tēr·fērd). Brit. field marshal.
—, Kenneth, 1885-1957. Am. nov.
—, Owen Jo·se'phus (jō·sē'fŭs), 1875-1955. Am. jurist.
Rob'ert·son (rŏb'ĕrt·s'n), William, 1721-1793. Scot. hist.
—, Sir William Robert, 1860-1933. Brit. field marshal.
Robe'son (rōb's'n), Paul, 1898– . Am. actor & singer.
Ro·bes·pierre', de (dĕ rō'bĕs'pyàr'; Angl. rōbz'pēr), Max'i'mi'lien' (mák'sē'mē'lyän') Fran'çois' (frän'swà') Ma'rie' (mà'rē') I'si'dore' (ē'zē'dôr'), 1758-1794. Fr. Revolutionist.
Rob'in·son (rŏb'ĭn·s'n), Edwin Ar'ling·ton (är'lĭng·tŭn), 1869-1935. Am. poet.
—, George Frederick Samuel, 1827-1909. 1st Marquis of Rip'on (rĭp'ŭn). Brit. statesman.
—, James Harvey, 1863-1936. Am. hist.
—, Sir Robert, 1886– . Eng. chem.
Ro'cham'beau', de (dĕ rō'shäN'bō'), Comte (kôNt), 1725-1807. Jean Bap'tiste' (bà'tēst') Do'na'tien' (dō'nà'syäN') de Vi'meur' (dĕ vē'mûr'). Fr. gen.; marshal of France (1791).
Rock'e·fel'ler (rŏk'ē·fĕl'ēr; rŏk'fĕl'ēr), John Da'vi·son (dā'vĭ·s'n), father, 1839-1937, and son, 1874– . Am. oil magnates & philanthropists.
Rock'ing·ham (rŏk'ĭng·ăm), 2d Marquis of, 1730-1782. Charles Wat'son-Went'worth (wŏt's'n-wĕnt'wûrth; -wērth). Eng. statesman.
Rock'ne (rŏk'nē), Knute (nōōt) Kenneth, 1888-1931. Norw.-born football coach.
Ro'de (rō'thĕ), Hel'ge (hĕl'gĕ), 1870-1937. Dan. poet.
Rodg'ers (rŏj'ĕrz), Richard, 1902– . Am. composer.
Ro'din' (rō'dăN'), Fran'çois' (frän'swà') Au'guste' (ō'güst') René (ō'güst') René, 1840-1917. Fr. sculptor.
Rod'ney (rŏd'nĭ), George Brydg'es (brĭj'ĕz; -ĭz), 1719-1792. 1st Baron Rodney. Eng. admiral.
Ro·dzin'ski (rō·jĭn'skĭ; Pol. rô·jēn'y'skĕ), Ar'tur (är'tŏŏr), 1894– . Am. conductor.
Roeb'ling (rōb'lĭng; Ger. rûb'-), John Augustus, 1806-1869. Am. (Ger.-born) civil engineer.
Roent'gen or **Rönt'gen** (rŭnt'gĕn; Angl. rĕnt'-, rŭnt'-, -yĕn), Wil'helm (vĭl'hĕlm) Kon'rad (kôn'rät), 1845-1923. Ger. physicist.
Roe'rich (rŏ'rĭk), Nicholas Kon·stan·tin' (kŭn·stŭn·tyēn'), 1874-1947. Russ. painter.
Rog'ers (rŏj'ērz), Bruce, 1870-1957. Am. printer & book designer.
—, Henry Hut'tle·ston (hŭt'l·stŭn) or Hud'dle·ston (hŭd'l-), 1840-1909. Am. financier.
—, Henry Huddleston, 1879-1935. Son of prec. Am. financier.
—, James Gam'ble (găm'b'l), 1867-1947. Am. architect.
—, Samuel, 1763-1855. Eng. poet.
—, William Penn A·dair' (à·dâr'), 1879-1935. Will. Am. actor & humorist.
Ro·get' (rō·zhā'; Brit. also rŏzh'ā), Peter Mark, 1779-1869. Eng. physician & scholar.
Ro·kos·sov'ski (rŭ·kŭ·sôf'skĭ), Kon·stan·tin' (kŭn·stŭn·tyēn'), 1893– . Russ. marshal.
Rolfe (rŏlf), John, 1585-1622. Husband of Pocahontas. Eng. colonist.
Rol'land (rō'läN'), Ro'main' (rō'măN'), 1866-1944. Fr. author.
Rol'lo (rŏl'ō) or **Hrolf** (rŏlf), 860?-?931. Norse chieftain.
Röl'vaag (rŏl'väg), O'le (ō'lĕ) Ed'vart (ĕd'värt; äd'-), 1876-1931. Norw.-born educ. & nov. in Am.
Ro'mains' (rō'măN'), Jules, 1885– . Pseud. of Louis Fa'ri'goule' (fà'rē'gōōl'). Fr. author.
Ro·ma'no (rō·mä'nō), Giu'lio (jōō'lyō), 1499-1546. Giulio Pip'pi de' Gia·nuz'zi (pēp'pē dä jä·nōōt'tsē). Ital. painter & architect.

Ro·ma'nov *or* Ro·ma'noff (rŭ·mä'nŭf; *Angl.* rō'má·nŏf), Mi·kha·il' (myĭ·κŭ·ēl') Fe·o'do·ro'vich (fyĭ·ô'dŭ·rō'vyĭch), 1596–1645. 1st tsar (1613–45) of Russ. Romanov dynasty (1613–1917).

Rom'berg (rŏm'bûrg), Sig'mund (sĭg'mŭnd), 1887–1951. Hung.-born composer in Am.

Ro·me'ro (rrô·mā'rō), Car'los (kär'lōs) O·roz'co (ô·rōs'kô), 1898– . Mex. caricaturist & painter.

Rom'mel (rŏm'ĕl), Er'win (ĕr'vĕn), 1891–1944. Ger. field marshal.

Rom'ney (rŏm'nĭ; rŭm'-), George, 1734–1802. Eng. painter.

Ron'sard', de (dĕ rôn'sàr'), Pierre, 1524–1585. Fr. poet.

Rönt'gen, Wilhelm Konrad. See ROENTGEN.

Roon, von (fôn rōn'), Count Al'brecht (äl'brĕkt) The'o·dor (tā'ô·dōr) E'mil (ā'mēl), 1803–1879. Prussian field marshal & statesman.

Roo'se·velt (rō'zĕ·vĕlt; -vĕlt; *formerly often, and still sometimes,* rōō'zĕ·vĕlt; *the usual pron. in both branches of the family is* rō'zĕ·vĕlt), Anna Eleanor, 1884– . Nee *Roosevelt. Wife of F. D.* Am. lecturer & writer.

—, Franklin Del'a·no (dĕl'á·nō), 1882–1945. 32d pres. of the U. S. (1933–45).

—, Theodore, 1858–1919. 26th pres. of the U. S. (1901–09).

—, Theodore, 1887–1944. *Son of prec.* Am. gen., explorer, & polit.

Root (rōōt), Elihu, 1845–1937. Am. lawyer & statesman.

Ropes (rōps), John Cod'man (kŏd'măn), 1836–1899. Am. hist.

Ro'rer (rōr'ēr), Sarah Ty'son (tī's'n), 1849–1937. Nee *Hes'ton* (hĕs'tŭn). Am. educ. & writer.

Ro'sa (rō'zä), Sal'va·tor' (säl'vä·tōr'), 1615–1673. Ital. painter & poet.

Rose'ber·y (rōz'bĕr·ĭ; rōz'brĭ), 5th Earl of, 1847–1929. *Archibald Philip Prim'rose* (prĭm'rōz). Eng. statesman.

Rose'crans (rōz'krăns), William Starke (stärk), 1819–1898. Am. gen.

Ro'sen·berg (rō'zĕn·bĕrk), Alfred, 1893–1946. Ger. Nazi & writer.

Ro'sen·wald (rō'z'n·wôld), Julius, 1862–1932. Am. merchant & philanthropist.

Ross (rôs), Betsy, 1752–1836. Nee *Gris'com* (grĭs'kŭm). Maker of first Am. flag.

—, Sir James Clark, 1800–1862. Scot. polar explorer.

—, Sir John, 1777–1856. *Uncle of prec.* Scot. arctic explorer.

—, Sir Ronald, 1857–1932. Brit. physician.

Ros·set'ti (rô·sĕt'ĭ; -zĕt'ĭ), Christina Georgina, 1830–1894. *Sister of D. G.* Eng. poet.

—, Dan'te (dän'tĕ) Gabriel, 1828–1882. Eng. painter & poet.

Ros'si (rôs'sē; *Angl.* rŏs'ĭ), Bruno, 1905– . Ital.-born physicist in Am.

Ros·si'ni (rôs·sē'nē), Gio·ac·chi'no (jō·äk·kē'nō) An·to'nio (än·tô'nyō), 1792–1868. Ital. composer.

Ros'tand' (rôs'tän'), Ed'mond' (ĕd'môn'), 1868–1918. Fr. poet & dram.

Ro·stov'tzeff (rŭ·stôf'tsĕf), Michael I·va'no·vich (ĭ·vä'nŭ·vyĭch), 1870–1952. Am. (Russ.-born) hist.

Roth'schild (*Ger.* rōt'shĭlt; *Eng.* rŏth[s]'chīld, rŏs'chīld), Mey'er (mī'ēr) Am'schel (äm'shĕl), 1743–1812. Ger. financier.

—, Nathan Meyer, 1777–1836. *Son of prec.* Financier in London.

Rou'get' de Lisle (rōō'zhĕ' dĕ lēl'), Claude (klōd) Jo'seph' (zhō'zĕf'), 1760–1836. Fr. army officer & composer.

Rous'seau' (rōō'sō'), Jean Jacques (zhäk), 1712–1778. Fr. (Swiss-born) philos. & writer.

—, The'o'dore' (tā'ō'dôr'), 1812–1867. Fr. painter.

Rowe (rō), Nicholas, 1674–1718. Eng. poet & dram.; poet laureate (1715–18).

Row'ley (rō'lĭ), William, 1585?–?1642. Eng. actor & dram.

Ro'xas y A·cu'ña (rrô'hās ē ä·kōō'nyä), Ma·nuel' (mä·nwĕl'), 1892–1948. Philippine statesman; pres. of the Philippine Republic (1946–48).

Roy'all (roi'ăl), Kenneth Clai'borne (klā'bĕrn), 1894– . Am. lawyer & statesman.

Royce (rois), Josiah, 1855–1916. Am. philos.

Ro·zhde'stven·ski (rŭ·zhdyä'stvyĕn·skĭ), Zi·no'vi (zyĭ·nō'vyĭ) Pe·tro'vich (pyĭ·trô'vyĭch), 1848–1909. Russ. admiral.

Ru'bens (*Angl.* rōō'bĕnz; *Flem.* rü'bĕns), Pe'ter (pā'tĕr) Paul (poul), 1577–1640. Flem. painter.

Ru'bin·stein (*Angl.* rōō'bĭn·stīn; *Russ.* rōō·byĭn·shtīn'), An·ton' (ŭn·tôn'), 1829–1894. Russ. pianist & composer.

Ru'dolf I of Haps'burg (rōō'dôlf, *Ger.* -dôlf; häps'bûrg), 1218–1291. Holy Rom. emp. (1273–91); 1st of the Hapsburgs.

Ru'dolf *or* Ru'dolph of Haps'burg, 1858–1889. Archduke & crown prince of Austria.

Ru'ger (rōō'gĕr), Thomas Howard, 1833–1907. Am. gen.

Ruis'dael *or* Ruys'dael (rois'däl), Ja'cob (yä'kôp), 1628?–1682, and his uncle Sa'lo·mon (sä'lō·mŏn), 1600?–1670. Du. painters.

Rum'ford, Count. See benjamin THOMPSON.

Ruml (rōōm''l), Beards'ley (bĕrdz'lĭ), 1894– . Am. businessman & financier.

Rund'stedt, von (fôn rōōnt'shtĕt), Karl Ru'dolf (rōō'dôlf) Gerd (gĕrt), 1875–1953. Ger. field marshal.

Ru'ne·berg (rōō'nĕ·bär'y), Jo'han (yōō'hän) Lud'vig (lŭd'vĭg), 1804–1877. Finnish poet.

Run'jit Singh. See RANJIT SINGH.

Run'yon (rŭn'yŭn), (Alfred) Da'mon (dā'mŏn), 1880–1946. Am. author.

Ru'pert (rōō'pĕrt; *Ger.* -pĕrt), Prince, 1619–1682. *Nephew of Charles I of Eng.* Ger.-Eng. gen. & admiral.

— *or* Rup'precht (rōōp'rĕkt), 1869–1955. Crown prince of Bavaria & Ger. field marshal.

Rush (rŭsh), Benjamin, 1745?–1813. Am. physician & Revolutionary patriot.

—, Richard, 1780–1859. *Son of prec.* Am. lawyer & statesman.

Rus'kin (rŭs'kĭn), John, 1819–1900. Eng. essayist, critic, & reformer.

Rus'sell (rŭs''l), Bertrand Arthur William, 3d Earl, 1872– . Eng. math. & philos.

—, Charles Taze (tāz), 1852–1916. Am. pastor.

—, Elizabeth Mary, Countess, 1866–1941. Pseud. *Elizabeth.* Australian-born nov.

—, George William, 1867–1935. Pseud. *Æ.* Irish author.

—, Lord John, 1792–1878. 1st Earl *Russell of Kings'ton Russell* (kĭng'stŭn). Brit. statesman.

—, Lillian, 1861–1922. *Helen Louise Leon'ard* (lĕn'ērd). Am. soprano.

Ruth'er·ford (rŭth'ēr·fērd), Ernest, 1871–1937. 1st Baron *Rutherford of Nel'son* (nĕl's'n). Brit. physicist.

—, Joseph Franklin, 1869–1942. *Judge.* Am. leader of Jehovah's Witnesses.

Rut'ledge (rŭt'lĭj), Ann, 1816–1835. Fiancée of Abraham Lincoln.

—, John, 1739–1800. Am. statesman.

—, Wiley Blount (blŭnt), 1894–1949. Am. jurist.

Ruys'dael. See RUISDAEL.

Ruy'ter *or* Rui'ter, de (dĕ roi'tēr), Mi'chel (mē'κĕl) A'dri·aans'zoon (ä'drē·än'sŭn; -sôn; -sôn), 1607–1676. Du. admiral.

Ru'žič'ka (rōō'zhĕch'kä), Le'o·pold (lā'ô·pôlt), 1887– . Yugoslavian chem.

Rys'kind (rĭs'kĭnd), Morris, 1895– . Am. dram.

S

Saa·ve'dra La'mas (sä·vä'thrä lä'mäs), Car'los (kär'lōs), 1880– . Argentine lawyer & diplomat.

Sa'ba·tier' (sä'bá·tyā'), Paul, 1854–1941. Fr. chem.

Sa·ba·ti'ni (sä'bä·tē'nē; säb'á·tē'nē), Raf'a·el (răf'á·ĕl, -ĭ·ĕl; rä'fä·ĕl, -fĭ-ĕl), 1875–1950. Ital. author.

Sachs (zäks), Hans, 1494–1576. Ger. cobbler & Meistersinger.

Sack'ville (săk'vĭl), Thomas, 1536–1608. 1st Earl of *Dor'set* (dôr'sĕt; -sĭt). Eng. poet & diplomat.

Sack'ville-West' (-wĕst'), Victoria Mary, 1892– . Eng. writer.

Sade, de (dĕ säd'), Comte (kônt) Do'na'tien' (dô'nà'syän') Al'phonse' (äl'fôns') Fran'çois' (frän'swà'), 1740–1814. Marquis *de Sade.* Fr. soldier & pervert.

Sage (sāj), Russell, 1816–1906. Am. financier.

Saint'-Cyr' (săn'sēr'), Marquis Lau'rent' (lō'rän') de Gou'vion' (dĕ gōō'vyôn'), 1764–1830. Fr. gen. under Napoleon; marshal of France (1812).

Sainte'-Beuve' (sănt'bûv'), Charles Au'gus'tin' (ō'güs'tăn'), 1804–1869. Fr. critic & author.

Saint-Gau'dens (sănt·gô'd'nz), Augustus, 1848–1907. Irish-born sculptor in Am.

St. John, Henry. See BOLINGBROKE.

Saint'-Just', de (dĕ săn'zhüst'), Louis An'toine' (än'twàn') Lé'on' (lā'ôn'), 1767–1794. Fr. Revolutionist.

St. Lau'rent' (săn' lō'rän'), Lou'is (lōō'ĭ) Ste'phen (stē'vĕn), 1882– . Canadian lawyer; prime min. (1948–).

Saint'-Pierre'. See BERNARDIN DE SAINT-PIERRE.

Saint'-Saëns' (săn'säns'), (Charles) Ca'mille' (kà'mē'y'), 1835–1921. Fr. composer.

Saints'bur·y (sănts'bĕr·ĭ; -brĭ), George Edward Bate'man (bāt'măn), 1845–1933. Eng. critic.

Saint'-Si'mon', de (dĕ săn'sē'môn'), Comte (kônt), 1760–1825. *Claude Hen'ri'* (än'rē') *de Rou'vroy'* (dĕ rōō'vrwà'). Fr. philos. & socialist.

—, Duc (dük), 1675–1755. *Louis de Rouvroy.* Fr. soldier, statesman, & writer.

Sai·on·ji (sī·ôn·jē), Marquis Kim·mo·chi (kēm·mô·chē), 1849–1940. Jap. statesman.

Sai·to (sī·tō), Ji·ro (jē·rō), 1893– . Jap. army officer.

Sal'a·din (săl[p]'s'n), 1138–1193. Sultan of Egypt and Syria.

Sa·la·zar' (sǎ·lǎ·zàr'), An·to'nio (än·tô'nyōō) de O·li·vei'ra (thĕ ô·lē·vā'ērá), 1889– . Port. statesman.

Sal'lust (săl'ŭst), 86–34 B.C. *Ga'ius* (gā'yŭs; gī'ŭs) *Sal·lus'ti·us Cris'pus* (sǎ·lŭs'chĭ·ŭs [-tĭ·ŭs] krĭs'pŭs). Rom. hist. & polit.

Sal·ve'mi·ni (säl·vā'mē·nē), Ga'e·ta'no (gä'ĕ·tä'nō), 1873–1957. Ital. hist.

Sal·vi'ni (säl·vē'nē), Tom·ma'so (tôm·mä'zō), 1829–1916. Ital. actor.

Samp'son (sămp[p]'s'n), William Thomas, 1840–1902. Am. admiral.

San'chez de Bus'ta·man'te y Sir·vén' (sän'chäs thä vōōs'tä·män'tä ē sēr·vän'), An·to'nio (än·tô'nyō), 1865–1951. Cuban jurist.

Sand (sänd; *Fr.* sänd), George, 1803–1876. Pseud. of *A'man'dine'* (ä'män'dēn') *Au'rore'* (ô'rôr') *Lu'cie'* (lü'sē'); nee *Du'pin'* (dü·păn'). Ba'ronne' (bä'rôn') *Du'de·vant'* (düd'vän'). Fr. writer.

Sand'burg (sănd'bûrg), Carl, 1878– . Am. author.

San'dra·cot'tus *or* San'dro·cot'tus. See CHANDRAGUPTA.

San·gal'lo, da (dä säng·gäl'lō), Giu·lia'no (jōō·lyä'nō), 1445–1516. Florentine architect & sculptor.

Sang'er (săng'ēr), Margaret, 1883– . Nee *Hig'gins* (hĭg'ĭnz). Am. leader of birth-control movement.

San'key (săng'kĭ), Ira David, 1840–1908. Am. evangelist & hymn writer.

San Mar·tín', de (thä sän' mär·tēn'), Jo·sé' (hō·sā'), 1778–1850. S. Am. soldier & statesman.

San'ta An'na *or* San'ta A'na, de (thä sän'tä ä'nä), An·to'nio (än·tô'nyō) Ló'pez (lō'pĕz), 1795?–1876. Mex. gen. & pres.

San'tan·der' (sän·tän·dĕr'), Fran·cis'co de Pau'la (frän·sēs'kō thä pou'lä), 1792–1840. Gen. & polit. of New Granada.

San'ta·ya'na (sän'tä·yä'nä), George (jôrj), 1863–1952. Am. (Span.-born) poet & philos.

San'tos-Du'mont' (sănn'tōōz·dü'môn'), Al·ber'to (äl·bâr'tōō), 1873–1932. Brazilian aeronaut in France.

Sap'pho (săf'ō), fl. ab. 600 B.C. Greek poet.

Sar'da·na·pa'lus (sär'd·n·á·pā'lŭs). King of Assyria (ab. 822 B.C.), sometimes identified with Ashurbanipal.

Sar'dou' (sär'dōō'), Vic'to'rien' (vĕk'tō'ryän'), 1831–1908. Fr. dram.

Sarg (särg), Anthony Frederick, 1882–1942. *To'ny* (tō'nĭ). Am. illustrator & marionette maker.

Sar'gent (sär'jĕnt), John Sing'er (sĭng'ēr), 1856–1925. Am. painter.

Sar'gon II (sär'gŏn), d. 705 B.C. King of Assyria (722–705).

Sa·ro'yan (sä·rō'yän), William, 1908– . Am. writer.

Sas·soon' (sǎ·sōōn'), Sieg'fried (sĕg'frēd), 1886– . Eng. writer.

Sa·to (sä·tō), Na·o·ta·ke (nä·ō·tä·kĕ), 1882– . Jap. diplomat.

Saun'ders (sôn'dĕrz; sän'-), La Verne (là vûrn'), 1903– . Am. gen.

Sav'age (săv'ĭj), Richard, 1697?–1743. Eng. poet.

Sa'vo·na·ro'la (sä'vō·nä·rō'lä; *Angl.* săv'ō·nà·rō'là), Gi·ro'la·mo (jĕ·rō'lä·mō), 1452–1498. Ital. reformer.

Saw'yer (sô'yĕr), Charles, 1887– . Am. lawyer & administrator.

Saxe, de (dĕ säks'), Comte (kônt) Her'mann' (ĕr'män') Maurice, 1696–1750. Fr. soldier; marshal of France (1744).

Sax'o Gram·mat'i·cus (săk'sō gră·măt'ĭ·kŭs), 1150?–?1220. Dan. hist.

Say'ers (sā'ērz; sârz), Dorothy Leigh (lē), 1893–1957. Eng. writer.

Scal'i·ger (skăl'ĭ·jẽr), Joseph Justus, 1540–1609. Ital.-born physician & scholar.

—, Julius Caesar, 1484–1558. *Father of prec.* Ital. physician.

Scan'der·beg (skăn'dẽr·bĕg); *Turk.* Is·ken·der' Bey (ĭs·kĕn·dẽr' bā'), 1403?–1468. *George Cas'tri·o'ta* (käs'trĭ·ō'tà). Albanian chieftain.

Scar·lat'ti (skär·lät'tē), A'les·san'dro (ä'läs·sän'drō), 1659–1725. Ital. composer.

Scar'ron' (skà'rôn'), Paul, 1610–1660. Fr. author.

Schacht (shäkt), (Hor'ace Gree'ley [hŏr'ĭs grē'lĭ]) Hjal'mar (yäl'mär), 1877– . Ger. financier.

Scharn'horst, von (fôn shärn'hôrst), Ger'hard (gĕr'härt) Jo·hann' (yō·hän') Da'vid (dä'vĕt; -vĭt; -fĕt; -fĭt), 1755–1813. Prussian gen.

Schar·wen'ka (shär·vĕng'kä), Phi'lipp (fē'lĭp; fĭl'ĭp), 1847–1917, and his bro. Xa'ver (ksä'vĕr; ksä·vär'), 1850–1924. Ger. pianists & composers.

Scheer (shär), Rein'hard (rīn'härt), 1863–1928. Ger. admiral.

Schei'de·mann (shī'dĕ·män), Phi'lipp (fē'lĭp; fĭl'ĭp), 1865–1939. Ger. polit.

Schel'ling, von (fôn shĕl'ĭng), Frie'drich (frē'drĭk) Wil'helm (vĭl'hĕlm) Jo'seph (yō'zĕf), 1775–1854. Ger. philos.

Schia'pa·rel'li (skyä'pä·rĕl'lē), Gio·van'ni (jō·vän'nē) Vir·gi'nio (vēr·jē'nyō), 1835–1910. Ital. astron.

Schick (shĭk), Bé'la (bā'là), 1877– . Am. (Hung.-born) pediatrician.

Schick'l·gru'ber. See HITLER.

Schil'ler, von (fôn shĭl'ẽr), Jo·hann' (yō·hän'; yō'hän) Chri'stoph (krĭs'tôf) Frie'drich (frē'drĭk), 1759–1805. Ger. poet & dram.

Schi'pa (skē'pä), Ti'to (tē'tō), 1890– . Ital.-born tenor in Am.

Schi'rach, von (fôn shē'räk), Bal'dur (bäl'dŏor), 1907– . Ger. Nazi polit.

Schle'gel, von (fôn shlā'gĕl), Au'gust (ou'gŏost) Wil'helm (vĭl'hĕlm), 1767–1845. Ger. author.

—, Frie'drich (frē'drĭk), 1772–1829. *Bro. of prec.* Ger. philos. & writer.

Schlei'cher, von (fôn shlī'kẽr), Kurt (kŏort), 1882–1934. Ger. soldier & statesman.

Schlei'er·ma'cher (shlī'ẽr·mä'kẽr), Frie'drich (frē'drĭk) Ernst (ĕrnst) Da'ni·el (dä'nĕ·ĕl), 1768–1834. Ger. theol. & philos.

Schley (slī), Win'field (wĭn'fēld) Scott, 1839–1911. Am. admiral.

Schlie'mann (shlē'män), Hein'rich (hīn'rĭk), 1822–1890. Ger. archaeologist.

Schmidt (shmĭt), Wil'helm (vĭl'hĕlm), 1868–1954. Austrian philologist & ethnographer.

Schna'bel (shnä'bĕl), Ar'tur (är'tŏor), 1882–1951. Am. (Austrian-born) pianist & composer.

Schnitz'ler (shnĭts'lẽr), Ar'thur (är'tŏor), 1862–1931. Austrian physician, dram., & nov.

Scho'field (skō'fēld), John Mc·Al'lis·ter (măk·ăl'ĭs·tẽr), 1831–1906. Am. gen.

Scho'pen·hau'er (shō'pĕn·hou'ẽr), Ar'thur (är'tŏor), 1788–1860. Ger. philos.

Schorr (shŏr), Frie'drich (frē'drĭk), 1888–1953. Hung.-born baritone in Am.

Schrö'ding·er (shrŭ'dĭng·ẽr), Er'win (ĕr'vēn), 1887– . Ger. physicist.

Schu'bert (shŏo'bĕrt), Franz (fränts) Pe'ter (pā'tĕr), 1797–1828. Austrian composer.

Schu'man' (shŏo'män'), Ro'bert' (rō'bâr'), 1886– . Fr. lawyer & polit.

Schu'mann (shŏo'män), Ro'bert (rō'bĕrt), 1810–1856. Ger. composer.

Schu'mann-Heink' (shŏo'män·hīngk'; *Ger.* shŏo'män-), Er'nes·ti'ne (ĕr'nĕs·tē'nĕ), 1861–1936. *Ne Roess'ler* (rûs'lĕr). Austrian-born contralto.

Schur'man (shŏor'män), Jacob Gould, 1854–1942. Am. philos. & diplomat; pres., Cornell U. (1892–1920).

Schurz (shŏorts), Carl, 1829–1906. Am. (Ger.-born) lawyer, gen., & polit.

Schusch'nigg, von (fôn shŏosh'nĭk), Kurt (kŏort), 1897– . Austrian statesman.

Schuy'ler (skī'lẽr), Philip John, 1733–1804. Am. gen. & statesman.

Schwab (shwŏb), Charles M., 1862–1939. Am. industrialist.

Schwein'furth (shvīn'fŏort), Ge·org' (gā·ôrk') Au'gust (ou'gŏost), 1836–1925. Ger. explorer in Africa.

Schwel'len·bach (shwĕl'ĕn·bäk), Lewis Baxter, 1894–1948. Am. lawyer & administrator.

Scip'i·o Ae·mil'i·a'nus Af·ri·ca'nus Nu'man·ti'nus (sĭp'ĭ·ō ē·mĭl'ĭ·ā'nŭs ăf'rĭ·kā'nŭs nū'măn·tī'nŭs), Pub'li·us (pŭb'lĭ·ŭs) Cornelius, 185–129 B.C. *Scipio the Younger.* Rom. gen.

Scip'i·o Af·ri·ca'nus (ăf'rĭ·kā'nŭs), Pub'li·us (pŭb'lĭ·ŭs) Cornelius, 237–183 B.C. *Scipio the Elder.* Rom. gen.

Scol'lard (skŏl'ẽrd), Clinton, 1860–1932. Am. poet.

Scopes (skōps), John Thomas, 1901– . Am. teacher.

Scott (skŏt), Dred (drĕd), 1795?–1858. Central figure in U. S. lawsuit.

—, Sir George Gilbert, 1811–1878. Eng. architect.

—, Robert Fal'con (fôl'kŭn; fô'-), 1868–1912. Eng. antarctic explorer.

—, Sir Walter, 1771–1832. Scot. poet & nov.

—, Win'field (wĭn'fēld), 1786–1866. Am. gen.

Sco'tus, Duns. See DUNS SCOTUS.

—, Johannes. See ERIGENA.

Scria'bin *or* Scria'bine (skryà'byĭn), A·le·xan'der (*Russ.* ŭ·lyĭ·ksàn'dẽr), 1872–1915. Russ. composer.

Scribe (skrēb), Au'gus'tin' (ō'güs'tăN') Eu'gène' (û'zhân'; ü'-), 1791–1861. Fr. dram.

Scud'der (skŭd'ẽr), Horace Elisha, 1838–1902. Am. author.

Scu·dé'ry, de (dĕ skü'dā'rē'), Mag'de·leine' (mȧg'dĕ·lĕn'), 1607–1701. *Sal'pho'* (sȧ'fō'). Fr. poet, nov., & lady of fashion.

Sea'borg (sē'bôrg), Glenn Theodore, 1912– . Am. chem.

Sedg'wick (sĕj'wĭk), Anne Douglas, 1873–1935. Am. writer.

See (sē), Thomas Jefferson Jackson, 1866– . Am. astron. & math.

Seeckt, von (fôn zäkt'), Hans, 1866–1936. Ger. army officer.

See'ger (sē'gẽr), Alan, 1888–1916. Am. poet.

Se·ja'nus (sē·jā'nŭs), Lucius Ae'li·us (ē'lĭ·ŭs), d. 31 A.D. Rom. polit. & conspirator.

Sel'den (sĕl'dĕn), George Baldwin, 1846–1922. Am. lawyer & inventor.

—, John, 1584–1654. Eng. jurist & antiquary.

Se·leu'cus I (sē·lū'kŭs), 358?–280 B.C. Ruler (306–280) of the Seleucid empire.

Sel'in·court, de (?dĕ sĕl'ĭn·kôrt; -kôrt), Hugh, 1878–1951. Eng. nov. & dram.

Sel'kirk (sĕl'kûrk), Alexander, 1676–1721. Scot. sailor; sole inhabitant of Juan Fernández islet (1704–09).

Sem'brich (zĕm'brĭk; *Angl.* sĕm'brĭk), Mar·cel'la (mär·tsĕl'ä; *Angl.* -sĕl'à), 1858–1935. *Prae·xe'de* (prā·ksā'dĕ) *Mar'cel·li'ne* (mär'tsĕ·lē'nĕ) *Ko·chan'ska* (kō·kän'y'skä). Austrian-born soprano.

Se·më'nov (syĭ·myô'nŭf), Gri·go'ri (gryĭ·gô'ryĭ), 1890?–1946. Russ. Cossack gen. & anti-Bolshevist.

Semmes (sĕmz), Raphael, 1809–1877. Am. Confed. admiral.

Sen'e·ca (sĕn'ĕ·kà), Lucius An·nae'us (ă·nē'ŭs), 4 B.C.?–65 A.D. Rom. statesman & philos.

Sen·nach'er·ib (sĕ·năk'ẽr·ĭb), d. 681 B.C. King of Assyria (705–681).

Se·quoy'a (sē·kwoi'à; -kwô'yà), 1770?–1843. Cherokee Indian scholar.

Ser'ra (sĕr'rä), Ju·ni'pe·ro (hōo·nē'pā·rō), 1713–1784. Orig. *Mi·guel'* (mē·gĕl') *Jo·sé'* (hō·sā'). Span. missionary in Mexico and California.

Ser·ra'no Su·ñer' (sĕr·rä'nō sōo·nyĕr'), Ra·món' (rä·mōn'), 1901– . *Bro.-in-law of Franco.* Span. lawyer & polit. & statesman.

Ser·to'ri·us (sûr·tō'rĭ·ŭs), Quin'tus (kwĭn'tŭs), d. 72 B.C. Rom. gen. & statesman.

Ser·ve'tus (sûr·vē'tŭs), Michael, 1511–1553. Span. theol. & martyr.

Ser'vice (sûr'vĭs), Robert William, 1874–1958. Canadian writer.

Se'ton (sē't'n), Ernest Thompson, 1860–1946. Orig. surname *Thomp'son* (tŏm[p]'s'n). Eng.-born writer & illustrator in Am.

Seu'rat' (sû'rä'), Georges (zhôrzh), 1859–1891. Fr. painter.

Se·ve'rus (sē·vē'rŭs), Lucius Sep·tim'i·us (sĕp·tĭm'ĭ·ŭs), 146–211. Rom. emp. (193–211).

Sé·vi·gné', de (dĕ sā'vē'nyā'), Mar'quise' (mär'kēz'), 1626–1696. Nee *Marie de Ra'bu'tin'-Chan'tal'* (dĕ rä'bü'tăN'shäN'täl'). Fr. writer & lady of fashion.

Sew'ard (sū'ẽrd), William Henry, 1801–1872. Am. statesman; secy. of state (1861–69).

Sey'mour (sē'mōr; -môr; -mẽr), Jane, 1509?–1537. *3d wife of Henry VIII of Eng. & mother of Edward VI.*

Seyss'-In'quart, von (fôn zīs'ĭng'kvärt), Ar'tur (är'tŏor), 1892–1946. Ger. Nazi polit.

Sfor'za (sfôr'tsä), Count Car'lo (kär'lō), 1873–1952. Ital. anti-Fascist statesman.

Shack'le·ton (shăk'l'tŭn; -t'n), Sir Ernest Henry, 1874–1922. Brit. antarctic explorer.

Shad'well (shăd'wĕl; -wĕl), Thomas, 1642?–1692. Eng. dram.; poet laureate (1689–92).

Shaf'ter (shăf'tẽr), William Rufus, 1835–1906. Am. gen.

Shaftes'bur·y (shăfts'bĕr·ĭ; -brĭ), 1st Earl of, 1621–1683. *Anthony Ashley Coo'per* (kōo'pẽr; kōop'ẽr). Eng. statesman.

Shah Ja·han' (shä' jȧ·hän'), 1592–1666. Mogul emp. of Hindustan (1628–58).

Shairp (shârp; shärp), John Campbell, 1819–1885. Scot. educ. & author.

Shake'speare *or* Shak'spere (shāk'spēr), William, 1564–1616. Eng. dram. & poet.

Sha'posh·ni·kov (shà'pŭsh·nyĭ·kŭf), Boris Mi·khai'lo·vich (myĭ·kī'lŭ·vyĭch), 1882–1945. Russ. field marshal.

Sharp (shärp), William, 1856?–1905. Pseud. *Fi·o'na* (fĭ·ō'nà; fĭ-) *Mac·leod'* (măk·loud'). Scot. author.

Shaw (shô), George Bernard, 1856–1950. Brit. author & socialist.

—, Thomas Edward. See T. E. LAWRENCE.

Shays (shāz), Daniel, 1747?–1825. Am. Revolutionist & rebel.

Shel'by (shĕl'bĭ), Joseph Or'ville (ôr'vĭl), 1830–1897. Am. Confed. gen.

Shel'don (shĕl'dŭn), Charles Monroe, 1857–1946. Am. clergyman & author.

Shel'ley (shĕl'ĭ), Mary Woll'stone·craft (wŏol'stŭn·krȧft), 1797–1851. Nee *God'win* (gŏd'wĭn); *wife of P. B.* Eng. nov.

—, Percy Bysshe (bĭsh), 1792–1822. Eng. poet.

Shen'stone (shĕn'stŭn; -stōn), William, 1714–1763. Eng. poet.

Sher'a·ton (shĕr'à·t'n; -tŭn), Thomas, 1751–1806. Eng. furniture maker & designer.

Sher'i·dan (shĕr'ĭ·d'n), Philip Henry, 1831–1888. Am. gen.

—, Richard Brins'ley (brĭnz'lĭ), 1751–1816. Irish dram. & orator.

Sher'riff (shĕr'ĭf), Robert Cedric, 1896– . Eng. writer.

Sher'man (shûr'mǎn), John, 1823–1900. *Bro. of W. T.* Am. statesman.

—, Roger, 1721–1793. Am. jurist & statesman.

—, Stuart Pratt, 1881–1926. Am. critic.

—, William Te·cum'seh (tĕ·kŭm'sĕ; -sĕ), 1820–1891. Am. gen.

Sher'ring·ton (shĕr'ĭng·tŭn), Sir Charles Scott, 1861–1952. Eng. physiol.

Sher'wood (shûr'wŏod), Robert Emmet, 1896–1955. Am. dram.

Shi·de·ha·ra (shē·dĕ·hä·rä), Baron Ki·ju·ro (kē·jŏo·rō), 1872–1951. Jap. diplomat & statesman.

Shi·ge·mi·tsu (shē·gĕ·mē·tsōō), Ma·mo·ru (mä·mō·rōō), 1887–1957. Jap. diplomat.

Shih Huang Ti (shĭr′ hwäng′ tē′), 259–210 B.C. Chin. emp.

Shi·ma·da (shē·mä·dä), Shi·ge·ta·ro (shē·gĕ·tä·rō), 1883– . Jap. admiral.

Shin′well (shĭn′wĕl; -wĕl), Emanuel, 1884– . Brit. laborite polit.

Shir′ley (shûr′lĭ), James, 1596–1666. Eng. dram.

Short (shôrt), Walter Campbell, 1880–1949. Am. gen.

Sho′sta·ko′vich (shŏs′tȧ·kô′vĭch; *Russ.* shŭ·stŭ·kô′vyĭch), Di·mi′tri (dĭ′·mē′trĭ; *Russ.* dyĭ′·myē′tryĭ) Di·mi′tri·e·vich (dyĭ′·myē′tryĭ·yĕ·vyĭch), 1906– . Russ. composer.

Shute (shōōt). Nev′il (nĕv′′l; -ĭl), 1899– . *Nevil Shute Nor′way* (nôr′wā). Eng. aeronautical engineer & writer.

Shver′nik (shvĕr′nĭk), Ni·ko·lai′ (nyĭ·kŭ·lī′), Mi·khai′lo·vich (myĭ·kī′lȧ·vyĭch), 1888– . Russ. polit.

Si·be′li·us (sĭ·bā′lĭ·ŏŏs; *Angl.* -ŭs), Jean (zhän; *Angl.* jēn), 1865–1957. Finnish composer.

Sick′les (sĭk′′lz), Daniel Edgar, 1825–1914. Am. gen. & polit.

Sid′dons (sĭd′′nz), Sarah, 1755–1831. Nee *Kem′ble* (kĕm′b′l). Eng. actress.

Sid′ney (sĭd′nĭ), Sir Philip, 1554–1586. Eng. poet, statesman, & soldier.

Sieg′bahn (sēg′bän), Karl (kärl) Man′ne′ (män′nĕ′) Ge′org (yā′ôr·y′), 1886– . Swed. physicist.

Sie′mens (sē′mĕnz; *Ger.* zē′mĕns), Sir William, 1823–1883. Brit. (Ger.-born) inventor.

Sien·kie′wicz (shĕn·kyĕ′vĕch), Hen′ryk (hĕn′rĭk), 1846–1916. Pol. nov.

Sie′vers (zē′fērs; -vērs), E′du·ard (ā′dōō·ärt), 1850–1932. Ger. philologist.

Sie′yès′ (syā′yäs′), Em′ma′nu·el′ (ē′mà′nü·ĕl′) Jo′seph′ (zhō′zĕf′), 1748–1836. Ab′bé′ (à′bā′) *Sieyès.* Fr. Revolutionist.

Sig′is·mund (sĭj′ĭs·mŭnd; sĭg′-; *Ger.* zē′gĭs·mŏŏnt), 1368–1437. Holy Rom. emp. (1411–37).

Sigs′bee (sĭgz′bē), Charles Dwight, 1845–1923. Am. admiral.

Si′gurds·son (sĭ′gûrths·sŏn), Jón (yōn), 1811–1879. Icelandic statesman & author.

Si·kor′sky (sĭ·kôr′skĭ; *Russ.* syĭ·kôr′skĭ), I′gor (ē′gôr·y′) Ivan, 1889– . Am. (Russ.-born) aeronautical engineer.

Sil′lan·pää′ (sĭl′län·pä′), Frans (fräns) Ee′mil (â′mĭl), 1888– . Finnish nov.

Sim′e·on Sty·li′tes (sĭm′ē·ŭn stī·lī′tēz; stĭ′-), Saint, 390?–459. Syrian ascetic & stylite.

Si′mon (sī′mŭn), John Allse′brook (?ôls′brŏŏk), 1st Viscount, 1873–1954. Brit. jurist & statesman.

Si·mon′i·des of Ce′os (sĭ·mŏn′ĭ·dēz, sē′ŏs), 6th–5th cent. B.C. Greek poet.

Simp′son (sĭm[p]′sn), William Hood, 1888– . Am. gen.

Sims (sĭmz), William Sow′den (sou′d′n), 1858–1936. Am. admiral.

Sin′clair (sĭng′klâr; sĭn′-; sĭn·klâr′), May, 1865?–1946. Eng. nov.

Sin·clair′ (sĭn·klâr′), Upton Beall (bĕl), 1878– . Am. writer & polit.

Sing′er (sĭng′ēr), Isaac Mer′rit (mĕr′ĭt), 1811–1875. Am. inventor.

Si·quei′ros (sē·kĕ′ē·rōs), David Al·fa′ro (äl·fä′rō), 1898– . Mex. muralist.

Si·raj′-ud-dau′la (sĭ·räj′ŏŏd·dou′lä) *or* **Su·ra′jah Dow′lah** (sŭ·rä′jà dou′lä), 1728?–1757. Nawab of Bengal (1756–57).

Sis′mon′di′, de (dē sĕs·môN′dē′; *Angl.* sĭs·mŏn′dĭ), Jean Charles Lé′o′nard′ (lā′ô′när′) Si′monde′ (sē′mônd′), 1773–1842. Swiss hist. & econ.

Sit′ter, de (dĕ sĭt′ēr), Wil′lem (vĭl′ĕm), 1872–1934. Du. astron.

Sit′ting Bull (sĭt′ĭng bŏŏl), 1834?–1890. Sioux Indian chief.

Sit′well (sĭt′wĕl; -wĕl), Sir George Reres′by (rĕrz′bĭ), 1860–1943, and his 3 children, Edith, 1887– , Sir Os′bert (ŏz′bērt), 1892– , and Sa·chev′er·ell (sȧ·shĕv′ēr·ĕl), 1897– . Eng. authors.

Skeat (skēt), Walter William, 1835–1912. Eng. philologist.

Skel′ton (skĕl′t′n; -tȧn), John, 1460?–1529. Eng. poet.

Skin′ner (skĭn′ēr), Cornelia Otis, 1901– . *Dau. of Otis.* Am. actress.

—, O′tis (ō′tĭs), 1858–1942. Am. actor.

Sko′da, von (fôn skō′dä), E′mil (ē′mĭl), 1839–1900. Czech engineer & industrialist.

Sla′ter (slā′tēr), Samuel, 1768–1835. Eng.-born industrialist in Am.

Sli′dell (slī′d′l; *popularly* slī·dĕl′), John, 1793–1871. Am. Confed. diplomat.

Sloan (slōn), John, 1871–1951. Am. painter, etcher, & illustrator.

Slo′cum (slō′kŭm), Henry Warner, 1827–1894. Am. gen.

Sme′ta·na (smĕ′tȧ·nà), Be′dřich (bĕ′dēr·zhĭk), 1824–1884. Czech pianist, conductor, & composer.

Smig′ly-Rydz′ (smēg′lĭ·rĭts′), Ed′ward (ĕd′värt), 1886– . Pol. gen.

Smiles (smīlz), Samuel, 1812–1904. Scot. writer.

Smith (smĭth), Adam, 1723–1790. Scot. econ.

—, Alfred Emanuel, 1873–1944. Am. polit.

—, Edmund Kirby. See KIRBY-SMITH.

—, Francis Hopkinson, 1838–1915. Am. author, painter, & engineer.

—, Gold′win (gōld′wĭn), 1823–1910. Brit. hist.

—, John, 1580–1631. Eng. colonist in Am.

—, Joseph, 1805–1844. Am. founder of Mormon Church.

—, Sydney, 1771–1845. Eng. clergyman & essayist

—, Walter Be·dell′ (bē·dĕl′), 1895– . Am. gen. & diplomat.

—, William, 1769–1839. Eng. geologist.

—, Win′chell (wĭn′chĕl), 1871–1933. Am. dram.

Smith′-Dor′ri·en (smĭth′dŏr′ĭ·ĕn), Sir Horace Lock′wood (lŏk′wŏŏd), 1858–1930. Brit. gen.

Smith′son (smĭth′s′n), James, 1765–1829. Brit. chem. & mineralogist.

Smol′lett (smŏl′ĕt; -ĭt), Tobias George, 1721–1771. Brit. author.

Smuts (smŭts; *S. Afr. Du.* smŭts), Jan (yän) Chris′ti·aan (krĭs′tē·än), 1870–1950. S. African field marshal; prime min. (1919–24; 1939–48).

Smyth (smĭth), Henry De Wolf (dē wŏŏlf′), 1898– . Am. physicist.

Snor′ri Stur′lu·son (snôr′rĭ stûr′lŭ·sŏn), 1178–1241. Icelandic statesman & hist.

Snow′den (snō′d′n), Philip, 1864–1937. 1st Viscount *Snowden of Ick′orn·shaw* (ĭk′ôrn·shô). Eng. econ. & polit.

Sny′der (snī′dēr), John Wesley, 1895– . Am. banker & administrator.

So·bies′ki, John. See JOHN III SOBIESKI.

So·ci′nus (sō·sī′nŭs), Faus′tus (fôs′tŭs), 1539–1604. *Fau′sto* (fou′stō) *Soz·zi′ni* (sŏt·tsē′nē). Ital. religious reformer.

Soc′ra·tes (sŏk′rȧ·tēz), 470?–399 B.C. Greek philos.

Sod′dy (sŏd′ĭ), Frederick, 1877–1956. Eng. chem.

Sö′der·blom′ (sû′dēr·blōōm′), Nathan, 1866–1931. Swed. theol.

So′do·ma, Il (ēl sō′dō·mä), 1477?–1549. *Gio·van′ni* (jō·vän′nē) *An·to′nio* (än·tō′nyō) *de′ Baz′zi* (dā bät′tsē). Ital. painter.

So·kol′ni·kov (sŭ·kôl′y·nyĭ·kŭf; *Russ.* sô·kôl′nĭ·kôf), Gri·go′ri (gryĭ·gô′ryĭ) Ya′kov·le·vich (yä′kŭv·lyĕ·vyĭch), 1888– . Russ. polit.

So·ko·lov′sky (sŭ·kŭ·lôf′skĭ), Va·si′li (vŭ·syē′lyĭ) Da·ni′lo·vich (dȧ·nyĭ′lȧ·vyĭch). Russ. marshal (ab. 1944).

So′lon (sō′lŏn; -lŭn), 638?–?559 B.C. Athenian lawgiver.

Sol′y·man. See SULEIMAN.

Som′er·vell (sŭm′ēr·vĕl; -vĕl), Bre′hon (brē′ŭn) Burke, 1892–1955. Am. gen.

Som′er·ville (sŭm′ēr·vĭl), Sir James Fownes (founz), 1882–1949. Brit. admiral of the fleet.

Soong (sōōng), Ai-ling (ī′lĭng′), 1888– . *Wife of H. H. Kung* (q.v.).

—, Ch′ing-ling (chĭng′lĭng′), 1890– . *Wife of Sun Yat-Sen* (q.v.).

—, Mei-ling (mā′lĭng′), 1898– . *Wife of Chiang Kai-shek* (q.v.).

—, Tse-ven *or* Tsŭ-wên (tsōō′wŭn′), 1891– . *T. V. Soong; bro. of the 3 prec.* Chin. financier & statesman.

Soph′o·cles (sŏf′ō·klēz), 496?–406 B.C. Greek dram.

Sor·del′lo (sŏr·dĕl′lō; *Angl.* sôr·dĕl′ō), 13th cent. Ital. troubadour.

So·rol′la y Bas·ti′da (sō·rō′lyä ē väs·tē′thä), Joa·quín′ (wä·kēn′), 1863–1923. Span. painter.

Soth′ern (sŭth′ērn), Edward Hugh, 1859–1933. Am. actor.

So′to, Hernando de. See DE SOTO.

Soult (sōōlt), Ni′co·las′ (nē′kô′lä′) Jean de Dieu (dĕ dyû′), 1769–1851. Duc (dük) *de Dal′ma′tie′* (dàl′mà′sē′). Fr. soldier; marshal of France (1804).

Sou′sa (sōō′sȧ; *popularly* -zȧ), John Philip, 1854–1932. *The March King.* Am. bandmaster & composer.

South (south), Robert, 1634–1716. Eng. clergyman & author.

Sou′they (sou′thĭ; sŭth′ĭ), Robert, 1774–1843. Eng. author; poet laureate (1813–43).

Soz·zi′ni, Fausto. See SOCINUS.

Spaak (späk), Paul Hen′ri′ (än′rē′), 1899– . Belg. lawyer & polit.; premier (1938–39; 1947–49).

Spaatz (späts), Carl, 1891– . Orig. *Spatz.* Am. gen.

Spal′ding (spôl′dĭng), Albert, 1888–1953. Am. violinist.

Sparks (spärks), Jar′ed (jär′ĕd; -ĭd), 1789–1866. Am. hist.

Spar′ta·cus (spär′tȧ·kŭs), d. 71 B.C. Rom. slave & insurrectionist.

Spee, von (fôn shpā′), Count Ma′xi·mi′li·an (mäk′sē·mē′lē·än), 1861–1914. Ger. admiral.

Spell′man (spĕl′mȧn), Francis Joseph, 1889– . Am. cardinal.

Spe′mann (shpā′män), Hans, 1869–1941. Ger. zool.

Spen′cer (spĕn′sēr), Herbert, 1820–1903. Eng. philos.

—, Stephen, 1909– . Eng. poet & critic.

Speng′ler (shpĕng′lēr), Os′wald (ôs′vält), 1880–1936. Ger. philos.

Spen′ser (spĕn′sēr), Edmund, 1552?–1599. Eng. poet; poet laureate (1591–99).

Sper′ry (spĕr′ĭ), Elmer Ambrose, 1860–1930. Am. inventor.

Spin′garn (spĭn′gärn), Joel Elias, 1875–1939. Am. author.

Spi·no′za (spĭ·nō′zä), Ba′ruch (bä′rōōk) *or* Be′ne·dict (bĕ′nē·dĭkt), 1632–1677. Du. philos.

Spit′te·ler (shpĭt′ē·lēr), Carl, 1845–1924. Pseud. *Fe′lix* (fā′lĭks) *Tan′den* (tän′dĕn). Swiss writer.

Spode (spōd), Josiah, 1754–1827. Eng. potter.

Spru′ance (sprōō′ăns), Raymond Ames, 1886– . Am. admiral.

Spur′geon (spûr′jŭn), Charles Had′don (hăd′′n), 1834–1892. Eng. Baptist preacher.

Spy′ri (shpē′rē), Jo·han′na (yō·hän′ä), 1827–1901. Nee *Heus′ser* (hoi′sēr). Swiss author.

Staël, de (dĕ stäl′), Mme. Anne (än; àn) Lou·ise′ (lwēz) Ger′maine′ (zhĕr′mân′), 1766–1817. Ba′ronne′ (bà′rôn′) *de Staël-Hols′tein′* (-ôls′tēn′); nee *Nec′ker* (nĕ′kâr′; *Angl.* nĕk′ēr). Fr. writer.

Ståhl′berg′ (stôl′bĕr′y), Kaar′lo (kär′lō) Ju′ho (yōō′hō), 1865–1952. Finnish statesman.

Stair, Viscount and Earl of. See under DALRYMPLE.

Sta′lin (stä′lyĭn; *Angl.* stä′lĭn, stäl′ĭn, -[l]ēn), Joseph, 1879–1953. *I·o′sif* (ē′ō·sēf; yô′syĭf) Vis·sa·ri·o′no·vich (vyĭs·sȧ·ryĭ·ô′nŭ·vyĭch) *Dzhu′ga·shvi′li* (jōō′gȧ·shvē′lĭ). Russ. polit. & dictator.

Stam′bo·lov′ (stäm′bô·lôf′), Ste′fan (stĕ′fän), 1855–1895. Bulgarian statesman.

Stan′dish (stăn′dĭsh), Myles *or* Miles, 1584?–1656. Eng. colonist in Am.

Stand′ley (stănd′lĭ), William Harrison, 1872– . Am. admiral & diplomat.

Stan′is·las I Lesz·czyń′ski (stăn′ĭs·lǎs [-läs] lĕsh·chĭn′y′·skē), 1677–1766. King of Poland (1704–09, 1733–35).

Stan′ley (stăn′lĭ), Arthur Pen′rhyn (pĕn′rĭn; pĕn·rĭn′), 1815–1881. Eng. prelate & author.

—, Sir Henry Morton, 1841–1904. Orig. *John Row′lands* (rō′lăndz). Brit. explorer in Africa.

—, Wendell Meredith, 1904– . Am. biochem.

Stan′ton (stăn′t′n), Edwin Mc·Mas′ters (mǔk·măs′tērz), 1814–1869. Am. jurist & polit.

—, Elizabeth, 1815–1902. Nee *Ca′dy* (kā′dĭ). Am. suffragist.

Sta·ra′ce (stä·rä′chä), A·chil′le (ä·kēl′lä), 1889–1945. Ital. Fascist soldier.

Star′hem·berg, von (fôn shtä′rĕm·bĕrк), Prince Ernst (ĕrnst) Rü′di·ger (rü′dĭ·gēr), 1899– . Austrian anti-Nazi statesman)

Stark (stärk), Harold Rayns'ford (rānz'fērd), 1880–1957. Am. admiral.

— (shtärk), Jo·han'nes (yō·hän'ĕs; -ĕs), 1874–1957. Ger. physicist.

— (stärk), John, 1728–1822. Am. Revolutionary gen.

Star·zyn'ski (stär·zĭn'y'skĕ), Ste'fan (stĕ'fän), 1893–?1940. Pol. polit. & hero.

Stas'sen (stäs'n), Harold Edward, 1907– . Am. lawyer & polit.

Sta'ti·us (stā'shĭ·ŭs; -shŭs), Pub'li·us (pŭb'lĭ·ŭs) Pa·pin'i·us (pȧ·pĭn'ĭ·ŭs), 45?–?96. Rom. poet.

Steed (stēd), Henry Wick'ham (wĭk'ăm), 1871–1956. Eng. journalist.

Steele (stēl), Sir Richard, 1672–1729. Brit. essayist & dram.

Steen (stān), Jan (yän), 1626–1679. Du. painter.

Ste'fans·son (stĕ'făns·sŏn; *Angl.* stĕf'n·s'n), Vil'hjal'mur (vĭl'hyoul'mĕr), 1879– . Canadian arctic explorer.

Stef'fens (stĕf'ĕnz), (Joseph) Lincoln, 1866–1936. Am. journalist & editor.

Stein (stīn), Gertrude, 1874–1946. Am. writer.

Stein, vom und zum (fôm ŏŏnt tsŏŏm [tsōōm] shtīn'), Baron Hein'rich (hīn'rĭk) Frie'drich (frē'drĭk) Karl, 1757–1831. Prussian statesman.

Stein'beck (stīn'bĕk), John Ernst (ûrnst), 1902– . Am. nov.

Stein'hardt (stīn'härt), Laurence Adolph, 1892–1950. Am. lawyer & diplomat.

Stein'metz (stīn'mĕts; *Ger.* shtīn'-), Charles Pro'teus (prō'tūs; -tē·ŭs), 1865–1923. Am. (Ger.-born) electrical engineer.

Sten'dhal' (stän'däl'), 1783–1842. Pseud. of *Ma'rie'* (mȧ'rē') *Hen'ri'* (äⁿ'rē') *Beyle* (bāl). Fr. writer.

Ste'phen (stē'vĕn), 1097?–1154. *Stephen of Blois* (blwä). King of England (1135–54).

—, Sir Leslie, 1832–1904. Eng. philos., critic, & biographer.

Ste'phens (stē'vĕnz), Alexander Hamilton, 1812–1883. Am. polit.; vice-pres. of the Confed. States.

—, James, 1882–1950. Irish poet & nov.

Ste'phen·son (stē'vĕn·s'n), George, 1781–1848. Eng. inventor & founder of railroads.

—, Robert, 1803–1859. *Son of George.* Eng. engineer.

Stern (stûrn), Otto (ôt'ō; *Angl.* ôt'ō), 1888– . Am. physicist.

Stern'berg (stûrn'bûrg), George Miller, 1838–1915. Am. physician & bacteriol.

Sterne (stûrn), Laurence, 1713–1768. Brit. nov.

Stet·tin'i·us (stĕ·tĭn'ĭ·ŭs; -tĭn'yŭs), Edward Rielley, 1900–1949. Am. financier & statesman.

Steu'ben, von (fôn stū'bĕn; *Ger.* shtoi'bĕn), Baron Frie'drich (frē'drĭk) Wil'helm (vĭl'hĕlm) Lu'dolf (lōō'dôlf) Ger'hard (gär'härt) Au'gu·stin' (ou'gŏŏs·tēn'), 1730–1794. Prussian-born gen. in Am.

Ste'vens (stē'vĕnz), John, 1749–1838. Am. inventor.

—, Thad'de·us (thăd'ē·ŭs; thă·dē'ŭs), 1792–1868. Am. lawyer & legislator.

Ste'ven·son (stē'vĕn·s'n), Ad'lai (ăd'lā; -lĭ) Ew'ing (ū'ĭng), 1900– . Am. lawyer & polit.

—, Robert Louis Balfour, 1850–1894. *R. L. S.* Scot. author.

Stew'art (stū'ĕrt), Du'gald (dōō'gŭld; dū'-), 1753–1828. Scot. philos.

—, Robert, 1769–1822. Viscount *Cas'tle·reagh* (kăs''l·rā). Eng. statesman.

Steyn (stān), Mar·ti'nus (mär·tē'nŭs) Theu'nis (tû'nĭs), 1857–1916. S. African lawyer & statesman.

Stieg'litz (stēg'lĭts), Alfred, 1864–1946. Am. photographer & editor.

Stil'i·cho (stĭl'ĭ·kō), Fla'vi·us (flā'vĭ·ŭs), 359?–408. Rom. gen. & statesman.

Still (stĭl), Andrew Taylor, 1828–1917. Am. physician; founder of osteopathy.

Stil'well (stĭl'wĕl; -wĕl), Joseph Warren, 1883–1946. Am. gen.

Stim'son (stĭm's'n), Henry Lewis, 1867–1950. Am. statesman.

Stin'nes (stĭn'ĕs), Hu'go (hōō'gō), 1870–1924. Ger. industrialist.

Stock'mar, von (*Ger.* fôn shtôk'mär; *Angl.* stôk'-), Baron Christian Frie'drich (frē'drĭk), 1787–1863. Anglo-Belg. statesman.

Stock'ton (stôk'tŭn), Francis Richard, 1834–1902. *Frank R.* Am. writer.

Stod'dard (stŏd'ĕrd), Lo'throp (lō'thrŭp), 1883–1950. Am. writer.

—, Richard Henry, 1825–1903. Am. poet & critic.

Stokes (stōks), Sir Frederick Wilfrid Scott, 1860–1927. Eng. engineer & inventor.

Sto·kow'ski (stō·kôf'skĕ; *Pol.* stô-), Le'o·pold (lē'ō·pōld) An·to'ni (än·tō'nyĭ) Sta·ni'slaw (stä·nē'släf), 1887– . Eng.-born conductor in Am.

Stone (stōn), Har'lan (här'lăn) Fiske, 1872–1946. Am. jurist.

—, Lucy, 1818–1893. Mrs. *Henry Brown Black'well* (blăk'wĕl; -wĕl). Am. suffragist.

Storm (shtôrm), The'o·dor (tā'ô·dôr), 1817–1888. Ger. writer.

Sto'ry (stō'rĭ), Joseph, 1779–1845. Am. jurist.

—, William Wet'more (wĕt'mōr), 1819–1895. *Son of Joseph.* Am. sculptor & writer.

Stow (stō), John, 1525?–1605. Eng. hist. & antiquary.

Stowe (stō), Harriet Elizabeth, 1811–1896. Nee *Bee'cher* (bē'chēr). Am. author.

Stra'bo (strā'bō), 63 b.c.?–?24 a.d. Greek geographer.

Stra'chey (strā'chĭ), Evelyn John St. Loe (sȧnt lō'), 1901– . Eng. socialist writer.

—, (Giles) Lytton, 1880–1932. Eng. biographer.

—, John St. Loe, 1860–1927. *Father of Evelyn.* Eng. journalist.

Stra·di·va'ri (strä·dē·vä'rē), An·to'nio (än·tō'nyō), 1644–1737. *An·to'ni·us* (än·tō'nĭ·ŭs; -tōn'yŭs) *Strad'i·var'i·us* (străd'ĭ·vâr'ĭ·ŭs). Ital. violinmaker.

Straf'ford (străf'ĕrd), 1st Earl of, 1593–1641. Sir *Thomas Went'worth* (wĕnt'wûrth; -wẽrth). Eng. statesman.

Strat'e·mey'er (străt'ē·mī'ẽr), George E., 1890– . Am. gen.

Strat'ford de Red'cliffe, Viscount. See CANNING.

Strath·co'na and Mount Roy'al (străth·kō'nȧ, mount roi'ăl), Baron, 1820–1914. *Donald Alexander Smith* (smĭth). Canadian (Scot.-born) railroad builder & administrator.

Straus (shtrous; *Angl.* strous), Os'kar (ôs'kär; *Angl.* ŏs'kẽr), 1870–1954. Fr. (Austrian-born) composer.

Strauss (shtrous; *Angl.* strous), Da'vid (dä'vĕt; -vĭt; -fĕt; -fĭt) Frie'drich (frē'drĭk), 1808–1874. Ger. theol. & philos.

—, Jo·hann' (yō·hän'), father, 1804–1849, and son, 1825–1899. Austrian composers.

—, Ri'chard (rĭk'ärt; *Angl.* rĭch'ẽrd), 1864–1949. Ger. composer.

Stra·vin'sky (*Angl.* strȧ·vĭn'skĭ; *Russ.* strŭ·vyēn'skĭ), I'gor (ē'gôr·y') Fē'do·ro'vich (fyô'dŭ·rô'vyĭch), 1882– . Am. (Russ.-born) composer.

Strei'cher (shtrī'kẽr), Ju'li·us (yōō'lē·ŏŏs), 1885–1946. Ger. Nazi administrator.

Stre'se·mann (shtrā'zĕ·män), Gu'stav (gŏŏs'täf), 1878–1929. Ger. statesman.

Strind'berg (strĭn'bĕr'y; *Angl.* strĭn[d]'bûrg), Au'gust (ou'gŭst; *Angl.* ô'gŭst), 1849–1912. Swed. dram. & nov.

Stritch (strĭch), Samuel Alphonsus, 1887–1958. Am. cardinal.

Strong (strŏng), George Vea'zey (vē'zĭ), 1880–1946. Am. gen.

Stru'en·see', **von** (fôn shtrŏŏ'ĕn·zā'), Count Jo·hann' (yō·hän'; yō'hän) Frie'drich (frē'drĭk), 1737–1772. Ger.-Dan. statesman & philos.

Struth'er (strŭth'ẽr), Jan (jän), 1901–1953. Pseud. of *Joyce Max'tone Gra'ham* (măks'tŭn grā'ăm; grâ'ăm); nee *An'struth'er* (ăn'·strŭth'ẽr). Eng. writer.

Strutt (strŭt), Joseph, 1749–1802. Eng. antiquary.

Stu'art (stū'ẽrt). See CHARLES I and MARY STUART.

—, Charles. *The Young Pretender.* See under CHARLES.

—, Gilbert Charles, 1755–1828. Am. painter.

—, James Ew'ell (ū'ĕl) Brown, 1833–1864. *Jeb* (jĕb). Am. Confed. gen.

—, James Francis Edward, 1688–1766. *The Old Pretender.* Eng. prince.

Stubbs (stŭbz), William, 1825–1901. Eng. hist. & prelate.

Stülp'na'gel, von (fôn shtülp'nä'gĕl), Ot'to (ôt'ō), 1880–1948. Ger. gen.

Stur'dee (stûr'dē), Sir Frederick Charles Dove'ton (?dŭv'tŭn), 1859–1925. Brit. admiral.

Stur'gis (stûr'jĭs), Russell, 1836–1909. Am. architect & writer.

Stur'lu·son. See SNORRI STURLUSON.

Štur'sa (shtŏŏr'sȧ), Jan (yän), 1880–1925. Czech sculptor.

Stuy've·sant (stī'vĕ·s'nt; *Du.* stoi'vĕ·sänt), Peter, 1592–1672. Du. administrator in Am.

Su'chet' (sü'shĕ'), Louis Ga'bri·el' (gȧ'brē'ĕl'), 1772–1826. Fr. gen.; marshal of France (1811).

Suck'ling (sŭk'lĭng), Sir John, 1609–1642. Eng. Cavalier poet.

Su'cre, de (sōō'krĕ), An·to'nio (än·tō'nyō) Jo·sé' (hō·sā'), 1795–1830. S. Am. liberator & gen.

Su'der·mann (zōō'dĕr·män), Her'mann (hĕr'män), 1857–1928. Ger. dram. & nov.

Sue (sü; *Angl.* sōō), Eu'gène' (û'zhân'; ü'zhân'), 1804–1857. *Ma'rie'* (mȧ'rē') *Jo'seph'* (zhō'zĕf'). Fr. nov.

Sue·to'ni·us (swē·tō'nĭ·ŭs), 2d cent. a.d. *Ga'ius* (gā'yŭs; gī'ŭs) *Suetonius Tran·quil'lus* (trăng·kwĭl'ŭs). Rom. biographer & hist.

Su·gi·ya·ma (sōō·gē·yä·mä), Ha·ji·me (hä·jĕ·mĕ), 1880–1945. Jap. field marshal.

Su·lei·man' (sü·lā·män') or **Sol'y·man I** (sŏl'ĭ·măn), 1496?–1566. *The Magnificent.* Ottoman sultan (1520–66).

Sul'la (sŭl'ȧ), 138–78 b.c. *Lucius Cornelius Sulla Fe'lix* (fē'lĭks). Rom. gen. & polit.

Sul'li·van (sŭl'ĭ·văn), Sir Arthur Seymour, 1842–1900. Eng. composer.

—, John, 1740–1795. Am. Revolutionary gen.

—, John Lawrence, 1899– . Am. lawyer & administrator.

Sul'ly (sŭl'ĭ), Thomas, 1783–1872. Eng.-born painter in Am.

Sul'ly', de (dĕ sŭl'ĭ'; *Angl.* sŭl'ĭ), Duc (dük), 1560–1641. *Max'i·mi'lien'* (mȧk'sē'mē'lyäⁿ') *de Bé'thune'* (dĕ bā'tün'). Baron *de Ros'ny'* (dĕ rō'nē'). Fr. statesman.

Sul'ly Pru'dhomme' (sü'lē' prü'dôm'), René Fran'çois' (frän'swä') Armand, 1839–1907. Fr. poet & critic.

Sum'ner (sŭm'nĕr), Charles, 1811–1874. Am. statesman & orator.

—, James Batch'el·ler (băch'ĕ·lẽr), 1887–1955. Am. biochem.

—, William Graham, 1840–1910. Am. sociol. & educ.

Sun'day (sŭn'dĭ), William Ashley, 1862–1935. *Billy.* Am. evangelist.

Sun Yat-sen (sōōn' yät'sĕn'), 1866–1925. *Father of the Revolution.* Chin. statesman.

Su·ra'jah Dow'lah. See SIRAJ-UD-DAULA.

Sur'rey, Earl of. See Henry HOWARD.

Sur'tees (sûr'tēz), Robert Smith, 1805–1864. Eng. nov. & editor.

Suth·er·land (sŭth'ẽr·lănd), Richard K., 1893– . Am. gen.

Sut'ter (sōō'tĕr; sŭt'ĕr), John Augustus, 1803–1880. Mex. (Ger.-born) pioneer in California.

Sutt'ner, von (fôn zōōt'nĕr), Ber'tha (bĕr'tä), 1843–1914. Nee Countess *Kin'sky* (kĭn'skē). Austrian writer & pacificist.

Su·vo'rov (sōō·vô'rŭf), Count A·le·ksan'dr (ȧ·lyĭ·ksän'dĕr) Va·sil'ie·vich (vȧ·syĕl'yĕ·vyĭch), 1729–1800. Russ. field marshal.

Sved'berg (sväd'bär'y'), The (tā) or The'o·dor (tā'ô·dôr), 1884– . Swed. chem.

Sver'drup (svär'drŏŏp), Ot'to (ôt'tō) Neu'mann (nû'ĭ·män), 1855–1930. Norw. arctic explorer.

Sver're (svär'rĕ), 1152?–1202. *Sverre Si'gurds·son* (sĭg'gŏŏrts·sŏn). King of Norway (1184–1202).

Swe'den·borg (svā'dĕn·bôr'y'; *Angl.* swē'd'n·bôrg), E·ma'nu·el (ĕ·mä'nŏŏ·ĕl; *Angl.* ĕ·măn'ū·ĕl), 1688–1772. Orig. *Sved'berg* (sväd'bär'y'). Swed. philos. & religious writer.

Sweet (swēt), Henry, 1845–1912. Eng. phonetician & philologist.

Swift (swĭft), Jonathan, 1667–1745. Eng. (Irish-born) satirist.

Swin'burne (swĭn'bûrn; -bẽrn), Algernon Charles, 1837–1909. Eng. poet.

Swin'ner·ton (swĭn'ẽr·t'n; -tŭn), Frank Arthur, 1884– . Eng. nov. & critic.

Swin'ton (swĭn't'n; -tŭn), 1st Viscount, 1884– . *Philip Cun'liffe-Lis'ter* (kŭn'lĭf-lĭs'tẽr). Eng. statesman.

Sy'fret (sī'frĕt; -frĭt), Sir Edward Neville, 1889– . Brit. admiral.

Sykes (sīks), George, 1822–1896. Am. gen.

Syl'va, Carmen. See ELIZABETH, Queen of Romania.

Sy′ming·ton (sī′mǐng·tŭn), William Stuart, 1901– . Am. industrialist & administrator.

Sym′onds (sǐm′ŭn[d]z), John Ad′ding·ton (ăd′ĭng·tŭn), 1840–1893. Eng. scholar.

Sy′mons (sī′mŭnz), Arthur, 1865–1945. Brit. poet & critic.

Synge (sĭng), John Mil′ling·ton (mĭl′ĭng·tŭn), 1871–1909. Irish poet & dram.

Szent-Györ′gyi von Nagy′ra′polt (sĕnt·dyûr′dyĭ fŏn nŏd′y′·rŏ′pŏlt), Al′bert (ŏl′bĕrt), 1893– . Hung. chem.

Szi′lard (sī′lôrd), Leo, 1898– . Am. (Hung.-born) physicist.

Szold (zōld), Henrietta, 1860–1945. Am. Zionist; founder of Hadassah.

T

Tac′i·tus (tăs′ĭ·tŭs), Cornelius, 55?–after 117. Rom. hist.

Tad′e·ma. See ALMA-TADEMA.

Taft (tăft), Lo·ra′do (lô·rä′dō), 1860–1936. Am. sculptor.
—, Robert Alphonso, 1889–1953. *Son of W. H.* Am. lawyer & polit.
—, William Howard, 1857–1930. 27th pres. of the U. S. (1909–13). Am.

Ta′gore (tä′gŏr; *freq. Angl.* tȧ·gōr′), Sir Ra·bin′dra·nath′ (rȧ·bēn′drȧ·nät′), 1861–1941. Hindu poet.

Taine (tĕn), Hip′po′lyte′ (ē′pô′lēt′) A′dolphe′ (ȧ′dôlf′), 1828–1893. Fr. philos. & critic.

Tal′ley·rand′-Pé′ri′gord′, de (dĕ tȧ′lā′rän′pā′rē′gôr′; *Angl.* tăl′ĭ·rănd-), Charles Maurice, 1754–1838. Prince *de Bé′né′vent′* (dĕ bā′nä′väN′). Fr. statesman.

Ta·ma′yo (tä·mä′yō), Ru·fi′no (rōō·fē′nō), 1899– . Mex. painter.

Tam′er·lane (tăm′ĕr·lān) *or* **Tam′bur·laine** (tăm′bĕr·lān), 1336?–1405. *Ti·mur′ Lenk* (tĭ·mōōr′ lĕngk′); *also Ti·mour′* (tĭ·mōōr′). Mongol conqueror.

Tan′cred (tăng′krĕd; -krĭd), 1078?–1112. Norman leader in the 1st Crusade.

Ta′ney (tô′nĭ), Roger Brooke, 1777–1864. Am. jurist.

Tar′bell (tär′bĕl; -bĕl), Ida Minerva, 1857–1944. Am. author.

Tar′dieu′ (tȧr′dyŭ′), An′dré′ (äN′drā′) Pierre Ga′bri′el′ (gȧ′brē′ĕl′) A′mé′dée′ (ȧ′mā′dā′), 1876–1945. Fr. statesman.

Tar′king·ton (tär′kĭng·tŭn), (Newton) Booth, 1869–1946. Am. nov.

Tas′man (tăs′män; *Angl.* tăz′măn), A′bel (*Du.* ȧ′bĕl) Jans′zoon (yän′sŭn; -sōn; -sōn), 1603–1659. Du. mariner.

Tas′si′gny′, de (dĕ tȧ′sē′nyē′), Jean de Lat′tre (zhäN de lȧ′tr′), 1890–1952. Fr. gen.

Tas′so (täs′sō; *Angl.* täs′ō), Tor·qua′to (tôr·kwä′tō), 1544–1595. Ital. poet.

Tate (tāt), Nahum, 1652–1715. Brit. dram.; poet laureate (1692–1715).

Tauch′nitz (touκ′nĭts; *Angl.* touк′-), Chri′sti·an (krĭs′tē·än) Bern′hard (bĕrn′härt), 1816–1895. Ger. publisher.

Taus′sig (tou′sĭg), Frank William, 1859–1940. Am. econ.

Tay′lor (tā′lĕr), Bay′ard (bī′ärd; -ĕrd; bā′-), 1825–1878. Am. writer.
—, Deems (dēmz), 1885– . Am. composer & music critic.
—, Jeremy, 1613–1667. Eng. prelate & author.
—, Lau·rette′ (lô·rĕt′), 1887–1946. Nee *Coo′ney* (kōō′nĭ). Am. actress.
—, My′ron (mī′rŭn) Charles, 1874– . Am. lawyer, businessman, & diplomat.
—, Tom, 1817–1880. Eng. dram.
—, Zachary, 1784–1850. *Old Rough-and-Ready.* 12th pres. of the U. S. (1849–50).

Tchai·kov′sky (chī·kôf′skĭ), Pëtr (pyô′tĕr) Il·ich′ (ĭl·yēch′), 1840–1893. Russ. composer.

Tche′khov. See CHEKHOV.

Teas′dale (tēz′dāl), Sara, 1884–1933. Am. poet.

Te·cum′seh (tĕ·kŭm′sĕ; -sĕ) *or* **Te·cum′tha** (-thȧ), 1768?–1813. Shawnee Indian chief.

Ted′der (tĕd′ĕr), Arthur William, 1st Baron, 1890– . Brit. air marshal.

Tek′a·kwith′a (tĕk′ȧ·kwĭth′ȧ), Ka′te·ri (kä′tĕ·rĭ), 1656–1680. *Lily of the Mohawks.* Am. Indian ascetic.

Tél′lez, Gabriel. See TIRSO DE MOLINA.

Tem′ple (tĕm′p′l), Sir William, 1628–1699. Eng. statesman & author.

Te·niers′ (*Flem.* tĕ·nērs′; *Angl.* tĕn′yĕrz; *often, as Fr.*, tȧ′nyā′), David, father, 1582–1649, and son, 1610–1690. Flem. painters.

Ten′niel (tĕn′yĕl), Sir John, 1820–1914. Eng. cartoonist & illustrator.

Ten′ny·son (tĕn′ĭ·s′n), Alfred, 1st Baron, 1809–1892. Eng. poet; poet laureate (1850–92).

Te·ra·u′chi (tĕ·rä·ōō·chĕ), Count Ju·i·chi (jōō·ē·chĕ), 1879–1946. Jap. gen.

Ter·borch′ *or* **Ter Borch** (tĕr·bôrk′), Ge′rard (kā′rärt), 1617–1681. Du. painter.

Ter′ence (tĕr′ĕns), 185–159 B.C. *Pub′li·us* (pŭb′lĭ·ŭs) *Te·ren′ti·us A′fer* (tĕ·rĕn′shĭ·ŭs [-shŭs] ā′fĕr′). Rom. dram.

Ter·hune′ (tûr·hūn′), Albert Pay′son (pā′s′n), 1872–1942. Am. author.

Ter′ry (tĕr′ĭ), Ellen Alicia *or* Alice, 1847–1928. Eng. actress.

Ter·tul′lian (tûr·tŭl′yăn; tĕr-), 160?–?230. *Quin′tus* (kwĭn′tŭs) *Sep′tim′i·us* (sĕp·tĭm′ĭ·ŭs) *Flo′rens* (flō′rĕnz) *Ter·tul′li·a′nus* (tûr·tŭl′ĭ·ā′nŭs; tĕr-). Latin church father.

Tes′la (tĕs′lȧ), Ni′ko·la (nē′kō·lä), 1857–1943. Am. (Austrian-born) electrician & inventor.

Te·traz·zi′ni (tä·trät·tsē′nē), Lu·i′sa (lōō·ē′zä), 1874–1940. Ital. coloratura soprano.

Tet′zel *or* **Te′zel** (tĕt′sĕl), Jo·hann′ (yō·hän′; yō′hän), 1465?–1519. Ger. Dominican monk.

Thack′er·ay (thăk′ĕr·ĭ), William Make′peace′ (māk′pēs′), 1811–1863. Eng. author.

Tha′les (thā′lēz), 640?–546 B.C. Greek philos.

Tha′net′, Octave. See Alice FRENCH.

Thax′ter (thăks′tĕr), Celia, 1835–1894. Nee *Laigh′ton* (lā′t′n). Am. poet.

Thayer (thâr), Sylvanus, 1785–1872. *Father of West Point.* Am. army officer & educ.
—, William Roscoe, 1859–1923. Am. hist. & biographer.

The·mis′to·cles (thē·mĭs′tō·klēz), 527?–?460 B.C. Athenian gen. & statesman.

The·oc′ri·tus (thē·ŏk′rĭ·tŭs), 3d cent. B.C. Greek poet.

The·od′o·ric (thē·ŏd′ō·rĭk), 454?–526. *The Great.* King of the Ostrogoths (474–526).

The′o·do′si·us I (thē′ō·dō′shĭ·ŭs; -shŭs), 346?–395. *The Great.* Rom. gen. & emp. (379–395).

The′o·phras′tus (thē′ō·frăs′tŭs), ab. 371–287 B.C. Greek philos. & naturalist.

The·re′sa *or* **Te·re′sa** (tĕ·rē′sȧ; -zȧ; *Span.* tä·rā′sä), Saint, 1515–1582. Span. Carmelite nun.

Thes′pis (thĕs′pĭs), 6th cent. B.C. Greek poet.

Thi′baud′ (tē′bō′), Jacques (zhȧk), 1880–1953. Fr. violinist.

Thiers (tyâr), Louis A′dolphe′ (ȧ′dôlf′), 1797–1877. Fr. statesman & hist.

Tho′ma, von (fôn tō′mä), Wil′helm (vĭl′hĕlm), 1891–1948. Ger. gen.

Thom′as (tŏm′ȧs), Augustus, 1857–1934. Am. dram.
—, George Henry, 1816–1870. Am. gen.
—, Norman Mat·toon′ (mȧ·tōōn′), 1884– . Am. socialist polit.
—, Seth, 1785–1859. Am. clock manufacturer.
—, Theodore, 1835–1905. Ger.-born conductor in Am.
— **à Beck′et.** See BECKET.
— **a Kem′pis** (ȧ [ä, ä] kĕm′pĭs), 1380–1471. Ger. ecclesiastic & writer.
— **of Er′cel·doune** (ûr′s′l·dōōn), fl. 1220–1297. *Thomas the Rhym′er* (rīm′ĕr). Scot. seer & poet.

Thom′a·son (tŏm′ȧ·s′n), John William, 1893–1944. Am. marine corps colonel & author.

Thomp′son (tŏm[p]′s′n), Benjamin, 1753–1814. Count *Rum′ford* (rŭm′fĕrd). Brit. (Am.-born) physicist & statesman.
—, Francis, 1859–1907. Eng. poet.

Thom′son (tŏm′s′n), George Pag′et (păj′ĕt; -ĭt), 1892– . Eng. physicist.
—, James, 1700–1748. Scot. poet.
—, James, 1834–1882. *B. V.* Scot. poet.
—, John Arthur, 1861–1933. Scot. biologist.
—, Sir Joseph John, 1856–1940. Eng. physicist.
—, William. See Baron KELVIN.

Tho′reau (thôr′ō; thō·rō′), Henry David, 1817–1862. Am. writer & philos.

Tho′rez′ (tô′râz′), Maurice, 1900– . Fr. Communist.

Thorn′dike (thôrn′dīk), Ashley Horace, 1871–1933, and his bro. Lynn, 1882– . Am. educators.

Thorn′ton (thôrn′t′n; -tŭn), William, 1759–1828. Am. architect.

Thor′wald′sen *or* **Thor′wald′sen** (tōōr′vȧl′s′n), Ber′tel (bär′tĕl), 1768–1844. Dan. sculptor.

Thras′y·bu′lus (thrăs′ĭ·bū′lŭs), d. 389 B.C. Athenian gen. & statesman.

Thu·cyd′i·des (thū·sĭd′ĭ·dēz), 471?–?400 B.C. Greek hist.

Thwing (twĭng), Charles Franklin, 1853–1937. Am. educ.

Thys′sen (tĭs′ĕn), Fritz, 1873–1951. Ger. industrialist.

Tib′bett (tĭb′ĕt; -ĭt), Lawrence Mer′vil (mûr′vĭl), 1896– . Am. baritone.

Ti·be′ri·us (tī·bēr′ĭ·ŭs), 42 B.C.–37 A.D. *Tiberius Claudius Ne′ro Cae′sar* (nē′rō [nĕr′ō] sē′zĕr). Rom. emp. (14–37).

Ti·bul′lus (tĭ·bŭl′ŭs), Al′bi·us (ăl′bĭ·ŭs), 54?–?18 B.C. Rom. poet.

Tieck (tēk), Lud′wig (lōōt′vĭk; lōōd′-), 1773–1853. Ger. author.

Tie′po·lo (tyä′pō·lō), Gio·van′ni (jô·vän′nē) Bat·ti′sta (bät·tēs′tä), 1696–1770. Ital. painter.

Tig′lath-pi·le′ser III (tĭg′lăth·pī·lē′zĕr; -pĭ·lē′zĕr), d. 727 B.C. King of Assyria (745–727).

Til′den (tĭl′dĕn), Samuel Jones, 1814–1886. Am. lawyer & polit.

Til′dy (tĭl′dĭ), Zol′tán (zōl′tän), 1889– . Hung. polit.; pres. of Hungary (1946–48).

Til′lot·son (tĭl′ŭt·s′n), John, 1630–1694. Eng. divine.

Til′ly (tĭl′ē), Count of, 1559–1632. *Jo·han′* (yō·hän′) *Tser·claes′* (tsĕr·kläs′). Flem. field marshal.

Ti·mo·shen′ko (tyĭ·mŭ·shĕn′kō; *Angl.* tĭm′ō·shĕng′kō), Se·mën′ (syĭ·myôn′) Kon·stan·ti′no·vich (kŭn·stŭn·tyē′nŭ·vyĭch), 1895– . Russ. marshal.

Ti·mour′, Ti·mur′, Ti·mur′ Lenk. See TAMERLANE.

Ting′ley (tĭng′lĭ), Katherine Augusta, 1847–1929. Nee *West′cott* (wĕs′kŭt). Am. theosophist.

Tin′ker (tĭng′kĕr), Clarence Leonard, 1887–1942. Am. gen.

Tin′to·ret′to, Il (tĭn′tô·rĕt′tō; *Ital.* ēl tēn·tô·rät′tō), 1518–1594. *Ja′co·po* (yä′kō·pō) *Ro·bu′sti* (rô·bōōs′tē). Ital. painter.

Ti′pu Sa′hib *or* **Tip′poo Sa′hib** (tē′pōō sä′hĭb), 1751–1799. Sultan of Mysore (1782–99).

Tir′pitz, von (fôn tĭr′pĭts), Alfred, 1849–1930. Ger. admiral.

Tir′so de Mo·li′na (tēr′sō thä mō·lē′nä), 1571?–1648. Pseud. of *Ga′bri·el′* (gä′vrē·ĕl′) *Tél′lez* (tā′lyäth). Span. dram.

Ti′so (tyĭ′sô), Jo′sef (yō′sĕf), 1887–1947. Slovakian clergyman & pro-Nazi polit.

Tis′sot′ (tē′sō′), James (zhămz; zhám) Jo′seph′ (zhō′zĕf′) Jacques (zhȧk), 1836–1902. Fr. painter & engraver.

Ti′tian (tĭsh′ăn), 1477–1576. *Ti·zia′no* (tē·tsyä′nō) *Ve·cel′lio* (vā·chĕl′lyō). Ital. painter.

Ti′to, Marshal. See Josip BROZ.

Ti′tus (tī′tŭs), 40?–81. *Titus Fla′vi·us* (flā′vĭ·ŭs) *Sa·bi′nus Ves·pa′si·a′nus* (sȧ·bī′nŭs vĕs·pā′zhĭ·ā′nŭs). Rom. emp. (79–81).

To′bin (tō′bĭn), Maurice Joseph, 1901–1953. Am. polit.

Tocque′ville′, de (dĕ tôk′vēl′), A′lex′is′ (ȧ′lĕk′sē′) Charles Hen′ri′ (äN′rē′) Maurice Clé′rel′ (klā′rĕl′), 1805–1859. Fr. statesman & author.

Todd (tŏd), David, 1855–1939. Am. astron.

Todt (tōt), Fritz (frĭts), 1891–1942. Ger. mil. engineer.

To·gliat′ti (tô·lyät′tē), Pal·mi′ro (päl·mē′rō), 1893?– . Ital. Communist.

To·go (tō·gō), Marquis Hei·ha·chi·ro (hä·hä·chē·rō), 1847–1934. Jap. admiral.
—, Shi·ge·no·ri (shē·gĕ·nō·rē), 1882–1950. Jap. diplomat & statesman.

To·jo (tō·jō), Hi·de·ki (hē·dĕ·kē), 1885–1948. Jap. gen. & statesman.

Tol·bu′khin (tŏl·bōō′kĭn), Fĕ′dor (fyô′dĕr) I·va′no·vich (ĭ·vä′nŭ-vyĭch), 1895?–1949. Russ. marshal.
Tol′ler (tôl′ĕr), Ernst (ĕrnst), 1893–1939. Ger. dram. & polit.
Tol·stoi′ (tŭl·stoi′; *Angl.* tŏl·stoi′, tŏl′stoi), Count Lev (lyăf) Ni·ko-la′e·vich (nyĭ·kṳ·lä′yĕ·vyĭch), 1828–1910. Russ. nov., philos., & mystic.
Tom·ma·si′ni (tôm·mä·zē′nē), Vi·cen′zo (vē·chĕn′tsō), 1880–1950. Ital. composer.
Tone (tōn), (Theobald) Wolfe, 1763–1798. Irish revolutionist.
Tooke (tŏŏk), (John) Horne (hôrn), 1736–1812. Eng. polit. radical & philologist.
Toombs (tōōmz), Robert Augustus, 1810–1885. Am. lawyer & Confed. statesman.
Tor′que·ma′da, de (thä tôr′kä·mä′thä), To·más′ (tō·mäs′), 1420?–1498. Span. grand inquisitor.
Tor·ri·cel′li (tôr·rē·chĕl′lē), E·van·ge·li′sta (ā·vän·jä·lēs′tä), 1608–1647. Ital. math. & physicist.
To·sca·ni′ni (tōs·kä·nē′nē; *Angl.* tŏs′kȧ·nē′nĭ), Ar·tu′ro (är·tōō′rō), 1867–1957. Ital. conductor.
Tot′le·ben *or* **Tod′le·ben** (tŏt′lyĕ·byĕn), Count Frants (frànts) E·du-ard′ (â·dōō·ärt′) I·va′no·vich (ĭ·vä′nŭ·vyĭch), 1818–1884. Russ. gen.
Tour′neur (tûr′nĕr), Cyril, 1575?–1626. Eng. dram.
Tous·saint′ L′Ou′ver′ture′ (tōō′săn′ lōō′vĕr′tür′), Pierre Do′mi′nique′ (dō′mē′nēk′), 1743–1803. Haitian gen. & liberator.
Tov′ey (tŭv′ĭ), John Cro′nyn (krō′nĭn), 1st Baron, 1885–   . Brit. admiral of the fleet.
Tow′ers (tou′ĕrz), John Henry, 1885–1955. Am. admiral.
Town′shend (toun′zĕnd), Sir Charles Vere (vēr) Fer′rers (fĕr′ĕrz), 1861–1924. Eng. gen.
Toyn′bee (toin′bē), Arnold Joseph, 1889–   . Eng. hist.
Tra′jan (trā′jăn), 52 or 53–117. *Marcus Ul′pi·us* (ŭl′pĭ·ŭs) *Tra·ja′-nus* (trȧ·jā′nŭs). Rom. emp. (98–117).
Tree (trē), Sir Herbert Beer′bohm (bẽr′bōm), 1853–1917. Eng. actor-manager.
Treitsch′ke, von (fôn trīch′kĕ), Hein′rich (hīn′rĭk), 1834–1896. Ger. hist.
Trench (trĕnch), Richard Chen′e·vix (shĕn′ĕ·vē), 1807–1886. Eng. poet & prelate.
Tren′chard (trĕn′chärd; -chĕrd), Hugh Montague, 1st Viscount, 1873–1956. Brit. air marshal.
Tre·vel′yan (trē·vĕl′yăn; -vĭl′yăn), George Macaulay, 1876–   . Eng. hist.
—, Sir George Otto, 1838–1928. *Father of prec.* Eng. polit., biographer, & hist.
Trol′lope (trŏl′ŭp), Anthony, 1815–1882. Eng. nov.
Tromp (trômp), Maar′ten (mär′tĕn) Har′perts·zoon (här′pĕrt·sⁱzän; -sōn; -sōn), 1597–1653. Du. admiral.
Trots′ky *or* **Trots′ki** (trŏts′kĭ; *Angl.* trŏt′skĭ), Le′on (lē′ŏn), 1877–1940. *Leib* (lāb) *or Lev* (lyăf) *Da·vy′do·vich* (dȧ·vī′dŭ·vyĭch) *Bron-stein′* (brŭn·shtīn′). Russ. Communist.
Troy′on′ (trwà′yôn′), Con′stant′ (kôn′stän′), 1813–1865. Fr. painter.
Tru·jil′lo Mo·li′na (trōō·hē′yō mō·lē′nä), Ra′fa·el′ (rä′fä·ĕl′) Le′o-ni′das (lē′ō·nē′thäs), 1891–   . Dominican gen.; pres. of Dominican Republic (1930–38; 1942–52).
Tru′man (trōō′măn), Harry S., 1884–   . 33d pres. of the U. S. (1945–53).
Trum′bull (trŭm′bŭl), John, 1756–1843. *Son of Jonathan.* Am. painter.
—, Jonathan, 1710–1785. Am. patriot & statesman.
Tsai Ting-kai (tsī′ tĭng′gī′), 1890–   . Chin. gen.
Tsal·da′res *or* **Tsal·da′ris** (tsäl·thä′rēs), Pa′na·ges′ *or* Pa′na·gis′ (pä′-nä·yēs′), 1868–1936. Greek statesman.
Tschai·kov′sky. Variant of TCHAIKOVSKY.
Tub′man (tŭb′măn), William Vac′a·nar′at (văk′ȧ·när′ăt) Shad′rach (shăd′răk), 1895–   . Liberian lawyer; pres. of Liberia (1944–   ).
Tul′si Das (tōōl′sĕ däs′), 1532–1623. Hindu poet.
Tu′renne′, de (dĕ tü·rĕn′), *Angl.* tṳ·rĕn′), Vi′comte′ (vē′kônt′), 1611–1675. *Hen′ri′* (än′rē′) *de La Tour d′Au′vergne′* (dĕ là tōōr′ dō′-vĕrn′y′). Fr. marshal.
Tur·ge′nev (tŏŏr·gā′nyĕf), Ivan Ser·ge′e·vich (syĭr·gā′yĕ·vyĭch), 1818–1883. Russ. nov.
Tur′got′ (tür′gō′), Anne (än; àn) Ro′bert′ (rō′bâr′) Jacques (zhàk), 1727–1781. Baron *de l′ Aulne* (dĕ lōn′). Fr. statesman & econ.
Tur′ner (tûr′nĕr), Frederick Jackson, 1861–1932. Am. hist.
—, Joseph Mal′lord (măl′ĕrd) William, 1775–1851. Eng. painter.
Tut′ankh·a′men (tōōt′ängk·ä′mĕn) *or* **Tut′enkh·a′mon** (tōōt′ĕngk-ä′mŏn), fl. ab. 1358 B.C. King of Egypt.
Twacht′man (twäkt′măn), John Henry, 1853–1902. Am. painter.
Twain, Mark. See S. L. CLEMENS.
Tweed (twēd), William Mar′cy (mär′sĭ), 1823–1878. Am. polit.
Tweeds′muir, Baron. See John BUCHAN.
Ty′ler (tī′lĕr), John, 1790–1862. 10th pres. of the U. S. (1841–45).
—, Wat (wŏt) *or* Walter, d. 1381. Eng. leader of Peasants′ Revolt (1381).
Tyn′dale (tĭn′d′l), William, 1492?–1536. Eng. reformer & martyr.
Tyn′dall (tĭn′d′l), John, 1820–1893. Brit. physicist.
Tyr′whitt (tĭr′ĭt), Sir Reginald Yorke (yôrk), 1870–1951. Eng. admiral of the fleet.
—-**Wil′son** (-wĭl′s′n), Gerald Hugh, 1883–1950. *Orig. Tyrwhitt.* 14th Baron Ber′ners (bûr′nĕrz). Eng. composer & painter.

U

U′dall (ū′d′l) *or* **Uve′dale** (ūv′dāl), Nicholas, 1505–1556. Eng. schoolmaster & dram.
U·gar′te (ōō·gär′tā), Ma·nuel′ (mä·nwĕl′), 1874–1951. Argentine writer.
Uh′land (ōō′länt), Jo·hann′ (yō·hän′; yō′hän) Lud′wig (lōōt′vĭk; lōōd′-), 1787–1862. Ger. poet & hist.
Ul′fi·las (ŭl′fĭ·läs; -lăs), **Ulf′i·la** (-lȧ), *or* **Wul′fi·la** (wŏŏl′fĭ·lȧ), 311?–381. Bishop of the Goths.
Ul′pi·an (ŭl′pĭ·ăn), 170?–228. *Do·mi′ti·us* (dō·mĭsh′ĭ·ŭs; -mĭsh′ŭs) *Ul′pi·a′nus* (ŭl′pĭ·ā′nŭs). Rom. jurist.

U′na·mu′no y Ju′go, de (dä ōō′nä·mōō′nō ē hōō′gō), Mi·guel′ (mĕ-gĕl′), 1864–1936. Span. philos. & writer.
Un′cas (ŭng′kȧs), 1588?–?1683. Pequot Indian chief.
Und′set (ōōn′sĕt), Si′grid (sĭ′grĭ), 1882–1949. Norw. nov.
Un′ter·mey′er (ŭn′tĕr·mī′ĕr), Louis, 1885–   . Am. poet & editor.
Up′ton (ŭp′tŭn), Emory, 1839–1881. Am. gen. & author.
Ur′ban (ûr′băn). Name of 8 popes; esp. **II** (*O′do* [ō′dō] *or U′do* [ōō′dō]), 1042?–1099 (pope 1088–1099).
U′rey (ū′rĭ), Harold Clay′ton (klā′t′n), 1893–   . Am. chem.
Ur′quhart (ûr′kĕrt; -kärt), Sir Thomas, 1611–1660. Scot. author & trans.
Ussh′er (ŭsh′ĕr), James, 1581–1656. Irish archbishop & Biblical chronologist.
Uve′dale. See UDALL.

V

Vail′lant′ (và′yän′), Jean Bap′tiste′ (bȧ′tēst′) Phi′li′bert′ (fē′lē′bâr′), 1790–1872. Fr. army officer; marshal of France (1851).
Val′de·mar. See WALDEMAR.
Val·di′via, de (thä väl·dē′vyä; 17), Pe′dro (pā′thrō), 1500?–1553. Span. conqueror of Chile.
Va′lens (vā′lĕnz), 328?–378. Rom. emp. of the East (364–378).
Val·en·tin′i·an (văl′ĕn·tĭn′ĭ·ăn; -tĭn′yăn); *Lat.* **Val′en·tin′i·a′nus** (văl′ĕn·tĭn′ĭ·ā′nŭs). Name of 3 Rom. emperors: **I**, 321–375 (reigned 364–375); **II**, 372–392 (reigned 375–392); **III**, 419–455 (reigned 425–455).
Va·le′ra, Eamon de. See DE VALERA.
Va·le′ra y Al′ca·lá′ Ga·lia′no, Juan (hwäm bä·lā′rä ē äl′kä·lä′ gä-lyä′nō; 17), 1824–1905. Span. writer & statesman.
Va·le′ri·an (vȧ·lēr′ĭ·ăn), d. ?269. *Pub′li·us* (pŭb′lĭ·ŭs) *Li·cin′i·us* (lĭ·sĭn′ĭ·ŭs) *Va·le′ri·a′nus* (vȧ·lēr′ĭ·ā′nŭs). Rom. emp. (253–260).
Va·lé′ry′ (và′lā′rē′), Paul Am′broise′ (än′brwàz′), 1871–1945. Fr. poet & philos.
Va′lin′ (và′lăn′), Mar′tial′ (màr′syàl′) Hen′ri′ (än′rē′), 1898–   . Fr. gen. & diplomat.
Val·lar′ta (bä·yär′tä; 17), Ma·nuel′ (mä·nwĕl′) San′do·val′ (sän′dō-väl′), 1899–   . Mex. physicist.
Val·le′jo (bä·lyĕ′hō; 17), Ma·ri′ano (mä·ryä′nō) Gua′da·lu′pe (gwä′-thä·lōō′pä), 1808–1890. Soldier & pioneer in California.
Van·brugh′ (văn·brōō′; *in Eng., commonly* văn′brṳ), Sir John, 1664–1726. Eng. dram. & architect.
Van Bu′ren (văn bū′rĕn), Martin, 1782–1862. 8th pres. of the U. S. (1837–41).
Van·cou′ver (văn·kōō′vĕr), George, 1758?–1798. Eng. navigator & explorer.
Van′de·grift (văn′dĕ·grĭft), Alexander Archer, 1887–   . Am. marine corps gen.
Van′den·berg (văn′dĕn·bûrg), Arthur Hen′drick (hĕn′drĭk), 1884–1951. Am. journalist & polit.
—, Hoyt San′ford (săn′fĕrd), 1899–1954. Am. gen.
Van′der·bilt (văn′dĕr·bĭlt), Cornelius, 1794–1877. Am. capitalist.
Van Dine, S. S. See under WRIGHT.
Van Do′ren (văn dō′rĕn), Carl, 1885–1950, and his bro. Mark, 1894–   . Am. writers & editors.
Van·dyke′ *or* **Van Dyck** (văn dīk′; *Flem.* vän), Sir Anthony, 1599–1641. Flem.-born painter in Eng.
van Dyke (văn dīk′), Henry, 1852–1933. Am. clergyman, educ., & writer.
Vane (vān), Sir Henry *or* Harry, 1613–1662. Eng. Puritan statesman.
Van Loon (văn lōn′), Hen′drik (hĕn′drĭk) Wil′lem (vĭl′ĕm), 1882–1944. Du.-born author & lecturer in Am.
Van Rens′se·laer (văn rĕn′sĕ·lĕr; -lēr), Stephen, 1764–1839. Am. gen. & polit.
Van·sit′tart (văn·sĭt′ĕrt), Robert Gilbert, 1881–1957. 1st Baron *Vansittart of Den′ham* (dĕn′ăm). Brit. diplomat.
van′t Hoff (vänt hôf′), Ja·co′bus (yȧ·kō′bŭs) Hen·dri′cus (hĕn·drē′kŭs), 1852–1911. Du. physical chem.
Van Zyl (fän zāl′), Gi′de·on (kĕ′dä·ôn) Brand (bränt), 1873–   . S. African lawyer; gov. gen. of Union of S. Africa (1946–50).
Var′gas (vär′gäs), Ge·tu′lio (zhĕ·tōō′lyōō) Dor·nel′les (thôor·nĕ′lĕz), 1883–1954. Brazilian lawyer; pres. of Brazil (1930–45; 1951–54).
Var′ro (văr′ō), Marcus Te·ren′ti·us (tĕ·rĕn′shĭ·ŭs; -shŭs), 116–27 B.C. Rom. scholar & author.
Va·sa′ri (vä·zä′rē), Gior′gio (jôr′jō; jôr′-), 1511–1574. Ital. painter, architect, & hist.
Vas′co da Ga′ma. See GAMA.
Va·si·lev′ski (vä·syĭ·lyĕf′skĭ; *Angl.* väs′ĭ·lĕf′skĭ), A·le·ksan′dr (ṳ·lyĭ-ksän′dĕr) Mi·khai′lo·vich (myĭ·kī′lŭ·vyĭch), 1905?–   . Russ. marshal.
Va·tu′tin (vṳ·tōō′tyĭn), Ni·ko·lai′ (nyĭ·kṳ·lī′), 1900?–1944. Russ. gen.
Vau′ban′, de (dĕ vō′bän′), Marquis, 1633–1707. *Sé′bas′tien′* (sā′-bàs′tyän′) *Le Pres′tre* (lĕ prâ′tr′). Fr. mil. engineer; marshal of France (1703).
Vaughan (vôn), Henry, 1622–1695. *The Sil′u·rist* (sĭl′ū·rĭst). Brit. poet.
Veb′len (vĕb′lĕn), Thor′stein (thôr′stīn) Bun′de (bōōn′dĕ), 1857–1929. Am. sociol. & econ.
Ved′der (vĕd′ĕr), Elihu, 1836–1923. Am. painter & illustrator.
Ve′ga, de (thä vā′gä; 17), Lo′pe (lō′pä), 1562–1635. *Lope Fé′lix* (fā′lēks) *de Vega Car′pio* (kär′pyō). Span. dram.
Ve·láz′quez (bä·läth′kāth; 17) *or* **Ve·lás′quez** (-läs′-), Die′go (dyā′gō) Ro·drí′guez de Sil′va y (rrō·thrē′gāth thä sēl′vä ē), 1599–1660. Span. painter.
Ven·dôme′, de (dĕ vän′dōm′), Duc (dük) Louis Jo′seph′ (zhō′zĕf′), 1654–1712. Fr. soldier; marshal of France.
Ve·ni·ze′los (vĕ·nyē·zā′lôs), E′leu·the′rios (ä′lyĕf·thä′ryōs), 1864–1936. Greek statesman.
Ven′ning (vĕn′ĭng), Sir Walter King, 1882–   . Brit. gen.
Ver′di (vâr′dē; *Angl.* vâr′-), Giu·sep′pe (jōō·zĕp′pä), 1813–1901. Ital. composer.
Ver′e·ker, John S. S. P. See Viscount GORT.

Ve·re·shcha′gin (vyĭ′·ryĭsh·chä′gĭn; *Angl.* vĕr′ĕsh·chä′gĭn), Va·si′li (vŭ·syē′lyĭ) Va·sil′ie·vich (vŭ·syĕl′yĕ·vyĭch), 1842–1904. Russ. painter.

Ver′gil *or* **Vir′gil** (vûr′jĭl), 70–19 B.C. *Pub′li·us* (pŭb′lĭ·ŭs) *Ver·gil′i·us Ma′ro* (vûr·jĭl′ĭ·ŭs mā′rō). Rom. poet.

Ver·laine′ (vĕr′lān′), Paul, 1844–1896. Fr. poet.

Ver·meer′ (vĕr·mār′), Jan (yän), 1632–1675. *Jan van der Meer van Delft* (vän dĕr mär′ van delft′). Du. painter.

Verne (vĕrn), Jules, 1828–1905. Fr. writer.

Ver′ner (vĕr′nĕr), Karl (kärl) A′dolph (ä′dŏlf), 1846–1896. Dan. philologist.

Ver′nier′ (vĕr′nyä′; *Angl.* vûr′nĭ·ĕr), Pierre, 1580–1637. Fr. math.

Ver′non (vûr′nŭn), Edward, 1684–1757. Eng. admiral.

Ve·ro·ne′se (vā·rō·nā′sā), Pa′o·lo (pä′ō·lō), 1528–1588. *Paolo Caglia′ri* (kä·lyä′rē). Ital. painter.

Ver·ra·za′no, da (dä vär·rä·tsä′nō), *or* **Ver·raz′za′no** (-rät·tsä′nō), Gio·van′ni (jō·vän′nē), 1485?–?1528. Florentine navigator.

Ver·roc′chio, del (dĕl vär·rôk′kyō), An·dre′a (än·drā′ä), 1435–1488. *Andrea di Mi′che·le Cio′ne* (dē mē·kā′lā chō′nä). Florentine sculptor & painter.

Ver′u·lam, Baron. See Francis BACON.

Ve′rus (vē′rŭs), Lucius Aurelius, 130–169. *Lucius Ce·io′ni·us* (sē·yō′nĭ·ŭs) *Com′mo·dus* (kŏm′ō·dŭs). Rom. emp. (161–169).

Ves·pa′sian (vĕs·pā′zhăn; -zhĭ·ăn), 9–79. *Titus Fla′vi·us* (flā′vĭ·ŭs) *Sa·bi′nus* (sà·bī′nŭs) *Ves·pa′si·a′nus* (vĕs·pā′zhĭ·ā′nŭs). Rom. emp. (69–79).

Ves·puc′ci (vĕs·pōō′chē; *Ital.* väs·pōōt′chē), A′me·ri′go (ä′mā·rē′gō), 1451–1512. *A·mer′i·cus Ves·pu′cius* (à·mĕr′ĭ·kŭs vĕs·pū′shŭs). Ital. navigator; eponym of *America.*

Vic′tor Em·man′u·el (vĭk′tĕr ĕ·măn′ū·ĕl; I-) **I,** 1759–1824. King of Sardinia (1802–21).

— **II,** 1820–1878. King of Sardinia (1849–61) & 1st king of Italy (1861–78).

— **III,** 1869–1947. King of Italy (1900–46).

Vic·to′ri·a (vĭk·tō′rĭ·à), Al′ex·an·dri′na (ăl′ĕg·zăn·drē′nà; ăl′ĭg-; *Brit. also* -zän-), 1819–1901. Queen of Gr. Britain (1837–1901).

Vi′da (vē′dä), Mar′co (mär′kō) Gi·ro′la·mo (jē·rō′lä·mō), 1480?–1566. Ital. poet.

Vi·de′la, Gabriel González. See GONZÁLEZ VIDELA.

Vi′ë·tor (fē′à·tôr), Wil′helm (vĭl′hĕlm), 1850–1918. Ger. philologist.

Vi′gée′-Le·brun′ (vē′zhä′lĕ·brŭn′), Marie Anne (än; àn) É′li′sa′beth′ (ā′lē′zä′bĕt′), 1755–1842. Fr. painter.

Vi·gno′la, da (dä vē·nyō′lä), Gia′co·mo (jä′kō·mō), 1507–1573. *Giacomo Ba·roc′chio* (bä·rôk′kyō) *or Ba·roz′zi* (bä·rôt′tsē). Ital. architect.

Vi′gny′, de (dē vē′nyē′), Comte (kÔNT) Alfred Vic′tor′ (vēk′tôr′), 1797–1863. Fr. poet & nov.

Vil′la (bē′yä; 17), Fran·cis′co (frän·sēs′kō), 1877–1923. *Pan′cho* (pän′chō). *Do′ro·te′o* (dō′rō·tā′ō) *A·ran′go* (ä·räng′gō). Mex. bandit & revolutionist.

Vil·lard′ (vĭ·lär′; -lärd′), Oswald Garrison, 1872–1949. Am. journalist.

Vil′lars′, de (dē vē′lär′), Duc (dük) Claude Louis Hec′tor′ (ĕk′tôr′), 1653–1734. Fr. soldier; marshal of France (1702).

Ville·neuve′, de (dē vēl′nûv′), Pierre Charles Jean Bap′tiste′ (bà·tēst′) Sil′ves′tre (sĕl′vĕs′tr′), 1763–1806. Fr. admiral.

Vil′liers (vĭl′ĕrz; vĭl′yĕrz), George, 1592–1628. 1st Duke of *Buck′ing·ham* (bŭk′ĭng·ăm). Eng. statesman & admiral.

— George, 1628–1687. 2d Duke of *Buckingham. Son of prec.* Eng. courtier & dram.

Vil′lon′ (vē′yôN′), Fran′çois′ (frän′swà′), 1431–after 1462. *François de Mont′cor′bier′* (dē môN′kôr′byä′). Fr. poet.

Vin′cent′ de Paul (văn′săN′ dē pôl′; *Angl.* vĭn′sĕnt dē pôl′), Saint, 1581?–1660. Fr. priest.

Vin′ci, da (dä vēn′chē), Le·o·nar′do (lā·ô·när′dō), 1452–1519. Florentine painter, sculptor, architect, & engineer.

Vi·no·gra′doff (vyĕ′nŭ·grä′dŏf), Sir Paul (pôl) Ga·vri′lo·vich (gŭ·vryē′lŭ·vyĭch), 1854–1925. Russ. jurist & hist. in Eng.

Vin′son (vĭn′s'n), Carl, 1883–   . Am. lawyer & administrator.

—, Frederick Moore, 1890–1953. Am. jurist & administrator.

Viol′let′-le-Duc′ (vyô′lĕ′lĕ·dük′), Eu′gène′ (û′zhän′; ü′-) Em′ma′nu·el′ (ĕ′mà′nü·ĕl′), 1814–1879. Fr. architect.

Vir′chow (fĭr′kō), Ru′dolf (rōō′dŏlf), 1821–1902. Ger. pathologist.

Vir′gil. See VERGIL.

Vir′ta·nen (vĭr′tà·nĕn), Art′tu·ri (ärt′tōō·rē) Il′ma·ri (ĭl′mà·rĭ), 1895–   . Finnish biochem.

Vi·tru′vi·us Pol′li·o (vĭ·trōō′vĭ·ŭs pŏl′ĭ·ō), Marcus, 1st cent. B.C. Rom. architect & engineer.

Vi′via′ni′ (vē′vyä′nē′), René Ra′pha′ël′ (rà′fà′ĕl′), 1863–1925. Fr. statesman.

Vi′vien′ de Saint′-Mar′tin′ (vē′vyäN′ dē săN′mär′tăN′), Louis, 1802–1897. Fr. geographer.

Viz′e·tel′ly (vĭz′ē·tĕl′ĭ), Frank Horace, 1864–1938. Am. lexicographer.

Vlad′i·mir (vlăd′ĭ·mĭr; *Russ.* vlŭ·dyē′myĭr), 956?–1015. *The Great.* Ruler of Russia (980–1015).

Vo′gler (fō′glĕr), Ge·org′ (gĕ·ôrK′) Jo′seph (yō′zĕf), 1749–1814. Abt (äpt) *or* Ab′bé (ab′ā) *Vogler.* Ger. musician.

Vol′i·va (vŏl′ĭ·vá), Wilbur Glenn, 1870–1942. Am. religious leader.

Vol′stead (vŏl′stĕd), Andrew John, 1860–1947. Am. legislator.

Vol′ta (vŏl′tä), Count A′les·san′dro (ä′läs·sän′drō), 1745–1827. Ital. physicist.

Vol·taire′ (vŏl·târ′; vŏl′târ; *Fr.* vôl′târ′), 1694–1778. *Fran′çois′* (frän′swà′) *Ma′rie′* (mà′rē′) *A′rou·et′* (à′rwĕ′). Fr. writer.

Vo·ro′nov (vô·rō′nŏf), Ni·ko·lai′ (nyĭ′kŭ·lī′) Ni·ko·la′e·vich (nyĭ·kŭ·lä′yĕ·vyĭch), 1899–   . Russ. marshal.

Vo·ro·shi′lov (vŭ·rŭ·shī′lŭf), Kli′ment (klyē′myĕnt) E·fre′mo·vich (yĭ·fryä′mŭ·vyĭch), 1881–   . Russ. marshal.

Voz·ne·sen′ski (vŏz·nyĭ·syĕn′skĭ; *Angl.* vŏz′nĕ·sĕn′skĭ), Ni·ko·lai′ (nyĭ·kŭ·lī′) A·lek·se′e·vich (ŭ·lyĭ·ksyä′yĕ·vyĭch), 1904–   . Russ. econ. & polit.

Vy·shin′sky (vĭ·shĭn′skĭ), An·drei′ Ya·nu·ar′ie·vich (ŭn·dryä′Ĭ yĭ·nōō·är′yĕ·vyĭch), 1883–1954. Russ. lawyer & statesman.

W

Waals, van der (vän dĕr väls′), Jo·han′nes (yō·hän′ĕs) Di′de·rik (dē′dĕ·rĭk), 1837–1923. Du. physicist.

Wace (*Angl.* wäs, wās; *mod. Fr.* wäs), 12th cent. Anglo-Norman poet.

Wag′ner (väg′nĕr), (Wil′helm [vĭl′hĕlm]) Ri′chard (rĭk′ärt; *Angl.* rĭch′ĕrd), 1813–1883. Ger. poet & composer.

— **von Jau′regg** (fŏn you′rĕk), Ju′li·us (yōō′lĕ·ŏŏs), 1857–1940. Austrian neurologist & psychiatrist.

Wain′wright (wān′rīt), Jonathan May′hew (mā′hū), 1883–1953. Am. gen.

—, Richard, father, 1817–1862, and son, 1849–1926. Am. naval officers.

Wal′de·mar (wôl′dĕ·mär); *Dan.* **Val′de·mar** (väl′dĕ·mär). Name of 4 kings of Denmark; esp. **I** (*the Great*), 1131–1182 (reigned 1157–82).

Wal′der·see, von (fŏn väl′dĕr·zā), Count Alfred, 1832–1904. Ger. field marshal.

Wal′do (wôl′dō; wŏl′-) *or* **Val′do** (väl′dō; *Fr.* väl′dō′), Peter, fl. 1173–1179. Fr. heretic.

Wald′teu′fel (väl′tû′fĕl′), É′mile′ (ā′mēl′), 1837–1915. Fr. composer.

Walk′er (wôk′ĕr), Francis Am′a·sa (ăm′à·sà), 1840–1897. Am. econ.

—, William, 1824–1860. Am. filibuster in Lower California and in Nicaragua.

Wal′lace (wŏl′ĭs), Alfred Rus′sel (rŭs′'l), 1823–1913. Eng. naturalist.

—, Henry A′gard (ā′gärd), 1888–   . Am. agriculturist, editor, & polit.

—, Lewis, 1827–1905. *Lew* (lū; lōō). Am. lawyer, gen., & nov.

—, Sir William, 1272?–1305. Scot. patriot.

Wal′lach (wŏl′äk), Ot′to (ŏt′ō), 1847–1931. Ger. chem.

Wal′len·stein, von (fŏn wŏl′ĕn·stīn; *Ger.* väl′ĕn·shtīn), Al′brecht (äl′brĕkt) Eu·se′bi·us (oi·zā′bē·ŏŏs) Wen′zel (vĕn′tsĕl), 1583–1634. Duke of *Fried′land* (frēt′länt) *and Meck′len·burg* (mĕk′lĕn·bōŏrk; mä′klĕn-). Prince of *Sa′gan* (zä′gän). Austrian gen.

Wal′ler (wŏl′ĕr), Edmund, 1606–1687. Eng. poet.

Wal′pole (wôl′pōl; wŏl′-), Horace *or* Horatio, 1717–1797. 4th Earl of *Or′ford* (ôr′fĕrd). Eng. author.

—, Sir Hugh Seymour, 1884–1941. Eng. nov.

—, Sir Robert, 1676–1745. 1st Earl of *Orford. Father of Horace.* Eng. statesman.

Wal′ter (väl′tĕr), Bru′no (brōō′nō), 1876–   . Orig. *Schle′sing·er* (shlä′zĭng·ĕr). Ger.-born conductor.

— (wôl′tĕr), Eugene, 1874–1941. Am. dram.

— (wôl′tĕr), John, 1739–1812. Eng. founder of *The* (London) *Times.*

Wal′ther von der Vo′gel·wei′de (väl′tĕr fŏn dĕr fō′gĕl·vī′dĕ), 1170?–?1230. Ger. minnesinger.

Wal′ton (wôl′t'n; -tŭn), I′zaak (ī′zàk; ī′zĭk), 1593–1683. Eng. writer.

Wan′a·ma′ker (wŏn′à·mā′kĕr), John, 1838–1922. Am. merchant.

Wang Ching-wei (wäng′ jĭng′wā′), 1884–1944. Chin. polit.

War′beck (wôr′bĕk), Per′kin (pûr′kĭn), 1474–1499. Walloon impostor; pretender to the Eng. throne.

War′burg (*Ger.* vär′bŏŏrk; *Eng.* wôr′bûrg), Ot′to (ôt′ō) Hein′rich (hīn′rĭk), 1883–   . Ger. physiol.

Ward (wôrd), Sir Adolphus William, 1837–1924. Eng. hist.

—, Ar′te·mas (är′tĕ·mǎs), 1727–1800. Am. Revolutionary gen.

—, Artemus (pseud.). See Charles Farrar BROWNE.

—, Sir Joseph George, 1856–1930. N. Z. statesman.

—, Mary Augusta, 1851–1920. *Mrs Humphry Ward; nee Ar′nold* (är′n'ld). Eng. nov.

War′ner (wôr′nĕr), Charles Dudley, 1829–1900. Am. editor & essayist.

—, Susan Bo′gert (bō′gĕrt), 1819–1885. Pseud. *Elizabeth Weth′er·ell* (wĕth′ĕr·ĕl). Am. nov.

War′ren (wŏr′ĕn; -ĭn), Earl, 1891–   . Am. lawyer & polit.; chief justice, U. S. Supreme Court (1953–   ).

—, Gou′ver·neur′ (gŭv′ĕr·nŷr′; gŭv′ĕr·nẽr) Kem′ble (kĕm′b'l), 1830–1882. Am. gen.

—, Joseph, 1741–1775. Am. physician & gen.

—, Robert Penn, 1905–   . Am. author & educ.

—, Whitney, 1864–1943. Am. architect.

War′ton (wôr′t'n), Thomas, 1728–1790. Eng. literary hist. & critic; poet laureate (1785–90).

War′wick (wŏr′ĭk), Earl of, 1428–1471. *Richard Nev′ille* (nĕv′'l; -ĭl). *The King′mak′er* (kĭng′māk′ĕr). Eng. soldier & statesman.

Wash′ing·ton (wŏsh′ĭng·tŭn), Book′er (bŏŏk′ĕr) Tal′ia·ferro (tŏl′ĭ·vĕr), 1856–1915. Am. educ.

—, George, 1732–1799. Am. gen.; 1st pres. of the U. S. (1789–97).

Was′ser·mann (väs′ĕr·män), Ja′kob (yä′kŏp), 1873–1934. Ger. nov.

Was′ser·mann, von (fŏn väs′ĕr·män), Au′gust (ou′gŏŏst), 1866–1925. Ger. bacteriol.

Wat′son (wŏt′s'n), John, 1850–1907. Pseud. *Ian Mac·lar′en* (măk·lär′ĕn). Scot. clergyman & author.

—, John Broa′dus (brō′dŭs), 1878–   . Am. psychol.

—, Sir William, 1858–1935. Eng. poet.

Watt (wŏt), James, 1736–1819. Scot. inventor.

—, Sir Robert Alexander Watson, 1892–   . Scot. physicist.

Wat′teau′ (vä′tō′; *Angl.* wŏ·tō′), Jean An′toine′ (än′twän′), 1684–1721. Fr. painter.

Wat′ter·son (wŏt′ĕr·s'n), Henry, 1840–1921. Am. journalist & polit.

Watts (wŏts), George Frederic, 1817–1904. Eng. painter & sculptor.

—, Isaac, 1674–1748. Eng. theol. & hymn writer.

Watts′-Dun′ton (wŏts′dŭn′t'n; -tŭn), Walter Theodore, 1832–1914. Eng. critic & poet.

Waugh (wô), Evelyn Arthur St. John (sănt jŏn′; *esp. Brit.,* sĭn′jŭn), 1903–   . Eng. writer.

—, Frederick Judd, 1861–1940. Am. painter.

Wa′vell (wā′vĕl), Archibald Percival, 1st Earl, 1883–1950. Brit. field marshal; viceroy of India (1943–47).

Wayne (wān), Anthony, 1745–1796. *Mad Anthony.* Am. Revolutionary gen.

Webb (wĕb), Beatrice, 1858–1943. Nee *Pot′ter* (pŏt′ĕr). *Wife of S. J.* Eng. econ. & socialist.

—, Sidney James, 1859–1947. 1st Baron *Pass′field* (pås′fēld). Eng. econ. & socialist.

We'ber (vā'bĕr), Ernst (ĕrnst) Hein'rich (hīn'rĭk), 1795–1878. Ger. physiol.

—, **von** (fôn), Baron Karl Ma·ri'a (mä·rē'ä) Frie'drich (frē'drĭk) Ernst, 1786–1826. Ger. composer & conductor.

—, Wil'helm (vĭl'hĕlm) E'du·ard (ā'dŏŏ·ärt), 1804–1891. *Bro. of E. H.* Ger. physicist.

Web'ster (wĕb'stĕr), Daniel, 1782–1852. Am. statesman & orator.

—, John, 1580?–?1625. Eng. dram.

—, Noah, 1758–1843. Am. lexicographer.

We'de·kind (vā'dĕ·kĭnt), Frank (frängk), 1864–1918. Ger. poet & dram.

Wedg'wood (wĕj'wŏŏd), Josiah, 1730–1795. Eng. potter.

Weems (wēmz), Mason Locke, 1759–1825. *Parson Weems.* Am. clergyman & biographer.

Weir (wēr), Robert Walter, 1803–1889, and his 2 sons, John Fer'gu·son (fûr'gŭ·s'n), 1841–1926, and Julian Alden, 1852–1919. Am. painters.

Weis'mann (vīs'män), Au'gust (ou'gŏŏst), 1834–1914. Ger. biologist.

Wei Tao-Ming (wā' dou'mĭng'), 1899– . Chin. lawyer & diplomat.

Weiz'mann (vīts'män), Cha'im (kī'yĭm), 1874–1952. Israeli (Russ.-born) chem.; 1st pres. of Israel (1948–52).

Welch (wĕlch; wĕlsh), William Henry, 1850–1934. Am. pathologist.

Welles (wĕlz), (George) Or'son (ôr's'n), 1915– . Am. actor & producer.

—, Gideon, 1802–1878. Am. polit. & writer.

—, Sumner, 1892– . Am. diplomat.

Welles'ley (wĕlz'lĭ), Richard Col'ley (kŏl'ĭ), 1760–1842. 1st Marquis *Wellesley.* Brit. statesman; gov. gen. of India (1797–1805).

Wel'ling·ton (wĕl'ĭng·tŭn), 1st Duke of, 1769–1852. *Arthur Wellesley. The Iron Duke.* Brit. gen. & statesman.

Wells (wĕlz), Carolyn, d. 1942. Am. writer.

—, Herbert George, 1866–1946. Eng. nov., hist., & sociol.

Wemyss (wēmz), Sir Henry Col'ville (kŏl'vĭl; kŏl'-) Barclay, 1891– . Brit. gen.

Wen'ces·laus (wĕn'sĕs·lôs); *Ger.* Wen'zel (vĕn'tsĕl), 1361–1419. King of Germany & Holy Rom. emp. (1378–1400), & (as Wenceslaus IV) king of Bohemia (1378–1419).

Wen'dell (wĕn'd'l), Bar'rett (bar'ĕt; -ĭt), 1855–1921. Am. scholar.

Went'worth (wĕnt'wûrth; -wĕrth), William Charles, 1793–1872. Australian statesman.

Wer'fel (vĕr'fĕl), Franz (fränts), 1890–1945. Ger. author.

Wer'ner (vĕr'nĕr), Al'fred (äl'frät), 1866–1919. Swiss chem.

Wer'ren·rath (wĕr'ĕn·räth), Rei'nald (rī'n'ld), 1883–1953. Am. baritone.

Wes'ley (wĕs'lĭ; wĕz'-), Charles, 1707–1788. *Bro. of John.* Eng. Methodist preacher & hymn writer.

—, John, 1703–1791. Eng. theol., evangelist, & founder of Methodism.

West (wĕst), Benjamin, 1738–1820. Am. painter in Eng.

—, Rebecca, 1892– . *Pseud. of Cic'i·ly* (sĭs'ĭ·lĭ) *Isabel Fair'field* (fâr'fēld). Eng. critic & nov.

West'cott (wĕs[t]'kŭt), Edward Noyes, 1846–1898. Am. banker & nov.

Wes'ter·marck (vĕs'tĕr·märk; *Angl.* wĕs'tĕr·märk), Edward Alexander, 1862–1939. Finnish philos. & anthropologist.

Wes'ting·house (wĕs'tĭng·hous'), George, 1846–1914. Am. inventor.

Wey'gand (vā'gäN'), Max'ime' (måk'sēm'), 1867– . Fr. gen.

Wey'man (wā'mǎn), Stanley John, 1855–1928. Eng. nov.

Whar'ton (hwôr't'n), Edith New'bold (nū'bōld), 1862–1937. Nee *Jones* (jōnz). Am. nov.

Whate'ly (hwāt'lĭ), Richard, 1787–1863. Eng. theol. & logician.

Wheat'stone (hwēt'stōn; *Brit. usu.* -stŭn), Sir Charles, 1802–1875. Eng. physicist & inventor.

Whee'ler (hwē'lĕr), Joseph, 1836–1906. Am. Confed. gen.

Whee'lock (hwē'lŏk), Eleazar, 1711–1779. Am. clergyman & educ.

Whew'ell (hū'ĕl), William, 1794–1866. Eng. philos. & math.

Whip'ple (hwĭp'l), George Hoyt, 1878– . Am. pathologist.

Whis'tler (hwĭs'lĕr), James Abbott Mc·Neill' (măk·nēl'), 1834–1903. Am. painter & etcher.

White (hwīt), Andrew Dick'son (dĭk's'n), 1832–1918. Am. educ. & diplomat.

—, Edward Douglass, 1845–1921. Am. jurist.

—, Gilbert, 1720–1793. Eng. clergyman & naturalist.

—, Stan'ford (stǎn'fĕrd), 1853–1906. Am. architect.

—, Stewart Edward, 1873–1946. Am. nov.

—, William Allen, 1868–1944. Am. journalist & writer.

White'field (hwīt'fēld), George, 1714–1770. Eng. Methodist revivalist.

White'head (hwīt'hĕd), Alfred North, 1861–1947. Eng. math. & philos.

—, William, 1715–1785. Eng. dram.; poet laureate (1757–1785).

Whit'man (hwĭt'mǎn), Marcus, 1802–1847. Am. missionary & pioneer in the Oregon region.

—, Walt (wôlt), 1819–1892. Orig. *Walter.* Am. poet.

Whit'ney (hwĭt'nĭ), Eli, 1765–1825. Am. inventor.

—, Josiah Dwight, 1819–1896. Am. scientist.

—, William Dwight, 1827–1894. *Bro. of J. D.* Am. philologist.

Whit'ti·er (hwĭt'ĭ·ĕr), John Green'leaf (grēn'lēf), 1807–1892. *The Quaker Poet.* Am. poet.

Wick'ard (wĭk'ĕrd), Claude Raymond, 1893– . Am. administrator.

Wic'lif *or* **Wick'liffe.** See WYCLIFFE.

Wi'dor (vē'dôr'), Charles Ma'rie' (må'rē'), 1845–1937. Fr. organist & composer.

Wi'du·kind. See WITTEKIND.

Wie'land (vē'länt), Chri'stoph (krĭs'tôf) Mar'tin (mär'tēn), 1733–1813. *The German Voltaire.* Ger. author.

—, Hein'rich (hīn'rĭk), 1877–1957. Ger. chem.

Wien (vēn), Wil'helm (vĭl'hĕlm), 1864–1928. Ger. physicist.

Wig'gin (wĭg'ĭn), Kate Douglas, 1856–1923. Nee *Smith* (smĭth). Am. writer & educ.

Wig'gins (wĭg'ĭnz), Carleton, 1848–1932, and his son Guy Carleton, 1883– . Am. painters.

Wig'ner (wĭg'nĕr), Eugene Paul, 1902– . Am. (Hung.-born) physicist.

Wil'ber·force (wĭl'bĕr·fôrs), William, 1759–1833. Eng. philanthropist & abolitionist.

Wil'bur (wĭl'bĕr), Ray Lyman, 1875–1949. Am. educ. & administrator.

Wilde (wīld), Oscar Fin'gal (fĭng'găl) O'Fla'her·tie (ō·flä'hĕr·tĭ; ō·flä'tĭ; ō·flä'[h]ĕr·tĭ) Wills (wĭlz), 1854–1900. Irish author.

Wil'der (wĭl'dĕr), Thorn'ton (thôrn't'n; -tŭn) Niv'en (nĭv'ĕn), 1897– . Am. author.

Wi'ley (wī'lĭ), Harvey Washington, 1844–1930. Am. chem. & food analyst.

Wil'hel·mi'na (wĭl'hĕl·mē'nà; wĭl'ĕ·mē'nà; *Du.* vĭl'hĕl·mē'nà), 1880– . Queen of the Netherlands (1890–1948).

Wilkes (wĭlks), Charles, 1798–1877. Am. naval officer & explorer.

—, John, 1727–1797. Eng. polit. reformer.

Wil'kins (wĭl'kĭnz), Sir George Hubert, 1888– . Australian polar explorer.

—, Mary Eleanor. See Mary E. FREEMAN.

Wil'kin·son (wĭl'kĭn·s'n), Ellen Cicely, 1891–1947. Eng. feminist & polit.

—, James, 1757–1825. Am. gen. & adventurer.

Wil'lard (wĭl'ĕrd), Emma, 1787–1870. Nee *Hart* (härt). Am. educ.

—, Frances Elizabeth Caroline, 1839–1898. Am. educ. & reformer.

Will'cocks (wĭl'kŏks), Sir William, 1852–1932. Brit. engineer.

Wil'liam (wĭl'yǎm). Name of 4 kings of Eng.: **I** (*the Conqueror*), 1027–1087 (reigned 1066–87); **II** (*Ru'fus* [rōō'fŭs]), 1056?–1100 (reigned 1087–1100); **III**, 1650–1702 (reigned 1689–1702; see MARY); **IV**, 1765–1837 (reigned 1830–37).

— **I**, 1533–1584. *The Silent.* Prince of Orange & founder of the Du. Republic.

— **I**, 1797–1888. King of Prussia (1861–88) & emp. of Germany (1871–88).

— **II**, 1859–1941. Emp. of Germany & king of Prussia (1888–1918).

—, 1882–1951. *Frie'drich Wil'helm Vic'tor Au'gust Ernst* (frē'-drĭk vĭl'hĕlm vĭk'tôr ou'gŏŏst ĕrnst). Crown prince of Germany (1888–1918).

— **of Malmes'bur·y** (mämz'bĕr·ĭ; -brĭ), between 1090 and 1096–?1143. Eng. hist.

Wil'liams (wĭl'yǎmz), Roger, 1603?–1683. Eng.-born clergyman; founder of Rhode Island colony.

Wil'lis (wĭl'ĭs), Sir Algernon Us'borne (?ŭz'bĕrn), 1889– . Brit. admiral.

—, Nathaniel Par'ker (pär'kĕr), 1806–1867. Am. editor & writer.

Will'kie (wĭl'kĭ), Wendell Lewis, 1892–1944. Am. lawyer, businessman, & polit.

Will'stät'ter (vĭl'shtĕt'ĕr), Ri'chard (rĭk'ärt), 1872–1942. Ger. chem.

Wil'son (wĭl's'n), Charles Thomson Rees (rēs), 1869– . Scot. physicist.

—, Sir Henry Hughes, 1864–1922. Brit. field marshal.

—, Henry Maitland, 1st Baron, 1881– . Brit. field marshal.

—, John, 1785–1854. Pseud. *Christopher North* (nôrth). Scot. author.

—, (Thomas) Wood'row (wŏŏd'rō), 1856–1924. 28th pres. of the U. S. (1913–21).

Winck'el·mann (vĭng'kĕl·män), Jo·hann' (yō·hän'; yō'hän) Jo'a·chim (yō'ä·kĭm; yō·ä'kĭm), 1717–1768. Ger. archaeologist & art hist.

Win'daus (vĭn'dous), A'dolf (ä'dôlf), 1876– . Ger. chem.

Win'disch-Graetz' (vĭn'dĭsh-grâts'), Prince Alfred Can'di·dus (kän'dĕ·dŏŏs) Fer'di·nand (fĕr'dĕ·nänt), 1787–1862. Austrian field marshal.

Wind'sor, Duke of. See EDWARD VIII.

Win'gate (wĭn'gĭt; -gāt), Sir Francis Reginald, 1861–1953. Brit. gen.

—, Orde (ôrd) Charles, 1903–1944. Brit. gen.

Win'kel·ried, von (fôn vĭng'kĕl·rēt), Ar'nold (är'nôlt), 14th cent. Swiss patriot.

Wins'low (wĭnz'lō), Edward, 1595–1655. Gov. of Plymouth colony (1633, 1636, 1644).

Win'sor (wĭn'zĕr), Justin, 1831–1897. Am. librarian & hist.

Win'throp (wĭn'thrŭp), John, 1588–1649. 1st gov. of Massachusetts Bay colony.

—, John, 1606–1676. *Son of prec.* Gov. of Connecticut colony.

—, John, 1638–1707. *Son of prec.* Gov. of Connecticut colony.

Wir'ta·nen, Ar'tu·ri. See Artturi VIRTANEN.

Wise (wīz), Stephen Samuel, 1874–1949. Am. (Hung.-born) rabbi.

Wise'man (wīz'mǎn), Nicholas Patrick Stephen, 1802–1865. Eng. cardinal & author.

Wiss'ler (wĭs'lĕr), Clark, 1870–1947. Am. anthropologist.

Wis'ter (wĭs'tĕr), Owen, 1860–1938. Am. nov.

With'er (wĭth'ĕr) *or* **With'ers** (-ĕrz), George, 1588–1667. Eng. poet & pamphleteer.

Wi'tos (vē'tôs), Win'cen·ty (vēn·tsĕn'tĭ), 1874–1945. Pol. statesman.

Wit'te (vyĕt'tyĕ), Count Ser·gei' (syĭr·gā'ĭ) Yul'ie·vich (yŏŏl'yĕ·vyĭch), 1849–1915. Russ. statesman.

Wit'te·kind (vĭt'ĕ·kĭnt) *or* **Wi'du·kind** (vē'dŏŏ·kĭnt), d. ab. 807. Saxon warrior.

Wode'house (wŏŏd'hous), Pel'ham (pĕl'ǎm) Grenville, 1881– . Eng. nov.

Wof'fing·ton (wŏf'ĭng·tŭn), Margaret, 1714?–1760. *Peg.* Irish-born actress.

Wol'cott (wŏŏl'kŭt), Oliver, 1726–1797. *Son of Roger.* Gov. of Connecticut (1796–97).

—, Oliver, 1760–1833. *Son of prec.* Gov. of Connecticut (1817–27).

—, Roger, 1679–1767. Gov. of Connecticut (1751–58).

Wolf (vôlf), Frie'drich (frē'drĭk) Au'gust (ou'gŏŏst), 1759–1824. Ger. philologist.

Wolfe (wŏŏlf), Charles, 1791–1823. Irish poet.

—, James, 1727–1759. Brit. gen.

—, Thomas Clayton, 1900–1938. Am. nov.

Wolff (vôlf), Kas'par (käs'pär) Frie'drich (frē'drĭk), 1733–1794. Ger. anatomist.

— *or* **Wolf, von** (fôn vôlf'), Baron Chri'sti·an (krĭs'tē·än), 1679–1754. Ger. philos. & math.

Wol'fram von E'schen·bach (vôl'främ fôn ĕsh'ĕn·bäк), 1170?–?1220. Ger. poet.

Wol'las·ton (wŏŏl'ăs·tŭn), William Hyde, 1766–1828. Eng. chem. & physicist.

Wolse'ley (wŏŏlz'lĭ), Gar'net (gär'nĕt; -nĭt) Joseph, 1st Viscount, 1833–1913. Brit. field marshal.

Wol'sey (wŏŏl'zĭ), Thomas, 1475?–1530. Eng. cardinal & statesman.

Wood (wŏŏd), Grant, 1892–1942. Am. painter.

—, Leonard, 1860–1927. Am. physician, gen., & colonial administrator.

Woolf (wŏŏlf), Virginia, 1882–1941. Nee *Ste'phen* (stē'vĕn). Eng. author.

Wooll'cott (wŏŏl'kŭt), Alexander, 1887–1943. Am. journalist & writer.

Wool'ley (wŏŏl'ĭ), Sir Charles Leonard, 1880– . Eng. archaeologist.

Wool'ton (wŏŏl't'n; -tŭn), 1st Baron, 1883– . *Frederick James Mar'quis* (mär'kwĭs). Eng. businessman & administrator.

Wool'worth (wŏŏl'wŭrth; -wẽrth), Frank Win'field (wĭn'fēld), 1852–1919. Am. merchant.

Worces'ter (wŏŏs'tẽr), Dean Co'nant (kō'nănt), 1866–1924. Am. administrator in the Philippines.

—, Joseph Emerson, 1784–1865. Am. lexicographer.

Words'worth (wûrdz'wûrth; -wẽrth), William, 1770–1850. Eng. poet; poet laureate (1843–50).

Wot'ton (wŏt'n), Sir Henry, 1568–1639. Eng. diplomat & poet.

Wran'gel (vrän'gĕl), Baron Pĕtr (pyŏ'tẽr) Ni·ko·la'e·vich (nyĭ·kŭ·lä'yĕ·vyĭch), 1878–1928. Russ. gen.

Wren (rĕn), Sir Christopher, 1632–1723. Eng. architect.

Wright (rīt), Frank Lloyd, 1869– . Am. architect.

—, Harold Bell, 1872–1944. Am. nov.

—, Joseph, 1855–1930. Eng. philologist.

—, Louis Book'er (bŏŏk'ẽr), 1899– . Am. educ. & librarian.

—, Or'ville (ôr'vĭl), 1871–1948, and his bro. Wilbur, 1867–1912. Am. pioneers in aviation.

—, Willard Huntington, 1888–1939. Pseud. *S. S. Van Dine* (văn dīn'). Am. writer.

—, William Al'dis (ôl'dĭs), 1836?–1914. Eng. scholar.

Wrong (rŏng), Humphrey Hume, 1894–1954. Canadian diplomat.

Wundt (vŏŏnt), Wil'helm (vĭl'hĕlm), 1832–1920. Ger. physiol. & psychol.

Wy'att *or* **Wy'at** (wī'ăt), Sir Thomas, 1503?–1542. Eng. poet & diplomat.

Wych'er·ley (wĭch'ẽr·lĭ), William, 1640?–1716. Eng. dram.

Wyc'liffe *or* **Wic'lif** (wĭk'lĭf), John, 1320?–1384. Eng. religious reformer & Bible trans.

Wyld (wīld), Henry Cecil Kennedy, 1870–1945. Eng. philologist & lexicographer.

Wy'lie (wī'lĭ), Elinor Morton, 1885–1928. Mrs. *William Rose Benét;* nee *Hoyt* (hoit). Am. poet & nov.

Wynd'ham (wĭn'dăm), Sir Charles, 1837–1919. *Charles Cul'ver·well* (kŭl'vẽr·wĕl; -wĕl). Eng. actor-manager.

—, George, 1863–1913. Eng. polit. & writer.

X

Xan·thip'pe (zăn·tĭp'ē; -thĭp'ē) *or* **Xan·tip'pe** (-tĭp'ē), 5th cent. B.C. *Wife of Socrates.*

Xa'vi·er (zā'vĭ·ẽr; zăv'ĭ·ẽr), Saint Francis, 1506–1552. *Fran·cis'co* (frän·thēs'kō) *Ja·vier'* (hä·vyẽr'). *Apostle of the Indies.* Span. Jesuit missionary.

Xe·noc'ra·tes (zĕ·nŏk'rà·tēz), 396–314 B.C. Greek philos.

Xe·noph'a·nes (zĕ·nŏf'à·nēz), 6th cent. B.C. Greek philos.

Xen'o·phon (zĕn'ō·fŭn), 434?–?355 B.C. Greek hist., essayist, & soldier.

Xer'xes I (zûrk'sēz), 519?–465 B.C. *The Great.* King of Persia (486–465).

Y

Yale (yāl), Elihu, 1649–1721. Eng. merchant in Am.

Ya·ma·da (yä·mä·dä), O·tsu·zo (ō·tsōō·zō), 1881– . Jap. gen.

Ya·ma·ga·ta (yä·mä·gä·tä), Prince A·ri·to·mo (ä·rē·tō·mō), 1838–1922. Jap. gen. & statesman.

Ya·ma·mo·to (yä·mä·mō·tō), I·so·ro·ku (ē·sō·rō·kōō), 1884–1943. Jap. admiral.

Ya·ma·shi·ta (yä·mä·shē·tä), To·mo·yu·ki (tō·mō·yōō·kē), 1885–1946. Jap. gen.

Ya·su·da (yä·sōō·dä), Ta·ke·o (tä·kĕ·ō), 1889– . Jap. gen.

Yeats (yāts), William Butler, 1865–1939. Irish poet & dram.

Yen (yĕn), W. W., 1877–1950. Orig. *Yen Hui-ch'ing* (yĕn' hwä'chĭng'). Chin. statesman.

Yen Hsi-shan (yĕn' shē'shän'), 1882– . Chin. gen.

Ye·re·men'ko (*Russ.* yĭ·ryĭ·myĕn'kŭ; *Ukrainian* yĭ·ryä'myĕn·kŭ), An·drei' (ŭn·dryä'ĭ) I·va'no·vich (ĭ·vä'nŭ·vyĭch), 1892– . Russ. gen.

Yer'kes (yûr'kĕs; -kĕz), Charles Ty'son (tī's'n), 1837–1905. Am. financier.

Yo·nai (yō·nī), Mi·tsu·ma·sa (mē·tsōō·mä·sä), 1880–1948. Jap. admiral & statesman.

York (yôrk), Alvin Cul'lum (kŭl'ŭm), 1887– . Am. soldier.

Yo·shi·da (yō·shē·dä), Zen·go (zĕn·gō), 1885– . Jap. admiral.

Yo·shi·hi·to (yō·shē·hē·tō), 1879–1926. Emp. of Japan (1912–26).

Young (yŭng), Brig'ham (brĭg'ăm), 1801–1877. Am. Mormon leader.

—, Edward, 1683–1765. Eng. poet.

—, Francis Brett, 1884–1954. Eng. nov.

—, Owen D., 1874– . Am. lawyer.

Young'hus'band (yŭng'hŭz'bănd), Sir Francis Edward, 1863–1942. Brit. explorer & author.

Yp'si·lan'ti (ĭp'sĭ·lăn'tĭ) *or* **Hy'pse·lan'tes** (ē'psĕ·län'dēs), Alexander, 1792–1828, and his bro. Demetrius, 1793–1832. Greek revolutionists.

Yüan Shih-k'ai (yü·än' shĭr'kī'), 1859–1916. Chin. statesman; pres. of China (1913–16).

Yu·de'nich (yōō·dyā'nyĭch), Ni·ko·lai' (nyĭ·kŭ·lī') Ni·ko·la'e·vich (nyĭ·kŭ·lä'yĕ·vyĭch), 1862–1933. Russ. gen.

Z

Zagh·lul' Pa'sha (zăg·lōōl' pä'shä), Saad (säd), 1860?–1927. Egyptian lawyer & statesman.

Za·ha'roff (zŭ·kä'rŭf; *Angl.* zà·hä'rŏf), Sir Bas'il (băz'l), 1850–1936. Brit. (Russ.-born) banker & armament contractor.

Za·i'mes *or* **Za·i'mis** (zä·ē'mēs), A·le'xan·dros (ä·lā'ksän·thrōs), 1855–1936. Greek statesman.

Za·les'ki (zä·lĕs'kē), Au'gust (ou'gōōst), 1883– . Pol. statesman.

Za·mo'ra y Tor'res (thä·mō'rä ē tôr'rās), Ni·ce'to (nē·thā'tō) Al'ca·lá' (äl'kä·lä'), 1877–1949. Span. polit.; pres. of Spain (1931–36).

Zan'gwill (zăng'gwĭl; zăng'wĭl), Israel, 1864–1926. Eng. dram. & nov.

Zar'a·thus'tra. See ZOROASTER.

Zee'man (zā'män), Pie'ter (pē'tẽr), 1865–1943. Du. physicist.

Zeitz'ler (tsīts'lẽr), Kurt (kōōrt), 1895– . Ger. gen.

Ze·lin'ski (zyĭ·lyĕn'skĭ; *Angl.* zĕ·lĭn'skĭ), Ni·ko·lai' (nyĭ·kŭ·lī') Di·mi'tri·e·vich (dyĭ·myē'tryĭ·yĕ·vyĭch), 1861–1953. Russ. chem.

Ze'no (zē'nō), 4th–3d cent. B.C. Greek philos.; founder of Stoic school.

—**of E'le·a** (ē'lē·à), 5th cent. B.C. Greek philos.

Ze·no'bi·a (zē·nō'bĭ·à), d. after 272. Queen of Palmyra (267–272).

Zep'pe·lin', von (fôn tsĕp'ē·lēn'; tsĕp'ĕ·lĕn; *Angl.* zĕp'ē·lĭn), Count Fer'di·nand (fẽr'dē·nänt), 1838–1917. Ger. gen. & aeronaut.

Zeux'is (zūk'sĭs), 5th cent. B.C. Greek painter.

Zhda'nov (zhdä'nŭf), An·drei' (ŭn·dryä'ĭ) A·le·ksan'dro·vich (ŭ·lyĭ·ksän'drô·vyĭch), 1896–1948. Russ. polit. & gen.

Zhu'kov (zhōō'kŭf), Ge·or'gi (gĭ·ôr'gĭ) Kon·stan·ti'no·vich (kŭn·stŭn·tyē'nŭ·vyĭch), 1894– . Russ. marshal.

Zim'ba·list (*Angl.* zĭm'bà·lĭst; *Russ.* zyĭm·bŭ·lyēst'), Ef'rem (*Angl.* ĕf'rĕm; *Russ.* yĭ·fryäm'), 1889– . Russ.-born violinist.

Zim'mer·mann (tsĭm'ẽr·män), Al'fred (äl'frät) F. M., 1859–1925. Ger. colonial statesman and hist.

—, Ar'thur (är'tōōr), 1864–1940. Ger. statesman, author of "Zimmermann Telegram."

Zim'mern (zĭm'ẽrn), Sir Alfred, 1879–1957. Eng. polit. scientist.

Zi·no'viev (zĭ·nô'vyĕf), Gri·go'ri (gryĭ·gô'ryĕf) E·vse'e·vich (yĭf·syā'yĕ·vyĭch), 1883–1936. Orig. *Hirsch Ap'fel·baum* (hĭrsh äp'fĕl·boum). Russ. Communist.

Zins'ser (zĭn'sẽr), Hans (häns), 1878–1940. Am. bacteriol.

Zin'zen·dorf, von (fôn tsĭn'tsĕn·dôrf), Count Ni·ko·la'us (nē'kō·lä'ōōs; nē·kô·lous) Lud'wig (lōōt'vĭk; lōōd'-), 1700–1760. Ger. leader of the Bohemian Brethren.

Žiž'ka (zhĭsh'kä; *Ger.* zhĭsh'kä), Jan (yän); *Ger.* Jo·hann' (yō·hän'; yō'hän), 1360?–1424. Bohemian gen. & Hussite.

Zog I (zôg) *or* **Zog'u I** (zô'g'w'), 1895– . *Scan'der·beg III* (skăn'dẽr·bĕg). Orig. *Ah·med'* (äk·mĕd') *Bey* (bā) *Zogu.* King of the Albanians (1928–46).

Zo'la' (zō'lä'; *Angl.* zō'là, zō·lä'), É'mile' (ā'mēl'), 1840–1902. Fr. nov.

Zorn (sôrn), An'ders (än'dẽrs) Le'on·hard (lā'ô·nàrd), 1860–1920. Swed. painter, etcher, & sculptor.

Zo'ro·as'ter (zō'rō·ăs'tẽr; zôr'ō-) *or* **Zar'a·thus'tra** (zăr'à·thōōs'trà), 6th cent. B.C. Founder of ancient Pers. religion.

Zor·ril'la y Mo·ral' (thôr·rē'lyä ē mō·räl'), Jo·sé' (hō·sā'), 1817–1893. Span. poet & dram.

Zsig'mon·dy (zhĭg'môn·dē), Ri'chard (rĭk'ärt), 1865–1929. Ger. chem.

Zu'lo·a'ga (thōō'lō·ä'gä), Ig·na'cio (ēg·nä'thyô), 1870–1945. Span. painter.

Zweig (tsvīk), Ar'nold (är'nôlt), 1887– . Ger. author.

—, Ste'fan (shtē'fän), 1881–1942. Brit. (Austrian-born) writer.

Zwing'li (tsvĭng'lē), Hul'dreich (hŏŏl'drīĸ) *or* Ul'rich (ōōl'rĭĸ), 1484–1531. Swiss Reformation leader.

A PRONOUNCING GAZETTEER

CONTAINING MORE THAN SEVEN THOUSAND
NAMES OF PLACES

The purpose of this section is to give basic information about the countries of the world and their most important regions, cities and towns, and natural features. The information includes the spelling, syllabication, and pronunciation of the names, the location of the place or natural feature, and for the more important entries the legal or political status (for example, town, city, urban district, commune, county, state) and statistical data. Population figures are given in round numbers to the nearest hundred. All incorporated urban centers in the United States having 15,000 or more inhabitants at the 1950 census have been included. Incorporated places in Canada having 12,000

or more inhabitants at the 1956 census have been included.

This section complements the general Vocabulary by listing many derivative forms, such as **Abyssinian** at ABYSSINIA and **Austronesian** at AUSTRONESIA, or by including references to related Vocabulary entries, such as the reference to ANNAMESE at Annam.

The abbreviations used are listed in the Abbreviations sections on pages xxi–xxii and pages 998–1007. The letters N, E, S, and W when not followed by a period indicate direction and are not part of a place name; thus, northern North Dakota appears as N North Dakota. The symbol ✳ denotes a capital.

A

Aa'chen (ä′κĕn), Fr. **Aix-la-Cha·pelle′** (āks′lä·shȧ·pĕl′) city, W Germany, on Belgian border; pop. 130,000.

Aaland. Var. of Åland: see AHVENANMAA.

Aal'borg (ôl′bôrg) seaport, Denmark, in NE Jutland; pop. 60,900.

Aa're (ä′rĕ) or **Aar** (är) river, Switzerland, flowing NW to the Rhine; 175 m. long.

Aar'gau′ (är′gou′), Fr. **Ar'go·vie′** (àr′gô′vē′) canton, N cen. Switzerland; ✳ Aarau; area 542 sq. m.; pop. 300,800.

Aar'hus (ôr′hōōs′) seaport, Denmark, in E Jutland; pop. 107,400.

A'ba·dan′ (ä′bä·dän′; Angl. ăb′à·dăn′) **1** island, W Iran, in Shatt-al-Arab delta. **2** town on Abadan I.; oil refineries; pop. with Khorramshahr 201,000.

Ab'bots·ford (ăb′ŭts·fĕrd) estate, SE Scotland, in Roxburgh co. on Tweed river W of Melrose; residence 1824–32 of Sir Walter Scott.

Ab'er·deen (ăb′ĕr·dēn′) **1** town, NE Maryland; nearby is **Aberdeen Proving Ground**, U.S. army reservation of 35,000 acres along W side of upper Chesapeake Bay. **2** city, W Washington, on Grays Harbor adjacent to Hoquiam; pop. 19,700. **3** city, NE South Dakota; pop. 21,100.

Ab'er·deen' (ăb′ĕr·dēn′; ăb′ĕr·dēn) **1** or **Ab'er·deen'shire** (ăb′ĕr·dēn′shīr; -shĕr) county, NE Scotland; 1971 sq. m.; pop. 308,100. **2** burgh, its ✳, on North Sea; pop. 182,700.

Ab'er·yst'wyth (ăb′ĕr·ĭst′wĭth) municipal borough, W Wales, on Cardigan Bay; ✳ of Cardiganshire; pop. 9300.

Ab'i·djan′ (ăb′ĭ·jän′) seaport, French West Africa, ✳ of Ivory Coast territory; pop. 128,200.

Abila. See MUSA, JEBEL.

Ab'i·lene (ăb′ĭ·lēn) **1** city, E cen. Kansas; pop. 5800. **2** city, NW cen. Texas; pop. 45,600.

Ab'in·ger (ăb′ĭn·jĕr) village, S England, in Surrey, at 51°12′N, 0°24′W; site of magnetic observatory and time clocks, removed from Greenwich in World War II.

Ab·kha'zi·a or **Ab·kha'si·a** (ăb·kä′zhĭ·à; -zhä), officially **Ab·kha'zian Autonomous Soviet Socialist Republic** (ăb·kä′zhŭn) autonomous republic, U.S.S.R., in NW Georgia on Black Sea; ✳ Sukhumi; 3358 sq. m.; pop. 293,100.

Abo. See TURKU.

Ab·ou·kir'. Var. of ABUKIR.

A·bruz'zi (ȧ·brōōt′tsē) region, cen. Italy, bordering on Adriatic Sea and including highest of Apennines; with Molise to the S, forms compartimento of **Abruzzi e Mo'li·se** (ā mô′lē·zā).

Ab'u·kir' or **A'bu Qir** (ăb′ōō·kĭr′; ȧ·bōō′kĕr) **1** bay, N Egypt, between Alexandria and the Rosetta mouth of the Nile; Battle of the Nile Aug. 1–2, 1798. **2** village on the bay.

A'bu Sim'bel (ä′bōō sĭm′bĕl) or **Ip'sam·bul'** (ĭp′săm·bōōl′) locality, cen. Egypt, on left bank of the Nile; site of two rock temples.

A·by'dos (ȧ·bī′dŏs) **1** ancient town, Asia Minor, on the Hellespont. **2** ancient town, Egypt, on left bank of the Nile; site of temples.

Abyla. See MUSA, JEBEL.

Ab'ys·sin'i·a (ăb′ĭ·sĭn′ĭ·à; -sĭn′yà). See ETHIOPIA. — **Ab'ys·sin'i·an**, adj. & n.

A·ca'di·a (ȧ·kā′dĭ·à), Fr. **A'ca'die'** (à′kà′dē′) Nova Scotia; — its original name. — **A·ca'di·an** (ȧ·kā′dĭ·ăn), adj. & n.

Acadia National Park, section of coast of Maine including areas on Mount Desert I. and Isle au Haut; established 1919.

A'ca·pul'co, in full **A'ca·pul'co de Juá'rez** (ä′kä·pōōl′kô thā hwä′rās) seaport, S Mexico, in Guerrero state on the Pacific S of Mexico City; resort; pop. 27,900.

Ac'ar·na'ni·a (ăk′är·nā′nĭ·à; ăk′ är-; -nän′yà), Mod. Gr. **A'kar·na·ni'a** (ä′kär·nä·nyē′à) region, W Greece, on Ionian Sea; ancient country loosely organized as Acarnanian League.

Accad. See AKKAD.

Accho. See ACRE.

Ac·cra' or **Ak·kra'** (ă·krä′; ăk′rà) seaport, ✳ of Ghana, on the Gulf of Guinea; pop. 135,900.

A·chae'a (ȧ·kē′à) or **A·cha'ia** (ȧ·kā′yà; ȧ·kī′à) region, S Greece, in N Peloponnesus, bordering on gulfs of Corinth and Patras; with Elis to the S, forms a department of modern Greece. See ACHAEAN, in Vocab.

Ack'ia Battleground National Monument (ăk′yà) site, NE Mississippi, near Tupelo, of battle 1736 in which Chickasaw Indians defeated French; established 1938.

Ac'on·ca'gua (ăk′ŭn·kä′gwà; -käg′wà; Span. ä′kông·kä′gwä) mountain, W Argentina, near Chilean border; highest peak of Andes and of Western Hemisphere, 22,835 ft.

Açores. See AZORES.

A'cre (Port. ä′krĕ; Span. ä′krä) territory, W Brazil, bordering on Peru and Bolivia; ✳ Rio Branco; area 57,153 sq. m.; pop. 116,100.

A'cre (ä′kĕr; ā′kĕr; ā′krĕ; ăk′ĕr; ăk′rĕ), Heb. **Ak·ko'** or **Ac·cho'** (ä·kō′), also once called **Ptol'e·ma'is** (tŏl′ĕ·mā′ĭs) and (by Crusaders) **Saint-Jean-d'A'cre** (săn′zhän′dà′kr′) seaport, NW Israel, at N end of bay (**Bay of Acre**) N of Mt. Carmel; pop. 9000.

Ac'ro·ce·rau'ni·a (ăk′rô·sē·rô′nĭ·à; -rŏn′yà) promontory, ancient Greece, in NW Epirus; now known as Cape Linguetta, in SW Albania.

Ac'te (ăk′tē; -tē), Mod. Gr. **Ak·ti'** (äk·tē′) peninsula, NE Greece, having at its tip Mount Athos.

Ac'ti·um (ăk′shĭ·ŭm; -tĭ·ŭm) promontory and ancient town, W Greece, in NW Acarnania; victory of Octavius.

Ac'ton (ăk′tŭn) municipal borough, SE England, in Middlesex, near London; pop. 67,400.

A'da (ā′dà) city, S cen. Oklahoma; pop. 16,000.

A'dak (ä′dăk) island, SW Alaska, in cen. Andreanof Is., Aleutian Is.

Adam's Peak, Singhalese **Sa'ma·na·la** (sŭ′mä·nȧ·là) mountain, S cen. Ceylon; 7365 ft. high.

A·da·na′ (ä·dä·nä′) or **Sey·han′** (sā·hän′) city, S Turkey, on Seyhan river; pop. 117,800.

Addar, Ras. See BON, CAPE.

Ad'dis Ab'a·ba (ăd′ĭs ăb′à·bà) town, ✳ of Ethiopia, on plateau at over 8000 ft.; pop. ab. 300,000.

A'de·laide (ăd′′l·ād) city, ✳ of South Australia; pop. 382,600.

A'dé'lie' Coast or **Land** (à′dā′lē′; Angl. ăd′′l-ē) region, Antarctica, on coast of Wilkes Land; placed under French sovereignty 1938.

A'den (ä′d′n; ā′d′n; ăd′′n) **1** protectorate, S Arabia, the coastal area from Yemen on W to Oman on E; ab. 112,000 sq. m.; includes also Socotra I.; constitutes numerous sheikdoms and sultanates under the protection of Great Britain; does not include area around Aden seaport. **2** colony, on coast of and surrounded by the protectorate, occupying Aden and Little Aden peninsulas and small part of hinterland; area 75 sq. m.; pop. 80,500; includes Perim I. **3** seaport, ✳ of Aden colony, on Aden Penin.; came under British 1839.

Aden, Gulf of, arm of Indian Ocean between Aden and Africa.

A'di·ge (ä′dē·jå) river, NE Italy, flowing S to Adriatic Sea; 220 m. long.

A·di·gey'. Var. of Adygei, in ADYGEI AUTONOMOUS REGION.

Ad'i·ron'dack Mountains (ăd′ĭ·rŏn′dăk) mountain group, NE New York; highest peak Mt. Marcy, 5344 ft.

Ad'mi·ral·ty Island (ăd′mĭ·răl·tĭ) island, SE Alaska, in N Alexander Archipelago; ab. 90 m. long by 20 m. wide.

Admiralty Islands, island group, W Pacific Ocean, N of New Guinea; part of Bismarck Archipelago; 800 sq. m.; pop. 13,700.

A'dri·an (ā′drĭ·ăn) city, SE Michigan; pop. 18,400.

Adrianople. See EDIRNE.

A'dri·at'ic Sea (ā′drĭ·ăt′ĭk; ăd′rĭ-) arm of Mediterranean E of Italy.

A'du·wa (ä′dŏŏ·wä), Ital. **A'do·ua** (ä′dōō·ä) town, N Ethiopia; scene of defeat of Italians 1896 by Emperor Menelik II.

A·dy·gei' Autonomous Region (ŭ·dĭ·gā′ī) autonomous region, S Soviet Russia, Europe; ✳ Maikop; 1505 sq. m.; pop. 254,100.

A·dzhar' (à·jär′; ä′jär) or **A·dzha'ri·a** (à·jär′ĭ·à), officially **Adzhar Autonomous Soviet Socialist Republic,** autonomous republic, SW Georgia, U.S.S.R., on Black Sea coast; ✳ Batum; area 1080 sq. m.; pop. 169,900. — **A·dzha'ri·an** (à·jär′ĭ·ăn), adj. & n.

Aegadian Isles, Aegates. See EGADI ISLANDS.

Ae·ge'an Islands (ē·jē′ăn) the islands of the Aegean Sea, including the Cyclades and the Northern and Southern Sporades.

Aegean Sea, arm of Mediterranean Sea between Asia Minor and Greece.

Ae·gi′na (ē·jī′nȧ), Mod. Gr. **Ai′gi·na** (â′yē·nä) island off coast of Greece, in the Saronic Gulf. — **Ae′gi·ne′tan** (ē′jī·nē′t'n), adj. & n.

Ae′gos·pot′a·mi (ē′gŏs·pŏt′ȧ·mī) or **Ae′gos·pot′a·mos** (-mŏs) river and town, ancient Thrace, in the Chersonese; naval battle 405 B.C.

Aemilia. See EMILIA.

Aeoliae Insulae. See LIPARI ISLANDS.

Ae′o·lis (ē′ō·lĭs) or **Ae·o′li·a** (ē·ō′lĭ·ȧ; ē·ōl′yȧ) ancient country, NW Asia Minor. See AEOLIAN, AEOLIC, in Vocab.

Aetna. See ETNA.

Ae·to′li·a (ē·tō′lĭ·ȧ; ē·tōl′yȧ), Mod. Gr. **Ai′to·li′a** (â′tô·lyē′ä) region, W cen. Greece, N of Gulf of Patras and E of Acarnania. — **Ae·to′li·an** (ē·tō′lĭ·ăn; -tōl′yăn), adj. & n.

Af·ghan′i·stan (ăf·găn′ĭ·stăn) country, W Asia; a constitutional monarchy; ✻ Kabul; area ab. 250,000 sq. m.; pop. ab. 12,000,000. See AFGHAN in Vocab.

Af′ri·ca (ăf′rĭ·kȧ) continent, Eastern Hemisphere, with equator crossing it just below the middle, and Greenwich meridian (0° long.) crossing it in the NW; adjoins Asia (Sinai Penin.) on NE at Isthmus of Suez; area ab. 11,596,000 sq. m. See AFRICAN, in Vocab.

Agade. See AKKAD.

A′ga·dir′ (ä′gȧ·dǐr′; ăg′ȧ-) seaport, SW Morocco; scene of incident 1911 (arrival of German warship) which brought on an international crisis.

A·ga′na (ä·gä′nyä) town, ✻ of Guam, on W coast of island; pop. 1300.

Ag′in·court (ăj′ĭn·kōrt) village, N France, WNW of Arras; scene of victory of Henry V of England over the French 1415.

A′gra (ä′grȧ; ä′grä) **1** region, N India; a presidency 1833–35, a province 1833–77 (called **North-West Provinces**), and since 1877 a unit with Oudh, the combined provinces being called 1902–50 the United Provinces of Agra and Oudh (now called Uttar Pradesh). **2** city, N India, in Uttar Pradesh on Jumna river; site of the Taj Mahal; pop. 284,100.

Agram. See ZAGREB.

Ağrı Dağı. See ARARAT.

A′guas·ca·lien′tes (ä′gwäs·kä·lyän′tās) **1** state, cen. Mexico; area 2499 sq. m.; pop. 188,100. **2** city, its ✻; pop. 82,200.

A·gul′has, Cape (ȧ·gŭl′ȧs; Port. ȧ·gōō′lyȧsh) southernmost point of Africa, at 34°50′S lat., 20°E long.

A·hag′gar Mountains (ȧ·hăg′ẽr; ä′hä·gär′) plateau region, S Algeria, in cen. Sahara; highest peaks 8000–10,000 ft.

Ah′med·a·bad′ or **Ah′mad·a·bad′** (ä′mȧd·ä·bäd′; -ȧ·băd′) city, W India, in N Bombay state on Sabarmati river; pop. 591,300.

Ah′ve·nan·maa′ (äk′vě·nän·mä′) or **Å′land′ Islands** (ō′lȧnd′) archipelago in S Gulf of Bothnia; a department of Finland; ✻ Maarianhamina; chief island **Ahvenanmaa** or **Åland.**

Ah·waz′ (ä·wäz′) town, SW Iran, on Karun river; pop. 53,000.

Aigina. See AEGINA.

Ain (ăN) river, E France, rising in Jura Mts. and flowing S to Rhone river; 118 m. long.

Aintab. See GAZIANTEP.

Aire (âr) river, N England, in W Yorkshire, flowing to Ouse river; its valley is called the **Aire′dale′** (âr′dāl′).

Aisne (ān) river, N France, flowing NW and W from Argonne Forest to Oise near Compiègne; ab. 175 m. long.

Aitolia. See AETOLIA.

Aix (āks) or **Aix-en-Pro′vence′** (ĕk′säN·prô′väNs′) city, SE France, N of Marseilles; pop. 46,100.

Aix-la-Chapelle. See AACHEN.

A·jac′cio (ä·yät′chō) seaport, France, ✻ of Corsica; pop. 31,400.

Aj′mer′ (ŭj·mẽr′; -mär′) **1** or **Ajmer-Mer·wa′ra** (-mẽr·wä′rä) former state, NW India, merged 1956 in Rajasthan state; area 2425 sq. m. **2** city, its ✻, SW of Delhi; pop. 147,300.

A′ka·ba, A′ka·bah. Vars. of 'AQABA.

A·ki·ta (ä·kē·tä) city, Japan, in NW Honshu; pop. 116,300.

Ak′kad or **Ac′cad** (ăk′ăd; äk′äd) **1** the northern division of ancient Babylonia. **2** anc. **A·ga′de** (ä·gä′dě; ȧ·gä′dě) ancient city, its ✻. — **Ak·ka′di·an, Ac·ca′di·an** (ă·kä′dĭ·ăn; ä·kä′-), adj. & n.

Akkerman. See BELGOROD-DNESTROVSKI.

Akko. See ACRE.

Akkra. See ACCRA.

Ak′ron (ăk′rŏn) city, NE Ohio; pop. 274,600.

Ak·sum or **Ax·um** (äk·sōōm) town, N Ethiopia; capital of ancient Ethiopian kingdom known as the Axumite Empire.

Ak·yab′ (äk·yäb′; äk′yäb) seaport, SW Burma, chief town of Arakan coast; pop. 38,100.

Al′a·bam′a (ăl′ȧ·băm′ȧ) **1** river, Alabama, flowing SW to join the Tombigbee river and form the Mobile and Tensaw rivers flowing into Mobile Bay; 315 m. long. **2** abbr. **Ala.**, state, SE United States, bordering on the Gulf of Mexico; ✻ Montgomery; area 51,609 sq. m.; pop. 3,061,700. — **Al′a·bam′i·an** (-băm′ĭ·ăn), **Al′a·bam′an** (-băm′ăn), adj. & n.

A′la·go′as (ä′lȧ·gō′ȧs) state, E Brazil; ✻ Maceió; area 11,031 sq. m.; pop. 1,106,500.

A·lai′ (ä·lī′) mountain range, Soviet Central Asia, in SW Kirgiz S.S.R.; highest peak 19,554 ft.

Al′a·me′da (ăl′ȧ·mē′dȧ; -mā′dȧ) city, W California, on island in San Francisco Bay; pop. 64,400.

Al′a·mo, the (ăl′ȧ·mō) fort in San Antonio, Texas; besieged by the Mexicans under Santa Anna Feb. 23–Mar. 6, 1836.

Al′a·mo·gor′do (ăl′ȧ·mō·gôr′dō) town, S New Mexico, near which is Holloman Air Force Base (in 1945 called Alamogordo Air Base), the base of operations for the trial of the first atomic bomb July 16, 1945, the explosion occurring 55 m. to the NW in the desert; pop. 6800.

Åland. Åland Islands. See AHVENANMAA.

A′la·se·hir′ (ä′lä·shě·hẽr′), anc. **Phil′a·del′phi·a** (fĭl′ȧ·děl′fĭ·ȧ; -fyȧ) city, W Turkey in Asia; ancient Philadelphia one of the Seven Churches of Asia Minor mentioned in the book of Revelation.

A·las′ka (ȧ·lăs′kȧ), abbr. (not official) **Alas.**, state of the United States, NW North America, including a wide peninsula (separated from the U.S.S.R. by Bering Strait, 56 m. wide), a coastal area to the SE, and the Aleutian Islands and the Alexander Archipelago; until 1958 a territory, purchased from Russia 1867; ✻ Juneau; area 586,400 sq. m.; pop. 128,600. — **A·las′kan**, adj. & n.

Alaska, Gulf of, inlet of Pacific Ocean, S Alaska, between Kenai Penin. and Cape Fairweather.

Alaska Peninsula, long narrow extension of SW Alaska, geographically a unit with Aleutian Is.

Alaska Range, mountain range, S Alaska, extending from Alaska Penin. to Yukon boundary; highest peak Mt. McKinley, 20,300 ft.

A′la Tau′ (ä′lä tou′) several ranges of the Tien Shan mountain system, Soviet Central Asia, in E Kazakh and Kirgiz republics around and NE of Issyk Kul; 10,000 to 18,000 ft. high.

Á′la·va (ä′lä·vä) province, N Spain, one of Basque Provinces; ✻ Vitoria; area 1175 sq. m.; pop. 118,000.

Al′a·va, Cape (ăl′ȧ·vä) cape, NW Washington, at 124°44′W long., 48°10′N lat.; most westerly point of United States mainland.

Al′ba·ce′te (äl′vä·thä′tā; -sä′tä) commune, SE Spain, in Murcia; pop. 71,800.

Al′ba Lon′ga (ăl′bȧ lŏng′gȧ) ancient city, Italy, SE of Rome; legendary birthplace of Romulus and Remus.

Al·ba′ni·a (ăl·bā′nĭ·ȧ; -bān′yȧ) **1** ancient country, Europe, in E Caucasus region on W side of Caspian Sea. **2** Albanian **Shqip·ni′** (shkyĭp·nē′) or **Shqip·ri′** (-rē′) country, S Europe, in Balkan Penin. on Adriatic Sea; a republic since 1946; ✻ Tirana; area 10,630 sq. m.; pop. 1,003,100. — **Al·ba′ni·an**, adj. & n.

Al′ba·ny (ôl′bȧ·nĭ) **1** city, W California, on San Francisco Bay; pop. 17,600. **2** city, SW Georgia; pop. 31,200. **3** city, ✻ of New York state, on Hudson river; pop. 135,000. **4** river, Canada, in N cen. Ontario, flowing E and NE into W James Bay; 610 m. long.

Al′be·marle Sound (ăl′bě·märl) inlet of Atlantic Ocean, NE North Carolina.

Al′bert′ (ȧl′bâr′) town, N France; destroyed in battles 1918.

Al′bert, Lake (ăl′bẽrt) lake, E Africa, between Uganda and Belgian Congo in course of the Nile; 100 m. long; elevation over 2000 ft.

Al·ber′ta (ăl·bûr′tȧ), abbr. **Alta.**, province, W Canada, E of Rocky Mts., ✻ Edmonton; area 248,800 sq. m.; pop. 1,123,100.

Al′bu·quer′que (ăl′bů·kûr′kē) city, cen. New Mexico, on the Rio Grande; pop. 96,800.

Al′ca·traz′ (ăl′kȧ·trăz′; ăl′kȧ·trăz) rocky island, California, in San Francisco Bay; U.S. fortification and penitentiary.

Al·dan′ (ŭl·dän′) **1** river, Soviet Russia, Asia, in SE Yakutsk A.S.S.R.; 1500 m. long. **2** town in Aldan valley; gold mining.

Al′der·ney (ôl′dẽr·nĭ), Fr. **Au′ri′gny′** (ō′rē′nyē′) island, English Channel, northernmost of Channel Is.; ✻ St. Anne; 3 sq. m.; pop. 1500.

Al′der·shot (ôl′dẽr·shŏt) municipal borough, S England, in Hampshire; military camp, established 1855; pop. 36,200.

A·le·ksan′drovsk (ŭ·lyĭ·ksän′drŭfsk) **1** or **Aleksandrovsk Grushevski**, city, SE Soviet Russia, Europe: see SHAKHTY. **2** city, U.S.S.R., in SE Ukraine: see ZAPOROZHE.

A′lep′ (ä′lěp′) or **A·lep′po** (ȧ·lěp′ō), Arab. **Ha′leb** (hä′lăb), anc. **Be·roe′a** (bě·rē′ȧ) city, NW Syria, near Turkish border; pop. 320,200.

A·lert′ (ȧ·lûrt′) weather station, N Canada, at NE tip of Ellesmere I.; run jointly by the U.S. and Canada; established 1950.

A′les·san′dri·a (ä′läs·sän′drē·ä; Angl. ăl′ě·săn′drĭ·ȧ) commune, NW Italy, in Piedmont; pop. 86,000.

A·leu′tian Islands (ȧ·lū′shăn; ȧ·lōō′-) chain of islands, SW Alaska, extending 1200 m. W from Alaska Penin.; chief island groups are Fox Is., Islands of the Four Mountains, Andreanof Is., Rat Is., and Near Is.

Aleutian Range, mountain range, SW Alaska, along E coast of Alaska Penin.; includes Mt. Katmai.

Al′ex·an′der Archipelago (ăl′ěg·zăn′dẽr; ăl′ĭg-; Brit. also -zän′-) group of ab. 1100 islands, SE Alaska; chief islands are Chichagof, Admiralty, Baranof, Kupreanof, Prince of Wales, and Revillagigedo.

Alexander I Island, island, Antarctica, W of base of Palmer Peninsula.

Alexandretta. See ISKENDERON.

Al′ex·an′dri·a (ăl′ěg·zăn′drĭ·ȧ; ăl′ĭg-; Brit. also -zän′-) **1** city, cen. Louisiana; pop. 34,900. **2** independent city, N Virginia, on Potomac river S of Washington, D.C.; pop. 61,800. **3** Arab. **al-Is·kan·da·rī′yah** (äl·ĭs·kän·dä·rē′yȧ) city, N Egypt, on the Mediterranean; pop. 925,100. See ALEXANDRIAN, in Vocab.

Alfiós. See ALPHEUS.

Al′föld (ŏl′fŭld) the central plain of Hungary.

Al Furāt. See EUPHRATES.

Al·gar′ve (äl·gär′vě) medieval Moorish kingdom, S Portugal; conquered 1251 by Alfonso III; later reduced to a province.

Al′ge·ci′ras (äl′jě·sēr′ȧs) seaport, SW Spain, W of Gibraltar; scene of conference, 1906; pop. 25,700.

Al·ge′ri·a (ăl·jẽr′ĭ·ȧ), Fr. **Al·gé′rie′** (ȧl′zhā′rē′) country in NW Africa, bordering on Mediterranean Sea; constitutes a government-general of the French Union; ✻ Algiers; 847,500 sq. m.; pop. 8,876,000. — **Al·ge′ri·an** (ăl·jẽr′ĭ·ȧn), adj. & n.

Al·giers′ (ăl·jẽrz′), Fr. **Al′ger′** (ăl′zhā′), Arab. **Al·je·za′ir** (ăl′jä·zä′ĭr) **1** former Barbary state, N Africa, now Algeria. **2** seaport, ✻ of Algeria, on Bay of Algiers; pop. 315,200.

Al·ham′bra (ăl·hăm′brȧ) city, SW California, ENE of Los Angeles; pop. 51,400.

A′li·can′te (ä′lě·kän′tā; Angl. ăl′ĭ·kăn′tě) seaport, SE Spain; pop. 104,100.

Al′ice (ăl′ĭs) city, S Texas; pop. 16,400.

A′li·garh′ (ü′lě·gŭr′h′; Angl. ăl′ĭ·gär′) or **Ko′il-Aligarh** (kō′ĭl-) city, N India, in Uttar Pradesh N of Agra; includes fortress of Aligarh and city of **Ko′il** (kō′ĭl) or **Kol** (kōl); pop. 112,700.

Al′i·quip′pa (ăl′ĭ·kwĭp′ȧ) borough, W Pennsylvania, on Ohio river; pop. 26,100.

Al Ku·wait′ (ăl kōō·wīt′; -wāt′) or **Kuwait**, seaport, ✻ of Kuwait principality, at head of Persian Gulf.

Al′lah·a·bad′ (äl′ȧ·hȧ·bäd′) city, N India, in Uttar Pradesh on Ganges river at junction with the Jumna; a holy city of the Hindus; pop. 260,600.

Al′lard′ Lake (ȧ′lär′) lake, E Canada, in province of Quebec N of Havre St. Pierre; titanium mines.

Al'le·ghe'ny (ăl'ē̇-gā'nĭ; ăl'ē̇-gā'nĭ) river, W Pennsylvania, uniting with Monongahela to form Ohio river at Pittsburgh; 325 m. long.

Allegheny Mountains, ranges of Appalachian system, E United States, in Pennsylvania, Maryland, Virginia, and West Virginia; vary in height from 2000 to over 4800 ft.

Allenstein. See OLSZTYN city, Poland.

Al'len·town (ăl'ĕn-toun; ăl'ĭn-) city, E Pennsylvania, pop. 106,800.

Al·li'ance (ă-lī'ăns) city, NE Ohio; pop. 26,200.

Al'lier' (ȧ'lyā') river, S cen. France, flowing NNW into Loire river; ab. 250 m. long.

Al'ma (ăl'mà; Russ. ȧl'y'mȧ) small river, S Soviet Russia, Europe, in SW Crimea; defeat of Russians by British and French 1854.

Al'ma-A·ta' (ăl'mä-ä-tä'), formerly **Ver'nyi** (vyĕr'nĭ) city, Soviet Central Asia, ✳ (since 1928) of Kazakh S.S.R.; pop. 230,500.

Al'ma·dén' (ăl'mä-thän') town, S cen. Spain, in the Sierra Morena; quicksilver mines.

Al'me·ri'a (ăl'mà-rē'ä) seaport, SE Spain, at head of Gulf of Almería; pop. 76,500.

A'lor (ä'lôr), formerly **Om·bai'** (ôm-bī') island, Indonesia, in Lesser Sundas N of Timor; with Pantar, forms **Alor Islands**.

Alor Star (stär) town, NW Federation of Malaya, ✳ of Kedah state; pop. 32,400.

Al·phe'us (ăl-fē'ŭs), Mod. Gr. **Al·fiós'** (ăl-fyôs') also **Rou·fiás'** (rōō-fyäs') river, S Greece, in W Peloponnesus, flowing NW into Ionian Sea; ab. 75 m. long.

Alps (ălps) mountain system of S cen. Europe, extending from Mediterranean coast between France and Italy into NW and W Yugoslavia; highest point Mont Blanc, France, 15,781 ft. See ALPINE in Vocab.

Al'sace (ăl'săs; ăl'sàs; ăl-săs'), anc. **Al·sa'ti·a** (ăl-sā'shĭ·à; -shà), Ger. **El'sass** (ĕl'zäs) region, N France, between Rhine river and Vosges Mts.; once a German province, under Louis XIV annexed to France; again part of Germany 1871–1918.

Alsace-Lor·raine' (ăl'săs-lŏ·rān'; ăl'săs-; -lō-), Ger. **Elsass-Lo'thring·en** (ĕl'zäs-lō'trĭng·ĕn) region, N France, including Alsace and part of Lorraine; in Germany 1871–1918.

Alt. See OLT.

Al'tai (ăl'tī; äl-tī') mountain system, cen. Asia, between Mongolia and Sinkiang prov., W China, and between Kazakh S.S.R. and the Russian S.F.S.R.; highest peak Belukha, 15,200 ft. See ALTAIC in Vocab.

Altai Territory, territory, SW Soviet Russia, Asia; ✳ Barnaul; 71,885 sq. m.; pop. 2,358,700.

Al'ta·mi'ra (äl'tä-mē'rä) cavern, NW Spain, WSW of Santander; prehistoric drawings, discovered 1879.

Alt'dorf (ält'dôrf) or **Al'torf** (äl'tôrf) town, cen. Switzerland, ✳ of Uri canton; connected with William Tell legend.

Al'ten·burg (äl'tĕn-bŏŏrk) city, E Germany, E of Weimar; pop. 51,800.

Altin Tagh. See ASTIN TAGH.

Al'ton (ôl't'n) city, SW Illinois, on Mississippi river; pop. 32,600.

Al·too'na (ăl-tōō'nà) city, S cen. Pennsylvania; pop. 77,200.

Altyn Tagh. See ASTIN TAGH.

Aluta. See OLT.

A·ma·ga·sa·ki (ä-mä-gä-sä-kē̇) city, Japan, in Honshu on Osaka Bay; pop. 233,200.

A·mal'fi (ä-mäl'fē̇) town, S Italy, in Campania on Gulf of Salerno; during Middle Ages an important port, notable for its maritime code.

A'ma·pá' (à'mà-pà') territory, N Brazil; ✳ Macapá; area 55,489 sq. m.; pop. 38,400.

Am'a·ril'lo (ăm'à-rĭl'ō; -rĭl'à) city, NW Texas; pop. 74,200.

'Amarna, Tell el. See TELL EL 'AMARNA.

Amatongaland. See TONGALAND.

Am'a·zon (ăm'à-zŏn; -zŭn) river, N South America, flowing from Peruvian Andes to the Atlantic in N Brazil; ab. 3900 m. long. See AMAZONIAN in Vocab.

Am·boi'na (ăm-boi'nà), Malay **Am'bon** (äm'bôn) island, E Indonesia, in the Moluccas S of Ceram; area 314 sq. m.; pop. 66,800.

Am'bridge (ăm'brĭj) borough, W Pennsylvania, on Ohio river; pop. 16,400.

Am'brose Channel (ăm'brōz) channel at entrance to New York harbor; 40 ft. deep, 2000 ft. wide.

Am·chit'ka (ăm-chĭt'kà) island, SW Alaska, in Aleutian Is. at E end of Rat Is.

A·mer'i·ca (ȧ-mĕr'ĭ-kȧ) **1** either continent of the Western Hemisphere (North America or South America). **2** the United States of America. **3** pl. the **A·mer'i·cas** (-kȧz) all the lands of the Western Hemisphere. See AMERICAN, in Vocab.

American, or **Eastern, Samoa**, group of islands of Samoa, SW cen. Pacific Ocean, E of long. 171°W; granted to U.S. by treaty of 1899; ✳ Pago Pago; 76 sq. m.; pop. 18,900.

A'mers·foort' (ä'mĕrs-fôrt') commune, cen. Netherlands; pop. 56,000.

Am·har'a (äm-här'ȧ; -hä'rä) province, NW Ethiopia; ✳ Gondar; former kingdom. See AMHARIC, in Vocab.

Ames (āmz) city, cen. Iowa; pop. 22,900.

Am'i·ens (ăm'ĭ-ĕnz; Fr. à'myăN') city, N France, on Somme river; pop. 84,800.

A'min·di'vi Islands (ŭ'mĭn-dē'vĭ) island group of the Laccadive Is.

Am·man' (äm-män'), Bib. **Rab'bah**, or **Rab'bath, Am'mon** (răb'ȧ [răb'ăth] ăm'ŏn), anc. Gr. **Phil'a·del'phi·a** (fĭl'à-dĕl'fĭ·à; -fyà) town, ✳ of Jordan; pop. 170,000.

Am'ne' Ma'chin' Shan (äm'nĕ' mä'jĭn' shän') range of the Kunlun Mts., W China, in E cen. Tsinghai; highest peak **Amne Machin** (99°45′E, 34°25′N), estimated at 25,000 ft.

Amnok. See YALU.

A·moy' (à-moi'; à-) or **Sze'ming'** (sŏŏ'mĭng') port, SE China, in Fukien prov. on Amoy I. and Kulangsu I.; pop. 220,000.

Am·rit'sar (ŭm-rĭt'sĕr) city, N India, in Punjab state; pop. 391,000.

Am'ster·dam (ăm'stĕr-dăm) **1** city, E New York, on Mohawk river; pop. 32,200. **2** (Du. pron. äm'stĕr-däm') city, ✳ of Netherlands; pop. 803,800.

A·mu' Dar·ya' (à-mōō' där-yä'; Angl. ä'mōō där'yà), anc. **Ox'us** (ŏk'-sŭs), Arab. **Jay·hun'** (jī-hōōn') river, cen. and W Asia, flowing from Pamir plateau to Lake Aral; over 1400 m. long.

A·mur' (ä-mōōr'), Chin. **Hei'lung'kiang'** (hā'lŏŏng'jĭ·äng') river, E

Asia, formed by junction of Shilka and Argun rivers and flowing to the Pacific at N end of Tatar Strait; forms boundary between Manchuria and Soviet Russia, Asia; length from junction ab. 1780 m.

An'a·con'da (ăn'à-kŏn'dà) city, SW Montana; pop. 11,300.

An'a·cos'ti·a (ăn'à-kŏs'tĭ·à) southeastern section of Washington, D.C., on Anacostia river; U.S. naval air station.

A·na·dyr' or **A·na·dir'** (ŭ-nŭ-dĭr') **1** river, Soviet Russia, Asia, flowing S and E to Gulf of Anadyr (Bering Sea); 450 m. long. **2** formerly **No'vo Ma·ri'insk** (nô'vŭ mȧ-rē'ĭnsk) town at mouth of the river.

A·ná'huac (ä-nä'wäk) the great central plateau of Mexico.

Anam. See ANNAM.

Anapurna. See ANNAPURNA.

An'a·to'lia (ăn'à-tōl'yà; -tō'lĭ·à), Turk. **A·na·do·lu'** (ä-nä-dō-lōō') that part of Turkey in Asia equivalent to the peninsula of Asia Minor. — **An'a·to'lian** (ăn'à-tōl'yăn; -tō'lĭ·ăn), adj. & n.

An'chor·age (ăng'kĕr-ĭj) seaport, Alaska, on Cook Inlet; pop. 11,100.

An·co'na (äng-kō'nà) seaport, cen. Italy, on Adriatic Sea; pop. 82,100.

Ancyra. See ANKARA.

An'da·lu'sia (ăn'dà-lōō'zhà; -shà), Span. **An'da·lu·ci'a** (än'dä-lōō-thē'ä; -sē'ä) region, S Spain, including the Sierra Nevada and the valley of Guadalquivir river. See ANDALUSIAN, in Vocab.

An'da·man Islands (ăn'dà-măn; -măn) group of islands, E Bay of Bengal; with Nicobar Is., constitute a territory, **Andaman and Nic'o·bar Islands** (nĭk'ō-bär), of Republic of India; ✳ Port Blair; area 3215 sq. m.; pop. 31,000.

An'der·lecht (än'dĕr-lĕkt) commune, cen. Belgium, WSW of Brussels; pop. 86,500.

An'der·son (ăn'dĕr-s'n) **1** city, cen. Indiana; pop. 46,800. **2** city, NW South Carolina; pop. 19,800.

An'der·son·ville (ăn'dĕrs·n-vĭl) village, cen. Georgia, SW of Macon; national cemetery; site of Confederate military prison 1864–65.

An'des (ăn'dēz) mountain system of South America extending along W coast from Tierra del Fuego to Panama; highest summit Aconcagua, 22,835 ft. See ANDEAN, in Vocab.

An'dhra Pra·desh (än'drà prà-dāsh') state, S India, N of Madras, bordering on Bay of Bengal; formed 1953 from part of Madras state; enlarged 1956 by addition of part of former Hyderabad state; ✳ (since 1956) Hyderabad; area 105,963 sq. m.; pop. 31,200,600.

An·dor'ra (ăn-dôr'à; -dôr'à), Fr. **An'dorre'** (äN'dôr') country, W Europe, in E Pyrenees between France and Spain; a coprincipality; 191 sq. m.; pop. 5200.

An'dre·a'nof Islands (ăn'drà-ä'nŭf; ăn'drē-ăn'ŭf, -än'ôf) island group, SW Alaska, in Aleutian Is.; chief islands Atka, Tanaga, Adak, Kanaga.

An'dri·a (än'drē-ä) commune, SE Italy, in Apulia; pop. 56,200.

An'dros (ăn'drŏs) island, Bahamas; largest of the group; 1600 sq. m.

An'dros (ăn'drŏs; Mod. Gr. än'drôs, -thrôs) island, Greece, in N Cyclades SE of Euboea.

An'dros·cog'gin (ăn'drŭs-kŏg'ĭn) river, NE New Hampshire and SW Maine, flowing into Kennebec river; 157 m. long.

A·ne'to, Pi'co de (pē'kô thă ä-nā'tô), Fr. **Pic de Né'thou'** (pēk' dĕ nā'-tōō') mountain, NE Spain, highest of the Pyrenees, 11,169 ft.

An·ga·ra' (ŭn-gŭ-rä') river, Soviet Russia, Asia, flowing from Lake Baikal to Yenisei river; 1100 m. long.

An'gel Falls (ăn'jĕl) waterfall, SE Venezuela, on Mt. Auyán-tepuí; highest known waterfall in the world, over 3200 ft.

An'gers' (äN'zhä'; Angl. ăn'jĕrz) city, W France, on Maine river 48 m. ENE of Nantes; pop. 94,400.

Ang'kor (äng'kôr), orig. **Angkor Thom** (tôm) ruins of ancient city, Indochina, in Cambodia NW of Tonle Sap; old capital of the Khmers; about 1 m. S is **Angkor Wat** or **Vat** (vät), ruins of temple.

An'gle·sey or **An'gle·sea** (ăng'g'l-sĭ) **1** anc. **Mo'na** (mō'nà) island, NW Wales. **2** county in Wales, including Anglesey I. and Holyhead I.; ✳ Llangefni; area 276 sq. m.; pop. 50,600.

Anglia. See ENGLAND.

Anglo-Egyptian Sudan. See SUDAN.

An·go'la (ăng-gō'là) or **Portuguese West Africa**, region, SW Africa, S of Congo river mouth; Portuguese colony; ✳ Luanda; area 481,351 sq. m.; pop. 3,738,000.

Angora. See ANKARA.

Angra Pequena. See LÜDERITZ.

An·guil'la (ăng-gwĭl'à) island, Leeward Is., West Indies Federation; part of St. Kitts-Nevis colony.

An'gus (ăng'gŭs), formerly **For'far** (fôr'fĕr) or **For'far·shire** (-shĭr; -shĕr) county, E Scotland; ✳ Forfar; 874 sq. m.; pop. 274,900.

An'halt (än'hält) former state, cen. Germany, ✳ Dessau.

An'hwei' or **An'hui'** (än'hwä') province, E China, crossed by lower course of the Yangtze river; capital Hofei; area 56,371 sq. m.; pop. 24,474,000.

An'i·ak'chak (ăn'ĭ-ăk'chăk) crater, SW Alaska, in Alaska Penin.; 6 m. in diameter.

An'jou' (äN'zhōō'; Angl. ăn'jōō) historical region of N France, watered by Loire river; ✳ Angers.

An'ka·ra (ăng'kà-rà; Turk. äng'kä-rä'), before 1930 **An·go'ra** (ăng-gō'rà; äng'gō-rà), anc. **An·cy'ra** (ăn-sī'rà) city, ✳ (since 1923) of Turkey; pop. 268,800.

An'king' (än'kĭng'), formerly (1912–49) **Hwai'ning'** (hwī'nĭng') city, E China, in Anhwei prov. on the Yangtze river; pop. 110,000.

Ann, Cape (ăn) peninsula, NE Massachusetts.

An Nafud. See NAFUD.

An Na'jaf (ăn nä'jäf) town, S cen. Iraq; starting point of pilgrimage route to Mecca; contains Ali's shrine.

An·nam' or **A·nam'** (ă-năm'; ăn'ăm) region, E Indochina, cen. part of Vietnam; formerly a kingdom and French protectorate; chief city Hué; 57,000 sq. m.; pop. 7,184,000. See ANNAMESE in Vocab.

An·nap'o·lis (ă-năp'ō-lĭs; ŭ-năp'lĭs) seaport, ✳ of Maryland, on Severn river near Chesapeake Bay; U.S. Naval Academy; pop. 10,000.

Annapolis Basin, inlet of Bay of Fundy, Canada, in W Nova Scotia.

Annapolis Roy'al (roi'ăl) town, Canada, in W Nova Scotia on Annapolis Basin; founded as **Port Roy'al** (pôrt roi'ăl) 1605.

An'na·pur'na or **An'a·pur'na** (ăn'à-pŏŏr'nà; ŭn'-) mountain range, Nepal, in Himalayas; highest peak (Annapurna I) 26,492 ft.

Ann Ar'bor (ăn' är'bĕr) city, SE Michigan; pop. 48,300.

An'nis·ton (ăn'ĭs·tŭn) city, NE Alabama; pop. 31,100.

An'shan' (än'shän') city, S Manchuria; pop. (1953 est.) 600,000.

An·so'ni·a (ăn·sō'nĭ·à; -sōn'yà) city, S Connecticut, WNW of New Haven; pop. 18,700.

An'ta·kya' (än'tä·kyä') or An'ta·ki'yah (än'tä·kē'yà), anc. An'ti·och (ăn'tĭ·ŏk) city, S Turkey in Asia, on Orontes river; pop. 30,400.

An'tal·ya' (än'täl·yä'), formerly A'da·li·a' (ä'dä·lē·yä') seaport, SW Turkey, on Gulf of Antalya; pop. 27,500.

Antananarivo. See TANANARIVE.

Ant·arc'ti·ca (ănt·ärk'tĭ·kà) or Ant·arc'tic Continent (-tĭk) the body of land around the South Pole; a plateau 6000 to 10,000 ft. high, covered by a great icecap; has mountain peaks 10,000 to 15,000 ft. high, some of which are volcanic; area ab. 5,000,000 sq. m.

Antarctic Archipelago. See PALMER ARCHIPELAGO.

An'ti·cos'ti Island (ăn'tĭ·kŏs'tĭ) island, E Canada, in St. Lawrence estuary and Gulf of St. Lawrence; belongs to Quebec prov.; 130 m. long.

An·tie'tam Creek (ăn·tē'tăm) creek, S Pennsylvania and N Maryland, flowing S into Potomac river N of Harpers Ferry; near its confluence with the Potomac is village of Antietam, 3 m. N of which, at Sharpsburg, was fought the battle of Antietam 1862.

An·ti'gua (ăn·tē'gà) island, Leeward Is., West Indies, forming (1958), with Barbuda and Redonda, a territory of the West Indies Federation; ✳ St. Johns; 108 sq. m.; pop. 52,500.

An·ti'gua (än·tē'gwä) or Antigua Gua'te·ma'la (gwä'tä·mä'lä) city, Guatemala; former ✳ of Guatemala; pop. 10,700.

An'ti-Leb'a·non (ăn'tĭ·lĕb'à·nŭn) mountain range, SW Asia, on Syria-Lebanon border; highest point Mt. Hermon, 9232 ft.

An·til'les, Greater and Lesser (ăn·tĭl'ēz; -ēz; Fr. äN'tē'y') two groups of islands in the West Indies: see WEST INDIES.

An'ti·och (ăn'tĭ·ŏk) 1 ancient city, Asia Minor, in Pisidia; at certain periods within the boundaries of Phrygia; its ruins lie near Yalvaç in modern Turkey. 2 ancient city, Syria; now Antakya, in Turkey.

An·tip'o·des (ăn·tĭp'ō·dēz) group of rocky islands, S Pacific Ocean, at 49°S, 180°E or W, belonging to New Zealand; almost exact antipodes of London, England.

An·ti·sa'na (än'tē·sä'nä) volcano, N cen. Ecuador, just SE of Quito; 18,885 ft. high.

An'to·fa·gas'ta (än'tō·fä·gäs'tä) seaport, N Chile; pop. 49,100.

An'trim (ăn'trĭm) county, NE Northern Ireland; ✳ Belfast; 1098 sq. m.; pop. 635,400.

An'tung' (än'dŏong') seaport, S Manchuria, at mouth of Yalu river; pop. 315,200.

Ant'werp (ănt'wûrp), Fr. An'vers' (äN'vâr'), Flem. Ant'wer'pen (änt'vĕr'pĕ[n]) city, N Belgium, on Schelde river; pop. 266,600.

A·nu·ra'dha·pu'ra (ŭ·nŏō·rä'dà·pŏō'rä) town, Ceylon; contains sacred Bo Tree, grown from a slip of the original sacred tree at Buddh Gaya.

An'zio (än'tsyō; Angl. ăn'zĭ·ō) town, Italy, on coast SSE of Rome, just W of Nettuno; bathing resort, once a port; scene of Allied landings January 1944; American military cemetery.

A'o·rang'i (ä'ō·räng'ē) or Mount Cook (kŏŏk) mountain, New Zealand, on South I.; highest peak in Southern Alps and New Zealand; 12,349 ft.

A·o'sta (ä·ôs'tä) commune, NW Italy, in Piedmont at junction of Great and Little St. Bernard passes; pop. 25,300; chief city of the Val d'Aosta (väl' dē·), Eng. Aosta Valley, which constitutes an autonomous province (since 1947).

Ap'a·lach'ee Bay (ăp'à·lăch'ē) inlet of Gulf of Mexico, N Florida.

Ap'a·lach·i·co'la (ăp'à·lăch'ĭ·kō'là) river, NW Florida; formed by Chattahoochee and Flint rivers in Georgia, flows S into Apalachicola Bay (Gulf of Mexico); 90 m. long.

A'pa·po'ris (ä'pä·pō'rēs) river, S Colombia, flowing SE into Japurá river on Colombia-Brazil boundary; ab. 500 m. long.

A'pel·doorn (ä'pĕl·dōrn) commune, Netherlands, N of Arnhem; pop. 83,400.

Ap'en·nines (ăp'ĕ·nīnz), Ital. Ap'pen·ni'no (äp'pän·nē'nō) chain of mountains, cen. Italy, extending the length of the peninsula; highest peak Monte Corno, 9585 ft.

A·pi'a (ä·pē'ä) seaport, Samoa, on island of Upolu; ✳ of Western Samoa.

A'po, Mount (ä'pō) mountain, highest in the Philippine Is., in SE Mindanao; 9689 ft.

Ap'pa·la'chian Mountains (ăp'à·lā'chăn; -lăch'ăn) mountain system of E North America, extending from the Canadian province of Quebec SW to N Alabama; highest peak Mount Mitchell, 6684 ft., in North Carolina.

Ap'pen·zell (äp'ĕn·tsĕl; Angl. ăp'ĕn·zĕl) canton, NE Switzerland; subdivided into demicantons: Appenzell Inner Rhodes (rōdz; Fr. rōd), ✳ Appenzell, area 61 sq. m., pop. 13,400; and Appenzell Outer Rhodes, ✳ Herisau, area 101 sq. m., pop. 47,900.

Ap'ple·ton (ăp'l·tŭn; -t'n) city, E Wisconsin, N of Oshkosh; pop. 34,000.

Ap'po·mat'tox (ăp'ō·măt'ŭks) 1 river, Virginia, flowing E to the James river; 150 m. long. 2 town, cen. Virginia, E of Lynchburg; at old Appomattox Court House nearby, on April 9, 1865, Confederates surrendered to Federal army; site now a national historical park.

A'pra Harbor (ä'prä), also Port Apra, harbor on W coast of island of Guam.

Ap·she·ron' (ŭp·shĕ·rŏn') peninsula, U.S.S.R., projecting into the Caspian Sea, on coast of E Azerbaidzhan Republic; oil fields.

A·pu'lia (à·pūl'yà; -pū'lĭ·à), Ital. Pu'glia (pŏō'lyä), pl. Le Pu'glie (lā pŏō'lyā) region, SE Italy, bordering on the Adriatic Sea and the Gulf of Taranto; forms spur and heel of Italian boot. — A·pu'lian (à·pūl'yăn; -pū'lĭ·ăn), adj. & n.

A·pu're (ä·pŏō'rā) river, W Venezuela, flowing E into Orinoco river; ab. 420 m. long.

A'pu·ri'mac (ä'pŏō·rē'mäk) river, S and cen. Peru; flows N to unite with Urubamba river and form Ucayali river; over 500 m. long.

'A'qa·ba or Qal''at el 'Aqaba (kŏl''ät ĕl 'ä'kà·bà), anc. E'lath (ē'lăth) seaport, SW Jordan, on border of Israel at head of NE arm, called Gulf of 'Aqaba, of the Red Sea.

A·quid'neck Island (à·kwĭd'nĕk) Rhode Island (the island); — its Indian name.

Aq'ui·taine (ăk'wĭ·tān; ăk'wĭ·tān'; Fr. à'kē'tĕn') historical region of SW France; ✳ Toulouse.

Aq'ui·ta'nia (ăk'wĭ·tăn'yà; -tä'nĭ·à) a Roman division of SW Gaul; under Caesar consisted of country between Pyrenees Mts. and Garonne river; under Augustus expanded to Loire and Allier rivers.

Arab, Shatt·al-. See SHATT-AL-ARAB.

'A'ra·ba, Wa'di el (wä'dē ăl ŭ'rŏ·bà), Bib. Ar'a·bah (ăr'à·bà) great valley extending S from Dead Sea to Gulf of 'Aqaba.

A·ra'bi·a (à·rā'bĭ·à; à·rāb'yà), Turk. A'ra·bi·stan' (ä'rä·bē·stän') peninsula of SW Asia; ab. 1400 m. long by 1250 m. wide; in early times divided into: Arabia Pe·trae'a (pē·trē'à), Eng. Rocky Arabia, the NW part; Arabia De·ser'ta (dē·zûr'tà), Eng. Desert Arabia, the N part; and Arabia Fe'lix (fē'lĭks), Eng. Fertile Arabia (on assumption that the interior was as fertile as the coastal strip), the main part of the peninsula, but by some geographers restricted to Yemen; now includes Saudi Arabia, Yemen, Oman, Trucial Oman, and Aden Protectorate. See ARAB, ARABIAN, ARABIC, in Vocab.

Arabian Desert, desert area, E Egypt, E of the Nile.

Arabian Sea, that section of the Indian Ocean lying between India on the E and Arabia on the W.

Arabistan. 1 See ARABIA. 2 See KHUZISTAN.

A'ra·ca·ju' (à'rà·kà·zhŏō') city, E Brazil, ✳ of Sergipe state; pop. 68,700.

A·rad' (ä·räd'; Hung. ŏ'rŏd) city, W Romania, on Mures river; pop. 75,700.

A'ra·fu'ra Sea (ä'rä·fŏō'rä) body of water between N Australia and West New Guinea.

Ar'a·gon (ăr'à·gŏn), Span. A'ra·gón' (ä'rä·gōn') region, NE Spain, bordering on France; once an independent kingdom. — Ar'a·go·nese' (ăr'à·gō·nēz'; -nēs'), adj. — Ar'a·go·nese', n. sing. & pl.

A'ra·guai'a (ä'rä·gwī'à) river, cen. Brazil, flowing N into Tocantins river; ab. 1100 m. long.

A·rak' (ä·räk'; à·răk') or I·raq' (ĭ·räk'; ĭ·răk'), also Sul·tan'a·bad' (sŏŏl·tän'à·bäd') city, W Iran; pop. 64,000.

A·ra·kan' (ä·rä·kän') region, SW Burma, on Bay of Bengal.

A·raks' (ä·räks'), Turk. A·ras' (ä·räs'), anc. A·rax'es (à·răk'sēz) river, W Asia, rising in mountains of Turkish Armenia and flowing E to join the Kura in E Azerbaidzhan, U.S.S.R.; 635 m. long.

Ar'al, Lake, or Aral Sea (ăr'ăl; Russ. ü·räl') inland sea, SW Soviet Central Asia, between Kazakh S.S.R. and Uzbek S.S.R.; area ab. 26,000 sq. m.

Ar'am (âr'ăm; ā'răm) ancient Syria; — its Hebrew name. — Ar'a·mae'an, Ar'a·me'an (ăr'à·mē'ăn), n. & adj. See ARAMAIC, in Vocab.

A·ran'sas Bay (à·răn'săs) inlet of Gulf of Mexico, S Texas, NE of Corpus Christi Bay between mainland and St. Joseph I.

Aransas Pass, chief entrance to Aransas Bay.

Ar'a·rat (ăr'à·răt), Turk. Ağ·rı Da·ğı' (à·rī' dä·Y') isolated mountain in E Turkey near Iranian border; 16,900 ft. high.

Aras, Araxes. See ARAKS.

Arbela, Arbil. See ERBIL.

Ar·ca'di·a (är·kā'dĭ·à) 1 city, SW California, ENE of Los Angeles; pop. 23,100. 2 Mod. Gr. Ar'ka·dhi'a (är'kä·thē'ä) region, S Greece in cen. Peloponnesus; a mountainous pastoral country; a department of modern Greece. See ARCADIA, in Vocab.

Archangel. See ARKHANGELSK.

Archangel, Gulf of. See DVINA GULF.

Arch'es National Monument (är'chĕz; -chĭz) wind-eroded natural arch formations, E Utah; established as national monument 1929.

Ar'co (är'kō) village, SE cen. Idaho, ab. 63 m. W of Idaho Falls; nuclear reactor testing station.

Ar'co·le (är'kō·lā) village, N Italy, SE of Verona, where Napoleon defeated the Austrians 1796.

Ar'cot (ûr'kŏt; Angl. är·kŏt') town, S India, in N Madras state; once capital of the Nawabs of the Carnatic.

Arc'tic Archipelago (ärk'tĭk), also Canadian Arctic Islands, group of islands, N Canada, in Arctic Ocean, constituting larger part of Franklin District, Northwest Territories.

Arctic Ocean, the ocean N of the Arctic Circle.

Ar'de·bil' or Ar'da·bil' (är'dà·bēl') city, NW Iran, in E Azerbaijan prov.; pop. 86,000.

Ar'den, Forest of (är'd'n) wooded region, cen. England, in N Warwickshire W of Stratford on Avon.

Ar·dennes' (är·dĕn'), often Forest of Ardennes, wooded plateau region, W Europe, E of Meuse river in N France, W Luxembourg, and SE Belgium; average height under 1600 ft.

Ard'more (ärd'mōr) city, S Oklahoma; pop. 17,900.

Arelas, Arelate. See ARLES.

Aremorica. See ARMORICA.

A're·qui'pa (ä'rā·kē'pä) city, S Peru; pop. 93,400.

A·rez'zo (à·rĕt'sō) commune, cen. Italy, in Tuscany SE of Florence; pop. 66,700.

Argenta. See NORTH LITTLE ROCK.

Ar'gen·tan' (är'zhäN·täN'; Angl. är'jĕn·tăn) town, NW France, in Normandy; in World War II the S anchor of Allied defense line that formed the Falaise pocket August 1944.

Ar'gen'teuil' (är'zhäN'tû'y) commune, N France, on Seine river NNW of Paris; pop. 53,500.

Ar·gen·ti·a (är·jĕn'shĭ·à; -shà) village, Canada, in SE Newfoundland on a peninsula extending into Placentia Bay; U.S. Air Force base.

Ar·gen·ti'na (är'jĕn·tē'nà) or Ar·gen·tine Republic (är'jĕn·tēn; -tīn) country, S South America, between the Andes and Atlantic Ocean S of Pilcomayo river; a federal republic; ✳ Buenos Aires; area 1,079,965 sq. m.; pop. 16,104,900. — Ar'gen·tine (är'jĕn·tēn; -tīn), adj. & n. — Ar'gen·tin'e·an (är'jĕn·tĭn'ē·ăn), n. — Ar'gen·tin'i·an, adj.

Ar'geş (är'jĕsh) river, S Romania, flowing S into the Danube; ab. 125 m. long.

Ar'gi·nu'sae (är'jĭ·nū'sē) group of small islands in Aegean Sea SE of Lesbos; last victory of Athens in Peloponnesian War 406 B.C.

Ar'go·lis (är'gō·lĭs) district, S Greece, the peninsula on E coast of Peloponnesus between Saronic Gulf and Gulf of Argolis (or Gulf of Nau'pli·a [nô'plĭ·à]). — Ar·gol'ic (är·gŏl'ĭk), adj.

Ar′gonne (är′gŏn; är·gŏn′), often **Argonne Forest**, wooded plateau, NE France, near Belgian border S of Ardennes and lying between Meuse and Aisne rivers; about 25 m. long and 10 m. wide.
Ar′gos (är′gŏs) city, Greece, in NE Peloponnesus at base of peninsula of Argolis; ancient city-state that dominated Argolis.
Argovie. See AARGAU.
Ar·guel′lo, Point (är·gwĕl′ō) cape, SW California, WNW of Santa Barbara; site of missile-launching center.
Ar′gun′ (är′gōōn′) river, NE Asia; flows NE, forming boundary between Manchuria and U.S.S.R., and unites with Shilka river to form Amur river; ab. 450 m. long.
Ar·gyll′ (är·gīl′) or **Ar·gyll′shire** (-shĭr; -shẽr) county, W Scotland; * Lochgilphead; 3110 sq. m.; pop. 63,300.
Ar′i·a (âr′ĭ·ȧ; ȧ·rī′ȧ) **1** an eastern province of ancient Persian Empire, now in NW Afghanistan and E Iran. **2** city: see HERAT.
A·ri′ca (ä·rē′kä) seaport, N Chile; once claimed also by Peru; by settlement of 1929 awarded to Chile but guaranteed as free port for Peru and as outlet for Bolivia; pop. 14,100.
Ar′i·ma·the′a (ăr′ĭ·mȧ·thē′ȧ), also **Ar′i·ma·thae′a** (-thē′ȧ) ancient town, Palestine; home of Joseph of Arimathea (see JOSEPH in Vocab.); not certainly identified. — **Ar′i·ma·the′an, Ar′i·ma·thae′an,** adj.
Ariminum. See RIMINI.
A′ri·pua·nã′ (ȧ′rē·pwȧ·näN′) river, W cen. Brazil; rises in N Mato Grosso state, flows N to the Madeira river; 600 m. long.
Ar′i·zo′na (ăr′ĭ·zō′nȧ), abbr. **Ariz.**, state, SW United States, bordering on Mexico; * Phoenix; area 113,909 sq. m.; pop. 749,600. — **Ar′i·zo′nan** (-năn), **Ar′i·zo′ni·an** (-nĭ·ăn), adj. & n.
Ar′kan·sas (in Arkansas, är′kăn·sô; elsewhere, esp. in Kansas, är·kăn′zăs also occurs, esp. for the river) **1** river, SW cen. United States, rising in cen. Colorado and flowing E through S Kansas, NE Oklahoma, and Arkansas; empties into Mississippi river; 1450 m. long. **2** abbr. **Ark.**, state, S cen. United States, just W of Mississippi river; * Little Rock; area 53,102 sq. m.; pop. 1,909,500. — **Ar·kan′san** (är·kăn′zăn), n.
Ar·khan′gelsk (ŭr·kȧn′gĕly′sk), Eng. **Arch′an′gel** (ärk′ān′jĕl) city, N Soviet Russia, Europe, on Northern Dvina river; pop. 281,100.
Arl′berg (ärl′bûrg; Ger. -bĕrk) Alpine valley, pass, and tunnel, W Austria, in the Tirol.
Arles (ȧrl; Angl. ärlz, ärl) **1** medieval kingdom, E and SE France; also called kingdom of Burgundy. **2** anc. **Ar′e·las** (ăr′ĕ·lăs) or **Ar′e·la′te** (ăr′ĕ·lā′tē) city, SE France, on the Rhone; pop. 35,000.
Ar′ling·ton (är′lĭng·tŭn) **1** county in Virginia, a suburb of Washington, D.C., across Potomac river; Arlington National Cemetery; Tomb of the Unknowns; pop. 135,400. **2** town, E Massachusetts, NW of Boston; pop. 44,400.
Ar·magh′ (är·mä′) county, S Northern Ireland; * Armagh; 489 sq. m.; pop. 108,800.
Ar·me′ni·a (är·mē′nĭ·ȧ; -mēn′yȧ) **1** Bib. **Min′ni** (mĭn′ī), ancient country in W Asia, now divided between the Soviet Union, Turkey, and Iran; centered in the mountainous region (highest point Mt. Ararat) SE of Black Sea and SW of Caspian Sea. **2** = ARMENIAN SOVIET SOCIALIST REPUBLIC. See ARMENIAN, in Vocab.
Armenian Soviet Socialist Republic, Armenian **Ha′yas·dan′** (hä′yäs·tän′; -dän′) a constituent republic of the U.S.S.R., in S Transcaucasia; * Yerevan; 11,580 sq. m.; pop. 1,346,700.
Ar′men·tières′ (är′mĕn·tyâr′; -tẽrz′) commune, N France, W of Lille; pop. 22,700.
Ar·mor′i·ca (är·mŏr′ĭ·kȧ), older **Ar′e·mor′i·ca** (ăr′ĕ·mŏr′ĭ·kȧ) **1** ancient name for region in NW France, between Seine and Loire rivers; NW part invaded in 5th cent. A.D. by Britons (Celtic peoples from Britain) and thereafter called Brittany; E part became Normandy. **2** often, Brittany.
Arn′hem (ärn′hĕm) commune, E Netherlands; pop. 97,400.
Arn′hem Land (är′nĕm·lănd′) or **Arn′hem·land′**, region, N Australia, on N coast of Northern Territory.
Ar′no (är′nō) river, cen. Italy, flowing W from the Apennines through Florence into Ligurian Sea; 140 m. long.
Aroe Islands. See ARU ISLANDS.
A·roos′took (ȧ·rōōs′tŏŏk; ȧ·rōōs′-; -tĭk) river, N Maine, flowing NE across New Brunswick border and into St. John river; 140 m. long.
Ar′ran (ăr′ăn) island off SW coast of Scotland, in Firth of Clyde; 165 sq. m.; pop. 4500.
Ar′ras (ăr′ăs; Fr. ȧ′räs′) city, N France, SSW of Lille; pop. 33,300.
Ar Rimal. See RUB′ AL KHALI.
Arroe Islands. See ARU ISLANDS.
Arsanias. See MURAT SUYU.
Ar·te′movsk (är·tĕm′ŭfsk), formerly **Bakh′mut** (bȧk′mōōt) city, U.S.S.R., in E Ukraine in the Donets Basin N of Stalino; pop. 55,200.
Ar′thur's Pass (är′thẽrz) mountain pass, New Zealand, in cen. South I., through Otira Gorge; railway tunnel 5.3 m. long.
Ar′tois′ (ȧr′twä′) historical region of N cen. France; * Arras.
A·ru′ba (ä·rōō′bä) island, Netherlands Antilles, off coast of NW Venezuela; chief town Oranjestad; 69 sq. m.; pop. 53,600.
A′ru Islands (ä′rōō), also **A′roe** or **Ar′roe** (ä′rōō) **Islands**, island group, E Indonesia, S of W New Guinea; 3305 sq. m.; pop. 18,200.
Ar′un·del (ăr′ŭn·d'l; -dĕl) municipal borough, England, in West Sussex; Arundel Castle, seat of dukes of Norfolk.
A′ru·wi′mi (ä′rōō·wē′mē) river, cen. Africa; rises in NE Belgian Congo, flows SW and W into Congo river; ab. 800 m. long.
Ar·vi′da (är·vī′dȧ; Fr. ȧr′vē′dȧ′) city, Canada, in S Quebec on the Saguenay W of Chicoutimi; pop. 12,900.
Ar·wad′ (ŭr·wăd′), Fr. **Île Rou·ad′** (ēl′ rwȧd′), anc. (Heb.) **Ar′vad** (är′văd) island, Syria, off coast of S Latakia.
A·sa·hi·ka·wa (ä·sä·hē·kä·wä) or **A·sa·hi·gawa** (-gä·wä) city, Japan, in cen. Hokkaido I.; pop. 107,500.
A·sa·ma (ä·sä·mä) or **A·sa·ma·ya·ma** (ä·sä·mä·yä·mä) active volcano, Japan, in cen. Honshu; 8340 ft. high.
As′bur′y Park (ăz′bĕr′ĭ; -bẽr·ĭ) city, New Jersey, on Atlantic Ocean; pop. 17,100.
Ascalon. See ASHKELON.
As·cen′sion (ȧ·sĕn′shŭn) **1** island in S Atlantic Ocean, at 7°55′S lat. and 14°25′W long.; since 1922 a part of British colony of St. Helena; 34 sq. m.; pop. under 200. **2** see PONAPE, Caroline Is.
A′sco·li Sa·tria′no (äs′kō·lē sä·tryä′nō), anc. **Aus′cu·lum Ap′u·lum** (ôs′kū·lŭm ăp′ū·lŭm) or **As′cu·lum** (ăs′kū·lŭm) town, SE Italy, in Apulia; site of Roman defeat by Pyrrhus, king of Epirus, 279 B.C.
As′cot (ăs′kŭt) village, S England, in Berkshire; race track (at **Ascot Heath**).
A·shan′ti (ȧ·shăn′tĭ; ăsh′ăn·tē′) region, central Ghana; former native kingdom, later a British colony; * Kumasi; 24,379 sq. m.; pop. 578,100. — **A·shan′ti, A·shan′tee** (ȧ·shăn′tĭ; ăsh′ăn·tē′), n.
Ash′bur′ton (ăsh′bûr′t'n; -bẽr·t'n) river, NW Western Australia, flowing NW to Indian Ocean; 500 m. long.
Ashe′ville (ăsh′vĭl) city, W North Carolina, on a plateau surrounded by mountains of the Blue Ridge; pop. 53,000.
Ash′ke·lon (ăsh′kĕ·lŏn) or **As′ca·lon** (ăs′kȧ·lŏn) ancient seaport, SW Palestine; a city-kingdom of Philistia; destroyed A.D. 1270.
Ashkh′a·bad (ăsh′kȧ·băd) city, Soviet Central Asia, * of Turkmen S.S.R.; pop. 126,600.
Ash′land (ăsh′lănd) city, NE Kentucky, on Ohio river; pop. 31,100.
Ash′ta·bu′la (ăsh′tȧ·bū′lȧ) city, NE Ohio, on Lake Erie; pop. 23,700.
Ashur. See ASSYRIA.
A′sia (ā′zhȧ; ā′shȧ) continent, Eastern Hemisphere, N of the equator; with Europe, forms one land mass, the conventional dividing line between Asia and Europe being the Ural Mts. (in the U.S.S.R.); area 16,235,000 sq. m. See ASIAN, ASIATIC, in Vocab.
Asia Mi′nor (mī′nẽr) the peninsula forming W extremity of Asia, between Black Sea on N, Mediterranean Sea on S, and Aegean Sea on W; forms the greater part of Turkey. See ANATOLIA.
A·sir′ (ä·sēr′) principality, SW Arabia, on the Red Sea; a dependency of the Nejd, Saudi Arabia; * As Sabya; 13,857 sq. m.; pop. ab. 750,000.
As·ma′ra (ăz·mä′rȧ) town, * of Eritrea; pop. 117,000.
As′nières′ (ȧ′nyâr′) commune, N France, NW of Paris; pop. 72,300.
A·so (ä·sō) or **A·so·san** (ä·sō·sän) volcanic mountain, Japan, in cen. Kyushu I.; highest of its five peaks 5225 ft.; has crater 10 to 15 m. in diameter with walls ab. 2000 ft. high.
As′pen (ăs′pĕn) city, W cen. Colorado; resort and cultural center.
A′spern (äs′pĕrn) former village, Austria, ENE of Vienna, where Napoleon was defeated by the Austrians 1809; since 1905 part of Vienna.
Asphaltites, Lacus. See DEAD SEA.
Aspinwall. See COLÓN.
As·sam′ (ȧ·săm′; ä·săm′; ăs′ăm) state, NE India, on edge of Himalayas; * Shillong; area 85,012 sq. m.; pop. 9,043,700.
As·sin′i·boine (ȧ·sĭn′ĭ·boin) river, S cen. Canada; rises in SE Saskatchewan, flows S and E across S Manitoba into Red river at Winnipeg; 450 m. long.
Assiout, Assiut. See ASYÛT.
As·si′si (ȧ·sē′zē) city, cen. Italy; place of birth and death of St. Francis of Assisi; pop. 22,500.
Assouan, Assuan. See ASWÂN.
As·syr′i·a (ȧ·sĭr′ĭ·ȧ), anc. **As′sur** (ä′sŏŏr; ăs′ẽr), **A′shur** (ä′shŏŏr; ăsh′ẽr), or **As′shur** (ä′shŏŏr; ăsh′ẽr) ancient empire, W Asia, extending along middle Tigris and over foothills to the E; under Babylonian rule c. 1950 to 1850 B.C.; early * Calah, later * Nineveh. See ASSYRIAN, in Vocab.
A′sti (äs′tē) commune, NW Italy, in Piedmont; pop. 53,100.
As′tin Tagh (äs′tĭn tä′), formerly **Al′tin**, or **Al′tyn, Tagh** (äl′tĭn) mountain range (tagh), W China, in S Sinkiang prov.; highest peak ab. 17,000 ft.
As′tra·khan (ăs′trȧ·kăn; -kăn) city, Soviet Russia, Europe, on the Volga at head of its delta; 50 ft. below sea level; pop. 253,700.
As·tu′ri·as (ăs·t[y]ŏŏr′ĭ·ăs) **1** region, NW Spain; once a kingdom. **2** city: see OVIEDO. — **As·tu′ri·an** (-ăn), adj. & n.
A′sun·ción′ (ä′sōōn·syôn′) city, * of Paraguay, on Paraguay river at confluence of the Pilcomayo; pop. 205,600.
As·wân′ or **As·wan′**, also **As·souan′** or **As·suan′** (ăs·wăn′; ăs·wŏn′) city, S Egypt, on right bank of the Nile; site of a dam 6400 ft. long; pop. 25,400.
As·yût′ or **As·yut′**, also **As·siout′** or **As·siut′** (ăs·yōōt′) city, cen. Egypt, on left bank of the Nile; pop. 90,400.
A′ta·ca′ma Desert (ä′tä·kä′mä) arid area in N cen. Chile, with borax lakes and saline and nitrate deposits.
At′ba·ra (ăt′bä·rä) river, NE Africa; rises in N Ethiopia, flows through E Anglo-Egyptian Sudan into the Nile; ab. 500 m. long.
A·tchaf′a·lay′a ([ȧ·]chăf′ȧ·lī′ȧ) river, S Louisiana, flowing S into Atchafalaya Bay, an inlet of Gulf of Mexico; 225 m. long.
Ath′a·bas′ca (ăth′ȧ·băs′kȧ), also **Ath′a·bas′ka**, river, W cen. Canada, in Alberta prov., flowing NE and N into Lake Athabasca; 765 m. long. — **Ath′a·bas′can** (-kăn), adj. & n.
Athabasca, Lake, lake, W cen. Canada, on Alberta-Saskatchewan boundary; area 3058 sq. m.
Ath′ens (ăth′ĕnz; -ĭnz) **1** city, NE Georgia; pop. 28,200. **2** anc. **A·the′nae** (ȧ·thē′nē), Mod. Gr. **A·thí′nai** (ä·thē′nā) city, * of Greece, in E near Saronic Gulf; pop. 559,300, with suburbs 1,368,100. — **A·the′ni·an** (ȧ·thē′nĭ·ăn; -thēn′yăn), adj. & n.
Ath′os (ăth′ŏs; ä′thŏs) mountain, NE Greece, at E end of Acte Penin.; site of Mount Athos republic; 6670 ft. high.
A′ti·tlán′ (ä′tē·tlän′) **1** lake, SW Guatemala, at 4700 ft. altitude, occupying a crater 1000 ft. deep; 24 m. long by 10 m. wide. **2** volcano, S of the lake; 11,562 ft. high. **3** town: see SANTIAGO ATITLÁN.
At′ka (ăt′kȧ) island, SW Alaska, in Aleutian Is.; largest of Andreanof group.
At·lan′ta (ăt·lăn′tȧ) city, * of Georgia; pop. 331,300.
At·lan′tic City (ăt·lăn′tĭk) city, SE New Jersey, on Atlantic Ocean; pop. 61,700.
Atlantic Ocean, body of water separating North and South America from Europe and Africa; area over 31,500,000 sq. m.
Atlantis. See in Vocab.
At′las Mountains (ăt′lăs) mountain system, NW and N Africa, extending from SW Morocco coast to NE Tunisia coast; its highest peaks (over 13,000 ft.) are in the **Grand**, or **High, Atlas** in W and S Morocco.

A·trek′ (ä·trĕk′) or **A·trak′** (ä·träk′) river, NE Iran, flowing into SE Caspian Sea in U.S.S.R.; ab. 300 m. long.

Atropatene. See AZERBAIJAN.

At′ti·ca (ăt′ĭ·kà) region, E Greece; as an ancient division and state its chief towns were Athens, Piraeus, and Eleusis. See ATTIC in Vocab.

At′tle·bor′o (ăt′l·bŭr′ŏ) city, SE Massachusetts; pop. 23,800.

At′tu (ăt′ōō) island, SW Alaska, most westerly of the Aleutian Is., in Near Is. group.

Aube (ōb) river, N cen. France, flowing NW and W into Seine river; ab. 125 m. long.

Au′ber·vil′liers′ (ō′bĕr′vē′lyā′) commune, N France, NNE of Paris; pop. 53,000.

Au′burn (ô′bĕrn) **1** city, SW Maine, on Androscoggin river opposite Lewiston; pop. 23,100. **2** city, cen. New York, on outlet of Lake Owasco; pop. 36,700.

Au′bus′son′ (ō′bü′sôn′) town, cen. France, on Creuse river; celebrated for its carpets and tapestries.

Auck′land (ôk′lănd) seaport, New Zealand, on North Island; pop. 329,000.

Audenarde. See OUDENAARDE.

Au·ghra′bies Falls (ô·krä′bĕs; -grä′-), also **King George's Falls** (jôr′jĭz) waterfall in Orange river, Union of South Africa, in NW Cape Province; 480 ft. high.

Augs′burg (ouks′bŏŏrk; Angl. ôgz′bûrg) city, W Germany, in Bavaria on Lech river; pop. 184,700.

Au·gus′ta (ô·gŭs′tà) **1** city, E Georgia, on Savannah river; pop. 71,500. **2** city, ✳ of Maine, on Kennebec river; pop. 20,900.

Au′lis (ô′lĭs) harbor, E Greece, in Boeotia on Euripus Strait; a traditional sailing place of Greek fleet against Troy at beginning of the Trojan War; scene of the sacrifice of Iphigenia.

Au′ri·gnac′ (ô′rē′nyàk′) village, S France, SW of Toulouse; caves with significant paleolithic remains.

Aurigny. See ALDERNEY.

Au·ro′ra (ô·rō′rà; ŭ·rô′-) city, NE Illinois; pop. 50,600.

Au·sa′ble (ô·sā′b'l) river, NE New York, flowing E into Lake Champlain; in its lower course flows through a deep scenic gorge, **Ausable Chasm**, ab. 2 m. long.

Auschwitz. See OŚWIĘCIM.

Aus′ter·litz (ôs′tĕr·lĭts; Ger. ous′-), Czech **Slav′kov** (släf′kôf) town, Czechoslovakia, ESE of Brno; battle Dec. 2, 1805.

Aus′tin (ôs′tĭn) **1** city, S Minnesota; pop. 23,100. **2** city, ✳ of Texas, on Colorado river; pop. 132,500.

Aus′tral·a′sia (ôs′trăl·ā′zhà; -shà) **1** that portion of Oceania between the equator and 47°S. **2** by extension, all of Oceania. — **Aus′tral·a′sian**, adj. & n.

Aus·tra′lia (ôs·trāl′yà; -trā′lĭ·à) island continent, Eastern Hemisphere, SE of Asia; entirely S of the equator and crossed by the Tropic of Capricorn; area 2,948,366 sq. m.; constitutes with Tasmania the **Commonwealth of Australia**, a dominion of the British Commonwealth of Nations, ✳ Canberra, area 2,974,581 sq. m., pop. (excluding aboriginals) 8,185,500. — **Aus·tra′lian**, adj. & n.

Australian Alps, mountain range, SE Australia, in E Victoria and SE New South Wales, forming S end of Great Dividing Range; highest peak Mt. Kosciusko, 7328 ft.

Australian Capital Territory, formerly known as **Federal Capital Territory**, territory, SE Australia, two enclaves in New South Wales, around Canberra and on Jervis Bay; area 939 sq. m.; pop. 20,800.

Austral Islands. See TUBUAI ISLANDS.

Aus·tra′sia (ôs·trā′zhà; -shà) or **Os·tra′sia** (ôs-) the eastern dominions of the Merovingian Franks, extending from Meuse river to Bohemian Forest. — **Aus·tra′sian**, adj. & n.

Aus′tri·a (ôs′trĭ·à), Ger. **O′ster·reich′** (û′stĕr·rīk′) country, cen. Europe, in and N of E Alps with the Danube crossing it in N; a republic; once an empire (1806–67) and part of dual monarchy of Austria-Hungary (1867–1918); ✳ Vienna; area 32,375 sq. m.; pop. 6,881,100. — **Aus′tri·an**, adj. & n.

Austria-Hun′ga·ry (-hŭng′gà·rĭ) dual monarchy 1867–1918, cen. Europe; included Austria, Hungary, Czechoslovakia, Bucovina and Transylvania in Romania, NW half of Yugoslavia, Galicia in Poland, and NE Italy. — **Aus′tro-Hun·gar′i·an** (ôs′trô-hŭng·gâr′ĭ·àn), adj. & n.

Aus′tro·ne′sia (ôs′trô-nē′zhà; -zhĭ·à; -shà; -shĭ·à) in general, the islands of the S Pacific Ocean; more accurately, the area from Madagascar in the W, through the Malay Penin. and Archipelago, to Hawaii and Easter I. in the E. — **Aus′tro·ne′sian**, adj. & n.

Au′teuil′ (ō′tû′y′) district in W Paris, France, at entrance to Bois de Boulogne; famous racecourse for steeplechasing.

Au′vergne′ (ō′vĕrn′y′) historical region of S cen. France, in NW Massif Central; ✳ Clermont (now Clermont-Ferrand); traversed N to S by the **Auvergne Mountains**, highest peak Puy de Sancy, 6185 ft.

Aux Cayes. See CAYES.

Aux Sources, Mont (mōn′-tō′ soors′) peak, E Union of South Africa, in N Basutoland on Natal border, in Drakensberg Mts.; highest mountain in the Union, 10,761 ft.

Au·yán′-te·pui′ (ou·yän′tà·pwē′) or **Dev′il Mountain** (dĕv′'l) mountain, SE Venezuela, E of Caroní river; actually a plateau ab. 20 m. long; site of Angel Falls.

Av′a·lon Peninsula (ăv′à·lŏn) the SE corner of Newfoundland, almost cut off from rest of island by Trinity and Placentia bays.

A′vel·la·ne′da (ä′vā·lä·nā′thä; Argentine pron. ä′vä·zhä-) city, E Argentina, a suburb of Buenos Aires; pop. 399,000.

A′venches′ (ä′vänsh′), anc. **A·ven′ti·cum** (à·vĕn′tĭ·kŭm) town, W Switzerland, in Vaud canton; the ancient Helvetia.

Aventine. See in Vocab.

A·ver′nus, Lake (à·vûr′nŭs), Ital. **La′go d'A·ver′no** (lä′gŏ dä·vĕr′nŏ), Lat. **La′cus A·ver′nus** (lā′kŭs à·vûr′nŭs) lake, S Italy, in crater of extinct volcano W of Naples. See AVERNUS, in Vocab.

A′vi′gnon′ (à′vē′nyôn′) city, SE France, near confluence of Rhone and Durance rivers; pop. 60,100. — **A·vign′on·ese′** (à·vĭn′yŭn·ēz′; -ēs′), adj.

Avlona. See VLONË.

A′von, 1 (ā′vŭn; ăv′ŭn) river, S England; rises near Devizes in Wiltshire, flows S into English Channel; 65 m. long. **2** (ā′vŭn) river, SW England; rises in Gloucestershire, flows S and W through city of Bristol into Bristol Channel at Avonmouth; 62 m. long. **3** (ā′vŭn; ăv′ŭn) river, cen. England; rises in Northamptonshire, flows WSW into the Severn at Tewkesbury; the "Shakespeare" Avon; 96 m. long.

A′vranches′ (à′vränsh′) town, NW France, in SW Normandy on inlet of Gulf of St-Malo; scene of decisive Allied breakthrough 1944.

A·wa·ji (ä·wä·jē) island, Japan, S of Honshu and NE of Shikoku I.

Ax. See DAX.

Ax′el Hei′berg (äk′s'l hī′bûrg) island, N Canada, one of the Sverdrup Is.; area 15,779 sq. m.

Axum. See AKSUM.

A′ya·cu′cho (ä′yä·kōō′chŏ) town, S Peru; scene of battle Dec. 9, 1824, in which Gen. Sucre won independence for Peru; pop. 18,300.

Áyion Óros. See MOUNT ATHOS.

Ay′ot St. Law′rence (ā′[y]ŭt sănt lô′rĕns; lŏr′ĕns) parish, cen. England, in Hertfordshire near Welwyn Garden City; residence of George Bernard Shaw.

Ayr (âr) **1** or **Ayr′shire** (âr′shĭr; -shēr) county, SW Scotland; 1132 sq. m.; pop. 321,200. **2** seaport, its ✳; pop. 43,000.

A·yu·dhy·a or **A·yu·thi·a** or **A·yut·tha·ya** (ä·yōōt·tä·yä) city, S Thailand, N of Bangkok, on an island in the lower Chao Phraya; Siamese capital 1350–1767; pop. ab. 50,000.

A′zer·bai·jan′ (ä′zĕr·bī·jän′; äz′ĕr-) **1** anc. **At′ro·pa·te′ne** or **Me′di·a Atropatene** (mē′dĭ·à ăt′rô·pà·tē′nē) province, NW Iran; ✳ Tabriz; area 41,150 sq. m. **2** or, usually, **A′zer·bai·dzhan′** (-jän′), in full **Azerbaidzhan Soviet Socialist Republic**, constituent republic of the U.S.S.R., E Transcaucasia, bordering on Caspian Sea and Azerbaijan province, Iran; ✳ Baku; area 33,200 sq. m.; pop. 3,372,800.

A·zores′ (à·zōrz′; ā′zōrz), Port. **A·ço′res** (à·sō′rĕsh) group of islands, N Atlantic Ocean, belonging to Portugal; chief town Ponta Delgada; 888 sq. m.; pop. 587,900.

A·zov′ or **A·zof′** (ŭ·zôf′; also, Angl., ăz′ôf, ā′zôf, ā′zôv) town, S Soviet Russia, Europe, near mouth of Don river; pop. 19,300.

Azov, or **Azof, Sea of**, sea, S Soviet Russia, Europe, N of Black Sea, with which it is connected by Kerch Strait; receives Don river; area ab. 14,520 sq. m.

Az′tec Ruins National Monument (ăz′tĕk) prehistoric pueblo, NW New Mexico; established 1929.

B

Ba′al·bek (bā′ăl·bĕk; bäl′bĕk), anc. **He′li·op′o·lis** (hē′lĭ·ŏp′ô·lĭs) village, E Lebanon; ancient city identified with worship of Baal.

Bab el Man′deb (băb′ ĕl măn′dĕb) strait between SW Arabia and Africa, uniting Red Sea and Gulf of Aden (Indian Ocean).

Ba′bel·thu′ap (bä′bĕl·tōō′äp) or **Ba′bel·do′ab** (-dō′äp), also **Pa·lau′** (pä·lou′) island, Palau Is., chief island of the group.

Bab′y·lon (băb′ĭ·lŏn) ancient city on Euphrates river near modern Hilla, Iraq; ✳ of **Bab′y·lo′ni·a** (-lō′nĭ·à; -lŏn′yà), ancient country in lower Euphrates valley. See BABYLON, BABYLONIAN, in Vocab.

Ba·co′lod (bä·kō′lôd) city, Philippine Is., on Negros I.; pop. 57,500.

Bactra. See BALKH.

Bac′tri·a (băk′trĭ·à), also **Bac′tri·a′na** (-ā′nà; -ăn′à) ancient country of SW Asia, between Hindu Kush Mts. and Oxus river; ✳ Bactra. See BACTRIAN, in Vocab.

Ba′da·joz′ (bä′thä·hôth′; -hôs′) city, SW Spain, on Guadiana river; pop. 87,900.

Ba′da·lo′na (bä′thä·lō′nä) seaport, NE Spain; pop. 58,600.

Ba′den (bä′dĕn) **1** region, SW Germany, bordering on Switzerland and France; includes Black Forest; grand duchy 1805–1918 and a state of Weimar Republic 1919–33, ✳ Karlsruhe; S part became a state of Bonn Republic 1949, ✳ Freiburg. **2** city: see BADEN-BADEN.

Ba′den-Ba′den (bä′dĕn-bä′dĕn) or **Baden**, city, SW Germany, in Baden SSW of Karlsruhe; pop. 33,000.

Bad′ Lands′, now usually **Bad′lands′**, orig. Fr. **Mau′vaises′ Terres** (mō′vāz′ târ′) or **Terres Mau′vaises′** (târ′ mō′vâz′) **1** any of several regions in W United States, esp. in the Dakotas, Nebraska, Montana, and Wyoming, having characteristic badlands topography, barren and eroded; **Badlands National Monument**, established 1939, is in SW South Dakota, E of Black Hills. **2** also, similar areas elsewhere; **Bad Lands Reserve** is in Canada, in S Alberta.

Baf′fin Bay (băf′ĭn) inlet of Atlantic Ocean between W Greenland and E Baffin I.

Baffin Island, formerly known as **Baffin Land**, island, NE Canada, largest in the Canadian Arctic Archipelago; area 178,700 sq. m.

Ba′fing′ (Fr. bà′fĕn′y′ or -făng′) river, French West Africa, the upper course of Senegal river; 350 m. long.

Bagh′dad or **Bag′dad** (băg′dăd) city, ✳ of Iraq, on the Tigris; pop. 400,000.

Ba′go (bä′gŏ) municipality, Philippine Is., on Negros I.; pop. 53,900.

Ba′guio (bä′gyŏ) city, Philippine Is., in NW cen. Luzon; summer ✳ of the Philippines; pop. 24,100.

Ba·ha′ma Islands (bà·hä′mà; in U.S., also -hā′-) or **Ba·ha′mas** (-máz) chain of islands in Atlantic Ocean SE of Florida; British colony; ✳ Nassau; area 4375 sq. m.; pop. 80,600. — **Ba·ha′mi·an** (-mĭ·ăn), n. & adj.

Ba·ha′wal·pur′ (bà·hä′măl·pŏŏr′) former princely state, NW India, in SW Punjab in Thar Desert; a province of Pakistan 1947–55; merged 1955 in province of West Pakistan.

Ba·hi′a (bà·ē′à) **1** ✳ See BAÍA. **2** See SALVADOR.

Ba·hi′a Blan′ca (bä·ē′ä vläng′kä) seaport, E Argentina, 350 m. SW of Buenos Aires; pop. 123,100.

Bah·rein′, also **Bah·rain′, Islands** (bà·rīn′; -rän′; bä-) archipelago, in Persian Gulf off coast of Arabia; nominally independent sultanate; ✳ Manama, on Bahrein I.; area 213 sq. m.; pop. 120,000.

Bahr el Abyad, Bahr el Azraq. See NILE.

Bahr el Gha·zal′ (bä′h'r äl gô·zäl′) river, SW Sudan (republic); flows E to unite at Lake No with the **Bahr el Je′bel** (jä′bäl) and form the White Nile; ab. 500 m. long.

Bahr en Nîl. See NILE.

Bahret el Hule. See MEROM, WATERS OF.

Ba'ia (bä'yä), anc. **Ba'iae** (bä'yē) village, S Italy, W of Naples; warm sulfur springs; ancient city a Roman resort.

Ba·i'a (bä·ē'ä) or **Ba·hi'a** (bä·ē'ä) **1** state, E Brazil; ✻ Salvador; area 215,329 sq. m.; pop. 4,900,400. **2** city: see SALVADOR.

Bai·kal', Lake (bī·kôl'; -käl') lake, S Soviet Russia, Asia, in mountains N of Mongolia; over 5710 ft. deep; area over 12,000 sq. m.

Baile Atha Cliath. See DUBLIN.

Bai·reuth'. Var. of BAYREUTH.

Baja California. See LOWER CALIFORNIA.

Bakan. See SHIMONOSEKI.

Ba'ker, Mount (bā'kēr) peak, NW Washington, in Cascade Range; 10,750 ft. high.

Baker Island, atoll, cen. Pacific Ocean near equator, at long. 176°31'W; formally proclaimed U.S. territory 1936.

Ba'kers·field (bā'kērz·fēld) city, S California, at S end of San Joaquin valley; pop. 34,800.

Bakhmut. See ARTEMOVSK.

Ba·ku' (bä·kōō') city, U.S.S.R., ✻ of Azerbaidzhan Republic, on W coast of Caspian Sea; center of oil region; pop. 809,300.

Bal'a·kla'va (băl'á·klä'vá; -klä̇v'á), also **Bal'a·cla'va,** seaport, S Soviet Russia, Europe, SE of Sevastopol; battle 1854 of Crimean War.

Bal'a·ton (bŏl'à·tŏn), Ger. **Plat'ten·see'** (plät'ĕn·zā') lake, W Hungary; largest lake in central Europe, area 266 sq. m.

Bal·bo'a (băl·bō'á) town, Panama Canal Zone, at Pacific entrance to the canal adjacent to Panama City; pop. 4100.

Balboa Heights, town, Panama Canal Zone, suburb of Balboa; administrative center of Canal Zone; pop. 400.

Bâle. See BASEL.

Bal·e·ar'ic Islands (băl'ē·ăr'ĭk), Span. **Is'las Ba'le·a'res** (ēz'läz vä'lä·ä'räs) island group, Spain, in W Mediterranean Sea, including Majorca and Minorca; constitutes a province, ✻Palma, area 1936 sq. m., pop. 422,100.

Ba'li (bä'lē) island, Indonesia, off E end of Java; chief town Singaradja; 2147 sq. m.; pop. 1,101,400. — **Ba'li·nese'** (bä'lē·nēz'; -nēs'), adj. & n. sing. & pl.

Ba'lik·pa'pan (bä'lĭk·pä'pän) seaport, Indonesia, in SE Borneo on inlet (**Balikpapan Bay**) of Macassar Strait; oil center; pop. 29,800.

Bal'kan Mountains (bôl'kăn), Bulg. **Sta'ra Pla'ni·na'** (stä'rä plä'nī·nä') range, cen. Bulgaria, extending from Yugoslav border to Black Sea; highest point ab. 7800 ft.

Balkan Peninsula, peninsula, SE Europe, between the Adriatic and Ionian seas on the W, the Mediterranean Sea on the S, and the Aegean and Black seas on the E.

Balkan States, also the **Bal'kans** (bôl'kănz) the countries occupying Balkan Peninsula: Yugoslavia, Romania, Bulgaria, Albania, Greece, and Turkey in Europe.

Balkaria. See KABARDINIAN A.S.S.R.

Balkh (bälk) **1** country of SW Asia, corresponding closely to ancient Bactria; now a district of N Afghanistan. **2** anc. **Bac'tra** (băk'trá) town, N Afghanistan; ✻ of ancient Bactria; pop. 10,000.

Bal·khash' (bäl·käsh') lake, Soviet Central Asia, in SE Kazakh S.S.R.; area ab. 6700 sq. m.

Bal·mor'al (băl·mŏr'ăl) castle, Scotland, in SW Aberdeen co.; Scottish residence of British sovereigns.

Bal'sas, Río de las (rē'ō thä läz väl'säs) river, Mexico, flowing from Tlaxcala state to Pacific Ocean on border between Michoacán and Guerrero states; 426 m. long.

Bal'tic Provinces (bôl'tĭk) the former Russian governments of Estonia, Livonia, and Kurland, which in 1918 were formed into the independent republics of Estonia and Latvia.

Baltic Sea, Ger. **Ost'see'** (ôst'zā') arm of the Atlantic Ocean, N Europe, enclosed by Denmark and the Scandinavian Penin.; area ab. 160,000 sq. m.

Baltic States, Estonia, Latvia, and Lithuania, which were independent states 1917–40, and sometimes also Finland and Poland; all situated on E side of Baltic Sea.

Bal'ti·more (bôl'tĭ·mōr; -mēr) independent city, Maryland, on Patapsco river near upper end of Chesapeake Bay; pop. 949,700.

Ba·lu'chi·stan' (bá·lōō'chĭ·stän'; -stän') country, S Asia, bordering on Arabian Sea, between Iran and India; now part of Pakistan; formerly divided into (1) **British Baluchistan,** province in NE, ✻ Quetta, area 45,144 sq. m., (2) agency territories and tribal areas, and (3) the **Baluchistan States:** Kalat, Kharan, and Las Bela.

Ba'ma'ko' (bä'mà'kō') town, French West Africa, ✻ of French Sudan territory, on Niger river; pop. 32,800.

Bam'berg (bäm'bĕrк; Angl. băm'bûrg) city, W Germany, in Bavaria; pop. 74,700.

Ba·nan'a River (bá·năn'á) lagoon, E Florida, W of Cape Canaveral.

Ba·na'ras (bá·nä'räs) or **Be·na'res** (bĕ·nä'rĕs; -rēz) or **Va·ra'na·si** (vä-rä'nǎ·sĭ) city, N India, in SE Uttar Pradesh on the Ganges; Holy City of the Hindus; pop. 255,700.

Ba·nat' (Romanian bä·nät'; Yugoslav bä'nät) region, cen. Europe, in Danube basin between Tisza and Mureş rivers and the Transylvanian Alps; once entirely in Hungary; divided (1919) between Yugoslavia and Romania.

Ban'da Islands (băn'dá) island group, Indonesia, in Moluccas S of Ceram.

Ban'da O'rien·tal' (băn'dä ō'ryän·täl') Uruguay; — its former name, used with reference to its position on E shore of the Río de la Plata.

Ban·dar' Shah·pur' (bän·dar' shä·h'·pōōr') seaport, SW Iran, at head of Persian Gulf.

Ban'djar·ma'sin or **Ban'jer·ma'sin** (bän'jĕr·mä'sĭn) town, Indonesia, in S Borneo on Martapura river; pop. 65,700.

Ban'dung or **Ban'doeng** (bän'dŏŏng) city, Indonesia, in W Java; pop. 166,800.

Banff (bămf) **1** town, W Canada, in SW Alberta; headquarters for **Banff National Park,** established 1885, on E slopes of Rocky Mts., including Lake Louise. **2** or **Banff'shire** (bămf'shĭr; -shĕr) county, NE Scotland; ✻ Banff; 630 sq. m.; pop. 50,100.

Ban'ga·lore' (băng'gà·lōr') city, S India, W of Madras; ✻ of Mysore state; pop. 248,300.

Bang'ka or **Ban'ka** (băng'ká) island, Indonesia, off SE Sumatra; tin mines; chief town Pangkalpinang; area 4609 sq. m.; pop. 205,400.

Bang'kok (băng'kŏk; băng·kŏk') city, ✻ of Thailand (since 1782), on the Chao Phraya ab. 20 m. above its mouth; pop. 681,200.

Ban'gor (băng'gôr; -gēr) city, E cen. Maine, on Penobscot river; pop. 31,600.

Bang'we·u'lu, Lake (băng'wĕ·ōō'lōō), N Northern Rhodesia; area gradually shrinking, once estimated as 1900 sq. m.

Banjermasin. Var. of BANDJARMASIN.

Banks Island (băngks) island, N Canada, at W end of Canadian Arctic Islands; area 23,230 sq. m.

Ban'nock·burn' (băn'ŭk·bûrn'; băn'ŭk·bûrn') town, cen. Scotland, in Stirling co. SSE of Stirling; battle June 23, 1314.

Ban'tam (băn'tăm; native bän·täm') village, Indonesia, in NW corner of Java; once capital of powerful Mohammedan sultanate of Bantam; site of first Dutch settlement in Indonesia 1596.

Ba'paume' (bá·pōm') town, N France, S of Arras; French victory 1871; heavy fighting in World War I.

Bar'a·nof (băr'á·nŏf) island, SE Alaska, S of Chichagof I.

Bar·a·tar'i·a Bay (băr'á·tär'ĭ·á) lagoon, SE Louisiana, W of mouth of Mississippi river.

Bar·ba'dos (bär·bā'dōz) island, West Indies Federation, in Lesser Antilles; ✻ Bridgetown; area 166 sq. m.; pop. 192,800.

Bar'ba·ry (bär'bá·rĭ) region, N Africa, on coast from Egyptian border to the Atlantic, including the former **Barbary States:** Morocco, Algiers, Tunis, and Tripoli.

Bar'bers Point (bär'bērz), also **Ka·la'e·lo'a Point** (kä·lä'á·lō'á) cape, Hawaii, on SW corner of Oahu I. W of Pearl Harbor.

Bar'ber·ton (bär'bēr·t'n; -tŭn) city, NE Ohio; pop. 27,800.

Bar·bu'da (bär·bōō'dá) island, West Indies Federation, in Leeward Islands N of Antigua, of which it is a dependency.

Bar·ce·lo'na (bär'sĕ·lō'ná) seaport, NE Spain; pop. 1,285,900.

Bar'dia (bär'dyä; bär·dē'à) town, Libya, in NE Cyrenaica near Egyptian border; several times captured in World War II.

Ba·reil'ly or **Ba·re'li** (bá·rä'lĭ) city, N India, in Uttar Pradesh; chief city of Rohilkhand; pop. 192,700.

Bar'ents Sea (bär'ĕnts) that part of Arctic Ocean between Spitsbergen and Novaya Zemlya.

Bar Har'bor (bär' här'bēr) town, SE Maine, on Mt. Desert I.

Ba'ri (bä'rē), in full **Bari del'le Pu'glie** (dāl'lā pōō'lyä) seaport, SE Italy, on Adriatic Sea; pop. 271,800.

Ba'ri·sal' (bŭ'rĭ·säl') town, E Pakistan, in East Bengal in Ganges delta; pop. 61,300.

Bar'king (bär'kĭng) urban district, SE England, in Essex E of London; pop. 78,200.

Bar·let'ta (bär·lĕt'á) seaport, SE Italy, in Apulia on Adriatic coast; pop. 62,000.

Bar·na·ul' (bēr·nŭ·ōōl') town, Soviet Russia, Asia, ✻ of Altai Territory, on the Ob; pop. 148,100.

Bar'net (bär'nĕt; -nĭt) urban district, SE England, in Hertfordshire N of London; battle 1471.

Barns'ley (bärnz'lĭ) county borough, N England, in West Riding, Yorkshire; pop. 75,600.

Ba·ro'da (bá·rō'dá) **1** former princely state, W India; merged in Bombay state 1949. **2** city, its ✻; pop. 152,300.

Ba·rot'se (bá·rŏt'sĕ) or **Ba·rot'se·land** (-länd') region, W Northern Rhodesia, inhabited by the Barotse people.

Bar'qui·si·me'to (bär'kē·sē·mā'tō) city, NW Venezuela; pop. 105,100.

Bar'ran·quil'la (bär'räng·kē'yä; Angl. băr'ăn·kē'[y]á) city, N Colombia, on Magdalena river; pop. 150,400.

Bar'rie (băr'ĭ) town, Canada, in SE Ontario on Lake Simcoe; pop. 16,900.

Bar'row (băr'ō) **1** village, N Alaska, at Point Barrow; Arctic Science Station, opened 1947. **2** or **Barrow in Fur'ness** (fûr'nĕs; -nĭs) county borough, NW England, in Lancashire; pop. 67,500.

Barrow, Point, most northerly point of Alaska, 71°20'N, 156°W.

Ba'sel (bä'zĕl), older **Basle** (bäl), Fr. **Bâle** (bäl) **1** canton, NW Switzerland; area 179 sq. m.; pop. 304,000. **2** city, NW Switzerland, ✻ of Basel-Stadt demicanton and of Basel canton; pop. 183,500.

Ba'shan (bā'shăn; -shän) region in ancient Palestine, E and NE of Sea of Galilee.

Ba'shi (bä'shē) **Channel,** strait between Philippine Is. and Formosa.

Bash·kir'i·a (bäsh·kĭr'ĭ·á) or **Bash'kir Republic** (băsh'kĭr; băsh·kĭr'), in full **Bashkir Autonomous Soviet Socialist Republic,** autonomous republic, E Soviet Russia, Europe, in S Ural Mts.; ✻ Ufa; area 54,233 sq. m.; pop. 3,304,500.

Ba·si'lan (bä·sē'län) island group, Philippine Is., SW of Mindanao; comprises Basilan I. and about 50 small islands.

Ba·si·li·ca'ta (bä·zē'lē·kä'tä) or **Lu·ca'ni·a** (lū·kä'nĭ·á; -kän'yá; Ital. lōō·kä'nyä) region, S Italy, on Gulf of Taranto.

Basque Provinces (băsk) region, N Spain, on Bay of Biscay; comprises provinces of Vizcaya, Álava, and Guipúzcoa. See BASQUE, in Vocab.

Bas'ra (bäs'rä; Angl. bŭs'rá), formerly **Bus'ra** or **Bus'rah** (bŭs'rá) port, S Iraq, at head of the Shatt-al-Arab; pop. 180,000.

Basse'terre' (bäs'târ') seaport, West Indies Federation, ✻ of St. Kitts I. and of St. Kitts-Nevis presidency; pop. 29,100.

Basse-Terre (bäs'târ') **1** island, French West Indies, the W part of Guadeloupe, or Guadeloupe proper. **2** seaport on SW coast of Basse-Terre I., ✻ of Guadeloupe; pop. 10,100.

Bass Strait (băs) strait separating Australia and Tasmania.

Bas'togne' (bás·tōn'y', Angl. bäs·tōn') town, SE Belgium, in the Ardennes, where an American division was surrounded December 1944.

Ba·su'to·land' (bá·sōō'tō·länd') territory, S Africa, just NW of Drakensberg Mts., containing sources of Orange river; under a British high commissioner; ✻ Maseru; area 11,716 sq. m.; pop. 563,900.

Ba·taan' (bá·tän'; bá·tän') peninsula, Philippine Is., in W Luzon on W side of Manila Bay; desperate fighting January–April 1942.

Batang. See PAAN.

Ba·ta'vi·a (bá·tā'vĭ·á; -tāv'yá) **1** city, W New York; pop. 17,800.
2 or **Batavian Republic,** Netherlands under the French 1795–1806.
3 city, Indonesia: see DJAKARTA. — **Ba·ta'vi·an,** adj. & n.

Bath (băth) city and county borough, SW England, in Somersetshire, on the Avon ESE of Bristol; pop. 79,300.

Bath'urst (băth'ûrst; -ẽrst) seaport, British West Africa, ✳ of Gambia colony and protectorate, on island of St. Mary in Gambia river.

Bat'on Rouge (băt'n rōōzh') city, ✳ of Louisiana, on Mississippi river; pop. 125,600.

Bat'ter·sea (băt'ẽr·sǐ) metropolitan borough, London, on the S bank of the Thames; pop. 117,100.

Bat'tle (băt''l) town, SE England, in East Sussex 6 m. NW of Hastings; named from the Battle of Hastings 1066.

Bat'tle Creek', city, S Michigan; pop. 48,700.

Ba·tum' (bȧ·tōōm') seaport, U.S.S.R., in SW Georgia; ✳ of Adzhar A.S.S.R., on Black Sea near Turkish border; pop. 70,800.

Ba·var'i·a (bȧ·vâr'ǐ·ȧ), Ger. **Bay'ern** (bī'ẽrn) region, S Germany, bordering on Austria and Czechoslovakia; formerly a duchy of Holy Roman Empire, an electorate from 1623, a kingdom 1805–1918, and a state of Weimar Republic 1919–33; became a state of Bonn Republic 1949; ✳ Munich. — **Ba·var'i·an**, adj. & n.

Bay City (bā) city, E Michigan, at head of Saginaw Bay; pop. 52,500.

Ba·yeux' (bȧ·yẽ'; Fr. bȧ·yû') town, NW France, in Normandy WNW of Caen; has museum containing the Bayeux tapestry.

Bay of Whales. See WHALES, BAY OF.

Bay·onne' (bā·ōn'; bā·yōn') city, NE New Jersey, on peninsula between Upper New York Bay and Newark Bay; pop. 77,200.

Ba'yonne' (bȧ'yôn'; Angl. bā-[y]ōn', -[y]ōn', bī-) city, SW France; pop. 32,600.

Bay·reuth' (bī·roit'; bī'roit) city, W Germany, in Bavaria NE of Nürnberg; pop. 55,600.

Bay'town' (bā'toun') city, SE Texas, on Galveston Bay; pop. 23,000.

Beach'y Head (bēch'ǐ) headland, S England, on coast of East Sussex; 575 ft. high.

Bear (bâr) river, SE Idaho and N Utah, emptying into Great Salt Lake; ab. 350 m. long.

Bé·arn' (bā'ȧr'; -ärn') historical region of SW France; part of Aquitaine under Romans; province of France 1620–1789; ✳ Pau.

Be'as or **Bi'as** (bē'äs) river, N India, in the Punjab, flowing to the Sutlej; 300 m. long.

Beau'fort Sea (bō'fẽrt) that part of the Arctic Ocean NE of Alaska and NW of Canada.

Beau'mont (bō'mŏnt) city, SE Texas, on Neches river; connected with Gulf of Mexico by Sabine-Neches Canal; pop. 94,000.

Beau'vais' (bō'vā') commune, N France, NNW of Paris; pop. 23,200.

Bea'ver Falls (bē'vẽr) city, W Pennsylvania; pop. 17,400.

Bea'ver·lodge, also **Beaver Lodge, Lake** (bē'vẽr·lŏj') lake, Canada, in NW Saskatchewan; uranium deposits.

Bech'u·a'na·land (běch'ōō·ä'nȧ·lănd; bĕ·chwä'nȧ-) **1** region, S Africa, N of Orange river and including Kalahari Desert. **2** British protectorate in the region N of Molopo river; seat of administration Mafeking, in Union of South Africa; area ab. 275,000 sq. m.; pop. 296,900. **3** or **British Bechuanaland**, former British colony in the region S of Molopo river; became part of Cape Province 1895.

Beck'en·ham (běk'n·ăm; běk'năm) urban district, SE England, in Kent, S suburb of London; pop. 74,800.

Beck'ley (běk'lǐ) city, S West Virginia; pop. 19,400.

Bed'ford (běd'fẽrd) **1** county in England: see BEDFORDSHIRE. **2** municipal borough, SE cen. England, ✳ of Bedfordshire; pop. 53,100.

Bed'ford·shire (-shǐr; -shẽr) or **Bedford** or **Beds** (bědz) county, SE cen. England; ✳ Bedford; 473 sq. m.; pop. 311,800.

Bed'loe's Island (běd'lōz), also **Lib'er·ty Island** (lǐb'ẽr·tǐ) island in New York Bay; site of Statue of Liberty.

Be'dzin (běn'jěn), Russ. **Ben'din** (byän'dyǐn), Ger. **Bend'zin** (běn'-tsĕn) commune, S Poland, in Silesia; pop. 50,700.

Be'er-she'ba (bē'ẽr·shē'bȧ; bẽr·shē'bȧ; bē·ẽr'shē·bȧ) city, S Israel, in N Negeb; in Bible times marked extreme S limit of Palestine; pop. (1950) 15,000. See DAN, in Vocab.

Behar. See BIHAR.

Be'his·tun' (bā'hǐs·tōōn') or **Bi'si·tun'** or **Bi'su·tun'** (bē'sŭ·tōōn') ruined town in W Iran; site of cuneiform inscriptions.

Beh'ring. Var. of BERING.

Bei'ra (bā'ẽ·rȧ) **1** old province, N cen. Portugal; ✳ Coimbra. **2** seaport, SE Mozambique; pop. 13,000.

Bei·rut' (bā·rōōt'), Fr. **Bey'routh'** (bā'rōōt'), anc. **Be·ry'tus** (bĕ·rī'tŭs) seaport, ✳ of Lebanon; pop. 201,500.

Bejraburana. See PHETCHABUN.

Bekáa. See BIKA, EL.

Bé'kés·csa'ba (bā'kásh·chō'bȯ) city, SE Hungary; pop. 50,000.

Be·lém' (bĕ·lĕm'), sometimes **Pa·rá'** (pȧ·rȧ') city, N Brazil, ✳ of Pará state, on Pará river at 1°28'S; pop. 230,200.

Bel'fast (běl'fȧst; běl·fȧst') county borough and seaport, ✳ of Northern Ireland and of co. Antrim; at head of **Belfast Lough** (lŏκ), inlet of North Channel; pop. 438,100.

Bel'fort' (běl'fôr'; bā'fôr') town, E France, commanding **Bel'fort Gap** (běl'fôr găp'), pass between the Vosges and the Jura Mts.

Bel'gian Con'go (běl'jăn [·jǐ·ăn] kŏŋ'gō), Fr. **Con'go' belge** (kôn'gō' bělzh'), Flem. **Bel'gisch Con'go** (běl'gǐs kŏŋ'gō), formerly **Congo Free State**, country, cen. Africa, occupying greater part of Congo river basin; Belgian colony; ✳ Léopoldville; area ab. 893,000 sq. m.; pop. 11,126,500.

Belgian East Africa. = RUANDA-URUNDI.

Bel'gium (běl'jǔm; -jǐ·ŭm), Fr. **Bel'gique'** (běl'zhēk'), Flem. **Bel'gi·ë** (běl'gĕ·ĕ) country, W Europe, bordering on North Sea; constitutional monarchy; ✳ Brussels; area 11,774 sq. m.; pop. 8,625,100. See BELGIAN, in Vocab.

Bel'go·rod-Dnes·trov'ski (byěl'gŭ·rŭt·d'nyěs·trôf'ski), formerly **Ak·ker·man'** (ŭk·kẽr·män'), Romanian **Ce·ta'tea Al'bă** (chĕ·tä'tyä äl'bȧ) city, U.S.S.R., in SW Ukraine on the Dniester estuary; pop. 33,500.

Bel'grade (běl'grād; běl'grād'), Serbian **Be'o·grad** (bě'ȯ·gräd) city, ✳ of Yugoslavia and of Serbia, on Danube river; pop. 389,100.

Belgravia. See in Vocab.

Belitung. See BILLITON.

Be·lize' (bě·lēz') seaport, ✳ of British Honduras.

Bell (běl) city, SW California, S of Los Angeles; pop. 15,400.

Bel'leau' (bě'lō') village, N France, NW of Château-Thierry; site of an American military cemetery.

Bel'leau' Wood (bě'lō'), Fr. **Bois de Bel'leau'** (bwäd' bě'lō'), since World War I also **Bois de la Bri'gade' Ma'rine'** (bwäd' lȧ brē'gȧd' mȧ'rēn') wood S of Belleau village, France; battle June 1918.

Belle Isle, Strait of (běl' īl') channel between N tip of Newfoundland and SE Labrador.

Belle'ville (běl'vǐl) **1** city, SW Illinois; pop. 32,700. **2** town, NE New Jersey, N of Newark; pop. 32,000. **3** city, E Canada, in SE Ontario on Bay of Quinte; pop. 20,600.

Bel'ling·ham (běl'ǐng·hăm) city, NW Washington, on Bellingham Bay; pop. 34,100.

Bel'lings·hau'sen Sea (běl'ǐngz·hou'z'n) inlet of S Pacific Ocean on coast of Antarctica W of Palmer Peninsula.

Bel'mont (běl'mŏnt) town, NE Massachusetts; pop. 27,400.

Beloe More. See WHITE SEA.

Be'lo Ho'ri·zon'te (bě'lō hȯr'ǐ·zȯn'tě) city, E Brazil, ✳ of Minas Gerais state; pop. 346,200.

Be·loit' (bě·loit') city, S Wisconsin, on Illinois border; pop. 29,600.

Belorussia, Belorussian S.S.R. See WHITE RUSSIA.

Belostok. See BIAŁYSTOK.

Bel'sen, in full **Ber'gen-Bel'sen** (běr'gĕn·běl'zĕn) locality in NW Germany, on Lüneburg Heath; site of Nazi concentration camp taken by Allies April 14, 1945, later destroyed.

Belts'ville (bělts'vǐl) village, Maryland, NE of Washington, D.C.; principal experiment station, U.S. Department of Agriculture.

Be·lu'kha (byĭ·lōō'kȧ) mountain, Soviet Russia, Asia; highest in Altai mountain system, 15,157 ft.

Be'mis Heights (bē'mǐs) hamlet, N New York, N of Stillwater; headquarters of Gen. Gates in battle of Saratoga 1777.

Benares. See BANARAS.

Bendin or **Bendzin.** See BĘDZIN.

Ben·gal' (běn·gôl'; běng·gôl'; attributively usu. běn'gal) region, NE Indian subcontinent, including delta of Ganges and Brahmaputra; formerly a presidency and (1937–47) a province of British India; divided 1947 between India (**West Bengal** state, area 33,945 sq. m.; pop. 26,306,600, ✳ Calcutta) and Pakistan (**East Bengal**, area 52,500 sq. m., pop. 35,276,000). —**Ben'ga·lese'** (běn'gȧ·lēz'; -lēs'; běng'-), adj. & n. sing. & pl. See BENGALI, in Vocab.

Bengal, Bay of, that part of the Indian Ocean between India and Ceylon on the W and Burma and Malay Penin. on the E.

Ben·ga'si (běn·gä'zē) or **Ben·ga'zi** or **Ben·gha'zi** or **Ben·gha'si**, anc. **Ber'e·ni'ce** (běr'ě·nī'sě) NE Libya, ✳ of Cyrenaica and a ✳ of Libya; pop. 64,600.

Be'ni (bā'nē) river, N and cen. Bolivia, flowing N to unite with Mamoré river and form the Madeira; over 1000 m. long.

Be'ni Ha'san (bā'nē hä'sän) village, N cen. Egypt, on Nile river; rock tombs (XIIth dynasty; c. 2000 B.C.).

Be·nin' (bě·nǐn'; -nēn'; bě-) **1** river, S Nigeria, W of the Niger, flowing into Bight of Benin. **2** province, SW Nigeria, W of Niger delta; powerful Negro kingdom 17th–19th cents.; ✳ Benin City.

Benin, Bight of, northern section of Gulf of Guinea, W Africa, off coast of SW Nigeria and Dahomey.

Be'ni Su·ef' (bā'nē sōō·wāf') city, S Egypt, on the Nile; pop. 57,500.

Ben Lo'mond (běn lō'mŭnd) mountain, S cen. Scotland, on E side of Loch Lomond; 3192 ft. high.

Ben Ne'vis (běn ně'vǐs; něv'ǐs) mountain, W Scotland, in Grampian Mts.; highest peak in Great Britain, 4406 ft.

Ben'ning·ton (běn'ǐng·tŭn) village, SW Vermont; battle of Bennington 1777 occurred nearby in New York state; Bennington College.

Be·no'ni (bě·nō'nǐ) town, NE Union of South Africa, in S Transvaal on the Witwatersrand; pop. 74,200.

Ben'ton Harbor (běn't'n) city, SW Michigan; pop. 18,800.

Be'nue (bā'nwā) or **Bin'ue** (bēn'wä) river, W Africa, chief tributary of Niger river from E; ab. 870 m. long.

Beograd. See BELGRADE.

Bep'pu (běp'ōō) city, Japan, in NE Kyushu on **Beppu Bay**, an arm of the Inland Sea; pop. 96,700.

Be·rar' (bě·rär') region, cen. India; once a Mohammedan kingdom, later part of Central Provinces and Berar; in Madhya Pradesh 1947–56, now part of Bombay state; chief city Amraoti.

Ber'be·ra (bûr'bẽr·ȧ) seaport, British Somaliland, ✳ until 1941.

Berch'tes·ga'den (běrκ'těs·gä'děn) town, W Germany, in Bavarian Alps S of Salzburg, Austria; Hitler's estate.

Berenice. See BENGASI.

Be·re'zi·na (bě·rě'zǐ·nȧ) river, U.S.S.R., in White Russia, flowing SE into Dnieper river; battle 1812 near Borisov; 350 m. long.

Bergama. See PERGAMUM.

Ber'ga·mo (běr'gä·mō) commune, N Italy, NE of Milan; pop. 107,200.

Bergen. See MONS.

Ber'gen (běr'gen; Angl. bûr'-) seaport, SW Norway; pop. 110,400.

Bergen-Belsen. See BELSEN.

Ber'gen·field (bûr'gĕn·fēld) borough, NE New Jersey, E of Paterson; pop. 17,600.

Be'ring Sea (bē'rǐng; bâr'-; bēr'-) that part of North Pacific Ocean between Alaska and NE Asia; area 878,000 sq. m.

Bering Strait, strait separating Asia (U.S.S.R.) from North America (Alaska); ab. 56 m. wide.

Berke'ley (bûrk'lǐ) city, W California, on San Francisco Bay N of Oakland; pop. 113,800.

Berk'ley (bûrk'lǐ) city, SE Michigan; pop. 17,900.

Berk'shire (bärk'shǐr; -shēr; rarely, in England, bûrk'-) or **Berks** (bärks; bûrks) county, S England, in Thames river basin; ✳ Reading; area 725 sq. m.; pop. 402,900.

Berkshire Hills (bûrk'shǐr; -shēr) range in W Massachusetts; highest peak Mount Greylock, 3505 ft.

Ber'lin (bûr'lǐn) city, N New Hampshire; pop. 16,600.

Ber·lin' (bûr·lǐn'; běr·lǐn'; bûr'lǐn) city, E Germany, on Spree river; before 1945 ✳ of Prussia and of Germany; under postwar occupation divided between East and West Germany, East Berlin being made ✳ of East German Republic 1949; pop. 3,187,500.

Ber·me′jo (bĕr·mĕ′hō) river, N Argentina, rising on Bolivian frontier and flowing SE into Paraguay river; 1000 m. long.

Ber·mu′da (bĕr·mū′dȧ), also **Bermuda Islands** or **Ber·mu′das** (-dȧz) island group, W North Atlantic; British colony; ✳ Hamilton; area 19 sq. m.; pop. 36,800. — **Ber·mu′di·an** (-dĭ·ăn), adj. & n.

Bern (bûrn; Ger. bĕrn) or **Berne** (bûrn; Fr. bĕrn) **1** canton, NW and W cen. Switzerland; area 2658 sq. m.; pop. 801,900. **2** city, ✳ of Bern canton and of Switzerland; pop. 146,500. — **Ber′nese** (bûr′nēz′; -nēs′), adj. & n.

Bern′burg (bĕrn′bŏŏrk) city, E Germany, W of Dessau; pop. 53,400.

Bernese Alps, Bernese Oberland. See OBERLAND.

Ber·ni′ci·a (bûr·nĭsh′ĭ·ȧ) Anglian kingdom of 6th cent. A.D., located between Tyne and Forth rivers, with ✳ at Bamborough.

Ber·ni′na (bĕr·nē′nä; Angl. bĕr·nē′nȧ) southern extension of Rhaetian Alps, on border between Italy and Switzerland; highest peak (highest in the Rhaetian Alps) **Piz Bernina** (pēts bĕr·nē′nä), 13,295 ft.

Be·roe′a or **Be·re′a** (bē·rē′ȧ) **1** Mod. Gr. **Vé′roia** (vâ′roià) town, W Greece, in Macedonia; one of first places in Europe where St. Paul preached. **2** ancient city, Syria: see ALEP.

Ber′ry′ or **Ber′ri′** (bĕ′rē′; Angl. bĕr′ĭ) historical region of cen. France; ✳Bourges.

Ber′wick (bĕr′ĭk) or **Ber′wick·shire** (-shĭr; -shĕr) county, SE Scotland; ✳ Duns; area 457 sq. m.; pop. 25,100.

Ber′wyn (bûr′wĭn) city, NE Illinois, W of Chicago; pop. 51,300.

Berytus. See BEIRUT.

Be·san′çon (bė·zäN′sôN′) city, E France, E of Dijon; pop. 63,500.

Bes′kids (bĕs′kĭdz; bĕs·kēdz′) mountain ranges, cen. Europe, in W Carpathians: **West Beskids**, in Poland and Czechoslovakia W of Tatra Mts., and **East Beskids**, in NE Czechoslovakia.

Bes′sa·ra′bi·a (bĕs′ȧ·rā′bĭ·ȧ; -räb′yȧ) region, SE Europe, between Dniester and Prut rivers; ceded by Turkey to Russia 1812; formed a government under Russia 1812–1917; joined Romania 1918; seized by Soviet Union 1940 and incorporated in the U.S.S.R. (see MOLDAVIAN REPUBLIC). — **Bes′sa·ra′bi·an**, adj. & n.

Bes′se·mer (bĕs′ĕ·mēr) city, cen. Alabama; pop. 28,400.

Beth′a·ny (bĕth′ȧ·nĭ) village, Palestine, just E of Jerusalem, in Jordan.

Beth′el (bĕth′ĕl; bĕth′ĕl; bĕth′ĕl′) ancient town, Palestine, N of Jerusalem; a holy place in early history of Israel. See BETHEL, in Vocab.

Be·thes′da (bė·thĕz′dȧ) village and district, cen. Maryland, just NW of Washington, D.C.; pop. (district) 45,800.

Beth′le·hem (bĕth′lĕ·ĕm; -hĕm) **1** city, E Pennsylvania, on Lehigh river; pop. 66,300. **2** town, Palestine, in Judaea SW of Jerusalem, in Jordan; birthplace of Christ.

Beth′nal Green (bĕth′n′l) metropolitan borough, E London; pop. 58,400.

Beth·sa′i·da of Gal′i·lee (bĕth·sā′ĭ·dȧ, găl′ĭ·lē) or **of Gau′lo·ni′tis** (gô′lō·nī′tĭs) ruined town, Palestine, on NE side of Sea of Galilee.

Be′ti·o (bā′tsĭ·ō; bāt′shĭ·ō) islet and village, Gilbert Is., at S end of Tarawa atoll.

Beuthen. See BYTOM.

Bev′er·ly (bĕv′ẽr·lĭ) city, NE Massachusetts, on coast; pop. 28,900.

Beverly Hills, city, SW California, W of Los Angeles; pop. 29,000.

Bex′ley (bĕks′lĭ) urban district, SE England, in Kent SE of London; pop. 88,800.

Bey′o·ğlu′ (bĕ′ĕ·ō·lōō′) division of İstanbul, Turkey in Europe, comprising the section N of the Golden Horn.

Beyrouth. See BEIRUT.

Bé′ziers′ (bā′zyā′) city, S France; pop. 64,600.

Bha·mo′ (bȧ·mō′) town, N Burma, on upper Irrawaddy river.

Bharat. See INDIA.

Bhat·pa′ra (bŭt′pä′rȧ) city, NE India, N of Calcutta; pop. 117,000.

Bhav·na′gar or **Bhau·na′gar** (bou·nŭg′ẽr) **1** former princely state, W India, in Kathiawar on Gulf of Cambay; became part of Saurashtra state 1948; to Bombay state 1956. **2** seaport, its ✳; pop. 102,900.

Bho·pal′ (bō·päl′) **1** former state, N cen. India, in and N of Vindhya Mts.; became 1956 part of Madhya Pradesh. **2** city, ✳ of Madhya Pradesh and of former Bhopal state; pop. 75,200.

Bhu·ba·nes′war or **Bhu′va·nesh′war** (bŏŏ′vȧ·näsh′wẽr) town, E India, ✳ of state of Orissa, S of Cuttack.

Bhu·tan′ (bŏŏ·tän′; bŏŏ·tän′), also **Bho·tan′** (bō·tän′) country, Asia, in Himalayas on NE border of India; semi-independent; ✳ Punakha; area 18,000 sq. m.; pop. 300,000. — **Bhu′tan·ese′** (bŏŏ′t′n·ēz′; -ēs′), adj. & n. sing. & pl.

Bi·a′fra, Bight of (bė·ä′frȧ) eastern section of Gulf of Guinea, W Africa.

Bi·ak′ (bė·yäk′) island off West New Guinea, largest of Schouten Is.

Bia·ly′stok (byä·lĭ′stôk), Russ. **Be·lo·stok′** (byĭ′lŭ·stôk′) city, NE Poland; pop. 105,300.

Bianco, Monte. See BLANC, MONT.

Biar′ritz′ (byä′rēts′) commune, SW France, on the Bay of Biscay; pop. 22,000.

Bias. See BEAS.

Bid′de·ford (bĭd′ĕ·fẽrd) city, SW Maine, on Saco river; pop. 20,800.

Biel (bēl), Fr. **Bienne** (byĕn) commune, NW Switzerland, in N Bern canton just NE of NE end of **Lake of Biel**; pop. 48,300.

Bie′le·feld (bē′lĕ·fĕlt) city, W Germany, E of Münster; pop. 153,100.

Big Bend, section of Columbia river, E cen. Washington, where river turns in its course S to make a wide bend W, S, and E.

Big Bend National Park, mountain and desert area, S Texas, in bend of the Rio Grande; established as national park 1944.

Big Black, river, W cen. Mississippi, flowing SW into Mississippi river; 330 m. long.

Big′horn′ (bĭg′hôrn′) river, N Wyoming and SE Montana, flowing N into Yellowstone river; 336 m. long.

Big′ Horn′ Mountains, range in N Wyoming, extending S from Montana border E of Bighorn river; highest point Cloud Peak, 13,165 ft.

Big Spring, city, W Texas; pop. 17,300.

Big Stone Lake, narrow lake between NE corner of South Dakota and W Minnesota; 35 m. long.

Big Thomp′son (tŏm[p]′s′n) river, N Colorado, flowing S to South Platte river; 75 m. long.

Bi·har′ (bė·här′) or **Be·har′** (bė-) **1** state, NE India, bordering on Nepal; ✳ Patna; area 67,164 sq. m.; pop 38,779,600. **2** town in cen. Bihar state, SE of Patna; pop. 54,600.

Bihar and O·ris′sa (ō·rĭs′ȧ) province 1912–36 of British India; ✳ Patna.

Biisk. See BISK.

Bijanagar. See VIJAYANAGAR.

Bi·ka′, El (äl bĭ·kä′), also **Be·káa′** (bĭ·kä′), anc. **Coe′le-Syr′i·a** or **Coe′le·syr′i·a** (sē′lē·sĭr′ĭ·ȧ) valley in Lebanon and Syria, between the Lebanon and Anti-Lebanon mountain ranges.

Bi′ka·ner′ (bē′kŭ·när′; Angl. bĭk′ȧ·nẽr′) **1** former princely state, NW India, in Thar Desert; became part of Rajasthan state 1948. **2** city, its ✳; pop. 127,200.

Bi·ki′ni (bĭ·kē′nĭ) native bĭk′ĭ·nĭ) atoll, Marshall Is., at NW end of Ratak chain; scene of atomic-bomb tests July 1946.

Bil·ba′o (bĭl·bä′ō) city, N Spain, ✳ of Vizcaya prov.; pop. 235,500.

Bill′ings (bĭl′ĭngz) city, S cen. Montana, on Yellowstone river; pop. 31,800.

Bil·li′ton (bĭ·lē′tŏn) or **Be·li′tung** (bĭ·lē′tŏŏng) island, Indonesia, between Bangka and Borneo; area 1866 sq. m.; pop. 73,400.

Bi·lox′i (bĭ·lŭk′sĭ; -lŏk′sĭ) city, SE Mississippi, on Gulf of Mexico; pop. 37,400.

Bim′i·ni (bĭm′ĭ·nĭ) or **Bim′i·nis** (-nĭz) two small islands of the Bahamas; area 9 sq. m.

Bing′en (bĭng′ĕn) city, W Germany, at confluence of Rhine and Nahe rivers; pop. 16,500.

Bing′ham·ton (bĭng′ăm·tŭn) city, S New York, at confluence of Chenango and Susquehanna rivers; pop. 80,700.

Binh Dinh (bĭn′y′ dĭn′y′) city, Indochina, in S Annam; pop. 147,200.

Binue. See BENUE.

Bi′o-Bi′o (bē′ō·vē′ō) river, S cen. Chile, flowing into the Pacific at Concepción; 238 m. long.

Bir′ken·head (bûr′kĕn·hĕd; bûr′kĕn·hĕd′) county borough, NW England, on the Mersey estuary opposite Liverpool; pop. 142,400.

Bir′ming·ham (bûr′mĭng·hăm; Brit. and occas. U.S., -mĭng·ăm) **1** city, N cen. Alabama; pop. 326,000. **2** city, SE Michigan; pop. 15,500. **3** city and county borough, W cen. England; pop. 1,112,300.

Bi′ro·bi·dzhan′ or **Bi′ro-Bi·djan′** (bĭr′ō·bĭ·jän′). See JEWISH AUTONOMOUS REGION.

Bisayas. See VISAYAN ISLANDS.

Bis′cay (bĭs′kā; -kĭ) or **Bis·ca′ya** (bĕs·kä′yä). See VIZCAYA.

Biscay, Bay of, inlet of Atlantic Ocean on W coast of France and N coast of Spain.

Bis′cayne Bay (bĭs·kān′; bĭs·kān′) inlet of Atlantic Ocean, SE Florida, at N end of Florida Keys.

Bish′op Rock (bĭsh′ŭp) islet, SW England; one of the Scilly Isles; lighthouse.

Bisitun. See BEHISTUN.

Bisk (byĕsk) or **Biisk** (byē′ĭsk) town, Soviet Russia, Asia, in E Altai Territory; pop. 80,200.

Bis′kra (bĭs′krō) town, NE Algeria, at an oasis on S edge of Atlas Mts.; pop. 18,900.

Bis′marck (bĭz′märk) city, ✳ of North Dakota, on Missouri river; pop. 18,600.

Bismarck Archipelago, island group in W Pacific Ocean N of E end of New Guinea, including islands of New Britain, New Ireland, New Hanover, and Admiralty Is.; part of Territory of New Guinea; area 22,930 sq. m.; pop. 202,000.

Bismarck Sea, that part of the W Pacific Ocean enclosed by the islands of the Bismarck Archipelago.

Bisutun. See BEHISTUN.

Bi·thyn′i·a (bĭ·thĭn′ĭ·ȧ) ancient country in NW Asia Minor, bordering on the Propontis and Euxine; became Roman province 74 B.C. — **Bi·thyn′i·an**, adj. & n.

Bit′ter Lakes (bĭt′ẽr) two lakes, Great and Little Bitter Lake, NE Egypt, just N of Suez; connected and traversed by the Suez Canal.

Bit′ter·root′, or **Bitter Root, Range** (bĭt′ẽr·rōōt′; -rōot′) range of the Rocky Mts. on Idaho-Montana boundary; highest peak 10,900 ft.

Bi·wa (bē·wä) lake, Japan, in Honshu NE of Kyoto; 40 m. long.

Bi·zerte′ (bė′zẽrt′; Angl. bĭ·zûrt′, bĭ·zûr′tĕ) or **Bi·zer′ta** (bĭ·zûr′tȧ) seaport, N Tunisia; pop. 28,500.

Black′burn (blăk′bẽrn) county borough, NW England, in Lancashire; pop. 111,200.

Black Canyon, 1 canyon of the Colorado river between Arizona and Nevada, S of Hoover Dam. **2** canyon of the Gunnison river, W Colorado; 50 m. long; most picturesque part is now the **Black Canyon of the Gun′ni·son National Monument** (gŭn′ĭ·s′n), established 1933.

Black Forest, Ger. **Schwarz′wald′** (shvärts′vält′) mountainous region, SW Germany, along upper Rhine from the Neckar to Swiss border; higher parts thickly forested.

Black Hills, group of mountains, W South Dakota and NE Wyoming; highest mountain Harney Peak, 7242 ft., in South Dakota.

Black Mountains, range of Blue Ridge Mts. in W North Carolina; highest peak Mount Mitchell, 6684 ft.

Black′pool′ (blăk′pōōl′) county borough, NW England, in Lancashire on Irish Sea; pop. 147,100.

Black River. See Bo.

Black Sea, also **Eux′ine Sea** (ūk′sĭn; Brit. usu. -sīn), anc. **Pon′tus** or **Pontus Eux·i′nus** (pŏn′tŭs ūk·sī′nŭs) sea between Europe and Asia, connected with Aegean Sea through the Bosporus, Sea of Marmara, and Dardanelles; 168,500 sq. m.

Black Warrior, river, cen. Alabama, flowing into Tombigbee river; 178 m. long.

Blackwells Island. See WELFARE ISLAND.

Bla′dens·burg (blā′d′nz·bûrg) town, S cen. Maryland, 7 m. ENE of Washington, D.C.; site of battle Aug. 24, 1814.

Bla′go·vesh′chensk (blăg′ō·vĕsh′chĕnsk) city, E Soviet Russia, Asia, on Amur river; pop. 58,800.

Blanc, Cape (kăp bläN′; Angl. blängk′, blăngk′) cape, N Africa, on N tip of Tunisia; northernmost point of the continent, 37°14′N.

Blanc, Mont (môn′ blän′; Angl. mŏnt′ blängk′, blăngk′), Ital. **Mon′te Bian′co** (mŏn′tā byäng′kō) mountain, SE France, on Italian border; highest of the Alps, 15,781 ft.

Blan′ca Peak (blăng′kà) mountain, S Colorado; highest in Sangre de Cristo Mts., 14,390 ft.

Blar′ney (blär′nĭ) town, SW Ireland, in cen. co. Cork NW of Cork; in its 15th-cent. Blarney Castle is the Blarney stone.

Bled (blĕd) village, NW Yugoslavia, NW of Ljubljana; mountain resort.

Blen′heim (blĕn′ĭm; -ĕm), Eng. and French form of German **Blind′-heim** (blĭnt′hīm) village, W Germany, in Bavaria NNW of Augsburg; battle 1704, called also battle of Höchstädt.

Blen′ner·has′sett Island (blĕn′ẽr-hăs′ĕt; -ĭt) island, West Virginia, in Ohio river below Parkersburg.

Blgariya. See BULGARIA.

Block Island (blŏk) island, Rhode Island, SSW of Point Judith.

Bloem′fon·tein′ (blōōm′fŏn-tān′) city, Union of South Africa, ✳ of Orange Free State; pop. 67,200.

Blois (blwà) city, France, on Loire river SW of Orléans; pop. 26,800.

Bloom′field (blōōm′fēld) town, NE New Jersey; pop. 49,300.

Bloom′ing·ton (blōōm′ĭng-tŭn) **1** city, cen. Illinois; pop. 34,200. **2** city, S cen. Indiana; pop. 28,200.

Blue′field′ (blōō′fēld′) **1** town, SW Virginia, on border adjoining Bluefield, West Virginia; pop. 4200. **2** city, S West Virginia, in Blue Ridge Mts.; pop. 21,500.

Blue′fields′ (blōō′fēldz′) town, Nicaragua, on SE coast at mouth of Escondido river; pop. 10,300.

Blue Island, city, NE Illinois, S of Chicago; pop. 17,600.

Blue Mountains, range, NE Oregon and SE Washington; highest peak Rock Creek Butte, 9097 ft.

Blue Nile, river, Anglo-Egyptian Sudan: see NILE.

Blue Ridge, also **Blue Ridge Mountains**, the eastern range of the Appalachian Mts., E United States, from near Harpers Ferry, West Virginia, into N Georgia; by some considered to include the N extension into Maryland, Pennsylvania, and New York.

Blythe′ville (blīth′vĭl) city, NE Arkansas; pop. 16,200.

Bo (bō) or **Song Bo** (sŏng′ bō′), Eng. **Black River**, river, SE Asia, rising in cen. Yunnan, China, and flowing SE to the Coi, in Indochina; nearly 500 m. long.

Bo·bruisk′ (bŭ-brōō′ĭsk) city, U.S.S.R., in White Russia on Berezina river; pop. 84,100.

Bo′ca Chi′ca (bō′kà chē′kà) island, Florida Keys, adjacent to Key West; U.S. Naval Air Station.

Bo′ca Ra·ton′ (bō′kà rà-tōn′) town, SE Florida, on coast N of Fort Lauderdale; radar training center of U.S. Air Force.

Bo′chum (bō′Koom) city, W Germany, in Ruhr valley; pop. 290,400.

Boden See. See CONSTANCE, LAKE.

Bodrum. See HALICARNASSUS.

Boe·o′tia (bē-ō′shà; -shĭ-à), Mod. Gr. **Voi·o·ti′a** (vyô-tē′à) district, E cen. Greece, just NW of Attica; an ancient republic. — **Boe·o′tian** (bē-ō′shăn), adj. & n.

Boetoeng. See BUTON.

Bo′ga·lu′sa (bō′gà-lōō′sà) city, E Louisiana; pop. 17,800.

Bo′gor (bō′gôr), formerly **Bui′ten·zorg** (boi′tĕn-zôrk) city, Indonesia, in W Java S of Djakarta; botanic gardens; pop. 65,400.

Bo′go·tá′ (bō′gō-tä′; bō′gō-tô′) city, ✳ of Colombia; on plateau of eastern Andes; altitude 8563 ft.; pop. 325,700.

Bo·he′mi·a (bō-hē′mĭ-à), Czech **Če′chy** (chĕk′ĭ), Ger. **Böh′men** (bû′mĕn) region, W Czechoslovakia; once a kingdom; a province 1918–39 and 1945–48; ✳ Prague; area 20,101 sq. m.; pop. 7,109,400. See BOHEMIAN, in Vocab.

Bo·he′mi·an Forest (bō-hē′mĭ-ăn), Ger. **Böh′mer Wald** (bû′mẽr vält′), Czech **Čes′ký Les** (chĕs′kē lĕs′) region, Czechoslovakia and Germany, along boundary between E Bavaria and SW Bohemia; mountainous and forested; highest peak 4780 ft.

Bo·hol′ (bō-hôl′) island, S cen. Philippine Is., one of the Visayan Is.

Bois de Belleau. See BELLEAU WOOD.

Bois de Bou·logne′ (bwä′ dĕ bōō·lôn′; bōō·loin′; Fr. bwäd′bōō′lôn′y′), familiarly **Bois** (bwä) park, France, just W of Paris; 2155 acres.

Boi′se (boi′sĭ; -zĭ) city, ✳ of Idaho, on Boise river; pop. 34,400.

Bois-le-Duc. See ′s HERTOGENBOSCH.

Bokhara. See BUKHARA.

Boks′burg (bŏks′bûrg) town, NE Union of South Africa, in S Transvaal E of Johannesburg; pop. 53,400.

Bo·lan′ Pass (bō-län′) mountain pass, Pakistan, in N Baluchistan; 5900 ft. high.

Bolbitine. See ROSETTA.

Bo·lí′var (bō-lē′vär), formerly **La Pa·ri′da** (lä pä-rē′thä) hill (Span. cerro), SE Venezuela, containing iron ore; ab. 6 m. long, 2000 ft. high.

Bo·liv′i·a (bō-lĭv′ĭ-à) country, W cen. South America; republic; administrative ✳ La Paz, constitutional ✳ Sucre; area 424,200 sq. m.; pop. (1956 est.) 3,235,000. — **Bo·liv′i·an**, adj. & n.

Bo·lo′gna (bō-lō′nyà; Angl. bō-lōn′yà, -lō′nà) commune, N Italy, in Emilia at foot of the Apennines; pop. 346,100. — **Bo′lo·gnese′** (bō′-lō·nyēz′; -nyēs′), adj. & n. sing. & pl.

Bolshaya. See McKINLEY, MOUNT.

Bol′ton (bōl′t′n), in full **Bolton-le-Moors** (-lĕ-mōōrz′) county borough, NW England, NW of Manchester; pop. 167,200.

Bol·za′no (bōl-tsä′nō) commune, NE Italy, in S Tirol; pop. 78,000.

Bo′ma (bō′mà) town, W Belgian Congo, on Congo river; until 1923 ✳ of Belgian Congo.

Bom·bay′ (bŏm-bā′; bŏm′bā′) **1** state, W India, on W coast extending to the N and E of Gulf of Cambay; formerly a presidency and (1937–47) a province of British India; boundaries re-established 1956; area 190,919 sq. m.; pop. 48,263,500. **2** city, its ✳, on coastal island (**Bombay Island**); pop. 1,489,900.

Bo′mi Hills (bō′mĭ) group of low hills, N Liberia, 40 m. N of Monrovia; iron mines.

Bo′mu (bō′mōō) or **Mbo′mu** (′m-bō′mōō) river, cen. Africa, forming boundary between N Belgian Congo and E French Equatorial Africa; unites with Uele river to form Ubangi river; 500 m. long.

Bon, Cape (kăp bŏn′; Fr. bôn′) or **Ras Ad·dar′** (räs äd-där′) peninsula, NE Tunisia; 50 m. long.

Bon′aire′ (bō′nâr′), Span. **Buen Ai′re** (bwän ī′rā) island, Netherlands Antilles, E of Curaçao; 95 sq. m.; pop. 5800.

Bône (bōn) seaport, NE Algeria; pop. 102,800.

Bo′nin (bō′nĭn), or **O·ga·sa·wa·ra** (ō-gä·sä·wä-rä), **Islands**, island group, W Pacific Ocean; belonged to Japan 1876–1945.

Bonn (bŏn) city, W Germany, on the Rhine; made ✳ of West German Federal Republic (often called the Bonn Republic) 1949; pop. 111,300.

Boo′thi·a, Gulf of (bōō′thĭ-à) gulf, N Canada, between Boothia Penin. and Melville Penin.

Boothia Peninsula, N Canada; its N tip is northernmost point of mainland of North America.

Boo′tle (bōō′t′l) county borough, NW England, suburb of Liverpool; pop. 74,300.

Bo·rås′ (bōō-rôs′) town, SW Sweden; pop. 57,000.

Bor′deaux′ (bôr′dō′) seaport, SW France, on the Garonne river 13 m. from Gironde estuary; pop. 253,800.

Bor′ger (bôr′gẽr) city, NW Texas, in the panhandle; pop. 18,100.

Bor′ger·hout (bôr′kẽr-hout) commune, N Belgium, E suburb of Antwerp; pop. 51,600.

Bo·ri′sov (bŭ-ryē′sôf) town, U.S.S.R., in N cen. White Russia on Berezina river; battle 1812.

Bor′ne·o (bôr′nē-ō) **1** island, Malay Archipelago; area 290,012 sq. m.; divided administratively between British dependencies in N (sometimes called collectively **British Borneo**: see NORTH BORNEO, SARAWAK, BRUNEI) and a part of the Republic of Indonesia in S (ab. 72 per cent of the island, formerly **Dutch Borneo**), which is called by the Indonesians **Ka′li·man′tan** (kä′lē-män′tän). **2** the S part of the island. — **Bor′ne·an** (bôr′nē-ăn), adj. & n.

Born′holm (bôrn′hōlm) island, Denmark; ✳ Rönne; 228 sq. m.; pop. 45,900.

Bor′nu (bôr′nōō) province of Nigeria, including part of Cameroons trust territory; with territory now in French West Africa, once constituted a Mohammedan native kingdom.

Bo′ro·bu·dur′, also **Bo′ro·boe·doer′** (bō′rō-bōō-dōōr′) Buddhist stupa, Indonesia, in Java S of Magelang; about 1000 years old.

Bo·ro·di·no′ (bŭ-rŭ-dyĭ-nô′) village, Soviet Russia, Europe; 70 m. SW of Moscow; battle 1812 in which Napoleon defeated Gen. Kutuzov.

Bos′ni·a (bŏz′nĭ-à), Yugoslav **Bos′na** (bôs′nä) region, cen. Yugoslavia, once a kingdom; in 1878 made part of Austrian province of **Bosnia and Her′ze·go·vi′na** (hûr′tsĕ-gō-vē′nà), which became a province of Yugoslavia 1918 and in 1945 a federated republic of Yugoslavia, ✳ Sarajevo, area 19,904 sq. m., pop. 2,565,300. — **Bos′ni·an** (bŏz′nĭ-ăn), adj. & n.

Bos′po·rus (bŏs′pō-rŭs), Turk. **Ka′ra·de·niz′ Bo′ğa·zı′** (kä′rä-dĕng-ĕz′ bō′ä-zĭ′) strait between Turkey in Europe and Turkey in Asia, connecting the Sea of Marmara with the Black Sea; 20 m. long.

Bosporus, Cim·me′ri·an (sĭ-mẽr′ĭ-ăn), anc. **Bosporus Cim·me′ri·us** (sĭ-mẽr′ĭ-ŭs) Kerch Strait.

Bos·sier′ City (bō-sẽr′) town, NW Louisiana; pop. 15,500.

Bos′ton (bŏs′tŭn) seaport, ✳ of Massachusetts, on Massachusetts Bay; pop. 801,400.

Boston Mountains, ridge, NW Arkansas, in Ozark Plateau; 1000 to 2000 ft. high.

Bos′worth Field (bŏz′wûrth; -wẽrth) battlefield, cen. England, in Leicestershire; final battle 1485 in Wars of the Roses.

Bot′a·ny Bay (bŏt′à-nĭ) inlet of South Pacific Ocean, SE Australia, in New South Wales; 6 m. at greatest width.

Both′ni·a, Gulf of (bŏth′nĭ-à) northern arm of Baltic Sea, between Sweden and Finland.

Bot′trop (bôt′rôp) city, W Germany, NNW of Essen; pop. 80,700.

Bot′wood (bŏt′wŏŏd) town, Canada, in E Newfoundland; seaplane base.

Bou′gain·ville (bōō′găn-vĭl; bō′-) island, Solomon Is., largest of the group; chief town Kieta; 3500 sq. m.; pop. 46,300.

Bouil′lon′ (bōō′yôn′) town, SE Belgium, in the Ardennes; made ✳ (1088) of small duchy belonging to the crusader Godfrey of Bouillon.

Boul′der (bōl′dẽr) city, N cen. Colorado; pop. 20,000.

Boulder Canyon, canyon of Colorado river between Arizona and Nevada; now covered by Lake Mead.

Boulder Dam. See HOOVER DAM.

Bou·logne′ (bōō·lōn′; -loin′) or **Bou·logne′-sur-Mer** (bōō·lôn′y′-sür-mär′) seaport, N France, on English Channel; pop. 34,900.

Bou′logne′-Bil′lan′court′ (bōō·lôn′y′-bē′yän′kōōr′) commune, N France, SW of Paris on Seine river; pop. 79,400.

Bourbon. See RÉUNION.

Bourges (bōōrzh) commune, cen. France; pop. 51,000.

Bourget, Le. See LE BOURGET.

Bourgogne. See BURGUNDY.

Bourne′mouth (bôrn′mŭth; bōōrn′-) county borough, S England, in Hampshire on English Channel; pop. 144,700.

Bou·vines′ (bōō′vēn′) village, NE France, SE of Lille; battle 1214.

Bow (bō) river, Canada, in SW Alberta; rises in Banff National Park, joins the Oldman to form South Saskatchewan river; 315 m. long.

Bowl′ing Green (bōl′ĭng) city, S Kentucky; pop. 18,300.

Boyne (boin) river, E Ireland, in Leinster prov., flowing into Irish Sea; battle July 1, 1690, on its banks near Drogheda.

Boz′ca·a·da′ (bōz′jä-ä-dä′), anc. **Ten′e·dos** (tĕn′ĕ-dŏs) island, Turkey, in NE Aegean Sea 12 m. S of the Dardanelles.

Boze′man (bōz′măn) city, S Montana; pop. 11,300.

Bra·bant′ (brà-bănt′) **1** old duchy of the Netherlands, covering what is now S Netherlands (province of **North Brabant**, ✳ ′s Hertogenbosch) and cen. and N Belgium. **2** province, cen. Belgium, part of the old duchy of Brabant; ✳ Brussels.

Brad′dock (brăd′ŭk) borough, SW Pennsylvania; pop. 16,500.

Brad′ford (brăd′fẽrd) **1** city, N Pennsylvania; pop. 17,400. **2** city and county borough, N England, in Yorkshire; pop. 292,400.

Bra·gan′ça (brà-gän′sà) or **Bra·gan′za** (brà-gän′zà) town, NE Portugal, near Spanish border; castle of dukes of Braganza.

Brah′ma·pu′tra (brä′mà-pōō′trà) river, S Asia, flowing from the Himalayas in Tibet, where it is called the **Tsang′po′** (tsäng′pō′) to the Ganges delta in NE Indian subcontinent, its lower course being called the **Ja′mu·na** (jŭ′mŏŏ-nä); 1680 m. long.

Bră·i′la (brȧ·ē′lä) city, E Romania, on Danube river; pop. 68,600.

Brain′tree (brān′trē; -trĕ) town, E Massachusetts; pop. 23,200.

Brak′pan (brăk′păn) town, NE Union of South Africa, in S Transvaal on the Witwatersrand; pop. 83,500.

Bramp′ton (brăm[p]′tŭn) town, Canada, in SE Ontario; pop. 12,600.

Bran′den·burg (brăn′dĕn·bûrg; Ger. brän′dĕn·bŏork) **1** region, NE cen. Germany; formerly a Prussian province; once a margraviate and electorate; its elector became king of Prussia 1701. **2** city, E Germany, on Havel river WSW of Berlin; pop. 70,600.

Bran′don (brăn′dŭn) city, Canada, in SW Manitoba on Assiniboine river; pop. 24,800.

Bran′dy·wine′ (brăn′dĭ·wīn′) creek, Pennsylvania and Delaware; battle of 1776 occurred in Pennsylvania NW of Wilmington, Delaware.

Brant′ford (brănt′fẽrd) city, Canada, in SE Ontario; pop. 51,900.

Brasil. See BRAZIL.

Bra·sí′lia or **Bra·zí′lia** (brȧ·zēl′yȧ) city, SE cen. Brazil, in E Goiás state; projected ✳ of Brazil.

Bra·sov′ (brä·shôv′), Hung. **Bras′só** (brŏsh′shō), Ger. **Kron′stadt** (krōn′shtät), now officially **Sta·lin′** (stä·lēn′) city, cen. Romania; pop. 61,800.

Bra′ti·sla′va (brät′ĭ·slä′vȧ), Ger. **Press′burg** (prĕs′bŏŏrk), Hung. **Po′zsony** (pō′zhŏn·y′) city, Czechoslovakia, chief city of Slovakia, on the Danube; pop. 172,700.

Braunschweig. See BRUNSWICK, Germany.

Bravo, Río. See RIO GRANDE.

Bra·zil′ (brȧ·zĭl′), officially **The United States of Brazil**, Port. **Es·ta′dos U·ni′dos do Bra·sil′** (ăsh·tä′thŏŏz ōō·nē′thŏŏz thŏŏ brȧ·zĭl′), Span. **Bra·sil′** (brä·sēl′) country, E and cen. South America; federal republic; ✳ Rio de Janeiro; area 3,286,169 sq. m.; pop. 52,645,500. — **Bra·zil′ian** (brȧ·zĭl′yăn), adj. & n.

Brazilia. See BRASÍLIA.

Braz′os (brăz′ŭs) river, cen. Texas, flowing SE into Gulf of Mexico; 870 m. long.

Braz′za·ville (brăz′ȧ·vĭl) port, ✳ of French Equatorial Africa and of Middle Congo territory, on Stanley Pool in the Congo river; pop. 83,600.

Breck′nock·shire (brĕk′nŏk·shĭr; -shẽr) or **Brec′on·shire** (brĕk′ŭn-), also **Brecknock** or **Brecon**, county, SE Wales; ✳ Brecknock; 733 sq. m.; pop. 56,500.

Bre·da′ (brā·dä′) commune, S Netherlands; pop. 85,300.

Breed's Hill. See BUNKER HILL.

Bre′genz (brā′gĕnts) commune, W Austria, on Lake Constance; ✳ of the Vorarlberg; pop. 20,700.

Brei′ten·feld (brī′tĕn·fĕlt) village, E Germany, in Saxony NNW of Leipzig; battles 1631 and 1642.

Bre′men (brā′mĕn; in English, also brĕm′ĕn) **1** former archbishopric and duchy, N Germany, between lower Weser and lower Elbe rivers. **2** state, NW Germany, comprising district around city of Bremen. **3** city, ✳ of Bremen state, on Weser river; pop. 444,200.

Brem′er·ha′ven (brĕm′ẽr·hä′vĕn; Ger. brä′mẽr·hä′fĕn) seaport, W Germany, at mouth of the Weser; port of Bremen; pop. 113,900.

Brem′er·ton (brĕm′ẽr·t′n; -tŏn) city, W Washington, on Puget Sound; site of Puget Sound Navy Yard; pop. 27,700.

Bren′ner Pass (brĕn′ẽr) mountain pass, Alps, between Austria and Italy; 4494 ft. high.

Brent′ford and Chis′wick (brĕnt′fẽrd, chĭz′ĭk) municipal borough, SE England, in Middlesex, on the Thames; pop. 59,400.

Bre′scia (brā′shä) commune, N Italy, in E Lombardy; pop. 151,800.

Breslau. See WROCŁAW.

Brest (brĕst) **1** seaport, NW France, in Brittany; pop. 75,000. **2** or **Brest Li·tovsk′** (brĕst′ lĭ·tôfsk′), Pol. **Brześć nad Bu′giem** (bzhĕsts′y′ näd bŏŏ′gyĕm) city, U.S.S.R., in SW White Russia on Bug river; pop. 55,400.

Bretagne. See BRITTANY.

Bret′ton Woods (brĕt′′n) resort, N New Hampshire, in White Mts.; site of United Nations conference July 1944.

Briansk. See BRYANSK.

Bridge′port (brĭj′pōrt) city, SW Connecticut; pop. 158,700.

Bridges Creek. See WAKEFIELD.

Bridge′ton (brĭj′tŭn) city, SW New Jersey; pop. 18,400.

Bridge′town (brĭj′toun) seaport, West Indies Federation, ✳ of Barbados; pop. 15,000.

Bri·enz′ (brē·ĕnts′) town, Switzerland, in SE Bern canton at NE end of **Lake of Brienz**, lake 9 m. long in course of Aare river.

Brigh′ton (brī′t′n) county borough, S England, in East Sussex on English Channel; pop. 156,400.

Brin′di·si (brĭn′dĭ·zĭ; brēn′-) seaport, SE Italy, on Strait of Otranto; pop. 60,000.

Bris′bane (brĭz′băn [locally]; -bän) city, Australia, ✳ of Queensland, on Brisbane river near its mouth; pop. with suburbs 402,200.

Bris′tol (brĭs′t′l) **1** city, N Connecticut, WSW of Hartford; pop. 36,000. **2** city, NE Tennessee, on border, contiguous to Bristol, Virginia; pop. 16,800. **3** independent city, SW Virginia, contiguous to Bristol, Tennessee; pop. 16,000. **4** city and county borough, SW England, on Avon River ab. 7 m. from Severn estuary; pop. 442,300.

Bristol Channel, arm of Atlantic Ocean, between S Wales and SW England.

Brit′ain (brĭt′′n) Anglicized form of Latin **Bri·tan′ni·a** (brĭ·tăn′ĭ·ȧ; -tăn′yȧ), applied historically to island of Great Britain.

Bri·tan′ni·a (brĭ·tăn′ĭ·ȧ; -tăn′yȧ) **1** see BRITAIN. **2** now, poetically, Great Britain and the Dominions.

British America, 1 specif. **British North America**, the British possessions N of United States, that is, Canada. **2** sometimes, all British possessions in, and adjacent to, North and South America.

British Baluchistan. See BALUCHISTAN.

British Bechuanaland. See BECHUANALAND.

British Borneo. See BORNEO.

British Columbia, abbr. **B.C.**, province, W Canada, on Pacific coast; ✳ Victoria; land area 359,279 sq. m.; pop. 1,398,500.

British Commonwealth of Nations. See in Vocab.

British East Africa, 1 Kenya; — a former name. **2** British dependencies in E Africa, including Kenya colony and protectorate, Uganda and Zanzibar protectorates, and Tanganyika Territory.

British Guiana, country, N South America, on Atlantic coast; British colony; ✳ Georgetown; area 89,480 sq. m.; pop. 361,800.

British Honduras, country, Central America, bordering on Caribbean Sea; British colony; ✳ Belize; area 8688 sq. m.; pop. 62,500.

British India, that part of India formerly under direct British administration, that is, the Indian Empire exclusive of the Indian States.

British Isles, the, island group, W Europe, comprising Great Britain, Ireland, and adjacent islands.

British Malaya, dependencies of Great Britain on Malay Penin. and in Malay Archipelago, including the Federation of Malaya, the colonies of Singapore, North Borneo, and Sarawak, and the protectorate of Brunei.

British North America. See BRITISH AMERICA.

British North Borneo. See NORTH BORNEO.

British Solomon Islands, British protectorate comprising Solomon Islands (except Bougainville, Buka, and adjacent small islands) and Santa Cruz Islands; ✳ Tulagi.

British Somaliland, officially **Somaliland Protectorate**, region, E Africa, bordering on Gulf of Aden; British protectorate; ✳ (since 1941) Hargeisa; area 67,936 sq. m.; pop. 350,000.

British West Africa, the British dependencies in W Africa, including the Federation of Nigeria, Gambia (colony and protectorate), Sierra Leone (colony and protectorate), Cameroons (trust territory), and, formerly, the Gold Coast (Gold Coast and Ashanti colonies and Northern Territories) and Togoland.

British West Indies, islands of the West Indies forming colonies of Great Britain, including Jamaica, Bahama Is., Leeward Is., Windward Is., Barbados, Trinidad, and Tobago. See WEST INDIES.

Brit′ta·ny (brĭt′n·ĭ), Fr. **Bre·tagne′** (brē·tän′y′) region of NW France, comprising peninsula W of Normandy; incorporated in France 1532; up to Revolution, a province. See BRETON, in Vocab.

Brize Nor′ton (brīz′ nôr′t′n) village, S England, in Oxfordshire; Royal Air Force base.

Br′no (bûr′nō), Ger. **Brünn** (brün) city, cen. Czechoslovakia, chief city of Moravia; pop. 273,100.

Broads, the (brôdz) low-lying district, E England, in Norfolk (**Norfolk Broads**) and Suffolk (**Suffolk Broads**).

Brock′en (brŏk′ĕn) mountain, E Germany; highest in Harz Mts.; 3747 ft.

Brock′ton (brŏk′tŭn) city, SE Massachusetts; pop. 62,900.

Brock′ville (brŏk′vĭl) town, E Canada, in Ontario on the St. Lawrence; pop. 13,900.

Bro′ken Hill (brō′kĕn) **1** city, SE Australia, in W New South Wales; center of district producing lead, zinc, and silver; pop. 27,100, **2** town, cen. Northern Rhodesia; mining (lead, zinc, vanadium).

Bromberg. See BYDGOSZCZ.

Brom′ley (brŭm′lĭ; brŏm′-) municipal borough, SE England, in Kent SE of London; pop. 64,200.

Bronx (brŏngks) or **the Bronx**, borough, New York City, on the mainland; 41 sq. m.; pop. 1,451,300.

Brook′field (-fēld) village, NE Illinois, W of Chicago; site of Chicago Zoological Park (Brookfield Zoo); pop. 15,500.

Brook′line (brŏŏk′līn) town, E Massachusetts; pop. 57,600.

Brook′lyn (brŏŏk′lĭn) borough, New York City, in SW extremity of Long Island; 71 sq. m.; pop. 2,738,200.

Brooks Range (brŏŏks) mountain range, N Alaska, extending from Kotzebue Sound to Canadian border.

Browns′ville (brounz′vĭl) city, S Texas, on the Rio Grande; pop. 36,100.

Brown′wood (broun′wŏŏd) city, cen. Texas; pop. 20,200.

Brug′ge (brŭg′ĕ) or **Bruges** (brōōzh; brōō′jĭz) commune, NW Belgium; pop. 53,000.

Bru·nei′ (brōō·nī′; brōō·nā′) **1** sultanate, NW Borneo, a British protectorate; 2226 sq. m.; pop. 38,000. **2** seaport, its ✳.

Brünn. See BRNO.

Bruns′wick (brŭnz′wĭk) city, SE Georgia, on coast; pop. 18,000.

Brunswick, Ger. **Braun′schweig** (broun′shvīk) **1** former German state, cen. Germany. **2** older German **Bruns′wick** (brŏŏns′vĭk) city, cen. Germany; ✳ of free state of Brunswick until 1935; pop. 223,300.

Brusa, Brussa. See BURSA.

Brus′sels (brŭs′′lz), Fr. **Bru′xelles′** (brü′sĕl′; locally brük′sĕl′), Flemish **Brus′sel** (brŭs′ĕl) city, ✳ of Belgium; pop. with suburbs 960,700.

Bruttium. See CALABRIA.

Bry′an (brī′ăn) city, E cen. Texas; pop. 18,100.

Bryansk, also **Briansk** (bryȧnsk; Angl. brĭ·ănsk′) city, SW Soviet Russia, Europe; pop. 87,500.

Bryce Canyon National Park (brīs) box canyon, S Utah, with fantastic eroded pinnacles; established as national park 1928.

Brześć nad Bugiem. See BREST.

Bu′cha·rest (bōō′kȧ·rĕst; bū′-), Romanian **Bu′cu·reş′ti** (bōō′kōō·rĕsht′; -rĕsh′tē) city, ✳ of Romania; pop. 648,200.

Bu′chen·wald′ (bōō′kĕn·vält′) village, E Germany, near Weimar; site of concentration camp 1937–45.

Buck′ing·ham·shire (bŭk′ĭng·ăm·shĭr; -shẽr) or **Buck′ing·ham** or **Bucks** (bŭks) county, SE cen. England; ✳ Aylesbury; 749 sq. m.; pop. 386,200.

Bu·co·vi′na or **Bu′ko·vi′na** (bōō′kô·vē′nȧ) region, E cen. Europe, in foothills of E Carpathians; a province of Romania 1918–40; N half became part of Ukrainian S.S.R. 1945.

Bucureşti. See BUCHAREST.

Bu′da·pest′ (bōō′dȧ·pĕst′; bū′-) autonomous city, ✳ of Hungary, on the Danube; pop. 1,115,900.

Budweis. See ČESKÉ BUDĚJOVICE.

Buen Aire. See BONAIRE.

Bue′na·ven·tu′ra (bwā′nä·vän·tōō′rä; Angl. bwĕn′ȧ·vĕn·tōōr′ȧ) seaport, W Colombia, on Pacific Ocean; pop. 14,500.

Bue′na Vis′ta (bwā′nä vēs′tä) battlefield, NE Mexico, near Saltillo; defeat of Santa Anna February 1847 by U.S. forces.

Bue′nos Ai′res (bwā′nŭs âr′ĕz; bō′nŭs; ī′rĕz) city, ✳ of Argentina, on Río de la Plata; pop. 3,000,400.

Buf′fa·lo (bŭf′ȧ·lō) city, W New York, at NE point of Lake Erie and on Niagara river, SE of Niagara Falls; pop. 580,100.

Bug (boog; Pol. book) river, cen. Poland, rising in W Ukraine, U.S.S.R., and flowing to the Vistula; over 450 m. long.

Bug (boog; Russ. book) river, U.S.S.R., in SW Ukraine, flowing SE to the Dnieper estuary; ab. 500 m. long.

Bu·gan'da (bŭ-gän'dȧ) native kingdom, E Africa, in SE Uganda protectorate; ✻ Kampala.

Buitenzorg. See BOGOR.

Bu'ka (boo'kȧ) island, Solomon Islands, just N of Bougainville.

Bu·kha'ra (boo-kä'rȧ; -kär'ȧ) or **Bo·kha'ra** (bō-) **1** former emirate, W Asia, occupying region around city of Bukhara. **2** city, Soviet Central Asia, in W Uzbek S.S.R. E of the Amu Darya; pop. 50,400.

Bu'kit·ting'gi (boo'kĭ-tĭng'gē), formerly, under the Dutch, **Fort de Kock** (fôrt' dě kôk') town, Indonesia, in W cen. Sumatra N of Padang; pop. 14,700.

Bukovina. See BUCOVINA.

Bu'la·wa'yo or **Bu'lu·wa'yo** (boo'lŭ-wä'yō) town, SW Southern Rhodesia, chief town of Matabeleland; pop. 39,800.

Bul·gar'i·a (bŭl-gâr'ĭ-ȧ; bool-), Bulgarian **Bl·ga'ri·ya** (bŭl-gä'rĕ-yä) country, SE Europe, bordering on Black Sea; republic; ✻ Sofia; 42,796 sq. m.; pop. 7,160,000. — **Bul·gar'i·an** (-gâr'ĭ-ȧn), adj. & n.

Bull Run (bool' rŭn') stream, NE Virginia, flowing into Potomac river; scene of Civil War battles July 21, 1861, and Aug. 29–30, 1862.

Bun'del·khand (boon'děl-kŭnd) region, N India, in hilly area containing tributaries of Jumna river; part of Madhya Pradesh.

Bun'ker Hill (bŭng'kẽr) height in Charlestown, Boston, Mass.; gave name to battle June 17, 1775, on adjacent **Breed's Hill** (brēdz), where Bunker Hill monument now stands.

Bur'bank (bûr'băngk) city, SW California; pop. 78,600.

Bur·gas' (boor-gäs') seaport, SE Bulgaria; pop. 36,200.

Bur'gen·land (boor'gĕn-länt) region, E Austria, W of Vienna on Hungarian border; constitutes a province, ✻ Eisenstadt; belonged to Hungary 1647–1921.

Bur'gos (boor'gōs) city, N Spain; once ✻ of Old Castile; pop. 72,600.

Bur'gun·dy (bûr'gŭn-dĭ), Fr. **Bour'gogne** (boor'gôn'y') region, E France; once a kingdom, duchy, and (1477 to the Revolution) province; for Free County of Burgundy, see FRANCHE-COMTÉ. — **Bur·gun'di·an** (bûr-gŭn'dĭ-ăn; bẽr-), adj. & n.

Bur'lin·game (bûr'lĭn-gām; -lĭng-gām) city, W California, on San Francisco Bay; pop. 19,900.

Bur'ling·ton (bûr'lĭng-tŭn) **1** city, SE Iowa, on Mississippi river; pop. 30,600. **2** city, N cen. North Carolina; pop. 24,600. **3** city, NW Vermont, on Lake Champlain; pop. 33,200.

Bur'ma (bûr'mȧ), officially **Union of Burma**, country, SE Asia, bordering on Bay of Bengal; formerly a province of British India and (1937–47) a British colony; since 1948 a federal republic; ✻ Rangoon; area 261,789 sq. m.; pop. 16,823,800. See BURMESE, in Vocab.

Burn'ley (bûrn'lĭ) county borough, NW England, in Lancashire N of Manchester; pop. 85,000.

Bur·sa' (boor-sä'), formerly **Bru·sa'** or **Brus·sa'** (broo-sä') city, NW Turkey in Asia; pop. 100,000.

Bur'ton·wood (bûr't'n-wood') parish, NW England, in Lancashire NW of Warrington; site of a U.S. Air Force base.

Bur'y (bĕr'ĭ) county borough, NW England, NNW of Manchester; pop. 58,800.

Bur·yat'-Mon'gol (boor-yät'mŏng'gŏl), or **Bur·iat'-Mon·go'lian** (boor-yät'mŏng-gōl'yăn; -gō'lĭ·ăn; -mŏn-), **Autonomous Soviet Socialist Republic**, autonomous republic, Soviet Russia, Asia, E of Lake Baikal; ✻ Ulan Ude; 127,020 sq. m.; pop. 569,700.

Busra, Busrah. See BASRA.

Butaritari. See MAKIN.

Bute (būt) **1** island, SW Scotland, in Firth of Clyde. **2** or **Bute'shire** (būt'shĭr; -shẽr) county, SW Scotland, comprising a number of islands in Firth of Clyde, chiefly Bute, Arran, and the Cumbraes; ✻ Rothesay, on Bute; 218 sq. m.; pop. 19,300.

But'ler (bŭt'lẽr) city, W Pennsylvania; pop. 23,500.

Bu'ton (boo'tŏn) or **Boe'toeng** (boo'toong) island, Indonesia, off SE Celebes.

Butte (būt) city, SW Montana; pop. 33,300.

Buz'zards Bay (bŭz'ẽrdz) inlet of Atlantic Ocean, SE Massachusetts.

Byd'goszcz (bĭd'gŏshch), Ger. **Brom'berg** (brōm'bẽrk) city, Poland, NE of Poznań; pop. 156,100.

Byel-, literally "white" in Russian; for names beginning Byel-, see BEL-, as BELAYA, BELGOROD; for **Byelorussia** see WHITE RUSSIA.

By·tom (bĭ'tôm), Ger. **Beu·then** (boi'těn) city, SW Poland, in Silesia; pop. 112,300.

By·zan'tine Empire (bĭ-zăn'tĭn; -tĭn; bĭ-; bĭz'ăn-) empire 5th to 15th cents. in S Europe and W Asia; originated as **Eastern Roman Empire** (395–474); lasted until destruction 1453, of its capital, Constantinople, earlier called **By·zan'ti·um** (bĭ-zăn'shĭ-ŭm; bĭ-; -shăm; -tĭ-ŭm): see ISTANBUL. See BYZANTINE, in Vocab.

C

For many names such as **Caraman**, **Cattegat**, and **Carlsruhe**, etc., see KARAMAN, KATTEGAT, and KARLSRUHE, etc., the preferable forms.

Ca'ba·na·tuan' (kä'bä-nä-twän') municipality, Philippine Is., in S cen. Luzon; pop. 46,600.

Ca·bin'da (kȧ-bĭn'dȧ) Portuguese territory, W Africa, N of Congo river; exclave belonging to Angola; area 3000 sq. m.

Ca'bo Yu'bi (kä'vō yoo'vē) or **Cabo Ju'by** (hoo'-) town, Southern Morocco; seat of administration of Spanish Sahara and Ifni.

Cá'diz (Span. kä'thēth, -thěs), Angl. **Ca·diz'** (kȧ-dĭz'; kā'dĭz; kăd'ĭz) seaport, SW Spain, on Bay of Cádiz; pop. 100,200.

Caelian. See in Vocab.

Caen (kän) city, NW France, in Normandy; pop. 51,400.

Caer·nar'von·shire (kär-när'vŭn-shĭr; -shẽr) or **Caernarvon**, county, NW Wales; ✻ Caernarvon; 569 sq. m.; pop. 124,100.

Cae'sa·re'a (sē'zȧ-rē'ȧ; sĕs'ȧ-; sēz'ȧ-) **1** ancient seaport, Palestine, 22 m. S of Haifa; site of a settlement founded 1940. **2** Caesarea Mazaca, chief city of ancient Cappadocia: see KAYSERI.

Caesarea Phi·lip'pi (fĭ-lĭp'ī; fĭl'ĭ-pī) ancient city, N Palestine, at foot of Mt. Hermon; now modern village of **Ba'ni·yas'** (bä'nĭ-yäs') in SW Syria.

Caesena. See CESENA.

Ca'ga·yan' (kä'gä-yän') **1** or **Ri'o Gran'de de Cagayan** (rē'ō grän'dä thä) river, Philippine Is., in NE Luzon, flowing N; 220 m. long. **2** municipality, Philippine Is., in E Mindanao; pop. 48,100.

Ca'glia·ri (kä'lyä-rē) seaport, Italy, ✻ of Sardinia; pop. 138,200.

Caicos Islands. See TURKS AND CAICOS ISLANDS.

Caird Coast (kârd) section of Antarctica, on SE coast of Weddell Sea; part of Coats Land and included in Falkland Islands Dependencies.

Cairn'gorm' (kârn'gôrm') mountain, NE cen. Scotland, in the Grampians in W Banff co.; 4084 ft. high.

Cai'ro (kâr'ō; kā'rō) city, SW Illinois, at confluence of Ohio and Mississippi rivers; pop. 12,100.

Cai'ro (kī'rō) city, ✻ of the United Arab Republic and of Egypt, in N Egypt on the Nile; pop. 2,100,500.

Caith'ness (kāth'něs; kăth-něs') county, N Scotland; ✻ Wick; area 686 sq. m.; pop. 22,700.

Ca·la'bri·a (kȧ-lä'brĭ-ȧ) **1** region of ancient Italy; a peninsula, forming the heel of Italian boot; now the S part of Apulia. **2** Ital. **Calabria** (kä-lä'brē-ä), pl. **Le Ca·la'bri·e** (lā kä-lä'brē-ě), anc. **Brut'ti·um** (brŭt'ĭ·ŭm) region occupying toe of Italian boot. — **Ca·la'bri·an** (kȧ-lä'brĭ-ăn), adj. & n.

Ca'lah (kā'lȧ), mod. **Nim·rud'** (nĭm-rood'), Biblical name of **Ka'lakh** (kä'läk) an ancient capital of Assyria, on Tigris river.

Ca'lais' (kă'lě'; Angl. kăl'â, kă-lā') seaport, N France, on Strait of Dover; pop. 50,000.

Cal·cut'ta (kăl-kŭt'ȧ) city and port, NE India, ✻ of West Bengal, on Hooghly river; pop. 2,108,900.

Cal'e·do'nia (kăl'ĕ-dōn'yȧ; -dō'nĭ·ȧ) Scotland; — its ancient name, still used poetically. — **Cal'e·do'nian**, adj. & n.

Cal'ga·ry (kăl'gȧ-rĭ) city, W Canada, in S Alberta; pop. 181,800.

Ca'li (kä'lē) city, W Colombia, on the Cauca river; pop. 88,400.

Cal'i·cut (kăl'ĭ-kŭt; -kŭt) or **Ko'zhi·kode** (kō'zhĭ-kōd') city, S India, in Kerala state on Malabar Coast; pop. 158,700.

Cal'i·for'nia (kăl'ĭ-fôrn'yȧ; -fôr'nĭ·ȧ), abbr. **Calif.** or **Cal.**, state, W United States, bordering on Pacific Ocean; ✻ Sacramento; area 158,693 sq. m.; pop. 10,586,200. — **Cal'i·for'nian**, adj. & n.

California, Gulf of, arm of Pacific Ocean, NW Mexico, between Lower California and the states of Sonora and Sinaloa.

California, Lower. See LOWER CALIFORNIA.

Cal·la'o (kä-yä'ō) seaport, Peru, on Callao Bay W of Lima; pop. 84,400.

Ca'lo·o'can (kä'lō-ō'kän) municipality, Philippine Is., in Luzon just N of Manila; pop. 58,200.

Ca·loo'sa·hatch'ee (kȧ-loo'sȧ-hăch'ē) river, S Florida, flowing W into Gulf of Mexico; connected by canal with Lake Hicpochee.

Calpe. See GIBRALTAR, ROCK OF.

Cal'ta·nis·set'ta (kăl'tä-nĭ-sět'ȧ) commune, Italy, in cen. Sicily; pop. 56,100.

Cal'u·met City (kăl'ū-mĕt; -mĭt) city, NE Illinois; pop. 15,800.

Calvary. See in Vocab.

Cal'y·don (kăl'ĭ-dŏn) ancient city, cen. Greece, in S Aetolia near Gulf of Patras. — **Cal'y·do'ni·an** (-dō'nĭ·ăn), adj.

Calydon, Gulf of. See PATRAS, GULF OF.

Cam (kăm) river, E cen. England, in Cambridgeshire, flowing into the Ouse; 40 m. long.

Ca'ma·güey (kä'mä-gwä') city, E cen. Cuba; pop. 78,500.

Cam·bay' (kăm-bā') former state, W India, at head of **Gulf of Cambay** (inlet of Arabian Sea); now part of Bombay state.

Cam'ber·well (kăm'bẽr-wĕl; -wěl) **1** city, Australia, E of Melbourne; pop. 50,100. **2** metropolitan borough, S London; pop. 179,700.

Cam·bo'di·a (kăm-bō'dĭ·ȧ), also formerly **Cam·bo'ja** (kăm-bō'jä), Fr. **Cam'bodge'** (kän'bôj') country, S Indochina, bordering on Gulf of Siam; a kingdom; formerly a French dependency; gained independence 1955; ✻ Pnompenh; area 69,866 sq. m.; pop. 3,046,000. — **Cam·bo'di·an** (kăm-bō'dĭ·ăn), adj. & n.

Cam'brai', older **Cam'bray'** (kän'brā'; Angl. kăm-brā') city, N France, on Schelde river; pop. 26,100.

Cam'bri·a (kăm'brĭ·ȧ) Wales; — its Latin name. See CAMBRIAN, in Vocab.

Cam'bridge (kām'brĭj) **1** city, NE Massachusetts, W of Boston; pop. 120,700. **2** see CAMBRIDGESHIRE. **3** Lat. **Can'ta·brig'i·a** (kăn'tȧ-brĭj'ĭ·ȧ) municipal borough, E England, ✻ of Cambridgeshire, on the Cam; pop. 81,500. See CANTABRIGIAN, in Vocab.

Cam'bridge·shire (-shĭr; -shẽr) or **Cambridge, 1** formerly, and still as a postal and geographical name, a county in E England comprising the modern administrative counties of Cambridge and the Isle of Ely. **2** administrative county, E England; ✻ Cambridge; 492 sq. m.; pop. 166,900.

Cam'den (kăm'děn) **1** city, SW New Jersey, on Delaware river opposite Philadelphia; pop. 124,600. **2** city, N cen. South Carolina; battle Aug. 16, 1780.

Camelot. See in Vocab.

Cam'er·oon' (kăm'ẽr-oon') or **Fa'ko** (fä'kō) mountain, W Africa, in British Cameroons near coast; 13,353 ft. high.

Cam'er·oons' (kăm'ẽr-oonz'), Port. **Ca·ma·rões'** (kȧ-mȧ-rōěnsh'), Ger. **Ka'me·run'** (kä'mě-roon'), Fr. **Ca'me·roun'** (käm'roon') region, W Africa, bordering NE Gulf of Guinea; German protectorate 1884 to World War I; in 1920 divided between British mandate (the NW portion, 34,081 sq. m., made a UN trust territory 1946) and French mandate (see CAMEROUN).

Ca'me·roun' (käm'roon') that part of the Cameroons administered by the French since 1920; became UN trust territory 1946; ✻ Yaoundé; area 166,489 sq. m.; pop. 2,516,600.

Ca'mi·guin' (kä'mě-gēn') **1** island, N Philippine Is., N of Luzon; has Camiguin volcano, 2750 ft. high. **2** island, S Philippine Is., off N coast of Mindanao; site of Hibokhibok volcano.

Cam·pa'gna di Ro'ma (käm-pä'nyä dē rō'mä), Eng. often **Roman Campagna** (rō'măn) region, Italy, around Rome; about 800 sq. m.

Cam·pa'nia (kăm-pān'yȧ, -pä'nĭ·ȧ) Ital. (käm-pän'yä) region S Italy, bordering on Tyrrhenian Sea. — **Cam·pa'nian** (kăm-pān'yăn; -pä'nĭ·ăn), adj. & n.

Cam·pe'che (kăm·pē'chē; Span. käm·pā'chā) **1** state, SE Mexico; area 19,670 sq. m.; pop. 121,400. **2** city, its ✳, on W coast of Yucatán penin.; pop. 23,300.
Campeche, Bay of, southwest section of Gulf of Mexico.
Cam'per·down (kăm'pẽr·doun), Du. **Kam'per·duin** (käm'pẽr·doin) region, W Netherlands, on coast around village of **Camp** (kämp); naval battle nearby 1797.
Cam·pi'na Gran'de (kăNm·pē'nȧ grăNn'dĕ) city, E Brazil, in E Paraíba state; pop. 73,800.
Cam·pi'nas (kăNm·pē'nȧs) city, SE Brazil; pop. 101,700.
Cam'po·bel'lo (kăm'pō·bĕl'ō) island, E Canada, in SW New Brunswick.
Cam'po·for'mi·do (kăm'pō·fôr'mĭ·dō), formerly **Cam'po·for'mi·o** (kăm'pō·fôr'mĭ·ō) village, NE Italy, SW of Udine; treaty 1797.
Cam'pos (kăNm'po͞os) city, SE Brazil; pop. 63,400.
Cam'ranh' Bay (käm'rän'y'; Angl. kăm'răn') inlet of South China Sea, Indochina, in SE Annam (Central Vietnam).
Ca'na (kā'nȧ), often **Cana of Galilee**, village, N Palestine, NE of Nazareth, where Christ performed his first miracle.
Canaan. See in Vocab.
Can'a·da (kăn'ȧ·dȧ) country, N North America, including Newfoundland and Arctic islands N of the mainland; a dominion of British Commonwealth; ✳ Ottawa; area 3,562,857 sq. m.; pop. 16,080,800. — **Ca·na'di·an** (kȧ·nā'dĭ·ăn), adj. & n.
Ca·na'di·an (kȧ·nā'dĭ·ăn) river, S United States, flowing from N New Mexico to Arkansas river in E Oklahoma; 906 m. long.
Canadian Arctic Islands. See ARCTIC ARCHIPELAGO.
Çanakkale Boğazı. See DARDANELLES.
Ca·nal' Zone (kȧ·năl') strip of territory, Panama, under perpetual lease to United States for Panama Canal; 10 m. wide, area 553 sq. m. (including 191 sq. m. of water); pop. 52,800.
Can'an·dai'gua Lake (kăn'ăn·dā'gwȧ) lake, W New York, one of the Finger Lakes; 15 m. long, 2 m. wide.
Ca·nar'y Islands (kȧ·nâr'ĭ) or **Ca·nar'ies** (kȧ·nâr'ĭz), Span. **Islas Ca·na'rias** (ēz'läs kä·nä'ryäs) island group in Atlantic Ocean off NW coast of Africa, belonging to Spain; area 2807 sq. m.; pop. 776,900.
Ca·nav'er·al, Cape (kȧ·năv'ẽr·ăl) cape, E Florida, on E coast of **Canaveral Peninsula**, strip of land enclosing the Indian River; Patrick Air Force Base; long-range missile test center.
Can'ber·ra (kăn'bẽr·ȧ) city, SE Australia, in Australian Capital Territory; ✳ of Commonwealth of Australia; pop. 15,200.
Can'di·a (kăn'dĭ·ȧ) **1** island: see CRETE. **2** or **He·rak'li·on** (hē·răk'lĭ·ŏn; hĕr'ȧ·klī'ŏn), Mod. Gr. **I·rá'kli·on** (ē·rä'klē·ôn) seaport, Greece, on N coast of Crete; pop. 53,500. — **Can'di·ot** (kăn'dĭ·ŏt), **Can'di·ote** (-ōt), adj. & n.
Ca·ne'a (kȧ·nē'ȧ; Ital. kä·nâ'ä), Mod. Gr. **Kha·niá'** (kä·nyä'), anc. **Cy·do'ni·a** (sĭ·dō'nĭ·ȧ; -dōn'yȧ) seaport, Greece, ✳ of Crete, on N coast of island; pop. 26,600.
Caney. See EL CANEY.
Can'nae (kăn'ē) battlefield, SE Italy; Hannibal's victory 216 B.C.
Cannes (kăn) seaport, SE France, SW of Nice; pop. 45,500.
Can'non Mountain (kăn'ŭn) mountain, N New Hampshire, in White Mts.; site of the Old Man of the Mountain; 4077 ft. high.
Ca·no'pus (kȧ·nō'pŭs) ancient city, N Egypt, E of Alexandria at Abukir. — **Ca·no'pic** (kȧ·nō'pĭk), adj.
Can'so, Cape (kăn'sō) easternmost point of Nova Scotia, SE Canada.
Can·ta'bri·an Mountains (kăn·tā'brĭ·ăn) range, N and NW Spain; highest peak Torre de Cerredo, 8787 ft.
Cantabrigia. See CAMBRIDGE, England.
Can'ter·bur'y (kăn'tẽr·bẽr'ĭ; esp. Brit., -bẽr·ĭ, -brĭ) **1** city, SE Australia, SW suburb of Sydney; pop. 79,100. **2** city and county borough, SE England, in Kent; pop. 27,800. — **Can'ter·bu'ri·an** (kăn'tẽr·bū'rĭ·ăn), adj.
Can'ti'gny' (käN'tē'nyē') village, N France, S of Amiens; battle 1918.
Can'ton (kăn't'n; -tŭn) city, NE Ohio; pop. 116,900.
Can·ton' (kăn·tŏn'; kăn'tŏn) **1** officially **Kwang'chow'** (kwäng'jō') city and port, SE China, ✳ of Kwangtung prov., on Pearl river; pop. 1,122,600. **2** river: see PEARL river. See CANTONESE, in Vocab.
Can'ton Island (kăn't'n; -tŭn) atoll, Phoenix Is.; controlled jointly by the United States and Great Britain; international airport.
Can'yon de Chel'ly National Monument (kăn'yŭn dĕ shā') cliff-dweller ruins, NE Arizona; established as national monument 1931.
Cap de la Ma'de·leine' (kȧp' dĕ lȧ mȧ'dlĕn') city, E Canada, in S Quebec on St. Lawrence river ENE of Three Rivers; pop. 22,900.
Cape Bret'on Island (brĭt''n; brĕt''n) island, SE Canada, off E end of Nova Scotia; area 3970 sq. m.; pop. 150,200.
Cape Canaveral. See CANAVERAL, CAPE.
Cape Cod (kŏd) **1** peninsula, SE Massachusetts; 1 to 20 m. wide, ab. 65 m. long. **2** the N tip of the peninsula.
Cape Cod Bay, south end of Massachusetts Bay, enclosed by Cape Cod.
Cape Fear (fẽr) **1** river, North Carolina, flowing SE into Atlantic Ocean; 202 m. long. **2** see FEAR, CAPE.
Cape Gi·rar'deau (jĭ·rä[r]'dō; -dŭ) city, SE Missouri, on Mississippi river; pop. 21,600.
Cape May (mā) **1** cape, S New Jersey: see MAY, CAPE. **2** city, S New Jersey, on Atlantic Ocean; one of the oldest Atlantic coast resorts.
Cape of Good Hope, 1 see GOOD HOPE, CAPE OF. **2** often called **Cape Province**, before 1910 **Cape Colony**, province, S Union of South Africa; ✳ Cape Town; area 277,169 sq. m.; pop. 4,053,800.
Ca·per'na·um (kȧ·pûr'nā·ŭm; -nĭ·ŭm) ruined city of ancient Palestine, on NW shore of Sea of Galilee.
Cape Sa'ble Island (sā'b'l) island, Canada, in Atlantic Ocean off SW tip of Nova Scotia; Cape Sable is its S point.
Cape Town or **Cape'town'** (kāp'toun') seaport, Union of South Africa, ✳ of Cape Province and seat of legislature of the Union, on Table Bay; pop. 383,800.
Cape Verde Islands (vûrd), Port. **I'lhas do Ca'bo Ver'de** (ē'lyȧzh tho͞o kȧ'vo͞o vär'dĕ) island group in Atlantic Ocean, belonging to Portugal; ✳ Praia, on São Tiago; 1557 sq. m.; pop. 181,300.
Cape York Peninsula (yôrk) peninsula, NE Australia, forming NE part of Queensland; terminates in Cape York.
Cap Hai'tien (kăp hā'shĕn), Fr. **Cap'-Ha'ï'tien'** (kȧ'pȧ'ē'syăN'; -tyăN'), locally **Le Cap** (lẽ kȧp') seaport, N Haiti; pop. 25,000.
Capital Federal. See FEDERAL DISTRICT, Argentina.
Capitan, El. See EL CAPITAN.
Capitoline. See in Vocab.
Ca'po·ret'to (kăp'ō·rĕt'ō), Ger. **Kar'freit** (kär'frīt), Yugoslav **Ko'ba·rid** (kō'bä·rēd) village, NW Yugoslavia, on the Isonzo; formerly in Italy; defeat of Italian forces 1917.
Cap'pa·do'ci·a (kăp'ȧ·dō'shĭ·ȧ; -shȧ) ancient district, E Asia Minor; Roman province A.D. 17. — **Cap'pa·do'ci·an**, adj. & n.
Ca'pri (kä'prē), anc. **Cap're·ae** (kăp'rē·ē) island, Italy, in Bay of Naples; 5 sq. m.
Cap'u·a (kăp'ū·ȧ; Ital. kä'pwä) town, S Italy, on Volturno river N of Naples, SE of site of the original ancient city of **Capua** (kăp'ū·ȧ).
Ca·ra'cas (kȧ·răk'ȧs; Span. kä·rä'käs) city, N Venezuela, ✳ of Venezuela, pop. 695,100.
Car'bon·dale (kär'bŭn·dāl) city, NE Pennsylvania; pop. 16,300.
Car'cas'sonne' (kȧr'kȧ'sôn') city, S France, 54 m. SE of Toulouse; pop. 38,100.
Car'che·mish (kär'kĕ·mĭsh; kär·kē'-) ruined city, S Turkey, on the Euphrates at Syrian border; battle 605 B.C.
Car'diff (kär'dĭf) county borough and seaport, SE Wales, ✳ of Glamorganshire; pop. 243,600.
Car'di·gan Bay (kär'dĭ·găn) inlet of St. George's Channel on W coast of Wales.
Car'di·gan·shire (-shĭr; -shẽr) or **Cardigan**, county, W Wales; ✳ Aberystwyth; 692 sq. m.; pop. 53,300.
Ca'ren'tan' (kȧ'räN'täN') town, NW France, at base of Cotentin Penin.; has small port; severe battle June 8–12, 1944.
Car'i·a (kâr'ĭ·ȧ) ancient division of SW Asia Minor, bordering on Aegean Sea; ✳ Halicarnassus. — **Car'i·an**, adj. & n.
Car'ib·be'an Sea (kăr'ĭ·bē'ăn; kȧ·rĭb'ē·ăn) arm of Atlantic Ocean, bounded by West Indies on N and E, South America on S, and Central America on W; 750,000 sq. m. See CARIBBEAN, in Vocab.
Caribbees. See WEST INDIES.
Car'i·boo Mountains (kăr'ĭ·bo͞o) range of the Rocky Mts., Canada, in E cen. British Columbia; highest point 11,750 ft.
Ca·rin'thi·a (kȧ·rĭn'thĭ·ȧ) region, cen. Europe, in E Alps; once a duchy, became Austrian crownland 1849; divided between Yugoslavia and Austria 1918. — **Ca·rin'thi·an**, adj. & n.
Car·lisle' (kär·līl'; kär'līl) **1** borough, S Pennsylvania; pop. 16,800. **2** city and county borough, NW England, ✳ of Cumberland; pop. 67,900.
Car'low (kär'lō) **1** county, SE Ireland, in Leinster prov.; 346 sq. m.; pop. 34,200. **2** urban district, its ✳; pop. 7700.
Carls'bad (kärlz'băd) city, SE New Mexico, on Pecos river; pop. 18,000.
Carlsbad Caverns, limestone caves, SE New Mexico, near Carlsbad; set aside as national park 1930.
Carmana, Carmania. See KERMAN.
Car·mar'then·shire (kär·mär'thĕn·shĭr; -shẽr; kẽr-) or **Carmarthen**, county, S Wales; ✳ Carmarthen; 919 sq. m.; pop. 171,700.
Car'mel, Mount (kär'mĕl) mountain, NW Palestine, near coast, extending 15 m. along Qishon river; 1800 ft. high. See CARMELITE, in Vocab.
Carnarvon, Carnarvonshire. Vars. of CAERNARVON, CAERNARVONSHIRE.
Car·nat'ic (kär·năt'ĭk) or **Kar·na'tik** (kẽr·nä'tĭk) region, SE India, between Eastern Ghats and Coromandel Coast.
Car'nic Alps (kär'nĭk) mountain range, E Alps, between Austria and Italy; highest peak Kellerwand, 9217 ft.
Car·nio'la (kärn·yō'lȧ; kär'nĭ·ō'lȧ), Ger **Krain** (krīn) region, S Europe, NE of Istrian Penin.; divided between Italy and Yugoslavia 1919–47; went entirely to Yugoslavia 1947. — **Car·nio'lan**, adj.
Car'o·li'na (kăr'ō·lī'nȧ) English colony 1663–1729, E coast of North America; divided 1729 into North Carolina and South Carolina (the **Car'o·li'nas** [-nȧz]). — **Car'o·lin'i·an** (-lĭn'ĭ·ăn), adj. & n.
Car'o·line Islands (kăr'ō·līn) or **Car'o·lines** (-līnz) archipelago, W Pacific Ocean, E of S Philippine Is.; part of trust territory assigned to U.S. 1947; area 550 sq. m.; pop. 48,000.
Ca'ro·ni' (kä'rō·nē') river, E Venezuela, flowing N into the Orinoco; 373 m. long.
Car·pa'thi·an Mountains (kär·pā'thĭ·ăn) mountain system, cen. Europe, along boundary between Czechoslovakia and Poland; highest peak Gerlachovka, 8737 ft.
Carpathian Ru·the'ni·a (ro͞o·thē'nĭ·ȧ; -thēn'yȧ), Czech. **Pod'kar·pat'ská Rus** (pôt'kär·pȧt'skä ro͞os') region, E cen. Europe, S of Carpathian Mts.; before World War I part of Hungary; became province of Czechoslovakia 1918; part of Hungary 1939–45; ceded 1945 to the Russians, who call it **Za'kar·pat'ska·ya** (zȧ'kŭr·pȧt'skȧ·yȧ).
Car'pen·tar'i·a, Gulf of (kär'pĕn·târ'ĭ·ȧ) gulf, NE Australia, ab. 480 m. N to S and 420 m. E to W.
Car·ra'ra (kȧ·rär'ȧ) commune, N Italy, E of La Spezia on edge of Apuan Alps; marble quarries; pop. 58,500.
Car·shal'ton (kẽr·shôl't'n; kär-; kăs·hô[l]'-; kā·shô'-) urban district, S England, in Surrey; pop. 62,800.
Car'so (kär'sō), Yugoslav **Kras** (kräs), Ger. **Karst** (kärst) limestone plateau, NW Yugoslavia, N of Trieste; before 1947 in Italy.
Car'son City (kär's'n) city, ✳ of Nevada, S of Reno; pop. 3100.
Car'stensz, Mount (kär'stĕnz), Du. **Car'stensz Top'pen** (kär'stĕns tôp'ĕn) mountain, West New Guinea; highest in New Guinea, 16,404 ft.
Car'ta·ge'na (kär'tȧ·jē'nȧ; -gā'nȧ) **1** seaport, NW Colombia, on Caribbean Sea; pop. 73,200. **2** seaport, SE Spain; pop. 120,200.
Car'thage (kär'thĭj), anc. **Car·tha'go** (kär·thā'gō; -tä'gō) ancient city, N Africa, near modern Tunis; near small modern community on the site is an American military cemetery. — **Car'tha·gin'i·an** (kär'thȧ·jĭn'ĭ·ăn; -jĭn'yăn), adj. & n.
Cas'a·blan'ca (kăs'ȧ·blăng'kȧ; kä'sȧ·bläng'kȧ), Arab. **Dar el Bei·da'** or **Dar-al-Bai·da'** (där' ăl bī·dä'; bā·dä') seaport, W Morocco; Churchill-Roosevelt conference Jan. 1943; pop. 569,500.
Cas'a Gran'de National Monument (kăs'ȧ grăn'dē) prehistoric ruins, S Arizona; discovered 1694, made a national monument 1918.
Cas·cade' Range (kăs·kād'; kăs'kād') mountain range, NW United States, extending N from Lassen Peak, NE California, across Oregon and Washington; highest peak Mt. Rainier, 14,408 ft.

Cas'co Bay (kăs'kō) inlet of Atlantic Ocean, S Maine; Portland is on it.

Cashmere. See KASHMIR.

Ca'si·quia're (kä'sē·kyä'rā) river, S Venezuela, connecting the upper course of Rio Negro with the Orinoco river; 125 m. long.

Cas'per (kăs'pẽr) city, cen. Wyoming; pop. 23,700.

Cas'pi·an Sea (kăs'pĭ·ăn) inland salt lake between Europe and Asia; about 85 ft. below sea level; 169,381 sq. m.

Cas·si'no (kȧ·sē'nō), before 1871 **San Ger·ma'no** (sän' jär·mä'nō) town, cen. Italy, ESE of Frosinone. See MONTE CASSINO.

Cas'tel·lón', in full **Castellón de la Pla'na** (käs·tĕl·[l]yōn' dä lä plä'nä) seaport, E Spain; pop. 56,700.

Castellorizo, Castelrosso. See KASTELORRIZON.

Cas·tile' (kăs·tēl'), Span. **Cas·til'la** (käs·tē'[l]yä) region and ancient kingdom, cen. and N cen. Spain; divided by the Sierra de Guadar-rama into Old Castile and, in the S, New Castile; area 53,500 sq. m.

Cas'tries' or **Port Castries** (kăs'trē'; käs'trēs) seaport, West Indies Federation, ✳ of colony of Saint Lucia, on NW Saint Lucia I.

Ca'strop-Rau'xel (käs'trôp-rouk'sĕl) city, W Germany, SSW of Mün-ster; pop. 63,800.

Ça'tal·ca' (chä'täl·jä'), Angl. **Cha'tal·ja'**, town, Turkey in Europe, W of İstanbul; Turks made final stand November 1912.

Catalina. See SANTA CATALINA.

Cat'a·lo'nia (kăt'ȧ·lō'nĭ·ȧ), Span. **Ca'ta·lu'ña** (kä'tä·lōō'nyä), Catalan **Ca·ta·lu'nya** (kȧ·tȧ·lōō'nyä) region, NE Spain, bordering on France and the Mediterranean; autonomous region 1932–34, 1936–39; area 12,431 sq. m. See CATALAN, in Vocab. — **Cat'a·lo'nian** (kăt'ȧ·lōn'yȧn; -lō'nĭ·ȧn), adj.

Ca·ta'nia (kä·tän'yä; Ital. kä·tä'nyä) commune, Italy, in E Sicily on Gulf of Catania at foot of Mt. Etna; pop. 295,000.

Ca'tan·za'ro (kä'tän·dzä'rō) city, S Italy, in Calabria; pop. 58,500.

Ca·taw'ba (kä·tô'bȧ) river, flowing from W North Carolina S into South Carolina, where it is known as the Wateree; 250 m. long.

Cathay. See in Vocab.

Catherine, Mount. See KATHERINA, GEBEL.

Cats'kill Mountains (kăts'kĭl) group of the Appalachian system, SE New York, along W bank of Hudson; highest peak Slide Mt., 4204 ft.

Cattaro. See KOTOR.

Cau'ca (kou'kä) river, W Colombia, flowing N into Magdalena river; 600 m. long.

Cau·ca'sia (kô·kā'zhä; -shä) or **Cau'ca·sus** (kô'kȧ·sŭs) region, U.S.S.R., between the Black and Caspian seas, containing the **Caucasus Mountains**, range including Mt. Elborus, 18,481 ft., highest point in Europe. See CAUCASIAN, in Vocab.

Caucasus Indicus. See HINDU KUSH.

Cau'dine Forks (kô'dĭn) mountain passes, S Italy, on road between Capua and Beneventum; defeat of Romans by the Samnites 321 B.C.

Caul'field (kōl'fēld) city, SE Australia, in S Victoria, SE suburb of Melbourne; pop. 65,300.

Cau've·ry (kô'vẽr·ĭ) or **Ka've·ri** (kä'vẽr·ĭ) river, S India, in Madras state, entering Bay of Bengal in a wide delta; 475 m. long; on border of Mysore state are the **Cauvery Falls**, descending 300 ft.

Cav'an (kăv'ȧn) county, N Republic of Ireland, in Ulster prov.; ✳ Cavan; area 730 sq. m.; pop. 66,400.

Ca·vi'te (kä·vē'tā) city, Philippine Is., in Luzon on Manila Bay SW of Manila; naval base; pop. 38,300.

Cawnpore. See KANPUR.

Caxias. See DUQUE DE CAXIAS.

Cay·enne' (kī·ĕn'; kä·ĕn'; attributively, also kī'ĕn, kä'ĕn) city, ✳ of French Guiana, on island formed by Cayenne river; pop. 11,700.

Cayes or **Aux Cayes** (ō kā'y'; ō kā') seaport, SW Haiti; pop. 11,800.

Cay'man' Islands (kā·măn'; kā'măn) island group, West Indies Federation, 200 m. NW of Jamaica, of which it is a dependency; 104 sq. m.; pop. 6700.

Cay·u'ga Lake (kā·[y]ōō'gȧ; kĭ·ōō'gȧ; kū'gȧ) lake, W cen. New York; one of the Finger Lakes; 40 m. long and 2 m. wide.

Cazes (kä'zĕz) airfield, Morocco, near Casablanca.

Ce·a·rá' (sā·ȧ·rä') **1** state, NE Brazil; ✳ Fortaleza; area 57,371 sq. m.; pop. 2,735,700. **2** city: see FORTALEZA.

Ce·bu' (sā·bōō') **1** island, Philippine Is., one of the Visayan Is.; area 1707 sq. m. **2** city on E coast of Cebu I.; pop. 146,800.

Čechy. See BOHEMIA.

Cedar Breaks National Monument (brāks) government reservation, SW Utah, N of Zion National Park, site of a vast, highly colored natural amphitheater; established as national monument 1933.

Cedar Rapids, city, E Iowa, on Cedar river; pop. 72,300.

Cel'e·bes (sĕl'ē·bēz; sĕl·lē'bēz), by Indonesians called **Su'la·we'si** (sōō'lä·wä'sĕ) island, Indonesia, E of Borneo; ✳ Makassar; 72,967 sq. m.; pop. 4,231,900. — **Cel'e·be'sian** (sĕl'ē·bē'zhȧn), adj.

Celebes Sea, that part of the Pacific Ocean enclosed on N by the Philippine Is., on S by Celebes, and on W by Borneo.

Celestial Empire. See in Vocab.

Cel'le (tsĕl'ĕ) city, W Germany, NE of Hannover; pop. 52,300.

Ce·nis', Mont (môⁿs'nē'), Ital. **Mon'te Ce·ni'sio** (môn'tä chā·nē'zyō) **1** mountain pass between France and Italy, over Mont Cenis massif, Graian Alps; altitude 6831 ft. **2** tunnel SW of the pass, piercing the Fréjus massif.

Central Africa, the British dependencies Northern Rhodesia, Southern Rhodesia, and Nyasaland, lying in the interior of S Africa.

Central America, the S portion of North America, from S boundary of Mexico to South America (NW Colombia); includes Guatemala, Honduras, El Salvador, Nicaragua, Costa Rica, Panama, and British Honduras.

Central Asia, Soviet, that part of cen. Asia belonging to the U.S.S.R.; comprises the Uzbek, Turkmen, Tadzhik, Kazakh, and Kirgiz Soviet Socialist Republics.

Central Falls, city, N Rhode Island, N of Pawtucket; pop. 23,600.

Cen·tra'lia (sĕn·trāl'yȧ; -trā'lĭ·ȧ) city, SW cen. Illinois; explosion of coal mine 1947; pop. 13,900.

Central India, former British agency, cen. India, comprising 89 states including Indore, Bhopal, and Rewa.

Central Provinces and Be·rar' (bā·rär') Madhya Pradesh state, India; — so called when it was a province of British India and until 1950.

Central Valley, valley of Sacramento and San Joaquin rivers, N California; over 400 m. long.

Ceos. See KEOS.

Ceph'a·lo'ni·a (sĕf'ȧ·lō'nĭ·ȧ; -lōn'yȧ), Mod. Gr. **Ke'fal·li·ni'a** (kyä'fä-lyē·nyē'ä), anc. **Ceph'al·le'ni·a** (sĕf'ȧ·lē'nĭ·ȧ; -lēn'yȧ) island, W Greece, one of Ionian Is.; area 277 sq. m.; pop. 57,600.

Ce'ram (sā'räm) island, E Indonesia, in Moluccas; area 6621 sq. m.; pop. 83,000.

Ce'ri·go (chā'rē·gō), Mod. Gr. **Ki'thi·ra** (kyē'thē·rä), anc. **Cy·the'ra** (sĭ·thēr'ȧ) island, W Greece, southernmost of the Ionian Is.; ✳ Kithira; 110 sq. m.; pop. 9100.

Cernăuți. See CHERNOVTSY.

Cer·re'do, Tor're de (tôr'rĕ thä thĕr·rĕ'thō [sĕr·rĕ'-]) mountain, N Spain, highest in the Cantabrian Mts., 8787 ft.

Cer'ro de Pas'co (sĕr'rō thä päs'kō) **1** mountain, cen. Peru; 15,100 ft. high. **2** town near the mountain, in mining district; pop. 19,200.

Cer'ro Gor'do (sĕr'ō gôr'dō) mountain pass, E Mexico, between Vera-cruz and Jalapa; battle April 18, 1847.

Cervin, Mont. See MATTERHORN.

Ce·se'na (chā·zā'nä), anc. **Cae·se'na** (sē·zē'nȧ) commune, N Italy, SE of Forlì; pop. 61,300.

Čes'ké Bu'dě·jo·vi·ce (chĕs'kâ bōō'dyĕ·yô'vĭ·tsĕ), Ger. **Bud'weis** (bōōt'vīs) city, W Czechoslovakia, in S Bohemia; pop. 38,200.

Český Les. See BOHEMIAN FOREST.

Cetatea Albă. See BELGOROD-DNESTROVSKI.

Ce'ti·nje (tsĕ'tē·nyĕ) town, Yugoslavia, former ✳ of Montenegro.

Cette. See SÈTE.

Ceu'ta (thä'ōō·tä; sā'ōō·tä) seaport, N Morocco, opposite Gibraltar, Spanish enclave, in former Spanish zone; pop. 58,900.

Cé'vennes' (sā'vĕn') mountain range, S France, W of the Rhone; highest peak Mt. Mézenc, 5753 ft.

Cey·lon' (sē·lŏn'), Arab. **Ser'en·dib** (sĕr'ĕn·dĭb), Lat. and Gr. **Ta·prob'a·ne** (tȧ·prŏb'ȧ·nē) island in Indian Ocean off SE India; formerly a British crown colony, became a dominion of British Commonwealth 1948; ✳ Colombo; area 25,332 sq. m.; pop. 6,657,300. — **Cey'lon·ese'** (sē'lŭn·ēz'; -ēs'), adj. & n. sing. & pl. See also SINGHA-LESE, in Vocab.

Cha'co (chä'kō), Span. **Chaco** (chä'kō) or **El Chaco** (ĕl) or **Gran Chaco** (grän) region, S cen. South America; drained by Paraguay river and its chief W tributaries the Pilcomayo and Bermejo; divided between Bolivia, Paraguay, and Argentina.

Cha'co Canyon National Monument (chä'kō) cliff-dweller ruins, NW New Mexico; established as national monument 1907.

Chad (chăd), officially **Tchad** (Fr. chäd) territory, N French Equatorial Africa; ✳ Fort-Lamy; 495,752 sq. m.; pop. 2,011,000.

Chad, Lake, lake, NW cen. Africa, at junction of boundaries of French West Africa, French Equatorial Africa, and NE Nigeria; area often only half its maximum of ab. 8000 sq. m.

Chaer'o·ne'a (kĕr'ō·nē'ȧ; kẽr'ō-) or **Chaer·o·nei'a** (-nī'ȧ) ancient city, E cen. Greece, in W Boeotia SE of Mt. Parnassus; battles 338 B.C. and 86 B.C.

Cha'gua·ra'mas (chä'gwä·rä'mäs) tract of land, NW Trinidad, West Indies Federation, on Chaguaramas Bay, inlet of Gulf of Paria, W of Port of Spain; site of naval base, leased 1940 to U.S.

Cha'har' (chä'här') former province, N China, on border of Inner Mongolia; ✳ Kalgan; partitioned 1950 and 1952 among other provinces.

Chalcedon. See KADIKÖY. — **Chal'ce·do'ni·an** (kăl'sĕ·dō'nĭ·ăn), adj.

Chal·cid'i·ce (kăl·sĭd'ĭ·sē) or **Khal'ki·di·ki'** (kăl'kyĕ·thĕ·kyē') peninsula, NE Greece, in E Macedonia; ends in three peninsulas.

Chal'cis (kăl'sĭs) or **Chal'kis** (kăl'kĭs), Mod. Gr. **Khal·kís** (kăl·kyēs') city, Greece, on W coast of Euboea I. on Euripus Strait; pop. 26,100.

Chal·de'a (kăl·dē'ȧ), also **Chal·dae'a** (-dē'ȧ) ancient region, SW Asia, on Euphrates river and Persian Gulf. — **Chal·de'an** (kăl·dē'ȧn), adj. & n. — **Chal·da'ic** (kăl·dā'ĭk), **Chal·dee'** (kăl·dē'; kăl'dē), adj. & n.

Cha·leur' Bay (shȧ·lōōr'; -lŭr') inlet of Gulf of St. Lawrence, SE Canada.

Chalk River (chôk) village, Canada, in SE Ontario near Ottawa river NW of Pembroke; site of atomic energy research establishment.

Chal'na (chŭl'nŭ) seaport, E Pakistan; opened Dec. 1950.

Châ'lons'-sur-Marne (shä'lôⁿ'sür·märn') town, NE France, on Marne river; Attila defeated by Aëtius in battle 451 A.D.

Cha'mar·tín' de la Ro'sa (chä'mär·tēn' dä lä rrō'sä) commune, cen. Spain, NNE of Madrid; pop. 64,500.

Cham'bal (chŭm'bäl) river, cen. India, flowing into the Jumna; 650 m.

Cham'bers·burg (chăm'bẽrz·bûrg) borough, S Pennsylvania; pop. 17,200.

Cha'mo·nix (shăm'ō·nē) or **Cha'mou·ni** (shăm'ōō·nē) valley, E France, NW of Mont Blanc.

Cham·pagne' (shăm·pān') region, NE France; a medieval county; came to French crown 1284; province until 1789; ✳ Troyes.

Cham·paign' (shăm·pān') city, E cen. Illinois; pop. 39,600.

Cham·plain', **Lake** (shăm·plān') lake, between Vermont and New York; extends 6 m. into Canada; 125 m. long; area 600 sq. m.

Chan'cel·lors·ville (chăn'sĕl·ẽrz·vĭl), now **Chan'cel·lor** (chăn'sĕl·ẽr) locality, Virginia, just W of Fredericksburg; battle May 2–3, 1863.

Chan'der·na·gore' (chŭn'dẽr·nȧ·gōr') or **Chan'der·na·gor'** (-gōr'), also **Chan'dar·na·gar** (chŭn'dẽr·nŭg'ẽr) town, NE India, in West Bengal N of Calcutta; before 1952 part of French India; pop. 38,300.

Chan'di·garh' (chŭn'dē·gär') town, N India, newly-constructed ✳ of Punjab state, inaugurated 1953.

Chang-chêng. See GREAT WALL.

Changchow. See LUNGKI.

Chang'chun' (chäng'chōōn') or **Hsin'king'** (shĭn'jĭng') city, S cen. Manchuria, ✳ of Kirin province; pop. 544,200.

Chang·jin (chäng·jĭn) or **Cho·shin** (chō·shĭn) reservoir, N Korea, formed by dam in Changjin river, tributary of the Yalu.

Changkiakow. See KALGAN.

Chang'sha' (chäng'shä') city and port, SE cen. China, ✳ of Hunan prov., on the Siang; pop. 311,600.

Chang'teh' (chäng'dŭ') city, SE cen. China, in N Hunan prov.; pop. 300,000.

Chan'nel Islands (chăn'ĕl; -'l) group of islands in English Channel, including Jersey, Guernsey, Alderney, and Sark; belong to Great Britain; ✳ St. Helier; area 75 sq. m.; pop. 93,200.

Chao'an' (chou'än') or **Chao'chow'** (chou'jō') city, SE China, in E Kwangtung prov. on Han river above Swatow; pop. 300,000.

Chao Phra·ya (chou prä·yä) formerly **Me Nam** or **Me·nam** (mā-näm) river, Thailand; flows S to Gulf of Siam; 160 m. long.

Cha·pul'te·pec (chä·pōōl'tĕ·pĕk) fortress, Mexico, on hill SW of Mexico City; battle 1847; Inter-American Conference 1945.

Cha'rente' (shä'ränt') river, W France, flowing W into Bay of Biscay; 225 m. long.

Cha'ri (shä'rē') or **Sha'ri** (shä'rē) river, French Equatorial Africa, flowing from Ubangi-Shari NW into Lake Chad; 1400 m. long.

Char'le·roi' or **Char'le·roy'** (shär'lĕ·rwä') town, SW Belgium, in Hainaut prov.; battle 1914; pop. 26,300.

Charles (chärlz) river, E Massachusetts, flowing into Boston Bay; its estuary separates Boston and Cambridge; 47 m. long.

Charles, Cape, cape, Virginia, N of entrance to Chesapeake Bay.

Charles'ton (chärlz'tŭn; chärl'stŭn) **1** seaport, SE South Carolina; pop. 70,200. **2** city, ✳ of West Virginia; pop. 73,500.

Charleston Peak, mountain, SE Nevada; 10,874 ft. high.

Charles'town (chärlz'toun) section of Boston, Massachusetts; before 1874 a city; U.S. Navy Yard; state prison (until 1956).

Char'lotte (shär'lŏt) city, S North Carolina; pop. 134,000.

Charlotte A·ma'lie (shär'lŏt ä·mäl'yĕ), formerly **Saint Thom'as** (sänt tŏm'ås) seaport, ✳ of the Virgin Is. of the U.S., on S coast of St. Thomas I.; pop. 11,500.

Char'lottes·ville (shär'lŏts·vĭl) independent city, cen. Virginia; pop. 26,000.

Char'lotte·town (shär'lŏt·toun) city, Canada, ✳ of Prince Edward I.; pop. 16,700.

Char'tres (shär'tr') city, N cen. France, 48 m. SW of Paris; cathedral; pop. 26,400.

Châ'teau·roux' (shä'tō·rōō') commune, cen. France, on Indre river; pop. 34,600.

Châ'teau·-Thier'ry (shä'tō·tyĕ'rē') town, N France, on Marne river; battle 1918; American military cemetery.

Chat'ham (chăt'ăm) **1** city, Canada, in SE Ontario; pop. 22,300. **2** municipal borough, SE England, in Kent; pop. 46,900.

Chatham Island. See SAN CRISTÓBAL.

Chatham Islands, two islands, Chatham and Pitt, in S Pacific Ocean; belong to New Zealand; total area 372 sq. m.; pop. 700.

Chatham Strait, passage, SE Alaska, between Admiralty I. and Kuiu I. on E and Baranof I. and Chichagof I. on W.

Châ'til·lon' (shä'tē'yôN') town, N France, just S of Paris; site of Fort de Châtillon, French atomic-energy headquarters.

Chat'ta·hoo'chee (chăt'å·hōō'chē) river, SE United States; rises in NE Georgia, joins Flint river to form Apalachicola river; 410 m. long.

Chat'ta·noo'ga (chăt'å·nōō'gå) city, SE Tennessee, on Tennessee river; pop. 131,000.

Chau·tau'qua (shå·tô'kwå) town, SW New York, on **Chautauqua Lake** (18 m. long); Chautauqua movement inaugurated 1874.

Che'foo' (jŭ'fōō') or **Yen'tai'** (yĕn'tī') city and port, NE China, on Shantung Penin.; pop. 131,700.

Che'ju' (chŭ'jōō') or **Sai·shu** (sī·shōō), formerly **Quel'part** (kwĕl'-pärt) island, S Korea, in East China Sea; pop. 276,100.

Che'kiang (jŭ'jĭ·äng') province, E China, on coast; ✳ Hangchow; 39,768 sq. m.; pop. 19,761,000.

Chelly, Canyon de. See CANYON DE CHELLY NATIONAL MONUMENT.

Chelms'ford (chĕlms'fĕrd; chĕmz'-; chĕlmz'-) municipal borough, SE England, ✳ of Essex; pop. 37,900.

Chel'sea (chĕl'sĭ) **1** city, E Massachusetts, NNE of Boston; pop. 38,900. **2** metropolitan borough, London, on N bank of Thames; pop. 50,900.

Chel'ten·ham (chĕlt'năm; chĕl't'n·ăm) municipal borough, SW cen. England, in Gloucestershire; pop. 62,800.

Che·lya'binsk (chĭ·lyä'byĭnsk) city, W Soviet Russia, Asia; pop. 273,100.

Che·lyus'kin, Cape (chĭ·lyoōs'kĭn) point of land, NW Soviet Russia, Asia; northernmost point of Asia, 77°35'N, 105°E.

Chem'nitz (kĕm'nĭts), renamed (1953) **Karl-Marx-Stadt** (kärl'-märks'shtät') city, E Germany, SE of Leipzig; pop. 250,200.

Chemulpo. See INCHON.

Che·nab' (chĕ·näb') river, N Indian subcontinent, in Kashmir and the Punjab; unites with the Sutlej to form the Panjnad; 590 m. long.

Chengchiatun. See LIAOYÜAN.

Cheng'teh' (chŭng'dŭ') or **Je·hol'** (jĕ·hōl') city, NE China, ✳ of former Jehol prov.; pop. 47,000.

Cheng'tu' (chŭng'dōō') city, S cen. China, ✳ of Szechwan prov.; pop. 441,000.

Chenstokhov. See CZĘSTOCHOWA.

Cher (shâr) river, cen. France, flowing NW into Loire river; 220 m. long.

Cher'bourg (shâr'bŏŏrg; -bōōr; Fr. shĕr'bōōr') seaport, NW France, on N coast of Cotentin Penin.; pop. 40,000.

Cheribon. See TJIREBON.

Cher·kess' Autonomous Region (chĕr·kĕs') autonomous region, SE Soviet Russia, Europe; ✳ Cherkessk; 1273 sq. m.; pop. 97,200.

Cher·ni'gov (chĭr·nyē'gŭf) city, U.S.S.R., in N Ukraine; pop. 67,400.

Cher·nov'tsy (chĕr·nôf'tsĭ), Romanian **Cer'nă·u'ţi** (chĕr'nå·ŏŏts'; -ōō'tsĕ), Ger. **Czer'no·witz** (chĕr'nō·vĭts) city, U.S.S.R., in W Ukraine on Prut river; former ✳ of Bucovina; pop. 109,700.

Cherry Valley, village, cen. New York, NE of Cooperstown; massacre Nov. 11, 1778.

Cher'so·nese, the (kûr'sō·nēz; -nēs), anc. **Cher'so·ne'sus** (-nē'sŭs) peninsula, that is, any of several peninsulas, as: (1) the Malay Peninsula, the **Golden Chersonese**; (2) the Crimea, the **Tau'ric** (tô'rĭk) **Chersonese**; (3) Jutland, the **Cim'bri·an** (sĭm'brĭ·ăn), or **Cim'bric** (sĭm'brĭk) **Chersonese**; and (4) Gallipoli Peninsula, the **Thra'cian** (thrā'shăn) **Chersonese**.

Ches·a·peake Bay (chĕs·å·pēk') inlet of Atlantic Ocean in Virginia and Maryland; 200 m. long, 4 to 40 m. wide.

Chesh'ire (chĕsh'ĕr; -ĭr) or **Ches'ter** (chĕs'tĕr) county, NW England; ✳ Chester; 973 sq. m.; pop. 1,258,050.

Ches'ter (chĕs'tĕr) **1** city, SE Pennsylvania, on Delaware river; pop. 66,000. **2** county in England: see CHESHIRE. **3** anc. **De'va** (dē'vå) or **De·va'na Cas'tra** (dē·vā'nå kăs'trå) city and county borough, NW England, ✳ of Cheshire, on the Dee; pop. 48,200.

Ches'ter·field (chĕs'tĕr·fēld) municipal borough, N cen. England, in Derbyshire; pop. 68,500.

Chev'i·ot Hills (chĕv'ĭ·ŭt; chē'vĭ-; chĭv'ĭ-) range along English-Scottish border; highest peak **Cheviot**, 2676 ft.

Chey·enne' (shī·ĕn'; -ăn') **1** river, South Dakota, flowing NE into Missouri river; 290 m. long. **2** city, ✳ of Wyoming; pop. 31,900.

Chia'i' (jǐ·ä'ē'), Jap. **Ka·gi** (kä·gē) city, S Formosa; pop. 73,000.

Chiamussu. See KIAMUSZE.

Chiang Mai (chē·äng' mī') or **Chieng'mai'** (chē·ĕng'mī') city, NW Thailand, on Ping river; pop. 50,000.

Chia'pas (chyä'päs) state, SE Mexico; ✳ Tuxtla Gutiérrez; 28,729 sq. m.; pop. 903,200.

Chi'ba (chē'bå) city, Japan, in Honshu on Tokyo Bay; pop. 122,000.

Chi·ca'go (shǐ·kä'gō; -kô'gō) **1** river, Chicago, Illinois; connected with Des Plaines river at Lockport by Sanitary and Ship Canal. **2** city, NE Illinois, on Lake Michigan; pop. 3,621,000.

Chicago Heights, city, NE Illinois, S of Chicago; pop. 24,600.

Chich'a·gof (chĭch'å·gŏf) island, SE Alaska, N of Baranof I.

Chi·chén' It·zá' (chē·chän' ēt·sä') village, Mexico, in Yucatán state W of Valladolid; once a principal center of the Mayas.

Chick'a·hom'i·ny (chĭk'å·hŏm'ĭ·nĭ) river, E Virginia; flows SE to James river; 90 m. long.

Chick'a·mau'ga (chĭk'å·mô'gå) village, NW Georgia, near **Chicka-mauga Creek** (tributary of Tennessee river); battle Sept. 1863.

Chick'a·sha (chĭk'å·shä) city, cen. Oklahoma; pop. 15,800.

Chic'o·pee (chĭk'ỉ·pē; -pē) city, SW Massachusetts, on Connecticut river N of Springfield; pop. 49,200.

Chi·cou'ti·mi (shĭ·kōō'tĭ·mĭ; Fr. shē'kōō'tē'mē') port, Canada, in Quebec on Saguenay river at mouth of Chicoutimi river; pop. 24,900.

Chiengmai. See CHIANG MAI.

Chihli, Gulf of. See Po HAI, GULF OF.

Chi·hua'hua (chē·wä'wä) **1** state, N Mexico; area 94,822 sq. m.; pop. 841,100. **2** city, its ✳; pop. 56,800.

Chilachap. Var. of TJILATJAP.

Chil'e (chĭl'ē) country, SW South America, between the Andes and Pacific Ocean; republic; ✳ Santiago; area 286,396 sq. m.; pop. 5,237,400. — **Chil'e·an** (-ăn), adj. & n.

Chil'i. English var. of CHILE.

Chil'koot Pass (chĭl'kōōt) mountain pass, from SE Alaska to Yukon Territory, Canada; highest point 3502 ft.

Chil'li·coth'e (chĭl'ĭ·kŏth'ē) city, S Ohio, on Scioto river; pop. 20,100.

Chil'lon' (shē'yôN'; Angl. shĭ·lŏn', shĭl'ŭn) castle, W Switzerland, in Vaud at E end of Lake Geneva.

Chim'bo·ra'zo (chĭm'bō·rä'zō; -rä'-; shĭm'-) peak, W cen. Ecuador; 20,702 ft. high.

Chim·kent' (chĭm·kĕnt') town, S Kazakh S.S.R.; pop. 74,200.

Chi'na (chī'nå), Chinese **Chung-Hua Min-Kuo** (chōōng'hwä' mĭn'-kwō') country, E Asia; formerly an empire, since 1912 a republic; ✳ Peking (✳ Nanking 1928–37, 1946–49; ✳ Chungking 1937–46); area (1950, including Formosa but not Tibet) 3,166,020 sq. m.; pop. 452,548,000. See CHINESE, in Vocab.

China Sea, 1 that part of Pacific Ocean reaching from Japan to S end of Malay Penin.; divided by Formosa into **East China Sea** and **South China Sea. 2** the South China Sea.

Chin'dwin' (chĭn'dwĭn') river, NW Burma, flowing to the Irrawaddy; 550 m. long.

Chinese Turkistan or **Kash·gar'i·a** (kăsh·gâr'ĭ·å) that part of Turkistan under Chinese control; the W and cen. parts of Sinkiang.

Chinese Wall. See GREAT WALL.

Chinghai. See TSINGHAI.

Chin Hills (chĭn) range, W Burma; highest point 7998 ft.

Chin'hsien' (jĭn'shyĕn') or **Chin'chow'** (jĭn'jō') town, S Manchuria, at head of Gulf of Po Hai; pop. 142,600.

Chin·ju (jĭn·jōō) or **Shin·shu** (shĭn·shōō) town, S Korea, W of Pusan; pop. 77,500.

Chin'kiang' (chĭn'kǐ·äng') city and port, E China, in Kiangsu prov., on the Yangtze at junction with the Grand Canal; pop. 199,800.

Chin·men. See QUEMOY.

Chin·nam·po (chĕn·näm·pō) seaport, N Korea, on W coast; pop. 61,500.

Chinnereth, Sea of. See GALILEE, SEA OF.

Chi'os (kī'ŏs), Mod. Gr. **Khí'os** (kē'ôs), Turk. **Sa·kis'-A·da·si'** (sä-kĭz'ä·dä·sĭ'), Ital. **Sci'o** (shē'ō) **1** island off W coast of Turkey in Asia, belonging to Greece; 355 sq. m.; pop. 82,900. **2** or **Ká'stron** (kä'strŏn) city on Chios I.; pop. 24,200. — **Chi'an** (kī'ăn), adj. & n.

Chip'pe·wa (chĭp'ē·wä; -wô) river, W cen. Wisconsin, flowing into Mississippi river; 183 m. long.

Chire. See SHIRE.

Chishima Retto. See KURIL ISLANDS.

Chişinău. See KISHINEV.

Chis'le·hurst and Sid'cup (chĭz'l·hûrst, sĭd'kŭp) urban district, SE England, in Kent SE of London; pop. 83,800.

Chiswick. See BRENTFORD AND CHISWICK.

Chi·ta' (chĭ·tä') city, SW Soviet Russia, Asia; on Trans-Siberian Railroad; pop. 102,600.

Chi·tral' (chĭ·träl') **1** river, Pakistan and Afghanistan, flowing into Kabul river; 300 m. long. **2** former state, NW Pakistan, in former North-West Frontier Province on Afghan border; ✳ Chitral; area 4500 sq. m.

Chit'ta·gong (chĭt'å·gŏng) seaport, E Pakistan, in East Bengal; pop. 294,000.

Chiu'si (kyoō'sē), anc. **Clu'si·um** (klōō'zhǐ·ŭm; -zǐ·ŭm) town, cen. Italy; one of the twelve cities of ancient Etruria.

Chka'lov (ch'kä'lŏf), before 1938 **O'ren·burg** (ō'rĕn·bŏŏrg) city, E Soviet Russia, Europe, on Ural river; pop. 172,900.

Choaspes. See KARKHEH.

Choi'seul' (shwä'zûl') island, Solomon Is.; area 1500 sq. m.

Cho'lon' (chō'lôn') seaport, S Indochina, in Cochin China SW of Saigon; pop. 481,000.

Cho·lu′la (chō·lōō′lä) town, SE cen. Mexico, W of Puebla; truncated Pyramid of Quetzalcoatl.

Chomolungma. See EVEREST, MOUNT.

Chong·jin (chông·jǐn) or **Sei·shin** (sā·shěn) port, NE Korea, on Sea of Japan; pop. 197,900.

Chong·ju (chông·jōō) or **Sei·shu** (sā·shōō) city, S Korea, in cen. part; pop. 64,600.

Chon·ju (jŭn·jōō) or **Zen·shu** (zěn·shōō) city, SW Korea, SW of Taejon; pop. 100,600.

Cho·ras′mi·a (kō·răz′mǐ·à) region, W Asia, a province of ancient Persia, on the Oxus, extending W to Caspian Sea; in 12th cent. about equivalent to empire of Khwarizm.

Cho′rzów (kō′zhōōf) city, SW Poland, in Silesia NNW of Katowice; pop. 130,900.

Chosen. See KOREA.

Choshin. See CHANGJIN.

Cho′ta Nag′pur (chō′tà näg′pŏŏr) region, E India, a plateau N of Mahanadi basin in N Orissa and S Bihar.

Christ′church (krīs[t]′chûrch) city, New Zealand, on South I.; pop. with suburbs 174,100.

Christiania. See OSLO.

Chris′tians·haab′ (krēs′tyàns·hôp′) Danish settlement, W coast of Greenland; founded 1734.

Chris′tian·sted′ (krīs′chǎn·stěd′) town, Virgin Is. of the United States, on NE coast of St. Croix I.; pop. 4100.

Christ′mas Island (krǐs′màs) **1** island, E Indian Ocean; formerly administered by the British from Singapore; to Australia Oct. 1958; 64 sq. m. **2** atoll, Line Is., Pacific Ocean, belonging to the British; largest atoll in the Pacific; area (including lagoon) 234 sq. m.

Chu (chōō) river, Soviet Central Asia, in SE Kazakh S.S.R., flowing W into the desert; 600 m. long.

Chu·but′ (chōō·vōōt′) river, S Argentina, flowing E across Patagonia into Atlantic Ocean; 500 m. long.

Chuck′chee Sea (chŏŏk′chē), Russ. **Chu·kot′sko·e Mo′re** (chŏŏ·kôt′-skŭ·yě mô′ryě) part of Arctic Ocean N of Bering Strait.

Chudskoe Ozero. See PEIPUS, LAKE.

Chu′gach Mountains (chōō′găk) range, S Alaska, extending along coast from Cook Inlet to St. Elias Range.

Chu-kiang. See PEARL river.

Chu·kot′ski (chōō·kôt′skǐ), or **Chu·kot′** (chōō·kôt′), **Peninsula**, peninsula, NE Soviet Russia, Asia; its E point is East Cape.

Chu′la Vis′ta (chōō′là vǐs′tà) city, SW California, S of San Diego; pop. 15,900.

Chu·lym′ or **Chu·lim′** (chōō·lǐm′) river, Soviet Russia, Asia, flowing N and W into Ob river; 700 m. long.

Chun·chon (chōōn·chôn) or **Shun·sen** (shōōn·sěn) city, S Korea, NE of Seoul just S of 38th parallel; pop. 54,500.

Chung′king (chōŏng′kǐng′), officially **Pa′hsien′** (bä′shyěn′) city, S China, in S Szechwan prov. on the Yangtze; 1937–46 ☀ of China; pop. 1,062,000.

Chuquisaca. See SUCRE.

Chur (kŏŏr), Fr. **Coire** (kwàr) commune, E Switzerland, ☀ of Graubünden canton; pop. 19,400.

Church·ill (chûrch′[h]ĭl) **1** river, Canada, flowing E across Saskatchewan and N Manitoba provinces into Hudson Bay; 1000 m. long. **2** seaport on Hudson Bay at mouth of Churchill river.

Chu′ru·bus′co (chōō′rŏŏ·vŏōs′kō) locality near Mexico City, Mexico; battle Aug. 20, 1847.

Chu′vash Republic (chōō′väsh) or **Chu·vash′i·a** (chōō·väsh′ǐ·à), officially **Chuvash Autonomous Soviet Socialist Republic**, autonomous republic, E cen. Soviet Russia, Europe, S of the Volga; ☀ Cheboksary; 6909 sq. m.; pop. 1,110,600.

Chu·zen·ji (chōō·zěn·jē) lake, Japan, in cen. Honshu; alt. 4375 ft.

Cic′er·o (sǐs′ěr·ō) town, NW Illinois, W suburb of Chicago; pop. 67,500.

Cieszyn. See TESCHEN.

Ci·li′ci·a (sǐ·lǐsh′ǐ·à; -lǐsh′à) ancient country, SE Asia Minor, extending along coast S of Taurus Mts.; as a modern region in Turkey, called also **Lesser Armenia.** — **Ci·li′cian** (sǐ·lǐsh′àn), adj. & n.

Ci·li′cian Gates, anc. **Ci·li′ci·ae Py′lae** (sǐ·lǐsh′ǐ·ē pī′lē), Turk. **Gü·lek′ Bo·ğaz′** (gü·lěk′ bō·äz′) mountain pass, S Turkey in Asia, through the Taurus Mts.

Cim′ar·ron (sǐm′à·rŏn; -rŏn) river, SW United States, flowing from NE New Mexico across Oklahoma to Arkansas river in NE Oklahoma; 600 m. long.

Cin′cin·nat′i (sǐn′sǐ·năt′ǐ; -năt′à) city, SW Ohio, on Ohio river; pop. 504,000.

Cinque Ports (sǐngk) old seaport towns, SE England; originally five: Dover, Sandwich, Hastings, Hythe, and Romney.

Cintra. See SINTRA.

Ci·pan′go (sǐ·pǎng′gō) Japan; — a name used poetically.

Circars. See NORTHERN CIRCARS.

Cirenaica, Cirene. See CYRENAICA, CYRENE.

Cis′cau·ca′sia (sǐs′kô·kā′zhà; -shà) region, Soviet Russia, N of the Caucasus Mts.

Ci·thae′ron (sǐ·thē′rŏn) or **El′a·te′a** (ěl′à·tē′à) mountain, Greece, on NW border of ancient Attica; sacred to Dionysus and the Muses.

Ci′tlal·te′petl (sē′tläl·tā′pět·'l) or **O′ri·za′ba** (ō′rĭ·zä′bà) volcanic peak, Mexico, in cen. Veracruz state; highest point in Mexico, 18,700 ft.

Città del Vaticano. See VATICAN CITY.

Ciu·dad′ Bo·lí′var (syōō·thäth′ vō·lē′vär) river port, SE Venezuela, on the Orinoco river; pop. 31,000.

Ciudad Juá′rez (hwä′räs) city, N Mexico, in Chihuahua state opposite El Paso, Texas; pop. 48,900.

Ciu·dad′ Tru·jil′lo (syōō·thäth′ trōō·hē′yō), before 1936 **San′to Do·min′go** (sän′tō dō·mǐng′gō) city, ☀ of the Dominican Republic, on S coast; pop. 181,500.

Ci·vi·ta·vec′chia (chē·vē·tä·věk′kyä) seaport, cen. Italy, on Tyrrhenian Sea; port for Rome; pop. 31,900.

Clack·man′nan (klǎk·măn′àn) or **Clack·man′nan·shire** (-shǐr; -shěr) county, cen. Scotland, bordering on Forth river where it widens into Firth of Forth; ☀ Clackmannan; area 55 sq. m.; pop. 37,500.

Clair′ton (klâr′t'n) city, SW Pennsylvania; pop. 19,700.

Clare (klâr) county, W Ireland, in Munster prov.; ☀ Ennis; 1231 sq. m.; pop. 81,400.

Clark Fork (klärk) river (not to be confused with Clarks Fork), rising in SW Montana and flowing NW to Pend Oreille Lake in N Idaho; 300 m. long.

Clarks′burg (klärks′bûrg) city, N West Virginia; pop. 32,000.

Clarks′dale (klärks′dāl) city, NW Mississippi; pop. 16,500.

Clarks Fork (klärks) river (not to be confused with Clark Fork), NW Wyoming and S Montana, flowing into Yellowstone river in Montana; 120 m. long.

Clarks′ville (klärks′vǐl) city, N Tennessee; pop. 16,200.

Clay′ton (klā′t'n) city, E Missouri, W of St. Louis; pop. 16,000.

Clear, Cape (klēr) headland, off SW Ireland, on S Clear I.

Clear′wa′ter (klēr′wô′tĕr; -wŏt′ĕr) city, W Florida, on Gulf of Mexico NW of St. Petersburg; pop. 15,600.

Cler′mont′-Fer′rand′ (klěr′môn′fě′räN′) city, cen. France, on edge of the Auvergne Mts. in Allier valley; pop. 108,100.

Cle′ve or **Kle′ve** (klā′vě), Eng. **Cleves** (klēvz) city, W Germany, near Rhine river; seat of old duchy; pop. 23,200.

Cleve′land (klēv′lånd) **1** city, N Ohio, on Lake Erie; pop. 914,800. **2** district, N England, in Yorkshire; yields iron.

Cleveland Heights, city, N Ohio, E of Cleveland; pop. 59,100.

Oli′chy′ (klē′shē′) or **Clichy-la-Ga′renne′** (-là·gà′rěn′) commune, N France, NW of Paris; pop. 53,000.

Cliff′side′ Park (klǐf′sǐd′) borough, NE New Jersey, on Hudson river; pop. 17,100.

Clif′ton (klǐf′t'n) city, N New Jersey, NNW of Passaic; pop. 64,500.

Cli′max (klī′măks) village, cen. Colorado, in Rocky Mts. NE of Leadville; site of molybdenum mine.

Clinch (klǐnch) river, E Tennessee; flows SW from SW Virginia and joins the Tennessee river; 200 m. long.

Cling′mans Dome (klǐng′mănz) mountain in Great Smoky Mts., on Tennessee–North Carolina boundary; highest point in Tennessee, 6642 ft.

Clin′ton (klǐn′t'n) **1** city, E Iowa, on Mississippi river; pop. 30,400. **2** town, E Tennessee, NE of Oak Ridge; pop. 3700.

Clip′per·ton (klǐp′ĕr·t'n; -tŭn) uninhabited island, E Pacific Ocean, in 10°N lat. and 109°W long.; turned over to France 1932.

Clo′vis (klō′vǐs) city, E New Mexico; pop. 17,300.

Cluj (klōŏzh), Ger. **Klau′sen·burg** (klou′zěn·bŏŏrk), Hung. **Ko′lozs·vár′** (kō′lōzh·vär′) city, NW cen. Romania, in Transylvania; pop. 100,300.

Clu′ny (klōō′nǐ; Fr. klü′nē′) town, E cen. France; remains of Benedictine abbey of Cluny.

Clusium. See CHIUSI.

Clu′tha (klōō′thà) river, New Zealand, in SE South I., flowing SE into Pacific Ocean; 210 m. long.

Clyde (klīd) river, S Scotland; 106 m. long; flows NW to the **Firth of Clyde**, an estuary 64 m. long.

Clydes′dale′ (klīdz′dāl′) the valley of the upper Clyde; 50 m. long.

Cni′dus (nī′dŭs) ancient town, SW Asia Minor, at end of long promontory of Caria.

Cnossus. See KNOSSOS.

Co′a·hui′la (kō′à·wē′lä) state, NE Mexico; ☀ Saltillo; area 58,062 sq. m.; pop. 720,100.

Coast Ranges, mountains, W North America, extending along Pacific coast from S California into Vancouver I. and W British Columbia; the **Coast Mountains** of British Columbia are not a continuation of the U.S. Coast Ranges but of the Cascade Range.

Co′balt (kō′bôlt) town, Canada, in SE Ontario; mining.

Cobh (kōv), formerly **Queens′town** (kwēnz′toun) seaport, SW Ireland, on Great I. in Cork Harbour; formerly a British naval base; pop. 5700.

Co′cha·bam′ba (kō′chä·väm′bä) city, W cen. Bolivia; pop. 60,000.

Co′chin (kō′chǐn; kōch′ǐn) former state, SW India, on coast N of Travancore; ☀ Ernakulam; united with Travancore 1949 to form Travancore and Cochin state; became 1956 part of Kerala state.

Cochin China, region, S Indochina, the S end of the peninsula; once a French colony; part of Vietnam since 1949; ☀ Saigon; area 29,974 sq. m.; pop. 4,616,000.

Co′coa (kō′kō) city, E Florida, on Indian River, on the mainland SW of Cape Canaveral.

Co′cos (kō′kŭs), or **Kee′ling** (kē′lǐng), **Islands**, group of small islands, E Indian Ocean; formerly part of Singapore colony; transferred to Australia 1955.

Co′co So′lo (kō′kō sō′lō) village, N Panama Canal Zone, just E of Colón; U.S. naval reservation and air base.

Cod, Cape. See CAPE COD.

Coele-Syria, Coelesyria. See BIKA, EL.

Coet′qui′dan′ (kwět′kē′dǎN′) military camp, NW France, in Brittany 30 m. SW of Rennes; St. Cyr military school since 1945.

Cof′fey·ville (kôf′ǐ·vǐl) city, SE Kansas; pop. 17,100.

Co·hoes′ (kō·hōz′) city, E New York, at confluence of Mohawk and Hudson rivers; pop. 21,300.

Coi (koi) or **Song Koi** (sông′ koi′), also, literally, **Red** (Fr. **Rouge** [rōōzh]) **River**, river (song), SE Asia; rises in cen. Yunnan, S China, flows SE across Tonkin, N Indochina, into Gulf of Tonkin; 500 m. long.

Coim′ba·tore′ (koim′bà·tōr′) city, S India, in S Madras state on S slope of Nilgiri Hills; pop. 130,300.

Co·im′bra (kō·ǐm′brà) city, W cen. Portugal; ☀ of Portugal 1139–c. 1260; pop. 35,400.

Coire. See CHUR.

Col′ches·ter (kōl′chěs′tĕr; -chǐs·tĕr) municipal borough, SE England, in Essex; pop. 57,400.

Col′chis (kōl′kǐs) ancient country, S Europe, on Black Sea S of Caucasus Mts., corresponding to W part of Soviet republic of Georgia.

Cold Harbor (kōld) locality, E cen. Virginia, N of the Chickahominy river ENE of Richmond; site of battles 1862 (Gaines′ Mill) and 1864.

Co·li′ma (kō·lē′mä) **1** volcano, W cen. Mexico, in Jalisco state; 12,792 ft. high. **2** state, SW Mexico; area 2009 sq. m.; pop. 112,300. **3** city, its ☀; pop. 22,600.

Col′lings·wood (kōl′ĭngz·wŏŏd) borough, SW New Jersey, SE of Camden; pop. 15,800.

Col′mar (kōl′mär), Ger. **Kol′mar** (kōl′mär) commune, NE France, at E edge of Vosges Mts.; pop. 46,100.

Co·logne′ (kō·lōn′), Ger. **Köln**, less often **Cöln** (kŭln) city, W Germany, on Rhine river; pop. 590,800.

Co′lombes′ (kō′lōnb′) commune, N France, NW of Paris; pop. 61,000.

Co·lom′bi·a (kō·lŭm′bĭ·á) country, NW South America, bordering on Caribbean Sea and Pacific Ocean; republic; ✳ Bogotá; area 439,825 sq. m.; pop. 9,905,400. — **Co·lom′bi·an**, adj. & n.

Co·lom′bo (kō·lŭm′bō) seaport, ✳ of Ceylon, on W coast; pop. 362,100.

Co·lón′ (kō·lōn′), formerly **As′pin·wall** (ăs′pĭn·wôl) city, Panama, on Limon Bay at N entrance to Panama Canal; pop. 62,400.

Colón Archipelago. See GALÁPAGOS ISLANDS.

Col′o·phon (kŏl′ō·fŏn) ancient city, Asia Minor, one of the 12 Ionian Cities.

Col′o·ra′do (kŏl′ō·rä′dō; -răd′ō) **1** river, SW United States; rises in N Colorado, flows to Gulf of California (for 90 m. in Mexico); 1450 m. long. **2** river, cen. Texas, flowing SE into Matagorda Bay (Gulf of Mexico); 840 m. long. **3** abbr. **Colo.**, state, W United States; ✳ Denver; area 104,247 sq. m.; pop. 1,325,100. — **Col′o·ra′dan** (-rä′d′n; -răd′′n), adj. & n.

Colorado Desert, arid region, SE California, W of the Colorado river.

Colorado Springs, city, Colorado, at foot of Pikes Peak; pop. 45,500; N of city is U.S. Air Force Academy, transferred 1958 from Lowry Air Force Base, Denver, Colorado.

Co·los′sae (kō·lŏs′ē) ancient city, cen. Asia Minor, in SW Phrygia; seat of an early Christian church. See COLOSSIANS, in Vocab.

Co·lum′bi·a (kō·lŭm′bĭ·á) **1** river, SW Canada and NW United States; rises in SE British Columbia, flows into Pacific; 1270 m. long. **2** city, cen. Missouri; pop. 32,000. **3** city, ✳ of South Carolina, on Congaree river; pop. 86,900. — **Co·lum′bi·an**, adj. & n.

Columbia, Cape, cape, N Canada, on N coast of Ellesmere I. at 83°07′ N lat.

Columbia, District of. See DISTRICT OF COLUMBIA.

Co·lum′bus (kō·lŭm′bŭs) **1** city, W Georgia, on Chattahoochee river; pop. 79,600. **2** city, cen. Indiana; pop. 18,400. **3** city, E Mississippi; pop. 17,200. **4** city, ✳ of Ohio, on the Scioto river; pop. 375,900.

Col′ville (kŏl′vĭl) river, N Alaska, flowing to Beaufort Sea; 320 m. long.

Commander Islands. See KOMANDORSKIE ISLANDS.

Co′mo (kō′mō) commune, N Italy, in Lombardy at SW end of **Lake Como** (35 m. long, 3 m. wide); pop. 76,100.

Co′mo·do′ro Ri′va·da′via (kō′mō·thō′rō rē′vä·thä′vyä) seaport, S Argentina, in petroleum region; a military district, pop. 51,500.

Com′o·rin, Cape (kŏm′ō·rĭn) cape, S tip of India, in Kerala.

Com′o·ro Islands (kŏm′ō·rō), Fr. **Îles Co′mores′** (ēl kō′mōr′) group of islands off SE Africa, between Mozambique and Madagascar; belong to France; area 790 sq. m.; pop. 128,600.

Com′piègne (kôN′pyĕN′y′) town, N France, on Oise river; armistice 1918.

Compostela, Santiago de. See SANTIAGO.

Comp′ton (kŏmp′tŭn) city, SW California; pop. 48,000.

Con′a·kry or **Kon′a·kri** (kŏn′á·krī) seaport, ✳ of French Guinea, French West Africa; pop. 8900.

Con·cep·ción′ (kôn′sĕp·syôn′; Angl. kŏn·sĕp′shŭn) city, S cen. Chile; pop. 85,800.

Con′cord, 1 (kŏng′kẽrd) town, NE Massachusetts, S of Lowell; scene of battle April 19, 1775. **2** (kŏng′kẽrd) city, ✳ of New Hampshire, on Merrimack river; pop. 28,000. **3** (kŏn′kôrd; kŏng′-) city, S cen. North Carolina; pop. 16,500.

Co′ney Island (kō′nĭ) pleasure resort, New York City, in Brooklyn borough; formerly an island, now part of Long Island.

Con′ga·ree (kŏng′gá·rē) river, cen. South Carolina; unites with Wateree river to form Santee river; 60 m. long.

Con′go (kŏng′gō) **1** river, Africa, crossing equator twice as it makes wide curve in its course to Atlantic Ocean; 2500–3000 m. long. **2** region on both sides of Congo river.

Congo Free State. See BELGIAN CONGO.

Conjeeveram. See KANCHIPURAM.

Con′nacht (kŏn′ŭkt; -ät), formerly **Con′naught** (kŏn′ôt; kŭ·nôt′) province, NW Ireland; 6611 sq. m.; pop. 472,000.

Con·nect′i·cut (kŏ·nĕt′ĭ·kŭt) **1** river, NE United States; rises in N New Hampshire, flows S into Long Island Sound; 407 m. long. **2** abbr. **Conn.**, state, NE United States, bordering on Long Island Sound; ✳ Hartford; area 5009 sq. m.; pop. 2,007,300.

Con′ners·ville (kŏn′ẽrz·vĭl) city, E Indiana; pop. 15,600.

Con′stance, Lake (kŏn′stăns), Ger. **Bo′den See** (bō′dĕn zā′) lake, W Europe, between Germany, Austria, and Switzerland; 207 sq. m.

Con·stan′ţa or **Con·stan′tsa** (kôn·stän′tsä), Turk. **Küs′ten·ja′** (küs′tĕn·jä′) seaport, SE Romania, on Black Sea; pop. 61,400.

Con′stan·tine (kŏn′stăn·tēn) city, NE Algeria; pop. 106,800.

Constantinople. See İSTANBUL.

Con·tre′ras (kôn·trä′räs) town, cen. Mexico, 14 m. SSW of Mexico City; battle 1847.

Coo. See Kos.

Cooch Be·har′ (kōōch′ bē·här′) former state, NE India, N of East Bengal; since 1947 attached to Indian Republic's state of West Bengal.

Cook, Mount (kōōk). See AORANGI.

Cook Inlet, arm of Pacific Ocean, S Alaska; 220 m. long.

Cook Islands, group of islands, S Pacific, SW of Society Is.; a dependency of New Zealand; ✳ Avarua, on Rarotonga; 84 sq. m.; pop. 10,200.

Cook Strait, channel between North I. and South I., New Zealand.

Coomassie. See KUMASI.

Coo′pers·town (kōō′pẽrz·toun; kōōp′ẽrz-) village, cen. New York, SE of Utica at S end of Otsego Lake; National Baseball Museum.

Coorg or **Kurg** (kōōrg) former state, S India, merged 1956 with Mysore state; ✳ Mercara; a province of British India until 1947.

Coo′sa (kōō′sá) river, Alabama, flowing from NW Georgia into Alabama to join Tallapoosa river and form Alabama river; 286 m. long.

Co·pán′ (kō·pän′) ruined city of the Mayas, in W Honduras.

Co′pen·ha′gen (kō′pĕn·hā′gĕn), Danish **Kö′ben·havn′** (kö′p′n·houn′) city, ✳ of Denmark, on E coast of Sjælland I. and N Amager I.; pop. 731,700, with suburbs 1,078,900.

Co′pia·pó′ (kō′pyä·pō′) volcano, N cen. Chile; 19,947 ft. high.

Cop′per·mine′ (kŏp′ẽr·mīn′) river, N Canada, flowing NW and N to Arctic Ocean; 525 m. long.

Cor′al Ga′bles (kŏr′ăl gā′b′lz) city, SE Florida, on Biscayne Bay; pop. 19,800.

Coral Sea, part of the Pacific Ocean between Queensland, Australia, on the W and the New Hebrides and New Caledonia on the E; scene of naval battle May 1942.

Corantijn. See COURANTYNE.

Co′ra·op′o·lis (kō′rĭ·ŏp′ō·lĭs) borough, SW Pennsylvania; Greater Pittsburgh Airport; pop. 10,500.

Cor′co·va′do (kôr′kō·vä′dō) **1** peak, SE Brazil, on S side of city of Rio de Janeiro; 2310 ft. high. **2** peak, S Chile; 7550 ft. high.

Cór′do·ba (kôr′thō·vä) **1** city, N cen. Argentina; pop. 287,600. **2** Eng. **Cordo·va** (kôr′dō·vá) city, S Spain, on Guadalquivir river; pop. 164,400. — **Cor′do·van** (kôr′dō·văn), adj. & n.

Cor·en·tyne (kôr′ĕn·tīn). Var. of COURANTYNE.

Cor·fu′ (kôr·fōō′; kôr′fū), Mod. Gr. **Kér′ky·ra** (kyär′kyĕ·rä), anc. ✳; pop. 103,200. **2** seaport, its ✳; pop. 30,700.

Cor′inth (kŏr′ĭnth) **1** city, NE Mississippi; battle 1862; pop. 9800. **2** Mod. Gr. **Kó′rin·thos** (kô′rĕn·thōs) city, Greece, in NE Peloponnesus on Gulf of Corinth at S end of Isthmus of Corinth, 3 m. NE of site of ancient city of Corinth. See CORINTHIAN in Vocab.

Corinth, or **Le·pan′to** (lē·păn′tō; Ital. lä′pän·tō), **Gulf of**, the inner part of the gulf W of the **Isthmus of Corinth**, the neck of land connecting the Peloponnesus with the rest of Greece.

Cork (kôrk) **1** county, SW Ireland, in Munster prov.; 2881 sq. m.; pop. 341,200. **2** city and county borough, its ✳, at head of Cork Harbour; pop. 74,600.

Cor′ner Brook′ (kôr′nẽr) town, E Canada, in W Newfoundland; pop. 23,200.

Cor′ning (kôr′nĭng) city, S New York, W of Elmira; pop. 17,700.

Cor′no, Mon′te (mōn′tä kôr′nō) mountain, cen. Italy, in the Abruzzi Apennines; highest peak in the Apennines, 9585 ft.

Corn′wall (kôrn′wôl; -wôl) **1** city, Canada, in SE Ontario on St. Lawrence river; pop. 18,200. **2** county, extreme SW England; ✳ Truro; 1357 sq. m.; pop. 345,600.

Cor′o·man′del Coast (kôr′ō·măn′d′l) coast of SE India, S of mouths of Kistna river.

Co′ro·nel′ (kō′rō·nĕl′) seaport, S cen. Chile, S of Concepción; naval battle 1914.

Cor′pus Chris′ti (kôr′pŭs krĭs′tĭ) city, S Texas, on Corpus Christi Bay; pop. 108,300.

Cor·reg′i·dor (kŏ·rĕg′ĭ·dôr) island, Philippine Is., in entrance to Manila Bay; rocky, with extensive tunnels; area about 2 sq. m.

Cor·rien′tes (kôr·ryän′tās) city, NE Argentina, on Paraná river; pop. 59,300.

Cor′si·ca (kôr′sĭ·ká), Fr. **Corse** (kôrs) island, France, in Mediterranean Sea N of Sardinia; ✳ Ajaccio; area 3367 sq. m.; pop. 322,900. — **Cor′si·can** (kôr′sĭ·kăn), adj. & n.

Cor′si·can′a (kôr′sĭ·kăn′á) city, NE cen. Texas; pop. 19,200.

Cort′land (kôrt′lănd) city, cen. New York; pop. 18,200.

Coruña, La; Corunna. See LA CORUÑA.

Cor·val′lis (kôr·văl′ĭs) city, W Oregon, on Willamette river; pop. 16,200.

Cos. See Kos.

Co′se·giü′na (kō′sĕ·gwē′nä) volcano, Nicaragua, on Gulf of Fonseca; 3830 ft. high; eruptions 1835, 1951.

Co·sen′za (kō·zĕn′tsä) commune, S Italy, in Calabria; pop. 60,600.

Cos′ta Ri′ca (kŏs′tá rē′ká) country, Central America, between Nicaragua and Panama; republic; ✳ San José; area 19,238 sq. m.; pop. 800,900. — **Cos′ta Ri′can**, adj. & n.

Côte d′A′zur′ (kōt′ dà′zūr′) the Mediterranean coast of France, esp. its E end; the French Riviera.

Côte d′Ivoire. See IVORY COAST.

Côte d′Or (kōt′ dôr′) range of hills, E France, in Burgundy SW of Dijon; noted for rich vineyards.

Co′ten′tin′ Peninsula (kō′täN′tăN′) peninsula, NW France, SW of mouth of the Seine.

Co′to·pax′i (kō′tō·păk′sĭ; Span. -pä′hĕ) volcano, N cen. Ecuador; 19,498 ft. high.

Cots′wold Hills (kŏts′wōld; -wŭld) or **Cots′wolds** (-wōldz; -wŭldz) range of hills, SW cen. England, in Gloucestershire.

Cot′ti·an Alps (kŏt′ĭ·ăn) range of W Alps, France and Italy; highest peak Mount Viso, 12,605 ft.

Couls′don and Pur′ley (kōlz′dŭn, pûr′lĭ) urban district, S England, in Surrey S of London; pop. 63,800.

Council Bluffs, city, SW Iowa, on Missouri river; pop. 45,400.

Cour′an·tyne′ (kûr′ăn·tēn′), Du. **Co′ran·tijn′** (kō′rän·tīn′) river, N South America; flows N to Atlantic Ocean, forming boundary between British Guiana and Surinam; 300 m. long.

Cour′be·voie′ (kōōr′bĕ·vwá′) commune, N France, on the Seine NW of Paris; pop. 55,100.

Courland. See KURLAND.

Courtrai. See KORTRIJK.

Cov′en·try (kŏv′ĕn·trĭ) city and county borough, cen. England, in Warwickshire; pop. 258,200.

Cov′ing·ton (kŭv′ĭng·tŭn) city, N Kentucky, on Ohio river opposite Cincinnati; pop. 64,500.

Cow′pens′ (kou′pĕnz′) town, NW South Carolina, ENE of Spartanburg; battle 1781.

Crab Island. See VIEQUES.

Cracow. See KRAKÓW.

Cra·io′va (krä·yô′vä) city, S Romania; pop. 55,400.

Cran′ston (krăn′stŭn) city, N Rhode Island; pop. 55,100.

Cra′ter Lake (krā′tẽr) lake, S Oregon, in Cascade Mts., in crater of extinct volcano; 2000 ft. deep; **Crater Lake National Park** established 1902.

Cré′cy′ (krā′sē′), in full **Cré′cy′-en-Pon′thieu′** (-äN·pôN′tyŭ′), Eng. **Cres′sy** (krĕs′ĭ) town, N France, N of Abbeville; battle 1346.

Cre·mo′na (krĕ·mō′ná) commune, N Italy, on Po river; pop. 71,700.

Crete (krēt), Mod. Gr. **Kri′ti** (krē′tē), anc. **Cre′ta** (krē′tá), also often **Can′di·a** (kăn′dĭ·á) island in E Mediterranean Sea, belonging to Greece; ✳ Canea; 3199 sq. m.; pop. 441,700. — **Cre′tan** (krē′t′n), adj. & n.

Crewe (krōō) municipal borough, NW England, in Cheshire; pop. 52,400.

Cri·me′a (krī·mē′à; krĭ-), Russ. **Krim** (krĭm) peninsula, S Soviet Russia, Europe, extending into the Black Sea; from 1921 to 1945 constituted an autonomous soviet socialist republic, ✻ Simferopol; 10,036 sq. m.; pop. 1,184,100. — **Cri·me′an** (krī·mē′ăn; krĭ-), adj.

Crip′ple Creek (krĭp′'l krēk′) city, cen. Colorado, SW of Colorado Springs; in gold-producing district.

Cris·to′bal (krĭs·tō′bäl), Span. **Cris·tó′bal** (krĕs·tō′väl) town, NW Panama Canal Zone; adjoins Colón, Panama.

Crna Gora. See MONTENEGRO.

Croa′tan′ Sound (krō′tăn′) strait, E North Carolina, between Roanoke I. and mainland.

Cro·a′ti·a (krō·ā′shǐ·à; -shà) **1** region, SE Europe, bordering on NE Adriatic Sea; in medieval times a kingdom, later a crownland (of Austria 1849–1867, of Hungary 1867–1918); part of Yugoslavia since 1918. **2** constituent republic, Yugoslavia, including Croatia, Slavonia, most of Istria and the Dalmatian coast; ✻ Zagreb; area 21,726 sq. m.; pop. 3,756,800. — **Cro·a′tian** (krō·ā′shăn), adj. & n.

Croc′o·dile (krŏk′ô·dīl). See LIMPOPO river.

Crooked Lake. See KEUKA LAKE.

Cros′by (krŏz′bĭ) or **Great Crosby**, municipal borough, NW England, in Lancashire at mouth of the Mersey; pop. 58,400.

Cross (krŏs) river, W Africa, in British Cameroons and SE Nigeria, flowing to Gulf of Guinea; 300 m. long.

Crown Point (kroun) village, NE New York, on W shore of S Lake Champlain S of Ticonderoga.

Croy′don (kroi′d'n) county borough, S England, S of London; pop. 249,600.

Ctes′i·phon (tĕs′ĭ·fŏn; tē′sĭ-) ancient city, cen. Iraq, on the Tigris SSE of Baghdad; ✻ of ancient kingdom of Parthia.

Cuan′za (kwän′zä) river, SW Africa, in cen. Angola, flowing NW into Atlantic Ocean; 500 m. long.

Cu′ba (kū′bà) island, West Indies; republic; ✻ Havana; area (with adjacent islands) 44,164 sq. m.; pop. 4,227,600. — **Cu′ban**, n. & adj.

Cubango. See OKOVANGGO.

Cuen′ca (kwäng′kä) city, S Ecuador; pop. 52,500.

Cu′fra, Oases of (Ital. kōō′frä), Arab. **Ku′fa·ra** (kōō′fà·rà) group of five oases, SE Libya, in Libyan Desert.

Culebra Cut. See GAILLARD CUT.

Cul·lod′en Moor (kŭ·lŏd′'n; -lō′d'n) moor in NW Scotland; battle April 16, 1746.

Cul′ver City (kŭl′vẽr) city, SW California, SW of Los Angeles; pop. 19,700.

Cu′mae (kū′mē) ancient town, S Italy, on coast W of Neapolis (Naples); oldest Greek colony in Italy or Sicily. — **Cu·mae′an** (kū·mē′ăn), adj.

Cu′ma·ná′ (kōō′mä·nä′) seaport, N Venezuela; settled 1520; pop. 46,400.

Cum′ber·land (kŭm′bẽr·lănd) **1** river, S Kentucky and N Tennessee, flowing into Ohio river in Kentucky; 687 m. long; **Cumberland Falls** (63 ft. high, over 100 ft. wide) are in Kentucky. **2** city, NW Maryland, on Potomac river; pop. 37,700. **3** county, NW England; ✻ Carlisle; area 1511 sq. m.; pop. 285,300.

Cumberland Gap, pass, NE Tennessee, through Cumberland Plateau; alt. 1315 ft.

Cumberland Plateau or **Mountains**, tableland, the SW portion of the Appalachian Mts., extending from S West Virginia to NE Alabama; average height 2000 ft.

Cum′bri·an Mountains (kŭm′brĭ·ăn) range of hills, NW England, in Cumberland, Westmorland, and Lancashire; highest peak Scafell Pike (highest in England), 3210 ft.

Cu·nax′a (kū·năk′sà) town, ancient Babylonia; battle 401 B.C.

Cu·ne′ne (kōō·nā′nĕ) river, SW Angola, flowing to Atlantic Ocean; 700 m. long.

Cuquenán. See KUKENAAM.

Cu′ra·ça′o (kōō′rä·sä′ô; Angl. kū′rà·sō′) island, Netherlands Antilles; chief town Willemstad (✻ of Netherlands Antilles); area 210 sq. m.; pop. 70,000.

Cu·ri·ti′ba (kōō′rē·tē′và) city, S Brazil, ✻ of Paraná state; pop. 141,300.

Cur′ragh (kûr′à) plain, E Ireland, in co. Kildare on the Liffey; racecourse.

Cusco. See CUZCO.

Cush or **Kush** (kŭsh) ancient country in Nile valley adjoining Egypt, S of about lat. 24°N.

Cüstrin. See KOSTRZYN.

Cutch. See KUTCH.

Cut′tack (kŭt′ăk) city, E India, in Orissa on Mahanadi river; former ✻ of Orissa; pop. 74,300.

Cux·ha′ven (kōōks·hä′fĕn) seaport, W Germany, on North Sea at mouth of Elbe river; pop. 42,500.

Cuy·a·hog′a Falls (kà·hŏg′à; kī-; -hô′gà; -hō′gà) city, NE Ohio, N of Akron; pop. 29,200.

Cu·yu′ni (kōō·yōō′nē) river, N South America; rises in E Venezuela, flows to the Essequibo river in British Guiana; 300 m. long.

Cuz′co (kōōs′kō), sometimes written **Cus′co** (kōōs′-) city, S Peru; once ✻ of Inca empire; pop. 45,200.

Cyc′la·des (sĭk′là·dēz), Mod. Gr. **Ki·klá′dhes** (kyĕ·klä′thâs) group of islands, Greece, in S Aegean Sea; ✻ Ermoúpolis; 996 sq. m.; pop. 147,000.

Cyd′nus (sĭd′nŭs) river, S Turkey (in ancient Cilicia), flowing past Tarsus to the Mediterranean.

Cydonia. See CANEA.

Cyn′os·ceph′a·lae (sĭn′ô·sĕf′à·lē; sī′nŭ-) two hills, NE Greece, in SE Thessaly; battles 364 B.C. and 197 B.C.

Cy′prus (sī′prŭs) island, E Mediterranean Sea; a British colony; ✻ Nicosia; 3572 sq. m.; pop. 389,500. — **Cyp′ri·ot** (sĭp′rĭ·ăn), adj. & n. — **Cyp′ri·ote** (sĭp′rĭ·ōt), **Cyp′ri·ot** (-ŏt), adj. & n.

Cyr′e·na′i·ca (sĭr′ē·nā′ĭ·kà; sī′rē-), Ital. **Ci·re·na′i·ca** (chē·rā·nä′ē·kä) **1** or **Cy·re′ne** (sī·rē′nē) region, NE Libya, N Africa, the coastal area dominated by ancient city of Cyrene. **2** region, E Libya, including

coastal area and extensive hinterland; became one of divisions of independent Libya 1951. — **Cyr′e·na′ic** (sĭr′ē·nā′ĭk; sī′rē-), adj. & n. — **Cy·re′ni·an** (sī·rē′nĭ·ăn), adj. & n.

Cy·re′ne (sī·rē′nē), Ital. **Ci·re′ne** (chē·rā′nä) **1** ancient region, N Africa: see CYRENAICA. **2** ancient city, N Africa, on coast S of Greece; chief city of ancient Cyrenaica. **3** modern town on site of the ancient city.

Cythera. See CERIGO.

Cyz′i·cus (sĭz′ĭ·kŭs) **1** modern **Ka′pı·da·ğı′** (kä′pĭ·dä·ĭ′) peninsula, NW Turkey in Asia, on Sea of Marmara. **2** ancient city, on isthmus leading to Cyzicus Penin.; naval battle 410 B.C.

Czech′o·slo·va′ki·a, also **Czech′o·Slo·va′ki·a** (chĕk′ô·slô·vä′kĭ·à; -väk′ĭ·à), Czech **Čes′ko·slo′ven·sko** (chĕs·kô·slô′vĕn·skô) country, cen. Europe; republic, created 1918 from territories formerly part of Austro-Hungarian Empire; ✻ Prague; area 49,373 sq. m.; pop. 12,-513,000. — **Czech′o·slo′vak** (chĕk′ô·slô′väk; -slô·väk′), adj. & n. — **Czech′o·slo·va′ki·an** (-slô·vä′kĭ·ăn; -väk′ĭ·ăn), adj. & n.

Czernowitz. See CHERNOVTSY.

Cze′sto·cho′wa (chĕn′stô·kô′vä), Russian **Chen·sto·khov′** (chĭn·stŭ·kôf′) city, S Poland; pop. 115,100.

D

Dac′ca (dăk′à) city, Pakistan, ✻ of East Pakistan prov.; pop. 411,000.

Da′chau (däk′ou) town, W Germany, in Bavaria NNW of Munich; in World War II site of concentration camp.

Da′ci·a (dā′shĭ·à; -shà) ancient country, cen. Europe, roughly equivalent to modern Romania including Bessarabia. — **Da′cian** (dā′shăn), adj. & n.

Dag′en·ham (dăg′năm) municipal borough, SE England, in Essex NE of London; pop. 114,600.

Dag′es·tan′ or **Dagh′es·tan′** (dăg′ĕs·tăn′), officially **Dagestan Autonomous Soviet Socialist Republic**, autonomous republic, SE Soviet Russia, Europe, on W shore of Caspian Sea; ✻ Makhachkala; 13,124 sq. m.; pop. 977,800.

Dagö. See KHIUMA.

Da·ho′mey (dà·hō′mĭ) territory, French West Africa, bordering on Gulf of Guinea; ✻ Porto-Novo; 44,749 sq. m.; pop. 1,474,000.

Daido. See TAEDONG.

Dai Nippon. See JAPAN.

Dai′ren′ (dī′rĕn′), Russ. **Dal′ny** (dàl′y·nyĭ), Chin. **Ta′lien′** (dä′-lĕ·ĕn′) seaport, Manchuria, on Liaotung Penin. See PORT ARTHUR.

Da·kar′ (dä·kär′; dà-) seaport, ✻ of French West Africa, on Cape Vert Penin. in Senegal territory; pop. 92,600.

Da·ko′ta (dà·kō′tà), usually called **James** (jāmz) river, North Dakota and South Dakota, flowing S into Missouri river; 710 m. long.

Dakota Territory, territory 1861–89, W United States, comprising the region on both sides of middle course of Missouri river and W of Red River of the North; admitted to the Union Nov. 2, 1889, by division into two states, the **Da·ko′tas** (-tàz): North and South Dakota.

Dal·hou′sie (dăl·hou′zĭ) seaport, Canada, in N New Brunswick on Chaleur Bay; pop. 4900.

Dal′las (dăl′ăs) city, NE Texas, on Trinity river; pop. 434,500.

Dal·ma′ti·a (dăl·mā′shĭ·à; -shà) region, W Yugoslavia, along Adriatic coast; once an Austrian crownland. — **Dal·ma′tian** (-shăn), adj. & n.

Dalny. See DAIREN.

Dal′ton (dôl′t'n) city, NW Georgia; pop. 16,000.

Da′ly City (dā′lĭ) city, W California, S of San Francisco; pop. 15,200.

Da·man′·hûr′ (dä′män·hōōr′) city, N Egypt; pop. 85,000.

Da·mão′ (dà·mouⁿ′) or **Da·man′** (dà·män′) **1** district of Portuguese India. **2** its chief town, a seaport on Gulf of Cambay.

Da·ma′ra·land′ (dà·mär′à·länd′; däm′à·rà-) or **Her·re′ro·land′** (hĕ·rä′rô·länd′) region, cen. South-West Africa.

Da·mas′cus (dà·măs′kŭs), Arab. **Esh Shâm** (ăsh shăm′) city, ✻ of Syria, on the Barada river; pop. 286,300.

Dam′i·et′ta (dăm′ĭ·ĕt′à; dăm·yĕt′à) seaport, N Egypt, at mouth of eastern (Damietta) branch of the Nile; pop. 53,600.

Da′mo·dar (dä′mô·där) river, NE India, in cen. Bihar and West Bengal, flowing ESE into Hooghly river; 350 m. long.

Dan. See 2d DAN, in Vocab.

Dan′bur′y (dăn′bĕr′ĭ; -bẽr·ĭ) city, SW Connecticut; pop. 22,100.

Danish West Indies. See VIRGIN ISLANDS.

Danmark. See DENMARK.

Dan·ne·mo′ra (dăn′ē·mō′rà; -mô′rà) village, NE New York, W of Plattsburg; site of Clinton State Prison.

Dantzig. = DANZIG.

Dan′ube (dăn′ūb), Ger. **Do′nau** (dō′nou), Hung. **Du′na** (dōō′nŏ), Romanian **Du′nă·rea** (dōō′nà·ryä), anc. **Da·nu′bi·us** (dà·nū′bĭ·ŭs) or **Is′ter** (ĭs′tẽr) river, cen. Europe, flowing from S Germany to the Black Sea; 1725 m. long. — **Da·nu′bi·an** (dà·nū′bĭ·ăn), adj.

Dan′vers (dăn′vẽrz) town, NE Massachusetts; pop. 15,700.

Dan′ville (dăn′vĭl) **1** city, E Illinois; pop. 37,900. **2** independent city, S Virginia, on Dan river; pop. 35,100.

Dan′zig (dăn[t]′sĭg; dăn′zĭg), Pol. **Gdańsk** (g'dän′y'sk) **1** city, N Poland, near Gulf of Danzig just W of mouth of the Vistula; pop. 169,700. **2** in full **Free City of Danzig**, territory 1920–39, N Poland, around the city of Danzig, constituting a free city (or state) under the League of Nations; area 754 sq. m.; before 1919 part of Germany; since 1945 part of Poland.

Danzig, Gulf or **Bay of**, inlet of Baltic Sea, N Poland.

Dapsang. See GODWIN AUSTEN.

Dar′da·nelles′ (där′d'n·ĕlz′), Turkish **Ça′nak·ka·le′ Bo′ğa·zı′** (chä′-näk·kä·lĕ′ bô′ä·zĭ′), anc. **Hel′les·pon′tus** (hĕl′ĕs·pŏn′tŭs), Angl. **Hel′les·pont** (hĕl′ĕs·pŏnt) strait, between Turkey in Europe (Gallipoli Penin.) and Turkey in Asia, connecting Sea of Marmara with Aegean Sea.

Dar el Beida. See CASABLANCA.

Dar es Sa·laam′ or **Dar′es·sa·lam′** (där′ ĕs sà·läm′) seaport, ✻ of Tanganyika Territory; pop. 74,000.

Dar′fur′ (där′fōōr′) province, W Sudan (republic); an independent kingdom until annexed by Egypt 1874; ✻ El Fasher.

Darial, or **Dariel, Pass.** See DARYAL PASS.

Dar'i·en' (dâr'ĭ·ĕn'; där'ĭ·ĕn), Span. **Da·rién'** (dä·ryän') Spanish colonial settlement, Central America, on N coast of Isthmus of Darien (now Isthmus of Panama); founded 1510.

Darien, Gulf of, inlet of Caribbean Sea, between E Panama and NW Colombia.

Darien, Isthmus of. See PANAMA, ISTHMUS OF.

Dar·jee'ling or **Dar·ji'ling** (där·jē'lĭng) town, NE India, in West Bengal on Sikkim border, at elevation of about 6000 ft.

Dar'ling (där'lĭng) river, SE Australia, in Queensland and New South Wales, flowing SW into Murray river; 1160 m. long.

Dar'ling·ton (där'lĭng·tŭn) county borough, N England, in Durham; pop. 84,900.

Darm'stadt (därm'shtät; Angl. därm'stăt) city, W Germany, in Hesse; pop. 76,300.

Dart'moor (därt'mŏŏr; -mōr) tableland, SW England, in S Devonshire; area 215 sq. m.

Dart'mouth (därt'mŭth) **1** town, Canada, in S Nova Scotia on Halifax harbor; pop. 21,100. **2** municipal borough, SW England, in Devonshire on English Channel; pop. 5800.

Dar'win (där'wĭn), also, formerly, **Port Darwin,** seaport, N Australia, ✳ of Northern Territory; pop. 2500.

Dar·yal' (dĕr·yäl'; där·yäl'), or **Dar'i·al'** (där'ĭ·äl'), **Pass,** also **Dar'i·el' Pass** (där'ĭ·ĕl') gorge, Soviet Russia, Europe, in Caucasus Mts., traversed by Terek river.

Dashan. = RAS DASHAN.

Daugava. See DVINA.

Dau'gav·pils (dou'gȧf·pĭls), Russ. **Dvinsk** (dvĭnsk), Ger. **Dü'na·burg** (dü'nä·bŏŏrk) city, E Latvia, on Dvina river; pop. 45,200.

Dau'phi·né' (dō'fē'nā') historical region, SE France; became appanage of eldest son of French king, who assumed title (dauphin) attached to the land; later formed a province, until the Revolution.

Da'vao (dä'vou) city, Philippine Is., in SE Mindanao on **Davao Gulf;** pop. 95,500.

Dav'en·port (dăv'ĕn·pōrt; dăv'm-) city, E Iowa, on Mississippi river across from Rock Island, Illinois; pop. 74,500.

Da'vis Strait (dā'vĭs) strait between SW Greenland and E Baffin I., connecting Baffin Bay with the Atlantic Ocean.

Da·vos' (dä·vōs') commune, E Switzerland, in Graubünden canton in Davos valley; pop. 10,400.

Daw'son (dô's'n) city, NW Canada, in Yukon Territory on Yukon river; former ✳ of the Territory; pop. 800.

Dax (däks) or **Ax** (äks) town, SW France, on Adour river; hot saline springs; mineral baths.

Day'ton (dā't'n) **1** city, SW Ohio, on Miami river; pop. 243,900. **2** city, E cen. Tennessee; scene of Scopes test-case evolution trial July 1925; William Jennings Bryan Univ.

Day·to'na Beach (dā·tō'nȧ) city, E Florida, on Atlantic Ocean; pop. 30,200.

Dead Sea, anc. **La'cus As'phal·ti'tes** (lā'kŭs ăs'făl·tī'tēz) salt lake on boundary between Palestine and Jordan; 46 m. long; 370 sq. m.; surface 1286 ft. below level of Mediterranean Sea.

Dean, Forest of (dēn) royal forest, SW England, in W Gloucestershire between the Severn and the Wye; area ab. 117,560 acres, including 15,000 acres set aside as a national forest park.

Dear'born (dēr'bôrn; -bērn) city, SE Michigan; pop. 95,000.

Death Valley, valley, E California, containing lowest point in the United States, 280 ft. below sea level; established 1933 as **Death Valley National Monument.**

Deau'ville (dō'vēl'; Angl. dō'vĭl) town, NW France, on Bay of the Seine; resort; racecourse.

De'bre·cen (dĕ'brĕ·tsĕn) autonomous city, E Hungary; pop. 122,500.

De·cap'o·lis (dĕ·kăp'ȯ·lĭs) region in N of ancient Palestine, extending from E end of Plain of Esdraelon to E and NE of Sea of Galilee.

De·ca'tur (dĕ·kā'tẽr) **1** city, N Alabama, on Tennessee river; pop. 20,000. **2** city, NW cen. Georgia, E of Atlanta; pop. 21,600. **3** city, cen. Illinois, on Sangamon river; pop. 66,300.

Dec'can (dĕk'ăn; dĕk'ăn) region, S India, constituting the plateau S of Narbada river; according to some, constitutes only that part of this region N of Kistna river.

de Chelly, Canyon. See CANYON DE CHELLY NATIONAL MONUMENT.

Ded'ham (dĕd'ăm) town, E Massachusetts; pop. 18,500.

Dee (dē) any of several rivers in Great Britain.

Deer'field (dēr'fēld) town, NW Massachusetts, S of Greenfield; Indian attacks 1675 (Bloody Brook massacre) and 1704; Deerfield Academy.

De·hi·wa'la—Mount La·vin'i·a (dā'hĭ·wä'lȧ mount' lȧ·vĭn'ĭ·ȧ) urban district, W Ceylon, on coast S of Colombo; pop. 56,900.

De'i·ra (dā'ē·rä) Anglian kingdom, NE England, which emerged in 6th cent. A.D. and extended from Tees river to the Humber.

Del·a·go'a Bay (dĕl'ȧ·gō'ȧ) inlet of Indian Ocean, SE Mozambique.

Del'a·ware (dĕl'ȧ·wâr; -wēr) **1** river, E United States, flowing S from S New York state to Delaware Bay; 296 m. long. **2** abbr. **Del.,** state, E United States, bordering on Delaware Bay and Atlantic Ocean; ✳ Dover; area 2057 sq. m.; pop. 318,100. — **Del'a·war'e·an** (-wâr'ē·ăn), adj. & n.

Delaware Bay, arm of Atlantic Ocean, between SW coast of New Jersey and E coast of Delaware.

Delaware Water Gap, gorge where Delaware river cuts through Kittatinny Mt., between Pennsylvania and New Jersey.

Delft (dĕlft) commune, SW Netherlands; pop. 62,000.

Del·ga'do, Cape (dĕl'gä'dō) cape, NE coast of Mozambique.

Del'hi (dĕl'ĭ) **1** territory, N India; area 578 sq. m.; pop. 1,744,100. **2** city, its ✳ and ✳ of India, comprising an old city, **Old Delhi,** and to the S a new city, **New Delhi,** containing the modern government buildings; total pop. with suburbs 521,800.

Del·mar'va (dĕl·mär'vȧ), or **Del·mar'vi·a** (-vĭ·ȧ), **Peninsula,** the peninsula, E United States, between Chesapeake and Delaware bays, including Delaware and parts of Maryland and Virginia.

De'los (dē'lŏs), Mod. Gr. **Dhi'los** (thē'lŏs) island, Greece, in the Cyclades; by ancient Greeks considered center of the archipelago. — **De'li·an** (dē'lĭ·ăn; dēl'yăn), adj. & n.

Del'phi (dĕl'fī), Mod. Gr. **Dhel·foi'** (thål·fē') town, cen. Greece, between Mt. Parnassus and Gulf of Corinth. See DELPHIAN, in Vocab.

Dem'a·vend (dĕm'ȧ·vĕnd) mountain, N Iran, NE of Tehran; highest in the Elburz Mts., over 18,600 ft.

Dem'e·rar'a (dĕm'ē·râr'ȧ; -rä'rȧ) river, British Guiana, flowing N to Atlantic Ocean; 200 m. long.

Den'bigh·shire (dĕn'bĭ·shĭr; -shẽr) or **Den'bigh,** county, N Wales; ✳ Ruthin; 669 sq. m.; pop. 170,700.

Den Hel'der (dĕn hĕl'dẽr) commune, W Netherlands; Dutch naval station; pop. 31,600.

Den'i·son (dĕn'ĭ·s'n) city, NE Texas; pop. 17,500.

Den'mark (dĕn'märk), Danish **Dan'mark** (dän'märk) country, N Europe, occupying most of Jutland and adjacent islands in the Baltic and in North Sea; kingdom; ✳ Copenhagen; area 16,576 sq. m.; pop. 4,045,200. See DANE, DANISH, in Vocab.

Denmark Strait, channel between SE Greenland and Iceland, connecting Arctic Ocean with the North Atlantic; 130 m. wide.

Den'ton (dĕn't'n; -tŭn) city, N Texas, NNW of Dallas; pop. 21,400.

D'En'tre·cas'teaux' Islands (dän'trĕ·kȧs'tō') island group, SW Pacific Ocean, off SE coast of New Guinea; attached to Territory of Papua; 1200 sq. m.; pop. 40,000.

Den'ver (dĕn'vẽr) city, ✳ of Colorado, on South Platte river on edge of Rocky Mts.; pop. 415,800.

Dept'ford (dĕt'fẽrd) metropolitan borough, London, on S bank of the Thames; pop. 75,700.

Der'by (dûr'bĭ; Brit. usu. där'bĭ) **1** see DERBYSHIRE. **2** county borough, England, ✳ of Derbyshire, on the Derwent; pop. 141,300.

Der'by·shire (-shĭr; -shẽr) or **Der'by,** county, N cen. England; ✳ Derby; area 1012 sq. m.; pop. 826,300.

Derry. See LONDONDERRY.

Der'went (dûr'wĕnt) **1** any of several rivers of England. **2** river, Tasmania; 130 m. long.

Der'went·wa'ter (-wô'tẽr; -wŏt'ẽr) lake, NW England, in Cumberland.

Des'chutes' (dā'shŏŏt') river, Oregon, flowing N into Columbia river; 250 m. long.

Des Moines (dĕ moin') **1** river, Iowa, flowing SE to the Mississippi; 327 m. long. **2** city, ✳ of Iowa, on Des Moines river; pop. 178,000.

Des·na' (dĕs·nä') river, U.S.S.R., flowing S to the Dnieper; 550 m. long.

Des Plaines (dĕs plānz') **1** river, NE Illinois, flowing S to unite with the Kankakee river and form the Illinois river; 150 m. long. **2** city, NE Illinois, NW of Chicago; pop. 15,000.

Des'sau (dĕs'ou) city, E Germany, on Mulde river; pop. 88,100.

Destêrro. See FLORIANÓPOLIS.

De·troit' (dĕ·troit') **1** river, SE Michigan, connecting Lake St. Clair with Lake Erie and forming section of U.S.-Canada boundary; 31 m. long. **2** city, SE Michigan, on Detroit river; pop. 1,849,600.

Detskoe Selo. See PUSHKIN.

Det'ting·en (dĕt'ĭng·ĕn) village, W Germany, in Bavaria; battle 1743.

Deur'ne (dûr'nĕ) commune, N Belgium, E of Antwerp; pop. 57,400.

Deutschland. See GERMANY.

Deva, Devana Castra. See CHESTER.

Devil Mountain. See AUYÁN-TEPUÍ.

Devil's Island, Fr. **Île du Dia'ble** (ēl' dü dyȧ'bl') island, French Guiana, one of Safety Is.; formerly a penal colony.

Dev'on (dĕv'ŭn). See DEVONSHIRE.

Devon Island, island, N Canada, N of Baffin I.; area 20,861 sq. m.

Dev'on·shire (dĕv'ŭn·shĭr; -shẽr) or **Devon,** county, SW England, between Bristol Channel and English Channel; ✳ Exeter; area 2612 sq. m.; pop. 798,300.

Dews'bur·y (dūz'bĕr·ĭ) county borough, N England, on the Calder S of Leeds; pop. 53,500.

Dezhnev, Cape. See EAST CAPE.

Dhah·ran' (dä·rän') town, E Saudi Arabia, on coast near Bahrein Is., in extensive oil region.

Dhau'la·gi'ri, Mount (dou'lȧ·gĭ'rĭ) mountain, W cen. Nepal, in the Himalayas; 26,800 ft. high.

Dhelfoi. See DELPHI.

Dhi'ban' (thē·bän') ruins, Jordan, E of Dead Sea, of ancient city of Moab, where Moabite stone was found 1868.

Dhilos. See DELOS.

Di'a·man·ti'na, 1 (dī'ȧ·măn·tē'nȧ) river, Australia, in SW Queensland, upper tributary of the Warburton; 470 m. long. **2** (dē·ȧ·männ·tē'nȧ) city, E Brazil, in cen. Minas Gerais state; diamond industry.

Di'a·mond, Cape (dī'ȧ·mănd) promontory, Canada, E end of city of Quebec; site of citadel.

Diamond Head, cape, Hawaii, on SE Oahu I.

Diarbekr. See DIYARBEKIR.

Dien Bien Phu (dyĕn' byĕn' fōō') village, SW Tonkin, N Vietnam; French military post in Indochina war; in 1954 besieged 55 days, fell to Vietminh May 7.

Di·eppe' (dē·ĕp') seaport, N France, N of Rouen; pop. 21,800.

Di'goel (dē'gōōl) or **Di'gul,** river, SE West Guinea, flowing S and W to Arafura Sea; 400 m. long.

Di'jon' (dē'zhôN') city, E France; pop. 100,700.

Diks·mui'de or **Dix·mui'de** (dĭks·moi'dĕ), Fr. **Dix'mude'** (dēks'müd'; dēs'-) town, Belgium, in W Flanders N of Ieper (Ypres); in World War I destroyed during heavy fighting 1914.

Di·nar'ic Alps (dĭ·năr'ĭk) range of E Alps, W Yugoslavia.

Di'o·mede Islands (dī'ō·mēd) two islands, Big Diomede (Russian) and Little Diomede (American) in Bering Strait, about 2 m. apart.

Diospolis. See THEBES, Egypt.

Discovery Bay, inlet of Indian Ocean, S Australia, at boundary between Victoria and South Australia.

Dis'mal Swamp (dĭz'măl) swamp area, SE Virginia and NE North Carolina; 30 m. long and 10 m. wide.

District of Co·lum'bi·a (kȯ·lŭm'bĭ·ȧ) federal district, E United States, on Potomac river; coextensive with city of Washington; area 69 sq. m.; pop. 802,200.

Di·yar'be·kir' (dē·yär'bĕ·kēr') or **Di·ar'bekr'** (dē·är'bĕk'ẽr) city, SE Turkey, on the Tigris; pop. 45,500.

Dj-. For some words beginning thus, see J-.

Djailolo. See HALMAHERA.

Dja·kar'ta (jȧ·kär'tȧ), formerly **Ba·ta'vi·a** (bȧ·tā'vĭ·ȧ; -täv'yȧ) city, ✳ of Indonesia, on NW coast of Java; pop. 1,200,000.

Djebel. See JEBEL.

Dji·bou′ti or **Ji·bu′ti** (jĭ·bōō′tĭ) city, ✳ of French Somaliland, on S shore of Gulf of Tadjoura; pop. 20,000.

Djok′ja·kar′ta (jŏk′yȧ·kär′tȧ; jŏk′yȧ) **1** native (Mohammedan) principality, Indonesia, in S Java; 1223 sq. m.; pop. 1,600,000. **2** city, its ✳; pop. 136,000.

Dne′pro·dzer·zhinsk′ (nĕp′rô·dĕr·zhĭnsk′) city, U.S.S.R., in E cen. Ukraine on the Dnieper; pop. 147,800.

Dne′pro·pe·trovsk′ (nĕp′rô·pĕ·trôfsk′), formerly **E·ka′te·ri′no·slav** (ĕ·kät′ẽr·ẽ′nō·släv) city, U.S.S.R., in Ukraine, on the Dnieper at its big bend; pop. 500,700.

Dne′pro·stroi′ (nĕp′rô·stroi′) dam, U.S.S.R., in the Ukraine, across the lower Dnieper below Dnepropetrovsk.

Dnie′per (nē′pẽr), Russ. **Dne′pr** (d′nyĕ′pr′), anc. **Bo·rys′the·nes** (bô·rĭs′thẽ·nēz) river, Soviet Russia, Europe, rising in S Valdai Hills near source of the Volga and flowing into the Black Sea; 1400 m. long.

Dnies′ter (nēs′tẽr), Russ. **Dnes′tr** (d′nyĕs′tr′), Romanian **Ni′stru** (nē′strōō), anc. **Ty′ras** (tī′răs) river, U.S.S.R.; rises on N slope of Carpathian Mts. and flows SE to the Black Sea; 850 m. long.

Do′bru·ja or **Do′bru·dja** (dô′brōō·jä), Bulgarian **Do′bru·dja** (dô′brōō·jä) region, S Europe, in Romania and Bulgaria on Black Sea coast; all in Romania 1913–40.

Do·dec·a·nese (dô·dĕk′ȧ·nēs; ·nēz) or **Do′dec·a·ne′sus** (dô′dĕk·ȧ·nē′sŭs; dô·dĕk′·) group of islands, SE Aegean Sea, belonging to Greece; belonged to Italy 1923–47; administrative center Rhodes; area 486 sq. m.; pop. 76,700.

Do·do′na (dô·dō′nȧ) town, NW Greece, in Epirus; site of ancient oracle.

Dog′ger Bank (dŏg′ẽr) submerged sandbank in cen. North Sea, near which naval battle was fought Jan. 24, 1915.

Dol′o·mites (dŏl′ô·mīts) range of E Alps, NE Italy, between valleys of Adige and Piave rivers.

Dôme, Puy de (pü·ē′ dōm′) mountain, S cen. France, in Auvergne Mts.; 4805 ft. high.

Dom′i·ni·ca (dŏm′ĭ·nē′kȧ; dô·mĭn′ĭ·kȧ) island, West Indies Federation, in Leeward Is.; administratively a colony attached to Windward Is.; ✳ Roseau; area 305 sq. m.; pop. 53,700.

Do·min′i·can Republic (dô·mĭn′ĭ·kȧn), officially **Re·pú′bli·ca Do·mi′ni·ca′na** (rĕ·pōō′vlē·kä thô·mē′nĕ·kä′nä) island country, West Indies, occupying E two thirds of Hispaniola; republic; ✳ Ciudad Trujillo; area 19,129 sq. m.; pop. 2,121,100.

Dom′re·my′-la-Pu′celle′ (dôₙr′mē′lȧ·pü′sĕl′) village, NE France, on the Meuse; birthplace of Joan of Arc.

Don (dŏn; Russ. dôn), Tatar **Du′na** (dōō′nä), anc. **Tan′a·is** (tăn′ȧ·ĭs) river, SE Soviet Russia, Europe, flowing to Sea of Azov; 1200 m. long.

Donau. See DANUBE.

Don′bas (dŏn′băs; Russ. dŭn·bȧs′) or **Do·nets′ Basin** (dô·nĕts′) region, U.S.S.R., in E Ukraine, in plain of Donets river and the lower Dnieper.

Don′cas·ter (dŏng′kȧs·tẽr) county borough, N England, in Yorkshire, on the Don; pop. 81,900.

Don′e·gal (dŏn′ĕ·gôl′; dŏn′ĕ·gôl′) county, N Republic of Ireland, in Ulster prov.; ✳ Lifford; 1865 sq. m.; pop. 131,500.

Do·nets′ (dô·nĕts′) river, U.S.S.R., in Soviet Russia, Europe, and the Ukraine; flows SE to the Don; 670 m. long.

Don′go·la (dŏng′gô·lȧ; popularly dŏng·gō′lȧ, dŏn·) town, N Sudan (republic), on the Nile; ✳ of former Dongola prov.; pop. 9000.

Doon (dōōn) river, SW Scotland, in Ayrshire, flowing through **Loch Doon** (lŏk) to Firth of Clyde.

Doone Valley (dōōn) valley, SW England, in N Devonshire.

Doorn (dōrn) town, cen. Netherlands, SE of Utrecht; residence (from 1920) of Kaiser William II of Germany.

Dor′dogne′ (dôr′dôn′y′) river, SW France, flowing SW and W to unite with Garonne river and form the Gironde estuary; 300 m. long.

Dor′drecht (dôr′drĕkt) or **Dort** (dôrt) commune, SW Netherlands, on Maas (Meuse) river; pop. 68,200.

Dore, Monts (môn′ dôr′) mountain group, S cen. France, in Auvergne Mts.; highest point Puy de Sancy, 6185 ft.

Do′ris (dô′rĭs; dŏr′ĭs) **1** anc. country, cen. Greece, between Mts. Oeta and Parnassus. **2** anc. district, SW Asia Minor, on coast of Caria.

Dorpat. See TARTU.

Dor′set·shire (dôr′sĕt·shĭr; ·shẽr; dôr′sĭt·) or **Dor′set**, county, S England; ✳ Dorchester; area 973 sq. m.; pop. 291,200.

Dort′mund (dôrt′mŏŏnt) city, W Germany, in the Ruhr; pop. 500,200.

Dor′val′ (dôr′väl′) city, Canada, in S Quebec on Montreal I. SW of Montreal; pop. 14,100.

Do′than (dō′thȧn) city, SE Alabama; pop. 21,600.

Dou′ai′, formerly **Dou′ay′** (dōō′ā′) city, N France, S of Lille; pop. 37,300. See DOUAY BIBLE, in Vocab.

Doubt, River of. See ROOSEVELT, RIO.

Dou′ro (dō′rōō), Span. **Due′ro** (dwā′rô) river, Spain and Portugal, flowing W into Atlantic Ocean; 485 m. long.

Do′ver (dō′vẽr) **1** city, ✳ of Delaware; pop. 6200. **2** city, SE New Hampshire; pop. 15,900. **3** municipal borough, SE England, in Kent on Strait of Dover; pop. 35,200.

Dover, Strait of, also **Straits of Dover**, Fr. **Pas de Ca′lais′** (päd′kȧ′lĕ′) channel between SE England and N France, the easternmost section of the English Channel; 20 m. wide at narrowest point.

Down (doun) county, SE Northern Ireland; ✳ Downpatrick; 952 sq. m.; pop. 210,700.

Downs, the (dounz) **1** hills, S England: see NORTH DOWNS, SOUTH DOWNS. **2** roadstead in English Channel along SE coast of Kent, protected by the Goodwin Sands; scene of battles 1652 and 1666.

Dra′chen·fels′ (dräk′ĕn·fĕls′) hill, W Germany, on the Rhine S of Bonn; one of the Siebengebirge; 1053 ft. high.

Dra′kens·berg Mountains (drä′kĕnz·bûrg) or **Quath·lam′ba** (kwät·läm′bȧ) mountain range, E Union of South Africa, in Cape Province and Natal; highest peak Mont aux Sources, 10,761 ft.

Drake Passage or **Strait** (drāk) strait, S South America, between Cape Horn and South Shetland Is.

Dra′va (drä′vä) or **Dra′ve** (drä′vĕ), Ger. **Drau** (drou) river, Austria and Yugoslavia, flowing E into Danube river; 450 m. long.

Dres′den (drĕz′dĕn) city, E Germany, chief city of Saxony, on Elbe river; pop. 468,000.

Dro′ghe·da (drô′ĕ·dȧ) municipal borough, NE Republic of Ireland, on Boyne river; massacre 1649; pop. 16,800.

Drum′mond·ville (drŭm′ȧnd·vĭl) city, Canada, in S Quebec on St. Francis river; pop. 26,300.

Druze, Jebel. See JEBEL ED DRUZE.

Du·bawnt′ (dŏŏ·bônt′; dōō′bônt) river, N cen. Canada, flowing N through **Dubawnt Lake** (1654 sq. m.) and E through Aberdeen Lake into Baker Lake; 580 m. long.

Dub′lin (dŭb′lĭn) **1** county, E Ireland, in Leinster prov.; 356 sq. m.; pop. 691,400. **2** Gael. **Bai·le A′tha Cli′ath** (blä′klē′ȧ) seaport and county borough, ✳ of Republic of Ireland and of co. Dublin, at mouth of Liffey river on Dublin Bay; pop. 521,300.

Du′brov·nik (dōō′brôv·nĕk), Ital. **Ra·gu′sa** (rä·gōō′zä) seaport, Yugoslavia, on Dalmatian coast; pop. 18,800.

Du·buque′ (dŭ·būk′) city, E Iowa, on Mississippi river; pop. 49,700.

Dud′ley (dŭd′lĭ) county borough, W cen. England, WNW of Birmingham; pop. 62,500.

Duero. See DOURO.

Duis′burg-Ham·born′ (düs′bŏŏrk·häm·bôrn′; ·häm′bôrn; Angl. dōōz′·bûrg·häm′bôrn, dōōs′·) city, W Germany, on Rhine river at confluence of the Ruhr; pop. 408,900.

Du·la′wan (dōō·lä′wän) municipality, Philippine Is., in Mindanao on Mindanao river; pop. 55,300.

Du·luth′ (dŭ·lōōth′) city, NE Minnesota, at W end of Lake Superior; pop. 104,500.

Dum·bar′ton (dŭm·bär′t'n) **1** burgh, W cen. Scotland, ✳ of Dunbartonshire, on Leven river near the Clude; pop. 23,700. **2** or **Dum·bar′ton·shire** (-shĭr; -shẽr). = DUNBARTON, DUNBARTONSHIRE.

Dumbarton Oaks, mansion in Georgetown, suburb of Washington, D.C.; conference 1944.

Dum·fries′ (dŭm·frēs′) or **Dum·fries′shire** (-frēsh′shĭr; -shẽr) county, S Scotland; ✳ Dumfries; area 1073 sq. m.; pop. 85,700.

Duna. See DANUBE; DON.

Düna. See DVINA.

Dinaburg. See DAUGAVPILS.

Du·na′jec (dōō·nä′yĕts) river, S Poland, flowing N from Carpathian Mts. into Vistula river; 130 m. long.

Du′na·pen′te·le (dōō′nô·pän′tä·lä) town, Hungary, S of Budapest.

Dunărea. See DANUBE.

Dun·bar′ (dŭn·bär′) burgh, SE Scotland, in East Lothian E of Edinburgh at mouth of the Firth of Forth; battle 1650.

Dun·bar′ton (dŭn·bär′t'n) or **Dun·bar′ton·shire** (-shĭr; -shẽr) county, W cen. Scotland; ✳ Dumbarton; area 244 sq. m.; pop. 164,300.

Dun′can (dŭng′kȧn) city, S Oklahoma; pop. 15,300.

Dun·dee′ (dŭn·dē′; dŭn′dē) seaport and burgh, E Scotland, in Angus co. on Firth of Tay; pop. 177,300.

Dun·e′din (dŭn·ē′d′n) city, New Zealand, in SE South I. at head of Otago Harbor; pop. with suburbs 95,300.

Dun·ferm′line (dŭn·fûrm′lĭn; dŭm·) burgh, E Scotland, in Fife co.; pop. 44,700.

Dunholme. See DURHAM, DUNELM.

Dun·kerque′ (dŭn′kẽrk′), Eng. **Dun′kirk** (dŭn′kûrk; dŭn·kûrk′), earlier French **Dun′querque′** (dûn′kẽrk′) seaport, N France, on Strait of Dover; Battle of the Dunes 1658; evacuation of Allies 1940.

Dun′kirk, 1 (dŭn′kûrk) city, SW New York, on Lake Erie; pop. 18,000. **2** see DUNKERQUE.

Dun Laoghai′re (dŭn lâ′rĕ) or **Dun·lea′ry** (dŭn·lēr′ĭ) city borough, E Ireland, in SE co. Dublin on S shore of Dublin Bay; pop. 48,000.

Dun·more′ (dŭn·mōr′; dŭn′mōr) borough, NE Pennsylvania, E of Scranton; pop. 20,300.

Dun′si·nane′ (dŭn′sĭ·nān′; dŭn′sĭ·nān′; dŭn·sĭn′ȧn) hill, cen. Scotland, in Sidlaw Hills, Perth co.; scene of defeat of Macbeth by Siward 1054.

Du′que de Ca·xi′as or **Caxias** (dōō′kĕ thĕ kȧ·shē′ȧs) city, SE Brazil, in Rio de Janeiro state; pop. 74,600.

Du·quesne′ (dōō·kān′) city, SW Pennsylvania; pop. 17,600.

Du·ran′go (dōō·räng′gô) **1** state, NW cen. Mexico; area 42,272 sq. m.; pop. 629,500. **2** officially **Vic·to′ria de Du·ran′go** (bĕk·tô′ryä thä thōō·räng′gô) city, its ✳; pop. 33,300.

Dur′ban (dûr′bȧn; -bȧn; dûr·bän′) seaport, E Union of South Africa, in E Natal on landlocked inlet of Indian Ocean; pop. 339,200.

Dur′ham (dûr′ȧm; Brit. dûr′-) **1** county, N England, bordering on North Sea; area 1015 sq. m.; pop. 1,463,400. **2** Saxon **Dun′holme** (dŭn′ȧm) municipal borough, its ✳, on the Wear S of Newcastle; pop. 19,300.

Durovernum. See CANTERBURY.

Dur′rës (dŏŏr′rĕs), Ital. **Du·raz′zo** (dōō·rät′tsô) seaport, W Albania, on Adriatic Sea; pop. 8700.

Düs′sel·dorf (düs′ĕl·dôrf; Angl. dōō′s'l·dôrf, dŏŏs′'l-, dĭs′'l-) city, W Germany, on Rhine river; pop. 498,300.

Dutch Borneo (dŭch). See BORNEO.

Dutch East Indies. = Netherlands Indies: see INDONESIA.

Dutch Guiana. See SURINAM.

Dutch Harbor, port, village, and U.S. naval station, SW Alaska, at E end of Aleutian Is. on island in Unalaska Bay.

Dutch New Guinea. = NETHERLANDS NEW GUINEA.

Dutch West Indies. = NETHERLANDS ANTILLES.

Dúvida, Rio da. See ROOSEVELT, RIO.

Dvi·na′ (dvē·nä′) **1** see NORTHERN DVINA. **2** Lettish **Dau′ga·va** (dou′gä·vä), Ger. **Dü′na** (dü′nä) river, N Europe, rising in Soviet Russia in the Valdai Hills and flowing to the Gulf of Riga; 630 m. long.

Dvina Gulf or **Bay**, formerly **Gulf of Arch′an′gel** (ärk′än′jĕl) southeast arm of White Sea, N Soviet Russia, Europe.

Dvinsk. See DAUGAVPILS.

Dyushambe. See STALINABAD.

Dzau·dzhi′kau (dzou·jē′kou), Russ. **Or′dzho·ni·kid′ze** (ôr′jŏn·ĭ·kĭd′zĕ) city, SE Soviet Russia, Europe, ✳ of North Ossetia, on the Terek river; pop. 127,200.

Dzer·zhinsk′ (dyẽr·zhĭnsk′) city, Soviet Russia, Europe, on Oka river just W of Gorki; pop. 103,400.

Dzun·gar′i·a ([d]zōōng·gâr′ĭ·ȧ; [d]zŭng-) or **Zun·gar′i·a** (zōōng-; zŭng-) region, W China, in N Sinkiang N of the Tien Shan.

E

Ea'ling (ē'lǐng) municipal borough, SE England, in Middlesex W of London; pop. 187,300.

East Africa Protectorate. See KENYA.

East An'gli·a (ăng'glǐ·à) region, E England, including Norfolk and Suffolk cos.; one of kingdoms of the Anglo-Saxon heptarchy.

East Bengal; East Beskids. See BENGAL; BESKIDS.

East'bourne (ēst'bōrn; -bẽrn) county borough, S England, in East Sussex on English Channel; pop. 57,800.

East Cape or **Cape Dezh'nev** (dĕzh'nĕf) cape, NE Soviet Russia, Asia, at E end of Chukotski Penin., projecting into Bering Strait.

East Chicago, city, NW Indiana, on Lake Michigan; pop. 54,300.

East China Sea. See CHINA SEA.

East Cleveland, city, N Ohio; pop. 40,000.

East Detroit, city, SE Michigan; pop. 21,500.

Eas'ter Island (ēs'tẽr), Span. **Pas'cua** (päs'kwä), native **Ra'pa Nu'i** (rä'pä nōō'ē) island in SE Pacific Ocean, 2000 m. W of Chilean coast; belongs to Chile; has gigantic statues of unknown origin.

Eastern Ghats. See GHATS.

Eastern Roman Empire. See BYZANTINE EMPIRE.

Eastern Rumelia, region, S Bulgaria, including Rhodope Mts. and Maritsa river valley; an autonomous province of Turkey 1878–85.

Eastern Samoa. See AMERICAN SAMOA.

Eastern Shore, 1 the eastern shore of Chesapeake Bay, including parts of Maryland and Virginia. **2** sometimes, the whole of the peninsula between Chesapeake and Delaware bays, including Delaware.

Eastern Thrace. See THRACE.

East Ham (ēst' hăm') county borough, SE England, in Essex, E London; pop. 120,900.

East Hartford, town, N Connecticut; pop. 29,900.

East In'dies (ĭn'dǐz; -dēz) **1** also **East In'di·a** (ĭn'dǐ·à) the islands of the Republic of Indonesia (formerly Netherlands Indies). **2** the islands of the Malay Archipelago. **3** sometimes, the Malay Archipelago, India, and Indochina. — **East In'di·an** (ĭn'dǐ·ăn), adj. & n.

East Lansing, city, S Michigan; pop. 20,300.

East Liverpool, city, E Ohio, on Ohio river; pop. 24,200.

East London, city, S Union of South Africa, in SE Cape Province at mouth of Buffalo river; pop. 76,100.

East Lothian, county, SE Scotland; ✳ Haddington; 267 sq. m.; pop. 52,200.

East'main' (ēst'mān') river, Canada, in W Quebec province, flowing W into James Bay; 375 m. long.

Eas'ton (ēs'tŭn) city, E Pennsylvania, at junction of Lehigh and Delaware rivers; pop. 35,600.

East Orange, city, NE New Jersey, WNW of Newark; pop. 79,300.

East Pakistan, the eastern division of Pakistan, comprising the predominantly Moslem portion of Bengal; from 1956 a province; ✳ Dacca; area 54,501 sq. m.; pop. 42,063,000.

East Paterson, borough, NE New Jersey, SE of Paterson; pop. 15,400.

East Point, city, NW cen. Georgia, SSW of Atlanta; pop. 21,100.

East'port (ēst'pōrt) city, SE Maine, on island in Passamaquoddy Bay; easternmost city in United States.

East Providence, town, N Rhode Island; pop. 35,900.

East Prussia, Ger. **Ost'preus'sen** (ōst'proi'sĕn) region, N Europe, bordering on Baltic Sea E of Pomerania; formerly a province of Prussia, for a time (1919–39) forming an exclave separated from rest of Prussia by Polish Corridor; since 1945 in Poland and the U.S.S.R.

East Punjab, region, NW India, comprising eastern section of the Punjab; one of the states (Punjab state) of the Republic of India.

East River, strait, SE New York, connecting Long Island Sound and Upper New York Bay; separates Manhattan from Long I.

East Saint Louis, city, SW Illinois, on Mississippi river opposite St. Louis, Mo.; pop. 82,300.

East Suffolk; East Sussex. See SUFFOLK; SUSSEX.

East'view' (ēst'vū') town, Canada, in SE Ontario NE of Ottawa; pop. 19,300.

Eau Claire (ō' klâr') city, W Wisconsin, on Chippewa river; pop. 36,100.

Eba, Mount. See MOUNT EBA.

Eboracum. See YORK, England.

E'bro (ā'brō) river, NE Spain; rises in Cantabrian Mts., flows ESE into Mediterranean Sea; 480 m. long.

Ecbatana. See HAMADAN.

Eckmühl. See EGGMÜHL.

E·corse' (ė·kôrs'; ē'kôrs) village, SE Michigan, on Detroit river; pop. 17,900.

Ec'ua·dor (ĕk'wà·dôr) country, W South America, on the equator; republic; ✳ Quito; area 104,510 sq. m.; pop. 3,171,400. — **Ec'ua·do'ri·an** (-dō'rǐ·ăn; -dôr'ǐ·ăn), **Ec'ua·do'ran** (-dō'răn; -dôr'ăn), adj. & n.

E'de (ā'dĕ) commune, E Netherlands, NW of Arnhem; pop. 42,600.

E'de (ā'dä) city, SW Nigeria; pop. 52,400.

Edge Hill or **Edge'hill'** ridge, cen. England, in S Warwickshire NW of Banbury; battle 1642.

Ed'in·burgh (ĕd'n·bûr'ō; Brit. -bŭ·rä, -brŭ) city and burgh, ✳ of Scotland and of Midlothian co., on Firth of Forth; pop. 466,800.

E·dir'ne (ė·dǐr'nė), formerly **A'dri·an·o'ple** (ā'drǐ·ăn·ō'p'l) city, NW Turkey in Europe; pop. 30,200.

Ed'mon·ton (ĕd'mŭn·tŭn) **1** city, Canada, ✳ of Alberta, on North Saskatchewan river; pop. 226,000. **2** municipal borough, SE England, in Middlesex just N of London; pop. 104,200.

Ed'munds·ton (ĕd'mŭn[d]·stŭn) town, Canada, in NW New Brunswick on Saint John river; pop. 12,000.

Edo. See TOKYO.

E'dom (ē'dŏm) in the Bible, the country of the Edomites, S of Judaea and the Dead Sea. See EDOMITE, in Vocab.

Ed'ward, Lake (ĕd'wẽrd) lake, E Africa between NE Belgian Congo and SW Uganda; area 830 sq. m.

Ed'wards Plateau (ĕd'wẽrdz) region, W Texas, comprising a level limestone plateau 2000–5000 ft. high SE of the Llano Estacado.

Eesti. See ESTONIA.

E·fa'te (ė·fä'tä) or **Va'té'** (Fr. và'tā') island, cen. New Hebrides Is.; chief town Vila, ✳ of the group.

E'ga·di Islands (ĕg'à·dǐ) or **Ae·ga'di·an Isles** (ē·gā'dǐ·ăn), anc. **Ae·ga'tes** (ė·gā'tēz) group of islands, Italy, off W coast of Sicily.

E'ger (ā'gẽr). See OHRE.

Egg'mühl (ĕk'mül) or **Eck'mühl,** village, W Germany, in Bavaria S of Regensburg; battle 1809.

Eg'mont (ĕg'mŏnt), Maori **Ta'ra·na'ki** (tä'rä·nä'kē) volcanic peak, New Zealand, in W cen. North I.; 8260 ft. high.

Egorevsk. See YEGOREVSK.

E'gypt (ē'jĭpt), anc. (Lat.) **Ae·gyp'tus** (ė·jĭp'tŭs), now often called by Arabic name **Misr** (mǐs'r'), the full form, conventionally transliterated, being **El Qutr el Mas'ri** (ăl kŏŏt'răl mǐs'rē) country, NE Africa, including small part (Sinai Penin.) of Asia, and bordering on Mediterranean Sea; a kingdom 1922–53, republic 1953–58; became a province of the United Arab Republic Feb. 1, 1958; ✳ Cairo; 386,198 sq. m.; pop. 19,087,300. — **E·gyp'tian** (ė·jĭp'shăn), adj. & n.

Eickel. See WANNE-EICKEL.

Ei'fel (ī'fĕl) region, W Germany, NW of Moselle river and NE of Luxembourg, containing limestone moors and many crater lakes.

Eilat. See ELATH.

Eind'ho'ven (īnt'hō'vĕ[n]) commune, S Netherlands; pop. 134,500.

Eire. See IRELAND.

Ei'se·nach (ī'zĕ·näk) city, E Germany, W of Erfurt; pop. 51,800.

Eisernes Tor. See IRON GATE.

Ekaterinburg. See SVERDLOVSK.

Ekaterinodar. See KRASNODAR.

Ekaterinoslav. See DNEPROPETROVSK.

E·klut'na, Lake (ė·klōōt'nà) lake, S Alaska, NE of Anchorage; source of Eklutna river.

El A·ghei'la (ĕl à·gā'là) town, N Libya, near SE end of Gulf of Sidra; scene of several battles 1941 and 1942.

El A'la·mein' (ĕl ăl'à·mān') village, N Egypt, N of NE corner of Qattara Depression; battle 1942.

E'lam (ē'lăm), also known as **Su'si·a'na** (sū'zǐ·ā'nà; -ăn'à) ancient kingdom, SW Asia, at head of Persian Gulf E of Babylonia, dating back possibly to 5th millennium B.C. — **E'lam·ite** (ē'lăm·īt), n. & adj.

Elatea. See CITHAERON.

E'lath (ē'lăth) **1** see 'AQABA. **2** or **Ei·lat'** (ā·lät') seaport, S Israel, W of 'Aqaba at head of Gulf of 'Aqaba; built since 1948.

El'ba (ĕl'bà) island, Italy, in Mediterranean Sea between mainland and Corsica; 86 sq. m.; pop. 27,000.

El Bahnasa. See OXYRHYNCHUS.

El'be (ĕl'bĕ; sometimes Angl. ĕlb), Czech **La'be** (lä'bĕ) river, Czechoslovakia and Germany; flows into North Sea; 720 m. long.

El Beqa', El Bika. See BIKA, EL.

El'bert, Mount (ĕl'bẽrt) mountain, cen. Colorado; highest peak in the Rocky Mts., 14,431 ft.

El'blag (ĕl'blôngg), Ger. **El'bing** (ĕl'bǐng) seaport, N Poland, near the Frisches Haff; pop. 90,000.

El'bo·rus' (ĕl'bō·rōōz') or **El·brus'** (ĕl·brōōz') mountain, U.S.S.R., in Georgia in N Caucasus Mts.; highest point in Europe, 18,481 ft.

El·burz' Mountains (ĕl·bŏŏrz') range, N Iran, parallel with S shore of Caspian Sea; highest peak Demavend, 18,600 ft.

El Ca·ney' (ĕl kä·nā') or **Ca·ney',** town, E Cuba; scene of battle July 1, 1898, in which American forces defeated the Spaniards.

El Cap'i·tan' (ĕl kăp'ǐ·tăn') mountain, cen. California, in Yosemite Valley; a monolith 7564 ft. high, rising 3604 ft. above the valley floor.

El Cer·ri'to (ĕl sĕ·rē'tō) city, W California, on San Francisco Bay N of Oakland; pop. 18,000.

El Chaco. See CHACO.

El'che (ĕl'chä) city, SE Spain, SW of Alicante; pop. 57,200.

El Do·ra'do (ĕl dō·rä'dō) city, S Arkansas; pop. 23,100.

E·lec'tric Peak (ė·lĕk'trĭk) mountain, S Montana, in Yellowstone National Park; highest in Gallatin Range, 11,155 ft.

El Es·co'ri·al (ĕl ĕs·kō'rǐ·ăl) town, cen. Spain, N of Madrid; site of the Escorial, vast structure built by Philip II.

Elets. See YELETS.

E·leu'sis (ė·lū'sǐs), Mod. Gr. **E'lev·sís'** (â'lâf·sēs') village, E Greece, in Attica NW of Athens, on inlet of Saronic Gulf; site of ruins of ancient city, seat of the Eleusinian mysteries (which see, in Vocab.).

E·leu'ther·a (ė·lū'thẽr·à) island, Bahama Is., E of New Providence I.

El Fai·yûm' or **El Fa·yum'** (ăl fä·yōōm'; fī-) town, N Egypt, SW of Cairo; pop. 74,300.

El Fer·rol' (ĕl fĕr·rōl') city, NW Spain, NE of La Coruña on coast; naval station; pop. 72,700.

El'gin, 1 (ĕl'jǐn) city, NE Illinois; pop. 44,200. **2** (ĕl'gǐn) or **El'gin·shire** (-shĭr; -shẽr) county, Scotland: see MORAY.

El Gizeh. See GIZA.

El'gon, Mount (ĕl'gŏn) volcanic peak, E Africa, on Uganda-Kenya boundary NE of Lake Victoria; 14,176 ft. high.

El Hamad. See SYRIAN DESERT.

El Hasa. See HASA, AL-.

E'lis (ē'lǐs), Mod. Gr. **I·lí'a** (ė·lyē'ä) region, S Greece, in NW Peloponnesus bordering on Ionian Sea, S of Achaea.

E·lis'a·beth·ville (ė·lǐz'à·bĕth·vǐl) town, SE Belgian Congo, near border of Northern Rhodesia; pop. 48,700.

Elisavetgrad. See KIROVOGRAD.

Elisavetpol. See KIROVABAD.

E·liz'a·beth (ė·lǐz'à·bĕth) city, NE New Jersey; pop. 112,800.

El Jezira. See GEZIRA.

Elk (ĕlk), Ger. **Lyck** (lǐk) city, NE Poland; pop. 56,400.

Elk'hart (ĕlk'härt; ĕl'kärt) city, N Indiana; pop. 35,600.

Ellas. See GREECE.

Elles'mere Island (ĕlz'mẽr) island, N Canada, its N point (in 83° N) being northernmost point of Canada; area 82,119 sq. m.

El'lice (ĕl'ĭs), or **La·goon'** (là·gōōn'), **Islands,** island group, W Pacific Ocean, N of Fiji Is. and SSE of Gilbert I.; belongs to British colony of Gilbert and Ellice Islands; area 14 sq. m.; pop. 4600.

El'lis Island (ĕl'ĭs) island, New York, in Upper New York Bay; U.S. immigration station 1891–1954.

El Maghreb el Aqsa. See MOROCCO.

El Man·sû'ra (ĕl măn·sŏŏr'à) city, N Egypt; pop. 102,700.

Elm'hurst (ĕlm'hûrst) city, NE Illinois, W of Chicago; pop. 21,300.

El Min'ya (ĕl mĭn'yà) city, cen. Egypt, on the Nile; pop. 69,700.

El·mi'ra (ĕl·mī'rà) city, S New York, on Chemung river; pop. 49,700.

El Mis'ti (ĕl mĕs'tē) volcano, S Peru; 19,110 ft. high.

Elm'wood Park (ĕlm'wood) village, NE Illinois, suburb of Chicago; pop. 18,800.

El Pa'o (ĕl pä'ō) mountain, E Venezuela, about 30 m. S of confluence of Caroní and Orinoco rivers; source of iron ore.

El Pas'o (ĕl păs'ō) city, W tip of Texas, on the Rio Grande; pop. 130,500.

El Quds esh Sherif. See JERUSALEM.

El Qutr el Masri. See EGYPT.

El Sal'va·dor (ĕl säl'và·dôr) country, Central America, bordering on Pacific Ocean; republic; ✳ San Salvador; area 13,176 sq. m.; pop. 1,858,700. — Sal'va·do'ran (säl'và·dō'răn; -dôr'ăn), Sal'va·do'ri·an (-dō'rĭ·ăn; -dôr'ĭ·ăn), adj. & n.

Elsass, Elsass-Lothringen. See ALSACE, ALSACE-LORRAINE.

Elsene. See IXELLES.

Elsinore. See HELSINGÖR.

El Uqsor. See LUXOR.

E'ly, Isle of (ē'lĭ) county, E England, largely comprising drained fenland; ✳ March; area 375 sq. m.; pop. 89,000.

E·lyr'i·a (ê·lĭr'ĭ·à) city, N Ohio; pop. 30,300.

Em'den (ĕm'dĕn) seaport, W Germany, at mouth of Ems river; pop. 31,400.

Emesa. See HOMS.

E·mi'lia (à·mē'lyà), anc. Æ·mil'ia (ê·mĭl'yà; -mĭl'ĭ·à) region, N Italy, between the Po river, the Adriatic Sea, and the Apennines; includes the fertile E·mil'ian Plain (ê·mĭl'yăn).

Em'men (ĕm'ĕ[n]) commune, NE Netherlands; pop. 54,100.

Em·po'ri·a (ĕm·pō'rĭ·à) city, E Kansas; pop. 15,700.

Empress Au·gus'ta Bay (ô·gŭs'tà) inlet of Solomon Sea, W Bougainville I., NW Solomon Is.: landing by U.S. Marines Nov. 1943.

Empty Quarter, the Rub 'al Khali desert, S Arabia.

Ems (ĕms; Angl. ĕmz) river, NW Germany, flowing to the North Sea, its mouth a wide estuary bordering the Netherlands; 160 m. long.

Ems (ĕms; āms; Angl. ĕmz), also Bad Ems (bät ĕms'; āms') town, W Germany, SE of Koblenz; watering place.

En'der·bur'y (ĕn'dēr·bĕr'ĭ; -bēr·ĭ) island, Phoenix Is.; an atoll; controlled jointly by Great Britain and the United States.

En'der·by Land (ĕn'dēr·bĭ) region, Antarctica, on coast E of Queen Maud Land, ab. 49°30'E to 57°20'E.

En'di·cott (ĕn'dĭ·kŭt) village, S New York, W of Binghamton; pop. 20,100.

En'field (ĕn'fēld) 1 town, N Connecticut, on Connecticut river on Massachusetts border; pop. 15,500. 2 urban district, SE England, in Middlesex N of London; pop. 110,500.

En'ga·dine (ĕng'gà·dēn) valley of the Inn river, E Switzerland, in Graubünden canton; 60 m. long.

En·ga'ño, Cape (ĕn·gä'nyō) cape, Philippine Is., at NE tip of Luzon; naval battle nearby 1944.

Eng'land (ĭng'glănd), Lat. An'gli·a (ăng'glĭ·à) country, S Great Britain; a division of the United Kingdom of Great Britain and Northern Ireland; ✳ London; area 51,356 sq. m.; pop. 41,572,600. See ENGLISH, in Vocab.

En'gle·wood (ĕng'g'l·wood) 1 city, NE cen. Colorado, S of Denver; pop. 16,900. 2 city, NE New Jersey, E of Paterson; pop. 23,100.

English Channel, often the Channel, Fr. La Manche (là mänsh') strait between S England and N France.

E'nid (ē'nĭd) city, N Oklahoma; pop. 36,000.

Enisei. See YENISEI.

E·ni'we·tok (ĕ·nē'wĕ·tŏk; popularly ĕn'ĭ·wē'tŏk) island, NW Marshall Is.; an atoll; since 1947 a proving ground for atomic weapons.

En Nasira. See NAZARETH.

En Nîl. See NILE.

Enns (ĕns; Angl. ĕnz) river, cen. Austria, flowing E and N from Styria into the Danube; 160 m. long.

En'sche·de' (ĕn'skĕ·dā') commune, E Netherlands, near German frontier; pop. 101,000.

En·teb'be (ĕn·tĕb'ĕ) town, E Africa, ✳ of Uganda, on N shore of Lake Victoria.

Eolie, Isole. See LIPARI ISLANDS.

Eph'e·sus (ĕf'ê·sŭs) ancient city, W Asia Minor, in Ionia near coast; one of the 12 Ionian Cities. See EPHESIANS, in Vocab.

E'phra·im (ē'frà·ĭm; ē'frĭ·ăm) 1 region, Palestine, N of Judaea; hilly country, sometimes called Mount Ephraim. 2 See ISRAEL.

E·pi'rus or E·pei'rus (ê·pī'rŭs), Mod. Gr. Ī'pi·ros (ē'pê·rŏs) region, NW Greece, bordering on Ionian Sea; once an independent kingdom and later (c. 200 B.C.) a republic.

Ep'ping (ĕp'ĭng) urban district, SE England, in Essex NE of London, on N edge of Epping Forest; pop. 6900.

Ep'som (ĕp'sŭm) town, S England, SW of London, just N of Epsom Downs (racecourse); part of Epsom and Ew'ell (ū'ĕl) municipal borough; pop. 68,000.

Er'bil (ĭr'bĭl) or Ar'bil (ĭr'bĭl), anc. Ar·be'la (är·bē'là) city, N Iraq; not scene of battle of Arbela, which was fought at Gaugamela, about 32 m. to the W.

Er·ci'yas' Da·ğ' (ĕr'jĕ·yäs' dä·ĭ') mountain, cen. Turkey; 12,848 ft. high.

Erevan. See YEREVAN.

Er'furt (ĕr'foort; -fērt) city, E Germany; pop. 174,600.

E'rie (ēr'ĭ) city, NW Pennsylvania, on Lake Erie; pop. 130,800.

Erie, Lake, lake, E cen. North America, between Canada and the United States; one of the Great Lakes; 241 m. long; area 9940 sq. m.

Erie Canal, canal, N New York, from Hudson river at Albany to Lake Erie at Buffalo; built 1817–25; now superseded by New York State Barge Canal.

Er'in (ĕr'ĭn; ēr'ĭn) Ireland; — now a poetic name.

Er·i·tre'a (ĕr'ĭ·trē'à) country, NE Africa, bordering on Red Sea N of Ethiopia; ✳ Asmara; area 46,000 sq. m.; pop. 1,000,000; before World War II an Italian dependency; federated with Ethiopia 1952. — Er·i·tre'an, adj.

Erivan. See YEREVAN.

Er Rif or Er Riff (ĕr rĭf') mountainous region, N Morocco, on coast in former Spanish zone. See RIFF, in Vocab.

Erz Ge·bir'ge (ĕrts' gĕ·bĭr'gĕ; ärts'), Eng. Erz Mountains (ĕrts') mountain range, Germany and Czechoslovakia, on border between Saxony and Bohemia.

Er'zu·rum' (ĕr'zū·room'; ĕrz·room'; ûr'zŭ-; ûrz-) city, NE Turkey, in mountains of W Turkish Armenia; pop. 54,400.

Es'ca·lan'te (ās'kä·län'tā) municipality, Philippine Is., in Negros on coast; pop. 60,200.

Es'ca·na'ba (ĕs'kà·nä'bà) city, Michigan, on Little Bay de Noc; pop. 15,200.

Escaut. See SCHELDE.

Escorial, El. See EL ESCORIAL.

Es'dra·e'lon (ĕz'drà·ē'lŏn; -drà-) plain, N Palestine, in valley of Qishon river.

E'sher (ē'shēr) urban district, S England, in Surrey; pop. 51,200.

Esh Sham. 1 See DAMASCUS. 2 See SYRIA.

Es'kils·tu'na (ĕs'kĭls·tōō'nä) city, SE Sweden; pop. 52,700.

Es'ki·şe·hir' (ĕs'kê·shĕ·hēr') or Es'ki·shehr' (ĕs'kê·shēr'h'r) city, W cen. Turkey, on tributary of Sakarya river; pop. 88,500.

España. See SPAIN.

Española. See HISPANIOLA.

Es·pí'ri·to San'to (ĕsh·pē'rē·tōō săn'tōō) state, E Brazil, on coast N of Rio de Janeiro state; ✳ Vitória; area 16,543 sq. m.; pop. 871,000.

Es·pí'ri·tu San'to (ås·pē'rē·tōō sän'tō) island, New Hebrides, in NW part of group; 76 m. long by 45 m. wide; 1875 sq. m.; pop. 7200.

Esquiline. See in Vocab.

Es·qui'malt (ĕs·kwī'môlt) seaport, W Canada, in British Columbia, in SE Vancouver I. W of Victoria; naval station.

Es'sen (ĕs'n) city, W Germany, in the Ruhr; pop. 605,100.

Es'se·qui'bo (ĕs'ê·kwē'bō) river, British Guiana; rises on Brazilian border, flows N into Atlantic Ocean through wide estuary; 600 m. long.

Es'sex (ĕks; -ĭks) county, SE England, bordering on North Sea and N shore of the Thames; ✳ Chelmsford; area 1528 sq. m.; pop. 2,043,600.

Ess'ling (ĕs'lĭng) village, Austria, near Vienna and Aspern; battle 1809.

Ess'lin·gen (ĕs'lĭng·ĕn) city, W Germany, on Neckar river SE of Stuttgart; pop. 64,900.

Es Sur. See TYRE.

Es'tes Park (ĕs'tĕz) valley, N Colorado, in Front Range in Rocky Mountain National Park.

Es·to'ni·a (ĕs·tō'nĭ·à; -tōn'yà), less correctly Es·tho'ni·a (ĕs·tō'nĭ·à; -tōn'yà; -thō'-; -thŏn'-), Estonian Ees'ti (ās'tĭ) country, N Europe, bordering on Baltic Sea; one of Baltic Provinces of Russia 1721–1917, independent republic 1918–40; since 1940 a constituent republic of the U.S.S.R. and called officially the Estonian Soviet Socialist Republic; ✳ Tallin; area 18,361 sq. m.; pop. 1,120,000. — Es·to'ni·an, Es·tho'ni·an, adj. & n.

Es'tre·ma·du'ra (ĕs'trĕ·mà·dōō'rà) 1 old province, W Portugal; ✳ Lisbon. 2 or Ex'tre·ma·du'ra (ĕks'trĕ-; ĕks'trĕ-) region, W cen. Spain, on Portuguese border.

E·thi·o'pi·a (ē'thĭ·ō'pĭ·à) 1 ancient country, NE Africa, bordering on Red Sea; included S Egypt, E Anglo-Egyptian Sudan, Eritrea, and N (modern) Ethiopia. 2 or Ab'ys·sin'i·a (ăb'ĭ·sĭn'ĭ·à; -sĭn'yà) country, E Africa; kingdom (or empire, nominally, from union of ancient kingdoms); ✳ Addis Ababa; area 350,000 sq. m.; pop. 9,450,000. See ERITREA. — E·thi·o'pi·an, adj. & n.

Et'na (ĕt'nà), Lat. Aet'na (ĕt'nà) volcano, Italy, in NE Sicily near the coast; destructive eruptions 1169, 1693, and 1832; 10,741 ft. high.

Et'on (ē't'n) urban district, SE cen. England, in Buckinghamshire, on the Thames; Eton College. See ETONIAN, in Vocab.

E·tru'ri·a (ê·trōō'rĭ·à) ancient country, cen. Italy, covering region now comprising Tuscany and part of Umbria. See ETRURIAN, ETRUSCAN, in Vocab.

Et'trick Forest (ĕt'rĭk) former forest and hunting ground, SE Scotland; now a pastoral region.

Eu·boe'a (ū·bē'à), Mod. Gr. Év'voi·a (ā'vyä), Ital. Ne·gro·pon'te (nä·grô·pōn'tä), Eng. Neg'ro·pont (nĕg'rô·pōnt) island, E Greece, in Aegean Sea NE of Attica and Boeotia; ✳ Chalcis; 90 m. long.

Eu'clid (ū'klĭd) city, N Ohio, adjoining Cleveland; pop. 41,400.

Eu·ga'ne·an Hills (ū·gā'nê·ăn; ū'gà·nē'ăn) range of hills, NE Italy, in Venetia between Padua and the Adige river; highest 1978 ft.

Eu·gene' (ū·jēn') city, W Oregon, on Willamette river; pop. 35,900.

Eu·phra'tes (ū·frā'tēz), Arab. Al Fu·rāt' (ăl fōō·rät') river, SW Asia, flowing from E Turkey to Persian Gulf; unites with the Tigris in Iraq to form the Shatt-al-Arab; 1700 m. long.

Eu·re'ka (ū·rē'kà) city, NW California, on Humboldt Bay; pop. 23,100.

Eu'rope (ū'rŭp) continent, Eastern Hemisphere; with Asia, forms one land mass often called Eur·a'sia (ūr·ā'zhà; -shà); area of Europe 3,800,000 sq. m. See EUROPEAN, EURASIAN, in Vocab.

Eu'taw Springs (ū'tô) locality, South Carolina; battle 1781.

Euxine Sea. See BLACK SEA.

Ev'ans·ton (ĕv'ăn·stŭn; -ănz·tŭn) city, NE Illinois; pop. 73,600.

Ev'ans·ville (ĕv'ănz·vĭl) city, SW Indiana, on Ohio river; pop. 128,600.

Ev'er·est, Mount (ĕv'ēr·ĕst; -ĭst), Tibetan Cho'mo·lung'ma (chō'mô·lōōng'mä) mountain, Asia, on border between Nepal and Tibet in the Himalayas; highest known in the world, 29,028 ft.

Ev'er·ett (ĕv'ēr·ĕt; -ĭt) 1 city, E Massachusetts, N of Boston; pop. 46,000. 2 city, Washington, on Puget Sound; pop. 33,800.

Ev'er·glades, the (ĕv'ēr·glādz) swamp region, S Florida, S of Lake Okeechobee; S part wilderness, set aside as national park 1947.

Eve'sham (ēv'shăm; ē'shăm; ē'săm) municipal borough, W cen. England, in Worcestershire; battle 1265.

Évros. See MARITSA.

Ex'e·ter (ĕk'sê·tēr) city and county borough, SW England, ✳ of Devonshire, on the Exe; pop. 75,500.

Ex'moor (ĕks'mōōr; -mōōr') moorland, SW England, in Somersetshire.

Extremadura. See ESTREMADURA, Spain.

By'lau (ī'lou) town, East Prussia, since 1945 in the U.S.S.R. on Polish border S of Kaliningrad; battle 1807.

Eyre, Lake (âr) lake bed, South Australia, a salt pan 39 to 60 ft. below sea level; usually dry, occasionally floods, as in 1950.

Eyre Peninsula, peninsula, S South Australia, W of Spencer Gulf.

F

Fa·en'za (fä·ĕn'tsä; Angl. -ĕn'zȧ) commune, N Italy; pop. 47,200.

Faer'oes (fâr'ōz), Dan. Faer'ö'er·ne (fâr'ṳ'ẽr·nĕ) island group, Atlantic Ocean, N of British Isles, belonging to Denmark; ✳ Thorshavn; 540 sq. m.; pop. 29,200. — Far'o·ese' (fâr'ȯ·ēz'; -ēs'), n. sing. & pl.

Faesulae. See FIESOLE.

Fa'id Pass (fä'ÿld) mountain pass, N Tunisia; battle 1943.

Fair'banks (fâr'băngks) town, cen. Alaska; pop. 5600.

Fair'field (fâr'fēld) town, SW Connecticut, on Long Island Sound; pop. 30,500.

Fair Lawn, borough, NE New Jersey, ENE of Paterson; pop. 23,900.

Fair'mont (fâr'mŏnt) city, N West Virginia; pop. 29,300.

Fair Oaks, locality, Virginia, just E of Richmond; battlefield (called also Seven Pines), May 31–June 1, 1862.

Fair'weath'er, Mount (fâr'wĕth'ẽr) mountain, Alaska-Canada border; highest point (over 15,300 ft.) in Fairweather Range.

Faiyûm, El. See EL FAIYÛM.

Faiz'a·bad (fīz'ȧ·bäd) 1 town, NE Afghanistan; pop. 62,500. 2 city, N India, in Uttar Pradesh; includes Ayodhya; pop. 55,200.

Fa·ka·ra'va (fä'kȧ·rä'vȧ) atoll, Tuamotu Archipelago; chief village Rotoava.

Fako. See CAMEROON.

Fa·laise' (fȧ·lāz') town, NW France, SE of Caen; seat of dukes of Normandy; captured by Canadians 1944.

Fal'kirk (fôl'kûrk) burgh, Scotland, in Stirling co. ENE of Glasgow; pop. 37,500.

Falk'land Islands (fôk'lănd; fôlk'-) island group, South Atlantic Ocean, 300 m. E of S end of Argentina; British crown colony; ✳ Port Stanley; area 4618 sq. m.; pop. 2300.

Falkland Islands Dependencies, islands and territories in South Atlantic Ocean and in Antarctica administered by the British from the Falkland Is., including South Georgia I., the South Orkney and South Sandwich Is., the Palmer Penin., and Palmer Archipelago.

Fall River (fôl) city, SE Massachusetts; pop. 112,000.

False Bay (fôls) bay, Union of South Africa, on SW coast of Cape Province E of Cape of Good Hope.

Fal'ster (fäl'stẽr) island, Denmark, S of island of Sjælland.

Fa'ma·gu'sta (fä'mȧ·gōōs'tȧ) seaport, E Cyprus, on Famagusta Bay.

Fan'ning Island (făn'ĭng) island, Line Is., lat. 4°N.

Fare'well', Cape (fâr'wĕl') the S tip of Greenland.

Far'go (fär'gō) city, SE North Dakota, on Red river; pop. 38,300.

Far'i·bault (fâr'ĭ·bō) city, S Minnesota; pop. 16,000.

Far'oe Islands (fâr'ō), also Far'oes (-ōz) the Faeroes.

Fars (färs) or Far'si·stan' (fär'sĕ·stän') province, SW Iran, corresponding closely with ancient Per'sis (pûr'sĭs); ✳ Shiraz.

Farther India. See INDOCHINA.

Fas. See FÈS.

Fashoda. See KODOK.

Fá'ti·ma (fá'tē·mȧ) village, cen. Portugal, NE of Lisbon; shrine of the Virgin (Our Lady of Fátima).

Fatshan. See NAMHOI.

Fa·yal' (fȧ·yäl') island, cen. Azores; 64 sq. m.; pop. 19,000.

Fay'ette·ville (fā'ĕt·vĭl) 1 city, NW Arkansas; pop. 17,100. 2 city, S cen. North Carolina, on Cape Fear river; pop. 34,700.

Fayum, El. See EL FAIYÛM.

Fear, Cape (fẽr) cape, North Carolina, on Smith I. at mouth of Cape Fear river.

Fe·da'la (fĕ·dä'lä) town, NW Morocco, on coast NE of Casablanca; one of landing places of American troops Nov. 7, 1942.

Federal Capital Territory. See AUSTRALIAN CAPITAL TERRITORY.

Federal District, Span. Dis·tri'to Fe'de·ral' (dĕs·trē'tŏ fā'thā·räl'), Port. Dis·tri'to Fe'de·ral' (dĕsh·trē'tōō fā'thĕ·räl') 1 or Federal Capital, Span. Ca'pi·tal' Federal (kä'pē·täl' fā'thā·räl') district, E Argentina, including city of Buenos Aires; area 74 sq. m.; pop. 3,000,400. 2 district, E Brazil, including city of Rio de Janeiro; area 451 sq. m.; pop. 2,413,200. 3 district, cen. Mexico, including Mexico City; area 573 sq. m.; pop. 2,942,600. 4 district, N Venezuela, including city of Caracas; area 745 sq. m.; pop. 700,100.

Federated Ma·lay' States (mȧ·lā'; mā'lā) the Malay states of Pahang, Perak, Selangor, and Negri Sembilan 1895–1945.

Federated Shan States. See SHAN STATE.

Federation of Malaya. See MALAYA, FEDERATION OF.

Feng'kieh' (fŭng'jĭ·ĕ') or Kwei'chow' (gwā'jō') city, S cen. China, in E Szechwan on Yangtze river at head of Yangtze Gorges; pop. 250,000.

Fengtien. 1 See LIAONING. 2 See MUKDEN.

Fen'no·scan'di·a or Fen'no-Scan'di·a (fĕn'ȯ·skăn'dĭ·ȧ) Finland and Scandinavia (Norway, Sweden, and Denmark).

Fens, the (fĕnz), also Fen Country (fĕn) low-lying districts, E England, esp. in Lincolnshire near shores of the Wash; once marshland.

Fer·ga'na or Fer·gha'na (fĕr·gä'nȧ) region, Soviet Central Asia, in Uzbek S.S.R. and Kirgiz S.S.R.

Fer·man'agh (fẽr·măn'ȧ) county, SW Northern Ireland; ✳ Enniskillen; 653 sq. m.; pop. 54,600.

Fer·nan'do de No·ro'nha (fẽr·năn'dōō the nōō·rō'nyȧ) island, Brazil, in Atlantic Ocean 300 m. NE of Natal; area 7 sq. m.; pop. 600.

Fer·nan'do Po'o (fẽr·năn'dō pō'ō) or Fer·nan'do Po (fẽr·năn'dō pō') island, Spanish Guinea, in Bight of Biafra; contains Santa Isabel, ✳ of Spanish Guinea.

Fern'dale (fûrn'dāl) city, SE Michigan, N of Detroit; pop. 29,700.

Fer·ra'ra (fĕ·rä'rȧ) commune, N Italy, in Emilian Plain near the Po; pop. 137,800.

Ferro. See HIERRO.

Ferrol, El. See EL FERROL.

Fès (fĕs) or Fez (fĕz), Arab. Fas (fäs) city, N cen. Morocco; one of sacred cities of Islam; pop. 202,000.

Fez·zan' (fĕ·zän') region, SW Libya, comprising mostly desert; one of three chief divisions of independent Libya; ✳ Sebha.

Fie'so·le (fyā'zō·lā), anc. Fae'su·lae (fē'zṳ·lē) town, cen. Italy, NE of Florence; ancient Etruscan town.

Fife (fīf) or Fife'shire (fīf'shĭr; -shẽr) county, E Scotland, between firths of Tay and Forth; ✳ Cupar; area 505 sq. m.; pop. 306,900.

Fi'ji (fē'jē; -jē) or Fiji Islands, island group, SW Pacific Ocean, lying across 180th meridian; over 250 islands (80 inhabited), constituting, with Rotuma, a British colony, ✳ Suva (on Viti Levu I.); area 7083 sq. m.; pop. 220,800. — Fi·ji'an (fē·jē'ăn; fē'jē·ăn), adj. & n.

Finch'ley (fĭnch'lĭ) municipal borough, SE England, in Middlesex NW of London; pop. 70,000.

Find'lay (fĭn'lĭ; fĭnd'lĭ) city, NW Ohio; pop. 23,800.

Fin'gal's Cave (fĭng'gȧlz) cave, Scotland, on Staffa I., Inner Hebrides.

Fin'ger Lakes (fĭng'gẽr) group of long narrow lakes, W New York, including lakes Seneca, Cayuga, Keuka, Canandaigua, Owasco, and Skaneateles.

Fin'is·terre', Cape (fĭn'ĭs·târ'; Span. fē'nĕs·tĕr'rĕ) cape, NW Spain, westernmost point of Spanish mainland, in 9°18'W long.

Fin'land (fĭn'lănd), Finnish Suo'mi (swô'mĭ) or Suo'men Ta'sa·val'ta (swô'mĕn tä'sä·väl'tä) country, N Europe, bordering on Gulf of Bothnia; republic; ✳ Helsinki; area 130,165 sq. m.; pop. 3,887,200. See FINN, FINNISH, in Vocab.

Finland, Gulf of, arm of Baltic Sea S of Finland and N of Estonia.

Fin'lay (fĭn'lĭ) river, Canada, in N British Columbia, flowing S to unite with Parsnip river and form Peace river; 250 m. long.

Fin'ster·aar'horn (fĭn'stẽr·är'hôrn) peak, S Switzerland, highest of the Bernese Alps, 14,026 ft.

Firenze. See FLORENCE, Italy.

Firth of Clyde; Firth of Forth. See CLYDE; FORTH.

Fitch'burg (fĭch'bûrg) city, cen. Massachusetts; pop. 42,700.

Fiume. See RIJEKA.

Fiumicino. See RUBICON.

Five Forks, locality, SE Virginia, just SW of Petersburg; battle 1865.

Flag'staff' (flăg'stàf') city, N Arizona; Lowell Observatory; pop. 7700.

Flam'bor'ough Head (flăm'bûr'ō; Brit. -bŭ·rȧ, -brȧ) promontory, N England, on E coast of Yorkshire.

Flan'ders (flăn'dẽrz; Brit. usu. flän'-), Fr. Flan'dre (flän'dr'), Flemish Vlaan'de·ren (vlän'dẽ·rĕ[n]) region, W Belgium and N France, bordering on the North Sea; once a county, ✳ Lille. See FLEMING, FLEMISH, in Vocab.

Flat'ter·y, Cape (flăt'ẽr·ĭ) cape, NW Washington, on S side of entrance to Juan de Fuca Strait.

Flens'burg (flĕns'bŏŏrk; Angl. flĕnz'bûrg) city, W Germany, in S Schleswig near Danish border on inlet of Baltic Sea; pop. 102,000.

Fletsch'horn' (flĕch'hôrn') or Ross'bo'den·horn' (rōs'bō'dĕn·hôrn') mountain, S Switzerland, S of Simplon Pass; 13,127 ft. high.

Fleu'rus' (flû'rüs') town, SW Belgium; battle 1794.

Flin'ders (flĭn'dẽrz) river, Australia, in N Queensland, flowing NW to Gulf of Carpentaria; 500 m. long.

Flinders Ranges, mountain ranges, E South Australia.

Flin Flon (flĭn' flŏn') town, Canada, in NW Manitoba; pop. 10,200.

Flint (flĭnt) 1 river, W Georgia, flowing S to unite with the Chattahoochee and form the Apalachicola river; 265 m. long. 2 city, SE cen. Michigan; pop. 163,100. 3 county of Wales: see FLINTSHIRE.

Flint'shire (flĭnt'shĭr; -shẽr) or Flint, county, NE Wales; ✳ Mold; 256 sq. m.; pop. 145,100.

Flod'den (flŏd'n) hill, N England, in N Northumberland near Scottish border; site of battle (also known as Flodden Field) Sept. 9, 1513.

Flor'ence (flôr'ĕns) 1 city, NW Alabama, on Tennessee river; pop. 23,900. 2 city, E South Carolina; pop. 22,500. 3 Ital. Fi·ren'ze (fē·rĕn'tsä) commune, cen. Italy, in Tuscany on Arno river; pop. 384,800. — Flor'en·tine (flôr'ĕn·tēn; -tīn), adj. & n.

Flo'res (flō'rĕs; -ĕz; flôr'-) 1 island, NW Azores; area 57 sq. m.; pop. ab. 7000. 2 island, Indonesia, in Lesser Sunda Is.; area 5500 sq. m.; pop. 500,000.

Flo'ri·a·nó'po·lis (flôr'ĭ·ȧ·nŏp'ȯ·lĭs), formerly Des·têr'ro (dĕsh·târ'rōō) city, S Brazil, ✳ of Santa Catarina state; pop. 49,300.

Flor'i·da (flôr'ĭ·dȧ), abbr. Fla., state, SE United States, comprising chiefly a peninsula between Atlantic Ocean and Gulf of Mexico; ✳ Tallahassee; area 58,560 sq. m.; pop. 2,771,300. — Flo·rid'i·an (flȯ·rĭd'ĭ·ăn), Flor'i·dan (flôr'ĭ·dăn), adj. & n.

Florida, Straits of (flôr'ĭ·dȧ), also Florida Strait, channel between Florida Keys (S end of Florida) and N coast of Cuba.

Florida Island (flôr'ĭ·dȧ; flō·rē'dȧ) or N'·Ge'la ('ng·gä'lä) island, SE Solomon Is., N of cen. Guadalcanal.

Florida Keys (flôr'ĭ·dȧ) chain of islands off S tip of Florida.

Flush'ing (flŭsh'ĭng) 1 section of New York City, on Long I. in Queens borough; formerly (before 1898) a village; includes Flushing Meadow, site of N.Y. World's Fair 1939–40 and of headquarters of United Nations 1946–51. 2 seaport, Netherlands: see VLISSINGEN.

Fly (flī) river, New Guinea, flowing into Gulf of Papua; 650 m. long.

Foc·şa'ni (fōk·shän'; -shä'nĕ) city, E cen. Romania, in S Moldavia; battles 1789, 1917; pop. 32,800.

Fog'gia (fôd'jä) commune, SE Italy, in Apulia; pop. 86,400.

Folke'stone (fōk'stŭn) municipal borough, SE England, in Kent on Strait of Dover WSW of Dover; pop. 45,200.

Fond du Lac (fŏn' dŭ lăk') city, E Wisconsin, at S end of Lake Winnebago; pop. 29,900.

Fon·se'ca, Gulf of (fŏn·sā'kä), or Fonseca Bay, inlet of Pacific Ocean, Central America, in El Salvador, Honduras, and Nicaragua.

Fon'taine·bleau (fôn't'n·blō; -tĭn-) commune, N France, SSE of Paris; château, former residence of kings of France; pop. 15,000.

Fon'te·noy' (fônt'nwä') 1 town, SW Belgium, ESE of Tournai; battle 1745. 2 formerly Fon'ta'net' (fôn'tà'nĕ') town, NE cen. France, S of Sens; battle 841.

Foo'chow' (fōō'jō') or Min'how' (mĭn'hō') seaport, China, ✳ of Fukien prov.; pop. 322,700.

For'a·ker, Mount (fôr'ȧ·kẽr; -ĭ·kẽr) mountain, S Alaska, in Alaska Range SW of Mt. McKinley; over 17,000 ft. high.

Forbidden City, 1 Lhasa, Tibet. 2 walled enclosure, Peiping, China, containing the Imperial Palace.

Forest Cantons, the Four, Uri, Schwyz, Unterwalden, and Lucerne cantons, Switzerland, surrounding Lake of Lucerne.

Forest Hill, village, Canada, in SE Ontario near Toronto; pop. 19,500.

Forest Hills, section of New York City, on Long I. in Queens borough; scene of national lawn tennis (grass-court) tournaments.

Forest Park, village, NE Illinois, suburb of Chicago; pop. 15,000.

For'far (fôr'fẽr) 1 or **For'far·shire** (-shĭr; -shẽr) county of Scotland: see ANGUS. 2 burgh, E Scotland, ✻ of Angus co.; pop. 10,000.
For·lì' (fôr·lē') commune, N Italy, in Emilia; pop. 74,800.
For·mo'sa (fôr·mō'sȧ) or **Tai·wan** (tī·wän) island, SE China, in China Sea off Fukien prov.; belonged to Japan 1895–1945; ✻ Taipeh; area 13,900 sq. m.; pop. (1950; with Pescadores) 6,384,600. — **For·mo'san**, adj. & n.
Fort Al'ba·ny (ôl'bȧ·nĭ) trading post, N Canada, in Ontario on James Bay at mouth of Albany river; established about 1670.
For'ta·le'za (fôr'tȧ·lā'zȧ), sometimes called **Ce'a·rá'** (sā'ȧ·rä') seaport, NE Brazil, ✻ of Ceará state; pop. 213,600.
Fort Bridg'er (brĭj'ẽr) village, SW Wyoming, near site of trading post built 1843 by James Bridger on Oregon Trail.
Fort Brown (broun) military reservation, S Texas, just E of Brownsville; fort established 1846.
Fort de Châ'til'lon' (fôr' dē shä'tē'yôɴ'). See CHÂTILLON.
Fort-de-France (fôr'dē·fräɴs') city, French West Indies, ✻ of Martinique, on SW coast of island; pop. 52,100.
Fort de Kock. See BUKITTINGGI.
Fort Dodge (fōrt dŏj) city, N cen. Iowa; pop. 25,100.
Fort Don'el·son (dŏn''l·s'n) former fort, NW Tennessee, on Cumberland river; captured by Grant 1862; site now a national military park, established 1928.
Fort Duquesne. See FORT PITT.
Fort Fish'er (fĭsh'ẽr) fort, SE North Carolina, near Cape Fear.
Fort Fred'er·i'ca (frĕd'ẽr·ē'kȧ; frĕd·rē'kȧ) fort, Georgia, on Saint Simon I.; built by Oglethorpe 1736; made a national monument 1945.
Forth (fōrth) river, S cen. Scotland; 114 m. long; flows E into **Firth of Forth**, an estuary extending inland 48 m. from North Sea.
Fort Hen'ry (hĕn'rĭ) fort, NW Tennessee, on Tennessee river, which was taken by Grant 1862; now only a commemorative site.
Fort Knox (nŏks) military reservation, N cen. Kentucky; location (since 1936) of U.S. Gold Bullion Depository.
Fort-La'my' (fôr'lá'mē') town, N French Equatorial Africa, ✻ of Chad territory, on Chari river; pop. 6000.
Fort Lau'der·dale (fōrt lô'dẽr·dāl) city, SE Florida; pop. 36,300.
Fort Leav'en·worth (lĕv'ĕn·wûrth) military reservation, E Kansas, adjoining Leavenworth; federal penitentiary.
Fort Mc·Hen'ry (mȧk·hĕn'rĭ; mȧ·kĕn'rĭ) fort, Maryland, at Baltimore; bombarded by the British 1814, the occasion of writing of Star-Spangled Banner; national monument and historic shrine.
Fort Mad'i·son (măd'ĭ·s'n) city, SE Iowa, on Mississippi river; pop. 15,000.
Fort Marion National Monument. See CASTILLO DE SAN MARCOS NATIONAL MONUMENT.
Fort Meigs (mĕgz) former fort, NW Ohio, at rapids in Maumee river; besieged unsuccessfully May 1–9, 1813, by British and Indians.
Fort Mims (mĭmz) temporary stockade, Alabama, near junction of Alabama and Tombigbee rivers; massacre Creek Indians Aug. 30, 1813.
Fort, or **Fortress, Mon·roe'** (mŭn·rō') military post, SE Virginia, at entrance to Hampton Roads.
Fort Moul'trie (mōōl'trĭ) fort, South Carolina, in Charleston harbor.
Fort Ni·ag'a·ra (nī·ăg'ȧ·rȧ; -ăg'rȧ) fort, New York, at mouth of Niagara river.
Fort Or'ange (ŏr'ĕnj; -ĭnj) Dutch fort, New York, on site of Albany.
Fort Pick'ens (pĭk'ĕnz) fort, Florida, on island at entrance to Pensacola harbor.
Fort Pitt (pĭt), before 1758 called **Fort Du·quesne'** (dōō·kān') fort, W Pennsylvania, on site of Pittsburgh; built by the French, captured by the British 1758.
Fort Prov'i·dence or **Providence** (prŏv'ĭ·dĕns) trading post, NW Canada, on Mackenzie river at its outlet from Great Slave Lake.
Fort Pu·las'ki (pū·lăs'kĭ; pŭ-) fort, Georgia, on island in mouth of Savannah river; built 1829–47; made a national monument 1924.
Fortress Monroe. See FORT MONROE.
Fort Simp'son or **Simpson** (sĭm[p]'s'n) trading post, NW Canada, on Mackenzie river where it is joined by the Liard.
Fort Slo'cum (slō'kŭm) military station, New York, on Davids I. in Long Island Sound, near New Rochelle, New York.
Fort Smith (smĭth) city, W Arkansas, on Arkansas river; pop. 47,900.
Fort Sum'ter (sŭm'tẽr) fort, South Carolina, at entrance to Charleston harbor; object of Confederate attack April 12–13, 1861, which began Civil War; established as national monument 1948.
Fort Wayne (wān) city, NE Indiana; pop. 133,600.
Fort Wil'liam (wĭl'yăm) city, Canada, in SW Ontario, on Lake Superior near Port Arthur; pop. 39,500.
Fort Worth (wûrth) city, N Texas, on Trinity river; pop. 278,800.
Foth'er·in·ghay' (fŏth'ẽr·ĭng·gā'; fŏth'rĭng-) village, England, in Northamptonshire; castle where Mary, Queen of Scots, was imprisoned Sept. 1586 to Feb. 8, 1587.
Four Forest Cantons, Lake of the. See LUCERNE, LAKE OF.
Four Forest Cantons, the. See FOREST CANTONS, THE FOUR.
Fow'liang' (fōō'lē·äng'; fō'-), formerly **King'teh'chen'** (jĭng'dŭ'jŭn') town, SE China, in NE Kiangsi prov.; pop. over 100,000.
Foxe Basin (fŏks), formerly **Fox Basin** (fŏks) body of water, N Canada, N of Hudson Bay and W of Baffin I.
Fox Islands (fŏks) island group, SW Alaska, in E Aleutian Is.
Foynes (foinz) town, SW Ireland, on Shannon estuary W of Limerick; former airfield, now superseded by Shannon.
Fra'ming·ham (frā'mĭng·hăm) town, E Massachusetts; pop. 28,100.
France (frăns) country, W Europe, bordering on English Channel and Mediterranean Sea; republic; ✻ Paris; area 212,655 sq. m.; pop. 40,502,500. See FRENCH, in Vocab.
Franche-Com'té' (fräɴsh'kôɴ'tā') region, E France, E of the Saône river; once constituted the Free County of Burgundy; formed a province of France 1678 to the Revolution; ✻ Besançon.
Fran·co'ni·a (frăng·kō'nĭ·ȧ; -kōn'yȧ), Ger. **Fran'ken** (främg'kĕn) 1 duchy of medieval Frankish dominions, in Austrasia (in S cen. modern Germany). 2 or **East Franconia**, after 12th cent., the eastern part of the old duchy. 3 after 1837, region, Bavaria, comprising districts of Upper, Middle, and Lower Franconia. — **Fran·co'ni·an** (frăng·kō'nĭ·ăn; -kōn'yăn), adj. & n.
Frank'fort (frăngk'fẽrt) 1 city, cen. Indiana; pop. 15,000. 2 city, ✻ of Kentucky, on Kentucky river; pop. 11,900. 3 see FRANKFURT.
Frank'furt (frăngk'fẽrt; Ger. frängk'fŏŏrt) 1 in full **Frankfurt am Main** (frängk'fŏŏrt äm mīn'), Eng. **Frank'fort on the Main** (frăngk'fẽrt; mān, mīn) city, W Germany, on Main river; pop. 523,900. 2 in full **Frankfurt an der O'der** (frängk'fŏŏrt än dẽr ō'dẽr), Eng. **Frankfort on the Oder** (frăngk'fẽrt, ō'dẽr) city, E Germany, on Oder river; pop. 51,600.
Frank'lin (frăngk'lĭn) district, N Canada, in Northwest Territories; includes Arctic islands and Boothia and Melville peninsulas.
Franklin D. Roo'se·velt Lake (dē' rō'zĕ·vĕlt; -vĕlt) lake, N cen. Washington, formed in Columbia river by Grand Coulee Dam; 151 m. long.
Franz Jo'sef Land (frănts jō'zĕf [-zĭf] lănd; Ger. fränts yō'zĕf länt) or **Fridt'jof Nan'sen Land** (frĭt'yôf nän'sĕn lănd) archipelago, N Soviet Russia, Europe, in Arctic Ocean N of Novaya Zemlya; ab. 70 islands, area 8000 sq. m.
Fra'ser (frā'zẽr; -zhẽr) river, W Canada, in S cen. British Columbia, flowing into Strait of Georgia just S of Vancouver; 700 m. long.
Fred'er·ick (frĕd'rĭk; -ẽr·ĭk) city, N Maryland; pop. 18,100.
Fred'er·icks·burg (frĕd'rĭks·bûrg; -ẽr·ĭks-) independent city, NE Virginia, on Rappahannock river; pop. 12,200.
Fredericksburg and Spot'syl·va'nia National Military Park (spŏt's'l·vān'yȧ; -vā'nĭ·ȧ) NE Virginia, including battlefields of Fredericksburg (1862), Chancellorsville, Spotsylvania Court House, and the Wilderness.
Fred'er·ic·ton (frĕd'rĭk·tŭn; -ẽr·ĭk-) city, SE Canada, ✻ of New Brunswick prov., on St. John river; pop. 18,300.
Fred'er·iks·berg (frĕd'rĭks·bûrg; frĕd'ẽr·ĭks-) city, Denmark, in Sjælland I., suburb of Copenhagen; pop. 113,600.
Free'port (frē'pōrt) 1 city, N Illinois; pop. 22,500. 2 village, SE New York, on Long I.; pop. 24,700.
Free Territory of Trieste. See TRIESTE.
Free'town' (frē'toun') seaport, W Africa, ✻ of Sierra Leone; pop. 80,000.
Frei'burg (frī'bŏŏrg; -bûrg; Ger. -bŏŏʀᴋ), also **Freiburg im Breis'gau** (ĭm brīs'gou) 1 city, W Germany, in Baden at W foot of Black Forest; pop. 109,800. 2 see FRIBOURG.
Fré'jus', Mas'sif' du (mȧ'sēf' dü frā'zhüs') mountain mass, on French-Italian border at SW end of Graian Alps; pierced by Mont Cenis Tunnel.
Fre·man'tle (frē·măn't'l) seaport, SW Western Australia, on Indian Ocean at mouth of Swan river; port for Perth.
Fre'mont (frē'mŏnt) city, N Ohio; pop. 16,500.
French Broad (frĕnch brôd) river, North Carolina and Tennessee, a headstream of the Tennessee river; 210 m. long.
French Equatorial Africa, formerly **French Congo**, country, W cen. Africa, N of Congo river, comprising a federation of French dependencies, including Gabon, Middle Congo, Ubangi-Shari, and Chad territories; ✻ Brazzaville; area 969,111 sq. m.; pop. 4,346,000.
French Guiana, Fr. **Guy'ane' fran'çaise'** (gü·ē'yȧn' fräɴ'sâz') country, N South America, bordering on Atlantic Ocean; an overseas department of France; ✻ Cayenne; area 34,740 sq. m.; pop. 37,000.
French Guinea, Fr. **Gui'née' fran'çaise'** (gē'nā' fräɴ'sâz') region, W Africa, bordering on Atlantic Ocean; formerly a territory of French West Africa, became an independent nation (**Guinea**) Oct. 1, 1958; ✻ Conakry; area 108,455 sq. m.; pop. 2,130,000.
French India, officially **É'ta'blisse'ments' fran'çais' dans l'Inde** (ā'tȧ'blēs'mäɴ' fräɴ'sĕ' däɴ lăɴd') former French possessions in India, including Chandernagore (to India 1950) and Pondichéry, Karikal, Yanaon, and Mahé (to India 1954); ✻ Pondichéry.
French Indochina. See INDOCHINA.
French'man, or **French'man's, Flat** (frĕnch'măn, -mănz) valley, S Nevada, 65 m. NW of Las Vegas; proving ground for atomic weapons.
French Morocco. See MOROCCO.
French Oceania, Fr. **É'ta'blisse'ments' (fran'çais') de l'O'cé'a'nie'** (ā'tȧ'blēs'mäɴ' [fräɴ'sĕ'] dē lô'sā'ȧ'nē') islands in South Pacific Ocean belonging to France, including Marquesas, Society, Gambier, and Tubuai Is. and Tuamotu Archipelago; ✻ Papeete, on Tahiti.
French Shore, the W and part of the N coast of Newfoundland; — so named in reference to the exclusive fishing rights (1713–1904) secured by France in the Treaty of Utrecht 1713.
French Somaliland, Fr. **Côte fran'çaise' des So'ma'lis'** (kōt'-fräɴ'sâz' dā sô'mȧ'lē') country, E Africa, on Gulf of Aden; a territory of France; ✻ Djibouti; area 8492 sq. m.; pop. 46,400.
French Sudan, Fr. **Sou'dan' fran'çais'** (sōō'däɴ' fräɴ'sĕ') region, W Africa; one of the territories of French West Africa; ✻ Bamako; area 461,389 sq. m.; pop. 3,137,000.
French Togo. See TOGO.
French Union, Fr. **U'nion' fran'çaise'** (ü'nyôɴ' fräɴ'sâz') the French Republic with its overseas departments, territories, and associated states, as reorganized under the Constitution 1946.
French West Africa, country, W Africa; a federation of French territories: Mauritania, French Sudan, Senegal, French Guinea, Ivory Coast, Dahomey, Upper Volta, and Niger; ✻ Dakar; area 1,805,287 sq. m.; pop. 16,375,000.
French West Indies, the islands of the West Indies belonging to France, including Guadeloupe, Martinique, Désirade, Les Saintes, Marie Galante, Saint Barthélemy, and part of Saint Martin.
Fres'no (frĕz'nō) city, S cen. California; pop. 91,700.
Fri'bourg (frē'bōōr; Fr. frē'bōōr'), Ger. **Frei'burg** (frī'bŏŏrg; -bûrg; Ger. -bŏŏʀᴋ) 1 canton, W cen. Switzerland; area 647 sq. m.; pop. 158,700. 2 commune, its ✻, SW of Bern; pop. 29,000.
Fridtjof Nansen Land. See FRANZ JOSEF LAND.
Friedland. See PRAVDINSK.
Friendly Islands. See TONGA ISLANDS.
Fries'land (frēz'lănd; -lănd'; frēs'-) 1 historical region, N Europe, bordering on North Sea. 2 province, N Netherlands, comprising part of the historical region; ✻ Leeuwarden.
Fri'sches Haff (frĭsh'ĕs häf), Russ. **Fri'shes Gaf** (fryē'shĕs gäf') lagoon, Poland and U.S.S.R., an inlet of Gulf of Danzig.
Fri'sian Islands (frĭzh'ăn; frĭz'ĭ·ăn), Du. **Frie'sche Ei'lan'den** (frē'sĕ ī'län'dĕ[n]) chain of islands, N Europe, in North Sea off coasts of Denmark, Germany, and the Netherlands.

Fri′u·li (frē′ōō-lē; frē-ōō′lē) district, N Italy, on Yugoslav border; part of what was once the duchy of Friuli.

Fro′bish·er Bay (frō′bĭsh-ẽr; frŏb′ĭsh-) bay, N Canada, an inlet of Atlantic Ocean, on SE coast of Baffin I.

Front Range (frŭnt) range of Rocky Mts., N cen. Colorado; highest point Grays Peak, 14,274 ft.

Frun′ze (frōōn′zĕ), formerly **Pish·pek′** (pĭsh-pĕk′) city, Soviet Central Asia, ✳ of Kirgiz S.S.R., on Kazakh border; pop. 92,700.

Fu′ji (fōō′jĭ; fū′-) or **Fu·ji·ya′ma** (fōō′jĭ-yä′mä; fū′-), more correctly **Fu·ji-no-Ya·ma** (fōō-jē-nō-yä-mä) or **Fu·ji·san** (fōō-jē-sän) mountain, Japan, in S cen. Honshu; highest in Japan, 12,388 ft.

Fu′kien′, also **Fuh′kien′** (fōō′kyĕn′) province, SE China, on coast; ✳ Foochow; area 46,332 sq. m.; pop. 11,150,600.

Fu′ku·o′ka (fōō′kōō-ō′kȧ) seaport, Japan, in N Kyushu on Hakata Bay; pop. 328,500.

Fu′na·fu′ti (fōō′nȧ-fōō′tĭ; fū′nȧ-fū′tĭ) island, cen. Ellice Is.; an atoll; contains chief village of the group.

Fun·chal′ (fōōn-shäl′) seaport, Portugal, on Madeira I.; pop. 54,000.

Fun′dy, Bay of (fŭn′dĭ) inlet of Atlantic Ocean, SE Canada, extending between S New Brunswick and Nova Scotia; 145 m. long, 48 m. wide at its mouth; tide sometimes over 50 ft.

Fundy National Park, region, SE Canada, in New Brunswick on upper Bay of Fundy; established as national park 1948.

Fünen. See FYN.

Fünfkirchen. See PÉCS.

Fur′neaux Group (fûr′nō) island group, Australia, off NE Tasmania; area 1031 sq. m.; pop. 1000.

Fur Seal Islands. See PRIBILOF ISLANDS.

Fürth (fürt) city, W Germany, NW of Nürnberg; pop. 95,400.

Fusan. See PUSAN.

Fusen. See PUJON.

Fushih. See YENAN.

Fu′shun′ (fōō′shōōn′) town, S Manchuria; pop. (1953 est.) 700,000.

Fu·tu′na Islands (fōō-tōō′nä) island group, SW Pacific Ocean, NE of Fiji Is.; a dependency, with Wallis Is., of New Caledonia.

Fyn (fün), Ger. **Fü′nen** (fü′nĕn) island, Denmark, between island of Sjælland and Jutland penin.; 1149 sq. m.; pop. 298,700.

Fyz′a·bad. Var. of FAIZABAD.

G

Ga′bès (gä′bĕs; Fr. gȧ′bĕs′) seaport, SE Tunisia, on the **Gulf of Gabès**, anc. **Syr′tis Mi′nor** (sûr′tĭs mī′nẽr).

Ga′bon′ (gȧ′bôn′) or **Ga·bun′** (gȧ·bōōn′), Eng. **Ga·boon′** (gȧ·bōōn′) **1** river, S French Equatorial Africa, just N of the equator; has an estuary 7 m. wide extending ab. 40 m. inland. **2** region, French Equatorial Africa, around the Gabon river; an overseas territory of France; ✳ Libreville; area 103,089 sq. m.; pop. 423,000.

Gad′a·ra (găd′ȧ-rȧ) ancient town, Palestine, on SE shore of Sea of Galilee. — **Gad′a·rene′** (găd′ȧ-rēn′; găd′ȧ-rēn), adj. & n.

Gads′den (gădz′dĕn) city, NE Alabama, on Coosa river; pop. 55,700.

Gadsden Purchase, tract of land, 29,640 sq. m., S of Gila river in present Arizona and New Mexico, purchased 1853 by U.S. from Mexico.

Ga·e′ta (gä-ā′tä) seaport, cen. Italy, on **Gulf of Gaeta**, an inlet of Tyrrhenian Sea N of Bay of Naples; pop. 18,300.

Gaf′sa (găf′sä) oasis, W cen. Tunisia; prehistoric discoveries nearby.

Gail·lard′ Cut (gĭl-yärd′), formerly **Cu·le′bra Cut** (kū-lā′brä; -lĕb′rȧ) southeast section of Panama Canal, through Culebra Mountain.

Gaines′ Mill (gānz) battlefield, Virginia, just ENE of Richmond; scene of battle 1862 sometimes known as Cold Harbor.

Gaines′ville (gānz′vĭl) city, N Florida; pop. 26,900.

Ga·lá′pa·gos Islands (gȧ·lä′pȧ·gŭs; -lăp′ȧ-) or **Co·lón′ Archipelago** (kō·lōn′) island group, Ecuador, in Pacific Ocean on the equator 600 m. W of mainland; ✳ San Cristóbal; 3029 sq. m.; pop. 661.

Gal′a·ta (găl′ȧ-tä) section of Istanbul, Turkey; a seaport.

Ga·la′ti (gä-läts′; gä-lä′tsē) or **Ga′latz** (gä′läts) city, E Romania, on lower Danube; pop. 102,000.

Ga·la′ti·a (gȧ-lā′shĭ·ȧ; -shä) ancient country, cen. Asia Minor; settled by Gauls in 3d cent. B.C.; became Roman province 25 B.C. See GALATIANS, in Vocab.

Gales′burg (gālz′bûrg) city, W Illinois; pop. 31,400.

Ga·li′ci·a (gȧ·lĭsh′ĭ·ȧ) region, E cen. Europe, including N slopes of Carpathian Mts. and the valleys of upper Vistula, Dniester, Bug, and Seret rivers; part of Poland between World War I and World War II; now divided between Poland and the U.S.S.R.

Ga·li′ci·a (gȧ·lĭsh′ĭ·ȧ; -lĭsh′ä) region, NW Spain, bordering on Atlantic Ocean and Portugal; a kingdom A.D. 411–585. See GALICIAN, in Vocab.

Gal′i·lee (găl′ĭ·lē) region, N Palestine, in hills N of plain of Esdraelon. See 1st GALILEAN, in Vocab.

Galilee, or **Ti·be′ri·as** (tĭ-bēr′ĭ·ăs), **Sea of**, also **Lake of Gen·nes′a·ret** (gĕ-nĕs′ȧ-rĕt) and **Sea of Chin′ne·reth** (kĭn′ĕ-rĕth), Heb. **Yam Kin·ne′ret** (yäm′ kĭ-nĕ′rĕt) lake, N Israel, on Syrian border; 14 m. long; 686 ft. below sea level.

Gal′la (găl′ȧ), also **Gal′la·land′** (-lănd′) region, W Ethiopia; chief town Gambela.

Gal′la·tin Range (găl′ȧ·t′n; -tĭn) mountains, S Montana; highest point Electric Peak, 11,155 ft.

Gallia. See GAUL.

Gal·li′nas, Point (gä-yē′näs) cape, N Colombia; northernmost point of South America, in 12°15′N.

Gal·lip′o·li (gä·lĭp′ō·lĭ), Turk. **Ge′li·bo·lu′** (gĕ′lē·bô·lōō′) seaport, Turkey in Europe, on **Gallipoli Peninsula**, on the Dardanelles at entrance to Sea of Marmara; pop. 9900.

Gal′lo·way (găl′ō·wā) district, SW Scotland, comprising the counties of Wigtown and Kirkcudbright. — **Gal·we′gian** (găl·wē′jăn), adj. & n.

Galt (gôlt) city, Canada, in SE Ontario; pop. 23,700.

Gal′ves·ton (găl′vĕs·tŭn) city, SE Texas, on **Galveston Island** (30 m. long) at entrance to **Galveston Bay**; pop. 66,600.

Gal′way (gôl′wä) **1** county, W Ireland, in Connacht prov. bordering on Atlantic Ocean; area 2293 sq. m.; pop. 160,100. **2** municipal borough and seaport, its ✳; pop. 21,300.

Gam′bi·a (găm′bĭ·ȧ) **1** river, W Africa, flowing from French Guinea to Atlantic Ocean; 460 m. long. **2** region, W Africa, around lower 200 m. of Gambia river; constitutes a British protectorate, a small area near mouth of river being designated a colony; ✳ (of colony and protectorate) Bathurst; total area 4000 sq. m.; pop. 199,200.

Gam′bier Islands (găm′bẽr) island group, S Pacific Ocean, SE of Tuamotu Archipelago, belonging to France; chief island Mangareva.

Gand. See GENT.

Gan′dak (gŭn′dŭk) river, Nepal and N India, flowing to the Ganges; 400 m. long.

Gan′der (găn′dẽr) airport, Canada, in E Newfoundland on Gander Lake.

Gandzha. See KIROVABAD.

Gan′ges (găn′jēz), Sanskrit and Hind. **Gan′ga** (gŭng′gä) river, N India, flowing from the Himalayas S and SE to Bay of Bengal; merges with Brahmaputra river to form a vast delta; over 1550 m. long.

Gang′tok (gŭng′tŏk) town, NE India, ✳ of Sikkim.

Gan′nett Peak (găn′ĕt; -ĭt) mountain, cen. Wyoming, in Wind River Range; highest point in the state, 13,785 ft.

Gar′da, Lake (gär′dä) lake, N Italy, in E Lombardy; 35 m. long.

Gar·de′na (gär-dē′nä) city, SW California, S suburb of Los Angeles; pop. 14,400.

Garden of the Gods, region, Colorado, near Colorado Springs, noted for numerous rock formations of red and white sandstone.

Gard′ner (gärd′nẽr) city, cen. Massachusetts; pop. 19,600.

Gar′field (gär′fēld) city, NE New Jersey, E of Paterson; pop. 27,600.

Garfield Heights, city, N Ohio, SSE of Cleveland; pop. 21,700.

Ga′ri·glia′no (gä′rē·lyä′nō) river, cen. Italy, flowing to Gulf of Gaeta; 100 m. long.

Gar′misch-Par′ten·kir′chen (gär′mĭsh-pär′tĕn-kir′kĕn) town, W Germany, in Bavaria, in foothills of Bavarian Alps near Oberammergau; winter Olympics 1936; pop. 24,600.

Garmo Peak. See STALIN PEAK.

Ga·ronne′ (gȧ·rŏn′) river, SW France, flowing NW to unite with the Dordogne and form Gironde estuary; 355 m. long.

Gar′y (gâr′ĭ) city, NW Indiana, on Lake Michigan; pop. 133,900.

Gas′co·ny (găs′kō·nĭ), Fr. **Gas′cogne′** (gäs·kôn′y′) historical region, SW France; ✳ Auch. See GASCON, in Vocab.

Ga′sher·brum (gŭ′shẽr·brōōm) mountain, N Kashmir, in Karakoram Range just SE of Mt. Godwin Austen; 26,470 ft. high.

Gas·pé Peninsula (găs·pā′; gäs·pā′) peninsula, SE Canada, in Quebec prov. S of mouth of St. Lawrence river and N of Chaleur Bay; site of Gaspé village.

Gas·pe′sian (găs·pē′zhŭn) **Park**, a provincial park.

Gas·to′ni·a (găs·tō′nĭ·ȧ; -tŏn′yȧ) city, SW North Carolina; pop. 23,100.

Gates′head (gāts′hĕd) county borough, N England, on the Tyne opposite Newcastle; pop. 115,000.

Ga·tun′ (gȧ·tōōn′), Span. **Ga·tún′** (gä·tōōn′) town, Panama Canal Zone, S of Colón; nearby are the **Gatun Locks** and **Gatun Dam**, the latter forming **Gatun Lake** (area 164 sq. m.).

Gau′ga·me′la (gô′gȧ·mē′lȧ) ancient village, Assyria, about 18 m. NE of Nineveh and 32 m. W of Erbil (Arbela); scene of battle 331 B.C. erroneously called the battle of Arbela.

Gaul (gôl), Fr. **Gaule** (gōl), Lat. **Gal′li·a** (găl′ĭ·ȧ) **1** ancient country, W Europe, comprising chiefly the region occupied by modern France; in earliest times included N Italy (N of the Apennines), which was called **Cis·al′pine Gaul** (sĭs·ăl′pĭn; -pĭn), the main part being called **Trans·al′pine Gaul** (trăns·ăl′pĭn; -pĭn). **2** sometimes, figuratively, modern France. See GALLIC, GALLICAN, in Vocab.

Ga·ya′ (gȧ·yä′) city, NE India, in cen. Bihar state; pop. 105,200.

Ga′za (gä′zä), Arab. **Ghaz′ze** (gäz′zĕ) seaport, S Palestine, on Mediterranean Sea; in ancient times one of five city-kingdoms of Philistia; since 1949, with surrounding coastal district (which adjoins Sinai in SW), administered by Egypt.

Ga′zi·an·tep′ or **Gazi Antep** (gä′zĕ·än·tĕp′), formerly **Ain·tab′** (īn-täb′) town, S Turkey in Asia; pop. 72,700.

Gdańsk. See DANZIG.

Gdy′nia (gȧ·dĭn′ĭ·ȧ; -dĭn′yȧ) seaport, Poland; pop. 111,100.

Gebel. See JEBEL.

Ge·diz′ (gĕ·dēz′) or **Sa′ra·bat′** (sä′rä·bät′) river, W Turkey in Asia, flowing W into Gulf of İzmir; 200 m. long.

Geel′vink Bay (kāl′vĭnk) inlet of Pacific Ocean, West New Guinea.

Gehenna. See in Vocab.

Gel′der·land (gĕl′dẽr·länd) province, E Netherlands, in region of ancient county and duchy of Gelder (or Gelre); ✳ Arnhem.

Gelibolu. See GALLIPOLI.

Gel′sen·kir′chen (gĕl′zĕn·kĭr′kĕn) city, W Germany, in the Ruhr W of Dortmund; pop. 310,100.

Gen′e·see (jĕn′ĕ·sē; jĕn′ĕ·sē′) river, W New York, flowing N into Lake Ontario; 144 m. long.

Ge·ne′va (jĕ·nē′vȧ) **1** city, W New York, at N end of Seneca Lake; pop. 17,100. **2** Fr. **Ge·nève′** (zhĕ·nâv′) canton, SW Switzerland; ✳ Geneva; area 107 sq. m.; pop. 202,900. **3** city, SW Switzerland, ✳ of Geneva canton, at S tip of Lake of Geneva on Rhone river; pop. 145,500. — **Ge·ne′van** (jĕ·nē′vȧn), adj. & n. — **Gen′e·vese′** (jĕn′ĕ·vēz′; -vēs′), adj. & n. sing. & pl.

Geneva, Lake of, or **Lake Le′man** (lē′măn; lēm′ăn; lĕ·män′) lake, SW Switzerland and E France; area 225 sq. m.

Gennesaret, Lake of. See GALILEE, SEA OF.

Gen′o·a (jĕn′ō·ȧ), Ital. **Ge′no·va** (jĕ′nō·vä) seaport, NW Italy, at foot of Apennines and at head of **Gulf of Genoa**, a part of Ligurian Sea; pop. 676,100. — **Gen′o·ese′** (jĕn′ō·ēz′; -ēs′), adj. & n. sing. & pl.

Gensan. See WONSAN.

Gent (kĕnt), Eng. **Ghent** (gĕnt), Fr. **Gand** (gän) city, NW cen. Belgium, at confluence of Schelde and Lys rivers; pop. 166,800.

Gen′tof′te (gĕn′tŭf′tĕ) city, Denmark, on Sjaelland; pop. 68,700.

Genzan. See WONSAN.

George, Lake (jôrj), by James Fenimore Cooper called **Lake Hor′i·con** (hôr′ĭ·kŏn) lake, E New York, S of Lake Champlain; 33 m. long.

George V Coast (jôrj) the ffffth′) region, Antarctica, on coast S of Australia.

George′town (jôrj′toun) city, ✳ of British Guiana, at mouth of Demerara river; pop. 72,400.

George Town (jôrj′ toun) or **Pe·nang′** (pē·năng′) seaport, Federation of Malaya, ✱ of Penang, on Penang I.; pop. 189,100.

Geor′gia (jôr′jȧ; -jyȧ; -jĭ·ȧ) **1**, abbr. **Ga.**, state, SE United States, bordering on Atlantic Ocean; ✱ Atlanta; area 58,876 sq. m.; pop. 3,444,600. **2** Georgian **Sa·kart′ve·lo** (sä·kärt′vĕ·lô), Russ. **Gru′zi·ya** (grōō′zyĭ·yȧ), officially **Georgian Soviet Socialist Republic**, constituent republic of the U.S.S.R., in region S of Caucasus Mts. bordering on Black Sea; in ancient and medieval times a kingdom; ✱ Tiflis; area 26,875 sq. m.; pop. 3,722,300. — **Geor′gi·an** (jôr′jĭ·ăn; -jăn; -jyăn), adj. & n.

Georgia, Strait of, channel, Canada and the United States, between Vancouver I. and the mainland.

Geor′gi·an Bay (jôr′jĭ·ăn; -jăn; -jyăn) inlet of Lake Huron, Canada, in SE Ontario; 125 m. long by 50 m. wide, with entrance 20 m. wide.

Ge′ra (gā′rä) city, E Germany; pop. 89,200.

Ger′la·chov′ka (gĕr′lȧ·KôF′kȧ), Ger. **Gerls′dor′fer Spit′ze** (gĕrls′dôr′fĕr shpĭt′sĕ) mountain, Czechoslovakia, in N Slovakia in Tatra Mts.; 8737 ft. high.

German East Africa. See TANGANYIKA TERRITORY.

Ger·ma′ni·a (jûr·mā′nĭ·ȧ; -mān′yȧ) **1** region of ancient Europe, E of the Rhine and N of the Danube, including territory of modern Germany. **2** under the Romans, region just W of the Rhine in what is now NE France and part of Belgium and the Netherlands.

German Ocean. See NORTH SEA.

German Southwest Africa. See SOUTH-WEST AFRICA.

Ger′man·town (jûr′măn·toun) a section of Philadelphia, Pennsylvania, originally a township; battle 1777.

Ger′ma·ny (jûr′mȧ·nĭ), Ger. **Deutsch′land′** (doich′länt′) country, cen. Europe, bordering on North Sea and Baltic Sea; since 1949 constitutes two republics: the West German Federal Republic, ✱ Bonn, area 94,634 sq. m., pop. 47,585,900; and the East German Democratic Republic, ✱ East Berlin, area 41,700 sq. m., pop. 17,313,700.

Ger′mis·ton (jûr′mĭs·tŭn) city, NE Union of South Africa, in S Transvaal E of Johannesburg; pop. 104,300.

Get′tys·burg (gĕt′ĭz·bûrg) borough, S Pennsylvania, 8 m. from Maryland border; site of battle July 1–3, 1863; pop. 7000.

Ge·zi′ra (jĕ·zē′rȧ), Arab. **El Je·zi′ra** (ăl jă·zē′rō) district, E cen. Sudan (republic), between Blue Nile and White Nile rivers.

Gha′na (gä′nȧ) **1** ancient empire, W Africa, in the W Sudan; flourished 4th–13th centuries. **2** its ✱, W of the Niger; exact location unknown. **3** country, W Africa, on Gulf of Guinea; formerly the Gold Coast; became Mar. 6, 1957 (as Ghana) independent member of British Commonwealth of Nations; area 78,802 sq. m.; pop. 4,191,000. — **Gha′na·ian** (gä′nȧ·yăn; gän′yăn), adj. & n.

Ghats, Eastern and **Western** (gôts) two mountain ranges, S India: Eastern Ghats (average height 1500–2000 ft.) extending for 500 m. along SE and E coast, and Western Ghats (average height 3000–5000 ft.) extending 800 m. along SW and W coast.

Ghaz′ni (gäz′nē) city, E cen. Afghanistan; once ✱ of a kingdom extending from the Tigris to the Ganges.

Ghazze. See GAZA.

Ghent. See GENT.

Gib′e·on (gĭb′ē·ŭn) city, ancient Palestine, 6 m. NW of Jerusalem. See GIBEONITES, in Vocab.

Gi·bral′tar, Rock of (jĭ·brôl′tĕr), anc. **Cal′pe** (kăl′pē) peninsula, S Spain, at E end of Strait of Gibraltar; a rocky headland less than 3 m. long by 1 m. wide; site of town and fortress of **Gibraltar**, belonging to the British since 1704 and constituting a colony and naval base.

Gibraltar, Strait (also **Straits**) **of,** passage between Spain and Africa, connecting Atlantic Ocean with Mediterranean Sea; 32 m. wide.

Gi·fu (gē·fōō) city, Japan, in cen. Honshu; pop. 167,000.

Gi·hulng′an (hē·hōōlng′än) municipality, Philippine Is., on NE coast of Negros; pop. 53,600.

Gi·jón′ (hē·hōn′) seaport, NW Spain, on Bay of Biscay; pop. 107,200.

Gi′la (hē′lȧ) river, New Mexico and Arizona, flowing to Colorado river in SW corner of Arizona; 630 m. long.

Gil′bert Islands (gĭl′bĕrt) island group, W Pacific Ocean, on the equator; British protectorate 1892–1914; since 1915 forms, with Ellice Is., a British colony, the **Gilbert and El′lice Islands** (ĕl′ĭs), ✱ Tarawa (since World War II), area 316 sq. m., pop. 34,400.

Gil′e·ad (gĭl′ē·ăd; -ăd) district, ancient Palestine (now in Jordan), in mountains E of valley of Jordan river; — Bible name.

Gil′git (gĭl′gĭt) town, NW Kashmir, on Gilgit river (150 m. long), a tributary of the Indus.

Gil′ling·ham (jĭl′ĭng·ăm) municipal borough, SE England, in Kent; pop. 68,100.

Gim′li (gĭm′lĭ) town, Canada, in Manitoba on Lake Winnipeg; site of Royal Canadian Air Force training school 1943–45 and since 1950.

Gi·ronde′ (jĭ·rŏnd′; Fr. zhē′rôɴd′) estuary, W France, formed by confluence of Garonne and Dordogne rivers; extends 45 m. inland.

Giuba. See JUBA.

Gi′za or **El Gi′zeh** (ăl [ĕl] gē′zȧ) city, N Egypt, on the Nile near Cairo and E of the pyramids and the Sphinx; pop. 68,500.

Glace Bay (glās) town, Canada, on Cape Breton I.; pop. 24,400.

Glacier National Park, 1 mountain region, NW Montana; established as national park 1910; since 1932 forms part of Waterton-Glacier International Peace Park. **2** mountain region, Canada, in SE British Columbia in Selkirk Mts.; made a national park 1886.

Glad′beck (glät′bĕk) city, W Germany; pop. 61,500.

Gla·mor′gan·shire (glȧ·môr′găn·shĭr; -shĕr) or **Gla·mor′gan**, county, SE Wales; ✱ Cardiff; area 813 sq. m.; pop. 736,400.

Gla′rus (glä′rōōs) canton, E cen. Switzerland; ✱ Glarus; area 267 sq. m.; pop. 37,700.

Glas′gow (glăs′kō; -gō; glăz′gō; Brit. also gläs′-, gläz′-) seaport and royal burgh, S cen. Scotland, on the Clyde; pop. 1,089,600.

Glas′ton·bur′y (glăs′tŭn·bĕr′ĭ; gläs′n-; esp. Brit., -bĕr·ĭ, -brĭ) municipal borough, SW England, in Somerset; ancient Celtic settlement.

Glen·coe′ (glĕn·kō′) valley, W Scotland, in Argyll co.; massacre 1692.

Glen Cove (glĕn kōv) city, SE New York, on Long I.; pop. 15,100.

Glen′dale (glĕn′dāl) city, SW California, N of Los Angeles; pop. 95,700.

Glenmore. See GREAT GLEN.

Glens Falls (glĕnz fôlz) city, E New York, on Hudson river; pop. 19,600.

Gli·wi′ce (glē·vē′tsĕ), Ger. **Glei′witz** (glī′vĭts) city, SW Poland, in Silesia; pop. 113,500.

Glom′ma (glôm′ä) river, E Norway, flowing S into the Skagerrak; 375 m. long.

Glossa, Cape. See LINGUETTA, CAPE.

Glouces′ter (glŏs′tĕr; glôs′-) **1** city, NE Massachusetts, on Cape Ann; pop. 25,200. **2** see GLOUCESTERSHIRE. **3** city and county borough, SW cen. England, ✱ of Gloucestershire, on the Severn; pop. 67,300.

Glouces′ter·shire (-shĭr; -shĕr) or **Gloucester**, county, SW cen. England; ✱ Gloucester; area 1257 sq. m.; pop. 938,600.

Glov′ers·ville (glŭv′ĕrz·vĭl) city, E New York; pop. 23,600.

Gnossus. See KNOSSOS.

Go′a (gō′ȧ), Port. **Gô′a** (gō′ȧ) **1** territory, Portuguese India, on SW coast of the subcontinent; ✱ Pangim; area 1301 sq. m. **2** or **Old Goa**, ruined town, formerly a seaport and ✱ of the territory; replaced in 18th century by New Goa (Pangim).

Goat Island (gōt) **1** island, New York, in Niagara river; divides Niagara Falls into American Fall and Horseshoe (or Canadian) Fall. **2** island, California: see YERBA BUENA.

Go′bi, the (gō′bē; -bĭ) desert, cen. Asia, mostly in Mongolia; area 500,000 sq. m.

Go·da′va·ri (gō·dä′vȧ·rē) river, cen. India, flowing SE across the Deccan and into Bay of Bengal through several mouths; 900 m. long.

Go′des·berg (gō′dĕs·bĕrK), also **Bad Godesberg** (bät) commune, W Germany, on the Rhine S of Bonn; pop. 38,700.

God′havn (gŏd′hä′vĕn; Dan. gōth·houn′) Danish settlement, W Greenland, on S coast of Disko I.

Godt′haab′ (gŏt′hôp′) town, ✱ of Greenland, on SW coast.

God′win Aus′ten (gŏd′wĭn ôs′tĕn; -tĭn) or **Dap′sang** (dŭp′sŭng) or **K²** (kā′tōō′) mountain, N Kashmir, near Sinkiang border; highest peak in Karakoram Range, 28,250 ft.

Goi·â′ni·a, formerly **Goy·a′ni·a** (goi·ä′nē·ȧ) city, SE cen. Brazil, ✱ of Goiás state; pop. 41,600.

Goi·ás′, also **Goi·az′** or **Goy·az′** (goi·äs′) state, SE cen. Brazil; ✱ Goiânia; area 244,330 sq. m.; pop. 1,234,700.

Gökcha. See SEVAN.

Gol·con′da (gŏl·kŏn′dȧ) ruined town and fortress, cen. India, in cen. Andhra Pradesh W of Hyderabad; capital 1512–1687 of ancient kingdom; famous for its diamonds. See also GOLCONDA, in Vocab.

Gold Coast, 1 section of coast, W Africa, on N shore of Gulf of Guinea; — so called from large quantities of gold formerly taken here. **2** region, W Africa, the Gold Coast and hinterland; former British territory including Northern Territories, the colonies of Ashanti and Gold Coast, and Togoland trust territory; ✱ Accra. See GHANA. **3** southern section of Gold Coast region, former British colony; ✱ Accra.

Golden Chersonese. See CHERSONESE, THE.

Golden Gate, strait, California, leading from Pacific Ocean into San Francisco Bay; ab. 2 m. wide.

Golden Horn, inlet of the Bosporus, Turkey in Europe, forming the harbor of İstanbul.

Gold′fields′ (gōld′fēldz′) village, Canada, in NW Saskatchewan on N shore of Lake Athabaska; uranium ore.

Golds′bor′o (gōldz′bûr′ō) city, E North Carolina; pop. 21,500.

Go′mel (gô′myĭl·y′; Angl. gō′mĕl) city, U.S.S.R., in SE White Russia; pop. 144,200.

Go·mor′rah (gō·mŏr′ȧ) in the Bible, a city in the plain of the Jordan which was destroyed for its wickedness. See SODOM.

Go′na′ïves′, Gulf of (gō′nȧ′ēv′) the wide bay on W coast of Haiti.

Gon′dar (gŏn′dĕr) city, NW Ethiopia, former ✱ of Ethiopia.

Good′e·nough (gŏŏd′′n·ŭf) island, D'Entrecasteaux Is.; has central peak, **Mount Goodenough**, 8419 ft. high.

Good Hope, Cape of, point of land, SW Union of South Africa, W of False Bay; in 34°21′S.

Good′win Sands (gŏŏd′wĭn) shoals in Strait of Dover 7 m. E of Deal, England, enclosing the Downs (roadstead).

Goose Bay, air base, E Canada, in Labrador on Hamilton Inlet.

Go′rée′ (gō′rā′) town, French West Africa, in Senegal on island off Cape Vert peninsula near Dakar; first ✱ of French West Africa.

Go·ri′zia (gō·rē′tsyä), Ger. **Görz** (gûrts) commune, NE Italy, on Isonzo river on Yugoslav border; pop. 38,100.

Gor′ki (gôr′kĭ; Russ. gôr′y′·kĭ), before 1932 **Nizh′ni Nov′go·rod** (nĭzh′nĭ nŏv′gō·rŏd) city, Soviet Russia, Europe, on Volga river; pop. 644,100.

Gör′litz (gûr′lĭts) city, E Germany, on the Neisse river; pop. 85,700.

Gor·lov′ka (gŭr·lôf′kȧ) city, U.S.S.R., in E Ukraine, in the Donbas just N of Stalino; pop. 108,700.

Gor′ner Grat (gôr′nĕr grät′) ridge, SW cen. Switzerland, in Valais canton; 10,289 ft. high.

Gor′no-Al·tai′ Autonomous Region (gôr′nŭ·ŭl·tī′), before 1948 **Oi′rot Autonomous Region** (oi′rŭt) autonomous region, Soviet Russia, Asia, in SE Altai Territory in Altai Mts.; ✱ Gorno-Altaisk (formerly Oirot-Tura); area 35,800 sq. m.; pop. 150,000.

Gor′no-Ba·dakh·shan′ (gôr′nŭ·bȧ·dŭK·shän′) autonomous region, Soviet Central Asia, in SE Tadzhik S.S.R. in the Pamirs bordering on Afghanistan and Sinkiang; ✱ Khorog; area 25,784 sq. m.; pop. 41,800.

Go′shen (gō′shĕn) district, ancient Egypt, E of the Nile delta. See GOSHEN, in Vocab.

Gos′port (gŏs′pōrt) municipal borough, S England, in Hampshire on Portsmouth harbor; pop. 58,200.

Gö′te·borg′ (yû′tĕ·bôr′y′) or **Goth′en·burg** (gŏth′′n·bûrg; gŏt′′n-) seaport, SW Sweden, at mouth of Göta river; pop. 349,100.

Go′tha (gō′tä; Angl. gō′thȧ, -tȧ) city, E Germany; pop. 57,600.

Got′land′ or **Gott′land′** (gŏt′lănd′; -lănd) island, Sweden, in Baltic Sea off SE coast; ✱ Visby; area 1225 sq. m.; pop. 59,600.

Göt′ting·en (gût′ĭng·ĕn) city, W Germany; pop. 68,600.

Governors Island, island, New York City, in New York Bay off S end of East river; U.S. military reservation; old fort, Castle William.

Goyania. See GOIÂNIA.

Goyaz. See GOIÁS.

Gra′ham Coast (grā′ăm), formerly **Graham Land**, region, Antarctica, on W side of Palmer Penin.

Gra'ian Alps (grā'yăn; grī'ăn) section of Alps on French-Italian border; highest peak Gran Paradiso, 13,324 ft.

Grain Coast, section of Guinea coast, W Africa, in Liberia; — so called from the old trade in grains of paradise.

Gram'pi·ans, the (grăm'pǐ·ănz) or **Gram'pi·an Hills** (-ăn) mountain system, N Scotland, between the Lowlands and the Great Glen; highest peak Ben Nevis, 4406 ft.

Gra·na'da (grà·nä'dà) **1** city, SW Nicaragua, on NW shore of Lake Nicaragua; pop. 26,200. **2** ancient kingdom, S Spain, founded by Moors in 13th cent. **3** city, S Spain, ✳ of ancient Moorish kingdom, in the Sierra Nevada; pop. 174,700.

Gran'by (grăn'bĭ; grăm'bĭ) city, Canada, in S Quebec; pop. 27,100.

Gran Chaco. See CHACO.

Grand (grănd) **1** the Colorado river from its source to its junction with Green river in SE Utah; — its former name. **2** river, SW Michigan, flowing N and W into Lake Michigan; 260 m. long. **3** river, NW Missouri, flowing SE into Missouri river; 300 m. long. **4** river, W Missouri, flowing SE into the Osage river; 140 m. long. **5** river, N South Dakota, flowing E into Missouri river; ab. 200 m. long. **6** see HAMILTON.

Grand Bank, shoal or banks in the Atlantic Ocean E and S of Newfoundland; great cod-fishing region; 500 m. from W to E, 200 m. wide.

Grand Ca·nar'y (grănd kà·nâr'ĭ), Span. **Gran Ca·na'ria** (gräng kä·nä'ryà) island, Spain, one of the Canary Is.; chief city Las Palmas; area 523 sq. m.; pop. 216,900.

Grand Can'yon (kăn'yŭn) gorge, NW Arizona, formed by Colorado river; 4 to 18 m. wide, over 1 m. deep; most of it a government reserve, comprising a national park, established 1919 and, adjacent to the park, a national monument, established 1932.

Grand Cou'lee (kōō'lǐ) valley, E Washington, extending SSW from S wall of valley of Columbia river where it turns W in forming Big Bend; over 50 m. long, 1½ to 5 m. wide, in places 1000 ft. deep.

Grand Coulee Dam, dam, Washington, in Columbia river; forms Franklin D. Roosevelt Lake; maximum height 550 ft.

Grande, Ri'o (rē'ō grănd'; rī'ō grănd'). See RIO GRANDE.

Gran'de, Ri'o (rē'ōō grăNn'dě) river, E Brazil, in Minas Gerais state, a headstream of the Paraná river; 680 m. long.

Grande-Terre (grän'târ'; Fr. grän'târ') island, French West Indies, forming E part of Guadeloupe.

Grand Falls (grănd fôlz) waterfall, E Canada, in W Labrador, in Hamilton river; 245 ft. high.

Grand Forks (fôrks) city, E North Dakota, on Red river; pop. 26,800.

Grand Island, city, SE cen. Nebraska, on Platte river; pop. 22,700.

Grand Lac. See TONLE SAP.

Grand Ma·nan' Island (mà·năn') island, SE Canada, off SW New Brunswick at entrance to Bay of Fundy; 20 m. long; pop. 3000.

Grand'·Mère (grän'mâr') city, Canada, in S Quebec; pop. 14,000.

Grand Pré (grän' prā'; Fr. grän' prā') village, Canada, in W Nova Scotia on Minas Basin; early home of the Acadians.

Grand Rap'ids (grănd răp'ĭdz) city, W Michigan; pop. 176,500.

Grand River. See GRAND.

Grand Te'ton (tē'tŏn) mountain, W Wyoming; highest point in Teton Range, 13,766 ft.; central feature of Grand Teton National Park, established 1929.

Gra·ni'cus (grà·nī'kŭs) river, NW Asia Minor, in ancient Mysia, flowing N into the Propontis; battle 334 B.C.

Granite City, city, SW Illinois; pop. 29,500.

Granja, La. See SAN ILDEFONSO.

Gran Sa·ba'na (grän' sä·vä'nä) region, SE Venezuela, in Guiana highlands bordering on British Guiana and Brazil.

Gras'mere (gräs'mēr) lake, NW England, in Westmorland.

Grau·bün'den (grou·bün'děn), Fr. **Gri'sons'** (grē'zôN') canton, E Switzerland; ✳ Chur; area 2774 sq. m.; pop. 137,100.

Graudenz. See GRUDZIĄDZ.

Gra've·lotte' (gräv'lôt') village, NE France, near Metz; battle 1870.

Gravenhage, 's. See HAGUE, THE.

Graves'end' (grāv'zěnd'; gräv'zěnd') municipal borough, SE England, in Kent, on Thames estuary; pop. 45,000.

Grays Harbor (grāz) inlet of Pacific Ocean, W Washington.

Grays Peak, mountain, Colorado, highest in Front Range, 14,274 ft.

Graz (gräts), earlier **Gratz**, city, S Austria, ✳ of Styria, on Mur river; pop. 229,800.

Great Australian Bight, wide bay on S coast of Australia.

Great Barrier Reef, coral reef, Australia, off NE coast of Queensland; 1250 m. long.

Great Basin, region, W United States, between the Sierra Nevada range and the Wasatch Mts., including most of Nevada and parts of California, Idaho, Utah, Wyoming, and Oregon; has no drainage to the ocean.

Great Bear Lake, lake, N Canada, with outlet, **Great Bear River**, flowing W 100 m. to Mackenzie river; area 12,000 sq. m.

Great Brit'ain (brǐt'n) **1** island, N Europe, N of France; constitutes a kingdom, with Northern Ireland comprising the **United Kingdom of Great Britain and Northern Ireland**; ✳ London; area 93,371 sq. m.; pop. 50,210,500. **2** sometimes, the United Kingdom of Great Britain and Northern Ireland.

Great Central Valley. = CENTRAL VALLEY.

Great Crosby. See CROSBY.

Great Dividing Range, mountain ranges, E Australia, in Queensland, New South Wales, and Victoria; from 100 to 200 m. wide.

Greater Antilles. See WEST INDIES.

Greater Walachia. See MUNTENIA.

Great Falls, city, cen. Montana, on Missouri river N of the **Great Falls of the Missouri** (92 ft. high); pop. 39,200.

Great Glen (glěn) or **Glen·more'** (glěn·môr') valley, N Scotland, cutting through the Highlands from SW to NE.

Great Lakes, chain of five lakes: Superior, Michigan, Huron, Erie, and Ontario, in cen. North America, through which (except for Lake Michigan, which is wholly within the U.S.) runs the U.S.–Canada boundary.

Great Plains, region, W cen. United States and Canada, E of the Rocky Mts.; smooth, treeless plains.

Great Rift Valley depression, SW Asia and E Africa, extending from valley of the Jordan S to Mozambique; in Africa S of Lake Rudolf, divides into two branches, an Eastern and a Western Rift Valley.

Great Saint Ber·nard' (sănt ber·närd') Alpine pass, Switzerland and Italy, 10 m. E of French border; altitude over 8100 ft.

Great Salt Lake, lake, N Utah, having strongly saline waters and no outlet; 80 m. long, 35 m. wide.

Great Slave Lake (slāv) lake, N Canada, receiving the Slave river on S and flowing out by way of Mackenzie river on W; area 11,170 sq. m.

Great Smoky Mountains, mountain range, North Carolina–Tennessee boundary; highest point Clingmans Dome, 6642 ft.; established as national park 1930.

Great Wall or **Chinese Wall**, Chin. **Chang-chêng** (jäng'chŭng') wall between China Proper and Mongolia; 1250 m. long, 20 to 50 ft. high, 15 to 25 ft. thick; built 3d cent. B.C.

Greece (grēs), Gr. **Hel'las** (hěl'ăs), Mod. Gr. **El·las'** (â·läs') country, S Europe, occupying S end of Balkan Penin.; a kingdom; ✳ Athens; area (with Ionian Is. and Crete) 50,147 sq. m.; pop. 7,602,600. — **Gre'cian** (grē'shăn), adj. — **Greek** (grēk), adj. & n.

Gree'ley (grē'lǐ) city, N Colorado; pop. 20,400.

Green, river, W United States, flowing from Wind River Mts., W Wyoming, to Colorado river in SE Utah; 730 m. long.

Green Bay, 1 inlet of Lake Michigan, Michigan and Wisconsin; 120 m. long. **2** city, E Wisconsin, on Green Bay; pop. 52,700.

Green'field (grēn'fēld) town, NW Massachusetts, on Connecticut river; pop. 15,100.

Green'land (grēn'lănd; -lănd'), Dan. **Grön'land** (grûn'lăn') island, N Atlantic Ocean, off NE North America; a Danish possession; ✳ Godthaab; area 839,800 sq. m.; pop. 18,400.

Green Mountains, range of the Appalachian system, E North America, extending from Canada through Vermont into W Massachusetts; highest peak Mount Mansfield (Vermont), 4393 ft.

Green'ock (grǐn'ŭk; grēn'-; grēn'-) seaport and burgh, SW Scotland, in Renfrew co. on Firth of Clyde; pop. 76,300.

Greens'bor'o (grēnz'bûr'ō) city, N cen. North Carolina; pop. 74,400.

Greens'burg (grēnz'bûrg) city, SW Pennsylvania; pop. 16,900.

Green'ville (grēn'vǐl) **1** city, W Mississippi, on Mississippi river; pop. 29,900. **2** town, E North Carolina; pop. 16,700. **3** city, NW South Carolina; pop. 58,200.

Green'wich (grēn'wǐch; grǐn'wǐch; grēn'ǐch) town, SW Connecticut, on Long Island Sound on New York border; pop. 40,800.

Green'wich (grǐn'ǐj; grēn'-; -ǐch) metropolitan borough, SE London, on S bank of the Thames; formerly site of Greenwich Observatory (see ABINGER; HERSTMONCEUX); pop. 91,500.

Green'wich Village (grēn'ǐch; grǐn'-; -ǐj) section of New York City, in Manhattan on lower W side; once a separate village.

Green'wood (grēn'wŏod) city, W Mississippi; pop. 18,100.

Gre·na'da (grē·nä'dà) island, West Indies Federation, southernmost of Windward Is.; with southern Grenadines constitutes a colony, ✳ St. George's, area 133 sq. m., pop. 90,100.

Gren'a·dines' (grěn'à·dēnz'; grěn'à·dēnz) group of islands, West Indies Federation, in Windward Is. just N of Grenada; divided administratively between colonies of Grenada and Saint Vincent.

Gre·no'ble (grě·nō'b'l) city, SE France, on Isère river; pop. 102,200.

Grey'lock', Mount (grā'lŏk') mountain, W Massachusetts, in Berkshire Hills; highest point in state, 3505 ft.

Grims'by (grǐmz'bǐ) county borough, E England, in Parts of Lindsey, Lincolnshire, near mouth of the Humber; pop. 94,500.

Gri'qua·land' East (grē'kwà·lănd'; grǐk'wà-) territory, Union of South Africa, in E Cape Province; one of the Transkeian Territories; chief town Kokstad; area 6602 sq. m.; pop. 328,500.

Gris-Nez, Cape (grē'nā') headland, N France, extending into Strait of Dover; point of European mainland nearest to Great Britain.

Grisons. See GRAUBÜNDEN.

Grod'no (grôd'nô) city, U.S.S.R., in W White Russia; pop. 57,300.

Gro'ning·en (grō'nǐng·ěn) **1** province, NE Netherlands, bordering on North Sea and the Ems estuary. **2** city, its ✳; pop. 132,000.

Grönland. See GREENLAND.

Gros Is'let Bay (grōs ī'lět; -lǐt) inlet, West Indies, on NW coast of Saint Lucia I.

Grosswardein. See ORADEA.

Groz'ny (grôz'nǐ) city, Soviet Russia, Europe, just N of Caucasus Mts.; pop. 172,500.

Gru'dziądz (grōō'jôNts), Ger. **Grau'denz** (grou'děnts) city, Poland, on Vistula river; pop. 58,500.

Gruziya. See GEORGIA, Russia.

Gua·la·ja'ra (gwä'thä·lä·hä'rä; Angl. gwŏd'à·là·här'à) city, W cen. Mexico, ✳ of Jalisco state; pop. 229,200.

Gua'dal·ca·nal' (gwŏd'l·kà·năl') island, SE Solomon Is.; site of Honiara, since World War II ✳ of British Solomon Is.; area 2500 sq. m.

Gua'dal·quiv'ir (gwŏd'l·kwǐv'ẽr) river, S Spain, flowing W and SW into Gulf of Cádiz; 374 m. long.

Gua'da·lupe (gwŏd'l·lōōp; gô'd'l-; wŏd'l-; gwŏd'l·lōō'pě) river, SE Texas, flowing into San Antonio river; 300 m. long.

Guadalupe Hi·dal'go (hĭ·däl'gō; Span. gwä'thä·lōō'pä ē·thäl'gō), officially **Gus·ta'vo A. Ma·de'ro** (gōōs·tä'vō ä' mä·thā'rō) city, cen. Mexico, just N of Mexico City; site of pilgrimage church of Our Lady of Guadalupe; pop. 25,900.

Guadalupe Mountains, mountain range, S New Mexico and SW Texas; highest point **Guadalupe Peak**, highest in Texas, 8751 ft.

Guadarrama, Sierra de. See SIERRA DE GUADARRAMA.

Gua'de·loupe' (Fr. gwäd'lōōp'; Angl. gwŏd'l·lōōp, gô'd'l-) two islands, Basse-Terre (or Guadeloupe proper) and Grande-Terre, French West Indies, separated by only a narrow channel and constituting a department of France; ✳ Basse-Terre; area 688 sq. m.; pop. 304,200.

Gua·dia'na (Span. gwä'thyä'nä; Port. gwä·thyä'nä) river, Spain and Portugal, emptying into Gulf of Cádiz; 515 m. long.

Guaira, La. See LA GUAIRA.

Guam (gwŏm) or **Gua·han'** (gwä·hän') island, Mariana Is., belonging to United States since 1898; ✳ Agana; area 206 sq. m.; pop. 59,500. — **Guam·a'ni·an** (gwŏ·mä'nǐ·ǎn), adj. & n.

Gua'na·ba'ra Bay (gwä'nà·và'rà), also **Rio de Janeiro Bay**, inlet of

Atlantic Ocean, SE Brazil, the site of Rio de Janeiro; over 16 m. long, 11 m. wide, entrance 1 m. wide.

Gua'na·ha'ni (gwä'nä·hä'nē) island, Bahama Is., which was Columbus's first landfall in the New World; thought to be San Salvador.

Gua'na·jua'to (gwä'nä·hwä'tō) **1** state, cen. Mexico; area 11,804 sq. m.; pop. 1,317,600. **2** city, its *; pop. 23,500.

Guan·tá'na·mo Bay (gwän·tä'nä·mō) inlet, E Cuba, on SE coast; site of U.S. naval station; landing place of U.S. naval units June 1898.

Gua·po·ré' (gwä'pōō·rā') **1** or **I·té'nez** (ē·tā'nās) river, W Brazil and NE Bolivia, chiefly on boundary; flows NW to Mamoré river; 950 m. long. **2**, since 1956 called **Ron·dô'nia** (rōn·dōn'yà) territory, W Brazil, bordering on Bolivia; * Pôrto Velho; area 96,986 sq. m.; pop. 37,400.

Guar'da·fui', Cape (gwär'dà·fwē'; -fōō'ī) cape, E Africa, at N tip of Italian Somaliland at entrance to Gulf of Aden.

Gua·te·ma'la (gwä'tĕ·mä'là) **1** country, Central America, just S of Mexico; a republic; * Guatemala City; area 42,044 sq. m.; pop. 2,787,000. **2** or **Guatemala City**, city, its *; pop. 283,100. — **Gua'te·ma'lan**, adj. & n.

Guatemala Antigua. = ANTIGUA GUATEMALA.

Gua·via're (gwä·vyä'rā) river, Colombia, flowing E into Orinoco river; 450 m. long.

Gua'ya·quil' (gwä'yä·kēl'; Angl. gwī'à·kēl, -kwĭl), officially **San·tia'go de Gua'ya·quil'** (sän·tyä'gō thä gwä'yä·kēl') seaport, SW Ecuador, on Guayas river, an arm of the **Gulf of Guayaquil**; pop. 172,900.

Guelph (gwĕlf) city, Canada, in SE Ontario; pop. 33,900.

Guer·ni'ca (gĕr·nē'kà) town, N Spain, in Vizcaya prov. (one of the Basque Provinces), E of Bilbao; once seat of a Basque parliament.

Guern'sey (gûrn'zĭ) island, English Channel, one of the Channel Is.; * St. Peter Port; area 25 sq. m.; pop. 40,600.

Guer·re'ro (gĕr·rā'rō) state, S Mexico, bordering on Pacific Ocean; * Chilpancingo; area 24,885 sq. m.; pop. 917,700.

Gui·a'na (gē·ä'nà; -ăn'à) region, N South America, bordering on Atlantic Ocean and bounded on W and S by the Orinoco, Negro, and Amazon rivers; includes parts of Venezuela and Brazil and all of Surinam, British Guiana, and French Guiana. — **Gui·a'nan**, adj. & n.

Gui'enne' or **Guy'enne'** (gü·ĕ'yĕn'; gē') historical region, SW France, bordering on Atlantic Ocean; part of Aquitaine, the name Guienne being often used interchangeably with Aquitaine.

Guil'ford Courthouse (gĭl'fērd) locality, N cen. North Carolina, near Greensboro; battle 1781.

Guin'ea (gĭn'ĭ) **1** region, W Africa, on Atlantic coast; includes Guinea proper, the SW and S coast of the great bulge of the continent from Gambia to the Cameroons, and Lower Guinea, the coast from S Cameroons to S Angola. **2** see FRENCH GUINEA.

Guinea, Gulf of, inlet of Atlantic Ocean, W Africa, S of the great western bulge of the continent; includes bights of Benin and Biafra.

Guinée française. See FRENCH GUINEA.

Gu'ja·rat' (gōō'jà·rät') region, W India, including areas in Kathiawar Penin. and around Gulf of Cambay where Gujarati is spoken.

Gülek Boğaz. See CILICIAN GATES.

Gulf'port (gŭlf'pōrt) city, SE Mississippi; pop. 22,700.

Gulf States, the states of the United States bordering on the Gulf of Mexico: Florida, Alabama, Mississippi, Louisiana, and Texas.

Gulf Stream, warm ocean current in North Atlantic Ocean flowing from Gulf of Mexico along coast of United States to Nantucket, thence eastward.

Gum'ti (gŏŏm'tē) river, N India, flowing SE to the Ganges; 500 m. long.

Gun'ni·son (gŭn'ĭ·s'n) river, W cen. Colorado, flowing W and NW into Colorado river; 150 m. long.

Gunzan. See KUNSAN.

Gu'sev (gōō'syĕf), Ger. **Gum·bin'nen** (gŏŏm·bĭn'ĕn) city, Soviet Russia, Europe, in NW East Prussia; battle 1914.

Gustavo A. Madero. See GUADALUPE HIDALGO.

Guyane française. See FRENCH GUIANA.

Guyenne. See GUIENNE.

Gwa'li·or (gwä'lǐ·ôr) **1** former state, N cen. India; * Lashkar; part of Madhya Bharat 1948–56; in Madhya Pradesh from 1956. **2** town in the state, site of medieval Hindu fort.

Gyang'tse' (gyäng'tsē') town, SE Tibet; junction of caravan routes.

Györ (dyûr), Ger. **Raab** (räp) autonomous city, NW Hungary; pop. 56,600.

H

Ha'a·bai' (hä'ä·bī') or **Ha'a·pai'** (-pī') island group, cen. Tonga Is.; about 50 islands; pop. 6900.

Haar'lem (här'lĕm) city, W Netherlands; pop. 156,900.

Habana, La. See HAVANA.

Hab·ba'ni·ya (häb·bä'nǐ·yà) **1** lake, cen. Iraq, just S of the Euphrates. **2** air base, Iraq, on the lake; accommodates seaplanes.

Hack'en·sack (häk'ĕn·săk) city, NE New Jersey; pop. 29,200.

Ha·dhra·maut' or **Ha·dra·maut'** (hŏ·drŏ·mōōt'; -mout') region, S Arabia, part of Aden Protectorate, bordering on Indian Ocean; chief town Mukalla; area 58,500 sq. m.; pop. 150,000.

Hadrumetum. See SOUSSE.

Hae·ju (hī·jōō) or **Kai·shu** (kī·shōō) city, W Korea, just N of 38th parallel on Haeju Bay; pop. 62,700.

Ha'gen (hä'gĕn) city, W Germany, ENE of Düsseldorf; pop. 146,100.

Ha'gers·town (hä'gĕrz·toun) city, N Maryland; pop. 36,300.

Hague, Cape La. See LA HAGUE.

Hague, The (häg), Du. **'s Gra'ven·ha'ge** (sKrä'vĕn·hà'Kĕ) city, SW Netherlands, 4 m. inland from North Sea; pop. 533,000.

Haidarabad. See HYDERABAD.

Hai'fa (hī'fà; Arab. hä'fä) seaport, NW Israel, on Bay of Acre at foot of Mt. Carmel; pop. (1949) 120,700.

Hai'nan' (hī'nän') island, SE China; belongs to Kwangtung prov.; * Kiungshan; area 13,000 sq. m.; pop. 3,000,000.

Hai'naut' (ĕ'nō') **1** medieval county, Low Countries, in region of SW Belgium and N France, SE of Flanders. **2** province of modern Belgium, part of the medieval county; * Mons.

Hai'phong' (hī'fông'), Fr. **Ha'ï'phong'** (à'ē'fôn') seaport, Indochina, in Tonkin in delta of Coi river; pop. 188,600.

Hai'ti (hā'tĭ) **1** see HISPANIOLA. **2** Fr. **Ha'ï'ti'** (à'ē'tē') island country, West Indies, at W end of Hispaniola I.; republic; * Port-au-Prince; area 10,850 sq. m.; pop. 3,112,000. — **Hai'ti·an, Hay'ti·an** (hā'tĭ·ăn), adj. & n.

Ha·ko·da·te (hä·kô·dä·tĕ) seaport, Japan, in SW Hokkaido; pop. 211,400.

Ha·le·a'ka·la' (hä'lä·ä'kä·lä') mountain, Hawaii, in E Maui I.; an extinct volcano; over 10,000 ft. high.

Haleb. See ALEP.

Hal·fa'ya Pass (hăl·fä'yà) pass, NW Egypt, through the range of hills just S of Salûm; battles January and November 1942.

Hal'i·car·nas'sus (hăl'ĭ·kär·năs'ŭs), mod. **Bo·drum'** (bô·drōōm') ancient city, Asia Minor, in SW Caria on coast; tomb of Mausolus.

Hal'i·fax (hăl'ĭ·făks) **1** city, Canada, * of Nova Scotia, on Atlantic Ocean; pop. 93,300. **2** county borough, N England, NE of Manchester; pop. 98,400.

Hal'le (häl'ĕ) city, E Germany, on Saale river; pop. 222,500.

Hall'statt (häl'shtät) village, W cen. Austria, on shore of **Hall'stät'ter Lake** (häl'shtĕt'ĕr); site of an early iron-age culture.

Hal'ma·he'ra (häl'mà·hĕr'à), Du. **Djai·lo'lo** (jī·lō'lō) island, Indonesia, largest of the Moluccas, lying on the equator; 6928 sq. m.

Häl'sing·borg' (hĕl'sĭng·bôr'y') seaport, SW Sweden; pop. 71,200.

Halys. See KIZIL IRMAK.

Ha'ma (hä'mä; hä·mä'), Bib. **Ha'math** (hā'măth) city, W Syria, on the Orontes; pop. 71,400.

Hamad, El. See SYRIAN DESERT.

Ha'ma·dan (hăm'à·dăn), anc. **Ec·bat'a·na** (ĕk·băt'n·à) city, W Iran, in plain at foot of Mt. Alwand; pop. 122,000.

Ha·ma·ma·tsu (hä·mä·mä·tsōō) city, Japan, in S Honshu; pop. 125,800.

Hamborn. See DUISBURG-HAMBORN.

Ham'burg (hăm'bûrg; Ger. häm'bŏŏrk) city, NW Germany, on Elbe river 90 m. from its mouth; from 13th cent. until 1935 a free city and, with surrounding area, a free state; reconstituted as a state of Bonn republic 1948; area 288 sq. m.; pop. 1,604,600.

Ham·hung (häm·hŏŏng) or **Kan·ko** (kän·kō) city, NE Korea, just NW of Hungnam; pop. 75,300.

Hami. See QOMUL.

Ham'il·ton (hăm'ĭl·tŭn; -t'n) **1** city, SW Ohio, N of Cincinnati; pop. 58,000. **2** seaport, * of Bermuda Is.; pop. 3200. **3** city, Canada, in SE Ontario at W end of Lake Ontario; pop. 239,600. **4** river, E Canada, in S cen. Labrador, flowing E into Atlantic Ocean by estuary, **Hamilton Inlet**, 14 to 25 m. wide; total length of river ab. 600 m.

Hamilton, Mount, mountain, W California, E of San Jose; site of Lick Observatory; over 4200 ft. high.

Hamm (häm) **1** city, W Germany, on Lippe river; pop. 49,800. **2** village, Luxembourg; site of American military cemetery.

Ham'mer·fest' (häm'ĕr·fĕst') city, N Norway, on Kvalöy I., at 70°38'N; pop. 3600.

Ham'mond (hăm'ŭnd) city, NW Indiana; pop. 87,600.

Hamp'shire (hăm[p]'shǐr; -shĕr) or **Hants** (hănts) **1** formerly, a county in S England, comprising the modern administrative counties of Southampton and the Isle of Wight. **2** officially **South·amp'ton** (sou·thăm[p]'tŭn; -ăm[p]'-) county, S England, bordering on English Channel; * Winchester; area 1503 sq. m.; pop. 1,196,600.

Hamp'stead (hăm[p]'stĕd; -stǐd) metropolitan borough, NW London, including **Hampstead Heath**; pop. 95,100.

Hamp'ton (hăm[p]'tŭn) independent city, SE Virginia, on Hampton Roads; pop. 6000.

Hampton Roads, channel, E Virginia, through which the James, Elizabeth, and Nansemond rivers flow into Chesapeake Bay.

Ham·tramck' (häm·trăm'ĭk) city, SE Michigan, entirely within city of Detroit; pop. 43,400.

Han (hän) **1** river, E cen. China, in Shensi and Hupeh provs., flowing SE into Yangtze river; 900 m. long. **2** or **Kan** (kän) river, S Korea, flowing WNW into Yellow Sea; 220 m. long.

Han Cities. See WUHAN.

Ha·ne'da (hä·nĕd'à) town, Japan, in Honshu on Tokyo Bay; airport.

Hang'chow' (häng'chou'; Chin. häng'jō') city, E China, * of Chekiang prov., at head of Hangchow Bay; pop. 485,100.

Hangchow Bay, inlet of East China Sea, China, in Chekiang prov. at mouth of Fuchun river; 60 m. wide at entrance, extends inland 70 m.

Hang'ö' (häng'ü'), Finnish **Han'ko** (häng'kô) seaport, S Finland; pop. 6800.

Hanka. See KHANKA.

Han'kow' (häng'kou'; Chin. hän'kō') city, E cen. China, in SE Hupeh prov. on the Yangtze E of the Han; pop. 804,500.

Han'ni·bal (hăn'ǐ·băl) city, NE Missouri, on Mississippi river; boyhood home of Mark Twain; pop. 20,400.

Han·no'ver (hä·nō'vĕr; -fĕr), Eng. **Han'o·ver** (hăn'ō·vĕr) city, W Germany, on the Leine river; pop. 441,600.

Ha·noi' (hä·noi'), Fr. **Ha'no'ï'** (à'nô'ē') city, Indochina, chief city of Tonkin, on Coi river; * in N Vietnam, formerly * of Indochina; pop. 297,900.

Hanseatic League. See HANSE, in Vocab.

Hants. See HAMPSHIRE.

Han'yang' (häng'yäng') city, E cen. China, in SE Hupeh prov. on the Yangtze W of Han river mouth; pop. 450,000.

Har'bin (här'bǐn), Chin. **Pin'kiang'** (bǐn'jǐ·äng') city, cen. Manchuria, on Sungari river; * of Heilungkiang prov.; pop. 638,000.

Har'bour Grace (här'bēr grās') seaport, Canada, in SE Newfoundland on Conception Bay; pop. 2300.

Har·gei'sa (här·gā'sà) town, * of British Somaliland.

Har'lem (här'lĕm) **1** river, SE New York, NE of Manhattan I.; with Spuyten Duyvil creek, connects Hudson and East rivers. **2** district, New York City, in N Manhattan bordering on Harlem and East rivers. **3** var. of HAARLEM.

Har'ling·en (här'lǐng·ĕn) city, S Texas; pop. 23,200.

Har'ney Peak (här'nǐ) mountain, SW South Dakota, in Black Hills; highest point in state, 7242 ft.

Har'pers Ferry (här'pĕrz) town, NE West Virginia, at confluence of Potomac and Shenandoah rivers; John Brown's raid 1859.

Har'ris·burg (här'ĭs·bûrg) city, ✱ of Pennsylvania, on Susquehanna river; pop. 89,500.

Har'ro·gate (här'ŏ·gĭt; -gāt) municipal borough, N England, in West Riding, Yorkshire; pop. 50,500.

Har'row (här'ō), officially **Harrow on the Hill**, urban district, SE England, in Middlesex NW of London; school; pop. 219,500.

Hart'ford (härt'fĕrd) city, ✱ of Connecticut, on Connecticut river; pop. 177,400.

Har'vey (här'vĭ) city, NE Illinois, S of Chicago; pop. 20,700.

Har'well (här'wĕl; -wĕl) village, S England, in Berkshire S of Oxford; site of first atomic pile established in England.

Har'wich (här'ĭj; -ĭch) municipal borough, SE England, in Essex, on North Sea; naval station; pop. 13,500.

Harz (härts) mountains, cen. Germany, between Elbe and Leine rivers; highest peak 3747 ft.

Ha'sa, al- (äl hä'sä), Angl. **El Ha'sa** (ĕl häs'à) district, Saudi Arabia, in E Nejd bordering on Persian Gulf; chief town Hofuf.

Has'tings (hās'tĭngz) **1** city, S Nebraska; pop. 20,200. **2** county borough, S England, at entrance to Strait of Dover; one of the Cinque Ports; battle of Hastings 1066 (see SENLAC); pop. 65,500.

Hat'ter·as, Cape (hăt'ĕr·ăs) cape, North Carolina, on SE **Hatteras Island**, a long, narrow sand bar in Atlantic Ocean off coast.

Hat'ties·burg (hăt'ĭz·bûrg) city, SE Mississippi; pop. 29,500.

Hau·rak'i Gulf (hou·räk'ĭ; -rä'kĭ) inlet of Pacific Ocean, New Zealand, on N coast of North I.

Haute-Volta See UPPER VOLTA.

Ha·van'a (hà·văn'à), Span. **La Ha·ba'na** (lä ä·vä'nä) seaport, ✱ of Cuba, on NW coast; pop. 676,400.

Ha'vel (hä'fĕl) river, E Germany, flowing to the Elbe; ab. 225 m. long.

Ha'ver·hill (hä'vrĭl; hä'vĕr·ĭl) city, NE Massachusetts; pop. 47,300.

Havre, Le. See LE HAVRE.

Hav're de Grace (hăv'ĕr dĕ grăs'; grās') city, NE Maryland, at mouth of Susquehanna river; pop. 7800.

Havre-de-Grâce, Le. See LE HAVRE.

Ha'vre Saint Pierre (hȧ'vr̃e săn' pyâr') town, E Canada, in Quebec prov. on St. Lawrence river; port developed since 1949.

Ha·wai'i (hȧ·wī'ē; -wō'yē; -wō'yä; -vī'ē) **1** or **Hawaiian Islands**, formerly **Sand'wich Islands** (săn[d]'wĭch; Brit. also -wĭj) chain of islands, N cen. Pacific Ocean, on Tropic of Cancer; belongs to United States and forms the **Territory of Hawaii**; ✱ Honolulu; area 6451 sq. m.; pop. 499,800. **2** island, Hawaiian Is., largest of the group; chief town Hilo; area 4021 sq. m.; pop. 67,700. — **Ha·wai'ian** (hȧ·wī'[y]ăn; -wō'yăn), adj. & n.

Hawaii National Park, volcanic area, Hawaiian Is., on islands of Hawaii and Maui, including Kilauea and Mauna Loa; established as national park 1916.

Ha'wash (hä'wäsh) or **A'wash** (ä'-) river, E Ethiopia, flowing NE into the desert; 500 m. long.

Haw'thorne (hô'thôrn) city, SW California, SW of Los Angeles; pop. 16,300.

Hayasdan. See ARMENIA.

Hayes and Har'ling·ton (här'lĭng·tŭn) urban district, SE England, in Middlesex; pop. 65,600.

Hay'ti. Var. of HAITI.

Ha'zel Park (hä'z'l) city, SE Michigan; pop. 17,800.

Ha'zle·ton (hä'z'l·tŭn; -t'n) city, E Pennsylvania; pop. 35,500.

Heathrow. See LONDON AIRPORT.

Heb'ri·des (hĕb'rĭ·dēz) or **Western Islands**, islands, W Scotland, constituting two groups: the **Inner Hebrides**, near the mainland, and the **Outer Hebrides**; total area 2900 sq. m.; pop. 61,800.

He'bron (hē'brŭn), anc. **Kir'jath-Ar'ba** (kir'jăth·är'bȧ; kĭr'-) town, Palestine, SSW of Jerusalem, in Arab (Jordanian) Palestine; an ancient Jewish town, home of Abraham; pop. 23,100.

Hec·a'te Strait (hĕk'à·tē; -tē) channel, W Canada, between British Columbia and the Queen Charlotte Is.

Hec'la. Var. of HEKLA.

He·djaz'. Var. of HEJAZ.

Heer'len (här'lĕ[n]) commune, SE Netherlands, just NE of Maastricht near German border; pop. 56,600.

Hei'del·berg (hī'd'l·bûrg; Ger. -bĕrk) city, W Germany, on Neckar river ESE of Mannheim; university; pop. 115,800.

Heijo. See PYONGYANG.

Heiko. See PYONGGANG.

Heil'bronn' (hīl'brôn') city, W Germany, on Neckar river; pop. 52,500.

Hei'lung'kiang' (hā'lŏong'ji·äng') **1** see AMUR. **2** province, N Manchuria; ✱ Harbin; area 179,000 sq. m.; pop. 11,897,000.

He·jaz' (hē·jăz') region, W Arabia, on Red Sea coast; for a time after World War I an independent kingdom; became part of Saudi Arabia 1932; ✱ Mecca; area 150,000 sq. m.; pop. 2,000,000.

Hek'la (hĕk'lä) volcano, SW Iceland; 4747 ft. high.

Helder, Den. See DEN HELDER.

Hel'e·na (hĕl'ĕ·nà) city, ✱ of Montana; pop. 17,600.

Hel'go·land (hĕl'gō·länd'; Ger. -länt'), Eng. **Hel'i·go·land** (hĕl'ĭ·gō·länd') island, W Germany, in North Sea 28 m. from mainland.

Hel'i·con (hĕl'ĭ·kŏn; -kŏn) mountain, Greece, in SW Boeotia near Gulf of Corinth; 5738 ft. high.

Hel'i·go·land' Bight (hĕl'ĭ·gō·länd') or Ger. **Hel'go·län'der Bucht** (hĕl'gō·lĕn'dĕr bŏŏkt') arm of North Sea between island of Helgoland and German mainland; scene of naval battle Aug. 28, 1914.

He·li·op'o·lis (hē'lĭ·ŏp'ō·lĭs) **1** Bib. **On** (ŏn) ancient city, N Egypt, NE of site of modern Cairo; dedicated to worship of the sun god Ra. **2** ancient city, N Egypt, S of site of modern Cairo. **3** see BAALBEK.

Hellas. See GREECE.

Hel'les, Cape (hĕl'ēz) cape, Turkey in Europe, at S tip of Gallipoli Peninsula.

Hellespont, Hellespontus. See DARDANELLES.

Hell Gate, section of East river, New York, a channel 200 ft. wide at narrowest part.

Hell's Canyon, canyon of Snake river on Idaho-Oregon border; 40 m. long, deepest point over 7000 ft.

Hel'mand or **Hel'mund** (hĕl'mŭnd) river, SW Afghanistan, flowing SW and W into morass on Iranian border; river 650 m. long.

Helm'stedt (hĕlm'shtĕt) city, W Germany, E of Brunswick; on border of East German Republic after 1945; pop. 25,600.

Hel'sing·ör' (hĕl'sĭng·ûr'), Eng. **El'si·nore** (ĕl'sĭ·nōr) seaport, Denmark, in N Sjælland I.; pop. 18,900.

Hel'sin·ki (hĕl'sĭng·kĭ), Swedish **Hel'sing·fors** (hĕl'sĭng·fôrz) seaport, ✱ of Finland, on Gulf of Finland; pop. 368,500.

Helvetia. See SWITZERLAND.

Hemp'stead (hĕm[p]'stĕd; -stĭd) village, SE New York, on Long I.; pop. 29,100.

Hen'der·son (hĕn'dĕr·s'n) city, NW Kentucky, on Ohio river; pop. 16,800.

Hen'don (hĕn'dŭn) urban district, SE England, in Middlesex NW of London; pop. 155,800.

Heng'yang' (hŭng'yäng'), formerly **Heng'chow'** (-jō') town, SE cen. China, in S cen. Hunan prov. on Siang river; pop. 181,400.

Hen'ley or **Henley on Thames** (hĕn'lĭ, tĕmz) municipal borough, cen. England, in Oxfordshire; annual regatta; pop. 8000.

Hen·lo'pen, Cape (hĕn·lō'pĕn) cape, Delaware, at entrance to Delaware Bay.

Hen'ry, Cape (hĕn'rĭ) cape, Virginia, S of entrance to Chesapeake Bay.

Her'a·cle'a (hĕr'à·klē'à) ancient city, S Italy; battle 280 B.C.

Heraklion. See CANDIA.

He·rat' (hĕ·rät'), anc. **Ar'i·a** (âr'ĭ·à; à·rī'à) city, NW Afghanistan, on the Hari Rud; pop. 85,000.

Hercegovina. See HERZEGOVINA.

Her'cu·la'ne·um (hûr'kū·lā'nē·ŭm) ancient city, Italy, at NW foot of Mt. Vesuvius; destroyed by eruption A.D. 79.

Her'e·ford (hĕr'ĕ·fĕrd) **1** see HEREFORDSHIRE. **2** municipal borough, W England, ✱ of Herefordshire, on the Wye; pop. 32,500.

Her'e·ford·shire (-shĭr; -shĕr) or **Hereford**, county, W England, on border of Wales; ✱ Hereford; area 842 sq. m.; pop. 127,100.

Hermannstadt. See SIBIU.

Her'mon, Mount (hûr'mŭn) mountain, Syria and Lebanon, in Anti-Lebanon Mts. just N of Palestine; 9232 ft. high.

Her'ne (hĕr'nĕ) city, W Germany, in the Ruhr; pop. 111,200.

Herreroland. See DAMARALAND.

Herst'mon·ceux' (hûrs[t]'mŭn·sōō') village, S England, in East Sussex NE of Eastbourne; site of Royal Observatory since 1949.

Hert'ford·shire (här'fĕrd·shĭr; -shĕr; härt'-) or **Hert'ford** or **Herts** (härts; hûrts) county, SE England, NW of London; ✱ Hertford; area 632 sq. m.; pop. 609,700.

Hertogenbosch, 's. See 's HERTOGENBOSCH.

Her'ze·go·vi'na (hûr'tsĕ·gō·vē'nȧ; Ger. hĕr'tsä·gō'vē·nä, -gō·vē'nä), Serb. **Her'ce·go'vi·na** (hĕr'tsĕ·gō'vē·nä) region, Yugoslavia; once (10th–14th cents.) an independent principality and in 15th cent. a duchy; since 1878, under Austria and as part of independent Yugoslavia, forms a political unit with Bosnia.

Hesse (hĕs; hĕs'ĕ), Ger. **Hes'sen** (hĕs'ĕn) **1** region, SW Germany, E of the Rhine and N of the Main; in Middle Ages a landgraviate; divided 1567, the two principal divisions being: (1) **Hesse-Cas'sel** (-kăs'l), Ger. **Hessen-Kas'sel** (hĕs'ĕn·käs'ĕl), in N, which was united with Prussia 1866 as part of the province of **Hesse-Nas'sau** (-năs'ô), Ger. **Hessen-Nas'sau** (hĕs'ĕn·näs'ou), along with duchy of Nassau and city of Frankfurt; and (2) **Hesse-Darm'stadt** (-därm'stăt), Ger. **Hessen-Darm'stadt** (hĕs'ĕn·därm'shtät), in S, which became a state of Weimar republic. **2** Hesse-Darmstadt as a state of the Weimar republic. **3** state of the Bonn republic, including larger part of Hesse-Darmstadt along with part of Hesse-Nassau; ✱ Wiesbaden.

Hes'ton and I'sle·worth (hĕs'tŭn [hĕs''n], ī'z'l·wûrth) municipal borough, SE England, in Middlesex W of London; pop. 106,600.

Hi'a·le'ah (hī'à·lē'à) city, SE Florida; race track; pop. 19,700.

Hib'bing (hĭb'ĭng) village, NE Minnesota, in the Mesabi Range; pop. 16,300.

Hibernia. See in Vocab.

Hi'bok·hi'bok (hē'bŏk·hē'bŏk) volcano, Philippine Is., on Camiguin I. (N of Mindanao); had violent eruptions 1948, 1951; height 5620 ft.

Hic'po·chee, Lake (hĭk'pō·chē') lake, S cen. Florida, W of Lake Okeechobee; a link in the Cross-Florida Waterway.

Hi·dal'go (hĭ·dăl'gō; Span. ĕ·thäl'gō) state, cen. Mexico; ✱ Pachuca; area 8057 sq. m.; pop. 840,800.

Hierosolyma. See JERUSALEM.

Hier'ro (yĕr'rō), formerly **Fer'ro** (fĕr'rō) island, Spain, westernmost of Canary Is.; 107 sq. m.; pop. 8100.

Highland Park, 1 city, NE Illinois, on Lake Michigan; pop. 16,800. **2** city, SE Michigan, N of Detroit; pop. 46,400.

Highlands, the, that portion of Scotland in and N of the Grampians.

Highlands of the Hudson, region, SE New York, comprising hills on both sides of Hudson river; includes Storm King, 1340 ft. high.

High Point, city, N cen. North Carolina; pop. 40,000.

Hiiumaa. See KHIUMA.

Hil'des·heim (hĭl'dĕs·hīm) city, W Germany, SSE of Hannover; pop. 59,000.

Hil'la (hĭl'à) town, cen. Iraq, near site of ancient Babylon.

Hi'lo (hē'lō) city, Hawaiian Is., on E coast of Hawaii I.; pop. 27,000.

Hil'ver·sum (hĭl'vĕr·sŭm) commune, W Netherlands, a suburb of Amsterdam; pop. 85,100.

Hi·ma'chal Pra·desh' (hĭ·mä'chȧl prȧ·däsh') territory, N India, bordering on Tibet; a union of former Punjab hill states; ✱ Simla; area 10,904 sq. m.; pop. 1,109,500.

Hi·ma'la·yas, the (hĭ·mä'lȧ·yȧz; -mäl'yȧz; Anglicized hĭm'ȧ·lā'ȧz), more correctly, **the Hi·ma'la·ya** (-[y]ȧ) mountain system, Asia, on border between India and Tibet and in Nepal; highest point Mt. Everest, over 29,000 ft. — **Hi·ma'la·yan**, adj.

Hi·me·ji (hĭ·mĕ·jĕ) city, Japan, in W Honshu; pop. 197,300.

Hindenburg. See ZABRZE.

Hin'du Kush (hĭn'dōō kōōsh'; kŭsh'), known to historians of Alexander's time as **Par'o·pa·mi'sus** (păr'ō·pȧ·mī'sŭs) or **Cau'ca·sus In'di·cus** (kô'kȧ·sŭs ĭn'dĭ·kŭs) mountain range, cen. Asia, on border of Kashmir and in Afghanistan; highest point Tirich Mir, 25,263 ft.

Hin'du·stan' (hĭn'dōō·stän'; -stän') or **Hin'do·stan'** (-dō-) **1** region,

N India, including the great plain drained by the Indus in the W and the Ganges and Brahmaputra in the E; place where Hindi is chiefly spoken. **2** more specifically, the area within this region comprising East Punjab, Rajputana (Rajasthan), and most of Uttar Pradesh (United Provinces). **3** sometimes, the Republic of India.

Hi·ro'shi·ma (Jap. hē̇·rōsh'mä; Angl. hē̇'rō·shē̇'mä, hē̇·rō'shĭ·mä) city, Japan, in Honshu at W end of Inland Sea; pop. 224,100.

Hispania. See in Vocab.

His'pan·io'la (hĭs'păn·yō'lä), orig. Span. **Es'pa·ño'la** (äs'pä·nyō'lä), also **Hai'ti** (hā'tĭ) island, West Indies; divided into two independent countries, Haiti and the Dominican Republic; area 30,000 sq. m.

His·sar·lik' (hĭ·sär·lĭk') site of ancient Troy, NW Turkey in Asia.

Hi'va O'a or **Hi'va·o'a** (hē̇'vȧ·ō'ȧ) island, Marquesas Is.; chief village Atuana, ✱ of the group.

Hi·was'see (hī·wŏs'ē) river flowing from NE Georgia into SE Tennessee to empty into Tennessee river; 150 m. long.

Ho'bart (hō'bärt; -bẽrt) city, ✱ of Tasmania; pop. 76,600.

Ho'bo'ken (hō'bō'kĕn) city, NE New Jersey, on Hudson river adjoining Jersey City; pop. 50,700.

Höch'städt (hük'shtĕt) town, W Germany, in Bavaria on the Danube; battles 1703, 1704 (often called battle of Blenheim), and 1800.

Ho·dei'da (hō·dā'dä; -dī'-) seaport, SW Arabia, in W Yemen; the port of San'a; pop. 40,000.

Hodg'en·ville (hŏj'ĕn·vĭl) town, cen. Kentucky; Lincoln's birthplace.

Hód'me·zö·vá'sár·hely (hŏd'mĕ·zŭ·vä'shär·hã) autonomous city, SE Hungary, near Tisza river; pop. 61,700.

Hoek van Holland. See HOOK OF HOLLAND.

Hof (hōf) city, W Germany, in Bavaria near border of Czechoslovakia and after 1945 on border of East Germany; pop. 54,600.

Ho·fuf' (hō·fōōf') town, Saudi Arabia, chief town of al-Hasa district.

Hogue, La. See LA HOGUE.

Ho'hen·lin'den (hō'ĕn·lĭn'dĕn) village, W Germany, in Bavaria E of Munich; battle 1800.

Ho'hen·zol'lern (hō'ĕn·tsŏl'ẽrn; Angl. hō'ĕn·zŏl'ẽrn) region, SW Germany; formerly a province of Prussia; with S part of Württemberg and S part of Baden, forms a state of the Bonn republic.

Hok·kai'do (hŏ·kī'dō) or **Ye·zo** (yĕ·zō) island, N Japan; chief city Sapporo; area 30,000 sq. m.; pop. 3,852,800.

Holin. See KARAKORUM.

Hol'land (hŏl'ănd) **1** city, W Michigan, on Lake Michigan; pop. 15,900. **2** medieval county of Holy Roman Empire, on North Sea coast; region forms two provinces of the Netherlands, North and South Holland. **3** kingdom: see NETHERLANDS. — **Hol'land·er,** n.

Hol·lan'di·a (hŏ·lăn'dĭ·ȧ) town, West New Guinea, on N coast 25 m. from border of North-East (British) New Guinea.

Hol'ly·wood' (hŏl'ĭ·wŏŏd) district in city of Los Angeles, California; center of U.S. motion-picture industry.

Hol'stein (hōl'stīn) region, NW Germany, just S of the peninsula of Jutland and adjoining Schleswig; once a fief of Denmark and a duchy (from 1474); became part of Prussia 1866.

Hol'ston (hōl'stŭn) river, E Tennessee, flowing SW to unite with French Broad river and form the Tennessee river; 140 m. long.

Holy Cross, Mount of the, mountain, NW cen. Colorado, in Sawatch Range; 13,996 ft. high; on side has two crevices which when filled with snow form a Greek cross, central feature of **Holy Cross National Monument,** established 1929.

Hol'y·head' (hŏl'ĭ·hĕd') island, NW Wales, in St. George's Channel off W coast of island of Anglesey.

Hol'yoke (hōl'yōk) city, SW Massachusetts, on Connecticut river N of Springfield; pop. 54,700.

Holy Roman Empire. See in Vocab.

Homs (hŏms), anc. **Em'e·sa** (ĕm'ē̇·sȧ) city, W Syria; pop. 100,100.

Ho'nan' (hō'nän') province, E cen. China, just S of the Hwang Ho; ✱ Kaifeng; area 59,459 sq. m.; pop. 30,465,000.

Hondo. See HONSHU.

Hon·du'ras (hŏn·dōōr'ăs; -dūr'-) country, Central America; a republic; ✱ Tegucigalpa; area 59,160 sq. m.; pop. 1,201,300. — **Hon·du'ran** (-ăn), adj. & n.

Honduras, British, see BRITISH HONDURAS.

Honduras, Gulf of, inlet of Caribbean Sea between S British Honduras, E Guatemala, and N Honduras.

Hon'fleur' (ôN'flûr') seaport, NW France, on Seine estuary opposite Le Havre; in 18th cent. supplanted in importance by Le Havre.

Hong Kong (hŏng' kŏng') island, SE China, just E of mouth of Pearl river; with adjacent area on mainland, constitutes a British crown colony; ✱ Victoria; area 391 sq. m.; pop. 1,860,000.

Ho'ni·a'ra (hō'nĭ·ä'rȧ) town, Solomon Is., on Guadalcanal; ✱ of British Solomon Is. protectorate since World War II.

Hon'o·lu'lu (hŏn'ō·lōō'lōō; hō'nō·lōō'lōō) seaport, ✱ of Hawaii, on SE Oahu I.; pop. 245,600.

Hon'shu (hŏn'shōō) or **Hon'do** (hŏn'dō) island, chief island of Japan, site of Tokyo; area 87,000 sq. m.

Hood, Mount (hŏŏd) mountain, NW Oregon, in Cascade Range; highest point in state, 11,245 ft.

Hoogh'ly or **Hug'li** (hōōg'lĭ) river, NE India, the most westerly channel of Ganges river in delta; 120 m. long, nearly 10 m. wide at mouth.

Hook of Hol'land (hŏŏk, hŏl'ănd), Du. **Hoek van Hol'land** (hŏŏk' vän hŏl'änt) cape, SW Netherlands, SW of The Hague.

Hoo'sac Range (hŏŏ'săk) range, W Massachusetts, part of the Green Mts.; highest peak 2588 ft.

Hoo'ver Dam (hŏŏ'vẽr), formerly **Boul'der Dam** (bōl'dẽr) dam in Colorado river, between Nevada and Arizona; 726 ft. high; forms Lake Mead.

Ho'peh' or **Ho'pei'** (hō'pā'), formerly **Chih'li'** (chē'lē') province, NE China; ✱ Paoting; area 54,826 sq. m.; pop. 29,790,000.

Ho'qui·am (hō'kwĭ·ăm) seaport, W Washington, on Grays Harbor adjacent to Aberdeen; pop. 11,100.

Hor, Mount (hôr) mountain, SW Jordan; 4430 ft. high.

Ho'reb (hō'rĕb) in the Bible, the mountain where the law was given to Moses; also called Sinai (which see).

Horicon, Lake. See GEORGE, LAKE.

Hor'muz (hôr'mŭz; native hôr·mōōz'), also **Or'muz** (ôr'mŭz; native

ôr·mōōz') island, Iran, in **Strait of Hormuz,** the strait between Iran and N tip of Trucial Oman.

Horn, Cape (hôrn), often, colloquially, **the Horn,** cape, southernmost point of South America, in Tierra del Fuego, at 55°59'S lat.

Horn'church' (hôrn'chûrch') urban district, SE England, in Essex ENE of London; pop. 104,100.

Hor·nell' (hôr·nĕl') city, S New York; pop. 15,000.

Horn'sey (hôrn'zĭ) municipal borough, SE England, in Middlesex N of London; pop. 98,100.

Hos·pi·ta·let' (ōōs·pē·tȧ·lĕt') city, NE Spain, SW of Barcelona; pop. 73,600.

Hotien. See KHOTAN.

Hot Springs, 1 city, W cen. Arkansas, in Ouachita Mts.; pop. 29,300; site of mineral springs, feature of **Hot Springs National Park,** established 1921. **2** city, SW South Dakota, in S foothills of Black Hills; thermal and mineral springs; pop. 5000. **3** village, western Virginia; in Allegheny Mts.; mineral springs.

Houf'fa'lize' (ōō'fä'lēz') village, SE Belgium, N of Bastogne; taken by Germans December 1944, retaken by Allies Jan. 16, 1945.

Hou'sa·ton'ic (hōō'sȧ·tŏn'ĭk) river, Massachusetts and Connecticut, flowing from Berkshire Hills S to Long Island Sound; ab. 150 m. long.

Hous'ton (hūs'tŭn) city, SE Texas, 25 m. NW of Galveston Bay; connected with Gulf of Mexico by ship channel over 50 m. long; pop. 596,200.

Hove (hōv) municipal borough, S England, in East Sussex on English Channel; W suburb of Brighton; pop. 69,400.

How'rah (hou'rȧ) city, NE India, in West Bengal on Hooghly river opposite Calcutta; pop. 379,300.

Hra'dec Krá'lo·vé (hrä'dĕts krä'lō·vä), Ger. **Kö'nig·grätz'** (kû'nĭk·gräts') city, W Czechoslovakia, in E Bohemia on Labe (Elbe) river; battle (Königgrätz or Sadowa) 1866; pop. 51,500.

Hsiang. See SIANG river.

Hsinking. See CHANGCHUN.

Hual·la'ga (wä·yä'gä) river, W and N Peru, flowing N into Marañón river; 700 m. long.

Huas'ca·rán' (wäs'kä·rän') or **Huas·cán'** (wäs·kän') mountain, W Peru; highest in the country, 22,205 ft.

Hud'ders·field (hŭd'ẽrz·fēld) county borough, N England, NE of Manchester; pop. 129,000.

Hud'son (hŭd's'n) river, E New York, flowing S into New York Bay; 306 m. long.

Hudson Bay, inland sea, N Canada, forming an indentation in mainland 850 m. long by 600 m. wide.

Hudson Strait, NE Canada, between S Baffin I. and N Quebec prov., connecting Atlantic Ocean with Hudson Bay; 50 to 100 m. wide.

Hué (hū·ā') seaport, Indochina, chief city of Annam; pop. 96,400.

Huel'va (wĕl'vä) commune, SW Spain; pop. 65,600.

Hueneme. See PORT HUENEME.

Hues'ca (wäs'kä) commune, NE Spain; once ✱ of kingdom of Aragon; pop. 21,300.

Hugli. See HOOGHLY.

Hule, Lake. See MEROM, WATERS OF.

Hull (hŭl) **1** city, E Canada, in Quebec, on Ottawa river opposite Ottawa, Ontario; pop. 49,200. **2** or **Kings'ton upon Hull** (kĭng'stŭn) city and county borough, N England, in East Riding, Yorkshire, on the Humber where it is joined by the Hull river; pop. 299,100.

Hum'ber (hŭm'bẽr) estuary, E England, formed by Ouse and Trent rivers; flows into North Sea.

Hum'boldt (hŭm'bōlt) river, N Nevada, flowing W and SW into Humboldt Lake; 290 m. long.

Hu'nan' (hōō'nän') province, SE cen. China, S of the Yangtze river; ✱ Changsha; area 79,537 sq. m.; pop. 29,998,000.

Hun'ga·ry (hŭng'gȧ·rĭ), Hung. **Ma'gyar·or'szág** (mŏ'dyŏr·ōr'säg), Ger. **Un'garn** (ŏŏng'gärn) country, cen. Europe; formerly a kingdom, the extensive plain crossed N–S by the Danube; since 1946 a republic; ✱ Budapest; area 35,900 sq. m.; pop. 9,201,200. — **Hun·gar'i·an** (hŭng·gâr'ĭ·ăn), adj. & n.

Hung·nam' (hōōng·näm') or **Ko·nan** (kō·nän) seaport, N Korea, on E coast; pop. 85,000.

Hung'shui' (hŏŏng'shwä') river, S China, rising in E Yunnan and uniting in E Kwangsi with Siang river to form Si river; 700 m. long.

Hun'ter (hŭn'tẽr) river, SE Australia, in E New South Wales, flowing E to S Pacific Ocean; 300 m. long.

Hun'ting·don·shire (hŭn'tĭng·dŭn·shĭr; -shẽr) or **Hun'ting·don** or **Hunts** (hŭnts) county, E cen. England; ✱ Huntingdon; area 366 sq. m.; pop. 69,300.

Hun'ting·ton (hŭn'tĭng·tŭn) **1** city, NE Indiana; pop. 15,100. **2** city, W West Virginia, on Ohio river; pop. 86,400.

Huntington Park, city, SW California, S of Los Angeles; pop. 29,500.

Hunts'ville (hŭnts'vĭl) city, N Alabama; Redstone Arsenal situated just S; pop. 16,400.

Hu'peh' or **Hu'pei'** (hōō'pā') province, E cen. China; ✱ Wuchang; area 71,845 sq. m.; pop. 21,470,000.

Hu'ron, Lake (hū'rŭn) lake on United States–Canada border between Michigan and Ontario; one of the Great Lakes; area 23,000 sq. m.

Hürt'gen (hûrt'gĕn) town, W Germany, E of Aachen; nearby **Hürtgen Forest** scene of severe fighting September 1944.

Hutch'in·son (hŭch'ĭn·s'n) city, cen. Kansas, on Arkansas river; pop. 33,600.

Hutt (hŭt) city, New Zealand, NE of Wellington; pop. 74,900.

Huy'ton with Ro'by (hī't'n, rō'bĭ) urban district, NW England, in Lancashire E of Liverpool; pop. 55,800.

Hwa·chon (hwä·chôn') or **Ka·sen** (kä·sĕn) town, N Korea, just N of 38th parallel on Pukhan river, which is dammed up to form **Hwachon Reservoir,** 15 m. long.

Hwai (hwī) river, E China, in S Honan and NW Anhwei provs., flowing into the Hwang Ho; 350 m. long.

Hwaining. See ANKING.

Hwang Hai. See YELLOW SEA.

Hwang Ho (hwäng' hō') or **Yel'low River** (yĕl'ō) river, N China, flowing from Kunlun Mts. to Gulf of Po Hai; 2700 m. long.

Hwang Pu (hwäng' pōō'), also **Whang'poo'**, river, E China, in S Kiangsu prov., flowing past Shanghai to the Yangtze; 100 m. long.

Hy'bla (hī'blà) ancient town in Sicily, on S slope of Mt. Etna; famous for its honey.

Hydaspes. See JHELUM.

Hy'der·a·bad' or **Hai'dar·a·bad'** (hī'dẽr·à·bäd'; -bäd') **1** former state, S India, in the Deccan; from 1713 to 1948 governed by rulers called nizams and hence often referred to as the **Ni·zam's' Dominions** (nĭ·zämz'; -zämz'). **2** city, ✴ of Andhra Pradesh, formerly ✴ of Hyderabad state; on Musi river; pop. 739,200. **3** city, W Pakistan, in Sind on Indus river; pop. 241,800.

Hydraotes. See RAVI.

Hy·met'tus (hī·mĕt'ŭs) mountain ridge, Greece, just E and SE of Athens; known for its honey.

Hyr·ca'ni·a (hũr·kā'nĭ·à; -kān'yà) ancient province, N Persia, SE of Caspian Sea; often residence of Parthian kings. — **Hyr·ca'ni·an**, adj.

I

Ia'și (yäsh; yä'shĕ) or **Jas'sy** (yäs'ē) city, NE Romania, in Moldavia; pop. 104,500.

I·ba'dan (ē·bä'dän) city, W Nigeria; pop. 387,100.

I·be'ri·a (ī·bẽr'ĭ·à) **1** ancient Hispania; the Iberian Peninsula. **2** ancient region between Caucasus Mts. and Armenia; modern Georgia, U.S.S.R.

I·be'ri·an Peninsula (-ăn) peninsula, SW Europe, occupied by Spain and Portugal.

I'bi·cuí' (ē'vē·kwē') river, S Brazil, in Rio Grande do Sul state, flowing W to Uruguay river on Argentina boundary; 400 m. long.

Içá. See PUTUMAYO.

Icaria. See IKARÍA.

Içel. See MERSIN.

Ice'land (īs'lănd), Dan. **Is'land** (ēs'län), Icelandic **Ís'land** (ēs'länt) island, NE North Atlantic Ocean; belonged to Denmark 1380–1944, for a time (1918–44) an independent kingdom in personal union with Denmark; now a republic; ✴ Reykjavík; area 39,709 sq. m.; pop. 144,500. — **Ice'land·er** (īs'lăn'dẽr; -lăn·dẽr), n. See also ICELANDIC, in Vocab.

I'chang' (ē'chäng') city, S China, in S Hupeh prov. on the Yangtze just below the gorges; pop. 107,900.

Iconium. See KONYA.

I'da (ī'dà) **1** Turk. **Kaz'da·ği'** (käz'dà·ĭ') mountain, NW Asia Minor, SE of site of ancient Troy; actually a range; highest point 5810 ft. **2** Mod. Gr. **I'dhi** (ē'thē) or **Psi·lo·rí'tis** (psē·lô·rē'tēs) mountain, Greece; highest on island of Crete, 8195 ft.

I'da·ho (ī'dà·hō), abbr. (not official) **Ida.**, state, NW United States, bordering on Canada; ✴ Boise; area 83,557 sq. m.; pop. 588,600. — **I'da·ho'an** (-hō'ăn), adj. & n.

Idaho Falls, city, SE Idaho, on Snake river; pop. 19,200.

Id'fu (ĭd'foo) or **Ed'fu** (ĕd'foo) town, S Egypt, on Nile river at lat. 25°N; ancient ruins.

I'dle·wild' (ī'd'l·wīld') locality, New York City, in Queens borough on Jamaica Bay; site of **New York International Airport**.

Id'u·mae'a or **Id·u·me'a** (ĭd'ữ·mē'à; ī'dữ-) ancient Edom; — so called by the Romans.

Ie'per (yä'pẽr), Fr. **Y'pres** (ē'pr') commune, NW Belgium; pop. 17,100.

If (ēf) island, S France, near Marseilles; site of fortress-prison Château d'If.

If'ni (ĭf'nĭ) town, SW Morocco; with surrounding district (741 sq. m.), administered by Spain from Cabo Yubi; pop. (district) 20,000.

I·gua·çu' (ē·gwä·sōō'), Span. **I'gua·zú'** (ē'gwä·sōō') river, S Brazil, in Paraná state, flowing W to the Alto Paraná; contains waterfall (**Iguaçu Falls**) over 2 m. wide with more than 20 cataracts averaging 200 ft. high.

I·guas·sú'. Var. of IGUAÇU.

IJs'sel (ī'sĕl), Eng. **Ijs'sel** or **Ys'sel** (ī'sĕl), anc. **Sa'la** (sā'là) river, Netherlands, flowing N out of Neder Rijn to IJsselmeer; 70 m. long.

IJs'sel·meer' (ī'sĕl·mār'), Eng. **Lake Ijssel**, formerly **Zui'der Zee** (zī'dẽr zā'; zē') lake, N Netherlands, separated from North Sea by a dike and bordered by reclaimed lands.

I·ka·rí'a (ē·kä·rē'à) or **Ni·ka·rí'a** (nyē-), anc. **I·car'i·a** (ī·kâr'ĭ·à) island, Greece, in Aegean Sea WSW of Samos.

Île-de-France or **Isle-de-France** (ēl'dẽ·fräns') historical region, N cen. France, around Paris; a province mid-15th cent. to 1790.

Il'ford (ĭl'fẽrd) municipal borough, SE England, in Essex NE of London; pop. 184,700.

I'li' (ē'lē') river, cen. Asia, in NW Sinkiang and SE Kazakh S.S.R., flowing into SW end of Lake Balkhash; its valley subject of 19th-cent. Russian-Chinese dispute settled 1881 by treaty.

Ilía. See ELIS.

Ilion, Ilium. See TROY.

Il·lam'pu (ē·yäm'pōō) mountain, W Bolivia; over 23,000 ft. high.

Il'li·ma'ni (ē'yē·mä'nē) mountain, W Bolivia; 22,579 ft. high.

Il'li·nois' (ĭl'ĭ·noi'; less often, -noiz') **1** river, Illinois, flowing SW to Mississippi river; 273 m. long. **2** abbr. **Ill.**, state, N cen. United States, bordering Lake Michigan in NE; ✴ Springfield; area 56,400 sq. m., not including 1526 sq. m. of Lake Michigan; pop. 8,712,200. — **Il'li·nois'an** (-noi'ăn; -noiz'n), adj. & n.

Il·lyr'i·a (ĭ·lĭr'ĭ·à) ancient country, SW Europe, comprising E Adriatic coast and its hinterland. — **Il·lyr'i·an**, adj. & n.

Il·lyr'i·cum (-kŭm) Roman province in ancient Illyria, established A.D. 9.

Il'men (ĭl'mĕn; Russ. ēl'y·myĕn·y') lake, NW Soviet Russia, Europe, S of Lake Ladoga.

I'lo·i'lo (ē'lô·ē'lô) city, Philippine Is., on Panay; pop. 90,500.

Imbros. See IMROZ.

Im·jin (ĭm·jĭn) or **Rin·shin** (rĭn·shĭn) river, cen. Korea, flowing SW across 38th parallel to mouth of Han river.

Imperial Valley, valley, SE California; mostly below sea level; formerly desert, now rendered fertile by irrigation.

Imp'hal (ĭmp'hŭl) city, NE India, ✴ of Manipur terr.; pop. 99,700.

Îm·roz' (ĭm·rôz'), Gr. **Imbros** (ĭm'brŏs) island, Turkey, in NE Aegean Sea W of Gallipoli Peninsula.

In·chon (ĭn·chŏn) or **Che·mul·po** (jĕ·mōōl·pô), also **Jin·sen** (jĕn·sĕn) seaport, S Korea, on W coast SW of Seoul; pop. 265,800.

In·de·pend'ence, city, W Missouri, E of Kansas City; pop. 37,000.

In'di·a (ĭn'dĭ·à; esp. Brit., -dyà) **1** peninsula, often called a subcontinent, S Asia, since 1947 including two independent countries, India and Pakistan. **2** or **Bha'rat** (bŭ'rŭt) country, comprising the larger part of the subcontinent; formerly part of the British Empire, since 1947 independent and since January 1950 a republic; ✴ New Delhi; area 1,266,900 sq. m.; pop. 361,151,700. **3** or **Indian Empire**, before 1947 those parts of India under British rule or protection, before 1937 including Burma and Aden; comprised British India and the princely states (Indian States). See INDIAN, in Vocab.

In'di·an'a (ĭn'dĭ·ăn'à), abbr. **Ind.**, state, N cen. United States, bordering Lake Michigan in NW; ✴ Indianapolis; area 36,291 sq. m., not including 228 sq. m. of water in Lake Michigan; pop. 3,934,200. — **In'di·an'i·an** (-ăn'ĭ·ăn), adj. & n.

In'di·an·ap'o·lis (ĭn'dĭ·ăn·ăp'ô·lĭs; -ăp'lĭs) city, ✴ of Indiana; pop. 427,200.

Indian Desert. See THAR DESERT.

Indian Ocean, body of water E of Africa, S of Asia, W of Australia, and N of Antarctica; area 28,375,000 sq. m.

Indian River, lagoon, E Florida, extending between mainland and coastal islands for 165 m.

Indian States, before 1947, the 562 semi-independent states of India that were ruled by native princes.

Indian Territory, former territory in present state of Oklahoma.

In'dies (ĭn'dĭz; -dēz) usually, the East Indies; sometimes, the West Indies.

In'di·gir'ka (ĭn'dữ·gĭr'kà) river, Soviet Russia, Asia, in NE Yakutsk Republic, flowing N to East Siberian Sea; 850 m. long.

In'do·chi'na (ĭn'dô·chī'nà) **1** or **Farther India**, the southeast peninsula of Asia, including Burma, Thailand, and the states of Laos, Vietnam, and Cambodia. **2** before 1946 usually called **French Indochina**, former country in E part of Indochina peninsula, bordering on South China Sea and Gulf of Siam; a federation of associated states (Vietnam, Cambodia, and Laos, often referred to as the **Associated States of Indochina**) of the French Union; since 1954, the region including Vietnam, Cambodia, and Laos. See INDO-CHINESE, INDO-CHINESE, in Vocab.

In'do·ne'sia (ĭn'dô·nē'zhà; -zhĭ·à; -shà; -shĭ·à) **1** island country, SE Asia, comprising the islands of the Malay Archipelago (Java, Sumatra, etc., but not West New Guinea) which, as the **Netherlands Indies**, belonged before December 1949 to the Netherlands; a republic; ✴ Djakarta; area 583,479 sq. m.; pop. 76,260,000. **2** the Malay Archipelago; — an occasional name. — **In'do·ne'sian**, adj. & n.

In·dore' (ĭn·dōr') **1** former state, cen. India, in the Narbada valley; part of state of Madhya Bharat 1948–56; part of Madhya Pradesh from 1956. **2** city, its ✴, later ✴ of Madhya Bharat; pop. 138,100.

In'dus (ĭn'dŭs) river, NW Indian subcontinent, rising in Tibet and flowing through W Pakistan to the Arabian Sea; over 1700 m. long.

In'gle·wood (ĭng'g'l·wood) city, SW California; pop. 46,200.

I'ni'ni', Territory of (ē'nē'nē') inland section of French Guiana.

In'ker·man (ĭng'kẽr·măn; Russ. ĭn·kẽr·màn') village, Soviet Russia, Europe, in SW Crimea just E of Sevastopol; battle 1854.

Ink'ster (ĭngk'stẽr) village, SE Michigan; pop. 16,700.

Inland Empire, region, NW United States, between Cascade Range and Rocky Mts., including E Washington, NE Oregon, N Idaho, and extreme W Montana.

Inland Sea, Jap. **Se·to Nai·kai** (sĕ·tô nī·kī) or **Seto no U·chi** (nô ōō·chē) body of water, Japan, between Honshu I. on N and Shikoku and Kyushu Is. on S.

Inn (ĭn) river, W Europe, in Switzerland, Austria, and Germany; flows NE to the Danube; 320 m. long.

Inner Hebrides. See HEBRIDES.

Inner Mongolia. See MONGOLIA, INNER.

Inns'bruck (ĭnz'brŏŏk; Ger. ĭns'-) city, W Austria, in the Tirol on Inn river; pop. 96,900.

In'ter·la'ken (ĭn'tẽr·lä'kĕn; ĭn'tẽr·lä'kĕn) town, Switzerland, in Bern canton on Aare river, between Lake of Thun and Lake of Brienz.

In'ver·ness' (ĭn·vẽr·nĕs'; ĭn'vẽr·nĕs') **1** or **In'ver·ness'-shire** (-vẽr·nĕs'shĭr; -nĕsh'-; -shẽr) county, NW Scotland; ✴ Inverness; area 4211 sq. m.; pop. 84,900. **2** burgh, its ✴; pop. 28,100.

In'yo·kern' (ĭn'yô·kûrn') town, S California, in NW Mojave Desert; site of a naval ordnance research station.

Io·an'ni·na (yô·ä'nyē·nä), also **Yan'ni·na** (yä'nē·nä), Serb. **Ja'ni·na** (yä'nē·nä) city, NW Greece, near Albanian frontier; pop. 20,500.

I·o'na (ī·ō'nà) island, Scotland, in Inner Hebrides off SW tip of Mull I.; early center of the Celtic church.

I·o'ni·a (ī·ō'nĭ·à; -ōn'yà) ancient district, W Asia Minor, bordering on Aegean Sea; never a political unit, had religious league of 12 cities. — **I·o'ni·an**, adj. & n. See also IONIC, in Vocab.

Ionian Islands, group of 7 islands, W Greece, in Ionian Sea; area 853 sq. m.; pop. 259,600.

Ionian Sea, body of water between SE Italy and W Greece.

I'o·wa (ī'ô·wà; locally also -wä) **1** river, Iowa, flowing SE into the Mississippi; 291 m. long. **2**, abbr. (not official) **Ia.**, state, N cen. United States, just W of the Mississippi river; ✴ Des Moines; area 56,280 sq. m.; pop. 2,621,100. — **I'o·wan** (ī'ô·wăn), adj. & n.

Iowa City, city, E Iowa; pop. 27,200.

I'pin' (ē'pĭn'), formerly **Su'chow'** (sü'jō'; shü'-) or **Sui'fu'** (swä'foo') city, S cen. China, in SW Szechwan prov. on Yangtze river at its junction with the Min; pop. 125,000.

Ípiros. See EPIRUS.

I'poh (ē'pō) city, Federation of Malaya, in cen. Perak state; pop. 80,900.

Ipsambul. See ABU SIMBEL.

Ip'sus (ĭp'sŭs) ancient village, Asia Minor, in S Phrygia; battle 301 B.C.

Ips'wich (ĭps'wĭch) county borough, E England, ✴ of East Suffolk, at head of Orwell estuary; pop. 104,800.

Íráklion. See CANDIA.

I·ran' (ē·rän'; ĭ·rän', ĭ-) or (before 1935, officially) **Per'sia** (pûr'zhà; -shà) country, SW Asia, bordering on Caspian Sea and Persian Gulf; kingdom; ✴ Tehran; area 628,000 sq. m.; pop. 15,000,000.

I·raq′ (ĭ-räk′; ĭ-răk′) **1** also **I·rak′** or **'I·raq′**, country, SW Asia, in Mesopotamia; formerly a kingdom, became a republic 1958; ✱ Baghdad; 116,600 sq. m.; pop. 3,800,000. **2** see ARAK. See IRAQI, in Vocab.

Ire′land (īr′lănd) **1** island, N Europe, one of the British Isles; includes the Republic of Ireland and Northern Ireland (see NORTHERN IRELAND); total area 31,840 sq. m. **2** Gael. **Ei′re** (Ir. ā′rĕ; in English, also ā′rĕ, âr′ĕ, âr′ĕ, ī′rĕ, ī′rĕ), also 1922–37 **I′rish Free State** (ī′rĭsh), Gael. **Saor′stat′ Eir′eann** (sâr′stŏt′ âr′ĭn) country occupying most of the island of Ireland; formerly (1922–37) a dominion of the British Commonwealth; proclaimed independent state 1937 and Republic of Ireland 1949; ✱ Dublin; area 26,602 sq. m.; pop. 2,958,900. See HIBERNIA, HIBERNIAN, IRISH, in Vocab.

Irian. See NETHERLANDS NEW GUINEA.

Irish Sea, body of water between England and Ireland.

Ir·kutsk′ (ĭr·kōōtsk′) city, S Soviet Russia, Asia, on Angara river; pop. 243,400.

I′ron Gate or **Gates** (ī′ẽrn), Romanian **Por·ţi′le de Fier** (pôr·tsē′lĕ dĕ fyĕr′), Ger. **Ei′ser·nes Tor** (ī′zĕr·nĕs tōr′) gorge in Danube river, on border between Romania and Yugoslavia at place where the river cuts around end of Transylvanian Alps; 2 m. long.

I′ron·ton (ī′ẽrn·tŭn) city, S Ohio, on Ohio river; pop. 16,300.

Ir′ra·wad′dy (ĭr′ȧ·wŏd′ĭ) river, cen. Burma, flowing S into Bay of Bengal through several mouths; 1350 m. long.

Ir·tysh′ or **Ir·tish′** (ĭr·tĭsh′) river, cen. Asia, flowing from Altai Mts. in Sinkiang, China, to the Ob river in Russia; over 2000 m. long.

Ir′ving·ton (ûr′vĭng·tŭn) **1** town, NE New Jersey, W of Newark; pop. 59,200. **2** village, SE New York, on Hudson river S of Tarrytown.

Isabel. See SANTA ISABEL.

I′sar (ē′zär) river, S Germany, in Bavaria; rises in the Tirol and flows NW into the Danube; 219 m. long.

I·sau′ri·a (ī·sô′rĭ·ȧ) ancient district, Asia Minor, on N slope of W Taurus Mts. — **I·sau′ri·an,** adj. & n.

Is′chi·a (ĭs′kĭ·ȧ; Ital. ēs′kyä) island, Italy, in Tyrrhenian Sea between Gulf of Gaeta and Bay of Naples.

I·se Bay (ē·sĕ) ocean inlet, Japan, on S coast of Honshu.

I′sère (ē′zâr′) river, SE France; flows SW to the Rhone; 150 m. long.

Is′fa·han (ĭs′fȧ·hän; -hän), formerly **Is′pa·han** (-pȧ-) city, W cen. Iran, former ✱ of Persia; pop. 192,000.

I·shim′ (ĭ·shĭm′) river, Soviet Russia, Asia, rising in Kazakh S.S.R. and flowing N to the Irtysh; 1330 m. long.

Iskandarîyah, al-. See ALEXANDRIA.

Is′ken·de·ron′ (ĕs′kĕn·dĕ·rōōn′), formerly **Al′ex·an·dret′ta** (ăl′ĕg·zăn·drĕt′ȧ; ăl′ĭg-; Brit. also -zän-) seaport, S Turkey; pop. 22,900.

Island, Ísland. See ICELAND.

Isle-de-France. See ÎLE-DE-FRANCE.

Isle of Ely; Isle of Man. See ELY, ISLE OF; MAN, ISLE OF.

Isle of Pines (īl, pīnz) **1** Span. **Is′la de Pi′nos** (ēz′lä thä pē′nŏs) island, West Indies, S of W Cuba; area 1180 sq. m.; pop. 9500. **2** island in Pacific Ocean: see KUNIE.

Isle of Wight. See WIGHT, ISLE OF.

Isle Roy′ale (īl roi′ăl) island, Michigan, in NW Lake Superior; forested wilderness; site of old copper mines; since 1940 a national park.

Is′ling·ton (ĭz′lĭng·tŭn) metropolitan borough, London, NW of the City; pop. 235,600.

Is′ma·il′i·a (ĭz′mä·ĭl′ē′ȧ) town, NE Egypt, on Lake Timsah; halfway station on Suez Canal.

Isole Eolie. See LIPARI ISLANDS.

I·son′zo (ē·zōn′tsō) river, NW Yugoslavia and NE Italy, flowing S into Gulf of Trieste; 75 m. long.

Ispahan. See ISFAHAN.

Is′ra·el (ĭz′rĭ·ĕl; -rå·ĕl) **1** ancient kingdom, Palestine, comprising lands occupied by the Hebrew people; first established c. 1025 B.C.; divided c. 933 B.C. into a southern kingdom of Judah and a northern kingdom of Israel. **2 or Northern Kingdom,** sometimes called **E′phra·im** (ē′frä·ĭm; ē′frĭ·ăm) the northern part of the Hebrew kingdom after the division. **3** modern country, comprising the larger part of Palestine; before World War I part of the Ottoman Empire; a British mandate 1923–48; since 1948 a republic; ✱ Jerusalem; area about 7800 sq. m.; pop. 1,400,000. See ISRAELI, ISRAELITE, in Vocab.

Is′sus (ĭs′ŭs) ancient town, S Asia Minor, 20 m. N of modern İskenderon; battles 333 B.C. and A.D. 194.

Is′syk Kul (ĭs′ĭk kŭl′), also **Is′siq Köl** (ĭs′ĭk kŭl′) lake, Soviet Central Asia, in NE Kirgiz Republic; area over 2200 sq. m.

İs′tan·bul′ (ĭs′tăm·bŏŏl′, formerly **Con′stan·ti·no′ple** (kŏn′stăn·t'n·ō′p'l), anc. **By·zan′ti·um** (bĭ·zăn′shĭ·ŭm; bĭ-; -shŭm; -tĭ·ŭm) city, Turkey in Europe, on the Bosporus and Sea of Marmara; former ✱ of Turkey; pop. 1,000,000.

Ister. See DANUBE.

Is′tri·a (ĭs′trĭ·ȧ) or **Is′tri·an Peninsula** (-ȧn) peninsula, SW Europe, at head of Adriatic Sea; belongs to Yugoslavia (since 1947) except for area around Trieste.

I·ta·bi′ra (ē·tȧ·vē′rȧ) town, SE Brazil, in Minas Gerais state; built on a hill containing iron ore.

Italian East Africa, former Italian possessions in East Africa, including Eritrea, Ethiopia, and Italian Somaliland.

Italian Somaliland or **So·ma′li·a** (sō·mä′lĕ·ȧ), Ital. **So·ma′lia I·ta·li·a′na** (sō·mä′lyä ē·tä·lĕ·ä′nä) country, E Africa, constituting since 1950 a trust territory under Italian administration; formerly an Italian colony; ✱ Mogadiscio; area 194,000 sq. m.; pop. 1,150,000.

It′a·ly (ĭt′'l·ĭ; -ȧ·lĭ), Ital. **I·ta′lia** (ē·tä′lyä), Lat. **I·tal′i·a** (ĭ·tăl′ĭ·ȧ; -tăl′yȧ) country, S Europe, comprising a boot-shaped peninsula 760 m. long; formerly a kingdom, since 1946 a republic; ✱ Rome; area 119,764 sq. m.; pop. 46,452,000. See ITALIAN, in Vocab.

I·tas′ca, Lake (ī·tăs′kȧ) lake, N Minnesota; source of Mississippi river.

Iténez. See GUAPORÉ.

Ith′a·ca (ĭth′ȧ·kȧ) city, New York, on Cayuga Lake; pop. 29,300.

Ithaca, Mod. Gr. **I·thá′ki** (ē·thä′kyē) island, W Greece, one of Ionian Is.; area 36 sq. m.; pop. 8800.

I·va′no·vo (ĭ·vä′nŭ·vŭ), formerly **Ivanovo Voz·ne·sensk′** (vŭz·nyĭ·syĕnsk′) city, Soviet Russia, Europe, S of the Volga; pop. 285,100.

Ivory Coast, Fr. **Côte d'Ivoire′** (kōt′ dē′vwàr′) **1** region, W Africa, along Atlantic coast W of Gold Coast; — so named because it was once source of ivory. **2** region, W Africa, including Ivory Coast and hinterland; one of territories of French West Africa; ✱ Abidjan; area 129,807 sq. m.; pop. 2,031,000.

I′vry′-la-Ba′taille′ (ē′vrē′lȧ-bȧ′tä′y′) town, N France, on Eure river W of Paris; scene of victory of Huguenots Mar. 14, 1590.

I′wo (ē′wō) city, W Nigeria, just NE of Ibadan; pop. 57,200.

I′wo Ji′ma (ē′wō jē′mȧ) island, Volcano Is., 660 nautical m. S of Tokyo; scene of heavy fighting February–March 1945.

Ix′elles′ (ĕk′sĕl′), Flem. **El′se·ne** (ĕl′sĕ·nĕ) commune, cen. Belgium, a suburb of Brussels; pop. 92,200.

I′za·bal′, Lake (ē′sä·väl′) lake, E Guatemala; 25 m. long.

I′zhevsk (ē′zhĕfsk) town, Soviet Russia, Europe, ✱ of Udmurt Republic; pop. 175,700.

Iz′ma·il (ĭz′mä·ĭl; Russ. ĭz·mŭ·ēl′) city, U.S.S.R., in the Ukraine on N side of Danube delta; pop. 26,100.

İz·mir′ (ĭz·mĭr′), formerly **Smyr′na** (smûr′nȧ) seaport, W Turkey in Asia, at head of Gulf of İzmir; pop. 230,500.

İz·nik′ (ĭz·nĭk′), anc. **Ni·cae′a** (nĭ·sē′ȧ), Angl. **Nice** (nīs) village, NW Turkey in Asia, at end of İznik Lake; ancient Nicaea a great city of Byzantine Empire.

Iz′tac·ci′huatl (ēs′täk·sē′wä·t'l) or **Ix′ta·ci′huatl** (ēs′tä·sē′wä·t'l) mountain, Mexico, N of Popocatepetl; 17,343 ft. high.

J

Jabal. See JEBEL.

Jabalpur. See JUBBULPORE.

Já′chy·mov (yä′kĭ·môf), Ger. **Sankt Jo′a·chims·thal′** (zängkt yō′ä·kĭms·täl′; yō·äk′ĭms-) town, Czechoslovakia, in NW Bohemia in Erz Gebirge; uranium mines.

Jack′son (jăk′s'n) **1** city, S Michigan; pop. 51,100. **2** city, ✱ of Mississippi; pop. 98,300. **3** city, ✱ of Tennessee; pop. 30,200.

Jack′son·ville (jăk′s'n·vĭl) **1** seaport, NE Florida, near mouth of St. Johns river; pop. 204,500. **2** city, W cen. Illinois; pop. 20,400.

Jacques Car′tier′ (zhäk′ kär′tyä′) town, Canada, in Quebec near mouth of Jacques Cartier river SW of city of Quebec; pop. 33,100.

Ja·én′ (hä·ān′) commune, S Spain; pop. 64,400.

Jaf′fa (jăf′ȧ; yăf′ȧ), Heb. **Ya·fo′** (yä·fō′), Lat. **Jop′pa** (jŏp′ȧ) seaport, Israel; incorporated 1950 in Tel Aviv.

Jaff′na (jäf′nȧ) town, N Ceylon; pop. 62,500.

Jagannath. See PURI.

Jai′pur (jī′pŏŏr) **1** former state, NW India; now part of Rajasthan state. **2** city, its ✱, now ✱ of Rajasthan; pop. 175,800.

Ja·kar′ta. = DJAKARTA.

Ja·la′pa (hä·lä′pä) city, E Mexico, ✱ of Veracruz state; pop. 39,500.

Ja·lis′co (hä·lēs′kō) state, W cen. Mexico; ✱ Guadalajara; area 31,149 sq. m.; pop. 1,744,700.

Jal′u·it (jäl′ōō·ĭt) island, Marshall Is., in Ralik chain; largest of the Marshall Is., an atoll 38 m. long by 21 m. wide.

Ja·mai′ca (jȧ·mā′kȧ) **1** section of New York City, on Long I. in Queens borough; formerly a town. **2** island, West Indies, one of Greater Antilles; a British colony, with dependencies (Turks and Caicos Is., Cayman Is., etc.), since 1958 a territory of the West Indies Federation; area 4722 sq. m.; pop. 1,249,400; area of island 4450 sq. m.; pop. 1,237,400. — **Ja·mai′can,** adj. & n.

James (jāmz) **1** see DAKOTA river. **2** river, cen. Virginia, flowing E into Chesapeake Bay at Hampton Roads; 340 m. long.

James Bay, southern extension of Hudson Bay, NE Canada, between NE Ontario and W Quebec provs.; 280 m. long and 150 m. wide.

James′town (jāmz′toun) **1** city, SW New York, at S end of Chautauqua Lake; pop. 43,400. **2** ruined village, E Virginia; first permanent English settlement in America, founded May 13, 1607.

Jammu and Kashmir. See KASHMIR.

Jam′shed·pur′ (jäm′shĕd·pŏŏr′) city, NE India, in S Bihar; pop. 148,700.

Janes′ville (jānz′vĭl) city, S Wisconsin, N of Beloit; pop. 24,900.

Ja·nic′u·lum (jȧ·nĭk′ū·lŭm) hill, Rome, Italy, on the Tiber opposite the Seven Hills.

Janina. See IOANNINA.

Jan May′en Island (yän mī′ĕn) island in Arctic Ocean 300 m. E of Greenland and 360 m. NNE of Iceland; belongs to Norway.

Ja·pan′ (jȧ·păn′), Japanese **Nip·pon** (nĕp·pŏn′ or Ni·hon (nĕ·hŏn), also **Dai Nippon** (dī) island country, E Asia, in Pacific Ocean E of Korea and SE Soviet Russia, Asia; includes chiefly the four main islands of Honshu, Hokkaido, Kyushu, and Shikoku; an empire; ✱ Tokyo; area 146,690 sq. m.; pop. 83,199,600. See JAPANESE, in Vocab.

Japan, Sea of, body of water between Japan and Asiatic mainland.

Ja′pu·rá′ (zhä′pŏŏ·rä′) river, Colombia and Brazil, flowing SE into Amazon river; 1750 m. long.

Jar′vis Island (jär′vĭs) island, Line Is., just S of the equator; occupied by the United States since 1935.

Jas′per National Park (jăs′pẽr) mountain region, W Canada, in W Alberta; established as national park 1907.

Jasper Place, town, Canada, W suburb of Edmonton, Alberta; pop. 16,000.

Jassy. See IAŞI.

Ja′va (jä′vȧ; jăv′ȧ) island, Indonesia, chief island of the republic; site of Djakarta; with Madura, 50,942 sq. m.; pop. 50,000,000. — **Java·nese′** (jăv′ȧ·nēz′; -nēs′), adj. & n.

Ja′va·rí′ (zhä′vȧ·rē′) or **Ya′ca·ra′na** (yä′kȧ·rä′nȧ) river, Peru and Brazil, flowing NE on the boundary and into the Amazon; 650 m. long.

Java Sea, body of water, Indonesia, between Java and Borneo.

Jaxartes. See SYR DARYA.

Jean·nette′ (jĕ·nĕt′) city, SW Pennsylvania; pop. 16,200.

Je′bel, Ja′bal, Ge′bel, or (Fr. transliteration) **Dje′bel** (jĕb′ĕl; Arab. jä′băl) mountain or hill; — various transliterations of the Arabic word; for names of mountains containing these forms, see the second element, as Jebel Musa, see MUSA, JEBEL.

Je′bel ed Druz (jĕb′ĕl ĕd drōōz′) or **Jebel Druze** (jĕb′ĕl drōōz′) region, S Syria, on border of Jordan; formerly (1921–42) autonomous; ✱ Es Suweida; area 2700 sq. m.; pop. 71,000.

Jedda. See JIDDA.

Jef′fer·son City (jĕf′ẽr·s'n) city, ✱ of Missouri, on Missouri river; pop. 25,100.

Jeh′lam. Var. of JHELUM.

Je·hol′ (jĕ·hōl′) **1** former province, N China, N of the Great Wall, between Inner Mongolia and Manchuria; administered 1949–56 as part of Manchuria; divided 1956 between Liaoning and Hopeh provinces and Inner Mongolia Autonomous Region; ✱ Chengteh (Jehol). **2** city: see CHENGTEH.

Je·mappes′ (zhĕ·màp′) town, SW Belgium, W of Mons; battle 1792.

Je′na (yā′nä) city, E Germany, on Saale river E of Erfurt; pop. 82,700.

Jen′nings (jĕn′ĭngz) city, E Missouri, suburb of St. Louis; pop. 15,300.

Je·qui′ti·nho′nha (zhĕ·kē′tē·nyō′nyà) river, E Brazil, flowing NE and E into Atlantic Ocean; 500 m. long.

Je·rez′ or **Jerez de la Fron·te′ra** (hã·rãth′ [-rãz′] thã lä frôn·tā′rä) formerly **Xe′res** (old pron. shã′rãs, shē′rĕs; mod. hã′rãs) city, SW Spain, NE of Cádiz; pop. 107,000.

Jer′i·cho (jĕr′ĭ·kō) ancient city, Palestine, just N of Dead Sea.

Jer′sey (jûr′zĭ) **1** New Jersey. **2** island, English Channel, one of Channel Is.; ✱ St. Helier; area 45 sq. m.; pop. 50,500.

Jersey City, city, NE New Jersey, on Hudson river and Upper New York Bay; pop. 299,000.

Je·ru′sa·lem (jĕ·rōō′så·lĕm), Arab. **El Quds esh She·rif′** (ăl kōōts′ ăsh shã·rēf′), anc. **Hi′er·o·sol′y·ma** (hī′ĕr·ō·sŏl′ĭ·mà) city, S Palestine, ancient ✱ of Israel and Judah and in modern times ✱ of Palestine; since 1948 divided between Jordan (old city) and the republic of Israel (new city, ✱ of the Republic since 1950); pop. 1,247,000.

Jer′vis Bay (jär′vĭs; jûr′-) inlet of Pacific Ocean, SE Australia, on SE coast of New South Wales.

Jes′sel·ton (jĕs′'l·tŭn; -t'n) seaport, ✱ of North Borneo, on China Sea; pop. 11,700.

Jewish Autonomous Region, also **Bi′ro·bi·dzhan′** or **Bi′ro-Bi·djan′** (bē′rō·bĭ·jän′) autonomous region, E Soviet Russia, Asia, bordering on Amur river; ✱ Birobidzhan; 14,085 sq. m.; pop. 198,400.

Jezira, El. See GEZIRA.

Jez′re·el (jĕz′rē·ĕl; -rēl) town, ancient Palestine, in Samaria in **Valley of Jezreel,** at E end of plain of Esdraelon, NW of Mt. Gilboa.

Jhan′si (jän′sĭ) city, N India, in Uttar Pradesh; pop. 103,300.

Jhe′lum (jā′lŭm), anc. **Hy·das′pes** (hī·dăs′pēz) river, NW Indian subcontinent, flowing from Kashmir to West Punjab and into the Chenab river; 450 m. long.

Jibuti. See DJIBOUTI.

Jid′da (jĭd′à) or **Jed′da** (jĕd′à) seaport, W Saudi Arabia, in Hejaz on coast of Red Sea; the port of Mecca; pop. 30,000.

Jinsen. See INCHON.

João Pes·so′a (zhwouɴm pĕ·sō′à), sometimes called **Pa′ra·i′ba** (pä′rä·ē′và) city, E Brazil, ✱ of Paraíba state; pop. 90,900.

Jodh′pur (jŏd′pĕr) **1** or **Mar′war** (mär′wär) former state, NW India, bordering on Thar Desert and Rann of Kutch; since 1949 part of Rajasthan state. **2** city, its ✱; pop. 126,800.

Jog′ja·kar′ta. Var. of DJOKJAKARTA.

Jo·han′nes·burg (jō·hăn′ĭs·bûrg; -ĭz-; yŏ·hän′ĕs-) city, NE Union of South Africa, in S Transvaal; pop. with suburbs 606,000.

John o′ Groat′s or **John o′ Groat′s House** (jŏn′ ŭ grōts′) point, N Scotland, on N coast of Caithness county.

John′son City (jŏn′s'n) **1** village, S New York, W of Binghamton; pop. 19,200. **2** city, NE Tennessee; pop. 27,900.

John′ston (jŏn′stŭn; jŏn′s'n) island, cen. Pacific Ocean, 700 m. SW of Honolulu; belongs to the United States; naval air station.

Johns′town (jŏnz′toun) city, SW cen. Pennsylvania, on Conemaugh river; pop. 63,200.

Jo·hore′ (jō·hōr′) state, Federation of Malaya, at S end of Malay Penin.; ✱ Johore Bahru; area 7321 sq. m.; pop. 738,300.

Jok′ya·kar′ta. Var. of DJOKJAKARTA.

Jo′li·et (jō′lĭ·ĕt; jō′lĭ·ĕt′) city, NE Illinois; pop. 51,600.

Jo′liette (zhō′lyĕt′) city, Canada, in Quebec prov. N of Montreal; pop. 16,900.

Jo·lo′ (hō·lō′; Angl. hō′lō) or **Su′lu** (sōō′lōō) island, Philippine Is., chief island of Sulu Archipelago; area 345 sq. m.

Jones′bor′o (jōnz′bŭr′ŏ) city, NE Arkansas; pop. 16,300.

Jon·quière′ (zhôn′kyär′) town, Canada, in S Quebec; pop. 25,600.

Jop′lin (jŏp′lĭn) city, SW Missouri; pop. 38,700.

Joppa. See JAFFA.

Jor′dan (jôr′d'n) **1** river, Palestine, flowing from Anti-Lebanon Mts. W of Mt. Hermon S to the Dead Sea; traverses Waters of Merom and Sea of Galilee; 200 m. long. **2** formerly **Trans·jor′dan** (trăns·jôr′d'n) country, SW Asia, chiefly E of the Jordan river, since 1950 including a portion of Palestine W of the Jordan; a Hashimite kingdom; ✱ Amman; area 39,460 sq. m.; pop. 1,400,000. — **Jor·da′ni·an** (jôr·dā′nĭ·ăn; -dän′yăn), adj. & n.

Juan de Fu′ca Strait (hwän′ dĕ fōō′kà) strait between Vancouver I., Canada, and the Olympic Penin., NW Washington; 100 m. long.

Juan Fer·nán′dez (hwäm′ fĕr·nän′dãs; Angl. jōō′ăn fĕr·năn′dĕz) three islands, S Pacific Ocean, 400 m. W of Chile, to which they belong.

Ju′ba (jōō′bà), Ital. **Giu′ba** (jōō′bà) river, E Africa; rises in Ethiopia, flows S across SW Italian Somaliland to Indian Ocean; 1000 m. long.

Jub′bul·pore (jŭb′ŭl·pōr) or **Ja′bal·pur** (jŭb′ăl·pōōr) city, cen. India, in Madhya Pradesh near Narbada river; pop. 104,300.

Juby, Cape. See YUBI, CAPE.

Ju′car (hōō′kär) river, E Spain, flowing S and E into Mediterranean Sea; 300 m. long.

Ju·dae′a or **Ju·de′a** (jōō·dē′à) ancient region, S Palestine, constituting the southern division of the country under Persian, Greek, and Roman rule. — **Ju·dae′an, Ju·de′an,** adj. & n.

Ju′dah (jōō′dà) ancient kingdom, S Palestine, the southern kingdom of the Jews after N part had broken away c. 933 B.C.; ✱ Jerusalem.

Juggernaut. See PURI.

Jugoslavia, Jugoslavija. See YUGOSLAVIA.

Juiz de Fo′ra (zhwēzh′ thĕ fô′rà) city, E Brazil, in S Minas Gerais state; pop. 86,800.

Jul′ian Alps (jōōl′yăn) section of E Alps, NW Yugoslavia, N of Istria.

Ju′li·a′ne·haab′ (yōō′lē·ä′nĕ·hôp′) seaport, S Greenland.

Julian Venetia. See VENETIA.

Jul′lun·dur (jŭl′ŭn·dĕr) city, NW India, in Punjab state (East Punjab); pop. 135,300.

Jum′na (jŭm′nà) river, N India, in Uttar Pradesh, flowing from the Himalayas S and SE to the Ganges; 860 m. long.

Ju′neau (jōō′nō) seaport, ✱ of Alaska, in SE on mainland; pop. 5800.

Jung′frau (yŏŏng′frou′) mountain, SW cen. Switzerland, in Bernese Alps on border between Bern and Valais cantons; 13,668 ft. high.

Ju′ni·at′a (jōō′nĭ·ăt′à) river, S cen. Pennsylvania, flowing into Susquehanna river; 150 m. long.

Ju·nín′ (hōō·nēn′) town, Peru, at S end of Lake Junín; battle 1824.

Ju′ra (jŏŏr′à) **1** (Fr. zhü′rà′) mountains, France and Switzerland, extending 200 m. along the boundary; highest peak Reculet, 5642 ft. **2** island, W Scotland, in the Inner Hebrides. See JURASSIC, in Vocab.

Juramento, Río del. See SALADO, RÍO.

Ju·ruá′ (zhōō·rwà′) river, NW cen. South America; rises in E cen. Peru and flows NE to the Solimões in NW Brazil; over 1200 m. long.

Ju·rue′na (zhōō·rwä′nà) river, W cen. Brazil; flows N and unites with the São Manoel to form the Tapajoz; 600 m. long.

Jut′land (jŭt′lŏnd), Dan. **Jyl′land** (yül′än) **1** peninsula, N Europe, most of which constitutes mainland of Denmark, the extreme S portion belonging to Germany. **2** the mainland of Denmark.

K

For many names such as **Kabinda, Karnatic, Kanea,** etc., see CABINDA, CARNATIC, CANEA, etc., the usual forms.

K². See GODWIN AUSTEN.

Kab′ar·din′i·an Autonomous Soviet Socialist Republic (kăb′ẽr·dĭn′ĭ·ăn; -dē′nĭ·ăn) autonomous republic, Soviet Russia, Europe, in N Caucasus region; before World War II known as the **Kab′ar·di′no-Bal·kar′i·an A.S.S.R.** (kăb′ẽr·dē′nō·băl·kär′ĭ·ăn) and included **Bal·kar′i·a** (băl·kär′ĭ·à), now mostly in the Georgian S.S.R.; ✱ Nalchik; area (since World War II) 4600 sq. m.; pop. 300,000.

Ka′bul (kä′bŏŏl; kà·bōōl′) **1** river, Afghanistan and Pakistan, flowing to the Indus; 360 m. long. **2** city, ✱ of Afghanistan, on Kabul river; pop. 120,000.

Ka·chin′ State (kà·chĭn′) region, N Burma, around Myitkyina and Bhamo; made state of Union of Burma 1947.

Kadiak. See KODIAK.

Ka′di·köy′ (kä′dĭ·kû′ē), anc. **Chal′ce·don** (kăl′sĕ·dŏn; -dŭn; kăl·sē′d'n) district of İstanbul, Turkey, on Asiatic side of the Bosporus.

Kae·song (kä·sŏng) or **Kai·jo** (kī·jō) city, S Korea, NW of Seoul and just S of 38th parallel; pop. 88,700.

Kaf·frar′i·a (kà·frär′ĭ·à) region, Union of South Africa, in E Cape Province S of Natal, bordering on Indian Ocean.

Kaf′i·ri·stan′ (käf′ĭ·rĭ·stän′; kà·fĭr′ĭ·stän′; kä′fĭ·rĭ·stän′) district, E Afghanistan, S of Hindu Kush Mts., inhabited by the Kafirs.

Ka·fu′e (kä·fōō′à) river, Northern Rhodesia, flowing to the Zambezi river; 500 m. long.

Ka·ge′ra (kä·gā′rä) river, NW Tanganyika Territory; flows N, then turns E and empties into Lake Victoria; 430 m. long.

Kagi. See CHIAI.

Ka·go·shi·ma (kä·gō·shē·mä) seaport, Japan, on Kyushu; pop. 170,400.

Kai·e·teur′ Falls (kī′ĕ·tōōr′) waterfall, cen. British Guiana, in Potaro river; 741 ft. high, 350 ft. wide.

Kai′feng′ (kī′fŭng′) city, E cen. China, ✱ of Honan prov., in Hwang Ho valley; pop. 223,000.

Kair′ouan′ (Fr. kĕr′wän′) or **Kair·wan′** (kĭr·wän′) city, NE Tunisia, a holy city of the Moslems; capital of the Aghlabite dynasty 800–909.

Kai′sers·lau′tern (kī′zẽrs·lou′tẽrn) city, W Germany, W of Ludwigshafen; pop. 62,200.

Kaishu. See HAEJU.

Kalaeloa Point. See BARBERS POINT.

Ka′la·ha′ri Desert (kä′lä·hä′rē) region, S Africa, N of Orange river and S of Lake Ngami, in Bechuanaland.

Kalakh. See CALAH.

Kal′a·ma·zoo′ (kăl′à·mà·zōō′) city, SW Michigan; pop. 57,700.

Ka·lat′ or **Khe·lat′** (kà·lät′) state, Pakistan, in E Baluchistan; ✱ Kalat; area 72,503 sq. m.; pop. 287,100.

Kal′gan′ (kăl′gän′) or **Chang′kia′kow′** (jäng′jĭ·ä′kō′), formerly (before 1947) also called **Wan′chuan′** (wän′chü·än′) city, N China, ✱ of Inner Mongolian Autonomous Region; pop. 130,000.

Kalimantan. See BORNEO.

Ka·li′nin (kà·lē′nĭn; Russ. kŭ·lyē′nyĭn), before 1932 **Tver** (tà·vĕr′; Russ. tvyĕr′y′) city, W cen. Soviet Russia, Europe, on the Volga; pop. 216,100.

Ka·li′nin·grad (kà·lē′nĭn·grăd), Ger. **Kö′nigs·berg** (kû′nĭks·bĕrk; Angl. kā′nĭgz·bûrg) seaport, W Soviet Russia, Europe, on Pregel river near the Frisches Haff; formerly ✱ of East Prussia; pop. 368,400.

Ka′lisz (kä′lĕsh), Ger. **Ka′lisch** (kä′lĭsh) commune, cen. Poland; pop. 80,200.

Ka·lu′ga (kà·lōō′gà) city, Soviet Russia, Europe, WNW of Tula on Oka river; pop. 89,500.

Ka′ma (kä′mà) river, E Soviet Russia, Europe, flowing from the Ural Mts. to the Volga river; 1200 m. long.

Ka·ma·ku·ra (kä′mä·kōō·rä) city, Japan, in Honshu on Sagami Sea S of Yokohama; colossal statue of Buddha; pop. 55,200.

Kam·chat′ka (kăm·chăt′kä) peninsula, NE Soviet Russia, Asia, extending S between Sea of Okhotsk and Bering Sea; 750 m. long.

Kamerun. See CAMEROONS.

Ka′met (kŭ′mŭt) mountain, N India, in Uttar Pradesh on Tibet border; 25,447 ft. high.

Kam·pa′la (käm·pä′lä) town, Uganda, ✱ of Buganda, N of Entebbe.

Kamperduin. See CAMPERDOWN.

Kan, 1 (gän) river, in Kiangsi prov., flowing N through Poyang Hu into the Yangtse; 350 m. long. **2** (kän) river, Korea: see HAN.

Ka·na′wha (kà·nô′[w]à; also, local and colloq., -nô′ĭ) river, W West Virginia, flowing NW into the Ohio river; 97 m. long.

Ka·na·za·wa (kä·nä·zä·wä) seaport, Japan, in W Honshu; pop. 231,400.

Kan'chen·jun'ga (kŭn'chĕn·jŭng'gä) or **Kin'chin·jun'ga** (kĭn'chĭn-jŭng'gä) mountain, Nepal and Sikkim, in Himalayas; 28,146 ft. high.

Kan·chi'pu·ram (kän·chē'pŏō·rȧm), Brit. corruption **Con·jee've·ram** (kŏn·jē'vĕr·ȧm) town, S India, in Madras state; pop. 74,600.

Kan'da·har (kän'dȧ·här) city, SE Afghanistan, once (under Ahmad Shah, 1747–73) a ✳; pop. 32,000.

Kan'dy (kän'dĭ) town, cen. Ceylon; pop. 51,300.

Ka'nem (kä'nĕm) region, French Equatorial Africa, in Chad territory NE of Lake Chad; once a powerful sultanate.

Ka'ne·o'he Bay (kä'nā·ō'hä) inlet, Hawaii, on E coast of Oahu I.

Kang'ting' (käng'dĭng') or **Ta'tsien'lu'** (dä'jĭ·ĕn'lōō') city, S China, in Sikang prov., in valley of Tatsienlu river near Szechwan border.

Kan'ia·pis'kau (kän'yȧ·pĭs'kou) river, E Canada, in N Quebec prov., flowing from **Lake Kaniapiskau** (area 441 sq. m.) N to unite with the Larch river and form Koksoak river; 445 m. long.

Kan'ka·kee' (käng'kȧ·kē') **1** river, Indiana and Illinois, flowing SW and W to unite with the Des Plaines river and form the Illinois river; 225 m. long. **2** city, NE Illinois, on Kankakee river; pop. 25,900.

Kanko. See HAMHUNG.

Kan·nap'o·lis (kȧ·năp'ō·lĭs; -năp'lĭs) town, S cen. North Carolina; pop. 28,400.

Ka'no (kä'nō) city, N cen. Nigeria; pop. 97,000.

Kan'pur (kän'pŏŏr) or **Cawn'pore** (kôn'pōr) city, N India, in Uttar Pradesh on the Ganges; pop. 487,300.

Kan'sas (kän'zȧs) **1** in Kansas usually **Kaw** (kô) river, E Kansas, flowing E into Missouri river; 169 m. long. **2**, abbr. **Kans.** or **Kan.**, state, cen. United States, W of the Mississippi river; ✳ Topeka; area 82,276 sq. m.; pop. 1,905,300. — **Kan'san** (kän'zȧn), adj. & n.

Kansas City, 1 city, NE Kansas, at confluence of Kansas and Missouri rivers, adjacent to Kansas City, Missouri; pop. 129,600. **2** city, W Missouri, on Missouri river; pop. 456,600.

Kan'su' (kän'sŏō') province, NW China, between Outer Mongolia and Tsinghai; includes former Ningsia province; ✳ Lanchow; area 257,000 sq. m.; pop. 12,928,000.

Kanto Plain. See KWANTO PLAIN.

Kao'hsiung' (gou'shyŏōng'), Jap. **Ta·ka·o** (tä·kä·ō) seaport, SW Formosa; pop. 100,000.

Kaolan. See LANCHOW.

Kapıdağı. See CYZICUS.

Ka·ra'chi (kȧ·rä'chĭ) seaport, ✳ of Pakistan, on arm of Arabian Sea just NW of mouths of the Indus; pop. 1,126,400.

Karadeniz Boğazı. See BOSPORUS.

Ka·ra'fu·to (kä·rä'fŏō·tō; Angl. kär'ȧ·fōō'tō) Sakhalin I.; — its Japanese name.

Ka'ra·gan·da' (kä'rä·gän·dä') city, Soviet Central Asia, in Kazakh S.S.R.; pop. 165,900.

Ka'ra-Kal'pak' (kä'rä·käl·päk'), officially **Kara-Kalpak Autonomous Soviet Socialist Republic,** autonomous area, Soviet Central Asia, in NW Uzbek S.S.R. along the Amu Darya SE of Lake Aral; ✳ Nukus; area 61,600 sq. m.; pop. 435,000.

Kar'a·ko'ram, or **Kar'a·ko'rum, Pass** (kär'ȧ·kō'rŭm) mountain pass through Karakoram Range, NE Kashmir, E of Mount Godwin Austen; altitude 18,290 ft.

Karakoram, or **Karakorum, Range,** mountain range, cen. Asia, in N Kashmir and Tibet; highest peak Godwin Austen, 28,250 ft.

Karakorum, Chin. **Ho'lin'** (hŭ'lĭn') ruins of ancient ✳ of Mongolia, on upper Orkhon river.

Ka'ra Kum (kä'rä kŏōm') desert, Soviet Central Asia, in Turkmen S.S.R., extending from the Caspian Sea to the Amu Darya.

Ka'ra Sea (kä'rȧ) arm of Arctic Ocean off Soviet Russia N of Ural Mts.

Karashahr. See QARA SHAHR.

Kar'ba·la (kär'bȧ·lä) or **Ker'be·la** (kŭr'bĕ·lä) town, cen. Iraq; holy city for Moslems of the Shiite branch; pop. 65,000.

Ka·re'li·a (kȧ·rē'lĭ·ȧ; -rēl'yȧ) **1** region, NW Soviet Russia, Europe, between Gulf of Finland and White Sea. **2** formerly (1923–40) the Karelian Autonomous Republic, an administrative unit of Soviet Russia in this region. **3** the Karelo-Finnish Soviet Socialist Republic.

Ka·re'li·an Isthmus (kȧ·rē'lĭ·ȧn; -rēl'yȧn) strip of land, NW Soviet Russia, Europe, between Lake Ladoga and the Gulf of Finland.

Ka·re'lo-Finn'ish Soviet Socialist Republic (kȧ·rē'lō·fĭn'ĭsh) constituent republic of the U.S.S.R., bordering on Finland and the White Sea; formed 1940 from the Karelian Autonomous S.S.R. (1923–40) and some of the territory acquired from Finland; ✳ Petrozavodsk; area 68,900 sq. m.; pop. 600,000.

Ka·ren'ni State (kȧ·rĕn'ĭ) region, E Burma, the country of the Karens; made state of Union of Burma 1947.

Karfreit. See CAPORETTO.

Ka'ri·kal' (kä'rĭ·käl') city, settlement of former French India, on E coast of India, in Madras state 150 m. S of Madras; pop. 70,500.

Kar·kheh' (kär·kä') or **Ker·kheh'** (kär·kä'), anc. **Cho·as'pes** (kō·ăs'pēz) river, W Iran, flowing SW to marshlands E of the Tigris in SE Iraq; 340 m. long.

Karl-Marx-Stadt. See CHEMNITZ.

Kar'lov·ci Srem'ski (kär'lŏv·tsĭ srĕm'skĭ), Ger. **Kar'lo·witz** (kär'lō·vĭts) town, NE Yugoslavia, in N Serbia; Treaty of Karlowitz 1699.

Kar'lo·vy Va'ry (kär'lō·vĭ vä'rĭ), Ger. **Karls'bad** (kärlz'bäd; Ger. kärls'bäd) town, W Czechoslovakia, in NW Bohemia 15 m. from German border; sulfur springs; pop. 30,900.

Karls·kro'na (kärls·krōō'nä) city, S Sweden, on the mainland and nearby islands in Baltic Sea; naval base; pop. 30,800.

Karls'ru'he (kärls·rōō'ĕ; kärls·rōō'ĕ; Angl. kärlz'rōō'ȧ) city, W Germany, in Baden on Rhine river; pop. 198,000.

Kar'nak (kär'näk) village, S Egypt, on the Nile; on N part of site of ancient Thebes, just N of Luxor; temple of Amenhotep III.

Kar'pa·thos (kär'pȧ·thŏs), Ital. **Scar'pan·to** (skär'pän·tō) island, Greece, one of the Dodecanese, between Rhodes and Crete.

Kar·roo' (kȧ·rōō') region, Union of South Africa, in Cape Province between coastal mountains and the Orange river; includes in S two E–W troughs, the **Little,** or **Southern, Karroo** and the **Great,** or **Central, Karroo,** and in N the **Northern,** or **Upper, Karroo,** constituting a large plateau sloping to the Orange river.

Kars (kärs) city, NE Turkey in Asia; ✳ of an independent Armenian principality in 9th and 10th cents; pop. 20,500.

Karst. See CARSO.

Ka·run' (kä·rōōn') river, W Iran; empties into the Shatt-al-Arab at N end of Abadan I.; 450 m. long.

Ka·saan' (kȧ·sän') Haida Indian village, SE Alaska, on Prince of Wales I.; feature of **Old Kasaan National Monument,** established 1916.

Ka·sai' (kä·sī') river, SW Africa; rises in cen. Angola, flows through S cen. and W Belgian Congo to empty into Congo river; 1200 m. long.

Kaschau. See KOŠICE.

Kasen. See HWACHON.

Ka·shan' (kä·shän') city, cen. Iran, N of Isfahan; pop. 55,000.

Kash'gar (käsh'gär), Chin. **Shu'fu'** (shōō'fōō') town, W China, in W Sinkiang at oasis on Kashgar river; pop. 80,000.

Kashgaria. See CHINESE TURKISTAN.

Kash'mir (käsh'mĭr; käsh'mĭr', Eng. **Cash'mere** (käsh'mēr; käsh-mēr') **1** region, N Indian subcontinent, including valley (Vale of Kashmir) watered by Jhelum and Kishenganga rivers. **2** officially **Jam'mu and Kashmir** (jŭm'ŏō) state, including the Kashmir region and Jammu (valley of the Chenab) to the S; borders on Tibet and China (Sinkiang); after 1947 in dispute between Pakistan and Republic of India; ✳ Srinagar; area 92,780 sq. m.; pop. 4,410,000. — **Kash·mir'i·an** (käsh·mĭr'ĭ·ȧn), adj. & n. See also KASHMIRI, in Vocab.

Kas·kas'ki·a (käs·käs'kĭ·ȧ) **1** river, SW Illinois, flowing SW into Mississippi river; 300 m. long. **2** township, SW Illinois, at junction of Kaskaskia river with the Mississippi; site of town founded 1703.

Kassa. See KOŠICE.

Kas'sa·la (käs'ȧ·lä) town, NE Sudan (republic); pop. 31,200.

Kas'sel (käs'ĕl; Angl. käs'l), also **Cas'sel,** city, W Germany, on Fulda river; pop. 161,300.

Kas'se·rine Pass (käs'ĕr·ēn; Arab. käs'rīn) mountain pass, Tunisia; scene of American defeat Feb. 14, 1943.

Ka'ste·lor'ri·zon (käs·tä·lô'rē·zŏn), Angl. **Ca'stel·lo'ri·zo** (käs·tä·lô'-rē·zō), Ital. **Ca·stel'ros'so** (käs·tĕl'rôs'sō) island, Greece, one of the Dodecanese, 2 m. off SW coast of Turkey.

Kastro. MYTILENE city.

Kastron. See CHIOS.

Kastrop-Rauxel. See CASTROP-RAUXEL.

Ka·tah'din, Mount (kȧ·tä'd'n; -dĭn) mountain, N cen. Maine; highest point in the state, 5268 ft.

Ka·tan'ga (kȧ·täng'gȧ) region, S Belgian Congo, having rich deposits of copper, uranium, and other minerals.

Kath'er·i'na, Ge'bel (jĕb'ĕl käth'ĕr'ĭ·nä), or **Mount Cath'er·ine** (käth'ĕr·ĭn; käth'rĭn) mountain, NE Egypt, in Sinai Penin.; highest in the Gebel Musa, 8652 ft.

Ka'thi·a·war' (kä'tĭ·ȧ·wär') peninsula, W India, between Gulf of Cambay and Gulf of Kutch; comprised a number of princely states merged 1947 to form Saurashtra state; became part of Bombay 1956.

Kat'mai, Mount (kät'mī) volcano, S Alaska, at N end of Alaska Penin.; 700 ft. high; eruption 1912; included, with Valley of Ten Thousand Smokes, in **Katmai National Monument,** established 1918.

Kat'man·du' (kät'män·dōō') city, ✳ of Nepal; pop. 108,800.

Ka'to·wi'ce (kä'tô·vē'tsĕ), Ger. **Kat'to·witz** (kät'ō·vĭts) city, S Poland, in Silesia; pop. 156,000.

Kat'rine, Loch (lŏk kät'rĭn) lake, cen. Scotland, in SW Perth co. E of Loch Lomond; over 9 m. long.

Kat'te·gat (kät'ĕ·gät; kät'ĕ·gät) arm of North Sea, between Sweden and the peninsula of Jutland, Denmark.

Ka'tyn (kä'tĭn) town, Soviet Russia, Europe, just NW of Smolensk; forest here scene of massacre of Polish soldiers 1939.

Kau'ai (kou'ī) island, NW Hawaii, WNW of Oahu; area 551 sq. m.; pop. 35,600.

Kau'nas (kou'näs), Russ. **Kov'no** (kôv'nŭ), Pol. **Kow'no** (kôv'nô) city, cen. Lithuania; ✳, 1918–40; pop. 152,400.

Ka·val'la (kä·väl'ä), Mod. Gr. **Ka·vál'la** (kä·vä'lä) seaport, NE Greece, in NE Macedonia at head of Gulf of Kavalla; pop. 42,300.

Kaveri. See CAUVERY.

Ka'vi·eng' (kä'vĭ·ĕng') town, Bismarck Archipelago, ✳ of New Ireland, on NW tip of the island.

Kaw. See KANSAS.

Ka·wa·gu·chi (kä·wä·gŏō·chē) city, Japan, in SE Honshu just N of Tokyo; pop. 116,000.

Ka·wa·sa·ki (kä·wä·sä·kē) city, Japan, in SE cen. Honshu, a S suburb of Tokyo; pop. 252,900.

Kay'se·ri' (kī'sĕ·rē'), anc. **Cae'sa·re'a Maz'a·ca** (sē'zȧ·rē'ȧ [sĕs'ȧ-; sēz'ȧ-] mäz'ȧ·kȧ) city, cen. Turkey; pop. 65,500.

Ka·zakh' Soviet Socialist Republic (kä·zäk') or **Ka'zakh·stan'** (kä'zäk·stän') or **Ka'zak·stan'** (kä'zäk·stän') constituent republic of the U.S.S.R., in Soviet Central Asia, extending from the Caspian sea to the Altai Mts. and bordering on China (Sinkiang) in the E; ✳ Alma Ata; area 1,061,600 sq. m.; pop. 6,000,000.

Ka·zan' (kȧ·zän') **1** river, N cen. Canada, flowing NNE through a series of lakes to Baker Lake; 450 m. long. **2** (Russ. kŭ·zän'y') city, E Soviet Russia, Europe, ✳ of Tatar Republic; pop. 401,700.

Kazan Retto. See VOLCANO ISLANDS.

Kazdağı. See IDA.

Kaz·vin' (käz·vēn') city, NW Iran, S of Elburz Mts.; pop. 80,000.

Kear'ny (kär'nĭ) town, NE New Jersey, N of Newark; pop. 40,000.

Kecs'ke·mét' (käch'kä·māt') autonomous city, cen. Hungary; pop. 83,700.

Ke'dah (kā'dä) state, N Federation of Malaya, bordering on Thailand; ✳ Alor Star; area 3660 sq. m.; pop. 554,400.

Kedron. See KIDRON.

Keeling Islands. See COCOS ISLANDS.

Kee'lung' (kē'lŏōng') or **Ki·run** (kē·rōōn) seaport, N Formosa, NE of Taipeh; pop. 100,000.

Keene (kēn) city, SW New Hampshire; pop. 15,600.

Kee·wa'tin (kē·wä't'n; -tĭn) district, N Canada, in Northwest Territories on NW side of Hudson Bay; area 228,160 sq. m.

Kefallinía. See CEPHALONIA.

Keigh'ley (kēth'lĭ) municipal borough, N England, in West Riding, Yorkshire, in the Aire valley; pop. 56,900.

Keijo. See SEOUL.

Ke·lan'tan (kĕ·län'tăn; -län'tän) state, Federation of Malaya, bordering on Thailand; ✱ Kota Bahru; area 5746 sq. m.; pop. 448,600.

Keltsy. See KIELCE.

Ke'me·ro'vo (kĕm'ĕ·rô'vō) city, Soviet Russia, Asia, in Kuznetsk Basin on Tom river; pop. 133,000.

Ke'nai Peninsula (kē'nī) peninsula, S Alaska, between Cook Inlet and Prince William Sound; 160 m. long, 130 m. wide.

Keng'tung (kĕng'tŏŏng) state, E Burma, in S Shan State, bordering on China, Laos, and Thailand; since 1947 part of the Shan State.

Ken'il·worth (kĕn'l·wûrth) urban district, cen. England, in Warwickshire; ruined castle.

Kénitra. See PORT LYAUTEY.

Ken'more (kĕn'mōr) village, W New York, on Niagara river N of Buffalo; pop. 20,100.

Ken'ne·bec (kĕn'ĕ·bĕk) river, S Maine, flowing S from Moosehead Lake to Atlantic Ocean; 164 m. long.

Ken'ne·saw Mountain (kĕn'ĕ·sô) mountain, NW Georgia, near Atlanta; scene of battle 1864; now a national battlefield site.

Ke·no'sha (kĕ·nō'shà) city, SE Wisconsin, on Lake Michigan; pop. 54,400.

Ken'sing·ton (kĕn'zĭng·tŭn) metropolitan borough, London, N of the Thames; pop. 168,100.

Kent (kĕnt) county, SE England; ✱ Maidstone; area 1525 sq. m.; pop. 1,563,300. — **Kent'ish**, adj.

Ken·tuck'y (kĕn·tŭk'ĭ; kĭn-) **1** river, N cen. Kentucky, flowing NW into Ohio river; 259 m. long. **2**, abbr. **Ky.**, state, E cen. United States, between Appalachian Mts. and Mississippi river just S of Ohio river; ✱ Frankfort; area 40,395 sq. m.; pop. 2,944,800. — **Ken·tuck'i·an** (-ĭ·ăn), adj. & n.

Ken'ya (kĕn'yà; locally also kēn'yà), formerly **East Africa Protectorate**, country, E Africa, NE of Lake Victoria; British crown colony and protectorate; ✱ Nairobi; area 224,960 sq. m.; pop. 3,866,500.

Kenya, Mount, mountain, cen. Kenya, near the equator; an extinct volcano; 17,040 ft. high.

Ke'o·kuk (kē'ô·kŭk) city, SE Iowa, on Mississippi river; pop. 16,100.

Ke'os (kē'ŏs) or **Ze'a** (Ital. tsā'ä), Mod. Gr. **Ké'os** (kyā'ŏs), anc. **Ce'os** (sē'ŏs) island, Greece, in NW Cyclades.

Ke·ra·la (kā'rà·là) state, SW India, bordering on Arabian Sea; formed 1956 from Travancore and Cochin state and part of Madras state; ✱ Trivandrum; area 15,035 sq. m.; pop. 13,550,600.

Kerbela. See KARBALA.

Kerch (kĕrch) **1** peninsula, Soviet Russia, Europe, extending E from the Crimea; separated by narrow **Kerch Strait** from point of land on mainland opposite. **2** seaport on Kerch Strait; pop. 104,500.

Ker'gue·len (kûr'gĕ·lĕn; -lĕn) **Island**, island, S Indian Ocean, belonging to France; area 1318 sq. m.

Kerkheh. See KARKHEH.

Kérkyra. See CORFU.

Ker·mad'ec Islands (kĕr·măd'ĕk; -ĭk) island group, Pacific Ocean, 600 m. NNW of New Zealand, to which it belongs; uninhabited.

Ker·man' (kĕr·män') **1** anc. **Car·ma'ni·a** (kär·mā'nĭ·à; -mān'yà) province, SE Iran, bordering on Pakistan and Gulf of Oman. **2** anc. **Car·ma'na** (kär·mā'nà) city, its ✱; pop. 53,000.

Ker·man'shah (kĕr·män'shä') city, W Iran; pop. 106,000.

Kern (kûrn) river, cen. California, flowing from the Sierra Nevada into Buena Vista Lake at S end of Central Valley; 200 m. long.

Ker'ry (kĕr'ĭ) county, SW Ireland, in Munster prov.; ✱ Tralee; area 1815 sq. m.; pop. 126,600.

Kes'wick (kĕz'ĭk) village, NW England, in Cumberland near N end of Derwentwater.

Ketch'i·kan' (kĕch'ĭ·kăn') town, SE Alaska, on Revillagigedo I.; pop. 5200.

Keu'ka (kū'kà; kà·ū'kà), or **Crook'ed** (krŏŏk'ĕd; -ĭd), **Lake**, lake, W New York; one of the Finger Lakes; 18 m. long.

Kew (kū) parish, S England, in Surrey; suburb of London, on the Thames; Royal Botanic Gardens.

Ke·wa'nee (kĕ·wŏn'ē) city, NW Illinois; pop. 16,800.

Ke'wee·naw Peninsula (kē'wĕ·nô) projection of Upper Peninsula, Michigan, extending into Lake Superior; on E side is deep indentation of Upper Peninsula, **Keweenaw Bay.**

Key West (kē' wĕst') city, Florida, on **Key West**, island, one of Florida Keys, SW of S tip of Florida; pop. 26,400.

Kha·ba'rovsk (ků·bä'růfsk) city, Soviet Russia, Asia, ✱ of Khabarovsk Territory, on Amur river; pop. 199,400.

Khabarovsk Territory, territory, E Soviet Russia, Asia, bordering on Sea of Okhotsk and Bering Sea; area 965,400 sq. m.; pop. 1,250,000.

Kha·kass' Autonomous Region (ků·kăs') autonomous region, Soviet Russia, Asia, in SW Krasnoyarsk Territory just N of the Sayan Mts.; ✱ Abakan; area 24,000 sq. m.; pop. 300,000.

Khalkidiki. See CHALCIDICE.

Khalkís. See CHALCIS.

Khan'ba·lik' (kän'bä·lĕk') ancient city, China; Kublai Khan's capital, corresponding to modern Peking; — a Mongol name.

Khaniá. See CANEA.

Khan'ka (kăng'kà) or **Han'ka** (häng'kà) lake, on boundary between Manchuria and Soviet Russia, Asia.

Khar'kov (kär'kôf; Russ. кȧr'у'kȧf) city, U.S.S.R., in NE Ukraine on edge of the Donbas; pop. 833,400.

Khar·toum' or **Khar·tum'** (kär·tōōm') city, ✱ of Republic of the Sudan, at junction of White Nile and Blue Nile; pop. 92,800.

Khartoum North, suburb of the city of Khartoum.

Kha'si Hills (kä'sĭ) region, NE India, in NW cen. Assam; with Jaintia Hills, constitutes an autonomous district of Republic of India.

Kha·tan'ga (ků·täng'gà) river, Soviet Russia, Asia, in NE Krasnoyarsk Territory, flowing SE and N to Laptev Sea; 800 m. long.

Khelat. See KALAT.

Kher·son' (kĕr·sôn') seaport, U.S.S.R., in S Ukraine on the Dnieper 19 m. from its mouth; pop. 97,200.

Khing'an' (shĭng'än') mountains, E Asia, chiefly in Manchuria, the **Great Khingan Mountains** extending N and S in W Manchuria and E Inner Mongolia.

Khíos. See CHIOS.

Khi'u·ma (kē'ŏŏ·mȧ), Estonian **Hii'u·maa** (hē'ŏŏ·mä), Ger. **Dag'ö'** (däg'ŭ') island, Estonia, in Baltic Sea N of Sarema I.

Khi'va (kē'vȧ) **1** or **Kho·rezm'** (kŏ·rĕz'm) oasis, Soviet Central Asia, in Uzbek S.S.R. on the lower Amu Darya. **2** anc. **Cho·ras'mi·a** (kŏ·răz'mĭ·à) and **Khwa·razm'** (kwŏ·räz'm) former khanate, cen. Asia, including Khiva oasis; conquered by the Russians 1873. **3** town in the oasis, once ✱ of the khanate.

Khokand. Var. of KOKAND.

Khor'ram·shahr' (kŏŏr'răm·shär') town, W Iran, ✱ of Khuzistan prov., on the Karun at its junction with the Shatt-al-Arab. See ABADAN.

Kho'tan' (kō'tän'), Chin. **Ho'tien'** (hō'tyĕn') town, W China, in SW Sinkiang at foot of Kunlun Mts., on S edge of the Takla Makan.

Khu'ra·san (kŏŏr'à·sän) or **Kho'ra·san** (kō'rà·sän) province, NE Iran, bordering on Afghanistan and the U.S.S.R.; ✱ Meshed.

Khu'zi·stan' (kŏŏ'zĭ·stän'), formerly **A'ra·bi·stan'** (ä'rà·bĭ'·stän') province, SW Iran, bordering on Persian Gulf, in extent corresponding closely to ancient Elam or Susiana; ✱ Khorramshahr.

Khwarazm. See KHIVA.

Khy'ber Pass (kī'bĕr) mountain pass, on border between Afghanistan and Pakistan, in the Safed Koh; over 30 m. long.

Kia'mu'sze' (jĭ·ä'mŏŏ'sŏ') or **Chia'mus'su'** (jĭ·ä'mŏŏ'sŏ') city, E Manchuria, on lower Sungari river; pop. 128,700.

Ki'an' (jē'än'), formerly **Lu'ling'** (lōō'lĭng') town, SE China, in S cen. Kiangsi prov. on Kan river; pop. 100,000.

Kiang'ling' (jĭ·äng'lĭng') or **King'chow'** (jĭng'jō') city, E cen. China, in S Hupeh prov. on the Yangtze just W of Shasi; pop. 300,000.

Kiang'si' (jĭ·äng'sē') province, SE China, in basin of the Khan river; ✱ Nanchang; area 66,795 sq. m.; pop. 12,684,000.

Kiang'su' (jĭ·äng'sōō') province, E China, on coast just S of Shantung; ✱ Nanking; area 34,363 sq. m.; pop. 32,231,000.

Kiangtu. See YANGCHOW.

Kiating. See LOSHAN.

Kid'ron (kĭd'rŏn; kī'drŏn) or **Ked'ron** (kĕd'rŏn; kē'drŏn) valley, Palestine, between Jerusalem and Mount of Olives.

Kiel (kēl) seaport, W Germany, ✱ of Schleswig-Holstein; on SE side of base of peninsula of Jutland; pop. 253,900.

Kiel Canal, canal, N Germany, across base of peninsula of Jutland (in Schleswig-Holstein); connects Baltic Sea with North Sea; 61 m. long.

Kiel'ce (kyĕl'tsĕ), Russ. **Kel'tsy** (kĕl'tsĭ) city, S Poland; pop. 68,800.

Ki'ev (kē'yĕf; Angl. kē'ĕf) city, U.S.S.R., ✱ of the Ukrainian S.S.R., on the Dnieper; pop. 846,300.

Ki'lau·e'a (kē'lou·ā'à) crater, Hawaii, on E side of Mauna Loa; 2 m. wide and at a height of 4088 ft.

Kil·dare' (kĭl·dâr') county, E Ireland, in Leinster prov.; ✱ Naas; area 654 sq. m.; pop. 66,400.

Kil·i'man·ja'ro, Mount (kĭl'ĭ·mȧn·jä'rō) mountain, NE Tanganyika; highest peak Kibo, 19,565 ft., the highest point in Africa.

Kil·ken'ny (kĭl·kĕn'ĭ) county, SE Ireland, in Leinster prov.; ✱ Kilkenny; area 796 sq. m.; pop. 65,100.

Kil·lar'ney, Lakes of (kĭ·lär'nĭ) three lakes, SW Ireland, in co. Kerry.

Kill Devil Hill. See KITTY HAWK.

Kil'lie·cran'kie (kĭl'ĭ·krăng'kĭ) mountain pass, cen. Scotland, in Perth co. in SE part of the Grampians; battle 1689.

Kim'ber·ley (kĭm'bĕr·lĭ) town, Union of South Africa, in N Cape Province near border of Orange Free State; pop. 52,600.

Kin'a·bu·lu' (kĭn'à·bŭ·lōō'), formerly **Kin'i·ba·lu'** (kĭn'ĭ·bà·lōō') mountain, British North Borneo; highest on the island, 13,455 ft.

Kin·car'dine (kĭn·kär'dĭn; -dĭn; kĭng-) or **Kin·car'dine·shire** (-shĭr; -shĕr), formerly **The Mearns** (mûrnz) county, E Scotland, bordering on North Sea; ✱ Stonehaven; area 382 sq. m.; pop. 47,300.

Kinchinjunga. See KANCHENJUNGA.

Kingchow. See KIANGLING.

King George's Falls. See AUGHRABIES FALLS.

Kings Canyon National Park, mountain wilderness, S cen. California, in the Sierra Nevada; established as national park 1940.

King's Lynn (lĭn') municipal borough, E England, in Norfolk near the Wash; pop. 26,200.

Kings Mountain, ridge, North Carolina and South Carolina, the part in South Carolina being site of American victory Oct. 7, 1780.

Kings Point, village, New York, on NW Long I.; U.S. Merchant Marine Academy.

Kings'port (kĭngz'pōrt) city, NE Tennessee; pop. 19,600.

Kings'ton (kĭng'stŭn) **1** city, SE New York, on Hudson river N of Poughkeepsie; pop. 28,800. **2** borough, E Pennsylvania, in N of Wilkes-Barre; pop. 21,100. **3** city, Canada, in SE Ontario on Lake Ontario near head of St. Lawrence river; pop. 48,600. **4** seaport, West Indies Federation, ✱ of Jamaica; pop. 109,000.

Kingston upon Hull. See HULL.

Kings'town (kĭngz'toun; kĭng'stŭn) seaport, West Indies Federation, ✱ of colony of St. Vincent, on island of St. Vincent; pop. 4300.

Kings'ville (kĭngz'vĭl) city, S Texas, SW of Corpus Christi; pop. 16,900.

Kingtehchen. See FOWLIANG.

Kinmen. See QUEMOY.

Kinneret, Yam. See GALILEE, SEA OF.

Kin·ross' (kĭn·rŏs') or **Kin·ross'-shire** (-rŏs'shĭr; -shĕr; -rŏsh'-) county, E cen. Scotland; ✱ Kinross; area 82 sq. m.; pop. 7400.

Kinsen. See KUMCHON.

Kin'ston (kĭn'stŭn) city, E North Carolina; pop. 18,300.

Kin·tyre' (kĭn·tīr') peninsula, SW Scotland, extending S on W side of Firth of Clyde; terminates in **Mull** (mŭl; mŏŏl) **of Kintyre** (cape).

Kioga; Kioto. See KYOGA; KYOTO.

Kirgiz, or **Kirghiz**, **Soviet Socialist Republic** (kĭr·gēz'), also **Kir·gi'zi·a** (kĭr·gē'zĭ·à; -zhĭ·à; -zhà) constituent republic of the U.S.S.R., Soviet Central Asia; ✱ Frunze; area 76,100; pop. 1,490,000.

Kirgiz Steppe (stĕp) or **the Steppes** (stĕps) steppe region of cen. Kazakh S.S.R., Soviet Central Asia.

Ki'rin' (kē'rĭn') **1** province, cen. Manchuria; ✱ Changchun; area 73,000 sq. m.; pop. 11,290,000. **2** formerly (1929–37) **Yung'ki'** (yŏŏng'jē') city, in Kirin prov., on Sungari river; pop. 173,000.

Kirjath-Arba. See HEBRON.

Kirk·cal′dy (kûr·kôl′dĭ; -kô′dĭ; -kä′dĭ) seaport, E Scotland, in Fife co. on Firth of Forth; pop. 49,000.

Kirk·cud′bright (kûr·kŏŏ′brĭ) or **Kirk·cud′bright·shire** (-shĭr; -shĕr) county, S Scotland; 899 sq. m.; ✳ Kirkcudbright; pop. 30,700.

Kir·kuk′ (kĭr·kŏŏk′) town, NE Iraq; center of oil fields.

Kirk′wood (kûrk′wŏŏd) city, E Missouri, W of St. Louis; pop. 18,600.

Ki′rov (kē′rŭf), formerly **Vyat′ka** (vyät′kȧ) city, Soviet Russia, Europe, on Vyatka river; pop. 143,200.

Ki·ro′va·bad (kĭ·rō′vȧ·bäd), known 1921–c. 1935 as **Gan′dzha** (gän′jä) and 1813–1920 as **E·li′sa·vet·pol′** (ĕ·lĭz′ȧ·vĕt·pôl′) city, U.S.S.R., in W Azerbaidzhan S of Kura river; pop. 98,700.

Ki·ro′vo·grad (kĭ·rō′vŏ·gräd), formerly **Zi·nov′ievsk** (zĭ·nôv′yĕfsk) and **E·li′sa·vet·grad′** (ĕ·lĭz′ȧ·vĕt·gräd′) city, U.S.S.R., in Ukraine on Ingul river; pop. 100,300.

Kirun. See KEELUNG.

Ki′shi·nev (kĭsh′ĭ·nĕf; Russ. kĭ·shĭ·nyôf′), Romanian **Chi′și·năŭ′** (kē′shĕ·nŭ′ŏŏ) city, U.S.S.R., ✳ of Moldavian S.S.R., in Bessarabia; pop. 112,500.

Kishm, Kishon. See QISHM, QISHON.

Kis′ka (kĭs′kȧ) island, SW Alaska, in Rat Is. group, W Aleutian Is.

Kis′pest′ (kĭsh′pĕsht′), Ger. **Klein-Pest** (klīn′pĕst′) city, cen. Hungary, SE of Budapest; pop. 62,800.

Kist′na (kĭst′nȧ) river, S India, flowing from the Western Ghats across the Deccan into the Bay of Bengal; 800 m. long.

Kitch′e·ner (kĭch′ĕ·nẽr) city, Canada, in SE Ontario; pop. 59,600.

Kíthira. See CERIGO.

Kit′ta·tin′ny Mountain (kĭt′ȧ·tĭn′ĭ) ridge, N New Jersey, extending into New York and Pennsylvania; flat-topped; altitude under 2000 ft.

Kit′ter·y (kĭt′ẽr·ĭ) town, SW Maine, across bay from Portsmouth, New Hampshire; site of Portsmouth Navy Yard; pop. 6700.

Kit′ty Hawk (kĭt′ĭ hôk′) village, E North Carolina, on sand barrier opposite Albemarle Sound; nearby is Kill Devil Hill (now a national memorial) scene of first airplane flight in U.S. Dec. 17, 1903.

Kiung′shan′ (chĭ·ŏŏng′shän′) city, SE China, ✳ of Hainan I.; pop. 45,800.

Kiushu. See KYUSHU.

Ki′vu, Lake (kē′vŏŏ) lake, E Belgian Congo, in Great Rift Valley; contains many islands; over 60 m. long, 30 m. wide.

Kı·zıl′ Ir·mak′ (kẽ·zĭl′ ĭr·mäk′), anc. **Ha′lys** (hā′lĭs) river, N cen. Turkey in Asia, flowing into the Black Sea; 600 m. long.

Kjel′ler (kĕl′ẽr) suburb of Oslo, Norway; site of an atomic pile.

Kjö′len Mountains (chû′lĕn) range along boundary between NE Norway and NW Sweden; highest peak Kebnekaise, 6963 ft.

Kla′gen·furt (klä′gĕn·fŏŏrt) city, Austria, ✳ of Carinthia, near Yugoslav border; pop. 63,800.

Klaipeda. See MEMEL.

Klam′ath (klăm′ăth) river, S Oregon and NW California, flowing from Upper Klamath Lake SW into the Pacific Ocean; 250 m. long.

Klamath Falls, city, S Oregon, at S end of Upper Klamath Lake; pop. 15,900.

Klamath Lakes, two lakes, **Upper Klamath Lake** in S Oregon, and **Lower Klamath Lake,** now dry, in S Oregon and N California.

Klausenburg; See CLUJ, KISPEST.

Klon′dike (klŏn′dīk) region, NW Canada, in Yukon river basin on both sides of **Klondike River,** 90 m. long, a tributary of the Yukon.

Klu·ane′ Lake (klŏŏ·än′) lake, N Canada, in S Yukon Territory along N slope of St. Elias Range; area 184 sq. m.

Knos′sos or **Cnos′sus** or **Gnos′sus** (nŏs′ŭs) city of ancient Crete.

Knox′ville (nŏks′vĭl) city, E Tennessee, on Tennessee river; pop. 124,800.

Kobarid. See CAPORETTO.

Ko′be (kō′bĕ; kō′bä) seaport, Japan, in Honshu on Osaka Bay; pop. 607,100.

København. See COPENHAGEN.

Ko′blenz or **Co′blenz** (kō′blĕnts) city, W Germany, at confluence of Moselle and Rhine rivers; pop. 91,000.

Ko′chi (kō′chē) seaport, Japan, on S coast of Shikoku I.; pop. 147,100.

Ko′di·ak (kō′dĭ·ăk), also, sometimes, **Ka·diak′** (Russ. kŭ·dyăk′) island, S Alaska, in Gulf of Alaska off Alaska Penin.; area over 5000 sq. m.

Ko′dok (kō′dŏk), formerly **Fa·sho′da** (fȧ·shō′dȧ) town, SE Sudan (republic); seized by the French 1898.

Koedoes. See KUDUS.

Ko′fu (kō′fŏŏ) city, Japan, in S cen. Honshu; pop. 105,000.

Koil, Koil-Aligarh. See ALIGARH.

Ko·kand′ or **Kho·kand′** (kŏ·känd′) **1** region, Soviet Central Asia, in E Uzbek S.S.R.; once a powerful khanate; conquered by Russians 1875–76. **2** city in the region; pop. 84,700.

Ko′ko·mo (kō′kŏ·mō) city, N cen. Indiana; pop. 38,700.

Koko Nor. See TSINGHAI.

Ko·ku·ra (kō·kŏŏ·rä) seaport, Japan, in N Kyushu I.; pop. 168,100.

Ko′la Peninsula (kō′lä) projection of NE end of Scandinavian Penin., N Europe, forming a region, ✳ Murmansk (on **Kola Bay**), of Soviet Russia; 250 m. long, 150 m. wide.

Ko·lar′ Gold Fields (kō·lär′) city, S India, in E Mysore state; gold mines; pop. 133,800.

Kol′ha·pur (kō′lȧ·pŏŏr) **1** former state, W India, in Western Ghats and E Deccan; now in Bombay state. **2** city, its ✳; pop. 93,000.

Kolmar. See COLMAR.

Köln. See COLOGNE.

Kolozsvár. See CLUJ.

Ko·ly′ma or **Ko·li′ma** (kŏ·lē′mȧ) river, Soviet Russia, Asia; rises in **Kolyma Range** (parallel to coast N of Sea of Okhotsk) and flows N and NE into Arctic Ocean; 1110 m. long.

Ko·man·dor′ski·e Islands (kŏ·mŭn·dôr′skĭ·yĕ; Angl. kŏm′ăn·dôr′skĭ), Eng. **Com·mand′er Islands** (kŏ·măn′dẽr) island group, Soviet Russia, Asia, E of Kamchatka Penin. in SW Bering Sea.

Ko·ma′ti (kŏ·mä′tē) river, S Africa; rises in N Drakensberg Mts., SE Transvaal, and flows into Delagoa Bay, Mozambique; 500 m. long.

Ko′mi Republic (kō′mĭ), formerly **Zyr′i·an Autonomous Area** (zĭr′ĭ·ăn), officially **Komi Autonomous Soviet Socialist Republic,** autonomous republic, NE Soviet Russia, Europe, W of the Northern Urals; ✳ Syktyvkar; area 145,221 sq. m.; pop. 335,200.

Kom′so·molsk′ (kŏm′sô·môlsk′) city, E Soviet Russia, Asia, on Amur river; pop. 70,700.

Konakri. See CONAKRY.

Konan. See HUNGNAM.

Königgrätz. See HRADEC KRÁLOVÉ.

Königsberg. See KALININGRAD.

Kon′stanz (kôn′stänts), Eng. **Con′stance** (kŏn′stȧns) commune, W Germany, on Lake Constance; pop. 38,000.

Kon·ya′ or **Kon·ia′** (kôn·yä′), anc. **I·co′ni·um** (ī·kō′nĭ·ŭm) city, SW cen. Turkey; pop. 64,500.

Koo′te·nay (kŏŏ′t·nā; kŏŏt′nā), in U.S. spelled **Koo′te·nai,** river, SW Canada and NW United States, crossing the border twice; flows from Rocky Mts. through **Kootenay Lake** (in British Columbia) and into the Columbia river; 400 m. long.

Kootenay National Park, Canada, in SE British Columbia around section of upper course of Kootenay river; established 1920.

Ko·re′a (kô·rē′ȧ) or **Cho·sen** (chō·sĕn) country, E Asia, occupying a peninsula extending S of Manchuria; once a kingdom and, from 1910 to 1945, a dependency of Japan, ✳ Seoul; after World War II divided at 38th parallel into two zones of occupation, Russian in N and American in S, in which were set up (1948) the North Korean People's Republic, ✳ Pyongyang, and the South Korean Republic, ✳ Seoul; total area 85,225 sq. m.; pop. 29,238,600. — **Ko·re′an,** adj. & n.

Korea Strait, channel between S Korea and SW Japan, connecting SW Sea of Japan with East China Sea.

Kórinthos. See CORINTH.

Korintji. See KERINTJI.

Kort′rijk (kôrt′rīk), Fr. **Cour′trai′** (kŏŏr′trā′) commune, NW Belgium, on Leie (Lys) river NNE of Lille, France; pop. 40,100.

Kos (kŏs; kôs) or **Cos** (kŏs), Ital. **Co′o** (kô′ō) island, Greece, one of the Dodecanese.

Kos′ci·us′ko, Mount (kŏz′ĭ·ŭs′kō) mountain, SE Australia, in New South Wales near Victoria border; highest point in Australia, 7305 ft.

Koshu. See KWANGJU.

Ko′ši·ce (kô′shĭ·tsĕ), Hung. **Kas′sa** (kŏsh′shŏ), Ger. **Ka′schau** (käsh′ou) city, Czechoslovakia, in SE Slovakia; pop. 58,100.

Ko′so·vo or **Kos′so·vo** (kô′sô·vô) plain, S Yugoslavia, containing sources of streams flowing N to the Morava river and S to the Vardar; with the Metohija to the W, constitutes an autonomous region.

Ko·stro·ma′ (kŭ·strô·mä′) city, Soviet Russia, Europe, on the Volga where it is joined by the Kostroma river; pop. 121,200.

Ko′tor (kō′tôr) or **Cat′ta·ro** (kät′tä·rō) seaport, S Yugoslavia, in Montenegro on **Gulf of Kotor,** an inlet of Adriatic Sea.

Kot′ze·bue (kŏt′sĕ·bū) village, NW Alaska, on **Kotzebue Sound,** an inlet of Chukchee Sea, 40 to 65 m. wide, just N of Bering Strait.

Kovno. See KAUNAS.

Koweit. See KUWAIT.

Kow′loon′ (kou′lŏŏn′) **1** peninsula, SE China, opposite Hong Kong I.; part of British colony of Hong Kong. **2** town on the peninsula.

Kowno. See KAUNAS.

Kozhikode. See CALICUT.

Kozlov. See MICHURINSK.

Kra, Isthmus of (krä) section of Malay Penin. in SW Thailand; 40 m. wide at its narrowest part.

Krain. See CARNIOLA.

Krak′a·to′a (kräk′ȧ·tō′ȧ) or **Kra′ka·tau′** (-tou′) island volcano, Indonesia, between Sumatra and Java; great eruption 1883.

Kra′ków (krä′kŏŏf), Eng. **Cra′cow** (krä′kō), Ger. **Kra′kau** (krä′kou) city, S Poland, on Vistula river; pop. 347,000.

Kras. See CARSO.

Kras′no·dar (kräs′nŏ·där), formerly **E·ka′te·ri′no·dar** (ĕ·kät′ẽr·ē′nô·där) city, S Soviet Russia, Europe, ✳ of Krasnodar Territory, on Kuban river; pop. 203,900.

Krasnodar Territory, territory, S Soviet Russia, Europe, in N Caucasus region; ✳ Krasnodar; area 32,800 sq. m.; pop. 3,000,000.

Kras′no·yarsk (kräs′nŏ·yärsk) town, Soviet Russia, Asia, ✳ of Krasnoyarsk Territory, on upper Yenisei river; pop. 190,000.

Krasnoyarsk Territory, territory, Soviet Russia, Asia, extending from Arctic Ocean to Sayan Mts.; area 928,000 sq. m.; pop. 2,100,000.

Kre′feld, formerly also **Kre′feld-Uer′ding·en** (krä′fĕlt-ûr′dĭng·ĕn) city, W Germany, on Rhine river WSW of Essen; pop. 170,500.

Krim. See CRIMEA.

Kris′tian·sand′ (krĭs′chȧn·sänd′) seaport, SW Norway, on the Skagerrak SW of Oslo; pop. 24,300.

Kríti. See CRETE.

Kri·voi′ Rog (krȳ·voi′ rôk′; Angl. krĭv′oi rōg′) city, U.S.S.R., in SE cen. Ukraine on Ingulets river; pop. 197,600.

Kron′shtadt or **Kron′stadt** (krōn′stät; Russ. krŭn·shtát′) fortress, Soviet Russia, Europe, on Kotlin I. at E end of Gulf of Finland near Leningrad; naval station.

Kronstadt. 1 See BRAȘOV. **2** See KRONSHTADT.

Kru′ger National Park (krŏŏ′gẽr) game reserve, NE Union of South Africa, in E Transvaal on Mozambique frontier; established 1926.

Kru′gers·dorp (krŏŏ′gẽrz·dôrp) town, NE Union of South Africa, in S Transvaal W of Johannesburg; pop. 71,900.

K². See GODWIN AUSTEN.

Kua′la Lum′pur (kwä′lȧ lŏŏm′pŏŏr) city, ✳ of Federation of Malaya and ✳ of Selangor state; pop. 176,000.

Ku·ban′ (kŏŏ·bän′; Russ. kŏŏ·bàn′y′) river, SE Soviet Russia, Europe, in region NW of Caucasus Mts.; has three mouths — two on the Sea of Azov and one on the Black Sea; 520 m. long.

Ku·ban′go. Var. of Cubango: see OKOVANGGO.

Ku′dus or **Koe′does** (kŏŏ′dŏŏs) town, Indonesia, in cen. Java NE of Semarang; pop. 55,000.

Kuenlun Shan. See KUNLUN SHAN.

Kufara. See CUFRA, OASES OF.

Kui′by·shev (kŏŏ′ĭ·bĭ·shĕf; Angl. kwē′bĭ·shĕf), before 1935 **Sa·ma′ra** (sȧ·mä′rȧ) city, Soviet Russia, Europe, on the Volga where Samara river joins it; pop. 390,300.

Ku·ke·naam′ (kŏŏ′kĕ·näm′) or **Cu′que·nán′** (kŏŏ′kĕ·nän′) mountain, N South America, on border between British Guiana and Venezuela, near Roraima; 8620 ft. high, has waterfall 2000 ft. high.

Kuku-khoto. See KWEISUI.

Ku'la Gulf (kōō'lå) body of water, Solomon Is.; battles 1943.

Kulun. See URGA.

Ku-ma-mo-to (kōō-mä-mō-tō) city, Japan, in Kyushu I. on W coast; pop. 245,800.

Ku-ma'si (kōō-mä'sǐ), formerly **Coo-mas'sie** (kōō-mǎs'ǐ) city, Ghana, ✱ of Ashanti; pop. 78,500.

Kum-chon (kŏŏm-chŭn) or **Kin-sen** (kǐn-sĕn) 1 town, S Korea, NW of Taegu; pop. 51,300. 2 town, N Korea, near 38th parallel.

Kum-gang (kŏŏm-gäng) or **Kon-go** (kŏn-gō) mountains, N Korea, near E coast SE of Wonsan; the Diamond Mts.; highest point 5374 ft.

Kumpo. See KIMPO.

Kun'chin-jun'ga. Var. of KANCHENJUNGA.

Ku'nie (kōō'nyä), Fr. **Île des Pins** (ēl' dā pǎn'), Eng. **Isle of Pines** (īl' ŭv pīnz') island, SW Pacific Ocean, SE of S end of New Caledonia, to which it belongs.

Kun'lun', or **Kuen'lun', Shan** (kŏŏn'lŏŏn' shän') mountain ranges, cen. Asia, on N edge of Tibetan plateau and S of Sinkiang, extending from the Pamirs and Karakoram Range on W to SE Tsinghai.

Kun'ming' (kŏŏn'mǐng'), formerly **Yun-nan'** (yōō-nän') city, SW China, ✱ of Yunnan prov.; pop. 90,000.

Kun-san (kŏŏn-sän) or **Gun-zan** (gōōn-zän) seaport, SW Korea, at mouth of Kum river; pop. 74,400.

Ku'pre-a'nof (kōō'prē-ä'nŏf; -än'ŏf) island, SE Alaska.

Ku-ra' (kŏŏ-rä') river, Soviet Russia, Europe, in Georgia and Azerbaidzhan; flows from mountains of Turkish Armenia E into Caspian Sea; 825 m. long.

Kur'di-stan' (kŏŏr'dǐ-stän'; kûr'dǐ-stăn') region, SW Asia, in SE Turkey, NW Iran, and NE Iraq; inhabited by the Kurds.

Ku're (kŏŏr'ĕ; kōō'rä) city, Japan, in SW Honshu on Inland Sea; pop. 185,700.

Kurg. See COORG.

Ku'ri-a Mu'ri-a Islands (kōōr'ǐ-å mōōr'ǐ-å) group of islets in Arabian Sea off SW coast of Oman; ceded 1854 to Great Britain.

Ku'ril, or **Ku'rile, Islands** (kōō'rēl; -rǐl; kōō-rēl'), Jap. **Chi-shi-ma Ret-to** (chē-shē-mä rĕt-tō) chain of islands, E Asia, between S tip of Kamchatka Penin. and main islands of Japan; belonged to Japan 1875–1945, now in U.S.S.R.; about 32 islands, total area 3960 sq. m.

Kur'land or **Cour'land** (kōōr'lǎnd) region, W Latvia, bordering on Baltic Sea and Gulf of Riga; once a Polish duchy and in 19th cent. a government of Russia.

Kurland Gulf, lagoon, U.S.S.R., in Kaliningrad region and SW Lithuania; separated from Baltic Sea by **Kurland Spit**.

Kursk (kŏŏrsk) city, Soviet Russia, Europe; pop. 120,000.

Kush. See CUSH.

Kus'ko-kwim (kŭs'kô-kwǐm) river, SW Alaska, flowing SW to **Kusko-kwim Bay**, an inlet of Bering Sea; 550 m. long.

Küstenja. See CONSTANŢA.

Küstrin. See KOSTRZYN.

Kut-al-I-ma'ra or **Kut-el-A-ma'ra** (kōōt'ǎl[ĕl]-å-mä'rå) town, SE cen. Iraq, on the Tigris; besieged by Turks 1915–16.

Kutch or **Cutch** (kŭch) former state, W India, now in Bombay state, on coast E of Indus river, including Rann of Kutch; a kingdom 13th–19th cents.; ✱ Bhuj.

Kutch, Rann of (rŭn) salt marsh, W India, extending in an arc from mouth of the Indus to head of **Gulf of Kutch**.

Ku-wait' or **Ku-weit'** (kōō-wīt'; -wāt'), also **Ko-weit'** (kō-) 1 region, Arabia, at NW corner of Persian Gulf between Iraq and Saudi Arabia; a principality; ✱ Al Kuwait; area 1930 sq. m.; pop. 60,000. 2 see AL KUWAIT.

Kuz-netsk' Basin (kŏŏz-nĕtsk') or **Kuz'bas** (kŏŏz'bǎs; Russ. kŏŏz-bäs') basin of Tom river, S Soviet Russia, Asia.

Kwa'ja-lein (kwŏj'å-līn; -län) island, W Marshall Is., in Ralik chain; an atoll with 18 islets; taken Jan. 30–Feb. 6, 1944, by Americans; since 1945 a U.S. naval base.

Kwan'do (kwän'dō) river, S Africa, flowing from cen. Angola SE and E into Zambezi river on border between Northern Rhodesia and Southern Rhodesia; 600 m. long.

Kwangchow. 1 See CANTON. 2 See KWANGCHOWAN.

Kwang'cho'wan' (gwäng'jō'wän') or **Kwang'chow'** (gwäng'jō') French leased territory 1898–1946, S China, on Luichow Penin.; ✱ Fort Bayard (now Siying).

Kwang-ju (gwäng-jōō) or **Ko-shu** (kō-shōō) city, SW Korea; pop. 138,900.

Kwang'si' (gwäng'sē') province, SE China, bordering on Indochina; ✱ Nanning; area 81,467 sq. m.; pop. 14,971,000.

Kwang'tung' (gwäng'dŏŏng') province, SE China, bordering on South China Sea and Indochina; ✱ Canton; area 85,328 sq. m.; pop. 26,683,000.

Kwan-to (kwän-tō), also **Kan-to** (kän-tō), **Plain**, sometimes **Tokyo Plain**, region, Japan, in Honshu around Tokyo; the largest area of level land in Japan, 5000 sq. m.

Kwan'tung' (gwän'dŏŏng') or **Kwantung Leased Territory**, former territory, S Manchuria, at tip of Liaotung Penin.; under lease to Russia 1898–1905, to Japan 1905–45, to Russia again 1945–55; includes Port Arthur–Dairen; area 1444 sq. m.; pop. 1,750,000.

Kwei'chow' (gwā'jō') 1 province, S China, between the Yangtze and Si rivers; ✱ Kweiyang; 67,954 sq. m.; pop. 10,487,000. 2 city, S Szechwan: see FENGKIEH.

Kwei'lin' (gwā'lǐn') city, SE China, in NE Kwangsi prov. on Kwei river; pop. 100,000.

Kwei'sui' (gwā'swā'), formerly **Kwei'hwa'-Sui'yuan'** (gwā'hwä'swā'yü-än'), Mongol. **Ku'ku-Kho'to** (kü'kü-kō'tō) town, N China, ✱ of Inner Mongolian Autonomous Region; pop. 65,000.

Kwei'yang' (gwā'yäng') or **Kwei'chu'** (-jōō') city, S China, ✱ of Kweichow prov.; pop. 116,000.

Kyo'ga or **Kio'ga** (kyō'gå) lake, E Africa, in Uganda N of Lake Victoria; traversed by the Victoria Nile; area 1000 sq. m.

Kyongsong. See SEOUL.

Kyo'to or **Kio'to** (kyō'tō) city, Japan, in W cen. Honshu; pop. 999,700.

Kyu'shu, also **Kiu'shu** (kyōō'shōō) island, Japan, southernmost of the four main islands; area 16,240 sq. m.; pop. 10,028,900.

L

Laaland. See LOLLAND.

Laatokka. See LADOGA.

Labe. See ELBE.

Lab'ra-dor (lăb'rå-dôr) 1 peninsula, E Canada, divided between Quebec and Newfoundland provs. 2 the section of the peninsula belonging to Newfoundland; area 110,000 sq. m.; pop. 10,800.

La'bu-an' (lä'bŏŏ-än') island off NW Borneo; since 1946 part of British colony of North Borneo; area 35 sq. m.; pop. 9300.

Lac'ca-dive Islands (lǎk'å-dīv) or **Lac'ca-dives** (-dīvz) group of islands, India, in Arabian Sea; constituted 1956 **Laccadive and Amindivi Islands** territory of Republic of India; pop. 21,200.

Lacedaemon. See SPARTA.

La-chine' (lå-shēn') city, Canada, on Montreal I. just above the Lachine Rapids of St. Lawrence river; pop. 34,500.

La'chish (lä'kǐsh) ancient city, S Palestine, in W Judah W of Hebron.

Lach'lan (lǎk'lǎn) river, SE Australia, in cen. New South Wales, flowing W to the Murrumbidgee river; 800 m. long.

Lack'a-wan'na (lǎk'å-wŏn'å) city, New York, on Lake Erie S of Buffalo; pop. 27,700.

La-co'ni-a (lå-kō'nǐ-å; -kōn'yå) or **La-con'i-ca** (lå-kŏn'ǐ-kå), Mod. Gr. **La'ko-ni'a** (lä'kō-nyē'ä) region, S Greece, in SE Peloponnesus bordering on Aegean and Mediterranean seas; an ancient country, ✱ Sparta. — **La-co'ni-an** (lå-kō'nǐ-ǎn; -kōn'yǎn) adj. & n.

La Co-ru'ña (lä kō-rōō'nyä), Eng. **Co-run'na** (kō-rŭn'å) seaport, NW Spain; pop. 129,600.

La Crosse (lå krŏs') city, W Wisconsin; pop. 47,500.

La Cumbre. See USPALLATA PASS.

Lacus Asphaltites. See DEAD SEA.

La-dakh' (lå-däk') district, E Kashmir, on Tibetan frontier; ✱ Leh; area 45,762 sq. m.; pop. 192,100.

Lad'o-ga (lǎd'ō-gå), Finnish **Laa'tok-ka** (lä'tôk-kå') lake, NW Soviet Russia, Europe, NE of Gulf of Finland, to which it drains; before 1940 partly in Finland; area 7000 sq. m.

Ladrone Islands. See MARIANA ISLANDS.

La'dy-smith (lā'dǐ-smǐth) town, E Union of South Africa, in W Natal; besieged 1899–1900; pop. 14,200.

La'e (lä'å) town, North-East New Guinea, on Huon Gulf; airfield.

La'fay-ette' (lä'fǐ-ĕt'; lǎf'ǐ-'; lǎf'ǐ-; in sou. U.S., often lå-fā'ĕt, lå-fāt', lå-fĕt') 1 city, W cen. Indiana, on Wabash river; site of Purdue Univ.; pop. 35,600. 2 city, S Louisiana; pop. 33,500.

La'gash (lā'gǎsh) ancient city of Sumer, S Babylonia; a city-state, flourished c. 3000 B.C. to 2300 B.C.

La'gens (lå'zhǎnsh) airfield, Azores, on Terceira I.; used jointly by the Portuguese and U.S. air forces.

Lagoa dos Patos. See PATOS, LAGOA DOS.

Lagoon Islands. See ELLICE ISLANDS.

La'gos (lā'gŭs; lä'gōs) seaport, ✱ of Nigeria; pop. 167,000.

La Grange (lå gränj') city, W Georgia; pop. 25,000.

La Granja. See SAN ILDEFONSO.

La Guai'ra (lä gwī'rä) seaport, N Venezuela; port for Caracas.

La Habana. See HAVANA.

La Hague, Cape (lå häg'), Fr. **Cap de la Hague** (kåp' dĕ lä åg') headland on coast of NW France, W of Cherbourg.

La Hogue (lå hōg'; Fr. lä ôg') roadstead, NW France, off Point Barfleur; naval battle 1692.

La-hore' (lå-hōr') city, Pakistan, ✱ of West Pakistan province, near Ravi river; pop. 671,700.

Laibach. See LJUBLJANA.

Laichow. See YEHSIEN.

La Jol'la (lå hoi'å) community, S California; part of San Diego.

Lake Charles (chärlz) city, SW Louisiana; pop. 41,300.

Lake District, region, NW England, in Cumberland, Westmorland, and Lancashire, containing many lakes and mountains.

Lake'hurst (lāk'hûrst) borough, E New Jersey, NW of Toms River; U.S. naval air station.

Lake'land (lāk'lǎnd) city, cen. Florida; pop. 30,900.

La'ken-heath (lä'kĕn-hēth) airfield, SE England, in NW Suffolk; Royal Air Force base.

Lake of the Ozarks. See OZARKS, LAKE OF THE.

Lake of the Woods, lake, N Minnesota and extending into Canadian provinces of Manitoba and Ontario; area 1346 sq. m.

Lake Plac'id (plǎs'ǐd) village, NE New York, in Adirondack Mts. on Mirror Lake, near Lake Placid; resort.

Lake Success, village, SE New York, in W Long Island E of Flushing; headquarters of United Nations Security Council 1946–50.

Lake'wood (lāk'wŏŏd) city, N Ohio, W of Cleveland; pop. 68,100.

La Man'cha (lä män'chä) region, S cen. Spain, in New Castile; level, arid, treeless plateau.

La Manche. See ENGLISH CHANNEL.

Lam'beth (lǎm'bĕth; -bĕth) metropolitan borough, London, on S bank of the Thames; pop. 230,100.

Lam'mer-muir (lǎm'ẽr-mūr'), or **Lam'mer-moor** (-mŏŏr'), **Hills**, range of hills, SE Scotland; highest point Says Law, 1749 ft.

Lam'pe-du'sa (läm'pĕ-dōō'sä; -zå; Ital. läm'pā-dōō'zä) island, Italy, in Mediterranean Sea, one of the Pelagian Is.

La-na'i (lä-nä'ē) island, cen. Hawaii, W of Maui I.

Lan'ark (lǎn'ẽrk) or **Lan'ark-shire** (-shǐr; -shẽr) county, S cen. Scotland; ✱ Lanark; area 892 sq. m.; pop. 1,614,100.

Lan'ca-shire (lǎng'kå-shǐr; -shẽr) or **Lan'cas-ter** (lǎng'kǎs-tẽr) county, NW England, bordering on Irish Sea; ✱ Lancaster; area 1875 sq. m.; pop. 5,116,000. See LANCASTRIAN b, in Vocab.

Lan'cas-ter (lǎng'kǎs-tẽr; in U.S., also lǎng'kǎs'tẽr, lǎn'kǎs'tẽr) 1 city, S cen. Ohio; pop. 24,200. 2 city, SE Pennsylvania; pop. 63,800. 3 city, Canada, in S New Brunswick; pop. 12,400. 4 county of England: see LANCASHIRE. 5 municipal borough, NW England, ✱ of Lancashire; pop. 51,700.

Lan'chow' (län'jō') or **Kao'lan'** (kou'län') city, N cen. China, ✱ of Kansu prov., on the Hwang Ho near the Great Wall; pop. 500,000.

Lands End or **Land's End** (lǎndz ĕnd) cape, SW England, on SW coast of Cornwall; westernmost land of England.

Lang′chung′ (läng′jŏong′), formerly **Pao′ning′** (bou′nĭng′) city, S cen. China, in N Szechwan prov. on Kialing river; pop. 100,000.

Lan·gre′o (läng·grā′ŏ) commune, NW Spain; pop. 52,900.

Lan′gue·doc′ (läng′dŏk; läng′gwĕ·dŏk′) historical region, S France, extending from Auvergne to the Mediterranean Sea.

Lan′sing (lăn′sĭng) city, * of Michigan; pop. 92,100.

Lantsang. See MEKONG.

La·od′i·ce′a (lā·ŏd′ĭ·sē′à) **1** ancient city, Asia Minor, near site of modern Denizli, Turkey. See LAODICEAN, in Vocab. **2** see LATAKIA.

Laoigh′is (lā′ĭsh) or **Leix** (lāks) county, cen. Ireland, in Leinster prov.; * Maryborough; 664 sq. m.; pop. 48,400.

Laos (louz) country, NW Indochina; a kingdom, formerly (1949–54) an associated state of the French Union; administrative * Vientiane, royal * Luang Prabrang; area 89,320 sq. m.; pop. 1,021,000. — **La·o′tian** (lā·ō′shăn; lou′shăn) adj. & n.

La Pal′ma (lä päl′mä; Angl. là päl′mà) island, Spain, one of the Canary Is.; chief town Santa Cruz de la Palma; area 280 sq. m.; pop. 51,800.

La Parida. See BOLÍVAR.

La Paz (lä päs′; Angl. là päz′) city, a * of Bolivia; pop. 301,000.

Lap′land (lăp′lănd; -lănd) region, N Europe, extending over N Norway, N Sweden, N Finland, and the Kola Penin. in NW Soviet Russia, above the Arctic Circle. See LAPLANDER, in Vocab.

La Plata (lä plä′tä) seaport, E Argentina, SE of Buenos Aires; pop. 256,400.

La Porte (là pōrt′) city, N Indiana; pop. 17,900.

Lap′tev Sea (läp′tĕf), formerly **Nor′den·skjöld′ Sea** (nōōr′dĕn·shŭld′) part of Arctic Ocean along N coast of Soviet Russia, Asia, between Severnaya Zemlya on W and New Siberian Is. on E.

Lar′a·mie (lăr′à·mĭ) **1** river, SE Wyoming; rises in N Colorado, flows N into North Platte river; 200 m. long. **2** city, SE Wyoming, on Laramie river; pop. 15,600.

La·re′do (là·rā′dō) city, S Texas, on the Rio Grande; pop. 51,900.

La Ro′chelle′ (là rō′shĕl′) seaport, W France, on Bay of Biscay; pop. 48,900.

La Salle (là săl′) town, Canada, on Montreal I.; pop. 19,000.

Las Be′la (lŭs bā′lä) state, W Pakistan, in Baluchistan; formerly under suzerainty of Kalat; * Bela; area 7043 sq. m.; pop. 69,100.

Lash′kar (lŭsh′kĕr) city, N cen. India, in Madhya Pradesh; pop. 113,700.

La Sou·frі′ère′ (là sōō′frē′âr′) or **Soufrière**, volcano, British West Indies, on island of St. Vincent; violent eruption May 7, 1902.

Las Pal′mas (läs päl′mäs) seaport, Spain, on Grand Canary I.; pop. 151,400.

La Spe′zia (lä spä′tsyä) seaport, NW Italy, on **Gulf of La Spezia** (inlet of Ligurian Sea); pop. 124,500.

Lassa. Var. of LHASA.

Las′sen Peak (lăs′n) volcano, NE California, in Cascade Range; 10,453 ft. high; eruptions 1914–21; central feature of Lassen Volcanic National Park, established 1916.

Las Ve′gas (läs vā′gäs) **1** city, SE Nevada; pop. 24,600. **2** community, NE cen. New Mexico, comprising city of Las Vegas, pop. 7500, and town of Las Vegas, pop. 6300.

Lat′a·ki′a (lăt′à·kē′à) **1** region, NW Syria, on coast N of Lebanon; autonomous 1922–42. **2** anc. **La·od′i·ce′a** (là·ŏd′ĭ·sē′à) seaport, W Syria, in Latakia; pop. 36,700.

Latin America, Spanish America and Brazil (a Portuguese-speaking country).

Latin Empire, also known as **Ro·ma′nia** (rō·mān′yà; -mā′nĭ·à) the Byzantine Empire under the Crusaders 1204–61, including most of the lands around the Aegean and the Sea of Marmara.

La′ti·um (lā′shĭ·ŭm), Ital. **La′zio** (lä′tsyŏ) region, Italy, in cen. part bordering on Tyrrhenian Sea; traversed by the Tiber river.

Lat′vi·a (lăt′vĭ·à), Lettish and Lithuanian **Lat′vi·ja** (lăt′vĭ·yä) country, N Europe, bordering on Baltic Sea; an independent republic 1918–40; since 1940 a constituent republic of the U.S.S.R. and called officially the **Latvian Soviet Socialist Republic**; * Riga; area 24,600 sq. m.; pop. 1,800,000. — **Lat′vi·an** (lăt′vĭ·ăn), adj. & n. See also LETT, LETTIC, LETTISH, in Vocab.

Lau′rel (lô′rĕl; lŏr′ĕl) city, SE Mississippi; pop. 25,000.

Lau·ren′tian Highlands or **Upland** (lô·rĕn′shăn) region, E Canada, N of St. Lawrence river and around Hudson Bay; on S border, just N of St. Lawrence river, are the **Laurentian**, or **Lau′ren·tide** (lô′rĕn·tīd), **Hills** (sometimes, **Mountains**), having steep slopes on the S.

Lau·sanne′ (lō·zän′) commune, W Switzerland, * of Vaud canton, on Lake of Geneva; pop. 106,800.

Lausitz. See LUSATIA.

Lausitzer Neisse. See NEISSE.

La Vendée (là). = VENDÉE region.

Lavongai. See NEW HANOVER.

Law′rence (lô′rĕns; lŏr′ĕns) **1** city, E Kansas, on Kansas river; pop. 23,400. **2** city, NE Massachusetts; pop. 80,500.

Law′ton (lô′t′n) city, SW Oklahoma; pop. 34,800.

Lead′ville (lĕd′vĭl) city, cen. Colorado, in Rocky Mts. at altitude of 10,190 ft.; a mining center.

Lea′side (lē′sīd) town, Canada, N suburb of Toronto; pop. 16,500.

Leav′en·worth (lĕv′ĕn·wûrth) city, NE Kansas, on Missouri river (Fort Leavenworth is just N); pop. 20,600.

Leb′a·non (lĕb′à·nŏn) **1** city, SE cen. Pennsylvania; pop. 28,200. **2** or **Leb′a·nese′ Republic** (lĕb′à·nēz′; -nēs′) country, W Asia, bordering on Mediterranean Sea N of Palestine; under French mandate 1920–44; republic since 1944; * Beirut; area 3470 sq. m.; pop. 1,143,000. — **Leb′a·nese′** (lĕb′à·nēz′; -nēs′; 2), adj. & n.

Lebanon Mountains, range of mountains, Lebanon, extending parallel with coast for 100 miles; highest point over 10,000 ft.

Le Bour′get′ (lĕ bŏŏr′zhā′) town, N France, NE of Paris; airport.

Le Cap. See CAP HAITIEN.

Lec′co (lĕt′chä) commune, SE Italy, in Apulia; pop. 60,800.

Lech (lĕk) river, Austria and Germany, rising in the Vorarlberg and flowing N into the Danube; 177 m. long.

Le·duc′ (lĕ·dŭk′) town, Canada, in Alberta S of Edmonton; oil field.

Leeds (lēdz) city and county borough, N England, in West Riding, Yorkshire, on the Aire; pop. 505,000.

Leeu′war′den (lā′vär′dĕ[n]) commune, N Netherlands, * of Friesland; pop. 76,700.

Lee′ward Islands (lē′wĕrd; lū′ĕrd, lōō′-) **1** island group, West Indies, the N part of the Lesser Antilles, extending from Dominica on S to Virgin Is. on N. **2** territory, West Indies Federation, comprising the British islands (Antigua, Barbuda, Montserrat, St. Kitts, Nevis, Anguilla, etc.) in the Leeward Is., excepting Dominica; * St. Johns, on Antigua; total area 414 sq. m.; pop. 98,100.

Leg′horn (lĕg′hôrn), Ital. **Li·vor′no** (lē·vôr′nō) seaport, cen. Italy, on Tyrrhenian Sea; pop. 147,200.

Le Ha′vre (lĕ ä′vr′; Angl. hä′vr′, -vrĕ, -vĕr), Eng. **Havre**, formerly (Fr.) **Le Havre-de-Grâce** (lĕ ä′vrĕ·dĕ·gräs′) seaport, N France, on English Channel on N side of Seine estuary; pop. 106,900.

Le′high (lē′hī) river, E Pennsylvania, flowing SW and SE to the Delaware river; 100 m. long.

Leh′man Caves (lē′măn) limestone caverns, E Nevada; established as national monument 1922.

Leices′ter (lĕs′tĕr) **1** county of England: see LEICESTERSHIRE. **2** city and county borough, cen. England, * of Leicestershire; pop. 285,100.

Leices′ter·shire (-shĭr; -shĕr) or **Leicester**, county, cen. England; * Leicester; area 832 sq. m.; pop. 630,900.

Lei′den or **Ley′den** (lī′d′n; Du. usu. lā′ĕ·yĕ) commune, SW Netherlands, on Oude Rijn river; pop. 86,900.

Leie. See LYS.

Lein′ster (lĕn′stĕr; Ir. lĭn′-) province, SE Ireland, bordering on Irish Sea; area 7581 sq. m.; pop. 1,334,800.

Leip′zig (līp′sĭg; -sĭk; Ger. līp′tsĭk), also **Leip′sic** (līp′sĭk) city, E Germany; pop. 607,700.

Lei′tha (lī′tä) river, E Austria and NW Hungary, flowing into the Rába river; 112 m. long.

Lei′trim (lē′trĭm) county, N Republic of Ireland, in Connacht prov.; * Carrick on Shannon; area 589 sq. m.; pop. 41,300.

Leix. See LAOIGHIS.

Lek (lĕk) river, Netherlands, the northern branch of the Lower Rhine.

Le Maine. See MAINE.

Leman, Lake. See GENEVA, LAKE OF.

Le Mans (lĕ män′) city, NW France, on Sarthe river; pop. 100,500.

Le Marche. See MARCHES.

Lemberg. See LVOV.

Lem′nos (lĕm′nŏs), Mod. Gr. **Lím′nos** (lyēm′nŏs) island, Greece, in Aegean Sea off W coast of Turkey; * Kástron.

Le′na (lē′nà; Russ. lyĕ′-) river, Soviet Russia, Asia; flows into Laptev Sea through a delta 250 m. wide; 3000 m. long.

Len′in·grad (lĕn′ĭn·grăd), from 1703–1914 **Saint Pe′ters·burg** (sănt pē′tĕrz·bûrg), from 1914–1924 **Pet′ro·grad** (pĕt′rō·grăd) city, N Soviet Russia, Europe, at E end of Gulf of Finland in Neva delta; * of Russian empire 1712–1917; pop. 3,191,300.

Len′in Peak (lĕn′ĭn; Russ. lyä′nyĭn) mountain, Soviet Central Asia, in Tadzhik S.S.R. in Trans Alai Range; 23,386 ft. high.

Leom′in·ster (lĕm′ĭn·stĕr) city, cen. Massachusetts; pop. 24,100.

Le·ón′ (lā·ŏn′) **1** city, cen. Mexico, in Guanajuato state; pop. 74,200. **2** region, NW Spain, traversed by Duero river; an ancient kingdom. **3** city, NW Spain, * of ancient kingdom; pop. 54,300.

Leopold II, Lake, lake, W Belgian Congo; area 900 to 3200 sq. m. according to the season.

Lé′o′pold′ville′ (lā′ō·pōld′vēl′; Angl. lē′ō·pōld·vĭl) city, * of Belgian Congo, at outlet of Stanley Pool in the Congo river; pop. 116,500.

Lepanto, Gulf of. See CORINTH, GULF OF.

Le′pa·ya (lyĕ′pä·yä), Latvian **Lie′pā·ja** (lyĕ′pä·yä), Ger. **Li′bau** (lē′bou) seaport, W Latvia, on Baltic Sea; naval base; pop. 57,100.

Le·pon′tine Alps (lē·pŏn′tīn) range of cen. Alps, on border between Switzerland and Italy; highest point Monte Leone, 11,684 ft.

Le Puglie. See APULIA.

Les′bos (lĕz′bŏs) or **Myt′i·le′ne** (mĭt′l·ē′nē) island, Greece, in Aegean Sea off NW Turkey in Asia; area 623 sq. m. See LESBIAN, in Vocab.

Lesser Antilles. See WEST INDIES.

Lesser Armenia. See CILICIA.

Lesser Slave Lake (slāv) lake, Canada, in cen. Alberta; its outlet is **Lesser Slave River**, a tributary of the Athabaska; 480 sq. m.

Leth′bridge (lĕth′brĭj) city, Canada, in S Alberta; pop. 29,500.

Le·ti′cia (lā·tē′syä; Angl. lē·tĭsh′ĭ·à) town, SE Colombia, on the Amazon river; border town, claimed by Peru and Colombia until 1934.

Leu′cas (lū′kăs) or **Leu·ca′di·a** (lū·kā′dĭ·à), Mod. Gr. **Lev·kás′** (lăf·käs′), Ital. **San′ta Mau′ra** (sän′tä mou′rä) island, W Greece, in Ionian Is. S of entrance to Ambracian Gulf.

Leuc′tra (lūk′trà) ancient village, Greece, in Boeotia SW of Thebes; battle 371 B.C.

Le·val′lois′-Per′ret′ (lĕ·và′lwä′pĕ′rĕ′) commune, N France, NW of Paris on Seine river; pop. 61,700.

Le·vant′ (lĕ·vănt′). See in Vocab.

Levant States, 1 the divisions of Syria under French mandate, 1920–44, comprising Syria, Lebanon, Latakia, and Jebel ed Druz. **2** sometimes, all of the states of the Levant, that is, states washed by, or near to, the eastern Mediterranean.

Le′ven, Loch (lŏk lē′vĕn) lake, E cen. Scotland, in Kinross co.

Le′ver·ku·sen (lā′vĕr·kōō′zĕn) city, W Germany, on Rhine river SE of Düsseldorf; pop. 55,400.

Le′vis (lē′vĭs), Fr. **Lé′vis′** (lā′vĭs′) city, Canada, in S Quebec on St. Lawrence river opposite city of Quebec; pop. 13,600.

Le′wes (lū′ĭs; lōō′ĭs) river, N Canada: see YUKON.

Lew′is·ton (lū′ĭs·tŭn; lōō′-) city, SW Maine, on Androscoggin river; pop. 41,000.

Lew′is with Har′ris (lū′ĭs [lōō′-], hăr′ĭs) island, W Scotland, most northerly of the Outer Hebrides; area 770 sq. m.

Lex′ing·ton (lĕks′ĭng·tŭn) **1** city, NE Kentucky; pop. 55,500. **2** town, E Massachusetts, NW of Boston; battle April 19, 1775.

Leyden. See LEIDEN.

Ley′te (lā′tĕ) island, Philippine Is., in the Visayan Is.; almost one island with Samar, from which it is separated by a narrow strait; * Tacloban; area 3084 sq. m.; pop. 915,900.

Leyte Gulf, inlet of Pacific Ocean, E Philippine Is., on E coast of Leyte I. and enclosed on N by Samar I.

Ley'ton (lā't'n) municipal borough, SE England, in Essex NE of London; pop. 105,200.

Lha'sa (lä'sȧ; lăs'ȧ), also **Las'sa** (lăs'ȧ) city, ✻ of Tibet, in SE part near the Indian border; pop. 50,000.

Liao (lĭ·ou') river, S Manchuria, flowing NE, then SW to the Gulf of Liaotung; 700 m. long.

Liao'ning' (lĭ·ou'nĭng'), originally **Feng'tien'** (fung'tĭ·ĕn') province, S Manchuria, ✻ Mukden; area 56,000 sq. m.; pop. 20,444,000.

Liao'si' (lĭ·ou'shē') former province (1948–54) of S Manchuria.

Liao'tung' Peninsula (lĭ·ou'dōōng') peninsula, S Manchuria, extending SW towards Shantung penin. and enclosing the **Gulf of Liaotung**, the NE arm of the Gulf of Po Hai.

Liao'yang' (lĭ·ou'yäng') city, S Manchuria; pop. 100,200.

Liao'yüan' (lĭ·ou'yü·än'), formerly **Cheng'chia'tun'** (jŭng'jĭ·ä'dōōn') city, cen. Manchuria, N of Mukden; pop. 191,100.

Li'ard (lē'ärd) river, W Canada, flowing from Stikine Mts. in Yukon Territory E and NW to Mackenzie river; 550 m. long.

Libau. See LEPAYA.

Li'be·rec (lĭ'bĕ·rĕts), Ger. **Rei'chen·berg** (rī'kĕn·bĕrk) city, W Czechoslovakia, in N Bohemia; pop. 52,800.

Li·be'ri·a (lī·bēr'ĭ·ȧ) country, W Africa, bordering on Atlantic Ocean; republic, established 1847; ✻ Monrovia; area 43,000 sq. m.; pop. 1,250,000. — **Li·be'ri·an**, adj. & n.

Liberty Island. See BEDLOE'S ISLAND.

Lib'y·a (lĭb'ĭ·ȧ) **1** north Africa, excepting Egypt; — its ancient Greek name. **2** Ital. **Li'bia** or **Libia I·ta·li·a'na** (lē'byä ē·tä·lē·ä'nä) country, N Africa; includes Tripolitania, Cyrenaica, and the Fezzan; a colony of Italy from 1912 to World War II; since December 1951 an independent kingdom, joint capitals Tripoli and Bengasi; area 679,358 sq. m.; pop. 1,177,000. — **Lib'y·an** (lĭb'ĭ·ăn), adj. & n.

Libyan Desert, desert, N Africa, at E end of the Sahara in Egypt, Libya, and Republic of Sudan; bordered on E by lower Nile.

Lick'ing (lĭk'ĭng) river, NE Kentucky, flowing NW into Ohio river; 350 m. long.

Lidd. See LYDDA.

Li'di·ce (lĭd'ĭ·sĕ; -ĭt·sĕ; Czech lĭ'dyĭ·tsĕ) village, Czechoslovakia, in W cen. Bohemia 10 m. WNW of Prague; destroyed 1942 by Germans.

Li'do (lē'dō) island, Italy, separating the Lagoon of Venice from the Gulf of Venice; at N end is **the Lido**, noted bathing resort.

Liech'ten·stein (lĭk'tĕn·shtīn) country, Europe, between Switzerland and Austria, on the Rhine; an independent principality; ✻ Vaduz; area 62 sq. m.; pop. 11,100.

Li·ége' (lē·āzh'; lē·ĕzh'), Flemish **Luik** (loik) **1** province, E Belgium; once an independent church state. **2** city, its ✻, at confluence of the Ourthe and Meuse rivers; pop. 156,700.

Liepāja. See LEPAYA.

Lietuva. See LITHUANIA.

Lif'fey (lĭf'ĭ) river, E Ireland, flowing into Dublin Bay; 50 m. long.

Li·gu'ri·a (lĭ·gū'rĭ·ȧ) region, N Italy, bordering on Mediterranean Sea and France. — **Li·gu'ri·an**, adj. & n.

Ligurian Sea, section of Mediterranean Sea off coast of Liguria.

Lille (lēl), formerly **Lisle** (lēl; Angl. līl) city, N France; pop. 188,900.

Li'ma (lī'mȧ) city, NW Ohio; pop. 50,200.

Li'ma (lē'mȧ) city, ✻ of Peru, 8 m. E of its port, Callao; pop. 533,600.

Lim'burg (lĭm'bûrg) region, W Europe, on E side of the Meuse; now divided between Netherlands and Belgium.

Lime'house' (līm'hous'; locally sometimes lĭm'ŭs) parish, E London, in E Stepney metropolitan borough, on the Thames.

Lim'er·ick (lĭm'ĕr·ĭk) **1** county, SW Ireland, in Munster prov.; area 1037 sq. m.; pop. 141,300. **2** city and county borough, its ✻, on the Shannon; pop. 50,800.

Li·moges' (lē·mōzh') city, W cen. France; pop. 107,900.

Li·món' or **Puer'to Limón** (pwĕr'tō lē·mōn') seaport, Costa Rica, on Caribbean Sea; pop. 11,300.

Li'mou'sin' (lē'mōō'zăɴ'; Angl. lĭm'ŏŏ·zēn') historical region, cen. France, W of Auvergne; before the Revolution a province, ✻ Limoges.

Lim·po'po (lĭm·pō'pō) or **Croc'o·dile** (krŏk'ō·dīl) river, SE Africa; rises in Transvaal, flows N and NE, turns SE across S Mozambique and empties into Indian Ocean; 1000 m. long.

Li·na'res (lē·nä'rās) commune, S Spain, N of Jaén; pop. 52,000.

Lin'coln (lĭng'kŭn) **1** city, ✻ of Nebraska; pop. 98,900. **2** county in England: see LINCOLNSHIRE. **3** city and county borough, E England, in Lincolnshire, ✻ of Parts of Lindsey; pop. 69,400.

Lincoln Park, city, SE Michigan, SW of Detroit; pop. 29,300.

Lin'coln·shire (lĭng'kŭn·shĭr; -shĕr) or **Lincoln**, or **Lincs** (lĭngks) county, E England, bordering on North Sea between the Wash and the Humber river; divided into: the Parts of Holland, ✻ Boston, area 420 sq. m., pop. 101,500; the Parts of Kesteven, ✻ Sleaford, area 724 sq. m., pop. 131,600; and the Parts of Lindsey, ✻ Lincoln, area 1520 sq. m., pop. 473,500.

Lin'den (lĭn'dĕn) city, NE New Jersey, S of Elizabeth; pop. 30,600.

Lin'des·nes' (lĭn'dĕs·nās') or **the Naze** (nāz) cape, S Norway, projecting into the North Sea at 57°59'N.

Line Islands (līn) group of islands, cen. Pacific Ocean, on the equator; divided between the United States (Kingman Reef and Palmyra) and Great Britain (Washington, Fanning, and Christmas islands, all part of Gilbert and Ellice Is. colony); includes also some islands which are claimed by both the U.S. and Great Britain.

Lin'ga·yen' Gulf (lĭng'gä·yĕn') inlet of South China Sea, Philippine Is., in NW Luzon; 35 m. long and 23 m. wide at entrance.

Lin·guet'ta (lĭng·gwĕt'ȧ) or **Glos'sa** (glŏs'ȧ), **Cape**, cape, SW Albania, the ancient Acroceraunia.

Lin'kö'ping (lĭn'chû'pĭng) city, SE Sweden; pop. 53,200.

Linn'he, Loch (lŏk lĭn'ē) inlet of the sea, W Scotland, between Argyll co. and Inverness, at SW end of the Great Glen; 20 m. long.

Linz (lĭnts) city, Austria, on Danube river; pop. 185,000.

Li'ons, Gulf of (lī'ŭnz), Fr. **Golfe du Lion** (gôlf' dü lyôɴ') inlet of Mediterranean Sea, S France.

Lip'a·ri Islands (lĭp'ȧ·rĭ), Ital. **I'so·le E·o'lie** (ē'zō·lā ā·ô'lyā), anc. **Ae·o'li·ae In'su·lae** (ē·ō'lĭ·ē ĭn'sū·lē) group of islands, Italy, in SE Tyrrhenian Sea off coast of Sicily; includes the islands Vulcano and Stromboli, and the chief island, Lipari.

Lip'pe (lĭp'ĕ) **1** river, W Germany, flowing from the Teutoberger Wald W into the Rhine; 150 m. long. **2** former state, Germany, between the Teutoberger Wald and the Weser river; ✻ Detmold.

Li'ri (lē'rē) river, cen. Italy, flowing SE between parallel ranges of cen. Apennine Mts. and then S to enter Gulf of Gaeta; 100 m. long.

Lis'bon (lĭz'bŭn), Port. **Lis·bo'a** (lēzh·vō'ȧ) seaport, ✻ of Portugal, on estuary of the Tagus river; pop. 709,200.

Lis'burne, Cape (lĭz'bĕrn) cape, NW Alaska, at 166°W.

Lisle. See LILLE.

Lith'u·a'ni·a (lĭth'ū·ā'nĭ·ȧ; -ān'yȧ), Lithuanian **Lie·tu'va** (lyĕ·tōō'vä), Russ. **Lit·va'** (lyĭt·vä') country, N Europe, bordering on Baltic Sea; remnant of a medieval principality extending from Baltic Sea to Black Sea; an independent republic 1918–40; since 1940 a constituent republic of the U.S.S.R. and called officially the **Lithuanian Soviet Socialist Republic**, ✻ Vilnyus; area 31,200 sq. m.; pop. 2,700,000. — **Lith'u·a'ni·an**, adj. & n.

Little America, base, Antarctica, on Ross Shelf Ice near the Bay of Whales; used by Byrd expeditions and by other explorers.

Little Big'horn' (bĭg'hôrn') river, S Montana; rises in N Wyoming, flows N into Bighorn river; 80 m. long.

Little Colorado, river, NE Arizona, flowing NW into the Colorado river; 300 m. long.

Little Missouri, river, W United States, flowing from NE Wyoming N into the Missouri river in W North Dakota; 560 m. long.

Lit'tle Rock', city, ✻ of Arkansas, on Arkansas river; pop. 102,200.

Little Saint Bernard, mountain pass, France and Italy, S of Mont Blanc and SW of Great Saint Bernard Pass; altitude over 7170 ft.

Little Walachia. See OLTENIA.

Liukiu Islands. See RYUKYU ISLANDS.

Liv'er·pool (lĭv'ĕr·pōōl) county borough and city, NW England, in Lancashire on the Mersey estuary; pop. 789,500.

Liv'ing·stone (lĭv'ĭng·stŭn) town, S Northern Rhodesia, on Zambezi river near Victoria Falls; until 1931 ✻ of Northern Rhodesia.

Li·vo'ni·a (lĭ·vō'nĭ·ȧ; -vōn'yȧ) **1** region, N Europe, on Baltic Sea in Latvia and Estonia; formed a government of Russia 1721–1918. **2** city, SE Michigan; pop. 17,500. — **Li·vo'ni·an**, adj. & n.

Livorno. See LEGHORN.

Liz'ard, the (lĭz'ĕrd) peninsula, SW England, in S Cornwall; its S end is extreme S point of Great Britain, **Lizard Point** or **Lizard Head**, 49°57'30"N, 5°12'W.

Lju'blja·na (lyōō'blyä·nä), Ger. **Lai'bach** (lī'bäk) city, NW Yugoslavia, ✻ of Slovenia, on Sava river; pop. 121,100.

Llan·ber'is (lăn·bĕr'ĭs; hlăn-) village, NW Wales, near foot of Mt. Snowdon, at entrance to the **Pass of Llanberis**, a rocky defile.

Llan·dud'no (lăn·dĭd'nō; -dŭd'-; hlăn-) urban district, NW Wales, in Caernarvonshire on coast; watering place; pop. 16,700.

Lla·nel'ly (lă·nĕl'ĭ; hlă·nĕ'hlĭ) seaport, S Wales, in Carmarthenshire; pop. 34,300.

Llan'o Es'ta·ca'do (lăn'ō ĕs'tȧ·kä'dō) or **Staked Plain** (stākt) region in SE New Mexico and W Texas; a section of the high plains.

Loanda. See LUANDA.

Lo·an'ge (lō·ăng'gĕ), Port. **Lu·an'gue** (lwäɴg'gĕ) river, S cen. Africa; rises in NE cen. Angola, flows N into Kasai river in SW Belgian Congo; 425 m. long.

Lo·car'no (lō·kär'nō) town, SE cen. Switzerland, in Ticino canton on N shore of Lake Maggiore; Locarno Pact 1925.

Lock'port (lŏk'pōrt) **1** city, NE Illinois, at end of the Chicago Sanitary and Ship Canal; pop. 5000. **2** city, W New York, ENE of Niagara Falls on N.Y. State Barge Canal; pop. 25,100.

Lo'cris (lō'krĭs; lŏk'rĭs) region of ancient Greece, in area between N Gulf of Euboea and the Gulf of Corinth.

Lod. See LYDDA.

Lo'di (lō'dī) borough, NE New Jersey, SE of Paterson; pop. 15,400.

Łódź (lōōj), Russ. **Lodz** (lôts'y') city, cen. Poland; pop. 592,600.

Lo'fo'ten (lō'fōō't'n, almost lōō'fōō't'n) island group, Norway, off NW coast; principal islands Austvågöy, Vestvågöy, and Maskenes.

Lo'gan (lō'găn) city, N Utah, N of Ogden; pop. 16,800.

Logan, Mount, mountain, NW Canada, in SW Yukon Territory, in St. Elias Range near Alaska boundary; 19,850 ft. high.

Lo'gans·port (lō'gănz·pōrt) city, N cen. Indiana; pop. 21,000.

Lo·gro'ño (lō·grō'nyō) commune, N Spain, on Ebro river; pop. 53,900.

Loire (lwär) river, France, flowing from the Massif Central N, NW, and W into the Bay of Biscay; 625 m. long.

Lol'land (lŏl'ănd) or **Laa'land** (lô'làn) island, Denmark, S of Sjælland.

Lo·ma'mi (lō·mä'mē) river, Belgian Congo; flows N and empties into the Congo; 900 m. long.

Lo'mas (lō'mäs) or **Lo'mas de Za·mo'ra** (lō'mäz thā sä·mō'rä) town, E Argentina, a suburb of Buenos Aires; pop. 100,000.

Lom'bar·dy (lŏm'bĕr·dĭ; -bär'dĭ; lŭm'-), Ital. **Lom·bar·di'a** (lôm·bär·dē'ä) region, N Italy, bordering on Switzerland; includes section of Po river valley; once a kingdom. See LOMBARD, in Vocab.

Lom·blen' (lŏm·blĕn') island, Indonesia, E of Flores I.

Lom·bok' (lŏm·bŏk') island, Indonesia, E of Bali I.; ✻ Mataram.

Lom'bok' Strait (lŏm'bŏk') channel, Indonesia, between Bali I. and Lombok I.; 22 m. wide.

Lo'mé' (lô'mā') seaport, W Africa, ✻ of French Togo.

Lomond, Ben. See BEN LOMOND.

Lo'mond, Loch (lŏk lō'mŭnd) lake, cen. Scotland, in Stirling and Dunbarton cos.; area over 27 sq. m.

Lon'don (lŭn'dŭn) **1** or **the City**, anc. **Lon·din'i·um** (lŏn·dĭn'ĭ·ŭm) city, S England, on the Thames river 40 m. from its mouth; with surrounding 28 metropolitan boroughs, constitutes county of London, ✻ of the United Kingdom of Great Britain and Northern Ireland, area 117 sq. m., pop. 3,348,300; and county of London with the Outer Ring (Middlesex and parts of Kent, Surrey, and Hertfordshire) forms Greater London, total area 693 sq. m., pop. 8,346,000. **2** city, Canada, in SE Ontario on Thames river; pop. 101,700.

London Airport, also **Heath'row** (hēth'rō) airport, S England, W of London in Middlesex; developed after World War II.

Lon'don·der'ry (lŭn'dŭn·dĕr'ĭ; in Ireland, usu. lŭn'dŭn·dĕr'ĭ) or **Der'ry** (dĕr'ĭ) **1** county, NW Northern Ireland; area 804 sq. m.; pop. 142,700. **2** county borough, its ✻; pop. 47,800.

Long Beach, 1 city, SW California, on San Pedro Bay; pop. 250,800. **2** city, SE New York, on island off S shore of Long I.; pop. 15,600.

Long Branch, city, E New Jersey, on Atlantic Ocean; pop. 23,100.

Long'champ' (lôṅ'shäṅ') race track, France, near Paris in the Bois de Boulogne.

Long'ford (lŏng'fẽrd) county, E cen. Ireland; ✻ Longford; area 403 sq. m.; pop. 34,600.

Long Island, island, SE New York, in Atlantic Ocean just E of mouth of Hudson river; total area (including water) 1723 sq. m.; land area 1401 sq. m.

Long Island Sound, body of water between Connecticut and Long I.

Longs Peak (lŏngz) mountain, N cen. Colorado, in Rocky Mountain National Park; 14,255 ft. high.

Lon·gueuil' (lôṅ·gû'y') city, Canada, in S Quebec on St. Lawrence river across from Montreal; pop. 14,300.

Long'view' (lŏng'vū') **1** city, NE Texas; pop. 24,500. **2** city, SW Washington, on Columbia river; pop. 20,300.

Long'xuyên' (loung'swē'ŭn) town, S Vietnam, in SW Cochin China on S side of Mekong delta; pop. 148,000.

Lookout Mountain, ridge, SE Tennessee, extending into Georgia and Alabama; highest point 2126 ft., near Chattanooga, battle 1863.

Lo·rain' (lō·rān') city, N Ohio, on Lake Erie; pop. 51,200.

Lor'ca (lôr'kä) commune, SE Spain, SW of Murcia; pop. 81,000.

Lord Howe Island (hou) island, N Tasman Sea, 436 m. ENE of Sydney, Australia; belongs to Australia.

Lo'reng·au' (lō'rĕng·ou') seaport, Admiralty Is., on E tip of Manus I.

Lo'rient' (lô'ryäṅ') seaport, NW France, on the Bay of Biscay; naval station and marine arsenal.

Lorne, Firth of (lôrn) strait, W Scotland, between mainland and island of Mull.

Lor·raine' (lŏ·rān'; lō-), Ger. **Lo'thring·en** (lō'trĭng·ĕn) region, N France, around the upper Moselle and Meuse rivers; remnant (Upper Lorraine) of medieval kingdom of **Lo'tha·rin'gi·a** (lō'thȧ·rĭn'jĭ·ȧ) including territory to the N (Lower Lorraine) between the Rhine and Schelde rivers; a duchy 10th to 18th cents.; a province of pre-Revolutionary France; divided 1871 and NE section (including Metz) became part of Germany 1871–1918.

Los Al'a·mos (lŏs ăl'ȧ·mōs) town, N New Mexico, 40 m. NW of Santa Fe; since 1942 site of atomic-bomb laboratory; pop. 9900.

Los An'ge·les (lŏs ăn'jĕ·lĕs; ăng'gĕ·lĕs), often called **L.A.** (ĕl'ā') city, SW California, near coast; pop. 1,970,400.

Lo'shan' (lō'shän') or **Kia'ting'** (jĭ·ä'dĭng') city, S cen. China, in SW Szechwan prov. on Min river; pop. 150,000.

Lot (lŏt) river, S France, flowing W into Garonne river; 300 m. long.

Lo'thi·an (lō'thĭ·ăn) region, S Scotland, bordering on Firth of Forth; now divided into 3 counties, **the Lothians:** East Lothian, Midlothian, and West Lothian.

Loualaba. See LUALABA.

Lou'is·burg or **Lou'is·bourg** (lōō'ĭs·bûrg) town, Canada, in Cape Breton I. on coast; founded by French 1713; strongly fortified (1720–40); site of the fort and its remains now preserved as a national historic park (**Fortress of Louisbourg**).

Lou·ise', Lake (lōō·ēz') lake, W Canada, in SW Alberta in Banff National Park; altitude 5670 ft.

Lou'i·si·an'a (lōō'ĭ·zĭ·ăn'ȧ; lōō'ĭ·zĭ-; lōō'zĭ-; chiefly by outsiders, lōō·ĕ'zĭ-), abbr. **La.,** state, S United States, bordering on Gulf of Mexico at mouth of Mississippi river; ✻ Baton Rouge; area 48,523 sq. m.; pop. 2,683,500. — **Lou'i·si·an'i·an** (-ăn'ĭ·ăn), **Lou'i·si·an'an** (-ăn'-ăn), adj. & n.

Louisiana Purchase, territory, W cen. United States, between Mississippi river and the Rocky Mts. extending from Gulf of Mexico to Canada; area 885,000 sq. m.; purchased by the U.S. from France 1803.

Lou'is·ville (lōō'ĭ·vĭl) city, N Kentucky, on Ohio river; pop. 369,100.

Loup (lōōp) river, E cen. Nebraska, flowing E into Platte river; 300 m. long (including North Loup headstream).

Lourdes (lōōrd) town, SW France, on the Gave de Pau SSW of Tarbes; shrine of the Virgin (Our Lady of Lourdes).

Lou·ren'ço Mar·ques' (lō·rāṅ'sōō mēr·käsh') seaport, ✻ of Mozambique, on Delagoa Bay; pop. 47,400.

Louth (louth; louth) county, NE Ireland, in Leinster prov.; ✻ Dundalk; 317 sq. m.; pop. 68,700.

Lou'vain' (lōō'văn') Flem. **Leu'ven** (lû'vĕ[n]) commune, cen. Belgium, E of Brussels; ✻ of Brabant; pop. 37,200.

Low Archipelago. See TUAMOTU ARCHIPELAGO.

Low Countries (lō) district, W Europe, bordering on North Sea, now comprising the Netherlands, Belgium, and Luxembourg.

Low'ell (lō'ĕl) city, NE Massachusetts; pop. 92,100.

Lower California, Span. **Ba'ja Ca'li·for'nia** (bä'hä kä'lē·fôr'nyä) peninsula, NW Mexico; divided into a N section, the state of **Baja California** (before 1952 a territory), ✻ Mexicali, area 27,653 sq. m., pop. 227,000; and a S section, the territory of **Baja California Sur** (sōōr'), ✻ La Paz, area 27,976 sq. m., pop. 60,900.

Lower Canada, Quebec province, Canada, 1791–1841.

Lower Saxony. See SAXONY.

Loyalty Islands, Fr. **Îles Loy·au'té'** (ēl' lwà·yō'tā') chain of islands, SW Pacific Ocean, E of New Caledonia (French), with which it is administered; total area 1059 sq. m.; pop. 10,100.

Lu'a·la'ba (lōō'ȧ·lä'bȧ), Fr. **Lou·a'la'ba'** (lwä'lä'bä') river, SE Belgian Congo; a headstream of the Congo river; 400 m. long.

Lu·an'da (lōō·än'dȧ) or **Lo·an'da** (lō·än'dȧ), also **São Pau'lo de Lo·an'da** (souṅ pou'lōō thĕ lwän'dȧ) seaport, ✻ of Angola; pop. 40,000.

Luangue. See LOANGE.

Lub'bock (lŭb'ŭk) city, NW Texas; pop. 71,700.

Lü'beck (lü'bĕk; Angl. lōō'-) city, W Germany, NE of Hamburg; formerly (before 1933) a free city; pop. 237,900.

Lu'blin (lōō'blēn), Russ. **Lyu'blin** (lyōō'blyĭn) city, E Poland; pop. 101,900.

Lucania. See BASILICATA.

Luc'ca (lōōk'kä) commune, cen. Italy, NE of Pisa; pop. 88,200.

Lu·cerne' (lŭ·sûrn'), Ger. **Lu·zern'** (lōō·tsĕrn') **1** canton, cen. Switzerland; area 579 sq. m.; pop. 223,200. **2** commune, its ✻, on Lake of Lucerne; pop. 60,500.

Lucerne, or the Four Forest Cantons, Lake of, lake, cen. Switzerland, enclosed by Schwyz, Uri, Unterwalden, and Lucerne cantons; 24 m. long.

Luchu Islands. See RYUKYU ISLANDS.

Luck'now (lŭk'nou) city, N India, ✻ of Uttar Pradesh; pop. 387,200.

Lü'de·ritz (lü'dĕ·rĭts), formerly **An'gra Pe·que'na** (äng'grä pĕ·kwē'nä) town, SW South-West Africa, on Atlantic Ocean; seaport; railroad terminus.

Lu'dhi·a'na (lōōd'hĭ·ä'nä) town, NW India, in Punjab state near Sutlej river; pop. 111,600.

Lud'wigs·ha'fen or **Ludwigshafen am Rhein** (lōōt'vĭks·hä'fĕn [lōōd'-] äm rīn') city, W Germany, on Rhine river; pop. 122,300.

Luf'kin (lŭf'kĭn) city, E Texas; pop. 15,100.

Lugansk. See VOROSHILOVGRAD.

Lu'go (lōō'gō) commune, NW Spain, on Miño river; pop. 54,200.

Luik. See LIÉGE.

Lü'le·bur·gaz' (lü'lĕ·bōōr·gäz'; -gäs') or **Lüle Burgas,** town, Turkey in Europe; scene of battle of the First Balkan War Oct. 28–30, 1912.

Luling. See KIAN.

Lun'dy's Lane (lŭn'dĭz) roadway, Canada, in Ontario prov. near Niagara Falls; battle July 25, 1814.

Lü'ne·burg (lü'nĕ·bōōrk) city, W Germany, SE of Hamburg and NE of **Lüneburg Heath** (hēth); pop. 49,200.

Lü'nen (lü'nĕn) city, W Germany, S of Münster; pop. 52,000.

Lu·né·ville (lü'nā'vēl') city, NE France, on Meurthe river SE of Nancy; treaty 1801; pop. 20,400.

Lung'ki' (lōōng'kē') or **Chang'chow'** (jäng'jō') city, SE China, in S Fukien prov.; pop. 100,000.

Lungkiang. See TSITSIHAR.

Lu·ray' (lū·rā') town, N Virginia, in Blue Ridge Mts.; caverns.

Lu·sa'ti·a (lū·sā'shĭ·ȧ; -shä), Ger. **Lau'sitz** (lou'zĭts) region, E Germany, between Elbe and Oder rivers NW of Silesia; in Middle Ages (from 10th cent.) a margraviate.

Lüshun. See PORT ARTHUR.

Lusitania. See PORTUGAL.

Lutetia. See PARIS.

Lu'ton (lū't'n) municipal borough, SE cen. England, in Bedfordshire; pop. 110,400.

Lüt'zen (lüt'sĕn) town, E Germany, in Saxony; battles 1632 and 1813.

Lux'em·bourg or **Lux'em·burg** (lŭk'sĕm·bûrg; lōōk'sĕm·bōōrg) **1** country, W Europe, between SE Belgium and W Germany; grand duchy; ✻ Luxembourg; area 999 sq. m.; pop. 298,600. **2** city, its ✻; pop. 61,600. — **Lux'em·burg'i·an** (lŭk'sĕm·bûr'gĭ·ăn; lōōk'sĕm·bōōr'-), adj. — **Lux'em·burg·er** (lŭk'sĕm·bûr'gẽr; lōōk'sĕm·bōōr'gẽr), n.

Lux'or (lŭk'sôr; lōōk'-), Arab. **El Uq'sor** (ĕl ōōk'sōr') town, S Egypt, the S part of site of ancient Thebes; tombs, temple ruins.

Luzern. See LUCERNE.

Lu·zon' (lōō·zŏn'; Span. lōō·sôn') island, N Philippine Is., the chief island of the group; area 40,420 sq. m.; pop. 3,800,000.

Lvov (lȧ·vôf'), Pol. **Lwów** (lȧ·vōōf'), Ger. **Lem'berg** (lĕm'bûrg; Ger. lĕm'bĕrk), Ukrainian **Lwiw** (ly'vēf) city U.S.S.R., in W Ukraine; pop. 318,100.

Lya'khov Islands (lyä'kŭf) two islands, N Soviet Russia, Asia, in Laptev Sea S of New Siberian Is.

Ly'all·pur (lī'ȧl·pōōr) town, W Pakistan, in the Punjab; pop. 179,100.

Lyc'a·o'ni·a (lĭk'ä·ō'nĭ·ȧ; lī'kä-; -ōn'yȧ) ancient district, S Asia Minor, on the inner plateau; became a separate province of Rome A.D. 371.

Ly'ci·a (lĭsh'ĭ·ȧ; lĭsh'ȧ) ancient district, S Asia Minor, on coast; a Roman province. — **Ly'ci·an** (lĭsh'ĭ·ăn; lĭsh'ăn), adj. & n.

Lyck. See EŁK.

Lyd'da (lĭd'ȧ), Arab. **Lidd** (lĭd), Heb. **Lod** (lōd) city, Israel, SE of Jaffa; international airport.

Lyd'i·a (lĭd'ĭ·ȧ) ancient country, W Asia Minor, bordering on the Aegean Sea; once a kingdom; ✻ Sardis. — **Lyd'i·an,** adj. & n.

Lyn'brook (lĭn'brŏōk) village, SE New York, on Long I.; pop. 17,300.

Lynch'burg (lĭnch'bûrg) independent city, S cen. Virginia, on James river in foothills of Blue Ridge Mts.; pop. 47,700.

Lynd'hurst (lĭnd'hûrst) town, NE New Jersey; pop. 20,000.

Lynn (lĭn) city, NE Massachusetts, on Lynn Harbor; pop. 99,700.

Lynn Canal, fiord, SE Alaska, indenting the mainland at N end of Alexander Archipelago; 80 m. long, 6 m. wide.

Lyn'wood (lĭn'wōōd) city, SW California, S of Los Angeles; pop. 25,800.

Ly·on·nais' or **Ly·o·nais'** (lē'ô·nā') historical region, SE cen. France, NE of Auvergne and W of the Saône and Rhone rivers; before the Revolution a province; ✻ Lyons.

Ly'ons' (lē'ôN'; lī'ŭnz), Fr. **Ly'on'** (lē'ôN') city, E cen. France, at confluence of Rhone and Saône rivers; pop. 460,700.

Lys (lēs), Flemish **Leie** (lī'ĕ) river, France and Belgium, flowing NE to join the Schelde river; 120 m. long.

Lyublin. See LUBLIN.

M

M'-, Mc-, abbreviated forms of MAC-. Names beginning with this prefix are all alphabetized as if spelled MAC. M' is sometimes written M', esp. in British references.

Maas (mäs) the section of the Meuse river in the Netherlands.

Maas·tricht' or **Maes·tricht'** (mäs·trĭkt') commune, SE Netherlands, on Maas (Meuse) river near the frontier of Belgium; pop. 74,400.

Mc·Al'es·ter (măk·ăl'ĕs·tẽr) city, SE Oklahoma; pop. 17,900.

Mc·Al'len (măk·ăl'ĕn; -ĭn) city, S Texas; pop. 20,100.

Ma·cao' (mȧ·kou'), Port. **Ma·cau'** (mȧ·kou') **1** island, SE China, in Kwantung prov., in Si delta W of mouth of Pearl river. **2** Portuguese colony on peninsula of SE Macao I.; area 6 sq. m.; pop. 374,700. **3** town, ✻ of colony; pop. 148,500.

Macassar. See MAKASSAR.

Mc·Cluer' Gulf (mȧ·klōōr') inlet, W New Guinea, on W side at base of Vogelkop Penin., almost cutting peninsula off from rest of the island.

M'·Clure' Strait (mȧ·klōōr') channel, N Canada, between Banks I. and Melville I.; opens on W into Arctic Ocean.

Mac′e·do′ni·a (măs′ĕ·dō′nĭ·à; -dōn′yà) **1** region, S Europe, in Balkan Penin. in NE Greece, SE Yugoslavia, and SW Bulgaria; includes territory of ancient kingdom of Macedonia, or **Mac′e·don** (măs′ĕ·dŏn), which reached its height under Alexander the Great in 4th cent. B.C. **2** Yugoslav section of Macedonia, a federated republic; ✳ Skoplje; area 10,229 sq. m.; pop. 1,153,000.

Ma′cei·ó′ (mà′sà·ô′) city, E Brazil; ✳ of Alagoas state; pop. 102,300.

Ma′chu Pic′chu (mä′chŏŏ pēk′chŏŏ) site of ancient Inca city, Peru, on a mountain NW of Cuzco.

Mc·Kees′port (mà·kēz′pōrt) city, SW Pennsylvania; pop. 51,500.

Mc·Kees′ Rocks (mà·kēz′) borough, SW Pennsylvania; pop. 16,200.

Mac·ken′zie (mà·kĕn′zĭ) **1** river, N Canada, flowing from Great Slave Lake NNW into Beaufort Sea; sometimes considered to include the Finlay, Peace, and Slave rivers, flowing into Great Slave Lake from the S; total length 2635 m., length from Great Slave Lake 1120 m. **2** district, N Canada, in North-West Territories around the Mackenzie river; area 527,490 sq. m.

Mack′i·nac, Straits of (măk′ĭ·nô) channel, Michigan, connecting Lake Huron and Lake Michigan; 4 m. wide at narrowest point.

Mack′i·nac Island (măk′ĭ·năk; -nô) island in Straits of Mackinac.

Mc·Kin′ley, Mount (mà·kĭn′lĭ), Russ. **Bol·sha′ya** (bŭl·y′·shä′yà) mountain, S cen. Alaska, in Alaska Range; highest peak in North America, 20,300 ft.; central feature of Mount McKinley National Park, established 1917.

Ma′con (mā′kŭn) city, cen. Georgia, on Ocmulgee river; pop. 70,300.

Mac·quar′ie (mà·kwôr′ĭ) river, Australia, in E cen. New South Wales, flowing NNW to Darling river; 750 m. long.

Mad′a·gas′car (măd′à·găs′kẽr) island, W Indian Ocean, off E coast of Africa; belongs to France; ✳ Tananarive; area 227,678 sq. m.; pop. 4,350,700. — **Mad·a·gas′can** (-kăn), adj. & n.

Ma·dei′ra (mà·dēr′à) **1** river, W Brazil; formed at Bolivian border by confluence of Mamoré and Beni rivers, flows NE into the Amazon; length with the Mamoré 2100 m. **2** island group in Atlantic Ocean N of the Canary Is.; belongs to Portugal; ✳ Funchal; area 302 sq. m.; pop. 250,100. **3** island, largest of the Madeira Is. and site of Funchal, ✳ of the group; 34 m. long, 12 m. wide.

Madeleine, Îles de la. See MAGDALEN ISLANDS.

Ma′dhya Bha′rat (mŭ′dyà bä′rät) or **United State of Gwa′li·or, In·dore′** and **Mal′wa** (gwä′lĭ·ôr, ĭn·dōr′, mäl′wä) former state, cen. India; a union of 20 states, formed 1948; ✳ Indore; became 1956 part of Madhya Pradesh.

Madhya Pra·desh′ (prà·dāsh′) state, cen. India; originally the Central Provinces and Berar; boundaries re-established 1956, other areas added; ✳ (from 1956) Bhopal; area 171,201 sq. m.; pop. 26,072,300.

Mad′i·son (măd′ĭ·s′n) city, ✳ of Wisconsin; pop. 96,100.

Ma·dras′ (mà·drăs′; -dräs′) **1** state, S India, bordering on Bay of Bengal; formerly a presidency and province of British India; area 50,110 sq. m.; pop. 29,974,200. **2** city, its ✳, on Bay of Bengal; pop. 777,500.

Ma′dre de Dios (mä′thrà thä thyôs′) river, Peru and Bolivia, rising in SE Peru and flowing E into Beni river; 900 m. long.

Ma·drid′ (mà·drĭd′; Span. mä·thrē[th]′) city, ✳ of Spain, on the Meseta; pop. 1,609,500. — **Mad′ri·le′ni·an** (măd′rĭ·lē′nĭ·ăn), adj. & n.

Mad′u·ra (măd′ṳ·rà; mà·dŏŏr′à) or **Ma·du·rai** (mŭ′dŏŏ·rī′) city, S India, in SE Madras state; pop. 239,100.

Ma·du′ra or **Ma·doe′ra** (mà·dŏŏr′à) island, Indonesia, off coast of NE Java; area (with adjacent islands) 2113 sq. m.

Maeander. See MENDERES.

Maestricht. See MAASTRICHT.

Maf′e·king (măf′ĕ·kĭng) town, S Union of South Africa, in N Cape Province near W Transvaal border; seat of administration of Bechuanaland Protectorate; pop. 5900.

Magallanes. See PUNTA ARENAS.

Mag′da·le′na (măg′dà·lē′nà) Span. măg′thä·lä′nä) river, Colombia, flowing N into the Caribbean Sea; 950 m. long.

Mag′da·len Islands (măg′dà·lĕn), Fr. **Îles de la Ma′de·leine′** (ēl′ dĕ lä mà′dlĕn′) island group, Canada, in Gulf of St. Lawrence.

Mag′de·burg (măg′dĕ·bûrg; Ger. mäk′dĕ·bŏŏrk) city, E Germany, on Elbe river; pop. 236,300.

Ma′ge·lang′ (mä′gà·läng′) city, Indonesia, in cen. Java; pop. 52,900.

Ma·gel′lan, Strait of (mà·jĕl′ăn; Brit. -gĕl′-) strait at S extremity of South America, between the mainland and Tierra del Fuego Archipelago; 370 m. long.

Ma·gen′ta (mà·jĕn′tà) town, N Italy, W of Milan; battle 1859.

Ma′gers·fon·tein′ (mä′gẽrs·fôn·tān′) battlefield, E cen. Union of South Africa, in W Orange Free State; battle 1899.

Mag·gio′re, Lake (mäd·jō′rà) lake, N Italy and S Switzerland, traversed by Ticino river; 40 m. long and 2 m. wide.

Ma′ghreb or **Ma′ghrib, the** (mŭ′grĭb) **1** northwest Africa and, at the time of the Moorish occupation, Spain; now includes Morocco, Algeria, Tunis, and, sometimes, Libya; — an Arabic name. **2** = EL MAGHREB AL AQSA: see MOROCCO. — **Ma′ghre·bi** or **Ma′ghri·bi** (mŭ′grĭ·bĭ), **Ma·ghreb′i·an** (mŭ·grĕb′i·ăn) or **Ma·ghrib′i·an** (-grĭb′ĭ·ăn), adj. or n.

Maghreb el Aqsa, El. See MOROCCO.

Magnesia. See MANISA.

Mag·ni′to·gorsk (măg·nē′tŏ·gôrsk) city, Soviet Russia, Asia, on the Ural river; pop. 145,900.

Ma′gog (mā′gŏg) town, Canada, in S Quebec on Lake Memphremagog; pop. 12,700.

Magyarország. See HUNGARY.

Ma·hal′la el Ku′bra (mà·hăl′à ĕl kŏŏ′brà) city, N Egypt; pop. 115,500.

Ma·ha′na·di (mà·hä′nà·dĭ) river, E India, flowing into Bay of Bengal through several mouths in Orissa; 512 m. long.

Ma·hé′ (mä′[h]ā′) **1** island, one of the Seychelles. **2** formerly **May·ya′li** (mī·yä′lĭ) city, India, on SW coast of the subcontinent, in Kerala; a settlement of French India until 1954; pop. 14,100.

Mähren. See MORAVIA.

Mährisch-Ostrau. See MORAVSKÁ OSTRAVA.

Maid′stone (mād′stŏn; Brit. usu. -stŭn) municipal borough, SE England, ✳ of Kent, on the Medway; pop. 54,000.

Mai·kop′ (mī·kôp′) city, S Soviet Russia, Europe, ✳ of Adygei Autonomous Region; pop. 67,300.

Main (mān; Ger. mīn) river, W Germany, rising in N Bavaria in the Fichtel Gebirge and flowing W into the Rhine; 305 m. long.

Maine (mān), abbr. **Me.**, state, NE United States, bordering on Canada and the Atlantic Ocean; ✳ Augusta; area 33,215 sq. m.; pop. 913,800.

Maine (mān) or **Le Maine** (lĕ) historical region, NW France, bordering on Normandy and Brittany; ✳ Le Mans.

Main′land′ (mān′lănd′; -lănd) **1** Honshu, the chief island of Japan. **2** Pomona I., N Scotland, largest of the Orkney Is. **3** island, N Scotland, chief of the Shetland Is.

Mainz (mīnts), Fr. **Ma′yence′** (mà′yäns′) city, W Germany, on Rhine at mouth of Main river; pop. 87,000.

Ma·jor′ca (mà·jôr′kà), Span. **Mal·lor′ca** (mä·[l]yôr′kä) island, Spain, the largest of the Balearic Is.; ✳ Palma; area 1352 sq. m.; pop. 292,400. — **Ma·jor′can** (mà·jôr′kăn), adj. & n.

Ma·ju′ba Hill (mà·jŏŏ′bà) height, Union of South Africa, in NW Natal; scene of Boer victory Feb. 27, 1881.

Ma·kas′sar or **Ma·cas′sar** (mà·kăs′ẽr) seaport, Indonesia, ✳ of Celebes (Sulawesi), on SW coast of the island; pop. 85,000.

Makassar Strait, passage, Indonesia, between E Borneo and W Celebes.

Ma′ka·té′a (mä′kà·tā′à) island, Tuamotu Archipelago.

Ma·ke′ev·ka (mŭ·kā′yĕf·kà) city, U.S.S.R., in E Ukraine, in the Donbas NE of Stalino; pop. 240,100.

Ma′khach·ka·la′ (mä′käch·kà·lä′), formerly **Pe·trovsk′** (pĕ·trôfsk′) city, Soviet Russia, on Caspian Sea; ✳ of Dagestan; pop. 86,800.

Ma′kin (mä′kĭn; mä′-) or **Bu·ta′ri·ta′ri** (bŏŏ·tä′rĕ·tä′rĕ) island at N end of Gilbert Is.; an atoll.

Makka. See MECCA.

Mal′a·bar Coast (măl′à·bär) region, SW India, on the Arabian Sea in Kerala and Mysore states.

Ma·lac′ca (mà·lăk′à) **1** settlement, Federation of Malaya, on W coast; formerly in Straits Settlements; area 633 sq. m.; pop. 239,400. **2** seaport, its ✳, on Strait of Malacca; pop. 54,500.

Malacca, Strait of, sometimes **Straits of Malacca**, channel between S Malay Penin. and island of Sumatra; 500 m. long.

Má′la·ga (măl′à·gà; Span. mä′lä·gä) seaport, S Spain, on Mediterranean Sea; pop. 261,200.

Ma·lai′ta (mà·lä′tà) island, SE Solomon Is.; area 2500 sq. m.

Ma·lak′ka. Var. of MALACCA.

Ma·lang′ (mä·läng′) city, Indonesia, in E Java; pop. 87,000.

Mä′lar·en (mâ′lär·ĕn) lake, SE Sweden, extending from Baltic Sea inland 70 m.

Ma·lay′a (mà·lā′à) **1** the Malay Peninsula. **2** British Malaya. **3** the Federation of Malaya. — **Ma·lay′an**, adj.

Malaya, Federation of, country, SE Asia, at S end of Malay Penin.; a former British protectorate comprising a federation of Malay states and the settlements of Penang and Malacca; became a dominion of the British Commonwealth Aug. 31, 1957; limited constitutional monarchy; ✳ Kuala Lumpur; area 50,600 sq. m.; pop. 4,908,100.

Ma·lay′ Archipelago (mà·lā′; mä′lä) or **Ma·lay′sia** (mà·lā′zhà; -zhĭ′à; -shà; -shĭ′à) island group, SE Asia, comprising the islands of Indonesia and the Philippines and including all of Borneo, Timor, and New Guinea. — **Ma·lay′sian** (mà·lā′zhăn; -shăn), adj. & n.

Malay Peninsula, peninsula, SE Asia; divided between Thailand and the Federation of Malaya.

Malay States, the native states of the Malay Penin., esp., those states constituting the larger part of the Federation of Malaya: Pahang, Perak, Selangor, Negri Sembilan, Johore, Kedah, Kelantan, Perlis, and Trengganu.

Mal′den (môl′dĕn) **1** city, E Massachusetts, N of Boston; pop. 59,800. **2** island, one of the Line Is.; claimed by both U.S. and Great Britain.

Mal′dive Islands (măl′dīv; môl′-) group of atolls in Indian Ocean, 400 m. SW of Ceylon; sultanate, under British protection.

Ma·le′a, Cape (mà·lē′à) cape, S Greece, at extremity of the E peninsula of Peloponnesus.

Mal′e·ku′la (măl′ĕ·kŏŏ′là) or **Mal′li·co′lo** (măl′ĭ·kō′lō) island, one of the New Hebrides.

Malines. See MECHELEN.

Mallorca. See MAJORCA.

Mal′mé′dy (mäl′mā′dē′) town, E Belgium, forming a district with Eupen; before 1919 in Germany.

Malmö′ (mäl′mŭ′) seaport, SW Sweden, on Öresund opp. Copenhagen, Denmark; pop. 189,200.

Mal′pla·quet′ (măl′plà·kā′) hamlet, N France, SE of Lille; scene of Marlborough's victory over the French Sept. 11, 1709.

Mal′ta (môl′tà) **1** or **Mal′tese′ Islands** (môl′tēz′; -tēs′) group of three islands in Mediterranean Sea S of Sicily; a British colony; ✳ Valletta; area 122 sq. m.; pop. 241,600. **2** island, chief of the Malta group, site of Valletta; area 95 sq. m.; pop. 235,000.

Maluku. See MOLUCCAS.

Mal′vern Hill (măl′vẽrn) plateau, Virginia, on the James SE of Richmond; battle 1862.

Mal′vern Hills (mô[l]′vẽrn) hills, W England, between Worcestershire and Herefordshire; highest point 1395 ft.

Ma·mar′o·neck (mà·măr′ō·nĕk) village, SE New York, on Long Island Sound NE of New York; pop. 15,000.

Mam′be·ra′mo (mäm′bà·rä′mō) river, West New Guinea, flowing NW into Pacific Ocean; 500 m. long.

Mam′moth Cave (măm′ŭth) series of underground chambers, SW cen. Kentucky; 150 m. explored; set aside as a national park 1936.

Mammoth Hot Springs, hot springs, Wyoming, in Yellowstone National Park; terraces of calcareous deposits covering 200 acres.

Ma′mo·ré′ (mä′mō·rā′) river, Bolivia, flowing N to unite with Beni river on Brazilian border and form Madeira river; 1200 m. long.

Man, Isle of (măn), anc. **Mo·na′pi·a** (mō·nā′pĭ·à) or **Mo′na** (mō′nà) island, England, off NW coast in Irish Sea; has own language (Manx), legislature, and laws. See MANX, in Vocab.

Ma·na′gua (mä·nä′gwà) city, ✳ of Nicaragua, on Lake Managua; pop. 93,000.

Ma·na′ma (mä·nä′mà) town, Arabia, ✳ of Bahrein Is., on Bahrein I.

Man′a·sa·ro′war (mŭn′à·sà·rō′ẽr) lake, SW Tibet; altitude 15,000 ft.

Ma·nas′sas (må·năs′ås) town, NE Virginia, W of Alexandria; battles of Bull Run (called Manassas by Confederates) 1861 and 1862.

Ma·naus′ (må·nous′) or **Ma·na′os** (må·nous′) city, W Brazil, ✻ of Amazonas state, on Rio Negro 12 m. from the Amazon; pop. 110,700.

Mancha, La. See LA MANCHA.

Manche, La. See ENGLISH CHANNEL.

Man′ches′ter (măn′chĕs′tẽr; -chĭs·tẽr) **1** town, N Connecticut; pop. 34,100. **2** city, S New Hampshire, on Merrimack river; pop. 82,700. **3** county borough and city, NW England, in Lancashire; pop. 703,200. — **Man·cu′ni·an** (măn·kū′nĭ·ăn), adj. & n.

Man·chu′ri·a (măn·chŏŏr′ĭ·å), Chin. **Man′chow′** (măn′jō′) also called by the Chinese the **Eastern**, or **Northeastern, Provinces**, region, NE China, bordering on Russia and Korea; under the Japanese 1931–45 constituted, with Jehol, the puppet state of **Man′chu′kuo′** (măn′chōō′kwō′; măn·chōō′kwō), ✻ Changchun (Hsinking); taken over 1949 by Communists, who set up the People's Government of the Northeast and attached the W part to the Inner Mongolian Autonomous Region; ✻ (since 1949) Mukden; area 308,000 sq. m.; pop. 43,600,000. — **Man·chu′ri·an** (măn·chŏŏr′ĭ·ăn), adj. & n.

Man′da·lay′ (măn′då·lā′) city, cen. Burma, on the Irrawaddy river; pop. 135,000.

Mang′a·re′va (mäng′å·rā′vä) island, chief of the Gambier Is.

Man·hat′tan (măn·hăt′'n; măn-) **1** island, SE New York, at mouth of Hudson river; constitutes a borough of New York City; area 22 sq. m.; pop. 1,960,100. **2** city, Kansas, on Kansas river; pop. 19,100.

Manhattan Beach, city, SW California, on Pacific Ocean SW of Los Angeles; pop. 17,300.

Ma′ni·hi′ki Islands (mä′nē·hē′kē), sometimes called **Northern Cook Islands** (kŏŏk) group of islands, S Pacific Ocean, belonging to New Zealand; chief island **Manihiki**, an atoll.

Ma·nil′a (må·nĭl′å) city, ✻ (see QUEZON CITY) of the Republic of the Philippines, on W coast of Luzon on **Manila Bay** (area 770 sq. m.); pop. 983,900.

Ma′ni·pur (mä′nĭ·pŏŏr) **1** river, NE India and W Burma, rising in India and flowing into Chindwin river; 210 m. long. **2** territory, NE India, around upper Manipur river; borders on Burma S of Assam; ✻ Imphal; area 8628 sq. m.; pop. 577,600.

Ma′ni·sa′ or **Ma′nis·sa′** (mä′nē·sä′), anc. **Mag·ne′sia** (măg·nē′zhå; -zhĭ·å) city, W Turkey in Asia, in Gediz valley; pop. 35,000.

Man′i·to′ba (măn′ĭ·tō′bå), abbr. **Man.**, province, cen. Canada, easternmost of the Prairie Provinces; ✻ Winnipeg; area 219,723 sq. m.; pop. 850,000. — **Man′i·to′ban**, adj. & n.

Manitoba, Lake, lake, Canada, in Manitoba; area 1817 sq. m.

Man′i·tou′lin Island (măn′ĭ·tōō′lĭn) island, Canada, in N Lake Huron, in Ontario prov.; 80 m. long.

Man′i·to·woc′ (măn′ĭ·tō·wŏk′) city, E Wisconsin, on Lake Michigan; pop. 27,600.

Man′i·za′les (măn′ĭ·zä′lĕs; -zäl′ĕs) city, Colombia; pop. 51,000.

Man·ka′to (măn·kā′tō) city, S Minnesota; pop. 18,800.

Man·nar′, Gulf of (må·när′) that part of Indian Ocean between Ceylon and the S point of India.

Mann′heim (măn′hīm; Ger. män′-) city, W Germany, on the Rhine at confluence of Neckar river; pop. 244,000.

Mans, Le. See LE MANS.

Mans′field (mănz′fēld; mănz′-) **1** city, N cen. Ohio; pop. 43,600. **2** municipal borough, N cen. England, in Nottinghamshire N of Nottingham; pop. 51,300.

Mansfield, Mount, mountain, N Vermont, in Green Mts.; highest point in Vermont, 4393 ft.

Man′ston (măn′stŭn) airfield, SE England, in Kent WNW of Ramsgate in Isle of Thanet; Royal Air Force base.

Mansûra, El. See EL MANSÛRA.

Man′tu·a (măn′tū·å), Ital. **Man′to·va** (măn′tō·vä) commune, N Italy, on Mincio river; pop. 56,300. — **Man′tu·an** (măn′tū·ăn), adj. & n.

Ma·nu′a Islands (må·nōō′å) three islands, American Samoa; area 22 sq. m.; pop. 2800.

Ma′nus (mä′nŏŏs) island, largest of the Admiralty Is.; area 600 sq. m.

Maple Heights, city, N Ohio, SE of Cleveland; pop. 15,600.

Mar, Serra do. See SERRA DO MAR.

Mar′a·cai′bo (mär′å·kī′bō) city, NW Venezuela, on channel between Lake Maracaibo and Gulf of Venezuela; pop. 232,500.

Maracaibo, Gulf of. See VENEZUELA, GULF OF.

Maracaibo, Lake, south extension of Gulf of Venezuela, NW Venezuela; area 6300 sq. m.

Maracanda. See SAMARKAND.

Ma′ra·cay′ (mä′rä·kī′) city, N Venezuela; pop. 65,800.

Ma′ra·nhão′ (mä′rä·nyoun′) state, NE Brazil, bordering on Atlantic Ocean; ✻ São Luis; area 133,674 sq. m.; pop. 1,600,400.

Ma′ra·ñón′ (mä′rä·nyôn′) river, Peru, joining the Ucayali to form the Amazon; 800 m. long.

Mar′a·thon (măr′å·thŏn; -thǔn) **1** plain, E Greece, in Attica NE of Athens, bordering on Aegean Sea. **2** ancient town on this plain; scene of battle 490 B.C.

Mar′ble·head′ (mär′b'l·hĕd′; -hĕd′) town, NE Massachusetts, on Atlantic Ocean NE of Boston; pop. 13,800.

March (märk), Czech **Mo′ra·va** (mō′rä·vä) river, Czechoslovakia, in Moravia, flowing SW and S into Danube river; 180 m. long.

Marche (märsh) historical region, cen. France, N of Limousin and NW of Auvergne; in pre-Revolutionary France a province; ✻ Guéret.

March′es (mär′chĕz; -chĭz), Ital. **Le Mar′che** (lā mär′kā) region, cen. Italy, bordering the Adriatic Sea between Abruzzi and Emilia.

Mar′cus Island (mär′kŭs) island, W Pacific Ocean, NE of the Marianas; formerly occupied by Japan.

Mar′cy, Mount (mär′sĭ) mountain, NE New York, in the Adirondack Mts.; highest peak in New York state, 5344 ft.

Mar del Pla′ta (mär′ thĕl plä′tä) city, E Argentina, S of Buenos Aires, on coast; pop. 94,500.

Mare Island (mâr) island, California, in San Pablo Bay; U.S. navy yard.

Ma·ren′go (må·rĕng′gō) village, NW Italy; battle June 14, 1800.

Mar′gra′ten (mär′grä′tĕ[n]) village, E Netherlands, E of Maastricht; site of American military cemetery for World War II dead.

Mar′ham (măr′ăm) airfield, E England, in Norfolk; RAF base.

Mar′i·an′a Islands (mär′ĭ·ăn′å; măr′-; -ä′nå), formerly **La·drone′ Islands** (lå·drōn′) island group, W Pacific Ocean, including Saipan and Guam; once belonged to the Spanish, who ceded Guam to the U.S. in 1898 and sold the rest of the islands to Germany in 1899; a Japanese mandate (except Guam) 1919–45, since 1947 part of the Trust Territory of the Pacific Islands, administered by the United States.

Ma′ri·a·na′o (mä′ryä·nä′ō) city, W Cuba, W of Havana; pop. 114,700.

Ma′ri·an·ské Láz′ně (mä′rĭ·än·skå läz′nyĕ), Ger. **Ma·ri′en·bad** (mä·rē′ĕn·bät) town, W Czechoslovakia, in NW Bohemia SE of Cheb; mineral springs.

Maria-Theresiopel. See SUBOTICA.

Ma′ri·bor (mä′rē·bôr), Ger. **Mar′burg** (mär′bŏŏrk; Angl. -bûrg) city, NW Yugoslavia, in Slovenia on Drava river; pop. 66,800.

Ma·rie′ Byrd Land (må·rē′ bûrd′) section of Antarctica E of Ross Shelf Ice and Ross Sea; claimed for the U.S. by Richard E. Byrd 1929.

Marienwerder. See KWIDZYŃ.

Mar′i·et′ta (mär′ĭ·ĕt′å) **1** city, NW Georgia, NW of Atlanta; pop. 20,700. **2** city, SE Ohio, on Ohio river; pop. 16,000.

Marignano. See MELEGNANO.

Ma′rin·du′que (mä′rĕn·dōō′kå) island, Philippine Is., S of Luzon.

Mar′i·on (măr′ĭ·ŭn; măr′-) **1** city, N cen. Indiana; pop. 30,100. **2** city, cen. Ohio; pop. 33,800.

Ma′ri Republic (mä′rĭ), officially **Mari Autonomous Soviet Socialist Republic**, autonomous republic, E cen. Soviet Russia, Europe; ✻ Ioshkar Ola; area 8900 sq. m.; pop. 600,000.

Mar′i·time Alps (măr′ĭ·tīm; -tĭm; -tēm) section of the Alps, SE France, on Italian border, extending to Mediterranean coast.

Maritime Provinces, often the **Mar′i·times** (-tīmz; -tĭmz; -tēmz) the Canadian provinces of New Brunswick, Nova Scotia, and Prince Edward Island.

Maritime Territory, Russ. **Pri·mor′ski Krai** (prĭ·môr′skĭ krī) territory, E Soviet Russia, Asia, bordering on Sea of Japan and Manchuria; ✻ Vladivostok; area 64,900 sq. m.; pop. 1,475,000.

Ma·ri′tsa (mä·rē′tsä), Turk. **Me·riç′** (mĕ·rĕch′), Mod. Gr. **Év′ros** (ĕv′rŏs) river, S Europe, flowing from W end of Rhodope Mts. in S Bulgaria to the Aegean Sea between Greece and Turkey; 320 m. long.

Mariupol. See ZHDANOV.

Ma′ri·ve′les (mä′rē·vä′lås) municipality, Philippine Is., in Luzon on coast of Bataan Penin.; military reservation, by treaty of 1947 retained by United States as permanent base.

Mark′ham (mär′kăm) river, E North-East New Guinea, flowing S and SE to Huon Gulf; 200 m. long.

Marl′bor′o or **Marl′bor′ough** (märl′bûr′ō; môl′bǔ·rǔ, -brǔ) city, E Massachusetts; pop. 15,800.

Mar′ly′-le-Roi (mär′lē′lẽ·rwä′) village, N France, NW of Versailles and on E side of the **Marly Forest** (area 5000 acres), site since 1951 of SHAPE (Supreme Headquarters, Allied Powers in Europe), which occupies 60 acres in SE corner near village of Rocquencourt.

Mar′ma·ra (mär′må·rå) or **Mar′mo·ra** (mär′mō·rå), **Sea of,** anc. **Pro·pon′tis** (prō·pŏn′tĭs) sea, NW Turkey, between Europe and Asia, connected with the Black Sea through the Bosporus and with the Aegean Sea through the Dardanelles.

Mar′mo·la′da (mär′mō·lä′dä) mountain, NE Italy; highest in the Dolomites, 10,965 ft.

Marne (märn) river, NE France, flowing W into the Seine; 325 m. long.

Maroc. See MOROCCO.

Ma·ro′ni (må·rō′nĭ), Du. **Ma′ro·wij′ne** (mä′rō·vī′nĕ) river, N South America; forms boundary between Surinam and French Guiana and empties into Atlantic Ocean; 420 m. long.

Maros. See MUREŞ.

Mar·que′sas Islands (mär·kā′säs), Fr. **Îles Mar′quises′** (ēl′ mär′kēz′) group of islands, S Pacific Ocean, belonging to France; ✻ Atuana, on Hiva Oa I.; 13 islands, total area 480 sq. m.; pop. 2700.

Mar·quette′ (mär·kĕt′) city, Michigan, in Upper Peninsula on Lake Superior; pop. 17,200.

Mar·ra′kech or **Mar·ra′kesh** (må·rä′kĕsh), also, formerly, **Mo·roc′co** (mō·rŏk′ō) city, Morocco, in N foothills of the Grand Atlas; pop. 239,200.

Marruecos. See MOROCCO.

Mar·sa′la (mär·sä′lä) seaport, Italy, in Sicily; pop. 62,200.

Mar·seilles′ (mär·sālz′), Fr. **Mar·seille′** (mär·sā′; Fr. màr′sâ′y′), anc. **Mas·sil′i·a** (mă·sĭl′ĭ·å; -sĭl′yå) seaport, SE France; pop. 636,300.

Mar′shall (mär′shǎl) city, NE Texas; pop. 22,300.

Marshall Islands, group of islands, W Pacific Ocean, comprising two chains, the Ratak chain and the Ralik chain; belonged to Germany 1899 to World War I, mandated to Japan 1920, assigned to the United States 1947 as a UN trust territory; chief island Jaluit, in Ralik chain; total land area 66 sq. m.

Mar′shall·town (mär′shǎl·toun) city, cen. Iowa; pop. 19,800.

Mars-la-Tour (màrs′là·tōōr′) village, NE France, SW of Metz; battle 1870.

Mars′ton Moor (märs′tŭn) battlefield (1644), N England, W of York.

Mar′ta·ban′, Gulf of (mär′tå·bän′) inlet of Bay of Bengal, S Burma, E of the Irrawaddy delta.

Mar′tha's Vine′yard (mär′thåz vĭn′yẽrd) island, SE Massachusetts, between Elizabeth Is. and Nantucket.

Mar′ti·nique′ (mär′t'n·ēk′) island, West Indies; an overseas department of France; ✻ Fort-de-France; area 385 sq. m.; pop. 246,700.

Mar′tins·burg (mär′t'nz·bûrg; -tĭnz-) city, NE West Virginia; pop. 15,600.

Mar′tins·ville (mär′t'nz·vĭl; -tĭnz-) independent city, S Virginia; pop. 17,300.

Marwar. See JODHPUR.

Mar′y·land (mĕr′ĭ·lǎnd), abbr. **Md.**, state, E United States, bordering on Chesapeake Bay; ✻ Annapolis; area 10,577 sq. m.; pop. 2,343,000. — **Mar′y·land·er** (-lǎn′dẽr), n.

Marylebone. = SAINT MARYLEBONE.

Mar′ys·vale (mĕr′ĭz·vāl) village, S cen. Utah; uranium discovered 1948.

Ma·san (mä·sän), formerly **Ma·sam·po** (mä·säm·pō) seaport, S Korea, on S coast NW of Pusan; pop. 91,300.

Mas·ba′te (mäs·bä′tä) island, cen. Philippine Is., S of SE Luzon.

Mashhad. See MESHED.

Ma·sho'na·land' (má·shō'ná·lănd') region, NE Southern Rhodesia, inhabited by the Mashona, a Bantu people.

Ma'son City (mā's'n) city, N Iowa; pop. 28,000.

Masqat and Oman. See OMAN.

Mas'sa·chu'setts (măs'á·chōō'sĕts; -sĭts), abbr. **Mass.**, state, NE United States, bordering on Atlantic Ocean; ✳ Boston; area 8257 sq. m.; pop. 4,690,500.

Massachusetts Bay, inlet of Atlantic Ocean, E Massachusetts, 50 m. long by 25 m. wide.

Mas'sa·nut'ten, or **Mas'a·nut'ton, Mountain** (măs'á·nŭt'n) ridge, N Virginia, in Shenandoah Valley.

Mas·sa'ua (mä·sä'wá; -sou'á) or **Mas·sa'wa** (má·sä'wá) seaport, Eritrea, on the **Bay of Massaua,** an inlet of the Red Sea.

Mas'sif' Cen'tral' (má'sēf' säN'trál') region, cen. France, constituting a central plateau rising sharply just W of the Rhone-Saône valley and sloping N to the Paris basin and W to the basin of Aquitaine.

Massilia. See MARSEILLES.

Mas'sil·lon (măs'l·lŭn) city, NE Ohio, W of Canton; pop. 29,600.

Ma·su'ri·a (má·zŏŏr'ĭ·á; -sŏōr'-), Ger. **Ma·su'ren** (mä·zŏō'rĕn), Pol. **Ma·zu'ry** (mä·zŏō'rĭ) region, N Europe, in area S of Gulf of Danzig, now in Poland; formerly part of East Prussia, Germany; site of many lakes, the **Ma·su'ri·an Lakes** (má·zŏōr'ĭ·ăn; -sŏōr'-).

Mat'a·be'le·land' (măt'á·bē'lē·lănd') region, SW Southern Rhodesia, between the Limpopo and Zambezi rivers; chief town Bulawayo.

Mat'a·mo'ros (măt'á·mō'rŏs) town, NE Mexico, on the Rio Grande opposite Brownsville, Texas; pop. 15,700.

Mat'a·nus'ka (măt'á·nŏōs'ká) village, S Alaska, NE of Anchorage at foot of valley of **Matanuska River** (90 m. long).

Mat'a·pan (măt'á·păn) or **Ma'ta·pás'** (mä'tä·päs'), also **Taí'na·ron** (tä'nä·rŏn) southernmost point of mainland of Greece, 36°24'N.

Ma'teur' (mä'tûr') town, N Tunisia; occupied by Germans December 1942; taken by Americans May 3, 1943, in battle for Bizerte.

Ma'to Gros'so (mät'ŭ grō'sō), formerly spelled **Mat'to Gros'so,** state, SW Brazil, bordering on Bolivia; includes the **Plateau of Mato Grosso;** ✳ Cuiabá; area 485,405 sq. m.; pop. 528,500.

Ma·trûh' (mä·trōō'), also **Mer·sa' Matrûh** (mĕr·sä') village, NW Egypt; taken and retaken several times 1942–43.

Ma'tsu' (mä'tsōō') island, China, off E coast ENE of Foochow (Minhow).

Ma·tsu·ya·ma (mä·tsŏō·yä·mä) city, Japan, in W Shikoku I.; pop. 148,000.

Mat'ter·horn (măt'ĕr·hôrn; Ger. mät'-) or **Mont Cer'vin'** (môN' sĕr'văN') mountain on Swiss-Italian border; 14,780 ft. high.

Mat·toon' (mă·tōōn') city, E cen. Illinois; pop. 17,500.

Mau'beuge' (mō'bûzh') city, N France, on Sambre river near Belgian border; siege 1914; pop. 20,900.

Mau'i (mou'ē) island, Hawaii; area 728 sq. m.

Mau'na Ke'a (mou'nä kā'ä) extinct volcano, Hawaii, in N cen. Hawaii I.; 13,784 ft. high.

Mauna Lo'a (lō'ä) volcano on island of Hawaii; 13,680 ft. high.

Mau're·ta'ni·a (mô'rē·tä'nĭ·á; -tän'yá) ancient country, N Africa; included modern Morocco and part of Algeria. — **Mau're·ta'ni·an, Mau'ri·ta'ni·an,** adj. & n.

Mauritania, 1 Fr. **Mau'ri·ta'nie'** (mô'rē'tá'nē') territory, W French West Africa, N of Senegal river; area 364,092 sq. m.; pop. 524,000. **2** see MAURETANIA.

Mau·ri'ti·us (mô·rĭsh'ĭ·ŭs; -rĭsh'ŭs), formerly **Île de France** (ēl' dĕ fräns') island, Indian Ocean; a colony of Great Britain; ✳ Port Louis; area 720 sq. m.; pop. 408,400. — **Mau·ri'tian** (mô·rĭsh'ăn), adj. & n.

May, Cape (mā) cape at extreme S point of New Jersey.

May'a·gua'na (mä'ä·gwä'nä; -gwô'ná) island, one of the Bahama Is., E of Acklins I.; area 96 sq. m.

Ma'ya·giez' (mä'yä·gwäs') city, W Puerto Rico; pop. 58,700.

Mayence. See MAINZ.

May'o (mā'ō) county, NW Republic of Ireland, in Connacht prov. bordering on Atlantic Ocean; ✳ Castlebar; area 2084 sq. m.; pop. 141,900.

Ma·yon', Mount (mä·yôn') volcano, Philippine Is., in SE Luzon; eruptions 1814, 1897, and 1928; 7943 ft. high.

May'wood (mā'wŏŏd) village, NE Illinois, W of Chicago; pop. 27,500.

Mayyali. See MAHÉ.

Mbomu. See BOMU.

Mazury. See MASURIA.

Mead, Lake (mēd) reservoir, NW Arizona and SE Nevada, formed by Hoover Dam in Colorado river; area 227 sq. m.

Mead'ville (mēd'vĭl) city, NW Pennsylvania; pop. 19,000.

Mearns, The. See KINCARDINE.

Meath (mēth; Ir. mēth) county, E Ireland, in Leinster prov.; ✳ Trim; area 903 sq. m.; pop. 66,300.

Meaux (mō) town, N France, NNE of Melun; fighting 1914.

Mec'ca (mĕk'á), Arab. **Mak'ka** (mäk'ká), anc. **Mac'o·ra'ba** (măk'ō·rä'bá) city, a ✳ of Saudi Arabia, in the Hejaz; birthplace of Mohammed A.D. 570; pop. 80,000. — **Mec'can** (mĕk'ăn), adj. & n.

Me·chan'ics·ville (mē·kăn'ĭks·vĭl) locality, Virginia, 7 m. NE of Richmond; battle June 26, 1862.

Me'che·len (mĕk'ĕ·lĕ[n]), Fr. **Ma·lines'** (má·lēn'), Eng. **Mech'lin** (mĕk'lĭn) commune, N Belgium; pop. 60,700.

Meck'len·burg (mĕk'lĕn·bŏŏrk; Angl. -bûrg) region, E Germany, SE of Jutland Penin. and of the Elbe; in 18th and 19th cents. divided into the duchies of **Mecklenburg-Schwe·rin'** (-shvä·rēn') and **Mecklenburg-Stre'litz** (-shträ'lĭts), which became grand duchies 1815 and states of Weimar republic 1918.

Me·dan' (mā·dän') city, Indonesia, in NE Sumatra; pop. 77,000.

Me'del·lín' (mā·dhā·yēn'; Angl. mĕd''l·ēn', mĕd'l·ĭn) city, NW Colombia, NW of Bogotá; pop. 144,000.

Med'ford (mĕd'fērd) **1** city, E Massachusetts, N of Boston; pop. 66,100. **2** city, SW Oregon; pop. 17,300.

Me'di·a (mē'dĭ·á) ancient country, SW Asia, in NW part of modern Iran; at one time an independent kingdom, at another a province of Persia; after conquest of Persia by Alexander, divided into **Media At'ro·pa·te'ne** (ăt'rō·pá·tē'nē) in N (see also AZERBAIJAN) and **Media Mag'na** (măg'ná). — **Me'di·an,** adj. & n. See also MEDE, in Vocab.

Medicine Hat, city, Canada, in SE Alberta; pop. 20,800.

Me·di'na (mĕ·dē'ná) city, Saudi Arabia, in E cen. Hejaz; contains tomb of Mohammed.

Med'i·ter·ra'ne·an Sea (mĕd'ĭ·tĕ·rā'nē·ăn) body of water between S Europe and N Africa, connecting with Atlantic Ocean through Strait of Gibraltar and with Red Sea through Suez Canal; 2330 m. long.

Mé'doc' (mā'dôk') district, SW France, N of Bordeaux; vineyards.

Mee'rut (mā'rŭt) city, N India, in Uttar Pradesh; pop. 169,300.

Meg'a·ra (mĕg'á·rá), Mod. Gr. **Mé'ga·ra** (mā'gä·rä) seaport, Greece, on Saronic Gulf W of Athens; ancient ✳ of **Meg'a·ris** (mĕg'á·rĭs), the E part of Isthmus of Corinth.

Me·gid'do (mĕ·gĭd'ō) ancient city, N Palestine, on S side of Plain of Esdraelon.

Méjico. See MEXICO.

Mek·nes' (mĕk·nĕs'), Fr. **Mek'nès'** (mĕk'nĕs'), Span. **Me'qui·nez'** (mā'kĕ·nās'; -näth') city, N Morocco, WSW of Fès; a former ✳ of Morocco; pop. 162,400.

Me·kong (mā·kông), Chin. **Lan'tsang'** (län'tsäng) river, SE Asia; rises in E Tibet, flows SE through S China, and empties into the South China Sea through several mouths in SE Indochina; 2600 m. long.

Mel'a·ne'sia (mĕl'á·nē'zhá; -zhĭ·á) the islands in the Pacific Ocean NE of Australia. See MELANESIAN, in Vocab.

Mel'bourne (mĕl'bĕrn) city, SE Australia, in S Victoria on Port Phillip Bay at mouth of Yarra Yarra river; pop. with suburbs 1,226,900.

Me·le·gna'no (mā·lā·nyä'nō), formerly **Ma'ri·gna'no** (mä'rē-) town, N Italy, SE of Milan; destroyed 1239; battles 1515 and 1859.

Me·lil'la (mā·lē'[l]yá) city, Morocco; Spanish enclave, on coast in Er Rif region; pop. 81,200.

Me·li·to'pol (mĕl'ĭ·tô'p'l) town, U.S.S.R., in S Ukraine; pop. 75,700.

Me'los (mē'lŏs), Mod. Gr. **Mí'los** (mē'lôs), Ital. **Mi'lo** (mē'lō) island, Greece, one of the Cyclades.

Mel'rose (mĕl'rōz) **1** city, E Massachusetts, N of Boston; pop. 27,000. **2** burgh, SE Scotland, in N Roxburgh co.; ruins of a Cistercian abbey.

Melville, Lake (mĕl'vĭl) lake, E Canada, in SE Labrador, the inner basin of Hamilton Inlet; area 1133 sq. m.

Melville Island, 1 island, N Australia, at mouth of Van Diemen Gulf; area 2400 sq. m. **2** island, N Canada, in Parry Is.; area 16,141 sq. m.

Melville Peninsula, projection of N Canada, NW of Hudson Bay.

Me'mel (mā'mĕl) **1** Lithuanian **Klai'pe·da** (klī'pĕ·dä) seaport, Lithuania, on Baltic Sea at mouth of Neman (Memel) river; before World War I belonged to Germany as part of East Prussia; with surrounding area, made autonomous territory 1924; seized by Germany 1939; pop. 38,900. **2** see NEMAN.

Mem'phis (mĕm'fĭs) **1** city, SW Tennessee, on Mississippi river; pop. 396,000. **2** ancient city, N Egypt, now a village on the Nile S of Cairo. See MEMPHIAN, in Vocab.

Mem'phre·ma'gog, Lake (mĕm'frē·mä'gŏg) lake, United States and Canada, in N Vermont and S Quebec.

Men'ai Strait or **Straits** (mĕn'ī) channel, N Wales, between Anglesey I. and mainland.

Me Nam or **Menam.** See CHAO PHRAYA.

Men'de·res' (mĕn'dĕ·rĕs') **1** anc. **Mae·an'der** (mē·ăn'dĕr) river, W Turkey in Asia, flowing SW and W into Aegean Sea; 240 m. long. **2** anc. **Sca·man'der** (ská·măn'dĕr) river, NW Turkey in Asia, flowing W and NW into the Dardanelles across the plain of ancient Troy.

Men'do·ci'no, Cape (mĕn'dō·sē'nō) extreme W point of California, at 124°8'W long.

Men·do'za (mĕn·dō'zà; Span. mǎn·dō'sä) city, W Argentina, 60 m. SE of Mt. Aconcagua; pop. 100,400.

Meng'tsz' (mŭng'dzŭ'), also **Meng-tseu** (mŭng'dzŭ') and **Meng'tseu'** (mŭng'dzŭ') city, S China, in S Yunnan prov. near Tonkin border; tin-mining region.

Me·nom'i·nee Range (mē·nŏm'ĭ·nē) iron range, Upper Peninsula, Michigan, and NE Wisconsin.

Menorca. See MINORCA.

Men'ton' (mäN'tôN'), Ital. **Men·to'ne** (mĕn·tō'nä) town, SE France, on Mediterranean Sea ENE of Nice; independent republic 1848–60.

Mequinez. See MEKNES.

Mer·ced' (mĕr·sĕd') **1** river, cen. California; flows W through the Yosemite Valley and into the San Joaquin river; 150 m. long. **2** city, cen. California, in valley of the San Joaquin; pop. 15,300.

Mer'ci·a (mûr'shĭ·á; -shá) ancient Anglian kingdom, cen. England. — **Mer'ci·an** (-shĭ·ăn; -shăn), adj. & n.

Meric. See MARITSA.

Mé'ri·da (mā'rē·thä) city, SE Mexico, ✳ of Yucatán state; pop. 98,900.

Mer'i·den (mĕr'ĭ·d'n; -dĕn) city, S Connecticut, NE of New Haven; pop. 44,100.

Me·rid'i·an (mē·rĭd'ĭ·ăn) city, E Mississippi; pop. 41,900.

Merín. See MIRIM, LAKE.

Mer'i·on'eth·shire (mĕr'ĭ·ŏn'ĕth·shĭr; -shĕr) county, W Wales; area 660 sq. m.; pop. 41,500.

Mer'o·ë (mĕr'ō·ē) ancient city on the Nile, site now in N Sudan (republic); once capital of a kingdom which included the **Isle of Meroë,** the region between the Nile, Blue Nile, and Atbara rivers.

Me'rom, Waters of (mē'rŏm) or **Lake Hu'le** (hōō'lĕ), Arab. **Bah'ret el Hule** (bä'h'·rŏt ăl) lake, N Israel, N of Sea of Galilee in course of Jordan river.

Mer'o·we (mĕr'ō·wĕ). Var. of MEROË.

Mer'ri·mack (mĕr'ĭ·măk) river, S New Hampshire and NE Massachusetts, flowing into the Atlantic Ocean; 110 m. long.

Mersa Matrûh. See MATRÛH.

Mers-el-Ke·bir' (mĕrs'ĕl·kĕ·bĭr') town, NW Algeria, on coast just W of Oran; French naval base; battle 1940.

Mer'sey (mûr'zĭ) river, NW England, flowing NW and W into the Irish Sea through a large estuary; 70 m. long.

Mer·sin' (mĕr·sēn') or **İ·çel'** (ē·chĕl') seaport, S Turkey; pop. 37,500.

Mer'thyr Tyd'fil (mûr'thĕr tĭd'vĭl) county borough, SE Wales, in Glamorganshire; pop. 61,100.

Mer'ton and Mor'den (mûr'd'n, môr'd'n) urban district, S England, in Surrey SW of London; pop. 74,600.

Me'sa (mā'sá) city, SW cen. Arizona; pop. 16,800.

Me·sa'bi Range (mĕ·sä'bī) iron range, NE Minnesota.

Me′sa Verde National Park (mā′sȧ vûrd′) site, SW Colorado, of prehistoric cliff dwellings; established as national park 1906.
Me·se′ta (mā·sā′tä) the central plateau of Spain.
Me·shed′ (mĕ·shĕd′), Iranian **Mash·had′** (măsh·hȧd′) city, NE Iran, site of a Shiite shrine; pop. 191,000.
Me′so·lón′gi·on (mâ′sô·lông′gyôn) or **Mis′so·lon′ghi** (mĭs′ō·lŏng′gĭ) city, cen. Greece, on Gulf of Patras; the place where Byron died 1824.
Mes′o·po·ta′mi·a (mĕs′ō·pō·tā′mĭ·ȧ; -tām′yȧ) region, SW Asia, between the Tigris and Euphrates rivers, extending from the mountains of Asia Minor to the Persian Gulf. — **Mes′o·po·ta′mi·an**, adj.
Mes·se′ne (mĕ·sē′nē), Mod. Gr. **Mes·sí′ni** (mâ·sē′nyē) town, S Greece, in SW Peloponnesus; ancient ✻ of Messenia.
Mes·se′ni·a (mĕ·sē′nĭ·ȧ; -sēn′yȧ) region, S Greece, in SW Peloponnesus, bordering on Ionian Sea; ancient country, subjugated by Sparta.
Mes·si′na (mĕ·sē′nȧ), anc. **Zan′cle** (zăng′klē) seaport, Italy, in NE Sicily on Strait of Messina; pop. 228,600.
Messina, Strait of, channel between S Italy and NE Sicily.
Mes′sines′ (mĕ′sēn′) village, NW Belgium, near Ieper (Ypres) on **Messines Ridge**; battles Nov. 1, 1914, and June 7–14, 1917.
Mes·ta′ (mĕs·tä′), Turk. **Ka′ra Su** (kä′rä sōō′), in Greece called **Nes′tos** (nĕs′tŏs) river, SW Bulgaria and NE Greece, flowing from W end of Rhodope Mts. SE into Aegean Sea; 130 m. long.
Me·tau′ro (mā·tou′rō), anc. **Me·tau′rus** (mĕ·tô′rŭs) river, E cen. Italy, flowing E into Adriatic Sea; site of battle of Metaurus 207 B.C.
Me·thu′en (mĕ·thū′ĕn) town, NE Massachusetts; pop. 24,500.
Met′la·kat′la or **Met′la·kaht′la** (mĕt′lȧ·kăt′lȧ) village, SE Alaska, on Annette I.; has U.S. Air Force base.
Me·to′hi·ja (mĕ·tō′hē·yä) district, SW Yugoslavia, on Albanian border; with Kosovo district, constitutes an autonomous region.
Metz (mĕts; Fr. mâs) city, NE France, on Moselle river; pop. 70,100.
Meurthe (mûrt) river, NE France, flowing from Vosges Mts. NW to the Moselle; 100 m. long.
Meuse (mûz; Angl. mūz), Du. **Maas** (măs) river, W Europe, flowing from NE France to the North Sea in the Netherlands; 575 m. long.
Mewar. See UDAIPUR.
Mex′i·co (mĕk′sĭ·kō), Span. **Mé′ji·co** (mĕ′hē·kō), Mex. Span. **Mé′xi·co** (mĕ′hē-) **1** officially **Es·ta′dos U·ni′dos Me′xi·ca′nos** (ās·tä′thōs ōō·nē′thōz mĕ′hē·kä′nōs) country, S North America, S of the United States, bordering on Caribbean Sea and Pacific Ocean; republic; ✻ Mexico City; area 761,830 sq. m.; pop. 25,581,300. **2** state, cen. Mexico; ✻ Toluca; area 8267 sq. m.; pop. 1,383,600. **3** or **Mexico City,** officially **México, D.F.** (mĕ′hē·kō, dĕs·trē′tō fā′thä·räl′) city, ✻ of republic of Mexico, in Federal District, an area surrounded on three sides by state of Mexico; pop. 2,527,300. — **Mex′i·can** (mĕk′sĭ·kăn), adj. & n.
Mexico, Gulf of, gulf on SE coast of North America, between the peninsula of Florida and Yucatán peninsula.
Mi·am′i (mī·ăm′ĭ; -ȧ) **1** river, W Ohio, flowing S into the Ohio river; 160 m. long. **2** city, SE Florida, on Biscayne Bay; pop. 249,300.
Miami Beach, city, SE Florida, on island across Biscayne Bay from Miami; pop. 46,300.
Mi·am′is·burg (mī·ăm′ĭz·bûrg) city, SW Ohio, S of Dayton; site of Mound Laboratory, atomic research center; pop. 6300.
Mich′i·gan (mĭsh′ĭ·găn), abbr. **Mich.**, state, N cen. United States, comprising the Lower Peninsula (the main part of the state, in this Gazetteer always referred to simply as Michigan), between lakes Michigan and Huron, and the Upper Peninsula, between lakes Michigan and Superior; ✻ Lansing; area 58,216 sq. m., not including 38,575 sq. m. of water of the Great Lakes; pop. 6,371,800. — **Mich′i·gan·ite** (-īt) or **Mich′i·gan′der** (-găn′dẽr), n.
Michigan, Lake, lake, N cen. United States, one of the Great Lakes; over 300 m. long, area 22,400 sq. m.
Michigan City, city, N Indiana, on Lake Michigan; pop. 28,400.
Mi′cho·a·cán′ (mē′chō·ä·kän′) state, SW Mexico, bordering on Pacific Ocean; ✻ Morelia; area 23,200 sq. m.; pop. 1,412,800.
Mi′cro·ne′sia (mī′krō·nē′zhȧ; -zhĭ·ȧ; -shĭ·ȧ), the islands of the W Pacific E of Philippine Is. See MICRONESIAN, in Vocab.
Middle America, region, Western Hemisphere, including Mexico and Central America and, usually, the islands of the Caribbean Sea.
Middle Congo, territory, French Equatorial Africa; ✻ Brazzaville; area 132,046 sq. m.; pop. 631,000.
Mid′dles·brough (mĭd′′lz·brŭ) county borough, N England, on the Tees estuary; pop. 147,300.
Mid′dle·sex (mĭd′′l·sĕks) county, SE England, comprising NW part of London section; area 232 sq. m.; pop. 2,268,800.
Mid′dle·town (mĭd′′l·toun) **1** city, S Connecticut, on Connecticut river S of Hartford; pop. 29,700. **2** city, SE New York; pop. 22,600. **3** city, SW Ohio; pop. 33,700.
Mid′land (mĭd′lănd) **1** city, W Texas, NE of Odessa; pop. 21,700. **2** town, Canada, in SE Ontario on Georgian Bay; site of Jesuit martyrs′ shrine; pop. 7200.
Mid′lands, the (mĭd′lăn[d]z) the central counties of England, esp. Derbyshire, Nottinghamshire, Leicestershire, Rutlandshire, Northamptonshire, Warwickshire, and Staffordshire.
Mid·lo′thi·an (mĭd·lō′thĭ·ăn; -thyăn) county, SE Scotland; ✻ Edinburgh; area 366 sq. m.; pop. 565,700.
Mid′way′ (mĭd′wā′) island, cen. Pacific Ocean, 1300 m. WNW of Honolulu; an atoll containing two islets, Sand and Eastern; belongs to United States; attacked by Japanese Dec. 1941 and Jan. 1942.
Mie′res (myā′rās) commune, NW Spain, SSE of Oviedo; pop. 51,700.
Mi·lan′ (mĭ·lăn′; mĭl′ăn), Ital. **Mi·la′no** (mē·lä′nō) commune, N Italy, in Lombardy in plain between Adda and Ticino rivers; pop. 1,289,300. — **Mil′a·nese′** (mĭl′ȧ·nēz′; -nēs′), adj. & n.
Mi·laz′zo (mē·lät′tsō), anc. **My′lae** (mī′lē) seaport, Italy, in NE Sicily W of Messina; victory of Garibaldi 1860; naval battle 260 B.C.
Mi·le′tus (mī·lē′tŭs; mĭ-) ancient city on W coast of Asia Minor, in Caria near mouth of the Maeander; chief of the 12 Ionian Cities.
Mil′ford (mĭl′fẽrd) **1** town, S Connecticut, on Long Island Sound; pop. 26,900. **2** town, cen. Massachusetts; pop. 15,400.
Milk (mĭlk) river, Canada and the United States, in Alberta and Montana; flows into Missouri river; 625 m. long.
Mill′ville (mĭl′vĭl) city, SW New Jersey; pop. 16,000.
Milo, Mílos. See MELOS.
Mil′ton (mĭl′t′n; -tŭn) town, E Massachusetts; pop. 22,400.
Mil·wau′kee (mĭl·wô′kē) city, SE Wisconsin, on Lake Michigan; pop. 637,400.
Mim′i·co (mĭm′ĭ·kō) town, Canada, in SE Ontario, on Lake Ontario W of Toronto; pop. 13,700.
Min (mĭn) **1** or **Min-kiang** (mĭn′jĭ·äng′) river, S cen. China, in Szechwan prov., flowing SE through the Red Basin into Yangtze river; 350 m. long. **2** or **Min-kong** (mĭn′kông′) river, SE China, in Fukien prov., flowing SE into East China Sea; 250 m. long.
Mi′nas Basin (mī′năs) northeast extension of Bay of Fundy, in cen. Nova Scotia, connected by **Minas Channel** with the Bay of Fundy.
Mi′nas de Ri′o·tin′to (mē′näz thā rē′ō·tēn′tō) commune, SW Spain, on Tinto river; rich copper mines.
Mi′nas Ge·rais′ (mē′nȧ zhā·rīs′) state, E Brazil; ✻ Belo Horizonte; area 226,179 sq. m.; pop. 7,839,800.
Min′cio (mēn′chō), anc. **Min′ci·us** (mĭn′shĭ·ŭs; -shŭs) river, N Italy; issues from Lake Garda, empties into Po river; 115 m. long.
Min′da·na′o (mĭn′dȧ·nä′ō) island, S Philippine Is.; area (including adjacent islands) 36,537 sq. m.; pop. 1,997,300.
Mindanao Sea, body of water, S Philippine Is., bordered on N by islands of Negros, Cebu, Bohol, and Leyte, and on S by Mindanao.
Min·do′ro (mĭn·dō′rō) island, cen. Philippine Is., SW of Luzon; area 3759 sq. m., with adjacent islands 3891 sq. m.; pop. 131,600.
Mi′nho (mē′nyōō), Span. **Mi′ño** (mē′nyō) river, Spain and Portugal; flows S and SW into Atlantic Ocean on the boundary; 171 m. long.
Minhow. See FOOCHOW.
Min′i·coy (mĭn′ĭ·koi) island, southernmost of the Laccadives.
Min-kiang, Min-kong. See MIN.
Min′ne·ap′o·lis (mĭn′ē·ăp′ō·lĭs; -ăp′lĭs) city, SE cen. Minnesota, on Mississippi river at the Falls of Saint Anthony; pop. 521,700.
Min′ne·ha′ha (mĭn′ē·hä′hä) creek, SE cen. Minnesota, flowing from Lake Minnetonka to the Mississippi river; falls, 54 ft. high.
Min′ne·so′ta (mĭn′ĕ·sō′tȧ) **1** river, Minnesota, flowing from Big Stone Lake on South Dakota border to the Mississippi river; 332 m. long. **2**, abbr. **Minn.**, state, N cen. United States, bordering on Canada and Lake Superior; ✻ St. Paul; area 84,068 sq. m., not including 2212 sq. m. of Lake Superior; pop. 2,982,500. — **Min′ne·so′tan** (-t′n), adj. & n.
Mi·nor′ca (mĭ·nôr′kȧ), Span. **Me·nor′ca** (mā·nôr′kä) island, Spain, in the Balearic group; area 264 sq. m.; pop. 41,500. — **Mi·nor′can** (mĭ·nôr′kăn), adj. & n.
Mi′not (mī′nŭt) city, North Dakota, on Souris river; pop. 22,000.
Minsk (mĭnsk) city, U.S.S.R., ✻ of White Russia; pop. 238,800.
Min′ya Kon′ka (mĭn′yȧ kŏng′kȧ) mountain, S China, in E Sikang prov.; 24,900 ft. high.
Miq′ue·lon Island (mĭk′ĕ·lŏn; Fr. mē′klôɴ′) island off S coast of Newfoundland, belonging to France. See SAINT PIERRE.
Mir′a·flo′res (mĭr′ȧ·flō′rĕs) village, lake, and double locks in the Panama Canal Zone, 5 m. NW of Panama.
Mi·rim′, Lake (mē·rēɴ′), Span. **Me·rín′** (mā·rēn′) lake, E Uruguay, separating Uruguay from extreme S tip of Brazil; 108 m. long.
Mish′a·wa′ka (mĭsh′ȧ·wô′kȧ) city, N Indiana; pop. 32,900.
Mis′kolc (mĭsh′kōlts) autonomous city, NE Hungary, on the Sajó river; pop. 73,500.
Mis′la·ko·wi′ce. Var. of MYSŁACHOWICE.
Misr. See EGYPT.
Missionary Ridge, ridge extending NE to SW in Tennessee and Georgia; a section near Chattanooga was site of a Union victory 1863.
Mis′sis·sip′pi (mĭs′ĭ·sĭp′ĭ) **1** river, cen. United States, flowing from N Minnesota to the Gulf of Mexico; 2470 m. long; about midway in its course, receives the Missouri river from the W, the combined Mississippi-Missouri river having a length of over 3800 m. **2**, abbr. **Miss.**, state, S United States, bordering on Gulf of Mexico E of Mississippi river; ✻ Jackson; area 47,716 sq. m.; pop. 2,178,900. — **Mis′sis·sip′pi·an** (-ĭ·ăn), adj. & n.
Missolonghi. See MESOLÓNGION.
Mis·sou′la (mĭ·zōō′lȧ) city, W Montana; pop. 22,500.
Mis·sou′ri (mĭ·zōōr′ĭ; -zōōr′ȧ) **1** river, W United States, flowing from SW Montana to the Mississippi river in state of Missouri; over 2700 m. long. **2**, abbr. **Mo.**, state, W cen. United States, just W of Mississippi river; ✻ Jefferson City; area 69,674 sq. m.; pop. 3,954,700. — **Mis·sou′ri·an** (-ĭ·ăn), adj. & n.
Mis′tas·si′ni (mĭs′tȧ·sē′nĭ) **1** lake, Canada, in S cen. Quebec prov.; drains W into James Bay; area 840 sq. m. **2** river, Canada, in S Quebec prov., flowing S into Lake St. John; 185 m. long.
Misti, El. See EL MISTI.
Mitch′am (mĭch′ăm) municipal borough, S England, in Surrey SSW of London; pop. 67,300.
Mitch′ell, Mount (mĭch′ĕl) mountain, W North Carolina, in Black Mts.; highest point E of Mississippi river, 6684 ft.
Mitlíni. See MYTILENE.
Mi·ya·ji·ma (mē·yä·jē·mä) island, Japan, in Inland Sea; temples, shrines.
Mi·ya·za·ki (mē·yä·zä·kē) seaport, Japan, on SE coast of Kyushu; pop. 92,100.
Mo, in full **Mo i Ra′na** (mō′ ē rä′nä) seaport, N Norway, just S of Arctic Circle at mouth of Rana river.
Mo′ab (mō′ăb) region, Jordan, E of Dead Sea, in Biblical times a kingdom between Edom and the country of the Amorites. See MOABITE, in Vocab.
Mo·bile′ (mō·bēl′; mō′bēl′) **1** river, SW Alabama; formed by Tombigbee and Alabama rivers, flows S into Mobile Bay; 38 m. long. **2** seaport, SW Alabama, at mouth of Mobile river; pop. 129,000.
Mobile Bay, inlet of Gulf of Mexico, SW Alabama; battle 1864.
Moçambique. See MOZAMBIQUE.
Mo′cha (mō′kȧ), Arab. **Mu·kha′** (mōō·kä′) seaport, SW Arabia, in SW Yemen on the Red Sea; formerly noted for its export of coffee.
Mod′der (mŏd′ẽr) river, Union of South Africa, in Orange Free State, a tributary of the Vaal; 180 m. long.
Mo′de·na (mô′dā·nä; Angl. -d′n·ȧ) commune, N Italy, in Emilia; pop. 116,900.

Mo·des'to (mŏ·dĕs'tō) city, cen. California; pop. 17,400.

Moe'si·a (mē'shǐ·à) ancient country, SE Europe, S of Danube river; made Roman province c. A.D. 15 and later divided into two provinces.

Mog'a·di'sci·o (mŏg'à·dĭsh'ĭ·ō; -dĭsh'ō) or **Mog'a·di'shu** (-dĭsh'ōō) seaport, ✳ of Italian Somaliland; pop. 55,000.

Mo'gi·lev (mŏg'ǐ·lĕf; Russ. mŭ·gǐ·lyôf') or **Mogilev on the Dnieper**, city, U.S.S.R., in E White Russia on the Dnieper; pop. 99,400.

Mo'hács (mō'häch) city, S Hungary, on Danube river; battle 1526.

Mo'hawk (mō'hôk) river, E cen. New York, flowing E into Hudson river; 148 m. long.

Mo·hen'jo-Da'ro (mō·hĕn'jō·dä'rō) prehistoric city, Pakistan, in S Sind 140 m. NE of Karachi; extensive excavations.

Mo·ja've, or **Mo·ha've, Desert** (mō·hä'vē) S California, SE of S end of the Sierra Nevada.

Mo·ji (mō·jē) seaport, Japan, in N Kyushu I.; pop. 109,600.

Mok'po (môk'pō or **Mop'po** (mŏk'pō) seaport, SW corner of Korea; pop. 111,100.

Moldau. 1 See MOLDAVIA. 2 See VLTAVA.

Mol·da'vi·a (mŏl·dā'vǐ·à; -dāv'yà), Romanian **Mol·do'va** (mŏl·dô'vä), Ger. **Mol'dau** (mŏl'dou; Angl. mŏl'-) region, E Europe, between Transylvania and the Dniester river; once a principality.

Mol·da'vi·an Soviet Socialist Republic (mŏl·dā'vǐ·ăn) constituent republic, U.S.S.R., bordering on Romania; created 1940; ✳ Kishinev; area 13,100 sq. m.; pop. 2,660,000.

Mo'len·beek or **Molenbeek-Saint-Jean** (mō'lĕn·bāk·săn'zhän'), Flem. **Sint-Jans-Molenbeek** (sĭnt yäns') commune, Belgium, near Brussels; pop. 63,900.

Mo·line' (mō·lēn') city, NW Illinois, on Mississippi river; pop. 37,400.

Mo'li·se (mô'lē·zā) region, cen. Italy, between the Apennines and the Adriatic Sea S of the Abruzzi.

Mo'lo·kai' (mŏl'ō·kī'; mō'lō-) island, cen. Hawaii; area 259 sq. m.

Mo·lo'po (mō·lō'pō) river bed, S Africa, usually dry; forms S boundary of Bechuanaland Protectorate, joins Orange river.

Mol'o·tov (mŏl'ŭ·tôf; Russ. mô'lŭ·tŭf), formerly, and since 1957, **Perm** (pyĕrm) city, Soviet Russia, W of Ural Mts. on Kama river; pop. 255,200.

Mo·luc'cas (mō·lŭk'àz) or **Spice Islands** (spīs) Indonesian **Ma·lu'ku** (mä·lōō'kōō) island group, E Indonesia, between Celebes and New Guinea; area 32,300 sq. m.; pop. 600,000.

Mom·ba'sa (mŏm·bä'sà) island, Kenya, on coast in a bay surrounded on three sides by mainland, arms of the bay forming the harbors of Mombasa (on NE of the island) and Kilindini (on SW).

Mona. See ANGLESEY; MAN, ISLE OF.

Mon'a·co (mŏn'à·kō; mō·nä'kō) 1 independent principality on Mediterranean coast of France near Italian border; 368 acres; pop. 24,000. 2 commune, ✳ of the principality; pop. 1900.

Mo·nad'nock, Mount (mō·năd'nŏk) mountain, SW New Hampshire; 3186 ft. high.

Mon'a·ghan (mŏn'à·găn; -hăn) county, NE Republic of Ireland, in Ulster prov.; ✳ Monaghan; area 498 sq. m.; pop. 55,400.

Mo'na Passage (mō'nà) strait between Hispaniola and Puerto Rico.

Monapia. See MAN, ISLE OF.

Monc'ton (mŭngk'tŭn) city, Canada, in SE New Brunswick on Petitcodiac river; pop. 36,000.

Mo·nes'sen (mō·nĕs'n) city, SW Pennsylvania; pop. 17,900.

Mon·go'lia (mŏn[g]·gōl'yà; -gōl'ǐ·à) region, E cen. Asia, W of the Khingan Mts.; includes Gobi Desert in E and part of Altai Mts. in W. — **Mon'gol** (mŏng'gŏl), n. — **Mon·go'lian** (mŏn[g]·gōl'yăn; -gō'lǐ·ăn), adj. & n.

Mongolia, Inner, the SE section of Mongolia; part of Chinese Republic since 1911; constituted 1947 the **Inner Mongolian Autonomous Region**; boundaries repeatedly changed; ✳ Kweisui.

Mongolian People's Republic or **Outer Mongolia**, country, cen. Asia, occupying greater part of Mongolia, including Gobi Desert; once dependent on China and, 1912–19, Russia; claimed independence 1921; independence formally recognized by China 1945; ✳ Urga (Ulan Bator); area 580,158 sq. m.; pop. 900,000.

Mong-tseu. See MENGTSZ.

Mon'mouth (mŏn'mŭth; in England, also mŭn'-) 1 see MONMOUTH COURT HOUSE. 2 see MONMOUTHSHIRE.

Mon'mouth Court House (mŏn'mŭth) Freehold, New Jersey; — its name 1715–95; scene of battle of Monmouth 1778.

Mon'mouth·shire (mŏn'mŭth·shǐr; -shēr; mŭn'-) or **Monmouth**, county, W England, on the border of Wales; ✳ Newport; area 546 sq. m.; pop. 319,400.

Mo·noc'a·cy (mō·nŏk'à·sǐ) battlefield (1864) along Monocacy river, Maryland, near city of Frederick.

Mo·non'ga·he'la (mō·nŏn'gà·hē'là; -hä'là) river, N West Virginia and SW Pennsylvania; flows N and unites with the Allegheny river to form the Ohio river; 128 m. long.

Mon·roe' (mŭn·rō') 1 city, N Louisiana; pop. 38,600. 2 city, SE Michigan, on Lake Erie at mouth of Raisin river; pop. 21,500.

Mon·ro'vi·a (mŭn·rō'vǐ·à) 1 city, SW California, ENE of Los Angeles; pop. 20,200. 2 seaport, ✳ of Liberia; pop. 10,000.

Mons (môns; Angl. mônz), Flem. **Ber'gen** (bĕr'gĕ[n]) commune, SW Belgium, ✳ of Hainaut prov.; pop. 25,700.

Mon·tan'a (mŏn·tăn'à), abbr. **Mont.**, state, NW United States, bordering on Canada; ✳ Helena; area 147,138 sq. m.; pop. 591,000. — **Mon·tan'an**, adj. & n.

Mon'tauk' Point (mŏn'tôk') point, New York, at E end of Long I.

Mont aux Sources. See AUX SOURCES, MONT.

Mont Blanc; Mont Cenis. See BLANC, MONT; CENIS, MONT.

Mont Cervin. See MATTERHORN.

Mont·clair' (mŏnt·klâr'; mŏnt'klâr) town, NE New Jersey, NNW of Newark; pop. 43,900.

Mon'te·bel'lo (mŏn'tē·bĕl'ō) city, SW California; pop. 21,700.

Mon'te Bel'lo Islands (mŏn'tē bĕl'ō) island group off NW coast of Western Australia; atomic weapon test Oct. 1952.

Mon'te Car'lo (mŏn'tē kär'lō) commune, Monaco; pop. 8500.

Mon'te Cas·si'no (mŏn'tē kä·sē'nō) monastery, Italy, in SE Latium near Cassino; sacked by Lombards 589, destroyed by Saracens 884; destroyed by Allied bombing 1944.

Mon'te·ne'gro (mŏn'tē·nē'grō), native **Cr'na Go'ra** (tsûr'nä gō'rä) region, Yugoslavia, bordering on N Albania; a kingdom 1910–18; since 1918 part of Yugoslavia, since 1946 a Yugoslav republic; ✳ Titograd; area 5343 sq. m.; pop. 377,200. — **Mon'te·ne'grin** (-grĭn), adj. & n.

Mon'te·rey' (mŏn'tē·rā') 1 city, W California, at S end of Monterey Bay; pop. 16,200. 2 see MONTERREY, Mexico.

Monterey Bay, inlet of Pacific Ocean, California, S of the San Francisco Peninsula.

Monterey Park, city, SW California, E of Los Angeles; pop. 20,400.

Mon'ter·rey' (mŏn'tĕ·rā'), sometimes, Anglicized, **Mon'te·rey'** (mŏn'tē·rā') city, NE Mexico, ✳ of Nuevo León state; pop. 185,800.

Mon'te·vi·de'o (mŏn'tē·vǐ·dā'ō; -vǐd'ē·ō) seaport, ✳ of Uruguay, on N La Plata estuary; pop. 708,200.

Mont·gom'er·y (mŏn[t]·gŭm'ĕr·ǐ; -gŭm'rǐ; -gŏm'-) 1 city, ✳ of Alabama, on Alabama river; pop. 106,500. 2 county in Wales: see MONTGOMERYSHIRE.

Mont·gom'er·y·shire (-shǐr; -shēr) or **Montgomery,** county, E Wales; ✳ Welshpool; area 797 sq. m.; pop. 46,000.

Mon'ti·cel'lo (mŏn'tǐ·chĕl'ō) estate of Thomas Jefferson, Virginia, 3 m. SE of Charlottesville.

Mont·mar'tre (môn·màr'tr') section of Paris, France, occupying a hill on right bank of the Seine river.

Mont'mo·ren'cy (mŏnt'mō·rĕn'sǐ) river, Canada, in S Quebec prov., flowing S into St. Lawrence river; in its course are the **Montmorency Falls**, dropping over 270 ft.

Mont·pe'lier (mŏnt·pēl'yēr) city, ✳ of Vermont; pop. 8600.

Mont'pel'lier (mŏnt·pĕl'yā') city, S France; pop. 93,100.

Mont're·al' (mŏn'trē·ôl'), Fr. **Mont're'al'** (môn'rā'äl') city, Canada, in Quebec prov. on island (**Montreal Island**) in St. Lawrence river; seaport, 1000 m. from open sea; pop. 1,109,400.

Montreal North. Fr. **Montréal-Nord** (-nôr') town, Canada, in S Quebec on Montreal I.; pop. 25,400.

Mont'treuil' (môn'trû'y') commune, N France, E of Paris; pop. 69,800.

Mont'treux' (môn'trû') group of villages, W Switzerland, at E end of Lake of Geneva.

Mont Royal. See MOUNT ROYAL.

Mont-Saint-Mi'chel' (môn'săn'mē'shĕl') island, NW France, in Gulf of St-Malo; a rock 234 ft. high, crowned with an abbey.

Mont'ser·rat' (mŏnt'sĕ·răt') island, British West Indies, in Leeward Is.; ✳ Plymouth; area 33 sq. m.; pop. 12,900.

Monument Valley, region, N Arizona and SE Utah, a sandy plain from which rise monumentlike buttes 1000 ft. high, also mesas and arches, all of red sandstone.

Mon'za (môn'tsä) commune, N Italy, NE of Milan; pop. 63,900.

Moon. See MUHU island, Estonia.

Moon, Mountains of the. See RUWENZORI, MOUNT.

Mo'o·ré'a (mō'ō·rā'à) island, Society Is., W of Papeete.

Moose'head' Lake (mōōs'hĕd') lake, NW cen. Maine, source of Kennebec river; 35 m. long, 10 m. wide.

Moose Jaw (mōōs' jô') city, Canada, in S Saskatchewan; pop. 29,600.

Moppo. See MOKPO.

Mo·rad'a·bad (mō·räd'à·bäd; mō·räd'à·băd) city, N India, in NW cen. Uttar Pradesh on Ramganga river; pop. 142,400.

Mo·ra'tu·wa (?·mō·rä'tōō·wà) town, W Ceylon, on Indian Ocean S of Colombo; pop. 50,700.

Mo'ra·va (Czech mô'rà·và; Yugoslav mō'rä·vä) 1 see MARCH river. 2 see MORAVIA. 3 river, Yugoslavia; formed by confluence of **Southern Morava** and **Western Morava,** flows NNW into Danube river; 100 m. long.

Mo·ra'vi·a (mō·rā'vǐ·à), Czech **Mo'ra·va** (mô'rà·và), Ger. **Mäh'ren** (mâ'rĕn) region, cen. Czechoslovakia, S of Silesia. — **Mo·ra'vi·an** (mō·rā'vǐ·ăn), adj. & n.

Moravian Gap, mountain pass, cen. Europe, along upper courses of Oder and Vistula rivers between SE Sudeten and W Carpathian Mts.

Mo'rav·ská O'stra·va (mô'räf·skä ô'strà·và), Ger. **Mäh'risch-Os'trau** (mâ'rǐsh·ôs'trou) city, cen. Czechoslovakia, near Moravian Gap; pop. 181,000.

Mor'ay (mûr'ǐ) or **El'gin** (ĕl'gǐn) or **El'gin·shire** (-shǐr; -shēr) county, NE Scotland, bordering on North Sea at mouth of Moray Firth; ✳ Elgin; area 476 sq. m.; pop. 48,200.

Mord·vin'i·an Autonomous Soviet Socialist Republic (môrd·vǐn'-ǐ·ăn; -vǐn'yăn) autonomous republic, cen. Soviet Russia, Europe, W of Sura river; ✳ Saransk; area 10,100 sq. m.; pop. 1,200,000.

Morea. See PELOPONNESUS.

Mo·re'lia (mō·rā'lyà) city, SW Mexico, ✳ of Michoacán state; pop. 44,300.

Mo·re'los (mō·rā'lôs) state, S cen. Mexico; ✳ Cuernavaca; area 1916 sq. m.; pop. 268,900.

Morena, Sierra. See SIERRA MORENA.

Mor'gan·town (môr'găn·toun) city, N West Virginia; pop. 25,500.

Mo·ri'ah (mō·rī'à) hill, Palestine, in E part of Jerusalem, on which Solomon built the Temple.

Mo·ri·o·ka (mō·rē·ō·kä) city, Japan, in N Honshu; pop. 107,100.

Mo·ro'be (mō·rō'bä) seaport, SE North-East New Guinea.

Mo·roc'co (mō·rŏk'ō) 1 Arab. **El Ma'ghreb el Aq'sa** (ăl mū'grĭb ăl ŭk'sä), Fr. **Ma'roc'** (mà'rôk'), Span. **Mar·rue'cos** (mär·rwä'kōs) country, N Africa, bordering on Atlantic Ocean and W end of Mediterranean Sea; a sultanate; ✳ Rabat; area 174,553 sq. m.; pop. 9,700,000; divided 1911–56 between the French and the Spanish: **French Morocco** (area 153,870 sq. m., ✳ Rabat; gained independence 1956) bordering on Atlantic Ocean, and **Spanish Morocco** (area 7589 sq. m., ✳ Tetuan; sovereignty relinquished 1957 by Spain except for cities of Ceuta and Melilla and several small garrisoned areas) on Mediterranean coast; included also an international zone around Tangier and the Spanish protectorate of Southern Morocco. 2 city: see MARRAKECH. — **Mo·roc'can** (mō·rŏk'ăn), adj. & n.

Mo'ro Gulf (mō'rō) body of water at S end of Philippine Is. between Mindanao and the Sulu Archipelago, the N section of Celebes Sea.

Mor'ris Jes'up, Cape (môr'ĭs jĕs'ŭp) most northerly point of Greenland, 83°39'N.

Morrison, Mount. See NIITAKA.

Mor′ris·town (môr′ĭs·toun) town, N New Jersey; pop. 17,100.

Mos′cow (mŏs′kou; -kō), Russ. **Mos·kva′** (mŭs·kvä′) city, ✳ of the U.S.S.R., in Soviet Russia, Europe, on Moskva river; in Middle Ages ✳ of principality, later grand duchy, of Moscow; ✳ of grand duchy of Russia 1547–1712, ✳ of Soviet Union since 1917; pop. 4,137,000.

Mo·selle′ (mō·zĕl′), Ger. **Mo′sel** (mō′zĕl) river, W Europe, flowing from Vosges Mts. in France to the Rhine in Germany; 320 m. long.

Mo′ses Lake (mō′zĭz; -zĭs) lake, E cen. Washington, in Big Bend region S of the Grand Coulee; 16 m. long, less than half a mile wide.

Mos·kva′ (mŭs·kvä′) **1** river, Soviet Russia, Europe, flowing E to join the Oka river; 315 m. long. **2** see Moscow.

Mos·qui′ti·a (mŭs·kē′tĭ·à) **1** territory, E Honduras, N of Segovia river; claimed by Nicaragua. **2** see Mosquito Coast.

Mosquito Coast or **Mos·qui′ti·a** (mŭs·kē′tĭ·à) region, E Nicaragua, on Caribbean coast; once a British protectorate; 300 m. long, 40 m. wide.

Mo·sul′ (mō·sōōl′; Arab. mō′sōōl) city, N Iraq, on the Tigris; pop. 260,000.

Moth′er·well and Wish′aw (mŭth′ẽr·wĕl [-wĕl], wĭsh′ô) burgh, S cen. Scotland, in Lanark co. on the Clyde SE of Glasgow; pop. 68,100.

Mouk′den′. Var. of Mukden.

Moul·mein′ (mōōl·mān′; môl-; -mīn′) city, S Burma, at mouth of Salween river on Gulf of Martaban; pop. 65,500.

Mountains of the Moon. See Ruwenzori, Mount.

Mount Ath′os (ăth′ŏs; ā′thŏs),Mod. Gr. **Á′yi·on Ó′ros** (ä′yôn ô′rŏs) autonomous republic, NE Greece, at tip of Acte Penin.; comprises 20 monasteries.

Mount Clem′ens (klĕm′ĕnz) city, SE Michigan; pop. 17,000.

Mount Des′ert (dĕz′ẽrt; older pron. dĕ·zûrt′) island, Maine, in Atlantic Ocean E of Penobscot Bay; 14 m. long, 8 m. wide.

Mount E′ba (ē′bà) district, cen. South Australia, 100 m. NW of Port Augusta; head of range for testing rockets and supersonic aircraft.

Mount Lavinia. See Dehiwala–Mount Lavinia.

Mount of the Holy Cross. See Holy Cross, Mount of the.

Mount Roy′al (mount roi′àl) or **Mont Roy′al** (môn′ rwä′yàl′) town, Canada, in S Quebec on Montreal I.; pop. 17,000.

Mount Ver′non (vûr′nŭn) **1** city, S Illinois, SE of Centralia; pop. 15,600. **2** city, SE New York, on Bronx river adjacent to New York City; pop. 71,900. **3** home and burial place of George Washington, in Virginia, on Potomac river 15 m. below Washington, D.C.

Mouse. See Souris river.

Mo′zam·bique′ (mō′zăm·bēk′; mō′zăm·bĕk′), Port. **Mo·çam·bi′que** (mōō·säm·bē′kẽ), also called **Portuguese East Africa**, country, SE Africa, bordering on Indian Ocean; belongs to Portugal; ✳ Lourenço Marques; area 297,654 sq. m.; pop. 5,081,300.

Mozambique Channel, strait between the island of Madagascar and the SE African mainland (Mozambique).

Muang-Thai. See Thailand.

Mu·gu′, Point (mŭ·gōō′) cape, California, W of Los Angeles and S of Oxnard; site of naval air-missile test center.

Mu′hu (mōō′hōō), Ger. **Moon** (mōn), Russ. **Mu′khu** (mōō′kōō) island, Estonia, in Baltic Sea between Sarema I. and the mainland.

Muk′den′ (mōōk′dĕn′; mōōk′-; -dĕn), Chin. **Shen′yang′** (shŭn′yäng′), formerly **Feng′tien′** (fŭng′tyĕn′) city, ✳ of Manchuria 1644–1912 and since 1949 and of Liaoning prov. since 1956; pop. 2,300,000.

Mukha. See Mocha.

Mul′ha·cén′ (mōō′lä·thän′; -sän′) or **Mu·ley′-Ha·cén′** (mōō·lä′ä-) mountain, S Spain, in the Sierra Nevada; 11,420 ft. high.

Mül′heim an der Ruhr (mül′hīm än dẽr rōōr′) city, W Germany, on Ruhr river near its mouth; pop. 148,600.

Mul′house′ (mü′lōōz′), Ger. **Mül·hau′sen** (mül·hou′zĕn) commune, NE France, in Alsace on Ill river; pop. 87,700.

Mull (mŭl) island, W Scotland, largest of Inner Hebrides; 351 sq. m.

Mul·tan′ (mōōl·tän′) city, W Pakistan; pop. 142,800.

Mult·no′mah Falls (mŭlt·nō′mà) waterfall, NW Oregon, E of Portland, in a small tributary of the Columbia river; 620 ft. high.

Mün′chen-Glad′bach (mün′kĕn-glät′bäk) city, W Germany, W of Düsseldorf; pop. 122,400.

Mun′cie (mŭn′sĭ) city, E cen. Indiana; pop. 58,500.

Mun′hall (mŭn′hôl) borough, SW Pennsylvania; pop. 16,400.

Mu′nich (mū′nĭk), Ger. **Mün′chen** (mün′kĕn) city, Germany, ✳ of Bavaria, on Isar river; pop. 831,000.

Mun′ster (mŭn′stẽr) province, S Ireland; area 9317 sq. m.; pop. 898,900.

Mün′ster (mün′stẽr; Angl. mŭn′-, mĭn′-) city, W Germany; formerly ✳ of Westphalia; pop. 119,800.

Mun·te′ni·a (mōō·tē′nĭ·à; Romanian mōōn·tē′nyä) or **Greater Wa·la′chi·a** (wō·lā′kĭ·à) region, S Romania, the E part of Walachia; formerly a province.

Mur (mōōr), Slavic **Mu′ra** (mōō′rä) river, Austria and N Yugoslavia; flows into Drava river; 230 m. long.

Mu·rat′ Su·yu′ (mōō·rät′ sōō·yōō′), anc. **Ar·sa′ni·as** (är·sä′nĭ·ăs) river, Turkey, a headstream of the Euphrates river.

Mur′chi·son (mûr′chĭ·s′n) river, W Western Australia, flowing W to Indian Ocean; 400 m. long.

Murchison Falls, waterfall, E Africa, in Uganda, in Victoria Nile just above Lake Albert; 120 ft. high.

Mur′ci·a (mûr′shĭ·à; -shä) **1** region, SE Spain, bordering on Mediterranean Sea between Andalusia and Valencia; once a kingdom. **2** commune, SE Spain, ✳ of ancient kingdom; pop. 201,300.

Mu′res or **Mu′resh** (mōō′rĕsh), Hung. **Ma′ros** (mô′rŏsh) river, Hungary and Romania, flowing W into Tisza river; 400 m. long.

Mur′frees·bor′o (mûr′frēz·bûr′ō) city, cen. Tennessee, on West Fork of Stones river; pop. 13,100.

Mur·man′, or **Mur·mansk′, Coast** (mōōr·màn′, -mänsk′) also, earlier, **Nor′man Coast** (nôr′măn) region, NW Soviet Russia, Europe, on N coast of Kola Peninsula.

Mur·mansk′ (mōōr·mänsk′) city, NW Soviet Russia, Europe, on Kola Bay; ice-free port all the year round; pop. 117,100.

Mu′roc (mū′rŏk) locality, S California, in Mojave Desert on **Muroc Dry Lake** SE of Bakersfield; U.S. Air Force base.

Mu·ro·ran (mōō·rō·rän) seaport, Japan, in SW Hokkaido I.; pop. 96,700.

Mur′ray (mûr′ĭ) river, SE Australia, flowing from Kosciusko Plateau in E Victoria to the Indian Ocean in SE South Australia; 1200 m. long, with the Darling river 2310 m. long.

Mur′rum·bidg′ee (mûr′ŭm·bĭj′ē) river, SE Australia, in New South Wales, flowing to the Murray river; 100 m. long.

Murua. See Woodlark.

Murviedro. See Sagunto.

Mu′sa, Ge′bel (jĕb′ĕl mōō′sä) mountain group, NE Egypt, in S Sinai Penin.; highest point Gebel Katherina, 8652 ft.

Mu′sa, Je′bel (jĕb′ĕl mōō′sä), anc. **Ab′i·la** or **Ab′y·la** (ăb′ĭ·là) mountain, N Morocco, opposite Gibraltar; 2775 ft. high.

Mus′ca·tine (mŭs′kà·tēn; mŭs′kà·tēn′) city, E Iowa; pop. 19,000.

Mus′cle Shoals (mŭs′'l shōlz′) rapids, N Alabama, in Tennessee river, now submerged (Wilson Dam at W end and Wheeler Dam at E end).

Mus′co·vy (mŭs′kô·vĭ) Russia; — an old name. See Moscow.

Mus·ke′gon (mŭs·kē′gŭn) city, W Michigan; pop. 48,400.

Muskegon Heights, city, W Michigan, S of Muskegon; pop. 18,800.

Mus·ko′gee (mŭs·kō′gē) city, E Oklahoma; pop. 37,300.

Mus·ko′ka, Lake (mŭs·kō′kà) lake, E Canada, in SE Ontario E of Georgian Bay and N of Lake Simcoe; area 54 sq. m.

Mus′sel·shell′ (mŭs′'l·shĕl′) river, cen. Montana, flowing into Missouri river; 300 m. long.

Mu′tan′kiang′ (mōō′dän′jĭ·äng′) city, E Manchuria, on Mutan river; pop. 179,200.

Mu·tsu Bay (mōō·tsōō) bay, Japan, at N extremity of Honshu I.

Mwe′ru (mwä′rōō) lake, cen. Africa, between SE Belgian Congo and Northern Rhodesia, W of S tip of Lake Tanganyika; 80 m. long.

Myc′a·le (mĭk′à·lē; -lē) promontory, Asia Minor, in Caria opposite island of Samos; — its ancient name; battle 479 B.C.

My·ce′nae (mī·sē′nē; -nē) ancient city, S Greece, in NE Peloponnesus N of Argos; at height c. 1400 B.C. See Mycenaean, in Vocab.

Myit′kyi′na′ (myī′chē′nä′) town, N Burma, on upper Irrawaddy river near China border; center of a district now part of the Kachin State.

Mylae. See Milazzo.

My′men·singh (mī′mĕn·sĭng) town, E Pakistan; pop. 53,000.

My′ra (mī′rà) ancient city, Asia Minor, on coast of Lycia; ruins.

My′si·a (mĭsh′ĭ·à) ancient country, NW Asia Minor, bordering on the Propontis (Sea of Marmara). — **My′si·an,** adj. & n.

Mys′ła·cho·wi′ce (mĭs′lä·kô·vē′tsĕ) locality, S Poland, near Kraków; place where Cominform was organized October 1947.

My·sore′ (mī·sōr′) **1** state, S India, at S end of the Deccan, bordering on Arabian Sea; ✳ Bangalore; area 74,326 sq. m.; pop. 19,399,300. **2** city in S Mysore state; pop. 150,400.

Myt′i·le′ne (mĭt′ĭ·lē′nē), Mod. Gr. **Mi′ti·li′ni** (mē′tē·lyē′nyē) **1** island: see Lesbos. **2** formerly **Ka′stro** (käs′trō) city, Greece, chief town on Lesbos I., on coast; pop. 27,100.

N

Nab′lus (năb′lŭs; nä′blŭs), anc. **She′chem** (shē′kĕm), Gr. **Ne·ap′o·lis** (nē·ăp′ō·lĭs) town, cen. Palestine, in Samaria; now in W Jordan.

Na·fud′ or **An Nafud** (än nä·fōōd′) desert, N Saudi Arabia, in N Nejd.

Na′ga Hills (nä′gä; nä·gä′) hills, NE India (Assam) and W Burma.

Na′ga·land′ (nä′gà·lănd′) administrative division of India, in Naga Hills N of Manipur; organized Dec. 1957.

Na′ga·sa′ki (nä′gä·sä′kē) seaport, Japan, in W Kyushu on inlet of East China Sea; pop. 198,600.

Na·gor′no-Ka·ra·bakh′ Autonomous Region (nŭ·gôr′nŭ·kà·rŭ·bàk′) autonomous region, U.S.S.R., in SW Azerbaidzhan S.S.R.; ✳ Stepanakert; area 1700 sq. m.; pop. 130,000.

Na·go·ya (nä·gô·yä) city, Japan, in S Honshu on Ise Bay; pop. 853,100.

Nag′pur (näg′pōōr) city, cen. India, in Madhya Pradesh (formerly Central Provinces and Berar); pop. 302,000.

Nagyszeben. See Sibiu.

Nagyvárad. See Oradea.

Na·ha (nä·hä) or **Na·wa** (nä·wä) seaport, Ryukyu Is., ✳ of Okinawa; pop. 65,800.

Na·huel′ Hua·pí′, Lake (nä·wĕl′ wä·pē′) lake, SW Argentina, in Andes near Chilean border; area 300 sq. m.

Nairn (nârn) or **Nairn′shire** (nârn′shĭr; -shẽr) county, NE Scotland, S of Moray Firth; ✳ Nairn; area 163 sq. m.; pop. 8700.

Nai·ro′bi (nī·rō′bĭ) city, ✳ of Kenya, at 1°15′S lat.; pop. 54,600.

Naissus. See Niš.

Najd. See Nejd.

Na·jin (nä·jēn) or **Ra·shin** (rä·shĕn) city, N Korea, on NE coast near Russian border; pop. 38,300.

Na′khi·che·van′ (nä′kē·chĕ·văn′) **1** officially **Nakhichevan Autonomous Soviet Socialist Republic,** autonomous republic, U.S.S.R., in Azerbaidzhan S.S.R.; ✳ Nakhichevan; area 2100 sq. m.; pop. 160,000. **2** town, its ✳, on Araks river. **3** or **Nakhichevan on Don,** town, Soviet Russia, Europe, on Don river near Rostov; pop. 71,000.

Nak·tong (näk·tông) or **Ra·ku·to** (rä·kô·tō) river, S Korea, flowing S to Korea Strait near Pusan; 260 m. long.

Na·ma′qua·land′ (nà·mä′kwä·länd′) or **Na′ma·land** (nä′mä·länd′) region, SW Africa, on coast; divided by Orange river into Great Namaqualand to the N (in South-West Africa) and Little Namaqualand to the S (in Union of South Africa); ✳ Springbok.

Nam′hoi′ (năm′hoi′) or **Fat′shan′** (fät′shän′) city, SE China, in cen. Kwangtung prov. above Canton in Si delta; pop. 500,000.

Nam′pa (năm′pà) city, SW Idaho, W of Boise; pop. 16,200.

Na·mur′ (nà·mōōr′; nà-; Fr. nà′mür′), Flem. **Na′men** (nä′mĕ[n]) commune, Belgium, on Meuse and Sambre rivers; pop. 31,600.

Nan (nän) river, W Thailand, a headstream of the Chao Phraya; 350 m. long.

Na·nai′mo (nà·nī′mō) city, Canada, in SW British Columbia on SE Vancouver I.; opp. Vancouver; pop. 12,700.

Nan′chang′ (nän′chäng′) city, SE China, ✳ of Kiangsi prov., on Kan river just SW of Poyang Hu (lake); pop. 206,400.

Nan′cy (năn′sĭ; Fr. näN′sē′) city, NE France, on Meurthe river; pop. 113,500.

Nan′da De′vi (nŭn′dä dā′vē) mountain, N India, in Uttar Pradesh in Himalayas; 25,645 ft.

Nan′ga Par′bat (nŭng′gä pŭr′bät) mountain, NW Kashmir, in W Himalayas; 26,660 ft. high.

Nan′king′ (nän′kĭng′) city, E China, in W Kiangsu prov. on Yangtze river; ✻ of Kiangsu, ✻ of China 1928–37, 1946–49; pop. 1,019,100.

Nan Ling (nän′ lĭng′) or **Nan Shan** (nän′ shän′) mountain system, S China, roughly separating Kwangtung and Kwangsi provs. from Hunan and Kweichow provs.

Nan′ning′ (nän′nĭng′), formerly **Yung′ning′** (yŏong′nĭng′) city, S China, in Kwangsi prov. on Siang river; pop. 202,700.

Nansei Islands. See RYUKYU ISLANDS.

Nan Shan or **Nanshan** (nän′shän′) **1** mountain range, cen. China, on border between Tsinghai and Kansu provs. **2** see NAN LING.

Nantes (nänts; Fr. näNt) city, NW France, on Loire river; pop. 200,300.

Nan′ti·coke (nän′tĭ·kōk) city, E Pennsylvania; pop. 20,200.

Nan·tuck′et (nän·tŭk′ĕt; -ĭt) island, Massachusetts, in Atlantic Ocean S of Cape Cod; area 57 sq. m.

Nan′tung′ (nän′tŏong′), formerly **Tung′chow′** (tŏong′jō′) seaport, E China, in SE Kiangsu prov. on Yangtze estuary; pop. 150,000.

Na′ples (nā′p'lz), Ital. **Na′po·li** (nä′pō·lē), anc. **Ne·ap′o·lis** (nē·ăp′ō-lĭs) seaport, S Italy, on **Bay of Naples** (inlet of Tyrrhenian Sea); pop. 1,029,800. — **Ne′a·pol′i·tan** (nē′à·pŏl′ĭ·tăn), adj. & n.

Na′po (nä′pō) river, NW South America; rises near Cotopaxi Mt. in N cen. Ecuador, flows E and SE and empties into Amazon river; 550 m. long.

Nar·ba′da (nẽr·bŭd′à) river, cen. India, flowing W between the Vindhya Mts. and the Satpura Range into the Gulf of Cambay; 800 m. long.

Na′rew (nä′rĕf), Russ. **Na·rev′** (nŭ·ryôf′) river, NE Poland, flowing W and SW into Bug river; 285 m. long.

Nar′ra·gan′sett Bay (năr′à·găn′sĕt; -sĭt) inlet of Atlantic Ocean, SE Rhode Island.

Nar′rows, the (năr′ōz) **1** strait, SE New York, between W end of Long I. and Staten I., connecting Upper New York Bay with Lower New York Bay. **2** section of the Dardanelles, its narrowest part.

Nar′sars·su′ak (när′sẽr·sŏo′äk) village, S Greenland, at about 61°10′N; airport.

Nar′va (när′và) city, NE Estonia; battle 1700; pop. 24,500.

Nar′vik (när′vĭk) seaport, N Norway; ice-free harbor; pop. 10,300.

Nase′by (nāz′bĭ) parish, England, in Northamptonshire; battle 1645.

Nash′u·a (năsh′û·à; locally also -à·wä) city, S New Hampshire, on Merrimack river S of Manchester; pop. 34,700.

Nash′ville (năsh′vĭl) city, ✻ of Tennessee, on Cumberland river; pop. 174,300.

Nasira, En. See NAZARETH.

Nas′sau (năs′ô) **1** city, ✻ of Bahama Is., on NE coast of New Providence I.; pop. 29,400. **2** (Ger. näs′ou) region, W Germany, N and E of the Rhine; once a duchy; chief city Wiesbaden.

Na·tal′ (nà·tăl′) **1** (Port. nà·täl′) seaport, NE Brazil, ✻ of Rio Grande do Norte state; pop. 97,700. **2** province, E Union of South Africa, between Drakensberg Mts. and Indian Ocean; ✻ Pietermaritzburg; area 35,284 sq. m.; pop. 2,202,400.

Natch′ez (năch′ĕz; -ĭz) city, SW Mississippi, on Mississippi river; pop. 22,700.

Na′tick (nā′tĭk) town, E Massachusetts, WSW of Boston; pop. 19,800.

National City, city, SW California, on San Diego Bay; pop. 21,200.

Natural Bridge, village, W Virginia, S of Lexington; natural bridge (over Cedar Creek) 215 ft. high, 50–100 ft. wide, 90-ft. span.

Natural Bridges National Monument, site of three natural bridges, SE Utah; established as national monument 1908.

Natzweiler. See STRUTHOF.

Nau′cra·tis (nô′crà·tĭs) ancient Greek city, N Egypt, in Nile delta W of Rosetta branch.

Nau′ga·tuck (nô′gà·tŭk) borough, S Connecticut; pop. 17,500.

Na·u′ru (nä·ōō′rōō), formerly **Pleasant Island,** island, W Pacific Ocean, 26 m. S of the equator; a joint British, New Zealand, and Australian trust territory; has phosphate deposits.

Nav′a·jo Mountain (năv′à·hō) mountain, SE Utah; 10,416 ft. high.

Navarino. See PYLOS.

Na·varre′ (nà·vär′), Span. **Na·var′ra** (nä·vär′rä), Fr. **Na′varre′** (nà′-vär′) region, N Spain, bordering on France; once an independent kingdom; for a time (1235–1328) an appanage of France. — **Na′var·rese′** (nä′và·rēz′; -rēs′; näv′à-), adj. & n. sing. & pl.

Navigators Islands. See SAMOA.

Náv′pak·tos (näf′päk·tôs), Ital. **Le′pan·to** (lâ′pän·tō; Angl. lê·păn′tō), anc. **Nau·pac′tus** (nô·păk′tŭs) seaport, Greece, on the strait connecting the gulfs of Corinth and Patras; naval battle (Lepanto) in nearby strait 1571.

Nawa. See NAHA.

Nax′os (năk′sŏs), Mod. Gr. **Ná′xos** (nä′ksôs) island, Greece, largest of the Cyclades Is.; area 171 sq. m.

Na′ya·rit′ (nä′yä·rēt′) state, W Mexico, bordering on Pacific Ocean; ✻ Tepic; area 10,444 sq. m.; pop. 292,300.

Naz′a·reth (năz′à·rĕth; năz′rĕth), Heb. **Na·tsrat** (nä·tsĕ′rĕt), Arab. **En Na′si·ra** (ăn nä′sĭ·rŏ) city, N Israel, in Galilee; pop. (1949) 20,100. See NAZARENE, in Vocab.

Naze, the (nāz) **1** headland, SE England, on E coast of Essex. **2** cape, S Norway: see LINDESNES.

Neapolis. See NABLUS; NAPLES.

Nearer Tibet. See TIBET, NEARER.

Near Islands (nẽr) westernmost of the Aleutian Is.; chief island Attu.

Nebo. See PISGAH, MOUNT.

Ne·bras′ka (nē·brăs′kà), abbr. **Nebr., Neb.,** state, cen. United States, in Great Plains just W of Missouri river; ✻ Lincoln; area 77,237 sq. m.; pop. 1,325,500. — **Ne·bras′kan,** adj. & n.

Nech′es (nĕch′ĕz; -ĭz) river, E Texas, flowing S and SE into Sabine Lake; 280 m. long.

Neck′ar (nĕk′är; Angl. -ẽr) river, SW Germany, rising in the Black Forest and flowing N and W into the Rhine; 246 m. long.

Need′ham (nēd′ăm) town, E Massachusetts; pop. 16,300.

Neer·win′den (när·vĭn′dĕ[n]) village, E Belgium, NW of Liége; battles 1693 and 1793.

Ne·fud′ (nē·fōōd′). Var. of NAFUD.

Neg′eb (nĕg′ĕb; nē·gĕb′) or **Negev** (nĕg′ĕv; nē·gĕv′) region, S Israel, a triangular wedge of desert; touches Gulf of 'Aqaba in S.

Ne·gri′ Sem·bi′lan (nē·grē′ sĕm·bē′län) state, Federation of Malaya, on Strait of Malacca; ✻ Seremban; area 2550 sq. m.; pop. 267,700.

Ne′gro, Ri′o (Port. rē′ōō nä′grōō), Span. **Rí′o Ne′gro** (rē′ō nä′grō) river, NW South America, flowing from E Colombia to the Amazon in N Brazil; 1400 m. long.

Ne′gro, Rí′o (rē′ō nä′grō) **1** river, S cen. Argentina, flowing E into Atlantic Ocean; 630 m. long. **2** river, cen. Uruguay, rising in S Brazil and flowing SW into the Uruguay river; 290 m. long.

Negropont, Negroponte. See EUBOEA.

Ne′gros (nā′grōs) island, Philippine Is., one of the Visayan Is.; area 4905 sq. m.; pop. (with adjacent small islands) 1,219,500.

Neis′se (nī′sĕ) **1** or **Lau′sit·zer Neisse** (lou′zĭt·sẽr), Pol. **Ny′sa Łu·życ′ka** (nī′sä lōō·zhĭts′kä) river, N Europe, flowing from N Czechoslovakia N to the Oder river; 140 m. long. **2** see NYSA.

Nejd (nĕjd), Arab. **Najd** (näjd) region, cen. Arabia; relatively fertile; nucleus of kingdom of Nejd (proclaimed 1905), ✻ Riyadh, area 447,000 sq. m., pop. 4,000,000, now the dominant unit of Saudi Arabia.

Nel′son (nĕl′s'n) river, Canada, in Manitoba; flows from N end of Lake Winnipeg to S end of Hudson Bay; 400 m. long, including Saskatchewan and Bow rivers 1600 m. long.

Ne′man (nĕm′ăn; Russ. nyĕ′mán), Pol. **Nie′men** (nē′mĕn; Pol. nyĕ′mĕn) river, E cen. Europe, flowing from cen. White Russia into Baltic Sea (Kurland Gulf); formerly known as the **Me′mel** (mā′mĕl) river in East Prussia; total length 500 m.

Ne′me·a (nē′mē·à) valley, Greece, in ancient Argolis; scene of battle 394 B.C. See NEMEAN, NEMEAN LION, in Vocab.

Ne·o′sho (nē·ō′shō; -shà) river, SE Kansas and NE Oklahoma, flowing SE and S into Arkansas river; 460 m. long.

Ne·pal′ (nē·pôl′) country, Asia, on NE border of India in the Himalayas; a kingdom; ✻ Katmandu; area 54,000 sq. m.; pop. 5,600,000. — **Nep′a·lese′** (nĕp′à·lēz′; -lēs′), adj. & n. sing. & pl.

Nestos. See MESTA.

Neth′er·lands (nĕth′ẽr·lăndz), Dutch **Ne′der·land** (nā′dẽr·länt), called also **Hol′land** (hŏl′ănd) country, NW Europe, bordering on North Sea; kingdom; ✻ Amsterdam, seat of government The Hague; land area 12,504 sq. m.; pop. 10,200,300.

Netherlands Antilles, the islands of the West Indies belonging to the Netherlands: Curaçao, Bonaire, Aruba, Saba, St. Eustatius, and S part of St. Martin; an overseas territory; ✻ Willemstad; area 403 sq. m.; pop. 150,000.

Netherlands Guiana. See SURINAM.

Netherlands India. = Netherlands Indies: see INDONESIA.

Netherlands Indies. See INDONESIA.

Netherlands New Guinea or **West New Guinea,** the western half of New Guinea, W of 141st meridian; claimed by the Indonesians, who call it, and sometimes the whole island, **I′ri·an** (ē′rē·än); area with adjacent islands 159,334 sq. m.; pop. 333,400.

Netherlands Timor. See TIMOR.

Netherlands West Indies, the Netherlands Antilles.

Néthou, Pic de. See ANETO, PICO DE.

Net·tu′no (nät·tōō′nō) town, Italy, on Tyrrhenian Sea 32 m. SSE of Rome, adjoining Anzio; American forces landed here January 1944.

Neu·châ′tel′ (nû′shä′tĕl′) **1** canton N Switzerland, in Jura Mts.; area 312 sq. m.; pop. 128,200. **2** commune, its ✻, on **Lake of Neuchâtel** (84 sq. m.); pop. 28,000.

Neuil′ly′-sur-Seine (nû′yē′sür·sâN′) commune, N France, NW of Paris near the Bois de Boulogne; pop. 60,200.

Neu-Mecklenburg. See NEW IRELAND.

Neu′mün′ster (noi′mün′stẽr) city, W Germany, SSW of Kiel; pop. 66,200.

Neupest. See ÚJPEST.

Neu·quén′ (nā′ōō·kān′) river, W Argentina, flowing from the Andes E to join the Limay river and form the Río Negro; 375 m. long.

Neusatz. See NOVI SAD.

Neuse (nūs) river, E cen. North Carolina, flowing SE into Pamlico Sound; 260 m. long.

Neuss (nois) city, W Germany, W of Düsseldorf; pop. 55,000.

Neus′tri·a (nūs′trĭ·à) **1** the western part of the dominions of the Franks after the conquest by Clovis in 511, comprising then the NW part of modern France between the Meuse, the Loire, and the Atlantic Ocean. **2** after A.D. 912, Normandy. — **Neus′tri·an,** adj. & n.

Neuve-Cha′pelle′ (nûv′shä′pĕl′) town, N France, NE of Béthune; scene of battle Mar. 10–13, 1915.

Neu′ville′, in full **Neuville-en-Con′droz′** (nû′vēl′äN·kôN′drōz′) village, E Belgium, SW of Liége; American military cemetery.

Ne′va (nē′và; Russ. nyĕ·vá′) river, N Soviet Russia, Europe, flowing from Lake Ladoga to Gulf of Finland at Leningrad; ab. 40 m. long.

Ne·vad′a (nē·văd′à; -vä′dà), abbr. **Nev.,** state, W United States, in W part of region between the Rocky Mts. and the Sierra Nevada; ✻ Carson City; area 110,540 sq. m.; pop. 160,100. — **Ne·vad′an** (-văd′'n; -vä′d'n), adj. & n.

Ne′ves (nā′vĕs) city, SE Brazil, on Guanabara Bay; pop. 53,100.

Ne′vis (nē′vĭs; nĕv′ĭs) island, West Indies Federation; part of Saint Kitts–Nevis colony in colony of Leeward Is.

Nevis, Ben. See BEN NEVIS.

New Al′ba·ny (ôl′bà·nĭ) city, S Indiana, on Ohio river; pop. 29,300.

New Am′ster·dam (ăm′stẽr·dăm) the Dutch city on Manhattan I. which became the city of New York; founded 1625.

New′ark (nū′ẽrk) **1** city, NE New Jersey, on Passaic river and Newark Bay; pop. 438,800. **2** city, cen. Ohio, E of Columbus; pop. 34,300.

New Bed′ford (bĕd′fẽrd) city, SE Massachusetts, on Buzzards Bay; pop. 109,200.

New Bern (nū′bẽrn) city, SE North Carolina; pop. 15,800.

New Brit′ain (brĭt′'n) **1** city, N Connecticut, SW of Hartford; pop. 73,700. **2** island, Bismarck Archipelago, largest of the group; chief town Rabaul; area 14,600 sq. m.; pop. 81,200.

New Bruns′wick (brŭnz′wĭk) **1** city, cen. New Jersey, on Raritan river W of Perth Amboy; pop. 38,800. **2,** abbr. **N.B.,** province, SE Canada, bordering on Gulf of St. Lawrence and Bay of Fundy; ✻ Fredericton; area 27,985 sq. m.; pop. 554,600.

New′burgh (nū′bûrg) city, SE New York, on Hudson river S of Poughkeepsie; pop. 32,000.

New Cal′e·do′nia (kăl′ē·dōn′yȧ; -dō′nĭ·ȧ) **1** Fr. **Nou′velle′ Ca′lé′do′nie′** (nōō′vĕl′ kȧ′lā′dô′nē′) island, SW Pacific Ocean, 700 m. E of Queensland, Australia; belongs to France and with other nearby islands (Loyalty Is., Kunie, etc.) constitutes an overseas territory, ✻ Nouméa, area 7756 sq. m., pop. 55,000; area of island 6300 sq. m.; pop. 53,200. **2** British Columbia; — its former name.

New Cas·tile′ (kăs·tēl′), Span. **Cas·til′la la Nue′va** (käs·tē′[l]yä lä nwā′vä) region, cen. Spain; chief city Toledo.

New′cas′tle (nū′kȧs′'l) **1** city, SE Australia, in E New South Wales on Pacific Ocean at mouth of Hunter river; pop. with suburbs 127,200. **2** or **Newcastle upon Tyne** (nū′kȧs′'l [locally nū·kȧs′'l], tīn) city and county borough, N England, in Northumberland, on the Tyne; pop. 291,700. **3** or **Newcastle under Lyme** (līm) municipal borough, W cen. England, in Staffordshire; pop. 70,000.

New Cas′tle (nū kȧs′'l; nū′ kȧs′'l) **1** city, E cen. Indiana; pop. 18,300. **2** city, W Pennsylvania on the Shenango river; pop. 48,800.

Newchwang. See Yingkow.

New Delhi. See Delhi.

New England, **1** northeast section of the United States, comprising the states of Maine, New Hampshire, Vermont, Massachusetts, Rhode Island, and Connecticut. **2** mountain range and plateau (**New England Plateau**), SE Australia, in NE New South Wales, part of Great Dividing Range; highest point 5000 ft.

New Forest, district, S England, in Hampshire; set aside 1079 as royal hunting ground, now partly in private ownership.

New′found·land′ (nū′fŭn[d]·lănd′ — the usu. local pron.; nū′fŭn[d]lănd, -lănd′; nonlocally also nū·foun[d]′lănd) **1** island, E Canada, in Atlantic Ocean E of mouth of St. Lawrence; area 42,734 sq. m.; pop. 404,300. **2** abbr. **Nfld.**, province, E Canada, including Newfoundland and Labrador; ✻ St. John's; area 154,734 sq. m.; pop. 415,100.

New France, the possessions of France in North America from the time of the discoveries of Cartier 1534–41 to 1763.

New Georgia, **1** group of islands, cen. Solomon Is.; part of British Solomon Is. protectorate. **2** chief island of the group; 50 m. long.

New Goa. See Pangim.

New Gra·na′da (grȧ·nä′dȧ) in colonial times, a Spanish viceroyalty in NW South America, occupying region now in Venezuela, Colombia, Panama, and Ecuador.

New Guin′ea (gĭn′ĭ) or **Pap′u·a** (păp′ū·ȧ) **1** island, Malay Archipelago, N of Australia; divided between the Dutch territory of West New Guinea, officially Netherlands New Guinea, and the Australian territories of North-East New Guinea and Papua; total area 306,600 sq. m. **2** any of the three sections of New Guinea. **3** the Territory of New Guinea.

New Guinea, Territory of, North-East New Guinea together with the Bismarck Archipelago and Bougainville, Buka, and adjacent small islands; a UN trust territory under Australian administration; since World War II administered with Territory of Papua from Port Moresby; area 93,000 sq. m.; pop. 985,000.

New Hamp′shire (hăm[p]′shẽr; -shĭr), abbr. **N.H.**, state, NE United States, bordering on Canada and the Atlantic Ocean; ✻ Concord; area 9304 sq. m.; pop. 533,200.

New Han′o·ver (hăn′ō·vẽr) or **La·von′gai** (lȧ·vông′gī) island, Bismarck Archipelago, NW of New Ireland.

New Ha′ven (hā′vĕn) city, S Connecticut, on New Haven Harbor (Long Island Sound); pop. 164,400.

New Heb′ri·des (hĕb′rĭ·dēz), Fr. **Nou′velles′ Hé′brides′** (nōō′vĕl′-zā′-brēd′) group of islands in SW Pacific Ocean NE of New Caledonia and W of Fiji Is.; under joint British and French administration; ✻ Vila; area 5700 sq. m.; pop. 4700.

New I·be′ri·a (ī·bēr′ĭ·ȧ) city, S Louisiana; pop. 16,500.

New Ire′land (īr′lănd), formerly **Neu-Meck′len·burg** (noi′mĕk′lĕn-bōōrk) island, Bismarck Archipelago; area 2800 sq. m.; pop. 20,500.

New Jer′sey (jûr′zĭ), abbr. **N.J.**, state, E United States, bordering on Atlantic Ocean; ✻ Trenton; area 7836 sq. m.; pop. 4,835,300.

New Ken′sing·ton (kĕn′zĭng·tŭn) city, SW Pennsylvania; pop. 25,100.

New Land. See Novaya Zemlya.

New Lon′don (lŭn′dŭn) city, SE Connecticut, on Long Island Sound at mouth of Thames river; Coast Guard Academy; naval station and submarine base; pop. 30,600.

New Mex′i·co (mĕk′sĭ·kō), abbr. **N. Mex.**, state, SW United States, bordering on Mexico; ✻ Santa Fe; area 121,666 sq. m.; pop. 681,200.

New Neth′er·land (nĕth′ẽr·lănd) Dutch colony in North America 1613–64, occupying lands bordering on the Hudson river and later also on the lower Delaware river.

New Or′le·ans (ôr′lē·ănz; locally also ôr′lănz; nonlocally often ôr·lēnz′, ẽr-) city, SE Louisiana, between the Mississippi river and Lake Pontchartrain; pop. 570,400.

New′port (nū′pōrt) **1** city, N Kentucky, on Ohio river just E of Covington; pop. 31,000. **2** city, SE Rhode Island, on Rhode I. (island) at mouth of Narragansett Bay; naval base; pop. 37,600. **3** municipal borough, S England, ✻ of Isle of Wight; pop. 20,400. **4** county borough, W England, ✻ of Monmouthshire, on the Usk; pop. 105,300.

Newport News (nūz) independent city, SE Virginia, at mouth of James river at entrance to Hampton Roads; pop. 42,400.

New Providence, island, Bahama Is.; site of Nassau, ✻ of the group.

New Quebec, region, NE Canada, in N Quebec prov. between Hudson Bay and Labrador.

New Ro·chelle′ (rō·shĕl′) city, SE New York, on Long Island Sound NE of New York; pop. 59,700.

New Sarum. See Salisbury.

New Siberian Islands, group of islands, N Soviet Russia, Asia, in Arctic Ocean; belong to Yakutsk Republic.

New South Wales, abbr. **N.S.W.**, state, SE Australia, bordering on Pacific Ocean; ✻ Sydney; area 309,432 sq. m.; pop. 3,225,200.

New Spain, in colonial times, a viceroyalty of Spain including territory now in SW United States, Mexico, Central America N of Panama, the West Indies, and the Philippines; ✻ Mexico City.

New Sweden, Swedish colony in North America 1638–55, W of lower Delaware river.

New′ton (nū′t'n) city, E Massachusetts, W of Boston; includes 14 villages; total pop. 82,000.

New Toronto, town, Canada, in SE Ontario; pop. 11,600.

New Wa′ter·ford (wô′tẽr·fẽrd; wŏt′ẽr-) town, E Canada, on Cape Breton I.; pop. 10,400.

New West′min′ster (wĕs[t]′mĭn′stẽr) city, Canada, in SW British Columbia on Fraser river; pop. 31,600.

New Windsor. See Windsor.

New York (yôrk′) **1**, abbr. **N.Y.**, state, E United States, bordering on Canada and the Atlantic Ocean; ✻ Albany; area 49,576 sq. m., not including 4376 sq. m. of water in lakes Erie and Ontario; pop. 14,-830,200. **2** or **New York City**, city, New York, at mouth of Hudson river, occupying Manhattan I., Staten I., the W end of Long I., and a section of the mainland; seat (since 1951) of the United Nations organization; pop. 7,892,000.

New York Bay, inlet of Atlantic Ocean, SE New York, at mouth of Hudson river, forming harbor of New York City; the inner part, **Upper New York Bay**, is connected with the outer part, **Lower New York Bay**, by the Narrows, between Staten I. and the W end of Long I.

New York International Airport. See Idlewild.

New York State Barge Canal, canal system, N New York state, its main waterway connecting Lake Erie with the Hudson river; branches extend to Lake Ontario (Oswego Canal) and Lake Champlain (Champlain Canal).

New Zea′land (zē′lănd), abbr. **N.Z.**, island country, S Pacific Ocean, comprising chiefly North I., South I., Stewart I., and the Chatham Is.; a dominion of the British Commonwealth; ✻ Wellington; area 103,410 sq. m.; pop. 1,940,700.

Nga′mi ('ng·gä′mē) marshy depression, S Africa, in NW Bechuanaland Protectorate; once a lake.

N′Gela. See Florida Island.

Ni·ag′a·ra Falls (nī·ăg′ȧ·rȧ; -ăg′rȧ) **1** falls of the **Niagara River** (flowing from Lake Erie to Lake Ontario) on United States–Canada boundary in New York and Ontario; in two parts: American Fall, 167 ft. high and 1060 ft. wide at crest; Horseshoe, or Canadian, Fall, 158 ft. high and 3010 ft. wide. **2** city, W New York, on Niagara river at the falls; pop. 90,900. **3** city, Canada, in SE Ontario on Niagara river just below the falls; pop. 23,600.

Ni·cae′a (nī·sē′ȧ) **1** see Iznik. **2** see Nice.

Nic′a·ra′gua (nĭk′ȧ·rä′gwȧ; Brit. also -răg′ū·ȧ) country, Central America; a republic; ✻ Managua; area 57,143 sq. m.; pop. 1,048,600.

Nicaragua, Lake, lake, S Nicaragua; area over 3000 sq. m.

Nice, **1** (nēs), Ital. **Niz′za** (nēt′tsä), anc. **Ni·cae′a** (nī·sē′ȧ) seaport, SE France; pop. 211,200. **2** (nīs) = Nicaea. **3** (nīs) see Iznik.

Nicholas II Land. See Severnaya Zemlya.

Nic′o·bar Islands (nĭk′ō·bär) or **Nic′o·bars** (-bärz) group of islands, SE Bay of Bengal, SW of Burma; with Andaman Is., form **Andaman and Nicobar Islands** territory of the Republic of India.

Ni·cop′o·lis (nĭ·kŏp′ō·lĭs; nī-) **1** see Nikopol. **2** ancient city, NW Greece, in Epirus on Ambracian Gulf; founded 31 B.C. by Octavian.

Nic′o·si′a (nĭk′ō·sē′ȧ) town, ✻ of Cyprus; pop. 29,400.

Nictheroy. See Niterói.

Niedersachsen. See Saxony.

Niemen. See Neman.

Nieuw′poort (nē′ōō·pōrt) or **Nieu′port** (nē′ōō·pōrt; Fr. nyû′pôr′) town, NW Belgium, SW of Oostende; many battles.

Ni′ger (nī′jẽr) **1** river, W Africa, in French West Africa and Nigeria, flowing into the Gulf of Guinea; 2600 m. long. **2** region, E cen. French West Africa, N of Nigeria; formerly a colony, since 1946 a territory; ✻ Niamey; area 493,822 sq. m.; pop. 2,041,000.

Ni·ge′ri·a (nī·jēr′ĭ·ȧ) region, W Africa, bordering on Gulf of Guinea; British colony and protectorate; became a federation of British Commonwealth 1954; ✻ Lagos; area 338,593 sq. m.; pop. 19,110,900. — **Ni·ge′ri·an**, adj. & n.

Nihon. See Japan.

Ni·i·ga·ta (nē·ē·gä·tä) seaport, Japan, in N Honshu; pop. 204,500.

Ni·i·ta·ka (nē·ē·tä·kä), also **Mount Mor′ri·son** (mŏr′ĭ·s'n) mountain, S cen. Formosa; 13,599 ft. high.

Nij′me′gen (nī′mā′gĕn) or **Nim′we′gen** (Ger. nĭm′vā′gĕn) or **Ni′me′guen** (nī′mā′gĕn) commune, E Netherlands; pop. 106,500.

Nikaría. See Ikaría.

Nik′ko (nĭk′ō) village, Japan, in cen. Honshu in **Nikko Range**, E of Lake Chuzenji; shrines, temples.

Ni·ko·la′ev (nyĭ·kŭ·lȧ′yĕf), also **Ver′no·le′ninsk** (vĕr′nō·lĕn′ĭnsk) seaport, U.S.S.R., in S Ukraine at confluence of the Bug and Ingul rivers, 20 m. from Black Sea; pop. 167,100.

Ni·ko′pol (nyĭ·kô′pŭl·y′) city, U.S.S.R., in E cen. Ukraine on Dnieper river; pop. 57,800.

Nile (nīl), Arab. fr. Greek, **En Nîl** (ăn nēl′), modern Egyptian **El Bahr** (ăl bä′h′r) or **Bahr en Nîl**, river, Africa, flowing N from Lake Victoria in Uganda to the Mediterranean Sea in Egypt; in different sections called specifically: **Vic·to′ri·a** (vĭk·tō′rĭ·ȧ), or **Som′er·set** (sŭm′ẽr-sĕt; -sĭt), **Nile**, between Lake Victoria and Lake Albert; **Al′bert Nile** (ăl′bẽrt), between Lake Albert and Sudan (republic); **White Nile**, Arab. **Bahr el Ab′yad** (bä′h′r ăl ăb′yŏd), from Lake No, in the Sudan, to Khartoum, where it receives the **Blue Nile**, Arab. **Bahr el Az′raq** (ăz′rŏk), also, in Ethiopia, **Ab·bai′** (äb·bī′), a tributary 850 m. long rising in Ethiopia; total length from remotest headstream (the Kagera, rising in Tanganyika and flowing N to Lake Victoria) 4037 m. See Nilotic, in Vocab.

Niles (nīlz) city, NE Ohio, NNW of Youngstown; pop. 16,800.

Nil′gi·ri Hills or **Nil′gi·ris** (nĭl′gĭ·rĭ[z]) plateau, S India, in W Madras state; highest point Mt. Dodabetta, 8760 ft.

Nîmes (nēm), older **Nismes** (nēm) city, S France; pop. 91,700.

Nimrud. See Calah.

Nin′e·veh (nĭn′ē·vē), also **Ni′nus** (nī′nŭs) ancient city, capital of Assyria; its ruins in Iraq on the Tigris river opposite Mosul

Ning′po′ (nĭng′pō′), 1911–49 **Ning′hsien′** (nĭng′shĭ·ĕn′) city, E China, in NE Chekiang prov. just S of Hangchow Bay; pop. 218,800.

Ning′sia′ or **Ning′hsia′** (nĭng′shĭ·ä′) former province, N China, in Inner Mongolia; ✻ Yinchwan (called Ningsia before 1945); now merged with Kansu prov.

Ni′o·brar′a (nī′ō·brâr′ȧ) river, E Wyoming and N Nebraska, flowing E to Missouri river; 431 m. long.

Nip'i·gon, Lake (nĭp'ĭ·gŏn), also **Lake Nep'i·gon** (nĕp'-) lake, Canada, in SW Ontario; area 1870 sq. m.

Nip'is·sing, Lake (nĭp'ĭ·sĭng), also **Lake Nep'is·sing** (nĕp'-) lake, Canada, in SE Ontario NE of Georgian Bay; area 330 sq. m.

Nippon. See JAPAN.

Nip·pur' (nĭ·pŏŏr') ancient city of Sumer, S Babylonia.

Niš or **Nish** (nĭsh), anc. **Na·is'sus** (nā·ĭs'ŭs) or **Nis'sa** (nĭs'à) city, E Yugoslavia, in E Serbia on Nišava river; pop. 50,700.

Ni·shi·no·mi·ya (nē·shē·nô·mē·yä) city, Japan, in Honshu I. E of Kobe on Osaka Bay; pop. 108,900.

Nismes. See NÎMES.

Nistru. See DNIESTER.

Ni'te·rói (nē'tě·roi'), formerly **Nic'the·roy'** (nē'tě·roi') city, SE Brazil, * of Rio de Janeiro state, on Guanabara Bay; pop. 174,500.

Ni·u'a·fo'o (nē·ōō'ȧ·fō'ō) island, Pacific Ocean, in extreme N Tonga Archipelago.

Ni·u'e (nē·ōō'ā) or **Sav'age Island** (săv'ĭj) island, S cen. Pacific Ocean, E of Tonga Is.; a New Zealand dependency.

Ni'ver·nais' (nĭv'ẽr·nā') historical region of cen. France, E of the upper Loire; a province before the Revolution, * Nevers.

Nizam's Dominions. See HYDERABAD.

Nizhni Novgorod. See GORKI.

Nizh'ni Ta·gil' (nĭzh'nĭ tȧ·gĭl') city, Soviet Russia, Asia, on E slopes of Ural Mts.; pop. 159,900.

Nizza. See NICE.

No, Lake (nō) lake, S cen. Sudan (republic), where Bahr el Jebel and Bahr el Ghazal join to form the White Nile.

Noc, Big Bay de (bā' dě nŏk') inlet of Lake Michigan, on S shore of Upper Peninsula, Michigan; just W is **Little Bay de Noc.**

Noem'foor (nōōm'fōr) or **Num'for** (nōōm'fôr) island, West New Guinea, in Geelvink Bay; one of Schouten Is.

No·gal'es (nô·gäl'ĕs; Span. nô·gä'läs) **1** city, S Arizona, on Mexican border; pop. 6200. **2** town, NW Mexico, in Sonora state adjacent to Nogales, Arizona; pop. 13,900.

Nome (nōm) city, W Alaska, on S coast of Seward Penin. on Norton Sound W of **Cape Nome.**

Non'ni' (nŭn'nĭ') river, N Manchuria, flowing to the Sungari river; 660 m. long.

Noot'ka Sound (nōōt'kȧ; nōōt'-) inlet of Pacific Ocean, Canada, in W Vancouver I.

Nordenskjöld Sea. See LAPTEV SEA.

Nord'kyn', Cape (nōr'kün'; nōōr'-) cape, NE Norway, E of North Cape, in 71°8'N lat.

Nore, the (nōr) sandbank in mouth of Thames river, England, off Sheerness on Kent coast.

Nor'folk (nôr'fŭk; in U.S., also -fôk) **1** independent city and seaport, SE Virginia, on Elizabeth river just S of Hampton Roads; pop. 213,500. **2** county, E England, bordering on North Sea; * Norwich; area 2055 sq. m.; pop. 546,600.

Norge. See NORWAY.

Nor'i·cum (nŏr'ĭ·kŭm) ancient country, S cen. Europe, N of N end of Adriatic Sea; a Roman province.

Nor'man (nôr'mǎn) city, cen. Oklahoma; pop. 27,000.

Norman Coast. See MURMAN COAST.

Nor'man·dy (nôr'mǎn·dĭ), Fr. **Nor'man'die'** (nôr'män'dē') historical region, NW France, comprising Cotentin Penin. and region to the SE and E including the lower Seine; a province before Revolution, * Rouen. See NORMAN, in Vocab.

Nor'ris·town (nôr'ĭs·toun) borough, SE Pennsylvania; pop. 38,100.

Norr'kö'ping (nôr'chü'pĭng) seaport, SE Sweden, SW of Stockholm at head of a long inlet of **Norrköping Bay;** pop. 84,000.

North Ad'ams (ăd'ǎmz) city, W Massachusetts; pop. 21,600.

North Albanian Alps, mountain range in N Albania and S Yugoslavia (Montenegro); highest point 8715 ft.

North America, continent, Western Hemisphere, N of the equator; adjoins South America (Colombia) on the SE (Isthmus of Panama).

North·amp'ton (nôr·thăm[p]'tŭn; nôrth·hăm[p]'-) **1** city, W Massachusetts, on Connecticut river; pop. 29,100. **2** county borough, cen. England, * of Northamptonshire; pop. 104,400. **3** see NORTH-AMPTONSHIRE.

North·amp'ton·shire (-shĭr; -shẽr) or **Northampton,** also **Northants'** (nôr·thănts') county, cen. England; * Northampton; area 914 sq. m.; pop. 359,600.

North Arlington, borough, NE New Jersey; pop. 16,000.

North Bay, city, Canada, in SE Ontario on Lake Nipissing; pop. 21,000.

North Borneo, the northeast part of island of Borneo; a British colony; * Jesselton; area 29,500 sq. m.; pop. 302,000.

North Canadian, river, NW and cen. Oklahoma, flowing E and SE into Canadian river; 760 m. long.

North Cape, 1 cape, New Zealand, at N end of North I. **2** cape, N Norway, on Mageröy I.; northernmost point of Europe, 71°10'N lat.

North Car'o·li'na (kăr'ô·lī'nȧ), abbr. **N.C.,** or **N. Car.,** state, E United States, bordering on Atlantic Ocean; * Raleigh; area 52,712 sq. m.; pop. 4,061,900. — North Car'o·lin'i·an (-lĭn'ĭ·ǎn), adj. & n.

North Da·ko'ta (dȧ·kō'tȧ), abbr. **N. Dak.,** state, NW United States, bordering on Canada; * Bismarck; area 70,665 sq. m.; pop. 619,600.

North Downs (dounz) range of hills, S England, chiefly in Kent, extending from Strait of Dover on E into Surrey on W.

Northeastern Provinces. See MANCHURIA.

North-East New Guinea, the northeast section of island of New Guinea; part of Territory of New Guinea, administered by Australia.

Northeast Passage, a passage by sea between the Atlantic and Pacific oceans along N coast of Europe and Asia.

Northern Cir·cars' (sẽr·kärz'; sûr'kärz) historically, the four northern districts of Madras province (now state), India.

Northern Cook Islands. See MANIHIKI ISLANDS.

Northern Dvi·na' (dvē·nä'), Russ. **Se'ver·na·ya Dvi·na'** (syä'vyĭr·nä·yȧ dvyĭ·nä') river, N Soviet Russia, Europe, flowing NW into the White Sea; 1100 m. long including longest tributary.

Northern Ireland, northeast section of Ireland, a subdivision of United Kingdom of Great Britain and Northern Ireland; * Belfast; area 5238 sq. m.; pop. 1,369,600.

Northern Kingdom. See ISRAEL.

Northern Land. See SEVERNAYA ZEMLYA.

Northern Rhodesia, country, S cen. Africa; a British crown colony, federated 1953 with Southern Rhodesia and Nyasaland; * Lusaka; area 290,320 sq. m.; pop. 1,381,800.

Northern Territories, region, N Ghana; formerly a British protectorate, administered as part of the Gold Coast; * Tamale; area 30,486 sq. m.; pop. 717,300.

Northern Territory, territory, cen. and N Australia; * Darwin; area 523,620 sq. m.; pop. 15,300.

North Island, island, New Zealand; area 44,280 sq. m.; pop. 1,077,900.

North Land. See SEVERNAYA ZEMLYA.

North Little Rock, formerly **Ar·gen'ta** (är·jĕn'tȧ) city, cen. Arkansas, on Arkansas river opposite Little Rock; pop. 44,100.

North'olt (nôr'thōlt) airfield, S England, in Middlesex W of London.

North Ossetia, officially **North Ossetian Autonomous Soviet Socialist Republic,** autonomous republic, SE Soviet Russia, Europe, on N slopes of cen. Caucasus Mts.; * Dzaudzhikau; area 3500 sq. m.; pop. 450,000.

North Platte, 1 river, W United States, flowing from N Colorado through Wyoming into Nebraska to unite with South Platte river; 618 m. long. **2** city, SW cen. Nebraska, at confluence of North Platte and South Platte rivers; pop. 15,400.

North River, estuary of Hudson river between New York City (Manhattan I.) and New Jersey.

North Sea or **German Ocean,** arm of the Atlantic Ocean between the European continent and Great Britain; 600 m. long and 350 m. wide, mostly under 300 ft. in depth.

North Ton'a·wan'da (tŏn'ȧ·wŏn'dȧ) city, W New York, E of Niagara Falls; pop. 24,700.

North·um'ber·land (nôr·thŭm'bẽr·lǎnd) county, N England; * Newcastle (upon Tyne); area 2019 sq. m.; pop. 798,200.

North·um'bri·a (nôr·thŭm'brĭ·ȧ) Anglo-Saxon kingdom of Britain, between the Humber and the Firth of Forth. — **North·um'bri·an,** adj. & n.

North Vancouver, city, W Canada, in S British Columbia on Burrard Inlet across from Vancouver; pop. 20,000.

North-West Frontier Province, former province, W Pakistan, on Afghanistan frontier; * Peshawar; became 1955 part of new province of West Pakistan.

Northwest Passage, a passage by sea between the Atlantic and Pacific oceans along N coast of North America.

Northwest Territories, abbr. **N.W.T.,** region, N Canada, comprising the mainland area N of 60°N lat. between Yukon Territory and Hudson Bay, and the Canadian Arctic Islands; land area 1,258,217 sq. m.; pop. 12,500.

Nor'ton Sound (nôr't'n) inlet of Bering Sea, W Alaska, between Seward Penin. and mouths of the Yukon.

Nor'walk (nôr'wôk) town, SW Connecticut, on coast; pop. 49,500.

Nor'way (nôr'wā), Norw. **Nor'ge** (nôr'gě) country, NW Europe, occupying W part of Scandinavian Penin.; a kingdom; * Oslo; area 119,085 sq. m.; pop. 3,157,300. — **Nor·we'gian** (nôr·wē'jǎn), adj. & n. See NORSE, in Vocab.

Norwegian Sea, that part of Arctic Ocean between Greenland and Iceland on the W and Spitsbergen and Norway on the E.

Nor'wich (nôr'wĭch; Brit. nôr'ĭj, -ĭch) **1** town, SE Connecticut, on Shetucket river; pop. 23,400. **2** city and county borough, E England, * of Norfolk; pop. 121,200.

Nor'wood (nôr'wŏŏd) **1** town, E Massachusetts; pop. 16,600. **2** city, SW Ohio, NE of (and almost surrounded by) Cincinnati; pop. 35,000.

Not'ta·way (nŏt'ȧ·wā) river, Canada, in SW Quebec, flowing NW into James Bay; 400 m. long.

Not'ting·ham (nŏt'ĭng·ǎm; in U.S., commonly -hǎm) **1** see NOTTINGHAMSHIRE. **2** city and county borough, N cen. England, * of Nottinghamshire, on the Trent; pop. 306,000.

Not'ting·ham·shire (-ǎm·shĭr; -shẽr) or **Nottingham** or **Notts** (nŏts) county, N cen. England; * Nottingham; 844 sq. m.; pop. 841,100.

Nouas'seur' (nwä'sûr') village, Morocco, S of Casablanca; site of U.S. air base.

No'va I·gua·çu' (nō'vȧ ē·gwä·sōō') city, SE Brazil, in Rio de Janeiro state NW of Rio de Janeiro; pop. 58,700.

No·va'ra (nô·vä'rä) commune, NW Italy, W of Milan; pop. 72,100.

No'va Sco'tia (skō'shȧ), abbr. **N.S.,** peninsula, SE Canada, SE of mouth of St. Lawrence river; with Cape Breton I., constitutes a province of Canada, * Halifax, area 21,103 sq. m., pop. 694,700. — **No'va Sco'tian** (-shǎn), adj. & n.

No'va·ya Zem·lya' (nō'vȧ·yȧ zyĭm·lyä'), Eng. **New Land,** two islands, NE Soviet Russia, Europe, in Arctic Ocean; area 36,000 sq. m.

Nov'go·rod (nŏv'gô·rŏd) city, NW Soviet Russia, Europe, on the Volkhov just N of Lake Ilmen; in 11th–15th cents. * of the principality of Novgorod extending from Lithuania to the Ural Mts.

No'vi Sad (nō'vē säd'), Hung. **Új'vi'dék** (ōō'y·vĭ'dāk) city, NE Yugoslavia, on Danube river, chief town of the Voivodina; pop. 77,700.

Novo Kuznetsk. See STALINSK.

Novo Mariinsk. See ANADYR.

No'vo·si·birsk' (nō'vô·sĭ·bĭrsk'), formerly **No'vo·ni·ko·la'evsk** (nō'vŭ·nyĭ·kŭ·lä'yĕfsk) city, Soviet Russia, Asia, 390 m. E of Omsk on the Ob river; pop. 405,600.

Nu'bi·a (nū'bĭ·ȧ) region in Nile valley, NE Africa, N of about 16°N lat., in Anglo-Egyptian Sudan and Egypt. — **Nu'bi·an,** adj. & n.

Nubian Desert, desert area, NE Sudan (republic), E of the Nile.

Nu·e'ces (nū·ā'sĕs) river, S Texas, flowing S and SE into **Nueces Bay,** at head of Corpus Christi Bay; 338 m. long.

Nue'vo La·re'do (nwā'vō lä·rā'thō) city, E Mexico, in Tamaulipas state on the Rio Grande opposite Laredo, Texas; pop. 28,900.

Nuevo Le·ón' (lā·ôn') state, NE Mexico, mostly in the Sierra Madre Oriental; * Monterrey; area 25,134 sq. m.; pop. 743,300.

Nûgs'su·aq (nōōg'sōō·äk) peninsula, W Greenland, N of Disko I.

Nu'ku Hi'va (nōō'kōō hē'vȧ) island, largest of the Marquesas Is.

Numfor. See NOEMFOOR.

Nu·mid'i·a (nū·mĭd'ĭ·ȧ) ancient country, N Africa, its territory nearly that of modern Algeria. — **Nu·mid'i·an,** adj. & n.

Nun (nōōn) or **Nun Entrance**, a mouth of the Niger river, S Nigeria.
Nun·ea′ton (nŭ-nē′t'n) municipal borough, cen. England, in Warwickshire E of Birmingham; pop. 54,400.
Nu′ni·vak (nōō′nĭ-văk) island, W Alaska, in Bering Sea; 50 m. long.
Nürn′berg (nürn′bĕrk), Angl. **Nu′rem·berg** (nū′rĕm-bûrg) city, W Germany, in Bavaria on Pegnitz river; pop. 360,000.
Nut′ley (nŭt′lĭ) town, NE New Jersey, N of Newark; pop. 27,000.
Ny·as′a, Lake (nĭ-ăs′ȧ; nī-) lake, SE Africa, in Great Rift Valley in Nyasaland and Tanganyika; area 11,000 sq. m.
Ny·as′a·land′ (-lănd′) country, SE Africa, W and S of Lake Nyasa; a British protectorate, federated 1953 with Northern Rhodesia and Southern Rhodesia; ✻ Zomba; land area 37,374 sq. m.; pop. 1,680,000.
Nyí′regy·há′za (nyē′rĕd-y'-hä′zŏ) city, NE Hungary; pop. 56,100.
Ny′sa (nĭ′sä), Ger. **Neis′se** (nī′sĕ), Ger. also **Glat′zer Neisse** (glät′-sĕr) river, SW Poland, rising on the Czechoslovak border and flowing NE to join the Odra (Oder); 120 m. long.
Nysa Łużycka. See NEISSE river.

O

O·a′hu (ō-ä′hōō) island, Hawaiian Is.; chief island of the group, site of Honolulu; area 600 sq. m.
Oak′land (ōk′lănd) city, W California, on San Francisco Bay; pop. 384,600.
Oak Park, village, NE Illinois, W of Chicago; pop. 63,500.
Oak Ridge, city, E Tennessee, W of Knoxville; site of research and training laboratories in nuclear studies; pop. 30,200.
Oa·xa′ca (wä-hä′kä) **1** state, SE Mexico, bordering on Pacific Ocean; area 36,371 sq. m.; pop. 1,444,900. **2** in full **Oaxaca de Juá′rez** (thā hwä′räs) city, its ✻; pop. 29,300.
Ob (ŏb; Russ. ôp′y') river, W Soviet Russia, Asia, flowing NW and N into the Gulf of Ob; 2500 m. long, with the Irtysh 3200 m.
Ob, Gulf of, inlet of Arctic Ocean, NW Soviet Russia, Asia, E of N end of Ural Mts.; 550 m. long.
O′ber·am′mer·gau (ō′bĕr-äm′ĕr-gou) village, Germany, in Bavaria 42 m. SSW of Munich; famous for its Passion play.
O′ber·hau′sen (ō′bĕr-hou′zĕn) city, W Germany, in the Ruhr WNW of Essen; pop. 202,300.
O′ber·land′ (ō′bĕr-lănd′; Ger. -länt′), specifically, the **Ber′nese′ Oberland** (bûr′nēz′ [-nēs′] ō′bĕr-lănd′), Ger. **Ber′ner Oberland** (bĕr′nĕr ō′bĕr-länt′), also called the **Bernese Alps**, section of the Alps, S Switzerland, in Bern and Valais cantons, between the Lakes of Thun and Brienz on the N and the valley of the upper Rhone river on the S.
O′ce·an′i·a (ō′shē-ăn′ĭ-ȧ; -ā′nĭ-ȧ) or **O′ce·an′i·ca** (-ăn′ĭ-kȧ) **1** the lands of the central and S Pacific Ocean, including Micronesia, Melanesia, and Polynesia, and sometimes also Australia, New Zealand, and the Malay Archipelago. **2** see FRENCH OCEANIA. — **O′ce·an′i·an** (-ăn′ĭ-ăn; -ā′nĭ-ăn), adj. & n.
Ocean Island, island, W Pacific Ocean, 57 m. (52′) S of the equator, between the Gilbert Is. and island of Nauru; has deposits of phosphate.
Oc·mul′gee (ōk-mŭl′gē) river, cen. Georgia, flowing S and SE to join the Oconee and form the Altamaha river; 255 m. long.
O·co′nee (ō-kō′nē) river, cen. Georgia, flowing S and SE to join the Ocmulgee and form the Altamaha river; 250 m. long.
Ödenburg. See SOPRON.
O′den·se (ō′thĕn-sĕ) city, Denmark, in N Fyn I.; pop. 92,400.
O′der (ō′dĕr), Czech and Polish **O′dra** (ô′drä) river, cen. Europe, rising in the mountains of Silesia, Czechoslovakia, and flowing N to join the Neisse, thence N into the Baltic Sea; 563 m. long.
O·des′sa (ō-dĕs′ȧ) **1** city, W Texas; pop. 29,500. **2** seaport, U.S.S.R., in S Ukraine on **Odessa Bay** (inlet of Black Sea); pop. 604,200.
Oesel. See SAREMA.
Oe′ta (ē′tȧ) mountain chain, cen. Greece, on E spur of the Pindus Mts.; in ancient times on E border of Aetolia.
Of′fa·ly (ŏf′ȧ-lĭ) county, cen. Ireland, in Leinster prov.; ✻ Tullamore; area 771 sq. m.; pop. 52,600.
Of′fen·bach (ôf′ĕn-bäk) city, W Germany; pop. 75,500.
Ogasawara Islands. See BONIN ISLANDS.
Og′bo·mo′sho (ŏg′bō-mō′shō) city, W Nigeria; pop. 86,700.
Og′den (ŏg′dĕn) city, N Utah, N of Salt Lake City; pop. 57,100.
Og′dens·burg (ŏg′dĕnz-bûrg) city, N New York; pop. 16,200.
O·gee′chee (ō-gē′chē) river, E Georgia, flowing SE into Atlantic Ocean; 250 m. long.
O·hi′o (ō-hī′ō) **1** river, E United States, flowing from junction of Allegheny and Monongahela rivers in W Pennsylvania to the Mississippi river on border between Illinois and Kentucky; 981 m. long. **2**, abbr. (not official) **O.**, state, E United States, between Ohio river and Lake Erie; ✻ Columbus; area 41,222 sq. m., not including 3457 sq. m. of water in Lake Erie; pop. 7,946,600. — **O·hi′o·an** (-ō-ăn), adj. & n.
O′hře (ô′h'r-zhĕ), Ger. **E′ger** (ā′gĕr) river, S Germany and W Czechoslovakia, flowing into the Elbe river; 193 m. long.
Oil City, city, NW Pennsylvania, on Allegheny river; pop. 19,600.
Oil Rivers, the delta of the Niger river, S Nigeria; region governed 1890–93 by British as the **Oil Rivers Protectorate**.
Oi′mya·kon (oi′myȧ-kŭn) town, Soviet Russia, Asia, in SE Yakutsk Republic on the upper Indigirka river; Soviet weather station.
Oirot Autonomous Region. See GORNO-ALTAI AUTONOMOUS REGION.
Oise (wäz) river, N France, flowing SW into Seine river; 186 m. long.
O·ka′ (ŭ-kä′) **1** river, Soviet Russia, Asia, flowing N from the Sayan Mts. to the Angara river; 530 m. long. **2** river, cen. Soviet Russia, Europe, flowing to the Volga; 950 m. long.
O′ka·nog′an (ō′kȧ-nŏg′ăn), in Canada **O′ka·na′gan** (-nä′găn) river, United States and Canada, flowing from Okanagan Lake in British Columbia to Columbia river in Washington; 300 m. long.
O·ka·ya·ma (ō-kä-yä-mä) seaport, Japan, in W Honshu; pop. 140,600.
O′kee·cho′bee, Lake (ō′kē-chō′bē) lake, S cen. Florida; 40 m. long, 25 m. wide.
O′ke·fi·no′kee, or **O′ke·fe·no′kee, Swamp** (ō′kĕ-fĭ-nō′kē; local & colloq., -fĭ-nŏk′) swamp, SE Georgia and NE Florida; area 660 sq. m.
O·khotsk′, Sea of (ō-kŏtsk′) inlet of Pacific Ocean, Soviet Russia, Asia, W of Kamchatka Penin. and the Kuril Is.; area 582,000 sq. m.
O′ki·na′wa (ō′kĭ-nä′wȧ) **1** island group, cen. Ryukyu Is. **2** island in the group; scene of severe fighting March–June 1945.
O′kla·ho′ma (ō′klȧ-hō′mȧ), abbr. **Okla.**, state, S cen. United States, in plains region between Rocky Mts. and Mississippi river; ✻ Oklahoma City; area 69,919 sq. m.; pop. 2,233,400. — **O′kla·ho′man**, adj. & n.
Oklahoma City, city, ✻ of Oklahoma, on North Canadian river; pop. 243,500.
Ok·mul′gee (ōk-mŭl′gē) city, E cen. Oklahoma; pop. 18,300.
O′ko·vang′go (ō′kō-văng′gō), Port. **Cu·ban′go** (kōō-vănng′gōō) river, SW cen. Africa; rises in cen. Angola, flows S and then E and empties into **Okovanggo Basin**, a great marsh N of Lake Ngami in N Bechuanaland Protectorate; 1000 m. long.
Ö′land (û′lănd) island, Sweden, in Baltic Sea off SE coast; chief town Borgholm; area 519 sq. m.; pop. 26,300.
Old′bur·y (ōld′bĕr-ĭ; -brĭ) municipal borough, W cen. England, in Worcestershire W of Birmingham; pop. 53,900.
Old Cas·tile′ (kăs-tēl′), Span. **Cas·til′la la Vie′ja** (käs-tē′[l]yä lä vyĕ′hä) region, cen. Spain; chief city Burgos.
Old Delhi. See DELHI.
Ol′den·burg (ōl′dĕn-bûrg; Ger. ôl′dĕn-bŏŏrk) **1** former state, NW Germany, bordering on North Sea (Heligoland Bight) W of Weser river. **2** city, ✻ of the former state, on Hunte river; pop. 121,600.
Old Goa. See GOA.
Old′ham (ōl′dăm) county borough, NW England, in Lancashire NE of Manchester; pop. 121,200.
Old Harbour Bay or **Port′land Bight** (pōrt′lănd) gulf, British West Indies, in SE coast of Jamaica; site of United States naval and air base.
Old Kasaan National Monument. See KASAAN.
Old Point Com′fort (kŭm′fĕrt) point, SE Virginia, on N shore of Hampton Roads.
Old Sar′um (sâr′ŭm) extinct borough and city, England, in Wiltshire 2 m. N of Salisbury; only a few ruins.
O′le·an (ō′lē-ăn; ō′lē-ăn′) city, SW New York; pop. 22,900.
O·lek′ma (ŭ-lyĕk′mȧ; ŭ-lyĕk-mä′) river, E Soviet Russia, Asia, rising in Yablonoi Mts. and flowing N to the Lena river; 700 m. long.
O·le·nek′ (ŭ-lyĭ-nyôk′) river, Soviet Russia, Asia, flowing NE into Laptev Sea W of the Lena; 1325 m. long.
O′lé′ron′, Île d′ (ēl′ dō′lā′rôN′) island, W France, in E Bay of Biscay.
Ol′i·fants (ŏl′ĭ-fănts) river, Union of South Africa and Mozambique, flowing from the Transvaal into Limpopo river; 350 m. long.
Ol′ives, Mount of (ŏl′ĭvz), or **Ol′i·vet** (ŏl′ĭ-vĕt) ridge, Palestine, running N and S on E side of Jerusalem.
O′lo·mouc (ô′lô-mōts), Ger. **Ol′mütz** (ôl′müts) city, Czechoslovakia, in cen. Moravia on March (Morava) river near the Moravian Gap; pop. 58,600.
Olsz′tyn (ôlsh′tĭn), Ger. **Al′len·stein** (äl′ĕn-shtīn; Angl. ăl′ĕn-stīn) city, N Poland, on Łyna (Alle) river; pop. 57,200.
Olt (ôlt) or **A·lu′ta** (ä-lōō′tä), Ger. **Alt** (ält) river, S Romania, flowing S through the Transylvanian Alps to the Danube; 308 m. long.
Ol·te′ni·a (ŏl-tē′nĭ-ȧ; Romanian ôl-tĕ′nyä) or **Little Walachia**, region, S Romania, the W division of Walachia, W of the Olt river; formerly a province.
O·lym′pi·a (ō-lĭm′pĭ-ȧ) **1** city, ✻ of Washington, at S extremity of Puget Sound; pop. 15,800. **2** plain, S Greece, in NW Peloponnesus on Alpheus river; a center of religious worship of ancient Greece. See OLYMPIAN, OLYMPIC, in Vocab.
O·lym′pic Mountains (ō-lĭm′pĭk) mountain mass, NW Washington, in cen. Olympic Penin.; highest peak **Mount O·lym′pus** (-pŭs), 7954 ft.; feature of **Olympic National Park**, established 1938.
Olympic Peninsula, region, NW Washington, between Puget Sound and Pacific Ocean.
O·lym′pus (ō-lĭm′pŭs) mountain range, NE Greece, in Thessaly near Gulf of Salonica; in ancient Greek mythology, the home of the gods; highest peak 9570 ft. See OLYMPIAN, in Vocab.
O·lyn′thus (ō-lĭn′thŭs) ancient town, NE Greece, in Macedonia on the Chalcidice Penin.
O′ma·ha (ō′mȧ-hô; -hä) city, E Nebraska, on the Missouri river; pop. 251,100.
Omaha Beach, section of the coast of Normandy, NW France, on Bay of the Seine; one of landing places of American forces June 1944.
O·man′ (ō-măn′), officially **Mas′qat and Oman** (mŭs′kăt) country, SE Arabia, bordering on Arabian Sea; an independent sultanate; ✻ Masqat; area 82,000 sq. m.; pop. 500,000.
Oman, Gulf of, body of water between Oman and SE coast of Iran.
Ombai. See ALOR.
Om′dur·man′ (ŏm′dĕr-măn′) city, NE cen. Sudan (republic), on White Nile opposite Khartoum; pop. 114,500.
O·mo·lon′ (ŭ-mŭ-lôn′) river, Soviet Russia, Asia, flowing from the Kolyma Range N into Kolyma river; 600 m. long.
Omsk (ômsk) city, Soviet Russia, Asia, at confluence of Irtysh and Om rivers; pop. 280,700.
O·mu·ta (ō-mōō-tä) city, Japan, in NW Kyushu; pop. 166,400.
On. See HELIOPOLIS.
O·ne′ga (ō-nĕg′ȧ) lake, NW Soviet Russia, Europe, in S Karelo-Finnish S.S.R.; area 3764 sq. m.
O·nei′da (ō-nī′dȧ) city, cen. New York, SE of Oneida Lake; pop. 11,300.
Ong·jin (ông-jĭn) or **O·shin** (ō-shĭn) town, S Korea, near W coast on peninsula (**Ongjin Peninsula**) just S of 38th parallel.
On′on·da′ga Lake (ŏn′ŭ[n]-dô′gȧ) lake, cen. New York, NE of the Finger Lakes; 5 m. long.
On·tar′i·o (ŏn-târ′ĭ-ō) **1** city, SE California, W of San Bernardino; pop. 22,900. **2**, abbr. **Ont.**, province, E Canada, between Great Lakes and Hudson Bay; ✻ Toronto; land area 363,282 sq. m.; pop. 5,404,900. — **On·tar′i·an** (-ăn), adj. & n.
Ontario, Lake, lake, United States and Canada, in New York and Ontario; easternmost of the Great Lakes; area 7540 sq. m.
Oost·en′de (ōst-ĕn′dĕ), Fr. **Os′tende′** (ôs′tänd′), Eng. **Ost·end′** (ŏs-tĕnd′; ŏs′tĕnd) seaport, NW Belgium; pop. 50,300.
O·po′le (ō-pô′lĕ), Ger. **Op′peln** (ôp′ĕln) city, SW Poland, in Silesia on the Oder (Odra) river; pop. 53,000.
O·por′to (ō-pōr′tō), Port. **Pôr′to** (pōr′tōō) seaport, NW Portugal, on the Douro river 2 m. from its mouth; pop. 262,300.

O·ra'dea (ô·rä'dyä) or Oradea Ma're (mä'rĕ), Hung. Nagy'vá'rad (nŏd'y'·vä'rŏd), Ger. Gross'war·dein' (grōs'vär-dīn') city, NW Romania, in Transylvania near Hungarian border; pop. 80,900.

O·ran' (ô-rän'; ô·rän') seaport, NW Algeria; pop. 194,700.

Or'ange (ŏr'ĕnj; -ĭnj) 1 city, NE New Jersey, adjoining Newark; pop. 38,000. 2 city, E Texas, on Sabine river; pop. 21,200. 3 river, S Africa, flowing from the Drakensberg in Basutoland W to the Atlantic Ocean; 1300 m. long.

O'range' (ŏ'ränzh'; Angl. ŏr'ĕnj, -ĭnj) city, SE France, N of Avignon; once ✱ of principality; gave name to Dutch princes of Orange.

Or'ange·burg (ŏr'ĕnj·bûrg; -ĭnj-) city, South Carolina, 35 m. SE of Columbia; pop. 15,300.

Orange Free State, S. Afr. Du. O·ran'je Vry'staat (ô-rän'yĕ frē'stät) province, E cen. Union of South Africa, between Orange river and the Vaal; ✱ Bloemfontein; area 49,647 sq. m.; pop. 879,100.

Oraşul Stalin. See BRAŞOV.

Ordzhonikidze. See DZAUDZHIKAU.

Ö're·bro' (û'rĕ·broo') city, S cen. Sweden, on Lake Hjälmaren; pop. 65,700.

Or'e·gon (ŏr'ĕ·gŏn) 1 the Columbia river; — its earlier name. 2, abbr. Oreg. or Ore., state, W United States, bordering on Pacific Ocean; ✱ Salem; area 96,981 sq. m.; pop. 1,521,300. — Or'e·go'ni·an (-gō'nĭ·ăn; -gŏn'yăn), adj. & n.

Oregon Country, region, W North America, between Pacific coast and Rocky Mountains extending from N border of California to Alaska; — often so called c. 1818–46.

Oregon Trail, route to the Northwest used especially 1804–60, from Independence, Missouri, to Fort Vancouver on Columbia river; 2000 m. long.

O·rel' (ô-rĕl'; Russ. ŭ·ryôl') city, Soviet Russia, Europe, on Oka river; pop. 110,600.

Orenburg. See CHKALOV.

O·ren'se (ô-rĕn'sä) commune, NW Spain; pop. 52,800.

Ö're·sund' (û'rĕ·sŭn'), Eng. the Sound (sound) strait between Sjælland I., Denmark, and S Sweden, connecting Kattegat with Baltic Sea.

Orfani, Gulf of. See STRYMONIC GULF.

O·ril'lia (ô-rĭl'yà) town, Canada, in SE Ontario; pop. 13,900.

O'ri·no'co (ō'rĭ·nō'kō) river, Venezuela, flowing from mountains in S on Brazilian border to the Atlantic Ocean; has wide delta; 1700 m. long.

O·ris'ka·ny (ô-rĭs'kà·nĭ) village, cen. New York, on Mohawk river WNW of Utica; scene of battle Aug. 6, 1777.

O·ris'sa (ô-rĭs'à) state, E India, bordering on Bay of Bengal; ✱ Bhubaneswar; area 60,136 sq. m.; pop. 14,645,900. See BIHAR AND ORISSA.

O'ri·za'ba (ō'rĭ·zä'bä) 1 see CITLALTEPETL. 2 city, E Mexico, in Veracruz state; pop. 47,900.

Or'khon (ŏr'kŏn) river, N Outer Mongolia, flowing NE from N edge of the Gobi to the Selenga river; 450 m. long.

Ork'ney Islands (ôrk'nĭ) or Ork'neys (-nĭz) group of islands, N Scotland, off NE tip of mainland; constitute a county; ✱ Kirkwall; area 376 sq. m.; pop. 21,300.

Or·lan'do (ôr-lăn'dō) city, cen. Florida; pop. 52,400.

Or·lé·a'nais (ôr'lā·ä'nĕ') historical region of France; ✱ Orléans.

Or'le·ans' (ôr'lā'äⁿ') commune, N cen. France, on Loire river; pop. 70,200.

Or'ly' (ôr'lē') town, N France, SSE suburb of Paris; airport.

Or·moc' (ôr-môk') municipality, Philippine Is., on NW coast of Leyte I., on Ormoc Bay, an inlet of Camotes Sea; pop. 77,300.

Ormuz. See HORMUZ.

O·ron'tes (ô-rŏn'tēz) river, Syria and Turkey; rises in Lebanon in El Bika (Coele-Syria), flows N, and in S Turkey turns W to the Mediterranean Sea; 246 m. long.

Or'ping·ton (ôr'pĭng·tŭn) urban district, SE England, in Kent SE of London; pop. 63,300.

Or'te·gal', Cape (ôr'tā·gäl') cape, NW Spain.

O·ru'ro (ô-rōō'rō) city, W Bolivia, formerly a ✱ of Bolivia; pop. 50,000.

Or·vie'to (ôr-vyā'tō), anc. Vel·su'na (vĕl-sū'nà) or Vol·sin'i·i (vŏl-sĭn'ĭ-ī) town, cen. Italy, WNW of Terni; one of 12 cities of ancient Etruria.

O·sage' (ô-sāj'; ō'sāj) river, E Kansas and Missouri, flowing E into the Missouri river; 500 m. long. See OZARKS, LAKE OF THE.

O'sa·ka (ō'sä·kä) seaport, Japan, on S coast of Honshu on NE shore of Osaka Bay; pop. 1,559,300.

Osh'a·wa (ŏsh'à·wà; -wô; -wä) city, Canada, in SE Ontario on Lake Ontario; pop. 50,400.

Oshin. See ONGJIN.

Osh'kosh (ŏsh'kŏsh) city, E Wisconsin, on Lake Winnebago; pop. 41,100.

O'si·jek (ō'sĕ·yĕk) city, N Yugoslavia, in Slavonia (the E part of Croatia federated republic), on the Drava river; pop. 50,400.

Os'lo (ŏz'lō; ŏs'lō), formerly Chris'ti·an'i·a (krĭs'chĭ·ăn'ĭ·à; krĭs'tĭ-) city, ✱ of Norway, at N end of Oslo Fjord (inlet of the Skagerrak extending inland 80 m.); pop. 418,400.

Os'na·brück' (ŏs'nä·brük'; Angl. ŏz'nà·brŏŏk) city, W Germany, NE of Münster; pop. 108,900.

Os'sa (ŏs'à) mountain, NE Greece, in E Thessaly near the coast; 6490 ft. high. See also in Vocab.

Os·se'ti·a (ŏ-sē'shǐ·à; -shà) region, SE Soviet Russia, Europe, in cen. Caucasus; divided into North Ossetian Autonomous Soviet Republic and South Ossetian Autonomous Region.

Os'si·ning (ŏs'ĭ·nĭng), formerly Sing Sing (sĭng' sĭng') village, SE New York, on Hudson river overlooking Tappan Zee; site of Sing Sing state prison; pop. 16,100.

Ostende, Ostend. See OOSTENDE.

Österreich. See AUSTRIA.

Os'ti·a (ŏs'tĭ·à) village, Italy, at mouth of the Tiber river just E of the ancient town of the same name, the port of Rome.

Ostpreussen. See EAST PRUSSIA.

Ostrasia. See AUSTRASIA.

Ostrava, Moravská. See MORAVSKÁ OSTRAVA.

Os·we'go (ŏs·wē'gō; ŭ·swē'-; -gŭ) city, cen. New York, on Lake Ontario at mouth of Oswego river; pop. 22,600.

Oś·wię'cim (ōsh-vyĕn'tsēm), Ger. Ausch'witz (oush'vĭts) town, S Poland, W of Kraków; site of German concentration camp 1940–45.

Otaheite. See TAHITI.

O·ta·ru (ô-tä·rōō) city, Japan, on W coast of Hokkaido I.; pop. 164,900.

O·ti'ra Gorge (ô-tēr'à) cleft in Southern Alps, New Zealand; place where the mountains are crossed by Arthur's Pass (road) and Otira Tunnel (railroad, 5.25 m. long).

O'tran·to (ō'trän·tō; Angl. ô-trän'tō) town, S Italy, on coast at end of the heel of the boot; once an important seaport; destroyed 1480.

Otranto, Strait of, strait between SE Italy and W Albania.

Ot'ta·wa (ŏt'à·wà; -wô; -wä) 1 city, N Illinois, on Illinois river; pop. 17,000. 2 river, E Canada, in SE Ontario and S Quebec provs.; flows E into St. Lawrence river; 696 m. long. 3 originally By'town (bī'toun) ✱ of Canada, in SE Ontario on Ottawa river; pop. 222,100.

Ot'ter·burn (ŏt'ĕr·bûrn) parish, N England, in N cen. Northumberland; scene of battle 1388 in which English were defeated by the Scots.

Ot'to·man (ŏt'ô·măn), or Turkish, Empire, former sultanate in Europe, Asia, and Africa, including at greatest extent Syria, Egypt, Iraq, Barbary States, Balkan States, and parts of Russia and Hungary; ✱ Constantinople.

Ot·tum'wa (ô·tŭm'wà; ô-) city, SE Iowa, on Des Moines river; pop. 33,600.

Ouach'i·ta or Wash'i·ta (wŏsh'ĭ·tô) river, SW Arkansas and E Louisiana, flowing E and then SE and S to the Black river; 605 m. long.

Ouachita Mountains, group of mountains, W Arkansas and E Oklahoma, S of the Arkansas river.

Ouadaï. See WADAI.

Oubangui, Oubangui-Chari. See UBANGI, UBANGI-SHARI.

Ou'de·naar'de (ou'dĕ·när'dĕ), Fr. Au'de·narde' (ōd'närd') town, Belgium, in E Flanders on Schelde river; scene of French defeat 1708.

Oudh (oud) region, N India, in Uttar Pradesh (formerly United Provinces of Agra and Oudh); once a kingdom, ✱ Lucknow.

Ouessant, Île d'. See USHANT.

Ouse (ōōz) 1 or Great Ouse, river, cen. and E England, flowing into the Wash; 160 m. long. 2 river, NE England, flowing SE to unite with the Trent river and form the Humber; 57 m. long.

Outer Hebrides. See HEBRIDES.

Outer Mongolia. See MONGOLIAN PEOPLE'S REPUBLIC.

Ou'tre·mont (ōō'trĕ·mŏnt; Fr. ōō'trĕ·môⁿ') city, Canada, in S Quebec on Montreal I.; pop. 30,000.

O'ver·ijs'sel (ō'vĕr·ī'sĕl) province, E Netherlands, N of Gelderland and between IJsselmeer and the German border; ✱ Zwolle.

O·vie'do (ō·vyä'thō) city, NW Spain; once ✱ of Asturias; pop. 103,000.

Ow'en Falls (ō'ĕn; -ĭn) waterfall, E Africa, in Uganda in the Nile river just N of Lake Victoria; 65 ft. high.

Ow'ens (ō'ĕnz; -ĭnz) river, E California, formerly flowing into Owens Lake (now dry), now supplying water to city of Los Angeles by way of Los Angeles Aqueduct.

Ow'ens·bor'o (ō'ĕnz·bûr'ō; ō'ĭnz-) city, NW Kentucky, on Ohio river; pop. 33,700.

Ow'en Sound (ō'ĕn; -ĭn) city, Canada, in SE Ontario on Owen Sound (inlet of Georgian Bay); pop. 17,000.

Owen Stan'ley Range (stăn'lĭ) mountain range, E New Guinea; highest peak 13,240 ft.

O·wos'so (ô-wŏs'ō) city, S cen. Michigan, W of Flint; pop. 15,900.

O·wy'hee (ô-wī'[h]ē) river, SE Oregon, flowing NW into Snake river; 250 m. long.

Ox'ford (ŏks'fĕrd) 1 county in England: see OXFORDSHIRE. 2 Lat. Ox·o'ni·a (ŏk-sō'nĭ·à) city and county borough, cen. England, ✱ of Oxfordshire, on the Thames 52 m. WNW of London; site of Oxford Univ.; pop. 98,700. See OXONIAN, in Vocab.

Ox'ford·shire (-shĭr; -shĕr) or Oxford or Ox'on (ŏk'sŏn; -s'n) county, cen. England; ✱ Oxford; area 749 sq. m.; pop. 275,800.

Ox'nard (ŏks'närd) city, SW California, NW of Los Angeles near coast; pop. 21,600.

Oxus. See AMU DARYA.

Ox'y·rhyn'chus (ŏk'sĭ·rĭng'kŭs), Arab. El Bah'na·sa (ăl bä'h'·nǎ·sà) archaeological site, Egypt, N of El Minya and S of El Faiyûm.

O'zark Plateau (ō'zärk), also Ozark Mountains, tableland, W cen. United States, W of Mississippi river and N of Arkansas river, in SW Missouri, NW Arkansas, and NE Oklahoma; 1500–2500 ft. high.

O'zarks, Lake of the (ō'zärks) lake, cen. Missouri, formed by dam in Osage river; 130 m. long, shore line 1300 m.

P

Paar'de·berg (pär'dĕ·bĕrk; -bûrg) battlefield (1900), Union of South Africa, in W Orange Free State on the Modder river SE of Kimberley.

Pa'bia·ni'ce (pä'byä·nē'tsĕ) commune, cen. Poland; pop. 52,000.

Pa·chu'ca (pä-chōō'kä) city, cen. Mexico, ✱ of Hidalgo state; pop. 53,400.

Pa·cif'ic Islands, Trust Territory of the (pá·sĭf'ĭk) the Caroline Is. (with Palau Is.), Marshall Is., and Mariana Is. (except Guam); assigned to the U.S. 1947.

Pacific Ocean, body of water extending from the Arctic circle to the Antarctic Regions and from W North America and W South America to Australia and E Asia; area 70,000,000 sq. m.

Pac·to'lus (păk·tō'lŭs) river, Asia Minor, in ancient Lydia flowing to the Hermus (mod. Gediz) near Sardis; famed for its gold-bearing sands.

Pa'dang (pä'däng) seaport, Indonesia, in W Sumatra; pop. 52,100.

Pad'ding·ton (păd'ĭng·tŭn) metropolitan borough, NW London; pop. 125,300.

Pad'u·a (păd'ū·à), Ital. Pa'do·va (pä'dô·vä) commune, NE Italy, W of Venice; pop. 169,400.

Pa·du'cah (pà·dū'kà) city, W Kentucky, on Ohio river; pop. 32,800.

Padus. See Po.

Paes'tum (pĕs'tŭm; pēs'-), mod. Pe'sto (pĕs'tō) ancient Greek city, S Italy, in W Lucania on Gulf of Salerno (anc. Bay of Paestum).

Pa'go Pa'go (päng'ō päng'ō; pä'gō pä'gō; päng'gō päng'gō), formerly also Pang'o·pang'o, town, ✱ of American Samoa, on Tutuila I. on long sea inlet (Pago Pago Harbor); pop. 1600.

Pa·hang′ (pȧ·hŭng′; Angl. pȧ·hăng′) state, E Federation of Malaya; ✱ Kuala Lipis; area 13,873 sq. m.; pop. 250,200.
Pahsien. See CHUNGKING.
Painted Desert, region, N cen. Arizona, E of Colorado and Little Colorado rivers; erosion has exposed many-colored rock surfaces.
Pain′ter, Mount (pān′tẽr) mountain, South Australia, in Flinders Ranges; site of uranium deposit.
Pais′ley (pāz′lĭ) burgh, SW Scotland, ✱ of Renfrew co.; pop. 93,700.
Pak′i·stan′ (păk′ĭ·stăn′; pä′kĭ·stän′) country, S Asia comprising two areas in Indian subcontinent, one in NW bordering on Afghanistan and one in NE bordering on Bay of Bengal; created 1947; a dominion until 1956, when it became a republic within the British Commonwealth [NOTE: Pakistan is not politically a part of India; it is a completely separate political unit]; ✱ Karachi; area 364,737 sq. m.; pop. 75,842,200. — **Pak′i·stan′i** (-ĭ), adj. & n.
Pa·lat′i·nate (pȧ·lăt′ĭ·nāt), Ger. **Pfalz** (pfälts) two districts, SW Germany, once ruled by counts palatine of the Holy Roman Empire: **Rhen′ish** (rĕn′ĭsh), or **Rhine, Palatinate,** Ger. **Rhein′pfalz′** (rīn′pfälts′), on the Rhine E of Saarland, and **Upper Palatinate,** on the Danube around Regensburg.
Pa·lau′ (pä·lou′), formerly **Pe·lew′** (pē·lōō′) **1** group of islands, W Pacific Ocean, generally considered a part of the Caroline Is. (Western Carolines); 100 islands, total area 184 sq. m.; pop. 12,800. **2** see BABELTHUAP.
Pa·la′wan (pä·lä′wän) island, SW Philippine Is.; area 4550 sq. m.; pop. with adjacent islands 93,700.
Pa′lem·bang′ (pä′lĕm·bäng′) city, Indonesia, in SE Sumatra on the Moesi river; pop. 108,100.
Pa·len′que (pä·lāng′kā) village, S Mexico, in N Chiapas state; ruins of an ancient city nearby.
Pa·ler′mo (pȧ·lûr′mō; -lĕr′-) seaport, Italy, ✱ of Sicily; pop. 497,000.
Pal′es·tine (păl′ĕs·tīn), Lat. **Pal′aes·ti′na** (păl′ĕs·tī′nȧ) **1** in ancient times, region, SW Asia, bordering on Mediterranean Sea and extending E of Jordan river in Bashan and Gilead. **2** in modern times, country between Jordan river and Mediterranean Sea, site of ancient kingdoms of Israel and Judah; a British mandate 1923–48, since 1948 divided between Jewish republic of Israel and Arab territory: the region around Gaza administered by Egypt, the region just W of the Jordan part of kingdom of Jordan (formerly Transjordan) since 1950. — **Pal′es·tin′i·an** (păl′ĕs·tĭn′ĭ·ăn; -tĭn′yăn), adj.
Pal′i·sades′ (păl′ĭ·sādz′) line of cliffs, New York and New Jersey, on W bank of Hudson river; 15 m. long, 13 m. of it included in Palisades Interstate Park.
Palk Strait (pôk; pôlk) channel between N Ceylon and SE India.
Pal′ma or **Palma de Mal·lor′ca** (päl′mä thā mä·[]yôr′kä) seaport, Spain, ✱ of Balearic Is., on Majorca I.; pop. 136,800.
Palma, La. See LA PALMA.
Pal′mas, Cape (päl′mȧs) cape, Liberia, on extreme S coast.
Palmas, Las. See LAS PALMAS.
Palm Beach (päm) town, SE Florida, on offshore island opposite West Palm Beach; pop. 3900.
Palm′er Archipelago (päm′ẽr), formerly **Antarctic Archipelago,** island group between South America and Antarctica; includes islands off NW coast of Palmer Peninsula.
Palmer Peninsula, the tongue of land, Antarctica, extending toward the S end of South America.
Palm′er·ston (päm′ẽr·stŭn) island, cen. Pacific Ocean, an atoll 270 m. NW of Rarotonga (Cook Is.); belongs to New Zealand.
Pal·my′ra (păl·mī′rȧ), Bib. **Tad′mor** (tăd′môr) or **Ta′mar** (tā′mẽr) ancient city, Syria, at an oasis on N edge of Syrian Desert; now a small village.
Palmyra Island, island, Pacific Ocean, one of the Line Is.
Pal′o Al′to (păl′ō ăl′tō) **1** city, W California, NW of San José; pop. 25,500. **2** battlefield, S Texas, NE of Brownsville; battle 1846.
Pal′o·mar, Mount (păl′ō·mär) mountain, S California, NNE of San Diego; site of astronomical observatory having a 200-inch telescope.
Pa·louse′ (pȧ·lōōs′) or **Pe·louse′,** river, Idaho and Washington, flowing W and S into Snake river; 220 m. long.
Pa·mirs′ (pȧ·mĭrz′) region, cen. Asia, in Tadzhik S.S.R. and on borders of Sinkiang, Kashmir, and Afghanistan; a number of valleys over 12,000 ft. high, each surrounded by high mountains.
Pam′li·co (păm′lĭ·kō) river, E North Carolina, the estuary of the Tar river; flows into **Pamlico Sound,** a body of water between mainland and islands off coast.
Pam′pa (păm′pȧ) city, NW Texas, in the panhandle; pop. 16,600.
Pam·phyl′i·a (păm·fĭl′ĭ·ȧ; -fĭl′yȧ) ancient district, S Asia Minor.
Pam·plo′na (päm·plō′nä), formerly **Pam′pe·lu′na** (päm′pā·lōō′nä) city, N Spain; once ✱ of kingdom of Navarre; pop. 72,500.
Pan′a·ma (păn′ȧ·mô; -mä; păn′ȧ·mô′; -mä′), Span. **Pa′na·má′** (pä′nä·mä′) **1** country, Central America, bordering on Colombia, South America; before 1903 part of Colombia; now a republic; ✱ Panama City; area 28,576 sq. m.; pop. 801,300. **2** or **Panama City,** city, ✱ of republic of Panama; pop. 111,900. — **Pan′a·ma′ni·an** (păn′ȧ·mā′nĭ·ăn; -mä′-), adj. & n.
Panama, Isthmus of, formerly **Isthmus of Dar′i·en′** (dâr′ĭ·ĕn′; dâr′ĭ·ĕn) the neck of land, S Central America, linking North America with South America; comprises the republic of Panama.
Panama Canal, ship canal, Central America, connecting Atlantic Ocean (Caribbean Sea) with Pacific Ocean at the Isthmus of Panama, in a band of territory (the Canal Zone) 10 m. wide, leased to the United States by the republic of Panama; completed 1914; length 51 m.
Panama Canal Zone. = CANAL ZONE.
Panama City, 1 city, NW Florida, on Gulf of Mexico; pop. 25,800. **2** see PANAMA city.
Pan′a·mint Mountains (păn′ȧ·mĭnt) mountain range, E California, W of Death Valley; highest point Telescope Peak, 11,045 ft.
Pa·nay′ (pä·nī′) island, Philippine Is., one of the Visayan Is.; chief town Iloilo; area 4446 sq. m.; pop. 1,310,200.
Pan·gim′ or **Pan·jim′** (päɴ·zhēɴ′) or **New Go′a** (gō′ȧ) town, ✱ of Portuguese India and of Goa territory, on Arabian Sea at mouth of Mandavi river; pop. 14,200.
Pangopango. See PAGO PAGO.
Pa′ni·pat′ (pä′nē·pŭt′) town, NW India, in Punjab state near Jumna river; scene of three great battles: 1526, 1556, and 1761.
Panj·nad′ (pŭnj·näd′) river, W Pakistan, the combined streams of the Chenab and Sutlej, flowing into the Indus; 50 m. long.
Pan·mun·jom (pän·mōōn·jŭm) village, S Korea, 6 m. SE of Kaesong; truce ending Korean fighting signed here July 27, 1953.
Pan·no′ni·a (pă·nō′nĭ·ȧ; -nōn′yȧ) Roman province, Europe, including territory now mostly in Hungary and Yugoslavia.
Pan′tel·le·ri′a (pän′tăl·lā·rē′ä) island, Italy, in Mediterranean Sea E of NE Tunisia.
Pá′nu·co (pä′nōō·kō) river, cen. Mexico, rising in Hidalgo state and flowing NE into Gulf of Mexico; 240 m. long.
Pao, El. See EL PAO.
Pão de A·çú′car (pouɴ′ thĕ [ē·]ȧ·sōō′kẽr), Eng. **Sug′ar·loaf′ Mountain** (shŏŏg′ẽr·lōf′) peak, Brazil, in city of Rio de Janeiro on W side of entrance to Guanabara Bay.
Paoning. See LANGCHUNG.
Pao′ting′ (bou′dĭng′), formerly (1913–49) **Tsing′yuan′** (chĭng′yü·än′) city, NE China, ✱ of Hopeh prov.; pop. 100,000.
Papal States. See STATES OF THE CHURCH.
Pa′pe·e′te (pä′pā·ā′tā; popularly pȧ·pē′tē) seaport, ✱ of Society Is. and of French Oceania, on island of Tahiti; pop. 11,600.
Paph′la·go′ni·a (păf′lȧ·gō′nĭ·ȧ; -gōn′yȧ) ancient country, N Asia Minor, on the Black Sea.
Pa′phos (pā′fŏs) town, SW coast of Cyprus; the old town seat of worship of Aphrodite (Cypris). See PAPHIAN in Vocab.
Pap′u·a (păp′ū·ȧ) **1** New Guinea; — the name for the whole island used in some older sources. **2** now, usually, the southeast section of the island. — **Pap′u·an,** adj. & n.
Papua, Territory of, the southeast section of the island of New Guinea with adjacent islands (Trobriand, D'Entrecasteaux, etc.); territory, to Australia; since World War II administered jointly with Territory of New Guinea, ✱ Port Moresby; area 90,540 sq. m.; pop. 303,200.
Papua and New Guinea, the joint territories of Papua and New Guinea, administered as a unit since World War II.
Pa·rá′ (pȧ·rä′) **1** river, Brazil, the S channel in delta of the Amazon; 200 m. long, 40 m. wide at mouth. **2** state, Brazil, S of the Amazon and including Pará river; ✱ Belém; area 470,752 sq. m.; pop. 1,142,800. **3** see BELÉM.
Par′a·guay (păr′ȧ·gwī; -gwā) **1** river, South America, flowing from SW Brazil in Plateau of Mato Grosso to the Paraná river at SW corner of Paraguay; 1500 m. long. **2** country, South America, on both sides of Paraguay river; republic; ✱ Asunción; area 157,000 sq. m.; pop. 1,405,600. — **Par′a·guay′an** (păr′ȧ·gwī′ăn; -gwā′ăn) adj. & n.
Pa′ra·í′ba (pä′rȧ·ē′vȧ) **1** or **Paraíba do Nor′te** (thōō nôr′tē) river, E Brazil, flowing E to Atlantic Ocean in the bulge on E coast; 240 m. long. **2** or **Paraíba do Sul** (sōōl′) river, SE Brazil, flowing NE into Atlantic Ocean; 660 m. long. **3** state, E Brazil, bordering on Atlantic Ocean in region of the Paraíba do Norte; ✱ João Pessoa; area 21,591 sq. m.; pop. 1,730,800. **4** see JOÃO PESSOA.
Par′a·mar′i·bo (păr′ȧ·măr′ĭ·bō) seaport, ✱ of Surinam; pop. 56,200.
Pa′ra·ná′ (Span. pä′rä·nä′; Port. pȧ′rȧ·nä′) **1** in upper course **Al′to Paraná** (Span. äl′tō; Port. -tōō) river, South America, flowing from junction of Rio Grande and Paranaíba rivers in SW Brazil to the Río de la Plata in Argentina; 2040 m. long. **2** state, S Brazil, in region E of Paraná river (Alto Paraná); ✱ Curitiba; area 82,741 sq. m.; pop. 2,149,500. **3** city, NE Argentina, on Paraná river; pop. 76,000.
Pa′ra·na·í′ba (pȧ′rȧ·nȧ·ē′vȧ), older spelling **Pa′ra·na·hi′ba** (-nȧ·ē′vȧ) river, Brazil, flowing W and SW to unite with the Rio Grande and form Paraná river; 530 m. long.
Pa′ria, Gulf of (pä′ryä) inlet of Atlantic Ocean between W coast of Trinidad and the Venezuelan mainland; enclosed on N by **Paria Peninsula,** extending E from NE coast of Venezuela.
Pa·rí′cu·tin (pä·rē′kōō·tēn) volcano, Mexico, in Michoacán state; started Feb. 20, 1943, in a cornfield.
Parida, La. See BOLÍVAR.
Par′is (păr′ĭs) **1** (Fr. pȧ′rē′), anc. **Lu·te′ti·a** (lū·tē′shĭ·ȧ; -shȧ) city, ✱ of France, on Seine river 107 m. from the sea; pop. 2,725,400. **2** city, NE Texas; pop. 21,600.
Par′kers·burg (pär′kẽrz·bûrg) city, W West Virginia; pop. 29,700.
Park Range (pärk) range of Rocky Mts., N Colorado; highest peak Mt. Lincoln, 14,284 ft.
Park Ridge, city, NE Illinois, N of Chicago; pop. 16,600.
Par′ma (pär′mȧ) **1** city, N Ohio, S of Cleveland; pop. 28,900. **2** commune, N Italy, in Emilia; pop. 123,300.
Par′na·í′ba (pär′nȧ·ē′vȧ), formerly **Par′na·hy′ba** (-ē′vȧ) river, NE Brazil; flows NE, forming boundary between Piauí and Maranhão states, and into Atlantic Ocean; 900 m. long.
Par·nas′sus (pär·năs′ŭs), Mod. Gr. **Par·nas·sós′** (pär·nä·sôs′) mountain, cen. Greece, N of Gulf of Corinth. See also in Vocab.
Par′os (pâr′ŏs; pä′rŏs), Mod. Gr. **Pá′ros** (pä′rôs) island, Greece, in cen. Cyclades; a mountain over 2500 ft. high. See PARIAN in Vocab.
Par′ris Island (păr′ĭs) island, South Carolina, one of the Sea Is.; Marine Corps training station.
Par′ry Islands (păr′ĭ) group of islands, N Canada, N of Victoria I.
Partenkirchen. See GARMISCH-PARTENKIRCHEN.
Par′thi·a (pär′thĭ·ȧ) ancient country, W Asia, in what is now NE Iran; formed a province of the Assyrian and Persian empires and, later, of Alexander's empire; new Parthian kingdom founded c. 250 B.C., at its height at beginning of 1st cent. B.C. — **Par′thi·an,** adj. & n.
Pas, The. See THE PAS.
Pas′a·de′na (păs′ȧ·dē′nȧ) **1** city, SW California, NE of Los Angeles; pop. 104,600. **2** town, SE Texas, E of Houston; pop. 22,500.
Pa·sar′ga·dae (pȧ·sär′gȧ·dē) city of ancient Persia; ✱ of Cyrus the Great; its ruins in the plain N of Lake Niriz.
Pa′say. See RIZAL.
Pasco, Cerro de. See CERRO DE PASCO.
Pascua. See EASTER ISLAND.
Pas de Calais. See DOVER, STRAIT OF.
Pas·sa′ic (pă·sā′ĭk) **1** river, NE New Jersey, flowing into Newark Bay; at Paterson are the Great Falls of the Passaic, 70 ft. high; river 100 m. long. **2** city, N New Jersey, on Passaic river; pop. 57,700.

Pas'sa·ma·quod'dy Bay (păs'ȧ·mȧ·kwŏd'ĭ) inlet of Bay of Fundy between SW New Brunswick, Canada, and SE Maine, at mouth of St. Croix river.

Pas'se·ro, Cape (päs'sā·rō) cape, Italy, at SE point of Sicily.

Pas·ta'za (päs·tä'sä) river, Ecuador and Peru, flowing S into the Marañón; 400 m. long.

Pas'to (päs'tō) volcano, SW Colombia, near Ecuadorian border; 13,900 ft. high.

Pat'a·go'nia (păt'ȧ·gōn'yȧ; -gō'nĭ·ȧ) region, South America, in Chile and Argentina, a barren tableland between the Andes and the Atlantic Ocean. — **Pat'a·go'nian**, adj. & n.

Pa'tan (pä'tăn) town, Nepal, adjoining Katmandu; pop. 104,900.

Pa·taps'co (pȧ·tăps'kō) river, N cen. Maryland, flowing SE into Chesapeake Bay; 80 m. long.

Pat'er·son (păt'ẽr·s'n) city, N New Jersey, on the Passaic river; pop. 139,300.

Pa'ti·a'la (pŭ'tĭ·ä'lȧ) **1** former state, NW India; became 1948 chief unit of the **Patiala and East Punjab States,** or **Pep'su** (pĕp'sōō), merged 1956 with Punjab state. **2** city, ✷ of former state, 70 m. SSW of Simla; pop. 69,900.

Pat'mos (păt'mŏs), Ital. **Pat'mo** (pät'mō) island, Greece, one of the Dodecanese.

Pat'na (pŭt'nȧ) city, NE India, ✷ of Bihar state, on Ganges river; pop. 175,700.

Pa'tos, La·go'a dos (lȧ·gō'ȧ thōōsh pä'tōōs) lagoon, S Brazil, in Rio Grande do Sul state; 124 m. long, 37 m. wide.

Pa·tras' (pȧ·träs'; pä'trȧs), Mod. Gr. **Pa'trai** (pä'trä) seaport, Greece, in NW Peloponnesus on Gulf of Patras; pop. 88,400.

Patras, Gulf of, or **Gulf of Cal'y·don** (kăl'ĭ·dŏn) inlet of Ionian Sea, W Greece, N of the Peloponnesus and W of the Gulf of Corinth.

Patrimony of Saint Peter. See ROME, DUCHY OF.

Patuxent River (pȧ·tŭk's'nt) government reservation, Maryland, at mouth of Patuxent river; naval air station, established 1943–44.

Pau (pō) commune, SW France, on the Gave de Pau (mountain stream); once ✷ of Béarn; pop. 46,200.

Paumotu Archipelago. See TUAMOTU ARCHIPELAGO.

Pa·vi'a (pä·vē'ä) commune, N Italy, S of Milan; pop. 65,700.

Paw·tuck'et (pô·tŭk'ĕt; -ĭt) city, N Rhode Island, NE of Providence, on Blackstone river at **Pawtucket Falls;** pop. 81,400.

Paz, La. See LA PAZ.

Pea'bod'y (pē'bŏd'ĭ; -bŭd·ĭ) city, NE Massachusetts; SE of Lowell; pop. 22,600.

Peace (pēs) river, Canada, flowing to Slave river just N of W end of Lake Athabaska; with headstream (the Finlay river) 1195 m. long.

Pearl (pûrl) **1** river, cen. and S cen. Mississippi; flows SW, then S into the Gulf of Mexico; 490 m. long. **2** or **Can·ton'** (kăn·tŏn'; kăn'tŏn), Chin. **Chu-kiang** (jōō'jĭ·äng') river, SE China, in Si delta; flows from city of Canton to South China Sea.

Pearl Harbor, inlet, Hawaii, on S coast of Oahu 6 m. W of Honolulu; a U.S. naval base; attacked by Japanese Dec. 7, 1941.

Pea'ry Land (pēr'ĭ), also **Pea'ry·land',** region of N Greenland, forming a mountainous peninsula.

Pe·chen'ga (pĕ·chĕng'gȧ), formerly **Pet'sa·mo** (pĕt'sȧ·mō) town, NW Soviet Russia, Europe, on inlet of Barents Sea near Norwegian border, in district (Petsamo Territory) which belonged to Finland 1920–44.

Pe·cho'ra (pĕ·chô'rä) river, NE Soviet Russia, Europe; rises in Ural Mts., flows N into Pechora Bay, inlet of Barents Sea; 1125 m. long.

Pe'cos (pā'kŭs) or **Ri'o Pecos** (rē'ō) river, E New Mexico and W Texas, flowing SE into the Rio Grande; 735 m. long.

Pécs (pāch), Ger. **Fünf'kir'chen** (fünf'kĭr'ḱĕn) municipality, S Hungary, W of the Danube; pop. 70,500.

Pe'dro Mi·guel' (pā'thrō mē·gĕl'; Angl. locally pē'tẽr mĭ·gĭl') town, Panama Canal Zone, at double locks in Panama Canal.

Pee'bles (pē'b'lz) or **Pee'bles·shire** (-shĭr; -shẽr) or **Tweed'dale'** (twēd'dāl') county, SE Scotland, including upper course of the river Tweed; ✷ Peebles; area 347 sq. m.; pop. 15,200.

Pee Dee (pē' dē') river, North Carolina and South Carolina, flowing SE into Winyah Bay; 233 m. long.

Peeks'kill (pēks'kĭl) city, SE New York, on Hudson river; pop. 17,700.

Peel (pēl) river, NW Canada; rises in W Yukon Territory, flows E and then N into Mackenzie river; 365 m. long.

Pee'ne·mün'de (pā'nĕ·mün'dĕ) village, NE Germany, on inlet at mouth of Peene river; in World War II became center for development and manufacture of robot bombs; destroyed by Russians 1945 but later reactivated.

Peiping. See PEKING.

Pei'pus (pī'pŏŏs), Estonian **Peip'si** (pāp'sĭ), Russ. **Chud'sko·e** (chōōt'skŭ·yĕ) lake in E Estonia and NW Soviet Russia; area 1357 sq. m.

Pei·rae'us. See PIRAEUS.

Pe·ka'long'an (pĕ·kä'lông'än) city, Indonesia, in cen. Java on N coast; pop. 66,000.

Pe'kin (pē'kĭn) city, cen. Illinois, S of Peoria; pop. 21,900.

Pe'king' (pē'kĭng') or **Pei'ping'** (bā'pĭng') city, NE China, ✷ of Hopeh prov. and ✷ of China before 1928 and after 1949; pop. 1,688,000.

Pe·lée', Mount (pĕ·lā') volcano, French West Indies, in N Martinique; erupted 1902.

Pel'e·liu (pĕl'ĕ·lū; popularly pĕl'ĕ·lē'ōō) island, Pacific Ocean, at S end of Palau Is.; captured by American forces October 1944.

Pelew. See PALAU.

Pe'li·on (pē'lĭ·ŏn), Mod. Gr. **Pi'li·on** (pē'lyŏn) mountain, NE Greece, in E Thessaly; in Greek legend, home of the centaurs. See also in Vocab.

Pel'la (pĕl'ȧ) ancient city, NE Greece; ancient ✷ of Macedonia.

Pel'ly (pĕl'ĭ) river, NW Canada, in Yukon Territory, flowing W to the Yukon river; 330 m. long.

Pel'o·pon·ne'sus (pĕl'ō·pŏ·nē'sŭs) or **Pel'o·pon·ne'sos** (pĕl'ō·pŏ·nē'sŏs), also (pĕl'ō·pŏ·nēs'; -nēz'), since 12th cent. often called **Mo·re'a** (mō·rē'ä) peninsula forming S part of the mainland of Greece. — **Pel'o·pon·ne'sian** (-nē'zhăn; -shăn), adj. & n.

Pe·lo'tas (pĕ·lō'tȧs) city, S Brazil, in SE Rio Grande do Sul state at S end of Lagoa dos Patos; pop. 79,600.

Pelouse. See PALOUSE.

Pem'ba (pĕm'bȧ) island in Indian Ocean, off NE coast of Tanganyika N of island of Zanzibar; included in the Zanzibar protectorate.

Pem'broke (pĕm'brŏk; -brŭk; in Great Britain usually -brŏŏk) **1** town, Canada, in SE Ontario on Allumette Lake; pop. 15,400. **2** county in Wales: see PEMBROKESHIRE.

Pem'broke·shire (-shĭr; -shẽr) or **Pembroke,** county, SW Wales; ✷ Haverfordwest; area 614 sq. m.; pop. 90,900.

Pe·nang' (pē·năng') **1** island, Federation of Malaya, in N end of Strait of Malacca; before 1948 one of the Straits Settlements; ✷ George Town; area 108 sq. m. **2** see GEORGE TOWN.

Peneus. See SALAMBRIA.

Peng'hu' (pŭng'hōō') **1** see PESCADORES. **2** island, largest of the Pescadores group.

Pen'ki' (pŭn'chē') or **Pen'hsi'hu'** (bŭn'shē'hōō') city, S Manchuria, S of Mukden; pop. (1953 est.) 500,000.

Pen'nine Alps (pĕn'īn) section of Alps, on border between Switzerland and Italy, NE of Graian Alps; highest point Monte Rosa, 15,217 ft.

Pennine Chain, mountains, N England, extending S from Scottish border to Derbyshire and Staffordshire; highest point 2930 ft.

Penn'syl·va'nia (pĕn'sĭl·vān'yȧ; -vā'nĭ·ȧ), abbr. **Pa.** or **Penna.,** state, E United States, between Lake Erie and Delaware river; ✷ Harrisburg; 45,333 sq. m.; pop. 10,498,000. — **Penn'syl·va'nian,** adj. & n.

Pe·nob'scot (pē·nŏb'skŏt; -skŭt) river, cen. Maine, flowing S into **Penobscot Bay,** inlet of Atlantic Ocean; 101 m. long.

Penrhyn. See TONGAREVA.

Pen'sa·co'la (pĕn'sȧ·kō'lȧ) city, NW Florida, on **Pensacola Bay,** inlet of Gulf of Mexico; pop. 43,500.

Pen·tap'o·lis (pĕn·tăp'ō·lĭs) any one of several groups of five ancient cities, in Italy, Asia Minor, and N Africa (Cyrenaica).

Pen·tel'i·kon (pĕn·tĕl'ĭ·kŏn), Mod. Gr. **Pen'de·li·kón'** (pân'dâ·lyĕ·kón') or **Pen·dé'li** (pân·dä'lyē) mountain, E Greece, in Attica NE of Athens; source of marble.

Pen·tic'ton (pĕn·tĭk'tŭn) city, Canada, in S British Columbia on Okanagan Lake; pop. 11,900.

Pen'za (pĕn'zä) city, Soviet Russia, Europe, on Sura river; pop. 157,100.

Pen·zance' (pĕn·zăns'; locally pĕn·zăns') municipal borough, SW England, in Cornwall on English Channel; pop. 20,600.

Pe·o'ri·a (pē·ō'rĭ·ȧ) city, NW cen. Illinois; pop. 111,900.

Pepsu. See PATIALA.

Pe·rae'a or **Pe·re'a** (pē·rē'ä) region in ancient Palestine (in New Testament times), E of Jordan river.

Pe'rak (pā'räk; pär'ȧ; pĕr'ȧ) state, W Federation of Malaya, on Strait of Malacca; ✷ Kuala Kangsar; area 7890 sq. m.; pop. 953,900.

Perche (pĕrsh) region, N France, in old province of Maine.

Peremyshl. See PRZEMYŚL.

Per'ga·mum (pûr'gȧ·mŭm) or **Per'ga·mus** (-mŭs) **1** ancient Greek kingdom, at its height 263–133 B.C., covering most of W Asia Minor. **2** mod. **Ber'ga·ma'** (bĕr'gä·mä') ancient city, ✷ of the kingdom of Pergamum and for a time ✷ of the Roman province of Asia.

Pé'ri'gord' (pā'rē'gôr') old division of N Guienne, SW France; ✷ Périgueux.

Pé'ri'gueux' (pā'rē'gŏŏ') commune, SW cen. France; pop. 40,900.

Pe·rim' (pĕ·rĭm') island in Bab el Mandeb Strait at entrance to Red Sea; belongs to Aden colony.

Per'lis (pûr'lĭs) state, N Federation of Malaya, bordering on Thailand and Andaman Sea; ✷ Kangar; area 310 sq. m.; pop. 70,500.

Perm. See MOLOTOV.

Per'nam·bu'co (pûr'năm·bū'kō; -bōō'-) **1** state, E Brazil, bordering on Atlantic; ✷ Recife; 38,315 sq. m.; pop. 3,430,600. **2** see RECIFE.

Pé'ronne' (pā'rŏn') town, N France, NE of Amiens on Somme river; besieged 1536; captured 1815 and 1871 and again 1914.

Per'pi'gnan' (pĕr'pē'nyän') city, S France, near Mediterranean Sea; pop. 75,000.

Per·sep'o·lis (pĕr·sĕp'ō·lĭs) ancient ✷ of Persia, residence of the Achaemenid kings; its ruins lie 30 m. NE of Shiraz in SW cen. Iran.

Per'sia (pûr'zhȧ; -shä) Iran; — its name before official change 1935; still often used, especially in British sources and in references to the ancient kingdom and empire. — **Per'sian,** adj. & n.

Persian Gulf, arm of the Arabian Sea, between Iran and the peninsula of Arabia.

Persis. See FARS.

Perth (pûrth) **1** city, ✷ of Western Australia, in SW part on Swan river 10 m. from its mouth; pop. with suburbs 272,600. **2** or **Perth'shire** (pûrth'shĭr; -shẽr) county, cen. Scotland, between the Grampians and the Firth of Tay; ✷ Perth; area 2493 sq. m.; pop. 128,100. **3** city, Scotland, ✷ of Perth co., on the river Tay; pop. 40,500.

Perth Am'boy (pûrth ăm'boi) city, cen. New Jersey, on Raritan Bay at mouth of Raritan river; pop. 41,300.

Pe·ru' (pē·rōō'; pā·rōō') country, W South America, bordering on Pacific Ocean; republic; ✷ Lima; area 482,257 sq. m.; pop. 7,023,100. — **Pe·ru'vi·an** (-vĭ·ȧn), adj. & n.

Pe·ru'gia (pā·rōō'jä; Angl. pĕ·rōō'jȧ, -jĭ·ȧ) commune, cen. Italy, between Tiber river and Lake Trasimeno; in ancient times one of 12 cities of Etruria; pop. 93,900.

Perugia, Lake. See TRASIMENO, LAKE.

Pe'sa·ro (pā'zä·rō) seaport, cen. Italy, on Adriatic Sea; pop. 52,500.

Pes'ca·do'res (pĕs'kȧ·dō'rēz; -rĕs), Chin. **Peng'hu'** (pŭng'hōō') island group off China, near Formosa; to Japan 1895–1945. See FORMOSA.

Pe·sca'ra (pās·kä'rä) seaport, cen. Italy, on Adriatic Sea; pop. 65,300.

Pe·sha'war (pĕ·shä'wẽr; pĕ·shour') city, W Pakistan, E of Khyber Pass; pop. 131,000.

Pe·sha'wa·run' (pä·shä'vä·rōōn') ancient city, SW Afghanistan, in what is now a desert area; extensive ruins; discovered 1949.

Pesto. See PAESTUM.

Pest'szent·er'zsé·bet (pässht'sänt·är'zhä·bĕt) town, Hungary, near Budapest; pop. 71,200.

Pe'ter·bor'ough (pē'tẽr·bûr'ō; Brit. usu. -bŭ·rŭ, -brŭ) **1** city, Canada, in SE Ontario N of Rice Lake; pop. 42,700. **2** municipal borough, cen. England, ✷ of Soke of Peterborough; pop. 53,400.

Peterborough, Soke of (sōk) northeast section of Northamptonshire, E cen. England; ✷ Peterborough; area 84 sq. m.; pop. 63,800.

Pe'ters·berg (pā'tĕrs·bĕrk) mountain, W Germany, one of the Siebenge-birge, on E side of the Rhine 6 m. above Bonn; 1095 ft. high.

Pe'ters·burg (pē'tĕrz·bûrg) independent city, SE Virginia, on Appomat-tox river S of Richmond; pop. 35,100.

Pet'it·co'di·ac (pĕt'ĭ·kō'dĭ·ăk) river, SE Canada, in SE New Bruns-wick, flowing to head of Bay of Fundy; 60 m. long.

Pe'tra (pē'trà; pĕt'rà) ancient city, ruins now in SW Jordan kingdom, on slope of Mt. Hor; ancient ✳ of Edomites and of Nabataeans.

Pet'ri·fied Forest National Monument (pĕt'rĭ·fīd) region, E Arizona, containing natural exhibit of petrified wood and a section of Painted Desert; established as national monument 1906.

Petrikau, Petrokov. See PIOTRKÓW.

Petrograd. See LENINGRAD.

Pet'ro·pav'lovsk (pĕt'rō·pāv'lôfsk) city, Soviet Central Asia, in Kazakh S.S.R.; pop. 91,700.

Pe·tró'po·lis (pĕ·trŏp'ô·lĭs) city, SE Brazil, in Rio de Janeiro state; pop. 61,800.

Petrovsk. See MAKHACHKALA.

Pet'ro·za·vodsk' (pĕt'rō·zà·vŏtsk') city, U.S.S.R., ✳ of Karelo-Finnish S.S.R., on Lake Onega; pop. 69,700.

Petsamo. See PECHENGA.

Pha'ros (fā'rŏs; fâr'ŏs) peninsula, N Egypt; in ancient times an island on which was located a lighthouse; now part of the city of Alexandria.

Phar·sa'lus (fär·sā'lŭs), Mod. Gr. **Phár'sa·los** (fär·sä·lôs) or **Phár'sa·la** (fär·sä·lä) town, NE Greece, in E Thessaly; battle 48 B.C. called also the battle of **Phar·sa'lia** (fär·sāl'yà; -sā'lĭ·à), from the name of the district surrounding the town.

Phenice, Phenicia. See PHOENICIA.

Phe'nix City (fē'nĭks) city, E Alabama, on Chattahoochee river oppo-site Columbus, Georgia; pop. 23,300.

Phil'a·del'phi·a (fĭl'à·dĕl'fĭ·à; -fyà) **1** city, SE Pennsylvania, at con-fluence of Delaware and Schuylkill rivers; pop. 2,071,600. **2** see AMMAN. **3** see ALAŞEHIR. — **Phil·a·del'phi·an**, adj. & n.

Phi'lae (fī'lē) island, Egypt, in Nile river in lat. 24°N; now submerged except July to October when the sluices of Aswân Dam are open.

Phi·lippe'ville' (fē'lēp'vēl'; Angl. fĭl'ĭp·vĭl) seaport, NE Algeria, N of Constantine; pop. 64,900.

Phi·lip'pi (fĭ·lĭp'ī; fĭl'ĭ·pī) ancient town, NE Greece, in N cen. Mace-donia 10 m. from the coast. See PHILIPPIANS, in Vocab.

Phil'ip·pine Islands (fĭl'ĭ·pēn) or **Phil'ip·pines** (-pēnz) group of is-lands, Malay Archipelago; once a Spanish possession and 1898–1945 a United States possession; since 1946 a republic (**Republic of the Philippines**); ✳ Manila, until completion of Quezon City, the official ✳; 7100 islands, total land area 114,830 sq. m.; pop. 19,557,000. — **Phil'ip·pine**, adj. See also FILIPINO, in Vocab.

Philippopolis. See PLOVDIV.

Phi·lis'ti·a (fĭ·lĭs'tĭ·à) ancient country, SW Palestine, on the coast; the land of the Philistines. See PHILISTINE, in Vocab.

Phil'lips·burg (fĭl'ĭps·bûrg) town, NW New Jersey, on Delaware river opposite Easton, Pennsylvania; pop. 18,900.

Phnom Penh. See PNOMPENH.

Pho·cae'a (fō·sē'à) ancient city, Asia Minor, on Aegean Sea in N Ionia; an important maritime state c. 1000–600 B.C.

Pho'cis (fō'sĭs) region, cen. Greece, N of Gulf of Corinth.

Phoe·ni'ci·a, also **Phe·ni'ci·a** (fē·nĭsh'ĭ·à; -nĭsh'à), or **Phe·ni'ce** (fē-nī'sē) ancient country, W Asia, at E end of Mediterranean Sea in what is now Syria and Lebanon; a group of city-states that flourished c. 1200–1000 B.C. — **Phoe·ni'cian** (-nĭsh'ăn), adj. & n.

Phoe'nix (fē'nĭks) city, ✳ of Arizona, on Salt river; pop. 106,800.

Phoenix Islands, group of islands, cen. Pacific ocean, 4°S of the equator and ESE of Gilbert Is.; belong to the British except for Canton and Enderbury, which are under joint U.S.–British control.

Phryg'i·a (frĭj'ĭ·à) ancient country, W cen. Asia Minor; divided c. 400 B.C. into **Greater Phrygia**, the inland region, and **Lesser Phrygia**, along the Hellespont. — **Phryg'i·an** (-ĭ·ăn), adj. & n.

Pia·cen'za (pyä·chĕn'tsä), anc. **Pla·cen'tia** (plà·sĕn'shà; -shĭ·à) com-mune, N Italy, on Po river; pop. 80,600.

Pi·au·í' (pyou·ē'), formerly spelled **Pi·au·hy'** (pyou·ē') state, NE Brazil, bordering on Atlantic Ocean E of Parnaíba river; ✳ Teresina; area 94,819 sq. m.; pop. 1,064,400.

Pia've (pyä'vä) river, NE Italy, flowing S and SE into the Adriatic Sea; 137 m. long.

Pic'ar·dy (pĭk'ĕr·dĭ), Fr. **Pi'car'die'** (pē'kár'dē') historical region, N France, bordering on English Channel N of Normandy; a province 1477 to Revolution. — ✳ Amiens. — **Pic'ard** (pĭk'ĕrd; pē'kär), adj. & n.

Pied'mont (pēd'mŏnt) **1** Ital. **Pie·mon'te** (pyä·môn'tä) region, N Italy, bordering on France and Switzerland, in foothills of the Alps. **2** region, E United States, just E of the Appalachian Mts. — **Pied'-mon·tese'** (pēd'môn·tēz'; -tēs'), adj. & n.

Pi·e'ri·a (pī·ē'rĭ·à) ancient region, NE Greece, in Macedonia W of Gulf of Salonica. See PIERIAN, PIERIAN SPRING, in Vocab.

Pierre (pēr) city, ✳ of South Dakota, on Missouri river; pop. 5700.

Pie'ter·mar'itz·burg (pē'tĕr·mär'ĭts·bûrg) town, E Union of South Africa, ✳ of Natal; pop. with suburbs 60,600.

Pikes Peak (pīks) mountain, E cen. Colorado, at S end of Front Range; 14,110 ft. high.

Pi·la'tus (pē·lä'tōos) mountain, cen. Switzerland, in Unterwalden can-ton; 6995 ft. high.

Pil'co·ma'yo (pēl'kō·mä'yō) river, S cen. South America; rises in Bolivia, flows SE into Paraguay river in Paraguay; 1000 m. long.

Pilion. See PELION.

Pil'lars of Her'cu·les (pĭl'ĕrz, hûr'kū·lēz) two promontories at E end of Strait of Gibraltar: the Rock of Gibraltar in Europe, and Jebel Musa at Ceuta in Africa. See also in Vocab.

Pilsen. See PLZEŇ.

Pin'dus Mountains (pĭn'dŭs) mountain system, N Greece, between Epirus and Thessaly; highest point over 7500 ft.

Pine Bluff, city, SE cen. Arkansas, on Arkansas river; pop. 37,200.

Pines, Isle of. **1** See ISLE OF PINES. **2** see KUNIE.

Ping (pĭng) river, W Thailand, flowing SSE to join with the Nan and form the Chao Phraya; 360 m. long.

Ping'yuan' (pĭng'yü·än') former province, N China, surrounded by Shansi, Hopeh, Shantung, and Honan; created by Communist regime 1949, ✳ Sinsiang; abolished 1952.

Piniós. See SALAMBRIA.

Pinkiang. See HARBIN.

Pinsk Marshes. See PRIPET.

Pio'tr·ków (pyô'tĕr·kōōf), Russ. **Pe·tro·kov'** (pyĭ·trŭ·kôf'; Angl. pĕt'-rō·kôf), Ger. **Pe'tri·kau** (pā'trĕ·kou) commune, Poland, SSE of Łódź; pop. 52,900.

Piq'ua (pĭk'wä; -wà) city, W Ohio, N of Dayton; pop. 17,400.

Pi·rae'us (pī·rē'ŭs), Mod. Gr. **Pi'rai·évs'** (pē'rà·âfs') seaport, E Greece, on Saronic Gulf; the port of Athens; pop. 184,800.

Pirineos. See PYRENEES.

Pir'ma·sens (pĭr'mä·zĕns) city, W Germany, near French border E of the Saar; pop. 50,600.

Pi'sa (pē'zà; Ital. -sä) commune, cen. Italy, on Arno river; pop. 84,000. — **Pi'san** (-z'n), adj. & n.

Pis'gah (pĭz'gà) or **Ne'bo** (nē'bō) mountain, Jordan, E of N end of Dead Sea; 2644 ft. high.

Pishpek. See FRUNZE.

Pi·sid'i·a (pĭ·sĭd'ĭ·à; pī-) ancient country, S Asia Minor, cut off from the Mediterranean by Pamphylia. — **Pi·sid'i·an**, adj.

Pi·sto'ia (pēs·tō'yä) commune, cen. Italy, NW of Florence; pop. 75,400.

Pit'cairn Island (pĭt'kârn) island, S Pacific Ocean, S of Tropic of Cap-ricorn; a British colony, founded 1790 by mutineers from the British ship *Bounty*.

Pitch Lake (pĭch) deposit of natural asphalt, SW Trinidad; extends over 114 acres.

Pitts'burg (pĭts'bûrg) city, SE Kansas; pop. 19,300.

Pitts'burgh (pĭts'bûrg) city, SW Pennsylvania; pop. 676,800.

Pittsburg Landing, hamlet, SW Tennessee, on Tennessee river; scene of battle, usually called battle of Shiloh, April 6–7, 1862.

Pitts'field (pĭts'fēld) city, W Massachusetts, on Housatonic river; pop. 53,300.

Pitts'ton (pĭts'tŭn) city, E Pennsylvania; pop. 15,000.

Pla·cen'tia (plà·sĕn'shà; -shĭ·à) **1** see PIACENZA. **2** town, Canada, in SE Newfoundland, on **Placentia Bay**, an inlet 75 m. long.

Plac'id, Lake (plăs'ĭd) **1** see LAKE PLACID. **2** lake, NE New York, in the Adirondack Mts.; 5 m. long.

Plain'field (plān'fēld) city, NE New Jersey; pop. 42,400.

Plains of A'bra·ham (ā'brà·hăm) plateau, Canada, W of old city of Quebec; battle 1759, in which the British defeated the French.

Plas'sey (plăs'ĭ) village, NE India, in West Bengal; battle 1757.

Pla'ta, Rí'o de la (rē'ō thä lä plä'tä), Brit. **River Plate** (plāt') estuary of Paraná and Uruguay rivers, South America, between Uruguay and Argentina; 225 m. long.

Pla·tae'a (plà·tē'à) or **Pla·tae'ae** (-tē'ē) ancient city, Greece, in SE Boeotia S of Thebes and near Attica border; scene 479 B.C. of defeat of Persians by the Greeks. — **Pla·tae'an** (-ăn), adj. & n.

Platte (plăt) river, cen. Nebraska; formed by confluence of North Platte and South Platte, flows E into Missouri river; 310 m. long (with North Platte 900 m.).

Plattensee. See BALATON.

Platts'burgh or **Platts'burg** (plăts'bûrg) city, NE New York, on W Lake Champlain 20 m. S of Canadian border; pop. 17,700.

Plau'en (plou'ĕn), also **Plauen im Vogt'land** (ĭm fōkt'länt) city, E Germany, on Weisse Elster SW of Zwickau; pop. 102,700.

Pleasant Island. See NAURU.

Plo·eş'ti (plô·yĕsht'; -yĕsh'tĕ) city, SE cen. Romania, in E foothills of Transylvanian Alps; pop. 77,400.

Plov'div (plôv'dĭf), Gr. **Phil'ip·pop'o·lis** (fĭl'ĭ·pŏp'ô·lĭs) city, S Bul-garia, on the Maritsa river N of the Rhodope Mts.; pop. 99,900.

Plym'outh (plĭm'ŭth) **1** town, SE Massachusetts, on Plymouth Bay; site of first permanent white settlement in New England, founded by Pilgrims 1620; pop. 13,600. **2** city and county borough, SW Eng-land, in Devonshire on Plymouth Sound; naval base; pop. 209,000.

Pl'zeň (pǔl'zĕn·y'), Ger. **Pil'sen** (pĭl'zĕn) city, Czechoslovakia, in Bo-hemia; pop. 117,800.

Pnom'penh' (p'nôm'pĕn'), also **Phnom Penh** (p'nôm'-) city, ✳ of Cambodia, on the Mekong; pop. 102,700.

Po (pō), anc. **Pa'dus** (pā'dŭs) river, N Italy, flowing from slopes of Mount Viso E into Adriatic Sea through several mouths; 418 m. long.

Po·ca·tel'lo (pō'kà·tĕl'ō; -tĕl'à) city, SE Idaho; pop. 26,100.

Podgorica or **Podgoritsa.** See TITOGRAD.

Podkarpatská Rus. See CARPATHIAN RUTHENIA.

Po·do'lia (pō·dōl'yà; -dō'lĭ·à), Russ. **Po·dolsk'** (pō·dôlsk'; Russ. pŭ-dôl'y'sk) region, U.S.S.R., in W Ukraine N of middle Dniester river.

Po·dolsk' (pō·dôlsk'; Russ. pǔ·dôl'y'sk) **1** see PODOLIA. **2** town, Soviet Russia, Europe, S of Moscow; pop. 72,400.

Po Hai, Gulf of (bō' hī'), formerly **Gulf of Chih'li'** (chē'lē') the NW arm of the Yellow Sea, NE China, enclosed by S Manchuria and Hopeh and Shantung provs.

Poictiers. See POITIERS.

Point Arguello. See ARGUELLO, POINT.

Pointe-à-Pi'tre (pwăN'-tȧ-pē'tr') seaport, French West Indies, in SW Grande-Terre I., E Guadeloupe; pop. 43,600.

Pointe-aux-Trem'bles (pwăN'-tō-träN'bl') town, Canada, in Quebec on Montreal I. NNE of Montreal; pop. 12,000.

Pointe-Claire (point'klâr'; Fr. pwăNt'klâr') town, Canada, in Quebec on Montreal I. SW of Montreal; pop. 15,200.

Point Mugu. See MUGU, POINT.

Poi'tiers' (pwä'tyä'), formerly spelled **Poic'tiers'** (pwä'-) city, W cen. France; battles 732 and 1356; pop. 48,500.

Poi'tou' (pwä'tōō') historical region, W cen. France, SE of Brittany; a province of France from 1416 until Revolution; ✳ Poitiers.

Pola. See PULJ.

Po'land (pō'lănd), Pol. **Pol'ska** (pôl'skä) country, E Europe, bordering on Baltic Sea; in Middle Ages a kingdom, at one time extending to the lower Dnieper river; partitioned 1772, 1793, 1795, among Russia, Prussia, and Austria; again a kingdom (Congress Poland or Russian Poland) 1815–30; lost autonomy 1831–1918; since 1918 a republic; ✳ Warsaw; area (1952) 119,703 sq. m.; pop. (1950) 24,976,900. See POLE, POLISH, in Vocab.

Polish Corridor, strip of land, N Europe, in Poland, which, between World War I and World War II, separated East Prussia from main part of Germany; before 1919 part of Germany.
Pol·ta′va (pŭl·tä′vȧ) city, U.S.S.R., in Ukraine on Vorskla river; battle 1709; pop. 130,300.
Pol′y·ne′sia (pŏl′ĭ·nē′zhȧ; -zhĭ·ȧ; -shȧ; -shĭ·ȧ) islands of the cen. Pacific Ocean, between 30°N and 47°S lat. See POLYNESIAN, in Vocab.
Pom′er·a′nia (pŏm′ẽr·ān′yȧ; -ā′nĭ·ȧ), Ger. **Pom′mern** (pôm′ẽrn) **1** historical region, N Europe, on Baltic Sea, formerly in Germany, now mostly in Poland; once a duchy. **2** former province of Prussia. See POMERANIAN, in Vocab.
Pom′er·e′lia (pŏm′ẽr·ēl′yȧ; -ē′lĭ·ȧ), Ger. **Pom′me·rel′len** (pôm′ĕ·rĕl′ĕn) ancient region on the Baltic Sea W of the Vistula; originally part of Pomerania.
Po·mo′na (pō·mō′nȧ) **1** city, SW California, E of Los Angeles; pop. 35,400. **2** or **Main′land′** (mān′lănd′; -lănd) island, N Scotland, largest of the Orkney Is.; area 190 sq. m.
Pom·pe′ii (pŏm·pā′ē; -pā′; -pē′[y]ī) ancient city, S Italy, SE of Naples near foot of Mt. Vesuvius; destroyed by eruption of Vesuvius A.D. 79. — **Pom·pe′ian** (pŏm·pā′[y]ăn; -pē′[y]ăn), adj. & n.
Po′na·pe (pō′nȧ·pā), formerly **As·cen′sion** (ȧ·sĕn′shŭn) island, Pacific Ocean, in E Caroline Is.; 134 sq. m.; pop. 11,500.
Pon′ca City (pŏn[g]′kȧ) city, N Oklahoma; pop. 20,200.
Pon′ce (pôn′sā) seaport, S Puerto Rico; pop. 99,200.
Pon′di·cher′ry (pŏn′dĭ·chĕr′ĭ; -shĕr′ĭ) or **Pon′di′ché′ry′** (pôN′dē′shā′rē′) **1** settlement, French India, on Coromandel Coast; area 112 sq. m.; pop. 204,700; became part of India 1954. **2** seaport, ✻ of former French India, chief town of settlement; pop. 53,100.
Pon′do·land′ (pŏn′dō·lănd′) territory, Union of South Africa, one of the Transkeian Territories, between Umtata river and Natal prov.
Pon′ta Del·ga′da (pôNn′tȧ thĕl·gä′thȧ) seaport, Portugal, in the Azores on SW coast of São Miguel I.; chief town of the Azores; pop. 21,000.
Pont′char·train′, Lake (pŏn′chẽr·trān′) lake, SE Louisiana, E of Mississippi river; area 600 sq. m.
Pon′te·ve′dra (pôn′tā·vā′thrä) commune, NW Spain, on coast; pop. 51,900.
Pon′ti·ac (pŏn′tĭ·ăk) city, SE Michigan; pop. 73,700.
Pon′ti·a′nak (pŏn′tē·ä′näk) city, Indonesia, on SW coast of Borneo; pop. 45,000.
Pon′tine Marshes (pŏn′tēn; -tīn) district, cen. Italy, in SW Latium; separated from sea by low sand hills which prevent natural drainage; now reclaimed and site of several cities.
Pon′tus (pŏn′tŭs) **1** ancient country, NE Asia Minor; a kingdom 4th cent. B.C. to 66 B.C., then a Roman province. **2** or **Pontus Euxinus**: see BLACK SEA. — **Pon′tic** (-tĭk), adj.
Poole (pōōl) municipal borough, S England, in Dorsetshire on English Channel; pop. 83,000.
Poo′na (pōō′nȧ) city, W India, in Bombay state; pop. 258,200.
Po′o·pó′, Lake (pō′ō·pō′) lake, W cen. Bolivia, S of Lake Titicaca; 60 m. long, 30 m. wide; altitude 12,000 ft.
Poplar Bluff, city, SE Missouri; pop. 15,100.
Po·po′ca·te′petl (pō·pō′kä·tā′pĕt·'l; Angl. pō′pō·kăt′ĕ·pĕt′'l) volcano, SE cen. Mexico, in Puebla state; contains crater over half a mile in circumference and 250 ft. deep; 17,887 ft. high.
Por′cu·pine (pôr′kū·pīn) river, Canada, and Alaska, flowing into Yukon river in Alaska; 400 m. long.
Pork′ka·la Peninsula (pôrk′kȧ·lȧ) tongue of land, S Finland, projecting into Gulf of Finland W of Helsinki; to Russia 1944–56.
Port Apra. See APRA HARBOR.
Port Ar′thur (är′thẽr) **1** city, SE Texas, on Sabine Lake S of Beaumont; pop. 57,500. **2** city, Canada, in SW Ontario on Lake Superior N of Fort William; pop. 38,100. **3** Jap. **Ryo·jun** (ryō·jōōn), Chin. **Lü′shun′** (lü′shōōn′) seaport, S Manchuria, on Liaotung Penin. SW of Dairen; in Kwantung Leased Territory 1905–45; joint Chinese-Russian naval base 1945–55; now combined with Dairen and other territory in Kwantung to form city of **Port Ar′thur-Dai′ren′** (dī′rĕn′), pop. (1953 est.) 1,200,000.
Port-au-Prince (pōrt′ō·prĭns′) seaport, ✻ of Republic of Haiti; pop. 142,800.
Port Castries. See CASTRIES.
Port Ches′ter (pōrt chĕs′tẽr) village, SE New York, on Long Island Sound near Connecticut boundary; pop. 24,000.
Port Col′borne (kōl′bẽrn) town, Canada, in SE Ontario on Lake Erie; pop. 14,000.
Port Dar′win (där′wĭn) **1** see DARWIN. **2** inlet of Clarence Strait, N Australia, on which Darwin is situated.
Port E·liz′a·beth (ē·lĭz′ȧ·bĕth) town, S Union of South Africa, in SE Cape Province on Algoa Bay; pop. with suburbs 133,400.
Port Hue·ne′me or **Hueneme** (wī·nē′mē) seaport, S California, on Santa Barbara Channel 40 m. W of Los Angeles; naval base.
Port Hu′ron (hū′rŏn) city, SE Michigan, at Lake Huron end of St. Clair river; pop. 35,700.
Port Jack′son (jăk′s'n) inlet of S Pacific Ocean, SE Australia, in New South Wales; forms harbor of Sydney.
Port Jin′nah (jĭn′ȧ) the port of Chalna, E Pakistan.
Port′land (pōrt′lănd) **1** seaport, SW Maine, on Casco Bay; pop. 77,600. **2** city, NW Oregon, on Willamette river; pop. 373,600.
Portland Bight. See OLD HARBOUR BAY.
Port Lou′is (pōrt lōō′ĭ[s]) seaport, ✻ of Mauritius; pop. 57,000.
Port Lyau′tey′ (pôr′ lyō′tā′; Angl. pōrt lē′ō·tā′), formerly, and since Feb. 1958, **Ké′ni′tra′** (kā′nē′trä′) town, Morocco, NE of Rabat; a river port, 10 m. from Atlantic Ocean; pop. 57,800.
Port Mores′by (pōrt mōrz′bĭ) seaport, SE New Guinea, ✻ of joint territories of Papua and New Guinea, on Gulf of Papua.
Pôrto. See OPORTO.
Pôr′to A·le′gre (pōr′tōō ȧ·lâ′grĕ) seaport, S Brazil, ✻ of Rio Grande do Sul state, at N end of Lagoa dos Patos; pop. 382,000.
Por′to·be′lo (pôr′tō·vā′lō), also **Por′to Bel′lo** (pōr′tō bĕl′ō) and **Puer′to Bel′lo** (pwĕr′tō bĕl′ō) seaport, Panama, on Caribbean coast; the great emporium of South American trade in 16th and 17th cents.
Port of Spain or **Port-of-Spain**, seaport, NW Trinidad, ✻ of Trinidad and Tobago colony; pop. 100,600.
Por′to-No′vo (pōr′tō·nō′vō) seaport, French West Africa, ✻ of Dahomey; pop. 27,500.
Porto Rico. See PUERTO RICO.
Port Phil′lip Bay (pōrt fĭl′ĭp) the harbor of Melbourne, Australia.
Port Roy′al (roi′ăl) **1** town, South Carolina, on **Port Royal Island**, one of the Sea Is.; site of Huguenot colony founded 1562. **2** town, British West Indies, on Jamaica at entrance to Kingston Harbor; early ✻ of Jamaica. **3** see ANNAPOLIS ROYAL.
Port Said′ (sīd′; sād′) seaport, NE Egypt, on Mediterranean Sea at N end of Suez Canal; pop. 178,400.
Ports′mouth (pōrts′mŭth) **1** seaport, SE New Hampshire; treaty 1905; pop. 18,800. **2** city, S Ohio, on Ohio river at mouth of Scioto river; pop. 36,800. **3** independent city, SE Virginia, on Elizabeth river across from Norfolk; pop. 80,000. **4** city and county borough, S England, in Hampshire; naval base; pop. 233,500.
Por′tu·gal (pōr′tū·găl; pôr′-), anc. **Lu′si·ta′nia** (lū′sĭ·tān′yȧ; -tā′nĭ·ȧ) country, W Europe, in W Iberian Penin. between Spain and the Atlantic Ocean; before 1910 a kingdom, now a republic; ✻ Lisbon; area 34,240 sq. m. (not including the Azores and Madeira Is.); pop. 8,618,000. — **Por′tu·guese** (-gēz; -gēs), adj. & n. sing. & pl.
Portuguese East Africa. See MOZAMBIQUE.
Portuguese Guinea, country, W Africa, on Guinea coast; a Portuguese colony; ✻ Bissau; area 13,944 sq. m.; pop. 351,100.
Portuguese India, Portuguese possessions on W coast of Indian subcontinent, comprising the territory of Goa and the districts of Damão and Diu; ✻ Pangim, in Goa; 1537 sq. m.; pop. 601,000.
Portuguese Timor, the eastern half of the island of Timor, belonging to Portugal; ✻ Dili; area 7330 sq. m.; pop. 463,800.
Portuguese West Africa. See ANGOLA.
Posen. See POZNAŃ.
Po·to′mac (pō·tō′măk) river, E United States, flowing from West Virginia to Chesapeake Bay, forming S boundary of Maryland; 287 m. long, with South Branch headstream 400 m. long.
Po′to·sí′ (pō′tō·sē′) city, Bolivia, at altitude of 13,600 ft.; pop. 40,000.
Pots′dam (pŏts′dăm) city, E Germany, SW of Berlin; pop. 113,600.
Potts′town (pŏts′toun) borough, SE Pennsylvania; pop. 22,600.
Potts′ville (pŏts′vĭl) city, E cen. Pennsylvania; pop. 23,600.
Pough·keep′sie (pō·kĭp′sĭ) city, SE New York, on Hudson river; pop. 41,000.
Pow′der (pou′dẽr) **1** river, E Oregon, flowing into Snake river; 150 m. long. **2** river, N Wyoming and SE Montana, flowing N into Yellowstone river; 375 m. long.
Po′yang′ Hu (pō′yäng′ hōō′) lake, SE China, in N Kiangsi prov.; 90 m. long and 20 m. wide.
Poz′nań (pôz′nän·y′), Ger. **Po′sen** (pō′zĕn) city, Poland, on Warta river; pop. 291,600.
Pozsony. See BRATISLAVA.
Prague (präg; prāg), Czech **Pra′ha** (prä′hä), Ger. **Prag** (präκ) city, ✻ of Czechoslovakia, in Bohemia on the Vltava river; pop. 922,300.
Prairie Provinces, the Canadian provinces of Manitoba, Saskatchewan, and Alberta.
Prav′dinsk (präv′dēnsk), Ger. **Fried′land** (frēt′länt) town, Poland, formerly in East Prussia, Germany; scene of battle June 14, 1807.
Presque Isle (prĕsk′ īl′) city, N Maine; site of air base; pop. 10,000.
Pressburg. See BRATISLAVA.
Pres′ton (prĕs′tŭn) county borough, NW England, in Lancashire, on the Ribble; pop. 119,200.
Pres′ton·pans′ (prĕs′tŭn·pănz′) burgh, SE Scotland, in East Lothian E of Edinburgh; scene of a battle Sept. 21, 1745.
Prest′wick (prĕst′wĭk) burgh, SW Scotland, in Ayr co. N of Ayr; international airport; pop. 11,400.
Pre·to′ri·a (prē·tō′rĭ·ȧ) city, administrative ✻ of Union of South Africa, in S cen. Transvaal; pop. with suburbs 168,100.
Preussen. See PRUSSIA.
Prib′i·lof Islands (prĭb′ĭ·lŏf), also **Fur Seal Islands**, group of islands, Alaska, in SE Bering Sea.
Prich′ard (prĭch′ẽrd) city, SW Alabama, NW of Mobile; pop. 19,000.
Primorski Krai. See MARITIME TERRITORY.
Prince Al′bert (ăl′bẽrt) city, Canada, in S cen. Saskatchewan on North Saskatchewan river; pop. 20,400.
Prince Albert National Park, Canada, in cen. Saskatchewan; forested region with many lakes and waterways; established 1927.
Prince Ed′ward Island (ĕd′wẽrd), abbr. **P.E.I.**, island, SE Canada, in Gulf of St. Lawrence off E New Brunswick and N Nova Scotia; constitutes a province; ✻ Charlottetown; area 2184 sq. m.; pop. 99,300.
Prince of Wales, Cape (wālz) cape, Alaska, at W tip of Seward Penin.; most westerly point of mainland of North America, at 168°W long.
Prince of Wales Island, 1 island, SE Alaska, largest in Alexander Archipelago; area 1500 sq. m. **2** island, N Canada, between Victoria I. and Somerset I.; area 12,830 sq. m.
Prince Ru′pert (rōō′pẽrt) city, Canada, in British Columbia on Pacific Ocean at head of Dixon Entrance; pop. 10,500.
Prince′ton (prĭns′tŭn) borough, W cen. New Jersey, NNE of Trenton; site of Princeton Univ.; pop. 12,200.
Prince Wil′liam Sound (wĭl′yăm) inlet of Gulf of Alaska, S Alaska, E of Kenai Penin.; 90 to 100 m. across.
Prip′et (prĭp′ĕt), Russ. **Pri′pyat** (pryē′pyȧt·y′), Pol. **Pry′peć** (prĭ′pĕch) river, E cen. Europe, in the U.S.S.R. in NW Ukraine and S White Russia, flowing E through marshes, the **Pripet**, or **Pinsk** (pĭnsk), **Marshes**, to the Dnieper river; 500 m. long.
Profile Mountain. See CANNON MOUNTAIN.
Pro·ko′pevsk (prŭ·kô′pyĕfsk) city, Soviet Russia, Asia, at S end of Kuznetsk Basin, adjacent to Stalinsk; pop. 107,200.
Prom′on·to′ry Point (prŏm′ŭn·tō′rĭ) point of land, Utah, on Great Salt Lake at S end of **Promontory Mountains**.
Propontis. See MARMARA, SEA OF.
Pro′vence′ (prô′väNs′) historical region, SE France, bordering on Mediterranean Sea; once a kingdom; one of pre-Revolutionary provinces; ✻ Aix. See PROVENÇAL, in Vocab.
Prov′i·dence (prŏv′ĭ·dĕns) **1** city, ✻ of Rhode Island; pop. 248,700. **2** see FORT PROVIDENCE.
Providence Plantations. See RHODE ISLAND.

Prov'ince·town' (prŏv'ĭns·toun') town, SE Massachusetts, on N tip of Cape Cod; first landing place of Pilgrims 1620.

Pro'vo (prō'vō) city, N cen. Utah, on Provo river; pop. 28,900.

Prus'sia (prŭsh'à), Ger. **Preus'sen** (proi'sĕn) **1** originally, region in N Germany bordering on Baltic Sea; the E half (East Prussia), from creation of duchy in 16th cent. and union with Brandenburg in 18th cent., developed into kingdom of Prussia; the W half (West Prussia) belonged to Poland 1466–1772 and again after World War II. **2** kingdom (1701–1918) and state (1918–33) of Germany; ✻ Berlin; area (1933) 114,120 sq. m.; pop. (1933) 39,934,000. — **Prus'sian** (prŭsh'ăn), adj. & n.

Prut (prŏŏt), Ger. **Pruth** (prŏŏt) river, E Europe, flowing from Carpathian Mts. SSE into Danube river; forms boundary between Moldavia and Bessarabia and, since World War II, the boundary between Romania and the U.S.S.R.; 500 m. long.

Prypeć. See PRIPET.

Prze'myśl (pshĕ'mĭsh), Russ. **Pe're·myshl'** (pĕr'ĕ·mĭsh'l) city, SE Poland, near Ukraine border; pop. 58,500.

Psilorítis. See IDA.

Pskov (pskôf) city, Soviet Russia, Europe, near **Lake Pskov** (southern arm of Lake Peipus, area 400 sq. m.); pop. 59,900.

Ptolemaïs. See ACRE.

Pue'bla (pwä'vlä; Angl. pṳ·ĕb'là) **1** state, S cen. Mexico; area 13,124 sq. m.; pop. 1,595,900. **2** city, its ✻; pop. 138,500.

Pu·eb'lo (pṳ·ĕb'lō) city, SE cen. Colorado; pop. 63,700.

Puer'to Bar'rios (pwĕr'tō vär'ryŏs) seaport, E Guatemala, on Gulf of Honduras; pop. 15,700.

Puerto Bello. See PORTOBELO.

Puerto Ca·bel'lo (kä·vä'yō) seaport, N Venezuela; pop. 16,800.

Puerto Limón. See LIMÓN.

Puerto Montt (mônt') seaport, S cen. Chile, S of Lake Llanquihue; pop. 21,400.

Puer'to Ri'co (pwĕr'tṳ rē'kō), before 1932 **Por'to Rico** (pōr'tṳ), abbr. **P.R.**, island, West Indies; a United States possession 1898–1952; became 1952 a commonwealth freely associated with the United States; ✻ San Juan; area 3435 sq. m.; pop. 2,210,700. — **Puer'to Ri'can** (rē'kăn), adj. & n.

Pu'get Sound (pū'jĕt; -jĭt) arm of Pacific Ocean, W Washington, extending S from E end of Juan de Fuca Strait; 80 m. long.

Puglia; Puglie, Le. See APULIA.

Pu·jon (pŏŏ·jŏn) or **Fu·sen** (fŏŏ·sĕn) reservoir, N Korea, formed by dam in Pujon river, tributary of the Changjin.

Puk·han (pŏŏk·hän) river, cen. Korea, flowing SW, across 38th parallel, to Han river; 110 m. long.

Pu'la (pŏŏ'là), Ital. **Po'la** (pō'là) seaport, NW Yugoslavia, at tip of Istrian Penin.; pop. 22,700.

Pul·to'va, Pul·to'wa (pŏŏl·tō'và). Vars. of POLTAVA.

Punch'bowl' (pŭnch'bōl') crater of extinct volcano, Hawaii, in Oahu overlooking city of Honolulu; site of National Memorial Cemetery of the Pacific, established 1949.

Pun·jab' (pŭn·jäb'; pŭn'jäb; -jäb[']) **1** region, NW Indian subcontinent, in Pakistan (West Punjab) and India (East Punjab), occupying valleys of the Indus and its five tributaries; formerly a province of British India, ✻ Lahore. **2** state, NW India, in the East Punjab; ✻ Chandigarh; area 47,456 sq. m.; pop. 16,134,900. **3** the West Punjab. — **Pun·ja'bi** (pŭn·jä'bē; -jäb'ē), n.

Pun'ta A·re'nas (pŏŏn'tä ä·rā'näs), before 1938 **Ma'gal·la'nes** (mä'gä·yä'näs) seaport, S Chile, on Strait of Magellan; pop. 29,900.

Pu'ra·cé' (pŏŏ'rä·sā') volcano, SW cen. Colombia; eruption during earthquake of 1827; recent eruption May 26, 1949; 15,420 ft. high.

Pu'ri (pŏŏr'ē) or **Ja'gan·nath** (jŭ'găn·nät'h') or **Jug'ger·naut** (jŭg'ĕr·nôt) seaport, E India, in SE Orissa on Bay of Bengal; site of temple.

Pu·rús' (pŏŏ·rŏŏs') river, NW cen. South America, rising in Andes Mts. in SE Peru and flowing NE into Amazon river in Brazil; 2000 m. long.

Pu·san (pŏŏ·sän) or **Fu·san** (fŏŏ·sän) seaport, SE Korea, on Korea Strait; pop. 473,600.

Push'kin (pŏŏsh'kĭn), formerly **Tsar'sko·e Se·lo'** (tsär'skṳ·yĕ syĕ·lô') and **Det'sko·e Selo** (dyĕt'skṳ·yĕ) town, NW Soviet Russia, Europe, S of Leningrad; former court residence.

Put-in-Bay (pŏŏt'ĭn'-) inlet of Lake Erie, Ohio, in South Bass I.; scene of Commodore Perry's victory over the British Sept. 10, 1813.

Pu'tu·ma'yo (pŏŏ'tŏŏ·mä'yō) river, NW South America; rises in SW Colombia, flows SE into Brazil, where it is known as the **I·çá'** (ē·sä'), and empties into Amazon river; 980 m. long.

Puy de Dôme; Puy de Sancy. See DÔME; SANCY.

Pyd'na (pĭd'nà) ancient town, N Greece, in Macedonia; ruins on Gulf of Salonica; scene of battle 168 B.C.

Py'los (pī'lŏs), Mod. Gr. **Pi'los** (pē'lôs), Ital. **Na'va·ri'no** (nä'vä·rē'nō; Angl. năv'à-) seaport, SW Greece, in SW Peloponnesus; naval battle (Navarino) 1827.

Pyong·yang (pyŭng·yäng) or **Hei·jo** (hā·jō) city, ✻ of North Korea; in 39°01′N lat., on Taedong river; pop. 286,000.

Pyr'e·nees (pĭr'ē·nēz), Fr. **Py'ré·nées'** (pē'rā'nā'), Span. **Pi'ri·ne'os** (pē'rē·nā'ōs) mountain range along the French-Spanish border from Bay of Biscay to the Gulf of Lions; highest peak Pico de Aneto, 11,169 ft. — **Pyr'e·ne'an** (pĭr'ĕ·nē'ăn), adj. & n.

Q

For many names beginning with Q-, especially those of Arabic or Turkish origin, see the more usual forms in English beginning with K-; as, for **Qandahar, Qara Qum, Qirghiz**, etc., see KANDAHAR, KARA KUM, KIRGHIZ, etc.

Qa'ra Shahr or **Ka'ra·shahr'** (kä'rä·shä'h'r), Chin. **Yen'ki'** (yĕn'jē') town, W China, in cen. Sinkiang on N border of Takla Makan Desert.

Qa'tar or **Ka'tar** (kŏ'tŏr) peninsula, E Arabia, projecting into SW Persian Gulf; a sheikdom; ✻ Doha; area 8500 sq. m.; pop. 25,000.

Qat·ta'ra Depression (kŏt·tä'rŏ) region, NW Egypt, a low area 40 m. from the coast; lowest point 440 ft. below sea level.

Qe'na (kē'nà; kä'-) city, S Egypt, N of Luxor; pop. 34,400.

Qishm, also **Kishm** (kĭsh'm) island, Iran, in Strait of Ormuz.

Qi'shon or **Ki'shon** (kī'shŏn; kĭsh'ŏn) river, N Palestine, flowing NW through plain of Esdraelon to the Mediterranean Sea; 50 m. long.

Qo·mul' (kō·mŏŏl') or **Ha'mi'** (hä'mē') oasis, W China, in E Sinkiang N of the Takla Makan Desert.

Quan'ti·co (kwŏn'tĭ·kō) town, NE Virginia, on Potomac river NNE of Fredericksburg; U.S. Marine Corps base.

Quathlamba. See DRAKENSBERG MOUNTAINS.

Qua'tre Bras (kà'tr'ĕ brä') village, cen. Belgium, SSE of Brussels; battle 1815, just before Waterloo.

Que·bec' (kwĕ·bĕk'; kwĕ'-), Fr. **Qué'bec'** (kā'bĕk') **1**, abbr. **Que.** or **P.Q.**, province, E Canada, extending from Hudson Bay to the Gaspé Penin.; land area 523,860 sq. m.; pop. 4,628,400. **2** city, its ✻, on N bank of St. Lawrence river; pop. 170,700.

Queen Char'lotte Islands (shär'lŏt) group of islands, Canada, off W British Columbia; total area 3970 sq. m.; pop. 2400.

Queen E·liz'a·beth Islands (ē·lĭz'à·bĕth) islands of N Canada N of water passage extending from M'Clure Strait to Lancaster Sound; include Parry Is., Sverdrup Is., Devon, and Ellesmere.

Queen Mar'y Coast (mâr'ĭ) section of coast of Antarctica, on Indian Ocean; claimed by the British.

Queen Maud Land (môd) section of Antarctica, on Atlantic Ocean; claimed by Norway.

Queens (kwēnz) borough of New York City, on Long I.; pop. 1,550,800.

Queens'land (kwēnz'lănd; -lănd) state, NE Australia; ✻ Brisbane; area 670,500 sq. m.; pop. 1,183,800.

Queenstown. See COBH.

Quelpart. See CHEJU.

Que·moy' (kē·moi'), also **Kin'men'** or **Chin·men** (jĭn'mŭn') island, China, off E coast E of Amoy; area ab. 50 sq. m.; with Little Quemoy I. and other islets nearby, comprises **Quemoy Islands** group.

Que·ré'ta·ro (kā·rā'tä·rō) **1** state, cen. Mexico; area 4432 sq. m.; pop. 282,600. **2** city, its ✻; pop. 33,600.

Quet'i·co Park (kwĕt'ĭ·kō) provincial park, Canada, in W Ontario on Minnesota border; established 1913.

Quet'ta (kwĕt'à) town, W Pakistan, in Baluchistan; pop. 60,300.

Que'zon City (kā'sŏn) city, Philippine Is., in Luzon adjoining Manila; official ✻ (since 1948) of the Philippines; pop. 108,000.

Qui'be·ron' (kē'brôɴ') town, NW France, in Brittany on S coast, at tip of **Quiberon Peninsula**, a peninsula 6 m. long forming W side of **Quiberon Bay**, site of naval battle Nov. 20, 1759.

Quil'mes (kēl'mäs) city, E Argentina, SE of Buenos Aires; pop. 50,000.

Quin'cy, 1 (kwĭn'sĭ) city, W Illinois, on Mississippi river; pop. 41,500. **2** (kwĭn'zĭ) city, E Massachusetts, S of Boston; pop. 83,800.

Quin·ta'na Ro'o (kēn·tä'nä rrô'ô) territory, SE Mexico, in E Yucatán; ✻ Chetumal; area 19,438 sq. m.; pop. 27,000.

Quirinal. See in Vocab.

Qui'to (kē'tō) city, ✻ of Ecuador, almost on the equator; pop. 165,900.

Qum (kŏŏm) city, NW cen. Iran; pop. 86,000.

R

Raab. See GYÖR.

Ra·bat' (rà·bät') seaport, ✻ of Morocco; pop. 161,600.

Ra·baul' (rä·boul') town, Bismarck Archipelago, on E end of New Britain I.; before 1942 ✻ of Territory of New Guinea.

Rabbah, or **Rabbath, Ammon.** See AMMAN.

Race, Cape (räs) the southeast point of Newfoundland, Canada.

Ra·ci'bórz (rä·tsē'bŏŏsh), Ger. **Ra'ti·bor** (rät'ē·bôr; Ger. rä'tē-) city, SW Poland, in Silesia on Odra (Oder) river; pop. 52,000.

Ra·cine' (rà·sēn'; rà-) city, SE Wisconsin; pop. 71,200.

Radak. See RATAK.

Ra'di·um Hill (rā'dĭ·ŭm) town, E South Australia, near border of New South Wales 50 m. from Broken Hill; uranium field.

Rad'nor·shire (răd'nĕr·shĭr; -shēr) or **Rad'nor**, county, E Wales; ✻ Llandrindod Wells; area 471 sq. m.; pop. 20,000.

Ra'dom (rä'dŏm) commune, Poland, NE of Kielce; pop. 77,900.

Rae'ti·a or **Rhae'ti·a** (rē'shĭ·à; -shà) ancient Roman province, Europe, S of Danube river, including most of what is now the Tirol and the Vorarlberg region of Austria, and Graubünden canton, E Switzerland.

Ra·gu'sa (rä·gŏŏ'zä) **1** commune, Italy, in SE Sicily; pop. 53,600. **2** see DUBROVNIK.

Rah'way (rô'wā) city, NE New Jersey, SSW of Elizabeth; pop. 21,300.

Rai·a·te'a (rī'yä·tā'à) island, Pacific Ocean, one of the Society Is.

Rainbow Bridge National Monument, natural bridge, SE Utah; established as national monument 1910.

Rai·nier', Mount (rà·nēr'; rà·nēr'; rän'yĕr), Indian name **Ta·co'ma** (tà·kō'mà) mountain, W cen. Washington; highest in Cascade Range, 14,408 ft.; extinct volcano; central feature of Mount Rainier National Park, established 1899.

Rain'y Lake (rān'ĭ) lake, Canada and the United States, on border between Ontario and Minnesota; area 366 sq. m.

Rai'sin (rā'z'n) river, SE Michigan, flowing into Lake Erie; 150 m. long.

Ra'ja·sthan (rä'jà·stän) **1** formerly also **Greater Rajasthan Union**, state, NW India, comprising a union of former states; ✻ Jaipur; area 132,077 sq. m.; pop. 15,972,000. **2** see RAJPUTANA.

Raj'kot (räj'kōt) **1** former state, W India, in N cen. Kathiawar penin. **2** town, its ✻; pop. 52,200.

Raj'pu·ta'na (räj'pŏŏ·tä'nà) or **Ra'ja·sthan** (rä'jà·stän) region, NW India, including part of Thar Desert; the country of the Rajputs.

Rakuto. See NAKTONG.

Ra'leigh (rô'lĭ) city, ✻ of North Carolina; pop. 65,700.

Ra'lik (rä'lĭk) western chain of the Marshall Is.

Ram·gan'ga (räm·gŭng'gä) river, N India, in Uttar Pradesh, flowing into the Ganges; 370 m. long.

Ra'mil'lies' (rà·mē'yē'; Angl. răm'ĕ·lĭz, -lēz) village, cen. Belgium, NE of Namur; scene of battle 1706.

Ram'pur (räm'pŏŏr) **1** former state, N India, E of the Ganges river; now part of Uttar Pradesh. **2** city, its ✻, on Kosi river; pop. 89,300.

Rams'gate (rămz'gāt; Brit. -gĭt) municipal borough, SE England, in Kent on North Sea N of Dover; pop. 35,700.

Rand, the. = WITWATERSRAND.

Range'ley Lakes (rānj'lĭ) chain of lakes, W Maine; area 80 sq. m.

Ran·goon' (răng·gōon'; răng'gōon) seaport, ✳ of Burma, on Rangoon river 21 m. from its mouth; pop. 400,400.

Ran'noch, Loch (lŏk rän'ŭk) lake, cen. Scotland, in Perth co.; 9 m. long.

Ra·pal'lo (rä·päl'lō) commune, NW Italy, ESE of Genoa on **Gulf of Rapallo**, an inlet of Ligurian Sea; treaties 1920 and 1922.

Rapa Nui. See EASTER ISLAND.

Rap'i·dan' (răp'ĭ·dăn'; răp'ĭ·dăn) river, N Virginia, rising in Blue Ridge Mts. and flowing E into Rappahannock river; 70 m. long.

Rap'id City (răp'ĭd) city, W South Dakota; pop. 25,300.

Rap'pa·han'nock (răp'á·hăn'ŭk) river, NE Virginia, forming a long estuary emptying into Chesapeake Bay; 185 m. long.

Rap'ti (räp'tē) river, Nepal and N India, flowing SE to Gogra river; 400 m. long.

Rar'i·tan (răr'ĭ·tăn) river, N cen. New Jersey, flowing E into **Raritan Bay**, S of Staten I.; 75 m. long.

Rar'o·ton'ga (răr'ō·tŏng'gä) island, Cook Is.; site of Avarua, ✳ of the group.

Ras Da·shan' (räs' dä·shän') mountain, N Ethiopia, NE of Lake Tana; highest point in Ethiopia, 15,160 ft.

Rashin. See NAJIN.

Ra'tak (rä'täk) or **Ra'dak** (-däk) eastern chain of the Marshall Is.

Ratibor. See RACIBÓRZ.

Ratisbon. See REGENSBURG.

Rat Islands (răt) group of islands, SW Alaska, in W Aleutian Is.

Ra·ven'na (rá·vĕn'à) commune, N Italy, formerly a seaport and ancient Roman naval base; now connected with Adriatic by canal; pop. 86,800.

Ra'vi (rä'vē), anc. **Hy'dra·o'tes** (hī'drá·ō'tēz; hĭd'rá-) river, NW Indian subcontinent, flowing SW to the Chenab and forming part of boundary between East Punjab (Republic of India) and West Punjab (Pakistan); 450 m. long.

Ra·wal·pin'di (rä'vál·pĭn'dē; Angl. rôl·pĭn'dĭ) city, W Pakistan, in West Punjab; pop. 237,200.

Ray, Cape (rā) southwest point of Newfoundland, Canada.

Read'ing (rĕd'ĭng) **1** city, SE Pennsylvania; pop. 109,300. **2** county borough, S England, ✳ of Berkshire; pop. 114,200.

Re·ci'fe (rĕ·sē'fĕ), formerly **Per'nam·bu'co** (pûr'năm·bū'kō; -bōo'-) seaport, E Brazil, ✳ of Pernambuco state; pop. 522,500.

Reck'ling·hau'sen (rĕk'lĭng·hou'zĕn) city, W Germany, SW of Münster; pop. 104,900.

Red Deer, city, Canada, in S Alberta; pop. 12,300.

Red'lands (rĕd'lăndz) city, SE California; pop. 18,400.

Re·don'do Beach (rĕ·dŏn'dō) city, SW California; pop. 25,200.

Red River, 1 river, S cen. United States, flowing E on border between Oklahoma and Texas and into Mississippi river in Louisiana; 1018 m. long. **2** or **Red River of the North,** river, N cen. United States and S cen. Canada, flowing from junction of Otter Tail and Bois de Sioux rivers on Minnesota–North Dakota border N into Lake Winnipeg; 310 m. long, with Sheyenne river 545 m. long. **3** see COI.

Red Sea, body of water between Arabia and NE Africa; 1450 m. long, area 178,000 sq. m.

Redwood City, city, W California, SE of San Francisco; pop. 25,500.

Re'gens·burg (rā'gĕnz·bûrg; Ger. rā'gĕns·bōork), formerly in Eng. **Rat'is·bon** (răt'ĭs·bŏn; -ĭz-) city, W Germany, on Danube river; pop. 117,000.

Reg'gio di Ca·la'bri·a (rĕd'jō dē kä·lä'brē·ä), often shortened to **Reggio** or **Reggio Calabria**, seaport, S Italy, on Strait of Messina; pop. 142,700.

Reggio nel·l'E·mi'lia (nĕl'lä·mē'lyä), often shortened to **Reggio** or **Reggio Emilia**, commune, N Italy, in Emilia; pop. 105,200.

Re·gi'na (rĕ·jī'ná) city, Canada, ✳ of Saskatchewan prov.; pop. 71,300.

Reichenberg. See LIBEREC.

Reichs'land (rīks'länt) **1** 1806–71, all German crownlands. **2** 1871–1918, Alsace-Lorraine.

Reims, older **Rheims** (rēmz; Fr. răns) city, NE France; pop. 110,700.

Reindeer Lake, Canada, in Saskatchewan and Manitoba; 2444 sq. m.

Reisui. See YOSU.

Re'ma'gen (rā'mä'gĕn) town, W Germany, on the Rhine NW of Koblenz; site of the Ludendorff bridge, which collapsed Mar. 17, 1945, just after being crossed by Allied troops.

Rem'scheid (rĕm'shīt) city, W Germany, ESE of Düsseldorf; pop. 102,900.

Ren·do'va (rĕn·dō'vá) island, Solomon Is., off New Georgia I.

Ren'frew (rĕn'frōo) or **Ren'frew·shire** (-shǐr; -shĕr) county, SW Scotland, bordering on lower Clyde river and Firth of Clyde; ✳ Paisley; area 227 sq. m.; pop. 324,700.

Rennes (rĕn) city, NW France, at junction of Ille and Vilaine rivers; pop. 113,800.

Re'no (rē'nō) city, W Nevada, N of Lake Tahoe; pop. 32,500.

Rens'se·laer' (rĕn'sĕ·lĕr'; rĕns·lĕr'; rĕn'sĕ·lĕr; rĕns'lĕr) city, E New York, on the Hudson river opposite Albany; pop. 10,900.

Ren'ton (rĕn't'n; -tŭn) city, W cen. Washington; pop. 16,000.

Re·pub'li·can (rĕ·pŭb'lĭ·kăn) river, Nebraska and Kansas, with headstreams in Colorado; flows E to unite with Smoky Hill river and form Kansas river; 445 m. long.

Re·sa'ca (rĕ·sä'ká) town, NW Georgia; battle 1864.

Re·sa'ca de la Pal'ma (rĕ·sä'kä thä lä päl'mä) battlefield, S Texas, N of Brownsville; American victory over Mexicans 1846.

Resht (rĕsht) city, NW Iran, near shore of Caspian Sea; pop. 111,000.

Res'o·lute (rĕz'ô·lūt) weather station, N Canada, on S coast of Cornwallis I. on **Resolute Bay**; maintained jointly by Canada and U.S.

Re·thondes' (rĕ·tônd') village, N France, near Compiègne; place where armistice of World War I was signed Nov. 11, 1918.

Ré·u'nion' (rā'ü'nyôn'; Angl. rē·ūn'yŭn), formerly **Bour'bon** (bōor'bŭn; Fr. bōor'bôn') island, Indian Ocean, one of the Mascarene Is., belonging to France; ✳ St-Denis; area 970 sq. m.; pop. 208,900.

Reval, Revel. See TALLIN.

Rev'el·stoke, Mount (rĕv'l·stōk) mountain, W Canada, in SE British Columbia on W side of Selkirk Mts.; its summit, at about 6000 ft., is a plateau occupied by Mount Revelstoke National Park, government reservation established 1914.

Re·vere' (rĕ·vēr') city, E Massachusetts, NE of Boston; pop. 36,800.

Re·vil'la·gi·ge'do Island (rĕ·vĭl'á·gĭ·gē'dō) island, SE Alaska, E of Prince of Wales I. in SE Alexander Archipelago.

Rey'kja·vik' (rā'kyä·vēk') seaport, ✳ of Iceland; pop. 44,300.

Rezaieh. See RIZAIYEH.

Rhaetia. See RAETIA.

Rhae'tian Alps (rē'shăn) section of Alps, E Switzerland, in E Graubünden canton; highest point Piz Bernina, 13,295 ft.

Rheims. See REIMS.

Rheinfall. See SCHAFFHAUSEN FALLS.

Rhein falz, Rhenish Palatinate. See PALATINATE.

Rheydt (rīt) city, W Germany, S of München-Gladbach; pop. 68,900.

Rhine (rīn), Ger. **Rhein** (rīn), Fr. **Rhin** (răN), Du. **Rijn** (rīn) river, W Europe, flowing from SE Switzerland to the North Sea in the Netherlands; 820 m. long. — **Rhen'ish** (rĕn'ĭsh), adj.

Rhine'land' (rīn'lănd'; -lănd), English form of Ger. **Rhein'land** (rīn'länt) **1** the part of W Germany W of the Rhine river. **2** formerly, Rhine Province, Prussia.

Rhine Palatinate. See PALATINATE.

Rhine Province, also **Rhen'ish Prussia** (rĕn'ĭsh) formerly, a province of Prussia, Germany, bordering on Belgium; ✳ Koblenz.

Rhio. See RIOUW.

Rhode Is'land (rōd ī'lănd; rō·dī'lănd) **1** island, SE Rhode Island (state), in Narragansett Bay. **2,** abbr. **R.I.,** officially **Rhode Island and Providence Plantations,** state, E United States, on Atlantic coast; ✳ Providence; area 1214 sq. m.; pop. 791,900. — **Rhode Is'land·er** (-lăn·dĕr), n.

Rhodes (rōdz), Mod. Gr. **Ró'dhos** (rô'thôs), Ital. **Ro'di** (rô'dē) **1** island, Greece, chief island of the Dodecanese; area 545 sq. m.; pop. 61,900. **2** city, its ✳; pop. 21,700. — **Rho'di·an** (rō'dĭ·ăn), adj. & n.

Rho·de'sia (rō·dē'zhá; -zhĭ·á) region, cen. South Africa, S of Belgian Congo, now forming British territories of Northern Rhodesia and Southern Rhodesia. — **Rho·de'sian** (-zhăn), adj. & n.

Rhod'o·pe Mountains (rŏd'ô·pē; Mod. Gr. rô·thô'pē) mountain range, S Bulgaria, on border of Greece; highest point Musala, 9595 ft.

Rhon'dda (rŏn'dá), formerly **Ys'trad·y·fod'wg** (ŭs'träd·ĭ·vŏd'ŏog) urban district, SE Wales, in Glamorganshire; pop. 111,400.

Rhone (rōn), Fr. **Rhône** (rōn) river, Switzerland and France, flowing from the Alps through Lake of Geneva to the Mediterranean Sea; 500 m. long.

Ria·zan'. Var. of RYAZAN.

Ri·bei·rão' Prê'to (rē·vā·roun' prā'tōō) city, SE Brazil, in N cen. São Paulo state; pop. 65,100.

Rich'field (rĭch'fēld) village, SE cen. Minnesota, S of Minneapolis; pop. 17,500.

Rich'land (rĭch'lănd) unincorporated community, S Washington; Hanford Engineer Works for separation of plutonium; pop. 21,800.

Rich'mond (rĭch'mŭnd) **1** city, W California, on San Francisco Bay; pop. 99,500. **2** city, E Indiana; pop. 39,500. **3** borough of New York City, coextensive with Staten I.; pop. 191,600. **4** independent city, ✳ of Virginia, on James River; pop. 230,300.

Richmond Heights, city, E Missouri, W of St. Louis; pop. 15,000.

Ridge'wood (rĭj'wŏod) village, NE New Jersey; pop. 17,500.

Rid'ing Mountain (rīd'ĭng) plateau, Canada, in SW Manitoba; 2200 ft. high; forms main part of Riding Mountain National Park, government reservation established 1929.

Rie'sen Ge·bir'ge or **Rie'sen·ge·bir'ge** (rē'zĕn·gĕ·bĭr'gĕ) mountain range, on boundary between Germany and Czechoslovakia; section of Sudeten Mts.; highest point Schneekoppe, 5266 ft.

Rif, Riff. See ER RIF.

Rift Valley. = GREAT RIFT VALLEY.

Ri'ga (rē'gá) seaport, ✳ of Latvia, on Dvina river; pop. 385,900.

Riga, Gulf of, inlet of Baltic Sea between Estonia and Latvia; 100 m. long, 60 m. wide

Ri'gi (rē'gē) or **Ri'ghi** (rē'gē) mountain mass, cen. Switzerland, between lakes of Lucerne and Zug; highest peaks 5905 ft. and 5462 ft.

Ri·je'ka (rē·yĕ'kä), Ital. **Fiu'me** (fyōo'mä) seaport, NW Yugoslavia, at N end of Adriatic Sea; before 1947 in Italy; pop. (with Sušak) 73,000.

Rijn. See RHINE.

Rijs'wijk (rīs'vīk), Eng. **Rys'wick** (rĭz'wĭk; rīz'-) commune, SW Netherlands, near The Hague; Treaty of Ryswick 1697; pop. 23,200.

Ri'mi·ni (rīm'ĭ·nĭ; Ital. rē'mē·nē), anc. **A·rim'i·num** (á·rĭm'ĭ·nŭm) seaport, N Italy, on the Adriatic ESE of Forlì; pop. 64,700.

Ri·mous'ki (rĭ·mōos'kĭ) town, Canada, in Quebec on St. Lawrence river; pop. 14,600.

Rin'e·an'na (rĭn'ē·ăn'á) village, SW Ireland, in co. Clare W of Limerick, on the Shannon; site of Shannon airport.

Rinshin. See IMJIN.

Ri'o (rē'ō; Port. rē'ōō) **1** Span. **Rí'o** (rē'ō) a word meaning river; for most names containing this word, see the distinguishing element, as, for **Rio Pecos,** see PECOS. **2** see RIO DE JANEIRO.

Ri'o Bran'co (rē'ōō vräng'kōō) **1** see BRANCO, RIO. **2** territory, NW Brazil, region around the Rio Branco bordering on Venezuela and British Guiana; ✳ Boa Vista; area 97,438 sq. m.; pop. 17,600.

Ri'o de Ja·nei'ro (rē'ō dĕ já·nā'rō; zhá-; -nâr'ō; -nīr'ō) **1** state, SE Brazil; ✳ Niterói; area 16,372 sq. m.; pop. 2,326,200. **2** colloq. **Rio,** seaport, ✳ of Brazil, on Guanabara Bay; in the Federal District, surrounded by state of Rio de Janeiro; pop. 2,335,900.

Rio de Janeiro Bay. = GUANABARA BAY.

Ri'o de O'ro (rē'ō thä ō'rō) **1** region, W Africa, including Spanish Sahara and Southern Morocco. **2** the southern zone of Spanish Sahara; area 73,362 sq. m.

Ri'o Grande (rē'ō grän'dĕ; grän'dā; rī'ō gränd'), Mex. **Ri'o Bra'vo** (rē'ō vrä'vō) river, SW United States, forming more than half of boundary between the United States and Mexico; flows from San Juan Mts. in SW Colorado to Gulf of Mexico; 1800 m. long.

Ri'o Gran'de (rē'ōō gränd'dĕ) **1** see GRANDE, RIO. **2** or **São Pe'dro do Rio Grande do Sul** (soun' pā'thrōō thōō rē'ōō gränd'dĕ thōō sōōl') city, S Brazil, in SE Rio Grande do Sul state W of entrance to the Lagoa dos Patos; pop. 64,200.

Rio Grande de Cagayan. See CAGAYAN.

Ri′o Gran′de do Nor′te (rē′ōō grăɴn′dĕ thōō nôr′tĕ) state, NE Brazil; ✻ Natal; area 20,236 sq. m.; pop. 983,600.
Rio Grande do Sul (sōōl′) state, SE Brazil, bordering on Uruguay and the Atlantic Ocean; ✻ Pôrto Alegre; area (including lagoons covering 5062 sq. m.) 100,150 sq. m.; pop. 4,213,300.
Riom (ryôɴ) town, S cen. France; ancient ✻ of duchy of Auvergne.
Rí′o Mu′ni (rē′ō mōō′nē) the mainland part of Spanish Guinea, W Africa; area 10,040 sq. m.; pop. 138,800.
Río Pie′dras (pyā′thräs) city, NE Puerto Rico, SE of San Juan near the coast; seat of Univ. of Puerto Rico; pop. 132,400.
Riotinto, Minas de. See MINAS DE RIOTINTO.
Ri′ouw (rē′ou), or **Rhi′o** (rē′ō), **Archipelago**, island group, Indonesia, just S of Singapore; chief island Bintan (sometimes called **Riouw Island**); total area 2279 sq. m.; pop. 77,000.
Rip′on Falls (rĭp′ŭn) waterfall, Uganda, in the Victoria Nile near where it issues from Lake Victoria; 13 ft. high and 1310 ft. across.
Rivadavia. = COMODORO RIVADAVIA.
River of Doubt. See ROOSEVELT, RIO.
River Rouge (rōōzh′; rōōj′) city, SE Michigan; pop. 20,500.
Riv′er·side′ (rĭv′ẽr·sīd′) **1** city, SE California; pop. 46,800. **2** town, Canada, in SE Ontario E of Windsor; pop. 13,300.
Ri·vie′ra (rē·vyâ′rä; Angl. rĭv′ĭ·âr′ȧ) region, SE France and NW Italy, bordering on Mediterranean Sea from Cannes to La Spezia.
Ri·yadh′ (rĭ·yäd′) city, ✻ of Saudi Arabia and of the Nejd; pop. 60,000.
Ri·za′i·yeh′ (rē·zä′ē·yā′) or **Re·za′i·eh′** (rā·zä′ē·yā′), formerly **Ur′mi·a** (ōōr′mĭ·ȧ) city, NW Iran, in Azerbaijan prov.; pop. 51,000.
Ri·zal′ (rē·säl′; Angl. rĭ·zäl′), formerly **Pa′say** (pä′sī) city, Philippines, in Luzon on Manila Bay; pop. 88,700.
Rju′kan (ryōō′kän) town, S Norway, 75 m. W of Oslo, near the Rjukan waterfall, 345 ft. high; hydroelectric station; manufactures nitrate and heavy water.
Ro′a·noke (rō′ȧ·nōk) **1** river, S Virginia and NE North Carolina, flowing E and SE into Albemarle Sound; 380 m. long. **2** independent city, W cen. Virginia; pop. 91,900.
Roanoke Island, island, North Carolina, S of entrance to Albemarle Sound; at N end is Fort Raleigh, site of first English settlement in North America 1585.
Rob′son, Mount (rŏb′s′n) mountain, W Canada, in E British Columbia; highest in Canadian Rockies, 12,972 ft.
Ro′ca, Cape (rô′kȧ), Port. **Ca′bo da Roca** (kȧ′vōō thȧ) cape, Portugal, westernmost point in continental Europe, at long. 9°30′ W.
Roch′dale (rŏch′dāl) county borough, NW England, in Lancashire NNE of Manchester; pop. 87,700.
Roche′fort′ (rôsh′fôr′), unofficially **Rochefort-sur-Mer** (-sür·mâr′) city, W France, SSE of La Rochelle; naval station; pop. 29,500.
Rochelle, La. See LA ROCHELLE.
Roch′es′ter (rŏch′ĕs′tẽr; -ĭs·tẽr) **1** city, SE Minnesota; pop. 29,900. **2** city, W New York, on Genesee river near Lake Ontario; pop. 332,500. **3** municipal borough, SE England, in Kent, on the Medway river; pop. 43,900.
Rock, the. **1** = GIBRALTAR, ROCK OF. **2** = CORREGIDOR.
Rock′ford (rŏk′fẽrd) city, N Illinois; pop. 92,900.
Rock Hill, city, N South Carolina; pop. 24,500.
Rock Island, city, NW Illinois, on Mississippi river; pop. 48,700.
Rock′ville Centre (rŏk′vĭl) village, SE New York, on Long I.; pop. 22,400.
Rocky Mount, city, NE North Carolina; pop. 27,700.
Rocky Mountain National Park, government reservation, N cen. Colorado, in Rocky Mts.; includes Longs Peak; established 1915.
Rocky Mountains or **Rock′ies** (rŏk′ĭz) mountain system, W North America, extending from the Mexican frontier to the Arctic; highest peak in U.S. section Mount Elbert, 14,431 ft., highest in Canadian section Mt. Robson, 12,972 ft.
Rocky Mountains National Park. = BANFF NATIONAL PARK.
Roc′quen′court′ (rô′kän′kōōr′) village, N France, N of Versailles and SE of Marly Forest. See MARLY-LE-ROI.
Ródhos, Rodi. See RHODES.
Rogue (rōg) river, SW Oregon, rising in Crater Lake National Park and flowing S and SW into Pacific Ocean; 220 m. long.
Ro′hil·khand′ (rō′hĭl·kŭnd′) or **Ba·reil′ly** (bȧ·rā′lĭ) region, N India, in Uttar Pradesh; inhabited chiefly by the Rohilla tribe of Afghans.
Ro·ma′gna (rō·män′yä), anc. **Ro·ma′nia** (rō·mān′yȧ; -mā′nĭ·ȧ) before 1860, a province of the States of the Church, Italy; ✻ Ravenna.
Roman Campagna. See CAMPAGNA DI ROMA.
Roman Empire. See in Vocab.
Ro·ma′nia (rō·mān′yȧ; -mā′nĭ·ȧ), also frequently **Rou·ma′nia** (rōō-) and **Ru·ma′nia** (rōō-) country, E Europe, bordering on Black Sea; one of the Balkan States; formerly a kingdom, since 1948 a republic; ✻ Bucharest; area 91,934 sq. m.; pop. 15,872,600. — **Ro·ma′nian, Rou·ma′nian, Ru·ma′nian**, adj. & n.
Ro·ma′nia (rō·mān′yȧ; -mā′nĭ·ȧ) **1** the Roman Empire, especially the Byzantine Empire; — so called by its neighbors. **2** the Latin Empire. **3** see ROMAGNA.
Rom·blon′ (rôm·blôn′) island group, Philippine Is., in Visayan Is.
Rome (rōm) **1** city, NW Georgia; pop. 29,600. **2** city, cen. New York, on Mohawk river WNW of Utica; pop. 41,700.
Rome (rōm), Ital. **Ro′ma** (rō′mä), anc. **Ro′ma** (rō′mȧ) city, ✻ of Italy, in Latium on Tiber river 16 m. from its mouth; pop. 1,665,700. See ROMAN, in Vocab.
Rome, Duchy of, division of Byzantine Empire 6th cent. to 8th cent., in cen. Italy, comprising most of modern Latium; later a province of the States of the Church, called the **Patrimony of Saint Pe′ter** (sānt pē′tẽr).
Rom′ford (rŭm′fẽrd; rŏm′-) municipal borough, SE England, in Essex ENE of London; pop. 88,000.
Ron′ces·val′les (rôn′thāz·vä′lyās; rôn′sāz·vä′yās), Fr. **Ron′ce·vaux′** (rôɴs′vō′) hamlet, N Spain, in Navarre, in the Pyrenees 5 m. from French boundary, near the **Pass of Roncesvalles**; battle A.D. 778.
Rondônia. See GUAPORÉ.
Rong′e·rik (rông′ĕ·rĭk) island, Marshall Is., in Ratak chain E of Bikini.
Roo′de·poort′-Ma·rais′burg (rōō′dĕ·pōōrt′mȧ·rāz′bûrg) town, Union of South Africa, in Transvaal W of Johannesburg; pop. 72,200.
Roo′se·velt, Ri′o (rē′ōō rō′zĕ·vĕlt), formerly **Ri′o da Dú′vi·da** (thȧ thōō′vē·thȧ), Eng. **River of Doubt**, river, Brazil, flowing from W Mato Grosso state N into the Aripuanã river in Amazonas state; with the Aripuanã (sometimes called Roosevelt) 900 m. long.
Roosevelt Roads (rō′zĕ·vĕlt) United States government reservation, E Puerto Rico, on coast; naval airstrip and drydock.
Ro·rai′ma (rō·rī′mȧ) mountain, N South America, on boundary between Venezuela, British Guiana, and Brazil; has flat top 9 m. long, 3 m. wide; highest point 8620 ft.
Ro′sa, Mon′te (môn′tā rō′zä) mountain on Swiss-Italian border; highest summit Dufourspitze, highest point in Pennine Alps, 15,217 ft.
Ro·sa′rio (rrō·sä′ryō) city, Argentina, on Paraná river; pop. 521,200.
Ros·com′mon (rŏs·kŏm′ŭn) **1** county, N cen. Ireland, in Connacht prov.; area 951 sq. m.; pop. 68,100. **2** town, its ✻; pop. 2000.
Ro·selle′ (rō·zĕl′) borough, NE New Jersey, W of Elizabeth; pop. 17,700.
Ro·set′ta (rō·zĕt′ȧ), anc. **Bol′bi·ti′ne** (bŏl′bĭ·tī′nē) **1** western branch of the Nile in its delta, N Egypt. **2** city, N Egypt, on the Rosetta branch of the Nile; near place where Rosetta stone was found 1799.
Rose′ville (rōz′vĭl) village, SE Michigan, NE of Detroit; pop. 15,800.
Ross and Crom′ar·ty (rŏs, krŏm′ẽr·tĭ) county, N Scotland; ✻ Dingwall; area 3089 sq. m.; pop. 60,500.
Rossbodenhorn. See FLETSCHHORN.
Ross Dependency, section of Antarctica lying S of 60°S lat. and between 160°E and 150°W long.; administered by New Zealand.
Rossiya. See RUSSIA.
Ross Sea, body of water, Antarctica, in deep indentation of the continent which is partly filled by the **Ross Shelf Ice**.
Ros′tock (rŏs′tŏk; Ger. rôs′tôk) seaport, E Germany, on Warnow river 8 m. from the Baltic; pop. 114,900.
Ros′tov (rŏs′tŏv; Russ. rŭ·stôf′), also frequently **Rostov-on-Don** (-ŏn-dŏn′) city, SE Soviet Russia, Europe, on the Don river 28 m. from its mouth; pop. 510,200.
Ros′well (rŏz′wĕl; -wĕl) city, SE New Mexico; pop. 25,700.
Roth′er·ham (rŏth′ẽr·ăm) county borough, N England, in Yorkshire, at confluence of Rother and Don rivers NE of Sheffield; pop. 82,300.
Ro′to·ru′a (rō′tō·rōō′ȧ) borough, New Zealand, in N cen. North I. at SW end of Rotorua Lake; center of a volcanic region; pop. 6500.
Rot′ter·dam (rŏt′ẽr·dăm; Du. rôt′ẽr·däm′) seaport, W Netherlands, 15 m. from the North Sea; pop. 646,200.
Rouad, Île. See ARWAD.
Rou′baix′ (rōō′bĕ′) city, N France, NE of Lille; pop. 101,000.
Rou·en′ (rōō·än′; rōō·äɴ′) city, N France, on Seine river; pop. 107,700.
Roufiás. See ALPHEUS.
Roumania. See ROMANIA.
Rou·me′lia. = RUMELIA.
Rous′sil′lon′ (rōō′sē′yôɴ′) historical region, S France, bordering on the Pyrenees and the Mediterranean; a pre-Revolutionary province, ✻ Perpignan.
Rou·yn′ (rwăɴ; Angl. rōō′ĭn) city, Canada, in SW Quebec; pop. 17,100.
Rovuma. See RUVUMA.
Rox′burgh (rŏks′bûr′ō; -bŭ·rŭ; -brŭ) or **Rox′burgh·shire** (-shĭr; -shẽr) county, SE Scotland; ✻ Jedburgh; area 666 sq. m.; pop. 45,600.
Royal Gorge, gorge, S cen. Colorado, in the Grand Canyon of the Arkansas river just W of Canon City; 4.5 m. long.
Royal Oak, city, SE Michigan, N of Detroit; pop. 46,900.
Ru·an′da (rōō·än′dä) district, E Africa, between Belgian Congo and Tanganyika; formerly part of German East Africa; since 1919 associated with Urundi as **Ruanda-U·run′di** (-ōō·rōōn′dē) and administered by Belgium, as a League of Nations mandate 1919–45, as a UN trust territory since 1946, ✻ Usumbura, area 21,234 sq. m., pop. 3,752,700.
Rub ′al Kha′li (rōōb′ ăl kä′lē) or **Ar Ri·mal′** (ŭr rĭ·măl′) desert region, S Arabia, extending from Nejd S to Hadhramaut; area 300,000 sq. m.
Ru′bi·con (rōō′bĭ·kŏn), mod. **Fiu′mi·ci′no** (fyōō′mē·chē′nō) river, N cen. Italy, flowing E into Adriatic Sea just N of Rimini; on N boundary of Italy at time of the ancient Roman republic.
Ru′dolf, Lake (rōō′dŏlf) lake, N Kenya, in Great Rift Valley; area 3500 sq. m.
Rug′by (rŭg′bĭ) municipal borough, cen. England, in Warwickshire, on the Avon; site of Rugby School; pop. 45,400.
Rü′gen (rü′gĕn) island, Germany, in Baltic Sea off coast of Pomerania; area 374 sq. m.
Ruhr (rōōr) **1** river, W Germany, flowing NW and W to the Rhine; 144 m. long. **2** region around the Ruhr river; source of coal and iron.
Ruis′lip (rīs′lĭp) town, S England, in Middlesex W of London; with Northwood, constitutes **Ruislip North′wood** (nôrth′wŏŏd) urban district; pop. 68,300.
Rum (rōōm) or **Roum** (rōōm) the late Byzantine Empire; — the name applied to it by the Moslems.
Rumania. See ROMANIA.
Ru·me′lia (rōō·mēl′yȧ; -mē′lĭ·ȧ) a European division of the old Turkish empire; included Albania, Macedonia, and Thrace.
Rum Jungle (rŭm) settlement, N Australia, in Northern Territory 35 m. S of Darwin; uranium deposits.
Run′ny·mede (rŭn′ĭ·mēd) meadow, S England, in Surrey on S bank of the Thames; Magna Charta signed here 1215.
Ru′se (rōō′sā), Turk. **Rus·chuk′** (rōōs·chōōk′) city, NE Bulgaria, on Danube river; pop. 49,400.
Rush′more, Mount (rŭsh′mōr) mountain, W South Dakota, in Black Hills, on which are carved the faces of Washington, Lincoln, Jefferson, and Theodore Roosevelt.
Rus′sia (rŭsh′ȧ), Russ. **Ros·si′ya** (rŭ·syē′yȧ) **1** former empire, E Europe and N and W Asia; its territories (except for Finland and Kars) now comprised in the Union of Soviet Socialist Republics; ✻ St. Petersburg (Petrograd). **2** popularly, the Union of Soviet Socialist Republics. See RUSSIAN, in Vocab.
Russian So′vi·et Federated Socialist Republic (sō′vĭ·ĕt; sō′vĭ·ĕt′; sō·vyĕt′; sŏv′ĭ·ĕt), commonly shortened to **Soviet Russia**, constituent republic of the U.S.S.R., occupying territory in E Europe and N cen. and NE Asia, bordering on Arctic and Pacific oceans and having outlet on Baltic Sea by way of Gulf of Finland; ✻ Moscow; area 6,501,500 sq. m.; pop. 111,000,000.

Russian Turkistan. See TURKISTAN.

Ruthenia. = CARPATHIAN RUTHENIA.

Ruth′er·ford (rŭth′ẽr·fẽrd) borough, NE New Jersey; pop. 17,400.

Rut′land (rŭt′lănd) **1** city, W Vermont; pop. 17,700. **2** see RUT-LANDSHIRE.

Rut′land·shire (-shĭr; -shêr) or **Rutland**, county, E cen. England; ✳ Oakham; area 152 sq. m.; pop. 20,500.

Ru·vu′ma (rōō-vōō′mä), Port. **Ro·vu′ma** (rōō-) river, SE Africa; rises in S Tanganyika, flows E into Indian Ocean on Mozambique border; 400 m. long.

Ru″wen·zo′ri, Mount (rōō″[w]ĕn·zō′rē) mountain group, E cen. Africa, between Uganda and Belgian Congo; Ptolemy's Mountains of the Moon; highest peak 16,795 ft.

Rya·zan′ (rē′à·zän′; Russ. ryĕ·zàn′y′) city, cen. Soviet Russia, Europe, on Oka river; pop. 95,400.

Rybinsk. See SHCHERBAKOV.

Ry′binsk Reservoir (rĭ′byĭnsk), also called **Sea of Rybinsk**, lake, N cen. Soviet Russia, Europe, formed 1941 by dam in upper Volga.

Rye (rī) town, S England, in East Sussex; one of the Cinque Ports.

Ryswick. See RIJSWIJK.

Ryu′kyu Islands (rĭ·ōō′kū), also **Liu′kiu′** (lĭ·ōō′kĭ·ōō′) or **Lu′chu′** (lōō′chōō′) **Islands**, also **Nan·sei Islands** (nän·sā) chain of islands, E Asia, S of Japan; from 1895 to World War II an integral part of Japan; after 1945 occupied by the United States.

S

Saa′le (zä′lĕ) river, Germany, rising in NE Bavaria in the Fichtel Gebirge and flowing N into the Elbe river; 226 m. long.

Saar (zär; sär), Fr. **Sarre** (sár) river, Europe, flowing from Vosges Mts. in France N to the Mosel in Germany; 84 m. long.

Saar, the, also **Saar′land** (zär′länt; Angl. sär′lănd) region, W Europe, in basin of Saar river, between France and Germany; once part of Lorraine, became part of Germany in 19th cent.; administered by League of Nations 1919–35; became a state of Germany 1935; came under control of France after World War II; to West Germany Jan. 1, 1957 by plebiscite; ✳ Saarbrücken; area 898 sq. m.; pop. 925,000.

Saar′brück′en (zär′brük′ĕn), Fr. **Sar′re·bruck′** (sá′rĕ·brük′) city, ✳ of the Saar; pop. 135,100.

Saaremaa. See SAREMA.

Sa′ba (sä′bá) island, NE West Indies, in Netherlands Antilles; ✳ the Bottom, built on a crater floor 800 ft. above sea level.

Saba, Saba′. See SHEBA.

Sabana, Gran. See GRAN SABANA.

Sa′bar·ma′ti (sä′bẽr·mŭ′tē) river, W India, flowing S into head of Gulf of Cambay; 200 m. long.

Sabi. See 1st SAVE.

Sa·bine′ (sá·bēn′) river, E Texas and W Louisiana; flows SE and empties through **Sabine Lake** and **Sabine Pass** into the Gulf of Mexico; 380 m. long.

Sa′ble, Cape (sā′b'l) **1** cape at SW tip of Florida; southernmost point of the U.S., about 25°7′N. **2** southern point of Cape Sable I., Canada, 43°40′N.

Sachsen. See SAXONY.

Sa′clay (sá·klā′) town, N France, SW of Paris near Versailles; site of atomic energy research laboratory.

Sac′ra·men′to (săk′rá·mĕn′tō) **1** river, N California; rises near Mt. Shasta and flows S into Suisun Bay (San Francisco Bay); 382 m. long. **2** city, ✳ of California, on Sacramento river; pop. 137,600.

Sa·do′wa (zä·dō′vä; zä′dô·vä) village, Czechoslovakia, in Bohemia NW of Königgrätz (Hradec Králové); battle 1866.

Safe′ty Islands (sāf′tĭ), Fr. **Îles du Sa′lut′** (ēl′ dü sá′lü′) three islands off coast of French Guiana, including Devil's I.

Sa′fi (sä′fĭ) seaport, French Morocco, SW of Casablanca; pop. 51,600.

Sa·ga·mi Sea (sä·gä·mē) inlet of Pacific Ocean, Japan, in SE Honshu.

Sa·gay′ (sä·gī′) municipality, Philippine Is., in Negros; pop. 53,800.

Saghalien. See SAKHALIN.

Sag′i·naw (săg′ĭ·nô) city, cen. Michigan, NW of Flint; pop. 92,900.

Saginaw Bay, inlet of Lake Huron, on coast of Michigan.

Saguache Range. See SAWATCH RANGE.

Sag′ue·nay′ (săg′ĕ·nā′; săg′ĕ·nā) river, Canada, in S Quebec prov., flowing from Lake St. John E into St. Lawrence river; 125 m. long.

Sa·gun′to (sä·gōōn′tō), formerly **Mur·vie′dro** (mōōr·vyä′thrō) town, E Spain, NNE of Valencia; siege 219–218 B.C.; pop. 20,300.

Sa·har′a (sá·hâr′á; sá·hä′rá), Arab. **Sah′ra** (sä′hrä) region of deserts and oases in N Africa, ranging from 100 ft. below sea level to 11,200 ft. above (in Tibesti region).

Sa·ha′ran·pur (sá·hä′rän·pōōr) city, N India, in Uttar Pradesh; pop. 108,300.

Saïda or **Saida.** See SIDON.

Sai·gon′ (sī·gŏn′; sī′gŏn), Fr. **Sa′ï′gon′** (sà′ē′gôn′) city, Indochina, ✳ of S Vietnam, in Cochin China; pop. 698,000.

Sai′maa, Lake (sī′mä) lake, SE Finland; area 680 sq. m.

Saint Au′gus·tine (ô′gŭs·tēn) city, NE Florida, on Atlantic Ocean; founded 1565; pop. 13,600.

Saint Ber·nard′ (sänt bẽr·närd′) two Alpine passes: see GREAT SAINT BERNARD, LITTLE SAINT BERNARD.

Saint Bon′i·face (bŏn′ĭ·făs) city, Canada, in S Manitoba on Red river opposite Winnipeg; pop. 28,900.

Saint Cath′a·rines (kăth′ẽr·ĭnz; kăth′rĭnz) city, Canada, in SE Ontario on Welland Ship Canal; pop. 39,700.

Saint Christopher. See SAINT KITTS.

Saint Clair (klâr′) river on United States-Canada border between Michigan and Ontario, connecting **Lake Saint Clair** (area 460 sq. m.) with Lake Huron; 40 m. long.

Saint Clair Shores, village, SE Michigan NE of Detroit; pop. 19,800.

Saint Cloud (kloud′) city, cen. Minnesota; pop. 28,400.

Saint Croix (sänt kroi′) **1** river on border between Canada (New Brunswick) and the United States (Maine), flowing S into Passama-quoddy Bay; 75 m. long. **2** river, NW Wisconsin and E Minnesota, flowing SW into Mississippi river; 164 m. long. **3** island, Maine, in St. Croix river near its mouth; site of settlement by French under

---

Champlain 1604. **4** or **San′ta Cruz** (săn′tá krōōz′) island, West Indies, largest of the Virgin Is. of the United States; chief town Christiansted; area 82 sq. m.; pop. 12,100.

Saint-Cyr-l′É′cole′ (săn′sēr′lā′kôl′) town, N France, W of Versailles; site of military school from 1808 to World War II, after which it was transferred to Coetquidan, Brittany.

Saint Da′vid's Island (sänt dā′vĭdz) NE Bermuda Is.; site of Kindley Field, U.S. Air Force base.

Saint-De·nis′ (săn′d·nē′; Angl. sănt dĕn′ĭs) commune, N France, NNE of Paris; pop. 69,900.

Sainte Anne de Beau′pré′ (sänt ăn′ dĕ bō′prä′) village, Canada, in S Quebec on St. Lawrence river NE of Quebec; shrine to Saint Anne.

Sainte Foy (sänt′ fwä′) city, Canada, in Quebec SW of Quebec city; pop. 14,600.

Saint E·li′as, Mount (ê·lī′ăs) mountain on Alaska-Canada boundary, in Saint Elias Range; 18,008 ft. high.

Saint-É′tienne (săn′-tā′tyĕn′) city, SE cen. France; pop. 178,000.

Saint Eu·sta′ti·us (sänt ū·stā′shĭ·ŭs; -shŭs) island, West Indies, in Netherlands Antilles.

Saint Fran′cis (sänt frăn′sĭs) **1** river, SE Missouri and E Arkansas, flowing S into Mississippi river; 425 m. long. **2** Fr. **Saint Fran′-çois′** (săn′ frän′swä′) river, Canada, in S Quebec prov., flowing NW into St. Lawrence river at Lake St. Peter; 165 m. long.

Saint Gal′len (sänt gäl′ĕn; gäl′ĕn), Ger. **Sankt Gal′len** (zängkt gäl′ĕn), Fr. **Saint-Gall** (săn′gàl′; Angl. sänt-gôl′, -gäl′) **1** canton, NE Switzerland; area 800 sq. m.; pop. 309,100. **2** commune, its ✳; pop. 68,000.

Saint George's Channel (sänt jôr′jĭz) strait, British Isles, between Wales and Ireland.

Saint-Ger·main′ (sänt·jẽr·mān′; Fr. săn′zhẽr′măn′), in full **Saint-Ger′main′-en-Laye** (săn′zhẽr′măn′-näx·lā′) commune, N France, WNW of Paris; treaties 1570, 1632, 1679, 1919; pop. 22,000.

Saint-Gilles (săn′zhēl′), Flemish **Sint-Gil′lis** (sĭnt·kĭl′ĭs) commune, cen. Belgium, near Brussels; pop. 62,000.

Saint Gott′hard (sänt gŏt′ẽrd; Ger. [zängkt] gôt′härt) or **Saint Got′-hard** (sänt gŏt′ẽrd; gŏth′ẽrd; Fr. săn′ gô′tár′) **1** mountain range, Switzerland, in Lepontine Alps between Uri and Ticino cantons. **2** mountain pass in St. Gotthard range; altitude 6935 ft.

Saint He·le′na (sänt′·lê′ná; sänt′ hĕ·lê′ná) island, S Atlantic Ocean; a British colony; ✳ Jamestown; area 47 sq. m.; pop. 4500.

Saint Hel′ens (sänt hĕl′ĕnz; -ĭnz) county borough, NW England, in Lancashire ENE of Liverpool; pop. 110,300.

Saint Hel′ier (sänt hĕl′yẽr) town, ✳ of Channel Is., on island of Jersey; pop. 25,800.

Saint Hy′a·cinthe (sänt hī′á·sĭnth; Fr. săn′·tyà′sănt′) city, Canada, in Quebec prov. 34 m. ENE of Montreal; pop. 20,400.

Saint James (sänt jämz′) city, Canada, in cen. Manitoba; pop. 26,500.

Saint-Jean-d'Acre. See ACRE.

Saint Jé′rôme (săn′ zhä′rōm′) city, Canada, in SW Quebec; pop. 20,600.

Saint John (sänt jŏn′) **1** river, NE United States and SE Canada, flowing from Maine to Bay of Fundy in New Brunswick; 450 m. long. **2** seaport, Canada, in New Brunswick at mouth of St. John river; pop. 52,500. **3** island, West Indies, one of Virgin Is. of the United States; area 19 sq. m.; pop. 700.

Saint John, Cape, cape, Canada, on N coast of Newfoundland.

Saint Johns (sänt jŏnz′) **1** river, Florida, flowing N into Atlantic Ocean; 276 m. long. **2** town, British West Indies, ✳ of Leeward Is. colony, on Antigua; pop. 10,000. **3** Fr. **Saint Jean** (săn′ zhän′) city, Canada, in S Quebec on Richelieu river; pop. 24,400.

Saint John's (sänt jŏnz′) city, Canada, ✳ of Newfoundland, on SE coast; pop. 57,100.

Saint Jo′seph (jō′zĕf; -zĭf) city, NW Missouri, on Missouri river; pop. 78,600.

Saint Jo′vite′ (săn′ zhō′vēt′) village, Canada, in S Quebec, in the Laurentians; resort; pop. 12,200.

Saint Kitts (kĭts′) or **Saint Chris′to·pher** (krĭs′tō·fẽr) island, West Indies Federation, in Leeward Is. colony; with Nevis and Anguilla, forms a colony (Saint Kitts-Nevis), ✳ Basseterre, area 152 sq. m., pop. 46,300; area of St. Kitts 68 sq. m., pop. 18,500.

Saint Lau′rent′ (săn′ lô′rän′) town, Canada, on Montreal I.; pop. 38,300.

Saint-Lau′rent′-sur-Mer (săn′lô′rän′sür·mâr′) town, NW France, in Normandy NW of Bayeux; an American beachhead June 1944.

Saint Law′rence (sänt lô′rĕns; lô′rĕns) river, E Canada, in Ontario and Quebec provs., flowing from Lake Ontario to Atlantic Ocean; 760 m. long; at its mouth is wide bay, the **Gulf of Saint Lawrence**.

Saint Lawrence Island, island, W Alaska, in N Bering Sea; 95 m. long.

Saint Lawrence Seaway, waterway, Canada and United States, along upper St. Lawrence river from Montreal to Lake Ontario, affording deep-draft navigation between Atlantic Ocean and Great Lakes; includes hydroelectric project; construction begun 1955.

Saint-Lô (sänt·lō′; Fr. săn′lō′) town, NW France, in Normandy W of Caen; center of heavy fighting July 1944.

Saint Lou′is (sänt lōō′ĭs) **1** river, NE Minnesota, flowing into W tip of Lake Superior on Wisconsin border; 220 m. long. **2** independent city, Missouri, on Mississippi river; pop. 856,800.

Saint-Lou·is′ (săn′lwē′) city, French West Africa, ✳ of Senegal territory, on island at mouth of Senegal river; pop. 40,300.

Saint Lou′is Park (sänt lōō′ĭs) village, SE Minnesota; pop. 22,600.

Saint Lu′cia (lōō′shá; lū·sē′á) island, West Indies Federation, in Windward Is.; ✳ Castries; area 233 sq. m.; pop. 73,700.

Saint-Ma′lo′ (săn′má′lō′) seaport, NW France, in Brittany on island at mouth of Rance river, on the **Gulf of Saint-Malo**, inlet of English Channel between peninsulas of Normandy and Brittany.

Saint Mar′tin (sänt mär′tĭn; -t′n; Fr. săn′ mär′tăn′) island, West Indies, E of Virgin Is.; N part belongs to France, S part to Netherlands; total area 38 sq. m.; pop. 8000.

Saint Mar′y·le·bone′, commonly **Marylebone** (sänt mär′ĭ·lĕ·bōn′; without 'St.,' mär′[ĭ·]lĕ·bŭn, mär′ĭ·bŭn) metropolitan borough, London, N of Hyde Park; pop. 75,800.

Saint Mar′ys (mâr′ĭz) **1** river on Georgia-Florida border; flows from

Okefinokee Swamp E into Atlantic Ocean; 175 m. long. **2** river between U.S. and Canada, in Ontario and Upper Peninsula, Michigan; flows from Lake Superior, descending 20 ft. in a mile at **Saint Marys Falls**, into N end of Lake Huron; 63 m. long.
Saint-Maur-des-Fos′sés′ (săN′môr′dā·fô′sā′) commune, N France, SE of Paris on the Marne; pop. 55,500.
Saint Mau′rice (sānt mô′rĭs; mŏr′ĭs; Fr. săN′ mô′rēs′) river, Canada, in S Quebec prov., flowing S into the St. Lawrence river; 325 m. long.
Saint Mi′chel′ (săN′ mē′shĕl′) town, Canada, on Montreal I.; pop. 24,700.
Saint-Mi′hiel′ (săN′mē′yĕl′) town, NE France, on the Meuse; battle Sept. 12–14, 1918.
Saint-Mo·ritz′ (sānt′mô·rĭts′; Fr. săN′mô′rēts′), Ger. **Sankt Mo·ritz′** (zängkt′ mō·rĭts′; often in Switzerland, säm′mō·rĭts′; by non-Swiss German speakers, often zängkt mō′rĭts) town, E Switzerland, in Graubünden canton on Inn river SSE of Chur; resort.
Saint-Na′zaire′ (săN′ná′zâr′) seaport, NW France, at mouth of Loire river; port of debarkation and supply base for American Expeditionary Force 1917–18; in World War II German U-boat base after 1940.
Sain′tonge′ (săN′tôNzh′) ancient province of France, on Bay of Biscay N of the Gironde.
Saint Paul (sānt pôl′) city, ✻ of Minnesota, on Mississippi river 10 m. E of Minneapolis; pop. 311,300.
Saint Pe′ter, Lake (pē′tẽr) expansion of St. Lawrence river, Canada, in Quebec; area 130 sq. m.
Saint Pe′ters·burg (pē′tẽrz·bûrg) **1** city, W Florida, on Tampa Bay; pop. 96,700. **2** see LENINGRAD.
Saint Pierre (sānt pēr′; Fr. săN′ pyâr′) island in Atlantic Ocean off S Newfoundland; with nearby island of Miquelon, constitutes French territory of **Saint Pierre and Miq′ue·lon** (mĭk′ĕ·lŏn; Fr. mē′klôN′), total area 93 sq. m., pop. 4700.
Saint-Quen′tin′ (săN′käN′tăN′; Angl. sānt·kwĕn′t'n, -tĭn) commune, N France, on Somme river NW of Laon; pop. 48,600.
Saint Thom′as (sānt tŏm′ăs) **1** island, West Indies, one of Virgin Is. of the United States; area 32 sq. m.; pop. 13,800. **2** see CHARLOTTE AMALIE. **3** city, Canada, in SE Ontario S of London; pop. 19,100. **4** see SÃO TOMÉ.
Saint Ubes. See SETÚBAL.
Saint Vin′cent (sānt vĭn′sĕnt) island, West Indies Federation, in Windward Is.; with northern Grenadines, constitutes a colony, ✻ Kingstown; area 133 sq. m.; pop. 44,300.
Saint Vincent, Cape, Port. **Ca′bo de São Vi·cen′te** (kȧ′vōō thē souN′ vē·sāNn′tē) cape, SW Portugal; battle 1797.
Saint Yves. See SETÚBAL.
Sai·pan′ (sī·păn′; sī·păn′; sī′păn) island, S cen. Mariana Is.; under the Japanese developed as naval base; taken by Americans July 1944.
Sa′ïs (sā′ĭs) city, ancient Egypt, ✻ of Lower Egypt, in Nile delta.
Saishu. See CHEJU.
Sa·kai (sä·kī) city, Japan, in Honshu on Osaka Bay; pop. 194,000.
Sakartvelo. See GEORGIA.
Sa·kar′ya (sä·kär′yä) river, NW Turkey in Asia, flowing into the Black Sea 80 m. E of the Bosporus; 300 m. long.
Sa′kha·lin (săk′ȧ·lēn; -lĭn), formerly **Sa′ghal·ien′** (să′găl·yĕn′), Jap. **Ka·ra·fu·to** (kä·rä·fōō·tō) island, E Asia, off coast of Soviet Russia, Asia, N of Japan; formerly (1905–45) divided between Russia and Japan (S half), since 1945 controlled by the U.S.S.R.; area 24,560 sq. m.; pop. 420,000.
Sakhar. See SUKKUR.
Sakis-Adasi. See CHIOS.
Sa·ki·shi·ma Islands (sä·kē·shē·mä) group of islands, S Ryukyu Is.
Sak·ka′ra. = SAQQARA.
Sala. See IJSSEL river. See SALIAN, in Vocab.
Salaberry de Valleyfield. See VALLEYFIELD.
Sa·la′do (sä·lä′thō) **1** river, Argentina, in upper course known as the **Rí′o del Ju′ra·men′to** (rē′ō thĕl hōō′rä·män′tō); flows from the Andes SE into Paraná river; 1120 m. long. **2** river, Argentina, in upper course known as the **Des′a·gua·de′ro** (dās′ä·gwä·thā′rō); flows into Colorado river; 850 m. long.
Sa·la′jar or **Sa·la′yar** (sä·lä′yär) island, Indonesia, off SW Celebes I.; area 256 sq. m.; pop. 76,100.
Sal′a·man′ca (săl′ȧ·măng′kȧ; Span. sä′lä·mäng′kä) commune, W Spain; once center of Arab learning in Europe; pop. 79,800.
Sal′a·mau′a (săl′ȧ·mou′ȧ) town, E North-East New Guinea, on Huon Gulf; formerly port for Morobe gold fields; destroyed 1942–1943.
Sa·lam′bri·a (sȧ·lăm′brĭ·ȧ; Ital. sä·läm′brē·ä), Mod. Gr. **Sa′lam·vrí′as** (sä′läm·vrē′äs) or **Pi·niós′** (pē·nyôs′), anc. Gr. **Pe·ne′us** (pē·nē′ŭs) river, Greece, in Thessaly, flowing to Gulf of Salonica; 125 m. long.
Sal′a·mis (săl′ȧ·mĭs) **1** ancient city, Cyprus; naval battle 449 B.C. **2** island, Greece, in Saronic Gulf off Attica; naval battle 480 B.C.
Salayar. See SALAJAR.
Sa′lé′ (sȧ′lā′), Arab. **Sla** (slă), Eng. **Sal′i** or **Sal′lee** (săl′ē) seaport, NW Morocco, just NE of Rabat; pop. 58,200.
Sa′lem (sā′lĕm) **1** city, NE Massachusetts, on Atlantic Ocean NE of Boston; pop. 41,900. **2** see WINSTON-SALEM. **3** city, ✻ of Oregon, on Willamette river SSW of Portland; pop. 43,100. **4** city, S India, in Madras state; pop. 129,700. **5** Jerusalem; — an ancient name.
Sa·ler′no (sä·lĕr′nō; Angl. sȧ·lûr′nō) seaport, S Italy, on **Gulf of Salerno** (inlet of Tyrrhenian Sea) ESE of Naples; pop. 90,400.
Sal′ford (sôl′fẽrd) city and county borough, NW England, in Lancashire, on the Irwell river adjacent to Manchester; pop. 178,000.
Sa·li′na (sȧ·lī′nȧ) city, cen. Kansas, on Smoky Hill river; pop. 26,200.
Salis′bur′y (sôlz′bĕr′ĭ; -bẽr·ĭ; -brĭ) **1** city, SE Maryland; pop. 15,100. **2** city, cen. North Carolina; pop. 20,100. **3** town, ✻ of Southern Rhodesia and of Mashonaland; pop. 32,800. **4** or **New Sar′um** (sâr′ŭm) municipal borough, S England, in Wiltshire, on the Avon; pop. 32,900; nearby is **Salisbury Plain**, site of Stonehenge.
Salm′on (săm′ŭn) river, cen. Idaho, flowing into Snake river; 420 m. long.
Sal′o·ni′ca or **Sal′o·ni′ka** (săl′ō·nē′kȧ; sȧ·lŏn′ĭ·kȧ; săl′ō·nī′kȧ), also **Thes′sa·lo·ni′ca** (thĕs′ȧ·lō·nī′kȧ; -lŏn′ĭ·kȧ), Mod. Gr. **Sa′lo·ní′ki** (sä′lô·nyē′kyē) or **Thes′sa·lo·ní′ki** (thä′sä·lô·nyē′kyē) seaport, NE Greece, in Macedonia at head of Gulf of Salonica; pop. 216,100.
Salonica, Gulf of, arm of Aegean Sea, NE Greece, between W Chalcidice and mainland.
Salop. **1** See SHROPSHIRE. **2** See SHREWSBURY. — **Sa·lo′pi·an** (sȧ·lō′pĭ·ăn), adj. & n.
Salt (sôlt) **1** river, Arizona, flowing W into Gila river; 200 m. long. **2** river, N cen. Kentucky, flowing into Ohio river; 100 m. long. **3** river, NE Missouri, flowing SE into Mississippi river; 200 m. long.
Sal·til′lo (säl·tē′yō) city, NE Mexico, ✻ of Coahuila state; pop. 49,400.
Salt Lake City, city, ✻ of Utah, SE of Great Salt Lake; pop. 182,100.
Sal′ton Sea (sôl′t'n; -tŭn), formerly **Salton Sink**, lake, S California; formed 1905–07 by diversion of water from Colorado river into a depression (sink) 280 ft. below sea level.
Sa·lu′da (sȧ·lōō′dȧ) river, W cen. South Carolina; flows SE and unites with Broad river to form Congaree river; 200 m. long.
Sal′va·dor (săl′vȧ·dôr), formerly **São Sal′va·dor′** (souN säl′vȧ·thōr′) or **Ba·í′a** (bȧ·ē′ȧ) seaport, E Brazil, ✻ of Baía state, on All Saints Bay; pop. 396,000.
Salvador, El. See EL SALVADOR.
Sal′ween (săl′wēn) river, SE Asia, flowing from E Tibet to Gulf of Martaban in Burma; 1750 m. long.
Salz′burg (zälts′bōōrk; Angl. sôlz′bûrg) city, Austria, on Salzach river; pop. 102,100.
Samanala. See ADAM'S PEAK.
Sa′mar (sä′mär) island, Philippine Is., in the Visayan Is. just NE of Leyte; ✻ Catbalogan; area 5050 sq. m.
Samara. See KUIBYSHEV.
Samarang. See SEMARANG.
Sa·mar′i·a (sȧ·mâr′ĭ·ȧ) **1** region, cen. Palestine, between Galilee and Judaea. **2** the ancient kingdom of Israel, the Northern Kingdom. **3** mod. **Se·bas′tye** (sĕ·bŏs′tĭ·yȧ) city, ✻ of ancient kingdom; modern village in Jordan. See SAMARITAN, in Vocab.
Sam′ar·kand (săm′ẽr·kănd; săm′ẽr·kănd′), Turki **Sa′mar·qand′** (sä′mär·känd′), anc. **Mar′a·can′da** (măr′ȧ·kăn′dȧ) city, Soviet Central Asia, in Uzbek S.S.R.; once ✻ of Sogdiana; pop. 134,400.
Sam′bre (säN′br′), Flem. **Sam′ber** (säm′bẽr) river, France and Belgium, flowing ENE into the Meuse; 100 m. long.
Sam′ni·um (săm′nĭ·ŭm) ancient country, cen. Italy, bordering on Adriatic Sea; conquered by Rome c. 290 B.C. See SAMNITE, in Vocab.
Sa·mo′a (sȧ·mō′ȧ) or **Samoa Islands**, formerly **Nav′i·ga′tors Islands** (năv′ĭ·gā′tẽrz) group of islands, SW cen. Pacific Ocean, divided by 171st W meridian into American, or Eastern, Samoa and the Territory of Western Samoa, administered by New Zealand; total area 1209 sq. m.; pop. 78,000. See SAMOAN, in Vocab.
Sa′mos (sā′mŏs), Turk. **Su·sam′-A·da·si′** (sōō·säm′ä·dä·sĭ′) island, Greece, in Aegean Sea off coast of Turkey N of the Dodecanese; area 171 sq. m.; pop. 58,600. — **Sa′mi·an** (sā′mĭ·ăn), adj. & n.
Sam′o·thrace (săm′ō·thrās), Mod. Gr. **Sa′mo·thrá′ki** (sä′mô·thrä′kyē) island, Greece, in NE Aegean Sea. See SAMOTHRACIAN, in Vocab.
San·′a′ or **San·aa′** (sŏn·ä′) city, SW Arabia, ✻ of Yemen; pop. 25,000.
San An′ge·lo (săn ăn′jĕ·lō) city, W cen. Texas; pop. 52,100.
San An·to′ni·o (săn′ ăn·tō′nĭ·ō) city, S cen. Texas, on San Antonio river; pop. 408,400.
San Ber′nar·di′no (săn bûr′nȧ·dē′nō) **1** city, SE California, in a valley W of N end of the San Bernardino Mts.; pop. 63,100. **2** mountain pass, SE Switzerland, in Graubünden canton in Lepontine Alps; alt. 6767 ft.
San Bernardino Mountains, mountain range, S California, S of Mojave Desert; highest peak San Gorgonio, 11,485 ft.
San Blas, Gulf of (săn blăs′) inlet of Caribbean Sea on N coast of Panama, E of Panama Canal.
San Blas, Isthmus of, narrowest section of Isthmus of Panama.
San Buenaventura. See VENTURA.
San Car′los (săn kär′lŭs) **1** municipality, Philippine Is., in Luzon SE of Lingayen; pop. 47,300. **2** municipality, Philippine Is., in Negros ESE of Bacolod; pop. 70,000.
San Cris·to′bal (săn′ krĭs·tō′b'l) island, S Solomon Is., SE of Guadalcanal.
San Cris·tó′bal (săn′ krĭs·tō′b'l) **1** also known as **Chat′ham Island** (chăt′ăm) island, Ecuador, one of the Galápagos Is.; only town is San Cristóbal, ✻ of the islands. **2** city, W Venezuela; pop. 56,100.
San′cy′, Puy de (pü·ēt′ säN′sē′) mountain, cen. France; highest point in the Monts Dore and in the Auvergne Mts., 6185 ft.
San·da′kan (sän·dä′kän) seaport, former ✻ of British North Borneo; pop. 13,800.
Sandalwood Island. See SUMBA.
Sand′hurst (sănd′hûrst) civil parish, S England, in Berkshire; site of Sandhurst Royal Military Academy, founded 1799, merged 1946 with Royal Military Academy at Woolwich.
San·di′a (săn·dē′ȧ) locality, New Mexico, adjoining Albuquerque on E; atomic energy laboratory and special weapons project.
San Di·e′go (săn′ dĭ·ā′gō) seaport, SW California, on San Diego Bay 12 m. N of Mexican border; naval and marine base; pop. 334,400.
San Domingo. See SANTO DOMINGO.
San′dring·ham (săn′drĭng·ăm) village, E England, in Norfolk, near the Wash; Sandringham House, royal residence.
San·dus′ky (săn·dŭs′kĭ; săn-) city, N Ohio, on Lake Erie S of entrance to Sandusky Bay; pop. 29,400.
Sand′wich (săn[d]′wĭch; Brit. also -wĭj) municipal borough, SE England, in Kent; one of the Cinque Ports.
Sandwich Islands. See HAWAII.
Sandy Hook, peninsula, E New Jersey, extending N along coast toward New York Bay.
San′ford, Mount (săn′fẽrd) mountain, S Alaska, at W end of Wrangell Mts.; 16,208 ft. high.
San Fran·cis′co (săn′ frŏn·sĭs′kō) **1** seaport, W California, on San Francisco Bay and Pacific Ocean; pop. 775,400. **2** = SÃO FRANCISCO.
San Francisco Bay, inlet of Pacific Ocean, California; 40 m. long and 3 to 12 m. wide; entrance (Golden Gate) 2 m. wide.
San Francisco Peaks, also **San Francisco Mountain**, three peaks, N Arizona, including highest point in Arizona, 12,611 ft.
San Ga′bri·el (săn gā′brĭ·ĕl) city, SW California; pop. 20,300.
San′ga·mon (săng′gȧ·mŭn) river, cen. Illinois, flowing SW and W into Illinois river; 225 m. long.

San·gay′ (säng·gī′) mountain, cen. Ecuador; active volcano; 17,749 ft.

San Germano. See CASSINO.

Sang′ihe Islands (säng′ĭr), island group, Indonesia, N of Celebes, including **Sangihe Island**, formerly **Great Sang′ir** (säng′ĭr), site of Awu volcano.

San′gre de Cris′to Mountains (säng′grĕ dĕ krĭs′tō) range of the Rocky Mts., extending from cen. Colorado to N cen. New Mexico; highest point Blanca Peak, 14,390 ft.

San Il′de·fon′so (sän ĭl′dĕ·fŏn′sō) or **La Gran′ja** (lä gräng′hä) town, cen. Spain, SE of Segovia; palace; scene of treaties 1796 and 1800.

San I·si′dro (sän′ ĕ·sē′thrō) town, E Argentina, near Buenos Aires; pop. 61,600.

San Ja·cin′to (sän′ jȧ·sĭn′tō) river, SE Texas, flowing into Galveston Bay; 100 m. long; near its mouth is site of battle 1836.

San Joa·quin′ (sän′ wō·kēn′) river, California, flowing SW out of the Sierra Nevada, then NW into Sacramento river; 350 m. long.

San Joaquin Valley, valley of the San Joaquin river and region S of it between the Sierra Nevada and the Coast Ranges.

San Jo·se′ (sän′ [h]ō·zā′) city, W California, SE of S end of San Francisco Bay; pop. 95,300.

San Jo·sé′ (sän′ [h]ō·zā′) city, ✳ of Costa Rica; pop. 86,900.

San Juan (sän wŏn′) **1** river, SW United States, rising in S Colorado and flowing into Colorado river in SE Utah; 360 m. long. **2** city, W Argentina; pop. 80,000. **3** seaport, ✳ of Puerto Rico; pop. 223,900.

San Juan Bautista. See VILLAHERMOSA.

San Juan Hill (sän wŏn′) elevation, E Cuba, near Santiago de Cuba; captured by American troops 1898.

San Juan Islands (sän wŏn′) group of islands, NW Washington, between Vancouver I. and the mainland.

San Juan Mountains, range of the Rocky Mts., SW Colorado; highest point Uncompahgre Peak, 14,306 ft.

Sankt Gallen. See SAINT GALLEN.

Sankt Joachimsthal. See JÁCHYMOV.

Sankt Moritz. See SAINT-MORITZ.

San Le·an′dro (sän′ lĕ·ăn′drō) city, W California, SE of Oakland; pop. 27,500.

San Luis Po′to·sí′ (sän lwēs′ pō′tō·sē′) **1** state, cen. Mexico; area 24,415 sq. m.; pop. 855,300. **2** city, its ✳; pop. 77,200.

San Ma·ri′no (sän′ mȧ·rē′nō) country, S Europe, on Italian penin. SSW of Rimini (Italy); an independent republic; ✳ San Marino city; area 38 sq. m.; pop. 14,500.

San Ma·te′o (sän′ mȧ·tā′ō) city, W California, on San Francisco Bay; pop. 41,800.

San Nic′o·las (sän nĭk′ō·lȧs) island, S California; one of the Santa Barbara group, W of Santa Catalina I.; missile-launching site.

San Pab′lo Bay (sän păb′lō) north extension of San Francisco Bay, California.

San Pe′dro (sän pē′drō) section of Los Angeles, California, on coast; formerly a city; military and naval base.

San Re′mo (sän rā′mo; rē′mō) seaport, NW Italy; pop. 31,800.

San Sal′va·dor (sän săl′vȧ·dôr) **1** known also, esp. formerly, as **Wat′lings Island** (wŏt′lĭngz) island, Bahama Is.; Columbus's first landfall in the New World. **2** city, ✳ of El Salvador; pop. 160,400.

San Se′bas·tián′ (sän sā′vȧs·tyän′; Angl. săn sĕ·băs′chȧn) seaport, N Spain, ✳ of Guipúzcoa prov., on Bay of Biscay; pop. 113,800.

San Ste′fa·no (sän stĕf′ȧ·nō), Turk. **Ye′şil·köy′** (yĕ′shĕl·kû′ĕ) village, Turkey in Europe, on Sea of Marmara W of İstanbul; treaty 1878.

San′ta An′a (sän′tȧ än′ȧ) **1** city, SW California, E of Long Beach; pop. 45,500. **2** city, NW El Salvador; pop. 51,700.

San′ta Bar′ba·ra (sän′tȧ bär′bȧ·rȧ; bär′brȧ) city, SW California, on Santa Barbara Channel; pop. 44,900.

Santa Barbara Islands, chain of islands off SW California.

San′ta Cat′a·li′na (sän′tȧ kăt′ȧ·lē′nȧ) or **Catalina**, island, California, in SW Santa Barbara Is.; area 70 sq. m.

San′ta Cat′a·ri′na (sän′tȧ kät′ȧ·rē′nȧ) state, S Brazil, bordering on Atlantic Ocean; ✳ Florianópolis; area 31,118 sq. m.; pop. 1,578,200.

San′ta Cruz (sän′tȧ krōōz′) **1** city, W California, on Monterey Bay; pop. 22,000. **2** see SAINT CROIX island, Virgin Is. of the U.S. **3** river, S Argentina, flowing E into Atlantic Ocean; 250 m. long.

San′ta Cruz de Te′ne·ri′fe (sän′tȧ krōōth′ [krōōz′] thā tā′nȧ·rē′fä) seaport, Spain, in Canary Is. on Tenerife I.; pop. 102,400.

San′ta Cruz Islands (sän′tȧ krōōz′) island group, SW Pacific Ocean, N of the New Hebrides and 240 m. E of S part of Solomon Is.; administratively attached to British Solomon Is.; chief island Ndeni.

San′ta Fe (sän′tȧ fā′) **1** city, ✳ of New Mexico; pop. 28,000. **2** city, cen. Argentina, on Salado river; pop. 149,900.

Santa Fe Trail, route to the Southwest used especially 1821–80, from vicinity of Kansas City, Missouri, to Santa Fe, New Mexico.

San′ta Is′a·bel (sän′tȧ ĭz′ȧ·bĕl) or **Isabel**, island, E cen. Solomon Is., E of SE Choiseul I.

San′ta Ma·rí′a (sän′tȧ mȧ·rē′ȧ) volcano, Guatemala, in Sierra Madre range; frequent eruptions between 1900 and 1930.

Santa Maura. See LEUCAS.

San′ta Mon′i·ca (sän′tȧ mŏn′ĭ·kȧ) city, SW California, on **Santa Monica Bay**, W of Los Angeles; pop. 71,600.

San′tan·der′ (sän′tän·dĕr′) **1** province, N Spain, bordering on Bay of Biscay. **2** seaport, its ✳; pop. 102,500.

San′ta·rém′ (sän′tȧ·rĕm′) city, N Brazil, in W Pará state on Amazon river where the Tapajoz joins it; pop. 14,600.

San′ta Ro′sa (sän′tȧ rō′zȧ) **1** city, W California; pop. 17,900. **2** in full **San′ta Ro′sa de Co·pán′** (Span. sän′tä rrō′sä thä kō·pän′) town, W Honduras; to the W is ruined city of Copán.

San·tee′ (sän·tē′; sän′tē′) river, South Carolina; flows SE into Atlantic Ocean; 143 m. long.

San′ti·a′go (sän′tĭ·ä′gō) **1** island, Cape Verde Is.: see SÃO TIAGO. **2** or **San′ti·a′go de Chi′le** (sän′tĭ·ä′gō dĕ chĭl′ĕ) city, ✳ of Chile; pop. 952,100. **3** = SANTIAGO DE CUBA. **4** or **San·tia′go de los Ca′bal·le′ros** (sän·tyä′gō thä lōs kä′vä·yā′rōs) city, N cen. Dominican Republic; pop. 56,200. **5** or **San·tia′go de Com′pos·te′la** (sän·tyä′gō thä kōm′pōs·tā′lä) commune, NW Spain; pop. 49,200.

San′ti·a′go de Cu′ba (sän′tĭ·ä′gō dĕ kū′bä) seaport, S Cuba; scene of destruction of Spanish fleet July 3, 1898; pop. 120,600.

Santiago de Guayaquil. See GUAYAQUIL.

San·tia′go del Es·te′ro (sän·tyä′gō thĕl äs·tä′rō) city, N Argentina, on Dulce river; pop. 58,900.

San′to Do·min′go (sän′tō dō·mĭng′gō), **1** also **San Domingo** (sän′ dō·mĭng′gō) the Dominican Republic; — its former name. **2** see CIUDAD TRUJILLO.

San′to·rin′ (sän′tō·rēn′), anc. **The′ra** (thēr′ȧ) island, Greece, in S Cyclades.

San′tos (sän′tŭs) seaport, SE Brazil, in SE São Paulo state; pop. 201,700.

São Ca·e·ta′no do Sul (souǹg′ kä·ĕ·tä′nŏō thōō sōōl′) city, S Brazil, in São Paulo state; pop. 55,800.

São Fran·cis′co (souǹ′ frän·sēsh′kōō) river, E Brazil; rises in S cen. Minas Gerais state, flows into Atlantic Ocean; 1800 m. long.

São Luís (soun lwēs′) seaport, NE Brazil, ✳ of Maranhão state, on Maranhão I.; pop. 81,400.

São Ma·nuel′ (soun′ mä·nwäl′) river, cen. Brazil; flows NW and joins the Juruena river to form the Tapajoz; 600 m. long.

São Mi·guel′ (soun′ mē·gäl′) island, Portugal, in E Azores; chief town Ponta Delgada; area 297 sq. m.; pop. 117,000.

Saône (sōn) river, E France, flowing SSW into Rhone river; 300 m. long.

São Pau′lo (sounm pou′lōō) **1** state, SE Brazil; area 95,459 sq. m.; pop. 9,242,600. **2** city, its ✳, on Tietê river; pop. 2,041,700.

São Paulo de Loanda. See LUANDA.

São Pedro do Rio Grande do Sul. See RIO GRANDE.

Saorstat Eireann. See IRELAND.

São Salvador. See SALVADOR.

São Tia′go (soun tyä′gōō), also **San′ti·a′go** (sän′tĭ·ä′gō) island, largest of Cape Verde Is.; chief town Praia, ✳ of the group; 359 sq. m.

São To·mé′ or **São Tho·mé′** (sounn′ tōō·mâ′) island, W Africa, in Gulf of Guinea on the equator; with Principe I., forms Portuguese colony of **São Tomé e Prin′ci·pe** (ĕ prĕn′sĕ·pĕ), 377 sq. m., pop. 60,500.

São Vicente, Cabo de. See SAINT VINCENT, CAPE.

Sap·po·ro (säp·pō·rō) city, Japan, on Hokkaido I.; pop. 259,600.

Saq·qa′ra (sŭk·kä′rō) village, N Egypt, just SW of ruins of Memphis; site of necropolis of ancient Memphis.

Sarabat. See GEDIZ.

Sar′a·gos′sa (săr′ȧ·gŏs′ȧ), Span. **Za′ra·go′za** (thä′rä·gō′thä; sä′rä·gō′sä) city, NE Spain, on Ebro river; pop. 261,100.

Sa′ra·je·vo (sä′rä·yĕ·vō) or **Se′ra·je·vo** (sĕ′-) city, cen. Yugoslavia, ✳ of Bosnia and Herzegovina; pop. 118,800.

Sar′a·nac Lake (săr′ȧ·năk) village, NE New York, in the Adirondack Mts. near Lower Saranac Lake; sanatoria for tuberculous patients; pop. 6900.

Sar′a·so′ta (săr′ȧ·sō′tȧ) city, W Florida, S of Tampa Bay; pop. 18,900.

Sar′a·to′ga (săr′ȧ·tō′gȧ), since 1831 called **Schuy′ler·ville** (skī′lẽr·vĭl) village, E New York, on Hudson river E of Saratoga Springs; scene of Burgoyne's surrender Oct. 17, 1777, after battles of Sept. 19 and Oct. 7, which occurred to the S at Stillwater.

Saratoga Springs, city, E New York, in Adirondack foothills; pop. 15,500.

Sa·ra′tov (sŭ·rä′tŭf) city, SE Soviet Russia, Europe, on the Volga; pop. 375,900.

Sa·ra′wak (sȧ·rä′wä[k]) country, NW Borneo; British colony; ✳ Kuching; area 50,000 sq. m.; pop. 490,000.

Sardica. See SOFIA.

Sar·din′i·a (sär·dĭn′ĭ·ȧ; -dĭn′yȧ), Ital. **Sar·de′gna** (sär·dān′yä) **1** island, Italy, in Mediterranean Sea; area 9283 sq. m.; pop. 1,239,600. **2** kingdom 1720–1860 including the island and (except for period 1792–1815) Piedmont and Savoy; ruled by house of Savoy.

Sar′dis (sär′dĭs) or **Sar′des** (-dēz) ancient city, Asia Minor, in Hermus valley 50 m. E of Smyrna; ✳ of ancient kingdom of Lydia.

Sa′re·ma (sä′ryĭ·mä), Estonian **Saa′re·maa** (sä′rĕ·mä), Ger. **Oe′sel** (û′zĕl) island, Estonia, at mouth of Gulf of Riga; area 1010 sq. m.

Sark (särk), Fr. **Sercq** (sĕrk) island, English Channel, one of the Channel Is.; area 2 sq. m.; pop. 600.

Sar·ma′tia (sär·mā′shá; -shĭ·á) ancient region, NE Europe, in what is now Poland and Russia between the Vistula and Volga rivers.

Sar′ni·a (sär′nĭ·ȧ) city, Canada, in SE Ontario on St. Clair river; pop. 43,500.

Sa·ron′ic Gulf (sȧ·rŏn′ĭk) inlet of Aegean Sea, SE Greece, between Attica and the Peloponnesus.

Sa′ros Gulf (sä′rŏs; sär′ōs) inlet of Aegean Sea, SW Turkey in Europe, at base of Gallipoli Peninsula.

Sarre. See SAAR river.

Sarum, New. See SALISBURY.

Sarum, Old. See OLD SARUM.

Sa·se·bo (sä·sĕ·bō) seaport, Japan, in NW Kyushu I.; pop. 175,200.

Saseno. See SAZAN.

Sas·katch′e·wan (săs·kăch′ĕ·wŏn; săs·; -wŏn) **1** river, Canada, flowing from Rocky Mts. in W Alberta to Lake Winnipeg in cen. Manitoba; formed by confluence in cen. Saskatchewan of the **North Saskatchewan**, 760 m. long, and the **South Saskatchewan**, 865 m. long; length to head of Bow river, headstream of the South Saskatchewan, 1205 m. **2**, abbr. **Sask.**, province, W cen. Canada; ✳ Regina; land area 237,975 sq. m.; pop. 880,700.

Sas′ka·toon′ (săs′kȧ·tōōn′) city, Canada, in S cen. Saskatchewan on South Saskatchewan river; pop. 72,900.

Sas′sa·ri (säs′sä·rē) commune, Italy, in Sardinia; pop. 69,000.

Sat′pu·ra Range (sät′pōō·rȧ) range of hills, W cen. India, between the Narbada and Tapti rivers; average elevation 3000 ft.

Sa′tu·Ma′re (sä′tōō·mä′rĕ), Hung. **Szat′már-Né′me·ti** (sŏt′mär·nä′mä·tĭ) city, NW Romania, near Hungarian border; pop. 51,700.

Sa·u′di Arabia (sä·ōō′dĭ; sä-) country, SW Asia, occupying most of peninsula of Arabia; includes former kingdoms of Nejd and Hejaz and principality of Asir; a kingdom, formed 1932; ✳✳ Riyadh and Mecca; area 597,000 sq. m.; pop. 6,000,000.

Sau′gus (sô′gŭs) town, NE Massachusetts; pop. 17,200.

Sault Sainte Ma·rie′ (sōō′ sänt mȧ·rē′) **1** city, N Michigan, in Upper Peninsula on Saint Marys river at the rapids; pop. 17,900. **2** city, Canada, in Ontario on St. Marys river opposite Sault Sainte Marie, Michigan; pop. 37,300.

Sault Sainte Marie Canals or **Soo Canals** or **Soo Locks** (sō͞o) three ship canals, two in the United States (four parallel locks) and one in Canada (one lock), at rapids in Saint Marys river, connecting Lake Superior with Lake Huron.

Sau·rash'tra (sou·rä͝sh'trȧ) former state, W India, in Kathiawar penin.; formed 1948; became 1956 part of Bombay state.

Sa'va (sä'vä), Fr. **Save** (sàv), Ger. **Sau** (zou) river, N Yugoslavia, flowing from Italian border E to the Danube; 450 m. long.

Savage Island. See NIUE.

Sav'age's Station (săv'ĭj·ĭz) battlefield near Richmond, Virginia; unsuccessful Confederate attack June 29, 1862.

Sa·vai'i (sä·vī'ē) island, Western Samoa; area 703 sq. m.

Sa·van'nah (sȧ·văn'ȧ) **1** river, E Georgia; flows SE, forming Georgia–South Carolina boundary, into Atlantic Ocean; 314 m. long. **2** seaport, SE Georgia, at mouth of Savannah river; pop. 119,600.

Savannah River, government reserve, South Carolina, along Savannah river below Augusta, Georgia; site of plant, started 1951, for manufacturing atomic materials.

Sa've (sä'vě), Eng. **Sa'bi** (sä'bĭ) river, SE Africa; rises in cen. Southern Rhodesia, flows E across S Mozambique into Mozambique Channel; 400 m. long.

Sa'vo (sä'vō) island, SE Solomon Is., N of W end of Guadalcanal I.; naval and air battles Aug. 8–9 and Nov. 12–13, 1942.

Sa·vo'na (sȧ·vō'nä) seaport, NW Italy, SW of Genoa; pop. 72,200.

Sa·voy' (sȧ·voi'), Fr. **Sa'voie'** (sà'vwä'), Ital. **Sa·vo'ia** (sä·vō'yä) historical region, SE France, bordering on Italy; duchy 1416–1720; part of kingdom of Sardinia 1720–1860; became part of France 1860. — **Sa·voy'ard** (sȧ·voi'ĕrd), n.

Sa·watch', or **Sa·guache', Range** (sȧ·wŏch') range of Rocky Mts., cen. Colorado; highest peak Mount Elbert, 14,431 ft.

Saxe (săks) Saxony; — its French form, used in English chiefly in names of former duchies in Thuringia; as, **Saxe-Al'ten·burg** (săks'-äl'tĕn·bo͝ork), **Saxe-Wei'mar-Ei'se·nach** (-vī'·mär·ī'zĕ·näk), **Saxe-Mei'ning·en** (-mī'nĭng·ĕn), **Saxe-Go'tha** (-gō'thä; -tà), and **Saxe-Co'burg** (-kō'bûrg).

Sax'o·ny (săk's'n·ĭ), Ger. **Sach'sen** (zäk'sĕn) **1** originally, region, NW Germany, S of Jutland and between the Elbe and Rhine rivers; a duchy 9th to 12th cents.; part of this region, now called **Lower Sax'ony,** Ger. **Nie'der·sach'sen** (nē'dĕr·zäk'sĕn), is a state of the Bonn Republic, ✻ Hannover. **2** region, E Germany, bordering on Czechoslovakia, in 15th cent. a duchy and electorate; in 1806 became a kingdom; N part became province of Prussia 1815, the remainder formed a state of Germany after 1871. See SAXON, in Vocab.

Sa·yan' Mountains (sä·yän') mountain range, Soviet Russia, Asia, on border of Tuva Autonomous Region; highest point 11,453 ft.

Sa'zan (sä'zän), Ital. **Sa·se'no** (sä·zā'nō) island, Albania, at entrance to Bay of Vlonë; Italian naval base 1914–47; after 1947 developed as submarine base by Soviets.

Sca'fell' Pike (skô'fĕl') mountain, England, in Cumberland; highest in England, 3210 ft.

Scamander. See MENDERES.

Scan'di·na'vi·a (skăn'dĭ·nā'vĭ·ȧ; -nāv'yȧ) **1** or **Scandinavian Peninsula,** the peninsula, N Europe, occupied by Norway and Sweden. **2** Norway, Sweden, and Denmark; also, sometimes, Iceland.

Scap'a Flow (skăp'ȧ flō') sea basin, N Scotland, in Orkney Is.; chief British naval base in World War I; place where Germans scuttled their own fleet June 21, 1919.

Scarpanto. See KARPATHOS.

Scebeli, Uebi. See SHIBELI, WEBBE.

Schaer'beek or **Schaar'beek** (skär'bāk) commune, cen. Belgium, NE of Brussels; pop. 124,300.

Schaff·hau'sen (shäf'hou'zĕn) **1** canton, N Switzerland, bordering on Germany; area 114 sq. m.; pop. 57,500. **2** commune, its ✻, on Rhine river near the falls; pop. 26,000.

Schaffhausen Falls or **Falls of the Rhine,** Ger. **Rhein'fall** (rīn'fäl) waterfall in Rhine river, in N Switzerland; 370 ft. wide, with two principal falls, 50 and 60 ft. high.

Schaum'burg-Lip'pe (shoum'bo͝oʀk·lĭp'ĕ) state of Germany 1918–33, in NW between Westphalia and Hannover; once a principality.

Schei'degg (shī'dĕk) village, cen. Switzerland, in Bernese Alps, on the **Little Scheidegg,** mountain pass leading from Lauterbrunnen to Grindelwald, altitude 6770 ft.; to NE is **Great Scheidegg,** pass leading from Grindelwald to valley of the Aare, altitude 6434 ft.

Schel'de (skĕl'dĕ) or **Scheldt** (skĕlt), Fr. **Es'caut'** (ĕs'kō') river, W Europe, flowing from N France through Belgium and into North Sea in Netherlands; 270 m. long.

Sche·nec'ta·dy (skĕ·nĕk'tȧ·dĭ) city, E New York, on Mohawk river; pop. 91,800.

Sche've·ning'en (sKä'vĕ·nĭng'ĕ[n]) town, SW Netherlands, in The Hague commune; scene of British naval victory over the Dutch 1653.

Schie·dam' (sKē·däm') commune, SW Netherlands; pop. 69,700.

Schip'hol (sKĭp'hôl) airfield, Netherlands, near Amsterdam; international airport.

Schles'wig (shlĕs'wĭg; Ger. shläs'vĭk, shlĕs'-), Dan. **Sle'svig** (slĭ'svĕ) historical region, NW Germany, in S Jutland; a mark of Holy Roman Empire; became part of Denmark 1027; came to be ruled by Holstein in 14th cent.; part of Germany (Prussia) from 1865; N part awarded to Denmark by plebiscite 1920.

Schles'wig-Hol'stein (-hōl'shtīn) the regions of Schleswig and Holstein united as a province of Prussia from 1866 and as a state of West Germany after 1945, ✻ Kiel.

Schmal'kal'den (shmäl'käl'dĕn), Eng. **Smal'kald** or **Smal'cald** (smôl'kôld) city, E Germany, SW of Erfurt; league formed 1531.

Schou'ten Islands (sKou'tĕ[n]) island group, West New Guinea, in mouth of Geelvink Bay; area 1230 sq. m.

Schuylerville. See SARATOGA.

Schuyl'kill (skō͞ol'kĭl; locally usu. skō͞o'k'l) river, SE Pennsylvania, flowing SE into Delaware river; 131 m. long.

Schwaben. See SWABIA.

Schwarzwald. See BLACK FOREST.

Schwein'furt (shvīn'fo͞ort) city, W Germany, on Main river; pop. 37,300.

Schweiz. See SWITZERLAND.

Schwe·rin' (shvä·rēn') city, E Germany, in Mecklenburg; pop. 88,200.

Schwyz (shvēts), also **Schwiz** (shvēts) **1** canton, E cen. Switzerland; area 351 sq. m.; pop. 71,100. **2** commune, its ✻, 22 m. E of Lucerne; pop. 10,300.

Scil'la (shīl'à; Ital. shēl'lä), anc. **Scyl'la** (sĭl'ä) headland, S Italy, projecting into Strait of Messina. See SCYLLA, in Vocab.

Scil'ly Isles or **Islands** (sĭl'ĭ) group of islands off Lands End, SW England; 140 islands, total area 6 sq. m.

Scio. See CHIOS.

Sci·o'to (sī·ō'tō; -tŭ) river, Ohio, flowing S into the Ohio river; 237 m. long.

Scone (skō͞on) parish, Scotland, just NE of Perth; place where Scottish kings were crowned.

Sco'pus, Mount (skō'pŭs) mountain, Palestine; Israeli exclave in Jordan, just E of Jerusalem; former site of Hebrew University.

Scores'by Sound (skōrz'bĭ) inlet of Norwegian Sea, E Greenland, just N of 70°N; at entrance is settlement of **Scores'by·sund'** (-so͝on').

Sco'tia (skō'shä) Scotland; — its medieval Latin name.

Scot'land (skŏt'lănd) country, N Great Britain, a division of the United Kingdom of Great Britain and Northern Ireland; before 1707 an independent kingdom; ✻ Edinburgh; area 29,794 sq. m.; pop. 5,096,000. See SCOT, SCOTCH, SCOTSMAN, and SCOTTISH, in Vocab.

Scran'ton (skrăn't'n; -tŭn) city, NE Pennsylvania; pop. 125,500.

Scul'thorpe (skŭl'thôrp) village, E England, in Norfolk 16 m. NE of King's Lynn; made site of U.S. bomber base 1948.

Scun'thorpe (skŭn'thôrp) municipal borough, E England, in Parts of Lindsey, Lincolnshire, WSW of Hull; pop. 54,200.

Scutari. See ÜSKÜDAR.

Scu'ta·ri, Lake (skō͞o'tȧ·rĭ), also **Lake Ska'dar** (skä'där) lake, SW Yugoslavia and NW Albania; area 130 sq. m.

Scylla. See SCILLA. See also in Vocab.

Scyth'i·a (sĭth'ĭ·à; sĭth'-) the country of the ancient Scythians, comprising sections of Europe and Asia now in the U.S.S.R., in region N and NE of Black Sea and E of Aral Sea. See SCYTHIAN, in Vocab.

Sea Islands, chain of islands, SE United States, off coast between the Santee river, South Carolina, and the St. Johns river, N Florida.

Sea'scale' (sē'skāl') village, NW England, in Cumberland on coast; nearby is Sellafield atomic energy plant.

Se·at'tle (sê·ăt''l) seaport, W cen. Washington, between Puget Sound and Lake Washington; pop. 467,600.

Sebaste, Sebastia. See SIVAS.

Sebastopol. See SEVASTOPOL.

Sebastye. See SAMARIA.

Se·cun'der·a·bad' or **Si·kan'dar·a·bad'** (sê·kŭn'dĕr·ä·bäd') town, S cen. India, in Andhra Pradesh just NE of city of Hyderabad; pop. 120,800.

Se·da'lia (sê·dāl'yȧ) city, W cen. Missouri; pop. 20,400.

Se·dan' (sê·dăn'; Fr. sê·dän') city, NE France, on Meuse river ESE of Mézières; scene of French defeat Sept. 2, 1870.

Sedge'moor (sĕj'mo͝or) tract of moorland, SW England, in Somersetshire; scene of Duke of Monmouth's defeat July 6, 1685.

Se·go'via (sâ·gō'vyä; Angl. sê·gō'vĭ·ȧ) commune, cen. Spain; once a residence of kings of Castile and León; pop. 29,300.

Seihun. See SEYHAN.

Seilun. See SHILOH.

Seim (sām), also **Seym,** river, SW cen. Soviet Russia, Europe, flowing W to the Desna river; 435 m. long.

Seine (sān) river, N France, flowing NW into English Channel; 480 m. long.

Seine, Bay of the, Fr. **Baie de la Seine** (bäd' là sân') inlet of English Channel, NW France, between Cotentin Penin. and mouth of the Seine.

Seishin. See CHONGJIN.

Seishu. See CHONGJU, South Korea.

Seis·tan' (sās·tän') region, E Iran and SW Afghanistan; a marshy depression; formerly a province of Iran.

Se·lang'or (sê·lăng'êr) state, Federation of Malaya, on Strait of Malacca; ✻ Kuala Lumpur; area 3166 sq. m.; pop. 710,800.

Se'len·ga' (sĕ'lĕng·gä') river, N cen. Asia, rising in W Outer Mongolia and flowing to Lake Baikal; 750 m. long.

Se·leu'ci·a (sê·lū'shĭ·ȧ; -shä) **1** or **Seleucia Tra'che·o'tis** (trä'kê·ō'tĭs) ancient city, SE Asia Minor, in Cilicia SW of Tarsus. **2** ancient city, ruins now in Iraq on Tigris river SSE of Baghdad; once chief city of Seleucid Empire. **3** ancient seaport, Asia Minor, N of mouth of the Orontes; the port of Antioch.

Sel'kirk (sĕl'kûrk) **1** or **Sel'kirk·shire** (-shîr; -shêr) county, SE Scotland; area 267 sq. m.; pop. 21,700. **2** burgh, its ✻; pop. 5900.

Selkirk Mountains or **Sel'kirks** (sĕl'kûrks) range of Rocky Mts., Canada, in SE British Columbia; highest point Mount Sir Donald, 11,123 ft.

Sel'la·field (sĕl'à·fēld) locality, NW England, in Cumberland near coast; site of an atomic energy plant.

Sel'ma (sĕl'mà) city, SW cen. Alabama, on Alabama river; pop. 22,800.

Se·ma'rang or **Sa·ma'rang** (sȧ·mä'räng) seaport, Indonesia, in cen. Java on N coast; pop. 218,000.

Se'mi·pa·la'tinsk (sĕ'mĭ·pȧ·lät'ĭnsk) city, Soviet Central Asia, in NE Kazakh S.S.R. on Irtysh river; pop. 109,800.

Semlin. See ZEMUN.

Sem'pach (zĕm'päK) town, cen. Switzerland, in Lucerne canton on Lake of Sempach; scene of victory of Swiss over Austrians 1386.

Sen·dai (sĕn·dī) city, Japan, in N Honshu near E coast; pop. 293,800.

Sen'e·ca Lake (sĕn'ê·kȧ) lake, W New York; one of the Finger Lakes; 35 m. long, 1 to 3 m. wide.

Sen'e·gal' (sĕn'ê·gôl'; sĕn'ê·gôl), Fr. **Sé'né'gal'** (sā'nā'gàl') **1** river, French West Africa, flowing from French Guinea N and NW into Atlantic Ocean; 1050 m. long. **2** territory, French West Africa, bordering on Atlantic Ocean between Senegal river and Portuguese Guinea, surrounding Gambia; area 81,081 sq. m.; ✻ Saint-Louis; pop. 1,994,000. — **Sen'e·gal·ese'** (sĕn'ê·gôl·ēz'; -ēs'), adj. & n.

Sen'e·gam'bi·a (sĕn'ê·găm'bĭ·à) region, W Africa, around the Senegal and Gambia rivers. — **Sen'e·gam'bi·an,** adj. & n.

Sen'lac (sĕn'lăk) hill, S England, in Sussex near Hastings; battle of Hastings 1066.

Sen·nar' or **Sen·naar'** (săn·när') region, E Sudan (republic), chiefly between the White Nile and the Blue Nile; ancient kingdom.

Seoul (sōl; să·ōōl') or **Kyong·song** (kyông·sông), also **Kei·jo** (kā·jō) city, S Korea, near W coast on Han river; formerly ✳ of Korea; became ✳ of South Korean Republic 1948; pop. 1,446,000.

Se'pik (sā'pĭk) river, North-East New Guinea, flowing E into Pacific Ocean; 600 m. long.

Sept Îles. See SEVEN ISLANDS.

Se·quoi'a National Park (sĕ·kwoi'ȧ) government reservation, California, in the Sierra Nevada adjoining Kings Canyon National Park; includes Mt. Whitney; established 1890.

Serajevo. See SARAJEVO.

Ser'bi·a (sûr'bĭ·ȧ), formerly **Ser'vi·a** (sûr'vĭ·ȧ), Serb. **Sr'bi·ja** (sûr'bĕ·yä) region, Yugoslavia; once an independent kingdom; since 1918 part of Yugoslavia, since 1946 a federated republic; ✳ Belgrade; area (with Voivodina and Kosovo-Metohija) 34,080 sq. m., pop. 6,528,000. See SERB, SERBIAN, in Vocab.

Serbs, Croats, and Slovenes, Kingdom of the. See YUGOSLAVIA.

Sercq. See SARK.

Serdica. See SOFIA.

Serendib. See CEYLON.

Ser·gi'pe (sĕr·zhē'pĕ) state, E Brazil, bordering on Atlantic Ocean; ✳ Aracajú; area 8321 sq. m.; pop. 650,100.

Se·rin'ga·pa·tam' (sĕ·rĭng'gȧ·pȧ·täm') or **Sri·ran'ga·pat·nam'** (srē·rŭng'gȧ·pȧt·näm') town, S India, in Mysore state N of city of Mysore; under Tipu Sahib ✳ of Mysore.

Se·row'e (sĕ·rō'ā) town, South Africa, in E Bechuanaland Protectorate; ✳ of Bamangwato tribe.

Serra da Es·trel'la (thȧ ĕsh·trā'lȧ) mountain range, Portugal; highest point 6532 ft., highest in Portugal.

Serra do Mar (thōō màr') mountain range, S Brazil, along coast, chiefly in Santa Catarina, Paraná, and São Paulo states; highest point 7323 ft.

Servia. See SERBIA.

Ses'tos (sĕs'tŏs) ruined town, Turkey in Europe, on the Dardanelles (Hellespont) at narrowest point; scene of legend of Hero and Leander.

Sète (sĕt), formerly **Cette** (sĕt) seaport, S France, on strip of land separating Étang de Thau from the Mediterranean; pop. 31,200.

Seto Naikai, Seto no Uchi. See INLAND SEA.

Se·tu'bal (sĕ·tōō'b'l), formerly called in English **Saint Ubes** (sānt ūbz') or **Saint Yves** (īvz') seaport, SW Portugal, on **Bay of Setubal** (receiving the Sado river) SE of Lisbon; pop. 35,100.

Se·van' (sĕ·vän') or **Se·vang'** (sĕ·väng'), Turk. **Gök'cha** (gûk'chä) lake, U.S.S.R., in N Armenian S.S.R.; 540 sq. m.

Se·vas'to·pol (sĕ·văs'tō·pōl; sĕv'ăs·tō'p'l), formerly **Se·bas'to·pol** (sĕ·băs'tō·pōl; sĕb'ăs·tō'p'l) seaport, Soviet Russia, Europe, in SW Crimea; naval base; sieges 1854–55, 1941–42; pop. 111,900.

Seven Islands, Fr. **Sept Îles** (sĕ'-tĕl') town, Canada, in SE Quebec on St. Lawrence river; port under development as outlet for new iron ore fields on Labrador-Quebec border.

Severnaya Dvina. See NORTHERN DVINA.

Se'ver·na·ya Zem·lya' (syä'vyĭr·nȧ·yȧ zyĭm·lyȧ'), Eng. **Northern,** or **North, Land,** formerly known as **Nich'o·las II Land** (nĭk'ō·lȧs thĕ sĕk'ŭnd) island group, Soviet Russia, Asia, in Arctic Ocean N of Taimyr Peninsula.

Sev'ern River (sĕv'ẽrn) **1** inlet of Chesapeake Bay, Maryland; 10 m. long. **2** river, Canada, in NW Ontario, flowing NE into Hudson Bay; 610 m. long. **3** river, Great Britain, flowing from E cen. Wales into Bristol Channel in England; 210 m. long.

Se·ville' (sĕ·vĭl'; esp. Brit., sĕv''l), Span. **Se·vil'la** (sā·vē'[l]yä) city, SW Spain, on Guadalquivir river; pop. 375,400.

Sè'vres (sĕ'vr') town, N France, on Seine river SW of Paris; treaty 1920.

Sew'ard (sū'ẽrd) town, S Alaska, on inlet of Gulf of Alaska on SE Kenai Peninsula; pop. 2100.

Seward Peninsula, projection of land, W Alaska; ends in Cape Prince of Wales; 180 m. long, 130 m. wide.

Sey·chelles' (sā·shĕl'; -shĕlz') group of islands, W Indian Ocean; a British colony; ✳ Victoria, on Mahé I.; area 156 sq. m., pop. 32,200.

Sey·han' (sā·hän') or **Sei·hun'** (sā·hōōn') **1** river, Turkey, flowing SSW into Mediterranean Sea; 780 m. long. **2** see ADANA.

Seym. See SEIM.

Sfax (sfäks) seaport, Tunisia, on Gulf of Gabès; pop. 43,300.

's Gravenhage. See HAGUE, THE.

Shaftes'bur·y (shäfts'bẽr·ĭ; -brĭ) town, S England, in N Dorsetshire; site of an ancient abbey and, since 1948, of a U.S. Air Force base.

Shahi. See URMIA, LAKE.

Shah·ja·han'pur (shä'jȧ·hän'pōōr) city, N India, in Uttar Pradesh; pop. 110,200.

Shah·pur' (shä·pōōr') ancient city, SW Iran, W of Shiraz; famous ruins.

Shak'er Heights (shāk'ẽr) city, N Ohio, E of Cleveland; pop. 28,200.

Shakh'ty (shäk'tĭ), formerly **A·le·ksan'drovsk Gru·shev'ski** (ŭ·lyĭ·ksän'drŭfsk grōō·shĕf'skĭ) city, Soviet Russia, Europe, NE of Rostov; pop. 155,100.

Sha·mo'kin (shȧ·mō'kĭn) borough, E Pennsylvania; pop. 16,900.

Shang'hai (shăng'hī') city, E China, in SE Kiangsu prov. on Hwang Pu (Whangpoo river 13 m. from its mouth; pop. 4,630,400.

Shan'non (shăn'ŭn) **1** river, Ireland, flowing from N co. Cavan S through a number of lakes, then turning W to the Atlantic Ocean through long estuary; 240 m. long. **2** airfield, Ireland, on Shannon estuary at Rineanna; international airport.

Shan'si' (shän'sē') province, NE China, bordering on Inner Mongolia; ✳ Taiyuan; area 52,124 sq. m.; pop. 10,799,000.

Shan State (shän; shăn) state, E Burma, including the former Federated Shan States; set up 1947 on formation of Union of Burma.

Shan'tung' (shän'tŭng'; -tōōng') province, NE China, including peninsula extending into Yellow Sea; ✳ Tsinan; area 38,610 sq. m.; pop. 40,503,000.

Shao'hing' (shou'shĭng') city, E China, in N Chekiang prov. ESE of Hangchow; pop. 300,000.

Shari. See CHARI.

Shar'on (shăr'ŭn) city, W Pennsylvania, on Ohio border; pop. 26,500.

Sharon, Plain of, region, Israel, on coast from Mt. Carmel to Jaffa.

Sharps'burg (shärps'bûrg) village, N Maryland, on Antietam Creek; nearby is Antietam Battlefield Site, commemorating battle of 1862.

Sha'si' (shä'sē') city, E cen. China, in S Hupeh prov. on the Yangtze; pop. 113,500.

Shas'ta, Mount (shăs'tȧ) mountain, N California, at S end of Cascade Range; an isolated volcanic cone; 14,162 ft. high.

Shatt-al-Ar'ab (shăt'äl-är'ăb) river, SE Iraq, formed by the Tigris and Euphrates rivers, flowing SE into Persian Gulf; 120 m. long.

Sha·win'i·gan Falls (shȧ·wĭn'ĭ·găn) city, Canada, in S Quebec on St. Maurice river NNW of Three Rivers; pop. 28,600.

Shaw·nee' (shô·nē'; shō'nē) city, cen. Oklahoma, on North Canadian river; pop. 22,900.

Shcher·ba·kov' (shchĭr·bŭ·kôf'), formerly **Ry'binsk** (rĭ'byĭnsk) city, Soviet Russia, Europe, on the Volga at SE end of Rybinsk Reservoir; pop. 139,000.

She'ba (shē'bȧ), more correctly **Sa'ba** (sä'bä), Arab. **Sa'ba'** (sä'bä) ancient country, S Arabia; — a Biblical name.

She·be'li. Var. of SHIBELI.

She·boy'gan (shĕ·boi'găn) city, E Wisconsin, on Lake Michigan; pop. 42,400.

Shechem. See NABLUS.

Shed'i·ac (shĕd'ĭ·ăk) town, Canada, in SE New Brunswick on Northumberland Strait; transatlantic airport.

Sheer'ness' (shēr'nĕs') urban district, SE England, in Kent at mouth of the Thames; seaport, government dockyard; pop. 15,700.

Shef'field (shĕf'ēld) city and county borough, N England, in West Riding, Yorkshire, on the Don; pop. 512,800.

Shel'by (shĕl'bĭ) city, SW North Carolina, W of Gastonia; pop. 15,500.

Shel'i·kof Strait (shĕl'ĭ·kôf) strait, S Alaska, between mainland (Alaska Penin.) and islands of Kodiak and Afognak.

Shem'ya (shĕm'yȧ) island, SW Alaska, in Semichi Is., Aleutian Is.; U.S. Air Force base.

Shen'an·do'ah (shĕn'ȧn·dō'ȧ; locally often shăn'ȧ·dō'ȧ) **1** river, N Virginia, flowing NE across NE tip of West Virginia and into Potomac river; 55 m. long. **2** borough, E cen. Pennsylvania; pop. 15,700.

Shenandoah National Park, government reservation, Virginia, in the Blue Ridge Mts.; established 1935.

Shenandoah Valley, valley, Virginia and West Virginia, drained by the Shenandoah river, between the Alleghenies and Blue Ridge Mts.; 110 m. long and 25 m. wide.

Shen'si' (shĕn'sē') province, NE cen. China, between Szechwan and Inner Mongolia; ✳ Sian; area 74,131 sq. m.; pop. 10,459,000.

Shenyang. See MUKDEN.

Sher'brooke (shûr'brŏŏk) city, Canada, in S Quebec 85 m. E of Montreal; pop. 58,700.

Sher'iff·muir (shĕr'ĭf·mūr; shĕr'ĭ·mūr') battlefield, cen. Scotland, in Perth co. just W of Ochil Hills; battle 1715.

Sher'man (shûr'măn) city, N Texas; pop. 20,200.

's Her'to'gen·bosch' (sĕr'tō'kĕn·bôs'), Fr. **Bois-le-Duc** (bwä'lĕ·dŭk') commune, S Netherlands; pop. 53,900.

Sher'wood Forest (shûr'wŏŏd) ancient royal forest, cen. England, chiefly in Nottinghamshire.

Shet'land (shĕt'lănd) or **Zet'land** (zĕt'lănd) or **Shetland Islands,** group of islands, N Scotland, NE of the Orkney Is.; constitutes a county of Scotland; ✳ Lerwick; area 550 sq. m.; pop. 19,300.

Shey·enne' (shī·ĕn'; -ăn') river, cen. and SE North Dakota, flowing E, then S and again E into Red River of the North; 325 m. long.

Shi·be'li, Web'be (wĕb'ȧ shĭ·bā'lĭ), Ital. **Ue'bi Sce·be'li** (wâ'bĕ shä·bā'lĕ) river, E Africa, rising in cen. Ethiopia and flowing to a swamp near Juba river in Italian Somaliland; 700 m. long.

Shi·ga'tse (shē·gä'tsĕ) town, SE Tibet, on Tsangpo river; residence of the Teshu Lama.

Shi·kar'pur (shĭ'kär'pŏŏr) city, W Pakistan, in N Sind; pop. 62,700.

Shi·ko'ku (shĭ·kō'kōō) island, Japan, E of Kyushu; area 7246 sq. m.

Shil'ka (shĭl'kä) river, Soviet Russia, Asia, flowing NE to unite with the Argun and form the Amur river; 300 m. long.

Shi'loh (shī'lō), mod. **Sei·lun'** (sī·lōōn'; sä-) village, Palestine, on E slope of Mt. Ephraim; in the Bible, a sanctuary of the Israelites.

Shiloh National Military Park, government reservation, SW Tennessee, at Pittsburg Landing; national military park since 1894.

Shi·mi·zu (shē·mē·zōō) seaport, Japan, in Honshu on Suruga Bay; pop. 80,500.

Shi'mo·no·se'ki (shĭm'ō·nō·sĕk'ĭ), popularly called **Ba·kan** (bä·kän) seaport, Japan, in Honshu on Shimonoseki Strait; pop. 176,700.

Shimonoseki Strait, channel, Japan, separating SW Honshu I. from N Kyushu I.

Shi'nar (shī'nẽr; -när) in the Bible, a country known to the early Hebrews as a plain in Babylonia; probably equivalent to Sumer.

Shingishu. See SINUIJU.

Shin·kol'o·bwe (shĭng·kŏl'ō·bwā) town, SE Belgian Congo, in Katanga region NW of Elisabethville; uranium mines.

Shinshu. See CHINJU.

Ship'ka, or **Sip'ka, Pass** (shĭp'kȧ) mountain pass, cen. Bulgaria, in Balkan Mts.; altitude 4376 ft.

Shi·raz' (shē·räz'; Angl. -räz') city, SW cen. Iran; pop. 114,000.

Shi're or **Shi'ré** (shē'rā), Port. **Chi're** (shē'rĕ) river, E Africa, flowing from Lake Nyasa S into Zambezi river; 370 m. long.

Shi·zu·o·ka (shē·zōō·ō·kä) city, Japan, in Honshu; pop. 205,700.

Sho'a (shō'ȧ) province, cen. Ethiopia; former kingdom; ✳ Addis Ababa.

Sho·ka (shō·kä) city, W coast of Formosa; pop. 51,200.

Sho'la·pur (shō'lä·pōŏr) city, W India, in SE Bombay state; pop. 212,600.

Shore'wood (shōr'wŏŏd) village, SE Wisconsin, on Lake Michigan; pop. 16,200.

Short'land Islands (shôrt'lănd) group of islands, Solomon Is., off S end of Bougainville; in British Solomon Islands Protectorate.

Sho·sho'ne (shō·shō'nē) river, NW Wyoming, flowing NE into Bighorn river; with longest headstream, 120 m. long.

Shoshone Falls, waterfall, S Idaho, in Snake river; 210 ft. high.

Shqipni, Shqipri. See ALBANIA.

Shreve'port (shrēv'pōrt) city, NW Louisiana, on Red river; pop. 127,200.

Shrews'bur'y (shrōōz'bĕr'ĭ; -bĕr-ĭ; -brĭ; in England, also shrōz'-) or **Sal'op** (săl'ŏp) municipal borough, W England, ✻ of Shropshire, on the Severn; pop. 44,900.

Shrop'shire (shrŏp'shĭr; -shĕr) or **Sal'op** (săl'ŏp) county, W England, on border of Wales; ✻ Shrewsbury; area 1347 sq. m.; pop. 289,800.

Shufu. See KASHGAR.

Shunsen. See CHUNCHON.

Shush, Shushan. See SUSA.

Si (shē) or **Si-kiang** (shē'jĭ-äng'), Eng. **West River**, river, SE China, flowing from confluence of Hungshui and Siang rivers in Kwangsi E to the China Sea; 300 m. long, with the Hungshui over 1000 m. long.

Si·al'kot (sĭ·äl'kōt) city, W Pakistan, in West Punjab near Chenab river; pop. 167,600.

Si·am' (sĭ·ăm'; sī'ăm). See THAILAND.

Siam, Gulf of, inlet of South China Sea between the peninsulas of Indochina and Malaya.

Si'an' (shē'än') city, NE cen. China, ✻ of Shensi prov., on Wei river; pop. 1,000,000.

Siang (shĭ-äng'), also **Hsiang** (shĭ-äng') **1** river, SE cen. China, flowing from NE Kwangsi N into the Tungting Hu (lake); 350 m. long. **2** or **Si·yang'** (shĭ-yäng'), formerly **Yu** (yü) river, S China; joins the Hungshui in Kwangsi to form the Si river; 400 m. long.

Siang'tan' (shĭ-äng'tän') city, SE cen. China, in E Hunan prov. on Siang river S of Changsha; pop. 300,000.

Si·be'ri·a (sī·bēr'ĭ·ȧ) the N part of Asia, constituting larger portion of Soviet Russia, Asia. — **Si·be'ri·an,** adj. & n.

Si·biu' (sĕ·byoō'), Hung. **Nagy'sze'ben** (nŏd'y'·sā'bĕn) city, W cen. Romania, in Transylvania; pop. 50,200.

Sic'i·lies, the Two (sĭs'ĭ·lĭz) kingdom 11th to 14th cent. consisting of S Italy and the island of Sicily.

Sic'i·ly (sĭs'ĭ·lĭ), Italian and anc. **Si·ci'lia** (Ital. sē·chēl'yä; anc. sĭ-sĭl'yȧ, -sĭl'ĭ·ȧ), anc. also **Tri·nac'ri·a** (trĭ·năk'rĭ·ȧ; trī-) island, Italy, in Mediterranean Sea off toe of Italian boot; ✻ Palermo; area 9926 sq. m.; pop. 4,413,000. — **Si·cil'ian** (sĭ·sĭl'yȧn; -sĭl'ĭ·ȧn), adj. & n.

Si'cy·on (sĭsh'ĭ·ŏn; sĭs'ĭ-), Gr. **Sik'y·on** (sĭk'ĭ·ŏn) ancient city, S Greece, in NE Peloponnesus NW of Corinth.

Sidcup. See CHISLEHURST and SIDCUP.

Si'di Bar·râ'ni (sē'dĭ bȧ·rä'nĭ) village, NW Egypt, on coast W of Matrûh; in World War II scene of much fighting.

Si'di-bel-Ab·bès' (sē'dĭ·bĕl·ȧ·bĕs') commune, NW Algeria, S of Oran; pop. 51,100.

Si'di Sli'mane (sē'dĭ slĭ'mān) village, N Morocco, NE of Rabat; site of U.S. air base.

Si'don (sī'd'n) or **Zi'don** (zī'-), Fr. **Sa'i'da'** (sä'ē'dà'), Arab. **Sai'da** (sī'dȧ) seaport, SW Lebanon; a chief city of ancient Phoenicia. — **Si·do'ni·an** (sī·dō'nĭ·ȧn), adj. & n.

Sid'ra, Gulf of (sĭd'rȧ), anc. **Syr'tis Ma'jor** (sûr'tĭs mā'jĕr) inlet of Mediterranean Sea on coast of Libya.

Sie'ben·ge·bir'ge (zē'bĕn·gĕ·bĭr'gĕ) group of hills, W Germany, along the Rhine.

Sie'na (syä'nä; Angl. sĭ·ĕn'ȧ) commune, cen. Italy, S of Florence; pop. 52,800.

Sier'ra de Cór'do·ba (syĕr'rä thä kôr'thô·vä) mountain range, cen. Argentina, in western pampas; highest peak 9350 ft.

Sier'ra de Gre'dos (syĕr'rä thä grā'thōs) mountain range, W cen. Spain; SW extension of the Sierra de Guadarrama.

Sierra de Gua'dar·ra'ma (gwä'thär·rä'mä) mountain range, cen. Spain; highest peak Pico de Peñalara, 7890 ft.

Si·er'ra Le·one' (sĭ·ĕr'ä lē·ōn'; sĭ·rä) **1** river, W Africa, the estuary of the Rokel river. **2** region, W Africa, on coast between Liberia and French Guinea; includes the Sierra Leone river and the **Sierra Leone Peninsula,** at the river mouth; the peninsula and several coastal islands constitute a British colony, established in latter part of 18th cent. for former slaves, ✻ Freetown; area 271 sq. m., pop. 117,300; the remainder of the region constitutes a British protectorate, area 27,669 sq. m., pop. 1,733,600.

Sier'ra Ma'dre del Sur (syĕr'rä mä'thrä thĕl soōr') range of mountains, S Mexico, along coasts of Guerrero and Oaxaca states.

Sierra Madre Oc'ci·den·tal' (ŏk'sĕ·thän·täl') range of mountains, W Mexico, running parallel to the Pacific coast.

Sierra Madre O'rien·tal' (ō'ryän·täl') range of mountains, E Mexico, running parallel to the shore of the Gulf of Mexico.

Si·er'ra Mo·re'na (sĭ·ĕr'ä mô·rā'nä) mountain range, SW Spain, between the Guadiana and Guadalquivir rivers; highest peak 8000 ft.

Si·er'ra Ne·vad'a (sĭ·ĕr'ä nĕ·väd'ȧ; -vä'dȧ) **1** mountain range, E California, extending N to S for over 400 m.; highest peak Mount Whitney, 14,495 ft. **2** mountain range, S Spain; highest peak Mulhacén, 11,420 ft.

Sier'ra Ne·va'da de San'ta Mar'ta (syĕr'rä nä·vä'thä thä sän'tä mär'tä) mountain range, N Colombia, on Caribbean coast; highest peak 19,030 ft.

Sikandarabad. See SECUNDERABAD.

Si'kang' (shē'käng') province, S China, bordering on India and Tibet; ✻ Yaan; area 170,000 sq. m. (including a Tibetan Autonomous District, formed 1950, area 60,000 sq. m.); pop. 1,756,000.

Si'kho·te A·lin' (sē'kō·tä ä·lēn') mountain range, Soviet Russia, Asia, along E coast of Maritime Territory.

Si-kiang. See SI.

Sik'kim (sĭk'ĭm) territory, Asia, on border between India and Tibet; a protectorate of Republic of India; ✻ Gangtok; area 2745 sq. m.; pop. 135,600.

Sikyon. See SICYON.

Si·le'sia (sī·lē'zhȧ; -zhĭ·ȧ; -shȧ; -shĭ·ȧ; sĭ-) region, E Europe, in the Sudeten Mts. (Austrian Silesia) and N of the mountains in basin of the Oder river (Prussian Silesia) Austrian Silesia, once a separate crownland, since World War I part of Czechoslovakia; Prussian Silesia, seized from Austria 1742, after World War II assigned almost entirely to Poland, which had already occupied the SE section (Polish Silesia) since 1921. — **Si·le'sian,** adj.

Sil'ler·y (sĭl'ĕr·ĭ; Fr. sē'lĕ·rē') city, Canada, SW of city of Quebec, on the St. Lawrence; pop. 13,200.

Simbirsk. See ULYANOVSK.

Sim'coe, Lake (sĭm'kō) lake, E Canada, in SE Ontario SE of Georgian Bay; area 280 sq. m.

Sim'fer·o'pol (sĭm'fĕr·ō'p'l) city, S Soviet Russia, Europe, in the Crimea; ✻ of Crimean S.S.R. before its dissolution 1945; pop. 142,700.

Sim'la (sĭm'lȧ) town, N India, ✻ of Himachal Pradesh; pop. 18,300.

Sim'plon (sĭm'plŏn) **1** mountain pass between Switzerland and Italy in Valais and Piedmont. **2** tunnel near pass through Monte Leone in Lepontine Alps; 12.3 m. long.

Simpson. See FORT SIMPSON.

Si'nai (sī'nĭ; sī'nä·ĭ) peninsula, W Asia, NW of Arabia between Mediterranean Sea and Red Sea; belongs to Egypt. — **Si'na·it'ic** (sī'nä·ĭt'ĭk), adj.

Sinai, Mount, in the Bible, the place where the Law was given to Moses; thought to be one of the Gebel Musa group, Sinai Peninsula.

Si'na·lo'a (sē'nä·lō'ä) state, W Mexico, bordering on Gulf of California; ✻ Culiacán; area 22,580 sq. m.; pop. 618,400.

Sind (sĭnd) former province, W Pakistan, on Arabian Sea between Baluchistan and Republic of India; ✻ Karachi.

Sin'ga·pore (sĭng'gȧ·pōr; sĭng'ȧ-; -pōr') **1** island, Malaya, off S end of Malay Penin.; with Christmas I., constitutes a British colony; area of island 217 sq. m. **2** seaport, ✻ of colony of Singapore, on Singapore I.; pop. 679,700.

Singapore, Strait of, channel between Singapore I. and islands of the Riouw Archipelago; connects South China Sea with Strait of Malacca.

Sing Sing. See OSSINING.

Sin'kiang' (shĭn'jĭ·äng') province, W China, between Mongolia and Tibet; borders on Soviet Central Asia; ✻ Urumchi (Tihwa); area 700,000 sq. m.; pop. 3,730,000.

Sint-Gillis. See SAINT-GILLES.

Sint Jans Molenbeek. See MOLENBEEK.

Sin'tra (sēn'trȧ) older **Cin'tra** (sēn'trȧ) town, W Portugal, NW of Lisbon; Moorish castle, royal palace; convention signed here 1808.

Sin·ui·ju (shĭn·ē·jōō) or **Shin·gi·shu** (shĕn·gē·shōō) city, NW Korea, on Yalu river near its mouth; pop. 61,100.

Sioux City (soō) city, W Iowa, on Missouri river; pop. 84,000.

Sioux Falls, city, SE South Dakota, on Big Sioux river; pop. 52,700.

Sipka Pass. See SHIPKA PASS.

Síra. See SYROS.

Siracusa. See SYRACUSE.

Syr Darya. See SYR DARYA.

Si·ret' (sĕ·rĕt') Ger. **Se'reth** (zā'rĕt) river, E Romania, flowing from Carpathian Mts. to the Danube; 270 m. long.

Síros. See SYROS.

Sit'ka (sĭt'kȧ) town, SE Alaska, on Baranof I.; naval base; pop. 2100.

Sitsang. See TIBET.

Sit'tang (sĭt'täng) river, E cen. Burma, flowing S into head of Gulf of Martaban; 350 m. long.

Si·vas' (sĭ·väs'), anc. **Se·bas'te** (sĕ·băs'tē) or **Se·bas'ti·a** (sĕ·băs'chĭ·ȧ; -tĭ-ȧ) city, E cen. Turkey, on upper Kızıl Irmak; pop. 52,300.

Si·wa'lik Range or **Hills** (sĭ·wä'lĭk) the foothills of the Himalayas, N India; highest point 5000 ft.

Siyang. See SIANG.

Sjæl'land (shĕl'làn), Eng. **Zea'land** (zē'lănd) island, largest of the islands of Denmark; site of Copenhagen; area 2709 sq. m.

Skadar. See SCUTARI.

Skag'er·rak or **Skag'e·rak** (skăg'ĕr·ăk; skăg'ĕ·răk) arm of the North Sea, between Norway and Denmark.

Skag'way (skăg'wā) city, SE Alaska, at head of Lynn Canal; boom town in the Klondike gold rush 1897–98.

Skan'e·at'e·les (skăn'ē·ăt'lĕs; locally usu. skĭn'ē-) village, cen. New York, at N end of **Skaneateles Lake,** one of the Finger Lakes.

Skaw, the (skô), or **Cape Ska'gen** (skä'gĕn) cape, Denmark, on N extremity of Jutland.

Skee'na (skē'nȧ) river, Canada, in W British Columbia, flowing S and then W into Hecate Strait; 335 m. long.

Skid'daw (skĭd'ô; skĭ·dô') mountain, NW England, in cen. Cumberland; 3054 ft. high.

Skop'lje (skŏp'lyĕ), Turk. **Üs·küb'** (ūs·küb') city, S Yugoslavia, ✻ of Macedonia, on Vardar river; pop. 91,500.

Sku'ta·ri. Var. of SCUTARI.

Skye (skī) island, Scotland, one of the Inner Hebrides; area 670 sq. m.

Sky'ros (skī'rŏs) or **Scy'ros** (sī'rŏs), Mod. Gr. **Ský'ros** (skyē'rŏs) island, Greece, in the Northern Sporades E of Euboea.

Slave (slāv), also **Great Slave,** river, Canada, flowing from W end of Lake Athabaska N into Great Slave Lake; 265 m. long.

Slave Coast, region, W Africa, on coast of Upper Guinea along Bight of Benin and between the Benin and Volta rivers.

Slavkov. See AUSTERLITZ.

Sla·vo'ni·a (slȧ·vō'nĭ·ȧ; -vōn'yȧ), Serb. **Sla·vo'ni·ja** (slä·vō'nē·yä) region, NE Yugoslavia, E of Croatia between the Sava, Drava, and Danube rivers. — **Sla·vo'ni·an** (slä·vō'nĭ·ăn; -vōn'yăn), adj. & n.

Slesvig. See SCHLESWIG.

Sles'wick (slĕs'wĭk). Var. of SCHLESWIG.

Slide Mountain (slīd) mountain, New York; highest in the Catskill Mts.; 4204 ft.

Sli'go (slī'gō) **1** county, N Republic of Ireland, in Connacht prov.; area 694 sq. m.; pop. 60,500. **2** municipal borough and seaport, its ✻, on Sligo Bay; pop. 13,500.

Slough (slou) urban district, England, in Buckinghamshire W of London; pop. 66,400.

Slo·va'ki·a (slō·vä'kĭ·ȧ; -văk'ĭ·ȧ), Czech **Slo'ven·sko** (slô'vĕn·skô) region, E cen. Czechoslovakia; formerly a province, ✻ Bratislava. — **Slo'vak** (slō'văk; slō·väk'), **Slo·va'ki·an** (slō·vä'kĭ·ăn; -văk'ĭ·ăn), adj. & n.

Slo·ve'ni·a (slō·vē'nĭ·ȧ; -vēn'yȧ), Serb. **Slo·ve'ni·ja** (slō·vē'nē·yä) region, NW Yugoslavia, bordering on Austria and Hungary; a constituent republic of Federal People's Republic of Yugoslavia; ✻ Ljubljana; area 7708 sq. m. pop. 1,391,900. — **Slo·ve'ni·an** (slō·vē'nĭ·ăn; -vēn'yăn), adj. & n.

Słu.bi′ce (sloō-bē′tsĕ), Ger. **Frank′furt** (frăngk′fĕrt; Ger. frängk′-foŏrt) city, W Poland, on the Oder; before 1945 part of Frankfurt on the Oder, Germany; pop. 77,000.

Smalcald, Smalkald. See SCHMALKALDEN.

Smeth′wick (smĕth′ĭk) county borough, W cen. England, W of Birmingham; pop. 76,400.

Smí′chov (smē′kôf), Ger. **Smi′chow** (smĭk′ō) city, Czechoslovakia, in Bohemia on Vltava river SW of Prague; pop. 56,300.

Smith Sound (smĭth) channel separating NW Greenland from SE Ellesmere I.

Smoky Hill, river, cen. Kansas, flowing E to unite with Republican river and form the Kansas river; 540 m. long.

Smoky Mountains. = GREAT SMOKY MOUNTAINS.

Smo.lensk′ (smô-lĕnsk′) city, Soviet Russia, Europe, on upper Dnieper river; once ✱ of Smolensk principality; pop. 156,700.

Smyrna. See İZMIR.

Snake (snāk) river, NW United States, flowing from Yellowstone National Park in NW Wyoming across S Idaho and into Columbia river in Washington; 1038 m. long.

Snow′don (snō′d'n) mountain massif, N Wales; highest point in Wales, 3560 ft.

Snow Mountains (snō), Du. **Sneeuw Ge.berg′te** (snā′oō kĕ·bĕrk′tĕ) range of mountains, West New Guinea; highest point Carstensz Toppen, 16,404 ft.

So′bat (sō′băt) river, Africa; flows W into the White Nile; 460 m. long.

Soche. See YARKAND.

So′chi (sō′chĭ) city, Soviet Russia, Europe, on Black Sea; pop. 50,000.

So.ci′e.ty Islands (sô·sī′ĕ·tĭ), Fr. **Îles de la So′ciété′** (ēl′ dĕ lä sô′syā′tā′) island group, S Pacific Ocean, belonging to the French; comprises two groups, the Windward Is. and the Leeward Is.; ✱ Papeete, on Tahiti; area 650 sq. m.; pop. 37,300.

So.co′tra or **So.ko′tra** (sô·kō′trä) island in Indian Ocean S of Arabia; belongs to Sultan of Qishn on coast of Aden Protectorate; area 1400 sq. m.; pop. 12,000.

Sod′om (sŏd′ŭm) in the Bible, a city in the plain of the Jordan which was destroyed for its wickedness. See SODOM, SODOMITE, in Vocab.

Soemba, Soembawa, Soenda Isles, Soerabaja, Soerakarta, etc. See SUMBA, SUMBAWA, SUNDA ISLES, SURABAJA, SURAKARTA, etc.

So′fia (sō′fĭ·à; sô·fē′à), Bulgarian **So′fi.ya** (sō′fĭ·yä) formerly **Sre′-dets** (srĕ′dĕts), anc. **Ser′di.ca** (sûr′dĭ·kà) or **Sar′di.ca** (sär′-) city, ✱ of Bulgaria; pop. 401,300.

Sog′di.a′na (sŏg′dĭ·ā′nà; -ăn′à) province of Persian Empire, 525 B.C.; ✱ Maracanda (mod. Samarkand). — **Sog′di.an** (sŏg′dĭ·ăn), adj. & n.

Sog′ne Fjord (sông′nĕ fyôr′; fyoōr′) inlet of Norwegian Sea, W Norway.

Sois′sons′ (swä′sôn′) commune, N France, on Aisne river SW of Laon; many battles, esp. 1486, 1918; pop. 18,200.

So′ko.to (sō′kô·tô) **1** province, NW Nigeria, bordering on Niger territory. **2** town, its ✱; once ✱ of the empire of the Fulah.

Sokotra. See SOCOTRA.

So′lent, the (sō′lĕnt) channel, S England, between Isle of Wight and the mainland.

Sol′fe.ri′no (sŏl′fĕ·rē′nō) village, N Italy, W of Mincio river; battle 1859.

So.li.mões′ (soō-lê-moẽNs′) the upper Amazon, Brazil, from Peruvian border to the Rio Negro.

So′ling.en (zō′lĭng·ĕn) city, W Germany, in the Ruhr; pop. 147,800.

Solo. See SURAKARTA.

Sol′o.mon Islands (sŏl′ô·mŭn) group of islands, W Pacific Ocean, E of New Guinea; the islands in the N, including Bougainville, belong to Australian Territory of New Guinea; the rest, including Guadalcanal, form major portion of British Solomon Islands Protectorate, ✱ Honiara (on Guadalcanal), area 12,780 sq. m.; pop. 95,000.

Solomon Sea, body of water, S Pacific; the N part of Coral Sea.

So′lo.thurn (zō′lô·toōrn) **1** canton, NW Switzerland; area 306 sq. m.; pop. 170,500. **2** commune, its ✱, on Aare river; pop. 16,700.

Sol′way Firth (sŏl′wä) inlet of Irish Sea, Great Britain, on boundary between England and Scotland; extends inland 38 m.

Somalia. See ITALIAN SOMALILAND.

So.ma′li.land′ (sô·mä′lē·länd′) region, E Africa, between the equator and the Gulf of Aden, including territories of French, Italian, and British Somaliland and SE Ethiopia. See SOMALI, in Vocab.

Somaliland Protectorate. See BRITISH SOMALILAND.

Somerset Nile. See NILE.

Som′er.set.shire (sŭm′ĕr·sĕt·shīr; -shĕr) or **Som′er.set,** county, SW England; ✱ Taunton; area 1620 sq. m.; pop. 551,200.

Som′er.ville (sŭm′ĕr·vĭl) city, E Massachusetts; pop. 102,400.

So.meş′ (sô·mĕsh′), Hung. **Sza′mos** (sō′mŏsh) river, NE Hungary and NW Romania, flowing NW into Tisza river; 200 m. long.

Somme (sôm) river, N France, flowing NW into the English Channel; battles 1916, 1944; 147 m. long.

Song Bo. See BO.

Song Koi. See COI.

So.no′ra (sô·nō′rà) **1** river, NW Mexico, in Sonora state; flows SW and W into upper Gulf of California; 300 m. long. **2** state, NW Mexico, bordering on United States and Gulf of California; ✱ Hermosillo; area 70,477 sq. m.; pop. 503,100.

Soo Canals, Soo Locks. See SAULT SAINTE MARIE CANALS.

Soo′chow′ (soō′jō′), formerly (1912–49) **Wu′hsien′** (woō′shĭ′ĕn′) city, E China, in S Kiangsu prov. E of the Tai Hu; pop. 260,000.

Sop′ron (shôp′rŏn), Ger. **Ö′den.burg** (û′dĕn·boŏrk) autonomous city, W Hungary, near Austrian boundary; pop. 36,000.

So′rel′ (sô′rĕl′) city, Canada, in S Quebec on the St. Lawrence; pop. 16,500.

So′ro.ca′ba (sō′roō·kà′và) city, SE Brazil, in SE São Paulo state; pop. 69,600.

Sor.ren′to (sŏr·rĕn′tō), anc. **Sur.ren′tum** (sŭ·rĕn′tŭm) seaport, S Italy, on Bay of Naples S of Naples; pop. 27,300.

Sos.no′wiec (sôs·nô′vyĕts), also, unofficially, **Sos′no.wi′ce** (sôs′nô·vē′tsĕ) city, SW Poland, NE of Katowice; pop. 130,000.

Soudan; Soudan français. See SUDAN; FRENCH SUDAN.

Sou.fri.ère′ (soō′frē′âr′) **1** mountain, British West Indies, in S Montserrat; highest point on island, 3002 ft. **2** see LA SOUFRIÈRE.

Sound, the. See ÖRESUND.

Sou′ris (soō′ĭs; Fr. soō′rē′) river, S Canada and North Dakota (where it is called the **Mouse** [mous] river), flowing to the Assiniboine in Manitoba; 450 m. long.

Sousse (soōs) or **Su′sa** (soō′sà), anc. **Had′ru.me′tum** (hăd′roō·mē′-tŭm) town, NE Tunisia, on Gulf of Hammamet; pop. 28,500.

South Africa. = UNION OF SOUTH AFRICA.

South African Republic. See TRANSVAAL.

South′all (south′ôl) municipal borough, S England, in Middlesex W of London; pop. 55,900.

South America, continent, Western Hemisphere, with the equator crossing it in its N quarter; extends farthest S of all inhabited continents; adjoins North America (Panama) on the NW; area 7,035,357 sq. m. — **South American,** adj. & n.

South.amp′ton (sou·thăm[p]′tŭn; south·hăm[p]′-) **1** administrative county, S England: see HAMPSHIRE. **2** seaport and county borough, S England, in Hampshire at head of **Southampton Water,** estuary of the Test River; pop. 178,300.

South Australia, state, S Australia; ✱ Adelaide; area 380,070 sq. m.; pop. 700,300.

South Bend (bĕnd′) city, N Indiana; pop. 115,900.

South′bridge (south′brij) town, cen. Massachusetts; pop. 17,500.

South Car′o.li′na (kăr′ô·lī′nà), abbr. **S.C.,** state, SE United States, bordering on Atlantic Ocean; ✱ Columbia; area 31,055 sq. m.; pop. 2,117,000. — **South Car′o.lin′i.an** (-lĭn′ĭ·ăn), adj. & n.

South Carpathians, the Transylvanian Alps.

South Charleston, town, West Virginia; pop. 16,700.

South China Sea. See CHINA SEA.

South Da.ko′ta (dà·kō′tà), abbr. **S. Dak.,** state, NW cen. United States, in plains region on both sides of Missouri river; ✱ Pierre; area 77,047 sq. m.; pop. 652,700. — **South Da.ko′tan** (-kō′t'n), adj. & n.

South Downs, range of hills, S England, chiefly in Sussex.

South′end′ on Sea (south′ĕnd′) county borough, SE England, in Essex at mouth of the Thames estuary; pop. 151,800.

Southern Alps, mountain range, New Zealand, in W South I., extending almost entire length of the island; highest peak Aorangi, 12,349 ft.

Southern Morava. See MORAVA.

Southern Morocco, former Spanish protectorate, W Africa, S of former French Morocco; area 10,039 sq. m.; ceded 1958 by Spain to Morocco; pop. 12,000.

Southern Rhodesia, country, S Africa, in cen. plateau S of Zambezi river; British self-governing territory; federated 1953 with Northern Rhodesia and Nyasaland; ✱ Salisbury; 150,333 sq. m.; pop. 61,800.

Southern Territories, Fr. **Ter′ri.toires′ du Sud** (tĕ′rē′twär′ dü süd′) the S part of Algeria, in the Sahara; area 770,158 sq. m.; pop. 642,700.

South Euclid, village, N Ohio, E of Cleveland; pop. 15,400.

South′gate (south′gĭt; -gāt) municipal borough, SE England, in Middlesex N of London; pop. 73,400.

South Gate (south′ gāt) city, SW California, 7 m. S of Los Angeles; pop. 51,100.

South Island, island, New Zealand; area 58,092 sq. m.; pop. 558,300.

South Mountain, mountain ridge, S Pennsylvania and W Maryland; battle 1862 occurred at Boonsboro, Maryland.

South Orange, village, NE New Jersey, W of Newark; pop. 15,200.

South Orkney Islands or **South Orkneys,** group of islands, S Atlantic Ocean; one of the Falkland Islands Dependencies.

South Os.se′ti.a (ŏs·sē′shĭ·à; -shà), officially **South Os.se′tian Autonomous Region** (ŏ·sē′shăn) autonomous region, U.S.S.R., in N Georgia on S slopes of the Caucasus Mts.; ✱ Stalinir; area 1500 sq. m.; pop. 120,000.

South Pasadena, city, SW California, NE of Los Angeles; pop. 16,900.

South Platte, river, Colorado and Nebraska; flows SE, then NE to join the North Platte river and form the Platte river; 424 m. long.

South Pole, the southern extremity of the earth's axis, in the center of a lofty plateau, W cen. Antarctica.

South′port (south′pôrt) county borough, NW England, in Lancashire on coast N of Liverpool; pop. 84,100.

South Portland, city, SW Maine, SE of Portland; pop. 21,900.

South Saint Paul, city, SE Minnesota; pop. 15,900.

South Sandwich Islands, island group, S Atlantic Ocean, in Falkland Islands Dependencies.

South Sea, 1 the Pacific Ocean — so named by Balboa on his discovery of it 1513. **2** pl. **South Seas,** the waters of the Southern Hemisphere, esp. the South Pacific Ocean.

South Sea Islands, islands of the South Pacific Ocean.

South Shetland Islands or **South Shetlands,** group of islands, S Atlantic Ocean, off tip of Palmer Penin., Antarctica; one of the Falkland Islands Dependencies.

South Shields (shēldz) county borough, N England, on North Sea at mouth of the Tyne E of Newcastle; pop. 106,600.

South′wark (sŭth′ĕrk; south′wĕrk) metropolitan borough, London, on S bank of the Thames; pop. 97,200.

South-West Africa, S. Afr. Dutch **Suid′wes′-A′fri.ka** (soit′vĕs′ä′-frĭ·kä), formerly **German Southwest Africa,** territory, SW Africa, bordering on Atlantic Ocean; before 1919 belonged to Germany, assigned as mandate to Union of South Africa 1919; ✱ Windhoek; area 318,099 sq. m.; pop. 430,400.

So.vetsk′ (sŭ·vyĕtsk′), Ger. **Til′sit** (tĭl′zĭt; in English, also -sĭt) city, Soviet Russia, Europe, on Neman river; pop. 50,800.

So.vet′ska.ya Ga′van (sŭ·vyĕt′skà·yà gà′vän·y′) seaport, SE Soviet Russia, Asia, in Khabarovsk Territory on Tatar Strait; naval base.

Soviet Central Asia. See CENTRAL ASIA, SOVIET.

So′vi.et Russia (sō′vĭ·ĕt; sō′vĭ·ĕt′; sŏ·vyĕt′; sŏv′ĭ·ĕt) the Russian Soviet Federated Socialist Republic.

Soviet Union, the Union of Soviet Socialist Republics.

Spa (spä; Angl. spä, spô) town, E Belgium, SE of Liége; mineral springs.

Spain (spān), Span. **Es.pa′ña** (ĕs·pä′nyä) country, SW Europe, occupying greater part of Iberian Penin.; nominally a kingdom; ✱ Madrid; area 193,144 sq. m.; pop. 28,286,500. See SPANIARD, SPANISH, in Vocab.

Spalato. See SPLIT.

Span'dau (shpän'dou) western suburb of Berlin, Germany; formerly a separate city; once residence of electors of Brandenburg.
Spanish Africa, the colonial possessions of Spain in Africa: Spanish Guinea, Spanish Sahara, Ifni, and, formerly, Spanish Morocco and Southern Morocco.
Spanish America, those parts of America settled by Spaniards and now governed or occupied chiefly by their descendants; includes most of South America (except Brazil and the Guianas), Central America (except British Honduras), Mexico, Cuba, Puerto Rico, Dominican Republic, and some small islands in the West Indies.
Spanish Guinea, Span. **Ter'ri·to'rios Es'pa·ño'les del Gol'fo de Gui·ne'a** (tĕr'rē·tō'ryōs ās'pä·nyō'lās thĕl gôl'fō thä gē·nā'ä) territory, W Africa, on Gulf of Guinea, including Río Muni on the mainland and several islands; a Spanish colony; ✻ Santa Isabel; area 10,852 sq. m.; pop. 170,600.
Spanish Main, the mainland of Spanish America, especially the N coast of South America; improperly, the S portion, or the whole, of the Caribbean Sea.
Spanish Morocco. See MOROCCO.
Spanish Peaks, two mountains, East and West Spanish Peak, S Colorado, E of Sangre de Cristo Mountains; west peak 13,623 ft. high.
Spanish Sahara, region, W Africa, on coast S of Morocco; includes Río de Oro; area 105,409 sq. m.; pop. 25,000.
Spar'ta (spär'tȧ) or **Lac'e·dae'mon** (lăs'ē·dē'mŏn) ancient city, S Greece, in the Peloponnesus; ✻ of Laconia and, 404–371 B.C., the chief city of Greece. See SPARTAN, in Vocab.
Spar'tan·burg (spär't'n·bûrg) city, NW South Carolina; pop. 36,800.
Spen'cer Gulf (spĕn'sẽr), also **Spen'cer's Gulf** (-sẽrz) inlet of Indian Ocean, SE South Australia; 175 m. long, 90 m. wide in widest part.
Spey'er (shpī'ẽr), Anglicized **Spires** (spīrz) city, W Germany, on the Rhine; formerly ✻ of the Rhine Palatinate; diet 1592; pop. 27,700.
Spezia, La. See LA SPEZIA.
Spice Islands. See MOLUCCAS.
Spi·on' Kop (spē·ôn' kŏp'; Angl. spī'ŭn kŏp') hill, Union of South Africa, in Natal WSW of Ladysmith; battle 1900.
Spit'head' (spĭt'hĕd'; -hĕd') roadstead on S coast of England, off Portsmouth harbor; connects with the Solent on the W.
Spits'ber'gen (spĭts'bûr'gĕn) group of islands, Arctic Ocean, belonging to Norway; chief island West Spitsbergen; area 24,280 sq. m.
Split (splĭt) or **Spljet** (splyĕt), Ital. **Spa'la·to** (spä'lä·tō) seaport, Yugoslavia, on the Dalmatian coast in Croatia; pop. 50,000.
Spo·kane' (spō·kăn') **1** river, E Washington, flowing W into Columbia river; 120 m. long. **2** city at falls of Spokane river; pop. 161,700.
Spo·le'to (spō·lā'tō) commune, cen. Italy, SE of Perugia; a leading city of ancient Umbria; pop. 32,300.
Spor'a·des (spŏr'ȧ·dēz) two island groups of Greece, in Aegean Sea: the **Northern Sporades**, N of Euboea and E of Thessaly, and the **Southern Sporades**, off SW Turkey, comprising chiefly the Dodecanese.
Spot'syl·va'nia (spŏt'sĭl·văn'yȧ; -vā'nĭ·ȧ) village, NE Virginia, SW of Fredericksburg; battles of **Spotsylvania Court House** May 1864.
Spree (shprā) river, E Germany, flowing N to the Havel; 220 m. long.
Spring'field (sprĭng'fēld) **1** city, ✻ of Illinois, on Sangamon river; pop. 81,600. **2** city, SW Massachusetts; pop. 162,400. **3** city, SW Missouri; pop. 66,700. **4** city, W Ohio, NE of Dayton; pop. 78,500.
Springs (sprĭngz) city, NE Union of South Africa, in S Transvaal; pop. 111,000.
Squaw Valley (skwô) valley, California, on Squaw Peak in the Sierra Nevada W of Lake Tahoe; ski resort.
Srbija. See SERBIA.
Sri·na'gar (srē·nŭg'ẽr) city, ✻ of Kashmir; pop. 207,800.
Srirangapatnam. See SERINGAPATAM.
Staf'fa (stăf'ȧ) island, W Scotland, in Inner Hebrides W of Mull.
Staf'ford·shire (stăf'ẽrd·shĭr; -shẽr) or **Staf'ford** or **Staffs** (stăfs) county, W cen. England; ✻ Stafford; area 1153 sq. m.; pop. 1,621,000.
Staked Plain. See LLANO ESTACADO.
Stalin. **1** See STALINO. **2** See VARNA. **3** See BRAŞOV.
Stalin, Mount. See GERLACHOVKA.
Sta'lin·a·bad' (stä'lĭn·ä·bäd'), formerly **Dyu·sham'be** (dū·shȧm'bĕ) city, Soviet Central Asia, ✻ of Tadzhik S.S.R.; pop. 82,500.
Sta'lin·grad (stä'lĭn·grăd; stăl'ĭn-), formerly **Tsa·ri'tsyn** (tsŭ·ryē'tsĭn) city, Soviet Russia, Europe, on the Volga; pop. 445,500.
Sta'li·no (stȧ'lyĭ·nŭ) or **Sta'lin** (stä'lĭn; -lēn; stăl'ĭn; stăl'ēn; Russ. stȧ'lyĭn), formerly **Yu'zov·ka** (yōō'zŭf·kȧ) city, U.S.S.R., in E Ukraine in the Donbas; pop. 462,400.
Sta'lin Peak (stä'lĭn; -lēn; stăl'ĭn; stăl'ēn; Russ. stȧ'lyĭn), formerly **Gar·mo' Peak** (gär·mō') mountain, Soviet Central Asia, in SE Tadzhik S.S.R. in the Pamirs; highest in Soviet Union, 24,590 ft.
Sta'linsk (stȧ'lyĭnsk), formerly **No'vo Kuz·netsk'** (nō'vō kōōz·nĕtsk') city, Soviet Russia, Asia, at S end of Kuznetsk Basin; pop. 169,500.
Stam·boul' (stăm·bōōl') İstanbul; — a once common variant now sometimes applied to the old part of the city S of the Golden Horn.
Stam'ford (stăm'fẽrd) city, SW Connecticut, on Long Island Sound on New York state border; pop. 74,300.
Stamford Bridge, village, N England, in East Riding, Yorkshire, ENE of York; scene of battle Sept. 25, 1066, just before battle of Hastings.
Stan'i·slav' (stăn'ĭ·slăv'), Pol. **Sta'ni·sła'wów** (stä'nē·slä'vōōf), Ger. **Sta'nis·lau** (shtä'nĭs·lou; stä'-) city, U.S.S.R., in SW Ukraine; pop. 71,200.
Stan'ley Falls (stăn'lĭ) seven cataracts of the upper Congo river, Belgian Congo, on the equator.
Stanley Pool, expansion of Congo river, cen. Africa, on border between Belgian Congo and French Equatorial Africa.
Stan'o·voi Range (stăn'ō·voi), Russ. **Sta·no·voi' Khre·bet'** (stȧ·nŭ·voi' kryĭ·byĕt') mountain range, E Soviet Russia, Asia, E of the Olekma river; highest point 8143 ft.
Stan'thorpe (stăn'thôrp) town, E Australia, in SE Queensland on New South Wales border; tin mines and uranium deposits.
Stara Planina. See BALKAN MOUNTAINS.
State College, borough, cen. Pennsylvania; pop. 17,200.
Stat'en Island (stăt''n) island, New York, just SW of mouth of Hudson river off New Jersey coast; part of New York City, constituting Richmond borough (which see); area 60 sq. m.
States of the Church or **Papal States**, temporal domain of the popes in cen. Italy 755–1870; area 16,000 sq. m.
States'ville (stāts'vĭl) city, cen. North Carolina; pop. 16,900.
Statue of Liberty National Monument, government reservation, New York City, on Bedloe's I. in Upper New York Bay; site of Bartholdi's statue Liberty Enlightening the World (unveiled 1886); made national monument 1924.
Staun'ton (stăn't'n; -tŭn) independent city, Virginia, in Shenandoah Valley; pop. 19,900.
Sta·vang'er (stä·väng'ẽr) seaport, SW Norway; pop. 50,300.
Stav'ro·pol (stăv'rō·pôl; stăv·rô'pŭl) city, Soviet Russia, Europe, ✻ of Stavropol Territory; pop. 85,100.
Stavropol Territory, territory, SE Soviet Russia, Europe, N of the Caucasus; ✻ Stavropol; area 29,600 sq. m.; pop. 1,500,000.
Stębark. See TANNENBERG.
Steep Rock Lake, Canada, in SW Ontario N of Quetico Park; drained since 1942, now site of open-pit iron mines.
Steiermark. See STYRIA.
Step'ney (stĕp'nĭ) metropolitan borough, London; pop. 98,600.
Steppes, the. See KIRGIZ STEPPE.
Stet·tin' (shtĕ·tēn'), Pol. **Szcze·cin'** (shchĕ·tsēn') seaport, NW Poland, near mouth of Oder river; pop. 159,100.
Steu'ben·ville (stū'bĕn·vĭl) city, E Ohio, on Ohio river; pop. 35,900.
Ste'vens Point (stē'vĕnz) city, cen. Wisconsin; pop. 16,600.
Stew'art Island (stū'ẽrt) island, New Zealand, S of South I.
Sti·kine' (stĭ·kēn') river, Canada and Alaska, flowing from **Stikine Mountains** (British Columbia and Yukon, highest point 8676 ft.) to Pacific Ocean; 335 m. long.
Still'wa'ter (stĭl'wô'tẽr; -wŏt'ẽr) **1** village, E New York, on Hudson river 21 m. N of Albany and just S of Saratoga (Schuylerville); battles of Saratoga 1777. **2** city, N cen. Oklahoma; pop. 20,200.
Stir'ling (stûr'lĭng) **1** or **Stir'ling·shire** (-shĭr; -shẽr) county, cen. Scotland; area 451 sq. m.; pop. 187,400. **2** burgh, its ✻, on Forth river; castle; battle 1297; pop. 27,000.
Stock'holm (stŏk'hōm; Swed. stôk'hôlm') seaport, ✻ of Sweden, on Baltic Sea; pop. 733,600.
Stock'port (stŏk'pōrt) county borough, NW England, S of Manchester; pop. 141,700.
Stock'ton (stŏk'tŭn) **1** city, cen. California, on San Joaquin river; pop. 79,900. **2** or **Stockton on Tees** (tēz) municipal borough, N England, in Durham; pop. 74,000.
Stoke on Trent (stōk, trĕnt) city and county borough, W cen. England, in Staffordshire; pop. 275,100.
Stoke Po'ges (pō'jĭs; -jĭz) parish, SE cen. England, in Buckinghamshire; generally considered the scene of Gray's "Elegy."
Stone'henge (stōn'hĕnj; stōn'hĕnj') an assemblage of upright stones, S England, in Salisbury Plain, indicating use by an early people.
Stone Mountain, mountain, NW cen. Georgia, near Atlanta; Confederate memorial.
Stones River (stōnz) river, cen. Tennessee, flowing N into Cumberland river; on West Fork, one of its headstreams, is site of battle (also called battle of Murfreesboro) Dec. 31, 1862–Jan. 2, 1863.
Stony Point, village, SE New York, on Hudson river nearly opposite Peekskill; site of fort taken by Gen. Anthony Wayne 1779.
Stour (stour; stōōr; stōr) any of several rivers in England, especially the one flowing past Canterbury into the North Sea through two arms which cut off the Isle of Thanet.
Straits, the (strāts) **1** the passageway between the Mediterranean and the Black Sea, including the Bosporus and the Dardanelles. **2** the Strait of Malacca. **3** the Strait of Gibraltar. **4** also, sometimes, other straits, as Bass Strait, Torres Strait.
Straits Settlements, before 1946, a group of British possessions in Malaya on Strait of Malacca which constituted a crown colony; included Singapore (now a separate colony), and Penang and Malacca (now part of Federation of Malaya).
Stral'sund (shträl'zōōnt; shträl·zōōnt') seaport, E Germany, opposite Rügen I.; pop. 50,400.
Stras'bourg (străs'bûrg; sträz'-; Fr. străz'bōōr'), Ger. **Strass'burg** (străs'bûrg; sträz'-; Ger. shträs'bōōrk) city, NE France, on Ill river W of its confluence with the Rhine; pop. 175,500.
Strat'ford (străt'fẽrd) **1** town, SW Connecticut, on Long Island Sound at mouth of Housatonic river; pop. 33,400. **2** city, Canada, in SE Ontario W of Kitchener; pop. 20,000.
Stratford on Avon, municipal borough, cen. England, in Warwickshire SSE of Birmingham; birthplace and burial place of William Shakespeare; pop. 15,000.
Strath·clyde' (străth·klīd') medieval Celtic kingdom of Scotland, S of the Clyde river; ✻ Dumbarton.
Strath·more' (străth·mōr') the great valley of cen. Scotland S of the Grampians.
Strea'tor (strē'tẽr) city, N Illinois; pop. 16,500.
Stre'sa (strā'zä) town, NW Italy, on Lake Maggiore; international conferences 1932, 1935.
Stret'ford (strĕt'fẽrd) municipal borough, NW England, in Lancashire; pop. 61,500.
Strom'bo·li (strŏm'bō·lĭ), anc. **Stron'gy·le** (strŏn'jĭ·lē) island, Italy, one of the Lipari Is.; has an active volcano **Stromboli**, 3040 ft. high.
Strouds'burg (stroudz'bûrg) borough, E Pennsylvania, near Delaware Water Gap; pop. 6400.
Strut'hof' (strü'tôf') section of village of **Natz'wei'ler'** (nȧts'vā'lâr'), NE France, in Vosges Mts. W of Strasbourg; site of concentration camp 1941–44.
Stry'mon (strī'mŏn), Mod. Gr. **Stri·món'** (strē·môn'), Bulg. **Stru'ma** (strōō'mȧ) river, Bulgaria and Greece, flowing S and SE into Strymonic Gulf; 225 m. long.
Stry·mon'ic Gulf (strī·mŏn'ĭk) or **Gulf of Stri·món'** (strē·môn'), also **Gulf of Or·fa'ni** (ôr·fä'nyē) inlet of Aegean Sea, NE Greece, NE of Chalcidice Penin.
Stutt'gart (shtōōt'gärt; Angl. stŭt'gärt) city, W Germany, on Neckar river; chief city of Württemberg; pop. 481,800.
Styr (stĭr) river, U.S.S.R., in NW Ukraine, flowing N into Pripyat river in the marshes; 300 m. long.

Styr′i·a (stĭr′ĭ·*ȧ*), Ger. **Stei′er·mark** (shtī′ẽr·märk) region, cen. and SE Austria; noted for iron mines; constitutes a province.

Su′bic (so͞o′bĭk) or **Su′big** (-bĭg) municipality, Philippine Is., in Luzon at head of **Subic Bay**, inlet NW of Bataan Penin.; U.S. naval base.

Su′bo·ti·ca (so͞o′bō·tē·tsä) or **Su′bo·ti·tsa**, Hung. **Sza′bad·ka′** (sŏ′bŏd-kŏ′), Ger. **Ma·ri′a-The·re′si·o′pel** (mä·rē′ä·tā·rā′zē·ō′pĕl) city, NE Yugoslavia, in N Voivodina near Hungarian frontier; pop. 112,500.

Su′chow′ (so͞o′jō′) **1** formerly (1912–45) also **Tung′shan′** (to͝ong′-shän′) city, E China, in SW Shantung prov. (before 1949 in Kiangsu); pop. 339,500. **2** = Soochow.

Su′cre (so͞o′krā), formerly **Chu′qui·sa′ca** (cho͞o′kē·sä′kä) city, constitutional ✻ of Bolivia; pop. 30,000.

Su·dan′ (so͞o·dăn′), Fr. **Sou′dan′** (so͞o′däɴ′) **1** region, Africa, between Atlantic Ocean and the upper Niger river, including basins of the Nile river, Lake Chad, and upper Nile river. **2** formerly **An′glo-E·gyp′-tian Sudan** (ăng′glō·ē·jĭp′shăn) country, NE Africa, S of Egypt; formerly under joint British and Egyptian rule, gained independence 1956; republic; ✻ Khartoum; area 967,500 sq. m.; pop. (1955 est.) 8,961,000. — **Su′da·nese′** (so͞o′d*ȧ*·nēz′; -nēs′), adj. & n. sing. & pl. See also Sudanic, in Vocab.

Sud′bur′y (sŭd′bĕr·ĭ; -bĕr·ĭ; -brĭ) city, Canada, in SE Ontario N of Georgian Bay; pop. 46,500.

Su·de′ten (so͞o·dā′t'n; Ger. zo͞o-), also **Su·de′tes** (so͞o·dē′tēz) or **Su-det′ic Mountains** (so͞o·dĕt′ĭk) mountain ranges, E cen. Europe, W of the Carpathians, forming the N border of Bohemia, Czechoslovakia.

Su·ez′ (so͞o·ĕz′; so͞o′ĕz; esp. Brit., so͞o′ĭz) seaport, NE Egypt, at S end of Suez Canal on Gulf of Suez; pop. 108,300.

Suez, Isthmus of, neck of land connecting NE Africa with Asia, in NE Egypt between Mediterranean Sea and NW arm (**Gulf of Suez**) of Red Sea; crossed by the **Suez Canal**, built 1859–69; nationalized 1956 by Egypt; 92 m. long.

Suf′folk (sŭf′ŭk; in U.S., also -ōk) **1** independent city, SE Virginia, on Nansemond river; pop. 12,300. **2** county, E England, bordering on North Sea; divided into **East Suffolk**, ✻ Ipswich, area 871 sq. m., pop. 321,800; and **West Suffolk**, ✻ Bury St. Edmunds, area 611 sq. m., pop. 120,600.

Sugarloaf Mountain. See Pão de Açúcar.

Suidwes-Afrika. See South-West Africa.

Suigen. See Suwon.

Suisse. See Switzerland.

Sui·sun′ Bay (s*ŭ*·so͞on′) inlet of San Francisco Bay, cen. California.

Sui′yuan′ (swā′yü·än′) former province, N China, N of the Great Wall; ✻ Kweisui; included 1954 in Inner Mongolian Autonomous Region.

Su′khu·mi (so͞o′ko͝o·mĭ) seaport, U.S.S.R., ✻ of Abkhazian A.S.S.R.

Suk′kur (so͝ok′ko͝or) or **Sa′khar** (sŭk′hẽr) town, W Pakistan, in N Sind on Indus river; pop. 66,500.

Sulawesi. See Celebes.

Sultanabad. See Arak.

Sulu. See Jolo.

Su′lu Archipelago (so͞o′lo͞o) chain of islands, SW Philippine Is.; chief island Jolo. See Sulu, in Vocab.

Su·ma′tra (so͝o·mä′tr*ȧ*) island, W Indonesia, S of Malay Penin.; lies across the equator; chief city Palembang; area 166,789 sq. m.; pop. 7,601,700. — **Su·ma′tran**, adj. & n.

Sum′ba or **Soem′ba** (so͞om′b*ȧ*), Eng. **San′dal·wood′ Island** (săn′d'l-wo͝od′) island, Indonesia, in Lesser Sunda Is. S of Flores.

Sum·ba′wa or **Soem·ba′wa** (so͞om·bä′w*ȧ*) island, Indonesia, in Lesser Sunda Is. E of Lombok.

Su′mer (so͞o′mẽr) the southern division of ancient Babylonia. See Sumerian, in Vocab.

Sum′mit (sŭm′ĭt) city, NE New Jersey, W of Newark; pop. 17,900.

Sum′ter (sŭm′tẽr) city, E cen. South Carolina; pop. 20,200.

Sun′bur′y (sŭn′bĕr′ĭ; -bĕr·ĭ; -brĭ) city, E Pennsylvania; pop. 15,600.

Sun′da (sŭn′d*ȧ*), or **Soen′da** (so͞on′dä), **Isles**, island group, Malay Archipelago, comprising the **Greater Sunda Islands**: Java, Sumatra, Borneo, and Celebes; and the **Lesser Sunda Islands**, the islands extending E from Java; except for British Borneo and Portuguese Timor, they belong to the Republic of Indonesia.

Sunda, or **Soenda, Strait**, channel between Java and Sumatra.

Sun′der·land (sŭn′dẽr·l*ă*nd) county borough, N England, in Durham on North Sea at mouth of the Wear; pop. 181,500.

Sun′ga′ri′ (so͞on′gä′rē′) or **Sung′hwa′** (so͝ong′hwä′) river, E Manchuria, flowing from mountains on Korean border to the Amur; 800 m. long; upper part is dammed, forming the **Sungari Reservoir**.

Sung′kiang′ (so͝ong′jĭ·äng′) former province, E Manchuria; formed 1950 merged 1956 with Heilungkiang prov.; ✻ Harbin.

Sunset Crater, volcanic crater, N cen. Arizona; central feature of Sunset Crater National Monument, established 1930.

Sun Valley, village, cen. Idaho, in Sawtooth Mts.; resort center.

Suomen Tasavalta, Suomi. See Finland.

Su·pe′ri·or (sū·pḗr′ĭ·ẽr; s*ŭ*-) city, NW Wisconsin, at W end of Lake Superior just S of Duluth, Minnesota; pop. 35,300.

Superior, Lake, lake, United States and Canada; largest, northernmost, and westernmost of the Great Lakes; area 31,820 sq. m.

Su′ra·ba′ja or **Soe′ra·ba′ja** (so͝or′*ȧ*·bä′y*ȧ*) seaport, Indonesia, in NE Java on **Surabaja Strait** (between Java and W end of Madura); naval base; pop. 342,000.

Su′ra·kar′ta or **Soe′ra·kar′ta** (so͝or′*ȧ*·kär′t*ȧ*) **1** native (Mohammedan) principality, Indonesia, in S cen. Java. **2** also **So′lo** (sō′lō) city, its ✻; pop. 165,000.

Su·rat′ (so͝o·răt′; native so͞o′r*ȧ*t) city, W India, in N Bombay state on Tapti river near its mouth; pop. 171,400.

Sur′bi·ton (sûr′bĭ·t'n) municipal borough, S England, in Surrey WSW of London; pop. 60,700.

Su′ri·ba′chi, Mount (so͝or′ĭ·bä′chĭ) volcano, Volcano Is., at S end of Iwo Jima; taken by Americans Feb. 23, 1945.

Su′ri·nam (so͝or′ĭ·năm), Du. **Su′ri·na′me** (sü′rē·nä′mĕ), often called **Netherlands**, or **Dutch, Guiana**, country, N South America, bordering on Atlantic Ocean in Guiana; a territory of the Netherlands; ✻ Paramaribo; area 55,142 sq. m.; pop. 183,700.

Su′ri·na′me (sü′rē·nä′mĕ) river, N Surinam, flowing N into Atlantic Ocean; 400 m. long.

Sur′ma (so͝or′mä) river, NE Indian subcontinent, flowing from Manipur territory, Republic of India, into East Bengal, Pakistan, where it forms the Meghna river; 560 m. long.

Sur′rey (sûr′ĭ) county, S England, SW of London; ✻ Kingston on Thames; area 722 sq. m.; pop. 1,601,600.

Su·ru·ga Bay (so͞o·ro͝o·gä) coastal inlet, Japan, in SE Honshu.

Su′sa, **1** (sū′z*ȧ*; -s*ȧ*), Biblical **Shu′shan** (sho͞o′shăn; -shăn) ancient city, ✻ of Elam; ruins in SW Iran. **2** (so͞o′s*ȧ*) see Sousse.

Su′šak (so͞o′shäk) seaport, NW Yugoslavia, suburb of Rijeka.

Susam-Adasi. See Samos.

Su′si·a′na (sū′zĭ·ā′n*ȧ*; -ăn′*ȧ*) ancient Elam; — occasionally so called from Susa, its ✻.

Sus′que·han′na (sŭs′kwē·hăn′*ȧ*) river, E United States, flowing from cen. New York S through Pennsylvania and into N end of Chesapeake Bay in Maryland; 444 m. long,

Sus′sex (sŭs′ĕks; -ĭks) **1** Anglo-Saxon kingdom, S England; became part of Wessex A.D. 825. **2** county, S England, on the English Channel; divided into **East Sussex**, ✻ Lewes, area 829 sq. m., pop. 618,100; and **West Sussex**, ✻ Chichester, area 628 sq. m., pop. 318,700.

Suth′er·land (sŭth′ẽr·l*ă*nd) or **Suth′er·land·shire** (-shĭr; -shẽr) county, N Scotland; ✻ Dornoch; area 2028 sq. m.; pop. 13,700.

Sutherland Falls, waterfall, New Zealand, in SW South I.; 1904 ft.

Sut′lej (sŭt′lĕj) river, N Indian subcontinent, flowing from Tibet W and SW through the Punjab to join the Chenab; 900 m. long.

Sut′ton and Cheam (sŭt′'n, chēm) municipal borough, S England, in Surrey S of London; pop. 80,700.

Su′va (so͞o′v*ȧ*) seaport, ✻ of Fiji Is., on Viti Levu I.; pop. 15,500.

Su·wał′ki (so͝o·väl′kē), Russ. **Su·val′ki** (so͝o·väl′kĭ), Lith. **Su·val′kai** (so͝o·väl′kī) district, Poland, just E of Masurian Lakes, formerly in Soviet Russia; battles Feb. to July 1915.

Su·wan′nee (so͝o·wô′nē; -wŏn′ē) river, SE Georgia and N Florida, flowing SW into Gulf of Mexico at Suwannee Sound; 240 m. long.

Su·won (so͝o·wôn) or **Sui·gen** (syĭ·gĕn) city, S Korea, S of Seoul; pop. 52,800.

Sval′bard (sväl′bär) the Norwegian islands in the Arctic Ocean between 74° and 81°N lat. and 10° and 35°E long., including Spitsbergen, Bear I., and other small islands; total area 25,000 sq. m.

Sverd·lovsk′ (svẽrd·lôfsk′), before 1924 **E·ka′te·rin·burg′** (ē·kăt′ẽr·ĭn-bûrg′) city, W Soviet Russia, Asia, in Ural Mts.; pop. 425,500.

Sver′drup Islands (svăr′dro͞op) group of islands, N Canada, W of Ellesmere I.; includes Axel Heiberg I. and the Ringnes Is.

Sverige; Svizzera. See Sweden; Switzerland.

Swa′bi·a (swā′bĭ·*ȧ*), Ger. **Schwa′ben** (shvä′bĕn) region, SW Germany, the territory inhabited by the ancient Suevi; in Middle Ages (from 10th cent.) a duchy. — **Swa′bi·an** (swā′bĭ·*ă*n), adj. & n.

Swan (swŏn) river, SW Western Australia, flowing W to Indian Ocean; 150 m. long.

Swan′sea (swŏn′zē; -sē) county borough and seaport, SE Wales, in Glamorganshire; pop. 160,800.

Swat (swät) **1** river, W Pakistan, in North-West Frontier Province, flowing SW and SE into Kabul river; 400 m. long. **2** native state in valley of upper Swat river.

Swa′tow′ (swä′tou′) seaport, SE China, in Kwangtung at mouth of Han river; pop. 178,600.

Swa′zi·land′ (swä′zē·lănd′) country, SE Africa, N of Natal between Transvaal and Mozambique; British protectorate; ✻ Mbabane; area 6705 sq. m.; pop. 156,700. See Swazi, in Vocab.

Swe′den (swē′d'n), Swedish **Sve′ri·ge** (svăr′yĕ) country, N Europe, occupying E section of Scandinavian Peninsula bordering on Baltic Sea; kingdom; ✻ Stockholm; area 173,349 sq. m.; pop. 6,597,300. See Swede, Swedish, in Vocab.

Swin′don (swĭn′d*ŭ*n) municipal borough, S England, in Wiltshire; pop. 68,900.

Świ′no·ujś′cie (shvē′nô·o͞o′ēsh·chĕ), Ger. **Swi′ne·mün′de** (svē′nĕ-mün′dĕ) seaport, NW Poland, on N coast of Uznam I. at mouth of Swine river; pop. 26,600.

Swiss′vale (swĭs′vāl) borough, SW Pennsylvania; pop. 16,500.

Swit′zer·land (swĭt′sẽr·l*ă*nd), Fr. **Suisse** (sü·ēs′), Ger. **Schweiz** (shvīts), Ital. **Sviz′ze·ra** (zvēt′tsā·rä), Latin **Hel·ve′ti·a** (hĕl·vē′-shĭ·*ȧ*; -sh*ȧ*) country, W Europe, in the Alps; a federal republic; ✻ Bern; area 15,940 sq. m.; pop. 4,715,000. See Swiss, in Vocab.

Syb′a·ris (sĭb′*ȧ*·rĭs) ancient Greek city, S Italy, on Gulf of Tarentum. See Sybarite, Sybaritic, in Vocab.

Syd′ney (sĭd′nĭ) **1** city, SE Australia, ✻ of New South Wales, on Port Jackson; pop. with suburbs 1,484,400. **2** city, Canada, on Cape Breton I. on an inlet of Atlantic Ocean; pop. 32,200.

Syr′a·cuse (sĭr′*ȧ*·kūs; for 2, also sĭr′*ȧ*·kūz and, esp. Brit., sī′r*ȧ*·kūz) **1** city, cen. New York, at head of Onondaga Lake; pop. 220,600. **2** Ital. **Si·ra·cu′sa** (sē·rä·ko͞o′zä), anc. **Syr′a·cu′sae** (sĭr′*ȧ*·kū′sē; -zē) seaport, Italy, in SE Sicily; pop. 69,500.

Syr Dar·ya′ (sĭr′ där·yä′; Angl. där′y*ȧ*), Turki **Sir Darya** (sēr′), anc. **Jax·ar′tes** (jăk·sär′tēz) river, Soviet Central Asia, flowing from the Tien Shan in Kazakh S.S.R. into Lake Aral; 1500 m. long.

Syr′i·a (sĭr′ĭ·*ȧ*), Heb. **A′ram** (ā′răm; âr′*ă*m), Arab. **Esh Shâm** (ăsh shăm′) **1** ancient country, W Asia, at E end of Mediterranean Sea, covering modern Syria, Lebanon, Palestine, and Jordan, and, according to some, N Arabia. **2** Fr. **Sy′rie′** or **La Syrie** (lȧ sē′rē′) modern country N of Palestine and Jordan (kingdom); between World Wars constituted part of a French mandate including Lebanon; an independent republic 1941–58, ✻ Damascus; became Feb. 1, 1958 a province of the United Arab Republic; area 73,587 sq. m.; pop. 3,252,700. **3** Syria and Lebanon under French mandate 1920–41; ✻ Beirut. — **Syr′i·an** (sĭr′ĭ·*ă*n), adj. & n.

Syrian Desert, desert region, W Asia, in N Arabia, SE Syria, W Iraq, and NE Jordan; its W part known as **El Ha·mad′** (ăl hă·măd′), a name applied by some to the entire desert.

Sy′ros (sī′rŏs) or **Sy′ra** (sī′r*ȧ*), Mod. Gr. **Sí′ros** (sē′rôs) or **Sí′ra** (sē′-rä) island, Greece, in Cyclades Is.; site of Ermoúpolis, ✻ of group.

Syrtis Major; Syrtis Minor. See Sidra, Gulf of; Gabès, Gulf of.

Szabadka. See Subotica.

Szamos. See Someş.

Szatmár-Németi. See Satu-Mare.

Szá·va. See SAVA.

Szczecin. See STETTIN.

Sze'chwan' or **Sze'chuan'** (sŭ'chwän'; Angl. sĕ'-) province, S cen. China; ✳ Chengtu; area 133,977 sq. m.; pop. 46,438,000.

Sze'ged (sĕ'gĕd), Ger. **Sze'ge·din** (sā'gā-dēn) autonomous city, S Hungary, on the Yugoslav border; pop. 131,900.

Szeming. See AMOY.

T

Ta·bas'co (tȧ·băs'kō) state, SE Mexico, on Caribbean Sea SW of Yucatán Penin.; ✳ Villahermosa; area 9782 sq. m.; pop. 351,100.

Ta'blas (tä'vläs) island, cen. Philippine Is., largest in Romblon group.

Ta'ble Bay (tā'b'l) harbor of Cape Town, Union of South Africa.

Table Mountain, mountain, Union of South Africa, S of Cape Town; 3550 ft. high.

Ta'bor, Mount (tā'bĕr) mountain, N Palestine, in Valley of Jezreel.

Ta·briz' (tȧ·brēz'), anc. **Tau'ris** (tô'rĭs) city, NW Iran, ✳ of Azerbaijan prov.; pop. 272,000.

Tac'na (täk'nä) department, S Peru; part of **Tacna-A·ri'ca** (-ȧ·rē'kä) region, which was occupied by Chile 1884–1930.

Ta·co'ma (tȧ·kō'mȧ) **1** seaport, Washington, on Puget Sound S of Seattle; pop. 143,700. **2** see RAINIER, MOUNT.

Ta·con'ic Mountains (tȧ·kŏn'ĭk) mountain ridges along Massachusetts-New York boundary and in Vermont; highest peak Equinox, 3816 ft., in SW Vermont.

Ta'cu·ba'ya (tä'kōō-vä'yä) city, cen. Mexico, SW of Mexico City; pop. 105,800.

Tadmor. See PALMYRA.

Tad'ous·sac (tăd'ōō·săk; Fr. tȧ'dōō'sȧk') village, Canada, in SE Quebec on St. Lawrence river at mouth of the Saguenay; settled 1600.

Ta·dzhik' Soviet Socialist Republic (tȧ·jĭk'; -jēk') or **Ta·dzhik'i·stan'** (tä·jĭk'ĭ·stän'; -stän'; tä·jē'kĭ'-), also **Ta·jik' S.S.R.** or **Ta·jik'i·stan'**, constituent republic, U.S.S.R., in Soviet Central Asia, bordering on China (Sinkiang) and Afghanistan; ✳ Stalinabad; area 54,900 sq. m.; pop. 1,455,000. — **Ta·dzhik', Ta·jik',** n. sing. & pl.

Tae·dong (tă·dŏong) or **Dai·do** (dī·dō) river, N Korea, flowing SSW to Yellow Sea; 200 m. long.

Tae·gu (tă·gōō) or **Tai·kyu** (tī·kyōō) city, SE Korea; pop. 313,700.

Tae·jon (tă·jŏn) or **Tai·den** (tī·dĕn) city, S Korea; pop. 126,700.

Ta'fi·lelt' (tä'fĭ·lĕlt') or **Ta'fi·lalt'** (-lält') or **Ta'fi·let'** (tä'fĭ·lĕt') oasis, SE Morocco; celebrated for its dates.

Ta'gan·rog (täg'ȧn·rŏg) city, Soviet Russia, Europe, on **Gulf of Taganrog** (NE arm of Sea of Azov); pop. 188,800.

Ta'gus (tā'gŭs), Span. **Ta'jo** (tä'hō), Port. **Te'jo** (tā'zhōō) river, Spain and Portugal, flowing W to the Atlantic Ocean; 566 m. long.

Ta·hi'ti (tȧ·hē'tē), formerly **O'ta·hei'te** (ō'tä·hē'tĕ; -hā'-), Fr. **Ta·ï'ti** (tä'ē'tē') island, Society Is.; site of Papeete; 402 sq. m.; pop. 23,100.

Ta'hoe, Lake (tä'hō) lake on California–Nevada boundary.

Tai'an' (tī'än') town, NE China, in W Shantung prov. S of Tai Shan (a sacred mountain); pop. 90,000.

Tai·chung (tī·chŏong), Jap. **Tai·chu** (tī·chōō) city, W Formosa; pop. (1935) 70,500.

Taihoku. See TAIPEH.

Tai Hu (tī' hōō') lake, E China, in Kiangsu and Chekiang provinces.

Taikyu. See TAEGU.

Tai·myr', or **Tai·mir'**, **Peninsula** (tī·mĭr'; tī'mĭr) peninsula, NW Soviet Russia, Asia, between the Yenisei and Khatanga rivers.

Tai·nan (tī·nän) city, on SW coast of Formosa; pop. 112,000.

Taínaron. See MATAPAN.

Tai'peh' (tī'bä') or **Tai'pei'** (tī'bā'), Jap. **Tai·ho·ku** (tī·hō·kōō) city, ✳ of Formosa; pop. (1940) 340,100.

Taiwan; Taiwan Strait. See FORMOSA; FORMOSA STRAIT.

Tai'yuan' (tī'yü·än'), formerly (1912–47) **Yang'ku'** (yäng'chü') city, NE China, ✳ of Shansi prov.; pop. 230,000.

Tajik, Tajikistan. See TADZHIK, TADZHIKISTAN.

Tajo. See TAGUS.

Ta'ju·mul'co (tä'hōō·mōōl'kō) or **Ta'ja·mul'co** (tä'hä-) mountain, W Guatemala; highest point in Central America, 13,816 ft.

Ta·ka·ma·tsu (tä·kä·mä·tsōō) city, Japan, in NE Shikoku I.; pop. 101,400.

Takao. See KAOHSING.

Ta·ka·o·ka (tä·kä·ō·kä) city, Japan, in Honshu; pop. 133,900.

Ta'kla Ma·kan' (tä'klä mä·kän') desert, W China, in cen. Sinkiang between the Tien Shan and the Kunlun Shan.

Ta'ku' (tä'kōō') town, NE China, in E Hopeh prov. on Hai river E of Tientsin; formerly site of forts guarding approach to Tientsin.

Ta'laud (tä'lout), or **Ta'laur** (tä'lour), **Islands**, island group, Indonesia, NE of Celebes.

Ta'la·ve'ra de la Rei'na (tä'lä·vā'rä thä lä rrē'ē·nä) commune, cen. Spain, on Tagus river; battle 1809; pop. 18,600.

Tal'ca (täl'kä) city, cen. Chile, 155 m. S of Santiago; pop. 50,500.

Talien. See DAIREN.

Tal'la·has'see (tăl'ȧ·hăs'ē) city, ✳ of Florida; pop. 27,200.

Tal'lin or **Tal'linn** (täl'ĭn), Russ. **Tal'lin** (täl'yĭn), formerly **Re'vel** (rā'vĕl), Ger. **Re'val** (rā'väl) seaport, ✳ of Estonia; pop. 145,800.

Tam'al·pais', Mount (tăm'ăl·pī's) mountain, W California, overlooking Pacific Ocean and San Francisco Bay; 2606 ft. high.

Tamar. See PALMYRA.

Ta'ma·tave' (tä'mä·täv') seaport, NE Madagascar; pop. 28,700.

Ta'mau·li'pas (tä'mou·lē'päs) state, E Mexico, bordering on United States and Gulf of Mexico; ✳ Ciudad Victoria; area 30,731 sq. m.; pop. 716,000.

Tam'bo·ra (täm'bō·rä) volcano, Indonesia, on Sumbawa I.; eruption 1815; 9354 ft. high.

Tam·bov' (tŭm·bôf') city, cen. Soviet Russia, Europe; pop. 121,300.

Tam'pa (tăm'pȧ) city, Florida, on **Tampa Bay**, inlet of Gulf of Mexico; pop. 124,700.

Tam'pe·re (täm'pĕ·rĕ), Swed. **Tam'mer·fors'** (täm'ĕr·fôrs') city, SW Finland, on Lake Näsijärvi; pop. 99,700.

Tam·pi'co (täm·pē'kō) seaport, E Mexico, in S Tamaulipas state on Pánuco river 7 m. from its mouth; pop. 81,300.

Ta'na (tä'nä) or **Tsa'na** (tsä'-), **Lake**, lake, N Ethiopia; 1100 sq. m.

Tan'a·gra (tăn'ȧ·grȧ; tȧ·năg'rȧ) ancient town, E cen. Greece, in E Boeotia E of Thebes; scene of battle 457 B.C.

Tanais. See DON.

Ta'na·na (tăn'ȧ·nô) river, E and cen. Alaska, flowing NW to the Yukon; 475 m. long.

Ta'na'na'rive' (Fr. tȧ'nȧ'nȧ'rēv'), Malagasy **Ta·na'na·ri'vo** (tä·nä'nä·rē'vō), Eng. **An'ta·nan'a·ri'vo** (än'tȧ·năn'ȧ·rē'vō) city, ✳ of Madagascar; pop. 174,200.

Tan'djung·pri'ok or **Tan'djoeng·pri'ok** (tän'jŏong·prē'ôk) seaport, Indonesia, in NW Java; the port of Djakarta.

Tan'gan·yi'ka (tăn'gȧn·yē'kä; täng'gȧn-) or **Tanganyika Territory**, before 1920 **German East Africa**, country, E Africa, between Lake Tanganyika and Indian Ocean; before World War I belonged to the Germans; became British mandate 1920, trust territory 1946; ✳ Dar es Salaam; area 360,000 sq. m.; pop. 5,300,000.

Tanganyika, Lake, lake, E Africa, in Great Rift Valley between Belgian Congo and Tanganyika; 4700 ft. deep; area 12,700 sq. m.

Tan·gier' (tăn·jēr'; tăn'jēr), sometimes **Tan·giers'** (tăn·jērz'; tăn'-jērz), Fr. and Ger. **Tan'ger** (Fr. tän'zhā'; Ger. tän'jĕr, täng'ĕr), Span. **Tán'ger** (täng'hĕr) seaport, N Morocco, at W end of Strait of Gibraltar; summer ✳ of Morocco since 1957; with surrounding territory, constituted 1925–56 **Tangier Zone** or **International Zone**, area 225 sq. m., pop. 100,000; became a province of Morocco Jan. 1, 1957.

Ta·nim'bar (tȧ·nĭm'bär; tän'ĭm·bär'), or **Ti'mor·laoet'** (tēmôr'-lout'), **Islands**, island group, Indonesia, in SE Moluccas.

Ta'nis (tā'nĭs), Bib. **Zo'an** (zō'ăn) ancient city, N Egypt, in Nile delta near **Tanis Lake** (now Lake Manzala).

Tan'nen·berg (tăn'ĕn·bûrg; Ger. tän'ĕn·bĕrk), Pol. **Ste'bark** (stĕnm'-bärk) village, NE Poland, SE of Ostróda (Osterode); formerly in East Prussia; battles 1410 and 1914.

Tannu Tuva. See TUVA.

Tan'ta (tŏn'tŏ) city, N Egypt, in Nile delta; pop. 140,000.

Taos (tous) town, N New Mexico, NNE of Santa Fe; actually three villages: Taos, Taos Pueblo, and Ranches of Taos; resort, art colony.

Ta'pa·joz' (tȧ'pȧ·zhôs') river, N Brazil, flowing NE into Amazon river; 500 m. long.

Tap'pan Zee (tăp'ăn zē') expansion of Hudson river, SE New York.

Taprobane. See CEYLON.

Tap'ti (täp'tē) river, W India, S of Satpura Range, flowing W into Gulf of Cambay; 436 m. long.

Ta'qua·rí' (tä'kwä·rē') river, S cen. Brazil; rises in S cen. Mato Grosso state, flows WSW into Paraguay river; 450 m. long.

Tar'a (tär'ȧ) ancient capital (until 6th cent.) of Ireland; site, the Hill of Tara, in co. Meath NW of Dublin.

Taranaki. See EGMONT.

Ta·ran·to (tä'rän·tō; Angl. tăr'ăn·tō, tȧ·răn'tō), anc. **Ta·ren'tum** (tȧ·rĕn'tŭm) seaport, SE Italy, on **Gulf of Taranto** (inlet between toe and heel of the boot); naval base; pop. 194,800.

Ta·ra'wa (tȧ·rä'wä; tä'rȧ·wä; native tä'rä·wä') island, N cen. Gilbert Is.; ✳ of Gilbert and Ellice Is. colony; battle Nov. 21–24, 1943.

Ta'rim' (dä'rēm') river, W China, S of the Tien Shan, flowing E and SE into Lop Nor; 1250 m. long.

Tar'lac (tär'läk) municipality, Philippine Is., in Luzon; pop. 55,700.

Tarn (tärn) river, S France, flowing W into Garonne river; 233 m. long.

Tar'nów (tär'nōōf) city, Poland, on Biala river; pop. 55,000.

Tar'pon Springs (tär'pŭn) city, W Florida, on coast N of St. Petersburg; sponge fisheries.

Tar·qui'nia (tär·kwē'nyȧ), anc. **Tar·quin'i·i** (tär·kwĭn'ĭ·ī) town, cen. Italy, in N Latium; ancient Tarquinii chief of the 12 Etruscan cities.

Tar'ra·go'na (tăr'ȧ·gō'nä) commune, NE Spain; pop. 38,800.

Tar'ry·town (tăr'ĭ·toun) village, SE New York, on Hudson river 24 m. N of New York City; pop. 8900.

Tar'shish (tär'shĭsh) in the Bible, an ancient maritime country, by some located in S Spain and identified with Tartessus.

Tar'sus (tär'sŭs) town, S Turkey, near Cilician Gates; pop. 33,800.

Tartary. See TATARY.

Tar·tes'sus or **Tar·tes'sos** (tär·tĕs'ŭs) ancient kingdom on SW coast of Hispania (Spain) near mouth of the Guadalquivir.

Tar'tu (tär'tōō), Ger. **Dor'pat** (dôr'pät), Russ., formerly **Yur'ev** (yōōr'yĕf) city, E Estonia, W of Lake Peipus; pop. 60,000.

Tash·kent' or **Tash·kend'** (tȧsh·kĕnt') city, Soviet Central Asia, ✳ of Uzbek S.S.R., E of the Syr Darya; pop. 585,000.

Tas·ma'ni·a (tăz·mā'nĭ·ȧ; -mān'yȧ), formerly **Van Die'men's Land** (văn dē'mĕnz) island, S Pacific Ocean, S of Australia; a state of the Commonwealth of Australia; ✳ Hobart; area 26,215 sq. m.; pop. 279,400. — **Tas·ma'ni·an**, adj. & n.

Tas'man Sea (tăz'măn) that part of S Pacific Ocean between SE Australia and W New Zealand.

Ta'tar Republic (tä'tĕr), officially **Tatar Autonomous Soviet Socialist Republic**, also called **Ta'tar·stan'** (tä'tĕr·stän') autonomous republic, E Soviet Russia, Europe, at bend of middle Volga; ✳ Kazan; area 26,100 sq. m.; pop. 2,850,000.

Tatar Strait, body of water between Asiatic mainland and Sakhalin I.

Ta'ta·ry (tä'tȧ·rĭ) or, less correctly, **Tar'ta·ry** (tär'tȧ·rĭ) historically, an indefinite region in Asia and Europe, extending from the Sea of Japan to the Dnieper river. See TATAR, TARTAR, in Vocab.

Ta'tra or **High Tatra** (tä'trä), Czech **Ta'try** (tä'trĭ) mountains, E Czechoslovakia, a section of the Carpathian Mts.; highest point Gerlachovka, 8737 ft.

Tatsienlu. See KANGTING.

Taun'ton (tän't'n; tôn'-; -tŭn) **1** city, SE Massachusetts; pop. 40,100. **2** municipal borough, SW England, ✳ of Somerset; pop. 33,600.

Tauric Chersonese. See CHERSONESE, THE.

Tauris. See TABRIZ.

Tau'rus Mountains (tô'rŭs), Turk. **To·ros' Dag'la·ri'** (tô·rôs' dä'lä·rĭ') mountain chain, S Turkey, running parallel to Mediterranean coast; has peaks above 11,000 ft.

Tay (tā) river, cen. Scotland, flowing into North Sea through **Firth of Tay**, an estuary 25 m. long; river 120 m. long.

Tbilisi. See TIFLIS.

Tchad. See CHAD.

Tees (tēz) river, N England; flows E along boundary between Yorkshire and Durham, empties into North Sea; 70 m. long.

Te·gu′ci·gal′pa (tē·gōō′sĭ·gäl′på) city, ✳ of Honduras; pop. 47,200.

Te·hran′ (tě·hrän′) or **Te′he·ran′** (tě′hě·rän′; tĕ′ě·rän′, -rän′) city, ✳ of Iran, at foot of S slope of Elburz Mts.; pop. 1,010,000.

Teh′ri (tā′rē) or **Tehri Garh·wal′** (gŭr·wäl′) former state, N India, on Tibet border; established 1815, merged with Uttar Pradesh 1949.

Te·huan′te·pec, Isthmus of (tā·wän′tě·pěk) the narrowest section of Mexico, between **Gulf of Tehuantepec** (on Pacific side) and the Bay of Campeche; 130 m. wide.

Tejo. See TAGUS.

Tel A·viv′ (tĕl′ å·vēv′) city, Israel, on coast NW of Jerusalem; founded 1909; pop. 363,500.

Tell el ′A·mar′na (tĕl′ ĕl′ å·mär′nå) station, Egypt, on Nile river, in ancient times midway between Thebes and Memphis; site of capital of Amenhotep IV.

Tell el-Ke·bir′ (tĕl′ ĕl′kě·bïr′) village, N Egypt; battle 1882.

Temagami, Lake. See TIMAGAMI, LAKE.

Tem′bu·land′ (tĕm′bōō·lănd′) region, Union of South Africa; one of the Transkeian Territories; ✳ Umtata.

Temesvár. See TIMISOARA.

Tem′pe (tĕm′pē), Mod. Gr. **Tém′bi** (tâm′bě), **Vale of,** valley, Greece, in NE Thessaly between mounts Olympus and Ossa.

Tem′pel·hof′ (tĕm′pěl·hōf′) southeast district of Berlin, Germany; airfield.

Tem′ple (tĕm′p'l) city, cen. Texas; pop. 25,500.

Tenedos. See BOZCAADA.

Ten′er·ife (tĕn′ěr·ĭf; -ēf; Span. tā′nå·rē′fā), older **Ten′er·iffe** (tĕn′ěr·ĭf; -ēf) island, Spain, largest of the Canary Is.; area 782 sq. m.

Teng′ri Khan (tĕng′rē kän′) mountain, cen. Asia, on border between Kirgiz S.S.R. and Sinkiang; highest point in the Tien Shan, 23,620 ft.

Ten′nes·see′ (tĕn′ě·sē′; tĕn′ě·sē) **1** river, E United States, in Tennessee, Alabama, and Kentucky, flowing into Ohio river; 652 m. long. **2,** abbr. **Tenn.,** state, E United States, between Appalachian Mts. and Mississippi river; ✳ Nashville; area 42,246 sq. m.; pop. 3,291,700. — **Ten′nes·see′an** (-sē′ăn), adj. & n.

Te·noch′ti·tlán′ (tå·nôch′tē·tlän′) Mexico City; — its name when it was capital of the Aztec Empire.

Ten′saw or **Ten′sas** (tĕn′sô) river, SW Alabama; formed by Tombigbee and Alabama rivers, flows S into Mobile Bay; 40 m. long.

Ten Thousand Smokes, Valley of. See VALLEY OF TEN THOUSAND SMOKES.

Te′quen·da′ma Falls (tā′kän·dä′mä) waterfall, Colombia, S of Bogotá; 450 ft. high.

Ter·cei′ra (těr·sā′ē·rå) island, cen. Azores; area 233 sq. m.; pop. 48,000.

Te′rek (tā′rěk) river, Soviet Russia, Europe, N of Caucasus Mts., flowing into Caspian Sea; 380 m. long.

Te′re·si′na (tā′rě·sē′nå) city, NE Brazil, ✳ of Piauí state; pop. 53,400.

Ter·na′te (těr·nä′tå) island, Indonesia, in the Moluccas off W Halmahera.

Ter′ni (těr′nē) commune, cen. Italy, on Nera river near Marmore Falls; pop. 80,300.

Terre′bonne′ (těr′bŏn′; -bôn′) bayou, SE Louisiana, flowing S into **Terrebonne Bay,** inlet of Gulf of Mexico just W of Mississippi delta.

Ter′re Haute (těr′ě hōt′) city, W Indiana, on Wabash river; pop. 64,200.

Terres Mauvaises. See BAD LANDS.

Te′schen (tĕsh′ěn) Czech **Tě′šín** (tyě′shěn), Pol. **Cie′szyn** (chě′shĭn) region, cen. Europe, in Silesia; once an Austrian duchy; divided 1920 between Poland and Czechoslovakia.

Tes′lin Lake (tĕz′lĭn) lake, NW Canada, between British Columbia and Yukon Territory; area 161 sq. m.

Te′ton Range (tē′tŏn) mountain range, NW Wyoming; highest peak Grand Teton, 13,766 ft.

Te·tuán′ (tå·twän′) city, N Morocco, in former Spanish Zone; pop. 49,500.

Teu′to·bur′ger Wald (toi′tŏ·bŏŏr′gěr vält′) range of hills, W Germany, in region between the Ems and the Weser rivers; highest point 1530 ft.

Tevere. See TIBER.

Tewkes′bur·y (tūks′běr·ĭ; -brĭ) municipal borough, SW cen. England, in Gloucestershire on Avon and Severn rivers; battle 1471; pop. 5300.

Tex′ar·kan′a (tĕk′sär·kăn′å; tĕk′sěr-) twin cities on Arkansas-Texas border: (1) city, SW Arkansas; pop. 15,900; (2) city, NE Texas; pop. 24,800.

Tex′as (tĕk′săs), abbr. **Tex.,** state, SW United States, bordering on Mexico and Gulf of Mexico; ✳ Austin; area 267,339 sq. m.; pop. 7,711,200. — **Tex′an** (tĕk′săn), adj. & n.

Texas City, city, SE Texas, on Galveston Bay; pop. 16,600.

Tex·co′co (tås·kō′kō) or **Tez·cu′co** (tås·kōō′kō) town, cen. Mexico, just E of Mexico City on **Lake Texcoco** (12 m. long); in Aztec times seat of Tezcucan kings.

Thai′land (tī′lănd) or **Si·am′** (sī·ăm′; sī′ăm), Siamese **Mu′ang-Thai** (mōō′äng·tī′) country, SE Asia, bordering on South China Sea (Gulf of Siam), and including part of Malay Penin.; kingdom; ✳ Bangkok; area 198,247 sq. m.; pop. 18,836,000. — **Thai** (tī), adj. See also SIAMESE, THAI, in Vocab.

Thames (tĕmz) **1** (locally also thāmz, tāmz) river, SE Connecticut, a tidal estuary flowing S into Long Island Sound; 15 m. long. **2** river, Canada, in SE Ontario, flowing S and SW to Lake St. Clair; 135 m. long. **3** river, S England, flowing from the Cotswold Hills in Gloucestershire E into the North Sea; 209 m. long.

Than′et, Isle of (thăn′ět; -ĭt) tract of land, SE England, in NE Kent, cut off from mainland by arms of river Stour; area 42 sq. m.

Thap′sus (thăp′sŭs) ancient town, N Africa, site on E coast of Tunisia SE of Sousse; battle 46 B.C.

Thar (tär), or **Indian, Desert,** region of desert, NW Indian subcontinent, in Pakistan and Republic of India between Aravalli Range and Indus river; area over 100,000 sq. m.

Tha′sos (thā′sŏs), Mod. Gr. **Thá′sos** (thä′sôs) island, Greece, in N Aegean Sea; area 152 sq. m.; pop. 12,000.

The·ba′id (thē·bā′ĭd; thē′bå·ĭd) the district about Thebes (either in Egypt or in Boeotia).

Thebes (thēbz) **1** classical **The′bae** (thē′bē), later **Di·os′po·lis** (dī·ŏs′pō·lĭs) ancient city, Egypt, on the Nile S of modern Qena; once ✳ of Upper (S) Egypt. **2** Mod. Gr. **Thí′vai** (thē′vä) ancient city, E Greece, on site of modern village 33 m. NNW of Athens; once leading city of Greece (379–362 B.C.). — **The′ban** (thē′băn), adj. & n.

The Hague. See HAGUE, THE.

Theiss. See TISZA.

The Pas (thě pä′) town, Canada, in W Manitoba on Saskatchewan river; pop. 4000.

Thera. See SANTORIN.

The·re·zi′na. = TERESINA.

Ther·mop′y·lae (thěr·mŏp′ĭ·lē) mountain pass, E Greece, between Mt. Oeta and S shore of Maliac Gulf; scene of battles 480 B.C., 279 B.C., 191 B.C., and A.D. 1941.

Thessalonica. See SALONICA.

Thes′sa·ly (thĕs′å·lĭ), Gr. **Thes′sa·li′a** (thĕs′å·lī′å) region, E Greece, between Pindus Mts. and Aegean Sea. — **Thes·sa′li·an** (thĕ·sā′lĭ·ăn), adj. & n.

Thet′ford Mines (thĕt′fěrd mīnz′) city, Canada, in S Quebec; asbestos mines; pop. 19,500.

Thi·bet′ (tĭ·bĕt′). Var. of TIBET.

Thing′vel′lir (thĕng′g′·vět′lĭr) plain, SW Iceland, near Thingvalla Water; once meeting place of the Althing, parliament of Iceland.

Thomp′son (tŏm[p]′s'n) river, Canada, in S British Columbia; flows S (as **North Thompson River,** 185 m. long) and turns W and SW to the Fraser river; joined at Kamloops by a branch (120 m. long) usually known as the **South Thompson River;** total length 270 m.

Thorn. See TORUŃ.

Thousand Islands, island group, Canada and the United States, in St. Lawrence river in Ontario prov. and New York state.

Thrace (thrās) region, SE Europe, in Balkan Penin. N of Aegean Sea; as ancient country, **Thra′ce** (as a Latin name, thrā′sē) or **Thra′ci·a** (thrā′shĭ·å; -shå), extended to the Danube; modern remnant divided between Greece (**Western Thrace**) and Turkey (**Eastern Thrace,** constituting Turkey in Europe). — **Thra′cian** (thrā′shăn), adj. & n.

Thracian Chersonese. See CHERSONESE, THE.

Three Rivers, 1 city, S Michigan; pop. 6800. **2** Fr. **Trois Ri′vières′** (trwä′ rē′vyâr′) city, Canada, in S Quebec; pop. 50,500.

Thu′le (tōō′lē) settlement, NW Greenland, N of Cape York; founded 1910; U.S. Air Force base (begun 1951). See also in Vocab.

Thun, Lake of (tōōn), Ger. **Thu′ner·see′** (tōō′něr·zā′) lake, cen. Switzerland, an expansion of Aare river.

Thur′gau (tōōr′gou) canton, NE Switzerland, bordering on Lake Constance; ✳ Frauenfeld; area 397 sq. m.; pop. 149,700.

Thu·rin′gi·a (thū·rĭn′jĭ·å), Ger **Thü′ring·en** (tü′rĭng·ěn) region, E Germany, including the **Thu·rin′gi·an Forest** (thū·rĭn′jĭ·ăn), Ger. **Thü′ring·er Wald** (tü′rĭng·ĕr vält′), a wooded mountain range extending from upper Werra river SE toward the Czech border; a state of Weimar republic, ✳ Weimar.

Thur′rock (thŭr′ŭk) urban district, England, in Essex; pop. 81,600.

Thurs′day Island (thûrz′dĭ) island, NE Australia, off N Queensland in Torres Strait; now incorporated as a town; pearl fishing.

Tia Juana. See TIJUANA.

Tian Shan. See TIEN SHAN.

Ti′ber (tī′běr), Ital. **Te′ve·re** (tā′vå·rå), anc. **Ti′ber·is** (tī′běr·ĭs) river, cen. Italy, flowing S and SW to the Tyrrhenian Sea; 244 m. long.

Tiberias, Sea of. See GALILEE, SEA OF.

Ti·bes′ti Mountains (tĭ·bĕs′tĭ) mountain group, N French Equatorial Africa, in Sahara region in NW Chad territory; highest 11,201 ft.

Ti·bet′ (tĭ·bĕt′), Chin. **Si′tsang′** (sē′tsäng′) country, cen. Asia, in high plateau (average altitude 16,000 ft.) N of the Himalayas; formerly nominally independent, claimed since 1950 by China as an autonomous region; ✳ Lhasa; area 469,294 sq. m.; pop. 3,000,000.

Tibet, Nearer, region, W China, comprising E and NE portions of Tibetan plateau in Tsinghai and Sikang provs.

Ti·ci′no (tē·chē′nō) **1** river, Switzerland and Italy, flowing from slopes of Saint Gotthard range SE and then SW through Lake Maggiore and into Po river; 154 m. long. **2** canton, Switzerland, bordering on Italy; ✳ Bellinzona; area 1088 sq. m.; pop. 175,100.

Ti′con·der·o′ga (tī′kŏn·děr·ō′gå; tī·kŏn′-) village, NE New York, at N end of Lake George just W of Lake Champlain; site of fort built by French 1755.

Tien Shan (tĭ·ĕn′ shän′) or **Tian Shan** (tĭ·än′) mountain chain, cen. Asia, in Kirgiz S.S.R. and Sinkiang prov., W China; highest peak Tengri Khan, 23,620 ft.

Tien′tsin′ (tĭ·ĕn′tsĭn′; Chin. tĭ·ĕn′jĭn′) city, NE China, in E Hopeh prov. at junction of the Pei river and Grand Canal; pop. 1,292,000.

Ti·er′ra del Fu·e′go (tĭ·ĕr′å dĕl′ fōō·ā′gō; fū-) **1** archipelago off S South America, S of Strait of Magellan; divided between Chile and Argentina; area 27,600 sq. m. **2** island, chief island of the archipelago; divided between Chile and Argentina; area 18,530 sq. m.

Tif′fin (tĭf′ĭn) city, N Ohio, ENE of Findlay; pop. 19,000.

Tif′lis (tĭf′lĭs; tĭ·flēs′), officially, Georgian **Tpi′li·si** or **Tbi′li·si** (t′pĭ′lĭ·sĭ) city, U.S.S.R., ✳ of Georgia, on Kura river; pop. 519,200.

Ti·gre′ (tē·grā′; tĭg′rā) region, N Ethiopia, bordering on Eritrea; former kingdom; ✳ Aduwa.

Ti′gris (tī′grĭs) river, Iraq and SE Turkey; flows SSE and unites with the Euphrates to form the Shatt-al-Arab; 1150 m. long.

Ti′hua′. Var. of TIHWA.

Tihwa. See URUMCHI.

Ti·jua′na (tē·hwä′nå) or **Tí′a Jua′na** (tē′å wä′nå) town, NW Mexico, in N Lower California on United States border; pop. 16,500.

Til′burg (tĭl′bûrg; Dutch. -bûrk) commune, S Netherlands, SE of Rotterdam; pop. 114,300.

Tilisit. See SOVETSK.

Ti·ma′ga·mi or **Te·ma′ga·mi, Lake** (tĭ·mä′gå·mĭ) lake, Canada, in Ontario prov. N of Lake Nipissing; area 90 sq. m.

Tim·buk′tu (tĭm·bŭk′tōō; tĭm′bŭk·tōō′), Fr. **Tom′bouc′tou′** (tôn′bōōk′tōō′) town, French West Africa, in French Sudan near Niger river; in 15th and 16th cents. a great city of the Songhai.

Tim·gad' (tĭm·găd'), anc. **Tham'u·ga'di** (thăm'ū·gä'dĭ) or **Tham'u·ga'dis** (-dĭs) ancient city, NE Algeria, founded A.D. 100 by Trajan.
Ti'mi·şoa'ra (tē'mē·shwä'rä), Hung. **Te'mes·vár'** (tă'măsh·vär') city, SW Romania, near Timiş river and Yugoslav border; pop. 89,900.
Tim'mins (tĭm'ĭnz) town, Canada, in E Ontario; pop. 27,600.
Ti'mor (tē'môr; tē·môr') island, SE Malay Archipelago; ab. 300 m. long; W half (**Timor**, formerly **Netherlands Timor**, area 5764 sq. m., pop. 350,000, ✻ Kupang) belongs to Indonesia, E half to Portugal (see PORTUGUESE TIMOR).
Timorlaoet Islands. See TANIMBAR ISLANDS.
Timor Sea, body of water between Timor I. and NW Australia.
Ti'ni·an' (tē'nē·än'; Angl. tĭn'ĭ·ăn') island, S Mariana Is., SSW of Saipan; contains ruins of colossal columned tombs.
Tin·tag'el Head (tĭn·tăj'ĕl) cape, SW England, on W coast of Cornwall; castle ruins.
Tin'tern Abbey (tĭn'tĕrn) ruins of a Cistercian abbey, W England, in Monmouthshire on the Wye.
Tip'pe·ca·noe' (tĭp'ē·kȧ·nōō') river, N Indiana; rises in **Tippecanoe Lake**, flows W and S into Wabash river; 200 m. long.
Tip'pe·rar'y (tĭp'ĕ·râr'ĭ) **1** county, S Ireland, in Munster prov.; ✻ Clonmel; 1643 sq. m.; pop. 133,300. **2** urban district, SW co. Tipperary, SE of Limerick; pop. 5100.
Ti·ra'na (tē·rä'nä) or **Ti·ra'në** (-nē) town, ✻ of Albania; pop. 30,800.
Ti'rich Mir (tē'rĭch mēr') mountain, Pakistan, in Chitral state on Afghan border; highest point in the Hindu Kush, 25,263 ft.
Ti·rol' or **Ty·rol'** (tĭ·rōl'; tĭr'ōl; tī'rōl), Ital. **Ti·ro'lo** (tē·rô'lō) region, Europe, in E Alps, chiefly in Austria, the section S of Brenner Pass belonging since 1919 to Italy; includes valley of Inn river; chief city Innsbruck. — **Tir'o·lese'**, **Tyr'o·lese'** (tĭr'ō·lēz'; -lēs'), adj. & n. sing. & pl. — **Ti·ro'le·an**, **Ty·ro'le·an** (tĭ·rō'lē·ăn, tī-; tĭr'ō·lē'ăn), adj. & n.
Ti·ru'chi·rap'al·li (tĭ·rōōch'ĭ·räp'ȧ·lĭ), also **Trich'i·nop'o·ly** (trĭch'ĭ·nŏp'ō·lĭ) city, S India, in Madras on Cauvery river; pop. 159,600.
Ti'sza (tĭ'sō), Ger. **Theiss** (tīs), Serb. **Ti'sa** (tē'sä) river, E Europe, flowing from Carpathian Mts. in W Ukraine W and SW into Danube river; 800 m. long.
Ti'ti·ca'ca, Lake (tĭt'ĭ·kä'kȧ) lake on Peru-Bolivia boundary; area 3200 sq. m.; altitude 12,500 ft.
Ti'to·grad (tē'tō·gräd), before 1945 **Pod'go·ri'ca** or **Pod'go·ri'tsa** (pŏd'gō·rē'tsä) town, S Yugoslavia, ✻ of Montenegro; pop. 12,300.
Tji·la'tjap (chē·lä'chäp) seaport, Indonesia, in S Java; pop. 28,000.
Tji're·bon' (chē'rē·bôn') or **Cher'i·bon'** (chĕr'ĭ·bŏn') city, Indonesia, in W Java on N coast E of Djakarta; pop. 54,100.
Tlax·ca'la (tläs·kä'lä) **1** state, cen. Mexico; area 1555 sq. m.; pop. 282,500. **2** town, its ✻; pop. 3300.
Tlem·cen' or **Tlem·sen'** (tlĕm·sĕn') city, NW Algeria; pop. 51,500.
To·ba'go (tō·bā'gō) island, West Indies Federation; part of colony of Trinidad and Tobago; ✻ Scarborough; area 116 sq. m.; pop. 25,400.
To·bol' (tō·bôl') river, U.S.S.R., flowing from SE foothills of Ural Mts. NNE into Irtysh river; 800 m. long.
To'bruk (tō'brŏŏk), Ital. **To'bruch** (tō'brŏŏk) town, NE Libya, in NE Cyrenaica on coast; taken by British December 1940, besieged by Germans March–November 1941.
To'can·tins' (tō'kănn·tēns') river, E cen. and NE Brazil, rising in S cen. Goiás state and flowing N into Pará river; 1700 m. long.
To'go (tō'gō) region, W Africa, on Atlantic Ocean between Gold Coast and Dahomey; until 1919 a German protectorate, then divided into two trust territories: British **To'go·land'** (tō'gō·lănd') in W, area 13,041 sq. m., pop. 392,000, which became 1957 part of Ghana; and **French Togo** in E, ✻ Lomé, area 21,893 sq. m., pop. 780,500.
To'ke·lau' (tō'kĕ·lou') or **Un'ion** (ūn'yŭn) island group, cen. Pacific Ocean; administered by New Zealand.
To·ku·shi·ma (tō·kōō·shē·mä) seaport, Japan, on E coast of Shikoku I.; pop. 103,300.
To'ky·o (tō'kĭ·ō), formerly **E·do** (ĕ·dō) or **Ye·do** (yĕ·dō) city, ✻ of Japan, in SE Honshu on Tokyo Bay; pop. 5,385,100.
Tokyo Plain. See KWANTO PLAIN.
To·le'do (tō·lē'dō) city, NW Ohio, on Lake Erie; pop. 303,600.
To·le'do (tō·lē'dō; Span. tō·lā'thō) commune, cen. Spain, on Tagus river SSW of Madrid; once ✻ of Roman Spain; independent Moorish state 1035–85; ✻ of New Castile and of León and Castile 1087–1560; pop. 39,400.
To·lu'ca (tō·lōō'kȧ), in full **Toluca de Ler'do** (tō·lōō'kä thā lĕr'thō) city, cen. Mexico, ✻ of Mexico state; pop. 43,400.
Tom (tŏm) river, Soviet Russia, Asia; rises in NW Altai Mts. and flows NNW into the Ob river; 450 m. long.
Tom·big'bee (tŏm·bĭg'bē) river, Alabama; flows S to join the Alabama river and form the Mobile and Tensaw rivers; 409 m. long.
Tombouctou. See TIMBUKTU.
Tomb'stone' (tōōm'stōn') town, SE Arizona, former mining center.
Tomsk (tŏmsk) city, Soviet Russia, Asia, on Tom river near the Ob; pop. 141,200.
Ton'ga (tŏng'gȧ), or **Friend'ly** (frĕnd'lĭ), **Islands**, archipelago, SW cen. Pacific Ocean, E of Fiji Is.; a British protectorate; ✻ Nukualofa; 150 islands; total area 250 sq. m.; pop. 34,100.
Ton'ga·land' (tŏng'gȧ·lănd') or **Am'a·ton'ga·land'** (ăm'ȧ-) region, Union of South Africa, in Natal on coast, bordering on Mozambique.
Ton'ga·re'va (tŏng'gȧ·rēv'ȧ) or **Pen'rhyn** (pĕn'rĭn) island, one of the Manihiki Is.; an atoll, land area 3 sq. m., lagoon area 108 sq. m.
Ton'ga·ri'ro (tŏng'[g]ȧ·rē'rō) volcano, New Zealand, in cen. North I.; central feature of a national park; 6458 ft. high.
Tonk (tŏngk) former state, NW India; since 1948 part of Rajasthan.
Ton'kin' (tŏn[g]'kĭn') or **Tong'king'** (tŏng'kĭng'), region, N Indochina, bordering on China; since 1946 forms N part of Vietnam; chief city Hanoi; area 44,660 sq. m.; pop. 8,700,000.
Tonkin, Gulf of, arm of South China Sea between Indochina and island of Hainan.
Ton'le Sap (tŏn'lā săp'), Fr. **Grand Lac** (grän' lák') lake, SW Indochina, in W Cambodia; 87 m. long.
To·pe'ka (tō·pē'kȧ) city, ✻ of Kansas, on Kansas river; pop. 78,800.
Tor'de·sil'las (tôr'thā·sē'[l]yäs) village, N Spain, on the Duero; treaty 1494.
Torino. See TURIN.
Tor'ne (tŏr'nĕ), Finnish **Tor'ni·o** (tôr'nĭ·ō) river, N and NE Sweden, flowing S into head of Gulf of Bothnia; 250 m. long.
To·ron'to (tŭ·rŏn'tō) city, Canada, ✻ of Ontario prov., near W end of Lake Ontario; pop. 667,700.
Toros Dağları. See TAURUS MOUNTAINS.
Tor·quay' (tôr·kē') municipal borough, SW England, in Devonshire on Torbay, an inlet of English Channel; pop. 53,200.
Tor'rance (tŏr'ăns) city, SW California; pop. 22,200.
Tor're An'nun·zia'ta (tŏr'rā än'nōōn·tsyä'tä) commune, S Italy, on Bay of Naples SE of Naples; pop. 72,900.
Torre del Gre'co (dāl grā'kō) commune, S Italy, on Bay of Naples; pop. 51,400.
Tor'rens (tŏr'ĕnz) salt lake, E South Australia, N of Spencer Gulf; 25 ft. below sea level.
Tor're·ón' (tôr'rē·ôn') city, NE Mexico, in Coahuila state; pop. 75,800.
Tor'res Strait (tôr'ĕs) strait between island of New Guinea and N tip of Cape York Penin., Australia; 80 m. wide.
Tor'res Ve'dras (tŏr'rĕzh vâ'thrȧsh) town, W Portugal, N of Lisbon; fighting 1810.
Tor'ring·ton (tŏr'ĭng·tŭn) city, NW cen. Connecticut; pop. 27,800.
Tor'toise Islands (tôr'tŭs; -tĭs) the Galápagos Is.
Tor·to'la (tôr·tō'lȧ) island, British West Indies, chief of the British Virgin Is.; site of Road Town; area 24 sq. m.; pop. 4000.
To'ruń (tô'rōōn·y'), Ger. **Thorn** (tôrn) city, N Poland, on Vistula river; pop. 81,200.
Toscana. See TUSCANY.
Tot'ten·ham (tŏt'nȧm; tŏt''n·ȧm) municipal borough, SE England, in Middlesex N of London; pop. 126,900.
Toug·gourt' or **Tug·gurt'** (tōō·gōōrt') **1** territory, Algeria, S of Atlas Mts., bordering on Tunisia. **2** oasis, its ✻; pop. 61,200.
Tou·lon' (tōō·lôn'; tōō'lŏn; Fr. tōō'lôɴ') seaport, SE France; naval base; pop. 125,700.
Tou'louse' (tōō'lōōz') city, S France, on Garonne river; pop. 264,400.
Tou·raine' (tōō·rān') historical region, NW cen. France, one of pre-Revolutionary provinces; ✻ Tours.
Tour'coing' (tōōr'kwăɴ') city, N France, NE of Lille; pop. 76,100.
Tours (tōōr) city, NW cen. France; battle 732; pop. 80,000.
Tow'ton (tou't'n) parish, N England, in Yorkshire; battle 1461.
To·ya·ma (tō·yä·mä) city, Japan, on Honshu near **Toyama Bay**, inlet of Sea of Japan; pop. 137,800.
To·yo·ha·shi (tō·yō·hä·shē) city, Japan, in S Honshu; pop. 129,400.
Tpilisi. See TIFLIS.
Trab·zon' (träb·zôn') or **Treb'i·zond** (trĕb'ĭ·zŏnd) seaport, NE Turkey, on Black Sea; once seat of empire of Trebizond; pop. 34,000.
Tra·fal'gar, Cape (trȧ·făl'gẽr; trăf''l·gär) cape, SW Spain, SE of Cádiz and WNW of the Strait of Gibraltar; Nelson's victory 1805.
Trail (trāl) city, Canada, in SE British Columbia on Columbia river; pop. 11,400.
Tra·lee' (trȧ·lē') seaport, SW Ireland, ✻ of co. Kerry, at head of **Tralee Bay**, inlet of Atlantic Ocean; pop. 11,000.
Trans A·lai' (trăns' ä·lī') mountain range, Soviet Central Asia, in the Pamirs; highest point Lenin Peak, 23,386 ft.
Trans'cau·ca'sia (trăns'kô·kā'zhȧ; -shȧ) region, U.S.S.R., S of the Caucasus Mts., embracing the three constituent republics Georgia, Azerbaidzhan, and Armenia. — **Trans'cau·ca'sian**, adj. & n.
Transjordan. See JORDAN kingdom.
Trans·kei' (trăns·kā') territory, E Union of South Africa; one of the Transkeian Territories; ✻ Butterworth.
Trans·kei'an Territories (trăns·kā'ăn) region, Union of South Africa, in E Cape Province, comprising that part of Kaffraria N of the Great Kei river; includes territories of Transkei, Tembuland, Griqualand East, and Pondoland; ✻ Umtata.
Trans·vaal' (trăns·väl') province, NE Union of South Africa, between the Vaal and Limpopo rivers; in 19th cent. a Boer republic (the **South African Republic**); ✻ Pretoria; area 110,450 sq. m.; pop. 4,283,000.
Tran'syl·va'nia (trăn'sĭl·vān'yȧ; -vā'nĭ·ȧ), Romanian **Tran'sil·va'nia** (trän'sēl·vä'nyä) region, W Romania, shut in on N, E, and S by mountains (the Carpathians and the **Tran'syl·va'nian** [trăn'sĭl-vān'yăn; -vā'nĭ·ăn] **Alps**, a S extension of the Carpathians); once a principality; part of Hungary 1867–1918.
Tra'pa·ni (trä'pä·nē) seaport, Italy, at NW tip of Sicily; pop. 74,800.
Tra'si·me'no (trä'zē·mâ'nō) or **Pe·ru'gia** (pā·rōō'jä; Angl. pĕ·rōō'jȧ, -jĭ·ȧ), **Lake**, anc. **Tras'i·me'nus** (trăs'ĭ·mē'nŭs) lake, cen. Italy, W of Perugia; scene of Hannibal's victory over the Romans 217 B.C.
Trav'an·core (trăv'ăn·kōr) former state, SW India, bordering on Indian Ocean; a part 1949–56 of former state of **Travancore and Co'chin** (kō'chĭn; kŏch'ĭn), ✻ Trivandrum. See KERALA.
Trav'erse, Lake (trăv'ẽrs) lake, NE South Dakota and W Minnesota; outlet on N is Bois de Sioux river; 30 m. long.
Traverse City, city, NW Michigan, on Grand Traverse Bay; pop. 17,000.
Treasure Island, man-made island, California, in San Francisco Bay; Golden Gate International Exposition 1939; now a naval base.
Treb'bia (trĕb'byä) river, NW Italy, flowing N into Po river; battles 218 B.C. and A.D. 1799.
Treb'i·zond (trĕb'ĭ·zŏnd) **1** Greek empire, 1204–1461, an offshoot of Byzantine Empire; at greatest extent included Georgia, Crimea, and the S shore of Black Sea E of Sakarya river; ✻ Trebizond (mod. Trabzon). **2** see TRABZON.
Treng·ga'nu (trĕng·gä'nōō) state, Federation of Malaya, bordering on South China Sea; ✻ Kuala Trengganu; area 5050 sq. m.; pop. 226,000.
Trent (trĕnt) **1** river, Canada, in SE Ontario, flowing from Kawartha Lakes through Rice Lake and into Bay of Quinte; sections of it form part of canal system (**Trent Canal**) connecting Lake Ontario with Georgian Bay; river 150 m. long. **2** river, cen. England, flowing NNE and uniting with the Ouse to form the Humber; 170 m. long. **3** Ital. **Tren'to** (trĕn'tō), Ger. **Tri·ent'** (trē·ĕnt'), anc. **Tri·den'tum** (trī·dĕn'tŭm) commune, NE Italy, on Adige river; seat of Council of Trent 1545–63; pop. 63,600. See TRIDENTINE, in Vocab.
Tren·ti'no (trĕn·tē'nō) region, NE Italy, around Trent; the Italian-speaking portion of S Tirol; belonged to Austria 1814–1919.

Tren′ton (trĕn′t′n; -tŭn) **1** city, * of New Jersey, on Delaware river; pop. 128,000. **2** town, Canada, in SE Ontario; pop. 11,500.
Tre·vi′so (trā·vē′zō) commune, NE Italy, NW of Venice; pop. 65,900.
Trichinopoly. See TIRUCHIRAPALLI.
Tridentum, Trient. See TRENT.
Trier (trēr), Eng. **Treves** (trēvz), Fr. **Trèves** (trâv) city, SW Germany, on Moselle river near Luxembourg border; pop. 88,000.
Tri·e′ste (trē·ĕs′tā; Angl. trē·ĕst′), Ger. **Tri·est′** (trē·ĕst′), Yugoslav **Trst** (tûrst) seaport between Italy and Yugoslavia, at head of Adriatic Sea on **Gulf of Trieste**, inlet on W side of Istrian Penin.; once belonged to Austria; part of Italy 1919–47; in 1947 made with surrounding area the **Free Territory of Trieste**, under administration of United Nations, area 293 sq. m., pop. 345,000; port (pop. 278,000) with N part of Free Territory returned to Italy 1953, S part of territory having already been absorbed into Yugoslavia.
Trinacria. See SICILY.
Trin′co·ma·lee′ or **Trin′ko·ma·li′** (trĭng′kō·mȧ·lē′) seaport, E Ceylon; pop. 32,500.
Trin′i·dad (trĭn′ĭ·dăd) island, West Indies Federation off coast of Venezuela; with Tobago, forms colony of **Trinidad and Tobago**, * Port of Spain, area 1980 sq. m., pop. 522,200; area of Trinidad 1864 sq. m.
Trin′i·ty (trĭn′ĭ·tĭ) river, E Texas, flowing SE into Galveston Bay; 360 m. long.
Trip′o·li (trĭp′ō·lĭ) **1** see TRIPOLITANIA. **2** city, NW Libya, * of Tripolitania and a * of independent Libya; pop. 108,200. **3** anc. **Trip′o·lis** (trĭp′ō·lĭs) seaport, NW Lebanon; pop. 37,300. — **Tri·pol′i·tan** (trĭ·pŏl′ĭ·tăn), adj. & n.
Trip′o·lis (trĭp′ō·lĭs) either of two ancient Phoenician confederations, one in N Africa (see TRIPOLITANIA), the other in Phoenicia (modern Lebanon), * Tripolis (modern Tripoli).
Trip′o·li·ta′nia (trĭp′ō·lĭ·tān′yȧ; trĭ·pŏl′ĭ-) region, NW Libya, bordering on Mediterranean Sea; once site of three Phoenician colonies, hence the ancient name of **Trip′o·lis** (trĭp′ō·lĭs); as **Trip′o·li** (trĭp′ō·lĭ), became one of the Barbary States; conquered by Italians 1912–19; became one of chief subdivisions of independent Libya 1952; * Tripoli. — **Trip′o·li·ta′nian** (trĭp′ō·lĭ·tān′yăn; trĭ·pŏl′ĭ-), adj. & n.
Tri′pu·ra (trĭ′pŏŏ·rä) territory, NE India, between East Bengal (Pakistan) and Assam; * Agartala; area 4032 sq. m.; pop. 639,000.
Tris′tan da Cu′nha (trĭs′tăn dȧ kōōn′yȧ) island, S Atlantic Ocean, chief of a group (Tristan da Cunha Islands) belonging to British colony of St. Helena; 45 sq. m.
Tri·van′drum (trĭ·văn′drŭm) seaport, SW India, * of Kerala state and of former Travancore and Cochin state; pop. 128,400.
Tro′as (trō′ăs) or **the Tro′ad** (trō′ăd) territory surrounding ancient city of Troy, in NW Mysia, Asia Minor.
Tro′bri·and Islands (trō′brē·änd) group of islands, Solomon Sea, N of New Guinea; attached to Territory of Papua and New Guinea.
Trois-Rivières. See THREE RIVERS.
Trom·be′tas (trōɴm·bā′tȧs) river, N Brazil, in NW Pará state, flowing S to Amazon river; 350 m. long.
Trom′sö′ (trŏm′sû′; trōōm′sû′; Angl. trŏm′sō′) seaport, N Norway; pop. 11,000.
Trond′heim (trôn′hām), formerly **Trond′hjem** (trôn′yĕm) seaport, cen. Norway, on **Trondheim Fjord** (80 m. long); pop. 57,100.
Tros′sachs (trŏs′ăks; -ăks) valley, cen. Scotland, in Perth co. between lochs Katrine and Achray.
Troy (troi) **1** city, E New York, on Hudson river NE of Albany; pop. 72,300. **2** or **Il′i·um** (ĭl′ĭ·ŭm), anc. **Tro′ia** (trō′yȧ) or **Tro′ja** (trō′jȧ) or **Il′i·on** (ĭl′ĭ·ŏn) ancient city, NW Asia Minor, S of the Dardanelles; subject of Greek legend. See TROJAN, in Vocab.
Troyes (trwä) city, NE France, on Seine river; pop. 58,800.
Trst. See TRIESTE.
Tru′chas (trōō′chȧs) mountain, N New Mexico, NE of Santa Fe; three peaks, the highest (North Truchas Peak) 13,110 ft.
Tru′cial O·man′ (trōō′shăl ō·măn′) or **Trucial Coast**, region, SE Arabia, along S coast of Persian Gulf between Qatar Penin. and Cape Musandam; * Sharja; comprises seven Arab states (sheikdoms) in treaty with Great Britain.
Trujillo. See CIUDAD TRUJILLO.
Truk Islands (trŏŏk; trōōk; Angl. trŭk) island group, cen. Caroline Is., encircled by a reef; formerly site of Japanese naval base.
Tru′ro (trŏŏr′ō) **1** seaport, Canada, in cen. Nova Scotia at head of Minas Basin; pop. 12,300. **2** municipal borough, SW England, * of Cornwall; pop. 12,900.
Trust Territory, the, the Trust Territory of the Pacific Islands: see PACIFIC ISLANDS.
Tsana, Lake. See TANA, LAKE.
Tsang′po′ (tsäng′pō′) the upper Brahmaputra river in S Tibet.
Tsaritsyn. See STALINGRAD.
Tsarskoe Selo. See PUSHKIN.
Tsi′nan′ (jē′nän′) city, NE China, * of Shantung prov.; pop. 472,300.
Tsing′hai′ or **Ching′hai′** (chĭng′hī′), also **Ko′ko Nor** (kō′kō nôr′) **1** province, W cen. China, bordering on Tibet; * Sining; area 318,533 sq. m.; pop. 1,317,000. **2** lake in NE Tsinghai, between the Nan Shan and E end of Kunlun Shan; area 2300 sq. m.
Tsing′tao′ (chĭng′dou′), Ger. **Tsing′tau′** (tsĭng′tou′) city, NE China, on S coast of Shantung Penin.; pop. 60,000.
Tsingyuan. See PAOTING.
Tsi′tsi·har (tsē′tsē·här), formerly (1913–47) **Lung′kiang′** (lŏŏng′jĭ·äng′) city, N Manchuria, in Heilungkiang prov.; pop. 133,500.
Tsu·ga·ru Strait (tsŏŏ·gä·rŏŏ) channel, Japan, between islands of Honshu and Hokkaido.
Tsu·shi·ma (tsŏŏ·shē·mä) island, Japan, in Korea Strait, separated from Kyushu by **Tsushima Strait**; area 271 sq. m.; pop. 52,000.
Tu′a·mo′tu (tōō′ä·mō′tōō), or **Pa′u·mo′tu** (pä′ōō·mō′tōō), or **Low** (lō), **Archipelago**, group of islands, S Pacific Ocean, E of Society Is.; belongs to the French; * Apataki; area 330 sq. m.; pop. 4700.
Tü′bing·en (tü′bĭng·ĕn) city, W Germany, on Neckar river S of Stuttgart; university; pop. 28,700.
Tu′bu·ai′ (tōō′bōō·ī′), or **Aus′tral** (ôs′trăl), **Islands**, chain of islands, S Pacific Ocean; belongs to France; area 115 sq. m.; pop. 3600.
Tuc·son′ (tōō·sŏn′; tōō′sŏn) city, S Arizona; pop. 45,500.
Tu′cu·mán′ (tōō′kōō·män′) city, N Argentina; pop. 109,600.
Tu·ge′la (tōō·gā′lȧ) river, E Union of South Africa, in cen. Natal, flowing E to Indian Ocean; 300 m. long; near its source on Mont aux Sources are the **Tugela Falls**, 2810 ft. high.
Tuggurt. See TOUGGOURT.
Tu′la (tōō′lȧ) **1** town, cen. Mexico, in SW Hidalgo state N of Mexico City; ruins of ancient capital of the Toltecs. **2** city, Soviet Russia, Europe, on a tributary of the Oka river; pop. 272,400.
Tu·la′gi (tōō·lä′gē) island, S cen. Solomon Is., off S coast of Florida I. and N of Guadalcanal; formerly * of British Solomon Islands.
Tu′le Lake (tōō′lē) lake, N California, near Oregon border.
Tul′la·ho′ma (tŭl′ȧ·hō′mȧ) town, Tennessee, ENE of Fayetteville; Arnold Engineering Development Center of the USAF; pop. 7600.
Tul′sa (tŭl′sȧ) city, NE Oklahoma, on Arkansas river; pop. 182,700.
Tu′men′ (tōō′mŭn′) river on NE border of Korea; flows N and NE, in its lower course turns sharply SE to Sea of Japan; 220 m. long.
Tu·muc′-Hu·mac′ Mountains (tōō·mōōk′ōō·mäk′) mountain range, NE Brazil, on boundary with Surinam and French Guiana.
Tungchow. See NANTUNG.
Tung′kiang′ (tōōng′jĭ·äng′) town, E Manchuria, on the Sungari at its junction with the Amur; pop. 96,700.
Tungshan. See SUCHOW.
Tung′ting′ Hu (dōōng′tĭng′ hōō′) lake, SE cen. China, in NE Hunan.
Tun·gu′ska (tōōn·gōō′skȧ) three rivers in Soviet Russia, Asia, tributaries of Yenisei river: **Lower Tunguska**, 2000 m. long; **Stony Tunguska**, 1000 m. long; and **Upper Tunguska**, lower course of Angara river.
Tu′nis (tū′nĭs) **1** see TUNISIA. **2** city, * of Tunisia, near site of ancient Carthage; pop. 219,600.
Tu·ni′si·a (tū·nĭzh′ĭ·ȧ; -nĭzh′ȧ) or **Tu′nis** (tū′nĭs), Fr. **Tu′ni′sie′** (tü′nē′zē′) country, N Africa, bordering on Mediterranean Sea, the region W and S of ancient Carthage; formerly one of the Barbary States (usually called Tunis); a French protectorate 1881–1956, gained independence 1956; monarchy 1956–57, republic since 1957; * Tunis; area 48,300 sq. m.; pop. 2,608,300. — **Tu·ni′sian** (-nĭzh′ăn), adj. & n.
Tu·ol′um·ne (tōō·ŏl′ŭ·mē) river, cen. California; flows W from Yosemite National Park into San Joaquin river; 155 m. long.
Tu′pe·lo (tū′pĕ·lō) city, NE Mississippi; battle 1864; pop. 11,500.
Tur′fan′ (tōōr′fän′) depression, W China, in E Sinkiang in NE part of Tarim basin; over 900 ft. below sea level.
Tu′rin (tū′rĭn; tū·rĭn′), Ital. **To·ri′no** (tō·rē′nō) commune, NW Italy, on Po river; pop. 730,600.
Tur′key (tûr′kĭ), Turk. **Tür′ki·ye′** (tür′kĭ·yĕ′) country, W Asia, between Mediterranean Sea and Black Sea and including small area in Europe; formerly center of an empire (Ottoman Empire, * İstanbul), since 1923 a republic; * Ankara; area 296,185 sq. m.; pop. 20,902,600. See TURKISH, in Vocab.
Tur′ki·stan′ (tûr′kĭ·stăn′; -stän′) or **Tur′ke·stan′** (tûr′kĕ-) region, cen. Asia, now divided between Russia, China, and Afghanistan: **Russian**, or **Western, Turkistan**, comprising the republics of Soviet Central Asia; **Chinese**, or **Eastern, Turkistan**, comprising part of Sinkiang province; and **Afghan Turkistan**, in the NE part of Afghanistan bordering on Uzbek S.S.R. See TURKI, TURKIC, in Vocab.
Turk′men Soviet Socialist Republic (tûrk′mĕn; -mĕn) or **Turk·me′ni·a** (tûrk·mē′nĭ·ȧ; -mēn′yȧ) constituent republic, U.S.S.R., in cen. Asia, bordering on Afghanistan, Iran, and the Caspian Sea; * Ashkhabad; area 187,200 sq. m.; pop. 1,170,000. See TURKMAN, TURKOMAN, in Vocab.
Turks and Cai′cos Islands (tûrks, kā′kŭs) two groups of islands (Turks Is. and Caicos Is.), West Indies Federation, at SE end of Bahamas; administered from Jamaica; chief island Grand Turk; total area 166 sq. m.; pop. 5300.
Tur′ku (tōōr′kōō), Swedish **Å′bo** (ō′bōō) seaport, SW Finland; pop. 99,900.
Tus′ca·loo′sa (tŭs′kȧ·lōō′sȧ) city, W cen. Alabama; pop. 46,400.
Tus′ca·ny (tŭs′kȧ·nĭ), Ital. **To·sca′na** (tōs·kä′nä) region, cen. Italy, bordering on Tyrrhenian and Ligurian seas; chief city Florence. See TUSCAN, in Vocab.
Tus′cu·lum (tŭs′kū·lŭm) ancient town, Italy, in Latium SE of Rome and just N of Lake Albano and the Alban Hills.
Tu′tu·i′la (tōō′tōō·ē′lä) island, chief island of American Samoa.
Tu′va (tōō′vȧ), in full **Tuva Autonomous Region**, formerly (1921–44) **Tan′nu Tu′va** (tăn′ōō tōō′vȧ) or **Tu·vin′i·an People's Republic** (tōō·vĭn′ĭ·ăn) autonomous region, Soviet Russia, Asia, on NW border of Outer Mongolia; an independent republic 1921–44, since 1945 part of the Soviet Union; * Kyzyl (Kizil Khoto); area 66,100 sq. m.; pop. 150,000.
Tver. See KALININ.
Tweed (twēd) river, SE Scotland and NE England; flows E into North Sea; 96 m. long.
Tweeddale. See PEEBLES.
Twick′en·ham (twĭk′′n·ăm; twĭk′năm) municipal borough, SE England, in Middlesex, on the Thames SW of London; pop. 105,600.
Twin Falls, city, S Idaho, SW of Twin Falls (125 ft.) in Snake river; pop. 17,600.
Ty′ler (tī′lẽr) city, NE Texas; pop. 39,000.
Tyne (tīn) river, N England, in Northumberland, flowing E into North Sea; 35 m. long.
Tyne′mouth (tīn′mouth; -mŭth; tĭn′mŭth) county borough, N England, on North Sea at mouth of the Tyne E of Newcastle; pop. 66,500.
Tyras. See DNIESTER.
Tyre (tīr), Arab. **Es Sur** (ăs sōōr′), Heb. **Zor** (tsōr; zōr) town, S Lebanon, on the coast; ancient maritime city, * of Phoenicia. See TYRIAN, in Vocab.
Tyrnau. See TRNAVA.
Tyrol. See TIROL.
Ty·rone′ (tĭ·rōn′) county, Northern Ireland; * Omagh; area 1218 sq. m.; pop. 127,600.
Tyr·rhe′ni·an Sea (tĭ·rē′nĭ·ăn) that part of the Mediterranean Sea SW of Italy, N of Sicily, and E of Sardinia and Corsica.
Tyu·men′ (tū·mĕn′; Russ. -myăn′y′) city, Soviet Russia, Asia, on Tura river; pop. 75,500.

U

Uap. See YAP.
Uau·pés' (wou·pās'), Span. **Vau·pés'** (bou·pās') river, Colombia and Brazil, flowing ESE into the Rio Negro; 700 m. long.
U·ban'gi (ū·băng'[g]ē; ōō·băng'[g]ē), Fr. **Ou'ban'gui'** (ōō'bäN'gē') river, cen. Africa, on border between Belgian Congo and French Equatorial Africa; flows W and S into Congo river; 700 m. long, with longest headstream 1400 m.
Ubangi-Sha'ri (-shä'rē), Fr. **Ou'ban'gui'-Cha'ri'** (ōō'bäN'gē'shà'rē') territory, French Equatorial Africa, between Cameroun and Anglo-Egyptian Sudan; ✻ Bangui; area 238,224 sq. m.; pop. 1,065,000.
U'be (ōō'bē; Jap. ōō·bĕ) seaport, Japan, in SW Honshu; pop. 108,700.
U'ca·ya'li (ōō'kä·yä'lē) river, cen. and N Peru; flows N to unite with Marañón river and form Amazon river; 1200 m. long.
Uc'cle (ük'l') or **Uk'kel** (ûk'ĕl) commune, cen. Belgium; pop. 56,900.
U·dai'pur (ōō·dī'pōōr; ōō'dī·pōōr'), also **Me·war'** (mā·wär') **1** former state, NW India, in S Rajasthan; since 1948 part of Rajasthan state. **2** city, its ✻; pop. 59,600.
U'di·ne (ōō'dē·nā) commune, NE Italy, NE of Venice; pop. 79,400.
Ud'murt Republic (ōōd'mōōrt), officially **Udmurt Autonomous Soviet Socialist Republic**, formerly **Vo·tyak'** (vŭ·tyäk') autonomous republic, E Soviet Russia, Europe, in W foothills of Ural Mts.; ✻ Izhevsk; area 16,200 sq. m.; pop. 1,200,000.
Uebi Scebeli. See SHIBELI, WEBBE.
Ue'le (wē'lā), also **Wel'le** (wĕ'lā) river, cen. Africa, flowing W across N Belgian Congo to unite with Bomu river and form Ubangi river; 700 m. long.
U·fa' (ōō·fä') city, Soviet Russia, Europe, ✻ of Bashkir Republic, at junction of Belaya and Ufa rivers; pop. 245,900.
U·gan'da (ū·găn'dȧ; ōō·gän'dä) country, E Africa, N of Lake Victoria; British protectorate; ✻ Entebbe; area 93,981 sq. m., including 13,680 sq. m. of Lake Victoria; pop. 3,930,700.
U·in'ta Mountains (ū·ĭn'tȧ) range, NE Utah; highest point Kings Peak, 13,498 ft.
Új'pest (ōō'y'·pĕsht), Ger. **Neu'pest** (noi'pĕst) city, cen. Hungary, on Danube river N of Budapest; pop. 72,900.
Újvidék. See NOVI SAD.
Ukkel. See UCCLE.
U·kraine' (ū·krān'; ū'krān; ū·krīn'; ū'krīn), Russ. **U·krai'na** (ōō·krī'nȧ), officially **U·krai'ni·an Soviet Socialist Republic** (ū·krā'nĭ·ăn; -krī'-) constituent republic of the U.S.S.R., in E cen. Europe on N shore of Black Sea; ✻ Kiev (✻ Kharkov 1921–34); area 222,600 sq. m.; pop. 40,500,000. See UKRAINIAN, in Vocab.
Ulan Bator, Ulan Bator Khoto. See URGA.
U'lan U·de' (ōō'län ōō·dĕ'), formerly **Verkh'ne·u'dinsk** (vyĕrK'nyĕ·ōō'dyĭnsk) city, Soviet Russia, Asia, ✻ of Buryat-Mongol Republic, on Selenga river; pop. 129,400.
U·li'thi (ōō·lē'thē) atoll, W Caroline Is.
Ulm (ōōlm) city, W Germany, on Danube river; pop. 58,100.
Ul'ster (ŭl'stẽr) **1** region, N Ireland (island), in Northern Ireland and Republic of Ireland; ancient Irish kingdom, later a province comprising nine counties, three of which (two in S one in NW) in 1921 joined Irish Free State (now Republic of Ireland) while the rest stayed with United Kingdom. **2** province, N Republic of Ireland, comprising counties Donegal, Cavan, and Monaghan; area 3093 sq. m.; pop. 253,300. **3** commonly, Northern Ireland, comprising counties Antrim, Armagh, Down, Fermanagh, Londonderry, and Tyrone.
U'lugh Muz·tagh' (ōō'lōō mōōz·tä') mountain, W China, in S Sinkiang on Tibet border; highest in Kunlun Mts., 25,340 ft.
Ul·ya'novsk (ōōl·yä'nŭfsk), also **Ul·ia'novsk**, before 1924 **Sim·birsk'** (sĭm·bĭrsk') city, Soviet Russia, Europe, on the Volga; pop. 102,100.
Um'bri·a (ŭm'brĭ·ȧ; Ital. ōōm'brē·ä) region, cen. Italy, in the Apennines; chief city Perugia. See UMBRIAN, in Vocab.
Um'nak (ōōm'năk) island, SW Alaska, in Aleutian Is. in Fox Is. group.
Un'a·las'ka (ŭn'ȧ·lăs'kȧ) island, SW Alaska, in Fox Is. group of the Aleutian Is.; area 1074 sq. m.; on N coast is **Unalaska Bay**.
Un'com·pah'gre Peak (ŭn'kŭm·pä'grē) mountain, SW Colorado; highest in the San Juan Mts., 14,306 ft.
Ungarn. See HUNGARY.
Un·ga'va (ŭn[g]·gä'vȧ; -gā'vȧ) region, NE Canada, in N Quebec prov. E of Hudson Bay; includes **Ungava Peninsula**, between Hudson Bay and **Ungava Bay** (inlet of Hudson Strait).
U'ni·mak (ū'nĭ·măk) island, SW Alaska, in Aleutian Is. in Fox group; 65 m. long.
Union City, city, NE New Jersey, adjoining Jersey City; pop. 55,500.
Union Islands. = TOKELAU islands.
Union of South Africa, Afrikaans **U'nie van Suid-A'fri·ka** (ü'nē fän soit'ä'frĭ·kä) country, S Africa, S of the Limpopo, Molopo, and Orange rivers, bordering on Atlantic and Indian oceans; a dominion of the British Commonwealth; administrative ✻ Pretoria, seat of legislature Cape Town; area 472,550 sq. m.; pop. 11,418,300.
Union of So'vi·et Socialist Republics (sō'vĭ·ĕt; sō'vĭ·ĕt'; sō·vyĕt'; sŏv'ĭ·ĕt), commonly shortened to **Soviet Union** or **U.S.S.R.**, often popularly **Russia**, country, Europe and Asia, bordering on Baltic Sea, Black Sea, Caspian Sea, and Arctic and Pacific oceans; ✻ Moscow; area 8,354,198 sq. m.; pop. 191,595,000.
Un'ion·town (ūn'yŭn·toun) city, SW Pennsylvania; pop. 20,500.
United Arab Republic, abbr. **U.A.R.**, country, NE Africa and SW Asia; a union of Egypt and Syria, formed Feb. 1, 1958; ✻ Cairo; allied 1958 with Yemen in United Arab States.
United Kingdom, abbr. **U.K.**, **1** in full **United Kingdom of Great Britain and Northern Ireland**, since 1922, Great Britain (including England, Scotland, and Wales) and Northern Ireland. **2** in full **United Kingdom of Great Britain and Ireland**, from 1801 to 1921, Great Britain and all of Ireland.
United Nations, abbr. **UN** or **U.N.**, international territory, a small enclave in New York City, in cen. Manhattan overlooking East River; seat, since 1951, of permanent headquarters of the United Nations. See UNITED NATIONS, in Vocab.
United Provinces, United Provinces of Agra and Oudh. See UTTAR PRADESH.
United States of America, abbr. **U.S.A.**, commonly **United States**, abbr. **U.S.**, or often **America**, country, North America, bordering on Atlantic and Pacific oceans; a federal republic; ✻ Washington, D.C.; area 3,022,387 sq. m.; pop. 150,697,400.
University City, city, E Missouri, WNW of St. Louis; pop. 39,900.
University Park, city, NE Texas, N of Dallas; pop. 24,300.
Un'ter·wal'den (ōōn'tẽr·väl'dĕn) canton, cen. Switzerland; subdivided into demicantons Nidwalden and Obwalden.
U·per'na·vik or **U·per'ni·vik** (ōō·pûr'nȧ·vēk) Danish settlement, W coast of Greenland, N of Disko I.
U·po'lu (ōō·pō'lōō) island, Western Samoa, 38 m. NW of Tutuila.
Upper Canada, British province, 1791–1841, in North America, N of the Great Lakes; equivalent to S Ontario.
Upper Peninsula, north part of Michigan, between lakes Superior and Michigan.
Upper Vol'ta (vŏl'tȧ), Fr. **Haute-Vol'ta'** (ōt'vôl'tà') territory, French West Africa, including upper courses of headstreams of the Volta river; ✻ Ougadougou; area 121,892 sq. m.; pop. 3,044,000.
Upp'sa'la or **Up'sa'la** (up'sä'lȧ) city, E Sweden; pop. 61,500.
Up'ton (ŭp'tŭn) locality, New York, on Long I.; site of Brookhaven National Laboratory for Nuclear Research.
Uqsor, El. See LUXOR.
Ur (ûr), Bib. **Ur of the Chal·dees'** (kăl·dēz'; kăl'dēz) city in ancient Sumer, S Babylonia; site in S Iraq; dates back to at least 3000 B.C.
U'ral (ū'răl; Russ. ōō·räl') river, U.S.S.R.; rises at S end of Ural Mts., flows S to the Caspian Sea; 1400 m. long.
Ural Mountains, mountain range, U.S.S.R., extending from the Kara Sea S to steppes N of Lake Aral; usually considered the dividing line between Europe and Asia; highest point under 6000 ft.
U·ralsk' (ū·rălsk'; Russ. ōō·räl'y'sk) town, Soviet Central Asia, in W Kazakh S.S.R. on Ural river; pop. 66,200.
U·ra'ri·coe'ra (ōō·rȧ'rē·kwā'rȧ) or **U·ra'ri·cue'ra** (-kwā'rȧ) river, N Brazil; a headstream of the Rio Branco; 360 m. long.
U·ra'wa (ōō·rä'wȧ) city, Japan, in Honshu N of Tokyo; pop. 106,200.
Ur·ban'a (ûr·băn'ȧ) city, E cen. Illinois, ENE of Decatur; pop. 22,800.
Ur'ga (ōōr'gä) or **U'lan Ba'tor** (ōō'län bä'tôr), also **Ulan Bator Kho'to** (kō'tō), Chin. **Ku'lun'** (kōō'lōōn') town, ✻ of Mongolian People's Republic; pop. 100,000.
U'ri (ōō'rē) canton, cen. Switzerland, S of Lake of Lucerne; ✻ Altdorf; area 415 sq. m.; pop. 28,600.
Ur'mi·a, Lake (ōōr'mĭ·ȧ), Pers. **Sha·hi'** (shä·hē') or **U'ru·mi·yeh'** (ōō'rōō·mē·yĕ') lake, NW Iran; area varies between 1500 and 2300 sq. m. according to the season.
U'ru·bam'ba (ōō'rōō·väm'bä) river, cen. Peru, flowing NNW to unite with Apurímac river and form Ucayali river; 450 m. long.
U'ru·guay (ū'rŭ·gwī; -gwā; ōōr'ŭ-) **1** river, SE South America, rising in Brazil and flowing into the Río de la Plata; 980 m. long. **2** officially **Re·pú'bli·ca O'rien·tal' del U'ru·guay'** (rrē·pōō'vlē·kä ō'ryān·täl' dĕl ōō'rōō·gwī') country, SE South America, between the lower Uruguay river and Atlantic Ocean; republic; ✻ Montevideo; area 72,172 sq. m.; pop. 2,650,000. — **U'ru·guay'an** (ū'rŭ·gwī'ăn; -gwā'ăn; ōōr'ŭ-), adj. & n.
U·rum'chi (ōō·rōōm'chē) or **Ti'hwa'** (dē'hwä'), also **U·rum'tsi** (ōō·rōōm'chē) city, W China, ✻ of Sinkiang prov.; pop. 70,000.
U·run'di (ōō·rōōn'dē) district, E Africa, part of Ruanda-Urundi trust territory.
Ush'ant (ŭsh'ănt), Fr. **Île d'Oues'sant'** (ēl' dwĕ'säN') island, NW France, off tip of Brittany.
Us·hua'ia (ōōs·wä'yä) town, S Argentina, ✻ of Tierra del Fuego territory, on S coast of Tierra del Fuego I. at 54°50'S.
Üs'kü·dar' (üs'kü·där'), formerly **Scu'ta·ri** (skōō'tȧ·rĭ) suburb of İstanbul, Turkey, on Asiatic side of the Bosporus.
Üsküp. = Üsküb: see SKOPLJE.
Us'pal·la'ta (ōōs'pä·yä'tä; -pä·zhä'-), or **La Cum'bre** (lä kōōm'brā), **Pass**, mountain pass, W Argentina, on road from Mendoza to Santiago, Chile; altitude over 12,000 ft.
Us·su'ri (ōō·sōōr'ĭ) river, E Soviet Russia, Asia, on Manchurian border; flows N into the Amur; 450 m. long.
Ú'stí or **Ústí nad La·bem'** (ōō'styē nàd' lȧ·byĕm') city, W Czechoslovakia, in N Bohemia on Labe (Elbe) river; pop. 56,300.
U'tah (ū'tô; ū'tä), abbr. (not official) **Ut.**, state, W United States, including E portion of Great Basin; ✻ Salt Lake City; area 84,916 sq. m.; pop. 688,900. — **U'tah·an** (ū'tô·ăn; -tä·ăn), adj. & n.
Utah Beach, section of coast, NW France, in Normandy N of Carentan; landing place of American forces June 1944.
U'ti·ca (ū'tĭ·kȧ) **1** city, cen. New York, on Mohawk river; pop. 101,500. **2** ancient city, N Africa, on coast NW of Carthage.
U'trecht (ū'trĕkt; Du. ü'trĕKt) **1** province, cen. Netherlands, S of the IJsselmeer. **2** city, its ✻; pop. 185,200.
Ut'tar Pra·desh' (ōōt'ẽr prȧ·dāsh'), formerly **United Provinces of A'gra and Oudh** (ä'grȧ, ä'grä; oud) or **United Provinces**, state, N India, bordering on Tibet and Nepal and including upper course of Ganges river; a unit since consolidation of provinces of Agra and Oudh 1902; ✻ Lucknow; area 113,409 sq. m.; pop. 63,215,700.
Ux'bridge (ŭks'brĭj) urban district, SE England, in Middlesex WNW of London; pop. 55,900.
Ux·mal' (ōōz·mäl') ancient city, SE Mexico, in Yucatán state S of Mérida; ✻ of the later Maya empire.
Uz'bek Soviet Socialist Republic (ōōz'bĕk; ŭz'-) or **Uz'bek·i·stan'** (ōōz'bĕk·ĭ·stăn'; ŭz'-; -stän') constituent republic, U.S.S.R., in cen. Asia E of the Amu Darya, between Lake Aral and Afghanistan; ✻ Tashkent; area 157,400 sq. m.; pop. 6,000,000. — **Uz'bek**, n.

V

Vaal (väl) river, Union of South Africa; rises in SE Transvaal, flows W into Orange river in N Cape Province; 700 m. long.
Vaa'sa (vä'sȧ), Swedish **Va'sa'** (vä'sä') seaport, W Finland; pop. 34,500.
Va·duz' (fä·dōōts') commune, ✻ of Liechtenstein; pop. 2800.
Váh (väK), Hung. **Vág** (väg), Ger. **Waag** (väK) river, Czechoslovakia; rises in the Tatra Mts., flows W and S into the Danube; 210 m. long

Va'lais' (và'lĕ'), Ger. **Wal'lis** (väl'ĭs) canton, SW cen. Switzerland, bordering on France and Italy; ✳ Sion; area 2026 sq. m.; pop. 159,200.

Val·dai' Hills (vŭl·dī') hills and plateau, W Soviet Russia, Europe, SE of Lake Ilmen; highest point 1053 ft.

Val·dos'ta (văl·dŏs'tà) city, S Georgia, pop. 20,000.

Va·len'ci·a (và·lĕn'shĭ·à; -shà) **1** region, E Spain, bordering on Mediterranean Sea; ancient Moorish kingdom. **2** commune, Spain, ✳ of ancient kingdom of Valencia; pop. 509,100. **3** city, N Venezuela, near Lake Valencia; pop. 88,700.

Val'la·do·lid' (väl'à·dō·lĭd'; -lē[th]'; Span. bä'[l]yä·thō·lē[th]') commune, NW cen. Spain; capital of Castile 1454–1598; pop. 124,200.

Val·le'cas (bä·[l]yä'käs) commune, cen. Spain, SE suburb of Madrid; pop. 60,600.

Val·le'jo (và·lā'ō) city, cen. California, on San Pablo Bay; pop. 26,000.

Val·let'ta (và·lĕt'à) seaport, ✳ of Malta; pop. 22,800.

Val'ley·field (văl'ĭ·fēld), formerly **Sal'a·ber'ry de Valleyfield** (săl'à·bĕr'ĭ dě) city, Canada, in S Quebec on Lake St. Francis; pop. 23,600.

Valley Forge (fôrj; fōrj) locality, SE Pennsylvania, on Schuylkill river SE of Phoenixville; winter headquarters of Washington 1777–78.

Valley of Ten Thousand Smokes, volcanic region, SW Alaska, in Katmai National Monument; formed at eruption of Katmai 1912.

Valley Stream, village, SE New York, on Long I.; pop. 26,900.

Val'lom·bro'sa (văl'ŏm·brō'sà; -zà) resort, cen. Italy, ESE of Florence in forested region; abbey, founded in 11th cent.

Val'my (väl'mī; -mē; Fr. val'mē') village, NE France; battle 1792.

Va'lois' (val'wä'; Angl. väl'wä) medieval county and duchy, N France, in NE Île-de-France; ✳ Crépy-en-Valois.

Valona. See VLONE.

Val'pa·rai'so (văl'pà·rā'zō) city, NW Florida, on Choctawhatchee Bay; Eglin Air Force Base, with air proving ground.

Val'pa·ra·i'so (bäl'pä·rä·ē'sō), Eng. **Val'pa·rai'so** (văl'pà·rā'zō; -rī'-) seaport, cen. Chile, 75 m. WNW of Santiago; pop. 209,900.

Van (vän; Angl. văn) lake, E Turkey, in mountains of Armenia at over 5000 ft. altitude; area 1425 sq. m.

Van·cou'ver (văn·kōō'vēr) **1** city, SW Washington, on Columbia river; pop. 41,700. **2** city, Canada, in S British Columbia at mouth of Burrard Inlet; pop. 365,800.

Vancouver, Mount, mountain, NW Canada, in Yukon Territory near Alaska border in St. Elias Range; 15,700 ft. high.

Vancouver Island, island, W Canada, off SW coast of British Columbia; chief city Victoria; area 12,408 sq. m.

Van Die'men Gulf (văn dē'mĕn) inlet of Arafura Sea, N Australia, in N Northern Territory.

Van Diemen's Land. See TASMANIA.

Vä'nern (vä'nērn) or **Ve'ner** (vä'nēr) lake, SW Sweden; 2141 sq. m.

Va·nu'a Le'vu (và·nōō'à lĕ'vōō) island, Fiji Is.; area 2128 sq. m.

Varanasi. See BANARAS.

Va·rang'er Fjord (vä·räng'ēr) inlet of Arctic Ocean, NE Norway.

Var'dar (vär'där; Angl. -dēr), Mod. Gr. **Var·dá'ris** (vär·thä'rēs) or **A·xiós'** (äk·syōs'), anc. **Ax'i·us** (ăk'sĭ·ŭs) river, SE Yugoslavia and N Greece, flowing S into Gulf of Salonica; 200 m. long.

Va·re'se (vä·rā'sā) commune, N Italy, NW of Milan; pop. 57,400.

Var'na (vär'nà), since 1949 officially **Sta'lin** (stä'lĭn) seaport, Bulgaria, on inlet of Black Sea; pop. 69,900.

Vasa. See VAASA.

Väs'ter·ås' (věs'tēr·ōs') city, E Sweden, on Lake Mälaren; pop. 57,800.

Vaté. See EFATE.

Vat'i·can City (văt'ĭ·kăn), Ital. **Cit·tà' del Va'ti·ca'no** (chēt·tä' däl vä'tē·kä'nō) independent papal state within commune of Rome, Italy; created Feb. 11, 1929; area 108.7 acres; pop. 1000.

Vät'tern (vět'ērn) or **Vet'ter** (vět'ēr) lake, S Sweden; 733 sq. m.

Vaud (vō), Ger. **Waadt** (vät) canton, W Switzerland, N of Lake of Geneva; ✳ Lausanne; area 1256 sq. m.; pop. 377,600. — **Vau'dois'** (vō'dwä'; Angl. vō'dwä), n. sing. & pl.

Vaupés. See UAUPÉS.

Ve'ii (vē'[y]ī) ancient city, Italy; one of the 12 cities of Etruria.

Vel'la Gulf (vĕl'à) body of water, Solomon Is., SE of Vella Lavella I. and NW of Kolombangara I.; American naval victory Aug. 6, 1943.

Vel'sen (vĕl'sĕ[n]) commune, W Netherlands; outer port of Amsterdam; pop. 41,300.

Velsuna. See ORVIETO.

Ven·dée' (vän'dā') region, W France, bordering on Bay of Biscay S of Brittany; larger portion constitutes a department; scene of Wars of the Vendée 1793–96. — **Ven·de'an** (vĕn·dē'ăn), adj. & n.

Vener. See VÄNERN.

Ve·ne'ti·a (vē·nē'shǐ·à; -shà), Ital. **Ve·ne'zia** (vā·nā'tsyä) **1** ancient division of Roman Empire in what is now NE Italy and NW Yugoslavia, including territory from lower Po river N and NE to the Alps; later divided into three parts (the Three Venetias), which continued until after World War II as divisions of modern Italy: **Venezia Euga'ne·a** (ā·ōō·gä'nä·ä) or simply **Venezia**, the S portion, bordering on the Po and the Adriatic; **Venezia Tri·den·ti'na** (trē·dĕn·tē'nä), the NW portion, N of Lake Garda and including the upper Adige river; and **Venezia Giu'lia** (jōō'lyä), Eng. **Venetia Jul'ia** (jōō'yà; jōō'lǐ·à) or **Jul'ian Venetia** (jōō'yàn), the NE portion (now mostly in Yugoslavia), including Julian Alps and Istria. **2** see VENICE.

Ven'e·zu·e'la (vĕn'ē·zwē'là, -zwē'-; -zwā'-, -zwä'-) country, N South America; republic; ✳ Caracas; area 352,141 sq. m.; pop. 5,034,800.

Venezuela, Gulf of, inlet of Caribbean Sea, NW Venezuela; its S extension is Lake Maracaibo.

Ven'ice (vĕn'ĭs), Ital. **Ve·ne'zia** (vā·nā'tsyä), Lat. **Ve·ne'ti·a** (vē·nē'shǐ·à; -shà) seaport, NE Italy, on islands in Lagoon of Venice, shallow inlet of Gulf of Venice; pop. 321,100. — **Ve·ne'tian** (vē·nē'shăn), adj. & n.

Venice, Gulf of, Ital. **Gol'fo di Ve·ne'zia** (gōl'fō dě vä·nā'tsyä) north section of the Adriatic Sea, between Po delta and Istria Peninsula.

Vents'pils (vĕnts'pĭls), Ger. **Win'dau** (vĭn'dou) seaport, Latvia, at mouth of Venta river; pop. 15,700.

Ven·tu'ra (vĕn·tŏŏr'à), officially **San Buen'a·ven·tu'ra** (săn bwĕn'à·věn·tŏŏr'à) seaport, SW California, NW of Los Angeles; pop. 16,500.

Venue, Ben. See BEN VENUE.

Ve'ra·cruz' (vĕr'à·krōōz') **1** state, E Mexico, bordering on Gulf of Mexico; ✳ Jalapa; area 27,736 sq. m.; pop. 2,057,200. **2** seaport, E Mexico, in Veracruz state on Gulf of Mexico; pop. 71,700.

Verde, Cape. See VERT, CAPE.

Verde Islands, Cape. See CAPE VERDE ISLANDS.

Ver·dun' (vĕr·dŭn'; vûr-) **1** city, Canada, on Montreal I.; pop. 78,300. **2** or **Ver·dun'-sur-Meuse** (vĕr·dŭn'sür-mûz') city, NE France, on Meuse river; treaty A.D. 843; battles 1916, 1917.

Ver'en·drye National Monument (vĕr'ĕn-drǐ) government reservation, NW North Dakota; point from which La Vérendrye first saw beyond Missouri river 1743; established 1917.

Verkhneudinsk. See ULAN UDE.

Ver·me'jo. Var. of BERMEJO.

Ver·mont' (vēr·mŏnt'), abbr. **Vt.**, state, NE United States, bordering on Canada; ✳ Montpelier; area 9609 sq. m.; pop. 377,700.

Vernoleninsk. See NIKOLAEV.

Vernyi. See ALMA-ATA.

Véroia. See BEROEA.

Ve·ro'na (vē·rō'nà; Ital. vä·rō'nä) commune, NE Italy, on Adige river; once an independent republic; pop. 198,200. — **Ver'o·nese'** (vĕr'ŏ·nēz'; -nēs'), adj. & n. sing. & pl.

Ver·sailles' (vēr·sālz'; vēr·sī'; vēr·sī') city, N France, WSW of Paris; site of palace built by Louis XIV; pop. 70,100.

Vert (vûrt) or **Verde** (vûrd), **Cape**, promontory, French West Africa, in Senegal; westernmost point of Africa, at 17°30'W long.

Ves'ter·å'len (věs'tēr·ô'lĕn) island group off NW Norway.

Ve·su'vi·us (vē·sū'vǐ·ŭs), Ital. **Ve·su'vio** (vā·zōō'vyō) volcano, Italy, on Bay of Naples; 3877 ft. high; many eruptions, notably A.D. 79, 1631, and 1906. — **Ve·su'vi·an** (vē·sū'vǐ·ăn), adj. & n.

Vet·lu'ga (vět·lōō'gà) river, cen. Soviet Russia, Europe, flowing S to the Volga; 500 m. long.

Vetter. See VÄTTERN.

Viatka. Var. of VYATKA.

Viborg. See VYBORG.

Vi·cen'te Ló'pez (bē·sän'tā lō'pās) city, E Argentina, just N of Buenos Aires; pop. 95,800.

Vi·cen'za (vē·chĕn'tsä), anc. **Vi·cen'ti·a** (vǐ·sĕn'shǐ·à) commune, NE Italy, W of Venice; pop. 78,500.

Vi·cha'da (vǐ·chä'dä) river, cen. and E Colombia, flowing ENE into Orinoco river; 335 m. long.

Vichegda. Var. of VYCHEGDA.

Vi'chy (vǐsh'ǐ; vē'shǐ; Fr. vē'shē') commune, cen. France, on Allier river; spa; seat of French government July 1940–November 1942; pop. 29,400. See VICHYITE, in Vocab.

Vicks'burg (vĭks'bûrg) city, W Mississippi, on Mississippi river; besieged 1862–63; pop. 27,900.

Vic·to'ri·a (vĭk·tō'rǐ·à) **1** city, S Texas, WNW of Matagorda Bay; pop. 16,100. **2** river, Australia, in NW Northern Territory, flowing N and NW to Timor Sea; 400 m. long. **3** state, SE Australia; ✳ Melbourne; area 87,884 sq. m.; pop. 2,202,900. **4** city, Canada, ✳ of British Columbia, on SE Vancouver I.; pop. 54,600. **5** seaport, ✳ of Hong Kong colony, on NW Hong Kong I.

Victoria, Lake, lake, E Africa, in Tanganyika and Uganda in region between E and W branches of Great Rift Valley; over 26,200 sq. m.

Victoria de Durango. See DURANGO.

Vic·to'ri·a Falls (vĭk·tō'rǐ·à) waterfall, S Africa, in Zambezi river on border between Northern and Southern Rhodesia; 350 ft. high.

Victoria Island, island, N Canada; area 81,930 sq. m.

Victoria Land, section of Antarctica on W shore of Ross Sea and Ross Shelf Ice.

Victoria Nile. See NILE.

Vic·to'ri·a·ville (vĭk·tō'rǐ·à·vǐl) town, Canada, in S Quebec; pop. 16,000.

Vi·en'na (vē·ĕn'à), Ger. **Wien** (vēn) city, ✳ of Austria, on Danube; pop. 1,737,900. — **Vi·en·nese'** (vē'ĕ·nēz'; -nēs'), adj. & n. sing. & pl.

Vienne (vyĕn) **1** river, SW cen. France, flowing NW into the Loire; 217 m. long. **2** city, SE France, on the Rhone; ancient ✳ of the Vien'nois' (vyĕ'nwä'), in the Dauphiné; pop. 23,500.

Vien'tiane' (vyän'tyän') town, Indochina, administrative ✳ of Laos, on the Mekong.

Vie'ques (byā'kās) or **Crab Island** (krăb) island, West Indies, off E Puerto Rico; belongs to Puerto Rico, E half leased by U.S. Navy.

Vi·et'nam', also **Viet-Nam** (vē·ĕt'näm'; -năm'; vēt'-; vē'ĕt-) country, SE Asia, in Indochina; state, including Tonkin and N Annam, set up 1945–46; recognized 1950, with S Annam and Cochin China added, as associated state of the French Union; on cessation of civil war 1954 divided at 17th parallel into N Vietnam (✳ Hanoi) and S Vietnam (✳ Saigon); total area 127,259 sq. m.; pop. 22,973,000. — **Vi·et'nam·ese'** (vē·ĕt'nă·mēz'; vēt'-; vē'ĕt-; -mēs'), adj. & n.

Vi'go (vē'gō) seaport, NW Spain, on the **Estuary of Vigo**, an inlet of Atlantic Ocean S of Pontevedra; pop. 125,300.

Viipuri. See VYBORG.

Vi'ja·ya·na'gar (vǐj'à·yà·nŭg'ēr) or **Bi'ja·na'gar** (bǐj'à·nŭg'ēr) Hindu kingdom, S India, S of the Kistna; established 1336, overthrown 1565.

Vi'la (vē'là) seaport, ✳ of New Hebrides, in SW Efate I.

Vil·la·her·mo'sa (bē'lyä·ĕr·mō'sä), formerly **San Juan Bau·tis'ta** (säng hwäm' bou·tēs'tä) city, SE Mexico, ✳ of Tabasco state, on the Grijalva river; pop. 25,100.

Ville'ur'banne' (vēl'ür'bàn') commune, E France; pop. 82,400.

Vil'ny·us or **Vil'ni·us** (vǐl'nǐ·ŭs), Pol. **Wil'no** (vǐl'nō), Russ. **Vil'na** (vǐl'nà) or **Vil'no** (vǐl'nō), Ger. **Wil'na** (vǐl'nä) city, ✳ of Lithuania; pop. 208,800.

Vi·lyui' (vǐ·lǐ'ūǐ) river, Soviet Russia, Asia, flowing E to the Lena; 1500 m. long.

Viminal. See in Vocab.

Vi'my Ridge (vīm'ǐ; vē'mǐ) ridge near Vimy commune, N France, N of Arras; captured by Canadians April 9–10, 1917.

Vi'ña del Mar (bē'nyä dĕl' mär') city, cen. Chile, E of Valparaíso; noted beach resort; pop. 65,900.

Vin·cennes' (vǐn·sĕnz'; vǐn'sĕnz) **1** city, SW Indiana, on Wabash river; pop. 18,800. **2** commune, N France, E of Paris; pop. 49,200.

Vin'dhya Mountains (vǐnd'hyà) range, N cen. India, N of and parallel to Narbada river.

Vindhya Pra·desh′ (prŭ·dāsh′) former state of the Republic of India, NE cen. India; ✻ Rewa; became 1956 part of Madhya Pradesh.

Vin′land (vĭn′lănd), also **Wine′land** (wīn′-) or **Vine′land** (vīn′-) a portion of the coast of North America; — so called by Norse voyagers.

Vin′ni·tsa (vĭn′ĭt·sà) city, U.S.S.R., in W cen. Ukraine; pop. 92,900.

Vir′gin (vûr′jĭn) river, SW Utah and SE Nevada; flows to Lake Mead; 200 m. long.

Vir·gin′ia (ver·jĭn′yà), abbr. **Va.**, state, E United States, bordering on Atlantic Ocean and Chesapeake Bay; ✻ Richmond; area 40,815 sq. m.; pop. 3,318,700. — **Vir·gin′ian**, adj. & n.

Virginia Capes, capes Charles and Henry, Virginia, forming the entrance to Chesapeake Bay.

Virginia City, **1** town, SW Montana; once an important gold-mining town. **2** village, W Nevada, SSW of Reno; site of Comstock lode, discovered 1859.

Vir′gin Islands (vûr′jĭn) group of islands, West Indies, just E of Puerto Rico; divided between Great Britain and the United States: **British Virgin Islands**, ✻ Road Town on Tortola I., area 58 sq. m., pop. 7100; and **Virgin Islands of the United States**, before 1917 **Danish West Indies**, ✻ Charlotte Amalie on St. Thomas I., area 133 sq. m., pop. 26,700.

Vi·sa′yan Islands (vē·sä′yăn) or **Bi·sa′yas** (bĕ·sä′yäz) islands, cen. Philippines, including islands of Panay, Samar, Leyte, Cebu, Negros, Bohol, Masbate, and the Romblon group.

Vis′by (vĭz′bĭ; Swed. vēs′bü), Ger. **Wis′by** (wĭz′bĭ; Ger. vĭs′bĕ) seaport, Sweden, on Gotland I. in Baltic Sea.

Vis′tu·la (vĭs′tȯͦlà), Pol. **Wis′la** (vēs′lä), Russ. **Vis′la** (vyes′là), Ger. **Weich′sel** (vīk′sĕl) river, Poland, flowing from Carpathian Mts. N into Gulf of Danzig; 630 m. long.

Vistula Lagoon, the Frisches Haff.

Vi′tebsk (vē′tĕpsk) city, U.S.S.R., in NE White Russia on the Dvina river; pop. 167,400.

Vi′ti Le′vu (vē′tē lĕ′vȯͦ) island, Fiji Is., site of Suva, ✻ of the colony.

Vi·tim′ (vĭ·tēm′) river, S Soviet Russia, Asia, flowing NE and N to the Lena; 1100 m. long.

Vi·to′ri·a (vĭ·tō′rĭ·à) city, N Spain, ✻ of Álava prov.; pop. 52,200.

Vi·tó′ri·a (vē·tō′rĭ·à) seaport, E Brazil, ✻ of Espírito Santo state, on Espírito Santo I.; pop. 51,300.

Viz·ca′ya (bēth·kä′yä), also **Bis·ca′ya** (bēs·kä′yä), Eng. **Bis′cay** (bĭs′kā; -kĭ) province, N Spain, bordering on Bay of Biscay; ✻ Bilbao; one of the Basque Provinces.

Vlaanderen. See FLANDERS.

Vlad′i·mir (vlăd′ĭ·mĭr; Russ. vlŭ·dyē′myĭr) city, Soviet Russia, Europe, on Klyazma river; pop. 66,800.

Vla′di·vos·tok′ (vlăd′ĭ·vŏs·tŏk′; -vŏs′tŏk) seaport, SE Soviet Russia, Asia, ✻ of Maritime Territory; pop. 206,400.

Vlis′sing·en (vlĭs′ĭng·ĕ[n]), Eng. **Flush′ing** (flŭsh′ĭng) seaport, SW Netherlands, on Walcheren I.; pop. 20,200.

Vlo′në (vlō′nĕ) or **Vlo′na** (-nä), also **Vlo′rë** (-rĕ) and **Vlo′ra** (-rä), Ital. **Va·lo′na** (vá·lō′nà) seaport, S Albania, on **Bay of Vlonë**, a harbor sheltered by island of Sazan (Saseno) and Cape Linguetta.

Vlotslavsk. See BOEOTIA.

Vl′ta·va (vŭl′tà·và), Ger. **Mol′dau** (mŏl′dou; Angl. mŏl′-) river, Czechoslovakia, in Bohemia, flowing to the Labe (Elbe) river; 270 m. long.

Vo′gel·kop (vō′gĕl·kŏp′) peninsula, NW New Guinea.

Voiotia. See BOEOTIA.

Voi′vo·di′na (voi′vō·dē′nä) region, NE Yugoslavia, N of Danube river; since 1945 an autonomous territory; pop. 1,663,200.

Vol·ca′no Islands (vŏl·kā′nō), Jap. **Ka·zan Ret·to** (kä·zän rĕt·tō) three islands, W Pacific Ocean, S of Bonin Is., including Iwo Jima.

Vol′ga (vŏl′gà) river, Soviet Russia, Europe; rises in Valdai Hills and flows to the Caspian Sea; 2325 m. long.

Vo′log·da (vō′lŏg·dà) city, Soviet Russia, Europe; pop. 95,200.

Vo′los (vō′lŏs), Gr. **Vó′los** (vō′lôs) seaport, NE Greece; pop. 41,700.

Volsinii. See ORVIETO.

Vol′ta (vŏl′tà) river, W Africa; formed by confluence of **Black Volta** (540 m. long) and **White Volta** (450 m. long) in N cen. Ghana, flows S into Bight of Benin; 250 m. long; the **Red Volta**, chiefly in French West Africa, flows to the White Volta.

Vol·ta Re·don′da (vōl′tà rĕ·thōn′dá) town, E Brazil, on Paraíba river near city of Rio de Janeiro; pop. 33,100.

Vol·tur′no (vōl·tȯͦr′nō) river, S cen. Italy; flows S and SE out of the Apennines, then turns W into the Gulf of Gaeta; 110 m. long.

Vor′arl′berg (fōr′ärl′bĕrk) region, W Austria, NW of the Tirol; constitutes a province; ✻ Bregenz.

Vo·ro′nezh (vȯ·rō′nĕsh) city, Soviet Russia, Europe, on Voronezh river near the Don; pop. 326,800.

Vo′ro·shi′lov·grad (vō′rō·shē′lĭf·grăd), formerly, and again since 1958, **Lu·gansk′** (lȯͦ·gänsk′) city, U.S.S.R., in E Ukraine in the Donbas; pop. 213,000.

Vosges (vōzh; vôzh) mountain range, NE France, forming W side of Rhine valley; highest point Ballon de Guebwiller, 4667 ft.

Votyak. See UDMURT REPUBLIC.

Vrangelya, Ostrov. See WRANGEL ISLAND.

Vyat′ka or **Viat′ka** (vyăt′kà) **1** river, E Soviet Russia, Europe, flowing W, S, and SE into Kama river; 800 m. long. **2** see KIROV.

Vy′borg (vē′bôrg; Russ. vī′bĕrk), Swedish **Vi′borg** (vē′bôrg; Swed. vē′bôr·y′), Finnish **Vii′pu·ri** (vē′pȯͦ·rĭ) seaport, Soviet Russia, Europe, on arm of Gulf of Finland; belonged to Finland 1917–40; pop. 74,200.

Vy′cheg·da or **Vi′cheg·da** (vī′chĕg·dá) river, N Soviet Russia, Europe, flowing W to the Northern Dvina river; 700 m. long.

W

Waadt. See VAUD.

Waag. See VÁH.

Waal (väl) river, Netherlands, the S branch of the Lower Rhine.

Wa′bash (wô′băsh) river, Indiana and Illinois, flowing W and SW into Ohio river; 475 m. long.

Wa′co (wā′kō) city, cen. Texas, on Brazos River; pop. 84,700.

Wa·dai′ (wä·dī′), Fr. **Oua′dai′** (wä′dī′) former independent sultanate, NE French Equatorial Africa, in E Chad territory; ✻ Abéché.

Wad′ding·ton, Mount (wŏd′ĭng·tŭn) mountain, W Canada, in SW British Columbia; highest in province, 13,260 ft.

Wa′gram (vä′gräm) village, Austria, NE of Vienna; battle 1809.

Wai′ki·ki′ Beach (wī′kĭ·kē′) resort, Hawaii, on SE Oahu I.

Wai·pa′hu (wī·pä′hȯͦ) city, Hawaii, on Pearl Harbor; pop. 7200.

Wa·ka·ya·ma (wä·kä·yä·mä) seaport, Japan, in SW Honshu; pop. 171,800.

Wake′field (wāk′fēld) **1** town, NE Massachusetts; pop. 19,600. **2** or **Bridg′es Creek** (brĭj′ĕz; -ĭz) estate, Virginia, on Potomac river; birthplace of George Washington. **3** city and county borough, N England, ✻ of West Riding, Yorkshire; pop. 60,400.

Wake Island (wāk) island, N Pacific Ocean, at lat. 19°18′N and long. 166°35′E; belongs to U.S.; taken by Japanese Dec. 23, 1941.

Wa·la′chi·a or **Wal·la′chi·a** (wŏ·lā′kĭ·à) region, S Romania, between Transylvanian Alps and the Danube; formerly (before 1861) a principality, ✻ Bucharest. — **Wa·la′chi·an, Wal·la′chi·an**, adj. & n.

Wal′brzych (väl′bzhĭk), Ger. **Wal′den·burg** (väl′dĕn·bȯͦrk) city, SW Poland, in Silesia on Bobr river; pop. 66,400.

Wal′che·ren (väl′Kĕ·rĕ[n]) island, SW Netherlands; area 82 sq. m.

Wal′deck (väl′dĕk) former state (1918–29) of Germany, between Westphalia and Hesse-Nassau; ✻ Arolsen.

Wales (wālz) section of Great Britain, a wide peninsula W of England; a principality forming part of United Kingdom of Great Britain and Northern Ireland; area 7469 sq. m.; pop. 2,172,300. See WELCH, WELSH, in Vocab.

Wal′la·sey (wŏl′à·sĭ) county borough, NW England, on coast W of Liverpool; pop. 101,300.

Wal′la Wal′la (wŏl′à wŏl′à) city, SE Washington; pop. 24,100.

Wallis. See VALAIS.

Wal′lis (wŏl′ĭs) island group, SW Pacific Ocean, NE of Fiji Is.; with Futuna Is., constitute **Wallis and Fu·tu′na Islands** (fȯͦ·tȯͦ′nä) colony of France, administered from New Caledonia.

Wal′sall (wŏl′sôl; -s′l) county borough, W cen. England, in Staffordshire NW of Birmingham; pop. 114,500.

Wal′tham (wôl′thăm [the usual local pron.]; -thăm) city, E Massachusetts, W of Boston; pop. 47,200.

Wal′tham·stow (wôl′thăm·stō; wôl′tăm-) municipal borough, SE England, in Essex NE of London; pop. 121,100.

Wal′vis Bay (wŏl′vĭs) **1** also **Wal′fish Bay** (wŏl′fĭsh) inlet of Atlantic Ocean, South-West Africa. **2** town on the bay; with surrounding territory (total area 374 sq. m.) an exclave of Cape Province.

Wanchuan. See KALGAN.

Wands′worth (wŏn[d]z′wûrth; -wĕrth) metropolitan borough, London, S of the Thames; pop. 330,300.

Wang′a·nu′i (wŏng′à·nȯͦ′ē) seaport, New Zealand, in North I. on Cook Strait, at mouth of Wanganui river; pop. 26,000.

Wan′hsien (wän′shĭ·ĕn′) city, China, in E Szechwan prov. on the Yangtze; pop. 210,800.

Wan′ne·Eick′el (vän′ĕ·ī′kĕl) city, W Germany, in the Ruhr N of Bochum; pop. 73,800.

Wan′stead and Wood′ford (wŏn′stĕd, -stĭd; wȯͦd′fĕrd) municipal borough, S England, in Essex NE of London; pop. 61,000.

Warm Springs, village, W Georgia; site of establishment founded 1927 by Franklin D. Roosevelt for treatment of infantile paralysis patients.

War′re·go (wŏr′ĕ·gō) river, Australia, flowing SSW from S cen. Queensland to the Darling in New South Wales; 400 m. long.

War′ren (wŏr′ĕn; -ĭn) city, NE Ohio, NW of Youngstown; pop. 49,900.

War′ring·ton (wŏr′ĭng·tŭn) county borough, NW England, on the Mersey E of Liverpool; pop. 80,700.

War′saw (wôr′sô), Pol. **War·sza′wa** (vär·shä′vä) city, ✻ of Poland, on the Vistula river; pop. 800,800.

War′ta (vär′tä), Ger. **War′the** (vär′tĕ) river, Poland, flowing NW and W into the Oder; 445 m. long.

Wart′burg (värt′bȯͦrk; Angl. wôrt′bûrg) castle, E Germany, Thuringia, near Eisenach; Luther translated New Testament 1521–22.

War′wick (wŏr′ĭk; wôr′wĭk — in England, the first only) **1** city, cen. Rhode Island, on Narragansett Bay S of Providence; pop. 43,000. **2** county in England: see WARWICKSHIRE.

War′wick·shire (wŏr′ĭk·shĭr; -shĕr) or **War′wick** (wŏr′ĭk) county, cen. England; ✻ Warwick; area 976 sq. m.; pop. 1,860,900.

Wa′satch Range (wô′săch) mountain range, Idaho and Utah; highest peak Mount Timpanogos, in Utah, 12,008 ft.

Wash, the (wŏsh) inlet of North Sea, E England, in Norfolk and Lincolnshire.

Wash′ing·ton (wŏsh′ĭng·tŭn) **1**, abbr. **Wash.**, state, NW United States, bordering on Canada and Pacific Ocean; ✻ Olympia; area 68,192 sq. m.; pop. 2,379,000. **2** city, ✻ of the United States, coextensive with District of Columbia; pop. 802,200. **3** city, SW Pennsylvania; pop. 26,300. — **Wash′ing·to′ni·an** (-tō′nĭ·ăn), adj. & n.

Washington, Lake, lake in state of Washington, E of Seattle; U.S. naval air station; connected with Puget Sound by ship canal 8.5 m. long.

Washington, Mount, mountain, N New Hampshire; highest in White Mts., 6288 ft.

Wash′i·ta (wŏsh′ĭ·tô) **1** river, Oklahoma; rises in NW Texas, flows E, then SE into Red river; 500 m. long. **2** var. of OUACHITA.

Wa′ten·stedt·Salz′git′ter (vä′tĕn·shtĕt·zälts′gĭt′ĕr) city, W Germany, SW of Brunswick; pop. 100,600.

Wa′ter·bur′y (wô′tĕr·bĕr′ĭ; -bĕr·ĭ; wŏt′ĕr-) city, SW Connecticut; pop. 104,500.

Wa′ter·ee′ (wô′tĕr·ē′; wŏt′ĕr·ē′) river, South Carolina, lower course of Catawba river, North Carolina; headstream of the Santee river.

Wa′ter·ford (wô′tĕr·fĕrd; wŏt′ĕr-) **1** county, S Ireland, in Munster prov.; area 710 sq. m.; pop. 75,100. **2** seaport, its ✻; pop. 27,000.

Wa′ter·loo′ (wô′tĕr·lȯͦ′; wŏt′ĕr-; -′—′) **1** city, NE cen. Iowa, on Cedar river; pop. 65,200. **2** (Flem. vä′tĕr·lō′) town, cen. Belgium, S of Brussels; battle June 18, 1815. **3** town, Canada, in SE Ontario NW of Kitchener; pop. 16,400.

Waters oi Merom. See MEROM, WATERS OF.

Wa′ter·ton Lakes National Park (wô′tĕr·t′n: -tŭn; wŏt′ĕr-) government reservation, Canada, in S Alberta; established 1895; since 1932 forms, with adjoining Glacier National Park in NW Montana, the **Waterton-Glacier International Peace Park.**

Wa′ter·town (wô′tẽr·toun; wŏt′ẽr-) **1** town, E Massachusetts, W of Boston; pop. 37,300. **2** city, N New York; pop. 34,400.

Wa′ter·ville (wô′tẽr·vĭl; wŏt′ẽr-) city, SW Maine; pop. 18,300.

Wa′ter·vliet (wô′tẽr-vlēt; wŏt′ẽr-) city, New York, on the Hudson opposite Troy; U.S. arsenal; pop. 15,200.

Wat′ford (wŏt′fẽrd) municipal borough, SE England, in Hertfordshire NW of London; pop. 73,100.

Watlings Island. See SAN SALVADOR island.

Wat′ten·scheid (vät′ĕn-shīt) city, W Germany, E of Essen; pop. 59,500.

Wau (wou) town, SE North-East New Guinea; center of gold fields.

Wau·ke′gan (wô-kē′găn) city, NE Illinois; pop. 38,900.

Wau′ke·sha (wô′kĕ-shô) city, SE Wisconsin; pop. 21,200.

Wau′sau (wô′sô) city, cen. Wisconsin, on Wisconsin river; pop. 30,400.

Wau′wa·to′sa (wô′wá-tō′sá) city, SE Wisconsin; pop. 33,300.

Way′cross (wā′krôs) city, SE Georgia; pop. 18,900.

Wa·zir′i·stan′ (wä·zẽr′ĭ-stän′) region, W Pakistan, on border of Afghanistan; inhabited by the Wazirs, a Pathan tribe.

Weald, the (wēld) region, S England, in Kent, Surrey, and Sussex, between North Downs and South Downs; once heavily forested.

Webbe Shibeli. See SHIBELI.

Web′ster Groves (wĕb′stẽr) city, E Missouri; pop. 23,400.

Wed′dell Sea (wĕd′′l) arm of S Atlantic Ocean in Antarctica SE of Palmer Peninsula.

Wei (wā) river, China, flowing from Kansu prov. to the Hwang Ho in Shensi; 400 m. long.

Weichsel. See VISTULA.

Wei′hai′wei′ (wā′hī′wā′) seaport, NE China, in NE Shantung; with adjoining territory, leased by Great Britain 1898–1930; pop. 214,100.

Wei′mar (vī′mär) city, E Germany, chief city of Thuringia; scene of German national assembly after World War I; pop. 66,700.

Weir′ton (wẽr′t'n) city, N West Virginia, on Ohio river; pop. 24,000.

Weis′sen·fels (vī′sĕn-fĕls) commune, E Germany; pop. 51,000.

Weiss′horn′ (vīs′hôrn′) mountain, Switzerland, in Valais canton in Pennine Alps; 14,804 ft. high.

Wel′fare′ Island (wĕl′fâr′), before 1921 known as **Black′wells Island** (blăk′wĕlz; -wĕlz) island, New York City, in East River.

Wel′land (wĕl′ănd) city, Canada, in SE Ontario; pop. 16,400; situated on **Welland Ship Canal**, waterway connecting Lake Erie with Lake Ontario, 27.6 m. long.

Welle. See UELE.

Welles′ley (wĕlz′lĭ) town, E Massachusetts; pop. 20,500.

Wel′ling·ton (wĕl′ĭng·tŭn) city, ✱ of New Zealand, in S North I. on Port Nicholson; pop. with suburbs 133,400.

Wells (wĕlz) municipal borough, SW England, in Somersetshire S of Bristol; cathedral; pop. 5800.

Wel′wyn Garden City (wĕl′ĭn) urban district, SE England, in Hertfordshire; established 1920; pop. 18,300.

Wem′bley (wĕm′blĭ) municipal borough, SE England, in Middlesex W of London; pop. 131,400.

Wen′chow′ (wŭn′jō′) city, E China, in SE Chekiang prov. at mouth of Wu river; pop. 631,300.

We′ner, Wen′ner (vä′nẽr). = VÄNERN.

We′ser (vā′zẽr) river, W Germany, flowing into North Sea; 280 m. long.

Wes′sex (wĕs′ĕks; -ĭks) **1** Anglo-Saxon kingdom in S Britain; ✱ Winchester. **2** region, S England, corresponding to ancient kingdom; approximately modern Berkshire, Dorsetshire, Hampshire, Somersetshire, and Wiltshire.

West Al′lis (ăl′ĭs) city, SE Wisconsin, SW of Milwaukee; pop. 43,000.

West Bengal. See BENGAL.

West Brom′wich (brŭm′ĭj; -ĭch; brŏm′-; -wĭch) county borough, W cen. England, in Staffordshire NW of Birmingham; pop. 43,000.

West Ches′ter (wĕst′ chĕs′tẽr) borough, SE Pennsylvania; pop 15,200.

Western Australia, state, Australia, W of 129°E long.; ✱ Perth; area 975,920 sq. m.; pop. 557,900.

Western Ghats. See GHATS.

Western Islands. See HEBRIDES.

Western Morava. See MORAVA.

Western Samoa, Territory of, group of islands of Samoa, W of long. 171°W; administered by New Zealand; ✱ Apia; area 1133 sq. m.; pop. 64,700.

Western Thrace. See THRACE.

West′field (wĕst′fēld) **1** city, SW Massachusetts, W of Springfield; pop. 21,000. **2** town, NE New Jersey, W of Elizabeth; pop. 21,200.

West Ham (hăm) county borough, SE England, in Essex; suburb of London; pop. 171,000.

West Hartford, town, Connecticut; pop. 44,400.

West Har′tle·pool (här′t'l-pŏŏl; härt′lē-) county borough, N England, in Durham on North Sea; pop. 72,600.

West In′dies (ĭn′dĭz; -dēz) **1** islands between SE North America and N South America, comprising the **Greater Antilles**, including Cuba, Hispaniola, Jamaica, and Puerto Rico, and two groups of smaller islands: the Bahama Is. and the **Lesser Antilles** or **Car′ib·bees** (kăr′ĭ-bēz). **2** or **West Indies Federation,** also **Federation of the West Indies,** country, including all of British West Indies except Bahama Is. and British Virgin Is. colonies; a dominion of the British Commonwealth, established April 1958; ✱ on Trinidad; permanent site unsettled; area 8005 sq. m.; pop. (1956 est.) 2,990,100. — **West In′di·an** (ĭn′dĭ·ăn; ĭn′dyăn), adj. & n.

West Lothian, county, SE Scotland, bordering on Firth of Forth; ✱ Linlithgow; area 120 sq. m.; pop. 88,600.

West′meath′ (wĕst′mēth′; Ir. -mĕth′) county, N cen. Ireland, in Leinster prov.; ✱ Mullingar; area 681 sq. m.; pop. 54,500.

West Mif′flin (mĭf′lĭn) borough, SW Pennsylvania; pop. 18,000.

West′min′ster (wĕs[t]′mĭn′stẽr) city and metropolitan borough, London, England, on N bank of the Thames; includes Houses of Parliament and Buckingham Palace; pop. 98,900.

West′mor·land (wĕs[t]′mẽr·lănd) county, NW England; ✱ Kendal; 789 sq. m.; pop. 67,400.

West′mount (wĕst′mount) city, Canada, enclosed by city of Montreal; pop. 24,800.

West New Guinea. See NETHERLANDS NEW GUINEA.

West New York, town, NE New Jersey; pop. 37,700.

West Orange, town, NE New Jersey, NW of Newark; pop. 28,600.

West Pakistan, 1 the division of Pakistan in NW Indian subcontinent; area 310,236 sq. m.; pop. 33,779,000. **2** a province of Pakistan, comprising all of the western division of Pakistan except a federal capital area around Karachi; formed 1955; ✱ Lahore.

West Palm Beach, city, SE Florida, on Lake Worth; pop. 43,200.

West·pha′lia (wĕst-fāl′yá; -fä′lĭ·á), Ger. **West′fa′len** (vĕst′fä′lĕn) region, W Germany, bordering on the Netherlands E of the Rhine; includes Ruhr valley; a province of Prussia 1816–1945, ✱ Münster. — **West·pha′lian** (wĕst-fāl′yăn; -fä′lĭ·ăn), adj. & n.

West Point, military post, SE New York, on Hudson river at the Highlands; U.S. Military Academy (founded 1802).

West Prussia, Ger. **West′preus′sen** (vĕst′proi′sĕn) region, N Europe, now in Poland; the W part of the original region of Prussia.

West Punjab, region, W Pakistan; western part of the Punjab; a province of Pakistan 1947–55.

West Quod′dy Head (kwŏd′ĭ) cape, NE Maine, at entrance to Passamaquoddy Bay; easternmost point of the U.S., at 66°57′W long.

West River. See SI.

West Spitsbergen, island, Spitsbergen; area 14,600 sq. m.

West Springfield, town, SW Massachusetts; pop. 20,400.

West University Place, town, SE Texas, near Houston; pop. 17,100.

West Virginia, abbr. **W. Va.,** state, E United States, bounded on NW by Ohio river; ✱ Charleston; area 24,181 sq. m.; pop. 2,005,600.

We′tar (wĕ′tär) island, Indonesia, N of Portuguese Timor.

Wet′ter·horn (vĕt′ẽr·hôrn) mountain, Switzerland, in Bernese Alps N of the Finsteraarhorn; 12,149 ft. high.

Wex′ford (wĕks′fẽrd) **1** county, SE Ireland, in Leinster prov.; area 908 sq. m.; pop. 90,000. **2** seaport, its ✱; pop. 12,000.

Wey′mouth (wā′mŭth) town, E Massachusetts; pop. 32,700.

Whales, Bay of (hwālz) inlet of Ross Sea, Antarctica, in Ross Shelf Ice.

Wham′po·a′ (hwäm′pō′á′) seaport, SE China; outport of Canton.

Whangpoo. See HWANG PU.

Whee′ling (hwē′lĭng) city, N West Virginia; pop. 58,900.

White (hwīt) **1** river, Arkansas, flowing into the Mississippi; 690 m. long. **2** river, South Dakota, flowing NE into Missouri river; 325 m. long.

White′horse′ or **White Horse** (hwīt′hôrs′) city, NW Canada, ✱ of Yukon Territory, on upper Yukon river; pop. 2600.

White Mountains, 1 mountains, E California and SW Nevada; contain Boundary Peak, 13,145 ft., highest peak in Nevada. **2** mountains, N New Hampshire; highest point Mt. Washington, 6288 ft.

White Nile. See NILE.

White Oak, locality, cen. Maryland, NE of Washington, D.C.; naval ordnance laboratory.

White Pass, mountain pass, SE Alaska, N of Skagway; altitude 2885 ft.

White Plains, city, SE New York; battle 1776, pop. 43,500.

White River. See WHITE.

White Russia, Russ. **Be·lo·rus′si·a** or **Bye·lo·rus′si·a** (byĭ·lŭ·rōōs′-syĭ·yá) **1** former region, E Europe, inhabited by the White Russians. **2** also **White Russian Soviet Socialist Republic** or **Be′lo·rus′sian Soviet Socialist Republic** (byĕ′lŏ-rŭsh′ăn) a constituent republic of the U.S.S.R., bordering on Poland, Lithuania, and Latvia; ✱ Minsk; area 80,100 sq. m.; pop. 7,220,000.

White Sands National Monument, government reservation, S New Mexico; region of gypsum sand dunes; established 1933.

White Sands Proving Ground, military reservation, S New Mexico, adjacent to White Sands National Monument; rocket and guided missile testing; Holloman Air Force Base adjacent.

White Sea, Russ. **Be′lo·e Mo′re** (byĕ′lŭ·yĕ mô′ryĕ) gulf of the Barents Sea, Soviet Russia, Europe, enclosed on N by Kola Peninsula.

White Volta. See VOLTA.

Whit′ney, Mount (hwĭt′nĭ) mountain, California, in S Sierra Nevada in Sequoia National Park; highest point in continental United States outside of Alaska, 14,495 ft.

Whit′ti·er (hwĭt′ĭ-ẽr) **1** city, SW California, ESE of Los Angeles; pop. 23,800. **2** seaport, S Alaska, on Prince William Sound.

Wich′i·ta (wĭch′ĭ-tô) **1** river, N Texas, flowing ENE into Red river; 230 m. long. **2** city, S cen. Kansas, on Arkansas river; pop. 168,300.

Wichita Falls, city, N Texas, on Wichita river; pop. 68,000.

Wick′low (wĭk′lō) county, E Ireland, in Leinster prov.; ✱ Wicklow; area 782 sq. m.; pop. 62,500.

Wien. See VIENNA.

Wieprz (vyĕpsh) river, cen. Poland; flows into the Vistula; 150 m. long.

Wies′ba·den (vēs′bä′dĕn; local pron. vīs′-) city, W Germany, on the Rhine W of Frankfurt am Main; pop. 218,300.

Wig′an (wĭg′ăn) county borough, NW England; pop. 84,500.

Wight, Isle of (wīt) island, S England, in English Channel off Hampshire; constitutes a county; ✱ Newport; area 147 sq. m.; pop. 95,600.

Wig′town (wĭg′tŭn; -toun) or **Wig′town·shire** (-shĭr; -shẽr) county, SW Scotland; ✱ Wigtown; area 487 sq. m.; pop. 31,600.

Wil′der·ness (wĭl′dẽr·nĕs; -nĭs) region, N Virginia, S of Rapidan river; battles 1863 (Chancellorsville) and May 5–7, 1864.

Wil·helms·ha′ven (vĭl′hĕlms·hä′fĕn) seaport, W Germany, W of Weser river; pop. 100,900.

Wilkes-Bar′re (wĭlks′băr′ē; -bär′ē) city, E Pennsylvania; pop. 76,800.

Wilkes Land (wĭlks) region of Antarctica, along Indian Ocean; in Australian claim except for Adélie Coast (which see).

Wil′kins·burg (wĭl′kĭnz·bûrg) borough, SW Pennsylvania, E of Pittsburgh; pop. 31,400.

Wil·lam′ette (wĭ·lăm′ĕt; -ĭt) river, NW Oregon; 190 m. long.

Wil′lem·stad (vĭl′ĕm-stät) city, ✱ of Netherlands Antilles, on Curaçao; pop. 33,100.

Willes′den (wĭlz′dĕn) municipal borough, SE England, in Middlesex W of London; pop. 179,600.

Wil′liams Bay (wĭl′yămz) village, S Wisconsin; Yerkes Observatory.

Wil′liams·burg (wĭl′yămz·bûrg) independent city, SE Virginia, NNW of Newport News; once (1699–1780) ✱ of Virginia; pop. 6700.

Wil′liams·port (wĭl′yămz·pôrt) city, N cen. Pennsylvania; pop. 45,000.

Wil·mette′ (wĭl·mĕt′) village, NE Illinois; pop. 18,200.

Wil′ming·ton (wĭl′mĭng·tŭn) **1** city, N Delaware, on Delaware river; pop. 110,400. **2** city, SE North Carolina; pop. 45,000.

Wilna, Wilno. See VILNYUS.

Wil'son (wĭl's'n) town, E North Carolina; pop. 23,000.

Wilson, Mount, mountain, California, in San Gabriel Mts. just NE of Pasadena; site of observatory; 5704 ft. high.

Wilt'shire (wĭlt'shĭr; -shẽr) or **Wilts** (wĭlts) county, S England; ✳ Trowbridge; area 1345 sq. m.; pop. 387,400.

Wim'ble·don (wĭm'b'l·dŭn) municipal borough, S England, in Surrey SW of London; pop. 58,200.

Win'ches'ter (wĭn'chĕs'tẽr; -chĭs·tẽr) **1** town, E Massachusetts, NW of Boston; pop. 15,500. **2** independent city, N Virginia, in Shenandoah Valley; pop. 13,800. **3** municipal borough, S England, ✳ of Hampshire; ancient ✳ of Wessex; pop. 25,700.

Windau. See VENTSPILS.

Wind Cave (wĭnd) limestone cavern, SW South Dakota, in Black Hills; intermittent air current; a national park since 1903.

Win'der·mere (wĭn'dẽr·mẽr) lake, NW England, on Westmorland-Lancashire border; over 10 m. long.

Wind'hoek (vĭnt'hŏŏk) town, ✳ of South-West Africa; pop. 20,500.

Wind River Range (wĭnd) range of the Rocky Mts., W cen. Wyoming; highest point Gannett Peak, 13,785 ft.

Wind'sor (wĭn'zẽr) **1** city, Canada, in SE Ontario on Detroit river opposite Detroit, Michigan; pop. 122,000. **2** officially **New Windsor,** municipal borough, S England, in Berkshire, on the Thames W of London; site of Windsor Castle; pop. 23,200.

Wind'ward Islands (wĭnd'wẽrd) **1** islands, West Indies, the S part of Lesser Antilles excepting Barbados, Trinidad, and Tobago. **2** administrative subdivision of British West Indies, comprising colonies of St. Lucia, St. Vincent, and Grenada in Windward Is. and Dominica in Leeward Is.; ✳ St. George's, on Grenada.

Windward Passage, channel, between Cuba and Hispaniola.

Wineland. See VINLAND.

Win'ne·ba'go, Lake (wĭn'ē·bā'gō) lake, E Wisconsin, traversed by Fox river; 30 m. long.

Win·net'ka (wĭ·nĕt'kä) village, NE Illinois, N of Chicago; famous school system; pop. 12,100.

Win'ni·peg (wĭn'ĭ·pĕg) **1** river, Canada, flowing from Lake of the Woods in SW Ontario to **Lake Winnipeg** (area 9398 sq. m.) in Manitoba; 140 m. long. **2** city, Canada, ✳ of Manitoba, at confluence of Assiniboine and Red rivers; pop. 255,100.

Win'ni·peg·o'sis, Lake (wĭn'ĭ·pĕg·ō'sĭs) lake, Canada, in W Manitoba W of Lake Winnipeg; area 2086 sq. m.

Win'ni·pe·sau'kee, Lake (wĭn'ĭ·pĕ·sô'kē), formerly **Win'ne·pe·sau'kee,** lake, cen. New Hampshire; area 71 sq. m.

Wi·no'na (wĭ·nō'nä) city, SE Minnesota, on Mississippi river; pop. 25,000.

Win'ston-Sa'lem (wĭn'stŭn-sā'lĕm) city, N cen. North Carolina; pop. 87,800.

Win'ter·thur' (vĭn'tẽr·tōōr') commune, Switzerland, in Zurich canton; pop. 66,900.

Win'throp (wĭn'thrŭp) town, E Massachusetts; pop. 19,500.

Win'yah Bay (wĭn'yô) inlet of Atlantic Ocean, South Carolina.

Wisby. See VISBY.

Wis·con'sin (wĭs·kŏn's'n; -sĭn) **1** river, Wisconsin, flowing S and W to Mississippi river; 430 m. long. **2,** abbr. **Wis.,** state, N United States, S of Lake Superior and W of Lake Michigan; ✳ Madison; area 56,154 sq. m., not including 10,062 sq. m. of water in Great Lakes; pop. 3,434,600. — **Wis·con'sin·ite,** n.

Wisła. See VISTULA.

Wis'mar (vĭs'mär) seaport, E Germany; pop. 42,000.

Wit'ten (vĭt'ĕn) city, W Germany, on Ruhr river; pop. 69,400.

Wit'ten·berg (vĭt'ʼn·bûrg; Ger. vĭt'ĕn·bĕrk) city, E Germany, on Elbe river E of Dessau; pop. 41,300.

Wit·wa'ters·rand (wĭt·wô'tẽrz·ränd; -wŏt'ẽrz-), colloquially **the Rand** (ränd); 62 m. long, 23 m. wide. ridge of auriferous rock, NE Union of South Africa, in S Transvaal;

Wło·cła'wek (vlô·tslä'vĕk), Russ. **Vlo·tslavsk'** (vlŭ·tsläfsk') commune, N cen. Poland, on Vistula river; pop. 66,700.

Wo'burn (wō'bẽrn; wōō'-) city, E Massachusetts; pop. 20,500.

Wolds (wōldz) chalk hills, NE England, in E Yorkshire and NE Lincolnshire, on both sides of the Humber.

Wol'lon·gong (wŏŏl'ŭn·gŏng) seaport, SE Australia, in E New South Wales; pop. 18,100.

Wol'ver·hamp'ton (wŏŏl'vẽr·hăm[p]'tŭn) county borough, W cen. England, in Staffordshire NW of Birmingham; pop. 162,700.

Won·san (wŭn·sän), also **Gen·zan** (gĕn·zän) or **Gen·san** (gĕn·sän) seaport, N Korea, on E coast; pop. 79,300.

Wood Green, municipal borough, SE England, in Middlesex N of London; pop. 52,200.

Wood'lark' (wŏŏd'lärk') or **Mu'ru·a** (mōōr'ōō·ä) island in Solomon Sea, NE of SE end of New Guinea; attached to Territory of Papua.

Woods, Lake of the. See LAKE OF THE WOODS.

Woods Hole (wŏŏdz) village, SE Massachusetts, on S coast of Cape Cod in town of Falmouth; Oceanographic Institution.

Wood'stock (wŏŏd'stŏk) city, Canada, in SE Ontario; pop. 18,300.

Wool'wich (wŏŏl'ĭj; -ĭch) metropolitan borough, London, on S bank of the Thames; pop. 147,200.

Woo'mer·a (wŏŏ'mẽr·ä) town, South Australia, in region W of Lake Torrens; base for rocket range.

Woon'sock'et (wŏŏn'sŏk'ĕt; -ĭt; wŏŏn'sŏk'-) city, N Rhode Island; pop. 50,200.

Worces'ter (wŏŏs'tẽr) **1** city, cen. Massachusetts; pop. 203,500. **2** county in England: see WORCESTERSHIRE. **3** city and county borough, W cen. England, ✳ of Worcestershire; pop. 59,700.

Worces'ter·shire (-shĭr; -shẽr) or **Worcester,** county, W cen. England; ✳ Worcester; area 699 sq. m.; pop. 523,000.

Worms (vôrms; Angl. wûrmz) city, W Germany, on the Rhine NNW of Mannheim; seat of Diet of Worms 1521; pop. 51,300.

Wörth (vûrt) town, NE France, near Strasbourg; battle 1870.

Worth, Lake (wûrth) **1** lagoon, SE Florida; 18 m. long. **2** lake, N Texas, near Fort Worth; formed by dam in West Fork of Trinity river.

Wor'thing (wûr'thĭng) municipal borough, S England, in West Sussex on coast; pop. 69,400.

Wran'gel Island (răng'gĕl), Russ. **O'strov Vran'ge·lya** (ô'strŭf vrän'-gĭ·lyä) island, U.S.S.R., in Arctic Ocean; lies across 180th meridian.

Wran'gell (răng'gĕl) island, SE Alaska, NE of Prince of Wales I.

Wrangell Mountains, range, S Alaska, near Yukon border; highest point over 16,000 ft.; includes **Mount Wrangell,** 14,000 ft.

Wrath, Cape (răth) extreme NW point of Scotland, at 58°35'N.

Wro'cław (vrô'tsläf), Ger. **Bres'lau** (brĕs'lou; in English, also brĕz'-) city, SW Poland, chief city of Silesia; pop. 279,400.

Wu (wōō) river, cen. China; rises in W Kweichow, flows NE, N, and NW through Szechwan into Yangtze river; 500 m. long.

Wu'chang' (wōō'chäng') city, E cen. China, ✳ of Hupeh prov., on the Yangtze; pop. 250,000.

Wu'han' (wōō'hän') group of three cities, SE China, the **Han Cities** (hän) — Hankow, Hanyang, and Wuchang — at the confluence of the Han with the Yangtze.

Wuhsien. See SOOCHOW.

Wu'hu' (wōō'hōō') city, E China, in E Anhwei on the Yangtze; pop. 135,400.

Wup'per·tal (vŏŏp'ẽr·täl) city, W Germany; pop. 362,100.

Würt'tem·berg (vür'tĕm·bĕrk; Angl. wûr'tĕm·bûrg) region, SW Germany, between Baden and Bavaria; once a duchy; kingdom 1813–1918; state 1918–34; divided after World War II, S part being joined to Hohenzollern and N part to N Baden.

Würz'burg (vürts'bŏŏrk; Angl. wûrts'bûrg) city, W Germany, on Main river; pop. 55,600.

Wu'sih' (wōō'shē') city, E China, in S Kiangsu prov.; pop. 200,000.

Wu'wei' (wōō'wā'), formerly **Liang'chow'** (lĭ·äng'jō') city, N cen. China, in cen. Kansu prov.; pop. 200,000.

Wy'an·dotte (wī'ăn·dŏt) city, SE Michigan, on Detroit river; pop. 36,800.

Wye (wī) river, E Wales and W England; flows into Severn estuary; 130 m. long.

Wy·o'ming (wī·ō'mĭng; Angl. wī'ō'-), abbr. **Wyo.,** state, W United States, in Rocky Mts.; ✳ Cheyenne; area 97,914 sq. m.; pop. 290,500. — **Wy·o'ming·ite** (wī·ō'mĭng·īt), n.

Wyoming Valley, valley, E Pennsylvania, along Susquehanna river; scene of attack on settlers by British and Indians 1778.

X–Y

Xan'thus (zăn'thŭs) ancient city, Asia Minor, in Lycia at mouth of Xanthus (mod. **Ko·ca'** [kō·jä']) river.

Xeres. See JEREZ.

Xin·gú' (shēng·gōō') river, cen. and N Brazil; rises in Plateau of Mato Grosso and flows N into the Amazon near its mouth; 1300 m. long.

Xo'chi·mil'co (sō'chē·mēl'kō) town, cen. Mexico, SE of Mexico City on Lake Xochimilco; floating gardens; pop. 14,400.

Ya·blo·noi' (yĭ·blȯ·noi'), or **Ya·blo·no·voi'** (yĭ·blä·nŭ·voi'), **Mountains,** range, S Soviet Russia, Asia; highest peak Sokhondo, 8228 ft.

Yacarana. See JAVARÍ.

Yad'kin (yăd'kĭn) river, cen. North Carolina, a headstream of Pee Dee river; 202 m. long.

Yafo. See JAFFA.

Yahata. See YAWATA.

Yak'i·ma (yăk'ĭ·mô) **1** river, S cen. Washington, flowing SE into Columbia river; 200 m. long. **2** city, S Washington, on Yakima river; pop. 38,500.

Ya·kutsk' Autonomous Soviet Socialist Republic (yĕ·kōōtsk'), also **Ya·kut' A.S.S.R.** (yĕ·kōōt') and **Ya·ku'ti·a** (yä·kōō'shĭ·ä) autonomous republic, E cen. Soviet Russia, Asia; ✳ Yakutsk; area 1,182,300 sq. m.; pop. 463,000.

Yal'ta (yŏl'tä; yäl'tä) town, Soviet Russia, Europe, on S coast of Crimea; scene of international conference 1945; pop. 28,800.

Ya'lu' (yä'lōō') or **Am'nok** (äm'nŏk) river, SE Manchuria and Korea, flowing N, W, and SW to Korea Bay; 300 m. long.

Ya'lung' (yä'lŏŏng') river, S China, in E Sikang prov., flowing S into the Yangtze; 725 m. long.

Yal·vac' (yäl·väch') town, SW Turkey; ruins of Pisidian Antioch.

Ya·mal' (yĕ·mäl') peninsula, NW Soviet Russia, Asia, at N end of Ural Mts. between Gulf of Ob and Kara Sea.

Yam Kinneret. See GALILEE, SEA OF.

Ya'na (yä'nä) river, Soviet Russia, Asia, flowing N into Laptev Sea; 750 m. long.

Ya'na·on' (yä'nä·ôn'; Angl. yä·noun') or **Ya·nam'** (yä·näm') city, India, on E coast in the Godavari delta, in Andhra Pradesh; until 1954 part of French India; pop. 5700.

Yang'chow' (yäng'jō', formerly (1912–49) **Kiang'tu'** (jĭ·äng'dōō') city, E China, in Kiangsu prov. on Grand Canal; pop. 100,000.

Yangku. See TAIYUAN.

Yang'tze' (yäng'[t]sē') or **Yangtze Kiang** (kĭ·äng') river, S China, flowing from Kunlun Shan in SW Tsinghai prov. E into East China Sea; 3100 m. long.

Ya'ni·na, Yan'ni·na. = IOANNINA.

Yan'tra (yän'trä) river, NE cen. Bulgaria, flowing N into Danube river; 110 m. long.

Ya'oun·dé' (yä·ōōn'dā') or **Yaun'de** (youn'dā) town, W Africa, ✳ of French Cameroun; pop. 16,600.

Yap (yäp; yăp) or **Uap** (wäp) island, W Caroline Is.; archaeological remains.

Ya'pu·rá' (yä'pōō·rä'). = JAPURÁ.

Ya·quí' (yä·kē') river, NW Mexico, in Sonora; flows SW into Gulf of California; 420 m. long.

Yar·kand' (yär·känd') **1** river, S cen. Asia, flowing N from Karakoram Range in Kashmir to join the Khotan in W Sinkiang, China, and form Tarim river; 500 m. long. **2** Turki **Yar·kend'** (yär·kĕnd'), Chin. **So'che'** (swä'chŭ') town and oasis, W China, in SW Sinkiang on Yarkand river at edge of Takla Makan Desert; pop. 70,000.

Yar'mouth (yär'mŭth) **1** town, SE Massachusetts, on Cape Cod; resort. **2** town, Canada, in SW Nova Scotia on Atlantic Ocean; pop. 8100. **3** or **Great Yarmouth,** county borough, E England, in Norfolk on North Sea; pop. 51,100.

Ya·ro·slavl' (yä'rô·släv''l) city, Soviet Russia, Europe, on the Volga; pop. 298,100.

Ya·va·ri' (yä'vä·rē'). = JAVARÍ.

Ya·wa·ta (yä·wä·tä), also **Ya·ha·ta** (yä·hä·tä) seaport, Japan, in N Kyushu; pop. 167,800.

Yaz'oo (yăz'ōō) river, Mississippi; flows SW into Mississippi river; 188 m. long.

Yedo. See TOKYO.

Ye·gor'evsk or **E·gor'evsk** (yĕ·gôr'yĕfsk) city, W cen. Soviet Russia, Europe; pop. 56,300.

Ye'hsien' (yĕ'shǐ·ĕn'), formerly **Lai'chow'** (lī'jō') city, NE China, in N Shantung prov.; pop. 100,000.

Yel'low·knife' (yĕl'ō·nīf') village, N Canada, on Great Slave Lake.

Yellow River. See HWANG HO.

Yellow Sea, Chin. **Hwang Hai** (hwäng' hī') inlet of Pacific Ocean between NE China and Korea.

Yel'low·stone' (yĕl'ō·stōn') river, NW Wyoming and S and E Montana, flowing N, E, and NE into Missouri river; 671 m. long; in NW Wyoming flows through the **Grand Canyon of the Yellowstone** (2000 ft. wide, 1200 ft. deep) and forms the **Yellowstone Falls** (upper fall 109 ft., lower fall 308 ft.)

Yellowstone Lake, lake, NW Wyoming, in Yellowstone National Park; area 139 sq. m.; altitude 7731 ft.

Yellowstone National Park, government reservation, NW Wyoming, including Grand Canyon of the Yellowstone; established 1872.

Yem'en (yĕm'ĕn) country, SW Arabia, bordering on Red Sea; kingdom; member (1958, with United Arab Republic) of United Arab States. ✱ San'a; area 75,000 sq. m.; pop. 4,000,000. — **Yem'en·ite,** n.

Yen'an' (yĕn'än'), formerly (1913–48) **Fu'shih'** (fōō'shǐr') town, NE cen. China, in N Shensi prov.; Communist headquarters 1937–47.

Ye'ni·sei' or **E'ni·sei'** (yĕn'ĭ·sā') river, Soviet Russia, Asia, flowing N into Arctic Ocean through **Yenisei Bay**; 2800 m. long.

Yenki. See QARA SHAHR.

Yentai. See CHEFOO.

Yer'ba Bue'na Island (yĕr'bȧ bwā'nä; yûr'bȧ), formerly **Goat Island** (gōt) island, California, in San Francisco Bay.

Ye·re·van' (yĕ·rĕ·vän') or **E·re·van'** (ĕ·rĕ·vän'), also **E·ri·van'** (Russ. ĕ·ryĭ·vän'y') city, U.S.S.R., ✱ of Armenian S.S.R.; pop. 200,000.

Ye·sil' Ir·mak' (yĕ·shĕl' ĭr·mäk') river, N Turkey in Asia, flowing N into Black Sea; 200 m. long.

Yeşilköy. See SAN STEFANO.

Yezd (yĕzd) city, cen. Iran; pop. 56,000.

Yezo. See HOKKAIDO.

Ying'kow' (yĭng'kō'), formerly also **New'chwang'** (nū'chwäng') city, S Manchuria, on Liao river; pop. 180,900.

Yo'ho National Park (yō'hō) government reservation, W Canada, in SE British Columbia on Alberta border; established 1886.

Yok·kai·chi (yōk·kī·chē) city, Japan, in S Honshu; pop. 112,400.

Yo'ko·ha'ma (yō'kō·hä'mä) seaport, Japan, in SE Honshu on Tokyo Bay S of Tokyo; pop. 814,400.

Yo'ko·su'ka (yō'kō·sōō'kä; Jap. yō·kōs·kä) seaport, Japan, in Honshu at entrance to Tokyo Bay; pop. 261,800.

Yon'kers (yŏng'kĕrz) city, SE New York; pop. 152,800.

York (yôrk) **1** city, S Pennsylvania; pop. 60,000. **2** county in England: see YORKSHIRE **3** anc. **Eb'o·ra'cum** (ĕb'ô·rā'kŭm) city and county borough, N England, in Yorkshire; pop. 105,300.

York, Cape, 1 cape, N Australia, at tip of Cape York Penin. **2** cape, NW Greenland, on N shore of Baffin Bay.

Yorke (yôrk), or **Yorke's** (yôrks), **Peninsula,** SE South Australia, between Spencer Gulf and Gulf of St. Vincent.

York River, estuary, E Virginia, formed by confluence of Pamunkey and Mattaponi rivers; flows SE into Chesapeake Bay; 40 m. long.

York'shire (yôrk'shǐr; -shẽr) or **York,** county, N England; borders on North Sea; comprises: North Riding, ✱ Northallerton, area 2128 sq. m., pop. 525,500; East Riding, ✱ Beverley, area 1172 sq. m., pop. 510,800; West Riding, ✱ Wakefield, area 2781 sq. m., pop. 3,480,100.

York'town (yôrk'toun) town, SE Virginia, on York river N of Newport News; surrender of Cornwallis 1781; naval base since 1917.

Yo·sem'i·te Valley (yō·sĕm'ĭ·tē) valley of Merced river, California, on W slope of Sierra Nevada in **Yosemite National Park** (established 1890); at edge of the valley are many waterfalls, including **Yosemite Falls** (upper fall 1430 ft., lower fall 320 ft.).

Yo·su (yō·sōō) or **Rei·sui** (rā·syȳ) port, S Korea; pop. 60,300.

Yough'io·ghe'ny (yŏk'ō·gā'nĭ; attributively, usu. yŏk'ō·gā'nĭ) river, NW Maryland and SW Pennsylvania, flowing N and NW into Monongahela river; ab. 150 m. long.

Youngs'town (yŭngz'toun) city, NE Ohio; pop. 168,300.

Ypres. See IEPER.

Yp'si·lan'ti (ĭp'sĭ·lăn'tĭ) city, SE Michigan; pop. 18,300.

Y'ser' (ē'zâr') river, France and Belgium, flowing into North Sea; 55 m. long.

Yssel. See IJSSEL.

Ystradyfodwg. See RHONDDA.

Yu. See SIANG.

Yuan (yü·än') or **Yuen** (yü·än') river, SE cen. China, flowing from Kweichow prov. NE to the Tungting Hu; 500 m. long.

Yu'bi (yōō'bĭ), or **Ju'by** (jōō'bĭ), **Cape,** cape, NW Africa, on NW coast of Spanish Sahara.

Yu·ca·tán' (yōō'kȧ·tän'; -tän') **1** peninsula, SE Mexico and N Central America, including British Honduras and part of Guatemala. **2** state, SE Mexico, at NW end of the peninsula; ✱ Mérida; area 23,926 sq. m.; pop. 515,300.

Yucatán Channel, channel between Yucatán and W end of Cuba.

Yuc'ca Flat (yŭk'ȧ) valley, SW Nevada, in region N of Las Vegas.

Yu'go·sla'vi·a (yōō'gō·slä'vĭ·ȧ; -släv'ĭ·ȧ), Serb. **Ju'go·sla'vi·ja** (yōō'gō·slä'vē·yä), from 1918 to 1929 called **Kingdom of the Serbs, Cro'ats, and Slo'venes** (sûrbz', krō'ăts, slō'vēnz) country, SE Europe, bordering on Adriatic Sea; formed 1918 as kingdom; proclaimed federal republic Nov. 1945; ✱ Belgrade; area 99,044 sq. m.; pop. 15,772,100. — **Yu'go·sla'vi·an** (yōō'gō·slä'vĭ·ăn; -släv'ĭ·ăn), **Yu'go·slav'** (yōō'gō·släv'; -släv'), adj. & n.

Yu'kon (yōō'kŏn) **1** river, NW Canada and Alaska, flowing NW into Alaska, then SW into Bering Sea; 1979 m. long; its upper course, S of junction with Pelly river, formerly called the **Lew'es** (lū'ĭs; lōō'-'). **2** or **Yukon Territory,** abbr. **Y.T.,** territory NW Canada, around upper Yukon river; borders on Arctic Ocean; ✱ Whitehorse; area 205,346 sq. m.; pop. 12,200.

Yu'ma (yōō'mä) city, SW Arizona, on Colorado river; pop. 9100.

Yungki. See KIRIN.

Yungning. See NANNING.

Yun·nan' (yōō·nän') **1** formerly also **Yün'nan'** (yün'nän') province, S China, bordering on Indochina and Burma; ✱ Kunming; area 154,054 sq. m.; pop. 10,853,000. **2** see KUNMING.

Yurev. See TARTU.

Yuzovka. See STALINO.

Y've·tot' (ēv'tō') town, N France, NW of Rouen; small monarchy 15th–16th cents.

Z

Zab'rze (zäb'zhĕ), Ger. **Hin'den·burg** (hĭn'dĕn·bûrg; Ger. -bōōrk) city, SW Poland, in Silesia; pop. 128,000.

Za·ca·te'cas (sä'kä·tā'käs) **1** state, cen. Mexico; area 28,122 sq. m.; pop. 664,400. **2** city, its ✱; pop. 21,800.

Zacynthus. See ZANTE.

Za'dar (zä'där), Ital. **Za'ra** (dzä'rä; Angl. zä'rȧ) seaport, W Yugoslavia, in Croatia federated republic; held by Italy 1920–47; pop. 20,100.

Zag'a·zig (zăg'ȧ·zĭg), Arab. **Za·qa·zîq'** (zŭ·kä·zēk') city, N Egypt; pop. 82,900.

Za'greb (zä'grĕb), Hung. **Zá'gráb** (zä'gräb), Ger. **A'gram** (ä'gräm) city, NW Yugoslavia, ✱ of Croatia federated republic; pop. 290,700.

Zag'ros Mountains (zăg'rŏs) mountain system, W and S Iran, bordering on Turkey, Iraq, and Persian Gulf; highest point over 14,900 ft.

Zakarpatskaya. See CARPATHIAN RUTHENIA.

Zákinthos, Zakynthos. See ZANTE.

Za'ma (zä'mä) ancient town, N Africa, SW of Carthage; battle 202 B.C.

Zam·be'zi or **Zam·be'si** (zăm·bē'zĭ), Port. **Zam·be'ze** (zănm·bā'zĕ) river, S cen. and SE Africa, flowing from NW Northern Rhodesia into Mozambique Channel; 1650 m. long.

Zam'bo·an'ga (säm'bō·äng'gä) city, Philippine Is., on SW coast of Mindanao; pop. 131,500.

Zancle. See MESSINA.

Zanes'ville (zānz'vĭl) city, Ohio, on Muskingum river; pop. 40,500.

Zan'te (zăn'tē; Ital. dzän'tä), also **Za·kyn'thos** (zȧ·kĭn'thŏs) and **Za·cyn'thus** (zȧ·sĭn'thŭs) or, Mod. Gr., **Zá'kin·thos** (zä'kyĕn·thŏs) island, W Greece, one of the Ionian Is.

Zan'zi·bar (zăn'zĭ·bär) **1** island, E Africa, off NE Tanganyika; ruled by a sultan; with Pemba and adjacent islands, forms British protectorate; area of island 640 sq. m., pop. 137,700. **2** seaport, ✱ of island and of protectorate; pop. 45,300.

Za'po·rozh'e (zä'pŭ·rô'zhĕ; Russ. zȧ·pô·rôzh'yĕ), formerly **A·le·ksan'drovsk** (ŭ·lyĭ·ksän'drŏfsk) city, U.S.S.R., in SE Ukraine on the Dnieper; pop. 289,200.

Zaqazîq. See ZAGAZIG.

Zara. See ZADAR.

Zaragoza. See SARAGOSSA.

Zea. See KEOS.

Zealand. See SJÆLLAND.

Zee'brug'ge (zā'brŭg'ĕ) seaport, NW Belgium, port for Brugge.

Zee'land (zē'lănd; Du. zā'länt) province, SW Netherlands, composed of several islands on coast and a part of mainland S of Schelde estuary.

Zem'po·al·te·pec' (säm'pō·äl'tä·pĕk') or **Zem'po·al·te'petl** (-äl·tā'pĕt-'l) mountain, SE Mexico, in Oaxaca state; 11,138 ft. high.

Ze'mun (zĕ'mōōn), Ger. **Sem·lin'** (zĕm·lēn'), Hung. **Zi'mony** (zĭ'mōn·y') section of Belgrade, Yugoslavia; formerly a separate city.

Zenshu. See CHONJU.

Zer·matt' (tsĕr·mät') village, SW cen. Switzerland, in Valais canton in Pennine Alps NE of the Matterhorn; elevation 5315 ft.

Zetland. See SHETLAND.

Zhda'nov (zhdä'nŭf), formerly **Ma'ri·u'pol** (mär'ĭ·ōō'pôl) city, U.S.S.R., in E Ukraine on Sea of Azov; pop. 222,400.

Zhi·to'mir (zhĭ·tô'myĭr) city, U.S.S.R., in W Ukraine; pop. 95,100.

Zim·ba'bwe (zĭm·bä'bwä) archaeological site, NE Southern Rhodesia.

Zinovievsk. See KIROVOGRAD.

Zi'on (zī'ŭn). See in Vocab.

Zion National Park, government reservation, SW Utah; canyon of Virgin river, with multicolored sandstone cliffs; established 1919; adjoining it is **Zion National Monument,** established 1937.

Zi·pan'gu (zĭ·păng'gōō) Japan; — Marco Polo's name for it.

Zla·to·ust' (zlä·tô·ōōst') city, Soviet Russia, Asia, in S Ural Mts.; pop. 99,300.

Zoan. See TANIS.

Zon'gul·dak' (zŏng'gōōl·däk') seaport, NW Turkey in Asia, on Black Sea; pop. 35,600.

Zor. See TYRE.

Zug (tsōōk) **1** canton, N cen. Switzerland; area 92 sq. m.; pop. 42,200. **2** commune, in canton; ✱; on Lake of Zug S of Zurich; pop. 14,500.

Zug, Lake of, Ger. **Zu'ger·see'** (tsōō'gĕr·zā') lake, N cen. Switzerland, in Zug and Schwyz cantons N of Lake of Lucerne; area 15 sq. m.

Zug'spit'ze (tsōōk'shpĭt'sĕ) mountain, SW Germany; highest in Bavarian Alps, 9719 ft.

Zuider Zee. = Zuider Zee: see IJSSELMEER.

Zu'lu·land' (zōō'lōō·lănd') territory, E Union of South Africa, in NE Natal, bordering on Indian Ocean; area 10,427 sq. m.; pop. 362,400.

Zungaria. See DZUNGARIA.

Zu'rich (zŏōr'ĭk), Ger. **Zü'rich** (tsü'rĭk) **1** canton, NE cen. Switzerland; area 665 sq. m.; pop. 777,000. **2** city, its ✱, at end of Lake of Zurich; pop. 390,000.

Zurich, Lake of, Ger. **Zü'rich·see'** (tsü'rĭk·zā') or **Zü'ri·cher See** (tsü'rĭ·kĕr zā') lake, N cen. Switzerland; 25 m. long.

Zuy'der Zee. = Zuider Zee; see IJSSELMEER.

Zwick'au (tsvĭk'ou) city, E Germany, S of Leipzig; pop. 122,900.

Zwol'le (zvôl'ĕ) commune, E Netherlands, ✱ of Overijssel prov., on IJssel river; pop. 47,500.

Zyrian Autonomous Area. See KOMI REPUBLIC.

A PRONOUNCING VOCABULARY OF COMMON ENGLISH GIVEN NAMES

The purpose of the following vocabulary is to present a list of such given names as are most frequent in English use. The list is not exhaustive either of the names themselves or of the variant spellings of those names which are entered. Compound or double names and surnames used as given names are not entered except in cases where long-continued or common use gives them an independent character.

Besides the pronunciations of the names, the lists below usually provide one or more of the following kinds of information at each entry: (1) Etymology, indicating the language source but not the original form of the name. (2) The meaning of the name, where known or ascertainable with reasonable certainty. (3) Foreign-language equivalents of each name in general use. (4) Diminutives that are well established or etymologically important.

NOTE: (1) Foreign-language equivalents of given names are added only when they are in frequent use among English-speaking peoples. If any of these forms has acquired an English pronunciation, it is given independent entry in these lists. (2) Diminutives are usually given in only one form when they follow the name from which they are derived; thus, *Fred* and *Fritz* are given at FREDERICK, but *Freddy* and *Fritzie*, which can be readily understood from the other forms, are not. If, however, the spelling of a diminutive is so different from that of the parent entry as to require its re-entry in its own alphabetical place, all of its forms are listed at this re-entry except variants in -*ie* or -*y*. (3) Some diminutives and contracted forms which are now used as given names (for example, *Madge* and *Maud*) are given independent entry regardless of their alphabetical position with respect to the parent name.

I. NAMES OF MEN

A

Aar'on (âr'ŭn). [Heb.]

A'bel (ā'bĕl). [Heb.] Breath; vanity.

Ab'ner (ăb'nẽr). [Heb.] My father is Ner.

A'bra·ham (ā'brȧ·hăm). [Heb.] Of uncertain meaning. — Dim. *Abe* (āb), *A'bie* (ā'bĭ).

A'bram (ā'brăm). [Heb.] Probably, exalted father. — Dim. *Abe*.

Ad'am (ăd'ăm). [Heb.] — Dim. *Ade* (ād).

Ad'el·bert (ăd'ĕl·bẽrt; ȧ·dĕl'bẽrt). = ALBERT.

Ad'olf, Ad'olph (ăd'ŏlf; ā'dŏlf; ȧ·dŏlf'), **A·dol'phus** (ȧ·dŏl'fŭs). [Teut.] Noble wolf; *i.e.*, noble hero. F. Adolphe (ȧ'dŏlf'); G. Adolf (ä'dŏlf); It. & Sp. Adolfo (*It.* ä·dŏl'fō; Sp. ä·thŏl'fō). — Dim. *Dolf, Dolph, Dol'phus.*

A'dri·an (ā'drĭ·ăn). [L.]

A'dri·en (ā'drĭ·ĕn; *F.* ȧ'drẽ'ăN'). French form of ADRIAN.

Al (ăl). Dim. of ALBERT, ALFRED, etc.

Al'an (ăl'ăn). [ML.]

Al'a·ric (ăl'ȧ-rĭk). [Gothic.] All-ruler.

Al'as·tair (ăl'ăs·târ). Scot. contr. of ALEXANDER.

Al'ban (ôl'băn; ăl'-). [L.]

Al'bert (ăl'bẽrt). [Teut.] Illustrious through nobility. F. Albert (ȧl'bâr'); G. Adalbert (ä'däl·bẽrt); It. & Sp. Alberto (äl·bẽr'tō). — Dim. *Al, Alb, Bert* (bûrt).

Al'bin (ăl'bĭn). [L.] White.

Al'den (ôl'dĕn). [AS.] Old friend.

Al'ex·an'der (ăl'ĕg·zăn'dẽr; ăl'ĭg-; *Brit. also* -zăn'-). [Gr.] A defender of men. Russ. Aleksandr, Alexander (ŭ·lyĭ·ksăn'dẽr). — Dim. *Al'ec* (ăl'ĕk; -ĭk), *Al'eck, Al'ex, El'lick* (ĕl'ĭk), *San'der* (săn'dẽr; săn'-), *San'dy.*

A·lex'is (ȧ·lĕk'sĭs). [Gr.] Help.

Al'fred (ăl'frĕd; -frĭd; *F.* ȧl'frĕd'; *G.* äl'frät). [AS.] Elf in council; *i.e.*, good counselor. — Dim. *Al, Alf, Fred.*

Al'ger·non (ăl'jẽr·nŭn). [F.] — Dim. *Al'gie* (ăl'jĭ).

Al'is·ter (ăl'ĭs·tẽr). Scot. contr. of ALEXANDER.

Al'lan (ăl'ăn), **Al'len** (-ĕn; -ĭn). Vars. of ALAN.

A·lon'so (ȧ·lŏn'zō; *It. & Sp.* ä·lōn'sō), **A·lon'zo** (ȧ·lŏn'zō). [Sp.] = ALPHONSO.

Al'o·y'si·us (ăl'ō·ĭsh'ĭ·ŭs, -ĭsh'ŭs). [ML.]

Al·phon'so (ăl·fŏn'sō; -zō). [Teut.] Al. phonsus (ăl·fŏn'sŭs); F. Alphonse (ȧl'fôNs'; *Angl.* ăl'fŏns, -fŏnz); It. & Sp. Alfonso (äl·fōn'sō).

Al'vah (ăl'vȧ), **Al'van** (-văn). [Heb.]

Al'vin (ăl'vĭn), **Al'win** (ăl'wĭn). [Teut.] Probably, noble and friend.

Am'brose (ăm'brōz). [Gr.] Immortal; divine.

A'mos (ā'mŏs). [Heb.] Borne (by God).

An'drew (ăn'drōō). [Gr.] Strong; manly. F. André (äN'drā'); Sp. Andrés (än·drās'). — Dim. *An'dy.*

An'gus (ăng'gŭs). [Celtic.]

An'selm (ăn'sĕlm), **An'sel** (ăn's'l). [Teut.] With divine helmet.

An'tho·ny (ăn'thō·nĭ; ăn'tō-), **An'to·ny** (ăn'tō-). [L.] F. Antoine (äN'twän'); It. & Sp. Antonio (*It.* än·tô'nyō; *Sp.* -tō'nyō; *Angl.* ăn·tō'nĭ·ō, -tōn'yō). — Dim. *To'ny* (tō'nĭ).

Ar'cher (är'chẽr). From a surname.

Ar'chi·bald (är'chȧ·bôld; -b'ld). [Teut.] Nobly bold. — Dim. *Ar'chy, Ar'chie* (är'chĭ), *Bald'ie* (bôl'dĭ).

Ar'mand (är'mănd; -mänd; *F.* är'mäN'). French form of HERMAN.

Ar'nold (är'n'ld). [Teut.] Strong as an eagle.

Ar'thur (är'thẽr). [Prob. W.] — Dim. *Art, Art'ie.*

A'sa (ā'sȧ). [Heb.] Healer; physician.

A'saph (ā'săf; -sȧf; ăs'ăf; ăz'ăf). [Heb.] Gatherer.

Ash'ley (ăsh'lĭ). From a surname.

Ath'el·stan (ăth'ĕl·stăn), **Ath'el·stane** (-stān). [AS.] Noble stone.

Au'brey (ô'brĭ). [Teut.] Elf ruler.

Au·gus'tin (ô·gŭs'tĭn), **Au'gus·tine** (ô'gŭs·tēn; ô·gŭs'tĭn). [L.] Belonging to Augustus.

Au·gus'tus (ô·gŭs'tŭs), **Au'gust** (ô'gŭst). [L.] August; majestic. G. August (ou'gōōst). — Dim. *Gus, Gus'tus.*

Au·re'lius (ô·rēl'yŭs; -rē'lĭ·ŭs). [L.] Golden.

Aus'tin (ôs'tĭn). Short form of AUGUSTIN.

A'ver·y (ā'vẽr·ĭ; ā'vrĭ). From a surname.

B

Bald'ie (bôl'dĭ). Dim. of ARCHIBALD.

Bald'win (bôld'wĭn). [Teut.] Bold or courageous friend.

Bal·tha'sar, Bal·tha'zar (băl·thä'zẽr; -thăz'ẽr). [Gr.] A baptizer. F. Baptiste (bȧ'tēst').

Bar'na·bas (bär'nȧ·băs), **Bar'na·by** (bär'nȧ·bĭ). [Aram.] Son of exhortation. — Dim. *Bar'ney.*

Bar'nard. See BERNARD.

Bar'ney (bär'nĭ). Dim. of BARNABAS, BERNARD.

Bar'ry (băr'ĭ). [Ir.]

Bar·thol'o·mew (bär·thŏl'ō·mū). [Aram.] Son of Talmai. F. Barthélemy (bȧr'tāl'mē'). — Dim. *Bart, Bat.*

Bas'il (băz''l; băs''l; bā'z'l; bā's'l). [Gr.] Kingly; royal.

Bay'ard (bā'ẽrd; bī'-; -ärd). [OF.]

Ben·e·dict (bĕn'ê·dĭkt; *Brit. also* bĕn'ĭt). [L.] Blessed.

Ben'ja·min (bĕn'jȧ·mĭn). [Heb.] Son of the right hand. — Dim. *Ben, Ben'ny, Ben'jy.*

Ben'net (bĕn'ĕt; -ĭt). [OF.] = BENEDICT.

Ben'o'ni (bĕn·ō'nī). [Heb.] Son of my sorrow.

Ber'nard (bûr'nẽrd, -närd; bẽr·närd', bûr-), **Bar'nard** (bär'nẽrd). [Teut.] Bold as a bear. G. Bernhard (bẽrn'härt). — Dim. *Bar'ney* (bär'nĭ), *Ber'nie, Ber'ny*, etc.

Bert (bûrt), **Ber'tie.** Dims. of ALBERT, BERTRAM, GILBERT, HERBERT, HUBERT, etc.

Ber'thold (bẽr'tōld; *G.* -tŏlt). [G.] Ruling in splendor.

Ber'tram (bûr'trăm). [Teut.] Bright raven. — Dim. *Bert.*

Ber'trand (bûr'trănd; *F.* bẽr'träN'). French form of BERTRAM.

Bill (bĭl), **Bil'ly.** Dims. of WILLIAM.

Bob (bŏb), **Bob'bie, Bob'by.** Dims. of ROBERT.

Bon'i·face (bŏn'ĭ·fās). [L.] Prob., lucky; fortunate.

Bo'ris (bō'rĭs; bŏr'ĭs; *Russ.* bŭ·ryēs'). [Russ.]

Bri'an (brī'ăn). [Ir.]

Bruce (brōōs). From a surname.

Bru'no (brōō'nō). [Teut.] Brown.

Bry'an (brī'ăn). Var. of BRIAN.

By'ron (bī'rŭn). [F.] From a surname.

C

Cad·wal'la·der (kăd·wŏl'ȧ·dẽr). [Welsh.] Battle arranger.

Cae'sar (sē'zẽr). [L.]

Ca'leb (kā'lĕb). [Heb.] Dog.

Cal'vin (kăl'vĭn). [L.] — Dim. *Cal.*

Carl (kärl). Variant of *Karl*, Ger. form of CHARLES.

Carl'ton, Carle'ton (kärl'tŭn; -t'n). From a surname.

Car'ol (kăr'ŭl). Anglicized form of CAROLUS (L. form of CHARLES).

Cas'par, Cas'per (kăs'pẽr). [G.] G. Kaspar (käs'pär).

Ce'cil (sē's'l; sĕs''l; sĕs'ĭl; sĭs''l). [L.] Dimsighted.

Ced'ric (sĕd'rĭk; sē'drĭk). [AS.]

Charles (chärlz). [Teut.] Strong; manly. F. Charles (shärl); It. Carlo (kär'lō); Sp. Carlos (kär'lōs); G. Carl, Karl (kärl). — Dim. *Char'lie, Char'ley.*

Chaun'cey (chôn'sĭ; chän'-). From a surname.

Ches′ter (chĕs′tẽr). From a surname.
Chris′tian (krĭs′chăn; krĭst′yăn). [L.] — Dim. *Chris′tie*.
Chris′to·pher (krĭs′tṓ·fẽr). [Gr.] Christ-bearer. — Dim. *Chris*, *Kit*.
Clare (klâr). [L.] Bright.
Clar′ence (klăr′ĕns). [From the English dukedom.]
Claude (klôd; F. klōd), **Claud** (klôd), **Clau′di·us** (klô′dĭ·ŭs). [L.] Lame. It. & Sp. Claudio (*It.* klou′dyṓ; *Sp.* -thyṓ).
Clay′ton (klā′t'n). From a surname.
Clem′ent (klĕm′ĕnt). [L.] Mild; merciful. — Dim. *Clem*.
Clif′ford (klĭf′ẽrd). From a surname.
Clif′ton (klĭf′tŭn). From a surname.
Clin′ton (klĭn′t'n; -tŭn). From a surname.
Clive (klīv). From a surname.
Clyde (klīd). From a surname.
Col′in (kŏl′ĭn; kō′lĭn). Orig., dim. of NICHOLAS.
Con (kŏn), **Con′nie** (kŏn′ĭ). Dims. of CONRAD, CORNELIUS.
Con′rad (kŏn′răd; -răd). [Teut.] Bold counsel. G. Konrad (kōn′rät). — Dim. *Con′nie*.
Con′stant (kŏn′stănt). [L.] Firm; faithful; true.
Con′stan·tine (kŏn′stăn·tīn; -tēn). [L.]
Cor·ne′lius (kôr·nēl′yŭs; -nē′lĭ·ŭs). [L.] — Dim. *Con* (kŏn), *Con′nie*, *Neil* (nēl).
Craig (krāg). From a surname.
Cur′tis (kûr′tĭs). [OF.] Courteous.
Cuth′bert (kŭth′bẽrt). [AS.] Noted splendor.
Cyr′il (sĭr′ĭl). [Gr.] Lordly.
Cy′rus (sī′rŭs). [Per.]

D

Dan (dăn). [Heb.] A judge.
Dan′iel (dăn′yĕl). [Heb.] God is my judge. — Dim. *Dan*.
Da·ri′us (dȧ·rī′ŭs). [Per.] Possessing wealth.
Da′vid (dā′vĭd). [Heb.] Beloved. — Dim. *Dave* (dāv), *Da′vy*.
Da′vis (dā′vĭs). From a surname.
Dean, Deane (dēn). From a surname.
De·me′tri·us (dē·mē′trĭ·ŭs). [Gr.] Belonging to Demeter.
Den′is (dĕn′ĭs), **Den′nis** (-ĭs). [F.] = DIONYSIUS. — Dim. *Den′ny*.
Der′ek (dĕr′ĕk; -ĭk), **Der′rick** (dĕr′ĭk). [D.] — Dim. *Dirk* (dûrk; *Du.* dĭrk).
De·witt′, De Witt (dē·wĭt′). From a surname.
Dex′ter (dĕks′tẽr). [L.] On the right hand; fortunate.
Dick (dĭk). Dim. of RICHARD.
Di′on (dī′ŏn; -ŭn). Short form of DIONYSIUS.
Di·o·ny′si·us (dī′ṓ·nĭsh′ĭ·ŭs; -nĭsh′ŭs; -nĭs′ĭ·ŭs; -nī′sĭ·ŭs). [Gr.] Belonging to Dionysus, the god of wine. F. Denys, or Denis (dē·nē′).
Dob (dŏb), **Dob′bin** (dŏb′ĭn). Dims. of ROBERT.
Dode (dōd). Dim. of THEODORE.
Dolf, Dolph (dŏlf), **Dol′phus** (dŏl′fŭs). Dims. of ADOLPH, RUDOLPH, etc.
Dom′i·nic (dŏm′ĭ·nĭk). [L.] Belonging to the Lord.
Don′ald (dŏn′ld). [Gael.] World ruler. — Dim. *Don*.
Doug′las (dŭg′lăs). From a surname. — Dim. *Doug*.
Dud′ley (dŭd′lĭ). From a surname.
Duke (dūk; 114). 1. [AS.] Leader. 2. Dim. of MARMADUKE.
Dun′can (dŭng′kăn). [Gael.] Brown warrior.
Dun′stan (dŭn′stăn). [AS.]
Dwight (dwīt). From a surname.

E

Earl (ûrl). [AS.] Man; noble.
Eb′en·e′zer (ĕb′ĕn·ē′zẽr). [Heb.] The stone of help. — Dim. *Eb′en* (ĕb′ĕn).
Ed (ĕd), **Ed′die**. Dims. of EDGAR, EDMUND, EDWARD, EDWIN.
Ed′gar (ĕd′gẽr). [AS.] A javelin (or protector) of property. — Dim. *Ed*.
Ed′mund (ĕd′mŭnd). [AS.] Defender of property. F. Edmond (ĕd′mōn′; *Angl.* ĕd′mŭnd). — Dim. *Ed*, *Ed′die*, *Ned*.
Ed′ward (ĕd′wẽrd). [AS.] Guardian of property. — Dim. *Ed*, *Ed′die*, *Ned*, *Ted*, *Ted′dy*.
Ed′win (ĕd′wĭn). [AS.] Gainer of property. — Dim. *Ed*.

Eg′bert (ĕg′bẽrt). [AS.] Probably, bright sword.
El′bert (ĕl′bẽrt). = ALBERT.
Ei′dred (ĕl′drĕd; -drĭd). [AS.]
El′e·a′zar, El′e·a′zer (ĕl′ė·ā′zẽr). [Heb.] God has helped.
E′li (ē′lī). [Heb.] High.
E·li′as (ē·lī′ăs). = ELIJAH.
El′i·hu (ĕl′ĭ·hū; ė·lī′hū). [Heb.] God is He.
E·li′jah (ē·lī′jȧ). [Heb.] Jehovah is God.
El′i·ot, El′li·ott (ĕl′ĭ·ŭt; ĕl′yŭt). From a surname.
E·liph′a·let (ē·lĭf′ȧ·lĕt; -lĭt). [Heb.] God is (a) deliverance.
E·li′sha (ē·lī′shȧ). [Heb.] God is salvation.
El′lick (ĕl′ĭk). Dim. of ALEXANDER.
El′lis (ĕl′ĭs). Var. of ELIAS.
El′mer (ĕl′mẽr). [AS.] Noble and famous.
El′ton (ĕl′t'n; -tŭn). From a surname.
Em′er·ich (ĕm′ẽr·ĭk), **Em′er·y** (ĕm′ẽr·ĭ).
Em′o·ry (ĕm′ṓ·rĭ). [Teut.] It. Amerigo (ä′mā·rē′gṓ).
E′mil (ā′mĭl; ē′mĭl; ĕm′ĭl), **E·mile′** (ȧ·mēl′). [F.] F. Émile (ā′mēl′); G. Emil (ā′mēl).
Em·man′u·el, E·man′u·el (ē·măn′ū·ĕl; ĭ-). [Heb.] God with us. Sp. Manuel (mä-nwēl′); Pg. Manoel, Manuel (mȧ·nwäl′).
E′noch (ē′nŭk). [Heb.] Dedicated.
E′nos (ē′nŏs). [Heb.] Man.
En·ri′co (ĕn·rē′kṓ; *It.* än·rē′kṓ). It. form of HENRY.
E′phra·im (ē′frä·ĭm; ē′frĭ·ŭm). [Heb.] Very fruitful.
E·ras′mus (ē·răz′mŭs). [Gr.] Lovely; worthy of love.
E·ras′tus (ē·răs′tŭs). [Gr.] Beloved.
Er′ic (ĕr′ĭk; ẽr′ĭk). [Scand.]
Er′nest (ûr′nĕst; -nĭst). [G.] Earnest. G. Ernst (ẽrnst).
Er′win (ûr′wĭn). From a surname.
Es′mé (ĕz′mē). [OF.] Probably, esteemed.
E′than (ē′thăn). [Heb.] Firmness; strength.
Eth′el·bert (ĕth′ĕl·bẽrt). [AS.] Noble and bright.
Eu·gene′ (ū·jēn′; ū′jēn). [Gr.] Well-born; of noble race. — Dim. *Gene*.
Eus′tace (ūs′tĭs). [Gr.] F. Eustache (ûs′-tȧsh′; ŭs′tȧsh′).
Ev′an (ĕv′ăn). [Welsh.]
Ev′e·lyn (ĕv′ė·lĭn; ēv′lĭn; ĕv′lĭn; ē′vė·lĭn). Prob., youth.
Ev′er·ard (ĕv′ẽr·ärd). [Teut.] Strong as a wild boar.
Ev′er·ett (ĕv′ẽr·ĕt, -ĭt; ĕv′rĕt, -rĭt). From a surname.
E·zek′iel (ē·zēk′yĕl; -zē′kĭ·ĕl; 58). [Heb.] God makes strong. — Dim. *Zeke*.
Ez′ra (ĕz′rȧ). [Heb.] Help.

F

Fe′lix (fē′lĭks). [L.] Happy; prosperous.
Fer′di·nand (fûr′dĭ·nănd; -d′n·ănd; *F.* fĕr′-dė′nän′; *G.* fĕr′dė·nänt). [Teut.] Sp. Fernando (fẽr·nän′dṓ).
Fer′gus (fûr′gŭs). [Gael.]
Flor′ence (flŏr′ĕns). See FLORENCE, under *Names of Women*.
Floyd (floid). From a surname.
Fran′cis (frăn′sĭs). [Teut.] Free. F. François (frän′swȧ′); G. Franz (fränts); Sp. Francisco (frän·thēs′kṓ; -sēs′-). — Dim. *Frank* (frăngk).
Frank′lin (frăngk′lĭn). [ME.] A freeman; a freeholder.
Fred (frĕd), **Fred′dy**. Dims. of ALFRED, FREDERIC(K), WILFRED.
Fred′er·ic, Fred′er·ick (frĕd′rĭk; frĕd′ẽr·ĭk). [Teut.] G. Friedrich (frē′drĭk), Fritz (frĭts). — Dim. *Fred*, *Fritz*.

G

Ga′bri·el (gā′brĭ·ĕl). [Heb.] Man of God. — Dim. *Gabe* (gāb).
Ga·ma′li·el (gȧ·mā′lĭ·ĕl; -māl′yĕl). [Heb.] Recompense of God.
Gar′di·ner (gärd′nẽr; gär′d'n·ẽr), **Gard′ner** (gärd′nẽr). From a surname.
Gar′ret, Gar′rett (găr′ĕt).
Gas′par (găs′pär). Cf. CASPAR.
Gas′ton (găs′tŭn; *F.* gȧs′tôn′).
Gene (jēn). Dim. of EUGENE.
Geof′frey (jĕf′rĭ). [Teut.]
George (jôrj). [Gr.] A husbandman. — Dim. *Geor′gie* (jôr′jĭ), *Geor′die* (jôr′dĭ).
Ger′ald (jĕr′ăld). [Teut.] Spear wielder. — Dim. *Jer′ry* (jĕr′ĭ).
Ge·rard′ (jĕ·rärd′ *or*, *esp. Brit.*, jĕr′ärd, -ẽrd).

[Teut.] Strong with the spear. G. Gerhard (gär′härt). — Dim. *Jer′ry* (jĕr′ĭ).
Ger′vase (jûr′vȧs). [LL.] F. Gervais (zhẽr′vē′).
Gib (gĭb). Dim. of GILBERT.
Gid′e·on (gĭd′ē·ŭn). [Heb.] Hewer; feller.
Gif′ford (gĭf′ẽrd). From a surname.
Gil′bert (gĭl′bẽrt). [Teut.] Prob., bright wish. — Dim. *Gil* (gĭl), *Bert*, *Gib*.
Giles (jīlz). [OF.] Aegis.
Glenn (glĕn). From a surname.
God′dard (gŏd′ẽrd). [Teut.] God-strong; pious; virtuous.
God′frey (gŏd′frĭ). [Teut.] Prob., peace of God. G. Gottfried (gôt′frēt).
God′win (gŏd′wĭn). [AS.] Friend of God.
Gor′don (gôr′d'n). From a surname.
Gou′ver·neur′ (gŭv′ẽr·nẽr′; gŭv′ẽr·nẽr). From a surname.
Gra′ham (grā′ăm). From a surname.
Grant (grȧnt). From a surname.
Greg′o·ry (grĕg′ṓ·rĭ; grĕg′rĭ). [Gr.] Vigilant. — Dim. *Greg*.
Grif′fith (grĭf′ĭth). [Welsh.]
Gro′ver (grō′vẽr).
Gus (gŭs). Dim. of AUGUSTUS, GUSTAVUS.
Gus·ta′vus (gŭs·tā′vŭs; -tä′vŭs). [Sw.] F. Gustave (gŭs·täv′); G. Gustav (gōōs′täf). — Dim. *Gus*.
Gus′tus (gŭs′tŭs). Dim. of AUGUSTUS.
Guy (gī). [F.] A leader. It. Guido (gwē′dṓ).

H

Hal (hăl). Dim. of HAROLD, HENRY.
Ham′il·ton (hăm′ĭl·tŭn; -t'n). From a surname.
Hank (hăngk). Dim. of HENRY.
Han′ni·bal (hăn′ĭ·băl). [Punic.] Grace of Baal.
Hans (hänz; *G.* häns). German form of JOHN.
Har′ley (här′lĭ). From a surname.
Har′old (hăr′ŭld). [AS.] Army leader. — Dim. *Hal* (hăl).
Har′ry (hăr′ĭ). Orig., dim. of HAROLD, HENRY.
Har′vey (här′vĭ). From a surname.
Hec′tor (hĕk′tẽr). [Gr.] Holding fast.
He′man (hē′măn). [Heb.] Faithful.
Hen′ry (hĕn′rĭ). [Teut.] Ruler of an enclosure, or private property. F. Henri (än′-rē′); It. Enrico (än·rē′kṓ; *Angl.* ĕn·rē′kṓ); G. Heinrich (hīn′rĭk); D. Hendrik (hĕn′drĭk). — Dim. *Hal* (hăl), *Hank* (hăngk), *Har′ry* (hăr′ĭ), *Hen*.
Her′bert (hûr′bẽrt). [AS.] Glory of the army. — Dim. *Bert*, *Ber′tie*, *Herb*.
Her′man (hûr′măn). [Teut.] A warrior. G. Hermann (hĕr′män).
Hez′e·ki′ah (hĕz′ė·kī′ȧ). [Heb.] God has strengthened.
Hil′a·ry (hĭl′ȧ·rĭ). [L.] Cheerful; merry. F. Hilaire (ē′lâr′).
Hi′ram (hī′răm). [Phoenician.] Most noble.
Ho′bart (hō′bẽrt; -bärt). From a surname.
Hodge (hŏj), **Hodg′kin** (hŏj′kĭn). Dims. of ROGER.
Ho′mer (hō′mẽr). [Gr.]
Hor′ace (hŏr′ĭs). = HORATIO.
Ho·ra′tio (hṓ·rā′shṓ; -shĭ·ṓ). [L.]
Ho·se′a (hṓ·zē′ȧ; -zā′ȧ). [Heb.] Salvation.
How′ard (hou′ẽrd).
How′ell (hou′ĕl). [Welsh.]
Hu′bert (hū′bẽrt). [Teut.] Bright in spirit; soul-bright.
Hugh (hū), **Hu′go** (hū′gō). [Teut.] Prob., mind.
Hum′bert (hŭm′bẽrt). [Teut.] High and bright.
Hum′phrey, Hum′phry (hŭm′frĭ). [AS.]

I

I′an (ē′ăn; ī′ăn; ē′än). Gaelic form of JOHN.
Ich′a·bod (ĭk′ȧ·bŏd). [Heb.] Inglorious.
Ig·na′ti·us (ĭg·nā′shĭ·ŭs; -shŭs). [L.] F. Ignace (ē′nyȧs′); Sp. Ignacio (ĕg·nä′thyṓ; -syṓ).
I′ra (ī′rȧ). [Heb.] Watchful.
Ir′ving (ûr′vĭng), **Ir′vin** (-vĭn). From a surname.
Ir′win (ûr′wĭn). From a surname.
I′saac (ī′zȧk; -zĭk). [Heb.] Laughter. — Dim. *Ik* (ĭk), *Ike*, *Ike′y*.
Is′a·dore (ĭz′ȧ·dōr), **Is′a·dor** (-dôr). Vars. of ISIDORE, ISIDOR.
I·sai′ah (ī·zā′[y]ȧ; ī·zī′ȧ). [Heb.] Salvation of the Lord.

Is'i·dore (ĭz'ĭ·dōr), **Is'i·dor** (-dôr). [Gr.] Gift of Isis.

Is'ra·el (ĭz'rā·ĕl; -rĭ·ĕl). [Heb.] Contender with God.

I'van (ī'văn; -văn; *Russ.* ĭ·vän'). Russian form of JOHN.

I'vor (ē'vẽr; ī'-). [Celt.]

J

Ja'bez (jā'bĕz; -bĭz). [Heb.] He will cause pain.

Jack (jăk). Familiar form of JOHN (but derived from OF. *Jacques*, fr. LL. *Jacobus*, James).

Ja'cob (jā'kŭb). [Heb.] A supplanter. F. Jacques (zhäk). — Dim. *Jake* (jāk). See JAMES.

Ja'i·rus (jā'ĭ·rŭs; jā·ī'rŭs). [Heb.] He will enlighten.

James (jāmz). = JACOB, through Sp. *Jaime* (hī'mā). — Dim. *Jem, Jim, Jim'mie, Jim'my*.

Ja'pheth (jā'fĕth; -fĭth), **Ja'phet** (-fĕt; -fĭt). [Heb.] Enlargement.

Jar'ed (jăr'ĕd; -ĭd). [Heb.] Descent.

Jar'vis (jär'vĭs), **Jer'vis** (jŭr'vĭs or, *esp. Brit.*, jär'-). From a surname.

Ja'son (jā's'n). [Gr.] Prob., a healer.

Jas'per (jăs'pẽr). [F.] Cf. CASPAR.

Jay (jā).

Jean (jēn; *F.* zhän). French form of JOHN.

Jef'frey (jĕf'rĭ). = GEOFFREY.

Jem (jĕm), **Jem'my**. Dims. of JAMES.

Jer'e·mi'ah (jĕr'ē·mī'à), **Jer'e·my** (jĕr'ē·mĭ). [Heb.] Exalted of the Lord. — Dim. *Jer'ry*.

Je·rome' (jē·rōm'; *Brit. also* jĕr'ŭm). [Gr.] Bearing a holy name.

Jer'ry (jĕr'ĭ). Dim. of GERALD, GERARD, JEREMIAH, JEREMY, JEROME.

Jes'se (jĕs'ē). [Heb.]

Jim (jĭm), **Jim'mie**, **Jim'my**. Dims. of JAMES.

Jo (jō). Dim. of JOSEPH.

Jo'ab (jō'ăb). [Heb.] Jehovah is his father.

Job (jōb). [Heb.] Afflicted; persecuted.

Jock (jŏk). Scottish form of JACK.

Joe (jō). Dim. of JOSEPH.

Jo'el (jō'ĕl; -ĕl). [Heb.] The Lord is God.

John (jŏn). [Heb.] God is gracious. F. Jean (zhän; *Angl.* jēn); It. Giovanni (jō·vän'nē); Sp. Juan (hwän; *Angl.* jōō'än); G. Johann (yō·hän'; yō'hän), Johannes (yō·hän'ĕs; -ĕs), Hans (häns; *Angl* hănz); D. Jan (yän); Russ. Ivan (ĭ·vän'; *Angl.* ī'văn, -văn). — Dim. *John'ny*. See JACK, JOCK.

Jo'nah (jō'nà). [Heb.] A dove.

Jo'nas (jō'năs). = JONAH.

Jon'a·than (jŏn'à·thǎn). [Heb.] God has given.

Jo'seph (jō'zĕf; -zĭf). [Heb.] He shall add. It. Giuseppe (jōō·zĕp'pā); Sp. José (hō·sā'; *Angl.* -zā'). — Dim. *Jo, Joe* (jō).

Josh'u·a (jŏsh'ū·à). [Heb.] Jehovah is deliverance. — Dim. *Josh*.

Jo·si'ah (jō·sī'à), **Jo·si'as** (jō·sī'ăs). [Heb.] Jehovah supports.

Ju'dah (jōō'dà). [Heb.] Praised.

Jude (jōōd; 114). [Heb.]

Jules (jōōlz; *F.* zhül). French form of JULIUS.

Jul'ian (jōōl'yăn; 58). Sprung from, or belonging to, Julius. — Dim. *Jule*.

Jul'ius (jōōl'yŭs; 58). [L.] F. Jules (zhül; *Angl.* jōōlz). — Dim. *Jule*.

Jun'ius (jōōn'yŭs; jōō'nĭ·ŭs; 58). [L.]

Jus'tin (jŭs'tĭn), **Jus'tus** (-tŭs). [L.] Just.

K

Karl (kärl). German form of CHARLES.

Keith (kēth). From a surname.

Kel'vin (kĕl'vĭn). From a surname.

Ken'elm (kĕn'ĕlm). [AS.] Bold helmet.

Ken'neth (kĕn'ĕth; -ĭth). [AS.]

Kit (kĭt). Dim. of CHRISTOPHER.

L

La'ban (lā'băn). [Heb.] White.

La'fa·yette' (lä'fī·ĕt'; lăf'ĭ-; lä'fĭ-). From a surname.

Lam'bert (lăm'bẽrt). [Teut.] Illustrious with landed possessions.

Lan'ce·lot (lăn'sē·lŏt; läns'lŏt), **Laun'ce·lot** (lôn'sē·lŏt, län'-; lôns'lŏt, läns'-). [F.] — Dim. *Lance*.

Lar'ry (lăr'ĭ). Dim. of LAURENCE, LAWRENCE.

Lars (lärz). [Etruscan.] Lord.

Lau'rence, **Law'rence** (lô'rĕns; lŏr'ĕns). [L.] F. Laurent (lō'rän'); It. Lorenzo (lō·rĕn'tsō; *Angl.* lō·rĕn'zō); G. Lorenz (lō'rĕnts). — Dim. *Lar'ry* (lär'ĭ), *Lau'rie, Law'rie* (lô'rĭ).

Laz'a·rus (lăz'à·rŭs). [Heb.] = ELEAZER.

Le·an'der (lē·ăn'dẽr). [Gr.]

Lee, Leigh (lē). From a surname.

Lem'u·el (lĕm'ū·ĕl). [Heb.] Consecrated to God.

Le'o (lē'ō). [L.] Lion.

Le'on (lē'ŏn; -ŭn). [L.] Lion.

Leon'ard (lĕn'ẽrd). [G.] Strong or brave as a lion.

Le·on'i·das (lē·ŏn'ĭ·dăs). [Gr.] Lionlike.

Le'o·pold (lē'ō·pōld; *formerly* lĕp'ŭld). [Teut.] Bold for the people.

Le·roy' (lē·roi'; lē·roi'; lē'roi). [OF.] Royal.

Les'lie (lĕs'lĭ; *esp. Brit.*, lĕz'-). From a surname.

Les'ter (lĕs'tẽr). From a surname.

Le'vi (lē'vī). [Heb.] Joining.

Lew'is (lū'ĭs; lōō'-). = LOUIS.

Lin'coln (lĭng'kŭn). From a surname.

Li'nus (lī'nŭs). [Gr.] Flaxen-haired.

Li'o·nel (lī'ō·n'l; -nĕl). [F.] Young lion.

Lisle (līl). Var. of LYLE.

Llew·el'lyn (lōō·ĕl'ĭn; lōō-). [Welsh.]

Lloyd (loid). From a surname.

Lo·ren'zo (lō·rĕn'zō; *It.* -tsō). See LAURENCE.

Lot, Lott (lŏt). [Heb.] An envelope; wrap.

Lou'is (lōō'ĭs; lōō'ĭ; *F.* lwē). [Teut.] Famous warrior. Sp. Luis (lōō·ēs'); G. Ludwig (lŏŏt'vĭk; lōōd'-). — Dim. *Lew* (lū; lōō).

Lou (lōō).

Lov'ell (lŭv'ĕl). [ME.] Beloved.

Low'ell (lō'ĕl). Var. of LOVELL.

Lu'cian (lū'shăn; -shĭ·ăn). [L.] F. Lucien (lü'syăn'; *Angl.* lū'shĕn).

Lu'cius (lū'shŭs; lū'shĭ·ŭs). [L.] Light.

Luke (lūk). [Gr.] L. Lucas (lū'kăs).

Lu'ther (lū'thẽr). [G.] Illustrious warrior. F. Lothaire (lō'târ'); It. Lotario (lō·tä'ryō).

Lyle (līl). From a surname.

Ly'man (lī'măn).

Lynn (lĭn). From a surname.

M

Mal'a·chi (măl'à·kī). [Heb.] Messenger.

Mal'colm (măl'kŭm). [Gael.] Servant of (St.) Columba.

Man'u·el (măn'ū·ĕl; *Sp.* mä·nwĕl'; *Pg.* mä·nwäl'). See EMMANUEL.

Mar·cel'lus (mär·sĕl'ŭs). [L.] Orig., dim. of MARCUS.

Mar'cus (mär'kŭs), **Mark** (märk). [L.] F. Marc (màrk); It. Marco (mär'kō).

Mar'i·on (măr'ĭ·ŭn; mâr'-). [F.]

Mar'ma·duke (mär'mà·dūk). — Dim. *Duke*.

Mar'shall, Mar'shal (mär'shăl). From a surname.

Mar'tin (mär'tĭn; -t'n). [L.] Of Mars; warlike.

Mar'vin (mär'vĭn). [Teut.] Prob., sea friend.

Mat'thew (măth'ū). [Heb.] Gift of Jehovah. — Dim. *Mat, Matt*.

Mat·thi'as (mà·thī'ăs). [Gr.] = MATTHEW.

Mau'rice (mô'rĭs; mŏr'ĭs; mô·rēs'; *F.* mō·rēs'). [L.] Moorish; dark-colored.

Max·i·mil'ian (măk'sĭ·mĭl'yăn; -mĭl'ĭ·ăn). [L.] — Dim. *Max*.

May'nard (mā'nẽrd; -närd). [Teut.]

Mer'e·dith (mĕr'ē·dĭth). [?Welsh.]

Mer'vin (mûr'vĭn). Var. of MARVIN.

Mi'cah (mī'kà). [Heb.] Who is like God?

Mi'chael (mī'kĕl; -k'l). [Heb.] Who is like God? F. Michel (mē'shĕl'); Sp. & Pg. Miguel (Sp. mē·gĕl'; Pg. mē·gäl'). — Dim. *Mike* (mīk), *Mick'y* (mĭk'ĭ).

Miles (mīlz). [Teut.]

Mil'ton (mĭl't'n; -tŭn). From a surname.

Mitch'ell (mĭch'ĕl). From a surname.

Mon·roe' (mŭn·rō'; *Brit. also* mŭn'rō). From a surname.

Mon'ta·gue (mŏn'tà·gū; mŭn'-). From a surname.

Mor'gan (môr'găn). [Welsh.] A dweller on the sea.

Mor'ris (mŏr'ĭs). = MAURICE.

Mor'ti·mer (môr'tĭ·mẽr).

Mor'ton (môr't'n). [AS.] From a surname.

Mo'ses (mō'zĕz; mō'zĭs). [Perh. Egypt.] Perh., child. — Dim. *Mose*.

Moss (môs). Var. of MOSES.

Mur'doch (mûr'dŏk). [Celt.] Sea man.

Mur'ray (mŭr'ĭ). 1. From a surname. 2. In modern usage, also a var. of MAURICE.

Myles (mīlz). = MILES.

N

Na'a·man (nā'à·măn). [Heb.] Pleasantness.

Na'hum (nā'[h]ŭm; -hŭm). [Heb.] Comforter.

Na·po'le·on (nà·pō'lē·ŭn; -pōl'yŭn). [It.]

Nat (năt), **Nate** (nāt). Dims. of NATHAN, NATHANIEL.

Na'than (nā'thăn; -th'n). [Heb.] Given; gift.

Na·than'iel (nà·thăn'yĕl; -ĭ·ĕl), **Na·than'a·el** (nà·thăn'ā·ĕl). [Heb.] Gift of God.

Neal, Neil (nēl). [Gael.] Prob., courageous. See CORNELIUS.

Ned (nĕd), **Ned'dy**. Dims. of EDMUND, EDWARD, EDWIN.

Ne·he·mi'ah (nē'[h]ē·mī'à). [Heb.] Comfort of Jehovah.

Nel'son (nĕl's'n). From a surname.

Nev'ille (nĕv'ĭl; -ĭl). From a surname.

New'ton (nū't'n). From a surname.

Nich'o·las, Nic'o·las (nĭk'ō·lăs). [Gr.] Victorious army. — Dim. *Nick*.

Ni'gel (nī'jĕl). [Gael.]

No'ah (nō'à). [Heb.] Rest; comfort.

No'el (nō'ĕl). [L.] Christmas. F. Noël (-ĕl').

Nor'bert (nôr'bẽrt). [Teut.] Njord's brightness.

Nor'man (nôr'măn). [Scand.] A Northman.

O

O'ba·di'ah (ō'bà·dī'à). [Heb.] Servant of the Lord. L. O'ba·di'as.

Oc·ta'vi·us (ŏk·tā'vĭ·ŭs). [L.] The eighth born.

O'laf (ō'läf; *Dan.* ō'läf; *Norw.* ō'läf; *Swed.* ōō'läf', ōō'läv'). [Scand.]

Ol'i·ver (ŏl'ĭ·vẽr). [F., of uncert. origin.]

Or·lan'do (ôr·lăn'dō; *It.* ôr·län'dō). [It.] See ROLAND.

Os'bert (ŏz'bẽrt). [AS.] Godly-bright.

Os'car (ŏs'kẽr). [Prob. AS.]

Os'mond, Os'mund (ŏz'mŭnd). [AS.] Protection of God.

Os'wald (ŏz'wăld), **Os'wold** (-wōld). [AS.] Power of God.

Ot'to (ŏt'ō). [G.]

Ow'en (ō'ĕn; -ĭn). [Welsh.]

P

Pad'dy (păd'ĭ). Dim. of PATRICK.

Pad'raic (pôth'rĭg). Irish form of PATRICK.

Pat'rick (păt'rĭk). [L.] Noble; a patrician. — Dim. *Pad'dy, Pat, Pat'sy*.

Paul (pôl; *F.* pōl; *G.* poul). [L.] Little. L. Paulus (pô'lŭs); It. Paolo (pä'ō·lō); Sp. Pablo (pä'vlō).

Pearce (pērs). = PETER.

Per'ci·val (pûr'sĭ·văl), **Per'ce·val** (pûr'sĕ-). [OF.]

Per'cy (pûr'sĭ). Dim. of PERCIVAL; also, from a surname.

Per'ry (pĕr'ĭ). From a surname.

Pe'ter (pē'tẽr). [Gr.] A rock. F. Pierre (pyâr; *Angl. also* pēr); It. Pietro (pyâ'trō); Sp. & Pg. Pedro (Sp. pā'thrō; Pg. pā'thrōō). — Dim. *Pete* (pēt), *Pe'ter·kin*.

Phi·lan'der (fĭ·lăn'dẽr). [Gr.] A lover of men.

Phi·le'mon (fĭ·lē'mŏn; fī-). [Gr.] Loving.

Phil'ip (fĭl'ĭp). [Gr.] A lover of horses. — Dim. *Phil, Pip* (pĭp).

Phin'e·as (fĭn'ē·ăs). [Heb.] Mouth of brass.

Pierce (pērs). = PETER.

Pierre (pyâr; *Angl. also* pēr). French form of PETER.

Pip (pĭp). Dim. of PHILIP.

Pi'us (pī'ŭs). [L.] Pious; filial.

Q

Quin'cy (kwĭn'sĭ; -zĭ).

Quin'tin (kwĭn't'n; -tĭn). Also **Quen'tin** (kwĕn'-). [L.] The fifth.

R

Ralph (rălf; *British also* rāf, rä[l]f). [AS.] F. Raoul (rà'ōōl').

Ran'dolph (răn'dŏlf; -d'lf). From a surname.

Ra'oul' (rà'ōōl'). French form of RALPH, RUDOLPH.

Raph'a·el (răf'ā·ĕl, -ĭ·ĕl; rā'fā·ĕl, -fĭ·ĕl). [Heb.] God hath healed.
Ray (rā). Orig., dim. of RAYMOND.
Ray'mond, Ray'mund (rā'mŭnd). [Teut.] Wise protection.
Reg'i·nald (rĕj'ĭ·n'ld). [Teut.] Strong ruler. — Dim. *Rex, Reg'gie* (rĕj'ĭ).
Re·né' (rĕ·nā'; *also* rā'nĕ, rĕn'ĕ, rē'nĕ, rĕn'ā). [F., fr. L.] Reborn.
Reu'ben (rōō'bĕn). [Heb.] Behold, a son!
Reu'el (rōō'ĕl). [Heb.] God is his friend.
Rex (rĕks). 1. [L.] King. 2. Dim. of REGINALD.
Reyn'old (rĕn''ld). = REGINALD.
Rich'ard (rĭch'ĕrd). [Teut.] Strong like a ruler; powerful. — Dim. *Dick.*
Rob'ert (rŏb'ĕrt). [Teut.] Bright in fame. G. Ruprecht (rōō'prĕkt). — Dim. *Bob, Bob'by, Dob, Dob'bin, Rob, Rob'bie, Rob'in.*
Rod'er·ic, Rod'er·ick (rŏd'ĕr·ĭk; rŏd'rĭk). [Teut.] Rich in fame.
Rod'ney (rŏd'nĭ). From a surname.
Ro'dolph (rō'dŏlf), **Ro·dol'phus** (rō·dŏl'fŭs). = RUDOLPH.
Rog'er (rŏj'ĕr). [Teut.] Famous with the spear. — Dim. *Hodge* (hŏj), *Hodg'kin* (hŏj'kĭn).
Ro'land (rō'lănd), **Row'land** (rō'lănd). [Teut.] Fame of the land. It. Orlando (ȏr·län'dȏ).
Rol'lo (rŏl'ō), **Rolf** (rŏlf), **Rolph.** Short forms of RUDOLPH.
Ron'ald (rŏn''ld). Old Norse form of REGINALD.
Ro'ry (rō'rĭ). Irish form of RODERIC.
Ros'coe (rŏs'kō). From a surname.
Ross (rŏs). From a surname.
Roy (roi). [OF.] King.
Ru'dolph (rōō'dŏlf), **Ru·dol'phus** (rōō·dŏl'fŭs). [Teut.] F. Rodolphe (rō·dȏlf'), Raoul (rȧ'ōōl'); G. Rudolf (rōō'dȏlf). — Dim. *Ru'dy.*
Ru'fus (rōō'fŭs). [L.] Red; red-haired.
Ru'pert (rōō'pĕrt). = ROBERT.
Rus'sell (rŭs''l). From a surname.

S

Sam'son (săm's'n), **Samp'son** (sămp's'n; săm'-). [Heb.] Solar; sun's man.
Sam'u·el (săm'ū·ĕl). [Heb.] His name is El (God). — Dim. *Sam, Sam'my.*
San'der (săn'dĕr; săn'-), **San'dy** (săn'dĭ). Dims. of ALEXANDER.
Saul (sȏl). [Heb.] Asked for.
Schuy'ler (skī'lĕr). From a surname.
Scott (skŏt). From a surname.
Sean (shŏn; shän). Irish form of JOHN.
Se·bas'tian (sē·băs'chăn). [Gr.]
Seth (sĕth). [Heb.] Appointed.

Sew'ard (sū'ĕrd; *Brit. also* sē'wĕrd). From a surname.
Sey'mour (sē'mōr; -môr; -mĕr). From a surname.
Shaun, Shawn (shôn). Irish forms of JOHN.
Shel'don (shĕl'dŭn). From a surname.
Sid'ney (sĭd'nĭ).
Sieg'fried (sēg'frēd; *G.* zēk'frēt). [G.]
Sig'is·mund (sĭj'ĭs·mŭnd; sĭg'-). [Teut.] Conquering protection. G. Sigmund (zēk'mōont; *Angl.* sĭg'mŭnd).
Si'las (sī'lăs). [L.]
Sil·va'nus (sĭl·vā'nŭs). [L.] Living in a wood.
Sil·ves'ter (sĭl·vĕs'tĕr). [L.] Bred in the country; rustic.
Sim'e·on (sĭm'ē·ŭn). [Heb.] Hearing. — Dim. *Sim* (sĭm).
Si'mon (sī'mŭn). = SIMEON.
Sin'clair (sĭn[g]'klâr; sĭn·klâr'). From a surname.
Sol'o·mon (sŏl'ō·mŭn). [Heb.] Peaceable.
Stan'ley (stăn'lĭ). From a surname.
Ste'phen, Ste'ven (stē'vĕn). [Gr.] Crown. — Dim. *Steve, Ste'vie; Steen'ie* (stēn'ĭ) (*Chiefly Scot.*).
Stew'art, Stu'art (stū'ĕrt). From a surname.
Sum'ner (sŭm'nĕr). From a surname.
Syd'ney (sĭd'nĭ). = SIDNEY.
Syl·va'nus (sĭl·vā'nŭs). = SILVANUS.
Syl·ves'ter (sĭl·vĕs'tĕr). = SILVESTER.

T

Tad (tăd). Dim. of THEODORE.
Ted (tĕd), **Ted'dy.** Dims. of EDWARD, THEODORE.
Ter'ence (tĕr'ĕns). [L.] — Dim. *Ter'ry.*
Thad'de·us (thăd'ē·ŭs). [Gr.] — Dim. *Thad, Thad'dy, Tha'dy.*
The'o·bald (thē'ō·bȏld; *now rarely* tĭb'ȏld). [Teut.] Bold for the people.
The'o·dore (thē'ō·dōr). [Gr.] Gift of God. — Dim. *Tad, Dode* (dōd), *Ted, Ted'dy.*
The·od'o·ric (thē·ŏd'ō·rĭk). [Teut.] Ruler of the people.
The·oph'i·lus (thē·ŏf'ĭ·lŭs). [Gr.] Dear to the gods or to God.
Thom'as (tŏm'ăs). [Heb.] A twin. — Dim. *Tom, Tom'my.*
Thurs'ton (thûrs'tŭn). [Scand.] Thor's stone.
Tim'o·thy (tĭm'ō·thĭ). [Gr.] Honoring God. — Dim. *Tim.*
Ti'tus (tī'tŭs). [Gr.]
To·bi'ah (tō·bī'ȧ), **To·bi'as** (tō·bī'ăs). [Heb.] The Lord is (my) good. — Dim. *To'by* (tō'bĭ).
Tod, Todd (tŏd).
Tom (tŏm), **Tom'my.** Dims. of THOMAS.

To'ny (tō'nĭ). Dim. of ANTHONY.
Tris'tan (trĭs'tăn), **Tris'tram** (trĭs'trăm).

U

U·lys'ses (ū·lĭs'ēz). [Gr.] A hater.
Ur'ban (ûr'băn). [L.] Of the city; courteous. F. Urbain (ür'băn').
U·ri'ah (ū·rī'ȧ). [Heb.] Flame of Jehovah, *or* my light is Jehovah

V

Val'en·tine (văl'ĕn·tīn). [L.] Strong; healthy; powerful.
Van (văn). From a surname.
Ver'gil, Vir'gil (vûr'jĭl). [L.]
Ver'non (vûr'nŭn).
Vic'tor (vĭk'tĕr). [L.] A conqueror.
Vin'cent (vĭn'sĕnt). [L.] Conquering.
Viv'i·an (vĭv'ĭ·ăn; vĭv'yăn). [F.] F. Vivien (vē'vyăN'). Full of life.

W

Wal'do (wŏl'dō; wŏl'-). [Teut.]
Wal'lace (wŏl'ĭs). From a surname.
Wal'ter (wŏl'tĕr). [Teut.] Ruling the host. — Dim. *Walt, Wat* (wŏt).
War'ren (wŏr'ĕn; -ĭn). From a surname.
Wes'ley (wĕs'lĭ; *esp. Brit.*, wĕz'-). From a surname.
Wil'bur, Wil'ber (wĭl'bĕr). [Teut.]
Wil'fred (wĭl'frĕd; -frĭd), **Wil'frid** (-frĭd). [Teut.] Prob., desire for peace. — Dim. *Fred.*
Will (wĭl), **Wil'lie, Wil'ly.** Dims. of WILLIAM.
Wil'lard (wĭl'ĕrd). From a surname.
Wil'liam (wĭl'yăm). [Teut.] Resolute helmet, *or* helmet of resolution. G. Wilhelm (vĭl'hĕlm). — Dim. *Bill, Bil'ly, Will, Wil'lie, Wil'ly.*
Wil'lis (wĭl'ĭs). From a surname.
Win'fred (wĭn'frĕd; -frĭd). [AS.] Win peace. — Dim. *Win.*
Win'ston (wĭn'stŭn). [OE.]

Z

Zach'a·ri'ah (zăk'ȧ·rī'ȧ), **Zach'a·ri'as** (-rī'ăs), **Zach'a·ry** (zăk'ȧ·rĭ). [Heb.] Jehovah hath remembered. — Dim. *Zach* (zăk).
Zeb'e·dee (zĕb'ē·dē). [Heb.]
Zech'a·ri'ah (zĕk'ȧ·rī'ȧ). [Heb.] = ZACHARIAH.
Zeke (zēk). Dim. of EZEKIEL.

II. NAMES OF WOMEN

A

Ab'i·gail (ăb'ĭ·gāl). [Heb.] My father is joy. — Dim. *Ab'by, Nab'by.*
A'da, A'dah (ā'dȧ). [Heb.]
Ad'a·line (ăd'ȧ·līn). = ADELINE.
Ad'die (ăd'ĭ), **Ad'dy.** Dims. of ADA, ADELA, ADELAIDE, ADELINA, ADELINE.
Ad'e·la (ăd'ē·lȧ). Also **A·dele'** (ȧ·dĕl'). F. Adèle (à·dĕl').
Ad'e·laide (ăd'ē·lād). [Teut.] Of noble rank.
Ad'e·li'na (ăd'ē·lī'nȧ), **Ad'e·line** (ăd'ē·lĭn; -lēn; -līn). [Teut.] Of noble birth. — Dim. *Ad'die, Ad'dy.*
A'dri·enne (ā'drĭ·ĕn; F. à'drē'ĕn'). [F.] Fem. of ADRIAN.
Ag'a·tha (ăg'ȧ·thȧ). [Gr.] Good; kind. — Dim. *Ag'gie.*
Ag'nes (ăg'nĕs; -nĭs). [Gr.] Chaste; pure. — Dim. *Ag'gie.*
Ai·leen' (ī·lēn'; ī'lēn; ā·lēn'; ā'lēn). Var. of EILEEN.
Al·ber'ta (ăl·bûr'tȧ), **Al'ber·ti'na** (ăl'bĕr·tē'nȧ), **Al'ber·tine** (ăl'bĕr·tēn). Fem. of ALBERT.
Al·bi'na (ăl·bī'nȧ; -bē'nȧ). Fem. of ALBIN.

Al'e·the'a (ăl'ē·thē'ȧ; ȧ·lē'thē·ȧ). [Gr.] Truth.
Al'ex·an'dra (ăl'ĕg·zăn'drȧ; ăl'ĭg-; *Brit. also* -zän'-), **Al'ex·an·dri'na** (ăl'ĕg·zăn·drē'na; ăl'ĭg-; *Brit. also* -zän-). [Gr.] Fem. of ALEXANDER.
Al·fre'da (ăl·frē'dȧ). Fem. of ALFRED.
Al'ice (ăl'ĭs), **A·li'ci·a** (ȧ·lĭsh'ĭ·ȧ; -lĭsh'ȧ). [Gr.] Truth. — Dim. *Al'lie or Al'ly.*
A·line' (ȧ·lēn'; ăl'ēn). [L.] Contr. of ADELINE.
Al'i·son (ăl'ĭ·s'n).
Al'ix (ăl'ĭks). = ALICE.
Al'ma (ăl'mȧ). [L.] Nourishing; cherishing.
Al·mi'ra (ăl·mī'rȧ).
Al·phon'sine (ăl·fŏn'sēn; -zēn). [F.] Fem. of ALPHONSO.
Al·the'a (ăl·thē'ȧ). [Gr.] A healer.
Al·vi'na (ăl·vī'nȧ; -vĭ'-). Fem. of ALVIN.
Am'a·bel (ăm'ȧ·bĕl). [L.] Lovable. — Dim. *Mab* (măb).
A·man'da (ȧ·măn'dȧ). [L.] Worthy to be loved. — Dim. *Man'dy.*
A·me'lia (ȧ·mēl'yȧ; ȧ·mēl'ĭ·ȧ). [Teut.] Industrious. F. Amélie (à'mā'lē'). — Dim. *Mil'lie.*

A'my (ā'mĭ). [L.] Beloved.
An'as·ta'si·a (ăn'ăs·tā'shĭ·ȧ; -shȧ; -zhĭ·ȧ; -zhȧ). [LL.] Of the Resurrection.
An'dre·a (ăn'drē·ȧ; *It.* än·drā'ä). [It.] Fem. of ANDREW.
An'ge·la (ăn'jē·lȧ), **An'ge·li'na** (ăn'jē·lē'nȧ; -lī'nȧ). = ANGELICA.
An·gel'i·ca (ăn·jĕl'ĭ·kȧ). [Gr.] Lovely; angelic. F. Angélique (äN'zhā'lēk').
A·ni'ta (ȧ·nē'tȧ; *Sp.* ä·nē'tä). Dim. of *Ana,* Spanish form of ANNA.
Ann, Anne (ăn), **An'na** (ăn'ȧ). [Heb.] Grace. = HANNAH. — Dim. *An'nie, Nan, Nan'cy, Nan'ny, Ni'na* (nī'nȧ; nē'nȧ).
An·na·bel, An'na·belle (ăn'ȧ·bĕl).
An·nette' (ȧ·nĕt'; ă-; F. à'nĕt'). [F.] Orig., dim. of ANNE.
An'toi·nette' (ăn't[w]ȯ·nĕt'; F. äN'twà'nĕt'). [F.] Dim. of ANTONIA. — Dim. *Net'tie, Net'ty.*
An·to'ni·a (ăn·tō'nĭ·ȧ; -tōn'yȧ). [L.] Fem. of *Antonius,* Latin form of ANTONY. It. & Sp. Antonina (än'tō·nē'nä).
A'pril (ā'prĭl). From the name of the month.
Ar'a·bel'la (ăr'ȧ·bĕl'ȧ), **Ar'a·bel** (ăr'ȧ·bĕl). [Origin uncertain.] F. Arabelle (à'rà'bĕl'; *Angl.* ăr'ȧ·bĕl). — Dim. *Bell, Bel'la, Belle.*

Ar·line' (är·lēn'; 2).

As·pa'sia (ăs·pā'zhà; -zhǐ·à). [L., fr. Gr.] Welcome.

As'trid (ăs'trĭd; *Dan.* às'trēth; *Swed.* às'trĭd). [Scand.]

A·the'na (à·thē'nà). [Gr.]

Au'drey (ô'drĭ).

Au·gus'ta (ô·gŭs'tà). [L.] Fem. of AUGUSTUS. — Dim. *Gus'sie* (gŭs'ĭ), *Gus'ta* (gŭs'tà).

Au·re'lia (ô·rēl'yà; ô·rē'lĭ·à). [L.] Golden. F. Aurélie (ō'rā'lē').

A'vis (ā'vĭs). [L.] Bird.

B

Bab (băb), Babs (băbz). Dims. of BARBARA.

Ba·bette' (bă·bĕt'; *F.* bá'bĕt'). Orig., French dim. of ELIZABETH.

Bap·tis'ta (băp·tĭs'tà). [Gr.] Fem. of BAPTIST.

Bar'ba·ra (bär'bà·rà; -brà). [Gr.] Foreign; strange. — Dim. *Bab, Babs* (băbz), *Bab'bie.*

Be·a'ta (bē·ā'tà). [L.] Blessed.

Be·a'trice (bē'à·trĭs). Also Be'a·trix (bē'à·trĭks). [L.] She that makes happy. F. Beatrix (bē·ā'trĭks). — Dim. *Bea* (bē), *Bee, Trix'ie* (trĭk'sĭ), *Trix'y.*

Beck'y (bĕk'ĭ). Dim. of REBECCA.

Be·lin'da (bē·lĭn'dà).

Bel'la (bĕl'à), Bell. Dims. of ARABELLA, ISABELLA, etc.

Belle (bĕl). [F.] Beautiful. See also ARABELLA, ISABEL.

Ben·e·dic'ta (bĕn'ē·dĭk'tà). [L.] Fem. of BENEDICT.

Ber'e·ni'ce (bĕr'ē·nī'sē), Ber·nice' (bĕr·nēs'; bûr-; bûr'nĭs). [Gr.]

Ber'na·dette' (bûr'nà·dĕt'; *F.* bĕr'nà'dĕt'). Ber'na·dine (bûr'nẽr·dē'nà; -när-), Ber'nar·dine (bûr'nẽr·dēn). [Teut.] Fem. of BERNARD.

Ber'tha (bûr'thà). [Teut.] Bright. F. Berthe (bĕrt). — Dim. *Ber'tie* (bûr'tĭ), *Ber'ty.*

Ber'yl (bĕr'ĭl). [Gr., fr. Skr.]

Bess (bĕs), Bes'sie (bĕs'ĭ), Beth (bĕth), Bet's(e)y (bĕt'sĭ), Bet'te (bĕt'ĕ), Bet·ti'na (bĕ·tē'nà), Bet'ty (bĕt'ĭ). Dims. of ELIZABETH.

Beu'lah (bū'là). [Heb.] Married.

Bid'dy (bĭd'ĭ). Dim. of BRIDGET.

Blanch, Blanche (blănch). [Teut.] White. It. Bianca (byäng'kä).

Bob'bie, Bob'by (bŏb'ĭ). Dim. of ROBERTA.

Bon'ny (bŏn'ĭ), Bon'nie. [ME.] Good.

Bren'da (brĕn'dà). [Scand.]

Bridg'et (brĭj'ĕt; -ĭt), Brig'id (brĭj'ĭd; brē'ĭd). [Ir.] Lofty; august. G. Brigitte (brē·gĭt'ĕ). — Dim. *Bid'dy, Bri'die* (brī'dĭ).

C

Ca·mil'la (kà·mĭl'à). [L.] A freeborn girl, esp. one attendant at a sacrifice. F. Camille (kà'mē'y'; *Angl.* kà·mēl').

Can·da'ce (kăn·dā'sē; kăn'dà·sē). [Gr.]

Can'di·da (kăn'dĭ·dà). [L.] Shining white.

Car'la (kär'là). [It.]

Car·lot'ta (kär·lŏt'à; *It.* kär·lôt'tä). Italian form of CHARLOTTE.

Car'mel (kär'mĕl). [Heb.]

Car·mel'a (kär·mĕl'à).

Car'men (kär'mĕn). [Sp., fr. Latin.] Song.

Car'ol (kär'ŭl). [ML.]

Car'o·line (kär'ô·lĭn; -lĭn), Car'o·lyn (-lĭn). Fem. of CHARLES. It. & Sp. Carolina (kä'rō·lī'nä; *Angl.* kăr'ō·lī'nà; -lē'nà). — Dim. *Car'rie.*

Cas·san'dra (kă·săn'drà). [Gr.] — Dim. *Cass, Cas'sie.*

Cath'er·ine (kăth'ẽr·ĭn; kăth'rĭn), Cath'a·ri'na (kăth'à·rē'nà). [Gr.] G. Katharine (kä'tä·rē'nĕ), Katrina (kä·trē'nä; *Angl.* kà·trē'nà). — Dim. *Cath'y* or *Kath'y, Kate* (kāt), *Kat'rine* (kăt'rĭn; -rēn; kà·trēn'), *Kay* (kā), *Kit* (kĭt), *Kit'ty.*

Cath'leen (kăth'lēn; kăth·lēn'). Var. of KATHLEEN.

Ce·cile' (sē·sēl'). Var. of CECILIA.

Ce·cil'ia (sē·sĭl'yà; -sĭl'ĭ·à; sĕ·sēl'-), Cec'i·ly (sĕs'ĭ·lĭ). [L.] Fem. of CECIL. F. Cécile (sā'sēl'). — Dim. *Cis* (sĭs), *Cis'sy, Sis.*

Ce·leste' (sē·lĕst'). [F.] Heavenly. F. Céleste (sā'lĕst').

Ce·les'tine (sē·lĕs'tĭn; sĕl'ĕs·tĭn, -tēn). Heavenly.

Ce'lia (sē'lĭ·à). [L.]

Cha·ris'sa (kà·rĭs'à). [Gr.] Grace.

Char'i·ty (chăr'ĭ·tĭ). [F., fr. L.] Dearness.

Char·lene' (shär·lēn'). 1. Fem. of CHARLES. 2. Var. of CAROLINE.

Char'lotte (shär'lŏt). Fem. of *Charlot,* French dim. of CHARLES. It. Carlotta (kär·lŏt'tä; *Angl.* kär·lŏt'à). — Dim. *Lot'tie* (lŏt'ĭ), *Lot'ta.*

Cher'ry (chĕr'ĭ).

Cher'yl (chĕr'ĭl).

Chlo'ë, Chlo'e (klō'ē). [Gr.] Young verdure; herb.

Chris (krĭs). Short for CHRISTIANA, etc.

Chris'ta·bel (krĭs'tà·bĕl).

Chris'ti·an'a (krĭs'tĭ·ăn'à). [Gr.] Fem. of CHRISTIAN.

Chris·ti'na (krĭs·tē'nà), Chris·tine' (krĭs·tēn'; krĭs'tēn). [Gr.] — Dim. *Chris'sie* (krĭs'ĭ), *Chris'tie* (krĭs'tĭ), *Xi'na* (zē'nà).

Cic'e·ly (sĭs'ē·lĭ). = CECILIA.

Cin'dy (sĭn'dĭ). Dim. of LUCINDA.

Cis (sĭs), Cis'sy. Dims. of CECILIA, etc.

Ciar'a (klăr'à; klăr'à). [L.] Bright; illustrious. F. Claire (klâr).

Clare (klâr). = CLARA.

Clar'i·bel (klăr'ĭ·bĕl). [L.] Brightly fair.

Clar'ice (klăr'ĭs; *F.* klà'rēs'), Cla·ris'sa (klà·rĭs'à). [L.] Deriv. of CLARA.

Cla·rin'da (klà·rĭn'dà).

Clau·dette' (klô·dĕt'; *F.* klō'dĕt'). [F.] Fem. of CLAUDE.

Clau'di·a (klô'dĭ·à). [L.] Fem. of *Claudius,* Latin form of CLAUDE.

Clau·dine' (klô·dēn'; *F.* klō'dēn'). = CLAUDIA.

Clem'ence (klĕm'ĕns), Clem'en·ti'na (klĕm'ĕn·tē'nà), Clem'en·tine (klĕm'ĕn·tēn; -tĭn). [L.] Fem. of CLEMENT.

Cle'o (klē'ō). Orig., dim. of CLEOPATRA.

Cle'o·pat'ra (klē'ō·păt'rà; -pā'trà; -pä'trà). [Gr.]

Clo·thil'da (klō·tĭl'dà), Clo·til'da (klō·tĭl'dà). [Teut.] F. Clothilde (klō'tēld').

Co·lette' (kô·lĕt'; *F.* kô'lĕt'). [F.] Fem. dim. of NICHOLAS.

Col'leen (kŏl'ēn; kŏ·lēn'). [Ir.] Girl.

Con'stance (kŏn'stăns). [L.] Firmness; constancy. — Dim. *Con'nie.*

Con·suel'o (kôn·swĕl'ō; *Sp.* kôn·swä'lō). [Sp.] Consolation.

Co'ra (kō'rà). [Gr.] Maiden.

Cor·de'lia (kôr·dēl'yà; -dē'lĭ·à). [L.]

Co·rin'na (kô·rĭn'à). [Gr.] Maiden. F. Corinne (kô'rēn'; *Angl.* kô·rĭn', -rēn').

Cor·ne'lia (kôr·nēl'yà; -nē'lĭ·à). [L.] Fem. of CORNELIUS.

Crys'tal (krĭs'tăl; -t'l). [ME.]

Cyn'thi·a (sĭn'thĭ·à). [Gr.]

D

Dag'mar (dăg'mär). [Dan.]

Dai'sy (dā'zĭ). Sometimes, dim. of CANDACE, MARGARET, etc.

Dale (dāl). [AS.]

Daph'ne (dăf'nē). [Gr.] Laurel.

Dawn (dôn). [Prob. Scand.]

Deb'o·rah (dĕb'ō·rà). [Heb.] A bee. — Dim. *Deb, Deb'by.*

Deir'dre (dēr'drĕ; -drä; dâr'-). From a heroine of old Irish legend.

De'lia (dēl'yà; dē'lĭ·à; 58). [Gr.] Of Delos.

Del'la (dĕl'à). Orig., a dim. of ADELA, ADELINA, etc.

Del·phine' (dĕl·fēn'). [F.]

De·nise' (dĕ·nēz'). [F.] Fem. of DENIS.

Di·an'a (dĭ·ăn'à). [L.] Goddess. F. Diane (dyàn; *Angl.* dĭ·ăn'). — Dim. *Di* (dī).

Di'nah (dī'nà). [Heb.] Judged.

Dol(l) (dŏl), Dol'ly. Dims. of DOROTHEA, DOROTHY.

Do·lo'res (dô·lō'rĕs; -rĭs). [Sp.] Sorrows.

Don'na (dŏn'à). [It.] Lady.

Do'ra (dō'rà). [L.] Orig., dim. of DOROTHY, EUDORA, THEODORA.

Dor'cas (dôr'kăs). [Gr.] A gazelle.

Do·reen' (dô·rēn'; dō'rēn). Prob., Irish dim. of DORA.

Dor'is (dŏr'ĭs; dō'rĭs). [Gr.]

Dor'o·the·a (dŏr'ô·thē'à), Dor'o·thy (dôr'ō·thĭ). [Gr.] Gift of God. — Dim. *Dol(l), Dol'ly, Dot, Dot'ty.*

Dru·sil'la (droo·sĭl'à). [L.]

Dul'ce (dŭl'sē), Dul'cie (-sĭ). Charming; dear.

E

E'dith (ē'dĭth). [AS.] L. Editha (ĕd'ĭ·thà; ē'dĭ·thà). — Dim. *E'die* (ē'dĭ).

Ed'na (ĕd'nà). [Heb.] Rejuvenation.

Ed·wi'na (ĕd·wē'nà; -wĭn'à). Fem. of EDWIN.

Ef'fie (ĕf'ĭ). Dim. of EUPHEMIA.

Ei·leen' (ī·lēn'; ī'lēn; ā·lēn'; ā'lēn). [Ir.] = HELEN.

E·laine' (ē·lān'). [OF., fr. Gr.] = HELEN.

El'ea·nor (ĕl'à·nẽr; -nôr), El'i·nor (ĕl'ĭ·nẽr; -nôr), El'ea·no'ra (ĕl'ē·nō'rà; ĕl'ē·à-). [F.] F. Eléonore (ā'lā'ō'nôr'); It. Eleonora (â·lā·ō·nō'rä; *Angl.* ĕl'ē·ō·nō'rä); G. Eleonore (ā'lā·ō·nō'rĕ). — Dim. *El'la, El'lie, Nell, Nel'lie, Nel'ly, No'ra.*

El'e·na (ĕl'ē·nà; ĕ·lē'nà). Var. of HELENA.

É·lise' (ā'lēz'). French form of ELIZABETH, etc.

E·liz'a·beth (ē·lĭz'à·bĕth), E·lis'a·beth (ē·lĭz'à·bĕth), E·li'za (ē·lī'zà). [Heb.] Consecrated to God. F. Élise (ā'lēz'); It. Elisa (â·lē'zä). — Dim. *Bess, Bes'sie, Beth, Bet's(e)y, Bet'te, Bet'ty, Lib'by, Li'sa, Liz'zie, Liz'zy.*

El'la (ĕl'à), El'lie. Dims. of ELEANOR, etc.

El'len (ĕl'ĕn; -ĭn). = HELEN.

El·o·ise' (ĕl'ō·ēz'; ĕl'ō·ēz). Var. of HELOISE.

El'sa (ĕl'sà; *G.* -zä). [G.]

El'sie (ĕl'sĭ). Orig., dim. of ALICE, ELIZABETH, ELSA.

El'speth (ĕl'spĕth; -spĕth). Scot. var. of ELIZABETH.

El'va (ĕl'và). [?Teut.] Elf.

El·vi'ra (ĕl·vī'rà; -vēr'à). [Sp.]

Em'e·line, Em'me·line (ĕm'ē·lĭn; -lēn). Deriv. of EMILY.

Em'i·ly (ĕm'ĭ·lĭ), Em'i·lie. [F.] F. Émilie (ā'mē'lē'); It. & Sp. Emilia (â·mē'lyä).

Em'ma (ĕm'à). [G.] — Dim. *Em(m), Em'mie.*

E'nid (ē'nĭd). [Celtic.]

Er'i·ca (ĕr'ĭ·kà). [Scand.] Fem. of ERIC.

Er'ma (ûr'mà). [Teut.] Dim. of ERMENGARDE, ERMINIA.

Er'men·garde (ûr'mĕn·gärd). [Teut.]

Er·min'i·a (ûr·mĭn'ĭ·à; -mĭn'yà), Er·mi'na (ûr·mē'nà), Er'mi·nie (ûr'mĭ·nĭ). [It.]

Er'nes·tine (ûr'nĕs·tēn; ûr'nĭs-). Fem. of ERNEST.

Es'sie (ĕs'ĭ). Dim. of ESTHER.

Es·tel'la (ĕs·tĕl'à), Es·telle' (ĕs·tĕl'; ĕs'tĕl; *F.* ĕs'tĕl'). [L.] = STELLA.

Es'ther (ĕs'tẽr). [Heb.] — Dim. *Es'sie, Het'ty.*

Eth'el (ĕth'ĕl). [AS.] Noble.

Eth'e·lind (ĕth'ĕ·lĭnd), Eth'e·lin'da (-lĭn'dà). [Teut.]

Et'ta (ĕt'à), Et'tie (ĕt'ĭ). Orig., dims. of HENRIETTA, HARRIET.

Eu·do'ra (û·dō'rà). [Gr.] Generous.

Eu·ge'ni·a (û·jē'nĭ·à; -jēn'yà). Fem. of EUGENE. F. Eugénie (û'zhā'nē'; ü'zhā'nē'). — Dim. *Ge'nie* (jē'nĭ), *Gene* (jēn).

Eu·la'li·a (û·lā'lĭ·à; -lāl'yà). [Gr.] Fair speech. F. Eulalie (û'là'lē'; ü'là'lē'; *Angl.* ū'là·lē).

Eu'nice (ū'nĭs; *L.* û·nī'sē). [L., fr. Gr.] Happy victory.

Eu·phe'mi·a (û·fē'mĭ·à). [Gr.] Of good report. F. Euphémie (ū'fā'mē'; ü'fā'mē'). — Dim. *Ef'fie, Phe'mie.*

E'va (ē'và). [Heb.] = EVE.

E·vad'ne (ē·văd'nē). [Gr.] Fortunate.

E·van'ge·line (ē·văn'jē·lĭn; -lĭn; -lēn). [Gr.] Bringing good news.

Eve (ēv). [Heb.] Life; living.

Eve·li'na (ĕv·ē·lī'nà; -lē'nà), Ev'e·line (ĕv'ē·lĭn; ĕv'lĭn; ĕv'ē·lēn; ē'vē·lēn'). Orig., dims. of EVA.

Ev'e·lyn (ĕv'ē·lĭn; ēv'lĭn; ēv'ē·lĭn; ē'vē·lĭn). Probably, youth.

F

Faith (fāth). [L.] — Dim. *Fay.*

Fan'nie, Fan'ny (făn'ĭ). Sometimes, dims. of FRANCES.

Faus·ti'na (fôs·tī'nà; -tē'nà). [L.] Lucky. F. Faustine (fōs'tēn'; *Angl.* fôs·tēn').

Fay (fā). Sometimes, dim. of FAITH.

Fe·li'ci·a (fē·lĭsh'ĭ·à; fē·lĭsh'à; -lē'shà), Fe·lice' (fē·lēs'). [L.] Happiness.

Fi·de'li·a (fī·dēl'ĭ·à; fī·dēl'yà; fī-). [L.] Faithful.

Fi·o'na (fī·ō'nà; fī-). [Celt.] Probably, white.

Fla'vi·a (flā'vĭ·à). [L.] Yellow; blonde.

Flo (flō). Dim. of FLORENCE.

Flo'ra (flō'rà). [L.] Flowers.

Flor'ence (flŏr'ĕns). [L.] Bloom; prosperity. — Dim. *Flo* (flō), *Flor'rie* (flŏr'ĭ), *Flos'sie* (flŏs'ĭ).

Fran'ces (frăn'sĕs; -sĭs). Fem. of FRANCIS. F. Francesca (frän·chĕs'kä). — Dim. *Fan'nie, Fan'ny, Fran'cie, Frank.*

Fran·cine', Fran·cene' (frän·sēn'; 2).

Fred'er·i'ca (frĕd'ēr·ē'kà; frĕd·rē'kà). Fem. of FREDERIC. — Dim. *Fred'die.*
Frie'da, Fre'da (frē'dà). [G.] Peace.

G

Ga'bri·el'la (gā'brĭ·ĕl'à), **Ga'bri·elle'** (gā'-brĭ·ĕl'; găb'rĭ-; 2). Fem. of GABRIEL.
Gail (gāl). Short for ABIGAIL.
Gene (jēn), **Ge'nie** (jē'nĭ). Dims. of EUGENIA.
Gen'e·vieve' (jĕn'ĕ·vēv'; jĕn'ĕ·vēv). [Prob. Celtic.]
Geor'gia (jôr'jà; -jyà; -jĭ·à). Fem. of GEORGE.
Geor'gi·an·a (jôr'jĭ·ăn'à; -ä'nà), **Geor·gi'na** (jôr·jē'nà). Fem. of GEORGE.
Ger'al·dine (jĕr'ál·dēn). Fem. of GERALD. — Dim. *Ger'ry, Jer'ry* (jĕr'ĭ).
Ger·maine' (jûr·mān'; jĕr·-). [Fr., ír. L.] German.
Ger'trude (gûr'trōōd). [Teut.] Spear maiden. — Dim. *Ger'tie* (gûr'tĭ), *Tru'dy* (trōō'dĭ).
Gil'da (gĭl'dà). [Celtic.]
Gi·nev'ra (jĭ·nĕv'rà), **Ge·nev'ra** (jĕ-). [It.] = GUINEVERE.
Glad'ys (glăd'ĭs). [L.]
Glen'na (glĕn'à). Fem. of GLENN.
Glo'ri·a (glō'rĭ·à; 70). [L.] Glory.
Grace (grās), **Gra'ci·a, Gra'ti·a** (grā'shĭ·à; -shà). [L.] Favor; grace.
Gre'ta (grē'tà; grĕt'à). Dim. of MARGARET.
Gretch'en (grĕch'ĕn; -ĭn; *G.* grāt'ken), **Gre'tel, Gre'thel** (grā'tĕl; *Angl.* grĕt''l). Dim. of *Margarete*, German form of MARGARET.
Gri·sel'da (grĭ·zĕl'dà). [Teut.] — Dim. *Gris'sel* (grĭs''l).
Guin'e·vere (gwĭn'ē·vēr). Also **Guen'e·ver** (gwĕn'ē·vēr), **Guin'e·ver** (gwĭn'-). [Celtic.]
Gus'sie (gŭs'ĭ). Dim. of AUGUSTA.
Gwen'do·len (gwĕn'dō·lĕn; -lĭn), **Gwen'do·line** (-lĭn; -lēn). **Gwen'do·lyn** (-lĭn). [Celtic.] — Dim. *Gwen.*

H

Han'nah (hăn'à). [Heb.] = ANN.
Har'ri·et, Har'ri·ot (hăr'ĭ·ŭt). Fem. of HARRY. — Dim. *Hat'ty.*
Ha'zel (hā'z'l). [AS.]
Heath'er (hĕth'ēr). [ME.] From a plant name.
Hed'da (hĕd'à). [G.] War.
Hed'wig (hĕd'wĭg). [G.] Strife.
Hel'en (hĕl'ĕn; -ĭn), **Hel'e·na** (hĕl'ē·nà; hĕ·lē'nà). [Gr.] F. Hélène (ā'lĕn') It. Elena (â'lā·nä). — Dim. *Nell, Nel'lie, Nel'ly.*
Hel'ga (hĕl'gà). [Teut.] Holy.
Hel'o·ise' (hĕl'ō·ēz'; hĕl'ō·ēz). [F.] F. Héloïse (ā'lō'ēz').
Hen'ri·et'ta (hĕn'rĭ·ĕt'à). Fem. of HENRY. F. Henriette (än'ryĕt'). — Dim. *Et'ta, Het'ty, Net'tie, Ret'ta.*
Heph'zi·bah (hĕf'zĭ·bà; hĕf'sĭ-; hĕp'sĭ-). [Heb.] My delight in her.
Her·mi'o·ne (hûr·mī'ō·nē). [Gr.]
Hes'ter (hĕs'tēr). = ESTHER. — Dim. *Het'ty.*
Het'ty (hĕt'ĭ). Dim. of ESTHER, HENRIETTA, HESTER.
Hil'a·ry (hĭl'à·rĭ). [L.] Cheerful; merry.
Hil'da (hĭl'dà). [AS.] Battle maid.
Hil'de·garde (hĭl'dĕ·gärd). [Teut.] Battle maiden.
Ho·no'ra (hō·nō'rà), **Ho·no'ri·a** (hō·nō'rĭ·à). [L.] Honorable. — Dim. *No'rah, No'ra.*
Hope (hōp). [Teut.]
Hor·ten'si·a (hôr·tĕn'sĭ·à; -shĭ·à; -shà). [L.] Also **Hor·tense'** (hôr·tĕns'; hôr'tĕns; *F.* ôr'täns'). [F.] A lady gardener.
Hul'da (hŭl'dà). [Scand.]
Hul'dah (hŭl'dà). [Heb.] A weasel.
Hy'a·cinth (hī'à·sĭnth). [Gr.]

I

I'da (ī'dà). [Teut.]
Il'se (ĭl'sĕ; *G.* ĭl'zĕ). Ger. dim. of ELIZABETH.
Im'o·gen (ĭm'ō·jĕn; -jĕn), **Im'o·gene** (-jēn).
I'na (ī'nà).
I'nez (ī'nĕz; ē'nĕz; -nĭz; ĭ·nĕz'; *Sp.* ē·nāth', -näs'). [Sp. & Pg.] = AGNES.
I·one' (ī·ōn'; ī·ō'nē). [Gr.]
I·rene' (ī·rēn'; 2; *esp. Brit.,* and *Lat.,* ī·rē'nē). [Gr.] Peace.
I'ris (ī'rĭs). [Gr.] Rainbow.
Ir'ma (ûr'mà). = ERMA.
Is'a·bel (ĭz'à·bĕl), **Is'a·bel'la** (-bĕl'à), **Is'o-**

bel (ĭz'ō·bĕl). F. Isabelle (ē'zà'bĕl'). — Dim. *Bell, Bel'la, Belle.*
Is'a·do'ra (ĭz'à·dō'rà; 70). [Gr.] Gift of Isis.
I·solde' (ĭ·sōld'). [OF.]
I'vy (ī'vĭ). [AS.]

J

Jac'que·line, Jaq'ue·line (jăk'wĕ·lĭn; -lēn). Fem. of *Jacques,* French form of JACOB.
Jane (jān). [F.] = JOAN.
Ja·net' (jà·nĕt'; jăn'ĕt, -ĭt). Orig., dim. of JANE.
Jan'ice (jăn'ĭs).
Jean (jēn). Also **Jeanne** (jēn; *F.* zhän). [F.] = JANE. See JOAN.
Jean·nette' (jĕ·nĕt'). [F.] Orig., dim. of JEANNE.
Je·mi'ma (jē·mī'mà). [Heb.] A dove.
Jen'ni·fer (jĕn'ĭ·fēr). Perh. a deriv. of GUINEVERE.
Jen'ny (jĕn'ĭ). Familiar form of JANE.
Jer'ry (jĕr'ĭ). Dim. of GERALDINE.
Jes'sa·mine (jĕs'à·mĭn). [F.]
Jes'si·ca (jĕs'ĭ·kà).
Jes'sie (jĕs'ĭ). [Scot.] — Dim. *Jess.*
Jew'el (jōō'ĕl; jū'-; -ĭl). [ME.]
Jill (jĭl).
Jo (jō). Dim. of JOSEPHINE.
Joan (jōn; jō'ăn; jō·ăn'), **Jo·an'na** (jō·ăn'à), **Jo·han'na** (-hăn'à). [Heb.] Fem. of JOHN. F. Jeanne (zhän); It. Giovanna (jō·vän'nä).
Joc'e·lin, Joc'e·lyn, Joc'e·line (jŏs'ē·lĭn; jŏs'lĭn). [L.]
Jo·se'pha (jō·sē'fà). = JOSEPHINE.
Jo'se·phine (jō'zĕ·fēn; jō'zĕ·fĕn'). Fem. of JOSEPH. — Dim. *Jo, Jo'sie, Jo'zy, Phe'ny.*
Joy (joi).
Joyce (jois).
Jua·ni'ta (wä·nē'tà; *Sp.* hwä·nē'tä). [Sp.]
Ju'dith (jōō'dĭth). [Heb.] Praised. — Dim. *Ju'dy.*
Jul'ia (jōōl'yà; 58). [L.] Fem. of JULIUS. F. Julie (zhü'lē'; *Angl.* jōō'lĭ).
Ju'li·an·a (jōō'lĭ·ăn'à; -ä'nà). [L.] Fem. of JULIAN. F. Julienne (zhü'lyĕn').
Ju'lie (jōō'lĭ; *F.* zhü'lē'). See JULIA.
Ju'li·et (jōō'lĭ·ĕt; -ĕt; jōō'lĭ·ĕt'; *or, esp. Brit.,* jōōl'yĕt). Orig., dim. of JULIA.
June (jōōn; 114). [L.] Perhaps, fem. of JUNIUS, or from the name of the month.
Jus·ti'na (jŭs·tī'nà; -tē'nà). [L.] Fem. of JUSTIN. F. Justine (zhüs·tēn'; *Angl.* jŭs·tēn'; 2).

K

Kar'en (kär'ĕn; kä'rĕn). Danish and Norwegian form of CATHERINE.
Kate (kāt). Dim. of CATHERINE.
Kath'a·rine (kăth'à·rĭn), **Kath'a·ri'na** (-rē'nà), **Kath'er·ine** (kăth'ēr·ĭn; kăth'rĭn), **Kath'ryn** (kăth'rĭn). Vars. of CATHERINE.
Kath'leen (kăth'lēn; kăth·lēn'). Irish dim. of CATHERINE.
Ka·tri'na (kà·trē'nà). Var. of CATHERINE.
Kat'rine (kăt'rĭn; -rēn; kà·trēn'), **Kay** (kā). Dims. of CATHERINE.
Ke·zi'a, Ke·zi'ah (kē·zī'à). [Heb.] Cassia.
Kir'sten (kûr'stĕn; *Norw.* kĭsh't'n, kĭr'st'n). Scandinavian form of CHRISTINE.
Kit (kĭt), **Kit'ty** (kĭt'ĭ). Dims. of CATHERINE.

L

Lau'ra (lô'rà). [L.] Laurel.
Lau·ret'ta (lô·rĕt'à). Var. of LORETTA; dim. of LAURA.
Lau·rin'da (lô·rĭn'dà). [L.] Deriv. of LAURA.
La·verne' (là·vûrn').
La·vin'i·a (là·vĭn'ĭ·à). [L.]
Le'ah (lē'à). [Heb.]
Lei'la, Lei'lah (lē'là). [Ar.] Dark as night.
Le'li·a (lē'lĭ·à; lēl'yà). [L.]
Le'na (lē'nà). Orig., dim. of HELENA, MAGDALENE.
Le·no'ra (lē·nō'rà; 70), **Le·nore'** (lē·nōr'). Vars. of LEONORA.
Le·o'na (lē·ō'nà). Fem. of LEO, LEON. F. Léonie (lā'ō'nē').
Le·o·no'ra (lē'ō·nō'rà). = ELEANOR. G. Leonore (lā'ō·nō'rĕ; *Angl.* lē'ō·nōr), Lenore (lē-nō'rĕ). — Dim. *No'ra.*
Les'lie, Les'ley (lĕs'lĭ; *esp. Brit.,* lĕz'-). From a surname.
Le·ti'ti·a (lē·tĭsh'ĭ·à; -tĭsh'yà; -tĭsh'à). [L.] Happiness. — Dim. *Let'ty* (lĕt'ĭ).
Let'tice (lĕt'ĭs). Anglicized form of LETITIA.

Let'ty (lĕt'ĭ). Dim. of LETITIA.
Lib'by (lĭb'ĭ). Dim. of ELIZABETH.
Lil'i·an, Lil'li·an (lĭl'ĭ·ăn; lĭl'yăn), **Lil'y** (lĭl'ĭ). [L.] Lily.
Lin'da (lĭn'dà). Orig., short for BELINDA, etc.
Li'sa (lī'zà; lē'zà; *It.* lē'zä). Orig., dim. of ELIZABETH.
Li'se (lē'zĕ). [G.] Orig., dim. of ELIZABETH.
Li·sette', Li·zette' (lĭ·zĕt'). Orig., dims. of ELIZABETH.
Liz'zie, Liz'zy (lĭz'ĭ). Dims. of ELIZABETH.
Lo'is (lō'ĭs). [Gr.]
Lo'la (lō'là; *Sp.* lō'lä). [Sp.] Dim. of DOLORES.
Lo·li'ta (lō·lē'tà; *Sp.* lō·lē'tä). [Sp.] Dim. of LOLA.
Lo·ret'ta (lō·rĕt'à). — Dim. *Ret'ta.*
Lo·rin'da (lō·rĭn'dà). Var. of LAURINDA.
Lor'na (lôr'nà).
Lor·raine' (lŏ·rān'; lō-).
Lot'ta (lŏt'à), **Lot'tie** (lŏt'ĭ). Dims. of CARLOTTA, CHARLOTTE.
Lou·el'la (lōō·ĕl'à). Var. of LUELLA.
Lou·i'sa (lōō·ē'zà), **Lou·ise'** (lōō·ēz'). Fem. of LOUIS. G. Luise (lōō·ē'zĕ). — Dim. *Lou, Lou'ie, Lu, Lu'lu* (lōō'lōō).
Lu'cia (lū'shà; -shĭ·à). [L.] Fem. of LUCIUS. See LUCY.
Lu·cile', Lu·cille' (lū·sēl'). [F.]
Lu·cin'da (lū·sĭn'dà). [L.] = LUCY. — Dim. *Cin'dy* (sĭn'dĭ).
Lu·cre'ti·a (lū·krē'shĭ·à; -shà). [L.]
Lu'cy (lū'sĭ). [L.] F. Lucie (lü'sē') It. Lucia (lōō·chē'ä).
Lu·el'la (lū·ĕl'à), **Lou·el'la** (lōō-).
Lu'lu (lōō'lōō). Dim. of LOUISA, LOUISE.
Lyd'i·a (lĭd'ĭ·à). [Gr.] A native of Lydia.

M

Ma'bel (mā'bĕl). = AMABEL. — Dim. *Mab* (măb).
Mad'e·leine (măd''l·ĭn; -än; *F.* mà'dlĕn'). French form of MAGDALENE.
Mad'e·line (măd''l·ĭn; -ĭn). = MAGDALENE.
Madge (măj). Short for MARGARET.
Mae (mā). Var. of MAY.
Mag (măg), **Mag'gie** (măg'ĭ). Dims. of MARGARET.
Mag'da·lene (măg'dà·lēn; măg'dà·lē'nĕ). [Heb.] Belonging to Magdala. F. Magdelaine (măg'dĕ·lĕn'), Madeleine (mà'dlĕn'; *Angl.* măd''l·ĭn, -än), Madelon (mà'dlôn') It. Maddalena (mäd'dä·lā'nä); Sp. Magdalena (măg'thä·lā'nä). — Dim. *Le'na* (lē'nà).
Mai'sie (mā'zĭ). 1. Scot. dim. of MARGARET. 2. Dim of MARY.
Mal·vi'na (măl·vī'nà; -vē'nà).
Ma'mie (mā'mĭ). Dim. of MARGARET.
Man'dy (măn'dĭ). Dim. of AMANDA.
Mar·cel'la (mär·sĕl'à). [L.] Fem. of MARCELLUS. F. Marcelle (mär·sĕl').
Mar'cia (mär'shà). [L.] Fem. of Latin *Marcius.*
Mar'ga·ret (mär'gà·rĕt; -rĭt). [Gr.] A pearl. F. Marguerite (mär'gē·rēt'; *Angl.* mär'gĕ·rēt') It. Margherita (mär'gä·rē'tä); Sp. Margarita (mär'gä·rē'tä); G. Margarete (-rā'tĕ). — Dim. *Gre'ta* (grē'tà; grĕt'à), *Mag* (măg), *Mag'gie, Ma'mie, Mar'gie* (mär'jĭ), *Meg* (mĕg), *Me'ta* (mē'tà), *Peg* (pĕg), *Peg'gy.*
Mar'ger·y (mär'jēr·ĭ), **Mar'jo·rie, Mar'jo·ry** (-jō·rĭ). = MARGARET. — Dim. *Mar'gie* (mär'jĭ).
Mar'got (mär'gō; -gŭt; *F.* mår'gō'). [F.] Short for MARGARET.
Mar'gue·rite' (mär'gĕ·rēt'; *F.* mår'gĕ·rēt'). [F.] = MARGARET.
Ma·ri'a (mà·rī'à; -rē'à). See MARY.
Mar'i·an (mâr'ĭ·ăn; măr'-). = MARIANNE, MARION.
Mar'i·anne' (mâr'ĭ·ăn'), **Mar'i·an'na** (-ăn'à). [F.] A compound of Mary and Anne, Anna.
Ma·rie' (mà·rē'; *Brit.* also mä'rĭ, mâr'ĭ; mà'rē'). See MARY.
Mar'i·et'ta (mâr'ĭ·ĕt'à; măr'ĭ-). Orig., dim. of MARY, MARIA.
Mar'i·on (măr'ĭ·ăn; mâr'-). Var. of MARY.
Mar'jo·rie, Mar'jo·ry (mär'jō·rĭ). Vars. of MARGERY.
Mar'tha (mär'thà). [Aramaic.] Lady; mistress. F. Marthe (màrt) It. & Sp. Marta (mär'tä). — Dim. *Mar'ty, Mat'ty, Pat'ty.*
Mar'y (mâr'ĭ; 6). Also **Ma·ri'a** (mà·rī'à; -rē'à), **Ma·rie'** (mà·rē'; *Brit.* also mä'rĭ, mâr'ĭ). [Heb.] F. Marie (mà'rē') G. Maria (mä·rē'ä); Sp. María (mä·rē'ä). — Dim. *May, Moll, Mol'ly, Poll, Pol'ly.*

Ma·thil'da (mȧ·tĭl'dȧ), **Ma·til'da** (mȧ·tĭl'dȧ). [Teut.] Mighty battle maid; heroine. F. Mathilde (mä'tēld'). — Dim. *Mat'ty, Pat'ty, Til'da, Til'lie, Til'ly.*

Mat'ty (măt'ĭ). Dim. of MARTHA, MATHILDA.

Maud, Maude (môd). Orig., contraction of MAGDALENE.

Mau'ra (mô'rȧ), **Maur'ya** (môr'yȧ). Irish forms of MARY. — Dim. *Mau·reen'* (mô·rēn').

Ma'vis (mā'vĭs). [F., prob. fr. Celt.]

Max·ine' (măk·sēn'; măk'sēn). [F.] Fem. dim. of MAX.

May (mā). Contraction of MARY.

Meg (mĕg). Dim. of MARGARET.

Mel'a·nie (mĕl'ȧ·nĭ). [Gr.] Black.

Me·lis'sa (mė·lĭs'ȧ). [Gr.] Bee.

Mer·ce'des (mûr·sē'dēz; -sā'dĕs; mûr'sė·dēz; *Sp.* mĕr·thā'thäs, -sā'-). [Sp.] Mercies.

Mer'cy (mûr'sĭ). [L.]

Me'ta (mē'tȧ). Orig., dim. of MARGARET.

Mi'gnon' (*F.* mē'nyôn'). [F.] Dainty; darling.

Mil'dred (mĭl'drĕd; -drĭd). [AS.] Dim. *Mil'lie.*

Mil'i·cent, Mil'li·cent (mĭl'ĭ·sĕnt). [Teut.]

Mil'lie, Mil'ly (mĭl'ĭ). Dims. of AMELIA, MILDRED, MIL(L)ICENT.

Mi'mi (mē'mē; -mē).

Mi'na (mē'nȧ). Dim. of WILHELMINA.

Mi·ner'va (mĭ·nûr'vȧ). [L.]

Min'na (mĭn'ȧ). Prob. short for WILHELMINA.

Min'nie (mĭn'ĭ). Remembrance; love; — often a nickname for MARY.

Mi·ran'da (mĭ·răn'dȧ). [L.] Admirable.

Mir'i·am (mĭr'ĭ·ăm). [Heb.] = MARY.

Moi'ra (moi'rȧ). Var. of MAURA.

Moll (mŏl), **Mol'ly**. Dims. of MARY.

Mo'na (mō'nȧ).

Mon'i·ca (mŏn'ĭ·kȧ). [LL.]

Mor'na (môr'nȧ). [Gael.]

Mu'ri·el (mū'rĭ·ĕl). [Gr.]

My'ra (mī'rȧ).

Myr'na (mûr'nȧ).

Myr'tle (mûr't'l). [Gr.]

N

Nab'by (năb'ĭ). Dim. of ABIGAIL.

Na·dine' (nȧ·dēn'; nȧ-; *F.* nȧ'dēn'). [F., fr. Russ.] Hope.

Nan (năn), **Nan'ny**. Dims. of ANN, etc.

Nan'cy (năn'sĭ). Familiar form of ANN. — Dim. *Nan, Nance.*

Nan·nette' (nă·nĕt'; *F.* nȧ'nĕt'). [F.] Dim. of ANNE.

Na·o'mi (nā·ō'mĭ; nā'ō·mĭ; *less often*, -mĭ). [Heb.] My sweetness.

Na·ta'lia (nȧ·tāl'yȧ; -täl'-), **Nat'a·lie** (năt'-'l·ĭ; *F.* nȧ'tȧ'lē'). [L.]

Nell (nĕl), **Nel'lie, Nel'ly** (nĕl'ĭ). Dims. of ELLEN, HELEN, ELEANOR.

Ne·ris'sa (nê·rĭs'ȧ).

Net'tie (nĕt'ĭ). Dim. of ANTOINETTE, HENRI-ETTA, JEANNETTE.

Ni'na (nī'nȧ; nē'-; *Russ.* nyē'nȧ). Orig., dim. of ANN.

Ni'ta (nē'tȧ; *Sp.* nē'tä). [Sp.]

No'ra, No'rah (nō'rȧ). Dims. of HONORA, LEONORA, ELEANOR.

No'reen (nō'rēn; nō·rēn'). Prob., Irish dim. of NORA.

Nor'ma (nôr'mȧ).

O

Oc·ta'vi·a (ŏk·tā'vĭ·ȧ; -tāv'yȧ). [L.] Fem. of OCTAVIUS.

Ol'ga (ŏl'gȧ; *Russ.* ôl'y'·gȧ). [Russ.] [L.]

Ol'ive (ŏl'ĭv), **O·liv'i·a** (ȯ·lĭv'ĭ·ȧ; -lĭv'yȧ).

O·lym'pi·a (ȯ·lĭm'pĭ·ȧ). [Gr.] Heavenly.

O'pal (ō'pȧl).

O·phe'lia (ȯ·fēl'yȧ). [Gr.]

Ot'ti·lie (ŏt'ĭ·ĭ). [G.] Fem. of OTTO.

P

Pam'e·la (păm'ė·lȧ; pȧ·mē'lȧ). — Dim. *Pam.*

Pan'sy (păn'zĭ). [F.]

Pat (păt). Dim. of MARTHA, MATHILDA, PATRICIA.

Pa'tience (pā'shĕns). [L.] — Dim. *Pat'ty.*

Pa·tri'cia (pȧ·trĭsh'ȧ; -ĭ·ȧ). Fem. of PATRICK. — Dim. *Pat, Pat'ty.*

Pat'ty (păt'ĭ), **Pat'sy** (păt'sĭ). Dims. of MARTHA, MATHILDA, PATIENCE, PATRICIA.

Pau'la (pô'lȧ). [L.] Fem. of PAUL.

Pau·li'na (pô·lī'nȧ; -lē'nȧ). [L.]

Pau·line' (pô·lēn'; 2). [F.]

Pearl (pûrl).

Peg, Peg'gy (pĕg'ĭ). Dims. of MARGARET.

Pe·nel'o·pe (pê·nĕl'ō·pē). [Gr.] A weaver. — Dim. *Pen'ny.*

Per'sis (pûr'sĭs). [Gr.] A Persian woman.

Phe'mie (fē'mĭ). Dim. of EUPHEMIA.

Phe'ny (fē'nĭ). Dim. of JOSEPHINE.

Phi·lip'pa (fĭ·lĭp'ȧ; fĭl'ĭ·pȧ). Fem. of PHILIP.

Phoe'be, Phe'be (fē'bē). [Gr.] Shining.

Phyl'lis, Phil'lis (fĭl'ĭs). [Gr.] A green bough.

Pol'ly (pŏl'ĭ). Dim. of MARY.

Po·mo'na (pȯ·mō'nȧ). [L.]

Por'ti·a (pōr'shĭ·ȧ; -shȧ; 70). [L.]

Pris·cil'la (prĭ·sĭl'ȧ). [L.]

Pru'dence (prōō'dĕns; -d'ns). [L.] Discretion. — Dim. *Prue, Pru'dy.*

Q

Queen'ie (kwēn'ĭ). Usually, dim. of REGINA.

R

Ra'chel (rā'chĕl). [Heb.] A ewe. — Dim. *Ray.*

Ra·mo'na (rȧ·mō'nȧ).

Re'ba (rē'bȧ). Short for REBECCA.

Re·bec'ca (rê·bĕk'ȧ), **Re·bek'ah** (rê·bĕk'ȧ). [Heb.] — Dim. *Beck'y.*

Re·gi'na (rê·jī'nȧ; -jē'nȧ). [L.] Queen. — Dim. *Queen'ie* (kwēn'ĭ).

Re'na (rē'nȧ).

Re·née' (rė·nā'; *also* rā'nĕ, rĕn'ĕ, rē'nĕ, rĕn'ā). [F., fr. L.] Reborn.

Ret'ta (rĕt'ȧ). Dim. of HENRIETTA, LORETTA.

Rhe'a (rē'ȧ). [Gr.]

Rho'da (rō'dȧ). [Gr.] A rose.

Ri'ta (rē'tȧ). [It.]

Ro·be'na (rȯ·bē'nȧ).

Ro·ber'ta (rȯ·bûr'tȧ). Fem. of ROBERT. — Dim. *Bob'by.*

Rom'o·la (rŏm'ō·lȧ). [It.]

Ron'ny (rŏn'ĭ). Dim. of VERONICA.

Ro'sa (rō'zȧ), **Rose** (rōz). [L.] A rose.

Ro'sa·bel (rō'zȧ·bĕl; rōz'ȧ-), **Ro'sa·bel'la** (-bĕl'ȧ). [L.] A fair rose.

Ro·sa'lia (rō·zā'lyȧ; -zā'lĭ·ȧ), **Ro'sa·lie** (rō'zȧ·lē; rōz'ȧ-). [L.]

Ro'sa·lind (rō'zȧ·lĭnd; rōz'ȧ-; *in Shak., also* -lĭnd). [Sp.] Prob., pretty rose.

Ro'sa·line (rō'zȧ·lĭn; rōz'ȧ-; -lĭn; -lēn).

Ro'sa·mond, Ro'sa·mund (rō'zȧ·mŭnd; rōz'ȧ-). [Teut.]

Rose (rōz). See ROSA.

Rose'mar'y (rōz'mâr'ĭ; -mêr·ĭ; 3).

Ro·we'na (rȯ·wē'nȧ). [Celtic.]

Rox·an'a (rŏks·ăn'ȧ; -ā'nȧ). [Per.] F. Roxane (rŏk'sän'). — Dim. *Rox'y.*

Ru'by (rōō'bĭ). [L.]

Ruth (rōōth). [Heb.]

S

Sa·bi'na (sȧ·bī'nȧ). [L.] A Sabine woman.

Sa·bri'na (sȧ·brī'nȧ). [L.]

Sa'die (sā'dĭ). Orig., dim. of SARA(H).

Sal'ly (săl'ĭ). Orig., dim. of SARA(H).

Sa·lo'me (sȧ·lō'mē). [Heb.] Peace.

San'dra (săn'drȧ; sän'-). Short for ALEXANDRA.

Sar'a, Sar'ah (sâr'ȧ; sā'rȧ). [Heb.] A princess. — Dim. *Sa'die* (sā'dĭ), *Sal'ly.*

Se·li'na (sė·lē'nȧ; -lī'nȧ).

Sel'ma (sĕl'mȧ).

Se·re'na (sė·rē'nȧ). [L.]

Shei'la (shē'lȧ). Irish form of CECILIA.

Shir'ley (shûr'lĭ). From a surname.

Sib'yl (sĭb''l; -ĭl). [Gr.] A sibyl.

Sid'ney (sĭd'nĭ).

Sig'rid (sĭg'rĭd; *G.* zē'grĭt, -grēt; *Norw.* sĭ'grĭ; *Swed.* sē'grĭd).

Sil'vi·a. Var. of SYLVIA.

Sis (sĭs). Dims. of CECILIA, etc.

So'nia, So'nya (sō'nyȧ; *Russ.* sō'nyȧ). Russian dims. of SOPHIA.

So·phi'a (sō·fī'ȧ; sō'fĭ·ȧ). [Gr.] Wisdom. F. Sophie (sō'fē'; *Angl.* sō'fĭ). — Dim. *So'phy.*

So·phro'ni·a (sō·frō'nĭ·ȧ; -frŏn'yȧ). [Gr.] Sensible.

Stel'la (stĕl'ȧ). [L.] A star. F. Estelle (ĕs'tĕl'; *Angl.* ĕs·tĕl'; ĕs'tĕl).

Steph·a·na (stĕf'ȧ·nȧ), **Steph'a·nie** (stĕf'ȧ·nĭ). [Gr.] Fem. of STEPHEN. F. Stéphanie (stā'fȧ'nē').

Su'san (sū'z'n), **Su·san'na** (sū·zăn'ȧ), *or* **Su·san'nah** (-zăn'ȧ). [Heb.] A lily. F. Suzanne (sü'zän'; *Angl.* sü·zăn'). — Dim. *Sue, Suke, Su'ky, Su'sie, Su'sy.*

Su·sanne' (sü·zăn'). Var. of *Suzanne*, French form of SUSAN.

Syb'il. Var. of SIBYL.

Syl'vi·a (sĭl'vĭ·ȧ). [L.] Fem. of SYLVANUS.

T

Tab'i·tha (tăb'ĭ·thȧ). [Aramaic.] A gazelle.

Te·re'sa (tė·rē'sȧ; -zȧ; *It.* tā·rā'zä; *Sp.* tā·rā'sä). = THERESA.

Ter'e·si'na (tĕr'ė·sē'nȧ; -zē'nȧ). [It. & Sp.] Dim. of TERESA.

Ter'ry (tĕr'ĭ). Dim. of THERESA.

Tess (tĕs), **Tes'sie**. Dims. of THERESA.

Tha'is (thā'ĭs; tä·ēs'). [Gr.]

Tha'lia (thăl'yȧ; thȧ·lī'ȧ). [Gr.] Blooming; luxuriant.

The'a (thē'ȧ). [Gr.] Goddess.

Thec'la, Thek'la (thĕk'lȧ). [Gr.]

Thel'ma (thĕl'mȧ).

The·o·do'ra (thē'ō·dō'rȧ). [Gr.] Fem. of THEODORE. — Dim. *Do'ra, The'o* (thē'ō).

The·o·do'sia (thē'ō·dō'shȧ; -shĭ·ȧ). [Gr.] Gift of God.

The·oph'i·la (thē·ŏf'ĭ·lȧ). [Gr.] Fem. of THEOPHILUS.

The·re'sa (tė·rē'sȧ; -zȧ). [L.] F. Thérèse (tā'râz'); It. & Sp. Teresa (It. tā·rā'zä; Sp. tā·rā'sä). — Dim. *Ter'ry, Tess.*

Thir'za, Thyr'za (thûr'zȧ). [Heb.] Pleasantness.

Thom'a·sa (tŏm'ȧ·sȧ), **Thom'a·sine** (-sēn). Fems. of THOMAS.

Til'da (tĭl'dȧ), **Til'lie, Til'ly** (tĭl'ĭ). Dims. of MATHILDA.

Ti'na (tē'nȧ). Dim. of ALBERTINA, CHRISTINA.

Trix (trĭks), **Trix'ie, Trix'y** (trĭk'sĭ). Dims. of BEATRICE, BEATRIX.

Tru'dy (trōō'dĭ). Dim. of GERTRUDE.

U

Ul·ri'ca (ŭl·rē'kȧ). [Teut.] Rich.

U'na (ū'nȧ). [L.] One.

Un·dine' (ŭn·dēn'; ŭn'dēn). [L.] Watery.

U·ra'ni·a (û·rā'nĭ·ȧ; -rān'yȧ). [Gr.] Heavenly. F. Uranie (ü'rȧ'nē').

Ur'su·la (ûr'sû·lȧ). [L.] She-bear.

V

Va·le'ri·a (vȧ·lēr'ĭ·ȧ). [L.] Fem. of Latin VALERIUS. F. Valérie (vȧ'lā'rē').

Va·nes'sa (vȧ·nĕs'ȧ). [Gr.]

Ve'ra (vēr'ȧ).

Ver'na (vûr'nȧ).

Ve·ron'i·ca (vė·rŏn'ĭ·kȧ). [ML.] — Dim. *Ron'ny* (rŏn'ĭ).

Vic·to'ri·a (vĭk·tō'rĭ·ȧ; 70). [L.] Victory. F. Victoire (vēk'twär'). — Dim. *Vick'y* (vĭk'ĭ).

Vi'o·la (vī'ō·lȧ; vē·ō'lȧ; vĭ·ō'-; vē'ō-). [L.] A violet.

Vi'o·let (vī'ō·lĕt; -lĭt). [OF., fr. L.]

Vir·gin'ia (vēr·jĭn'ĭ·ȧ; -jĭn'yȧ). [L.] F. Virginie (vēr'zhē'nē').

Viv'i·an (vĭv'ĭ·ăn; vĭv'yăn), **Viv'i·en** (-ĕn; -yĕn). [F.] F. Vivienne (vē'vyĕn'). Full of life.

W

Wan'da (wŏn'dȧ). [Teut.]

We·no'nah (wė·nō'nȧ). [Am. Ind.] = WI-NONA.

Wil'hel·mi·na (wĭl'hĕl·mē'nȧ; wĭl'ė·mē'nȧ; *Du.* vĭl'hĕl·mē'nä; *G.* vĭl'hĕl·mē'nä). [Teut.] Fem. of *Wilhelm*, German form of WILLIAM. F. Wilhelmine (vē'lĕl'mē'n'). — Dim. *Mi'na* (mē'nȧ), *Wil'mot* (wĭl'mŭt).

Wil'la (wĭl'ȧ).

Wil'ma (wĭl'mȧ). Var. of *Wilmot* (see WILHELMINA).

Win'i·fred (wĭn'ĭ·frĕd; -frĭd). [ML.] — Dim. *Win'nie.*

Wi·no'na (wĭ·nō'nȧ).

X, Y, Z

Xi'na (zē'nȧ). Dim. of CHRISTINA.

Yo·lan'da (yȯ·lăn'dȧ), **Yo·lan'de** (-dĕ; *F.* yȯ'länd'). [?OF.]

Y·vonne' (ĭ·vŏn'; *F.* ē'vŏn'). [F.]

Ze·no'bi·a (zė·nō'bĭ·ȧ). [Gr.] Having life from Jupiter.

Zo'ë, Zo'e (zō'ē). [Gr.] Life.

Zo'na (zō'nȧ).

VOCABULARY OF RHYMES

The purpose of this vocabulary of rhymes is to list only such words and pronunciations as are in current good use and as are in keeping with the practice of good poets who have exercised freedom in observing the rules of rhyming. Obsolete, dialectal, and illiterate words and pronunciations are not recognized. A few foreign words of frequent occurrence in English speech and writing have been entered. As a rule rhymes "to the eye," as *bough* and *though*, are very sparingly given.

There are two common forms of rhymes: rhymes of monosyllables or of final accented syllables (called *single*, or *masculine*, rhymes); rhymes of two syllables the first of which is accented (called *double*, or *feminine*, rhymes), such as *pastor, faster, aiding, fading*. Single, or masculine, rhymes are the more common, and are the only ones listed freely in this vocabulary.

MASCULINE RHYMES

Theory and practice in rhyming. Theoretically, a rhyme is the correspondence, in two or more words or verses, of terminal sounds beginning with an accented vowel, which, in modern English usage, must be preceded by different consonant sounds, or by a consonant sound or sounds in one case and none in the other. In strict rhyme there is, therefore, exact correspondence in sound and also exact correspondence in accent. In practice, however, these theoretical standards are not always strictly observed and more or less freedom is exercised even by careful poets. This vocabulary includes many rhymes sanctioned by good usage under the extensions of the rules noted in the following paragraphs.

Correspondence in accent. Strictly speaking, single rhymes consist only of monosyllables or of final syllables having a primary accent. There are, however, many polysyllables which, having a primary accent on the antepenult, receive on the final syllable a secondary accent of sufficient strength to make it proper to use these words in single rhymes; thus, *accumulate* may be used to rhyme with *date* or *create, expedite* to rhyme with *sight* or *benight*. In polysyllables, such common terminations as *-an, -ant,* etc., are usually slighted in pronunciation, so that the vowel quality is obscured, as in *pelican*. Consequently under -AN, -ANT, etc., this vocabulary restricts its choice of words of more than one syllable to those which have a primary accent on the last syllable or, in the case of polysyllables accented on the antepenult, an unslurred final syllable, as in *sedan, caravan, supplant, epitaph*. Furthermore, only monosyllables which, because of their importance to the thought, are likely to carry the speech accent are entered. Certain monosyllabic words usually slurred over in speech, as prepositions and articles, are therefore excluded as not proper to serious verse. The chief principle to be observed in exercising freedom regarding correspondence of accent is that no rhyme be forced and that accepted pronunciations and customary speech accents be respected. In this connection, it should be noted that in many words of the same spelling and derivation, as *contract*, the accent is not placed on the same syllable in each part of speech, and that in others, as the noun *recess*, a change in sense may mean a change in accent. For this reason, use of the main vocabulary of the dictionary will sometimes be necessary in determining the part of speech or the sense in which a word may be used as a rhyme.

Correspondence in sound. Strictly speaking, the terminal vowel sounds should exactly correspond, but poets sometimes use rhymes in which the vowels are not exact homophones. In the vocabulary of rhymes, broad differences in terminal sounds, as in words ending in *-age*, are shown by multiple entries and multiple lists of words, but slight differences in the quality of terminal vowels are not so differentiated. Words differing but slightly are usually, as at -ANT, included under one entry. Those who seek close or delicate correspondence in sounds should consult the main vocabulary and the numbered sections of the Guide to Pronunciation to which cross reference is made.

Rhymes by contraction, elision, etc. The final two syllables of a word are often pronounced like a single syllable with a long vowel sound, by slurring over or slighting one of the syllables in the pronunciation, or by dropping a consonant or vowel. Thus *plyer, higher*, as ordinarily pronounced, may be used to rhyme with *lyre, fire;* the poetical *o'er* to rhyme with *lore, roar;* the poetical *ne'er* to rhyme with *care, stair*.

Words differently pronounced. For some words, more than one pronunciation is recognized as being in good usage, and the more common of these, when they can be used in single rhymes in either or both pronunciations, are given in this vocabulary in each group with which they may rhyme; thus, *trait* (see pron. in main vocab.) is given under -ATE and -AY, *wrath* under -ATH and -OTH, etc. This rule does not hold for foreign words that have two pronunciations.

Vocabulary arrangement. Only that part of the word or last syllable is considered which corresponds in sound with that of its rhymes, and this part of each word is treated as a termination or ending. All of these terminations must, therefore, begin with the last sounded vowel or diphthong of the word; hence any particular word with its rhymes can be readily found in this vocabulary by looking for such ending. Thus in the case of *band, made, brain, league, due, blight, amend, pontoon, terminus*, etc., look in the lists below for -AND, -ADE, -AIN, -EAGUE, -UE, -IGHT, -END, -OON, -US, etc., respectively, and under those entries will be found either the rhyming words or references to the headings under which they are given. Rhyme groups are in all cases given under the accented vowel sound. Thus *done* and its rhymes will be found under -UN, *sign* under -INE, *warn* under -ORN, *yacht* under -OT, etc.

Rhyming lists can also be extended by consulting entries to which there is a "Cf." reference. Thus under the entry -OOP will be found a reference "Cf. -UPE."

FEMININE RHYMES

Theoretically, feminine rhymes occur at the ends of lines in trochaic, amphibrachic, and dactylic meter; actually, they often also occur when the poet, for one reason or another, wishes to add a hypermetrical syllable or syllables. They are also called double (or triple) rhymes because there must be correspondence in sound and accent between the last accented syllable and the following syllable or syllables. The rule for masculine rhymes requiring a consonantal difference (sometimes by omission of one consonant) before the rhyming sounds holds good here for the accented syllables of the feminine rhyme but not for the unaccented syllables, which must be identical in sound; thus *tabard* rhymes with *scabbard, feather* with *heather, pastor* with *master, furious* with *penurious*. Because of this rule, it is not easy to find many words which serve as feminine rhymes.

It is well for the versifier in need of a group of rhyming

words, or of words to complete a rhyme already begun, to remember that the unaccented syllables of feminine rhymes frequently correspond in sound, even if not in spelling, to well-known suffixes. Such rhymes are usually most frequently found among inflected forms and derivative nouns, adjectives, adverbs, and verbs ending in *-er*, *-ify*, *-ing*, *-ious*, *-ly*, *-ment*, *-y*, and the like. To get at many words of this kind consult the list for the accented syllable as given under the masculine rhymes and select the words to which the desired suffix can be added (sometimes by doubling a final consonant, sometimes by dropping a final *-e*, and so on). Thus, -AB supplies *crab*, from which *crabbed* may be formed; -AND supplies *brand*, from which *branded* may be formed.

If, as frequently happens, several double rhymes are needed, it will be wise to choose, at least as a beginning, a derivative of this sort, especially one in which the accented syllable corresponds to an entry in the masculine rhymes that has a long list of words. For example, the list at -ECT will be very rewarding in such a situation; for it will suggest, among others, feminine rhymes ending in *-ion* (as, *effection, objection, protection, section, selection*), in *-ive* (as, *effective, objective, protective, selective*), and in *-ful* (as, *neglectful, respectful*). Similarly, the list at -AY will suggest many words to which can be added *-al* (as, *betrayal, de-*

frayal, portrayal) or *-ment* (as, *allayment, displayment, payment*). Moreover, to most such lists can be added words of which there is no counterpart in the masculine rhymes: for example, *insurrection, invective, Baal, raiment, claimant*.

Greater difficulty will be encountered by the versifier who has already started his rhyme but fails in an attempt to discover words with equivalent endings. If his accented syllable is not given under the masculine rhymes, he will not succeed by the method described above, even though his terminal syllable corresponds to a common suffix like *-er*. Such an instance is *sever* — unless such obvious words as *clever, endeavor, ever, never* will satisfy his needs. If, however, he requires a rhyme for *booty* or *water* or *plastered* he will find *fruity* suggested by the -OOT (-ōōt) list, *tauter* by the -AUT list, *mastered* by the -AST list. The return will often be much greater. If he has *attar* to start with, the list at -AT (-ăt) will give him *batter, chatter, fatter, flatter, hatter, matter*, and *patter*, which in turn may make him think of others, such as *satyr, shatter, tatter*. Thus, the pronunciation of *daisy* leads one to the masculine rhyme -AZE, where the listed words will suggest several rhymes, such as *hazy* and *mazy;* the pronunciation of *fuel* and *gruel* lead to the list at -EW, which by addition of the suffix *-al* will suggest *accrual, imbual, renewal, reviewal*.

-ab (ăb). Bab, blab, cab, crab, dab, drab, gab, grab, jab, Mab, nab, scab, slab, stab, -tab.
-abe (āb). Babe; astrolabe.
-ac (ăk). See -ACK.
-ace (ās). Ace, base, bass, brace, case, chase, face, grace, lace, mace, pace, place, race, space, trace, vase; abase, apace, debase, deface, disgrace, displace, efface, embrace, encase, erase, footpace, grimace, misplace, outface, outpace, replace, retrace, ukase; boniface, commonplace, interlace, interspace.
-ach (ăch). See -ATCH.
-ache (āk). See -AKE.
-acht (ŏt). See -OT.
-ack (ăk). Back, black, clack, claque, crack, hack, jack, knack, lac, lack, pack, plaque, quack, rack, sac, sack, sacque, shack, slack, smack, snack, stack, tack, thwack, track, whack, wrack; aback, ack-ack, alack, attack, bivouac, gimcrack, knickknack, ransack, shellac, ticktack; almanac, bric-a-brac, cardiac, cul-de-sac; demoniac, symposiac.
-act (ăkt). Act, bract, fact, pact, tact, tract; abstract, attract, compact, contract, detract, diffract, distract, enact, entr'acte, exact, extract, impact, infract, intact, protract, react, redact, refract, retract, subtract, transact; cataract, counteract, re-enact, retroact; *also, past tenses and past participles of verbs in* -ack, *as* backed, hacked.
-ad (ăd). Add, bad, bade, brad, cad, clad, dad, egad, fad, gad, glad, had, lad, mad, pad, plaid, sad, scad, shad; begad, forbade.
-ad (ŏd). See -OD.
-ade (äd). Ballade, façade, roulade; accolade, promenade. Cf. -OD.
-ade (ād). Aid, blade, braid, fade, glade, grade, jade, lade, laid, made, maid, raid, shade, spade, staid, suede, trade, wade; abrade, afraid, arcade, blockade, brigade, brocade, cascade, charade, cockade, crusade, degrade, dissuade, evade, grenade, invade, parade, persuade, pervade, stockade, tirade, upbraid; ambuscade, balustrade, barricade, cannonade, cavalcade, colonnade, enfilade, escalade, escapade, esplanade, fusillade, lemonade, marmalade, masquerade, palisade, renegade, retrograde, serenade; harlequinade, rodomontade; *also, past tenses and past participles of verbs in* -ay, -ey, -eigh, *as* paid, played, obeyed, weighed.
-adge (ăj). Badge, cadge.
-afe (āf). Chafe, safe, waif; vouchsafe.
-aff (ăf; àf; 9). Chaff, gaff, graph, quaff, staff; carafe, giraffe; autograph, cenotaph, epitaph, lithograph, monograph, paragraph, phonograph, photograph, telegraph.
-aft (àft; 9). Aft, craft, daft, draft, draught, graft, haft, raft, shaft, waft; abaft, aircraft, ingraft; handicraft, overdraft; *also, past tenses and past participles of verbs in* -aff, *as* chaffed, quaffed.
-ag (ăg). Bag, brag, crag, drag, fag, flag, gag, hag, jag, lag, nag, quag, rag, sag, scrag, shag,

slag, snag, stag, swag, tag, wag; ragtag, wigwag, zigzag; bullyrag, scalawag.
-age (āj). Age, cage, gauge, page, rage, sage, stage, swage, wage; assuage, engage, enrage, outrage, presage; disengage.
-age (äzh). Barrage, garage, ménage, mirage; badinage, persiflage.
-age (ĭj). Anchorage, average, cartilage, equipage, foliage, heritage, hermitage, parentage, parsonage, pasturage, patronage, personage, pilgrimage, privilege, tutelage, vicarage.
-agm (ăm). See -AM.
-agne (ān). See -AIN.
-ague (āg). Plague, vague.
-ah (ä). Ah, bah, ha, ma, shah, spa; huzza.
-aid (ād). See -ADE.
-aif (āf). See -AFE.
-aight (āt). See -ATE.
-aign (ān). See -AIN.
-ail (āl). Ail, ale, bail, bale, dale, fail, flail, frail, Gael, gale, grail, hail, hale, jail, mail, male, nail, pail, pale, quail, rail, sail, sale, scale, snail, stale, swale, tail, tale, trail, vale, veil, wail, wale, whale; assail, avail, bewail, curtail, detail, entail, exhale, impale, inhale, prevail, regale, retail, travail, unveil; countervail, nightingale.
-aim (ām). See -AME.
-ain (ān). Bane, blain, brain, Cain, cane, chain, crane, Dane, deign, drain, fain, fane, feign, gain, grain, lain, lane, main, mane, pain, pane, plain, plane, rain, reign, rein, sane, skein, slain, Spain, sprain, stain, strain, swain, ta'en, thane, thegn, train, twain, vain, vane, vein, wain, wane; abstain, airplane, amain, arraign, attain, campaign, champagne, chicane, complain, constrain, contain, demesne, detain, disdain, distrain, domain, enchain, explain, germane, humane, inane, insane, maintain, obtain, ordain, pertain, profane, refrain, regain, remain, restrain, retain, sustain, urbane; aeroplane, appertain, ascertain, chatelaine, counterpane, entertain, hurricane.
-ain (ĕn). See -EN.
-ainst (ĕnst). Against, 'gainst; *also, past tenses and past participles of verbs in* -ence, -ense, *as* commenced, sensed.
-aint (ānt). Faint, feint, paint, plaint, quaint, saint, taint; acquaint, attaint, complaint, constraint, distraint, restraint.
-air, -aire (âr). See -ARE.
-airn (ârn). Bairn, cairn.
-aise (āz). See -AZE.
-ait (āt). See -ATE.
-aith (āth). Faith, wraith.
-aize (āz). See -AZE.
-ake (āk). Ache, bake, brake, break, cake, drake, fake, flake, hake, lake, make, quake, rake, sake, shake, slake, snake, spake, stake, steak, strake, take, wake; betake, forsake, mistake, opaque, partake; overtake, undertake.
-al, -ale (ăl). Banal, cabal, canal, corral, locale, morale, timbale; musicale.

-ald (ôld). Bald, scald; *also, past tenses and past participles of verbs in* -all, -aul, -awl, *as* called, mauled, scrawled.
-ale (āl). See -AIL.
-alf (ăf; àf; 9). Calf, half, laugh; behalf. Cf. -OFF.
-alk (ôk). Balk, calk, chalk, gawk, hawk, squawk, stalk, talk, walk; Mohawk; tomahawk.
-all (ôl). See -AWL.
-alm (äm). Balm, calm, palm, psalm, qualm; embalm, salaam.
-alp (ălp). Alp, palp, scalp.
-alt (ôlt). Fault, halt, malt, salt, smalt, vault; assault, basalt, cobalt, default, exalt.
-alt (ălt). Alt, shalt.
-alve (ăv; àv; 9). Calve, halve, salve, Slav, suave.
-am, -amb (ăm). Am, cam, clam, cram, dam, damn, dram, gram, ham, jam, jamb, lam, lamb, ram, scram, sham, slam, swam, tram, yam; anagram, cablegram, diagram, diaphragm, dithyramb, epigram, monogram, telegram; aerogram, radiogram.
-ame (ām). Aim, blame, came, claim, dame, fame, flame, frame, game, lame, maim, name, same, shame, tame; acclaim, became, declaim, defame, exclaim, inflame, misname, nickname, proclaim, reclaim, surname; overcame.
-amp (ămp). Camp, champ, clamp, cramp, damp, guimpe, lamp, ramp, scamp, stamp, tamp, tramp, vamp; decamp, encamp.
-amp (ŏmp). See -OMP.
-an (ăn). Ban, bran, can, clan, fan, man, pan, plan, ran, scan, span, tan, van; began, divan, foreran, japan, pecan, rattan, sedan, trepan, unman; artisan, caravan, courtesan, partisan.
-an (ŏn). See -ON.
-ance (àns; ăns; 9). Chance, dance, France, glance, lance, manse, prance, trance; advance, askance, enhance, entrance, expanse, finance, mischance, perchance, romance; circumstance.
-anch (ànch; ănch; 9). Blanch, branch, ranch, stanch; avalanche.
-and (ănd; ànd; 9). Band, bland, brand, gland, grand, hand, land, rand, sand, stand, strand; command, demand, disband, expand, remand, withstand; contraband, countermand, reprimand, saraband, understand; *also, past tenses and past participles of verbs in* -an, *as* planned.
-and (ŏnd). See -OND.
-ane (ān). See -AIN.
-ang (ăng). Bang, clang, fang, gang, hang, pang, rang, sang, slang, sprang, whang; harangue, meringue; boomerang.
-ange (ānj). Change, grange, mange, range, strange; arrange, derange, estrange, exchange; disarrange, interchange.
-angue (ăng). See -ANG.
-ank (ăngk). Bank, blank, clank, crank, dank, drank, flank, frank, hank, lank, plank, prank, rank, sank, shank, shrank, spank,

stank, swank, tank, thank, yank; disrank, embank, outflank, outrank.
-anse (ăns). See -ANCE.
-ant (ȧnt; ănt; 9). Ant, cant, chant, grant, pant, plant, rant, scant, slant; aslant, decant, descant, displant, enchant, gallant, implant, Levant, recant, supplant, transplant; adamant, commandant.
-ant (ônt; ŏnt). See -AUNT.
-ap (ăp). Cap, chap, clap, flap, gap, hap, lap, map, nap, pap, rap, sap, scrap, slap, snap, strap, tap, trap, wrap; entrap, enwrap, mishap, unwrap.
-ape (āp). Ape, cape, chape, crepe, drape, grape, jape, nape, rape, scrape, shape, tape; agape, escape, shipshape.
-aph (ȧf; 9). See -AFF.
-apse (ăps). Apse, craps, lapse; collapse, elapse, perhaps, relapse; *also, plurals of nouns, and third person sing. present of verbs, in* -ap, *as* caps, laps, saps.
-apt (ăpt). Apt, rapt, wrapt; adapt; *also, past tenses and past participles of verbs in* -ap, *as* slapped, tapped.
-aque (ăk). See -ACK.
-ar (är). Bar, car, char, far, jar, mar, par, scar, spar, star, tar, tsar; afar, bazaar, bizarre, catarrh, debar, disbar, guitar, hussar, lascar; avatar, caviar, registrar, samovar, seminar.
-ar (ôr). See -OR.
-arb (ärb). Barb, garb.
-arce (ärs). See -ARSE.
-arch (ärch). Arch, larch, march, parch, starch.
-arch (ärk). See -ARK.
-ard (ärd). Bard, card, chard, guard, hard, lard, nard, pard, sard, shard, yard; bombard, canard, discard, petard, placard, regard, retard; boulevard, disregard, interlard; *also, past tenses and past participles of verbs in* -ar, *as* barred, scarred.
-ard (ôrd). See -ORD.
-are (âr; ăr). Air, bare, bear, blare, care, chair, dare, e'er, ere, fair, fare, flair, flare, glair, glare, hair, hare, heir, lair, mare, ne'er, pair, pare, pear, prayer, rare, scare, share, snare, spare, square, stair, stare, swear, tare, tear, their, there, ware, wear, where; affair, aware, beware, compare, declare, despair, ensnare, forbear, forswear, howe'er, impair, prepare, repair, whate'er, whene'er, where'er; debonair, doctrinaire, millionaire.
-ares (ârz). Theirs; unawares; *also, plurals of nouns, and third person sing. present of verbs, in* -are, -air, -eir, -ear, *as* cares, pairs, heirs, bears.
-arf (ôrf). Dwarf, wharf.
-arge (ärj). Barge, charge, large, marge; discharge, enlarge, surcharge.
-ark (ärk). Arc, ark, bark, cark, dark, hark, lark, mark, park, sark, shark, spark, stark; debark, embark, remark; hierarch, patriarch.
-arl (ärl). Carl, gnarl, snarl.
-arm (ärm). Arm, barm, charm, farm, harm; alarm, disarm, gendarme, unarm.
-arm (ôrm). See -ORM.
-arn (ärn). Barn, darn, tarn, yarn.
-arn (ôrn). See -ORN.
-arp (ärp). Carp, harp, scarp, sharp; escarp; counterscarp, pericarp.
-arp (ôrp). See -ORP.
-arse (ärs). Farce, parse, sparse.
-arsh (ärsh). Harsh, marsh.
-art (ärt). Art, cart, chart, dart, hart, heart, mart, part, smart, start, tart; apart, depart, dispart, impart, sweetheart, upstart.
-art (ôrt). See -ORT.
-arth (ôrth). See -ORTH.
-arve (ärv). Carve, starve.
-as (ŏz). Boz, was.
-as (ăs). Bass, gas; amass, crevasse, cuirass, morass; sassafras. Cf. -ASS.
-ase (ās; āz). See -ACE, -AZE.
-ash (ăsh). Ash, bash, brash, cache, cash, clash, crash, dash, flash, gash, gnash, hash, lash, mash, plash, rash, sash, slash, smash, thrash, trash; abash, calash; balderdash, calabash.
-ash (ŏsh). Quash, squash, swash, wash; awash, galosh; mackintosh.
-ask (ȧsk; ăsk; 9). Ask, bask, cask, flask, mask, masque, Pasch, task; unmask.
-asm (ăz'm). Chasm, spasm; cataplasm, protoplasm; enthusiasm, iconoclasm.
-asp (ȧsp; 9). Asp, clasp, gasp, grasp, hasp, rasp; enclasp, unclasp.
-ass (ȧs; ăs; 9). Ass, brass, class, glass, grass, lass, mass, pass; alas, repass, surpass. Cf. -AS.
-ast (ȧst; ăst; 9). Bast, blast, cast, caste, fast, last, mast, past, vast; aghast, avast, contrast, forecast, outcast, repast; overcast; *also, past tenses and past participles of verbs in* -ass, *as* amassed.
-aste (āst). Baste, chaste, haste, paste, taste, waist, waste; distaste; *also, past tenses and past participles of verbs in* -ace, *as* faced, placed.
-at (ăt). At, bat, brat, cat, chat, fat, flat, gnat, hat, mat, pat, plat, rat, sat, slat, spat, sprat, tat, that, vat; cravat, whereat.
-at (ŏt). See -OT.
-atch (ăch). Batch, catch, hatch, latch, match, patch, scratch, snatch, thatch; attach, detach, dispatch.
-atch (ŏch). See -OTCH.
-ate (āt). Bait, bate, crate, date, eight, fate, fete, freight, gait, gate, grate, great, hate, late, mate, pate, plait, plate, prate, rate, sate, skate, slate, state, straight, strait, trait, wait, weight; abate, await, belate, collate, create, debate, dilate, elate, estate, inflate, ingrate, innate, irate, rebate, relate, sedate, translate; abdicate, advocate, aggravate, agitate, animate, antiquate, arbitrate, calculate, candidate, captivate, celebrate, circulate, congregate, consecrate, cultivate, dedicate, delegate, deprecate, derogate, dissipate, educate, elevate, emulate, estimate, extricate, generate, hesitate, imitate, imprecate, innovate, instigate, intimate, irritate, laureate, liberate, lubricate, magistrate, mediate, mitigate, moderate, nominate, opiate, penetrate, perpetrate, potentate, profligate, propagate, radiate, regulate, reprobate, separate, simulate, stimulate, stipulate, subjugate, suffocate, supplicate, terminate, tolerate, venerate, vindicate, violate; abominate, accelerate, accommodate, accumulate, adulterate, annihilate, anticipate, articulate, assassinate, capacitate, capitulate, commemorate, commiserate, communicate, compassionate, congratulate, contaminate, degenerate, denominate, discriminate, evaporate, exaggerate, exasperate, facilitate, illuminate, intimidate, intoxicate, invalidate, inviolate, matriculate, participate, pontificate, precipitate, predestinate, predominate, premeditate, prevaricate, regenerate, reiterate, rejuvenate.
-ath (ȧth; ăth; 9). Bath, hath, lath, path, snath, wrath; aftermath, allopath.
-ath (ôth). See -OTH.
-athe (āth). Bathe, lathe, scathe, swathe; unswathe. Cf. -AITH.
-auce (ôs). Hawse, sauce. Cf. -OSS, -AUSE.
-aud (ôd). Bawd, broad, fraud, gaud, laud; abroad, applaud, belaud, defraud, maraud; *also, past tenses and past participles of verbs in* -aw, *as* gnawed, sawed.
-augh (ăf; ȧf). See -ALF.
-aught (ôt; ȧft). See -OUGHT, -AFT.
-aul (ôl). See -AWL.
-aulm (ôm). Haulm, shawm.
-ault (ôlt). See -ALT.
-aunch (ônch; änch). Craunch, haunch, launch, paunch, staunch.
-aunt (ônt; änt). Aunt, daunt, flaunt, gaunt, haunt, jaunt, taunt, vaunt, want; avaunt.
-ause (ôz). Cause, clause, gauze, hawse, pause, yaws; applause, because; *also, plurals of nouns, and third person sing. present of verbs, in* -aw, *as* laws, saws.
-aust (ôst). Exhaust; holocaust.
-aut (ôt). Taut; aeronaut.
-ave (āv). Brave, cave, crave, gave, glaive, grave, knave, lave, nave, pave, rave, save, shave, slave, stave, waive, wave; behave, concave, deprave, engrave, enslave, forgave, misgave; architrave.
-aw (ô). Awe, caw, claw, craw, daw, draw, flaw, gnaw, haw, jaw, law, maw, paw, raw, saw, squaw, straw, thaw, yaw; foresaw, macaw, papaw, withdraw.
-awd (ôd). See -AUD.
-awk (ôk). See -ALK.
-awl (ôl). All, awl, ball, bawl, brawl, call, crawl, drawl, fall, gall, hall, haul, maul, pall, pawl, scrawl, shawl, small, sprawl, squall, stall, tall, thrall, trawl, wall, yawl; appall, befall, enthrall, forestall, install.
-awm (ôm). See -AULM.
-awn (ôn). Awn, brawn, dawn, drawn, faun, fawn, lawn, pawn, prawn, spawn, yawn.
-ax (ăks). Ax, flax, lax, tax, wax; relax; battle-ax, parallax; *also, plurals of nouns, and third person sing. present of verbs, in* -ack, *as* backs, lacks, packs.
-ay (ā). Aye, bay, bray, clay, day, dray, eh, fay, fey, flay, fray, gay, gray, hay, jay, lay, may, nay, neigh, pay, play, pray, prey, ray, say, slay, sleigh, spay, splay, spray, stay, stray, sway, trait, tray, trey, way, weigh, whey; affray, allay, array, assay, astray, away, belay, betray, bewray, bouquet, convey, croquet, decay, defray, delay, dismay, display, essay, gainsay, inlay, inveigh, mislay, obey, portray, purvey, relay, repay, risqué, sachet, survey, waylay; émigré(e), matinee, negligee, protégé(e), roundelay, virelay.
aze (āz). Blaze, braise, braze, chaise, craze, daze, faze, gaze, glaze, graze, haze, maze, phrase, praise, raise, raze; ablaze, amaze, dispraise; chrysoprase, Marseillaise, paraphrase; *also, plurals of nouns, and third person sing. present of verbs, in* -ay, -eigh, -ey, *as* days, inveighs, obeys.
-e (ē). See -EE.
-ea (ē). See -EE.
-eace (ēs). See -EASE (ēs).
-each (ēch). Beach, beech, bleach, breach, breech, each, leech, peach, preach, reach, screech, speech, teach; beseech, impeach.
-ead (ēd; ĕd). See -EED, -ED.
-eaf (ēf; ĕf). See -IEF, -EF.
-eague (ēg). Klieg, league; colleague, enleague, fatigue, intrigue, renege.
-eak (ēk). Beak, bleak, cheek, clique, creak, creek, eke, freak, Greek, leak, leek, meek, peak, pique, reek, seek, shriek, sleek, sneak, speak, squeak, streak, teak, tweak, weak, week, wreak; antique, bezique, critique, oblique, physique, unique.
-eak (āk). See -AKE.
-eal (ēl). Ceil, deal, eel, feel, heal, heel, keel, kneel, leal, meal, peal, peel, reel, seal, squeal, steal, steel, teal, veal, weal, wheel, zeal; anneal, appeal, conceal, congeal, genteel, repeal, reveal.
-eald (ēld). See -IELD.
-ealm (ĕlm). See -ELM.
-ealth (ĕlth). Health, stealth, wealth; commonwealth.
-eam (ēm). Beam, bream, cream, deem, dream, fleam, gleam, ream, scheme, scream, seam, seem, steam, stream, team, teem, theme; beseem, blaspheme, esteem, extreme, redeem, supreme.
-ean (ēn). Bean, clean, dean, e'en, glean, green, keen, lean, lien, mean, mien, preen, queen, scene, screen, seen, sheen, spleen, wean, ween, yean; baleen, between, canteen, careen, convene, cuisine, demean, demesne, foreseen, machine, marine, obscene, poteen, ravine, routine, sardine, serene, subvene, tontine, unclean; submarine.
-eant (ĕnt). See -ENT.
-eap (ēp). See -EEP.
-ear (ẽr; âr). See -EER, -ARE.
-earch (ûrch). See -URCH.
-eard (ẽrd). Beard, weird; *also, past tenses and past participles of verbs in* -ear, -ere, *as* feared, revered.
-eard (ûrd). See -URD.
-earl (ûrl). See -URL.
-earn (ûrn). See -URN.
-earse (ûrs). See -ERSE.
-eart (ärt). See -ART.
-earth (ûrth). See -IRTH.
-ease (ēs). Cease, crease, fleece, geese, grease, lease, niece, peace, piece; decease, decrease, increase, obese, police, release, surcease; frontispiece.
-ease (ēz). Breeze, cheese, ease, freeze, frieze, grease, lees, please, seize, sneeze, squeeze, tease, these, wheeze; appease, disease, displease; *also, plurals of nouns in* -ea, *as* pleas, teas, *and third person sing. present of verbs in* -ee, *as* frees, sees.
-east (ēst). Beast, east, feast, least, priest, yeast; artiste; *also, past tenses and past participles of verbs in* -ease, *as* ceased, increased.
-eat (ēt). Beat, bleat, cheat, eat, feat, feet, fleet, greet, heat, meat, meet, mete, neat, peat, pleat, seat, sheet, sleet, street, suite, sweet, teat, treat, wheat; compete, complete, conceit, concrete, deceit, defeat, delete, deplete, discreet, effete, entreat, receipt, replete, retreat, secrete.
-eat (āt). See -ATE.
-eat (ĕt). See -ET.
-eath (ĕth). Breath, death, Seth; *also, archaic third person sing. forms of verbs, as* saith, lingereth.
-eath (ēth). Heath, sheath, teeth, wreath; beneath; underneath.
-eathe (ēth). Breathe, seethe, sheathe, teethe, wreathe; bequeath, enwreathe.
-eau (ō). See -ow (ō).
-eave (ēv). Breve, cleave, eve, grieve, heave, leave, peeve, reave, sleeve, thieve, weave; achieve, aggrieve, believe, bereave, conceive, deceive, naïve, perceive, receive, relieve, reprieve, retrieve.
-eb (ĕb). Bleb, deb, ebb, neb, web.
-eck (ĕk). Beck, check, deck, fleck, neck, peck, reck, speck, trek, wreck.

-ect (ĕkt). Sect; abject, affect, collect, connect, correct, defect, deflect, deject, detect, direct, dissect, effect, eject, elect, erect, expect, infect, inject, inspect, neglect, object, project, protect, reflect, reject, respect, select, subject, suspect; architect, circumspect, dialect, intellect, intersect, recollect; *also, past tenses and past participles of verbs in* -eck, *as* checked, decked.

-ed (ĕd). Bed, bled, bread, bred, dead, dread, fed, fled, head, lead, led, read, red, said, shed, shred, sled, sped, spread, stead, ted, thread, tread, wed; abed, behead, inbred, instead, misled.

-ede (ēd). See -EED.

-edge (ĕj). Dredge, edge, fledge, hedge, kedge, ledge, pledge, sedge, sledge, wedge; allege; sacrilege, sortilege.

-ee (ē). Be, bee, fee, flea, flee, free, glee, he, key, knee, lea, lee, me, pea, plea, quay, sea, see, she, spree, tea, tee, thee, three, tree, we, ye; agree, bohea, debris, decree, degree, foresee; absentee, cap-a-pie, coterie, jubilee, pedigree, referee, refugee; Gethsemane.

-eece (ēs). See -EASE (ēs).

-eech (ēch). See -EACH.

-eed (ēd). Bead, bleed, breed, cede, creed, deed, feed, freed, greed, heed, knead, lead, mead, meed, need, plead, read, reed, seed, speed, steed, tweed, weed; concede, exceed, impede, indeed, precede, proceed, recede, stampede, succeed; intercede, supersede.

-eef (ēf). See -IEF.

-eek (ēk). See -EAK.

-eel (ēl). See -EAL.

-eem (ēm). See -EAM.

-een (ēn). See -EAN.

-eep (ēp). Cheap, cheep, creep, deep, heap, keep, leap, neap, peep, reap, seep, sheep, sleep, steep, sweep, weep; asleep.

-eer (ẽr). Beer, bier, blear, cheer, clear, dear, deer, drear, ear, fear, fleer, gear, hear, here, jeer, leer, mere, near, peer, pier, queer, rear, sear, seer, sere, shear, sheer, smear, sneer, spear, sphere, steer, tear, tier, veer, year; appear, austere, career, cohere, compeer, revere, severe, sincere; buccaneer, chanticleer, disappear, domineer, engineer, hemisphere, interfere, mountaineer, mutineer, persevere, pioneer, sonneteer; charioteer.

-eese (ēs). See -EASE (ēs).

-eet (ēt). See -EAT.

-eethe (ēth). See -EATHE.

-eeze (ēz). See -EASE (ēz).

-ef (ĕf). Chef, clef, deaf, feoff.

-eft (ĕft). Cleft, deft, eft, heft, left, reft, theft, weft; bereft.

-eg (ĕg). Beg, dreg, egg, keg, leg, peg, skeg.

-ège (ĕzh). Barège, cortege, manège.

-ege (ĭj). See -AGE (ĭj).

-egm (ĕm). See -EM.

-eigh (ā). See -AY.

-eight (āt; īt). See -ATE, -ITE.

-eign (ān). See -AIN.

-eil (āl; ēl). See -AIL, -EAL.

-ein (ān). See -AIN.

-eint (ānt). See -AINT.

-eir (âr). See -ARE.

-eird (ẽrd). See -EARD.

-eive (ēv). See -EAVE.

-eize (ēz). See -EASE (ēz).

-eke (ēk). See -EAK.

-el (ĕl). Bell, belle, cell, dell, dwell, ell, fell, hell, knell, quell, sell, shell, smell, spell, swell, tell, well, yell; befell, compel, dispel, excel, expel, foretell, gazelle, impel, rebel, repel; asphodel, bagatelle, citadel, demoiselle, hydromel, parallel, philomel, sentinel.

-eld (ĕld). Eld, geld, held, weld; beheld, upheld, withheld; *also, past tenses and past participles of verbs in* -ell, *as* felled, swelled.

-elf (ĕlf). Delf, elf, pelf, self, shelf.

-elk (ĕlk). Elk, whelk.

-ell, -elle (ĕl). See -EL.

-elm (ĕlm). Elm, helm, realm, whelm; overwhelm.

-elp (ĕlp). Help, kelp, whelp, yelp.

-elt (ĕlt). Belt, Celt, dealt, dwelt, felt, knelt, melt, pelt, smelt, spelt, svelte, welt.

-elve (ĕlv). Delve, helve, shelve, twelve.

-elves (ĕlvz). *Plurals of nouns in* -elf, -elve, *as* shelves, twelves.

-em (ĕm). Em, gem, hem, phlegm, stem, them; begem, condemn, contemn; apothegm, diadem, requiem, stratagem.

-eme (ēm). See -EAM.

-emn (ĕm). See -EM.

-empt (ĕmpt). Dreamt, tempt; attempt, contempt, exempt, pre-empt, unkempt.

-en (ĕn). Ben, den, fen, glen, hen, ken, men, pen, ten, then, wen, when, wren, yen; again; citizen, denizen, regimen.

-ence (ĕns). Cense, dense, fence, hence, pence, sense, tense, thence, whence; commence, condense, defense, dispense, expense, immense, incense, intense, offense, pretense, suspense; abstinence, affluence, confidence, consequence, continence, difference, diffidence, diligence, eloquence, eminence, evidence, excellence, immanence, imminence, impotence, impudence, indigence, indolence, inference, influence, innocence, negligence, penitence, preference, providence, reference, reverence, sapience, violence, virulence; beneficence, benevolence, grandiloquence, inconsequence, intelligence, magnificence, munificence, obedience, omnipotence.

-ench (ĕnch). Bench, blench, clench, drench, flench, French, quench, stench, tench, trench, wench, wrench; intrench, retrench.

-end (ĕnd). Bend, blend, end, fend, friend, lend, mend, rend, send, spend, tend, trend, vend, wend; amend, ascend, attend, befriend, commend, contend, defend, depend, descend, distend, emend, expend, extend, forefend, impend, intend, offend, portend, pretend, suspend, transcend, unbend; apprehend, comprehend, condescend, dividend, recommend, reprehend; *also, past tenses and past participles of verbs in* -en, *as* kenned, penned.

-ends (ĕndz). Amends; *also, plurals of nouns, and third person sing. present of verbs, in* -end, *as* friends, sends.

-ene (ēn). See -EAN.

-enge (ĕnj). Avenge, revenge.

-ength (ĕngth). Length, strength.

-ense (ĕns). See -ENCE.

-ense (ĕnz). Cleanse, gens, lens; *also, plurals of nouns, and third person sing. present of verbs, in* -en, *as* hens, kens.

-ent (ĕnt). Bent, blent, cent, dent, leant, lent, meant, pent, rent, scent, sent, spent, tent, vent, went; absent, anent, ascent, assent, augment, cement, comment, consent, content, descent, dissent, event, extent, ferment, foment, frequent, indent, intent, invent, lament, misspent, portent, present, prevent, relent, repent, resent, torment, unbent, unspent; abstinent, accident, aliment, argument, banishment, battlement, blandishment, chastisement, competent, complement, compliment, confident, continent, detriment, different, diffident, diligent, document, element, eloquent, eminent, evident, excellent, exigent, firmament, fraudulent, government, immanent, imminent, implement, impotent, impudent, incident, indigent, innocent, insolent, instrument, languishment, management, monument, negligent, nourishment, nutriment, occident, opulent, orient, ornament, parliament, penitent, permanent, pertinent, precedent, president, prevalent, provident, punishment, ravishment, redolent, regiment, represent, resident, reverent, rudiment, sacrament, sentiment, settlement, subsequent, supplement, tenement, testament, vehement, violent, virulent, wonderment; acknowledgment, astonishment, belligerent, benevolent, experiment, impenitent, impertinent, imprisonment, improvident, intelligent, irreverent, magnificent.

-ep (ĕp). Nep, pep, rep, step, steppe; footstep.

-ept (ĕpt). Crept, kept, sept, slept, stepped, swept, wept; accept, adept, except, inept, y-clept.

-er (ẽr; ûr). Blur, bur, cur, err, fir, fur, her, myrrh, per, purr, shirr, sir, slur, spur, stir, were, whir; aver, bestir, chasseur, chauffeur, concur, confer, defer, demur, deter, hauteur, incur, infer, inter, occur, prefer, recur, refer, transfer; amateur, arbiter, chorister, connoisseur, harbinger, Jupiter, Lucifer, presbyter, sepulcher, voyageur; administer, idolater; *also, comparatives of adjectives and agent nouns accented on the antepenult, as* cosier, kindlier, flatterer.

-erb (ûrb). Curb, herb, verb; acerb, disturb, perturb, superb.

-erce (ûrs). See -ERSE.

-erch (ûrch). See -URCH.

-erd (ûrd). See -URD.

-ere (ẽr). See -EER.

-erf (ûrf). See -URF.

-erg (ûrg). Berg, burgh; exergue, iceberg.

-erge (ûrj). Dirge, merge, purge, scourge, serge, spurge, surge, urge, verge; converge, diverge, emerge, immerge, submerge; demiurge, thaumaturge.

-erm (ûrm). See -IRM.

-ern (ûrn). See -URN.

-err (ûr). See -ER.

-erse (ûrs). Burse, curse, Erse, hearse, herse, nurse, purse, terse, verse, worse; accurse, adverse, amerce, asperse, averse, coerce, converse, disburse, disperse, diverse, imburse, immerse, inverse, perverse, rehearse, reverse, transverse; intersperse, universe.

-ert (ûrt). Blurt, curt, dirt, flirt, girt, hurt, pert, shirt, spurt, squirt, wert, wort; advert, alert, assert, avert, concert, convert, desert, dessert, divert, exert, expert, inert, insert, invert, pervert, revert, subvert.

-erth (ûrth). See -IRTH.

-erve (ûrv). Curve, nerve, serve, swerve, verve; conserve, deserve, observe, preserve, reserve, unnerve.

-es, -esce (ĕs). See -ESS.

-ese (ēz; ēs). See 1st & 2d -EASE.

-esh (ĕsh). Flesh, fresh, mesh, thresh; afresh, enmesh, immesh, refresh.

-esk, -esque (ĕsk). Desk; burlesque, grotesque, Moresque; arabesque, picturesque, statuesque.

-ess, -esse (ĕs). Bless, cess, chess, cress, dress, guess, less, mess, press, stress, tress, yes; access, address, assess, caress, compress, confess, depress, digress, distress, egress, excess, express, finesse, impress, ingress, noblesse, obsess, oppress, possess, profess, progress, recess, redress, repress, success, suppress, transgress, unbless, undress, unless; acquiesce, coalesce, comfortless, convalesce, effervesce, motherless, motionless, pitiless, poetess, prophetess, shepherdess, sorceress, spiritless, votaress, wilderness; *also, many abstract nouns ending in* -ness, *as* sacredness.

-est (ĕst). Best, blest, breast, chest, crest, guest, jest, lest, nest, pest, quest, rest, test, vest, west, wrest, zest; abreast, attest, behest, bequest, congest, contest, detest, digest, divest, infest, invest, molest, protest, request, suggest, unblest, unrest; alkahest, anapaest, manifest; *also, past tenses and past participles of verbs in* -ess, *as* dressed, expressed, *and the superlatives of adjectives accented on the antepenult, as* loveliest.

-et (ĕt). Bet, debt, fret, get, jet, let, met, net, pet, set, stet, sweat, threat, tret, wet, whet, yet; abet, aigrette, beget, beset, cadet, coquette, curvet, duet, forget, gazette, grisette, regret, rosette, soubrette, vignette; alphabet, amulet, annulet, bayonet, cabinet, cigarette, coronet, epaulet, epithet, etiquette, mignonette, minaret, parapet, rivulet, silhouette, violet.

-etch (ĕch). Etch, fetch, ketch, retch, sketch, stretch, vetch, wretch.

-ete (ēt). See -EAT.

-eth (ĕth). See -EATH.

-ette (ĕt). See -ET.

-euce (ūs). See -USE.

-eud (ūd). See -UDE.

-eur (ûr). See -ER.

-euth (ōōth). See -OOTH.

-eve (ēv). See -EAVE.

-ew (ōō; ū; 114). Blew, blue, brew, chew, clue, crew, cue, dew, drew, due, few, flew, glue, grew, hew, hue, Jew, knew, mew, new, pew, rue, screw, shrew, skew, slew, stew, strew, sue, thew, threw, true, view, yew; accrue, adieu, askew, bedew, debut, endue, ensue, eschew, imbue, pursue, renew, review, subdue, withdrew; interview, residue, retinue. Cf. -oo.

-ewd (ūd). See -UDE.

-ewt (ūt). See -UTE.

-ex (ĕks). Flex, sex, vex; annex, complex, convex, perplex; circumflex; *also, plurals of nouns, and third person sing. present of verbs, in* -eck, *as* checks, decks, wrecks.

-ext (ĕkst). Next, text; pretext; *also, past tenses and past participles of verbs in* -ex, *as* annexed, vexed.

-ey (ā; ē). See -AY, -EE.

-ib (ĭb). Bib, crib, fib, glib, jib, nib, rib, sib, squib.

-ibe (īb). Bribe, gibe, scribe, tribe; ascribe, describe, imbibe, inscribe, prescribe, proscribe, subscribe, transcribe; circumscribe, diatribe.

-ic (ĭk). See -ICK.

-ice (īs). Dice, ice, lice, mice, nice, price, rice, slice, spice, splice, thrice, trice, twice, vice, vise; advice, concise, device, entice, precise; paradise, sacrifice.

-ich (ĭch). See -ITCH.

-ick (ĭk). Brick, chick, click, crick, flick, kick, lick, nick, pick, prick, quick, rick, sick, snick, stick, thick, tick, trick, wick; bailiwick, catholic, choleric, heretic, politic, rhetoric; arithmetic.

-ict (ĭkt). Pict, strict; addict, afflict, convict, depict, inflict, predict, restrict; benedict, contradict, derelict; *also, past tenses and past participles of verbs in* -ick, *as* kicked, licked.

-id (ĭd). Bid, chid, did, grid, hid, kid, lid, mid, quid, rid, skid, slid, squid; amid, forbid, outbid, outdid, undid; invalid, pyramid, underbid.
-ide (īd). Bide, bride, chide, glide, guide, hide, pied, pride, ride, side, slide, stride, tide, wide; abide, aside, astride, beside, bestride, betide, collide, confide, decide, deride, divide, elide, misguide, noontide, outside, preside, provide, reside, subside, Yuletide; fratricide, homicide, matricide, parricide, regicide, suicide; *also, past tenses and past participles of verbs in* -ie, -igh, -y, *as* died, sighed, replied.
-ides (īdz). Ides; besides; *also, plurals of nouns, and third person sing. present of verbs, in* -ide, *as* rides.
-idge (ĭj). Bridge, midge, ridge; abridge. Cf. -AGE (ĭj).
-idst (ĭdst). Bidst, didst, hidst, midst, ridst; amidst, forbidst.
-ie, -y (ī). Ay, aye, buy, by, cry, die, dry, dye, eye, fie, fly, fry, guy, hie, high, I, lie, lye, my, nigh, pie, ply, pry, rye, shy, sigh, sky, sly, spry, spy, sty, thigh, thy, tie, try, vie, why, wry; ally, apply, awry, belie, comply, decry, defy, deny, descry, espy, imply, July, outcry, outvie, rely, reply, supply, untie; amplify, beautify, butterfly, certify, crucify, dignify, edify, fortify, glorify, gratify, justify, lullaby, magnify, modify, mollify, multiply, occupy, pacify, prophesy, purify, qualify, ratify, rectify, sanctify, satisfy, signify, terrify, testify, verify.
-iece (ēs). See -EASE (ēs).
-ied (īd). See -IDE.
-ief (ēf). Beef, brief, chief, fief, grief, leaf, lief, reef, sheaf, thief; belief, relief; disbelief, unbelief.
-iege (ēj). Liege, siege; besiege.
-ield (ēld). Field, shield, weald, wield, yield; afield; *also, past tenses and past participles of verbs in* -eal, *as* healed, sealed.
-ien (ēn). See -EAN.
-iend (ēnd). Fiend; *also, past tenses and past participles of verbs in* -ean, *as* gleaned, weaned.
-iend (ĕnd). See -END.
-ier (ēr). See -EER.
-ierce (ērs). Fierce, pierce, tierce; transpierce.
-iest (ēst). See -EAST.
-ieu (ū). See -EW.
-ieve (ēv). See -EAVE.
-iew (ū). See -EW.
-ieze (ēz). See EASE (ēz).
-if, -iff (ĭf). Cliff, glyph, griffe, if, miff, skiff, sniff, stiff, tiff, whiff; hieroglyph.
-ife (īf). Fife, knife, life, rife, strife, wife.
-ift (ĭft). Drift, gift, lift, rift, shift, shrift, sift, swift, thrift; adrift, uplift; *also, past tenses and past participles of verbs in* -iff, *as* whiffed.
-ig (ĭg). Big, brig, dig, fig, gig, grig, jig, pig, prig, rig, sprig, swig, twig, Whig, wig; periwig, whirligig.
-igh (ī). See -IE.
-ight (īt). See -ITE.
-ign (īn). See -INE.
-igue (ēg). See -EAGUE.
-ike (īk). Dike, hike, like, pike, shrike, spike, strike, tyke; alike, dislike, Vandyke.
-il (ĭl). See -ILL.
-ilch (ĭlch). Filch, milch.
-ild (īld). Aisled, child, mild, wild; *also, past tenses and past participles of monosyllabic or finally accented verbs in* -ile, *as* piled, reviled.
-ild (ĭld). Build, gild, guild; rebuild, regild, self-willed, unskilled; *also, past tenses and past participles of verbs in* -ill, *as* filled, killed, milled, swilled, willed.
-ile (īl). Aisle, bile, chyle, file, guile, isle, lisle, mile, pile, rile, smile, spile, stile, style, tile, vile, while, wile; awhile, beguile, compile, defile, erewhile, revile; juvenile, reconcile.
-ilk (ĭlk). Bilk, ilk, milk, silk.
-ill (ĭl). Bill, brill, chill, dill, drill, fill, frill, gill, grill, hill, ill, kill, mill, nil, pill, quill, rill, shrill, sill, skill, spill, squill, still, swill, thill, thrill, till, trill, twill, will; distill, fulfill, instill, quadrille; codicil, daffodil, whippoorwill; *also, many words, ending in* -ile, *with primary accent on the antepenult, as* volatile. See Guide to Pron., § 56.
-ilt (ĭlt). Built, gilt, guilt, hilt, jilt, kilt, lilt, milt, quilt, silt, spilt, stilt, tilt, wilt.
-ilth (ĭlth). Filth, spilth, tilth.
-im (ĭm). Brim, dim, glim, grim, him, hymn, limb, limn, prim, rim, skim, slim, swim, trim, vim, whim; bedim; cherubim, interim, paradigm, seraphim.
-imb (ĭm; īm). See -IM, -IME.
-ime (īm). Chime, chyme, climb, clime, crime, cyme, dime, grime, lime, mime, prime, rhyme, slime, thyme, time; begrime, berhyme, sublime, upclimb; maritime, pantomime.
-imes (īmz). Betimes, ofttimes, sometimes; *also, plurals of nouns, and third person sing. present of verbs, in* -ime, -yme, *as* chimes, rhymes.
-imp (ĭmp). Blimp, crimp, gimp, imp, limp, pimp, primp, scrimp, shrimp, skimp.
-impse (ĭmps). Glimpse; *also, plurals of nouns, and third person sing. present of verbs, in* -imp, *as* imps, limps.
-in (ĭn). Been, bin, chin, din, fin, gin, grin, in, inn, jinn, kin, pin, shin, sin, skin, spin, thin, tin, twin, whin, win; akin, begin, chagrin; discipline, feminine, genuine, heroine, mandolin, masculine, moccasin, paladin, violin.
-inc (ĭngk). See -INK.
-ince (ĭns). Chintz, mince, prince, quince, rinse, since, wince; convince, evince.
-inch (ĭnch). Chinch, cinch, clinch, finch, flinch, inch, lynch, pinch, winch.
-inct (ĭngkt). Tinct; distinct, extinct, instinct, precinct, succinct; *also, past tenses and past participles of verbs in* -ink, *as* linked, pinked.
-ind (īnd). Bind, blind, find, grind, hind, kind, mind, rind, wind; behind, mankind, remind, unkind; *also, past tenses and past participles of verbs in* -ine, *as* refined.
-ind (ĭnd). Wind; prescind, rescind; *also, past tenses and past participles of verbs in* -in, *as* pinned, tinned.
-ine (īn). Brine, chine, dine, fine, kine, line, mine, nine, pine, shine, shrine, sign, sine, spine, stein, swine, thine, tine, trine, twine, vine, whine, wine; align, assign, benign, combine, condign, confine, consign, decline, define, design, divine, enshrine, entwine, incline, opine, outshine, recline, refine, repine, resign, sunshine, supine; anodyne.
-ine (ēn; ĭn). See -EAN, -IN.
-ing (ĭng). Bring, cling, ding, fling, king, ping, ring, sing, sling, spring, sting, string, swing, thing, wing, wring; *also, present participles in* -ing, *and diminutives in* -ling, *with accent on the antepenult, as* covering, fosterling.
-inge (ĭnj). Binge, cringe, fringe, hinge, singe, springe, swinge, tinge, twinge; impinge, infringe, syringe.
-ink (ĭngk). Blink, brink, chink, clink, drink, ink, kink, link, pink, shrink, sink, skink, slink, stink, think, wink, zinc; bethink, forethink, hoodwink; bobolink.
-inse (ĭns). See -INCE.
-int (ĭnt). Dint, flint, glint, hint, lint, mint, print, splint, sprint, squint, stint, tint; asquint, footprint, imprint.
-inth (ĭnth). Plinth; hyacinth, labyrinth.
-inx (ĭngks). Lynx, minx, sphinx; methinks; *also, plurals of nouns, and third person sing. present of verbs, in* -ink, *as* drinks, winks.
-ip (ĭp). Chip, clip, dip, drip, flip, grip, grippe, hip, kip, lip, nip, pip, quip, rip, scrip, ship, sip, skip, slip, snip, strip, tip, trip, whip; equip, transship; *also, polysyllables in* -ship, *with accent on the antepenult, as* authorship.
-ipe (īp). Gripe, pipe, ripe, snipe, stipe, stripe, swipe, tripe, type, wipe; unripe; archetype, prototype; stereotype.
-ipse (ĭps). Eclipse, ellipse; apocalypse; *also, plurals of nouns, and third person sing. present of verbs, in* -ip, *as* lips, strips.
-ique (ēk). See -EAK.
-ir (ûr). See -ER.
-irch (ûrch). See -URCH.
-ird (ûrd). See -URD.
-ire (īr). Byre, choir, dire, fire, gyre, hire, ire, lyre, mire, pyre, quire, shire, sire, spire, squire, tire, wire; acquire, admire, aspire, attire, conspire, desire, entire, expire, inquire, inspire, perspire, require, respire, retire, transpire; *also, nouns formed from verbs ending in* -ie *or* -y, *as* crier, dyer, *and such comparatives of adjectives as* nigher, shyer.
-irge (ûrj). See -ERGE.
-irk (ûrk). See -URK.
-irl (ûrl). See -URL.
-irm (ûrm). Firm, germ, squirm, term, worm; affirm, confirm, infirm; pachyderm.
-irp (ûrp). Burp, chirp; usurp.
-irr (ûr). See -ER.
-irst (ûrst). See -URST.
-irt (ûrt). See -ERT.
-irth (ûrth). Berth, birth, dearth, earth, firth, girth, mirth, worth.
-is (ĭz). Fizz, friz, frizz, his, is, quiz, whiz.
-is (ĭs). See -ISS.
-ise (īs; īz). See -ICE, -IZE.
-ish (ĭsh). Dish, fish, swish, wish.
-isk (ĭsk). Bisque, brisk, disk, frisk, risk, whisk; basilisk, obelisk, tamarisk.
-ism (ĭz'm). Chrism, prism, schism; altruism, barbarism, cataclysm, criticism, egoism, egotism, heroism, mysticism, optimism, organism, realism, solecism, syllogism, witticism.
-isp (ĭsp). Crisp, lisp, wisp.
-iss (ĭs). Bliss, hiss, kiss, miss, this; abyss, amiss, dismiss, remiss; chrysalis, nemesis, synthesis.
-ist (ĭst). Cyst, fist, gist, grist, hist, list, mist, schist, tryst, twist, whist, wist, wrist; assist, consist, desist, exist, insist, persist, resist, subsist; alchemist, amethyst, annalist, colonist, egoist, egotist, eucharist, humorist, journalist, loyalist, moralist, novelist, optimist, pessimist, realist, royalist, satirist, socialist, vocalist; *also, past tenses and past participles of verbs in* -iss, *as* hissed, missed.
-it (ĭt). Bit, chit, fit, flit, grit, hit, kit, knit, lit, pit, quit, sit, slit, smit, spit, split, sprit, tit, twit, whit, wit, writ; acquit, admit, befit, commit, emit, omit, outwit, permit, remit, submit, transmit; apposite, benefit, definite, exquisite, infinite, opposite, perquisite.
-itch (ĭch). Bitch, ditch, fitch, flitch, hitch, itch, niche, pitch, rich, stitch, switch, twitch, which, witch; bewitch.
-ite (īt). Bight, bite, blight, bright, cite, dight, fight, flight, fright, height, hight, kite, knight, light, might, mite, night, plight, quite, right, rite, sight, site, sleight, slight, smite, spite, sprite, tight, trite, white, wight, wright, write; affright, alight, aright, bedight, benight, contrite, delight, despite, excite, ignite, incite, indict, indite, invite, polite, recite, requite, tonight, unite; acolyte, aconite, appetite, dynamite, expedite, oversight, parasite, proselyte, satellite, underwrite.
-ith (ĭth). Frith, kith, myth, pith, smith, withe.
-ith (ĭth). With, withe; forthwith, herewith, therewith, wherewith.
-ithe (īth). Blithe, lithe, scythe, tithe, withe, writhe.
-ive (īv). Dive, drive, five, gyve, hive, live, rive, shive, shrive, strive, thrive, wive; arrive, connive, contrive, deprive, derive, revive, survive.
-ive (ĭv). Give, live, sieve; forgive, misgive, outlive; amative, formative, fugitive, negative, positive, primitive, relative, sedative, sensitive, tentative, transitive.
-ix (ĭks). Fix, mix, pyx, six, Styx; affix, commix, prefix, prolix, transfix; crucifix, intermix, politics; *also, plurals of nouns, and third person sing. present of verbs, in* -ick, *as* licks, picks.
-ixt (ĭkst). Twixt; betwixt; *also, past tenses and past participles of verbs in* -ix, *as* fixed.
-iz (ĭz). See -IS.
-ize (īz). Guise, prize, rise, size, wise; advise, apprise, arise, assize, baptize, chastise, comprise, demise, despise, devise, disguise, emprise, excise, incise, revise, surmise, surprise, uprise; advertise, authorize, canonize, civilize, colonize, criticize, enterprise, equalize, exercise, idolize, lionize, localize, moralize, organize, patronize, recognize, solemnize, sympathize, temporize, tyrannize, utilize, vitalize; *also, plurals of nouns, and third person sing. present of verbs, in* -ie *or* -y, *as* lies, pies, flies.
-o (ō; ōō). See -OW, -OO.
-oach (ōch). Broach, brooch, coach, loach, poach, roach; abroach, approach, encroach, reproach.
-oad (ôd; ōd). See -AUD, -ODE.
-oaf (ōf). Oaf, loaf.
-oak (ōk). See -OKE.
-oal (ōl). See -OLE.
-oam (ōm). See -OME.
-oan (ōn). See -ONE.
-oap (ōp). See -OPE.
-oar (ōr). See -ORE.
-oard (ōrd). See -ORD (ōrd).
-oast (ōst). See -OST (ōst).
-oat (ōt). See -OTE.
-oath (ōth). See -OTH (ōth).
-oax (ōks). Coax, hoax; *also, plurals of nouns, and third person sing. present of verbs, in* -oak, -oke, *as* oaks, smokes.
-ob (ŏb). Blob, bob, cob, fob, hob, job, knob, lob, mob, rob, snob, sob, squab, swab, throb.
-obe (ōb). Globe, Job, lobe, probe, robe; conglobe, disrobe, enrobe, unrobe.
-ock (ŏk). Block, clock, cock, crock, dock, flock, frock, hock, knock, lock, mock, pock, rock, shock, smock, sock, stock; unlock.
-oct (ŏkt). Concoct, decoct; *also, past tenses and past participles of verbs in* -ock, *as* blocked, locked.

-od (ŏd). Clod, cod, God, hod, nod, odd, plod, pod, prod, quad, quod, rod, shod, sod, squad, tod, trod, wad; demigod, goldenrod. Cf. -ADE (ăd).

-ode (ōd). Bode, code, goad, load, lode, mode, node, ode, road, rode, strode, toad, woad; abode, commode, corrode, explode, forebode, unload; episode; *also, past tenses and past participles of verbs in* -ow, *as* owed.

-odge (ŏj). Dodge, lodge, podge, stodge.

-oe (ō; ōō). See -ow, -oo.

-oes (ūz). See -uzz.

-off (ŏf; ŏf; 74). Cough, doff, off, scoff, trough. Cf. -ALF.

-oft (ŏft; 74). Croft, loft, oft, soft; aloft; *also, past tenses and past participles of verbs in* -off, *as* scoffed.

-og (ŏg; ôg; 74). Bog, clog, cog, dog, flog, fog, frog, grog, hog, jog, log, nog, slog; catalogue, decalogue, dialogue, epilogue, monologue, pedagogue, synagogue.

-oge (ōj). Doge; gamboge.

-ogue (ōg). Brogue, rogue, vogue; prorogue; disembogue.

-ogue (ŏg; 74). See -OG.

-oice (ois). Choice, voice; rejoice.

-oid (oid). Void; avoid, devoid; aneroid, asteroid; *also, past tenses and past participles of verbs in* -oy, *as* cloyed, toyed.

-oil (oil). Boil, broil, coil, foil, moil, oil, roil, soil, spoil, toil; despoil, embroil, recoil, uncoil.

-oin (oin). Coign, coin, groin, join, loin, quoin; adjoin, conjoin, disjoin, enjoin, purloin, rejoin, subjoin.

-oint (oint). Joint, point; anoint, appoint, aroint, conjoint, disjoint; counterpoint, disappoint.

-oir (wär). Devoir; reservoir.

-oise (oiz). Noise, poise; counterpoise, equipoise; avoirdupois; *also, plurals of nouns, and third person sing. present of verbs, in* -oy, *as* boys, cloys.

-oist (oist). Foist, hoist, joist, moist; *also, past tenses and past participles of verbs in* -oice, *as* rejoiced.

-oit (oit). Adroit, exploit.

-oke (ōk). Broke, choke, cloak, coke, folk, joke, poke, smoke, soak, spoke, stoke, stroke, woke, yoke, yolk; awoke, bespoke, convoke, invoke, provoke, revoke.

-ol (ŏl). Doll, loll, Sol; extol; folderol, protocol.

-ol (ōl). See -OLE.

-old (ōld). Bold, cold, fold, gold, hold, mold, mould, old, scold, sold, told, wold; behold, enfold, foretold, unfold, untold, uphold, withhold; manifold, marigold; *also, past tenses and past participles of verbs in* -oll, -ole, -oal, *as* rolled, cajoled, foaled.

-ole (ōl). Bole, bowl, coal, dole, droll, foal, goal, hole, jowl, knoll, mole, pole, role, roll, scroll, shoal, sole, soul, stole, stroll, toll, troll, whole; cajole, condole, console, control, enroll, parole.

-olk (ōk). See -OKE.

-oll (ŏl; ōl). See -OL, -OLE.

-olt (ōlt). Bolt, colt, dolt, holt, jolt, molt, poult; revolt; thunderbolt.

-olve (ŏlv). Solve; absolve, convolve, devolve, dissolve, evolve, involve, resolve, revolve.

-om (ŏm). Bomb, from, Tom.

-om (ōōm). See -OOM.

-omb (ōm; ŏm; ōōm). See -OM, -OME, -OOM.

-ome (ōm). Chrome, comb, dome, foam, home, loam, ohm, roam, tome; aerodrome, catacomb, hippodrome.

-omp (ŏmp). Romp, pomp, swamp.

-ompt (ŏmpt). Prompt, romped, swamped.

-on (ŏn; ŏn; 74). Con, don, gone, on, shone, swan, wan, yon; anon, begone, upon; Amazon, paragon, Rubicon; phenomenon.

-on (ŭn). See -UN.

-once (ŏns). Nonce, sconce; ensconce, response.

-once (ŭns). See -UNCE.

-onch (ŏngk). Conch, honk.

-ond (ŏnd). Blond(e), bond, fond, frond, pond, wand, yond; abscond, beyond, despond, respond; correspond, vagabond; *also, past tenses and past participles of verbs in* -on, *as* conned, donned.

-one (ōn). Bone, cone, crone, drone, flown, groan, grown, hone, known, loan, lone, moan, mown, own, prone, roan, shown, sown, stone, throne, thrown, tone, zone; alone, atone, condone, dethrone, enthrone, intone, postpone.

-one (ŭn). See -UN.

-one (ŏn). See -ON.

-ong (ŏng; 74). Gong, long, prong, song, strong, thong, throng, wrong; along, belong, prolong, Souchong.

-ong (ŭng). See -UNG.

-ongue (ŭng). See -UNG.

-onk (ŏngk; ŭngk). See -ONCH, -UNK.

-onse (ŏns). See -ONCE.

-ont (ŏnt). Font, want. Cf. -AUNT.

-ont (ŭnt). See -UNT.

-oo (ōō; 114). Coo, do, loo, shoe, sou, through, to, too, two, who, woo, you; ado, bamboo, canoe, halloo, Hindu, outdo, ragout, shampoo, taboo, tattoo, undo; rendezvous. Cf. -EW.

-ood (ōōd; 114). Brood, crude, food, mood, prude, rood, rude, snood; conclude, exclude, include, intrude, obtrude, preclude, protrude, seclude; *also, past tenses and past participles of verbs in* -oo, *as* cooed, wooed, *and of many verbs in* -ue, -ew, *as* rued, strewed. Cf. -UDE.

-ood (ōōd). Could, good, hood, should, stood, wood, would; brotherhood, livelihood, maidenhood, motherhood, neighborhood, sisterhood, understood, womanhood.

-oof (ōōf; 85). Hoof, proof, roof, woof; aloof, behoof, disproof, reproof.

-ook (ōōk). Book, brook, cook, crook, hook, look, nook, rook, shook, took; forsook, mistook; overlook.

-ook (ōōk; 114). Snook, spook; caoutchouc, peruke. Cf. -UKE.

-ool (ōōl; 114). Cool, drool, fool, pool, rule, school, spool, stool, tool, tulle; befool; overrule. Cf. -ULE.

-oom (ōōm; 85; 114). Bloom, boom, broom, doom, gloom, groom, loom, room, tomb, whom, womb; entomb. Cf. -UME (ōōm).

-oon (ōōn; 114). Boon, coon, croon, June, loon, moon, noon, prune, rune, soon, spoon, swoon; baboon, balloon, bassoon, buffoon, cartoon, cocoon, dragoon, festoon, galloon, harpoon, lagoon, lampoon, maroon, monsoon, platoon, pontoon, raccoon, typhoon; honeymoon. Cf. -UNE.

-oop (ōōp; 85; 114). Coop, croup, droop, drupe, group, hoop, jupe, loop, poop, scoop, sloop, soup, stoop, swoop, troop, whoop. Cf. -UPE.

-oor (ōōr; 84). Boor, moor, poor, tour, your; amour, assure, contour, insure; paramour. Cf. -URE.

-oor (ōr). See -ORE.

-oors (ōōrz). See -OURS.

-oose (ōōs; 114). Goose, juice, loose, moose, noose, sluice, spruce, truce; abstruse, burnoose, recluse. Cf. -USE (ūs).

-oose (ōōz). See -OOZE.

-oot (ōōt; 114). Boot, bruit, brute, chute, coot, flute, fruit, hoot, loot, moot, root, route, shoot, toot; recruit, uproot; parachute. Cf. -UTE.

-oot (ōōt). Foot, put, soot.

-ooth (ōōth). Booth, smooth, smoothe, soothe.

-ooth (ōōth; 114). Booth, ruth, sleuth, sooth, tooth, truth, youth; forsooth, insooth, uncouth.

-oove (ōōv). See -OVE.

-ooze (ōōz; 114). Booze, bruise, choose, cruise, lose, ooze, ruse, snooze, whose; peruse; *also, plurals of nouns, and third person sing. present of many verbs, in* -oo, -ue, *as* coos, rues. Cf. -USE (ūz).

-op (ŏp). Chop, cop, crop, drop, flop, fop, hop, lop, mop, prop, shop, slop, sop, stop, strop, swap, top; eavesdrop, overstop.

-ope (ōp). Cope, grope, hope, mope, ope, pope, rope, scope, slope, soap, tope, trope; elope; antelope, horoscope, interlope, telescope; heliotrope.

-opt (ŏpt). Copt; adopt; *also, past tenses and past participles of verbs in* -op, *as* hopped, lopped.

-or (ōr). Dor, war; abhor; *also, words ending in* -or, *as* bailor, donor, lessor, vendor, *when used in contrast with correlatives in* -ee.

-or (ōr). See -ORE.

-orb (ôrb). Orb, sorb, Sorb; absorb.

-orce (ōrs). See -ORSE (ōrs).

-orch (ôrch; ōrch; 70). Scorch, porch, torch.

-ord (ôrd). Chord, cord, lord, sward, ward; abhorred, accord, award, record, reward.

-ord (ōrd; 70). Board, ford, hoard, sword; aboard, afford; *also, past tenses and past participles of verbs in* -ore, *as* bored.

-ore (ōr). Boar, bore, core, corps, door, floor, fore, four, gore, lore, more, oar, o'er, ore, pore, pour, roar, score, shore, snore, soar, sore, store, swore, tore, wore, yore; adore, afore, ashore, before, deplore, explore, forbore, forswore, galore, ignore, implore, restore; evermore, nevermore, sophomore, sycamore. Cf. -OR.

-orge (ôrj; ōrj; 70). Forge, gorge; disgorge, engorge.

-ork (ôrk; ōrk; 70). Cork, fork, pork, stork, torque.

-orld (ûrld). Curled, furled, hurled, swirled, world.

-orm (ôrm). Form, norm, storm, swarm, warm; conform, deform, inform, perform, reform, transform; chloroform, cruciform, uniform.

-orm (ûrm). See -IRM.

-orn (ôrn). Born, corn, horn, lorn, morn, scorn, thorn, warn; adorn, forewarn, forlorn, suborn; unicorn.

-orn (ōrn; 70). Borne, bourn, mourn, shorn, sworn, torn, worn; forsworn.

-orp (ôrp). Dorp, thorp, warp.

-orse (ôrs). Corse, gorse, horse, morse, torse; endorse, remorse, unhorse.

-orse (ōrs; 70). Coarse, course, force, hoarse, source; discourse, divorce, enforce, perforce, recourse, resource.

-orst (ûrst). See -URST.

-ort (ôrt). Mort, ort, short, sort, swart, thwart, tort, wart; abort, assort, athwart, consort, distort, escort, exhort, extort, resort, retort.

-ort (ōrt; 70). Court, fort, port, sport; comport, disport, export, import, rapport, report.

-orth (ôrth; ōrth; 70). Forth, fourth, north, swarth.

-ose (ōs). Close, dose, gross; engross, globose, jocose, morose, verbose; bellicose, comatose, grandiose, otiose.

-ose (ōz). Chose, close, doze, froze, gloze, nose, pose, prose, rose, those; arose, compose, depose, disclose, dispose, enclose, expose, foreclose, impose, oppose, propose, repose, suppose, transpose; *also, plurals of nouns, and third person sing. present of verbs, in* -ow, -oe, -o, *as* glows, foes, goes.

-osk, -osque (ŏsk). Bosk, mosque; kiosk.

-oss (ŏs; ōs; 74). Boss, cross, dross, floss, fosse, gloss, joss, loss, moss, toss; across, emboss, lacrosse.

-ost (ôst; ōst; 74). Cost, frost, lost, wast; accost; Pentecost; *also, past tenses and past participles of verbs in* -oss, *as* crossed, embossed.

-ost (ōst). Boast, coast, ghost, host, most, post, roast, toast; *also, polysyllabic superlatives ending in* -most, *and accented on the antepenult, as* uttermost.

-ot (ŏt). Blot, clot, cot, dot, got, grot, hot, jot, knot, lot, not, plot, pot, rot, sot, shot, slot, sot, spot, squat, tot, trot, what, wot, yacht; allot, besot, forgot, gavotte, unknot; polyglot.

-otch (ŏch). Blotch, botch, crotch, notch, scotch, splotch, watch.

-ote (ōt). Bloat, boat, coat, cote, dote, float, gloat, goat, groat, moat, mote, note, oat, quote, rote, shoat, smote, stoat, throat, tote, vote, wrote; afloat, denote, devote, promote, remote; anecdote, antidote, table d'hôte.

-oth (ŏth; 74). Broth, cloth, froth, Goth, moth, swath, troth, wroth; betroth.

-oth (ōth). Both, growth, loath, oath, quoth, sloth, wroth.

-oth (ôth). Swath, wrath.

-othe (ōth). Betroth, clothe, loathe.

-ou (ou). See -OW.

-ou (ū). See -EW.

-oubt (out). See -OUT.

-ouch (ouch). Couch, crouch, grouch, ouch, pouch, slouch, vouch; avouch.

-ouch (ŭch). See -UTCH.

-ouche (ōōsh). Douche, ruche; barouche, cartouche, debouch.

-oud (oud). Cloud, crowd, loud, proud, shroud; aloud, becloud, enshroud; *also, past tenses and past participles of verbs in* -ow, *as* bowed.

-ough (ŏf; ou; ō; ŭf). See -OFF, -OW, -UFF.

-ought (ôt). Aught, bought, brought, caught, fought, fraught, naught, nought, ought, sought, taught, taut, thought, wrought; besought, distraught, inwrought, methought; Argonaut, Juggernaut, overwrought.

-oul (ōōl; ōl). See -OWL, -OLE.

-ould (ōōd). See -OOD.

-oun (oun). See -OWN.

-ounce (ouns). Bounce, flounce, frounce, ounce, pounce, trounce; announce, denounce, pronounce, renounce.

-ound (ound). Bound, found, ground, hound, mound, pound, round, sound, wound; abound, aground, astound, compound, confound, expound, profound, propound, rebound, redound, resound, surround; *also, past tenses and past participles of verbs in* -own (oun), *as* frowned.

-ound (oōnd; 114). Wound; *also, past tenses and past participles of verbs in* -oon, -une, *as* crooned, pruned. Cf. -UNED.

-ount (ount). Count, fount, mount; account, amount, discount, dismount, miscount, recount, remount, surmount; catamount, paramount, tantamount.

-oup (oōp). See -OOP.

-our (our). Flour, hour, our, scour, sour; devour; *also, words ending in* -ower, *when these syllables are pronounced as one, as* bower, cower, flower, glower, lower, power, shower, tower.

-ourge (ûrj). See -ERGE.

-ourn (ōrn; ûrn). See -ORN (ōrn), -URN.

-ours (ourz). Ours; *also, plurals of nouns, and third person sing. present of verbs, in* -our *and* -ower, *as* hours, scours, bowers, showers.

-ours (oōrz). Yours; *also, plurals of nouns, and third person sing. present of verbs, in* -oor, -our (ōōr), *and* -ure, *as* moors, tours, cures, endures.

-ourse (ōrs). See -ORSE.

-ourt (ōrt). See -ORT.

-ourth (ōrth). See -ORTH.

-ous (ŭs). See -US.

-ouse (ous). Blouse, douse, grouse, house, *n.*, louse, mouse, *n.*, souse.

-ouse (ouz). Blouse, browse, drowse, house, *v.*, mouse, *v.*, rouse, spouse; arouse, carouse, espouse; *also, plurals of nouns, and third person sing. present of verbs, in* -ow (ou), *as* brows, plows.

-out (out). Bout, clout, doubt, drought, flout, gout, grout, knout, lout, out, pout, rout, scout, shout, snout, spout, sprout, stout, tout, trout; about, devout, redoubt, without.

-outh (outh). Drouth, mouth, *n. & adj.*, south, *n. & adj.*

-outh (outh). Mouth, *v.*, south, *v.*

-outh (ōōth). Mouth, *v.*, south, *v.*

-ove (ōv). Clove, cove, dove, *v.*, drove, grove, hove, Jove, mauve, rove, shrove, stove, strove, throve, wove; inwove; interwove.

-ove (ōōv). Groove, move, prove; approve, behoove, disprove, improve, reprove; disapprove.

-ove (ŭv). Dove, glove, love, shove; above, belove, unglove; turtledove.

-ow (ou). Bough, bow, brow, cow, how, mow, now, plow, prow, row, scow, slough, sow, *n.*, thou, vow; allow, avow, endow, kotow.

-ow (ō). Beau, blow, bow, crow, doe, dough, floe, flow, foe, fro, glow, go, grow, hoe, know, lo, low, mot, mow, no, O, oh, owe, roe, row, sew, show, sloe, slow, snow, so, sow, *v.*, stow, strow, throe, throw, toe, tow, trow, woe; aglow, ago, below, bestow, château, foreknow, foreshow, outgrow, rainbow, tableau, trousseau; buffalo, bungalow, calico, overflow, overgrow, overthrow.

-owd (oud). See -OUD.

-owl (oul). Cowl, foul, fowl, growl, howl, jowl, owl, prowl, scowl, yowl; befoul.

-own (oun). Brown, clown, crown, down, drown, frown, gown, noun, town; adown, embrown, renown.

-owse (ouz). See -OUSE.

-owth (ōth). See -OTH (ōth).

-ox (ŏks). Box, fox, ox, phlox; equinox, orthodox, paradox; heterodox; *also, plurals of nouns, and third person sing. present of verbs, in* -ock, *as* locks, stocks.

-oy (oi). Boy, buoy, cloy, coy, joy, toy, troy; alloy, annoy, convoy, decoy, deploy, destroy, employ, enjoy.

-oze (ōz). See -OSE.

-ub (ŭb). Chub, club, cub, drub, dub, grub, hub, rub, scrub, shrub, snub, stub, tub; hubbub; sillabub.

-ube (ūb). Cube, tube.

-uce (ūs). See -USE (ūs).

-uch (ŭch). See -UTCH.

-uck (ŭk). Buck, chuck, cluck, duck, luck, muck, pluck, puck, ruck, shuck, struck, stuck, suck, truck, tuck; amuck.

-uct (ŭkt). Duct; abduct, conduct, construct, deduct, induct, instruct, obstruct; aqueduct, viaduct; *also, past tenses and past participles of verbs in* -uck, *as* plucked.

-ud (ŭd). Blood, bud, cud, flood, mud, rudd, scud, spud, stud, thud.

-ude (ūd; 114). Dude, feud, lewd, nude; al-

lude, collude, delude, denude, elude, exude; altitude, aptitude, desuetude, fortitude, gratitude, habitude, interlude, lassitude, latitude, longitude, magnitude, multitude, plenitude, promptitude, quietude, servitude, similitude, solicitude, solitude, turpitude; vicissitude; *also, past tenses and past participles of many verbs in* -ew *and* -ue, *as* stewed, subdued. Cf. -OOD.

-ude (ōōd). See -OOD.

-udge (ŭj). Budge, drudge, fudge, grudge, judge, nudge, sludge, smudge, trudge; adjudge, begrudge, misjudge.

-ue (ū; ōō). See -EW, -OO.

-uff (ŭf). Bluff, buff, chough, clough, cuff, fluff, gruff, huff, luff, muff, puff, rough, ruff, scruff, scuff, slough, snuff, sough, stuff, tough, tuff; enough, rebuff; overstuff.

-uft (ŭft). Tuft; *also, past tenses and past participles of verbs in* -uff, -ough (ŭf), *as* bluffed, sloughed.

-ug (ŭg). Bug, drug, dug, hug, jug, lug, mug, plug, pug, rug, shrug, slug, smug, snug, thug, tug.

-uge (ūj). Huge; febrifuge, subterfuge, vermifuge.

-uice (ūs). See -USE (ūs).

-uise (īz). See -IZE.

-uke (ūk; 114). Duke, fluke, puke; rebuke; Mameluke. Cf. -OOK (ōōk).

-ul, -ull (ŭl). Cull, dull, gull, hull, lull, mull, null, scull, skull, trull; annul, mogul; disannul.

-ul, -ull (ōōl). Bull, full, pull, wool; *also, polysyllabic adjectives and nouns in* -ful, *with accent on the antepenult, as* masterful, bucketful.

-ulch (ŭlch). Gulch, mulch.

-ule (ūl; 114). Mule, pule, yule; molecule, reticule, ridicule. Cf. -OOL.

-ulge (ŭlj). Bulge; divulge, effulge, indulge, promulge.

-ulk (ŭlk). Bulk, hulk, skulk, sulk.

-ulp (ŭlp). Gulp, pulp, sculp.

-ulse (ŭls). Pulse; appulse, convulse, repulse.

-ult (ŭlt). Cult; adult, consult, exult, insult, occult, result; catapult, difficult.

-um (ŭm). Chum, come, crumb, drum, dumb, glum, grum, gum, hum, mum, numb, plum, plumb, rum, scum, slum, some, strum, stum, sum, swum, thrum, thumb; become, benumb, succumb; *also, polysyllables in* -dom, -some, -um, *with accent on the antepenult, as* Christendom, cumbersome, vacuum.

-ume (ūm; 114). Fume, spume; assume, consume, costume, exhume, illume, legume, perfume, presume, relume, resume.

-ume (ōōm; 114). Brume, flume, glume, plume, rheum. Cf. -OOM.

-ump (ŭmp). Bump, chump, clump, dump, hump, jump, lump, plump, pump, rump, slump, stump, thump, trump.

-un (ŭn). Bun, done, dun, fun, gun, Hun, none, nun, one, pun, run, shun, son, spun, stun, sun, ton, tun, won; begun, outrun, undone.

-unce (ŭns). Dunce, once.

-unch (ŭnch). Bunch, crunch, hunch, lunch, munch, punch, scrunch.

-unct (ŭngkt). Defunct, disjunct; *also, past tenses and past participles of verbs in* -unk, *as* funked.

-und (ŭnd). Bund, fund; obtund, refund, rotund; moribund, orotund, rubicund; *also, past tenses and past participles of verbs in* -un, *as* punned.

-une (ūn; 114). Dune, hewn, June, tune; attune, commune, impugn, oppugn; importune, opportune, picayune. Cf. -OON.

-une (ōōn). See -OON.

-uned (ūnd; 114). Tuned; attuned, communed, impugned. Cf. -OUND (ōōnd).

-ung (ŭng). Bung, clung, dung, flung, hung, lung, rung, slung, sprung, strung, stung, sung, swung, tongue, wrung, young; among, unstrung, unsung.

-unge (ŭnj). Lunge, plunge, sponge; expunge.

-unk (ŭngk). Bunk, chunk, drunk, funk, hunk, junk, monk, punk, shrunk, skunk, slunk, spunk, sunk, trunk.

-unt (ŭnt). Blunt, brunt, bunt, front, grunt, hunt, punt, runt, shunt, stunt, wont.

-up (ŭp). Cup, pup, scup, sup, tup, up.

-upe (ūp; 114). Dupe, stupe. Cf. -OOP.

-upt (ŭpt). Cupped, supped, tupped, upped;

abrupt, corrupt, disrupt, erupt; interrupt.

-ur (ûr). See -ER.

-urb (ûrb). See -ERB.

-urch (ûrch). Birch, church, lurch, perch, search, smirch; research.

-urd (ûrd). Bird, curd, gird, heard, herd, surd, third, word; *also, past tenses and past participles of many verbs in* -er, -ir, -ur, *as* averred, bestirred, demurred.

-ure (ūr; 114). Cure, lure, pure; allure, demure, endure, immure, impure, manure, mature, obscure, procure, secure; aperture, epicure, forfeiture, furniture, immature, overture, premature, sinecure; miniature, temperature. Cf. -OOR.

-ures (ūrz). See -OURS (ōōrz).

-urf (ûrf). Scurf, serf, surf, turf.

-urge (ûrj). See -ERGE.

-urk (ûrk). Burke, clerk, dirk, irk, jerk, kirk, perk, quirk, shirk, smirk, Turk, work.

-url (ûrl). Burl, churl, curl, earl, furl, girl, hurl, knurl, pearl, purl, swirl, twirl, whirl; uncurl, unfurl.

-urn (ûrn). Burn, churn, earn, fern, kern, learn, quern, spurn, tern, turn, urn, yearn; adjourn, concern, discern, return, sojourn.

-urnt (ûrnt). Burnt, learnt, weren't.

-urp (ûrp). See -IRP.

-urse (ûrs). See -ERSE.

-urst (ûrst). Burst, curst, durst, erst, first, thirst, versed, verst, worst; accurst, athirst.

-urt (ûrt). See -ERT.

-urve (ûrv). See -ERVE.

-us (ŭs). Bus, buss, fuss, muss, plus, pus, truss, us; discuss; blunderbuss, omnibus; *also, polysyllables in* -ous, -us, *with accent on the antepenult, as* fabulous, impetus.

-use (ūs; 114). Deuce, puce, use, *n.*, Zeus; abuse, *n.*, adduce, conduce, deduce, diffuse, *adj.*, disuse, *n.*, excuse, *n.*, induce, misuse, *n.*, obtuse, produce, profuse, reduce, seduce, traduce; introduce. Cf. -OOSE.

-use (ōōz; 114). See -OOZE.

-use (ūz; 114). Fuse, muse, news, use, *v.*; abuse, *v.*, accuse, amuse, confuse, diffuse, *v.*, disuse, *v.*, excuse, *v.*, infuse, misuse, *v.*, refuse, suffuse, transfuse; *also, plurals of nouns, and third person sing. present of verbs, in* -ew *and* -ue, *as* dews, imbues. Cf. -OOZE.

-ush (ŭsh). Blush, brush, crush, flush, gush, hush, lush, mush, plush, rush, slush, thrush, tush; ablush, ahush.

-ush (ōōsh). Bush, push.

-usk (ŭsk). Brusque, busk, cusk, dusk, husk, musk, rusk, tusk.

-ust (ŭst). Bust, crust, dost, dust, gust, joust, just, lust, must, rust, thrust, trust; adjust, adust, august, disgust, distrust, intrust, mistrust, robust, unjust; *also, past tenses and past participles of verbs in* -uss, *as* discussed, trussed.

-ut (ŭt). But, butt, cut, glut, gut, hut, jut, nut, putt, rut, shut, slut, smut, strut, tut; abut, rebut, uncut.

-ut (ōōt). See -OOT.

-utch (ŭch). Clutch, crutch, Dutch, hutch, much, smutch, such, touch.

-ute (ūt; 114). Butte, cute, lute, mute, newt, suit; acute, astute, commute, compute, confute, depute, dilute, dispute, impute, minute, pollute, pursuit, refute, repute, salute, transmute, volute; absolute, attribute, constitute, destitute, dissolute, execute, institute, persecute, prosecute, resolute, substitute. Cf. -OOT (ōōt).

-uth (ōōth). See -OOTH.

-ux (ŭks). Crux, flux; *also, plurals of nouns, and third person sing. present of verbs, in* -uck, *as* ducks, trucks.

-uzz (ŭz). Buzz, coz, does, fuzz.

-y (ī). See -IE.

-ymn (ĭm). See -IM.

-ymph (ĭmf). Lymph, nymph.

-yne (īn). See -INE.

-ynx (ĭngks). See -INX.

-ype (īp). See -IPE.

-yph (ĭf). See -IFF.

-ypse (ĭps). See -IPSE.

-yre (īr). See -IRE.

-yrrh (ûr). See -ER.

-ysm (ĭz'm). See -ISM.

-yst (ĭst). See -IST.

-yve (īv). See -IVE.

-yx (ĭks). See -IX.

ORTHOGRAPHY

Spelling changes advocated by Noah Webster in his *Dictionary* (1828) have had considerable influence upon orthography, especially in the United States. These changes were proposed by him chiefly on the basis of etymology and of analogy with the dual object, first, of making the words correspond, as far as practicable, with their primitive forms in order to reveal more obviously their etymological affinities, and second, of reducing the number of anomalies and exceptional cases.

It is to be observed that many of these deviations from the usage of his time were not innovations, but restorations of older forms which were once generally employed. For example, the spelling with the termination *-er* of words often written with *-re*, as *meter*, and the spelling with *-or* of words often written with *-our*, as *color*, are but restorations of older spellings.

Presented below are some of Noah Webster's spelling rules as they have been modified in American practice.

RULES FOR SPELLING

§ 1. Words ending in c have a k inserted when adding a termination beginning with *e*, *i*, or *y*, to prevent the *c* from being pronounced like *s*: as, *shellac, shellacked; picnic, picnicker; panic, panicky.* Exceptions: *arc, arced, arcing; disc, disced, discing; zinc, zincic.*

§ 2. Final consonant doubled. Monosyllables and words accented on the last syllable, when ending in a single consonant *b, d, f, g, k, l, m, n, p, r, s, t, v* preceded by a single vowel, double the consonant before adding a termination beginning with a vowel or the suffix *-y*: as, *club, clubbed, clubby; forbid, forbidding; if, iffy; rebel', rebellious; plan, planned, plan'ning, plan'ner; bag, bag'-gage; hot, hot'ter, hot'test; abet', abet'ted, abet'ting, abet'tor; infer', inferred'; rev, revved.* The consonant is doubled to preserve the vowel sound of the base. Thus, *plănned, hŏttest,* and *abĕtted* would naturally be pronounced *plāned, hōtest,* and *abēted* if the consonant were not doubled. Derivatives of a few words having a long vowel sound in the accented final syllable follow the rule, as *control, controlled, controllable, controller; extol, extolled; patrol, patrolled, patroller.*

Verbs ending in *r* with few exceptions follow the rule in uniting with *-able, -al, -er,* as *averrable, barrable, conferrable, conferral, conferrer, deferrable, deterrable, incurrable, slurrable, spurrable, stirrable,* but the few compounds with *r* doubled before *-ible* are not preferred spellings.

EXCEPTIONS: (1) Derivatives of *gas* (except *gassed, gas'sing,* and *gassy*): as, *gas'eous, gas'ify.* (2) Derivatives in which the accent of the base is thrown back on another syllable: as, *infer', in'ference; refer', ref'erable; defer', def'erence; prefer', pref'erable.* (3) *Chagrin, chagrined, chagrining.* Since *chagrin,* which in British use rhymes with *green,* rhymes in the U. S. with *grin, chagrinned, chagrinning* would be justifiable in the U. S.

§ 3. Final consonant not doubled. Words having primary accent on any syllable but the last, words ending in more than one consonant, and words ending in a single consonant preceded by a diphthong or vowel digraph do not double the final consonant before adding a termination beginning with a vowel or the suffix *-y*: as, *revel, reveled, reveling, reveler; profit, profited; catalog, cataloged; act, acted, actor; daub, daubed; need, needy; brief, briefer, briefest; tread, treading.*

EXCEPTIONS: (1) *Humbug, humbugged, humbugging.* (2) Derivatives of *kidnap, benefit, carburet,* and *program,* whose ultima has a secondary accent, are spelled properly either with or without the final consonant doubled: as, *kid'naped'* or *kid'napped', kid'nap'ing* or *kid'nap'-ping, kid'nap'er* or *kid'nap'per; benefited* or *benefitted; carbureted* or *carburetted; programed* or *programmed* (but only *programmatic*). (3) *Worship, worshiped* or *worshipped, worshiper* or *worshipper.*

NOTE. According to some lexicographers, a large class of words ending in a single consonant and accented on some other syllable than the last (including all verbs ending in unaccented *el*) double the final consonant before a vowel in derivatives: for example, *apparel, bevel, cancel, cavil, counsel, cudgel, dial, dishevel, duel, empanel, enamel, equal, gambol, grovel, imperil, jewel, label, level, libel, marshal, marvel, medal, metal, model, parcel, pencil, quarrel, ravel, revel, rival, shrivel, travel, yodel.* See § 27, below.

§ 4. Double consonant retained. Words ending in a double consonant commonly retain both consonants when adding terminations: as, *ebb, ebbing; odd, oddly; stiff, stiffness; will, willful, willfulness; dull, dullness.* So also the double *l* is retained in the preferred forms of the words *installment, enthrallment, thralldom,* and *enrollment,* in order to prevent an erroneous pronunciation with short ă or short ŏ. See § 27, below.

EXCEPTIONS: (1) The adjective forms of *pontiff* have a single *f: pontific, pontifical.* (2) The adverbs *illy, dully, fully.* (3) *Skilless* and similar derivatives in *-less* of words ending in *ll,* which are alternate forms to the commoner forms ending in *ll-less,* as *skill-less.*

§ 5. Silent e retained. Words ending with silent *e* generally retain this *e* when the termination begins with a consonant: as, *awesome, doelike, hateful, incitement, issueless, judgeship, paleness, ropelike, shapely.*

EXCEPTIONS: (1) A few words ending in silent *e* immediately preceded by another vowel (except *e*) drop the *e* in forming derivatives: as, *due, duly; argue, argument; true, truly.* (2) *Abridgment, acknowledgment, fledgling, lodgment, judgment, wholly.* Cf. § 28, below.

§ 6. Silent e omitted. Words ending with silent *e* generally drop the *e* before terminations beginning with a vowel: as, *base, basal; force, forcible; guide, guidance; hoe, hoed; plume, plumage; scale, scalable; shape, shaping; statue, statuesque; sue, sued; true, truism.*

EXCEPTIONS: (1) The *e* is retained in *hoeing, shoeing,* and *toeing,* but is generally excluded from *shoer.* (2) The *e* is retained in *dyeing, singeing, swingeing, tingeing* (from *dye, singe, swinge, tinge*), to distinguish them from *dying, singing, swinging, tinging* (from *die, sing, swing, ting*), but no *e* is needed in *cringing* or *impinging* because there is no verb *cring* or *imping* to be confused with *cringe* or *impinge.* (3) Words ending in *ce* or *ge* retain the *e* before terminations beginning with *a* or *o,* to prevent the *c* or *g* from being pronounced with the hard sound: as, *notice, noticeable; manage, manageable; advantage, advantageous. Mortgagor,* pronounced *mor'-gajor',* from *mortgage,* is exceptional. (4) *Mileage.* (5) A few derivatives in *-able* in which *e* is regularly retained by many writers: as, *likeable, useable, saleable.*

§ 7. Ending -ing added to ie. Words ending in *ie* generally drop the *e* and change the *i* to *y* when adding *-ing*, so as to prevent two *i*'s from coming together: as, *die, dying; tie, tying* or *tieing; hie, hying* or *hieing.*

§ 8. y preceded by a consonant. Words ending in *y* preceded by a consonant usually change the *y* to *i* before any termination except one beginning with *i:* as, *icy, iciest, icily, iciness; mercy, merciless; modify, modifiable, modifies; pity, pitiable, pitiful;* but *thirty, thirtyish.*

EXCEPTIONS: (1) Adjectives of one syllable have comparative and superlative forms in both *-ier, -iest* and *-yer, -yest:* as, *shy, shier* or *shyer, shiest* or *shyest; spry, sprier* or *spryer, spriest* or *spryest;* but *drier, driest* are commoner than *dryer, dryest,* and the noun *dryer* is preferred for an apparatus in distinction from *drier* for a chemical. (2) Adjectives of one syllable usually retain the *y* before *-ly* and *-ness:* as, *shy, shyly, shyness; wry, wryly, wryness;* but *dryly* and *drily* are about equally common, also *slyly* and *slily.* (3) *Flier* and *flyer* are both in good use. (4) Before *-ship* and *-like,* as *secretaryship, citylike,* and in derivatives formed from *baby* and *lady,* the *y* is retained: as, *babyish, ladykin.* (5) The *y* is retained in the plural of proper names: the *Storys.* (6) The *y* is retained in *busyness* (busy state). (7) The *y* is retained in the possessive case: as, *everybody's.*

§ 9. y preceded by a vowel. Words ending in *y* preceded by a vowel generally retain the *y* unchanged before all terminations: as, *obey, obeying; joy, joyful; gay, gayer, gayest; gluey, glueyness* (but *gluier, gluiest*).

EXCEPTIONS: *Daily, laid, said, slain* (from *day, lay, say, slay*). *Gaily* and *gayly* are in equally good use, likewise *gaiety* and *gayety.*

§ 10. Spelling of a final vowel sound retained. Words ending with a vowel sound retain the letter or letters representing such sound before a termination beginning with a vowel: as, *toga, togaed; agree, agreeable; weigh, weighing; ski, skied, skier; taxi, taxied, taxiing; charivari, charivaried; veto,* (he) *vetoes; dough, doughy; cameo, cameoed; bow, bowed; shampoo, shampooed.*

NOTE 1. The 3d person singular present indicative of verbs ending in two vowels takes *-s,* not *-es:* as, (he) *radios,* (a cow) *moos,* (it) *hoodoos.*

NOTE 2. Words ending in *ee* drop the final *e* before a termination beginning with *e:* as, *free, freer, freest.*

§ 11. Compound words formed by joining two or more words (in distinction from certain above-mentioned derivatives and from portmanteau words) commonly retain all of the letters of the simple words: as, *airstrip, beachhead, carryall, rove-over, flare-up.*

PLURALS

For irregular plurals, as of *foot, mouse, ox,* and for plurals retained from foreign languages, as of *genus, crisis, focus,* see the individual words and also the *Note* under the word PLURAL in the *Vocabulary.*

§ 12. The plural of English nouns regularly ends in -s, or, in certain classes of words, in -es.

When the singular ends in a sound with which *s* can unite and be pronounced without forming a separate syllable, *-s* only is added in forming the plural: as, *bays, woes, virtues, claws, chiefs, paths, aches, plagues, acts.*

When the singular ends in a sound (as that of *ch* in *much, sh, j, s, x,* or *z*) with which *s* cannot unite in pronunciation but must form a separate syllable, *e* is inserted before *-s* in forming the plural, unless the word ends with silent *e,* which then forms a separate syllable with *-s:* as, *church, churches; rush, rushes; edge, edges; gas, gases; case, cases; box, boxes; maze, mazes.*

The plural ending *-s* following a vowel or voiced consonant (pronounced *b, m, v, d, n, g, ng, l, r*) and the plural ending *-es* are both pronounced with the voiced sound *z;* the plural ending *-s* following a voiceless consonant (pronounced *p, f, t, th* as in *thin, k*) is pronounced with the voiceless sound *ss.* For nouns ending in a voiceless sound in the singular and the voiced sound in the plural (*life, lives*), see *Guide to Pronunciation,* § 99.

Plurals of nouns ending in o. All nouns ending in *o* preceded by a vowel add *-s* only: as, *cameo, radio, zoo.* Proper names ending in *o* add *-s* only: as, *Filipino, Eskimo, Romeo.* Nouns ending in *o* preceded by a consonant fall into four classes: (1) Taking *-s* only, including infrequently used nouns, infrequently pluralized nouns, very long nouns, nouns bearing the stamp of foreign origin, as well as many others: as, *albino, chromo, credo, crescendo, ditto, dynamo, electro, embryo, kimono, lean-to, magneto, medico, mestizo, octavo, photo, piano, poncho, pro, pueblo, shako, silo, solo, two, tyro.* (2) Taking *-s* usually but sometimes *-es:* as, *avocado, banjo, commando, flamingo, gecko, halo, indigo, junco, lasso, memento, palmetto, politico, pronunciamento, proviso, salvo, tobacco, tuxedo, zero.* (3) A small number of nouns taking *-es* usually but sometimes *-s:* as, *archipelago, buffalo, calico, cargo, desperado, dido, fresco, grotto, hobo, lingo, mango, manifesto, mosquito, motto, peccadillo, portico, stucco, virago, volcano.* (4) A small number of nouns taking *-es* only: as, *dingo, echo, embargo, go, hero, innuendo, jingo, mulatto, Negro, potato, tomato, tornado, torpedo, veto.*

Plurals of nouns ending in i are preferably formed by adding *-s:* as, *rabbi, rabbis; alibi, alibis.*

Plurals of letters, figures, signs, abbreviations, and words named merely as words are formed by adding *-s.* An apostrophe which according to the older convention regularly preceded the *-s* is omitted by more and more writers and printers where no ambiguity is likely: as, the three *Rs* or *R's;* dotted both *i's;* two *l's* in *all;* hisses his *s's* (or *esses*); the two *Os* or *O's* in *400;* a group of *B-29s* or *B-29's;* in the *1920s* or *1920's;* a man in his *30s* or *30's; GIs* or *GI's* or *G.I.'s* or *G.I.s; Ph.D.'s* or *Ph.D.s;* three *its* or *it's* in one sentence.

Plurals of a certain few abbreviations are formed by doubling the (final) consonant; as, *cc.,* chapters; *ff.,* folios; *MM.,* Messieurs; *pp.,* pages; *Qq.,* quartos; *spp.,* species; *vv.,* verses, violins.

§ 13. Nouns ending in y preceded by a consonant or by u pronounced as a consonant form their plurals by adding *-es* and changing *y* into *i:* as, *mercy, mercies; sky, skies; soliloquy, soliloquies.* But proper names usually take *-s:* as, three Hail *Marys;* two *Germanys.*

Nouns ending in y preceded by a, e, o, or u (except *u* pronounced as a consonant) form their plurals by adding *-s* only: as, *key, keys; alloy, alloys; guy, guys.*

§ 14. Nouns ending in f, fe, or ff for the most part form their plurals by the addition of *-s* only: as, *belief, chief, grief, handkerchief, motif, oaf, proof, reef, roof, serif, waif; fife, safe, strife; cuff, cutoff, gaff, mastiff, plaintiff, sheriff.* A few, however, change *f* or *fe* into *ves:* as, *calf, elf, half, leaf, loaf, self, sheaf, shelf, thief, wolf; knife, life, wife.* The nouns *beef, scarf,* and *wharf* regularly add *ves,* sometimes *-s; hoof* and *turf* regularly add *-s,* sometimes *ves.* See STAFF in the *Vocabulary.*

VARIATIONS IN USAGE

§ 15. em- or im-, en- or in-. Among words beginning with *em-* or *im-,* as *embed* or *imbed,* and *en-* or *in-,* as *endorse* or *indorse,* usage varies. In some *em-* is preferred, as *empower;* in some *en-* is preferred, as *enclose, entrust;* in some *im-,* as *impale;* in some *in-,* as *incrust, inquire;* in some *en-* is preferred for certain senses, *in-* for other senses, as *ensure, insure.*

§ 16. -er or -re. American usage prefers *-er* for words of the *center, meter, theater* class, but many American writers prefer *-re* in particular words, especially *theatre.* (Cf. § 23, below, for British usage.) *Acre, chancre, lucre, nacre, massacre, ogre,* and *euchre* retain the termination *-re,* to show the hard sound of the *c, g,* and *ch.*

§ 17. -id or -ide. Chemical *-ide* is preferred to *-id.*

§ 18. -ize or -ise. Two classes of verbs having *i* as the next-to-last sound and *z* as the last sound are distinguished in taking the *-ize* or *-ise* spelling: (1) Verbs derived from Greek verbs in *-izein* (as *euphemize, ostracize, paralogize, prologize, syllogize, synchronize*) or through Latin or Old French or French from Greek (as *anathematize, baptize, catechize, cauterize, characterize, evangelize, stigmatize, tyrannize*) properly have the termination *-ize*. Those verbs having a similar Latin background, as with a Late Latin ending *-izare* or an Old French ending *-ir, -iss*, but derived from French (as *amortize, dramatize, naturalize, pulverize, satirize, temporize*) likewise have the termination *-ize*. Exception: *exorcise*, though ultimately from Greek *exorkizein*, commonly has *-ise* corresponding to *exercise*. Verbs formed by adding *-ize* or *-ise* to English words are by analogy spelled with *-ize* (as *animalize, botanize, criticize, legalize, memorize, modernize, oxidize, patronize, sterilize*). Exception: *chastise*, derived from *chasten* + *-ize*. The verbs of this class have in older British usage followed the French spelling with *-ise* (see § 21, below) in contrast

to American spelling with *-ize*. Spellings with *-ise* are not generally given in this dictionary where they are mere variants of *-ize* forms.

(2) The following verbs and corresponding nouns borrowed from Old French or French end in *-ise*, with rare instances of variant forms in *-ize: advertise, advise, franchise, affranchise, disfranchise, disenfranchise, enfranchise, compromise, demise, despise, devise, disguise, excise* (duty), *improvise, merchandise, revise, surmise;* likewise *circumcise, excise* (cut out), and *supervise*, borrowed from Latin. Verbs and nouns derived from compounds of the French verb *prendre* (participle *pris* or *prise*) regularly end in *-ise: apprise* (inform), *comprise, emprise, enterprise, surprise*. *Apprize* (appraise), from Old French *aprisier*, is preferred to *apprise*.

BRITISH SPELLING PREFERENCES

Certain differences are noticeable between the spelling practices of books and papers published in the British Commonwealth and American practices. The main points of divergence that persist despite interchange of publications are outlined in the following paragraphs.

§ 19. ae, oe. In common words derived from the Latin or Greek in which American usage has pretty generally replaced *ae* or *oe* by *e*, British usage prefers the forms with *ae* or *oe*, often written as ligatures: as, *aestivate* (or *œstivate*), *encyclopaedia, palaeontology, oecology, oecumenical, homoeopathy*. And in such semitechnical words as *anaemia, anaesthetic, faeces, orthopaedic, oedema, oesophagus, asafoetida* British usage permits only *ae* or *oe*, whereas these forms in American usage have been superseded by *anemia, anesthetic*, etc.

§ 20. em-, en-, im-, in-. British usage favors the *em-* and *en-* forms practically to the exclusion of *im-* and *in-* forms, which are in certain cases still the commoner in American usage: as, Brit. *empanel, encase, encrust, enfold;* U. S. *impanel, incase, incrust, infold*. A few British exceptions using *in-* are: *incrustation, ingrained, inquire, inquiry, insure* (financial sense), *inure, inweave*.

§ 21. -ise, -ize. In British printing the forms in *-ise* have in the past been the commoner, but the trend of usage, influenced by the *Oxford English Dictionary* and the practice of the *Encyclopædia Britannica* and the London *Times*, is to adopt more generally the *-ize* forms and their derivatives in *-ization, -izer, -izable*. Thus, whereas *apologize, capitalize, dramatize, satirize, visualize, visualization*, etc., are the exclusive American forms, both forms *apologize* and *apologise, capitalize* and *capitalise*, etc., are in use in Great Britain. In Canadian official and literary usage *-ize* has been adopted; Indian, South African, and Australian usage favors *-ise*. The words of this class are not to be confused with the verbs not etymologically related which are always spelled *-ise*. See paragraph (2) of § 18, above.

§ 22. -our, -or. In words of the *colour, color* and *honour, honor* class, the forms in *-or* are regarded as non-British, thus differing from particular words, as *horror, pallor, squalor, torpor, tremor*, always spelled *-or,* which are indistinguishable in form and origin from this class. Among the derivatives of *colour, honour*, etc., those in *-able, -er, -ite, -less* are regarded as formed from English words and retain the *u*, but those in *-ation, -ific, -ize* (*-ise*), *-ism, -ist, -ous, -ously, -ousness* drop the *u*.

British preferences:

armour	armourer, armoury	
clamour	clamouring	clamorous
colour	colourable, colourist	coloration, colorific
favour	favourite, favourless	
honour	honourable	honorary, honorific
humour	humourless	humorous
labour	labourer, Labourite	laborious
odour	odourless	odorous, odorific
vapour	vapourish	vaporize, vaporise
vigour	vigourless	invigorate

Agent nouns (except *saviour* and *paviour*) in British use have now generally gone over to *-or*, as *governor*.

§ 23. -re, -er. The British predilection for *centre, metre, theatre*, etc., is invariable. Thus: Brit. *calibre, centring, fibre, lustre, mitre, sabre, sceptre, sombre, spectre;* U. S. *caliber, centering, fiber, luster*, etc.

§ 24. -ou-, -o-. British usage prefers *mould, moult, smoulder* to *mold, molt, smolder*, which are commoner in American use; likewise, British *plough*, U. S. *plow*.

§ 25. -ce, -se. The nouns spelled *defense, license, offense*, and *pretense* in American use are in British use more often spelled *defence, licence* (but *license*, verb), *offence*, and *pretence;* in their derivatives the British spell with *c* before suffixes beginning with a consonant, as *defenceless*, but with *s* before suffixes beginning with a vowel, as *offensive, pretension*. British usage shows only *practise* for the verb; American usage is *practice*.

§ 26. -xion, -ction. The British prefer *connexion, deflexion, inflexion* (derived from Latin nouns in *-xio*) to American *connection, deflection, inflection* (influenced by the corresponding verbs in *ct* and by analogy with nouns in *-tion*); they also use *reflexion* in the scientific sense (throwing back of light, heat, etc.) but generally use *reflection* in all other senses.

§ 27. **Doubling and retaining final l.** (1) In British use, words of more than one syllable ending in *l*, in forming derivatives, double the *l* before a vowel, as before *-ed, -ing, -ery, -ist, -ize* (*-ise*), whereas the more consistent American usage authorizes the doubling of the final *l* only when the accent is on the final syllable. (Cf. §§ 2 & 3, above.) Thus: Brit. *apparelled, councillor, jewellery, levelled, libelled, medallist, quarrelled, totalled, travelled, woollen;* U. S. *appareled, councilor, jewelry, leveled, libeled, medalist, quarreled, totaled, traveled, woolen;* but both Brit. and U. S. *annulled* because *annul* has the accent on the final syllable. The *Oxford English Dictionary* prefers the forms with the doubled letters. Exception: Brit. *paralleled*. (2) A number of verbs accented on the final syllable have preferably a single final *l* in British usage and double final *l* in American usage in the present tense and present infinitive. Thus: Brit. *enrol, enrols, enthral, fulfil, instil;* U. S. *enroll, enrolls*, etc., but both Brit. and U. S. *enrolled, enrolling*. Exception: Brit. *install*. (3) In British printing it is customary in forming derivatives of two-syllable verbs ending in *l*, and a few nouns ending in *ll*, to use a single *l* before a consonant. Thus: Brit. *thraldom, enrolment, instalment, skilful, wilful;* U. S. *thralldom, enrollment, installment, skillful, willful*. *Dulness* and *fulness* prevail in British printing; otherwise *ll* is retained before *-ness*.

§ 28. **Silent e retained.** The former British preferred forms *abridgement, acknowledgement, fledgeling, judgement, lodgement* are yielding in favor of the forms *abridgment, acknowledgment, fledgling, judgment, lodgment*, long standard in the United States.

§ 29. **Sulphur** and **sulpha** are British preferences.

PUNCTUATION, COMPOUNDS, CAPITALS, ETC.

PUNCTUATION

The chief marks of punctuation and reference, with their names.

,	Comma.	**`** (è)	Grave accent.	**/**	Virgule.
;	Semicolon.	**∧** or **⌃** or **~**	Circumflex.	**{** or **}**	Brace.
:	Colon.	**~** (ñ)	Tilde.	*** * *** or ———	Ellipsis.
.	Period, *or* full stop.	**⁻** (ō)	Macron.	**. . .**	Ellipsis; *also*, leaders.
—	Dash.	**˘** (ŏ)	Breve.	*****	Asterisk.
?	Interrogation point.	**··** (oö)	Diaeresis.	**†**	Dagger.
!	Exclamation point.	**ç** (ç)	Cedilla.	**‡**	Double dagger.
( )	Parentheses, *or* curves.	**∧**	Caret.	**§**	Section; *also*, numbered clause.
[ ]	Brackets.	**" "** *also* **" "**	Quotation marks.	**‖**	Parallels.
'	Apostrophe.	**« »**	Quotation marks, French.	**¶** or **⁋**	Paragraph.
-	Hyphen.	**» «** or **„ "**	Quotation marks, German.	**☞**	Index, *or* fist.
'	(é) Acute accent.	**' '** *also* **' '**	Quotation marks, single.	******* or ***⁎***	Asterism.

The chief uses of the most important punctuation marks are explained in the numbered sections below.

These directions represent preferred American usage; permissible alternatives and British differences are sometimes but not always shown below. The directions represent usage in continuous textual matter; these practices may be varied for special purposes in display printing, in tabulated matter, or in certain condensed styles of compilation.

1. THE PERIOD, OR FULL STOP [.]

A period is used at the end of a sentence, or any expression standing for a sentence, that is neither interrogative nor exclamatory.

Society is a wave. The wave moves onward, but the water of which it is composed does not. The same particle does not rise from the valley to the ridge.

Please close the door. Certainly.

A period is used after an abbreviation.

Reedville, Montg. Co., pop. 879; cap. or l. c.; n. masc.; 7 a.m.; 30 mins.; lg. pkg.; no. 72; 5s. 6d.; 50 m.p.h.; bks. marked o.p. [or op]; dept. bulls.; *Tech. Bull.*, mo., 50 pp.; U.S.S. *Wyoming;* Dr. and Mrs. Jas. Brown, 7 Pine St., Bath, Ohio; David Livingstone, LL.D. (b. 1813, d. 1873); raid of Apr. 18, 1942 led by Lt. Col. James H. Doolittle.

Exceptions. Abbreviations of compound names of international organizations and government agencies, official abbreviations designating equipment, and a large number of similar compound abbreviations are preferably written without periods and without spaces:

ABCD powers; ILO; UNRRA; UN; USSR; MVD; MGB; SEC; TVA; Pfc; GI; PX; PT; TD; VT fuze; IOU; ESP; IPA; MS.

NOTE 1. Many common contractions (with omission of medial letters) are preferably written as abbreviations with periods:

secy. (preferred to sec'y); advt.; mfg.; recd.; Dr. (debtor).

NOTE 2. A period is sometimes omitted by some publishers, chiefly British, from *Mr, Mrs,* and *Dr;* as, *Dr* Brown.

NOTE 3. No period is used after symbols of chemical elements, as *Al, Cu, U* 235.

NOTE 4. The terms *1st, 2d, 3d, 8vo, 12mo,* etc., are not abbreviations and take no period.

NOTE 5. Isolated letters of the alphabet used as designations take no period; as, **T** square; *A* 1; I beam.

A period is used before a decimal and between dollars and cents (in figures); as, 16.63 ft.; .32 cal.; $12.17. In British use the decimal point is centered: 16·63.

The Roman numerals I, IV, xxii, etc., designating the serial number of a thing, as a page or chapter, are used with or without a period; as, 2 *Sam.* xix. 12; after names, without a period; as, George VI of England.

After titles of books and articles, after headings, and in display printing the period is omitted at the ends of lines, as well as other punctuation except an essential interrogation or exclamation mark.

An ellipsis or a suspension may be indicated by a row of spaced periods, commonly three periods (in the use of some authorities four periods) in addition to punctuation marks required at the beginning and end of the ellipsis; thus, four periods (or five) are used when the omitted words constitute a whole sentence or the last words of a sentence or when the omission falls at the end of the quotation and at the same time at the end of the main sentence.

As ellipsis marks these periods are used to indicate intentional omission of one or more words or sentences from quoted matter as nonessential to the present purpose, also to indicate illegible or unquotable words, dashes being commoner for this last purpose.

"Now that wars . . . have become far more horrible and . . . insane."
Dean Inge.
"A good deal . . . hangs on the meaning . . . of this short word."
T. S. Eliot.

We quote from Keats's *Endymion:*
Now with aught else can our souls interknit
So wingedly . . . . [not the end of sentence in Keats]

Belial's well-known lines:
Sad cure! for who would lose
Though full of pain, this intellectual being . . . ?
Paradise Lost II. 146

Omission of one or more complete lines of poetry may be indicated by a full line of spaced periods or, much less frequently, asterisks.

Thus driven
By the bright shadow of that lovely dream,
. . . .
He fled.
Shelley.

As suspension periods, called also suspension points, three spaced periods are used at points other than structural division points to indicate an interrupted sentence or an unfinished sentence with a suspensive effect, carrying over the emphasis toward the immediately succeeding words. Suspension periods often have a more continuative effect than the dash, which is the chief suspension point. Three spaced periods are usual except when a new sentence succeeds.

He traces S—a— . . . and she sees her name Sara as well as written.
I'll write to Marie . . . . Or perhaps they named her Jane. The voice weakened, trailed off . . . . Only silence.

Centered periods are used in many dictionaries to indicate division between syllables where division is not otherwise indicated by accent marks or hyphens.

symp'tom·a·tol'o·gy; ul'tra·a·tom'ic

2. THE COMMA [,]

Of all the marks of punctuation, the comma offers the most difficulty in use, and is used with the least uniformity. The most marked divergence in accepted practice lies in the use for ordinary descriptive and narrative writing of the *open* system of punctuation, that is, a minimum of pointing without causing ambiguity, and for more compact involved composition in which clearness and precision are the first requisites, of a *close* system of punctuation, providing abundant points, esp. commas. Though often, as formerly, marking rhetorical or elocutionary pauses, the comma is used primarily as a mark of separation to make clear the grouping of words, phrases, and clauses in respect to the grammatical structure of the sentence.

Words, phrases, and clauses that are appositional, or parenthetical, or independent, as nouns of direct address, exclamations, absolute phrases, are set off by a comma or commas.

A control plan was proposed by Bernard Baruch, elder statesman.
Mr. Chairman, I yield. Pshaw, I am in no hurry.
His true ambition, and a lofty one it must be counted, was to affect the course of events by affecting the course of thought.
A man in black, stately and old, rose slowly.

NOTE. The comma is *not* used between a noun and its appositive when so closely connected in thought as to form one idea.

Edward the Confessor; the American architect Ralph Adams Cram; the aircraft carrier USS *Coral Sea;* a figure eight; the demon Rum; that expression *in the groove.*

Dependent adverbial clauses preceding their principal clauses, and most initial adverbial phrases including a verbal, are set off by a comma.

If we were always candid, woe to self-esteem!
Immediately upon reaching the surface, he struck out boldly.
To gain popularity, he yielded his convictions.

NOTE 1. A short introductory adverbial clause may need no comma after it, provided that there can be no slightest uncertainty, without a comma, where the main clause begins, as is likely to be the case where the subject of both clauses is the same.

But if peace is to be paramount it must before all things be a peace of peoples.... *Sir Bernard Pares.*
If we all came to talk alike there would no longer be any point in our not writing alike.... *T. S. Eliot.*

NOTE 2. When a dependent adverbial clause follows the main clause, the comma is usually omitted, except when the clause is plainly nonrestrictive, that is, adds a reason or concession introduced by *because, since, as, though.*

He has bought a new car, though I doubt if he can afford it.

Adverbs and adverbial phrases that modify an entire clause or sentence rather than one word are set off by a comma.

In the first place, he will tell you a fairy story.
Unfortunately, we shall have to decline.
It was, in fact, regarded among the faculty as a case of juvenile overenthusiasm that could, after all, be overlooked.

Transitional phrases and conjunctive adverbs used transitionally (as *therefore, moreover, however, nevertheless, then, consequently, accordingly*) are set off by commas except in very short sentences in which they are logically close to the verb (as in, consequently I shall resign).

The question, therefore, is still open.
On the contrary, under the rules a vote is in order.
Still, I doubt the wisdom of retrenching.

Nonrestrictive (called also descriptive, or appositive, or additive) **relative clauses and participial phrases** are set off by commas.

I visited Cardiff, which is in Wales.
Fishes, that tipple in the deep, Know no such liberty.
Richard Lovelace.
The senators voted assent, which was to be expected of them.
Dick, feeling bitter, turned away from the scene.

NOTE. A restrictive (called also limiting or essential) relative clause must not be set off by a comma.

A man who beats a horse is discharged.

In giving dates and places an added defining year or place name is set off by a comma or commas in formal style, but in lighter styles year or place name may have no following comma; in the United States a postal zone number is not set off from the name of the city, only from what follows.

George Catlett Marshall, born December 31, 1880, at Uniontown, Pennsylvania, became Secretary of State January 21, 1947, and advanced a plan for European relief at Cambridge, Massachusetts, in June, 1947. British style: 21 January, 1951.
Apply for information to Public Information Division, Department of the Army, Washington 25, D. C.

Exception. Usage is evenly divided between using and not using a comma in dates when no day is given:

June, 1944 or June 1944.

Before "of" in phrases indicating residence, position, or title, a comma is ordinarily used.

President James Bryant Conant, of Harvard University.
Senator Joseph Christopher O'Mahoney, of Wyoming.

Words placed out of their natural position, as for clearness or emphasis, and elements obviously added as an afterthought or suspended for emphasis but not so distinct an interruption as to call for a dash, are ordinarily set off by a comma.

To the wise and upright, old age brings many joys.
That the mine is rich, I concede.
Conditions for large production and ready sales continue favorable, for the present at least.
She made her husband her whole life, she idealized him, but she did not know him at all, really.

Contrasted words and phrases are set off by a comma.

Work, not words, is what is needed.
The greater the security, the less the yield.

Words, phrases, and clauses of like construction used in a series, also pairs of words in a series, are separated by commas.

The estate was left to John, Robert, and William.
Trees, trees, trees were all we could see.
Old and young, rich and poor, wits and morons came out for the baseball classic.

NOTE 1. Before *and* or *or* introducing the final term in a series such as *a, b,* and *c* the comma called for by this rule is omitted by some publications in a series of single words or simple phrases. Scientific, technical, and learned periodicals and university presses in the United States show a predominance of those uniformly using this comma over those uniformly omitting it and over those sometimes using the comma and sometimes omitting it in the same publication; United States government publications quite uniformly use this comma. Journalistic, literary, and popular publications that regularly use this comma, that regularly do not use this comma, and that sometimes use and sometimes omit this comma are about equally divided. This comma is not omitted between clauses and scarcely ever between phrases.

NOTE 2. Two adjectives preceding a noun are not separated by a comma when the second adjective relates more closely to the noun than the first, or when the first adjective modifies the second adjective and the noun, thought of as a unit.

A vivid red tie; a brilliant military strategist; a limpid trout brook.

NOTE 3. *Etc., or the like, and so on,* when terminating a series but not terminating a sentence, are preferably followed by a comma unless other sentence punctuation is called for.

Any agency promoting, selling, using, etc., these records and transcriptions is eligible.

Independent clauses joined by a co-ordinating conjunction are separated by a comma when the clauses are closely connected in thought and are not broken up with commas (cf. § 3, below).

He seemed inattentive, but no word escaped him.
His face showed his chagrin, for he was conscious of failure.

NOTE. In less formal writing, when both clauses are brief and esp. when the subject of both clauses is the same, the comma may be omitted before the co-ordinating conjunction.

He will suffer but he will recover.

A short informal quotation or question or a maxim is separated from the rest of the sentence by a comma (cf. § 4, below).

"Make way for liberty," he cried.
He asked abruptly, "Which way do you vote?"
As Prior says, "Virtue is its own reward."

Ellipsis of a word (common to two parts of a sentence but not repeated) is indicated by a comma.

Reading maketh a full man; conference, a ready man; and writing, an exact man.

After *namely, viz., that is, i.e., as, e.g.*, etc., introducing an illustration or example, not an enumeration, a comma is used.

There are three genders in Latin: namely, masculine, feminine, and neuter.
The chief aim of censorship, namely, to eliminate inartistic pandering to base appetites, is frustrated by stupid and literal-minded censors.

Inverted names in bibliographies and reference lists are set off by a comma.

Holmes, Oliver Wendell, Jr. [*or* jr.]

A proper name and an academic or honorary title, also two or more such titles in succession, are separated by a comma.

James K. Jones, M.A., Ph.D., President.

After the salutation in personal letters and after the complimentary closing in all letters the comma is the regular mark.

Dear Jack, ... Sincerely yours, Ted.

Two adjacent sets of figures or identical words are separated by a comma.

In the year 1934, 967 students were enrolled.
Whatever is, is right.   *Pope.*

In numbers the comma normally separating thousands, millions, and other groups of three digits is omitted in dates, page numbers, and street numbers, and may properly be omitted in numbers of four digits in accordance with the practice of some of the best authorities; as, an altitude of 7525 feet; at 3600 rpm.

3. THE SEMICOLON [;]

A semicolon is used to separate the clauses of a compound sentence:

(1) In the absence of any connective.

Make no terms; resist until the last breath.

(2) When an antithesis exists between the clauses.

A fool babbles continually; a wise man holds his tongue.
A soft answer turneth away wrath; but grievous words stir up anger.

(3) When there is a marked change in thought.

You must practice, practice, practice day after day; else you will retrograde and become mediocre.

(4) Where the connective is one of the conjunctive adverbs *accordingly, also, consequently, furthermore, hence, however, indeed, moreover, nevertheless, otherwise, so, still, then, therefore, thus,* yet.

You recommend this man; therefore I will give him a trial
He is a graduate of Oxford; hence we expect a learned discussion.

(5) When the clauses themselves contain commas.

The seasons come and go, and the years pass on; but love abides.

A semicolon is used to separate the members of a series of clauses or phrases introduced by a colon.

The yield was: 1925, 660 bbls.; 1935, 886 bbls.

A semicolon (so also a colon, a dash, or a comma) **is used before** *namely, to wit, that is, i.e., viz., e.g., as, for instance, for example,* when introducing an illustrative example or explanation or an enumeration of particulars not felt as parenthetical (cf. § 2, above).

The Navy is the first line of defense; that is to say, it is not until the Navy has been beaten that our shores can be invaded.
'Small' is overworked as well as 'great'; for example: in "a small particle of gold" 'small' adds nothing to the meaning.

A semicolon is used in lists of names with addresses, titles, or figures, where a comma alone would not separate items or references clearly.

Deut. 3:1–10; 4:4–16.

4. THE COLON [:]

A colon is used to introduce a formal direct quotation or direct question.

He cited this line from Pope:
When Ajax strives some rock's vast weight to throw.

A colon is used to introduce a formal enumeration of particulars, regularly after "the following" (but disapproved by some after "are"), regularly to introduce a numbered series, less commonly before a short informal series; and inversely, in formal context, before a final clause summarizing the preceding series (cf. the dash for similar service in less formal context, § 7, below).

His favorite themes may be classified under three heads: the folly of pacifism, public waste, and the spread of communism.
To make an early prognosis of possible dissension; to diagnose the potential crisis; to administer a drastic purge: these steps are imperative for a dictator.

A colon is used to set off an appositive clause or phrase that constitutes a restatement of the preceding clause, with or without *to wit, that is,* or the like.

His recipe for health is a program of simple living: he prescribes only plain food, abundant exercise, and bodily exposure to the sun.
And here Machiavellism must live or die: there is no alternative offered.   *Richard Christopherson.*
But in its best and fullest sense this kind of intellectuality must encompass the whole poem: it must fuse the poem into a tight logical structure.   *Wallace C. Brown.*

A colon is used after the salutation in a business letter or an address.

Sirs: Mr. Chairman, Ladies, and Gentlemen: Mr. President:

A colon is used to separate the parts of numerical ratios.

The ratios 12:19 and x:57.

A proportion, commonly written $12:19 = x:57$ or $12:19 :: x:57$, is often written by scientists $12/19 = x/57$.

A colon is used between Biblical chapter and verse numbers, and between volume and page numbers, in references using Arabic numerals and between place of publication and publisher's name in bibliographical references and footnotes. These uses of the colon are paralleled by equally common use of the period. The comma is commoner in styles using Roman numerals to indicate volume number of periodicals and in styles using the abbreviations "chap." or "v." with the numerals. See Bibliographies, page 1156.

1 Corinthians 13:4–13.
J. Am. Chem. Soc. 72:127 (1950).
Brock, Werner. *An Introduction to Contemporary German Philosophy.* Cambridge: Cambridge University Press, 1947.

A centered colon is used to separate corresponding words apposed in pairs or sets for comparison, for example, rhyming words or words linguistically compared.

Seventeenth-century rhymes include prayer : afar and brass : was : ass.
We learn that the stature in the two sexes shows very nearly the same female : male proportions.
Examples in Gothic of a feminine abstract from an o/ā adjective are *managei : manags, hauhei : hauhs, audagei : audags.*

A centered colon is regularly used between hours and minutes and seconds in representing twelve-hour clock time, but in British practice and frequently in American publications a period is used; in charts and timetables the hours and minutes are usually spaced without punctuation mark; in representing twenty-four-hour clock time hours and minutes are regularly set without spacing or punctuation mark.

2:31:30 P.M.
When it is 9:32 P.M. by the city-hall clock, it is 2132 aboard a submarine in the harbor.

5. THE EXCLAMATION POINT [!]

An exclamation point is used after an ejaculation, and after any phrase or sentence of wish, command, irony, or the like to indicate forceful utterance or strong feeling.

Egad! I had no such intention.
Oh that those lips had speech!
Is the writer to become the slave of the publishers!
"Stop! Class dismissed!" he bit off the words.

6. THE INTERROGATION POINT [?]

An interrogation point is used at the end of a direct question, even if in declarative form.

What after that? You say you will persist?
How can he expect reinstatement? now or later? — with a record of insubordination, obstruction, and insolence marked down against him.
An Oxford degree — or was it Cambridge? — lured him.

NOTE 1. A request put for courtesy's sake in interrogative form takes a period.

Will you kindly fill out and return this questionnaire.

NOTE 2. Used as a terminal mark of a direct quotation, the interrogation point, as well as the exclamation point, usually obviates need for comma or period (other than ellipsis or suspension periods).

After he had affixed the title "Why the comma?" he slipped away.

An interrogation point, enclosed in parentheses, is used after a word, phrase, or date to indicate uncertainty of its accuracy or conjecture or irony, or to mark a gap in available information.

Omar Khayyám, Persian poet (?–1123?).
The Ophir of the Bible, rich in gold, was Arabia (?).
He offered to sell me a bag of real (?) pearls.

7. THE DASH [—]

A dash is used to mark an abrupt suspension of the sense, an unexpected turn of the thought, or a sudden change in the construction; also a faltering in speech.

Carranza's answer was — obey.
If you will listen, I will explain — but perhaps you do not care to hear.
To revert to sensuously insistent jungle rhythms with smashing or stinging discords — that is what jazz offered a war-weary generation.
The past has been a failure; the present — what can it matter in the light of the perfecting future? *Lionel Trilling.*
"Yes, but I — er — I'll have to —" and he stopped.

A dash is used to introduce a repetitive phrase, a summing-up word or words like *namely*, or an afterthought, with more or less emphasis (cf. § 3, above, for use of a semicolon before words like *namely*).

I will never — never, I say — agree to this iniquitous proposal.
Breadth of culture, practicality, frankness, astuteness, inflexibility, leniency — all are requisites of a teacher.
Sports develop two valuable traits — viz., quick decision and self-control.
He is recommended merely as a graduate of high rank — as if scholarly achievement gave assurance of teaching ability.

Dashes are used in pairs to set off interpolations when the matter is brief and calls for some emphasis, that is, when it is subordinate and incidental to a less degree than is indicated by parentheses.

I saw her — my pulse even now stops at the thought — in the path of the careening automobile.

Dashes enclose parenthetical matter in text that is itself inside brackets inside parentheses.

A dash (en dash) **is used as the equivalent of *to and including* between extreme dates or numbers**, also often in compounding capitalized two-word names.

Pages 40–89; the decade 1941–1950; a New York–Lisbon plane.

A dash (usually a two-em dash) **is used to indicate ellipsis of a word or letters in a word.**

Yelling —— loudly; Mr. M—— of New York; the d——l.

8. PARENTHESES, OR CURVES [( )]

Parentheses, or marks of parenthesis, are used to set off a word, phrase, or sentence which is inserted by way of comment, explanation, translation, etc., in a sentence but which is structurally independent of it.

Know, then, this truth (enough for man to know): Virtue alone is happiness below.
We were now nearing our destination (after five days on the river), and our spirits rose.
Nil desperandum (Never despair)!

9. BRACKETS [[ ]]

Brackets are used to set off inserted matter as extraneous or merely incidental to the context, esp. editorial interpolations and other comments not by the author of the text.

"He is just as cheerful as when you was [were] here."

"The ensuing winter [1789] promised to be a turning point."
Gypsum and barites are mentioned as sulfates [*sic*].
A fly is said to be a two-winged dipterous [does that make four wings?] insect.

Brackets are used for parentheses within parentheses.

Bowman Act (22 Stat. L., ch. 4, § [or sec.] 4, p. 50).

10. QUOTATION MARKS [" "]

Quotation marks are used to enclose all direct quotations, that is, quotations in which the exact phraseology of another or of a text is directly cited.

"When I am dead," said one of the keenest of modern minds, one of the greatest of modern poets, "lay a sword on my coffin, for I was a soldier in the war for the liberation of humanity."

NOTE 1. In all quotations, excepting extracts from plays, quotation marks are put at the beginning of every paragraph occurring within the quotation, in addition to those at the beginning and at the end of the extract.

NOTE 2. No quotation marks are used when the quoted matter is set in smaller type or in paragraphs indented on both sides.

NOTE 3. No quotation marks are used to enclose oft-quoted familiar phrases, such as *to err is human.*

Single quotation marks are used to indicate a quotation within a quotation and are preferred by some, esp. in British usage, to indicate quoted matter, in which case double quotation marks are used for a quotation within a quotation.

The witness said: "I distinctly heard him say, 'Don't be late'; and then I heard the door close."

Quotation marks are used ordinarily to enclose titles of short plays and poems, paintings, lectures, articles, and parts of books; whereas titles of whole books, periodicals, and newspapers are in present usage italicized in context.

He read a paper on "The Influence of Poe in European Literature."
The "To be or not to be" soliloquy. The title story "Sold Out."

Quotation marks, often single quotation marks, are used to enclose technical terms expected to be unfamiliar to the reader or words used in an unusual or ironical or humorous sense; or coined words, colloquialisms, trade or shop jargon, or the like, for which the writer offers a slight apology. Quotation marks are often equivalent to affixing *so-called* to a term.

The plates of copper are hung by 'corrosion hooks' in the acid.
This venture is plainly a "wildcat" intended to prey upon the unwary.
We've had enough of your "unshrinkable" shirts.
His request for a "freeze" order on construction.
Compensated by exports to the U.S.A. and by "invisible" exports.
The exterior "overhang" of the living-room window.

Quotation marks are often used to enclose the names of ships or words used as words, though italic type for these uses is generally preferred.

Lost with the "Titanic," which sank April 15, 1912.
It is well to use a dash before and a colon after the word "namely" when introducing a full clause.

Quotation marks with other punctuation marks.

(1) Terminal quotation marks are accompanied by only one other mark, whether the quotation and the whole sentence call for the same mark repeated or different marks.

Did he keep asking you, "What is your number?"
We exclaim with Wat Tyler, "When Adam delved and Eve span, who was then the gentleman?"
Just as he shouted, "I will not!" he slammed the door.
Is this the acknowledgment I get, to have you bellow "Barefaced Philistine! Sniveling time-serving extortionist!"

(2) A period or comma is regularly placed inside closing quotation marks whether logically belonging to the quoted matter or to the whole sentence, according to the predominant American practice.

We accept a nicely unified and definable compartment labeled "Man."
The first principle of existentialism, "Existence is prior to essence," is easy to remember.

NOTE. A logical distinction is often applied in printing U. S. Congressional matter and in the British and Canadian style of punctuation, and advocated by some American writers, whereby a period or comma is placed outside the quotation marks when it belongs not to the quotation but to the whole sentence or the clause containing the quotation.

This act may be cited as the "Army-Navy Medical Services Corps Act of 1947".

The Prime Minister, after reporting the negotiations, declared resolutely, "Our only course is to resist aggression".

Replying with the one word "Bunk", he subsided.

(3) A colon or semicolon is regularly placed outside quotation marks. A terminal colon or semicolon of quoted matter incorporated into a sentence regularly gives place to appropriate sentence punctuation.

"Fame is proof that people are gullible"; with this quotation from Emerson he retired in silence.

"Don't be nervous," we urged; "you can beat him." [Compare the original of the quotation: Don't be nervous; you can beat him.]

Exception.   A colon or semicolon may be placed inside the quotation marks in exceptional cases in which it belongs inseparably to the quotation, as in:

"Sirs:" is the salutation used in letters to the editor.

(4) An interrogation or exclamation point is regularly placed inside or outside the quotation marks according as it belongs to the quoted matter or to the whole sentence or clause including the quotation.

Can you forget his angry exit after shouting "Include me out"?

"And what do *you* think of 'The Wings of Death'?" Mrs. Roby abruptly asked her.   *Edith Wharton.*

11. THE APOSTROPHE [']

The possessive case of singular nouns and plural nouns not ending in an *s* or *z* sound is formed by adding an apostrophe and *s.*

A book's chances of success; carpenter's; dog's; motorist's; owl's; president's; at his wit's end; fish's tail; garage's responsibility; Senator Edge's constituency; the church's philosophy; men's; oxen's; children's; Des Moines's press; Descartes's philosophy; Dumas's novels; Delacroix's painting.

The possessive of singular common and proper nouns of one syllable ending in an *s* or *z* sound is formed by adding an apostrophe and *s.*

The class's outburst; the press's description; boss's; bus's; fox's; fuzz's; the Times's; Charles's; King James's reign; Court of St. James's; Brooks's; Marx's; Burns's; Keats's sonnets; Strauss's waltzes.

NOTE.   An apostrophe and *s* are usually added to a noun to form the possessive case.   This form is a survival of the *es* ending in Old and Middle English, from which the vowel sound has disappeared in Modern English except in nouns ending in an *s* or *z* sound.   In early Modern English this *s* or *z* sound was often dropped from the possessive of nouns ending in an *s* or *z* sound, both in speaking and writing, leaving only the apostrophe in writing, as is evident in certain idioms and in poetry.   Since the middle of the nineteenth century, however, the form with apostrophe and *s* (pron. -ĕz or -ĭz) has been generally adopted for the possessives in which the extra syllable is not awkward to pronounce in the context.

The possessive of singular common and proper nouns of two or more syllables ending in an *s* or *z* sound and having an accent (primary or secondary) on the final syllable is formed by adding an apostrophe and *s.*

Our advance's speed; the marquise's jewels; a showcase's protection; a strongbox's weight; a pickax's imprint; the enterprise's success; Laplace's; Alphonse's; Hortense's; Berlioz's.

The possessive of singular common nouns and modern proper nouns of more than one syllable that end in an *s* or *z* sound and have no accent (primary or secondary) on the final syllable may be formed by adding an apostrophe and *s* or an apostrophe only according as the *s* is intended by the author to be pronounced or omitted.   Eminent literary publications show consistency in the use of the apostrophe and *s,* scientific and technical publications in the use of the apostrophe alone.   The form with apostrophe and *s* is appropriate as long as it is readily pronounceable in

the context.   An apostrophe alone is added by some writers and speakers when an *s* or *z* sound closely precedes that in the final syllable or when the immediately following word has an initial *s* or *z* sound.   The antipathy to several successive sibilants often set up as a reason for omitting the *s* in the possessive is not evident when the same sequence of sounds includes the verb *is,* pronounced the same as *'s* (thus: an *octopus's* snaky appearance; an *octopus is* snaky in appearance).   The reluctance to duplicate a final *-ez* or *-iz* sound by adding apostrophe and *s* is a genuine reason for using the apostrophe only (thus: Bill *Jeffries'* sister).   A practical reason for using apostrophe and *s* is that the shorter form with apostrophe only is ambiguous (*Roberts'* being indistinguishable in pronunciation from *Robert's, Paris' sight* similar to *parasite*).

An audience's (or audience') reaction; an acquaintance's (or acquaintance') sickness; a governess's (or governess') fault; an heiress' (or heiress's) estate; whether you drink at your host's or hostess's; the postmistress's (or postmistress') zeal; out of the waitress's (or waitress') sight; the business' (or business's) status; the axis's (or axis') ends; the Foreign Office's traditional fears; the service's age limit; arthritis's (or arthritis') true cause; the phoenix' (or phoenix's) nest; the universe's galaxy population.

Dr. Adams's (or Adams') services; Ben Andrews's (or Andrews') daughter; Chambers's (or Chambers'); Dickens's (or Dickens'); Alice's (rarely Alice'); Robert Service's (or Service') verse; Horace's (sometimes Horace'); Harris's (or Harris'); Felix's (or Felix'); Furness's (or Furness'); Dos Passos' (or Passos's); Cervantes' (or Cervantes's); Columbus's (or Columbus'); Linnaeus's (or Linnaeus'); Stettinius's (or Stettinius'); Col. Ephraim Williams's (or Williams').

NOTE.   Before the word *sake* the possessive of such nouns formed by the apostrophe without an *s* is correct in set expressions and closely analogous expressions.

For goodness' sake; for conscience' sake; for convenience' sake; for righteousness' sake; violence for violence' sake.

Preferred: For appearance's sake; for science's sake.

The possessive of ancient classical and Biblical proper names and some foreign proper names ending in an *s* or *z* sound may be formed, as often in poetry and usually in classical works, by an apostrophe without an *s,* though some authorities for present use prefer the apostrophe and *s* when readily pronounceable.

(1) Such names of one syllable are better spelled in the possessive, like modern proper names, with an apostrophe and *s.*

Zeus's son; Mars's help [but Mars' Hill].

(2) Such names of two or more syllables having the accent on the penult more often take an apostrophe without an *s.*

Brutus' (or Brutus's); Phoebus' (or Phoebus's); St. Agnes' (or St. Agnes's); Aeneas' (or Aeneas's); Aquinas' (or Aquinas's); Catullus' (or Catullus's); Epicurus' (or Epicurus's); Menelaus' (or Menelaus's); Odysseus' (or Odysseus's).

(3) Such names of two or more syllables having the accent on the penult and ending in *-es* (pron. ēz) take the apostrophe without *s.*

Achilles'; Ceres'; Ulysses'; Xerxes'; Archimedes'.

(4) Such names of three or more syllables having the accent on the antepenult may take the apostrophe and *s* or the apostrophe only; those ending in *-es* (pron. ēz) usually take the apostrophe only.

Pythagoras's (or Pythagoras'); Aeschylus's (or Aeschylus'); Democritus's (or Democritus'); Herodotus's (or Herodotus'); Oedipus's (or Oedipus'); Tacitus's (or Tacitus'); Theophrastus's (or Theophrastus').

Aristophanes' (or Aristophanes's); Diogenes' (or Diogenes's); Euripides' (or Euripides's); Hercules' (or Hercules's); Miltiades' (or Miltiades's); Pericles' (or Pericles's); Socrates' (or Socrates's); Sophocles' (or Sophocles's); Themistocles' (or Themistocles's); Thucydides' (or Thucydides's).

(5) More familiar classical names of this class are usually spelled in the possessive like modern proper names, that is, preferably with apostrophe and *s* as long as the extra syllable is readily pronounceable (see paragraphs above).

Cyrus's; Venus's; Judas's; Marcus's.

But: Moses'; Jesus'.

The possessive of all plurals ending in an *s* or *z* sound is formed by adding the apostrophe only, including a number of French plurals ending in *-x* that are pronounced in English with a final *z* sound.

Consumers' resistance; foxes' holes; a bumblebees' nest; the Henrys' invitation; the Joneses' doing; the two chateaux' destruction; the tableaux' effect; Farquhar's "The Beaux' Stratagem."

Exceptions: geese's; lice's; mice's.

The possessive of titles, firm names, initials, abbreviations, acronyms, and the like, may be formed by adding apostrophe and *s*.

Charles I's; the Edison Co.'s; RFC's; CIO's; C. D. K. Jr.'s; UNRRA's; DDT's.

The possessive of compound nouns is formed as the possessive of the concluding noun would be if it were standing alone; the possessive of a compound not concluding in a noun, by an apostrophe with an *s*.

Cutpurse's; scapegallows'; sons-in-law's; passers-by's; the Adjutant General's Department.

The possessive of two or more nouns in apposition or in the same construction is indicated by an apostrophe with an *s* added to the last noun.

The Representative from Utah's vote.
In our representative Mr. Burns's car.
Bring the matter to Mr. Robert Burns, our Chicago representative's attention.
At Smith's, the stationer in K Street.
At Smith, the stationer's in K Street.
At Smith the stationer's office.

The possessive form of time words is used in idiomatic expressions of duration, in the singular or plural form according to the context.

A week's delay; a two hours' ride; thirty days' grace.

NOTE. A nonpossessive form with hyphen is likewise proper.

A two-week delay; a two-hour ride; (infrequently) a two-hours ride.

The possessive form is used in a number of idiomatic expressions of measure, rate, or worth.

A boat's length; at arm's length; a hand's breadth; a stone's throw; at two streets' remove; at a snail's pace; a dollar's worth; five cents' worth.

The apostrophe with an added *s* is used with each of two or more possessives joined by a co-ordinate conjunction, when referring to separate possessions and with only the last possessive when referring to joint ownership.

George's and William's answers are equally informative (each answering independently). The centuries of her family's and England's history.
From papa and mamma's bedroom came the sound of grief.
It is George and William's turn to row (together).

No apostrophe is used in the possessive pronouns *his*, *hers*, *its*, *ours*, *yours*, *theirs*.

The apostrophe is often omitted in titles and geographic names.

The form of the corporate title or authorized or official title is to be followed.

Citizens Bank; The Authors Club; St. Anthonys Retreat; Smiths Market; Harpers Ferry; Eastern State Teachers College; Joyce's *Finnegans Wake*.

An apostrophe followed by a *d* is used to form the past and past participle of arbitrarily coined verbs.

Thee'd; O.K.'d; K.O.'d; LL.D.'d; influenza'd.

The apostrophe is commonly used before *s* in the plurals of exclamations, imperatives, conjunctions, adverbs, numbers, and abbreviations used substantively but may be omitted as long as no ambiguity is likely to result. Cf. *Orthography* § 12, last paragraph.

The yes's (better yeses) equal the no's (better noes); the dos and don'ts of poultry raising; heavy with ifs and buts; told of whys and hows; arranged in twos and threes; a battery of 88s (or 88's); IOUs (or I.O.U.'s); a guard of MPs (or M.P.'s).

An apostrophe followed by an *s* is used to form the plurals of figures and letters and signs, and of words when used as words only, but forms omitting the apostrophe are gaining ground. Cf. *Orthography* § 12, last paragraph.

A million is expressed by 1 followed by six 0's.
The sentence has three *and's* in it. A's, B's. Two Cs and a D.

The omission of a letter or letters from a word or of one or more figures from a date is marked by an inserted apostrophe.

Don't; I've; he's; who'd; 'tis; 'gainst; o'er; o'clock; you'll; you're; I'd; the class of '49; ass'n.

COMPOUNDS AND HYPHENATION

Though authorities differ widely as to which compounds are to be written solid, which separate, and which with a hyphen, the following generalizations represent the trend of the best usage in regard to the use of the hyphen in compounding. Forms prescribed below are preferred for general use; in some categories separate-word forms or hyphened forms are retained in conservative or formal style, while solid forms have been adopted in technical style.

Compounds are usually solid when the first element is a prefix (*unconscious*) or a combining form (*telegraph*), or when the last element is a suffix (*slowly*) or a combining form (*geology*).

Compounds are hyphened:

(1) When the second element is capitalized or thought of as representing something official or institutional.

Russo-Finnish; pro-United Nations; ex-governor.

(2) When consisting of impromptu formations, reduplicating terms, or temporary combinations.

Clickety-clack; clomp-clomp; a kind of *caught-in-the-act* look.

(3) When based upon a syntactical relation.

All-inclusive; tax-exempt; fire-eater; fire-resistant; flea-bitten; God-descended; hate-inspired; heat-treat; Latin-derived.

(4) When containing a prepositional phrase.

Behind-the-scenes agreements; a *between-the-acts* intermission; a *heart-to-heart* talk; *Jack-in-the-pulpit; mother-in-law;* an *off-center* axis; *off-white* satin; *out-of-door* exercise; *over-the-counter* stocks; *up-to-dately* recorded; *up-to-the-minute* information.

(5) When the first element is self-.

Self-love; self-determination; self-inflicted; self-starter.

(6) To distinguish a compound from a word of different meaning that would be otherwise identical.

Re-creation (cf. recreation); *re-form* (cf. reform).

(7) When the same letter occurs three times in succession.

Bell-like; skill-less; cross-stitch.

(8) When otherwise a vowel would be confusingly doubled in combination.

Anti-imperialist; co-owner; intra-atomic; pre-empt; re-enter; semi-independent; you-uns.

Exceptions: *Cooperate* and *coordinate* and their derivatives are often written thus as solid forms, because of their great frequency and familiarity.

(9) To avoid an ambiguous situation, as when two adjacent vowels might be mistaken for a diphthong:

Cave-in; drive-in; flare-up; freeze-out; mop-up; tie-in.

Exceptions: Compounds, esp. scientific nouns and adjectives, in which combining forms (as well as prefixes) constitute the first element, are usually written solid (*autointoxication, frontoauricular, genitourinary, microorganism, nasoorbital, paleethnology, zooid*).

COMPOUND NOUNS

Compound nouns are usually solid (*blackboard*) or separate (*school year*). They have often become solid when the meaning is specialized or figurative and when the accent is partly or altogether lost on the second element, esp. when the first element is of one or two syllables and the second is of one syllable.

Beekeeper; blackbird; choirmaster; mineowner; plateholder; playwright; summertime; voltmeter.

Certain words, mostly of one syllable (*ache, bane, berry, board, book, boy, bush, craft, fish, flower, foot, head, hound, house, man, mouth, room, shop, weed, woman, wood, work, wort, yard*), form solid compounds if the meaning is specific.

Toothache; baneberry; cardboard; notebook; bellboy; woodcraft; blackfish; sunflower; arrowhead; deerhound; workman; bathroom; bindweed; needlewoman; handwork; shipyard.

Compound nouns formed from a one-syllabled verb and a short adverb are mostly solid except when an ambiguous situation would result.

Blowout; breakup; hangover; hideaway; smashup. But: *sit-in.*

The following classes of compound nouns are hyphened:

(1) Compound agent nouns formed by adding -er to a verb, plus an adverb.

Bucker-up; cutter-off; hanger-on; listener-in; rubber-down; tapper-out.

(2) Compound nouns naming the same person or thing under two aspects.

Actor-manager; city-state; man-brute; poet-statesman.

(3) Compound nouns consisting of three or more words, esp. of a noun plus a prepositional phrase.

Jack-in-the-pulpit; mother-in-law; will-o'-the-wisp; forget-me-not; give-and-take; merry-go-round.

Exceptions: Noun expressions containing the phrases *at arms, at large, in chief,* or *of* phrases are usually not hyphened; thus, *attorney at law, commander in chief, sergeant at arms, chief of staff, bill of fare.* But: *man-of-war.*

(4) Compound nouns consisting of a verb plus a noun (or pronoun), or a verb plus a verb.

Cure-all; has-been; know-nothing; make-believe.

(5) Compound nouns naming a technical unit of measurement ending in *year, day, hour, minute, second, mile, foot, inch, pound, ton.*

Light-year; foot-pound; degree-day.

(6) Most compound nouns consisting of a possessive case and a noun, naming usually a flower or plant, or having a fanciful meaning.

Adder's-tongue; bull's-eye; cat's-paw; mare's-tail.
Exceptions: *cockscomb, coltsfoot, monkshood, wolfsbane.*

NOTE.   Terms consisting of a capital letter and a noun are not hyphened except when used as attributive adjectives (*G string;* I *beam;* L *head;* T *rail,* T *square;* X *ray;* Y *chromosome*).
But: L-*head* cylinder; *X-ray* tube.

COMPOUND ADJECTIVES

Most compound adjectives consisting of two or more words are hyphened, though in several classes particular adjectives having specialized or figurative meaning of long standing are written as solid words. Thus: *boneheaded, shamefaced, tightfisted, crackbrained, underwitted, stouthearted, backbreaking, faultfinding, laborsaving, everbearing, slowgoing, bloodthirsty, headstrong,* and most compounds ending in *-born, -bred, -proof, -sick, -tight,* or *-worthy.*

The following classes are regularly hyphened in both attributive and predicative uses.

(1) An adjective or noun prefixed to a noun plus the suffix -ed.

Bull-necked; double-faced; full-bodied; saber-toothed.

(2) An adjective plus a participle.

Atrocious-smelling; sinister-looking; dark-colored; quiet-spoken.

(3) A noun standing as object of a following present participle.

Fun-loving boys; normal boys are *fun-loving;* a spectacle *awe-inspiring* to the multitude; *breath-taking; health-giving; soul-stirring; heart-rending.*

(4) Compound numerals and fractions used as adjectives.

Twenty-one persons; until he was *twenty-one;* a *two-thirds* majority.

But: *Two thirds* of those present were Scandinavian, the rest German; a tolerance of *two thousandths.*

The following classes are regularly hyphened in at-

tributive use but in predicative use are hyphened (rather than written as separate words) only when ambiguity as to their syntactical relation would result from omission of the hyphen.

(1) A noun plus a prepositional phrase.

A *face-to-face* interview; *door-to-door* calls; *run-of-the-mill* performers; make the canvass *door to door;* these novels seem only *run of the mill.*

(2) The first word modifying the second.

Bluish-gray eyes; *dark-green* shadows; *quick-fire* guns; *secondary-school* education; *well-made* tools; *wide-open* door; the sky was *dark blue;* find the door *wide open.*

(3) An adverb not ending in -ly plus a present or past participle.

A *slow-growing* shrub; a shrub usually *slow-growing* in this climate; *hard-working; far-flung; fine-sewn;* the breach is *ever widening;* a remark *often repeated.*

But: An adverb in *-ly* used with a present or past participle is regularly written as a separate word (a *quietly spoken* warning) because its syntactical relation is evident without a hyphen.

(4) A noun in some syntactical relation to an adjective or to a present or past participle. There is a recognizable trend toward hyphening compounds of this class in predicative uses as well as attributive uses.

A *pitch-black* room; a *stem-winding* watch; *terror-crazed* occupants; he found the room *pitch black;* whether the mechanism is *hand* or *spring winding;* mines chiefly *British owned.*

Exception: Compound adjectives consisting of a two-word proper noun or adjective are not hyphened.

New Jersey rivers; *New Testament* period; *Old French* words.

COMPOUND ADVERBS

Compound adverbs consisting of two or more words are mostly hyphened, esp. newly formed compounds.

Go *cross-lots;* buy a house *dirt-cheap;* cut *end-grain;* sing *full-throatedly;* manipulate *left-handedly;* scratched *skin-deep;* prices rose *sky-high;* played only *so-so.*

NOTE 1.   Some compound adverbs are written solid, such as those compounds established in older English and many in common use consisting of two monosyllables, one of which is thought of as a prefix or suffix.

Henceforth; outdoors; thereon; throughout; whereto; downtown; inshore; nearby; offhand; overnight; upstate.

NOTE 2.   Adverbial combinations of words whose syntax in any context is evident on first reading are preferably not hyphened (as, situated *hard by;* move *close in;* turn *inside out;* go *out of date*).

COMPOUND VERBS

Compound verbs formed with prefixes are mostly solid.

Coextend; defrost; overhang; prefabricate; recap; sublet; underestimate.

Compound verbs formed from an adjective plus a noun or an adjective plus a verb are mostly hyphened.

Cold-chisel; double-tongue; dry-clean; quick-freeze; still-hunt.

THE DIVISION HYPHEN

The hyphen is used in printing and writing as a mark of separation or division chiefly as follows:

(1) At the end of a line which terminates with a syllable of a word, the remainder of which is carried to the next line.

mill- [end of line] *stone; pas- sion; fa- ther; liv- id.*

(2) Between letters or syllables repeated to give the effect of stuttering, sobbing, or halting expression.

S-s-sammy; ah-ah-ah.

(3) With suspensive effect.

A *six-* or *eight-cylindered* motor; in *ten-* and twenty-dollar bills.

(4) To indicate a word as spelled out letter by letter.

p-r-o-b-a-t-i-o-n.

THE USE OF CAPITALS

The essential distinction in the use of capitals and lower-case letters beginning words lies in the particularizing or individualizing significance of capitals as against the generic or generalizing significance of non-capitals. A capital is used with all proper nouns, that is, nouns that distinguish some individual person, place, or thing from others of the same class, and with all proper adjectives, that is, adjectives that take their descriptive meaning from what is characteristic of the person, place, or thing named by the noun. Most proper nouns and proper adjectives used not in the primary signification but in a derived, secondary, or special sense (as *cashmere*, the fabric; *utopia, utopian*) are written without capitalization.

The directions below represent normal practice in continuous textual matter; the practice may be varied for special reasons in display printing, in tabular matter, or in certain condensed styles of compilation.

A capital is used as the initial letter or letters of:

(1) **The first word of a sentence or an expression standing for a sentence, a direct formal quotation, or a line of verse**; also, a direct question within a sentence even though not quoted.

> You urge in vain. Recant my views? Never!
> Our fears in Banquo
> Stick deep; and in his royalty of nature
> Reigns that which would be fear'd. *Shak.*
> The eighteenth century asked of any action, Is it decorous?

(2) **Proper nouns, words used as proper nouns**, and (generally) their derivatives used in the primary sense.

> George, Georgian; Spain, Spanish; Americanize, Americanism; Californian; Roman customs. But: roman type.

(3) **Names of peoples, races, tribes, and languages.**

> Mongolian; Phoenician; Vietnamese; Iroquois; Indo-European; Latin; Mayan.

(4) **Titles of honor, academic and religious titles, and professional and business titles used with proper nouns**; also, epithets used in place of proper nouns.

> Queen Mary, Dean Inge, His Eminence the Cardinal Archbishop of New York; Iron Chancellor; Citizen King; Old Hickory; the Hoosier Poet; All-America team.
> Associate Professor E. F. Brown, Emeritus; Chief Engineer J. L. Coe; David Williams, Chairman of the Labor Board; Treasurer C. D. Smith of the Union Trust Company.

(5) **Official and government titles and titles of nobility**, as President, Governor, Senator, Speaker of the House, Secretary for Defense, Postmaster General, Prime Minister, Prince of Wales, when accompanying a proper name or used in direct address; as, John Doe, U. S. Minister to Spain; Secretary Trygve Lie; His Honor the Mayor; Mr. President; Your Honor. Also, often, the adjective *Presidential* when used specifically of the president of the United States.

(6) **Official names of national or international governmental bodies or documents**, also sometimes short forms of these used specifically or with a capitalized name, but not usually any short forms or modified forms of them in general reference:

> The Constitution of the United States; the Eightieth Congress; the Federal Reserve System; Federal Reserve banks; the Federal Communications Commission; the National Advisory Committee for Aeronautics; Charter of the United Nations (*or*, the Charter); the Security Council (*or*, the Council); the International Bank.
> But: according to the constitution; administration policies; federal agency.

(7) Nouns and often also adjectives that refer to the Deity; and pronouns and pronominal adjectives referring to the Deity when not closely preceding or following their antecedent naming Deity.

> God; the Supreme Being; the Almighty; Allah; Great Manito; Providence; Lord; the Trinity; Holy Ghost; Son of Man.
> Trust Him who doeth all things well; take time to think about God and his beneficence.
> The Almighty has his own purposes. *Abraham Lincoln.*
> So lonely 'twas, that God himself
> Scarce seemèd there to be. *Coleridge.*
> Lamb of God, who takest away the sins of the world, only in thy grace shall my soul be healed. *Katherine Anne Porter.*

NOTE. Some writers and a few hymnals capitalize a pronoun or pronominal adjective referring to Deity, even when close to the antecedent naming Deity and thus not requiring a capital for clarity of reference (as, a personal God, creator and governor of all, Who will bring His children into fellowship with Himself; Jesus and His disciples; "My Jesu, as Thou wilt").

> Teach me, my God and King,
> In all things Thee to see. *George Herbert.*
> God's in His heaven —
> All's right with the world. *Robert Browning.*
> All Thy works, O Lord, shall bless Thee *Oxford Amer. Hymnal.*

(8) **Names for the Bible or parts, versions, or editions of it**, and names of other sacred books, and derivative adjectives when the adjective refers explicitly to the Bible, Scriptures, Talmud, etc. (otherwise not capitalized).

> Bible; Talmud, Talmudic; Vedas; the Scriptures; Old Testament; Pentateuch; Apocrypha; Gospel of Mark; Apocalypse.

(9) **Names of creeds and confessions, religious denominations, monastic orders**, and *Church* when used to designate a specific body or edifice.

> Apostles' Creed; the Thirty-nine Articles of the Church of England; Hunt Memorial Church.

(10) **Holidays and holydays generally**; also, the months of the year and the days of the week.

> Fourth of July; Good Friday; Yom Kippur; Labor Day; January.

(11) **Names of congresses, councils, and expositions**; of organizations and institutions; of governmental departments; of political parties [but not the word *party*].

> The Yalta Conference; the Security Council of the United Nations; Louisiana Purchase Exposition; the Progressive party; the Smithsonian Institution; Bureau of Engraving and Printing; Congress of Industrial Organizations; the Olympic Games.

(12) **Names of courts of law.**

> Circuit Court of the United States for the 2d Circuit (*but* the circuit court); the Michigan Court of Appeals (*but* the state court of appeals).

(13) **Names of treaties, laws, acts, important events, historical epochs, literary periods, etc.**

> Versailles Treaty; the Crusades; Middle Ages; the Enlightenment.

(14) **Names of geological eras, periods, epochs, strata, etc.**, and names of prehistoric divisions.

> Carboniferous; Upper Jurassic; Age of Reptiles; Neolithic age.

(15) **Names of genera but not of species**, in binomial scientific names in zoology and botany.

> The marine worm *Nereis diversicolor; Spiraea latifolia.*

(16) **New Latin names of classes, families, and all other groups above genera**, in zoology and botany, but not derivative adjectives or nouns.

> Gastropoda, *but* gastropod; Ranunculaceae, *but* ranunculaceous.

(17) **Names of planets, constellations, asteroids, stars, and groups of stars**, but not sun, earth, and moon unless listed with other astronomical names.

(18) **Generic geographical terms that form an integral part of a specific proper name**, such as *bay, borough, colony, continent, county, district, hemisphere, island, lake, mountain, ocean, pass, peninsula, river, sea;* and likewise *avenue, boulevard, bridge, park, road, square, street.*

> Cook County, Illinois; the Japan Current; the Northern Hemisphere; the Marquesas Islands; the Indian Ocean; the Red Sea; Park Drive.
> But: the Atlantic coast of Labrador; Pacific islands; Swiss mountains; the Ohio River valley; the Continent or continent (the mainland of Europe).

NOTE 1. In some publications, such a generic term may be written without capitalization even when following a specific name, seldom when preceding.

> Ceding the Hangö peninsula in exchange for a lease of the Porkkala peninsula; born in Chekiang province; on the Ohio river; Oak avenue; Wise county. Cape Sable; but county Sligo or Cork.

NOTE 2. When such a generic term accompanies two or more specific names, usage is divided between a capital and lower-case initial.

The Leeward and Windward islands or Islands; at the confluence of the Allegheny and Monongahela rivers or Rivers.

(19) **Generic political terms that form an integral part of a specific proper name**, denoting a political division, such as *colony, department, dominion, empire, kingdom, republic, state, territory*, etc.

The Holy Roman Empire; the Province of Quebec; the State of Ohio; the Third Republic.

(20) **Names of definite geographical divisions.**

The Orient; the Old World; the Middle East; the Middle West.

(21) **Points of the compass used to designate geographical portions of a country or divisions of the world**, also nouns or adjectives derived therefrom.

The South; the Northwest; a Northerner; cooked Southern style.

NOTE. When used to denote direction only, points of the compass are not capitalized (due east; go west).

(22) **Abstract ideas or inanimate objects personified and names of seasons only when personified** or sometimes when referred to specifically or with special connotations.

Do the bidding of Nature; the Winter at Valley Forge; the Plague Year of 1665; where Spring her verdant mantle cast.

(23) **All words in titles of books, periodicals, essays, poems**, except unemphatic prepositions, conjunctions and articles; **academic degrees** and the abbreviations.

Shakespeare's *Taming of the Shrew;* the *Journal of the American Medical Association;* "Phosphorus: Bearer of Light and Life," *Scientific American* 178:101 *ff.;* Doctor of Laws (LL.D.).

NOTE. In cataloguing and often in bibliographies only the first word and proper names are capitalized in titles of publications.

(24) **The article** *the* **when part of a proper name or title or when incorporated as part of the legal name**, but usually not in referring to newspapers and magazines in running text, only in citations of references.

The Honorable William E. Borah; *but,* the *Chicago Daily News;* the *Saturday Evening Post.*

(25) **Particles in American names but in foreign names only when not preceded by a forename**, a professional title, or title of nobility or of courtesy:

Reginald De Koven; Della Crusca; Von Moltke (Count von Moltke).

(26) **German common nouns that have not been Anglicized, when used in English text.**

Frau; Kamerad; Kultur; Lawine; Junker; Luftwaffe; Turnverein; Weltschmerz.

NOTE. Anglicized German nouns may be written with a small initial letter (blitzkrieg; gestalt; kriegspiel; leitmotiv; pumpernickel; rathskeller; sauerkraut; stein; ablaut; umlaut).

(27) **Names of registered trademarks.**

MISCELLANEOUS

THE USE OF ITALIC TYPE

Italicize unnaturalized foreign words and phrases used in an English text. In manuscript a single underscore indicates italics.

Ancien régime; Anschluss; Autobahn; Bushido; cognoscente; de trop; dolce far niente; jeu d'esprit; mañana; noblesse oblige; rapprochement; Te Deum; Zeitgeist.

Italicize titles of books (not parts of books), plays (having book format), works of art, symphonies, magazines, newspapers, also names of ships and aircraft (cf. rules for quotation marks, above), but not the Bible or its books.

Robert Penn Warren's *All the King's Men;* Michelangelo's *David;* the *Christian Science Monitor;* Lindbergh's *Spirit of St. Louis.*

Italicize a word spoken of as a word, a phrase as a phrase, a letter as a letter (except that a letter indicating shape is printed in type most nearly depicting the shape; thus, V-shaped; I beam).

The pronoun *that;* avoid the solecism *he don't;* insert a capital *S.*

Italicize New Latin scientific names of genera, species, subspecies, and varieties (but not groups of higher rank, as phyla, classes, orders) in botanical and zoological names.

The quahog (*Venus mercenaria*) has a thick shell.

BIBLIOGRAPHIES

In making bibliographies, catalogues, and the like, the author's last name comes first, followed by his other names in full or his initials or his first name when he has only one; followed by the title of the book usually in italics; followed by the place of publication, the name of the publisher, and the date. Before a second work by an author, the author's name is represented by a prolonged dash, and a second listed edition of a particular work by two long dashes or the abbreviation *Ibid.* in italics. Citations of periodicals or newspapers include the author's name, the title in italics, the volume, paging, and date. Arrangement of items in a bibliography may be by classification of subject, or chronological, or alphabetical. Practice varies between capitalizing all important words in titles or only the first word and proper names. In strict practice an initial *the, a,* or *an* of a title is used, but in common

practice the definite or indefinite article is omitted, as it is usually omitted in cataloguing, except in cases where the article has essential meaning.

Indention varies according to the relative fullness of entries and the relative importance of the author's name, the title of the work, and any added annotation. In the full form the author's name stands alone, the title being indented on the next line; in the brief form the title follows the author's name on the same line. Indention of the author's name, with the next line beginning flush with the margin, giving the entry the form of a paragraph of text, is permitted by some authorities.

The *Macbeth* item below is shown first arranged according to the full form and second according to the brief form. The succeeding items, each unrelated to the others, may serve to illustrate various approved adaptations of the basic formula:

Shakespeare, William.
　　Macbeth; ed. by John Dover Wilson. Macmillan, 1948. (New Shakespeare)

or

Shakespeare, William. *Macbeth;* ed. by John Dover Wilson. Macmillan, 1948. (New Shakespeare)
Webb, Sidney, and Webb, Beatrice.
　　Soviet communism: a new civilization? 3d ed. Longmans, 1945.
　　[Permissibly: Webb, Sidney and Beatrice Webb.]
Toynbee, A. J. *Study of history;* ed. by D. C. Somervell. Oxford, 1947.
Dictionary of American history. James Truslow Adams, ed. in chief. N.Y., Scribner, 1940, v. 4, p. 222–223, under Patent Office, the United States.
Jaspers, Karl. *Philosophie* (3 vols.; Berlin: Julius Springer, 1932), Vol. I: *Philosophische Weltorientierung.*
Shapiro, K. J. *Trial of a poet, and other poems.* Reynal, 1947.
Aiken, C. P. *Kid* [poem]. Duell, 1947.
Conant, J. B. Role of Science in our Unique Society. *Science* 107:77–83 Ja 23 '48.
Nichols, W. T. "The technical report bugaboo" *Chem & Eng News* 26:602–4 Mar 1, 1948.
Mann, William. Phosphorus: Bearer of Light and Life; *Scientific American,* v178, p101–104, 157–160 (Mar, Apr, '48).

For incunabula:

Cicero, Marcus Tullius. De oratore. [Subiaco, C. Sweynheym & A. Pannartz, before 30 Sept. 1465]. 4to. (Pembroke-Murray). (H*5098; GW 6742)
———— [Venice, P. Pincius] 15 July 1495. fol. (C. H. Weir-W. C. H. Vere). (H 5110; GW 6752)
———— Orationes Philippicae. Rome, U. Han [c. 1470]. 4to. (Pembroke-J. A. Brooke). (H 5134; BMC. IV. 21; GW 6794)

PREPARATION OF COPY FOR THE PRESS

GENERAL SUGGESTIONS

1. **Copy should be prepared on single sheets of paper** of a uniform size, *one side only* being used. Sheets of the ordinary commercial letterhead size (8½ × 11 inches) are the most convenient. The sheets should be numbered, and plain white or neutral (gray, yellow, or brown) paper is best.

2. **Copy should be typewritten and double-spaced**, except that quotations and footnotes that go in smaller type may be single-spaced. A duplicate should be kept for reference and as a safeguard against loss in transmission, but no carbon or mimeographed copy should be sent to the printer. The first line of each page should begin not less than an inch from the top of the page, and there should be a blank margin of an inch and a half at the left side of the page. Sheets should be numbered consecutively. Any necessary insertions of more than a sentence should be on sheets of the same size as the rest of the copy, labeled 'Insert 41-A' or the like and included immediately after the page on which the proper point of insertion is marked 'Insert A.'

3. **Copy should embody the final ideas of the author**. Allowance must be made for some changes, but, to avoid expense, the copy as sent to the compositor should be as complete and perfect as possible.

4. **Footnotes.** A reference from the text of a work to a note that is to appear at the foot of the printed page should be indicated by a superior figure following the word to which the note refers and corresponding with the superior figure preceding the note. The figures should run consecutively through each chapter or article. The material constituting the footnote should be entered immediately below the line to which it refers and should be separated from the text by lines running entirely across the page. Names of publications should be abbreviated in the references only after giving the full title and data at the first appearance of each title.

5. **All proper names, technical and scientific words, references, quotations, and figures** that appear in the MS should be verified.

6. **Spelling should be uniform.** For words that have two or more accepted spellings, one form should be adopted and adhered to throughout. When two spellings are shown in this dictionary, separated by a comma or by an italic *or*, the one printed first is in general to be preferred but the second is acceptable, sometimes equally acceptable with the first.

7. **Capitalization and punctuation should be used according to a uniform style.** For rules see the preceding sections on *Punctuation* and *Use of Capitals*.

8. **Paragraphing** should be indicated on copy, not left to the compositor or proofreader. To indicate a new paragraph the symbol ¶ is used.

9. **The title page, preface, table of contents, and list of illustrations or tables** should accompany the MS.

10. **The kind of type to be used**, if not ordinary roman, is indicated by underscoring. Underscore once for *italics*, twice for SMALL CAPITALS, three times for CAPITALS, and once with a wavy line for **bold-faced type.**

11. **Manuscript should be kept and mailed flat.** If necessary, it may be folded, but it should never be rolled.

CORRECTION OF PROOFS

12. **Corrections on proof sheets should be made by means of the standard proofreaders' marks** in the margins directly opposite the indicated errors, usually in the nearer margin. For every correction marked in the text there must be a corresponding direction or mark in the margin, either the same mark as is used in the text or an abbreviation representing the direction. These marks must be kept strictly in order of occurrence and marks in the same horizontal line separated from each other by a diagonal mark, or virgule (/), or a similar vertical mark. This mark is made after every punctuation mark inserted and is often made after every marginal mark.

13. **Queries on proof sheets must be answered.** If the proposal is approved, striking out the query mark is sufficient; otherwise write the answer.

14. **All final changes should be made on the galley proof** because changes on subsequent proofs are more expensive; subsequent proofs are for verification only. In making changes the author should keep in mind that the alteration of a few words at the opening of a paragraph may require the resetting of the whole paragraph, and in linotype work the alteration of a single comma requires the resetting of the whole line.

15. **The original manuscript should be returned** unchanged with the corrected galley proof.

16. **An index should be compiled** — if the book is likely to be used for reference — beginning with the arrival of the first page proofs and should be sent to the printer immediately following the final page proofs.

PRINTING TERMS

body. — The solid rectangular metal base supporting the face of a printing type. Sizes of type are determined by the measurement of the type body from the front (containing the nick) to the back. See TYPE, *Illust.*, in *Vocabulary.*

electrotype. — A facsimile plate, esp. for use in printing, made by taking an impression in a special kind of wax or a sheet of soft lead, depositing in this mold a thin shell of copper, nickel, or the like, by an electrolytic process, and backing this shell with molten metal. The wax mold is rendered conductive for electroplating by coating it with graphite.

em. — The portion of a line occupied by any square type body (formerly by the letter *m*, then a square type) used as a unit of measure for printed matter. The em, now usually an em pica, approximately ⅙ of an inch (see TYPE, in the *Vocabulary*), is the unit of measure for printed matter, esp. of column width.

en. — A type body, unit of measure, etc., one half the width of an em (which see).

end paper. — A sheet of paper folded and pasted to the first or last leaf of a book to give an extra flyleaf and a paste-down (that is, a leaf that is pasted to the inside of the cover to secure it to the book).

flush. — (Set) even with the edge of the type page, usually the left margin; without indention.

font. — A complete assortment of any particular size and style of type; — in British use often *fount.*

half title. — The name alone of a book, placed on a separate page or at the head of the first page of text; also, any similar sectional title.

indention. — The setting of a line or lines in from the margin; the beginning of a line or series of lines a little within the flush line of the text. In **hanging indention** all the lines of a paragraph except the first line are indented.

lead (lĕd). — A thin strip of type metal, used to separate lines of type in printing; hence, a similar strip of brass. Leads vary in thickness from one half point (1/144 of an inch) to three points (1/24 of an inch) (from twenty-four to four to a pica). The commonest in use is the 2-point.

Linotype. — A trademark applied to a kind of typesetting machine which produces slugs, each of which corresponds to a line of separate pieces of type.

make-up. — Arrangement of type lines and illustrations into page form for printing.

Monotype. — A trademark applied to a typesetting machine consisting of two units. One, the keyboard, perforates a roll of paper which, when fed through the other, the caster, causes it to cast individual pieces of type and set them in justified lines.

pie *or* **pi.** — To upset or disarrange, as set type.

plate. — A page of stereotype, electrotype, or the like, to be printed from.

proof. — A trial impression from type, taken for correction or examination; — called also **proof sheet.** — **author's proof.** The clean proof sent to an author, after correction of the compositors' errors. — **galley proof.** A proof from type on a galley (the printer's steel tray holding type that has been set) before it is made up in pages. The first author's proof is generally a galley proof. — **page proof.** A proof of type that has been made up into page form. — **foundry proof.** A proof for a final reading before the electrotype or stereotype plates are made. — **plate proof.** A proof taken from a plate.

quad (quadrat). — A block of type metal lower than the letters, and half a one em, or two, or three ems in width, — used in spacing and in blank lines.

recto. — The right-hand (odd-numbered) page.

register. — Exact correspondence in position of lines, columns, or pages on the two sides of the sheet, or of the several impressions in a design printed in parts, as in process printing.

rule. — A thin type-high plate of type metal with a line or lines as its face. **single rule** has one light line; **parallel rule,** two light lines; **double rule,** a light and a heavy line; **dotted rule,** a line of dots; **wave rule,** a wavy line.

run in. — To make (matter) continuous without a paragraph or break.

serif. — One of the fine lines of a letter, esp. one of the fine cross strokes at the top or bottom. See TYPE, *Illust.,* in the *Vocabulary.*

sidehead. — A subhead placed at or in the side of printed matter. In bookwork, it is usually placed in the left side of the first line of a paragraph.

signature. — (1) A letter or figure placed at the bottom of the first page of each sheet of a book or pamphlet, as a direction to the binder in arranging and folding the sheets; — called also **signature mark.** (2) A printed sheet containing a number of pages, as 4, 8, 12, 16, etc., folded as one unit and forming a section of a book or pamphlet; hence, in bookbinding, such a printed sheet or set of sheets folded into four, or some multiple of four, pages; — called also *section.*

small capital. — A letter in the form of, but about two thirds the size of, a capital. Small capitals are used chiefly to mark principal parts, plurals, and cross references (as, See TYPE, *n.,* 8 b). See § 10, p. 1157. Abbr. *s.c., s. caps.,* or *sm. cap.*

stereotype. — A plate made by taking a mold or matrix of a printing surface in plaster of Paris, paper pulp, or the like, and making from this a cast in type metal, commonly with more than the usual percentage of lead. Stereotypes are chiefly used in newspaper and magazine printing, electrotypes for printing books.

verso. — The left-hand (even-numbered) page.

PROOFREADERS' MARKS

ℬ *or* ℐ *or* ℐ (L. *dele*). Dele, *or* delete; take out, or expunge.

ℬ Take out a letter and close up.

⌒ Print as a ligature; thus, a͡e (i. e., print æ); also, close up.

∨ *or* ⌄ Less space.

◡ Close up entirely; no space.

Ɔ *or* ℔ Turn a reversed letter.

∧ *or* > caret. Insert at this point the marginal addition.

or ≠ Space, or more space.

Eq. # Space evenly; — in margin.

∟ *or* ⌐ *or* ⊏ Carry farther to the left.

⌐ *or* ⌐ *or* ⌐ Carry farther to the right.

⌐ Elevate a letter or word.

⌣ Sink or depress a letter or word.

□ Em quad space; or, indent one em.

1/m̄, |—|, 1/em̄ *or* |—| One-em dash.

‖ *or* | Straighten ends of lines.

≡ *or* /// *or* \\\ Straighten a crooked line or lines.

⊥ *or* ⊥ Push down a space which prints as a mark.

✕ *or* + *or* ⊗ Broken or imperfect type; — used in the margin.

¶ Make a new paragraph.

○ (That is, a ring drawn around an abbreviation, figure, etc.) spell out; — used in the text.

ⓢⓟ Spell out; — used in the margin.

⊙ Period.

⋀ *or* ⁄ Comma.

:⁄ *or* ⊙ Colon.

;⁄ Semicolon.

⌄ *or* ⌄ Apostrophe or single quotation mark.

⌄⌄ Double quotation mark.

=⁄ *or* -⁄ Hyphen.

[⁄] Brackets. (⁄) Parentheses.

wf or *w.f.* Wrong font; — used when a character is of a wrong size or style.

ital. Put in italic type; — in margin, with _____ under text matter.

rom. Put in roman type; — in margin, with text matter underscored or circled.

bf. Put in bold-faced type; — in margin, with ⌇⌇⌇ under text matter.

⌐__⌐ Transpose.

tr. Transpose; — used in the margin.

l.c. Lower case; — used in the margin, with a slanting line drawn through the letter in the text.

=, s.c., *s. caps.,* or *sm.c.* Put in small capitals; — the double lines being drawn under the letters or word.

≡ *or caps.* Put in capitals; — the triple lines being drawn under the letters or word.

ld. Insert a lead between lines.

stet Restore words crossed out; — usually written in the margin (with dots under the words to be kept).

See following page for illustration of the application of these marks.

PROOFS OF LINCOLN'S GETTYSBURG ADDRESS WITH CORRECTIONS
MARKED (*above*) AND MADE (*below*)

"Four score and 7 years ago our fathers brought fourth on this continent a new nation, conceived in ~~in~~ liberty, and dedicated to the proposition, that all men are created equal. Now we're engaged in a great Civil War, testing whether that nation, or any nation conceived so and dedicated so, can long endure.

We are met on a great battle field of that war we have come to dedicate a portion of ~~this~~ field, as a final resting place for those who here ~~have given~~ their lives that this nation might live. it is altogether proper and fitting that we should do this. But, in a larger sense, we can not dedicate—we cannot consecrate—we cannot hallow—this ground. The brave men, living and dead, who struggled here, have ~~have~~ consecrated it, far above our power to ~~de-tract~~ or ~~add~~. The world will little note, nor long remember, what we say here, but it can never forget what ~~we~~ did here. It is for us the living, rather, to be dedicated here to the great Task remaining before us,—that from these honored dead we take increased devotion to that cause for which they gave the last full measure of devotion—that we ~~now highly~~ resolve that these dead shall not have died in vain—that this nation under God, shall have a new birth of freedom—and Government of the people, by the people, for the people, shall ~~never~~ perish from the earth.

"Fourscore and seven years ago our fathers brought forth on this continent a new nation, conceived in liberty, and dedicated to the proposition that all men are created equal. Now we are engaged in a great civil war, testing whether that nation, or any nation so conceived and so dedicated, can long endure. We are met on a great battlefield of that war. We have come to dedicate a portion of that field, as a final resting place for those who here gave their lives that that nation might live. It is altogether fitting and proper that we should do this. But, in a larger sense, we cannot dedicate—we cannot consecrate—we cannot hallow—this ground. The brave men, living and dead, who struggled here, have consecrated it, far above our poor power to add or detract. The world will little note, nor long remember, what we say here, but it can never forget what they did here. It is for us the living, rather, to be dedicated here to the unfinished work which they who fought here have thus far so nobly advanced. It is rather for us to be here dedicated to the great task remaining before us,—that from these honored dead we take increased devotion to that cause for which they gave the last full measure of devotion—that we here highly resolve that these dead shall not have died in vain—that this nation, under God, shall have a new birth of freedom—and that government of the people, by the people, for the people, shall not perish from the earth."

COLLEGES AND UNIVERSITIES IN THE UNITED STATES AND CANADA

The first list contains all institutions of higher education in the United States and Territories, according to information available at the date of compilation. It includes some (but not all) branches which retain by general recognition their individual names, but no attempt is made to indicate relationship of one institution to another or connection with a state university system. Recurrent institutional designations are abbreviated as follows:

A. & M.	Agricultural and Mechanical	Mech.	Mechanical
Acad.	Academy	Med.	Medical
Agric.	Agriculture	Sch.	School
C.	College	Sem.	Seminary
Ed.	Education	Tech.	Technology
Inst.	Institute	Theol.	Theological
		U.	University

The entry gives pronunciation, location, kind of student body, and date. Pronunciations not given may be found elsewhere in this dictionary. The location is that of the main administrative center or campus only. The state, or sometimes the city, is omitted when it is part of the title and when no uncertainty is likely. The abbreviation *coed.* (for *coeducational*) is used for institutions which regularly admit women to any one of their academic divisions; otherwise *men* or *women* is used. The word *junior*, as used when not a part of the name, indicates a junior college. The date is intended to be the earliest assignable to the institution's establishment; it is not always the year when the current name was adopted.

Similarly, the second list, beginning on page 1172, contains Canadian institutions.

UNITED STATES COLLEGES AND UNIVERSITIES

Ab′i·lene Christian C. (ăb′ĭ·lēn). Abilene, Texas; coed.; 1906.
A′bra·ham Bald′win Agricultural C. (ā′brȧ·hăm bôld′wĭn). Tifton, Ga.; junior coed.; 1907.
Ad′ams State C. (ăd′ămz). Alamosa, Colo.; coed.; 1921.
A·del′bert C. (ȧ·dĕl′bẽrt). Cleveland, Ohio; men; 1826.
A·del′phi C. (ȧ·dĕl′fĭ). Garden City, N. Y.; coed.; 1896.
A′dri·an C. (ā′drĭ·ăn). Adrian, Mich.; coed.; 1845.
Advanced International Studies, Sch. of. Washington, D. C.; coed.; 1943.
Advanced Study, Inst. for. Princeton, N. J.; coed.; 1930.
Aeronautical U. Chicago, Ill.; men; 1929.
Aeronautics, Acad. of. La Guardia Field, N. Y.; men; 1939.
Ag′nes Scott C. (ăg′nĕs [-nĭs] skŏt′). Decatur, Ga.; women; 1889.
Agricultural, Mech., and Normal C. Pine Bluff, Ark.; coed.; 1873.
Air Force Inst. of Tech. Dayton, Ohio; men; 1920.
Air U. See UNITED STATES AIR FORCE U.
Ak′ron, U. of (ăk′rŏn). Ohio; coed.; 1870.
Al′a·bam′a, U. of (ăl′ȧ·băm′ȧ). University; coed.; 1831.
Alabama A. & M. C. Normal; coed.; 1873.
Alabama State C. Montevallo; women; 1893.
Alabama Polytechnic Inst. Auburn; coed.; 1872.
Alabama State C. Montgomery; coed.; 1874.
A·las′ka, U. of (ȧ·lăs′kȧ). College; coed.; 1915.
Al′ba·ny State C. (ôl′bȧ·nĭ). Albany, Ga.; coed.; 1903.
Al·ber′tus Mag′nus C. (ăl·bũr′tŭs măg′nŭs). New Haven, Conn.; women; 1925.
Al′bi·on C. (ăl′bĭ·ŭn). Albion, Mich.; coed.; 1835.
Al′bright C. (ôl′brīt). Reading, Pa.; coed.; 1856.
Al′corn A. & M. C. (ôl′kôrn). Lorman, Miss.; coed.; 1871.
Al′der·son–Broad′dus C. (ôl′dẽr·s'n·brŏd′ŭs). Philippi, W. Va.; coed.; 1871.
Al′fred U. (ăl′frĕd; -frĭd). Alfred, N. Y.; coed.; 1836.
Al′lan Han′cock C. (ăl′ăn hăn′kŏk). Santa Maria, Calif.; junior coed.; 1920.
Al′le·ghe′ny C. (ăl′ĕ·gā′nĭ; ăl′ē·gā′nĭ). Meadville, Pa.; coed.; 1815.
Al′len Military Acad. and Junior C. (ăl′ĕn; -ĭn). Bryan, Texas; men; 1947.
Allen U. Columbia, S. C.; coed.; 1870.
Al·li′ance C. (ȧ·lī′ăns). Cambridge Springs, Pa.; coed.; 1912.
All Saints′ Episcopal Junior C. Vicksburg, Miss.; women; 1908.
Al′ma C. (ăl′mȧ). Alma, Calif.; men; 1934.
Alma C. Alma, Mich.; coed.; 1886.
Alma White C. (hwīt). Zarephath, N. J.; coed.; 1921.
Al·pe′na Community C. (ăl·pē′nȧ). Alpena, Mich.; junior coed.; 1952.
Al·ver′no C. (ăl·vûr′nō). Milwaukee, Wis.; women; 1887.
Al′vin Junior C. (ăl′vĭn). Alvin, Texas; coed.; 1949.
Am′a·ril′lo C. (ăm′ȧ·rĭl′ō; -ú). Amarillo, Texas; junior coed.; 1929.
American Acad. of Art. Chicago, Ill.; coed.; 1923.
American Conservatory of Music. Chicago, Ill.; coed.; 1886.
American Inst. for Foreign Trade. Phoenix, Ariz.; coed.; 1946.
American International C. Springfield, Mass.; coed.; 1885.
American U. Washington, D. C.; coed.; 1891.
Am′herst C. (ăm′ẽrst; -ûrst). Amherst, Mass.; men; 1821.
An·cil′la Do′mi·ni C. (ăn·shĭl′ȧ dō′mĭ·nē). Donaldson, Ind.; junior women; 1937.
An′der·son C. (ăn′dẽr·s'n). Anderson, S. C.; junior women; 1911.
Anderson C. and Theol. Sem. Anderson, Ind.; coed.; 1917.
An′do·ver New′ton Theol. Sch. (ăn′dō′vẽr nū′t'n). Newton Centre, Mass.; coed.; 1807.
An′drew C. (ăn′drōō). Cuthbert, Ga.; junior coed.; 1854.

An′na Ma·ri′a C. (ăn′ȧ mȧ·rē′ȧ). Paxton, Mass.; women; 1946.
An·nap′o·lis (ȧ·năp′ō·lĭs; ŭ·năp′lĭs). See UNITED STATES NAVAL ACAD.
Ann′hurst C. (ăn′hûrst). South Woodstock, Conn.; women; 1941.
An′te·lope Valley Junior C. (ăn′t'l·ōp). Lancaster, Calif.; coed.; 1929.
An′ti·och C. (ăn′tĭ·ŏk). Yellow Springs, Ohio; coed.; 1852.
Apostolic C. Tulsa, Okla.; junior coed.; 1938.
Ap′pa·lach′i·an State Teachers C. (ăp′ȧ·lăch′ĭ·ăn; -lȧ′chĭ·ăn; -lăch′-ăn; -lȧ′chăn). Boone, N. C.; coed.; 1903.
Apprentice School. Newport News, Va.; junior men; 1886.
A·qui′nas C. (ȧ·kwī′năs). Grand Rapids, Mich.; coed.; 1886.
Ar′i·zo′na, U. of (ăr′ĭ·zō′nȧ). Tucson; coed.; 1885.
Arizona State C. Flagstaff; coed.; 1899.
Arizona State C. Tempe; coed.; 1885.
Ar′kan·sas, U. of (är′kăn·sô). Fayetteville; coed.; 1871.
Arkansas A. & M. C. College Heights; coed.; 1909.
Arkansas Baptist C. Little Rock; coed.; 1884.
Ar·kan′sas City Junior C. (är·kăn′zăs). Arkansas City, Kans.; coed.; 1922.
Ar′kan·sas C. (är′kăn·sô). Batesville; coed.; 1872.
Arkansas Polytechnic C. Russellville; coed.; 1909.
Arkansas State C. State College; coed.; 1909.
Arkansas State Teachers C. Conway; coed.; 1907.
Ar′ling·ton State C. (är′lĭng·tăn). Arlington, Texas; junior coed.; 1917.
Arm′strong C. (ärm′strông). Berkeley, Calif.; coed.; 1918.
Armstrong C. of Savannah. Ga.; junior coed.; 1935.
A·roos′took State Teachers C. (ȧ·rōōs′tōōk; ȧ·rōōs′-; -tĭk). Presque Isle, Me.; coed.; 1903.
Art Center Sch. Los Angeles, Calif.; coed.; 1930.
As′bur·y C. (ăz′bẽr·ĭ). Wilmore, Ky.; coed.; 1890.
Asbury Theol. Sem. Wilmore, Ky.; coed.; 1923.
Ashe′ville–Bilt′more C. (ăsh′vĭl·bĭlt′mōr; 70). Asheville, N. C.; junior coed.; 1927.
Ash′land C. (ăsh′lănd). Ashland, Ohio; coed.; 1878.
Ashland Junior C. Ashland, Ky.; coed.; 1938.
As·sump′tion Abbey Sem. (ȧ·sŭm[p]′shŭn). Richardson, N. Dak.; men; 1899.
Assumption C. Worcester, Mass.; men; 1904.
Assumption Junior C. Mendham, N. J.; women; 1953.
Ath′ens C. (ăth′ĕnz; -ĭnz). Athens, Ala.; coed.; 1842.
At·lan′ta Art Inst. (ăt·lăn′tȧ). Ga.; junior coed.; 1926.
Atlanta U. Ga.; coed.; 1865.
At·lan′tic Christian C. (ăt·lăn′tĭk). Wilson, N. C.; coed.; 1902.
Atlantic Union C. South Lancaster, Mass.; coed.; 1882.
Atonement Sem. of the Holy Ghost. Washington, D. C.; men; 1924.
Au′burn Community C. (ô′bẽrn). Auburn, N. Y.; junior coed.; 1953.
Auburn Theol. Sem. New York, N. Y.; coed.; 1818.
Augs′burg C. and Theol. Sem. (ôgz′bûrg). Minneapolis, Minn.; coed.; 1869.
Au·gus′ta, Junior C. of (ô·gŭs′tȧ). Augusta, Ga.; coed.; 1925.
Au·gus·tan′a C. (ô′gŭs·tăn′ȧ). Rock Island, Ill; coed.; 1860.
Augustana C. Sioux Falls, S. Dak.; coed.; 1860.
Augustana Theol. Sem. Rock Island, Ill.; men; 1860.
Au·gus·tin′i·an Acad. (ô′gŭs·tĭn′ĭ·ăn). Staten Island, N. Y.; junior men; 1899.
Augustinian C. Washington, D. C.; men; 1923.
Augustinian Scholasticate. Villanova, Pa.; junior men; 1842.
Au·ro′ra C. (ô·rō′rȧ; ŭ·rō′rȧ). Aurora, Ill.; coed.; 1893.
Aus′tin C. (ôs′tĭn). Sherman, Texas; coed.; 1849.
Austin Junior C. Austin, Minn.; coed.; 1940.

Austin Peay State C. (pē'). Clarksville, Tenn.; coed.; 1929.
Austin Presbyterian Theol. Sem. Austin, Texas; men; 1902.
A'ver-ett C. (ă'vĕr-ĕt; -ĭt). Danville, Va.; junior women; 1859.
Bab'son Inst. of Business Administration (băb's'n). Babson Park, Mass.; men; 1919.
Ba-cone' C. (bȧ-kōn'). Bacone, Okla.; junior coed.; 1880.
Ba'kers-field C. (bā'kĕrz-fēld). Bakersfield, Calif.; junior coed.; 1913.
Ba'ker U. (bā'kĕr). Baldwin City, Kans.; coed.; 1858.
Bald'win-Wal'lace C. (bôld'wĭn-wŏl'ĭs). Berea, Ohio; coed.; 1845.
Ball State Teachers C. (bôl). Muncie, Ind.; coed.; 1918.
Bal'ti-more, U. of (bôl'tĭ-mōr). Md.; coed.; 1925.
Baltimore C. of Commerce. Md.; coed.; 1909.
Baltimore Junior C. Md.; coed.; 1947.
Bank Street C. of Ed. (bĭngk' strēt'). New York, N. Y.; coed.; 1930.
Baptist Bible Sem. Johnson City, N. Y.; junior coed.; 1932.
Baptist Theol. Sem. and Bible Inst. Grand Rapids, Mich.; coed.; 1941.
Ba'rat' C. of the Sa'cred Heart (bȧ'rȧ'). Lake Forest, Ill.; women; 1858.
Bar'ber-Sco'tia C. (bär'bĕr-skō'shȧ). Concord, N. C.; women; 1867.
Bard C. (bärd). Annandale-on-Hudson, N. Y.; coed.; 1860.
Bar'nard C. (bär'nĕrd). New York, N. Y.; women; 1889.
Bar'ry C. (băr'ĭ). Miami, Fla.; women; 1940.
Bates C. (bāts). Lewiston, Me.; coed.; 1863.
Bay City Junior C. (bā' sĭt'ĭ). Bay City, Mich.; coed.; 1922.
Bay'lor U. (bā'lĕr). Waco, Texas; coed.; 1845.
Bay Path Junior C. (bā' păth'). Longmeadow, Mass.; women; 1897.
Bea'ver C. (bē'vĕr). Jenkintown, Pa.; women; 1853.
Beck'ley C. (bĕk'lĭ). Beckley, W. Va.; junior coed.; 1933.
Bel-ha'ven C. (bĕl-hā'vĕn). Jackson, Miss.; coed.; 1894.
Bel'lar-mine C. (bĕl'ĕr-mĭn). Louisville, Ky.; men; 1950.
Bellarmine C. Plattsburg, N. Y.; men; 1952.
Belle'view C. (bĕl'vū). Denver, Colo.; coed.; 1926.
Belle'ville Township Junior C. (bĕl'vĭl). Belleville, Ill.; coed.; 1946.
Bel'mont Abbey C. (bĕl'mŏnt). Belmont, N. C.; men; 1878.
Belmont C. Nashville, Tenn.; coed.; 1951.
Be-loit' C. (bĕ-loit'). Beloit, Wis.; coed.; 1846.
Be-midj'i State C. (bĕ-mĭj'ĭ). Bemidji, Minn.; coed.; 1913.
Ben'e-dict C. (bĕn'ē-dĭkt). Columbia, S. C.; coed.; 1870.
Ben'e-dic'tine Heights C. (bĕn'ē-dĭk'tĭn). Guthrie, Okla.; coed.; 1889.
Benedictine Mission Sem. Newton, N. J.; junior men; 1932.
Ben'ja-min Frank'lin U. (bĕn'jȧ-mĭn frăngk'lĭn). Washington, D. C.; coed.; 1925.
Ben'nett C. (bĕn'ĕt; -ĭt). Greensboro, N. C.; women; 1873.
Bennett Junior C. Millbrook, N. Y.; women; 1891.
Ben'ning-ton C. (bĕn'ĭng-tŭn). Bennington, Vt.; women; 1925.
Be-re'a C. (bĕ-rē'ȧ). Berea, Ky.; coed.; 1855.
Berke'ley Baptist Divinity Sch. (bûrk'lĭ). Berkeley, Calif.; coed.; 1889.
Berkeley Divinity Sch. New Haven, Conn.; men; 1854.
Ber'ry C. (bĕr'ĭ). Mount Berry, Ga.; coed.; 1902.
Beth'a-ny Biblical Sem. (bĕth'ȧ-nĭ). Chicago, Ill.; coed.; 1905.
Bethany C. Lindsborg, Kans.; coed.; 1881.
Bethany C. Bethany, W. Va.; coed.; 1840.
Bethany Lutheran C. and Theol. Sem. Mankato, Minn.; junior coed.; 1911.
Bethany Nazarene C. (năz'ȧ-rēn'). Bethany, Okla.; coed.; 1899.
Beth'el C. (bĕth'ĕl). North Newton, Kans.; coed.; 1887.
Bethel C. Hopkinsville, Ky.; junior coed.; 1854.
Bethel C. McKenzie, Tenn.; coed.; 1842.
Bethel C. and Sem. St. Paul, Minn.; coed.; 1871.
Be-thune'–Cook'man C. (bĕ-thūn'kŏok'măn). Daytona Beach, Fla.; coed.; 1872.
Bible, C. of the. Lexington, Ky.; coed.; 1865.
Bible Baptist Sem. Arlington, Texas; coed.; 1939.
Bible Inst. of Los Angeles. Calif.; coed.; 1908.
Biblical Sem. in N. Y. New York City; coed.; 1900.
Birmingham–Southern C. Birmingham, Ala.; coed.; 1856.
Bish'op C. (bĭsh'ŭp). Marshall, Texas; coed.; 1880.
Bis'marck Junior C. (bĭz'märk). Bismarck, N. Dak.; coed.; 1939.
Black'burn C. (blăk'bĕrn). Carlinville, Ill.; coed.; 1835.
Black Hills Teachers C. Spearfish, S. Dak.; coed.; 1883.
Black Mountain C. Black Mountain, N. C.; coed.; 1933.
Blinn C. (blĭn). Brenham, Texas; junior coed.; 1883.
Bliss Electrical Sch. (blĭs). Takoma Park, Md.; men; 1893.
Bloom'field C. and Theol. Sem. (blōom'fēld). Bloomfield, N. J.; coed.; 1868.
Blue'field C. (blōo'fēld). Bluefield, Va.; junior coed.; 1922.
Bluefield State C. (blōo'fēld). Bluefield, W. Va.; coed.; 1895.
Blue Mountain C. Blue Mountain, Miss.; women; 1873.
Bluff'ton C. (blŭf'tŭn). Bluffton, Ohio; coed.; 1900.
Bob Jones U. (bŏb' jōnz'). Greenville, S. C.; coed.; 1927.
Boi'se Junior C. (boi'sĭ; -zĭ). Boise, Idaho; coed.; 1932.
Boone Junior C. (bōon). Boone, Iowa; coed.; 1927.
Bos'ton C. (bŏs'tŭn). Chestnut Hill, Mass.; coed.; 1863.
Boston Conservatory of Music. Mass.; coed.; 1867.
Boston Sch. of Occupational Therapy. Mass.; coed.; 1918.
Boston U. Mass.; coed.; 1839.
Bou'vé–Bos'ton Sch. (bōo'vȧ-bŏs'tŭn). Medford, Mass.; women; 1913.
Bow'doin C. (bō'd'n). Brunswick, Me.; men; 1794.
Bowl'ing Green C. of Commerce (bōl'ĭng grēn'). Bowling Green, Ky.; coed.; 1874.
Bowling Green State U. Bowling Green, Ohio; coed.; 1910.
Brad'ford Dur'fee C. of Tech. (brăd'fĕrd dûr'fē). Fall River, Mass.; coed.; 1904.
Bradford Junior C. Bradford, Mass.; women; 1803.
Brad'ley U. (brăd'lĭ). Peoria, Ill.; coed.; 1896.
Brai'nerd Junior C. (brā'nĕrd). Brainerd, Minn.; coed.; 1938.
Bran'deis U. (brăn'dīs). Waltham, Mass.; coed.; 1947.
Brant'ley–Draughon C. (brănt'lĭ-drôn'). Fort Worth, Texas; junior coed.; 1894.

Bre-nau' C. (brē-nou'). Gainesville, Ga.; women; 1878.
Bre'scia C. (brĕsh'ȧ). Owensboro, Ky.; coed.; 1874.
Bre-vard' C. (brē-värd'). Brevard, N. C.; junior coed.; 1934.
Brew'ton–Par'ker Junior C. (brōo't'n-pär'kĕr). Mount Vernon, Ga.; coed.; 1904.
Bri'ar Cliff C. (brī'ĕr klĭf'). Sioux City, Iowa; women; 1930.
Bri'ar-cliff' C. (brī'ĕr-klĭf'). Briarcliff Manor, N. Y.; junior women; 1904.
Bridge'port, U. of (brĭj'pōrt). Conn.; coed.; 1927.
Bridgeport Engineering Inst. Conn.; coed.; 1924.
Bridge'wa'ter C. (brĭj'wô'tĕr; -wŏt'ĕr). Bridgewater, Va.; coed.; 1880.
Brig'ham Young U. (brĭg'ăm yŭng'). Provo, Utah; coed.; 1875.
Brite C. of the Bible (brīt). Fort Worth, Texas; coed.; 1906.
Brook'lyn, Polytechnic Inst. of (brŏok'lĭn). N. Y.; men; 1854.
Brooklyn C. N. Y.; coed.; 1930.
Brooklyn Law School. N. Y.; coed.; 1901.
Broome Technical Community C. (brōom). Binghamton, N. Y.; junior coed.; 1946.
Brown Military Acad. (broun). San Diego, Calif.; junior men; 1928.
Brown U. Providence, R. I.; coed.; 1764.
Bry'ant & Strat'ton Business Inst. (brī'ănt, străt'n). Buffalo, N. Y.; junior coed.; 1854.
Bryant C. Providence, R. I.; coed.; 1863.
Bryn Mawr C. (brĭn' mär'). Bryn Mawr, Pa.; women; 1880.
Buck-nell' U. (bŭk-nĕl'). Lewisburg, Pa.; coed.; 1846.
Bue'na Vis'ta C. (bū'nȧ vĭs'tȧ). Storm Lake, Iowa; coed.; 1891.
Buf'fa-lo, U. of (bŭf'ȧ-lō). N. Y.; coed.; 1846.
Bur-dett' C. (bĕr-dĕt'). Boston, Mass.; junior coed.; 1912.
Bur'ling-ton C. (bûr'lĭng-tŭn). Burlington, Iowa; junior coed.; 1920.
Business Training C. Pittsburgh, Pa.; junior coed.; 1933.
But'ler C. (bŭt'lĕr). Tyler, Texas; coed.; 1927.
Butler U. Indianapolis, Ind.; coed.; 1850.
Cald'well C. for Women (kôld'wĕl; -wĕl; kôld'-). Caldwell, N. J.; 1939.
Cal'i-for'nia, U. of (kăl'ĭ-fôrn'yȧ; -fôr'nĭ-ȧ). Berkeley; coed.; 1855.
California at Los Angeles, U. of. Coed.; 1881.
California Baptist Theol. Sem. Covina; coed.; 1944.
California C. of Arts and Crafts. Oakland; coed.; 1907.
California C. of Chiropody. San Francisco; coed.; 1914.
California Con-cor'di-a C. (kŏn-kôr'dĭ-ȧ). Oakland; junior coed.; 1906.
California Flyers Sch. of Aeronautics. Inglewood; men; 1930.
California Inst. of Tech. Pasadena; men; 1891.
California Maritime Acad. Vallejo; men; 1929.
California Sch. of Fine Arts. San Francisco; coed.; 1874.
California State Polytechnic C. San Luis Obispo; men; 1901.
Cal'vin C. (kăl'vĭn). Grand Rapids, Mich.; coed.; 1876.
Calvin Coo'lidge C. of Liberal Arts (kōo'lĭj). Boston, Mass.; coed.; 1934.
Calvin Coolidge Law Sch. Boston, Mass.; men; 1939.
Calvin Sem. Grand Rapids, Mich.; men; 1876.
Cam'bridge Junior C. (kăm'brĭj). Cambridge, Mass.; coed.; 1934.
Cam'er-on State Agricultural C. (kăm'ĕr-ŭn). Lawton, Okla.; junior coed.; 1908.
Camp'bell C. (kăm'(b)ĕl). Jackson, Miss.; junior coed.; 1890.
Campbell C. (kăm'ĕl). Buies Creek, N. C.; junior coed.; 1887.
Camp'bells-ville C. (kăm'bĕlz-vĭl). Campbellsville, Ky.; coed.; 1906.
Ca-nal' Zone Junior C. (kȧ-năl' zōn'). Balboa Heights; coed.; 1933.
Ca'ney Junior C. (kā'nĭ). Pippapass, Ky.; coed.; 1923.
Ca-ni'sius C. (kȧ-nĭsh'ŭs; -nē'shŭs). Buffalo, N. Y.; coed.; 1870.
Cap'i-tal U. (kăp'ĭ-tăl; -t'l). Columbus, Ohio; coed.; 1850.
Cap'i-tol Radio Engineering Inst. (kăp'ĭ-tŏl; -t'l). Washington, D. C.; men; 1927.
Cap'u-chin C. (kăp'ū-shĭn). Washington, D. C.; men; 1917.
Capuchin Franciscan Friary. Milton, Mass.; men; 1945.
Car'bon C. (kär'bŏn). Price, Utah; junior coed.; 1937.
Car'di-nal Stritch C. (kär'dĭ-năl strĭch). Milwaukee, Wis.; women; 1932.
Carle'ton C. (kärl'tŭn; -t'n). Northfield, Minn.; coed.; 1866.
Car-ne'gie Inst. of Tech. (kär-nā'gĭ; -nĕg'ĭ; kär'nĕ-gĭ). Pittsburgh, Pa.; coed.; 1900.
Car'roll C. (kär'ŭl). Helena, Mont.; coed.; 1909.
Carroll C. Waukesha, Wis.; coed.; 1840.
Car'son–New'man C. (kär's'n-nū'măn). Jefferson City, Tenn.; coed.; 1851.
Car'thage C. (kär'thĭj). Carthage, Ill.; coed.; 1846.
Car'ver C. (kär'vĕr). Charlotte, N. C.; junior coed.; 1949.
Carver Sch. of Missions and Social Work. Louisville, Ky.; coed.; 1907.
Cas-cade' C. (kăs-kād'; kăs'kād). Portland, Ore.; coed.; 1918.
Case Inst. of Tech. (kās). Cleveland, Ohio; coed.; 1880.
Cas'per Junior C. (kăs'pĕr). Casper, Wyo.; coed.; 1945.
Ca-taw'ba C. (kȧ-tô'bȧ). Salisbury, N. C.; coed.; 1851.
Cathedral C. New York, N. Y.; junior men; 1903.
Cathedral C. of the Immaculate Conception. Brooklyn, N. Y.; men; 1914.
Catholic Sisters C. Washington, D. C.; coed.; 1911.
Catholic Teachers C. Providence, R. I.; women; 1929.
Catholic U. of A-mer'i-ca. Washington, D. C.; coed.; 1887.
Catholic U. of Puer'to Ri'co. Santa María, Ponce; coed.; 1948.
Caz'e-no'vi-a Junior C. (kăz'n-ō'vĭ-ȧ). Cazenovia, N. Y.; women; 1824.
Ce'dar Crest C. (sē'dĕr krĕst'). Allentown, Pa.; women; 1867.
Ce'dar-ville Baptist C. and Bible Inst. (sē'dĕr-vĭl). Cedarville, Ohio; coed.; 1887.
Cen'te-nar'y C. of Louisiana (sĕn'tē-nĕr'ĭ). Shreveport; coed.; 1825.
Centenary Junior C. Hackettstown, N. J.; women; 1867.
Cen'ter-ville Community C. (sĕn'tĕr-vĭl). Centerville, Iowa; junior coed.; 1930.

Central Baptist Theol. Sem. Kansas City, Kans.; coed.; 1902.
Central Bible Inst. Springfield, Mo.; coed.; 1922.
Central Christian C. Bartlesville, Okla.; junior coed.; 1950.
Central C. Pella, Iowa; coed.; 1853.
Central C. McPherson, Kans.; junior coed.; 1914.
Central C. Fayette, Mo.; coed.; 1854.
Cen·tra'lia Junior C. (sĕn·trāl'yá). Centralia, Wash.; coed.; 1925.
Centralia Township Junior C. Centralia, Ill.; coed.; 1940.
Central Michigan C. Mount Pleasant; coed.; 1892.
Central Missouri State C. Warrensburg; coed.; 1870.
Central State C. Wilberforce, Ohio; coed.; 1887.
Central State C. Edmond, Okla.; coed.; 1890.
Central Technical Inst. Kansas City, Mo.; coed.; 1937.
Central Washington C. of Ed. Ellensburg; coed.; 1891.
Cen'tre C. of Ken·tuck'y (sĕn'tĕr). Danville; coed.; 1819.
Chaf'fey C. (chǎf'ĭ). Ontario, Calif.; junior coed.; 1883.
Cha·nute' Junior C. (shá·nōōt'). Chanute, Kans.; coed.; 1935.
Chap'man C. (chǎp'mǎn). Orange, Calif.; coed.; 1861.
Charles'ton, C. of (chärlz'tǔn). S. C.; coed.; 1770.
Char'lotte C. (shär'lŏt). Charlotte, N. C.; junior coed.; 1946.
Chat'ham C. (chǎt'ǎm). Pittsburgh, Pa.; women; 1869.
Chat'ta·noo'ga, U. of (chǎt'á·nōō'gá). Tenn.; coed.; 1886.
Chest'nut Hill C. (chĕs'nŭt hĭl'; chĕst'-; -nŭt). Philadelphia, Pa.; women; 1871.
Chicago, Sch. of the Art Inst. of. Ill.; coed.; 1866.
Chicago, U. of. Ill.; coed.; 1891.
Chicago Acad. of Fine Arts. Ill.; coed.; 1902.
Chicago City Junior C. Ill.; coed.; 1931.
Chicago C. of Osteopathy. Ill.; coed.; 1913.
Chicago Conservatory. Ill.; coed.; 1857.
Chicago Evangelistic Inst. University Park, Iowa; coed.; 1910.
Chicago–Kent C. of Law (-kĕnt'). Chicago, Ill.; coed.; 1887.
Chicago Lutheran Theol. Sem. Maywood, Ill.; men; 1891.
Chicago Med. Sch. Ill.; coed.; 1912.
Chicago Teachers C. Ill.; coed.; 1867.
Chicago Technical C. Ill.; men; 1904.
Chicago Theol. Sem. Ill.; coed.; 1855.
Chi'co State C. (chē̄'kō). Chico, Calif.; coed.; 1887.
Chi·po'la Junior C. (chĭ·pō'lá). Marianna, Fla.; coed.; 1947.
Choui·nard' Art Inst. (shĭ·närd'). Los Angeles, Calif.; coed.; 1921.
Cho·wan' C. (chô·wŏn'). Murfreesboro, N. C.; junior coed.; 1848.
Christian Brothers C. Memphis, Tenn.; men; 1871.
Christian C. Columbia, Mo.; junior women; 1851.
Christ the King Sem. St. Bonaventure, N. Y.; men; 1859.
Church Divinity Sch. of the Pacific. Berkeley, Calif.; men; 1893.
Cincinnati, U. of. Ohio; coed.; 1819.
Cis'co Junior C. (sĭs'kō). Cisco, Texas; coed.; 1940.
Cit'a·del, The (sĭt'á·dĕl; -d'l). Charleston, S. C.; men; 1842.
Cit'rus Junior C. (sĭt'rŭs). Azusa, Calif.; coed.; 1915.
City C. New York, N. Y.; coed.; 1847.
City C. of San Francisco. Calif.; junior coed.; 1935.
Claf'lin U. (klǎf'lĭn). Orangeburg, S. C.; coed.; 1869.
Clare'mont Graduate Sch. (klâr'mŏnt). Claremont, Calif.; coed.; 1926.
Claremont Men's C. Claremont, Calif.; 1947.
Clar'en·don Junior C. (klär'ĕn·dŏn). Clarendon, Texas; coed.; 1927.
Cla·re'tian (Do·min'guez) Major Sem. (klă·rē'shǎn, dô·mĭng'gĕz). Compton, Calif.; men; 1924.
Cla·rin'da Junior C. (klă·rĭn'dá). Clarinda, Iowa; coed.; 1923.
Clark C. (klärk). Atlanta, Ga.; coed.; 1869.
Clark C. Vancouver, Wash.; junior coed.; 1933.
Clarke C. (klärk). Dubuque, Iowa; women; 1843.
Clarke Memorial C. Newton, Miss.; junior coed.; 1908.
Clark'son C. of Tech. (klärk's'n). Potsdam, N. Y.; men; 1896.
Clark U. Worcester, Mass.; coed.; 1887.
Clea'ry C. (klēr'ĭ). Ypsilanti, Mich.; coed.; 1883.
Clem'son Agricultural C. (klĕm's'n). Clemson, S. C.; coed.; 1889.
Cleveland Inst. of Music. Ohio; coed.; 1920.
Clin'ton Junior C. (klĭn't'n; -tŭn). Clinton, Iowa; coed.; 1946.
Co'a·ho'ma Junior C. (kō'á·hō'má). Clarksdale, Miss.; junior coed.; 1926.
Coa·lin'ga C. (kō·lĭng'gá). Coalinga, Calif.; junior coed.; 1932.
Coe C. (kō). Cedar Rapids, Iowa; coed.; 1881.
Cof'fey·ville C. of Arts, Science, and Vocations (kôf'ĭ·vĭl). Coffeyville, Kans.; junior coed.; 1923.
Cogs'well Polytechnical C. (kŏgz'wĕl). San Francisco, Calif.; junior coed.; 1930.
Co'ker C. (kō'kĕr). Hartsville, S. C.; women; 1894.
Col'by C. (kōl'bĭ). Waterville, Me.; coed.; 1813.
Colby Junior C. for Women. New London, N. H.; 1837.
Col'gate–Roch'es'ter Divinity Sch. (kōl'gāt·rŏch'ĕs'tĕr; -ĭs·tĕr). Rochester, N. Y.; coed.; 1817.
Colgate U. Hamilton, N. Y.; men; 1819.
College Conservatory of Music. Cincinnati, Ohio; coed.; 1867.
Colorado, U. of. Boulder; coed.; 1861.
Colorado C. Colorado Springs; coed.; 1874.
Colorado Sch. of Mines. Golden; coed.; 1874.
Colorado State C. Greeley; coed.; 1889.
Colorado State U. Fort Collins; coed.; 1870.
Colorado Woman's C. Denver; junior; 1909.
Co·lum'bi·a Bible C. (kō·lŭm'bĭ·á). Columbia, S. C.; coed.; 1923.
Columbia C. Chicago, Ill.; coed.; 1890.
Columbia C. Columbia, S. C.; women; 1854.
Co·lum'bi·an C. (kō·lŭm'bĭ·ǎn). Washington, D. C.; coed.; 1821.
Columbia Theol. Sem. Decatur, Ga.; men; 1828.
Columbia U. New York, N. Y.; coed.; 1754.
Community C. and Technical Inst. Benton Harbor, Mich.; junior coed.; 1946.
Comp'ton Junior C. (kŏmp'tŭn). Compton, Calif.; coed.; 1927.
Con'cord C. (kŏn[g]'kôrd; kŏng'kĕrd). Athens, W. Va.; coed.; 1872.
Con·cor'di·a C. (kŏn·kôr'dĭ·á). Moorhead, Minn.; coed.; 1891.
Concordia C. St. Paul, Minn.; junior coed.; 1893.

Concordia C. Portland Ore.; junior coed.; 1905.
Concordia C. Milwaukee, Wis.; junior men; 1881.
Concordia Collegiate Inst. Bronxville, N. Y.; junior coed.; 1881.
Concordia Sem. St. Louis, Mo.; coed.; 1839.
Concordia Senior C. Fort Wayne, Ind.; men; 1839.
Concordia Teachers C. River Forest, Ill.; coed.; 1864.
Concordia Teachers C. Seward, Nebr.; coed.; 1894.
Concordia Theol. Sem. Springfield, Ill.; men; 1846.
Connecticut, Teachers C. of. New Britain; coed.; 1849.
Connecticut, U. of. Storrs; coed.; 1881.
Connecticut C. New London; women; 1911.
Con'nors State Agricultural C. (kŏn'ĕrz). Warner, Okla.; junior coed.; 1908.
Con'roe Normal & Industrial C. (kŏn'rō). Conroe, Texas; junior coed.; 1903.
Conservative Baptist Theol. Sem. Denver, Colo.; coed.; 1950.
Con'verse C. (kŏn'vûrs; -vĕrs). Spartanburg, S. C.; coed.; 1889.
Coo'per Union (kōō'pĕr; kōōp'ĕr). New York, N. Y.; coed.; 1859.
Co·pi'ah–Lin'coln Junior C. (kô·pī'á·lĭng'kŭn). Wesson, Miss.; coed.; 1915.
Cop'pin State Teachers C. (kŏp'ĭn). Baltimore, Md.; coed.; 1900.
Cor·nell' C. (kôr·nĕl'; kôr'nĕl'). Mount Vernon, Iowa; coed.; 1852.
Cornell U. Ithaca, N. Y.; coed.; 1865.
Cor'pus Chris'ti, U. of (kôr'pŭs krĭs'tĭ). Corpus Christi, Texas; coed.; 1947.
Cosmopolitan Sch. of Music. Chicago, Ill.; coed.; 1906.
Cot'tey C. (kŏt'ĭ). Nevada, Mo.; junior women; 1884.
Creigh'ton U. (krā't'n). Omaha, Nebr.; coed.; 1878.
Cres'ton Junior C. (krĕs'tŭn). Creston, Iowa; coed.; 1926.
Cro'sier Sem. (krō'zhĕr). Onamia, Minn.; junior men; 1922.
Cro'zer Theol. Sem. (krō'zĕr). Chester, Pa.; coed.; 1867.
Cul'ver–Stock'ton C. (kŭl'vĕr·stŏk'tŭn). Canton, Mo.; coed.; 1853.
Cum'ber·land C. (kŭm'bĕr·lǎnd). Williamsburg, Ky.; junior coed.; 1888.
Cumberland U. Lebanon, Tenn.; coed.; 1842.
Cur'ry C. (kûr'ĭ). Milton, Mass.; coed.; 1879.
Cur'tis Inst. of Music (kûr'tĭs). Philadelphia, Pa.; coed.; 1924.
Cus'ter County Junior C. (kŭs'tĕr). Miles City, Mont.; coed.; 1939.
Da·ko'ta Wesleyan U. (dá·kō'tá). Mitchell, S. Dak.; coed.; 1883.
Dal'las Theol. Sem. and Graduate Sch. of Theology (dǎl'ǎs). Texas; men; 1924.
Dan'a C. (dǎn'á). Blair, Nebr.; coed.; 1884.
Dan'bur'y State Teachers C. (dǎn'bĕr'ĭ; -bĕr·ĭ). Danbury, Conn.; coed.; 1904.
Dan'ville Junior C. (dǎn'vĭl). Danville, Ill.; coed.; 1946.
Dart'mouth C. (därt'mŭth). Hanover, N. H.; men; 1769.
David Lips'comb C. (lĭps'kŭm). Nashville, Tenn.; coed.; 1891.
Da'vid·son C. (dā'vĭd·s'n). Davidson, N. C.; men; 1837.
Da'vis and El'kins C. (dā'vĭs. ĕl'kĭnz). Elkins, W. Va.; coed.; 1903.
Daw'son County Junior C. (dô's'n). Glendive, Mont.; coed.; 1940.
Day'ton, U. of (dā't'n). Ohio; coed.; 1850.
De·ca'tur Baptist C. (dê·kā'tĕr). Decatur, Texas; junior coed.; 1891.
Deep Springs C. Deep Springs, Calif.; junior men; 1917.
De·fi'ance C. (dê·fī'ǎns). Defiance, Ohio; coed.; 1850.
De La Salle Normal Sch. (dē̓ lá săl'). Lafayette, La.; men; 1923.
Del'a·ware, U. of (dĕl'á·wâr; -wĕr). Newark; coed.; 1743.
Delaware State C. Dover; coed.; 1891.
Del Mar C. (dĕl mär'). Corpus Christi, Texas; junior coed.; 1935.
Del'ta State C. (dĕl'tá). Cleveland, Miss.; coed.; 1924.
De Maz'e·nod Scholasticate (dĕ mǎz'n·ŏd). San Antonio, Texas; men; 1928.
Den'i·son U. (dĕn'ĭ·s'n). Granville, Ohio; coed.; 1831.
Den'ver, U. of (dĕn'vĕr). Colo.; coed.; 1864.
De Paul U. (dĕ pôl'). Chicago, Ill.; coed.; 1898.
De·Pauw' U. (dĕ·pô'). Greencastle, Ind.; coed.; 1832.
Des Moines Still C. of Osteopathy and Surgery (dĕ moin'). Des Moines, Iowa; coed.; 1898.
Detroit, U. of. Mich.; coed.; 1877.
Detroit Bible Inst. Mich.; coed.; 1945.
Detroit C. of Law. Mich.; coed.; 1891.
Detroit Inst. of Musical Art. Mich.; coed.; 1914.
Detroit Inst. of Tech. Mich.; coed.; 1891.
Devils Lake Junior C. Devils Lake, N. Dak.; coed.; 1941.
Dick'in·son C. (dĭk'ĭn·s'n). Carlisle, Pa.; coed.; 1773.
Dickinson Sch. of Law. Carlisle, Pa.; coed.; 1834.
Dil'lard U. (dĭl'ĕrd). New Orleans, La.; coed.; 1869.
Diocesan Normal School. Brooklyn, N. Y.; coed.; 1920.
District of Columbia Teachers C. Wash., D. C.; coed.; 1851.
Divine Savior Sem. Lanham, Md.; men; 1941.
Divinity Sch. of the Protestant Episcopal Church. Philadelphia, Pa.; coed.; 1857.
Dix'ie Junior C. (dĭk'sĭ). St. George, Utah; coed.; 1911.
Doane C. (dōn). Crete, Nebr.; coed.; 1872.
Dodge City C. (dŏj). Dodge City, Kans.; junior coed.; 1935.
Do·min'i·can C. (dô·mĭn'ĭ·kǎn). Racine, Wis.; coed.; 1935.
Dominican C. of San Ra·fael' (săn' rá·fĕl'). San Rafael, Calif.; women; 1850.
Dominican Junior C. of Blau'velt (blô'vĕlt). Blauvelt, N. Y.; women; 1952.
Don Bos'co C. (dŏn bŏs'kō). Newton, N. J.; men; 1929.
Don'nel·ly C. (dŏn''l·ĭ). Kansas City, Kans.; junior coed.; 1949.
Doug'lass C. (dŭg'lǎs). New Brunswick, N. J.; women; 1918.
Drake U. (drāk). Des Moines, Iowa; coed.; 1881.
Draughon's Business C. (drônz). Abilene, Amarillo, Dallas, Lubbock, and Wichita Falls, Texas; junior coed.; 1884.
Draughon's Business C. San Antonio, Texas; junior coed.; 1888.
Draughon Sch. of Business. Little Rock, Ark.; junior coed.; 1901.
Drew U. (drōō). Madison, N. J.; coed.; 1867.
Drex'el Inst. of Tech. (drĕk's'l). Philadelphia, Pa.; coed.; 1891.
Drop'sie C. for Hebrew and Cognate Learning (drŏp'sĭ). Philadelphia, Pa.; coed.; 1907.
Dru'ry C. (drōōr'ĭ). Springfield, Mo.; coed.; 1873.

D. T. Wat'son Sch. of Physiatrics (wŏt′s′n). Leetsdale, Pa.; coed.; 1920.

Du·buque′, U. of (dŭ·būk′). Dubuque, Iowa; coed.; 1852.

Du·chesne′ C. (dōō·shän′). Omaha, Nebr.; women; 1880.

Duke U. (dūk). Durham, N. C.; coed.; 1838.

Dun·bar′ton C. of Holy Cross (dŭn·bär′t′n). Washington, D. C.; women; 1935.

Duns Sco′tus C. (dŭnz skō′tŭs). Detroit, Mich.; junior men; 1930.

Du·quesne′ U. (dōō·kān′). Pittsburgh, Pa.; coed.; 1878.

Dur′ham's Business Junior C. (dûr′ămz). Austin, Ft. Worth, Harlingen, Houston, and San Antonio, Texas; coed.; 1936.

D'You′ville C. (dū′vĭl). Buffalo, N. Y.; women; 1908.

Eagle Grove Junior C. Eagle Grove, Iowa; coed.; 1928.

Earl′ham C. (ûr′lăm). Richmond, Ind.; coed.; 1847.

East Carolina C. Greenville, N. C.; coed.; 1907.

East Central Junior C. Decatur, Miss.; coed.; 1914.

East Central State C. Ada, Okla.; coed.; 1909.

East Con′tra Cos′ta Junior C. (kŏn′trà kŏs′tà). Concord, Calif.; coed.; 1949.

Eastern Arizona Junior C. Thatcher; coed.; 1891.

Eastern Baptist C. St. Davids, Pa.; coed.; 1952.

Eastern Baptist Theol. Sem. Philadelphia, Pa.; coed.; 1925.

Eastern Illinois State C. Charleston; coed.; 1895.

Eastern Kentucky State C. Richmond; coed.; 1906.

Eastern Mennonite C. Harrisonburg, Va.; coed.; 1917.

Eastern Michigan C. Ypsilanti; coed.; 1849.

Eastern Montana C. of Ed. Billings; coed.; 1925.

Eastern Naz′a·rene C. (năz′à·rēn). Wollaston, Mass.; coed.; 1900.

Eastern New Mexico U. Portales; coed.; 1934.

Eastern Oklahoma A. & M. C. Wilburton; junior coed.; 1909.

Eastern Oregon C. La Grande; coed.; 1925.

Eastern Pilgrim C. Allentown, Pa.; coed.; 1921.

Eastern Washington C. of Ed. Cheney, Wash.; coed.; 1890.

East Los Angeles Junior C. Los Angeles, Calif.; coed.; 1945.

East′man Dental Dispensary and Sch. for Dental Hygienists (ĕst′măn). Rochester, N. Y.; women; 1915.

East Mississippi Junior C. Scooba; coed.; 1927.

East Tennessee State C. Johnson City; coed.; 1909.

East Texas Baptist C. Marshall; coed.; 1914.

East Texas State C. Commerce; coed.; 1889.

E′den Theol. Sem. (ē′d′n). Webster Groves, Mo.; coed.; 1850.

Edge′wood C. of the Sacred Heart (ĕj′wŏŏd). Madison, Wis.; women; 1927.

Ed′wards Military Inst. (ĕd′wĕrdz). Salemburg, N. C.; junior men; 1935.

Edward Wa′ters C. (wô′tĕrz; wŏt′ĕrz). Jacksonville, Fla.; junior coed.; 1942.

El Ca·mi′no C. (ĕl′ dō·rā′dō). El Camino College, Calif.; junior coed.; 1946.

El Do·ra′do Junior C. (ĕl′ dō·rā′dō). El Dorado, Kans.; coed.; 1927.

El′gin Community C. (ĕl′jĭn). Elgin, Ill.; junior coed.; 1949.

E·liz′a·beth City State Teachers C. (ĕ·lĭz′à·bĕth). Elizabeth City, N. C.; coed.; 1891.

E·liz′a·beth·town′ C. (ĕ·lĭz′à·bĕth·toun′). Elizabethtown, Pa.; coed.; 1899.

Ells′worth Junior C. (ĕlz′wûrth; -wĕrth). Iowa Falls, Iowa; coed.; 1890.

Elm′hurst C. (ĕlm′hûrst). Elmhurst, Ill.; coed.; 1865.

El·mi′ra C. (ĕl·mī′rà). Elmira, N. Y.; women; 1853.

E′lon C. (ē′lŏn). Elon College, N. C.; coed.; 1889.

El Re′no C. (ĕl rē′nō). El Reno, Okla.; junior coed.; 1938.

E′ly Junior C. (ē′lĭ). Ely, Minn.; coed.; 1922.

Em′bry–Rid′dle Sch. of Aviation (ĕm′brĭ·rĭd′′l). Miami, Fla.; men; 1926.

Em′er·son C. (ĕm′ĕr·s′n). Boston, Mass.; coed.; 1880.

Em·man′u·el C. (ĕ·măn′û·ĕl; ĭ-). Franklin Springs, Ga.; junior coed.; 1933.

Emmanuel C. Boston, Mass.; women; 1919.

Emmanuel Missionary C. Berrien Springs, Mich.; coed.; 1874.

Em′mets·burg Junior C. (ĕm′ĕts·bûrg; ĕm′ĭts-). Emmetsburg, Iowa; coed.; 1930.

Em′o·ry and Hen′ry C. (ĕm′ô·rĭ, hĕn′rĭ). Emory, Va.; coed.; 1838.

Emory at Oxford. Oxford, Ga.; junior men; 1836.

Emory Junior C. Valdosta, Ga.; men; 1928.

Emory U. Emory University, Ga.; coed.; 1836.

Em·po′ri·a, C. of (ĕm·pō′rĭ·à; 70). Emporia, Kans.; coed.; 1882.

En′di·cott Junior C. (ĕn′dĭ·kŭt). Beverly, Mass.; women; 1939.

Epiphany Apostolic C. New Windsor, N. Y.; junior men; 1888.

Episcopal Theol. Sch. Cambridge, Mass.; men; 1867.

E′rie County Technical Inst. (ēr′ĭ). Buffalo, N. Y.; junior coed.; 1946.

Er′skine C. (ûr′skĭn). Due West, S. C.; coed.; 1839.

Es′ther·ville Junior C. (ĕs′tĕr·vĭl). Estherville, Iowa; coed.; 1924.

Eu·re′ka C. (û·rē′kà). Eureka, Ill.; coed.; 1848.

Evangelical and Reformed Church, Theol. Sem. of the. Lancaster, Pa.; coed.; 1825.

Evangelical Theol. Sem. Naperville, Ill.; coed.; 1873.

Ev′ans·ville C. (ĕv′ănz·vĭl). Evansville, Ind.; coed.; 1854.

Ev′e·leth Junior C. (ĕv′ĕ·lĕth). Eveleth, Minn.; coed.; 1918.

Ev′er·ett Junior C. (ĕv′ĕr·ĕt; -ĭt). Everett, Wash.; coed.; 1941.

Ey′mard Sem. (ā′märd). Hyde Park, N. Y.; junior men; 1904.

Fair′bur′y Junior C. (fâr′bĕr′ĭ). Fairbury, Nebr.; coed.; 1941.

Fair′fax Hall Junior C. (fâr′făks). Waynesboro, Virginia; women; 1920.

Fair′field U. (fâr′fēld). Fairfield, Conn.; men; 1942.

Fair′leigh Dick′in·son U. (fâr′lĭ dĭk′ĭn·s′n). Rutherford, N. J.; coed.; 1942.

Fair′mont State C. (fâr′mŏnt). Fairmont, W. Va.; coed.; 1867.

Faith Theol. Sem. Philadelphia, Pa.; coed.; 1937.

Farm′ing·ton State Teachers C. (fär′mĭng·tŭn). Farmington, Me.; coed.; 1864.

Fashion Inst. of Tech. New York, N. Y.; junior coed.; 1944.

Fay′ette·ville State Teachers C. (fā′ĕt·vĭl). Fayetteville, N. C.; coed.; 1867.

Fe·li′cian C., The (fĕ·lĭsh′ăn). Chicago, Ill.; junior women; 1926.

Fenn C. (fĕn). Cleveland, Ohio; coed.; 1881.

Fer′ris Inst. (fĕr′ĭs). Big Rapids, Mich.; coed.; 1884.

Fer′rum Junior C. (fĕr′ŭm). Ferrum, Va.; coed.; 1914.

Finch C. (fĭnch). New York, N. Y.; women; 1900.

Find′lay C. (fĭn[d]′lĭ). Findlay, Ohio; coed.; 1882.

Fish′er Junior C. (fĭsh′ĕr). Boston, Mass.; women; 1903.

Fisk U. (fĭsk). Nashville, Tenn.; coed.; 1866.

Flat River, Junior C. of (flăt). Flat River, Mo.; coed.; 1922.

Fletch′er Sch. of Law and Diplomacy (flĕch′ĕr). Medford, Mass.; coed.; 1933.

Flint Junior C. (flĭnt). Flint, Mich.; coed.; 1923.

Flo′ra Mac·don′ald C. (flō′rà măk·dŏn′′ld). Red Springs, N. C.; women; 1896.

Flora Stone Math′er C. (măth′ĕr). Cleveland, Ohio; women; 1888.

Florida, U. of. Gainesville; coed.; 1853.

Florida A. & M. U. Tallahassee; coed.; 1887.

Florida Christian C. Tampa; junior coed.; 1944.

Florida Normal and Industrial Memorial C. St. Augustine; coed.; 1892.

Florida Southern C. Lakeland; coed.; 1885.

Florida State U. Tallahassee; coed.; 1857.

Fond du Lac C. (fŏn′ dŭ lăk′). Fond du Lac, Wis.; junior coed.; 1944.

Font′bonne C. (fŏnt′bŏn). St. Louis, Mo.; women; 1923.

Ford′ham U. (fôr′dăm). New York, N. Y.; coed.; 1841.

Foreign Mission Sem. of Holy Cross. Wash., D. C.; men; 1924.

For′syth Sch. for Dental Hygienists (fôr′sĭth). Boston, Mass.; women; 1916.

Fort Dodge Junior C. (dŏj). Fort Dodge, Iowa; coed.; 1922.

Fort Hays Kansas State C. (hāz). Hays, Kans.; coed.; 1901.

Fort Kent State Normal Sch. (kĕnt). Fort Kent, Me.; coed.; 1878.

Fort Lew′is A. & M. C. (lū′ĭs; lōō′-). Durango, Colo.; coed.; 1911.

Fort Scott Junior C. (skŏt). Fort Scott, Kans.; coed.; 1919.

Fort Smith Junior C. (smĭth). Fort Smith, Ark.; coed.; 1928.

Fort′ Val′ley State C. (văl′ĭ). Fort Valley, Ga.; coed.; 1895.

Fort′ Wayne′ Art Sch. (wān′). Fort Wayne, Ind.; coed.; 1880.

Fort Wayne Bible C. Fort Wayne, Ind.; coed.; 1904.

Franciscan Preparatory Sem. Hollidaysburg, Pa.; junior men; 1929.

Franciscan Theol. Sem. Santa Barbara, Calif.; men; 1896.

Francis T. Nich′olls State C. (nĭk′ŭlz; -′lz). Thibodaux, La.; coed.; 1948.

Frank′lin and Mar′shall C. (frăngk′lĭn, mär′shăl). Lancaster, Pa.; men; 1787.

Franklin C. of Indiana. Franklin; coed.; 1834.

Franklin Junior C. Columbus, Ohio; coed.; 1918.

Franklin Technical Inst. Boston, Mass.; coed.; 1908.

Franklin U. Columbus, Ohio; coed.; 1902.

Frank Phil′lips C. (fĭl′ĭps). Borger, Texas; junior coed.; 1946.

Freed–Har′de·man C. (frēd′här′dĕ·măn). Henderson, Tenn.; junior coed.; 1908.

Free′man Junior C. (frē′măn). Freeman, S. Dak.; coed.; 1900.

Fres′no Junior C. (frĕz′nō). Fresno, Calif.; coed.; 1910.

Fresno State C. Fresno, Calif.; coed.; 1911.

Friends Bible C. Haviland, Kans.; junior coed.; 1917.

Friendship Junior C. Rock Hill, S. C.; coed.; 1891.

Friends U. Wichita, Kans.; coed.; 1898.

Ful′ler Theol. Sem. (fŏŏl′ĕr). Pasadena, Calif.; coed.; 1947.

Ful′ler·ton Junior C. (fŏŏl′ĕr·t′n; -tŭn). Fullerton, Calif.; coed.; 1913.

Fur′man U. (fûr′măn). Greenville, S. C.; coed.; 1825.

Gaines′ville Junior C. (gānz′vĭl). Gainesville, Texas; coed.; 1924.

Gal·lau·det′ C. (găl′û·dĕt′; 2). Washington, D. C.; coed.; 1864.

Gam′mon Theol. Sem. (găm′ŭn). Atlanta, Ga.; coed.; 1883.

Gan′non C. (găn′ŭn). Erie, Pa.; men; 1933.

Garden City Junior C. Garden City, Kans.; coed.; 1919.

Gard′ner–Webb Junior C. (gärd′nĕr·wĕb′). Boiling Springs, N. C.; coed.; 1905.

Gar′land Sch., a Junior C. (gär′lănd). Boston, Mass.; women; 1872.

Gar′rett Biblical Inst. (găr′ĕt). Evanston, Ill.; coed.; 1853.

General Bea′dle State Teachers C. (bē′d′l). Madison, S. Dak.; coed.; 1881.

General Motors Inst. Flint, Mich.; men; 1919.

General Theol. Sem. New York, N. Y.; men; 1817.

Ge·ne′va C. (jĕ·nē′và). Beaver Falls, Pa.; coed.; 1848.

George Fox C. (fŏks). Newberg, Ore.; coed.; 1891.

George Pea′bod′y C. for Teachers (pē′bŏd′ĭ; -bŭd·ĭ). Nashville, Tenn.; coed.; 1875.

George Pep′per·dine C. (pĕp′ĕr·dīn). Los Angeles, Calif.; coed.; 1937.

George′town C. (jôrj′toun). Georgetown, Ky.; coed.; 1787.

Georgetown U. Washington, D. C.; coed.; 1789.

Georgetown Visitation Junior C. Washington, D. C.; women; 1799.

George Wash′ing·ton U. Washington, D. C.; coed.; 1821.

George Wil′liams C. (wĭl′yămz). Chicago, Ill.; coed.; 1890.

Geor′gia, Medical C. of (jôr′jà; -jyà; -jĭ·à). Augusta; coed.; 1828.

Georgia, U. of. Athens; coed.; 1785.

Georgia Inst. of Tech. Atlanta; coed.; 1885.

Georgia Military C. Milledgeville; junior men; 1879.

Geor′gi·an Court C. (jôr′jĭ·ăn [-jăn; -jyăn] kōrt′). Lakewood, N. J.; women; 1908.

Georgia Southwestern C. Americus; junior coed.; 1906.

Georgia State C. for Women. Milledgeville; 1889.

Georgia State C. of Business Administration. Atlanta; coed.; 1914.

Georgia Teachers C. Collegeboro; coed.; 1908.

Get′tys·burg C. (gĕt′ĭz·bûrg). Gettysburg, Pa.; coed.; 1832.

Glen′dale C. (glĕn′dāl). Glendale, Calif.; junior coed.; 1927.

Glen′ville State C. (glĕn′vĭl). Glenville, W. Va.; coed.; 1872.

God′dard C. (gŏd′ĕrd). Plainfield, Vt.; coed.; 1938.

Go·ge′bic Community C. (gŏ·gē′bĭk). Ironwood, Mich.; junior coed.; 1932.

Golden Gate Baptist Theol. Sem. Berkeley, Calif.; coed.; 1944.

Golden Gate C. San Francisco, Calif.; coed.; 1901.

Gon·zag'a U. (gŏn·zăg'à). Spokane, Wash.; coed.; 1887.
Good Counsel C. White Plains, N. Y.; women; 1923.
Gor'don C. (gôr'd'n). Beverly Farms, Mass.; coed.; 1889.
Gordon Military C. Barnesville, Ga.; junior coed.; 1852.
Gor'ham State Teachers C. (gôr'ăm). Gorham, Me.; coed.; 1878.
Go'shen C. (gō'shĕn). Goshen, Ind.; coed.; 1894.
Gou'cher C. (gou'chĕr). Baltimore, Md.; women; 1885.
Grace Bible Inst. (grās). Omaha, Nebr.; coed.; 1943.
Grace'land C. (grās'lănd). Lamoni, Iowa; coed.; 1895.
Grace Theol. Sem. and Grace C. Winona Lake, Ind.; coed.; 1937.
Gram'bling C. (grăm'blĭng). Grambling, La.; coed.; 1929.
Grand Canyon C. Phoenix, Ariz.; coed.; 1949.
Grand Rapids Baptist Theol. Sem. and Bible Inst. Mich.; coed.; 1941.
Grand Rapids Junior C. Mich.; coed.; 1914.
Grand View C. Des Moines, Iowa; junior coed.; 1896.
Gratz C. (grāts). Philadelphia, Pa.; coed.; 1895.
Grays Harbor C. (grāz). Aberdeen, Wash.; junior coed.; 1930.
Great Falls, C. of. Great Falls, Mont.; coed.; 1932.
Green'bri'er C. (grēn'brī'ẽr). Lewisburg, W. Va.; junior women; 1808.
Green Mountain Junior C. Poultney, Vt.; women; 1834.
Greens'bor'o C. (grēnz'bŭr'ō). Greensboro, N. C.; women; 1838.
Green'ville C. (grēn'vĭl). Greenville, Ill.; coed.; 1892.
Grin·nell' C. (grĭ·nĕl'). Grinnell, Iowa; coed.; 1846.
Grove City C. (grōv). Grove City, Pa.; coed.; 1876.
Guam, Territorial C. of (gwŏm). Agana; junior coed.; 1952.
Guil'ford C. (gĭl'fẽrd). Guilford College, N. C.; coed.; 1834.
Gulf Park C. Gulfport, Miss.; junior women; 1919.
Gus·ta'vus A·dol'phus C. (gŭs·tā'vŭs à·dŏl'fŭs). St. Peter, Minn.; coed.; 1862.
Guz'man Hall (gŭz'măn). Providence, R. I.; men; 1926.
Gwyn'edd—Mer'cy Junior C. (hă'gẽrz·toun). Gwynedd Valley, Pa.; women; 1948.
Ha'gers·town Junior C. (hă'gẽrz·toun). Hagerstown, Md.; coed.; 1946.
Hah'ne·mann Medical C. and Hospital (hä'nĕ·măn). Philadelphia, Pa.; coed.; 1848.
Ham'il·ton C. (hăm'ĭl·tŭn; -t'n). Clinton, N. Y.; men; 1793.
Ham'line U. (hăm'lĭn). St. Paul, Minn.; coed.; 1854.
Hamp'den—Syd'ney C. (hăm'dĕn·sĭd'nĭ). Hampden-Sydney, Va.; men; 1776.
Hamp'ton Inst. (hăm[p]'tŭn). Hampton, Va.; coed.; 1868.
Han'ni·bal—La Grange C. (hăn'ĭ·băl·là·grănj'). Hannibal, Mo.; junior coed.; 1858.
Han'o·ver C. (hăn'ō·vẽr). Hanover, Ind.; coed.; 1827.
Har'cum Junior C. (här'kŭm). Bryn Mawr, Pa.; women; 1915.
Har'ding C. (här'dĭng). Searcy, Ark.; coed.; 1924.
Har'din—Sim'mons U. (här'd'n·sĭm'ŭnz; här'dĭn-). Abilene, Texas; coed.; 1891.
Har'pur C. (här'pẽr). Endicott, N. Y.; coed.; 1946.
Har'ris Teachers C. (här'ĭs). St. Louis, Mo.; coed.; 1857.
Hart'ford Art Sch. (härt'fẽrd). Hartford, Conn.; coed.; 1877.
Hartford C. West Hartford, Conn.; women; 1933.
Hartford Sem. Foundation. Hartford, Conn.; coed.; 1834.
Hart'nell C. (härt'nĕl). Salinas, Calif.; junior coed.; 1920.
Hartt C. of Music (härt). Hartford, Conn.; coed.; 1920.
Hart'wick C. (härt'wĭk). Oneonta, N. Y.; coed.; 1928.
Har'vard U. (här'vẽrd). Cambridge, Mass.; coed.; 1636.
Has'tings C. (hăs'tĭngz). Hastings, Nebr.; coed.; 1882.
Hav'er·ford C. (hăv'ẽr·fẽrd). Haverford, Pa.; men; 1833.
Ha·wai'i, U. of (hà·wī'ē; -wō'yà; -vī'ē). Honolulu; coed.; 1907.
Hebrew Teachers C. Brookline, Mass.; coed.; 1918.
Hebrew Union C.—Jewish Inst. of Religion. Cincinnati, Ohio, and New York, N. Y.; men; 1875.
Hei'del·berg C. (hī'd'l·bûrg). Tiffin, Ohio; coed.; 1850.
Hen'der·son County Junior C. (hĕn'dẽr·s'n). Athens, Texas; coed.; 1946.
Henderson State Teachers C. Arkadelphia, Ark.; coed.; 1890.
Hen'drix C. (hĕn'drĭks). Conway, Ark.; coed.; 1876.
Hen'ry Ford Community C. (hĕn'rĭ fôrd'; 70). Dearborn, Mich.; junior coed.; 1938.
Her'shey Junior C. (hûr'shĭ). Hershey, Pa.; coed.; 1938.
Hess'ton C. and Bible Sch. (hĕs'tŭn). Hesston, Kans.; junior coed.; 1909.
Hib'bing Junior C. (hĭb'ĭng). Hibbing, Minn.; coed.; 1916.
High'land Junior C. (hī'lănd). Highland, Kans.; coed.; 1858.
Highland Manor Junior C. W. Long Branch, N. J.; women; 1928.
Highland Park Junior C. Highland Park, Mich.; coed.; 1918.
High Point C. High Point, N. C.; coed.; 1924.
Hills'dale C. (hĭlz'dāl). Hillsdale, Mich.; coed.; 1844.
Hill'yer C. (hĭl'yẽr). Hartford, Conn.; coed.; 1879.
Hinds Junior C. (hĭndz). Raymond, Miss.; coed.; 1917.
Hi'ram C. (hī'răm). Hiram, Ohio; coed.; 1849.
Hi·was'see C. (hī·wŏs'ē). Madisonville, Tenn.; junior coed.; 1849.
Ho'bart C. (hō'bẽrt). Geneva, N. Y.; men; 1822.
Hof'stra C. (hŏf'strä). Hempstead, N. Y.; coed.; 1935.
Hol'lins C. (hŏl'ĭnz). Hollins College, Va.; women; 1842.
Holmes Junior C. (hōmz). Goodman, Miss.; coed.; 1911.
Hol'ton—Arms Sch. and Junior C. (hōl't'n·ärmz'). Washington, D. C.; women; 1901.
Holy Cross, C. of the. Worcester, Mass.; men; 1843.
Holy Cross C. Washington, D. C.; men; 1895.
Holy Cross Preparatory Sem. Dunkirk, N. Y.; junior men; 1920.
Holy Cross Sem. Canon City, Colo.; men; 1925.
Holy Cross Sem. Notre Dame, Ind.; junior men; 1893.
Holy Family C. Manitowoc, Wis.; women; 1869.
Holy Family Missionary Sem. St. Louis, Mo.; men; 1944.
Holy Family Sem. Oldenburg, Ind.; men; 1866.
Holy Ghost Missionary C. Cornwells Heights, Pa.; junior men; 1897.
Holy Ghost Novitiate. Ridgefield, Conn.; men; 1922.
Holy Name C. Washington, D. C.; men; 1930.
Holy Names, C. of the. Oakland, Calif.; women; 1868.
Holy Names C. Spokane, Wash.; women; 1907.

Hol'yoke Junior C. (hōl'yōk). Holyoke, Mass.; coed.; 1946.
Holy Trinity Missionary Cen'a·cle (sĕn'à·k'l). Silver Spring, Md.; men; 1926.
Holy Trinity Orthodox Sem. Jordanville, N. Y.; men; 1930.
Hood C. (hŏŏd). Frederick, Md.; women; 1893.
Hope C. (hōp). Holland, Mich.; coed.; 1851.
Hough'ton C. (hō't'n). Houghton, N. Y.; coed.; 1883.
Hous'ton, U. of (hūs'tŭn). Texas; coed.; 1934.
Houston Conservatory of Music. Texas; coed.; 1917.
How'ard C. (hou'ẽrd). Birmingham, Ala.; coed.; 1841.
Howard County Junior C. Big Spring, Texas; coed.; 1945.
Howard Payne C. (pān). Brownwood, Texas; coed; 1889.
Howard U. Washington, D. C.; coed.; 1867.
Hud'son Valley Technical Inst. (hŭd's'n). Troy, N. Y.; junior coed.; 1953.
Hum'boldt State C. (hŭm'bōlt). Arcata, Calif.; coed.; 1913.
Hun'ter C. (hŭn'tẽr). New York, N. Y.; coed.; 1870.
Hun'ting·don C. (hŭn'tĭng·dŭn). Montgomery, Ala.; coed.; 1854.
Hun'ting·ton C. (hŭn'tĭng·tŭn). Huntington, Ind.; coed.; 1897.
Hu'ron C. (hū'rŭn). Huron, S. Dak.; coed.; 1883.
Hus'son C. (hŭs'n). Bangor, Maine; coed.; 1898.
Hus'ton—Til'lot·son C. (hūs'tŭn·tĭl'ŭt·sŭn). Austin, Texas; coed.; 1877.
Hutch'in·son Junior C. (hŭch'ĭn·s'n). Hutchinson, Kans.; coed.; 1928.
I'da·ho, C. of (ī'dà·hō). Caldwell; coed.; 1891.
Idaho, U. of. Moscow; coed.; 1889.
Idaho State C. Pocatello; coed.; 1901.
I'liff Sch. of Theol. (ī'lĭf). Denver, Colo.; coed.; 1892.
Il·li·nois', U. of (ĭl'ĭ·noi'; -noiz'). Urbana; coed.; 1867.
Il'li·nois' C. Jacksonville; coed.; 1829.
Illinois C. of Chiropody and Foot Surgery. Chicago; coed.; 1912.
Illinois C. of Optometry. Chicago; coed.; 1872.
Illinois Inst. of Tech. Chicago; coed.; 1892.
Illinois State Normal U. Normal; coed.; 1857.
Illinois Wesleyan U. Bloomington; coed.; 1850.
Im·mac'u·la'ta C. (ĭ·măk'û·lä'tà). Immaculata, Pa.; women; 1920.
Immaculata Junior C. Washington, D. C.; women; 1905.
Immaculate Conception, C. of the. Washington, D. C.; men; 1905.
Immaculate Conception, Pontifical Faculty of the. Washington, D. C.; men; 1905.
Immaculate Conception, Sem. of the. Huntington, N. Y.; men; 1926.
Immaculate Conception Junior C. Lodi, N. J.; women; 1923.
Immaculate Conception Monastery. Chicago, Ill.; men; 1909.
Immaculate Conception Monastery. Hastings, Nebr.; men; 1931.
Immaculate Conception Monastery. Jamaica, N. Y.; men; 1930.
Immaculate Conception Sem. Cedar Lake, Ind.; men; 1938.
Immaculate Conception Sem. Darlington, N. J.; men; 1856.
Immaculate Heart C. Los Angeles, Calif.; women; 1916.
Immaculate Heart of Mary Sem. Winona, Minn.; men; 1948.
Im·man'u·el Lutheran C. (ĭ·măn'û·ĕl). Greensboro, N. C.; junior coed.; 1903.
Imperial Valley C. El Centro, Calif.; junior coed.; 1922.
Incarnate Word C. San Antonio, Texas; women; 1881.
Independence Community C. Independence, Kans.; junior coed.; 1925.
Indiana Central C. Indianapolis; coed.; 1902.
Indiana State Teachers C. Terre Haute; coed.; 1865.
Indiana Technical C. Fort Wayne; men; 1930.
Indiana U. Bloomington; coed.; 1820.
I·o'la Junior C. (ī·ō'là). Iola, Kans.; coed.; 1923.
I·o'na C. (ī·ō'nà). New Rochelle, N. Y.; men; 1940.
I'o·wa, State U. of (ī'ō·wà; *locally also* -wā). Iowa City; coed.; 1847.
Iowa State C. of Agric. and Mechanic Arts. Ames; coed.; 1858.
Iowa State Teachers C. Cedar Falls; coed.; 1876.
Iowa Wesleyan C. Mount Pleasant; coed.; 1842.
I·tas'ca Junior C. (ĭ·tăs'kà). Coleraine, Minn.; coed.; 1922.
It'a·wam'ba Junior C. (ĭt'à·wŏm'bà). Fulton, Miss.; coed.; 1948.
Ith'a·ca C. (ĭth'à·kà; -ĭ·kà). Ithaca, N. Y.; coed.; 1892.
Jack'son C. (jăk's'n). Medford, Mass.; women; 1910.
Jackson Junior C. Jackson, Mich.; coed.; 1928.
Jackson State C. Jackson, Miss.; coed.; 1877.
Jack'son·ville C. (jăk's'n·vĭl). Jacksonville, Texas; junior coed.; 1899.
Jacksonville C. of Music. Jacksonville, Fla.; coed.; 1923.
Jacksonville U. Jacksonville, Fla.; coed.; 1934.
James'town C. (jāmz'toun). Jamestown, N. Dak.; coed.; 1883.
Jamestown Community C. Jamestown, N. Y.; junior coed.; 1934.
Jar'vis Christian C. (jär'vĭs). Hawkins, Texas; coed.; 1912.
Jef'fer·son City Junior C. (jĕf'ẽr·s'n). Jefferson City, Mo.; coed.; 1926.
Jefferson Medical C. of Philadelphia. Pa.; men; 1825.
Jer'sey City Junior C. (jûr'zĭ). Jersey City, N. J.; coed.; 1946.
Jewish Inst. of Religion. See HEBREW UNION C.
Jewish Theol. Sem. of America. New York, N. Y.; coed.; 1886.
John Brown U. (broun). Siloam Springs, Ark.; coed.; 1919.
John Car'roll U. (kär'ŭl). Cleveland, Ohio; coed.; 1886.
John Her'ron Art Sch. (hĕr'ŭn). Indianapolis, Ind.; coed.; 1878.
John Marshall Law Sch. Chicago, Ill.; coed.; 1899.
Johns Hop'kins U. (jŏnz' hŏp'kĭnz). Baltimore, Md.; coed.; 1867.
John'son Bible C. (jŏn's'n). Kimberlin Heights, Tenn.; coed.; 1893.
Johnson C. Smith U. (smĭth). Charlotte, N. C.; coed.; 1867.
Jo'li·et Junior C. (jō'lĭ·ĕt[']). Joliet, Ill.; coed.; 1902.
Jones County Junior C. (jōnz). Ellisville, Miss.; coed.; 1911.
Jop'lin Junior C. (jŏp'lĭn). Joplin, Mo.; coed.; 1937.
Jo'se·phi'num, Pontifical C. of (jō'zĕ·fē'nŭm). Worthington, Ohio; men; 1888.
Jud'son C. (jŭd's'n). Marion, Ala.; women; 1838.
Juil'liard Sch. of Music (jōōl'yärd). New York, N. Y.; coed.; 1905.
Ju'ni·at'a C. (jōō'nĭ·ăt'à). Huntingdon, Pa.; coed.; 1876.
Kal'a·ma·zoo' C. (kăl'à·mà·zōō'). Kalamazoo, Mich.; coed.; 1833.

Kansas, U. of. Lawrence; coed.; 1864.
Kansas City, Conservatory of Music of. Mo.; coed.; 1907.
Kansas City, U. of. Mo.; coed.; 1929.
Kansas City Art Inst. and Sch. of Design. Mo.; coed.; 1887.
Kansas City Bible C. Mo.; coed.; 1932.
Kansas City C. of Osteopathy and Surgery. Mo.; coed.; 1916.
Kansas City Kansas Junior C. Coed.; 1923.
Kansas City, Missouri, The Junior C. of. Coed.; 1915.
Kansas State C. of Agric. and Applied Science. Manhattan; coed.; 1862.
Kansas State Teachers C. Emporia; coed.; 1863.
Kansas State Teachers C. Pittsburg; coed.; 1903.
Kansas Wesleyan U. Salina; coed.; 1886.
Keene Teachers C. (kēn). Keene, N. H.; coed.; 1909.
Kem'per Military Sch. (kĕm'pẽr). Boonville, Mo.; junior men; 1844.
Ken'dall C. (kĕn'd'l). Evanston, Ill.; junior coed.; 1934.
Ken'rick Sem. (St. Louis Roman Catholic Theol. Sem.) (kĕn'rĭk). St. Louis, Mo.; men; 1818.
Kents Hill Sch. (kĕnts). Kents Hill, Me.; coed.; 1824.
Kent State U. (kĕnt). Kent, Ohio; coed.; 1910.
Kentucky, U. of. Lexington; coed.; 1865.
Kentucky State C. Frankfort; coed.; 1886.
Kentucky Wesleyan C. Owensboro; coed.; 1866.
Ken'wood Normal Training Sch. (kĕn'wo͝od). Albany, N. Y.; women; 1899.
Ken'yon C. (kĕn'yŭn). Gambier, Ohio; men; 1824.
Ke'o·kuk Community C. (kē'ô·kŭk). Keokuk, Iowa; junior coed.; 1950.
Keu'ka C. (kū'ká; kȧ·ū'kȧ). Keuka Park, N. Y.; women; 1890.
Keystone Junior C. La Plume, Pa.; coed.; 1868.
Kil'gore C. (kĭl'gōr). Kilgore, Texas; junior coed.; 1935.
King C. Bristol, Tenn.; coed.; 1867.
King's C. Wilkes-Barre, Pa.; men; 1946.
King's C., The. Briarcliff Manor, N. Y.; coed.; 1938.
Kirks'ville C. of Osteopathy and Surgery (kûrks'vĭl). Kirksville, Mo.; coed.; 1892.
Kit·trell' C. (kĭ·trĕl'). Kittrell, N. C.; coed.; 1886.
Knox C. (nŏks). Galesburg, Ill.; coed.; 1836.
Knox'ville C. (nŏks'vĭl). Knoxville, Tenn.; coed.; 1863.
La'dy·cliff' C. (lā'dĭ·klĭf'). Highland Falls, N. Y.; women; 1933.
La'fa·yette' C. (lä'fī·ĕt'). Easton, Pa.; men; 1826.
La Grange C. (lȧ gränj'). La Grange, Ga.; coed.; 1831.
Lain Technical Inst. (lān). Indianapolis, Ind.; junior coed.; 1941.
Lake E'rie C. (ẽr'ĭ). Painesville, Ohio; women; 1856.
Lake For'est C. (fŏr'ĕst; -ĭst). Lake Forest, Ill.; coed.; 1857.
Lake'land C. (lāk'lănd). Sheboygan, Wis.; coed.; 1862.
La·mar' Junior C. (lȧ·mär'). Lamar, Colo.; coed.; 1937.
Lamar State C. of Tech. Beaumont, Texas; coed.; 1923.
Lam'buth C. (lăm'bŭth). Jackson, Tenn.; coed.; 1924.
La Men·nais' C. (lä' mĕ·nā'). Alfred, Me.; coed.; 1939.
Lan'der C. (lăn'dẽr). Greenwood, S. C.; coed.; 1872.
Lane C. (lān). Jackson, Tenn.; coed.; 1882.
Lang'ston U. (lăng'stŭn). Langston, Okla.; coed.; 1897.
La·re'do Junior C. (lȧ·rā'dō). Laredo, Texas; coed.; 1947.
La Sa·lette' Sem. (lä' sȧ·lĕt'). Olivet, Ill.; men; 1942.
La Salette Sem. Enfield, N. H.; men; 1927.
La Salle C. (lȧ săl'). Philadelphia, Pa.; men; 1863.
La Salle–Pe·ru'–O'gles·by Junior C. (-pĕ·rōō'ō'g'lz·bĭ). La Salle, Ill.; coed.; 1924.
La·sell' Junior C. (lȧ·sĕl'). Auburndale, Mass.; women; 1851.
La Si·er'ra C. (lä' sĭ·ĕr'ȧ). Arlington, Calif.; coed.; 1922.
Las'sen Junior C. (lăs'n). Susanville, Calif.; coed.; 1925.
La Verne C. (lȧ vûrn'). La Verne, Calif.; coed.; 1891.
Law'rence C. (lô'rĕns; lŏr'ĕns). Appleton, Wis.; coed.; 1847.
Lawrence Inst. of Tech. Highland Park, Mich.; men; 1932.
Lay'ton Sch. of Art (lā't'n). Milwaukee, Wis.; coed.; 1920.
Leb'a·non Valley C. (lĕb'ȧ·nŭn). Annville, Pa.; coed.; 1866.
Lee C. (lē). Cleveland, Tenn.; junior coed.; 1918.
Lee C. Baytown, Texas; junior coed.; 1934.
Lees Junior C. (lēz). Jackson, Ky.; coed.; 1883.
Lees'–Mc·Rae' C. (lēz'mȧ·krā'). Banner Elk, N. C.; junior coed.; 1900.
Le'high U. (lē'hī). Bethlehem, Pa.; coed.; 1865.
Le'land C. (lē'lănd). Baker, La.; coed.; 1870.
Le Moyne C. (lĕ moin'). Syracuse, N. Y.; coed.; 1946.
Le-Moyne' C. (lĕ·moin'). Memphis, Tenn.; coed.; 1870.
Le·noir' Rhyne C. (lĕ·nôr' rīn'). Hickory, N. C.; coed.; 1891.
Les'ley C. (lĕs'lĭ). Cambridge, Mass.; women; 1909.
Le·Tour'neau Technical Inst. of Texas (lĕ·tûr'nō). Longview; men; 1946.
Lew'is and Clark C. (lū'ĭs, lōō'ĭs; klärk). Portland, Ore.; coed.; 1867.
Lewis C. Lockport, Ill.; coed.; 1930.
Lick'–Wil'mer·ding Sch. (lĭk'wĭl'mẽr·dĭng). San Francisco, Calif.; junior men; 1895.
Limestone C. Gaffney, S. C.; women; 1845.
Lin'coln Bible Inst. (lĭng'kŭn). Lincoln, Ill.; coed.; 1944.
Lincoln C. Lincoln, Ill.; junior coed.; 1865.
Lincoln Memorial U. Harrogate, Tenn.; coed.; 1897.
Lincoln C. Jefferson City, Mo.; coed.; 1866.
Lincoln U. Lincoln University, Pa.; men; 1854.
Lin'den Hall Junior C. (lĭn'dĕn). Lititz, Pa.; women; 1935.
Lin'den·wood' C. (lĭn'dĕn·wo͝od'). St. Charles, Mo.; women; 1820.
Lind'sey Wil'son C. (lĭn'zĭ wĭl's'n). Columbia, Ky.; junior coed.; 1903.
Lin'field C. (lĭn'fēld). McMinnville, Ore.; coed.; 1857.
Little Rock U. Little Rock, Ark.; coed.; 1927.
Liv'ing·stone C. (lĭv'ĭng·stŭn). Salisbury, N. C.; coed.; 1879.
Long Beach City C. Long Beach, Calif.; junior coed.; 1913.
Long Beach State C. Long Beach, Calif.; coed.; 1949.
Long Island U. Brooklyn, N. Y.; coed.; 1926.
Long'wood C. (lŏng'wo͝od). Farmville, Va.; women; 1884.
Lon Mor'ris C. (lŏn mŏr'ĭs). Jacksonville, Texas; junior coed.; 1873.

Lo'ras C. (lō'răs; 70). Dubuque, Iowa; coed.; 1839.
Lo·ret'to Heights C. (lô·rĕt'ō). Loretto, Colo.; women; 1891.
Loretto Junior C. Nerinx, Ky.; women; 1936.
Los Angeles City C. Calif.; junior coed.; 1929.
Los Angeles C. Calif.; junior men; 1926.
Los Angeles C. of Optometry. Calif.; coed.; 1904.
Los Angeles Conservatory of Music and Arts. Calif.; coed.; 1883.
Los Angeles Harbor Junior C. Wilmington, Calif.; coed.; 1949.
Los Angeles Junior C. of Business. Calif.; coed.; 1935.
Los Angeles Pacific C. Calif.; coed.; 1903.
Los Angeles Pierce Junior C. (pẽrs). Woodland Hills, Calif.; coed.; 1947.
Los Angeles State C. of Applied Arts and Sciences. Calif.; coed.; 1947.
Los Angeles Trade–Technical Junior C. Calif.; coed.; 1949.
Los Angeles Valley Junior C. Van Nuys, Calif.; coed.; 1949.
Lou'is·burg C. (lōō'ĭs·bûrg). Louisburg, N. C.; junior coed.; 1787.
Louisiana C. Pineville; coed.; 1906.
Louisiana Polytechnic Inst. Ruston; coed.; 1894.
Louisiana State U. and A. & M. C. Baton Rouge; coed.; 1860.
Lou'is·ville, U. of (lōō'ĭ·vĭl). Ky.; coed.; 1798.
Louisville Municipal C. Ky.; coed.; 1931.
Louisville Presbyterian Theol. Sem. Ky.; men; 1853.
Low'ell Technological Inst. (lō'ĕl). Lowell, Mass.; coed.; 1895.
Lower Columbia Junior C. Longview, Wash.; coed.; 1934.
Loy·o'la C. (loi·ō'lȧ). Baltimore, Md.; coed.; 1852.
Loyola U. Chicago, Ill.; coed.; 1869.
Loyola U. New Orleans, La.; coed.; 1849.
Loyola U. of Los Angeles. Calif.; coed.; 1865.
Lutheran Theol. Sem. Gettysburg, Pa.; coed.; 1826.
Lutheran Theol. Sem. Philadelphia, Pa.; men; 1864.
Lutheran Theol. Southern Sem. Columbia, S. C.; men; 1830.
Lu'ther C. (lū'thẽr). Decorah, Iowa; coed.; 1861.
Luther Junior C. Wahoo, Nebr.; coed.; 1883.
Luther Theol. Sem. St. Paul, Minn.; men; 1876.
Ly·com'ing C. (lī·kŭm'ĭng). Williamsport, Pa.; coed.; 1812.
Lynch'burg C. (lĭnch'bûrg). Lynchburg, Va.; coed.; 1903.
Ly'ons Township Junior C. (lī'ŭnz). La Grange, Ill.; coed.; 1929.
Mac·al'es·ter C. (măk·ăl'ĕs·tẽr). St. Paul, Minn.; coed.; 1853.
Mc·Cook' C. (mȧ·ko͝ok'). McCook, Nebr.; junior coed.; 1926.
Mc·Cor'mick Theol. Sem. (mȧ·kôr'mĭk). Chicago, Ill.; coed.; 1829.
Mc·Coy' C. (mȧ·koi'). Baltimore, Md.; coed.; 1909.
Mc·Kech'nie–Lung'er Sch. of Commerce (mȧ·kĕk'nĭ·lŭng'ẽr). Rochester, N. Y.; junior coed.; 1917.
Mc·Ken'dree C. (mȧ·kĕn'drē). Lebanon, Ill.; coed.; 1828.
Mac·Mur'ray C. (măk·mûr'ĭ). Jacksonville, Ill.; coed.; 1846.
Mc·Mur'ry C. (măk·mûr'ĭ). Abilene, Texas; coed.; 1923.
Mc·Neese' State C. (măk·nēs'). Lake Charles, La.; coed.; 1939.
Mac·Phail' C. of Music (măk·fāl'). Minneapolis, Minn.; coed.; 1907.
Mc·Pher'son C. (măk·fûr's'n). McPherson, Kans.; coed.; 1887.
Mad'i·son C. (măd'ĭ·s'n). Madison College, Tenn.; coed.; 1904.
Madison C. Harrisonburg, Va.; women; 1908.
Ma·don'na C. (mȧ·dŏn'ȧ). Livonia, Mich.; women; 1937.
Maine, U. of. Orono; coed.; 1865.
Maine Maritime Acad. Castine; men; 1941.
Mal'linck·rodt C. (măl'ĭn·krŏt). Wilmette, Ill.; junior women; 1918.
Ma·lone' C. (mȧ·lōn'). Canton, Ohio; coed.; 1892.
Man'ches'ter C. (măn'chĕs'tẽr; -chĭs·tẽr). North Manchester, Ind.; coed.; 1889.
Man·hat'tan Bible C. (măn·hăt'n; măn-). Manhattan, Kans.; coed.; 1927.
Manhattan C. New York, N. Y.; men; 1853.
Manhattan Sch. of Music. New York, N. Y.; coed.; 1917.
Man·hat'tan·ville C. of the Sacred Heart (măn·hăt'n·vĭl; măn-). Purchase, N. Y.; coed.; 1841.
Man·ka'to State C. (măn·kā'tō). Mankato, Minn.; coed.; 1866.
Man'nes C. of Music (măn'ĕs). New York, N. Y.; coed.; 1916.
Man'or C. (măn'ẽr). Philadelphia, Pa.; junior women; 1947.
Margaret Mor'ri·son Car·ne'gie C. (môr'ĭ·s'n kär·nā'gĭ). Pittsburgh, Pa.; women; 1900.
Mar'i·an C. (măr'ĭ·ăn; -ȧn). Indianapolis, Ind.; coed.; 1937.
Marian C. Poughkeepsie, N. Y.; men; 1946.
Marian C. Fond du Lac, Wis.; women; 1936.
Marian Hills Sem. Hinsdale, Ill.; men; 1926.
Mar'i·et'ta C. (măr'ĭ·ĕt'ȧ; măr'ĭ-). Marietta, Ohio; coed.; 1797.
Ma·rin' C. of (mȧ·rĭn'). Kentfield, Calif.; junior coed.; 1926.
Mar'i·on C. (măr'ĭ·ăn; măr'-). Marion, Ind.; coed.; 1920.
Marion C. Marion, Va.; junior women; 1873.
Marion Inst. Marion, Ala.; junior men; 1842.
Mar'ist C. (măr'ĭst). Washington, D. C.; men; 1900.
Marist C. and Sem. Framingham Center and Bedford, Mass.; men; 1939.
Marjorie Webster Junior C. Washington, D. C.; women; 1920.
Marl'bor·o C. (märl'bûr·ō; mô̂l'brō). Marlboro, Vt.; coed.; 1946.
Mar·quette' U. (mär·kĕt'). Milwaukee, Wis.; coed.; 1857.
Mar'shall C. (mär'shăl). Huntington, W. Va.; coed.; 1837.
Mar'shall·town Junior C. (mär'shăl·toun). Marshalltown, Iowa; coed.; 1927.
Mars Hill C. (märz). Mars Hill, N. C.; junior coed.; 1856.
Mar'tin C. (mär'tĭn; -t'n). Pulaski, Tenn.; junior coed.; 1870.
Mary Al'len C. (ăl'ĕn; -ĭn). Crockett, Texas; women; 1944.
Mary Bald'win C. (bôld). Staunton, Va.; women; 1842.
Mar'y·crest' C. (măr'ĭ·krĕst'). Davenport, Iowa; women; 1939.
Mar'y·grove' C. (măr'ĭ·grōv'). Detroit, Mich.; women; 1906.
Mary Har'din–Bay'lor C. (här'd'n·bā'lĕr; -). Belton, Texas; women; 1845.
Mary Holmes Junior C. (hōmz). West Point, Miss.; coed.; 1892.
Mar'y·hurst' Normal Sch. (măr'ĭ·hûrst'). Kirkwood, Mo.; men; 1922.
Mary Immaculate, Sem. of. Garrison, N. Y.; men; 1932.
Mary Immaculate of West Hartford, C. of. Conn.; women; 1940.
Mary Immaculate Sem. Northampton, Pa.; men; 1939.

Maryknoll Junior Sem. Mountain View, Calif.; men; 1926.
Maryknoll Sem. Glen Ellyn, Ill.; men; 1949.
Maryknoll Sem. Ossining, N. Y.; men; 1911.
Maryknoll Teachers C. Maryknoll, N. Y.; women; 1931.
Maryland, U. of. College Park; coed.; 1807.
Maryland Inst. Baltimore; coed.; 1825.
Maryland State C. Princess Anne; coed.; 1886.
Maryland State Teachers C. Bowie; coed; 1908.
Maryland State Teachers C. Frostburg; coed.; 1902.
Maryland State Teachers C. Salisbury; coed.; 1925.
Maryland State Teachers C. Towson; coed.; 1865.
Mar'yl·hurst' C. (mär'ĭl·hûrst'). Marylhurst, Ore.; women; 1893.
Mary Manse C. (măns). Toledo, Ohio; women; 1873.
Mar'y·mount' C. (mâr'ĭ·mount'). Los Angeles, Calif.; women; 1933.
Marymount C. Salina, Kans.; women; 1922.
Marymount C. Tarrytown, N. Y.; women; 1907.
Marymount Junior C. Arlington, Va.; women; 1950.
Mar'y·ville C. (mâr'ĭ·vĭl). Maryville, Tenn.; coed.; 1819.
Maryville C. of the Sacred Heart. St. Louis, Mo.; women; 1846.
Mary Wash'ing·ton C. (wŏsh'ĭng·tŭn). Fredericksburg, Va.; women; 1908.
Mar'y·wood' C. (mâr'ĭ·wŏŏd'). Scranton, Pa.; women; 1915.
Ma'son City Junior C. (mā's'n). Mason City, Iowa; coed.; 1918.
Massachusetts, U. of. Amherst; coed.; 1863.
Massachusetts C. of Optometry. Boston; coed.; 1894.
Massachusetts C. of Pharmacy. Boston; coed.; 1823.
Massachusetts Inst. of Tech. Cambridge; coed.; 1859.
Massachusetts Maritime Acad. Buzzards Bay; men; 1891.
Massachusetts Sch. of Art. Boston; coed.; 1874.
Massachusetts State Teachers C. Boston; coed.; 1852.
Massachusetts State Teachers C. Bridgewater; coed.; 1840.
Massachusetts State Teachers C. Fitchburg; coed.; 1894.
Massachusetts State Teachers C. Framingham; women; 1839.
Massachusetts State Teachers C. Lowell; coed.; 1894.
Massachusetts State Teachers C. North Adams; coed.; 1894.
Massachusetts State Teachers C. Salem; coed.; 1854.
Massachusetts State Teachers C. Westfield; coed.; 1839.
Massachusetts State Teachers C. Worcester; coed.; 1871.
Mead'ville Theol. Sch. (mēd'vĭl). Chicago, Ill.; coed.; 1844.
Medical Evangelists, C. of. Loma Linda, Calif.; coed.; 1907.
Me·har'ry Med. C. (mē·här'ĭ). Nashville, Tenn.; coed.; 1876.
Memphis State U. Tenn.; coed.; 1909.
Men'lo C. (mĕn'lō). Menlo Park, Calif.; men; 1915.
Mer'cer U. (mûr'sẽr). Macon, Ga.; coed.; 1833.
Mercy C. Detroit, Mich.; women; 1941.
Mer'cy·hurst' C. (mûr'sĭ·hûrst'). Erie, Pa.; women; 1871.
Mercy Junior C. Webster Groves, Mo.; women; 1952.
Mercy Junior C. Tarrytown, N. Y.; women; 1950.
Mer'e·dith C. (mĕr'ẽ·dĭth). Raleigh, N. C.; women; 1891.
Me·rid'i·an Municipal Junior C. (mẽ·rĭd'ĭ·ăn). Meridian, Miss.; coed.; 1937.
Mer'rill–Palm'er Sch. (mĕr'ĭl·päm'ẽr). Detroit, Mich.; coed.; 1920.
Mer'ri·mack C. (mĕr'ĭ·măk). North Andover, Mass.; coed.; 1947.
Me'sa County Junior C. (mā'sà). Grand Junction, Colo.; coed.; 1925.
Messiah C. Grantham, Pa.; coed.; 1909.
Mi·am'i, U. of (mī·ăm'ĭ; -à). Coral Gables, Fla.; coed.; 1925.
Miami–Ja'cobs C. (-jā'kŭbz). Dayton, Ohio; junior coed.; 1860.
Miami U. Oxford, Ohio; coed.; 1809.
Michigan, U. of. Ann Arbor; coed.; 1817.
Michigan C. of Mining and Tech. Houghton; coed.; 1885.
Michigan State U. of Agric. and Applied Science. East Lansing; coed.; 1855.
Mid'dle·bur'y C. (mĭd'l·bĕr'ĭ; -bẽr·ĭ). Middlebury, Vt.; coed.; 1800.
Middle Georgia C. Cochran; junior coed.; 1884.
Middle Tennessee State C. Murfreesboro; coed.; 1909.
Mid'dle·town Collegiate Center (mĭd'l·toun). Middletown, N. Y.; junior coed.; 1946.
Mid'land C. (mĭd'lănd). Fremont, Nebr.; coed.; 1887.
Mid'way' Junior C. (mĭd'wā'). Midway, Ky.; women; 1847.
Midwest Christian C. Oklahoma City, Okla.; coed.; 1946.
Midwestern U. Wichita Falls, Texas; coed.; 1922.
Miles C. (mīlz). Birmingham, Ala.; coed.; 1907.
Mil'ford Novitiate (mĭl'fẽrd). Milford, Ohio; junior men; 1925.
Mil'lard Fill'more C. (mĭl'ẽrd fĭl'mōr; 70). Buffalo, N. Y.; coed.; 1923.
Mil'li·gan C. (mĭl'ĭ·găn). Milligan College, Tenn.; coed.; 1882.
Mil'li·kin U. (mĭl'ĭ·kĭn). Decatur, Ill.; coed.; 1901.
Mill'saps C. (mĭl'săps). Jackson, Miss.; coed.; 1890.
Mills C. (mĭlz). Oakland, Calif.; women; 1852.
Mills C. of Ed. New York, N. Y.; women; 1909.
Mil'ton C. (mĭl't'n; -tŭn). Milton, Wis.; coed.; 1844.
Mil'ton·vale' Wesleyan C. (mĭl't'n·vāl'; -tŭn-). Miltonvale, Kans.; junior coed.; 1909.
Milwaukee–Dow'ner C. (-dou'nẽr). Milwaukee, Wis.; women; 1851.
Milwaukee Inst. of Tech. Wis.; junior coed.; 1923.
Milwaukee Sch. of Engineering. Wis.; men; 1903.
Milwaukee Vocational and Adult Schools. Wis.; junior coed.; 1934.
Minneapolis C. of Music. Minn.; coed.; 1927.
Minneapolis Sch. of Art. Minn.; coed.; 1886.
Minnesota, U. of. Minneapolis; coed.; 1851.
Minnesota Bible C. Minneapolis; coed.; 1913.
Mi·ser'i·cor'di·a C. (mĭ·sẽr'ĭ·kôr'dĭ·à). Dallas, Pa.; women; 1923.
Mississippi, U. of. University; coed.; 1844.
Mississippi C. Clinton; coed.; 1826.
Mississippi Industrial C. Holly Springs; coed.; 1905.
Mississippi Southern C. Hattiesburg; coed.; 1910.
Mississippi State C. State College; coed.; 1878.
Mississippi State C. for Women. Columbus; 1884.
Mississippi Vocational C. Itta Bena; coed.; 1946.
Missouri, U. of. Columbia; coed.; 1839.
Missouri Sch. of Mines. Rolla; coed.; 1870.

Missouri Valley C. Marshall, Mo.; coed.; 1888.
Mitch'ell C. (mĭch'ĕl). New London, Conn.; junior coed.; 1938.
Mitchell C. Statesville, N. C.; junior coed.; 1853.
Mo'ber·ly Junior C. (mō'bẽr·lĭ). Moberly, Mo.; coed.; 1927.
Modern Sch. of Music. Washington, D. C.; coed.; 1935.
Mo·des'to Junior C. (mō·dĕs'tō). Modesto, Calif.; coed.; 1921.
Mo'hawk Valley Technical Inst. (mō'hôk). New Hartford, N. Y.; junior coed.; 1946.
Mo·line' Community C. (mō·lēn'). Moline, Ill.; junior coed.; 1946.
Mon'mouth C. (mŏn'mŭth). Monmouth, Ill.; coed.; 1853.
Monmouth C. West Long Branch, N. J.; coed.; 1933.
Montana Sch. of Mines. Butte; coed.; 1893.
Montana State C. Bozeman; coed.; 1893.
Montana State U. Missoula; coed.; 1893.
Mon'te·rey' Peninsula C. (mŏn'tẽ·rā'; 2). Monterey, Calif.; junior coed.; 1947.
Mon'te·zu'ma Sem. (mŏn'tẽ·zōō'mà). Montezuma, N. Mex.; men; 1937.
Mont'fort Preparatory Sem. (mŏnt'fẽrt). Bay Shore, N. Y.; junior men; 1921.
Montgomery Bible C. Montgomery, Ala.; junior coed.; 1942.
Montgomery Junior C. Takoma Park, Md.; coed.; 1946.
Mon'ti·cel'lo C. (mŏn'tĭ·sĕl'ō). Alton, Ill.; junior women; 1835.
Mon·treat' C. (mŏn·trēt'). Montreat, N. C.; coed.; 1916.
Moo'dy Bible Inst. (mōō'dĭ). Chicago, Ill.; junior coed.; 1886.
Moore Inst. of Art, Science, and Industry (mōr; 70). Philadelphia, Pa.; women; 1844.
Moor'head State C. (mōr'hĕd; mōōr'-; 70). Moorhead, Minn.; coed.; 1885.
Moravian C. Bethlehem, Pa.; coed.; 1807.
Mo'reau Sem. (mō'rō; 70). Notre Dame, Ind.; junior men; 1920.
More'head City Technical Inst. (mōr'hĕd; 70). Morehead City, N. C.; junior men; 1947.
Morehead State C. Morehead, Ky.; coed.; 1923.
More'house C. (mōr'hous; 70). Atlanta, Ga.; men; 1867.
Morgan State C. Baltimore, Md.; coed.; 1867.
Morn'ing·side' C. (môr'nĭng·sīd'). Sioux City, Iowa; coed.; 1889.
Morris Brown C. Atlanta, Ga.; coed.; 1881.
Morris C. Sumter, S. C.; coed.; 1908.
Morris Har'vey C. (här'vĭ). Charleston, W. Va.; coed.; 1888.
Mor'ris·town Normal and Industrial C. (môr'ĭs·toun). Morristown, Tenn.; junior coed.; 1881.
Morse Junior C. (môrs). Hartford, Conn.; coed.; 1860.
Mor'ton Junior C. (môr't'n). Cicero, Ill.; coed.; 1924.
Mount Al'o·y'sius Junior C. (ăl'ō·ĭsh'ŭs). Cresson, Pa.; women; 1848.
Mount Al·ver'nia Sem. (ăl·vûrn'yà). Wappingers Falls, N. Y.; men; 1944.
Mount An'gel Sem. (ăn'jĕl). St. Benedict, Ore.; men; 1887.
Mount Angel Women's C. Mount Angel, Ore.; 1887.
Mount Car'mel Normal School (kär'mĕl). New Orleans, La.; women; 1924.
Mount Hol'yoke C. (hōl'yōk). South Hadley, Mass.; women; 1836.
Mount I'da (ī'dà). Newton, Mass.; junior women; 1899.
Mount Mar'ty C. (mär'tĭ). Yankton, S. Dak.; women; 1922.
Mount Mary C. Milwaukee, Wis.; women; 1872.
Mount Mercy C. Pittsburgh, Pa.; women; 1929.
Mount Mercy Junior C. Cedar Rapids, Iowa; women; 1875.
Mount Saint Agnes C. Baltimore, Md.; women; 1867.
Mount St. Clare C. (klâr). Clinton, Iowa; junior women; 1895.
Mount St. Joseph–on–the–Ohio, C. of. Mount St. Joseph, Ohio; women; 1854.
Mount St. Joseph Teachers C. Buffalo, N. Y.; women; 1937.
Mount St. Mary C. Hooksett, N. H.; women; 1934.
Mount Saint Mary Normal and Training Sch. Newburgh, N. Y.; women; 1930.
Mount St. Mary's C. Los Angeles, Calif.; women; 1925.
Mount St. Mary's C. Emmitsburg, Md.; men; 1808.
Mount St. Michael's Scholasticate. Hillyard, Wash.; men; 1916.
Mount St. Scho·las'ti·ca C. (skō·lăs'tĭ·kà). Atchison, Kans.; women; 1863.
Mount St. Vincent, C. of. New York, N. Y.; women; 1847.
Mount San An·to'ni·o C. (săn' ăn·tō'nĭ·ō; săn' ăn-). Walnut, Calif.; junior coed.; 1945.
Mount Union C. Alliance, Ohio; coed.; 1846.
Mount Ver'non Junior C. (vûr'nŭn). Washington, D. C.; women; 1875.
Muh'len·berg C. (mū'lĕn·bûrg). Allentown, Pa.; coed.; 1848.
Mult·no'mah C. (mŭlt·nō'mà). Portland, Ore.; junior coed.; 1897.
Multnomah Sch. of the Bible. Portland, Ore.; coed.; 1936.
Mun'de·lein C. (mŭn'dẽ·līn). Chicago, Ill.; women; 1930.
Mur'ray State Agricultural C. (mûr'ĭ). Tishomingo, Okla.; junior coed.; 1908.
Murray State C. Murray, Ky.; coed.; 1922.
Mus'ca·tine Junior C. (mŭs'kà·tēn). Muscatine, Iowa; coed.; 1929.
Mus·ke'gon Community C. (mŭs·kē'găn). Muskegon, Mich.; junior coed.; 1926.
Mus·kin'gum C. (mŭs·kĭng'[g]ŭm). New Concord, Ohio; coed.; 1837.
Mus·ko'gee Junior C. (mŭs·kō'gĕ). Muskogee, Okla.; coed.; 1920.
Nac'og·do'ches Business C. (năk'ŏ·dō'chĕz; -chĭz). Nacogdoches, Texas; junior coed.; 1944.
Nap'a C. (năp'à). Napa, Calif.; junior coed.; 1941.
Na·sho'tah House (nà·shō'tà). Nashotah, Wis.; men; 1842.
Nas·son' C. (nà·sŏn'; năs'ŏn). Springvale, Me.; coed.; 1912.
Natch'ez Junior C. (năch'ĕz; ·ĭz). Miss.; coed.; 1885.
National Agricultural C. Doylestown, Pa.; men; 1896.
National C. Kansas City, Mo.; coed.; 1899.
National C. of Ed. Evanston, Ill.; coed.; 1886.
National Schools. Los Angeles, Calif.; men; 1905.
Na·var'ro Junior C. (nà·văr'ō). Corsicana, Texas; coed.; 1946.
Naz'a·reth C. (năz'à·rĕth). Louisville, Ky.; women; 1829.
Nazareth C. Nazareth, Mich.; women; 1897.

Nazareth C. Rochester, N. Y.; women; 1924.
Nazareth C. and Acad. Nazareth, Ky.; women; 1814.
Nazareth Hall C. and Sem. St. Paul, Minn.; junior men; 1923.
Nebraska, U. of. Lincoln; coed.; 1869.
Nebraska State Teachers C. Chadron; coed.; 1911.
Nebraska State Teachers C. Kearney; coed.; 1905.
Nebraska State Teachers C. Peru; coed.; 1867.
Nebraska State Teachers C. Wayne; coed.; 1891.
Nebraska Wesleyan U. Lincoln; coed.; 1887.
Ner Israel Rabbinical C. (nŭr). Baltimore, Md.; men; 1933.
Nevada, U. of. Reno; coed.; 1874.
Newark C. of Engineering. N. J.; coed.; 1881.
Newark Colleges. N. J.; coed.; 1946.
New Bed'ford Inst. of Tech. (bĕd'fẽrd). Mass.; coed.; 1895.
New'ber'ry C. (nŭ'bĕr'ĭ; -bẽr-ĭ). Newberry, S. C.; coed.; 1856.
New Bruns'wick Theol. Sem. (brŭnz'wĭk). New Brunswick, N. J.; men; 1784.
New Church, Acad. of the. Bryn Athyn, Pa.; coed.; 1876.
New'comb C. (nŭ'kŭm). New Orleans, La.; women; 1886.
New England C. of Pharmacy. Boston, Mass.; coed.; 1927.
New England Conservatory of Music. Boston, Mass.; coed.; 1867.
New Hampshire, U. of. Durham; coed.; 1866.
New Haven State Teachers C. Conn.; coed.; 1893.
New Haven YMCA Junior C. New Haven, Conn.; coed.; 1920.
New Jersey State Teachers C. Glassboro; coed.; 1917.
New Jersey State Teachers C. Jersey City; coed.; 1929.
New Jersey State Teachers C. Newark; coed.; 1855.
New Jersey State Teachers C. Paterson; coed.; 1855.
New Jersey State Teachers C. Trenton; coed.; 1855.
New Jersey State Teachers C. Upper Montclair; coed.; 1908.
New Mel'ler·ay Abbey (mĕl'ẽr·ā). Peosta, Iowa; men; 1849.
New Mexico, U. of. Albuquerque; coed.; 1889.
New Mexico C. of Agric. and Mechanic Arts. State College; coed.; 1889.
New Mexico Highlands U. Las Vegas; coed.; 1893.
New Mexico Inst. of Mining and Tech. Socorro; coed.; 1889.
New Mexico Military Inst. Roswell; men; 1893.
New Mexico Western C. Silver City; coed.; 1893.
New Orleans Baptist Theol. Sem. La.; coed.; 1917.
New Ro·chelle', C. of (rō·shĕl'). New Rochelle, N. Y.; women; 1904.
New Sch. for Social Research. New York, N. Y.; coed.; 1919.
New Su'bi·ac'o Abbey Sem. (sōō'bĭ·ăk'ō). Subiaco, Ark.; men; 1878.
New'ton C. of the Sacred Heart (nū't'n). Newton, Mass.; women; 1946.
Newton Junior C. Newtonville, Mass.; coed.; 1946.
New York Agricultural and Technical Inst., State U. of. Alfred; junior coed.; 1909.
New York Agricultural and Technical Inst., State U. of. Canton; junior coed.; 1907.
New York Agricultural and Technical Inst., State U. of. Cobleskill; junior coed.; 1911.
New York Agricultural and Technical Inst., State U. of. Delhi; junior coed.; 1913.
New York Agricultural and Technical Inst., State U. of. Farmingdale; junior coed.; 1912.
New York Agricultural and Technical Inst., State U. of. Morrisville; junior coed.; 1908.
New York City Community C. of Applied Arts and Sciences. Brooklyn; junior coed.; 1946.
New York C. for Teachers, State U. of. Albany; coed.; 1844.
New York C. for Teachers, State U. of. Buffalo; coed.; 1872.
New York C. of Agric., State U. of. Ithaca; coed.; 1904.
New York C. of Ceramics, State U. of. Alfred; coed.; 1900.
New York C. of Forestry, State U. of. Syracuse; coed.; 1911.
New York C. of Home Economics, State U. of. Ithaca; coed.; 1925.
New York Downstate Medical Center, State U. of. Brooklyn; coed.; 1930.
New York Law Sch. New York, N. Y.; coed.; 1891.
New York Mar'i·time C., State U. of (măr'ĭ·tīm). Fort Schuyler; men; 1874.
New York Med. C. New York City; coed.; 1860.
New York Sch. of Industrial & Labor Relations, State U. of. Ithaca; coed.; 1944.
New York Teachers C., State U. of. Brockport; coed.; 1842.
New York Teachers C., State U. of. Cortland; coed.; 1863.
New York Teachers C., State U. of. Fredonia; coed.; 1866.
New York Teachers C., State U. of. Geneseo; coed.; 1867.
New York Teachers C., State U. of. New Paltz; coed.; 1833.
New York Teachers C., State U. of. Oneonta; coed.; 1889.
New York Teachers C., State U. of. Oswego; coed.; 1861.
New York Teachers C., State U. of. Plattsburg; coed.; 1889.
New York Teachers C., State U. of. Potsdam; coed.; 1866.
New York U. New York City; coed.; 1831.
New York Upstate Medical Center, State U. of. Syracuse; coed.; 1812.
New York Veterinary C., State U. of. Ithaca; coed.; 1894.
Ni·ag'a·ra U. (nī·ăg'a·rá; -ăg'rá). Niagara University, N. Y.; coed.; 1856.
Nich'ols Junior C. (nĭk'ŭlz; -'lz). Dudley, Mass.; men; 1815.
Nor'folk Junior C. (nôr'fôk). Norfolk, Nebr.; coed.; 1927.
Nor'man C. (nôr'măn). Norman Park, Ga.; junior coed.; 1900.
North Carolina, Agricultural and Technical C. of. Greensboro; coed.; 1891.
North Carolina, U. of. Chapel Hill; coed.; 1789.
North Carolina C. at Durham. Coed.; 1910.
North Carolina State C. of Agric. and Engineering. Raleigh; coed.; 1887.
North Central C. Naperville, Ill.; coed.; 1861.
North Dakota, U. of. Grand Forks; coed.; 1883.
North Dakota Agricultural C. State College; coed.; 1890.
North Dakota Sch. of Forestry. Bottineau; junior coed.; 1889.

North Dakota State Normal and Industrial C. Ellendale; coed.; 1889.
North Dakota State Sch. of Science. Wahpeton; junior coed.; 1889.
Northeast Agricultural Junior C. Sheridan, Wyo.; coed.; 1948.
Northeastern Junior C. of Colorado. Sterling; coed.; 1941.
Northeastern Oklahoma A. & M. C. Miami, Okla.; junior coed.; 1919.
Northeastern State C. Tahlequah, Okla.; coed.; 1846.
Northeastern U. Boston, Mass.; coed.; 1898.
Northeast Louisiana State C. Monroe, La.; coed.; 1931.
Northeast Mississippi Junior C. Booneville; coed.; 1948.
Northeast Missouri State Teachers C. Kirksville; coed.; 1867.
Northern Baptist Theol. Sem. Chicago, Ill.; coed.; 1913.
Northern Conservatory of Music. Bangor, Me.; coed.; 1929.
Northern Illinois U. De Kalb; coed.; 1895.
Northern Michigan C. Marquette; coed.; 1899.
Northern Montana C. Havre; coed.; 1913.
Northern Oklahoma Junior C. Tonkawa; coed.; 1901.
Northern State Teachers C. Aberdeen, S. Dak.; coed.; 1899.
North Georgia C. Dahlonega; coed.; 1873.
North Green'ville Junior C. (grēn'vĭl). Taylors, S. C.; coed.; 1892.
North Idaho Junior C. Coeur d'Alene; coed.; 1939.
North'land C. (nôrth'lănd). Ashland, Wis.; coed.; 1892.
North Park C. Chicago, Ill.; junior coed.; 1891.
Nor'throp Aeronautical Inst. (nôr'thrŭp). Inglewood, Calif.; men; 1942.
North Texas State C. Denton; coed.; 1890.
Northwest Bible C. Seattle, Wash.; coed.; 1934.
Northwest Christian C. Eugene, Ore.; coed.; 1895.
Northwestern C. Minneapolis, Minn.; coed.; 1902.
Northwestern C. Watertown, Wis.; coed.; 1865.
Northwestern Junior C. Orange City, Iowa; coed.; 1882.
Northwestern Lutheran Theol. Sem. Minneapolis, Minn.; men; 1920.
Northwestern Michigan C. Traverse City; junior coed.; 1951.
Northwestern State C. Alva, Okla.; coed.; 1897.
Northwestern State C. of Louisiana. Natchitoches; coed.; 1884.
Northwestern U. Evanston, Ill.; coed.; 1851.
Northwest Mississippi Junior C. Senatobia; coed.; 1915.
Northwest Missouri State C. Maryville; coed.; 1905.
Northwest Naz'a·rene C. (năz'á·rēn). Nampa, Idaho; coed.; 1913.
Nor'wich U. (nôr'wĭch). Northfield, Vt.; men; 1819.
No'tre Dame, C. of (nō'trĕ dăm'). Belmont, Calif.; women; 1851.
No'tre Dame, U. of (nō'tĕr dăm'). Notre Dame, Ind.; men; 1842.
No'tre Dame C. (nō'tĕr dăm'). St. Louis, Mo.; women; 1896.
No'tre Dame C. (nō'trĕ dăm'). Manchester, N. H.; women; 1950.
No'tre Dame C. (nō'trĕ dăm'). Cleveland, Ohio; women; 1922.
No'tre Dame C. of Staten Island (nŭt'rĕ dăm'). Grymes Hill, N. Y.; women; 1931.
No'tre Dame of Maryland, C. of (nō'trĕ dăm'). Baltimore; women; 1848.
No'tre Dame Sem. (nō'tĕr dăm'). New Orleans, La.; men; 1923.
Ny'ack Missionary C. (nī'ăk). Nyack, N. Y.; coed.; 1882.
Oak'land City C. (ōk'lănd). Oakland City, Ind.; coed.; 1885.
Oakland Junior C. Oakland, Calif.; coed.; 1927.
Oak Ridge Military Inst. Oak Ridge, N. C.; junior men; 1852.
Oak'wood C. (ōk'wŏŏd). Huntsville, Ala.; coed.; 1896.
O'ber·lin C. (ō'bẽr·lĭn). Oberlin, Ohio; coed.; 1832.
Ob'late C. and Sem. (ŏb'lāt). Bar Harbor, Me.; men; 1941.
Oblate C. and Sem. Natick, Mass.; men; 1927.
Oblate Preparatory Sch. Newburgh, N. Y.; junior men; 1926.
Oblate Scholasticate. Washington, D. C.; men; 1904.
Occidental C. Los Angeles, Calif.; coed.; 1887.
O'cean·side'–Carls'bad C. (ō'shăn·sīd'kärlz'băd). Oceanside, Calif.; junior coed.; 1934.
O·des'sa C. (ō·dĕs'á). Odessa, Texas; junior coed.; 1946.
Office Training Sch. Columbus, Ohio; coed.; 1911.
O'gle·thorpe U. (ō'g'l·thôrp). Oglethorpe University, Ga.; coed.; 1913.
Ohio C. of Chiropody. Cleveland; coed.; 1916.
Ohio Mechanics Inst. Cincinnati; men; 1828.
Ohio Northern U. Ada; coed.; 1871.
Ohio State U. Columbus; coed.; 1864.
Ohio U. Athens; coed.; 1804.
Ohio Wesleyan U. Delaware; coed.; 1841.
Oklahoma, U. of. Norman; coed.; 1890.
Oklahoma State U. of Agriculture and Applied Science. Stillwater; coed.; 1890.
Oklahoma Baptist U. Shawnee; coed.; 1906.
Oklahoma City U. Okla.; coed.; 1911.
Oklahoma C. for Women. Chickasha; 1908.
Oklahoma Military Acad. Claremore; junior men; 1910.
O'ko·lo'na C. (ō'kō·lō'ná). Okolona, Miss.; junior coed.; 1902.
Old Mission San'ta Bar'ba·ra Sem. (săn'tá bär'bá·rá; bär'brá). Santa Barbara, Calif.; men; 1896.
Ol'i·vet C. (ŏl'ĭ·vĕt). Olivet, Mich.; coed.; 1844.
Olivet Naz'a·rene C. (năz'á·rēn). Kankakee, Ill.; coed.; 1907.
O·lym'pic C. (ō·lĭm'pĭk). Bremerton, Wash.; junior coed.; 1946.
Omaha, Municipal U. of. Nebr.; coed.; 1908.
Orange Coast C. Costa Mesa, Calif.; coed.; 1947.
Orange County Community C. Middletown, N. Y.; junior coed.; 1950.
Oregon, U. of. Eugene; coed.; 1872.
Oregon C. of Ed. Monmouth; coed.; 1856.
Oregon State C. Corvallis; coed.; 1858.
Oregon Technical Inst. Oretech; junior coed.; 1947.
Or·lan'do Junior C. (ôr·lăn'dō). Orlando, Fla.; coed.; 1941.
Osteopathic Physicians and Surgeons, C. of. Los Angeles, Calif.; coed.; 1896.
O·ter'o Junior C. (ō·târ'ō). La Junta, Colo.; coed.; 1941.
Ottawa U. Ottawa, Kans.; coed.; 1865.
Ot'ter·bein C. (ŏt'ẽr·bīn). Westerville, Ohio; coed.; 1847.
Ot·tum'wa Heights C. (ō·tŭm'wá; ō-). Ottumwa, Iowa; junior women; 1925.

Ouach'i·ta Baptist C. (wŏsh'ĭ·tô). Arkadelphia, Ark.; coed.; 1885.

Our Lady of An'gels Sem. (ăn'jĕlz). Niagara University, N. Y.; men; 1856.

Our Lady of Angels Sem. Cleveland, Ohio; men; 1907.

Our Lady of Car'ey Sem. (kâr'ĭ). Carey, Ohio; men; 1936.

Our Lady of Cincinnati C. Cincinnati, Ohio; women; 1935.

Our Lady of Fat'i·ma Sem. (făt'ĭ·má). Holliston, Mass.; men; 1946.

Our Lady of Hope Mission Sem. Newburgh, New York; junior men; 1900.

Our Lady of La Sa·lette', Sem. of (lä' sȧ·lĕt'). Ipswich, Mass.; men; 1945.

Our Lady of La Sa·lette', Sem. of (lä' sȧ·lĕt'). Altamont, N. Y.; men; 1852.

Our Lady of Mercy Sem. Lenox, Mass.; junior men; 1948.

Our Lady of Mount Car'mel, C. of (kär'mĕl). Washington, D. C.; men; 1940.

Our Lady of Providence, Sem. of. Warwick Neck, R. I.; junior men; 1939.

Our Lady of the Elms, C. of. Chicopee, Mass.; women; 1928.

Our Lady of the Forest Sem. Lake Bluff, Ill.; men; 1945.

Our Lady of the Holy Ghost Abbey. Conyers, Ga.; men; 1944.

Our Lady of the Lake C. San Antonio, Texas; coed.; 1896.

Our Lady of the Lake Sem. Wawasee, Ind.; junior men; 1948.

Our Lady of the O'zarks Sem. (ō'zärks). Carthage, Mo.; junior men; 1944.

Our Lady of the Valley, Abbey of. Valley Falls, R. I.; men; 1815.

Our Lady of Victory C. Fort Worth, Texas; junior women; 1930.

O·wos'so Bible C. (ō·wŏs'ō). Owosso, Mich.; coed.; 1909.

O'zarks, C. of the (ō'zärks). Clarksville, Ark.; coed.; 1891.

Pace C. (pās). New York, N. Y.; coed.; 1906.

Pacific, C. of the. Stockton, Calif.; coed.; 1851.

Pacific Bible C. Portland, Ore.; coed.; 1922.

Pacific Bible C. of A·zu'sa (á·zōō'sá). Azusa, Calif.; coed.; 1899.

Pacific Bible Inst. of Fres'no (frĕz'nō). Fresno, Calif.; coed.; 1944.

Pacific Lutheran C. Parkland, Wash.; coed.; 1894.

Pacific Lutheran Theol. Sem. Berkeley, Calif.; men; 1950.

Pacific Sch. of Religion. Berkeley, Calif.; coed.; 1866.

Pacific Union C. Angwin, Calif.; coed.; 1882.

Pacific U. Forest Grove, Ore.; coed.; 1849.

Pack'er Collegiate Inst., Junior C. of the (păk'ĕr). Brooklyn, N. Y.; women; 1845.

Pa·du'cah Junior C. (pȧ·dū'kȧ). Paducah, Ky.; coed.; 1932.

Paine C. (pān). Augusta, Ga.; coed.; 1883.

Pal'lot·tine Fathers Preparatory Sem. (păl'ŭ·tīn). Sag Harbor, N. Y.; junior men; 1942.

Pallottine House of Studies. Washington, D. C.; men; 1927.

Palm Beach Junior C. Lake Worth, Fla.; coed.; 1933.

Pal'o·mar C. (păl'ō·mär). San Marcos, Calif.; junior coed.; 1946.

Pal'o Ver'de Junior C. (păl'ō vûr'dĕ). Blythe, Calif.; coed.; 1947.

Pan American C. Edinburg, Texas; coed.; 1927.

Panhandle A. & M. C. Goodwell, Okla.; coed.; 1909.

Pa·no'la County Junior C. (pȧ·nō'lȧ). Carthage, Texas; coed.; 1947.

Pan'zer C. of Physical Ed. and Hygiene (păn'zĕr). East Orange, N. J.; coed.; 1917.

Paper Chemistry, Inst. of. Appleton, Wis.; men; 1929.

Par'is Junior C. (păr'ĭs). Paris, Texas; coed.; 1924.

Park C. (pärk). Parkville, Mo.; coed.; 1875.

Par'sons C. (pär's'nz). Fairfield, Iowa; coed.; 1875.

Parsons Junior C. Parsons, Kans.; coed.; 1923.

Parsons Sch. of Design. New York, N. Y.; coed.; 1896.

Pas'a·de'na City C. (păs'ȧ·dē'ná). Pasadena, Calif.; junior coed.; 1924.

Pasadena C. Pasadena, Calif.; coed.; 1901.

Passionist Preparatory Sem. St. Louis, Mo.; junior men; 1890.

Paul Quinn C. (kwĭn). Waco, Texas; coed.; 1881.

Paul Smith's C. Paul Smiths, N. Y.; junior coed.; 1937.

Pea'bod·y Inst. of the City of Baltimore (pē'bŭd·ĭ). Md.; coed.; 1857.

Peace C. Raleigh, N. C.; junior women; 1857.

Pearl River Junior C. Poplarville, Miss.; coed.; 1909.

Pem'broke C. (pĕm'brōk). Providence, R. I.; women; 1891.

Pembroke State C. Pembroke, N. C.; coed.; 1887.

Penn Hall Junior C. (pĕn). Chambersburg, Pa.; women; 1906.

Pennsylvania, U. of. Philadelphia; coed.; 1740.

Pennsylvania Military C. Chester; men; 1862.

Pennsylvania State C. of Optometry. Philadelphia; coed.; 1919.

Pennsylvania State U. University Park; men; 1855.

Pen'sa·co'la Junior C. (pĕn'sȧ·kō'lȧ). Pensacola, Fla.; coed.; 1948.

Pe·o'ri·a Junior C. (pē·ō'rĭ·ȧ; 70). Peoria, Ill.; coed.; 1946.

Per'kins·ton Junior C. (pûr'kĭn·stŭn; -kĭnz·tŭn). Perkinston, Miss.; coed.; 1911.

Pes'ta·loz'zi Froe'bel Teachers C. (pĕs'tȧ·lŏt'sĕ frā'bĕl). Chicago, Ill.; coed.; 1896.

Pfeif'fer C. (fī'fĕr). Misenheimer, N. C.; coed.; 1887.

Philadelphia Bible Inst. Pa.; junior coed.; 1913.

Philadelphia C. of Osteopathy. Pa.; coed.; 1898.

Philadelphia C. of Pharmacy and Science. Pa.; coed.; 1821.

Philadelphia Museum Sch. of Art. Pa.; coed.; 1876.

Philadelphia Musical Acad. Pa.; coed.; 1870.

Philadelphia Textile Inst. Pa.; coed.; 1883.

Phi·lan'der Smith C. (fĭ·lăn'dĕr). Little Rock, Ark.; coed.; 1868.

Phil'lips U. (fĭl'ĭps). Enid, Okla.; coed.; 1906.

Phoe'nix C. (fē'nĭks). Phoenix, Ariz.; junior coed.; 1920.

Physicians and Surgeons, C. of. San Francisco, Calif.; coed.; 1896.

Pied'mont C. (pēd'mŏnt). Demorest, Ga.; coed.; 1897.

Pike'ville C. (pīk'vĭl). Pikeville, Ky.; coed.; 1889.

Pine'land' C. (pīn'lănd'). Salemburg, N. C.; junior coed.; 1926.

Pine Manor Junior C. Wellesley, Mass.; women; 1911.

Pin'ey·wood' Business Junior C. (pĭn'ĭ·wŏŏd'). Lufkin, Texas; coed.; 1944.

Pin'ey Woods Country Life Sch. (pĭn'ĭ). Piney Woods, Miss.; junior coed.; 1934.

Pittsburgh, U. of. Pa.; coed.; 1787.

Pittsburgh–Xe'nia Theol. Sem. (-zēn'yȧ). Pittsburgh, Pa.; coed.; 1794.

Plym'outh Teachers C. (plĭm'ŭth). Plymouth, N. H.; coed.; 1870.

Po·mo'na C. (pō·mō'nȧ). Claremont, Calif.; coed.; 1887.

Port Arthur C. Port Arthur, Texas; junior coed.; 1909.

Por'ter·ville C. (pōr'tĕr·vĭl). Porterville, Calif.; junior coed.; 1927.

Port Hu'ron Junior C. (hū'rŭn). Port Huron, Mich.; coed.; 1923.

Port'land, U. of (pōrt'lănd; 70). Ore.; coed.; 1901.

Portland Junior C. Portland, Me.; men; 1933.

Portland Sch. of Music. Portland, Ore.; coed.; 1917.

Portland State C. Portland, Ore.; coed.; 1946.

Post Junior C. (pōst). Waterbury, Conn.; coed.; 1890.

Po·teau' Junior C. (pō·tō'). Poteau, Okla.; coed.; 1943.

Po·to'mac State C. (pō·tō'măk). Keyser, W. Va.; junior coed.; 1902.

Prairie View A. & M. C. Prairie View, Texas; coed.; 1876.

Pratt Inst. (prăt). Brooklyn, N. Y.; coed.; 1887.

Pratt Junior C. Pratt, Kans.; coed.; 1938.

Pren'tiss Normal and Industrial Inst. (prĕn'tĭs). Prentiss, Miss.; junior coed.; 1907.

Presbyterian C. Clinton, S. C.; coed.; 1880.

Presbyterian General Assembly's Sch. for Lay Workers. Richmond, Va.; coed.; 1914.

Presbyterian Junior C. Maxton, N. C.; coed.; 1929.

Prince'ton Theol. Sem. (prĭns'tŭn). Princeton, N. J.; coed.; 1812.

Princeton U. Princeton, N. J.; men; 1746.

Prin·cip'i·a C., The (prĭn·sĭp'ĭ·ȧ). Elsah, Ill.; coed.; 1910.

Protestant Episcopal Theol. Sem. in Virginia. Alexandria; men; 1823.

Providence–Barrington Bible C. Providence, R. I.; coed.; 1900.

Providence C. R. I.; men; 1917.

Pu·eb'lo Junior C. (pŭ·ĕb'lō). Pueblo, Colo.; coed.; 1933.

Puerto Rico, Inter American U. of. San Germán; coed.; 1912.

Puerto Rico, U. of. Río Piedras; coed.; 1900.

Puerto Rico Junior C. Río Piedras; coed.; 1949.

Pu'get Sound, C. of (pū'jĕt; -jĭt). Tacoma, Wash.; coed.; 1888.

Pur·due' U. (pẽr·dū'; pûr-). Lafayette, Ind.; coed.; 1865.

Put'ney Graduate Sch. of Teacher Ed. (pŭt'nĭ). Putney, Vt.; coed.; 1950.

Queen of the Apostles Sem. Madison, Wis.; junior men; 1949.

Queen of the Holy Rosary C. Mission San Jose, Calif.; women; 1930.

Queens C. (kwēnz). Flushing, N. Y.; coed.; 1937.

Queens C. Charlotte, N. C.; women; 1857.

Quig'ley Preparatory Sem. (kwĭg'lĭ). Chicago, Ill.; junior men; 1905.

Quin'cy C. (kwĭn'sĭ). Quincy, Ill.; coed.; 1860.

Quin'ni·pi·ac' C. (kwĭn'ĭ·pĭ·ăk'). Hamden, Conn.; coed.; 1929.

Rad'cliffe C. (răd'klĭf). Cambridge, Mass.; women; 1879.

Rad'ford C. (răd'fĕrd). Radford, Va.; coed.; 1910.

Ran'dolph–Ma'con C. (răn'dŏlf·mā'kŭn). Ashland, Va.; coed.; 1830.

Randolph–Macon Woman's C. Lynchburg, Va.; 1891.

Rang'er Junior C. (răn'jĕr). Ranger, Texas; coed.; 1926.

RCA Institutes. New York, N. Y.; coed.; 1909.

Red'lands, U. of (rĕd'lăndz). Redlands, Calif.; coed.; 1907.

Reed C. (rēd). Portland, Ore.; coed.; 1904.

Reed'ley C. (rēd'lĭ). Reedley, Calif.; junior coed.; 1926.

Re'gis C. (rē'jĭs). Denver, Colo.; men; 1877.

Regis C. Weston, Mass.; women; 1927.

Rein'hardt C. (rīn'härt). Waleska, Ga.; junior coed.; 1883.

Rens'se·laer' Polytechnic Inst. (rĕn'sĕ·lẽr'; rĕns·lẽr'; rĕn'sĕ·lĕr; rĕns'-lẽr). Troy, N. Y.; coed.; 1824.

Resurrection Scholasticate. Washington, D. C.; men; 1936.

Rhode Island, U. of. Kingston; coed.; 1892.

Rhode Island C. of Ed. Providence; coed.; 1854.

Rhode Island Sch. of Design. Providence; coed.; 1877.

Rice Inst. (rīs). Houston, Texas; coed.; 1891.

Rich'mond, U. of (rĭch'mŭnd). Va.; coed.; 1832.

Richmond Professional Inst. Va.; coed.; 1917.

Rick'er C. (rĭk'ĕr). Houlton, Me.; coed.; 1848.

Ricks C. (rĭks). Rexburg, Idaho; junior coed.; 1888.

Ri'der C. (rī'dĕr). Trenton, N. J.; coed.; 1865.

Ri'o Grande C. (rĭ'ō gränd'). Rio Grande, Ohio; coed.; 1876.

Rip'on C. (rĭp'ŭn). Ripon, Wis.; coed.; 1850.

Riverside City C. Riverside, Calif.; junior coed.; 1916.

Ri'vi·er' C. (rē'vē·ā'). Nashua, N. H.; women; 1933.

Ro'a·noke C. (rō'ȧ·nōk). Salem, Va.; coed.; 1842.

Roberts Wesleyan C. (rŏb'ĕrts). North Chili, N. Y.; coed.; 1866.

Rochester, U. of. N. Y.; coed.; 1850.

Rochester Business Inst. N. Y.; junior coed.; 1863.

Rochester Inst. of Tech. N. Y.; coed.; 1829.

Rochester Junior C. Rochester, Minn.; coed.; 1915.

Rock'ford Colleges (rŏk'fĕrd). Rockford, Ill.; coed.; 1847.

Rock'hurst C. (rŏk'hûrst). Kansas City, Mo.; men; 1910.

Rock'mont C. (rŏk'mŏnt). Longmont, Colo.; coed.; 1945.

Rocky Mountain C. Billings, Mont.; coed.; 1883.

Roger Ba'con C. (bā'kŭn). El Paso, Texas; men; 1940.

Roger Wil'liams Junior C. (wĭl'yȧmz). Providence, R. I.; coed.; 1948.

Rol'lins C. (rŏl'ĭnz). Winter Park, Fla.; coed.; 1885.

Roo'se·velt U. (rō'zĕ·vĕlt; -vĕlt). Chicago, Ill.; coed.; 1945.

Rosary C. River Forest, Ill.; women; 1848.

Rosary Hill C. Buffalo, N. Y.; women; 1948.

Rose'mont C. (rōz'mŏnt). Rosemont, Pa.; women; 1921.

Rose Polytechnic Inst. (rōz). Terre Haute, Ind.; men; 1874.

Rus'sell Sage C. (rŭs''l sāj'). Troy, N. Y.; women; 1916.

Rust C. (rŭst). Holly Springs, Miss.; coed.; 1866.

Rut'gers U. (rŭt'gĕrz). New Brunswick, N. J.; coed.; 1766.

Sac'ra·men'to Junior C. (săk'rȧ·mĕn'tō). Sacramento, Calif.; coed.; 1916.

Sacramento State C. Sacramento, Calif.; coed.; 1947.

Sacred Heart, C. of the. Santurce, Puerto Rico; women; 1935.

Sacred Heart C. Wichita, Kans.; women; 1933.

Sacred Heart Dominican C. Houston, Texas; women; 1946.
Sacred Heart Junior C. Cullman, Ala.; women; 1940.
Sacred Heart Junior C. Belmont, N. C.; women; 1892.
Sacred Heart Mission Sem. Geneva, Ill.; junior men; 1925.
Sacred Heart Monastery. Hales Corners, Wis.; men; 1928.
Sacred Heart Retreat. Louisville, Ky.; men; 1936.
Sacred Heart Sch. of Ed. Fall River, Mass.; women; 1934.
Sacred Heart Sem. Fort Wayne, Ind.; men; 1938.
Sacred Heart Sem. Detroit, Mich.; men; 1921.
Sacred Heart Sem. Shelby, Ohio; men; 1934.
Sacred Hearts Sem. Washington, D. C.; men; 1932.
Sacred Hearts Sem. Wareham, Mass.; junior men; 1946.
Saint Albert the Great, C. of. Oakland, Calif.; men; 1932.
Saint Ambrose C. Davenport, Iowa; coed.; 1882.
Saint Andrew on Hudson Sem. Poughkeepsie, N. Y.; junior men; 1950.
Saint Andrew's Preparatory Sem. Rochester, N. Y.; junior men; 1870.
Saint Ann's Monastery. Scranton, Pa.; men; 1905.
Saint An'selm's C. (ăn'sĕlmz). Manchester, N. H.; men; 1889.
Saint An'tho·ny—on—Hudson Sem. (ăn'thô-nĭ-). Rensselaer, N. Y.; men; 1912.
Saint Anthony's Apostolic Sch. San Antonio, Texas; junior men; 1903.
Saint Anthony's Monastery. Marathon, Wis.; men; 1918.
Saint Anthony's Sem. Santa Barbara, Calif.; junior men; 1896.
Saint Anthony's Sem. Catskill, N. Y.; junior men; 1908.
Saint Anthony's Sem. El Paso, Texas; men; 1936.
Saint Au·gus'tine's C. (ô·gŭs'tĭnz). Raleigh, N. C.; coed.; 1867.
Saint Augustine's Sem. Kansas City, Kans.; men; 1935.
Saint Augustine's Sem. Bay St. Louis, Miss.; men; 1923.
Saint Bas'il's C. (băz''lz). Stamford, Conn.; men; 1939.
Saint Bede C. (bēd). Peru, Ill.; junior men; 1890.
Saint Ben'e·dict, C. of. (bĕn'ê·dĭkt). St. Joseph, Minn.; women; 1912.
Saint Benedict C. Ferdinand, Ind.; women; 1914.
Saint Benedict's C. Atchison, Kans.; men; 1857.
Saint Ber'nard C. (bûr'nẽrd). St. Bernard, Ala.; men; 1892.
Saint Ber'nard·ine of Si·en'a C. (bûr'nẽr-dĕn, sĭ-ĕn'à). Loudonville, N. Y.; coed.; 1937.
Saint Ber'nard's Sem. and C. (bûr'nẽrdz). Rochester, N. Y.; men; 1893.
Saint Bon'a·ven'ture U. (bŏn'à·vĕn'tụr; bŏn'à·vĕn'tụr). St. Bonaventure, N. Y.; coed.; 1859.
Saint Cath'a·rine Junior C. (kăth'à·rĭn; kăth'rĭn). Springfield, Ky.; coed.; 1932.
Saint Cath'er·ine, C. of (kăth'ẽr·ĭn; kăth'rĭn). St. Paul, Minn.; women; 1906.
Saint Charles Bor'ro·me'o, C. of (bŏr'ô·mā'ō). Columbus, Ohio; men; 1923.
Saint Charles Borromeo Sem. Philadelphia, Pa.; men; 1832.
Saint Charles C. Grand Coteau, La.; men; 1838.
Saint Charles C. Catonsville, Md.; junior men; 1830.
Saint Charles Sem. Carthagena, Ohio; men; 1861.
Saint Clem'ent's Hall (klĕm'ĕnts). Brighton, Mass.; junior men; 1940.
Saint Cloud State C. (kloud). St. Cloud, Minn.; coed.; 1866.
Saint Co·lum'ban's Sem. (kô·lŭm'bǎnz). St. Columbans, Nebr.; men; 1923.
Saint Columban's Sem. Silver Creek, N. Y.; junior men; 1924.
Saint Columban's Sem. Bristol, R. I.; men; 1933.
Saint Edward's Sem. Kenmore, Wash.; men; 1930.
Saint Edward's U. Austin, Texas; men; 1876.
Saint Elizabeth, C. of. Convent Station, N. J.; women; 1899.
Saint Elizabeth Teacher Training Inst. Allegany, N. Y.; women; 1945.
Saint Fi·del'is C. and Sem. (fĭ·dĕl'ĭs; fê·dā'lĭs). Herman, Pa.; men; 1877.
Saint Francis, C. of. Joliet, Ill.; women; 1874.
Saint Francis Cap'u·chin C. (kăp'ủ·shĭn). Washington, D. C.; men; 1917.
Saint Francis C. Fort Wayne, Ind.; women; 1890.
Saint Francis C. Brooklyn, N. Y.; men; 1858.
Saint Francis C. Loretto, Pa.; coed.; 1847.
Saint Francis C. Burlington, Wis.; men; 1930.
Saint Francis C. Biddeford, Me.; men; 1953.
Saint Francis Sem. Staten Island, N. Y.; junior men; 1928.
Saint Francis Sem. Milwaukee, Wis.; men; 1856.
Saint Gabriel's Monastery. Des Moines, Iowa; men; 1922.
Saint Gabriel's Monastery. Brighton, Mass.; junior men; 1911.
Saint Gregory Minor Sem. Cincinnati, Ohio; junior men; 1891.
Saint Gregory's C. Shawnee, Okla.; junior men; 1915.
Saint Henry's Preparatory Sem. Belleville, Ill.; junior men; 1925.
Saint Hy'a·cinth Sem. (hī'à·sĭnth). Granby, Mass.; men; 1927.
Saint John Can'tius Sem. (kăn'shǔs). St. Louis, Mo.; men; 1918.
Saint John C. of Cleveland. Ohio; women; 1928.
Saint John Fish'er C. (fĭsh'ẽr). Rochester, N. Y.; men; 1952.
Saint John's Atonement Sem. Montour Falls, N. Y.; junior men; 1913.
Saint John's Catholic Sem. Kansas City, Mo.; junior men; 1928.
Saint John's C. Camarillo, Calif.; men; 1939.
Saint John's C. Winfield, Kans.; junior coed.; 1893.
Saint John's C. Annapolis, Md.; coed.; 1696.
Saint John's Provincial Sem. Plymouth, Mich.; men; 1949.
Saint John's Sem. Brighton, Mass.; men; 1884.
Saint John's Sem. San Antonio, Texas; men; 1915.
Saint John's U. Collegeville, Minn.; men; 1857.
Saint John's U. Brooklyn, N. Y.; coed.; 1870.
Saint Jo'sa·phat's Sem. (jŏ'sà·făts). Washington, D. C.; men; 1941.
Saint Joseph, C. of. Framingham, Mass.; women; 1947.
Saint Joseph and the Little Flower, Little Sem. of. Buffalo, N. Y.; men; 1925.

Saint Joseph C. West Hartford, Conn.; women; 1925.
Saint Joseph C. Emmitsburg, Md.; women; 1809.
Saint Joseph Junior C. St. Joseph, Mo.; coed.; 1915.
Saint Joseph on the Ri'o Gran'de, C. of (rē'ô grän'dê). Albuquerque, N. Mex.; coed.; 1940.
Saint Joseph's C. Mountain View, Calif.; junior men; 1898.
Saint Joseph's C. Collegeville, Ind.; men; 1889.
Saint Joseph's C. North Windham, Me.; coed.; 1915.
Saint Joseph's C. Princeton, N. J.; junior men; 1938.
Saint Joseph's C. Philadelphia, Pa.; men; 1851.
Saint Joseph's C. for Women. Brooklyn, N. Y.; 1916.
Saint Joseph Sem. Teutopolis, Ill.; men; 1862.
Saint Joseph Sem. Westmont, Ill.; junior men; 1862.
Saint Joseph Sem. St. Benedict, La.; junior men; 1891.
Saint Joseph's Normal Sch. Metuchen, N. J.; men; 1901.
Saint Joseph's Pas'sion·ist Monastery (păsh'ŭn-ĭst). Baltimore, Md.; men; 1867.
Saint Joseph's Preparatory C. Kirkwood, Mo.; junior men; 1888.
Saint Joseph's Preparatory Sem. Holy Trinity, Ala.; junior men; 1925.
Saint Joseph's Priory. Somerset, Ohio; men; 1818.
Saint Joseph's Sem. Washington, D. C.; men; 1892.
Saint Joseph's Sem. Elgin, Ill.; men; 1937.
Saint Joseph's Sem. Grand Rapids, Mich.; junior men; 1909.
Saint Joseph's Sem. Yonkers, N. Y.; men; 1839.
Saint Joseph's Sem. Cleveland, Ohio; men; 1931.
Saint Joseph's Seraphic Sem. Callicoon, N. Y.; junior men; 1901.
Saint Joseph Teacher Training Inst. St. Augustine, Fla.; junior women; 1939.
Saint Jude Sem. (jōōd). Momence, Ill.; junior men; 1933.
Saint Lawrence Sem. Mt. Calvary, Wis.; junior men; 1860.
Saint Lawrence U. Canton, N. Y.; coed.; 1856.
Saint Leo Abbey Scholasticate. St. Leo, Fla.; men; 1890.
Saint Louis C. of Pharmacy and Allied Sciences. Mo.; coed.; 1864.
Saint Lou'is de Mont'fort Sem. (lōō'ĭs, mŏnt'fẽrt). Litchfield, Conn.; men; 1947.
Saint Louis Inst. of Music. Mo.; coed.; 1924.
Saint Louis Preparatory Sem. Webster Groves, Mo.; junior men; 1900.
Saint Louis U. St. Louis, Mo.; coed.; 1818.
Saint Mar'tin's C. (mär'tĭnz; -t'nz). Olympia, Wash.; men; 1895.
Saint Mary, C. of. Omaha, Nebr.; women; 1923.
Saint Mary C. Xavier, Kans.; women; 1882.
Saint Mary of the Angels Sem. Green Bay, Wis.; men; 1913.
Saint Mary of the Lake Sem. Mundelein, Ill.; men; 1920.
Saint Mary of the Plains C. Dodge City, Kans.; coed.; 1913.
Saint Mary of the Springs, C. of. Columbus, Ohio; women; 1911.
Saint Mary–of–the–Wa'satch, C. of (-wô'săch). Salt Lake City, Utah; women; 1895.
Saint Mary–of–the–Woods C. Saint Mary-of-the-Woods, Ind.; women; 1840.
Saint Mary's C. Notre Dame, Ind.; women; 1844.
Saint Mary's C. St. Marys, Kans.; men; 1869.
Saint Mary's C. St. Mary, Ky.; men; 1821.
Saint Mary's C. Winona, Minn.; men; 1912.
Saint Mary's C. North East, Pa.; junior men; 1881.
Saint Mary's C. of California (mâr'ĭz). St. Mary's College; men; 1863.
Saint Mary's Dominican C. New Orleans, La.; women; 1910.
Saint Mary's Junior C. St. Mary's City, Md.; women; 1839.
Saint Mary's Junior C. O'Fallon, Mo.; women; 1929.
Saint Mary's Junior C. Raleigh, N. C.; women; 1842.
Saint Mary's Manor. Penndel, Pa.; junior men; 1920.
Saint Mary's Mission Sem. Techny, Ill.; men; 1900.
Saint Mary's Monastery. Morristown, N. J.; men; 1927.
Saint Mary's Monastery. Dunkirk, N. Y.; men; 1862.
Saint Mary's Sem. Norwalk, Conn.; men; 1906.
Saint Mary's Sem. Cleveland, Ohio; men; 1848.
Saint Mary's Sem. La Porte, Texas; men; 1901.
Saint Mary's Sem. Randolph, Vt.; men; 1931.
Saint Mary's Sem. and U. Roland Park, Md.; men; 1791.
Saint Mary's U. of San Antonio. Texas; coed.; 1852.
Saint Mein'rad Sem. (mīn'răd). St. Meinrad, Ind.; men; 1854.
Saint Michael's C. Santa Fe, N. Mex.; men; 1947.
Saint Michael's C. Winooski Park, Vt.; men; 1904.
Saint Michael's Pas'sion·ist Monastery (păsh'ŭn-ĭst). Union City, N. J.; men; 1866.
Saint Nor'bert C. (nôr'bẽrt). West De Pere, Wis.; coed.; 1893.
Saint O'laf C. (ō'làf). Northfield, Minn.; coed.; 1874.
Saint Patrick's Monastery. Wilmington, Del.; men; 1937.
Saint Patrick's Sem. Menlo Park, Calif.; men; 1898.
Saint Paul Bible C. Minn.; coed.; 1916.
Saint Paul's C. Washington, D. C.; men; 1889.
Saint Paul's C. Concordia, Mo.; junior men; 1884.
Saint Paul's C. Lawrenceville, Va.; coed.; 1888.
Saint Paul Sem. Minn.; men; 1895.
Saint Paul's Monastery. Detroit, Mich.; men; 1929.
Saint Pe'ters·burg Bible Inst. (pē'tẽrz·bûrg). St. Petersburg, Fla.; junior coed.; 1947.
Saint Pe'ters·burg Junior C. St. Petersburg, Fla.; coed.; 1927.
Saint Peter's C. Jersey City, N. J.; coed.; 1872.
Saint Philip Ne'ri, Sch. of (nā'rê; nẽr'ĭ). Boston, Mass.; junior men; 1946.
Saint Philip's C. San Antonio, Texas; junior coed.; 1902.
Saint Pi'us X Sem. (pī'ǔs). Saranac Lake, N. Y.; men; 1956.
Saint Pro·co'pi·us C. (prô·kō'pǐ·ǔs). Lisle, Ill.; men; 1885.
Saint Rose, C. of (rōz). Albany, N. Y.; women; 1920.
Saint Scho·las'ti·ca, C. of (skô·lăs'tĭ·kà). Duluth, Minn.; women; 1912.
Saints Cyr'il and Me·tho'di·us Sem. (sĭr'ĭl, mê·thō'dǐ·ǔs). Orchard Lake, Mich.; men; 1885.

Saint Stan'is·laus Sem. (stăn'ĭs·lôs). Florissant, Mo.; junior men; 1823.
Saint Stephen's Friary. Croghan, N. Y.; junior men; 1896.
Saint Te·re'sa, C. of (tĕ·rē'sȧ; ·zȧ). Winona, Minn.; women; 1907.
Saint Teresa, C. of. Kansas City, Mo.; women; 1866.
Saint Thomas, C. of. St. Paul, Minn.; men; 1885.
Saint Thomas, U. of. Houston, Texas; coed.; 1947.
Saint Thomas A·qui'nas, C. of (ȧ·kwī'nȧs). River Forest, Ill.; men; 1925.
Saint Thomas Sem. Denver, Colo.; men; 1907.
Saint Thomas Sem. Bloomfield, Conn.; junior men; 1897.
Saint Vincent C. Latrobe, Pa.; men; 1840.
Saint Vlad'i·mir's Orthodox Theol. Sem. (vlăd'ĭ·mĭrz). New York, N. Y.; men; 1938.
Saint Xav'i·er C. (zăv'ĭ·ẽr). Chicago, Ill.; women; 1846.
Sa'lem C. (sā'lĕm). Winston-Salem, N. C.; coed.; 1772.
Salem C. Salem, W. Va.; coed.; 1888.
Sa·le'sian C. (sȧ·lē'zhȧn). Aptos, Calif.; men; 1948.
Sa·li'nas Evening Junior C. (sȧ·lē'nȧs). Salinas, Calif.; coed.; 1919.
Salm'on P. Chase C. (săm'ŭn, chās'). Cincinnati, Ohio; coed.; 1920.
Sal'va·to'ri·an Sem. (săl'vȧ·tō'rĭ·ȧn; 70). St. Nazi, Wis.; junior men; 1909.
Sal've Re·gi'na C. (săl'vā rā·gē'nä). Newport, R. I.; women; 1934.
Sam Hous'ton State Teachers C. (hūs'tŭn). Huntsville, Texas; coed.; 1879.
San An'ge·lo C. (săn ăn'jĕ·lō). San Angelo, Texas; junior coed.; 1928.
San Antonio C. Texas; junior coed.; 1925.
San Be·ni'to County Junior C. (săn' bĕ·nē'tō). Hollister, Calif.; coed.; 1919.
San Ber'nar·di'no Valley C. (săn bûr'nẽr·dē'nō). San Bernardino, Calif.; junior coed.; 1926.
San Diego C. for Women. Calif.; 1952.
San Diego Junior C. Calif.; coed.; 1914.
San Diego State C. Calif.; coed.; 1897.
San Francisco, U. of. Calif.; coed.; 1855.
San Francisco C. for Women. Calif.; 1930.
San Francisco State C. Calif.; coed.; 1899.
San Francisco Theol. Sem. San Anselmo, Calif.; coed.; 1871.
San Jo·se' Junior C. (săn' [h]ō·zā'). San Jose, Calif.; coed.; 1921.
San Jose State C. San Jose, Calif.; coed.; 1857.
San Lu'is O·bis'po Junior C. (săn lōō'ĭs ō·bĭs'pō). San Luis Obispo, Calif.; coed.; 1936.
San Luis Rey C. (rā). San Luis Rey, Calif.; men; 1930.
San Ma·te'o, C. of. (săn' mȧ·tā'ō). San Mateo, Calif.; junior coed.;1922.
San'ta An'a C. (săn'tȧ ăn'ȧ). Santa Ana, Calif.; junior coed.; 1915.
San'ta Bar'ba·ra C. (săn'tȧ bär'bȧ·rȧ; bär'brȧ). Santa Barbara, Calif.; coed.; 1909.
Santa Barbara Junior C. Santa Barbara, Calif.; coed.; 1946.
Santa Clar'a, U. of (klăr'ȧ; klăr'ȧ). Santa Clara, Calif.; men; 1777.
Santa Mon'i·ca City C. (mŏn'ĭ·kȧ). Santa Monica, Calif.; junior coed.; 1929.
Santa Ro'sa Junior C. (rō'zȧ). Santa Rosa, Calif.; coed.; 1918.
Sarah Law'rence C. (lô'rĕns; lŏr'ĕns). Bronxville, N. Y.; women; 1926.
Sa·van'nah State C. (sȧ·văn'ȧ). Savannah, Ga.; coed.; 1890.
Saw'yer Sch. of Business (sô'yẽr). Los Angeles, Calif.; junior coed.; 1916.
Sayre Junior C. (sâr). Sayre, Okla.; coed.; 1938.
Scar'ritt C. for Christian Workers (skăr'ĭt). Nashville, Tenn.; coed.; 1924.
Schrei'ner Inst. (shrī'nẽr). Kerrville, Texas; junior coed.; 1923.
Scotts'bluff' C. (skŏts'blŭf'). Scottsbluff, Nebr.; junior coed.; 1926.
Sco'tus C. (skō'tŭs). Hebbronville, Texas; men; 1932.
Scran'ton, U. of (skrăn't'n; ·tŭn). Scranton, Pa.; coed.; 1888.
Scripps C. (skrĭps). Claremont, Calif.; women; 1926.
Sea'bur·y–Western Theol. Sem. (sē'bẽr·ĭ·). Evanston, Ill.; men; 1858.
Seattle Pacific C. Seattle, Wash.; coed.; 1891.
Seattle U. Wash.; coed.; 1892.
Sel'ma U. (sĕl'mȧ). Selma, Ala.; coed.; 1878.
Sen'e·ca, Colleges of the (sĕn'ē·kȧ). = HOBART C.; WILLIAM SMITH C.
Se·quoi'as, C. of the (sē·kwoi'ȧz). Visalia, Calif.; junior coed.; 1926.
Se'ton Hall U. South Orange, N. J.; coed.; 1856.
Seton Hill C. Greensburg, Pa.; women; 1883.
Seventh–day Adventist Theol. Sem. Wash., D. C.; coed.; 1936.
Shas'ta C. (shăs'tȧ). Redding, Calif.; junior coed.; 1949.
Shaw U. (shô). Raleigh, N. C.; coed.; 1865.
Shel'don Jack'son Junior C. (shĕl'dŭn jăk's'n). Sitka, Alaska; coed.; 1878.
Shel'ton C. (shĕl't'n; ·tŭn). Ringwood, N. J.; coed.; 1907.
Shen'an·do'ah C. (shĕn'ăn·dō'ȧ). Dayton, Va.; junior coed.; 1875.
Shenandoah Conservatory of Music. Dayton, Va.; coed.; 1875.
Shep'herd C. (shĕp'ẽrd). Shepherdstown, W. Va.; coed.; 1871.
Sher'wood Music Sch. (shûr'wŏŏd). Chicago, Ill.; coed.; 1895.
Shi'mer C. (shī'mẽr). Mount Carroll, Ill.; coed.; 1853.
Shor'ter C. (shôr'tẽr). North Little Rock, Ark.; coed.; 1884.
Shorter C. Rome, Ga.; coed.; 1873.
Si·en'a C. (sĭ·ĕn'ȧ). Memphis, Tenn.; coed.; 1921.
Siena Heights C. Adrian, Mich.; women; 1919.
Si·er'ra C. (sĭ·ĕr'ȧ). Auburn, Calif.; junior coed.; 1914.
Sim'mons C. (sĭm'ŭnz). Boston, Mass.; women; 1899.
Simp'son Bible C. (sĭm[p]'s'n). San Francisco, Calif.; coed.; 1921.
Simpson C. Indianola, Iowa; coed.; 1860.
Sin'clair C. (sĭn'klâr). Dayton, Ohio; junior coed.; 1887.
Sioux Falls C. (sōō' fôlz). Sioux Falls, S. Dak.; coed.; 1883.
Sisters of Mercy Normal Sch. Albany, N. Y.; coed.; 1928.
Skag'it Valley Junior C. (skăj'ĭt). Mount Vernon, Wash.; coed.; 1926.
Skid'more C. (skĭd'mōr). Saratoga Springs, N. Y.; women; 1911.
Smith C. Northampton, Mass.; women; 1871.
Snead Junior C. (snēd). Boaz, Ala.; coed.; 1898.
Snow C. (snō). Ephraim, Utah; junior coed.; 1888.
South, U. of the. Sewanee, Tenn.; men; 1857.
South Carolina, Med. C. of. Charleston; coed.; 1824.

South Carolina, U. of. Columbia; coed.; 1801.
South Carolina State C. Orangeburg; coed.; 1896.
South Dakota, State U. of. Vermillion; coed.; 1862.
South Dakota Sch. of Mines and Tech. Rapid City; coed.; 1885.
South Dakota State C. of Agric. and Mechanic Arts. Brookings; coed.; 1881.
Southeastern Baptist Theol. Sem. Wake Forest, N. C.; coed.; 1951.
Southeastern Bible C. Birmingham, Ala.; coed.; 1934.
South–Eastern Bible C. Lakeland, Fla.; coed.; 1935.
Southeastern Louisiana C. Hammond; coed.; 1925.
Southeastern State C. Durant, Okla.; coed.; 1909.
Southeastern U. Washington, D. C.; coed.; 1917.
Southeast Missouri State C. Cape Girardeau; coed.; 1873.
Southern Baptist C. Walnut Ridge, Ark.; junior coed.; 1941.
Southern Baptist Theol. Sem. Louisville, Ky.; coed.; 1859.
Southern California, U. of. Los Angeles; coed.; 1879.
Southern California Bible C. Costa Mesa; coed.; 1920.
Southern C. of Fine Arts. Houston, Texas; coed.; 1937.
Southern C. of Optometry. Memphis, Tenn.; coed.; 1932.
Southern C. of Pharmacy. Atlanta, Ga.; coed.; 1903.
Southern Illinois U. Carbondale; coed.; 1874.
Southern Methodist U. Dallas, Texas; coed.; 1910.
Southern Missionary C. Collegedale, Tenn.; coed.; 1893.
Southern Oregon C. Ashland; coed.; 1926.
Southern Sem. and Junior C. Buena Vista, Va.; women; 1868.
Southern State C. Magnolia, Ark.; coed.; 1909.
Southern State Teachers C. Springfield, S. Dak.; coed.; 1881.
Southern Union C. Wadley, Ala.; junior coed.; 1934.
Southern U. and A. & M. C. Scotlandville, La.; coed.; 1880.
South Georgia C. Douglas; junior coed.; 1907.
South Texas C. Houston; coed.; 1925.
Southwest Baptist C. Bolivar, Mo.; junior coed.; 1878.
Southwestern at Memphis. Tenn.; coed.; 1848.
Southwestern Baptist Theol. Sem. Fort Worth, Texas; coed.; 1905.
Southwestern Bible Inst. Waxahachie, Texas; coed.; 1927.
Southwestern Christian C. Terrell, Texas; junior coed.; 1950.
Southwestern C. Winfield, Kans.; coed.; 1885.
Southwestern Junior C. Keene, Texas; coed.; 1893.
Southwestern Louisiana Inst. Lafayette; coed.; 1900.
Southwestern Pentecostal Holiness C. Oklahoma City, Okla.; junior coed.; 1946.
Southwestern State C. Weatherford, Okla.; coed.; 1901.
Southwestern U. Georgetown, Texas; coed.; 1840.
Southwest Mississippi Junior C. Summit; coed.; 1918.
Southwest Missouri State C. Springfield; coed.; 1905.
Southwest Texas Junior C. Uvalde; coed.; 1946.
Southwest Texas State Teachers C. San Marcos; coed.; 1899.
Spar'tan·burg Junior C. (spär't'n·bûrg). Spartanburg, S. C.; coed.; 1911.
Spel'man C. (spĕl'mȧn). Atlanta, Ga.; women; 1881.
Spring Arbor Junior C. Spring Arbor, Mich.; coed.; 1873.
Springfield C. Springfield, Mass.; coed.; 1885.
Springfield Junior C. Springfield, Ill.; coed.; 1929.
Spring Garden Inst. Philadelphia, Pa.; junior coed.; 1850.
Spring Hill C. Spring Hill, Ala.; coed.; 1830.
Sta'ley C. of the Spoken Word (stā'lĭ). Brookline, Mass.; coed.; 1900.
Stan'ford U. (stăn'fẽrd). Stanford, Calif.; coed.; 1885.
State Teachers C. Florence, Ala.; coed.; 1830.
State Teachers C. Jacksonville, Ala.; coed.; 1883.
State Teachers C. Livingston, Ala.; coed.; 1880.
State Teachers C. Troy, Ala.; coed.; 1887.
State Teachers C. Dickinson, N. Dak.; coed.; 1916.
State Teachers C. Mayville, N. Dak.; coed.; 1889.
State Teachers C. Minot, N. Dak.; coed.; 1913.
State Teachers C. Valley City, N. Dak.; coed.; 1889.
State Teachers C. at Blooms'burg (blŏŏmz'bûrg). Pa.; coed.; 1839.
State Teachers C. at California. Pa.; coed.; 1852.
State Teachers C. at Chey'ney (chā'nĭ). Pa.; coed.; 1837.
State Teachers C. at Clar'i·on (klăr'ĭ·ŭn). Pa.; coed.; 1866.
State Teachers C. at East Strouds'burg (stroudz'bûrg). Pa.; coed.; 1893.
State Teachers C. at Ed'in·bor'o (ĕd'n·bûr'ō). Pa.; coed.; 1859.
State Teachers C. at Indiana. Pa.; coed.; 1871.
State Teachers C. at Kutz'town (kŏŏts'toun). Pa.; coed.; 1860.
State Teachers C. at Lock Haven. Pa.; coed.; 1870.
State Teachers C. at Mans'field (măns'fēld; mănz'-). Pa.; coed.; 1857.
State Teachers C. at Mil'lers·ville (mĭl'ẽrz·vĭl). Pa.; coed.; 1854.
State Teachers C. at Ship'pens·burg (shĭp'ĕnz·bûrg). Pa.; coed.; 1873.
State Teachers C. at Slippery Rock. Pa.; coed.; 1889.
State Teachers C. at West Ches'ter (chĕs'tẽr). Pa.; coed.; 1812.
State Technical Inst. Hartford, Conn.; junior coed.; 1946.
Stel'la Ni·ag'a·ra Normal School (stĕl'ȧ nī·ăg'ȧ·rȧ; ·äg'rȧ). Buffalo, N. Y.; women; 1931.
Stephen F. Aus'tin State C. (ôs'tĭn). Nacogdoches, Texas; coed.; 1917.
Ste'phens C. (stē'vĕnz). Columbia, Mo.; junior women; 1833.
Ster'ling C. (stûr'lĭng). Sterling, Kans.; coed.; 1887.
Stet'son U. (stĕt's'n). De Land, Fla.; coed.; 1883.
Steu'ben·ville, C. of (stū'bĕn·vĭl). Steubenville, Ohio; coed.; 1946.
Ste'vens Inst. of Tech. Hoboken, N. J.; men; 1867.
Stig'ma·tine Juniorate (stĭg'mȧ·tēn). Waltham, Mass.; men; 1923.
Stigmatine Major Sem. Wellesley, Mass.; men; 1940.
Still'man C. (stĭl'mȧn). Tuscaloosa, Ala.; coed.; 1876.
Stock'ton C. (stŏk'tŭn). Stockton, Calif.; junior coed.; 1935.
Stone'hill' C. (stōn'hĭl'). North Easton, Mass.; coed.; 1948.
Stout Inst. (stout). Menomonie, Wis.; coed.; 1893.
Strat'ford C. (străt'fẽrd). Danville, Va.; junior women; 1852.
Strayer C. of Accountancy (strär). Wash., D. C.; coed.; 1928.
Sue Ben'nett C. (bĕn'ĕt; ·ĭt; 30). London, Ky.; junior coed.; 1896.

Suf'folk U. (sŭf'ŭk; -ôk). Boston, Mass.; coed.; 1906.
Sul'lins C. (sŭl'ĭnz). Bristol, Va.; junior women; 1870.
Sul Ross State C. (sŭl' rŏs'). Alpine, Texas; coed.; 1920.
Sunflower Junior C. Moorhead, Miss.; coed.; 1911.
Suo'mi C. and Theol. Sem. (swō'mē). Hancock, Mich.; coed.; 1896.
Sus'que·han'na U. (sŭs'kwĕ·hăn'à). Selinsgrove, Pa.; coed.; 1858.
Swarth'more C. (swôrth'mōr; *locally usu.* swŏth'·). Swarthmore, Pa.; coed.; 1864.
Sweet' Bri'ar C. (swēt' brī'ēr). Sweet Briar, Va.; women; 1901.
Syr'a·cuse U. (sĭr'à·kūs). Syracuse, N. Y.; coed.; 1849.
Ta'bor C. (tā'bēr). Hillsboro, Kans.; coed.; 1908.
Ta·co'ma Catholic Junior C. (tà·kō'mà). Tacoma, Wash.; women; 1942.
Taft C. (tăft). Taft, Calif.; junior coed.; 1922.
Tal'la·de'ga C. (tăl'à·dē'gà). Talladega, Ala.; coed.; 1867.
Tam'pa, U. of (tăm'pà). Tampa, Fla.; coed.; 1931.
Tar'ki·o C. (tär'kĭ·ō). Tarkio, Mo.; coed.; 1883.
Tarle'ton State C. (tärl'tŭn). Stephenville, Texas; junior coed.; 1899.
Tay'lor U. (tā'lēr). Upland, Ind.; coed.; 1846.
Teachers C. New York, N. Y.; coed.; 1888.
Temple Junior C. Temple, Texas; coed.; 1926.
Temple U. Philadelphia, Pa.; coed.; 1884.
Tennessee, U. of. Knoxville; coed.; 1794.
Tennessee Agricultural and Industrial State U. Nashville; coed.; 1909.
Tennessee Polytechnic Inst. Cookeville; coed.; 1915.
Tennessee Wesleyan C. Athens; coed.; 1866.
Tex'ar·kan'a C. (tĕk'sär·kăn'à; tĕk'sēr·). Texarkana, Texas; junior coed.; 1927.
Texas, A. & M. C. of. College Station; men; 1862.
Texas, U. of. Austin; coed.; 1881.
Texas Christian U. Fort Worth; coed.; 1873.
Texas C. Tyler; coed.; 1894.
Texas C. of Arts and Industries. Kingsville; coed.; 1917.
Texas Lutheran C. Seguin; coed.; 1891.
Texas Southern U. Houston; coed.; 1927.
Texas South'most C. (south'mōst). Brownsville; junior coed.; 1926.
Texas Technological C. Lubbock; coed.; 1923.
Texas Wesleyan C. Fort Worth; coed.; 1890.
Texas Western C. El Paso; coed.; 1913.
Texas Woman's U. Denton; 1901.
Textile Technology, Inst. of. Charlottesville, Va.; men; 1944.
Thiel C. (tēl). Greenville, Pa.; coed.; 1866.
Thorn'ton Junior C. (thôrn't'n; -tŭn). Harvey, Ill.; coed.; 1927.
Tif'fin U. (tĭf'ĭn). Tiffin, Ohio; junior coed.; 1924.
Tift C. (tĭft). Forsyth, Ga.; women; 1847.
Toc·co'a Falls C. (tŏ·kō'à). Toccoa Falls, Ga.; coed.; 1911.
Toledo, U. of. Ohio; coed.; 1872.
Tou'ga·loo Southern Christian C. (tōō'gà·lōō). Tougaloo, Miss.; coed.; 1869.
Tran'syl·va'nia C. (trăn'sĭl·văn'yà; -vā'nĭ·à). Lexington, Ky.; coed.; 1780.
Trenton Junior C. Trenton, Mo.; coed.; 1925.
Trenton Junior C. Trenton, N. J.; coed.; 1947.
Tre·vec'ca Nazarene C. (trĕ·vĕk'à). Nashville, Tenn.; coed.; 1901.
Trin'i·dad State Junior C. (trĭn'ĭ·dăd). Trinidad, Colorado; coed.; 1925.
Trinity C. Hartford, Conn.; men; 1823.
Trinity C. Washington, D. C.; women; 1897.
Trinity C. Burlington, Vt.; women; 1925.
Trinity Sem. and Bible C. Chicago, Ill.; coed.; 1897.
Trinity U. San Antonio, Texas; coed.; 1869.
Tri–State C. (trī'stāt'). Angola, Ind.; coed.; 1884.
Tru'ett–Mc·Con'nell Junior C. (trōō'ĕt[Ĭt]·mà·kŏn'l). Cleveland, Ga.; coed.; 1947.
Tufts U. (tŭfts). Medford, Mass.; coed.; 1852.
Tu·lane' U. of Louisiana (tū·lān'). New Orleans; coed.; 1834.
Tul'sa, U. of (tŭl'sà). Okla.; coed.; 1894.
Tus'cu·lum C. (tŭs'kū·lŭm). Greeneville, Tenn.; coed.; 1794.
Tus·ke'gee Inst. (tŭs·kē'gē). Tuskegee Institute, Ala.; coed.; 1881.
Ty'ler Commercial C. (tī'lēr). Tyler, Texas; coed.; 1904.
Tyler Junior C. Tyler, Texas; coed.; 1926.
Union C. Barbourville, Ky.; coed.; 1879.
Union C. Lincoln, Nebr.; coed.; 1891.
Union C. and U. Schenectady, N. Y.; men; 1785.
Union Junior C. Cranford, N. J.; coed.; 1933.
Union Theol. Sem. New York, N. Y.; coed.; 1836.
Union Theol. Sem. in Virginia. Richmond; men; 1812.
Union U. Jackson, Tenn.; coed.; 1834.
United States Air Force Acad. Colorado Springs, Colorado; men; 1954.
United States Air Force Air U. Maxwell Air Force Base, Ala.; men; 1945.
United States Coast Guard Acad. New London, Conn.; men; 1876.
United States Department of Agriculture Graduate Sch. Washington, D. C.; coed.; 1921.
United States Merchant Marine Acad. Kings Point, N. Y.; men; 1938.
United States Military Acad. West Point, N. Y.; men; 1802.
United States Naval Acad. Annapolis, Md.; men; 1845.
United States Naval Postgraduate Sch. Monterey, Calif.; men; 1909.
United Theol. Sem. Dayton, Ohio; coed.; 1871.
Up'land C. (ŭp'lănd). Upland, Calif.; coed.; 1920.
Upper Iowa U. Fayette; coed.; 1857.
Up·sa'la C. (ŭp·sä'là). East Orange, N. J.; coed.; 1893.
Ur·ban'a Junior C. (ûr·băn'à). Urbana, Ohio; coed.; 1850.
Ur·si'nus C. (ûr·sī'nŭs). Collegeville, Pa.; coed.; 1869.
Ur'su·line C. (ûr'sū·lĭn). Louisville, Ky.; women; 1938.
Ur'su·line C. (-lĭn). Cleveland, Ohio; women; 1871.
Utah, U. of. Salt Lake City; coed.; 1850

Utah State U. of Agriculture and Applied Science. Logan; coed.; 1888.
Utica C. Utica, N. Y.; coed.; 1946.
Val·dos'ta State C. (văl·dŏs'tà). Valdosta, Ga.; coed.; 1906.
Val·le'jo Junior C. (vă·lā'ō). Vallejo, Calif.; coed.; 1945.
Valley Forge Military Junior C. Wayne, Pa.; men; 1928.
Val'pa·rai'so Tech. Inst. (văl'pà·rā'zō). Valparaiso, Ind.; coed.; 1934.
Valparaiso U. Valparaiso, Ind.; coed.; 1859.
Van'der·bilt U. (văn'dēr·bĭlt). Nashville, Tenn.; coed.; 1872.
Van'der·Cook' C. of Music (văn'dēr·kŏŏk'). Chicago, Ill.; coed.; 1909.
Van'port Extension Center (văn'pōrt; 70). Portland, Ore.; junior coed.; 1946.
Vas'sar C. (văs'ēr). Poughkeepsie, N. Y.; women; 1861.
Ven·tu'ra C. (vĕn·tōōr'à). Ventura, Calif.; junior coed.; 1925.
Vermont and State Agricultural C., U. of. Burlington; coed.; 1791.
Vermont Junior C. Montpelier, Vt.; women; 1834.
Vermont State Teachers C. Castleton; coed.; 1787.
Vermont State Teachers C. Johnson; coed.; 1867.
Vermont State Teachers C. Lyndon Center; coed.; 1911.
Vi'a·to'ri·an House of Studies (vī'à·tō'rĭ·ăn; 70). Davenport, Iowa; men; 1938.
Viatorian Sem. Washington, D. C.; men; 1928.
Victoria C. Victoria, Texas; junior coed.; 1925.
Vil'la Ma·don'na C. (vĭl'à mà·dŏn'à). Covington, Ky.; coed.; 1921.
Villa Ma·ri'a C. (mà·rē'à). Erie, Pa.; women; 1882.
Vil·la·no'va U. (vĭl'à·nō'và). Villanova, Pa.; coed.; 1842.
Villa Walsh C. (wŏlsh). Morristown, N. J.; junior women; 1928.
Vin'cennes U. (vĭn'sĕnz; 2). Vincennes, Ind.; junior coed.; 1804.
Virginia, Med. C. of. Richmond; coed.; 1838.
Virginia, U. of. Charlottesville; coed.; 1819.
Virginia In'ter·mont C. (ĭn'tēr·mŏnt). Bristol; junior women; 1884.
Virginia Junior C. Virginia, Minn.; coed.; 1921.
Virginia Military Inst. Lexington; men; 1839.
Virginia Polytechnic Inst. Blacksburg; coed.; 1872.
Virginia State C. Petersburg; coed.; 1882.
Virginia Theol. Sem. and C. Lynchburg; coed.; 1888.
Virginia Union U. Richmond; coed.; 1865.
Vi·ter'bo C. (vĭ·tûr'bō). La Crosse, Wis.; women; 1931.
Vocational Junior C. Milwaukee, Wis.; coed.; 1934.
Voor'hees Sch. and Junior C. (vōr'hēz). Denmark, S. C.; coed.; 1897.
Wa'bash C. (wô'băsh). Crawfordsville, Ind.; men; 1832.
Wag'ner Lutheran C. (wăg'nēr). Staten Island, N. Y.; coed.; 1883.
Wake Forest C. (wāk). Winston-Salem, N. C.; coed.; 1833.
Wal'dorf C. (wŏl'dôrf). Forest City, Iowa; junior coed.; 1903.
Walk'er Junior C. (wôk'ēr). Jasper, Ala.; coed.; 1938.
Wal'la Wal'la C. (wŏl'à wŏl'à). College Place, Wash.; coed.; 1892.
Warren Wilson C. Swannanoa, N. C.; junior coed.; 1893.
Wart'burg C. (wôrt'bûrg). Waverly, Iowa; coed.; 1868.
Wartburg Theol. Sem. Dubuque, Iowa; men; 1854.
Wash'burn U. of Topeka (wŏsh'bērn; -bûrn). Kans.; coed.; 1865.
Washington, State C. of. Pullman; coed.; 1890.
Washington, U. of. Seattle; coed.; 1861.
Washington and Jef'fer·son C. (jĕf'ēr·s'n). Washington, Pa.; men; 1780.
Washington and Lee U. (lē). Lexington, Va.; men; 1749.
Washington C. Chestertown, Md.; coed.; 1706.
Washington Junior C. Pensacola, Fla.; coed.; 1949.
Washington Missionary C. Takoma Park, Md.; coed.; 1904.
Washington Musical Inst. Washington, D. C.; coed.; 1928.
Washington Sch. of Psychiatry. D. C.; coed.; 1936.
Washington Square C. of Arts and Science. New York, N. Y.; coed.; 1913.
Washington State Teachers C. Machias, Me.; coed.; 1909.
Washington U. St. Louis, Mo.; coed.; 1853.
Way'land Baptist C. (wā'lănd). Plainview, Texas; coed.; 1909.
Waynes'burg C. (wānz'bûrg). Waynesburg, Pa.; coed.; 1850.
Wayne State U. (wān). Detroit, Mich.; coed.; 1868.
Weath'er·ford C. of Parker County (wĕth'ēr·fērd). Weatherford, Texas; junior coed.; 1869.
Web'ber C. (wĕb'ēr). Babson Park, Fla.; junior women; 1927.
Webb Inst. of Naval Architecture (wĕb). Glen Cove, N. Y.; men; 1889.
We'ber C. (wē'bēr). Ogden, Utah; junior coed.; 1889.
Webster City Junior C. Webster City, Iowa; coed.; 1926.
Webster C. Webster Groves, Mo.; women; 1915.
Welles'ley C. (wĕlz'lĭ). Wellesley, Mass.; women; 1870.
Wells C. (wĕlz). Aurora, N. Y.; women; 1868.
We·natch'ee Junior C. (wĕ·năch'ē). Wenatchee, Wash.; coed.; 1939.
Went'worth Inst. (wĕnt'wûrth; -wērth). Boston, Mass.; men; 1904.
Wentworth Military Acad. Lexington, Mo.; junior men; 1880.
Wes'ley·an C. (wĕs'lĭ·ăn). Macon, Ga.; women; 1836.
Wesleyan Methodist C. Central, S. C.; coed.; 1906.
Wesleyan U. Middletown, Conn.; men; 1831.
Wes'ley Junior C. (wĕs'lĭ). Dover, Del.; coed.; 1873.
Wesley Theol. Sem. Westminster, Md.; coed.; 1881.
Wes'sing·ton Springs C. (wĕs'ĭng·tŭn). Wessington Springs, S. Dak.; junior coed.; 1887.
West Ba'den C. (bā'd'n). West Baden Springs, Ind.; men; 1934.
West'brook Junior C. (wĕst'brŏŏk). Portland, Me.; women; 1831.
West'ches'ter Community C. (wĕst'chĕs'tēr). White Plains, N. Y.; junior coed.; 1946.
West Coast U. Los Angeles, Calif.; men; 1909.
West Con'tra Cos'ta Junior C. (kŏn'trà kŏs'tà). San Pablo, Calif.; coed.; 1949.
Western Carolina C. Cullowhee, N. C.; coed.; 1889.
Western C. for Women. Oxford, Ohio; 1853.
Western Evangelical Sem. Portland, Ore.; coed.; 1945.
Western Illinois U. Macomb; coed.; 1899.
Western Kentucky State C. Bowling Green; coed.; 1906.
Western Maryland C. Westminster; coed.; 1867.

Western Michigan U. Kalamazoo; coed.; 1903.
Western Montana C. of Ed. Dillon; coed.; 1893.
Western New England C. Springfield, Mass.; coed.; 1919.
Western Pennsylvania Horological Inst. Pittsburgh; men; 1936.
Western Re·serve′ U. (rē·zûrv′). Cleveland, Ohio; coed.; 1826.
Western State C. of Colorado. Gunnison; coed.; 1911.
Western Theol. Sem. Holland, Mich.; men; 1866.
Western Theol. Sem. Pittsburgh, Pa.; coed.; 1825.
Western Washington U. of Ed. Bellingham, Wash.; coed.; 1893.
West Georgia C. Carrollton; junior coed.; 1933.
West′hamp′ton C. (wĕst′hăm[p]′tŭn). Richmond, Va.; women; 1914.
West Liberty State C. West Liberty, W. Va.; coed.; 1837.
West′mar C. (wĕst′mär). Le Mars, Iowa; coed.; 1900.
West′min′ster Choir C. (wĕs[t]′mĭn′stẽr). Princeton, N. J.; coed.; 1926.
Westminster C. Fulton, Mo.; men; 1851.
Westminster C. New Wilmington, Pa.; coed.; 1852.
Westminster C. Salt Lake City, Utah; coed.; 1875.
Westminster Theol. Sem. Chestnut Hill, Pa.; men; 1929.
West′mont C. (wĕst′mŏnt). Santa Barbara, Calif.; coed.; 1940.
Wes′ton C. (wĕs′tŭn). Weston, Mass.; men; 1857.
West Point. See UNITED STATES MILITARY ACAD.
West Texas State C. Canyon; coed.; 1909.
West Virginia Inst. of Tech. Montgomery; coed.; 1895.
West Virginia State C. Institute; coed.; 1891.
West Virginia U. Morgantown; coed.; 1867.
West Virginia Wesleyan C. Buckhannon; coed.; 1890.
Whar′ton County Junior C. (hwôr′t′n). Wharton, Texas; coed.; 1946.
Whea′ton C. (hwē′t′n). Wheaton, Ill.; coed.; 1853.
Wheaton C. Norton, Mass.; women; 1834.
Whee′ling C. (hwē′lĭng). Wheeling, W. Va.; coed.; 1954.
Whee′lock C. (hwē′lŏk). Boston, Mass.; women; 1889.
White′fri′ars Hall (hwīt′frī′ẽrz). Washington, D. C.; men; 1926.
Whit′man C. (hwĭt′mǎn). Walla Walla, Wash.; coed.; 1859.
Whit′ti·er C. (hwĭt′ĭ·ẽr). Whittier, Calif.; coed.; 1891.
Whitworth C. Spokane, Wash.; coed.; 1890.
Wich′i·ta, U. of (wĭch′ĭ·tô). Kans.; coed.; 1892.
Wil′ber·force U. (wĭl′bẽr·fôrs; 70). Wilberforce, Ohio; coed.; 1856.
Wi′ley C. (wī′lĭ). Marshall, Texas; coed.; 1873.
Wilkes C. (wĭlks). Wilkes-Barre, Pa.; coed.; 1933.
Wil·lam′ette U. (wĭ·lăm′ĕt; -ĭt). Salem, Ore.; coed.; 1842.
William and Mary, C. of. Williamsburg, Va.; coed.; 1693.
William Car′ey C. (kâr′ĭ). Hattiesburg, Miss.; women; 1911.
William Jen′nings Bry′an U. (jĕn′ĭngz brī′ăn). Dayton, Tenn.; coed.; 1930.
William Jew′ell C. (jōō′ĕl; jū′-; -ĭl). Liberty, Mo.; coed.; 1849.
William Mitch′ell C. of Law (mĭch′ĕl). St. Paul, Minn.; coed.; 1900.
William Penn C. (pĕn). Oskaloosa, Iowa; coed.; 1873.
Wil′liams C. (wĭl′yămz). Williamstown, Mass.; men; 1785.
William Smith C. Geneva, N. Y.; women; 1908.

William Woods C. (wŏŏdz). Fulton, Mo.; junior women; 1890.
Wil′li·man′tic State Teachers C. (wĭl′ĭ·măn′tĭk). Willimantic, Conn.; coed.; 1889.
Wil′ming·ton C. (wĭl′mĭng·tŭn). Wilmington, N. C.; junior coed.;1947.
Wilmington C. Wilmington, Ohio; coed.; 1863.
Wil′son C. (wĭl′s′n). Chambersburg, Pa.; women; 1869.
Win′gate Junior C. (wĭn′gāt). Wingate, N. C.; coed.; 1896.
Win·net′ka, Graduate Teachers C. of (wĭ·nĕt′kà). Winnetka, Ill.; coed.; 1932.
Wi·no′na State C. (wĭ·nō′nà). Winona, Minn.; coed.; 1858.
Win′ston–Sa′lem Teachers C. (wĭn′stŭn·sā′lĕm). Winston-Salem, N. C.; coed.; 1892.
Win′throp C. (wĭn′thrŭp). Rock Hill, S. C.; women; 1886.
Wisconsin, U. of. Madison; coed.; 1836.
Wisconsin Conservatory. Milwaukee; coed.; 1899.
Wisconsin Inst. of Tech. Platteville; men; 1907.
Wisconsin State C. at Eau Claire (ō′klâr′). Coed.; 1916.
Wisconsin State C. at La Crosse (là krôs′). Coed.; 1909.
Wisconsin State C. at Osh′kosh (ŏsh′kŏsh). Coed.; 1871.
Wisconsin State C. at Platte′ville (plăt′vĭl). Coed.; 1866.
Wisconsin State C. at River Falls. Coed.; 1875.
Wisconsin State C. at Stevens Point (stē′vĕnz). Coed.; 1894.
Wisconsin State C. at Superior. Coed.; 1896.
Wisconsin State C. at White′wa′ter (hwīt′wô′tẽr; -wŏt′ẽr). Coed.; 1868.
Wit′ten·berg C. (wĭt′′n·bûrg). Springfield, Ohio; coed.; 1842.
Wof′ford C. (wŏf′ẽrd). Spartanburg, S. C.; men; 1851.
Woman′s C. of the U. of North Carolina. Greensboro; 1891.
Woman′s Med. C. of Pennsylvania. Philadelphia; 1850.
Wood′bur′y C. (wŏŏd′bĕr′ĭ; -bĕr·ĭ). Los Angeles, Calif.; coed.; 1884.
Wood Junior C. (wŏŏd). Mathiston, Miss.; coed.; 1886.
Wood′stock C. (wŏŏd′stŏk). Woodstock, Md.; men; 1867.
Woos′ter, C. of (wŏŏs′tẽr). Wooster, Ohio; coed.; 1866.
Worces′ter Junior C. (wŏŏs′tẽr). Mass.; coed.; 1905.
Worcester Polytechnic Inst. Mass.; men; 1865.
Wor′thing·ton Junior C. (wûr′thĭng·tŭn). Worthington, Minn.; coed.; 1936.
Wyoming, U. of. Laramie; coed.; 1886.
Wy′o·mis′sing Polytechnic Inst. (wī′ô·mĭs′ĭng). Wyomissing, Pa.; coed.; 1927.
Xa·ve′ri·an C. (zà·vẽr′ĭ·ǎn). Silver Spring, Md.; junior men; 1931.
Xav′i·er U. (zăv′ĭ·ẽr). New Orleans, La.; coed.; 1915.
Xa′vi·er U. (zā′vĭ·ẽr). Cincinnati, Ohio; coed.; 1831.
Yak′i·ma Valley Junior C. (yăk′ĭ·mô). Yakima, Wash.; coed.; 1928.
Yale U. (yāl). New Haven, Conn.; coed.; 1701.
Yank′ton C. (yăngk′tŭn). Yankton, S. Dak.; coed.; 1881.
Ye·shi′va U. (yĕ·shē′và). New York, N. Y.; coed.; 1886.
York Junior C. York, Pa.; coed.; 1941.
Young L. G. Harris C. Young Harris, Ga.; junior coed.; 1886.
Youngs′town U. (yŭngz′toun). Youngstown, Ohio; coed.; 1908.
Ys·let′a C. (ĭz·lĕt′à). El Paso, Texas; junior men; 1925
Yu′ba C. (yōō′bà). Marysville, Calif.; junior coed.; 1927.

CANADIAN COLLEGES AND UNIVERSITIES

Abbreviations used in the preceding list are used here except that French names require the following spellings: *Acad.* A′ca′dé′mie′ (à′kà′dä′mē′); *C.* Col′lège′ (kô′lâzh′); *Inst.* In′sti′tut′ (ăn′stē′tü′); *Sém.* Sé′mi′naire′ (sā′mē′nâr′); and *U.* U′ni′ver′si′té′ (ü′nē′vẽr′sē′tā′).

A·ca′di·a U. (à·kā′dĭ·à). Wolfville, N. S.; coed.; 1838.
A′gri′cul′ture′, É′cole′ Su′pé′rieure′ d′ (ā′kôl′ sü′pā′ryûr′ dà′grē′kül′tür′). Ste. de la Pocatière, P. Q.; men; 1859.
Al·ber′ta, U. of (ăl·bûr′tà). Edmonton; coed.; 1906.
Alberta Sch. of Agric. Vermillion; junior coed.; 1913.
Al′ma C. (ăl′mà). St. Thomas, Ont.; junior women; 1881.
A′mos′, C. d′ (dà′mōs′). Amos, P. Q.; men; 1940.
Anglican Theol. C. Vancouver, B. C.; men; 1912.
Anglican Women′s Training C. Toronto, Ont.; 1892.
Ap′ple·by C. (ăp′′l·bĭ). Oakville, Ont.; men; 1911.
Ar′pen′tage′, É′cole′ d′ (ā′kôl′ dàr′pän′tàzh′). Quebec, P. Q.; men; 1907.
Assumption U. Windsor, Ont.; men; 1857.
Banff Sch. of Fine Arts (bămf). Banff, Alta.; coed.; 1933.
Ba′sile′–Mo′reau′, C. (bá′zĭl′mô′rō′). St. Laurent, P. Q.; women; 1929.
Beaux–Arts, É′cole′ des (ā′kôl′ dä bō′-zàr′). Montreal, P. Q.; coed.; 1921.
Beaux–Arts, École des. Quebec, P. Q.; coed.; 1922.
Bishop′s U. Lennoxville, P. Q.; coed.; 1843.
Bour′get′ C. (bōōr′zhĕ′). Rigaud, P. Q.; men; 1850.
Bran′don C. (brăn′dǔn). Brandon, Man.; coed.; 1899.
British Columbia, U. of. Vancouver; coed.; 1890.
British Columbia Provincial Normal Sch. Vancouver; coed.; 1900.
British Columbia Provincial Normal Sch. Victoria; coed.; 1915.
Cam′pi·on C. (kăm′pĭ·ǔn). Regina, Sask.; junior men; 1917.
Cam′rose Lutheran C. (kăm′rōz). Camrose, Alta.; coed.; 1911.
Canadian Credit Inst. Toronto, Ont.; coed.; 1927.
Canadian Memorial Chiropractic C. Toronto, Ont.; coed.; 1945.
Canadian Sch. of Missions. Toronto, Ont.; coed.; 1921.
Canadian Union C. Lacombe, Alta.; junior coed.; 1906.
Carle′ton C. (kärl′tŭn; -t′n). Ottawa, Ont.; coed.; 1942.
Chi′cou′ti′mi′, Pen′sion′nat′ (păn′syô′nà′ shē′kōō′tē′mē′). Chicoutimi, P. Q.; women; 1864.
Chicoutimi, Sém. de (dĕ). Chicoutimi, P. Q.; men; 1873.
Christ the King, C. of. Toronto, Ont.; men; 1930.

Cis′ter′ciens′ de l′Im′ma′cu′lée′–Con′cep′tion′, Pri′eu′ré′ des (prē′û′rā′ dä sĭs′tẽr′syǎN′ dē lĭm′mà′kü′lā′kôN′sĕp′syôN′). St. Michel de Rougemont, P. Q.; men; 1932.
Com′merce′, É′cole′ Su′pé′rieure′ de (ā′kôl′ sü′pā′ryûr′ dē kô′mẽrs′). Quebec, P. Q.; coed.; 1924.
Con·cor′di·a C. (kŏn·kôr′dĭ·à). Edmonton, Alberta; junior coed.; 1921.
Dal·hou′sie U. (dăl·hou′zĭ). Halifax, N. S.; coed.; 1818.
Dié′té′tique′ et de Nu′tri′tion′, Inst. de (dē dyā′tā′tĭk′ ād nü′trē′syôN′). Montreal, P. Q.; women; 1942.
Do′mi′ni′cains′, C. des (dä dô′mē′nē′kăN′). Ottawa, Ont.; men; 1900.
Doon Sch. of Fine Arts (dōōn). Doon, Ont.; coed.; 1947.
Emmanuel C. Toronto, Ont.; coed.; 1841.
Emmanuel C. Saskatoon, Sask.; men; 1879.
Evangelical Lutheran Sem. Waterloo, Ont.; men; 1924.
Fran′cis′cains′, C. d′Ap′pren′tis′sage′ des (dà′prăn′tē′sàzh′ dä frän′sēs′kăN′). Sorel, P. Q.; junior men; 1946.
Frères—Mi′neurs′ Ca′pu′cins′, No′vi′ciat′ des (nô′vē′syà′ dä frär′mē′nûr′ kà′pü′säN′). Cacouna, P. Q.; junior men; 1903.
Gas′pé′, C. de (dĕ gàs′pā′). Gaspé, P. Q.; men; 1926.
Gra′vel′bourg′, C. Ca′tho′lique′ de (kà′tô′lĭk′ dĕ grà′vĕl′bōōr′). Gravelbourg, Sask.; men; 1917.
Hal′i·fax Conservatory of Music (hăl′ĭ·făks). N. S.; coed.; 1887.
Ham′il·ton C. (hăm′ĭl·tǔn; -t′n). Hamilton, Ont.; coed.; 1948.
Hamilton Normal Sch. Hamilton, Ont.; coed.; 1908.
Hautes É′tudes′ Com′mer′ciales′, É′cole′ des (ā′kôl′ dä ōt-zā′tüd′ kô′mẽr′syàl′). Montreal, P. Q.; coed.; 1907.
Hav′er·gal C. (hăv′ẽr·gǎl). Toronto, Ont.; junior coed.; 1894.
Holy Heart Sem. Halifax, N. S.; men; 1894.
Holy Names C. Windsor, Ont.; women; 1934.
Holy Rosary Scholasticate. Orleans, Ont.; men; 1930.
Hu′ron C. (hū′rǔn). London, Ont.; men; 1863.
Hy′giene′ So′ciale′ Ap′pli′quée′, É′cole′ d′ (ā′kôl′ dē′zhyân′ sô′syàl′ à′plē′kā′). Montreal, P. Q.; women; 1925.
Im′ma′cu′lée′ Con′cep′tion′, Sco′las′ti′cat′ de l′ (skô′làs′tē′kà′ dē lĭm′mà′kü′lā′ kôN′sĕp′syôN′). Montreal, P. Q.; men; 1884.

Jacques–Car′tier′, É′cole′ Nor′male′ (ä′kôl′ nôr′mål′ zhäk′kår′tyä′). Montreal, P. Q.; men; 1939.

Jean–de–Bré′beuf′, C. (zhän′dĕ·brä′bûf′). Montreal, P. Q.; men; 1928.

Jé′suites′, C. des (dä zhä′zü·ĭt′). Quebec, P. Q.; men; 1930.

Jé′sus′–Ma′rie′, C. (zhā′zü′må′rē′). Outremont, P. Q.; women; 1933.

Jo′liette, Sém. de (dĕ zhô′lyĕt′). Joliette, P. Q.; men; 1846.

Kempt′ville Agricultural C. (kĕm[p]t′vĭl). Kemptville, Ont.; junior coed.; 1917.

King′s College, U. of. Halifax, N. S.; coed.; 1789.

Kitch′e·ner Conservatory of Music (kĭch′ĕ·nĕr). Kitchener, Ont.; coed.; 1913.

Knox C. (nŏks). Toronto, Ont.; men; 1843.

Lake′head′ C. (lāk′hĕd′). Port Arthur, Ont.; junior coed.; 1948.

La Ré′pa′ra′tion′, Mai′son′ d′É′tudes′ du Mo′nas′tère′ de (mä′zôN′ dä′tüd′ dü mô′nás′tår′ dĕ lä rä′på′rä′syôN′). Pointe aux Trembles, P. Q.; men; 1922.

L′As′somp′tion′, C. de (dĕ lå·sôNp′syôN′). L′Assomption, P. Q.; men; 1832.

La′val′, É′cole′ Nor′male′ (ä′kôl′ nôr′mål′ lå′vål′). Quebec, P. Q.; coed.; 1857.

La′val′, U. (lå′vål′). Quebec, P. Q.; coed.; 1852.

Lé′vis′, C. de (dĕ lā′vē′). Levis, P. Q.; men; 1853.

London Normal Sch. London, Ont.; coed.; 1899.

Lo·ret′to Abbey (lō·rĕt′ō). Toronto, Ont.; women; 1847.

Lorne Park C. (lôrn). Port Credit, Ont.; junior coed.; 1924.

Loy·o′la C. (loi·ō′lá). Montreal, P. Q.; men; 1896.

Lutheran C. and Sem. Saskatoon, Sask.; men; 1913.

Lutheran Theol. Sem. Saskatoon, Sask.; men; 1939.

Lu′ther C. (lü′thĕr). Regina, Sask.; junior coed.; 1926.

Mac·don′ald C. (måk·dŏn′ld). Ste. Anne de Bellevue, P. Q.; coed.; 1907.

Mc·Gill′ U. (må·gĭl′). Montreal, P. Q.; coed.; 1821.

Mc·Mas′ter U. (måk·mås′tĕr). Hamilton, Ont.; coed.; 1887.

Manitoba, U. of. Winnipeg; coed.; 1877.

Manitoba Normal Sch. Tuxedo; coed.; 1890.

Manitoba Technical Inst. Winnipeg; junior coed.; 1948.

Mar′gue·rite′–Bour′geoys′, C. (mär′gĕ·rēt′bŏŏr′zhwä′). Montreal, P. Q.; women; 1908.

Marguerite d′You′ville′, C. (dü′vĭl′). Montreal, P. Q.; women; 1935.

Mar′i·a·nop′o·lis C. (mär′ĭ·à·nŏp′ō·lĭs; mär′·). Montreal, P. Q.; women; 1943.

Ma′rie′–Anne′, C. (må′rē′än′). Lachine, P. Q.; women; 1932.

Ma′rie′ de France, C. (må′rē′ dĕ fräNs′). Montreal, P. Q.; women; 1939.

Marie de l′In′car′na′tion′, C. (dĕ lăN′kår′nä′syôN′). Trois–Rivières, P. Q.; women; 1697.

Ma′rie′–Im′ma′cu′lée′, Sém. Ob′lat′ de (ô′blä′ dĕ må′rē′ĭm′må′kü′lā′). Chambly, P. Q.; men; 1926.

Ma′rie′–Mé′dia′trice′, Sém. (må′rē′mā′dyä′trĭs′). Montreal, P. Q.; men; 1938.

Maritime C. of Pharmacy. Halifax, N. S.; coed.; 1911.

Maritime Sch. of Social Work. Halifax, N. S.; coed.; 1940.

Mé′de·cine′ Vé′té′ri′naire′, É′cole′ de (ä′kôl′ dĕ mĕt′sĭn′ vä′tā′rē′nâr′). St. Hyacinthe, P. Q.; men; 1886.

Memorial U. C. St. John′s, Newf.; coed.; 1925.

Men′non·ite Brethren Bible C. (mĕn′ŏn·īt). Winnipeg, Manitoba; coed.; 1944.

Meu′ble, É′cole′ du (ä′kôl′ dü mû′bl′). Montreal, P. Q.; coed.; 1935.

Mis′sion′naires′ d′A′frique′, Sém. des (dä mĭ′syô′när′ då′frĭk′). Eastview, Ont.; men; 1938.

Mis′sions′ É′tran′gères′, Sém. des (dä mĭ′syôN′–nä′träN′zhâr′). Pont Viau, P. Q.; men; 1921.

Mont′for′tains′, Sco′las′ti′cat′ des (skô′làs′tē′kå′ då môN′fôr′tăN′). Eastview, Ont.; men; 1890.

Mont–Lau′rier′, Sém. de (dĕ môN′lô′ryä′). Mont Laurier, P. Q.; men; 1915.

Mont′ré′al′, C. de (dĕ môN′rā′àl′). P. Q.; men; 1767.

Montréal, Grand Sém. de (gräN′). P. Q.; men; 1840.

Montréal, U. de. P. Q.; coed.; 1876.

Mont′re·al′ Diocesan C. (mŏn′trē·ôl′; mŭn′·). P. Q.; men; 1873.

Montreal Presbyterian C. P. Q.; men; 1865.

Moose Jaw Bible C. Moose Jaw, Sask.; coed.; 1940.

Mount Al′li·son U. (ăl′ĭ·s′n). Sackville, N. B.; coed.; 1839.

Mount Car′mel C. (kär′mĕl). Niagara Falls, Ont.; junior men; 1864.

Mount Royal C. Calgary, Alta.; junior coed.; 1910.

Mount St. Ber′nard C. (sånt bûr′nĕrd). Antigonish, N. S.; women; 1894.

Mount St. Lou′is C. (sånt lŏŏ′ē). Montreal, P. Q.; junior men; 1888.

Mount St. Vin′cent C. (sånt vĭn′sĕnt). Rockingham, N. S.; women; 1873.

New Brunswick, U. of. Fredericton; coed.; 1785.

New Brunswick Teachers′ C. Fredericton; coed.; 1876.

Ni′co′let′, Pen′sion′nat′ de (pän′syô′nä′ dĕ nē′kô′lĕ′). Nicolet, P. Q.; women; 1853.

Nicolet, Sém. de. Nicolet, P. Q.; men; 1801.

North Bay Normal Sch. North Bay, Ont.; coed.; 1909.

No′tre Dame C. (nō′tĕr däm′). Ottawa, Ont.; women; 1932.

Notre Dame C. Wilcox, Sask.; coed.; 1933.

No′tre–Dame′–de–Belle′vue′, Pen′sion′nat′ de (pän′syô′nä′ dĕ nô′-trĕ·däm′dĕ·bĕl′vü′). Quebec, P. Q.; women; 1931.

No′tre–Dame′ de l′As′somp′tion′, C. (nô′trĕ·däm′ dĕ lå·sôNp′syôN′). Nicolet, P. Q.; women; 1937.

No′tre–Dame′ du Lac, Ab′ba′ye′ (å′bä′yē′ nô′trĕ·däm′ dü låk′). La Trappe, P. Q.; men; 1881.

Nova Scotia Agricultural C. Truro; junior coed.; 1905.

Nova Scotia C. of Art. Halifax; coed.; 1887.

Nova Scotia Normal C. Truro; coed.; 1855.

Nova Scotia Tech. C. Halifax; men; 1907.

Ob′lats′, No′vi′ciat′ des (nô′vē′syä′ dä–zô′blä′). Richelieu, P. Q.; men; 1930.

O′ka′, Inst. A′gri′cole′ d′ (å′grē′kôl′ dô′kå′). La Trappe, P. Q.; men; 1893.

Ontario C. of Agriculture. Guelph; coed.; 1874.

Ontario C. of Art. Toronto; coed.; 1876.

Ontario C. of Ed. Toronto; coed.; 1906.

Ontario C. of Pharmacy. Toronto; coed.; 1871.

Ontario Ladies C. Whitby; junior; 1874.

Ontario Veterinary C. Guelph; coed.; 1862.

Op′to′mé′trie′, É′cole′ d′ (ä′kôl′ dôp′tô′mä′trē′). Montreal, P. Q.; coed.; 1910.

Optometry of Ontario, C. of. Toronto; coed.; 1925.

Os′goode Hall Law Sch. (ŏz′gŏŏd). Toronto, Ont.; coed.; 1873.

Osh′a·wa Missionary C. (ŏsh′å·wô). Oshawa, Ont.; coed.; 1903.

Ot′ta′wa′, Grand Sém. d′ (gräN′ sä′mē′när′ dô′tä′wä′). Ont.; men; 1848.

Ottawa, Sém. d′. Ont.; men; 1926.

Ottawa, U. d′. Ont.; coed.; 1848.

Our Lady of the Sacred Heart Convent. Ottawa, Ont.; women; 1869.

Pê′che·ries′, É′cole′ des (ä′kôl′ dä pĕsh′rē′). Ste. Anne de la Pocatière, P. Q.; men; 1938.

Pé′da′go′gique′, Inst. (pä′dä′gô′zhĭk′). Montreal, P. Q.; women; 1926.

Pédagogique St.–Georges, Inst. (săN′zhôrzh′). Montreal, P. Q.; men; 1929.

Pères Ma′ristes′, Ju′vé′nat′ des (zhü′vä′nä′ dä pâr′ må′rĭst′). Sillery, P. Q.; junior men; 1929.

Pères Mont′for′tains′, Sém. des (dä pâr′ môn′fôr′tăN′). Papineauville, P. Q.; junior men; 1908.

Pe′ter·bor′ough Normal Sch. (pē′tĕr·bûr′ô). Peterborough, Ont.; coed.; 1909.

Phar′ma′cie′, É′cole′ de (ä′kôl′ dĕ får′må′sē′). Quebec, P. Q.; coed.; 1873.

Pine Hill Divinity Hall. Halifax, N. S.; men; 1820.

Po′ly′tech′nique′, É′cole′ (ä′kôl′ pô′lē′tĕk′nĭk′). Montreal, P. Q.; coed.; 1873.

Pontifical Inst. of Mediaeval Studies. Toronto, Ont.; coed.; 1929.

Prince of Wales C. and Normal Sch. Charlottetown, P. E. I.; junior coed.; 1860.

Provincial Inst. of Mining. Haileybury, Ont.; junior men; 1945.

Provincial Inst. of Tech. and Art. Calgary, Alta.; junior coed.; 1916.

Provincial Inst. of Textiles. Hamilton, Ont.; junior coed.; 1946.

Qué′bec′, Sém. de (dĕ kā′bĕk′). Quebec, P. Q.; men; 1663.

Queen′s U. Kingston, Ont.; coed.; 1841.

Radio Arts, Acad. of. Toronto, Ont.; coed.; 1945.

Reformed Episcopal Theol. C. Toronto, Ont.; men; 1948.

Re·gi′na Cle′ri Sem. (rĕ·jī′ná klâ′rē). Regina, Sask.; men; 1932.

Re·gi′na C. (rĕ·jī′ná). Regina, Sask.; junior coed.; 1911.

Ri′mous′ki′, Sém. de (dĕ rē′mŏŏs′kē′). Rimouski, P. Q.; men; 1855.

Royal Military C. Kingston, Ont.; men; 1875.

Royal Roads C. Royal Roads, B. C.; junior men; 1942.

Royal Victoria C. Montreal, P. Q.; women; 1899.

Ry′er·son Inst. of Tech. (rī′ĕr·s′n). Toronto, Ont.; junior coed.; 1948.

Sa′cré′–Coeur′, C. du (dü så′krā′kûr′). Bathurst, N. B.; men; 1879.

Sacré–Coeur, C. du. Sudbury, Ont.; men; 1913.

Sacré–Coeur, C. du. Sherbrooke, P. Q.; women; 1945.

Sacré–Coeur, É′cole′ A′pos′to′lique′ du (ä′kôl′ å′pôs′tō′lĭk′ dĕ). Beauport, P. Q.; men; 1920.

Sacré–Coeur, Sco′las′ti′cat′ de Phi′lo′so′phie′ des Mis′sion′naires′ du (skô′làs′tē′kä′ dĕ fē′lō′zō′fē′ dä mĭ′syô′när′ dü). Waterloo, Ont.; men; 1933.

Sacré–Coeur, Scholasticat du. Lebret, Sask.; men; 1926.

Sacré–Coeur, Sém. du. St. Victor, P. Q.; men; 1910.

Sacred Heart C. Regina, Sask.; junior women; 1927.

Sacred Heart, Convent of the. Halifax, N. S.; women; 1849.

Saint–A′lex′an′dre, C. (säN′–tä′lĕk′säN′dr′). Limbour, P. Q.; men; 1912.

Saint–Al′phonse′, Sém. (säN′–tål′fôNs′). Ste. Anne de Beaupré, Quebec; men; 1896.

Saint Al·phon′sus Sem. (sänt ăl·fŏn′sŭs). Woodstock, Ont.; men; 1930.

Saint Andrew′s C. Aurora, Ont.; junior men; 1899.

Saint Andrew′s C. Saskatoon, Sask.; coed.; 1912.

Saint–An′toine′, Sém. (săN′–tän′twän′). Trois–Rivières, P. Q.; men; 1860.

Saint Au·gus′tine′s Sem. (sänt ô·gŭs′tĭnz). Toronto, Ont.; men; 1913.

Saint Bas′il′s Sem. (băs′lz). Toronto, Ont.; men; 1852.

Saint–Be·noît′–du–Lac, Pri′eu′ré′ de (prē′ö′rā′ dĕ săN′bĕ·nwä′dü·låk′). St. Benoit du Lac, P. Q.; men; 1912.

Saint–Bo′ni′face′, C. de (dĕ săN′bô′nē′fäs′). St. Boniface, Man.; men; 1818.

Saint Chad′s C. (chădz). Regina, Sask.; men; 1907.

Saint–Charles, Sco′las′ti′cat′ (skô′làs′tē′kå′ săN′shärl′). Joliette, P. Q.; men; 1930.

Saint–Charles–Gar′nier′, C. (·går′nyä′). Quebec, P. Q.; men; 1930.

Saint Dun′stan′s U. (sänt dŭn′stänz). Charlottetown, P. E. I.; coed.; 1855.

Sainte–Anne, C. (săN′tän′). Church Point, N. S.; men; 1891.

Sainte–Anne, C. de (dĕ). Ste. Anne de la Pocatière, P. Q.; men; 1827.

Sainte–Croix, Ex′ter′nat′ Clas′sique′ (ĕks′tĕr′nä′ klä′sĭk′ săNt′·krwä′). Montreal, P. Q.; men; 1927.

Sainte–Croix, Sco′las′ti′cat′ de la Con′gré′ga′tion′ de (skô′làs′tē′kä′ dĕ lä kôN′grä′gä′syôN′ des săN′t·krwä′). Montreal, P. Q.; men; 1900.

Sainte–Croix, Sém. de. St. Laurent, P. Q.; men; 1893.

Sainte–Croix, Sém. de Phi′lo′so′phie′ (fē′lô′zō′fē′). Montreal, P. Q.; men; 1893.

Sainte–Ma′rie′, C. (săNt′må′rē′). Montreal, P. Q.; men; 1848.

Sainte–Ma′rie′ des Pères Blancs, No′vi′ciat′ (nô′vē′syä′ săNt′·må′rē′ dä pâr′ bläN′). St. Martin, P. Q.; men; 1937.

Sainte–Thé′rèse′, Sém. de (dĕ săNt′tā′räz′). Ste. Thérèse, P. Q.; men; 1825.

Saint Francis Xa·vi·er Sem. (zā′vĭ·ẽr). Scarboro Bluffs, Ont.; men; 1924.

Saint Francis Xav′i·er U. (zăv′ĭ·ẽr; *occas.* zā′vĭ·ẽr). Antigonish, N. S.; coed.; 1853.

Saint–Ger′main′, Sém. de (dẽ săN′zhẽr′măN′). Rimouski, P. Q.; men; 1870.

Saint–Hya′cinthe′, Sém. de (dẽ săN′-tyà′săNt′). St. Hyacinthe, P. Q.; men; 1811.

Saint–I′gnace′, C. (săN′-tē′nyàs′). Montreal, P. Q.; junior men; 1927.

Saint–Jean, C. (săN′zhäN′). Edmonton, Alta.; men; 1908.

Saint–Jean, C. de (dẽ). Saint Jean, P. Q.; men; 1911.

Saint–Jean, Sco′las′ti′cat′ (skö′làs′tē′kà′). Eastview, Ont.; men; 1901.

Saint–Jean–Eudes, C. (-zhäN′-nûd′). Quebec, P. Q.; men; 1937.

Saint–Jean Vian′ney′, Sém. (-zhäN′ vyà′nā′). Ottawa, Ont.; men; 1926.

Saint Je·rome′s′ C. (sànt jẽ·rōmz′). Kitchener, Ont.; men; 1864.

Saint John′s C. Winnipeg, Man.; coed.; 1829.

Saint–Jo′seph′, Mai′son′ (mā′zôN′ săN′zhō′zẽf′). Sault-au-Récollet, P. Q.; junior men; 1880.

Saint–Joseph, Sco′las′ti′cat′ (skö′làs′tē′kà′). Ottawa, Ont.; men; 1885.

Saint–Joseph, Sém. Mont Laurier, P. Q.; men; 1915.

Saint–Joseph, Sém. Trois-Rivières, P. Q.; men; 1663.

Saint–Joseph, U. St. Joseph, N. B.; men; 1864.

Saint Jo′seph′s C. (sànt jō′zẽfs; -zĭfs). Edmonton, Alta.; men; 1927.

Saint Joseph′s C. Toronto, Ont.; women; 1911.

Saint Joseph′s Sem. Edmonton, Alta.; men; 1927.

Saint–Lau′rent′, C. de (dẽ săN′lô′räN′). St. Laurent, P. Q.; men; 1847.

Saint Martha′s Sch. of Nursing. Antigonish, N. S.; women; 1926.

Saint Mary′s C. Winnipeg, Man.; women; 1874.

Saint Mary′s C., U. of. Halifax, N. S.; men; 1841.

Saint–Mau′rice′, C. (săN′mô′rēs′). St. Hyacinthe, P. Q.; women; 1935.

Saint Michael′s C. Toronto, Ont.; men; 1852.

Saint Patrick′s C. Ottawa, Ont.; coed.; 1928.

Saint–Paul, Sém. (săN′pôl′). Ottawa, Ont.; men; 1937.

Saint Paul′s C. (sànt pôlz′). Winnipeg, Man.; men; 1926.

Saint Peter′s C. Muenster, Sask.; junior men; 1922.

Saint Peter′s Sem. London, Ont.; men; 1912.

Saint–Sa′cre·ment′, Sém. du (dü săN′sà′krẽ·măN′). Terrebonne, P. Q.; junior men; 1902.

Saints–Anges, Ju′vé′nat′ des (zhü′vā′nà′ dā săN′-zänzh′). Berthierville, P. Q.; junior men; 1892.

Saint Stan′is·laus Noviciate (stăn′ĭs-lôz). Guelph, Ont.; junior men; 1913.

Saint Stephen′s C. Edmonton, Alta.; coed.; 1910.

Saint Thom′as C. (sànt tŏm′ăs). Chatham, N. B.; coed.; 1876.

Saint Thomas C. North Battleford, Sask.; men; 1932.

Saint Thomas More C. (mōr; 70). Saskatoon, Sask.; coed.; 1936.

Saint–Vic′tor′, Sém. de (dẽ săN′vēk′tôr′). St. Victor, P. Q.; men; 1910.

Saskatchewan, U. of. Saskatoon; coed.; 1907.

Saskatchewan Normal Sch. Moose Jaw; coed.; 1927.

Saskatchewan Normal Sch. Saskatoon; coed.; 1912.

Sciences Do′mes′tiques′, É′cole′ de (ā′kôl′ dẽ syäns′ dô′mẽs′tĭk′). Quebec, P. Q.; women; 1941.

Ser′vice′ So′cial′, É′cole′ de (ā′kôl′ dẽ sẽr′vĭs′ sô′syàl′). Montreal, P. Q.; coed.; 1939.

Sil′le·ry′, C. de (dẽ sē′y′·rē′). Quebec, P. Q.; women; 1857.

Sir George William C. Montreal, P. Q.; coed.; 1873.

Sta′nis′las′, C. (stà′nĭs′läs′). Montreal, P. Q.; men; 1938.

Stan′stead Wesleyan C. (stăn′stĕd; -stĭd). Stanstead, P. Q.; junior coed.; 1872.

Strat′ford Normal Sch. (străt′fẽrd). Stratford, Ont.; coed.; 1908.

Stu′dium′ Fran′cis′cain′ de Thé′o′lo′gie′ (stü′dyôm′ frän′sĭs′kăN′ dẽ tā′ô′lô′zhē′). Montreal, P. Q.; men; 1892.

Tech′no′lo′gie′ Mé′di′cale′, É′cole′ de (ā′kôl′ dẽ tĕk′nô′lô′zhē′ mā′-dē′kàl′). Montreal, P. Q.; coed.; 1942.

The′ve·net′, C. (tĕv′nĕ′). Gravelbourg, Sask.; women; 1915.

Toronto, U. of. Ont.; coed.; 1827.

Toronto Baptist Sem. Ont.; coed.; 1926.

Toronto Normal Sch. Ont.; coed.; 1847.

Très–Saint–Sa′cre·ment′, Sco′las′ti′cat′ des Re·li′gieux′ du (skö′-làs′tē′kà′ dā rē·lē′zhyû′ dü trē′săN′sà′krẽ·măN′). Montreal, P. Q.; men; 1890.

Trinity C., U. of. Toronto, Ont.; coed.; 1852.

Trois–Ri′vières′, Sém. de (dẽ trwä′rē′vyâr′). Trois-Rivières, P. Q.; men; 1860.

Union C. Vancouver, B. C.; men; 1927.

United Church Training Sch. Toronto, Ont.; women; 1893.

United C. Winnipeg, Man.; coed.; 1871.

United Theological C. Montreal, P. Q.; coed.; 1925.

Ursuline C. London, Ont.; women; 1919.

Ur′su′lines′, C. des (dā-zür′sü′lĭn′). Rimouski, P. Q.; women; 1906.

Val′ley·field, Sém. de (dẽ vàl′ĭ·fēld). Valleyfield, P. Q.; men; 1893.

Vancouver Sch. of Art. B. C.; coed.; 1925.

Vic·to′ri·a C. (vĭk·tō′rĭ·à). Victoria, B. C.; junior coed.; 1902.

Victoria U. Toronto, Ont.; coed.; 1832.

Wa′ter·loo′ C. (wô′tẽr·lōō′; wŏt′ẽr-). Waterloo, Ont.; coed.; 1924.

Western Ontario, U. of. London; coed.; 1878.

Wyc′liffe C. (wĭk′lĭf). Toronto, Ont.; men; 1879.
